RECORD COLLECTOR

RARE RECORD PRICE GUIDE 2002

PUBLISHER
Sean O'Mahony

MANAGING EDITOR
Peter Doggett

EXECUTIVE EDITOR
Andy Davis

EDITOR
Jack Kane

ASSISTANT
Joe Geesin

ADDITIONAL RESEARCH
James Blandford
Tim Jones
Joel McIver
Martin O'Gorman

PRODUCTION MANAGER
Peter Phillips

ART DIRECTOR
Ian Gray

RECORD COLLECTOR

RARE RECORD PRICE GUIDE 2002

PUBLISHED BY
RECORD COLLECTOR MAGAZINE
THE WORLD'S LEADING PUBLICATION FOR
COLLECTORS OF RARE RECORDS AND MEMORABILIA

Published in the United Kingdom 2000
by Parker Mead Limited for Parker Publishing
45 St. Mary's Road, Ealing, London W5 5RQ

Printed in England

ISBN No. 0 9532601 1 9

CONTENTS

THE BIBLE
OF THE BEAT

This is the sixth edition of the world's biggest and best price guide for collectable records, compiled by *Record Collector*, the world's best-selling magazine in the field. It's been fully updated to include all the latest values for an astonishing variety of vinyl singles, EPs and LPs, CDs, cassettes, 78s, and even reel-to-reel tapes and 8-track cartridges.

The majority of entries included in this book are vinyl singles, EPs and LPs, as vinyl was the most important format from the 50s to the late 80s. But the *Rare Record Price Guide* also reflects the fact that Compact Discs have become increasingly dominant in the market over the last decade. CDs are not only the best-selling format of the 90s and beyond, but they are also the standard currency for anyone who started buying records in that period, so it's only natural that they are now playing a significant role in the collecting market as well.

From Aardvark to Zzy, you'll find listings of thousands of rare records which have been issued in this country over the past five decades. Each record is dated, with full details of its label, catalogue number, and format (whether it's a single, LP, CD, cassette or 78). Unlike other price guides, in the case of singles we list *both* sides. Finally, the current value of the disc is given, for copies in Mint (absolutely perfect) condition.

It's a real challenge to keep track of all the collectable records and CDs which have been released over the years, and discover which of them now attract premium prices. Hence the need for this book, which has been a vital tool for collectors ever since the first, slim volume appeared in 1987. No wonder dealers have nicknamed the *Rare Record Price Guide* 'The Bible'!

QUEEN

THE CONTINUING STORY OF VINYL

Ever since the CD was launched in the mid-80s, both the record and hi-fi industries have been declaring that vinyl was dead, or at least sitting in the condemned cell. It's certainly true that far fewer new releases are now sold on vinyl than they were ten years ago. But all the industry predictions about the death of the format have proved to be false, both for current releases and especially for collector's items from the past.

Although CDs have taken over as the most common format for buying new singles and albums, vinyl has become synonymous with collecting. Besides the limited 12" singles which have been the staple diet of dance DJs for more than two decades, there are a number of other areas in which new vinyl continues to play an important part — and they are all likely to have an impact on collectors in years to come.

In the indie rock market, limited 7" singles are still a vital way of launching new bands, and of allowing more established acts a chance to experiment outside their normal contracts. In fact, many bands these days have deals which allow them to issue limited edition vinyl singles for any label they choose, as long as they continue to release their mainstream albums with the record company who own their contract. The result is that there has been a steady stream of instant collectables over the last decade, either as part of indie-label singles clubs, or as 'split' singles, combining two acts from different labels on the same record. All these items are likely to rise in value in the future, and many are already appearing in the *Rare Record Price Guide*.

The other area where vinyl continues to play an important, if minor, role is in the reissue market. Once again, CDs dominate proceedings these days, but collectors of soul, dance, R&B, film soundtracks and other specialist genres have been delighted to see limited edition vinyl LPs making an appearance in the shops and mail-order lists. As soon as these releases sell out, they immediately become collector's items.

Vinyl rarities have also left their mark in a more surprising arena — the regular auctions of rock and pop memorabilia staged in London by Christie's and Sotheby's. Signed albums, one-off acetates and ultra-rare collectables regularly turn up in these sales, often fetching remarkably high prices.

FROM STREET MARKETS TO THE NET

The record collecting market began to take shape in the late 60s, when the first professional dealers began to sell rare rock'n'roll and beat group releases at street markets in London. In the early 70s, the first collector's shops appeared across the country, and the path was set for the multi-million-pound international business that exists today. The world of collecting has expanded in other ways as well, and it now covers every imaginable form of popular music, from the early 1950s to the present day.

Over the last five years, collecting has taken another giant leap, onto the internet. Websites like *Record Collector*'s own **www.rcsetsale.com** now offer the chance to browse through tens of thousands of collectable records.

There are now many rare record auctions being conducted online, although many collectors who use the net have expressed reservations about buying records this way, as they are put off by the high reserve prices being asked for many quite common items, and also worry that some dealers may be bidding against themselves to artificially inflate the prices. Certainly there is no sign at the moment that the net will replace the traditional marketplace of shops, fairs and mail-order adverts, but the power of the web is obviously bringing the pleasures of collecting to a new international audience.

PRICING RECORDS

There is no fixed price for any secondhand record. The price is determined by what the buyer is prepared to pay, and what the seller will accept.

What's more, values can fluctuate wildly from region to region. Funk records, for example, tend to sell for more in London than in the north of England, while the reverse is true of heavy metal.

It's also true that the asking price for a particular record might

ELVIS PRESLEY

vary depending on whether it is sold through a shop, online, a record fair or through the pages of *Record Collector*. There are no hard-and-fast rules governing the valuation of a record. But with our long experience of the market, stretching back over more than 20 years, we've been able to work out the fairest possible price for each release.

There's one more important thing to remember: if you're selling to a shop or dealer, you can't expect to get more than 50% of the price listed here. That's a standard mark-up that applies right across the collecting scene. Professional dealers have their overheads to cover and a profit margin to make. If you want the top price, you should sell privately to another collector, through the pages of *Record Collector*.

THE EXPANDING MARKET

As the number of collectable records has grown, so has the market. Each new generation of record-buyers has spawned its own hard core of collectors, many of them inspired to investigate music from the past by the quantity and quality of reissue CDs which are being released every month. These days, there are almost as many reissues reaching the shelves as there are new recordings. These have helped to focus attention on the original releases.

But collecting isn't always about the past. This book features thousands of records from the last few years which have already become collector's items. Some of these are limited editions, cleverly marketed by record companies to capitalise on the collecting boom. Others are early releases by artists who have gone on to enjoy some kind of fame or notoriety over the next few years. Collectors new and old relish the challenge and excitement of tracking down these releases. Whether you're hunting for rare rock'n'roll singles from the 50s, or the latest limited edition singles, the *Rare Record Price Guide* will help you get the most out of your collecting.

HOW TO USE THE GUIDE

PRICING YOUR RECORDS

Although the *Rare Record Price Guide 2002* contains a comprehensive listing of collectable U.K. releases, it does NOT list all the recordings made by the artists we've included. Complete discographies of important artists can be found every month in *Record Collector* magazine.

MINIMUM VALUES FOR INCLUSION

ONLY THOSE RELEASES WHICH ARE CURRENTLY SOLD AT THE MINIMUM VALUES LISTED BELOW HAVE BEEN INCLUDED.

Any other releases obviously sell for less than these prices.

```
7" SINGLES, MAXI-SINGLES, CASSETTE SINGLES,
   DOUBLE PACKS & FLEXIDISCS ........................................£4
78s ...................................................................................£5
10" SINGLES: ....................................................................£5
EPs, 12" SINGLES, CASSETTE EPs AND CD SINGLES ......£7
LPs.....................................................................................£10
DOUBLE-LPs .....................................................................£14
CD ALBUMS........................................................................£15
```

NOTE: EPs from the 1950s and 1960s usually sold at around twice the retail price of a 7" single. But most so-called EPs released since 1976 actually retailed at the same price as 7" singles. These records have been included in the Guide if they are worth £4 or more.

CURRENT MINT VALUES

The prices listed in this book are for the original issues of records, cassettes and CDs in MINT condition. Bear in mind that most records which turn up from the 1950s, 60s and even the early 1970s are NOT in Mint condition and their value will be affected accordingly. To find out the value of any item which is in less than Mint condition, consult our Grading System on page 1534 and the Ready Reckoner on page 1535.

ALPHABETICAL ORDER

The artists in this Guide are listed in alphabetical order, from A to Z. After the alphabetical listings, there is a section of Various Artists compilation releases, divided into several sections covering singles and 50s & 60s EPs, 70s, 80s & 90s EPs, LPs, film soundtrack LPs and original cast recordings from theatrical shows.

The alphabetical order within the Guide has been determined by the first letter of a group name or an artist's surname. The word 'the' has not been included when placing artists in alphabetical order; for instance, 'The Verve' are listed under 'V', rather than 'T'.

The order follows the usual alphabetical principle of 'reading through' an artist's name or title, so that (for example) 'Peter Gabriel' is listed before 'Gabriel's Angels', and 'Generation X' is listed before 'Gen X'. Names and titles which include numbers appear as if the number was spelt out in full; e.g. the band '2.3' are listed as if their name was 'Two.Three'.

CHRONOLOGICAL ORDER

Within each artist entry, records are listed in chronological order of release. Singles (including 7", 10", 12", CD, cassette, and double packs) are listed first; then EPs; and finally LPs (including cassette and CD albums).

In the case of long entries, different formats of releases have also been grouped together under separate headers to make them easier to find.

PACKAGING AND INSERTS

All prices refer to records with all their original packaging and inserts (where applicable) intact. Wherever possible, we have provided details of inserts and special items of packaging for each entry — pointing out gatefold sleeves, lyric sheets and other bonus items like posters, for example.

Any record with some or all of these additional items missing will obviously be worth less than the values listed here. The level of depreciation depends on the missing items: in some cases, the value of an album can be dramatically reduced without its collectable insert (as in the case of the Who's "The Who Sell Out" LP, for example), while in others, it is the record itself that is desirable, and the insert is only of secondary importance (as with the two various-artists albums, "Samantha Promotions").

DOUBLE PRICES: PICTURE SLEEVES

Since 1978, all U.K. 7", 10" and 12" singles have usually been issued in picture sleeves. Before 1978, however, picture covers were definitely the exception rather than the rule.

All those singles which originally appeared in a picture sleeve are listed with the abbreviation '(p/s)'. Where the picture sleeve was only available with the first batch of singles, there are two prices listed: the first refers to the record with its picture sleeve, the second without. If only one price is listed, then the single has to have its picture sleeve intact and in Mint condition to quality for this value.

Most singles from the 1950s, 1960s and early 1970s were issued in 'company' sleeves, carrying the name and logo of the label which issued the record. Unless a picture sleeve is indicated, the prices listed in this guide are for singles with their company sleeves intact and, like the records themselves, in Mint condition. Most collectors are not too concerned about company sleeves — although in isolated cases (like the cult 60s label Planet), the company sleeves can be harder to find than the records themselves.

Company sleeves don't usually have much effect on a record's value. For example, an original Kinks single from 1966, valued at £5, may only be worth £4.50 without its Pye company sleeve. At the other extreme, no rock'n'roll collector is going to be bothered if a copy of a rarity like Bobby Charles' "See You Later Alligator", valued at £2750, comes in a plain sleeve, or indeed, no sleeve at all — what matters here is that the record is in Mint condition.

DOUBLE PRICES: FREEBIES & INSERTS

Two prices have been listed for those items which were available in more than one form. 'Freebie' singles given away with newspapers and magazines have two values: the first for the record with the publication, the second for the disc itself. Records which were issued only briefly with an insert, like a poster or lyric sheet, are often priced both with and without the extra packaging.

DOUBLE PRICES: CHANGES IN DESIGN

Two or more prices have been given for records which were released more than once with the same catalogue number, but in slightly different form — with a change of label colour or sleeve design (for instance, the substitution of triangular centres by round centres on late 1950s singles), or the manufacture of more recent singles in a variety of different coloured vinyls.

These variations of packaging and presentation can make an enormous difference to the value of a record, which is why we have documented them here. They help collectors identify the first pressing or edition of each release, which is almost always more sought-after than later issues of the same record. One notable example is the first edition of the Beatles' "Please Please Me" LP, which featured the black-and-gold Parlophone label for a few weeks, before the introduction of the more modern-looking yellow-and-black label. Black-and-gold copies of the stereo version of this LP are worth £1750, as against £100 for the first yellow-and-black edition issued a few weeks later.

Occasionally, second pressings can be worth more than the originals, as is the case with early Shadows and Cliff Richard singles. Green label copies of these 45s sold in their millions, while later re-pressings on black labels are much scarcer. So always check which pressing of any record you are buying before parting with your money.

MONO AND STEREO

In the case of EPs and LPs from the 1950s and 1960s, mono and stereo releases often have different values — and different catalogue numbers. Both prices are listed, together with the separate catalogue numbers for the two versions of each release (mono first, then stereo). Where the mono and stereo editions are worth the same amount, only one price has been listed.

The last few years have seen a polarisation in the prices between mono and stereo pressings — increasingly so for those late mono releases from 1968 to 1970, when the single-channeled format was being phased out in favour of the twin-tracked stereo. Similarly, early stereo editions should prove to be sound investments.

U.K. RELEASES AND EXPORT ISSUES

Only U.K. releases are included in the *Rare Record Price Guide*, not overseas issues. The exceptions to this rule are a handful of folk releases, U2 singles and Boyzone releases, all from the Irish Republic, which were heavily imported into Britain, but not officially issued here. The other exceptions are 'Export Releases'. These were manufactured in the U.K. in the 1950s and 1960s by companies like EMI and Decca for distribution to countries which didn't have their own pressing plants. Because they were pressed in very small quantities, and then distributed to the furthest corners of the globe, export records by artists like the Beatles and the Rolling Stones are often worth many times the values of similar items pressed for the U.K.

U.K. RELEASES PRESSED OVERSEAS

Although the great majority of the records we've listed were manufactured in the U.K., not all U.K. releases were made in this country — or vice versa. For example, a large proportion of the Rolling Stones' U.S. singles on the London label in the 1960s were actually manufactured in Britain. More recently, many British releases by major labels — notably WEA — have been made in Europe, and sent in identical form to Britain and many other countries. In these cases, the record sleeves often carry many different catalogue numbers, to cater for every country where the records are being distributed.

The problem of identifying the country where a particular record has been issued has grown more difficult with the advent of CDs. In these cases, it is the packaging that helps you identify the origin of a particular CD, rather than the disc itself.

78rpm RELEASES

The market for 78rpm singles has undergone a revival in recent years. The common misconception about 78s is that they are more valuable than 7" singles. In fact, the opposite is true in most cases, as far more 78s were sold in the 1950s than 45rpm 7" singles.

The last batches of 78s issued from 1958 to 1960 are the main exception to this rule (see Elvis Presley's entry, for example). As these were often only available in small quantities (as the public switched to 45s), or even by special order, they can prove to be much harder to find than their 45rpm equivalents.

All these collectable 78s from the 1950s are included in this edition of the *Rare Record Price Guide*, although we've removed those titles issued prior to 1950 because, these represent a completely different era of popular music. The vast majority of 78s, it should be added, are worth less than £5.

COMMERCIAL RELEASES, NOT PROMOS

In general, this Guide only includes records which were manufactured for commercial release, or for distribution in some way to the public — as a freebie with a magazine, for example.

Promotional records, demos, acetates and test pressings have not usually been included, apart from exceptional cases where these items actually reached the public, or where (as with artists like Blinky & Edwin Starr) one promo single has become so famous among collectors that it would have been misleading for it not to be mentioned. The major exceptions to this rule are artists like the Beatles, and modern artists like U2 and Oasis, whose promos are often more valuable than many of their commercial releases.

Full details of the values of non-commercial rarities like promos, demos, acetates and test pressings can be found in the articles and discographies in *Record Collector* every month.

IMPORTANT NOTE

Every effort has been taken to ensure that the information contained in this Price Guide is as accurate and up-to-date as possible. However, the publishers cannot take any responsibility for any errors or omissions; nor can they be held responsible or liable for any loss or damage to any person acting on the information in this Guide. The publishers welcome any corrections or additions to the Guide, which will be considered for future editions.

THE HISTORY OF THE
RARE RECORD PRICE GUIDE

RECORD COLLECTOR MAGAZINE

Record Collector was first published in 1979, and over the last twenty years, the magazine has established itself as the bible of Pop and Rock history. When the magazine was born, record collecting was a small, rather disorganised business, which wasn't making much effort to encourage new people to get involved.

From the start, *Record Collector* set out to provide the information that collectors needed, whether they'd been buying and selling records for years, or were just starting to build up a collection. There were two vital things they wanted to know: what records had been released by their favourite artists, and how much were they worth?

Every issue of *Record Collector* has provided complete discographies (lists of record releases, complete with full catalogue numbers, release dates and current Mint values) for an amazing variety of performers, from pre-rock stars like Frank Sinatra to the latest chart-bound arrivals like Travis and Geri Halliwell, via every imaginable style and genre along the way. Our in-depth features have provided the essential information to help readers get the most out of their music — by explaining the history of the artists and the records.

A DOZEN YEARS OF THE
RARE RECORD PRICE GUIDE

In 1987, we published our first price guide — a slim volume which was designed as a quick and easy reference source to records by around 2,000 important artists.

That was only the beginning, though. We soon began work on the first edition of the book you're holding. Published in late 1992, the first *Rare Record Price Guide* filled 960 pages and listed 60,000 rare and collectable records.

The response to that book was tremendous, but we quickly realised that the collecting market was changing so fast that we couldn't rest on our laurels. Every year, thousands of new records reach the shops, in a bewildering variety of formats — everything from 7" singles and cassettes to expensive multi-CD boxed sets.

A small but sizeable proportion of these new releases became instant collector's items. Over the last twenty years, it's been common for record companies to issue special limited editions — anything from a few hundred to a few thousand copies — which sell out in a few days. The most sought-after of these records can triple or quadruple their value within a few months.

At the same time, interest in vinyl from the past continues to grow. As collectors track down all the records they want in a particular genre, they start to broaden their horizons. As a result, obscure items from the 50s, 60s, 70s and 80s become much-wanted treasures on the collector's market — and their prices rise to reflect the new demand.

That's why we published a second edition, a year later, which grew to 1,152 pages, with 70,000 records listed. And this was expanded again for the 1995 edition (over 75,000 entries and 1,252 pages) and 1997/98 edition (85,000 entries and 1,440 pages), to take in all the latest collectable release The Millennium Edition ran to 1,504 pages, and now, another two years on, the *Rare Record Price Guide 2002* is bigger than ever.

THE BIRTH OF COLLECTING

When the collecting scene was in its infancy in the 1970s, the market was focused on particular artists or genres. All the early attention was concentrated on 1950s rock'n'roll, and 1960s beat music. In addition, major artists like the Beatles, the Rolling Stones, Elvis Presley and David Bowie began to attract specialist collectors. But the whole collecting scene blossomed during the 1980s and it's now true to say that there aren't any musical styles which *aren't* collectable. Folk, jazz, techno, rap, blues, heavy metal, punk, psychedelia, progressive rock, film soundtracks, soul, funk, reggae, disco, mainstream rock and pop, even classical — each genre boasts its share of in-demand rarities.

LIMITED EDITIONS

In the late 1970s, the arrival of punk spawned scores of new, independent record labels, which had fresh views about the way to market their releases. It became common for singles to appear in picture sleeves, as they had done overseas since the 1960s.

Records also began to appear on coloured vinyl or as picture discs, in an attempt to attract more buyers. Never slow to cash in on a marketing trend, the major record companies soon joined in. By the early 1980s, they were issuing a bewildering variety of editions of the same record in slightly different formats.

This sudden change in marketing techniques helped to trigger an entirely new development on the collecting scene. For the first time, records were becoming instant collector's items. A limited-edition single could be released one week, and sell for twice its retail price a fortnight later.

That opened the floodgates. No longer were 1950s and 1960s records the only things you'd find in the collector's shops. Now, it was open season, for anything and everything from Elvis Presley to Madonna.

COMPACT DISCS

The arrival of CDs in the mid-1980s was greeted with doom and gloom in some quarters. But some CDs — notably compilations of old, obscure 45s — have actually helped to increase the market for old vinyl releases. So many vintage recordings are available on CD that record-buyers today have a wider musical choice than ever before.

If you grew up in the 1960s, you probably remember that it was difficult to find the records that had been hits only a few years earlier. Now, you can go into most record stores and buy compilations of music from every era of pop and rock history. For thousands of collectors, however, owning the music on a new CD isn't enough — and they track down the original releases of music made before they were born.

Fifteen years later, the CD is well established as a collectable format — particularly for promotional items, limited edition singles, and CD issues by 80s artists which have yet to be reissued.

STATE OF THE MARKET

The arrival of a new century has coincided with many changes in the state of the record collecting market. In this sixth edition of the *Rare Record Price Guide*, we cover all the rare and collectable releases issued in Britain from 1950 (when rock'n'roll wasn't even on the horizon) to the latest instant collector's items in the pop, indie, rock and dance fields.

One of the most important developments in recent years has been the way that promotional releases — which in theory are only given to DJs, journalists and other music business insiders, to promote a new release or artist — have begun to dominate the market as far as modern artists are concerned. There has always been a steady market for rare promo items, especially those which included recordings that weren't available on commercial releases. But these days almost all of the most collectable items by the major contemporary pop and rock artists, from the Spice Girls to Travis, are promos.

As a result, we have decided to include many of these promo rarities in the *Rare Record Price Guide*, particularly for those artists who have a strong following among collectors, but whose commercial releases have produced very few real rarities. This trend, which is noticeable among many of the artists who emerged in the 90s, seems likely to continue in the future. In this edition, artists like Geri Halliwell, Oasis, Travis and Stereophonics are heavily represented by promos, while their releases that were commercially available over the counter are much less important in the collector's market. The exception that proves the rule is Boyzone, whose early Irish singles have become their prime collectables in recent months.

THE BEATLES — the world's most collectable group.

THE CARDIGANS

Because of the potential rarity value of many promos, some collectors assume that any promotional item is automatically worth more than a commercial release by the same artist. But that's not always true. Though it's often the case that promos sell for two or three times the value of normal releases, there are many promos which are actually easier to find than their commercial equivalents. And while their 80s and 90s counterparts are fascinated by promos, most collectors of 50s releases still tend to prefer commercial releases instead.

Every new edition of the *Rare Record Price Guide* gives us the opportunity to revise and update the entries for the major artists who dominate the collecting scene. The Beatles are still by far the most collectable artists of all time, and their entry has been completely re-organised for this edition. Much new information has emerged in recent years about the different pressings of the 60s releases, and the Beatles entry in this book will enable collectors to tell at a glance whether they have an original single or LP in their hands. While the general financial trend for Beatles collectables is always up, it's noticeable that the demand for later pressings of their 60s releases has dropped quite considerably, so it is very important that you study the small print in the Beatles entry — and indeed on their records, as tiny alterations in the copyright wording or label design of Beatles singles can make a sizeable difference to their value.

Besides making the Beatles entry the most comprehensive listing of Fab Four rarities ever published, we've also included photographs of all the different variations in Parlophone company sleeves, to make the job of locating originals that much easier.

Prices for Elvis Presley rarities are generally keeping pace with inflation, and that's also true for 50s rock'n'roll items in general. Demand for 78rpm singles has been relatively static in recent times, although we have unearthed some more rarities and included them in the Guide for the first time.

THE BEAUTIFUL SOUTH

As we noted in our Millennium Edition, one real growth area for both 50s and 60s music is in the field of British modern jazz. Prices are still rising after the huge increases we noticed last time, and jazz purists may be surprised to learn that British performers like Tubby Hayes, Ronnie Scott and the London Jazz Orchestra are now much more collectable than their more famous US counterparts, like Miles Davis and John Coltrane.

Much of the demand for these British jazz records has come from Japan — in fact, Japanese collectors helped to fuel a 90s price boom in many other areas of collecting as well. More recently, of course, the Japanese economy has suffered something of a downturn, and there seems to be less Japanese money coming into the UK market at the moment. Surprisingly, though, this doesn't seem to have had an adverse effect on prices in areas like UK jazz, progressive rock and 60s psychedelia, all of which were popular with Japanese collectors in the past.

This edition includes expanded coverage of many other genres, including oi!, virtually the only punk/new wave genre to show a marked increase in prices; soul, especially from the early 70s; NWOBHM, the critically despised heavy metal explosion of the early 80s (note the remarkable price of the recently discovered compilation, "Kent Rocks"); folk and progressive folk; and Christian rock, where almost everything on 70s labels like Myrrh is attracting interest from collectors; like the 90s boom in private pressings, this trend has been inspired by collectors who have already tracked down the more mainstream rarities, and are now searching for something more esoteric.

Despite the media hype about a 70s revival, it's the 80s which is showing most sign of a nostalgic rise in interest. Groups like Blancmange, A Flock Of Seagulls and the Thompson Twins, who were almost laughable in collector's circles a year ago, have made a strong comeback over the last few months. The effect has been noticeable across the board, with the Associates, ABC and even Level 42 benefiting. But the revival has so far ignored Spandau Ballet.

While 80s pop has been enjoying a boom period, the mid-to-late 80s indie music that followed it has dipped in popularity — as have some of the 90s artists in the same field. Interest in acts like the Wedding Present and the Weather Prophets has definitely waned over the last two years, while Britpop acts like Cornershop, Sleeper and Menswear have effectively vanished off the collecting map. But it can't be too long before we're due for a 90s revival, which would rekindle enthusiasm for bands like these.

In keeping with trends over the last five years, it's true that the rarer an item is, the more quickly its value continues to rise — and vice versa. Many standard 7" and 12" singles by late 80s and early 90s stars, like the Wonder Stuff, Madonna and Prince, have lost some of their value; but their CD equivalents, which were much scarcer at the time, have soared by comparison. Some artists from this era have made a remarkable impact on the collecting scene in recent months, like the Beautiful South (who have a sizeable new entry in this edition) and the Cardigans, now one of the most popular European bands — especially, yet again, in Japan.

Some areas of collecting never lose their appeal, and the demand for rarities in the psych, prog, industrial and soul genres is as heavy as ever. There has also been heavy demand for 'cool' jazz releases by Hammond organ exponents like Jimmy Smith, while the constant search by DJs for new breakbeats recently fuelled a revival in early Ska star Jackie Mittoo. Brazilian club music, particularly from the Tropicalia era, is also proving very popular, while by contrast the Easy boom of the last five years is showing signs of settling down.

Besides pinpointing the trends and artists who are pulling in the collectors, this edition of the *Rare Record Price Guide* also provides the answer to many queries which have puzzled collectors for years. We've finally been able to prove, for example, that the legendary David Bowie "Space Oddity" picture sleeve from 1969 is a legitimate item, manufactured for in-house use at Philips, and now worth in excess of £3,000. But another elusive collectable, the 1982 reissue of the LP "The Beatles' First", has been omitted from this edition — for the simple reason that it definitely doesn't exist!

DAVID BOWIE

ACKNOWLEDGEMENTS

CONSULTANTS
Jonathan Benton-Hughes, Mark Brennan, Bob Brooks (Reggae Revive), Johnny Chandler (Division 1), Ben Cree (Mole Jazz), John Esplen (Overground Records), John Fisher (Recent & Rare Records), Chris Giles (The Elvis Shop), Dizzy Holmes (Detour Records), Mark Hosken (Hedonizm), Terry Hunt, Nigel Ince, Michael De Koningh, Nigel Lees, Mark Mastrangelo (Beano's), Andrew Neill (On The Beat), Vince Oldham, Alan Ould (Good Humour Records), Alan Parker, Ray Platt, Lee & Paul Phelps (Energy Mail Order), Mark Powell, John Reed, Nick Salomon, Philip Spelman, Spencer Streeter (G & S Music), Neil Thompson, Mark 'Nathan Detroit' Troster, David Wells, Deke Wheeler, Eric White, Dave Wilson

THANKS ALSO TO
Mike Atherton, Tony Boothroyd (Vinyl Tap), Rob Caiger, Laurence Cane-Honeysett, Ian Chapman, Martin Edmunds, Dave Ferguson, John Gray, Jason Hodgson, Adrian Horton (Madhouse Music), Chris Jones (Rock Of Ages), Dave Lewis, Ade Macrow, Dave McFeat, Terry McLaughlin, Steve Pafford, Paul Pelletier, Martin Pike, Glenn Povey, Tim Sinzenich, Greg Vandike, Adam Walton, Huw Williams

SPECIAL THANKS FOR THEIR HELP
Walter Geertson, Alex Hogg, Marshall Jarman, Jon Jemmett, Phil Lee (Norman Records), Rob Jovanovich, Diane Le Page, Des McMahon, Peter Nash, Wolfram Roddewig, Phil Smee (Waldo's/Strange Things), Lee Stevens, Johnny Tree, Mike Vandenbosch (More Than Music), Filip De Volder

THANKS TO THE FOLLOWING FANZINES
Nova Lepidoptera (Barclay James Harvest), Blur FC, Blues Matters!/ Shades Of Savoy Brown, Secret Public (Buzzcocks), Sidetaulk (Capercaillie), The Caravan Newsletter, North South East & West (The Church), Where's Eric! (Eric Clapton), Friends Of The Dave Clark Five, The Crickets File, The Deep Purple Appreciation Society, Donovan's Friends, Isis (Bob Dylan), Return Of Voodoo (Echo & Bunnymen), Twangsville (Duane Eddy), The Biggest Library Yet (The Fall), Crystal (Fleetwood Mac), Free Appreciation Society, About Lake Five (IQ), MJ News International (Michael Jackson), Change Of Scenery (James), We Will Let You Know (King Crimson), The Official Kinks Fan Club, Goin' Blind (Kiss), Nut Inc. (Madness), Brave Hearts Collection (Marillion), Official Meat Loaf Fan Club, Head (The Monkees), Motörheadbangers, Mungo Jerry International Fan Club, The Side Parting Is Dead (Gary Numan), Voyage 35 (Porcupine Tree), Ramones UK Fan Club, Spirit Of Rush, Darlings Of Wapping Wharf (Small Faces), Looks Aren't Everything (Sparks), Dusty Springfield Bulletin, Cut Above The Rest (The Sweet), Voyager (Tangerine Dream), Ventures . . . Resurgence, Naked Eye (The Who), Neil Young Appreciation Society, T'Mershi Duween (Frank Zappa)

THANKS ALSO TO THE FOLLOWING FANZINES AND FAN CLUBS (PAST AND PRESENT) FOR THEIR ASSISTANCE

Agnetha, Benny, Bjorn, Frida Fanclub (Abba), Electric Outlaws (AC/DC), A-Ha Fanclub, Grit & Glitter (Marc Almond/Soft Cell), Why Are We Sleeping (Kevin Ayers), Banglemania (Bangles), Chapter 24 (Syd Barrett), Jeff Beck Bulletin, B-Hive (B-52's), The Tony Bennett Appreciation Society, On The Run (Blackfoot), Southern Cross (Black Sabbath), Oasis (Blondie/Debbie Harry), Marc Bolan Liberation Front, Photograph (Colin Blunstone), James Bond Collector's Club, Late For The Sky (Jackson Browne), Sabre Dance (Budgie), Late For The Real World (Buzzcocks), Full Circle (Byrds), Open House (John Cale), Belinda Mania Fraternity (Belinda Carlisle), Carterzine (Carter USM), The Man In Black (Johnny Cash), Talk Is Cheap (Cheap Trick), Cheap Trickzine, Lightning Strikes (Lou Christie), Petula (Petula Clark), Petula & Company (Petula Clark), Leonard Cohen Information Service, So Far . . . (Crosby, Stills & Nash), Sheer Cult (Cult), George O'Dowd Fanclub (Culture Club/Boy George), Mystery Of The Damned, International Chrysis (Dead Or Alive), UHCK (Deviants/Pink Fairies), Keep On Running (Dexy's Midnight Runners), Curbjob (Dickies), Yo Frankie (Dion), Donovan's Friends, The Soft Parade (Doors), Pink Moon (Nick Drake), A Kind Of Love In (Julie Driscoll), The Dutch Go Duran (Duran Duran), The Krush Brothers (Duran Duran), Crossfire (Echo & Bunnymen/Electrafixion), The Duane Eddy Circle, Extreme Li'l Fanzine, Friends Of Fairport (Fairport Convention), Back On The Road (Fleetwood Mac/Stevie Nicks), Lonely Is . . . (4AD), Official International Billy Fury Appreciation Society, Kontakt (Peter Gabriel), Queerest (Garbage), The Waiting Room (Genesis), Proclamation (Gentle Giant), The Debbie Gibson Fanzine, Airwaves (Gordon Giltrap), Rebels Without Applause (Sid Griffin), In Touch (Daryl Hall & John Oates), My Only Vice (Steve Harley), Hors d'Oeuvres (Roy Harper), Hawkeye (Hawkwind), Jimpress (Jimi Hendrix), Univibes (Jimi Hendrix), Brenda Of The Lightbulb Eyes (Robyn Hitchcock), Carousel Newsletter (Hollies), Friends Of Holly Society (Buddy Holly), The Factory (Hothouse Flowers), The Outsider (Ian Hunter/Mick Ronson/Mott The Hoople), Wild Youth (Billy Idol), Pipeline (instrumental music), Billie Jean (Michael Jackson), Man In The Mirror (Michael Jackson), Jackson (Michael Jackson), Jackson — The Black & White Billboard (Michael Jackson), Start! (Jam), Spirit (Brian Jones), Virtual Vortex (k.d. lang), Barefoot (k.d. lang), Angel With An Attitude (k.d. lang), Raymond Paul (Kiss Army International), Kiss Kollector, Aktivitat (Kraftwerk), Fire-Ball Mail (Jerry Lee Lewis), Love Is In The Air (Lindisfarne), Apollox (Love & Rockets/Bauhaus), Dita (Madonna), Stay Beautiful (Manic Street Preachers), 4-Real (Manic Street Preachers), Distant Drums (Bob Marley), The Dean Martin Association, Rising Sun (Medicine Head), Word Is Out! (Kylie/Dannii Minogue), Guy Mitchell Appreciation Society, Band 6 (Monkees UK Fan Club), And Now For Something Completely Different (Monty Python), Emerald Blues (Gary Moore), Razamanewz (Nazareth), Only Olivia (Olivia Newton-John), Stevie Nicks Fanzine, In Bloom (Nirvana), Asylum (Gary Numan), World Storm (Gary Numan), Headshrinker (Oasis), Splishin' (Oasis), Hiawatha (Mike Oldfield), Dark Star (Mike Oldfield), Airborne (Mike Oldfield), View From A Beacon (Mike Oldfield), Paradis Club (Vanessa Paradis), Why? (Pearl Jam), Shire News (Steve Peregrine Took Appreciation Society), Makin' Some Noise (Tom Petty), Brain Damage (Pink Floyd), Interstellar Overdrive (Pink Floyd), The Amazing Pudding (Pink Floyd), Suzi & Other Four Letter Words (Suzi Quatro), Princes Of The Universe (Queen), Radiohead World Service, Ramones Ramones, Destiny (Johnnie Ray), Cliff United (Cliff Richard), Constantly Cliff (Cliff Richard), Shattered International Fan Club (Rolling Stones), Tumbling Dice (Rolling Stones), Scarred For Life (Rose Tattoo), Never Trust A Hippy (Sex Pistols), Shadsfax (Shadows), A Rough Guide To Rarities (Siouxsie & Banshees), Ogden's Newsletter (Small Faces), Miserable Lies (Smiths/Morrissey), Frankly Charming (Smiths/Morrissey), World Service (Spear Of Destiny/Theatre Of Hate), The Jersey Devil (Bruce Springsteen), The Ragamuffin Gunner's Club (Bruce Springsteen), Soul Deep (Lisa Stansfield), Smiler (Rod Stewart), Ride On! (Stone Roses), A Blast Of Pop (Take That), Strangled (Stranglers), Suave (Suede), Everything Changes (Take That), Voyager (Tangerine Dream), The Whole Point (James Taylor Quartet), Telex UK Fan Club, Looney Tunes (Telex), Simply The Best (Tina Turner), Misty Green & Blue (UFO Appreciation Society), Official Uriah Heep Appreciation Society, Silver & Gold (U2), Pilgrims (Van Der Graaf Generator), Bobby Vee Connection, Walkerpeople (Walker Brothers), The Walkers (Walker Brothers), Waves (Clifford T. Ward), Weller Is Back! (Paul Weller/TSC/Jam), Boys About Town (Paul Weller/TSC/Jam), The Wilde Connection (Kim Wilde), Coloured Rain (Stevie Winwood/Traffic), Hot Ash (Wishbone Ash), The Revealing (Yes), Broken Arrow (Neil Young).

USING THE GUIDE
A BRIEF SUMMARY

ALL PRICES REFER TO RECORDS
AND PACKAGING IN MINT CONDITION

(See pages 1534/1535 for Grading System and Ready Reckoner)

ARTISTS AND GROUPS are listed in alphabetical order.

Numerical names (e.g. 2.3) are listed as if the numbers are spelt in full (i.e. Two.Three).

ALL RECORDS LISTED ARE
U.K. COMMERCIAL RELEASES

with the following exceptions:

> (1) Records pressed in the U.K. for export overseas.
>
> (2) Important demo or promo releases.
>
> (3) Records or flexidiscs included as freebies with magazines, books and other records.

In general, promo and demo editions are not included, except when these records contain unique material and/or packaging, or are by major collectable artists.

EACH ENTRY includes:

> SINGLES (7" 45s & cassettes) valued at £4 or more
>
> 78s and 10" singles valued at £5 or more
>
> EPs, 12" singles & CD singles valued at £7 or more
>
> LPs valued at £10 or more
>
> DOUBLE-LPs valued at £14 or more
>
> CD ALBUMS valued at £15 or more
>
> Records worth less than these prices have not been included.

WITHIN EACH ENTRY, records are listed in chronological

order of release, within each of the following categories (where applicable):

78s, SINGLES, EPs, LPs, CDs, PROMOS. The exceptions are major artists like the Beatles, the Rolling Stones and Elvis Presley, where the entry is further divided into originals, reissues and label variations.

Where TWO PRICES are listed for a single item, they refer to

> (a) the record with and without a special insert or piece of packaging
>
> (b) mono and stereo editions of EPs and LPs
>
> (c) pressings of the same record with different label or sleeve designs.

IMPORTANT TERMS
USED IN THIS GUIDE

acetate	one-off disc cut by hand in a mastering studio, used for demonstration purposes
adaptor	plastic outer disc clipped onto 3" CDs to make them compatible with 5" CD players
art sleeve	pictorial cover using graphics rather than photographs or drawings
artwork	original design for sleeves or labels
audiophile pressing	high quality pressing for hi-fi enthusiasts
blister pack	shaped outer PVC packaging, usually for 3" CDs
bonus disc	disc given away free with another disc
bootleg	illegal pressing of material not intended for official release
box set	records or CDs in presentation case
budget release	pressing which retailed below full-price
catalogue number	manufacturer's reference number on record labels and sleeves
CD-R	one-off CD, digital equivalent of acetate
CD-ROM	audio/visual computer-compatible CD
CD Video	5" CD containing several audio tracks and (usually) one video track; now obsolete
company sleeve	standard non-picture sleeve for singles, printed with name or logo of label
counterfeit	illegal reproduction of official release
DAT	digital audio tape
deleted	no longer commercially available
demo	record issued for demonstration purposes; not commercially available
die-cut sleeve	sleeve with circular hole cut into the centre
digipak	gatefold CD sleeve with plastic inner tray
DJ-only	record issued for radio airplay only
double groove	record with two grooves pressed concentrically on same side
double pack	two singles issued together as one package
8-track cartridge	1970s tape format, popular for in-car entertainment; now obsolete
EP	extended play disc, with four or more tracks, usually in a picture sleeve
EPK	electronic press kit; i.e. short promo-only documentary available on video
envelope p/s	large mailing-type cover with envelope-style foldover flap
etched disc	one-sided vinyl record with laser-etched graphics (e.g. group's signatures) on other side
export issue	record or CD pressed in the U.K. for sale exclusively overseas
factory custom pressing	unofficial record pressed after hours (usually on coloured vinyl) at official pressing plant
flexidisc	thin, flexible record, usually issued free with magazine, etc.
flipback sleeve	LP or EP cover glued together with card flaps from the front folded over onto the back
foldaround/foldout/ foldover sleeve	sleeve which opens out as a poster, etc.
freebie	record given away free of charge
gatefold sleeve	double-size sleeve opening out like a book
import	record or CD pressed abroad but sold in the U.K.
inlay	printed paper booklet with CD packaging
inner sleeve	protective sleeve inside main cover
insert	loose item included as part of a record's packaging, e.g. postcard, poster, lyric sheet, etc.
interview album	spoken word record, often used as promo
jewel case	standard clear plastic case for cassettes and CDs

jukebox centre	plastic centre inserted into record with large centre hole
jukebox issue	record issued exclusively to jukebox franchise holders
laminated sleeve	cover with high-gloss plastic coating
large centre hole	$1\frac{1}{2}$ inch (3.8 cm) hole in singles
long box	tall, rectangular outer card packaging for CDs
LP	long playing vinyl record; standard album format superseded by CDs
matrix number	master tape number, scratched into the 'land' or run-off groove area; sometimes also found on the record label
maxi-single	early 70s term for an EP, featuring more than two tracks, often in a picture sleeve
megamix	medley of different tracks, often linked by dance beats
mid-price release	record which retails at a discount
mispressing	record or CD pressed with incorrect material
mono	one-channelled playback system
numbered (no'd)	individually numbered, limited edition release
obi	sealed paper strip wrapped around sleeve of disc; originated in Japan where obis were printed with Japanese translations of foreign titles
one-sided	vinyl record which plays on one side only
picture disc	novelty record made by sealing a picture within clear vinyl
picture sleeve	pictorial paper or card sleeve, used specifically for one particular record
plain sleeve	single sleeve without special printing or artwork
premium	record available via a special offer with another product — e.g. food or drink
press kit	information pack with photos and biography, used by record companies to promote new releases
private pressing	record issued and distributed by private individuals rather than a company
promo	promotional record or item sent out to the media for publicity purposes
push-out centre	centre of a single connected to the rest of the disc at 3 or 4 points, so it can be pushed out for use on jukeboxes, etc.
quadrophonic	four-channelled playback system, now obsolete
reel-to-reel tape	1960s tape format, superseded by cassette
reissue	re-release of a deleted disc
remix	different version of existing track created by rearranging its component parts
removeable/ replaceable centre	centre which can be removed from a record without damage and later replaced (not to be confused with jukebox or 'spider' centres)
re-pressing	a second run of a record or CD which hasn't been deleted
run-off groove	groove between end of playing surface and record label
sampler	compilation showcasing an artist or label
sealed/shrinkwrapped	machine-wrapped in cellophane
shaped disc	any non-circular record
shellac	brittle material used to press 78s
slipcase	small card cover used for some CDs and cassette singles
solid centre	centre of record which cannot be removed, as on LPs
stickered sleeve	sleeve with sticker as an integral part of its packaging
stereo	two-channelled playback system
test pressing	manufacturer's sample record, pressed for quality control
tri-centre	push-out triangular centre found on some 1950s singles and EPs
tri-fold	triple fold-out sleeve
unissued/unreleased	disc not made commercially available; may or may not have been pressed
vinyl	material from which records are made
warp	buckle in vinyl caused by heat
white label	usually blank, perhaps printed or handwritten labels, often for promo purposes; term also used for demo, promo or test pressing
withdrawn	record deliberately removed from sale by its manufacturer

AARDVARK
70	Deram Nova SDN 17	AARDVARK (LP)	45

ABACUS
74	York YR 207	Indian Dancer/Be That Way	5
72	Polydor 2371 215	ABACUS (LP)	35

A BAND CALLED DORIS
(see under Doris)

ABBA
73	Epic EPC 1793	Ring Ring/Rock'N'Roll Band (yellow label)	45
74	Epic EPC 2452	Ring Ring (second version)/Rock'N'Roll Band (yellow label)	8
74	Epic EPC 2848	So Long/I've Been Waiting For You (yellow label)	15
75	Epic EPC 3229	I Do I Do I Do I Do I Do/Rock Me (yellow label)	7
79	Epic EPC 7499	Voulez Vous/Angeleyes (p/s)	7
79	Epic EPC 8088	I Have A Dream/Take A Chance On Me (live) (gatefold p/s)	12
80	Epic EPC 8835	The Winner Takes It All/Elaine (p/s)	8
80	Epic EPC 12-8835	The Winner Takes It All/Elaine (12", gatefold pop-up p/s)	40
81	Epic EPCA 13-1456	Lay All Your Love On Me/On & On & On (12" p/s)	10
81	Epic EPCA 11-1740	One Of Us/Should I Laugh Or Cry (picture disc)	12
82	Epic EPCA 11-2971	Under Attack/You Owe Me One (picture disc)	25
82	Lyntone LYN 11763	Konica Pop Flexi (1-sided flexidisc, p/s, featuring edits of Abba's "Lay All Your Love On Me" & tracks by Stars On 45 & Nolan Sisters)	7
82	Lyntone LYN 12570/1	Happy Xmas From The Stars (with other artists, flexidisc, some with *Smash Hits* magazine)	12/8
82	Epic EPCA 2618	GREATEST ORIGINAL HITS (EP)	10
82	Epic EPCA 2618	GREATEST ORIGINAL HITS (EP, cassette)	10
83	Epic A 3894	Thank You For The Music/Our Last Summer (poster p/s)	15
83	Epic WA 3894	Thank You For The Music/Our Last Summer (shaped picture disc)	25
84	Kelloggs KELL 1	I Have A Dream/SHAKIN' STEVENS: Oh Julie ('Rice Krispies' premium)	8
84	Epic ABBA 26	ANNIVERSARY BOXED SET (26 x blue vinyl 7", numbered, 2,000 only)	350
84	Epic ABBA 26	ANNIVERSARY BOXED SET (26 x black vinyl 7")	100
86	Readers Digest (no cat. no.)	The Best Of Abba (flexidisc sampler)	8
93	Polydor 859 085-2	MORE ABBA GOLD (4-track CD, promo only)	75
93	Polydor ABBA 1DJ	Summer Night City/Eagle/Ring Ring (12", 1-sided sampler, promo only)	40
94	Polydor 853 891-2	DREAM WORLD (CD, 4-track sampler, promo only)	100
99	No label ABBA 1	MAMMA MIA (4-track CD)	20
99	Polydor 563 213-2	Waterloo (CD, 1 track, promo-only)	45
99	Polydor 563 286-2	ABBA Singles Collection 1974-1982 (29 CD singles in card sleeves & 1-track CD picture disc, with booklet, in silver tin, 20,000 only)	80
74	Epic EPC 32009	WATERLOO (LP, yellow label)	15
75	Epic EPC 80835	ABBA (LP, yellow label)	15
76	Epic EPC 69218	GREATEST HITS (LP, gatefold sleeve, yellow label, some with "Fernando" sticker)	15
78	Epic EPC 86052	THE ALBUM (LP, gatefold sleeve, some with sticker)	15/12
79	Epic EPC 11-86086	VOULEZ VOUS (LP, picture disc)	70
80	Epic EPC 86123	GRACIAS POR LA MUSICA (LP)	18
80	Epic ABBOX 1	SUPER TROUPER (LP, box set with book & poster)	60
83	Epic ABBOX 11-2/ ABBA-11-10	THE SINGLES — THE FIRST TEN YEARS (2-LP, picture discs, with poster, ticket & booklet in box)	60
83	Epic EPC 10043	THANK YOU FOR THE MUSIC — A COLLECTION OF LOVE SONGS (LP)	20
83	Epic CDEPC 10022	SUPER TROUPER (CD, original issue)	20
83	Epic CDEPC 10032	THE VISITORS (CD, original issue)	20
84	St. Michael 1361/5704	THE HIT COLLECTION (cassette, with 64-page book *Their Story*, available via Marks & Spencer)	40
86	R. Digest GABA-A-112	THE BEST OF ABBA (5-LP box set)	40
86	R. Digest GABC-C-112	THE BEST OF ABBA (5-cassette box set)	50
99	Polar Music Int. ABBA.INT	THE INTERVIEW ... (CD, 12-page booklet with unique artwork)	70

(see also Hep Stars, Hootenanny Singers, Northern Lights, Agnetha Faltskog, Frida)

BILLY ABBOTT & JEWELS
63	Cameo Parkway P 874	Groovy Baby/Come On And Dance With Me	15

ABC
83	Lyntone MADDOX 1	Selections From "Beauty Stab" (flexidisc sampler, yellow or blue vinyl)	5
84	Neutron NTP 106	S.O.S./United Kingdom (picture disc)	5
85	Neutron NTD 108	Be Near To Me/A To Z//Poison Arrow (U.S. Remix)/The Look Of Love (U.S. Remix) (double pack, gatefold PVC sleeve with sticker)	6
85	Neutron NTP 109	Vanity Kills/Judy's Jewels (cartoon-shaped picture disc, PVC sleeve)	7
85	Neutron NTD 110	Ocean Blue/Tower Of London//All Of My Heart/The Look Of Love (double pack, stickered PVC gatefold p/s)	6
85	Neutron NT 110/NT 102	Ocean Blue/Tower Of London//Poison Arrow/Theme From "Mantrap" (p/s, shrinkwrapped double pack)	6
85	Neutron NTX 107	How To Be A Zillionaire (The Bond Street Mix)/How To Be A Billionaire/How To Be A Millionaire (12", p/s)	8
87	Neutron NTXG 113	King Without A Crown (Monarchy Mix)/The Look Of Love (live)/Poison Arrow (live) (12", 'gold' p/s)	8

87	Neutron NTXRG 113	King Without A Crown (The Mendelson Mix)/The Look Of Love (live)/ Poison Arrow (live)/All Of My Heart (live) (12", 'gold' p/s)	8
87	Neutron NTCD 113	King Without A Crown/The Look Of Love (live)/Poison Arrow (live)/ King Without A Crown (Monarchy Mix — Abridged Version) (CD, card p/s)	8

(see also Vice Versa)

ABH
78	Music Bank BECK 694	Geoffrey/Colt 45 Rock (no p/s)	10

SHIRLEY ABICAIR
56	Parlophone MSP 6224	Willie Can/Happy Trails	12
57	Parlophone R 4347	Bimini/Where The Sun Always Shines (with Humphrey Lyttleton)	7
64	Piccadilly 7N 35364	I Will Be There/Am I Losing You	8
66	Pye 7N 17119	Flowers Never Bend With The Rainfall/I Know	6
67	Pye 7N 17389	So Goes Love/Carnival	6
67	Piccadilly 7N 35383	This Girl/You Can't Hide (A Broken Heart)	6
57	Parlophone GEP 8612	FAIR DINKUM (EP)	12
65	Decca DFE 8640	ON THE NURSERY BEAT (EP)	8

MICK ABRAHAMS (BAND)
71	Chrysalis ILPS 9147	(A MUSICAL EVENING WITH) THE MICK ABRAHAMS BAND (LP, g/fold sleeve)	20
72	Chrysalis CHR 1005	AT LAST (LP, circular foldout sleeve)	30
75	SRT SRTM 73313	HAVE FUN LEARNING THE GUITAR WITH MICK ABRAHAMS (LP, solo, initally with typed insert)	18/15

(see also Blodwyn Pig, Jethro Tull, Mighty Flyers)

ABRASIVE WHEELS
81	Abrasive ABW 1	Army Song/Juvenile/So Low (p/s)	10
82	Riot City RIOT 4	VICIOUS CIRCLE (EP, p/s)	5
82	Riot City RIOT 9	Army Song/Juvenile/So Slow (p/s, reissue, red vinyl)	5
82	Riot City RIOT 16	Burn The Schools/Urban Rebels/Burn 'Em Down (p/s)	6
83	Clay CLAY 24	Jailhouse Rock/Scenic Ocean (p/s)	5
83	Clay CLAY 28	Banner Of Hope/Law Of The Jungle (p/s)	5
82	Riot City CITY 001	WHEN THE PUNKS GO MARCHING IN (LP)	15
84	Clay CLAYLP 9	BLACK LEATHER GIRL (LP, with lyric inner sleeve)	12

MIKE ABSALOM
60s	Sportsdisc ILP 1081	THE MIGHTY ABSALOM SINGS BATHROOM BLUES (LP)	12
69	Saydisc SDL 162	SAVE THE LAST GHERKIN FOR ME (LP)	40
71	Vertigo 6360 053	MIKE ABSALOM (LP, spiral label, poster sleeve)	50
72	Philips 6308 131	HECTOR AND OTHER PECCADILLOS (LP)	15

ABSOLUTE
85	Reset 7REST 5	TV Glare/At The Third Stroke (p/s)	25
85	Reset 12 REST 5	TV Glare/At The Third Stroke (12", p/s)	40
87	Reset 7REST 8	Can't You See/Love In My Heart (release cancelled)	150

ABSOLUTE ELSEWHERE
76	Warner Bros K 16697	Earthbound/Gold Of The Gods (p/s)	5
76	Warner Bros K 56192	IN SEARCH OF THE ANCIENT GODS (LP, with booklet)	12

ABSOLUTELY FABULOUS
94	Parlophone CDR 6332	Absolutely Fabulous (7" Mix)/(Our Tribe Tongue-In-Cheek Mix)/ Absolutely Dubious/This Wheel's On Fire (CD, withdrawn)	20

(see also Pet Shop Boys)

ABYSSINIAN BAPTIST CHOIR
63	Philips 847095 BY	ABYSSINIAN BAPTIST CHOIR (LP)	30

ABYSSINIANS
73	Harry J. HJ 6652	Yim Mas Gan/JOHN CROW GENERATION: Crank Shaft	12
75	Grounation GR 2029	Love Comes And Goes/(Version)	6
76	Soundtrack TST 109	African Race/Satta A Massagana	5
77	Klik KL 631	Forward On To Zion/Satta A Massagana	5
79	Different HAVE 18	Declaration Of Rights/African Race	5

ACADEMY
69	Morgan Bluetown BTS 2	Rachel's Dream/Munching The Candy (as Academy featuring Polly Perkins)	12
69	Morgan Bluetown BT 001	POP-LORE ACCORDING TO THE ACADEMY (LP)	80

(see also Polly Perkins)

ACCELERATORS
81	Spiv ACCEL EP	POPGUNS AND GREEN LANTERNS (12" EP)	8

ACCENT
67	Decca F 12679	Red Sky At Night/Wind Of Change	140

(see also Rick Hayward)

ACCENTS
59	Coral Q 72351	Wiggle, Wiggle/Dreamin' And Schemin'	30
59	Coral Q 72351	Wiggle, Wiggle/Dreamin' And Schemin' (78)	40

ACCIDENT
84	Flicknife SHARP 016	A CLOCKWORK LEGION (LP)	12

(see also Major Accident)

ACCIDENTS
80	H. Line 'n' Sinker HOOK 1	Blood Spattered With Guitars/Curtains For You (p/s)	15
80	Hook Line 'n' Sinker	KISS ME ON THE APOCALYPSE (LP, unreleased; 6 test pressings only, some supposedly with proof sleeves)	100/50

ACCIDENTS ON EAST LANCS.
81	Roach RR 1	The Back End Of Nowhere/Rat Race (p/s)	18
81	Roach SPLIFF 001	Tell Me What You Want/We Want It Legalised (no p/s)	18

AC/DC

ACCOLADE
70	Columbia DB 8688	Natural Day/Prelude To A Dawn	6
70	Columbia SCX 6405	ACCOLADE (LP)	20
72	Regal Zono. SLRZ 1024	ACCOLADE 2 (LP)	25

(see also Gordon Giltrap, Wizz Jones, Pauline Filby, Don Partridge)

ACCURSED
79	Wrek 'Em ACC 3	Going Down (p/s)	8
83	Wrek 'Em ACC 1	AGGRESSIVE PUNK (LP)	20

AC/DC
76	Atlantic K 10745	It's A Long Way To The Top (If You Wanna Rock'N'Roll)/ Can I Sit Next To You, Girl? (no p/s)	15
76	Atlantic K 10805	Jailbreak/Fling Thing (original issue with running times on label, dark label, heavy print, no p/s)	20
76	Atlantic K 10860	High Voltage/Live Wire (some in p/s)	80/15
77	Atlantic K 10899	Dirty Deeds Done Dirt Cheap/Big Balls/The Jack (maxi-single, 'schoolboy' p/s)	35
77	Atlantic K 11018	Let There Be Rock (edit)/Problem Child (initially with small label lettering & 3.06 timing, no p/s)	10/5
78	Atlantic K 11142	Rock'N'Roll Damnation/Sin City (initially with small label lettering & 3.05 timing, no p/s)	7
78	Atlantic K 11142T	Rock'N'Roll Damnation/Sin City (12", p/s)	20
78	Atlantic K 11207	Whole Lotta Rosie (live)/Hell Ain't A Bad Place To Be (live) (dark labels; later reissued with lighter labels; no p/s)	8/6
78	Atlantic K 11207T	Whole Lotta Rosie (live)/Hell Ain't A Bad Place To Be (live) (12", no p/s)	20
79	Atlantic K 11321	Highway To Hell/If You Want Blood (You've Got It) ('1979' on p/s)	8
79	Atlantic K 11406	Girl's Got Rhythm/Get It Hot (p/s, initially without 'Elephant Head' motif)	12/8
79	Atlantic K 11406E	Girl's Got Rhythm/If You Want Blood (You've Got It)/Hell Ain't A Bad Place To Be (live)/Rock'N'Roll Damnation (EP, gatefold envelope p/s)	10
80	Atlantic K 11435	Touch Too Much/Live Wire (live)/Shot Down In Flames (live) (p/s)	7
80	Atlantic K 11435	Touch Too Much/Live Wire (live)/Shot Down In Flames (live) (p/s, misprinted back-to-front)	10
80	Atlantic K 10805	Jailbreak/Fling Thing (reissue, light label, fine print; initially without 'Elephant Head' motif on p/s)	18/12
80	Atlantic K 11018	Let There Be Rock (edit)/Problem Child (reissue, no p/s, large label lettering)	6
80	Atlantic K 11142	Rock'N'Roll Damnation/Sin City (reissue, initially without 'Elephant Head' motif on p/s)	10
80	Atlantic K 11321	Highway To Hell/If You Want Blood (You've Got It) (reissue, '1980' on p/s)	6
80	Atlantic HM 1	High Voltage/Live Wire (reissue, p/s)	5
80	Atlantic HM 2	Dirty Deeds Done Dirt Cheap/Big Balls/The Jack (reissue, p/s)	5
80	Atlantic HM 3	It's A Long Way To The Top (If You Wanna Rock'N'Roll)/ Can I Sit Next To You? (p/s, reissue)	5
80	Atlantic HM 4	Whole Lotta Rosie (live)/Hell Ain't A Bad Place To Be (live) (p/s, reissue)	5
80	Atlantic K 11600	You Shook Me All Night Long/Have A Drink With Me (p/s)	7
80	Atlantic K 11600	You Shook Me All Night Long/Have A Drink With Me (p/s, mispressing, A-side plays "Shake A Leg")	100
80	Atlantic K 11630	Rock'N'Roll Ain't Noise Pollution/Hell's Bells (some with large production credit on p/s)	each 5
80	Atlantic K 11630T	Rock'N'Roll Ain't Noise Pollution/Hell's Bells (12", p/s, with badge)	12/8
82	Atlantic K 11706	Let's Get It Up/Back In Black (live) (p/s)	5
82	Atlantic K 11706T	Let's Get It Up/Back In Black (live)/TNT (live) (12", p/s)	10
82	Atlantic K 11721	For Those About To Rock (We Salute You)/Let There Be Rock (live) (p/s)	5
82	Atlantic K 11721T	For Those About To Rock (We Salute You)/Let There Be Rock (ext'd live) (12", p/s)	10

MINT VALUE £

82	Atlantic SAM 143	For Those About To Rock (We Salute You)/C.O.D. (12", p/s, promo only) 65
83	Atlantic A 9774	Guns For Hire/Landslide (p/s) 5
83	Atlantic A 9774P	Guns For Hire/Landslide (logo-shaped picture disc) 20
84	Atlantic A 9651	Nervous Shakedown/Rock'N'Roll Ain't Noise Pollution (live) (p/s; some with silver labels) . . . . each 5
84	Atlantic A 9651C	Nervous Shakedown/Rock'N'Roll Ain't Noise Pollution (live)/ Sin City (live)/This House Is On Fire (live) (cassette) 7
84	Atlantic A 9651P	Nervous Shakedown/Rock'N'Roll Ain't Noise Pollution (live) (shaped picture disc) 20
84	Atlantic A 9651T	Nervous Shakedown/Rock'N'Roll Ain't Noise Pollution (live)/ Sin City (live)/This House Is On Fire (live) (12", p/s). 8
85	Atlantic A 9532	Danger/Back In Business (p/s) 4
85	Atlantic A 9532W	Danger/Back In Business (poster p/s) 6
85	Atlantic A 9532P	Danger/Back In Business (fly-shaped picture disc) 20
85	Atlantic A 9532T	Danger/Back In Business (12", p/s) 8
86	Atlantic A 9474	Shake Your Foundations/Stand Up (p/s) 5
86	Atlantic A 9474C	Shake Your Foundations/Stand Up ('calendar' poster p/s) 7
86	Atlantic A 9474P	Shake Your Foundations/Stand Up (Angus-shaped picture disc) 15
86	Atlantic A 9474T	Shake Your Foundations/Stand Up/Jailbreak (live) (12", p/s) 10
86	Atlantic A 9425P	Who Made Who/Guns For Hire (live) (shaped picture disc) 18
86	Atlantic A 9425TW	Who Made Who (remix)/Guns For Hire (live) (12", some with stickered p/s & poster) 15/8
86	Atlantic A 9377G	You Shook Me All Night Long/She's Got Balls (live) (gatefold p/s) 4
86	Atlantic A 9377P	You Shook Me All Night Long/She's Got Balls (live) (shaped picture disc). 15
88	Atlantic A 9136	Heatseeker/Go Zone (p/s, silver labels). 4
88	Atlantic A 9136TP	Heatseeker/Go Zone/Snake Eye (12", picture disc) 12
88	Atlantic A 9136TW	Heatseeker/Go Zone/Snake Eye (12", gatefold p/s) 8
88	Atlantic A 9136CD	Heatseeker/Go Zone/Snake Eye (3" CD) 10
88	Atlantic A 9098TP	That's The Way I Wanna Rock'N'Roll/Kissin' Dynamite/Borrowed Time (12", picture disc). 10
88	Atlantic A 9098CD	That's The Way I Wanna Rock'N'Roll/Kissin' Dynamite/Shoot To Thrill/ Whole Lotta Rosie (3" CD with adaptor, 5" case) 10
90	Atco B 8907P	Thunderstruck/Fire Your Guns (10", picture disc). 8
90	Atco SAM 693	Thunderstruck/Mistress For Christmas/Moneytalks/ Fire Your Guns (12", red vinyl with insert, promo only) 18
90	Atco B 8886P	Moneytalks/Mistress For Christmas (picture disc w/ insert) . . 8
91	Atco 8830X	Are You Ready/Got You By The Balls (numbered p/s, with patch) 5
91	Atco 8830W	Are You Ready/Got You By The Balls (numbered 'satchel' p/s). 5
92	Atco SAM 1089	Highway To Hell (live) (4.57)/Highway To Hell (live) (3.58) (12", with insert, no p/s, promo only) 10
92	Atco SAM 1127	Dirty Deeds Done Cheap (live)/Shoot To Thrill (live) (12", with 2 tracks by Screaming Jets; no p/s, promo only) 12
95	East West 3BALLCD	Hail Caesar/Hard As A Rock/Ballbreaker (CD, no'd hologram p/s, promo only) . . 25
76	Atlantic K 50257	HIGH VOLTAGE (LP, 'cartoon' sleeve) 12
77	Atlantic K 50366	LET THERE BE ROCK (LP, with Shorewood Packaging-printed sleeve) 12
77	Atlantic K 50366	LET THERE BE ROCK (LP, mispressing, both sides play Side 1). 200
79	Atlantic K 50628	HIGHWAY TO HELL (LP, test pressing in alternative "live" proof sleeve). . . . . 300+
81	Atlantic SAM 155	JAPAN TOUR '81 (LP, picture disc, promo only, clear or black rim) 120/100
81	Atlantic 60149	BOX SET (3-LP, including "High Voltage", "Dirty Deeds Done Cheap" & "Powerage", promo 7" & poster; export issue) 25
91	Atco WX 364P	THE RAZOR'S EDGE (LP, picture disc with inlay card) 15
95	East West SAM 1693	BALLBREAKERS (CD, promo only compilation). 30

(see also Geordie, A II Z, Home)

BUDDY ACE

68	Action ACT 4504	Got To Get Myself Together/Darling Depend On Me 12
64	Vocalion VEP 1-70164	BUDDY ACE (EP) 70

CHARLIE ACE

70	High Note HS 051	Creation (Version)/GAYTONES: Creation (Version Three). 6
70	Punch PH 49	Silver And Gold/PHILL PRATT ALLSTARS: Bump And Bore 6
70	Punch PH 53	Book Of Books/WINSTON HARRIS: Musical Dove 10
70	Punch PH 62	Love (You) I Madly/Especially For You. 6
70	Punch PH 67	Do Something/MAYTONES: Run Babylon. 6
71	G.G. GG 4507	Ontarius Version/G.G. ALL STARS: Ontarius Version 2 7
71	G.G. GG 4518	Do Something/MAYTONES: Groove Me. 15
71	Upsetter US 359	The Creeper/UPSETTERS: The Creeper (Version). 15
71	Smash SMA 2325	Need No Whip/Grine Grine. 15

(see also Charles, Paulette & Gee, Gaytones, Phil Pratt Allstars, Maytones, G.G. Allstars, Upsetters, Gaby Wilton & Charlie Ace)

JOHNNY ACE

61	Vogue V 9180	Pledging My Love/Anymore. 65
61	Vocalion V 9180	Pledging My Love/Anymore (reissue) 35
62	Vogue VE 1-70150	JOHNNY ACE (EP) 110
61	Vocalion VA 160177	THE MEMORIAL ALBUM (LP) 110

MARTIN ACE

81	C.J.'s CJS 1	Sad Party/Eating (p/s) 6

(see also Man, Motors)

RICHARD ACE (& SOUND DIMENSIONS)

67	Coxsone CS 7031	Don't Let The Sun Catch You Crying/VICEROYS: Magadown 20
67	Studio One SO 2022	I Need You/SOUL VENDORS: Cool Shade 20
69	Studio One SO 2072	More Reggae (with Sound Dimensions)/GLADIATORS: Hello Carol. 20
69	Trojan TR 654	Hang 'Em High (with Sound Dimensions)/BLACK & GEORGE: Candy Lady. 6
70	Sugar SU 104	Sound Of The Reggae/Got To Build A Wall 5

(see also Viceroys, Soul Vendors, Gladiators, Ken Boothe)

A CERTAIN RATIO

79	Factory FAC 5	All Night Party/The Thin Boys (p/s, 5,000 only, 1,000 with sticker stating "ltd. edition on poor quality vinyl") 10/5
80	Factory FAC 22	Blown Away/Flight/And Then Again (12", p/s, with inner sleeve) 7
81	Factory FAC 52	Waterline/Funaezekea (12", p/s) 7
82	Factory FAC 62-7	Knife Slits Water/Tumba Rumba (p/s) 5
82	Factory FAC 62T	Knife Slits Water/Kether — Hot Knives Mix-In Special (12", p/s) 7
83	Factory FAC 72-7	I Need Someone Tonite (edit)/Don't You Worry 'Bout A Thing (edit) (promo)...... 7
84	Factory FAC 112	Life's A Scream/There's Only This (12", p/s, with 'obi'). 7
84	Factory FAC 112P	Life's A Scream (edit)/There's Only This (edit) (promo pack including 7", photo & biography in custom ACR envelope)........................... 10
85	Factory FAC 128	Wild Party/Sounds Like Something Dirty (12", p/s) 7
79	Factory FAC 16C	THE GRAVEYARD AND THE BALLROOM (cassette, 4 different coloured plastic wallets, with insert)............................. 10
85	private label	A CERTAIN RATIO LIVE IN AMERICA (cassette, sold at gigs) 15

(see also Sir Horatio)

ACES

| 63 | Parlophone R 5094 | Wait Until Tomorrow/The Last One .... 10 |
| 64 | Parlophone R 5108 | I Count The Tears/But Say It Isn't So .... 10 |

ACES

| 82 | Etc ETC 01 | One Way Street/Why Should It Be Mine (p/s) .... 18 |

(see also Menace)

ACHES & PAINS

| 66 | Page One POF 008 | There's No Other Like Your Mother/Again And Again........................ 6 |

ACHILLES & HIS HEELS

| 61 | Fontana H 340 | Brigitte Bardo/Acapulco .... 8 |

ACHOR

| 76 | Cedar CEDAR 1 | END OF MY DAY (LP).. 50 |
| 78 | Dove Tail DOVE 54 | HOSANNA TO THE SON OF DAVID (LP) .... 25 |

(see also Wine Of Lebanon, Valley Of Achor)

ACID GALLERY

| 69 | CBS 4608 | Dance Around The Maypole/Right Toe Blues .... 40 |

(see also Epics, Carl Wayne & Vikings, Roy Wood, Outer Limits)

DAVID ACKLES

68	Elektra EKSN 45039	La Route A Chicago/Down River 6
69	Elektra EKSN 45054	Laissez Faire/Blue Ribbons... 6
70	Elektra EKSN 45079	Subway To The Country/That's No Reason To Cry 6
68	Elektra EKL 4022	DAVID ACKLES (LP, orange label, also stereo EKS 74022) 25
70	Elektra EKS 74060	SUBWAY TO THE COUNTRY (LP, orange label)........................... 18
72	Elektra K 42112	AMERICAN GOTHIC (LP).. 12
73	CBS 32466	FIVE AND A DIME (LP)... 15

BARBARA ACKLIN

68	MCA MU 1038	Love Makes A Woman/Come And See Me Baby 8
69	MCA MU 1071	Am I The Same Girl/Be By My Side 7
69	MCA MU 1102	Love Makes A Woman/Come And See Me Baby (reissue) 5
69	MCA MU 1103	Am I The Same Girl/Be By My Side (reissue) 5
75	Brunswick BR 26	Love Makes A Woman/Am I The Same Girl 5
69	MCA MUP(S) 366	LOVE MAKES A WOMAN (LP) 25
71	MCA MUPS 410	SEVEN DAYS OF NIGHT (LP)... 25
71	MCA MUPS 416	SOMEBODY ELSE'S ARMS (LP) 20
75	Capitol E-ST 11377	A PLACE IN THE SUN (LP)... 12

(see also Gene Chandler & Barbara Acklin)

A.C. MARIAS (A.C.)

81	Dome DOM 45 1	Drop/So (as A.C. Marias A.C., plain black sleeve)......................... 8
87	Mute MUTE 50	Just Talk/Just Talk (No Talk Instrumental) (DJ-only) 6
90	Mute MUTE 105	One Of Our Girls Is Missing/(same) (DJ-only, stickered plain sleeve) 5

(see also Dome, Gilbert & Lewis)

ACME ATTRACTIONS

| 81 | Orchid OR1 | Eve Of Destruction/It's OK (p/s, with Bonnie Parker) .... 20 |

SEPH ACRE & PETS

| 58 | Pye International 7N 25001 | You Are My Love/Rock And Roll Cha Cha.................................. 10 |
| 58 | Pye International N 25001 | You Are My Love/Rock And Roll Cha Cha (78) .... 12 |

(see also Pets)

ACRYLIC TONES

| 94 | Detour DR 010 | Girl/The Theme From The Acrylic Tones/The Rainbow Song (p/s, 1,000 only, 100 on pink vinyl; 500 with laminated p/s)............................... 8/5 |

ACT

67	Columbia DB 8179	Cobbled Streets/One Heart 25
67	Columbia DB 8261	Here Come Those Tears Again/Without You 20
68	Columbia DB 8331	Just A Little Bit/The Remedies Of Doctor Brohnicoy 30

ACT

87	ZTT 12 ZTAS 28	Snobbery And Decay (That's Entertainment)/Poison/ I'd Be Surprisingly Good For You (12", p/s). 8
87	ZTT 12 ZACT 28	Snobbery And Decay (That's Entertainment)/Poison/I'd Be Surprisingly Good For You (12", gatefold p/s). 8
87	ZTT 12 XACT 28	Snobbery And Decay (Naked Civil Remix)/Strong Poison/Theme From Snobbery And Decay (12", gatefold p/s, some with poster) 18/10
87	ZTT CTIS 28	SNOBBERY AND DECAY CABARET CASSETTE (cassette EP) 6

87	ZTT CID 28	Emotional Highlights From Snobbery And Decay: Snobbery And Decay (Extended For Stephanie Beecham)/I'd Be Surprisingly Good For You/Poison/ (Theme From) Snobbery And Decay (CD, gatefold card sleeve) 15
87	ZTT CT 01	Snobbery And Decay (Moonlighting Mix)/Instant 1/Instant 2 (12", plain black die-cut sleeve)........................ 40
87	ZTT VIMM 1	Absolutely Immune 2/Bloodrush/States Of Logic (12", p/s) 20
87	ZTT CD IMM 2	I Can't Escape From You (Love And Hate)/Heaven Knows I'm Miserable Now/ Dear Life/I Can't Escape From You (CD) 15
88	ZTT BET 1	Chance/Winner '88 (p/s, withdrawn) 50
88	ZTT BETT 1	Chance (12 To 1 Mix)/Winner '88/Chance (We Give You Another Chance) (12", p/s, withdrawn) 80
88	ZTT BETCD 1	Chance (12 To 1 Mix)/Winner '88/Chance (We Give You Another Chance) (CD, unissued)
88	ZTT ZQCD 1	LAUGHTER, TEARS AND RAGE (CD) 25

(see also Propaganda, Claudia Brücken, Glenn Gregory & Claudia Brücken, Thomas Leer)

ACTION

65	Parlophone R 5354	Land Of 1000 Dances/In My Lonely Room 40
66	Parlophone R 5410	I'll Keep On Holding On/Hey Sah-Lo-Ney 45
66	Parlophone R 5474	Baby You've Got It/Since I Lost My Baby 45
67	Parlophone R 5572	Never Ever/Twenty Fourth Hour 45
67	Parlophone R 5610	Shadows And Reflections/Something Has Hit Me 50
81	Edsel E 5001	I'll Keep On Holding On/Wasn't It You? (p/s)................. 10
81	Edsel E 5002	Since I Lost My Baby/Never Ever/Wasn't It You (p/s) 10
82	Edsel E 5003	Shadows And Reflections/Something Has Hit Me (p/s) 10
84	Edsel E 5008	Hey Sah-Lo-Ney/Come On, Come With Me (p/s) 10
80	Edsel ED 101	THE ULTIMATE ACTION (LP, with inner sleeve) 15
85	Dojo DOJO LP 3	ACTION SPEAKS LOUDER THAN. . . (mini-LP)............... 15

(see also Boys, Sandra Barry & Boys, Mighty Baby, Reg King, Stone's Masonry)

ACTION PACT

81	Subversive ANARCHO 1	HEATHROW TOUCHDOWN (EP, 1 side by Dead Man's Shadow) 6
82	Fallout FALL 003	Suicide Bag/Stanwell/Blue Blood (p/s) 5
83	Fallout FALL 010	People/Times Must Change/Sixties Flix (p/s)................. 5
83	Fallout FALL 019	Question Of Choice/Hook Line & Sinker (p/s)................ 5
83	Fallout FALL 026	Yet Another Dole Queue Song/Rockaway Beach (p/s)............ 5
83	Fallout FALL 029	Cocktail Credibility/Consumer Madness (p/s)................ 5

ACTIVE RESTRAINT

83	Sticky PEEL OFF 3	Terror In My Home/Turns Out Roses (p/s)................... 4

(see also Mighty Lemon Drops)

ACTIVES

84	Quiet QS 001	RIOT (EP, p/s) 4

ACTRESS

69	CBS 4016	It's What You Give/Good Job With Prospects 45

ROY ACUFF & SMOKY MOUNTAIN BOYS

57	Brunswick 05635	I Like Mountain Music/It's Hard To Love (And Not To Be In Love) 8
57	Brunswick 05635	I Like Mountain Music/It's Hard To Love (And Not To Be In Love) (78).... 10
65	Capitol T 2276	THE VOICE OF COUNTRY MUSIC (LP) 12
65	Hickory LPM 101	ONCE MORE (LP) 12
65	Hickory LPM 117	HAND CLAPPING GOSPEL SONGS (LP).................. 12
66	Hickory LPM 125	GREAT TRAIN SONGS (LP) 12
68	London HAB 8361	SINGS FAMOUS OPRY FAVOURITES (LP)................. 12

ADAM & THE ANTS

78	Decca F 13803	Young Parisians/Lady (p/s, original with paper labels)........... 6
81	Lyntone LYN 9285	A.N.T.S. (1-sided blue flexidisc with *Flexipop* magazine issue 4) 6
89	Damaged Goods FNARR 7	Young Parisians/Lady/(interview) (12", white vinyl, p/s, 2,000 with no'd fanzine) 10
89	Damaged Goods FNARR 7	Young Parisians/Lady/(interview) (12", picture disc, with postcard) 10

(see also Adam Ant, Maneaters, Models)

ADAM, MIKE & TIM

64	Decca F 12040	Little Baby/You're The Reason Why...................... 5
65	Decca F 12112	That's How I Feel/It's All Too True 5
65	Decca F 12221	Little Pictures/Summer's Here Again 5
66	Columbia DB 7836	Flowers On The Wall/Give That Girl A Break 6
66	Columbia DB 7902	A Most Peculiar Man/Wedding Day 7

(see also Mike Sedgewick)

ADAMO

64	Columbia DB 7273	Another Love Affair/Make Tonite Last Forever 5
64	Columbia DB 7329	She Was An Angel/The Stars Will Shine (Vous Permettez Monsieur)....... 5
66	HMV POP 1499	Nobody Ever Told Sandy/Tears Come (The Hurt Has Begun)......... 6
67	HMV POP 1601	Inch Allah (God Willing)/The Tramp With A Beard............... 5
67	HMV POP 1609	Let's Stop The World From Turning/Hitch Hiker 5
63	HMV 7EG 8860	BELGIUM'S TOP RECORDING STAR ADAMO (EP)............. 8
66	HMV CLP 3601	THE HITS OF ADAMO (LP)......................... 12
67	HMV CLP 3635	THE SENSATIONAL ADAMO (LP) 12
68	Columbia SCX 6254	SALVATORE ADAMO (LP) 12

ALICIA ADAMS

61	Capitol CL 15195	Love Bandit/Oom Dooby Doom Lovey Dovey Sh' Boom 10

ARTHUR K. ADAMS

68	Blue Horizon 57-3136	She Drives Me Out Of My Mind/Gimme Some Of Your Lovin'......... 15

BILLY ADAMS

60	Capitol CL 15107	Count Every Star/Peggy's Party 15

MINT VALUE £

BILLY ADAMS
69 London HL 10258   I Need Your Love/Why Don't You Believe Me 8

BRYAN ADAMS
79	A&M AMS 7460	Let Me Take You Dancing/Don't Turn Me Away (no p/s)	18
79	A&M AMSP 7460	Let Me Take You Dancing (Extended)/Don't Turn Me Away (12", no p/s)	25
80	A&M AMS 7520	Hidin' From Love/Wait And See (p/s)	18
81	A&M AMS 8183	Lonely Nights/Don't Look Now (p/s)	12
83	A&M AM 103	Straight From The Heart/Lonely Nights (p/s)	5
83	A&M AMX 103	Straight From The Heart/Lonely Nights (12", p/s)	8
83	A&M AM 129	Cuts Like A Knife/Fits Ya Good (p/s)	5
83	A&M AMP 129	Cuts Like A Knife/Fits Ya Good/Hidin' From Love (12", p/s)	8
84	A&M AM 170	One Good Reason (unissued, existence unconfirmed)	
84	A&M AM 224	Run To You/I'm Ready//Cuts Like A Knife/Lonely Nights (p/s, double pack)	7
84	A&M AMY 224	Run To You (Remix)/I'm Ready/Cuts Like A Knife (12", poster p/s)	15
85	A&M AMP 236	Somebody/Long Gone (picture disc)	12
85	A&M AMY 236	Somebody/Long Gone (12", p/s, with tour poster)	10
85	A&M AMS 256/FREE 3	Heaven/Diana//Straight From The Heart/You Want It, You Got It (double pack, stickered p/s)	5
85	A&M AM 285	It's Only Love (with Tina Turner)/The Best Was Yet To Come// Somebody/Long Gone (p/s, double pack)	5
86	A&M AMS 322	Straight From The Heart/Fits Ya Good//Run To You/Somebody (p/s, dble pack)	5
87	A&M ADAM 3	Hearts On Fire/Run To You (red vinyl, stickered p/s)	12
87	A&M AMF 407	Victim Of Love/Heat Of The Night (live) (box set with postcards & patch)	5
87	A&M ADAM 12	Heat Of The Night (remixes) (12", p/s)	10
91	A&M AM 789	Everything I Do (I Do It For You) (p/s)	5
80	A&M AMLH 64800	BRYAN ADAMS (LP)	12
81	A&M AMLH 64864	YOU WANT IT, YOU GOT IT (LP)	12

(see also Rock Aid Armenia)

CLIFF ADAMS ORCHESTRA
60 Pye International 7N 25056   The Lonely Man Theme/Trigger Happy 7

DANNY ADAMS & CHALLENGERS
64 Philips BF 1346   Bye Bye Baby, Bye Bye/I'm So Proud Of You 7

DERROLL ADAMS
72 Village Thing VTS 17   FEELIN' FINE (LP, with inner sleeve) 20

EDITH ADAMS
55 Brunswick 05406   Ohio (with Rosalind Russell)/A Little Bit In Love 6

EVE ADAMS
61 Qualition PSP 7131   Kookie Talk/My Love Dear 5

FAYE ADAMS
56 London HLU 8339   I'll Be True/Happiness To My Soul 650
56 London HLU 8339   I'll Be True/Happiness To My Soul (78) 65

GLADSTON ADAMS
69 Trojan TR 659   Dollars And Cents/TOMMY McCOOK: Popcorn Regay 12
(see also Gladstone Anderson)

GLEN ADAMS
67	Island WI 3072	Silent Lover/I Remember	18
67	Island WI 3083	She (actually titled "I'm Shocking")/SONNY BURKE: Some Other Time	18
67	Island WI 3099	Grab A Girl/DELROY WILSON: This Heart Of Mine	18
67	Island WI 3100	Hold Down Miss Winey/VINCENT GORDON: Sounds And Soul	30
67	Island WI 3106	That New Girl/UNIQUES: Speak No Evil	18
67	Island WI 3120	She's So Fine/ROY SHIRLEY: Girlie	18
68	Blue Cat BS 126	She Is Leaving/UNIQUES: Girls Like Dirt	15
68	Trojan TR 621	Rent Too High/Every Time	12
68	Collins Downbeat CR 006	Cool Cool Rocksteady (act. D. Tony Lee)/OWEN GRAY: Girl I Will Be Leaving . . .	35
68	Duke DU 58	My Girl/GLADIATORS: You Were To Be	8
68	Bullet BU 414	Cat Woman/PETER TOUCH: Selassie Serenade (B-side actually by Peter Tosh) . .	20
68	Collins Downbeat CR 010	King Sized/I'm Gonna Take You Back (B-side actually by Owen Gray)	30
68	Giant GN 33	Lonely Girl/ROY SHIRLEY: Warming Up The Scene	10
69	Amalgamated AMG 837	She's So Fine/ERNEST WILSON: Private Number	8
70	Gas GAS 141	Leaving On A Jet Plane/REGGAE BOYS: Phrases	6
71	Big BG 321	Weary Version 3/TONY BREVETT: Hills And Valleys	12
71	Explosion EX 2048	Never Fall In Love/JET SCENE: Jet 747	8

(see also Glen Amams, Reggae Boys, Roy Shirley, Maxie & Glen, Delroy Wilson, Derrick Morgan, Ernest Wilson, Owen Gray)

JOHNNY ADAMS (& GONDOLIERS)
59 Top Rank JAR 192   Come On/Nowhere To Go (as Johnny Adams & Gondoliers) 8
69 Polydor 56775   Reconsider Me/If I Could See You One More Time 10
72 Atlantic K 10245   I Wish It Would Rain/You're A Lady 5

JUNE ADAMS
66 King KG 1038   River Keep Movin'/Heavenly Father 15

MARIE ADAMS
59 Capitol CL 14963   A Fool In Love/What Do You Want To Make Those Eyes At Me For 20
(see also Johnny Otis)

PAUL & LINDA ADAMS
75 S. Folk & Country SFA 27   FAR OVER THE FELL (LP) 15

RAY ADAMS
61 Pye International 7N 25099   You Belong To My Heart/Hear My Song, Violetta 6
61 Pye International 7N 25117   Soria Moria/Little Rosemarie 5
62 Pye International 7N 25129   Walk Hand In Hand/Crying Cloud 5

Ray ADAMS

62	Decca F 11507	Venus In Blue Jeans/He's Got My Sympathy	6
62	Pye 7N 15481	Gypsy/Brother Bill	5

RITCHIE ADAMS
60	London HLU 9200	Back To School/Don't Go My Love, Don't Go	30

RUSH ADAMS
54	Parlophone MSP 6101	I'm Sorry Dear/No One To Cry To	12
55	Parlophone CMSP 33	Then I'll Be Happy/Arizona (with Ace Dooley & Son) (export issue)	15
56	MGM SP 1162	Love Plays The Strings Of My Banjo/Kiss! Kiss! Kiss!	7
56	MGM SP 1176	The Birds And The Bees (with Loulie Jean Norman)/My Buddy's Girl	10

(see also David Rose)

WOODROW ADAMS
65	Blue Horizon BH 1001	Baby You Just Don't Know/Wine Head Woman (99 copies only)	150

ADAM'S APPLES
77	Brunswick BR 42	Don't Take It Out On This World/Don't You Want To Take Me Home	5

BARRY ADAMSON
91	Mute MUTE 119	These Boots Are Made For Walking/Go Johnny (p/s)	6
94	Mute 12MUTE 188	Achieved In The Valley Of The Dolls (Glass Dolls Mix) (featuring Billy MacKenzie)/Achieved In The Valley Of The Dolls (Original Version)/Dirty Barry/Farewell My Lovely (12", p/s, unreleased)	
94	Mute CDMUTE 188	Achieved In The Valley Of The Dolls (Single Mix) (featuring Billy MacKenzie)/Dirty Barry/Everybody's Sleeping But Me/Farewell My Lovely (CD, unreleased)	
94	Mute LCDMUTE 188	Achieved In The Valley Of The Dolls (Glass Dolls Mix) (featuring Billy MacKenzie)/Hear The Angels/Trouble Asunder/Achieved In The Valley Of The Dolls (Original Version) (CD, unreleased)	
96	Mute RCDSTUMM 134	Achieved In The Valley Of The Dolls (Radio Edit)/Achieved In The Valley Of The Dolls (Album Version) (CD, as Barry Adamson featuring Billy MacKenzie, promo only)	8

(see also Magazine, Nick Cave & Bad Seeds, Billy MacKenzie)

AD CONSPIRACY
79	Diamond	AD CONSPIRACY (LP)	20

CANNONBALL ADDERLEY
60	Riverside RIV 106900 RIF	This Here Parts 1 & 2	5
61	Riverside RIV 45-457	African Waltz Parts 1 & 2	5
61	Riverside RIV 33-457	African Waltz Parts 1 & 2 (33rpm)	5
63	Riverside RIV 45415	The Sidewalks Of New York/Things Are Getting Better	5
67	Capitol CL 15489	Mercy Mercy Mercy/Games	5
67	Capitol CL 15500	Why (Am I Treated So Bad)/I'm On My Way	6
62	Riverside RLP 12-311	THE CANNONBALL ADDERLEY QUINTET IN SAN FRANCISCO (LP)	15
62	Riverside RLP 12-318	WORK SONG (LP, actually by Nat Adderley)	15
65	Fontana FJL 107	WOW! (LP)	15
65	Fontana FJL 117	WHAM! (LP)	12
68	Capitol ST 2987	ACCENT ON AFRICA (LP)	12

(see also Nancy Wilson, Miles Davis, John Coltrane)

ADDICTS
64	Decca F 11902	That's My Girl/Here She Comes	20

JOHN ADDISON
64	United Artists UP 1053	The Girl With Green Eyes/Love Theme From "Tom Jones"	5

ADDIX
79	Zig Zag ZZ 22002	Too Blind To See/(No Such Thing As A) Bad Boy (p/s)	5

ADDRISSI BROTHERS
59	London HL 8922	Cherrystone/Lilies Grow High	25
59	London HL 8922	Cherrystone/Lilies Grow High (78)	30
59	London HL 8973	Un Jarro/Saving My Kisses	10
59	London HL 8973	Un Jarro/Saving My Kisses (78)	25
59	Columbia DB 4370	Back To The Old Salt Mine/It's Love	12

BOBBY ADENO
66	Vocalion V 9279	The Hands Of Time/It's A Sad World	20

ADICTS
81	Dining Out TUX 1	LUNCH WITH THE ADICTS (EP, with insert & screen-printed p/s)	20
82	Fall Out FALL 002	Viva La Revolution/Steamroller (p/s)	7
82	Razor RZS 101	Chinese Takeaway/You'll Never Walk Alone (p/s)	7
83	Razor RZS 104	Bad Boy/Shake, Rattle, Bang Your Head (p/s)	5
83	Razor RZLP 104	Bad Boy/Shake, Rattle, Bang Your Head (shaped picture disc)	7
84	Sire W 9298	Tokyo/The Odd Couple (p/s)	5
85	Fall Out FALL 12038	BAR ROOM BOP (12" EP)	8
81	Dwed SMT 008	SONGS OF PRAISE (LP)	12
81	Fall Out FALL LP 006	SONGS OF PRAISE (LP, reissue, yellow vinyl, 2,000 only)	12
81	Fall Out FALL LP 006P	SONGS OF PRAISE (LP, reissue, picture disc)	12
82	Razor RAZ 2	SOUND OF MUSIC (LP)	12

(see also A.D.X.)

BETH ADLAM with BUZZ & BOYS
60	Starlite ST45 024	Seventeen/I'll Walk Into The Sea	12

LARRY ADLER
56	Columbia SCM 5217	Rififi/Malaguena	7
57	HMV POP 405	Weeping Willows/Theme On Four Notes	10

ADLIBS (U.K.)
65	Fontana TF 584	Neighbour Neighbour/Lovely Ladies	35

AD-LIBS

AD-LIBS (U.S.)
66	Red Bird RB 10-102	The Boy From New York City/Kicked Around	30
69	Deep Soul DS 9102	Giving Up/Appreciation	15
75	Contempo CS 9029	The Boy From New York City/Johnny My Boy	6
79	Inferno HEAT 1	New York In The Dark/The Boy From New York City (p/s, coloured vinyl)	5

ADMIRALS
65	Fontana TF 597	Promised Land/Palisades Park	35

AD NAUSEUM
83	Flicknife FLS 12	BRAINSTORM (EP, p/s)	5

A.D. 1984
79	Voyage VOY 005	The Russians Are Coming/New Moon Falling (p/s)	8
81	Grand Prix GP003	The Clockwork Generation/Melody In The Key Of Time (p/s)	6

DALE ADRIATICO
67	Parlophone R 5583	I Hurt Too Easy/All (Una Moglie Americana)	12

ADVENTURERS
60	Capitol CL 15108	Trail Blazer/Rip Van Winkle	6

ADVERTISING
77	EMI EMI 2710	Lipstick/Lonely Guys (p/s)	6
77	EMI EMI 2754	Stolen Love/Suspender Fun (p/s)	6
78	EMI EMC 3253	ADVERTISING JINGLES (LP, with inner sleeve)	12

(see also Secret Affair, Innocents, Simon Boswell)

ADVERTS
77	Stiff BUY 13	One Chord Wonders/Quickstep (p/s, 1st pressing with push-out centre)	15
77	Stiff BUY 13	One Chord Wonders/Quickstep (p/s, re-pressing with solid centre)	6
77	Anchor ANC 1043	Gary Gilmore's Eyes/Bored Teenagers (p/s, some with blanked-out eyes on label, white or pink lettering on p/s, push-out or solid centre)	6/5
77	Anchor ANC 1047	Safety In Numbers/We Who Wait (p/s)	5
78	Bright BR 1	No Time To Be 21/New Day Dawning (p/s)	5
78	RCA PB 5128	Television's Over/Back From The Dead (p/s)	5
79	RCA PB 5160	My Place/New Church (live) (p/s)	5
79	RCA PB 5191	Cast Of Thousands/I Will Walk You Home (p/s)	5
83	Bright BULB 1	Gary Gilmore's Eyes/We Who Wait/New Day Dawning (p/s)	7
78	Bright BRL 201	CROSSING THE RED SEA WITH THE ADVERTS (LP, 5,000 on red vinyl)	20/15
81	Butt/Bright ALSO 002	CROSSING THE RED SEA WITH THE ADVERTS (LP, reissue, red vinyl)	15
90	Link Classics CLINK 1	CROSSING THE RED SEA WITH THE ADVERTS (LP, 2nd reissue, clear vinyl)	12
90	Link Classics CLINK 1	CROSSING THE RED SEA WITH THE ADVERTS (LP, 2nd reissue, green vinyl)	12

(see also TV Smith's Explorers)

A.D.X.
85	Sire W 9070	Falling In Love Again/Come Along (p/s)	5

(see also Adicts)

AEROSMITH
73	CBS 1898	Dream On/Somebody	12
76	CBS 4000	Dream On/Somebody (reissue)	5
76	CBS 4452	Last Child/Combination	5
77	CBS 4878	Walk This Way/Uncle Salty	5
77	CBS S AR 2	Draw The Line/Bright, Light, Fright (p/s)	8
78	CBS 6584	Come Together/Kings And Queens	5
80	CBS 8220	Remember (Walking In The Sand)/Bone To Bone (p/s)	5
87	Geffen GEF 29TP	Dude (Looks Like A Lady)/Simoriah/Once Is Enough (12", picture disc)	12
88	Geffen GEF 34TP	Angel/Girl Keeps Coming Apart (12", picture disc)	10
88	Geffen GEF 34CD	Angel (A.O.R. Remix)/Angel/Girl Keeps Coming Apart/Dude (Looks Like A Lady) (3" CD, with adaptor in 5" case)	8
89	Geffen GEF 63	Love In An Elevator/Young Lust (p/s, with patch)	7
89	Geffen GEF 63TP	Love In An Elevator/Young Lust/Ain't Enough (p/s)	8
89	Geffen GEF 63CD	Love In An Elevator (Edit)/Ain't Enough/Young Lust (3" CD, gatefold p/s)	8
89	Geffen GEF 68P	Janie's Got A Gun/Voodoo Medicine Man (shaped picture disc)	12
89	Geffen GEF 68CD	Janie's Got A Gun/Rag Doll (Live!)/Voodoo Medicine Man (3" CD, gatefold p/s)	8
90	Geffen GEF 72P	Dude (Looks Like A Lady)/Monkey On My Back (shaped picture disc)	12
90	Geffen GEF 72CD	Dude (Looks Like A Lady) (Extended Rockin' Dude)/Love In An Elevator (live)/Walk This Way (live) (CD)	8
90	Geffen GEF 76CD	Rag Doll/Mama Kin (live)/Dream On (live) (CD)	8
89	CBS 4607038	GREATEST HITS (LP, 'European Tour' picture disc)	12

(see also Run DMC, Flame)

A FAIR SET
65	Decca F 12168	Honey And Wine/Runaround	12

AFEX
67	King KG 1058	She Got The Time/I Never Knew Love Was Like This	40

AFFINITY
70	Vertigo 6059 007	I Wonder If I Care As Much/Three Sisters	12
70	Vertigo 6360 004	AFFINITY (LP, gatefold sleeve, spiral label)	70

(see also Linda Hoyle, Ice)

AFFLICTED
81	Bonk AFF 1	I'm Afflicted/Be Aware (rubber-stamped white labels, plain sleeve, some with insert)	12/10
82	Bonk AFF 2	All Right Now/Who Can Tell (p/s, stamped white labels)	10
82	Bonk AFF 4	Afflicted (untitled single in stamped striped bag)	8
82	Bonk AFF 3	THE AFFLICTED MAN'S MUSICAL BAG (LP, stamped white label in stamped bag sleeve)	12
82	Bonk AFF 6	HIGH SPEED AND THE AFFLICTED MAN — GET STONED (LP)	12

A FLOCK OF SEAGULLS

81	Cocteau COQ 3	It's Not Me Talking/Factory Music (p/s)	7
82	Jive JIVEP 14	I Ran/Pick Me Up/Messages (picture disc)	5
82	Jive JIVEP 17	Space Age Love Song/Windows (picture disc)	5
83	Jive JIVEP 33	Nightmares/Rosen Montag (picture disc)	5
83	Jive JIVEP 41	Transfer Affection/I Ran (picture disc)	5
84	Jive JIVEP 62	The More You Live The More You Love/Lost Control (square picture disc)	5
85	Jive AFOS 1	COLLECTION (10 x 7" pack)	18
85	Jive AFLOCK 1	COLLECTION (10 x 12" pack)	20
83	Jive HOPX 201	A FLOCK OF SEAGULLS (LP, picture disc)	12
83	Jive HIPX 4	LISTEN (LP, picture disc)	12

AFRICAN

72	Sioux SI 006	Cock Mouth Kill Cock/ERROL T.: I Need To Know	5

AFRICAN BEAVERS

65	RCA RCA 1447	Find My Baby/Jungle Fever	6

AFRICAN MUSIC MACHINE

72	Mojo 2092 046	Black Water Gold (Pearl)/Making Nassau Fruit Drink	8
73	Contempo CR 13	Tropical/The Girl In France	8
73	Contempo CR 25	Never Name A Baby/Dapp	5
74	Contempo CS 2025	Mr Brown/Camel Time	5

AFRIQUE

73	Pye International 7N 25616	Soul Makossa/Hot Mud	8
74	Mainstream MSL 1018	SOUL MAKOSSA (LP)	20

AFRO

71	Punch PH 89	Lonely World/ALTON ELLIS ALL STARS: Put It On	6

AFRO ENCHANTERS

63	Island WI 071	Peace And Love/Wayward African	15

AFRO RHYTHM KINGS

54	Lyragon J 732	Skokiaan/Bantu Boogie (78)	10

AFROTONES

69	Trojan TR 655	Things I Love/ERIC FATTER: Since You've Been Gone	8
69	Duke DU 19	Freedom Sound/BOYS: Easy Sound	5
69	High Note HS 023	All For One/BELTONES: Broken Heart	5

(see also Delroy Wilson)

AFTER DARK

81	After Dark AD 001	Evil Woman/Johnny/Lucy (p/s)	80
83	Lazer PROMO 1	Deathbringer/Call Of The Wild (picture disc, promo only)	50

AFTER TEA

68	Ace Of Clubs SCL-R 1251	AFTER TEA (LP)	30

(see also Ray Fenwick)

AFTER THE FIRE

79	CBS 7025	One Rule For You/Joy (p/s, red vinyl)	5
79	CBS 7769	Laser Love/Your Love Is Alive (p/s, red vinyl)	5
80	Epic EPC 8394	Love Will Always Make You Cry/Every Mother's Son (p/s, withdrawn)	7
75	Rapid RR 001	SIGNS OF CHANGE (LP, with insert)	25
80	Epic EPC 84545	80-F (LP, with original mix, unreleased, only on cassette with white labels)	15
82	Epic EPC 85135	BATTERIES NOT INCLUDED (LP, withdrawn version with different sleeve)	12

(see also Narnia, Waiting For The Sun)

AFX

(see under Aphex Twin)

AGENTS

79	Grapevine GRP 142	Trouble/The Love I Hold	5

AGE OF LOVE

92	React REACT 9	JAM AND SPOON MIXES (12")	8

AGGROVATORS

70	Jackpot JP 751	Sex Machine/You Left Me And Gone (both act. by Dave Barker & Aggrovators)	6
70	Smash SMA 2302	Big Red Ball Parts 1 & 2 (A-side actually "Big Red Bumble" by Lloyd Tyrell; B-side actually "Big Bumble Version" by Lloyd & Devon)	7
71	Smash SMA 2312	One More Bottle Of Beer/Beer Version	5
73	Smash SMA 2339	Straight To Jackson Head/You Are My Angel	10
73	Downtown DT 500	Dreadlocks Man/Rasta Wants Peace (both actually by Rasta Twins)	10

(see also Dave Barker, Dennis Alcapone, Jerry Lewis [Jamaica], Delroy Wilson, John Holt, Alton Ellis, Cornell Campbell)

AGINCOURT

70	Merlin HF 3	FLY AWAY (LP, with insert)	400

(see also Friends, Ithaca, Alice Through The Looking Glass, Tomorrow Come Someday, BBC Radiophonic Workshop/Peter Howell)

AGNES STRANGE

75	Birdsnest BN 1	Give Yourself A Chance/Clever Fool	7
77	Baal BDN 38048	Can't Make Up My Mind/Johnny B. Goode	7
75	Birdsnest BRL 9000	STRANGE FLAVOUR (LP)	60

AGONY BAG

80	Monza MON 2	Rabies Is A Killer/Never Never (p/s)	15

(see also Pesky Gee, Black Widow)

AGONY COLUMN

80	Back Door DOOR 8	Love In The Head/Free Of Love (p/s)	5

AGROS
71	Punch PH 56	What Do You Fall In Love For/SLICKERS: Too Much 6

A GUY CALLED GERALD
88	Rham RX 8804	Voodoo Ray/Escape/Rhapsody In Acid/Blow Your House Down (12", p/s) 12

A-HA
84	Warner Bros W 9146	Take On Me/And You Tell Me (silver/blue p/s) 40
84	Warner Bros W 9146T	Take On Me (Extended)/And You Tell Me/Stop And Make Your Mind Up (12", silver/blue p/s, some with poster & stickers).................. 120/80
85	Warner Bros W 9006T	Take On Me/Love Is The Reason (12", black & white p/s)................... 8
85	Warner Bros W 9006	Take On Me/Love Is The Reason (reissue, colour p/s with gatefold booklet) 7
86	Warner Bros W 8846P	The Sun Always Shines On T.V./Driftwood (shaped picture disc) 12
86	Lyntone	The Sun Always Shines On T.V. (U.S. Remix) (square picture flexidisc with *No. 1* magazine) 10/5
86	Warner Bros W 8736T	Train Of Thought (Extended)/(7" Remix)/And You Tell Me (12", p/s) ... 8
86	Warner Bros W 8736P	Train Of Thought (Remix)/And You Tell Me (train-shaped picture disc) 12
86	Warner Bros W 8663TP	Hunting High And Low (Extended)/Hunting High And Low (Remix)/ The Blue Sky (Demo) (12", picture disc)............................. 10
86	Warner Bros W 8663T	Hunting High And Low (Extended)/Hunting High And Low (Remix)/ The Blue Sky (Demo) (12", p/s with 'Morten', 'Pal' or 'Mags' poster)....... each 10
86	Warner Bros W 8500TP	Cry Wolf (Extended)/Cry Wolf (7" Version)/Maybe Maybe (12", picture disc) 10
87	Warner Bros W 8405W	Manhattan Skyline/We're Looking For The Whales (poster p/s)............... 5
87	Warner Bros W 8405TP	Manhattan Skyline (Extended Remix)/Manhattan Skyline (LP Version)/ We're Looking For The Whales (12", picture disc)....................... 10
87	Warner Bros W 8305TP	The Living Daylights (Extended)/(7" Remix)/Manhattan Skyline (12", picture disc) ... 12
88	Warner Bros W 7936TP	Stay On These Roads (Extended Remix)/Soft Rains Of April (Original Mix) (12", picture disc).. 10
88	Warner Bros W 7936CD	Stay On These Roads (Extended Remix)/Soft Rains Of April (Original Mix)/ Take On Me/Cry Wolf (3" CD with adaptor in 5" case) 8
88	Warner Bros W 7840W	The Blood That Moves The Body/There's Never A Forever Thing (with pack of 3 postcards in card wallet) 5
88	Warner Bros W 7840TP	The Blood That Moves The Body (Extended)/The Blood That Moves The Body (LP Version)/There's Never A Forever Thing (12", picture disc) 10
88	Warner Bros W 7840CD	The Blood That Moves The Body/There's Never A Forever Thing/ The Blood That Moves The Body (Extended Version)/The Living Daylights (3" CD with adaptor in 5" case)................................... 8
88	Warner Bros W 7749W	Touchy!/Hurry Home (felt p/s) 5
88	Warner Bros W 7749WW	Touchy!/Hurry Home ('liquid' poster p/s) 8
88	Warner Bros W 7749CD	Touchy! (Go-Go Mix)/Hurry Home/Hunting High And Low (3" CD, 5" case) 8
88	Warner Bros W 7636V	You're The One (Remix)/Out Of The Blue Comes Green (Xmas card pack) 5
88	Warner Bros W 7636TP	You're The One (12" Remix)/You're The One (Instrumental)/ Out Of The Blue Comes Green (12", picture disc) 10
88	Warner Bros W 7636CD	You're The One (7" Remix)/Scoundrel Days (LP Version)/Out Of The Blue Comes Green (LP Version) (3" CD with adaptor in 5" case).............. 8
90	Warner Bros W 9547EP	CRYING IN THE RAIN (EP, gatefold p/s) 5
91	Warner Bros W 0012	Early Morning (box set with postcards & tour pass) 5
94	Warner Bros W 0236CDX	Shapes That Go Together/Slender Frame (live)/Touchy (live)/Rolling Thunder (live) (CD, with 3 photographic prints, numbered) 8
88	Warner Bros 925 616-2	STAY ON THESE ROADS (CD, picture disc) 18

(see also Phenomena)

AHAB
82	Chicken Jazz JAZZ 5	Party Girl/Don't Give Up On Us (p/s)............................... 8

(see also Another Pretty Face, Waterboys)

AHAB & WAILERS
63	Pye 7N 15553	Cleopatra's Needle/Neb's Tune 12

A HOUSE
87	Rip ARIP 1	Kick Me Again Jesus/I Want You (p/s) 5
87	Rip ARIPT 1	Kick Me Again Jesus/I Want You/When I Change (12", p/s) 8

AIM
94	Detour DR 018	Call Your Name/Out On The Streets (p/s,1,000 only, 100 on blue vinyl)........ 8/5

ALISON & JILL
73	Profile GMOR 103	ALISON AND JILL (LP).. 20

ALYN AINSWORTH
59	Parlophone R 4533	Bedtime For Drums/The Cobbler's Song (with His Orchestra)................ 6
59	Parlophone R 4533	Bedtime For Drums/The Cobbler's Song (with His Orchestra) (78) 12
59	Parlophone R 4594	18th-Century Rock/Hell's Bells (with Rock-A-Fellas) 7

AIRBRIDGE
82	Carve Up CU 3	PARADISE MOVES (LP) 15

AIRMAIL
79	Graffiti GIT 001	No Human Feeling/In A Moment (p/s) 5

AIR LIQUIDE
94	Smile/Profile SM 9008	ROBOT WARS (10", picture disc).................................. 12

AIRPORT & DEAN
81	Polydor POSP 312	Lost In Space/Window In the Sky (p/s) 5

(see also X-Ray Spex)

AIRTO
71	Buddah 2318 040	SEEDS TO THE GROUND — THE NATURAL SOUNDS OF AIRTO (LP)........... 12
73	CTI CTI 18	FINGERS (LP)... 12
74	CTI CTI 21	IN CONCERT (LP, with Deodato) 12
74	CTI CTI 23	VIRGIN LAND (LP) 12

(see also Deodato)

AIR TRAFFIC CONTROL

77	Epic EPC 5665	Gotta Get A Message Back To You/Move On Up	5

BOBBY AITKEN (& CARIBBEATS)

62	Island WI 028	Baby Baby (actually with Patsy)/Lonely Boy	18
62	Blue Beat BB 93	Never Never (South Virginia)/Isabella	16
63	Blue Beat BB 146	Don't Leave Me/Mom And Dad (both as Bobby Aitken & Tinse)	16
63	Rio R 14	I've Told You/Please Go Back	15
63	Rio R 15	It Takes A Friend/LAUREL AITKEN: Sunshine	15
64	Rio R 34	Rolling Stone/LESTER STERLING'S GROUP: Man About Town	15
64	Rio R 40	Garden Of Eden/Whiplash	15
64	Rio R 50	Little Girl/Together	15
65	Rio R 52	Rain Came Tumbling Down/SHENLEY LUNAN: Something Is On Your Mind	15
65	Rio R 64	Mr Judge/BINZ: Times Have Changed	15
65	Black Swan WI 441	Jerico/LESTER STERLING: Lunch Time	20
66	Blue Beat BB 369	Shame And Scandal/Coconut Woman	16
66	Ska Beat JB 252	Thunderball/ORIGINATORS: Chelip Chelip	16
67	Doctor Bird DB 1071	Keep On Pushing/You Won't Regret It	15
67	Doctor Bird DB 1072	Let Them Have A Home/Temptation (with Caribbeats)	15
67	Doctor Bird DB 1077	Sweets For My Sweet/How Sweet It Is (with Caribbeats)	15
67	Island WI 3028	Kiss Bam Bam/CYNTHIA RICHARDS: How Could I	60
67	Giant GN 11	What A Fool/Curfew (with Caribbeats)	10

(see also Caribbeats, Laurel Aitken, Frank Cosmo, Lloyd & Glen)

LAUREL AITKEN (& BLUE BEATS)

60	Kalypso XX 15	Sweet Chariot/Nebuchnezer	15
60	Kalypso XX 16	Aitken's Boogie/Cherrie	18
60	Kalypso XX 19	Baba Kill Me Goat/Tribute To Collie Smith	12
60	Starlite ST45 011	Boogie In My Bones/Little Sheila	25
60	Starlite ST45 014	Honey Girl (with Caribs)/Drinkin' Whisky (with Bluebeats)	25
60	Melodisc M 1570	Mary Lee/Lonesome Lover (with Bluebeats)	18
60	Blue Beat B 1	Boogie Rock/Heavenly Angel (white label)	20
60	Blue Beat BB 1	Boogie Rock/Heavenly Angel (blue label)	20
60	Blue Beat BB 10	Jeannie Is Back/If It's Money You Need	18
60	Blue Beat BB 14	Judgment Day/Yea Yea Baby	12
60	Blue Beat BB 22	Railroad Track/Tell Me Darling	12
60	Blue Beat BB 25	More Whisky/LLOYD CLARKE: Parapinto Boogie	12
61	Starlite ST45 034	Love Me Baby/Stars Were Made	18
61	Blue Beat BB 40	Bartender/Mash Potato Boogie	15
61	Blue Beat BB 52	Bouncing Woman/Nursery Rhyme Boogie (with Blue Beats)	15
61	Blue Beat BB 70	Mighty Redeemer/Please Don't Leave Me	15
62	Blue Beat BB 84	Brother David/Back To New Orleans (with Blue Beats)	12
62	Blue Beat BB 109	Lucille/I Love You More Everyday	12
62	Blue Beat BB 120	Sixty Days And Sixty Nights/Going To Kansas City	12
62	Blue Beat BB 142	Jenny Jenny/Weary Wanderer (with Bandits and Ruddy & Sketto)	12
62	Dice CC 1	Mabel/You Got Me Rocking (with Hyacinth)	10
63	Dice CC 13	Sweet Jamaica/Bossa Nova Hop	10
63	Blue Beat BB 164	Zion/Swing Low Sweet Chariot	12
63	Blue Beat BB 194	Little Girl/Daniel Saw The Stone	12
63	Duke DK 1002	Low Down Dirty Girl/Pink Lane Shuffle	12
63	Island WI 092	I Shall Remove/We Got To Move	18
63	Island WI 095	What A Weeping/Zion City Wall	18
63	Island WI 099	In My Soul/One More River To Cross	18
63	Rio R 11	Adam & Eve/BOBBY AITKEN: Devil Woman	15
63	Rio R 12	Mary/Hometown	15
63	Rio R 13	Bad Minded Woman/Life	15
63	Rio R 17	Devil Or Angel/Fire	15
63	Rio R 18	Freedom Train/Peace Perfect Peace	15
64	Rio R 35	Rock Of Ages/The Mule	15
64	Rio R 36	Leave Me Standing/Bug A Boo	15
64	Rio R 37	John Saw Them Coming/Jericho	15
64	R&B JB 167	Yes Indeed/You Can't Stop Me From Loving You	15
64	R&B JB 170	Pick Up Your Bundle And Go/Let My People Go	15
64	R&B JB 171	Bachelor Life/You Was Up	15
64	Columbia DB 7280	Be Mine/Don't Stay Out Late	7
64	Blue Beat BB 249	This Great Day/I May Never See My Baby	12
64	J.N.A.C. 1	West Indian Cricket Test/3 Cheers For Worrell	8
64	Black Swan WI 401	Lion Of Judah/Remember My Darling (B-side with Cynthia Richards)	15
64	Black Swan WI 411	The Saint/Go Gal Go	15
64	Dice CC 28	Jamaica/I Don't Want No More	10
65	Dice CC 31	We Shall Overcome/You Left Me Standing	10
65	Rio R 53	Mary Don't You Weep/I Believe	12
65	Rio R 54	Mary Lou/Jump And Shout	12
65	Rio R 56	One More Time/Ring Don't Mean A Thing	12
65	Rio R 65	Let's Be Lovers/I Need You	12
65	Island WI 198	Boogie In My Bones/Little Sheila	15
65	Island WI 252	How Can I Forget You/Weeping And Crying (existence unconfirmed)	
66	Blue Beat BB 340	Clementine/Bongo Jerk	12
66	Ska Beat JB 232	Jumbie Jamboree/Looking For My Baby	15
66	Ska Beat JB 236	Propaganda/Shake	15
66	Ska Beat JB 239	Green Banana/Darling	15
66	Rio R 91	How Can I Forget You/I've Been Weeping And Crying	12
66	Rio R 92	Baby Don't Do It/That Girl	12
66	Rio R 97	We Shall Overcome/Street Of Glory	12
66	Rio R 99	Clap Your Hands/Revival	12
66	Rainbow RAI 101	Don't Break Your Promises/Last Night (with Soulmen)	12
66	Rainbow RAI 106	Voodoo Woman/Bewildered And Blue (B-side with Carols)	12

Laurel AITKEN

67	Rainbow RAI 111	Sweet Precious Love/I Want To Love You Forever (with Carols)	12
67	Columbia Blue Beat DB 102	Rock Steady/Blowin' In The Wind	10
67	Columbia Blue Beat DB 106	I'm Still In Love With You Girl/Blue Rhythm	10
67	Fab FAB 5	Never You Hurt/I Need You (as Laurel Aitken & Soulmen)	8
68	Fab FAB 45	For Sentimental Reasons/Last Waltz (as Laurel Aitken & Rainbows)	6
68	Doctor Bird DB 1160	Mr Lee/Birmingham Girl	15
68	Doctor Bird DB 1161	La La La (Means I Love You)/DETOURS: Sunnyside	15
69	Doctor Bird DB 1187	Fire In Your Wire/Quando Quando	15
69	Doctor Bird DB 1190	Rice And Peas/CLASSICS: Worried Over Me	15
69	Doctor Bird DB 1196	Reggae Prayer/Deliverance Will Come	15
69	Doctor Bird/J.J. DB 1197	The Rise And Fall (Of Laurel)/If You're Not Black	15
69	Doctor Bird DB 1202	Haile Haile (The Lion)/SEVEN LETTERS: Call Collect	15
69	Doctor Bird DB 1203	Carolina/Kingston Town	15
69	Junior JR 105	Think Me No Know/RECO: Trombone Man	10
69	Nu Beat NB 024	Woppi King/Mr Soul	8
69	Nu Beat NB 025	Suffering Still (with Girlie)/Reggae '69	8
69	Nu Beat NB 032	Haile Selassie/Blues Dance	8
69	Nu Beat NB 033	Lawd Doctor (with Girlie)/Big Fight In Hell Stadium	8
69	Nu Beat NB 035	Run Powell Run/RICO RODRIGUEZ: A Message To You	8
69	Nu Beat NB 039	Save The Last Dance/Walk Right Back	7
69	Nu Beat NB 040	Don't Be Cruel/John B	7
69	Nu Beat NB 043	Shoo Be Doo/Babylon Gone	7
69	Nu Beat NB 044	Landlords And Tenants/Everybody Sufferin'	8
69	Nu Beat NB 045	Jesse James/Freedom	8
69	Nu Beat NB 046	Pussy Price Gone Up/Gimme Back Me Dollar	8
69	Nu Beat NB 047	Skinhead Train/Kent People	12
70	Nu Beat NB 048	Skinhead Invasion/Benwood Dick (unissued, blank white label demos only)	15
70	Nu Beat NB 048	Mr Popcorn/GRUVY BEATS: Share Your Popcorn	7
70	Nu Beat NB 049	I've Got Your Love/GRUVY BEATS: Blue Mink	7
70	Nu Beat NB 050	Scandal In Brixton Market/Soul Grinder (both sides with Girlie)	8
70	New Beat NB 054	Nobody But Me/Baby Please Don't Go	7
70	New Beat NB 056	I'll Never Love Any Girl/The Best I Can	7
70	New Beat NB 057	Reggae Popcorn/Take Me Back	7
70	New Beat NB 063	Baby I Need Your Loving/Think It Over	7
70	New Beat NB 065	Sex Machine/Since You Left	7
70	New Beat NB 072	Pachanga/Version	7
70	Ackee ACK 104	Pussy Got Thirteen Life/Single Man	8
70	Ackee ACK 106	Sin Pon You/Everynight	8
70	Bamboo BAM 16	Moon Rock/Cut Up Munno	10
70	Pama PM 818	Mary's Boy Child/RUPIE EDWARDS ALLSTARS: Version	5
70	Pama Supreme PS 300	Why Can't I Touch You/Can't Turn Your Back On Me	5
71	Trojan TR 7826	It's Too Late/AITKEN'S BAND: Slow Rock	6
71	New Beat NB 078	True Love/The Best I Can	5
71	New Beat NB 089	I Can't Stop Loving You/El Paso	5
71	Black Swan BW 1408	If It's Hell Below/Just A Little Bit Of Love	5
72	Big Shot BI 605	Take Me In Your Arms/Two-Timing Woman	5
72	Camel CA 90	Africa Arise/GI GINGRI: Holy Mount Zion	5
72	Columbia DB 8914	Pretty Face In The Market Place/Come Back To My Lonely World	5
75	Camel CA 2007	La Vien Rose/Spanish Eyes	5
80	I-Spy SEE 4	Big Fat Man/It's Too Late (as Laurel Aitken & Unitone)	5
66	Rio LR 1	SKA WITH LAUREL (LP)	125
67	Doctor Bird DLM 5012	SAYS FIRE (LP)	90
69	Pama PSP 1012	THE HIGH PRIEST OF REGGAE (LP)	70
69	Pama ECO 8	SCANDAL IN BRIXTON MARKET (LP, with Girlie)	55
69	J.J.	RISE AND FALL (LP)	75

(see also Laurel & Owen, Girlie, King Horror, Lorenzo, Ruts, Bobby Aitken, Classics, Beresford Ricketts, Duke Reid, Tommy McCook)

A-JAES
64	Oak RGJ 132	I'm Leaving You/Kansas City	450

AKA & CHARLATANS
78	Vanity VANE 1	Heroes Are Losers/Lady Of The Night/Perhaps One Day (12", screen-printed die-cut p/s)	12

JEWEL AKENS
65	London HLN 9954	The Birds And The Bees/Tic Tac Toe	6
65	London HLN 9969	Georgie Porgie/Around The Corner	7
66	Ember EMB S 219	Dancin' Jenny/A Wee Bit More of Your Lovin'	8
65	London HA-N 8234	THE BIRDS AND THE BEES (LP)	18

AK 47
81	Output ORR 202	Stop! Dance!/Autobiography/Hilversum-Ao (p/s)	5

(see also AK Process, File Under Pop)

JAN AKKERMAN
73	Harvest HAR 8069	Blue Boy/Minstrel-Farmers Dance	6
74	Atlantic K 10427	House Of The King/Javeh	5
78	Atlantic K 11014	Crackers/Wings Of Strings	5
73	Harvest SHSP 4026	PROFILE (LP)	12
74	Atlantic K 40522	TABERNAKEL (LP)	12
78	CBS 81843	ARANJUEZ (LP)	12
78	Atlantic K 50420	JAN AKKERMAN (LP)	12

(see also Hunters [Holland], Brainbox, Focus)

AK PROCESS
79	Output OPQ 101	Electronic Music: After All Love/Post Town (p/s, handmade white labels)	6

(see also AK 47)

AKRYLYKZ
80	Double R RED 2	Spyderman/Smart Boy (p/s)	7
80	Polydor POSP 128	Spyderman/Smart Boy (reissue, p/s)	5
80	Polydor 2059 253	J.D./Ska'd For Life (p/s)	6

ROLANDO AL
(see under Roland Alphonso)

AL (Linval Martin) & EWAN (McDermott)
| 71 | Moodisc HM 107 | Let's Talk It Over/Set Me Free | 5 |

AL & VIBRATORS
67	Doctor Bird DB 1085	Move Up/Lone Lover	15
69	High Note HS 005	Check Up/I'll Come Back	10
69	High Note HS 007	Move Up Calypso/PATSY: Fire In Your Wire	8

(see also Vibrators, Patsy Todd, Lord Power)

ALABAMA JUG BAND
| 55 | Brunswick OE 9161 | ALABAMA JUG BAND (EP) | 15 |
| 67 | Ace Of Hearts AH 163 | JUGS AND WASHBOARDS (LP) | 12 |

STEVE ALAIMO
62	Pye International 7N 25161	My Friends/Going Back To Marty	7
63	Pye International 7N 25174	Little Girl/Every Day I Have To Cry	22
63	Pye International 7N 25199	It's A Long Long Way To Happiness/A Lifetime Of Loneliness	7
66	HMV POP 1531	So Much Love/Truer Than True	8
68	Atlantic 588 227	Watching The Trains Go By/Thank You For The Sunshine Days	5

ALARM
81	White Cross W 3/4	Unsafe Buildings/Up For Murder (gatefold p/s)	40
82	Illegal ILS 0032	Marching On/Across The Border/Lie Of The Land (p/s)	15
83	I.R.S. PFP 1014	The Stand/Third Light (p/s)	5
83	I.R.S. PFPC 1023	68 Guns Pts 1 & 2 (p/s, with free cassette: "The Stand"/"Across The Border"/ "Marching On"/"Lie Of The Land"/"For Freedom" (all live) [CS 70504])	8
84	I.R.S. IRS 103	The Deceiver/Reason 41 (p/s, clear vinyl)	5
84	I.R.S. IRS 103	The Deceiver/Reason 41 (p/s, mispress on mustard vinyl)	30
84	I.R.S. IRSD 103/103A	The Deceiver/Reason 41//Lie Of The Land/Legal Matter (double pack, gatefold p/s)	7
85	I.R.S. ALARMD 1	Absolute Reality/Blaze Of Glory//Room At The Top/Reason 36 (double pack)	5
86	I.R.S. IRMSP 112	Knife Edge (Edit)/Caroline Isenberg (poppy-shaped picture disc)	5
87	I.R.S. DIRM 144	Rain In The Summertime/Rescue Me/Presence Of Love/ Eye Of The Hurricane (CD, promo only)	8
88	I.R.S. IRMP 155	Presence Of Love (Laugherne)/Knife Edge (picture disc)	5
88	I.R.S. DIRM 155	Presence Of Love (Laugherne)/Knife Edge (live)/Rain In The Summertime (Through The Haze Mix) (CD, card sleeve, no'd, 5,000 only)	8
80s	Lyntone	flexidisc with tour magazine (red vinyl)	10

(see also Seventeen)

ALBA
| 77 | Rubber RUB 021 | ALBA (LP) | 12 |

BILLY ALBERT "THE KID"
| 56 | Vogue Coral Q 72214 | Black Jack/The Golden Touch | 12 |

EDDIE ALBERT
55	London HL 8136	I'm In Favour Of Friendship/Come Pretty Little Girl	30
55	London HL 8136	I'm In Favour Of Friendship/Come Pretty Little Girl (78)	15
56	London HLU 8241	Little Child (Daddy Dear) (with Sondra Lee)/Jenny Kissed Me	25
56	London HLU 8241	Little Child (Daddy Dear) (with Sondra Lee)/Jenny Kissed Me (78)	15

MEL ALBERT
| 59 | Top Rank JAR 178 | Sugar Plum/Never Let Me Go | 6 |
| 59 | Top Rank JAR 178 | Sugar Plum/Never Let Me Go (78) | 25 |

ALBERTO & RICARDO
| 64 | RCA RCA 1376 | Love's Made A Fool Of You/I'll Do It To You | 5 |

ALBERTO Y LOST TRIOS PARANOIAS
76	Big T BIG 541	Dread Jaws/De Version	6
77	Stiff LAST 2	SNUFF ROCK (EP, p/s)	10
78	Logo GO(D) 323	DEAD MEAT EP (double pack, gatefold p/s)	8
82	New Hormones ORG 30	Cruisin' With Santa/Unfunny Art-School Parody Band (p/s)	5
76	Transatlantic TRA 316	ALBERTO Y LOST TRIOS PARANOIAS (LP)	15
77	Transatlantic TRA 349	ITALIANS FROM OUTER SPACE (LP)	15
78	Logo LOGO 1009	SKITE (LP)	12
80	New Hormones	RADIO SWEAT (cassette, with booklet & stickers in plastic 'radio' bag)	15

(see also Mothmen, Charlie Parkas)

AL ALBERTS
58	Coral Q 72344	Things I Didn't Say/God's Greatest Gift (78)	12
59	Coral Q 72352	Willingly/My Love (78)	15
59	Coral Q 72363	How Soon? (Will I Be Seeing You)/Taking A Chance On Love (78)	20

(see also Four Aces [U.K.])

ALBINO GORILLA
| 72 | Ember EMBS 321 | Shake Me Wake Me/Going To A Go Go | 5 |
| 72 | Ember NR 5060 | DETROIT SOUNDS (LP) | 12 |

ALBION BAND
76	Harvest HAR 5113	Hopping Down In Kent/Merry Sherwood Rangers (as Albion Dance Band)	5
77	Harvest HAR 5128	The Postman's Knock/La Sexte Estample Real (as Albion Dance Band)	5
78	Harvest HAR 5156	Poor Old Horse/Ragged Heroes (p/s)	5
79	Harvest HAR 5175	Pain And Paradise/Lay Me Low (p/s)	6

MINT VALUE £

76	Island HELP 25	BATTLE OF THE FIELD (LP, as Albion Country Band)	12
76	Harvest SHSP 4059	THE PROSPECT BEFORE US (LP, as Albion Dance Band)	12
78	Harvest SHSP 4092	RISE UP LIKE THE SUN (LP)	12

(see also Shirley Collins, Fairport Convention, Keith Dewhurst & Albion Band)

MICHAEL ALBUQUERQUE

| 69 | United Artists UP 35037 | Better Men Than Me/Burn Burn Burn | 6 |
| 70 | United Artists UP 35098 | Roll Him Over/Blind Man | 6 |

(see also Michael D'Albuquerque, E.L.O.)

DENNIS ALCAPONE

70	Explosion EX 2039	Revelation Version/Marka Version	10
70	Supreme SUP 214	You Must Believe Me (with Niney)/	
		RUPIE EDWARDS ALLSTARS: Funk The Funk	10
70	Big Shot BI 565	Shades Of Hudson/Spanish Amigo	15
71	Treasure Isle TI 7069	The Great Woggie/TOMMY McCOOK & SUPERSONICS: Buttercup Version	12
71	Treasure Isle TI 7074	Wake Up Jamaica (with Joya)/TOMMY McCOOK & SUPERSONICS: Version	12
71	Banana BA 328	Duppy Serenade/Sunshine Version	12
71	Banana BA 341	(Love Me) Forever Version/I Don't Want To See You Cry	12
71	Upsetter US 373	Well Dread/UPSETTERS: Dread Version	8
71	Upsetter US 377	Alpha And Omega/JUNIOR BYLES: Beat Down Babylon	8
71	Duke DU 125	Medley Version/Version Two	6
71	Prince Buster PB 8	Sons Of Zion/ANSELL COLLINS: Short Circuit	6
71	Prince Buster PB 12	Let It Roll (with Max Romeo)/ANSELL COLLINS: Clear Blue (w/l demos only)	7
71	Jackpot JP 773	Jumping Jack (with John Holt)/AGGROVATORS: King Of The Track	6
71	Jackpot JP 775	Togetherness (Black & White) (with John Holt)/DELROY WILSON: Live Good	6
71	Jackpot JP 776	Tell It Like It Is/Come Along	5
71	Dynamic DYN 421	Horse And Buggy/ROLAND ALPHONSO & DENZIL LAING: Buggy And Horse	5
71	Dynamic DYN 422	Ripe Cherry/INNER CIRCLE: Red Cherry	5
71	Dynamic DYN 427	Alcapones Guns Don't Bark/Alcapones Guns Don't Bark Version	5
71	Camel CA 74	This A Butter/PHIL PRATT ALLSTARS: Version	5
71	Tropical AL 003	False Prophet/MAX ROMEO: Rude Medley	5
72	Tropical AL 019	Worldwide Love (with Twinkle Brothers)/CARL MASTERS: Gable Up	5
72	Ackee ACK 146	Power Version/BLUESBLASTERS: Martie (B-side actually titled "Margie")	8
72	Prince Buster PB 24	Giant/PRINCE BUSTER: Science	7
72	Upsetter US 381	Wonderman (with Dave Barker, actually by Dave Barker)/	
		Place Called Africa (with Dave Barker & Junior Byles)	12
72	Upsetter US 388	Master Key/UPSETTERS: Keyhole	12
72	Grape GR 3035	Rasta Dub/UPSETTERS: Rasta Version	7
72	Attack ATT 8027	Fine Style/WINSTON SCOTLAND: On The Track	6
72	Duke DU 131	The Sky's The Limit/HUDSON'S ALLSTARS: Limit Version	7
72	Duke DU 147	Get In The Groove (with Dennis Brown)/DYNAMITES: Version	7
72	Techniques TE 918	Look Into Yourself/TECHNIQUES ALLSTARS: Yourself Version	6
72	Green Door GD 4041	Rub Up A Daughter/TONY'S ALLSTARS: Daughter Version	5
72	Jackpot JP 808	Cassius Clay/SLIM SMITH: Love And Affection	8
72	Bullet BU 509	Dub Up A Daughter/PRINCE TONY'S ALL STARS: Version	5
73	Downtown DT 508	You Don't Say/TONY'S ALLSTARS: Version	8
73	Treasure Isle TI 7074	Wake Up Jamaica/Version (with Tommy McCook)	8
73	Jackpot JP 808	Cassius Clay/SLIM SMITH: Love And Affection	5
73	Bread BR 1121	Musical Liquidator/Lorna Banana (B-side with Prince Jazzbo)	6
73	G.G. GG 4538	Musical Alphabet/BUCKLEY ALLSTARS: Things Gonna Change	
		(B-side actually by Maytones)	5
73	Pyramid PYR 7008	Belch It Off/Jack Horner	5
71	Trojan TBL 187	GUNS DON'T ARGUE (LP)	25
73	Magnet MGT 001	KING OF THE TRACK (LP)	25
74	Attack ATLP 1005	DENNIS ALCAPONE (LP)	15
75	Live And Love LALP 104	DREAD CAPONE (LP)	20
77	Third World TWS 801	SIX MILLION DOLLAR MAN (LP)	15
77	Third World TWS 911	INVESTIGATOR ROCK (LP)	15

(see also El Paso, Dennis & Lizzy, Mad Roy, D. Smith, Wailing Souls, Innkeepers, GG Allstars, Stranger Cole, Lizzy & Dennis, Lee)

CRAIG ALDEN

| 60 | London HLW 9224 | Crazy Little Horn/Goggle-Eye'd | 8 |

STEVE ALDO (& CHALLENGERS)

| 64 | Decca F 12041 | Can I Get A Witness/Baby What You Want Me To Do (with Challengers) | 40 |
| 66 | Parlophone R 5432 | Everybody Has To Cry/You're Absolutely Right (solo) | 50 |

RONNIE ALDRICH

54	Decca F 10248	Coach Call Boogie/Donegal Cradle Song	8
54	Decca F 10274	Wolf On The Prowl/Mudhopper	8
55	Decca F 10494	Ko Ko Mo (I Love You So)/Rock Love (with Squads)	10
55	Decca F 10494	Ko Ko Mo (I Love You So)/Rock Love (with Squads) (78)	10
55	Decca F 10544	Rock Candy/Boom, Boom Boomerang (with Squads)	10
55	Decca F 10544	Rock Candy/Boom, Boom Boomerang (with Squads) (78)	10
55	Decca F 10564	Rhythm 'N Blues/Where Ya Gone, Baby? (with Squads)	10
55	Decca F 10564	Rhythm 'N Blues/Where Ya Gone, Baby? (with Squads) (78)	10
57	Columbia DB 3882	Right Now, Right Now/Rock And Roll Boogie (with Squadronaires)	12
57	Columbia DB 3882	Right Now, Right Now/Rock And Roll Boogie (with Squadronaires) (78)	10
57	Columbia DB 3945	Crazy Bear/The Big Band Beat (with Squadronaires)	8
60	Decca F 11283	Friendly Persuasion/Our Concerto (with Dreamers)	5
60	Decca F 11310	The Singer Not The Song/Pepe (with Dreamers)	5
69	Decca F 12909	Ride My See-Saw/Romance On The North Sea (with London Festival Orch.)	5

(see also Squadronaires, Joan Regan)

URIE ALDRIDGE

| 71 | Harry J. HJ 6634 | Set Me Free/LLOYD WILLIS: Free Version | 5 |

(see also John Holt)

ALEANNA
78   Inchrecronin INC 7421   ALEANNA (LP) 30

AKI ALEONG
61   Reprise R 20021   Trade Winds, Trade Winds/Without Your Love 8

DON ALESSI
66   Salvo SLO 5521 LP   GUITAR SPECTACULAR! (LP) 25

ALETHIONS
70s   Myrrh Gold MYR 1002   R.S.V.P. (LP) 15

ARTHUR ALEXANDER
62   London HLD 9523   You Better Move On/A Shot Of Rhythm And Blues 30
63   London HLD 9566   Where Have You Been/Soldier Of Love 30
63   London HLD 9641   Anna/I Hang My Head And Cry 30
63   London HLD 9667   Go Home Girl/You're The Reason 25
64   London HLD 9899   Black Night/Ole John Amos... 20
66   London HLU 10023   (Baby) For You/The Other Woman 20
76   Buddah BDS 439   Everyday I Have To Cry/Everybody Needs Somebody To Love 6
63   London RE-D 1364   ALEXANDER THE GREAT (EP) 100
63   London RE-D 1401   ARTHUR ALEXANDER (EP)... 100
62   London HA-D 2457   YOU BETTER MOVE ON (LP) 165

DAVID ALEXANDER
74   Rare Earth RES 112   Love Love Love/Missy 5

JEFF ALEXANDER & HIS ORCHESTRA
58   London HA-P 2130   ALFRED HITCHCOCK PRESENTS — MUSIC TO BE MURDERED BY
                                    (LP, also stereo SH-P 6012)....................................... 40/30

TEXAS ALEXANDER
61   Fontana 467 136TE   TREASURES OF NORTH AMERICAN NEGRO MUSIC VOLUME 7 (EP) 15

ALFALFA
77   EMI EMC 3213   ALFALFA (LP, with inner sleeve) 12

ALFI & HARRY
56   London HLU 8242   Trouble With Harry/A Little Beauty (triangular centre, gold lettering on label) ... 20
57   London HLU 8494   Closing Time/Safari 10
57   London HLU 8494   Closing Time/Safari (78)... 12
      (see also David Seville)

CLEM ALFORD
74   Columbia SCX 6571   MIRROR IMAGE — THE ELECTRONIC SITAR OF CLEM ALFORD (LP) 40
75   KPM KPM 1183   INDIA (LP, music library album, side 2 only).......................... 45
      (see also Sagram, Magic Carpet)

SANDRA ALFRED
58   Oriole CB 1408   Rocket And Roll/Six Day Rock 60
58   Oriole CB 1408   Rocket And Roll/Six Day Rock (78) 50
      (see also Sandra Barry, Slack Alice)

ALFRED & MELMOTH
68   Island WI 3130   I Want Someone/ALFRED BROWN: One Scotch One Bourbon One Beer 12

LYNN ALICE
76   K&B KB 5520   (You Keep Me) Hanging On/(You Keep Me) Hanging On 7

ALICE COOPER
      (see under 'C')

ALICE IN CHAINS
93   Columbia 659 365-7   Angry Chair (snakeskin wallet sleeve) 8
93   Columbia 659 751-7   Down A Hole (picture disc) 8
93   Columbia 659 751-6   Down A Hole (12", die cut p/s)..................................... 10
93   Columbia 659 751-2   Down A Hole (CD) 8
93   Columbia 658 888-7   Would?/Man In The Box (picture disc, numbered) 8
93   Columbia 658 888-6   Would?/Man In The Box (12", green vinyl, numbered die cut sleeve) 12
93   Columbia 659 090-6   Them Bones/We Die Young/Got Me Wrong/Am I Inside (12", no'd, blue vinyl).... 15

ALICE ISLAND BAND
74   Warren WAR 341   SPLENDID ISOLATION (LP, with insert).............................. 175

ALICE THROUGH THE LOOKING GLASS
69   H&F Recording/SNP   ALICE THROUGH THE LOOKING GLASS (LP, private pressing,
      (no cat. no.)   handmade sleeve, actually by Peter Howell & John Ferdinando).......... 400
97   Tenth Planet TP 032   ALICE THROUGH THE LOOKING GLASS (LP, reissue, no'd, 1,000 only) 12
      (see also Ithaca, Friends, Agincourt, Tomorrow Come Someday, BBC Radiophonic Workshop/Peter Howell)

ALIEN MUTATION
93   Amb. Space Acid ASA 1201 STARSHIP HEART OF GOLD (12") 8
93   Amb. Space Acid ASA 1203 BRIAN VORTEX EP (12", purple vinyl).................................. 8

ALIENS
80   Alien ALI 001   When The River Runs Dry (no p/s) 5

ALIEN SEX FIEND
83   Anagram ANA 11   Ignore The Machine/The Gurl At The End Of My Gun
                                    (p/s, green or pink print on sleeve)................................. 5
84   Anagram ANA 18   R.I.P./New Christian Music (cream & black p/s & red vinyl or b&w poster p/s) .. 6/7
84   Anagram 10 ANA 18   R.I.P./New Christian Music/Crazee (10", p/s)......................... 6
84   Anagram ANA 23   Dead And Buried/Attack (p/s, red vinyl) 5
84   Anagram PANA 23   Dead And Buried/Attack (picture disc) 5
84   Anagram 11 ANA 25   E.S.T. (Trip To The Moon)/Boneshaker Baby/I Am A Product (live)
                                    (11", PVC sleeve with insert)....................................... 8

MINT VALUE £

85	Anagram PANA 11	Ignore The Machine/The Gurl At The End Of My Gun (picture disc)	5
86	Flicknife DLEP 106	I Walk The Line/School's Out//Here She Comes/Can't Stop Smoking (double pack, gatefold p/s)	5
87	Anagram ANA 40	Stuff The Turkey/They Call Me Crazee (p/s, red or green vinyl)	6
87	Anagram CD GRAM 25	THE FIRST ALIEN SEX FIEND COMPACT DISC (CD, with poster)	18
90	Windsong 02	ASF BOX (box set, export issue, 4,000 only, with 3 coloured vinyl singles [12", 11" & 10"], poster, T-shirt & imitation dog turd)	25

(see also Demon Preacher, Demons)

(Dr.) ALIMANTADO
70s	Sun & Star ST 003	Best Dress Chicken/She Wreng-Ep	5

ALIVE 'N KICKING
70	Roulette RO 517	Tighter, Tighter/Sunday Morning	5
70	Roulette 2097 002	Tighter, Tighter/Sunday Morning (reissue)	5

ALKATRAZ
76	Rockfield UAS 30001	DOING A MOONLIGHT (LP)	12

(see also Man)

ALKATRAZZ
82	RCA RCAP 183	Think It Over/Halfway There (picture disc)	5
81	RCA RCALP 5023	YOUNG BLOOD (LP)	12
82	RCA RCALP 3066	RADIO 5 (LP)	12

ALL ABOUT EVE
85	Eden EDEN 1	D For Desire/Don't Follow Me (12", p/s)	20
86	Eden EDEN 2	In The Clouds/End Of The Day/Love Leads Nowhere (12", p/s, some with poster)	18/8
87	Eden EVEN 3	Our Summer/Lady Moonlight (p/s)	5
87	Eden EVENX 3	Our Summer (extended)/Lady Moonlight/Shelter From The Rain (12", p/s)	8
87	Eden EVEN 4	Flowers In Our Hair/Paradise (p/s)	5
87	Eden EVENX 4	Flowers In Our Hair/Paradise/Devil Woman (12", p/s)	8
88	Mercury EVEN 710	Every Angel (extended)/Candy Tree/Wild Flowers/More Than This Hour (10", numbered envelope p/s with poster)	6
88	Mercury EVNXB 8	Martha's Harbour/Another Door/In The Clouds (live)/Shelter From The Rain (live) (12", numbered pack with poster, 2,000 autographed)	10/7
91	Mercury EVCX 13	In The Clouds/Never Promise/Scarlet/More Than The Blues/Road To Your Soul (live fan club cassette, some including "She Moves Through The Fair")	12/7
80s	fan club	LIVE AT THE BRIXTON ACADEMY (live cassette)	15

(see also Ghost Dance)

ALLAM
73	Fab FAB 190	Hide & Seek/Version (actually by Allen & Mr. Lonely)	7

JOHNNIE ALLAN
74	Oval 1001	Promised Land/SHELTON DUNAWAY: Betty And Dupree	6
78	Oval/Stiff LOT 1	Promised Land/PETE FOWLER: One Heart One Song (p/s)	5

RICHARD ALLAN/ALLEN
60	Parlophone R 4634	As Time Goes By/Only Love	6
60	Parlophone R 4673	Everyday/Doctor In Love (as Richard Allen)	5
60	Parlophone R 4711	Don't Ever Say You're Gonna Leave Me/Poetry In Motion	5

ALL DAY
73	private pressing	YORK POP MUSIC PROJECT (LP)	175

ANNISTEEN ALLEN
55	Capitol CL 14264	Fujiyama Mama/Wheels Of Love	150
55	Capitol CL 14264	Fujiyama Mama/Wheels Of Love (78)	40
57	Brunswick 05639	Don't Nobody Move/The Money Tree	18
57	Brunswick 05639	Don't Nobody Move/The Money Tree (78)	10

BARBARA ALLEN
59	Felsted AF 115	Tommy's Song/Never Let Me Go	6
59	Felsted AF 115	Tommy's Song/Never Let Me Go (78)	15

BOBBY ALLEN (& COMMANCHES)
62	Fontana 267252 TF	I'll Forget About You/Your Cheatin' Heart	7
63	Fontana TF 401	Here Comes The Bride/Nothing's Impossible	6
64	Fontana TF 429	Half As Much As You/So In Love With You (with Commanches)	6

(see also Commanches)

CLAY ALLEN
62	Starlite ST45 086	This Time It's Really Goodbye/Broken Home	10
63	Starlite ST45 096	I Can't Stop The Blues From Moving/You've Got The Cleanest Mind	10
63	Starlite ST45 106	Crazy Crazy World/Just A Stone's Throw Away	10

DAEVID ALLEN
75	Virgin VS 123	Fred The Fish/It's The Time Of Your Life (p/s, promo only)	10
79	Charly CY 51056	Much Too Old/I Am A Freud (with New York Gong, p/s with insert)	6
83	Charly CY 2101	ALIEN IN NEW YORK (12" EP)	8
75	Caroline C 1512	BANANA MOON (LP)	12
76	Virgin V 5024	GOOD MORNING! (LP, by Daevid Allen & Euterpe)	12
81	Shanghai HAI 201	THE DEATH OF ROCK AND OTHER ENTRANCES (mini-LP, with poster)	12

(see also Gong, Planet Gong, New York Gong, Here And Now, Soft Machine)

DAVE ALLEN
69	Philips BF 1748	The Good Earth/A Way Of Life	5

DEAN ALLEN
58	London HLM 8698	Rock Me To Sleep/Ooh-Ooh Baby Baby	30
58	London HLM 8698	Rock Me To Sleep/Ooh-Ooh Baby Baby (78)	30

HENRY 'RED' ALLEN
66 CBS BPG 62400   FEELING GOOD (LP) 12

JEFF ALLEN
57 HMV JO 477   That'll Be The Day/Guilty Mind (export issue)........................ 25

JERRY ALLEN & HIS TRIO
54 Decca F 10248   S'Posin'/When I Needed You Most........................ 6
55 Decca F 10443   Kind/Delaunay's Dilemma 6

LEE ALLEN (& HIS BAND)
58 HMV POP 452   Walkin' With Mr. Lee/Promenade 35
58 HMV POP 452   Walkin' With Mr. Lee/Promenade (78)................. 45
59 Top Rank JAR 265   Cat Walk/Creole Alley............................. 12
82 NoLa 4   Zabo/Walkin' With Mr Lee.......................... 5
59 Top Rank JKR 8020 WALKIN' WITH MR LEE (EP) 30
62 Ember ELR 3312   MOOD MUSIC LIBRARY (LP, uncredited library issue, generic sleeve) 50
78 NoLa LP 16   DOWN ON BOURBON STREET (LP) 12
(see also Huey 'Piano' Smith & Clowns)

MAURICE ALLEN
58 Pye 7N 15128   Ooh Baby/Rockhearted 12
58 Pye N 15128   Ooh Baby/Rockhearted (78)......................... 12

RAY ALLEN TRIO
54 Parlophone MSP 6134 Love My Love/Why Should I Love You 6
55 Parlophone MSP 6163 Amapola/Love In Rhyme 6

RED ALLEN
62 Longhorn BLH 0005   Trouble Round My Door/Beautiful Brown Eyes........ 8

REX ALLEN
52 Brunswick 04871   Ragtime Melody/Tuck Me To Sleep In My Old 'Tucky Home (78) 7
52 Brunswick 04955   Rack Up The Balls Boy/Till The Well Runs Dry (78)........ 7
52 Brunswick 05003   Jambalaya/Two-Faced Clock (78) 7
53 Brunswick 05162   Crying In The Chapel/I Thank The Lord (78) 8
54 Brunswick 05341   This Ole House/They Were Doin' The Mambo (with Tex Williams) 15
57 Brunswick 05675   The Little White Horses/Drango.................... 8
57 Brunswick 05677   Wringle Wrangle/Westward Ho The Wagons 8
57 Brunswick 05699   Flower Of San Antone/Money, Marbles And Chalk 7
59 Top Rank JAR 188   One More Sunrise (Morgen)/The Little Old Church In The Valley 6
59 Top Rank JAR 188   One More Sunrise (Morgen)/
                       The Little Old Church In The Valley (78) 12
62 Mercury AMT 1191   Don't Go Near The Indians/Touched So Deeply 6
57 Brunswick OE 9317 WESTWARD HO THE WAGONS (EP) 15
64 Mercury 10011MCE   COUNTRY AND WESTERN ACES (EP) 15
(see also Tex Williams)

STEVE ALLEN (& HIS ORCHESTRA)
56 Vogue Coral Q 72118 The Ballad Of Davy Crockett/Very Square Dance..... 15
58 Vogue Coral Q 72310 Pretend You Don't See Her/But I Haven't Got Him ... 7
58 Vogue Coral Q 72310 Pretend You Don't See Her/But I Haven't Got Him (78)... 12
58 London HL 8742   Almost In Your Arms (Love Song From "Houseboat")/Hula Hoop 7
58 London HL 8742   Almost In Your Arms (Love Song From "Houseboat")/Hula Hoop (78)....... 20
(see also George Cates)

TONY ALLEN
62 Philips BBE 12522 Time To Swing (EP) 20

VERNON ALLEN
64 R&B JB 169   Fari Come/Babylon................................ 15

(Vernon) ALLEN & (Milton) HAMILTON
66 Blue Beat BB 348   It Is I/Baby What's More 12
66 Blue Beat BB 353   You're The Angel/Someone Like You................ 12

WOODY ALLEN
64 Colpix PX 775   Spot Floyd/The Bullet 7
64 Colpix PXL 488   WOODY ALLEN VOLUME 2 (LP) 18
65 Colpix PXL 518   WOODY ALLEN (LP)............................... 18

ALLEY CATS
59 Vogue V 9155   Last Night/Snap-Crackle And Pop.................. 20
59 Vogue V 9155   Last Night/Snap-Crackle And Pop (78) 70

ALLIES
80 Harp HSP 1025   Plush Living/Computer (p/s) 5

BOB ALLISON
64 Solar SRP 103   You've Got Everything/Change Your Mind........... 12

CLAY ALLISON
85 Bucketfull Of Brains SR 1 Fell From The Sun/All Souls
                       (free with *Bucketfull Of Brains* magazine) 6/5

GENE ALLISON
58 London HLU 8605   Hey, Hey, I Love You/You Can Make It If You Try 75
58 London HLU 8605   Hey, Hey, I Love You/You Can Make It If You Try (78)... 40

JERRY ALLISON & CRICKETS
65 Liberty LIB 10196 Now Hear This/Everybody's Got A Little Problem...... 12
(see also Crickets, Ivan)

LUTHER ALLISON
71 Delmark DS 625   LOVE ME MAMA (LP, blue label) 12

MINT VALUE £

LYNN ALLISON

57	Columbia DB 3867	Mama From The Train (A Kiss, A Kiss)/Song Of The Sparrow	8
57	Columbia DB 3906	If Only/The Sky	8

MOSE ALLISON

61	Fontana H 292	Baby Please Don't Go/Deed I Do	12
64	Columbia DB 7330	I Love The Life I Live/Life Is Suicide	10
59	Esquire EP 214	PARCHMAN FARM (EP)	20
59	Esquire EP 221	BACK COUNTRY SUITE (EP)	20
60	Esquire EP 224	BLUEBERRY HILL (EP)	20
61	Esquire EP 231	THAT MAN MOSE AGAIN (EP)	30
64	Columbia SEG 8353	ALLISON SINGS THE BLUES (EP)	20
59	Esquire 32-051	BACK COUNTRY SUITE (LP)	15
59	Esquire 32-071	LOCAL COLOUR (LP)	15
59	Esquire 32-083	YOUNG MAN MOSE (LP)	20
60	Esquire 32-094	CREEK BANK (LP)	25
61	Esquire 32-131	AUTUMN SONG (LP)	25
62	Esquire 32-171	RAMBLIN' WITH MOSE (LP)	18
63	London HA-K 8083	SWINGIN' MACHINE (LP, as Mose Allison Jazz Group)	25
64	Columbia SX 6058	V-8 FORD (LP)	25
64	Stateside SL 10106	MOSE ALLISON SINGS (LP)	20
66	Atlantic 587/588 007	MOSE ALIVE (LP)	15
66	CBS Realm RM(S) 52318	I LOVE THE LIFE I LIVE (LP)	35
66	Atlantic 587/588 031	WILD MAN ON THE LOOSE (LP)	15
67	Transatlantic PR 7189	AUTUMN SONG (LP)	15
68	Transatlantic PR 7279	MOSE ALLISON (LP)	12
72	Atlantic 2400 205	WESTERN MAN (LP)	12
72	Prestige PR 24002	MOSE ALLISON (2-LP)	15
73	Atlantic K 40460	MOSE IN YOUR EAR (LP)	12

ALLISONS (U.K.)

61	Fontana H 294	Are You Sure/There's One Thing More (as Allisons [Bob & John])	5
61	Fontana H 304	Words/Blue Tears	6
61	Fontana H 336	What A Mess!/Lorraine (some in p/s)	10/6
61	Fontana H 362	Lesson In Love/Oh, My Love	6
62	Fontana 267 231TF	Sweet And Lovely/Sugar Love	7
62	Fontana 267 255TF	I'll Cross My Fingers/You Should Be Sorry	7
69	Fontana TF 1021	Are You Sure/There's One Thing More (p/s)	8
61	Fontana TFE 17339	THE ALLISONS (EP)	25
61	Fontana TFL 5135	ARE YOU SURE (LP, also stereo STFL 558)	30/40

ALLISONS (U.S.)

64	Stateside SS 289	Surfer Street/Money	10

(see also Blossoms, Darlene Love)

ALLMAN BROTHERS BAND

73	Capricorn/Sound For Industry SFI 165	Ramblin' Man/MARSHALL TUCKER BAND: Take The Highway (flexidisc free with *Rolling Stone* magazine)	8/5
70	Atco 228 033	THE ALLMAN BROTHERS BAND (LP)	15
71	Atco 2400 032	IDLEWILD SOUTH (LP)	12

(see also Duane Allman, Gregg Allman, Duane & Gregg Allman, Allman Joys, Hourglass)

DUANE ALLMAN

72	Capricorn K 67502	AN ANTHOLOGY (2-LP)	18

(see also Allman Brothers, Duane & Gregg Allman)

DUANE & GREGG ALLMAN

73	Polydor 2310 235	DUANE & GREGG ALLMAN (LP)	12

(see also Allman Brothers, Duane Allman, Gregg Allman)

GREGG ALLMAN

73	Capricorn K 47508	LAID BACK (LP)	12

(see also Allman Brothers, Duane & Gregg Allman)

ALLMAN JOYS

73	Mercury 6398 005	ALLMAN JOYS (LP)	15

ALLNIGHT BAND

79	Contact CON 5	Lovely Ladies/It's My Life	12

ALLNIGHT BAND

79	Casino Classics CC 5/6-12	The Wigan Joker/Six By Six/RON GRAINER ORCH.: A Touch Of Velvet — A Sting Of Brass/Theme From "Joe 90" (12", p/s, crimson vinyl, Disco DJ Version)	8

ALL SAINTS (1.9.7.5.)

94	ZTT SAM 1372	Silver Shadow (Shadow '94)/(UK Swing One)/(Club Sax)/(B-Bop)/(UK Swing Two)/(Jungle)/(Rap Dub)/(Underground Mix)/(Rare Groove)/(Bogle Dub) (12", as All Saints 1.9.7.5., double-pack, stickered title sleeve, promo only)	25
95	ZTT ZANG 53	Silver Shadow/(UK Swing One) (p/s, as All Saints 1.9.7.5.)	8
95	ZTT ZANG 53C	Silver Shadow/(UK Swing One) (cassette, as All Saints 1.9.7.5.)	5
95	ZTT ZANG 53T	SILVER SHADOW (12" EP, as All Saints 1.9.7.5., remixes)	12
95	ZTT ZANG 53CD	SILVER SHADOW (CD EP, as All Saints 1.9.7.5., remixes)	15
95	ZTT ZANG 63C	LET'S GET STARTED (cassette, as All Saints 1.9.7.5., remixes)	5
95	ZTT ZANG 63T	LET'S GET STARTED (12" EP, as All Saints 1.9.7.5., remixes)	12
95	ZTT ZANG 71T	LET'S GET STARTED (12" EP)	10
95	ZTT SAM 1521	LET'S GET STARTED (Love To Infinity Mixes) (12" EP, doublepack, stickered sleeve, promo only)	18
95	ZTT SAM 1603	Let's Get Started (Full Krew Mix)/(Love To Infinity R'n'B Mix) (12", stickered sleeve, promo only)	12
95	ZTT ZANG 63CD	LET'S GET STARTED (CD EP, as All Saints 1.9.7.5., remixes)	15
95	ZTT ZANG 71C	If You Wanna Party (I Found Lovin')/Let's Get Started (Full Krew Mix) (cass.)	5

95	ZTT ZANG 71CD	If You Wanna Party (I Found Lovin')/Let's Get Started (Full Krew Mix)/ (Classic Paradise Club Mix)/(R'N'B Edit) (CD, slimline case)	10
97	London RED 1	I Know Where It's At (Cutfather & Joe's Alternative Mix)/(Original Mix)/ (K-Gee's Bounce Mix)/(Bounce Mix)/(Bounce Instrumental) (12", p/s, promo)	8
97	London BLUE 1	I Know Where It's At (Nu Birth Vocal Mix)/(Nu Birth Riddum Dub)/ (Colour System Inc. Vox)/(Colour System Inc. Dub) (12", p/s, promo)	8
97	London LOCDP 398	I Know Where It's At (K-Gee's Bounce Mix)/(Nu Birth Riddum Dub)/ (Colour System Inc. Vox)/Alone (CD, gatefold card sleeve)	12
97	London LXDJ 407	Never Ever/(Booker T's Vocal Mix)/(Booker T's Down South Dub)/ (Booker T's Down South Dub) (12", white label promo)	8
97	London LOCDP 407	Never Ever/(Booker T's Vocal Mix)/(Booker T's Down South Dub)/ (Booker T's Down South Dub) (CD, gatefold card sleeve)	12
98	London LXXDJ 408	Lady Marmalade (Remixes) (12", p/s, promo)	8
97	London (no cat. no.)	ALL SAINTS (box set w/ CD, cassette, EPK, 4 prints & 3 inserts, promo only)	40
97	London ASINT 1	AN OPEN ENDED INTERVIEW WITH (CD, promo only)	25
97	London (no cat. no.)	I KNOW WHERE IT'S AT (CD & videotape, in All Saints wrap, stickered, promo)	20

(see also Drive)

TOMMY ALLSUP
65	London HA-U 8218	BUDDY HOLLY SONG BOOK (LP)	40

TONY ALMERICO'S DIXIELAND JAMBOREE ALLSTARS
55	London RE-P 1019	DIXIELAND (EP, reissued as RE-D 1019)	12/10

JOHNNY ALMOND MUSIC MACHINE
69	Deram DM 266	Solar Level/To R.K.	6
69	Deram DML/SML 1043	PATENT PENDING (LP)	25
70	Deram SML 1057	HOLLYWOOD BLUES (LP)	20

(see also Alan Price Set, Zoot Money, Paul Williams Set, John Mayall & Bluesbreakers, Mark-Almond, Jon Mark)

MARC ALMOND
SINGLES
84	Some Bizzare BZS 23	The Boy Who Came Back/Joey Demento (p/s)	5
84	Some Bizzare BZS 2310	The Boy Who Came Back (Extended)/Joey Demento (Extended) (10", p/s)	15
84	Some Bizzare BZS 2312	The Boy Who Came Back (Loud Cut)/Joey Demento (Extended) (12", p/s)	8
84	Some Bizzare BZS 24	You Have/Split Lip (p/s)	6
84	Some Bizzare BZS 2410	You Have (Ext.)/Black Mountain Blues/Split Lip (Ext.) (10", p/s, with lyric sheet)	12
84	Some Bizzare BZS 2412	You Have (Long Version)/Joey Demento/Split Lip (Long Version) (12", p/s)	12
84	Some Bizzare BZS 25	Tenderness Is A Weakness/Love For Sale (p/s)	5
84	Some Bizzare BZS 2510	Tenderness Is A Weakness (Extended)/Love For Sale/Pink Shack Blues (live)/ The Heel (live) (10", p/s, with lyric insert)	15
85	Some Bizzare BONK 1	Stories Of Johnny/Stories Of Johnny (with choir)//Blond Boy/ Take My Heart (double pack, stickered gatefold p/s)	6
85	Some Bizzare BONK 1	Stories Of Johnny/Stories Of Johnny (with choir) (p/s)	5
85	Some Bizzare BONK 1-10	Stories Of Johnny/(with choir)/Blond Boy/Take My Heart (10", p/s)	10
85	Some Bizzare BONK 1-12	Stories Of Johnny/(with choir)/Blond Boy/Take My Heart (12", p/s, with poster)	8
85	Some Bizzare BONK P2	Love Letter/Love Letter (with choir) (stickered p/s with poster)	5
85	Some Bizzare BONK 2-10	Love Letter (Cabaret Voltaire Mix)/Love Letter (with choir) (10", stickered p/s)	10
85	Some Bizzare GLOWD 1	The House Is Haunted (By The Echo Of Your Last Goodbye)/Broken Bracelets//Cara A Cara/Medley (double pack, gatefold p/s)	6
85	Some Bizzare GLOW 1-12	The House Is Haunted (Ectoplasmix)/Broken Bracelets/ Cara A Cara/Heart Medley/Burning Books (12", p/s)	8
86	Some Bizzare GLOW 2	A Woman's Story/For One Moment (p/s)	5
86	Some Bizzare TGLOW 2-12	A Woman's Story/For One Moment/The Heel/A Salty Dog/The Plague/ The Little White Cloud That Cried/Just Good Friends (cassette)	5
86	Some Bizzare GLOWY 2-10	A Woman's Story/The Heel/A Salty Dog/The Plague/The Little White Cloud That Cried/For One Moment/Just Good Friends (10", picture disc, stickered PVC sl.)	15
86	Some Bizzare GLOWY 2-12	A Woman's Story/The Heel/A Salty Dog/The Plague/The Little White Cloud That Cried/For One Moment/Just Good Friends (12", p/s, with inner & outer sleeve)	15
86	Some Bizzare GLOW 3	Ruby Red/I'm Sick Of You Tasting Of Somebody Else (p/s)	5
86	Some Bizzare GLOW 3-12	Ruby Red (Anarcoma)/I'm Sick Of You Tasting Of Somebody Else/Jackal Jackal (Mustapha Tomb Stone Teeth)/Brokenhearted And Beautiful (12", p/s)	8
86	Some Bizzare GLOW 3-13	Ruby Red (Re-recorded Extended Dance Mix)/(Instrumental)/ I'm Sick Of You Tasting Of Somebody Else (12", stickered p/s; some mispressed with same track repeated on Side 1)	20/15
87	Some Bizzare GLOWD 4	Melancholy Rose/Gyp The Blood//Pirate Jenny/Surabaya Johnny (double pack, gatefold p/s)	7
87	Some Bizzare GLOW 4-12	Melancholy Rose/Gyp The Blood/A World Full Of People/Black Lullaby (12", p/s with postcard)	8
88	Parlophone RX 6186	Tears Run Rings/Everything I Wanted Love To Be (box set with booklet, cards & badge)	5
88	Parlophone 12RS 6186	Tears Run Rings (Extended)/Tears Run Rings (7" Mix)/ Everything I Wanted Love To Be (12", p/s)	8
88	Parlophone CDR 6186	Tears Run Rings (Extended)/Everything I Wanted Love To Be/ Tears Run Rings (7" Version) (CD)	15
88	Parlophone RG 6194	Bitter-Sweet/King Of Fools (gatefold p/s)	6
88	Parlophone RC 6194	Bitter-Sweet/King Of Fools (clear vinyl, p/s)	5
88	Parlophone CDR 6194	Bitter-Sweet (12" Version)/King Of Fools/Tears Run Rings (The Justin Strauss Mix) (CD)	10
89	Parlophone RX 6201	Something's Gotten Hold Of My Heart (with "Special Guest Star Gene Pitney")/ Something's Gotten Hold Of My Heart (numbered box set with booklet, 2 cards & badge & sticker)	8
89	Parlophone CDR 6201	Something's Gotten Hold Of My Heart (with "Special Guest Star Gene Pitney")/ Something's Gotten Hold Of My Heart/The Frost Comes Tomorrow (CD)	8
89	Parlophone PSR 500	Kept Boy (etched B-side, no p/s, cancelled freebie intended for "The Stars We Are" LP)	25
89	Parlophone R 6210	Only The Moment/Real Evil (clear vinyl, p/s)	6

Marc ALMOND

MARC ALMOND

HERB ALPERT

90	Parlophone RPD 6229	A Lover Spurned (Full Length Version)/Exotica Rose (square-shaped picture disc, printed PVC sleeve) 8
91	Mercury SOFCP 1	Say Hello Wave Goodbye '91/Numbers (Original Version)/Torch (Original Extended Version) (CD, picture disc) 10
91	Mercury SOFCD 2	Tainted Love (Original 7" Version)/Where The Heart Is (Remix)/Tainted Love (Remixed By Mendelsohn) (CD in leather wallet, various colours) 12
92	WEA YZ 638T	Extract From "Trois Chanson De Bilitis"/The Days Of Pearly Spencer/ Dancing In A Golden Cage/Dancing In A Golden Cage (Reflection In A Golden Eye) (12", withdrawn, 300 only) 15
92	WEA YZ 638CDX	Extract From "Trois Chanson De Bilitis"/The Days Of Pearly Spencer/ Dancing In A Golden Cage (CD, no'd holographic disc in metallic card p/s)...... 8

FLEXIDISCS & FREEBIES

82	Lyntone LYN 12505	Discipline (as 'Marc Almond & Friends', flexidisc with *Flexipop* issue 23) 12/7
84	Gutter Hearts LYN 14210	My Death (fan club flexidisc) 12
86	MM Vinyl Conflict 1	Oily Black Limousine (b/w 3 songs by others, free with *Melody Maker*) 6
86	(no label or cat. no.)	Your Aura (live) (fan club flexidisc) 10
89	Offbeat 1	Tears Run Rings (La Magia Dance Mix) (3" CD, with *Offbeat* magazine) 10
92	(no label or cat. no.)	Christmas In Vegas (fan club flexidisc)............................. 5
95	(no label or cat. no.)	When I Was A Young Man (fan club cassette)......................... 10

PROMOS

85	Some Bizzare GLOW DJ 1	The House Is Haunted (By The Echo Of Your Last Goodbye) (Time Expanded DJ Version)/The House Is Haunted 10
88	Parlophone PSR 500	Kept Boy (1-sided, B-side etched)................................. 25
88	Parlophone 12RX 6186	Tears Run Rings (The Justin Strauss Mix)/Tears Run Rings (La Magia Dance Mix)/Everything I Wanted Love To Be (12", plain stickered sleeve)........ 8
90	Parlophone RDJ 6229	A Lover Spurned (Radio Version)/Exotica Rose (with matrix no.: A-1-1-1) 6
90	Parlophone RDJ 6229	A Lover Spurned (Radio Version 'New Mix')/Exotica Rose (with matrix no.: A-2-1, with sticker) 6
90	Parlophone RDJ 6263	Waifs & Strays (12" Grid Mix)/Waifs & Strays (The Grid Twilight Mix) (12"). 8
91	Mercury SOFT DJ 112	Say Hello Wave Goodbye '91 (The Long Goodbye Ext. Mendelsohn Remix)/ Memorabilia '91 (Extended Grid Remix) (12", p/s) 12
91	Mercury SOFT DJ 212	Tainted Love (Mendelsohn Remix)/Tainted Love (The Grid Remix) (12", p/s) 12
91	Mercury SOFT DJ 3	Bedsitter (Grid Remix)/Torch (Original) (p/s)......................... 25
91	Mercury SOFT DJ 312	Tainted Love (MegaMix '91)/Bedsitter (Original 12" Version) (12", p/s)................................ 20
91	WEA YZ 633 DJ	My Hand Over My Heart (DJ Edit)/Deadly Serenade (p/s)................. 5
92	WEA YZ 633 CDDJ	The Days Of Pearly Spencer/Bruises/Dancing In A Golden Cage (CD) 12
95	Mercury MRXDJ 431	Adored And Explored (Andy Meecham Big Long Club Mix)/(X-Press 2 Supervox Mix)/(X-Press 2 Extreme Excess Mix)/(Kung-Fu Mix)/(Kung-Fu Instrumental Mix)/(Beatmasters Master Dub) (12", double pack, red vinyl)..... 15
95	Mercury MRRDJ 431	Adored And Explored (Andy Meecham Slow Fat Dub) (12", 1-sided w.l.) 40
95	Mercury MRXDJ 437	The Idol (Tin Tin Out Mix)/(Idolised)/(Teenage Dream Mix)/(Mad Dog Mix) (12", double pack, white vinyl)................................. 15
96	Mercury MXDJ 444	Out There (Non Eric Remix)/(B-Flats Northern Soul Mix)/(House Of Usher Remix)/(DA Clubheroes Remix)/(DA Clubheroes Rework) (12")............... 10
96	Mercury MERDJ 444	Out There (Tony De Vit Mix Parts 1 & 2)/(Space Cat Mix)/(F*** TheCustomsMix)/ (Sticky Black Plastic Mix)/(Valerie Singleton Mix)/ (Cabaret Mix) (12" double pack) 15
96	EMI PJDJ 25	Yesterday Has Gone (Balearico Mix)/Yesterday Has Gone (with P.J. Proby) (12")................................... 12
96	EMI MARC PJDJ 25	Yesterday Has Gone (with My Life Story Orchestra & P.J. Proby) (12")........ 12

LPs

84	Gutter Hearts GH 1	BITE BACK + BLUES (fan club-only LP, credited to "Raoul & The Ruined") 30
84	Some Bizzare BIZL 8	VERMIN IN ERMINE (LP, with inner sleeve & lyric sheet)................... 12

85	Some Bizzare FAITH 1	STORIES OF JOHNNY (LP, embossed sleeve with lyric book)	12
93	Some Bizzare SBZLP 021	ABSINTHE (LP, gatefold sleeve)	15
95	EMI CDMATBOX 1	TREASURE BOX 1 (2-CD, box set)	20
97	Some Bizzare SBZCD 022	VIOLENT SILENCE/FLESH VOLCANO (CD, withdrawn)	20

(see also Soft Cell, Marc & Mambas, Burmoe Brothers, Vicious Pink Phenomena, Flesh Volcano, Annie Hogan, Sally Timms, Bronski Beat, Gene Pitney)

ALMOND LETTUCE

| 68 | Columbia DB 8442 | The Tree Dog Song/To Henry With Hope | 5 |
| 69 | Philips BF 1764 | Magic Circle/Twenty Weary Miles | 12 |

ALMOND MARZIPAN

| 70 | Trend TNT 53 | Open Up Your Heart/Summer Love | 5 |
| 70 | Trend TNT 55 | Marie Take A Chance/I'll Forget You | 5 |

ALONE AGAIN OR

| 84 | All One ALG 1 | Drum The Beat (In My Soul)/Smartie Edit (p/s) | 7 |

(see also Shamen)

HERB ALPERT (& TIJUANA BRASS)

64	Stateside SS 286	Mexican Drummer Man/The Great Manolette	7
67	Pye International 7N 25419	Casino Royale (From The Film)/The Wall Street Rag (unissued)	
68	A&M AMS 700	Casino Royale (From The Film)/The Wall Street Rag (p/s)	7
69	A&M AMS 755	Without Her/Sandbox (p/s)	5
80	A&M AMSP 7500	Rotation/Behind The Rain (12")	8
62	Stateside SE 1007	THE LONELY BULL (EP)	8
63	Stateside SL 10027	THE LONELY BULL (LP)	12
64	Stateside SL 10072	HERB ALPERT'S TIJUANA BRASS (VOL. 2) (LP)	12

ALPHAVILLE

84	WEA X 9264T	Forever Young (12", p/s)	8
86	WEA X 8643T	Universal Daddy (Aquarian Dance Mix)/Next Generation (12", p/s)	10
86	WEA X 8747T	DANCE WITH ME (12", p/s)	10

CARLTON ALPHONSO

| 67 | Pama PM 700 | Where In This World/Peace Makers | 12 |
| 69 | Grape GR 3000 | Belittle Me/Keep Your Love | 6 |

CLYDE ALPHONSO

| 69 | Studio One SO 2076 | Good Enough/Let The Music Play | 20 |

ORVILLE ALPHONSO

| 65 | Caribou CRC 1 | Belly Lick/Inspiration | 8 |

ROLAND ALPHONSO (alias ROLAND AL)

61	Blue Beat BB 58	Blackberry Brandy/ALVIN & CECIL: Marjorie	15
62	Blue Beat BB 112	Four Corners Of The World (with Alley Cats)/SHINERS: Romantic Shuffle	15
64	R&B JB 164	Crime Wave/MAYTALS: Hello Honey	25
65	Island WI 217	El Pussy Cat/LORD BRYNNER: Tiger In Your Tank	15
65	Ska Beat JB 210	Nimble Foot/ANDY & JOEY: Love Is Stronger	35
65	Ska Beat JB 216	Nuclear Weapon (& Baba Brooks)/STRANGER COLE: Love Thy Neighbour	35
65	Rio R 58	Jazz Ska/HYACINTH: Oh Gee	12
66	Blue Beat BB 356	Just A Closer Walk/Jericho Train	15
66	Island WI 259	James Bond/LEE PERRY: Just Keep It Up	35
66	Doctor Bird DB 1010	From Russia With Love/Cleopatra (with Soul Brothers)	18
66	Doctor Bird DB 1011	Sufferer's Choice (with Soul Brothers)/SOULETTES: I Want To Be	18
66	Doctor Bird DB 1013	WAILERS: Rude Boy/ROLANDO AL & SOUL BROTHERS: Ringo's Theme (This Boy)	60
66	Doctor Bird DB 1017	Sugar And Spice/Get Out Of My Life (with Soul Brothers)	18
66	Doctor Bird DB 1020	Phoenix City (with Soul Brothers)/DEACONS: Men Alone	25
66	Doctor Bird DB 1023	Doctor Ring-A-Ding/FREDDIE & HEARTACHES: Here Is My Heart	25
66	Doctor Bird DB 1039	WAILERS: Rasta Put It On/ROLAND AL & SOUL BROTHERS: Ska With Ringo	60
66	Ska Beat JB 231	Rinky Dink (So Good) (with Studio One Orchestra)/SCRATCH & DYNAMITES: Deacon Johnson	15
67	Pyramid PYR 6003	Middle East/Wise Man	10
67	Pyramid PYR 6004	El Torro/007 (Shanty Town)	8
67	Pyramid PYR 6005	Women Of The World (& Beverley's Allstars)/SPANISHTONIANS: Kisses	12
67	Pyramid PYR 6006	On The Move (& Beverley's Allstars)/DESMOND DEKKER & ACES: It's A Shame	10
67	Pyramid PYR 6007	Jungle Bit (& Beverley's Allstars)/NORMAN GRANT: Somebody Please Help Me	12
67	Pyramid PYR 6008	The Cat/DESMOND DEKKER & ACES: Rudy Got Soul	10
67	Pyramid PYR 6009	Guantanamera Ska (& Beverley's Allstars)/SPANISHTONIANS: Suffer Me Not	10
67	Pyramid PYR 6011	Nothing For Nothing/DESMOND DEKKER & ACES: Rude Boy Train	10
67	Pyramid PYR 6018	Sock It To Me (& Beverley's Allstars)/SPANISHTONIANS: Rudie Gets Plenty	10
68	Pyramid PYR 6022	Whiter Shade Of Pale/On The Move	8
68	Pyramid PYR 6030	Dreamland MAYTALS: 54-46, Was My Number	25
68	Pyramid PYR 6043	Stream Of Life/MAYTALS: Struggle	10
68	Coxsone CS 7077	Reggae In The Grass/ROY RICHARDS: Get Smart	40
69	Gas GAS 112	A Thousand Tons Of Megaton (actually by Derrick Morgan)/Musical Resurrection	10
69	Jackpot JP 704	Zapatoo The Tiger/Music House	6
70	Punch PH 39	Roll On (& Upsetters)/CARL DAWKINS: True Love	5
71	Banana BA 340	Mellow Mood (Way To My Heart)/MAYTALS: Marching On	20

(see also Eric Morris, Bob Marley/Wailers, Prince Buster, Hopeton Lewis, Joe White, Johnny Melody, Monty & Roy, Derrick Morgan, Niney, Jackie Opel, Owen & Leon, Kentrick Patrick, Duke Reid, Roy & Millie, Slickers, Lou Sparkles, Jack Sparrow, Austin Faithful, Clancy Eccles, Charmers, Denny & Wilson, Dennis Alcapone, Ken Boothe, Larry Marshall)

ALPINES

| 68 | Double D DD 110 | Get Ready/CARIBBEATS: Come Back Charlie | 10 |

ALQUIN

| 73 | Polydor 2480 152 | MARKS (LP) | 12 |

MINT VALUE £

RITA ALSTON
70	Trojan TR 7751	Popcorn Funky Reggae/NAT COLE: My Love	6
70	Trojan TR 7752	All Kinds Of Everything/CARL LEVEY: Instrumental Version	6

(see also Rita, Nat Cole)

SHIRLEY ALSTON
75	London HLA 10477	Medley: I Hear Those Church Bells Ringing-Chapel Of Love/I Do Love You	5
75	London SHA 8491	WITH A LITTLE HELP FROM MY FRIENDS (LP)	10

(see also Shirelles)

ALTECS
61	London HLU 9387	Easy/Recess	10

ALTERED IMAGES
81	Epic EPC A 1023	Dead Pop Stars/Sentimental (p/s)	5
81	Epic EPC 40A 1023	Dead Pop Stars/Sentimental/Leave Me Alone (cassette)	5
83	Lyntone LYN 10795	Happy New Year/Real Toys/Leave Me Alone (red vinyl flexi with *Flexipop* 14)	6/5

ALTERNATIVE TV
77	Sniffing Glue SG 75 RPS	Love Lies Limp (1-sided flexidisc with *Sniffing Glue* fanzine issue 12)	20/5
77	Deptford Fun City DFC 02	How Much Longer/You Bastard (p/s)	8
77	Deptford Fun City DFC 02	How Much Longer/You Bastard (p/s, labelled 'alternate versions')	7
78	Deptford Fun City DFC 04	Life After Life/Life After Dub (p/s)	5
78	Deptford Fun City DFC 06	Life/Love Lies Limp (p/s)	5
78	Deptford Fun City DFC 07	Action Time Vision/Another Coke (live p/s)	6
79	Deptford Fun City DFC 10	The Force Is Blind/Lost In Room (Vibing Up The Senile Man) (p/s, last track uncredited)	5
80	Nice NICE 2	Knights Of The Future/(Deluxe Green)/Alternatives To Normal Eating (live Italian 7", no p/s, 2nd track uncredited, free with *Red Ronnie's Bazar No. 4* fanzine)	20/15
87	Anagram ANA 36	My Baby's Laughing (Empty Summer's Dream)/Look At Her Eyes/I Had Love In My Hands	5
78	Deptford Fun City DLP 01	THE IMAGE HAS CRACKED (LP)	12
78	Deptford Fun City DLP 02	WHAT YOU SEE IS … WHAT YOU ARE (LP, 1 side by Here & Now)	12
78	Deptford Fun City DLP 03	VIBING UP THE SENILE MAN (PART ONE) (LP)	12
79	Crystal CLP 01	LIVE AT THE RAT CLUB '77 (authorised bootleg) (LP)	12
80	Deptford Fun City DLP 05	ACTION TIME VISION (LP, with inner sleeve)	12
80	Weird Noise WEIRD 001	SCARS ON SUNDAY (shared C60 cassette, 1 side by Good Missionaries)	15
80	Conventional CON 14	AN YE AS WELL (cassette, shared with Good Missionaries)	15

(see also Mark Perry, Good Missionaries, The Door & The Window, Reflections, Jools Holland, Alex Fergusson, Rat & Whale)

ALTERNATORS
78	Energy NRG 001	No Answers/The Kid Don't Know (no p/s)	15

ALTERN 8
91	Network NWKT 24	VERTIGO EP (12", silver vinyl)	8

ALTERNOMEN UNLIMITED
79	Object OM 06	Facade/Connections (p/s)	4

(see also Spherical Objects)

ALTON (Ellis) & EDDY
60	Blue Beat BB 17	Muriel/CLUE J. & HIS BLUES BLASTERS: Silky	18
62	Island WI 009	My Love Divine/Let Me Dream	18

(see also Alton Ellis)

ALTON & FLAMES
(see under Alton Ellis)

ALVARO
77	Squeaky Shoes SSRM 1	DRINKING MY OWN SPERM (LP)	18
79	Squeaky Shoes SSRM 2	MUM'S MILK NOT POWDER (LP)	15
81	Squeaky Shoes SSRM 3	THE WORKING CLASS (LP)	15

(see also 101'ers)

ALVYN
69	Morgan Bluetown MR 18S	You've Gotta Have An Image/Mind The Gap	6

AMALGAM
69	Transatlantic TRA 196	A PRAYER FOR PEACE (LP)	30
73	A Records A 002	PLAY BLACKWELL & HIGGINS (LP)	15

GLEN AMAMS
69	Escort ES 804	Rich In Love/WOODPECKERS: Zumbelly	6

(see also Glen Adams)

AMAZIAH
74	Sunrise SR 001	STRAIGHT TALKER (LP, private pressing with insert)	150

AMAZING BLONDEL
72	Island WIP 6153	Alleluia (Cantus Firmus To Counterpoint)/Safety In God Alone	6
75	DJM DJS 407	Be So Happy/Queen	6
76	DJM DJS 661	I'll Go The Way I Came/Liberty Belle	6
76	DJM DJX 503	Mulgrave Street/Sad To See You Go/Hole In The Head	6
70	Bell SBLL 131	THE AMAZING BLONDEL AND A FEW FACES (LP)	60
70	Island ILPS 9136	EVENSONG (LP, gatefold sleeve)	15
71	Island ILPS 9156	FANTASIA LINDUM (LP, with inner lyric sleeve)	15
72	Island ILPS 9205	ENGLAND (LP, gatefold sleeve)	12
73	Island ILPS 9257	BLONDEL (LP, gatefold sleeve)	12
75	DJM DJLPS 443	MULGRAVE STREET (LP)	12
76	DJM DJLPS 446	INSPIRATION (LP)	12

MINT VALUE £

76	DJM DJLPS 472	BAD DREAMS (LP)	12
77	DJM DJF 20203	LIVE IN TOKYO (LP)	12

(see also Dimples, Gospel Garden)

AMAZING CATSFIELD STEAMERS
83	Fat Hen FH 002LP	UNITED FRIENDS (LP)	12

AMAZING DANCING BAND
68	Verve VS 567	Deep Blue Train/Simon Smith & His Amazing Dancing Bear	15
67	Verve SVLP 9214	AMAZING DANCING BAND (LP)	15

AMAZING FRIENDLY APPLE
69	Decca F 12887	Water Woman/Magician	40

AMAZING SPACE FROGS
79	Ribbett RIB 1	THE DIRTY HABITS EP (EP)	25
99	Bin Liner RUBBISH 7002	(I'm Into) Necrophilia/Popcorn And Bubblegum (p/s)	6

AMAZORBLADES
77	Chiswick CHIS 20	Common Truth/Messaround (p/s)	6

AMBERGRIS
70	Paramount SPFL 262	AMBERGRIS (LP)	12

AMBER SQUAD
80	Sound Of Leicester ST 1	(I Can't) Put My Finger On You/Tell You A Lie (p/s)	20
80	Dead Good DEAD 17	Can We Go Dancing?/You Should See (What I Do To You In My Dreams) (p/s)	18

(AMERICAN) AMBOY DUKES
68	Fontana TF 971	Let's Go Get Stoned/It's Not True	15
68	Fontana (S)TL 5468	THE AMBOY DUKES (LP)	40
68	London HA-T/SH-T 8378	JOURNEY TO THE CENTER OF THE MIND (LP, as American Amboy Dukes)	30
69	London HA-T/SH-T 8392	MIGRATION (LP, as American Amboy Dukes)	25
74	Discreet DS 2203	TOOTH, FANG AND CLAW (LP)	25

(see also Ted Nugent)

AMBOY DUKES (U.K.)
66	Polydor 56149	Turn Back To Me/I Never Complain About You	6
67	Polydor 56172	All I Need/Doing The Best I Can	7
67	Polydor 56190	High Life In Whitley Wood (Parts 1 & 2)	6
68	Polydor 56228	Judy In Disguise/Who's Foolin' Who	6
68	Polydor 56243	Simon Says/The Marquis	6
68	Polydor 56281	He Came To See Me Yesterday/Easy Going Me	5

AMBROSE & HIS ORCHESTRA
55	MGM SPC 2	Chelsea/My Guy's Come Back (export issue)	10
55	MGM SPC 3	Chee Chee-oo Chee (Sang The Little Bird) (export issue)	10
55	MGM SPC 4	Whistling Willie/Get Happy (export issue)	10
55	MGM SPC 9	Slide Rule/Tango Capriccioso (export issue)	10
56	MGM SP 1151	Lilacs In The Rain/Deep Purple	10

AMANDA AMBROSE
63	RCA Victor RD 7605	THE AMAZING AMANDA AMBROSE (LP)	12

SAMMY AMBROSE
65	Stateside SS 385	This Diamond Ring/Bad Night	70
65	Stateside SS 399	Monkey See Monkey Do/Welcome To Dreamsville	85

AMBROSE SLADE
69	Fontana TF 1015	Genesis/Roach Daddy	150
69	Fontana STL 5492	BEGINNINGS (LP, laminated sleeve, black label with silver print; beware of counterfeits with matt sleeve & black & white label)	200
75	Contour 6870 678	BEGINNINGS OF SLADE (LP, reissue, different cover & running order, withdrawn)	50

(see also Slade, 'N Betweens)

AMBROSIA
75	20th Century BT 434	AMBROSIA (LP)	15
76	20th Century BT 519	SOMEWHERE I'VE NEVER TRAVELLED (LP, with inner sleeve)	15
78	Warner Bros K 56252	LIFE BEYOND L.A. (LP)	12
80	Warner Bros K 56811	ONE EIGHTY (LP)	12

AMEBIX
82	Spiderleg SDL 6	Who's The Enemy/Carnage/No Gods No Masters (p/s)	5
83	Spiderleg SDL 10	Winter/Beginning Of The End (p/s)	5

LOLA AMECHE
53	Oriole CB 1143	Rock The Joint/Don't Let The Stars Get In Your Eyes (78)	12
53	Oriole CB 1172	The Knockin' Song/So Far So Good (78)	10

AMEN CORNER
67	Deram DM 136	Gin House Blues/I Know	7
67	Deram DM 151	The World Of Broken Hearts/Nema	6
68	Deram DM 172	Bend Me Shape Me/Satisnek The Job's Worth	6
68	Deram DM 197	High In The Sky/Run, Run, Run	6
69	Deram DM 228	The World Of Broken Hearts/Gin House Blues	6
69	Immediate IM 073	(If Paradise Is) Half As Nice/Hey Hey Girl	6
69	Immediate IM 081	Hello Susie/Evil Man's Gonna Win	6
69	Immediate IM 084	Get Back/Farewell To The Real Magnificent Seven	6
69	Immediate AS 3	So Fine (promo only 'single sampler' for IMSP 023)	18
76	Immediate SV 104	(If Paradise Is) Half As Nice/Bend Me Shape Me//Hello Susie/High In The Sky (double pack, gatefold p/s)	5
68	Deram DML/SML 1021	ROUND AMEN CORNER (LP)	20

AMEN CORNER

69	Immediate IMSP 023	THE NATIONAL WELSH COAST LIVE EXPLOSION COMPANY (LP, g/fold sl.) 18
69	Immediate IMSP 028	FAREWELL TO THE REAL MAGNIFICENT SEVEN (LP, gatefold sleeve). 16
69	Decca SPA 33	WORLD OF AMEN CORNER (LP) 12

(see also Andy Fairweather-Low, Fairweather, Mayfield's Mule, Judas Jump)

AMERICAN BREED

67	CBS 2888	Step Out Of Your Mind/The Same Old Thing 8
67	CBS 2972	Step Out Of Your Mind/The Same Old Thing (reissue) 5
68	Stateside SS 2078	Bend Me Shape Me/Mindrocker. 6
68	Dot DOT 101	Green Light/Don't It Make You Cry 6
68	Dot DOT 106	Ready, Willing And Able/Take Me If You Want Me 6
67	Dot DOLP 255	AMERICAN BREED (LP). 18
68	Dot (S)LPD 502	BEND ME, SHAPE ME (LP) 18
68	Dot (S)LPD 507	NO WAY TO TREAT A LADY (LP, soundtrack) 25
68	Dot (S)LPD 518	PUMPKIN, POWDER, SCARLET AND GREEN (LP) 15
69	Dot (S)LPD 526	THE LONELY SIDE OF THE CITY (LP) 15

AMERICAN GYPSY

71	CBS 7027	Gypsy Queen Pt 1/Dead & Gone 5
75	BTM SBT 101	Angel Eyes/Lady Eleanor. 5
75	BTM BTM 1001	AMERICAN GYPSY (LP). 25

(AMERICAN) POETS

| 66 | London HLC 10037 | She Blew A Good Thing/Out To Lunch (as American Poets) . . . . 75 |
| 71 | United Artists UP 35308 | She Blew A Good Thing/Out To Lunch (reissue, as Poets). . . . . 6 |

AMERICAN SPRING

72	United Artists UP 35376	Good Time/Sweet Mountain. 5
72	United Artists UP 35421	Mama Said/Tennessee Waltz 5
73	CBS 1590	Shyin' Away/Falling In Love 6
72	United Artists UAG 29363	AMERICAN SPRING (LP) 15

(see also Beach Boys, Honeys)

AMERICAN YOUTH CHOIR

| 71 | Polydor 2066 013 | Together We Can Make It/Keep Your Fine Self Near Me . . . . 15 |

EDDIE AMES

| 57 | HMV POP 311 | The Bean Song/I'd Give You The World . . . . 6 |

NANCY AMES

| 66 | Columbia DB 7809 | Friends And Lovers Forever/I've Got A Lot Of Love. 8 |
| 66 | Columbia DB 8039 | Cry Softly/I Don't Want To Talk About It. . . . . 40 |

AMES BROTHERS

53	HMV 7M 153	You, You, You/My Life, My Love, My Happiness. 12
54	HMV 7M 179	I Can't Believe That You're In Love/Boogie Woogie Maxine 10
54	HMV 7M 209	The Man With The Banjo/Man, Man, Is For The Woman Made. 8
54	HMV 7M 253	Hopelessly/One More Time 8
55	HMV 7M 281	The Naughty Lady Of Shady Lane/Addio 20
55	HMV 7M 310	Sweet Brown-Eyed Baby/Sympathetic Eyes 8
55	HMV 7M 322	Wrong Again/Merci Beaucoup. 8
55	HMV 7M 331	So Will I/My Bonnie Lassie 7
55	HMV POP 121	So Will I/My Bonnie Lassie (78) 8
56	HMV 7M 410	My Love, Your Love/If You Wanna See Mamie Tonight 6
56	HMV POP 218	My Love, Your Love/If You Wanna See Mamie Tonight (78) 8
56	HMV 7MC 46	If You Wanna See Mamie Tonight/It Only Hurts For A Little While
		(export issue) 10
56	HMV POP 242	I'm Gonna Love You/It Only Hurts For A little While 8
56	HMV POP 264	49 Shades Of Green/Summer Sweetheart. 5
57	RCA RCA 1015	Rocking Shoes/Tammy 10
57	RCA RCA 1015	Rocking Shoes/Tammy (78) 10
57	RCA RCA 1021	So Little Time/Melodie D'Amour 5
57	RCA RCA 1021	So Little Time/Melodie D'Amour (78) 8
58	RCA RCA 1049	In Love/A Very Precious Love 5
58	RCA RCA 1049	In Love/A Very Precious Love (78). 8
58	RCA RCA 1091	No One But You (In My Heart)/Pussy Cat 5
58	RCA RCA 1091	No One But You (In My Heart)/Pussy Cat (78) 8
59	RCA RCA 1104	Red River Rose/When The Summer Comes 5
59	RCA RCA 1104	Red River Rose/When The Summer Comes (78). 8
59	RCA RCA 1118	(Yes, I Need) Only Your Love/Dancin' In The Streets 5
59	RCA RCA 1118	(Yes, I Need) Only Your Love/Dancin' In The Streets (78) 8
59	RCA RCA 1135	Someone To Come To/Mason-Dixon Line 5
59	RCA RCA 1135	Someone To Come To/Mason-Dixon Line (78). 12
57	HMV 7EG 8237	EXACTLY LIKE YOU (EP) 10
59	RCA RCX 1047	BEST OF THE AMES BROTHERS (EP) 10
56	Coral LVA 9071	THE SOUNDS OF CHRISTMAS HARMONY (LP) 12

IDI AMIN

| 73 | Transatlantic BIG 527 | Amazin' Man/Findin' De Lady. . . . . 5 |

AMITY

| 76 | Red Rag RRR 001 | AMITY (LP) . . . . 20 |

AMM

| 66 | Incus EP 1 | AT THE ROUNDHOUSE (EP) . . . . 150 |
| 67 | Elektra EUKS 7256 | AMM MUSIC (LP) . . . . 120 |

(see also Eddie Provost Band)

ALBERT AMMONS

| 52 | Vogue V 2109 | Boogie Woogie Stomp/Boogie Woogie Blues (78) . . . . 10 |
| 54 | Vogue V 2201 | Chicago In Mind (with Meade 'Lux' Lewis)/Two And Few (78) . . . . 10 |

MINT VALUE £

54	Vogue V 2213	Bass Goin' Crazy/Suitcase Blues (78)	12
55	Vogue EPV 1071	ALBERT AMMONS (EP)	50
57	Brunswick OE 9325	BOOGIE WOOGIE STOMP (EP)	30
54	Mercury MG 25012	ALBERT AMMONS (10" LP)	35
62	Storyville SLP 184	BOOGIE WOOGIE TRIO (LP)	15

(see also [Big] Joe Turner)

ALBERT AMMONS & PETE JOHNSON
| 55 | HMV DLP 1011 | EIGHT TO THE BAR (10" LP) | 35 |

ALBERT AMMONS, PETE JOHNSON & MEADE 'LUX' LEWIS
| 55 | Columbia SEG 7528 | SHOUT FOR JOY (EP) | 30 |
| 63 | Riverside RLP 12-106 | GIANTS OF BOOGIE WOOGIE (LP) | 25 |

(see also Pete Johnson, Meade 'Lux' Lewis)

GENE AMMONS (BAND)
60	Starlite ST45 017	Echo Chamber Blues/Ammons' Boogie	50
63	Starlite ST45 097	Anna/Cae' Cae'	10
62	Esquire EP 249	BOSSA NOVA BY THE BOSS (EP)	12
59	Esquire 32-047	HI FI JAM SESSION (LP)	25
59	Esquire 32-077	FUNKY (LP)	25
60	Esquire 32-097	JAMMIN' WITH GENE (LP)	25
62	Esquire 32-147	BLUE GENE (LP)	25
63	Esquire 32-177	BOSS TENOR (LP)	25
63	Esquire 32-178	BAD! BOSSA NOVA (LP)	40
72	Prestige PR 24021	JUG & DODO (LP, with Dodo Marmarosa)	12
73	Prestige PR 10019	YOU TALK THAT TALK (LP)	12
73	Prestige PR 10021	BROTHER JUG (LP)	12
74	Prestige PR 24036	JUGANTHOLOGY VOL. 1 (LP)	12

AMON DÜÜL II
70	Liberty LBF 15355	Archangel's Thunderbird/Burning Sister	10
69	Liberty LBS 83279	PHALLUS DEI (LP)	35
70	Liberty LSP 101/LBS 83359	YETI (2-LP, gatefold sleeve)	25
71	United Artists UAD 60003/4	DANCE OF THE LEMMINGS (2-LP, gatefold sleeve)	18
72	Sunset SLS 50257	PHALLUS DEI (LP, reissue)	12
72	United Artists UAG 23927	CARNIVAL IN BABYLON (LP, gatefold sleeve)	18
72	United Artists UAG 29406	WOLF CITY (LP, gatefold sleeve)	15
73	United Artists USP 102	LIVE IN LONDON (LP)	12
73	United Artists UAS 29504	VIVE LA TRANCE (LP, with inner sleeve)	12
75	Atlantic K 50136	HIJACK (LP)	12
82	Illuminated JAMS 024	HAWK MEETS PENGUIN (LP)	12
84	Illuminated JAMS 27	MEETING WITH MEN MACHINES (LP, as Amon Düül [UK])	12

(see also Utopia)

AMORPHOUS ANDROGYNOUS
| 93 | Quigley LPEBV 1 | TALES OF EPHIDRINA (LP) | 18 |
| 93 | Quigley CDEBV 1 | TALES OF EPHIDRINA (CD) | 18 |

(see also Future Sound Of London)

ADAM AMOS & NOEL ROCKS
| 60s | Celtic Music CM 011 | CASUAL ON THE BALCONY (LP) | 15 |
| 60s | Celtic Music CM 026 | ADAM AMOS & NOEL ROCKS (LP) | 15 |

TORI AMOS
91	East West YZ 618T	ME AND A GUN EP (12")	15
91	East West YZ 618CD	ME AND A GUN EP (CD)	25
91	East West YZ 618	Silent All These Years/Me And A Gun (p/s)	12
91	East West YZ 618C	Silent All These Years/Me And A Gun (cassette)	5
91	East West YZ 618T	Silent All These Years/Upside Down/Me And A Gun/Thoughts (12", p/s)	12
91	East West YZ 618CD	Silent All These Years/Upside Down/Me And A Gun/Thoughts (CD)	10
92	East West A 7531	China/Sugar (p/s)	5
92	East West A 7531T	China/Sugar/Flying Dutchman/Humpty Dumpty (12", p/s)	12
92	East West A 7531CD	China/Sugar/Flying Dutchman/Humpty Dumpty (CD)	15
92	East West A 7504	Winter/The Pool (p/s)	5
92	East West A 7504CD	Winter/The Pool/Take To The Sky/Sweet Dreams (CD, jewel case)	8
92	East West A 7504CDX	Winter/Angie/Smells Like Teen Spirit/Thank You (CD, digipak)	25
92	East West A 7479CD	Crucify (Remix)/Here In My Head/Mary/Crucify (LP version) (CD)	8
92	East West A 7479CDX	CRUCIFY LIVE EP (CD, box set, with art prints, some sealed)	50/40
92	East West A 7433	Silent All These Years/Ode To The Banana King Part 1 (p/s)	6
92	East West A 7433CD	Silent All These Years/Me And A Gun/Upside Down/Thoughts (CD)	10
92	East West A 7433CDX	Silent All These Years/Ode To The Banana King Part 1/Song For Eric/Happy Phantom (CD, digipak)	25
94	East West A 7281CD	Cornflake Girl/Sister Janet/Piano Suite: All The Girls Hate Her/Over It (CD)	8
94	East West A 7281CDX	Cornflake Girl/A Case Of You/If 6 Were 9/Strange Fruit (CD, digipak)	20
94	East West A 7263CDX	Pretty Good Year/Home On The Range (with Cherokee addition)/Daisy Dead Petals (CD, digipak)	8
94	East West A 7257CDX	PAST THE MISSION EP: Upside Down (live)/Past The Mission (live)/Icicle (live)/Flying Dutchman (live)	8
94	East West A 7521P	God/God (Acappella Vocal & Rain Mix) (picture disc)	5
96	East West A 5524CD2	Caught A Lite Sneeze/London Girls/That's What I Like Mick (The Sandwich Song)/Samurai (CD, picture disc, digipak)	8
96	East West A 5494CD	Hey Jupiter (Dakota Version)/Professional Widow (Armand's Star Trunk Funkin' Mix)/Honey (live) (CD)	8
98	East West AT 0045C	Raspberry Swirl (Lip Gloss Version)/(Sticky Extended Vocal Mix) (cassette, withdrawn)	10
98	East West AT 0045C	Raspberry Swirl (Lip Gloss Version)/(Sticky Extended Vocal Mix)/(Scarlet Spectrum Feels) (CD, withdrawn)	10
96	East West 82862-1	BOYS FOR PELE (2-LP, clear vinyl)	15
97	East West PROP 100	BOYS FOR PELE (CD, promo, card sleeve)	40

MINT VALUE £

AMOS & SARA
81	private release	THE PRIVATE WORLD OF AMOS (cassette)	8
82	It's War Boys £9	Go Home Soldier/Enough Is Enough/Surveillance O.H.M.S. (12", screenprint p/s)	8

(see also Homosexuals)

AMPS
95	4AD AMP 1	Bragging Party/Bragging Party (no p/s, promo only)	8

(see also Pixies, Breeders)

MOREY AMSTERDAM
54	MGM SP 1086	Somebody Bad Stole De Wedding Cake/I Wish I Was A Peanut	5

ANAL FLEAS
82	Rectal FLEA 45	Psych/Over the Edge/Landlord/Go Down (p/s, with insert)	20

ANAN
68	Pye 7N 17571	Haze Woman/I Wonder Where My Sister's Gone	25
68	Pye 7N 17642	Madena/Standing Still	20

ANCIENT GREASE
71	Mercury 6338 033	WOMAN AND CHILDREN FIRST (LP)	30

(see also Eyes Of Blue, Big Sleep, Man, Gary Pickford-Hopkins)

AND ALSO THE TREES
84	Reflex RE 3	The Secret Sea/Secrecy (p/s)	8
84	Reflex 12 RE 6	The Secret Sea/Secrecy/There Were No Bounds/The Tease The Tear/ Midnight Garden/Wallpaper Dying (12", p/s)	10
84	Reflex FS 9	Shantell/Wallpaper Dying (p/s)	10
85	Reflex 12 RE 8	A Room Lives In Lucy/There Was A Man Of Double Deed/Scarlet Aran (12", p/s)	8
87	Reflex 12 RE 12	The Critical Distance/Scythe And Spade/The Renegade (12", p/s)	8
87	Reflex 12 RE 13	Shaletown/Needle Street/L'Unica Strada (12", p/s)	8
84	Reflex LEX 1	AND ALSO THE TREES (LP)	12

ALISTAIR ANDERSEN
72	Trailer LER 2074	PLAYS ENGLISH CONCERTINA (LP)	10

ERIC ANDERSEN
65	Fontana TFL 6061	TODAY IS THE HIGHWAY (LP)	16
68	Fontana STFL 6068	'BOUT CHANGES AND THINGS TAKE 2 (LP)	15

CARLEEN ANDERSON
90s	Circa YR12	DUSKY SAPPHO EP (12", p/s)	15

CAROL ANDERSON
79	Grapevine GRP 133	Sad Girl/I'll Get Off At the Next Stop	5

ERNESTINE ANDERSON
59	Mercury AMT 1035	Be Mine/I Don't See Me In Your Eyes Any More	6
59	Mercury AMT 1073	My Love Will Last/Call Me Darling	5
60	Mercury AMT 1082	There Are Such Times/You, You, You	5
60	Mercury AMT 1103	A Kiss To Build A Dream On/Come On, Baby, Let's Go	5
61	Mercury AMT 1137	A Lover's Question/That's All I Want From You	5
64	Sue WI 309	Keep An Eye On Love/Continental Mind	25
65	Stateside SS 455	Somebody Told You/How Many Times	8
65	Mercury MF 912	Jerk & Twine/You Can't Buy Love	8
60	Mercury ZEP 10057	RUNNING WILD (EP)	10
60	Mercury ZEP 10089	WELCOME TO THE CLUB (EP)	10
61	Mercury ZEP 10105	AZURE-TE (EP)	8
61	Mercury ZEP 10124	JUST A SWINGIN' (EP)	8
64	Mercury 10007 MCE	ERNESTINE ANDERSON (EP)	10
58	Pye Nixa NPT 19025	BY SPECIAL REQUEST (LP)	16
59	Mercury MMC 14016	RUNNIN' WILD (LP)	22
60	Mercury MMC 14037	THE FASCINATING ERNESTINE (LP)	16
61	Mercury MMC 14062	MOANIN' (LP)	16
64	Sue ILP 911	THE NEW SOUND OF ERNESTINE ANDERSON (LP, unissued)	80+
67	Columbia S(C)X 6145	ERNESTINE ANDERSON (LP)	15

GLADSTONE ANDERSON (& FOLLOWERS)
69	Blue Cat BS 172	Judas/The World Come To An End (with Followers)	10
74	Ashanti ASH 413	It May Sound Silly/Gladdy's Workshop	5
73	Ashanti SHAN 103	IT MAY SOUND SILLY (LP)	12

(see also Stranger & Gladdy, Tommy McCook)

IAN ANDERSON
83	Chrysalis CHS 2746	Fly By Night/End Game (p/s)	5

(see also Jethro Tull)

IAN (A.) ANDERSON
71	Village Thing VTSX 1002	One More Chance/Policeman's Ball	12
69	Saydisc EP SD 134	ALMOST THE COUNTRY BLUES (EP, with Elliot Jackson)	25
68	Saydisc Matchbox SDM 159	THE INVERTED WORLD (LP, with Mike Cooper)	40
69	Liberty LBS 83242E	STEREO DEATH BREAKDOWN (LP, as Ian Anderson Country Blues Band)	30
70	Fontana STL 5542	BOOK OF CHANGES (LP)	22
70	Village Thing VTS 3	ROYAL YORK CRESCENT (LP)	12
72	Village Thing VTS 9	A VULTURE IS NOT A BIRD YOU CAN TRUST (LP)	12
72	Village Thing VTS 18	SINGER SLEEPS ON AS BLAZE RAGES (LP)	12

(see also Mike Cooper; Anderson Jones Jackson)

JON ANDERSON
76	Atlantic K 10840	Flight Of The Moorglade/To The Runner	5
80	Atlantic K 11641	Take Your Time/Hear It	5
82	Polydor POSP 393	Surrender/Spider (p/s)	5

MINT VALUE £

85	Elektra EKR 31T	Easier Said Than Done/Three Ships/Oh Holy Night (12", p/s)	8
88	Epic 651 514-6	Hold On To Love/In A Lifetime/Sundancing (12", p/s)	8
76	Atlantic K 50261	OLIAS OF SUNHILLOW (LP, gatefold sleeve with booklet & inner sleeve)	10

(see also Hans Christian, Warriors, Yes, Mike Oldfield, Jon & Vangelis; Anderson, Bruford, Wakeman & Howe)

KIP ANDERSON
67	President PT 163	You'll Lose A Good Thing/I'm Out Of Love	6

LEROY ANDERSON & HIS "POPS" CONCERT ORCHESTRA
55	Brunswick 05375	Song Of The Bells/Sandpaper Ballet	6
55	Brunswick 05485	Forgotten Dreams/The Last Rose Of Summer	6

MILLER ANDERSON
71	Deram DM 337	Bright City/Another Time, Another Place	6
71	Deram SDL 3	BRIGHT CITY (LP)	20

(see also Voice, At Last The 1958 Rock'n'Roll Show, Keef Hartley Band, Hemlock, Dog Soldier, Lyn Dobson)

REUBEN ANDERSON
66	Doctor Bird DB 1045	Christmas Time Again/DESMOND TUCKER: Oh Holy Night	8

SONNY ANDERSON
60	London HLP 9036	Lonely Lonely Train/Yes, I'm Gonna Love You	45

UDELL T. ANDERSON
69	Direction 58-4212	Love Ain't Love/Funky Walk	5

VICKI ANDERSON
71	Polydor 2001 150	Super Good/Super Good (Version)	7
73	Mojo 2093 005	I'm Too Tough For Mr Big Stuff/Sound Funky	6
74	Mojo 2093 028	Don't Throw Your Love In The Garbage Can/Land Of Milk And Honey/BOBBY BYRD: Sayin' It And Doin' It Are Two Different Things	6

(see also Bobby Byrd, James Brown)

ANDERSON, BRUFORD, WAKEMAN & HOWE
89	Arista 612 379	Brother Of Mine/Themes (gatefold p/s)	5
89	Arista 260 018	Brother Of Mine/Vultures In The City (10", p/s with print)	6
89	Arista 162 379	Brother Of Mine/Themes (Sound/Attention/Soul Warrior)/Vultures In The City (3" CD, gatefold sleeve)	8
89	Arista 662 379	Brother Of Mine/Themes (Sound/Attention/Soul Warrior)/Vultures In the City (CD, picture disc)	8
89	Arista 612 618	Order Of The Universe (Long Edit)/Fist Of Fire/Order Of The Universe (Short Edit) (12", gatefold p/s)	8
90	Arista 662 770	I'm Alive/Let's Pretend/Birthright (Live Version) (CD)	8
91	Arista 209 970	ANDERSON, BRUFORD, WAKEMAN & HOWE (LP, gatefold sleeve with print)	12

(see also Yes, Asia, Jon Anderson, Steve Howe)

ANDERSON, HARLEY & BATT
88	Epic PEEPS 1	Whatever You Believe/Whatever You Believe (live) (p/s)	10
88	Epic PEEPS 12P 1	Whatever You Believe (live)/Whatever You Believe/Deep Is My Yearning (12", p/s)	10

(see also Steve Harley, Mike Batt)

ANDERSON, JONES, JACKSON
68	Saydisc 33 SD 125	ANDERSON, JONES, JACKSON (EP)	20

(see also Ian A. Anderson, Al Jones)

ANDERSON'S ALLSTARS
68	Blue Cat BS 133	Intensified Girls/Jump And Shout	12

BARBARA ANDREWS
70	Escort ERT 838	Lonesome Feeling/RAINY BOP: Hop Scotch	5

BARRY ANDREWS
79	Virgin VS 260	TOWN AND COUNTRY (EP)	6
80	Virgin VS 378	Rossmore Road (NW1)/Win A Night Out With A Well Known Paranoiac (p/s)	8
81	Virgin VS 428	Rossmore Road (NW1)/Pages Of My Love (p/s)	6

(see also XTC, Shriekback, Robert Fripp)

CATHERINE ANDREWS
80	Cat Tracks PURR LP 2	FRUITS (LP, with lyric sheet & poster sleeve)	50

(see also Gordon Giltrap, Inner City Unit)

CHRIS ANDREWS
65	Decca F 12236	Yesterday Man/Too Bad You Don't Want Me	5
65	Decca F 22285	To Whom It Concerns/It's All Up To You Now	5
66	Decca F 22365	Something On My Mind/I'll Do The Best I Can	5
66	Decca F 22404	Whatcha Gonna Do Now?/Lady Oh Lady	5
66	Decca F 22472	Stop That Girl/I'd Be Far Better Off Without You	5
66	Decca F 22521	That's What She Said/Write It Down	5
67	Decca F 22597	I'll Walk To You/They've All Got Their Eyes On You	5
67	Decca F 22668	Hold On/Easy	5
68	Pye 7N 17617	The Man With The Red Balloon/Keep Your Mind On The Right Side	5
69	Pye 7N 17727	Pretty Belinda/Maker Of Mistakes	5
70	Pye 7N 17958	Yo Yo/Hey Babe	5

(see also Chris Ravel & Ravers)

DAVE ANDREWS & SUGAR
68	Jewel JL 04	I'm On My Way/Beatin' Of My Heart	45

EAMONN ANDREWS
56	Parlophone R 4234	High Wind/The Legend Of Wyatt Earp	7
57	Parlophone R 4318	The Ship That Never Sailed/The Magic Tree	7

Ernie ANDREWS

MINT VALUE £

ERNIE ANDREWS
60	Vogue V 9166	'Round Midnight/Lover Come Back To Me	12
65	Capitol CL 15407	Where Were You/What Do I See In The Girl	15
76	Capitol CL 15873	Fine Young Girl/Then I'll Know	5

HARVEY ANDREWS
72	Cube BUG 20	In The Darkness/Soldier	5
72	Cube BUG 26	Learning The Game/Don't Know The Time	5
65	Transatlantic TRAEP 133	HARVEY ANDREWS (EP)	18
70	Decca Nova SDN 9	PLACES AND FACES (LP)	25
72	Cube HIFLY 10	WRITER OF SONGS (LP, with lyric insert)	12
73	Fly HIFLY 15	FRIENDS OF MINE (LP, gatefold sleeve)	12
75	Transatlantic TRA 298	FANTASIES FROM A CORNER SEAT (LP)	12
76	Transatlantic TRA 329	SOME DAY (LP)	12

INEZ ANDREWS & ANDREWETTES
65	Vogue EDVP 1283	INEZ ANDREWS & ANDREWETTES (EP)	30

JOHN ANDREWS & LONELY ONES
66	Parlophone R 5455	A Rose Growing In The Ruins/It's Just Love	30

(see also Supertramp)

LEE ANDREWS (& HEARTS)
57	London HL 7031	Teardrops/Girl Around The Corner (solo, export issue)	165
58	London HLM 8546	Teardrops/Girl Around The Corner (solo)	275
58	London HLM 8546	Teardrops/Girl Around The Corner (solo) (78)	50
58	London HLU 8661	Try The Impossible/Nobody's Home (as Lee Andrews & Hearts)	400
58	London HLU 8661	Try The Impossible/Nobody's Home (as Lee Andrews & Hearts) (78)	75

PATTY ANDREWS
55	Capitol CL 14324	Without Love/Where To My Love?	5
55	Capitol CL 14374	Suddenly There's A Valley/Booga Da Woog	6

(see also Bing Crosby, Jimmy Durante)

TIM ANDREWS
67	Parlophone R 5656	Sad Simon Lives Again/You Won't Be Seeing Me Anymore	6
68	Parlophone R 5695	Your Tea Is Strong/(Something About) Suburbia	5
70	Parlophone R 5824	Tiny Goddess/Josephine	5

(see also Fleur De Lys, Rupert's People)

TIM ANDREWS & PAUL KORDA
68	Parlophone R 5714	Smile If You Want To/Makin' Love To Him	5
68	Parlophone R 5746	Angel Face/Waiter Get Me A Drink	5
69	Parlophone R 5769	How Many Hearts Must Be Broken/Discovery	5

(see also Paul Korda)

ANDREWS SISTERS
57	Capitol CL 14705	Rum And Coca-Cola/No, Baby	12
57	Capitol CL 14705	Rum And Coca-Cola/No, Baby (78)	12
57	Capitol CL 14807	I'm Goin' Home/By His Word	6
58	Capitol CL 14826	One Mistake/Melancholy Moon	6
58	Capitol CL 14878	Torero/Sunshine	6
58	Capitol CL 14878	Torero/Sunshine (78)	12
59	Brunswick 05782	I'll Be With You In Apple Blossom Time/Oh! Johnny	5
59	Brunswick 05782	I'll Be With You In Apple Blossom Time/Oh! Johnny (78)	12
59	Capitol CL 14998	I've Got An Invitation To A Dance/My Love Is A Kitten	5
60	Capitol CL 15170	Rum And Coca-Cola/I'll Be With You In Apple Blossom Time	5

ANDROIDS OF MU
80	Fuck Off FLP 001	BLOOD ROBOTS (LP)	15

ANDROMEDA
69	RCA RCA 1854	Go Your Way/Keep Out 'Cos I'm Dying	18
69	RCA SF 8031	ANDROMEDA (LP)	100
90	Reflection MM 06	SEVEN, LONELY STREET (LP, numbered & signed, 500 only)	15
95	Kissing Spell KSLP 9497	LIVE 1967 (LP)	12

(see also Attack, Five Day Week Straw People, Hard Stuff, Atomic Rooster, John Du Cann, Fuzzy Duck)

AND THE NATIVE HIPSTERS
79	Heater Volume HVR 003	There Goes Concorde Again.../Stands, Still The Building.../ I Wanna Be Around (several different coloured photocopied foldaround sleeves with insert in poly bag)	each 5
82	Illuminated/Glass HIP 1	TENDERLY HURT ME (Poor Prince/Hang Ten/Tenderly Hurt Me/Stuck) (12" EP, p/s)	8

ANDWELLA('S DREAM)
69	CBS 4301	Sunday/Midday Sun (as Andwella's Dream)	25
69	CBS 4469	Mrs. Man/Felix (as Andwella's Dream)	15
69	CBS 4634	Mr. Sunshine/Shades Of Grey (as Andwella's Dream)	15
70	Reflection HRS 1	Every Little Minute/Michael Fitzhenry (as Andwella)	7
70	Reflection HRS 3	Hold Onto Your Mind/Shadow Of The Night (as Andwella)	7
71	Reflection HRS 6	People's People/Are You Ready (as Andwella)	6
69	CBS 63673	LOVE AND POETRY (LP, as Andwella's Dream)	220
70	Reflection REFL 10	WORLD'S END (LP, as Andwella, with poster)	20
71	Reflection REF 1010	PEOPLE'S PEOPLE (LP, as Andwella)	20

(see also David Lewis, David Baxter)

BOB ANDY
67	Island WI 3040	I've Got To Get Back Home/SONNY BURKE: Rudy Girl	18
68	Studio One SO 2063	Too Experienced/Let Them Stay	18
68	Coxsone CS 7074	Born A Man/MARCIA GRIFFITHS: Mark My Word	20
69	Doctor Bird DB 1183	The Way I Feel/ETHIOPIANS: Long Time Now	18

MINT VALUE £

69	Studio One SO 2075	I'm Going Home/SOUND DIMENSION: Straight Flush	18
70	Harry J. HJ 6612	Peace Of Mine/Weep	6
71	Trojan TR 7809	Green Green Valley/Peace Of Mind	5
71	Trojan TR 7821	One Woman/You Don't Know (B-side actually "Save Me Version" by Bob Andy Band)	5
71	Trojan TR 7840	One Woman/You Don't Know	5
71	London HLJ 7127	Games People Play/GAYLETTES: Son Of A Preacher Man (export issue)	8
72	Sioux SI 019	Baby I Need Your Loving/CIRCLES: Mammy Blue	5
72	Sioux SI 020	Everyday People/HONG GANG: Smoking Wild	5
72	Green Door GD 4047	Life/HARRY J. ALL STARS: Version	8
73	Green Door GD 4059	You Don't Know/The Border Song	15
73	Horse HOSS 31	One Woman/Second Hand Love	5
75	Fab FAB 241	Feeling Soul/SOUND DIMENSION: Part 2	10

(see also Bob & Marcia, Larry & Alvin)

HORACE ANDY

72	Attack ATT 8026	Feel Good All Over/PHIL PRATT ALLSTARS: Feel Good (Version)	5
73	Bread BR 1170	Don't Try To Use Me/Goddess Of Love	5
73	Randy's RAN 533	Don't Think About Me (with Earl Flute)/DINO PERKINS: Skin Him Alive	15
74	Ackee ACK 530	Til/IMPACT ALLSTARS: Version	5
75	Fab FAB 260	Oh Lord Why Lord/SOUND DIMENSION: Part 2	10
72	Trojan TBL 197	YOU ARE MY ANGEL (LP)	18

(seel also Jon Cuno, Big Youth & Keith Hudson)

ANDY & BEY SISTERS

59	Fontana H 174	Pretty Baby/Sweeter Than Sweet	8
59	Fontana H 174	Pretty Baby/Sweeter Than Sweet (78)	25
59	Fontana H 197	Scoubidou/Don't Get Around Much Anymore	8
59	Fontana H 197	Scoubidou/Don't Get Around Much Anymore (78)	25

ANDY & CLYDE

65	Rio R 62	Never Be A Slave/Magic Is Love	15
65	Rio R 69	I'm So Lonesome/WINSTON STEWART: Day After Day	15
65	Rio R 71	We All Have To Part/UPSETTERS: Scandalizing	15

ANDY & JOEY

62	Island WI 056	Have You Ever/Cross My Heart	18
64	Port-O-Jam PJ 4009	I Want To Know/My Love Has Gone	15
64	Ska Beat JB 162	You're Wondering Now/You'll Never (copies also exist on R&B label)	15

(see also Roland Alphonso)

ANGEL

| 74 | Cube BUG 41 | Good Time Fanny/Who D'Ya Think You're Foolin' | 6 |
| 74 | Cube BUG 51 | Little Boy Blue/Tragedy Queen | 10 |

ANGEL

| 76 | Casablanca CBC 4007 | ANGEL (LP, with insert) | 20 |
| 76 | Casablanca CBC 4010 | HELLUVA BAND (LP) | 15 |

JOHNNY ANGEL

60	Parlophone R 4642	Chinese Butterfly/My Very Good Friend The Milkman	8
60	Parlophone R 4679	Too Young To Go Steady/You're Thrilling	8
61	Parlophone R 4750	What Happens To Love/Luna Luna Luna Lu	8
61	Parlophone R 4795	Trocadero-Double-Nine-One-O/Web Of Love	8
62	Parlophone R 4874	Look, Look Little Angel/Jenny From Missouri	8
62	Parlophone R 4948	Better Luck Next Time/The Power Of You	8
63	Parlophone R 5026	A Touch Of Venus/The Two Together	8

MARIAN ANGEL

65	Columbia DB 7537	It's Gonna Be Alright/Tomorrow's Fool	10
65	Columbia DB 7705	You Can't Buy My Love/One Way Only	8
66	CBS 202391	Little Bit Of Sunshine/All The Time In The World	6

ANGELA & FANS

| 66 | Pye 7N 17108 | Love Ya Illya/I Know You | 10 |

(see also Alma Cogan)

ANGEL CORPUS CHRISTI & DEAN WAREHAM

| 98 | Via Satellite V-SAT 1966 | Je T'aime — I Wanna Boogie With You/ANGEL CORPUS CHRISTI & ALAN VEGA: Cheree/Surfer Girl (pink vinyl, PVC sleeve with postcard, 1,000 only) | 5 |

(see also Alan Vega)

ANGELFISH

| 93 | Wasteland WSLD 92002 | Suffocate Me/You Can Love Her/Kimberley/Trash It (cassette) | 5 |

(see also Goodbye Mr MacKenzie, Garbage)

ANGELIC UPSTARTS

78	Dead IS/AU/1024	Murder Of Liddle Towers/Police Oppression (p/s, 1,000 only)	30
78	Rough Trade RT/SW 001	Murder Of Liddle Towers/Police Oppression (reissue, p/s)	5
79	Warner Bros K 17354	I'm An Upstart/Leave Me Alone (p/s)	5
79	Warner Bros K 17354	I'm An Upstart/Leave Me Alone (green vinyl, no p/s)	5
79	Warner Bros K 17354T	I'm An Upstart/Leave Me Alone (12", p/s)	8
79	Warner Bros K 17426	Teenage Warning/The Young Ones (p/s)	5
79	Warner Bros K 17426C	Teenage Warning/The Young Ones (red vinyl, no p/s)	5
79	Warner Bros K 17476	Never 'Ad Nothin'/Nowhere Left To Hide (p/s)	5
80	Warner Bros K 17558	Out Of Control/Shotgun Solution (p/s)	5
80	Warner Bros K 17586	We Gotta Get Out Of This Place/Unsung Heroes Part 2 (p/s)	5
80	Warner Bros SPZ 2	I'm An Upstart/Never 'Ad Nothin' (cassette single)	6
80	Zonophone Z 7	Last Night Another Soldier/The Man Who Came In From The Beano (p/s)	5
81	Zonophone Z 12	England/Stick's Diary (p/s)	10
81	Zonophone Z 16	Kids On The Street/The Sun Never Shines (p/s)	5
81	Zonophone Z 22	I Understand/Never Come Back (p/s)	5

MINT VALUE £

81	Zonophone Z 25	Different Strokes/Different Dub (p/s)	5
82	Zonophone Z 28	Never Say Die/We Defy You (p/s)	5
82	Anagram ANA 3	Woman In Disguise/Lust For Glory (p/s)	5
82	Anagram 12 ANA 3	Woman In Disguise/Lust For Glory (12", p/s)	8
83	Anagram ANA 7	Solidarity/Five Flew Over (p/s)	5
83	Anagram 12 ANA 7	Solidarity/Five Flew Over (12", p/s)	8
83	Anagram ANA 12	The Burglar (p/s, unissued)	
83	Anagram ANA 13	Not Just A Name/The Leech (p/s)	5
83	Anagram 12 ANA 13	Not Just A Name/The Leech/Leave Me Alone/Liddle Towers (12", p/s)	8
84	Picasso PIK 001	Machine Gun Kelly/Paint It In Red (p/s)	6
85	Gas GM 3010	Brighton Bomb/Thin Red Line/Soldier (12", banned 'Maggie Thatcher' p/s)	10
79	Warner Bros K 56717	TEENAGE WARNING (LP)	15
80	Warner Bros K 56806	WE GOTTA GET OUT OF THIS PLACE (LP)	15
81	Zonophone ZEM 102	LIVE (LP, some with free live flexidisc: "We're Gonna Take The World"/ "Leave Me Alone"/"The Young Ones"/"White Riot" [no cat. no.])	15/12
81	Zonophone ZONO 104	2,000,000 VOICES (LP)	12
85	Gas GLP 4012	THE POWER OF THE PRESS (LP)	12

ANGELINA
65	Fontana TF 648	I Just Don't Know How/Wishing My Life Away	6

ANGELIQUE
66	Pye 7N 17066	Mio Amore Sta Lontano/LORENZO & HIS ORCHESTRA: Cipolline	5

BOBBY ANGELO & TUXEDOS
61	HMV POP 892	Baby Sitting/Skinny Lizzie	15
61	HMV POP 982	Don't Stop/I Gotta Have You	30
	(see also Innocents [UK], End)		

JERRY ANGELO
59	Parlophone R 4548	Crush Me/Mary Lou	6
59	Parlophone R 4561	If You Change Your Mind/I Love You My Love	6
59	Parlophone R 4561	If You Change Your Mind/I Love You My Love (78)	12
60	Parlophone R 4656	Maria Elena/Old Man River	7
62	Palette PG 9031	Lonely Hill/Make Her Mine	6
62	Palette PG 9034	Innocent Angel/The Boy Who Walks Alone	6

MICHAEL ANGELO & HIS ORCHESTRA
61	Columbia DB 4705	Rocco's Theme/Spinneree	12
62	Columbia DB 4800	Tears/The Roman Spring Of Mrs Stone	15
	(see also John Barry)		

MAYA ANGELOU
57	London HA-U 2062	MISS CALYPSO (LP)	12

ANGEL PAVEMENT
69	Fontana TF 1059	Baby You've Gotta Stay/Green Mello Hill	8
70	Fontana TF 1072	Tell Me What I've Got To Do/When Will I See June Again	8
	(see also Fortes Mentum, Pussy)		

ANGELS
62	Pye International 7N 25150	Everybody Loves A Lover/Blow Joe	7
63	Mercury AMT 1211	My Boyfriend's Back/Now	6
63	Mercury AMT 1215	I Adore Him/Thank You And Goodnight	10
64	Philips BF 1312	Wow Wee Wee/Snowflakes And Teardrops	8
	(see also Beachnuts)		

ANGEL STREET
79	Motor MTR 003	Midnight Man/Running Away (blue vinyl, no p/s)	8

ANGEL WITCH
80	EMI EMI 5064	Sweet Danger/Flight Nineteen (p/s)	12
80	EMI 12EMI 5064	Sweet Danger/Flight Nineteen/Hades Paradise (12", p/s)	30
80	Bronze BRO 108	Angel Witch/Gorgon (p/s)	10
81	Bronze BRO 121	Loser/Suffer/Dr Phibes (p/s)	15
85	Killerwatt KIL 3001	Goodbye/Reawakening (no p/s)	8
80	Bronze BRON 532	ANGELWITCH (LP)	15

ANGIE
79	Stiff BUY 51	Peppermint Lump/ANGIE'S ORCHESTRA: Breakfast In Naples (p/s)	5
	(see also Pete Townshend)		

ANGLETRAX
79	Ariola AHA 554	Things To Make And Do/Nuclear Power (die-cut plain orange sleeve)	5

ANGLIANS
67	CBS 202489	A Friend Of Mine/Daytime Lover	8
	(see also Moving Finger)		

ANGLOS
65	Fontana TF 561	Incense/You're Fooling Me (unissued)	
65	Brit WI 004	Incense/You're Fooling Me	22
65	Fontana TF 589	Incense/You're Fooling Me (reissue)	12
67	Sue WI 4033	Incense/You're Fooling Me (unissued)	
69	Island WIP 6061	Incense/You're Fooling Me (2nd reissue)	8
	(see also Spencer Davis Group, Stevie Winwood)		

ANGRY YOUNG MEN
59	Fontana H 187	Big Daddy/Ciribiribin	8
59	Fontana H 187	Big Daddy/Ciribiribin (78)	25

ANIMALS
64	Columbia DB 7247	Baby Let Me Take You Home/Gonna Send You Back To Walker	6
64	Columbia DB 7301	The House Of The Rising Sun/Talkin' 'Bout You	6

64	Columbia DB 7354	I'm Crying/Take It Easy 6
65	Columbia DB 7445	Don't Let Me Be Misunderstood/Club-A-Go Go (standard issue, matrix: '2N') 6
65	Columbia DB 7445	Don't Let Me Be Misunderstood/Club-A-Go Go (mispressing, with 'demo' version of A-side, matrix: '1N') 15
65	Columbia DB 7539	Bring It On Home To Me/For Miss Caulker 6
65	Columbia DB 7639	We've Gotta Get Out Of This Place/I Can't Believe It 6
65	Columbia DB 7741	It's My Life/I'm Going To Change The World 6
66	Decca F 12332	Inside Looking Out/Outcast. 7
66	Decca F 12407	Don't Bring Me Down/Cheating 7
82	Rak RRP 1	The House Of The Rising Sun/Don't Let Me Be Misunderstood/I'm Crying (picture disc) 5
63	Graphic Sound ALO 10867	I JUST WANNA MAKE LOVE TO YOU (12" EP, 1-sided, 99 only, as Alan Price Rhythm & Blues Group or as Animals, private pressing, blank white cover, typed label) 375
64	Columbia SEG 8374	THE ANIMALS IS HERE (EP) 25
65	Columbia SEG 8400	THE ANIMALS (EP) 30
65	Columbia SEG 8439	THE ANIMALS NO. 2 (EP) 30
65	Columbia SEG 8452	THE ANIMALS ARE BACK (EP) 30
65	Decca DFE 8643	IN THE BEGINNING THERE WAS EARLY ANIMALS (EP, reissue of Graphic Sound EP) 30
66	Columbia SEG 8499	ANIMAL TRACKS (EP) 30
64	Columbia 33SX 1669	THE ANIMALS (LP) 35
64	EMI Regal SREG 1104	THE ANIMALS (LP, export issue). 25
65	Columbia 33SX 1708	ANIMAL TRACKS (LP) 40
65	Columbia TA-SX 1708	ANIMAL TRACKS (reel-to-reel tape) 20
66	Columbia SX 6035	THE MOST OF THE ANIMALS (LP) 20
66	Columbia TA-SX 6035	THE MOST OF THE ANIMALS (reel-to-reel tape). 12
66	Decca LK 4797	ANIMALISMS (LP) 35
76	DJM DJSL 069	IN CONCERT FROM NEWCASTLE (LP) 12

(see also Eric Burdon & Animals, Alan Price, Danny McCullough)

ANIMALS & MEN

| 80 | Strange Days DAYS 1 | The Terraplane Fixation/Shell Shock (p/s). . . . . 5 |
| 80 | TW HIT 101 | Don't Misbehave In The New Age/Machines (p/s) . . . . 5 |

ANIMATED EGG

| 69 | Marble Arch MAL 890 | ANIMATED EGG (LP) . . . . 20 |

PAUL ANKA

78s

58	Columbia DB 4063	You Are My Destiny/When I Stop Loving You (78). 8
58	Columbia DB 4110	Crazy Love/Let The Bells Keep Ringing (78). 8
58	Columbia DB 4172	Midnight/Verboten! (Forbidden) (78) 10
58	Columbia DB 4199	Just Young/So It's Goodbye (78) 10
59	Columbia DB 4241	(All Of A Sudden) My Heart Sings/That's Love (78) 15
59	Columbia DB 4286	I Miss You So/Late Last Night (78) 15
59	Columbia DB 4324	Lonely Boy/Your Love (78). 15
59	Columbia DB 4355	Put Your Head On My Shoulder/Don't Ever Leave Me (78) 20
60	Columbia DB 4390	It's Time To Cry/Something Has Changed Me (78) 35

SINGLES

57	Columbia DB 3980	Diana/Don't Gamble With Love (mauve label). 7
57	Columbia DB 3980	Diana/Don't Gamble With Love (re-pressings on green or black label) 12
57	Columbia DB 4022	I Love You, Baby/Tell Me That You Love Me (mauve or green label) 6/7
58	Columbia DB 4063	You Are My Destiny/When I Stop Loving You (mauve or green label). 6/7
58	Columbia DB 4110	Crazy Love/Let The Bells Keep Ringing (green label). 6
58	Columbia DB 4172	Midnight/Verboten! (Forbidden). 6
58	Columbia DB 4199	Just Young/So It's Goodbye 5
59	Columbia DB 4241	(All Of A Sudden) My Heart Sings/That's Love 5
59	Columbia DB 4286	I Miss You So/Late Last Night 6
59	Columbia DB 4324	Lonely Boy/Your Love 6
59	Columbia DB 4355	Put Your Head On My Shoulder/Don't Ever Leave Me 5
60	Columbia DB 4390	It's Time To Cry/Something Has Changed Me 5
60	Columbia DB 4434	Puppy Love/Adam And Eve. 7
60	Columbia DB 4472	My Home Town/Waiting For You. 6
60	Columbia DB 4504	Hello Young Lovers/I Love You In The Same Old Way 6
60	Columbia DB 4524	Summer's Gone/I'd Have To Share 6
61	Columbia DB 4582	The Story Of My Love/Don't Say You're Sorry 6
61	Columbia DB 4629	Tonight My Love, Tonight/I'm Just A Fool Anyway 6
61	Columbia DB 4669	I Talked To You (On The Telephone)/Dance On Little Girl 6
61	Columbia DB 4702	Cinderella/Kissin' On The Phone 7
62	Columbia DB 4772	The Bells At My Wedding/Loveland 7
62	RCA RCA 1276	Love Me Warm And Tender/I'd Like To Know. 6
62	RCA RCA 1318	Eso Beso/Give Me Back My Heart 6
65	RCA RCA 1434	To Wait For Love/Behind My Smile (some in p/s). 8/5
67	RCA RCA 1567	I Don't Wanna Catch Him Round You Anymore/Sunrise, Sunset 5
68	RCA RCA 1676	Can't Get You Out Of My Mind/When We Get There 25

EPs

57	Columbia SEG 7747	DIANA (EP). 20
58	Columbia SEG 7801	ANKA AGAIN (EP) 18
59	Columbia SEG 7890	SING SING SING (EP). 18
60	Columbia SEG 7985	SINGS SONGS FROM 'GIRLS' TOWN' AND OTHER SUCCESSES (EP). 18
64	RCA RCX 7127	FLY ME TO THE MOON (EP) 15
64	RCA RCX 7152	FOUR GOLDEN HITS (EP) 15
64	RCA RCX 7170	SYLVIE (EP) 15

LPs

| 58 | Columbia 33SX 1092 | PAUL ANKA (LP, green label). . . . . 45 |
| 59 | Columbia 33SX 1196 | MY HEART SINGS (LP) . . . . 25 |

Paul ANKA

MINT VALUE £

60	Columbia 33SX 1268	ANKA SWINGS FOR YOUNG LOVERS (LP)	25
60	Columbia 33SX 1282	PAUL ANKA SINGS HIS BIG 15 (LP)	18
60	Columbia 33SX 1287	IT'S CHRISTMAS EVERYWHERE (LP)	30
61	Columbia 33SX 1395	PAUL ANKA SINGS HIS BIG 15 VOL. 2 (LP)	20
62	Columbia 33SX 1432	PAUL ANKA SINGS HIS BIG 15 VOL. 3 (LP)	20
62	RCA RD 27257/SF 5129	YOUNG ALIVE AND IN LOVE (LP, mono/stereo; add £5 with photo insert)	18/20
62	RCA RD/SF 7533	LET'S SIT THIS ONE OUT (LP, mono/stereo)	18/20
63	RCA RD/SF 7547	OUR MAN AROUND THE WORLD (LP, mono/stereo)	18/20
63	RCA RD/SF 7573	ANKA'S 21 GOLDEN HITS (LP, mono/stereo)	18/20
63	RCA RD/SF 7613	SONGS I WISH I'D WRITTEN (LP, mono/stereo)	18/20
64	RCA RD 7700	EXCITEMENT ON PARK AVENUE — LIVE AT THE WALDORF ASTORIA (LP)	18
68	RCA RD/SF 7956	TIMELESS (LP)	15

(see also Micki Marlo & Paul Anka, Neil Sedaka)

ANNALISE

99	Boss Tunage BOSTAGE 701	Signposts And Alleyways/Empire Builder (p/s, 1-sided green vinyl with free CD, numbered, 250 copies only)	10

ANNETTE (& AFTERBEATS)

59	Top Rank JAR 137	Lonely Guitar/Wild Willie	10
59	Top Rank JAR 137	Lonely Guitar/Wild Willie (78)	25
59	Top Rank JAR 233	First Name Initial/My Heart Became Of Age (with Afterbeats)	8
60	Top Rank JAR 343	It Took Dreams/O Dio Mio	8
60	Pye International 7N 25061	Pineapple Princess/Luan Cha Cha Cha (with Afterbeats)	7
64	HMV POP 1270	Muscle Beach Party/I Dream About Frankie	10
64	HMV POP 1322	Scrambled Egghead/Merlin Jones	7
65	HMV POP 1447	The Monkey's Uncle (with Beach Boys)/How Will I Know My Love	20
59	Gala 45XP 1046	TALL PAUL (EP)	15
64	HMV CLP 1782	ANNETTE'S BEACH PARTY (LP)	40
60s	Buena Vista BV 3305	DANCE ANNETTE (LP)	15

ANNETTE & KEYMEN

64	King KG 1006	Look Who's Blue/How Can I Tell Him	7

ANNIS

79	GTO GT 266	Don't Play Your Games/After Me	8

ANNIVERSARY

78	Aerco AERE 102	GIVE ME A SMILE (EP)	30

ANN-MARGRET

61	RCA RCA 1245	I Just Don't Understand/I Don't Hurt Anymore	6
61	RCA RCA 1267	It Do Me So Good/Gimme Love	7
64	RCA RCA 1396	Man's Favourite Sport/Hey Little Star	7
64	RCA RCX 7148	THE VIVACIOUS ONE (EP)	40
62	RCA RD 27239/SF 5116	AND HERE SHE IS (LP, mono/stereo)	30/35
62	RCA Victor RD/SF 7503	ON THE WAY UP (LP, mono/stereo)	25/30
63	RCA Victor RD/SF 7580	BYE BYE BIRDIE (LP, mono/stereo)	25/30
64	RCA Victor RD/SF 7632	BEAUTY AND THE BEARD (LP, mono/stereo, with Al Hirt)	20/25
64	RCA Victor RD/SF 7649	BACHELORS' PARADISE (LP, mono/stereo)	25/30
64	RCA Victor RD/SF 7591	"ANNE MARGRET" (LP, mono/stereo)	25/30

(see also Al Hirt)

ANNO DOMINI

71	Deram SML-R 1085	ON THIS NEW DAY (LP)	80

ANONYMOUSLY YOURS

69	Trojan TR 680	Get Back/ERNIE SMITH: Not For Sale	6
69	Trojan TR 681	It's Your Thing/'69 (B-side actually by Wallace Wilson)	6
69	Duke DU 40	Organism/Itch	6

ANOREXIA

80	Slim SJP 812	Rapist In The Park/I'm A Square/Pets	25

ANOTHER DREAM

84	Sticky PEEL OFF 2	Forever In Darkness/Human Life (p/s)	8

(see also Mighty Lemon Drops)

ANOTHER PRETTY FACE

79	New Pleasures Z1	All The Boys Love Carrie/That's Not Enough (green & white foldout p/s)	12
79	New Pleasures Z1	All The Boys Love Carrie/That's Not Enough (red & white p/s)	8
80	Virgin VS 320	Whatever Happened To The West?/Goodbye 1970's (p/s)	6
80	Chicken Jazz JAZZ 1	Only Heroes Live Forever/Heaven Gets Closer Everyday (poster p/s)	10
81	Chicken Jazz JAZZ 2	I'M SORRY THAT I BEAT YOU, I'M SORRY THAT I SCREAMED, FOR A MOMENT THERE I REALLY LOST CONTROL (8-track cassette, some with fanzine; add £5 if also with badge)	40/25

(Some copies of the above cassette exist with tracks from DNV single taped onto the end.)

81	Chicken Jazz JAZZ 3	Soul To Soul/A Woman's Place/God On The Screen (foldout p/s)	15

(see also DNV, Funhouse, Waterboys, Ahab)

ANOTHER SUNNY DAY

88	Sarah SARAH 003	Anorak City (5¾" flexidisc free with *Are You Scared To Get Happy* fanzine [SARAH 004], 1,500 only)	25/10
88	Sarah SARAH 007	I'm In Love With A Girl Who Doesn't Know I Exist/Things Will Be Nice/The Centre Of My Little World (14" x 10" foldout poster p/s)	15
89	Caff CAFF 7	Genetic Engineering/Kilburn Towers (p/s, with inner)	20

BRETT ANSELL

62	Oriole CB 1701	That's Where Lonesome Lives/The Door Is Open	6
62	Oriole CB 1725	The Outsider/Rosalita	6

ANSELL (Collins) & ELAINE

72	Camel CA 98	Presenting Cheater/RON WILSON: Official Trombone	12

ANSWERS

66	Columbia DB 7847	It's Just A Fear/You've Gotta Believe Me	80
66	Columbia DB 7953	That's What You're Doing To Me/Got A Letter From My Baby	20

(see also Misunderstood, High Tide)

ADAM ANT

82	CBS A 2367	Goody Two Shoes/Red Scab (p/s, credited to 'Adam & the Ants')	10
82	CBS A 2367	Goody Two Shoes/Red Scab (poster p/s)	5
82	CBS A 2892	Desperate But Not Serious/Why Do Girls Love Horses? (non-gatefold p/s, existence unconfirmed)	25+
83	CBS WA 3614	Puss In Boots/Kiss The Drummer (picture disc)	8
84	CBS A 3589	Strip/Yours, Yours, Yours (standard or 'calendar' poster p/s)	each 8
84	CBS WA 3589	Strip/Yours, Yours, Yours (picture disc)	8
84	CBS TA 4719	Apollo 9 (Splashdown Remix)/Instrumental Splashdown (12", p/s)	10
85	CBS A 6367	Vive Le Rock/Greta X (p/s, mispressing, both sides play "Vive Le Rock")	6
90	MCA MCAR 1387	Room At The Top/Bruce Lee (poster p/s)	5
90	MCA DMCAX 1387	Room At The Top (7" Version)/(House Vocal)/Bruce Lee (CD in no'd tin)	8
90	MCA MCA 1404	Can't Set Rules About Love/How To Steal The World (p/s)	5
85	CBS CD 26583	VIVE LE ROCK (CD, with extra track "Human Bondage Den")	75
94	Arcade ARC 310 000-2	THE VERY BEST OF ADAM ANT (CD, with free live CD)	18

(see also Adam & Ants, Maneaters)

ANTEEEKS

66	Philips BF 1471	I Don't Want You/Ball And Chain	65

PAUL ANTELL

65	Pye International 7N 25329	The Times They Are A-Changin'/Yesterday And Tomorrow	5

BILLIE ANTHONY

54	Columbia SCM 5143	This Ole House/Oh, What A Dream	20
54	Columbia SCM 5155	Teach Me Tonight/Don't Let The Kiddygeddin	12
55	Columbia SCM 5164	Butterscotch Hop/No More	10
55	Columbia SCM 5174	Tweedlee Dee/Shake The Hand Of A Stranger	18
55	Columbia SCM 5184	Something's Gotta Give/Boom Boom Boomerang	10
55	Columbia SCM 5191	The Banjo's Back In Town (with Big Ben Banjo Band)/Ten Little Kisses	10
55	Columbia SCM 5210	Bring Me A Bluebird/The Old Pi-anna Rag	10
56	Columbia SCM 5286	A Sweet Old Fashioned Girl/The Treasure Of Love	8
56	Columbia DB 3818	Lay Down Your Arms/One Finger Piano	8
57	Columbia DB 3874	I Dreamed/The Charge Of The Light Brigade (B-side with ex-R.S.M. Brittain)	5
57	Columbia DB 3935	Rock-A-Billy/A Needle And Thread	15
57	Columbia DB 3935	Rock-A-Billy/A Needle And Thread (78)	8
57	Columbia DB 3970	One/It's Fun Finding Out About London (with Big Ben Banjo Band)	5
57	Columbia DB 4021	Love And Kisses/Everybody's Buddy	5
58	Columbia DB 4141	You/Careful, Careful (Handle Me With Care)	5
59	Columbia DB 4279	Too Late Now/Yes, We Have No Bananas	5
60	Columbia DB 4394	Sure Fire Love/A Handful Of Gold	5

(see also Big Ben Banjo Band)

DAVE ANTHONY'S MOODS

66	Parlophone R 5438	New Directions/Give It A Chance	20

(see also David Anthony)

DAVID ANTHONY

68	Island WI 3148	All Night/Out Of My Mind	15

(see also Dave Anthony's Moods)

LITTLE JOHN ANTHONY

60	Ember EMB 3302	TEENAGE DANCE PARTY (LP)	12

MARC ANTHONY

63	Stateside SS 210	Let's All Cheer Again/Why Do I Love You	5

MARK ANTHONY & JETS

70	Unity UN 565	More Balls/TONY KING: Bum Ball (Chapter II)	6

RAY ANTHONY

53	Capitol CL 13983	Dragnet/Bye Bye Baby (78)	8
55	Capitol CL 14205	I Don't Hurt Anymore/Woman's World	6
55	Capitol CL 14243	Juke Box Special/Heat Wave	10
55	Capitol CL 14243	Juke Box Special/Heat Wave (78)	15
55	Capitol CL 14275	Baby You/Happy Hornblowers (with Dick Stabile Orchestra)	6
55	Capitol CL 14306	Sluefoot/Something's Gotta Give	6
55	Capitol CL 14321	Learnin' The Blues/Mmmm Mamie	7
55	Capitol CL 14345	Pete Kelly's Blues/DC-7	8
55	Capitol CL 14354	Hernando's Hideaway/The Bunny Hop	10
56	Capitol CL 14525	Flip-Flop/Hurricane Anthony	10
56	Capitol CL 14553	Cry Me A River/Bullfighter's Lament	6
56	Capitol CL 14567	Rockin' Through Dixie/Madeira	8
56	Capitol CL 14588	The Sleep Walker/Braziliera (Mexican Storm Song)	6
56	Capitol CL 14648	I Love You, Samantha/I Am In Love	6
56	Capitol CL 14670	Love Is Just Around The Corner/Dancing Lovers	6
57	Capitol CL 14689	Rock Around The Rock Pile/The Girl Can't Help It	18
57	Capitol CL 14689	Rock Around The Rock Pile/The Girl Can't Help It (78)	18
57	Capitol CL 14703	Plymouth Rock/Calypso Dance	7
57	Capitol CL 14740	The Incredible Shrinking Man/This Could Be The Night	6
57	Capitol CL 14752	The Lonely Trumpet/Cello-phane	6
57	Capitol CL 14769	The Bunny Hop/The Hokey Pokey	7
57	Capitol CL 14775	Drive-In/Show Me The Way To Go Home	6
58	Capitol CL 14929	Peter Gunn/Tango For Two (Mmm Shall We Dance?)	6
58	Capitol CL 14929	Peter Gunn/Tango For Two (Mmm Shall We Dance?) (78)	15
59	Capitol CL 15019	The Bunny Hop Rock/Walkin' To Mother's	6

Ray ANTHONY

57	Capitol EAP 1-823	THE GIRL CAN'T HELP IT (EP)	25
57	Capitol EAP 1-958	ROCK AND ROLL WITH RAY ANTHONY (EP)	20
57	Capitol EAP 1008	THE LONGEST WALK (EP)	12
53	Capitol LC 6570	RAY ANTHONY'S ORCHESTRA (10" LP)	15
53	Capitol LC 6615	SWEET AND LOVELY (10" LP)	15
53	Capitol LC 6617	HOUSE PARTY (10" LP)	15
54	Capitol LC 6653	I REMEMBER GLENN MILLER (10" LP)	15
55	Capitol LC 6692	ARTHUR MURRAY SWING FOXTROTS (10" LP)	15

(see also Gordon MacRae & Ray Anthony)

RAYBURN ANTHONY
| 60 | London HLS 9167 | Who's Gonna Shoe Your Pretty Little Feet/There's No Tomorrow | 30 |

RICHARD ANTHONY
62	Columbia DB 4933	J'Entends Siffler Le Train/J'Irai Twister Le Blues	5
63	Columbia DB 7073	Too Late To Worry/Music Maker	5
63	Columbia DB 7133	Walking Alone/C'Est Ma Fete (It's My Party)	5
64	Columbia DB 7235	If I Loved You/More Than Words Could Say	5
64	Columbia DB 7383	A World Of My Own/Every Hour And Ev'rywhere	5
64	Columbia DB 7326	Cry/While I Live	5
65	Columbia DB 7569	I'm Crying In The Rain/I Don't Know What To Do	5
66	Columbia DB 7945	Cloudy/I Only Dream Of You	5
66	Columbia DB 7864	You Gave Me Somebody To Love/Night (La Nuit)	5
67	Columbia DB 8143	Put Your Head On My Shoulder/I Wish I Could Be There	5
63	Columbia SEG 8319	WALKING ALONE (EP)	8
65	Columbia 33SX 1763	RICHARD ANTHONY (LP)	12

VAL ANTHONY
| 53 | Columbia SCM 5079 | Walk With The Wind/No Tears, No Regrets | 8 |
| 54 | Columbia SCM 5103 | The Heart Of A Fool/The Portuguese Fishermen | 8 |

ANTHONY & IMPERIALS
(see under Little Anthony & Imperials)

ANTHRAX (U.K.)
| 83 | Small Wonder SMALL 27 | THEY'VE GOT IT ALL WRONG (EP, p/s) | 8 |
| 83 | Crass 221984/9 | CAPITALISM IS CANNIBALISM (EP, foldout p/s) | 6 |

ANTHRAX (U.S.)
86	Island 12ISP 285	Madhouse/Air/God Save The Queen (12", picture disc)	15
86	Island 12IS 285	Madhouse/Air/God Save The Queen (12", p/s with patch)	10
87	Megaforce MRS 05(P)	Armed And Dangerous (12" EP, import, some as picture disc)	15/10
87	Island LAWP 1	I Am The Law/Bud E. Luvbomb And Satan's Lounge Band (picture disc)	8
87	Island ISX 316	I Am The Law (live)/Bud E. Luvbomb And Satan's Lounge Band/	
		Madhouse (live) (red vinyl, p/s)	8
87	Island 12IS 316	I Am The Law/Bud E. Luvbomb And Satan's Lounge Band	
		(12", poster p/s)	15
87	Island ISP 325	Indians/Sabbath Bloody Sabbath (picture disc with sticker)	6
87	Island IS 325	Indians/Sabbath Bloody Sabbath (p/s, orange vinyl)	5
87	Island IS 325	Indians/Sabbath Bloody Sabbath (p/s, orange vinyl, mispress)	6
87	Island 12IS 325	Indians/Sabbath Bloody Sabbath/Taint (12", poster p/s)	8
87	Island 12ISP 325	Indians/Sabbath Bloody Sabbath/Taint (12", picture disc)	8
87	Island ISP 338	I'm The Man/Caught In The Mash (logo-shaped picture disc)	5
88	Island CIDP 379	Make Me Laugh/Friggin' In The Riggin'/Anti-Social (live)	
		(CD, 7" 'pyramid' card pack)	8
89	Island CIDX 409	Anti-Social/Parasite/Le Sects (3" CD)	8
90	Island ISP 476	Got The Time/Who Put This Together (picture disc)	5
86	Music For Nations MFN62P	SPREADING THE DISEASE (LP, picture disc)	15
87	Music For Nations MFN14P	FISTFUL OF METAL (LP, picture disc)	15
87	Island PILPS 9865	AMONG THE LIVING (LP, picture disc)	15
88	Island PILPS 9916	STATE OF EUPHORIA (LP, picture disc, die-cut sleeve)	12

ANTI ESTABLISHMENT
80	Charnel House CADAV 1	1980/Mechanical Man (p/s)	10
82	Glass GLASS 022	Future Girl/No Trust (p/s)	5
83	Glass GLASS 023	Anti Men/Misunderstood (p/s)	5

ANTI GROUP
85	Sweatbox SOX09	Zulu/Ha (12", die-cut white embossed sleeve, with 8-page booklet)	8
86	Sweatbox SOX 010	ShT (EP, black die-cut embossed sleeve)	7
87	Sweatbox OX 011	Big Sex/The Ocean (printed plastic sleeve, 2,000 only)	6
87	Sweatbox SOX 011	Big Sex/The Ocean (12", red embossed die-cut sleeve)	7
86	Sweatbox SOX 012	DIGITARIA (LP, with inner sleeve)	10
88	Sweatbox SACD 012	DIGITARIA (CD)	15

(see also Clock DVA)

ANTI NOWHERE LEAGUE
82	WXYZ ABCD 1	So What/Streets Of London (p/s, withdrawn)	8
82	WXYZ ABCD 1T	So What/Streets Of London (12", p/s, withdrawn)	10
82	WXYZ ABCD 2	I Hate ... People/Let's Break The Law (p/s)	8
82	WXYZ ABCD 4	Woman/Rocker (picture disc)	10

ANTI PASTI
80	Rondelet ROUND 2	FORE SORE POINTS (EP)	10
81	Rondelet ROUND 5	Let Them Free/Another Dead Soldier (p/s, red or black vinyl)	5
81	Rondelet ROUND 10	Six Guns/Now's The Time/Call the Army (p/s)	5
82	Rondelet ROUND 18	East To The West/Burn In Your Own Flames (p/s)	5
82	Rondelet ROUND 26	Caution To The Wind/Last Train (p/s, with sticker)	5

ANTI SOCIAL
| 77 | Dynamite DRO 1 | Traffic Lights/Teacher Teacher (no p/s) | 150 |

ANTI SOCIAL

82	Lightbeat SOCIAL 1	MADE IN ENGLAND (EP)	10
82	Beat The System BTS 2	Battle Scarred Skinheads/Sewer Rat/Official Hooligan (p/s)	6
82	Beat The System FIT 2	Too Many People/Let's Have Some (p/s)	5
82	Lightbeat	THE NEW PUNKS EP (cassette)	8

ANTI SYSTEM

83	Paragon/Pax PAX 11	DEFENCE OF THE REALM (EP)	5

ANTOINE

66	Vogue VRS 7009	Les Elucubrations D'Antoine/J'ai Oublié La Nuit	5
66	Vogue VRS 7017	Before The Good Thing/Elephants Looking At Me	5
66	Vogue VRS 7022	Ma Fete Forraine/Only These Few Snowflakes	5
68	Vogue VRS 7028	La Tramontana/10 Voglic Andaré In Guerra	5
69	Vogue VRS 7031	The Football Match/Where Did Everyone Go To	5
68	Vogue VRL 3032	ANTOINE (LP)	15

ANTOINETTE

64	Decca F 11820	Jenny Let Him Go/Please Don't Hurt Me Anymore	10
64	Piccadilly 7N 35201	There He Goes (The Boy I Love)/Little Things Mean A Lot	10
65	Piccadilly 7N 35223	Thank You For Loving Me/If You Really Love Me	7
65	Piccadilly 7N 35252	Our House/What's A-Happening To Me	6
66	Piccadilly 7N 35293	Why Don't I Run Away From You/There's No-One In The Whole Wide World	6
66	Piccadilly 7N 35310	Lullaby Of Love/I'm For You	6

(see also Toni Daly)

REY ANTON

62	Oriole CB 1771	Hey Good Looking/Mary Lou	10
63	Oriole CB 1811	Peppermint Man/Can't Say More Than That (with Batons)	10
63	Oriole CB 1843	How Long Can This Last/If You Don't Want Me Now	10
64	Parlophone R 5132	You Can't Judge A Book By The Cover/It's Cold Outside (with Peppermint Men)	25
64	Parlophone R 5172	Heard It All Before/I Want You (with Peppermint Men)	15
65	Parlophone R 5245	Wishbone/Kingsway (with Peppermint Men)	15
65	Parlophone R 5274	Girl You Don't Know Me/Don't Treat Me Bad (with Peppermint Men)	15
65	Parlophone R 5310	Nothing Comes Easy/Breakout (with Peppermint Men)	15
65	Parlophone R 5358	Premeditation/Now That It's Over (with Pro Form)	15
66	Parlophone R 5420	Don't You Worry Boy/Hold It Babe (with Pro Formula)	15
66	Parlophone R 5487	Things Get Better/Newsboy (with Pro Form)	15

TERRY ANTON

65	Pye 7N 15857	Leave A Little Love/Don't Say Goodbye	7

ANTHONY ANTONIO

82	Elite DAZZ 15	Lifeline/Vibeline (12", p/s)	7

DAVE ANTONY

68	Mercury MF 1031	Race With The Wind/Hide And Seek	8

(see also Dave Anthony['s Moods])

MARK ANTONY & AVENGERS

60s	Malconi MCD LP 17	MARK ANTONY & THE AVENGERS (LP, private pressing, plain sleeve)	25

ANTS

63	Parlophone R 5082	Christmas Star/Wandering	7

ANVIL FLUTES & CAPRICORN VOICES

68	Deram DM 208	April Showers/Jolie Gendarme	5
68	Deram DML/SML 1026	SOMETHING NEW IS COMING (LP)	12

ANY TROUBLE

79	Pennine PSS 165	Yesterday's Love/(Where Are All The) Nice Girls (p/s)	15
80	Stiff TRUBZ 1	LIVE AT THE VENUE (LP)	12

(see also Tickawinda)

APARTMENT

80	Heartbeat PULSE 7	The Car/Winter (p/s)	5

APEMEN

94	Detour DR021	Love Train/Let The Good Times Surround You (p/s, 1,000 only, 100 on purple or pink vinyl; 2nd pressing of 500 copies on clear vinyl; 3rd pressing 500 on black vinyl)	8/5/5/5

APEX RHYTHM & BLUES ALLSTARS

59	John Lever AP 100	Yorkshire Relish/Caravan	25
60s	John Lever JLEP 1	APEX RHYTHM & BLUES ALLSTARS (EP, no p/s)	200

(see also Ian Hunter)

APHEX TWIN

91	Mighty Force 01	ANALOGUE BUBBLEBATH VOL. 1 (12", with Schizophrenia, 4-track, label on 1 side only)	25
91	Rabbit City CUT 001	ANALOGUE BUBBLEBATH VOL. 1 (12" EP)	40
91	Rabbit City 009	Analogue Bubblebath Vol. 2 (Didgeridoo 'Aboriginal' Mix) (12", 1-sided, white label, 500 only)	40
92	Outer Rhythm/R+S RSUK	DIDGERIDOO (12", 4-track in stickered sleeve)	15
92	Outer Rhythm/R+S RSUK	DIDGERIDOO (CD EP)	75
93	Rabbit City CUT 002	ANALOGUE BUBBLEBATH VOL. 2 (12" EP, 1-sided, 500 only)	50
93	Rephlex CAT 008	ANALOGUE BUBBLEBATH VOL. 3 (12" EP, paper bag sleeve)	15
93	Rephlex CAT 008	ANALOGUE BUBBLEBATH VOL. 3 (CD EP, bubble wrap sleeve)	18
94	Rephlex CAT 019	ANALOGUE BUBBLEBATH VOL. 4 (12", 4-track, p/s)	8
95	Warp WAP 67	HANGABLE AUTOBULB I EP (12" EP, plain sleeve, 1,000 only)	40
95	Warp WAP 69	HANGABLE AUTOBULB II EP (12" EP, plain sleeve, 1,000 only)	30
97	Rephlex CAT 00897	ANALOGUE BUBBLEBATH VOL 3.1 (12" only, 4 different tracks)	8

(see also Caustic Window, Polygon Window, Q-Chastic, Kosmic Kommando)

MINT VALUE £

APHRODITE'S CHILD

68	Mercury MF 1039	Rain & Tears/Don't Try To Catch A River	45
69	Mercury MF 1079	End Of The World/You Always Stand In My Way	10
69	Polydor 56769	I Want To Live/Magic Mirror	8
69	Polydor 56785	Let Me Love, Let Me Live/Marie Jolie	5
70	Polydor 56791	It's Five O'Clock/Funky Mary	5
72	Vertigo 6032 900	Break/Babylon	8
68	Mercury SMCL 20140	END OF THE WORLD/RAIN AND TEARS (LP)	20
69	Mercury 138 351	IT'S FIVE O'CLOCK	15
72	Vertigo 6673 001	666 — THE APOCALYPSE OF JOHN (2-LP, spiral labels, black cover)	30
77	Vertigo 6641 581	666 (2-LP, reissue, as Aphrodite's Child with Demis Roussos & Vangelis, different sleeve, 'spaceship' labels)	15

(see also Vangelis, Demis Roussos, Forminx)

APOLLOS

60	Mercury AMT 1096	Rockin' Horses/Just Dreaming	10

APOLLO XI

91	Wau! Mr. Modo APOLLO 11	Peace (In The Middle East) (7" Mix 2)/Peace (Sea Of Tranquility Mix)/ Peace (Is This Really The Orb? Mix) (12")	10

(see also Orb)

A POPULAR HISTORY OF SIGNS

80	Melodia M 1	Justice Not Vengeance/Possession (p/s, with insert)	5
81	Melodia M 2	Crowds/Crossing The Border (stamped p/s with insert)	5
82	Melodia M 4	Dancing With Ideas (p/s)	5

APOSTOLIC INTERVENTION

67	Immediate IM 043	(Tell Me) Have You Ever Seen Me/Madame Garcia	130

(see also Small Faces, Humble Pie)

APPALACHIANS

63	HMV POP 1158	Bony Moronie/It Takes A Man	8
65	Mercury MF 930	Look Away/My Broken Heart	6

APPALOOSA

94	Recoil RCL 003	UNPLUGGED EP (12", 3-track, die-cut sleeve)	8

(see also Global Communications)

DAVE APPELL (& APPLEJACKS)

55	Brunswick 05396	Smarter/My Heart Will Wait For You (as Dave Appell & Applejacks)	20
55	Brunswick 05396	Smarter/My Heart Will Wait For You (as Dave Appell & Applejacks) (78)	12
57	Columbia DB 3894	Country Dance/Applejack (as Dave Appell & Applejacks)	50
57	Columbia DB 3894	Country Dance/Applejack (as Dave Appell & Applejacks) (78)	15
62	Columbia DB 4763	Happy Jose/Noivous (as Dave Appell & Orchestra)	8

(see also Applejacks [U.S.], John Zacherle)

APPLE

68	Page One POF 101	Let's Take A Trip Down The Rhine/Buffalo Billy Can	55
68	Page One POF 110	Doctor Rock/The Other Side	75
69	Page One POLS 016	AN APPLE A DAY (LP, some with 'apple' insert)	500/400

APPLE BOUTIQUE

88	Creation CRE 052T	Love Resistance/I Don't Even Believe In You/ The Ballad Of Jet Harris (12", p/s)	7

APPLEJACKS (U.S.)

58	London HLU 8753	Mexican Hat Rock/Stop, Stop Red Light	8
58	London HLU 8753	Mexican Hat Rock/Stop, Stop Red Light (78)	15
58	London HL 7063	Mexican Hat Rock/Stop, Stop Red Light (export issue)	10
59	London HLU 8806	Rocka-Conga/Am I Blue	15
59	London HLU 8806	Rocka-Conga/Am I Blue (78)	25
60	Top Rank JAR 273	Circle Dance/Love Scene	8

(see also Dave Appell)

APPLEJACKS (U.K.)

64	Decca F 11833	Tell Me When/Baby Jane	5
64	Decca F 11916	Like Dreamers Do/Everybody Fall Down	6
64	Decca F 11981	Three Little Words/You're The One For Me	7
65	Decca F 12050	Chim Chim Chiree/It's Not A Game Anymore (export, probably unissued)	100+
65	Decca F 12106	It's Not A Game Anymore/Bye Bye Girl	12
65	Decca F 12216	I Go To Sleep/Make Up Or Break Up	18
65	Decca F 12301	I'm Through/We Gotta Get Together	10
67	CBS 202615	You've Been Cheating/Love Was In My Eyes	15
64	Decca LK 4635	THE APPLEJACKS (LP)	120

APPLETREE THEATRE

68	Verve (S)VLP 6018	PLAYBACK (LP)	25
72	MGM 2353 051	PLAYBACK (LP, reissue)	12

CHARLIE APPLEWHITE

54	Brunswick 05358	No One But You/Parade	5
55	Brunswick 05411	Prize Of Gold/Mister Publisher (Have I Got A Song For You)	5
55	Brunswick 05416	Blue Star — The Medic Theme/A Prayer Was Born	15
55	Brunswick 05416	Blue Star — The Medic Theme/A Prayer Was Born (78)	8

APRIL WINE

72	Pye 7N 45163	Bad Side Of The Moon/Believe In Me	6
73	Pye 7N 45624	Weeping Widow/Just Like That	6

A PRIMARY INDUSTRY

85	Sweatbox SOX 007	Sicatrice/Obeah/Biting Back/Bled Dry (12", stamped p/s)	8
86	Temps Modernes CSBTVV	At Gunpoint/Perversion (p/s)	12

AQUARIAN AGE
| | 68 | Parlophone R 5700 | 10,000 Words In A Cardboard Box/Good Wizard Meets Naughty Wizard | 80 |

(see also Twink, Tomorrow, Clem Cattini Ork, Nicky Hopkins)

AQUARIANS
| 71 | Ackee ACK 135 | Circy Cap/Circy Version | 10 |
| 71 | Ackee ACK 137 | Rebel/Invasion Version | 10 |

(see also Augustus Pablo, Herman)

AQUATONES
| 58 | London HLO 8631 | You/She's The One For Me | 40 |
| 58 | London HLO 8631 | You/She's The One For Me (78) | 40 |

AQUILA
| 70 | RCA SF 8126 | THE AQUILA SUITE (LP, gatefold sleeve) | 35 |

(see also Patrick Campbell-Lyons)

ARABIS
| 69 | Doctor Bird DB 1204 | Jump High Jump Low/TONY SHABAZZ: Stool Pigeon | 12 |

ARAB STRAP
96	Chemikal Underground CHEM 007	The First Big Weekend/Gilded (700 only)	20
98	Too Many Cooks BROTH 001	Live: Packs Of Three/Blood	20
99	Go! Beat STRAP PRO	Sampler (CD, promo, 4-track, card sleeve)	15
99	Go! Beat 547387	MAD FOR SADNESS (LP, 1000 only)	12
99	Go! Beat 547387 2	MAD FOR SADNESS (CD, 3000 only)	18
99	Go! Beat 547 387-2 DJ	MAD FOR SADNESS (CD, promo, withdrawn)	20

ARANBEE POP SYMPHONY ORCHESTRA
| 66 | Immediate IMLP/IMSP 003 | TODAY'S POP SYMPHONY (LP) | 150 |

(see also Andrew Oldham Orchestra, Keith Richard[s])

ARBORS
66	CBS 202410	Symphony For Susan/Love Is The Light	5
68	CBS 3221	Valley Of The Dolls/You Are The Music	5
69	CBS 4137	The Letter/Most Of All	5
69	CBS 4379	I Can't Quit Her/Lovin' Tonight	5
69	CBS 4640	Motet Overture/Touch Me	6

ARC
| 71 | Decca SKL-R 5077 | ARC . . . AT THIS (LP) | 35 |

(see also Heavy Jelly, Skip Bifferty, Bell & Arc)

ARC
| 80 | Orchrist ORC 1 | Tribute (To Mike Hailwood) (p/s) | 60 |

ARCADIA
85	EMI NSR 1	Election Day/She's Moody And Grey (gatefold p/s)	5
85	EMI 12 NSR 1	Election Day (Consensus Mix)/Election Day (7" Version)/ She's Moody And Grey She's Mean And She's Restless (12", p/s)	8
85	EMI 12 NSR 1	Election Day (Consensus Mix)/Election Day (7" Version)/ She's Moody And Grey She's Mean And She's Restless (12", promo in foil sleeve, some sealed)	30/20
85	EMI 12 NSRA 1	Election Day (Cryptic Cut No Voice Mix)/Election Day (7" Mix)/ Election Day (Consensus Mix) (12", p/s)	10
85	EMI 12 NSRX 1	Election Day (The Fact And Story Mix) (12", 1-sided, white label, plain black black sleeve, promo only)	80
86	EMI 12 NSR 2	The Promise/Rose Arcana/The Promise (7" Mix) (12", stickered gold p/s, with poster)	18
86	EMI 12 NSR 2	The Promise/Rose Arcana/The Promise (7" Mix) (12", blue p/s)	8
86	EMI 12 NSR 3	The Flame (Extended Remix)/Flame Game (Yo Homeboy Mix)/ Election Day (Early Rough Mix) (12", p/s)	8

(see also Duran Duran)

ARCADIUM
| 69 | Middle Earth MDS 102 | Sing My Song/Riding Alone | 25 |
| 69 | Middle Earth MDLS 302 | BREATHE AWHILE (LP) | 150 |

ARCHIES
| 69 | RCA RD/SF 8073 | SUGAR SUGAR (LP) | 12 |

ARCHITECTS OF DISASTER
| 82 | Neuter NEU 1 | Cucumber Sandwich/Friendly Fire (6" x 6" insert in poly bag, no p/s) | 8 |

(see also Orange Disaster, Perfect Disaster, Varicose Veins)

TONI ARDEN
55	HMV 7M 314	Beware/I'll Step Aside	7
57	Brunswick 05645	Little By Little/Without Love (There Is Nothing)	8
57	Brunswick 05679	My Empty Heart/Like A Baby	7
58	Brunswick 05745	Padre/All At Once	7

NEIL ARDLEY
65	Decca SKL 4690	WESTERN UNION (LP)	80
69	Verve SVLP 9236	DEJEUNER SUR L'HERBE (LP)	80
70	Columbia SCX 6414	GREEK VARIATIONS (LP, with Ian Carr & Don Rendell)	80
72	Regal Zono. SLRZ 1028	A SYMPHONY OF AMARANTHS (LP)	80
74	Argo ZDA 164/5	WILL POWER (2-LP, with Ian Carr, Stan Tracey & Mike Gibbs)	80
75	Gull GULP 1018	KALEIDOSCOPE OF RAINBOWS (LP)	40
78	Decca TXS-R 133	HARMONY OF THE SPHERES (LP, featuring John Martyn)	20

(see also Ian Carr, Don Rendell, New Jazz Orchestra, Michael Gibbs)

COLIN AREETY
| 73 | Deram DM 383 | I Don't Want To Be Right/One Night Affair | 5 |

MINT VALUE £

ARGENT

ARENA TWINS
59	London HL 7071	Mama, Care Mama/Little Pig (export issue)...................................	15

ARGENT
71	Epic S EPC 5423	Celebration/Kingdom..	5
71	Epic S EPC 9135	Hold Your Head Up/Closer To Heaven/Keep On Rollin' (p/s)..................	5
72	Epic S EPC 8115	Tragedy..	5
73	Epic S EPC 1628	It's Only Money (Part 2)/Candle On The River............................	5
73	Epic S EPC 1243	God Gave Rock'N'Roll To You	5
70	CBS 63781	ARGENT (LP)..	15
71	Epic EPC 64190	RING OF HANDS (LP)	12
72	Epic EPC 64962	ALL TOGETHER NOW (LP, with booklet).................................	12
74	Epic EQ 32195/Q 65475	IN DEEP (LP, quadrophonic)	15
74	Epic EPC 88063	ENCORE (2-LP)	15

(see also Zombies, Unit 4 + 2, Roulettes, John Verity Band, Phoenix)

ARGONAUTS
85	Lyntone LYN 18249/50	Apeman/Under My Thumb (signed white label, no p/s)	10

(see also Madness)

ARGOSY
69	DJM DJS 214	Mr. Boyd/Imagine	10

(see also People Like Us, Supertramp)

ARIEL
94	De Construction AR 2	T-Baby (Dust Brothers Mix) (12", promo only)	12

A RIOT OF COLOUR
86	Lyntone LYN 17114/GIVE 1	Skink/Newtown (p/s, flexidisc free with various fanzines)...................	8/6
87	Dreamworld DREAM 009	Skink/Country/House/Newtown (12", p/s)................................	8

ARISTOCRATS
64	Oriole CB 1928	Girl With The Laughing Eyes/I Picked You..............................	8

ARIZONA BOYS' CHOIR
56	Columbia SCM 5215	Ballad Of Davy Crockett/Blue Shadows On The Trail	8

ARIZONA SWAMP COMPANY
70	Parlophone R 5841	Train Keeps Rollin'/Tennessee Woman	25

(see also Nashville Teens)

ARKADE
70	Stateside SS 8053	Sing Out The Love/Susan	5
71	Probe PRO 521	Morning Of Our Lives/Rhythm Of The People............................	5

A.R. KANE
86	One Little Indian 12 TP 2	WHEN YOU'RE SAD (12" EP)..	7
87	4AD BAD 704	Lolita/Sado-Masochism Is A Must/Butterfly Collector (12", p/s)............	8
88	Rough Trade RT 201	Baby Milk Snatcher/W.O.G.S. (plain black stickered sleeve, promo only)	6

WILLIAM ARKLE
80s	The Stand WAM 1	THE MUSIC OF WILLIAM ARKLE (cassette)	10

(see also Robert John Godfrey)

DEE ARLEN
59	Philips PB 950	Stay/Why Should We Wait Any Longer	8
59	Philips PB 950	Stay/Why Should We Wait Any Longer (78).............................	30

STEVE ARLEN

58	Melodisc M 1458	That's Love/Easy 'N' Free	10
58	Melodisc M 1458	That's Love/Easy 'N' Free (78)	8
60	HMV POP 835	Suddenly I'm In Love/Happy Days	5

DEKE ARLON (& OFFBEATS)

64	HMV POP 1340	I Need You/I Must Go And Tell Her	22
64	Columbia DB 7194	I'm Just A Boy/Can't Make Up My Mind	30
65	Columbia DB 7487	If I Didn't Have A Dime/Gotta Little Girl	10
65	Columbia DB 7753	Little Piece Of Paper/I've Been Away (solo)	8
66	Columbia DB 7841	Hard Times For Young Lovers/Little Boy (solo)	8

ARMAGEDDON

| 75 | A&M AMLH 64513 | ARMAGEDDON (LP, with inner sleeve) | 20 |

(see also Keith Relf, Steamhammer)

JOAN ARMATRADING

73	Cube BUG 31	Lonely Lady/Together In Words And Music	6
75	A&M AMS 7181	Back To The Night/So Good	5
76	Cube BUG 74	Alice/All The Kings' Gardens	5
78	A&M AMS 7365	Flight Of The Wild Geese/No Way Out	5
72	Cube HIFLY 12	WHATEVER'S FOR US (LP, original issue, gatefold sleeve)	12

ARMED FORCE

| 80 | Armed Force AF 1 | Pop Star/Attack (p/s) | 6 |

KAY ARMEN

| 55 | MGM SP 1146 | He/Suddenly There's A Valley | 6 |
| 58 | Brunswick 05729 | Ha! Ha! Ha! (Chella Lla!)/Till | 5 |

ARMENIAN JAZZ QUARTET

| 57 | London HLR 8454 | Pretty Girl/Harem Dance | 12 |
| 57 | London HLR 8454 | Pretty Girl/Harem Dance (78) | 8 |

RUSSELL ARMS

57	London HLB 8406	Cinco Robes (Five Oaks)/The World Is Made Of Lisa (gold/silver label)	18/12
57	London HLB 8406	Cinco Robes (Five Oaks)/The World Is Made Of Lisa (78)	10
57	London HL 7018	Cinco Robes (Five Oaks)/The World Is Made Of Lisa (export issue)	10

ARMS & LEGS

76	MAM MAM 140	Janice/She'll Surprise You	8
76	MAM MAM 147	Heat Of The Night/Good Times	8
77	MAM MAM 156	Is There Any More Wine/She'll Surprise You	8

(see also Joe Jackson)

FRANKIE ARMSTRONG

| 72 | Topic 12TS 216 | LOVELY ON THE WATER (LP) | 15 |
| 75 | Topic 12TS 273 | SONGS AND BALLADS (LP) | 12 |

(see also A.L. Lloyd)

JACK ARMSTRONG

| 57 | Beltona SEP 43 | NORTHUMBRIAN PIPE MUSIC (EP) | 12 |
| 74 | Saydisc SDL 252 | CELEBRATED MINSTREL (LP) | 15 |

LOUIS ARMSTRONG

78s

50	Brunswick 04627	Life Is So Peculiar/You Rascal You (with Louis Jordan) (78)	8
52	Brunswick 04995	Takes Two To Tango/That's My Desire (B-side with Velma Middleton) (78)	8
55	Brunswick 05400	Ko Ko Mo (I Love You So)/Struttin' With Some Barbecue (with Gary Crosby) (78)	8
55	Brunswick 05415	Pledging My Love/Sincerely (78)	8
56	Brunswick 05512	Only You (And You Alone)/Moments To Remember (78)	8
56	Philips PB 604	The Faithful Hussar/The Memphis Blues (78)	8
58	Brunswick 05772	The Mardi Gras March/I Love Jazz (78)	8
59	Philips PB 967	Mack The Knife/The Faithful Hussar (78)	20
59	Pye International N 25043	The Formula For Love (with Nina & Frederick)/Struttin' With Some Barbecue (with Velma Middleton) (78)	10

SINGLES

53	Columbia SCM 5061	King Of The Zulus/Lonesome Blues	10
54	Columbia SCM 5118	Chicago Breakdown/Twelfth Street Rag	10
54	Columbia SCM 5142	I'm Not Rough/Put 'Em Down Blues	10
54	Brunswick 05303	Basin Street Blues (Parts 1 & 2)	10
54	Brunswick 05332	Skokiaan (Parts 1 & 2)	7
54	Brunswick 05347	Muskrat Ramble/Someday You'll Be Sorry (B-side with Commanders)	7
55	Brunswick 05364	Trees/Spooks	7
55	Brunswick 05400	Ko Ko Mo (I Love You So)/Struttin' With Some Barbecue (with Gary Crosby)	10
55	Brunswick 05460	Pretty Little Missy/Bye And Bye	7
55	Brunswick 05505	Christmas Night In Harlem/Christmas In New Orleans	8
56	Brunswick 05574	Easy Street/Lazybones (with Gary Crosby)	6
56	Capitol CL 14643	Now You Has Jazz (with Bing Crosby)/High Society Calypso	7
57	Brunswick 05649	This Younger Generation/In Pursuit Of Happiness	6
58	Brunswick 05772	The Mardi Gras March/I Love Jazz	6
59	MGM MGM 1035	The Beat Generation/Someday You'll Be Sorry	5
59	Philips PB 967	Mack The Knife/The Faithful Hussar	5
59	Pye International 7N 25043	The Formula For Love (with Nina & Frederick)/Struttin' With Some Barbecue (with Velma Middleton)	5
60	Philips JAZ 108	Mahogany Hall Blues Stomp/On The Sunny Side Of The Street (p/s)	6
60	Philips JAZ 112	Way Down Yonder In New Orleans/Do You Know What It Means To Miss (p/s)	6
60	MGM MGM 1107	Muskrat Ramble/Dardanella	5
69	United Artists UP 35059	We Have All The Time In The World/Pretty Little Missy	25
69	United Artists UA 3172	We Have All The Time In The World/Pretty Little Missy (reissue, p/s)	35

Louis ARMSTRONG

EPs

50s	Brunswick OE 9035	PRESENTING LOUIS ARMSTRONG AND THE MILLS BROTHERS (EP) 10
50s	Parlophone GEP 8627	LOUIS PLAYS THE BLUES (EP) 8
50s	Philips BBE 12035	TAKE IT SATCH (EP) 8
56	Philips 429 290 BE	LOUIS (EP) 8

LPs

51	Brunswick LA 8528	LOUIS ARMSTRONG CLASSICS (10" LP) 18
51	Brunswick LA 8534	JAZZ CONCERT (10" LP) 18
52	Brunswick LA 8537	NEW ORLEANS DAYS (10" LP) 18
52	Brunswick LAT 8017	SATCHMO AT SYMPHONY HALL (LP) 15
52	Brunswick LAT 8018	SATCHMO AT SYMPHONY HALL (LP) 15
52	Brunswick LAT 8019	SATCHMO AT PASADENA (LP) 15
53	Brunswick LA 8597	LOUIS ARMSTRONG JAZZ — CLASSICS (10" LP) 18
53	London AL 3501	PLAYS THE BLUES (10" LP) 25
53	Columbia 33S 1007	JAZZIN' WITH ARMSTRONG (10" LP) 18
53	HMV DLP 1015	NEW YORK TOWN HALL CONCERT 1947 (10" LP) 18
54	Columbia 33SX 1029	LOUIS ARMSTRONG AND HIS HOT FIVE (LP) 15
54	HMV DLP 1036	LAUGHIN' LOUIS (10" LP) 18
54	Columbia 33S 1041	LOUIS ARMSTRONG AND HIS HOT SEVEN (10" LP) 18
54	Brunswick LA 8679	SATCHMO SERENADES (10" LP) 18
54	Brunswick LA 8681	LOUIS ARMSTRONG AND THE MILLS BROTHERS (10" LP) 18
54	Brunswick LA 8691	BASIN STREET BLUES (10" LP) 18
55	Columbia 33S 1058	RENDEZVOUS AT THE SUNSET CAFE (10" LP) 18
55	Columbia 33S 1069	LOUIS ARMSTRONG (10" LP) 18
55	HMV DLP 1105	SATCHMO SESSION (10" LP) 18
55	Philips BBL 7017	SATCHMO PLAYS W.C. HANDY (LP) 12
55	Philips BBL 7046	LOUIS ARMSTRONG AND EARL HINES (LP) 12
55	Brunswick LA 8698	LOUIS' HOT FIVES AND SEVENS (10" LP) 18
55	Brunswick LA 8700	BLUEBERRY HILL (10" LP) 18
56	Philips BBL 7064	SATCH PLAYS FATS (LP) 12
56	Philips BBL 7091	AMBASSADOR SATCH (LP) 12
56	Brunswick LAT 8084	LOUIS ARMSTRONG AT THE CRESCENDO VOL. 1 (LP) 12
56	Brunswick LAT 8085	LOUIS ARMSTRONG AT THE CRESCENDO VOL. 2 (LP) 12
57	Philips BBL 7134	LOUIS ARMSTRONG STORY VOL. 1 (LP) 12
57	Philips BBL 7189	LOUIS ARMSTRONG STORY VOL. 2 (LP) 12
57	Brunswick LAT 8210	LOUIS AND THE ANGELS (LP) 12
57	Brunswick LAT 8211	SATCHMO — A MUSICAL AUTOBIOGRAPHY (LP) 12
57	Brunswick LAT 8212	SATCHMO — A MUSICAL AUTOBIOGRAPHY (LP) 12
57	Brunswick LAT 8213	SATCHMO — A MUSICAL AUTOBIOGRAPHY (LP) 12
57	Brunswick LAT 8214	SATCHMO — A MUSICAL AUTOBIOGRAPHY (LP) 12
58	Philips BBL 7202	LOUIS ARMSTRONG STORY VOL. 3 (LP, with Earl Hines) 12
58	Fontana TFR 6003	LOUIS ARMSTRONG AND HIS HOT FIVE (10" LP) 15
58	Philips BBL 7216	SATCHMO THE GREAT (LP, soundtrack) 12
58	Philips BBL 7218	LOUIS ARMSTRONG STORY VOL. 4 (LP) 12
58	Brunswick LAT 8243	SATCHMO SINGS (LP) 12
58	Brunswick LAT 8270	LOUIS AND THE GOOD BOOK (LP) 12
60	HMV CLP 1328	LOUIS ARMSTRONG MEETS OSCAR PETERSON (LP) 12
60	HMV CLP 1388/CSD 1317	I'VE GOT THE WORLD ON A STRING (LP, mono/stereo) 12/15

(see also Danny Kaye, Ella Fitzgerald & Louis Armstrong, Nina & Frederik, Bing Crosby, Earl 'Fatha' Hines, Red Onion Jazz Babies)

B.J. ARNAU

72	Mojo 2092 028	I Want To Go Back There Again/I Love You 5
72	Polydor 2058 238	The Big Hurt/Hey Brenda 5
73	RCA RCA 2365	Live And Let Die/In One Night 6

(see also Brenda Arnau)

BRENDA ARNAU

68	United Artists UP 2244	Gonna Spread Love/Christian 5
68	United Artists UP 2265	Yesterday I Heard The Rain/Where Do You Go 5

GINNY ARNELL

60	Brunswick 05836	Carnival/We 10
63	MGM MGM 1217	Dumb Head/How Many Times Can One Heart Break 15
63	MGM MGM 1243	I Wish I Knew What Dress To Wear/He's My Little Devil 10
65	MGM MGM 1270	Just Like A Boy/Portrait Of A Fool 10
65	MGM MGM 1283	Little Bit Of Love/B-I-I-I-Why 8

CHICO ARNEZ & HIS LATIN AMERICAN ORCHESTRA

59	Pye 7N 15196	Yashmak/Ain't She Sweet 25
59	Pye N 15196	Yashmak/Ain't She Sweet (78) 50
59	Pye NPL 18035	THIS IS CHICO (LP) 30
68	Columbia S(C)X 6265	FROM CHICO WITH LOVE (LP) 15
72	Contour 2870 153	THE NEW SOUNDS OF CHICO ARNEZ (LP) 12

(see also Jackie Davies)

CALVIN ARNOLD

68	MGM MGM 1378	Funky Way/Snatchin' Back 6
68	MGM MGM 1449	Mama In Law/Mini Skirt 7

EDDY ARNOLD

50	HMV MH 96	One Kiss Too Many/Don't Rob Another Man's Castle (78, export issue) 8
50	HMV MH 100	That Wonderful Mother Of Mine/Mother (78, export issue) 8
53	HMV MH 162	There's Been A Change In Me/My Mother's Sweet Voice (78, export issue). 8
53	HMV MH 167	Call Her Your Sweetheart/Bundle Of Southern Sunshine (78, export issue) 8
53	HMV MH 175	Eddy's Song/Condemned Without Trial (78, export issue) 8
53	HMV MH 180	I'd Trade All My Tomorrows/Older And Bolder (78, export issue) 8
53	HMV JO 381	My Desire/I Want To Thank You Lord (78, export issue) 10
53	HMV JO 396	Prayer/Robe Of Calvary (78, export issue) 8

MINT VALUE £

53	HMV JO 400	I Really Don't Want To Know/I'll Never Get Over You (78, export issue) 10
54	HMV 7MC 10	Prayer/Robe Of Calvary (export issue) 15
54	HMV 7MC 16	Free Home Demonstrations/If I Never Get To Heaven (export issue) 15
54	HMV 7MC 19	Second Fling/My Everything (export issue) 15
54	HMV 7MC 22	Hep Cat Baby/This Is The Thanks I Get (For Loving You) (export issue) 15
55	HMV 7MC 32	In Time/Two Kinds Of Love (export issue) 15
55	HMV 7M 339	I Walked Alone Last Night/The Richest Man (In The World) 7
55	HMV POP 134	I Walked Alone Last Night/The Richest Man (In The World) (78) 8
57	RCA RCA 1008	Gonna Find Me A Bluebird/Little Bit 6
57	RCA RCA 1008	Gonna Find Me A Bluebird/Little Bit (78) 8
57	RCA RCA 1017	Scarlet Ribbons/Bayou Baby (A Cajun Lullaby) 5
57	RCA RCA 1017	Scarlet Ribbons/Bayou Baby (A Cajun Lullaby) (78) 8
58	RCA RCA 1057	Little Miss Sunbeam/My Darling, My Darling 5
58	RCA RCA 1057	Little Miss Sunbeam/My Darling, My Darling (78) 8
59	RCA RCA 1138	Tennessee Stud/What's The Good (Of All This Love) 6
59	RCA RCA 1138	Tennessee Stud/What's The Good (Of All This Love) (78) 15
60	RCA RCA 1212	Just Out Of Reach/Before This Day Ends 5
54	HMV 7EG 8020	EDDY ARNOLD (EP) 15
55	HMV 7EG 8080	CHAPEL ON THE HILL (EP) 15
59	RCA Camden CDN 133	EDDY ARNOLD (LP) 12
60	RCA RD 27155	THEREBY HANGS A TALE (LP) 12
62	RCA Victor RD 7796	I WANT TO GO WITH YOU (LP) 12
63	RCA Victor RD 7804	CATTLE CALL (LP) 12

KOKOMO ARNOLD
69	Saydisc Matchbox SDR 163	KOKOMO ARNOLD (LP) 20

PAUL ARNOLD
67	Pye 7N 17317	Somewhere In A Rainbow/Got A Feeling 5
68	Pye 7N 17473	Bon Soir Dame/Don't Leave. 5
(see also Overlanders)		

P.P. ARNOLD
66	Immediate IM 040	Everything's Gonna Be Alright/Life Is But Nothin' 65
67	Immediate IM 047	The First Cut Is The Deepest/Speak To Me 8
67	Immediate IM 055	The Time Has Come/If You See What I Mean 6
68	Immediate IM 061	(If You Think You're) Groovy/Though It Hurts Me Badly 12
68	Immediate IM 067	Angel Of The Morning/Life Is But Nothin' 7
69	Immediate IM 079	The First Cut Is The Deepest/The Time Has Come 5
69	Polydor 56350	Bury Me Down The River/Give A Hand, Take A Hand 5
70	Polydor 2058 061	Likely Piece Of Work/May The Winds Blow 5
76	Virgin/NEMS SV 103	Angel Of The Morning/Everything's Gonna Be Alright/The First Cut Is The Deepest/Groovy/The Time Has Come (double pack, gatefold p/s) 8
67	Immediate IMLP/IMSP 011	THE FIRST LADY OF IMMEDIATE (LP) 60
68	Immediate IMSP 017	KAFUNTA (LP, gatefold sleeve) 35
(see also Ikettes, Nice, Small Faces, Spectrum, P.P. & Primes)		

ARRIVAL
70	Decca SKL 5055	ARRIVAL (LP) 12

ARRIVALS
69	Pye 7N 17761	Scooby Doo/She's About A Mover 6

ARROWS (U.S.)
65	Capitol CL 15386	Apache '65/Blue Guitar 7

ARROWS (U.K.)
69	Pye 7N 17756	Mercy/See Saw 12

ARS NOVA
68	Elektra EKSN 45029	Zoroaster/Pavan For My Lady 7
68	Elektra EKSN 45034	Fields Of People/Song To The City 7
68	Elektra EKS 74020	ARS NOVA (LP, orange label, gatefold sleeve) 25
69	Atlantic 588 196	SUNSHINE AND SHADOWS (LP) 15

ART
67	Island WIP 6019	What's That Sound (For What It's Worth)/Rome Take Away Three 10
69	Island WIP 6048	Room With A View/SPOOKY TOOTH: Nobody There At All (promo only) 35
75	Island WIP 6224	What's That Sound (For What It's Worth)/Flying Anchors. 6
67	Island ILP 967	SUPERNATURAL FAIRY TALES (LP, pink label, laminated sleeve). 60
75	Island ILP 967	SUPERNATURAL FAIRY TALES (LP, reissue, matt sleeve, 'palm tree' label) 20
(see also V.I.P.'s, Baron With His Pounding Piano, Spooky Tooth, Luther Grosvenor, Hapshash & Coloured Coat)		

ART & LANGUAGE/RED CRAYOLA
80	Rough Trade RT 054	Born In Flames/Sword Of God (p/s) 5
81	Rough Trade ROUGH 19	KANGAROO (LP) 12
81	Rough Trade COPY 005	KANGAROO (cassette, with 2 extra tracks) 12
(see also Red Crayola)		

ART ATTACKS
78	Albatross TIT 1	I'm A Dalek/Neutron Bomb (p/s) 18
79	Fresh FRESH 3	First And Last: Punk Rock Stars/Rat City/First And Last (p/s). 15
(see also Monochrome Set, Tagmemics, Kray Cherubs)		

ART BEARS
81	Recommended RE 6622	CODA TO "MAN AND BOY" (EP, live, 1-sided clear vinyl, silk-screened p/s, 1,750 only, 500 signed & numbered for subscribers). 12/10
78	Recommended REC 2188	HOPES AND FEARS (LP, gatefold sleeve with poster & booklet). 12
79	Recommended REC 0618	WINTER SONGS (LP, with booklet) 12
81	Recommended RE 6622	THE WORLD AS IT IS TODAY (LP, 45rpm, with booklet) 12
(see also Henry Cow, Slapp Happy)		

MINT VALUE £

ART ENSEMBLE OF CHICAGO
72	Polydor 2383 098	SPIRITUAL (LP)	10

ARTERY
79	Limited Edition TAKE 1	Mother Moon/Pretends/Heinz (p/s)	12
80	Aardvark STEAL 3	Unbalanced/The Slide (p/s, some with EP [Perhaps/Turtle/Toytown/Heinz])	10/6
81	Aardvark AARD 5	Cars In Motion/Life And Death (p/s)	6
81	Armageddon AS 026	Afterwards/Into The Garden (p/s)	6
82	Red Flame RF 704	The Clown/The Clown (p/s)	6
82	Red Flame RFM 4	OCEANS (LP, with insert)	12

(see also Mission)

DAVE & TONI ARTHUR
70	Trailer LER 1	Bushes And Briars/Lazio Feher	5
67	Transatlantic TRA 154	MORNING STANDS ON TIPTOE (LP)	25
69	Topic 12T 190	THE LARK IN THE MORNING (LP, blue label)	25
71	Trailer LER 2017	HEARKEN TO THE WITCHES' RUNE (LP, red label)	30

(see also Strollers)

ANDY ARTHURS
77	EMI EMI 2618	Listen To My Brain (Kapounding)/Come To The Party (custom p/s)	5
78	Radar ADA 7	I Can Detect You For 1,000,000 Miles/I Am A Machine (p/s, unissued)	12
78	TDS TDS 3	I Can Detect You For 1,000,000 Miles/I Am A Machine (p/s)	5
79	TDS TDS 6	I Feel Flat/Play The Music	5

ARTISTICS
66	Coral Q 72488	I'm Gonna Miss You/Hope We Have	25
67	Coral Q 72492	Girl I Need You/I'm Glad I Met You	22
70	MCA MU 1117	I'm Gonna Miss You/Hope We Have (reissue)	6
76	Brunswick BR 39	I'm Gonna Miss You/GENE CHANDLER: There Was A Time	6
66	Columbia	GET MY HANDS ON SOME LOVIN' (LP)	175

ART MOVEMENT
68	Decca F 12768	I Love Being In Love With You/The Game Of Love	7
68	Decca F 12836	Loving Touch/Happy Song	6
69	Columbia DB 8602	Yes Sir . . . No Sir/Sally Goes Round The Moon	5
70	Columbia DB 8651	For As Long As You Need Me/Nice 'n' Easy	5
70	Columbia DB 8697	The Sooner I Get To You/Morning Girl	5

ART NOUVEAUX
64	Fontana TF 483	Extra Terrestrial Visitations/The Way To Play It	12

ART OBJECTS
80	Heartbeat PULSE 10	Showing Off To Impress The Girls/Our Silver Sister (live) (p/s)	5
81	Fried Egg EGG 007	Hard Objects/Bibliotheque/Fit Of Pique (p/s)	5
81	Heartbeat HB 5	BAGPIPE MUSIC (LP)	12

ART OF NOISE
83	ZTT ZTIS 100	INTO BATTLE WITH THE ART OF NOISE (12" EP)	8
84	ZTT P ZTPS 01	Close (To The Edit)/A Time To Hear (Who's Listening) (picture disc)	5
84	ZTT 12 P ZTPS 01	Edited/A Time To Clear (It Up) (12", picture disc)	8
85	ZTT 12 ZTPS 1	CLOSE TO THE EDIT (12, stamped green label, unreleased)	8
85	ZTT P ZTPS 02	Moments In Love/Beatbox (tortoise-shaped picture disc)	6
91	China CHINX 23	Art Of Love/Ambience Of Love Mix (12", some in p/s)	10/8

ART OF NOISE WITH DUANE EDDY
86	China WOKP 6	Peter Gunn/Something Always Happens (shaped picture disc)	7

(see also Duane Eddy)

ART SCIENCE TECHNOLOGY
90	Debut DEBTX 3100	A.S.T./Esus Flow (2 mixes) (12", p/s)	12

(see also Future Sound Of London, Stakker)

ARTWOODS
64	Decca F 12015	Sweet Mary/If I Ever Get My Hands On You	45
65	Decca F 12091	Oh My Love/Big City	40
65	Decca F 12206	Goodbye Sisters/She Knows What To Do	40
66	Decca F 12384	I Take What I Want/I'm Looking For A Saxophonist Doubling French Horn Wearing Size 37 Boots	45
66	Decca F 12465	I Feel Good/Molly Anderson's Cookery Book	50
67	Parlophone R 5590	What Shall I Do/In The Deep End	100
66	Decca DFE 8654	JAZZ IN JEANS (EP)	300
66	Decca LK 4830	ART GALLERY (LP)	250
70	Decca Eclipse ECM 2025	ART GALLERY (LP, reissue in different sleeve, also stereo [ECS 2025])	35
73	Spark SRLM 2006	THE ARTWOODS (LP)	45
83	Edsel ED 107	100 OXFORD STREET (LP, with foldout insert)	15

(see also St. Valentine's Day Massacre, Keef Hartley Band, Jon Lord, Dog Soldier, Lucas & Mike Cotton Sound)

ARZACHEL
69	Evolution Z 1003	ARZACHEL (LP)	225

(see also Egg, Steve Hillage, Khan, Hatfield & the North, National Health, Gong)

A.S.A.P.
(see under Adrian Smith & Project)

ASGARD
72	Threshold TH 10	Where Are Your Friends/Children Of A New Born Age	5
73	Threshold TH 15	In The Realm Of Asgard/Town Cryer	5
72	Threshold THS 6	IN THE REALM OF ASGARD (LP, gatefold sleeve)	25

ASH
94	La La Land LA LA 001	Jack Names The Planets/Don't Know (wraparound p/s in poly bag, 5,000 only)	15
94	Infectious INFECT 13S	Petrol/The Little Pond/A Message From Oscar Wilde And Patrick The Brewer (p/s, 500 only)	18

94	Infectious INFECT 16S	Uncle Pat/Different Today (p/s, 1,000 only)	18
95	Infectious INFECT 21J	Kung Fu/Day Of The Triffids (p/s, 'Japanese' wraparound no'd p/s in poly bag)	10
95	Infectious INFECT 21S	Kung Fu (mispressed, 1-sided only, p/s)	7
95	Infectious INFECT 21C	Kung Fu/Kung Fu (red vinyl promo)	12
95	Infectious INFECT 27C	Angel Interceptor/Angel Interceptor (blue vinyl, promo only, hand-stamped p/s)	12
95	Infectious INFECT 27J	Angel Interceptor/Girl From Mars (jukebox issue)	8
95	Fantastic Plastic FP 004	Get Ready/Zero Zero Zero (red vinyl, 1,000 only)	10
94	Infectious INFECT 14LP	TRAILER (LP, with yellow vinyl 7", "Silver Surfer"/"Jazz '59" [INFECT 14S])	30
98	MPO IRL 01	OH YEAH (CD, 'Heineken Rock Awards' issue free with *Hot Press* magazine, with Neil Hannon & other artists)	18

IRVING ASHBY & HIS COMBO

58	London HLP 8578	Big Guitar/Motatin'	20
58	London HLP 8578	Big Guitar/Motatin' (78)	22

JOHNNY ASHCROFT

59	Felsted AF 118	A Pub With No Beer/Bouquet For The Pride	6
59	Felsted AF 118	A Pub With No Beer/Bouquet For The Pride (78)	12
60	HMV POP 759	Little Boy Lost/My Love Is A River	8

ASHFORD & SIMPSON

74	Warner Brothers K 16373	Have You Ever Tried It?/Time	5
78	Warner Brothers 12K 17096	Don't Cost You Nothing/Let Love Use Me (12")	10
78	Warner Brothers 12K 17237	It Seems To Hang On (12")	8

ASHKAN

70	Decca Nova (S)DN-R 1	IN FROM THE COLD (LP)	40

MICKEY ASHMAN

60	Pye Jazz NJL 25	TAKING THE MICKEY (LP)	15
61	Pye Jazz NJL 29	THROUGH DARKEST ASHMAN (LP)	25

VIC ASH QUARTET

55	Jazz Today JTS 1501	Jeepers Creepers/Cocktails For Two (78)	8
56	Tempo A 135	Blue Lou/Doxy	6
56	Tempo A 135	Blue Lou/Doxy (78)	7
56	Tempo A 137	Early Morning/Just One Of Those Things	6
56	Tempo A 137	Early Morning/Just One Of Those Things (78)	7
55	Jazz Today JTE 100	SESSION FOR FOUR (EP)	30
56	Nixa NJE 1002	HOAGY (EP)	12
56	Nixa NJE 1032	VIC ASH & FOUR (EP)	20
56	Columbia SEG 7634	CLARINET VIRTUOSO (EP)	15
56	Tempo EXA 44	MODERN JAZZ SCENE (EP)	15

(see also Maxine Sullivan, Jazz Five)

ASH RA (TEMPLE)

77	Virgin V 2080	NEW AGE OF EARTH (LP)	12
77	Virgin V 2091	BLACKOUTS (LP)	12
79	Virgin V 2117	CORRELATIONS (LP)	12

BUD ASHTON (& HIS GROUP)

59	Embassy WB 355	40 Miles Of Bad Road/PAUL RICH: 'Til I Kissed You (78)	8
60	Embassy WB 396	Shazam!/PAUL RICH: Green Fields (78)	10
60	Embassy WB 409	Because They're Young/Apache	5
60	Embassy WB 409	Because They're Young/Apache (78)	10
60	Embassy WB 422	Kommotion/STEVE STANNARD: Rockin' Goose (78)	12
61	Embassy WB 436	FBI/Wheels	5
61	Embassy WB 451	The Frightened City/DORIS LEE: You'll Never Know	5
61	Embassy WB 462	Kon-Tiki/HAPPY KNIGHTS JAZZ BAND: That's My Home	5
61	Embassy WB 483	The Savage/PAUL RICH: Give Us A Kiss For Christmas	5
62	Embassy WB 518	Guitar Tango/PAUL RICH: Roses Are Red	5
62	Embassy WB 525	Telstar/RIKKI HENDERSON: Don't That Beat All	5
62	Embassy WB 543	Dance On! (as Bud Ashton & His Group)/KAY BARRY: Like I Do	5
62	Embassy WB 558	Foot Tapper/Robot (as Bud Ashton & His Group)	5
64	Embassy WB 564	Rhythm & Greens/It's Gonna Be Alright	5
62	Embassy WB 569	Atlantis (as Bud Ashton & His Group)/HANK ROGERS: Deck Of Cards	5
62	Embassy WB 582	Wipe Out (as Bud Ashton & His Group)/RAY PILGRIM: I'm Telling You	5
63	Embassy WB 593	Shindig/DON DUKE: Blue Velvet	5
63	Embassy WB 605	Geronimo/TYPHOONS: I Want To Hold Your Hand	5
64	Embassy WB 622	Theme For Young Lovers/MIKE REDWAY: Little Children	5
64	Embassy WB 632	The Rise And Fall Of Flingel Bunt/Baby, Let Me Take You Home	5
61	Embassy WEP 1058	SWINGING GUITARS (EP)	8
63	Embassy WEP 1088	MORE SWINGING GUITARS (EP)	8

(see also Pearls, Typhoons, Jaybirds, Paul Rich)

TONY ASHTON

72	Purple PUR 109	Celebration/Sloeback	7

(see also Green Bullfrog)

(TONY) ASHTON & (JON) LORD

74	Purple PUR 121	We're Gonna Make It/Band Of The Salvation Army Band	7
74	Oyster OYR 101	Ballad Of Mr Giver/TONY ASHTON: The Resurrection Shuffle	6
74	Purple TPS 3507	FIRST OF THE BIG BANDS (LP)	12

(see also Tony Ashton, Ashton Gardner & Dyke, Paice Ashton & Lord, Jon Lord, Deep Purple)

ASHTON, GARDNER & DYKE

69	Polydor 56306	Maiden Voyage/See The Sun In My Eyes	35
70	Polydor 583 081	ASHTON, GARDNER & DYKE (LP)	12
71	Capitol E-ST 563	THE WORST OF ASHTON, GARDNER AND DYKE (LP)	12
72	Capitol EA-ST 22862	WHAT A BLOODY LONG DAY IT'S BEEN (LP)	12

(see also Ashton & Lord, Remo Four, Creation, Birds, Mike Hurst & Method, Badger, Medicine Head, Family)

ASIA

82	Geffen A 2228	Only Time Will Tell/Ride Easy (p/s)	6
82	Geffen A 11-2228	Only Time Will Tell/Ride Easy (picture disc)	8
82	Geffen A 2494	Heat Of The Moment/Time Again (p/s)	5
82	Geffen A 2884	Sole Survivor/Here Comes The Feeling (p/s)	5
82	Geffen A 3580	Don't Cry/True Colours (p/s)	6
82	Geffen WA 3580	Don't Cry/True Colours (blue or green logo-shaped picture disc)	12/10
83	Geffen TA 3836	The Smile Has Left Your Eyes/Lying To Yourself/Midnight Sun (12", p/s, red vinyl)	8
85	Geffen TA 6737	Go (Remix)/Go (Instrumental)/After The War (12", p/s)	8
92	Musidisc 109527	Who Will Stop The Rain/Aqua Pt. 1 (p/s)	5
92	Musidisc 109521	Who Will Stop The Rain/Aqua Pt. 1/Heart Of Gold (10", picture disc)	10
92	Musidisc 109526	Who Will Stop The Rain/Aqua Pt. 1/Heart Of Gold (12", p/s)	8
92	Musidisc 109522	Who Will Stop The Rain/Aqua Pt. 1/Heart Of Gold/Obsessing (CD)	8
94	Bullet Proof CDVEST 1001	Anytime/Reality/Anytime (Extended)/Feels Like Love (CD)	8
82	Geffen GEF 11-85577	ASIA (LP, picture disc)	18

(see also Yes, Emerson Lake & Palmer, Steve Howe, Anderson Bruford Wakeman & Howe)

ED ASKEW

69	Fontana STL 5519	ED ASKEW (LP)	12

ARTHUR ASKEY

57	HMV 7EG 8294	HELLO! PLAYMATES (EP)	10
57	Oriole MG 20017	HELLO! PLAYMATES (LP)	20

ASLAN

76	Profile GMOR 006	PAWS FOR THOUGHT (LP)	125
77	Profile GMOR 144	SECOND HELPINGS (LP)	150

SVEND ASMUSSEN

54	Philips PB 343	Sh-Boom/Do, Do, Do, Do, Do, Do It Again (78)	12

MONICA ASPELUND

77	RCA PB 9044	Lapponia/La-La, Sing A Song	8

VERA ASPEY

77	Topic 12TS 356	THE BLACKBIRD (LP)	12

VERA & GARY ASPEY

75	Topic 12TS 255	FROM THE NORTH (LP, blue label)	12
76	Topic 12TS 299	A TASTE HOTPOT (LP, blue label)	12

ASPHALT RIBBONS

88	Lily LILY 002	PASSION, COOLNESS, INDIFFERENCE (12", p/s)	8
89	In Tape IT 063	THE ORCHARD EP (p/s)	5
89	In Tape ITTI 063	THE ORCHARD EP (12", p/s)	5
89	In Tape IT 068	Good Love/Long Lost Uncle/The Day I Turned Bad (p/s)	5
89	In Tape ITTI 068	Good Love/Long Lost Uncle/The Day I Turned Bad (12", p/s)	8
89	In Tape IT 6545 1	Over Again/EVA: Unquenchable (p/s, promo only)	8

(see also Tindersticks)

MARY ASQUITH

78	Mother Earth MUM 1204	CLOSING TIME (LP)	30

ASSAGAI

71	Vertigo 6059 034	Telephone Girl/I'll Wait For You	6
71	Vertigo 6360 030	ASSAGAI (LP, gatefold sleeve, spiral label)	18
72	Philips 6308 079	ZIMBABWE (LP)	15
70s	Sounds Superb SPR 90054	AFRO ROCK (LP)	15

ASSEMBLED MULTITUDE

70	Atlantic 2091 002	Overture From Tommy/Mud	5

LYS ASSIA

54	Decca F 10097	O Mein Papa/Ponylied	5
57	Decca DFE 6383	A CONTINENTAL STAR PRESENTS FOUR CONTINENTAL HITS (EP)	10

ASSOCIATES

79	Double Hip DHR 1	Boys Keep Swinging/Mona Property Girl (no p/s, 500 only)	50
79	MCA MCA 537	Boys Keep Swinging/Mona Property Girl (no p/s, demos more common, £25)	30
80	Fiction FICS 11	The Affectionate Punch/You Were Young (p/s)	6
81	Fiction FICSX 13	A/Would I … Bounce Back (p/s)	6
81	RSO RSO 78	Kites/A Girl Named Property (p/s, band on A-side credited as "39 Lyon St.")	5
81	RSO RSOX 78	Kites/A Girl Named Property (12", p/s, A-side credited as "39 Lyon St.")	8
82	Lyntone LYN 11649	Even Dogs In The Wild (clear 1-sided flexi free with *Flexipop* mag, issue 20)	8/5
82	Lyntone LYN 11649	Even Dogs In The Wild (one-sided hard vinyl test pressing)	30
82	Beggars Banquet BEG 86	Tell Me Easter's On Friday/Straw Towels (unreleased, white labels only)	25
84	WEA YZ 16T	Waiting For The Loveboat (Extended Version)/(John Peel Session Version)/Schampout (Extended Version) (12", stickered p/s)	8
85	WEA YZ 28P	Breakfast/Breakfast Alone (picture disc, stickered PVC sleeve)	5
85	Sounds/WEA CRACKER 1	CHRISTMAS CRACKER 45 (cassette, includes "Breakfast [live at Ronnie Scott's]", free with *Sounds*)	5
85	WEA YX 47TE	Take Me To The Girl/Perhaps/God Bless The Child (live)/Even Dogs In The Wild (live)/The Boy That Santa Claus Forgot (live) (10", p/s)	10
88	WEA YZ 310 TX	Heart Of Glass (The Temperament Mix)/Heart Of Glass/Her Only Wish/Heaven's Blue (12", 3-D p/s, shrinkwrapped with 3-D glasses)	10
88	WEA YZ 310CD	Heart Of Glass/Her Only Wish/Breakfast/Those First Impressions (3" CD in 5" case, with adaptor)	10
88	WEA YZ 329B	Country Boy/Just Can't Say Goodbye (12" Mix)/Take Me To The Girl/Heart Of Glass (Dub Mix) (33rpm, p/s, unissued)	
88	WEA YZ 329T	Country Boy/Heart Of Glass (Dub Mix)/Just Can't Say Goodbye (12" Mix) (12", p/s, unissued, white labels only)	60

88	WEA YZ 329CD	Country Boy/Just Can't Say Goodbye (12" Mix)/Take Me To The Girl/ Heart Of Glass (Dub Mix) (3" CD with adaptor in jewel case, unissued)	50
89	Strange Fruit SFPSC 075	PEEL SESSIONS: It's Better This Way/Nude Spoons/Me, Myself And The Tragic Story/A Matter Of Gender/Ulcragyceptemol (cassette)	5
90	Circa YRTB 46	Fever (Album Version)/Green Tambourine/Groovin' With Mr. Bloe (12", p/s, with 2 prints)	8
90	Circa YRTB 46	Fever (Single Version)/Green Tambourine/Groovin' With Mr. Bloe (12", p/s, with different B-sides, unreleased, handwritten white label, test pressings only)	12
90	Circa YRTX 49	Fire To Ice/The Glamour Chase/Green Tambourine/Groovin' With Mr. Bloe (10", p/s)	7
90	WEA YZ 534	POPERETTA EP: Waiting For The Loveboat (Slight Return)/ Club Country Club (p/s)	5
90	WEA YZ 534C	POPERETTA EP: Waiting For The Loveboat (Slight Return)/ Club Country Club (cassette)	5
90	WEA YZ 534T	POPERETTA EP: Waiting For The Loveboat (Extended Voyage)/ Club Country Club/Club Country Club (Time Unlimited)/ Waiting For The Loveboat (Slight Return) (12", p/s)	8
90	WEA YZ 534CD	POPERETTA EP: Waiting For The Loveboat (Slight Return)/Club Country Club/ Waiting For The Loveboat (Extended Voyage)/Club Country Club (Time Unlimited) (CD)	8
91	Circa YRTPR 56	Just Can't Say Goodbye (Extended Mix)/(Club Mix) (12", unreleased, white label test pressing, label credits "I Never Can Say Goodbye")	10
90	Circa BILLY 1	WILD AND LONELY (12" sampler, p/s)	8
90	Circa BILLYC 1	WILD AND LONELY (cassette sampler, card sleeve)	10
90	Circa BILLYCD 1	WILD AND LONELY (CD sampler, printed PVC sleeve)	12
93	Amnesty Intl. DSAPC 71	Amnesty International (picture disc, PVC sleeve, Billy MacKenzie features on photograph but not on recording, promo only)	15
82	Beggars Banquet BEGA 43	FOURTH DRAWER DOWN (LP, gatefold sleeve with poster, label also credits SITU 2)	12
82	WEA 240 005-4 (WX 24C)	SULK (cassette, includes U.S. edition, U.K. edition, extra tracks & exclusive remixes)	12
88	WEA WX 222C	THE GLAMOUR CHASE (unreleased, advance cassette only; with extra track "Take Me To The Girl")	40
88	WEA 244 619-2	THE GLAMOUR CHASE (CD, with extra track "Take Me To The Girl", unissued)	
88	WEA K 240 005-2	SULK (CD)	18

(see also Billy MacKenzie, Jih)

ASSOCIATION

66	London HLT 10054	Along Comes Mary/Your Own Love	7
66	London HLT 10074	Cherish/Don't Blame It On Me	6
66	London HLT 10098	Pandora's Golden Heebie Jeebies/Standing Still	8
67	London HLT 10118	No Fair At All/Looking Glass	6
67	London HLT 10140	Windy/Sometime	6
67	London HLT 10157	Never My Love/Requiem For The Masses	6
68	Warner Bros WB 7163	Everything That Touches You/We Love Us	6
68	Warner Bros WB 7195	Time For Livin'/Birthday Morning	6
68	Warner Bros WB 7229	Six Man Band/Like Always	6
69	Warner Bros WB 7267	Goodbye Columbus/The Time It Is Today	6
70	Warner Bros WB 7372	Just About The Same/Look At Me, Look At You	6
67	London HA-T 8305	AND THEN . . . ALONG COMES THE ASSOCIATION (LP)	22
67	London HA-T 8313	RENAISSANCE (LP)	22
67	London HA-T/SH-T 8342	INSIGHT OUT (LP)	22
68	Warner Bros W(S) 1733	BIRTHDAY (LP)	18
69	Warner Bros W(S) 1767	GREATEST HITS (LP)	18
69	Warner Bros W(S) 1786	GOODBYE COLUMBUS (LP, soundtrack)	18
69	Warner Bros W(S) 1800	THE ASSOCIATION (LP)	18

FRED ASTAIRE

57	HMV POP 337	Funny Face/AUDREY HEPBURN: How Long Has This Been Going On	10
57	MGM MGM 963	Paris Loves Lovers (with Cyd Charisse & Carol Richards)/All Of You	8
57	MGM MGM 964	The Ritz Roll And Rock/JANIS PAIGE: Satin And Silk	15
57	MGM MGM 964	The Ritz Roll And Rock/JANIS PAIGE: Satin And Silk (78)	15
57	MGM EP 601	SHOES WITH WINGS ON (EP)	12

(see also Judy Garland, Bing Crosby)

ASTERIX

70	Decca F 13075	Everybody/If I Could Fly	10

EDWIN ASTLEY ORCHESTRA

63	Oriole CB 1880	The World Ten Times Over/Soho	20
65	RCA RCA 1492	Danger Man Theme/Saint Theme	55

(see also Ted Astley)

TED ASTLEY

66	Decca F 12389	The Baron/Drop Head	40

(see also Edwin Astley)

ASTON & YEN

66	Doctor Bird DB 1064	Skillamy/BABA BROOKS & BAND: Party Time	15

ASTON HALL

80	Tamebeat TAME 001	The Daily Sun/Popular People (p/s)	6

ASTORS

65	Atlantic AT 4037	Candy/I Found Out	25
69	Atlantic 584 245	Candy/I Found Out (reissue)	5

ASTRALASIA

90s	Magic Eye PROMO 1	UTOPIA EP (12", promo)	8
90	Fungus BUBBLE LP 7	ASTRALASIA (LP)	15

ASTRAL NAVIGATIONS

71	Holyground HG 114/ NSR 172	ASTRAL NAVIGATIONS (LP, actually by Lightyears Away & Thundermother, poster cover & booklet, 250 copies only, some numbered)	225
89	Magic Mixture MM 2	ASTRAL NAVIGATIONS (LP, reissue with booklet, 425 copies only)	30
90s	Holyground HBG 122/1 CD	ASTRAL NAVIGATIONS (CD)	18

(see also Bill Nelson, David John & Mood)

ASTRONAUTS

63	RCA Victor RCA 1349	Baja/Kuk	12
63	RCA Victor RD 7662	ORBIT KAMPUS (LP)	40

ASTRONAUTS

66	Hala Gala HG 9	Before You Leave/Syncopate	10
67	Island WI 3065	Before You Leave/Syncopate (reissue)	8

ASTRONAUTS (U.K.)

79	Bugle BLAST 1	THE ASTRONAUTS EP (All Night Party/Back Soon/ Everything Stops The Baby/Survivors) (p/s)	12
80	Bugle BLAST 5	PRANKSTERS IN REVOLT (EP)	10
81	Bugle GENIUS 001	PETER PAN HITS THE SUBURBS (LP)	40
82	Bugle GENIUS 002	IT'S ALL DONE BY MIRRORS (LP)	35
86	All The Madmen MAD 5	IT'S ALL DONE BY MIRRORS (LP, reissue)	12

(see also Restricted Hours, Syndicate)

A SUDDEN SWAY

(see under Sudden Sway)

ASYLUM CHOIR

68	Mercury SMCL 21041	A LOOK INSIDE THE ASYLUM CHOIR (LP)	15

(see also Leon Russell)

ATACAMA

71	Charisma CAS 1039	ATACAMA (LP)	15
72	Charisma CAS 1060	THE SUN BURNS UP ABOVE (LP)	15

ATHENIANS

64	ESC ESC 1	You Tell Me/Little Queenie (custom sleeve)	35
64	Waverley SLP 532	I've Got Love If You Want It/I'm A Lover Not A Fighter (some in p/s)	100/60
65	Waverley SLP 533	Thinking Of Your Love/Mercy Mercy (some in custom sleeve)	50/35

GLENN ATHENS & TROJANS

65	Spot 7E 1018	GLENN ATHENS & TROJANS (EP)	400

PETE ATKIN

70	Philips 6006 050	Be Careful When They Offer You The Moon/Master Of The Revels	5
70	Fontana 6309 011	BEWARE THE BEAUTIFUL STRANGER (LP)	15
71	Philips 6308 070	DRIVING THROUGH MYTHICAL AMERICA (LP)	12
73	RCA SF 8336	A KING AT NIGHTFALL (LP)	12

BENNY ATKINS

60	Mercury AMT 1113	Lipstick On Your Lips/I'm Following You	7

CHET ATKINS

59	RCA Victor RCA 1153	Boo Boo Stick Beat/Django's Castle	7
59	RCA Victor RCA 1153	Boo Boo Stick Beat/Django's Castle (78)	20
60	RCA Victor RCA 1174	Teensville/One Mint Julep	7
60	RCA Victor RCA 1174	Teensville/One Mint Julep (78)	40
60	RCA Victor RCA 1209	"The Dark At The Top Of The Stairs" Theme/Hocus Pocus	6
64	RCA Victor RCA 1382	Susie Q/Windy & Warm	5
65	RCA Victor RCA 1441	Cloudy And Cool/Travelin'	5
65	RCA Victor RCA 1464	Yakety Axe/Letter Edged In Black	6
66	RCA Victor RCA 1515	From Nashville With Love/Rhythm Guitar	5
68	RCA Victor RCA 1773	Light My Fire/Mrs Robinson	5
69	RCA Victor RCA 1797	Those Were The Days/"Zorba The Greek" Theme	5
63	RCA Victor RCX 7118	GUITAR GENIUS (EP)	15
60	RCA Victor RD 27168	TEENSVILLE (LP)	18
60	RCA Victor RD 27194	THE OTHER CHET ATKINS (LP)	16
60	RCA Victor RD 27214	CHET ATKINS' WORKSHOP (LP)	16
62	RCA Victor RD 7507	GENIUS WITH CHET ATKINS (LP)	15
62	RCA Victor RD 7519	CARIBBEAN GUITAR (LP)	15
62	RCA Camden CDN 160	CHET ATKINS AND HIS GUITAR (LP)	15
62	RCA Camden CDN 165	DOWN HOME (LP)	15
63	RCA Victor RD/SF 7529	OUR MAN IN NASHVILLE (LP, mono/stereo)	15/18
63	RCA Victor RD 7557	TRAVELIN' (LP)	15
63	RCA Victor RD/SF 7602	TEENSCENE (LP, mono/stereo)	15/18
63	RCA Victor RD/SF 7647	PROGRESSIVE PICKING (LP, mono/stereo)	15/18
63	RCA Victor RD 7664	BEST OF CHET ATKINS (LP)	15
64	RCA Victor RD 7691	REMINISCING (LP, with Hank Snow)	15
65	RCA Victor RD 7710	MY FAVOURITE GUITARS (LP)	15
65	RCA Victor RD 7763	MORE OF THAT GUITAR COUNTRY (LP)	15
66	RCA Victor RD 7805	POPS GO COUNTRY (LP, with Boston Pops Orchestra)	12
66	RCA Victor RD/SF 7813	CHET ATKINS PICKS ON THE BEATLES (LP, mono/stereo)	15/18
67	RCA Victor RD 7838	FROM NASHVILLE WITH LOVE (LP)	15
67	RCA Victor RD 7882	IT'S A GUITAR WORLD (LP)	15
68	RCA Victor RD/SF 7934	SOLO FLIGHTS (LP)	15
69	RCA Victor SF 8064	PICKS ON THE POPS (LP)	12
60s	RCA Camden CDN 5110	GUITAR GENIUS (LP)	12
70	RCA Victor SF 8092	SOLD GOLD 70 (LP)	12
70	RCA Victor SF 8130	YESTERGROOVIN' (LP)	12

(see also Country Hams, Hank Snow, Mark Knopfler)

SWEETPEA ATKINSON

82	Ze ILPS 7018	DON'T WALK AWAY (LP, with lyric inner sleeve)	12

ATLANTIC BRIDGE
71	Dawn DNX 2507	I Can't Lie To You/Hilary Dickson/Childhood Room (p/s)	6
70	Dawn DNLS 3014	ATLANTIC BRIDGE (LP, gatefold sleeve)	12

ATLANTIC DRUM & PIPE BAND
76	Riva RIVA 2	Skye Boat Song/Skye Boat Song (Instrumental)	15

(see also Rod Stewart)

ATLANTICS
64	Windsor WPS 129	Don't Say No/Send Him To Me	7

ATLANTIS
73	Vertigo 6360 609	ATLANTIS (LP, spiral label)	12

ATLAS
78	Emerging WIL 001	AGAINST ALL THE ODDS (LP, private pressing)	25

AT LAST THE 1958 ROCK & ROLL SHOW
68	CBS 3349	I Can't Drive/Working On The Railroad	12

(see also Ian Hunter, Mott The Hoople, Freddie 'Fingers' Lee, Miller Anderson, Charles Woolfe)

ATMOSFEAR
79	Elite DAZZ 4	Journey To The Powerline (Remix)/LEVEL 42: Sandstorm (12", w/l promo)	100
79	Elite	Dancing In Outer Space/Dancing In Outer Space (Version) (12")	10
79	MCA 12 MCA 543	Dancing In Outer Space/Dancing In Outer Space (Version) (12", co. sleeve)	8
80	Elite DAZZ 2	Motivation/Extract (12", p/s)	8
83	Elite DAZZ 23	What Do We Do? (Club Mix)/What Do We Do?/Xtra Special (12", p/s)	8
81	MCA MCF 3110	ENTRANCE (LP)	12

(see also Level 42)

ATMOSPHERES
59	London HLW 8977	Kabalo/The Fickle Chicken	20
59	London HLW 8977	Kabalo/The Fickle Chicken (78)	20
60	London HLW 9091	Telegraph/Caravan	15

A TO AUSTR
70	Holy Ground HG 113	A TO AUSTR — MUSICS FROM HOLY GROUND (LP, with booklet, 99 only)	325
89	Magic Mixture MM 1	A TO AUSTR (LP, reissue, 425 only)	35
95	Holyground 010101LP	A TO AUSTR (LP, second reissue, foldover gatefold sleeve)	20
95	Kissing Spell KSG 002	A TO AUSTR (CD)	15

(see also Bill Nelson)

ATOMIC ROOSTER
70	B&C CB 121	Friday The 13th/Banstead (initial copies in p/s)	15/8
70	B&C CB 131	Tomorrow Night/Play The Game	7
71	B&C CB 157	Devil's Answer/Rock	7
72	Dawn DNS 1027	Stand By Me/Never To Lose	6
72	Dawn DNS 1029	Save Me/Close Your Eyes	6
74	Decca FR 13503	Tell Your Story (Sing Your Song)/O.D. (as Vincent Crane's Atomic Rooster)	8
80	EMI EMI 5084	Do You Know Who's Looking For You/Throw Your Life Away (p/s)	6
80	EMI 12EMI 5084	Do You Know Who's Looking For You (Ext.)/Throw Your Life Away (12", p/s)	10
81	Polydor POSP 334	Play It Again/Start To Live (p/s)	5
81	Polydor POSPX 334	Play It Again/Start To Live/Devil's Answer (live) (12", p/s)	8
82	Polydor POSP 408	End Of The Day/Living Underground (p/s)	5
82	Polydor POSPX 408	End Of The Day/Living Underground/Tomorrow Night (live) (12", p/s)	8
70	B&C CAS 1010	ATOMIC ROOSTER (LP)	25
70	B&C CAS 1026	DEATH WALKS BEHIND YOU (LP, gatefold sleeve)	20
71	Pegasus PEG 1	IN HEARING OF ATOMIC ROOSTER (LP, gatefold sleeve)	15
72	Dawn DNLS 3038	MADE IN ENGLAND (LP, limited 'denim' cover)	30
73	Dawn DNLS 3038	MADE IN ENGLAND (LP, re-pressing, standard cover)	15
73	Dawn DNLS 3049	NICE'N'GREASY (LP)	30
83	Towerbell TOWLP 004	HEADLINE NEWS (LP)	12

(see also Crane/Farlowe, Chris Farlowe, Crazy World Of Arthur Brown, Hard Stuff, Leaf Hound, Andromeda, John Du Cann)

ATOMS
79	Rinka R 23	Max Bygraves Killed My Mother/Beatles Jacket (colour silk-screened p/s in poly bag with inserts)	10

A II Z
81	Polydor POSP 243	No Fun After Midnight/Treason (no p/s)	12
81	Polydor POSPX 243	No Fun After Midnight/Treason/Valhalla's Force (12", p/s, red vinyl)	18
81	Polydor POSP 314	I'm The One Who Loves You/Ringside Seat (p/s)	15
80	Polydor 2383 587	THE WITCH OF BERKELEY — LIVE (LP, initially sealed with sew-on patch)	25/20

(see also AC/DC)

ATTACK (U.S.)
67	Philips BF 1585	Washington Square/Please Phil Spector	20

ATTACK (U.K.)
67	Decca F 12550	Try It/We Don't Know	60
67	Decca F 12578	Any More Than I Do/Hi-Ho Silver Lining	25
67	Decca F 12631	Created By Clive/Colour Of My Mind	35
68	Decca F 12725	Neville Thumbcatch/Lady Orange Peel	50
72	Decca F 13353	Hi-Ho Silver Lining/Any More Than I Do (reissue, unissued)	
90	Reflection MM 08	MAGIC IN THE AIR (LP)	20

(see also Andromeda, Five Day Week Straw People, Nice)

ATTAK
82	No Future OI 17	Today's Generation: Murder In The Subway/Future Dreams (p/s)	8
83	No Future PUNK 6	ZOMBIES (LP)	15

ATTEMPTED MOUSTACHE
78	Skeleton SKL 003	Superman/No Way Out (folded p/s)	5

(see also Half Man Half Biscuit)

ATTIC
79	Attic ATT 1	Yes I Want To/We're At War (white labels, stamped plain sleeve with insert)	6
80	Brain Booster BB 003	ALL PLANS EXIST (EP, stickered white labels)	5

ATTILA THE STOCKBROKER
81	No Wonder E 1	PHAZING OUT CAPITALISM (EP)	5
82	Cherry Red CHERRY 46	COCKTAILS (EP)	5

ATTRACTION
66	Columbia DB 7936	Stupid Girl/Please Tell Me	30
66	Columbia DB 8010	Party Line/She's A Girl	40

ATTRACTIONS
80	F-Beat XXLP 8	MAD ABOUT THE WRONG BOY (LP, with free EP [COMB 1])	10
	(see also Elvis Costello)		

ATTRITION
81	Sound For Industry SFI 671/A.R.R. 002	Fear/Devoid (flexidisc, p/s, some with *Adventures In Reality* fanzine, issue 5)	20/10
84	Uniton Recordings 1984-1	MONKEY IN A BIN (12" EP, poster p/s, split with tracks by Schamanen Circel)	15
84	Third Mind TMS 03	THE VOICE OF GOD (12" EP)	12
85	Third Mind TMS 04	Shrinkwrap/Pendulum Turns (12", p/s with insert)	12
87	Hamster HAM 18	DEATH HOUSE (mini-LP)	12
87	Hamster HAM 18	DEATH HOUSE (cassette)	12

ATTRIX
78	Attrix RB 01	Lost Lenore/Hard Times (p/s, stamped white labels)	6
81	Scoff DT 011	Procession/11th Hour (p/s)	5

WINIFRED ATWELL
55	Decca F 10448	Song Of The Sea/The Black Mask Waltz	6
55	Decca F 10476	Big Ben Boogie/Winnie's Waltzing Rag	6
55	Decca F 10496	17th Century Boogie/Stranger In Paradise	7
55	Decca F 10634	"Let's Have A Ding-Dong" Medley	8
56	Decca F 10681	Poor People Of Paris (Poor John)/Piano Tuners Boogie	12
56	Decca F 10727	Port-Au-Prince/Startime	8
56	Decca F 10762	Left Bank (C'est A Hambourg)/Rampart Street Rock	8
56	Decca F 10785	Bumble Boogie/St. Louis Blues	6
56	Decca F 10796	Make It A Party (medley, both sides)	7
56	Decca F 10825	The Garden Of Eden/Moonlight Gambler	5
57	Decca F 10852	Let's Rock 'N' Roll (medley, both sides)	7
57	Decca F 10886	Spaceship Boogie/Jane Street	7
57	Decca F 10886	Spaceship Boogie/Jane Street (78)	10
57	Decca F 10956	"Let's Have A Ball" Medley	5
58	Decca F 10987	Raunchy/Dugga Dugga Boom Boom	5
65	CBS 202006	Snow Bells/Flea-Market Of Paris (Vlooien Circus)	5
55	Decca DFE 6099	BOOGIE WITH WINIFRED ATWELL (EP)	8
50s	Decca	10" LPs	12

AUBREY SMALL
72	Polydor 2058 204	Loser/Oh What A Day It's Been	7
71	Polydor 2383 048	AUBREY SMALL (LP, with insert)	50
	(see also Sons Of Man)		

AUDIENCE
71	Charisma CB 126	Belladonna Moonshine/The Big Spell	6
71	Charisma CB 141	Indian Summer/It Brings A Tear/Priestess (some in p/s)	8/5
71	Charisma CB 156	You're Not Smiling/Eye To Eye	5
72	Charisma CB 185	Stand By The Door/Thunder And Lightnin'	5
72	Charisma CB 196	Raviole/Hard Cruel World	5
69	Polydor 583 065	AUDIENCE (LP)	60
70	Charisma CAS 1012	FRIEND'S FRIEND'S FRIEND (LP)	12
71	Charisma CAS 1032	THE HOUSE ON THE HILL (LP, gatefold sleeve with lyric inner sleeve)	12
72	Charisma CAS 1054	LUNCH (LP, gatefold sleeve)	12
	(see also Howard Werth & Moonbeams)		

AUDREY
69	Downtown DT 414	Love Me Tonight/BROTHER DAN ALLSTARS: Show Them Amigo	7
69	Downtown DT 418	Lover's Concerto/BROTHER DAN ALLSTARS: Along Came Roy	7
69	Downtown DT 436	You'll Lose A Good Thing/DESMOND RILEY: If I Had Wings	7
70	Downtown DT 452	Sweeter Than Sugar/The Way You Move	7
70	Downtown DT 454	Oh I Was Wrong/Let's Try It Again (B-side with Dandy)	7
70	Downtown DT 457	Someday We'll Be Together/MUSIC DOCTORS: Sunset Rock	7
70	Downtown DT 463	How Glad I Am/DANDY & AUDREY: I'm So Glad	7
70	Trend 6099 006	Getting Ready For A Heartache/M Y O B: Leave Me Alone	7
	(see also Dandy)		

BRIAN AUGER (&) TRINITY
65	Columbia DB 7590	Fool Killer/Let's Do It Tonight (as Brian Auger Trinity)	30
65	Columbia DB 7715	Green Onions '65/Kiko (as Brian Auger Trinity)	25
67	Columbia DB 8163	Tiger/Oh Baby, Won't You Come Back Home To Croydon, Where Everybody Beedle's And Bo's (solo)	30
67	Marmalade 598 003	Red Beans And Rice Pts 1 & 2	10
68	Marmalade 598 006	I Don't Know Where You Are/A Kind Of Love In (with Julie Driscoll, unissued in favour of "This Wheel's On Fire")	
69	Marmalade 598 015	What You Gonna Do/Bumpin' On Sunset	7
70	RCA RCA 1947	I Want To Take You Higher/Just Me Just You	6
71	Polydor 2058 119	This Wheel's On Fire/Road To Cairo (as Brian Auger & Julie Driscoll)	5
71	Polydor 2058 133	Marie's Wedding/Tomorrow City (as Brian Auger's Oblivion Express)	5
73	CBS 1444	Inner City Blues/Light Of The Path (as Brian Auger's Oblivion Express)	5
74	CBS 2309	Straight Ahead/Change	5

MINT VALUE £

68	Marmalade 608 004	DON'T SEND ME NO FLOWERS (LP, w/ Jimmy Page & Sonny Boy Williamson) . . 40
69	Marmalade 607/608 003	DEFINITELY WHAT! (LP) 30
70	RCA SF 8101	BEFOUR (LP) 20
70	Polydor 2334 004	THE BEST OF BRIAN AUGER, JULIE DRISCOLL & THE TRINITY (LP) 15
71	RCA SF 8170	OBLIVION EXPRESS (LP) 15
71	Polydor 2383 062	BETTER LAND (LP) 12
72	Polydor 2383 104	SECOND WIND (LP, as Brian Auger's Oblivion Express) 12
73	CBS 65625	CLOSER TO IT (LP) 12
74	CBS 80058	STRAIGHT AHEAD (LP) 12

(see also Julie Driscoll Brian Auger & Trinity, Shotgun Express, Jimmy Page, Sonny Boy Williamson)

AU GO-GO SINGERS

| 65 | Columbia DB 7493 | San Francisco Bay Blues/Pink Polemoniums . . . . 8 |
| 64 | Columbia 33SX 1696 | THEY CALL US AU GO-GO SINGERS (LP) . . . . 45 |

(see also Buffalo Springfield, Stephen Stills, Poco)

GEORGIE AULD

| 54 | Vogue Coral Q 2002 | Manhattan/Solitaire . . . . 5 |
| 60 | Top Rank JAR 281 | Hawaiian War Chant/Sleepy Lagoon . . . . 5 |

(see also Lancers, Modernaires)

AUM

| 69 | London HA-K/SH-K 8401 | BLUESVIBES (LP) . . . . 25 |

CLIFF AUNGIER

68	Polydor 56250	Time/Fisherboy 5
68	RCA RCA 1730	My Love And I/Abigail 5
69	Pye 7N 17753	Lady From Baltimore/Back On The Road Again 5
69	Pye NSPL 18294	LADY FROM BALTIMORE (LP) 12

(see also Royd Rivers & Cliff Aungier)

AUNTIEPUS

| 79 | Septic AUNT 1 | Half-Way To Venezuela/Marmalade Freak (p/s) . . . . 6 |

(see also Damned)

AUNT FORTESCUE'S BLUESROCKERS

| 76 | Vole VOLE 01 | Not Getting Caught Again/Cannard's Grave . . . . 5 |

(see also Graham Larkbey)

AU PAIRS

80	021 OTO 2	You/Domestic Departure/Kerb Crawler (p/s, with lyric insert) 5
81	Human HUMAN 1	PLAYING WITH A DIFFERENT SEX (LP) 12
82	Kamera KAM 010	SENSE AND SENSUALITY (LP, with insert) 12
83	AKA AKA 6	LIVE IN BERLIN (LP) 12

AURAL EXCITERS

| 79 | Ze ZE 700 | Spooks In Space '4'/Spooks In Space (die-cut p/s, luminous vinyl) . . . . 5 |

AURORA

| 82 | Aurora RAM 9 | I'll Be Your Fantasy (no p/s) . . . . 60 |

BURNER-LEE AUSTIN

| 73 | Mojo 2093 027 | Gimme Your Hand/Real Woman . . . . 5 |

GENE AUSTIN

| 51 | London L 567 | Ace In The Hole (with Les Paul Trio)/I'm Crying Just For You (78) . . . . 8 |

PATTI AUSTIN

69	United Artists UP 35018	The Family Tree/Magical Boy 5
70	United Artists UP 35097	Your Love Made The Difference In Me/It's Easier To Laugh Than Cry 5
71	CBS 7180	Are We Ready For Love/Now That I Know What Loneliness Is 10
74	Probe PRO 608	Music To My Heart/Love 'Em And Leave 'Em Kind Of Love 5

PETER AUSTIN

| 68 | Caltone TONE 125 | Your Love/Time Is Getting Harder . . . . 10 |

(see also Little Freddy, Mr. Foundation)

REG AUSTIN

| 65 | Pye 7N 15885 | My Saddest Day/I'll Find Her . . . . 45 |

SIL AUSTIN

57	Mercury MT 132	Slow Walk/Wildwood (78) 18
58	Mercury MT 189	Fall Out/Green Blazer (78) 18
58	Mercury 7MT 220	Don't You Just Know It/Rainstorm 15
58	Mercury MT 220	Don't You Just Know It/Rainstorm (78) 18
58	Mercury 7MT 225	Hey, Eula/The Last Time 15
58	Mercury MT 225	Hey, Eula/The Last Time (78) 20
58	Mercury MEP 9540	THE BAND WITH THE BEAT (EP) 35
58	Mercury MEP 9541	GO SIL GO (EP) 35
58	Mercury MPL 6534	SLOW WALK ROCK (LP) 40

AUSTRALIAN PLAYBOYS

| 67 | Immediate IM 054 | Black Sheep R.I.P./Sad . . . . 250 |

(see also Procession)

AUTECHRE

92	Hardcore HARD 003	Cavity Job/Accelera 1 + 2 (12", 1,000 only) 40
94	Warp 10WAP 11	BASECADET REMIXES (3 x 10" in box) 15
93	Warp LP 17LTD	INCUNABULA (2-LP set, silver vinyl) 35

(see also Gescom)

AUTO DAFÉ

82	Rewind REWIND 13	November November (p/s) 12
85	Spartan SP 18	All Is Yellow Hot Hot Hot (p/s) 10
85	Spartan SPP 18	All Is Yellow Hot Hot Hot (shaped picture disc) 20

MINT VALUE £

AUTOGRAPHS
| 78 | RAK RAK 281 | While I'm Still Young/Fabulous (p/s) .... 5 |

AUTOMATIC FINE TUNING (A.F.T.)
| 76 | Charisma CAS 1122 | AUTOMATIC FINE TUNING (LP) .... 12 |

AUTOMATIC DLAMINI
86	D For Drum DLAM 1	THE CRAZY SUPPER EP (p/s)................................... 5
87	D For Drum DLAM 2	I Don't Know You But... /I've Never Seen That Colour Anywhere Before (p/s, with insert) 5
87	Idea IDEA 009	Me And My Conscience (p/s)..................................... 5
87	Idea IDEAT 009	Me And My Conscience (12", p/s) 8
87	Idea IDEALP 001	THE D IS FOR DRUM (LP) 12
92	Big Intl. BOT 04	FROM A DIVA TO A DIVER (LP, also CD BOT 04CD) 12/20
	(see also P.J. Harvey)	

AUTOMATIC MAN
| 76 | Island WIP 6301 | My Pearl/Wallflower (p/s) .... 15 |

AUTOMATICS
| 78 | Island WIP 6433 | Wakin' With The Radio On/Watch Her Now (unissued) |
| 78 | Island WIP 6439 | When Tanks Roll Over Poland/Watch Her Now (p/s)...................... 10 |

GENE AUTRY
50	Columbia FB 3575	Have I Told You Lately That I Love You/Pretty Mary (78) 8
51	Columbia FB 3597	I Love You Because/Blue Canadian Rockies (78) 8
51	Columbia FB 3611	Mister And Mississippi (78).. 8
53	Philips PB 169	The Last Roundup/When It's Springtime In The Rockies (78) 8
54	Philips PB 273	Bimbo/Easter Mornin' (78) 8
59	London HLU 9001	Nine Little Reindeer/Buon Natale 8
59	London HLU 9001	Nine Little Reindeer/Buon Natale (78)............................... 20
66	Realm RM 52319	THE BEST OF GENE AUTRY (LP) 12
67	RCA Victor RD 7839	GOLDEN HITS (LP)... 12

AUTUMN VINE
| 70 | Evolution E 2447 | He Ain't No Superman/Maxi Baby .... 5 |

AVALANCHE
| 71 | Parlophone R 5890 | Finding My Way Home/Rabbits .... 30 |
| | *(see also Norman Haines Band)* | |

FRANKIE AVALON
58	HMV POP 453	Dede Dinah/Ooh-La-La. 18
58	HMV POP 453	Dede Dinah/Ooh-La-La (78) 35
58	London HL 8636	You Excite Me/Darlin' 30
58	London HL 8636	You Excite Me/Darlin' (78) 40
58	HMV POP 517	Ginger Bread/Blue Betty 10
58	HMV POP 517	Ginger Bread/Blue Betty (78)...................................... 25
59	HMV POP 569	I'll Wait For You/What Little Girl?.................................... 8
59	HMV POP 569	I'll Wait For You/What Little Girl? (78) 40
59	HMV POP 603	Venus/I'm Broke. 7
59	HMV POP 603	Venus/I'm Broke (78) 40
59	HMV POP 636	Bobby Sox To Stockings/A Boy Without A Girl. 7
59	HMV POP 636	Bobby Sox To Stockings/A Boy Without A Girl (78) 40
59	HMV POP 658	Just Ask Your Heart/Two Fools 6
59	HMV POP 658	Just Ask Your Heart/Two Fools (78). 40
60	HMV POP 688	Why/Swinging On A Rainbow 7
60	HMV POP 688	Why/Swinging On A Rainbow (78). 50
60	HMV POP 727	Don't Throw Away All Those Teardrops/Talk, Talk, Talk 6
60	HMV POP 742	The Faithful Kind/Gee Whizz — Whilikins — Golly Gee 6
60	HMV POP 766	Where Are You/Tuxedo Junction 6
60	HMV POP 794	Togetherness/Don't Let Love Pass Me By 6
60	HMV POP 816	Green Leaves Of Summer/Here's To The Ladies........................ 6
58	HMV 7EG 8471	FRANKIE AVALON (EP) 20
58	HMV 7EG 8482	FRANKIE AVALON NO. 2 (EP) 20
58	HMV 7EG 8507	FRANKIE AVALON NO. 3 (EP) 20
60	HMV 7EG 8632	SONGS OF THE ALAMO (EP)..................................... 15
59	HMV CLP 1346	SWINGIN' ON A RAINBOW (LP)................................... 25
60	HMV CLP 1423	SUMMER SCENE (LP) 25
60	HMV CLP 1440/CSD 1358	YOUNG AND IN LOVE (LP, mono/stereo) 25/30
64	United Artists ULP 1078	MUSCLE BEACH PARTY (LP) 25

AVALONS
| 66 | Island WI 263 | Everyday/I Love You. .... 12 |

AVANT-GARDE
| 68 | CBS 3704 | Naturally Stoned/Honey And Gall .... 7 |

AVANT GARDENER
| 77 | Virgin VEP 1003 | GOTTA TURN BACK (EP) .... 6 |

AVANT-GARDENERS
| 80 | Appaloosa AP 013 | THE AVANT-GARDENERS (LP) .... 10 |

AVAVA
| 91 | A5 AVA 5555 | AVAVA (LP, 500 only) .... 10 |

AVENGER
| 83 | Neat NEAT 31 | Too Wild To Tame/On The Rocks (p/s) .... 5 |
| 85 | Neat NEAT 1026 | KILLER ELITE (LP, with lyric insert) .... 15 |

AVENGERS
| 68 | Parlophone R 5661 | Everyone's Gonna Wonder/Take My Hand............................ 8 |
| | *(see also Vanity Fair)* | |

AVERAGE WHITE BAND
73	MCA MUS 1187	Put It Where You Want It/Reach Out	5
74	Atlantic K 10489	Pick Up The Pieces/You Got It	5

(see also Dream Police, Scots Of St. James, Hopscotch, Forever More)

AVIATOR
79	Harvest HAR 5180	Time Traveller/Rocking Chair (p/s)	5

AVIATOR
87	RCA PL 89934	AVIATOR (LP)	12

ENRIQUE AVILES
57	Melodisc 1402	Tan Sabrosona/Bombon Cha (78)	8

AVO-8
80	Stroppo STROP 1	Gone Wrong/Target One/No Hesitation (p/s)	10

ALAN AVON & TOY SHOP
70	Concord CON 005	These Are The Reasons/Night To Remember	90

(see also Hedgehoppers Anonymous)

VALERIE AVON
67	Columbia DB 8201	He Knows I Love Him Too Much/To Be Let	8

(see also Avons)

AVON CITIES' JAZZ BAND
56	Tempo A 151	Shim-Me Sha-Me Wabble/Hawaiian War Chant	8
56	Tempo A 151	Shim-Me Sha-Me Wabble/Hawaiian War Chant (78)	8
60	Tempo A 169	Upper Set/American Patrol	5
56	Tempo LAP 10	AVON CITIES JAZZ BAND (LP)	45
58	Tempo TAP 18	AVON CITIES JAZZ (LP, with Ray Bush)	30
60s	Eclipse ECS 2175	BRISTOL FASHION (LP)	15

(see also Ray Bush)

AVONS
59	Columbia DB 4363	Seven Little Girls Sitting In The Back Seat/Alone At Eight	6
59	Columbia DB 4363	Seven Little Girls Sitting In The Back Seat/Alone At Eight (78)	30
60	Columbia DB 4413	Pickin' Petals/We Fell In Love	6
60	Columbia DB 4461	We're Only Young Once/I Keep Dreaming	6
60	Columbia DB 4522	Four Little Heels/This Was Meant To Be	6
61	Columbia DB 4569	Rubber Ball/Cool And Cosy	6
61	Columbia DB 4700	Skin Divin'/Little Bo Peep	6
62	Columbia DB 4280	Tonight I Cannot Sleep/Gotta Go	6
62	Columbia DB 4899	A Wonderful Dream/Tonight You Belong To Me	7
63	Decca F 11588	Hey Paula/I Wanna Do It	6
63	Decca F 11641	Love Should Be True/All About You	5
64	Fontana TF 442	I Am The Girl/Once Upon A Summer's Day	6

(see also Valerie Avon, Avon Sisters)

AVON SISTERS
59	Columbia DB 4236	Jerri-Lee (I Love Him So)/Baby-O	8
59	Columbia DB 4236	Jerri-Lee (I Love Him So)/Baby-O (78)	30

AWAY FROM THE SAND
70s	Beaujangle DB 0003	AWAY FROM THE SAND (LP)	30

(see also Bev Pegg, Dave Cartwright, Brindley Brae)

A WITNESS
85	Ron Johnson ZRON 15	LOUDHAILER SONGS (12" EP)	8

DAVID AXELROD
68	Capitol ST 2982	SONGS OF INNOCENCE (LP)	50
73	MCA MCF 2664	THE AUCTION (LP)	30

AXIS
80	Metal Minded ISAX 1047	Lady/Messiah (p/s)	6
81	Axis	When You Hold Me	8
81	Neat NEAT 13	You Got It/One Step Ahead (p/s)	5

HOYT AXTON
64	Stateside SL 10082	GREENBACK DOLLAR (LP)	20
64	Stateside SL 10096	THUNDER 'N' LIGHTNIN' (LP)	20
66	London HA-F/SH-F 8276	THE BEST OF HOYT AXTON (LP)	20

KEVIN AYERS (& WHOLE WORLD)
70	Harvest HAR 5011	Singing A Song In The Morning/Eleanor's Cake Which Ate Her	10
70	Harvest HAR 5027	Butterfly Dance/Puis-Je? (with Whole World)	12
71	Harvest HAR 5042	Stranger In Blue Suede Shoes/Stars (with Whole World)	10
72	Harvest HAR 5064	Oh! Wot A Dream/Connie On A Rubber Band	10
73	Harvest HAR 5071	Caribbean Moon/Take Me To Tahiti (some in p/s)	20/5
74	Island WIP 6194	The Up Song/Everybody's Sometimes & Some People's All The Time Blues	6
74	Island WIP 6201	After The Show/Thank You Very Much	6
75	Harvest HAR 5100	Caribbean Moon/Take Me To Tahiti	6
76	Island WIP 6271	Falling In Love Again/Everyone Knows The Song	6
76	Harvest HAR 5107	Stranger In Blue Suede Shoes/Fake Mexican Tourist Blues (possibly some in p/s)	20/5
76	Harvest HAR 5109	Caribbean Moon/Take Me To Tahiti (reissue, some in different p/s)	20/5
77	Harvest HAR 5124	Star/The Owl	6
80	Harvest HAR 5198	Money, Money, Money/Stranger In Blue Suede Shoes (p/s)	6
83	Charly/Celluloid CYZ 7107	My Speeding Heart/Champagne & Valium (p/s)	10
86	Illuminated LEV 71	Stepping Out/Only Heaven Knows (no p/s)	15
70	Harvest SHVL 763	JOY OF A TOY (LP, gatefold sleeve)	30

Kevin AYERS

70	Harvest SHSP 4005	SHOOTING AT THE MOON (LP, with Whole World)	30
72	Harvest SHVL 800	WHATEVERSHEBRINGSWESING (LP, gatefold sleeve)	20
73	Harvest SHVL 807	BANANAMOUR (LP, gatefold sleeve, some with booklet)	30/15
74	Island ILPS 9263	THE CONFESSIONS OF DR. DREAM AND OTHER STORIES (LP, with inner)	15
75	Island ILPS 9322	SWEET DECEIVER (LP, with inner sleeve)	12
75	Harvest SHDW 407	JOY OF A TOY/SHOOTING AT THE MOON (2-LP, reissue, gatefold sleeve)	15
76	Harvest SHSP 2005	ODD DITTIES (LP)	12
76	Harvest SHSP 4057	YES WE HAVE NO MAÑANAS (LP, with inner sleeve)	12
78	Harvest SHSP 4085	RAINBOW TAKEAWAY (LP)	12
80	Harvest SHSP 4106	THAT'S WHAT YOU GET BABE (LP, with inner sleeve)	12
83	Charly CR 30224	DIAMOND JACK AND THE QUEEN OF PAIN (LP)	15
86	Illuminated AMA 25	AS CLOSE AS YOU THINK (LP)	25
92	Permanent PERM LP 5	STILL LIFE WITH GUITAR (LP)	15

(see also Soft Machine, Lady June, Lol Coxhill, David Bedford, Mike Oldfield, Bridget St. John)

AYERS, CALE, NICO & ENO
| 74 | Island ILPS 9291 | JUNE 1ST, 1974 (LP) | 15 |

(see also Kevin Ayers, John Cale, Nico, Brian Eno)

ROY AYERS (UBIQUITY)
76	Polydor 2066 671	Evolution/Mystique Voyage (as Roy Ayers' Ubiquity)	5
77	Polydor 2066 842	Running Away/Cincinnati Growl (as Roy Ayers' Ubiquity)	5
78	Polydor 2066 896	Freaky Dee Jay/You Came Into My Life	5
78	Polydor AYERS 12	Get On Up Get On Down/And Don't Say No (12")	8
79	Polydor POSP 53	Fever/Is It Too Late To Try	5
79	Polydor POSPX 53	Fever/Is It Too Late To Try (12")	8
80	Polydor STEPX 9	Don't Stop The Feeling (12")	8
80	Polydor POSP 135	Running Away/Can't You See Me	5
80	Polydor POSPX 135	Running Away/Can't You See Me (12")	12
80	Polydor POSPX 186	Sometimes, Believe In Yourself (12")	8
83	Polydor UM 1T	Silver Vibrations/Fast Money (12")	8
87	Urban URBX 6	Can't You See Me/Love Will Bring Us Back Together/Sweet Tears (12", p/s)	8
83	Uno Melodic UMLP 2	DRIVIN' ON UP (LP)	15

(see also Jack Wilson Quartet)

AYRSHIRE FOLK
| 74 | Deroy | AYRSHIRE FOLK (LP, private pressing) | 50 |

AYSHEA
65	Fontana TF 627	Eeny Meeny/Peep My Love	7
68	Polydor 56276	Celebration Of The Year/Only Love Can Save Me Now	15
69	Polydor 56302	Another Night/Taking The Sun From My Eyes	6
70	Polydor 2001 029	Mr White's White Flying Machine/Ship Of The Line	5
70	Polydor 2058 074	Who's Gonna Rescue Jesus/The Flowers Are Mine	5
71	MAM MAM 59	Old Fashioned Love Song/Family Of A Man	5
73	Harvest HAR 5073	Farewell/The Best Years Of My Life	5
70	Polydor 2384 026	AYSHEA (LP)	25
74	DJM DJLPS 445	LIFT OFF WITH AYSHEA (LP)	15

(see also Ayshea Brough)

AZTEC CAMERA
81	Postcard 81-3	Just Like Gold/We Could Send Letters (die-cut sleeve, some with card)	18/10
81	Postcard 81-8	Mattress Of Wire/Lost Outside The Tunnel (p/s)	15
82	Rough Trade RT 112	Pillar To Post/Queen's Tattoos (p/s)	5
82	Rough Trade RT 112P	Pillar To Post/Queen's Tattoos (picture disc)	6
83	Rainhill ACFC 1	Oblivious (Langer/Winstanley Remix)/Oblivious (Colin Fairley Remix) (fan club issue, no p/s)	15
83	WEA AZTEC 1	Oblivious/Orchid Girl/We Could Send Letters (live)/Back On Board (live) (double pack, numbered gatefold p/s, 10,000 only)	5
84	WEA AC 1 T	All I Need Is Everything (Remix)/Jump (Extended) (12", p/s, with poster)	15
87	WEA YZ 154 CD	Deep & Wide & Tall (Breakdown Mix)/Bad Education (3" CD, card sleeve)	10
88	WEA YZ 168 CD	How Men Are/The Red Flag/Killermont Street (live)/Pillar To Post (live) (3" CD, card sleeve)	10
88	WEA YZ 181	Somewhere In My Heart/Everybody Is A Number One (Boston '86 version) (p/s)	5
88	WEA YZ 181TE	Somewhere In My Heart/Everybody Is A Number One (Boston '86 version) (10", p/s)	8
88	WEA YZ 181 CD	Somewhere In My Heart/Everybody Is A Number One/Walk Out To Winter/Still On Fire (3" CD, card sleeve)	10
88	WEA YZ 199 TW	Working In A Goldmine/I Threw It All Away (live)/Working In A Goldmine (instrumental) (12", p/s, with badge)	10
88	WEA YZ 199 CD	Working In A Goldmine/I Threw It All Away (live)/How Men Are (live) (3" CD, card sleeve)	10
88	WEA YZ 154 TE	Deep & Wide & Tall/Bad Education/Working In A Goldmine (live)/Somewhere In My Heart (live) (10", p/s)	8
88	WEA YZ 154 CD	Deep & Wide & Tall (7" version)/Deep & Wide & Tall (Extended Remix)/Bad Education/More Than A Law (CD)	8

(see also French Impressionists)

AZYMUTH
79	Milestone MRC 101	Jazz Carnival/Fly Over The Horizon (12")	8
78	ECM ECM 1130	THE TOUCHSTONE (LP)	12
80	ECM ECM 1163	DEPART (LP, with Ralph Towner)	12
80	Milestone M 9097	OUTUBRO (LP)	12

BOB AZZAM & HIS ORCHESTRA
| 60 | Decca F 21235 | Mustapha/Tintarella Di Luna | 6 |
| 61 | Oriole CB 1599 | Couscous/Abuglubu | 6 |

IKE B & CRYSTALS
68	Island WI 3151	Try A Little Merriness/Patricia	15

B's
70s	private pressing	IN YOUR BONNET (LP)	30

MEHER BABA
70	Univ. Spiritual League 1	HAPPY BIRTHDAY (LP, with inserts, 6 Pete Townshend tracks, 100 only)	100
70	Univ. Spiritual League 2	I AM (LP, with inserts, features 5 Pete Townshend tracks)	60
76	Univ. Spiritual League 3	WITH LOVE (LP, features 3 Pete Townshend tracks)	50
70s	MBO MBO 1	STAR OF THE SILENT SCREEN ... MEHER BABA (LP, reissue of "Happy Birthday" without inserts)	20
70s	MBO MBO 2	I AM (LP, reissue, without inserts)	20

(see also Pete Townshend)

BABE RUTH
71	Decca F 13234	Rupert's Magic Feather/Flood	5
72	Harvest SHSP 4022	FIRST BASE (LP)	12
73	Harvest SHVL 812	AMAR CABALLERO (LP)	12
75	Harvest SHSP 4038	BABE RUTH (LP)	12

(see also Jenne Haan, Bernie Marsden, Wild Turkey)

ALICE BABS
63	Fontana TF 409	After You've Gone/St. Louis Blues Twist	6

MONTY BABSON
59	London HLJ 8877	All Night Long/The Things Money Cannot Buy	8
59	London HLJ 8877	All Night Long/The Things Money Cannot Buy (78)	30
60	London HAJ 2212	ALL NIGHT LONG (LP)	15

BABY
77	Chelsea CHL 517	WHERE DID ALL THE MONEY GO (LP)	12

BABY BIRD
96	Echo ECS 026	You're Gorgeous/Bebe Limonade (p/s, gold vinyl)	8
96	Echo ECSCX 026	You're Gorgeous/Bebe Limonade/Ooh Yeah/Car Crash (CD, mirrored silver digipak)	10
96	Echo ECS 031	Candy Girl/Farmer (picture disc)	5
97	Echo ECS 033	Cornershop/Death Of A Neighbourhood (picture disc)	5
95	Baby Bird LP 1	IF I WAS BORN A MAN (LP, 500 only)	10
95	Baby Bird LP 2	BAD SHAVE (LP, 500 only)	15
95	Baby Bird LP 3	FATHERHOOD (LP, 500 only)	12
95	Baby Bird CD 1	IF I WAS BORN A MAN (CD, 1,000 only)	15
95	Baby Bird CD 2	BAD SHAVE (CD, 1,000 only)	15

BABY DOLLS
60	Warner Bros WB 16	Quiet!/Hey, Baby!	6

BABY HUEY
71	Buddah 2365 001	LIVING LEGEND — THE BABY HUEY STORY (LP)	35

BABY JANE & ROCKABYES
63	United Artists UP 1010	How Much Is That Doggie In The Window/My Boy John	10

BABY LEMONADE
87	Sha La La 003	The Jiffy Neckware Creation/BACHELOR PAD: Girl Of Your Dreams (flexidisc, p/s, with *Are You Scared To Be Happy* fanzine)	10/6
87	Narodnik NRK 004	The Secret Goldfish/Real World (p/s)	7

BABYLON
69	Polydor 56356	Into The Promised Land/Nobody's Fault But Mine (some in p/s)	10/5

(see also Carole Grimes)

BABY SUNSHINE
75	Deroy DER 1301	BABY SUNSHINE (LP, with insert)	65

(see also Fairy's Moke)

BACCA
73	Grape GR 3048	George Foreman/Version	5

BURT BACHARACH (ORCHESTRA)
65	London HLR 9968	Trains And Boats And Planes/Wives And Lovers	6
65	London HLR 9983	What's New Pussycat/My Little Red Book (B-side with Tony Middleton)	20
69	A&M AMS 702	Bond Street/Alfie	15
65	London HAR/SHR 8233	HIT MAKER! (LP, 1st pressing, plum/blue label, mono/stereo)	15
68	London HAR/SHR 8233	HIT MAKER! (LP, 2nd pressing, plum/black label, mono/stereo)	12
67	RCA Victor RD/SF 7874	CASINO ROYALE (LP, soundtrack, mono/stereo)	50/65
68	A&M AMLS 908	REACH OUT (LP)	12
69	A&M AMLS 938	MAKE IT EASY ON YOURSELF (LP)	12
70	A&M AMLS 963	BUTCH CASSIDY AND THE SUNDANCE KID (LP, soundtrack)	12
71	A&M AMLH 63501	BURT BACHARACH (LP, gatefold sleeve)	10
71	A&M AMLS 2010	PORTRAIT IN MUSIC (LP)	10
72	MCA MUPS 450	HIT MAKER (LP)	10
73	A&M AMLS 63527	LIVING TOGETHER (LP)	10
73	A&M AMLS 68159	PORTRAIT IN MUSIC VOL. 2 (LP)	10

Burt BACHARACH Orchestra

74	A&M AMLS 68279	IN CONCERT (LP)	10
74	MCA MCF 2523	HITS (LP)	10

(see also Tony Middleton, Breakaways)

BACHDENKEL
77	Initial IRL 001	LEMMINGS (LP, some with bonus EP)	25/15
77	Initial IRL 002	STALINGRAD (LP, numbered)	15

JOHNNY BACHELOR
60	London HLN 9074	Mumbles/Arabella Jean	40

BACHELORS (U.K.)
58	Parlophone R 4454	Platter Party/Love Is A Two Way Street	25
58	Parlophone R 4454	Platter Party/Love Is A Two Way Street (78)	15
59	Parlophone R 4547	Please Don't Touch/Ding Dong	25
60	Decca F 11300	Lovin' Babe/Why Can't It Be Me	45

BACHELORS (Ireland)
72	Decca F 13248	Diamonds Are Forever/Where There's A Heartache	10

BACHMAN TURNER OVERDRIVE
74	Mercury 6167 071	Roll On Down The Highway/Sledgehammer	5
75	Mercury 6167 173	Hey You/Flat Broke Love	7
77	Mercury 6167 520	My Wheels Won't Turn	8
77	Mercury 6167 567	Shot Gun Rider	6
79	Mercury 6167 759	Heart Aches	7

BACH TWO BACH
71	Mushroom 100 MR 10	BACH TWO BACH (LP)	15

BACK ALLEY CHOIR
72	York SYK 517	Smile Born Of Courtesy/Why Are You Here	20
73	York FYK 406	BACK ALLEY CHOIR (LP, 500 only)	275

BACKBEAT PHILHARMONIC
61	Top Rank JAR 576	Rock And Roll Symphony Parts 1 & 2	10

BACK DOOR
72	Blakey BLP 5989	BACK DOOR (LP, sold at gigs)	35
73	Warner Bros K 46231	BACK DOOR (LP)	12
76	Warner Bros K 56243	ACTIVATE (LP)	12

MIRIAM BACKHOUSE
77	Mother Earth MUM 1203	GYPSY WITHOUT A ROAD (LP)	100

BACK PORCH MAJORITY
65	Columbia DB 7627	Ramblin' Man/Good Time Joe	5

BACKSEAT ROMEOS
80	Future Earth FER 007	Zero Ambition/In The Night (p/s)	6

BACK STREET CRAWLER
75	Atlantic K 50173	THE BAND PLAYS ON (LP)	12
76	Atlantic K 50267	SECOND STREET (LP, with inner sleeve)	12

(see also Paul Kossoff, Crawler, Beckett)

BACK TO ZERO
79	Fiction FICS 004	Your Side Of Heaven/Back To Back (p/s)	8

BACKYARD HEAVIES
73	Action ACT 4616	Just Keep On Truckin'/Never Can Say Goodbye	10

GAR BACON
58	Felsted AF 107	Mary Jane/Chains Of Love	15
58	Felsted AF 107	Mary Jane/Chains Of Love (78)	40
59	Fontana H 196	Marshal, Marshal/Too Young To Love	20
59	Fontana H 196	Marshal, Marshal/Too Young To Love (78)	30

BACON FAT
70	Blue Horizon 57-3171	Nobody But You/Small's On 53rd	12
70	Blue Horizon 57-3181	Evil/Blues Feeling	12
70	Blue Horizon 7-63858	GREASE ONE FOR ME (LP)	50
71	Blue Horizon 2431 001	TOUGH DUDE (LP)	55

(see also Dirty Blues Band, George 'Harmonica' Smith)

BAD ACTORS
80	Sophist. Noise SONO 1	Strange Love/Energy Society (p/s)	6
80	Plastic Speech	Love Song/Are They Hostile (p/s)	5

BAD BOYS
64	Piccadilly 7N 35208	The Owl And The Pussycat/That's What'll Do	25

BAD BRAINS
82	Alt. Tentacles VIRUS 13	I Luv Jah/Sailin' On/Big Takeover (12", p/s)	12
83	Food For Thought YUMT101	I And I Survive (An' T'ing)/Destroy Babylon (12", p/s)	15

BAD COMPANY
76	Island WIP 6263	Run With The Pack/Do Right By Your Woman	5
77	Island WIP 6381	Everything I Need/Too Bad	5
79	Swan Song SSK 19416	Rock'n'Roll Fantasy/Crazy Circles (p/s)	5
74	Island ILPS 9279	BAD CO. (LP, gatefold stickered sleeve)	12
75	Island ILPS 9304	STRAIGHT SHOOTER (LP, with inner sleeve)	12

(see also Free, Firm, King Crimson, Mott The Hoople, Boz, Rock Aid Armenia)

BADFINGER
70	Apple APPLE 20	Come And Get It/Rock Of All Ages (p/s)	8
70	Apple APPLE 31	No Matter What/Better Days (p/s)	15

71	Apple APPLE 35	Name Of The Game/Suitcase (unreleased)	
72	Apple APPLE 40	Day After Day/Sweet Tuesday Morning (p/s)	12
72	Apple APPLE 42	Baby Blue/Flying (unreleased in U.K.)	
74	Apple APPLE 49	Apple Of My Eye/Blind Owl	15
79	Elektra K 12345	Lost Inside Your Love/Come Down Hard	6
79	Elektra K 12369	Love Is Gonna Come At Last/Sail Away	7
70	Apple SAPCOR 12	MAGIC CHRISTIAN MUSIC (LP)	50
70	Apple SAPCOR 16	NO DICE (LP, gatefold sleeve)	45
72	Apple SAPCOR 19	STRAIGHT UP (LP)	50
73	Warner Bros K 56023	BADFINGER (LP, with insert)	15
74	Apple SAPCOR 27	ASS (LP, with inner sleeve)	35
74	Warner Bros K 56076	WISH YOU WERE HERE (LP, withdrawn)	60
89	Edsel ED 302	SHINE ON (LP)	15
91	Apple SAPCOR 12	MAGIC CHRISTIAN MUSIC (LP, reissue, gatefold sleeve with bonus 12" [SAPCOR 121])	20
92	Apple SAPCOR 16	NO DICE (LP, reissue, gatefold sleeve with bonus 12" [SAPCOR 161])	20
93	Apple SAPCOR 19	STRAIGHT UP (LP, reissue, gatefold sleeve with bonus 12" [SAPCOR 191])	20
95	Apple SAPCOR 28	COME AND GET IT — THE BEST OF BADFINGER (2-LP, gatefold sleeve)	25

(see also Iveys, Masterminds, Gary Walker & Rain, Dodgers, Natural Gas, Blue Goose)

BADGE
81	Metal Minded MM 2	Silver Woman/Something I've Lost (p/s)	25

BADGER
74	Epic EPC 2326	White Lady/Don't Pull The Trigger	5
73	Atlantic K 40473	ONE LIVE BADGER (LP, gatefold pop-up sleeve)	15
74	Epic EPC 80009	WHITE LADY (LP)	12

(see also Ashton Gardner & Dyke, Jackie Lomax)

BADLY DRAWN BOY
97	Twisted Nerve TN 001	EP1 (EP, 500 only)	50
98	Twisted Nerve TN 002	EP2 (EP, 1,000 only)	30
98	Twisted Nerve XL TN 001T	EP3 (EP, 1,000 only)	8
99	Twisted Nerve TNXL 002R	IT CAME FROM THE GROUND (10" EP, 500 only)	12

BAD MANNERS
80	Magnet MAG 180	Special Brew/Ivor The Engine (picture disc)	8
81	Flexipop 005	Just Pretendin'/No Respect (blue flexidisc free with *Flexipop* mag, issue 5)	7/5
81	Record Mirror	Runaway (flexidisc, die-cut printed sleeve, free with *Record Mirror* paper)	7/5

BAD NEWS
87	EMI EM 24X	Bohemian Rhapsody/Life With Brian (scratch'n'sniff p/s)	8
87	EMI EMP 24	Bohemian Rhapsody/Life With Brian (p/s, with sew-on patch)	7
87	EMI 12EM 24	Bohemian Rhapsody/Pretty Woman/Life With Brian (12", standard p/s)	8
87	EMI 12EM 24X	Bohemian Rhapsody/Pretty Woman/Life With Brian (12", scratch'n'sniff p/s)	10
87	EMI EM 36	Cashing In On Christmas/Bad News (p/s)	8
87	EMI EMG 36	Cashing In On Christmas/Bad News (Christmas card poster pack)	7
87	EMI 12EM 36	Cashing In On Christmas (Let's Bank Mix)/Bad News/Cashing In On Christmas (12", p/s)	8

(see also Brian May)

BAD TASTE
88	Newgate SRT#8KS 1554	Rockin' Girl (p/s, with insert)	15

JOAN BAEZ
65	Fontana TF 604	It's All Over Now Baby Blue/Daddy You've Been On My Mind	5
65	Fontana TF 639	Farewell Angelina/Queen Of Hearts	5
66	Vanguard VA 2	Love Minus Zero/Love Is Just A Four-Letter Word	5
63	Fontana TE 18012	WITH GOD ON OUR SIDE (EP)	8
60	Fontana (S)TFL 6002	JOAN BAEZ (LP)	12
61	Fontana (S)TFL 6025	JOAN BAEZ 2 (LP)	12
62	Fontana (S)TFL 6035	IN CONCERT 2 (LP)	12
64	Fontana (S)TFL 6043	JOAN BAEZ 5 (LP)	12
65	Fontana (S)TFL 6058	FAREWELL ANGELINA (LP)	12

(see also Earl Scruggs)

DOC BAGBY
58	Fontana H 106	Dumplin's/Sylvia's Calling (78)	12

BURR BAILEY (& SIX SHOOTERS)
63	Decca F 11686	San Francisco Bay/Like A Bird Without Feathers (with Six Shooters)	20
64	Decca F 11846	Chahawki/You Made Me Cry	35

CLIVE BAILEY & RICO'S GROUP
62	Blue Beat BB 92	Evening Train/Going Home	15

DAVE BAILEY SEXTET
69	Fontana SFJL 919	MODERN MAINSTREAM (LP)	12

DEREK BAILEY & TRISTAN HOSINGER
70s	Incus INCUS 2	DUO (LP, private pressing)	25

(see also Tony Oxley)

MILDRED BAILEY
57	Parlophone GEP 8600	MILDRED BAILEY AND HER ALLEY CATS (EP)	10
54	Brunswick LA 8692	THE ROCKIN' CHAIR LADY (10" LP)	30

PEARL BAILEY
54	Vogue Coral Q 2026	She's Something Spanish/What Happened To The Hair	8
56	HMV POP 244	Tired/Go Back Where You Stayed Last Night	5
56	London HLN 8354	That Certain Feeling/Hit The Road To Dreamland	12
56	London HLN 8354	That Certain Feeling/Hit The Road To Dreamland (78)	6
56	HMV POP 244	Tired/Go Back Where You Stayed Last Night (78)	8
56	London REU 1104	THAT CERTAIN FEELING (EP)	12

ROY BAILEY (U.K.)
| 71 | Trailer LER 3021 | ROY BAILEY (LP) | 12 |
| 76 | Fuse AC 262 | NEW BELL AWAKE (LP) | 12 |

(see also Leon Rosselson)

ROY BAILEY (Jamaica)
| 72 | Duke DU 146 | Run Away Child/Wedding March | 5 |

ZEDDIE BAILEY
| 73 | Grape GR 3037 | Babylon Gone/TONY KING: Speak No Evil | 6 |

ALY BAIN & MIKE WHELLANS
| 70s | Trailer LER 2022 | ALY BAIN & MIKE WHELLANS (LP) | 12 |

BOB BAIN & HIS MUSIC
| 58 | Capitol CL 14912 | Wagon Wheels/Strollin' Home | 6 |

ARTHUR BAIRD SKIFFLE GROUP
| 56 | Beltona BL 2669 | Union Train/Union Maid | 25 |
| 56 | Beltona BL 2669 | Union Train/Union Maid (78) | 25 |

BAJA MARIMBA BAND
| 63 | London HL 9828 | Comin' In The Back Door/December Child | 6 |

CHET BAKER (QUARTET)
56	Vogue V 2377	My Funny Valentine/But Not For Me	5
56	Vogue V 2381	Just Friends/Daybreak	5
56	Vogue V 2232	Winter Wonderland/This Time The Dream's On Me	5
56	Vogue V 2309	Long Ago And Far Away/Bea's Flat	5
54	Vogue EPV 1007	CHET BAKER QUARTET (EP)	10
55	Vogue EPV 1032	THE FABULOUS CHET BAKER QUARTET (EP)	10
56	Vogue EPV 1121	CHET BAKER (EP)	22
56	Vogue EPV 1131	CHET BAKER VOL. 1 (EP)	10
56	Vogue EPV 1132	CHET BAKER VOL. 2 (EP)	10
56	Vogue EPV 1137	CHET BAKER SINGS AND PLAYS (EP)	10
56	Vogue EPV 1138	CHET BAKER SINGS AND PLAYS (EP)	10
57	Vogue EPV 1186	CHET BAKER AND HIS CREW (EP)	10
57	Felsted ESD 3034	MYTH (EP)	10
59	Felsted ESD 3069	CHET BAKER PLAYS STANDARDS (EP)	10
54	Vogue LDE 045	CHET BAKER QUARTET (10" LP)	18
55	Philips BBL 7022	CHET BAKER AND STRINGS (LP)	15
55	Vogue LDE 116	CHET BAKER QUARTET (10" LP)	18
56	Vogue LAE 12018	CHET BAKER SINGS (LP)	15
56	Vogue LDE 159	CHET BAKER SEXTET (10" LP)	50
56	Vogue LDE 163	CHET BAKER ENSEMBLE (10" LP)	35
56	Vogue LDE 182	CHET BAKER SINGS (10" LP)	22
56	Felsted PDL 85008	CHET BAKER QUARTET VOL. 1 (LP)	15
56	Felsted PDL 85013	CHET BAKER QUARTET VOL. 2 (LP)	15
57	Felsted PDL 85036	I GET CHET (LP, as Chet Baker & His Combo)	50
57	Vogue LAE 12044	CHET BAKER QUARTET AT ANN ARBOR (LP)	15
57	Vogue LAE 12076	CHET BAKER AND HIS CREW (LP, mono)	25
58	Vogue LAE 12109	CHET BAKER — PHIL'S BLUES (LP)	15
59	Vogue SEA 5005	CHET BAKER AND HIS CREW (LP, stereo)	18
59	Vogue LAE 12164	CHET BAKER SINGS (LP)	12
59	Vogue LAE 12183	CHET BAKER AND ART PEPPER SEXTET — PLAYBOYS! (LP)	12
66	Fontana TL 5326	MICHELLE (LP, credited to Bud Shank featuring Chet Baker)	12

(see also Art Pepper, Russ Freeman & Chet Baker Quartet, Gerry Mulligan)

DESMOND BAKER & CLAREDONIANS
| 66 | Island WI 295 | Rude Boy Gonna Jail/SHARKS: Don't Fool Me | 18 |

(see also Claredonians)

DOROTHY BAKER
| 63 | Parlophone R 5040 | A Little Like Lovin'/Try Being Nice To Me | 5 |

GEORGE BAKER SELECTION
70	Penny Farthing PEN 717	Little Green Bag/Pretty Little Dreamer	8
70	Penny Farthing PEN 726	Dear Ann/Fly	5
70	Penny Farthing PELS 503	LITTLE GREEN BAG (LP)	15

GINGER BAKER('S AIRFORCE)
70	Polydor 56380	Man Of Constant Sorrow/Doin' It	5
71	Polydor 2058 107	Atunde! (We Are Here)/Part 2 (as Ginger Baker Drum Choir)	5
70	Polydor 2662 001	GINGER BAKER'S AIRFORCE (2-LP, gatefold sleeve)	20
70	Polydor 2383 029	AIRFORCE II (LP, gatefold sleeve, with insert)	15
72	Polydor 2383 133	STRATAVARIOUS (LP)	15

(see also Graham Bond Organisation, Cream, Blind Faith, Fela Ransome-Kuti [& Africa '70], Harold McNair, Griffin, Denny Laine)

GLEN BAKER
| 85 | The Stand THE STAND 3 | BRIEF ENCOUNTER (LP) | 20 |

(see also Enid)

HYLDA BAKER
| 59 | Decca F 11186 | She Knows Y'Know/Makin' Love | 7 |
| 59 | Decca F 11186 | She Knows Y'Know/Makin' Love (78) | 15 |

JEANETTE BAKER
| 59 | Vogue Pop V 9143 | Everything Reminds Me Of You/JEANETTE & DECKY: Crazy With You | 250 |
| 59 | Vogue Pop V 9143 | Everything Reminds Me Of You/JEANETTE & DECKY: Crazy With You (78) | 80 |

KENNY BAKER
| 53 | Parlophone MSP 6019 | Round About Midnight/Afternoon In Paris | 5 |
| 53 | Parlophone MSP 6057 | Hayfoot, Strawfoot/The Continental | 5 |

MINT VALUE £

54	Parlophone MSP 6062	Trumpet Fantasy/Melancholy Baby	5
54	Parlophone MSP 6082	That's My Desire/Stompin' At The Savoy	5
54	Parlophone MSP 6114	I Speak To The Stars/Wanted	5
54	Parlophone MSP 6121	Peg O' My Heart/The Other Side	5
55	Jazz Today JTS 1503	Blues In Thirds/Ding Dong Daddy (as Kenny Baker's After Hours Group) (78)	8
56	Pye Nixa N 15059	Blues I Love To Sing/Baker's Dozen (as Kenny Baker Dozen) (78)	8
55	Jazz Today JTL 1	OPERATION JAM SESSION (10" LP, with The Jazz Today Unit)	50
55	Jazz Today JTL 4	KENNY BAKER QUARTET/AFTER HOURS GROUP (10" LP)	25
55	Jazz Today JTL 5	TRIBUTE TO BENNY CARTER (10" LP, with The Jazz Today Unit)	20
56	Pye Nixa NPT 19003	BAKER'S DOZEN VOL. 1 (LP)	15
57	Pye Nixa NPT 19020	DATE WITH THE DOZEN (LP)	18
57	Pye Nixa NJL 10	PRESENTS THE HALF DOZEN (LP)	40
57	Pye Nixa NJT 517	BAKER PLAYS McHUGH (LP)	22
59	Columbia 33S1140	BLOWIN' UP A STORM (LP)	50
75	77 77S56	BAKER'S JAM (LP)	25

LAVERN BAKER (& GLIDERS)

55	Columbia SCM 5172	Tweedle Dee/Tomorrow Night (with Gliders)	375
55	Columbia DB 3591	Tweedle Dee/Tomorrow Night (with Gliders) (78)	60
55	London HLA 8199	Play It Fair/That Old Lucky Sun (with Gliders)	275
55	London HLA 8199	Play It Fair (with Gliders)/That Old Lucky Sun (78)	40
56	London HLE 8260	My Happiness Forever (with Gliders)/Get Up! Get Up! (You Sleepy Head)	250
56	London HLE 8260	My Happiness Forever (with Gliders)/Get Up! Get Up! (You Sleepy Head) (78)	40
57	Columbia DB 3879	Jim Dandy/Tra La La (with Gliders)	325
57	Columbia DB 3879	Jim Dandy/Tra La La (with Gliders) (78)	45
57	London HLE 8396	I Can't Love You Enough/Still	110
57	London HLE 8396	I Can't Love You Enough/Still (78)	40
57	London HLE 8442	Game Of Love/Jim Dandy Got Married	220
57	London HLE 8442	Game Of Love/Jim Dandy Got Married (78)	45
57	London HLE 8524	Humpty Dumpty Heart/Love Me Right	110
57	London HLE 8524	Humpty Dumpty Heart/Love Me Right (78)	40
58	London HLE 8638	Learning To Love/Substitute	80
58	London HLE 8638	Learning To Love/Substitute (78)	35
58	London HLE 8672	Whipper Snapper/Harbour Lights	65
58	London HLE 8672	Whipper Snapper/Harbour Lights (78)	35
59	London HLE 8790	I Cried A Tear/St. Louis Blues	35
59	London HLE 8790	I Cried A Tear/St. Louis Blues (78)	40
59	London HLE 8871	I Waited Too Long/You're Teasing Me	40
59	London HLE 8871	I Waited Too Long/You're Teasing Me (78)	45
59	London HLE 8945	So High So Low/If You Love Me (I Won't Care)	35
59	London HLE 8945	So High So Low/If You Love Me (I Won't Care) (78)	55
60	London HLE 9023	Tiny Tim/For Love Of You	35
60	London HLE 9252	Bumble Bee/My Turn Will Come	25
61	London HLE 9300	You're The Boss/I'll Never Be Free (with Jimmy Ricks)	18
61	London HLK 9343	Saved/Don Juan	25
61	London HLK 9468	Hey, Memphis/Voodoo Voodoo	55
63	London HLK 9649	See See Rider/The Story Of My Love (I Had A Dream)	30
65	Atlantic AET 6009	THE BEST OF LAVERN BAKER (EP)	50
58	London HA-E 2107	ROCK 'N' ROLL WITH LAVERN BAKER (LP)	475
58	London Jazz LTZK 15139	SINGS BESSIE SMITH (LP)	75
61	London HA-K 2422	SAVED (LP)	110
63	London HA-K 8074	SEE SEE RIDER (LP)	110
64	Atlantic ATL 5002	THE BEST OF LAVERN BAKER (LP, plum label)	75
68	Atlantic 587/588 133	SEE SEE RIDER (LP, reissue)	25

MICKEY BAKER

| 70 | Major Minor SMLP 67 | IN BLUNDERLAND (LP) | 15 |
| 75 | Big Bear BEAR 5 | TAKE A LOOK INSIDE (LP) | 12 |

(see also Mighty Flea)

SAM BAKER

| 68 | Monument MON 1009 | I Believe In You/I'm Number One | 10 |

TWO-TON BAKER

| 55 | London HL 8121 | Clink, Clank (In My Piggy Bank)/Mr. Froggie (Went A Courtin') | 50 |
| 55 | London HL 8121 | Clink, Clank (In My Piggy Bank)/Mr. Froggie (Went A Courtin') (78) | 20 |

VICKY BAKER

| 64 | London HLU 9856 | No More Foolish Stories/Darling Say The Word | 10 |

YVONNE BAKER

| 77 | London HLU 10553 | You Didn't Say A Word/BOBBY PARIS: Night Owl | 5 |

(see also Sensations, Bobby Paris)

BAKER-GURVITZ ARMY

74	Vertigo 9103 201	BAKER-GURVITZ ARMY (LP)	12
75	Mountain TOPS 101	ELYSIAN ENCOUNTER (LP)	12
76	Mountain TOPS 111	HEARTS ON FIRE (LP, with inner sleeve)	12

(see also Ginger Baker, Adrian Gurvitz, Three Man Army, Parrish & Gurvitz, Gun)

BAKERLOO

| 69 | Harvest HAR 5004 | Driving Backwards/Once Upon A Time | 20 |
| 69 | Harvest SHVL 762 | BAKERLOO (LP) | 60 |

(see also May Blitz)

BAKER STREET PHILHARMONIC

| 71 | Pye International 7N 25540 | The Last One/Theme From 'Love Story' | 6 |
| 70 | Pye Intl. NSPL 28131 | BY THE LIGHT OF THE MOON (LP) | 35 |

(see also Mike Vickers)

BAKER TWINS
| 64 | Pye 7N 15628 | He's No Good/Words Written On Water | 5 |

BALANCE
81	Portrait PRTA 1477	Breaking Away/It's So Strange	7
73	Incus INCUS 11	BALANCE (LP)	25
73	private pressing	IN FOR THE COUNT (LP)	20
81	Portrait	BALANCE (LP, reissue)	15
82	Portrait	IN FOR THE COUNT (LP, reissue)	12

BALDHEAD GROWLER
| 67 | Jump Up JU 531 | Sausage/Bingo Woman | 7 |

CHRIS BALDO
| 68 | Vogue VRS 7029 | Living For Your Love/Arretez – Vous A Saint Michel | 15 |

LONG JOHN BALDRY
64	United Artists UP 1056	Up Above My Head (I Hear Music In The Air)/You'll Be Mine (with Rod Stewart)	25
65	United Artists UP 1078	I'm On To You Baby/Goodbye Baby	8
65	United Artists UP 1107	How Long Will It Last/House Next Door	20
66	United Artists UP 1124	Unseen Hands/Turn On Your Lovelight	8
66	United Artists UP 1136	The Drifter/Only A Fool Breaks His Own Heart	30
66	United Artists UP 1158	Cuckoo/Bring My Baby Back To Me	6
67	United Artists UP 1204	Only A Fool Breaks His Own Heart/Let Him Go (And Let Me Love You)	12
67	Pye 7N 17385	Let The Heartaches Begin/Annabella (Who Flies To Me When She's Lonely)	5
68	Pye 7N 17455	Hold Back The Daybreak/Since I Lost You Baby	5
68	Pye 7N 17563	Mexico (Underneath The Sun In)/We're Together	5
68	Pye 7N 17593	When The Sun Comes Shining Thru'/Wise To The Ways Of The World	5
69	Pye 7N 17664	It's Too Late Now/Long And Lonely Nights	5
69	Pye 7N 17815	Wait For Me/Don't Pity Me	5
70	Pye 7N 17921	Setting The Tail Of A Fox On Fire/Well I Did	6
70	Pye 7N 45007	When The World Is Over/Where Are My Eyes?	5
71	Warner Bros K 16105	Rock Me When He's Gone/Flying (as John Baldry)	5
72	Warner Bros K 16175	Iko Iko/Mother Ain't Dead (with Rod Stewart)	6
72	Warner Bros K 16217	Everything Stops For Tea/Hambone	5
65	United Artists UEP 1013	LONG JOHN'S BLUES (EP, with Hoochie Coochie Men)	55
64	United Artists ULP 1081	LONG JOHN'S BLUES (LP, with Hoochie Coochie Men)	85
66	United Artists (S)ULP 1146	LOOKING AT LONG JOHN (LP)	35
67	Pye N(S)PL 18208	LET THE HEARTACHES BEGIN (LP)	20
68	Pye N(S)PL 18228	LET THERE BE LONG JOHN (LP, unissued)	
69	Hallmark HM 560	LONG JOHN BALDRY & THE HOOCHIE COOCHIE MEN (LP)	15
69	Pye N(S)PL 18306	WAIT FOR ME (LP)	20
71	Warner Bros K 46088	IT AIN'T EASY (LP)	15
72	Warner Bros K 46160	EVERYTHING STOPS FOR TEA (LP, Rod Stewart duets on 1 track)	15

(see also Rod Stewart, Alexis Korner, Bluesology)

BALIL
| 92 | Rhythmic Tech. ART 1 | NORT ROUTE (12") | 20 |

KEITH BALFOUR
| 69 | Studio One SO 2079 | Dreaming/Tired Of Waiting | 15 |

CANNON BALL (Carl Bryan) & JOHNNY MELODY (Moore)
| 69 | Big Shot BI 518 | Parapinto/Cool Hand Luke | 8 |

DAVE BALL
| 83 | Some Bizzare BIZL 5 | IN STRICT TEMPO (LP, with Genesis P. Orridge) | 15 |

(see also Soft Cell, Grid, Psychic TV)

KENNY BALL & HIS (JAZZ) BAND
59	Collector JDN 101	Waterloo/Wabash Cannonball	10
60	Pye 7N 15272	Teddy Bears' Picnic/Waltzing Matilda	10
59	Jazz Collector JEN 2	KENNY BALL & HIS BAND (EP)	20
59	Tempo EXA 83	KENNY BALL JAZZ BAND (EP)	20
60	Pye NJE 1086	KENNY BALL PLAYS (EP)	10
60	Pye Jazz NJL 24	INVITATION TO THE BALL (LP)	22
61	Pye Jazz NJL 28	KENNY BALL AND HIS JAZZMEN (LP)	15
62	Pye Jazz NJL 42	THE KENNY BALL SHOW (LP, as Kenny Ball & His Jazzmen)	15
64	Pye Jazz NJL 54	TRIBUTE TO TOKYO (EP)	25
70	Fontana 6438 032	FLEET STREET LIGHTNING (LP)	12
72	Pye NSPL 18306	HAVE A DRINK ON ME (LP)	15
72	Pye NSPL 18379	MY VERY GOOD FRIEND FATS WALLER (LP)	15
73	Pye NSPL 18415	LET'S ALL SING A HAPPY TUNE (LP)	15
77	Spiral SPJ 9000	SATURDAY NIGHT AT THE MILL (LP)	12

(see also Gary Miller)

BALLADEERS
| 59 | Columbia DB 4364 | Tom Gets The Last Laugh/Morning Star | 5 |

DAVE BALLANTYNE
| 66 | Columbia DB 7807 | I Can't Express It/Ginger Eyes | 5 |
| 66 | Columbia DB 7896 | Love Around The World/Wonder Full Of Women | 5 |

(see also Just Plain Jones, Esprit De Corps)

FLORENCE BALLARD
| 68 | Stateside SS 2113 | It Doesn't Matter How I Say It (It's What I Say That Matters)/Goin' Out Of My Head | 30 |

(see also Supremes)

HANK BALLARD (& MIDNIGHTER)S
| 59 | Parlophone R 4558 | The Twist/Kansas City | 35 |
| 60 | Parlophone R 4682 | Finger Poppin' Time/I Love You, I Love You So-o-o | 20 |

LONG JOHN BALDRY

RUSS BALLARD

60	Parlophone R 4688	The Twist/Teardrops On Your Letter.	25
60	Parlophone R 4707	Let's Go, Let's Go, Let's Go/If You'd Forgive Me	25
61	Parlophone R 4728	The Hoochie Coochie Coo/LITTLE WILLIE JOHN: Walk Slow.	25
61	Parlophone R 4762	Let's Go Again/Deep Blue Sea.	15
61	Parlophone R 4771	The Continental Walk/What Is This I See.	15
72	Mojo 2093 010	Annie Had A Baby/Teardrops On Your Letter	6
80s	Urban	From The Loveside (12")	10
61	Parlophone PMC 1158	SPOTLIGHT ON HANK BALLARD (LP)	75
63	London HA 8101	THE JUMPIN' HANK BALLARD (LP)	60

(see also Midnighters)

KAYE BALLARD
55	Brunswick 05376	Triumph Of Love/Where Were You Last Night?	7
55	Brunswick 05436	Don't You Tell Pa/In Love And Out Again	7
62	CBS BPG 62107	PEANUTS (LP, with Arthur Siegel).	20

RUSS BALLARD
74	Epic S EPC 3122	Loose Women.	10
78	Epic S EPC 6316	Treat Her Right.	6
84	EMI EA 185	Voices (p/s).	7

(see also Argent, Roulettes)

BALLOON BUSTERS
| 69 | Pye 7N 17748 | Alcock And Brown/Bluer Than Blue | 5 |

BALLOON FARM
| 68 | London HLP 10185 | A Question Of Temperature/Hurtin' For Your Love | 55 |

BALLS
| 71 | Wizard WIZ 101 | Fight For My Country/Janie Slow Down | 12 |

(see also Denny Laine, Lemon Tree, Trevor Burton, Uglys, Wizzard)

LORI BALMER
| 68 | Polydor 56293 | Treacle Brown/Four Faces West | 12 |

BALTIMORE & OHIO MARCHING BAND
| 67 | Stateside SS 2065 | Lapland/Condition Red | 70 |
| 68 | Stateside (S)SL 10231 | LAPLAND (LP). | 25 |

BAMA WINDS
| 69 | Island ILPS 9096 | WINDY (LP). | 15 |

BAMBIS
| 64 | Oriole CB 1965 | Not Wrong/Handle With Care. | 18 |
| 65 | CBS 201778 | Baby Blue/If This Is Love | 18 |

BAMBOO SHOOT
| 68 | Columbia DB 8370 | The Fox Has Gone To Ground/There And Back Again Lane. | 120 |

BAMBOOS OF JAMAICA
| 70 | Pye Intl. 7N 25515 | Reggae Man/Candy | 5 |

BANANA BUNCH
| 71 | DJM DJS 252 | Tra-La-La Song/Season Of The Rain | 5 |

(see also Nite People)

BANANAMEN
| 83 | Big Beat NS 88 | The Crusher/Love Me/Surfin' Bird (p/s). | 10 |

BANANARAMA
81	Demon D 1010	Aie A Mwana/Dubwana (p/s)	6
81	Deram DMX 446	Aie A Mwana (Extended)/Dubwana (Extended) (12", p/s).	10
83	London NANX 6	Robert De Niro's Waiting/Push (3 x 12", coloured vinyl with different labels).	10

MINT VALUE £

84	London NANAJ 8	Hotline To Heaven/State I'm In (p/s, with jigsaw)	5
86	London NANDP 11	More Than Physical (Alternate Mix)/Scarlett//Venus/White Train (double pack, gatefold p/s)	5
87	London NANCD 15	I Can't Help It (Extended Club Mix)/Ecstasy (Chicago House Stylee) (CD)	10
88	London NANCD 16	I Want You Back/Bad For Me/Amnesia (Extended 12" Version)/ (The Theme From The Roxy)/Love In The First Degree (House Remix) (CD)	10
88	London NANCD 17	Love, Truth And Honesty (Dance Hall Version)/Strike It Rich (Full Length Club Mix)/I Want You Back/Love, Truth And Honesty (CD)	8
93	London 828 415-2	PLEASE YOURSELF (CD, with free remix CD)	15

(see also Shakespear's Sister)

BANBARRA
76	United Artists UP 36113	Shack Up Parts 1 & 2	8

BAND
68	Capitol CL 15559	The Weight/I Shall Be Released	5
69	Capitol CL 15613	Up On Cripple Creek/The Night They Drove Old Dixie Down	5
72	Capitol CL 15737	Don't Do It/Rag Mama Rag	5
73	Capitol CL 15767	Ain't Got No Home/Get Up Jake	5
68	Capitol (S)T 2955	MUSIC FROM BIG PINK (LP, black/rainbow label)	15

(see also Levon & Hawks, Bob Dylan, Ronnie Hawkins, Robbie Robertson)

BAND AID
85	Mercury FEEDP 1	Do They Know It's Christmas?/Feed The World (shaped picture disc)	10

BAND OF ANGELS
64	United Artists UP 1049	Not True As Yet/Me	20
64	United Artists UP 1066	Gonna Make A Woman Of You/She'll Never Be You	20
66	Piccadilly 7N 35279	Leave It To Me/Too Late My Love	20
66	Piccadilly 7N 35292	Invitation/Cheat And Lie	18

(see also Mike D'Abo)

BAND OF MERCY & SALVATION
69	Duke DU 20	Suffering Stink/BOB MELODY: The Break (B-side actually by Winston Francis)	6

BAND OF SUSANS
88	Furthur FU-2-7	Hope Against Hope (Radio Edit) (white label)	5

(see also Robert Poss)

BANDOGGS
78	Transatlantic LTRA 504	BANDOGGS (LP)	12

(see also Peter & Chris Coe)

BANDWAGON
(see under Johnny Johnson & Bandwagon)

BANDY LEGS
74	WWW WWS 01	Ride Ride/Don't Play Games	20
76	Jet JET 783	Bet You Can't Dance/Circles	6

(see also Quartz)

HONEY BANE
81	Crass 521984/1	YOU CAN BE YOU (EP, stapled gatefold p/s)	4

(see also Fatal Microbes)

JAYASRI BANERJEE
67	Polydor 583 010	CLASSICAL INDIAN RAGAS (LP)	15

ED BANGER
78	Rabid TOSH 106	Kinnel Tommy/Baby Was A Baby (p/s)	5
78	EMI International INT 570	Kinnel Tommy/Baby Was A Baby (reissue, numbered p/s)	5
81	Spiv DIV 1	I've Just Had My Car Nicked/P.C. Plod/Sponge (p/s, with photo insert)	6
83	Cloud Nine CNS 01	Poor People/Vicars In The Dark (p/s)	5

(see also Nosebleeds, Slaughter & Dogs)

BANGOR FLYING CIRCUS
70	Stateside-Dunhill SSL 5022	BANGOR FLYING CIRCUS (LP)	12

BESSIE BANKS
64	Red Bird BC 106	Go Now/Sounds Like My Baby	40
67	Verve VS 563	I Can't Make It (Without You Baby)/Need You	40
68	Soul City SC 105	Go Now/Sounds Like My Baby (reissue)	10
75	Contempo CS 2070	Baby You Sure Know How To Get To Me/Try To Leave Me If You Can	5

DARRELL BANKS
66	London HL 10070	Open The Door To Your Heart/Our Love (Is In The Pocket) (demo only)	300
66	Stateside SS 536	Open The Door To Your Heart/Our Love (Is In The Pocket)	20
67	Atlantic 584 120	Angel Baby (Don't You Ever Leave Me)/Look Into The Eyes Of A Fool	25
69	Stax STAX 124	Just Because Your Love Is Gone/I'm The One Who Loves You	35
77	Atlantic K 10879	Angel Baby (Don't You Ever Leave Me)/Look Into The Eyes Of A Fool (reissue)	5
78	Contempo CS 8005	Open The Door To Your Heart/Angel Baby (Don't You Ever Leave Me)	5
69	Stax SXATS 1011	HERE TO STAY (LP)	45

HOMER BANKS
66	Liberty LIB 12028	A Lot Of Love/Fighting To Win	15
67	Liberty LIB 12047	60 Minutes Of Your Love/Do You Know What	20
67	Liberty LIB 12060	Hooked By Love/Lady Of Stone	20
68	Minit MLF 11004	Round The Clock Lover Man/Foolish Hearts Break Fast	7
68	Minit MLF 11007	60 Minutes Of Your Love/A Lot Of Love	10
69	Minit MLF 11015	Me Or Your Mama/I Know You Know I Know You Know	7
70	Liberty LBF 15392	60 Minutes Of Your Love/I Know You Know I Know You Know	5
72	United Artists UP 35360	Hooked By Love/Lady Of Stone (reissue)	5

LARRY BANKS
67	Stateside SS 579	I Don't Wanna Do It/I'm Coming Home	15

LLOYD BANKS
66   Reaction 591 008   We'll Meet Again/Look Out Girl 8

DR. MURRAY BANKS
69   Viva MB 104   DR. MURRAY BANKS SPEAKS ON THE DRAMA OF SEX (LP) 10

PETER BANKS
73   Sovereign SNVA 7256   PETER BANKS (LP, gatefold sleeve) 15
(see also Syndicats, Syn, Neat Change, Yes, Flash, Jan Akkerman, Phil Collins, Steve Hackett, Blodwyn Pig)

RON BANKS & DRAMATICS
75   ABC ABC 4052   Trying To Get Over Losing You/How Do You Feel 4

ROSIE BANKS
76   Tamla Motown TMG 1037   Darling Baby/Whole New Thing 8
(see also Sly & Family Stone)

TONY BANKS
80   Charisma CB 365   For A While (Remix)/A Curious Feeling (p/s) 6
83   Charisma BANKS 12   This Is Love (Extended)/Charm (Extended) (12", p/s) 7
83   Atlantic A 9825   The Wicked Lady/The Wicked Lady (Orchestral Version) (no p/s) 8
83   Charisma CBEP 415   You Call This Victory/Redwing/Line Of Symmetry (EP, p/s) 6
86   Charisma CB 426-12   Short Cut To Somewhere/Smilin' Jack Casey/K2 (12", p/s, with Fish) 7
(see also Genesis, Fish)

BANNED
77   Can't Eat EAT 1 UP   Little Girl/CPGJ's (stamped white labels, some in handmade p/s) 40/10

BANSHEES
64   Columbia DB 7361   Don't Say Goodnight And Mean Goodbye/I Got A Woman 30
65   Columbia DB 7530   Big Buildin'/Mockingbird 30
65   Columbia DB 7752   I'm Gonna Keep On Loving You/Yes Indeed 30
(this group does not include Bryan Ferry)

PATO BANTON
92   I.R.S. THRASH 1   BEAMS OF LIGHT (2 Orb mixes) (12") 10

BARBARA & BRENDA
68   Direction 58-3799   Never Love A Robin/Sally's Party 8

BARBARA & WINSTON
64   Island WI 418   The Dream/I Love You 15

BARBARA ANN
65   Piccadilly 7N 35221   You've Lost That Loving Feeling/Till The Summer Time 7
65   Piccadilly 7N 35244   Black Is The Colour Of My True Love's Hair/Since You've Loved Me 8

BARBARIANS
65   Stateside SS 449   Are You A Boy Or Are You A Girl/Take It Or Leave It 25
66   Stateside SS 497   Moulty/I'll Keep On Seeing You 25

PAUL BARBARIN & BAND/PUNCH MILLER & BAND
59   Tempo EXA 98   PAUL BARBARIN & HIS JAZZ BAND (EP) 8
64   London HA-K/SH-K 8164   JAZZ AT PRESERVATION HALL VOL. 4 (LP, with George Lewis) 12

BARBECUE BOB
67   Kokomo K 1002   GEORGIA BLUES NO. 1 (LP, 99 copies only) 100

JOHN HENRY BARBEE
65   Storyville 670 171   PORTRAITS IN BLUES VOLUME 9 (LP) 15

CHRIS BARBER('S JAZZ BAND)
78s
51   Esquire 12-013   Oh, Didn't He Ramble/CRANE RIVER JAZZ BAND: Eh La Bas! (78) 15
52   Tempo A 101   Camp Meeting Blues/Stomp Off, Let's Go (78) 10
52   Tempo A 102   When Erastus Plays His Old Kazoo/Misty Morning (78) 10
54   Columbia DC 672 10   White Christmas/On A Christmas Day (78) (with Lonnie Donegan, export issue). 10
55   Jazz Today JTS 1500   High Society/Papa De-Da-Da (78) 8
56   Tempo A 116   Precious Lord, Lead Me On (with Lonnie Donegan)/Tiger Rag (78) 8
56   Tempo A 132   Saratoga Swing/Ice Cream (78) 8
57   Tempo A 160   Ice Cream/Down By The Riverside (78) 8
58   Pye Jazz NJ 2004   Tuxedo Rag/Brown Skin Mama (78) 8
58   Pye Jazz NJ 2023   When The Saints Go Marching In (both sides) (78) 8
59   Pye Jazz NJ 2026   Petite Fleur/Bugle Boy March (78) 10
59   Columbia DB 4333   Lonesome (with Monty Sunshine)/There'll Be A Hot Time In The
                          Old Town Tonight (with Ottilie Patterson) 7

SINGLES
52   Tempo A 101   Camp Meeting Blues/Stomp Off, Let's Go. 5
54   Decca F 10417   Chimes Blues/Merrydown Rag 7
54   Columbia SCMC 10   White Christmas/On A Christmas Day (with Lonnie Donegan, export issue) 25
55   Decca F 10492   Bobby Shafto/The Martinique 7
55   Decca F 10666   It's Tight Like That/All The Girls Go Crazy About The Way I Walk 7
56   Decca FJ 10724   The World Is Waiting For The Sunrise/St. Louis Blues 7
56   Decca FJ 10790   I Never Knew Just What A Girl Could Do/Storyville Blues 7
56   Tempo A 116   Precious Lord, Lead Me On (with Lonnie Donegan)/Tiger Rag 15
56   Tempo A 132   Saratoga Swing/Ice Cream 8
57   Tempo A 160   Ice Cream/Down By The Riverside 8
58   Pye Jazz 7NJ 2011   Whistlin' Rufus/Hushabye 5
58   Pye Jazz 7NJ 2004   Tuxedo Rag/Brown Skin Mama 5
58   Pye Jazz 7NJ 2007   High Society/Papa De-Da-Da 5
58   Pye Jazz 7NJ 2023   When The Saints Go Marching In (both sides) 5
59   Pye Jazz 7NJ 2026   Petite Fleur/Bugle Boy March 5
59   Columbia DB 4333   Lonesome (with Monty Sunshine)/There'll Be A Hot Time In The
                          Old Town Tonight (with Ottilie Patterson) 5

Chris BARBER'(s Jazz Band)

60	Pye Jazz 7NJ 2030	Bill Bailey Won't You Please Come Home/Wild Cat Blues 5
60	Columbia DB 4501	Bohemia Rag/Swanee River 5
60	Columbia DB 4531	The Mountains Of Mourne/Real Old Mountain Dew (with Ottilie Patterson) 5
61	Columbia SCD 2156	Mama He Treats Your Daughter Mean/
		Swipsy Cakewalk (with Ottilie Patterson) 5

EPs

55	Columbia SEG 7568	PLAYS SPIRITUALS (EP) 12
55	Columbia SEG 7586	BARBER GOES TO TOWN WITH ELLINGTON (EP) 8
55	Tempo EXA 6	CHRIS BARBER'S NEW ORLEANS JAZZ BAND (EP) 10
55	Tempo EXA 22	CHRIS BARBER'S JAZZ BAND (EP) 10
55	Decca DFE 6238	JAZZ AT THE ROYAL FESTIVAL HALL (EP). 20
55	Decca DFE 6252	CHRIS BARBER AT THE ROYAL FESTIVAL HALL (EP). 12
56	Decca DFE 6344	CHRIS BARBER AT THE ROYAL FESTIVAL HALL NO. 2 (EP) 10
56	Decca DFE 6382	BARBER'S BEST (EP) 10
56	Jazz Today JTE 103	PLUS/MINUS 1 (EP) 18
56	Pye Jazz NJE 1013	PLUS/MINUS 1 (EP, reissue) 12
57	Decca DFE 6463	NEW ORLEANS BLUES (EP) 20
59	Esquire EP 206	CHRIS BARBER NOT IN HI FI (EP, with Washboard Wonders) 20
59	Columbia SEG 7980	BANDBOX VOL. 1 (EP, also stereo ESG 7789) 8/12
50s	Pye Jazz NJE 1007	CHRIS BARBER SPECIAL (EP) 8
50s	Pye Jazz NJE 1039	CHRIS BARBER IN CONCERT PT. 1 (EP) 8
50s	Pye Jazz NJE 1040	CHRIS BARBER IN CONCERT PT. 2 (EP) 8
50s	Pye Jazz NJE 1068	CHRIS BARBER JAZZ PARADE VOL. 1 (EP) 8
50s	Pye Jazz NJE 1073	CHRIS BARBER JAZZ PARADE VOL. 2 (EP) 8
50s	Pye Jazz NJE 1075	CHRIS BARBER JAZZ PARADE VOL. 3 (EP) 8
50s	Pye Jazz NJE 1076	CHRIS BARBER JAZZ PARADE VOL. 4 (EP) 8
50s	Pye Jazz NJE 1077	CHRIS BARBER JAZZ PARADE VOL. 5 (EP) 8
50s	Pye Jazz NJE 1078	CHRIS BARBER JAZZ PARADE VOL. 6 (EP) 8
50s	Pye Jazz NJE 1084	CHRIS BARBER JAZZ PARADE VOL. 8 (EP) 10
50s	Pye Jazz NJE 1088	CHRIS BARBER JAZZ PARADE VOL. 9 (EP) 8
50s	Storyville SEP 300	TIGER RAG (EP). 10
50s	Storyville SEP 306	MAKING WHOOPEE (EP) 8
50s	Storyville SEP 310	DOWN HOME RAG (EP) 8
50s	Storyville SEP 314	TRAD JAZZ SCENE IN EUROPE NO. 3 8
50s	Storyville SEP 340	MARYLAND (EP) 8
50s	Storyville SEP 360	LORD, YOU'VE SURE BEEN GOOD TO ME (EP) 8
50s	Storyville SEP 412	WILDCAT BLUES (EP) 8
60	Columbia SEG 7994	BANDBOX VOL. 1 No. 2 (EP, also stereo ESG 7801). 8/12
60	Columbia SEG 8030	EXTRACTS FROM BARBER IN BERLIN (EP, with Ottilie Patterson,
		also stereo ESG 7821). 8/12
61	Columbia SEG 8075	BARBER IN BERLIN VOL. 2 (EP) 8
61	Columbia SEG 8081	PAT (EP, with Pat Halcox, also stereo ESG 7846). 8/12
61	Columbia SEG 8110	INTRODUCING IAN (EP, with Ian Wheeler) 12
62	Columbia SEG 8182	INTERNATIONAL VOL. 2 PT. 1 — BARBER IN COPENHAGEN (EP) 10
60s	Columbia SEG 8214	BARBER'S BLUES BOOK VOL. 1 (EP). 10
60s	Columbia SEG 8224	IN BARBER'S CHAIR (EP) 12

LPs

54	Decca LF 1198	NEW ORLEANS JOYS (10" LP,
		with Lonnie Donegan's Skiffle Group). 50
55	Nixa Jazz Today NJL 1	ECHOES OF HARLEM (LP, with Ottilie Patterson) 30
55	Jazz Today JTL 3	CHRIS BARBER PLAYS VOL. 1 (10" LP) 35
56	Nixa Jazz Today NJT 500	CHRIS BARBER PLAYS VOL. 1 (10" LP, reissue) 35
56	Nixa Jazz Today NJT 502	CHRIS BARBER PLAYS VOL. 2 (10" LP) 35
57	Nixa Jazz Today NJT 505	CHRIS BARBER PLAYS VOL. 3 (10" LP) 35
57	Nixa Jazz Today NJT 508	CHRIS BARBER PLAYS VOL. 4 (10" LP) 30
57	Columbia 33S 1112	JAZZ SACRED AND SECULAR (10" LP, with Lonnie Donegan) 45
57	Nixa Jazz Today NJL 6	CHRIS BARBER IN CONCERT (LP, with Ottilie Patterson) 35
58	Pye Nixa Jazz NJL 15	CHRIS BARBER IN CONCERT VOL. 2 (LP, with Ottilie Patterson) 20
58	Pye Nixa Jazz NJL 17	CHRIS BARBER IN CONCERT VOL. 3 (LP, with Ottilie Patterson) 20
58	Decca LK 4246	BARBER'S BEST (LP) 20
59	Columbia 33SX 1158	BAND BOX VOL. 1 (LP). 30
59	Columbia 33SX 1189	BARBER IN BERLIN VOL. 1 (LP, with Ottilie Patterson) 40
59	Columbia 33SX	BARBER IN BERLIN VOL. 2 (LP, with Ottilie Patterson) 30
60	Columbia 33SX 1245	BAND BOX VOL. 2 — ELITE SYNCOPATIONS (LP, stereo SCX 3319) 30/35
60	Ace Of Clubs ACL 1037	THE BEST OF CHRIS BARBER
		(LP, with Ottilie Patterson & Lonnie Donegan) 25
61	Columbia 33SX 1274	BARBER IN COPENHAGEN (LP, also stereo SCX 3342) . . . . each 40
61	Columbia 33SX 1321	CHRIS BARBER'S AMERICAN JAZZ BAND
		(LP, also stereo SCX 3376) . . . . each 50
61	Columbia 33SX 1333	BLUES BOOK (LP, with Ottilie Patterson, also stereo SCX 3384) . . . . each 50
61	Columbia 33SX 1346	AT THE LONDON PALLADIUM (LP) 100
61	Columbia 33SX 1401	BEST YET! (LP) 45
64	Encore! ENC 135	JAZZ SACRED AND SECULAR (LP, reissue) 12
65	Columbia 33SX 1657	GOOD MORNIN' BLUES (LP) 60
65	Decca LK 4742	FOLK BARBER STYLE (LP, mono) 40
65	Phase 4 Stereo PFS 4070	FOLK BARBER STYLE (LP, as Chris Barber & His Jazz Band) 25
71	Polydor 2683 001	GET ROLLING (LP). 20
78	Black Lion BLP 12172	SIDEWAYS (LP) 30
78	Black Lion BLM 51003	STORY - VOLUME 1: IN THE BEGINNING (LP). 25
78	Black Lion BLM 51004	STORY - VOLUME 2: VISITING INFLUENCES (LP). 25
78	Black Lion BLM 51005	STORY - VOLUME 3: THE SEVENTIES (LP) 25
79	Black Lion BLP 12182	SWING IS HERE (LP) 20
82	Black Lion BLM 51008	COME FRIDAY (LP). 12
82	Black Lion 61003/4	BARBICAN BLUES (LP). 18

(see also Ottilie Patterson, Lonnie Donegan, Sonny Terry & Brownie McGhee, Kenneth Washington & Chris Barber, Dickie Bishop & Sidekicks)

CHRIS BARBER'S SKIFFLE GROUP

51	Esquire 10-180	Everybody Loves My Baby/Whoop It Up (with Washboard Wonders) (78)	20
58	Pye Jazz 7NJ 2014	Doin' My Time/Where Could I Go? (with Johnny Duncan)	6
58	Pye Jazz NJ 2014	Doin' My Time/Where Could I Go? (with Johnny Duncan) (78)	8
58	Pye Jazz 7NJ 2017	Can't You Line 'Em/Gipsy Dave (with Dickie Bishop)	7
58	Pye Jazz NJ 2017	Can't You Line 'Em/Gipsy Dave (with Dickie Bishop) (78)	8
57	Pye Jazz NJE 1025	CHRIS BARBER SKIFFLE GROUP (EP)	25

(see also Lonnie Donegan, Johnny Duncan & Blue Grass Boys)

CHRIS BARBER'S BAND

67	Marmalade 598 005	Catcall/Mercy Mercy Mercy	35
69	Marmalade 558 013	Battersea Rain Dance/Sleepy Joe	5
69	Marmalade 608 009	BATTERSEA RAIN DANCE (LP, as Chris Barber & His Band)	25

CHRIS BARBER SOUL BAND

65	Columbia DB 7461	Finishing Straight/Morning Train	20

(see also Louis Jordan & Chris Barber)

FRANK BARBER FIVE

62	Ember JBS 709	Flyover/Golden Shadows	6

(see also Frank & Barbarians)

GATO BARBIERI

72	Philips 6369 409	FENIX (LP)	12
73	Philips 6369 418	EL PAMPERO (LP)	12
73	Philips 6369 419	UNDER FIRE (LP)	12

DAVE BARBOUR & HIS ORCHESTRA

59	Oriole CB 1507	Tough/Bu Bam	7
59	Oriole CB 1507	Tough/Bu Bam (78)	15

EDDIE BARCLAY & HIS ORCHESTRA

57	Felsted ESD 3041	JAMES DEAN — MUSIC FROM HIS FILMS (EP)	25

RUE BARCLAY & PEGGY DUNCAN

54	London HL 8033	Tongue Tied Boy/River Of Tears	25

TIMOTHY BARCLAY

70	Penny Farthing PEN 740	Catch The Wind/The Girl From Indiana	5

(see also Mike Berry)

BARCLAY JAMES HARVEST

68	Parlophone R 5693	Early Morning/Mr. Sunshine	15
69	Harvest HAR 5003	Brother Thrush/Poor Wages	10
70	Harvest HAR 5025	Taking Some Time On/The Iron Maiden	10
71	Harvest HAR 5034	Mocking Bird/Vanessa Simmons	7
72	Harvest HAR 5051	I'm Over You/Child Of Man	7
72	Harvest HAR 5058	Thank You/Medicine Man	7
73	Harvest HAR 5068	Rock And Roll Woman/The Joker (BJH logo p/s)	8
74	Polydor 2058 474	Poor Boy Blues/Crazy City	6
74	Polydor (matrix: SH 1041/2)	Negative Earth/RARE BIRD: Diamonds (33rpm flexidisc free with *Sounds*)	10/6
75	Harvest HAR 5094	Mocking Bird/Galadriel	5
75	Polydor 2058 660	Titles/Song For You	5
77	Polydor 2229 198	LIVE (Rock'n'Roll Star/Medicine Man Part 1/Medicine Man Part 2) (EP, p/s)	6
77	Polydor 2058 904	Hymn/Our Kid's Kid (p/s)	5
78	Polydor 2059 002	Friend Of Mine/Suicide? (live)	5
78	Polydor POSP 012	Loving Is Easy/Polk Street Rag (blue or black vinyl)	5/7
79	Polydor POSP 097	Love On The Line/Alright Down Get Boogie (Mu Ala Rusic) (p/s)	5
80	Polydor POSP 140	Capricorn/Berlin (no p/s)	5
80	Polydor POSP 195	Life Is For Living/Shades Of B Hill (p/s)	5
81	Polydor BARC 1	Life Is For Living (jukebox version)/Hymn (no p/s, jukebox issue)	8
83	Polydor POPPX 585	Just A Day Away/Looking From The Outside (shaped picture disc)	8
83	Polydor POSP 640	Waiting For The Right Time/Blow Me Down	5
83	Polydor POSPX 640	Waiting For The Right Time (LP)/Waiting For The Right Time (edit)/ Blow Me Down (12", p/s)	8
84	Polydor POSP 674	Victims Of Circumstance/Victims Of Circumstance (instrumental) (p/s)	5
84	Polydor POSPP 674	Victims Of Circumstance/Victims Of Circumstance (instrumental) (shaped picture disc)	8
84	Polydor POSPX 674	Victims Of Circumstance/Victims Of Circumstance (instrumental) (12", p/s)	8
84	Polydor POSPX 674	Victims Of Circumstance/Victims Of Circumstance (instrumental)/Love On The Line (12", white label test pressing)	12
84	Polydor POSP 705	I've Got A Feeling/Rebel Woman (p/s)	5
86	Polydor POSP 834	He Said Love/On The Wings Of Love (p/s)	5
90	Polydor PO 67	Cheap The Bullet/Shadows On The Sky (p/s)	5
90	Polydor PZCD 67	Cheap The Bullet/Shadows On The Sky/Alone In The Night (live)/ Hold On (live) (CD)	8
91	Swallowtail SWALLOW 2	Too Much On Your Plate (fan club flexi)	10
70	Harvest SHVL 770	BARCLAY JAMES HARVEST (LP)	12
71	Harvest SHVL 788	ONCE AGAIN (LP)	12
71	Harvest SHVL 794	BARCLAY JAMES HARVEST AND OTHER SHORT STORIES (LP)	12
72	Harvest Q4SHVL 788	ONCE AGAIN (LP, quadrophonic)	20

(see also Bombadil, John Lees, Woolly Wolstenholme)

KENNY BARDELL

58	Oriole CB 1420	Salty Salty Is The Sea/My Darling, My Darling	5

PETER BARDENS

70	Transatlantic TRA 222	THE ANSWER (LP)	20
71	Transatlantic TRA 243	PETER BARDENS (LP, gatefold sleeve)	20
76	Transatlantic TRASAM 36	VINTAGE '69 (LP, featuring Peter Green, some on clear vinyl)	15

(see also Cheynes, Peter B's, Shotgun Express, Them, Village, Camel, Steve Tilston)

MINT VALUE £

BRIGITTE BARDOT
66	Vogue VRS 7018	Mister Sun/Gang Gang (some in p/s)	150/30
68	Pye International 7N 25450	Harley-Davidson/Contact (some in p/s)	75/15
63	Philips BL 7561	BRIGITTE BARDOT (LP)	80

BOBBY BARE
60	Top Rank JAR 310	I'm Hanging Up My Rifle/That's Where I Want To Be	12
63	RCA RCA 1352	Detroit City/Heart Of Ice	5
63	RCA RCA 1366	500 Miles Away From Home/It All Depends On Linda	5
64	RCA RCX 7139	DETROIT CITY (EP)	12
66	RCA RD 7783	CONSTANT SORROW (LP)	15
68	RCA RD 7918	THE ENGLISH COUNTRYSIDE (LP, with Hillsiders)	12

(see also Bill Parsons, Skeeter Davis & Bobby Bare)

BAREFOOT BLUES BAND
70	Beacon BEA 163	Can't You See/Sunday Morning Barefoot Blues	15
72	Deram DM 353	The Spirit Of Joe Hill/I Believe In Music	8
73	Deram DM 372	Getting Better All The Time/Half Of Me	6

MINOUCHE BARELLI
67	CBS 2806	Boum Badaboum/Let Me Take You	20

MARK BARKAN
67	Stateside SS 2064	A Great Day For The Clown/Pity The Woman	8

BAR-KAYS
67	Stax 601 014	Soul Finger/Knucklehead	10
68	Stax 601 036	A Hard Day's Night/I Want Someone	8
69	Atlantic 584 244	Soul Finger/Knucklehead (reissue)	8
69	Stax STAX 135	Midnight Cowboy/A.J. The House Fly	6
70	Stax STAX 146	Sing And Dance/I Thank You	6
69	Atco 228 030	SOUL FINGER (LP)	20
69	Stax SXATS 1009	GOTTA GROOVE (LP)	18
71	Stax 2362 003	BLACK ROCK (LP)	15
73	Stax 2325 087	DO YOU SEE WHAT I SEE? (LP)	15
76	Stax STX 1033	COLD BLOODED (LP)	20

(see also Otis Redding)

BUTCH BARKER
75	Creole CR 113	The Joker/Juicie Brucie	6

DAVE BARKER
70	Duke DU 74	Funkey Reggae/TOMMY McCOOK & SUPERSONICS: I Love You My Baby (B-side actually by Versatiles)	8
70	Punch PH 20	Prisoner Of Love/BUSTY & UPSETTERS: Soul Juice	7
70	Punch PH 22	You Betray Me/Will You Still Love Me Tomorrow?	7
70	Punch PH 25	Shocks Of Mighty Parts 1 & 2	7
70	Punch PH 42	Reggae Meeting/MARTIN ALL STARS: Soul Bone	6
70	Jackpot JP 736	The Fastest Man Alive/NORMAN GRANT: Bloodshot Eyes	7
70	Jackpot JP 742	Wet Version/I Got To Get Away	7
70	Jackpot JP 745	Girl Of My Dreams/On Broadway	7
70	High Note HS 049	She Want It/FIRST GENERATION: Give Him Up	6
70	Randy's RAN 503	October/RANDY'S ALLSTARS: Time Out	7
70	Unity UN 567	Blessed Are The Meek (with Slim Smith)/JEFF BARNES & UNIQUES: The People's Voice	6
70	Upsetter US 331	Shocks Of Mighty/Set Me Free (with Upsetters)	10
70	Upsetter US 344	Some Sympathy/UNTOUCHABLES: Tender Love	10
70	Upsetter US 347	Sound Underground/Don't Let The Sun Catch You Crying	10
71	Upsetter US 358	Shocks '71/HURRICANES: You've Got To Be Mine	10
71	Upsetter US 362	Groove Me/UPSETTERS: Screwdriver	18
71	Upsetter US 364	What A Confusion/UPSETTERS: Confusion — Version 2	10
71	Ackee ACK 113	Johnny Dollar/Version	10
71	Ackee ACK 119	Life Of A Millionaire/Version	8
71	Trojan TR 7851	Sex Machine/You Left Me And Gone (both sides with Aggrovators)	5
71	Punch PH 69	What A Confusion/BOB MARLEY: Small Axe	25
71	Supreme SUP 228	Double Heavy/Johnny Dollar	5
71	Downtown DT 482	Only The Strong Survive/Only The Strong — Version	5
72	Jackpot JP 803	You'll Be Sorry/Green Grow The Lilacs	5
72	Big Shot BI 614	Are You Sure/I Don't Know Why (B-side actually by Sensations)	5
72	Fab FAB 25	Green Grow The Lilacs/JIMMY RILEY: Keep An Eye (On Your Closest Friend) (white label)	5
76	Trojan TRL 127	PRISONER OF LOVE (LP)	25

(see also Glen & Dave, Dave & Ansell Collins, Bobby & Dave, Aggrovators, David Crooks, Dennis Alcapone, Don Drummond, Owen Gary, Lizzy & Dennis, Bob Marley, Lester Sterling, Busty Brown)

RONNIE BARKER
78	EMI EMI 2768	Going Straight/String Bean Queen	5

BARNABY RUDGE
68	CBS 3262	Joe, Organ & Co./Railway Jim	5

BARNEY J. BARNES & INTRO.
67	Decca F 12662	It Must Be Love/Can't Stand The Pain	10

BENNY BARNES
60	Mercury AMT 1094	Token Of Love/That-A-Boy Willie	5

DENA BARNES
80	Grapevine GRP 141	If You Ever Walked Out Of My Life/Who Am I	6

JEFF BARNES
70	Jackpot JP 735	Get In The Groove/JOHN HOLT: A Little Tear	7
70	Unity UN 568	1,000 Tons Of Version/Wake The Nation (B-side with Hugh Roy)	6

| 70 | Pama PM 802 | Jeff Barnes Thing/LENNOX BROWN: Lover's Mood | 5 |
| 71 | Smash SMA 2313 | Wake The Nation (with Hugh Roy)/1,000 Tons Of Version | 8 |

(see also Hugh Roy, Dave Barker, Darker Shade Of Blue, Delroy Wilson)

J.J. BARNES

67	Polydor 56722	Day Tripper/Deeper In Love	20
69	Stax STAX 130	Baby Please Come Back Home/Easy Living	20
73	Tamla Motown TMG 870	Real Humdinger/Please Let Me In/I Ain't Gonna Do It	10
74	Contempo CS 2009	To An Early Grave/To An Early Grave (Instrumental Version)	5
76	Contempo CX 16	The Errol Flynn/Guess I'l Try It Again (12")	8
75	Contempo CLP 520	THE GROOVESVILLE MASTERS (LP)	15
77	Contempo CLP 604	SARA SMILE (LP)	12

J.J. BARNES/STEVE MANCHA

| 69 | Stax SXATS 1012 | RARE STAMPS (LP) | 25 |

LLOYD BARNES

| 64 | Blue Beat BB 235 | Time Is Hard/BUSTER'S ALLSTARS: Reincarnation | 15 |

MYRA BARNES

| 88 | Urban | Message For The Soul Sisters/(Bobby Byrd track) (12") | 10 |

RICHARD BARNES

68	Columbia DB 8436	Woman, Woman/The Princess And The Soldier	5
68	Columbia DB 8507	Look Away/Mr In Between	5
70	Philips BF 1840	Take To The Mountains/But It's Now I Need Your Love	5
70	Philips 630 8027	RICHARD BARNES (LP)	15

(see also Quiet Five)

ERIC BARNET(T)

68	Gas GAS 100	The Horse (actually by Theo Beckford & Group)/Action Line (actually by Versatiles)	6
69	Gas GAS 106	Te Ta Toe (act. by Theo Beckford & Group)/MILTON BOOTHE: Lonely And Blue	6
69	Crab CRAB 37	Quaker City/Double Up (both actually by Theo Beckford & Group)	5
70	Gas GAS 130	Pink Shark/Swing Free (both actually by Theo Beckford & Group)	5
70	Gas GAS 147	Bumper To Bumper/Fat Turkey (both actually by Theo Beckford & Group)	5

(see also Theo[philus] Beckford)

BARRY BARNETT

58	HMV POP 487	The Book Of Love/All I Have To Do Is Dream	8
58	HMV POP 487	The Book Of Love/All I Have To Do Is Dream (78)	8
58	HMV POP 511	When/Secretly	7
58	HMV POP 511	When/Secretly (78)	8
58	HMV POP 521	My Lucky Love/Too Young To Love	7
58	HMV POP 521	My Lucky Love/Too Young To Love (78)	8
58	HMV POP 532	Susie Darlin'/Just A Dream	8
58	HMV POP 532	Susie Darlin'/Just A Dream (78)	10
59	HMV POP 579	The Diary/Only A Memory	6
59	HMV POP 579	The Diary/Only A Memory (78)	12
59	HMV POP 627	Cuckoo Girl/I'll String Along With You	5

BARNSTORMERS SPASM BAND

58	Parlophone R 4416	Whistling Rufus/Won't You Come Home, Bill Bailey?	8
58	Parlophone R 4416	Whistling Rufus/Won't You Come Home, Bill Bailey? (78)	20
59	Tempo A 168	Stormin' The Barn/That's All There Is (There Ain't No More)	8
59	Tempo A 168	Stormin' The Barn/That's All There Is (There Ain't No More) (78)	20

(see also Original Barnstormers Spasm Band)

H.B. BARNUM

61	Fontana H 299	Lost Love/Hallelujah	10
65	Capitol CL 15391	The Record (Baby I Love You)/I'm A Man	25
76	Capitol CL 15851	Heartbreaker/Searchin' For My Soul	6
79	Capitol CL 16067	Heartbreaker/BOBBY PARIS: I Walked Away	6
64	RCA Victor RCX 7147	THE GREAT H.B. BARNUM (EP)	150
62	RCA Victor RD/SF 7500	THE BIG VOICE OF BARNUM . . . H.B., THAT IS (LP, mono/stereo)	15/18
63	RCA Victor RD/SF 7543	EVERYBODY LOVES H.B. (LP, mono/stereo)	15/18

CARL BARON & CHEETAHS

| 63 | Columbia DB 7162 | This Is Only The Beginning/Beg Borrow Or Steal | 12 |

RIKKY BARON

| 60 | Parlophone R 4706 | Angry Young Man/My Lonely Heart | 5 |

BARON ROJO

| 81 | Kamaflage KAMLP 5 | LARGA VIDA AL ROCK'N'ROLL (LP) | 15 |

BARON WITH HIS POUNDING PIANO

| 65 | Sue WI 398 | Is A Blue Bird Blue/In The Mood | 18 |

(see also V.I.P.'s)

BARONS (U.S.)

| 57 | London HLP 8391 | Don't Walk Out/Once In A Lifetime | 2,100 |
| 57 | London HLP 8391 | Don't Walk Out/Once In A Lifetime (78) | 185 |

BARONS (U.K.)

| 61 | Oriole CB 1608 | Cossack/Summertime | 12 |
| 61 | Oriole CB 1620 | Samurai/Whirlwind | 15 |

BARRABAS

| 76 | Atlantic K 10716 | Checkmate/Four Seasons Woman | 4 |

BARRACUDAS

79	Cells CELLOUT 1	I Want My Woody Back/Subway Surfin' (p/s)	12
80	Zonophone Z 5	Summer Fun/Chevy Baby (p/s, with/without stickers)	15/6
80	Zonophone Z 8	His Last Summer/Barracuda Waver/Surfers Are Back (p/s)	8

BARRACUDAS

80	Zonophone Z 11	(I Wish It Could Be) 1965 Again/Rendezvous (p/s)	6
81	Zonophone Z 17	I Can't Pretend/The KGB (Made A Man Out Of Me) (p/s)	6
83	Lyntone BOB 7	Very Last Day/There's A World Out There (flexi with *Bucketfull Of Brains*)	6/5
80	Zonophone ZONO 103	DROP OUT WITH THE BARRACUDAS (LP)	12

BARRELHOUSE FIVE
50	Jazz Collect L 24	Endurance Stomp/Some Do And Some Don't (78)	8

DICKIE BARRETT
58	MGM MGM 976	Smoke Gets In Your Eyes/Remember Me	8
58	MGM MGM 976	Smoke Gets In Your Eyes/Remember Me (78)	8

JOE BARRETT
55	Brunswick 05432	I'm Sincere/Why Did You Break My Heart?	7

RICHARD BARRETT & CHANTELS
59	HMV POP 609	Come Softly To Me/Walking Through Dreamland	15

(see also Chantels)

RITCHIE BARRETT
62	London HLK 9552	Some Other Guy/Tricky Dicky	35

'SWEET EMMA' BARRETT
60s	Riverside RLP 364	THE BELL GAL AND HER DIXIELAND BOYS (LP)	12

SYD BARRETT
69	Harvest HAR 5009	Octopus/Golden Hair	75
88	Strange Fruit SFPS 043	THE PEEL SESSION (12", EP)	15
88	Strange Fruit SFPSCD 043	THE PEEL SESSION (CD EP)	12
70	Harvest SHVL 765	THE MADCAP LAUGHS (LP, laminated or matt gatefold sleeve)	25/18
70	Harvest SHSP 4007	BARRETT (LP, laminated or textured flipback sleeve)	30/15
70s	Harvest SHSP 4007	BARRETT (LP, textured non-flipback sleeve)	15
74	Harvest SHDW 404	SYD BARRETT (2-LP, reissue of "Madcap" & "Barrett", gatefold sleeve)	18
88	Harvest SHSP 4126	OPEL (LP, gatefold sleeve)	12

(see also Pink Floyd)

WILD WILLY BARRETT
77	Logo GO 105	Return Of Kong/Nice To Know You're My Friend (p/s)	5
79	Polydor 2059 067	Let's Play Schools/I Did It Otway (p/s)	5
86	Galvanised DIP 1	ORGANIC BONDAGE (LP, with Stephen Two Names; some in wooden sleeve)	20/10

(see also John Otway/Wild Willy Barrett)

RAY BARRETTO
63	Columbia DB 7051	El Watusi/Ritmo Sabroso	10
65	Columbia DB 7684	El Watusi/Swingin' Shepherd Blues	8
69	London HL 10262	Acid/Mercy Mercy Baby	12
67	Island ILP 946	EL WATUSI (LP)	35
69	London HA/SH 8383	ACID (LP)	40

BARRIER
68	Eyemark EMS 1013	Georgie Brown/Dawn Breaks Through (some in handmade p/s)	200/80
68	Philips BF 1692	The Tide Is Turning/Place In Your Heart	6
68	Philips BF 1731	Spot The Lights/Uh	20

BARRINO BROTHERS
72	Invictus INV 523	I Shall Not Be Moved/When Love Was A Child	8

BARRON KNIGHTS
62	Fontana H 368	Let's Face It/Never Miss A Chance	10
63	Columbia DB 7108	Jo-Anne/That's My Girl	6
64	Columbia DB 7188	Comin' Home Baby/Peanut Butter	6
64	Columbia DB 7317	Call Up The Groups Medley (both sides)	5
64	Columbia DB 7375	Come To The Dance/Choose Me Tonight	5
64	Columbia DB 7427	The House Of Johann Strauss/She's The One	5
65	Columbia DB 7525	Pop Goes The Workers Medley (both sides)	5
65	Columbia DB 7698	It Was A Very Good Year/Worry And Wonder	5
65	Columbia DB 7780	Merry Gentle Pops Medley (both sides)	5
66	Columbia DB 7884	Round The World Rhythm & Blues/Where There's A Will	5
66	Columbia DB 7933	Doing What She's Not Supposed To Do/Every Night	5
66	Columbia DB 8071	Under New Management Medley (both sides)	5
67	Columbia DB 8161	Lazy Fat People/In The Night	5
67	Columbia DB 8280	Here Come The Bees/It's A Sin	5
68	Columbia DB 8423	I Never Will Marry/Cold In My Nose	5
68	Columbia DB 8485	An Olympic Record/An Olympic Record	5
69	Columbia DB 8612	Love And The World Loves With You/Along Come Those Summer Days	5
69	Columbia DB 8679	Traces/Awake	5
64	Columbia SEG 8424	GUYING THE TOP POPS (EP)	12
66	Columbia SEG 8526	THOSE VERSATILE BARRON KNIGHTS (EP)	12
64	Columbia 33SX 1648	CALL UP THE GROUPS (LP)	25
66	Columbia SX 6007	BARRON KNIGHTS (LP)	18
67	Columbia S(C)X 6176	SCRIBED (LP)	18

BARROW POETS
68	Fontana TF 939	Letter In A Bottle (Music "Sleepy Lagoon")/Dynamite Barbee (Music "Barbee Song")	6
67	Barrow BR 1	AT THE PRINTER'S DEVIL (EP, private pressing)	25
63	Argo PLP 1072	PRESENT AN ENTERTAINMENT OF POETRY AND MUSIC (LP)	30
68	Fontana 6857 003	FINEST FOLK (LP)	20
70	RCA SF 8110	JOKER (LP)	20
72	Argo ZSW 508	OUTPATIENTS (LP)	25
72	Argo ZSW 511	MAGIC EGG (LP)	25

SYD BARRETT *JOHN BARRY*

AL BARRY
70	Duke DU 81	Ooh Wee/Hold It Baby	6
70	Doctor Bird DB 1502	Morning Sun/MARKONIANS: Over And Over	7

(see also Desmond Dekker & Aces)

DAVE BARRY
60	London HA-G 2313	LAUGHS FOR LOSERS (LP)	12

DAVE BARRY & SARA BERNER
56	London HLU 8324	Out Of This World With Flying Saucers Parts 1 & 2	40
56	London HLU 8324	Out Of This World With Flying Saucers Parts 1 & 2 (78)	15

JOE BARRY
61	Mercury AMT 1149	I'm A Fool To Care/I Got A Feeling	10
68	Stateside SS 2127	I Started Loving You Again/California Bound	8
62	Mercury ZEP 10130	A FOOL TO CARE (EP)	165

JOHN BARRY (SEVEN)

78s
57	Parlophone R 4363	Zip Zip/Three Little Fishes (as John Barry & The Seven) (78)	20
58	Parlophone R 4394	Every Which Way/You've Gotta Way (as John Barry Seven) (78)	12
58	Parlophone R 4418	Big Guitar/Rodeo (as John Barry Seven) (78)	12
58	Parlophone R 4453	Pancho/Hideaway (as John Barry Seven) (78)	12
58	Parlophone R 4488	Farrago/Bee's Knees (as John Barry Seven) (78)	12
59	Parlophone R 4530	Long John/Snap 'n' Whistle (as John Barry Seven) (78)	14
59	Parlophone R 4560	Little John/For Pete's Sake (as John Barry Seven) (78)	18

SINGLES
57	Parlophone R 4363	Zip Zip/Three Little Fishes (as John Barry & The Seven)	65
58	Parlophone R 4394	Every Which Way/You've Gotta Way (as John Barry Seven)	45
58	Parlophone R 4418	Big Guitar/Rodeo (as John Barry Seven)	25
58	Parlophone R 4453	Pancho/Hideaway (as John Barry Seven)	10
58	Parlophone R 4488	Farrago/Bee's Knees (as John Barry Seven)	10
59	Parlophone R 4530	Long John/Snap 'n' Whistle (as John Barry Seven)	8
59	Parlophone R 4560	Little John/For Pete's Sake (as John Barry Seven)	8
59	Parlophone R 4582	Twelfth Street Rag/Christella (as John Barry Seven)	15
60	Columbia DB 4414	Hit And Miss/Rockin' Already (as John Barry Seven)	7
60	Columbia DB 4446	Beat For Beatniks/Big Fella (as John Barry Orchestra)	7
60	Columbia DB 4480	Blueberry Hill/Never Let Go (as John Barry Orchestra)	7
60	Columbia DB 4505	Walk Don't Run/I'm Movin' On (as John Barry Seven)	6
60	Columbia DB 4554	Black Stockings/Get Lost Jack Frost (as John Barry Seven)	6
61	Columbia DB 4598	The Magnificent Seven/Skid Row (as John Barry Seven)	6
61	Columbia DB 4659	The Menace/Rodeo (as John Barry Orchestra)	6
61	Columbia DB 4699	Starfire/A Matter Of Who (as John Barry Seven)	6
61	Columbia DB 4746	Watch Your Step/Twist It (as John Barry Seven)	6
62	Columbia DB 4806	Cutty Sark/Lost Patrol (as John Barry Seven & Orchestra)	6
62	Columbia DB 4898	The James Bond Theme/The Blacksmith Blues (with Orchestra) (green or black label)	5/6
62	Columbia DB 4941	The Lolly Theme/March Of The Mandarins (as John Barry Seven & Orchestra)	10
63	Columbia DB 7003	The Human Jungle/Onward, Christian Spacemen (some in p/s)	15/6
63	Ember EMB S 178	Kinky/Fancy Dance	6
63	Ember EMB S 181	007/From Russia With Love (some in p/s)	15/6
63	Ember EMB S 183	Elizabeth/The London Theme	7
63	Ember EMB S 185	Zulu Stamp/Monkey Feathers (mauve/grey or red/yellow label; some in p/s)	12/5
63	Lyntone LYN 378	Theme Music From The Ingersoll Trendsetters T.V. Commercial (flexidisc; some with 8-page A4 promo booklet)	30/15
64	Columbia DB 7414	Twenty-Four Hours Ago/Seven Faces	22

John BARRY

64	United Artists UP 1060	Seance On A Wet Afternoon/Oublie Ça	22
64	United Artists UP 1068	Goldfinger/Troubador	8
64	Stateside SS 296	Barney's Blues/Theme From The Film "Man In The Middle" (No More)	18
65	CBS 201747	Man Alone (Ipcress File Theme)/Barbra's Theme	12
65	CBS 201822	The Syndicate/What A Question	15
66	CBS 202390	Vendetta/The Danny Scipio Theme	6
67	CBS 202451	Wednesday's Child (Quiller Memorandum)/Sleep Well My Darling	12
67	Ember EMB S 243	007/The Loneliness Of Autumn (some in p/s)	12/5
67	CBS 2825	You Only Live Twice/The Girl With The Sun In Her Hair	12
68	CBS Special Prod. WB 730	James Bond Theme/RAY CONNIFF: Love Is Blue (p/s)	7
69	CBS 3935	The Lion In Winter Parts 1 & 2	22
69	CBS 4468	Midnight Cowboy/Fun City	7
69	CBS 4680	On Her Majesty's Secret Service/We Have All The Time In The World	14
70	Probe PRO 518	The Last Valley/Main Title Theme	7
71	CBS 7469	Theme From "The Persuaders"/The Girl With The Sun In Her Hair	6
72	Polydor 2058 216	This Way Mary/Diamonds Are Forever	12
72	Polydor 2058 275	The Adventurer/Follow Follow	20
80	United Artists UP 634	Midnight Cowboy/Fun City	5
83	Cherry Red CHERRY 67	Cutty Sark/The Lolly Theme (p/s)	6

EPs

58	Parlophone GEP 8737	THE BIG BEAT (as John Barry Seven) (EP)	35
61	CBS WEP 1131	GREAT SCREEN THEMES (EP, shared with Percy Faith Orchestra, mail-order via Lyons Bakery)	10
61	Columbia SEG 8069	THE JOHN BARRY SOUND (EP, as John Barry Seven)	20
62	Columbia SEG 8138	BEAT GIRL (EP, as John Barry Seven, with Adam Faith)	35
63	Columbia SEG 8255	JOHN BARRY THEME SUCCESSES (EP)	22
63	United Artists UEP 1011	FROM RUSSIA WITH LOVE (EP, soundtrack)	22
64	Ember EMB EP 4544	LONELINESS OF AUTUMN (EP)	22
64	United Artists UEP 1012	GOLDFINGER (EP, soundtrack)	22
65	Ember EMB EP 4551	JAMES BOND IS BACK (EP)	22
65	United Artists UEP 1015	THUNDERBALL (EP, soundtrack)	22

LPs

60	Columbia 33SX 1225	BEAT GIRL (LP, soundtrack, with Adam Faith)	40
61	Columbia 33SX 1358	STRINGBEAT (LP, also stereo SCX 3401)	30/40
63	United Artists (S)ULP 1052	FROM RUSSIA WITH LOVE (LP, soundtrack, mono/stereo)	22/25
64	Ember NR 5012	ZULU (LP, yellow/orange label, flipback sleeve)	30
64	Stateside S(S)L 10087	MAN IN THE MIDDLE (LP, soundtrack, with Lionel Bart)	55
64	United Artists (S)ULP 1076	GOLDFINGER (LP, soundtrack, mono/stereo)	22/25
65	Ember NR 5025	JOHN BARRY PLAYS 007 (LP)	30
65	Ember NR 5032	JOHN BARRY MEETS CHAD & JEREMY (LP)	20
65	Ember NR 56088	FOUR IN THE MORNING (LP, soundtrack, mono/stereo)	35/45
65	CBS (S)BPG 62402	THE GREAT MOVIE SOUNDS OF JOHN BARRY (LP)	15
65	CBS BPG 62598	PASSION FLOWER HOTEL (LP, original cast, mono only)	35
65	CBS BPG 62530	THE IPCRESS FILE (LP, soundtrack, mono only)	60
65	United Artists ULP 1104	THE KNACK (AND HOW TO GET IT) (LP, soundtrack)	50
65	United Artists (S)ULP 1110	THUNDERBALL (LP, soundtrack, mono/stereo)	22/25
65	Fontana (S)TL 55021	KING RAT (LP, soundtrack)	40
66	CBS (S)BPG 62665	THE CHASE (LP, soundtrack, mono/stereo)	30/40
66	CBS (S)BPG 62869	THE QUILLER MEMORANDUM (LP, soundtrack, mono/stereo)	30/40
66	RCA RD 7860	FUNERAL IN BERLIN (LP, soundtrack)	25
66	MGM MGM-C 8010	BORN FREE (LP, soundtrack)	18
67	CBS 63038	JOHN BARRY CONDUCTS HIS GREATEST MOVIE HITS (LP)	15
67	United Artists (S)ULP 1168	THE WHISPERERS (LP, soundtrack)	50
67	United Artists (S)ULP 1171	YOU ONLY LIVE TWICE (LP, soundtrack)	20
67	United Artists LAS 29021	THE BEST OF BOND (LP, mono)	15
68	Stateside S(S)L 10263	DEADFALL (LP, soundtrack, Shirley Bassey on 1 track)	45
69	United Artists UAS 29020	ON HER MAJESTY'S SECRET SERVICE (LP, soundtrack, foldout sleeve)	35
69	United Artists UAS 29021	THE BEST OF BOND (LP, stereo)	15
69	CBS 70049	THE LION IN WINTER (LP, soundtrack)	30
69	MCA MUPS 360	BOOM (LP, soundtrack, with Georgie Fame)	90
70	CBS 63952	READY WHEN YOU ARE, JB (LP)	15
71	CBS 64816	THE PERSUADERS (LP)	15
71	United Artists UAS 29216	DIAMONDS ARE FOREVER (LP, soundtrack)	20
71	Probe SPB 1027	THE LAST VALLEY (LP, soundtrack, some with insert)	40/35
72	MCA MUPS 441	MARY QUEEN OF SCOTS (LP, soundtrack)	30
72	Sunset SLS 50291	FROM RUSSIA WITH LOVE (LP, soundtrack, reissue)	12
72	Ember SE 8008	JOHN BARRY REVISITED (LP, foldout sleeve, initially in 'nude' sleeve)	30/25
72	CBS 64816	FILM THEMES FROM JOHN BARRY (LP)	15
72	United Artists UAD 60027/8	THE JAMES BOND COLLECTION (2-LP, with booklet)	30
73	Polydor 2383 156	THE CONCERT JOHN BARRY (LP)	18
74	Polydor 2383 300	PLAY IT AGAIN (LP)	18
74	Phase 4 Stereo PFS 4339	THE DAY OF THE LOCUST (LP, soundtrack)	18
76	CBS 22014	THE MUSIC OF JOHN BARRY (2-LP)	22
76	Polydor 2383 405	AMERICANS (LP)	22
76	Reprise K 54090	KING KONG (LP, soundtrack with poster)	15
77	Casablanca CAL 2018	THE DEEP (LP, soundtrack)	15
77	Polydor 2383 461	THE VERY BEST OF JOHN BARRY (LP)	12
79	United Artists UAG 30247	MOONRAKER (LP, soundtrack)	12
81	RCA RCALP 5212	THE LEGEND OF THE LONE RANGER (LP, soundtrack)	12
83	A&R FILM 001	HIGH ROAD TO CHINA (LP, soundtrack)	22
83	A&M AMLX 64967	OCTOPUSSY (LP, soundtrack)	12
86	MCA MCF 3310	OUT OF AFRICA (LP, soundtrack)	12

(see also Alan Bown, Chad & Jeremy, Adam Faith, Michael D'andelo, Elizabeth Taylor, Desmond Lane, Johnny Pearson, Tony Bennett, Jim Lowe, Lyn Paul, Russ Conway, Lance Fortune, Alan Haven, Countdowns, Johnny De Little, Marion Ryan, Dick Kallman)

KAY BARRY
62	Embassy WB 534	Bobby's Girl/James (Hold The Ladder Steady)	5
63	Embassy WB 599	Be My Baby/Bye Bye Birdie	5
65	Embassy WB 674	Terry/Girl Don't Come	5

(see also Bud Ashton)

LEN BARRY
65	Cameo Parkway P 969	Hearts Are Trump/Little White House	12
65	Brunswick 05942	1-2-3/Bullseye	5
66	Brunswick 05949	Like A Baby/Happiness	6
66	Brunswick 05955	Somewhere/It's A Crying Shame	7
66	Brunswick 05962	It's That Time Of The Year/Happily Ever After	7
66	Brunswick 05966	I Struck It Rich/Love Is	7
67	RCA RCA 1588	The Moving Finger Writes/Our Love	8
68	Bell BLL 1022	4-5-6 Now I'm Alone/Funky Night	5
71	Now! NOW 1003	Now I'm Alone/Funky Night	6
72	MCA MU 1172	1-2-3/You Baby	5
73	Paramount PARA 3031	Heaven And Earth/I'm Marching To The Music	5
73	Paramount PARA 3039	It's Time To Fall In Love/Touching, Holding, Feeling	5
66	Cameo Parkway CPE 556	HAVIN' A GOOD TIME (EP)	18
65	Brunswick LAT 8637	1-2-3 (LP)	22
66	Cameo Parkway C 1082	LEN BARRY AND THE DOVELLS (LP)	18
69	Bulldog BDL 1013	MORE FROM THE 1-2-3 MAN (LP)	15
69	RCA Intl. INTS 1027	MY KIND OF SOUL (LP)	12

(see also Dovells, Electric Indian)

MARGARET BARRY (& MICHAEL GORMAN)
58	Topic 10T 6	STREET SONGS AND FIDDLE TUNES OF IRELAND (10" LP, mid-blue label, later buff/black or dark blue/silver labels)	20/15
60	Top Rank Intl. 25/020	IRELAND'S QUEEN OF THE TINKERS SONG (LP, Margaret Barry solo)	20
65	Topic 12T 123	HER MANTLE SO GREEN (LP, dark blue/silver label, or reissue in diff. sl.)	15/12
67	Xtra XTRA 5037	THE BLARNEY STONE (LP)	12
68	Emerald GEM 1003	COME BACK PADDY REILLY (LP)	15

SANDRA BARRY (& BOYS)
64	Decca F 11851	Really Gonna Shake/When We Get Married (as Sandra Barry & Boys)	30
65	Pye 7N 15753	The End Of The Line/We Were Lovers	10
65	Pye 7N 15840	Question/You Can Take It From Me	10
66	Pye 7N 17102	Stop! Thief/I Won't Try To Change Your Mind	10

(see also Boys, Sandra Alfred, Slack Alice)

TONY BARRY
66	Decca F 12431	When You're In Love With A Girl/Oh, My Love	5

BARRY & TAMERLANES
63	Warner Bros WB 116	I Wonder What She's Doing Tonight/Don't Go	30
64	Warner Bros WB 124	Roberta/Butterfly	10
64	Warner Bros WM 8145	I WONDER WHAT SHE'S DOING TONIGHT (LP)	25

(see also Barry De Vorzon)

BARRY & TONY
65	Decca F 12224	Lost Love/Make It Or Break It	6

(see also Brothers Grimm)

BARRY SISTERS (U.S.)
56	London HLA 8248	Cha Cha Joe/Baby Come A Little Closer	35
56	London HLA 8248	Cha Cha Joe/Baby Come A Little Closer (78)	18
56	London HLA 8304	Till You Come Back To Me/Intrigue	35
56	London HLA 8304	Till You Come Back To Me/Intrigue (78)	18
56	Columbia DB 3843	Sing Me A Sentimental Love Song/The Italian Theme	10
58	Columbia DB 4215	I Hear Bells/I Get Up Ev'ry Morning	8
58	Columbia DB 4215	I Hear Bells/I Get Up Ev'ry Morning (78)	14
60	Columbia DB 4562	Misty/Why Don't You Do Right?	7
60	Columbia 33SX 1309	SIDE BY SIDE (LP)	18

BARRY SISTERS (U.K.)
59	Decca F 11099	My Sweetie's Coming To Call/Little Boy Blue (78)	10

(see also Three Barry Sisters)

LIONEL BART
59	Decca LF 1324	BART FOR BART'S SAKE (10" LP)	15
67	Deram DML/SML 1028	ISN'T THIS WHERE WE CAME IN (LP)	20

CHRIS BARTLEY
67	Cameo Parkway P 101	The Sweetest Thing This Side Of Heaven/Love Me Baby	40
68	Bell BLL 1031	I Found A Goodie/Be Mine Forever	12
75	Right On RO 105	I See Your Name/I See Your Name (Instrumental)	5

BARTOK
82	On ON 1	Insanity/I Am The Bomb (p/s)	8

EVA BARTOK
67	Philips BF 1589	Broken Blossoms/Wait For Summer	5

RIA BARTOK
64	Columbia DB 7362	See If I Care/I Don't Wanna Leave You	7

EILEEN BARTON
55	Vogue Coral Q 72060	The Year We Fell In Love/I Don't Want To Mambo Polka	10
55	Vogue Coral Q 72075	Fujiyama Mama/I'd've Baked A Cake	35
55	Vogue Coral Q 72075	Fujiyama Mama/I'd've Baked A Cake (78)	10
56	Vogue Coral Q 72122	Cry Me A River/Come Home	12
56	Vogue Coral Q 72122	Cry Me A River/Come Home (78)	10

Eileen BARTON

56	Vogue Coral Q 72148	Teenage Heart/My Social Hot Dog	10
56	Vogue Coral Q 72148	Teenage Heart/My Social Hot Dog (78)	12
56	Vogue Coral Q 72205	Spring It Was/I Have To Tell You	8
56	Vogue Coral Q 72205	Spring It Was/I Have To Tell You (78)	10
57	Vogue Coral Q 72250	Too Close For Comfort/Here I Am In Love Again	8
57	Vogue Coral Q 72270	Without Love/The Scene Of The Crime	8
57	Vogue Coral Q 72270	Without Love/The Scene Of The Crime (78)	10

ROD BARTON (& THE LINCOLNAIRES)

| 62 | Salvo SLO 1812 | Dear Old San Francisco/Does A Chinese Chicken Have A Pigtail | 30 |

BASHERS

| 76 | Virgin 154 | The Womble Bashers/Womble Bashers Wock | 20 |

(see also Mike McGear)

BASHFUL ALLEY

| 81 | Ellie Jay BA 001 | Running Blind (p/s, black-and-white or black-and-yellow sleeve) | 40 |
| 82 | Graffiti BA 001 | Running Blind/My, My, My (p/s, reissue) | 35 |

COUNT BASIE & HIS ORCHESTRA

59	Columbia DB 4262	The Late Late Show/The M Squad Theme	5
59	Columbia DB 4262	The Late Late Show/The M Squad Theme (78)	8
59	Columbia SCD 2116	April In Paris/Party Blues (with Joe Williams)	5
60	HMV POP 733	April In Paris/The Midgets	5
60	Philips JAZ 109	The Golden Bullet/Bluebeard Blues (p/s)	5
67	Coral Q 72497	Green Onions/Hang On Sloopy	5
68	MCA MCA 1014	For Your Precious Love/Uptight (with Jackie Wilson)	7
68	Decca AD 1008	For Your Precious Love/Uptight (with Jackie Wilson, export issue)	10
53	Brunswick LA 8589	BASIE'S BEST (10" LP)	15
54	Oriole/Mercury MG 25015	COUNT BASIE/LESTER YOUNG (10" LP, 1 side each)	15
55	Columbia 33S 1054	THE COUNT (10" LP)	12
55	Philips BBR 8036	THE OLD AND THE NEW COUNT (10" LP)	12
55	Columbia Clef 33C 9010	THE COUNT BASIE SEXTET (10" LP)	12
55	Columbia Clef 33CX 10007	COUNT BASIE DANCE SESSION (LP)	12
56	Columbia Clef 33CX 10026	COUNT BASIE SWINGS AND JOE WILLIAMS SINGS (LP)	12
56	Columbia Clef 33CX 10044	COUNT BASIE DANCE SESSION NO. 2 (LP)	12
57	Columbia Clef 33CX 10065	BASIE (LP)	12
57	Columbia Clef 33CX 10088	APRIL IN PARIS (LP)	12
57	Vanguard PPL 11005	A NIGHT AT COUNT BASIE'S (LP, with Joe Williams)	12
57	Philips BBL 7141	BASIE'S BACK IN TOWN (LP)	12
57	Philips BBL 7190	BLUES BY BASIE (LP)	12
58	Columbia 33CX 10110	AT NEWPORT (LP)	12
58	Columbia 33SX 1084	THE ATOMIC MR. BASIE (LP, also stereo SCX 3265)	12/15
58	Columbia 33SX 1135	BASIE PLAYS HEFTI (LP)	12
59	Columbia 33SX 1151	SING ALONG WITH BASIE (LP)	12
59	Col. 33SX 1174/SCX 3278	COUNT BASIE SWINGS — TONY BENNETT SINGS (LP, mono/stereo)	12
59	Columbia 33SX 1175	MEMORIES AD-LIB (LP, also stereo SCX 3280)	12
59	Columbia 33SX 1183	BASIE (ONE MORE TIME) (LP, also stereo SCX 3284)	12
59	Fontana TFL 5046	ONE O'CLOCK JUMP (LP)	12
60	Fontana TFL 5077	COUNT BASIE CLASSICS (LP, with Jimmy Rushing)	12
60	Columbia 33SX 1209	BREAKFAST DANCE AND BARBECUE (LP, also stereo SCX 3294)	12
60	Columbia 33SX 1224	CHAIRMAN OF THE BOARD (LP, also stereo SCX 3304)	12
60	Columbia 33SX 1264	DANCE ALONG WITH BASIE (LP, also stereo SCX 3333)	12
61	Columbia 33SX 1293	NOT NOW, I'LL TELL YOU WHEN (LP, also stereo SCX 3356)	12
61	HMV CLP 1428	THE BAND OF DISTINCTION (LP)	12
61	Columbia 33SX 1316	THE COUNT BASIE STORY (VOL. 1) (LP, also stereo SCX 3372)	12
61	Columbia 33SX 1317	THE COUNT BASIE STORY (VOL. 2) (LP, also stereo SCX 3373)	12
61	Columbia 33SX 1326	JUST THE BLUES (LP, with Joe Williams, also stereo SCX 3380)	12
66	United Artists (S)ULP 1127	BASIE MEETS BOND (LP)	20

(see also Joe Williams, Jackie Wilson, Tony Bennett, Lester Young, Ella Fitzgerald)

BASIES

| 67 | Coxsone CS 7030 | River Jordan/SOUL VENDORS: Swing Easy | 18 |

BASKIN & COPPERFIELD

70	Decca F 13053	The Long And Winding Road/Beautiful Blue Eyes	5
70	Decca F 23079	I Never See The Sun/Stranger On The Ground	5
71	Decca F 23131	Moonbeams/Long Grass	5
71	Decca F 23174	Roly Poly/We Got Love	5

(see also Rubettes)

ALFIE BASS

| 60 | Pye 7N 15286 | Villikens And His Dinah/Rat Catcher's Daughter | 6 |

BILLY BASS

| 69 | Pama PM 761 | I Need Your Love So Bad/I'm Coming To | 10 |

FONTELLA BASS

65	Chess CRS 8007	Don't Mess Up A Good Thing (with Bobby McClure)/OLIVER SAIN: Jerk Loose	20
65	Chess CRS 8007	Don't Mess Up A Good Thing/Baby What You Want Me To Do (different B-side, existence unconfirmed)	
65	Chess CRS 8023	Rescue Me/Soul Of The Man	10
66	Chess CRS 8027	Recovery/Leave It In The Hands Of Love	10
66	Chess CRS 8032	I Can't Rest/Surrender	12
66	Chess CRS 8042	Safe And Sound/You'll Never Know	10
69	Chess CRS 8090	Rescue Me/I Can't Rest	7
69	Chess CRS 8023	Rescue Me/Soul Of The Man (reissue)	6
72	Mojo 2092 032	Who You Gonna Blame/Hold On This Time	6
72	Mojo 2092 045	I Want Everyone To Know/I Need To Be Loved	6
66	Chess CRE 6015	FONTELLA'S HITS (EP)	25

66	Chess CRE 6020	I CAN'T REST (EP)	25
66	Chess CRE 6025	FONTELLA BASS AND BOBBY McCLURE (EP)	25
66	Chess CRL 4517	THE NEW LOOK (LP)	25
72	Mojo 2916 018	FREE (LP)	18

(see also Bobby McClure)

SHIRLEY BASSEY
78s
59	Philips PB 917	Love For Sale/Crazy Rhythm (78)	15
59	Philips PB 919	My Funny Valentine/How About You? (78)	15
59	Philips PB 975	Night And Day/The Gypsy In My Soul (78)	25
59	Columbia DB 4344	If You Love Me/Count On Me (78)	15

SINGLES
57	Philips JK 1006	The Banana Boat Song/Tra La La (jukebox issue)	25
57	Philips JK 1018	If I Had A Needle And Thread/Tonight My Heart She Is Crying (jukebox issue)	15
57	Philips JK 1034	Puh-leeze! Mister Brown/Take My Love, Take My Love (jukebox issue)	15
58	Philips PB 845	As I Love You/Hands Across The Sea	5
58	Philips PB 860	Kiss Me, Honey Honey, Kiss Me/There's Never Been A Night	7
59	Philips PB 917	Love For Sale/Crazy Rhythm	5
59	Philips PB 919	My Funny Valentine/How About You?	5
59	Philips PB 975	Night And Day/The Gypsy In My Soul	5
59	Columbia DB 4344	If You Love Me/Count On Me	6
60	Columbia DB 4421	With These Hands/The Party's Over	5
61	Philips BF 1091	Birth Of The Blues/The Careless Love Blues	5
62	Columbia DB 4777	Tonight/Let's Start All Over Again	5
62	Columbia DB 4816	You'll Never walk Alone/Ave Maria	5
62	Columbia DB 4836	Far Away/My Faith	5
63	Columbia DB 4974	What Kind Of Fool Am I/Till	5
64	Columbia DB 7185	My Special Dream/You	5
64	Columbia DB 7248	Gone/Your Love	5
64	Columbia DB 7337	Who Can I Turn To?/To Be Loved By A Man	5
64	Columbia DB 7360	Goldfinger/Strange How Love Can Be	7
66	United Artists UP 1134	Don't Take The Lovers From The World/Takeaway	10
67	United Artists UP 1192	Big Spender/Dangerous Game	5
68	United Artists UP 2254	To Give/My Love Has Two Faces	12
72	United Artists UP 35293	Diamonds Are Forever/Pieces Of Dreams	5
77	United Artists UP 36247	I Let You Let Me Down/Razzle Dazzle (withdrawn)	5

EPs
57	Philips BBE 12113	AT THE CAFE DE PARIS LONDON (EP)	8
58	Philips BBE 12212	AS I LOVE YOU (EP)	8
59	Philips BBE 12232	BLUES BY SHIRLEY BASSEY (EP)	10
59	Philips BBE 12321	LOVE FOR SALE (EP)	8
60	Philips BBE 12408	BLUES BY SHIRLEY BASSEY NO. 2 (EP)	8
61	Columbia ESG 7819	FABULOUS SHIRLEY BASSEY (EP, stereo)	10
61	Columbia ESG 7840	FABULOUS SHIRLEY BASSEY (EP, stereo)	10
61	Columbia ESG 7854	SHIRLEY NO. 1 (EP, stereo)	10
62	Columbia ESG 7865	SHIRLEY NO. 2 (EP, stereo)	10
62	Columbia ESG 7869	SHIRLEY NO. 3 (EP, stereo)	10
62	Columbia ESG 7879	SHIRLEY BASSEY (EP, stereo)	10
62	Columbia ESG 7889	SHIRLEY BASSEY NO. 2 (EP, stereo)	10
63	Columbia SEG 8252	HITS OF SHIRLEY BASSEY (EP)	8
63	Columbia ESG 7899	LET'S FACE THE MUSIC (EP, stereo)	10
64	Columbia SEG 8315	SHIRLEY'S MOST REQUESTED SONGS (EP)	8
64	Columbia SEG 8369	THE DYNAMIC SHIRLEY (EP)	8

LPs
58	Philips BBR 8130	BORN TO SING THE BLUES (10" LP)	20
60	Columbia 33SX 1286	SHIRLEY (LP, also stereo SCX 3352)	15/18
62	Columbia 33SX 1454	LET'S FACE THE MUSIC (LP, also stereo SCX 3454)	12
70	United Artists UAS 29100	SOMETHING (LP)	12
71	United Artists UAG 29149	SOMETHING (LP, reissue)	12

(see also Yello, Nelson Riddle Orchestra, John Barry)

BASSIX
| 90 | Champion CHAMP 12 | CLOSE ENCOUNTERS (12") | 12 |

BAS-SHEVA
| 55 | Capitol CL 14218 | Flame Of Love/I Just Wanna Be Your Loving Baby | 8 |

JOE BATAAN
75	RCA RCA 2457	Latin Strut/Peace, Friendship And Solidarity	15
75	RCA RCA 2553	The Bottle/When You're Down	12
69	London HA/SH 8386	RIOT! (LP)	25

JUNE BATEMAN
| 64 | Sue WI 347 | I Don't Wanna/NOBLE 'THIN MAN' WATTS & HIS BAND: Noble's Theme | 30 |

COLLIN BATES TRIO
| 68 | Fontana SFJ 2913 | BREW (LP) | 125 |

JON BATES
| 65 | CBS 202818 | Where Were You Last Night/If Anything Goes Wrong | 5 |

MARTYN BATES
| 82 | Cherry Red TRED 38 | LETTERS WRITTEN (10" EP) | 10 |
| 80s | Ambivalent Scale | IMAGINATION FEELS LIKE POISON (CD, with book, 500 only) | 20 |

(see also Eyeless In Gaza)

BATMAN THEME
| 88 | Bam Caruso NRIC 107 | Batman Theme/Batman Theme (Instrumental Mix) (p/s) | 5 |

MINT VALUE £

STIV BATORS
79	London/Bomp HLZ 10575	It's Cold Outside/The Last Year (p/s)	10

(see also Dead Boys, Lords Of The New Church, Wanderers)

BATS
64	Columbia DB 7429	Accept It/Lovers Lie Sleeping	8
66	Decca F 22534	Listen To My Heart/Stop Don't Do It	10
67	Decca F 22568	You Will Now, Won't You?/You Look Good Together	8
67	Decca F 22616	Hard To Get Up In The Morning/Take Me As I Am	8

MIKE BATT
68	Liberty LBF 15093	Mister Poem/Fading Yellow	7
68	Liberty LBF 15122	I See Wonderful Things In You/Mary Goes Round	5
69	Liberty LBF 15210	Your Mother Should Know/Suddenly	5

(see also Phase 4, Hapshash & Coloured Coat, Anderson Harley & Batt)

BATTERED ORNAMENTS
70	Harvest HAR 5013	Goodbye We Loved You (Madly)/CHRIS SPEDDING: Rock'n'Roll Band	15
69	Harvest SHVL 758	MANTLE-PIECE (LP)	85

(see also Pete Brown & His Battered Ornaments, Chris Spedding, People Band)

BATTERSEA
78	Anchor ANC 1060	Always Something There To Remind Me/Split Image (p/s)	5

SKIP BATTIN
72	Signpost SGP 756	Central Park/St. Louis Browns	5
72	Signpost SG 4255	SKIP (LP)	15

(see also Skip & Flip, Byrds, Flying Burrito Brothers, Evergreen Blueshoes)

JEAN BATTLE
72	Mojo 2027 010	Love Making/When A Woman Loves A Man	6

BATTLEAXE
82	Guardian GRC 132	Burn This Town/Battleaxe (no p/s)	18

ERIC BATTY
57	Esquire 10-493	One Sweet Letter From You/Whispering Pines Of Nevada (78)	8

BAUHAUS
79	Small Wonder TEENY 2	Bela Lugosi's Dead/Boys/Dark Entries (12", p/s, black vinyl, later white vinyl)	7/15
88	Small Wonder TEENY 2P	Bela Lugosi's Dead/Boys/Dark Entries (12", reissue, picture disc)	10
88	Small Wonder TEENY 2CD	Bela Lugosi's Dead/Boys/Dark Entries (CD, no'd reissue, 2,000 only)	10
89	Small Wonder TEENY 2	Bela Lugosi's Dead/Boys/Dark Entries (12", reissue, green or blue vinyl, p/s)	12/10
91	Small Wonder TEENY 2	Bela Lugosi's Dead/Boys/Dark Entries (12", reissue, pink, clear or purple vinyl, in corresponding coloured p/s)	each 10
80	Axis AXIS 3	Dark Entries/Untitled (brown label, p/s)	18
80	Axis AD 3	Dark Entries/Untitled (blue label, p/s)	8
80	4AD BEG 37	Dark Entries/Untitled (p/s, blue 4AD labels, lists BEG 37 on sleeve)	10
80	Beggars Banquet BEG 37	Dark Entries/Untitled (p/s, red Beggars Banquet labels)	10
82	Beggars Banquet AD 3	Dark Entries/Untitled (reissue, 'nudes' label, no contact address on p/s)	7
80	4AD AD 7	Terror Couple Kill Colonel/Scopes/Terror Couple Kill Colonel II (p/s)	5
80	4AD AD 7	Terror Couple Kill Colonel/Scopes/Terror Couple Kill Colonel II (version) (mispressed with 'rejected' version of third track, p/s)	25
80	4AD AD 17	Telegram Sam/Crowds (p/s)	5
81	Beggars Banquet BEG 54	Kick In The Eye/Satori (p/s)	5
81	Beggars Banquet BEG 54T	Kick In The Eye/Satori (12", white label in stamped plain sleeve)	8
81	Beggars Banquet BEG 59	The Passion Of Lovers/David J: Peter Murphy: Kevin Haskins: Daniel Ash (p/s, with lyric insert)	5
82	Beggars Banquet BEG 74	Kick In The Eye/Harry/Earwax (p/s)	5
82	Beggars Banquet BEG 74T	Kick In The Eye/Poison Pen/Harry/Earwax (12" mispressing, p/s, matrix: A1)	30
82	Beggars Banquet BEG 79	Spirit/Terror Couple Kill Colonel (live) (p/s, with Beggars labels)	5
82	Beggars Banquet BEG 79	Spirit/Terror Couple Kill Colonel (live) (p/s, mispressed, A-side plays Gary Numan's "We Take Mystery [To Bed]")	10
82	Beggars Banquet BEG 79P	Spirit/Terror Couple Kill Colonel (live) (picture disc in printed PVC sleeve)	8
82	Beggars Banquet BEG 83	Ziggy Stardust/Third Uncle ('Bauhaus' label with p/s, or Beggars label, no p/s)	5
82	Beggars Banquet BEG 83T	Ziggy Stardust/Party Of The First Part/Third Uncle/Waiting For The Man (12", p/s, with stickered poster p/s)	10
82	Lyntone LYN 12106	A God In An Alcove (Early Version) (blue flexidisc with *Flexipop*, issue 23)	12/7
82	Lyntone LYN 12106	A God In An Alcove (Early Version) (hard vinyl test pressing)	30
83	Lyntone LYN 13777/8	The Sanity Assassin/Spirit In The Sky (fan club freebie, 320 only)	125
84	Beggars Banquet BEG 91P	She's In Parties/Departure (picture disc in PVC sleeve)	8
88	Beggars Banquet BBP 4CD	THE SINGLES 1981-1983 (CD EP)	10
82	Beggars Banquet BEGA 38	PRESS THE EJECT AND GIVE ME THE TAPE (LP, with bonus 45 "Satori In Paris" [BH 1] & poster)	12
82	Beggars Banquet BEGA 42	THE SKY'S GONE OUT (LP, with bonus LP "Press The Eject And Give Me The Tape" [BEGA 38] & inner sleeves)	12
83	B. Banquet BEGA 45P	BURNING FROM THE INSIDE (LP, picture disc)	12
85	Beggars Banquet BEGA 64	1979-1983 (LP, with numbered inserts)	12
88	B. Banquet BAUCD BOX 1	1979-1983 (2-CD, boxed set with book & badge, no'd, 2,000 only, export issue)	30

(see also Sinister Ducks, Peter Murphy, Tones On Tail, David J., Love & Rockets, Dali's Car)

ART BAXTER
56	Philips PB 652	Jingle Rock/Rock And Roll Rag (78)	18
57	Philips PB 666	Don't Knock The Rock/Rock Rock Rock (78)	18
57	Philips BBR 8107	ROCK YOU SINNERS (10" LP)	120

DAVID BAXTER
70	Reflection REFL 9	GOODBYE DAVE (LP)	25

(see also David Lewis)

LES BAXTER & HIS ORCHESTRA

55	Capitol CL 14237	Cherry Pink And Apple Blossom White/Play Me Hearts And Flowers 10
55	Capitol CL 14239	Earth Angel/Happy Baby (as Les Baxter & Bombers) 18
55	Capitol CL 14249	I Ain't Mad At You (with Bombers)/Blue Mirage 10
55	Capitol CL 14257	Unchained Melody/Blue Star (The Medic Theme) 15
55	Capitol CL 14344	Wake The Town And Tell The World/I'll Never Stop Loving You. 10
56	Capitol CL 14533	Poor John/"Helen Of Troy" Theme 6
56	Capitol CL 14546	The Trouble With Harry/Havana 5
57	Capitol CL 14677	Giant/There's Never Been Anyone Else But You. 5
59	Capitol CL 15055	Sabre Dance/Milord 5
60	Capitol CL 15140	Ooch-I-Baba/Boomada (as Les Baxter Drums). 5
66	Pye International 7N 25351	Michelle/Little Girl Lonely 5
59	Capitol T/ST 1248	WILD GUITARS (LP) 12
60	Capitol (S)T 1355	TEEN DRUMS (LP) 18

RONNIE BAXTER

60	Top Rank JAR 293	I Finally Found You/Is It Because? 6

FRANCIS BAY

59	Philips PB 899	Manhattan Spiritual/Eso Es El Amour (78) 12

BAYTOWN SINGERS

65	Decca F 12160	Walkin' Down The Line/Let My Feet Fall On The Ground 5

B.B. BLUNDER

71	United Artists UP 35203	Sticky Living/Rocky Yagbatee Yagbag. 6
71	United Artists UP 35204	Little Boy/10,000 Miles 6
71	United Artists UAG 29156	WORKERS' PLAYTIME (LP) 15

(see also Reg King & B.B. Blunder, Action, Julie Driscoll Brian Auger & Trinity, Kevin Westlake, Mark Charig)

BBC RADIOPHONIC WORKSHOP/PETER HOWELL

64	Decca F 11837	Doctor Who/BRENDA & JOHNNY: This Can't Be Love (unboxed Decca logo). . . . 18
72	Decca F 11837	Doctor Who/BRENDA & JOHNNY: This Can't Be Love (reissue, boxed logo) 8
73	BBC RESL 11	Doctor Who/Reg (blue/white label, credits 'Delia Derbyshire', 'TARDIS' p/s). . . . 10/6
76	BBC RESL 11	Doctor Who/Reg (reissue, no p/s, silver label) 6
78	BBC RESL 11	Doctor Who/Reg (2nd reissue, in 'TARDIS' p/s, blue label, white rim) 6
80	PRT RESL 80	Doctor Who/The Astronauts ('Tom Baker' p/s,
		as 'Peter Howell & BBC Radiophonic Workshop') 10
82	PRT RESL 80	Doctor Who/The Astronauts (reissue, 'Peter Davison' p/s). 10
84	PRT RESL 80	Doctor Who/The Astronauts (2nd reissue, 'Colin Baker' p/s) 7
72	BBC REC 93S	TEST CARD MUSIC (LP) 12
78	BBC REC 316	DOCTOR WHO SOUND EFFECTS No. 19 (LP). 12

(see also Dr. Who, Jon Pertwee, Ray Cathode, Radiophonic Workshop, Ithaca, Alice Through The Looking Glass, Agincourt, Blossom Toes)

BEA & DEE

59	Capitol CL 15066	Jerry/Wishing Time 5

BEACH BOYS

SINGLES

62	Capitol CL 15273	Surfin' Safari/409 25
63	Capitol CL 15285	Ten Little Indians/County Fair 60
63	Capitol CL 15305	Surfin' USA/Shut Down 18
64	Capitol CL 15339	Fun, Fun, Fun/Why Do Fools Fall In Love 40
64	Capitol CL 15350	I Get Around/Don't Worry Baby 7
64	Capitol CL 15361	When I Grow Up (To Be A Man)/She Knows Me Too Well 7
65	Capitol CL 15370	Dance, Dance, Dance/The Warmth Of The Sun 7
65	Capitol CL 15384	All Summer Long/Do You Wanna Dance 7
65	Capitol CL 15392	Help Me Rhonda/Kiss Me Baby 6
65	Capitol CL 15409	California Girls/Let Him Run Wild 6
65	Capitol CL 15425	The Little Girl I Once Knew/There's No Other (Like My Baby) 8
66	Capitol CL 15432	Barbara Ann/Girl Don't Tell Me 5
66	Capitol CL 15441	Sloop John B/You're So Good To Me 5
66	Capitol CL 15459	God Only Knows/Wouldn't It Be Nice 6
66	Capitol CL 15475	Good Vibrations/Wendy 6
67	Capitol CL 15502	Then I Kissed Her/Mountain Of Love 6
67	Capitol CL 15510	Heroes And Villains/You're Welcome 6
67	Capitol CL 15521	Wild Honey/Wind Chimes 6
68	Capitol CL 15527	Darlin'/Country Air. 6
68	Capitol CL 15545	Friends/Little Bird 6
68	Capitol CL 15554	Do It Again/Wake The World. 6
68	Capitol CL 15572	Bluebirds Over The Mountain/Never Learn Not To Love. 6
69	Capitol CL 15598	Break Away/Celebrate The News 6
70	Capitol CL 15640	Cottonfields/The Nearest Faraway Place (black label) 6
70	Stateside SS 2181	Tears In The Morning/It's About Time 6
71	Stateside SS 2190	Long Promised Road/Deirdre 6
71	Stateside SS 2194	Don't Go Near The Water/Student Demonstration Time
		(demos in p/s £18) 6
72	Reprise K 14173	You Need A Mess Of Help To Stand Alone/Cuddle Up (p/s) 10
72	Capitol CMS 1	Wouldn't It Be Nice/Fun Fun Fun/California Girls (printed sleeve). 6
72	Capitol CMS 2	Barbara Ann/Dance Dance Dance/You're So Good To Me (printed sleeve) 6
74	Reprise K 14346	California Saga: California/Sail On Sailor/Marcella/I'm The Pied Piper
		(printed sleeve) 5
76	Reprise K 14411	Child Of Winter/Susie Cincinnati (withdrawn). . . . . 40+
76	Reprise K 14440	Rock And Roll Music/The T.M. Song (p/s) 5
76	Capitol PSR 402	Good Vibrations/Interview With Carl Wilson (promo only) 10
77	Reprise K 14481	Mona/Rock And Roll Music/Sail On Sailor/Marcella (p/s) 5
78	Capitol CL 15969	Little Deuce Coupe/SUNRAYS: I Live For The Sun/SUPERSTOCKS:
		Hot Rod High (p/s) 5

MINT VALUE £

| 79 | Caribou 12-7204 | Here Comes The Night/(Disco Version)/Baby Blue (12", p/s, blue vinyl) . . . . 8 |
| 79 | Capitol BBP 26 | SINGLES COLLECTION (26 x 7" box set) . . . . 60 |

EPs

63	Capitol EAP 1-20540	SURFIN' USA (EP) 20
64	Capitol EAP 1-20603	FUN, FUN, FUN (EP) 18
64	Capitol EAP 5267	FOUR BY THE BEACH BOYS (EP) 15
64	Capitol EAP 4-2198	BEACH BOYS CONCERT (EP) 18
64	Capitol EAP 1-20781	THE BEACH BOYS HITS (EP) 15
67	Capitol EAP 6-2458	GOD ONLY KNOWS (EP) 15

LPs

62	Capitol T 1808	SURFIN' SAFARI (LP, mono only) 30
63	Capitol (S)T 1890	SURFIN' USA (LP, mono/stereo) 25/30
63	Capitol (S)T 1981	SURFER GIRL (LP, mono/stereo) 22/25
63	Capitol (S)T 1998	LITTLE DEUCE COUPE (LP, mono/stereo) 18/22
63	Capitol (S)T 2027	SHUT DOWN VOLUME 2 (LP, mono/stereo) 18/22
64	Capitol (S)T 2164	THE BEACH BOYS' CHRISTMAS ALBUM (LP, mono/stereo) 30/25
64	Capitol (S)T 2198	BEACH BOYS CONCERT (LP, mono/stereo) 18/22
64	Capitol (S)T 2110	ALL SUMMER LONG (LP, mono/stereo) 18/22
65	Capitol (S)T 2398	BEACH BOYS' PARTY! (LP, mono/stereo) 15/18
65	Capitol (S)T 2269	BEACH BOYS TODAY! (LP, mono/stereo) 15/18
65	Capitol (S)T 2354	SUMMER DAYS (AND SUMMER NIGHTS!!) (LP, mono/stereo) 15/18
66	Capitol (S)T 2458	PET SOUNDS (LP) 25
66	Capitol (S)T 20856	THE BEST OF THE BEACH BOYS (LP) 12
67	Capitol (S)T 1981	SURFER GIRL (LP, reissue, non-flipback sleeve) 12
67	Capitol (S)T 20956	THE BEST OF THE BEACH BOYS VOL. 2 (LP) 12
67	Capitol (S)T 9001	SMILEY SMILE (LP) 18
68	Capitol (S)T 2859	WILD HONEY (LP, mono/stereo) 20/15
68	Capitol (S)T 2895	FRIENDS (LP, mono/stereo) 20/15

(The above LPs were originally issued with flipback sleeves & rainbow-rim black labels; later copies are worth half the value.)

69	Capitol (S)T 21142	THE BEST OF THE BEACH BOYS VOL. 3 (LP, mono/stereo) 15/12
69	Capitol E T/ST 133	20-20 (LP, mono/stereo, gatefold sleeve) 20/15
70	Stateside SSLA 8251	SUNFLOWER (LP, gatefold sleeve) 15
71	Stateside SSL 10313	SURF'S UP (LP, textured sleeve, some with gatefold insert) 18/12
73	Reprise K 54008	HOLLAND (LP, with insert & bonus EP "Mount Vernon And Fairway" [K 54008/7] in p/s) 16
73	Reprise K 54008	HOLLAND (LP) 12
77	EMI EMTV 1	20 GOLDEN GREATS (LP, blue vinyl) 12
78	Brother K 54102	M.I.U. ALBUM (LP, with inner sleeve) 12
79	Caribou CRB 11-86081	L.A. (LIGHT ALBUM) (LP, picture disc) 15
70s	Capitol ST 2458	PET SOUNDS (LP, reissue, green or orange label) 12
81	WRC SM 651-657	THE CAPITOL YEARS (7-LP box set) 50
86	EMI ENS 1179	PET SOUNDS (LP, remastered reissue) 12

REEL-TO-REEL TAPES

64	Capitol TA-T 1981	SURFER GIRL (mono only) 12
64	Capitol TA-T 1998	LITTLE DEUCE COUPE (mono only) 12
65	Capitol TA-T 2198	BEACH BOYS CONCERT (mono only) 12
65	Capitol TA-T 2398	BEACH BOYS' PARTY! (mono only) 12
66	Capitol TA-T 2458	PET SOUNDS (mono only) 12
66	Capitol TA-T 20856	THE BEST OF THE BEACH BOYS (mono only) 12
67	Capitol TA-T 20956	THE BEST OF THE BEACH BOYS VOL. 2 (mono only) 12
67	Capitol TA-T 9001	SMILEY SMILE (mono only) 12
68	Capitol TA-T 2859	WILD HONEY (mono only) 12
68	Capitol TA-T 2895	FRIENDS (mono only) 12
69	Capitol TA-E-T 133	20-20 (mono only) 12
69	Capitol TA-T 21142	THE BEST OF THE BEACH BOYS VOL. 3 (mono only) 12

(see also Brian Wilson, Dennis Wilson, Bruce Johnston, Legendary Masked Surfers, American Spring, Annette, Flame, Flames, California Music, Rutles, Moon, Murry Wilson)

BEACHCOMBER
| 70 | Parlophone R 5850 | Surfin' Soul/Nothing To Say . . . . 5 |

BEACHCOMBERS
| 63 | Columbia DB 7124 | Mad Goose/You Can't Sit Down . . . . 25 |
| 64 | Columbia DB 7200 | Night Train/The Keel Row . . . . 25 |

(the above singles do not feature Keith Moon)

BEACH-NUTS
| 65 | London HL 9988 | Out In The Sun (Hey-O)/Someday Soon . . . . 12 |

(see also Angels, Strangeloves)

BEACON STREET UNION
| 68 | MGM MGM 1416 | Blue Suede Shoes/Four Hundred And Five . . . . 6 |
| 68 | MGM MGM-C(S) 8069 | THE EYES OF THE BEACON STREET UNION (LP) . . . . 25 |

BEALE STREET BUSKERS
| 60 | Ember EMB S 107 | 'Fraidy Cat/Dusty . . . . 5 |

GEORGE BEAN
63	Decca F 11762	Secret Love/Lonely Weekends 8
64	Decca F 11808	Will You Be My Lover Tonight?/It Should Be You 15
64	Decca F 11922	A Sad Story/Er Um Er 15
65	Decca F 12228	She Belongs To Me/Why Must They Criticise? (as George Bean & Runners) 8
67	CBS 2801	The Candy Shop Is Closed/Smile From Sequin 8
68	CBS 3374	Bring Back Lovin'/Floatin' 20

(see also Trifle, Bean & Loopy's Lot)

BEAN & LOOPY'S LOT
66	Parlophone R 5458	A Stitch In Time/Haywire	18

(see also Alan Bown Set)

BEANO
74	Deram DM 424	Candy Baby/Rock And Roll (Gonna Save Your Soul)	6
75	Deram DM 427	Little Cinderella/Bye And Bye	5

BEANS
62	Starlite ST45 071	Jumping Beans/Salute To Fitz	8
62	Starlite ST45 076	Hey Janey/Crazy Dog	8

BEAR
68	Verve FTS 3059	GREETINGS CHILDREN OF PARADISE (LP)	30

DEAN BEARD & CREW CATS
57	London HLE 8463	Rakin' And Scrapin'/On My Mind Again	375
57	London HLE 8463	Rakin' And Scrapin'/On My Mind Again (78)	55

BEARS
79	Good Vibrations Intl. GVI 1	Insane/Decisions (p/s)	6
79	Waldo's JS 001	On Me/Wot's Up Mate (p/s, various designs, with insert)	8

BEARZ
80	Axis AXIS 2	She's My Girl/Girls Will Do (p/s)	15
84	Occult OCC 1	Darwin/Julie (p/s)	12

BEAS
68	Pama PM 744	Dr. Goldfoot And His Bikini Machine/Where Do I Go From You	15

BEASTIE BOYS
82	Rat Cage MOTR 21	POLLY WOG STEW (EP)	10
82	Rat Cage MOTR 21	POLLY WOG STEW (12" EP)	12
86	Rat Cage MOR 26	COOKY PUSS EP: Cooky Puss/Bonus Batter/Beastie Revolution/ Cookie Puss (Censored Version) (p/s)	5
86	Rat Cage MOTR 26CD	COOKY PUSS EP: Cooky Puss/Bonus Batter/Beastie Revolution/ Cooky Puss (Censored Version) (CD)	8
86	Def Jam A 7055	Hold It, Now Hit It/Acapulco (p/s)	5
86	Def Jam TA 7055	Hold It, Now Hit It/Acapulco (12", p/s)	8
86	Def Jam 650 114 7	She's On It/Slow'n'Low (p/s)	5
86	Def Jam 650 114 6	She's On It/Slow'n'Low/Hold On, Now Hit It (12", p/s)	8
87	Def Jam 650 169 7	It's The New Style/Paul Revere (p/s)	5
87	Def Jam 650 169 6	It's The New Style/It's The New Style (Instrumental)/Paul Revere/ Paul Revere (Instrumental) (12", p/s)	7
87	Def Jam 650 418 7	(You Gotta) Fight For Your Right (To Party)/Time To Get III (p/s)	5
87	Def Jam 650 418 6	(You Gotta) Fight For Your Right (To Party)/Time To Get III (12", p/s)	7
87	Def Jam BEASTP 1	No Sleep Till Brooklyn/Posse In Effect (plane-shaped picture disc)	12
87	Def Jam BEASTT 1	No Sleep Till Brooklyn/Posse In Effect (12", p/s)	8
87	Def Jam BEASTB 2	She's On It/Slow'n'Low (reissue, p/s, badge pack)	5
87	Def Jam BEASTT 2	She's On It/Slow'n'Low/Hold On, Now Hit It (12", reissue, p/s)	7
87	Def Jam BEASTP 3	Girls/She's Crafty (poster p/s)	5
87	Def Jam BEASTQ 3	Girls/She's Crafty (logo shaped picture disc)	10
88	Rat Cage MOTR 21T	POLLY WOG STEW (12" EP, reissue)	12
92	Capitol CDCL 653	PASS THE MIC (Netty's Girl/Something's Got To Give/Pass The Mic [Pt. 2, Skills To Pay The Bills]) (CD, slimline jewel case)	15
92	Capitol CDCL 665	Jimmy James (Single Version)/The Blue Nun/Jimmy James (Original Original Version)/Drinkin' Wine (CD, slimline jewel case)	18
92	Capitol 12CLS 665	Frozen Metal Head/Jimmy James (Single Version)/So What'cha Want (All The Way Live Freestyle Version)/Jimmy James (Original Original Version)/Drinkin' Wine (12", white p/s)	10
92	Capitol CDCLS 665	Frozen Metal Head/Jimmy James (Single Version)/So What'cha Want (All The Way Live Freestyle Version)/Jimmy James (Original Original Version)/Drinkin' Wine (CD)	18
87	Def Jam 450 062 1	LICENSED TO ILL (LP, with poster)	10
94	Grand Royal GRAND 1	THE SAMPLER (CD, digipak, promo only)	15

BEAT
79	2-Tone TT 6	Tears Of A Clown/Ranking Full Stop (paper label, company sleeve)	5

(see also Fine Young Cannibals)

NICKY BEAT & THE BEATNICKS
78	Rigid IS BEAT 1033	I Can Hear Voices/Split Second Love/Starstruck (p/s)	5

BEAT BOYS
63	Decca F 11730	That's My Plan/Third Time Lucky	30

(see also Rats)

BEAT BROTHERS
63	Polydor NH 52185	Nick Nack Hully Gully/Lantern Hully Gully	30

(see also Tony Sheridan & Beat Brothers, Bobby Patrick Big Six)

BEAT CHICS
64	Decca F 12016	Skinny Minnie/Now I Know	12

BEATHOVEN
88	CBS 651 626-7	Socrates/Socrates (withdrawn)	30

BEATLE HANS
90s	Fierce FRIGHT 049/KS 007	Violets Of Dawn/Me (p/s)	6

BEATLES

SINGLES
(Beatles' original Parlophone singles came in a variety of company sleeves, which are referred to here as "Type 1", etc., and are depicted in the illustrations accompanying this text. When a sleeve is not specified, details are unknown.)

1962
(with "The Parlophone Co. Ltd." in upper-lower case & "Recording first published 1962" label text, without "Sold in UK ..."; all issues before 1967 have push-out centres)

FIRST PRESSING
Parlophone 45-R 4949   **Love Me Do/P.S. I Love You** (red label, 'Ringo on drums & no tambourine' version; with or without "Made In Great Britain" credit; in sleeve Type A, B, or C) 50
(note: the 1982 red label repressing of "Love Me Do" includes the word "mono" on the label)

1963
(with "The Parlophone Co. Ltd." in either upper-lower or upper case & "Recording first published 1963" label text, without "Sold in UK ...")

FIRST PRESSINGS
Parlophone 45-R 4983   **Please Please Me/Ask Me Why** (red label; with or without "Made In Great Britain" credit; in sleeve Type a, b or c) 60
Parlophone R 5015   **From Me To You/Thank You Girl** (in Type 1 sleeve) 10
Parlophone R 5055   **She Loves You/I'll Get You** (in Type 1 sleeve) 8
Parlophone R 5084   **I Want To Hold Your Hand/This Boy** (with "The Parlophone Co. Ltd" in upper-case only; in Type 1 sleeve) 8

KNOWN SECOND PRESSINGS
Parlophone R 4949   **Love Me Do/P.S. I Love You** (black label, with "The Parlophone Co. Ltd" in upper-lower case, matrix suffixed with '1N' indicating 'Ringo on drums & no tambourine' version) .. 80
Parlophone 45-R 4983   **Please Please Me/Ask Me Why** (black label, with "The Parlophone Co. Ltd" in upper-lower case, with "45" prefix) 15

KNOWN THIRD PRESSING
Parlophone R 4983   **Please Please Me/Ask Me Why** (black label, with "The Parlophone Co. Ltd" in upper-lower case, without "45" prefix) 18

1964
FIRST PRESSINGS
(with "The Parlophone Co. Ltd." in either upper-lower, or upper case, "Recording first published 1964" & "Sold in UK ..." label text)
Parlophone R 5114   **Can't Buy Me Love/You Can't Do That** (with "The Parlophone Co. Ltd" in upper case; in Type 1 sleeve) 8
Parlophone R 5160   **A Hard Day's Night/Things We Said Today** (Type 1b sleeve) 8
Parlophone R 5200   **I Feel Fine/She's A Woman** (with "The Parlophone Co. Ltd" in upper case; in Type 1b sleeve) 8

KNOWN THIRD PRESSING
Parlophone R 4949   **Love Me Do/P.S. I Love You** (black label, with "The Parlophone Co. Ltd" in upper case, matrix suffixed with '1N' indicating 'Ringo on drums & no tambourine' version) .. 70

KNOWN FOURTH PRESSING
Parlophone R 4983   **Please Please Me/Ask Me Why** (with "The Parlophone Co. Ltd" in upper case) 18

1965
FIRST PRESSINGS
(with "The Parlophone Co. Ltd." in upper case, Ⓟ & "Sold in UK ..." label text)
Parlophone DP 562   **If I Fell/Tell Me Why** (domestic pressing of export issue; in Type 1b sleeve) 45
Parlophone R 5265   **Ticket To Ride/Yes It Is** (in Type 2 sleeve) 10
Parlophone R 5305   **Help!/I'm Down** (in Type 2 sleeve) 12
Parlophone R 5389   **We Can Work It Out/Day Tripper** (in Type 3 sleeve) 15

KNOWN SECOND PRESSINGS
(with "The Gramophone Co. Ltd" in upper case, Ⓟ & "Sold in UK ..." label text)
Parlophone R 5305   **Help!/I'm Down** 10
Parlophone R 5389   **We Can Work It Out/Day Tripper** 10

1966
(with "The Gramophone Co. Ltd" in upper case, Ⓟ & "Sold in UK ..." label text)

FIRST PRESSINGS
Parlophone R 5452   **Paperback Writer/Rain** (in Type 4 or 5 sleeve) 15
Parlophone R 5493   **Yellow Submarine/Eleanor Rigby** (in Type 5 or 6 sleeve) 10

1967
(all the pressings listed below have push-out or solid centres, with "The Gramophone Co. Ltd" in upper case, Ⓟ & "Sold in UK ..." label text)

FIRST PRESSINGS
Parlophone R 5570   **Strawberry Fields Forever/Penny Lane** (250,000 only in p/s) 35
Parlophone R 5620   **All You Need Is Love/Baby You're A Rich Man** (with no reference to "Live World Television Transmission"; in Type 8 sleeve) 40
Parlophone R 5655   **Hello, Goodbye/I Am The Walrus** (company sleeve, with "7/- to 50/-" on back) 10

KNOWN SECOND PRESSINGS
Parlophone R 5452   **Paperback Writer/Rain** (solid centre only) 12
Parlophone R 5493   **Yellow Submarine/Eleanor Rigby** (solid centre only) 8
Parlophone R 5570   **Strawberry Fields Forever/Penny Lane** (in Type 5, 6 or 7 sleeve). 10
Parlophone R 5620   **All You Need Is Love/Baby You're A Rich Man** (with reference to "Live World Television Transmission"; most in Type 8 sleeve) 10
Parlophone R 5655   **Hello, Goodbye/I Am The Walrus** (with 'Made In France' credit) 25

1968
FIRST PRESSINGS
Parlophone R 5675   **Lady Madonna/The Inner Light** (with Fan Club insert; sl. with "7/- to 50/-" on back). 50
(all Apple pressings except for early issues of "Let It Be" have black, glossy "Apple" sleeves)
Apple R 5722   **Hey Jude/Revolution** 15

Sleeve Type A: (left) coloured wavy lines with small box on front and (right) large box on back.

Sleeve Type B: (left) coloured wavy lines without box on front and (right) with large box on back.

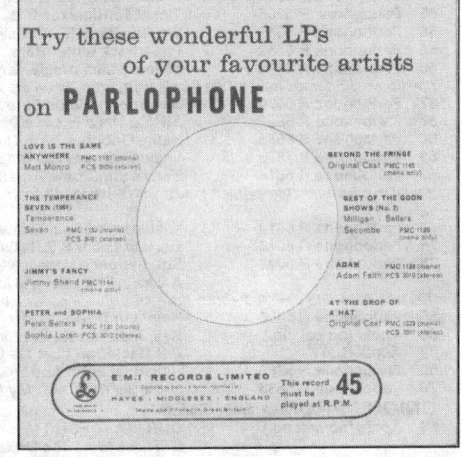

Sleeve Type C: (left) coloured shapes on front and (right) LP details on back.

KNOWN SECOND PRESSINGS

Parlophone R 5675	Lady Madonna/The Inner Light (no insert)	10
Parlophone R 5084	I Want To Hold Your Hand/This Boy (solid centre)	15
Apple R 5722	Hey Jude/Revolution (Philips pressing, with three-pronged push-out centre)	25

1969
FIRST PRESSINGS

Apple R 5777	Get Back/Don't Let Me Down (as "The Beatles with Billy Preston")	12
Apple R 5786	Ballad Of John And Yoko/Old Brown Shoe	12
Apple R 5814	Something/Come Together (without "Sold in UK..." label text)	18

KNOWN SECOND PRESSINGS
(without "Sold in UK ..." label text)

Apple R 5722	Hey Jude/Revolution	10
Apple R 5777	Get Back/Don't Let Me Down (as "The Beatles with Billy Preston")	8
Apple R 5786	Ballad Of John And Yoko/Old Brown Shoe	8

KNOWN THIRD PRESSING

Parlophone R 5305	Help!/I'm Down (with "The Parlophone Co. Ltd" label text)	12

1970
FIRST PRESSING

Apple R 5833	Let It Be/You Know My Name (Look Up The Number) (scratched-out B-side matrix: APPLES 1002, p/s)	20

KNOWN SECOND PRESSING

Apple R 5833	Let It Be/You Know My Name (Look Up The Number) (scratched-out B-side matrix: APPLES 1002)	8

KNOWN THIRD PRESSING

Apple R 5833	Let It Be/You Know My Name (Look Up The Number) (B-side matrix: 7YCE 21408)	6

(later 1970s copies with **EMI boxed logos** are of nominal value.
add £10 to the value for any singles with a red & white "Factory Sample Not For Sale" sticker)

EXPORT SINGLES

64	Parlophone DP 562	If I Fell/Tell Me Why (without "Sold in UK..." label text)	50
65	Parlophone DP 563	Yesterday/Dizzy Miss Lizzy	90
66	Parlophone DP 564	Michelle/Drive My Car	110
68	Parlophone DP 570	Hey Jude/Revolution (with or without Swedish p/s)	70/50
70	Parlophone P-R 5833	Let It Be/You Know My Name (Look Up The Number) (no p/s)	70

("Let It Be" was pressed with "Parlophone" label text on one side & "Gramophone" on the other)

70	Apple P-R 5833	Let It Be/You Know My Name (Look Up The Number) (no p/s)	120

FAN CLUB FLEXIDISCS

63	Lyntone LYN 492	The Beatles' Christmas Record (gatefold p/s)	80
64	Lyntone LYN 757	Another Beatles Christmas Record (p/s, with gatefold newsletter insert)	40
65	Lyntone LYN 948	The Beatles' Third Christmas Record (p/s, with gatefold newsletter insert)	45
66	Lyntone LYN 1145	Pantomime: Everywhere It's Christmas (p/s, with 7" x 7" newsletter insert)	60
67	Lyntone LYN 1360	Christmas Time (Is Here Again) (p/s, with 7" x 7" newsletter insert)	65
68	Lyntone LYN 1743/4	The Beatles' Sixth Christmas Record (p/s, some with 'Superpix' sales insert)	60/55
69	Lyntone LYN 1970/1-IL	The Beatles' Seventh Christmas Record (p/s, some with 2 x foolscap fan club newsletters)	60/50

(fan club flexidiscs are worth around £10 less without newsletters, and a third of the listed values without picture sleeves)

DEMO SINGLES

62	Parlophone 45-R 4949	Love Me Do/P.S. I Love You (McCartney misspelt "McArtney", 250 only)	1,200
63	Parlophone 45-R 4983	Please Please Me/Ask Me Why	700
63	Parlophone (45-)R 5015	From Me To You/Thank You Girl (with or without '45-' prefix)	each 500
63	Parlophone R 5055	She Loves You/I'll Get You	600
63	Parlophone R 5084	I Want To Hold Your Hand/This Boy	500
64	Parlophone R 5114	Can't Buy Me Love/You Can't Do That	500
64	Parlophone R 5160	A Hard Day's Night/Things We Said Today (red "A" on both sides)	500
64	Parlophone R 5200	I Feel Fine/She's A Woman	500
65	Parlophone R 5265	Ticket To Ride/Yes It Is	450
65	Parlophone R 5389	We Can Work It Out/Day Tripper (red "A" on both sides)	450
66	Parlophone R 5452	Paperback Writer/Rain	500
66	Parlophone R 5493	Yellow Submarine/Eleanor Rigby	600

(the above 12 demos have white labels with a red "A" on the A-side, unless otherwise stated)

67	Parlophone R 5570	Strawberry Fields Forever/Penny Lane (white "A" on both sides)	600
67	Parlophone R 5620	All You Need Is Love/Baby You're A Rich Man	400
67	Parlophone R 5655	Hello, Goodbye/I Am The Walrus	400
68	Parlophone R 5675	Lady Madonna/The Inner Light	400
69	Parlophone R 5814	Something/Come Together	700

(the above 5 demos have green labels with a white "A" on the A-side. Demos with centres missing are worth half the listed values)

76	Parlophone R 6013	Yesterday/I Should Have Known Better (green generic p/s)	30
76	Parlophone R 6016	Back In The U.S.S.R./Twist And Shout (green generic p/s)	30
78	Parlophone R 6022	Sgt. Pepper's Lonely Hearts Club Band/With A Little Help From My Friends/A Day In The Life (p/s)	30

(the last three demos listed above have silver/black paper labels with a silver "A")

65	Parlophone R 5305	Help!/I'm Down (existence unconfirmed)	
68	Apple (no cat. no.)	Hey Jude/Revolution (green & white Apple 'custom' label, handwritten details)	
69	Apple R 5777	Get Back/Don't Let Me Down (Apple 'custom' label, typed details)	650
69	Parlophone R 5786	Ballad Of John And Yoko/Old Brown Shoe (existence unconfirmed)	
70	Parlophone R 5833	Let It Be/You Know My Name (Look Up The Number) (existence unconfirmed)	

UNIQUE PROMO SINGLES

68	Apple (no cat. no.)	OUR FIRST FOUR (4 x 7" in presentation pack, including "Hey Jude" [R 5722] & "Those Were The Days" by Mary Hopkin [APPLE 2], "Sour Milk Sea" by Jackie Lomax [APPLE 3] & "Thingumybob" by Black Dyke Mills Band [APPLE 4]; each mounted in PVC pocket on printed dayglo card insert, in 10" x 12" card or plastic outer box)	1,000

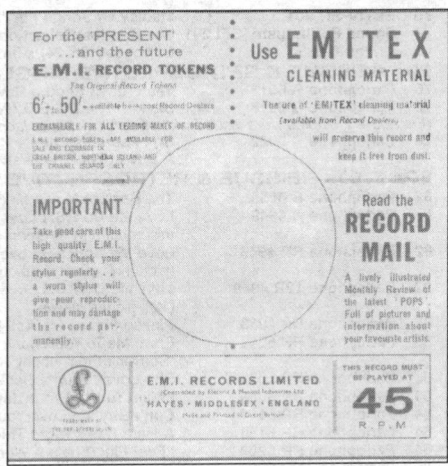

Green sleeve Type 1: (left) straight cut at top and (right) "6/- to 50/-" on back.

Green sleeve Type 1b: (left) wavy cut at top and (right) "6/- to 50/-" on back.

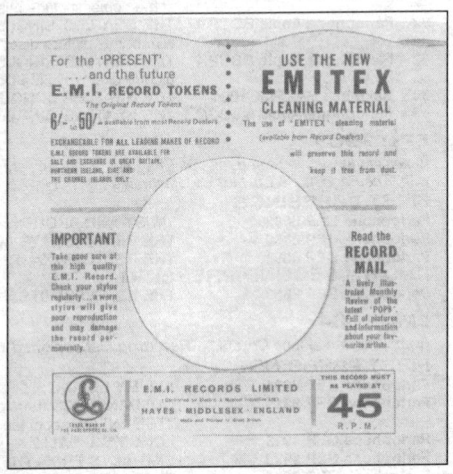

Green sleeve Type 2: (left) rectangular box on front and (right) "6/- to 50/-" on back.

BEATLES

MINT VALUE £

| 76 | EMI SPSR 401 | Medley Of Songs For "Rock'n'Roll Music" (excerpts) | 300 |
| 77 | Sound For Industry SFI 291 | The Beatles' Collection (Singles 1962-1970) (flexidisc "audition disc" sampler for box set [BS 24], with foldout p/s & "Dear Customer" letter) | 20 |

70s REISSUE & RETROSPECTIVE SINGLES, & PICTURE DISCS

| 76 | Parlophone R 6013 | Yesterday/I Should Have Known Better (p/s) | 5 |
| 76 | Parlophone R 6016 | Back In The U.S.S.R./Twist And Shout (black cross on reverse of p/s) | 5 |

(the above 2 singles were issued with silver/black paper labels & green generic picture sleeves)

| 78 | Parlophone R 6022 | Sgt. Pepper's Lonely Hearts Club Band/With A Little Help From My Friends/ A Day In The Life (p/s) | 5 |

80s & 90s REISSUE & RETROSPECTIVE SINGLES

82	Parlophone R 6055	The Beatles Movie Medley/I'm Happy Just To Dance With You (p/s)	6
82	Parlophone R 4949	Love Me Do/P.S. I Love You (p/s, red label reissue, with publishing miscredited to "Ardmore & Beechwood")	15
82	Parlophone RP 4949	Love Me Do/P.S. I Love You (picture disc, with/without publishing miscredit)	20/10
82	Parlophone 12R 4949	Love Me Do/P.S. I Love You/Love Me Do (Original Single Version) (12", picture sleeve)	12
83	Parlophone RP 4983	Please Please Me/Ask Me Why (picture disc)	10
83	Parlophone RP 5015	From Me To You/Thank You Girl (picture disc, some with "Souvenir From Abbey Road Studios" sticker on sleeve)	35/15
83	Parlophone RP 5055	She Loves You/I'll Get You (picture disc)	30
83	Parlophone RP 5084	I Want To Hold Your Hand/This Boy (picture disc)	10
84	Parlophone RP 5114	Can't Buy Me Love/You Can't Do That (picture disc)	10
84	Parlophone RP 5160	A Hard Day's Night/Things We Said Today (picture disc)	30
84	Parlophone RP 5200	I Feel Fine/She's A Woman (picture disc)	10
85	Parlophone RP 5265	Ticket To Ride/Yes It Is (picture disc)	10
85	Parlophone RP 5305	Help!/I'm Down (picture disc)	10
85	Parlophone RP 5389	We Can Work It Out/Day Tripper (picture disc)	10
86	Parlophone RP 5452	Paperback Writer/Rain (picture disc)	15
86	Parlophone RP 5493	Yellow Submarine/Eleanor Rigby (picture disc)	15
87	Parlophone RP 5570	Strawberry Fields Forever/Penny Lane (picture disc, later with slightly larger picture on disc)	each 15
87	Parlophone RP 5620	All You Need Is Love/Baby You're A Rich Man (picture disc)	10
87	Parlophone 12R 5620	All You Need Is Love/Baby You're A Rich Man (12", p/s)	10
87	Parlophone RP 5655	Hello, Goodbye/I Am The Walrus (picture disc)	10
88	Parlophone RP 5675	Lady Madonna/The Inner Light (picture disc, with "Past Masters" insert)	10
88	Apple RP 5722	Hey Jude/Revolution (picture disc, with "Apple" insert)	10
88	Apple 12R 5722	Hey Jude/Revolution (12", p/s)	12
88	Apple 12RP 5722	Hey Jude/Revolution (12", picture disc with "Apple" insert)	15
89	Apple RP 5777	Get Back/Don't Let Me Down (with Billy Preston, picture disc, with "20th Anniversary" insert)	10
89	Apple RP 5786	Ballad Of John And Yoko/Old Brown Shoe (picture disc, with "20th Anniversary" insert)	10
89	Apple RP 5814	Something/Come Together (picture disc, with "20th Anniversary" insert)	10
90	Apple RP 5833	Let It Be/You Know My Name (Look Up The Number) (picture disc, with "20th Anniversary" insert)	10

(all the picture discs listed above were issued in PVC sleeves)

SINGLES BOX SETS

76	Parlophone/Apple BS 24	THE BEATLES' SINGLES COLLECTION 1962-1970 (24 x 7", each in green p/s, green & white stickered box set)	35
76	Parlophone/Apple/ World Record Club	THE BEATLES' COLLECTION (24 x 7", mail-order black box set, later copies with "Sgt. Pepper's Lonely Hearts Club Band" [R 6022])	35
78	Parlophone/Apple BSC 1	THE BEATLES' SINGLES COLLECTION (26 x 7" blue box set, with insert; some copies include mispressing of "Get Back" [Apple R 5777])	35
82	Parlophone/Apple BSCP 1	THE BEATLES' SINGLES COLLECTION (27 x 7" blue box set, with bonus picture disc "Love Me Do" [RP 4949], export issue)	40
82	Parlophone/Apple BSCP 1	THE BEATLES' SINGLES COLLECTION (27 x 7" blue box set, with mispressed picture disc "Love Me Do"/"Love Me Do" [RP 4949], export issue)	40
89	Baktabak BAKPAK 1004	THE BEATLES CONQUER AMERICA (4 x 7" interview pack)	18
89	Parlophone/Apple CDBSC 1	THE BEATLES' SINGLES COLLECTION (22 x 3" CD single box set)	100

EPs: 1963

(unless otherwise indicated, all 60s EPs have push-out centres & laminated, flipback sleeves, with "The Parlophone Co. Ltd." & "Recording first published 1963" label text, but without "Sold in UK ...")

FIRST PRESSINGS

Parlophone GEP 8882	TWIST AND SHOUT	20
Parlophone GEP 8880	THE BEATLES' HITS (without "Recording first published 1963" label text)	22
Parlophone GEP 8883	THE BEATLES (No. 1)	20

KNOWN SECOND PRESSING

| Parlophone GEP 8880 | THE BEATLES' HITS | 18 |

EPs: 1964

(with "The Parlophone Co. Ltd.", "Recording first published 1964" & "Sold in UK ..." label text)

FIRST PRESSINGS

Parlophone GEP 8891	ALL MY LOVING	18
Parlophone GEP 8899	GOLDEN DISCS (unreleased, 2 x 1-sided test pressings [matrices: 7TCE-1N & 7TCE-1N] & 1 set of label proofs only; price does not include labels)	2,500
Parlophone GEP 8913	LONG TALL SALLY	18
Parlophone GEP 8920	EXTRACTS FROM THE FILM "A HARD DAY'S NIGHT"	20
Parlophone GEP 8924	EXTRACTS FROM THE ALBUM "A HARD DAY'S NIGHT"	35

KNOWN SECOND PRESSING

| Parlophone GEP 8882 | TWIST AND SHOUT | 18 |

Green sleeve Type 3: (left) wavy cut at top and (right) "Fran The Fan" advert on back .

Green sleeve Type 4: (left) wavy cut at top and (right) "Fran The Fan" advert on back.

 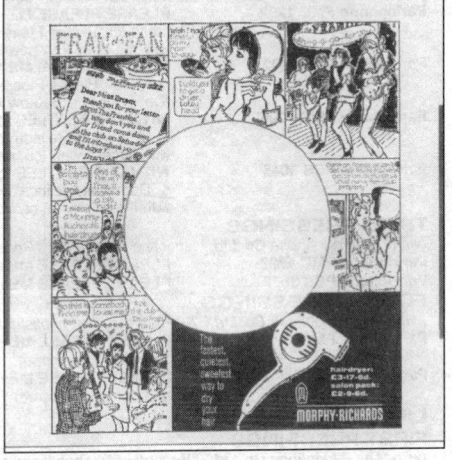

Green sleeve Type 5: (left) straight cut at top and (right) "Fran The Fan, Dear Miss Brown" ad. on back.

MINT VALUE £

EPs: 1965
(with "The Parlophone Co. Ltd.", ℗ *& "Sold in UK ..." label text)*

FIRST PRESSINGS
Parlophone GEP 8931	BEATLES FOR SALE	22
Parlophone GEP 8938	BEATLES FOR SALE (No. 2)	30

(with "The Gramophone Co. Ltd.", ℗ *& "Sold in UK ..." label text)*
Parlophone GEP 8946	THE BEATLES' MILLION SELLERS with "Golden Discs" label text)	22

KNOWN SECOND PRESSING
(with "The Gramophone Co. Ltd.", ℗ *& "Sold in UK ..." label text)*
Parlophone GEP 8883	THE BEATLES (No. 1)	18

KNOWN THIRD PRESSING
Parlophone GEP 8880	THE BEATLES' HITS	18
Parlophone GEP 8882	TWIST AND SHOUT	18

EPs: 1966
(with "The Gramophone Co. Ltd.", ℗ *& "Sold in UK ..." label text)*

FIRST PRESSINGS
Parlophone GEP 8948	YESTERDAY	40
Parlophone GEP 8952	NOWHERE MAN	60

KNOWN SECOND PRESSING
Parlophone GEP 8946	THE BEATLES' MILLION SELLERS (with "Million Sellers" label text)	25

EPs: 1967
(with "The Gramophone Co. Ltd." , ℗ *& "Sold in UK ..." label text)*

FIRST PRESSING
Parlophone MMT-1	MAGICAL MYSTERY TOUR (2-EP, gatefold sleeve, with booklet & blue lyric sheet; push-out or solid centre; mono)	25
Parlophone SMMT-1	MAGICAL MYSTERY TOUR (2-EP, gatefold sleeve, with booklet & blue lyric sheet; stereo)	30

KNOWN SECOND PRESSINGS
Parlophone GEP 8931	BEATLES FOR SALE (with "The Parlophone Co. Ltd" label text; solid centre)	20
Parlophone GEP 8952	NOWHERE MAN (solid centre)	45

(the above titles with "The Gramophone Co. Ltd." & ℗ *label text, but without "Sold in UK..." are 70s re-pressings, and are worth half the listed values. Later copies with "EMI" label text & varnished sleeves are worth approximately one-third the listed values)*

EPs: REISSUES & BOX SET
73	Parlophone SMMT-1	MAGICAL MYSTERY TOUR (2-EP, gatefold sleeve, with booklet & yellow lyric sheet)	12
81	Parlophone BEP 14	THE BEATLES EP COLLECTION (14-EP box set, with bonus stereo EP [SGE 1])	60

LPs: 1963
(with "The Parlophone Co. Ltd." label text but without "Sold in UK ...")

FIRST PRESSINGS
Parlophone PMC 1202	PLEASE PLEASE ME (black & gold label, with "Dick James Mus. Co." publishing credit for "Please Please Me", "I Saw Her Standing There", "Misery", "Do You Want To Know A Secret" & "There's A Place"; E. J. Day sleeve; mono)	350
Parlophone PCS 3042	PLEASE PLEASE ME (black & gold label, with "Dick James Mus. Co." publishing credit for "Please Please Me", "I Saw Her Standing There", "Misery", "Do You Want To Know A Secret" & "There's A Place"; E. J. Day sleeve; stereo)	1,750
Parlophone PMC 1206	WITH THE BEATLES (black & yellow label, with "Recording first published", & "Jobete" publishing credit for "Money"; G & L or E. J. Day sleeve, with large "mono" on front cover; mono)	45
Parlophone PCS 3045	WITH THE BEATLES (black & yellow label, with "Recording first published", & "Jobete" publishing credit for "Money"; G & L or E. J. Day sleeve, with large "stereo" on front cover; stereo)	90

(above pressings have polythene-lined, "Use Emitex" die-cut inner sleeves)

SECOND PRESSINGS
(with "The Parlophone Co. Ltd." label text but without "Sold in UK ...")
Parlophone PMC 1202	PLEASE PLEASE ME (black & gold label, with "Northern Songs" publishing credit for "Please Please Me", "I Saw Her Standing There", "Misery", "Do You Want To Know A Secret" & "There's A Place"; E. J. Day sleeve; mono)	350
Parlophone PCS 3042	PLEASE PLEASE ME (black & gold label, with "Northern Songs" publishing credit for "Please Please Me", "I Saw Her Standing There", "Misery", "Do You Want To Know A Secret" & "There's A Place"; E. J. Day sleeve; stereo)	1,750
Parlophone PMC 1206	WITH THE BEATLES (black & yellow label, with "Recording first published", & "Dominion, Belinda" publishing credit for "Money"; G & L or E. J. Day sleeve, with large "mono" on front cover; mono)	40
Parlophone PCS 3045	WITH THE BEATLES (black & yellow label, with "Recording first published", & "Dominion, Belinda" publishing credit for "Money"; G & L or E. J. Day sleeve, with large "stereo" on front cover; stereo)	75

THIRD PRESSINGS
(with "The Parlophone Co. Ltd." label text but without "Recording first published 1963" & "Sold in UK ...")
Parlophone PMC 1202	PLEASE PLEASE ME (with large "mono" on front cover; E. J. Day sleeve; mono)	100
Parlophone PCS 3042	PLEASE PLEASE ME (with large "stereo" on front cover; E. J. Day sleeve; stereo)	175

FOURTH PRESSINGS
(with "The Parlophone Co. Ltd." & "Recording first published 1963", label text but without "Sold in UK ...")
Parlophone PMC 1202	PLEASE PLEASE ME (G & L or E. J. Day sleeve, with large "mono" on front cover; mono)	40
Parlophone PCS 3042	PLEASE PLEASE ME (G & L or E. J. Day sleeve, with large "stereo" on front cover; stereo)	75

LPs: 1964

FIRST PRESSINGS
(with "The Parlophone Co. Ltd.", "Recording first published 1964" & "Sold in UK ..." label text)
Parlophone PMC 1230	A HARD DAY'S NIGHT (G & L or E. J. Day sleeve, mid-sized "mono" on front cover; mono)	40

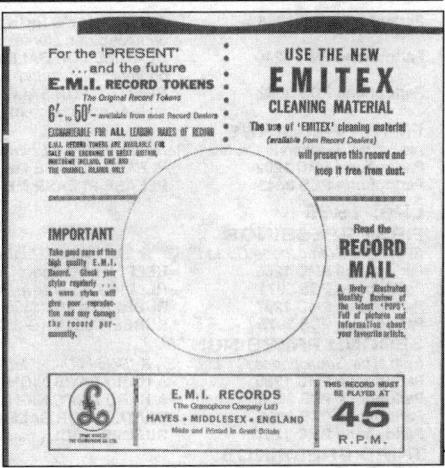

Green sleeve Type 6: (left) wavy cut, with rectangular box on front and (right) "6/- to 50/-" on back.

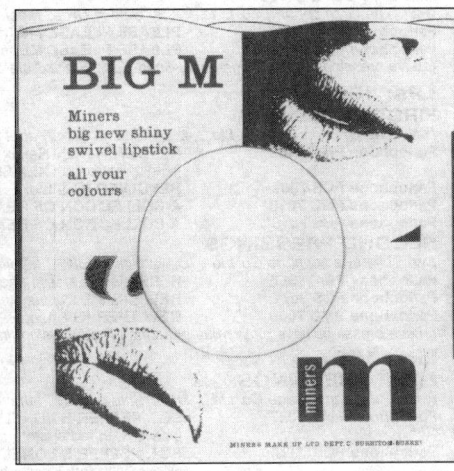

Green sleeve Type 7: (left) wavy cut at top and (right) "Big M" advert on back .

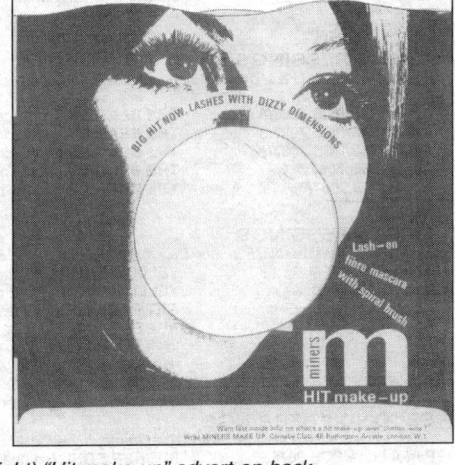

Green sleeve Type 8: (left) wavy cut at top and (right) "Hit make-up" advert on back.

MINT VALUE £

Parlophone PCS 3058	**A HARD DAY'S NIGHT** (G & L sleeve, mid-sized "stereo" on front cover; stereo)	80
Parlophone PMC 1240	**BEATLES FOR SALE** (G & L gatefold sleeve, with outline "mono" on front cover; mono)	40
Parlophone PCS 3062	**BEATLES FOR SALE** (G & L gatefold sleeve, with outline "stereo" on front cover; stereo)	60

FIFTH PRESSINGS
(with "The Parlophone Co. Ltd.", "Recording first published 1963" & "Sold in UK ..." label text)

Parlophone PMC 1202	**PLEASE PLEASE ME** (G & L sleeve, with large "mono" on front cover; mono)	30
Parlophone PCS 3042	**PLEASE PLEASE ME** (G & L sleeve, with large "stereo" on front cover; stereo)	60

LPs: 1965
FIRST PRESSINGS
(with "The Gramophone Co. Ltd.", Ⓟ, & "Sold in UK ..." label text)

Parlophone PMC 1255	**HELP!** (G & L sleeve, with "mono" in outline on front cover; mono)	40
Parlophone PCS 3071	**HELP!** (G & L sleeve, with "stereo" in outline on front cover; stereo)	50
Parlophone PMC 1267	**RUBBER SOUL** ('loud' cut matrix: [XEX 579-1], G & L or E. J. Day sleeve; mono)	60
Parlophone PCS 3075	**RUBBER SOUL** (G & L or E. J. Day sleeve; stereo)	75

SECOND PRESSINGS
(with "The Gramophone Co. Ltd.", Ⓟ, & "Sold in UK ..." label text)

Parlophone PMC 1230	**A HARD DAY'S NIGHT** (small "mono" on front cover; mono)	30
Parlophone PCS 3058	**A HARD DAY'S NIGHT** (small "stereo" on front cover; stereo)	40
Parlophone PCS 3062	**BEATLES FOR SALE** (outline "stereo" on front cover; gatefold sleeve; stereo)	40
Parlophone PMC 1267	**RUBBER SOUL** (matrix: [XEX 579-4 or 5]; mono)	45

THIRD PRESSINGS
(with "The Gramophone Co. Ltd.", Ⓟ, & "Sold in UK ..." label text)

Parlophone PCS 3045	**WITH THE BEATLES** (small "stereo"on front cover; stereo)	40

SIXTH PRESSINGS
(with "The Gramophone Co. Ltd.", Ⓟ, & "Sold in UK ..." label text)

Parlophone PMC 1202	**PLEASE PLEASE ME** (mono, with small "mono" on front cover)	30
Parlophone PCS 3042	**PLEASE PLEASE ME** (stereo, with small "stereo" on front cover)	40

(above pressings have tracing-paper-lined ,"Use Emitex" die-cut inner sleeves)

LPs: 1966
FIRST PRESSINGS
(with "The Gramophone Co. Ltd.", Ⓟ, & "Sold in UK ..." label text)

Parlophone PMC 7009	**REVOLVER** (with 'Remix 11' of **"Tomorrow Never Knows"** [side 2 matrix no.: **XEX 606-1**], G & L or E. J. Day sleeve; mono only)	175
Parlophone PCS 7009	**REVOLVER** (G & L or E. J. Day sleeve; stereo)	60
Parlophone PMC 7016	**A COLLECTION OF BEATLES OLDIES** (G & L or E. J. Day sleeve; mono)	40
Parlophone PCS 7016	**A COLLECTION OF BEATLES OLDIES** (G & L or E. J. Day sleeve; stereo)	50

SECOND PRESSINGS
(with "The Gramophone Co. Ltd.", Ⓟ, & "Sold in UK ..." label text)

Parlophone PMC 1255	**HELP!** (G & L sleeve; mono, with small solid black "mono" on front cover)	30
Parlophone PCS 3071	**HELP!** (G & L sleeve; stereo, with small solid black "stereo" on front cover)	45
Parlophone PMC 7009	**REVOLVER** (G & L or E. J. Day sleeve; mono)	60

(above pressings have plain white or sepia "LP advertising" inner sleeves)

LPs: 1967
FIRST PRESSINGS
(with "The Gramophone Co. Ltd.", Ⓟ, & "Sold in UK ..." label text)

Parlophone PMC 7027	**SGT. PEPPER'S LONELY HEARTS CLUB BAND** (G & L laminated gatefold sleeve, with red & white inner & cut-out insert; mono)	60
Parlophone PCS 7027	**SGT. PEPPER'S LONELY HEARTS CLUB BAND** (G & L laminated gatefold sleeve, with red & white inner & cut-out insert; stereo)	55

SECOND PRESSING

Parlophone PMC 7027	**SGT. PEPPER'S LONELY HEARTS CLUB BAND** (G & L laminated gatefold sleeve, with plain white inner & insert, Side 2 label omits "A Day In The Life" credit; mono only)	125

LPs: 1968
FIRST PRESSINGS
(with top-opening G & L gatefold sleeve, black inners, poster & 4 colour prints. Dark green label with Ⓟ & "Sold in UK ..." label text)

Apple PMC/PCS 7067/8	**THE BEATLES** (mono or stereo, numbered below 0000010)	5,000-8,000+
Apple PMC/PCS 7067/8	**THE BEATLES** (mono or stereo, numbered below 0001000)	1,000
Apple PMC/PCS 7067/8	**THE BEATLES** (mono or stereo, numbered below 0010000)	500
Apple PMC 7067/8	**THE BEATLES** (mono, numbered above 0010000)	200
Apple PCS 7067/8	**THE BEATLES** (stereo, numbered above 0010000)	120

1969
FIRST PRESSINGS
(with G & L sleeve & black inners. Dark green label with Ⓟ & "Sold in UK ..." text)

Apple PMC 7070	**YELLOW SUBMARINE** (with red lines above & below rear sleevenote; mono)	250
Apple PCS 7070	**YELLOW SUBMARINE** (with red lines above & below rear sleevenote; stereo)	75
Apple PCS 7080	**GET BACK** (LP, unreleased, acetates only)	
Apple PCS 7088	**ABBEY ROAD** (black or plain white inner sleeve, with Apple logo aligned to Side 1 track listing on rear sleeve; with or without "Her Majesty" credit on label)	25/30
Apple PCS 7088	**ABBEY ROAD** (black or plain white inner sleeve, Apple logo misaligned to Side 1 track listing on rear sleeve; with or without "Her Majesty" credit on label)	35/40

SECOND PRESSINGS
(with G & L sleeve. Label text with "The Gramophone Co. Ltd." & Ⓟ, but without "Sold in UK ...")

Parlophone PCS 3075	**RUBBER SOUL** (some with E. J. Day sleeve; stereo)	40
Parlophone PCS 7009	**REVOLVER** (stereo)	40
Parlophone PMC 7016	**A COLLECTION OF BEATLES OLDIES** (mono)	35

MINT VALUE £

Parlophone PCS 7016	A COLLECTION OF BEATLES OLDIES (stereo)	40
Parlophone PCS 7027	SGT. PEPPER'S LONELY HEARTS CLUB BAND (gatefold sleeve, with white inner & cut-out insert; stereo)	45

(above pressings have plain white or sepia "LP advertising" inner sleeves)
(with G & L sleeve, black inners. Label text with ℗ but without "Sold in UK ...")

Apple PCS 7067/8	THE BEATLES (top-opening, numbered g/fold sl., poster & 4 colour prints; stereo)	50
Apple PCS 7070	YELLOW SUBMARINE (with red lines above & below rear liner note; stereo)	45

THIRD PRESSINGS

(with G & L sleeve. Label text with "The Gramophone Co. Ltd." & ℗, but without "Sold in UK ...")

Parlophone PMC 1230	A HARD DAY'S NIGHT (small "mono" on front cover; mono)	35
Parlophone PCS 3058	A HARD DAY'S NIGHT (small "stereo" on front cover; stereo)	40
Parlophone PCS 3062	BEATLES FOR SALE (gatefold sleeve; stereo)	40
Parlophone PMC 1255	HELP! (small solid black "mono" on front cover; mono)	40
Parlophone PCS 3071	HELP! (small solid black "stereo" on front cover; stereo)	40
Parlophone PMC 1267	RUBBER SOUL (mono)	30
Parlophone PCS 7009	REVOLVER (mono)	35
Parlophone PMC 7027	SGT. PEPPER'S LONELY HEARTS CLUB BAND (laminated gatefold sleeve, & cut-out insert; mono)	35

(above pressings have plain white or sepia "LP advertising" inner sleeves)

FOURTH PRESSINGS

(with G & L sleeve. Label text with "The Gramophone Co. Ltd." & ℗, but without "Sold in UK ...")

Parlophone PCS 3045	WITH THE BEATLES (small "stereo" on front cover; stereo)	40

(above pressings have plain white or sepia "LP advertising" inner sleeves)

SEVENTH PRESSINGS

(with G & L sleeve & sepia "LP advertising" inner. Label has "The Gramophone Co. Ltd." & ℗, but no "Sold in UK ...")

Parlophone PMC 1202	PLEASE PLEASE ME (small "mono" on front cover; mono)	35
Parlophone PCS 3042	PLEASE PLEASE ME (small "stereo" on front cover; stereo)	40

*(Please Please Me, With The Beatles, A Hard Day's Night, Help!, Rubber Soul, Revolver, A Collection Of Beatles Oldies & Yellow Submarine have **flipback** sleeves. Beatles For Sale, Sgt. Pepper's Lonely Hearts Club Band & The Beatles have **visible** flaps inside the gatefold sleeves. Abbey Road has **internal** flaps)*

LPs: 1970

FIRST PRESSINGS

(with G & L sleeve & dark green label with ℗)

Apple PXS 1	LET IT BE (box set, red Apple logo on rear sleeve & white inner, with *Get Back* book housed in black card tray ['PXS 1' not listed on package])	225
Apple/Lyntone LYN 2154	FROM THEN TO YOU (THE BEATLES' CHRISTMAS ALBUM) (fan club issue, some with labels reversed)	260

SECOND PRESSING

Apple PCS 7096	LET IT BE (green Apple logo on rear sleeve, plain white inner)	15

EXPORT LPs: ORIGINALS

(with yellow/black labels, unless otherwise stated)

65	Parlophone CPCS 101	SOMETHING NEW (1st pressing, with "Parlophone Co. Ltd." label text)	700
65	Parlophone CPCS 101	SOMETHING NEW (2nd pressing, with "Gramophone Co. Ltd." label text)	600
66	Parlophone CPCS 103	THE BEATLES' SECOND ALBUM	600
66	Parlophone CPCS 104	BEATLES VI	650
68	Parlophone P-PCS 7067/8	THE BEATLES (2-LP, numbered, top opening 'mono' gatefold sleeve with "stereo" sticker & black inners, poster & 4 colour prints)	1,500
69	Odeon PPCS 7070	YELLOW SUBMARINE (Odeon sticker on rear of Apple sleeve)	2,000
69	Parlophone P-PCS 7088	ABBEY ROAD (Parlophone sticker on rear of Apple sleeve)	1,500
70	Parlophone P-PCS 7096	LET IT BE.	1,500
70	Parlophone CPCS 106	HEY JUDE (silver/black label, one EMI boxed logo, laminated sleeve)	600

EXPORT LPs: REISSUES

(with silver/black labels, unless otherwise stated.)

69	Parlophone CPCS 101	SOMETHING NEW (one EMI boxed logo)	300
69	Parlophone CPCS 103	THE BEATLES' SECOND ALBUM (one EMI boxed logo)	300
69	Parlophone CPCS 104	BEATLES VI (one EMI boxed logo)	300
69	Parlophone P-PCS 7088	ABBEY ROAD (Parlophone sticker on rear of Apple sleeve; one EMI boxed logo)	400
70	Parlophone P-PCS 7096	LET IT BE (one EMI boxed logo)	400
70	Parl./Apple (P-)PCS 7096	LET IT BE (2nd reissue, Apple label [PCS 7096] in Parlophone sleeve)	50
70	Parlophone CPCS 103	THE BEATLES' SECOND ALBUM (2nd reissue, two EMI boxed logos)	275
70s	Parl./Apple (P-)CPCS 106	HEY JUDE (Apple label [CPCS 106] in Parlophone sleeve [P-CPSC 106])	75
71	Apple CPCS 106	HEY JUDE (2nd reissue, dark green label)	65
73	Apple CPCS 106	HEY JUDE (3rd reissue, light green label)	40
78	Parlophone PCTC 255	MAGICAL MYSTERY TOUR (transparent yellow vinyl)	40
78	Apple PCS 7067/8	THE BEATLES (2-LP, white vinyl, gatefold sleeve)	60
78	Apple PCS 7088	ABBEY ROAD (green vinyl)	40
78	Apple PCS 7096	LET IT BE (white vinyl)	40

LPs: 1969 RE-PRESSINGS

*(with laminated flipback sleeves & silver/black labels with **one** boxed EMI logo)*

69	Parlophone PMC 1202	PLEASE PLEASE ME (mono)	25
69	Parlophone PCS 3042	PLEASE PLEASE ME (stereo)	18
69	Parlophone PCS 3045	WITH THE BEATLES (stereo only)	18
69	Parlophone PCS 3058	A HARD DAY'S NIGHT (stereo only)	18
69	Parlophone PCS 3062	BEATLES FOR SALE (gatefold sleeve, stereo only)	18
69	Parlophone PMC 1255	HELP! (mono)	25
69	Parlophone PCS 3071	HELP! (stereo)	18
69	Parlophone PCS 3075	RUBBER SOUL (stereo only)	18
69	Parlophone PCS 7009	REVOLVER (stereo only)	18
69	Parlophone PCS 7016	A COLLECTION OF BEATLES OLDIES (stereo only)	18
69	Parlophone PMC 7027	SGT. PEPPER'S LONELY HEARTS CLUB BAND (laminated gatefold sleeve, with cut-out insert, mono)	25

BEATLES

69	Parlophone PCS 7027	**SGT. PEPPER'S LONELY HEARTS CLUB BAND**	
		(laminated gatefold sleeve, with cut-out insert, stereo)	18

LPs: 1970s RE-PRESSINGS
*(with laminated non-flipback sleeves, with silver/black labels with **two** boxed EMI logos)*

73	Parlophone PCS 3042	**PLEASE PLEASE ME**	10
73	Parlophone PCS 3045	**WITH THE BEATLES**	10
73	Parlophone PCS 3058	**A HARD DAY'S NIGHT**	10
73	Parlophone PCS 3062	**BEATLES FOR SALE** (gatefold sleeve)	10
73	Parlophone PCS 3071	**HELP!**	10
73	Parlophone PCS 3075	**RUBBER SOUL**	10
73	Parlophone PCS 7009	**REVOLVER**	10
73	Parlophone PCS 7016	**A COLLECTION OF BEATLES OLDIES**	10
73	Parlophone PCS 7027	**SGT. PEPPER'S LONELY HEARTS CLUB BAND**	
		(gatefold sleeve with cut-out insert)	10
73	Apple PCS 7067/8	**THE BEATLES** (2-LP, un-numbered, laminated, side-opening gatefold sleeve, with poster & 4 soft card colour prints, stereo only)	18
73	Apple PCS 7070	**YELLOW SUBMARINE** (laminated non-flipback sleeve, stereo only)	10
79	Parlophone PHO 7027	**SGT. PEPPER'S LONELY HEARTS CLUB BAND** (picture disc, die-cut sleeve)	15

LPs: 1980s RE-PRESSINGS
(lightweight vinyl with yellow/black labels listing "mono", unless otherwise stated)

82	Parlophone PMC 1202	**PLEASE PLEASE ME** (mono)	12
82	Parlophone PMC 1206	**WITH THE BEATLES** (mono)	12
82	Parlophone PMC 1230	**A HARD DAY'S NIGHT** (mono)	12
82	Parlophone PMC 1240	**BEATLES FOR SALE** (gatefold sleeve, mono)	12
82	Parlophone PMC 1255	**HELP!** (mono)	12
82	Parlophone PMC 1267	**RUBBER SOUL** (mono)	12
82	Parlophone PMC 7009	**REVOLVER** (mono)	12
82	Parlophone PMC 7027	**SGT. PEPPER'S LONELY HEARTS CLUB BAND**	
		(gatefold sleeve with cut-out inserts, mono)	12
82	Apple PMC 7067/8	**THE BEATLES** (2-LP, un-numbered, side-opening gatefold sleeve, with poster & 4 prints, light green Apple label; mono)	18
82	Apple PMC 7070	**YELLOW SUBMARINE** (light green Apple label; mono)	12

LPs: RETROSPECTIVES

77	EMI EMTV 4	**THE BEATLES AT THE HOLLYWOOD BOWL** (gatefold sleeve with inner)	10
78	Apple PCSPR 717	**THE BEATLES 1962-1966** (2-LP, red vinyl, gatefold stickered sleeve with lyric inners; without sticker £12)	18
78	Apple PCSPB 718	**THE BEATLES 1967-1970** (2-LP, blue vinyl, gatefold stickered sleeve with lyric inners; without sticker £12)	18
79	Parlophone PCS 7184	**HEY JUDE** (black/silver label with two boxed EMI logos)	12
82	Parlophone EMTVS 34	**THE BEATLES' GREATEST HITS** (2-LP, unreleased)	

REEL-TO-REEL TAPES: ORIGINALS

63	Parlophone TA-PMC 1202	**PLEASE PLEASE ME** (mono only)	20
64	Parlophone TA-PMC 1206	**WITH THE BEATLES** (mono only)	20
64	Parlophone TA-PMC 1230	**A HARD DAY'S NIGHT** (mono only)	20
65	Parlophone TA-PMC 1240	**BEATLES FOR SALE** (mono only)	20
65	Parlophone TA-PMC 1255	**HELP!** (mono only)	20
66	Parlophone TA-PMC 1267	**RUBBER SOUL** (mono only)	25
66	Parlophone TA-PMC 7009	**REVOLVER** (mono only)	25
67	Parlophone TA-PMC 7016	**A COLLECTION OF BEATLES OLDIES** (mono only)	25
67	Parlophone TA-PMC 7027	**SGT. PEPPER'S LONELY HEARTS CLUB BAND** (mono only)	25

(issued on 4" spools with printed leaders, and housed in card trays in card boxes)

69	Apple DTA-PMC 7067/8	**THE BEATLES** (5" spool, mono)	80
69	Apple DTD-PCS 7067/8	**THE BEATLES** (5" spool, stereo)	80
70	Apple TA-PMC 7088	**ABBEY ROAD** (mono)	100
70	Apple TD-PCS 7088	**ABBEY ROAD** (stereo)	80
70	Apple TA-PMC 7096	**LET IT BE** (mono)	100
70	Apple TD-PCS 7096	**LET IT BE** (stereo)	80

(unless otherwise stated, the above issues were on 4" spools with printed leaders, and were housed in jewel cases with inlays)

REEL-TO-REEL TAPES: REISSUES
(issued on 4" spools with printed leaders, and housed in jewel cases with inlays)

68	Parlophone TA-PMC 1202	**PLEASE PLEASE ME** (mono)	30
68	Parlophone TD-PCS 3042	**PLEASE PLEASE ME** (stereo)	30
68	Parlophone TA-PMC 1206	**WITH THE BEATLES** (mono)	30
68	Parlophone TD-PCS 3045	**WITH THE BEATLES** (stereo)	30
68	Parlophone TA-PMC 1230	**A HARD DAY'S NIGHT** (mono)	30
68	Parlophone TD-PCS 3058	**A HARD DAY'S NIGHT** (stereo)	30
68	Parlophone TA-PMC 1240	**BEATLES FOR SALE** (mono)	30
68	Parlophone TD-PCS 3062	**BEATLES FOR SALE** (stereo)	30
68	Parlophone TA-PMC 1255	**HELP!** (mono)	30
68	Parlophone TD-PCS 3071	**HELP!** (stereo)	30
68	Parlophone TA-PMC 1267	**RUBBER SOUL** (mono)	35
68	Parlophone TD-PCS 3075	**RUBBER SOUL** (stereo)	35
68	Parlophone TA-PMC 7009	**REVOLVER** (mono)	35
68	Parlophone TD-PCS 7009	**REVOLVER** (stereo)	35
68	Parlophone TA-PMC 7016	**A COLLECTION OF BEATLES OLDIES** (mono)	35
68	Parlophone TD-PCS 7016	**A COLLECTION OF BEATLES OLDIES** (stereo)	35
68	Parlophone TA-PMC 7027	**SGT. PEPPER'S LONELY HEARTS CLUB BAND** (mono)	35
68	Parlophone TD-PCS 7027	**SGT. PEPPER'S LONELY HEARTS CLUB BAND** (stereo)	35

CASSETTES

68	Parlophone TC-PMC 7027	**SGT. PEPPER'S LONELY HEARTS CLUB BAND** (mono, yellow paper labels)	35
73	Parlophone TC-PCS 3077	**MAGICAL MYSTERY TOUR** (with 'gold band' inlay & "Baby You're A Rich Man" in 'true' stereo)	20
84	St Michael 1361/5701	**THEIR GREATEST HITS** (12" box set, with 64-page book, some shrinkwrapped)	45
86	EMI SMMC 151	**ONLY THE BEATLES** (promotional cassette available via Heineken offer, withdrawn)	15

8-TRACK CARTRIDGES

70	Apple 8X-CPCS 106	HEY JUDE (export only)	30
73	Parlophone 8X PCS 3077	MAGICAL MYSTERY TOUR (jewel case with 'gold band' inlay, with "Baby You're A Rich Man" in 'true' stereo)	25

ALBUM BOX SETS

78	Parlophone BC 13	THE BEATLES COLLECTION (13 x LP, stereo, some with poster)	100
80	WRC SM 701/708	THE BEATLES' BOX (8 x LP, mail-order only)	25
82	Parlophone BMC 10	THE BEATLES MONO COLLECTION (10 x LP, red box)	300

CD ALBUMS & BOX SETS

87	HMV BEACD 25/1	PLEASE PLEASE ME/WITH THE BEATLES/A HARD DAY'S NIGHT/ BEATLES FOR SALE (4 x CD, numbered 12" black box set with "Book Of Beatles Lists" paperback book)	60
87	HMV BEACD 25/2	HELP!/RUBBER SOUL/REVOLVER (3 x CD, numbered 12" red box set with insert & reprint of Beatles Book Monthly, issue 12)	40
87	HMV BEACD 25/3	SGT. PEPPER'S LONELY HEARTS CLUB BAND (CD, numbered 12" box set with booklet, cut-outs & badge)	20
87	HMV BEACD 25/4	THE BEATLES (2-CD, numbered 12" box set with booklet & badge)	25
87	HMV BEACD 25/5	YELLOW SUBMARINE (CD, numbered 12" box set with insert, cut-outs & badge)	30
87	HMV BEACD 25/6	MAGICAL MYSTERY TOUR (CD, numbered 12" box set with booklet, poster & badge)	30
87	HMV BEACD 25/7	ABBEY ROAD (CD, numbered 12" box set with 2 posters, booklet & badge)	15
87	HMV BEACD 25/8	LET IT BE (CD, numbered 12" box set with booklet & badge)	15
88	HMV BEACD 25/9	PAST MASTERS VOL. 1 (CD, numbered 12" box set with booklet & badge)	15
88	HMV BEACD 25/10	PAST MASTERS VOL. 2 (CD, numbered 12" box set with booklet & badge)	15

POLYDOR RECORDINGS

SINGLES

(with push-out centres & orange labels, unless otherwise stated)

62	Polydor NH 66833	My Bonnie/The Saints (When The Saints Go Marching In) (as Tony Sheridan & The Beatles; 1st pressing, 'broad' title & "Made In England" label text)	50
63	Polydor NH 66833	My Bonnie/The Saints (When The Saints Go Marching In) (as Tony Sheridan & The Beatles; 2nd pressing, push-out or solid centre, 'narrow' title & "Made In England" label text)	45
64	Polydor NH 52906	Sweet Georgia Brown/Nobody's Child (German import only, unissued in U.K.)	
64	Polydor NH 52275	Cry For A Shadow (A-side credited to 'Beatles')/TONY SHERIDAN & BEATLES: Why (Can't You Love Me Again) ('scroll' label, with "Made In England" text	40
64	Polydor NH 52317	Ain't She Sweet (A-side as 'Beatles', vocal: John Lennon')/If You Love Me, Baby (B-side credited to 'Beatles with Tony Sheridan, vocal'; 1st pressing, 'scroll' label with "Made In England" text)	40
64	Polydor NH 52317	Ain't She Sweet/If You Love Me, Baby (2nd pressing, red label, with "Made In England" text)	15

EPs

64	Polydor EPH 21 610	TONY SHERIDAN WITH THE BEATLES (1st pressing, German import in U.K. p/s, orange 'scroll' label; "Why" songwriting credit as 'Sheridan' or 'Sheridan-Crompton')	40
64	Polydor EPH 21 610	TONY SHERIDAN WITH THE BEATLES (2nd pressing, German import in U.K. p/s, red label; "Why" songwriting credit as 'Sheridan' or 'Sheridan-Crompton')	25

LPs

64	Polydor Hi-Fi 46 432	THE BEATLES' FIRST (purple/black sleeve, Germany only, unissued in U.K.)	
67	Polydor Special 236 201	THE BEATLES' FIRST (as Tony Sheridan & The Beatles, 1st pressing, without 'stereo' on label or sleeve, 'pop art' sleeve)	60
67	Polydor Special 236 201	THE BEATLES' FIRST (later pressings with 'stereo' on label & sleeve, minor label variations, 'pop art' sleeve)	40
71	Contour 2870 111	THE EARLY YEARS (as Beatles featuring Tony Sheridan, reissue of "The Beatles' First", 'cobblestone' sleeve)	10
82	Charly CFM 701	THE SAVAGE YOUNG BEATLES (10")	12
83	Phoenix PXS 339P	FIRST MOVEMENT (picture disc)	10

(see also John Lennon, Paul McCartney/Wings, George Harrison, Ringo Starr, Pete Best Four, Quarry Men, Tony Sheridan, George Martin, Billy Preston, Yoko Ono)

BEATMEN

64	Pye 7N 15659	You Can't Sit Down/Come On Pretty Baby	12
65	Pye 7N 15792	Now The Sun Has Gone/Please Believe	8

BEAT MERCHANTS

64	Columbia DB 7367	Pretty Face/Messin' With The Man	40
65	Columbia DB 7492	So Fine/She Said Yeah	40

BEAT SIX

64	Decca F 12011	Bernadine/The River And I	10

(see also Guys)

BEATSTALKERS

65	Decca F 12259	Ev'rybody's Talking 'Bout My Baby/Mr. Disappointed	12
66	Decca F 12352	Left Right Left/You'd Better Get A Better Hold On	15
66	Decca F 12460	A Love Like Yours/Base Line	18
67	CBS 2732	My One Chance To Make It/Ain't No Soul (Left In These Old Shoes)	20
67	CBS 3105	Silver Treetop School For Boys/Sugar Coated Man	30
68	CBS 3557	Rain Coloured Roses/Everything Is For You	25
69	CBS 3936	When I'm Five/Little Boy	30

PAUL BEATTIE

57	Parlophone R 4385	I'm Comin' Home/Nothing So Strange	6
58	Parlophone R 4429	Me, Please Me/Wanderlust	5
58	Parlophone R 4429	Me, Please Me/Wanderlust (78)	10
58	Parlophone R 4468	A House, A Car, And A Wedding Ring/Banana	5
58	Parlophone R 4468	A House, A Car, And A Wedding Ring/Banana (78)	10

E.C. BEATTY
59	Felsted AF 127	Ski King/I'm A Lucky Man	12
59	Felsted AF 127	Ski King/I'm A Lucky Man (78)	30

BEAU
69	Dandelion S 4403	1917 Revolution/Sleeping Town	5
69	Dandelion S 63751	BEAU (LP)	20
71	Dandelion DAN 8006	CREATION (LP, with The Way We Live)	20

(see also Way We Live)

BEAU BRUMMEL
82	Moonlight MNS 004	Hot George/Oscar (p/s)	6

(see also Paul Roland, Weird Strings)

BEAU BRUMMELS
65	Pye International 7N 25293	Laugh, Laugh/Still In Love With You Baby	10
65	Pye International 7N 25306	Just A Little/They'll Make You Cry	10
65	Pye International 7N 25318	You Tell Me Why/I Want You	10
65	Pye International 7N 25333	Don't Talk To Strangers/In Good Time	10
66	Pye International 7N 25342	Good Time Music/Sad Little Girl (unissued)	
65	Pye International NPL 28062	INTRODUCING THE BEAU BRUMMELS (LP, mono only)	40

BEAU-MARKS
60	Top Rank JAR 377	Clap Your Hands/Daddy Said	15

(see also Del-Tones, Milton De Lugg Orchestra)

JIMMY BEAUMONT
66	London HLZ 10059	You Got Too Much Going For You/I Never Loved Her Anyway	40

BEAUMONT & HANNANT
93	GPR GENP(X) 14	TASTES AND TEXTURES VOLUME 1 EP (12", p/s)	8
93	GPR GPRLP 2	BASIC DATA MANIPULATION: TASTES & TEXTURES VOL. 2 (12" EP, double pack)	10
93	GPR GENP(X) 21	TASTES AND TEXTURES VOL. 3 (12" EP, p/s)	8
94	GPR GENP(X) 33	ORMEAU EP (12", custom sleeve)	8
94	GPR GENP(R) 33	ORMEAU EP (with Joseph Johnson) (12", custom sleeve)	8
94	GPR GENP(CD) 33	ORMEAU EP (with Lisa Husik) (CD)	8
95	GPR GENP(X) 37	PSI - ONYX EP (12", double pack, custom sleeve)	8
95	GPR GENP(CD) 37	PSI - ONYX CONCEPT EP (CD)	8
95	GPR GENP(X) 39	NOTIONS OF TONALITY VOL. 1 (12" EP, custom sleeve)	8
95	GPR GENP(R) 39	NOTIONS OF TONALITY VOL. 1 (12" EP, custom sleeve)	8
95	GPR GENP(CD) 39	NOTIONS OF TONALITY VOL. 1 (CD EP, compilation of above 12"s)	8
96	GPR GENP(X) 40	NOTIONS OF TONALITY VOL. 2 (12" EP, custom sleeve)	8
96	GRP GENP(R) 40	NOTIONS OF TONALITY VOL. 2 (12" EP, custom sleeve)	8
96	GPR GENP(CD) 40	NOTIONS OF TONALITY VOL. 2 (CD EP, compilation of above 12"s)	8

BEAUTIFUL SOUTH
89	Go! Discs GOD 32	Song For Whoever/Straight In At 37	5
89	Go! Discs GODP 32	Song For Whoever/Straight In At 37 (envelope pack, with 5 cards and sticker)	8
89	Go! Discs GODX 32	Song For Whoever/Straight In At 37/You And Your Big Ideas (12", p/s)	8
89	Go! Discs GODXCD 32	Song For Whoever/Straight In At 37/You And Your Big Ideas (CD)	10
89	Go! Discs GOD 35	You Keep It All In/I Love You (But You're Boring) (no p/s)	8
89	Go! Discs GOD 35	You Keep It All In/I Love You (But You're Boring) (p/s)	4
89	Go! Discs GODS 35	You Keep It All In/I Love You (But You're Boring) (p/s with poster)	5
89	Go! Discs GODX 35	You Keep It All In/You Just Can't Smile It Away/I Love You (But You're Boring)/It's Instrumental (12", p/s)	8
89	Go! Discs GODCD 35	You Keep It All In/You Just Can't Smile It Away/I Love You (But You're Boring)/It's Instrumental (CD)	8
89	Go! Discs GODP 38	I'll Sail This Ship Alone/But 'til Then (envelope pack with 4 postcards)	8
89	Go! Discs GODW 38	I'll Sail This Ship Alone/But 'til Then/I'll Sail This Ship Alone (orchestral mix) (10", white vinyl)	8
89	Go! Discs GODCD 38	I'll Sail This Ship Alone/But 'til Then/I'll Sail This Ship Alone (orchestral mix) (CD)	8
90	Go! Discs GODP 47	A Little Time/In Other Words I Hate You (numbered pack with 2 postcards & badge)	6
90	Go! Discs GODCD 47	A Little Time/In Other Words I Hate You/What You See Is What You Get (CD)	8
90	Go! Discs GODP 48	My Book/Big Beautiful South (no'd pack with postcards & badge)	6
90	Go! Discs GOCD 48	My Book/Big Beautiful South/Bigger Doesn't Mean Better/Speak To Me (CD)	8
91	Go! Discs GODP 53	Let Love Speak Up Itself/Danielle Steele (The Enemy Within) (numbered pack with postcards & badge)	6
91	Go! Discs GODCD 66	Old Red Eyes Is Back/Fleet St. B.C./Diamonds (CD)	8
92	Go! Discs GOD 78	Bell Bottomed Tear/A Thousand Lies/They Used To Wear Black (p/s, with postcards)	5
99	Mercury 562 1662	The Table/Don't Marry Her, Fuck Me (acoustic)/Look What I Found In My Beer (acoustic) (CD, promo, digipak)	8
89	Go! Discs FGOLP 16	WELCOME TO THE BEAUTIFUL SOUTH (LP, 'furry rabbit' sleeve)	15
89	Go! Discs FGOCD 16	WELCOME TO THE BEAUTIFUL SOUTH (CD, 'furry rabbit' sleeve)	18
94	Go! Discs 828 569 1	CARRY ON UP THE CHARTS: THE BEST OF THE BEAUTIFUL SOUTH (2-LP, limited edition with 'B-sides')	15
94	Go! Discs 828 569 2	CARRY ON UP THE CHARTS: THE BEST OF THE BEAUTIFUL SOUTH (2-CD, limited edition with 'B-sides')	18

(see also Housemartins)

BEAVER & KRAUSE
72	Warner Bros K 46130	GANDHARVA (LP)	15
72	Warner Bros K 46184	ALL GOOD MEN (LP)	15

BEAVERS
58	Capitol CL 14909	Road To Happiness/Low As I Can Be	6

JACKIE BEAVERS
75	Buddah BDS 423	Mr Bump Man/Somebody Help The Bigger Man	6
76	Jay Boy BOY 102	Trying To Get Back To You Girl/Trying To Get Back To You Girl (Version)	6

BEAZERS
64	Decca F 11827	The Blue Beat/I Wanna Shout	20

(see also Chris Farlowe, Little Joe Cook)

BE-BOP DELUXE
73	Smile LAFS 001	Teenage Archangel/Jets At Dawn (mono, 1,000 only)	25
74	Harvest HAR 5081	Jet Silver (And The Dolls Of Venus)/Third Floor Heaven	8
75	Harvest HAR 5091	Between The Worlds/Lights (withdrawn)	40
75	Harvest HAR 5098	Maid In Heaven/Lights	5
76	Harvest HAR 5110	Kiss Of The Light/FUNKY PHASER & HIS UNEARTHLY MERCHANDISE: Shine	5
77	Harvest HAR 5135	Japan/Futuristic Manifesto	5
78	Harvest HAR 5147	Panic In The World/Blue As A Jewel	5
78	Harvest HAR 5158	Electrical Language/Surreal Estate (p/s)	5
77	Harvest SHVL 816	LIVE! IN THE AIR AGE (LP, with bonus EP "Live! In The Air Age" [PSR 412])	12

(see also Bill Nelson)

BE-BOP PRESERVATION SOCIETY
71	Dawn DNLS 3027	THE BE-BOP PRESERVATION SOCIETY (LP, gatefold sleeve with insert)	30

GILBERT BECAUD
59	HMV POP 574	The Day The Rains Came/Les Marches De Provence	6
59	HMV POP 574	The Day The Rains Came/Les Marches De Provence (78)	10

SIDNEY BECHET
50	Esquire 10-76	Who/September Song (78)	8
51	Decca C 16169	King Porter Stomp/DUTCH SWING COLLEGE: Dutch Swing College Blues (78, export issue)	8
54	Vogue V 2246	Joshua Fit De Battle Of Jericho/Tailgate Ramble (78)	8
58	Vogue V 2394	Theme From The "Threepenny Opera"/Army Song	5
59	Vogue V 9141	Petit Fleur/Dans La Rue D'Antibes	7
59	Vogue V 9141	Petit Fleur/Dans La Rue D'Antibes (78)	20
59	Vogue V 9157	Le Marchand de Poissons/Si Tu Vois Ma Mere	5
59	Vogue V 9157	Le Marchand de Poissons/Si Tu Vois Ma Mere (78)	12
60	Philips JAZ 110	My Woman's Blues/What A Dream (p/s)	5
55	Melodisc EPM 7-51	SIDNEY BECHET WITH HUMPHREY LYTTELTON'S BAND (EP)	20
55	Melodisc EPM 7-62	BECHET/SPANIER BIG FOUR (EP, with Mugsy Spanier)	8
56	Melodisc EPM 7-68	BECHET-SPANIER IN NEW YORK, BECHET-LYTTELTON IN LONDON (EP)	8
56	Melodisc EPM 7-79	IN MERENGUE MOOD (EP)	7
64	Melodisc MLP 12-148	REQUIEM A BECHET (LP)	25

(see also Humphrey Lyttelton, Mezz Mezzrow)

SIDNEY BECHET & CLAUDE LUTER
51	Vogue V 2005	Temptation Rag/Riverboat Shuffle (78)	8
51	Vogue V 2014	Careless Love/Down Home Rag (78)	8
51	Vogue V 2027	Maryland, My Maryland/Lastic (78)	8

BECK
94	Geffen GFS 67	Loser/Alcohol/Fume (p/s)	12
94	Geffen GFSJB 67	Loser/Loser (jukebox issue, no p/s)	12
94	Geffen GFSTD 67	Loser/Totally Confused/Corvette Bummer/MTV Makes Me Want To Smoke Crack (Lounge Act Version) (CD)	15
94	Geffen GFS 74	Pay No Mind (Snoozer)/Special People (unreleased)	
94	Geffen GFSC 74	Pay No Mind (Snoozer)/Special People (cassette, unreleased)	
94	Geffen GFST 74	Pay No Mind (Snoozer)/Special People/Trouble All My Days/ Super Golden (Sunchild) (12", p/s, withdrawn)	20
94	Geffen GFST 74	Pay No Mind (Snoozer)/Special People/Trouble All My Days/ Super Golden (Sunchild) (CD, withdrawn)	10
96	Geffen GFS 22183	Devil's Haircut/Lloyd Price Express (p/s)	7
96	Geffen GFS 22205	The New Pollution/Electric Music And The Summer People (p/s)	7
97	Geffen GFS 22253	Sissyneck/Feather In Your Cap (p/s)	7
96	Geffen GED 24908	ODELAY (CD, with bonus track "Diskobox" & unlisted track "Clock")	15

GORDON BECK (QUARTET)
68	Morgan MJ 1	GYROSCOPE (LP)	300
69	M. Minor MMLP/SMLP 21	EXPERIMENTS WITH POPS (LP, as Gordon Beck Quartet)	20
69	M. Minor MMLP/SMLP 22	HALF A JAZZ SIXPENCE (LP)	70
69	Major Minor SMLP 88	DR. DOOLITTLE LOVES JAZZ (LP)	45
72	Dire FO 341	BECK-MATTHEWSON-HUMAIR TRIO (LP)	25

(see also Seven Ages Of Man)

JEFF BECK
67	Columbia DB 8151	Hi-Ho Silver Lining/Beck's Bolero	10
67	Columbia DB 8227	Tallyman/Rock My Plimsoul	10
68	Columbia DB 8359	Love Is Blue (L'Amour Est Bleu)/I've Been Drinking	8
69	Columbia DB 8590	Plinth (Water Down The Drain)/Hangman's Knee (unissued)	
72	Epic EPC 7720	Got The Feeling/Situation	7
75	Epic EPC 3334	She's A Woman/It Doesn't Really Matter	10
80	Epic EPC 8806	The Final Peace/Space Boogie	7
80	Epic EPCA 1009	The Final Peace/Scatter Brain/Too Much To Lose/Led Boots (12", p/s)	10
82	Rak RRP 3	Hi Ho Silver Lining/Beck's Bolero/Rock My Plimsoul (picture disc)	6
85	Epic EPCA 6387	People Get Ready/Back On The Street (p/s)	5
85	Epic TA 6387	People Get Ready/Back On The Street/You Know, We Know (12", p/s)	8
85	Epic EPCA 6981	Ambitious/Escape (p/s)	5
85	Epic TA 6981	Ambitious/Escape (12", p/s)	8
86	Epic EPCA 7271	Wild Thing/Gets Us All In The End (p/s)	5
86	Epic TA 7271	Wild Thing/Nighthawks/Gets Us All In The End (12", p/s)	8
86	Epic EPCA 6587	Stop, Look And Listen/You Know We Know (p/s)	5
86	Epic TA 6587	Stop, Look And Listen/You Know We Know/Stop, Look And Listen (Remix) (12", p/s)	8
89	Epic BECK 1	Day In The House/People Get Ready (p/s)	5
89	Epic BECK 1T	Day In The House/Guitar Shop (Special Mix)/Cause We've Ended As Lovers (12", p/s)	8

Jeff BECK

89	Epic BECK 1CD	Day In The House/People Get Ready/Cause We've Ended As Lovers/ Blue Wind (CD)........8
68	Columbia S(C)X 6293	TRUTH (LP, 1st pressing, blue/black labels, mono/stereo)............40/30
69	Columbia S(C)X 6351	BECK-OLA (LP, 1st pressing, blue/black labels, mono/stereo)............25/20
69	Columbia SCX 6293	TRUTH (LP, 2nd pressing, silver/black labels, mono/stereo)............12
69	Columbia SCX 6351	BECK-OLA (LP, 2nd pressing, silver/black labels, mono/stereo)............12
72	Epic EPC 64619	ROUGH AND READY (LP, yellow label)............15
72	Epic EPC 64899	JEFF BECK GROUP (LP, yellow label)............18
72	Epic EQ 30973	ROUGH AND READY (LP, quadrophonic)............20
74	CBS EQ 31331	JEFF BECK GROUP (LP, quadrophonic)............22

(see also Yardbirds, Beck Bogert Appice, Donovan, Rod Stewart, Cozy Powell, Honeydrippers)

BECK, BOGERT & APPICE
73	Epic S EPC 1251	Black Cat Moan/Livin' Alone............6
73	CBS EPC 22001	BECK, BOGERT & APPICE (LP)............6
75	CBS EQ 32140/Q 65455	BECK, BOGERT & APPICE (LP, quadrophonic)............18

(see also Jeff Beck, Vanilla Fudge, Cactus)

BECKETT
| 74 | Raft/Lyntone LYN 2842 | My Lady (clear flexidisc, given away at gigs)............5 |
| 74 | Raft RA 48502 | BECKETT (LP, with lyric insert)............10 |

(see also Back Street Crawler, Crawler)

HAROLD BECKETT
71	Philips 6308 026	FLARE UP (LP)............100
72	RCA SF 8225	WARM SMILES (LP)............60
73	RCA SF 8264	THEME FOR FEGA (LP)............22
75	Cadillac SGC 1004	JOY UNLIMITED (LP)............25
76	Ogun OG 800	MEMORIES OF BACARES (LP)............12

(see also Graham Collier, Galliard, Ninesense)

STUART BECKETT
| 60s | Sherwood SRS 1001 | Kariline/Breakthrough............25 |

JENNY BECKETT
| 65 | Parlophone R 5373 | My Love And I/Lock Away Your Love............6 |

LYN BECKFORD
68	Island WI 3144	Combination/Hey Little Girl............15
69	Jackpot JP 707	Kiss Me Quick/MRS. MILLER: Feel It............6
69	Big Shot BI 521	Suzie Wong (as K. Beckford)/SWINGING KINGS: Deebo............5
71	G.G. GG 4514	Groove Me/Groove Version (as Keeling Beckford)............5

THEO(PHILUS) BECKFORD
61	Blue Beat BB 33	Jack And Jill Shiffle/Little Lady (as Theophilus Beckford & Clue J. & His Blues Blasters)............12
61	Blue Beat BB 50	Georgie And The Old Shoe/That's Me (as Theo Beckford & City Slickers)............12
62	Blue Beat BB 87	Walking Down King Street/The Clock (B-side actually by Sir D's Group)............12
62	Blue Beat BB 132	Bringing In The Sheep (song actually "Bringing In The Sheaves")/Run Away....12
62	Island WI 026	I Don't Want You (actually by King Edward's All Stars)/Seven Long Years............15
63	Island WI 106	Daphney/Boller Man............15
64	Blue Beat BB 250	She's Gone/Old Flame (as Cotheo Beckford, B-side act. by Frederick Hibbert)..15
64	Blue Beat BB 257	Don't Worry To Cry/Love Me Or Leave Me (as Theophilus Beckford, B-side actually by Lloyd Clarke)............15
64	Blue Beat BB 287	On Your Knees/Now You're Gone (with Yvonne Harrison)............12
65	Blue Beat BB 303	Dig The Dig (as Basil Gabbidon)/Don't Let Me Cry No More............12
65	Black Swan WI 452	Take Your Time/STRANGER COLE: Happy-Go-Lucky............15
65	Island WI 238	Trench Town People/PIONEERS: Sometime............15
65	Island WI 243	You Are The One Girl/Grudgeful People............12
65	Island WI 246	If Life Was A Thing/L. CLARKE: Parro Saw The Light (B-side actually "Pharaoh Saw The Light" by Lloyd Clarke)............12
65	Island WI 248	What A Whoe/Bajan Girl............12
68	Nu Beat NB 009	Easy Snappin'/ERIC MORRIS: My Lonely Days............8
69	Crab CRAB 25	Brother Ram Goat (as T. Beckford)/STARLIGHTS: What A Condition............12

(see also Eric Barnet[t], Maytels, Clue J & His Bluesblasters)

BOB BECKHAM
59	Brunswick 05808	Just As Much As Ever/Your Sweet Love............5
59	Brunswick 05808	Just As Much As Ever/Your Sweet Love (78)............10
60	Brunswick 05822	Crazy Arms/Beloved............6
60	Brunswick 05835	Mais Oui/Only The Broken Hearted............5
60	Brunswick 05837	Nothing Is Forever/Two Wrongs Don't Make A Right............5
60	Brunswick 05837	Nothing Is Forever/Two Wrongs Don't Make A Right (78)............15

DAVID BEDFORD
70	Argo ZRG 638	MUSIC FOR ALBION MOONLIGHT (LP, 1 side by Elizabeth Lutyens)...22
72	Dandelion 2310 165	NURSE'S SONG WITH ELEPHANTS (LP, gatefold sleeve)............22
74	Virgin V 2020	STARS END (LP)............12
75	Virgin V 2026	ORCHESTRAL TUBULAR BELLS (LP)............12
75	Virgin V 2038	RIME OF THE ANCIENT MARINER (LP)............12
76	Virgin V 2070	THE ODYSSEY (LP, with inner sleeve)............12
77	Virgin V 2090	INSTRUCTIONS FOR ANGELS (LP, with inner sleeve)............12

(see also Coxhill/Bedford Trio, Kevin Ayers & Whole World, Mike Oldfield)

BEDLAM
73	Chrysalis CFB 1	I Believe In You/Whiskey And Wine............8
73	Chrysalis CHR 1048	BEDLAM (LP)............20
85	Metal Masters METALP 104	BEDLAM (LP, reissue)............12

(see also Cozy Powell, Ace Kefford Stand, Big Bertha)

BEDROCKS
| 68 | Columbia DB 8516 | Ob-La-Di, Ob-La-Da/Lucy............5 |

EDWIN BEE
68	Decca F 12781	I've Been Loving You/Call For My Baby	6

MOLLY BEE
57	London HLD 8400	Since I Met You, Baby/I'll Be Waiting For You	40
57	London HLD 8400	Since I Met You, Baby/I'll Be Waiting For You (78)	18
58	Capitol CL 14849	Going Steady (With A Dream)/Magic Mirror	6
58	Capitol CL 14880	Don't Look Back/Please Don't Talk About Me When I'm Gone	6
58	Capitol CL 14949	After You've Gone/Five Points Of A Star	6
65	MGM MGM 1280	Single Girl Again/Keep It A Secret	5

BEE BEE CEE
77	Rel RE 48-S	You Gotta Know Girl/We Ain't Listening (p/s)	60

BEEFEATERS
64	Pye International 7N 25277	Please Let Me Love You/Don't Be Long	80
70	Elektra 2101 007	Please Let Me Love You/Don't Be Long (reissue)	25
	(see also Byrds)		

BEEHEEHEE
70s	Hunny BZ 001	I've Got A Laugh Like A Bee/Bees Are Really Funny	6

BEE GEES
67	Polydor 56727	Spicks And Specks/I Am The World	8
67	Polydor 56161	New York Mining Disaster 1941/I Can't See Nobody	6
67	Polydor 56178	To Love Somebody/Close Another Door	6
67	Polydor 56192	Massachusetts/Barker Of The U.F.O.	6
67	Polydor 56220	World/Sir Geoffrey Saved The World	6
68	Polydor 56229	Words/Sinking Ships	6
68	Polydor 56242	Jumbo/The Singer Sang His Song	6
68	Polydor 56273	I've Gotta Get A Message To You/Kitty Can	6
69	Polydor 56304	Odessa (Parts 1 & 2) (unissued)	
69	Polydor 56304	First Of May/Lamplight	6
69	Polydor 56331	Tomorrow Tomorrow/Sun In The Morning	6
69	Polydor 56343	Don't Forget To Remember/The Lord	6
70	Polydor 56377	I.O.I.O./Sweetheart	6
70	Polydor 2001 104	Lonely Days/Man For All Seasons	6
71	Polydor 2058 115	How Can You Mend A Broken Heart/Country Woman	6
77	RSO 2090224	Children Of The World/Boogie Child	5
67	Polydor 582/583 012	BEE GEES FIRST (LP)	15
68	Polydor 582/583 020	HORIZONTAL (LP)	15
68	Polydor 236 221	RARE PRECIOUS AND BEAUTIFUL (LP)	15
68	Polydor 236 513	RARE PRECIOUS AND BEAUTIFUL VOL. 2 (LP)	15
68	Polydor 582/583 036	IDEA (LP)	15
69	Polydor 236 556	RARE PRECIOUS AND BEAUTIFUL VOL. 3 (LP)	15
69	Polydor 582 049/050	ODESSA (2-LP, felt cover)	25
70	Polydor 2383 010	CUCUMBER CASTLE (LP)	12
70	Polydor 2310 069	TWO YEARS ON (LP)	12
71	Polydor 2383 052	TRAFALGAR (LP)	12
72	Polydor 2383 139	TO WHOM IT MAY CONCERN (LP)	12
73	RSO 2394 102	LIFE IN A TIN CAN (LP, unissued)	
	(see also Barry Gibb, Robin Gibb, Maurice Gibb, Humpy Bong, Fut)		

BEEKEEPERS
81	Rundown ACE 40	PLATFORM FIVE EP	10

MARK BEER
80	Waste WAS 001	ISOLATIONS (EP, with printed info sheet)	5
81	My China TAO 001	DUST ON THE ROAD (LP)	15

BEES
67	Blue Beat BB 386	Jesse James Rides Again/The Girl In My Dreams	10
68	Columbia Blue Beat DB 111	The Prisoner From Alcatraz/The Ska's The Limit	7

BEES MAKE HONEY
73	EMI EMI 2078	Knee Trembler/Caldonia	5
72	EMI EMC 3013	MUSIC EVERY NIGHT (LP)	15

BEE VAMP
81	Monsters In Orbit TVEYE 2	Valium Girls/Lucky Grills/Without Barry In Bengal (p/s)	5

BEEZ
79	Edible SNACK 001	Easy/Vagrant (gatefold p/s)	25
79	Edible SNACK 002	THE BEEZ EP (no p/s)	25

B.E.F. (British Electric Foundation)
91	Ten TEN 386	Free (Edit)/Secret Life Of Arabia (stickered p/s, as B.E.F. featuring Billy MacKenzie, unissued, 200 copies only)	50
80	Virgin V 2888	MUSIC FOR STOWAWAYS (LP, unissued, w/l test pressing w/ press release)	30
81	Virgin BEF 1	MUSIC FOR LISTENING TO (LP, export issue)	12
82	Virgin VV 2219	MUSIC OF QUALITY & DISTINCTION VOL. 1 (5 x 7" box set & insert)	12
	(see also Heaven 17, Billy MacKenzie)		

BEGGARS FARM
84	White Rabbit WR 1001	THE DEPTH OF A DREAM (LP)	25

BEGGARS HILL
76	Moonshine MS 60	BEGGARS HILL (LP, private pressing)	125

BEGGARS OPERA
70	Vertigo 6059 026	Sarabande/Think	10
72	Vertigo 6059 060	Hobo/Pathfinder	8
73	Vertigo 6059 088	Two Timing Woman/Lady Of Hell Fire	7
74	Vertigo 6059 105	Classical Gas/Sweet Blossom Woman	6
70	Vertigo 6360 018	ACT ONE (LP, spiral label, gatefold sleeve)	20
71	Vertigo 6360 054	WATERS OF CHANGE (LP, spiral label, gatefold sleeve)	18
72	Vertigo 6360 073	PATHFINDER (LP, spiral label, foldout poster cover)	25
73	Vertigo 6360 090	GET YOUR DOG OFF ME! (LP, 'spaceship' label)	15

BEGINNING OF THE END
| 71 | Atlantic 2091 097 | Funky Nassau (Parts 1 & 2) (initially red label) | 10/6 |
| 71 | Atlantic K 40304 | FUNKY NASSAU (LP, gatefold sleeve) | 20 |

BRENDAN BEHAN
| 60 | HMV 7EG 8491 | THE HOSTAGE (EP) | 12 |
| 60 | Argo RG 239 | THE HOSTAGE (LP) | 15 |

DOMINIC BEHAN
59	Decca F 11147	The Bells Of Hell/The Captains And The Kings	5
59	Decca F 11147	The Bells Of Hell/The Captains And The Kings (78)	10
60	Topic STOP 115	The Patriot Game/Erin Go Brath (p/s)	5
64	Piccadilly 7N 35172	Liverpool Lou/Love Is Where You Find It	5
58	Collector JEL 3	SONGS OF THE STREETS (EP)	18
60	Topic 12T 35	DOWN BY THE LIFFEYSIDE — IRISH STREET BALLADS (LP)	18
61	Topic 12T 44	EASTER WEEK AND AFTER — SONGS OF "THE TROUBLES" (LP)	18
66	Pye NPL 18134	IRELAND SINGS (LP)	15
69	Marble Arch MAL 1123	ARKLE (LP)	12
	(see also Ewan MacColl)		

BIX BEIDERBECKE & HIS GANG
60	Philips JAZ 116	Since My Best Gal Turned Me Down/At The Jazz Band Ball	5
55	Columbia SEG 7523	BIX BEIDERBECKE AND HIS ORCHESTRA (EP)	12
56	Columbia SEG 7577	BIX BEIDERBECKE (EP)	12
55	Columbia 33SL 1035	THE GREAT BIX (10" LP)	20

(HARRY) BELAFONTE
54	HMV 7M 202	Hold 'Em Joe/Suzanne (Every Night When The Sun Goes Down)	12
54	HMV 7M 224	I'm Just A Country Boy/Pretty As A Rainbow	10
55	Capitol CL 14312	Close Your Eyes/I Still Get A Thrill (Thinking Of You)	10
57	HMV POP 308	Banana Boat Song (Day-O)/Jamaica Farewell	10
57	HMV POP 339	Mama Looka Boo Boo/Don't Ever Love Me	7
57	HMV POP 360	Scarlet Ribbons (For Her Hair)/Hold 'Em Joe	10
57	RCA RCA 1007	Island In The Sun/Coconut Woman	5
57	RCA RCA 1022	Mary's Boy Child/Eden Was Just Like This	5
58	RCA RCA 1033	Judy Drowned/Lucy's Door	5
58	RCA RCA 1033	Judy Drowned/Lucy's Door (78)	8
58	RCA RCA 1035	Lead Man Holler/Haiti Cherie	8
58	RCA RCA 1035	Lead Man Holler/Haiti Cherie (78)	8
58	RCA RCA 1089	Banana Boat Song (Day-O)/Jamaica Farewell (78, re-recording)	8
59	RCA RCA 1103	Times Are A Gettin' Hard/The Waiting Game (78)	8
59	RCA RCA 1116	Darlin' Cora/Turn Around (78)	10
56	Capitol EAP1 619	CLOSE YOUR EYES (EP)	8
57	HMV 7EG 8211	CALYPSO (EP)	8
57	HMV 7EG 8259	MATHILDA MATHILDA (EP)	8
57	HMV DLP 1147	THE VERSATILE MR. BELAFONTE (10" LP)	15
57	HMV CLP 1122	MARK TWAIN AND OTHER FOLK FAVOURITES (LP)	12
57	RCA RC 24005	BELAFONTE SINGS OF THE CARIBBEAN (10" LP)	12
59	RCA RD 27129	PORGY AND BESS (LP, with Lena Horne)	12
59	RCA SF 5050	BELAFONTE AT CARNEGIE HALL (LP, stereo)	12
60	RCA SF 5058	MY LORD, WHAT A MORNIN'! (LP, stereo)	12
61	RCA SF 5061	SWING DAT HAMMER (LP, stereo)	12
61	RCA SF 5088	BELAFONTE RETURNS TO CARNEGIE HALL (LP, stereo)	12
	(see also Lena Horne)		

BEL CANTO'S
| 65 | R&B MRB 5003 | Feel Aw Right (Parts 1 & 2) | 15 |

BELFAST GYPSIES
66	Island WI 3007	Gloria's Dream/Secret Police	25
77	Sonet SNTF 738	THEM BELFAST GYPSIES (LP)	20
	(see also Them, Jackie McAuley, Freaks Of Nature)		

BELIEVERS
| 67 | Master's Time MT 001 | Money In The Rock/JOYFUL SINGERS: Jesus Christ Is Risen | 5 |

ED 'TEX' BELIN
| 63 | Starlite STEP 39 | ED 'TEX' BELIN (EP) | 12 |
| 67 | Starlite GRK 509 | ED 'TEX' BELIN (EP, reissue) | 8 |

ALEXANDER BELL
| 67 | CBS 2977 | Alexander Bell Believes/Hymn ... With Love | 8 |

ARCHIE BELL & THE DRELLS
68	Atlantic 584 185	Tighten Up/Dog Eat Dog	8
68	Atlantic 584 217	I Can't Stop Dancing/You're Such A Beautiful Child	8
71	Atlantic 2091 156	Tighten Up/I Can't Stop Dancing/(There's Gonna Be A) Showdown	8
72	Atlantic K 10210	Here I Go Again/A World Without Music	6
73	Atlantic K 10263	There's Gonna Be A Showdown/Tighten Up	6
68	Atlantic	TIGHTEN UP (LP)	35
72	Atlantic K 40454	HERE I GO AGAIN (LP)	15

BELINDA BELL
73	Columbia DB 8995	If Only You Believe/Stone Valley	5
73	Columbia SCXA 9255	STONE VALLEY (LP, gatefold sleeve)	16
73	One Up OU 2009	MUSIC OF W. GULGOWSKI (LP)	12

BENNY BELL & BLOCK BUSTERS
| 57 | Parlophone R 4372 | The Sack Dress/Dr. Jazz | 10 |

CAREY BELL
| 60s | Delmark DS 622 | CAREY BELL'S BLUES HARP (LP) | 12 |

CHARLES BELL & CONTEMPORARY JAZZ QUARTET
| 63 | London HA-K/SH-K 8095 | ANOTHER DIMENSION (LP) | 12 |

ERIC BELL BAND

81	Hobo HOS 016	Lonely Man/Anyone Seen My Baby (p/s)	30

(see also Thin Lizzy, Noel Redding Band)

FREDDIE BELL & BELLBOYS

56	Mercury MT 122	Giddy-Up-A Ding Dong/I Said It And I'm Glad (78)	10
57	Mercury MT 141	Hucklebuck/Rompin' And Stompin' (78)	15
57	Mercury MT 146	Teach You To Rock/Take The First Train Out Of Town (78)	15
57	Mercury MT 149	Big Bad Wolf/Rockin' The Polonaise (78)	18
57	Mercury MT 159	Rockin' Is My Business/You're Gonna Be Sorry (78)	22
56	Mercury MEP 9508	ROCK WITH THE BELL BOYS (EP)	25
57	Mercury MEP 9512	ROCK WITH THE BELL BOYS VOL. 2 (EP)	40

FREDRICK BELL

68	Nu Beat NB 004	Rocksteady Cool/CARLTON ALPHONSO: I Have Changed	8

GARY BELL

67	CBS 202234	Is This What I Get For Loving You?/To Keep You	6
67	CBS 2646	Anyway That You Want Me/Leave It To Me	5

GRAHAM BELL

66	Polydor 56067	How Can I Say I Don't Love You/If You're Gonna Go	7
72	Charisma CB 201	Too Many People/Before You're A Man	5
73	Charisma CB 209	You Need A 60 Minute Man/The Whole Town Wants You Hung	5
75	Charisma CB 250	You Need A 60 Minute Man/That's The Way It Is	5
72	Charisma CAS 1061	GRAHAM BELL (LP)	12

(see also Heavy Jelly, Griffin, Every Which Way, Skip Bifferty, Bell & Arc)

MADELINE BELL

63	HMV POP 1215	I Long For Your Love/Because You Didn't Care	10
64	Columbia DB 7257	You Don't Love Me No More/Don't Cross Over To My Side Of The Street	10
65	Columbia DB 7512	Daytime/Don't Cry My Heart	6
65	Philips BF 1448	What The World Needs Now Is Love/I Can't Wait To See My Baby's Face	12
66	Philips BF 1501	Don't Come Running To Me/I Got Carried Away	10
66	Philips BF 1526	One Step At A Time/You Won't See Me	6
67	Philips BF 1611	Picture Me Gone/Go Ahead On	12
68	Philips BF 1656	I'm Gonna Make You Love Me/I'm Gonna Leave You	8
68	Philips BF 1688	Thinkin'/Don't Give Your Love Away	5
68	Philips BF 1726	Hold It/What Am I Supposed To Do?	5
71	Philips 6006 082	If You Didn't Hear Me The First Time/You Walked Away	5
67	Philips (S)BL 7818	BELLS A POPPIN' (LP)	15
68	Philips SBL 7865	DOIN' THINGS (LP)	15

(see also Seven Ages Of Man, Blue Mink, Underground, Ian Green [Revelation])

MAGGIE BELL

74	Polydor 2058 447	Oh My My/As The Years Go Passing By	5
73	Polydor 2383 239	QUEEN OF THE NIGHT (LP)	12
75	Polydor 2383 313	SUICIDE SAL (LP)	12

(see also Stone The Crows, Frankie & Johnny)

PADDIE BELL

68	Waverly (S)ZLP 2104	I KNOW WHERE I'M GOING (LP, with Finbar & Eddie Furey, mono/stereo)	12/15

WILLIAM BELL

67	Atlantic 584 076	Never Like This Before/Soldier's Goodbye	6
69	Atlantic 584 259	Everyday Will Be Like A Holiday/Ain't Got No Girl	5
67	Stax 601 019	Eloise (Hang On In There)/One Plus One	5
68	Stax 601 038	A Tribute To A King/Every Man Oughta Have A Woman	5
69	Stax STAX 110	I Forgot To Be Your Lover/Bring The Curtain Down	5
69	Stax STAX 121	My Whole World Is Falling Down/All God's Children Got Soul	6
69	Stax STAX 128	Happy/Johnny I Love You	10
69	Atco 228 003	A TRIBUTE TO A KING (LP)	22
69	Stax SXATS 1016	BOUND TO HAPPEN (LP)	18
71	Stax 2363 002	BOUND TO HAPPEN (LP, reissue)	12
71	Stax 2362 009	WOW ... WILLIAM BELL (LP)	15
72	Stax 2362 027	PHASES OF REALITY (LP)	20

(see also Judy Clay & William Bell)

BELLA & ME

67	Columbia DB 8243	Whatever Happened To The Seven Day Week/Help Me Break This Habit	8

GEORGE BELLAMY

65	Parlophone R 5282	Where I'm Bound/How Could I Ever	25
72	Chapter One CH 167	Maman/Come To The Party	10

(see also Tornados)

PETER BELLAMY

68	Argo	MAINLY NORFOLK (LP)	20
69	Xtra XTRA 1075	FAIR ENGLAND'S SHORE (LP)	30
69	Topic 12T 200	THE FOX JUMPS OVER THE PARSON'S GATE (LP, blue label)	15
70	Argo ZFB 11	OAK, ASH AND THORN (LP)	20
72	Argo ZFB 37	WON'T YOU GO MY WAY (LP)	15
72	Argo ZFB 81	MERLIN'S ISLE OF GRAMARYE (LP)	15
74	Trailer LER 2089	TELL IT LIKE IT IS (LP)	12
77	Free Reed FRR 014	BARRACK-ROOM BALLADS (LP)	10
79	Topic 12TS 400	BOTH SIDES THEN (LP)	10
83	Fellside FE 032	PETER BELLAMY WITH FRIENDS: KEEP ON KIPLING (LP)	15

(see also Young Tradition)

BELL & ARC

71	Charisma CB 170	She Belongs To Me/Dawn	6
71	Charisma CAS 1053	BELL & ARC (LP, gatefold sleeve)	20

(see also Skip Bifferty, Arc, Every Which Way, Graham Bell)

MINT VALUE £

BELL BROTHERS
68	Action ACT 4510	Tell Him No/Throw Away The Key	8

BELLE & SEBASTIAN
97	Jeepster JPR 7001	Dog On Wheels/The State I Am In (p/s, 1,000 only)	5
96	Elektric Honey EHRLP 5	TIGERMILK (LP, 1,000 only)	150

BELLES
70	President PT 311	Don't Pretend/Words Can't Explain	6

BELLFIELD
73	Downtown DT 514	Sugar Plum/Sugar Plum Dub	5

BELL NOTES
59	Top Rank JAR 102	I've Had It/Be Mine	6
59	Top Rank JAR 102	I've Had It/Be Mine (78)	20
59	Top Rank JAR 147	Old Spanish Town/She Went That-A-Way	6
59	Top Rank JAR 147	Old Spanish Town/She Went That-A-Way (78)	20
59	Top Rank JAR 201	That's Right/Betty Dear	6

BELLS OF JOY
55	Vogue V 2357	I'm Gonna Press On/How Sweet It Is (78)	12

BELL SOUNDS
59	HMV POP 685	Marching Guitars/Chloe	6

LOUIS BELLSON
50s	Columbia Clef LB 10080	Caxton Hall Swing/For Europeans Only (78)	7
56	Columbia Clef SEG 10030	BOOGIE WOOGIE PIANO AND DRUMS NO. 1 (EP)	22
56	Columbia Clef SEG 10052	BOOGIE WOOGIE PIANO AND DRUMS NO. 2 (EP)	25
70	Pye NSPL 18349	LOUIE IN LONDON (LP, as Louie Bellson)	25

(see also Duke Ellington)

BELL-TONES
62	Columbia DB 4848	Selina/Did You Ever See A Dream Walking?	10

TONY BELLUS
59	London HL 8933	Robbin' The Cradle/Valentine Girl	35
59	London HL 8933	Robbin' The Cradle/Valentine Girl (78)	18

BELLY
92	4AD AD 2018	Gepetto/Sexy S (p/s, with 2 postcards, 2,000 only)	5
93	4AD AD 3001	Feed The Tree/Dream On Me (p/s, with 2 postcards)	5
95	4AD BELLY ONE	Now They'll Sleep/King/Super-Connected (12", promo only, plain grey sleeve)	10
95	4AD BELLY 2	Seal My Fate (U.S. Radio Mix)/Judas Mon Coeur (12", grey sleeve, promo)	10
95	4AD CADD 5004CD	KING (CD, with A5 book pack)	20

(see also Throwing Muses, Tanya Donelly)

BELMONTS
61	Pye International 7N 25094	Tell Me Why/Smoke From Your Cigarette	25
62	Stateside SS 128	Come On Little Angel/How About Me?	15

(see also Dion & Belmonts)

BELOVED
86	Flim Flam HARP 2	A Hundred Words (Radio Mix)/Slow Drowning (freebie)	6
86	Flim Flam HARP 2T	A Hundred Words/Slow Drowning/In Trouble And Shame (12", p/s)	8
86	Flim Flam HARP 3T	This Means War/Let It Begin/Saints Preserve Us (12", p/s)	8
86	Flim Flam HARP 5T	Happy Now/Righteous Me/Kiss Goodbye/If Pennies Come (12", p/s)	8
87	Flim Flam HARP 7ET	Forever Dancing/Forever Dancing (Remix)/Surprise Me (12", p/s)	8
88	WEA YZ 311T	Loving Feeling (Feeling Lovely Mix)/Acid Love (Love & Ecstasy Mix) (12", p/s)	10
88	WEA YZ 311CD	Loving Feeling/Acid Love (Original Mix)/Loving Feeling (Feeling Lovely Mix) (3" CD with adaptor, picture case)	25
89	WEA YZ 357T	Your Love Takes Me Higher (Pod Went Pop Mix)/(Magic Jeans Sex Mix)/(Burning With DJ Desire Mix) (12", p/s)	8
89	WEA YZ 357TX	Your Love Takes Me Higher (Deep Joy)/(New Beats For Old)/(Simply Devine)/(Divinely Simple) (12", p/s with T-shirt transfer)	15
89	WEA YZ 357CD	Your Love Takes Me Higher/Paradise (My Darling, My Angel)/Your Love Takes Me Higher (Rise Up Higher)/(Beautiful Mix) (3" CD with adaptor, 5" case)	25
89	WEA YZ 414T	The Sun Rising/The Sun Rising (Gentle Night)/The Sun Rising (Eurovisionary)/The Sun Rising (Deeply Satisfying) (12", p/s)	10
90	WEA YZ 414TX	The Sun Rising (Remixes) (12" EP, p/s)	18
89	WEA YZ 414TP	The Sun Rising/The Sun Rising (Gentle Night)/The Sun Rising (Eurovisionary)/The Sun Rising (Deeply Satisfying) (12", picture disc)	12
89	WEA YZ 414CD	The Sun Rising/The Sun Rising (Gentle Night)/The Sun Rising (Eurovisionary)/The Sun Rising (Deeply Satisfying) (3" CD, gatefold card sleeve)	18
90	WEA YZ 426CD	Hello/Hello Honky Tonk/Godfrey's Tonic/Hello Dolly (CD)	8
90	WEA YZ 541CD	It's Alright Now (7" Mix)/(Rattling Good Time)/(Back To Basics Instrumental) (CD, slimline jewel case)	15
96	East West EW 043CD	Deliver Me (3.56)/Deliver Me (Extended)/(Eau De Livami Vocal)/(Salt Lake City Vocal)/(Coco Dub)/(Robodisco Dub) (CD, withdrawn)	15
87	Flim Flam HARPLP 2	WHERE IT'S AT (LP, with bonus 7")	15
87	Flim Flam HARPCD 2	WHERE IT'S AT (CD)	25

BELT & BRACES ROADSHOW BAND
75	Belt & Braces Roadshow	BELT & BRACES ROADSHOW BAND (LP, with lyric sheet)	15

BELTONES
68	Trojan TR 628	No More Heartaches/I'll Follow You	7
69	Duke DU 17	Home Without You/Why Pretend	5
69	High Note HS 017	Mary Mary/Going Away	6
69	High Note HS 023	A Broken Heart/AFROTONES: All For One	7
72	Ackee ACK 150	Wrapped Up In Love/SOUND DIMENSION: Pasero	8

(see Bop & Beltones, Trevor Shield)

JOHN BELTRAN
96	Peacefrog PF 049	TEN DAYS OF BLUE (2-LP)	18
96	Peacefrog PF 049CD	TEN DAYS OF BLUE (CD)	15

JESSE BELVIN
59	RCA RCA 1119	Guess Who/Funny	15
59	RCA RCA 1119	Guess Who/Funny (78)	12

BEN
71	Vertigo 6360 052	BEN (LP, gatefold sleeve, spiral label)	85

PAT BENATAR
79	Chrysalis CHS 2373	If You Think You Know How To Love Me/So Sincere (p/s)	7
79	Chrysalis CHS 2395	Heartbreaker/My Clone/Sleeps Alone (p/s)	5
80	Chrysalis CHS 2403	We Live For Love/I Need A Lover (p/s)	10
80	Chrysalis CHS 2474	Hit Me With Your Best Shot/You Better Run/Heartbreaker/ We Live For Love (p/s, some on red vinyl)	7/10
81	Chrysalis CHS 2511	Treat Me Right/Hell Is For Children (p/s, clear vinyl)	6
81	Sounds FREEBIE No. 1	Promises In The Dark (Edit)/MICHAEL SCHENKER GROUP: Let Sleeping Dogs Lie (flexidisc in red printed sleeve, free with *Sounds* magazine)	6/5
81	Chrysalis CHS 2529	Fire And Ice/Hard To Believe (p/s, clear vinyl)	6
81	Chrysalis CHSP 2529	Fire And Ice/Hard To Believe (picture disc)	6
83	Chrysalis CHSP 2662	Shadows Of The Night/The Victim (shaped picture disc)	15
83	Chrysalis CHS 12 2662	Shadows Of The Night (12", p/s, blue vinyl)	8
84	Chrysalis CHSP 2747	Love Is A Battlefield/Hell Is For Children (live) (picture disc)	7
84	Chrysalis CHSP 2821	We Belong/Suburban King (picture disc)	6
85	Chrysalis PATP 2	Shadows Of The Night/Hit Me With Your Best Shot (shaped pic disc & plinth)	5
88	Chrysalis PAT 5	All Fired Up (p/s)	5
88	Chrysalis PAT 6	Don't Walk Away (gatefold p/s, red vinyl)	6
81	Chrysalis CHR 1346	PRECIOUS TIME (LP, with poster)	15
82	Chrysalis PCHR 1396	GET NERVOUS (LP, picture disc)	18
83	Chrysalis CHRP 1451	LIVE FROM EARTH (LP, picture disc)	20

STEVE BENBOW
68	L'gue Against Cruel Sports	Tattered Doll (mail-order only)	6
59	Collector	STEVE BENBOW AND THE FOLK FOUR (EP)	10
62	HMV CLP 1603	STEVE BENBOW SINGS (LP)	15
63	HMV CLP 1687	I TRAVEL THE WORLD (LP)	15
67	Decca LK/SKL 4881	OF SITUATIONS AND PREDICAMENTS (LP)	14

RALF BENDIX & LITTLE ELIZABETH
65	Columbia DB 7774	Sag Mir Deine Sorgen/Baby Sittin' Boogie	6

BENDLE
81	own label (no cat. no.)	Optimism/Squirrel/Absurd (cassette)	12

TEX BENEKE & HIS ORCHESTRA
56	MGM SP 1158	'S Wonderful/Singin' In The Rain	6

ROGER BENNET
67	Polydor NH 56724	Night Flight To Tokyo/Memories	5

BENNY BENNETT
54	Seeco SV 2197	Mambo Boogie/Sax Mambo (78)	8
58	Vogue Pop V 9119	Stranger In Paradise (Cha Cha Cha)/Cha Cha Cha No. 5 (78)	8
58	Vogue Pop V 9121	Esmerelda/Mambo de Monaco (78)	8
50s	Seeco LDS 024	BENNY BENNETT AND HIS ORCHESTRA (LP)	12

BOBBY BENNETT (U.K.)
67	CBS 202511	Just Say Goodbye/She Believes In Me	6
68	Columbia DB 8435	All My Life Is You/To Give (The Reason I Live)	6
69	Columbia DB 8532	Music Mother Made/You're Ready Now	20

BOBBY BENNETT (U.S.)
69	London HL 10274	Big New York/Baby, Try Me	8

(BIG MOE WITH) BOYD BENNETT & HIS ROCKETS
78s
55	Parlophone R 4002	Everlovin'/Boogie At Midnight (78) (with Big Moe)	60
55	Parlophone R 4063	Seventeen/Little Ole You-All (78) (as Boyd Bennett & His Rockers)	20
56	Parlophone R 4121	My Boy — Flat Top/Banjo Rock And Roll (with Big Moe) (78)	20
56	Parlophone R 4167	Blue Suede Shoes/Oo-Oo-Oo (with Big Moe) (78)	20
56	Parlophone R 4214	The Groovy Age/Hit That Jive, Jack (78) (as Big Moe with Boyd Bennett & His Rockets)	30
56	Parlophone R 4252	The Most/Rockin' Up A Storm (78) (as Boyd Bennett & His Rockets)	30
58	Parlophone R 4423	Click Clack/Move (78) (as Boyd Bennett & His Rockers)	40
59	Mercury AMT 1031	Tear It Up/Tight Tights (78) (as Big Moe & His Orchestra)	75

SINGLES
55	Parlophone MSP 6161	Everlovin'/Boogie At Midnight (with Big Moe)	275
55	Parlophone MSP 6180	Seventeen/Little Ole You-All (as Boyd Bennett & His Rockers)	225
56	Parlophone MSP 6203	My Boy — Flat Top/Banjo Rock And Roll (with Big Moe)	275
56	Parlophone MSP 6233	Blue Suede Shoes/Oo-Oo-Oo (with Big Moe)	225
56	Parlophone R 4214	The Groovy Age/Hit That Jive, Jack (as Big Moe with Boyd Bennett & His Rockets)	225
56	Parlophone R 4252	The Most/Rockin' Up A Storm (as Boyd Bennett & His Rockets)	225
58	Parlophone R 4423	Click Clack/Move (as Boyd Bennett & His Rockers)	160
59	Mercury AMT 1031	Tear It Up/Tight Tights (as Big Moe & His Orchestra)	65

(see also Moon Mullican)

BRIAN BENNETT
67	Columbia DB 8294	Canvas/Slippery Jim De Grize	16
74	Fontana 6007 040	Chase Side Shoot-Up/Pegasus	12
76	DJM DJS 10714	Thunderbolt/Clearing Skies (promos in p/s)	10/5
77	DJM DJS 10756	Saturday Night Special/Farewell To A Friend (promos in p/s)	10/5

Brian BENNETT

77	DJM DJS 10791	The Girls Back Home/Jonty Jump	5
78	DJM DJS 10843	Pendulum Force/Ocean Glide	5
82	DJM DJS 10981	Top Of The World/Soul Ice	5
67	Columbia S(C)X 6144	CHANGE OF DIRECTION (LP)	30
69	Col. Studio Two TWO 268	THE ILLUSTRATED LONDON NOISE (LP)	50
77	DJM DJF 20499	ROCK DREAMS (LP)	12
78	DJM DJF 20532	VOYAGE (LP)	12

(see also Shadows, Thunder Company, Wasp, Marty Wilde, Krewcats, Collage, Alan Skidmore, Big Jim Sullivan, Heat Exchange, Julian [Scott])

BRUCE BENNETT
71	Big BG 311	If You Don't Mind/Lenore (both actually by Dobby Dobson)	6

CAROLE BENNETT
56	Capitol CL 14652	The Little Magician/I Was Your Only Love	7
57	Capitol CL 14692	Play The Music/Miser's Gold	6
57	Capitol CL 14725	Haunted Lover/Let The Chips Fall (Where They May)	6

CLIFF BENNETT & REBEL ROUSERS
61	Parlophone R 4793	You've Got What I Like/I'm In Love With You	25
61	Parlophone R 4836	That's What I Said/When I Get Paid	25
62	Parlophone R 4895	Poor Joe/Hurtin' Inside (Twist)	25
63	Parlophone R 5046	Everybody Loves A Lover/My Old Stand-By	30
63	Parlophone R 5080	You Really Got A Hold On Me/Alright	7
64	Parlophone R 5119	Got My Mojo Working/Beautiful Dreamer	7
64	Parlophone R 5173	One Way Love/Slow Down	6
65	Parlophone R 5229	I'll Take You Home/Do You Love Him?	6
65	Parlophone R 5259	Three Rooms Of Running Water/If Only You'd Reply	6
65	Parlophone R 5317	I Have Cried My Last Tear/As Long As She Looks Like You	6
66	Parlophone R 5406	You Can't Love 'Em All/Need Your Loving Tonight	6
66	Parlophone R 5466	Eyes For You/Hold On I'm Coming	6
66	Parlophone R 5489	Got To Get You Into My Life/Baby Each Day	5
66	Parlophone R 5534	Never Knew Lovin' Could Be So Doggone Good/Don't Help Me Out	6
67	Parlophone R 5565	I'm Sorry/I'll Take Good Care Of You	7
67	Parlophone R 5598	I'll Be There/Use Me	6
63	Parlophone DP 560	Poor Joe/Hurtin' Inside (Twist) (export issue, black label)	80
64	Parlophone DP 561	When I Get Paid/That's What I Said (export issue, black label)	80
64	Parlophone GEP 8923	CLIFF BENNETT AND THE REBEL ROUSERS (EP)	30
65	Parlophone GEP 8936	TRY IT BABY (EP)	30
66	Parlophone GEP 8955	WE'RE GONNA MAKE IT (EP)	60
64	Parlophone PMC 1242	CLIFF BENNETT AND THE REBEL ROUSERS (LP, yellow/black label)	50
66	M. For Pleasure MFP 1121	DRIVIN' YOU WILD (LP)	12
66	EMI Regal REG 1039	CLIFF BENNETT (LP, export issue)	25
67	Parlophone PMC/PCS 7017	GOT TO GET YOU INTO OUR LIFE (LP, yellow/black label)	40

CLIFF BENNETT BAND
68	Parlophone R 5666	Take Your Time/House Of A Thousand Dolls	5
68	Parlophone R 5691	You're Breaking Me Up (And I'm Wasting Away)/I Hear Her Voice	5
68	Parlophone R 5711	Lonely Weekends/Good Times	5
68	Parlophone R 5728	One More Heartache/Nobody Runs Forever	6
68	Parlophone R 5749	Back In The USSR/This Man	5
68	Parlophone PMC/PCS 7054	BRANCHES OUT (LP, yellow/black label)	30

CLIFF BENNETT'S REBELLION
71	CBS 7231	Amos Moses/Movin' And Travelin' On	5
71	CBS 64487	CLIFF BENNETT'S REBELLION (LP)	12

(see also Charles Hodges, Rebel Rousers, Toefat, Screaming Lord Sutch & Savages)

DICKIE BENNETT
55	Decca F 10595	There, But For The Grace Of God Go I/Stars Shine In Your Eyes	6
56	Decca F 10697	Dungaree Doll/Can't We Be Partners (After The Dance)	10
56	Decca F 10782	You Don't Know Me/Cry Upon My Shoulder	6

DUSTER BENNETT
68	Blue Horizon 57-3141	It's A Man Down There/Things Are Changing	12
69	Blue Horizon 57-3148	Raining In My Heart/Jumpin' For Joy	15
69	Blue Horizon 57-3154	Bright Lights, Big City/Fresh Country Jam (with His House Band)	12
69	Blue Horizon 57-3164	I'm Gonna Wind Up Endin' Up Or I'm Gonna End Up Windin' Up With You/ Rock Of Ages, Cleft For Me	18
70	Blue Horizon 57-3173	I Chose To Sing The Blues/If You Could Hang Your Washing Like You Hang Your Lines	10
70	Blue Horizon 57-3179	Act Nice And Gentle/I Want You To Love Me	10
74	Rak RAK 177	Comin' Home/Pretty Little Thing	15
68	Blue Horizon 7-63208	SMILING LIKE I'M HAPPY (LP, with His House Band, i.e. Fleetwood Mac)	50
69	Blue Horizon 7-63221	BRIGHT LIGHTS... (LP, gatefold sleeve)	60
70	Blue Horizon 7-63868	12 DB's (LP)	35

(see also Fleetwood Mac)

JOE BENNETT & SPARKLETONES
57	HMV POP 399	Black Slacks/Boppin' Rock Boogie	110
57	HMV POP 399	Black Slacks/Boppin' Rock Boogie (78)	35
58	HMV POP 445	Rocket/Penny Loafers And Bobby Socks	140
58	HMV POP 445	Rocket/Penny Loafers And Bobby Socks (78)	45

JO JO BENNETT
67	Doctor Bird DB 1097	The Lecture/Cantelope Rock (with Fugitives)	18
67	Doctor Bird DB 1117	Rocksteady/Real Gone Loser (with Fugitives)	18
70	Explosion EX 2029	Groovy Jo Jo/Ten Steps To Soul (both actually with Mudie's All Stars)	8
70	Trojan TR 7774	Leaving Rome/In The Nude (both with Mudie's All Stars)	6
71	Moodisc MU 3514	Snowbird/MUDIE'S ALLSTARS: Change The Tide	5
71	Moodisc HME 108	Poison Ivy/MUDIE'S ALLSTARS: Ivy Poison	5
70	Trojan TBL 133	GROOVY JO JO (LP, with Mudie's Allstars)	25

(see also Fugitives, I Roy)

KIM BENNETT

55	Decca F 10449	Softly Softly/ROLAND SHAW ORCHESTRA: Trumpeter's Lullaby	7
55	Decca F 10460	Melody Of Love/Ding Dong	7
55	Decca F 10599	The Kentuckian Song/Overnight	6
56	Decca F 10706	No, Not Much/You Can't Keep Running	6

(see also Roland Shaw)

LEE BENNETT & SUNLINERS

64	Decca F 12024	Poor Bachelor Boy/Fool, Fool, Fool	5

LORNA BENNETT

72	Blue Mountain BM 1013	Breakfast In Bed/SCOTTY: Skank In Bed	5
72	Blue Mountain BM 1013	Breakfast In Bed/Remember When (2nd issue with different B-side)	5
73	Blue Mountain BM 1025	Chapel Of Love/I Love Everything About You	5

NICK BENNETT

60	Columbia DB 4516	You Understand Me/Mr. Lonely	5

PETER E. BENNETT

71	RCA SF 8190	THE BALLAD OF GALDWAIN (LP)	10

RAY BENNETT

62	Decca F 11550	Go Away Little Girl/Twistin' To The Blues	5
62	Decca DFE 8516	INTRODUCING RAY BENNETT (EP)	12

ROY BENNETT

68	Blue Cat BS 146	I Dangerous/DEE SET: I Know A Place	10

RUDI BENNETT

68	Decca F 12741	I'm So Proud/WHISTLING JACK SMITH: Havah Nagilah	4

(see also Whistling Jack Smith)

TONY BENNETT

51	Columbia DB 2924	Because Of You/Cold, Cold Heart (78)	10
52	Columbia 38926	Our Lady Of Fatima/Just Say I Love Her (78)	15
53	Columbia SCM 5048	Congratulations To Someone/Take Me	10
53	Philips PB 689	Sold To The Man With The Broken Heart/One Kiss Away From Heaven	8
54	Philips PB 357	Madonna, Madonna/Not As A Stranger (78)	8
54	Columbia 39745	Here In My Heart/I'm Lost Again	10
55	Philips PB 420	Stranger In Paradise/Take me Back Again (78)	8
55	Philips PB 521	How Can I Replace You?/Tell Me That You Love Me (78)	8
56	Philips PB 501	Can You Find It In Your Heart/Forget Her (78)	8
57	Philips PB 710	One For My Baby (And One For The Road)/No Hard Feelings (78)	8
57	Philips JK 1008	Whatever Lola Wants/Heart (jukebox issue)	15
58	Philips PB 831	Young And Warm And Wonderful/Now I Lay Me Down To Sleep	6
58	Philips PB 831	Young And Warm And Wonderful/Now I Lay Me Down To Sleep (78)	8
58	Philips PB 855	Firefly/The Night That Heaven Fell	7
58	Philips PB 855	Firefly/The Night That Heaven Fell (78)	10
59	Philips PB 907	Being True To One Another/It's So Peaceful In The Country	5
59	Philips PB 907	Being True To One Another/It's So Peaceful In The Country (78)	12
59	Philips PB 961	Smile (Theme From "Modern Times")/You Can't Love 'Em All	5
59	Philips PB 961	Smile (Theme From "Modern Times")/You Can't Love 'Em All (78)	12
60	Philips PB 996	Love Look Away/The Cool School	5
60	Philips PB 1008	Ask Me (I Know)/I'll Bring You A Rainbow	5
60	Philips PB 1079	Till/Ask Anyone In Love	5
60	Philips PB 1089	Marriage-Go-Round/Somebody	5
62	Columbia 41127	You're So Right For Me/Alone At Last:My Foolish Heart	10
63	CBS 3370	A Fool Of Fools/The Glory Of Love	8
77	IMPROV TB711105	There's Always Tomorrow/I Wish I Were In Love Again (p/s)	8
53	Columbia B 2620	TONY BENNETT SPOTLITE (EP)	10
54	Columbia B 2079	TONY BENNETT (EP)	10
55	Philips BBE 12009	TONY BENNETT (EP)	12
57	Columbia B 2582	ONE FOR MY BABY (EP)	10
58	Philips BBE 12223	TONY BENNETT — PHILIPS TV SERIES (EP)	12
60	Philips BBE 12338	HOMETOWN, MY HOMETOWN (EP)	12
55	Philips BBR 8051	CLOUD 7 (10" LP)	20
56	Philips BBR 8089	THE VOICE OF YOUR CHOICE (10" LP)	20
57	Philips BBL 7138	TONY BENNETT SHOWCASE (LP)	15
57	Philips BBL 7219	THE BEAT OF MY HEART (LP)	15
58	Philips BBL 7219	LONG AGO AND FAR AWAY (LP)	15
60	Philips BBL 7308	IN PERSON! (LP, with Count Basie Orch., with fake audience noise, mono)	15
60	Philips SBBL 542	IN PERSON! (LP, with Count Basie Orch., with fake audience noise, stereo)	15
60	Philips BBL 7413	TO MY WONDERFUL ONE (LP)	15
60	Philips BBL 7452	ALONE TOGETHER (LP)	15
61	Philips BBL 7455	SINGS A STRING OF HAROLD ARLEN (LP, also stereo SBBL 609)	14/16
61	Philips BBL 7479	TONY SINGS FOR TWO (LP)	15
61	Philips BBL 7495	MY HEART SINGS (LP)	15
63	CBS BPG 62205	THIS IS ALL I ASK (LP)	12
64	CBS BPG 62245	THE MANY MOODS OF TONY (LP)	12
64	CBS BPG 62296	WHEN LIGHTS ARE LOW (LP)	12
64	CBS BPG 62486	WHO CAN I TURN TO (LP)	12

(see also Count Basie, John Barry)

VAL BENNETT

68	Island WI 3113	Jumping With Mr. Lee/ROY SHIRLEY: Keep Your Eyes On The Road	15
68	Island WI 3146	The Russians Are Coming (Take Five)/LESTER STERLING: Sir Lee's Whip	18
68	Trojan TR 611	Spanish Harlem/ROY SHIRLEY: If I Did Know	10
69	Trojan TR 640	Baby Baby/Barbara	10
69	Crab CRAB 6	Reggae City/CANNON KING: Mellow Trumpet (B-side actually by Carl 'King Cannon Ball' Bryan)	6
69	Camel CA 24	Midnight Spin/SOUL CATS: Money Money	6

(see also Roy Shirley, Max Romeo, Derrick Morgan, Clancy Eccles, Harry J Allstars, George A Penny, Lloyd Terrell, Uniques, Versatiles)

MINT VALUE £

JOHNNY BENNINGS & HIS RHYTHM & BLUES BAND
54 Esquire 10-376   Third Degree Blues/Timber (78). 25

BENNY & TINA
69 Mercury MF 1133   This Love Is Real/Over My Dead Body 6

BARRY BENSON
66 Parlophone R 5446   Stay A Little While/That's For Sure 12
66 Parlophone R 5484   Not A One Girl Guy/Sunshine Child 7
66 Parlophone R 5544   Always Waitin'/My Friend And I 6
67 Parlophone R 5578   Cousin Jane/Meet Jacqueline 5
67 Page One POF 034   I Can't Wait/Oh No 5

BOBBY BENSON & HIS COMBO
58 Philips PB 854   Taxi Driver, I Don't Care/Gentleman Bobby. 6
58 Philips PB 854   Taxi Driver, I Don't Care/Gentleman Bobby (78) 12

GEORGE BENSON (QUARTET)
66 CBS (S)BPG 62817   IT'S UPTOWN (LP, as George Benson Quartet). 12
67 CBS (S)BPG 62971   THE GEORGE BENSON COOKBOOK (LP) 12
68 CBS 63533   WILLOW WEEP FOR ME (LP). 12

HOAGY BENSON
68 CBM CBM 003   Kangaroo/Turn Me On 5

MARIE BENSON & LONDONAIRES
55 Decca F 10452   Mambo Italiano/Mobile. 8
55 Philips PB 528   Sooty/Mr. Dumpling (78). 10

MICHAEL BENTINE
72 Polydor 2058 294   Wine Tasting Man/Olympic Showjumping 5
62 Parlophone PMC 1179   IT'S A SQUARE WORLD (LP, also stereo PCS 3031) 20/22
67 RCA Victor RD 7885   SQUARE BASHING (LP). 15
(see also Goons)

BRIAN BENTLEY & BACHELORS
60 Philips PB 1085   Wishing Well/Please Make Up Your Mind 6
60 Philips PB 1086   First Flight East/Sunday Break 6
62 Salvo SLO 1813   Caramba/Nellie Dean (99 copies only). 12

JAY BENTLEY & JET SET
64 Vocalion VN 9230   Watusi '64/I'll Get You. 7

RAY BENTLEY
67 Disc-A-Fran AVE 44   RAY BENTLEY (EP, features uncredited tracks by other artists) 8

BENTLEY BROTHERS
59 Top Rank JAR 208   Ma (She's Making Eyes At Me)/Yes, We Have No Bananas. 5

BROOK BENTON
58 RCA RCA 1044   A Million Miles From Nowhere/Devoted 6
58 RCA RCA 1044   A Million Miles From Nowhere/Devoted (78) 10
58 Mercury AMT 1014   It's Just A Matter Of Time/Hurtin' Inside 6
58 Mercury AMT 1014   It's Just A Matter Of Time/Hurtin' Inside (78). 18
59 Mercury AMT 1043   Endlessly/So Close 6
59 Mercury AMT 1043   Endlessly/So Close (78) 30
59 Mercury AMT 1061   Thank You Pretty Baby/With All Of My Heart 6
59 Mercury AMT 1068   So Many Ways/I Want You Forever 6
60 Mercury AMT 1097   The Ties That Bind/Hither And Thither And Yon 6
60 Mercury AMT 1109   Kiddio/The Same One 6
60 Mercury AMT 1121   Fools Rush In/Somebody You'll Want Me To Want You 7
61 Mercury AMT 1134   For My Baby/Think Twice. 6
61 Mercury AMT 1148   The Boll Weevil Song/Your Eyes 6
61 Mercury AMT 1157   Frankie And Johnny/It's Just A House Without You 6
61 Mercury AMT 1168   Revenge/Really Really 5
62 Mercury AMT 1172   Walk On The Wild Side/Somewhere In The Used To Be 5
62 Mercury AMT 1178   Hit Record/Thanks To The Fool 5
62 Mercury AMT 1187   Lie To Me/The Touch Of Your Hand 5
62 Mercury AMT 1194   Hotel Happiness/Still Waters Run Deep 5
62 Mercury AMT 1203   I Got What I Wanted/Dearer Than Life 5
63 Mercury AMT 1208   My True Confession/Tender Years 5
63 Mercury AMT 1212   Two Tickets To Paradise/Don't Hate Me. 5
63 Mercury AMT 1217   Baby You Got It Made/Stop Foolin' (with Damita Jo) 5
64 Mercury MF 822   Too Late To Turn Back Now/Another Cup Of Coffee 5
64 Mercury MF 828   A House Is Not A Home/Come On Back 5
64 Mercury MF 842   Do It Right/Please, Please Make It Easy 5
68 Atlantic 584 222   Do Your Own Thing/I Just Don't Know What To Do With Myself 5
69 Atlantic 584 266   Touch 'Em With Love/She Knows What To Do For Me 5
69 Atlantic 584 267   Nothing Can Take The Place Of You/Woman Without Love. 5
58 RCA RCX 169   BROOK BENTON (EP, tri centre) 22
58 Fontana TFE 17151   BROOK BENTON AT HIS BEST (EP) 12
59 Mercury ZEP 10023   THE CARESSING VOICE OF BROOK BENTON (EP) 10
60 Mercury ZEP 10046   MAKE A DATE WITH BROOK BENTON (EP) 10
60 Mercury ZEP 10076   I'M IN THE MOOD FOR LOVE. 10
60 Mercury ZEP 10091   WHEN I FALL IN LOVE (EP, also stereo [SEZ 19009]) 8/10
61 Mercury ZEP 10107   WHEN YOU'RE IN LOVE (EP, also stereo [SEZ 19019]) 8/10
61 Mercury ZEP 10125   SO WARM (EP, also stereo [SEZ 19024]) 8/10
58 Mercury MMC 14015   IT'S JUST A MATTER OF TIME (LP). 22
59 Mercury MMC 14022   ENDLESSLY (LP) 22
59 RCA Camden CDN 143   BROOK BENTON (LP) 12
60 Mercury MMC 14042   I LOVE YOU IN SO MANY WAYS (LP). 18
60 Mercury MMC 14060   SONGS I LOVE TO SING (LP, also stereo [CMS 18041]). 15/18
61 Mercury MMC 14090   THE BOLL WEEVIL SONG (LP, also stereo [CMS 18060]) 15/18
61 Mercury MMC 14108   THERE GOES THAT SONG AGAIN (LP, also stereo [CMS 18068]). 15/18
62 Mercury MMC 14124   GOLDEN HITS (LP). 15
62 Mercury 20024 MCL   BORN TO SING THE BLUES (LP). 15
63 Mercury 20040 MCL   IT'S JUST A MATTER OF TIME (LP). 15
63 Mercury 20053 MCL   THIS BITTER EARTH (LP) 15

BROOK BENTON & DINAH WASHINGTON

60	Mercury AMT 1083	Baby (You've Got What It Takes)/I Do	10
60	Mercury AMT 1099	A Rockin' Good Way/I Believe	18
69	Mercury MF 1100	A Rockin' Good Way/I Do	5
61	Mercury ZEP 10120	A ROCKING GOOD WAY (EP, also stereo SEZ 19022)	30/35
64	Mercury 20069 MCL	THE TWO OF US (LP)	15

BENT WIND

95	Acme AC 8004 LP	SUSSEX (LP, reissue of Canadian LP, handmade sleeve, w/ insert, 500 only)	12

BERESFORD BAND

77	Leader LEA 2069	YORKSHIRE DALES DANCE NIGHT (LP)	12

BERETS

70	Avant Garde AVS 116	THE MASS FOR PEACE (LP, with insert)	20

BERKELEY KITES

68	Polydor 56742	Hang Up City/Mary-Go-Round	5
69	Polydor 56770	Alice In Wonderland/What Goes Up Must Come Down	5

MILTON BERLE

56	Vogue Coral Q 72197	In The Middle Of The House/Buffalo	12

BERLIN

80	Charisma CB 351	Over 21/Waiting For The Future (p/s)	5

BERLIN BLONDES

80	EMI EMI 5031	Science/Mannequin (p/s)	5
80	Scratch SCR 005	Marseille/The Poet (no p/s)	5

SHELLEY BERMAN

60	HMV POP 732	'On The Phone': Hold On/Nephew Trouble	5
60	HMV CLP 1300	INSIDE (LP)	12
60	HMV CLP 1407	THE EDGE OF SHELLEY BERMAN (LP)	12

BERMUDAS

64	London HLN 9894	Donnie/Chu Sen Ling	12

BERNADETTE

67	Rim RIM 2	Come Kiss Me Love/Let Me Do The Talking	6

KENNY BERNARD (& WRANGLERS)

65	Pye 7N 15920	The Tracker/You Gotta Give (with Wranglers)	12
66	Pye 7N 17131	Nothing Can Change This Love/What Love Brings	22
67	Pye 7N 17233	Ain't No Soul (Left In These Old Shoes)/Hey Woman	18
67	CBS 2936	Somebody/Pity My Feet	45
68	CBS 3860	Victim Of Perfume And Lace/A Change Is Gonna Come	10

(see also Kenny & Wranglers, Wranglers, Cat's Pyjamas)

ROD BERNARD

59	London HLM 8849	This Should Go On Forever/Pardon, Mr. Gordon	25
59	London HLM 8849	This Should Go On Forever/Pardon, Mr. Gordon (78)	60
59	Mercury AMT 1070	One More Chance/Shedding Teardrops Over You	8

BERNIE & BUZZ BAND

68	Decca F 22829	The House That Jack Built/PETE KELLY'S SOULUTION: Midnight Confessions (export issue)	15
68	Deram DM 181	When Something's Wrong With My Baby/Don't Knock It	6

(see also Pete Kelly's Soulution)

ELMER BERNSTEIN

56	Brunswick 05544	Clark Street (Parts 1 & 2) (gold or silver print on label)	10/6
59	Capitol CL 15101	Staccato's Theme/The Jazz At Waldo's	5
59	Capitol CL 15101	Staccato's Theme/The Jazz At Waldo's (78)	8
61	United Artists/HMV POP 889	The Magnificent Seven/The Lonely Rebel	6
63	MGM MGM 1238	Rat Race/Saints & Sinners	8
66	United Artists UP 1163	The Magnificent Seven/Return Of The Seven	5
60	Capitol EAP1 1287	STACCATO (EP)	8
57	London HA-P 2076	MEN IN WAR (LP, soundtrack)	65
58	London HA-D 2074/5	THE TEN COMMANDMENTS (2-LP, soundtrack)	35
58	London HA-D 2111	DESIRE UNDER THE ELMS (LP, soundtrack)	18
58	London HA-T 2125	GOD'S LITTLE ACRE (LP, soundtrack)	18
62	MGM MGM-C 891	WALK ON THE WILD SIDE (LP, soundtrack)	18
63	United Artists ULP 1041	THE GREAT ESCAPE (LP, soundtrack)	18
66	United Artists (S)ULP 1140	CAST A GIANT SHADOW (LP, soundtrack)	15
67	RCA Victor RD 7792	THE SILENCERS (LP, soundtrack)	35
67	Fontana TL 5306	BABY, THE RAIN MUST FALL (LP, soundtrack)	35
69	Paramount SPFL 254	WHERE'S JACK? (LP, soundtrack)	18
70	Capitol E-ST 263	TRUE GRIT (LP, soundtrack)	15

CHUCK BERRY

78s

56	London HLU 8275	No Money Down/Down Bound Train (78)	100
57	London HLN 8375	You Can't Catch Me/Havana Moon (78)	75
57	London HLU 8428	Roll Over Beethoven/Drifting Heart (78)	40
57	Columbia DB 3951	School Day (Ring! Ring! Goes The Bell)/Blue Feeling (78)	30
57	London HLM 8531	Rock And Roll Music/Blue Feeling (78)	50
58	London HLM 8585	Sweet Little Sixteen/Reelin' And Rockin' (78)	30
58	London HLM 8629	Johnny B. Goode/Around And Around (78)	40
58	London HL 8677	Beautiful Delilah/Vacation Time (78)	50
58	London HL 8712	Carol/Hey Pedro (78)	70
58	London HLM 8767	Sweet Little Rock And Roller/Joe Joe Gun (78)	80
59	London HLM 8853	Almost Grown/Little Queenie (78)	90
59	London HLM 8921	Back In The U.S.A./Memphis, Tennessee (78)	120

MINT VALUE £

CHUCK BERRY

SINGLES

56	London HLU 8275	No Money Down/Down Bound Train (gold lettering, existence unconfirmed) . . .	600
56	London HLU 8275	No Money Down/Down Bound Train (silver lettering on label,	
		triangular or round centre)	250/140
57	London HLN 8375	You Can't Catch Me/Havana Moon (gold lettering on label, later silver)	250/140
57	London HLU 8428	Roll Over Beethoven/Drifting Heart	85
57	Columbia DB 3951	School Day (Ring! Ring! Goes The Bell)/Blue Feeling	85
57	London HLM 8531	Rock And Roll Music/Blue Feeling	55
58	London HLM 8585	Sweet Little Sixteen/Reelin' And Rockin'	30
58	London HLM 8629	Johnny B. Goode/Around And Around	20
58	London HL 8677	Beautiful Delilah/Vacation Time	35
58	London HL 8712	Carol/Hey Pedro	35
58	London HL 7055	Carol/Hey Pedro (export issue)	40
58	London HLM 8767	Sweet Little Rock And Roller/Joe Joe Gun	22
59	London HLM 8853	Almost Grown/Little Queenie	22
59	London HLM 8921	Back In The U.S.A./Memphis, Tennessee	25

(The above London 45s were originally issued with triangular centres; later silver top label/round centre pressings are worth half to two-thirds these values.)

60	London HLM 9069	Let It Rock/Too Pooped To Pop	18
60	London HLM 9159	Bye Bye Johnny/Mad Lad	18
61	Pye International 7N 25100	I'm Talkin' 'Bout You/Little Star (blue label, later red/yellow)	15/12
63	Pye International 7N 25209	Go Go Go/Come On	6
63	Pye International 7N 25218	Memphis, Tennessee/Let It Rock	6
63	Pye International 7N 25228	Run Rudolph Run/Johnny B. Goode	7
64	Pye International 7N 25236	Nadine (Is It You?)/O Rangutang	6
64	Pye International 7N 25242	No Particular Place To Go/Liverpool Drive	6
64	Pye International 7N 25257	You Never Can Tell/Brenda Lee	7
64	Pye International 7N 25271	Little Marie/Go Bobby Soxer	6
65	Pye International 7N 25285	The Promised Land/The Things I Used To Do	6
65	Chess CRS 8006	Lonely School Days/I Got A Booking	7
65	Chess CRS 8012	Dear Dad/My Little Lovelight	7
65	Chess CRS 8022	It Wasn't Me/It's My Own Business	7
66	Chess CRS 8037	Ramona Say Yes/Lonely School Days	7
66	Mercury MF 958	Club Nitty Gritty/Laugh And Cry	5
67	Mercury MF 994	Back To Memphis/I Do Really Love You	5
68	Mercury MF 1057	St. Louis To Frisco/Ma Dear	5
68	Chess CRS 8075	Johnny B. Goode/Sweet Little Sixteen	6
69	Chess CRS 8089	No Particular Place To Go/It Wasn't Me	6
72	Chess 6145 007	Rock And Roll Music/Johnny B. Goode/School Days	5

EPs

56	London REU 1053	RHYTHM AND BLUES WITH CHUCK BERRY	
		(EP, maroon/gold label, triangular centre)	160
56	London REU 1053	RHYTHM AND BLUES WITH CHUCK BERRY	
		(EP, later pressing, maroon/silver label, round centre)	65
60	London REM 1188	REELIN' AND ROCKIN' (EP, maroon/silver label, tri or round centre)	160/75
63	Pye Intl. NEP 44011	CHUCK BERRY (EP)	15
63	Pye Intl. NEP 44013	THIS IS CHUCK BERRY (EP)	15
64	Pye Intl. NEP 44018	THE BEST OF CHUCK BERRY (EP)	15
64	Pye Intl. NEP 44028	CHUCK BERRY HITS (EP)	15
64	Pye Intl. NEP 44033	BLUE MOOD (EP)	15
65	Chess CRE 6002	THE PROMISED LAND (EP)	25
65	Chess CRE 6005	COME ON (EP)	25
66	Chess CRE 6012	I GOT A BOOKING (EP)	25
66	Chess CRE 6016	YOU CAME A LONG WAY FROM ST. LOUIS (EP)	25

LPs

58	London HA-M 2132	ONE DOZEN BERRYS (LP)	110
62	Pye Intl. NPL 28019	NEW JUKE BOX HITS (LP)	30
63	Pye Intl. NPL 28024	CHUCK BERRY (LP)	18
63	Pye Intl. NPL 28027	CHUCK BERRY ON STAGE (LP)	15
63	Pye Intl. NPL 28028	MORE CHUCK BERRY (LP)	15
64	Pye Intl. NPL 28031	THE LATEST AND THE GREATEST (LP)	18
64	Pye Intl. NPL 28039	YOU NEVER CAN TELL (LP)	18
65	Chess CRL 4005	CHUCK BERRY IN LONDON (LP)	15
65	Chess CRL 4506	FRESH BERRYS (LP)	15
66	Golden Guinea GGL 0352	CHUCK BERRY (LP)	12
67	Mercury 20110 (S)MCL	CHUCK BERRY IN MEMPHIS (LP)	12
67	Mercury 20112 (S)MCL	LIVE AT THE FILLMORE AUDITORIUM — SAN FRANCISCO (LP)	12
69	Mercury 20162 (S)MCL	CONCERTO IN B. GOODE (LP)	15
72	Chess 6641 018	GOLDEN DECADE (2-LP, gatefold sleeve)	15

CHUCK BERRY/BO DIDDLEY

63	Pye Intl. NEP 44009	CHUCK AND BO (EP)	15
63	Pye Intl. NEP 44012	CHUCK AND BO, VOL. 2 (EP)	15
64	Pye Intl. NEP 44017	CHUCK AND BO, VOL. 3 (EP)	18
64	Pye Intl. NPL 28047	TWO GREAT GUITARS (LP)	22

(see also Bo Diddley)

DAVE BERRY (& CRUISERS)

63	Decca F 11734	Memphis Tennessee/Tossin' & Turnin' (with Cruisers)	10
63	Decca F 11803	My Baby Left Me/Hoochie Coochie Man (B-side with Cruisers)	8
64	Decca F 11876	Baby It's You/Sweet And Lovely	7
64	Decca F 11937	The Crying Game/Don't Gimme No Lip Child	5
64	Decca F 12020	One Heart Between Two/You're Gonna Need Somebody	6
65	Decca F 12103	Little Things/I've Got A Tiger By The Tail	6
65	Decca F 12188	This Strange Effect/Now	8
65	Decca F 12258	I'm Gonna Take You There/Just Don't Know	6
66	Decca F 12337	If You Wait For Love/Hidden	6
66	Decca F 12435	Mama/Walk, Walk, Talk, Talk	5
66	Decca F 12513	Picture Me Gone/Ann	7
67	Decca F 12579	Stranger/Stick By The Book	6
67	Decca F 12651	Forever/And I Have Learned To Dream	6
68	Decca F 12739	Just As Much As Ever/I Got A Feeling	6
68	Decca F 12771	(Do I Figure) In Your Life/Latisha	6
69	Decca F 12905	Oh What A Life (by Dave Berry & Sponge)/Huma Luma	6
70	Decca F 12999	Change Our Minds/Long Walk To D.C.	6
70	Decca F 13080	Chaplin House/Trees	5
72	CBS 7780	Movin' On (Turn Around)/Don't Bring Me Down	5
88	Flagstaff 002	Out Of Time/Serenade To Alice (p/s, 200 only)	5
64	Decca DFE 8601	DAVE BERRY (EP)	25
65	Decca DFE 8625	CAN I GET IT FROM YOU (EP)	20
64	Decca LK 4653	DAVE BERRY (LP)	45
66	Decca LK 4823	THE SPECIAL SOUND OF DAVE BERRY (LP)	30
66	Ace Of Clubs ACL 1218	ONE DOZEN BERRIES (LP, also stereo SCL 1218)	18/22
68	Decca LK/SKL 4932	DAVE BERRY '68 (LP)	30
87	Butt BUTT 007	HOSTAGE TO THE BEAT (LP, 1,000 only)	12

(see also Cruisers)

HEIDI BERRY

91	4AD HB 1	EXTRACTS FROM "LOVE" (CD sampler, card sleeve, promo only)	15

MIKE BERRY (& OUTLAWS)

61	Decca F 11314	Will You Love Me Tomorrow/My Baby Doll (with Outlaws)	25
61	HMV POP 912	Tribute To Buddy Holly/What's The Matter (with Outlaws)	12
62	HMV POP 979	It's Just A Matter Of Time/Little Boy Blue (backing group miscredited as Admirals, actually Outlaws)	12
62	HMV POP 1042	Every Little Kiss/How Many Times	15
62	HMV POP 1105	Don't You Think It's Time/Loneliness (with Outlaws)	7
63	HMV POP 1142	My Little Baby/You'll Do It, You'll Fall In Love	15
63	HMV POP 1194	It Really Doesn't Matter/Try A Little Bit Harder	12
64	HMV POP 1257	This Little Girl/On My Mind	12
64	HMV POP 1284	Lovesick/Letter Of Love	12
64	HMV POP 1314	Who Will It Be/Talk (with Innocents)	12
64	HMV POP 1362	Two Lovers/Don't Try To Stand In My Way	7
65	HMV POP 1449	That's All I Ever Wanted From You/She Didn't Care	7
65	HMV POP 1494	It Comes And Goes/Gonna Fall In Love	7
66	HMV POP 1530	Warm Baby/Just Thought I'd 'Phone	7
67	Polydor 56182	Raining In My Heart/Eyes	7
72	York SYK 516	Going Down To Virginia/Love Her	5
72	York SYK 530	Drift Away/Keep Your Eyes On The Road	5
63	HMV 7EG 8793	IT'S TIME FOR MIKE BERRY (EP, with Outlaws)	30
63	HMV 7EG 8808	A TRIBUTE TO BUDDY HOLLY (EP)	35
72	York FYK 409	AMBUSH (LP)	15

(see also Outlaws, Timothy Barclay, Le Roys, Shepperton Flames, Innocents [U.K])

RICHARD BERRY & PHARAOHS

64	Ember EMB EP 4527	RHYTHM AND BLUES VOL. 3 (EP)	180

BERRY STREET STATION

75	Crystal CR 7024	Chocolate Sugar/All I Want Is You	8

JON BEST

65	Decca F 12077	Young Boy Blues/Living Without Love	12

MINT VALUE £

PETE BEST FOUR
64   Decca F 11929   I'm Gonna Knock On Your Door/Why Did I Fall In Love With You?............. 55
(see also Beatles, Lee Curtis & All Stars)

THE BETA BAND
97   Regal REG 16   CHAMPION VERSIONS EP: Dry The Rain/I Know/B+A/Dog's Got A Bone
(12", p/s, 1,000 only)... 20
98   Regal REG 18   THE PATTY PATTY SOUND EP: Inner Meet Me/The House/The Monolith/
She's The One (2 x 12", p/s, 1,000 only) 12
98   Regal REG 18   THE PATTY PATTY SOUND EP: Inner Meet Me/The House/The Monolith/
She's The One (CD, card slipcase) 8

BETHNAL
77   Bethnal VIOL 1   The Fiddler/This Just Ain't Another Love Song (p/s, gig freebie) 10
78   Vertigo BET 1   We've Gotta Get Out Of This Place/Outcome (p/s) 5
78   Vertigo BET 2   Don't Do It/Where Do We Stand (p/s) 5
78   Vertigo BET 12   Don't Do It/Where Do We Stand (12", p/s) 8
78   Vertigo 6059 213   Nothing New/Summer Wine (p/s, blue vinyl) 5

BET LYNCH'S LEGS
80   Absurd ABSURD 10   Riders In The Sky/High Noon (p/s) 4
80   Absurd ABSURD 11   Some Like It Hot/Some Don't (p/s) 4

BETTERDAYS
65   Polydor BM 56024   Don't Want That/Here 'Tis. 200
91   N.T.B. 001   HOWL OF THE STREETS (EP, numbered p/s) 8
92   N.T.B. 1002   DOWN ON THE WATERFRONT (EP, numbered p/s) 8

HAROLD BETTERS
65   Sue WI 378   Do Anything You Wanna (Parts 1 & 2) 15

BETWEEN PICTURES
80   A Side Records SON 2216   Treat Me Like An Equal/Life Of Your Own 5

BEVERLEY
66   Deram DM 101   Happy New Year/Where The Good Times Are 8
67   Deram DM 137   Museum/DENNY CORDELL ENSEMBLE: A Quick One For Sanity 8
(see also John & Beverley Martyn, Levee Breakers)

BEVERLEY SISTERS
54   Philips PB 370   Sisters/The Mama Doll Song (78) 10
54   Philips PB 378   It's Christmas All Over The World/I Saw Mummy Kissing Santa Claus (78)...... 10
55   Decca F 10539   I Remember Mama/I've Been Thinking 7
55   Decca F 10603   Humming Bird/Have You Ever Been Lonely? 7
55   Decca F 10641   My Heart Goes A-Sailing/Teddy Bear 7
56   Decca F 10705   Willie Can/I've Started Courtin' 10
56   Decca F 10729   Rickshaw Boy/You Ought To Have A Wife 6
56   Decca F 10770   Born To Be With You/It's Easy 7
56   Decca F 10813   Come Home To My Arms/Doodle-Doo-Doo 6
57   Decca F 10832   I Dreamed/Mama From The Train (A Kiss, A Kiss) 6
57   Decca F 10853   Greensleeves/I'll See You In My Dreams 6
57   Decca F 10893   Mr. Wonderful/Blow The Wind Southerly 6
57   Decca F 10909   Bye, Bye Love/It's Illegal, It's Immoral, Or It Makes You Fat 7
57   Decca F 10909   Bye, Bye Love/It's Illegal, It's Immoral, Or It Makes You Fat (78) 10
57   Decca F 10943   Riding Down From Bangor/The Young Cavaliero 6
58   Decca F 10971   Long Black Nylons/Without You 10
58   Decca F 10971   Long Black Nylons/Without You (78) 10
58   Decca F 10999   Always And Forever/Siesta 5
58   Decca F 11042   Left Right Out Of My Heart/I Would (Climb The Highest Mountain) 5
59   Decca F 11107   The Little Drummer Boy/Strawberry Fair. 5
59   Decca F 11172   Little Donkey/And Kings Come A-Calling 5
56   Columbia SEG 7602   THREE'S COMPANY (EP). 12
56   Decca DFE 6307   THE BEVERLEY SISTERS (EP). 12
57   Decca DFE 6401   THE BEVERLEY SISTERS NO. 2 (EP). 15
57   Decca DFE 6402   THE BEVERLEY SISTERS NO. 3 (EP) 10
58   Decca DFE 6512   THE BEVERLEY SISTERS NO. 4 (EP) 12
50s   Decca DFE 6611   THE BEVS FOR CHRISTMAS (EP). 10
55   Philips BBR 8052   A DATE WITH THE BEVS (10" LP) 25
60   Columbia 33SX 1285   THE ENCHANTING BEVERLEY SISTERS (LP, also stereo [SCX 3351])....... 12/15
60   Ace Of Clubs ACL 1048   THOSE BEVERLEY SISTERS (LP)....................................... 12

BEVERLEY'S ALLSTARS
65   Black Swan WI 449   Go Home/THEO BECKFORD: Ungrateful People 15
69   Trojan TR 683   Double Shot/Gimme Gimme Gal (B-side act. "Banana Water" by Mellotones)..... 8
70   Trojan TR 7729   Moon Dust/Fat Cat (both sides actually by Ansell Collins) 7
(see also Clarendonians, Gaylads, Ken Boothe, Glen Brown, Desmond Dekker, Bob Marley, Maytals, Melodians, Derrick Morgan, Pioneers, Rockstones, Bruce Ruffin, Delroy Wilson)

BEVERLY HILLBILLIES
66   Starlite GRK 602   THE FABULOUS BEVERLY HILLBILLIES (LP)............................. 15

BEVIS FROND
88   Freakbeat/Lyntone   African Violets (flexidisc free with *Freakbeat* fanzine)..................... 8/6
88   Bucketfull Of Brains BOB 21   High In A Flat/DREAM SYNDICATE: Blind Willie McTell (free with
Bucketfull Of Brains issue 27, 33rpm, yellow die-cut sleeve) 15/12
90   Clawfist PIS 1   Sexorcist/WALKINGSEEDS: Reflection In A Tall Mirror (p/s, mail-order only) 6
87   Woronzow WOO 3   MIASMA (LP) 15
87   Woronzow WOO 4   INNER MARSHLAND (LP) 10
87   Woronzow WOO 5 1/2   BEVIS THROUGH THE LOOKING GLASS — THE GREAT MAGNET DISASTER
(2-LP, 500 only, originals all signed, with booklet; counterfeits unsigned) 60
88   Woronzow WOO 8   TRIPTYCH (LP).. 15

MINT VALUE £

90	Woronzow WOO 13	MAGIC EYE (LP, featuring Twink, 200 only)	15
91	Woronzow WOO 16	NEW RIVER HEAD (2-LP, 1st 500 with EP & insert)	20/15
92	Woronzow WOO 18	LONDON STONE (LP)	15
92	Woronzow WOO 26	SUPERSEEDER (2-LP)	18
93	Woronzow WOO 21	IT JUST IS (2-LP, gatefold sleeve)	15
93	Woronzow WOO 22	SPRAWL (2-LP, gatefold sleeve, with insert)	18
97	Woronzow WOO 406	NORTH CIRCULAR (3-LP, with insert, 750 only, signed & numbered)	30

(see also Von Trap Family, Room 13)

RODNEY BEWES
| 69 | Revolution REV 1003 | Remember When/Dear Mother Love Albert | 6 |
| 70 | Revolution Pop REVP 1001 | Dear Mother Love Albert/Meter Maid | 6 |

(see also Highly Likely)

BEYOND
| 82 | MJB MEL 001 | Father's Name Was Dad/Grey (p/s) | 5 |

BEYOND
90	Big Cat ABB 15T	Eve Of My Release (12", p/s, with inserts)	10
90	Big Cat ABB 22T	No Excuse (12", p/s)	10
90	Big Cat ABB 22T	No Excuse (12", test pressing in proof sleeve)	15
90	Big Cat ABB SCD 22	No Excuse (CD)	8
91	Harvest 12 HAR 5300	Empire (12", poster p/s)	8
91	Harvest HARS 5301	RAGING (EP, p/s, with cards)	7

BEYOND THE IMPLODE
| 79 | Diverse 101 | LAST THOUGHTS EP (EP, limited edtion, numbered) | 8 |

B-52's
79	Island WIP 6527	6060-842/Hero Worship (p/s)	6
80	Island PWIP 6551	Planet Claire/There's A Moon In The Sky (Called The Moon) (picture disc)	5
80	Island WIP 6579	Give Me Back My Man/Give Me Back My Man (Version) (p/s, mispressed, B-side plays "Strobe Light")	8
80	Island WIP 6685	Strobe Light/Dirty Back Road (in blue/black plastic bag)	8
83	Island ISD 107	Future Generation/Future Generation (Instrumental)//Planet Claire/There's A Moon In The Sky (Called The Moon) (double pack, gatefold p/s)	6
86	Island BFTD 1	Rock Lobster/Planet Claire//Song For A Future Generation/52 Girls (double pack)	6
86	Island BFTR/BFTL/BFTP 1	Rock Lobster/Planet Claire (set of 3 x 10" x 7" picture discs ['rock'/'lobster'/ 'planet'], each with same tracks, in printed PVC folder)	12
90	Reprise W 9917X	Love Shack/Planet Claire (live)/Rock Lobster (live) (p/s, with 'Shack Pack')	6
90	Reprise W 9917P	Love Shack/Planet Claire (live)/Rock Lobster (live) (picture disc, promo only)	10
90	Reprise W 9737X	Channel Z/Roam (deluxe 'TV' pack)	4
92	Reprise W 0109	Good Stuff/Bad Stuff (p/s)	5
92	Reprise W 0141	Is That You Mo-Dean?/Good Stuff (p/s)	5
79	Island ILPS 9580	THE B-52's (LP, with bonus single "Rock Lobster"/"52 Girls" [PSR 438])	15
80	Island ILPS 9622	WILD PLANET (LP, in plastic bag with badge)	15

MAURICIO BIANCHI
| 81 | Sterile SR 2 | SYMPATHY FOR A GENOCIDE (LP, 200 only) | 70 |

GENE BIANCO GROUP
| 53 | London L 1209 | Limehouse Boogie/Harpin' Boogie (78) | 12 |
| 60 | Vogue V 9167 | Alarm Clock Rock/Harp Rock Boogie | 20 |

BIBBY
| 65 | Blue Beat BB 289 | Rub It Down/Wicked Man (actually by Harris Seaton) | 15 |

(see also B.B. Seaton, Horace Seaton)

BILL BICKELL TRIO
| 51 | MGM 411 | Signed Sealed And Delivered/Strange Little Girl (78) | 8 |

BIDDU
| 67 | Regal Zonophone RZ 3002 | Daughter Of Love/Look Out Here I Come | 6 |
| 69 | Polydor 56323 | Started Me Thinking/Where In The World | 5 |

(see also Headbangers)

BIELERFELDER KINDERCHOR
| 66 | Parlophone CPCS 105 | A GERMAN CHRISTMAS (LP, export issue, yellow/black label) | 12 |

BIFF BANG POW!
84	Creation CRE 003	Fifty Years Of Fun/Then When I Scream (foldaround sprayed p/s in poly bag)	8
84	Creation CRE 007	There Must Be A Better Life/The Chocolate Elephant Man (foldaround p/s in poly bag)	15
90	Caff CAFF 13	Sleep/TIMES: Extase (p/s, with insert)	20
89	Creation CRELP 046	THE ACID HOUSE ALBUM (LP, hand-sprayed sleeve)	10

(see also Laughing Apple, Times)

BIG AMONGST SHEEP
| 83 | Rock Solid RSS 01 | ASTROPOP (12" EP, p/s) | 12 |
| 82 | Rock Solid RSR 2001 | TERMINAL VELOCITY (LP) | 60 |

(see also Inner City Unit, Silverwing)

BIG BARON
| 60 | Top Rank JAR 404 | Swinging Bells (Oberon Jump)/Romance | 10 |

BIG BEN ACCORDIAN BAND
| 56 | Columbia DB 3835 | "Rock 'N' Roll (No. 1)" Medley (both sides) | 8 |
| 56 | Columbia DB 3856 | "Rock 'N' Roll (No. 2)" Medley (both sides) | 8 |

(see also Norrie Paramor & His Orchestra)

BIG BEN BANJO BAND
| 66 | Columbia DB 8069 | Beatle Medley For Mums And Pops (Parts 1 & 2) | 5 |

(see also Billie Anthony, Norrie Paramor & His Orchestra)

BIG BEN TRAD BAND

MINT VALUE £

61	Columbia 33SX 1356	BIG BEN TRAD BAND (LP)	40

BIG BERTHA featuring ACE KEFFORD
69	Atlantic 584 298	This World's An Apple/Gravy Booby Jamm	20

(see also Cozy Powell, Ace Kefford Stand, Bedlam, Youngblood)

BIG BLACK
86	Homestead HMS 042	Il Duce/Big Money (p/s)	15
87	Blast First BFFP 24	He's A Whore/The Model (p/s)	8
85	Homestead HMS 007	RACER-X (12" EP, with insert)	8
87	Blast First BFFP 14T	HEADACHE (12" p/s, 1,000 only in black vinyl bag, dark red vinyl, 12-page booklet, fold-out poster & free 45, "Heartbeat"/"Things To Do Today"/ "I Can't Believe", sealed with gold medallion, Blast First logo on back)	50
87	NOT 2 (BUT 1)	SOUND OF IMPACT (LP, matt sleeve, no'd up to 1,000, with 8-page booklet)	40
87	NOT 2 (BUT 1)	SOUND OF IMPACT (LP, laminated sleeve, numbered from 1,001-1,500, with 8-page booklet)	20
87	NOT 2 (BUT 1)	SOUND OF IMPACT (LP, unnumbered, with 8-page booklet)	10
92	Touch & Go TG 81	PIGPILE (LP, boxed set with video & T-shirt with insert)	30

(see also Rapeman)

BIG BOB
59	Top Rank JAR 185	Your Line Was Busy/What Am I	25

BIG BOPPER
58	Mercury AMT 1002	Chantilly Lace/The Purple People Eater Meets The Witchdoctor	12
58	Mercury AMT 1002	Chantilly Lace/The Purple People Eater Meets The Witchdoctor (78)	45
59	Mercury AMT 1017	Big Bopper's Wedding/Little Red Riding Hood	20
59	Mercury AMT 1017	Big Bopper's Wedding/Little Red Riding Hood (78)	55
59	Mercury AMT 1046	It's The Truth, Ruth/That's What I Am Talking About	22
59	Mercury ZEP 10004	THE BIG BOPPER (EP)	160
59	Mercury ZEP 10027	PINK PETTICOATS (EP)	260
58	Mercury MMC 14008	CHANTILLY LACE (LP)	200
74	Contour 6870 531	CHANTILLY LACE (LP)	15

BIG BORIS
72	RCA RCA 2197	Big Country/Devil's Drive	6

BIG BOY PETE
68	Camp 602 005	Cold Turkey/My Love Is Like A Spaceship	60
96	Tenth Planet TP 026	HOMAGE TO CATATONIA (LP)	12

(see also Miller, Pete Miller)

BIG BROTHER & HOLDING COMPANY
67	Fontana TF 881	Bye Bye Baby/All Is Loneliness	12
68	CBS 3683	Piece Of My Heart/Turtle Blues (some in p/s)	18/6
68	London HLT 10226	Down On Me/Call On Me	8
67	Fontana (S)TL 5457	BIG BROTHER & THE HOLDING COMPANY (LP, with Janis Joplin, mono/stereo)	35/30
68	CBS (S)63392	CHEAP THRILLS (LP, with Janis Joplin, laminated single sleeve, mono/stereo)	50/15
69	London HA-T/SH-T 8377	BIG BROTHER & THE HOLDING COMPANY (LP, reissue, mono/stereo)	20
71	CBS S 64118	BE A BROTHER (LP)	14
86	Edsel ED 170	JOSEPH'S COAT (LP)	12

(see also Janis Joplin, Nick Gravenites)

BIG CARROT
73	EMI EMI 2047	Blackjack/Squint Eye Mangle	30

(see also Marc Bolan/T. Rex)

BIG CHIEF
91	Snake Skin SS007	Friday Night Aug. 14th/Bong Wrench (p/s)	5

BIG COUNTRY
83	Mercury COUP 2	Fields Of Fire/Angle Park/Harvest Home (Scotland-shaped picture disc)	6
83	Mercury COUNT 313	In A Big Country (Pure Mix)/Heart And Soul/In A Big Country/All Of Us (12", red p/s)	7
84	Mercury COUP 4	Chance/The Tracks Of My Tears (live)/The Crossing (12", picture disc)	7
84	Mercury MERD 185	Where The Rose Is Sown/Belief In The Small Man//Wonderland/In A Big Country/Auld Lang Syne (double pack, gatefold p/s)	6
86	Mercury BIGCP 1	Look Away/Restless Natives (shaped picture disc)	5
88	Mercury BIGCD 5	King Of Emotion/The Travellers/Starred And Crossed/ Not Waving But Drowning (CD)	7
99	Track Records 0004/A	Fragile Thing/I Get Hurt/John Wayne's Dream (CD, promo)	12
83	Mercury MERS 27	THE CROSSING (LP, 1st pressing, red sleeve)	10

(see also Skids)

BIG DAVE (Cavanaugh) & HIS ORCHESTRA
54	Capitol CL 14156	Rock, Roll, Ball And Wall/The Big Goof (78)	18
54	Capitol CL 14195	Loosely With Feeling/The Cat From Coos Bay (triangular centre)	15
55	Capitol CL 14245	Rock And Roll Party/Your Kind Of Love (triangular centre)	30
55	Capitol CL 14245	Rock And Roll Party/Your Kind Of Love (78)	10

BIG FLAME
84	Laughing Gun PLAQUE 001	Sink/The Illness/Sometimes (p/s, with insert)	15

(see also Great Leap Forward)

BARRY BIGGS
70	Dynamic DYN 401	Got To Be Mellow/Love Grows	6

(see also Bob & Marcia)

BIG IN JAPAN
77	Eric's ERICS 0001	Big In Japan/CHUDDIE NUDDIES: Do The Chud (p/s)	10
78	Zoo CAGE 1	FROM Y TO Z AND NEVER AGAIN (EP, foldout p/s)	12

(see also Pink Industry/Military, Holly, Holly Johnson, Yachts, Bill Drummond, Creatures, Siouxsie & Banshees, Lightning Raiders, Original Mirrors)

BIG JOE (Joseph Spalding)
74	Dip DL 5007	Selassie Skank/Version	12
74	Dip DL 5008	Weed Specialist/CHERRY & DUB MASTER: Rub A Daughter	12
74	Dip DL 5027	Hog In A Me Minty/Sweet Melody	20
75	Fab FAB 243	American Pum Pum/Tape White Wash	5

BIG LUCKY, BIG AMOS & DONALD HINES
72	London SHU 8425	RIVER TOWN BLUES (LP)	12

BIG MAYBELLE
57	London HLC 8447	I Don't Want To Cry/All Of Me	40
57	London HLC 8447	I Don't Want To Cry/All Of Me (78)	18
59	London HLC 8854	Baby, Won't You Please Come Home/Say It Isn't So	22
59	London HLC 8854	Baby, Won't You Please Come Home/Say It Isn't So (78)	16
65	London HL 9941	Careless Love/My Mother's Eyes	12
67	CBS 2735	Turn The World Around The Other Way/I Can't Wait Any Longer	22
67	CBS 2926	Mama (He Treats Your Daughter Mean)/Keep That Man	15
68	Direction 58-3312	Quittin' Time/I Can't Wait Any Longer	22
67	CBS 62999	THE PURE SOUL OF BIG MAYBELLE (LP)	40

BIG MOE with BOYD BENNETT & ROCKETS
(see under Boyd Bennett)

BIG MOOSE (Walker)
60s	Python PKM 01	Ramblin' Woman/Puppy Howl Blues	12

BIG NOISE
90s	President PCOM 1111	BIG NOISE (CD)	15

(see also Gary Numan)

BIGROUP
70s	Peer Intl. Library PIL 009	BIG HAMMER (LP, library disc)	100

BIG SLEEP
71	Pegasus PEG 4	BLUEBELL WOOD (LP, gatefold sleeve)	30

(see also Eyes Of Blue, Ancient Grease, Gentle Giant, Man, Ritchie Francis, Gary Pickford-Hopkins)

BIG STAR
78	Stax STAX 504	September Gurls/Mod Lang	6
78	Aura AUS 103	Kizza Me/Dream Lover (p/s)	6
78	Aura AUS 107	Jesus Christ/Big Black Car	5
78	Stax SXSP 302	RADIO CITY/BIG STAR (2-LP)	15
78	Aura AUL 703	THIRD ALBUM (LP)	10

(see also Alex Chilton, Box Tops)

BIG STICK
89	EMI EM 88	Crack Attack/Crack Attack (Freakscene) (p/s)	5

BIG THREE (U.K.)
63	Decca F 11614	Some Other Guy/Let True Love Begin	12
63	Decca F 11689	By The Way/Cavern Stomp	8
63	Decca F 11752	I'm With You/Peanut Butter	12
64	Decca F 11927	If You Ever Change Your Mind/You've Got To Keep Her Under Hand	18
73	Polydor 2058 343	Some Other Guy/Let It Rock/If You Gotta Make A Fool Of Somebody	5
63	Decca DFE 8552	AT THE CAVERN (EP)	45
73	Polydor 2383 199	RESURRECTION (LP)	22

(see also Escorts, Paddy Klaus & Gibson, Johnny Gustafson, Faron's Flamingos, Johnny & John)

BIG THREE (U.S.)
68	Roulette RCP 5002	THE BIG THREE FEATURING MAMA CASS (LP)	18

(see also Mama Cass [Elliot], Mamas & Papas)

BIG YOUTH
72	Blue Beat BB 424	Chi Chi Run/JOHN HOLT: OK Fred	7
73	Downtown DT 497	Dock Of The Bay/CRYSTALITES: Bass And Drums (Version)	10
73	Gayfeet CS 206	Medicine Doctor/Facts Of Life	10
73	Prince Buster PB 46	Chi Chi Run/Drums And Bass (Version)	7
73	Prince Buster PB 48	Leggo Beast/Leave Your Skeng	12
73	Prince Buster PB 50	Cain And Abel/Cain And Abel (Version)	12
73	Grape GR 3040	Foreman Versus Frazier/Foreman Versus Frazier Round Two	8
73	Grape GR 3044	JA To UK/JA To UK (Version)	6
73	Grape GR 3051	Opportunity Rock/Double Attack	15
73	Grape GR 3061	Concrete Jungle/Screaming Tonight	7
73	Green Door GD 4051	Cool Breeze/CRYSTALITES: Windstorm	15
73	Summit SUM 8542	A So We Say (with Dennis Brown)/WINSTON SCOTLAND: Scarface	7
74	Harry J. HJ 6682	Ride On Ride On/Wild Goose Chase (both with Dennis Brown)	5
75	Attack ATT 8104	Mammy Hot And Daddy Cold/GROOVEMASTERS: Some Like It Dread	6
75	Dip DL 5097	Big Youth Dread/Another Version	6
75	Lucky DL 5103	Natty Warning/Version	6
76	Lucky LY 6001	Get Up Stand Up/Version (with Dennis Brown)	6
72	Fab MS 8	CHI CHI RUN (LP)	20
73	Trojan TRLS 61	SCREAMING TARGET (LP)	15
76	Trojan TRLS 123	NATTY CULTURAL DREAD (LP)	12
76	Trojan TRLS 137	HIT THE ROAD JACK (LP)	10

(see also Upsetters, Keith Hudson)

BIG YOUTH & KEITH HUDSON

73	Pyramid PYR 7055	Can You Keep A Secret/HORACE ANDY & EARL FLUTE: Peter And Judas	15

(see also Keith Hudson)

BIKINIS

58	Columbia DB 4149	Bikini/Boogie Rock And Roll	15
58	Columbia DB 4149	Bikini/Boogie Rock And Roll (78)	15

(Mr.) ACKER BILK (& HIS PARAMOUNT JAZZ BAND)

56	Tempo A 134	Dippermouth Blues/Where The River Shannon Flows	7
59	Columbia DB 4382	Summer Set/Acker's Away (78)	8
60	Pye 7NJ 2029	Marching Through Georgia/Delia Gone	5
60	Melodisc 1547	Goodnight Sweet Prince/East Coast Trot	20
60	Pye 7NJ 2033	The C.R.E. March (Wings)/Willie The Weeper	4
60	Pye 7NJ 2034	Blaze Away/Higher Ground (p/s)	6
60	Pye 7NJ 2035	Under The Double Eagle/Easter Parade (p/s)	6
61	Columbia SCD 2155	Stars And Stripes Forever/Creole Jazz (p/s)	8
62	Columbia SCD 2176	Gotta See Baby Tonight/If You Were The Only Girl In The World (p/s)	8
59	Esquire EP 213	MASTER ACKER BILK (EP)	10
59	Pye NJE 1067	ACKER BILK SINGS (EP)	8
59	Columbia SEG 7940	ACKER'S AWAY (EP)	10
60	Melodisc EPM 7 93	Mr. ACKER BILK & HIS PARAMOUNT JAZZ BAND Vol. 1 (EP)	10
60	Melodisc EPM 7 94	Mr. ACKER BILK & HIS PARAMOUNT JAZZ BAND Vol. 2 (EP)	10
60	Melodisc EPM 7 101	Mr. ACKER BILK & HIS PARAMOUNT JAZZ BAND Vol. 3 (EP)	10
60s	Melodisc EPM 7 106	ACKER BILK (EP)	10
62	Columbia SEG 8156	4 HITS AND A MISTER (EP)	8
62	Columbia SEG 8178	BAND OF THIEVES (EP)	15
58	77 LEU 12/1	ACKER'S EARLY DAYS (LP)	20
58	Pye Nixa NJT 513	ACKER BILK REQUESTS (10" LP)	25
59	Columbia 33S 1141	THE NOBLE ART OF ACKER BILK (10" LP)	15
60	Pye NJL 22	THE MR ACKER BILK OMNIBUS (LP)	35
60	Columbia 33SX 1205	SEVEN AGES OF ACKER (LP)	35
60	Columbia 33SX 1248	ACKER (LP)	35
60	Society SOC 908	MY EARLY DAYS (LP)	18
61	Columbia 33SX 1304	A GOLDEN TREASURY OF BILK (LP)	12
61	Columbia 33SX 1348	LANDSDOWNE FOLIO (LP)	35
62	Columbia 33SX 1456	BEAU JAZZ (LP)	12
63	Columbia 33SX 1525	CALL ME MISTER (LP)	30
65	Columbia 33SX 1747	ACK'S BACK (LP)	25
67	Columbia S(C)X 6241	THE VERITABLE MR BILK (LP)	40
70	Starline SRS 5026	EXPO' 70 (LP)	12

(see also Michael London)

BILL & COO

75	Bradley's BRAD 7513	Smoochy Smoochy/Always I Love You	5

(see also Twinkle)

BILLIE & EDDIE

59	Top Rank JAR 249	The King Is Coming Back/Come Back, Baby	12

BILLIE & ESSENTIALS

63	London HLW 9657	Over The Weekend/Maybe You'll Be There	50

BILLION DOLLAR BABIES

77	Polydor 2391 273	BATTLE AXES (LP)	12

(see also Alice Cooper)

TREVOR BILLMUSS

70	Charisma CB 130	Whoops Amour/Sunday Afternoon In Belgrave Square	5
71	Charisma CB 158	English Pastures/Fishing Songs	5
70	Charisma CAS 1017	FAMILY APOLOGY (LP)	12

BILLY & LILLIE (& Billy Ford & Thunderbirds)

58	London HLU 8564	La Dee Dah/BILLY FORD'S THUNDERBIRDS: The Monster	22
58	London HLU 8564	La Dee Dah/BILLY FORD'S THUNDERBIRDS: The Monster (78)	18
58	London HLU 8630	Creepin', Crawlin', Cryin'/Happiness (with Billy Ford & Thunderbirds)	30
58	London HLU 8630	Creepin', Crawlin', Cryin'/Happiness (with Billy Ford & Thunderbirds) (78)	35
58	London HLU 8689	The Greasy Spoon/Hangin' On To You (with Billy Ford & Thunderbirds)	20
58	London HLU 8689	The Greasy Spoon/Hangin' On To You (with Billy Ford & Thunderbirds) (78)	30
59	London HLU 8795	I Promise You/Lucky Ladybug	20
59	London HLU 8795	I Promise You/Lucky Ladybug (78)	35
59	Top Rank JAR 157	Bells, Bells, Bells/Honeymoonin' (as Billie & Lillie)	7
59	Top Rank JAR 157	Bells, Bells, Bells/Honeymoonin' (as Billie & Lillie) (78)	40

BIM & BAM

70	Crab CRAB 48	The Pill (with Clover)/TOMMY McCOOK: Spring Fever	5
70	Crab CRAB 49	Immigrant Plight (w/ Clover)/PETER AUSTIN & HORTENSE: Bang Shangalang	5
73	Gayfeet GS 201	Fatty/Landlord	5

BIM, BAM & CLOVER

70	Trojan TR 7754	Party Time (Parts 1 & 2)	5

BINGO

73	Polydor 2066 365	We Can't Get Enough/Mumblin' Man	10

SONNY BINNS (& RUDIES)

69	Downtown DT 420	The Untouchables/Lazy Boy	6
69	Downtown DT 424	Wheels/Night Train	6
70	Escort ES 818	Boss A Moon (as S. Binns)/BUNNY LEE ALLSTARS: Brotherly Love	7

(see also Rudies)

TONY BINNS
71	Explosion EX 2044	Love I Madly/Musical Shower	8
71	Explosion EX 2046	Humpty Dumpty/Got To Get A Message	10

BIONIC BOOGIE
(see under Gregg Diamond)

BIOTA
85	Recommended DYS 12 & 13	RACKABONES (LP, with inserts)	40

IVOR BIRD
78	RSO 2090 270	Over The Wall We Go/Beauty Queen	7

(see also Oscar, Paul Dean & Soul Savages, Paul Nicholas)

STANLEY & JEFFREY BIRD
60	HMV POP 702	Johnny At The Crossheads/Betty, Betty (Go Steady With Me)	7

BIRDHOUSE
80s	Strychnine STR 01	New Race (live)/MONKS: You Took Me By Surprise (33rpm flexidisc, free with *Strychnine* magazine)	5/4

BIRD LEGS & PAULINE
66	Sue WI 4014	Spring/In So Many Ways	15

BIRDS
64	Decca F 12031	You're On My Mind/You Don't Love Me (You Don't Care)	75
65	Decca F 12140	Leaving Here/Next In Line	60
65	Decca F 12257	No Good Without You Baby/How Can It Be	65
85	Demon WEST 901	THESE BIRDS ARE DANGEROUS (LP)	15

(see also Birds Birds, Ron Wood, Faces, Creation, Ashton Gardner & Dyke)

BIRDS & BRASS
70	Rediffusion ZS 57	SOUNDSATIONAL (LP)	12
74	Rediffusion 0100 171	...ARE BACK (LP)	12

BIRDS BIRDS
66	Reaction 591 005	Say Those Magic Words/Daddy Daddy	325

(see also Birds)

BIRDS OF A FEATHER
69	Page One POF 156	Blacksmith Blues/Sing My Song And Pray	6
70	Page One POF 179	All God's Children Got Soul/Get It Together	6
72	Jam JAM 23	You Know Me Better/Summer Has Gone	5
72	DJM DJS 243	Thank You/Baby Don't You Bring Me Down	5
70	Page One POLS 027	BIRDS OF A FEATHER (LP)	30

(see also Chanters, Chanter Sisters)

BIRDS WITH EARS
83	Laughing Man BONK 1	Mr Sneed/Doggy (p/s)	4

JANE BIRKIN & SERGE GAINSBOURG
69	Fontana TF 1042	Je T'Aime, Moi Non Plus/Jane B (initially with p/s)	10/6
69	Major Minor MM 645	Je T'Aime, Moi Non Plus/Jane B (reissue)	5
72	Philips 6009 201	La Decadanse/Les Langues De Chat	8
74	Antic K 11511	Je T'Aime, Moi Non Plus/Jane B (2nd reissue, 'nude' p/s)	10
69	Fontana STL 5493	JANE BIRKIN AND SERGE GAINSBOURG (LP)	30

BIRMINGHAM
71	Grosvenor GRS 1011	BIRMINGHAM (LP)	80

(see also Dave Peace Quartet)

BIRTH CONTROL
71	Charisma CAS 1036	BIRTH CONTROL (LP)	18

BIRTHDAY PARTY
80	4AD AD 12	The Friend Catcher/Waving My Arms/Cat Man (p/s)	8
81	4AD AD 111	Release The Bats/Blast Off (p/s)	8
81	4AD AD 114	Mr. Clarinet/Happy Birthday (p/s)	8
82	Masterbag BAG 005	Dead Joe (flexidisc free with *Masterbag* magazine issue 15)	8/6

(see also Nick Cave & Bad Seeds, Roland S. Howard & Lydia Lunch)

BIS
95	Chemikal U'ground CHEM 2	DISCO NATION (EP, 400 only, b&w sleeve, hand-printed label with insert)	4
96	Chemikal U'ground CHEM 3	THE SECRET VAMPIRE SOUNDTRACK (EP, with insert, 1st 3,000 with foil 'Bis' lettering)	4

DICKIE BISHOP & SIDEKICKS
57	Decca F 10869	Cumberland Gap/No Other Baby	12
57	Decca F 10869	Cumberland Gap/No Other Baby (78)	8
57	Decca F 10959	The Prisoner's Song/Please Remember Me	12
57	Decca F 10959	The Prisoner's Song/Please Remember Me (78)	10
58	Decca F 10981	Skip To My Lou/No Other Baby	8
58	Decca F 10981	Skip To My Lou/No Other Baby (78)	10
58	Decca F 11028	They Can't Take That Away From Me/Jumpin' Judy	8
58	Decca F 11028	They Can't Take That Away From Me/Jumpin' Judy (78)	15

(see also Chris Barber's Skiffle Group)

TOMMY BISHOP'S RICOCHETS
65	Decca F 12238	I Should Have Known/On The Other Hand	6

(see also Rock 'n' Roll Revival Show)

BISHOPS
(see under Count Bishops)

BITCH
| 79 | Hurricane FIRE 5 | Big City/Wild Kids (p/s) | 6 |

BITCH
| 81 | Rutland RX 101 | First Bite/Maggie (no p/s, some with promo insert) | 10/15 |

BITCHES SIN
81	Neat NEAT 09	Always Ready For Love/Sign Of The Times (p/s)	8
83	Quiet QT 001	No More Chances/Overnight/Ice Angels (12", p/s)	10
83	Terminal TCAS 21	OUT OF MY MIND (EP, cassette, 6-track)	8
82	Heavy Metal HMRLP 4	PREDATOR (LP)	15

BITCH MAGNET
| 91 | Caff CAFF 14 | Sadie/Ducks And Drakes (p/s, with insert) | 8 |

BITING TONGUES
| 85 | Factory FAC 134 | Trouble Hand/Panorama/Meat Mask Separatist/Boss Toyota Trouble/Probate (12", p/s) | 7 |
| 87 | Factory FAC 188 | Compressor/Compressor (promo only) | 6 |

(see also 808 State)

BITTER SPRINGS
| 97 | Wurlitzer Jukebox WJ 34 | It's Business/Planet Smackhead (p/s) | 4 |

BIZ
| 93 | Warp WARP LP 9 | ELECTRO SOMA (LP, orange vinyl) | 12 |

BIZET BOYS
| 89 | Parlophone RIDE 1 | Ride 'Em Cowboy/Ride 'Em Cowboy (Speechless) (p/s) | 5 |
| 89 | Parlophone 12RIDE 1 | Ride 'Em Cowboy (A Classic Mix)/Ride 'Em Cowboy (Opera House Mix)/Ride 'Em Cowboy (3 M's Much More Mix) (12", p/s) | 10 |

BJÖRK
93	One Little Indian BJDJ 101	One Day (Endorphin Mix)/(Springs Eternal Mix) (10", die-cut sleeve, promo only, 2,000 copies)	18
93	One Little Indian BJDJ 102	Violently Happy (12" Mix)/(Basso Hitto Dubo) (10", die-cut sleeve, promo only, 2,000 copies)	18
94	One Little Indian BJDJ 103	Come To Me (Black Dog Productions)/Anchor Song (Black Dog Productions) (10", die-cut sleeve, promo only, 2,000 copies)	18
93	One Little Indian BJDJ 104	Human Behaviour (The Underworld Dub 1)/(The Underworld Dub 2) (10", die-cut sleeve, promo only, 1,000 copies)	18
93	One Little Indian 112TP 12P	Human Behaviour (Speedy J. Close To Human Mix)/(Dom T. Mix)/(Bassheads Edit) (12", promo only)	15
93	One Little Indian 112TP 12DJ	Human Behaviour (The Underworld Mix)/(The Underworld Dub) (12", promo only)	15
93	One Little Indian BJDJ 123	One Day (Adrenalin — Far Removed) (12", 1-sided, promo only, 1,000 copies)	30
93	O. L. Indian BJDJ 124/125	BIG TIME SENSUALITY (12" EP, double pack, promo only, 500 copies)	25
93	O. L. Indian BJDJ 124/125g	BIG TIME SENSUALITY (12" EP, double pack, promo only, 1,000 copies)	30
95	One L. Indian 162 TP12P	ARMY OF ME (12" EP, remix double pack, single p/s, promo only)	15
95	One L. Indian 162 TP12GM	ARMY OF ME (Graham Massey Mix) (12", white label, no p/s, promo only)	15
96	O. Little Indian 193TP12DM	Enjoy/Possibly Maybe (12", 1,000 only, numbered p/s)	30
96	O. Little Indian 193TP12TD	POSSIBLY MAYBE (12" EP, 1,000 only, numbered p/s)	25
96	O. Little Indian 193TP7CD	POSSIBLY MAYBE (CD EP, with box)	8
96	O. Little Indian 193TP12MO	Possibly Maybe (Lucy Mix)/Enjoy (Further Over The Edge Mix) (12", p/s)	8
97	O. Little Indian 193TPGH	Isobel's Lonely Heart/Hyperballad (12", p/s)	8
97	O. Little Indian 193TP12PD	I Miss You/Cover Me (12", p/s)	8
97	O. Little Indian 193TP12PT	Big Time Sensuality/One Day (12", p/s)	8
97	O. Little Indian 193TPTT	Hyperballad (Towa Tei Remix)/Enjoy (The Beats Mix) (12", p/s)	8
97	O. L. Indian TPLP 81	JOGA (12" triple-pack, inner sleeves, p/s)	15
97	O. L. Indian 20 TP7 BOX	JOGA (CD box set, 3 x CD singles & 1-track video, 3,000 only)	40
97	O. L. Indian 20 TP7 BOX 212	BACHELORETTE (CD box set, 3 x CD singles & 1-track video, 3,000 only)	30
93	One Little Indian TPLP 31L	DEBUT (LP, with 16-page lyric booklet, 5,000 only)	12
93	One L. Indian TPLP 31CD	DEBUT (CD, with 16-page lyric booklet, 20,000 only)	15
94	One Little Indian 152TP 7	THE BEST MIXES FROM THE ALBUM "DEBUT" FOR THOSE PEOPLE WHO DON'T BUY WHITE LABELS (mini-LP)	15
95	One L. Indian TPLP 51L	POST (LP, pink vinyl, with inner sleeve)	12
95	One L. Indian TPLP 51CDX	POST (CD, digipak w/poster & lyric book, some copies in PVC purse)	20/15
96	One L. Indian BJORK FC1	CELEBRATING WOOD AND METAL (CD, 20,000 only, card sleeve)	15
97	O. L. Indian TPLP 71CD/X	HOMOGENIC (CD, digipak with poster & booklet)	15

(see also Sugarcubes, Kukl)

BLAB HAPPY
| 80s | Wisdom WIZ 1 | IT'S TURNED OUT NICE AGAIN (EP, p/s in bag, white labels) | 4 |

BLACK
| 81 | Rox ROX 17 | Human Features/Electric Church (p/s) | 10 |

BILL BLACK'S COMBO
59	Felsted AF 129	Smokie (Parts 1 & 2)	10
59	Felsted AF 129	Smokie (Parts 1 & 2) (78)	65
60	London HLU 9090	White Silver Sands/The Wheel	8
60	London HLU 9156	Josephine/Dry Bones	6
60	London HLU 9212	Don't Be Cruel/Rollin'	6
61	London HLU 9267	Blue Tango/Willie	7
61	London HLU 9306	Hearts Of Stone/Royal Blue	6
61	London HLU 9383	Ole Buttermilk Sky/Yogi	7
61	London HLU 9436	Movin'/Honky Train	10
61	London HLU 9479	Twist-Her/My Girl Josephine	6
62	London HLU 9594	So What/Blues For The Red Boy	6
62	London HLU 9645	Joey's Song/Hot Taco	6
63	London HLU 9721	Do It — Rat Now/Little Jasper	6

63	London HLU 9788	Monkey-Shine/Long Gone	6
64	London HLU 9855	Comin' On/Soft Winds	6
64	London HLU 9903	Tequila/Raunchy	7
64	London HLU 9925	Little Queenie/Boo-Ray	15
68	London HLU 10216	Turn On Your Love Light/Ribbon Of Darkness	5
60	London REU 1277	BILL BLACK'S COMBO (EP)	22
63	London REU 1369	THE UNTOUCHABLE SOUND OF BILL BLACK (EP)	22
62	London HA-U 2310	SOLID AND RAUNCHY (LP)	30
62	London HA-U 2427	LET'S TWIST (LP, also stereo SAH-U 6222)	20/25
62	London HA-U 2433	MOVIN' (LP)	22
63	London HA-U 8080	THE UNTOUCHABLE SOUND OF BILL BLACK (LP)	20
63	London HA-U 8113	GREATEST HITS (LP)	18
64	London HA-U 8187	PLAYS CHUCK BERRY (LP)	30
68	London HA-U/SH-U 8367	BILL BLACK'S BEAT GOES ON (LP)	15
69	London HA-U/SH-U 8373	TURN ON YOUR LOVE LIGHT (LP)	14
69	London HA-U/SH-U 8389	SOULIN' THE BLUES (LP)	14

(see also Elvis Presley)

CILLA BLACK

63	Parlophone R 5065	Love Of The Loved/Shy Of Love	8
64	Parlophone R 5101	Anyone Who Had A Heart/Just For You	5
64	Parlophone R 5133	You're My World/Suffer Now I Must	5
64	Parlophone R 5162	It's For You/He Won't Ask Me	6
65	Parlophone R 5225	You've Lost That Lovin' Feelin'/Is It Love?	5
65	Parlophone R 5265	I've Been Wrong Before/I Don't Want To Know	6
66	Parlophone R 5395	Love's Just A Broken Heart/Yesterday	5
66	Parlophone R 5427	Alfie/Night Time Is Here	5
66	Parlophone R 5463	Don't Answer Me/The Right One Is Left	5
66	Parlophone R 5515	A Fool Am I (Dimmelo Parlami)/For No One	6
67	Parlophone R 5608	What Good Am I?/Over My Head	6
67	Parlophone R 5652	I Only Live To Love You/From Now On	6
68	Parlophone R 5674	Step Inside Love/I Couldn't Take My Eyes Off You	5
68	Parlophone R 5706	Where Is Tomorrow/Work Is A Four Letter Word	7
69	Parlophone R 5759	Surround Yourself With Sorrow/London Bridge	5
69	Parlophone R 5785	Conversations/Liverpool Lullaby	5
69	Parlophone R 5820	If I Thought You'd Ever Change Your Mind/It Feels So Good	6
70	Parlophone R 5879	Child Of Mine/That's Why I Love You	7
71	Parlophone R 5924	Something Tells Me (Something's Gonna Happen Tonight)/La La La Lu	6
72	Parlophone R 5938	The World I Wish For You/Down In The City	6
72	Parlophone R 5972	You, You, You/Silly Wasn't I?	6
74	EMI EMI 2107	Baby We Can't Go Wrong/Someone	5
74	EMI EMI 2169	I'll Have To Say I Love You In A Song/Never Run Out (Of You)	5
74	EMI EMI 2227	He Was A Writer/Anything That You Might Say	5
75	EMI EMI 2278	Alfie Darling/Little Bit Of Understanding	5
75	EMI EMI 2328	I'll Take A Tango/To Know Him Is To Love Him	5
64	Parlophone GEP 8901	ANYONE WHO HAD A HEART (EP)	12
64	Parlophone GEP 8916	IT'S FOR YOU (EP)	15
66	Parlophone GEP 8954	CILLA'S HITS (EP)	15
67	Parlophone GEP 8967	TIME FOR CILLA (EP)	25
65	Parlophone PMC 1243	CILLA (LP, mono, yellow/black label)	18
65	Parlophone PCS 3063	CILLA (LP, stereo, yellow/black label)	22
66	Parlophone PMC 7004	CILLA SINGS A RAINBOW (LP, mono, yellow/black label)	18
66	Parlophone PCS 7004	CILLA SINGS A RAINBOW (LP, stereo, yellow/black label)	22
66	Parlophone TA-PMC 7004	CILLA SINGS A RAINBOW (reel-to-reel tape, mono only)	12
68	Parlophone PMC 7041	SHER-OO! (LP, mono, yellow/black label)	18
68	Parlophone PCS 7041	SHER-OO! (LP, stereo, yellow/black label)	18
68	Parlophone TA-PMC 7041	SHER-OO! (reel-to-reel tape, mono only)	12
68	Parlophone PMC/PCS 7065	THE BEST OF CILLA BLACK (mono/stereo, yellow/black label)	15
68	Parlophone TA-PCS 7065	THE BEST OF CILLA BLACK (reel-to-reel tape, mono only)	12
68	Parlophone PMC/PCS 7079	SURROUND YOURSELF WITH CILLA (LP, mono/stereo, yellow/black label)	15

(Any black and silver label reissues of the above LPs from the 70s are worth half these values.)

69	Parlophone PCS 7103	SWEET INSPIRATION (LP)	12
70	Parlophone PCS 7128	IMAGES (LP)	12
73	Parlophone PCS 7155	DAY BY DAY WITH CILLA (LP)	12

'FLIP' BLACK & BOYS UPSTAIRS

| 59 | Capitol CL 15037 | For You My Lover/Tell Her Mister Moon | 7 |

FRANK BLACK

| 93 | 4AD CADD 3004 | FRANK BLACK (LP, die-cut screen-printed sleeve) | 12 |

(see also Pixies)

JEANNE BLACK

| 60 | Capitol CL 15131 | He'll Have To Stay/JEANNE & JANIE: Under Your Spell Again | 7 |

(see also Janie, Jeanne & Janie)

MATT BLACK & DOODLEBUGS

| 76 | Punk BCS 0005 | Punky Xmas/Nightmare (no p/s) | 10 |

STANLEY BLACK & HIS PIANO ORCHESTRA

| 63 | Decca F 11624 | Hand In Hand/Lullaby Of The Stars | 15 |

BLACK ABBOTTS

70	Chapter One CH 123	She Looked Away/I Don't Mind	5
71	Evolution E 3001	How About Me/Everybody Needs A Little Sunshine	6
71	Evolution E 3004	Love Is Alive/The Painter	15

BLACK ACE

| 61 | XX MIN 701 | BLACK ACE (EP) | 15 |
| 62 | Heritage HLP 1006 | BLACK ACE (LP) | 35 |

BLACK ANGELS
| 84 | Gull GULP 1041 | KICKDOWN (LP) | 12 |

BLACK AXE
| 80 | Metal MELT 1 | Highway Rider/Red Lights (some in p/s) | 15/6 |

BLACK BEATLES
| 70 | Pama PM 804 | Reggae And Shout/LENOX BROWN: The Green Hornet | 7 |

BLACKBIRDS
| 68 | Saga OPP 3 | No Destination/Space (company sleeve, possibly promo only) | 25 |
| 68 | Saga FID 2113 | NO DESTINATION (LP) | 20 |

BLACK, BROWN & BEIGE
| 72 | Regal Zonophone RZ 3051 | We Are The Champions/What Is A Man | 5 |

TONY BLACKBURN
65	Fontana TF 562	Don't Get Off That Train/Just To Be With You Again	10
65	Fontana TF 601	Is There Another Way To Love You/Here Today Gone Tomorrow	5
66	Fontana TF 729	Green Light/Winter Is Through	5
67	MGM MGM 1375	So Much Love/In The Night	6
68	MGM MGM 1394	She's My Girl/Closer To A Dream	5
69	MGM MGM 1467	It's Only Love/Janie	5
69	Polydor 56360	Blessed Are The Lonely/Wait For Me	5
71	RCA RCA 2067	Is It Me Is It You/Happy	5
71	RCA RCA 2109	Chop Chop/If You Were A Dream	6
68	MGM C(S) 8062	TONY BLACKBURN SINGS (LP)	15
70	Fontana SFL 13161	TONY BLACKBURN MEETS MATT MONRO (LP)	12

BLACKBYRDS
74	Fantasy FTC 113	Do It Fluid/Summer Love	8
75	Fantasy FTC 114	Walking In Rhythm/Baby	6
75	Fantasy FTC 117	I Need You/All I Ask	6
76	Fantasy FTC 122	Rock Creek Park/Flying High	8
76	Fantasy FTC 129	Happy Music/Love So Fine	6
85	Streetwave SWAVE 3	Rock Creek Park/Walking In Rhythm (12")	12
75	Fantasy FT 9444	BLACKBYRDS (LP)	20
75	Fantasy FT 522	FLYING START (LP)	15
76	Fantasy FTA 3003	CITY LIFE (LP)	15
77	Fantasy FT 534	ACTION (LP)	15
79	Fantasy FT 555	NIGHT GROOVES — THE BEST OF THE BLACKBYRDS (LP)	15

(see also Donald Byrd)

BLACK CAT BONES
| 70 | Decca Nova SDN 15 | BARBED WIRE SANDWICH (LP) | 70 |

(see also Leaf Hound, Brian Short, Free, Foghat)

BLACK COUNTRY THREE
| 66 | Transatlantic TRA 140 | BLACK COUNTRY THREE (LP) | 40 |

(see also Jon Raven)

BLACK CROWES
90	Def American DEFA 4	Jealous Again/Thick'n'Thin (p/s)	6
90	Def American DEFA 412	Jealous Again/Thick'n'Thin/Waitin' Guilty (12", p/s)	10
90	Def American DEFAC 412	Jealous Again/Thick'n'Thin/Waitin' Guilty (12", picture disc)	15
90	Def American DEFAC 4	Jealous Again/Thick'n'Thin/Waitin' Guilty (CD)	10
90	Def American DEFA 612	Hard To Handle/Jealous Again (Acoustic)/Twice As Hard (live) (12", p/s)	8
90	Def American DEFAP 612	Hard To Handle/Jealous Again (Acoustic)/Twice As Hard (live) (12", crow-shaped picture disc with plinth)	15
90	Def American DEFAC 6	Hard To Handle/Jealous Again (Acoustic)/Twice As Hard (Remix) (CD)	10
91	Def American DEFA 712	Twice As Hard/Jealous Again (live)/Jealous Guy (live) (12", poster p/s)	8
91	Def American DEFAP 712	Twice As Hard/Jealous Again (live)/Could I've Been So Blind (live) (12", picture disc with insert)	10
91	Def American DEFAC 712	Twice As Hard/Jealous Again (live)/Jealous Guy (live) (CD)	10
91	Def American DEFA 812	Jealous Again/She Talks To Angels/She Talks To Angels (live) (12", p/s with patch, some sealed)	15/12
91	Def American DEFAC 812	Jealous Again/She Talks To Angels (live)/Could I've Been So Blind (live) (CD)	12
91	Def American DEFAP 10	Hard To Handle/Stare It Cold (live) (shaped picture disc)	10

BLACK DOG
91	GPR GENP(X) 2	PARALLEL EP (12", p/s)	20
92	Black Dog Prods BDP 001	VIRTUAL EP (12", p/s)	75
92	Black Dog Prods BDP 002	AGE OF SLACK (12", p/s)	75
92	Black Dog Prods BDP 003	BLACK DOG EP (12", p/s)	60
92	GPR GENP(X) 3	VIR 2 L (12", custom sleeve)	25
92	GPR GENP(X) 9	VANTOOL EP (12", custom sleeve)	20
93	GPR GENP(X) 17	COST II (12", custom sleeve)	15
93	Rising High RSN 046	BLACK DOG PRODUCTIONS (12", 4-track, p/s)	15
92	GPR GPRLP 1	TEMPLE OF TRANSPARENT BALLS (2-LP, some with poster)	20/18
93	GPR GPRCD 1	TEMPLE OF TRANSPARENT BALLS (CD)	20
95	GPR GPRLP 15	PARALLEL (2-LP)	20
95	GPR GPRCD 15	PARALLEL (CD)	20
95	Warp PUPLP 1	SPANNERS (2-LP)	20
95	Warp WAP LP 8LTD	BYTES (LP, bronze vinyl)	40

(see also Plaid, Repeat, Unexplored Beats, Shiva)

BLACK DYKE MILLS BAND
| 68 | Apple APPLE 4 | Thingumybob/Yellow Submarine | 40 |

BLACK DYNAMITES
| 60 | Top Rank JAR 319 | Brush Those Tears/Lonely Cissy | 22 |

BLACK EASTER
82   Illuminated KILL 13   READY TO ROCK (EP, p/s) 5

BLACK FLAG
81   Alt. Tentacles VIRUS 9   Six Pack/I've Heard It All Before/American Waste (p/s) 15
84   SST SST 12001   Family Man/I Won't Stick Any Of You Unless And Until I Can
                                   Stick All Of You (12", p/s) 15

BLACKFOOT
79   Atlantic K 11368   Highway Song/Road Fever 5
79   Atlantic K 11447   Train Train/Baby Blue 5
80   Atco K 11610   On The Run/Streetfighter (p/s) 7
80   Atco K 11636   Every Man Should Know (Queenie)/Highway Song 5
81   Atco K 11673   Good Morning/Payin' For It Now (p/s) 7
82   Atco K 11686T   Dry Country/Too Hard To Handle//On The Run/Train Train
                                   (double pack, gatefold sleeve) 5
82   Atco K 11760   Highway Song/Rollin' 'n' Tumblin'/Flyman (p/s, 6 different 45s, recorded live in
                                   Glasgow, Edinburgh, Newcastle, Liverpool, Manchester or Birmingham) . . . each 6
83   Atco B 9880P   Send Me An Angel/Driving Fool (shaped picture disc) 8
(see also Lynyrd Skynyrd)

J.D. BLACKFOOT
71   Mercury 6338 031   THE ULTIMATE PROPHECY (LP) 60

BLACKFOOT SUE
72   Jam JAM 13   Standing In The Road/Celestial Plain 5
72   Jam JAM 29   Sing Don't Speak/2 B Free 5
73   Jam JAM 44   Summer/Morning Light 5
73   Jam JAM 53   Get It All To Me/My Oh My 5
74   DJM DJS 296   Bye Bye Birmingham/Messiah 5
74   DJM DJS 326   You Need Love/Tobago Rose 5
75   DJM DJS 411   Moonshine/Corrie 5
73   Jam JAL 104   NOTHING TO HIDE (LP) 18
75   DJM DJLPS 455   GUN RUNNING (LP, withdrawn) 45

BLACK IVORY
74   Kwanza K 19500   What Goes Around Comes Around/No One Else Will Do 4

BLACKJACK
80   Polydor POSP 76   Without Your Love/Heart Of Mine (p/s) 20
79   Polydor 2391 411   BLACKJACK (LP) 20
80   Polydor   WORLDS APART (LP) 12
   (see also Michael Bolotin, Michael Bolton)

BLACKJACKS
63   Pye 7N 15586   Woo Hoo/Red Dragon 15
   (see also Pat Harris & Blackjacks)

BLACK KNIGHTS
65   Columbia DB 7443   I Gotta Woman/Angel Of Love 18

BLACK MAMBAZO
58   Columbia DB 4135   Fuzzy Night/Matshutshu 5
58   Columbia DB 4135   Fuzzy Night/Matshutshu (78) 10

HONOR BLACKMAN
68   CBS 3896   Before Today/I'll Always Be Loving You (some in p/s) 50/20
64   Decca LK/SKL 4642   EVERYTHING I'VE GOT (LP, mono/stereo) 40/50
   (see also Patrick MacNee & Honor Blackman)

RITCHIE BLACKMORE (ORCHESTRA)
65   Oriole CB 314   Getaway/Little Brown Jug 750
   (see also Outlaws, Neil Christian & Crusaders, Deep Purple, [Ritchie Blackmore's] Rainbow, Rally Rounders,
   Green Bullfrog, Rock Aid Armenia)

BLACK NASTY
80   Grapevine GRP 140   Cut Your Motor Off/Keep On Stepping 6

BLACK OAK ARKANSAS
75   Atlantic K 10621   Fancy Nancy/Keep On 7
71   Atlantic 2400 180   BLACK OAK ARKANSAS (LP) 12

BLACK RIDERS
85   Plastic Head GILP 555   CHOSEN FEW (LP) 12

BLACK ROSE
82   Teesbeat TB 5   No Point Runnin'/Sucker For Your Love (p/s) 40
83   Bullet BOLT 6   WE GONNA ROCK YOU (12" EP) 7
84   Bullet BOL 9   Boys Will Be Boys/Liar (p/s) 15
85   Neat NEAT 4812   Nightmare/Need A Lot Of Lovin'/Rock Me Hard (12", p/s) 7
84   Bullet BULP 3   BOYS WILL BE BOYS (LP) 10
87   Neat NEAT 1034   WALK IT LIKE YOU TALK IT (LP, with lyric insert) 10

BLACK SABBATH
70   Fontana TF 1067   Evil Woman/Wicked World 70
70   Vertigo V2   Evil Woman/Wicked World (reissue, Vertigo 'spiral' sleeve) 15
70   Vertigo 6059 010   Paranoid/The Wizard (Vertigo 'spiral' sleeve) 15
72   Vertigo 6059 061   Tomorrow's Dream/Laguna Sunrise (Vertigo 'spiral' sleeve) 12
72   Phonogram DJ 005   Children Of The Grave/STATUS QUO: Roadhouse Blues
                                   (100 promo copies only) 375
73   WWA WWS 002   Sabbath Bloody Sabbath/Changes (company sleeve) 8
75   NEMS 6165 300   Am I Going Insane? (Radio)/Hole In The Sky (no p/s) 10
78   Vertigo SAB 001   Never Say Die/She's Gone (p/s) 6

MINT VALUE £

78	Vertigo SAB 002	Hard Road/Symptom Of The Universe (purple or black vinyl)	each 6
80	Vertigo SAB 412	Die Young/Heaven And Hell (extended live) (12", p/s)	8
81	Vertigo SAB 512	Mob Rules/Die Young (live) (12", p/s)	10
82	Vertigo SABP 6	Turn Up The Night/Lonely Is The Word (picture disc)	5
82	Vertigo SABP 612	Turn Up The Night/Lonely Is The Word (12", picture disc)	8
86	Vertigo SABDJ 12	In For The Kill/Turn To Stone/Heart Like A Wheel (12", promo only)	15
87	Vertigo SABAF 1	4 SONGS FROM THE ETERNAL IDOL (12", p/s, promo only)	10
89	I.R.S. EIRS CB 107	Headless Cross (Edit)/Cloak And Dagger (signed label, stickered PVC sleeve)	6
89	I.R.S. EIRSPD 115	Devil And Daughter (1-sided picture disc)	5
89	I.R.S. EIRSB 115	Devil And Daughter (box set, 1-sided disc with stencil, insert & 2 postcards)	8
92	I.R.S. EIRSDJ 180	Master Of Insanity (edit)/Time Machine/Neon Knights (live)/TV Crimes (live)/Die (live)/Children Of The Sea (live) (CD, no p/s, promo only)	12
70	Vertigo VO 6	BLACK SABBATH (LP, gatefold sleeve, spiral label)	35
70	Vertigo 6360 011	PARANOID (LP, gatefold sleeve, spiral label)	35
71	Vertigo 6360 050	MASTER OF REALITY (LP in box cover, spiral label, some with poster)	60/25
72	Vertigo 6360 071	BLACK SABBATH VOL. 4 (LP, gatefold sleeve with booklet, initially with spiral label, later with 'spaceship' label)	30/15
88	Castle BSBCD 001	THE BLACK SABBATH CD COLLECTION (6-CD box set with badge & book, numbered, 3,000 only)	40
89	I.R.S. EIRSAPD 1002	HEADLESS CROSS (LP, picture disc, with bonus track "Cloak And Dagger")	12
90	I.R.S. EIRSACV 1038	TYR (LP, picture disc with insert & 2 bonus live tracks)	12

(see also Ozzy Osborne, Dio, Elf, Cozy Powell, Quartz, Phenomena, Rock Aid Armenia)

BLACK SHEEP
85	Rock Machine MACH 2	BLACK SHEEP (LP)	12

BLACKTHORN
77	WHM 1921	BLACKTHORN (LP)	60
78	WHM 1923	BLACKTHORN II (LP)	100

BLACK VELVET
69	Beacon BEA 129	African Velvet/Whatcha Gonna Do 'Bout It	5
69	Beacon BEA 137	Peace And Love Is The Message/Clown	5
70	Beacon BEA 151	Please Let Me In/Clown	15
70	Beacon BEA 162	What Am I To Do/Coal Mine	5
70	Beacon BEA 170	Thought I Had Me A Good Thing Going/Loves Makes The World Go Round	5
71	Mam MAM 22	See What You Get Out-A-Me/Can't Stand The Pain	5
72	Seven Sun SSUN 3	Children/Domestic Man	5
72	Pye 7N 45183	So Good To See You/Velvet Funk	5
73	Pye 7N 45228	There Must Be A Way/Domestic Man	5
73	Seven Sun SSUN 4	Groove Along/Can You Feel It	6
74	Seven Sun SSUN 6	There Goes My Heart Again/Cindy Cindy	6
71	Beacon BEAS 16	THIS IS BLACK VELVET (LP)	20
72	Pye NSPL 18392	PEOPLE OF THE WORLD (LP)	20
73	Seven Sun SUNLP 1	CAN YOU FEEL IT (LP)	25

(see also Ram John Holder)

CHARLES BLACKWELL ORCHESTRA
61	HMV POP 977	Taboo/Midnight In Luxembourg	25
62	Columbia DB 4839	Supercar/Persian Theme	18
62	Columbia DB 4919	Freight Train/Death Valley	8
63	Columbia DB 4994	High Noon/For Me And My Gal	6
63	Columbia DB 7066	El Toro/Hawaiian War Chant	6
63	Columbia DB 7139	The Hokey Croakey/Lost Patrol	6
65	Columbia DB 7501	Meditation/La Bamba	6
67	United Artists UP 1187	Sailor From Gibraltar (Joe Le Rouge)/Hoi	6
60	Triumph TRY 4000	THOSE PLUCKING STRINGS (LP, unreleased, white label test pressings only)	500

OTIS BLACKWELL
58	London HLE 8616	Make Ready For Love/When You're Around	40
58	London HLE 8616	Make Ready For Love/When You're Around (78)	40

RORY BLACKWELL & HIS BLACKJACKS
57	Parlophone R 4326	Bye Bye Love/Such A Shame	30
57	Parlophone R 4326	Bye Bye Love/Such A Shame (78)	20
70s	Rory SJP 763	Daddy Don't You Walk So Fast/Drum Rhapsody	5

SCRAPPER BLACKWELL
67	Collector JEN 7	SCRAPPER BLACKWELL (EP)	10
63	'77' LA 12/4	BLUES BEFORE SUNRISE (LP)	25
60s	Xtra XTRA 5011	MR SCRAPPER'S BLUES (LP)	18

BLACKWELLS (U.S.)
60	London HLW 9135	Unchained Melody/Mansion On The Hill	10
61	London HLW 9334	Love Or Money/Big Daddy And The Cat	10

BLACKWELLS (U.K.)
65	Columbia DB 7442	Why Don't You Love Me/All I Want Is Your Love	25

BLACK WIDOW
70	CBS 5031	Come To The Sabbat/Way To Power	15
71	CBS 7596	Wish You Would/Accident	12
70	CBS 63948	SACRIFICE (LP, gatefold sleeve)	22
70	CBS 64133	BLACK WIDOW II (LP)	22
72	CBS 64562	BLACK WIDOW III (LP, with inner)	25

(see also Pesky Gee, Agony Bag)

ANDY BLADE
80	SMS SMS 001	Break The News/Girl With The Goods (p/s)	5

(see also Eater)

BLADES

80	Energy NRG 3	Hot For You/The Reunion (p/s; Irish w/ paper labels, later UK w/ plastic)	8/6
81	Energy NRG 5	Ghost Of A Chance/Real Emotion (p/s; Irish w/ paper labels; UK w/ plastic)	8/6
84	Reekus RKS 013	The Last Man In Europe (p/s)	5
85	Reekus RKS 15	Those Were The Days (p/s)	5
85	Reekus RKSY 15	Those Were The Days (picture disc)	6
86	Reekus RKS 017	Downmarket/Truth Don't Hurt (as Blades with Paul Cleary)	5
84	Reekus RKLP 1	THE LAST MAN IN EUROPE (LP)	12
86	Reekus RKLP 3	RAY TOWN REVISITED (LP)	12
	(see also Partisans)		

BLADES OF GRASS

67	Stateside SS 2040	Happy/That's What A Boy Likes	6
68	Stateside SS 2101	Charlie And Fred/You Won't Find That Girl	6

BLAH BLAH BLAH

79	Absurd ABSURD 1	In The Army/Why Diddle? (p/s)	5
80s	Lyntone LYN 17627	Heavenly View/ST. VITUS DANCE: Meet Mohammed	
	Good Vibes H 002	(1-sided 33rpm flexidisc with *Helden* fanzine)	6/5
81	Some Bizzare	BLAH BLAH BLAH	
		(LP, unreleased, stickered sleeve, white label test pressings only)	40

HAL BLAINE (& YOUNG COUGARS)

64	RCA RCA 1379	Gear Stripper/Challenger II (with Young Cougars)	12
64	RCA RD/SF 7624	DEUCES, T'S, ROADSTERS AND DRUMS (LP, mono/stereo)	30/35

VIVIAN BLAINE

53	Brunswick 05100	A Bushel And A Peck/My Time Of Day/Luck Be A Lady (78)	20
54	Parlophone MSP 6070	Changing Partners/Lonely	8

BLAIR

79	Miracle M4	Night Life/Virgo Princess (12")	10

BEVERLEY BLAIR

58	Mercury 7MT 209	With Love We Live/Tony	6

HENRY BLAIR

50s	Capitol EAP 1-3003	SPARKY'S MAGIC PIANO (EP)	10

SALLY BLAIR

58	MGM MGM 1000	Whatever Lola Wants (Lola Gets)/Daddy	8
58	MGM MGM 1000	Whatever Lola Wants (Lola Gets)/Daddy (78)	10

GARRY BLAKE

66	Columbia DB 7885	Strawberries And Cream/Look Out Now!	5
66	Columbia DB 7977	Wait Until Dark/Jungle Juice	5
66	Columbia DB 8074	The Danny Scipio Theme/Celebration Day	7
68	Studio Two TWO 237	A SWINGING PARTY (LP)	15

KARL BLAKE

80	Daark Inc. 1	TANK DEATH (C-60 cassette)	15
81	Daark Inc. 2	THE NEW POLLUTION (C-60 cassette)	15
83	Glass GLASS 013	THE PREHENSILE TAPES (LP)	12
92	Tak Tak Tak TAK 07	MANDIBLES (cassette, 500 only)	12
	(see also Lemon Kittens, Shock Headed Peters, Underneath, Gland Shrouds, Homunculus, Fur Fur, Sol Invictus)		

KEITH BLAKE

68	Blue Cat BS 102	Musically/I'm Moving On	15
	(see also Overtakers, Uniques)		

SONNY BLAKE

80	Rooster R 706	HARMONICA BLUES (EP)	8

TIM BLAKE

78	Barclay Towers BAR 711	Generator Laserbeam/Woodland Voice (p/s)	8
78	Barclay Towers CLAY 7005	BLAKE'S NEW JERUSALEM (LP)	18
	(see also Gong, Hawkwind)		

WINSTON BLAKE & M-SQUAD

71	Green Door GD 4003	Carrol Street/ANSELL COLLINS & M-SQUAD: Carol St. Version	5

ART BLAKEY JAZZ MESSENGERS

60	Fontana TFE 17257	BLUES MARCH (EP)	10
61	Fontana TFE 17337	I REMEMBER CLIFFORD (EP)	10
61	Fontana TFE 17364	ARE YOU REAL (EP, with Lee Morgan & Benny Golson)	10
61	Fontana TFL 5116	OLYMPIA CONCERT (LP)	20
62	HMV CLP 1532	ART BLAKEY JAZZ MESSENGERS (LP, also stereo CSD 1423)	15/20
62	Fontana TFL 5184	DANGEROUS FRIENDSHIPS (LP, soundtrack)	20
63	United Artists (S)ULP 1017	THREE BLIND MICE (LP, mono/stereo)	15/20
64	Riverside RLP 438	CARAVAN (LP)	15
64	HMV CLP 1760	A JAZZ MESSAGE (LP)	15
64	Riverside RLP 464	UGETSU (LP)	15
65	Limelight (S)LML 4000	'S MAKE IT (LP)	12
66	Limelight (S)LML 4012	SOUL FINGER (LP)	12
66	Limelight (S)LML 4021	BUTTERCORN LADY (LP)	12
67	Limelight (S)LML 4023	HOLD ON, I'M COMIN' (LP)	12
67	Atlantic 590 009	BLUE MONK (LP, with Thelonious Monk)	15
69	Storyville 673 013	KYOTO (LP)	12
70	Polydor 545 116	RIGHT DOWN FRONT (LP)	12
74	Prestige PR 10047	CHILD'S DANCE (LP)	12
74	Milestone ML 47008	THERMO (LP)	12
	(see also Annie Ross)		

MINT VALUE £

ART BLAKEY/MILES DAVIS

66	Fontana FJL 135	L'ASCENSEUR POUR L'ECHAFAUD/FEMME DISPARAISSANTE (LP, soundtrack, 1 side each)	45

(see also Thelonious Monk, Miles Davis)

MEL BLANC

56	Capitol CJ 109	Woody Woodpecker Meets Davy Crockett/Davy Crockett (78)	8
56	Capitol CJ 110	Pied Piper Pussy Cat (Parts 1 & 2) (78)	8
56	Capitol CJ 117	Tweety Pie Pts 1 & 2 (78)	8
58	Capitol CL 14950	I Taut I Taw A Puddy Cat/K-K-K-Katy	12
60	Warner Bros WB 26	Tweety's Twistmas Twouble/I Keep Hearing Those Bells	5

BURT BLANCA

60	Zodiac ZR 004	Texas Rider/Shamash	15

BLANCMANGE

80	Blaah Music MFT-1	IRENE AND MAVIS (EP, gatefold p/s)	25
82	Lyntone LYN 1183/84	Living On The Ceiling/Sad Day (excerpt)/PASSAGE: Born Every Minute (33rpm black flexidisc free with *Melody Maker* magazine)	10/5
82	London BLANCX 1	I've Seen The World (Extended)/God's Kitchen (Extended) (12", p/s)	8
82	London BLAPD 2	Feel Me/Feel Me (Instrumental) (picture disc)	5
82	London BLANCX 2	Feel Me (Extended)/Feel Me (Instrumental) (12", p/s)	8
84	London BLATP 5	Blind Vision/Heaven Knows Where Heaven Is (clear vinyl, PVC sleeve w/ insert)	5
84	London BLAPD 6	That's Love That It Is/Vishnu (picture disc)	5
84	London BLAPD 7	Don't Tell Me/Get Out Of That (picture disc)	5
84	London BLAPD 8	(The) Day Before You Came/All Things Are Nice (picture disc)	5
84	London BLAPX 8	(The) Day Before You Came/Feel Me/All Things Are Nice (Version) (12", picture disc, existence unconfirmed)	15+
82	London SHPD 8552	HAPPY FAMILIES (LP, picture disc)	12
84	London SHPD 8554	MANGE TOUT (LP, picture disc)	12
85	London 820 301-2	BELIEVE YOU ME (CD)	25

BILLY BLAND

60	London HL 9096	Let The Little Girl Dance/Sweet Thing	15
71	Atlantic 2091 130	Let The Little Girl Dance/Chicken Hop	5

BOBBY BLAND

61	Vogue V 9178	Cry Cry Cry/I've Been Wrong So Long	22
61	Vogue V 9182	Lead Me On/Hold Me Tenderly	22
61	Vogue V 9188	Don't Cry No More/St. James Infirmary	20
62	Vogue V 9190	You're The One (That I Need)/Turn On Your Love Light	20
62	Vogue V 9192	Blue Moon/Who Will The Next Fool Be?	20
64	Vocalion VP 9222	Ain't Nothing You Can Do/Honey Child	15
64	Vocalion VP 9229	After It's Too Late/Share Your Love With Me	15
65	Vocalion VP 9232	Yield Not To Temptation/How Does A Cheating Woman Feel?	12
65	Vocalion VP 9251	These Hands (Small But Mighty)/Today	15
66	Vocalion VP 9262	I'm Too Far Gone (To Turn Around)/ If You Could Read My Mind	12
66	Vocalion VP 9273	Good Time Charlie/Good Time Charlie (Working His Groove Bag)	15
68	Sue WI 4044	That Did It/A Touch Of The Blues	25
69	Action ACT 4524	Rockin' In The Same Old Boat/Wouldn't You Rather Have Me?	12
69	Action ACT 4538	Gotta Get To Know You/Baby I'm On My Way	15
69	Action ACT 4548	Share Your Love With Me/Honey Child	12
69	Action ACT 4553	Chains Of Love/Ask Me 'Bout Nothing But The Blues	15
74	ABC ABC 4014	Ain't No Love In The Heart Of The City/Twenty Four Blues	8
75	ABC ABC 4030	I Wouldn't Treat A Dog (The Way You Treat Me)/ I Ain't Gonna Be The First To Cry	8
77	ABC ABC 4186	The Soul Of A Man/If I Weren't A Gambler	8
61	Vogue VAP 160183	TWO STEPS FROM THE BLUES (LP)	50
63	Vocalion VEP 170153	YIELD NOT INTO TEMPTATION (EP)	45
64	Vocalion VEP 170157	BOBBY BLAND (EP)	45
64	Vocalion VAP 8027	AIN'T NOTHING YOU CAN DO (LP)	50
65	Vocalion VAP 8034	CALL ON ME/THAT'S THE WAY LOVE IS (LP)	50
60s	Vogue VAP 8034	CALL ON ME/THAT'S THE WAY LOVE IS (LP, later issue)	35
66	Vocalion VAP 8041	HERE'S THE MAN (LP)	50
68	Island ILP 974	A TOUCH OF THE BLUES (LP)	40
69	Action ACLP 6006	A PIECE OF GOLD (LP)	35
73	ABC ABCL 5044	HIS CALIFORNIA ALBUM (LP)	12
74	ABC ABCL 5053	DREAMER (LP)	12
74	Polydor 2383 257	BLUES FOR MR. CRUMP (LP, with tracks by Junior Parker & Howlin' Wolf)	20
75	ABC ABCL 5139	GET ON DOWN WITH BOBBY BLAND (LP)	12

BOBBY BLAND & B.B. KING

74	ABC ABCD 605	TOGETHER FOR THE FIRST TIME (2-LP)	18

(see also B.B. King)

MARCIE BLANE

62	London HLU 9599	Bobby's Girl/A Time To Dream	18
63	London HLU 9673	What Does A Girl Do/How Can I Tell Him	10
63	London HLU 9744	Little Miss Fool/Ragtime Sound	10
63	London HLU 9787	You Gave My Number To Billy/Told You So	12
63	London REU 1393	MARCIE BLANE (EP)	80

BLANKS

79	Void SRTS/79/CUS/560	The Northern Ripper/Understand (p/s)	15

(see also Destructors)

BLAZER, BLAZER

78	Logo GO 362	Cecil B. Devine/Warsaw/Six O'Clock In The Morning (p/s)	25

BLAZERS
58   Fontana TFR 6010   ROCK AND ROLL (10" LP)... 80

BLAZING SONS
83   Cool Ghoul COOL 002   Chant Down The National Front/N.F. Dub (no p/s) 10
(see also Phantom)

BLEACH BOYS
78   Tramp THF 002   Chloroform/You've Got Nothing (no p/s)................................. 35
85   Zombie International   Stocking-Clad Nazi Death Squad Bitches/Death Before Disco/
     ZOMBO 103010   Gimme That Neutron Taste (12", p/s)................................... 25

BLEAK HOUSE
80s Buzzard BUZZ 1   Rainbow Warrior (some in p/s) 100/30
82   Buzzard BUZZ 2   LIONS IN WINTER (EP, p/s with insert) 50

BLEECHERS
69   Trojan TR 679   Ease Up/You're Gonna Feel It 8
69   Upsetter US 314   Come Into My Parlour/MELOTONES: Dry Up Your Tears..................... 8
70   Col. Blue Beat DB 118   Send Me The Pillow (That You Dream On)/Adam And Eve 8
71   Duke DU 118   Put It Good/J.J. ALLSTARS: Good Good Version 6
(see also Busty Brown, Upsetters)

PETER BLEGVAD
80   Recommended RRA 5.75   Alcohol (p/s, 1-sided, other side etched)........................... 4
(see also Slapp Happy)

BLENDELLS
64   Reprise RS 20291   La La La La La La/Huggies Bunnies 7
64   Reprise RS 20340   Dance With Me/Get Your Baby 7

BLESSINGS IN DISGUISE
89   Mooncrest DISGUISE 1   Crying In The Rain/Wild Nights (p/s).................................. 6
91   Gotham GOTH 2   Chance To Be/You're The Reason I'm Staying (p/s) 5
(see also Slade)

CARLA BLEY
72   JCOA JT 4001   ESCALATOR OVER THE HILL (3-LP, with Paul Haines & Jack Bruce) 20
74   Watt WATT 1   TROPIC APPETITES (LP)... 10
(see also Jazz Composers Orchestra, Michael Mantler, Jack Bruce)

PAUL BLEY TRIO
69   Fontana SFJL 929   TOUCHING (LP) 40
(see also Bley-Peacock Synthesizer Show, Annette Peacock)

ARCHIE BLEYER & HIS ORCHESTRA
54   London HL 8035   Amber/Julie's Jump 25
54   London HL 8035   Amber/Julie's Jump (78) 12
54   London HL 8111   The Naughty Lady Of Shady Lane/While The Vesper Bells Were Ringing .. 25
54   London HL 8111   The Naughty Lady Of Shady Lane/While The Vesper Bells Were Ringing (78).... 12
55   London HLA 8176   Hernando's Hideaway/S'il Vous Plait................................. 20
56   London HLA 8243   Nothin' To Do/JANET BLEYER: 'Cause You're My Lover.................. 15
56   London HLA 8243   Nothin' To Do/JANET BLEYER: 'Cause You're My Lover (78) 15
56   London HLA 8263   Bridge Of Happiness/You Tell Me Your Dream, I'll Tell You Mine...... 15
56   London HLA 8263   Bridge Of Happiness/You Tell Me Your Dream, I'll Tell You Mine (78) .. 15

BLEY-PEACOCK SYNTHESIZER SHOW
72   Polydor 2425 043   REVENGE (LP) 50
(see also Annette Peacock, Paul Bley)

BLIND BLAKE
50   Tempo R 23   Hey Hey Daddy Blues/Brownskin Mama Blues (78) 18
50   Tempo R 40   Southern Rag/CC Pill Blues (78) 18
54   Jazz Collector L 97   Hot Potatoes/Southbound Rag (78)................................... 12
58   Ristic LP 18   THE LEGENDARY BLIND BLAKE (10" LP) 50
50s Jazz Collector JLP 2001   THE LEGENDARY BLIND BLAKE (10" LP, reissue)........................ 35
67   Riverside RLP 8804   BLUES IN CHICAGO (LP).. 25
60s Whoopee 101   BLIND BLAKE 1927-30 (LP)... 15
(see also Paramount Allstars)

BLIND BLAKE/CHARLIE JACKSON
50s Heritage HLP 1011   BLIND BLAKE AND CHARLIE JACKSON (LP) 35

BLIND BLAKE/RAMBLIN' THOMAS
59   Jazz Collector JEL 4   THE MALE BLUES VOLUME 3 (EP)....................................... 14

BLIND FAITH
69   Island (no cat. no.)   Change Of Address From June 23rd 1969 (promo issue, 500 only)........... 100
69   Polydor 583 059   BLIND FAITH (LP, gatefold sleeve).................................. 18
(see also Stevie Winwood, Ginger Baker, Eric Clapton)

BLINKERS
69   Pye 7N 17752   Original Sin/Dreams Secondhand 50

BLINKY & EDWIN STARR
69   Tamla Motown TMG 720   Oh How Happy/Ooo Baby Baby (unissued, demos only) 120
70   Tamla Motown TMG 748   Oh How Happy/Ooo Baby Baby... 6
70   T. Motown (S)TML 11131   JUST WE TWO (LP, as Edwin Starr & Blinky) 18
(see also Edwin Starr)

BLISS
69   Chapter One CH 107   Courtyards In Castile/Lifetime 8

MELVIN BLISS
77   Contempo CS 2013   Reward/Synthetic Substitute 12

BLISTERS
80   Lyntone LYN 11074   Get Smart/Heatwave (live) (flexidisc) 5

MINT VALUE £

BLITZ
81	No Future OI 1	ALL OUT ATTACK (EP, rubber-stamped labels, 500 only)	25
81	No Future OI 1	ALL OUT ATTACK (EP, reissue, white labels, later printed labels)	8/6
82	No Future OI 6	Never Surrender/Razor In The Night (p/s)	8
82	No Future OI 16	Warriors/Youth (p/s)	8
83	Future FS 1	New Age/Fatigue (p/s)	5
83	Future FS 3	Telecommunication/Teletron (p/s)	5
82	No Future PUNK 1	VOICE OF A GENERATION (LP, with inner sleeve)	15

(see also Rose Of Victory)

BLITZ BOYS
80	Told You So TYS 001	Eddy's New Shoes/Eddie's Friend/She Told My Friends (foldover p/s)	50

BLITZKRIEG
81	Neat NEAT 10	Buried Alive/Blitzkrieg (p/s)	40
85	Neat NEAT 1023	A TIME OF CHANGES (LP)	20

BLITZKRIEG
82	No Future OI 8	LEST WE FORGET (EP)	10
83	Sexual Phonograph SPH 3	CONSCIOUS PRAYER (EP)	5

BLITZKRIEG BOP
77	Mortonsound MTN 3172/3	Let's Go/Nine Till Five/Bugger Off (p/s, 500 only)	55
77	Lightning GTL 504	Let's Go (re-recorded)/Life Is Just A So-So/Mental Case (p/s)	30
78	Lightning GTL 543	U.F.O./Bobby Joe (p/s)	25

BLOATED TOADS
79	Shattered SHAT 4	Why/Essential In Some Form/Happy Home/Yankee TV Victim (p/s, with insert)	4

BLODWYN PIG
69	Island WIP 6059	Dear Jill/Sweet Caroline	10
69	Island WIP 6069	Walk On The Water/Summer Day	10
70	Island WIP 6078	Same Old Story/Slow Down	10
89	private release	A TASTE OF THINGS TO COME (cassette, 50 only, sold at gigs)	25
69	Island ILPS 9101	AHEAD RINGS OUT (LP, gatefold sleeve, pink or 'pink rim palm tree' label)	20/12
70	Chrysalis ILPS 9122	GETTING TO THIS (LP, gatefold sleeve)	15

(see also Mick Abrahams, Jethro Tull, Peter Banks)

BLOND
69	Fontana TF 1040	(I Will Bring You) Flowers In The Morning/I Wake Up And Call	10
69	Fontana STL 5515	THE LILAC YEARS (LP, gatefold sleeve)	90

(see also Tages)

BLONDE ON BLONDE
69	Pye 7N 17637	All Day All Night/Country Life	40
70	Ember EMB S 279	Castles In The Sky/Circles (some in p/s)	15/8
72	Ember EMB S 316	Sad Song For An Easy Lady/Happy Families	6
69	Pye NSPL 18288	CONTRASTS (LP, gatefold sleeve)	40
70	Ember NR 5049	RE-BIRTH (LP, gatefold sleeve)	25
71	Ember NR 5058	REFLECTIONS ON A LIFE (LP, gatefold sleeve)	25
70s	Ember LP 7005	BLONDE ON BLONDE (LP, unissued, test pressings only)	100+

BLONDIE
77	Private Stock PVT 90	X Offender/In The Sun (unissued, promos or stock copies, no p/s)	750
77	Private Stock PVT 105	In The Flesh/X Offender (no p/s)	20
77	Chrysalis CHS 2180	Rip Her To Shreds/In The Flesh/X Offender (p/s)	8
77	Chrysalis CHS 2180-12	Rip Her To Shreds/In The Flesh/X Offender (12", green labels, '75p' p/s)	8
78	Chrysalis CHS 2204	Denis (Denee)/Contact In Red Square (red p/s)	5
78	Chrysalis CHS 2242	Picture This/Fade Away (And Radiate) (p/s, yellow vinyl)	5
78	Chrysalis CHE 2266	Hanging On The Telephone/Will Anything Happen (p/s, export issue)	6
78	Chrysalis CHE 2275	Heart Of Glass/Rifle Range (p/s, export issue with "pain in the ass" lyrics)	8
80	Flexi FLX 146	Speaking From The Studio (Blondie Fan Club flexidisc)	15
82	Lyntone LYN 10840/1	Yuletown Throwdown (Rapture) (with Freddie)/BRATTLES: The Christmas Song/ SNUKY TATE: Santa's Agent (33rpm blue vinyl flexi with *Flexipop* issue 15)	8/5
89	Chrysalis CHSP 12 3342	Call Me (Remix)/Backfired (Remix)/Call Me (1989) (12", picture disc)	8
98	EMI 12 ATOM 150	ATOMIC 98 (Remixes) (12", p/s, withdrawn)	15
98	EMI CD ATOM 150	ATOMIC 98 (Remixes) (CD, withdrawn)	15
76	Private Stock PVLP 1017	BLONDIE (LP)	15
82	Chrysalis PCDL 1384	THE HUNTER (LP, picture disc)	15
89	Chrysalis CHR 1658	THE 12" MIXES (2-LP)	15
89	Chrysalis CCD 1658	THE 12" MIXES (CD)	15
95	Chrysalis CD CHR 6105	BEAUTIFUL – THE REMIX ALBUM (CD)	15
98	Chysalis 4949962	ATOMIC (CD)	15

(see also Debbie Harry, New York Blondes, Wind In The Willows, Jimmy Destri, Rodney & Brunettes)

BLOOD
83	No Future OI 22	Megalomania/Calling The Shots/Parasite In Paradise (p/s)	10
83	Noise NOY 1	Stark Raving Normal/Mesrine (p/s)	8
82	Noise NOYZLP 1	FALSE GESTURES FOR A DEVIOUS PUBLIC (LP)	12
85	Conquest QUEST 3	SE PARARE NEX (LP)	12
89	Link Classics CLINK 5	FALSE GESTURES FOR A DEVIOUS PUBLIC (LP, reissue, red vinyl)	10

BLOOD DONOR
81	Safari SAFE 29	Doctor...?/Soap Box Blues (p/s)	5

(see also Jon Pertwee)

BLOODROCK
71	Capitol CL 15670	D.O.A./Children's Heritage	4
71	Capitol E-ST 491	BLOODROCK 2 (LP)	10
71	Capitol E-ST 765	BLOODROCK 3 (LP)	10

BLOODS
84	Exit Intl./021 OTO 9	Button Up/Raumen (p/s)	5

BLOOD, SWEAT & TEARS
68	CBS 3563	I Can't Quit Her/House In The Country	6
69	CBS 4220	Spinning Wheel/More And More	5
73	CBS 1142	Spinning Wheel/And When I Die (p/s, 'Hall Of Fame Hits' series)	5
68	CBS 63296	CHILD IS THE FATHER TO THE MAN (LP)	12
73	CBS CQ 31170/Q 64803	GREATEST HITS (LP, quadrophonic)	12

(see also Al Kooper, David Clayton-Thomas)

ROGER BLOOM'S HAMMER
67	CBS 202654	Out Of The Blue/Life's A Gamble	10
67	CBS 2848	Polly Pan/Fifteen Degree Temperature Rise	5

MIKE BLOOMFIELD
69	CBS 63652	IT'S NOT KILLING ME (LP)	15

(see also Barry Goldberg Reunion, Stephen Stills, K.G.B.)

MIKE BLOOMFIELD & AL KOOPER
69	CBS 4094	The Weight/59th Street Bridge Song	8
69	CBS 66216	THE LIVE ADVENTURES OF MIKE BLOOMFIELD AND AL KOOPER (2-LP)	15

(see also Al Kooper, Paul Butterfield Blues Band, Electric Flag)

BLOOMSBURY SET
80	Graduate GRAD 13	This Year Next Year/The Other Side Of You (p/s)	5
83	Stiletto STL 13	Hangin' Around With The Big Boys/Getting Away From It All (p/s)	5
83	Stiletto STL 15	Dress Parade/Serenade (p/s)	5

BLOSSOMS (U.S.)
58	Capitol CL 14833	Move On/He Promised Me	35
58	Capitol CL 14856	Little Louie/Have Faith In Me	40
58	Capitol CL 14947	No Other Love/Baby Daddy-O	40
71	Pama PM 814	Stand By/Soul And Inspiration	15
73	Mojo 2027 013	Touchdown/It's All Up To You	5

(see also Darlene Love, Allisons [U.S.])

BLOSSOMS (U.K.)
68	MGM MGM 1435	Tweedle Dee/You Got Me Hummin'	6

BLOSSOM TOES
67	Marmalade 598 002	What On Earth/Mrs Murphy's Budgerigar/Look At Me I'm You (some in p/s)	50/22
68	Marmalade 598 009	I'll Be Your Baby Tonight/Love Is	22
68	Marmalade 598 012	Postcard/Everyone's Leaving Me Now	20
69	Marmalade 598 014	Peace Loving Man/Up Above My Hobby Horse's Head	18
69	Marmalade 598 022	New Day/Love Bomb (unissued, existence unconfirmed)	
67	Marmalade 607/608 001	WE ARE EVER SO CLEAN (LP)	50
69	Marmalade 608 010	IF ONLY FOR A MOMENT (LP)	70

(see also B.B. Blunder, Stud, Kevin Westlake)

MICHAEL BLOUNT
70	CBS 7022	Sometimes/Angelina Baby	5
72	York SYK 519	Beautiful Morning/Feathered Cloud	5
72	York SYK 28	Tackle And Sack/Pretty Face	5
72	York SKY 535	Rosie/Trombone Man	5
71	CBS 64230	PATCHWORK (LP)	15
72	York FYK 401	SOUVENIRS (LP)	12
73	York FYK 414	FANTASIES (LP)	12

BLOW
91	Ten TENXDJ 384	CUTTER EP (12", p/s, promo only)	8

BLOW MONKEYS
87	RCA MONKX 6	(Celebrate) The Day After You (Election Mix)/It's Not Unusual (live)/Beautiful Child/The Smile On Her Face (Sweet Murder) (10", with Curtis Mayfield, withdrawn 'Thatcher' p/s, 'General Election Party Edition')	10
88	RCA PD 42232	It Pays To Be Short (4.40)/The Love Of Which I Dare Not Speak/Hingway!/It Pays To Belong (8.41) (CD, in numbered gold circular tin box)	7

(see also Curtis Mayfield)

BLOWZABELLA
70s	Special Delivery SPD 1028	VANILLA (LP)	20

BLUE
73	RSO 2090 109	Red Light Song/Look Around	5
73	RSO 2090 114	Little Jody/The Way Things Are	5
73	RSO 2394 105	BLUE (LP)	12

(see also Poets)

BABBITY BLUE
65	Decca F 12053	Don't Make Me/I Remembered How To Cry	7
65	Decca F 12149	Don't Hurt Me/Question	7

BOBBY BLUE
70	Duke DU 86	Going In Circles (actually by Lloyd Charmers)/Doggone Right (actually by Bobby Davis)	5

DAVID BLUE
67	Elektra EKL 4003	DAVID BLUE (LP, red label)	25
72	Asylum SYL 9001	STORIES (LP)	15
73	Asylum SYL 9009	NICE BABY AND THE ANGEL (LP)	15
75	Asylum SYL 9025	COMIN' BACK FOR MORE (LP)	12
76	Asylum K 53056	CUPID'S ARROW (LP)	12

PAMELA BLUE
63	Decca F 11761	My Friend Bobby/Hey There Stranger	90

TIMOTHY BLUE
68	Spark SRL 1014	The Room At The Top Of The Stairs/She Won't See The Light	12

BLUE ACES
64	Pye 7N 15672	Land Of Love/Love Song Of The Waterfall	7
64	Pye 7N 15713	I Beat You To It/I Just Can't Help Loving You	7
65	Pye 7N 15821	Ain't What You Say/You Don't Care	7
65	Columbia DB 7755	Tell Me What You're Gonna Do/All I Want	30
66	Columbia DB 7954	That's All Right/Talk About My Baby	55

(see also Riot Squad)

BLUE & FERRIS
68	Blue Cat BS 147	You Stole My Money/Tell Me The Reason	12

BLUE ANGEL
80	Polydor POSP 212	I'm Gonna Be Strong/Anna Blue (no p/s)	15
81	Polydor POSP 241	I Had A Love/Can't Blame Me	18
84	Polydor POSP 212	I'm Gonna Be Strong/Anna Blue (p/s, reissue)	10
80	Polydor 2391 486	BLUE ANGEL (LP)	20

(see also Cyndi Lauper)

BLUE BEARD
71	Ember EMB S 302	Country Man/Sly Willy (some in p/s)	15/8
71	Ember LT 7004	BLUE BEARD (LP, unreleased, test pressings only)	200
71	Ember ZCE 5054	BLUE BEARD (cassette)	10

BLUEBEATS
64	Ember EMB EP 4525	THE FABULOUS BLUEBEATS VOL. 1 (EP)	40
64	Ember EMB EP 4526	THE FABULOUS BLUEBEATS VOL. 2 (EP)	40

BLUEBEATERS
64	Piccadilly 7N 35181	Little David/Ain't Got A Care	6

BLUE-BELLES
62	HMV POP 1029	I Sold My Heart To The Junkman/Itty Bitty Twist	25

(see also Patti LaBelle & Blue Belles)

BLUEBELLS
82	London LON(F) 14/ Lyntone LYN 12361	Forevermore/Aim In Life (p/s, with free 33rpm clear vinyl flexidisc "Everybody's Somebody's Fool")	6
84	London LON 49	Young At Heart/Tender Mercy (bluebell-shaped disc)	6

(see also McClusky Brothers)

BLUEBERRIES
65	Mercury MF 894	It's Gonna Work Out Fine/Please Don't Let Me Know	20

BLUE BLOOD
70	Sonet SNTF 615	BLUE BLOOD (LP)	18

BLUE CHEER
68	Philips BF 1646	Summertime Blues/Out Of Focus	15
68	Philips BF 1684	Just A Little Bit/Gypsy Ball	6
68	Philips BF 1711	Feathers From Your Tree/Sun Cycle	6
69	Philips BF 1778	West Coast Child Of Sunshine/When It All Gets Old	7
71	Philips 6051 010	Pilot/Babaji	7
68	Philips (S)BL 7839	VINCEBUS ERUPTUM (LP, mono/stereo)	40/25
68	Philips SBL 7860	OUTSIDEINSIDE (LP, gatefold sleeve)	25
69	Philips SBL 7896	NEW! IMPROVED! (LP)	20
69	Philips 6336 001	BLUE CHEER (LP)	20
71	Philips 6336 004	B.C. #5 THE ORIGINAL HUMAN BEING (LP)	30

(see also Leigh Stephens, Group B)

BLUE CHIPS
60	Polydor NH 66950	Take Another Step/A Song And A Prayer	5

BLUE CHIPS
65	Pye 7N 15970	I'm On The Right Side/You're Good To Me	20
66	Pye 7N 17111	Some Kind Of Lovin'/I Know A Boy	20
66	Pye 7N 17155	Tell Her/Good Lovin' Never Hurt	20

BLUE DANUBE
80	EMI EMI 5070	You Are A Song/Du Bist Music/Let Me Hear That Song Again	5

BLUE DIAMONDS
60	Decca F 21292	Ramona/All Of Me	5
60	Decca DFE 6675	I'M FOREVER BLOWING BUBBLES (EP)	10

BLUE EPITAPH
74	Holyground HG 117	ODE (LP, 99 copies only)	225
91	Holyground HG 117	ODE (LP, reissue, folded gatefold sleeve)	18

(see also Magus)

BLUE FLAMES
63	R&B JB 114	J.A. Blues/Orange Street	35
63	R&B JB 126	Stop Right Here/Rik's Tune	35

(see also Georgie Fame & Blue Flames)

BLUE GOOSE
75	Anchor ANC 1015	Loretta/Call On Me	5
75	Anchor ANCL 2005	BLUE GOOSE (LP)	12

(see also Badfinger, Curtis Knight & Zeus, Motörhead)

BLUE JEANS
69	Columbia DB 8555	Hey Mrs. Housewife/Sandfly	20

(see also Swinging Blue Jeans, Ray Ennis & Blue Jeans)

BLUE MAGIC
74	Atlantic K 10494	Sideshow/Just Don't Want To Be Lonely	4
75	Atlantic K 10553	Three Ring Circus/Spell	4

(see also Margie Joseph)

BLUE MEN
60	Triumph RGXST 5000	I HEAR A NEW WORLD (PART ONE) (EP)	375
60	Triumph RGXST 5001	I HEAR A NEW WORLD (PART TWO) (EP, only sleeves exist)	sleeve 80
60	Triumph TRX ST 9000	I HEAR A NEW WORLD (LP, unreleased, white label demos only)	1,100

(see also Joe Meek, Peter Jay & Blue Men, Rodd-Ken & Cavaliers)

BLUE MINK
70	Philips SBL 7926	MELTING POT (LP)	10
71	Philips 6208 024	OUR WORLD (LP)	10

(see also Madeline Bell, Roger [James] Cook, Rumplestiltskin)

BLUE MOUNTAIN BOYS
63	Oriole CB 1774	Drop Me Gently/One Small Photograph Of You	7

BLUE MOVIES
79	ROK ROK9	Mary Jane/THE NOISE: Criminal (no p/s)	8

BLUE NILE
81	RSO RSO 84	I Love This Life/The Second Act (p/s)	25
84	Linn LKS 1	Stay/Saddle The Horses (white p/s)	8
84	Linn LKS 1-12	Stay/Saddle The Horses (12", white p/s)	12
84	Linn LKS 1	Stay (Remix)/Saddle The Horses (p/s)	5
84	Linn LKSD 1	Stay (Remix)/Saddle The Horses//Tinsel Town In The Rain/Heatwave (Instrumental) (p/s, double pack)	8
84	Linn LKS 1-12	Stay (Extended Remix)/Saddle The Horses (12", p/s)	8
84	Linn LKS 2	Tinsel Town In The Rain/Heatwave (Instrumental) (p/s)	5
84	Linn LKS 2-12	Tinsel Town In The Rain (Extended)/Regret/Heatwave (Instrumental) (12", p/s)	8
89	Linn LKSCD 3	The Downtown Lights/The Wires Are Down/Halfway To Paradise (3" CD, card sleeve)	10
89	Linn LKYCD 4	Headlights On The Parade (CD, collector's pack)	8
80s	Linn	flexidisc (demonstration disc)	20

BLUENOTES
60	Top Rank JAR 291	I Don't Know What It Is/You Can't Get Away From Love	6

BLUE ORCHIDS
81	Rough Trade RT 065	Disney Boys/The Flood (p/s)	4
81	Rough Trade RT 067	Work/The House That Faded Out (p/s)	4
82	Rough Trade RT 117T	AGENTS OF CHANGE (12" EP, in carrier bag)	7
84	Rough Trade ROUGH 37	GREATEST HITS (LP)	10

(see also Nosebleeds, Fall)

BLUE OYSTER CULT
76	CBS 4483	(Don't Fear) The Reaper/R U Ready 2 Rock	5
76	CBS 4483	(Don't Fear) The Reaper/Tattoo Vampire (promo with different B-side)	10
78	CBS 5689	Going Through The Motions/Searching For The Celine	5
78	CBS 12-6333	(Don't Fear) The Reaper (12")	8
79	CBS 7763	Mirrors/Lonely Teardrops (clear vinyl)	5
81	CBS A 1453	Burnin' For You/Heavy Metal (p/s)	5
81	CBS A 13 1453	Burnin' For You/Heavy Metal/The Black & Silver (12", p/s)	8
83	CBS A 3937	Take Me Away/Feel The Thunder (p/s)	5
83	CBS TA 3937	Take Me Away/Feel The Thunder/Burnin' For You/Doctor Music (12", p/s)	8
84	CBS A 4117	Shooting Shark/Dragon Lady (p/s)	5
84	CBS TA 4117	Shooting Shark/Dragon Lady (12", p/s)	8
89	CBS 652 985-2	Astronomy/Magna Of Illusion/(Don't Fear) The Reaper (CD, card sleeve)	8
73	CBS 64904	BLUE OYSTER CULT (LP)	12
80	CBS 86120	CULTOSAURUS ERECTUS (LP, with poster)	12

BLUE PEARL
92	Big Life BL RR 73	MOTHER DAWN — ORB REMIX (12", p/s)	8

BLUE PHANTOM
72	Kaleidoscope KAL 101	DISTORTIONS (LP)	50

BLUE RIDGE RANGERS
73	Fantasy FTC 105	Hearts Of Stone/Somewhere Listening For My Name	6
73	Fantasy FTC 110	You Don't Own Me/Back In The Hills	6
73	Fantasy FT 511	BLUE RIDGE RANGERS (LP)	15

(see also John Fogerty, Creedence Clearwater Revival)

BLUE RIVERS & MAROONS
67	Columbia Blue Beat DB 103	Witchcraft Man/Searching For You Baby	8
68	Spectrum SP 105	Take It Or Leave It/I've Been Pushed Around	6
68	Columbia S(C)X 6192	BLUE BEAT IN MY SOUL (LP)	25

BLUE RONDOS
64	Pye 7N 15734	Little Baby/Baby I Go For You	55
65	Pye 7N 15833	Don't Want Your Lovin' No More/What Can I Do	40

BLUES BAND
80	Arista BBBP 101	OFFICIAL BOOTLEG ALBUM (LP, with autographs)	12

(see also Paul Jones, McGuinness-Flint, Manfred Mann)

BLUESBREAKERS
(see under John Mayall & Bluesbreakers)

MINT VALUE £

BLUES BUSTERS (U.S.)
71   Jay Boy BOY 44   I Can't Stop/Inspired To Love You 5

BLUES BY FIVE
64   Decca F 12029   Boom Boom/I Cried 50

BLUES COUNCIL
65   Parlophone R 5264   Baby Don't Look Down/What Will I Do 60

BLUES 5
64   Studio 36 (no cat. no.)   Hey Baby/When You're In Love 75

BLUES IMAGE
70   Atlantic 2091 009   Ride Captain Ride/Pay My Dues 5
71   Atlantic 2400 120   RED, WHITE AND BLUES IMAGE (LP)...................................... 12

BLUES INCORPORATED
(see under Alexis Korner)

BLUES MAGOOS
66   Mercury MF 954   (We Ain't Got) Nothin' Yet/Gotta Get Away 25
67   Fontana TF 848   One By One/Love Seems Doomed 15
71   Probe PRO 522   Can't Get Enough Of You/Sea Breeze Express 4
66   Fontana (S)TL 5402   BLUES MAGOOS (LP, mono/stereo)................................... 50/40
71   Probe SPB 1024   GULF COAST BOUND (LP) 15

BLUES MASTERS
63   Island WI 078   5 O'Clock Whistle/African Blood (both sides actually by Baba Brooks) 15

BLUESOLOGY
65   Fontana TF 594   Come Back Baby/Time's Getting Tougher Than Tough 275
66   Fontana TF 668   Mister Frantic/Everyday (I Have The Blues)........................... 350
(see also Stu Brown & Bluesology, Elton John, Long John Baldry, Elton Dean, Mark Charig)

BLUES PROJECT
67   Verve Forecast VS 1505   I Can't Keep From Crying/The Way My Baby Walks 12
67   Verve (S)VLP 6004   PROJECTIONS (LP) 15
72   Capitol E-ST 11017   THE BLUES PROJECT (LP) 10
(see also Al Kooper, Tommy Flanders, Seatrain)

BLUE STARS
58   Felsted PDL 95037   MEET THE BLUE STARS (LP) 12

BLUE STARS
65   Decca F 12303   Please Be A Little Kind/I Can Take It 150

BLUE STEAM
78   Rip Off RIP 5   Lizard King/Cortina Cowboys (p/s) 10

BLUETONES
95   Superior Quality TONE 001   Slight Return/The Fountainhead (blue vinyl, plain white sleeve in stickered
                           polythene bag, 2,000 only, sold by mail-order & at gigs, some numbered).... 35/30
95   Superior Quality TONE 001   Slight Return/The Fountainhead (red vinyl, foldover p/s in poly bag,
                           1,000 only, export issue to Japan)................................... 45
95   Superior Quality BLUE 001X   Are You Blue Or Are You Blind?/String Along (p/s, numbered, 4,000 only) 8
95   Superior Quality BLUE 001T   Are You Blue Or Are You Blind?/String Along/Driftwood (12", p/s, 3,000 only) ... 15
95   Superior Q. BLUE 001CD   Are You Blue Or Are You Blind?/String Along/Driftwood (CD) 12
95   Superior Quality BLUE 002   Bluetonic/Glad To See Y'Back Again? (p/s, 5,000 only) 7
95   Superior Quality BLUE 002T   Bluetonic/Colorado Beetle/Glad To See Y'Back Again? (12", p/s, 2,000 only) 12
95   Superior Q. BLUE 002CD   Bluetonic/Colorado Beetle/Glad To See Y'Back Again? (CD).................. 8
96   Superior Quality BLUE 003X   Slight Return/Don't Stand Me Down (p/s, with plain inner sleeve, 10,000 only) .. 5
96   Superior Quality BLUE 003X   Slight Return/Don't Stand Me Down (red vinyl,
                           export issue to Japan with Japanese text on rear of p/s) 75
96   Superior Quality BLUE 001X   Are You Blue Or Are You Blind?/String Along
                           (p/s, blue vinyl export issue) 8
96   Superior Q. BLUE 005DJ   Cut Some Rug (CD, 1-track promo with 'classroom' inlay, withdrawn) 18
96   Superior Quality   EXPECTING TO FLY (LP, 5,000 copies with gatefold sleeve & booklet,
     BLUELPX 004   embossed PVC sleeve) 18

BLUE TRAIN
87   Dreamworld DREAM 007T   LAND OF GOLD (12" EP).. 8
(see also Go Service)

BLUEWATER FOLK
70s Folk Heritage   BLUEWATER FOLK (LP) 60
70s Moonraker MOO 1   BUGS, BLACK PUDDINGS AND CLOGS (LP, with insert).................... 12
70s Moonraker MOO 2   A LANCASHIRE LIFE (LP, with insert)................................. 12

BLUE YOGURT
70   Penny Farthing PEN 732   Lydia/Umbrella Man 8

BLUE ZONE
87   Rockin' Horse RHCD 116   On Fire (Extended)/(Conflagration Mix)/Be The Sugar
                           (3" CD & adaptor, 5" case).. 8
88   Rockin' Horse RHCD 115   Thinking About His Baby/Thinking About His Baby (Extended Dance)/
                           Big Thing (Extended) (3" CD, foldout p/s) 8

(see also Lisa Stansfield)

COLIN BLUNSTONE
71   Epic EPC 7095   Mary, Won't You Warm My Bed/I Hope I Didn't Say Too Much Last Night........ 5
71   Epic EPC 7520   Caroline Goodbye/Though You Are Far Away............................. 5
72   Epic EPC 7765   Say You Don't Mind/Let Me Come Closer (p/s) 7
72   Epic EPC 8434   I Don't Believe In Miracles/I've Always Had You 5
73   Epic EPC 1197   How Could We Dare To Be Wrong?/Time's Runnin' Out 5
73   Epic EPC 1775   Wonderful/Beginning.. 6

BLUR

74	Epic EPC 2413	It's Magical/Summersong.	6
76	Epic EPC 4576	When You Close Your Eyes/Good Guys Don't Always Win	5
76	Epic EPC 4752	Planes/Dancing In The Dark.	5
76	Epic EPC 5009	Beautiful You/It's Hard To Say Goodbye	5
77	Epic EPC 5199	Lovin' And Free/Dancing In The Dark	5
78	Epic EPC 6320	I'll Never Forget You/You Are The Way For Me	5
78	Epic EPC 6535	Ain't It Funny/Who's That Knocking	5
78	Epic EPC 6793	Photograph/Touch And Go	5
81	Panache PAN 1	Miles Away/MITCHELL-COE MYSTERIES: Excerpts From "Exiled" (p/s)	5
71	Epic EPC 64557	ONE YEAR (LP, textured sleeve)	15
72	Epic EPC 65278	ENNISMORE (LP, textured sleeve).	15
74	Epic EPC 65805	JOURNEY (LP)	12
76	Epic EPC 81592	PLANES (LP, with lyric insert)	12
78	Epic EPC 82835	NEVER EVEN THOUGHT (LP, with lyric insert)	15

(see also Zombies, Neil MacArthur, Mitchell-Coe Mysteries)

BLUNT INSTRUMENT

78	Diesel DCL 01	No Excuse/Interrogation (p/s)	5

BLUR

90	Food FOOD 26	She's So High (Edit)/I Know (p/s)	12
90	Food TCFOOD 26	She's So High (Edit)/I Know (cassette)	8
90	Food 12FOOD 26	She's So High (Definitive)/Sing/I Know (Extended) (12", p/s).	20
90	Food CDFOOD 26	She's So High/I Know (Extended)/Down (CD)	30
91	Food FOOD 29	There's No Other Way/Inertia (p/s).	10
91	Food TCFOOD 29	There's No Other Way/Inertia (cassette)	7
91	Food 12FOOD 29	There's No Other Way (Extended)/Inertia/Mr. Briggs/I'm All Over (12", p/s)	18
91	Food 12 FOODX 29	There's No Other Way (The Blur Remix)/Won't Do It/ Day Upon Day (live) (12", p/s lists '12 FOODDX 29').	25
91	Food CDFOOD 29	There's No Other Way/Inertia/Mr. Briggs/I'm All Over (CD)	30
91	Food FOOD 31	Bang/Luminous (p/s)	8
91	Food TCFOOD 31	Bang/Luminous (cassette).	7
91	Food 12FOOD 31	Bang (Extended)/Explain/Luminous/Uncle Love (12", p/s)	15
91	Food CDFOOD 31	Bang/Explain/Luminous/Beserk (CD)	30
91	Food 12BLUR 4	High Cool (Easy Listening Mix)/Bad Day (Leisurely Mix) (12", blue & gold company sleeve, promo, 1,000 only)	25
92	Food FOOD 37	Popscene/Mace (p/s)	15
92	Food TCFOOD 37	Popscene/Mace (cassette)	8
92	Food 12FOOD 37	Popscene/I'm Fine/Mace/Garden Central (12", p/s).	20
92	Food CDFOOD 37	Popscene/Mace/Badgeman Brown (CD)	40
92	Food BLUR 6	The Wassailing Song (1-sided gig freebie, no p/s, 500 only)	80
92	Food TCFOOD 40	For Tomorrow/Into Another/Hanging Over (cassette)	7
92	Food 12FOOD 40	For Tomorrow (Visit To Primrose Hill Extended)/Into Another/ Hanging Over/Peach (12", p/s).	15
92	Food CDFOOD 40	For Tomorrow (Visit To Primrose Hill Extended)/Peach/Bone Bag (CD, double jewel case).	25
92	Food CDSFOOD 40	For Tomorrow (Single Version)/When The Cows Come Home/ Beachcoma/For Tomorrow (Acoustic Version) (CD)	25
93	Food FOODS 45	Chemical World/Maggie May (red vinyl, paper labels, p/s)	15
93	Food 12FOOD 45	Chemical World/Es Schmecht/Young And Lovely/My Ark (12", p/s with print).	18
93	Food CDFOODS 45	Chemical World (Reworked)/Never Clever (live)/Pressure On Julian (live)/ Come Together (live) (CD, double jewel case).	25
93	Food CDFOOD 45	Chemical World/Young And Lovely/Es Schmecht/My Ark (CD)	25

93	Food FOODS 46	Sunday Sunday/Tell Me, Tell Me (B-side as Blur featuring Seymour) (yellow vinyl, p/s)	15
93	Food 12FOODS 46	Sunday Sunday/Long Legged/Mixed Up (B-sides as Blur featuring Seymour) (12", p/s with print)	15
93	Food CDFOOD 46	Sunday Sunday/Dizzy/Fried/Shimmer (CD, final 3 tracks as "B-sides as Blur featuring Seymour")	25
93	Food CDFOODX 46	THE SUNDAY SUNDAY POPULAR COMMUNITY SONG CD: Sunday Sunday/ Daisy Bell/Let's All Go Down The Strand (CD)	25
94	Food FOODS 47	Girls And Boys/Magpie/People In Europe (p/s, numbered)	6
94	Food CDFOOD 47	Girls And Boys/People In Europe/Peter Panic (CD, slimline jewel case)	10
94	Food CDFOODS 47	Girls And Boys/Magpie/Anniversary Waltz (CD, digipak)	10
94	Food CDFOOD 50	To The End/Girls And Boys (Pet Shop Boys 7" Remix)/Girls And Boys (Pet Shop Boys 12" Remix) (CD, slimline jewel case)	10
94	Food CDFOODS 53	Parklife/Supa Shoppa/Theme From An Imaginary Film (CD, slimline jewel case)	7
94	Food CDFOOD 53	Parklife/Beard/To The End (French Version) (CD, slimline jewel case)	7
95	Food CDFOODDJ 59	This Is A Low (CD, promo only, plain card sleeve with set of 4 stamps)	12
95	Food 12FOODDJ 63	Country House (12", promo only, 1-sided, die-cut p/s)	12
95	Food 12FOODDJ 69	The Universal/Entertain Me (Live It! Remix) (12", promo only, die-cut p/s)	12
96	Fan Club DEATH 1	Death Of A Party (demo) (CD, 1-track, card p/s, fan club issue, 3250 only)	10
97	Food 12BLURDJ 7	On Your Own (Crouch End Broadway Mix) (12", 1-sided, promo only)	15
97	Fan Club LOVE 001	I Love Her (CD, card p/s, fan club issue, 3,500 only)	10
97	Food CDFOODDJ 109	Death Of A Party (7" Remix)/(Well Blurred Remix)/(Billy Whiskers Mix)/ (Album Version) (CD, promo only, card p/s)	10
99	Food CD FOOD DJ 117	Tender (LP version)/(radio edit) (CD, silver foil pack, promo only)	15
97	Food CDIN 106	BLURB (CD, interview, promo only)	25
99	Food FOOD CDJX 29	13 (CD in duffelbag with folder, photos, ski-hat and biography, promo only)	100

BLURT

80	Test Pressing TP 1	My Mother Was A Friend Of An Enemy Of The People/Get (p/s)	4
81	Armageddon AS 013	The Fish Needs A Bike/This Is My Royal Wedding Souvenir (p/s)	4

HENRY BLYTHE

56	Oriole MG 20009	AN INVESTIGATION INTO REINCARNATION (LP)	20

JIMMY BLYTHE

54	London AL 3527	SOUTH SIDE BLUE PIANO (10" LP)	25
54	London AL 3529	SOUTH SIDE CHICAGO JAZZ (10" LP)	25

ENID BLYTON

57	HMV 7EG 8260	NODDY STORIES (EP)	10

B-MOVIE

80	Dead Good DEAD 9	TAKE THREE (EP)	25
80	Dead Good BIG DEAD 12	NOWHERE GIRL (12" EP, with insert)	20
81	Lyntone LYN 10410	Remembrance Day/SOFT CELL: Metro Mr X (red or green flexidisc with Flexipop magazine, issue 12)	12/6
81	Deram DM 443	Marilyn Dreams/Film Music (Part 1) (p/s)	5
81	Deram DMX 443	Marilyn Dreams/Film Music (Part 1) (12", p/s)	8
88	Wax 12 WAX 3	Nowhere Girl/Remembrance Day (12", p/s, 250 on orange vinyl, numbered)	10
88	Wax 12 WAX 3	Nowhere Girl/Remembrance Day (12", p/s, pink or black vinyl, numbered)	10/7
88	Wax 12 WAX 4	Polar Opposites/Taxi Driver (12", clear vinyl or picture disc)	each 8
88	Wax CD WAX 4	Polar Opposites/Taxi Driver (CD)	15
88	Wax WAXLP 1P	THE DEAD GOOD TAPES (LP, picture disc)	12
88	Wax WAXCD 4	THE DEAD GOOD TAPES (CD)	18
91	Dead Good GOOD 3	REMEMBRANCE DAYS (LP, with 7" "The Fool"/"Swinging Lights" [CHEAP 1])	12

BMX BANDITS

86	53rd & 3rd AGARR 3	Sad?/E102 (p/s, some with comic)	10/5
86	53rd & 3rd AGARR 312	Sad?/E102/The Cat From Outer Space (live)/Strawberry Sunday (live)/ Groovy Good Luck Friend (live) (12", p/s)	10
87	53rd & 3rd AGARR 6	What A Wonderful World/The Day Before Tomorrow (p/s)	6
87	53rd & 3rd AGARR 612	What A Wonderful World/The Day Before Tomorrow/ Johnny Alucard/Sad?/Sandy's Wallet (12", p/s)	8
92	Sunflower SUN 006	GORDON KEEN & HIS BMX BANDITS EP (p/s, red vinyl)	8

(see also Soup Dragons, Boy Hairdressers, Teenage Fanclub, Vaselines)

EDDIE BO

73	Action ACT 4609	Check Your Bucket (Parts 1 & 2)	20

BO & PEEP

64	Decca F 11968	Young Love/The Rise Of The Brighton Surf	30

(see also Andrew Oldham Orchestra)

BOARDS OF CANADA

96	Skam SKA 8	High Scores/Turquoise Hexagon Sun/Nlagon/June 9th/ See Ya Later/Everything You Do Is A Balloon (12", p/s)	10
98	Skam KMAS 1	Aquarius/Chinook (p/s, 1,000 only)	30

BOARDWALKERS

60s	own label J.C. 1	A Miracle/Any Man's Girl	150

(see also Warren Davis)

BOB (Relf) & EARL (Nelson)

65	Sue WI 374	Harlem Shuffle/I'll Keep Running Back	15
65	Sue WI 393	Baby I'm Satisfied/The Sissy	15
67	Sue WI 4030	Don't Ever Leave Me/Fancy Free	15
69	Island WI 6053	Harlem Shuffle/I'll Keep Running Back (reissue)	8
69	B&C CB 102	Dancin' Everywhere/Baby It's Over	5
69	Warner Bros WB 6059	Everybody Jerk/He's A Playbrother	6
70	Uni UN 519	Pickin' Up Love's Vibrations/Uh, Uh, Naw Naw Naw	5

MINT VALUE £

72	Jay Boy BOY 72	I Can't Get Away/I'll Keep Running Back	5
72	Jay Boy BOY 73	My Little Girl/His & Her Shuffle (as Bob & Earl Band)	5
73	Contempo C 4	Harlem Shuffle/Harlem Shuffle (Instrumental Version)	6
67	Sue ILP 951	HARLEM SHUFFLE (LP)	50
69	Joy JOYS 199	TOGETHER (LP)	15
69	B&C BCB 1	BOB AND EARL (LP)	15
71	Jay Boy JSX 2004	HARLEM SHUFFLE (LP)	15

(see also Bob Relf, Jackie Lee, Earl Nelson, Hollywood Flames)

BOB & JERRY

58	Pye International 7N 25003	Ghost Satellite/Nothin'	12
58	Pye International N 25003	Ghost Satellite/Nothin' (78)	15
61	Philips PB 1205	Dreamy Eyes/We're The Guys	6

BOB (Andy) & MARCIA (Griffiths)

70	Bamboo BAM 40	Really Together/BOB ANDY: Desperate Lover	10
70	Harry J. HJ 6605	Young, Gifted And Black/JAY BOYS: Young, Gifted & Black (Instrumental)	6
70	Escort ES 824	Young, Gifted And Black/BARRINGTON BIGGS: My Cheri Amour	6
71	Trojan TR 7818	Pied Piper/Save Me	5
72	Trojan TR 7854	But I Do/I Don't Care	5
70	Trojan TBL 122	YOUNG, GIFTED & BLACK (LP)	18
72	Trojan TRLS 26	PIED PIPER (LP)	15

(see also Bob Andy, Marcia Griffiths)

BOB & TYRONE

69	Coxsone CS 7086	I Don't Care/LASCELLES PERKINS: Little Green Apples	18

BOBBEJAAN

60	Palette PG 9009	I'm Cryin' In My Beer/A Little Bit Of Heaven	6

BOB(B)ETTES

57	London HLE 8477	Mr. Lee/Look At The Stars	45
57	London HLE 8477	Mr. Lee/Look At The Stars (78)	25
58	London HLE 8597	Come-A Come-A/Speedy	45
58	London HLE 8597	Come-A Come-A/Speedy (78)	30
60	London HLE 9173	I Shot Mr. Lee/Untrue Love	30
60	London HLE 9248	Have Mercy Baby/Dance With Me Georgie	25
60	Pye International 7N 25060	I Shot Mr. Lee/Billy (as Bobettes)	25
72	Action ACT 4603	That's A Bad Thing To Know/All In Your Mind	12

BOBBSEY TWINS

57	London HLA 8474	A Change Of Heart/Part-Time Gal	25
57	London HLA 8474	A Change Of Heart/Part-Time Gal (78)	25

BOBBY & DAVE

71	Ackee ACK 116	Build My World Around You/LIZZY & TONY BOP: Sammy Version	10

(see also Dave Barker, Lizzy & Dennis)

BOBBY & JIM

58	Capitol CL 14877	Carry My Books/A Lover Can Tell	6

BOBBY & LAURIE

66	Parlophone R 5480	Hitch Hiker/You'll Come 'Round	12

BOBBY & MIDNITES

84	CBS 26046	WHERE THE BEAT MEETS THE STREET (LP)	15

(see also Bob Weir, Grateful Dead)

BOBCATS

67	Pye 7N 17242	Can't See For Looking/Let Me Get By	12

BOBO MR. SOUL

73	London HLU 10418	Hitch Hiking To Heartbreak/She's My Woman	7

FRIDA BOCCARA

69	Philips BF 1765	Through The Eyes Of A Child/So Fair	15

BOCKY & VISIONS

65	Atlantic AT 4049	I Go Crazy/Good Good Lovin'	18

BODAST

81	Cherry Red BRED 12	THE BODAST TAPES FEATURING STEVE HOWE (LP)	10

(see also Steve Howe, Tomorrow)

IAN BODDY

83	Signal 1	THE CLIMB (LP)	12
84	New Media 001	SPIRITS (LP)	12
86	SER 001	PHOENIX (LP)	12

J.P. BODDY

73	Columbia DB 8989	Stop Me Spinning (Like A Top)/Song Without A Word	5

BODGER'S MATE

78	Cottage COT 521	BRIGHTER THAN USUAL (LP)	25

BODIES

79	Waldo's HS 007	Art Nouveau/Machinery (poster p/s, 5 different colours; later in standard p/s)	5/4

BODINES

85	Creation CRE 016	God Bless/Paradise (wraparound p/s with poly bag)	8
86	Creation CRE 030T	Heard It All/William Shatner/Clear (12", p/s)	7

BODKIN

72	West CSA 104	BODKIN (LP, private pressing in posthumously-designed sleeve)	300

BODY

81	Recession	THE BODY ALBUM (LP, private pressing with booklet)	50

BODYSNATCHERS
80	2-Tone CHS TT 9	Let's Do Rocksteady/Ruder Than You (paper label, company sleeve)	5
80	2-Tone CHS TT 12	Easy Life/Too Experienced (paper label, company sleeve)	5

BOEING DUVEEN & BEAUTIFUL SOUP
68	Parlophone R 5696	Jabberwock/Which Dreamed It (some with p/s)	120/60

BOFFALONGO
70	United Artists UP 35144	Dancing In The Moonlight/Endless Questions	5
71	United Artists UAG 29130	BEYOND YOUR HEAD (LP)	15

LUCILLE BOGAN
57	Jazz Collector L 90	Sweet Man, Sweet Man/Down In Boogie Alley (78)	8

DIRK BOGARDE
65	Fontana TF 615	Darling/MOVIE SOUNDS: Pavanne For Diane	6
60	Decca LK 4373	LYRICS FOR LOVERS (LP)	15

BOGDON
81	Black Label GB 3	Oh Eddie/Reet Petite (p/s)	10
81	Brilliant HIT 1	Who Do You Think You Are?/Take Me Back (p/s)	10

(see also Whitesnake, Bernie Marsden)

BOGEYMEN
93	Detour Records DR008	Let Me Give You My Love/You've Got No Scruples/Gimme A Little Sign (p/s, 1,000 only, 100 blue vinyl)	8/5

BOGIES
64	private press (no cat. no.)	THE BOGIES ON CAMPUS (LP)	200
64	private press (no cat. no.)	BYE BYE BOGIES (LP)	200

LEE BOGLE
71	Black Swan BW 1406	Tomorrow's Dreams/SWANS: Hot Pants Reggae	7

HAMILTON BOHANNON
75	Brunswick BR 16	South African Man/Have A Good Day	5
78	Mercury 6167 700	Let's Start The Dance/I Wonder Why	5
78	Mercury 9199 830	Let's Start The Dance/I Wonder Why (12")	10
75	Brunswick BRLS 3013	SOUTH AFRICAN MAN (LP)	12

HOUSTON BOINES
66	Blue Horizon 45 BH 1006	Superintendent Blues/Monkey Motion (99 copies only)	75

BOLA 1
95	Skam SKA 5	Forcasa 3/Krak Jakomo/Metalurg 2/Ballom (12", custom sleeve)	40

MARC BOLAN
65	Decca F 12288	The Wizard/Beyond The Rising Sun (some as Marc Bölan; demos £250)	300
66	Decca F 12413	The Third Degree/San Francisco Poet (demos £300)	350
66	Parlophone R 5539	Hippy Gumbo/Misfit (demos £350)	450
72	Track 2094 013	Jasper C. Debussy/Hippy Gumbo/The Perfumed Garden Of Gulliver Smith (p/s)	25
81	Rarn MBFS 001C	Sing Me A Song/Endless Sleep (Extended Version)/The Lilac Hand Of Menthol Dan (12", no p/s, clear vinyl, handwritten labels)	8
81	Rarn MBFS 001P	Sing Me A Song/Endless Sleep (Extended Version)/The Lilac Hand Of Menthol Dan (12" picture disc, misprinted with black rim; also white rim)	15/7
81	Rarn MBFS 001P	Sing Me A Song/Endless Sleep (Extended Version)/The Lilac Hand Of Menthol Dan (12", picture disc misprinted back-to-front)	20
81	Cherry Red CHERRY 29	You Scare Me To Death/The Perfumed Garden Of Gulliver Smith (initial copies with bronze label, glossy p/s & free flexidisc [Lyntone LYN 10086])	7
81	Cherry Red CHERRY 29	You Scare Me To Death/The Perfumed Garden Of Gulliver Smith (later pressing with silver label/matt p/s)	4
81	Cherry Red CHERRY P29	You Scare Me To Death/The Perfumed Garden Of Gulliver Smith (picture disc)	6
81	Cherry Red CHERRY 32	Cat Black/Jasper C. Debussy (p/s)	5
82	Cherry Red CHERRY 39	The Wizard/Beyond The Rising Sun/Rings Of Fortune (p/s)	5
72	Track 2406 101	HARD ON LOVE (LP, unreleased, 2 test pressing copies only)	500+
74	Track 2410 201	THE BEGINNING OF DOVES (LP)	20
81	Cherry Red PERED 20	YOU SCARE ME TO DEATH (LP, picture disc)	12
81	Cherry Red ERED 20	YOU SCARE ME TO DEATH (LP, gatefold sleeve; early copies with booklet stapled into sleeve; later copies with loose booklet) each	10
89	Media Motion MEDIA 2	THE BEGINNING OF DOVES (LP, reissue, 750 only, withdrawn)	10

(see also Marc Bolan/T. Rex, Marc Bolan & Gloria Jones, Toby Tyler, John's Children, Big Carrot, Dib Cochran & The Earwigs)

MARC BOLAN & GLORIA JONES
77	EMI EMI 2572	To Know You Is To Love You/City Port	14

(see also Gloria Jones)

MARC BOLAN/T. REX
SINGLES
70	Octopus OCTO 1	Ride A White Swan/Summertime Blues/Jewel (unreleased, handwritten white label, 2 test pressings only)	2,500
70	Fly BUG 1	Ride A White Swan/Is It Love/Summertime Blues (p/s, purple labels, later with mustard labels)	15/7
71	Fly BUG 6	Hot Love/Woodland Rock/King Of The Mountain Cometh (mustard labels, later with 'fly' design)	6/5
71	Fly BUG 10	Get It On/There Was A Time/Raw Ramp (p/s, black label with silver 'fly' logo)	12
70s	Fly BUG 10	Get It On/There Was A Time/Raw Ramp (p/s, black label with white 'fly' or later silver 'fly' text) each	4
71	Fly GRUB 1	Electric Warrior Preview Single: Jeepster/Life's A Gas (gig freebie, originally in pink envelope sleeve, later standard paper sleeve)	175/125

MINT VALUE £

71	Fly BUG 16	Jeepster/Life's A Gas (white 'fly' label, or scarce issue w/out 'GRUB 1A' ref.) . . . 5/4
72	EMI T REX 101	Telegram Sam/Cadillac/Baby Strange 4
72	Magni Fly ECHO 102	One Inch Rock/The Woodland Bop/The Throat Of Winter (unreleased, rejected 1-sided test pressing for B-side of "Debora"/"One Inch Rock", stamped white label) 125
72	EMI MARC 2	Children Of The Revolution/Jitterbug Love/Sunken Rags 4
72	EMI MARC 3	Solid Gold Easy Action/(5th Dimension track) (mispressing) 15
72	EMI MARC 3	Solid Gold Easy Action/(Partridge Family track) (mispressing) 15
72	EMI SPRS 346	Chariot Choogle/The Slider (promo only, 'T. Rex' picture label or white label) 350/250
72	Lyntone	Christmas Time/Wanna Spend My Christmas With You/Christmas/Everybody Knows It's Christmas (fan club flexi, some with letter in brown envelope) 40/25
73	EMI MARC 6	Truck On (Tyke)/Sitting Here 5
74	EMI MARC 7	Teenage Dream/Satisfaction Pony (credited to 'Marc Bolan & T. Rex' or 'Marc Bolan') 5/4
74	EMI MARC 8	Light Of Love/Explosive Mouth 4
74	EMI MARC 9	Zip Gun Boogie/Space Boss 5
75	EMI MARC 10	New York City/Chrome Sitar. 5
75	EMI MARC 11	Dreamy Lady/Do You Wanna Dance?/Dock Of The Bay (as T. Rex Disco Party). . . . 5
75	EMI MARC 12	Christmas Bop/Telegram Sam/Metal Guru (unreleased, A- & B-side paper labels exist, 2 sets only). 1,000
76	EMI MARC 13	London Boys/Solid Baby 5
76	Cube BUG 66	Hot Love/Get It On 5
76	EMI MARC 14	I Love To Boogie/Baby Boomerang 5
76	EMI MARC 15	Laser Love/Life's An Elevator 5
77	EMI MARC 16	The Soul Of My Suit/All Alone 5
77	EMI MARC 17	Dandy In The Underworld/Groove A Little/Tame My Tiger (p/s) 6
77	EMI MARC 18	Celebrate Summer/Ride My Wheels (p/s) 7
78	EMI MARC 19	Crimson Moon/Jason B. Sad (p/s). 5
77	Cube ANT 1	BOLAN'S BEST PLUS ONE (EP, p/s) 5
78	Cube ANT 2	Hot Love/Raw Ramp/Lean Woman Blues (p/s, misprinted "Raw Amp", sleeve credits 'Bolan', label credits 'T.Rex') 5
78	Cube BINT 1	Steve Dixon Interview (free with initial copies of compilation LP [HIFLD 1]) 7
79	Cube ANTS 001	Life's A Gas/Find A Little Wood/Once Upon The Seas Of Abyssinia/ Blessed Wild Apple Girl (12", p/s) 12
81	Cube/Dakota	Christmas Jingle/Sailors Of The Highway (MBFS fan club flexidisc). 4
82	Rarn MBFS RAP 1	Life's A Gas/Find A Little Wood/Once Upon The Seas Of Abyssinia/ Blessed Wild Apple Girl (12", p/s, reissue) 7
82	Marc ABOLAN 2	THE CHILDREN OF RARN (10" EP, p/s, 33rpm, gatefold sleeve with 12-page lyric book) 25
82	Marc SBOLAN 13	Mellow Love/Foxy Box/Lunacy's Back (p/s, blue vinyl, as Marc Bolan) 5
82	Rarn MBFS RAP 2	Deep Summer/Oh Baby/One Inch Rock (unreleased version) (12", p/s, blue vinyl) 10
83	Marc SBOLAN 12EP	CHRISTMAS BOP EP (12", p/s, OMBFS only, extra tracks: acoustic versions of "King Of The Rumbling Spires" & "Savage Beethoven") 7
83	Marc SBOLAN 14PD	Think Zinc/Till Dawn/Magical Moon (picture disc) 5
84	Marc On Wax SPS 1	Mister Motion (1-sided, from "Child Of The Revolution — 14 Greats" LP, p/s). 6
84	Cube BUG 99	Sailor Of The Highway/Do You Remember (white labels, promo only). 10
84	Cube HBUG 99	RARE MAGIC (12" EP) 7
85	Cambra MAIN 1	(Whatever Happened To The) Teenage Dream (Ext.)/Solid Gold Segue (picture disc free with "Mainman" LP) 5
85	Marc PTANX 1	Megarex 1/Megarex 1 (shaped picture disc, with free plinth) 8
85	Marc STANX 1	Megarex 3/Tame My Tiger/Chrome Sitar/Solid Baby (12", picture disc) 7
87	Marc MARCX 1	Children Of The Revolution (remix)/The Slider (remix)/Tear For The High Star (tribute by Dave Ash-B) (shaped picture disc) 8
94	Edsel MBPROMO 1	T. REX (CD, picture disc, 4-track sampler, tri-fold digipak, promo only) 18
97	Edsel MARC 20-50	20th Century Boy/Carsmile Smith & The Old One/All My Love/Dandy In The Underworld (CD, gig freebie) 12

LPs

70	Fly HIFLY 2	T. REX (LP, in semi-gatefold sleeve) 15
71	Fly HIFLY 6	ELECTRIC WARRIOR (LP, unreleased version with "Jeepster" on side 2, 1 test pressing copy only, with Marc's annotations on white sleeve) 600
71	Fly HIFLY 6	ELECTRIC WARRIOR (LP, with poster & inner sleeve; some with stickered sl.) . . 15
71	Fly HIFLY 8	BOLAN BOOGIE (LP, 1-sided test pressing with "The Visit" instead of "Jewel") 300
72	Fly HIFLY 8	BOLAN BOOGIE (LP) 12
72	EMI BLN 5001	THE SLIDER (LP, with lyric inner sleeve) 12
73	EMI BLN 5002	TANX (LP, with poster & inner sleeve). 15
73	EMI BLN 5003	GREAT HITS (LP, with poster) 12
74	EMI BNLA 7751	ZINC ALLOY AND THE HIDDEN RIDERS OF TOMORROW (LP, with 3-way numbered promo fold-out sleeve & inner, given as competition prize with letter from *Pink* or *Mirabelle* magazines, 1,000 only) 250
74	EMI BNLA 7751	ZINC ALLOY AND THE HIDDEN RIDERS OF TOMORROW (LP, with 3-way promo fold-out sleeve & inner, without letter; no'd or un-no'd copies) 200/175
74	EMI BNLA 7751	ZINC ALLOY AND THE HIDDEN RIDERS OF TOMORROW (LP, commercial gatefold sleeve with lyric inner sleeve) 15
75	EMI BNLA 7752	BOLAN'S ZIP GUN (LP, diamond-cut sleeve & inner sleeve) 18
76	EMI BLNA 5004	FUTURISTIC DRAGON (LP, with lyric inner sleeve) 12
77	EMI BLNA 5005	DANDY IN THE UNDERWORLD (LP, with round-cut sleeve & lyric inner sleeve). . 10
78	Cube HIFLD 1	MARC: THE WORDS AND MUSIC OF MARC BOLAN 1947-1977 (2-LP, gatefold sleeve, with free single [BINT 1]). 20
81	Marc ABOLAN 1P	T. REX IN CONCERT (LP, picture disc, 2 designs) 10
82	Cube/Dakota ICSX 1004	ACROSS THE AIRWAVES (LP, picture disc) 10
82	Marc ABOLAN 3P	ELECTRIC WARRIOR (LP, picture disc). 10
84	Marc ABOLAN 5	T. REXTASY (LP, with 12" "Jam (live)"/"Elemental Child (live)" [ABOLAN 5F], Official Fanclub only) 15
86	Marc On Wax WARRIOR 1/4	HISTORY OF T. REX (4-LP, numbered picture disc set, some with free fanclub T-shirt). 30/25

(see also Marc Bolan, Tyrannosaurus Rex, Dib Cochran & Earwigs, John's Children, Big Carrot)

TOMMY BOLIN
76	Nemperor K 10730/NE 4	The Grind/Homeward Strut	10
75	Atlantic K 50208	TEASER (LP, some stickered)	15/12
76	CBS S 81612	PRIVATE EYES (LP)	12

(see also James Gang, Deep Purple)

SIMON BOLIVAR ORCHESTRA
56	London HLG 8245	Meringue Holiday/Shy	15
56	London HLG 8245	Meringue Holiday/Shy (78)	10

BOLLARDS
70s	Bumkin Records	BOLLARDS (LP)	15

MICHAEL BOLOTIN
75	RCA SF 8451	MICHAEL BOLOTIN (LP)	15

(see also Blackjack, Michael Bolton)

MICHAEL BOLTON
88	CBS 651 387-2	(Sittin' On) The Dock Of The Bay (Lightning Bolton Mix)/(Perc-Apella Version)/ Call My Name (CD, card sleeve)	7
88	CBS 651 059-2	That's What Love Is All About/Take A Look At My Face/Fools Game/ Can't Hold On, Can't Let Go (CD, card sleeve)	7
89	CBS 654 946-3	Soul Provider/The Hunger/That's What Love Is All About (live) (3" CD, gatefold sleeve)	7

(see also Blackjack, Michael Bolotin)

BOMBADIL
72	Harvest HAR 5056	Breathless/When The City Sleeps (p/s)	8
75	Harvest HAR 5095	Breathless/When The City Sleeps (p/s, reissue)	5

(see also Barclay James Harvest)

BOMBAY DUCKS
80	Complete Control CON 1	Sympathy For The Devil/1-0-6-9 (p/s)	10
80s	United Dairies UD 05	DANCE MUSIC (LP)	20
80s	Erasehead C-60	ANYONE CAN BE ENO (cassette)	10
80s	Erasehead C-30	A RETROSPECTIVE LOOK AT THE BOMBAY DUCKS (cassette with mask)	10

BOMBERS
77	The Label TLR 006	I'm A Liar, Baby/2230 A.D. (p/s)	5

BON-BONS
55	London HL 8139	That's The Way Love Goes/Make My Dreams Come True	40
55	London HL 8139	That's The Way Love Goes/Make My Dreams Come True (78)	15
56	London HLU 8262	Circle/Frog On A Log	35
56	London HLU 8262	Circle/Frog On A Log (78)	15

BOBBY BOND
61	Pye International 7N 25081	You're A Livin' Doll/Sweet Love	10
69	Warner Bros WB 7292	One More Mile, One More Town/If You're Leaving Me	5

BRIGITTE BOND
64	Blue Beat BB 212	Oh Yeah Baby/Blue Beat Baby	10

GRAHAM BOND (ORGANISATION)
64	Decca F 11909	Long Tall Shorty/Long Legged Baby (as Graham Bond Organization)	40
65	Columbia DB 7471	Wade In The Water/Tammy (as Graham Bond Organisation)	30
65	Columbia DB 7528	Tell Me (I'm Gonna Love Again)/Love Come Shining Through (as Graham Bond Organisation)	25
65	Columbia DB 7647	Lease On Love/My Heart's In Little Pieces (as Graham Bond Organisation)	25
66	Columbia DB 7838	St James Infirmary/Soul Tango (as Graham Bond Organisation)	25
67	Page One POF 014	You've Gotta Have Love Babe/I Love You	30
70	Warner Bros WB 8004	Walking In The Park/Springtime In The City (solo)	10
71	Vertigo 6059 042	Twelve Gates To The City/Water Water (as Graham Bond with Magick)	8
65	Columbia SX 1711	THE SOUND OF '65 (LP, 1st pressing, blue/black label)	120
66	Columbia SX 1750	THERE'S A BOND BETWEEN US (LP, 1st pressing, blue/black label)	120
69	Columbia SX 1711	THE SOUND OF '65 (LP, 2nd pressing, silver/black label)	45
69	Columbia SX 1750	THERE'S A BOND BETWEEN US (LP, 2nd pressing, silver/black label)	45
71	Warner Bros WS 3001	SOLID BOND (2-LP)	35
71	Vertigo 6360 021	HOLY MAGICK (LP, gatefold sleeve, spiral label, as Graham Bond & Magick)	25
71	Vertigo 6360 042	WE PUT OUR MAGICK ON YOU (LP, gatefold sleeve, spiral label, as Graham Bond With Magick)	25
72	Philips 6382 010	BOND IN AMERICA (2-LP, solo [individual discs: 6499 200/1])	25
72	Philips 6382 010	THIS IS GRAHAM BOND (LP, solo)	12

(see also Jack Bruce, Dick Heckstall-Smith, Ginger Baker, Duffy Power, Who, Don Rendell, Steve York's Camelo Pardalis)

GRAHAM BOND & PETE BROWN
71	Greenwich GSS 104	Lost Tribe/Macumbe/Milk Is Turning Sour In My Shoes (maxi-single)	20
72	Chapter One CHSR 813	TWO HEADS ARE BETTER THAN ONE (LP)	60

(see also Pete Brown)

ISABEL BOND
68	Major Minor MM 565	Cry/When A Woman Loves A Man (some in p/s)	7/5
69	Major Minor MM 627	Don't Forget About Me/You'll Never Get The Chance Again	6
68	Major Minor MMLP 28	THE HEART AND SOUL OF ISABEL BOND (LP)	16

JACKI BOND
65	Columbia DB 7719	My Sister's Boy/Now I Know	6
66	Strike JH 302	Tell Him To Go Away/Don't You Worry	10
66	Strike JH 320	He Say/Why Can't I Love Him	20

JANE BOND & UNDERCOVER MEN
86	Dreamworld BIG DREAM 1	POLITICALLY CORRECT (LP)	10

JOHNNY BOND

50	MGM MGM 262	Music Music Music (Put Another Nickel In) (with Orchestra)/Rag Mop (78)	10
60	London HLU 9189	Hot Rod Jalopy/Five-Minute Love Affair	15
60	London HL 7100	Hot Rod Lincoln/Five-Minute Love Affair (export issue)	20
65	London HLB 9957	Ten Little Bottles/Eleven More Months And Ten More Days (B-side with Cowboy Copas)	10
62	Stateside SL 10008	THAT WILD, WICKED BUT WONDERFUL WEST (LP)	18
63	London HA-B 8098	LIVE IT UP (LP, as Johnny Bond & His Friends On Stage)	18
65	London HA-B 8228	THE SONGS THAT MADE HIM FAMOUS (LP)	22
66	London HA-B 8272	FAMOUS HOT RODDERS I HAVE KNOWN (LP)	18
67	London HA-B 8269	THE MAN WHO COMES AROUND (LP)	15

JOYCE BOND

67	Airborne NBP 0011	It's Alright/Mrs. Soul	15
66	Island WI 3019	Tell Me What It's All About/Tell Me Right Now	8
67	Island WIP 6010	Do The Teasy/Sugar	7
67	Island WIP 6018	This Train/Not So With Me	7
68	Island WIP 6051	Ob-La-Di, Ob-La-Da/Robin Hood Rides Again	6
68	Pama PM 718	Back To School/They Wish	7
69	Pama PM 771	Mr. Pitiful/Let's Get Married (as Joyce Bond & Little John)	7
70	Upfront UPF 5	Wind Of Change/First In Line	6
71	Trojan TR 7837	Help Me Make It Through The Night/Reconsider Our Love	10
68	Island ILP 968	SOUL AND SKA (LP, mono only)	100

MARGARET BOND

55	Decca F 10506	You'll Always Be My Lifetime Sweetheart/Where Is The One For Me	6
55	Decca F 10555	My Love's A Gentle Man/Mirror, Mirror	6
55	Decca F 10632	There's Always A First Time/Dancing In My Socks	6
57	Parlophone R 4283	Your Love Is My Love/Goodnight My Love, Pleasant Dreams	5
57	Parlophone R 4312	The Wind In The Willow/Young And In Love	5

OLIVER BOND

66	Parlophone R 5476	I Saw You All Alone/Let Me Love You	12
	(see also Oliver Bone)		

RONNIE BOND

69	Page One POF 123	Anything For You/Carolyn	30
	(see also Troggs)		

(GARY) 'U.S.' BONDS

60	Top Rank JAR 527	New Orleans/Please Forgive Me (as U.S. Bonds)	10
61	Top Rank JAR 566	Not Me/Give Me One More Chance (as U.S. Bonds)	10
61	Top Rank JAR 575	Quarter To Three/Time Ole Story (as U.S. Bonds)	7
61	Top Rank JAR 581	School Is Out/One Million Tears	10
61	Top Rank JAR 595	School Is In/Trip To The Moon	10
62	Top Rank JAR 602	Dear Lady Twist/Havin' So Much Fun	10
62	Top Rank JAR 615	Twist Twist Senora/Food Of Love	10
62	Stateside SS 111	Seven Day Weekend/Gettin' A Groove	10
62	Stateside SS 125	Copy Cat/I'll Change That Too	8
63	Stateside SS 144	Mixed Up Faculty/I Dig This Station	8
63	Stateside SS 179	Where Did That Naughty Little Girl Go?/Do The Limbo With Me	8
63	Stateside SS 219	What A Dream/I Don't Wanta Wait	8
64	Stateside SS 271	New Orleans/Quarter To Three	8
64	Stateside SS 308	My Sweet Baby Rose/Ella Is Yella	8
67	Stateside SS 2025	Send Her To Me/Workin' For My Baby	12
61	Top Rank 35/114	DANCE 'TIL QUARTER TO THREE WITH U.S. BONDS (LP)	55
62	Stateside SL 10001	TWIST UP CALYPSO (LP)	35
63	Stateside SL 10037	THE GREATEST HITS OF GARY (U.S.) BONDS (LP)	30

JOHNNY BOND'S RED RIVER VALLEY BOYS

51	Columbia DB 2844	Love Song In 32 Bars/CHAMP BUTLER: Dear, Dear, Dear (78)	10

OLIVER BONE & SOUNDS MAXIMUM

66	Parlophone R 5527	Knock On Wood/Jugger Tea	8
	(see also Oliver Bond)		

BROTHER BONES & HIS SHADOWS

60	Oriole CB 1030	Sweet Georgia Brown/Margie	7

BONGO HERMAN (Davis)

70	Songbird SB 1018	True Grit/True Grit Version 2 (both credited with Les Crystalites but actually with Les & Crystalites)	7
71	Songbird SB 1060	BONGO HERMAN & LES BUNNY: Know For I/CRYSTALITES: Version (B-side actually titled 'Know Fari')	6
71	Songbird SB 1066	BONGO HERMAN & LES & BUNNY: Salaam (Peace)/CRYSTALITES: Scraper	6
72	Big BG 332	Eternal Drums/ERROL DUNKLEY: Darling Ooh Wee (both actually by Hugh Roy Junior)	6
72	Green Door GD 4049	African Breakfast/BONGO HERMAN & LES AND BUNNY: Chairman Of The Board	6
72	Songbird SB 1069	We Are Praying/CRYSTALITES: Version	6

BONGO LES & HERMAN

71	Songbird SB 1050	Home Sweet Home/Hail I	8
	(see also Heptones, Scotty, Meditators)		

BONGOS

80	Fetish FET 003	Telephoto Lens/Glow In The Dark (p/s)	4
81	Fetish FR 2004	BONGOS (LP)	10

BON JOVI

Year	Label	Description	Value
84	Vertigo VER 11	She Don't Know Me/Breakout (p/s)	25
84	Vertigo VERX 11	She Don't Know Me/Breakout (12", p/s)	35
84	Vertigo VER 14	Runaway/Breakout (live) (p/s)	25
84	Vertigo VERX 14	Runaway/Breakout (live)/Runaway (live) (12", p/s)	35
85	Vertigo VER 19	In And Out Of Love/Roulette (live) (p/s)	12
85	Vertigo VERP 19	In And Out Of Love/Roulette (live) (picture disc)	40
85	Vertigo VERX 19	In And Out Of Love/Roulette (live)/Shot Through The Heart (live) (12", p/s)	18
85	Vertigo VER 22	The Hardest Part Is The Night/Always Run To You (p/s)	15
85	Vertigo VERDP 22	The Hardest Part Is The Night/Always Run To You//Tokyo Road (live)/Shot Through The Heart (live) (double pack, gatefold p/s)	20
85	Vertigo VERX 22	The Hardest Part Is The Night/Always Run To You/Tokyo Road (live) (12", p/s)	20
85	Vertigo VERXR 22	Red Hot And Two Parts Live: The Hardest Part Is The Night/Tokyo Road (live)/In And Out Of Love (live) (12", p/s, red vinyl)	35
86	Vertigo VERP 26	You Give Love A Bad Name/Let It Rock (10", shaped picture disc)	30
86	Vertigo VERX 26	You Give Love A Bad Name/Let It Rock/Borderline (12", p/s with poster)	15
86	Vertigo VERXR 26	You Give Love A Bad Name/Let It Rock/The Hardest Part Is The Night (live)/Burning For Love (live) (12", p/s, blue vinyl)	20
86	Vertigo VERPA 28	Livin' On A Prayer/Wild In The Streets (p/s, with patch)	12
86	Vertigo VERP 28	Livin' On A Prayer/Wild In The Streets (picture disc)	20
86	Vertigo VERXR 28	Livin' On A Prayer/Wild In The Streets/Edge Of A Broken Heart (12", green vinyl, p/s)	15
86	Vertigo VERXG 28	Livin' On A Prayer/Wild In The Streets/Only Lonely (live)/Runaway (live) (12", gatefold p/s)	20
88	Mercury 080 042-2	Livin' On A Prayer/Borderline/Let It Rock/Wild In The Streets (CD Video)	25
87	Vertigo JOVS 1	Wanted Dead Or Alive/Shot Through The Heart (p/s, with metal stickers)	10
87	Vertigo JOVPB 112	Wanted Dead Or Alive/Shot Through The Heart/Social Disease (12", poster p/s)	20
87	Vertigo JOVR 112	Wanted Dead Or Alive/Shot Through The Heart/Social Disease/Get Ready (live) (12", p/s, silver vinyl)	18
87	Vertigo JOVCD 1	Wanted Dead Or Alive (Full Version)/(Radio Edit)/(Acoustic) (CD, promo only)	35
87	Vertigo JOVR 212	Never Say Goodbye/Raise Your Hands/Wanted Dead Or Alive (Acoustic Version) (12", yellow vinyl, PVC sleeve)	15
87	Vertigo	Never Say Goodbye (CD video)	30
87	Vertigo	Wanted Dead Or Alive (CD video)	30
87	Vertigo 080 042-2	Livin' On A Prayer/Borderline/Let It Rock/Wild In The Streets (CD video)	30
88	Vertigo JOVS 3	Bad Medicine/99 In The Shade (fold-out photofile p/s)	10
88	Vertigo JOVR 312	Bad Medicine/You Give Love A Bad Name/Livin' On A Prayer (live) (12", embossed p/s)	10
88	Vertigo JOVCD 3	Bad Medicine/Lay Your Hands On Me/99 In The Shade (CD, card sleeve)	15
88	Vertigo JOVS 4	Born To Be My Baby/Love For Sale (gold 'calendar' card envelope pack)	10
88	Vertigo JOVR 412	Born To Be My Baby/Love For Sale/Wanted Dead Or Alive (live) (12", gatefold p/s)	10
88	Vertigo JOVP 412	Born To Be My Baby/Love For Sale/Wanted Dead Or Alive (live) (12", picture disc)	15
88	Vertigo JOVCD 4	Born To Be My Baby/Love For Sale/Runaway/Livin' On A Prayer (CD)	15
89	Vertigo JOVPB 5	I'll Be There For You/Homebound Train (p/s, with poster)	6
89	Vertigo JOVCD 5	I'll Be There For You/Homebound Train/Borderline/Edge Of A Broken Heart (CD, card sleeve)	15
89	Vertigo JOVS 661	Lay Your Hands On Me/Bad Medicine (live) (red vinyl, stickered PVC sleeve)	8
89	Vertigo JOVS 662	Lay Your Hands On Me/Bad Medicine (live) (white vinyl, stickered PVC sleeve)	8
89	Vertigo JOVS 663	Lay Your Hands On Me/Bad Medicine (live) (blue vinyl, stickered PVC sleeve)	8
89	Vertigo JOVS 661-663	Lay Your Hands On Me/Bad Medicine (live) (3 x 7", red, blue or white vinyl, paper box set)	25
89	Vertigo JOVP 610	Lay Your Hands On Me/Bad Medicine (live)/Blood On Blood (10", picture disc with insert)	15
89	Vertigo JOVG 612	Lay Your Hands On Me/Blood On Blood (live)/Born To Be My Baby (Acoustic) (12", gatefold p/s)	7
89	Vertigo JOVCD 6	Lay Your Hands On Me/You Give Love A Bad Name/Let It Rock (CD)	15
89	Vertigo JOVR 712	Living In Sin/Love Is War/The Boys Are Back In Town (12", white vinyl with stickered card insert)	15
89	Vertigo JOVCD 7	Living In Sin/Love Is War/Ride Cowboy Ride/Stick To Your Guns (CD, box set)	20
92	Vertigo JOVCB 8	Keep The Faith/I Wish Everyday Could Be Like Christmas/Living In Sin (CD, box set)	8
92	Vertigo JOVCD 8	Keep The Faith/I Wish Everyday Could Be Like Christmas/Little Bit Of Soul (CD, digipak)	12
92	Vertigo JOVLH 9	Bed Of Roses/Bed Of Roses (jukebox issue, no p/s)	8
92	Vertigo JOVCD 9	Bed Of Roses/Lay Your Hands On Me (live)/Tokyo Road (live)/I'll Be There For You (live) (CD, slimline jewel case)	12
93	Vertigo JOVMB 10	In These Arms/Bed Of Roses (Acoustic) (cassette, pull-apart outer card slip case with tour pass)	8
93	Vertigo JOVCD 10	In These Arms/Keep The Faith (live)/In These Arms (live) (CD, slimline case)	8
93	Vertigo JOVD 11	Sleep When I'm Dead/Blaze Of Glory/You Give Love A Bad Name/Bad Medicine (CD, digipak)	12
93	Vertigo JOVCD11	Sleep When I'm Dead/Blaze Of Glory (live)/Wild In The Streets (live) (CD)	8
94	Vertigo JOVBX 13	Dry County/Stranger In This Town (live)/Blood Money (live) (gold CD, digipak)	10
94	Vertigo JOVJB 14	Always (edit)/Always (jukebox issue, no p/s)	8
94	Vertigo JOVCD 14	ALWAYS (CD EP, digipak)	15
94	Vertigo JOVJB 15	Someday I'll Be Saturday Night/Always (live) (jukebox issue, no p/s)	8
94	Vertigo JOVP 15	Someday I'll Be Saturday Night (picture disc, with insert)	5
94	Vertigo JOVDD 15	Someday I'll Be Saturday Night/Good Guys Don't Always Wear White/Someday I'll Be Saturday Night (live) (CD, in red circular tin)	10
94	Vertigo JOVJB 16	Please Come Home For Christmas/Back Door Santa (jukebox issue, no p/s)	8
94	Vertigo JOVP 16	Please Come Home For Christmas/Back Door Santa (picture disc)	8
88	Vertigo VERHP 38	SLIPPERY WHEN WET (LP, picture disc with poster)	18
88	Vertigo VERHP 62	NEW JERSEY (LP, picture disc, stickered PVC sleeve)	18
89	Vertigo JOVI 1989	ESSENTIAL (CD, 8-track sampler, promo only)	30

JON BON JOVI
90	Vertigo JBJ 212	Miracle/Dyin' Ain't Much Of A Livin'/Interview With Jon Bon Jovi (12", p/s, with poster & numbered sticker)	15
90	Vertigo JBJP 212	Miracle/Dyin' Ain't Much Of A Livin'/Going Back (live) (12", picture disc with insert)	18

JUKE BOY BONNER
69	Blue Horizon 57-3163	Runnin' Shoes/Jackin' In My Plans	22
60s	Jan & Dil JR 451	MORE DOWN HOME BLUES (EP)	12
68	Flyright LP 3501	THE ONE MAN TRIO (LP)	25
69	Liberty LBS 83319	THINGS AIN'T RIGHT (LP)	18

GRAHAM BONNET
72	RCA RCA 2230	Rare Specimen/Whisper In The Night	8
73	RCA RCA 2380	Trying To Say Goodbye/Castles In The Air	5
74	DJM DJS 328	Back Row In The Stalls/Ghost Writer In My Eye	8
77	Ring O' 2017 105	It's All Over Now, Baby Blue/Heroes On My Picture Wall (company sleeve)	10
77	Ring O' 2017 106	Danny/Rock Island Line (company sleeve, some in promo p/s)	15/10
77	Ring O' 2017 110	Goodnight And Goodmorning/Wino Song (company sleeve)	10
78	Ring O' 2017 114/POSP 2	Warm Ride/10/12 Observation (company sleeve)	8
78	Ring O' POSP 002	Warm Ride/10/12 Observation (12", company sleeve)	15
81	Lyntone LYN 10138/9	Night Games/POLECATS: We Say Yeah/THIN LIZZY: Song For Jimmy/WAY OF THE WEST: Monkey Love (orange flexi with *Flexipop* mag, issue 10)	12/8
81	Vertigo VER 1	Night Games/Out On The Water (p/s)	5
81	Vertigo VER 2	Liar/Bad Days Are Gone (p/s)	5
81	Vertigo VER 4	That's The Way That It Is/Don't Tell Me To Go (p/s)	6
77	Ring O' 2320 103	GRAHAM BONNET (LP, with inner sleeve)	18
81	Vertigo 6302 151	LINE UP (LP, with inner sleeve)	12

(see also Marbles, Rainbow, Cozy Powell, Forcefield, Fut, Michael Schenker Group, Jon Lord)

GRAHAM BONNEY
65	Columbia DB 7773	My Little World Is All Blue/Why Can't We Be Friends	6
66	Columbia DB 7843	Super Girl/Hill Of Lovin'	7
66	Columbia DB 7934	Baby's Gone/Later Tonight	6
66	Columbia DB 8005	No One Knows/Mixed Up Baby Girl	8
67	Columbia DB 8111	Thank You Baby/Briony	6
67	Columbia DB 8142	Happy Together/That Bad Day	6
67	Columbia DB 8283	Papa Joe/My Jenny	6
68	Columbia DB 8338	By The Way I Love You/Devil's Child	6
68	Columbia DB 8382	I'll Be Your Baby Tonight/Back From Baltimore	6
68	Columbia DB 8464	Frenzy/Something I've Got To Tell You	6
69	Columbia DB 8531	Get Ready/Fly Me High Lorelei	8
69	Columbia DB 8592	Leanda Angeline/Mixing The Wine	6
70	Columbia DB 8648	Sign On The Dotted Line/Words We Said	8
70	Columbia DB 8687	When Evelyn Was Mine/Sunny Has Gone	5
66	Columbia SX 6052	SUPER GIRL (LP)	20

(see also Riot Squad)

BONNIE & SKITTO
63	Island WI 122	Get Ready (actually by Vikings [alias Maytals])/ DON DRUMMOND: The Rocket	18

BONNIE & TREASURES
65	London HLU 9998	Home Of The Brave/Our Song	30

BONO & GAVIN FRIDAY
94	Island CID 593	In The Name Of The Father (7" Edit)/(12" Remix)/(12" Beats Mix)/ (LP Instrumental) (CD)	15

(see also U2, Virgin Prunes)

BONZO DOG (DOO-DAH) BAND
66	Parlophone R 5430	My Brother Makes The Noises For The Talkies/ I'm Gonna Bring A Watermelon To My Gal Tonight	35
66	Parlophone R 5499	Alley Oop/Button Up Your Overcoat	30
67	Liberty LBF 15040	Equestrian Statue/The Intro And The Outro	8
68	Liberty LBF 15144	Urban Spaceman/Canyons Of Your Mind (initially with spoken intro to A-side)	10/5
69	Liberty LBF 15201	Mr. Apollo/Ready Mades	7
69	Liberty LBF 15273	I Want To Be With You/We Were Wrong	8
70	Liberty LBF 15314	You Done My Brain In/Mr Slater's Parrot	7
92	China WOK 2021	No Matter Who You Vote For The Government Always Gets In/ NEIL INNES: Them (promo only)	7
92	China WOK CD 2021	No Matter Who You Vote For The Government Always Gets In/ Urban Spaceman/The Intro/NEIL INNES: Them (CD)	12
67	Liberty LBL/LBS 83056	GORILLA (LP, some with booklet)	30/18
68	Liberty LBL/LBS 83158E	THE DOUGHNUT IN GRANNY'S GREENHOUSE (LP, gatefold sleeve, some with booklet)	30/18
69	Liberty LBS 83257	TADPOLES (LP, die-cut sleeve, some with insert)	30/18
69	Liberty LBS 83290	KEYNSHAM (LP, gatefold sleeve)	20
72	United Artists UAS 29288	LET'S MAKE UP AND BE FRIENDLY (LP)	15
74	United Artists UAD 60071/2	THE HISTORY OF THE BONZOS (2-LP, gatefold sleeve with booklet)	18

(see also Vivian Stanshall, Neil Innes, Grimms, Roger Ruskin Spear, Topo D. Bill, New Vaudeville Band)

BETTY BOO
79	Grapevine GRP 125	Say It Isn't So/Say It Isn't So (Instrumental)	6

BOOGALOOS
69	President PT 253	Rule Britannia/Love Is Blind	5

BOOGIE BOX HIGH
87	Hardback 7 BOSS 4	Jive Talkin'/Rhythm Talkin' (Part 1) (p/s)	4
87	Hardback BOSS 4	Jive Talkin'/Jive Talkin' (Fever Pitch Mix)/Rhythm Talkin' (Part 1) (12", p/s)	8

(see also George Michael, Nick Heyward)

James BOOKER

JAMES BOOKER
61	Vogue V 9177	Cool Turkey/Gonzo	15
63	Vocalion VEP 170154	GONZO (EP)	55

BOOKER T. & M.G.s
62	London HLK 9595	Green Onions/Behave Yourself	10
63	London HLK 9670	Jelly Bread/Aw' Mercy	10
63	London HLK 9784	Chinese Checkers/Plum Nellie	10
65	Atlantic AT 4033	Boot-Leg/Outrage	10
66	Atlantic AT 4063	Be My Lady/Red Beans And Rice	8
66	Atlantic 584 044	My Sweet Potato/Booker Loo	7
66	Atlantic 584 060	Jingle Bells/Winter Wonderland	7
67	Atlantic 584 088	Green Onions/Boot-Leg	10
67	Stax 601 009	Hip Hug Her/Summertime (initially dark blue label; later light blue)	8/5
67	Stax 601 018	Groovin'/Slim Jenkins' Place	6
67	Stax 601 026	Chinese Checkers/Plum Nellie (reissue)	6
68	Stax STAX 102	Soul Limbo/Heads Or Tails	5
69	Stax STAX 119	Time Is Tight/Hang 'Em High	5
69	Stax STAX 127	Soul Clap '69/Mrs. Robinson	5
69	Stax STAX 136	The Horse/Slum Baby	6
71	Stax 2025 026	Melting Pot/Kinda Easy Like	8
72	Stax 2025 074	Jamaica This Morning (as the MGs)/Fuquawi	5
63	London REK 1367	R&B WITH BOOKER T (EP)	20
64	Atlantic AET 6002	R&B WITH BOOKER T VOL. 2 (EP)	20
64	London HA-K 8182	GREEN ONIONS (LP)	40
65	Atlantic ATL 5027	SOUL DRESSING (LP)	25
66	Atlantic 587/588 033	GREEN ONIONS (LP, reissue)	15
67	Atlantic 587 047	SOUL DRESSING (LP, reissue)	15
67	Stax 589 002	AND NOW! (LP)	15
68	Stax 589 013	SOUL CHRISTMAS (LP)	15
68	Stax 230 002/231 002	DOIN' OUR THING (LP)	15
68	Stax (S)XATS 1001	SOUL LIMBO (LP)	15
69	Atco 228 004	GET READY (LP)	15
69	Stax (S)XATS 1005	UPTIGHT (LP, soundtrack, with Judy Clay)	15
69	Stax (S)XATS 1015	THE BOOKER T. SET (LP)	15
69	Atco 228 015	THE BEST OF BOOKER T. AND THE M.G.s (LP)	15
70	Stax SXATS 1031	McLEMORE AVENUE (LP)	15
71	Stax 2325 030	MELTING POT (LP)	12
71	Stax 2362 002	GREATEST HITS (LP)	12
71	Stax 2362 012	THE BOOKER T. SET (LP, reissue)	12
71	Stax 2362 016	McLEMORE AVENUE (LP, reissue)	12
75	Stax STX 1037	MEMPHIS SOUND (LP)	12

(see also Mar-Keys, Steve Cropper, Albert King, Judy Clay)

BOOMERANGS
64	Fontana TF 507	Rockin' Robin/Don't Let Her Be Your Baby	30
65	Fontana TF 555	Another Tear Falls/Fun Fun Fun	18

BOOMERANGS
66	Pye 7N 17049	Dream World/Upgraded	8

BOOMTOWN RATS
81	Flexipop 003	Dun Laoghaire (clear, green, yellow or red 1-sided flexi with *Flexipop*, issue 3)	5

PAT BOONE
78s
55	London HLD 8197	At My Front Door/No Arms Can Ever Hold You (78)	10
56	London HLD 8233	Gee Whittakers/Take The Time (78)	8
57	London HLD 8520	White Christmas/Jingle Bells (78)	10
59	London HLD 8775	I'll Remember Tonight/The Mardi Gras March (78)	10
59	London HLD 8824	There's Good Rockin' Tonight/With The Wind And The Rain In Your Hair (78)	15
59	London HLD 8855	For A Penny/Wang Dang Taffy-Apple Tango (78)	15
59	London HLD 8910	Rock Boll Weevil/Twixt Twelve And Twenty (78)	15
59	London HLD 8974	A Fool's Hall Of Fame/Brightest Wishing Star (78)	18
60	London HLD 9029	Beyond The Sunset/The Faithful Heart (78)	22
60	London HLD 9067	(Welcome) New Lovers/Words (78)	25
60	London HLD 9184	Delia Gone/Candy Sweet (78)	50

SINGLES
55	London HLD 8172	Ain't That A Shame/Tennessee Saturday Night	25
55	London HLD 8197	At My Front Door/No Arms Can Ever Hold You	30
56	London HLD 8233	Gee Whittakers/Take The Time	35
56	London HLD 8253	I'll Be Home/Tutti Frutti	15
56	London HLD 8291	Long Tall Sally/Just As Long As I'm With You	22
56	London HLD 8303	I Almost Lost My Mind/I'm In Love With You	15
56	London HLD 8316	Two Hearts, Two Kisses/Rich In Love	18
56	London HLD 8346	Friendly Persuasion (Thee I Love)/Chains Of Love	10

(The above 45s were originally issued with gold lettering labels; later silver lettering copies are worth two-thirds these values.)

57	London HLD 8370	Don't Forbid Me/Anastasia	10
57	London HLD 8404	Why Baby Why/I'm Just Waiting For You	10
57	London HLD 8445	Love Letters In The Sand/Bernadine	7
57	London HLD 8479	Remember You're Mine/There's A Goldmine In The Sky	7
57	London HLD 8512	April Love/When The Swallows Come Back To Capistrano	7
57	London HLD 8520	White Christmas/Jingle Bells	8
58	London HLD 8574	A Wonderful Time Up There/It's Too Soon To Know	6
58	London HLD 8640	Sugar Moon/Cherie, I Love You	6
58	London HLD 8675	If Dreams Came True/That's How Much I Love You	6

MINT VALUE £

58	London HLD 8739	Gee, But It's Lonely/For My Good Fortune 6
59	London HLD 8775	I'll Remember Tonight/The Mardi Gras March 6
59	London HLD 8824	There's Good Rockin' Tonight/With The Wind And The Rain In Your Hair 6
59	London HLD 8855	For A Penny/Wang Dang Taffy-Apple Tango 6
59	London HLD 8910	Rock Boll Weevil/Twixt Twelve And Twenty. 6
59	London HLD 8974	A Fool's Hall Of Fame/Brightest Wishing Star 6

(The above 45s were originally issued with triangular centres; later round centre copies are worth two-thirds these values.)

60	London HLD 9029	Beyond The Sunset/The Faithful Heart 5
60	London HLD 9067	(Welcome) New Lovers/Words 5
60	London HLD 9138	Walking The Floor Over You/Spring Rain 5
60	London HLD 9184	Delia Gone/Candy Sweet 5
60	London HLD 9238	Dear John/Alabam 5
61	London HLD 9299	The Exodus Song/There's A Moon Out Tonight 5
61	London HLD 9350	Moody River/A Thousand Years 6
61	London HLD 9420	Big Cold Wind/That's My Desire 5
61	London HLD 9461	Johnny Will/(If I'm Dreaming) Just Let My Dream 5
62	London HLD 9504	I'll See You In My Dreams/Pictures In The Fire 5
64	Dot DS 16658	Beach Girl/Little Honda 10
67	Dot DS 26752	As Tears Go By/Something About You 5
69	Polydor 56763	July, You're Just A Woman/Break My Mind 5

EXPORT SINGLES

56	London HL 7007	I'll Be Home/Tutti Frutti 15
56	London HL 7010	Long Tall Sally/Just As Long As I'm With You 15
56	London HL 7012	I Almost Lost My Mind/I'm In Love With You 10
56	London HL 7015	Friendly Persuasion (Thee I Love)/Chains Of Love. 10
57	London HL 7019	Love Letters In The Sand/Bernadine 10
58	London HL 7033	A Wonderful Time Up There/It's Too Soon To Know 10
58	London HL 7041	Sugar Moon/Cherie, I Love You 10
58	London HL 7051	If Dreams Came True/That's How Much I Love You 10
58	London HL 7059	Gee, But It's Lonely/For My Good Fortune 10
59	London HL 7070	With The Wind And The Rain In Your Hair/There's Good Rocking Tonight 10
59	London SLD 4002	For A Penny/Wang Dang Taffy-Apple Tango (both tracks stereo). 35
61	London HLD 7112	Moody River/The Exodus Song 10
63	London HL 7118	Send Me The Pillow You Dream On/(You've Got) Personality 15
63	London HLD 7121	Mexican Joe/In The Room 18

EPs

56	London RE-D 1063	PAT BOONE SINGS THE HITS (EP) 10
57	London RE-D 1069	PAT 'ON MIKE' (EP) 8
57	London RE-D 1086	PAT BOONE SINGS THE HITS NO. 2 (EP) 10
57	London RE-D 1095	A CLOSER WALK WITH THEE (EP) 8
57	London RE-D 1109	FOUR BY PAT (EP). 8
58	London RE-D 1112	PAT BOONE SINGS THE HITS NO. 3 (EP) 10
58	London RE-D 1128	WHITE CHRISTMAS (EP) 8
58	London RE-D 1132	PAT PART ONE (EP) 10
58	London RE-D 1133	PAT PART TWO (EP) 10
58	London RE-D 1139	PAT'S VOICE (EP, export issue) 10
58	London RE-D 1166	SINGS IRVING BERLIN (EP). 10
59	London RE-D 1244	JOURNEY TO THE CENTRE OF THE EARTH (EP) 12
61	London RE-D 1294	ALL HANDS ON DECK (EP). 8
62	London RE-D 1335	PAT BOONE'S LATEST AND GREATEST NO. 2 (EP) 10
63	London RE-D 1384	ALWAYS YOU AND ME (EP) 10
63	London RE-D 1391	PAT SINGS MOVIE THEMES (EP) 10

LPs

57	London HA-D 2024	PAT'S BIG HITS (LP). 20
57	London HA-D 2030	HOWDY! (LP) 15
57	London HA-D 2049	PAT! (LP) 15
58	London HA-D 2078	APRIL LOVE (LP, soundtrack, with Shirley Jones & Lionel Newman Orchestra). . 15
58	London HA-D 2082	SINGS IRVING BERLIN (LP, also stereo SAH-D 6038) 15/18
58	London HA-D 2098	PAT'S BIG HITS, VOL. 2 (LP) 15
58	London HA-D 2127	STARDUST (LP, also stereo SAH-D 6001). 15/18
59	London HA-D 2144	YES INDEED! (LP, also stereo SAH-D 6010). 15/18
59	London HA-D 2161	PAT SINGS (LP, stereo edition SAH-D 6013 unissued) 15/18
60	London HA-D 2204	TENDERLY (LP, also stereo SAH-D 6053). 15/18
60	London HA-D 2210	SIDE BY SIDE (LP, with Shirley Boone, also stereo SAH-D 6057) 15/18
60	London HA-D 2265	MOONGLOW (LP, also stereo SAH-D 6085). 15/18
61	London HA-D 2305	THIS AND THAT (LP) 15
61	London HA-D 2354	THE GREAT GREAT GREAT PAT BOONE (LP, also stereo SAH-D 6155) 15/18
61	London HA-D 2382	MOODY RIVER (LP, also stereo SAH-D 6182). 15/18
62	London HA-D 2452	I'LL SEE YOU IN MY DREAMS (LP, also stereo SAH-D 6240). 15/18
62	London HA-D/SH-D 8031	PAT BOONE'S GOLDEN HITS (LP, mono/stereo). 15/18
63	London HA-D/SH-D 8053	I LOVE YOU TRULY (LP, with Shirley Boone, mono/stereo) 15/18
63	London HA-D/SH-D 8073	DAYS OF WINE AND ROSES (LP, mono/stereo) 15/18
63	London HA-D/SH-D 8109	SINGS ... GUESS WHO? (LP, mono/stereo) 30/35
64	London HA-D/SH-D 8153	THE TOUCH OF YOUR LIPS (LP, mono/stereo). 15/18
65	Dot (D)DLP 3594	BOSS BEAT (LP) 15
66	Dot (D)DLP 3650	MY TENTH ANNIVERSARY WITH DOT RECORDS (LP). 12

(see also Fontane Sisters)

BOO RADLEYS

90	Rough Trade RTT 241	KALEIDOSCOPE (12" EP) 8
90	Rough Trade RTT 241CD	KALEIDOSCOPE (CD EP) 10
91	Rough Trade R 20112710	EVERY HEAVEN (12" EP). 7
91	Rough Trade R 20112713	EVERY HEAVEN (CD EP) 8
90	Action TAKE 4	ICHABOD AND I (LP) 15
92	Creation CRELP 120	EVERYTHING'S ALRIGHT FOREVER (LP, with inner sleeve & bonus 7", "Sunfly" [CREFRE 010], 3,000 only) 10

MINT VALUE £

ANTHONY BOOTH
69	Tangerine DP 0008	Till Death Do Us Part/September Days	5

BARRY BOOTH
68	Pye NPL 18216	DIVERSIONS! (LP)	15

(see also Monty Python)

KEN BOOTHE
66	Island WI 3020	The Train Is Coming/This Is Me	18
66	Island WI 3035	I Don't Want To See You Cry/Baby I Need You (B-side actually by Wailers)	60
66	Ska Beat JB 248	You're No Good/SOULETTES: Don't Care What The People Say	40
67	Doctor Bird DB 1110	Say You/LYN TAITT & JETS: Smokey Places	18
67	Coxsone CS 7006	Lonely Teardrops/Oowee Baby	18
67	Coxsone CS 7020	Home Home Home/SOUL BROTHERS: Windell.	18
67	Caltone TONE 107	The One I Love/You Left The Water Running.	20
67	Studio One SO 2000	Feel Good/Mustang Sally.	18
67	Studio One SO 2012	Puppet On A String/ROLAND ALPHONSO: Look Away	35
67	Studio One SO 2014	Fatty Fatty (actually Heptones)/Mother Word (actually by Delroy Wilson)	18
67	Studio One SO 2026	Why Did You Leave (actually by Leroy Sibbles)/Don't Try To Reach Me (actually by Gaylads)	18
68	Studio One SO 2039	When I Fall In Love/HEPTONES: Christmas Time	18
68	Studio One SO 2041	The Girl I Left Behind/TERMITES: My Last Love	18
68	Studio One SO 2053	Tomorrow/Movin' Away	18
68	Fab FAB 63	I Remember Someone/Can't You See?	75
68	Coxsone CS 7041	Everybody Knows/GAYLADS: I'm Free	18
69	Coxsone CS 7094	Sherry/I've Got You.	18
69	Studio One SO 2073	You're On My Mind/RICHARD ACE & SOUND DIMENSIONS: Love To Cherish	20
69	High Note HS 003	Lady With The Starlight/LESLIE BUTLER & COUNT OSSIE: Gay Drums	25
69	Bamboo BAM 4	Pleading/SOUND DIMENSION: Call 1143.	12
69	Bamboo BAM 8	Be Yourself/SOUND DIMENSION: Rathid.	10
70	Trojan TR 7716	Why, Baby Why/Keep My Love From Fading.	7
70	Trojan TR 7756	Freedom Street/BEVERLEY'S ALLSTARS: Freedom Version	7
70	Trojan TR 7772	It's Gonna Take A Miracle/Now I Know	6
70	Trojan TR 7780	Drums Of Freedom/BEVERLEY'S ALLSTARS: Version.	7
70	Gas GAS 169	Give To Me/Why	6
70	Jackpot JP 748	You Left The Water Running/PHIL PRATT ALL STARS: Cut Throat	15
70	Punch PH 30	Artibella/PRATT ALLSTARS: Version Of Artibella	10
70	Punch PH 33	Morning/Morning (Version)	6
71	Punch PH 70	Stop Your Crying/CONSCIOUS MINDS: Suffering Through The Nation	5
71	Banana BA 352	Original Six (Parts 1 & 2).	10
71	Summit SUM 8518	I Wish It Could Be Peaceful Again/BEVERLEY'S ALLSTARS: Peaceful Version	7
71	Summit SUM 8519	Your Feeling And Mine/BEVERLEY'S ALLSTARS: Your Feeling Version	6
71	Big Shot BI 590	So Nice/So Nice Version	5
71	Green Door GD 4002	Medley Version/Medley Version 2	5
71	Dynamic DYN 411	Hallelujah/Trying To Reach	7
72	Dynamic DYN 453	Tears From My Eyes/CONSCIOUS MINDS: Tears From My Eyes Version.	5
72	Pama Supreme PS 369	Look What You've Done/LLOYD CHARMERS: Look What You've Done Version	5
73	Trojan TR 7893	Is It Because I'm Black/Black, Gold And Green	7
73	Green Door GD 4053	Silver Words/Rasta God Version	6
74	Trojan TR 7920	Everything I Own/Drum Song	5
74	Trojan TR 7944	Crying Over You/Now You Can See Me Again	5
75	Fab FAB 270	Thinking/Moving Away.	20
67	Studio One SOL 9001	MR. ROCK STEADY (LP)	100
73	Trojan TRLS 58	BLACK, GOLD AND GREEN (LP).	15

(see also Stranger & Ken, Keith Hudson, Gaylads, Richard Ace, Lloyd & Ken)

PATRICK BOOTHE
82	Streetwave STRA 2213	Dance All Night/Dance All Night (Instrumental Version).	6
82	Streetwave STRA 13-2213	Dance All Night/Dance All Night (Instrumental Version) (12")	8
82	Streetwave STRA 2596	Never Knew Love Like This Before/(Version)	6
82	Streetwave STRA 13-2596	Never Knew Love Like This Before/(Version) (12")	8

BOOTLES
64	Vocalion VN 9216	I'll Let You Hold My Hand/Never Till Now.	15

BOOTS
68	CBS 3550	Even The Bad Times Are Good/The Animal In Me	12
68	CBS 3833	Keep Your Lovelight Burning/Give Me One More Chance	15
70	Youngblood YB 1018	You Better Run/A To D.	4

DAVE BOOTS
60s	Solent SM 013	GREEN SATIN AND GOLD (LP)	100

BOOTSY'S RUBBER BAND
77	Warner Bros K 16964T	Pinocchio Theory/Psychoticbumpschool/What's A Telephone (12")	10
78	Warner Bros K 17196T	Bootzilla/Hollywood Squares (12", p/s)	10
76	Warner Bros K 56200	STRETCHIN' OUT IN BOOTSY'S RUBBER BAND (LP)	12
77	Warner Bros K 56302	AHH... THE NAME IS BOOTSY, BABY! (LP, gatefold sleeve)	12
78	Warner Bros K 56424	BOOTSY? PLAYER OF THE YEAR (LP, gatefold sleeve)	12
79	Warner Bros K 56615	THE BOOT IS MADE FOR FONK-N (LP, with inner sleeve)	12
81	Warner Bros K 56998	THE ONE GIVETH, THE COUNT TAKETH AWAY (LP)	12

(see also Parliament, Funkadelic)

RANNY BOP
70	Gas GAS 155	Pipe Dream/Suck Suck	6

BOP & BELTONES
67	Coxsone CS 7012	Treat Me Good/PETER TOUCH & WAILERS: Dancing Time (B-side actually also by Bop & Beltones)	20

(see also Beltones, Soul Vendors, Jackie Mittoo)

VICTOR BORGE
60s	Phillips BBE 12154	PHONETIC PUNCTUATION (EP)	10

BILLY BORLYNN
60	Philips PB 1031	Baby Listens/Liebelei	6
60	Philips PB 1057	Every Step Of The Way/It Takes Time	6

BORN B.C.
82	Xcentric Noise FIRST 1	THE POWER & THE PRIVILEGE (EP)	8

BOSS
86	Power House (no cat. no.)	One Good Reason/Wake Up Children (p/s, with lyric sheet)	6

BOSS ATTACK
71	Fab FAB 187	Hell-El/TEARDROPS: Let Me Be Free	7

BOSS COMBO
62	Coral LVA 9205	GOLDEN ROCK AND ROLL INSTRUMENTALS (LP)	18

BOSS GUITARS
65	London HA-R/SH-R 8237	PLAY THE WINNERS (LP)	15

EARL BOSTIC (ORCHESTRA)
78s
54	Parlophone DP 345	The Song Is Ended/Cherokee (78, export issue)	8
55	Parlophone R 3976	Cracked Ice/The Sheik Of Araby (78)	8
55	Parlophone R 4049	Remember/Cherry Bean (78)	8
56	Parlophone R 4169	Ubangi Stomp/Time On My Hands (78)	10
56	Parlophone R 4187	Steamwhistle Jump/The Hour Of Parting (78)	10
56	Parlophone R 4208	The Bo-Do Rock (with Bill Doggett)/Mean To Me (78)	8
56	Parlophone R 4232	For All We Know/Beyond The Blue Horizon (78)	8
57	Parlophone R 4278	Bubbins Rock/Indiana (with Bill Doggett) (78)	10
57	Parlophone R 4305	Avalon/Too Fine For Crying (B-side with Bill Jones) (78)	8
57	Parlophone R 4370	Temptation/September Song (78)	8
58	Parlophone R 4460	Over The Waves Rock/Twilight Time (78)	10

SINGLES
54	Parlophone MSP 6075	Off Shore/What! No Pearls	15
54	Parlophone MSP 6089	Deep Purple/Smoke Rings	15
54	Parlophone MSP 6105	Melancholy Serenade/Don't You Do It	12
54	Parlophone MSP 6110	Jungle Drums/Danube Waves	12
54	Parlophone MSP 6119	Mambolino/Blue Skies	12
54	Parlophone MSP 6131	These Foolish Things/Mambostic	12
54	Parlophone CMSP 8	Cherokee/The Song Is Ended (export issue)	25
55	Parlophone MSP 6162	Melody Of Love/Sweet Lorraine	12
56	Vogue V 2145	Flamingo/Sleep	15
56	Vogue V 2148	Moonglow/Ain't Misbehaving	15
56	Parlophone R 4208	The Bo-Do Rock (with Bill Doggett)/Mean To Me	12
56	Parlophone R 4232	For All We Know/Beyond The Blue Horizon	8
57	Parlophone R 4263	I Hear A Rhapsody/Harlem Nocturne	8
57	Parlophone R 4278	Bubbins Rock/Indiana (with Bill Doggett)	10
57	Parlophone R 4305	Avalon/Too Fine For Crying (B-side with Bill Jones)	8
57	Parlophone R 4370	Temptation/September Song	6
58	Parlophone R 4460	Over The Waves Rock/Twilight Time	10
58	Wheeler WD 40	Stuck On You/The South Coast	18
62	Ember JBS 708	Tuxedo Junction/Air Mail Special	12
66	Island WI 271	Honeymoon Night/PATSY COLE: Disappointed Bride	12

EPs
54	Parlophone GEP 8506	FLAMINGO (EP)	12
55	Parlophone GEP 8513	LINGER AWHILE (EP)	12
55	Parlophone GEP 8520	EARL BOSTIC AND HIS ALTO SAX (EP)	12
55	Vogue EPV 1010	EARL BOSTIC (EP)	15
56	Vogue EPV 1111	VELVET SUNSET (EP)	12
56	Parlophone GEP 8539	WRAP IT UP (EP)	12
56	Parlophone GEP 8548	EARL'S IMAGINATION (EP)	10
56	Parlophone GEP 8565	ALTO SAX AND MAMBO STRINGS (EP)	10
56	Parlophone GEP 8571	MUSIC A LA BOSTIC NO. 1 (EP)	10
56	Parlophone GEP 8574	MUSIC A LA BOSTIC NO. 2 (EP)	10
57	Parlophone GEP 8603	MUSIC A LA BOSTIC NO. 3 (EP)	10
57	Parlophone GEP 8637	BOSTIC IN HARLEM (EP)	10
58	Parlophone GEP 8701	BOSTIC BEAT (EP)	8
58	Parlophone GEP 8741	ROCKING WITH BOSTIC (EP)	10
58	Parlophone GEP 8754	ALTO MAGIC (EP)	10

LPs
54	Vogue LDE 100	EARL BOSTIC AND HIS ORCHESTRA (10" LP)	25
54	Parlophone PMD 1016	EARL BOSTIC AND HIS ALTO SAX (10" LP)	25
56	Parlophone PMD 1040	EARL BOSTIC AND HIS ALTO SAX NO. 2 (10" LP)	25
58	Parlophone PMD 1054	BOSTIC MEETS DOGGETT (10", with Bill Doggett)	30
58	Parlophone PMD 1068	BOSTIC ROCKS (10" LP)	30
59	Parlophone PMD 1071	BOSTIC SHOWCASE OF SWINGING DANCE HITS (10" LP)	25
59	Parlophone PMD 1074	SWEET TUNES OF THE FANTASTIC FIFTIES (10" LP)	25
60	Parlophone PMC 1125	PLAYS THE HIT TUNES OF THE BIG BROADWAY SHOWS (LP)	18

(see also Bill Doggett, Sonny Carter)

BOSTON
78	Epic 12 6653	Don't Look Back/The Journey (12", p/s)	7
79	Epic EPC 7888	Don't Look Back/More Than A Feeling/Smokin' (p/s)	4
76	Epic EPC 81611	BOSTON (LP)	12
76	Epic EPCH 81611	BOSTON (LP, audiophile pressing)	15
76	Epic EPC 81611	BOSTON (LP, picture disc)	15

BOSTON

78	Epic E 9945050	DON'T LOOK BACK (LP, picture disc)............................	12
86	MCA MCGP 6017	THIRD STAGE (LP, picture disc)................................	18
92	MCA MC 19066	THIRD STAGE (CD, in slip case)................................	18
94	Epic EK 64402	BOSTON (CD, in slip case).....................................	18
94	MCA MCGP	WALK ON (LP, picture disc)....................................	18

BOSTON CRABS
65	Columbia DB 7586	Down In Mexico/Who?..	15
65	Columbia DB 7679	As Long As I Have You/Alley Oop..............................	15
66	Columbia DB 7830	Gin House/You Didn't Have To Be So Nice......................	12

BOSTON DEXTERS
64	Contemporary CR 101	Matchbox/La Bamba...	80
64	Contemporary CR 102	You've Been Talking About Me/Nothing's Gonna Change Me.......	80
64	Contemporary CR 103	What Kind Of Girl Are You/I've Got Troubles Of My Own........	80
65	Columbia DB 7498	I Believe To My Soul/I've Got Something To Tell You...........	25
65	Columbia DB 7641	Try Hard/No More Tears......................................	25

(see also Buzz, Tam White)

BOSTON POPS ORCHESTRA
68	RCA RCA 1683	And I Love Her/A Hard Day's Night............................	6

BO STREET RUNNERS
64	Decca F 11986	Bo Street Runner/Tell Me.....................................	40
65	Columbia DB 7488	Tell Me What You're Gonna Do/And I Do Just What I Want........	65
65	Columbia DB 7640	Baby Never Say Goodbye/Get Out Of My Way.....................	40
66	Columbia DB 7901	Drive My Car/So Very Woman (featuring Mike [Too Much] Patto)..	40
64	Oak RGJ 131	BO STREET RUNNERS (EP).....................................	1,000

(see also [Mike] Patto, Timebox, Chicago Line, Cheynes, Radical Sheiks, Fleetwood Mac)

CONNIE BOSWELL
54	Brunswick 05319	T-E-N-N-E-S-S-E-E (Spells ...)/If I Give My Heart To You.......	10
55	Brunswick 05397	How Important Can It Be?/Fill My Heart With Happiness.........	8

ERIC BOSWELL
70	Gayfeet GS 204	Little Donkey (actually by Lou & Maxine)/Hope And Joy (act. by Lou Sparkes)...	6

(see also Lou Sparkes)

EVE BOSWELL
78s
51	Parlophone R 3421	Would You/I'm In Love Again (78).............................	5
52	Parlophone R 3561	Sugar Bush/I'm Yours (78)....................................	7
54	Parlophone R 3913	On The Waterfront/Skokiaan (78)..............................	7
55	Parlophone R 3966	Open Your Heart/These Are The Things We'll Share (78).........	7
56	Parlophone R 4230	True Love/Where In The World Is Billy? (78)...................	7
57	Parlophone R 4275	Rock Bobbin' Boats/Tra La La (78)............................	7
57	Parlophone R 4299	Chantez, Chantez/She Said (Aunt Magnolia) (78)...............	6
57	Parlophone R 4328	With All My Heart/Sugar Candy (78)...........................	6
57	Parlophone R 4341	The Gypsy In My Soul/Stop Whistlin' Wolf (78).................	6
57	Parlophone R 4362	Swedish Polka (Chickadee)/Tell My Love (78)...................	6
58	Parlophone R 4455	Left Right Out Of Your Heart/Voom-Ba-Voom (78)...............	8
58	Parlophone R 4479	More Than Ever (Come Prima)/I Know Why (78)..................	8
58	Parlophone R 4492	Christmas Lullaby/The Christmas Tree (78)....................	8
59	Parlophone R 4517	If I Had A Talking Picture Of You/Piccaninny (78).............	10
59	Parlophone R 4555	Once Again/You Are Never Far Away From Me (78)...............	8

SINGLES
53	Parlophone MSP 6006	Sugar Bush/Moon Above Malaya (China Nights)..................	20
55	Parlophone MSP 6158	Ready, Willing And Able/Pam-Poo-Dey.........................	12
55	Parlophone MSP 6160	The Heart You Break (May Be Your Own)/Tika Tika Tok..........	12
56	Parlophone MSP 6208	Young And Foolish/Where You Are..............................	12
56	Parlophone MSP 6220	It's Almost Tomorrow/Cookie..................................	12
56	Parlophone MSP 6250	Saries Marias/Come Back My Love..............................	10
56	Parlophone R 4230	True Love/Where In The World Is Billy?.......................	10
57	Parlophone R 4275	Rock Bobbin' Boats/Tra La La.................................	15
57	Parlophone R 4299	Chantez, Chantez/She Said (Aunt Magnolia)...................	10
57	Parlophone R 4328	With All My Heart/Sugar Candy................................	8
57	Parlophone R 4341	The Gypsy In My Soul/Stop Whistlin' Wolf.....................	8
57	Parlophone R 4362	Swedish Polka (Chickadee)/Tell My Love.......................	6
58	Parlophone R 4401	(I Love You) For Sentimental Reasons/Bobby...................	6
58	Parlophone R 4414	I Do/Love Me Again..	8
58	Parlophone R 4455	Left Right Out Of Your Heart/Voom-Ba-Voom...................	6
58	Parlophone R 4479	More Than Ever (Come Prima)/I Know Why......................	6
58	Parlophone R 4492	Christmas Lullaby/The Christmas Tree.........................	8
59	Parlophone R 4517	If I Had A Talking Picture Of You/Piccaninny.................	6
59	Parlophone R 4544	Wimoweh Cha Cha/Boegoeberg Se Dam..........................	6
59	Parlophone R 4555	Once Again/You Are Never Far Away From Me...................	5
60	Parlophone R 4618	Misty/Turnabout Heart.......................................	5
69	Morgan MRS 19	This Is My Love/Lonely In A Crowd............................	5

EPs
57	Parlophone GEP 8601	THE ENCHANTING EVE (EP)...................................	15
58	Parlophone GEP 8690	EVE BOSWELL'S SHOWCASE (EP)................................	15
58	Parlophone GEP 8717	EVE BOSWELL'S SHOWCASE NO. 2 (EP)..........................	15

LPs
56	Parlophone PMD 1039	SUGAR AND SPICE (10" LP)...................................	35
57	Parlophone PMC 1038	SENTIMENTAL EVE (LP).......................................	30
59	Parlophone PMC 1105	FOLLOWING THE SUN AROUND (LP)..............................	30
76	EMI EMC 3147	SUGAR BUSH '76 (LP)..	12

SIMON BOSWELL
75	Transatlantic TRA 307	MIND PARASITES (LP)..	10

(see also Advertising)

BOTANY 500
86   Supreme Intl. Eds. 86-12   Bully Beef/My Silent Love/Chillshake (12", p/s) 7

BOTHY BAND
70   Polydor 2383 417   OLD HAG YOU HAVE KILLED ME (LP)....................... 12
79   Polydor 2383 530   AFTERHOURS (LP, with lyric insert) 10

PERRY BOTKIN
60   Brunswick 05838   The Executioner Theme/Waltz Of The Hunter 5
(see also Charles Boyer)

BOULEVARD
79   Chopper CHOP 5D   MAGIC MAN (12", red vinyl, no p/s)...................... 10
81   Boulevard VARD 1   Dawn Raid (p/s) 100

BOUNTY HUNTERS
80   EMI RIC 112   Coconut Shuffle (remix)/Barrelhouse 5

BOW BELLS
65   Polydor 56030   Not To Be Taken/I'll Try Not To Hold It Against You 4
66   Parlophone R 5520   Belinda/When You're In 6
(see also Nola York)

JIMMY BOWEN
57   Columbia DB 3915   Ever Lovin' Fingers/I'm Stickin' With You 50
57   Columbia DB 3915   Ever Lovin' Fingers/I'm Stickin' With You (78) 20
57   Columbia DB 3984   Warm Up To Me, Baby/I Trusted You 45
57   Columbia DB 3984   Warm Up To Me, Baby/I Trusted You (78).................. 20
57   Columbia DB 4027   Cross Over/It's Shameful............................. 25
57   Columbia DB 4027   Cross Over/It's Shameful (78) 20
58   Columbia DB 4184   The Two Step/By The Light Of The Silvery Moon 18
58   Columbia DB 4184   The Two Step/By The Light Of The Silvery Moon (78)............ 20
65   Reprise RS 23043   The Eagle (demos & some issues list "The Golden Eagle")/Spanish Cricket 22
67   Reprise RS 20592   Raunchy (w/ Chorus & Orchestra)/It's Such A Pretty World Today (w/ Singers) ... 4
58   Columbia SEG 7757   MEET JIMMY BOWEN (EP) 90
58   Columbia SEG 7793   MEET JIMMY BOWEN NO. 2 (EP)....................... 90

BEN BOWERS
55   Columbia SCM 5192   The Kentuckian Song/The Man From Laramie 12
56   Columbia SCM 5260   To You, My Love/I'm Still A King To You................... 8
57   Parlophone R 4317   Country Boy (with His Royal Jamaicans)/
                          Rum And Coconut Water (Rum And Coca-Cola)................ 8
57   Parlophone R 4317   Country Boy (with His Royal Jamaicans)/
                          Rum And Coconut Water (Rum And Coca-Cola) (78) 12
59   Pye N 15175   Naughty Little Flea/Donkey City (78)..................... 8
57   Pye Jazz NJE 1001   BIG BEN BLUES (EP, with His Bluesicians) 12
58   Pye NEP 24069   KINGS OF CALYPSO VOL. 4 (EP) 8

DAVID BOWIE
SINGLES
66   Pye 7N 17020   Can't Help Thinking About Me/And I Say To Myself (with Lower Third) 110
66   Pye 7N 17079   Do Anything You Say/Good Morning Girl 165
66   Pye 7N 17157   I Dig Everything/I'm Not Losing Sleep 165
66   Deram DM 107   Rubber Band/The London Boys 135
67   Deram DM 123   The Laughing Gnome/The Gospel According To Tony Day
                     (with inverted matrix no. on label) 55
67   Deram DM 135   Love You Till Tuesday/Did You Ever Have A Dream 135
69   Philips BF 1801   Space Oddity/Wild Eyed Boy From Freecloud (unreleased p/s,
                     only 2 or 3 copies known to exist) .... 3,000+
69   Philips BF 1801   Space Oddity/Wild Eyed Boy From Freecloud (mono or stereo)........... 10/15
70   Mercury MF 1135   The Prettiest Star/Conversation Piece................... 110
70   Mercury 6052 026   Memory Of A Free Festival (Parts 1 & 2)................. 110
71   Mercury 6052 049   Holy Holy/Black Country Rock 125
72   RCA RCA 2160   Changes/Andy Warhol 5
72   RCA RCA 2199   Starman/Suffragette City (some in p/s) 50/5
72   RCA RCA 2263   John, I'm Only Dancing/Hang Onto Yourself (original pressing with slow
                     'acoustic guitar' version; later pressings have faster version with sax [£3])...... 5
72   Pye 7NX 8002   Do Anything You Say/I Dig Everything/I Can't Help Thinking About Me/
                     I'm Not Losing Sleep (p/s) 10
72   RCA RCA 2302   The Jean Genie/Ziggy Stardust....................... 5
73   RCA RCA 2352   Drive-In Saturday/Round And Round 5
73   RCA RCA 2316   Life On Mars?/The Man Who Sold The World (some in p/s)............ 10/5
73   Deram DM 123   The Laughing Gnome/The Gospel According To Tony Day
                     (reissue, matrix number correct way up on label) 5
74   RCA RCA 2424   Sorrow/Amsterdam 5
74   RCA LPBO 5009   Rebel Rebel/Queen Bitch........................... 5
74   RCA LPBO 5021   Rock'N'Roll Suicide/Quicksand....................... 5
74   RCA APBO 0293   Diamond Dogs/Holy Holy........................... 5
74   RCA/Mainman/   Bowie's Greatest Hits (excerpts from Knock On Wood/Space Oddity/The Man
      Lyntone LYN 2929   Who Sold The World/Life On Mars?/Starman/Jean Genie/Sorrow/Diamond Dogs)
                     (33rpm 1-sided flexidisc with *Record Mirror/Popswop* magazine) 18/8
74   RCA RCA 2466   Knock On Wood/Panic In Detroit....................... 5
75   RCA RCA 2523   Young Americans/Suffragette City 5
75   Decca F 13579   The London Boys/Love You Till Tuesday.................. 5
75   RCA RCA 2579   Fame/Right.................................. 5
75   RCA RCA 2593   Space Oddity/Changes/Velvet Goldmine (p/s) 8
76   RCA RCA 2726   Suffragette City/Stay (p/s) 12
77   RCA BOW-1E   From The New Album 'Low" (excerpts from Speed Of Life, Breaking Glass,
                     What In The World, Sound And Vision, Be My Wife &
                     A New Career In A New Town; demo only) 500

David BOWIE

77	RCA PB 1017	Be My Wife/Speed Of Life	5
77	RCA PB 1121	'Heroes'/V-2 Schneider	5
78	RCA PB 1190	Beauty And The Beast/Sense Of Doubt (p/s)	8
79	RCA BOW 2	Boys Keep Swinging/Fantastic Voyage (p/s)	5
79	RCA BOW 3	DJ/Repetition (p/s, some on green vinyl)	15/5
79	RCA BOW 4	John, I'm Only Dancing (Again)/John, I'm Only Dancing (p/s)	5
79	RCA BOW 12-4	John, I'm Only Dancing (Again) (Extended)/John, I'm Only Dancing (12", p/s)	7
80	RCA BOW 5	Alabama Song/Space Oddity (poster p/s)	5
80	RCA BOW 6	Ashes To Ashes/Move On (with 3 different p/s & 4 different sheets of 9 stamps)	5
81	RCA BOW 8	Scary Monsters/Because You're Young (p/s)	5
81	RCA BOWC 8	Scary Monsters/Because You're Young (cassette, card sleeve)	8
81	RCA BOW 9	Up The Hill Backwards/Crystal Japan (p/s)	5
81	RCA BOWC 9	Up The Hill Backwards/Crystal Japan (cassette, card sleeve)	8
82	RCA BOW 11	IN BERTHOLT BRECHT'S "BAAL" (EP, foldout p/s)	6
82	RCA BOW 100	FASHIONS (10 x 7" picture discs in plastic wallet [BOWP 101-110], each £4)	40
82	RCA BOWT 12	Peace On Earth/Little Drummer Boy/Fantastic Voyage (12", p/s, picture labels, with Bing Crosby)	8
83	EMI America 45-TCEA 152	Let's Dance/Cat People (cassette)	5
83	EMI America EAP 157	China Girl/Shake It (picture disc)	6
83	EMI America 12 EA 158	Modern Love/Modern Love (Live) (12", p/s with poster)	8
84	EMI America EA 187	Tonight/Tumble And Twirl (poster p/s)	5
85	EMI America EAP 195	Loving The Alien (Remixed Version)/Don't Look Down (Remixed Version) (shaped picture disc)	8
85	EMI America 12 EAG 195	Loving The Alien (Extended Dance Mix)/Don't Look Down (Extended Dance Mix)/Loving The Alien (Extended Dub Mix) (12", gatefold p/s with poster)	7
86	Virgin VSS 838	Absolute Beginners/Absolute Beginners (Dub Mix) (square picture disc)	6
86	EMI America EAP 216	Underground (Edited Version)/Underground (Instrumental) (shaped picture disc)	8
86	Virgin VSS 906	When The Wind Blows/When The Wind Blows (Instrumental) (shaped pic disc)	5
87	EMI America 12 EAX 230	Day-In Day-Out (Remix)/(Extended Dub Mix)/Julie (12", stickered black p/s)	7
87	EMI America EAP 237	Time Will Crawl (Single Version)/Girls (Single Edit) (poster p/s)	6
87	EMI America 12 EAX 237	Time Will Crawl (Dance Crew Mix)/(Dub)/Girls (Japanese Version) (12", p/s)	7
87	EMI America EAP 239	Never Let Me Down/'87 And Cry (picture disc)	5
88	Virgin CDT 20	Absolute Beginners (Full Length Version)/(Dub Mix) (3" CD, card sleeve)	10
90	EMI USA CD FAME 90	FAME 90 (Remixes) (CD)	8
93	BMG Arista 136977	Jump They Say (Radio Edit)/Pallas Athena (Don't Stop Praying Mix) (jukebox issue, no p/s)	7
93	Arista 13942-2	Jump They Say (7" Version)/Pallas Athena (Don't Stop Praying Mix) (CD, double jewel case with booklet)	8
93	BMG Arista 177057	Buddha Of Suburbia/Dead Against It (p/s)	5
93	BMG Arista 18168-2	Buddha Of Suburbia/Dead Against It (CD, holographic disc)	8
97	RCA 307031	The Heart's Filthy Lesson (Alternative Mix)/(Bowie Mix)/(Rubber Mix)/(Simple Text Mix)/(Filthy Mix) (12", picture disc)	8
95	RCA 329407	Strangers When We Meet (Edit)/The Man Who Sold The World (live) (green vinyl, stickered card p/s)	5
95	RCA 353847	Hallo Spaceboy (Remix)/The Heart's Filthy Lesson (Radio Edit) (pink vinyl, stickered card p/s)	5
97	RCA 512347	Seven Years In Tibet (Edit)/Seven Years In Tibet (Mandarin Version) (p/s, clear vinyl)	5
97	RCA 51254-2	Seven Years In Tibet (Edit)/Seven Years In Tibet (Mandarin Version) Pallas Athena (Live) (CD, digipak)	8
97	RCA 39741-1	Telling Lies (Paradox Mix)/Telling Lies (Feelgood & Adam F Mix) (12", p/s)	8
99	Virgin VSP 1767	Survive/Seven (live) (picture disc)	10

LPs

67	Deram DML/SML 1007	DAVID BOWIE (LP, mono/stereo)	140/200
69	Philips SBL 7912	DAVID BOWIE (LP, gatefold sleeve)	165
70	Decca PA 58	THE WORLD OF DAVID BOWIE (LP, mono)	20
72	Decca SPA 58	THE WORLD OF DAVID BOWIE (LP, stereo, 'curly hair' cover)	12
71	Mercury 6338 041	THE MAN WHO SOLD THE WORLD (LP, with 'dress' cover)	275
71	Mercury 6338 041	THE MAN WHO SOLD THE WORLD (cassette, with 'dress' cover)	65
71	RCA SF 8244	HUNKY DORY (LP, orange label with lyric sheet)	12
72	RCA SF 8287	THE RISE AND FALL OF ZIGGY STARDUST AND THE SPIDERS FROM MARS (LP, orange label w/ lyric inner sleeve)	12
72	RCA LSP 4813	SPACE ODDITY (LP, reissue of SBL 7912 in different sleeve, orange label with lyric inner sleeve & poster)	15
72	RCA LSP 4816	THE MAN WHO SOLD THE WORLD (LP, orange label w/ inner sleeve & poster)	15
73	RCA RS 1001	ALADDIN SANE (LP, orange label, gatefold sleeve & lyric inner sleeve, some with fan club membership card)	16/12
74	RCA APL 1-0576	DIAMOND DOGS (LP, orange label, gatefold sleeve)	12
74	RCA APL 2-0771	DAVID LIVE (2-LP, gatefold sleeve, orange label, photos on inners)	15
76	RCA APLI 1327	STATION TO STATION (LP, with original colour proof sleeve)	500
76	RCA RS 1055	CHANGESONEBOWIE (LP, with 'sax' version of "John I'm Only Dancing")	25
78	RCA PL 02913	STAGE (2-LP, gatefold sleeve, yellow vinyl)	20
77	RCA BOW LP 1	LOW (LP, red vinyl, semi-official 'factory custom pressing')	600
80	RCA BOW LP 2	SCARY MONSTERS (AND SUPER CREEPS) (LP, purple vinyl, semi-official 'factory custom pressing')	600
83	EMI America AMLP 3029	LET'S DANCE (LP, picture disc)	10
84	RCA BOPIC 1	ALADDIN SANE (LP, picture disc with numbered insert)	15
84	RCA BOPIC 2	HUNKY DORY (LP, picture disc with numbered insert)	15
84	RCA BOPIC 3	ZIGGY STARDUST (LP, picture disc with numbered insert)	15
84	RCA BOPIC 4	PIN-UPS (LP, picture disc with numbered insert)	15
84	RCA BOPIC 5	DIAMOND DOGS (LP, picture disc with numbered insert)	15
95	RCA 307021	EXCERPTS FROM OUTSIDE (LP, with 12" booklet & lyric sheet)	15
97	RCA 44949	EARTHLING (LP, gatefold sleeve)	15

CDs

84	Deram 800 087-2	DAVID BOWIE (CD, withdrawn with white title)	70
85	RCA PD 84623	HUNKY DORY (CD, withdrawn)	25
85	RCA PD 84654	THE MAN WHO SOLD THE WORLD (CD, withdrawn)	30
85	RCA PD 84702	THE RISE AND FALL OF ZIGGY STARDUST AND THE SPIDERS FROM MARS (CD, withdrawn)	25
85	RCA PD 84813	SPACE ODDITY (CD, withdrawn)	30
85	RCA PD 84653	PIN-UPS (CD, withdrawn)	25
85	RCA PD 83890	ALADDIN SANE (CD, withdrawn)	25
85	RCA PD 80998	YOUNG AMERICANS (CD, withdrawn)	25
85	RCA PD 81327	STATION TO STATION (CD, withdrawn)	30
85	RCA PD 81732	CHANGESONEBOWIE (CD, withdrawn)	40
85	RCA PD 83856	LOW (CD, withdrawn)	25
85	RCA PD 83889	DIAMOND DOGS (CD, withdrawn)	25
85	RCA PD 83856	LOW (CD, withdrawn)	25
85	RCA PD 83857	HEROES (CD, withdrawn)	25
85	RCA PD 82743	PETER AND THE WOLF (CD)	20
85	RCA PD 89002	STAGE (2-CD, withdrawn)	50
85	RCA PD 84234	LODGER (CD, withdrawn)	20
85	RCA PD 83647	SCARY MONSTERS (AND SUPER CREEPS) (CD, withdrawn)	30
85	RCA PD 84202	CHANGESTWOBOWIE (CD, withdrawn)	35
85	RCA PD 94792	GOLDEN YEARS (CD, withdrawn)	30
85	RCA PD 84919	FAME AND FASHION (ALL TIME GREATEST HITS) (CD, withdrawn)	55
93	EMI BOWIE 1	SELECTIONS FROM THE SINGLES COLLECTION (CD, 10-track sampler, card p/s, promo only)	20
93	Arista 17822-2	THE BUDDHA OF SUBURBIA (CD, special edition in clear plastic case, with novel)	20
99	Virgin CDVX 2900	'hours...' (CD, hologram sleeve)	15

Promos

90	BMG BOW 908	SO FAR (CD, 8-track sampler for "Sound & Vision" box set)	35
93	BMG MEAT 1	Pallas Athena (12", white label, no p/s, includes two exclusive Meat Beat Manifesto remixes)	45
93	Back To Basics HOME 1	Night Flights/(B-side by Moodswings) (12")	20
95	RCA HALLO 2	Hallo Spaceboy (12" Remix) (12", 1-sided, no p/s)	20
95	BMG SOLO 1	EXCLUSIVE TOUR CD: Strangers When We Meet/MORRISSEY: The Boy Racer (Outside Tour CD)	70
96	RCA SPACE 2	Hallo Spaceboy (12" Remix) (1-sided 12", some copies listed as RCA HALLO 2, no p/s)	35
96	RCA SPACE 3	Hallo Spaceboy (Double Click Mix)/Hallo Spaceboy (Instrumental)/Hallo Spaceboy (Lost In Space Mix) (12", no p/s)	65
99	Virgin CDVDJ 2900	'hours...' (CD, card sleeve)	20
99	EMI CDLRL 015	ALBUM SAMPLER (CD, 17-track sampler, promo only)	25
99	EMI QUEENWL 28	Under Pressure (Remixes) (with Queen) (12", white label, unreleased mix, promo only)	60

(see also Davie Jones & King Bees, Davy Jones & Lower Third, Manish Boys, Arnold Corns, Spiders From Mars, Mick Ronson, Queen, Tin Machine, Tao Jones Index, Bing Crosby)

BOWMAN-HYDE PLAYERS

| 61 | Parlophone PMC 1155 | SING ME A SOUVENIR (LP) | 60 |

ALAN BOWN (SET)

65	Pye 7N 15934	Can't Let Her Go/I'm The One	12
66	Pye 7N 17084	Baby Don't Push Me/Everything's Gonna Be Alright	15
66	Pye 7N 17148	Headline News/Mister Pleasure	10
66	Pye 7N 17192	Emergency 999/Settle Down	12
67	Pye 7N 17256	Gonna Fix You Good (Everytime You're Bad)/I Really Really Care	18
67	Music Factory CUB 1	We Can Help You/Magic Handkerchief (as the Alan Bown!)	8
67	MGM MGM 1355	Toyland/Technicolour Dream	8
68	MGM MGM 1387	Story Book/Little Lesley	15
69	Deram DM 259	Still As Stone/Wrong Idea	7
69	Deram DM 278	Gypsy Girl/All I Can	7
70	Island WIP 6091	Pyramid/Crash Landing	6
75	CBS 3721	Rockford Files/I Don't Know	5
68	Music Factory CUB LM/LS 1	OUTWARD BOWN (LP)	25
69	Deram DML/SML 1049	THE ALAN BOWN! (LP)	15
70	Island ILPS 9131	LISTEN (LP)	12

(see also Robert Palmer, John Barry Seven, Bronco, Jonesy)

ALAN BOWN/JIMMY JAMES & VAGABONDS

| 68 | Pye N(S)PL 18156 | LONDON SWINGS — LIVE AT THE MARQUEE CLUB (LP, 1 side each) | 25 |

(see also Jimmy James & Vagabonds)

ANDREW BOWN

| 70 | Parlophone R 5856 | Tarot (Theme From 'Ace Of Wands')/Lulli Rides Again | 40 |

(see also Andy Bown)

ANDY BOWN

73	GM GMS 1	Sweet William/I Won't Let You Down	5
74	GM GMS 19	New York Satyricon Zany/Party Games	5
75	GM GMS 9039	Supersonic/Feeling Better	5
77	EMI EMI 2571	Love Love Love/Blood On The Keys	5
77	EMI EMI 2657	Good Enough Reason/317 Manhattan Blues	5
79	EMI EMI 2906	Another Shipwreck/Another Night With You	6
79	EMI EMI 2943	Good Advice/One More Chance	5
81	EMI EMI 5245	Say It Was Magic/One Forward Two Back Again (some in p/s)	10/5
82	EMI EMI 5312	Marianne/One Forward Two Back Again	5
82	EMI EMI 5372	Help Me/Marianne (p/s)	8

Andy BOWN

72	Mercury 6310 002	GONE TO MY HEAD (LP)	12
73	GM GML 1001	SWEET WILLIAM (LP)	12
77	EMI EMC 3176	COME BACK ROMANCE, ALL IS FORGIVEN (LP, with inner sleeve)	10
79	EMI EMC 3283	GOOD ADVICE (LP)	10

(see also Andrew Bown, Herd, Judas Jump, Status Quo, Rossi & Frost, Storyteller)

BOW WOW
| 83 | Heavy Metal Intl. HMINT 2 | You're Mine/Don't Cry Baby (live) (p/s) | 7 |

BOW WOW WOW
80	EMI EMI 5088	C-30 C-60 C-90 Go!/Sun Sea And Piracy (cassette, some in promo 'dog food' can with inserts)	15/5
81	EMI TCEMI 5153	W.O.R.K./C-30 ... Anda! (cassette)	5
81	RCA RCA 100	Prince Of Darkness/Orang Utan (poster p/s)	4
81	Tour D'Eiffel TE 001	The Mile High Club/C-30 C-60 C-90 Go! (plain white sleeve)	8
82	RCA RCA 238	I Want Candy (p/s, 1-sided, etched B-side)	5
82	RCA RCA 238	I Want Candy/King Kong (p/s)	4
82	RCA RCXK 004	I Want Candy/See Jungle/Go Wild In The Country/Chihuahua (cassette)	5
82	RCA RCA 263	Louis Quatorze (re-recorded)/Mile High Club (p/s)	4
82	Lyntone LYN 11358	Elimination Dancing (New Version)/King Kong (New Version) (green or clear 1-sided 33rpm flexidisc free with *Flexipop*, issue 18; with/without mag)	6/4
83	RCA RCA 314	Do You Wanna Hold Me?/What's The Time (Hey Buddy) (picture disc)	5
80	EMI WOW 1	BOW WOW WOW — YOUR CASSETTE PET (cassette, mini-LP)	7

BRENDAN BOWYER (& ROYALS)
65	HMV POP 1481	The Wonder Of You/Fun Fun Fun	5
66	HMV POP 1521	The Fly/Answer Me	5
67	King KG 1059	Sitting In The Sun/Da Doo Ron Ron (as Brendan Bowyer & Royals)	5
68	King KG 1078	Woman Woman/Lady Willpower (as Brendan Bowyer & Royals)	5

DAVID BOX
| 64 | London HLU 9874 | If You Can't Say Something Nice/Sweet Sweet Day | 15 |
| 64 | London HLU 9924 | Little Lonely Summer Girl/No One Will Ever Know | 15 |

(see also Crickets)

BOXER
| 75 | Virgin V 2049 | BELOW THE BELT (LP, with uncensored full-frontal back cover) | 12 |
| 76 | Virgin V 2073 | BLOODLETTING (LP, withdrawn) | 50 |

(see also Patto, Timebox)

BOXEROS
| 61 | Palette PG 9023 | El Senior Ping Pong/Y Viva El Cha Cha | 5 |

BOX TOPS
67	Stateside SS 2044	The Letter/Happy Times	7
67	Stateside SS 2070	Neon Rainbow/She Knows How	7
68	Bell BLL 1001	Cry Like A Baby/The Door You Closed To Me	6
68	Bell BLL 1017	Choo Choo Train/Fields Of Clover	6
68	Bell BLL 1035	I Met Her In Church/People Gonna Talk	6
69	Bell BLL 1045	Sandman/Sweet Cream Ladies, Forward March	6
69	Bell BLL 1063	I Shall Be Released/I Must Be The Devil	6
69	Bell BLL 1068	Soul Deep/The Happy Song	6
69	Bell BLL 1084	Turn On A Dream/Together	6
70	Bell BLL 1097	You Keep Tightening Up On Me/Come On Honey	6
73	London HLU 10402	Sugar Creek Woman/It's All Over	6
68	Stateside (S)SL 10218	THE LETTER/NEON RAINBOW (LP)	25
68	Stateside TA-SL 10218	THE LETTER/NEON RAINBOW (reel-to-reel tape, mono)	12
68	Bell MBLL/SBLL 105	CRY LIKE A BABY (LP)	18
69	Bell MBLL/SBLL 108	NON-STOP (LP)	18
69	Bell SBLL 120	DIMENSIONS (LP)	15
70	Bell MBLL/SBLL 129	SUPER HITS (LP)	15
70	Bell BELLS 149	BOX TOPS (LP)	15

(see also Big Star, Alex Chilton)

EL BOY
| 57 | Columbia DB 3927 | Jack, Jack, Jack/Tonight My Heart She Is Crying | 6 |

DENNY BOYCE & HIS ORCHESTRA/RHYTHM
57	Oriole CB 1358	One Man Went To Rock/Thunderstorm (78)	10
58	Oriole CB 1458	Bad Boy/When Your Hair Has Turned To Silver	8
58	Oriole CB 1458	Bad Boy/When Your Hair Has Turned To Silver (78)	10

TOMMY BOYCE
| 65 | MGM MGM 1287 | Pretty Thing/I Don't Have To Worry 'Bout You | 6 |

TOMMY BOYCE & BOBBY HART
67	A&M AMS 705	Out And About/My Little Chickadee	5
67	A&M AMS 710	Sometimes She's A Little Girl/Love Every Day	5
68	A&M AMS 714	I Wonder What She's Doing Tonight?/Ambushers	5
68	A&M AMS 722	Goodbye Baby/Where Angels Go Trouble Follows	5
68	A&M AMS 729	Alice Long (You're Still My Favourite Girlfriend)/P.O. Box 9847	5
67	A&M AML 907	TEST PATTERNS (LP)	12

(see also Monkees, Tommy Boyce)

EDDIE BOYD
66	Blue Horizon 45 BH 1009	It's So Miserable To Be Alone/Empty Arms	100
67	Blue Horizon 57-3137	The Big Boat/Sent For You Yesterday (with Fleetwood Mac)	20
62	Esquire EP 247	BOYD'S BLUES (EP, as Eddie Boyd Blues Combo)	60
65	Fontana STJL 905	FIVE LONG YEARS (LP)	35
67	Decca LK/SKL 4872	EDDIE BOYD AND HIS BLUES BAND FEATURING PETER GREEN (LP)	90
68	Blue Horizon 7-63202	7936 SOUTH RHODES (LP, with Fleetwood Mac)	65
68	Storyville SLP 4054	IN CONCERT (LP)	20

(see also Fleetwood Mac)

MINT VALUE £

EDDIE BOYD/BUDDY GUY
66	Chess CRE 6009	WITH THE BLUES (EP, 2 tracks each)	25

(see also Buddy Guy)

JIMMY BOYD
53	Columbia SCM 5072	I Saw Mommy Kissing Santa Claus/Little Train A-Chuggin' In My Heart	25

CHARLES BOYER
65	London HL 10002	Where Does Love Go/PERRY BOTKIN JR: Theme From Where Does Love Go	6
65	London HAT 8268	WHERE DOES LOVE GO (LP)	15

JACQUELINE BOYER
60	Columbia DB 4452	Tom Pillibi/FRANCOIS DEGUELT: Ce Soir-La	6

BOYFRIENDS
78	United Artists UP 36424	I'm In Love Today/Saturday Night (p/s)	5
78	United Artists UP 36442	Don't Ask Me To Explain/Jenny (p/s)	5
78	United Artists UP 36478	Last Bus Home/Romance (p/s)	5

(see also Vibrators)

BOYFRIENDS
82	Plastic PRES 001	Boyfriend/Give A Little, Take A Little (p/s)	25

BOY GEORGE
87	Virgin CDEP 9	To Be Reborn/Where Are You Now? (CD, gatefold card p/s)	15
87	Virgin BOY 102	Sold/Everything I Own (Go-Go Version) (box set)	5
88	Virgin BOY 105-12	Live My Life/Live My Life (Klub Mix)/Live My Life (12" Club Remix) (12", poster sleeve)	10
88	Virgin BOY 105-13	Keep Me In Mind/I Pray/State Of Love (Extended Version)/Everything I Own (12", picture disc)	8
88	Virgin BOYT 106	No Clause 28 (Space Face Full Remix)/(Space Face Full Dub)/ (Full Version) (3" CD, in 5" slimline jewel case, with adaptor)	12
88	Virgin BOYCD 106	No Clause 28 (5" CD)	10
89	Virgin BOYCD 107	Don't Cry/Leave In Love/Don't Cry (Full Version)/A Boy Called Alice (3" CD)	12
89	Virgin BOYCD 108	Don't Take My Mind On A Trip/I Go Where I Go/Girlfriend/ What Becomes Of The Broken Hearted (3" CD, card p/s)	15
94	Virgin VSCDG 1490	THE DEVIL IN SISTER GEORGE EP: Miss Me Blind (Return To Gender Mix)/ Generations Of Love (Ramp Club Mix)/Am I Losing Control (Metal Bird Mix)/ Love Hurts (Disco Moment Mix)/Everything I Own (Redemption Extension Mix) (CD, digipak)	12
95	Spaghetti CIO CD	THE CRYING GAME (CD EP)	10

(see also Culture Club, Jesus Loves You, JYL Posse)

BOY HAIRDRESSERS
88	53rd & 3rd AGARR T12	Golden Showers/Tidalwave/The Assumption As An Elevator (12", p/s)	18

(see also Teenage Fanclub, BMX Bandits, Clouds)

BILLY BOYLE
62	Decca F 11503	My Baby's Crazy 'Bout Elvis/Held For Questioning	25
63	Decca F 11709	I'm Coming Home/Sunday's Child	7
63	Columbia DB 7111	Lovers Hill/She's New To You	7
63	Columbia DB 7127	Hootin' In The Kitchen/Lover's Hill	7
64	Columbia DB 7294	Walk, Walk, Walkin'/My Baby Tonight (with Le Roys)	10

(see also Le Roys)

A. BOYNE
70	Punch PH 36	Oh My Darling (actually Audley Rollins)/DENNIS SMITH: Ball Of Confusion	5

BOYS (U.K.)
63	Parlophone R 5027	Polaris/Jumpin'	18

BOYS (U.K.)
64	Pye 7N 15726	It Ain't Fair/I Want You	45

(see also Sandra Barry & Boys, Action)

BOYS (Jamaica)
69	Duke DU 19	Easy Sound/AFROTONES: Freedom Sound	8

(see also Harry J. Allstars)

BOYS (U.K.)
77	NEMS NES 102	I Don't Care/Soda Pressing (p/s)	8
77	NEMS NES 111	First Time/Whatcha Gonna Do/Turning Grey (p/s)	8
78	NEMS NES 116	Brickfield Nights/Teacher's Pet (p/s)	6
79	Safari SAFE 21	Kamikaze/Bad Days (p/s, some with booklet)	7/5
80	Safari SAFE 23	Terminal Love/I Love Me (p/s)	5
80	Safari SAFE 27	You Better Move On/Schoolgirls (p/s)	5
80	Safari SAFE 31	Weekend/Cool (p/s)	5
80	Safari SAFE 33	Let It Rain/Lucy (p/s)	6
77	NEMS NES 6001	THE BOYS (LP)	15
78	NEMS NEL 6015	ALTERNATIVE CHARTBUSTERS (LP)	15
79	Safari 1-2 BOYS	TO HELL WITH THE BOYS (LP, with songbook & stickered sleeve)	12

(see also Yobs, Cockney 'N' Westerns, Rowdies, Hollywood Brats)

BOYS (U.K.)
88	private pressing	Happy Days/Standard Avenue/Learn How To Dance (p/s)	8

(see also Ocean Colour Scene)

BOYS BLUE
65	HMV POP 1427	You Got What I Want/Take A Heart	65

(see also Jeff Elroy & Boys Blue)

BOYS OF THE LOUGH
73	Trailer LER 2086	THE BOYS OF THE LOUGH (LP)	12
74	Trailer LER 2090	SECOND ALBUM (LP)	12

MINT VALUE £

BOYS TOWN STEEL ORCHESTRA
| 55 | Sagomes SG 126 | Woman Police/Is It Yes? Is It No? (78) | 8 |

BOYS WONDER
87	Sire W 8195	Shine On Me/Stop It (p/s)	6
87	Sire W 8293	What Now, Earthman?/Ten Million Ton Headache (p/s)	5
88	Boys Wonder BW 1	Goodbye Jimmy Dean/Hot Rod (p/s)	5
90	Flat OUTS OO1	Eat Me, Drink Me/Harley Davidson (p/s)	5
89	Flat OUTA OO2	RADIO WONDER (LP)	15

BOYZONE
94	Polydor 853 246-2	Working My Way Back To You (Radio Edit)/(12" POD Hi NRG Mix)/Father And Son (CD, Irish-only)	20
95	Polydor 851 278-2	Love Me For A Reason/Daydream Believer (CD, slimline jewel case)	8
95	Polydor 851 280-2	Love Me For A Reason/Daydream Believer (CD, digipak, with foldout poster)	10

BOZ
66	Columbia DB 7832	You're Just The Kind Of Girl I Want/Isn't That So	7
66	Columbia DB 7889	Meeting Time/No (Ah) Body Knows The Blues	7
66	Columbia DB 7941	Pinocchio/Stay As You Are	6
66	Columbia DB 7972	The Baby Song/Carry On Screaming	6
68	Columbia DB 8406	I Shall Be Released/Down In The Flood	5
68	Columbia DB 8468	Light My Fire/Back Against The Wall	7

(see also King Crimson, Bad Company)

JANET BRACE
| 55 | Brunswick 05272 | Teach Me Tonight/My Old Familiar Heartache | 8 |

BRACKEN
| 79 | Look LKLP 6438 | PRINCE OF THE NORTHLANDS (LP, private pressing, with insert) | 75 |

KIM & KELLY BRADEN
| 67 | Columbia DB 8312 | Didn't I/You're Leaving, She's Laughing | 5 |
| 68 | Columbia DB 8421 | Happiness Is/Sing A Rainbow | 5 |

BRADFORD
| 88 | Village VILS 101 | Skin Storm/Gatling Gun (white title p/s) | 4 |

PROF. ALEX BRADFORD
| 63 | London REU 1357 | TOO CLOSE TO HEAVEN (EP) | 16 |
| 63 | Stateside SL 10047 | ONE STEP (LP) | 15 |

(see also Bradford Singers)

BRADFORD SINGERS
| 62 | Stateside SL 10026 | BLACK NATIVITY (LP) | 20 |
| 64 | Stateside SL 10083 | ANGEL ON VACATION (LP) | 15 |

(see also Prof. Alex Bradford)

GEORGE BRADLEY & HIS BAND
| 65 | HMV POP 1459 | Breakout/Vendetta | 6 |

JAN BRADLEY
| 63 | Pye International 7N 25182 | Mama Didn't Lie/Lovers Like Me | 20 |

OWEN BRADLEY (ORCHESTRA/QUINTET)
56	Brunswick 05528	Theme From "The Threepenny Opera"/Lights Of Vienna (with Orchestra)	6
57	Brunswick 05700	White Silver Sands/Midnight Blues (as Owen Bradley Quintet)	7
58	Brunswick 05736	Big Guitar/Sentimental Dream (as Owen Bradley Quintet)	12
58	Brunswick 05736	Big Guitar/Sentimental Dream (as Owen Bradley Quintet) (78)	15
60	Brunswick LAT 8327	THE BIG GUITAR (LP)	30

BRADLEY STRYDER
| 92 | Rephlex CAT 001 | BRADLEY'S BEAT (12" EP, logo sleeve) | 20 |
| 96 | Rephlex CAT 020 | BRADLEY'S ROBOT (12" EP, poster p/s) | 10 |

DON BRADSHAW-LEATHER
| 72 | Distance DIST 101 | DISTANCE BETWEEN US (2-LP, gatefold sleeve, private pressing) | 40 |

(supposedly by Robert John Godfrey)

BUDDY BRADSHAW
| 59 | Capitol CL 15036 | Nothing You Can Say/Tonight I Walk Alone | 8 |

(see also Owen Gray)

SONNY BRADSHAW (& YOUNG JAMAICA)
| 61 | Duke DK 1003 | Yellow Birds/Festival Jump Up | 7 |
| 71 | Big Shot BI 576 | Wig Wam/Peace And Love (as Sonny Bradshaw & Young Jamaica) | 5 |

TINY BRADSHAW & HIS ORCHESTRA
52	Vogue V 2146	Breaking Up The House/Walk That Mess (78)	12
54	Parlophone CMSP 3	South Of The Orient/Later (export issue)	20
54	Parlophone MSP 6118	The Gypsy/Spider Web	15
54	Parlophone R 3894	The Gypsy/Spider Web (78)	10
55	Parlophone DP 418	Bradshaw Boogie/Walkin' The Chalk Line (78, export issue)	22
55	Parlophone MSP 6145	Overflow/Don't Worry 'Bout Me	15
55	Parlophone R 3959	Overflow/Don't Worry 'Bout Me (78)	18
55	Parlophone R 4062	Stomping Room Only/Cat Nap (78)	8
55	Parlophone R 4084	Pompton Turnpike/Come On (78)	8
54	Parlophone GEP 8507	TRAIN KEPT A ROLLING (EP)	30
56	Parlophone GEP 8552	POMPTON TURNPIKE (EP)	18

TINY BRADSHAW ORCHESTRA/WYNONIE HARRIS
| 70 | Polydor 623 273 | KINGS OF RHYTHM AND BLUES (LP, 1 side each) | 20 |

(see also Wynonie Harris)

BOB BRADY & CONCHORDS
68	Bell BLL 1025	Everybody's Goin' To The Love-In/It's Been A Long Time Between Kisses	10
70	Bell BLL 1114	Everybody's Goin' To The Love-In/It's Been A Long Time Between Kisses (reissue)	5

PHIL BRADY & RANCHERS
65	Rex R 11011	Little Rose/Just One More Time	6
	(see also Ranchers)		

VICTOR BRADY
70	Polydor	BROWN RAIN (LP)	20

BRADY BUNCH
73	Paramount SPFL 284	MEET THE BRADY BUNCH (LP)	12

RUBY BRAFF
71	Polydor 2460 127	HEAR ME TALKIN'! (LP)	10

BILLY BRAGG
87	Go! Discs/Flexi FLX 418	Back To Basics Audio Aid/Play In A Day The Billy Bragg Way (square flexidisc free with book *Back To Basics*)	6/4
	(see also Riff Raff)		

AL 'TNT' BRAGGS
66	Vocalion VP 9278	Earthquake/How Long (Do You Hold On)	12
68	Action ACT 4506	Earthquake/How Long (Do You Hold On) (reissue)	8
69	Action ACT 4526	I'm A Good Man/I Like What You Do To Me	10
65	Vocalion VEP 170163	AL 'TNT' BRAGGS (EP)	45

ERNEL BRAHAM
66	Rio R 79	Musical Fight/EDWARDS ALLSTARS: Pipeline	8
	(see also Kent Walker)		

BRAIN
67	Parlophone R 5595	Nightmares In Red/Kick The Donkey	45
87	Bam Caruso OPRA 63	Nightmares In Red/SRC: Black Sheep (jukebox edition, die-cut co. sleeve)	5
	(see also Giles Giles & Fripp, Trendsetters Ltd, League Of Gentlemen)		

BRAINBOX
69	Parlophone R 5775	Woman's Gone/Down Man	10
70	Parlophone R 5842	So Helpless/To You	7
70	Parlophone PCS 7094	BRAINBOX (LP)	35
	(see also Jan Akkerman, Hunters, Focus)		

BRAINCHILD
70	A&M AMS 805	Cage/Autobiography	5
70	A&M AMLS 979	HEALING OF THE LUNATIC OWL (LP)	30

BRAINIAC 5
80	Roach RR 5002	Working/Feel (p/s)	10
78	Roach RREP 5001	MUSHY DOUBT (EP, 33rpm, p/s)	10

BRAINSTORM
79	Miracle M5	Lovin' Is Really My Game/Stormin' (12", no p/s)	8

WILFRED BRAMBELL
63	Parlophone R 5058	Secondhand/Ragtime Ragabone Man	12
71	CBS 7062	The Decimal Song/Time Marches On	6

WILFRED BRAMBELL & HARRY H. CORBETT
63	Pye 7N 15588	Steptoe And Son At Buckingham Palace (Parts 1 & 2)	5
63	Pye NEP 24169	THE FACTS OF LIFE (EP)	8
64	Pye NPL 18081	STEPTOE AND SON (LP)	16
65	Pye NPL 18101	STEPTOE A LA CARTE (LP)	15
65	Pye NPL 18135	LOVE AND HAROLD STEPTOE (LP)	20
66	Pye NPL 18153	GEMS FROM THE STEPTOE SCRAP HEAP (LP)	20
67	Golden Guinea GGL 0373	STEPTOE A LA CARTE (LP, reissue)	12
	(see also Harry H. Corbett)		

DELANEY BRAMLETT
64	Vocalion VP 9227	Heartbreak Hotel/You Never Looked Sweeter	12
65	Vocalion VP 9237	Liverpool Lou/You Have No Choice	15
	(see also Delaney & Bonnie, King Curtis with Delaney & Friends)		

BRAM STOKER
72	Windmill WMD 117	HEAVY ROCK SPECTACULAR (LP)	30

BILL BRAMWELL
58	Starlite ST45 004	My Old Man/Shoutin' In That Amen Corner	7
60	Decca F 11309	Candid Camera Theme/Frederika	6

BRAN
74	Sain 1038M	AIL DDECHRA (LP)	30
70s	Sain 1070M	HEDFAN (LP)	25
78	Sain 1120M	GWRACH Y HOS (LP, with inner sleeve)	20

BRAND
64	Piccadilly 7N 35216	I'm A Lover Not A Fighter/Hear 'Em Talking (unissued)	
64	Piccadilly 7N 35216	I'm A Lover Not A Fighter/Zulu Stomp	90

MARLON BRANDO & JEAN SIMMONS
55	Brunswick OE 9241	GUYS AND DOLLS (EP)	10

BILL BRANDON
73	Mercury 6052 186	I Am Free Of Your Love/(Take Another Little) Piece Of My Heart	5

JOHNNY BRANDON

			MINT VALUE £
56	Parlophone MSP 6238	Rock-A-Bye Baby/Lonely Lips	10
56	Parlophone R 4207	Shim Sham Shuffle/I Didn't Know	15
56	Decca F 10778	Glendora/Song For A Summer Night	6
57	Decca F 10858	Nothing Is Too Good For You/A Sort-Of-A-Feeling	6
59	Top Rank JAR 241	Santa Claus Jnr./I Heard A Bluebird Sing	6
55	Pye NEP 24003	JOHNNY BRANDON HITS (EP)	18

KIRK BRANDON & PACK OF LIES

87	SS SS1N2/SS2N1	KIRK BRANDON AND THE PACK OF LIES (EP)	10

(see also Theatre Of Hate, Spear Of Destiny, Senate, Pack)

TONY BRANDON

68	MGM MGM 1401	Candy Kisses/Get Going Baby	5

VERN BRANDON

62	Decca F 11472	Let Me Be The One/Gotta Know The Reason	15

ANGELO BRANDUARDI

79	Ariola ARL 5016	HIGHDOWN FAIR (LP)	12

BRAND X

79	Charisma CB 340	Soho/Dance Of The Illegal Aliens (no p/s)	5
79	Charisma CB 340-12	Soho/Dance Of The Illegal Aliens/Noddy Goes To Sweden/Pool Room Blues (12", p/s)	8

(see also Phil Collins)

BRANDY BOYS

65	Columbia DB 7507	Gale Winds/Don't Come Knocking At My Door	10

BRANDY WINE BRIDGE

77	Cottage COT 311	THE GREY LADY (LP)	25
78	Cottage COT 321	AN ENGLISH MEADOW (LP, hand-drawn sleeve with insert)	25

JOHNNY BRANTLEY'S ALL STARS

58	London HLU 8606	The Place/Pot Luck	20
58	London HLU 8606	The Place/Pot Luck (78)	20

BRASS ALLEY

(see under Various Artists EPs)

ANDRÉ BRASSEUR

65	Pye International 7N 25332	Early Bird Satellite/Special 230	10
67	CBS 202557	The Kid/Holiday	8
71	CBS 2557	The Kid/Holiday (reissue)	5
66	CBS 62858	TASTY (LP)	12

BRASS INCORPORATED

70	Pye International 7N 25520	At The Sign Of The Swinging Cymbal/Just Like That	20

BRASS TACKS

68	Big T BIG 110	I'll Keep On Holding On/Let The Sunshine In	6
68	Big T BIG 114	Maxwell Ferguson/Sunshine After The Rain	15

BRATZ

80	A Famous Record AFR 1	The Bratz Are Coming/Coast To Coast/Everyone Wants To Be Elvis (p/s)	6

BOB BRAUN

62	Brunswick 05875	Till Death Do Us Part/So It Goes	5

STEVE BRAUN

85	Numa NU 12	When I See Your Eyes/Out To Play (p/s)	6
85	Numa NUM 12	When I See Your Eyes/Out To Play (12", p/s)	8
86	Numa NU 15	Love Could Be So Good/Red Light Districts (p/s)	6
86	Numa NUM 15	Love Could Be So Good/Red Light Districts (12", p/s)	8

RICHARD BRAUTIGAN

69	Zapple ZAPPLE 03	LISTENING TO RICHARD BRAUTIGAN (LP, unreleased, acetates exist)	

LOS BRAVOS

66	Decca F 22419	Black Is Black/I Want A Name	5
66	Decca F 22484	I Don't Care/Don't Be Left Out In The Cold	5
66	Decca F 22529	Going Nowhere/Brand New Baby	6
67	Decca F 22615	I'm All Ears/You'll Never Get The Chances Again	6
67	Decca F 22682	Like Nobody Else/Wearing A Smile	6
68	Decca F 22765	Bring A Little Lovin'/Make It Last	6
69	Decca F 22853	Save Me, Save Me/Baby I Love You Because I Need You	6
70	Decca F 13064	People Talking Around/Every Dog Has His Night	6
66	Decca LK 4822	BLACK IS BLACK (LP)	25
68	Decca LK/SKL 4905	LOS BRAVOS (LP)	25

(see also Mike Kennedy)

PRISCILLA BRAZIER

74	Dovetail DOVE 9	PRISCILLA BRAZIER (LP)	35
76	Key KL 038	SOMETHING BEAUTIFUL (LP)	30

BREAD

69	Elektra EKSN 45071	London Bridge/Dismal Day	5
69	Elektra EKS 74044	BREAD (LP)	12

(see also David Gates, Pleasure Fair)

BREAD & BEER BAND

69	Decca F 12891	Dick Barton Theme (The Devil's Gallop)/Breakdown Blues	110
72	Decca F 13354	Dick Barton Theme (The Devil's Gallop)/Breakdown Blues (reissue)	55
69	Rubbish (no cat. no.)	THE BREAD AND BEER BAND (LP, 1 copy known to exist)	2,000+

(see also Elton John, Caleb)

MINT VALUE £

BREAD, LOVE & DREAMS
69	Decca F 12958	Virgin Kiss/Switch Out The Sun	12
69	Decca LK/SKL 5008	BREAD, LOVE AND DREAMS (LP)	60
70	Decca LK/SKL 5048	THE STRANGE TALE OF CAPTAIN SHANNON AND	
		THE HUNCHBACK FROM GIGHA (LP)	60
71	Decca SKL 5081	AMARYLLIS (LP)	220

(see also Human Beast)

BREADWINNER
85	Ninth Wand DOG 1	BEST OF NINTH WAND RECORDS (private cassette with 'glitter' cover)	200
90	Ninth Wand DOG 2	GIVE US A LIGHT, YOU BASTARD (LP, private pressing)	150

(see also Mr Rubbish)

BREAKAWAYS
62	Pye 7N 15471	He's A Rebel/Wishing Star	8
63	Pye 7N 15585	That Boy Of Mine/Here She Comes	10
64	Pye 7N 15618	That's How It Goes/He Doesn't Love Me	10
65	Pye 7N 15973	Danny Boy/Your Kind Of Love	8
67	CBS 2833	Sacred Love/Don't Be A Baby	10
68	MCA MU 1018	Santo Domingo/So In Love Are We	7

(see also Vernons Girls, Burt Bacharach Orchestra, Mike Patto, Ken Cope, Sharades, De Laine Sisters)

BREAKDOWN
77	MCP 001	MEET ME ON THE HIGHWAY (LP, private pressing with insert)	20

BREAKTHRU'
68	Mercury MF 1066	Ice Cream Tree/Julius Caesar	10

BREAKWATER
86	Arista ARIST 12674	Say You Love Me Girl/Work It Out (12", p/s)	12

BREATHERS
80	Diversion DIV 111	Livin' In The Age Age/Count On Counting (p/s)	5

PATRICIA BREDIN
59	Top Rank JAR 257	Till The Right Times Comes/I Live To Love You	5

BREEDERS
93	4AD CADD 3014	LAST SPLASH (LP, with free 7" "Grungé New Year")	12

(see also Pixies, Amps)

JIMMY BREEDLOVE
57	London HLE 8490	Over Somebody Else's Shoulder/That's My Baby	80
57	London HLE 8490	Over Somebody Else's Shoulder/That's My Baby (78)	40
62	Pye International 7N 25121	You're Following Me/Fabulous	10
75	Pye Disco Demand DDS 110	I Can't Help Loving You/I Saw You	5

(see also Cues)

BUDDY BREGMAN & HIS ORCHESTRA
56	HMV 7MC 40	Theme From "Picnic"/Riviera (export issue)	12

JACQUES BREL
65	Fontana TL 5330	JACQUES BREL (LP)	15
66	Fontana TL 5391	JACQUES BREL VOL. 2 (LP)	15
67	Fontana TL 5429	JACQUES BREL '67 (LP)	15
68	Fontana SFJL 967	A L'OLYMPIA (LP)	18

BRELLO CABAL
67	CBS 3214	Margarine Flavoured Pineapple Chunk/Follow That	5

(see also Anita Harris)

BEVERLEY BREMERS
72	Wand WN 18	Get Smart Girl/Don't Say You Don't Remember	7
72	Wand WN 28	We're Free/Colours Of Love	5
72	Wand WN 34	I'll Make You Music/I Made A Man Out Of You Jimmy	5

BRENDA & TABULATIONS
67	London HL 10127	Dry Your Eyes/The Wash	12
67	London HL 10174	When You're Gone/Hey Boy	12
68	Direction 58-3678	Baby You're So Right For Me/To The One I Love	6
69	Action ACT 4541	That's In The Past/I Can't Get Over Her	20
70	London HL 10325	A Child No One Wanted/'Scuse Uz Y'all	5
71	CBS 7279	Right On The Tip of My Tongue/Always And Forever	5
73	Epic EPC 1361	One Girl Too Late/The Magic Of Your Love	6
69	Action ACLP 6003	DRY YOUR EYES (LP)	35

BRENDON
76	Magnet MAG 80	Gimme Some/Changing My Life Won't Do	15

BUDDY BRENNAN QUARTET
60	London HLU 9049	Big River/The Chase	6

ROSE BRENNAN
55	HMV B 10858	Pledging My Love/When I See A Ship (78)	10
55	HMV 7M 299	Ding Dong/Sincerely	10
55	HMV 7M 328	Wake The Town And Tell The People/Ten Little Kisses	7
56	HMV 7M 360	You Are My Love/My Dublin Bay	7
56	HMV 7M 383	Band Of Gold/My Believing Heart	7
56	HMV POP 180	Band Of Gold/My Believing Heart (78)	8
57	HMV POP 302	Without Love (There Is Nothing)/Tra La La	10
58	HMV POP 548	Mean To Me/Treasure Of Your Love	5
58	HMV POP 548	Mean To Me/Treasure Of Your Love (78)	8
59	Top Rank JAR 152	Johnny Let Me Go/My Summer Diary	5
59	Top Rank JAR 152	Johnny Let Me Go/My Summer Diary (78)	12
61	Philips PB 1193	Tall Dark Stranger/This Girl With The Wistful Eyes	5

Walter BRENNAN

WALTER BRENNAN
60	London HLD 9148	Dutchman's Gold/Back To The Farm	7
62	Liberty LIB 55436	Old Rivers/Epic Ride Of John H Glenn	6
62	Liberty LIB 55477	Houdini/The Old Kelly Place	5
63	Liberty LIB 55508	Mama Sang A Song/Who Will Take Gramma	5
64	Liberty LBY 1249	GUNFIGHT AT THE OK CORRAL (LP)	20

BERNIE BRENT'S COMBO
60s	Honey Hit TB 4501	BERNIE BRENT'S COMBO (EP)	7

FRANKIE BRENT
57	Pye N 15102	Rockin' Shoes/I Ain't Never Gonna Do You No Good (78)	22
57	Pye N 15103	Be My Girl/Rang Dang Doo (78)	22

TONY BRENT
53	Columbia SCM 5042	Have You Heard?/Strange Love	22
53	Columbia SCM 5057	Which Way The Wind Blows/My One And Only Heart	20
54	Columbia SCM 5135	I Understand Just How You Feel/The Magic Tango	18
54	Columbia SCM 5146	Nicolette/Tell Me, Tell Me	15
55	Columbia SCM 5160	It's A Woman's World/Give Me The Right To Be Wrong	18
55	Columbia SCM 5170	Open Up Your Heart (with Anne Warren)/Hearts Of Stone (with Coronets)	20
55	Columbia SCM 5188	Mirror, Mirror/Love And Kisses	15
55	Columbia SCM 5200	With Your Love/On A Little Balcony In Spain	15
56	Columbia SCM 5245	Sooner Or Later (Love Comes Along)/Pick Yourself A Star	12
56	Columbia SCM 5272	My Little Angel/What A Heavenly Night For Love	15
56	Columbia DB 3844	Cindy, Oh Cindy/Two Innocent Hearts	15
57	Columbia DB 3884	Amore/If Wishes Were Horses	12
57	Columbia DB 3918	Butterfly/How Lonely Can One Be?	15
57	Columbia DB 3950	Dark Moon/The Game Of Love (A-One And A-Two)	10
57	Columbia DB 3987	Deep Within Me/Why Ask For The Moon	10
57	Columbia DB 4043	Love By The Jukebox Light/We Belong Together	10
57	Columbia DB 4043	Love By The Jukebox Light/We Belong Together (78)	10
58	Columbia DB 4066	Don't Save Your Love (For Me)/The Clouds Will Soon Roll By	6
58	Columbia DB 4128	Chanson D'Amour/Little Serenade	6
58	Columbia DB 4128	Chanson D'Amour/Little Serenade (78)	10
58	Columbia DB 4177	Girl Of My Dreams/Don't Play That Melody	6
58	Columbia DB 4177	Girl Of My Dreams/Don't Play That Melody (78)	8
59	Columbia DB 4238	Call Me/I Surrender, Dear	6
59	Columbia DB 4238	Call Me/I Surrender, Dear (78)	8
59	Columbia DB 4304	Why Should I Be Lonely?/My Little Room	6
59	Columbia DB 4304	Why Should I Be Lonely?/My Little Room (78)	10
59	Columbia DB 4357	Forever, My Darling (Pledging My Love)/Worried Mind	6
60	Columbia DB 4402	Oh, So Wunderbar/Just As Much As Ever	6
60	Columbia DB 4478	Your Cheatin' Heart/Come On In	6
60	Columbia DB 4514	I'm Alone Because I Love You/Just A-Wearyin' For You	6
61	Columbia DB 4610	Until The Real Thing Comes Along/Ten Lonely Weekends	6
61	Columbia DB 4657	Is It Too Late?/You Made Me Care	6
58	Columbia SEG 7824	TONY CALLS THE TUNE (EP)	22
58	Columbia SEG 7869	TIME FOR TONY (EP)	22
59	Columbia SEG 8019	OFF STAGE (EP)	20
59	Columbia SEG 8040	OFF STAGE NO. 2 (EP)	20
58	Columbia 33S 1125	OFF STAGE (10" LP)	40
60	Columbia 33SX 1200	TONY TAKES FIVE (LP, also stereo SCX 3288)	30/35
60s	Columbia 33SX 5001	TONY'S BIG HITS (LP)	30

(see also Coronets)

TONY BRENT & JULIE DAWN
53	Columbia SCM 5029	Ding Dong Boogie/When Are We Gonna Get Married?	25

(see also Julie Dawn)

BRENT FORD & NYLONS
78	Brumbeat	19th Nervous Breakdown/Big Rock Candy Mountain (handmade foldout p/s)	30

BRENTWOOD ROAD ALLSTARS
70	Bamboo BAM 23	Love At First Sight/MAYTALS: Life Could Be A Dream	12
70	Bamboo BAM 25	Soul Shake/Moon Ride	10

GERRY BRERETON
53	Parlophone MSP 6056	From Here To Eternity/If You've Never Been In Love	8
53	Parlophone R 3639	A Fool Such As I/Broken Wings (78)	8
54	Parlophone MSP 6081	The Book/Somewhere Someone (Is Saying A Prayer)	7
55	Columbia SCM 5195	A Million Helping Hands/Fair Sets The Wind For Love	6

(see also Eddie Calvert)

BERNARD BRESSLAW
58	HMV POP 522	Mad Passionate Love/You Need Feet	5
58	HMV POP 522	Mad Passionate Love/You Need Feet (78)	7
59	HMV POP 599	Charlie Brown/The Teenager's Lament	5
59	HMV POP 599	Charlie Brown/The Teenager's Lament (78)	10
59	HMV POP 669	Ivy Will Cling/I Found A Hole	5
59	HMV POP 669	Ivy Will Cling/I Found A Hole (78)	20
59	HMV 7EG 8439	I ONLY ARSKED (EP)	15
68	Davjon DJ 1004	READS FROM HANS CHRISTIAN ANDERSEN (LP)	12

PAUL BRETT('S SAGE)
70	Pye 7N 17974	Three D Mona Lisa/Mediterranean Lazy Heat Wave	6
71	Dawn DNX 2508	Reason For Your Askin'/Everlasting Butterfly/Savannah Ladies/ To Everyman (Freedom) (p/s)	8
71	Dawn DNS 1010	Goodbye Forever/Good Old Fashioned Funky Kind Of Music	5
72	Dawn DNS 1021	Dahlia/Cottage Made For Two	5

PAUL BRETT | **TERESA BREWER**

73	Bradley's BRAD 301	Mr. Custer/Good Times, Hard Times	5
73	Bradley's BRAD 305	Summer Driftin'/Clocks (p/s)	6
70	Pye NSPL 18347	PAUL BRETT SAGE (LP)	18
71	Dawn DNLS 3021	JUBILATION FOUNDRY (LP, gatefold sleeve, as Paul Brett's Sage)	15
72	Dawn DNLS 3032	SCHIZOPHRENIA (LP, foldout sleeve, as Paul Brett's Sage)	22
73	Bradley's BRADL 1001	PAUL BRETT (LP, envelope sleeve with inner)	15
73	Bradley's BRADL 1004	CLOCKS (LP)	15
75	PF private pressing	PHOENIX FUTURE (LP, 500 only)	18
70s	private pressing	MUSIC MANIFOLD (LP, library issue)	22

(see also Elmer Gantry's Velvet Opera, Fire)

STEVE BRETT & MAVERICKS

65	Columbia DB 7470	Wishing/Anything That's Part Of You	55
65	Columbia DB 7581	Sad, Lonely And Blue/Candy	55
65	Columbia DB 7794	Sugar Shack/Chains On My Heart	85

(see also 'N Betweens, Slade)

TONY BREVETT

71	Supreme SUP 224	Don't Get Weary/BREVETT ALLSTARS: Version	10
74	Dip DL 5028	You Don't Love Me/Version	6

(see also Melodians, Glen Adams)

TERESA BREWER

78s

50	London L 562	Copper Canyon/'Way Back Home (with Bobby Wayne)	10
50	London L 563	Ol' Man Mose/I Beeped When I Shoulda Bopped!	8
50	London L 678	Choo'n Gum/Honky Tonkin' (with Johnny Lyttel)	8
50	London L 696	The Picnic Song/Let's Have A Party (B-side with Snooky Lanson, Claire Hogan & Bobby Wayne)	12
50	London L 768	Cincinnati Dancing Pig/Punky Punkin	8
50	London L 794	Molasses Molasses/Grizzly Bear	10
50	London L 873	The Thing/I Guess I'll Have To Dream The Rest	8
51	London L 878	A Penny A Kiss — A Penny A Hug/Hello (with Snooky Lanson)	10
51	London L 967	I've Got The Craziest Feeling/If You Want Some Lovin'	10
51	London L 970	Counterfeit Kisses/Lonesome Gal	10
51	London L 1085	I Wish I Wuz/If You Don't Marry Me	8
51	London L 969	The Picnic Song/Let's Have A Party (with Snooky Lanson)	10
54	Vogue Coral Q 2001	Jilted/Le Grand Tour De L'Amour	8
54	Vogue Coral Q 2011	Skinny Minnie (Fishtail)/I Had Someone Else Before I Had You	10
54	Vogue Coral Q 2029	Au Revoir/Danger Signs	8
55	Vogue Coral Q 72066	Tweedlee Dee/Rock Love	8
57	Vogue Coral Q 72278	Lula Rock-A-Hula/Teardrops In My Heart	8
57	Vogue Coral Q 72292	You Send Me/Born To Love	8
58	Coral Q 72301	Careless Caresses/Mutual Admiration Society	8
58	Coral Q 72320	Saturday Dance/I Think The World Of You	8
58	Coral Q 72336	Pickle Up A Doodle/The Rain Falls On Ev'rybody	8
58	Coral Q 72340	The Hula Hoop Song/So Shy	8
58	Coral Q 72349	I Like Christmas/Jingle Bell Rock	12
58	Coral Q 72354	Satellite/The One Rose (That's Left In My Heart)	10
59	Coral Q 72364	Heavenly Lover/Fair Weather Sweetheart	12
59	Coral Q 72375	Bye Bye Baby Goodbye/Chain Of Friendship	12
59	Coral Q 72383	Bill Bailey, Won't You Please Come Home/Mexicali Rose	12

SINGLES

54	Vogue Coral Q 2011	Skinny Minnie (Fishtail)/I Had Someone Else Before I Had You	25
54	Vogue Coral Q 2029	Au Revoir/Danger Signs	20
55	Vogue Coral Q 72043	Let Me Go, Lover (with Lancers)/Baby, Baby, Baby	22
55	Vogue Coral Q 72065	How Important Can It Be?/What More Is There To Say?	18
55	Vogue Coral Q 72066	Tweedlee Dee/Rock Love	22

Teresa BREWER

55	Vogue Coral Q 72077	Pledging My Love/I Gotta Go Get My Baby	18
55	Vogue Coral Q 72083	You're Telling Our Secret/Time	18
55	Vogue Coral Q 72098	The Banjo's Back In Town/How To Be Very, Very Popular	15
56	Vogue Coral Q 72130	A Good Man Is Hard To Find/It's Siesta Time	15
56	Vogue Coral Q 72139	Rememb'ring/My Sweetie Went Away	15
56	Vogue Coral Q 72146	A Tear Fell/Bo Weevil	15
56	Vogue Coral Q 72172	A Sweet Old-Fashioned Girl/Goodbye, John	10
56	Vogue Coral Q 72199	Keep Your Cotton Pickin' Paddies Offa My Heart/ So Doggone Lonely	8
56	Vogue Coral Q 72213	Crazy With Love/The Moon Is On Fire	10
57	Vogue Coral Q 72224	Nora Malone/When I Leave The World Behind	10
57	Vogue Coral Q 72239	I'm Drowning My Sorrows/How Lonely Can One Be	7
57	Vogue Coral Q 72251	Empty Arms/The Ricky-Tick Song	8
57	Vogue Coral Q 72278	Lula Rock-A-Hula/Teardrops In My Heart	12
57	Vogue Coral Q 72292	You Send Me/Born To Love	10
58	Coral Q 72301	Careless Caresses/Mutual Admiration Society	6
58	Coral Q 72320	Saturday Dance/I Think The World Of You	6
58	Coral Q 72336	Pickle Up A Doodle/The Rain Falls On Ev'rybody	6
58	Coral Q 72340	The Hula Hoop Song/So Shy	6
58	Coral Q 72349	I Like Christmas/Jingle Bell Rock	7
58	Coral Q 72354	Satellite/The One Rose (That's Left In My Heart)	5
59	Coral Q 72364	Heavenly Lover/Fair Weather Sweetheart	6
59	Coral Q 72375	Bye Bye Baby Goodbye/Chain Of Friendship	6
59	Coral Q 72383	Bill Bailey, Won't You Please Come Home/Mexicali Rose	5
60	Coral Q 72386	Peace Of Mind/Venetian Sunset	5
60	Coral Q 72396	How Do You Know It's Love/If There Are Stars In My Eyes	5
60	Coral Q 72405	Anymore/That Piano Man	5
60	Coral Q 72418	Have You Ever Been Lonely/When Do You Love Me	5

EPs

59	Coral FEP 2013	HULA HOOP TIME WITH TERESA BREWER (EP)	18
59	Coral FEP 2036	WHEN YOUR LOVER HAS GONE PART 1 (EP)	18
59	Coral FEP 2037	WHEN YOUR LOVER HAS GONE PART 2 (EP)	18
59	Coral FEP 2038	WHEN YOUR LOVER HAS GONE PART 3 (EP)	18
60	Coral FEP 2047	TERESA BREWER AND THE DIXIELAND BAND PART 1 (EP)	18
60	Coral FEP 2048	TERESA BREWER AND THE DIXIELAND BAND PART 2 (EP)	18
60	Coral FEP 2061	HOW DO YOU KNOW IT'S LOVE (EP)	18

LPs

51	London H-APB 1006	SHOWCASE (10" LP)	35
57	Coral LVA 9020	MUSIC! MUSIC! MUSIC! (LP)	25
58	Coral LVA 9075	FOR TEENAGERS IN LOVE (LP)	25
58	Coral LVA 9091	AT CHRISTMAS TIME (LP)	30
59	Coral LVA 9095	TIME FOR TERESA BREWER (LP)	20
59	Coral LVA 9100	WHEN YOUR LOVER HAS GONE (LP, also stereo SVL 3003)	20/22
59	Coral LVA 9107	TERESA BREWER AND THE DIXIELAND BAND (LP)	20
60	Coral LVA 9129	RIDIN' HIGH (LP)	20
60	Coral LVA 9131	MY GOLDEN FAVOURITES (LP)	20
60	Coral LVA 9138	NAUGHTY NAUGHTY NAUGHTY (LP)	20
61	Coral LVA 9145	SONGS EVERYBODY KNOWS (LP)	20
62	Coral LVA 9152	ALOHA FROM TERESA (LP)	20
62	Coral LVA 9204	DON'T MESS AROUND WITH TESS (LP)	20
67	Wing WL 1157	TERRIFIC TERESA BREWER! (LP)	12

(see also Snooky Lanson)

BREWER & SHIPLEY

70	Kama Sutra 2361 001	TARKIO ROAD (LP)	12
71	Kama Sutra 2361 005	WEEDS (LP)	12
72	Kama Sutra 2319 021	SHAKE OFF THE DEMON (LP)	10

BREWER'S DROOP

72	RCA RCA 2216	Sweet Thing/Heart Of Stone/It Ain't The Meat — It's The Motion (p/s)	5
72	RCA SF 8301	OPENING TIME (LP)	15

BRIAR

82	Happy Face MM 142	Rainbow (To The Skies)/Crying In The Rain (p/s)	12
87	PRT BRIAR 1	Edge Of A Broken Heart/Don't Forget Me When You're On Your Own (p/s)	5
87	PRT BRIARP 1	Edge Of A Broken Heart/La Bamba/Don't Forget Me When You're On Your Own (shaped picture disc)	10
89	Shotgun Charlie SCR 1	Gimme All You Got (some in p/s)	12/5
92	Shotgun Charlie SCR 2	All She Wants (p/s)	6
85	Heavy Metal HMRLP 41	TOO YOUNG (LP, with 7" & poster)	15

BRIDES OF FUNKENSTEIN

78	Atlantic K 50545	FUNK OR WALK (LP)	12

(see also Parliament, Funkadelic)

BOBBY BRIDGER

70	Beacon BEA 149	The World Is Turning On/Why Do I Love You	5
70	Beacon BEA 159	Sugar Shaker/You're In Love	5

(see also Errol Sobers)

DEE DEE BRIDGEWATER

80	Elektra K12 490	Lonely Disco Dancer/One In A Million Guy (12", no p/s)	12

MARC BRIERLEY

68	CBS 3857	Hold On, Hold On, The Garden Sure Looks Good Spread On The Floor/ Autograph Of Time	7
69	CBS 4191	Stay A Little Longer Merry Ann/Flaxen Hair	6
69	CBS 4632	Lady Of The Light/Sunny Weather	6
70	CBS 5266	Be My Brother/If You Took The Bandage Off	5
60s	Transatlantic TRAEP 147	MARC BRIERLEY (EP)	40
67	CBS 63478	WELCOME TO THE CITADEL (LP)	25
69	CBS 63835	HELLO (LP)	20

ANNE BRIGGS
63	Topic TOP 94	THE HAZARDS OF LOVE (EP, with leaflet)	150
71	Topic 12TS 207	ANNE BRIGGS (LP)	80
71	CBS 64612	THE TIME HAS COME (LP)	100

(see also A.L. Lloyd)

BILLY BRIGGS
51	Columbia DB 2938	Chew Tobacco Rag (No. 2)/Alarm Clock Boogie (78)	10

DUGGIE BRIGGS BAND
78	It IT 3	Punk Rockin' Granny/I'm A Flasher (p/s)	5
78	It ITEP 5	THE DUGGIE BRIGGS FLASHES ON IT AGAIN (EP, p/s)	8

LILLIAN BRIGGS
55	Philips PB 522	I Want You To Be My Baby/Give Me A Band And My Baby (78)	15
60	Coral Q 72408	Not A Soul (Blanket Roll Blues)/Smile For The People	6

GREG BRIGHT
69	private pressing	ROOM BY GREG (LP)	200

LEN BRIGHT COMBO
86	Empire LEN 1	Someone Must've Nailed Us Together/Mona (p/s)	6

(see also Wreckless Eric, Milkshakes)

BRIGHTON HORNS
66	Stateside SS 526	Surf Dell'amore/High Midnight	5

BRIGHTWATER
70s	Myrrh MYR 1030	A BAND FOR ALL SEASONS (LP)	15

BRILLIANT
81	Limelight LIME 7001	That's What Good Friends Are For/Push (p/s)	5
83	Rough Trade RTT 105	Colours/Colours (Monster Mix) (12", p/s)	8
85	Food FOOD 5	It's A Man's Man's Man's World/Crash The Car (picture disc)	5

(see also Youth, Killing Joke, J.A.M.s, KLF)

BRILLIANT CORNERS
84	SS20 SS21	She's Got Fever/Black Water (red or pink p/s)	15
84	SS20 SS22	Big Hip/Tangled Up In Blue (p/s)	5
84	SS20 SS23T	My Baby's In Black/Rope In My Hand/Sixteen Years (12", p/s)	7
87	SS20 SS27	Brian Rix/Trudy Is A Squeal (p/s)	4

BRILLS
79	Barclay Towers TB 1	Gang Of One/What Is Done/Burst Of Old Flames (p/s)	4

BRIMSTONE
71	Deram DM 322	Keyhole Jake/The Monkey Song	4
71	Decca D F 13222	If Ever You See Me/Work Out	4

LOS BRINCOS
67	Page One POF 023	Lola/Passport (1st 5,000 in p/s)	45/18
67	Page One POF 031	Nobody Wants You Now/Train	15

BRINDLEY BRAE
70s	Harmony DB 0002	VILLAGE MUSIC (LP, private pressing with insert)	30

(see also Bev Pegg, Away From The Sand)

BRINSLEY SCHWARZ
70	United Artists UP 35118	Shining Brightly/What Do You Suggest	7
71	Liberty LBY 15419	Country Girl/Funk Angel	8
72	United Artists UP 35312	Country Girl/Funk Angel (reissue)	6
73	United Artists UP 35588	Speedo/I Worry	5
74	United Artists UP 35642	I've Cried My Last Tear/Bringdown	5
74	United Artists UP 35700	(What's So Funny 'Bout) Peace, Love And Understanding/ Ever Since You're Gone	6
75	United Artists UP 35768	Everybody/I Like You, I Don't Love You	5
75	United Artists UP 35812	There's A Cloud In My Heart/I Got The Real Thing	5
70	United Artists UAS 29111	BRINSLEY SCHWARZ (LP, gatefold sleeve)	20
70	Liberty LBG 83427	DESPITE IT ALL (LP, gatefold sleeve)	20
72	United Artists UAS 29217	SILVER PISTOL (LP, some with poster)	18/12
72	United Artists UAS 29374	NERVOUS ON THE ROAD (LP)	15
73	United Artists UAS 29489	PLEASE DON'T EVER CHANGE (LP)	20
74	United Artists UAS 29641	THE NEW FAVOURITES OF BRINSLEY SCHWARZ (LP)	12

(see also Kippington Lodge, Hitters, Knees, Limelight, Nick Lowe, Ernie Graham, Rumour, Chilli Willi & Red Hot Peppers, Ducks Deluxe)

JOHNNY BRISTOL
75	MGM 2006 505	Leave My World/All Goodbyes Aren't Gone	4
80	Ariola Hansa AHAD 567	Love No Longer Has A Hold On Me/Till I See You Again (12")	7

BRITISH ELECTRIC FOUNDATION
(see under B.E.F.)

BRITISH LIONS
78	Vertigo 6059 192	One More Chance To Run/Booster (p/s)	5
78	Vertigo 6059 201	International Heroes/Eat The Rich	5
78	Vertigo 9102 019	BRITISH LIONS (LP, with inner sleeve)	12

(see also Mott The Hoople, Medicine Head)

BRITISH WALKERS
65	Pye International 7N 25298	I Found You/Diddley Daddy	25

BRITT (Ekland)
66	Piccadilly 7N 35273	You Really Have Started Something/Leave My Baby Alone	12

(see also Britt Ekland)

MINT VALUE £

MAY BRITT
59   Top Rank JAR 230   Falling In Love Again/Lola-Lola 6

TINA BRITT
65   London HLC 9974   The Real Thing/Teardrops Fell 30

BUDDY BRITTEN & REGENTS
62   Piccadilly 7N 35075   My Pride, My Joy/Long Gone Baby 10
62   Decca F 11435   Don't Spread It Around/The Beat Of My Heart 8
63   Oriole CB 1827   If You Gotta Make A Fool Of Somebody/Money 12
63   Oriole CB 1839   Hey There/I'll Cry No More 10
63   Oriole CB 1859   My Resistance Is Low/When I See You Smile 10
63   Oriole CB 1889   Money/Sorrow Tomorrow 12
64   Oriole CB 1911   I Guess I'm In The Way/Zip-A-Dee-Doo-Dah 12
65   Piccadilly 7N 35241   She's About A Mover/Since You've Gone 10
65   Piccadilly 7N 35257   Right Now/Jailer Bring Me Water 7
(see also Regents)

BOBBIE BRITTON (& KEYNOTES)
54   Decca F 10288   Wanted/Lost (as Bobbie Britton & Keynotes) 6
55   Decca F 10563   Learnin' The Blues/Strange Lady In Town (with Ted Heath Music) 6
56   Decca F 10777   Autumn Concerto/The Fool Of The Year (with Ted Heath Music) 6
59   Embassy WB 367   Red Indian Christmas Carol/The Village Of St. Bernadette (78) 8
(see also Ted Heath, Keynotes, Steve Stannard, Neville Taylor)

CHRIS BRITTON
69   Page One POLS 022   AS I AM (LP) 160
(see also Troggs)

BROADCAST
96   Wurlitzer Jukebox WJ 6   Accidentals/We've Got Time (p/s, some with sticker) 25/20
96   Duophonic DS 45-14   Living Room/Phantom (p/s, 1,500 only) 15
96   Duophonic DS 45-16   THE BOOK LOVERS EP (12", p/s, 2,000) 8
96   Duophonic DS 45-CD 16   THE BOOK LOVERS EP (CD, 2,500 only) 10
96   Warp   WORK AND NON-WORK (LP, promo-only die-cut sleeve) 15

BROADSIDE
71   Lincolnshire Ass. LA 4   THE GIPSY'S WEDDING DAY (10" LP) 50
75   Guildhall GHS 5   SONGS FROM THE STOCKS (LP) 70
75   Guildhall GHS 12   DRIVE THE DARK AWAY (LP) 50

DAVE BROCK
83   Flicknife FLS 024   Social Alliance/Raping Robots In The Street (p/s) 5
83   Flicknife FLS 024P   Social Alliance/Raping Robots In The Street (picture disc) 8
(see also Dr. Technical & Machines, Hawkwind)

NORAH BROCKSTEDT
60   Top Rank JAR 353   Big Boy/Tell Me No Lies 10

BROKEN BONES
85   Fall Out FALL 020   Decapitated/Problem/Liquidated Brains (p/s) 5
85   Fall Out FALL 034P   Seeing Through My Eyes/The Point Of Agony/It's Like (picture disc) 5
85   Fall Out FALL 10034   Seeing Through My Eyes/The Point Of Agony/It's Like/Decapitated/
                       Part 2/Death Is Imminent (10", p/s) 6

BROKEN GLASS
75   Capitol E-ST 11510   BROKEN GLASS (LP) 12

JOHN BROMLEY
68   Polydor 56224   What A Woman Does/My My 5
68   Polydor 56287   And The Feeling Goes/Sweet Little Princess 5
69   Polydor 56305   Melody Fayre/Sugar Love 5
69   Polydor 56340   Hold Me Woman/Weather Man 5
69   Atlantic 584 289   Kick A Tin Can/Wonderland Avenue U.S.A. 6
69   Polydor 583 048   SING (LP) 15
(see also Fleur De Lys, Three People)

BRONCO
70   Island ILPS 9124   COUNTRY HOME (LP, gatefold sleeve, pink or 'pink rim palm tree' label) 35/12
71   Island ILPS 9161   ACE OF SUNLIGHT (LP, gatefold sleeve, 'pink rim palm tree' label) 15
73   Polydor 2383 215   SMOKIN' MIXTURE (LP) 12
(see also Alan Bown Set)

BRONSKI BEAT
85   Forbidden Fruit BITET 4   Love To Love You Baby/I Feel Love/Johnny Remember Me Vocal (Cake Mix)/
                       Love To Love You Baby/I Feel Love/Johnny Remember Me Vocal Instrumental
                       (Fruit Mix) (10", with Marc Almond, red or green p/s) 10
(see also Communards, Marc Almond)

BRONX CHEER
70   Parlophone R 5865   Drive My Car/Foxtrot 6
71   Dawn DNX 2512   Barrelhouse Player/Surprising Find/Whether Or Not/Party For One (p/s) 7
72   Dawn DNS 1019   Hold On To Me/Late Date 5
72   Dawn DNLS 3004   GREATEST HITS VOLUME 3 (LP, gatefold sleeve) 12

BRONZ
84   Bronze BRO 178   Send Down An Angel/Tiger (p/s) 5
84   Bronze BROX 178   Send Down An Angel/Tiger/Stranded (12", p/s) 8
80s   Lyntone LYN 14383   Taken By Storm (flexidisc) 5

MICHAEL BROOK
92   4AD TAD 2011   LIVE AT THE AQUARIUM (CD, digipak) 15

PATTI BROOK (& DIAMONDS)

60	Pye 7N 15300	Since You've Been Gone/That's The Way It's Gonna Be (as Patti Brook & Diamonds)	7
61	Pye 7N 15339	When The Red Red Robin/Look What You've Done To Me	6
62	Pye 7N 15422	I Love You, I Need You/Unloved, Unwanted	15

TONY BROOK & BREAKERS

64	Columbia DB 7279	Meanie Genie/Ooh Poo Pah Doo (some in p/s)	100/55
65	Columbia DB 7444	Love Dances On/I Won't Hurt You	10

BROOK BROTHERS

60	Top Rank JAR 349	Green Fields/How Will It End?	7
60	Top Rank JAR 409	Please Help Me, I'm Falling/When Will I Be Loved	7
60	Pye 7N 15298	Say The Word/Everything But Love	5
61	Pye 7N 15333	Warpaint/Sometimes	6
61	Pye 7N 15352	Little Bitty Heart/Tell Her	5
61	Pye 7N 15369	Ain't Gonna Wash For A Week/One Last Kiss	6
61	Pye 7N 15387	Married/I Love Girls	5
62	Pye 7N 15409	He's Old Enough To Know Better/Win Or Lose	5
62	Pye 7N 15415	Too Scared/Tell Tale	5
62	Pye 7N 15441	Just Another Fool/Double Trouble	8
62	Pye 7N 15453	Welcome Home Baby/So Long	5
62	Pye 7N 15463	I Can't Make Up My Mind/Town Girl	5
63	Pye 7N 15498	Trouble Is My Middle Name/Let The Good Times Roll	5
63	Pye 7N 15527	I'm Not Jimmy/Side By Side (with RBQ)	5
63	Pye 7N 15570	Crosswords/Whistle To The Wind	5
61	Pye NEP 24140	BROOK BROTHERS HIT PARADE (EP)	25
61	Pye NEP 24148	BROOK BROTHERS HIT PARADE VOLUME 2 (EP)	25
62	Pye NEP 24155	BROOK BROTHERS (EP)	22
61	Pye NPL 18067	BROOK BROTHERS (LP)	45

(see also Brooks)

BROOKLYN

80	Rondelet ROUND 3	I Wanna Be A Detective (p/s)	12
81	Rondelet ROUND 6	Hollywood/Late Again (p/s)	15
80	Rondelet ABOUT 3	YOU NEVER KNOW WHAT YOU'LL FIND (LP)	18

BROOKLYN BRIDGE

68	Pye International 7N 25473	From My Window I Can See/Little Red Boat By The River	5
69	Buddah 201 029	The Worst That Could Happen/Your Kite, My Kite	5
70	Buddah 2011 010	Free As The Wind/He's Not A Happy Man	5
70	Buddah 2011 034	Down By The River/Look Again	5

(see also Johnny Maestro)

BROOKS

64	Decca F 11868	Once In A While/Poor Poor Man	6

(see also Brook Brothers)

BABA BROOKS

63	Island WI 078	5 O'Clock Whistle/African Blood (by Blues Masters)	20
63	Island WI 096	Bank To Bank (Parts 1 & 2)	20
63	Island WI 127	Three Blind Mice/BILLY & BOBBY: We Ain't Got Nothing	20
63	R&B JB 125	Water Melon Man/STRANGER COLE: Things Come To Those Who Wait	15
64	Black Swan WI 137	Portrait Of My Love/STRANGER COLE: Goodbye Peggy	18
64	Black Swan WI 412	Jelly Beans/ERIC MORRIS: Sampson	20
64	Black Swan WI 414	Key To The City/ERIC MORRIS: Solomon Grundie	20
64	Black Swan WI 434	Spider/Melody Jamboree	20
64	Black Swan WI 438	Cork Foot/HERSANG COMBO: B.B.C. Channel 2	20
65	Black Swan WI 442	Musical Workshop/DUKE WHITE: Be Wise	20
65	Black Swan WI 444	Bus Strike/DUKE WHITE: Sow Good Seeds	20
65	Black Swan WI 451	Ethiopia/ARCHIBALD TROTT: Promised Land	20
65	Black Swan WI 466	Baby Elephant Walk/DON DRUMMOND: Don's Special	20
65	Ska Beat JB 220	One Eyed Giant (with His Band)/DYNAMITES: Walk Out On Me	15
65	Island WI 229	Guns Fever/DOTTY & BONNIE: Don't Do It	20
65	Island WI 233	Independent Ska/STRANGER & CLAUDETTE: Seven Days	20
65	Island WI 235	Duck Soup/ZODIACS: Renegade	20
65	Island WI 239	Vitamin A/ALTON ELLIS: Dance Crasher	20
65	Island WI 241	Teenage Ska/ALTON ELLIS: You Are Not To Blame	15
65	Rio R 061	Skank J. Sheck (& Band)/SHENLEY & HIACYNTH: Set Me Free	15
66	Doctor Bird DB 1042	The Clock (& Band)/LYN TAITT & COMETS & SILVERTONES: Raindrops	15
66	Doctor Bird DB 1046	Jam Session (with His Band)/CONQUERORS: What A Agony	18
67	Ska Beat JB 268	One Eyed Giant (with His Band)/DYNAMITES: Walk Out On Me (reissue)	15

(see also Blues Masters, Eric Brooks, Stranger & Patsy, Riots, Joey Smith, Saints, Richard Brothers, Derrick Morgan, Lord Tanamo, Lord Brisco, Hippy Boys, Roy Panton, Higgs & Wilson, Vinley Gayle, Joe White, Stranger & Patsy)

CHUCK BROOKS

69	Soul City SC 116	Black Sheep/I've Got To Get Myself Together	10

D. BROOKS

70	Big BG 304	Oh Me Oh My (actually "Every Time" by Hi-Tals)/ANSEL COLLINS: Staccato (actually "Every Time Version" by Rupie Edwards Allstars)	7

DALE BROOKS

65	King KG 1025	Army Green/Reminds Me Of You	8
66	Stateside SS 553	I Wanna Be Your Girl/Like Other Girls Do	10

DONNIE BROOKS

60	London HLN 9168	Mission Bell/Do It For Me	8
60	London HLN 9168	Mission Bell/Do It For Me (78)	90
60	London HLN 9253	Doll House/Round Robin	8
61	London HLN 9361	That's Why/Memphis	7
62	London HLN 9572	Oh, You Beautiful Doll/Just A Bystander	7
61	London HA-N 2391	THE HAPPIEST DONNIE BROOKS (LP)	35

ELKIE BROOKS

64	Decca F 11928	Something's Got A Hold On Me/Hello Stranger	12
64	Decca F 11983	Nothing Left To Do But Cry/Strange Though It Seems	18
65	Decca F 12061	The Way You Do The Things You Do/Blue Tonight	15
65	HMV POP 1431	He's Gotta Love Me/When You Appear	22
65	HMV POP 1480	All My Life/Can't Stop Thinking Of You	12
66	HMV POP 1512	Baby Let Me Love You/Stop The Music	12
69	NEMS 56-4136	Come September/If You Should Go	6
74	Island WIP 6187	Rescue Me/Sweet Nuthin's	5
74	Chrysalis CHS 2069	Sacrifice/ALICE COOPER: I'm Flash	
		(p/s, unissued, promo only)	35

(see also Dada, Vinegar Joe, Steve York's Camelo Pardalis, Elki & Owen)

HADDA BROOKS

50	London L 684	I Hadn't Anyone 'Till You/Hadda's Boogie (78)	12
51	London L 865	Man Plays A Horn/All I Need is You (78)	10
51	London L 859	Vanity/It Hadda B Brooks (78)	10
51	London L 796	Maggie's Boogie/A Rendezvous With The Blues (78)	10

MEL BROOKS

78	Asylum K 13115	High Anxiety/Springtime For Hitler	5
81	Luggage LUG 2	It's Good To Be The King Rap/It's Good To Be The King Rap (Version) (p/s)	5
83	Island ISP 158	To Be Or Not To Be (Hitler Rap)/(Version)	
		(picture disc, 5000 only)	8

NORMAN BROOKS & G- BOYS

54	London L 1166	Hello Sunshine/You're My Baby	25
54	London L 1202	Somebody Wonderful/You Shouldn't Have Kissed Me The First Time	25
54	London L 1228	A Sky-Blue Shirt And A Rainbow Tie/This Waltz With You	30
54	London HL 8015	I'm Kinda Crazy/I'd Like To Be In Your Shoes, Baby	25
54	London HL 8041	I Can't Give You Anything But Love (solo)/GO-BOYS: Johnny's Tune	25
54	London HL 8041	I Can't Give You Anything But Love (solo)/GO-BOYS: Johnny's Tune (78)	10
54	London HL 8051	Candy Moon/My 3-D Sweetie	25
54	London HL 8051	Candy Moon/My 3-D Sweetie (78)	10
55	London HL 8115	Back In Circulation/Lou Lou Louisiana	25
55	London HL 8115	Back In Circulation/Lou Lou Louisiana (78)	10
54	London RE-P 1004	PRESENTING NORMAN BROOKS VOLUME 1 (EP)	40
55	London RE-P 1021	BABY MINE (EP)	40

PAM BROOKS

70	Big BG 307	Oh Me Oh My/ANSELL COLLINS: Staccato	15

BROOKS & JERRY

68	Direction 58-3267	I Got What It Takes (Parts 1 & 2)	5

MARK BROOM

92	GPR GENP(X) 4	SEAGULLS EP (12", custom sleeve)	7
92	GPR GENP(X) 6	GOLD CHEESE EP (12", custom sleeve)	7

BIG BILL BROONZY/CHICAGO BILL

51	Vogue V 2068	Back Water Blues/Lonesome Road Blues (78)	15
51	Vogue V 2073	In The Evenin'/Low Land Blues (78)	15
51	Vogue V 2074	John Henry/Blues In 1890 (78)	15
51	Vogue V 2075	Big Bill Blues/Hey Hey Baby (78)	15
51	Vogue V 2076	House Rent Stomp/The Moppin' Blues (78)	15
51	Vogue V 2077	Black, Brown And White/Feelin' Low Down (78)	15
52	Vogue V 2078	Make My Getaway/What I Used To Do (78)	15
52	Melodisc 1191	Keep Your Hands Off Her/Stump Blues	
		(78, as Chicago Bill)	15
52	Melodisc 1203	Five Foot Seven/Plough Hand Blues	
		(78, as Chicago Bill)	15
50s	private pressing	Keep Your Hand On Your Heart/T For Texas (78)	18
56	Pye Jazz NJ 2012	When Do I Get To Be Called A Man/Mindin' My Own Business (78)	15
57	Pye Jazz NJ 2016	Southbound Train/It Feels So Good (78)	15
58	Vogue V 2351	Guitar Shuffle/When Did You Leave Heaven	18
61	Storyville A 44053	Midnight Special/Black Brown And White	8
55	Vogue EPV 1024	HEY BUD BLUES (EP)	15
56	Vogue EPV 1074	SINGS THE BLUES (EP)	18
56	Vogue EPV 1107	GUITAR SHUFFLE (EP)	18
56	Pye Jazz NJE 1005	MISSISSIPPI BLUES VOLUME 1 (EP)	10
56	Pye Jazz NJE 1014	MISSISSIPPI BLUES VOLUME 2 (EP)	10
57	Pye Jazz NJE 1047	SOUTHERN SAGA (EP)	10
57	Columbia SEG 7674	BIG BILL BROONZY SINGS THE BLUES (EP)	15
57	Tempo EXA 61	BILL BAILEY WON'T YOU PLEASE COME HOME (EP)	10
58	Columbia SEG 7790	BIG BILL BROONZY SINGS THE BLUES NO. 2 (EP)	15
50s	Melodisc EPM7 65	KEEP YOUR HANDS OFF (EP)	10
60	Mercury ZEP 10065	WALKIN' DOWN A LONESOME ROAD (EP)	10
60	Mercury ZEP 10093	HOLLERIN' BLUES (EP)	10
62	Storyville SEP 383	BLUES ANTHOLOGY VOLUME 3 (EP)	10
64	Mercury 10003 MCE	BLUES-GOSPEL-SPIRITUAL (EP)	12
57	Vogue LAE 12009	BIG BILL BLUES (LP)	30
57	Philips BBL 7113	BIG BILL BROONZY (LP)	35
58	Vogue LAE 12063	THE BLUES (LP)	30
58	Pye Nixa Jazz NJL 16	TRIBUTE TO BIG BILL (LP)	25
59	Tempo TAP 23	AN EVENING WITH BIG BILL BROONZY (LP)	30
61	HMV CLP 1544	LAST SESSION PART 1 (LP)	18
62	HMV CLP 1551	LAST SESSION PART 2 (LP)	18
62	HMV CLP 1562	LAST SESSION PART 3 (LP)	18
65	Storyville SLP 143	AN EVENING WITH BROONZY (LP)	12

MINT VALUE £

65	Fontana 688 206ZL	TROUBLE IN MIND (LP)	20
66	Mercury 20044 MCL	REMEMBERING BROONZY — THE GREATEST MINSTREL OF THE AUTHENTIC BLUES (LP)	12
66	Storyville SLP 188	BLUES IN EUROPE (LP)	12
67	Storyville 670 154	PORTRAITS IN BLUES VOLUME 2 (LP)	18
69	CBS Realm 52648	BIG BILL'S BLUES (LP)	10
60s	Xtra XTRA 1093	SINGS COUNTRY BLUES (LP)	10
78	Spotlite SPJ 900	TROUBLE IN MIND (LP, reissue)	10

(see also Chicago Bill)

BIG BILL BROONZY & PETE SEEGER

| 64 | Xtra XTRA 1006 | IN CONCERT (LP) | 22 |
| 66 | Verve Folkways VLP 5006 | IN CONCERT (LP, reissue, also stereo SVLP 506) | 12/15 |

(see also Pete Seeger)

BIG BILL BROONZY/SONNY BOY WILLIAMSON [I]

| 65 | RCA Victor RD 7685 | BIG BILL AND SONNY BOY (LP) | 50 |

(see also Sonny Boy Williamson [I])

BIG BILL BROONZY, SONNY TERRY & BROWNIE McGHEE

| 64 | Xtra XTRA 1004 | BIG BILL BROONZY/SONNY TERRY/BROWNIE McGHEE (LP) | 25 |

(see also Sonny Terry & Brownie McGhee, Washboard Sam)

BROTH

| 71 | Mercury 6338 032 | BROTH (LP) | 20 |

BROTHER BARON

| 70s | Fab FAB 281 | Your Love/Your Love Version | 5 |

BROTHER BUNG

| 68 | Avenue BEV 1054 | BLUES CRUSADE (EP) | 22 |

(see also Bob Pearce, Fresh)

BROTHER DAN ALLSTARS

68	Trojan TR 601	Donkey Returns/Tribute To Sir K.B.	10
68	Trojan TR 602	Eastern Organ/JIVERS: Our Love Will Last	10
68	Trojan TR 603	Hold Pon Them/OWEN GRAY: Answer Me	10
68	Trojan TR 607	Read Up/Gallop	10
68	Trojan TR 608	Another Saturday Night/Bee's Knees	10
68	Trojan TBL 101	LET'S CATCH THE BEAT (LP)	35
69	Trojan TRL 1	FOLLOW THAT DONKEY (LP)	20

(see also Audrey, Pooch Jackson)

BROTHERHOOD

| 69 | Philips BF 1766 | Paper Man/Give It To Me Now | 8 |

BROTHERHOOD OF BREATH

| 74 | Ogun OG 100 | LIVE AT WILLISAU (LP, with Chris McGregor) | 15 |

(see also Chris McGregor's Brotherhood Of Breath, Mark Charig)

BROTHERHOOD OF MAN

69	Deram DM 276	Love One Another/A Little Bit Of Heaven	6
70	Deram DM 317	This Boy/You Can Depend On Me	5
71	Deram DM 327	Reach Out Your Hand/Better Tomorrow	5
71	Deram DM 335	You And I/Sing In The Sunshine	5
71	Deram DM 341	California Sunday Morning/Do Your Thing	5
72	Deram DM 361	Say A Prayer/Follow Me	5
72	Deram DM 366	Rock Me Baby/Hang On	5
73	Deram DM 385	Happy Ever After/We Can Make It	5
74	Dawn DNS 1055	When Love Catches Up With You/How Can You Love (p/s)	6
76	Pye 7N 45569	Save Your Kisses For Me/Let's Love Together (p/s)	5
70	Deram SML 1066	UNITED WE STAND (LP)	22
72	Deram SML 1089	BROTHERHOOD OF MAN (LP)	15
75	Dawn DNLS 3063	GOOD THINGS HAPPENING (LP)	12

(see also Sue & Sunny, Sue & Sunshine, Stockingtops, First Class)

BROTHERLY LOVE

| 67 | CBS 2978 | Ocean Of Tears/Mister Average Man | 5 |
| 73 | CBS 1403 | I Love Everything About You/Tip Of My Tongue | 5 |

(see also Car[r]ols)

BROTHERS

| 67 | London HLU 10158 | Love Story/The Girl's Alright | 6 |

BROTHERS

| 75 | People PEO 118 | In The Pocket/Everybody Loves A Winner | 5 |
| 75 | People PLEO 25 | DISCO SOUL (LP) | 15 |

BROTHERS & SISTERS (U.K.)

| 68 | private pressing | ARE WATCHING YOU (LP) | 125 |

BROTHERS & SISTERS (U.S.)

| 69 | CBS 4583 | Mighty Quinn/Chimes Of Freedom | 4 |
| 69 | CBS 63746 | DYLAN'S GOSPEL (LP) | 10 |

BROTHERS FOR "BOB"

| 93 | SUBG SUBG 23 | "Bob" Will Stop The Aliens From Killing Me/Yog Sothot Party Mix (p/s) | 8 |

BROTHERS FOUR

60	Philips PB 1009	Greenfields/East Virginia	5
60	Philips PB 1072	Beautiful Brown Eyes/The Green Leaves Of Summer	5
64	CBS BPG 62282	SIGNS OF OUR TIMES (LP)	12
66	CBS BPG 62313	GREATEST HITS (LP)	12

MINT VALUE £

BROTHERS GRIMM
65	Decca F 12224	Lost Love/Make It Or Break It	7
66	Ember EMB 222	A Man Needs Love/Looky Looky	55

(see also Barry & Tony)

BROTHERS KANE
66	Decca F 12448	Walking In The Sand/Won't You Stay Long	12

(see also Sarstedt Brothers, Peter Lincoln, Peter Sarstedt, Clive Sands, Wes Sands, Eden Kane)

BROTHERS TWO
68	Action ACT 4513	Here I Am, In Love Again/I'm Tired Of You Baby	15

BROTHERS WILLIAM
65	Parlophone R 5293	Linda Jane Blues/Honey Love	5

AYSHEA BROUGH
71	RCA RCA 2105	Master Jack/Both Sides Now	4

(see also Ayshea)

PETER BROUGH & ARCHIE ANDREWS
53	HMV BD 1306	The Little Fir Tree/I Saw Mommy Kissing Santa Claus (78, picture label)	8

EDGAR BROUGHTON BAND
69	Harvest HAR 5001	Evil/Death Of An Electric Citizen	7
70	Harvest HAR 5015	Out Demons Out/Momma's Reward	5
70	Harvest HAR 5021	Up Yours!/Officer Dan.	6
70	Harvest HAR 5032	Apache Drop Out/Freedom	5
71	Harvest HAR 5040	Hotel Room/Call Me A Liar	6
72	Harvest HAR 5049	Gone Blue/Someone/Mr. Crosby	6
69	Harvest SHVL 757	WASA WASA (LP, gatefold sleeve)	22
70	Harvest SHVL 772	SING BROTHER SING (LP, gatefold sleeve, with lyric insert)	22
71	Harvest SHVL 791	THE EDGAR BROUGHTON BAND (LP, gatefold sleeve)	18
72	Harvest SHTC 252	IN SIDE OUT (LP, gatefold sleeve with lyric sheet)	22
73	Harvest SHVL 810	OORA (LP, wraparound card sleeve in clear artwork plastic bag)	20
75	NEMS NEL 6006	BANDAGES (LP)	12

AL BROWN (Jamaica)
71	Banana BA 360	No Soul Today/RUFFIANS: Where Did I Go Wrong (B-side actually "Bang Shang Alang" by Peter Austin & Hortense Ellis)	10
71	Fab FAB 186	Ain't Got No Soul/TEARDROPS: I Got A Feeling	7

AL BROWN'S TUNETOPPERS (U.S.)
60	Top Rank JAR 374	The Madison/Mo' Madison	5

(CRAZY WORLD OF) ARTHUR BROWN
65	Lyntone LYN 770/1	You Don't Know (as Arthur Brown & Diamonds)/DIAMONDS: You'll Be Mine (Reading University Rag Week flexidisc)	60
67	Track 604 008	Devil's Grip/Give Him A Flower	10
68	Track 604 022	Fire!/Rest Cure (push-out or large centre)	6/5
68	Track 604 026	Nightmare/What's Happening (some copies list "Music Man" as B-side)	6
74	Gull GULS 4	Gypsies/Dance	5
75	Gull GULS 13	We Gotta Get Out Of This Place/Here I Am	5
77	Gull SIXPACK 4	SIX-PACK/SIX TRACK (EP, picture disc, die-cut sleeve with stand, 5,000 only)	6
68	Track 612 005/613 005	THE CRAZY WORLD OF ARTHUR BROWN (LP, mono/stereo)	25/20
70	Backtrack 2407 012	THE CRAZY WORLD OF ARTHUR BROWN (LP, reissue, different sleeve)	12
74	Gull GULP 1008	DANCE (LP, with insert)	12
77	Gull GUD 2003/4	THE LOST EARS (2-LP, gatefold sleeve, as Arthur Brown's Kingdom Come)	25
78	Gull GULP 1023	CHISHOLM IN MY BOSOM (LP)	12

(see also Kingdom Come, Nick Greenwood, Atomic Rooster, Crane/Farlowe)

BEN BROWN
67	Polydor 56198	Ask The Lonely/Sidewinder	20

BOOTS BROWN & HIS BLOCKBUSTERS
58	RCA RCA 1078	Cerveza/Juicy	8
58	RCA RCA 1078	Cerveza/Juicy (78)	12
59	RCA RCA 1102	Jim Twangy/Trollin'	7
59	RCA RCA 1102	Jim Twangy/Trollin' (78)	20

(see also Shorty Rogers)

BUNNY BROWN
72	Songbird SB 1073	Fat Boy/Fat Boy — Version	8

(see also Noel Brown, Winston Scotland)

BUSTER BROWN
60	Melodisc 1559	Fannie Mae/Lost In A Dream	50
65	Sue WI 368	Fannie Mae/Lost In A Dream (reissue)	18
67	Island WI 3031	My Blue Heaven/Two Women	20
69	Blue Horizon 57-3147	Sugar Babe/I'm Going, But I'll Be Back	15
60s	XX MIN 713	B. AND BUSTER BROWN (EP, with B. Brown)	15

BUSTY BROWN
68	Doctor Bird DB 1158	Here Comes The Night/Don't Look Back	15
69	Upsetter US 304	What A Price/How Can I Forget?	8
69	Upsetter US 308	To Love Somebody/BLEECHERS: Farmer's In The Den	8
69	Punch PH 10	Broken Heart/Tribute To A King	6
70	Punch PH 38	Greatest Love/I Love You Madly	5
70	Escort ES 822	Fight For Your Right/MEDETATORS: Soul Fight Busty Top A Pop (B-side actually "Soul Fight" by Busty Brown)	5
70	Escort ES 845	Man Short (with Gaytones)/DAVE BARKER: She Want It	5
70	Gas GAS 154	I Love You Madly/Greatest Love	5
70	High Note HS 048	Man Short (with Gaytones)/GAYTONES: Another Version	5
71	Punch PH 72	You Inspire Me/UPSETTERS: Version	5
71	Pama Supreme PS 356	Throw Away Your Gun/TWINKLE BROTHERS: Sad Song	12

(see also Llans Thelwell, John Holt, David Isaacs)

CHARLES BROWN (BAND)

56	Vogue V 9061	I'll Always Be In Love With You/Soothe Me	400
56	Vogue V 9061	I'll Always Be In Love With You/Soothe Me (78)	50
57	Vogue V 9065	Confidential/Trouble Blues	400
57	Vogue V 9065	Confidential/Trouble Blues (78)	50
61	Parlophone R 4848	It's Christmas All Year Round/Christmas Question	30

(see also Brown Brothers)

CLARENCE 'GATEMOUTH' BROWN

65	Vocalion VE 170161	CLARENCE 'GATEMOUTH' BROWN (EP)	60
72	Python PLP 26	CLARENCE 'GATEMOUTH' BROWN VOL. 1: 1948-1953 (LP)	30
72	Python PLP 27	CLARENCE 'GATEMOUTH' BROWN VOL. 2: 1956-1965 (LP)	30

CLIFFORD BROWN (& GROUP)

56	Emarcy ERE 1501	SWEET CLIFFORD (EP, as Clifford Brown & Group)	10
58	Emarcy ERE 1565	STUDY IN BROWN VOL. 1 (EP, as Clifford Brown & Group)	8
58	Emarcy ERE 1566	STUDY IN BROWN VOL. 2 (EP, as Clifford Brown & Group)	8
58	Emarcy ERE 1572	CLIFFORD BROWN AND MAX ROACH (EP)	8
54	Esquire EP 3	CLIFFORD BROWN & ART FARMER WITH THE SWEDISH ALLSTARS (EP)	8
54	Esquire EP 4	AND ART FARMER WITH THE SWEDISH ALLSTARS VOL. 2 (EP)	8
55	Esquire EP 71	CLIFFORD BROWN WITH TADD DAMERON'S BAND (EP)	8
55	Vogue EPV 1027	GIGI GRYCE — CLIFFORD BROWN ORCHESTRA (EP)	8
55	Vogue EPV 1041	CONCEPTION (EP)	8
56	Vogue EPV 1119	CLIFFORD BROWN ENSEMBLE (EP)	8
54	Vogue LDE 042	CLIFFORD "BROWNIE" BROWN QUARTET (10" LP)	18
55	Vogue LDE 121	THE CLIFFORD BROWN SEXTET (10" LP)	18
58	Emarcy EJL 1278	STUDY IN BROWN (LP)	15

(see also Art Farmer, Tadd Dameron, Sonny Rollins, Max Roach)

DENNIS BROWN

70	Bamboo BAM 56	Love Grows/SOUND DIMENSION: Less Problem	10
70	Banana BA 309	No Man Is An Island/SOUL SISTERS: Another Night	10
71	Banana BA 336	Never Fall In Love/Make It With You	10
71	Ocean OC 001	Little Green Apples/SOUND DIMENSION: Version	8
72	Duke DU 139	What About The Half/What About The Half Version	12
72	Explosion EX 2068	Black Magic Woman/PHILL PRATT ALL STARS: Black Magic Woman Pt 2	12
72	Pressure Beat PR 5513	Money In My Pocket/JOE GIBBS ALLSTARS: Money Love	6
72	Randy's RAN 526	Cheater/TOMMY McCOOK & IMPACT ALLSTARS: Harvest In The East	8
72	Randy's RAN 528	Meet Me On The Corner (actually unknown instrumental)/ IMPACT ALLSTARS: Version	6
72	Songbird SB 1074	Silhouettes/CRYSTALITES: Version	7
73	Ashanti ASH 402	It's Too Late/Song My Mother Used To Sing	8
73	Jackpot JP 813	He Can't Spell/CRYSTALITES: Acid Version	8
73	Smash SMA 2327	Concentration/Version	6
73	Trojan TRLS 57	SUPER REGGAE & SOUL HITS (LP)	15
75	Trojan TRLS 107	JUST DENNIS (LP)	12

(see also Big Youth & Dennis Brown, Hugh Roy, Big Youth, Sound Dimension)

DUSTY BROWN

61	Starlite ST45 058	Please Don't Go/Well You Know	25

ED BROWN

64	London HA 8149	THE JOHN FITZGERALD KENNEDY MEMORIAL ALBUM (LP, unissued)

ERROL BROWN & CHOSEN FEW

72	Songbird SB 1082	People Make The World Go Round/People Make The World Go Round (Version)	5

FAITH BROWN

70	CBS 4728	Lock Me In/The Game Of Love	5
71	Penny Farthing PEN 766	Any Way That You Want Me/City Wine	5
72	Regal Zonophone RZ 3063	Take Me With You/If We Only Have Love	5

(see also Carrolls)

FAY BROWN

55	Columbia SCM 5185	Unchained Melody/I Was Wrong	12

FRIDAY BROWN(E)

66	Parlophone R 5396	Getting Nowhere/And (To Me He Meant Everything) (as Friday Browne)	8
66	Fontana TF 736	32nd Love Affair/Born A Woman	7
67	Fontana TF 851	Ask Any Woman/Outdoor Seminar	7
69	Fontana TF 996	Stand By Your Man/I Want To Rain	5
72	Philips 6006 239	Shake A Hand/Everything's Alright	5
73	Philips 6006 324	Groovy Kind Of Love/Salford	5
71	Philips 6308 074	FRIDAY BROWN (LP)	12

(see also Marianne & Mike, High Society, Manchester Mob, Graham Gouldman)

FUNKY BROWN

72	Sioux SI 018	African (Indian Reservation)/JUMBO STERLING: Elizabethan Reggae	5

GABRIEL BROWN

77	Policy Wheel PW 4592	GABRIEL BROWN AND HIS GUITAR (LP, withdrawn)	15

GEORGIA BROWN

55	Decca F 10489	My Crazy L'il Mixed Up Heart/Before We Know It	7
55	Decca F 10551	I Love To Dance With You/That's All I Need	7
55	Decca F 10616	I Went To The Village/Wrong Again	7
72	Fly BUG 18	Turn Out The Light/I Scare Myself (p/s)	5
63	Decca SKL 4586	SINGS GERSHWIN (LP)	12

GERRY BROWN'S JAZZMEN

61	Fontana TFL 5165	IT'S TRAD TIME! (LP)	20

MINT VALUE £

GLEN BROWN
68	Blue Cat BS 131	Way Of Life (with Joe White & Trevor)/CARL BRYAN & LYN TAITT: I'm So Proud . 20
70	Summit SUM 8502	Collie And Wine/BEVERLEY'S ALLSTARS: Version 8
70	Songbird SB 1021	Love I/CRYSTALITES: Heavy Load 8
72	Songbird SB 1081	Smokey Eyes (with Crystalites)/Smokey Eyes (Version) 15
73	Downtown DT 507	Two Wedding Skank/BARRY SIMPSON: Sugar Down Deh 12

GLENMORE BROWN & HOPETON LEWIS
| 68 | Fab FAB 42 | Girl You're Cold/Soul Man . . . . 12 |

(see also Hopeton Lewis & Glenmore Brown)

HENRY BROWN
50s	Signature 909	Henry Brown Blues/Twenty-First Street Blues (78). 10
50s	Jazz Collector L 15	Henry Brown Blues/Twenty-First Street Blues (78, reissue). 5
50s	Jazz Collector L 31	Blues Stomp/Blind Boy Blues (78) 8
50s	Jazz Collector L 55	It Hurts So Good/Screenin' The Blues (78) 8
50s	Jazz Collector L 70	Deep Morgan Blues/Eastern Chimes Blues (78) 8
61	'77' LA 12-5	HENRY BROWN BLUES (LP) 25

HUX BROWN & SCOTTY
| 71 | High Note HS 056 | Unbelievable Sounds/GAYTONES: Unbelievable Sounds Version . . . . 15 |

HYLO BROWN (& TIMBERLINERS)
59	Capitol CL 15075	You Can't Relive The Past/Thunder Clouds Of Love. 5
60	Capitol CL 15139	I've Waited As Long As I Can/Just Any Old Love 5
63	London HAB/SHB 8094	BLUEGRASS GOES TO COLLEGE (LP). 12

IRVING BROWN
70	Bamboo BAM 36	Today/SOUND DIMENSION: Young Gifted And Black Version 10
70	Bamboo BAM 58	I'm Still Around/Run Come 10
70	Bamboo BAM 61	Let's Make It Up (actually by Larry Marshall)/BURNING SPEAR: Free. 15
71	Bamboo Now BN 1003	Now I'm Alone/Funky Night. 6

(see also Larry Marshall)

JACKIE BROWN
| 72 | High Note HS 057 | One Night/GAYTONES: One Night Version . . . . 6 |
| 72 | High Note HS 060 | Last Dance/GAYTONES: Last Dance Version . . . . 6 |

JAMES BROWN (& FAMOUS FLAMES)
SINGLES
60	Parlophone R 4667	Think/You've Got The Power (with Famous Flames). 25
60	Fontana H 273	This Old Heart/Wonder When You're Coming Home 25
62	Parlophone R 4922	Night Train/Why Does Everything Happen To Me (with Famous Flames). 30
62	Parlophone R 4952	Shout And Shimmy/Come Over Here (with Famous Flames). 25
63	London HL 9730	Prisoner Of Love/Choo-Choo (Locomotion) (with Famous Flames) 15
63	London HL 9775	These Foolish Things/(Can You) Feel It (Part 1) (with Famous Flames) 15
64	Philips BF 1368	Out Of Sight/Maybe The Last Time (& His Orchestra). 12
64	Sue WI 360	Night Train/Why Does Everything Happen To Me (with Famous Flames). 12
65	London HL 9945	Have Mercy Baby/Just Won't Do Right (with Famous Flames). 12
65	London HL 9990	Papa's Got A Brand New Bag (Parts 1 & 2) (with Famous Flames) 10
65	Ember EMB S 216	Tell Me What You're Gonna Do/Lost Someone (some in p/s). 25/15
65	Philips BF 1458	Try Me/Papa's Got A Brand New Bag 8
66	Philips BF 1481	New Breed (Parts 1 & 2). 8
66	Pye International 7N 25350	I Got You (I Feel Good)/I Can't Help It (I Just Do-Do-Do) (with Famous Flames). . . 8
66	Pye International 7N 25367	Ain't That A Groove (Parts 1 & 2) (with Famous Flames) 8
66	Pye International 7N 25371	It's A Man's Man's Man's World/Is It Yes Or Is It No? (with Famous Flames) . . . 8
66	Pye International 7N 25379	Money Won't Change You (Parts 1 & 2) (with Famous Flames) 10
66	Pye International 7N 25394	Don't Be A Drop-Out/Tell Me That You Love Me (with Famous Flames). 8
67	Pye International 7N 25411	Bring It Up/Nobody Knows (with Famous Flames). 7
67	Pye International 7N 25418	Kansas City/Stone Fox (with Famous Flames) 7
67	Pye International 7N 25423	Let Yourself Go/Good Rockin' Tonight (with Famous Flames) 7
67	Pye International 7N 25430	Cold Sweat (Parts 1 & 2) (with Famous Flames). 7
67	Pye International 7N 25441	Get It Together (Parts 1 & 2) (with Famous Flames) 7
68	Polydor 56740	I Can't Stand Myself/There Was A Time. 6
68	Polydor 56743	I Got The Feelin'/If I Ruled The World 6
68	Polydor 56744	Licking Stick, Licking Stick (Parts 1 & 2) 6
68	Polydor 56752	Say It Loud, I'm Black And I'm Proud (Parts 1 & 2) 7
68	Polydor 56540	That's Life/Please, Please, Please (with Famous Flames) 8
68	Polydor 56541	Say It Loud, I'm Black And I'm Proud (Parts 1 & 2) (reissue) 6
69	Polydor 56776	Mother Popcorn (Parts 1 & 2)`. 6
69	Polydor 56780	The World (Parts 1 & 2) 6
69	Polydor 56783	Let A Man Come In And Do The Popcorn/Sometimes 6
69	Polydor 56787	There Was A Time/I Can't Stand Myself (When You Touch Me). 6
70	Polydor 56793	Ain't It Funky Now (Parts 1 & 2) 6
70	Polydor 2001 018	It's A New Day/Georgia On My Mind 6
70	Polydor 2001 071	Get Up, I Feel Like Being A Sex Machine (Parts 1 & 2) (paper or plastic label) . . 6/5
70	Polydor 2001 097	Call Me Super Bad (Parts 1, 2 & 3) 6
71	Polydor 2001 163	Soul Power (Parts 1, 2 & 3) 6
71	Polydor 2001 190	I Cried/Get Up, Get Into It, Get Involved 6
71	Polydor 2001 213	Hot Pants (She Got To Use What She Got To Get What She Wants)
		(Parts 1, 2 & 3) 6
71	Polydor 2001 223	Make It Funky (Parts 1 & 2) 5
71	Mojo 2093 006	Hey America!/Brother Rapp (Part 1) 5
71	Polydor 2066 153	I'm A Greedy Man (Parts 1 & 2) 5
72	Polydor 2066 185	King Heroin/Theme From King Heroin 8
72	Polydor 2066 210	There It Is (Parts 1 & 2) 5
72	Polydor 2066 216	Honky Tonk (Parts 1 & 2) 5
72	Polydor 2066 231	Get On The Good Foot (Parts 1 & 2) 5

MINT VALUE £

72	Polydor 2066 283	What My Baby Needs Now Is A Little More Lovin'/This Guy's In Love With You (with Lyn Collins)	5
73	Polydor 2066 285	I've Got A Bag Of My Own/I Know It's True	5
73	Polydor 2141 008	Papa's Got A Brand New Bag/Out Of Sight/It's A Man's Man's Man's World (p/s)	6
73	Polydor 2066 296	I Got Ants In My Pants (Parts 1, 15 & 16)	5
73	Polydor 2066 329	Think/Something	5
73	Polydor 2066 370	Woman (Parts 1 & 2)	5
74	Polydor 2066 411	Stone To The Bone/Sexy, Sexy, Sexy	5
74	Polydor 2066 485	My Thang/The Payback	5
74	Polydor 2066 513	It's Hell/Papa Don't Take No Mess	5
75	Polydor 2066 520	Funky President (People It's Bad)/Cold Blooded	6
76	Polydor 2066 642	Hot (I Need To Be Loved, Loved, Loved)/Superbad, Superslick (Part 1)	5
76	Polydor 2066 687	Get Up Offa That Thing/Release The Pressure	5
77	Polydor 2066 763	Bodyheat (Parts 1, 15 & 16)	5
77	Polydor 2066 834	Honky Tonk/Brother Rapp	5
78	Polydor 2066 915	Eyesight/I Never, Never, Never Will Forget	5
78	Polydor 2066 984	Nature (Parts 1 & 2)	5
79	Polydor POSP 24	For Goodness Sakes, Look At Those Cakes/Get Up, I Feel Like Being A Sex Machine (red or silver label)	5
79	Polydor POSPX 24	Get Up, I Feel Like Being A Sex Machine/For Goodness Sakes, Look At Those Cakes (12")	10
79	Polydor POSPX 68	It's Too Funky In Here/Are We Really Dancing? (12")	10
79	Polydor STEP 2	Star Generation/Let The Boogie Do The Rest	5
79	Polydor STEPX 2	Star Generation/Let The Boogie Do The Rest (12")	8
80	Polydor POSP 121	Regrets/Stone Cold Drag	5
80	RCA RCAT 28	Rapp Payback (Where Iz Moses?) (Parts 1 & 2) (12")	8
81	RCA RCAT 44	Stay With Me/Smokin' And Drinkin' (12")	8
81	RCA RCAT 65	Funky Man (Parts 1 & 2)/Mashed Potatoes (12")	8
88	Urban URBX 13	She's The One/Funky President (People It's Bad)/Funky Drummer (9.13)/Funky Drummer (Bonus Beats Reprise) (12", die-cut title sleeve)	10
88	Urban URBA 13	She's The One (Funky Drummer Remix)/Funky President (People It's Bad)/Funky Drummer/Funky Drummer (Bonus Beats Reprise) (12")	10
88	Urban URBA 17	Payback (Final Mixdown)/Give It Up Or Turn It Loose/Coldsweat (12")	15
88	Urban URBX 17 DJ	Coldcut Meets The Godfather (12" promo, same as "The Payback Mix")	10
88	Polydor 080 430-2	Give It Up Or Turn It Loose (Remix)/The Payback Mix — Keep On Doing What You're Doing, But Make It Funky/Cold Sweat/The Payback — Part 1 (CDV)	8

EPs

64	London RE 1410	JAMES BROWN AND THE FAMOUS FLAMES (EP)	35
64	Ember EMB EP 4549	I DO JUST WHAT I WANT (EP)	30
66	Pye Intl. NEP 44059	I GOT YOU (EP)	22
66	Pye Intl. NEP 44068	I'LL GO CRAZY (EP)	22
67	Pye Intl. NEP 44072	PRISONER OF LOVE (EP)	22
67	Pye Intl. NEP 44076	HOW LONG DARLING (EP)	22
67	Pye Intl. NEP 44088	BRING IT UP (EP)	22
70	Polydor 580 701	TURN IT LOOSE (EP)	20

LPs

64	London HA 8177	PURE DYNAMITE! (LP, as James Brown & Famous Flames)	40
64	London HA 8184	LIVE AT THE APOLLO (LP, as James Brown & Famous Flames)	40
64	Ember EMB 3357	TELL ME WHAT YOU'RE GONNA DO (LP)	30
64	Philips BL 7630	SHOWTIME (LP)	30
65	London HA 8203	UNBEATABLE 16 HITS (LP)	35
65	London HA 8231	PLEASE, PLEASE, PLEASE (LP, as James Brown & Famous Flames)	40
65	Philips BL 7664	GRITS AND SOUL (LP)	25
65	London HA 8240	JAMES BROWN TOURS THE U.S.A. (LP, with Famous Flames)	40
66	London HA 8262	PAPA'S GOT A BRAND NEW BAG (LP, as James Brown & Famous Flames)	40
66	Philips BL 7697	JAMES BROWN PLAYS JAMES BROWN TODAY AND YESTERDAY (LP)	25
66	Pye Intl. NPL 28074	I GOT YOU (I FEEL GOOD) (LP)	30
66	Philips BL 7718	JAMES BROWN PLAYS NEW BREED (LP)	22
66	Pye Intl. NPL 28079	IT'S A MAN'S MAN'S MAN'S WORLD (LP)	25
66	Pye Intl. NPL 28097	THE JAMES BROWN CHRISTMAS ALBUM (LP)	40
67	Pye Intl. NPL 28093	MIGHTY INSTRUMENTALS (LP)	22
67	Philips (S)BL 7761	HANDFUL OF SOUL (LP)	22
67	Pye Intl. NPL 28099	PAPA'S GOT A BRAND NEW BAG (LP, reissue)	18
67	Pye Intl. NPL 28100	MR. EXCITEMENT (LP)	30
67	Polydor 582 703	THE JAMES BROWN SHOW (LP, live)	18
67	Pye Intl. NPL 28103	SINGS RAW SOUL (LP)	15
67	Pye Intl. NPL 28104	LIVE AT THE GARDEN (LP)	30
68	Philips (S)BL 7823	JAMES BROWN PLAYS THE REAL THING (LP)	22
68	Polydor 623 017	JAMES BROWN'S GREATEST HITS (LP)	15
68	Polydor 623 032	MR. DYNAMITE (LP)	18
68	Polydor 184 100	MR. SOUL (LP)	18
68	Polydor 184 136	I CAN'T STAND MYSELF (LP)	25
69	Polydor 184 148	SOUL FIRE (LP)	20
69	Polydor 184 159	KING OF SOUL (LP)	18
60s	Polydor 2852 002	THE SOUL OF JAMES BROWN (reissue of "I Can't Stand Myself") (LP)	25
69	Mercury 20133 SMCL	JAMES BROWN SINGS OUT OF SIGHT (LP)	35
69	Polydor 583 729/30	LIVE AT THE APOLLO VOLUME TWO (2-LP)	25
69	Polydor 583 741	SAY IT LOUD — I'M BLACK AND I'M PROUD (LP)	25
69	Polydor 583 765	THE BEST OF JAMES BROWN (LP)	15
69	Polydor 583 768	IT'S A MOTHER (LP)	30
69	Polydor 643 317	THIS IS … JAMES BROWN (LP)	18
70	Polydor 583 742	GETTIN' DOWN TO IT (LP)	25
70	Polydor 184 319	THE POPCORN (LP)	30
70	Polydor 2343 010	AIN'T IT FUNKY (LP)	35
70	Polydor 2612 005	LIVE AT THE APOLLO VOLUME TWO (2-LP, reissue)	18
70	Polydor 2334 009	PAPA'S GOT A BRAND NEW BAG (LP)	15

James BROWN

71	Polydor 2625 004	SEX MACHINE (2-LP)	25
71	Polydor 2310 022	SOUL ON TOP (LP)	25
71	Polydor 2310 029	IT'S A NEW DAY (LP)	25
71	Polydor 2310 089	SUPER BAD (LP)	20
71	Polydor 2343 036	SOUL BROTHER, NUMBER ONE (LP)	15
71	Polydor 2425 086	HOT PANTS (LP)	15
72	Philips 6336 201	THIS IS ... JAMES BROWN (LP, reissue)	12
72	Polydor 2659 011	REVOLUTION OF THE MIND: RECORDED LIVE AT THE APOLLO VOL. III (2-LP)	35
72	Polydor 2391 033	THERE IT IS (LP)	30
72	Phillips 6336 201	THIS IS ... JAMES BROWN (LP, reissue)	12
72	Contour 2870 116	PRISONER OF LOVE (LP)	15
73	Polydor 2659 018	GET ON THE GOOD FOOT (2-LP)	30
73	Polydor 2391 057	SOUL CLASSICS (LP, also issued as record club edition [ACB 00222])	15
73	Polydor 2490 117	BLACK CAESAR (LP, soundtrack)	35
73	Polydor 2391 084	SLAUGHTER'S BIG RIP-OFF (LP, soundtrack)	30
74	Polydor 2391 116	SOUL CLASSICS VOLUME TWO (LP)	15
74	Polydor 2659 030	THE PAYBACK (2-LP)	40
74	Polydor 2659 036	IT'S HELL (2-LP)	40
75	Polydor 2391 164	REALITY (LP)	15
75	Polydor 2391 166	SOUL CLASSICS VOLUME THREE (LP)	15
75	Polydor 2391 175	SEX MACHINE TODAY (LP)	15
75	Polydor 2482 184	LIVE AT THE APOLLO (LP, reissue of original live album)	12
75	Polydor 2391 197	EVERYBODY'S DOIN' THE HUSTLE AND DEAD ON THE DOUBLE BUMP (LP)	15
76	Polydor 2391 214	HOT (LP)	12
76	Polydor 2391 228	GET UP OFFA THAT THING (LP)	15
77	Polydor 2391 258	BODYHEAT (LP)	15
77	Polydor 2391 300	MUTHA'S NATURE (LP, by James Brown & the New J.B.'s)	12
78	Polydor 2391 342	JAM 1980s (LP)	12
79	Polydor 2391 384	TAKE A LOOK AT THOSE CAKES (LP)	12
79	Polydor 2391 412	THE ORIGINAL DISCO MAN (LP)	12
80	Polydor 2391 446	PEOPLE (LP)	12
80	RCA LP 5006	SOUL SYNDROME (LP)	12
81	Polydor POLS 1029	THE THIRD COMING (LP)	12
85	Polydor 821 231-1	AIN'T THAT A GROOVE — THE J.B. STORY 1966-69 (LP)	15
85	Polydor 821 232-1	DOING IT TOO DEATH — THE J.B. STORY 1970-73 (LP)	15
86	Boiling Point 827 439-1	DEAD ON THE HEAVY FUNK — THE J.B. STORY 1974-76 (LP)	15
86	Polydor 829 417-1	JAMES BROWN'S FUNKY PEOPLE VOL. 1 (LP, with other artists)	15
88	Urban URBLP 14	JAMES BROWN'S FUNKY PEOPLE VOL. 2 (LP, with other artists)	15
88	Urban URBLP 11	IN THE JUNGLE GROOVE (2-LP)	15
91	Polydor 849 108-2	STAR TIME (4-CD, with booklet)	35

(see also Lyn Collins, JBs, Maceo & All King's Men, Nat Kendrick & Swans)

JAMES BROWN (Jamaica)

71	Punch PH 76	Don't Say/TRANS AM ALLSTARS: Don't Say Version	6
72	Ashanti ASH 408	Mama Don't Want To See You/Mama Don't Want To See You Version	5

JERICHO BROWN

60	Warner Bros WB 14	Don'tcha Know (That I Love You)/Look For A Star	7
64	Warner Bros WB 141	I'm Watching You/Wisdom Of A Fool	6

JIM EDWARD BROWN

66	RCA RCX 7179	INTRODUCING JIM EDWARD BROWN (EP)	10

(see also Browns)

JIM EDWARD (BROWN) & MAXINE BROWN

55	London HL 8123	Itsy Witsy Bitsy Me/Why Am I Falling?	30
55	London HL 8123	Itsy Witsy Bitsy Me/Why Am I Falling? (78)	12
55	London HLU 8166	Your Love Is Wild As The West Wind/Draggin' Mainstreet	30
55	London HLU 8166	Your Love Is Wild As The West Wind/Draggin' Mainstreet (78)	25
55	London HLU 8200	You Thought I Thought/Here Today And Gone Tomorrow (B-side with Bonnie)	25
55	London HLU 8200	You Thought I Thought/Here Today And Gone Tomorrow (78, B-side with Bonnie)	12
55	London R-EP 1024	COUNTRY SONGS (EP)	25
55	London R-EU 1044	COUNTRY SONGS VOLUME 3 (EP)	25

JOE BROWN (& BRUVVERS)

59	Decca F 11185	People Gotta Talk/Comes The Day (solo, triangular centre)	15
59	Decca F 11185	People Gotta Talk/Comes The Day (78)	35
60	Decca F 11207	Darktown Strutter's Ball/Swagger (solo)	12
60	Decca F 11246	Jellied Eels/Dinah	10
60	Pye 7N 15322	Shine/The Switch	10
61	Piccadilly 7N 35000	Crazy Mixed Up Kid/Stick Around	6
61	Piccadilly 7N 35005	Good Luck & Goodbye/I'm Henery The Eighth I Am	8
62	Piccadilly 7N 35024	What A Crazy World We're Living In/Popcorn	6
62	Decca F 11496	Comes The Day/People Gotta Talk (reissue)	6
62	Piccadilly 7N 35047	A Picture Of You/A Lay-About's Lament	5
62	Piccadilly 7N 35058	Your Tender Look/The Other Side Of The Town	5
62	Piccadilly 7N 35082	It Only Took A Minute/All Things Bright And Beautiful	5
63	Piccadilly 7N 35106	That's What Love Will Do/Hava Nagila (The Hora)	5
63	Piccadilly 7N 35129	Nature's Time For Love/The Spanish Bit	6
63	Piccadilly 7N 35138	Sally Ann/There's Only One Of You	6
63	Piccadilly 7N 35150	Little Ukelele/Hercules Unchained	6
64	Piccadilly 7N 35163	You Do Things To Me/Everybody Calls Me Joe	6
64	Piccadilly 7N 35194	Don't/Just Like That	6
65	Pye 7N 15784	Teardrops In The Rain/Lonely Circus	6
65	Pye 7N 15888	Sicilian Tarantella/Thinkin' That I Loves You	6
65	Pye 7N 15983	Charlie Girl/My Favourite Occupation	6
66	Pye 7N 17074	Sea Of Heartbreak/Mrs O's Theme	6

MINT VALUE £

66	Pye 7N 17135	Little Ray Of Sunshine/Your Loving Touch	6
66	Pye 7N 17184	A Satisfied Mind/Stay A Little While	8
67	Pye 7N 17339	With A Little Help From My Friends/Show Me Around	5
68	MCA MU 1003	Bottle Of Wine/Blue Tuesday	5
68	MCA MU 1030	Davy The Fat Boy/Katerine	5
69	MCA MU 1082	Sweet Music/Suzanne	5
70	Penny Farthing PEN 718	Molly Perkins/Captain Of My Love Ship	5
70	Penny Farthing PEN 747	Come Up And See Me Sometime/Give Me Muddy Water	5
62	Decca DFE 8500	A PICTURE OF JOE BROWN (EP)	18
62	Piccadilly NEP 34025	JOE BROWN HIT PARADE (EP)	15
62	Piccadilly NEP 34026	ALL THINGS BRIGHT AND BEAUTIFUL (EP)	15
62	Ace Of Clubs ACL 1127	A PICTURE OF JOE BROWN (LP)	18
62	Golden Guinea GGL 0146	A PICTURE OF YOU (LP)	15
63	Piccadilly NPL 38006	JOE BROWN — LIVE! (LP)	22
63	Golden Guinea GGL 0231	HERE COMES JOE! (LP)	15
68	MCA MUPS 347	JOE BROWN (LP)	15
72	Bell BELLS 208	BROWN'S HOME BREW (LP)	15

JOE BROWN/MARK WYNTER

63	Piccadilly NEP 24167	JUST FOR FUN (EP, soundtrack, 2 tracks each)	12
64	Golden Guinea WO 1	BIG HITS OF JOE BROWN AND MARK WYNTER (EP)	10
63	Golden Guinea GGL 0179	JOE BROWN/MARK WYNTER (LP, 6 tracks each)	12

(see also Mark Wynter)

JOHNNY BROWN

| 61 | Philips PB 1119 | Walkin' Talkin' Kissin' Doll/Sundown | 7 |

J.T. BROWN

| 75 | Flyright LP 4712 | ROCKIN' WITH J.T. (LP) | 12 |

KAY BROWN

| 56 | Brunswick 05595 | Me 'N' You 'N' The Moon/What Do You Think It Does To Me? | 7 |

KENT BROWN & RAINBOWS

| 68 | Fab FAB 53 | When You Going To Show Me How/Come Ya Come Ya | 8 |

(see also Kent & Jeannie, Sir D's Group)

LAWRENCE BROWN'S ALL-STARS

| 65 | HMV CLP 1913 | INSPIRED ABANDON (LP) | 12 |

LENNOX BROWN

| 72 | Green Door GD 4023 | High School Serenade/WINSTON SCOTLAND: On The Track (1st issue) | 6 |
| 72 | Bullet BU 501 | High School Serenade/WINSTON SCOTLAND: On The Track (2nd issue) | 6 |

(see also Jeff Barnes, Peter Tosh)

LES BROWN & HIS BAND OF RENOWN

54	Vogue Coral Q 2034	Ramona/Hot Point	8
54	Vogue Coral Q 2042	St. Louis Blues Mambo/Moon Song	8
55	Vogue Coral Q 72049	The Man That Got Away/Doodle-Doo-Doo	8
55	Capitol CL 14331	Frenesi/Perfidia	7
55	Capitol CL 14350	He Needs Me/Simplicity	7
55	Vogue Coral Q 72107	Lullaby Of Birdland/Bernie's Tune	7
56	Vogue Coral Q 72123	Hong Kong Blues (with Hoagy Carmichael & Band Of Renown)/It's All Right With Me	8
56	Vogue Coral Q 72215	Flamingo/Midnight Sun	7
56	Capitol CL 14512	Sincerely Yours/Take Back Your Mink	5
56	Capitol CL 14611	That Certain Feeling/Hit The Road To Dreamland	5
56	Capitol CL 14631	Talk About A Party/Ancient History	6
57	Capitol CL 14675	Priscilla/The Best Years Of My Life	8
57	Capitol CL 14706	Original Joe/If I Had The Money	5
57	Vogue Coral Q 72242	Forty Cups Of Coffee/I'm Forever Blowing Bubbles	10
57	Vogue Coral Q 72242	Forty Cups Of Coffee/I'm Forever Blowing Bubbles (78)	10
59	Coral Q 72367	Boola/Say It With Music	5
59	Coral Q 72367	Boola/Say It With Music (78)	10
54	Vogue Coral LVC 10002	LES DANCE (10" LP)	15
55	Vogue Coral LVC 10017	INVITATION (10" LP)	15
55	Vogue Coral LVC 10033	LES BROWN (10" LP)	15

MAXINE BROWN

61	London HLU 9286	All In My Mind/Harry, Let's Marry	18
62	HMV POP 1102	Am I Falling In Love/Promise Me Anything	55
63	Stateside SS 188	Ask Me/Yesterday's Kisses	18
64	Pye International 7N 25272	Oh No Not My Baby/You Upset My Soul	15
65	Pye International 7N 25299	It's Gonna Be Alright/You Do Something To Me	10
65	Pye International 7N 25317	One Step At A Time/Anything For A Laugh	15
67	Pye International 7N 25410	I've Got A Lot Of Love Left In Me/Hold On (I'm Comin') (B-side with Chuck Jackson)	10
67	Pye International 7N 25434	Since I Found You/Gotta Find A Way	12
70	Major Minor MM 709	Reason To Believe/I Can't Get Along Without You	8
73	Avco 6105 022	Picked Up, Packed Up And Put Away/Bella Mia	5
75	Pye Disco Demand DDS 117	One In A Million/Let Me Give You My Lovin'	5

(see also Chuck Jackson & Maxine Brown)

NAPPY BROWN (& HIS BAND)

55	London HL 8145	Don't Be Angry/It's Really You	650
55	London HL 8145	Don't Be Angry/It's Really You (78)	50
55	London HLC 8182	Pitter Patter/There'll Come A Day	450
55	London HLC 8182	Pitter Patter/There'll Come A Day (78)	50
57	London HLC 8384	Little By Little/I'm Getting Lonesome (& His Band) (gold or silver lettering on label)	275/165
57	London HLC 8384	Little By Little/I'm Getting Lonesome (& His Band) (78)	35
58	London HLC 8760	It Don't Hurt No More/My Baby	55
58	London HLC 8760	It Don't Hurt No More/My Baby (78)	25

NOEL BROWN
68	Island WI 3149	Man's Temptation/Heartbreak Girl	18
69	Songbird SB 1012	By The Time I Get To Phoenix/Heartbreak Girl	7
70	Bullet BU 423	By The Time I Get To Phoenix/Heartbreak Girl (reissue)	6

(see also Bunny Brown)

OSCAR BROWN JNR
61	Philips PB 1097	But I Was Cool/Dat Dere	5
61	Philips BBL 7478	SIN AND SOUL (LP)	12
73	Atlantic K 40452	MOVIN' ON (LP)	12

PAMELA BROWN
70	Joe JRS 8	People Are Running/CRITICS: School Days	8

PETE BROWN('S PIBLOKTO)
69	Parlophone R 5767	The Week Looked Good On Paper/Morning Call (as Pete Brown & His Battered Ornaments, promo p/s)	70
69	Parlophone R 5767	The Week Looked Good On Paper/Morning Call (as Pete Brown & His Battered Ornaments)	18
69	Harvest HAR 5008	Living Life Backwards/High Flying Electric Bird (as Pete Brown & Piblokto!)	10
70	Harvest HAR 5023	Can't Get Off The Planet/Broken Magic (with His Battered Ornaments)	10
70	Harvest HAR 5028	Flying Hero Sandwich/My Last Band (as Pete Brown & Piblokto!)	20
69	Harvest SHVL 752	A MEAL YOU CAN SHAKE HANDS WITH IN THE DARK (LP, as Pete Brown & His Battered Ornaments, mono or stereo)	90
70	Harvest SHVL 768	THE ART SCHOOL DANCE GOES ON FOREVER (LP, as Pete Brown & Piblokto!)	70
70	Harvest SHVL 782	THOUSANDS ON A RAFT (LP, as Pete Brown & Piblokto!)	55
73	Deram SML 1103	THE NOT FORGOTTEN ASSOCIATION (LP, with Graham Bond)	65
77	Harvest SHSM 2017	MY LAST BAND (LP, as Pete Brown & Piblokto!)	18
82	Discs Intl. INTLP 1	PARTY IN THE RAIN (LP, with Ian Lynn, private pressing)	30

(see also Battered Ornaments, Graham Bond & Pete Brown, Deke Leonard)

PINEY BROWN
54	Esquire 10-330	That's Right Little Girl/EDDIE CHAMBLEE: Blues For Eddie (78)	15

POLLY BROWN
73	Pye NSPL 18396	POLLY BROWN (LP)	12

(see also Pickettywitch)

RANDY BROWN
80	Casablanca CANL	I Wanna Make Love To You/We Ought To Be Doin' It (12", p/s)	8
80	Casablanca CAL 2010	MIDNIGHT DESIRE (LP)	10

ROY BROWN
57	London HLP 8398	I'm Sticking With You/Party Doll (gold label print, later silver)	500/350
57	London HLP 8398	I'm Sticking With You/Party Doll (78)	55
57	London HLP 8448	Saturday Night/Everybody	650
57	London HLP 8448	Saturday Night/Everybody (78)	65

RUTH BROWN (& HER RHYTHMAKERS)
55	London HL 8153	Mambo Baby/Mama (He Treats Your Daughter Mean) (with Rhythmakers)	275
55	London HL 8153	Mambo Baby/Mama (He Treats Your Daughter Mean) (as Ruth Brown & Her Rhythmakers) (78)	35
55	London HLE 8210	As Long As I'm Moving/R.B. Blues (with Her Rhythmakers)	275
55	London HLE 8210	As Long As I'm Moving/R.B. Blues (with Her Rhythmakers) (78)	35
56	London HLE 8310	I Want To Do More/Sweet Baby Of Mine	165
56	London HLE 8310	I Want To Do More/Sweet Baby Of Mine (78)	35
57	London HLE 8401	Mom Oh Mom/I Want To Be Loved (But Only By You)	135
57	London HLE 8401	Mom Oh Mom/I Want To Be Loved (But Only By You) (78)	55
57	Columbia DB 3913	Lucky Lips/My Heart Is Breaking Over You	275
57	Columbia DB 3913	Lucky Lips/My Heart Is Breaking Over You (78)	45
57	London HLE 8483	When I Get You Baby/One More Time	70
57	London HLE 8483	When I Get You Baby/One More Time (78)	50
58	London HLE 8552	A New Love/Look Me Up	70
58	London HLE 8552	A New Love/Look Me Up (78)	35
58	London HLE 8645	Just Too Much/Book Of Lies	60
58	London HLE 8645	Just Too Much/Book Of Lies (78)	45
58	London HLE 8757	This Little Girl's Gone Rockin'/Why Me	60
58	London HL 7061	This Little Girl's Gone Rockin'/Why Me (export issue)	35
58	London HLE 8757	This Little Girl's Gone Rockin'/Why Me (78)	55
59	London HLE 8887	Jack O' Diamonds/I Can't Hear A Word You Say	45
59	London HLE 8887	Jack O' Diamonds/I Can't Hear A Word You Say (78)	65
59	London HLE 8946	I Don't Know/Papa Daddy	35
59	London HLE 8946	I Don't Know/Papa Daddy (78)	75
60	London HLE 9093	Don't Deceive Me/I Burned Your Letter	25
61	London HLK 9304	Sure 'Nuff/Here He Comes	30
64	Brunswick 05904	Yes Sir That's My Baby/What Happened To You	15
76	President PT 457	Sugar Babe/Stop Knocking	5
55	London REE 1038	THE QUEEN OF R&B (EP)	160
63	Philips BE 12537	GOSPEL TIME (EP)	40
60	London Jazz LTZ-K 15187	LAST DATE WITH RUTH BROWN (LP)	50
62	Philips 652 012 BL	ALONG COMES RUTH (LP)	35
63	Philips 652 020 BL	GOSPEL TIME (LP)	35
64	Atlantic ATL 5007	THE BEST OF RUTH BROWN (LP, plum label)	70
76	President PTLS 1067	SUGAR BABE (LP)	15

RUTH BROWN/JOE TURNER
56	London REE 1047	THE KING AND QUEEN OF R&B (EP, 2 tracks each)	200

SAMMI BROWN
68	Fontana TF 947	Daydream/Stop The Music	5

SANDY BROWN('S JAZZ BAND)

58	Tempo A 124	African Queen/Special Delivery (as Sandy Brown's Jazz Band)	7
53	Esquire EP 28	SANDY BROWN'S JAZZ BAND (EP)	15
55	Tempo EXA 13	SANDY BROWN'S JAZZ BAND (EP)	15
55	Tempo EXA 33	SANDY BROWN'S JAZZ BAND (EP)	15
56	Tempo EXA 49	TRADITIONAL JAZZ SCENE '56 (EP)	15
57	Nixa NJE 1054	BLUE McJAZZ (EP)	12
57	Nixa NJE 1056	AFRO McJAZZ (EP)	12
53	Esquire 20-022	SANDY BROWN (10" LP, with Bobby Mickleburgh)	20
56	Tempo TAP 3	SANDY'S SIDEMEN PLAYING COMPOSITIONS BY AL FAIRWEATHER (LP)	120
57	Nixa Jazz Today NJL 9	McJAZZ (LP)	18
66	Fontana TE1 7473	SANDY BROWN ALL STARS (LP)	20
69	Fontana SFJL 921	HAIR AT ITS HAIRIEST (LP, as Sandy Brown & His Gentlemen Friends)	45
71	77 SEU 12/49	WITH THE BRIAN LEMON TRIO (LP)	15

(see also Wally Fawkes, Sandy & Teachers, Al Fairweather)

SAVOY BROWN
(see under 'S')

SHIRLEY BROWN

75	Stax STXS 2019	Woman To Woman/Yes Sir, Brother	6
75	Stax STXS 2032	I Can't Give You Up/It Ain't No Fun	5
75	Stax STX 1031	WOMAN TO WOMAN (LP)	15

(see also Oliver Sain)

STU BROWN & BLUESOLOGY

67	Polydor 56195	Since I Found You Baby/Just A Little Bit	275

(see also Bluesology, Elton John)

TEDDY BROWN

70	Trojan TR 7793	What Greater Love/Lady Love	4
71	Trojan TR 7827	Walk The World Away/Senorita Rita	4

TINY BROWN

50	Capitol CL 13306	No More Blues/Slow-Motion Baby (78)	25

VEDA BROWN

74	Stax STXS 2008	Short Stopping/I Can See Every Woman's Man But Mine	4

VERNON BROWN

71	Mojo 2093 002	I'm A Lover/Of Your Life	5

VIC BROWN COMBO

63	Rio R 7	Swanee River/Robert E. Lee	10

(se also Alan Martin)

VINCENT BROWN

70	Gas GAS 128	Look What You're Going To Do/Hold On To What You Have Got	6

WATSON T. BROWN (& EXPLOSIVE)

68	President PT 207	Some Lovin'/Home Is Where Your Heart Lies	5
68	President PT 221	Crying All Night/I Close My Eyes	5
70	Bell BLL 1109	Will You Still Love Me Tomorrow/Save The Last Dance For Me (solo)	5

(see also Explosive)

WILLIAM BROWN

71	Ackee ACK 128	I'm Alone/BELTONES: Soul People	6

BROWN BROTHERS

59	Vogue V 9131	Let The Good Times Roll/You're Right, I'm Left	175
59	Vogue V 9131	Let The Good Times Roll/You're Right, I'm Left (78)	70

(see also Charles Brown)

DUNCAN BROWNE

68	Immediate IM 070	On The Bombsite/Alfred Bell	12
70	Bell BLL 1119	Resurrection Joe/Final Asylum	5
73	Rak RAK 162	Send Me The Bill/My Only Son	5
78	Logo GO 329	Wild Places/Camino Real	5
68	Immediate IMSP 018	GIVE ME, TAKE YOU (LP, with insert)	200
73	RAK SRKA 6754	DUNCAN BROWNE (LP, gatefold sleeve)	18

GEORGE BROWNE

54	Parlophone CMSP 6	Calypso Mambo/The Peanut Vendor (export issue)	10
54	Parlophone CMSP 17	Somebody Bad Stole De Wedding Bell (Who's Got De Ding Dong?)/ Matilda, Matilda! (export issue)	10
57	Columbia DB 3940	Sound Barrier/Te-Le-Le	7
57	Columbia DB 3940	Sound Barrier/Te-Le-Le (78)	10
56	Melodisc MLP 509	HE LIKE IT SHE LIKE IT (10" LP)	12

(see also Humphrey Lyttleton)

IVAN BROWNE & HIS CALYPSO MUSIC

54	London Calypso CAY 109	I'm My Own Grandpa/My Little Boy (78)	8

JACKSON BROWNE

82	Asylum K 13185	Somebody's Baby/The Crow On The Cradle (p/s)	4
83	Asylum E 9826	Lawyers In Love/Say It Isn't True//Tender Is The Night/On The Day (double pack, 1st 7" in p/s)	6
86	Elektra EKR 35P	For America (Edit)/Till I Go Down (Statue Of Liberty-shaped picture disc)	5
86	Elektra EKR 42P	In The Shape Of A Heart/Voice Of America (heart-shaped picture disc)	5
74	Asylum K2 43007	LATE FOR THE SKY (LP, quadrophonic)	15

(see also Clarence Clemons)

MINT VALUE £

SANDRA BROWNE (& BOYFRIENDS)

63	Columbia DB 4998	By Hook Or By Crook/Johnny Boy (as Sandra Browne & Boyfriends) 10
63	Columbia DB 7109	You'd Think He Didn't Know Me/Mama Never Told Me 8
65	Columbia DB 7465	Knock On Any Door/I Want Love.. 10

TEDDY BROWN(E)

| 59 | Capitol CL 15059 | A Corner In Paradise/The Everglades .... 8 |
| 61 | Starlite ST45 033 | Pretty Little Baby/Genevieve (as Teddy Brown) .... 12 |

THOMAS F. BROWNE

| 71 | Vertigo 6325 250 | WEDNESDAY'S CHILD (LP, gatefold sleeve, swirl label)..................... 40 |

(see also Gary Wright)

TOM BROWNE

| 80 | Arista ARIST 12357 | Funkin' For Jamaica (N.Y.)/Her Silent Smile (12") .... 8 |

DUKE BROWNER

| 79 | Grapevine GRP 145 | Crying Over You/Crying Over You (Instrumental) .... 6 |

(see also Kaddo Strings)

BROWNHILL'S STAMP DUTY

| 69 | Columbia DB 8625 | Maxwell's Silver Hammer/My Woman's Back .... 6 |

BROWNS

59	RCA RCA 1140	The Three Bells/Heaven Fell Last Night 5
59	RCA RCA 1140	The Three Bells/Heaven Fell Last Night (78)............................. 40
59	RCA RCA 1157	Scarlet Ribbons (For Her Hair)/Blue Bells Ring 5
59	RCA RCA 1157	Scarlet Ribbons (For Her Hair)/Blue Bells Ring (78)....................... 30
60	RCA RCA 1176	Teen-Ex/The Old Lamplighter 6
60	RCA RCA 1193	Margo (The Ninth Of May)/Lonely Little Robin 6
60	RCA RCA 1218	Send Me The Pillow You Dream On/You're So Much A Part Of Me 6
60	RCA RCX 587	IN THE COUNTRY (EP).. 18
59	RCA RD 27153/SF 5052	SWEET SOUNDS BY THE BROWNS (LP, mono/stereo) 25/30

(see also Jim Edward & Maxine Brown)

BROWN SUGAR

| 70s | Lovers Rock CJ 613 | I'm In Love With A Dreadlocks/Version .... 15 |

ANNETTE (Reis) & VICTOR BROX

| 65 | Fontana TF 536 | I've Got The World In A Jug/Wake Me And Shake Me...................... 5 |
| 74 | Sonet SNTF 663 | ROLLIN' BACK (LP) .... 18 |

(see also Aynsley Dunbar Retaliation)

DAVE BRUBECK (QUARTET)

53	Vogue 45-2156	A Foggy Day/Lyons Busy 8
53	Vogue 45-2157	Mam'selle/Me And My Shadow 8
53	Vogue 45-2158	Frenesi/At A Perfume Counter... 8
53	Vogue 45-2159	Body And Soul/Let's Fall In Love 8
53	Vogue 45-2160	I'll Remember April/Singin' In The Rain................................... 8
53	Vogue 45-2161	Lullaby In Rhythm/You Stepped Out Of A Dream 8
54	Vogue V 2171	At A Perfume Counter/Me And My Shadow 5
54	Vogue V 2171	At A Perfume Counter/Me And My Shadow (78) 8
54	Vogue V 2206	Frenesi/Mam'selle 5
54	Vogue V 2206	Frenesi/Mam'selle (78)... 8
60	Philips JAZ 106	I'm In A Dancing Mood/Lover (p/s) 5
61	Fontana H 339	Take Five/Blue Rondo A La Turk 4
61	CBS AAG 102	The Unsquare Dance/Camptown Races 5
54	Vogue LDE 090	DAVE BRUBECK TRIO (10" LP)... 18
54	Vogue LDE 095	DAVE BRUBECK QUARTET (10" LP)..................................... 18
54	Vogue LDE 104	DAVE BRUBECK QUARTET VOL. 2 (10" LP) 18
55	Vogue LDE 114	DAVE BRUBECK QUARTET VOL. 3 (10" LP) 18
57	Fontana TFL 5017	DAVE DIGS DISNEY (LP) 12
57	Philips BBL 7147	AT NEWPORT (LP, with J.J. Johnson and Kei Winding) 12
59	Vogue LAE 12008	THE FABULOUS DAVE BRUBECK TRIO AND OCTET (LP) 15
59	Fontana TFL 5071	GONE WITH THE WIND (LP, also stereo STFL 501)........................ 12
60	Vogue LAE 12114	DAVE BRUBECK QUARTET FEATURING PAUL DESMOND (LP) 15
60	Fontana TFL 5085	TIME OUT (LP, also stereo STFL 523) 12
60	Fontana TFL 5099	SOUTHERN SCENE (LP, also stereo STFL 530) 12
60	Fontana TFL 5101	THE RIDDLE (LP, also stereo STFL 532).................................. 12
60	Fontana TFL 5114	BERNSTEIN PLAYS BRUBECK PLAYS BERNSTEIN (LP, also stereo STFL 542).. 12
60	Philips BBL 7447	JAZZ GOES TO COLLEGE (LP) 12
61	Fontana TFL 5126	BRUBECK AND RUSHING (LP, with Jimmy Rushing, also stereo STFL 550) ... 12
61	Fontana TFL 5136	THE BEST OF BRUBECK (LP)... 12

(see also Paul Desmond, Jimmy Rushing, Carmen McRae)

ALLAN BRUCE

| 58 | Fontana H 169 | Mio Amor/Will Ye No Come Back Again (78)............................... 8 |
| 59 | Fontana H 216 | My Only Love/A Dangerous Game (78) .... 10 |

JACK BRUCE

65	Polydor BM 56036	I'm Getting Tired (Of Drinking And Gambling)/Rootin' Tootin' 45
71	Polydor 2058 153	The Consul At Sunset/Letter Of Thanks 10
74	RSO 2090 141	Keep It Down/Golden Days 5
69	Polydor 583 058	SONGS FOR A TAILOR (LP, gatefold sleeve)............................. 18
70	Polydor 2343 033	THINGS WE LIKE (LP) 15
71	Polydor 2310 070	THINGS WE LIKE (LP, reissue).. 12
71	Polydor 2310 107	HARMONY ROW (LP, gatefold sleeve) 12
74	RSO 2394 143	OUT OF THE STORM (LP, with insert) 12

(see also Alexis Korner's Blues Incorporated, Cream, Manfred Mann, Graham Bond Organisation, John Mayall, West Bruce & Laing, Lifetime, Rocket 88, Carla Bley, Duffy Power, Cozy Powell)

JACK BRUCE & ROBIN TROWER
81	Chrysalis CHS 2497	What It Is/Into Money (clear vinyl, p/s)	5

(see also Robin Trower)

LENNY BRUCE
69	Transatlantic TRA 195	BERKELEY CONCERT (2-LP)	25

TOMMY BRUCE (& BRUISERS)
60	Columbia DB 4453	Ain't Misbehavin'/Got The Water Boilin' (with Bruisers)	6
60	Columbia DB 4498	Broken Doll/I'm On Fire (with Bruisers)	8
60	Columbia DB 4532	On The Sunny Side Of The Street/My Little Girl (with Bruisers)	6
61	Columbia DB 4581	You Make Love So Well/I'm Crazy 'Bout My Baby (with Bruisers)	6
61	Columbia DB 4682	Love, Honour And Oh! Baby/I'm Gonna Sit Right Down And Write	6
62	Columbia DB 4776	Babette/Honey Girl, You're Lonely	6
62	Columbia DB 4850	Horror Movies/It's You	6
62	Columbia DB 4927	Buttons And Bows/London Boys	6
63	Columbia DB 7025	Let's Do It, Let's Fall In Love/Two Feet Left	6
63	Columbia DB 7132	Lavender Blue/Sixteen Years Ago Tonight	6
64	Columbia DB 7241	Let It Be Me/No More	6
64	Columbia DB 7387	Over Suzanne/It's Drivin' Me Wild	6
65	Polydor BM 56006	Boom Boom/Can Your Monkey Do The Dog (with Bruisers)	12
66	RCA RCA 1535	Monster Gonzales/I Hate Getting Up In The Morning	10
68	CBS CBS 3405	I've Been Around Too Long/Where The Colour Of The Soil Is Different	6
68	CBS CBS 3937	Heartbreak Melody/The Reason Why	5
61	Columbia SEG 8077	KNOCKOUT (EP)	120

BRUCE & ROBIN ROCKERS
66	Marble Arch MAL 626	THE BATMAN THEME (LP)	20

CLAUDIA BRÜCKEN
90	Island ISB 471	Absolute/Whisper (numbered box set with postcards)	5
90	Island 12ISX 471	Absolut[e] (Bastille Mix)/Absolut[e] (Shooting Star Mix) (12", remix, stickered title sleeve, promo only)	10
90	Island CID 471	Absolut[e] (Original)/Absolut[e] (Shooting Star)/Whisper (CD, g/fold card p/s)	15
91	Island CID 479	Kiss Like Ether (Electrical Embrace)/Kiss Like Ether (As Pure)/I, Dream (Recurring)/Kiss Like Ether (Earth Mood Magic) (CD, gatefold card p/s)	15
91	Island CID 9971	LOVE & A MILLION OTHER THINGS (CD)	25

(see also Propaganda, Act, Glenn Gregory & Claudia Brücken)

HEIDI BRÜHL
60	Philips PB 1095	Ring Of Gold/I'll Belong To You Forever (some in p/s)	10/5
63	Philips 345 579 BF	Marcel/Talk It Over With Someone	12

BRUISERS
63	Parlophone R 5042	Blue Girl/Don't Cry	8
63	Parlophone R 5092	Your Turn To Cry/Give It To Me	7

(see also [Peter] Lee Stirling & Bruisers)

BRUMBEATS
64	Decca F 11834	Cry Little Girl, Cry/I Don't Understand	18

BEAU BRUMMEL ESQUIRE
65	Columbia DB 7447	I Know Know Know/Shoppin' Around	7
65	Columbia DB 7538	The Next Kiss/Come And Get Me	7
65	Columbia DB 7675	A Better Man Than I/Teardrops	7
66	Columbia DB 7878	You Don't Know What You've Got/Take Me Like I Am	6

BRUNNING (HALL) SUNFLOWER BLUES BAND
68	Saga FID 2118	BULLEN STREET BLUES (LP, as Brunning Sunflower Blues Band)	18
69	Saga EROS 8132	TRACKSIDE BLUES (LP)	45
70	Saga EROS 8150	I WISH YOU WOULD (LP, as Brunning Sunflower Blues Band)	45
71	Gemini GM 2010	THE BRUNNING/HALL SUNFLOWER BLUES BAND (LP)	45
71	Boulevard 4032	BULLEN STREET BLUES (LP, reissue)	12

(see also Five's Company, Fleetwood Mac, Leaf Hound)

TONY BRUNO
68	Capitol CL 15534	What's Yesterday/Small Town, Bring Down	15

BRUTE FORCE
69	Apple APPLE 8	King Of Fuh/Nobody Knows (unissued)	500

BRUTUS
75	Purple PUR 126	Payroll/New Deal Princess	7

CARL BRYAN
69	Trojan TR 673	Red Ash/SILVERTONES: Bluebirds Flying Over	8
69	Duke DU 13	Soul Pipe/Overproof	8
69	Camel CA 22	Run For Your Life/TWO SPARKS: When We Were Young	6
69	Gas GAS 133	Stagger Back/The Creeper	7
69	Gas GAS 134	Walking The Dead/TREVOR & KEITH: Got What You Want	6

(see also Cannon Ball & Johnny Melody, King Cannon, Vincent Foster, Hugh Malcolm, King Cannonball, Glen Brown, Shenley Duffas, Alton Ellis, Kid Gungo, Jackie Mittoo, Johnny Moore, Joe White, Royals)

DORA BRYAN
55	HMV POP 133	My Only Love With Men/Why Did You Call Me Lily (78)	10
63	Fontana TF 427	All I Want For Christmas Is A Beatle/If I Were A Fairy	6

FITZVAUGHN BRYAN'S ORCHESTRA
60	Melodisc 45-1560	Evening News/Hold Up Your Head And Smile (with Kentrick Patrick)	8

RAD BRYAN
71	Techniques TE 909	Jumping Jack/ANSELL COLLINS: Point Blank	7
71	Bullet BU 463	Shock Attack/Cuban Waltz	6
71	Big Shot BI 559	Just Do The Right Things/Corpral Jones	6
71	Big Shot BI 591	I'll Be Right There (actually by Techniques)/PLAYBOYS: Hot Pants Rock	6
71	Big Shot BI 592	My Best Girl/My Best Girl Version	6
72	Attack ATT 8040	Standing In The Rain (actually by Neville Grant)/Standing In The Rain Version	5

V. BRYAN ORCHESTRA
55	Kay CRS 028	Tan Tan — Calypso/CYRIL DIAS: Brass Crown (Vocal: Lord Superior) (78)	10

WES BRYAN
58	London HLU 8607	Lonesome Love/Tiny Spaceman	30
58	London HLU 8607	Lonesome Love/Tiny Spaceman (78)	35
59	London HLU 8978	Honey Baby/So Blue Over You	40
59	London HLU 8978	Honey Baby/So Blue Over You (78)	45

BRYAN & BRUNELLES
65	HMV POP 1394	Jacqueline/Louie Louie	45

ANITA BRYANT
59	London HLL 8983	Six Boys And Seven Girls/The Blessings Of Love	8
59	London HLL 8983	Six Boys And Seven Girls/The Blessings Of Love (78)	18
60	London HLL 9075	Little George (Got The Hiccoughs)/Love Look Away	8
60	London HLL 9114	Paper Roses/Mixed Emotions	6
60	London HLL 9171	In My Little Corner Of The World/Just In Time	7
60	London HLL 9171	In My Little Corner Of The World/Anyone Would Love You (unissued)	
60	London HLL 9219	One Of the Lucky Ones/The Party's Over	6
60	London HLL 9247	Wonderland By Night/Pictures	6
61	London HLL 9281	Till There Was You/A Texan And A Girl From Mexico	6
61	London HLL 9353	Do-Re-Mi/An Angel Cried	6
61	Philips BF 1182	The Wedding/Seven Kinds Of Lonesome	6
66	CBS 202026	Another Year, Another Love/My Mind's Playing Tricks On Me Again	30
62	CBS AAG 20005	KISSES SWEETER THAN WINE (EP)	15
61	London HA-L 2381	IN MY LITTLE CORNER OF THE WORLD (LP)	40

BOOD & FILEECE (Boudleaux & Felice) BRYANT
51	MGM MGM 452	Overweight Blues/I Dreamed Of A Wedding (78)	7

BOUDLEAUX BRYANT
60	Polydor NH 66952	Hot Spot/Touché (with Sparks)	7
	(see also Bood & Fileece Bryant)		

DON BRYANT
70	London HA-U/SH-U 8409	PRECIOUS SOUL (LP)	15

LAURA K. BRYANT
58	London HLU 8551	Bobby/Angel Tears	25
58	London HLU 8551	Bobby/Angel Tears (78)	25

MARIE/MARGARET BRYANT
52	Lyragon J 701	Tomato/Rhumboogie Anna (78)	8
52	Lyragon J 709	Little Boy/STERLING BETTANCOURT: Blue Basin Sam (78)	8
52	Parlophone R 3592	Ain't Misbehavin'/Beale Street Blues (78)	8
54	London Calypso CAY 105	Don't Touch Me Nylon/Water Melon (78)	8
54	London Calypso CAY 107	Mary's Lamb/Noisy Spring (78)	8
54	Lyragon J 724	The Lost Watch (Tick Tick)/S. BETTANCOURT: Beater Pam (78)	10
54	Lyragon J 725	My Handy Man/RUSSEL HENDERSON: Bacchanal (78)	10
54	Lyragon J 726	Banana Woman/"SHAKE" KEANE: Creole Honey (78)	10
61	Kalypso XX 27	Water Melon/Tomato	6
61	Kalypso XX 28	Don't Touch Me Nylon/Little Boy	6
61	Kalypso XXEP 7	CALYPSOS TOO HOT TO HANDLE (EP)	12
60s	Melodisc MLP 12 132	DON'T TOUCH ME NYLONS (LP, with or without sleeve)	25/15
60s	Fab MLP 12 132	DON'T TOUCH ME NYLONS (LP, reissue)	12

MATT BRYANT & LINDA JOYCE
60	Embassy WB 420	Goodness Gracious Me/STEVE STANNARD & HIS GROUP: Man Of Mystery	5
	(see also Maureen Evans)		

RAY BRYANT TRIO/COMBO
60	Pye International 7N 25052	Little Susie (Parts 2 & 4)	5
60	Philips PB 1003	Little Susie (Parts 1 & 3)	5
60	Philips PB 1014	The Madison Time (Parts 1 & 2)	5

RUSTY BRYANT
57	London HB-D 1066	RUSTY BRYANT (10" LP)	75

SANDRA BRYANT
67	Major Minor MM 523	Girl With Money/Golden Hours	6
68	Major Minor MM 553	Out To Get You/There's No Lock Upon My Door	7

GAVIN BRYARS
75	Obscure 1	THE SINKING OF THE TITANIC (LP)	12
	(see also Brian Eno)		

BERYL BRYDEN'S BACK-ROOM SKIFFLE
56	Decca F 10823	Casey Jones/Kansas City Blues	18
56	Decca F 10823	Casey Jones/Kansas City Blues (78)	25
56	Melodisc EPM 7-69	BERYL BRYDEN WITH FATTY GEORGE'S JAZZ BAND (EP)	8
	(see also Alexis Korner, Cyril Davies)		

BETSY BRYE
59	Columbia DB 4350	Sleep Walk/Daddy Daddy (Gotta Get A Phone In My Room)	8

YUL BRYNNER
53	Brunswick 05171	A Puzzlement/GERTRUDE LAWRENCE: Getting To Know You (78)	10
53	Brunswick 05171	Shall We Dance (with Gertrude Lawrence)/The King And I (Instrumental) (78)	10

B.T.
94	Perfecto SAM 1517	EMBRACING THE SUNSHINE (Original & Sasha Mixes) (12", double pack, promo only)	12
94	Perfecto SAM 1652	LOVING YOU MORE (12", double pack, promo only)	10
95	Perfecto SAM 1688	TRIPPING THE LIGHT FANTASTIC (12", 1-sided LP sampler, promo only)	20
95	Perfecto SAM 1690	DIVINITY (12", 1-sided LP sampler, promo only)	15
95	Perfecto SAM 1691	QUARK (12", 1-sided LP sampler, promo only)	15

B.T.B.-4
68	Liberty LBF 15067	Do It To 'Em/Sparrows And Daisies	5

B.T. EXPRESS
75	Pye International 7N 25674	Express (Parts 1 & 2)	5
75	Pye International 7N 25682	Once You Get It/This House Is Smokin'	6
75	Pye Intl. NSPL 28207	DO IT (TIL YOU'RE SATISFIED) (LP)	12
75	EMI International INA 1501	NON-STOP (LP)	12
76	EMI International INA 1502	ENERGY TO BURN (LP)	12
77	EMI International INS 3009	FUNCTION AT THE JUNCTION (LP)	12
78	EMI International INS 3016	SHOUT (SHOUT IT OUT) (LP)	12

B.T.P. FOLDERS
80	Future Earth FER 005	Radio/All Of A Sudden (p/s)	12

B12
93	Warp LP 9LTD	ELECTRO — SOMA (2-LP, orange vinyl)	40
93	B12 09 CASSETTE	PRELUDE PART 1 (cassette, 400 only)	20
93	B12 09 CD	PRELUDE PT 1 (CD, 500 only)	25
93	B12 CD 1	REDCELL & STASIS (CD, 1500 only)	20
94	B12 15	B12 (12", 4-track promo only, 10 copies pressed)	40

(see also Redcell, Musicology)

BUBA & SHOP ASSISTANTS
85	Villa 21 002	Something To Do/Dreaming Backwards (p/s, with insert in poly bag)	30

(see also Shop Assistants, Pastels)

BUBBLE GUM
68	Philips BF 1677	Little Red Bucket/With The Sun In Your Hair	5

BUBBLEGUM SPLASH
87	Subway Org. SUBWAY 13	SPLASHDOWN (EP, foldaround p/s with insert in poly bag)	5

BUBBLES
63	Duke DK 1001	Bopping In The Barnyard/The Wasp	12
63	Duke DK 1001	The Wasp/Bopping In The Barnyard (matrix: DK 1001A-1, plays "Rocking Crickets" by Hot Toddy's)	12

BUCCA
82	Plant Life PLR 039	THE HOLE IN THE HARPERS HEAD (LP)	12

LINDSAY BUCKINGHAM
81	Mercury MER 85	Trouble/That's How We Do It In L.A. (p/s)	5
82	Mercury MER 96	The Visitor (Bwana)/A Satisfied Mind (p/s)	6
82	Mercury MER 102	Mary Lee Jones/September Song (p/s)	6
83	Mercury MER 150	Holiday Road/Mary Lee Jones (p/s)	8
84	Mercury MER 168	Go Insane/Play In The Rain (p/s)	5
84	Mercury MERX 168	Go Insane/Play In The Rain (12", p/s)	12
84	Mercury MER 176	Slow Dancing/D.W. Suite (p/s)	5
92	Mercury MER 371	Countdown/This Nearly Was Mine (p/s)	5
92	Mercury MERCD 371	Countdown/This Nearly Was Mine/Surrender The Rain/Trouble (CD)	8
92	Mercury MER 380	Soul Drifter/Say You'll Meet Again (p/s)	5
92	Mercury MER 380 CD	Soul Drifter/Say You'll Meet Again/This Nearly Was Mine (live)/ Street Of Dreams (live) (CD)	8

BUCKINGHAM-NICKS
74	Polydor 2066 398	Don't Let Me Down Again/Races Are Run	15
76	Polydor 2066 700	Don't Let Me Down Again/Crystal	10
73	Polydor 2391 013	BUCKINGHAM-NICKS (LP, with insert, some with stickered sleeve)	40/35
81	Polydor 2482 378	BUCKINGHAM-NICKS (LP, reissue with insert)	25

(see also Lindsay Buckingham, Stevie Nicks, Fleetwood Mac, Walter Egan)

BUCKINGHAMS (U.K.)
65	Pye 7N 15848	I'll Never Hurt You No More/She Lied	7
65	Pye 7N 15921	To Be Or Not To Be/I Was Your First Guy	6

BUCKINGHAMS (U.S.)
67	Stateside SS 588	Kind Of A Drag/You Make Me Feel So Good	6
68	CBS 2640	Don't You Care/Why Don't You Love Me	12
68	CBS 3559	Back In Love Again/You Misunderstand Me	6

SEAN BUCKLEY & BREADCRUMBS
65	Stateside SS 421	It Hurts Me When I Cry/Everybody Knows	70

TIM BUCKLEY
67	Elektra EKSN 45008	Aren't You The Girl/Strange Street Affair Under Blue	7
67	Elektra EKSN 45018	Morning Glory/Knight-Errant	6
68	Elektra EKSN 45023	Once I Was/Phantasmagoria In Two	6
68	Elektra EKSN 45031	Wings/I Can't See You	6
68	Elektra EKSN 45041	Pleasant Street/Carnival Song	6
70	Straight S 4799	Happy Time/So Lonely	6
66	Elektra EKL/EKS 4004	TIM BUCKLEY (LP, orange label)	40
67	Elektra EKL/EKS 318	GOODBYE AND HELLO (LP, orange label, gatefold sleeve)	25
68	Elektra EKS 74045	HAPPY SAD (LP, orange label)	25
69	Straight STS 1060	BLUE AFTERNOON (LP)	25

Tim BUCKLEY

70	Elektra 2410 005	LORCA (LP)	30
71	Straight STS 1064	STARSAILOR (LP)	25
72	Warner Bros K 46176	GREETINGS FROM L.A. (LP, gatefold sleeve)	20
74	Discreet K 49201	SEFRONIA (LP)	20
74	Discreet K 59204	LOOK AT THE FOOL (LP)	25

VERNON BUCKLEY

73	Grape GR 3057	Mr Softhand/G.G. ALLSTARS: Dub	5
73	Grape GR 3058	Ital Queen/G.G. ALLSTARS: Dub	5

MILT BUCKNER & HIS MUSIC

56	Capitol CL 14662	Night Mist/Good Time Express	8

TEDDY BUCKNER & HIS BAND

56	Vogue V 2369	Oh, Didn't He Ramble/Battle Hymn Of The Republic	7
56	Vogue V 2375	When The Saints Go Marching In/West End Blues	7
57	Vogue V 2414	Sweet Georgia Brown/That's My Home	7

BUCKY & STRINGS

62	Salvo SLO 1807	Lolita's On The Loose/Lonely Island (99 copies only)	18

BUD & HIS BUDDIES

58	Starlite ST45 006	June, July And August/Sing A Little Sweeter	8

BUD & TRAVIS

59	London HLU 8965	Bonsoir Dame/Truly Do	7
59	London HLU 8965	Bonsoir Dame/Truly Do (78)	15
60	London HLG 9211	The Ballad Of The Alamo/The Green Leaves Of Summer	7
61	London HA-G 2328	BUD AND TRAVIS IN CONCERT (LP, also stereo SAH-G 6128)	15/18

ROY BUDD

65	Pye 7N 15807	Birth Of The Budd/M'Ghee M'Ghee	8
66	Parlophone R 5514	Summer Samba/Bahama Sound	5
67	Pye 7N 17279	Mr Rose/Summer Rain	10
68	Pye 7N 17652	Pavanne/Whizz Ball	6
69	Pye 7N 17773	Tijuana Piano/Lead On	6
70	Pye 7N 17987	Borsalino (Theme)/It Only Goes To Show	8
70	Pye 7N 45051	Carter (Theme)/Plaything (some in p/s)	75/30
67	Pye N(S)PL 18177	PICK YOURSELF UP — THIS IS ROY BUDD (LP)	50
67	Pye N(S)PL 18195	THE SOUND OF MUSIC (LP)	20
68	Pye NPL 18212	AT NEWPORT (LP)	65
69	Pye N(S)PL 18305	LEAD ON (LP)	25
71	Pye NSPL 18348	PLAYS SOLDIER BLUE AND OTHER THEMES (LP)	80
71	Pye NSPL 18354	BUDD 'N' BOSSA (LP)	40
71	Pye NSPL 18373	GREAT SONGS AND THEMES FROM GREAT FILMS (LP)	80
72	Pye NSPL 18389	CONCERTO FOR HARRY — SOMETHING TO HIDE (LP, soundtrack)	45
72	Polydor 2383 102	KIDNAPPED (LP, soundtrack, with Mary Hopkin)	50
73	Pye NSPL 18398	FEAR IS THE KEY (LP, soundtrack)	70
76	Bradley's BRADS 8002	DIAMONDS (LP, soundtrack)	70
70s	Pye NSPL 19494	EVERYTHING'S COMING UP (LP)	50
80	EMI EMC 3340	THE SEA WOLVES (LP, soundtrack)	12

BUDDY & JUNIORS
(see under Buddy Guy)

BUDGIE

71	MCA MK 5072	Crash Course In Brain Surgery/Nude Disintegrating Parachutist Woman	15
72	MCA MK 5085	Whisky River/Guts	10
74	MCA MCA 133	Zoom Club (Edited Version)/Wondering What Everyone Knows	8
75	MCA MCA 175	I Ain't No Mountain/Honey	8
78	A&M AMS 7342	Smile Boy Smile/All At Sea	8
80	Active BUDGE	Wildfire/Wildfire (promo only)	12
80	Active BUDGE 1	IF SWALLOWED DO NOT INDUCE VOMITING (12" EP)	12
80	Active BUDGE 2	Crime Against The World/Hellbender (p/s)	8
81	RCA BUDGE 3	Keeping A Rendezvous/Apparatus (p/s)	5
81	RCA BUDGE 3	Keeping A Rendezvous/Apparatus (picture disc)	5
81	RCA BUDGE 4	I Turned To Stone (Part 1)/I Turned To Stone (Part 2) (orange vinyl, no p/s)	6
82	RCA RCA 271	Bored With Russia/Don't Cry (poster p/s)	6
82	RCA RCAP 271	Bored With Russia/Don't Cry (picture disc)	5
71	MCA MKPS 2018	BUDGIE (LP, pink/red label, initially with poster)	40/25
71	MCA MKPS 2018	BUDGIE (LP, later pressing with blue/black label)	20
73	MCA MCF 2506	BUDGIE (LP, reissue, rainbow label)	12
72	MCA MKPS 2023	SQUAWK (LP, blue/black label)	15
73	MCA MDKS 8010	NEVER TURN YOUR BACK ON A FRIEND (LP, blue/black label, g/fold sleeve)	15
74	MCA MCF 2546	IN FOR THE KILL (LP)	12
75	MCA MCF 2723	BANDOLIER (LP)	12
75	MCA MCF 2766	THE BEST OF BUDGIE (LP)	12
76	A&M AMLH 68377	IF I WAS BRITANNIA I'D WAIVE THE RULES (LP)	12
78	A&M AMLH 64675	IMPECKABLE (LP)	12
80	Active ACTLP 1	POWER SUPPLY (LP, with insert)	12
81	RCA RCALP 3046	POWER SUPPLY (LP, reissue, with different back sleeve)	12
81	RCA RCALP 6003	NIGHT FLIGHT (LP)	12
81	Cube HIFLY 36	BEST OF BUDGIE (LP)	12
82	RCA RCALP 6054	DELIVER US FROM EVIL (LP)	12

(see also Tredegar, Phenomena, George Hatcher Band)

DENNIS BUDLIMAR

67	Fontana TL 5307	THE CREEPER (LP)	15

BUENA VISTAS

66	Stateside SS 525	Hot Shot/T.N.T.	10

BUDGIE

BUFFALO
81	Heavy Metal HEAVY 3	Battle Torn Heroes/Women Of The Night (p/s)	15
82	Heavy Metal HEAVY 15	Mean Machine/The Rumour (p/s)	15

BUFFALO SPRINGFIELD
67	Atlantic 584 077	For What It's Worth (Stop Hey What's That Sound)/ Do I Have To Come Right Out And Say It	6
67	Atlantic 584 145	Rock'n'Roll Woman/A Child's Claim To Fame	6
68	Atlantic 584 165	Expecting To Fly/Everydays	7
68	Atlantic 584 189	Uno-Mundo/Merry-Go-Round	6
69	Atco 226 006	Pretty Girl Why/Questions	6
72	Atlantic K 10237	Bluebird/Mr Soul/Rock'n'Roll Woman/Expecting To Fly (p/s)	6
67	Atlantic 587/588 070	BUFFALO SPRINGFIELD (LP, plum label, mispressing, lists "For What It's Worth" but plays "Baby Don't Scold Me"; matrix no. ends '1'; mono/stereo)	55/45
67	Atlantic 587/588 070	BUFFALO SPRINGFIELD (LP, plum label, plays "For What It's Worth", m/s)	35/25
68	Atlantic 587/588 091	BUFFALO SPRINGFIELD AGAIN (LP, plum label, mono/stereo)	35/25
69	Atco 228 024	LAST TIME AROUND (LP, plum label, gatefold sleeve)	18
69	Atco 228 012	RETROSPECTIVE (LP, plum label)	12
70	Atlantic 2464 012	EXPECTING TO FLY (LP, plum label)	18
72	Atlantic K 40014	BUFFALO SPRINGFIELD AGAIN (LP, reissue, green & orange label)	18
72	Atlantic K 40077	LAST TIME AROUND (LP, reissue, green & orange label, gatefold sleeve)	12
73	Atlantic K 30028	BEGINNINGS (ATLANTIC MASTERS) (LP, green & orange label)	12
73	Midi MID 0020	STAR COLLECTION (LP)	12

(see also Neil Young, Stephen Stills, Poco, Au-Go-Go Singers, Crosby Stills Nash & Young)

BUFFALO TOM
89	Caff CAFF 6	Enemy/Deep In The Ground (p/s)	20

BUFFOONS
67	Columbia DB 8317	My World Fell Down/Tomorrow Is Another Day	10

BUGALOOS
71	Capitol E-SW 621	THE BUGALOOS (LP)	12

BULAWAYO SWEET RHYTHMS BAND
54	Decca F 10350	Skokiaan/In The Mood	6

BULLAMAKANKA
83	BBC REL 454	Dr Who Is Gonna Fix It/Harlequin	6

JOHN BULL BREED
66	Polydor BM 56065	Can't Chance A Breakup/I'm A Man	165

BULLDOG BREED
69	Deram DM 270	Portcullis Gate/Halo In My Hair	35
70	Deram Nova (S)DN 5	MADE IN ENGLAND (LP)	50

(see also Flies)

BULLDOGS
64	Mercury MF 808	John, Paul, George And Ringo/What Do I See	12

BULLET
71	Purple PUR 101	Hobo/Sinister Minister	8

(see also Hard Stuff)

BULLET
75	Contour 2870 437	THE HANGED MAN (LP, TV soundtrack)	45

MINT VALUE £

BULLSEYE
80	Kennet K1	No. 10, 553/Why Don't You Let Me Know (no p/s)	8

BULLY WEE (BAND)
75	Folksound	BULLYWEE (LP)	20
76	Red Rag RRR 007	THE ENCHANTED LADY (LP)	15
70s	Red Rag RRR 017	SILVERMINES (LP, as Bullywee Band)	12
81	Jigsaw SAW 1	THE MADMAN OF GOTHAM (LP)	20

B. BUMBLE & STINGERS
61	Top Rank JAR 561	Bumble Boogie/School Day Blues	8
62	Top Rank JAR 611	Nut Rocker/Nautilus	6
62	Stateside SS 113	Apple Knocker/The Moon And The Sea	7
62	Stateside SS 131	Dawn Cracker/Scales	7
63	Stateside SS 192	Baby Mash/Night Time Madness	7
67	Mercury MF 977	Silent Movies/Twelfth Street Rag	7
72	Pye International 7N 25597	Down At Mother's Place/Manhattan Spiritual	6
62	Stateside SE 1001	THE PIANO STYLINGS OF B. BUMBLE (EP)	30

(see also Kim Fowley)

BUMBLE BEE SLIM
60s	Fontana 688 138ZL	BEE'S BACK IN TOWN (LP)	20

BUMBLES
72	Purple PUR 107	Beep Beep/Buzz Off (some in promo only p/s)	25/8

BUNCH
67	CBS 202506	We're Not What We Appear To Be/You Never Came Home	45
67	CBS 2740	Don't Come Back To Me/You Can't Do This	18
67	CBS 3060	Looking Glass Alice/Spare A Shilling	60
68	CBS 3692	Birthday/Still	15
68	CBS 3709	Birthday/Still (reissue)	10

(see also Peter & The Wolves, Sounds Around, John Pantry)

BUNCH
69	Beacon BEA 128	Red Rover, Red Rover/Happy Like This	5

BUNCH
72	Island WIP 6130	When Will I Be Loved/Willie And The Hand Jive	7
72	Island ILPS 9189	ROCK ON (LP, some with 1-sided flexi: "Let There Be Drums" [WI 4002])	35/15

(see also Fairport Convention, Sandy Denny, Richard & Linda Thompson, Ashley Hutchings, Trevor Lucas)

BUNCH OF FIVES
66	Parlophone R 5494	Go Home Baby/At The Station	30

(see also Viv Prince, Egg, Hullaballoos, Junior's Eyes, Outsiders [U.K.])

BUNDLE
70	Polydor 2058 029	Dirty La Rue/Progressive Underground	5

ROGER BUNN
70	Major Minor SMLP 70	PIECE OF MIND (LP)	20

BUNNIES
66	Decca F 12350	Thumper/Ja Da	5

BINGY BUNNY & BONGO LES
73	Ackee ACK 506	International Scout/International Scout Version	5

(see also Bongo Les, Mediators)

BUNNY & RUDDY
68	Nu Beet NB 007	Rhythm & Soul/MONTY MORRIS: True Romance	10
68	Nu Beat NB 011	On The Town/MONTY MORRIS: Simple Simon	8

BOB BUNTING
68	Transatlantic TRA 166	YOU'VE GOT TO GO DOWN THIS WAY (LP)	35

VASHTI BUNYAN
70	Philips 6308 019	JUST ANOTHER DIAMOND DAY (LP)	250

(see also Vashti, Fairport Convention, Dave Swarbrick, Robin Williamson)

BUOYS
70	Wand WN 7	Timothy/It Feels Good	5

ERIC BURDON (BAND)
75	Capitol E-ST 11359	SUN SECRETS (LP, as Eric Burdon Band)	12
75	Capitol E-ST 11426	STOP (LP, as Eric Burdon Band)	12
78	Polydor 2302 078	SURVIVOR (LP, with 8-page booklet)	12
80	Polydor 2344 147	DARKNESS — DARKNESS (LP)	12

ERIC BURDON & ANIMALS
66	Decca F 12502	Mama Told Me Not To Come/See See Rider (unreleased)	
66	Decca F 12502	Help Me Girl/See See Rider (amended issue with new A-side)	6
67	MGM MGM 1340	When I Was Young/A Girl Named Sandoz	10
67	MGM MGM 1344	Good Times/Ain't That So	8
67	MGM MGM 1359	San Franciscan Nights/Gratefully Dead	8
68	MGM MGM 1373	Sky Pilot (Parts 1 & 2)	8
68	MGM MGM 1412	Monterey/Anything	10
69	MGM MGM 1461	Ring Of Fire/I'm An Animal	12
69	MGM MGM 1481	River Deep Mountain High/Help Me Girl	15
71	MGM 2006 028	Good Times/San Franciscan Nights	6
67	MGM C(S) 8052	WINDS OF CHANGE (LP)	20
68	MGM C(S) 8074	THE TWAIN SHALL MEET (LP)	20
68	MGM C(S) 8105	LOVE IS (LP)	20
71	MGM 2619 002	LOVE IS (2-LP; individual LP nos.: 2354 006/7)	30
71	MGM 2354 001	WINDS OF CHANGE (LP, reissue)	12

(see also Animals, Stud, Zoot Money's Big Roll Band)

ERIC BURDON & WAR
70	Polydor 2001 072	Spill The Wine/Magic Mountain	5
71	Liberty LBF 15434	They Can't Take Away Our Music/Home Cookin'	5
71	United Artists UP 35217	Paint It Black/Spirit	5
70	Polydor 2310 041	ERIC BURDON DECLARES WAR (LP)	18
70	Liberty LDS 8400	BLACKMAN'S BURDON (2-LP, some with banned track "P.C. 3")	30/25
76	ABC ABCL 5207	LOVE IS ALL AROUND (LP)	12

(see also War)

ERIC BURDON & JIMMY WITHERSPOON
71	United Artists UP 35287	Soledad/Headin' For Home	5
71	United Artists UAG 29251	GUILTY! (LP, gatefold sleeve)	18

(see also Jimmy Witherspoon)

DAVE BURGESS (TRIO)
55	London HLB 8175	I Love Paris/Five Foot Two, Eyes Of Blue (Has Anybody Seen My Girl)	35
55	London HLB 8175	I Love Paris/Five Foot Two, Eyes Of Blue (Has Anybody Seen My Girl) (78)	18
58	Oriole CB 1413	I'm Available/Who's Gonna Cry?	90
58	Oriole CB 1413	I'm Available/Who's Gonna Cry? (78)	45

JOHN BURGESS
69	Topic 12T 199	KING OF HIGHLAND PIPERS (LP)	12

SONNY BURGESS
60	London HLS 9064	Sadie's Back In Town/A Kiss Goodnight	225

JIM BURGETT
61	Philips PB 1133	Let's Investigate/The Living Dead	22

CHRIS DE BURGH
75	A&M AMS 7148	Hold On/Sin City	6
75	A&M AMS 7185	Flying/Watching The World	6
76	A&M AMS 7196	Lonely Sky/The Song For You	5
76	A&M AMS 7224	Patricia The Stripper/Old Friend	5
76	A&M AMS 7267	A Spaceman Came Travelling/Just A Poor Boy (initially in p/s)	7
77	A&M AMS 7320	Broken Wings/I Will	6
78	A&M AMS 7336	Discovery/Round And Around	6
78	A&M AMS 7347	Spanish Train/Perfect Day (initially in p/s)	6
80	A&M AMS 7546	Shadows And Lights/Walls Of Silence (initially in p/s)	6
80	A&M AMS 7562	The Traveller/Eastern Wind (initially in p/s)	6
81	A&M AMS 8160	Waiting For The Hurricane/Broken Wings (p/s)	5
82	A&M AMS 8268	The Getaway/Living On The Island (p/s)	5
84	A&M AMX 202	I Love The Night/Moonlight And Vodka (12", p/s)	8
80s	A&M C DE B 1	Sailor/Lonely Sky (p/s, clear vinyl, numbered)	7

KEVIN BURKE
78	Rockburgh ROC 105	IF THE CAP FITS (LP)	25

SOLOMON BURKE
61	London HLK 9454	Just Out Of Reach/Be Bop Grandma	25
62	London HLK 9512	Cry To Me/I Almost Lost My Mind	40
62	London HLK 9560	Down In The Valley/I'm Hanging Up My Heart For You	15
63	London HLK 9715	If You Need Me/You Can Make It If You Try	15
63	London HLK 9763	Can't Nobody Love You/Stupidity	15
64	London HLK 9849	He'll Have To Go/Rockin' Soul	15
64	London HLK 9887	Goodbye Baby (Baby Goodbye)/Someone To Love Me	15
64	Atlantic AT 4004	Everybody Needs Somebody To Love/Looking For My Baby	10
64	Atlantic AT 4014	The Price/More Rockin' Soul	10
65	Atlantic AT 4022	Got To Get You Off My Mind/Peepin'	8
65	Atlantic AT 4030	Maggie's Farm/Tonight's The Night	12
65	Atlantic AT 4044	Someone Is Watching/Dance, Dance, Dance	8
65	Atlantic AT 4061	Only Love (Can Save Me Now)/Little Girl That Loves Me	10
66	Atlantic AT 4073	Baby Come On Home/No, No, No, I Can't Stop Lovin' You Now	7
66	Atlantic 584 005	I Feel A Sin Comin' On/Mountain Of Pride	6
66	Atlantic 584 026	Keep Lookin'/Suddenly	6
67	Atlantic 584 100	Keep A Light In The Window Till I Come Home/Time Is A Thief	6
67	Atlantic 584 122	Take Me (Just As I Am)/I Stayed Away Too Long	6
68	Atlantic 584 191	I Wish I Knew (How It Would Feel To Be Free)/It's Just A Matter Of Time	6
68	Atlantic 584 204	Save It/Meet Me In Church	6
68	Bell BLL 1047	Uptight Good Woman/I Can't Stop (No No No)	6
69	Bell BLL 1062	Proud Mary/What Am I Living For	6
74	Anchor ABC 4002	Midnight And You/I Have A Dream	5
63	London REK 1379	TONIGHT MY HEART SHE IS CRYING (EP)	50
65	London AET 6008	ROCK'N'SOUL (EP)	40
63	London HA-K 8018	SOLOMON BURKE'S GREATEST (LP)	60
64	Atlantic ATL 5009	KING OF ROCK'N'SOUL (LP)	40
66	Atlantic 587/588 016	THE BEST OF SOLOMON BURKE (LP)	30
66	Atlantic 590 004	KING OF ROCK'N'SOUL (LP, reissue)	18
68	Atlantic 587 105	KING SOLOMON (LP)	25
68	Atlantic 587/588 117	I WISH I KNEW (LP)	18
69	Bell MBLL/SBLL 118	PROUD MARY (LP)	15
72	MGM 2315 048	THE ELECTRONIC MAGNETISM (LP)	12

(see also Soul Clan)

SONNY BURKE & HIS ORCHESTRA (U.S.)
55	Brunswick 05361	"Phffft" Mambo/Long Hair Mambo	5

SONNY BURKE (U.K.)
64	Black Swan WI 457	I Love You Still/It's Always A Pleasure	15
64	Black Swan WI 458	City In The Sky/Everyday I Love You More	15
65	Black Swan WI 469	Glad/Jeanie	15

Sonny BURKE

65	Black Swan WI 470	Dance With Me/My Girl Can't Cook	15
65	Black Swan WI 471	Wicked People/Good Heaven Knows	15
66	Blue Beat BB 363	Blue Island/You Came And Left	12
67	Blue Beat BB 371	Look In Her Eyes/LLOYD CLARKE: Love Is Strange	15
68	Island ILP 972	THE SOUNDS OF SONNY BURKE (LP, mono only)	70

(see also Bob Andy, Gaylads, Ken Parker, Eddie Thornton Outfit, Glen Adams, Stranger Cole, Gaylads, Sonny & Yvonne)

DAVE BURLAND

71	Trailer LER 2029	A DALESMAN'S LITANY (LP, red label)	20
72	Trailer LER 2082	DAVE BURLAND (LP)	18
75	Rubber RUB 012	SONGS AND BUTTERED HAYCOCKS (LP)	15
79	Rubber RUB 036	YOU CAN'T FOOL THE FAT MAN (LP)	12
80	Rubber RUB 012/036	DOUBLE TAKE (2-LP, reissue)	15

SASCHA BURLAND

61	Philips PB 1152	Gorilla Walk/Hole In My Soul	6

BURMOE BROTHERS

85	Wild Blue Yonder WBY 121	Skin/Leber Oder Lippenstift/Under The Blanket Of Love (12", p/s)	15

(see also Marc Almond, Nick Cave)

JEAN-JACQUES BURNEL

79	United Artists UP 36500	Freddie Laker (Concorde And Eurobus)/Ozymandias (p/s)	5
80	United Artists BP 361	Girl From The Snow Country/Ode To Joy (live)/Do The European (live) (p/s, unissued)	400+
88	Stranglers Information Service S.I.S. 003	Goebbels, Mosley, God And Ingrams (fan club flexidisc, with issue 27 of *Strangled* fanzine)	10/5
79	United Artists UAG 30214	EUROMAN COMETH (LP, with inner sleeve)	12
88	Mau Mau P MAU 601	EUROMAN COMETH (LP, picture disc reissue)	15

JEAN-JACQUES BURNEL & DAVE GREENFIELD

84	Epic EPCA 4076	Rain And Dole And Tea/Consequences (p/s)	6
84	Epic EPC 25707	FIRE AND WATER (LP)	12

(see also Stranglers)

FRANCES BURNETT

59	Coral Q 72374	Please Remember Me/How I Miss You So (triangular or round centre)	45/35
59	Coral Q 72374	Please Remember Me/How I Miss You So (78)	25

REV. J.C. BURNETT/REV. GATES/REV. MOSELEY

60	Fontana TFE 17265	TREASURES OF NORTH AMERICAN NEGRO MUSIC VOLUME 6: PREACHERS AND CONGREGATIONS (EP)	15

KING BURNETT

75	Dip DL 5056	I Man Free/UPSETTERS: Version	7
75	Dip DL 5073	Key Card/UPSETTERS: Domino Game	7

DORSEY BURNETTE

60	London HLN 9047	Juarez Town/(There Was A) Tall Oak Tree	18
60	London HLN 9160	Hey Little One/Big Rock Candy Mountain	20
61	London HLN 9365	(It's No) Sin/Hard Rock Mine	15
65	Tamla Motown TMG 534	Jimmy Brown/Everybody's Angel	55
69	Liberty LBF 15190	The Greatest Love/Thin Little, Simple Little, Plain Little Girl	10
63	London RE-D 1402	DORSEY BURNETTE SINGS (EP)	45
63	London HA-D 8050	DORSEY BURNETTE (LP)	70

(see also Johnny & Dorsey Burnette)

JOHNNY BURNETTE (TRIO)

78s

56	Vogue Coral Q 72177	Tear It Up/You're Undecided (as Johnny Burnette & Rock'N'Roll Trio) (78)	160
57	Vogue Coral Q 72227	Honey Hush/Lonesome Train (as Johnny Burnette Trio) (78)	130
57	Vogue Coral Q 72283	Touch Me/Eager Beaver Baby (as Johnny Burnette Trio) (78)	110
60	London HLG 9172	Dreamin'/Cincinnati Fireball (78)	550
96	Cruisin' The 50s CASB 003	The Train Kept A Rollin'/Sweet Love On My Mind (78, 300 copies only)	40

SINGLES

56	Vogue Coral Q 72177	Tear It Up/You're Undecided (as Johnny Burnette & Rock'N'Roll Trio)	550
57	Vogue Coral Q 72227	Honey Hush/Lonesome Train (as Johnny Burnette Trio)	550
57	Vogue Coral Q 72283	Touch Me/Eager Beaver Baby (as Johnny Burnette Trio)	250
60	London HLG 9172	Dreamin'/Cincinnati Fireball	7
60	London HLG 9254	You're Sixteen/I Beg Your Pardon	6
61	London HLG 9315	Little Boy Sad/Pledge Of Love	7
61	London HLG 9388	Girls/I've Got A Lot Of Things To Do	8
61	London HLG 9453	God Country And My Baby/Honestly I Do	12
61	London HLG 9458	Settin' The Woods On Fire/I'm Still Dreaming	12
61	London HLG 9473	Big Big World/The Fool	12
62	Liberty LIB 55416	Clown Shoes/The Way I Am	8
62	Liberty LIB 55489	Damn The Defiant/Lonesome Waters	8
66	Liberty LIB 10235	Dreamin'/Little Boy Sad	10
62	Pye International 7N 25158	I Wanna Thank Your Folks/The Giant	10
63	Pye International 7N 25187	Remember Me/Time Is Not Enough	10
63	Capitol CL 15322	All Week Long/It Isn't There	18
64	Capitol CL 15347	Sweet Suzie/Walking Talking Doll	25

EXPORT SINGLES

60	London HLG 7104	You're Sixteen/Settin' The Woods On Fire	25
61	London HL 7109	Little Boy Sad/I Go Down To The River	30

EPs

60	London RE-G 1263	DREAMING (EP)	70
61	London RE-G 1291	LITTLE BOY SAD (EP)	70
61	London RE-G 1309	BIG BIG WORLD (EP)	70
61	London RE-G 1327	GIRLS (EP)	70
63	Liberty LEP 2091	HIT AFTER HIT (EP)	45
64	Capitol EAP 20645	FOUR BY BURNETTE (EP)	120

LPs

56	Coral LVC 10041	ROCK AND ROLL TRIO (10" LP, as Johnny Burnette Trio)	1000
61	London HA-G 2306	DREAMIN' (LP)	80
61	London HA-G 2349	YOU'RE SIXTEEN (LP)	80
61	London HA-G 2375	JOHNNY BURNETTE SINGS (LP, also stereo SAH-G 6175)	80/100
62	Liberty LBY 1006	BURNETTE'S HITS AND OTHER FAVOURITES (LP)	40
64	Liberty LBY 1231	THE JOHNNY BURNETTE STORY (LP)	60
66	Ace Of Hearts AH 120	ROCK AND ROLL TRIO (LP, reissue, as Johnny Burnette Trio)	18
68	Sunset SLS 50007E	DREAMIN' (LP)	15
68	Coral CP 10	TEAR IT UP (LP, as Johnny Burnette Trio)	18
71	Coral CP 61	ROCK AND ROLL TRIO (LP, 2nd reissue, as Johnny Burnette Trio)	12
74	United Artists UAS 29643	TENTH ANNIVERSARY ALBUM (LP)	12

(see also Johnny & Dorsey Burnette)

JOHNNY & DORSEY BURNETTE
63	Reprise R 20153	Hey Sue/It Don't Matter Much	35

(see also Johnny Burnette, Dorsey Burnette)

SMILEY BURNETTE
50	Capitol CL 13388	Rudolph The Red-Nosed Reindeer/Grandaddy Frog (78)	12
54	London HL 8071	Lazy Locomotive/That Long White Line	45
54	London HL 8071	Lazy Locomotive/That Long White Line (78)	35
54	London HL 8085	Chuggin' On Down "66"/Mucho Gusto	50
54	London HL 8085	Chuggin' On Down "66"/Mucho Gusto (78)	35

BURNING SPEAR
75	Fab FAB 240	Foggy Road/Version	8
75	Island ILPS 9377	MARCUS GARVEY (LP)	15

(see also Irving Brown, King Cry Cry)

BURNIN' RED IVANHOE
71	Warner Bros K 44062	BURNIN' RED IVANHOE (LP)	20
72	Dandelion 2310 145	W.W.W. (LP, gatefold sleeve)	25

JAN BURNNETTE
62	Oriole CB 1716	I Could Have Loved You So Well/The Miracle Of Life	12
62	Oriole CB 1742	All At Once/Does My Heartache Show?	10
62	Oriole CB 1761	Teddy/Trust In Me	10
63	Oriole CB 1807	The Boy I Used To Know/Unimportant Things	12
63	Oriole CB 1841	Till I Hear The Truth From You/Fall In Love	8
64	Oriole CB 1905	Let Me Make You Smile Again/No Regrets	12
64	Oriole CB 1920	Too Young/The Four Winds And The Seven Seas	12
64	Oriole CB 1949	Love, Let Me Not Hunger/The One I Love (Belongs To Somebody Else)	10

DENNIS BURNS
(see Mark Perry)

EDDIE 'GUITAR' BURNS
72	Action ACMP 100	BOTTLE UP AND GO (LP)	18
75	Big Bear BEAR 7	DETROIT BLACKBOTTOM (LP)	12

JACKIE BURNS & BELLES
63	MGM MGM 1226	He's My Guy/I Do The Best I Can	60

JIMMY BURNS
79	Grapevine GRP 118	I Really Love You/I Love You Girl	6

LISA BURNS
78	MCA MCF 2849	LISA BURNS (LP)	12

RANDY BURNS
68	Fontana STL 5520	EVENING OF THE MAGICIAN (LP)	18

RAY BURNS
53	Columbia SCM 5077	Rags To Riches/Begorrah	7
54	Columbia SCM 5153	I Can't Tell A Waltz From A Tango/Lonely Nightingale	7
55	Columbia DB 3640	That's How A Love Song Was Born/The Voice (78)	14
56	Columbia DB 3811	Condemned For Life (With A Rock And Roll Life)/The Mare Piccola	12
57	Columbia DB 3966	Wonderful! Wonderful!/Bernadine	6
58	Columbia DB 4107	Are You Sincere/The Best Dream Of All	6
55	Columbia SEG 7594	RAY BURNS (EP)	18

(see also Ruby Murray, Ronnie Harris, Diana Decker, Ray Martin)

WILFRED BURNS
53	MGM SP 1059	There Was An Old Lady/Broken Horseshoe	6

HAROLD BURRAGE
65	Sue WI 353	I'll Take One/A Long Ways Together	22
68	President PT 130	You Made Me So Happy/Take Me Now	10

KENNY BURRELL
61	Esquire 32-140	ALL NIGHT LONG (LP, as Kenny Burrell All Stars)	18
64	Verve VLP 9058	BLUE BLASH (LP, with Jimmy Smith)	15
65	Verve VLP 9099	GUITAR FORMS (LP)	15
66	Stateside SL 10163	CRASH! (LP, with Brother Jack McDuff)	18
68	Verve (S)VLP 9217	BLUES, THE COMMON GROUND (LP)	18
69	Verve SVLP 9246	NIGHT SONG (LP)	15
70	Verve SVLP 9250	ASPHALT CANYON SUITE (LP)	12

(see also Brother Jack McDuff, Jimmy Smith)

STUART BURROWS
60s	Qualition QEP 4041	SINGS (EP)	8

WILLIAM S. BURROUGHS
80	Industrial IR 0016	NOTHING HERE NOW BUT THE RECORDINGS (LP)	30

BUDDY BURTON
(see under Dixie Four)

HAL BURTON
58	Embassy WB 290	Rave On/Big Man (78)	8
58	Embassy WB 308	Move It/Susie Darling	5
58	Embassy WB 308	Move It/Susie Darling (78)	10

GARY BURTON (QUARTET)
68	RCA Victor SF 7923	LOFTY FAKE ANAGRAM (LP)	18
60s	RCA Victor SF 8015	GENUINE TONGUE FUNERAL (LP)	18
71	Atlantic 2400 107	GOOD VIBES (LP)	15
72	Atlantic K 40305	ALONE AT LAST (LP)	12
72	Atlantic K 40378	PARIS ENCOUNTER (LP, with Stefan Grappelli)	12

(see also Michael Gibbs)

JAMES BURTON
71	A&M AMLS 64293	THE GUITAR SOUNDS OF JAMES BURTON (LP)	55

(see also Jim & Joe, Shindogs)

TOMMY BURTON COMBO
64	Blue Beat BB 237	Lavender Blue/I'm Walking	12

TREVOR BURTON
71	Wizard WIZ 103	Fight For My Country/Janie Slow Down	15

(see also Uglys, Move, Balls, Denny Laine, Danny King's Mayfair Set, Magic Christians, Idle Race)

BURUNDI STEPHENSON BLACK
71	Barclay BAR 3	Burundi Black (Parts 1 & 2) (some with p/s)	8/4

LOU BUSCH & HIS ORCHESTRA
56	Capitol CL 14504	Zambesi/Rainbow's End	12

(see also Joe 'Fingers' Carr)

KATE BUSH
78	EMI EMI 2719	Wuthering Heights/Kite (p/s)	40
78	EMI EMI 2806	The Man With The Child In His Eyes/Moving (p/s)	20
78	EMI EMI 2887	Hammer Horror/Coffee Homeground (p/s)	10
79	EMI EMI 2911	Wow/Fullhouse (p/s)	10
79	EMI MIEP 2991	KATE BUSH ON STAGE (EP, gatefold sleeve)	15
79	EMI PSR 442/3	KATE BUSH ON STAGE (EP, double pack, gatefold sleeve, promo only)	70
80	Sound For Industry SFI 562	Selected Highlights from "Never Forever" (flexidisc, black vinyl)	15
80	Sound For Industry SFI 562	Selected Highlights from "Never Forever" (square flexidisc, black vinyl)	15
81	EMI EMI 5201	Sat In Your Lap/Lord Of The Reedy River (p/s)	6
82	EMI EMI 5350	There Goes A Tenner/Ne T'Enfuis Pas (thick card, p/s)	10
84	EMI KBS 1	THE SINGLE FILE (13 x 7" box set with lyric booklet)	150
85	EMI KB 1	Running Up That Hill/Under The Ivy (gatefold p/s)	5
85	EMI 12 KB 2	Cloudbusting (Organon Mix)/Burning Bridges/My Lagan Love (12", p/s)	7
86	EMI KBP 4	The Big Sky (Single Mix)/Not This Time (picture disc)	15
89	EMI CDEM 102	The Sensual World/(Instrumental)/Walk Straight Down The Middle (CD)	10
89	EMI EMPD 119	This Woman's Work/Be Kind To My Mistakes (picture disc, with insert, PVC sl.)	5
89	EMI 12EMP 119	This Woman's Work/Be Kind To My Mistakes/I'm Still Waiting (12", poster p/s)	8
89	EMI CDEM 119	This Woman's Work/Be Kind To My Mistakes/I'm Still Waiting (CD)	10
90	EMI CDEM 134	Love And Anger/Ken/The Confrontation/One Last Look Around The House (CD)	10
91	Rocket TRICD 2	Rocket Man/Candle In The Wind/Rocket Man (Instrumental) (CD, digipak)	10
93	EMI GIRL 1	Rubberband Girl (CD, 1-track "lyrical teaser", promo only)	15
93	EMI EM 280	Eat The Music/Big Stripey Lie (p/s, picture labels, release cancelled, 17 copies only)	1,500
93	EMI 12EMPD 280	Eat The Music/Eat The Music (Madagascan Remix)/Big Stripey Lie (12", picture disc, unissued)	
93	EMI CDEM 280	Eat The Music/Eat The Music (Madagascan Remix)/Big Stripey Lie (CD, unissued)	
93	EMI MUSIC 1	Eat The Music (CD, 1-track promo for unissued single, no inlay, withdrawn)	150
93	EMI CDEM 297	Moments Of Pleasure/December Will Be Magic Again/Experiment IV (CD, box set with 4 prints)	8
94	EMI EMPD 355	And So Is Love/Rubberband Girl (USA Mix) (picture disc, PVC sleeve, with 60" x 40" poster, unnumbered or 5,000 numbered)	25/8
79	EMI EM CP 3223	THE KICK INSIDE (LP, picture disc, stickered sleeve)	50
79	EMI EM CP 3223	THE KICK INSIDE (LP, picture disc, stickered sleeve, second pressing with "manufactured in the U.K. by EMI Records Ltd" wording)	40
79	EMI EM CP 3223	THE KICK INSIDE (LP, picture disc, mispress with same picture both sides)	150
90	EMI KBBX 1	THIS WOMAN'S WORK (9-LP, box set)	100
90	EMI CKBBX 1	THIS WOMAN'S WORK (cassette, box set)	40
90	EMI CDKBBX 1	THIS WOMAN'S WORK (CD, box set)	100

(see also Peter Gabriel & Kate Bush, Lesley Duncan)

RAY BUSH & AVON CITIES' SKIFFLE
56	Tempo A 146	Hey Hey Daddy Blues/Green Corn	20
56	Tempo A 146	Hey Hey Daddy Blues/Green Corn (78)	20
56	Tempo A 149	Fisherman's Blues/This Little Light Of Mine	20
56	Tempo A 149	Fisherman's Blues/This Little Light Of Mine (78)	20
57	Tempo A 156	How Long, How Long, Blues/Julian Johnson	15
57	Tempo A 156	How Long, How Long, Blues/Julian Johnson (78)	20
57	Tempo A 157	Lonesome Day Blues/I Don't Know	12
57	Tempo A 157	Lonesome Day Blues/I Don't Know (78)	20
57	Tempo EXA 40	RAY BUSH & AVON CITIES' SKIFFLE (EP)	20
57	Tempo EXA 50	RAY BUSH & AVON CITIES' SKIFFLE NO. 2 (EP)	20

(see also Avon Cities Jazz Band)

BUSH BOYS
59	Capitol CL 15082	A Broken Vow/Never Before	6

BUSHIDO
| 84 | Third Mind TMS 02 | Among The Ruins/The First Cut/Beyond The Great Wall (12", p/s)............. 8 |
| 85 | Third Mind TMS 05 | VOICES (12" EP).. 7 |

BUSH TETRAS
81	Fetish FET 007	Things That Go Boom In The Night/Das Ah Riot (p/s).................... 6
82	Fetish FE 15	Can't Be Funky (unissued, stamped white label only, custom plain sleeve)..... 10
82	Fetish FET 16EP	RITUALS (12" EP)..................................... 15

BUSINESS
81	Secret SHH 123	Harry May/National Insurance Blacklist (p/s)....................... 12
82	Secret SHH 132	Smash The Disco/Disco Girls/Dayo (The Banana Boat Song) (p/s)......... 10
83	Secret SHH 150	OUT OF BUSINESS (12" EP, unissued, white label promo, 10 copies only).... 100+
85	Wonderful World Of... 121	Get Out Of My House/All Out Tonight/Foreign Girl/Outlaw (12", p/s)... 25
85	Diamond DIA 001	Drinking N Driving/H-Bomb (live) (p/s)......................... 15
85	Diamond DIA 001T	Drinking N Driving/H-Bomb (live)/Hurry Up Harry/Drinking 'N' Driving (original version) (12", p/s)............................... 25
80s	Link LINK 1201	DO A RUNNER (12" EP)................................ 12
83	Secret SEC 11	SUBURBAN REBELS (LP)............................... 20
83	Syndicate SYNLP 2	1980-81 OFFICIAL BOOTLEGS (LP)...................... 30
84	Syndicate SYNLP 6	LOUD, PROUD 'N' PUNK, LIVE (LP)...................... 20
85	Harry May SE 13	SATURDAY HEROES (LP)............................. 20
86	Dojo DOJO LP 35	SINGALONGABUSINESS (LP)........................... 15
88	Link LINK LP 035	WELCOME TO THE REAL WORLD (LP)..................... 12
90	Link LRMO 1	IN AND OUT OF BUSINESS (LP, mail-order, 550 only)................... 20

BUSKERS
| 73 | Rubber RUB 007 | LIFE OF A MAN (LP)................................. 15 |
| 75 | Hawk HALPX 142 | THE BUSKERS (LP).................................. 15 |

GEORGE HENRY BUSSEY/JIM BUNKLEY
| 71 | Revival RVS 1003 | GEORGE HENRY BUSSEY/JIM BUNKLEY (LP)................. 15 |

BUSTERS
| 63 | Stateside SS 231 | Bust Out/Astronauts................................. 10 |

BUSTER('S) ALLSTARS
64	Blue Beat BB 244	Prince Royal/COSMO: One God........................... 15
64	Blue Beat BB 269	The Tickler/COSMO: Rice And Badge....................... 15
65	Blue Beat BB 294	Eye For Eye/South Virginia............................. 15
65	Blue Beat BB 322	Happy Independence 65/STRANGER COLE: When The Party Is Over.......... 15
65	Blue Beat BB 333	When The Party Is Over/Matilda (with Stranger Cole)................. 15
66	Blue Beat BB 342	Cincinnatti Kid/Sammy Dead............................ 50
67	Blue Beat BB 372	Sounds And Pressure/My Darling (both actually by Hopeton Lewis)......... 30
67	Blue Beat BB 384	Take It Easy/Why Must I Cry (both actually by Hopeton Lewis)............. 15
69	Fab FAB 101	Pum Pum A Go Kill You/Oh Lady Oh......................... 8
70	Fab FAB 124	The Rebel/The Preacher.............................. 8

(see also Prince Buster, Teddy King, Little Darling, Khandars, Higgs & Wilson, Owen Gray, Charmers, Fitzroy D Long, Maytals, Derrick Morgan, Eric Morris, Personalities, Roy & Millie, Zoot Simms, Spanish Boys, Spanish Town Skabeats)

BUSTER'S GROUP
| 61 | Starlite ST45 052 | Buster's Shack/ERIC MORRIS: Search The World..................... 18 |

(see also Prince Buster, Rico, Owen Gray)

BUSTY & COOL
| 62 | Blue Beat BB 144 | Mr Policeman/What A World............................. 15 |

TONY BUTALA
| 62 | Salvo SLO 1801 | Long Black Stockings/Rumors (99 copies only)..................... 25 |

BUTCHER
82	Inept INEPT 002	On The Ground/Grow Up Don't Blow Up (p/s)....................... 8
83	Inept INEPT 003	Stand And Fight/Killing Groups (p/s, red vinyl)...................... 5
83	Chainsaw (no cat. no.)	Ain't It Great/RIOT SQUAD: Permanent Force (flexidisc with *Chainsaw* fanzine No. 13)........................ 6/4
84	Chainsaw (no cat. no.)	Get It On/Psycho Trend/MORNINGTON CRESCENT: Possession/B.G.K./ White Male Dominance (flexidisc with *Chainsaw* fanzine No. 14)............ 6/4

(see also Intestines)

EDDIE BUTCHER
| 76 | Free Reed FRR 003 | I ONCE WAS A DAYSMAN (LP, with insert)....................... 12 |
| 76 | Leader LED 2070 | SHAMROCK, ROSE AND THISTLE (LP, gatefold sleeve)................. 10 |

SAM BUTERA (& WITNESSES)
58	HMV POP 476	Good Gracious Baby/It's Better Than Nothing At All...................... 35
58	HMV POP 476	Good Gracious Baby/It's Better Than Nothing At All (78)................. 30
58	Capitol CL 14913	Bim Bam/Twinkle In Your Eye (as Sam Butera & Witnesses)............. 160
59	Capitol CL 14988	Handle With Care/French Poodle......................... 18
64	Prima PR 1003	Skinnie Minnie/Little Liza Jane........................... 6
56	HMV 7EG 8087	SAX SERENADE (EP)................................. 30
60	London HA-D 2288	THE RAT RACE (LP, as Sam Butera & Witnesses).................... 25

(see also Louis Prima)

BILLY BUTLER (& ENCHANTERS)
| 69 | Soul City SC 113 | The Right Track/Boston Monkey............................ 10 |
| 74 | Epic S EPC 2508 | The Right Track/Can't Live Without Her........................ 6 |

CHAMP BUTLER
| 56 | Vogue Coral Q 72163 | The Joshua Tree/Down In Mexico........................ 6 |

MINT VALUE £

JERRY BUTLER

58	London HL 8697	For Your Precious Love/Sweet Was The Wine (with Impressions)	125
58	London HL 8697	For Your Precious Love/Sweet Was The Wine (with Impressions) (78)	50
60	Top Rank JAR 389	I Found A Love/A Lonely Soldier	25
60	Top Rank JAR 531	He Will Break Your Heart/Thanks To You	45
61	Top Rank JAR 562	Find Another Girl/When Trouble Calls	20
61	Columbia DB 4743	Moon River/Aware Of Love	18
62	Stateside SS 121	Make It Easy On Yourself/It's Too Late	18
63	Stateside SS 158	You Can Run But You Can't Hide/I'm The One	18
63	Stateside SS 170	You Go Right Through Me/The Wishing Star	15
63	Stateside SS 195	Whatever You Want/You Won't Be Sorry	15
64	Stateside SS 252	Need To Belong/Give Me Your Love	15
64	Stateside SS 300	Giving Up On Love/I've Been Trying	15
65	Fontana TF 553	Good Times/I've Grown Accustomed To Her Face	12
65	Fontana TF 588	I Can't Stand To See You Cry/Nobody Needs Your Love	12
65	Mercury MF 932	Love (Oh, How Sweet It Is)/Loneliness	12
66	Sue WI 4003	I Stand Accused/I Don't Want To Hear Anymore	25
66	Sue WI 4009	Just For You/Believe In Me	20
67	Mercury MF 964	I Dig You Baby/Some Kinda Magic	10
67	Mercury MF 1005	Mr. Dream Merchant/'Cause I Love You So	8
68	Mercury MF 1035	Never Give You Up/Beside You	8
68	Mercury MF 1058	Hey Mr Western Union Man (Send A Telegram)/Just Can't Forget About You	10
69	Mercury MF 1078	Are You Happy/Strange I Still Love You	6
69	Mercury MF 1094	Only The Strong Survive/Just Because I Really Love You	8
69	Mercury MF 1122	Moody Woman/Go Away And Find Yourself	10
69	Mercury MF 1132	A Brand New Me/What's The Use Of Breaking Up	10
70	President PT 299	Make It Easy On Yourself/Moon River	7
72	Mercury 6052 036	One Night Affair/What's So Good About It (You're My Baby)	6
72	Mercury 6052 119	Moody Woman/A Brand New Me	6
72	Mercury 6052 155	I Only Have Eyes For You/Ain't Understanding Mellow	6
72	Mercury 6052 168	One Night Affair/What's So Good About It (You're My Baby) (reissue)	6
63	Stateside SL 10032	HE WILL BREAK YOUR HEART (LP)	50
63	Stateside SL 10050	FOLK SONGS (LP)	35
68	Fontana (S)TL 5264	LOVE ME (LP)	25
68	Mercury 20118 (S)MCL	MR. DREAM MERCHANT (LP)	20
69	Mercury 20144 (S)MCL	SOUL GOES ON (LP)	20
69	Mercury 20154 (S)MCL	THE ICE MAN COMETH (LP)	20
70	Joy JOYS 171	MAKE IT EASY ON YOURSELF (LP)	12
72	Mercury 6338 102	SPICE OF LIFE (LP)	15
72	Mercury 6430 401	THE VERY BEST OF JERRY BUTLER (LP)	12

(see also Betty Everett & Jerry Butler, Impressions, Gene & Jerry)

LESLIE BUTLER (& FUGITIVES)

67	Island WI 3069	Hornpipe Rock Steady/You Don't Have To Say You Love Me	25
67	Doctor Bird DB 1083	Winchester Rocksteady (with Fugitives)/	
		ASTON CAMPBELL & CONQUERORS: Ramona	25
68	High Note HS 008	Top Cat/WEBBER SISTERS: Stars Above	12
68	High Note HS 009	Revival/GAYLADS: Over The Rainbow's End	12

(see also Ken Boothe, Fugitives, Gaylads)

BUTTERCUPS

| 68 | Pama PM 742 | If I Love You/Loving You | 7 |
| 69 | Pama PM 760 | Come Put My Life In Order/If I Love You | 5 |

BILLY BUTTERFIELD & HIS ORCHESTRA

| 55 | London HLF 8181 | The Magnificent Matador/Sugar Blues Mambo | 18 |
| 55 | London HLF 8181 | The Magnificent Matador/Sugar Blues Mambo (78) | 15 |

(PAUL) BUTTERFIELD BLUES BAND

66	London HLZ 10100	Come On In/I Got A Mind To Give Up Living	12
67	Elektra EKSN 45007	All These Blues/Never Say No	6
67	Elektra EKSN 45020	Run Out Of Time/One More Heartache	6
68	Elektra EKSN 45047	Get Yourself Together/Mine To Love	6
69	Elektra EKSN 45069	Where Did My Baby Go/In My Own Dream	6
70	Elektra 2101 012	Love March/Love Disease	5
65	Elektra EKL/EKS 294	PAUL BUTTERFIELD BLUES BAND (LP, orange label)	30
66	Elektra EKL/EKS 315	EAST — WEST (LP, orange label)	35
67	Elek. EKL 4015/EKS 74015	THE RESURRECTION OF PIGBOY CRABSHAW (LP, orange label)	25
68	Elektra EKL 4025	IN MY OWN DREAM (LP, orange label, also stereo EKS 74025)	20
69	Elektra EKS 74053	KEEP ON MOVIN' (LP)	15
71	Elektra EKD 2001	LIVE (2-LP)	18
72	Elektra K 62011	GOLDEN BUTTER (LP, gatefold sleeve)	12

(see also John Mayall's Bluesbreakers, Mike Bloomfield)

BUTTERFLIES

| 68 | President PT 192 | Love Me Forever/He's Got Everything | 6 |

BUTTERFLYS

| 64 | Red Bird RB 10009 | Goodnight Baby/The Swim | 15 |

BUTTERSCOTCH

| 70 | RCA 1983 | Surprise, Surprise/In This World Of Loving You | 5 |

BUTTERSCOTCH CABOOSE

| 68 | Bell BLL 1023 | Melinda/Let A Little Sunshine In | 5 |

BUTTHOLE SURFERS

| 84 | Alt. Tentacles VIRUS 22 | BUTTHOLE SURFERS (mini-LP, black & white sleeve) | 8 |
| 91 | Rough Trade R 2081 2601 | PIOUGHD (LP, with bonus 12") | 12 |

BUTTONDOWN BRASS

| 67 | Fontana LPS 16255 | HA HA HA (HEE-HEE-HEE) (LP) | 15 |
| 76 | DJM DJS 22046 | FUNK IN HELL (LP) | 25 |

(see also Ray Davies)

SHEILA BUXTON

55	Columbia SCM 5193	Thank You For The Waltz/Just Between Friends	10
57	Columbia DB 3887	Perfect Love/I Love You Baby (My Baby Loves Me)	10
57	Columbia DB 4051	The In-Between Age/Charm	10
57	Columbia DB 4051	The In-Between Age/Charm (78)	10
59	Top Rank JAR 113	Soldier, Won't You Marry Me?/Li Per Li	7
59	Top Rank JAR 113	Soldier, Won't You Marry Me?/Li Per Li (78).	10
59	Top Rank JAR 144	The Valley Of Love/The Wonder Of You	7
59	Top Rank JAR 144	The Valley Of Love/The Wonder Of You (78)	15
59	Top Rank JAR 240	All I Do Is Dream Of You/Shakedown.	7
60	Top Rank JAR 356	Sixteen Reasons/Goodnight, God I Love You	8
	(see also Craig Douglas)		

BUZZ

66	Columbia DB 7887	You're Holding Me Down/I've Gotta Buzz	140
	(see also Boston Dexters, Tam White)		

BUZZ

79	Redball RR 06	Insanity/Him Not Me/Sick At Heart (p/s)	7

BUZZ

93	Detour Records DR004	Tell Her No/Well, I Think It's Already Dead (p/s, with insert)	5

BUZZ & BUCKY

65	Stateside SS 428	Tiger A Go Go/Bay City	18

BUZZCOCKS

77	New Hormones ORG 1	SPIRAL SCRATCH (EP, plastic labels, p/s doesn't credit Howard Devoto)	20
77	United Artists UP 36316	Orgasm Addict/Whatever Happened To...? (p/s).	7
78	United Artists UP 36348	What Do I Get?/Oh Shit (p/s)	5
78	United Artists UP 36386	I Don't Mind/Autonomy (p/s)	5
78	United Artists UP 36433	Love You More/Noise Annoys (p/s)	5
78	United Artists UP 36455	Ever Fallen In Love (With Someone You Shouldn't've?)/Just Lust (p/s)	5
78	United Artists UP 36455	Ever Fallen In Love (With Someone You Shouldn't've?)/Just Lust (p/s, mispressed with Gerry Rafferty track on B-side)	10
78	United Artists UP 36471	Promises/Lipstick (p/s)	5
78	New Hormones ORG 1	SPIRAL SCRATCH (EP, reissue, p/s credits Howard Devoto, paper label)	5
79	United Artists UP 36499	Everybody's Happy Nowadays/Why Can't I Touch It? (p/s, available in 3 different colours)	each 5
79	United Artists UP 36541	Harmony In My Head/Something's Gone Wrong Again (blue p/s)	5
79	United Artists UP 36541	Harmony In My Head/Something's Gone Wrong Again (red p/s)	5
79	United Artists BP 316	You Say You Don't Love Me/Raison D'Etre (p/s)	5
80	United Artists BP 365	Why She's A Girl From The Chainstore/Are Everything (p/s)	5
80	United Artists BP 371	Strange Thing/Airwaves Dream (p/s)	5
80	United Artists BP 382	Running Free/What Do You Know (p/s)	5
78	United Artists UALP 15	Moving Away From The Pulsebeat (12", 1-sided, die-cut co. sl., promo only)	20
91	New Hormones ORG 1	SPIRAL SCRATCH (EP, 2nd reissue, promo only 7")	10
93	Essential ESS 2025	Innocent (p/s)	5
95	One Stop Music ONE 7001	Noise Annoys/Isolation (live) (p/s, 1,500 only)	5
78	United Artists UAG 30159	ANOTHER MUSIC IN A DIFFERENT KITCHEN (LP, black inner sleeve, initially in printed carrier bag)	25/12
78	United Artists UAG 30159	ANOTHER MUSIC IN A DIFFERENT KITCHEN (LP, mispressing without "I Need")	15
78	United Artists UAG 30197	LOVE BITES (LP, with embossed sleeve with insert)	12
79	United Artists UAG 30260	A DIFFERENT KIND OF TENSION (LP, with inner sleeve).	12
89	Absolutely Free FREELP 02	LIVE AT THE ROXY (LP).	20
91	Document DLP 2	TIME'S UP (LP, mock bootleg, with bonus 33rpm interview single [FDLP 2])	20
	(see also Magazine, Steve Diggle, Flag Of Convenience, Pete Shelley, Things, Stevie's Buzz)		

JAKI BYARD

68	Transatlantic PR 7463	FREEDOM TOGETHER! (LP)	12

DON BYAS & HIS RHYTHM

56	Vogue V 2390	On The Way To Your Heart/The Portuguese Washerwomen	7

BYE LAWS

68	Pye 7N 17481	Then You Can Tell Me Goodbye/Come On Over To My Place	6
69	Pye 7N 17701	Run Baby Run/To Sir With Love	6

MAX BYGRAVES

53	HMV 7M 112	Cowpuncher's Cantata/True Loves And False Lovers	15
53	HMV 7M 113	Little Sir Echo/Bygraves Boogie	12
53	HMV 7M 114	The Travelling Salesman/Ten Bottles Of Gin.	12
53	HMV 7M 134	Lovely Dollar Lolly (with Peter Brough & Archie Andrews)/ The Red Robin Cantata	12
53	HMV 7M 145	Time To Dream/The Queen Of Ev'ryone's Heart	12
53	HMV 7M 154	Big 'Ead/Say "Si Si" (B-side with Peter Brough & Archie Andrews).	12
54	HMV 7M 180	She Was A Good Girl (As Good Girls Go)/The Jones Boy	12
54	HMV 7M 194	(The Gang That Sang) Heart Of My Heart/Once She's Got You Up (B-side with Tanner Sisters).	15
54	HMV 7M 220	Friends And Neighbours (with Tanner Sisters)/Chip Chopper Charlie.	12
54	HMV 7M 237	Gilly Gilly Ossenfeffer Katzenellen.../Third Little Turning On The Right	15
54	HMV 7M 238	Bank Of Sunshine/Little Johnny Rainbow	12
56	HMV 7M 357	The Ballad Of Davy Crockett/A Good Idea — Son	15
56	HMV 7M 368	Out Of Town/Fingers Crossed	15
56	HMV 7M 388	Nothin' To Do/Lift Boy	12
56	HMV 7M 400	Seventeen Tons/Try Another Cherry Tree	12
59	Decca F 11119	Napoli-Napoli/Old Tymes Square.	5
59	Decca F 11119	Napoli-Napoli/Old Tymes Square (78)	8

Max BYGRAVES

59	Decca F 11148	Last Night I Dreamed/Bobbikin's Lullaby	5
59	Decca F 11148	Last Night I Dreamed/Bobbikin's Lullaby (78)	8
59	Decca F 11176	Jingle Bell Rock/Who Made The Morning	5
59	Decca F 11176	Jingle Bell Rock/Who Made The Morning (78)	15
60	Decca F 11214	Fings Ain't Wot They Used To Be/When The Thrill Has Gone	6
60	Decca F 11214	Fings Ain't Wot They Used To Be/When The Thrill Has Gone (78)	15
55	HMV 7EG 8061	PETER BROUGH, ARCHIE ANDREWS AND MAX BYGRAVES (EP)	8
56	HMV 7EG 8203	A GOOD IDEA SON (EP)	10
50s	Lantern MB 103	SINGS CHRISTMAS GREETINGS (EP)	10
50s	Lantern MB 201	IT'S YOUR BIRTHDAY (EP)	10

(see also Joan Regan)

MAX BYGRAVES & TED HEATH

59	Decca LK 4317/SKL 4068	THE HITS OF THE TWENTIES (LP, mono/stereo)	12/15
60	Decca LK 4360/SKL 4106	THE HITS OF THE THIRTIES (LP, mono/stereo)	12/15

(see also Ted Heath)

JUNIOR BYLES

71	Bullet BU 499	Beat Down Babylon/UPSETTERS: Version	7
71	Upsetter US 365	Palace Called Africa/UPSETTERS: Earthquake	10
72	Upsetter US 387	Festival Da Da/UPSETTERS: Version	8
72	Pama PM 857	Fever/GROOVERS: Soul Sister (B-side actually by Heptones)	6
72	Dynamic DYN 432	Pharaoh Hiding/Hail To Power	6
72	Randy's RAN 523	King Of Babylon/UPSETTERS: Nebuchadnezzer	8
72	Punch PH 109	Pharaoh Hiding/UPSETTERS: Hail To Power	5
73	Pama PM 878	Education Rock/KEN McKAY: Nobody Knows	6
74	Magnet MAG 27	Curly Locks/Now Generation	7
74	Dip DL 5035	Curly Locks/Now Generation	8
75	Dip DL 5074	Long Way/All The Way	8
75	Ethnic ETH 26	Mumbling And Grumbling/King Size Mumble	7
72	Trojan TRL 52	BEAT DOWN BABYLON (LP, beware of Canadian imports)	35

(see also King Chubby, Lloyd Terrell, Dennis Alcapone, Upsetters, Bob Marley, Lee & Junior)

JAMES BYNUM

79	Grapevine GRP 117	Time Passes By/Love You	5

BOBBY BYRD

71	Mojo 2001 118	I Need Help (Parts 1 & 2)	6
71	Mojo 2027 003	I Know You Got Soul/If You Don't Work You Can't Eat	7
71	Mojo 2093 004	Hot Pants ... I'm Coming, I'm Coming, I'm Coming/Hang It Up	6
72	Mojo 2093 013	Keep On Doin' What You're Doin'/Let Me Know	6
72	Mojo 2093 017	If You Got A Love You'd Better Keep Hold Of It/You've Got To Change Your Mind	6
72	Mojo 2093 020	Never Get Enough/My Concerto	5
73	Warner Bros K 16291	Try It Again/I'm On The Move	5
73	Mojo 2093 028	Saying It And Doing It Are Two Different Things/VICKI ANDERSON: Don't Throw Your Love In Garbage/In The Land Of Milk And Honey	6
75	Seville SEV 1003	Back From The Dead/The Way To Get Down	5
75	Seville SEV 1005	Headquarters/Headquarters (Instrumental Version)	5
76	Contempo CS 2096	Here For The Party/Thank You For Your Love	8
87	Urban URB 8	I Know You Got Soul/Hot Pants	7
87	Urban URBX 8	I Know You Got Soul/Hot Pants ... I'm Coming, I'm Coming, I'm Coming/I Know You Got Soul (Version) (12", die-cut company sleeve)	15
72	Mojo 2918 002	I NEED HELP — LIVE (LP)	60

(see also JB's, James Brown, Anna King & Bobby Byrd, Vicki Anderson)

C. BYRD & SIR D.'s GROUP

60	Blue Beat BB 49	Baa Baa Black Sheep/LLOYD & CECIL: Come Over Here	15

CHARLIE BYRD

62	Riverside RLP 436	BOSSA NOVA PELOS PASSAROS (LP)	15
66	CBS 62610	TRAVELLIN' MAN LIVE (LP)	12
66	CBS 62958	BYRDLAND (LP)	12

DONALD BYRD

66	Verve VS 532	Boom Boom/See See Rider	8
80	United Artists UP 622	Dominoes/Wind Parade	8
80	United Artists 12 UP 622	Dominoes/Wind Parade (12")	15
81	Elektra K 12559T	Love Has Come Around/Only You (12")	8
50s	Esquire EP 139	DONALD BYRD'S JAZZ GROUP (EP)	8
50s	Esquire EP 149	DONALD BYRD JAZZ GROUP (EP)	8
59	Philips BBE 12274	DONALD BYRD & GIG GRYCE (EP)	8
62	Eros ERL 50067	AND THEN SOME (LP)	8
65	Vintage Jazz VLP 9104	UP WITH BYRD (LP)	12
67	Polydor 423/623 224	CHILD'S PLAY (LP, with Johnny Coles)	10
70s	Blue Note UAG 20001	PLACES AND SPACES (LP)	25
78	Blue Note UAG 20008	CARICATURES (LP)	15

(see also Blackbyrds, Art Farmer)

MICHAEL BYRD & COMMERCIALS

80	Another AN 002	SELL OUT BEFORE THE FALL OUT (EP, gatefold p/s, 500 copies only)	6

(see also Cardiac Arrest, Selecter)

RUSSELL BYRD

64	Sue WI 305	Hitch Hike (Parts 1 & 2)	30

BYRDS

65	CBS 201765	Mr. Tambourine Man/I Knew I'd Want You	6
65	CBS 201796	All I Really Want To Do/Feel A Whole Lot Better	6
65	CBS 202008	Turn! Turn! Turn! (To Everything There Is A Season)/	
		She Don't Care About Time	6
66	CBS 202037	Set You Free This Time/It Won't Be Wrong	10
66	CBS 202067	Eight Miles High/Why	7
66	CBS 202259	5D (Fifth Dimension)/Captain Soul	6
66	CBS 202295	Mr Spaceman/What's Happening?!?!	7
67	CBS 202559	So You Want To Be A Rock'n'Roll Star/Everybody's Been Burned	7
67	CBS 2648	My Back Pages/Renaissance Fair	6
67	CBS 2924	Lady Friend/Don't Make Waves	15
67	CBS 3093	Goin' Back/Change Is Now	6
68	CBS 3411	You Ain't Goin' Nowhere/Artificial Energy	6
68	CBS 3752	I Am A Pilgrim/Pretty Boy Floyd	6
69	CBS 4055	Bad Night At The Whiskey/Drug Store Truck Drivin' Man	7
69	CBS 4284	Lay Lady Lay/Old Blue	7
69	CBS 4572	Wasn't Born To Follow/Child Of The Universe	6
70	CBS 4753	Jesus Is Just Alright/It's All Over Now Baby Blue	6
71	CBS 5322	Chestnut Mare/Just A Season	6
71	CBS 7253	I Trust/This Is My Destiny	6
72	CBS 7712	America's Great National Pastime/Farther Along (unreleased)	
73	CBS 8210	Mr. Tambourine Man/Turn! Turn! Turn! (p/s, 'Hall Of Fame Hits' series)	5
73	Asylum AYM 516	Things Will Be Better/For Free (promos in p/s)	12/5
73	Asylum AYM 517	Full Circle/Long Live The King	5
66	CBS EP 6069	THE TIMES THEY ARE A' CHANGIN' (EP)	15
66	CBS EP 6077	EIGHT MILES HIGH (EP)	18
90	CBS 656544 5	FOUR DIMENSIONS EP (CD, picture disc)	8
65	CBS (S)BPG 62571	MR TAMBOURINE MAN (LP, mono/stereo)	30/25
66	CBS (S)BPG 62652	TURN! TURN! TURN! (LP, mono/stereo)	35/30
66	CBS (S)BPG 62783	FIFTH DIMENSION (LP, mono/stereo)	35/30
67	CBS (S)BPG 62988	YOUNGER THAN YESTERDAY (LP, mono/stereo)	35/30
68	CBS BPG 63107	THE BYRDS' GREATEST HITS (LP, mono)	15
68	CBS (S)BPG 63169	THE NOTORIOUS BYRD BROTHERS (LP, mono/stereo)	30/25
68	CBS 63353	SWEETHEART OF THE RODEO (LP, mono/stereo)	20/15
69	CBS 63545	DR BYRDS & MR HYDE (LP, mono)	12

(Original copies of the above LPs were issued with rough-textured, plain orange labels & laminated sleeves; later copies are worth two-thirds these values.)

71	Bumble GEXP 8001	PRE-FLYTE (LP)	20
73	Asylum SYLA 8754	THE BYRDS (LP, gatefold sleeve)	12

(see also Beefeaters, Roger McGuinn, David Crosby, Gene Clark, Gram Parsons, Gene Parsons, Skip Battin, Earl Scruggs, Flying Burrito Brothers, Evergreen Blueshoes, Dillard & Clark, Kentucky Colonels)

BOBBY BYRNE & ALL STAR ORCHESTRA

59	Top Rank TR 5011	Rhapsody In Blue/Adios	5

DAVID BYRNE

81	Sire SIR 4054	Big Blue Plymouth/Leg Bells (p/s)	4

(see also Brian Eno & David Byrne, Talking Heads, Dinosaur, Love Of Life Orchestra, Robert Fripp)

JERRY BYRNE

76	Speciality SON 5011	Lights Out/Honey Baby	6

PACKIE BYRNE (& BONNIE SHALJEAN)

69	EFDSS LP 1009	PACKIE BYRNE (LP)	20

EDD/EDWARD BYRNES

60	Warner Bros WB 5	Kookie, Kookie (Lend Me Your Comb) (with Connie Stevens)/	
		You're The Top	7
60	Warner Bros WB 27	Lonely Christmas/Yulesville (as Edd Byrnes)	7
60	Warner Bros WEP 6010	KOOKIE (EP, also stereo WSEP 2010)	15/18
63	Warner Bros W(S)EP 6108	KOOKIE VOLUME 2 (EP)	15
60s	Warner Bros	77 SUNSET STRIP (LP)	15

(see also Connie Stevens)

MARTIN BYRNES

70	Leader LEA 2004	BYRNES (LP)	12

PAUL BYRON

60	Decca F 11210	Pale Moon/Year Ago Tonight	8

SOL BYRON & IMPACTS

60s	Flamingo PR 5027	Pride And Joy/Thou Shall Not Steal	15

BYSTANDERS

65	Pylot WD 501	That's The End/This Time	140
66	Piccadilly 7N 35330	(You're Gonna) Hurt Yourself/Have I Offended The Girl	18
66	Piccadilly 7N 35351	My Love — Come Home/If You Walk Away	20
67	Piccadilly 7N 35363	98.6/Stubborn Kind Of Fellow	12
67	Piccadilly 7N 35382	Royal Blue Summer Sunshine Day/Make Up Your Mind	20
67	Piccadilly 7N 35399	Pattern People/Green Grass	15
68	Pye 7N 17476	When Jezamine Goes/Cave Of Clear Light	35
68	Pye 7N 17540	This World Is My World/Painting The Time	15

(see also Man)

BYZANTIUM

73	A&M AMS 7064	What A Coincidence/My Seasons Changing With The Sun	6
72	private pressing	LIVE AND STUDIO ('BLACK AND WHITE') (LP, 100 only)	150
72	A&M AMLH 68104	BYZANTIUM (LP, some with poster)	40/25
73	A&M AMLH 68163	SEASONS CHANGING (LP, poster sleeve)	40

(see also Ora)

MINT VALUE £

FANTASTIC JOHNNY C
67	London HL 10169	Boogaloo Down Broadway/Look What Love Can Make You Do	6
68	London HL 10212	Hitch It To The Horse/Cool Broadway	6
69	Action ACT 4543	Is There Anything Better Than Making Love/New Love	10
75	Island USA 8	Don't Depend On Me (Parts 1 & 2)	6
69	Action ACLP 6001	BOOGALOO DOWN BROADWAY (LP)	30

ROY C
66	Island WI 273	Shotgun Wedding/I'm Going To Make It	12
66	Island WI 273	Shotgun Wedding/High School Dropout (different B-side)	7
67	Ember EMB S 230	Twistin' Pneumonia/Tear Avenue	8
66	Ember NR 5055	THE SHOTGUN WEDDING MAN (LP)	30
75	Mercury 9100 017	SEX AND SOUL (LP)	12

CABARET VOLTAIRE
81	Rough Trade RT 096	Eddie's Out/Walls Of Jericho (12", p/s, with bonus 7" "Jazz The Glass"/ "Burnt To The Ground" [pink die-cut sleeve, RT 095] in plastic wallet)	8
82	Masterbag BAG 004	Gut Level (live) (flexidisc free with *Masterbag* magazine)	7/5
76	(no label or cat. no.)	LIMITED EDITION (private cassette)	40

(see also Richard H. Kirk, Hafler Trio, Peter Hope & Richard H. Kirk, Stephen Mallinder, UV Pop, Pressure Co., Eric Random)

CABLES
68	Coxsone CS 7072	What Kind Of World?/My Broken Heart	18
68	Studio One SO 2060	Baby Why?/Be A Man	18
68	Studio One SO 2071	Love Is A Pleasure/Cheer Up	18
69	Studio One SO 2085	Got To Find Someone/ALEXANDER HENRY: Please Be True	18
69	Bamboo BAM 12	So Long/PRESSURE BOYS: More Love	10
70	Bamboo BAM 19	How Can I Trust You?/SOUND DIMENSIONS: How Can I Trust You? (Inst.)	10
70	Trojan TR 7792	Salt Of The Earth/Ring A Bell	10
70	Harry J. HJ 6614	Didn't I/JAY BOYS: Tilly	6
70	Harry J. HJ 6620	Feel Alright/Equal Rights	6
71	Big Shot BI 598	A Sometime Girl/IN CROWD BAND: A Sometime Girl Version	5
72	Jackpot JP 787	Come On/Come On Version	5
73	Attack ATT 8053	Give Me A Chance/JAH FISH: King Of Zion	5

(see also K. Drummond, Dingle Brothers, Alton Ellis)

CABOOSE
| 70 | Stax STAX 151 | Black Hands, White Cotton/In My Hour Of Need | 5 |

CACOPHONY
| 87 | Roadrunner RR 349577 | SPEED METAL SYMPHONY (LP) | 12 |
| 88 | Roadrunner RR 9577 | GO OFF (LP, as Marty Friedman, Jason Becker & Cacophony) | 12 |

(see also Marty Friedman, Megadeth)

CACTUS
70	Atco 2400 020	CACTUS (LP)	15
71	Atco 2400 114	ONE WAY ... OR ANOTHER (LP, reissue of above LP)	12
72	Atlantic K 40307	RESTRICTIONS (LP)	12
72	Atlantic K 50013	'OT AND SWEATY (LP)	12

(see also Vanilla Fudge, Leaf Hound, Beck Bogert Appice)

ALAN CADDY
| 64 | HMV POP 1286 | Tornado/Workout | 30 |

(see also Tornados)

CADETS (U.S.)
| 56 | London HLU 8313 | Stranded In The Jungle/I Want You (gold or silver label lettering) | 550/300 |
| 56 | London HLU 8313 | Stranded In The Jungle/I Want You (78) | 30 |

CADETS (U.K.)
63	Decca F 11677	Hello Trouble/Our First Quarrel	7
64	Pye 7N 15693	Chapel Of Love/I Gave My Wedding Dress Away	7
65	Pye 7N 15769	Are You Teasing Me?/My Heart Skips A Beat	6
65	Pye 7N 15852	Jealous Heart/Right Or Wrong	6
65	Pye 7N 15947	Baby Roo/Raining In My Heart	6
66	Pye 7N 17024	If I Had My Life To Live Over/Best Of All	6
66	Pye 7N 17167	At The Close Of A Long Long Day/True Love	6
69	Pye 7N 17762	Dying Ranger/Storeen Bawn	6

CADILLAC
| 86 | CBS A 7180 | Valentino/Valentino (p/s) | 8 |

EARL CADILLAC & HIS ORCHESTRA
59	Vogue V 9133	Zon, Zon, Zon/Il Suffit D'Une Melodie	12
59	Vogue V 9133	Zon, Zon, Zon/Il Suffit D'Une Melodie (78)	20
59	Vogue V 9138	The Fish Seller/Tremendo Cha Cha Cha (Plegaria)	12
59	Vogue V 9138	The Fish Seller/Tremendo Cha Cha Cha (Plegaria) (78)	20

CADILLACS
| 59 | London HLJ 8786 | Peek-A-Boo/Oh, Oh, Lolita | 40 |
| 59 | London HLJ 8786 | Peek-A-Boo/Oh, Oh, Lolita (78) | 50 |

CADO BELLE
77	Anchor AN 1	THE CADO BELLE EP (12")	7
76	Anchor ANCL 2015	CADO BELLE (LP, with inner sleeve)	10

SUSAN CADOGAN
74	Dip DL 5030	Hurt So Good/UPSETTERS: Loving Is Good	6
75	Lucky LY 5078	Feeling Right/Congratulations	6

CAEDMON
78	private pressing	CAEDMON (LP, with insert, some with bonus 7": "Beyond The Second Mile"/"Give Me Jesus")	500/350

CAERN
70s	Gem DES 1015	A COLLECTION OF SCOTCH FOLK (LP)	15

CAESAR & CLEO
65	Reprise R 20419	Love Is Strange/Let The Good Times Roll (some in p/s)	14/7
65	Reprise R 30056	CAESAR AND CLEO (EP, 2 tracks each by Caesar & Cleo and Sonny & Cher)	18

(see also Sonny & Cher)

CAESARS
65	Decca F 12251	On The Outside Looking In/Can You Blame Me?	12
66	Decca F 12462	Five In The Morning/It's Superman	10

CAFE SOCIETY
75	Konk KOS 5	Whitby Two-Step/Maybe It's Me	5
75	Konk KONK 102	CAFE SOCIETY (LP, with inner sleeve)	12

(see also Tom Robinson Band, Claire Hamill)

BUTCH CAGE
78	Flyright LP 545	RAISE A RUCKUS TONIGHT (LP)	12

BUTCH CAGE/MABEL LEE WILLIAMS
60s	Storyville SLP 129	COUNTRY BLUES (LP)	15

AUBREY CAGLE
62	Starlite ST45 082	Come Along Little Girl/Blue Lonely World	375

JAMES CAGNEY
70	United Artists UP 36385	Yankee Doodle Dandy/Over There (B-side with Frances Langford) (p/s)	6

JEREMY CAHILL
70s	Solent	September Blues/Yesterday	15

(see also Shide & Acorn)

PATRICIA CAHILL
70	Deram DM 320	Little Altar Boy/Rain	5
71	Deram DM 324	Colm Ban/Eighteen	5
70	Deram Nova SDN 22	SUMMER'S DAUGHTER (LP)	20
72	Rex RPS 104	IRELAND (LP)	12

CAIN
68	Page One POF 054	Her Emotion/Take Me Back One Time	10

CAIN
80s	private pressing	CAIN (2-LP)	30

TUBAL CAINE
70	Attack ATT 8023	I'm A Drifter Part 1/CIMARONS: I'm A Drifter Part 2	6

AL CAIOLA (ORCHESTRA)
56	London HLC 8285	Flamenco Love/From The Heart	18
56	London HLC 8285	Flamenco Love/From The Heart (78)	5
61	London HLT 9294	The Magnificent Seven/The Lonely Rebel	7
61	London HLT 9325	Bonanza/Bounty Hunter	12
61	HMV POP 884	Bonanza/Bounty Hunter (as Al Caiola Orchestra, reissue)	5
61	HMV POP 889	The Magnificent Seven/The Lonely Rebel (as Al Caiola Orchestra)	5
62	Oriole CB 1732	Mambo Jambo/Twistin' At The Woodchoppers Mill	5
66	United Artists UEP 1018	HIT T.V. THEMES (EP)	12
56	London HA-C 2017	DEEP IN A DREAM (LP)	18
57	London HA-C 2022	SERENADE IN BLUE (LP)	18
64	United Artists ULP 1090	TUFF GUITAR (LP)	18
66	United Artists (S)ULP 1115	SOUNDS FOR SPIES AND PRIVATE EYES (LP)	25

JOHN CAIRNEY
57	HMV POP 424	Two Strangers/A Certain Girl I Know (with Sammy San)	6
68	Waverley SLP 543	Please/Deep Purple	5

FORRIE CAIRNS
62	Fontana 267240 TF	Salty Dog/Cockles And Mussels	6

CAIRO
80	Absurd ABSURD 7	I Like Blue Beat/Version (p/s)	4
80	Absurd ASK 15	Movie Stars/Cuthbert's Birthday Treat (p/s)	4

CAJUN MOON
76	Chrysalis CHR 1116	CAJUN MOON (LP)	15

CAKE
68	MCA MUPS 303	THE CAKE (LP)	18
69	MCA MUPS 390	A SLICE OF CAKE (LP)	18

J.J. CALE
66	Liberty LIB 55881	Outside Lookin' In/In Our Time	12
72	A&M AMS 7018	Cajun Moon/Starbound	5
72	A&M AMS 7022	After Midnight/Crazy Mama	5
72	A&M AMLS 68105	NATURALLY (LP, tan label)	12
72	A&M AMLS 68157	REALLY (LP, tan label)	12
79	Shelter ISA 5018	FIVE (LP, with bonus single "Katy Cool"/"Juan And Maria Juarez Blues" [JJ-1])	12

(see also Leathercoated Minds)

MINT VALUE £

JOHN CALE

74	Island WIP 6202	The Man Who Couldn't Afford To Orgy/Sylvia Said	8
77	Illegal IL 003	ANIMAL JUSTICE (EP)	5
77	Illegal IL 003	ANIMAL JUSTICE (12" EP)	8
77	Illegal IL 006	Jack The Ripper In The Moulin Rouge/Memphis (unissued, test pressings only)	25
81	A&M AMS 8130	Dead Or Alive/Honi Soit (no p/s)	5
83	Ze IS 113	Close Watch/I Keep A Close Watch (p/s)	5
84	Ze IS 157	Caribbean Sunset/(same) (unissued, no p/s, promo only)	8
84	Ze IS 197	Ooh La La/Magazines (p/s)	5
71	CBS 64256	VINTAGE VIOLENCE (LP, orange label)	15
71	CBS 64259	CHURCH OF ANTHRAX (LP, with Terry Riley)	15
72	Reprise K 44212	ACADEMY IN PERIL (LP)	12
73	Reprise K 44239	PARIS 1919 (LP, with lyric insert)	12
75	Island ILPS 9350	HELEN OF TROY (LP)	12
77	Island ILPS 9459	GUTS (LP)	12

(see also Velvet Underground, Nico, Terry Riley, Ayers Cale Nico & Eno, Judy Nylon)

CALEB (Quaye)

67	Philips BF 1588	Baby Your Phrasing Is Bad/Woman Of Distinction	225

(see also Mirage, Hookfoot, Bread & Beer Band, Elton John)

CALEDONIANS

69	Fab FAB 103	Funny Way Of Laughing/Don't Please	8

(see also Clarendonians, Prince Buster)

CALENDAR

75	All Platinum 6146 308	Hypertension (Parts 1 & 2)	6

RANDY CALIFORNIA

82	Beggars Banquet BEG 76	Hand Gun (Toy Guns)/This Is The End (p/s)	5
82	Beggars Banquet BEG 82	All Along The Watchtower/Radio Man (p/s)	5
82	Beggars Banquet BEG 82T	All Along The Watchtower/Killer Weed/Radio Man/Breakout (12", p/s)	8
85	Vertigo VER 16	Run To Your Lover/Second Child (p/s)	5
85	Vertigo VER 21	Jack Rabbit/Super Child (p/s)	5

(see also Spirit, Kapt. Kopter & Fabulous Twirly Birds)

CALIFORNIA IN-CROWD

66	Fontana TF 779	Questions And Answers/Happiness In My Heart	30

CALIFORNIA MUSIC

74	RCA RCA 2488	Don't Worry Baby/Ten Years Harmony	5
76	RCA RCA 2661	Jamaica Farewell/California Farewell	5

(see also Bruce Johnston, Beach Boys)

CALIFORNIANS

67	CBS 2263	Golden Apples/Little Ship With A Red Sail	20
67	Decca F 12678	Follow Me/What Love Can Do	8
67	Decca F 12712	Sunday Will Never Be The Same/Can't Get You Out Of My Mind	5
68	Decca F 12758	Congratulations/What Is Happy, Baby?	5
68	Decca F 12802	Out In The Sun/The Sound	5
69	Fontana TF 991	Mandy/The Cooks Of Cake And Kindness	40
69	Fontana TF 1052	Sad Old Song/Weep No More	6
69	Chapter One CH 112	You've Got Your Troubles/Early Morning Sun	5

(see also Warren Zevon)

CALLAN & JOHN

69	CBS 4447	House Of Delight/Long Shadow Day	15

CALL GIRLS

88	53rd & 3rd AGAR 001	Primal World/VATICAN SHOTGUN SCARE: Thick Fat Heat Source (p/s)	8

(MISSISSIPPI) JOE CALLICOTT

68	Blue Horizon 7-63227	PRESENTING THE COUNTRY BLUES (LP)	50
71	Revival RVS 1002	DEAL GONE DOWN (LP, as Joe Callicott)	20

TERRY CALLIER

79	Elektra K 12372	Sign Of The Times/Occasional Rain	8
90	Acid Jazz JAZID 27T	I Don't Want To See Myself (Without You)/(If I Could Make You) Change Your Mind (12")	10
78	Elektra K 52096	FIRE ON ICE (LP)	20
79	Elektra K 52140	TURN YOU TO LOVE (LP)	25
94	Charly ARC 514	THE VERY BEST OF TERRY CALLIER ON CADET (2-LP)	15

CALLIES

71	Rubber RUB 002	ON YOUR SIDE (LP, gatefold sleeve)	15

CALLINAN-FLYNN

72	Mushroom 150 MR 18	FREEDOM'S LAMENT (LP)	140

JO CALLIS

81	Pop: Aural POP 12	Woah Yeah/Sinistrale/Dodo Boys (p/s)	5

(see also Rezillos, Shake, Human League)

CAB CALLOWAY

50	London L 657	La Mucura/Pero Que Jelenque (78)	15
52	Brunswick 05022	Minnie The Moocher/Kickin' The Gong Around (78)	20
66	Stateside SS 509	History Repeats Itself/After Taxes	5
58	Gala 45XP 1016	CAB CALLOWAY (EP)	8
60	Fontana TFE 17216	CAB CALLOWAY (EP)	20
70s	Vintage Jazz VEP 22	CABULOUS CALLOWAY (EP)	8
70s	Vintage Jazz VEP 35	CABULOUS CALLOWAY VOL. 2 (EP)	8

CALUM BRYCE
68   Conder PS 1001   Love-Maker/I'm Glad 100

EDDIE CALVERT
53	Columbia SCM 5003	My Yiddishe Momme/Hora Staccato	6
53	Columbia SCM 5004	Ave Maria/Just A-Wearyin' For You (as Eddie Calvert Orchestra)	6
54	Columbia SCM 5129	My Son, My Son/Sherpa Song	6
55	Columbia SCM 5168	Cherry Pink And Apple Blossom White/Roses Of Picardy	12
56	Columbia SCM 5237	The Man With The Golden Arm/Memories Of You	5
56	Columbia SCM 5277	Moonglow & Theme From "Picnic"/If I Loved You	5
58	Melodisc EPM 7	MISERLOU (EP)	8
55	Columbia SEG 7591	GOLDEN MELODIES OF THE GOLDEN TRUMPET (EP)	8
56	Columbia SEG 7637	GOLDEN TRUMPET — GOLDEN MELODIES No. 2 (EP)	8

(see also Gerry Brereton)

ROBERT CALVERT
72	United Artists UP 35543	Ejection/Catch A Falling Starfighter (p/s)	15
79	Wake Up WUR 5	Cricket Star (p/s, 33rpm flexidisc, as Robert Calvert & 1st XI)	10
80	Flicknife FLS 204	Lord Of The Hornets/The Greenfly & The Rose (purple print p/s)	10
81	Flicknife FLS 204	Lord Of The Hornets/The Greenfly & The Rose (reissue, black print p/s)	5
74	United Artists UAG 29507	CAPTAIN LOCKHEED AND THE STARFIGHTERS (LP, gatefold sleeve, with booklet and inner sleeve)	25
75	United Artists UAG 29852	LUCKY LIEF AND THE LONGSHIPS (LP, gatefold sleeve)	20
81	A-Side IF 0311	HYPE (SONGS OF TOM MAHLER) (LP)	15
84	Flicknife SHARP 021	FREQ (LP)	12
86	Demi Monde DMLP 1010	TEST TUBE CONCEIVED (LP)	12
86	Harbour (no cat. no.)	THE CELLAR TAPES VOLUME ONE (cassette only)	15
86	Harbour (no cat. no.)	THE CELLAR TAPES VOLUME TWO (cassette only)	15
88	Harbour (no cat. no.)	ROBERT CALVERT READS THE EARTH RITUAL (cassette, limited edition)	15
88	Harbour (no cat. no.)	LIVE AT THE QUEEN ELIZABETH HALL (cassette, possibly unreleased)	20+
88	Beat Goes On BGOLP 2	LUCKY LIEF AND THE LONGSHIPS (LP, gatefold sleeve, reissue)	12
88	Beat Goes On BGOLP 5	CAPTAIN LOCKHEED AND THE STARFIGHTERS (LP, gatefold sleeve with booklet, reissue)	12
89	Clear BLACK 1	ROBERT CALVERT AT THE QUEEN ELIZABETH HALL (LP, mail order only, with badge, poster & T-shirt, gatefold sleeve)	40
92	Cyborg (no cat. no.)	REVENGE (cassette only)	12

(see also Hawkwind, Imperial Pompadours, Catapilla, Adrian Wagner, John Stevens Away)

TABBY CALVIN & ROUNDERS
56   Capitol CL 14640   False Alarm/I Came Back To Say I'm Sorry 7

CAMARATA
59	Top Rank JAR 160	Love Theme Sleeping Beauty/Medley Sleeping Beauty (as Walt Disney Studio Orchestra)	10
59	Top Rank JAR 160	Love Theme Sleeping Beauty/Medley Sleeping Beauty (78, as Walt Disney Studio Orchestra)	20
59	Top Rank JAR 162	On The Trail/Trumpeter's Prayer (as Tutti's Trumpets)	5
59	Top Rank JAR 162	On The Trail/Trumpeter's Prayer (78, as Tutti's Trumpets)	10
65	London SHU 8257	THINK YOUNG! (LP, as Camarata Orchestra)	15
70	Deram SML 1053	THE VELVET GENTLEMAN: THE MUSIC OF ERIK SATIE (LP)	80

CAMBODIANS
70   Duke DU 101   Coolie Man/J.J. ALLSTARS: Coolie Version 8

CAMBRIDGE BUSKERS
70s   Polydor 2371 984   DOUBLE CONCERTO (LP) 12

CAMEL
73	MCA MUPS 1177	Never Let Go/Curiosity	6
80	Decca FR 13871	Your Love Is Stranger Than Mine/Neon Magic (p/s)	6
84	Decca CAMEL 1	Cloak And Dagger Man/Pressure Point (p/s)	5
73	MCA MUPS 473	CAMEL (LP, black/blue label)	12
74	Deram SML 1107	MIRAGE (LP, with insert)	12
75	Decca Gama SKL-R 5207	MUSIC INSPIRED BY THE SNOW GOOSE (LP, with insert)	12
76	Decca Gama TXS-R 115	MOON MADNESS (LP, textured sleeve)	12

(see also Pete Bardens, Gong/Camel, Hatfield & The North)

CAMEL DRIVERS
68   Pye International 7N 25471   Sunday Morning 6 O'Clock/Give It A Try 6

CAMEO
78	Casablanca CAN 121	It's Serious/Inflation (12")	8
80	Casablanca CAN 199	On The One/Cameosis (12")	8
77	Casablanca CAL 2015	CARDIAC ARREST (LP)	12
78	Casablanca CAL 2026	WE ALL KNOW WHO WE ARE (LP)	12

CAMEOS
63	Columbia DB 7092	Powercut/High Low And Lonesomely	40
64	Columbia DB 7201	My Baby's Coming Home/Where E'er You Walk	35

CAMEOS
67	Toast TT 503	A Pretty Shade Of Blue/You Didn't Have To Be So Nice	6
68	Toast TT 508	On The Good Ship Lollipop/The Love Of A Boy	6

CAMERA OBSCURA
80   Small Wonder SMALL 28   Destitution/Race In Athens (p/s) 4

ANDY CAMERON
78   Klub KLUB 03   Ally's Tartan Army/I Want To Be A Punk Rocker (no p/s, different label colours) .. 5

DEBBIE CAMERON & TOMMY SEEBACH
81   EMI EMI 5173   Straight Or Curly Hair/Kroller Eller Eu 6

DION CAMERON & THREE TOPS
66   Rio R 111   Lord Have Mercy/Get Ready 10
(see also Dion & Three Tops)

G.C. CAMERON
76   Tamla Motown TMG 1033   Me And My Life/Act Like A Shotgun 5
(see also Detroit Spinners)

ISLA CAMERON
64   Transatlantic TRAEP 109   LOST LOVE (EP) 20
(see also Ewan MacColl)

JOHN CAMERON (QUARTET)
67   Columbia DB 8120   You Owe Me/Walk Small (solo) 6
69   Deram DM 256   Troublemaker/Off Centre 5
67   Columbia SCX 6116   COVER LOVER (LP) 45
69   Deram DML/SML 1044   OFF CENTRE (LP) 60

JOHNNY CAMERON
60   Top Rank JAR 396   I Double Dare You/Fantasy 7

RAY CAMERON
67   Island WIP 6003   Doin' My Time/Getaway, Getaway Car 7

CAMOUFLAGE
90   Atlantic   STRANGERS THOUGHTS (CD video) 50
90   Atlantic   THE GREAT COMMANDMENT (CD) 30

CAMPAG VELOCET
97   Fierce Panda NING 41   Drencrom [Velocet Synthemesc]/REGULAR FRIES: Dust It, Don't Bust It
      (p/s, 1,500 only) 8
97   Rabid Badger NANG 1   IT'S THE TEENAGE ARGOT ... EP (12", p/s, 1,000 only) 10

ALEX CAMPBELL
65   Transatlantic TRASP 4   Been On The Road So Long/The Night Visiting Song (some in p/s) 8/5
68   Saga OPP 2   Victoria Dines Alone/Pack Up Your Sorrows 5
63   Arc ARC 36   OUT WEST WITH ALEX CAMPBELL (EP) 7
63   Society SOC 912   WAY OUT WEST (LP) 15
63   Society SOC 960   FOLK SESSION (LP) 15
64   Fidelity FID 2171   FOLK SESSION (LP, reissue) 12
64   Xtra XTRA 1064   ALEX CAMPBELL (LP, with Martin Carthy) 20
65   Polydor 623 035   IN COPENHAGEN (LP) 15
67   Saga ERO 8021   ALEX CAMPBELL AND HIS FRIENDS (LP, with Sandy Denny) 30
71   Ad-Rhythm/Tepee ARPS 1   THIS IS ALEX CAMPBELL VOL. 1 (LP) 25
71   Ad-Rhythm/Tepee ARPS 2   THIS IS ALEX CAMPBELL VOL. 2 (LP) 25
76   Look LKLP 6043   NO REGRETS (LP) 12
79   Burlington BURL 002   ALEX CAMPBELL, ALAN ROBERTS AND DOUGIE MACLEAN (LP) 12
87   Sundown SDLP 2048   WITH THE GREATEST RESPECT (2-LP, reissue of "This Is..." Vols. 1 & 2) 15
(see also Sandy Denny)

BILL & PETE CAMPBELL
71   Duke DU 123   Come On Home Girl/You Are Mine 6

CAT CAMPBELL & NICKY THOMAS
72   Pressure Beat PB 5511   Hammering/PETER TOSH: Medicine Man 15

CHOKER CAMPBELL
65   Tamla Motown TMG 517   Mickey's Monkey/Pride And Joy (as Choker Campbell's Big Band) 80
65   Tamla Motown TML 11011   HITS OF THE SIXTIES (LP, as Choker Campbell & His 16-Piece Band) 100

CHRISTINE CAMPBELL
62   Parlophone R 4881   Wherever I Go/Near Your Heart (red label, later black) 6
63   Parlophone GEP 8874   WHEREVER I GO (EP) 12

CORNELL CAMPBELL
63   Island WI 039   Rosabelle/Turndown Date (B-side actually "Under The Old Oak Tree") 18
63   Island WI 083   Each Lonely Night/ROLAND ALPHONSO: Steamline 18
64   Port-O-Jam PJ 4008   Jericho Road (with Dimple Hinds)/DON DRUMMOND & GROUP:
      Roll On Sweet Don 50
64   Rio R 38   Gloria/I'll Be True 12
72   Dynamic DYN 446   My Confession/AGGROVATORS: Version 10
72   Green Door GD 4042   Dearest Darling/Star Dust 12
72   Jackpot JP 801   Queen And The Minstrel/Put Yourself In My Place 10
73   Jackpot JP 809   Pity The Children/You're No Good 12
73   Jackpot JP 814   Harry Hippy/Just One Kiss 5
73   Green Door GD 4057   Give Me Love/Help Them O Lord 10
73   Duke DU 158   Shotgun Wedding/Girl Of My Dreams 5
73   Duke DU 159   The Very Best I Can/Heading For The Mountains 5
73   Ackee ACK 513   Give Me A Love/SHORTY PERRY: Message Of Love 5
72   Trojan TBL 199   CORNELL CAMPBELL (LP) 30
(see also Eternals, Don Cornel & Eternals, Clarendon Ians, Charmers, Stranger & Patsy, GG Allstars)

DAVID CAMPBELL
67   Transatlantic TRA 141   DAVID CAMPBELL (LP) 20
72   Decca SKL 5139   SUN WHEEL (LP) 12

ETHNA CAMPBELL
64   Mercury MF 804   What's Easy For Two Is Hard For One/Again 12
64   Mercury MF 816   Girls Like Boys/Five Minutes More 7

GLEN CAMPBELL
61   Top Rank JAR 596   Turn Around, Look At Me/Brenda 12
62   Capitol CL 15268   Too Late To Worry, Too Blue To Cry/How Do I Tell My Heart Not To Break? 6
62   Capitol CL 15278   Here I Am/Long Black Limousine 6
63   Capitol CL 15295   Prima Donna/Oh My Darling 6

MINT VALUE £

67	Speciality SPE 1002	Satisfied Mind/Can't You See I'm Trying	5
68	Ember EMB S 252	I Wanna Live/Hey Little One	5
68	Ember EMB S 255	Dreams Of The Everyday Housewife/Combine	5
68	Ember EMB S 258	Straight Life/That's Not Home	5
69	Ember EMB S 261	Wichita Lineman/Back In The Race (p/s)	6
69	Ember EMB S 263	Galveston/Everytime I Itch I Wind Up Scratching You	5
66	London HA-F/SH-F 8291	SWINGING 12-STRING (LP)	15
75	Capitol E-SW 11336	REUNION (LP & inner sleeve, with Jimmy Webb)	12

(see also Sagittarius, Jimmy Slade)

IAN CAMPBELL (FOLK) GROUP

63	Topic STOP 102	The Sun Is Burning/The Crow On The Cradle (some in title p/s)	12/6
64	Decca F 11802	Marilyn Monroe/The Bells Of Rhymney	6
65	Transatlantic TRASP 2	Kelly From Killane/Boys Of Wexford (with Boys From Wexford)	6
65	Transatlantic TRASP 5	The Times They Are A-Changin'/Across The Hills	6
66	Transatlantic TRASP 6	Come Kiss Me/The First Time I Ever Saw Your Face (some in p/s)	10/6
66	Transatlantic TRASP 7	Guantanamera/Mary Anne	6
66	Transatlantic TRASP 10	One Eyed Reilly/Snow Is Falling (solo)	6
67	Big T BIG 103	Lover Let Me In/Private Harold Harris (as Ian Campbell Four)	6
69	Major Minor MM 639	Break My Mind/Govan Cross Special (solo)	6
62	Topic TOP 82	SONGS OF PROTEST (EP)	12
64	Decca DFE 8592	IAN CAMPBELL FOLK GROUP (EP)	12
65	Transatlantic TRAEP 128	SAMPLER (EP)	10
63	Transatlantic TRA 110	THIS IS THE IAN CAMPBELL FOLK GROUP (LP)	30
64	Transatlantic TRA 118	ACROSS THE HILLS (LP)	25
64	Contour 2870 314	PRESENTING THE IAN CAMPBELL FOLK GROUP (LP, reissue of 1st LP)	12
68	Transatlantic TRA 163	THE CIRCLE GAME (LP)	20
68	Xtra XTRA 1074	TAM O'SHANTER (LP, as Ian Campbell & John Dunkerley)	15
69	Transatlantic TRASAM 4	THE IAN CAMPBELL FOLK GROUP SAMPLER (LP)	15
69	Transatlantic TRASAM 12	SAMPLER 2 (LP, as Ian Campbell Folk Four)	12
69	MFP SMFP 1349	IAN CAMPBELL & FOLK GROUP WITH DAVE SWARBRICK (LP)	12
71	Argo ZFB 13	THE SUN IS BURNING (LP)	35
72	Pye PKL 5506	SOMETHING TO SING ABOUT (LP)	15

(see also Dave Swarbrick)

JEAN CAMPBELL

55	Parlophone R 4026	Two Hearts, Two Kisses/Dance With Me, Henry (78)	8
60	Embassy WB 372	The Big Hurt/I Can't Begin To Tell You (78)	8
60	Embassy WB 395	Sweet Nuthin's/PAUL RICH: Standing On The Corner (78)	8
60	Embassy WB 398	Robot Man/BOBBY BRENT: Lucky Five (78)	8
60	Embassy WB 407	I'm Sorry/Everybody's Somebody's Fool (78)	10
60	Embassy WB 408	Paper Roses/Train Of Love (78)	10
60	Embassy WB 417	My Heart Has A Mind Of It's Own/I Want To Be Wanted (78)	10

JIMMY CAMPBELL

69	Fontana TF 1009	On A Monday/Dear Marge (some in p/s)	8/5
70	Fontana TF 1076	Lyanna/Frankie Joe	5
70	Fontana 6007 025	Don't Leave Me Now/So Lonely Without You	5
69	Fontana STL 5508	SON OF ANASTASIA (LP)	15
70	Vertigo 6360 010	HALF BAKED (LP, gatefold sleeve, spiral label)	12
72	Philips 6308 100	JIMMY CAMPBELL'S ALBUM (LP)	12

(see also Kirkbys, 23rd Turnoff, Rockin' Horse)

JO-ANN CAMPBELL

58	London HLU 8536	Wait A Minute/It's True	35
58	London HLU 8536	Wait A Minute/It's True (78)	20
60	HMV POP 776	Bobby, Bobby, Bobby/A Kookie Little Paradise	10
61	HMV POP 873	Motorcycle Michael/Puka Puka Pants	10
62	HMV POP 1003	You Made Me Love You/I Changed My Mind Jack	10
62	Columbia DB 4889	Sloppy Joe/I'm The Girl From Wolverton Mountain	6
62	Cameo Parkway CP 237	Mr Fix It Man/Let Me Do It My Way	10
63	Cameo Parkway CP 249	Mother Please/Waiting For Love	10

JUNIOR CAMPBELL

71	Deram DM 344	Goodbye Baby Jane/If I Call Your Name	5
72	Deram DM 364	Hallelujah Freedom/Alright With Me	5
74	Deram SML 1106	SECOND TIME AROUND (LP)	15

(see also Marmalade, Clan, Dean Ford & Gaylords)

MURRAY CAMPBELL

58	Philips PB 880	Hey Cabby/One Day I'll Buy A Trumpet (78)	10
58	Philips PB 774	Shangri-La/Balmoral Melody (78)	8

PAT CAMPBELL

69	Major Minor 648	The Deal/The Mission	5
70	Starline MRS 55162	JUST A QUIET CONVERSATION (LP)	12

ROY CAMPBELL (& JAZZBO JASPERS)

68	Giant GN 41	Another Saturday Night/Wonderful World (with Jazzbo Jaspers)	6
68	Jolly JY 003	Suzette/Engine Engine Number Nine	6

PATRICK CAMPBELL-LYONS

73	Sovereign SOV 115	Everybody Should Fly A Kite/I Think I Want Him Too	12
73	Sovereign SOV 119	Out On The Road/Me And My Friend	12
77	Electric WOT 12	That's What My Guru Said Last Night/The Whistling Fiddler	5
81	Public PUB 006	Naked Robots Watching Breakfast TV	5
73	Sovereign SVNA 7258	ME AND MY FRIEND (LP, gatefold sleeve)	60
81	Public PUBL 1	THE ELECTRIC PLOUGH (LP)	15

(see also Nirvana [U.K.], Erewhon, Patrick O'Magick, Rock O'Doodle, Pica, Hat & Tie, Aquila)

MINT VALUE £

CAN

73	United Artists UP 35506	Spoon/I'm So Green	6
73	United Artists UP 35596	Moonshake/Future Days (Edit)	6
74	United Artists UP 35749	Dizzy Dizzy (Edit)/Splash (Edit)	6
76	Virgin VS 153	I Want More/... And More	5
76	Virgin VS 166	Silent Night/Cascade Waltz	5
77	Virgin VS 172	Don't Say No/Return	5
78	Lightning LIG 545	Can-Can/Can Be	5
69	United Artists UAS 29094	MONSTER MOVIE (LP, burgundy label)	25
70	United Artists UAS 29283	SOUNDTRACKS (LP)	20
71	Utd. Artists UAD 60009/10	TAGO MAGO (2-LP, flip-top sleeve)	25
72	United Artists UAS 29414	EGE BAMYASI (LP, with inner sleeve)	25
73	United Artists UAS 29505	FUTURE DAYS (LP)	12
74	United Artists UAG 29673	SOON OVER BABALUMA (LP, original silver sleeve)	15
74	United Artists USP 103	LIMITED EDITION (LP)	15
75	Virgin V 2041	LANDED (LP)	15
76	Caroline CAD 3001	UNLIMITED EDITION (2-LP, gatefold sleeve)	30
76	Sunset SLS 50400	OPENER (LP, reissue of "Monster Movie")	12
77	Virgin V 2081	FLOW MOTION (LP)	15
77	Virgin V 2079	SAW DELIGHT (LP, with insert)	15
78	United Artists UDM 105/6	CANNABALISM (2-LP, gatefold sleeve)	30
78	Laser LASL 2	CAN (LP)	12

CANAAN

73	Dovetail DOVE 3	CANAAN (LP)	30
76	Myrrh MYR 1042	OUT OF THE WILDERNESS (LP, with inner sleeve)	20

LOS CANARIOS

67	Major Minor MM 502	Three Two One Ah/What Can I Do For You	10
67	Major Minor MM 532	Get On Your Knees/Keep On The Right Side	8

CANDIDO

57	HMV	THE VOLCANIC (10" LP)	20
79	Salsoul SSLP 1517	DANCIN' AND PRANCIN' (LP)	12

CANDLE FACTORY

70s	CAVS	NIGHTSHIFT (LP, private pressing)	50

CONTE CANDOLI

56	London Jazz LZ-N 14010	SINCERELY, CONTE (10" LP)	15
56	London Jazz LTZ-N 15036	TOOTS SWEET (LP)	12

PETER CANDOLI & HIS ORCHESTRA

56	Capitol CL 14615	St. Louis Blues — Boogie/The Big Top (Entry Of The Gladiators)	8
60	Warner Bros WB 2	Sunset Strip Cha-Cha/DON RALKE: 77 Sunset Strip	5

CANDY

69	Grape GR 3017	Ace Of Hearts/BILLY JACK: Bet Yer Life I Do	6

PENNY CANDY

60	Top Rank JAR 328	Come On Over/They Said	5

CANDY & KISSES

65	Cameo Parkway C 336	The 81/Two Happy People	60
85	Kent TOWN 104	Mr Creator/CHUCK JACKSON: Hand It Over (withdrawn)	15

CANDY CHOIR

66	Parlophone R 5472	Silence Is Golden/Shake Hands (And Come Out Crying)	12
67	CBS 3061	Children And Flowers/Marianne	6
68	CBS 3305	Alexander's Ragtime Band/No Grey Skies	6
70	Polydor 56369	Why Do You Cry My Love/Lucky Jim	5
	(see also Summer Set, Barry Ryan)		

CANDY DATES

65	Pye 7N 15944	A Day Just Like That/Well I Do	6

CANDYMEN

67	HMV POP 1612	Georgia Pines/Movies In My Mind	7

CANE

78	Lightning GIL 531	3 X 3 (EP)	8

BOB CANN

70s	Topic 12TS 275	WEST COUNTRY MELODEON (LP)	15

CANNED HEAT

68	Liberty	Rollin' And Tumblin'/Bullfrog Blues (unreleased)	
68	Liberty LBF 15090	On The Road Again/The World In A Jug	6
69	Liberty LBF 15169	Going Up The Country/One Kind Favour	6
69	Liberty LBF 15200	Time Was/Low Down	6
69	Liberty LBF 15255	Poor Moon/Sic 'Em Pigs	6
69	Liberty LBF 15302	Let's Work Together/I'm Her Man	6
70	Liberty LBF 15350	Sugar Bee/Shake It And Break It	6
70	Pye International 7N 25513	Spoonful/Big Road Blues	6
70	Liberty LBF 15395	Future Blues/Skat	5
70	Liberty LBF 15429	Christmas Blues/Do Not Enter	5
71	Liberty LBF 15439	Wooly Bully/My Time Ain't Long	5
72	United Artists UP 35348	Rockin' With The King (with Little Richard)/I Don't Care What You Tell Me	5
73	United Artists UP 35562	Keep It Clean/You Can Run But You Sure Can't Hide	5
67	Liberty LBL/LBS 83059E	CANNED HEAT (LP)	20
68	Liberty LBL/LBS 83103	BOOGIE WITH CANNED HEAT (LP)	20

MINT VALUE £

69	Liberty LDS 84001E	LIVING THE BLUES (2-LP, gatefold sleeve)	25
69	Liberty LBS 83239	HALLELUJAH (LP, gatefold sleeve)	15
70	Pye Intl. NSPL 28129	VINTAGE HEAT (LP)	15
70	Liberty LBS 83303	CANNED HEAT COOKBOOK (LP)	15
70	Liberty LBS 83333	CANNED HEAT '70 CONCERT (RECORDED LIVE IN EUROPE) (LP, g/fold sleeve)	12
70	Liberty LBS 83364	FUTURE BLUES (LP, gatefold sleeve)	15
71	Liberty LPS 103/4	HOOKER'N'HEAT (2-LP, gatefold sleeve, with John Lee Hooker)	30
72	United Artists UAG 29304	HISTORICAL FIGURES AND ANCIENT HEADS (LP, gatefold sleeve)	12
73	United Artists UAS 29455	THE NEW AGE (LP)	12
74	Atlantic K 50026	ONE MORE RIVER TO CROSS (LP)	12

(see also Harvey Mandel)

CANNIBAL & HEADHUNTERS
| 65 | Stateside SS 403 | Land Of A Thousand Dances/I'll Show You How To Love Me | 18 |
| 67 | CBS 62942 | LAND OF A 1000 DANCES (LP) | 25 |

CANNIBALS
| 78 | Big Cock F-UK 1 | Good Guys/Nothing Takes The Place Of You (printed paper bag sleeve) | 6 |

(see also Count Bishops, Stoned Aid)

ACE CANNON
62	London HLU 9498	Tuff/Sittin'	6
62	London HLU 9546	Blues Stay Away From Me/Blues In My Heart	6
63	London HLU 9745	Cottonfields/Mildew	6
64	London HLU 9866	Searchin'/Love Letters In The Sand	6
67	London HLU 10105	Wonderland By Night/As Time Goes By	5
70	London HA-U/SH-U 8407	ACE OF SAX (LP)	15

CONROY CANNON
| 69 | Pama PM 769 | Oh Happy Day/Can't Get Along Without You | 5 |

FREDDY CANNON
59	Top Rank JAR 135	Tallahassee Lassie/You Know	7
59	Top Rank JAR 135	Tallahassee Lassie/You Know (78)	70
59	Top Rank JAR 207	Okefenokee/Kookie Hat	8
59	Top Rank JAR 247	Way Down Yonder In New Orleans/Fractured	5
60	Top Rank JAR 309	California, Here I Come/Indiana	6
60	Top Rank JAR 334	Chattanooga Shoeshine Boy/Boston (My Home Town)	6
60	Top Rank JAR 369	The Urge/Jump Over	6
60	Top Rank JAR 407	Happy Shades Of Blue/Guernavaca Choo Choo	6
60	Top Rank JAR 518	Humdinger/My Blue Heaven	6
61	Top Rank JAR 548	Muskrat Rumble/Two Thousand 88	5
61	Top Rank JAR 568	Buzz Buzz A Diddle It/Opportunity	15
61	Top Rank JAR 579	Transistor Sister/Walk To The Moon	7
61	Top Rank JAR 592	For Me And My Gal/Blue Plate Special	6
62	Top Rank JAR 609	Teen Queen Of The Week/Wild Guy	6
62	Stateside SS 101	Palisades Park/June July And August	5
62	Stateside SS 118	What's Gonna Happen When Summer's Done/Broadway	5
62	Stateside SS 134	If You Were A Rock & Roll Record/The Truth Ruth	6
63	Stateside SS 155	Come On And Love Me/Four Letter Man	6
63	Stateside SS 183	The Ups And Downs Of Love/It's Been Nice	6
63	Stateside SS 201	Patty Baby/Betty Jean	10
63	Stateside SS 220	Everybody Monkey/Oh Gloria	6
64	Stateside SS 260	That's The Way Girls Are/Do What The Hippies Do	6
64	Warner Bros WB 123	Abigail Beecher/All American Girl	6
64	Stateside SS 298	Sweet Georgia Brown/What A Party	6
65	Warner Bros WB 5645	Action/Beechwood City	6
66	Warner Bros WB 5693	The Dedication Song/Come On Come On	6
69	London HLK 10252	Beautiful Downtown Burbank/If You Give Me A Title	5
60	Top Rank JKP 2058	THE EXPLOSIVE FREDDY (BOOM! BOOM!) CANNON (EP)	30
60	Top Rank JKP 2066	FOUR DIRECT HITS (EP)	30
61	Top Rank JKP 3010	ON TARGET (EP)	25
62	Stateside SE 1002	BLAST OFF WITH FREDDY CANNON (EP)	25
60	Top Rank 25/018	THE EXPLOSIVE FREDDY CANNON (LP)	40
61	Top Rank 35/106	FREDDY CANNON SINGS HAPPY SHADES OF BLUE (LP)	50
61	Top Rank 35/113	FREDDY CANNON FAVOURITES (LP)	50
63	Stateside SL 10013	BANG ON (LP)	50
64	Stateside SL 10062	STEPS OUT (LP)	60
64	Warner Bros WM/WS 8153	FREDDY CANNON (LP)	30

(see also Danny & Juniors)

JUDY CANNON
| 65 | Pye 7N 15900 | The Very First Day I Met You/Hello Heartache | 35 |

RICHARD CANNON
| 59 | Capitol CL 15001 | You'll Never Walk Alone/Tonight I Am A King | 5 |

SEAN CANNON
| 77 | Cottage COT 411 | THE ROVING JOURNEY MAN (LP) | 10 |

CANNON BALL & JOHNNY MELODY
| 69 | Big Shot BI 518 | Parapinto/Cool Hand Luke | 8 |

(see also Carl Bryan, King Cannon, Johnny Moore, Jackie Mittoo, Royals)

CANNONBALLS
| 61 | Coral Q 72428 | Cannonball Caboose/New Orleans Beat | 12 |
| 61 | Coral Q 72431 | Lullaby Of Birdland/Calliope Boogie | 12 |

CANNON BROTHERS
| 65 | Brit WI 1003 | Turn Your Eyes To Me/Don't Stop Now | 12 |

MINT VALUE £

CANNONS
60	Decca F 11269	I Didn't Know The Gun Was Loaded/My Guy's Come Back	15
61	Columbia DB 4724	Bush Fire/Juicy	15

CANNON'S JUG STOMPERS
66	Tax LP 2	CANNON'S JUG STOMPERS/CLIFFORD'S LOUISVILLE JUG BAND (LP, 1 side each)	20

CANNY FETTLE
75	Tradition TSR 023	VARRY CANNY (LP)	25
77	Tradition TSR 027	TRIP TO HARROGATE (LP)	15

EDDIE CANTOR
61	Capitol EAP1 20113	MA HE'S MAKING EYES AT ME (EP)	10

CAPABILITY BROWN
72	Charisma CB 193	Wake Up Little Sister/Windfall	5
73	Charisma CB 207	Midnight Cruiser/Silent Sounds	5
73	Charisma CB 217	Liar/Keep Death Off The Road	5
70s	Charisma BCP 7	War (p/s)	5
72	Charisma CAS 1056	FROM SCRATCH (LP)	15
73	Charisma CAS 1068	VOICE (LP)	15

(see also Unit 4+2, Tony Rivers & Castaways)

JIM CAPALDI
74	Island WIP 6198	It's All Up To You/Whale Meat Again	5
72	Island ILPS 9187	OH HOW WE DANCED (LP, gatefold sleeve)	12
77	Island ILPS 9497	PLAY IT BY EAR (LP)	12

(see also Hellions, Traffic)

CAPE KENNEDY CONSTRUCTION CO.
69	President PT 265	The First Steps On The Moon/Armageddon	35

CAPERCAILLIE
91	Survival ZD 44594	Coisich A Ruin (Walk My Beloved) (7" Version)/Outlaws/The Islay Ranters' Reels (A & B)/Coisich A Ruin (Walk My Beloved) (Extended 12" Version) (CD)	8
92	Survival 74321-11587-2	Waiting For The Wheel To Turn/Breisleach (live)/Kenny McDonald's Jigs (live)/ Waiting For The Wheel To Turn (Edit) (CD, withdrawn, no inlay)	12
93	Survival (no cat. no.)	Four Stone Walls/Hi Ri'm Bo/Stinging Rain (CD, digipak, promo only)	8
84	Etive/SRT 4KL 178	CASCADE (LP)	20
87	Grampian TV GPN 1001	THE BLOOD IS STRONG (LP, with insert)	12

(see also Etives)

CAPES & MASKS
65	Nevis NEV R005	COMIC BOOK HEROES (LP)	18

CAPITOLS (U.K.)
66	Pye 7N 17025	Honey And Wine/Boulavogue	8

CAPITOLS (U.S.)
66	Atlantic 584 004	Cool Jerk/Hello Stranger	12
72	Atlantic K 10205	Ain't That Terrible/Zig-Zagging	4
76	Contempo CS 9030	Cool Jerk/Ain't That Terrible	6

(see also Three Caps)

CAPITOL SHOW BAND
67	Marble Arch MAL 694	THE CAPITOL SHOWBAND (LP)	12

ANDY CAPP
69	Treasure Isle TI 7052	Pop-A-Top/RICO: The Lion Speaks	8
70	Duke DU 69	The Law (Parts 1 & 2)	5
70	Duke DU 71	Poppy Show/Pop-A-Top (Part 2)	5

AL CAPPS
73	Stateside SS 2214	Shangri-La/Magician	5

CAPREEZ
79	Grapevine GRP 113	How To Make A Sad Man Glad/It's Good To Be Home Again	5

DANNY CAPRI
55	Capitol CL 14265	Desirable/I Do, I Do	5
55	Capitol CL 14302	Don't Make A Liar Out Of Me/Angelica	5

CAPRICORN
70	MCA MK 5050	Liverpool Hello/How Did You Find Me	5

(see also Marty Wilde)

CAPRIS
61	Columbia DB 4605	There's A Moon Out Tonight/Indian Girl	90

CAPTAIN BEEFHEART & HIS MAGIC BAND
SINGLES
68	Pye International 7N 25443	Yellow Brick Road/Abba Zabba	30
68	A&M AMS 726	Moonchild/Who Do You Think You're Fooling	40
73	Reprise K 14233	Too Much Time/My Head Is My Only House Unless It Rains	6
74	Virgin VS 110	Upon The My-Oh-My/Magic Be	5
78	Buddah BDS 466	Sure 'Nuff 'N Yes I Do/Electricity	7
78	MCA MCA 366	Hard Workin' Man (Jack Nitzsche featuring Captain Beefheart)/ JACK NITZSCHE: Coke Machine	6

EPs
71	A&M AME 600	DIDDY WAH DIDDY (EP, p/s, promo only)	375
79	Virgin SIXPACK 1	SIX-PACK/SIX TRACK (EP, picture disc, die-cut p/s with stand, 5,000 only)	18
82	Virgin VS 534 12	LIGHT REFLECTED OFF THE OCEANS OF THE MOON (12", p/s)	12
84	A&M AMY 226	THE LEGENDARY A&M SESSIONS (12" EP/mini-LP, "Diddy Wah Diddy" EP plus "Where I Am, I Always Am")	15
86	Edsel BLIMP 902	THE LEGENDARY A&M SESSIONS (12" EP, reissue)	15

CAPTAIN SENSIBLE   *CAPTAIN BEEFHEART*

ORIGINAL LPs

68	Pye Intl. NPL 28110	SAFE AS MILK (LP, mono, flipback sleeve)	35
68	Liberty LBL/LBS 83172	STRICTLY PERSONAL (LP, gatefold sleeve, mono/stereo)	35/30
69	Straight STS 1053	TROUT MASK REPLICA (2-LP, gatefold sleeve)	45
70	Straight STS 1063	LICK MY DECALS OFF, BABY (LP)	45
71	Buddah 2365 002	MIRROR MAN (LP, gatefold die-cut sleeve)	25
72	Reprise K 44162	THE SPOTLIGHT KID (LP, tan 'riverboat' label, some with lyric card insert)	20/18
72	Reprise K 54007	CLEAR SPOT (LP, PVC sleeve with card insert)	25
74	Virgin V 2015	UNCONDITIONALLY GUARANTEED (LP, 'two virgins' label)	20
74	Virgin V 2023	BLUEJEANS & MOONBEAMS (LP, 'two virgins' label)	15
79	Virgin V 2149	SHINY BEAST (BAT CHAIN PULLER) (LP)	18
80	Virgin V 2172	DOC AT THE RADAR STATION (LP)	18
82	Virgin V 2237	ICE CREAM FOR CROW (LP, with inner sleeve)	18

REISSUE LPs

68	Marble Arch MAL 1117	SAFE AS MILK (LP, mono, 10 tracks only)	15
70	Buddah 2349 002	DROPOUT BOOGIE (LP, stereo reissue of "Safe As Milk")	20
73	Sunset SLS 50208	STRICTLY PERSONAL (LP, 'Contemporary' series)	15
73	Reprise K 44244	LICK MY DECALS OFF, BABY (LP)	25
74	Buddah BDLP 4004	MIRROR MAN (LP)	20
75	Reprise K 64026	TROUT MASK REPLICA (2-LP, g/fold sleeve, tan 'riverboat' label, matt sleeve)	25
70s	Reprise K 64026	TROUT MASK REPLICA (2-LP, gatefold sleeve, 2nd re-pressing, tan 'riverboat' label, soft laminated sleeve)	20
76	Reprise K 84006	TWO ORIGINALS OF CAPTAIN BEEFHEART (2-LP, reissue of "Lick My Decals Off, Baby" & "The Spotlight Kid")	20
77	Pye FILD 008	THE FILE SERIES (2-LP, reissue of "Safe As Milk" & "Mirror Man", die-cut sleeve with inners)	15
79	Liberty LBR 1006	STRICTLY PERSONAL (LP, 2nd reissue)	15
82	PRT NCP 1004	SAFE AS MILK (LP)	15
82	PRT NCP 1006	MIRROR MAN (LP)	15
83	Buddah/PRT DOW 15	MUSIC IN SEA MINOR (10" LP, 6 tracks from "Safe As Milk" & "Mirror Man")	15
84	Design PIXLP 4	TOP SECRET (LP, picture disc, tracks from "Safe As Milk" & "Mirror Man")	12

(see also Mallard, Mu, Frank Zappa, Jack Nitzsche)

CAPTAIN BEYOND

72	Capricorn K 47503	CAPTAIN BEYOND (LP)	25

(see also Deep Purple)

CAPTAIN LOCKHEED & THE STARFIGHTERS

73	United Artists UP 35543	Ejection/Catch A Falling Starfighter (p/s)	25
73	United Artists UP 35543	Ejection/Catch A Falling Starfighter (different mix of A-side, no p/s)	10

(see also Robert Calvert)

CAPTAIN NOAH & HIS FLOATING ZOO

72	Argo ZDA 149	HOLY MOSES (LP, with Kings Singers)	12

CAPTAIN SCARLET

(see under Century 21)

CAPTAIN SENSIBLE

81	Crass 321984/5	THIS IS YOUR CAPTAIN SPEAKING (EP, foldout p/s)	5
82	Big Beat NS 77	Jet Boy, Jet Girl/SOFTIES: Children Of The Damned (p/s)	5

(see also Damned, Magic Michael, Maxim's Trash, Percy Pavillion)

C.A. QUINTET

83	Psycho PSYCHO 12	TRIP THROUGH HELL (LP, reissue of U.S. LP)	15

CARAVAN

69	Verve VS 1518	A Place Of My Own/Ride	35
70	Decca F 13063	Hello, Hello/If I Could Do It All Over Again, I'd Do It All Over You	12
71	Decca F 23125	Love To Love You (And Tonight Pigs Will Fly)/Golf Girl	12
75	Decca FR 13599	Stuck In A Hole/Lover	5
76	BTM SBT 104	All The Way (With John Wayne's Single-Handed Liberation Of Paris)/ Chiefs And Indians (p/s)	6
77	Arista ARIST 110	Better By Far/Silver Strings	5
80	Kingdom KV 8009	Heartbreaker/It's Never Too Late (p/s)	6
68	Verve (S)VLP 6011	CARAVAN (LP, 'pillar' sleeve, mono/stereo)	100
70	Decca SKL 5052	IF I COULD DO IT ALL OVER AGAIN, I'D DO IT ALL OVER YOU (LP)	25
71	Deram SDL-R 1	IN THE LAND OF GREY AND PINK (LP, gatefold sleeve)	25
72	Deram SDL 8	WATERLOO LILY (LP, gatefold sleeve)	25
72	MGM 2353 058	CARAVAN (LP, reissue)	30
73	Deram SDL-R 12	FOR GIRLS WHO GROW PLUMP IN THE NIGHT (LP, gatefold sleeve)	15
74	Deram SML 1110	CARAVAN AND THE NEW SYMPHONIA (LIVE AT DRURY LANE) (LP)	15
75	Decca SKLR 5210	CUNNING STUNTS (LP)	12
76	BTM BTM 107	BLIND DOG AT ST. DUNSTAN'S (LP)	12
77	Arista SPARTY 1008	BETTER BY FAR (LP)	12

(see also Gringo, Matching Mole, Hatfield & The North, Spiro Gyra)

CARAVELLES

63	Decca F 11697	You Don't Have To Be A Baby To Cry/The Last One To Know	5
63	Decca F 11758	I Really Don't Want To Know/I Was Wrong	6
64	Decca F 11816	Have You Ever Been Lonely?/Gonna Get Along Without Ya Now	6
64	Fontana TF 466	You Are Here/How Can I Be Sure?	7
64	Fontana TF 509	I Don't Care If The Sun Don't Shine/I Like A Man	6
64	Polydor NH 59034	True Love Never Runs Smooth/Georgia Boy	6
66	Polydor 56137	Hey Mama You've Been On My Mind/New York	10
67	Polydor 56156	I Want To Love You Again/I Had To Walk Home Myself	5
68	Pye 7N 17654	The Other Side Of Love/I Hear A New Kind Of Music	6
63	Decca LK 4565	THE CARAVELLES (LP)	30

(see also Lois Lane)

GUY CARAWAN

58	Pye Nixa 7N 15132	Old Man Atom (Talking Atomic Blues)/Michael Row The Boat Ashore	6
58	Pye Nixa N 15132	Old Man Atom (Talking Atomic Blues)/Michael Row The Boat Ashore (78)	12

(see also Peggy Seeger & Guy Carawan)

CARDALE TRIO

68	Pilgrim	FOLLOW ON (EP)	12

CARDBOARD ORCHESTRA

69	CBS 4176	Zebady Zak/Mary Tell Me Why	6
69	CBS 4633	Nothing But A Sad Sad Show/Yes I Heard A Little Bird	6

(see also Zior, Monument)

CARDIAC ARREST

79	Another Record AN 1	Running In The Street/T.V. Friends (p/s, 500 only)	10

(see also Michael Byrd & Commercials)

CARDIAC ARREST

79	Tortch TOR 002	A BUS FOR A BUS ON A BUS (EP)	15

(see also Cardiacs)

CARDIACS

81	private label	TOY WORLD (cassette)	20
81	private label	THE OBVIOUS IDENTITY (cassette)	20
80s	Alphabet ALPH 000	ARCHIVE CARDIACS (cassette, fan club issue, compilation of "Toy World" & "The Obvious Identity")	10
88	Alphabet ALPH 008	Is This The Life/I'm Eating In Bed (p/s)	7
88	Alphabet ALPH 009	Susannah's Still Alive (p/s)	5
86	Alphabet ALPH 002	SEASIDE TREATS (12" EP, with poster & lyric insert)	8
87	Alphabet ALPH 006	THERE'S TOO MANY IRONS IN THE FIRE (12" EP, with poster)	8
91	Alphabet ALPH 015	DAY IS GONE (12" EP, with lyric sheet)	8
83	Alphabet ALPH 01	THE SEASIDE (13-track cassette, colour inlay)	20
86	Alphabet ALPH 003	MR & MRS SMITH & MR DRAKE (cassette, fan club issue)	10
87	Alphabet ALPH 004	BIG SHIP (mini LP, with lyric insert)	12
87	Alphabet ALPH 005	RUDE BOOTLEG — LIVE AT READING '86 (LP, stamped sleeve with insert)	20
87	Alphabet ALPH MC005	RUDE BOOTLEG — LIVE AT READING '86 (cassette)	12
88	Torso CD 060	A LITTLE MAN AND A HOUSE AND THE WHOLE WORLD WINDOW (CD)	25

(see also Cardiac Arrest)

CARDIGANS

58	Mercury AMT 1007	Poor Boy/Each Other	10
58	Mercury AMT 1007	Poor Boy/Each Other (78)	20

CARDIGANS

95	Stockholm PO 345	Carnival/Mr. Crowley (Live) (p/s)	5
95	Stockholm PO 336	Sick & Tired/Plain Parade (p/s)	5
95	Stockholm PZCD 336	Sick & Tired/Plain Parade/Laika/Pooh Song (CD, card sleeve)	8
96	Stockholm 575 528 7	Lovefool/Nasty Sunny Beam (p/s, white vinyl)	5
99	Simply Vinyl SVLP 114	LIFE (LP, reissue)	15
96	Stockholm CARDBOXCD 1	FIRST BAND ON THE MOON (CD, box set with poster & T-shirt)	20

Promos

97	Motor 571 661 1	Your New Cuckoo/(remixes) (12", title sleeve)	8
99	Stockholm CARDI 5	Erase\Rewind (Cut La Rock Vocal Mix)/(NÂid Remix) (12", also as white label)	8
99	Stockholm CARDI 7	Hanging Around (NÂid Remix)/My Favourite Game (Faithless Mix) (12")	8
96	Stockholm	HIGHLIGHTS FROM THE CARDIGANS CATALOGUE (CD-R)	30
96	Stockholm MOON 1	FIRST BAND ON THE MOON ALBUM SAMPLER (CD, card sleeve)	15
98	Stockholm CARD INT 1	INTERVIEW DISC (CD, card sleeve, with outer plastic sleeve & 3 photo-cards)	25

CARDINALS
72	Nelmwood Audio	ON TOP OF THE WORLD (LP)	20

JACK CARDWELL
54	Parlophone CMSP 24	Whiskey, Women And Loaded Dice/Slap-Ka-Dab (export issue)	25
54	Parlophone DP 400	Whiskey, Women And Loaded Dice/Slap-Ka-Dab (78, export issue)	8
54	Parlophone CMSP 27	Blue Love/Diddle Diddle Dumpling (export issue)	25
54	Parlophone DP 406	Blue Love/Diddle Diddle Dumpling (78, export issue)	8

CARE
83	Arista KBIRD 2	Flaming Sword/Misericorde (picture disc)	7

(see also Wild Swans, Lotus Eaters, Lightning Seeds, Original Mirrors)

CAREFREES
63	Oriole CB 1916	We Love You Beatles/Hot Blooded Lover	15
64	Oriole CB 1931	Aren't You Glad You're You/Paddy Wack	8

CARETAKER RACE
88	Roustabout RST 004	Anywhere But Home/Gilda (unreleased, DJ-only)	12

(see also Loft)

BILL CAREY
55	Vogue Coral Q 72096	Heavenly Lover/My Fate Is In Your Hands	7
56	Vogue Coral Q 72151	Where Walks My True Love/Laughing Boy	7

DAVE CAREY (JAZZ BAND)
53	Columbia SCM 5030	Broken Wings/Oh, Happy Day (as David Carey)	8
56	Tempo A 122	Kater Street Rag/Kansas City Kitty	7
56	Tempo A 133	I've Found A New Baby/Brown Skin Mama	7
56	Tempo A 138	Sunset Cafe Stomp/Sweet Georgia Brown	7
56	Tempo A 150	Ida, Sweet As Apple Cider/Button Up Your Overcoat	7
61	Philips PB 1158	Bingo (I'm In Love)/Paddlin' Madelin' Home (some in p/s)	8/5
56	Tempo EXA 38	DAVE CAREY JAZZ BAND (EP)	15
56	Tempo EXA 43	DAVE CAREY JAZZ BAND (EP)	15
56	Tempo EXA 51	DAVE CAREY JAZZ BAND (EP)	10
55	Tempo LAP 4	DAVE CAREY JAZZ BAND (LP)	18
57	Tempo TAP 16	JAZZ AT THE RAILWAY ARMS (LP)	25

MARIAH CAREY
90	Columbia 655 932-0	Vision Of Love/Sent From Up Above (p/s)	5
90	Columbia 655 932-2	Vision Of Love/Sent From Up Above/Medley (CD)	12
90	Columbia 656 149-7	Love Takes Time/Sent From Up Above (p/s)	6
90	Columbia 656 364-6	Love Takes Time/You Need Me/Vanishing (12", p/s)	10
90	Columbia 656 364-2	Love Takes Time/Vanishing/You Need Me (CD)	10
90	Columbia 656 364-5	Love Takes Time/Vanishing/You Need Me/Vision Of Love (CD, picture disc)	30
91	Columbia 656 583-7	Someday/Alone In Love (p/s)	5
91	Columbia 656 583-6	Someday (7" House Mix)/(12" Jackswing Mix)/(Pianoapercaloopaperlla Mix) (12", p/s)	12
91	Columbia 656 583-2	Someday (7" Jackswing Mix)/(12" Jackswing Mix)/Love/Love Takes Time (CD)	15
91	Columbia 656 583-5	Someday (7" Jackswing Mix)/Vision Of Love/Love Takes Time/Alone In Love (CD, picture disc)	25
91	Columbia 656 931-2	There's Got To Be A Way (Album Version)/(12" Remix)/(ALT Vocal Club Mix) (CD)	15
91	Columbia 656 931-5	There's Got To Be A Way/(Album Version)/(7" Remix)/Someday (7" Jackswing Mix)/Vision Of Love (CD, picture disc)	25
91	Columbia 657 403-2	Emotions/Vanishing/Vision Of Love (CD)	15
92	Columbia 657 662-7	Can't Let Go (Edit)/To Be Around You (p/s)	5
92	Columbia 657 662-6	Can't Let Go (Edit)/To Be Around You/The Wind (12", p/s)	8
92	Columbia 657 662-2	Can't Let Go (Edit)/To Be Around You/The Wind (CD, slimline jewel case)	18
92	Columbia 657 941-7	Make It Happen/Emotions (Special Motion Edit) (p/s)	5
92	Columbia 657 941-6	Make It Happen (Extended Version)/(Dub Version)/(C&C Classic Mix)/(LP Version) (12", p/s)	10
92	Columbia 657 941-2	Make It Happen (Radio Edit)/(Ext. Version)/(Dub)/(C&C Classic Mix)/(LP Version) (CD)	18
92	Columbia 658 137-9	I'll Be There (live)/Vision Of Love (live)/If It's Over/All In Your Mind (CD, picture disc)	18
95	Columbia XPR 2129	Joy To The World (Celebration Mix)/(Flava Mix)/(Club Mix)/(Crash Dub Crash)/(LP Version)(12", title p/s, promo only)	15
97	Columbia XPR 2378	Fly Away (Fly Away Club Mix)/(Def 'B' Fly Mix) (12", p/s, promo only)	15
97	Columbia XPR 2380	The Roof (Remix With Mobb Deep)/Underneath The Stars/Breakdown/Babydoll (12", title p/s, promo only)	18
98	Columbia XPR 2396	The Roof (Full Crewe's Club Mix)/(Full Crewe Club Mix)/(Mobb Deep Remix)/(Full Crewe Radio Mix) (12", title p/s, promo only)	15
98	Columbia XPR 2398	The Roof (Funky Club Mix)/(Radio Mix)/(After Hours Mix)/(Bass Man Mix) (12", title p/s, promo only)	15
98	Columbia XPR 2409	My All (Full Crewe Main Mix)/(Full Crewe Radio Edit)/(Full Crewe Main Mix Without Rap)/(Full Crewe Main Mix Instrumental) (12", title p/s, promo only)	12

TONY CAREY
84	MCA MCA 873	Fine Fine Day/Say It's Over (p/s)	6
84	MCA MCFC 3212	SOME TOUGH CITY (LP, with inner sleeve)	12

(see also Rainbow, Planet P Project)

CAREY & LLOYD
72	Attack ATT 8032	Do It Again (as Carey/Lloyd)/GARY RANGLIN: Watch It	5
72	Grape GR 3025	Come Down Part 1/DYNAMITES: Come Down Part 2	5

(see also Carey Johnson, Lloyd Young, Lloyd & Carey)

HENSON CARGILL
68	Monument MON 1015	Skip A Rope/Very Well-Travelled Man	5

MINT VALUE £

PATRICK CARGILL
71 Hit HIT 16   Father Dear Father/Theme (Instrumental) 5

CARIBBEANS
69 Doctor Bird DB 1181   Let Me Walk By/AMBLINGS: Tell Me Why 12
69 Crab CR 14   Please Please/MATADORS: The Destroyer 7

CARIBBEATS
66 Ska Beat JB 246   The Bells Of St. Mary's/WINSTON RICHARDS: Loki 15
67 Double D DD 101   Highway 300/I Think Of You (actually by Merlene McKenzie) 10
67 Double D DD 103   I'll Try/If I Did Look 10
(see also Bobby Aitken, Itals)

CARIBS
60 Starlite ST45 012   Taboo/Mathilda Cha Cha Cha! 6

CARIFTA ALLSTARS
72 Green Door GD 4040   The Harder They Come (actually by Charlie Ace)/Time Is Still Here 7

CARL & COMMANDERS
61 Columbia DB 4719   Farmer John/Cleanin' Up 15

BELINDA CARLISLE
86 I.R.S. IRM 118   Mad About You/I Never Wanted A Rich Man (p/s) 8
86 I.R.S. IRMT 118   Mad About You/(Extended Mix)/I Never Wanted A Rich Man (12", p/s) 12
88 I.R.S. DIRM 118   Mad About You/I Never Wanted A Rich Man/Mad About You
                                 (Extended Mix) (3" CD) 50
87 Virgin VSCD 1036   Heaven Is A Place On Earth/We Can Change/Heaven Is A Place On Earth
                                 (Heavenly Version)/Heaven Is A Place On Earth (Acapella Version) (CD) 25
88 Virgin VSP 1046   I Get Weak/Should I Let You In (poster p/s) 10
88 Virgin VST 1046   I Get Weak (12" Version)/I Get Weak (7" Version)/Should I Let You In?
                                 (12", p/s, with poster) 15
88 Virgin VSCD 1046   I Get Weak (7" Version)/Should I Let You In/I Get Weak (12" Version)
                                 (CD, picture disc) 25
88 Virgin VSTY 1074   Circle In The Sand/(Beach Party Mix)/(Seaside Groove Mix)
                                 (12", picture disc) 18
88 Virgin VSCD 1074   Circle In The Sand (7" Version)/(Seaside Mood Groove Mix)/
                                 (Sandblast Multi-Mix)/(Beach Party Mix) (CD) 15
88 Virgin VSX 1114   World Without You (Remix)/Nobody Owns Me (box set, 2 cards & lyric sheet) ... 15
88 Virgin VSTP 1114   World Without You (Extended World-wide Mix)/World Without You
                                 (7" Remix)/Nobody Owns Me (12", poster p/s) 15
88 Virgin VSCD 1114   World Without You (Extended World-wide Mix)/World Without You (7" Remix)/
                                 World Without You (Panavision Mix) (CD) 15
88 Virgin VSTA 1150   Love Never Dies... (Full Length Version)/I Feel Free (live)/Heaven Is A Place
                                 On Earth (live) (12", p/s with advent calendar) 15
88 Virgin VSCD 1150   Love Never Dies... (Full Length Version)/I Feel Free (live)/Circle In The Sand
                                 (live)/Heaven Is A Place On Earth (live) (CD, with prints) 15
89 Virgin VSP 1210   Leave A Light On/Shades Of Michaelangelo/Leave A Light On (Extended Mix)
                                 (foldout poster p/s) 7
89 Virgin VSCD 1210   Leave A Light On (7" Version)/Shades Of Michaelangelo/Leave A Light On
                                 (Extended Mix) (3" CD in card sl., also 5" CD in jewel case [662 719/211], £25) .. 12
89 Virgin VSX 1230   La Luna/Whatever It Takes ('Xmas' pack, gatefold p/s) 8
89 Virgin VSTP 1230   La Luna/La Luna (Extended Dance Mix)/La Luna (12" Dub Mix) (12", poster p/s) . 15
89 Virgin VSCD 1230DJ   La Luna/Whatever It Takes (3" CD, picture disc, promo only) 70
89 Virgin VSCDT 1230   La Luna (Single Version)/La Luna (Extended Dance Mix)/La Luna (12" Dub Mix)
                                 (5" CD, slimline jewel case) 25
90 Virgin VSTP 1244   Runaway Horses/Heaven Is A Place On Earth (live)/Circle In The Sand
                                 (Beach Party Mix) (12", foldout poster pack) 15
90 Virgin VSCD 1244   Runaway Horses/Heaven Is A Place On Earth (live)/Circle In The Sand
                                 (Beach Party Mix) (3" CD, card sleeve) 10
90 Virgin VSCDT 1244   Runaway Horses/Heaven Is A Place On Earth (Live)/Circle In The Sand
                                 (Beach Party Mix) (5" CD, slimline jewel case) 20
90 Virgin VSTY 1264   Vision Of You/Leave A Light On (Kamikazee Mix)/I Feel Free (live)
                                 (12", picture disc, gatefold sleeve) 8
90 Virgin VSTD 1264   Vision Of You (7" Version)/Leave A Light On (Kamikaze Mix)/I Feel Free
                                 (12" Extended Mix) (CD) 10
90 Virgin VSTA 1291   (We Want) The Same Thing (Extended Summer Remix)/Circle In The Sand
                                 (Sand Blast Multi Mix) (12", box set with 6 stickers) 10
90 Virgin VSCDP 1291   (We Want) The Same Thing (Summer Mix)/Circle In The Sand
                                 (Sand Blast Multi Mix)/Shades Of Michaelangelo (CD, picture disc) 12
90 Virgin VSCDX 1323   Summer Rain/Summer Rain (Justin Strauss Mix)/Leave A Light On
                                 (Kamikazee Mix) (CD, digipak with prints in video-style case) 18
91 Virgin VSCDG 1370   Live Your Life Be Free/Loneliness Game/Live Your Life Be Free (Club Mix)
                                 (CD, digipak) 8
91 Virgin VSY 1383   Do You Feel Like I Feel/Do You Feel Like I Feel (Dance Mix)
                                 (picture disc with print in frame) 5
91 Virgin VSCDX 1388   Half The World/Vision Of You (Remix 91)/Circle In The Sand/Love Never Dies
                                 (CD, die-cut digipak, with pull-out poster calendar) 8
87 Virgin VSCD 1036   HEAVEN ON EARTH (CD, picture disc, stickered case) 40
(see also Go-Go's, Smithereens)

BILL CARLISLE & CARLISLES
55 Mercury MB 3215   Rusty Old Halo/It's Bedtime (78) 12
59 Mercury AMT 1063   Down Boy/Union Suit 30
64 Hickory 45-1254   Shanghai Rooster/Big John Henry's Girl 7

CARLISLE BROTHERS
59 Parlophone GEP 8799   FRESH FROM THE COUNTRY (EP) 20

DON CARLOS ORCHESTRA
53	HMV GV 183	Chilli Sauce — Samba/Maria Christina — Mambo (78, export issue)	10
54	HMV 7 MC 4	Delicado/Anything Can Happen (export issue)	10
56	HMV 7 MC 48	The Bandit/Mexicana (export issue)	10
60	Top Rank JAR 376	Mustapha/Josita	6
58	Pye Nixa NPT 19028	CHA-CHA-CHA-CARLOS (10" LP)	15

DAVE CARLSEN
73	Spark SRLP 110	A PALE HORSE (LP)	25

RAY CARLSON
67	MGM MGM 1362	Speak No Sorrow/It's Getting Me Down Girl	6

(LITTLE) CARL CARLTON
68	Action ACT 4501	Competition Ain't Nothin'/Three Way Love	25
68	Action ACT 4514	46 Drums 1 Guitar/Why Don't They Leave Us Alone	10
69	Action ACT 4537	Look At Mary Wonder/Bad For Each Other (as Carl Carlton)	10
75	ABC ABC 4040	Smokin' Room/Signed, Sealed, Delivered, I'm Yours (as Carl Carlton)	6

EDDIE CARLTON
76	Cream CRM 5001	It Will Be Done (Parts 1 & 2)	8

CARLTON & HIS SHOES
68	Coxsone CS 7065	Love Me Forever/Happy Land	25
68	Studio One SO 2062	This Feeling/You And Me (Love Is A Treasure)	15
70s	Studio One PSOL 003	LOVE ME FOREVER (LP)	45

(see also Lee 'Scratch' Perry, Roy & Enid)

CARMEN
74	Regal Zonophone RZ 3086	Flamenco Fever/Lonely House	5
74	Regal Zonophone RZ 3090	Bulerias/Stepping Stone	5
73	R. Zonophone SRZA 8518	FANDANGOS IN SPACE (LP, gatefold sleeve)	18
75	R. Zonophone SLRZ 1040	DANCING ON A COLD WIND (LP, with inner sleeve)	25

HOAGY CARMICHAEL
51	Brunswick 04710	My Resistance Is Low/Sacramento (78)	10
55	Vogue Coral Q 72078	Crazy Otto Rag/Happy Hoagy's Medley	10
55	Vogue Coral Q 72095	Lazy River/I'm Just Wild About Mary	8
56	Vogue Coral Q 72123	Hong Kong Blues/LES BROWN: It's All Right With Me	8
56	Vogue Coral Q 72206	I Walk The Line/Flight To Hong Kong	8
54	Brunswick OE 9023	THE STARDUST ROAD (EP)	12
58	Vogue VE 170113	HOAGY CARMICHAEL (EP)	15
50s	HMV 7EG 8037	STARDUST (EP)	10

IAN CARMICHAEL
57	HMV POP 406	Lucky Jim (How I Envy Him)/Tomorrow, Tomorrow	8

CARMITA
58	Fontana H 160	The Crowd/Waterwagon Blues	5
58	Fontana H 160	The Crowd/Waterwagon Blues (78)	10

JEAN CARN
77	Philadelphia Intl. PIR 5501	If You Wanna Go Back/You Are All I Need	5
80	Philadelphia Intl. PIR 8840	Was That All It Was/What's On Your Mind	5
80	Phil. Intl. PIR 13 8840	Was That All It Was/What's On Your Mind (12")	10

(see also Al Johnson & Jean Carn)

CARNABY
65	Piccadilly 7N 35272	Jump And Dance/My Love Will Stay	50

CARNABY STREET POP ORCHESTRA & CHOIR
69	Carnaby CNLS 6003	CARNABY STREET POP (LP)	45

CARNAGE
83	Creative Reality REAL 5	All The Sad People/Dismal 1984 (p/s)	5
84	Creative Reality REAL 6	Liars And Hypocrites/Vivisecting Bastards/Corrupt Youth (p/s)	5
85	Creative Reality REAL 10	Our Life In Their Hands/Land Of Make Believe/Every Six Seconds (p/s)	5

CARNATIONS
65	Blue Beat BB 285	Mighty Man/What Are You Selling	15

JUDY CARNE
61	Decca F 11347	Late Last Evening (with David Kernan)/A Plea For The Throne (with Betty Marsden & Pip Hinton) ('On The Brighter Side' cast)	7
69	Reprise RS 20680	Sock It To Me/Right, Said Fred	5

CARNEGY HALL
68	Polydor 56224	The Bells Of San Francisco/Slightly Cracked	10

CARNIVAL
67	Columbia DB 8255	The Big Bright Green Pleasure Machine/Silver Dreams And Scarlet Memories	6
70	Liberty LBF 15252	Son Of A Preacher Man/Walk On By	5
70	Liberty LBS 83305	THE CARNIVAL (LP)	12

CAROL & MEMORIES
66	CBS 202086	Tears On My Pillow/Crying My Eyes Out	8

BOBBI CAROL
63	Fontana 267 260TF	Will You Love Me Tomorrow/It Doesn't Matter	6

CAROLE & SHERRY
62	Fontana 270 107 TF	I Ain't Ready Yet/Like I Gotta Get Away	6

CAROLINA SLIM
72	Flyright LP 4702	CAROLINA BLUES AND BOOGIE (LP)	20

MINT VALUE £

CAROLINES
65	Polydor BM 56027	Love Made A Fool Of Me/Believe In Me	5

CAROLLS
65	Polydor BM 56046	Give Me Time/Darling I Want You So Much	6

(see also Carols, Carrolls)

CAROLS
70	Revolution REV 013	Everyday I Have To Cry Some/FIRE SESSION: Sleeping Reggae	5

(see also Carolls, Carrolls)

RENATO CAROSONE & HIS QUARTET
57	Parlophone R 4366	Ricordate Marcellino!/Lazzarella	5
58	Parlophone R 4433	Torero — Cha Cha Cha/Il Piccolo Montanaro	6

CAROUSEL
89	Cosmic English Music CTA 102	Strawberry Fayre/Evergreen/Halfpennies And Farthings/September Come Again (12", p/s)	8
90	Cosmic English Music CTA 104	Sorrow Is The Way To Love/Hand Me Down Green/Locks And Bolts/No Ticket For The Train (12", p/s)	7

(see also Talulah Gosh)

THELMA CARPENTER
61	Coral Q 72422	Yes, I'm Lonesome Tonight/Gimme A Little Kiss	7
61	Coral Q 72442	Back Street/I Ought To Know	7

CARPENTERS
71	A&M AMS 832	Love Is Surrender/For All We Know	6
71	A&M AMS 851	Rainy Days And Mondays/Saturday	5
71	A&M AMS 868	Merry Xmas Darling/Bless The Beasts And The Children	6
72	A&M AMS 885	Hurting Each Other/Maybe It's You	5
78	A&M AMS 7327	Sweet Sweet Smile/Two Sides	5

CARPENTER'S APPRENTICE
72	SRS 12107	CHANGES (LP, with insert)	100

CARPET BAGGERS
67	Spin SP 2006	Flea Teacher/On Sunday	8

CARPETTES
77	Small Wonder SMALL 3	RADIO WUNDERBAR (EP)	8
78	Small Wonder SMALL 9	Small Wonder?/2 Ne 1 (p/s)	8
79	Beggars Banquet BEG 27	I Don't Mean It/Easy Way Out (p/s)	7
80	Beggars Banquet BEG 32	Johnny Won't Hurt You/Frustration Paradise/Keys To Your Heart/Total Insecurity (double pack)	7
80	Beggars Banquet BEG 47	Nothing Ever Changes/You Never Realise/Frustration Paradise (live p/s)	7
80	Beggars Banquet BEG 49	The Last Lone Ranger/Love So Strong/Fan Club (p/s)	7
79	Beggars Banquet BEGA 14	FRUSTRATION PARADISE (LP)	12
80	Beggars Banquet BEGA 21	FIGHT AMONGST YOURSELVES (LP)	12

CATHY CARR
56	London HLH 8274	Ivory Tower/Please, Please Believe Me	40
56	Vogue Coral Q 72175	Heartbroken/I'll Cry At Your Wedding	6
59	Columbia DB 4270	First Anniversary/With Love	6
59	Columbia DB 4270	First Anniversary/With Love (78)	6
59	Columbia DB 4317	I'm Gonna Change Him/The Little Things You Do	6
60	Columbia DB 4408	Little Sister/Dark River	6
63	Stateside SS 147	Sailor Boy/The Next Time The Band Plays A Waltz	6

IAN CARR('S NUCLEUS)
60	Columbia	CHANGE IS 2 (LP, with Don Rendell)	60
71	Vertigo 6360 039	SOLAR PLEXUS (LP, gatefold sleeve, spiral or 'spaceship' label)	35/12
72	Vertigo 6360 076	BELLADONNA (LP, gatefold sleeve, spiral or 'spaceship' label)	45/12

(see also Nucleus, Don Rendell & Ian Carr Quintet, Neil Ardley, Centipede, Michael Garrick, New Jazz Orchestra)

JAMES CARR
66	Stateside SS 507	You've Got My Mind Messed Up/That's What I Want To Know	45
66	Stateside SS 535	Love Attack/Coming Back To Me Baby	15
66	Stateside SS 545	You're Pouring Water On A Drowning Man/Forgetting You	12
67	Stateside SS 2001	The Dark End Of the Street/Loveable Girl	12
67	Stateside SS 2038	Let It Happen/A Losing Game	15
67	Stateside SS 2052	I'm A Fool For You/Gonna Send You Back To Georgia	8
68	Bell BLL 1004	A Man Needs A Woman/Stronger Than Love	5
69	B&C CB 101	Freedom Train/That's The Way Love Turned Out For Me	5
72	Mojo 2092 053	Freedom Train/That's What I Want To Know	8
67	Stateside SL 10205	YOU GOT MY MIND MESSED UP (LP)	45
69	Bell MBLL/SBLL 113	A MAN NEEDS A WOMAN (LP)	25

JOE 'FINGERS' CARR
54	Capitol CL 14169	Piccadilly Rag/Fiddle-A-Delphia	12
55	Capitol CL 14359	The Barky-roll Stomp/Deep In The Heart Of Texas (with Carr-Hops)	10
55	Capitol CL 14372	Give Me A Band And My Baby/Zig-A-Zig (with Joy-Riders)	8
56	Capitol CL 14520	Memories Of You/Henderson Stomp (with Carr-Hops)	8
56	Capitol CL 14535	Let Me Be Your Honey, Honey/Ragtime Cowboy Joe (with Carr-Hops)	6
56	Capitol CL 14587	The Portuguese Washerwoman/Stumbling	6

(see also Lou Busch, Vicki Young)

JOHNNY CARR (& CADILLACS)
64	Decca F 11854	Remember That Night/Respectable	15
65	Fontana TF 600	Do You Love That Girl?/Give Him A Little Time	15
66	Fontana TF 681	Then So Do I/I'm Just A Little Bit Shy (solo)	8
67	Fontana TF 823	Things Get Better/You Got Me Baby (solo)	15

LEROY CARR

53	Jazz Collector L 58	Alki Blues/HOKUMBAND: Easy Rider (78)	8
54	Jazz Collector L 92	Barrelhouse Woman No. 2/I Believe I'll Make A Change (78)	8
58	Fontana TFE 17051	TREASURES OF NORTH AMERICAN NEGRO MUSIC VOLUME 1 (EP)	18
64	RCA RCX 7168	R.C.A. VICTOR RACE SERIES VOL. 2 (EP)	14
63	CBS BPG 62206	BLUES BEFORE SUNRISE (LP)	30

LINDA CARR

67	Stateside SS 2058	Everytime/Trying To Be Good For You	18

MIKE CARR

68	Columbia SCX 6248	UNDER PRESSURE (LP)	18
73	Ad-Rhythm ARPS	MIKE CARR (LP)	15

PETER CARR

69	DJM DJS 10213	Angel And The Woman/Imagine Yourself	5

ROMEY CARR

70	Columbia DB 8710	These Things Will Keep Me Loving You/Stand Up And Fight	15

VALERIE CARR

58	Columbia DB 4083	You're The Greatest/Over The Rainbow	5
58	Columbia DB 4131	When The Boys Talk About The Girls/Padre	5
58	Columbia DB 4225	Bad Girl/Look Forward	5
58	Columbia DB 4225	Bad Girl/Look Forward (78)	5
59	Columbia DB 4365	The Way To My Heart/I'm Only Asking	5
50s	Columbia 33S 1137	VALERIE CARR (10" LP)	20
61	Columbia 33SX 1228	EV'RY HOUR, EV'RY DAY OF MY LIFE (LP, also stereo SCX 3307)	18

VIKKI CARR

66	Liberty LIB 55917	It Must Be Him (Seul Sur Son E Tiole)/So Nice (Summer Samba)	5
64	Liberty LBY 1208	DISCOVERY (LP)	15
65	Liberty LBY 1284	ANATOMY OF LOVE (IP)	15
68	Liberty LBL 83037	IT MUST BE HIM (LP)	12
68	Liberty LBL 83099	VIKKI (LP)	12
69	Liberty LBS 83180	FOR ONCE IN MY LIFE (LP)	12
72	CBS 65121	SONG SUNG BLUE (LP)	12
73	United Artists UAD 60039/40	THE VIKKI CARR COLLECTION (2-LP)	15

WYNONA CARR

61	Reprise R 20033	I Gotta Stand Tall/My Faith	15

DAVID CARRADINE

75	Jet JET 756	Around/Cosmic Joke	5
76	Jet JET 778	Cosmic Joke/Chicken Song	5
75	Jet JETLP 10	GRASSHOPPER (LP)	15

CARRICK FOLK FOUR

65	Thistle TM 90	Radio Scotland/Blue Nose	5

ANDREA CARROLL

63	London HLX 9772	It Hurts To Be Sixteen/Why Am I So Shy	8

BARBARA CARROLL

59	London HLR 8981	North By Northwest/Far Away	10
59	London HLR 8981	North By Northwest/Far Away (78)	10

BERNADETTE CARROLL

64	Stateside SS 311	Party Girl/I Don't Wanna Know	8

BOB CARROLL

55	MGM SP 1132	I Love You So Much It Hurts/My Dearest, My Darling, My Love	7
56	London HLU 8299	Red Confetti, Pink Balloons And Tambourines/Handwriting On The Wall	35
56	London HLU 8299	Red Confetti, Pink Balloons And Tambourines/Handwriting On The Wall (78)	12
58	London HLT 8724	Hi Yo Silver/Tonto The Brave	15
58	London HLT 8724	Hi Yo Silver/Tonto The Brave (78)	12
59	London HLT 8888	I Can't Get You Out Of My Heart/Since I'm Out Of Your Arms	10
59	London HLT 8888	I Can't Get You Out Of My Heart/Since I'm Out Of Your Arms (78)	10

CATHY CARROLL

62	Warner Bros WB 72	Poor Little Puppet/Love And Learn	7

DIAHANN CARROLL

59	London HLT 8788	The Big Country/Guiding Light	10
59	London HLT 8788	The Big Country/Guiding Light (78)	20

DON CARROLL

57	Capitol CL 14812	At Your Front Door/The Gods Were Angry With Me	6
58	Capitol CL 14823	In My Arms/The Things I Might Have Been	6

GINA CARROLL

65	Decca F 12297	Bye Bye Big Boy/Down The Street	7

JACK CARROLL

58	Brunswick 05733	One Blade Of Grass/Bullfight	6
58	Brunswick 05733	One Blade Of Grass/Bullfight (78)	8

JOHNNY CARROLL & HOT ROCKS

56	Brunswick 05580	Corrine Corrina/Wild Wild Women	800
56	Brunswick 05580	Corrine Corrina/Wild Wild Women (78)	125
56	Brunswick 05603	Crazy, Crazy Lovin'/Hot Rock	800
56	Brunswick 05603	Crazy, Crazy Lovin'/Hot Rock (78)	125
74	UK USA 1	Black Leather Rebel/Be-Bop-A-Lula (as Johnny Carroll & Blue Caps)	5
79	Rollercoaster RRC 2002	Black Leather Rebel/Be-Bop-A-Lula (p/s, reissue)	5

PAT CARROLL
72 Pye International 7N 25592 To The Sun/Out Of My Mind. 6

RONNIE CARROLL
59 Philips PB 904 Sweet Music/Walk With Faith In Your Heart (78) 10
59 Philips PB 944 The Wonder Of You/Wonderful Love (78). 14
60 Philips PB 1004 Footsteps/Where My True Love Walks. 5
62 Philips PB 1222 Ring-A-Ding Girl/The Girls In Their Summer Dresses. 5
62 Philips 326 550 BF If Only Tomorrow/Think Of Her (p/s) 6
56 Philips BBE 12074 WALK HAND IN HAND (EP) 8
62 Philips BL 7563 SOMETIMES I'M HAPPY, SOMETIMES I'M BLUE (LP). 15
62 Philips (S)BL 7591 MR AND MRS IS THE NAME (LP, with Millicent Martin) 15
(see also Millicent Martin)

TONI CARROLL
58 MGM MGMm 987 Dreamsville/I've Never Felt This Way Before. 6
58 MGM MGMm 987 Dreamsville/I've Never Felt This Way Before (78) 7
58 MGM EP 689 THIS ONE IS TONI (EP). 12

CARROLLS
66 Polydor BM 56081 Surrender Your Love/The Folk I Love 8
68 CBS 3414 So Gently Falls The Rain/Nice To See You Darling 5
68 CBS 3710 Ever Since/Come On 7
68 CBS 3875 A Lemon Balloon And A Blue Sky/Make Me Belong To You 5
69 CBS 4401 We're In This Thing Together/We Know Better 5
(see also Carols, Carolls, Faith Brown, Brotherly Love)

BEN CARRUTHERS & DEEP
65 Parlophone R 5295 Jack O' Diamonds/Right Behind You. 35

CARS
78 Elektra K 12301 Just What I Needed/I'm In Touch With Your World
        (withdrawn; later issued as K 12312) 8
78 Elektra K 12301 My Best Friend's Girl/Living In Stereo (picture disc, printed PVC sleeve). 5
79 Elektra K 12312 Just What I Needed/I'm In Touch With Your World (picture disc) 5

CHAD CARSON
63 HMV POP 1156 They Were Wrong/Stop Picking On Me 40

DEL CARSON
59 Decca F 11135 Jean/I Told Myself A Lie. 5
59 Decca F 11135 Jean/I Told Myself A Lie (78) 12

JOHNNY CARSON
60 Fontana H 243 Fraulein/I Wish It Were You. 8
60 Fontana H 259 The Train Of Love/First Proposal. 8
·60 Fontana H 277 You Talk Too Much/Now And Always. 8
62 Ember EMB S 150 Teenage Bachelor/Are You Anyone's Girl? 10
63 Ember EMB S 161 The Tears Came Rolling Down/One Track Mind. 10

KAY CARSON
56 Capitol CL 14565 Those Who Have Loved/The Fellow Over There 7
56 Capitol CL 14634 There's A Shadow Between Us/This Man 7
(see also Kit Carson)

KEN CARSON
55 London HLF 8213 Hawkeye/I've Been Working On The Railroad 30
55 London HLF 8213 Hawkeye/I've Been Working On The Railroad (78). 15
56 London HLF 8237 Let Her Go, Let Her Go/The Song Of Daniel Boone (The Daddy Of Them All). . . 25
56 London HLF 8237 Let Her Go, Let Her Go/The Song Of Daniel Boone (The Daddy Of Them All)
        (78) 18

KIT CARSON
56 Capitol CL 14524 Band Of Gold/Cast Your Bread Upon The Waters 8
(see also Kay Carson)

MINDY CARSON
58 Philips PB 822 The Sentimental Touch/I Was Born 5

MINDY CARSON & GUY MITCHELL
53 Columbia SCM 5022 That's A Why/Train Of Love 30
(see also Guy Mitchell)

VINCE CARSON
55 HMV 7M 313 Sweetie, Sweet, Sweet Sue/My Possession 6

ANITA CARTER
58 London HLA 8693 Blue Doll/Go Away Johnnie. 18
60 London HLW 9102 Moon Girl/Mama Don't Cry At My Wedding. 12

BENNY CARTER
54 HMV 7M 189 Blue Mountain/Sunday Afternoon 6
(see also Helen Humes)

BETTY CARTER
63 London HLK 9748 The Good Life/Nothing More To Look Forward To 8
(see also Ray Charles)

CAROLINE CARTER
65 Decca F 12239 The Ballad Of Possibilities/We Want Love. 5

CAROLYN CARTER
65 London HL 9959 It Hurts/I'm Thru 15

CHRIS CARTER
81	Industrial IRC 32	THE SPACE BETWEEN (cassette)	12
85	C.T.I. CTILP 3	MONDO BEAT (LP)	12

(see also Throbbing Gristle, Chris & Cosey)

CLARENCE CARTER
68	Atlantic 584 154	Thread The Needle/Don't Make My Baby Cry	10
68	Atlantic 584 176	Looking For A Fox/I Can't See Myself (Crying About You)	10
68	Atlantic 584 187	Funky Fever/Slip Away	8
68	Atlantic 584 223	Too Weak To Fight/Let Me Comfort You	8
69	Atlantic 584 248	Snatchin' It Back/Making Love (At The Dark End Of The Street)	6
69	Atlantic 584 272	The Feeling Is Right/You Can't Miss When You Can't Measure	6
70	Atlantic 584 309	Take It Off Him And Put It On Me/The Few Troubles I've Had	8
70	Atlantic 2091 030	Patches/I Can't Leave Your Love Alone	8
71	Atlantic 2091 045	It's All In Your Mind/Willie And Laura Mae Jones	6
71	Atlantic 2091 093	The Court Room/Getting The Bills (But No Merchandise)	6
71	Atlantic 2091 139	Slipped, Tripped And Fell In Love/I Hate To Love And Run	6
68	Atlantic 588 152	THIS IS CLARENCE CARTER (LP)	15
69	Atlantic 588 172	THE DYNAMIC CLARENCE CARTER (LP)	15
69	Atlantic 588 191	TESTIFYIN' (LP)	15
70	Atlantic 2400 027	PATCHES (LP)	15

HAL CARTER FIVE
62	Oriole CB 1709	Come On And Twist Me/Twistin' Time Is Here	6

HERBIE CARTER
68	Duke DU 4	Happy Time (actually by Keble Drummond)/BOYS: Smashville	6

JACKIE CARTER
76	Atlantic K 10720	Treat Me Like A Woman/Mamma Don't Wait For Me	5

JEAN CARTER & CENTREPIECES
68	Stateside SS 2114	No Good Jim/And None	8
72	Stateside SS 2204	No Good Jim/And None (reissue)	5

JOHN CARTER & RUSS ALQUIST
68	Spark SRL 1017	The Laughing Man/Midsummer Dreaming	25

(see also Carter-Lewis & Southerners, Ivy League, Flowerpot Men)

LYNDA CARTER
80	Motown TMG 1207	The Last Song/What's A Little Love Between Friends (p/s)	8
78	Epic EPC 8305L	LYNDA CARTER (LP)	12

MARTIN CARTER
72	Tradition TSR 012	UPS & DOWNS (LP)	40

MEL CARTER
63	Pye International 7N 25212	When A Boy Falls In Love/So Wonderful	8
66	Liberty LIB 66113	Hold Me, Thrill Me, Kiss Me/Sweet Little Girl	20

MOTHER MAYBELLE CARTER
64	London HA-R 8214	QUEEN OF THE AUTOHARP (LP)	15

SHEILA CARTER & EPISODE SIX
66	Pye 7N 17194	I Will Warm Your Heart/Incense	30

(see also Episode, Episode Six)

SONNY CARTER with EARL BOSTIC & HIS ORCHESTRA
55	Parlophone MSP 6167	There Is No Greater Love/Oh Baby	25
55	Parlophone R 4015	There Is No Greater Love/Oh Baby (78)	8

(see also Earl Bostic)

SYDNEY CARTER
66	Elektra EPK 801	LORD OF THE DANCE (EP)	15

CARTER FAMILY
55	Brunswick OE 9168	MOUNTAIN MUSIC VOL. 2 (EP)	12
62	RCA RCX 7100	ORIGINAL AND GREAT CARTER FAMILY VOL. 1 (EP)	10
62	RCA RCX 7101	ORIGINAL AND GREAT CARTER FAMILY VOL. 2 (EP)	10
62	RCA RCX 7102	ORIGINAL AND GREAT CARTER FAMILY VOL. 3 (EP)	10
63	RCA RCX 7109	ORIGINAL AND GREAT CARTER FAMILY VOL. 4 (EP)	10
63	RCA RCX 7110	ORIGINAL AND GREAT CARTER FAMILY VOL. 5 (EP)	10
63	RCA RCX 7111	ORIGINAL AND GREAT CARTER FAMILY VOL. 6 (EP)	10
63	Ace Of Hearts AH 58	A COLLECTION OF FAVOURITES (LP)	12

CARTER-LEWIS & SOUTHERNERS
61	Piccadilly 7N 35004	So Much In Love/Back On The Scene	25
61	Ember EMB S 145	Two Timing Baby/Will It Happen To Me?	40
62	Piccadilly 7N 35085	Here's Hopin'/Poor Joe	30
62	Ember EMB S 165	Tell Me/My Broken Heart	40
63	Oriole CB 1835	Sweet And Tender Romance/Who Told You?	15
63	Oriole CB 1868	Your Momma's Out Of Town/Somebody Told My Girl	15
64	Oriole CB 1919	Skinny Minnie/Easy To Cry	25

(see also Ivy League, Flowerpot Men, White Plains, John Carter & Russ Alquist, Jimmy Page, Dawn Chorus, First Class)

CARTER THE UNSTOPPABLE SEX MACHINE
91	Rough Trade GIFT 1	Christmas Shoppers Paradise/G.I. Blues (gig freebie)	12
94	Chrysalis GIFT 2	Lonely This Christmas (1-sided, no p/s, fan club freebie)	6
90	Big Cat ABB 103X	HANDBUILT FOR PERVERTS (mini-LP, export issue)	12

MINT VALUE £

MARTIN CARTHY
76	Topic STOP 7002	The Bonny Lass Of Anglesey/Palaces Of Gold	5
65	Fontana (S)TL 5269	MARTIN CARTHY (LP)	30
71	Philips 6308 049	LANDFALL (LP)	25
72	Pegasus PEG 12	SHEARWATER (LP, with insert)	18
72	Philips 6282 022	THIS IS MARTIN CARTHY (LP)	15
74	Deram SML 1111	SWEET WIVELSFIELD (LP)	12
75	Mooncrest CREST 25	SHEARWATER (LP, reissue)	12

MARTIN CARTHY & DAVE SWARBRICK
67	Fontana TE 17490	NO SONGS (EP)	35
66	Fontana STL 5362	SECOND ALBUM (LP)	25
67	Fontana STL 5434	BYKER HILL (LP)	25
68	Fontana STL 5477	BUT TWO CAME BY (LP)	25
70	Fontana STL 5529	PRINCE HEATHEN (LP)	25
70s	Fontana 6852 003	ROUND UP (LP)	12
71	Pegasus PEG 6	SELECTIONS (LP, gatefold sleeve)	18

(see also Dave Swarbrick, Three City Four, Steeleye Span, Leon Rosselson, Alex Campbell, Nigel Denver)

BARBARA CARTLAND
78	State ETAT 22	BARBARA CARTLAND SINGS AN ALBUM OF LOVE SONGS (LP)	15

CARTOONE
69	Atlantic 584 240	Knick Knack Man/A Penny For The Sun	7
69	Atlantic 588 174	CARTOONE (LP)	20

(see also Jimmy Page)

FLIP CARTRIDGE
66	London HLU 10076	Dear Mrs Applebee/Don't Take The Lovers From The World	7

DAVE CARTWRIGHT
70	Harmony DB 0001	MIDDLE OF THE ROAD (LP, private pressing with insert)	25
72	Transatlantic TRA 255	A LITTLE BIT OF GLORY (LP)	12
73	Transatlantic TRA 267	BACK TO THE GARDEN (LP)	12
75	Transatlantic TRA 284	DON'T LET YOUR FAMILY DOWN (LP)	12

(see also Bev Pegg, Away From The Sand)

DICK CARUSO
60	MGM MGM 1077	Two Long Years/Yes Sir, That's My Baby	7
60	MGM MGM 1099	Pretty Little Dancin' Doll/We've Never Met	7

MARIAN CARUSO
55	Brunswick 05398	The Dove/Before We Know It	5
55	Brunswick 05442	A Man Called Peter/This Is The Thanks I Get	5
55	Brunswick 05462	The Boston Fancy/I Keep Telling Myself	5

MIKE CARVER
79	Venom SRTS/79/CUS/396	MURDER OF BLAIR PEACH (EP, 2 different sleeves)	5

CASABLANCA
74	Rocket PIGL 7	CASABLANCA (LP, die-cut sleeve with inner lyric sleeve)	15

(see also Trees)

CASCADES
63	Warner Bros WB 88	Rhythm Of The Rain/Let Me Be	6
63	Warner Bros WB 98	Shy Girl/The Last Leaf	7
63	Warner Bros WB 103	I Wanna Be Your Lover/My First Day Alone	7
63	RCA Victor RCA 1358	Cinderella/A Little Like Loving	6
64	RCA Victor RCA 1378	Jeannie/For Your Sweet Love	6
65	Liberty LIB 55822	I Bet You Won't Stay/She'll Love Again	6
66	Stateside SS 515	Cheryl's Goin' Home/Truly Julie's Blues	5
69	Uni UN 508	Maybe The Rain Will Fall/Naggin' Cries	5
63	Warner Bros WEP/WSE 6106	RHYTHM OF THE RAIN (EP, mono/stereo)	30
63	Warner Bros WM 8127	RHYTHM OF THE RAIN (LP)	45

CASE
83	SUS SUS 1	WHEAT FROM THE CHAFF (EP)	6

(see also Long Tall Shorty, Rage)

AL CASEY & K.C. ETTES
63	Pye International 7N 25215	Surfin' Hootenanny/Easy Picking	15

(see also Sanford Clark, Duane Eddy)

HOWIE CASEY & SENIORS
62	Fontana H 364	Double Twist/True Fine Mama	20
62	Fontana H 381	I Ain't Mad At You/Twist At The Top	15
63	Fontana TF 403	The Boll Weevil Song/Bony Moronie	15
62	Fontana TFL 5108	TWIST AT THE TOP (LP)	40
65	Wing WL 1022	LET'S TWIST (LP, reissue of "Twist At The Top")	25

(see also Freddie Starr)

ALVIN CASH (& REGISTERS)
65	Stateside SS 386	Twine Time/The Bump (as Alvin Cash & Crawlers)	20
66	Stateside SS 543	Philly Freeze/No Deposits, No Returns (as Alvin Cash & Registers)	15
68	President PT 115	Philly Freeze/No Deposits, No Returns (as Alvin Cash & Registers) (reissue)	8
68	President PT 119	Alvin's Boo-Ga-Loo/Let's Do Some Good Timing (as Alvin Cash & Registers)	8
68	President PT 129	Doin' The Ali Shuffle/Feel So Good	8
68	President PT 147	Charge/Diff'rent Strokes For Diff'rent Folks	10
71	President PT 351	Twine Time/Twine Awhile	8
72	President PT 383	Barracuda/Do It One More Time	8
67	President PTL 1000	THE PHILLY FREEZE (LP)	20

JOHNNY CASH (& TENNESSEE TWO)

78s

57	London HL 8358	I Walk The Line/Get Rhythm (78)	30
57	London HLS 8427	Train Of Love/There You Go (78)	30
57	London HLS 8461	Next In Line/Don't Make Me Go (78)	30
57	London HLS 8514	Home Of The Blues/Give My Love To Rose (78)	30
58	London HLS 8586	Big River (with Tennessee Two)/Ballad Of A Teenage Queen (78)	25
58	London HLS 8656	Guess Things Happen That Way/Come In, Stranger (78)	25
58	London HLS 8709	The Ways Of A Woman In Love/You're The Nearest Thing To Heaven (78)	30
59	Philips PB 874	All Over Again/What Do I Care (78)	40
59	Philips PB 897	Don't Take Your Guns To Town/I Still Miss Someone (78)	45
59	London HLS 8789	It's Just About Time/I Just Thought You'd Like To Know (78)	30
59	London HLS 8847	Luther Played The Boogie/Thanks A Lot (78)	35
59	Philips PB 928	Frankie's Man, Johnny/You Dreamer You (78)	20
59	London HLS 8928	Katy Too/I Forgot To Remember To Forget (78)	40
59	Philips PB 953	I Got Stripes/Five Feet High And Rising (78)	50
59	London HLS 8979	You Tell Me/Goodbye, Little Darlin', Goodbye (78)	45
59	Philips PB 979	The Little Drummer Boy/I'll Remember You (78)	60

SINGLES

57	London HL 8358	I Walk The Line/Get Rhythm (gold label lettering, later silver)	100/65
57	London HLS 8427	Train Of Love/There You Go	40
57	London HLS 8461	Next In Line/Don't Make Me Go	35
57	London HLS 8514	Home Of The Blues/Give My Love To Rose	30
58	London HLS 8586	Big River (with Tennessee Two)/Ballad Of A Teenage Queen	25
58	London HLS 8656	Guess Things Happen That Way/Come In, Stranger (with Tennessee Two)	12
58	London HLS 8709	The Ways Of A Woman In Love/You're The Nearest Thing To Heaven (with Tennessee Two)	12
59	Philips PB 874	All Over Again/What Do I Care	10
59	Philips PB 897	Don't Take Your Guns To Town/I Still Miss Someone	10
59	London HLS 8789	It's Just About Time/I Just Thought You'd Like To Know (with Tennessee Two)	15
59	London HLS 8847	Luther Played The Boogie/Thanks A Lot	15
59	Philips PB 928	Frankie's Man, Johnny/You Dreamer You	10
59	London HLS 8928	Katy Too/I Forgot To Remember To Forget	10
59	Philips PB 953	I Got Stripes/Five Feet High And Rising	10
59	London HLS 8979	You Tell Me/Goodbye, Little Darlin', Goodbye	8
59	Philips PB 979	The Little Drummer Boy/I'll Remember You	6
60	London HLS 9070	Straight A's In Love/I Love You Because	10
60	Philips PB 1017	Seasons Of My Heart/Smiling Bill McCall	6
60	London HLS 9182	Down The Street To 301/Story Of A Broken Heart	6
60	Philips PB 1075	Going To Memphis/Loading Coal	6
61	London HLS 9314	Oh Lonesome Me/Life Goes On	7
61	Philips PB 1148	The Rebel — Johnny Yuma/Forty Shades Of Green	6
61	Philips PB 1200	Tennessee Flat-Top Box/Tall Man	5
63	CBS AAG 159	Ring Of Fire/I'd Still Be There	5
63	CBS AAG 173	The Matador/Still In Town	5
63	CBS AAG 200	Understand Your Man/Dark As A Dungeon	5
65	CBS 201741	Orange Blossom Special/All God's Children Ain't Free	5
65	CBS 201760	It Ain't Me Babe/Time And Time Again	5
65	CBS 201809	Ring Of Fire/Streets Of Laredo	5
66	CBS 202046	The One On The Right Is On The Left/Cotton Pickin' Hands	5
66	CBS 202256	Everybody Loves A Nut/Austin Prison	5
67	CBS 202546	You Beat All I Ever Saw/Put The Sugar To Bed	5
67	CBS 3268	Rosanna's Going Wild/Long-Legged Guitar-Pickin' Man (with June Carter)	5
68	CBS 3438	Certain Kind Of Hurtin'/Another Song To Sing	5
68	CBS 3549	Folsom Prison Blues (live)/The Folk Singer	5
68	CBS 3878	Daddy Sang Bass/He Turned The Water Into Wine	5
69	CBS 4460	A Boy Named Sue (live) /San Quentin (live)	5
69	CBS 4638	Blistered/See Ruby Fall	5
76	CBS S 4287	One Piece At A Time/Go On Blues	5
83	Peach River BBPR-5	Love Me Tender (with Julie Andrews)/JULIE ANDREWS: Love Is Where Two People Fall	5
84	CBS A 4723	Chicken In Black/Battle Of Nashville	5

EXPORT SINGLES

57	London HL 7020	Next In Line/Don't Make Me Go	25
57	London HL 7023	Home Of The Blues/Give My Love To Rose	25
58	London HL 7032	Ballad Of A Teenage Queen/Big River	18
58	London HL 7053	The Ways Of A Woman In Love/You're The Nearest Thing To Heaven	18
57	London HL 7131	Folsom Prison Blues/I Walk The Line	18

EPs

58	London RES 1120	JOHNNY CASH (EP, triangular or round centre)	30/18
59	London RES 1193	JOHNNY CASH SINGS HANK WILLIAMS (EP, triangular or round centre)	30/18
59	London RES 1212	COUNTRY BOY (EP, triangular or round centre)	25/15
59	London RES 1230	JOHNNY CASH NO. 2 (EP, triangular or round centre)	25/15
60	Philips BBE 12377	THE TROUBADOR (EP)	15
60	Philips BBE 12318	GRANDFATHER'S CLOCK (EP)	15
60	Philips BBE 12395	SONGS OF OUR SOIL (EP)	15
61	Philips BBE 12494	STRICTLY CASH (EP)	15
64	CBS AGG 20050	FORTY SHADES OF GREEN (EP)	15
64	CBS EP 5576	FABULOUS JOHNNY CASH (EP)	12
64	CBS EP 5735	ORANGE BLOSSOM SPECIAL (EP)	12
64	CBS EP 5744	EVERYBODY LOVES A NUT (EP)	12
64	CBS EP 5964	RING OF FIRE (EP)	12
65	CBS EP 6061	IT AIN'T ME BABE (EP)	12
66	CBS EP 6073	MEAN AS HELL! — BALLADS FROM THE TRUE WEST (EP, with Statler Brothers & Carter Family)	12
65	CBS EP 6109	SONGS OF KATIE ELDER (EP)	12

Johnny CASH

65	CBS EP 6147	HAPPINESS IS YOU (EP)	12
69	CBS EP 6601	FOLSOM PRISON BLUES (EP)	12
72	CBS EP 9155	JOHNNY CASH (EP, with Little Fauss & Big Halsy)	10

LPs

59	London HA-S 2157	SINGS THE SONGS THAT MADE HIM FAMOUS (LP)	35
59	London HA-S 2179	WITH HIS HOT AND BLUE GUITAR (LP)	35
59	Philips BBL 7298	THE FABULOUS JOHNNY CASH (LP, also stereo SBBL 554)	20/25
59	Philips BBL 7353	SONGS OF OUR SOIL (LP)	20
59	Philips BBL 7373	HYMNS BY JOHNNY CASH (LP)	25
60	Philips BBL 7358	NOW THERE WAS A SONG! (LP, also stereo SBBL 580)	18/20
60	Philips BBL 7417	RIDE THIS TRAIN (LP)	15
61	CBS (S)BPG 62042	THE FABULOUS JOHNNY CASH (LP, mono/stereo)	12/15
62	CBS (S)BPG 62015	HYMNS FROM THE HEART (LP, mono/stereo)	12/15
62	CBS (S)BPG 62073	THE SOUND OF JOHNNY CASH (LP, mono/stereo)	12/15
63	CBS BPG 62119	BLOOD SWEAT AND TEARS (LP)	12
63	CBS (S)BPG 62171	RING OF FIRE (LP, mono/stereo)	12/15
63	CBS (S)BPG 62284	THE CHRISTMAS SPIRIT (LP, mono/stereo)	12/15
64	CBS (S)BPG 62371	I WALK THE LINE (LP, mono/stereo)	12/15
64	CBS (S)BPG 62463	BITTER TEARS (LP, mono/stereo)	12/15
65	CBS (S)BPG 62501	ORANGE BLOSSOM SPECIAL (LP, mono/stereo)	12/15
65	Fontana FJS 301	JOHNNY CASH'S COUNTRY ROUND-UP (LP, 4 tracks only)	12
65	London HA-S 8220	THE ORIGINAL SUN SOUND OF JOHNNY CASH (LP)	30
65	CBS (S)BPG 62538	BALLADS OF THE TRUE WEST VOL. 1 (LP)	15
65	CBS (S)BPG 62575	RIDE THIS TRAIN (LP)	12
65	CBS (S)BPG 62591	BALLADS OF THE TRUE WEST VOL. 2 (LP)	15
66	London HA-S 8253	LONESOME ME (LP)	30
66	CBS (S)BPG 62717	EVERYBODY LOVES A NUT (LP)	12
66	CBS (S)BPG 62760	HAPPINESS IS YOU (LP)	12
67	CBS (S)BPG 62972	FROM SEA TO SHINING SEA (LP)	12
67	CBS (S)BPG 63105	CARRYIN' ON (LP)	12
68	CBS 63308	AT FOLSOM PRISON (LP, mono)	12
68	CBS 63316	OLD GOLDEN THROAT (LP)	12
69	CBS 63428	THE HOLY LAND (LP)	15
69	CBS 63521	MORE OF OLD GOLDEN THROAT (LP)	12
70	CBS 63796	HELLO, I'M JOHNNY CASH (LP)	12
70	CBS 64089	THE JOHNNY CASH SHOW (LP)	12
71	CBS 64331	MAN IN BLACK (LP)	12
71	CBS 70083	I WALK THE LINE (LP, soundtrack)	12
71	CBS 70087	LITTLE FAUSS AND BIG HALSY (LP, soundtrack)	12
72	CBS 67201	STAR PORTRAIT (2-LP, gatefold sleeve)	15
73	CBS Q 63629	LIVE AT SAN QUENTIN (LP, quadrophonic)	12
74	CBS 80347	THE JUNKIE AND THE JUICEHEAD MINUS ME (LP)	12
75	CBS 88153	RIDING THE RAILS (2-LP)	18
83	Word WST 9629	A DIAMOND IN THE ROUGH (LP)	12
84	Charley SUN BOX-105	THE SUN YEARS (5-LP box set)	30

CASH PUSSIES
79	The Label TLR 010	99% Is Shit/Cash Flow (p/s)	6

(see also Sex Pistols)

CASINO
76	State ETAT 5	CASINO (LP)	12

CASINO ROYALES
67	London HLU 10122	When I Tell You That I Love You/Love In The Open Air	5

CASINOS
67	Ember EMB S 241	That's The Way/Too Good To Be True	25
67	President PT 123	Then You Can Tell Me Goodbye/I Still Love You	10
68	President PT 140	To Be Loved/Tailor Made	5
68	President PT 156	When I Stop Dreaming/Please Love Me	5
68	President PTL 1007	THEN YOU CAN TELL ME GOODBYE (LP)	20

TONY CASO
68	London HL 10178	Shadow On The Ground/I Don't Care Who Knows It	5

MAMA CASS
(see under Mama Cass Elliot, Mamas & Papas, Mugwumps, Big Three)

CASSANDRA COMPLEX
85	Complex CXD 001	March/Pickup (live)/Hcoma (12", p/s)	7

CASSETTE
79	1 track CAS 001	THE FAST FORWARD EP: What's The Point/Product/All The Rage	10

CASSETTES
81	Zip ZIP 101	Reverberate/Don't Label Me (diecut sleeve)	5

DAVID CASSIDY
71	Bell BELL 1189	Cherish/All I Wanna Do Is Touch You	5
85	Arista ARISD 589	The Last Kiss/The Letter (shaped picture disc with calendar, 6500 only)	6
85	Arista ARIST 12589	The Last Kiss/The Letter (12", signed p/s)	7
85	Arista ARISD 620	Romance (Let Your Heart Go)/(Instrumental Mix) (with Samantha Fox) (picture disc)	8

(see also Partridge Family, Samantha Fox)

STEVE CASSIDY
63	Ember EMB S 177	Ecstasy/I'm A Worrying	6

TED CASSIDY
65	Capitol CL 15423	The Lurch/Wesley	20

CAST
94	(no label) GRA 001	CAST SAMPLER (Sandstorm/Follow Me Down/Tell It Like It Is) (10", white label, white stamped sleeve, promo only, 700 copies)	80
95	Polydor 579 506-7	Finetime/Better Man/Satellites (p/s, green vinyl with stencil)	5
96	Polydor 577 903-2	Sandstorm/Hourglass/Back Of My Mind (live)/Alright (live) (CD in numbered tin, 2,500 only)	10
95	Polydor LEEDS 1	Tell It Like It Is (Live At Leeds University 30/10/95) (flexidisc, company sleeve, mail-order only)	6

(see also La's)

CASTANARC
74	Peninsula PENCIL 10	JOURNEY TO THE EAST (LP, private pressing)	15

CASTAWAYS
65	London HL 10003	Liar Liar/Sam	25

CASTE
68	President PT 211	Don't Cast Aside/One Step Closer	5

JOEY CASTELL
57	Decca F 10966	I'm Left, You're Right, She's Gone/Tryin' To Get To You	80
57	Decca F 10966	I'm Left, You're Right, She's Gone/Tryin' To Get To You (78)	40

CASTELLS
61	London HLN 9392	Sacred/I Get Dreamy	20
62	London HLN 9551	So This Is Love/On The Street Of Tears	25

CASTELLS
67	Masquerade MA 500	Two Lovers/Jerusalem	5

LEE CASTLE & BARONS
64	Parlophone R 5151	A Love She Can Count On/Foolin'	12

ROY CASTLE
58	Pye 7N 15173	In My Heart/Mister Music Man	5
58	Pye N 15173	In My Heart/Mister Music Man (78, vinyl pressing)	8
59	Pye 7N 15215	The Chosen Few/Bimbo	5
59	Pye N 15215	The Chosen Few/Bimbo (78, vinyl pressing)	8
60	Philips PB 1087	Little White Berry/Crazy Little Thorn	7
65	CBS 201736	Doctor Terror's House Of Horrors/Voodoo Girl	20
68	Olga OLE 12	Wonderful World/For All The World	6
71	United Artists UP 35254	Maybe That's Your Problem/Thick As Thieves (with Dilys Watling)	5
60s	Philips	EPs	each 8
61	Philips BBL 7457	CASTLEWISE (LP, also stereo SBBL 626)	15/18

CASTLE ROCK
73	FEST 002	NOTTINGHAM CASTLE FESTIVAL FRINGE (LP, private pressing)	75

CASTLE SISTERS (U.K.)
59	Columbia DB 4335	Drifting And Dreaming/Lucky Girl	8
59	Columbia DB 4335	Drifting And Dreaming/Lucky Girl (78)	15

CASTLE SISTERS (Jamaica)
66	Ska Beat JB 257	Stop Your Lying/Don't Be A Fool	15

CAST OF THOUSANDS
66	Stateside SS 546	My Jenny Wears A Mini/Girl Do What You Gonna Do	15

CASTON & MAJORS
75	Tamla Motown TMG 938	Child Of Love/No One Will Know	5

(see also Radiants)

JIMMY CASTOR (BUNCH)
66	Philips BF 1543	Hey Leroy, Your Mama's Callin'/Hamhock's Espanol	10
67	Philips BF 1590	Magic Saxophone/Just You Girl	15
71	Mercury 6052 110	Hey Leroy, Your Mama's Callin'/Hamhock's Espanol (reissue)	8
72	Mercury 6052 185	Bang Bang/Hey Willie	5
72	RCA Victor RCA 2226	Troglodyte (Cave Man)/I Promise To Remember	5
73	RCA Victor APD1 0103	DIMENSION III (LP, quadrophonic)	15
74	Atlantic K 50052	THE EVERYTHING MAN (LP)	12
75	Atlantic K 50120	BUTT OF COURSE (LP)	12
75	Atlantic K 50190	SUPERSOUND (LP)	12
76	Atlantic K 50295	E-MAN GROOVIN' (LP)	12

FRANKIE CASTRO
56	Mercury MT 114	Goodbye, So Long, I'm Gone/Too Much (78)	40

CASUAL FOUR
60s	Specially Made For Us 102	I Can Tell/Love Potion No. 9	40

CASUALS
65	Fontana TF 635	If You Walk Out/Please Don't Hide	8
68	Decca F 12737	Adios Amor (Goodbye My Love)/Don't Dream Of Yesterday	5
68	Decca F 22784	Jesamine/I've Got Something Too	5
68	Decca F 22852	Toy/Touched (some in p/s)	10/5
69	Decca F 22900	Fools Paradise/7 X 7	5
69	Decca F 22943	Sunflower Eyes/Never My Love	5
69	Decca F 22969	Caroline/Naughty Boy	5
70	Decca F 23027	My Name Is Love/I Can't Say	5
71	Decca F 23112	Someday Rock 'n' Roll Lady/A Letter Every Day	5
72	Parlophone R 5959	Tara Tiger Girl/Nature's Girl	5
74	Dawn DNS 1069	Witch/Good Times	5
69	Decca LK-R/SKL-R 5001	HOUR WORLD (LP)	25

Johnny CASWELL

JOHNNY CASWELL
85 Kent TOWN 106 You Don't Love Me No More/STEINWAYS: You've Been Leading Me On 10

CATAPILLA
71 Vertigo 6360 029 CATAPILLA (LP, gatefold sleeve, spiral label) 60
72 Vertigo 6360 074L CHANGES (LP, gatefold sleeve, spiral label) 135

CATATONIA
93 Crai C 039L FOR TINKERBELL EP (cassette) 7
93 Crai CD 039B FOR TINKERBELL EP (CD) 10
94 Crai CRAI C 039L Hooked/Fall Beside Her/Difrydreulyd (cassette) 5
94 Crai CRAICD 039 Hooked/Fall Beside Her/Difrydreulyd (CD) 8
94 Rough Trade 45rev33 Whale/You Can (p/s, 'Singles Club' release) 25
95 Nursery NYS 12L Bleed/This Boy Can't Swim (red vinyl, numbered p/s, 1,000 only) 20
95 Nursery NYSCD 12 Bleed/This Boy Can't Swim/Painful (CD) 20
95 Blanco Y Negro SAM 1746 Blow The Millennium Blow/Beautiful Sailor (p/s, white vinyl Xmas 45, freebie) . . . 25
95 Blanco Y Negro NEG 85X Sweet Catatonia/Tourist (no'd p/s, clear vinyl, 5,000 only) 5
96 Blanco Y Negro NEGAT 8X Lost Cat/Too And Fro (yellow vinyl, p/s) 5
96 Blanco Y Negro NEG 97 Bleed/This Boy Can't Swim (p/s, reissue, red vinyl) 5
96 Blanco Y Negro NEG 97CD1 Bleed/This Boy Can't Swim/Painful (CD, reissue, one of a pair) 8
99 Blanco Y Negro NEG 116CDDJ Karaoke Queen (CD, card sleeve, withdrawn, promo only) 20
96 Blanco Y Negro 16305-1 WAY BEYOND BLUE (LP, deleted after one week, with free 7") 20
98 Blanco Y Negro 20834-1 INTERNATIONAL VELVET (LP, 1,000 only, with free 12") 25

CATCH (featuring Marilyn Middleton)
76 London HLZ 10543 Mr. Nice Guy/Mephisto's Nightmare 6

CATCH
77 Logo GO 103 Borderline/Black Blood (no p/s) 40
(see also Tourists, Eurythmics)

GEORGE CATES & HIS ORCHESTRA
55 Vogue Coral Q 72106 Autumn Leave (with Steve Allen)/High And Dry 5
56 Vogue Coral Q 72162 Moonglow/Theme From "Picnic"/Rio Batucada 12
(see also Steve Allen & Orchestra)

CATFISH
70 CBS 64006 GET DOWN (LP, orange label) 15
71 Epic 64408 LIVE CATFISH (LP) 12

PHILIP CATHERINE
76 Atlantic K 50193 GUITARS (LP) 12
82 WEA K 58450 END OF AUGUST (LP) 12

CATHERINE WHEEL
91 Willde Club WILDE 4 SHE'S MY FRIEND (12", p/s) 12
91 Willde Club WILDE 5 PAINFUL THING EP (12", p/s) 10

RAY CATHODE (BBC RADIOPHONICS)
62 Parlophone R 4901 Time Beat/Waltz In Orbit 7
(see also BBC Radiophonic Workshop, George Martin)

CAT IRON
69 Xtra XTRA 1087 CAT IRON (LP) 12

CAT MOTHER & ALL NIGHT NEWSBOYS
69 Polydor 56543 Good Old Rock'N'Roll/Bad News 8
70 Polydor 2066 026 I Must Be Dreaming/Last Go Round 5
69 Polydor 184 300 THE STREET GIVETH AND THE STREET TAKETH AWAY (LP) 15
70 Polydor 2425 021 ALBION DOO-WAH (LP, gatefold sleeve) 12
72 United Artists UAG 29313 CAT MOTHER & ALL NIGHT NEWS BOYS (LP, gatefold sleeve) 12
73 United Artists UAG 29381 LAST CHANCE DANCE (LP) 12

CATS
69 Baf BAF 1 Swan Lake/Swing Low 5
69 Baf BAF 2 My Girl/The Hog 6
69 Baf BAF 3 The Hig/Blues For Justice 6
69 Baf BAF 4 William Tell/Love Walk Right In 6

CATS
67 Parlophone R 5558 What A Crazy Life/Hopeless Try 5
68 Parlophone R 5663 What Is The World Coming To/How Could I Be So Blind? 5
69 Columbia DB 8524 I Gotta Know What's Going On/Lea 5
69 Columbia DB 8571 Why/Mandy, My Dear 5
70 Columbia DB 8655 Marian/Somewhere Up There 5
71 Columbia DB 8748 I Love You, I Do/Where Have I Been Wrong 5
71 Columbia DB 8816 One Way Mind/Country Woman 5
72 Columbia DB 8850 Dance, Dance, Dance/My Friend Joe 5
72 Columbia DB 8909 Let's Dance/I've Been In Love Before 5
71 Columbia SCX 6459 TAKE ME WITH YOU (LP) 12

CAT'S ARSE
81 Fellix Mahone T002 Tabby Twat/Ginger Minge (Pussy Power) (p/s) 7

CATS EYES
68 Deram DM 190 Smile Girl For Me/In A Fantasy World 7
68 Deram DM 209 I Thank You Marianne/Turn Around 6
69 Deram DM 251 Where Is She Now?/Tom Drum 15
70 MCA MK 5028 Loser/Circus 5
70 MCA MK 5043 Circus/Come Away Melinda 5
70 MCA MK 5056 The Wizard/Hey (Open Your Eyes) 10

CAT'S PYJAMAS
68	Direction 58-3235	Virginia Waters/Baby I Love You	15
68	Direction 58-3482	Camera Man/House For Sale	20

(see also Kenny Bernard)

CLEM CATTINI ORK
65	Decca F 12135	No Time To Think/Impact	30

(see also Tornados, Aquarian Age, Rumplestiltskin, Spaghetti Head, Sounds Nice)

NADIA CATTOUSE
61	Parlophone R 4725	The Boy Without A Heart/Long Time, Boy	5
65	Parlophone R 5240	Port Mahon/A Little More Oil	5
66	Reality RE 503	Beautiful Barbados/Turn Around	7
60s	Church Miss. Soc. LIV/SP/81	The Larder/PAULINE FILBY: I'm Hungry	15
66	Reality RY 1001	NADIA CATTOUSE (LP)	100
70	RCA Victor SF 8070	EARTH MOTHER (LP)	35

CAUSTIC WINDOW
92	Rephlex CAT 004	JOYREX J4 EP (12", 6-track)	40
92	Rephlex CAT 005	JOYREX J5 EP (12, 4-track, black or white vinyl)	50/40
93	Rephlex CAT 009 i	JOYREX J9 EP (10", picture disc, with bonus track "HMNA", 300 only)	50
93	Rephlex CAT 009 ii	JOYREX J9 EP (12" 4-track, initially in card mailer with bag of "space dust")	20/15

(see slso Aphex Twin)

EDDIE CAVE & FYX
66	Pye 7N 17161	Fresh Out Of Tears/It's Almost Good	30

NICK CAVE (& BAD SEEDS)
84	Mute 7 MUTE 32	In The Ghetto/The Moon Is In The Gutter (p/s)	7
85	Mute 7 MUTE 30	Tupelo/The Six Strings That Drew Blood (p/s)	7
86	Lyntone LYN 18038	Scum (green vinyl flexidisc with poster, concert freebie)	15
88	Mute MUTE 86	Oh Deanna/The Girl At The Bottom Of My Class (no p/s, DJ-only)	10
92	Mute LMUTE 140	Straight To You/Jack The Ripper (Acoustic Version) (limited issue, p/s)	6
92	Mute MUTE 148	I Had A Dream, Joe/The Good Son (live) (numbered p/s, 2,000 only)	10
94	Mute MUTE 160	Do You Love Me? (Single Version)/Cassiel's Aong/Sail Away (silver vinyl, p/s, 1,000 copies)	10
94	Mute MUTE 169	Loverman (Single Version)/(I'll Love You) Till The End Of The World (picture disc, 2,000 only)	8
94	Mute MUTE 172	Red Right Hand/That's What Jazz Is To Me (red vinyl, p/s, with 2 different stickers & labels, 2,000 only)	8
97	Mute RCD STUMM 138	MURDER BALLADS (CD, 4-track sampler, promo only)	10
86	Mute STUMM 34	YOUR FUNERAL ... MY TRIAL (2 x 12", with lyric inner sleeves)	10
88	Mute LSTUMM 52	TENDER PREY (LP, with bonus spoken word 12" "And The Ass Saw The Angel" [P STUMM 52]: "Autumn"/"Animal Static"/"Mah Sanctum"/"Lamentation", 5,000 only)	15
90	Mute LSTUMM 76	THE GOOD SON (LP, with bonus 7" "Acoustic Versions From Tender Prey" [P STUMM 76]: "The Mercy Seat"/"City Of Refuge"/"Deanna")	12
90	Mute CDSTUMM 76	THE GOOD SON (CD, with bonus CD "Acoustic Versions From Tender Prey" [P STUMM 76]: "The Mercy Seat"/"City Of Refuge"/"Deanna")	18
92	Mute LSTUMM 92	HENRY'S DREAM (LP, with photographic print)	12
93	LCD STUMM 122	LIVE SEEDS (CD, with book in slip case)	15
94	Mute LSTUMM 123	LET LOVE IN (LP, with set of postcards or poster)	12
96	Mute CAVESPEAK 1CD	MURDER BALLADS: THE INTERVIEW (CD, promo only)	20
97	Mute CAVESPEAK 2CD	THE BOATMAN'S CALL: THE INTERVIEW (CD, promo only)	18

(see also Birthday Party, Annie Hogan, Burmoe Brothers)

ANDY CAVELL
62	HMV POP 1024	Hey There Cruel Heart/Lonely Soldier Boy	25
62	HMV POP 1080	Always On Saturday/Hey There, Senorita	25
63	Pye 7N 15539	Andy/There Was A Boy	35
64	Pye 7N 15610	Shut Up/Tell The Truth	30

JIMMY CAVELLO & HIS HOUSE ROCKERS
57	Vogue Coral Q 72226	Rock, Rock, Rock/The Big Beat	250
57	Vogue Coral Q 72226	Rock, Rock, Rock/The Big Beat (78)	60
57	Vogue Coral Q 72240	Foot Stompin'/Ooh-Wee	300
57	Vogue Coral Q 72240	Foot Stompin'/Ooh-Wee (78)	75

(see also Alan Freed)

CAVE OF THE LIVING STRINGS
74	UHC 1	SIXTEEN SONGS (LP, private pressing)	100

CAVERN
82	Kay Drum DRUM 2	No Reason To Cry/Cry For You/Won't Let You Go (p/s)	6

FRANCISCO CAVEZ
54	HMV 7 MC 11	Quien Sera/Mambo No. 5 (export issue)	6
55	Parlophone CMSP 35	Mambo In The Moonlight/Acapulco Joe (export issue)	6
56	Parlophone CMSP 37	El Viandero/Lamento Borincano (export issue)	6
56	Parlophone MSP 6205	Arriverderci Roma/Ecuador	5

CAY
98	Org ORG 048 CD	Better Than Myself/Hooked On That/Princes & Princesses/ Seven Schizos Sat On A Beach (CD, 1,000 only)	25
99	East West EW 200	Neurons Like Brandy/Ashley's Diary (hand-numbered p/s, 500 only)	10
99	East West EW 200 CD	Neurons Like Brandy/Ashley's Diary/Lucien (CD, hand-numbered, 2000 only)	8
99	East West EW 202	Princes & Princesses/Poppyhead (hand-numbered p/s, 500 only)	8

MONTE CAZAZZA
79	Industrial IR 0005	To Mom On Mother's Day/Candy Man (p/s, with insert, 2,500 only)	12
80	Industrial IR 0010	SOMETHING FOR NOBODY (EP)	8
81	Industrial IRC 28	LIVE AT LEEDS FAN CLUB (cassette)	10

(see also Psychic TV

MINT VALUE £

C.C.S. (Collective Consciousness Society)

70	Rak RAK 104	Whole Lotta Love/Boom Boom	5
72	Rak RAK 126	Brother/Mister What You Can't Have I Can Get	5
70	Rak SRKA 6751	C.C.S. (LP, gatefold sleeve)	18
72	Rak SRAK 503	C.C.S. (LP)	15
73	Rak SRAK 504	THE BEST BAND IN THE LAND (LP)	12

(see also Alexis Korner)

CEDARS

68	Decca F 22720	For Your Information/Hide If You Want To Hide	30
68	Decca F 22772	I Like The Way/I Don't Know Why	30

(see also Seaders)

CELIA & THE MUTATIONS

77	United Artists UP 36262	Mony Mony/Mean To Me (p/s)	6
77	United Artists UP 36318	You Better Believe Me/Round And Around (p/s)	8
81	S.I.S./Liberty FREE 18	Mony Mony/Mean To Me (reissue, promo only, no p/s)	7

(see also Stranglers, Tonight)

CELLOPHANE

(see under Selofane)

CELTIC FROST

84	Noise N 0017	MORBID TALES	
		(mini LP, with poster)	15

CENOTAPH CORNER

76	Cottage COT 501	UPS AND DOWNS (LP)	20
79	Cottage COT 031	EVERY DAY BUT WEDNESDAY (LP)	25

CENTIPEDE

71	RCA Neon NE 9	SEPTOBER ENERGY (2-LP)	50
74	RCA DPS 2054	SEPTOBER ENERGY	
		(2-LP, reissue, different cover)	20

(see also Mark Charig, Ian Carr, Elton Dean, Zoot Money, Alan Skidmore, Keith Tippett, Julie Tippetts, Mike Patto, Robert Wyatt)

CENTURION

82	Centurion 0001	Two Wheels (no p/s, private pressing)	50

CENTURY 21 (Gerry Anderson TV spin-offs)

65	Century 21 MA 100	JOURNEY TO THE MOON (EP)	12
65	Century 21 MA 101	INTO ACTION WITH TROY TEMPEST (EP)	12
65	Century 21 MA 102	A TRIP TO MARINEVILLE (EP)	12
65	Century 21 MA 103	INTRODUCING THUNDERBIRDS (EP)	12
65	Century 21 MA 104	MARINA SPEAKS (EP)	10
65	Century 21 MA 105	TV CENTURY 21 THEMES (EP)	15
66	Century 21 MA 106	THE DALEKS (EP)	40
66	Century 21 MA 107	F.A.B. (EP)	18
66	Century 21 MA 108	THUNDERBIRD 1 (EP)	18
66	Century 21 MA 109	THUNDERBIRD 2 (EP)	18
66	Century 21 MA 110	THE STATELY HOME ROBBERIES (EP)	20
66	Century 21 MA 111	LADY PENELOPE & OTHER TV THEMES (EP)	20
66	Century 21 MA 112	THUNDERBIRD 3 (EP)	20
66	Century 21 MA 113	THUNDERBIRD 4 (EP)	20
66	Century 21 MA 114	THE PERILS OF PENELOPE (EP)	20
66	Century 21 MA 115	TOPO GIGIO IN LONDON (EP)	40
67	Century 21 MA 116	GREAT THEMES FROM GERRY ANDERSON'S THUNDERBIRDS (EP)	25
67	Century 21 MA 117	SPACE AGE NURSERY RHYMES (EP)	30
67	Century 21 MA 118	LADY PENELOPE AND PARKER (EP)	30
67	Century 21 MA 119	BRAINS AND TIN TIN (EP)	30
67	Century 21 MA 120	INTERNATIONAL RESCUE (EP)	30
67	Century 21 MA 121	THUNDERBIRDS (EP)	30
67	Century 21 MA 122	LADY PENELOPE (EP)	30
67	Century 21 MA 123	BRAINS (EP)	30
67	Century 21 MA 124	BRINK OF DISASTER (EP)	30
67	Century 21 MA 125	ATLANTIC INFERNO (EP)	30
67	Century 21 MA 126	RICOCHET (EP)	30
67	Century 21 MA 127	TINGHA & TUCKER & THE WOMBAVILLE BAND (EP)	35
67	Century 21 MA 128	ONE MOVE & YOU'RE DEAD (EP)	30
67	Century 21 MA 129	30 MINUTES AFTER NOON (EP)	30
67	Century 21 MA 130	TINGHA & TUCKER IN NURSERY RHYME TIME (EP)	35
67	Century 21 MA 131	INTRODUCING CAPTAIN SCARLET (EP)	30
67	Century 21 MA 132	CAPTAIN SCARLET AND THE MYSTERONS (EP)	30
67	Century 21 MA 133	CAPTAIN SCARLET IS INDESTRUCTIBLE (EP)	25
67	Century 21 MA 134	CAPTAIN SCARLET OF SPECTRUM (EP)	25
67	Century 21 MA 135	CAPTAIN SCARLET VS. CAPTAIN BLACK (EP)	25
67	Century 21 MA 136	THEMES FROM GERRY ANDERSON'S CAPTAIN SCARLET (EP)	25
65	Century 21 LA 100	JOURNEY TO THE MOON (LP)	60
66	Century 21 LA 1	THE WORLD OF TOMORROW (LP)	45
66	Century 21 LA 2	LADY PENELOPE PRESENTS (LP)	40
66	Century 21 LA 3	JEFF TRACY INTRODUCES INTERNATIONAL RESCUE (LP)	40
66	Century 21 LA 4	LADY PENELOPE INVESTIGATES (LP)	40
66	Century 21 LA 5	THE TINGHA & TUCKER CLUB SONG BOOK (LP)	40
67	Century 21 LA 6	FAVOURITE TELEVISION THEMES (LP)	40
68	Marble Arch MAL 770	TV FAVOURITES VOL. 1 (LP)	20
68	Marble Arch MAL 771	TV FAVOURITES VOL. 2 (LP)	20
72	Hallmark HMA 227	THUNDERBIRDS AND CAPTAIN SCARLET (LP)	15

(see also Barry Gray, Dr. Who)

CERRONE
Year	Label	Title	Value
78	Atlantic K 11089	Supernature/Give Me Love	4
78	Atlantic K 11089T	Supernature/Give Me Love (12")	10
77	Atlantic K 50334	LOVE IN 'C' MINOR (LP)	10
77	Atlantic K 50377	CERRONE'S PARADISE (LP)	10
78	Atlantic K 50431	SUPERNATURE (LP)	10

FRANK CHACKSFIELD & HIS ORCHESTRA
Year	Label	Title	Value
53	Parlophone R 3658	Little Red Monkey/Roundabouts And Swings (as Frank Chacksfield's Tunesmiths) (78)	6
53	Parlophone MSP 6018	Quiet Rhythm Blues/Junior Miss	5
54	Decca F 10354	Smile (Theme From "Modern Times")/Piper In The Heather	5
56	Decca F 10689	In Old Lisbon (Lisboa Antigua)/Memories Of You	5
56	Decca F 10743	The Donkey Cart/The Banks Of The Seine	5
59	Decca F 11146	Java Boogie/A Paris Valentine	5
59	Decca F 11146	Java Boogie/A Paris Valentine (78)	10
62	Decca F 11439	The Sky At Night/Face To Face	5
58	Decca LK 4174	SOUTH SEA ISLAND MAGIC (LP)	15

CHAD (STUART) & JEREMY (CLYDE)
Year	Label	Title	Value
64	Ember EMB S 180	Yesterday's Gone/Lemon Tree (as Chad Stuart & Jeremy Clyde)	7
64	Ember EMB S 186	Early In The Morning/Like I Love You Today (as Chad Stuart & Jeremy Clyde)	7
64	United Artists UP 1062	Summer Song/No Tears For Johnnie (as Chad Stuart & Jeremy Clyde)	5
64	United Artists UP 1070	Willow Weep For Me/If She Was Mine	5
65	Ember EMB S 205	If I Loved You/No Tears For Johnnie	5
65	CBS 201769	Before And After/Evil-Hearted Me	10
65	CBS 201814	I Don't Want To Lose You/Pennies	7
66	Ember EMB S 217	What Do You Want With Me/Donna Donna	5
66	CBS 202035	Teenage Failure/Early Mornin' Rain	5
66	CBS 202279	Distant Shores/Last Night	5
66	CBS 202397	You Are She/I Won't Cry	5
64	Ember EMB EP 4543	YESTERDAY'S GONE (EP)	15
65	United Artists UEP 1008	CHAD STUART AND JEREMY CLYDE (EP)	15
65	Ember NR 5021	SING FOR YOU (LP)	20
66	Ember NR 5031	SECOND ALBUM (LP)	20
66	Ember (ST)NR 5036	THE BEST OF CHAD AND JEREMY (LP)	12

(see also John Barry, Jeremy Clyde)

ERNIE CHAFFIN
Year	Label	Title	Value
57	London HLS 8409	Feelin' Low/Lonesome For My Baby	140
57	London HLS 8409	Feelin' Low/Lonesome For My Baby (78)	50

CHAIN GANG
Year	Label	Title	Value
87	Supreme Intl. EDITION 8714	Makin' Tracks/Creepy Crawlies (p/s)	6

CHAINO
Year	Label	Title	Value
59	London SAH-D 6078	AFRICANA (LP)	15

CHAIN REACTION
Year	Label	Title	Value
76	Gull GULS 43	Never Lose Never Win/This Eternal Flame	5
77	Gull GULS 53	Why Can't We Be Lovers/Hogtied	8
76	Gull GULS 43	Never Lose Never Win/Chase A Miracle	5

CHAINSAW
Year	Label	Title	Value
80	Square SQSP 2	Police And Politicians (p/s)	70
80	Pot Belly EJSP 9462	Lonely Without You	35
84	GMC CS 001	Long Legged Woman	30
84	Thunderbolt THBE 1006	MASSACRE (12" EP)	8

CHAIRMEN OF THE BOARD
Year	Label	Title	Value
70	Invictus INV 501	Give Me Just A Little More Time/Since The Days Of Pigtails	5
70	Invictus INV 504	You've Got Me Dangling On A String/Patches	5
71	Invictus INV 507	Everything's Tuesday/Bless You	5
71	Invictus INV 511	Pay To The Piper/When Will She Tell Me She Needs Me?	5
71	Invictus INV 516	Chairman Of The Board/Hanging On To A Memory	5
71	Invictus INV 516	Chairman Of The Board/When Will She Tell Me She Needs Me? (different B-side)	5
72	Invictus INV 519	Working On A Building Of Love/Try On My Love For Size	5
72	Invictus INV 524	Elmo James/Bittersweet	5
72	Invictus INV 527	I'm On My Way To A Better Place/So Glad You're Mine	5
73	Invictus INV 530	Finders Keepers/Finders Keepers (Instrumental)	5
70	Invictus SVT 1002	CHAIRMEN OF THE BOARD (LP)	20
71	Invictus SVT 1003	IN SESSION (LP)	20
72	Invictus SVT 1006	BITTERSWEET (LP)	15
73	Invictus SVT 1009	GREATEST HITS (LP)	15
74	Invictus 65868	SKIN I'M IN (LP)	15

(see also Showmen, General Johnson, Norman Johnson)

CHAKACHAS
Year	Label	Title	Value
72	Polydor 2121 093	Jungle Fever/Chaka Cha	8
72	Polydor 2489 050	JUNGLE FEVER (LP)	15
73	Young Blood SYB 3003	CHAKACHAS (LP)	12

GEORGE CHAKIRIS
Year	Label	Title	Value
59	Saga SAG 45-2905	Cool/I Got Rhythm	8
60	Triumph RGM 1010	Heart Of A Teenage Girl/I'm Always Chasing Rainbows	35

BRYAN CHALKER('S NEW FRONTIER)
Year	Label	Title	Value
70	Amity OTS 502	Ned Kelly/Four Girls From The Town Of Boston	5
72	Columbia DB 8883	Daddy Sang Bass/Lot 69	5
72	Chapter One SCH 179	Help Me Make It Through The Night/Eskimo Song	5
73	Chapter One SCH 185	Daisy A Day/Life Gets Tee-jus, Don't It	5

71	Avenue AVE 071	THE HANGING OF SAMUEL HALL (LP, as Bryan Chalker's New Frontier)	30
72	Chapter One CMS 1010	BRYAN CHALKER'S NEW FRONTIER (LP)	20
73	Chapter One CMS 1017	BRYAN CHALKER (LP)	18
74	Chapter One CMS 1020	DADDY SING ME A SONG (LP, as Brian Chalker & The Road Band)	15
75	BBC REC 206	FROM WATERS OF THE MEDWAY (LP)	12
75	Sweet Folk & C. SFAO 20	EARLY DAYS (LP)	12
75	Sweet Folk & C. SFAO 25	SONGS AND BALLARDS WITH BRYAN CHALKER (LP)	12

CHALLENGER
| 81 | CMC CM 0001 | So Sure Of Yourself (no p/s) | 20 |

CHALLENGERS (U.K.)
| 61 | Parlophone R 4773 | Cry Of The Wild Goose/Deadline | 10 |

CHALLENGERS (U.S.)
63	Stateside SS 177	Torquay/Bulldog	10
65	Vocalion V 9253	The Man From U.N.C.L.E./The Streets Of London	15
66	Vocalion V 9270	Walk With Me/How Could I	8
63	Stateside SL 10030	SURFBEAT (LP)	40
67	Vocalion VA-N/SAV-N 8069	WIPE OUT (LP, mono/stereo)	35/40

(see also Surfaris)

RICHARD CHAMBERLAIN
62	MGM MGM-EP 776	HITS (EP)	8
62	MGM MGM-EP 778	I'LL BE AROUND (EP)	10
62	MGM MGM-EP 781	DREAM (EP)	10
63	MGM MGM-C 923	SINGS (LP)	15
64	MGM MGM-C 1009	JOY IN THE MORNING (LP)	15

CHAMBER POP ENSEMBLE
| 68 | Decca F 12789 | Walk Away Renee/59th Street Bridge Song (Feeling Groovy) | 5 |
| 68 | Decca LK/SKL 4933 | CHAMBER POP ENSEMBLE (LP) | 18 |

JAMES CHAMBERS
| 71 | Summit SUM 8523 | Bongo Man/KEN BOOTHE: Now I Know | 8 |

(see also Jimmy Cliff)

CHAMBERS BROTHERS
66	Vocalion VL 9267	Love Me Like The Rain/Pretty Girls Everywhere	10
66	Vocalion VL 9276	Call Me/Seventeen	10
67	CBS 202565	All Strung Out Over You/Falling In Love	6
68	Direction 58-3215	Up Town/Love Me Like The Rain	5
68	Direction 58-3671	Time Has Come Today/Dinah	5
68	Direction 58-3760	Time Has Come Today/Dinah (reissue)	5
68	Direction 58-3865	I Can't Turn You Loose/Do Your Thing	5
69	Direction 58-4098	Are You Ready/You Got The Power To Turn Me On	5
69	Direction 58-4318	People Get Ready/No, No, No, Don't Say Goodbye	5
69	Direction 58-4367	Wake Up/Everybody Needs Someone	5
70	Direction 58-4846	Love Peace And Happiness/If You Want Me To	5
70	Direction 58-5033	Let's Do It/To Love Somebody	5
71	CBS 5389	Funky/Love, Peace And Happiness	10
71	CBS 7689	By The Hair On My Chinny Chin Chin/Heaven	5
66	Vocalion VA-L/SAV-L 8058	PEOPLE GET READY (LP)	25
68	Direction 8-63407	THE TIME HAS COME (LP)	18
69	Direction 8-63451	A NEW TIME — A NEW DAY (LP)	18
70	Direction 8-66228	LOVE PEACE AND HAPPINESS (Live At Bill Graham's Fillmore West) (2-LP)	18
70	Liberty LBS 83276	FEELIN' THE BLUES (LP)	12
71	CBS 64156	A NEW GENERATION (LP)	12

EDDIE CHAMBLEE & HIS RHYTHM & BLUES BAND
53	Esquire 10-329	All Out/TOMMY DEAN R&B BAND: Scamon Boogie (78)	10
53	Esquire 10-330	Blues For Eddie/PINEY BROWN: That's Right, Little Girl (78)	15
54	Esquire 10-340	Cradle Rock/Back Street (78)	15

CHAMELEONS
82	Epic EPCA 2210	In Shreds/Less Than Human (p/s)	15
83	Statik STAT 30	As High As You Can Go/Pleasure And Pain (p/s)	6
83	Statik STAT 3012	As High As You Can Go/Pleasure And Pain/Paper Tigers (12", p/s)	8
83	Statik TAK 6	A Person Isn't Safe Anywhere These Days/Thursday's Child (p/s)	7
83	Statik TAK 6/12	A Person Isn't Safe Anywhere These Days/Thursday's Child/Prisoners Of The Sun (12", p/s)	8
85	Statik TAK 29	In Shreds/Nostalgia (p/s)	7
85	Statik TAK 29/12	In Shreds/Less Than Human/Nostalgia (12", p/s)	10
85	Statik TAK 35	Singing Rule Britannia (While The Walls Close In)/Singing Rule Britannia (Radio 1 'Saturday Live' Session Version) (p/s)	6
85	Statik TAK 35/12	Singing Rule Britannia (While The Walls Close In)/Singing Rule Britannia (Radio 1 'Saturday Live' Session Version) (12", p/s)	8
86	Geffen GEF 4	Tears/Paradiso (p/s)	5
86	Geffen GEF 4F/SAM 287	Tears/Paradiso//Swamp Thing/Inside Out (double pack, gatefold p/s)	8
86	Geffen GEF 4T	Tears/Paradiso/Inside Out (12", p/s)	8
86	Geffen GEF 10	Swamp Thing/John, I'm Only Dancing (p/s)	5
86	Geffen GEF 10T	Swamp Thing/John, I'm Only Dancing/Tears (Original Arrangement) (12", p/s)	8
90	Glass Pyramid EMC 1	TONY FLETCHER WALKED ON WATER (12" EP)	20
90	Glass Pyramid EMCD 1	TONY FLETCHER WALKED ON WATER (CD EP)	20
85	Statik STATLP 17	SCRIPT OF THE BRIDGE (LP, picture disc)	20
85	Statik STATLP 22	WHAT DOES ANYTHING MEAN? BASICALLY (LP, gatefold sleeve, with insert)	12

(see also Sun & Moon, Reegs)

TEDDY CHAMES
68   Blue Cat BS 141   I Want It Girl/She Is Gone (actually by Teddy Charmes) 7

CHAMPIONS
63   Oriole CB 1854   Circlorama/Pinky 10

CHAMPS (U.S.)
58	London HLU 8580	Tequila/Train To Nowhere.	12
58	London HLU 8580	Tequila/Train To Nowhere (78)	15
58	London HL 8655	Midnighter/El Rancho Rock.	12
58	London HL 8655	Midnighter/El Rancho Rock (78)	18
58	London HL 8715	Chariot Rock/Subway.	12
58	London HL 8715	Chariot Rock/Subway (78)	25
59	London HLH 8811	Beatnik/Gone Train.	10
59	London HLH 8811	Beatnik/Gone Train (78)	30
59	London HLH 8864	Caramba/Moonlight Bay.	10
59	London HLH 8864	Caramba/Moonlight Bay (78)	40
60	London HLH 9052	Too Much Tequila/Twenty Thousand Leagues.	7
61	London HLH 9430	Cantina/Panic Button.	7
62	London HLH 9506	Tequila Twist/Limbo Rock	7
62	London HLH 9539	Experiment In Terror/La Cucaracha	7
62	London HLH 9604	Limbo Dance/Latin Limbo	7
59	London RE 1176	FOUR BY THE CHAMPS (EP).	35
59	London RE-H 1209	ANOTHER FOUR BY THE CHAMPS (EP)	35
59	London RE-H 1223	STILL MORE BY THE CHAMPS (EP)	35
61	London RE-H 1250	KNOCKOUTS! (EP).	35
58	London HA-H 2152	GO CHAMPS GO! (LP)	40
59	London HA-H 2184	EVERYBODY'S ROCKIN' WITH THE CHAMPS (LP)	40
62	London HA-H 2451	GREAT DANCE HITS (LP, early issues with flipback cover).	30/25
77	London ZGH 141	BEST OF THE CHAMPS (LP)	12

CHAMPS (Jamaica)
64   Blue Beat BB 267   Walk Between Your Enemies/Do What I Say 15

JACQUI CHAN
60   Pye 7N 15273   But No One Knows/Gentlemen Please!. 5
    (see also Simon Dupree & Big Sound)

ROB CHANCE & CHANCES-R
67   CBS 3130   At The End Of The Day/I've Got The Power 8
    (see also Chances-R)

CHANCES ARE
67   Columbia DB 8144   Fragile Child/What Went Wrong 25

CHANCES-R
67   CBS 202614   Talking Out The Back Of My Head/I Aimed Too High 8
67   CBS 2940   Do It Yourself/Turn A New Leaf Over 8
    (see also Ron Chance & Chances-R)

DANY CHANDELLE
65   Columbia DB 7540   Lying Awake/I Love You 15

BARBARA CHANDLER
63   London HLR 9823   Do You Really Love Me Too?/I Live To Love You 8
64   London HLR 9861   I'm Going Out With The Girls/Lonely New Year 8

GENE CHANDLER
62	Columbia DB 4793	Duke Of Earl/Kissing In The Kitchen	25
63	Stateside SS 185	Rainbow/You Threw A Lucky Punch	18
64	Stateside SS 331	Just Be True/A Song Called Soul.	15
64	Stateside SS 364	Bless Our Love/London Town	12
65	Stateside SS 388	What Now/If You Can't Be True (Find A Part Time Love)	15
65	Stateside SS 401	You Can't Hurt Me No More/Everybody Let's Dance.	12
65	Stateside SS 425	Nothing Can Stop Me/The Big Lie	45
65	Stateside SS 458	Good Times/No One Can Love You (Like I Do)	15
66	Stateside SS 500	(I'm Just A) Fool For You/Buddy Ain't It A Shame	15
66	Chess CRS 8047	I Fooled You This Time/Such A Pretty Thing	35
67	Coral Q 72490	The Girl Don't Care/My Love	18
68	Soul City SC 102	Nothing Can Stop Me/The Big Lie (reissue)	10
69	Action ACT 4551	I Can't Save It/I Can Take Care Of Myself	30
69	President PT 234	Duke Of Earl/Stand By Me	5
70	Mercury 6052 033	Groovy Situation/Not The Marrying Kind	5
71	Mercury 6052 098	You're A Lady/Stone Cold Feeling.	5
76	Brunswick BR 39	There Was A Time/ARTISTICS: I'm Gonna Miss You	6
65	Fontana TL 5247	DUKE OF EARL (LP)	60
67	Coral LVA 9236	THE GIRL DON'T CARE (LP)	40
69	MCA MUPS 367	THERE WAS A TIME (LP)	20
69	Action ACLP 6010	LIVE ON STAGE (LP)	35
71	Mercury 6338 037	SITUATION (LP)	15
74	Joy JOYS 136	A GENE CHANDLER ALBUM (LP)	15

GENE CHANDLER & BARBARA ACKLIN
69   MCA Soul Bag BAG 1   Little Green Apples/Will I Find Love 5
74   Brunswick BR 30   From The Teacher To The Preacher/Little Green Apples 8
    (see also Barbara Acklin, Gene & Jerry)

JEFF CHANDLER
54   Brunswick 05264   I Should Care/More Than Anyone 12
55   Brunswick 05441   Foxfire/Shaner Maidel 8
57   London HLU 8484   Half Of My Heart/Hold Me 12
57   London HLU 8484   Half Of My Heart/Hold Me (78) 10
58   London HA-U 2100   JEFF CHANDLER SINGS TO YOU (LP). 40

MINT VALUE £

KAREN CHANDLER

55	Vogue Coral Q 72091	The Price You Pay For Love/The Man In The Raincoat	8
56	Brunswick 05570	Love Is The $64,000 Question/(I'm Just A) Beginner	8
56	Brunswick 05596	Tonight You Belong To Me/Crazy Arms (with Jimmy Wakely)	8
56	Brunswick 05596	Tonight You Belong To Me/Crazy Arms (with Jimmy Wakely) (78)	10
57	Brunswick 05662	Your Wild Heart/It's An International Language	6
57	Brunswick 05662	Your Wild Heart/It's An International Language (78)	10
62	Salvo SLO 1803	My Own True Love/You Made Me Love You (99 copies only)	18

(see also Jimmy Wakely)

KENNY CHANDLER

63	Stateside SS 166	Heart/Wait For Me	6
68	Stateside SS 2110	Beyond Love/Charity	45

LEN CHANDLER

67	CBS 62931	TO BE A MAN (LP)	12

LORRAINE CHANDLER

75	Black Magic BM 105	Love You Baby/What Can I Do	5

CHANDONS

68	RCA RCA 1704	Timber/Never Been Loved Before	5

CHANGE

81	WEA K12 1916	Paradise/Your Move (12")	8

CHANGIN' TIMES

68	Bell BLL 1009	When The Good Sun Shines/Show Me The Way To Go Home	5

BRUCE CHANNEL

62	Mercury AMT 1171	Hey! Baby/Dream Girl	6
62	Mercury AMT 1177	Number One Man/If Only I Had Known	6
62	Pye International 7N 25137	Run Romance Run/Don't Leave Me	6
63	London HLU 9776	I Don't Wanna/Blue And Lonesome	7
64	London HLU 9841	Going Back To Louisiana/Forget Me Not	7
67	Stateside SS 2066	Mr. Bus Driver/It's Me	6
68	Bell BLL 1010	Keep On/Barbara Allen	6
68	Bell BLL 1030	Try Me/Water The Family Tree	6
68	Bell BLL 1038	Mr. Bus Driver/Trouble With Sam	5
68	Sonet SON 2001	Hey! Baby '68/Come On Baby	5
62	Mercury MMC 14104	HEY! BABY! (LP)	50
68	Bell MBLL/SBLL 1110	KEEP ON (LP)	20

CHANNEL 4

79	Ripping RIP 1	Vampire/Channel 4 (numbered p/s with insert)	6

CHANNEL 3

82	No Future OI 11	I've Got A Gun/Manzanar/Mannequin (p/s)	10

CHANTAYS

63	London HLD 9696	Pipeline/Move It	8
64	King KG 1018	Beyond/I'll Be Back Someday	15
66	Dot DS 26757	Pipeline/Move It (reissue)	6
63	London RED 1397	PIPELINE (EP)	50
63	London HA-D/SH-D 8087	PIPELINE (LP, mono/stereo)	40/45
74	Contour 2870 389	PIPELINE (LP, reissue)	12

CHANTELLES

65	Parlophone R 5271	I Want That Boy/London My Home Town	12
65	Parlophone R 5303	The Secret Of My Success/Sticks And Stones	8
65	Parlophone R 5350	Gonna Get Burned/Gonna Give Him Some Love	10
66	Parlophone R 5431	I Think Of You/Please Don't Kiss Me	8
66	Polydor 56119	There's Something About You/Just Another Fool	12
67	CBS 2777	Blue Mood/The Man I Love	10

(see also Lana Sisters)

CHANTELS

58	London HLU 8561	Maybe/Come My Little Baby	425
58	London HLU 8561	Maybe/Come My Little Baby (78)	50
62	London HLL 9428	Look In My Eyes/Glad To Be Back	25
62	London HLL 9480	Well I Told You/Still	20
62	London HLL 9532	Here It Comes Again/Summertime	20
63	Capitol CL 15297	Swamp Water/Eternally	10
70	Roulette RO 514	Maybe/He's Gone	7

(see also Richard Barrett)

CHANTER

77	Expert ELP 1	SUBURBAN ETHNIA (LP, private pressing)	12

IRENE CHANTER

75	Polydor 2058 608	Make Me Happy/Funky Music	5

(see also Birds Of A Feather, Chanters, Chanter Sisters)

CHANTERS

66	CBS 202454	Every Night (I Sit And Cry)/Where	6
67	CBS 202616	You Can't Fool Me/All Day Long	12
68	CBS 3400	What's Wrong With You/Right By Your Side	5
68	CBS 3668	My Love Is For You/Mississippi Paddleboat	7

(see also Birds Of A Feather, Chanter Sisters, Irene Chanter)

CHANTER SISTERS

76	Polydor 2058 679	Halfway To Paradise/My Love	7

(see also Birds Of A Feather, Chanters, Irene Chanter)

CHANTS (U.S.)
58	Capitol CL 14876	Close Friends/Lost And Found	12

CHANTS (U.K.)
63	Pye 7N 15557	I Don't Care/Come Go With Me	8
64	Pye 7N 15591	I Could Write A Book/A Thousand Stars	8
64	Pye 7N 15643	She's Mine/Then I'll Be Home	8
64	Pye 7N 15691	Sweet Was The Wine/One Star	8
66	Fontana TF 716	Come Back And Get This Loving Baby/Love Light	8
67	Decca F 12650	A Lover's Story/Wearing A Smile	8
67	Page One POF 016	Ain't Nobody Home/For You	8
68	RCA Victor RCA 1754	A Man Without A Face/Baby I Don't Need Your Love	45
69	RCA Victor RCA 1823	I Get The Sweetest Feeling/Candy	8
76	Chipping Norton CHIP 2	I've Been Trying/Lucky Old Me	20

(see also Real Thing)

CHAOS
79	Chaotic Records VD 1	Summer Of Hate/I Want To Be Left Alone (wraparound xerox sleeve)	7

CHAOS & JULIA SET
93	Recoil RCL 001	VOL. 1 (12", plain sleeve)	10
93	Recoil RCL 002	VOL. 2 — FEAR OF THE FUTURE (12", plain sleeve)	10

(see also Global Communications)

CHAOS U.K.
82	Riot City RIOT 6	BURNING BRITAIN (EP)	5
82	Riot City RIOT 12	LOUD, POLITICAL AND UNCOMPROMISING (EP)	6

CHAOTIC DISCHORD
82	Riot City RIOT 10	FUCK THE WORLD (EP)	6
83	Riot City RIOT 22	NEVER TRUST A FRIEND (EP)	7
83	Beat The System	SAD SOCIETY (EP)	8

PAUL CHAPLAIN & HIS EMERALDS
60	London HLU 9205	Shortnin' Bread/Nicotine	20

MICHAEL CHAPLIN
65	Decca F 12142	I Am What I Am/Restless	6

CHARLES CHAPLIN
57	HMV POP 370	The Spring Song/Mandolin Serenade	8

GENE CHAPMAN
63	Starlite ST45 102	Oklahoma Blues/Don't Come Crying	250

GRADY CHAPMAN
60	Mercury AMT 1107	Sweet Thing/I Know What I Want	7

MICHAEL CHAPMAN
69	Harvest HAR 5002	It Didn't Work Out/Mozart Lives Upstairs	6
69	Harvest SHVL 755	RAINMAKER (LP, gatefold sleeve)	18
70	Harvest SHVL 764	FULLY QUALIFIED SURVIVOR (LP, gatefold sleeve)	18
71	Harvest SHVL 786	WINDOW (LP, gatefold sleeve)	18
71	Harvest SHVL 798	WRECKED AGAIN (LP, gatefold sleeve)	18
73	Deram SML 1105	MILLSTONE GRIT (LP)	15
74	Deram SML 1114	DEAL GONE DOWN (LP)	12
76	Decca SKL-R 5242	SAVAGE AMUSEMENT (LP, with lyric sheet)	12
70s	Standard ESL 146	GUITARS (LP, library issue)	40

ROGER CHAPMAN & SHORTLIST
79	Acrobat BAT 5	Who Pulled The Night Down/Shortlist (p/s)	5
79	Acrobat BAT 9	Let's Spend The Night Together/Shape Of Things (p/s)	5
79	Acrobat ACRO 6	LIVE IN HAMBURG (LP)	12

(see also Family, Farinas, Streetwalkers)

CHAPS
62	Parlophone R 4979	Poppin' Medley (Parts 1 & 2)	18

(see also Outlaws)

CHAPTER FIVE
66	CBS 202395	Anything You Do Is Alright/You Can't Mean It	325
67	CBS 2696	One In A Million/Hey Hey (unissued, demos only)	125

CHAPTER FOUR (U.S.)
66	United Artists UP 1143	In My Life/In Each Other's Arms	165

(see also Jay & Americans)

CHAPTER FOUR (U.K.)
60s	GSP 11009/10	CHAPTER FOUR (EP, no p/s)	75

CHAPTER FOUR (U.K.)
80	Bridge BR 001	HANGING AROUND STERLING (LP)	40

CHAPTERS
65	Pye 7N 15815	Can't Stop Thinking About Her/Dance Little Lady	40

CHAPTER THREE (U.K.)
67	CBS 2971	Cold And Lonely Hours/Wrecking Crew	5

CHAPTER THREE (U.S.)
75	Pye International 7N 25680	I'll Never Be The Same (Parts 1 & 2)	5

CHAQUITO & HIS ORCHESTRA
60	Fontana H 265	Never On Sunday/Song Of Orpheus	5
72	Philips 6006 225	Hawaii 5-0/Ironside	5

(see also Johnny Gregory)

CHARLATANS (U.K.)

CHARGE
70	private pressing	Zeugma/Boring Song (art sleeve)	20

CHARGE
73	SRT private pressing	CHARGE (LP, 1 known copy)	800
92	Kissing Spell KSLP 9205	CHARGE (LP, reissue, revised sleeve, 500 only)	10

CHARGE
81	Test Pressing	You Deserve More Than A Maybe (p/s, 500 only)	20
82	Test Pressing TP 3	Kings Cross/Brave New World (p/s)	15
82	Kamera ERA 003	DESTROY THE YOUTH (EP)	8
82	Kamera ERA 007	Fashion/Ugly Shadows (p/s, red vinyl)	6
82	Kamera ERA 015	Luxury/Madman In The North (p/s)	5

MARK CHARIG
77	Ogun OG 710	PIPEDREAM (LP)	12

(see also Bluesology, B.B. Blunder, Reg King, Centipede, Keith Tippett, Julie Tippett, Brotherhood Of Breath, Elton Dean, Ninesense)

CHARLATANS (U.S.)
69	Philips SBL 7903	THE CHARLATANS (LP)	50

(see also Mike Wilhelm, Tongue & Groove)

CHARLATANS (U.K.)
89	Dead Dead Good (no cat.no)	OCTOBER '89 (demo cassette, sold at gigs)	20
90	Dead Dead Good GOOD ONE TWELVE	Indian Rope/You Can Talk To Me/Who Wants To Know (12", 1st issue with barcode on p/s)	20
91	Dead Dead Good GOOD ONE T	Indian Rope/You Can Talk To Me/Who Wants To Know (12", 2nd issue without barcode on p/s)	10
91	D. D. G. GOOD 1CD	Indian Rope/You Can Talk To Me/Who Wants To Know (CD)	10
90	Situation Two SIT 70CD	The Only One I Know/Imperial 109 (Edit)/Everything Changed/You Can Talk To Me (CD)	8
90	Situation Two SIT 74	Then/Taurus Moaner (p/s)	5
90	Situation Two SIT 74T	Then/Taurus Moaner/Then (Alternate Take)/Taurus Moaner (Instrumental) (12", mispressing with vocal version of "Taurus Moaner" on both sides)	8
90	Situation Two SIT 74T	Polar Bear/Taurus Moaner (12", white label test pressing, around 10 only)	80
90	Situation Two SIT 74CD	Then/Taurus Moaner/Then (Alternate Take)/Taurus Moaner (Instrumental) (CD)	8
91	Situation Two SIT 76	Over Rising/Way Up There (p/s)	5
91	Situation Two SIT 76CD	Over Rising/Way Up There/Opportunity Three/Happen To Die (CD)	8
91	Situation Two SIT 84	Me. In Time/Occupation h. Monster (p/s)	5
91	Beggars Banquet CHAR 1	Happen To Die (1-sided, green die-cut sleeve, promo only)	10
92	Situation Two SIT 88	Weirdo/Theme From "The Wish" (p/s, with art print)	5
92	Situation Two SIT 88T	Weirdo/Theme From "The Wish"/Sproston Green (U.S. Version)/Weirdo (Alternate Take) (12", with art print)	8
92	Situation Two SIT 88CD	Weirdo/Theme From "The Wish"/Sproston Green (U.S. Version)/Weirdo (Alternate Take) (CD)	8
93	Beggars Banquet CHAR 7	Subterranean (live) (CD, free with 109 fan club magazine)	12/8
94	Beggars Banquet CHAR 9	I Never Want An Easy Life If Me And He Were Ever To Get There (12", promo only)	10
94	Beggars Banquet BBQ 31CD1	I Never Want An Easy Life If Me And He Were Ever To Get There/Only A Boho/Subterranean/Can't Get Out Of Bed (Demo Version) (CD, oblong box set with 3 postcards, numbered)	15
95	Beggars Banquet CHAR 13	THE CHEMICAL BROTHERS REMIXES (Nine Acre/Toothache [Chemical Risk Dub]/Toothache [Chemical Risk]) (12", 33rpm, black die-cut sleeve, promo only)	10

MINT VALUE £

92	Situation Two SIT 97CD2	LIVE APRIL '92 (CD EP, shrinkwrapped with plastic g/fold box [ONE CD TWO]). . . 8
90	Situation Two SITU 30L	SOME FRIENDLY (LP, 'some friendly edition' in white PVC sleeve with inner) . . . 12
91	Live Live Good CB 2	ISOLATION 21.2.91 (LP, official live bootleg, sold via fan club, 1,000 only). 20
92	Situation Two SITU 37	BETWEEN 10TH AND 11TH (CD, box set with cassette & video, promo only). . . . 35
94	Beggars Banquet BBCD 147	UP TO OUR HIPS (CD, box set with cassette & video, promo only) 35

(see also Electric Crayons, Makin' Time)

BOBBY CHARLES

56	London HLU 8247	See You Later, Alligator/On Bended Knee 2,750
56	London HLU 8247	See You Later, Alligator/On Bended Knee (78) 450
73	Bearsville K 15508	Small Town Talk/Grow Too Old 5
73	Chess 6145 024	See You Later, Alligator/JAMES 'SUGARBOY' CRAWFORD: Jock-o-mo (Iko Iko) . . 5
72	Bearsville K 45516	BOBBY CHARLES (LP) 15
77	Chess CXMP 2009	BOBBY CHARLES (LP) 12

DON CHARLES

62	Decca F 11424	Walk With Me My Angel/Crazy Man, Crazy 15
62	Decca F 11464	The Hermit Of Misty Mountain/Moonlight Rendezvous 15
62	Decca F 11528	It's My Way Of Loving You/Guess That's The Way It Goes 15
63	Decca F 11602	Angel Of Love/Lucky Star 18
63	Decca F 11645	Heart's Ice Cold/Daybreak 30
63	HMV POP 1271	Tower Tall/Look Before You Love 6
64	HMV POP 1307	If You Don't Know I Ain't Gonna Tell Ya/Voice On The Phone 6
64	HMV POP 1332	Big Talk From A Little Man/She's Mine 12
65	HMV POP 1382	Forgetting Me, Loving Him/A Long Time Ago 6
65	HMV POP 1420	Dream On Little Dreamer/We Only Live Once 6
65	HMV POP 1478	I Could Conquer The World/Time Will Tell 6
66	HMV POP 1542	Out Of This Cold/From The Beginning 6
67	Parlophone R 5564	So Let It Be/Bring Your Love To Me 6
67	Parlophone R 5596	Have I Told You Lately/Time Waits For Nobody 6
68	Parlophone R 5659	If I Had The Chance/(I've Got Everything) I've Got You 6
68	Parlophone R 5688	The Drifter/Great To Be Livin' 30
68	Parlophone R 5712	Your Name Is On My Heart/How Can I 6
63	Decca DFE 8530	DON CHARLES (EP) 100
67	Parlophone PMC/PCS 7021	HAVE I TOLD YOU LATELY (LP, mono/stereo) 25/30

JIMMY CHARLES

| 60 | London HLU 9206 | A Million To One/Hop Scotch Hop . . . . 10 |

RAY CHARLES

78s

58	London HLE 8768	Rockhouse (Parts 1 & 2) (78) 40
59	London HLE 8917	What'd I Say (Parts 1 & 2) (78) 75
59	London HLE 9009	I'm Movin' On/I Believe To My Soul (78) 90
60	HMV POP 792	Georgia On My Mind/Carry Be Back To Old Virginny (78) 100

SINGLES

58	London HLE 8768	Rockhouse (Parts 1 & 2) 25
59	London HLE 8917	What'd I Say (Parts 1 & 2) 15
59	London HLE 9009	I'm Movin' On/I Believe To My Soul 10
60	London HLE 9058	Let The Good Times Roll/Don't Let The Sun Catch You Cryin' 10
60	HMV POP 774	Sticks And Stones/Worried Life Blues 8
60	London HLK 9181	Tell The Truth/You Be My Baby 10
60	HMV POP 792	Georgia On My Mind/Carry Be Back To Old Virginny 6
60	London HLK 9251	Come Rain Or Come Shine/Tell Me You'll Wait For Me 8
61	HMV POP 825	Ruby/Hard Hearted Hannah 8
61	HMV POP 838	Them That Got/I Wonder 6
61	London HLK 9364	Early In The Mornin'/A Bit Of Soul 8
61	HMV POP 862	One Mint Julep/Let's Go 7
61	HMV POP 935	Hit The Road Jack/The Danger Zone 6
61	London HLK 9435	I Wonder Who/Hard Times 8
62	HMV POP 969	Unchain My Heart/But On The Other Hand Baby 6
62	HMV POP 1017	Hide Nor Hair/At The Club 7
62	HMV POP 1034	I Can't Stop Loving You/Born To Lose 5
62	HMV POP 1064	You Don't Know Me/Careless Love 5
62	HMV POP 1099	Your Cheating Heart/You Are My Sunshine 5
63	HMV POP 1133	Don't Set Me Free/The Brightest Smile In Town 5
63	HMV POP 1161	Take These Chains From My Heart/No Letter Today 5
63	HMV POP 1202	No One/Without Love (There Is Nothing) 5
63	HMV POP 1221	Busted/Making Believe 7
64	HMV POP 1251	That Lucky Old Sun/Mississippi Mud 5
64	HMV POP 1272	Baby Don't You Cry/My Heart Cries For You 5
64	HMV POP 1315	My Baby Don't Dig Me/Something's Wrong 5
64	HMV POP 1333	No One To Cry To/A Tear Fell 5
64	HMV POP 1350	Smack Dab In The Middle/I Wake Up Crying 6
65	HMV POP 1383	Makin' Whoopee/Move It On Over 5
65	HMV POP 1392	Cry/Teardrops From My Eye 5
65	HMV POP 1414	Light Out Of Darkness/Please Forgive And Forget 5
65	HMV POP 1437	I Gotta Woman/Without A Song 6
65	HMV POP 1457	Love's Gonna Live Here/I'm A Fool To Care 5
65	HMV POP 1484	The Cincinnati Kid/That's All I Am To You 5
66	HMV POP 1502	Crying Time/When My Dreamboat Comes Home 5
66	HMV POP 1519	Together Again/You're Just About To Lose Your Clown 5
66	HMV POP 1537	Let's Go Get Stoned/The Train. 5
66	HMV POP 1551	I Chose To Sing The Blues/Hopelessly 10
66	HMV POP 1566	Please Say You're Fooling/I Don't Need No Doctor 35
67	Atlantic 584 093	What'd I Say/I Got A Woman 5
67	HMV POP 1589	You Win Again/Bye Bye Love 5
67	HMV POP 1595	Somebody Oughta Write A Book About It/Here We Go Again 5

Ray CHARLES

67	HMV POP 1607	In The Heat Of The Night/Something's Got To Change	6
71	Tangerine 6121 001	Booty Butt/Zig Zag	5

EPs

59	London Jazz EZK 19043	THE GREAT RAY CHARLES (EP)	12
59	London Jazz EZK 19048	SOUL BROTHERS (EP, with Milt Jackson)	12
61	London REK 1306	WHAT'D I SAY (EP)	12
61	London REK 1317	RAY CHARLES AT NEWPORT (EP)	12
62	HMV 7EG 8729	HIT THE ROAD JACK (EP)	10
62	HMV 7EG 8781	I CAN'T STOP LOVING YOU (EP)	8
63	HMV 7EG 8783	THE BALLAD STYLE OF RAY CHARLES (EP)	8
63	HMV 7EG 8801	THE SWINGING STYLE OF RAY CHARLES (EP)	8
63	HMV 7EG 8807	BABY IT'S COLD OUTSIDE (EP, with Betty Carter)	8
63	HMV 7EG 8812	TAKE THESE CHAINS FROM MY HEART (EP)	8
63	London REB 1407	THE ORIGINAL RAY CHARLES VOLUME ONE (EP)	12
63	London REB 1408	THE ORIGINAL RAY CHARLES VOLUME TWO (EP)	12
63	London REB 1409	THE ORIGINAL RAY CHARLES VOLUME THREE (EP)	12
64	HMV 7EG 8841	BUSTED (EP)	8
64	HMV 7EG 8861	RAY CHARLES SINGS (EP)	8
64	Realm REP 4001	THE YOUNG RAY CHARLES (EP)	10
66	HMV 7EG 8932	RAY CHARLES LIVE IN CONCERT (EP)	8
66	HMV 7EG 8951	RAY CHARLES SINGS SONGS OF BUCK OWENS (EP)	8

LPs

58	London Jazz LTZ-K 15134	THE GREAT RAY CHARLES (LP)	35
59	London Jazz LTZ-K 15146	SOUL BROTHERS (LP with Milt Jackson, also stereo SAH-K 6030)	22/25
59	London Jazz LTZ-K 15149	RAY CHARLES AT NEWPORT (LP, also stereo SAH-K 6008)	25/30
59	London HA-E 2168	YES INDEED (LP)	20
59	London HA-E 2226	WHAT'D I SAY (LP)	25
60	London Jazz LTZ-K 15190	THE GENIUS OF RAY CHARLES (LP)	30
60	HMV CLP 1387/CSD 1320	THE GENIUS HITS THE ROAD (LP, mono/stereo)	15/18
60	London HA-K 2284	RAY CHARLES IN PERSON (LP)	20
61	HMV CLP 1449/CSD 1362	DEDICATED TO YOU (LP, mono/stereo)	15/18
61	HMV CLP 1475/CSD 1384	GENIUS + SOUL = JAZZ (LP, mono/stereo)	15/18
62	HMV CLP 1520/CSD 1414	RAY CHARLES AND BETTY CARTER (LP, mono/stereo)	15/18
62	London Jazz LJZ-K 15238	THE GENIUS SINGS THE BLUES (LP)	20
62	HMV CLP 1580/CSD 1451	MODERN SOUNDS IN COUNTRY & WESTERN (LP, mono/stereo)	22/25
63	HMV CLP 1613/CSD 1477	MODERN SOUNDS IN COUNTRY & WESTERN VOL. TWO (LP, mono/stereo)	15/18
63	London HA-K 8022	THE ORIGINAL RAY CHARLES (LP)	25
63	London HA-K 8023	THE RAY CHARLES STORY VOL. 1 (LP)	15
63	London HA-K 8024	THE RAY CHARLES STORY VOL. 2 (LP)	15
63	London HA-K 8035	THE GENIUS AFTER HOURS (LP)	20
63	HMV CLP 1626/CSD 1482	GREATEST HITS (LP, mono/stereo)	15/18
63	London HA-K/SH-K 8045	SOUL MEETING (LP, with Milt Jackson)	18
63	HMV CLP 1678	INGREDIENTS IN A RECIPE FOR SOUL (LP)	16
63	Realm RM 101	RAY CHARLES IN R&B GREATS (LP)	15
64	HMV CLP 1728/CSD 1537	SWEET AND SOUR TEARS (LP, mono/stereo)	15/18
64	HMV CLP 1795/CSD 1566	HAVE A SMILE WITH ME (LP, mono/stereo)	15/18
65	HMV CLP 1872/CSD 1696	LIVE IN CONCERT (LP, mono/stereo)	15/18
65	HMV CLP 1914/CSD 1630	C&W MEETS R&B (LP, mono/stereo)	15/18
66	HMV CLP/CSD 3533	CRYIN' TIME (LP, with Raelets)	15
66	HMV CLP/CSD 3574	RAY'S MOODS (LP)	15
67	Atlantic 587/588 056	HALLELUJAH I LOVE HER SO (LP)	12
67	HMV CLP/CSD 3630	RAY CHARLES INVITES YOU TO LISTEN (LP)	15
67	Saga FID 2103	RAY CHARLES (LP)	12
68	Stateside S(S)L 10241	GREATEST HITS (VOL. 2) (LP)	12
69	Stateside S(S)L 10269	A PORTRAIT OF RAY (LP)	12
69	Stateside S(S)L 10281	I'M ALL YOURS — BABY! (LP)	12
70	Stateside SSL 10293	DOING HIS THING (LP)	12
70	Probe SPB 1015	LOVE — COUNTRY STYLE (LP)	12
71	Xtra XTRA 1103	RAY CHARLES (LP)	12
71	Tangerine 6495 001	MY KIND OF JAZZ (LP)	12
71	Probe SPB 1039	VOLCANIC ACTION OF MY SOUL (LP)	12
72	Atlantic 2659 009	SALUTE TO RAY CHARLES (LP)	15
73	Probe PBSP 108	ALL TIME GREAT C&W HITS (LP)	12

(see also Raelets, Milt Jackson)

SONNY CHARLES (& CHECKMATES LTD)

67	Ember EMB S 240	Mastered The Art Of Love/Please Don't Take My World Away	18
69	A&M AMS 752	Black Pearl/Lazy Susan	5
70	A&M AMS 780	I Keep Forgettin'/Do You Love Your Baby	5
70	A&M AMS 787	It Takes A Little Longer/Welfare Man	5

(see also Checkmates Ltd)

CHARLES, PAULETTE & GEE

71	G.G. GG 4515	Shock And Shake (Version 3)/WINSTON WRIGHT: Roll On (Version 2) (as Charlie, Paulette & Gee)	6
71	G.G. GG 4517	Rock And Shake (Version 3) (actually "Lover's Affair" by Charlie Ace & Maytones)/Roll On (Version 2) (actually "My Love And I" by Winston Wright)	6

(see also Charlie Ace)

DICK CHARLESWORTH (& HIS CITY GENTS)

61	Top Rank JAR 558	Billy Boy/Night Fall	5
61	HMV POP 930	In The Doghouse/You're Just In Love (solo)	5
57	Melodisc EPM7-76	DICK CHARLESWORTH'S JAZZ BAND (EP)	8
61	Top Rank 35-104	MEET THE GENTS (LP)	15
62	HMV CLP 1495	YES INDEED IT'S THE GENTS (LP)	25

CHARLIE & MELODIANS

(see under Charlie Ace)

CHARLIE PARKAS
80	Paranoid Plastics PPS 1	The Ballad Of Robin Hood/Space Invaders (p/s)	8

(see also Alberto Y Lost Trios Paranoias)

CHARLIE, PAULETTE & GEE
(see under Charles, Paulette & Gee)

CHARLOTTES
88	Molesworth HUNTS 5	Are You Happy Now/How Can You Say (foldover p/s)	6
90	Subway Org. SUBWAY 27T	LOVE IN THE EMPTINESS (12" EP)	8

CHARME
84	RCA RCAT 484	Georgy Porgy/Rock The Boat (12", p/s)	8

CHARMER
56	Melodisc MEL 1353	Back To Back, Belly To Belly/Is She Is Or Is She Ain't (78)	12

CHARMERS (U.S.)
58	Vogue V 9095	He's Gone/Oh! Yes	425
58	Vogue V 9095	He's Gone/Oh! Yes (78)	75

CHARMERS (Jamaica)
61	Blue Beat BB 42	Lonely Boy/I Am Going Back Home	15
62	Blue Beat BB 114	Crying Over You/Now You Want To Cry	15
63	Blue Beat BB 157	Time After Time/Done Me Wrong (with Prince Buster's Band)	15
63	R&B JB 118	Angel Love/My Heart	12
63	R&B JB 121	Oh Why Baby/ROLAND ALPHONSO: Perhaps	12
64	R&B JB 151	What's The Use/I Am Through	12
64	R&B JB 156	In My Soul/Beware	12
64	Blue Beat BB 204	I'm Back/It's A Dream	15
64	Blue Beat BB 238	Waiting For You/You Are My Sunshine	15
64	Blue Beat BB 251	Dig Then Prince (act. Dip Them Prince)/Girl Of My Dreams (as The Charmer)	15
65	Blue Beat BB 279	Nobody Takes My Baby Away From Me/BUSTER ALLSTARS: Mules Mules Mules	15
66	Blue Beat BB 345	Oh My Baby/STRANGER COLE: When The Party Is Over	15
66	Ska Beat JB 237	Best Friend/MAYTALS: My Darling	15
66	Rio R 78	You Don't Know/CORNELL CAMPBELL & ROY PANTON: Sweetest Girl	15
68	Coxsone CS 7043	Things Going Wrong/KEN BOOTHE: You Keep Me Hanging On	18
68	Treasure Isle TI 7036	Keep On Going (actually by Lloyd Charmers)/SILVERTONES: Don't Say No	18
70	Duke DU 87	Colour Him Father/Version	10
70	Trojan TR 7773	Sweeter She Is (actually by Lloyd Charmers, Dave Barker & Slim Smith)/Fire Fire (actually by Lloyd Charmers)	5
70	Explosion EX 2026	Can I Get Next To You?/Big Five	6
70	Explosion EX 2035	Sweet Back/Music Talk (actually by Lloyd Charmers)	6
71	Explosion EX 2045	Skinhead Train/TONY & CHARMERS: Everstrong (B-side with Tony Binns)	15
71	Explosion EX 2055	Reggae In Wonderland/Wonder — Version (both actually by Byron Lee & Dragonaires)	6
71	Supreme SUP 220	Just My Imagination/Gotta Get A Message To You (actually by Dave Barker)	6
71	Green Door GD 4000	Rasta Never Fails (actually by Lloyd Charmers & Ken Boothe)/CHARMERS ALL STARS: Rasta Version	6
71	Green Door GD 4001	One Big Unhappy Family/CONSCIOUS MINDS: Africa Is Paradise	15
71	Pama Supreme PS 340	Red Head Duck/Jingle Jangle	5

(see also Spanishtown Skabeats, Lloyd & Ken, Lloydie & Lowbites, Lloyd Terrell)

LLOYD CHARMERS
67	Coxsone CS 7023	Time Is Getting Hard/TONY GREGORY: I Sit By The Shore	18
69	Duke DU 15	Cooyah/UNIQUES: Forever	12
69	Duke DU 16	Follow This Sound/Why Pretend	10
69	Duke DU 25	5 To 5/SOUL STIRRERS: Come See About Me	10
69	Duke DU 36	Safari (The Far East)/Last Laugh	10
69	Songbird SB 1001	Ling Ting Tong/LLOYD ROBINSON: Sweet Sweet	7
69	Songbird SB 1007	Duckey Luckey/In The Spirit	7
69	Camel CA 30	Confidential/TOMMY COWAN: House In Session	6
69	Explosion EX 2001	Death A Come/Zylon	7
70	Explosion EX 2032	Vengeance/Look A-Py-Py	8
70	Explosion EX 2034	Ready Talk/There Is Something About You	6
70	Trojan TR 7788	Oh Me Oh My/I Did It	10
70	Bullet BU 435	Dollars And Bonds/Sounds Familiar	6
70	Bullet BU 442	Reggae A Bye Bye/DAVE BARKER:Doctor Jekyll	6
70	Escort ES 836	Hi Shan/Soul At Large	10
70	Smash SMA 2302	Big Red Bum Ball/BUNNIE LEE ALLSTARS: Big Bum Ball Version	6
73	Green Door GD 4064	Save The People (as L. Charmers)/SCOTTY: Salvation Train	12
74	Harry J. HJ 6662	I'm Gonna Love You Just A Little Bit More/Have I Sinned	5
70	Trojan TTL 25	REGGAE IS TIGHT (LP)	20
70	Trojan TTL 30	REGGAE CHARM (LP)	20
70	Pama SECO 25	HOUSE IN SESSION (LP, with Hippy Boys)	35
71	Pama Supreme PS 339	Shaft/Harry's Mood	7
71	Pama Supreme PS 346	Show Business/DEBBY & LLOYD: Gloria	5
72	Pama Supreme PS 355	Desiderata/Desiderata Music	5

(see also Charmers, Lloyd Tyrell/Terrell, Ken Boothe, Hippy Boys, Wayne Howard, Martia Riley, Eric Donaldson)

CHARMETTES
63	London HLR 9820	Please Don't Kiss Me Again/What Is A Tear	15

CHARMS (U.S.)
55	Parlophone MSP 6155	Hearts Of Stone/Ko Ko Mo (I Love You So)	550
55	Parlophone R 3988	Hearts Of Stone/Ko Ko Mo (I Love You So) (78)	65
55	Parlophone DP 412	Hearts Of Stone/Bazoom, I Need Your Lovin' (78) (export issue)	75
55	Parlophone DP 423	Two Hearts/The First Time We Met (78) (export issue)	75

(see also Otis Williams & Charms, Tiny Topsy, Harmonizing Four)

CHARMS (Jamaica)
64	Island WI 154	Carry, Go, Bring Home (actually by Justin Hinds & Dominoes)/Hill And Gully (actually by L. Reid's Group)	10
66	Rio R 98	Everybody Say Yeah/This World Is Yours	10

CHARTBUSTERS
64	London HLU 9906	She's The One/Slippin' Thru Your Fingers	10
64	London HLU 9934	Why/Stop The Music	8

CHASE
71	CBS EQ 30472	CHASE (LP, quadrophonic)	12

LINCOLN CHASE
57	London HLU 8495	Johnny Klingeringding/You're Driving Me Crazy (What Did I Do)	18
57	London HLU 8495	Johnny Klingeringding/You're Driving Me Crazy (What Did I Do) (78)	12
61	Philips PB 1103	Miss Orangutang/Walking Slowly	6

CHASERS
65	Decca F 12302	Hey Little Girl/That's What They Call Love (some in p/s)	80/40
66	Parlophone R 5451	Inspiration/She's Gone Away	70
67	Philips BF 1546	The Ways Of A Man/Summer Girl	10

ROBERT CHAUVIGNY
59	Top Rank JAR 142	The Bottle Theme/French Rockin' Waltz (Eux)	5
59	Top Rank JAR 142	The Bottle Theme/French Rockin' Waltz (Eux) (78)	10

CHEAP BOOTS
70	Fontana 6001 020	Baby I Do Need You/Come And Stay With Me	5

CHEAP TRICK
77	Epic S EPC 5701	I Want You To Want Me/Oh Boy (Instrumental Version)	5
78	Epic S EPC 6199	So Good To See You/You're All Talk (withdrawn)	20
79	Epic S EPC 7144	Voices/Surrender (withdrawn)	5
79	Epic S EPC 7258	I Want You To Want Me (live)/I Want You To Want Me (studio) (DJ only)	6
79	Epic CT-1	Dream Police/Voice/I'll Be With You Tonight (sampler, promo only)	10
88	Epic 652 896-0	Don't Be Cruel (Remix)/I Know What I Want (shaped picture disc)	5
88	Epic 652 896-2	Don't Be Cruel (Remix)/I Know What I Want (live)/Ain't That A Shame (live)/California Man (CD)	8
88	Epic 653 005-3	Don't Be Cruel (Remix)/Dream Police/Way Of The World/I Know What I Want (live) (3" CD)	8
88	Epic 651 466-0	The Flame/Through The Night (shaped picture disc)	5
88	Epic 651 466-2	The Flame (Album Version)/Through The Night/I Want You To Want Me/If You Want My Love (CD, card sleeve)	8
88	Epic 654 851-3	Solid Gold: The Flame/I Want You To Want Me/Surrender (3" CD, gatefold p/s)	8
78	Epic EPC 86083	AT THE BUDOKAN (LP, yellow vinyl, with booklet)	12
79	Epic EPC 11-83522	DREAM POLICE (LP, picture disc)	12
82	Epic EPC 85740	ONE ON ONE (LP, red vinyl with insert)	12
82	Epic EPC 11-85740	ONE ON ONE (LP, picture disc)	15

CHEATERS
80	Parlophone R 6041	Nothing Ever Happens On Saturdays/Hard Work/Stop Pushing	5

OLIVER CHEATHAM
83	MCA MCA 828	Get Down Saturday Night/Something About You (12")	8

CHEATIN' HEARTS
66	Columbia DB 8048	Zip-Tease/The Bad Kind	8

CHUBBY CHECKER
59	Top Rank JAR 154	The Class/Schooldays, Oh, Schooldays	35
59	Top Rank JAR 154	The Class/Schooldays, Oh, Schooldays (78)	50
60	Columbia DB 4503	The Twist/Toot	8
60	Columbia DB 4541	The Hucklebuck/Whole Lotta Shakin' Goin' On	12
61	Columbia DB 4591	Pony Time/Oh Susanna	7
61	Columbia DB 4652	Good Good Loving/Mess Around	8
61	Columbia DB 4691	Let's Twist Again/Everything's Gonna Be All Right	5
61	Columbia DB 4728	The Fly/That's The Way It Goes	8
62	Columbia DB 4808	Slow Twistin'/The Lose Your Inhibitions Twist	6
62	Columbia DB 4876	Dancin' Party/Gotta Get Myself Together	6
62	Pye International 7N 25160	Dancin' Party/Gotta Get Myself Together (reissue)	6
62	Cameo Parkway P 806	What Do You Say/Something To Shout About	6
62	Cameo Parkway P 824	Let's Twist Again/The Twist	5
62	Cameo Parkway P 849	Limbo Rock/Hitch Hiker	6
63	Cameo Parkway P 862	Let's Limbo Some More/Twenty Miles	5
63	Cameo Parkway P 873	Black Cloud/Birdland	6
63	Cameo Parkway P 879	Twist It Up/Surf Party	7
64	Cameo Parkway P 890	Loddy Lo/Hooka Tooka	7
64	Cameo Parkway P 907	Hey Bobba Needle/Spread Joy	8
64	Cameo Parkway P 920	Lazy Elsie Molly/Rosie	6
64	Cameo Parkway P 922	She Wants T'Swim/You Better Believe It Baby	6
65	Cameo Parkway P 936	Lovely, Lovely/The Weekend's Here	10
65	Cameo Parkway P 949	(At The) Discotheque/Do The Freddie	30
65	Cameo Parkway P 959	Everything's Wrong/Cu Ma La Be Stay	18
65	Cameo Parkway P 965	Two Hearts Make One Love/You Just Don't Know (What You Do To Me)	100
65	Cameo Parkway P 989	Hey You Little Boogaloo/Pussy Cat	10
69	Buddah 201 045	Back In The U.S.S.R./Windy Cream	5
71	London HL 10331	Let's Go Down/Goodbye Victoria	5
76	London HLU 10515	(At The) Discotheque/Slow Twistin'	6
78	London HLU 10557	You Just Don't Know (What You Do To Me)/Two Hearts Make One Love (reissue)	6

MINT VALUE £

62	Columbia SEG 8155	KING OF THE TWIST (EP)	12
63	Cameo Parkway CPE 550	DANCING PARTY (EP)	12
61	Columbia 33SX 1315	TWIST WITH CHUBBY CHECKER (LP)	30
61	Columbia 33SX 1341	FOR TWISTERS ONLY (LP)	25
61	Columbia 33SX 1365	IT'S PONY TIME (LP)	25
62	Columbia 33SX 1445	TWIST ALONG WITH CHUBBY CHECKER (LP)	18
62	Golden Guinea GGL 0236	TWISTIN' ROUND THE WORLD (LP)	20
63	Cameo Parkway P 7014	ALL THE HITS (LP)	20
63	Cameo Parkway P 7020	LIMBO PARTY (LP)	18
63	Cameo Parkway P 7036	CHUBBY CHECKER (LP)	20
71	London SHZ 8419	CHEQUERED (LP)	12

CHUBBY CHECKER & BOBBY RYDELL

62	Columbia DB 4802	Teach Me To Twist/Swingin' Together	7
62	Cameo Parkway C 205	Jingle Bell Rock/What Are You Doing New Year's Eve?	7
64	Cameo Parkway CPE 554	CHUBBY CHECKER AND BOBBY RYDELL IN LONDON (EP)	20
62	Columbia 33SX 1424	CHECKER AND RYDELL (LP)	30
63	Cameo Parkway C 1063	GOLDEN HITS (LP)	18

CHUBBY CHECKER & DEE DEE SHARP

62	Cameo Parkway C 1029	DOWN TO EARTH (LP)	30

(see also Dream Lovers, Bobby Rydell, Dee Dee Sharp)

CHECKERS

54	Parlophone DP 403	Over The Rainbow/CECIL YOUNG QUARTET: Oooh-Diga-Gow (78, export issue)	60

CHECKMATES

61	Piccadilly 7N 35010	Rockin' Minstrel/Pompeii	8
63	Decca F 11603	You've Gotta Have A Gimmick Today/Westpoint	20
64	Decca F 11844	Sticks And Stones/Please Listen To Me	25
65	Decca F 12114	Around/I've Got To Know Now	12
65	Parlophone R 5337	Stop That Music/I've Been In Love Before	12
66	Parlophone R 5402	(You Got) The Gamma Goochie/It Ain't Right	15
66	Parlophone R 5495	Every Day Is Just The Same/I'll Be Keeping The Score	12
61	Pye NPL 18061	THE CHECKMATES (LP)	30

(see also Original Checkmates)

CHECKMATES LTD

67	Ember EMB S 235	Do The Walk (The Temptation Walk)/Glad For You	8
69	A&M AMS 747	Love Is All I Have To Give/I Never Should Have Lied	6
69	A&M AMS 769	Proud Mary/Spanish Harlem	5
69	A&M AMLS 943	LOVE IS ALL I HAVE TO GIVE (LP)	18
70	Ember NR 5048	LIVE AT CAESAR'S PALACE (LP)	12

(see also Sonny Charles & Checkmates Ltd)

CHEECH & CHONG

72	A&M AMLS 67010	CHEECH AND CHONG (LP)	15
72	A&M AMLH 67014	BIG BAMBU (LP, foldout sleeve)	12

CHEEKY

80	Woodbine St. WSR 005	Don't Mess Around/Get Outa My 'Ouse(no p/s)	60

CHEERS

54	Capitol CL 14189	Bazoom (I Need Your Lovin')/Arriverderci	35
54	Capitol CL 14189	Bazoom (I Need Your Lovin')/Arriverderci (78)	10
55	Capitol CL 14248	Bernie's Tune/Whodaya Want?	20
55	Capitol CL 14248	Bernie's Tune/Whodaya Want? (78)	10
55	Capitol CL 14280	Blueberries/Can't We Be More Than Friends	20
55	Capitol CL 14280	Blueberries/Can't We Be More Than Friends (78)	10
55	Capitol CL 14337	I Must Be Dreaming/Fancy Meeting You Here	30
55	Capitol CL 14337	I Must Be Dreaming/Fancy Meeting You Here (78)	10
55	Capitol CL 14377	Black Denim Trousers And Motorcycle Boots/Some Night In Alaska	40
55	Capitol CL 14377	Black Denim Trousers And Motorcycle Boots/Some Night In Alaska (78)	15
56	Capitol CL 14561	Chicken/Don't Do Anything	18
56	Capitol CL 14561	Chicken/Don't Do Anything (78)	20
56	Capitol CL 14601	Que Pasa Muchacha/BERT CONVY: Heaven On Earth	15
56	Capitol CL 14601	Que Pasa Muchacha/BERT CONVY: Heaven On Earth (78)	15
56	Capitol EAP1 584	THE CHEERS (EP)	65

(see also Bert Convy [& Thunderbirds])

CHEETAHS

64	Philips BF 1362	Mecca/Goodnight Kiss	10
65	Philips BF 1383	Soldier Boy/Johnny	10
65	Philips BF 1412	Goodbye Baby (Baby Goodbye)/That's How It Goes	10
65	Philips BF 1453	Whole Lotta Love/Party	10
66	Philips BF 1499	The Russian Boat Song/Gamble	10

(see also Carl Wayne & Cheetahs)

CHEETER

79	GTO GT 250	Goodbye Baby/That's How It Goes	5

(see also Wimple Winch)

KEITH CHEGWIN

73	Cherub CHUBS 002	I'll Take You Back Again/Sometimes I Think I'm Crazy	5

CHELSEA

77	Step Forward SF 2	Right To Work/The Loser (p/s)	7
77	Step Forward SF 5	High Rise Living/No Admission (p/s)	7
78	Step Forward SF 8	Urban Kids/No Flowers (p/s)	7
80	Step Forward SF 14	No One's Coming Outside/What Would You Do (p/s)	5
80	Step Forward SF 15	Look At the Outside/Don't Get Me Wrong (p/s)	5
80	Step Forward SF 16	No Escape/Decide (p/s)	5

MINT VALUE £

81	Step Forward SF 17	Rockin' Horse/Years Away (p/s)	5
81	Step Forward SF 18	Freemans/I.D. Parade/How Do You Know? (p/s)	5
81	Step Forward SF 20	Evacuate/New Era (p/s)	5
82	Step Forward SF 21	War Across The Nation/High Rise Living (Remix) (p/s)	5
82	Step Forward SF 22	Stand Out/Last Drink (p/s)	5
82	Step Forward SF 22	Stand Out/Last Drink (picture disc)	5
84	Chelsea CH 001	Give Me More/Sympathy For The Devil (p/s)	5
79	Step Forward SFLP 2	CHELSEA (LP, with inner sleeve)	20
81	Step Forward SFLP 5	ALTERNATIVE HITS (LP)	20
82	Step Forward SFLP 7	EVACUATE (LP)	15
84	Picasso PIK 003	LIVE AND WELL (LP)	12

(see also Gene October)

CHELSEA LADS
| 66 | CBS 202047 | English Tea/Hump A Dink | 5 |

CHEMICAL ALICE
| 81 | Acidic GNOME 1 | Goodnight Vienna (12", p/s) | 75 |

(see also Marillion)

CHEMICAL BROTHERS
91	Eastern Bloc	Sea Of Beats/Sea Of Beats (Justin Robertson Mix) (12", p/s, as Ariel)	25
91	Deconstruction PT 44888	Rollercoaster/Mustn't Grumble/Mustn't Grumble (God's Grumble Mix) (12", as Ariel)	15
93	Dust Brothers DB's 333	Song To The Siren (12", as Dust Brothers, no p/s, 500 only)	75
93	Junior Boys Own JBO 10	Song To The Siren/Song To The Siren (Sabres Of Paradise Mixes) (12", p/s)	25
94	Boys Own COLLECT 004	14TH CENTURY SKY EP (12", no p/s, as Dust Brothers)	20
94	Junior Boys Own JBO 20	MY MERCURY MOUTH EP (12", JBO sleeve, as Dust Brothers)	15
95	Junior Boys Own CHEMS TI	Leave Home/Leave Home (Sabres Of Paradise)/Let Me In Mate (12", p/s)	20
95	Junior Boys Own CHEMS TXI	Leave Home (Underworld Mix One)/Leave Home (Underworld Mix Two) (12", p/s)	20

CHEQUERED PAST
| 85 | Heavy Metal America HMUSA53 | CHEQUERED PAST (LP, picture disc, 1,000 only) | 30 |

(see also Steve Jones)

CLIFTON CHENIER
69	Action ACT 4550	Black Gal/Frogs Legs	8
70	Sonet SNTF 5012	BAYOU BLUES (LP)	15
70	Harvest MHSP 4002	CLIFTON CHENIER'S VERY BEST (LP)	25
79	Flyright FLY 539	ZYDECO BLUES (LP, with other artists)	12

CHER
65	Liberty LIB 66114	All I Really Want To Do/I'm Gonna Love You	5
66	Liberty LIB 66136	Where Do You Go/See See Rider	6
66	Liberty LIB 66160	Bang Bang (My Baby Shot Me Down)/Our Day Will Come	6
66	Liberty LIB 12034	I Feel Something In The Air/Come To Your Window	5
66	Liberty LIB 12038	Sunny/She's No Better Than Me	6
67	Liberty LIB 12046	Mama (When My Dollies Have Babies)/Behind The Door	6
67	Liberty LBF 15038	You Better Sit Down Kids/Elusive Butterfly	6
69	Atlantic 584 278	Walk On Gilded Splinters/Tonight I'll Be Staying Here With You	6
69	Atco 226 003	For What It's Worth/Hangin' On	6
71	MCA MU 1137	Classified 1A/Don't Put It On Me	5
72	MCA MU 1148	The Way Of Love/Fire And Rain	5
72	MCA MU 1158	Living In A House Divided/One Honest Man	5
72	MCA MU 1168	Don't Hide Your Love/First Time	5
75	Phil Spector Intl. 2010 006	A Love Like Yours (with Nilsson)/Hangin' On	5
76	Phil Spector Intl. 2010 013	A Woman's Story/Baby I Love You	6
87	Geffen GEF 31P	I Found Someone/Dangerous Times (picture disc)	5
88	Geffen GEF 35TP	We All Sleep Alone (Remix)/Working Girl/I Found Someone (12", picture disc)	8
88	Geffen GEF 35CD	We All Sleep Alone (Remix)/Working Girl/I Found Someone (3" CD with adaptor, 5" case)	8
88	Geffen GEF 44CD	Skin Deep (Extended Dance Mix)/Skin Deep (Dub Version)/Perfection (LP Version) (3" CD with adaptor, 5" case)	8
89	Geffen GEF 52CD	After All (Love Theme From 'Chances Are')/Dangerous Times/I Found Someone/Main Man (3" CD, with Peter Cetera, gatefold sleeve)	8
66	Liberty LEP 4047	THE HITS OF CHER (EP)	15
65	Liberty (S)LBY 3058	ALL I REALLY WANT TO DO (LP, mono/stereo)	15/18
66	Liberty (S)LBY 3072	THE SONNY SIDE OF CHER (LP, mono/stereo)	15/18
66	Liberty (S)LBY 3081	CHER (LP, mono/stereo)	15/18
68	Liberty LBL/LBS 83051	WITH LOVE, CHER (LP)	12
68	Liberty LBL/LBS 83105E	GOLDEN GREATS (LP)	12
69	Atco 226 026/228 026	3614 JACKSON HIGHWAY (LP, gatefold sleeve, mono/stereo)	15/12
71	MCA MUPS 438	CHER (LP)	12
72	MCA MUPS 459	FOXY LADY (LP)	12
73	MCA MUPS 484	BITTERSWEET WHITE LIGHT (LP)	12

(see also Sonny & Cher, Caesar & Cleo, Nilsson)

VIVIENNE CHERING
| 66 | Decca F 12360 | I'll Do My Crying Tomorrow/Make My Dreams Come True | 7 |

(see also Flip & Dateliners)

CHEROKEES (U.S.)
| 61 | Pye International 7N 25066 | Cherokee/Harlem Nocturne | 10 |

CHEROKEES (U.K.)
64	Decca F 11915	You've Done It Again Little Girl/Girl Girl Girl	8
64	Columbia DB 7341	Seven Daffodils/Are You Back In My World Now	8
65	Columbia DB 7473	Wondrous Place/Send Me All Your Love	8
65	Columbia DB 7704	I Will Never Turn My Back On You/Dig A Little Deeper	8
66	Columbia DB 7822	Land Of A 1000 Dances/Everybody's Needs	8

(see also Lee Diamond)

DON CHERRY
56	Brunswick 05538	Wanted Someone To Love/The Thrill Is Gone	7
56	Philips PB 608	Ghost Town/I'll Be Around (78)	8
57	Philips PB 755	I Keep Running Away From You/A Ferryboat Called Minerva (78)	8
58	Philips PB 816	The Golden Age/Another Time, Another Place (78)	8
57	Philips JK 1013	The Last Dance/Don't You Worry (jukebox edition)	12
58	Philips PB 816	Another Time, Another Place/The Golden Age	5
59	Philips PB 911	Hasty Heart/I Look For A Love	5
59	Philips PB 911	Hasty Heart/I Look For A Love (78)	18
66	London HLU 10045	I Love You Drops/Don't Change	5
56	Philips BBL 7128	SWINGIN' FOR TWO (LP)	12

(see also John Coltrane, Jazz Composers Orchestra)

CHERRY PEOPLE
68	MGM MGM 1438	And Suddenly/Imagination	25
69	MGM MGM 1472	Gotta Get Back/I'm The One Who Loves You	6
69	MGM MGM 1489	Light Of Love/On To Something New	6
75	Black Magic BM 112	And Suddenly/Imagination (reissue)	8

CHERRY PIES
64	Black Swan WI 448	Do You Keep Dreaming/Sweeter Than Cherry Pie	6

CHERRY SMASH
67	Track 604 017	Sing Songs Of Love/Movie Star	8
68	Decca F 12838	Goodtime Sunshine/Little Old Country Home Town	12
69	Decca F 12884	Fade Away Maureen/Green Plant	12

FRANKIE CHERVAL
62	MGM MGM 1183	How Come/Tag Along	10

CHEST
95	Mook MK 03	DESTINY PHONES EP (10", p/s)	6

PETE CHESTER
60	Pye 7N 15305	Ten Swinging Bottles/Whole Lotta Shakin' On The Range (with Consulates)	25
61	Pye International 7N 25074	Three Old Maids/Forest Fire (as Pete Chester & Group)	25

(see also Five Chesternuts)

VIC CHESTER
57	Decca F 10882	Rock-A-Billy/First Date, First Kiss, First Love	20
57	Decca F 10882	Rock-A-Billy/First Date, First Kiss, First Love (78)	10

CHESTERFIELDS
85	Subway Organisation GVP 007	Nose Out Of Joint/SHOP ASSISTANTS: Home Again (33rpm flexidisc, with *The Underground* issue 4, *Screed* or *The Legend!* fanzine)	8/6
86	Subway Org. SUBWAY 5	A GUITAR IN YOUR BATH (EP, wraparound p/s in poly bag)	7
87	Subway Org. SUBORG 003	KETTLE (LP)	12
87	Subway Org. SUBORG 005	WESTWARD HO (LP)	12

MORRIS CHESTNUT
79	Grapevine GRP 128	Too Darn Soulful/You Don't Love Me Anymore	8

MAURICE CHEVALIER
55	Decca F 10429	Mon P'tit Moustique/Deux Amoureux Sur Un Banc	6

CHEVIOT RANTERS
73	Topic 12TS 222	THE CHEVIOT HILLS (LP)	15
74	Topic 12TS 245	CHEVIOT BARN DANCE (LP)	15

CHEVLONS
66	Pye 7N 17145	Too Long Alone/It's My Problem	6

CHEVRONS
60	Top Rank JAR 308	Lullaby/Day After Forever	8

CHEVY
80	Avatar AAA 104	Too Much Loving/See The Light (company sleeve)	10
80	Avatar AAA 107	The Taker/Life On The Run (p/s)	15
81	Avatar AAA 114	Just Another Day/Rock On	12
80	Avatar AALP 5001	THE TAKER (LP, gatefold sleeve with inner sleeve)	18

CHEYNES
63	Columbia DB 7153	Respectable/It's Gonna Happen To You	55
64	Columbia DB 7368	Going To The River/Cheyne-Re-La	55
65	Columbia DB 7464	Down And Out/Stop Running Around	55

(see also Peter Bardens, Peter B's, Fleetwood Mac, Mark Leeman Five, Bo Street Runners)

CHEYNES
71	Bell BLL 1144	April Fool/Gotta Get Back	5

CHIC
84	Atlantic AT 9604	Chic Cheers/Savoir Faire/Dance Dance Dance (12")	8
86	Atlantic K 11209	Le Freak/Savoir Faire/Chic (12")	8
87	Atlantic AT 9198	Jack The Freak/Savoir Faire (12")	8
88	Atlantic AT 9107	Good Times/Warm Summer Nights (12", p/s)	8

CHICAGO
69	CBS 4381	Questions 67 And 68/Listen	5
69	CBS 4503	I'm A Man (Parts 1 & 2) (withdrawn)	15
73	CBS 1167	25 Or 6 To 4/Make Me Smile (p/s, 'Hall Of Fame Hits' series)	5
69	CBS 66221	CHICAGO TRANSIT AUTHORITY (2-LP, orange label)	15
71	CBS 66405	IV (AT CARNEGIE HALL) (4-LP, orange label)	20

CHICAGO BILL
52	Melodisc 1191	Keep Your Hands Off/Stump Blues (78)	20
52	Melodisc 1203	Five Foot Seven/Plough Hand Blues (78)	20
	(see also Big Bill Broonzy)		

CHICAGO LINE
66	Philips BF 1488	Shimmy Shimmy Ko Ko Bop/Jump Back	75
	(see also Mike Patto, Bo Street Runners, Viv Prince)		

CHICAGO LOOP
66	Stateside SS 564	(When She Needs Good Lovin') She Comes To Me/This Must Be The Place	5

CHICANES
81	Dinosaur DD 003	Further Thoughts/Cry A Little (p/s)	5

CHICK with TED CAMERON & D.J.'s
60	Pye 7N 15292	Early In The Morning/Cool Water	35

CHICKEN SHACK
67	Blue Horizon 57-3135	It's OK With Me Baby/When My Left Eye Jumps	12
68	Blue Horizon 57-3143	Worried About My Woman/Six Nights In Seven	12
68	Blue Horizon 57-3146	When The Train Comes Back/Hey Baby	8
69	Blue Horizon 57-3153	I'd Rather Go Blind/Night Life	8
69	Blue Horizon 57-3160	Tears In The Wind/The Things You Put Me Through	8
70	Blue Horizon 57-3168	Maudie/Andalucian Blues	8
70	Blue Horizon 57-3176	Sad Clown/Tired Eyes	8
73	Deram DM 381	Time Goes Passing By/Poor Boy	6
73	Deram DM 396	You Know You Could Be Right/The Loser	6
74	CBS 1832	I'd Rather Go Blind/Sad Clown	5
68	Blue Horizon 7-63203	FORTY BLUE FINGERS FRESHLY PACKED AND READY TO SERVE (LP)	30
69	Blue Horizon 7-63209	O.K. KEN? (LP, gatefold sleeve)	25
69	Blue Horizon 7-63218	100 TON CHICKEN (LP)	25
70	Blue Horizon 7-63861	ACCEPT CHICKEN SHACK (LP, gatefold sleeve)	25
72	Deram SDL 5	IMAGINATION LADY (LP, gatefold sleeve)	25
73	Deram SML 1100	UNLUCKY BOY (LP)	25
74	Deram SDL 8008	GOODBYE CHICKEN SHACK (LP)	18
	(see also Errol Dixon, Fleetwood Mac, Christine Perfect, Carmen Macrae)		

CHICKEN SHED
77	Colby AJ 370	ALICE (LP)	60

CHICKS
63	Oriole CB 1828	What Are Boys Made Of?/Over The Mountain	7

CHIEFS
58	London HLU 8624	Apache/Dee's Dream	25
58	London HLU 8624	Apache/Dee's Dream (78)	25
58	London HLU 8720	Enchiladas!/Moments To Remember	18
58	London HLU 8720	Enchiladas!/Moments To Remember (78)	20

CHIEFTAINS
64	Claddagh CC 2	THE CHIEFTAINS (LP)	12
69	Claddagh CC 7	THE CHIEFTAINS VOL. 2 (LP)	12
72	Claddagh CC 10	THE CHIEFTAINS VOL. 3 (LP)	12
73	Claddagh CC 14	THE CHIEFTAINS VOL. 4 (LP)	12

CHIFFONS
63	Stateside SS 172	He's So Fine/Oh! My Lover	7
63	Stateside SS 202	One Fine Day/Why Am I So Shy	7
63	Stateside SS 230	A Love So Fine/Only My Friend	7
64	Stateside SS 254	I Have A Boyfriend/I'm Gonna Dry Your Eyes	8
64	Stateside SS 332	Sailor Boy/When Summer's Through	8
65	Stateside SS 437	Nobody Knows What's Going On (In My Mind But Me)/The Real Thing	18
66	Stateside SS 512	Sweet Talkin' Guy/Did You Ever Go Steady	6
66	Stateside SS 533	Out Of This World/Just A Boy	10
66	Stateside SS 559	Stop, Look And Listen/March	10
67	Stateside SS 578	My Boyfriend's Back/I Got Plenty Of Nuttin'	12
64	Stateside SE 1012	THEY'RE SO FINE (EP)	60
63	Stateside SL 10040	THE CHIFFONS (LP)	60
66	Stateside S(S)L 10190	SWEET TALKIN' GUY (LP)	45
	(see also Four Pennies)		

LORRAINE CHILD
64	Decca F 11969	You/Not This Time	10

SONNY CHILDE (& T.N.T.)
65	Decca F 12218	Giving Up On Love/Mighty Nice	15
66	Polydor 56108	Two Lovers/Ain't That Good News	15
66	Polydor 56141	Heartbreak/I Still Love You (as Sonny Childe & T.N.T.)	15
66	Polydor 582 003	TO BE CONTINUED (LP)	15

CHILD HAROLDS
68	Trident TRA 201	Diary Of My Mind/Loophole	25

BILLY CHILDISH
87	Hangman HANG 9-UP	THE 1982 CASSETTES (LP, pink & black sleeve)	15
	(see also Milkshakes, Thee Mighty Caesars)		

DR. A.A. CHILDS & CONGREGATION
50s	Esquire 10-414	The Healing Prayer (Parts 1 & 2) (78)	10
60	Starlite ST45 009	The Healing Prayer (Parts 1 & 2)	5

CHI-LITES
69	Beacon BEA 119	Pretty Girl/Love Bandit	20
71	MCA MU 1138	(For God's Sake) Give More Power To The People/Trouble's A' Comin'	5
73	Brunswick BR 7	Stoned Out Of My Mind/Someone Else's Arms	8
70	MCA MUPS 397	GIVE IT AWAY (LP)	12
71	MCA MUPS 437	(FOR GOD'S SAKE) GIVE MORE POWER TO THE PEOPLE (LP)	12
72	MCA MUPS 457	A LONELY MAN (LP)	12

(see also Jackie Wilson)

CHILLIWACK
71	London HLU 10327	Everyday/Sundown	5
71	London SHU 8418	CHILLIWACK (LP)	12
72	A&M AMLH 63509	CHILLIWACK (LP)	12
75	Sire 9103 250	ROCKERBOX (LP)	12

(see also Collectors, Electric Prunes)

CHILLI WILLI & RED HOT PEPPERS
75	Mooncrest MOON 40	Breathe A Little/Friday Song	5
72	Revelation REV 002	KINGS OF THE ROBOT RHYTHM (LP)	18
74	Mooncrest CREST 21	BONGOS OVER BALHAM (LP)	12

(see also Brinsley Schwarz, Jo-Ann Kelly)

CHILLUM
71	Mushroom 100 MR 11	CHILLUM (LP, with photo insert)	50

(see also Secondhand)

ALEX CHILTON
80	Aura AUS 117	Hey! Little Child/No More The Moon Shines Lorena (p/s)	8

(see also Box Tops, Big Star)

CHIMES (U.S.)
61	London HLU 9283	Once In A While/Summer Night	22

CHIMES featuring DENISE (U.K.)
63	Decca F 11783	Say It Again/Can This Be Love?	6
64	Decca F 11885	I'll Be Waiting, I'll Be Here/Hello Heartache	7

(see also Little Frankie)

CHIMNEYS
80	Tagmemics 45-003	Do The Big Baby/Take Your Brain Out For A Walk (p/s, 500 only)	15

TSAI CHIN
59	Decca F 11192	The Ding Dong Song/The Second Spring	5
59	Decca F 11192	The Ding Dong Song/The Second Spring (78)	12
63	Decca F 11737	School In Cheltenham/Any Old Iron	5
64	Decca F 12039	Tokyo Melody/I Love A Man	5
62	Decca LK 4501	THE WORLD OF TSAI CHIN (LP)	15
65	Decca LK 4717	THE WESTERN WORLD OF TSAI CHIN (LP)	12

CHINA CRISIS
82	Inevitable INEV 10	African And White/Red Sails (p/s)	5

CHINA DOLLS
82	Speed FIRED 1	One Hit Wonder/Ain't Love Ain't Bad (p/s)	40

(see also Slade, Dummies)

CHINA DRUM
93	China Drum CC 193	Simple/On My Way/Meaning (Acoustic Version) (CD, 555 only)	20
95	Fluffy Bunny FLUFF 6	Great Fire/Biscuit Barrel (Acoustic Version)/Meaning/Down By The River (live) (10", p/s)	7
95	Fluffy Bunny FLUFF 6CD	Great Fire/Biscuit Barrel (Acoustic Version)/Meaning/Down By The River (live) (CD, foldout sleeve)	8
95	Fluffy Bunny FLUFF 8	The Barrier/Brain/One Way Down/Sleazeball (10", p/s)	8
95	Fierce Panda NING 06	Wuthering Heights/FLYING MEDALLIONS: Riot (p/s, stamped die-cut paper sleeve, 1,500 only, 1st 1,000 numbered)	15/8

CHINA STREET
78	Criminal CRM 1	You're A Ruin/(I Wanna Be) Your M.P. (foldout lyric p/s in poly bag & badge)	8

CHINATOWN
81	Airship AP 138	Short And Sweet/How Many Times (p/s)	35
81	Airship AP 343	PLAY IT TO DEATH (LP)	75

CHINAWITE
83	Future Earth FER 014	Blood On The Streets/Ready To Satisfy (p/s)	15

CHIN CHIN
88	53rd & 3rd AGAS 001	Stop! Your Crying/Dark Days/Never Surrender/Cry In Vain/Revolution/Stay With Me/My Guy/Jungle Of Fear (12", p/s)	8

CHING
66	Parlophone R 5325	My Hong Kong/You	5

KES CHINS
62	Starlite ST45 089	Annie/Moody	6

CHIPMUNKS
58	London HLU 8762	The Chipmunk Song/DAVID SEVILLE: Almost Good	5
59	London HLU 8916	Ragtime Cowboy Joe/DAVID SEVILLE: Flip Side (78)	8
60	London HLG 9243	Rudolph The Red-Nosed Reindeer/Lilly Of Laguna	5
64	Liberty LIB 10170	All My Loving/Please Please Me	7
64	Liberty LBY 1218	THE CHIPMUNKS SING THE BEATLES (LP)	15

(see also David Seville)

MINT VALUE £

GEORGE CHISHOLM & BLUENOTES
56	Beltona BL 2671	Honky Tonk/D.R. Rock (with Bert Weedon)	10
56	Beltona BL 2671	Honky Tonk/D.R. Rock (with Bert Weedon) (78)	12
50s	Decca LK 4147	CHIS (LP)	25
60s	Philips SBBL 612	TRAD TREAT (LP)	20
60s	Wing WL 1043	TRAD SPECIAL (LP)	20
60s	77 SEU 12/43	ALONG THE CHISHOLM TRAIL (LP)	25
60s	Philips BL 7694	MUSIC FOR ROMANTICS (LP)	18
60s	Columbia SCX 6195	THE MAGNIFICENT SEVEN (LP)	20
70s	Gold Star 1500001	GEORGE CHISHOLM (LP)	25
70s	Velvet VELP 1002	IN A MELLOW MOOD (LP)	25
70s	Line L 2030	TROMBONE SHOWCASE (LP)	50
80s	Zodiac ZR 1025	THAT'S A PLENTY (LP)	15
80s	Zodiac ZR 1026	THE SWINGIN' MR. C (LP)	12

(see also Bert Weedon)

CHITINIOUS ENSEMBLE
72	Deram SML 1093	CHITINIOUS ENSEMBLE (LP)	75

CHOCOLATE BOYS
74	Decca F 13556	El Bimbo/Voltaire Pier	6

CHOCOLATE FROG
68	Atlantic 584 207	Butchers And Bakers/I Forgive You	18

(see also Fleur De Lys)

CHOCOLATE MILK
75	RCA RCA 2592	Action Speaks Louder Than Words/Ain't Nothing But A Thing	10
75	RCA RCAT 2592	Action Speaks Louder Than Words/Ain't Nothing But A Thing (12")	20
77	RCA PL 11830	COMIN' (LP)	20

CHOCOLATE WATCH BAND (U.K.)
67	Decca F 12649	The Sound Of The Summer/The Only One In Sight	20
67	Decca F 12704	Requiem/What's It To You	20

CHOIR
68	Major Minor MM 537	It's Cold Outside/I'm Going Home	35
68	Major Minor MM 557	When You Were With Me/Changin' My Mind	25

(see also Raspberries)

CHOPYN
75	Jet JET 751	In The Midnight Hour/Funky Lady	5
75	Jet JET 752	Wasting Time/If It Feels Good Do It	5
75	Jet LPO 8	GRAND SLAM (LP)	15

(see also Ann Odell, Ray Russell)

CHORALERNA
70s	Myrrh 1047	LET THERE BE LIGHT (LP)	15

CHORDETTES
54	Columbia SCM 5158	Mr. Sandman/I Don't Wanna See You Cryin'	225
54	Columbia DB 3553	Mr. Sandman/I Don't Wanna See You Cryin' (78)	40
55	London HLA 8169	Humming Bird/Lonely Lips	40
55	London HLA 8169	Humming Bird/Lonely Lips (78)	18
56	London HLA 8217	Dudelsack Polka/I Told A Lie	35
56	London HLA 8217	Dudelsack Polka/I Told A Lie (78)	18
56	London HLA 8264	Eddie My Love/Our Melody (triangular or round centre)	50/25
56	London HLA 8264	Eddie My Love/Our Melody (78)	15
56	London HLA 8302	Born To Be With You/Love Never Changes	35
56	London HA 7011	Born To Be With You/Love Never Changes (export issue)	25
56	London HLA 8302	Born To Be With You/Love Never Changes (78)	10
56	London HLA 8323	Lay Down Your Arms/Teenage Goodnight	25
56	London HLA 8323	Lay Down Your Arms/Teenage Goodnight (78)	10
57	London HLA 8473	Echo Of Love/Just Between You And Me	30
57	London HLA 8473	Echo Of Love/Just Between You And Me (78)	15
57	Beltona HLA 8497	Like A Baby/Soft Sands	25
57	London HLA 8497	Like A Baby/Soft Sands (78)	18
58	London HLA 8566	Baby Of Mine/Photographs	18
58	London HLA 8566	Baby Of Mine/Photographs (78)	18
58	London HLA 8584	Lollipop/Baby, Come-A-Back-A	12
58	London HLA 8584	Lollipop/Baby, Come-A-Back-A (78)	18
58	London HLA 8654	Love Is A Two-Way Street/I Don't Know, I Don't Care	15
58	London HLA 8654	Love Is A Two-Way Street/I Don't Know, I Don't Care (78)	20
59	London HLA 8809	We Should Be Together/No Other Arms, No Other Lips	10
59	London HLA 8809	We Should Be Together/No Other Arms, No Other Lips (78)	30
59	London HLA 8926	A Girl's Work Is Never Done/No Wheels (B-side with Jeff Crom & Jackie Ertel)	20
59	London HLA 8926	A Girl's Work Is Never Done/No Wheels (78)	35
61	London HLA 9400	Never On Sunday/Faraway Star	7
62	London HLA 9519	The White Rose Of Athens/Adios (Goodbye My Love)	6
60	London RE-A 1228	THE CHORDETTES (EP)	60
58	London HA-A 2088	THE CHORDETTES (LP)	50
62	London HA-A 2441	THE CHORDETTES SING (LP)	45

CHORDS (U.S.)
54	Columbia SCM 5133	Sh-Boom (Life Could Be A Dream)/Little Maiden	1,750
54	Columbia DB 3512	Sh-Boom (Life Could Be A Dream)/Little Maiden (78)	125

CHORDS (U.K.)
79	Polydor 2059 141	Now It's Gone/Don't Go Back (p/s)	7
80	Polydor POSP 101	Maybe Tomorrow/I Don't Wanna Know/Hey Girl (p/s)	8
80	Polydor POSP 146	Something's Missing/This Is What They Want (p/s)	7
80	Polydor 2059 258	The British Way Of Life/The Way It's Got To Be (p/s)	8
80	Polydor POSP 185	In My Street/I'll Keep On Holding On (p/s)	7
81	Polydor POSP 270	One More Minute/Who's Killing Who (p/s)	8
81	Polydor POSP 288	Turn Away Again/Turn Away Again (Again) (p/s)	8
80	Polydor Super POLS 1019	SO FAR AWAY (LP, with 7" "Now It's Gone"/"Things We Said" [KRODS 1])	15

(see also Rage)

CHORDS FIVE
67	Island WI 3044	I'm Only Dreaming/Universal Vagrant	40
68	Polydor 56261	Same Old Fat Man/Hold On To Everythin' You've Got	35
69	Jay Boy BOY 6	Some People/Battersea Fair	15

(see also Smoke)

CHORUS
85	Aaz AAZ 3	These Stones/Diamond Mine/The Verse (p/s)	6

CHOSEN FEW (U.K.)
65	Pye 7N 15905	It Won't Be Around You Anymore/Big City	15
65	Pye 7N 15942	So Much To Look Forward To/Today, Tonight & Tomorrow	15

(see also Alan Hull, Lindisfarne, Skip Bifferty)

CHOSEN FEW (Jamaica)
70	Songbird SB 1031	Time Is Hard/CRYSTALITES: Time Is Hard Part Two	8
70	Songbird SB 1032	Going Back Home/CRYSTALITES: Going Back Home Part Two	7
70	Songbird SB 1046	Why Can't I Touch You/INNER CIRCLE BAND: Touch You Version	8
71	Songbird SB 1061	Shaft/Shaft (Version)	6
71	Songbird SB 1067	Everybody Just A Stall/Everybody (Version)	6
72	Songbird SB 1070	Do Your Thing/Your Thing (Version)	12
72	Trojan TR 7864	Ebony Eyes/Ebony Eyes (Version)	5
72	Trojan TR 7882	Everybody Plays The Fool/You're A Big Girl Now	10
73	Trojan TR 7894	Am I Black Enough For You/Message From A Blackman	5
73	Duke DU 162	Children Of The Night/LLOYD CHARMERS: For The Good Times	5
73	Duke DU 163	Stoned In Love/MIKE CHUNG & NOW GENERATION: Stoned In Love (Version)	6
73	Duke DU 164	It's Too Late/MIKE CHUNG & NOW GENERATION: It's Too Late (Version)	6
73	Trojan TRLS 56	HIT AFTER HIT (LP)	18

CHOSEN FEW (U.S.)
74	Action ACT 4623	Funky Butter/Wondering	5
76	Polydor 2058 721	I Can Make Your Dreams Come True/Pretty Face	10
78	Polydor 2058 975	You Mean Everything To Me/It Won't Be Long	10

CHOU PAHROT
79	Klub KEP 101	Buzgo Tram Chorus/Gwizgweela Gwamhnoo/Lemons (p/s)	10
79	Klub KLP 19	LIVE (LP, private pressing)	12

CHRIS & COSEY/CREATIVE TECHNOLOGY INSTITUTE
81	Rough Trade RT 078	October (Love Song)/Little Houses (p/s)	5
81	Rough Trade RTT 078	October (Love Song)/Little Houses (12", p/s)	7
80s	Electronic Sound Maker	Sweet Surprise (magazine with free cassette)	20
84	Intl. One CTI 002	Conspiracy International/The Gift Of Tongues/The Need (p/s)	7
84	C.T.I. CTI 1	HAMMER HOUSE EP (12")	10
84	C.T.I. CTI 2	GIFT OF TONGUES (12")	10
85	Rough Trade RTT 148	Sweet Surprise 1 (1984)/2 (1985) (12", p/s, with Annie Lennox & Dave Stewart)	8
91	World Serpent WS7 004	Passion (p/s, 1-sided, other side etched)	5
80s	Sinn And Form	City Of Spirit (cassette magazine)	10
81	Rough Trade ROUGH 34	HEARTBEAT (LP, with insert)	12
81	Rough Trade COPY 008	HEARTBEAT (cassette, with 2 extra tracks "Pressure Drop" & "Tight Fit")	12
82	Rough Trade ROUGH 44	TRANCE (LP)	12

(see also Throbbing Gristle, Chris Carter, Eurythmics, Cosey Fanni Tutti)

CHRIS & STUDENTS
61	Parlophone R 4806	Lass Of Richmond Hill/Ducks Away From My Fishin'.	20

PETER CHRIS & OUTCASTS
66	Columbia DB 7923	Over The Hill/The Right Girl For Me	30

BOBBY CHRISTIAN & HIS ORCHESTRA
57	Oriole CB 1384	Enough Man/Crickets On Parade (possibly unissued)	20+
57	Oriole CB 1384	Enough Man/Crickets On Parade (78)	15

CHRIS CHRISTIAN
70s	Myrrh MYR 1064	CHRIS CHRISTIAN (LP)	15

FUD CHRISTIAN ALL STARS
71	Big Shot BI 571	Never Fall In Love (actually by Winston Heywood)/Never Fall In Love Version	12

HANS CHRISTIAN
68	Parlophone R 5676	All Of The Time/Never My Love	50
68	Parlophone R 5698	(The Autobiography Of) Mississippi Hobo/Sonata Of Love	75

(see also Jon Anderson, Yes)

LIZ CHRISTIAN
67	CBS 202520	Suddenly You Find Love/Make It Work Out	45
69	Spark SRL 1004	Call My Name/Think Of You Baby	5

(see also James Royal)

MARIA CHRISTIAN
85	MCA MCA 974	Wait Until The Weekend Comes/(Instrumental) (p/s)	15

Neil CHRISTIAN

NEIL CHRISTIAN (& CRUSADERS)
62	Columbia DB 4938	The Road To Love/The Big Beat Drum	25
63	Columbia DB 7075	A Little Bit Of Someone Else/Get A Load Of This (with Crusaders)	10
66	Strike JH 301	That's Nice/She's Got The Action	7
66	Strike JH 313	Oops/She Said Yeah	7
66	Strike JH 319	Two At A Time/Wanna Lover	7
67	Pye 7N 17372	You're All Things Bright And Beautiful/I'm Gonna Love You Baby	10
73	Youngblood YB 1044	That's Nice/She's Got The Action	6
66	Columbia SEG 8492	A LITTLE BIT OF SOMETHING ELSE (EP)	60

(see also Christian's Crusaders, Guy Hamilton, Jimmy Page, Ritchie Blackmore, Nicky Hopkins, Miki Dallon, Screaming Lord Sutch)

CHRISTIAN DEATH
83	No Future FL 2	ONLY THEATRE OF PAIN (LP, with insert)	25
86	Jungle NOS 006	OFFICIAL ANTHOLOGY OF LIVE BOOTLEGS (LP, black & yellow sleeve)	25
86	Jungle NOS 006	OFFICIAL ANTHOLOGY OF LIVE BOOTLEGS (LP, pink vinyl)	12

JOHN CHRISTIAN DEE
68	Pye 7N 17566	Take Me Along/The World Can Pack Its Bags And Go Away	5
69	Decca F 12901	The World Can Pack Its Bags And Go Away/Stick To Your Guns	5
70	London HLH 10317	Come Forward The Man/Mr. & Mrs. Jones	5

CHRISTIAN'S CRUSADERS
64	Columbia DB 7289	Honey Hush/One For The Money	18

(see also Neil Christian & Crusaders)

CHRISTIE
71	CBS 9130	Everything's Gonna Be Alright/Freewheelin' Man/Magic Highway (p/s)	5
70	CBS 64108	CHRISTIE (LP)	12
71	CBS 64397	FOR ALL MANKIND (LP)	12

(see also Epics, Outer Limits)

JOHN CHRISTIE
74	Polydor 2058 496	4th Of July (written by Paul McCartney)/Old Enough To Know Better (some in p/s)	25/12
74	Polydor 2058 528	Everybody Knows/How Does It Feel (p/s)	5
77	EMI EMI 2726	Here's To Love/Here's To Rock'n'Roll	5

LOU CHRISTIE
63	Columbia DB 4983	The Gypsy Cried/Red Sails In The Sunset	12
63	Columbia DB 7031	Two Faces Have I/All That Glitters Isn't Gold	12
63	Columbia DB 7096	How Many Teardrops/You And I (Have A Right To Cry)	10
66	MGM MGM 1297	Lightnin' Strikes/Cryin' In The Streets	8
66	MGM MGM 1308	Rhapsody In The Rain/Trapeze	6
66	MGM MGM 1317	Painter/Du Ronda	7
66	MGM MGM 1325	If My Car Could Only Talk/Song Of Lita	10
66	Colpix PX 735	Merry Go Round/Guitars And Bongos	7
67	King KG 1036	Outside The Gates Of Heaven/All That Glitters Isn't Gold	7
67	CBS 2718	Shake Hands And Walk Away Cryin'/Escape	6
67	CBS 2922	Gina/Back To The Days Of The Romans	8
69	Buddah 201 057	I'm Gonna Make You Mine/I'm Gonna Get Married	6
69	Buddah 201 073	She Sold Me Magic/Are You Gettin' Any Sunshine?	6
69	MGM MGM 1492	Lightnin' Strikes/Cryin' In The Streets (reissue)	5
70	Buddah 201 081	Love Is Over/Generation	5
70	Buddah 2011 016	Sweet London Lady/Down When It's Up, Up When It's Down	5
70	Buddah 2011 052	Indian Lady/Glory River	5
71	Buddah 2011 074	Waco/Lighthouse	5
71	Buddah 2011 111	I'm A Song, Sing Me/Paper Me	5
71	Buddah 2011 127	Why Do Fools Fall In Love?/I'm Gonna Get Married	5
72	Buddah 2011 148	Shuffle On Down To Pittsburgh/I'm Gonna Get Married	7
73	CTI CTS 4002	Beyond The Blue Horizon/Hey You Cajun	7
75	Buddah BDS 431	I'm Gonna Make You Mine/Mickey's Monkey	5
75	Elektra K 12188	Summer Days/The One And Only Original Sunshine Kid	5
76	Elektra SEPC 4471	Riding In My Van/Summer In Malibu	5
76	Midland International MID 6	You're Gonna Make Love To Me/Fantasies	5
66	MGM MGM-C(S) 8008	LIGHTNIN' STRIKES (LP)	25
66	Colpix PXL 551	STRIKES AGAIN (LP)	20
69	Buddah 203 029	I'M GONNA MAKE YOU MINE (LP)	15
71	Buddah 2318 035	PAIN AMERICA LOVE (LP)	15
74	CTI CTL 24	LOU CHRISTIE (LP)	15

CHRISTIE BROTHERS STOMPERS
51	Melodisc 1173	Heebie Jeebies/Creole Song (78)	8
51	Melodisc 1196	Salutation Stomp/Bogalousa Moan (78)	8
51	Melodisc 1204	Black Cat/Hiawatha Rag (78)	8
51	Esquire 10-160	Ai Ai Ai/Bucket's Got A Hole In It (78)	8
52	Melodisc 1234	Old Fashioned Love/Fly Cat Boogie (78)	8
59	Parlophone GEP 8719	TOGETHER AGAIN (EP)	15
60	Esquire EP233	RUM & COCA COLA (EP)	25
60	Esquire EP243	STOMPIN' (EP)	25

KEITH CHRISTIE
54	Esquire 20-047	HOMAGE TO THE DUKE (LP)	40

TONY CHRISTIE (& TRACKERS)
66	CBS 202097	Life's Too Good To Waste/Just The Two Of Us	6
67	MGM MGM 1365	Turn Around/When Will I Ever Love Again?	6
68	MGM MGM 1386	I Don't Want To Hurt You Anymore/Say No More	6
68	MGM MGM 1440	My Prayer/I Need You	6
73	MCA MKS 5101	Avenues And Alleyways/I Never Was A Child	5

DEREK CHRISTIEN
70	Major Minor MM 676	When A Woman Has A Baby/Please Don't Go Away	6
70	Major Minor MM 713	Suddenly There's A Valley/I'll Be Coming Home	100

(see also Christien Brothers)

CHRISTIEN BROTHERS
69	Major Minor MM 628	I Reached For You/Answer Me	6

KEITH CHRISTMAS
69	RCA Victor SF 8059	STIMULUS (LP, with Mighty Baby)	50
70	B&C CAS 1015	FABLE OF THE WINGS (LP)	15
71	B&C CAS 1041	PIGMY (LP, gatefold sleeve)	15
74	Manticore K 53503	BRIGHTER DAY (LP, with inner sleeve)	15
76	Manticore K 53509	STORIES FROM THE HUMAN ZOO (LP, with insert)	15

(see also Mighty Baby, Esperanto Rock Orchestra, Magic Muscle)

JUNE CHRISTY
55	Capitol CL 14355	Pete Kelly's Blues/Kicks	6
55	Capitol EAP 516	SOMETHING COOL (EP)	10
54	Capitol LC 6682	SOMETHING COOL (10" LP)	20
56	Capitol T 725	JUNE CHRISTY (LP)	15
57	Capitol T 833	JUNE — FAIR AND WARMER (LP)	15
58	Capitol T 902	GONE FOR THE DAY (LP)	15
58	Capitol T 1006	JUNE CHRISTY (LP)	15
59	Capitol (S)T 1076	JUNE'S GOT RHYTHM (LP)	15
59	Capitol (S)T 1114	THE SONG IS JUNE (LP)	15
59	Capitol T 1202	JUNE CHRISTY RECALLS THOSE KENTON DAYS (LP)	15
60	Capitol (S)T 1308	BALLADS FOR NIGHT PEOPLE (LP)	15
61	Capitol (S)T 1398	COOL SCHOOL (LP, with Joe Castro Quartet)	15

(see also Stan Kenton)

CHROME
80	Siren/Red RS 12007	READ ONLY MEMORY (12" EP, some with poster)	12/10
80	Beggars Banquet BEG 36	New Age/Information (p/s)	6
81	D. F. O. T. Mountain Y3	INWORLDS (12" EP)	12
82	D. F. O. T. Mountain Z17	Firebomb/Shadows Of A Thousand Years (p/s)	8
80	Beggars Banquet BEGA 15	RED EXPOSURE (LP, with inner sleeve)	12
80	Beggars Banquet BEGA 18	HALF MACHINE LIP MOVES (LP, some with poster insert)	15/12
81	D. F. O. T. Mountain X6	BLOOD ON THE MOON (LP, with inner sleeve)	12
82	D. F. O. T. Mountain X18	3RD FROM THE SUN (LP, with insert)	12

CHRON GEN
81	Gargoyle GRGL 780	PUPPETS OF WAR (EP)	7
81	Gargoyle/Fresh GRGL 780	PUPPETS OF WAR (EP, reissue, silver & black label)	6
81	Step Forward SF 19	Reality/Subway Sadist (p/s)	5
82	Secret SEC 3	LIVING NEXT DOOR TO ALICE (EP, some with *Chronic Generation Oi* magazine No. 1)	8/5
82	Secret SHH 129	Jet Boy Jet Girl/Abortions/Subway Sadist (p/s)	5
82	Secret SHH 139	Outlaw/Behind Closed Doors/Disco (p/s)	5
83	Secret SEC 3	CHRONIC GENERATION (LP)	12

CHRONICLE
78	SRT SRTX 78 CUS 251	TWO SIDES OF CHRONICLE (LP, private pressing)	12

CHUBBY & HONEYSUCKERS
66	Rio R 75	Emergency Ward/LEN & HONEYSUCKERS: One More River	8

CHUBUKOS
73	Mainstream MSS 303	Witch Doctor Bump/House Of The Rising Funk	8

CHUCK & BETTY
59	Brunswick 05815	Sissy Britches/Come Back Little Girl	35
59	Brunswick 05815	Sissy Britches/Come Back Little Girl (78)	35

CHUCK (Josephs) & DOBBY (Dobson)
60	Blue Beat BB 19	Til The End Of Time/DUKE REID & HIS GROUP: What Makes Honey	15
60	Blue Beat BB 23	Cool School/DUKE REID & HIS GROUP: Joker	15
61	Starlite ST45 043	Sad Over You/Sweeter Than Honey	15
61	Starlite ST45 044	Lovey Dovey/Sitting Square	15
61	Blue Beat BB 39	Du Du Wap/I Love My Teacher (with Aubrey Adams & Du Droppers)	15
61	Blue Beat BB 59	Oh Fanny/Running Around	15
64	Blue Beat BB 246	Tell Me/I'm Going Home	15

CHUCK & GARY
58	HMV POP 466	Teenie Weenie Jeanie/Can't Make Up My Mind	50
58	HMV POP 466	Teenie Weenie Jeanie/Can't Make Up My Mind (78)	35

CHUCK & GIDEON
63	Parlophone R 5011	Cherry Berry Lips/The Tender Touch	6

CHUCK & JOE WHITE
64	Ska Beat JB 180	Punch You Down/TOMMY McCOOK: Cotton Tree	18
65	Island WI 201	Low Minded People/Irene	18

(see also Joe White & Chuck)

CHUCKLES
72	Duke DU 144	Reggae Limbo/ZAP POW: Broken Contract	10

CHUCK

MINT VALUE £

CHUCK
63	Decca F 11569	Loo Be Loo/Anytime Is The Right Time	6
63	Decca F 11617	Mulberry Bush/That's All I Needed	6
63	Decca F 11777	The Hitch Hiker/Humpity Dumpity	6
64	Decca DFE 8562	THE CHUCKS (EP)	30

CHUMBAWAMBA
85	Agitprop AGIT 001	REVOLUTION (EP)	8
86	Agitprop AGIT 002	We Are The World/State Of Mind (p/s)	6
88	Agitprop AGIT 003	Fight The Alton Bill/Smash Clause 28 (p/s)	5
94	One Little Indian 119TP 12	HOMOPHOBIA (12" EP, with 4 prints)	8
86	Agitprop PROP 001	PICTURES OF STARVING CHILDREN SELL RECORDS(LP)	12
87	Agitprop PROP 002	NEVER MIND THE BALLOT: HERE'S THE REST OF YOUR LIFE (LP)	12
88	Agitprop PROP 003	ENGLISH REBEL SONGS 1381 — 1914 (10" LP)	15

MIKIE CHUNG & NOW GENERATION
72	Green Door GD 4032	Breezing/NOW GENERATION: Breezing — Version	10
73	Duke DU 163	Stoned In Love/CHOSEN FEW: Stoned In Love	6
73	Duke DU 164	It's Too Late/CHOSEN FEW: It's Too Late	6

CHURCH
82	Carrere CAR 212	Unguarded Moment/Busdriver (p/s)	5
82	Carrere CAR 247	Almost With You/Life Speeds Up (p/s)	5
82	Carrere CAR EP 257	Unguarded Moment/Interlude/Golden Dawn/Sisters (10", p/s)	8
83	Carrere CHURCH R5A	Different Man/I Am A Rock (no p/s)	7
83	Carrere CHURCH 5	SING SONGS (12" EP)	10
86	Bucketfull Of Brains BOB 9	Warm Spell (flexidisc with *Bucketfull Of Brains* magazine)	6/5
86	Bucketfull Of Brains BOB 9	Warm Spell (hard vinyl test pressing, 20 copies only)	20
88	Bucketfull Of Brains BOB 19	Texas Moon (flexidisc with *Bucketfull Of Brains* magazine)	6/5
88	Arista 659 778CD	Under The Milky Way/Musk/The Warm Spell (CD, picture disc)	8
88	Arista 208895	STARFISH (LP, with bonus 5-track numbered 12")	15

EUGENE CHURCH
59	London HL 8940	Miami/I Ain't Goin' For That (triangular or round centre)	50/25
59	London HL 8940	Miami/I Ain't Goin' For That (78)	70

CHICK CHURCHILL
73	Chrysalis CHR 1051	YOU AND ME (LP)	15

(see also Ten Years After, Cozy Powell, Jethro Tull, Bernie Marsden)

SAVANNAH CHURCHILL
53	Brunswick 05218	Shake A Hand/Shed A Tear (78)	25
61	London HLW 9273	I Want To Be Loved/Time Out For Tears	8

SIR WINSTON CHURCHILL
65	HMV ALP 2081	THE STATE FUNERAL OF WINSTON CHURCHILL (LP)	15
65	Decca LXT 6200	THE VOICE OF WINSTON CHURCHILL (LP)	15

CHURCH OF RAISM
89	Creation CRELP 057	CHURCH OF RAISM (LP, with book, *Raism* by James Havoc)	12

CICCONE YOUTH
86	Blast First BFFP 8	Into The Groovy/Tuff Titty Rap (12", p/s)	8

(see also Sonic Youth)

CICERO
92	Spaghetti CIOCD 1	Heaven Must Have Sent You Back To Me/(Melt Mix)/Pukka (Elevation Mix) (CD)	12
92	Spaghetti CIOCD 3	Love Is Everywhere/Love Is Everywhere (Extended)/Mind Gap (Extended) (CD)	8
92	Spaghetti CIOCD 4	That Loving Feeling (7" Mix)/That Loving Feeling (Extended Mix)/	
		Splatt (Extended Mix) (CD)	8
92	Spaghetti CIAOCD 5	Heaven Must Have Sent You Back To Me (Remix)/	
		(Extended Remix)/Jungilism (CD)	8
93	Spaghetti 513 428-1	FUTURE BOY (LP)	12
93	Spaghetti 513 428-2	FUTURE BOY (CD)	18

(see also Pet Shop Boys)

CIGARETTES
78	Dead Good KEVIN 1	THE CIGARETTES (EP, unreleased)	
79	Company CIGCO 008	They're Back Again, Here They Come/I've Forgot My Number/	
		All We Want Is Your Money (gatefold p/s, red or later black labels)	30/25
80	Dead Good DEAD 10	Can't Sleep At Night/It's The Only Way To Live (Die) (p/s)	25

CIM(M)AR(R)ONS
70	Hot Rod HR 105	Grandfather Clock/Kick Me Or I Kick You (as Cimarrons)	8
70	Reggae REG 3003	Bad Day At Black Rock (with Cimmaron Kid)/Fragile	8
71	Big Shot BI 562	Funky Fight/You Turned Me Down	5
71	Spinning Wheel SW 107	Soul For Sale/Bogus-ism	6
71	Downtown DT 486	Oh Mammy Blue/Oh Mammy Blue — Version	5
71	Downtown DT 487	Holy Christmas/Silent Night/White Christmas	5
82	IMP IMPS 50	With A Little Luck/Peggy Sue (p/s)	10
82	Safari SAFE 49	Big Girls Don't Cry/How Can I Prove Myself To You	6
82	Safari SAFEL 49	Big Girls Don't Cry/How Can I Prove Myself To You/Poor People Of Paris (12")	12
82	Safari SAFELX 49	Big Girls Don't Cry/How Can I Prove Myself To You/	
		Poor People Of Paris (12", clear vinyl picture disc)	15
83	Cimarons CIM 001	Love And Affection/Bombs And Buns	10
83	Cimarons 12CIM 001	Love And Affection/Bombs And Buns (12", company sleeve)	15
82	Pickwick SHM 3106	REGGAEBILITY (LP)	15

(see also Reaction, Winston Groovy)

LOS CINCOS (RICARDOS)
65	Philips BF 1436	One Big Kiss/Something	5
65	Philips BF 1461	La Yenka/Too Big For Her Boots	5
66	Philips BF 1525	Most Exclusive Residence For Sale/It's All Over Now (as Los Cincos)	5

CINDERELLAS
59	Brunswick 05794	Mister Dee-Jay/Yum Yum Yum	30
59	Brunswick 05794	Mister Dee-Jay/Yum Yum Yum (78)	30
60	Philips PB 1012	The Trouble With Boys/Puppy Dog	12

CINDERELLAS
64	Colpix PX 11026	Baby, Baby (I Still Love You)/Please Don't Wake Me	50

(see also Cookies)

CINDERS
63	Warner Bros WB 86	The Cinnamon Cinder/C'mon Wobble	7

(see also Darlene Love)

CINDY & BARBIE DOLLS
80	Not Major NOTEM 1	ISN'T SHOWBIZ WONDERFUL (EP, foldout poster p/s)	6

CINDY & BERT
74	BASF BA 1004	Spanish Guitars/Our Summer Song Of Love	8

CINDY & LINDY
57	HMV POP 409	The Language Of Love/Tell Me Something Sweet	6
57	HMV POP 409	The Language Of Love/Tell Me Something Sweet (78)	10
59	Coral Q 72368	Saturday Night In Tiajuana/The Wonder That Is You	7
59	Coral Q 72368	Saturday Night In Tiajuana/The Wonder That Is You (78)	15

CINDYTALK
91	Fourth Dimension	In Sunshine/SPLINTERED: Mouth Clamp (numbered freebie with *Grim Humour* magazine, Vol. 2 No. 1)	7/5
95	Touched FEEL 01	Prince Of Lies (922 copies only)	6
84	Midnight CHIME 00.065	CAMOUFLAGE HEART (LP, with inner sleeve)	10

(see also This Mortal Coil)

CINEMATICS
80s	Pulsebeat CINE 001	FAREWELL TO THE PLAYGROUND (EP, foldover p/s)	25

(see also Razorcuts)

CINNAMON
69	Beacon BEA 111	You Won't See Me Leaving/Leaves Of Love	5

ROBERT CINNAMOND
75	Topic 12T 269	YOU RAMBLING BOYS OF PLEASURE (LP)	12

CINNAMON QUILL
69	Morgan MRS 17	Girl On A Swing/Take It Or Leave It	8
69	Morgan MRS 21	Candy/Hello, It's Me	8

GIGLIOLA CINQUETTI
64	Decca F 21882	Non Ho L'Eta Per Amarti/Sei Un Bravo Ragazzo	5
65	Decca F 12344	Dio Come Ti Amo/Vuoi	5

CIRCLE
60s	Circle GR 1	IN AID OF THE MILLFIELD BUILDING FUND (EP, private pressing)	225

CIRCLES
66	Island WI 279	Take Your Time/Don't You Love Me No More	55

(see also Plastic Penny, Savages, Tony Dangerfield & Thrills, Screaming Lord Sutch)

CIRCLES
72	Sioux SIOUX 017	Mammy Blue/POOCH JACKSON & HARRY J. ALLSTARS: King Of The Road	5

(see also Bob Andy)

CIRCLES
79	Graduate GRAD 4	Opening Up/Billy (p/s)	10
80	Vertigo ANGRY 1	Angry Voices/Summer Nights (p/s)	8
80	Chrysalis CHS 2418	Opening Up/Billy (p/s, reissue)	8
85	Graduate GRAD 17	Circles/Summer Nights (p/s)	10

CIRCUS
67	Parlophone R 5633	Gone Are The Songs Of Yesterday/Sink Or Swim	12
68	Parlophone R 5672	Do You Dream/House Of Wood	40
69	Transatlantic TRA 207	CIRCUS (LP, gatefold sleeve)	50

(see also Philip Goodhand-Tait)

CIRCUS MAXIMUS
67	Vanguard VSD 79260	CIRCUS MAXIMUS (LP)	20
68	Vanguard VSD 79274	NEVERLAND REVISITED (LP)	20

CIRKUS
80	Guardian GRCA 4	Melissa/Amsterdam/Pick Up A Phone (EP)	20
73	RCB 1	CIRKUS ONE (LP, private pressing with gatefold sleeve)	120
77	Shock SHOCK 1	FUTURE SHOCK (LP)	40
86	Five Hours Back TOCK 1	CIRKUS ONE (LP, reissue, gatefold sleeve)	12

CIRRUS
81	Jet JET 123	Rollin' On/Keep On Rolling (p/s, oblong-shaped brown vinyl)	12

CITATIONS
63	Columbia DB 7068	Moon Race/Slippin' And Slidin'	20

CITY OF WESTMINSTER STRING BAND
68	Pye 7N 17620	A Touch Of Velvet And A Sting Of Brass/Tommy Tucker	6

MINT VALUE £

CITY RAMBLERS SKIFFLE GROUP

57	Tempo A 158	Ella Speed/2.19 Blues	15
57	Tempo A 158	Ella Speed/2.19 Blues (78)	20
57	Tempo A 161	Mama Don't Allow/Tom Dooley	12
57	Tempo A 161	Mama Don't Allow/Tom Dooley (78)	18
57	Tempo A 165	Delia's Gone/Boodle-Am Shake	15
57	Tempo A 165	Delia's Gone/Boodle-Am Shake (78)	18
57	Storyville SEP 327	I WANT A GIRL (EP)	40
57	Storyville SEP 345	I SHALL NOT BE MOVED (EP)	40
57	Tempo EXA 59	I WANT A GIRL (EP)	30
57	Tempo EXA 71	GOOD MORNING BLUES (EP)	30
57	Tempo EXA 77	DELIA'S GONE (EP)	30

(see also Henrik Johansen)

CITY SMOKE
66	Mercury MF 971	Sunday Morning/A Little Bit Of Love	5

CITY WAITES
74	EMI EMI 2149	The Fox/One Of My Aunts	6
74	EMI EMC 3027	A GORGEOUS GALLERY OF GALLANT INVENTIONS (LP)	30
76	Decca SKL 5264	THE CITY WAITES (LP)	40
81	Hyperion A 66008	HOW THE WORLD WAGS (LP, gatefold sleeve, possibly some with insert)	70

C-JAM BLUES
66	Columbia DB 8064	Candy/Stay At Home Girl	15

CLAGUE
69	Dandelion S 4493	Mandy Lee/Bottle Up And Go (with Kevin Coyne)	7

(see also Coyne-Clague, Kevin Coyne, Siren)

GARY CLAIL
86	World WR 009	Half Cut For Confidence/Half A Gram A Shout (12", p/s)	8

CLAN
72	Deram DM 356	Pretty Belinda/Ode To Karen	5

(see also Junior Campbell)

CLANCY BROTHERS & TOMMY MAKEM
63	CBS (S)BPG 62164	THE BOYS WON'T LEAVE THE GIRLS ALONE (LP)	12
63	CBS BPG 62192	IN PERSON AT CARNEGIE HALL (LP)	12
66	CBS (S)BPG 62674	ISN'T IT GRAND BOYS (LP)	12
67	CBS (S) 62775	FREEDOM'S SONS (LP)	12
68	CBS 63393	SING OF THE SEA (LP)	18
69	CBS 63516	A SPONTANEOUS PERFORMANCE RECORDING (LP)	12

CLANCY'S ALLSTARS
68	Pama PM 722	C.N. Express (Parts 1 & 2) (B-side actually "You Were Meant For Me" by Lee Perry)	18

(see also Owen Gray)

CLANNAD
86	RCA PB 4035	In A Lifetime (with Bono)/Indoor (p/s)	6
86	RCA PB 4035T	In A Lifetime (with Bono)/Indoor (12", p/s, some with poster)	12/8
89	RCA PB 42995	In A Lifetime (with Bono)/Something To Believe In (p/s)	5
89	RCA PA 42995	In A Lifetime (with Bono)/Something To Believe In (picture disc)	10
89	RCA PB PD42995	In A Lifetime (with Bono)/Something To Believe In/Caislean Oir/ The Wild Cry/Atlantic Realm (CD)	10

(see also U2)

JIMMY CLANTON
58	London HLS 8699	Just A Dream/You Aim To Please (as Jimmy Clanton & His Rockets)	15
58	London HLS 8699	Just A Dream/You Aim To Please (78)	20
58	London HL 7066	A Letter To An Angel/A Part Of Me (as Jimmy Clanton & Aces) (export issue)	18
59	London HLS 8779	A Letter To An Angel/A Part Of Me (as Jimmy Clanton & Aces)	30
59	London HLS 8779	A Letter To An Angel/A Part Of Me (78)	35
59	Top Rank JAR 189	My Own True Love/Little Boy In Love	8
59	Top Rank JAR 189	My Own True Love/Little Boy In Love (78)	60
60	Top Rank JAR 269	Go, Jimmy, Go/I Trusted You	10
60	Top Rank JAR 382	Another Sleepless Night/I'm Gonna Try	7
60	Top Rank JAR 509	Come Back (To Me)/Wait	8
61	Top Rank JAR 544	What Am I Gonna Do/If I	10
62	Stateside SS 120	Venus In Blue Jeans/Highway Bound	10
63	Stateside SS 159	Darkest Street In Town/Dreams Of A Fool	8
65	Stateside SS 410	Hurting Each Other/Don't Keep Your Friends Away	20
69	London HLP 10289	Curly/I'll Never Forget Your Love	6
59	London RES 1224	JUST A DREAM (EP)	75

CLAP
79	SRTS SRTS/79/CUS	Hey Little Girl/20 Watts Of Power (p/s)	10

CLAPHAM SOUTH ESCALATORS
81	Upright UP YOUR 1	Get Me To The World On Time/Leave Me Alone/Cardboard Cut Outs (p/s)	15

(see also Meteors)

ERIC CLAPTON

66	Purdah 45-3502	Lonely Years/Bernard Jenkins (with John Mayall, 500 copies only)	250
70	Polydor 2001 096	I Am Yours (unissued)	
70	Polydor 2001 096	After Midnight/Easy Now	10
74	RSO 2090 139	Willie And The Hand Jive/I Can't Hold Out Much Longer (p/s)	6
76	RSO 2090 208	Hello Old Friend/All Our Pastimes (p/s)	12
80	RSO JON 1	Wonderful Tonight (live)/Further On Up The Road (live) (promo only)	15
80	RSO JONX 1	Wonderful Tonight (live)/Further On Up The Road (live) (12", numbered p/s)	15
81	RSO RSO 75	Another Ticket/Rita Mae (p/s)	8
83	Duck W 9651	Slow Down Linda/Crazy Mountain Hop (p/s)	6
83	Duck W 9701P	The Shape You're In/Crosscut Saw (picture disc)	8
85	Duck W 8954	She's Waiting/Jail Bait (p/s)	10
87	Duck W 8461F	Behind The Mask/Grand Illusion//Crossroads (live)/White Room (live) (double pack, gatefold p/s)	8
87	Duck W 8397F	It's In The Way That You Use It/Bad Influence//Behind The Mask/ Grand Illusion (double pack, shrinkwrapped with sticker)	10
87	Duck W 8299TP	Tearing Us Apart (with Tina Turner)/Hold On/Run (live) (12", p/s)	7
88	Polydor PZCD 8	After Midnight (Extended Version)/I Can't Stand It/Whatcha Gonna Do/ Sunshine Of Your Love (CD, card sleeve)	12
89	BBC RSL 178	Edge Of Darkness/Shoot Out (with Michael Kamen, p/s)	8
89	BBC 12 RSL 178	Edge Of Darkness/Shoot Out/Obituary/Escape From Northmoor/ Oxford Circus/Northmoor (with Michael Kamen, 12", p/s)	10
89	BBC CD RSL 178	Edge Of Darkness/Shoot Out/Obituary/Escape From Northmoor/ Oxford Circus/Northmoor (with Michael Kamen, 3" CD with adaptor, 5" case)	15
89	Duck W 2644B	Bad Love/I Shot The Sheriff (live) (box set with family tree & 2 colour prints)	6
90	Duck W 2644CD	Bad Love/Badge (live)/Let It Rain (live) (CD)	12
90	Duck W 9981B	No Alibis/Running On Faith (box set with 2 live photos & metal Strat badge)	6
90	Duck W 9981CD	No Alibis/Running On Faith/Behind The Mask (live)/Cocaine (CD)	10
90	Duck W 9970CD	Pretending/Hard Times/Knock On Wood/Behind The Sun (CD)	10
70	Polydor 2383 021	ERIC CLAPTON (LP)	12
73	RSO 2479 702	CLAPTON (LP, withdrawn)	45
74	RSO QD 4801	461 OCEAN BOULEVARD (LP, quadrophonic)	15
82	RSO RSDX 3	TIME PIECES (2-LP, unissued)	
83	WEA W 37734	MONEY AND CIGARETTES (cassette, with interview)	12
84	Aston PD 20118	TOO MUCH MONKEY BUSINESS (LP, picture disc, with Yardbirds)	15
99	Reprise SAM 00189	A SELECTION FROM THE BEST OF (CD, 9-track sampler, promo only)	20

(see also Yardbirds, John Mayall, Cream, Blind Faith, Delaney & Bonnie, Derek & The Dominos, Viv Stanshall, King Curtis, Randy Crawford)

ALAN CLARE GROUP

62	Parlophone R 4938	Screwball/Love For Sale	6
65	Pye 7N 15764	Dog's Body/Mulligatawny	6
56	Decca DFE 6368	THE IMPROVISATIONS OF... (EP)	60
56	Decca DFE 6391	ALAN CLARE TRIO WITH BOB BURNS (EP)	50
58	Decca LK 4260	JAZZ AROUND THE CLOCK (LP)	50
68	Decca SKL 4965	YOUNG GIRL (LP)	12

KENNY CLARE

67	Columbia DB 8216	If I Were A Buddy Rich Man/Hum-Drum	5

KENNY CLARE & RONNIE STEPHENSON

67	Studio Two TWO 146	DRUM SPECTACULAR (LP, also mono Columbia SX 6168)	12

CLARENDONIANS

65	Ska Beat JB 219	Muy Bien (My Friend)/You Are A Fool	15
66	Ska Beat JB 261	Doing The Jerk/You Won't See Me	15
66	Island WI 284	Try Me One More Time/Can't Keep A Good Man Down	18
66	Island WI 3005	I'll Never Change/Rules Of Life	18
67	Island WI 3032	Shoo-Be-Doo-Be (I Love You)/Sweet Heart Of Beauty	18
67	Island WI 3041	You Can't Be Happy/Goodbye Forever	18
67	Studio One SO 2004	The Table's Going To Turn/I Can't Go On	18
67	Studio One SO 2007	He Who Laughs Last/GAYLADS: Just A Kiss From You	18
67	Studio One SO 2017	Love Me With All Your Heart/Love Don't Mean Much To Me	18
67	Rio R 112	Rudie Bam Bam/Be Bop Boy	12
67	Rio R 115	Musical Train/Lowdown Girl	12
68	Caltone TONE 114	Baby Baby/Bye Bye Bye	12
69	Duke DU 97	Come Along/Try To Be Happy	8
69	Gas GAS 131	When I Am Gone/She Brings Me Joy	6
70	Trojan TR 7714	Lick It Back/BEVERLEY'S ALLSTARS: Busy Bee	7
70	Trojan TR 7719	Baby Don't Do It/BEVERLEY'S ALLSTARS: Touch Down	7
71	Green Door GD 4009	Seven In One (Medley) (both sides)	5
72	Attack ATT 8039	Bound In Chains/STUD ALLSTARS: Version	5
72	Pama PM 847	This Is My Story/VAL BENNETT: Caledonia	5
73	Pama PM 856	Good Hearted Woman/CORNELL CAMPBELL: What Happens	5
73	Techniques TE 925	Just One Look/Sinner Man	5
73	Dragon DRA 1006	Walking Up A One Way Street/DYNAMITES: Instrumental	6

(see also Lee & Clarendonians, Desmond Baker & Clarendonians, Four Aces, Prince Buster, Dennis Walks)

ALICE CLARK

69	Action ACT 4520	You Got A Deal/Say You'll Never	8

CHRIS CLARK

67	Tamla Motown TMG 591	Love's Gone Bad/Put Yourself In My Place	25
67	Tamla Motown TMG 624	From Head To Toe/The Beginning Of The End	20
68	Tamla Motown TMG 638	I Want To Go Back There Again/I Love You	15
68	T. Motown (S)TML 11069	SOUL SOUNDS (LP)	75

MINT VALUE £

CLAUDINE CLARK

62	Pye International 7N 25157	Party Lights/Disappointed	7
63	Pye International 7N 25186	Walk Me Home From The Party/Who Will You Hurt?	7
67	Sue WI 4039	The Strength To Be Strong/Moon Madness	18

DAVE CLARK FIVE

62	Ember EMB S 156	Chaquita/In Your Heart (grey/pink or red/yellow labels)	40/35
62	Piccadilly 7N 35088	First Love/I Walk The Line	35
62	Piccadilly 7N 35500	That's What I Said/I Knew It All The Time	35
63	Columbia DB 7011	The Mulberry Bush/Chaquita	25
63	Columbia DB 7112	Do You Love Me/Doo-Dah	6
63	Columbia DB 7154	Glad All Over/I Know You	5
64	Columbia DB 7210	Bits And Pieces/All Of The Time	5
64	Columbia DB 7291	Can't You See That She's Mine/Because	5
64	Columbia DB 7335	Thinking Of You Baby/Whenever You're Around	5
64	Columbia DB 7377	Any Way You Want It/Crying Over You	6
65	Columbia DB 7453	Everybody Knows/Say You Want Me	7
65	Columbia DB 7503	Reelin' And Rockin'/Little Bitty Pretty One	5
65	Columbia DB 7580	Come Home/Mighty Good Loving (some in p/s)	15/6
65	Columbia DB 7625	Catch Us If You Can/Move On	6
65	Columbia DB 7744	Over And Over/I'll Be Yours	6
66	Columbia DB 7863	Try Too Hard/All Night Long	7
66	Columbia DB 7909	Look Before You Leap/Please Tell Me Why	6
66	Columbia DB 8028	Nineteen Days/I Need Love	6
67	Columbia DB 8152	You Got What It Takes/Sitting Here Baby	6
67	Columbia DB 8194	Tabatha Twitchit/Man In A Pin-Striped Suit (some in export p/s)	15/6
67	Columbia DB 8286	Everybody Knows/Concentration Baby	6
68	Columbia DB 8342	No One Can Break A Heart Like You/You Don't Want My Lovin'	6
68	Columbia DB 8465	The Red Balloon/Maze Of Love	6
68	Columbia DB 8505	Live In The Sky/Children	6
69	Columbia DB 8545	The Mulberry Tree/Small Talk	7
69	Columbia DB 8591	Get It On Now/Maze Of Life (unreleased, acetates exist)	
69	Columbia DB 8624	Put A Little Love In Your Heart/34-06.	6
69	Columbia DB 8638	Good Old Rock'N'Roll Medley (Parts 1 & 2) (some in p/s)	8/5
70	Columbia DB 8660	Everybody Get Together/Darling I Love You	6
70	Columbia DB 8681	Julia/Five By Five	10
70	Columbia DB 8689	Here Comes Summer/Break Down And Cry	6
70	Columbia DB 8724	Play More Good Old Rock'N'Roll Medley (Parts 1 & 2) (some in p/s)	8/5
71	Columbia DB 8749	Southern Man/If You Wanna See Me Cry	7
71	Columbia DB 8791	Won't You Be My Lady/Into Your Life	7
72	Columbia DB 8963	All Time Greats Medley (Glad All Over/Do You Love Me/Bits & Pieces/ Glad All Over)/Wild Weekend (p/s).	12
75	EMI EMI 2307	Here Comes Summer/Break Down & Cry (reissue)	5
76	EMI EMI 2456	Glad All Over/Break Down And Cry	6
77	Polydor 2058 953	Everybody Knows/Always Me (some in p/s)	12/6
93	EMI EM 8	Glad All Over/Good Old Rock'n'Roll (p/s)	5
93	EMI EMCT 8	Glad All Over/Good Old Rock'n'Roll (cassette)	5
64	Columbia SEG 8289	THE DAVE CLARK FIVE (EP)	15
65	Columbia SEG 8381	THE HITS OF THE DAVE CLARK FIVE (EP)	25
65	Columbia SEG 8447	WILD WEEKEND (EP)	25
64	Columbia 33SX 1598	SESSION WITH THE DAVE CLARK FIVE (LP, blue/black label)	25
64	Ember FA 2003	DAVE CLARK FIVE AND THE WASHINGTON D.C.'s (LP)	35
65	EMI Regal REG 2017	IN SESSION (LP, export issue)	40
65	Columbia SX 1756	CATCH US IF YOU CAN (LP, soundtrack, blue/black label)	35
67	Columbia SX 6105	THE DAVE CLARK FIVE'S GREATEST HITS (LP, blue/black label)	25
68	Columbia SX 6207	EVERYBODY KNOWS (LP, blue/black label)	30
68	M. For Pleasure MFP 1260	A SESSION WITH THE DAVE CLARK FIVE (LP, reissue, different sleeve)	12
69	Columbia SX 6309	5 BY 5 1964-69: 14 TITLES BY THE DAVE CLARK FIVE (LP, blue/black label)	30
70	Columbia SCX 6437	IF SOMEBODY LOVES YOU (LP)	30
71	Starline SRS 5090	PLAYS GOOD OLD ROCK AND ROLL (LP)	12
93	EMI EMTV 751/2	GLAD ALL OVER AGAIN (2-LP)	15

(see also Dave Clark & Friends, Smith D'Abo, Mike Smith, Washington D.C.s)

DAVE CLARK & FRIENDS

71	Columbia DB 8834	Draggin' The Line/One Eyed, Blues Suited, Gun Totin' Man	6
72	Columbia DB 8862	Think Of Me/Right Or Wrong	8
72	Columbia DB 8907	Rub It In/I'm Sorry Baby	5
73	EMI EMI 2013	Sweet City Woman/Love Comes But Once	5
73	EMI EMI 2082	Sha-Na-Na/I Don't Know	5
74	EMI EMI 2205	Rub It In/I'm Sorry Baby (reissue)	5
72	Columbia SCX 6494	DAVE CLARK AND FRIENDS (LP)	20

(see also Dave Clark Five)

DEE CLARK

59	London HL 8802	Nobody But You/When I Call On You	20
59	London HL 8802	Nobody But You/When I Call On You (78)	35
59	London HL 8915	Just Keep It Up (And See What Happens)/Whispering Grass (Don't Tell The Trees)	25
59	London HL 8915	Just Keep It Up (And See What Happens)/Whispering Grass (Don't Tell The Trees) (78)	45
59	Top Rank JAR 196	Hey, Little Girl/If It Wasn't For Love	18
59	Top Rank JAR 196	Hey, Little Girl/If It Wasn't For Love (78)	60
60	Top Rank JAR 284	How About That/Blues Get Off My Shoulder	12
60	Top Rank JAR 373	At My Front Door/Cling-A-Ling	18
60	Top Rank JAR 501	Gloria/You're Looking Good	7
61	Top Rank JAR 551	Your Friends/Because I Love You	7
61	Top Rank JAR 570	Raindrops/I Want To Love You	12

MINT VALUE £

62	Columbia DB 4768	Don't Walk Away From Me/You're Telling Our Secrets	18
63	Stateside SS 180	I'm A Soldier Boy/Shook Up Over You	15
64	Stateside SS 355	Heartbreak/Warm Summer Breeze	10
65	Stateside SS 400	T.C.B./It's Impossible	15
70	Liberty LBF 15334	Where Did All The Good Times Go?/24 Hours Of Loneliness	10
60	Top Rank BUY 044	HOW ABOUT THAT! (LP)	35
70	Joy JOYS 130	YOU'RE LOOKING GOOD (LP)	12

DOTTY CLARK
| 61 | London HLX 9418 | It's Been A Long, Long Time/That's A Step In The Right Direction | 7 |

GENE CLARK
67	CBS 202523	Echoes/I Found You	15
74	Asylum AYM 536	No Other/The True One	5
74	Asylum AYM 540	Life's Greatest Fool/From A Silver Phial	5
88	Bucketfull of Brains BOB 18	Gypsy Rider/SEERS: Flyaway (flexidisc with *Bucketfull Of Brains* magazine, issue 24)	7/5
92	Demon GENE 1	GENE CLARK AND CARLA OLSON SING 3 SONGS BY THE BYRDS (CD, picture disc, no inlay, promo only)	12
67	CBS 62934	GENE CLARK WITH THE GOSDIN BROTHERS (LP)	25
72	A&M AMLS 64297	WHITE LIGHT (LP)	20
74	Asylum SYL 9020	NO OTHER (LP)	15
77	RSO 2394 175	TWO SIDES TO EVERY STORY (LP)	12
84	Making Waves SPIN 122	FIREBYRD (LP)	12

(see also Byrds, Dillard & Clark)

GUY CLARK
| 75 | RCA Victor APL1-130 | OLD NO. 1 (LP) | 15 |
| 76 | RCA Victor RS 1097 | TEXAS COOKIN' (LP) | 15 |

JAMES CLARK(E) + SOUNDS
| 68 | Fontana TF 918 | "A Man Of Our Times" T.V. Series Theme/Spring Bossa | 5 |
| 68 | Fontana SFJL 966 | A MAN OF OUR TIMES (LP) | 20 |

JIMMY 'SOUL' CLARK
| 76 | Black Magic BM 115 | Sweet Darlin'/Sweet Darlin' (Instrumental) | 5 |

LOUIS CLARK
79	Jet JET 151	Escape/Departure (p/s)	5
80	Jet JET 7031	Hooked On Christmas/Motif (p/s)	5
79	Jet JETLP 218	PER-SPEK-TIV (LP)	15

(see also E.L.O.)

MICHAEL CLARK
| 66 | Liberty LIB 5893 | None Of These Girls/Work Out | 10 |

PAUL CLARK & FRIENDS
| 77 | Myrrh MYR 1054 | GOOD TO BE HOME (LP, with inner sleeve) | 15 |
| 78 | Myrrh MYR 1059 | HAND TO THE PLOUGH (LP) | 15 |

PETULA CLARK
78s
50	Polygon P 1002	You Are My True Love/You're The Sweetest In The Land (B-side with Stargazers) (78)	8
51	Polygon P 1003	Beloved Be Faithful/Fly Away Peter, Fly Away Paul (78)	8
51	Polygon P 1004	Tennessee Waltz/Sleepy Eyes (78)	8
51	Polygon P 1005	Teasin'/Black Note Serenade (78)	8
51	Polygon P 1008	May Kway/Clickety Clack (78)	8
51	Polygon P 1009	Mariandl/Broken Heart (with Jimmy Young) (78)	8
51	Polygon P 1021	Cold Cold Heart/That's How A Love Song Is Born (78)	8
52	Polygon P 1022	Tell Me Truly/Song Of The Mermaid (78)	8
52	Polygon P 1043	It Had To Be You/The Card (78)	8
52	Polygon P 1048	A Boy In Love/Fly Away Peter, Fly Away Paul (78)	8
52	Polygon P 1057	Made In Heaven/Temptation Rag (78)	7
53	Polygon P 1063	My Love Is A Wanderer/Take Care Of Yourself (78)	7
53	Polygon P 1072	Christopher Robin At Buckingham Palace/Three Little Kittens (78)	7
53	Polygon P 1082	Poppa Piccolino/The Who-Is-It Song (78)	7
54	Polygon P 1121	A Long Way To Go/Meet Me In Battersea Park (78)	8
54	Polygon P 1135	Little Johnny Rainbow/Christmas Cards (78)	8
54	Polygon P 1146	Majorca/Fascinating Rhythm (78)	8
55	Polygon P 1164	Romance In Rome/Chee Chee-Oo-Chee (78)	8
55	Polygon P 1169	Crazy Otto Rag (with Joe Henderson)/Pendulum Song (78)	8
55	Polygon P 1179	How Are Things With You?/Tuna Puna Trinidad (78)	8
56	Pye Nixa N 15024	The Little Shoemaker/Someday (78)	8
56	Pye Nixa N 15026	Majorca/Fascinating Rhythm (78, reissue)	8
56	Pye Nixa N 15040	Band Of Gold/Memories Are Made Of This (78)	8
56	Pye Nixa N 15041	To You My Love/Fortune Teller (78)	8
56	Pye Nixa N 15073	A Million Stars Above/Another Door Opens (78)	8
57	Pye Nixa N 15086	Who Needs You?/The Sky (78)	8
57	Pye Nixa N 15135	Love Me Again/In A Little Moment (78)	8
58	Pye Nixa N 15126	Baby Lover/The Little Blue Man (78)	6
58	Pye Nixa N 15135	Love Me Again/In A Little Moment (78)	8
58	Pye Nixa N 15152	St. Tropez (Sur La Plage)/Devotion (78)	8
58	Pye Nixa N 15168	I Wish I Knew/Fibbin' (78)	8
59	Pye Nixa N 15182	Ever Been In Love/Lucky Day (78)	8
59	Pye Nixa N 15191	Watch Your Heart/Suddenly (78)	8
59	Pye Nixa N 15208	Where Do I Go From Here?/Mama's Talking Soft (78)	8
59	Pye Nixa N 15220	Adonis/If I Had My Way (78)	8
59	Pye Nixa N 15230	Dear Daddy/Through The Livelong Day (78)	10
59	Pye N 15244	I Love A Violin/Guitare Et Tambourin (78)	15

Petula CLARK

SINGLES

57	Pye Nixa 7N 15096	With All My Heart/Gonna Find Me A Bluebird	15
57	Pye Nixa 7N 15112	Alone/Long Before I Knew You	6
58	Pye Nixa 7N 15126	Baby Lover/The Little Blue Man	6
58	Pye Nixa 7N 15135	Love Me Again/In A Little Moment	7
58	Pye Nixa 7N 15152	St. Tropez (Sur La Plage)/Devotion	8
58	Pye Nixa 7N 15168	I Wish I Knew/Fibbin'	7
59	Pye Nixa 7N 15182	Ever Been In Love/Lucky Day	7
59	Pye Nixa 7N 15191	Watch Your Heart/Suddenly	7
59	Pye Nixa 7N 15208	Where Do I Go From Here?/Mama's Talking Soft	8
59	Pye Nixa 7N 15220	Adonis/If I Had My Way	8
59	Pye Nixa 7N 15230	Dear Daddy/Through The Livelong Day	10
59	Pye 7N 15244	I Love A Violin/Guitare Et Tambourin	12
60	Pye 7N 15281	Cinderella Jones/All Over Now	8
61	Pye 7N 15324	Sailor/My Heart	5
61	Pye 7N 15337	Something Missing/Isn't This A Lovely Day?	7
61	Pye 7N 15355	Welcome Home/Les Gens Diront	7
61	Pye 7N 15361	Romeo/You're Getting To Be A Habit With Me	5
61	Pye 7N 15389	My Friend The Sea/With All My Love	5
62	Pye 7N 15407	I'm Counting On You/Some Other World	6
62	Pye 7N 15437	Whistlin' For The Moon/Tender Love	6
62	Pye 7N 15448	Ya Ya Twist/Si C'est Oui, C'est Oui	5
62	Pye 7N 15456	Jumble Sale/Too Late	5
62	Pye 7N 15478	The Road/No Love, No Nothin'	6
63	Pye 7N 15495	I Will Follow Him/Darling Cheri	6
63	Pye 7N 15517	Valentino/Imagination	6
63	Pye 7N 15522	Chariot/Casanova	5
63	Pye 7N 15551	Let Me Tell You/Be Good To Me	6
63	Pye 7N 15573	Baby It's Me/This Is Goodbye	6
64	Pye 7N 15606	Thank You/Crying Through A Sleepless Night	8
64	Pye 7N 15639	In Love/Forgetting You (J'ai Tout Oublié)	6
64	Pye 7N 15668	True Love Never Runs Smooth/Saturday Sunshine	6
65	Pye 7N 15722	Downtown/You'd Better Love Me	5
65	Pye 7N 15772	I Know A Place/Jack And John	5
65	Pye 7N 15864	You'd Better Come Home/My Heart	5
65	Pye 7N 15945	Round Every Corner/Two Rivers	5
65	Pye 7N 15991	You're The One/Gotta Tell The World (some in export p/s)	15/5
66	Pye 7N 17038	My Love/Where I'm Going	5
66	Pye 7N 17071	A Sign Of The Times/Time For Love	6
66	Pye 7N 17133	I Wouldn't Live Without Your Love/Your Way Of Life	5
66	Pye 7N 17187	Who Am I/Love Is A Long Journey	6
66	Pye 7N 17218	Colour My World/I'm Begging You	6
67	Pye 7N 17258	This Is My Song/The Show Is Ours	5
67	Pye 7N 17325	Don't Sleep In The Subway/Here Comes The Morning	5
67	Pye 7N 17377	The Cat In The Window/Fancy Dancin' Man	6
67	Pye 7N 17416	The Other Man's Grass/At The Crossroads	5
68	Pye 7N 17466	Kiss Me Goodbye/I've Got Love Going For Me	5
68	Pye 7N 17580	Don't Give Up/Everytime I See A Rainbow	5
68	Pye 7N 17646	I Want To Sing With Your Band/Look To The Sky	5
69	Pye 7N 17733	Happy Heart/Love Is The Only Thing	5
69	Pye 7N 17779	Look At Mine/You And I	5
69	Pye 7N 17840	No One Better Than You/Things Bright And Beautiful	5
70	Pye 7N 17973	Melody Man/Big Love Sale	5
71	Pye 7N 45026	The Song Of My Life/For Love	5
71	Pye 7N 45091	The World Song/I Know What Love Is About	5
71	Pye 7N 45112	I Don't Know How To Love Him/Song Went Wrong	5
72	Polydor 2058 295	Wedding Song (There Is Love)/Song Without End	6
73	Polydor 2058 413	Lead Me On/Taking It On (both with Sacha Distel)	12
74	Polydor 2058 519	Let's Sing A Love Song/I'm The Woman You Need	8
75	Polydor 2058 560	I Am Your Song/Super Loving Lady	12
75	Pye 7N 45473	Wind Of Change (edit)/Memories Are Made Of This	6
75	Pye 7N 45506	What I Did For Love/I Believe In Love	6
76	Pye 7N 45650	Downtown (Disco Version)/Two Rivers	8
78	Lyntone	Put A Little Sunbeam In Your Life (flexidisc for Sunbeam cars)	6
78	CBS S 6103	I'm Not In Love/What Am I Doing Here?	5
78	CBS S 6245	Put A Little Sunbeam In Your Life/Songbird	5
78	CBS S 6781	(Life Is) Just A Dance With Time/Don't Stop The Music	6
81	Epic EPC A 1475	Edelweiss/Darkness	8
81	Scotti Bros DB 081	Edelweiss/Darkness	6
82	Scotti Bros SCTA 1645	Natural Love/Because I Love Him	6
82	Scotti Bros SCTA 2904	Dreamin' With My Eyes Wide Open/Afterglow	6
84	PRT 7P 323	Mr Orwell (English Language)/Glamoureuse	6
87	PRT PYS 1	Downtown/I Know A Place (p/s)	5
88	Fly EAGLE 2	Life's A Game/How (p/s)	6
89	Legacy LGYCD 100	I Couldn't Live Without Your Love ('89 Mix — Extended)/(7" Version)/(Original Version)/Come On Home/Call Me '89 ('65 Vocal) (CD)	20
90	First Night SCORE 23	Someone Like You (with Dave Willetts)/Getting The Right Thing Wrong (p/s)	7

EPs

56	Pye Nixa NEP 24006	CHILDREN'S CHOICE (EP)	30
56	Pye Nixa NEP 24016	PETULA CLARK HIT PARADE (EP)	20
57	Pye Nixa NEP 24056	PETULA CLARK HIT PARADE NO. 2 (EP)	10
57	Pye Nixa NEP 24060	YOU ARE MY LUCKY STAR PART 1 (EP)	18
57	Pye Nixa NEP 24061	YOU ARE MY LUCKY STAR PART 2 (EP)	18
57	Pye Nixa NEP 24062	YOU ARE MY LUCKY STAR PART 3 (EP)	18
58	Pye Nixa NEP 24080	PETULA CLARK HIT PARADE NO. 3 (EP)	10
58	Pye Nixa NEP 24089	PETULA CLARK SINGS IN FRENCH (EP)	15
58	Pye Nixa NEP 24094	A CHRISTMAS CAROL (EP, also stereo NSEP 85001)	15/25

59	Pye NEP 24121	ENCORE (EP)	10
61	Pye NEP 24137	PETULA CLARK HIT PARADE 4 (EP)	10
61	Pye NEP 24150	PETULA CLARK HIT PARADE 5 (EP)	10
61	Pye NEP 24163	PETULA CLARK'S HITS (EP)	8
62	Pye NEP 24157	PET-OOH-LA-LA (EP)	10
63	Pye NEP 24182	EN FRANÇAIS (EP)	15
64	Pye NEP 24189	ENCORE EN FRANÇAIS (EP)	15
64	Pye NEP 24194	PETULA SINGS 'HELLO DOLLY!' IN FRENCH (EP)	15
65	Pye NEP 24206	DOWNTOWN (EP)	10
65	Pye-Vogue VRE 5004	LES DISQUES D'OR DE LA CHANSON (EP)	12
65	Pye-Vogue VRE 5007	PETULA CLARK CHANTE EN ITALIEN (EP)	15
65	Pye NEP 24233	YOU'RE THE ONE (EP, existence unconfirmed)	30+
66	Pye NEP 24237	CALL ME (EP)	10
66	Pye NEP 24246	MY LOVE (EP)	8
66	Pye NEP 24259	JUST SAY GOODBYE (EP)	10
66	Pye NEP 24266	I COULDN'T LIVE WITHOUT YOUR LOVE (EP)	10
67	Pye NEP 24279	THIS IS MY SONG (EP)	8
66	Pye-Vogue VRE 5019	L'AGENT SECRET (EP)	12
66	Pye-Vogue VRE 5023	HELLO MISTER BROWN (EP)	12
67	Pye-Vogue VRE 5025	C'EST MA CHANSON (EP)	12
67	Pye NEP 24280	THE MANY FACES OF PETULA CLARK (EP)	10
67	Pye NEP 24286	HERE, THERE AND EVERYWHERE (EP)	10
68	Pye-Vogue VRE 5026	L'AMOUR VIENDRA (EP)	10
68	Pye-Vogue VRE 5028	DIS-MOI AU REVOIR (EP)	10
68	Pye NEP 24301	DON'T GIVE UP (EP)	10

LPs

56	Pye Nixa NPT 19002	PETULA CLARK SINGS (10" LP)	80
56	Pye Nixa NPT 19014	A DATE WITH PET (10" LP)	70
57	Pye Nixa NPL 18007	YOU ARE MY LUCKY STAR (LP)	50
59	Pye Nixa NPL 18039	PETULA CLARK IN HOLLYWOOD (LP)	45
62	Pye NPL 18070	IN OTHER WORDS — PETULA CLARK (LP)	35
63	Pye NPL 18098	PETULA (LP)	20
64	Pye-Vogue VRL 3001	LES JAMES DEAN (LP)	20
65	Pye NPL 18114	DOWNTOWN (LP)	12
65	Pye N(S)PL 18118	THE NEW PETULA CLARK ALBUM (LP)	12
65	Pye NPL 18123	SINGS THE INTERNATIONAL HITS (LP)	12
65	Pye-Vogue VRL 3010	PETULA '65 (LP, in French)	25
66	Pye-Vogue VRL 3016	HELLO PARIS VOL. 1 (LP)	20
66	Pye-Vogue VRL 3019	HELLO PARIS VOL. 2 (LP)	20
66	Pye NPL 18141	MY LOVE (LP)	12
66	Pye N(S)PL 18148	I COULDN'T LIVE WITHOUT YOUR LOVE (LP)	12
66	Pye-Vogue VRL 3022	PETULA '66 (LP)	15
67	Pye N(S)PL 18159	PETULA CLARK'S HIT PARADE (LP)	12
67	Pye N(S)PL 18171	COLOUR MY WORLD (LP, original track listing, with "England Swings" & "Reach Out I'll Be There")	15
67	Pye N(S)PL 18171	COLOUR MY WORLD (LP, revised track listing, with "This Is My Song" & "The Show Is Over")	12
67	Pye-Vogue VRL 3030	C'EST MA CHANSON (LP)	12
67	Pye N(S)PL 18197	THESE ARE MY SONGS (LP)	12
68	Pye N(S)PL 18211	THE OTHER MAN'S GRASS IS ALWAYS GREENER (LP)	12
68	Warner Bros WF(S) 2550	FINIAN'S RAINBOW (LP, soundtrack)	20
68	Pye-Vogue VRLS 3035	PETULA CLARK A PARIS (LP)	15
68	Pye N(S)PL 18235	PETULA (LP)	12
69	Pye N(S)PL 18282	PETULA CLARK'S HIT PARADE VOL. 2 (LP)	12
69	Pye NSPL 18292	PORTRAIT OF PETULA (LP)	12
69	MGM CS 8113	GOODBYE MR CHIPS (LP, soundtrack, gatefold sleeve)	20
69	Pye NSPL 18325	JUST PET (LP)	12
69	Pye-Vogue VRLS 3039	PETULA CLARK (LP, in French)	12
70	Pye NSPL 18345	MEMPHIS (LP)	12
71	Pye NSPL 18363	THE SONG OF MY LIFE (LP)	12
71	Pye Special PKL 5502	TODAY (LP)	12
71	Pye NSPL 18370	PETULA '71 (LP)	15
72	Pye NSPL 18391	LIVE AT THE ROYAL ALBERT HALL (LP)	12
73	Polydor 2383 170	NOW (LP)	12
75	Polydor 2384 068	JUST PETULA (LP)	12
74	Pye 11PP 101	DEVOTION (4-LP set)	25
74	Polydor 2383 279	COME ON HOME (LP)	12
74	Polydor 2383 303	LIVE IN LONDON (LP)	15
75	Polydor 2383 324	I'M THE WOMAN YOU NEED (LP)	18
75	Pet Projects PP 1	NOEL (LP, International Petula Clark Society issue)	50
76	Pet Projects PP 2	BEAUTIFUL SOUNDS (LP, International Petula Clark Society issue)	50
78	CBS 82608	DESTINY (LP)	12
81	Epic EPC 70212	THE SOUND OF MUSIC (THE ORIGINAL 1981 CAST ALBUM) (LP, gatefold sleeve)	12
87	PRT PYL 7002	THE HIT SINGLES COLLECTION (2-LP, gatefold sleeve)	15

ROY CLARK

59	HMV POP 581	Please Mr. Mayor/Puddin'	60
59	HMV POP 581	Please Mr. Mayor/Puddin' (78)	80
63	Capitol CL 15288	In The Mood/Texas Twist	8
63	Capitol CL 15317	Tips Of My Fingers/Spooky Movies	6
69	Dot DOT 126	Yesterday When I Was Wrong/Just Another Man	5
69	Dot DOT 131	September Song/For All The Life Of Me	5
62	Capitol (S)T 1780	THE LIGHTNING FINGERS OF ROY CLARK (LP)	20

MINT VALUE £

SANFORD CLARK

56	London HLD 8320	The Fool/Lonesome For A Letter (with Al Casey) (gold label print, later silver)	120/60
56	London HL 7014	The Fool/Lonesome For A Letter (with Al Casey) (export issue)	35
56	London HLD 8320	The Fool/Lonesome For A Letter (78)	25
59	London HLW 8959	Run, Boy Run/New Kind Of Fool (triangular or round centre)	25/15
59	London HLW 8959	Run, Boy Run/New Kind Of Fool (78)	60
60	London HLW 9026	Son-Of-A-Gun/I Can't Help It (If I'm Still In Love With You)	15
60	London HLW 9095	Go On Home/Pledging My Love	15
68	Ember EMB S 250	Shades/Once Upon A Time	8
68	Speciality SPE 1004	Shades/Once Upon A Time (reissue)	5
57	London RED 1105	PRESENTING SANFORD CLARK (EP)	75
60	London REW 1256	LOWDOWN BLUES (EP)	60
72	Ember CW 131	THEY CALL ME COUNTRY (LP)	18

(see also Al Casey)

TERRY CLARK

78	Myrrh MYR 1071	WELCOME (LP)	15

ALLAN CLARKE

72	RCA RCA 2244	You're Losing Me/A Coward By Name	8
73	EMI EMI 2024	Who/I Look In Your Eyes	5
74	EMI EMI 2133	Sideshow/Don't Let Me Down Again	5
75	EMI EMI 2352	Born To Run/Why Don't You Call	5
76	EMI EMI 2491	Living In Love/People Of That Kind	5
78	Polydor 2058 979	I Don't Know When I'm Beat/The Passenger	8
78	Polydor 2059 025	I'm Betting My Life On You/I Wasn't Born Yesterday	5
79	Aura AUS 108	Shadow In The Street/No Prisoner Taken	6
79	Aura AUS 109	I Wasn't Born Yesterday/New Blood	6
80	Aura AUS 121	The Only Ones/The Survivor	6
81	Aura AUS 125	Walls/Baby Blue	6
81	Aura AUS 129	Born To Run/If I Were The Priest	6
82	Aura AUS 130	Shadow In The Street/If You Walked Away	6
82	Forever FORE 3	Someone Else Will/Castles In The Wind	10
72	RCA SF 8283	MY REAL NAME IS 'AROLD (LP)	12
73	EMI EMA 752	HEADROOM (LP)	12
74	EMI EMC 3041	ALLAN CLARKE (LP)	12
76	EMI EMC 3130	I'VE GOT TIME (LP)	12
78	Aura AUL 704	I WASN'T BORN YESTERDAY (LP)	12
80	Aura AUL 711	THE ONLY ONES (LP)	12
81	Aura AUL 718	THE BEST OF ALLAN CLARKE (LP)	12

(see also Hollies)

ANNETTE CLARKE

73	Techniques TE 925	Just One Look/Sinner Man	6

DAVE CLARKE

94	Bush 1012	Red 1 (of 3) (Protective Custody)/Zeno Xero (12", p/s, red vinyl)	15
94	Bush 1015	Red 2 (of 3) (Wisdom To The Wise)/Gonk (12", p/s, red vinyl)	12

JOHN COOPER CLARKE

78	Rabid TOSH 103	INNOCENTS (EP, orange p/s, green labels)	5
78	Rabid TOSH 103	INNOCENTS (EP, 2nd pressing, blue foldout p/s, blue labels)	5
79	Epic S EPC 12 7009	¡Gimmix!/I Married A Monster From Outer Space (Third Version) (p/s, triangular disc, orange vinyl)	5
79	Epic S EPC 7982	Splat/Twat/Sleepwalk (double-grooved A-side, p/s, with Epic inner sleeve)	5
78	CBS 83132	DISGUISE IN LOVE (LP)	12
80	Epic EPC 84083	SNAP, CRACKLE [&] BOP (LP, with 48-page book in sleeve pocket)	12

JOHNNY CLARKE

74	Explosion EX 2089	None Shall Escape The Judgement/Every Rasta Is A Star	5
74	Pyramid PYR 7013	My Desire/Lemon Tree	5
75	Attack ATLP 1015	ENTER INTO HIS GATES WITH PRAISE (LP)	10
75	Vulcan VULP 001	PUT IT ON (LP)	10

KENNY CLARKE (with Francy Boland Big Band)

57	Columbia SEG 7830	KENNY CLARKE QT. (EP)	8
63	London HA-K 8085	JAZZ IS UNIVERSAL (LP, with Francy Boland Big Band)	15
71	Polydor 2460 131	AT HER MAJESTY'S PLEASURE (LP, with Francy Boland)	12
72	Polydor 2310 147	OFF LIMITS (LP)	12

LINDA CLARKE

67	Decca F 12709	Your Hurtin' Kinda Love/Send Me The Pillow You Dream On	5
68	Decca F 12787	Society's Child/Rain In My Heart	5

LLOYD CLARKE

62	Blue Beat BB 99	Good Morning/Now I Know A Reason (with Smithie's Sextet)	15
62	Blue Beat BB 104	Fool's Day/You're A Cheat (with Reco's All Stars)	15
62	Island WI 007	Love You The Most/LLOYD ROBINSON: You Said You Loved Me	18
62	Island WI 045	Japanese Girl/He's Coming	18
63	Rio R 16	Love Me/Half As Much	10
64	Rio R 23	Stop Your Talking/A Penny	10
64	Rio R 24	Fellow Jamaican/PATRICK & GEORGE: My Love	10
68	Island WI 3116	Summertime/VAL BENNETT: Soul Survivor	15
68	Blue Cat BS 136	Young Love/UNTOUCHABLES: Wall Flower	12
70	Escort ERT 849	Chicken Thief/STRANGER COLE: Tomorrow	6
71	Black Swan BW 1405	Love You The Most/LOW BITES:Version	12

(see also Derrick & Lloyd, Theo Beckford, Soulettes, Delroy Wilson, Laurel Aitken, Sonny Burke, Uniques)

CLASH

TONY CLARKE
64	Pye International 7N 25251	Ain't Love Good, Ain't Love Proud/Coming Back Strong	12
65	Chess CRS 8011	The Entertainer/This Heart Of Mine	15
69	Chess CRS 8091	The Entertainer/Ain't Love Good, Ain't Love Proud	10
74	Chess 6145 030	Landslide/The Entertainer	5

VINCE CLARKE & PAUL QUINN
85	Mute TAG 1	One Day/Song For (p/s)	5
85	Mute 12TAG 1	One Day (Extension)/Song For (Extension) (12", p/s)	8

(see also Erasure, Yazoo, Paul Quinn)

CLARK-HUTCHINSON
70	Decca Nova (S)DN-R 2	A = MH^2(LP)	25
70	Deram SML 1076	RETRIBUTION (LP)	25
71	Deram SML 1090	GESTALT (LP)	25

(see also Sam Gopal, Vamp, Upp)

CLARK SISTERS
59	London HLD 8791	Chicago/Opus 1	10
59	London HLD 8791	Chicago/Opus 1 (78)	10
58	London RE-D 1198	SING, SING, SING (EP)	15
58	London HA-D 2128	SING, SING, SING (LP)	20
59	London HA-D 2177	THE CLARK SISTERS SWING AGAIN (LP, also stereo SAH-D 6025)	18/22

CLASH
77	CBS S CBS 5058	White Riot/1977 (p/s, 'The Clash' or 'The CLASH' on label)	10
77	CBS CL 1	CAPITAL RADIO (EP, *NME* freebie, p/s)	40
77	CBS S CBS 5293	Remote Control/London's Burning (live) (p/s)	10
77	CBS S CBS 5664	Complete Control/The City Of The Dead (p/s)	6
78	CBS S CBS 5834	Clash City Rockers/Jail Guitar Doors (p/s)	5
78	CBS S CBS 6383	(White Man) In Hammersmith Palais/The Prisoner (initially green, then pink, blue or yellow die-cut sleeve)	5
78	CBS S CBS 6788	Tommy Gun/1, 2, Crush On You (p/s)	5
79	CBS S CBS 7082	English Civil War/Pressure Drop (p/s)	5
79	CBS S CBS 7324	THE COST OF LIVING (EP, gatefold p/s & inner sleeve)	8
79	CBS S CBS 8087	London Calling/Armagideon Time (p/s, green or red shaded sleeve, white or yellow/orange label)	5

(All the early Clash singles were re-pressed in 1979 with picture sleeves.)

81	CBS A12 1133	The Magnificent Seven/The Magnificent Dance (12", p/s with sticker sheet)	8
81	CBS S 2309	Know Your Rights/First Night Back In London (p/s, with free sticker)	5
82	CBS A 2479	Rock The Casbah/Long Time Jerk (p/s, with free stickers)	5
82	CBS A 11 2479	Rock The Casbah/Long Time Jerk (picture disc)	8
82	CBS A 2646	Should I Stay Or Should I Go/Straight To Hell (p/s, with free sticker)	5
82	CBS A 11 2646	Should I Stay Or Should I Go/Straight To Hell (picture disc)	5
82	CBS A 12 2646	Should I Stay Or Should I Go/Straight To Hell (12", p/s with stencil)	8
88	CBS CLASHB 2	London Calling/Brand New Cadillac/Rudie Don't Fail (box set)	7
91	Columbia 656 667-5	Should I Stay Or Should I Go/London Calling/Train In Vain/I Fought The Law (CD in tin)	10
91	Columbia 656 814-5	Rock The Casbah/Tommy Gun/(White Man) In Hammersmith Palais/Straight To Hell (CD in tin)	10
91	Columbia 656 946-5	London Calling/Clampdown/The Call Up/London's Burning (CD in tin)	8
78	CBS 82431	GIVE 'EM ENOUGH ROPE (LP, promo-only package with poster in folder)	50

(see also 101'ers, Big Audio Dynamite, Topper Headon, Janie Jones & Lash, Tymon Dogg, Ellen Foley, Futura 2000)

MINT VALUE £

CLASSICS (U.S.)
61	Mercury AMT 1152	Life Is But A Dream/That's The Way	70
63	Stateside SS 215	Till Then/Enie Minie Mo	15
66	Capitol CL 15470	Pollyanna/Cry Baby	8

CLASSICS (Jamaica)
69	Doctor Bird DB 1190	Worried Over Me/LAUREL AITKEN: Rice And Peas	12
70	New Beat NB 061	Same Old Feeling/So Much Love	7
70	New Beat NB 071	History Of Africa/Honeybee	6
70	Pama PM 830	Sex Education/POWER: Soul Flash	6
71	Punch PH 79	Cheerio Baby/Civilization	6

CLASSICS IV
68	Liberty LBF 15051	Spooky/Poor People	7
69	Liberty LBF 15177	Stormy/Twenty Four Hours Of Loneliness	8
69	Liberty LBF 15196	Traces/Mary, Mary Row Your Boat	5
69	Liberty LBF 15231	Everyday With You Girl/Sentimental Lady	5

(see also Dennis Yost & Classics IV)

CLASSIC SULLIVANS
| 74 | Kwanza K 19501 | Paint Yourself In The Corner/I Don't Want To Lose You | 6 |

CLASSMATES
63	Decca F 11736	Let's Get Together Tonight/It's No Game	6
63	Decca F 11779	Go Tell It On The Mountain/Give Me A Girl	6
64	Decca F 11806	In Morocco/I Feel	6
64	Decca F 12047	Go Away/Pay Day	10

CLATTERBOX
| 96 | Clear CLR 412 | CLATTERBOX (2 x 10", p/s) | 8 |

CLAUDETTE (& CORPORATION)
69	Jackpot JP 712	Let's Fall In Love/PROPHETS: Purple Moon	6
70	Grape GR 3020	Skinheads A Bash Them (with Corporation)/	
		CORPORATION: Walkin' Thru Jerusalem	20

(see also Corporation)

CASSIUS CLAY
64	CBS AAG 190	Stand By Me/I Am The Greatest	20
66	CBS 202190	Stand By Me/I Am The Greatest (reissue)	12
63	CBS BPG 62274	I AM THE GREATEST! (LP)	35

JEFFREY CLAY
55	Vogue Coral Q 72093	No Arms Can Ever Hold You/Come On Back, Come On Back	6
55	Vogue Coral Q 72113	Sweet Kentucky Rose/Unknown To Me	6
56	Vogue Coral Q 72143	These Hands/You'll Be Sorry (When Someone Else Is Glad)	6

JUDY CLAY
| 67 | Stax 601 022 | You Can't Run Away From Your Heart/It Takes A Lotta Good Love | 8 |

(see also Billy Vera & Judy Clay, Booker T. & M.G.'s)

JUDY CLAY & WILLIAM BELL
| 68 | Stax STAX 101 | Private Number/Love, Aye 'Tis | 6 |
| 69 | Stax STAX 115 | My Baby Specialises/Left Over Love | 6 |

(see also William Bell, Billy Vera & Judy Clay)

OTIS CLAY
67	President PT 121	It's Easier Said Than Done/Flame In Your Heart	5
68	President PT 132	I'm Satisfied/I Testify	5
68	President PT 148	That's How It Is/Show Place	5
68	President PT 176	A Lasting Love/Got To Find A Way	5
69	Atlantic 584 282	Baby Jane/You Hurt Me For The Last Time	40
72	London HLU 10397	Trying To Live My Life Without You/Let Me Be The One	5
74	London HLU 10467	You Did Something To Me/It Was Jealousy	5
73	London SH-U 8446	TRYING TO LIVE MY LIFE WITHOUT YOU (LP)	18

TOM CLAY
| 72 | Tamla Motown TMG 801 | What The World Needs Now/The Victors | 5 |

ALASDAIR CLAYRE
| 67 | Elektra EUK 255 | ALASDAIR CLAYRE (LP) | 45 |
| 76 | Acorn CF 252 | ADAM AND THE BEASTS (LP) | 20 |

ALAN CLAYSON & ARGONAUTS
78	Virgin VS 215	The Taster/Landwaster (live) (p/s)	5
82	Rackets ARG 36	LAST RESPECTS (EP, 33rpm, 500 only)	5
85	Butt BUTT 005	WHAT A DIFFERENCE A DECADE MADE (LP)	12

ADAM CLAYTON & LARRY MULLEN
96	Mother MUM 75	Theme From Mission: Impossible/Theme From Mission: Impossible	
		(Junior's Hard Mix Edit) (jukebox issue, no p/s, promo only)	8
96	Mother 12MUMDJ 75-1	THEME FROM MISSION: IMPOSSIBLE — REMIXES BY JUNIOR VASQUEZ	
		(12", brown die-cut sleeve with title sticker, promo only)	15
96	Mother 12MUMDJ 75-2	THEME FROM MISSION: IMPOSSIBLE — REMIXES BY GOLDIE &	
		ROB PLAYFORD (12", grey die-cut sleeve with title sticker, promo only)	15
96	Mother MUMCD 75DJ	Theme From Mission: Impossible/(Junior's Hard Mix)/(Junior's Hard Mix)/	
		Mission Accomplished — Cut The Red Not The Blue/(Dave Clarke's Remix)/	
		(Guru Mix) (CD, digipak, promo only)	12

(see also U2)

BUCK CLAYTON
60	Philips BBL 7317	SONGS FOR SWINGERS (LP)	12
66	77 LEU 12/11	LE VRAI BUCK CLAYTON VOLUME 1 (LP)	12
66	77 LEU 12/18	LE VRAI BUCK CLAYTON VOLUME 2 (LP)	12
68	CBS Realm RM 52078	A BUCK CLAYTON JAM SESSION (LP)	12

BUCK CLAYTON & JOE TURNER
73	Black Lion 2460 303	FEEL SO FINE (LP)	12

(see also Joe Turner)

DOCTOR CLAYTON
65	RCA Victor RCX 7177	RCA RACE SERIES VOLUME 6 (EP)	15
70	RCA Intl. INTS 1176	PEARL HARBOUR BLUES (LP)	15

MERRY CLAYTON
70	A&M AMS 802	Gimme Shelter/Good Girls	5
73	Ode ODS 66301	Acid Queen (p/s)	6
70	A&M AMLS 995	GIMME SHELTER (LP)	15
72	A&M AMLS 67012	MERRY CLAYTON (LP)	15

(see also Raelets)

PAUL CLAYTON
61	London HLU 9285	Wings Of A Dove/So Long (It's Been Good To Know You)	10
61	London REU 1276	PAUL CLAYTON (EP)	75

STEVE CLAYTON
56	Vogue Coral Q 72200	Two Different Worlds/It Happened Again	6
57	Vogue Coral Q 72253	The Boy With The Golden Kazoo/I Wanna Put My Arms Around You	6
60	London HLU 9033	Let's Tell Them Now/They Say In Time	6

VIKKI CLAYTON
88	Dambuster DAM 021	LOST LADY FOUND (LP)	20

(see also Fairport Convention)

CLAYTON SQUARES
65	Decca F 12250	Come And Get It/And Tears Fell	25
66	Decca F 12456	There She Is/Imagination	60

(see also Liverpool Scene, Andy Roberts, Mike Hart)

DAVID CLAYTON-THOMAS
72	CBS 64755	DAVID CLAYTON-THOMAS (LP, plain orange label)	15
72	CBS 65237	TEQUILA SUNRISE (LP, plain orange label)	15
73	RCA SF 8381	DAVID CLAYTON-THOMAS (LP, gatefold sleeve)	15

(see also Blood Sweat & Tears)

CLEANLINESS & GODLINESS SKIFFLE BAND
68	Vanguard SVRL 19043	GREATEST HITS (LP)	12

CLEAR BLUE SKY
71	Vertigo 6360 013	CLEAR BLUE SKY (LP, gatefold sleeve, spiral label)	40
90	Saturn SRLP 101	DESTINY (LP)	12

CLEAR LIGHT
67	Elektra EKSN 45019	Black Roses/She's Ready To Be Free	8
68	Elektra EKSN 45027	Night Sounds Loud/How Many Days Have Passed	6
67	Elektra EKL 4011	CLEAR LIGHT (LP, orange label, also stereo EKS 74011)	30

CLEARLIGHT
75	Virgin V 2029	FOREVER BLOWING BUBBLES (LP)	15
75	Virgin V 2039	SYMPHONY (LP, stickered sleeve)	15

(see also Gong, Steve Hillage)

CLEARWAYS
64	Columbia DB 7333	I'll Be Here/I've Just Got A Letter	6

JOHN CLEESE (& 1948 CHOIR)
67	Pye 7N 17336	The Ferret Song — From 'At Last The 1948 Show'/The Rhubarb Tart Song	7
67	Parlophone PMC 7024	I'M SORRY I'LL READ THAT AGAIN (LP)	18

(see also Monty Python)

CLEFS
62	Salvo SLO 1010	Don't Cry/The Dream Train Special (99 copies only)	18

CLEFTONES
56	Columbia DB 3801	You Baby, You/Little Girl Of Mine	450
56	Columbia DB 3801	You Baby, You/Little Girl Of Mine (78)	80
61	Columbia DB 4678	Heart And Soul/How Do You Feel	135
61	Columbia DB 4720	(I Love You) For Sentimental Reasons/Deed I Do	70
63	Columbia DB 4988	Lover Come Back To Me/There She Goes	70

PAT CLEMENCE
64	HMV POP 1360	While I Live/Since I Don't Have You	6

JACK CLEMENT
58	London HLS 8691	Ten Years/Your Lover Boy	45
58	London HLS 8691	Ten Years/Your Lover Boy (78)	40

SOUL JOE CLEMENTS
69	Plexium PXM 10	Smoke And Ashes/Ever, Ever	100

CLARENCE CLEMONS
86	CBS A 6681	You're A Friend Of Mine/Let The Music Say It (p/s, with Jackson Browne)	5
86	CBS TA 6681	You're A Friend Of Mine/Let The Music Say It (12", p/s, with Jackson Browne)	8

(see also Jackson Browne, Bruce Springsteen)

CLEO
64	Decca F 11817	To Know Him Is To Love Him/ANDREW OLDHAM ORCHESTRA: There Are But Five Rolling Stones	25

(see also Andrew Oldham Orchestra, This 'N' That)

CLERKS
80	Rok ROK VIII/VII	No Good For Me/HAZARD: Gotta Change My Life (company sleeve)	6
84	Puddisc SRT8 KS 1538	Dancing With My Girl/On The Telephone/All I Want Is You (p/s)	5

CLEVELANDS
64	Philips BF 1315	Big Town/Lonely, Weary And Blue	6
64	Philips BF 1342	Little Girl In Calico/Everything Is Fine	6

CLIENTELLE
79	Quest BRS 003	Can't Forget (p/s)	125
81	Banana BANANA 505	DESTINATION UNKNOWN (LP)	120

JIMMY CLIFF
62	Blue Beat BB 78	I'm Sorry (with Cavaliers Combo)/BLUE BEATS: Roarin' (with Red Price)	15
62	Island WI 012	Hurricane Hatty/Dearest Beverley	15
62	Island WI 016	Miss Jamaica/Gold Digger	15
62	Island WI 025	Since Lately/I'm Free	15
63	Island WI 062	My Lucky Day/One-Eyed Jacks	15
63	Island WI 070	King Of Kings/SIR PERCY: Oh Yeah	15
63	Island WI 112	Miss Universe/The Prodigal	15
63	Black Swan WI 403	The Man/You Are Never Too Old	15
64	Stateside SS 342	One Eyed Jacks/King Of Kings	12
66	Fontana TF 641	Call On Me/Pride And Passion	10
67	Island WIP 6004	Aim And Ambition/Give And Take	6
67	Island WIP 6011	I Got A Feeling/Hard Road To Travel	6
67	Island WIP 6024	That's The Way Life Goes/Thank You	6
68	Island WIP 6039	Waterfall/Reward	12
69	Trojan TR 690	Wonderful World, Beautiful People/Hard Road To Travel	5
70	Trojan TR 7722	Vietnam/She Does It Right	5
70	Trojan TR 7745	Suffering/Come Into My Life	5
70	Trojan TR 7745	Those Good Good Old Days/Pack Up Hang Ups	5
70	Trojan TR 7767	You Can Get It If You Really Want/Be Aware	5
70	Island WIP 6087	Wild World/Be Aware	5
70	Island WIP 6097	Synthetic World/I Go To Pieces	5
71	Island WIP 6103	Goodbye Yesterday/Breakdown	5
71	Island WIP 6100	Sitting In Limbo/The Bigger They Come	5
72	Island WIP 6132	Trapped/Struggling Man	5
68	Island ILP 962	HARD ROAD TO TRAVEL (LP)	45
69	Trojan TRLS 16	JIMMY CLIFF (LP)	18
71	Island ILPS 9159	ANOTHER CYCLE (LP)	12

(see also Jackie Edwards & Jimmy Cliff, James Chambers)

CLIFF & HANK
(see under Cliff Richard)

CLIFF DWELLERS
66	Polydor 56707	Hang On Stupid/I'm A Superman For You Baby	5

BUZZ CLIFFORD
61	Fontana H 297	Baby Sittin' Boogie/Driftwood (blue or black label)	10/8
61	Fontana H 312	Three Little Fishes/Simply Because	6
62	Columbia DB 4903	More Dead Than Alive/Nobody Loves Me Like You	8
61	Fontana TFL 5147	BABY SITTIN' WITH BUZZ CLIFFORD (LP, also stereo {STFL 567})	70/90

JOHN & JULIA CLIFFORD
77	Topic 12TS 311	THE HUMOURS OF LISHEEN (LP)	20

LINDA CLIFFORD
74	Paramount PARA 3051	After Loving You/Check Out Your Heart	5
78	Curtom K 17163	If My Friends Could See Me Now/Runaway Love	5
78	Curtom K 17163T	If My Friends Could See Me Now/Runaway Love (12")	8
79	RSO RSO 37	Don't Give It Up/Don't Let Me Have Another Bad Dream (12")	8

CLIFFTERS
62	Philips PB 1242	Django/Amapola (Pretty Little Poppy)	8

BILL CLIFTON
60	Melodisc 1554	You Don't Think About Me/Mail Carrier's Warning	6
63	Decca F 11793	Beatle Crazy/Little Girl Dressed In Blue	8
58	Mercury MEP 9546	BILL CLIFTON AND THE DIXIE MOUNTAIN BOYS (EP)	15
62	London HA-B 8004	CARTER FAMILY MEMORIAL ALBUM (LP)	18
62	London HA-B 8020	THE BLUEGRASS SOUND OF BILL CLIFTON (LP)	18
63	London HA-B 8070	SOLDIER SING ME A SONG (LP)	18
64	London HA-B 8193	CODE OF THE MOUNTAINS (LP)	18
67	London HA-U 8325	MOUNTAIN RAMBLINGS (LP)	18

BILL CLIFTON & JIM EANES
60s	Melodisc EPM 7102	BLUE RIVER HOEDOWN (EP)	15

CLIMAX (CHICAGO) BLUES BAND
69	Parlophone R 5809	Like Uncle Charlie/Loving Machine	15
70	Harvest HAR 5029	Reap What I've Sowed/Spoonful	5
71	Harvest HAR 5041	Towards The Sun/Everyday (as Climax Chicago)	5
72	Harvest HAR 5065	Mole On The Dole/Like Uncle Charlie (as Climax Chicago)	5
73	Harvest HAR 5067	Shake Your Love/You Make Me Sick	5
69	Parlophone PMC/PCS 7069	CLIMAX CHICAGO BLUES BAND (LP, yellow/black label)	30
70	Parlophone PCS 7084	PLAYS ON (LP)	25
70	Harvest SHSP 4009	A LOT OF BOTTLE (LP)	15
71	Harvest SHSP 4015	TIGHTLY KNIT (LP)	12
72	Harvest SHSP 4024	RICH MAN (LP)	12

PATSY CLINE

57	Brunswick 05660	A Poor Man's Roses (Or A Rich Man's Gold)/Walkin' After Midnight	50
57	Brunswick 05660	A Poor Man's Roses (Or A Rich Man's Gold)/Walkin' After Midnight (78)	40
61	Brunswick 05855	I Fall To Pieces/Lovin' In Vain	12
61	Brunswick 05861	Crazy/Who Can I Count On	20
62	Brunswick 05866	She's Got You/Strange	7
62	Brunswick 05869	When I Get Through With You/Imagine That	7
62	Brunswick 05874	So Wrong/You're Stronger Than Me	7
62	Brunswick 05878	Heartaches/Why Can't He Be You	6
63	Brunswick 05883	Leavin' On Your Mind/Tra Le La Le La Triangle	8
63	Brunswick 05888	Sweet Dreams/Back In My Baby's Arms	10
62	Brunswick OE 9490	SWEET DREAMS (EP)	25
62	Brunswick LAT 8394	SHOWCASE (LP)	25
62	Brunswick LAT/STA 8510	SENTIMENTALLY YOURS (LP, mono/stereo)	20/25
63	Brunswick LAT 8549	A TRIBUTE TO PATSY CLINE (LP)	25
64	Brunswick LAT/STA 8589	A PORTRAIT OF PATSY CLINE	
		(LP, mono/stereo)	20/25
65	Ember CW 16	IN MEMORIAM (LP)	18
65	Fontana FJL 302	TODAY TOMORROW AND FOREVER (LP)	18
66	Fontana FJL 309	I CAN'T FORGET YOU (LP)	18
68	Ember CW 134	WALKING AFTER MIDNIGHT (LP)	15
68	MCA MUP 316	THE SOUND OF PATSY CLINE (LP)	15
68	MCA MUP(S) 326	HEARTACHES (LP)	15
69	MCA MUP(S) 350	ALWAYS (LP)	15
70	MCA MUPS 378	THAT'S HOW A HEARTACHE BEGINS (LP)	15

CLINIC

97	Aladdin's Cave Of Golf GOLF 001	IPC Subeditors Dictate Our Youth/Porno/D.I.Y. (p/s, 500 copies only)	20
98	Aladdin's C.O.G. GOLF 002	Monkey On Your Back/D.T. (p/s, 500 copies only)	6
98	Aladdin's C.O.G. GOLF 003	Cement Mixer/Kimberley (p/s, 1,000 copies only)	5

BUDDY CLINTON

60	Top Rank JAR 287	Across The Street From Your House/How My Prayers Have Changed	6

GEORGE CLINTON

79	ABC ABC 4053	Please Don't Run From Me/Life And Breath	6
	(do not see also Parliament, Funkadelic)		

LARRY CLINTON

79	Grapevine GRP 120	She's Wanted In Three States/If I Knew	7

CLINTONES

73	Ackee ACK 515	Equal Rights/Version	5

CLIQUE (U.K.)

65	Pye 7N 15786	She Ain't No Good/Time Time Time	70
65	Pye 7N 15853	We Didn't Kiss, Didn't Love, But Now We Do/You've Been Unfair	140
	60s private pressing	THE CLIQUE (EP, no p/s)	500
	(see also Hammersmith Gorillas)		

CLIQUE (U.S.)

69	London HLU 10286	Sugar On Sunday/Superman	20

CLIQUE

93	Detour DR 006	THE EARLY DAYS EP (EP, purple, orange or blue p/s, 130 on green vinyl; rest on black, white or yellow vinyl	15/12
94	Detour DR 014	Reggie/She Doesn't Need You Anymore (p/s, some on red vinyl)	12/5
94	Detour DR 014	Reggie/She Doesn't Need You Anymore (pic disc, 200 only)	18

JIMMY CLITHEROE

65	Parlophone R 5387	They All Blame Jim/Jim Plays Hookies	5

CLIVE & GLORIA

63	R&B JB 113	Change Of Plan/Little Gloria	10
64	R&B JB 173	Money Money Money/Have I Told You Lately	10
64	King KG 1004	Do The Ska/You Made Me Cry	12

CLIVE & NAOMI

65	Ska Beat JB 181	You Are Mine/Open The Door	15
	(see also Desmond Dekker)		

CLOCK DVA

81	Fetish FET 008	Four Hours (Re-mixed)/Sensorium (p/s)	8
80	private cassette	DEEP FLOOR (cassette)	12
80	private cassette	FRAGMENT DVATION (cassette)	12
81	Fetish FR 2002	THIRST (LP, with insert)	12
81	Industrial IRC 31	WHITE SOULS IN BLACK SUITS (cassette, with booklet)	15
	(see also Anti Group)		

CLOCKWORK CRIMINALS

82	Ace ACE 38	YOUNG AND BOLD (EP)	12

CLOCKWORK ORANGES

66	Ember EMB S 227	Ready Steady/After Tonight	12

CLOCKWORK SOLDIERS

84	Rot ASS 5	Wet Dreams/Suicide/In The Name Of Science (p/s)	5

BETTY CLOONEY

55	HMV 7M 311	I Love You A Mountain/Can't Do Without You	8
	(see also Rosemary Clooney)		

MINT VALUE £

ROSEMARY CLOONEY

50	Columbia DB 2708	Me And My Teddy Bear/I Found My Mamma (78)	10
51	Columbia DB 2861	Shot Gun Boogie/Beautiful Brown Eyes (78)	10
51	Columbia DB 2892	Alice In Wonderland Medley (Parts 1 & 2)	10
53	Columbia DB 3240	On The First Warm Day/If Teardrops Were Pennies (78)	10
53	Columbia DB 3254	Eggbert, The Easter Egg/Little Johnny Chickadee (78)	10
53	Columbia DB 3368	Little Red Riding Hood's Xmas Tree/The Land Of Hatchy Milatchy (78)	10
53	Columbia SCM 5019	Half As Much/Botch-A-Me (Ba-Ba-Baciami Piccina)	18
53	Columbia SCM 5027	If I Had A Penny/You're After My Own Heart	10
53	Columbia SCM 5028	On The First Warm Day/If Teardrops Were Pennies	12
53	Columbia SCM 5040	(Remember Me) I'm The One Who Loves You/Lover's Gold	10
53	Columbia SCM 5049	Blues In The Night/Who Kissed Me Last Night?	12
54	Columbia SCM 5093	I Still Feel The Same About You (with Betty Clooney)/Why Fight The Feeling	10
56	Philips JB 100	The Teddy Bear's Picnic/Kitty Kat's Party (78, picture label)	10
57	Philips PB 744	You Can't Lose The Blues With Colours/That's How It Is (78)	10
57	Philips JK 1010	Mangos/All The Pretty Little Horses (jukebox issue)	15
58	Philips PB 792	I Can't Stop Crying/Love And Affection (78)	10
58	Philips PB 800	I Could Have Danced All Night/I've Grown Accustomed To Your Face	6
58	Philips PB 800	I Could Have Danced All Night/I've Grown Accustomed To Your Face (78)	10
58	MGM MGM 990	The Loudenboomer Bird/It's A Boy	6
58	MGM MGM 990	The Loudenboomer Bird/It's A Boy (78)	10
59	Philips PB 900	Tonight/Come Rain Or Come Shine	6
59	Philips PB 900	Tonight/Come Rain Or Come Shine (78)	20
59	Coral Q 72357	Diga Me (Deega May-Tell Me)/A Touch Of The Blues	6
59	Coral Q 72357	Diga Me (Deega May-Tell Me)/A Touch Of The Blues (78)	12
59	MGM MGM 1010	Love Eyes/Flattery (B-side with Jose Ferrer)	6
60	Coral Q 72388	Love, Love Away/I Wish I Were In Love Again	6
60	MGM MGM 1062	For You/I Wonder	5
60	RCA RCA 1203	Many A Wonderful Moment/Vaya, Vaya	5
54	Columbia SEG 7552	ROSEMARY CLOONEY AND HARRY JAMES (EP)	10
55	Philips BBE 12004	ROSEMARY CLOONEY (EP)	12
56	Philips BBE 12051	ROSEMARY CLOONEY (EP)	12
60	Coral FEP 2045	SWING AROUND ROSIE VOL. 1 (EP)	12
60	Coral FEP 2046	SWING AROUND ROSIE VOL. 2 (EP)	12
54	Philips BBR 8022	WHITE CHRISTMAS (10" LP)	30
55	Philips BBR 8047	ROSEMARY CLOONEY (10" LP)	25
56	Philips BBR 8073	AT THE LONDON PALLADIUM (10" LP)	25
56	Philips BBL 7090	HEY BABY (LP, with Duke Ellington)	18
57	Philips BBL 7156	RING AROUND ROSIE (LP, with Hi-Lo's)	18
57	Philips BBL 7191	CHILDREN'S FAVOURITES (LP)	18
59	Philips BBL 7301	SHOWCASE OF HITS (LP)	18
59	Coral LVA 9112	SWING AROUND ROSIE (LP)	15
61	RCA RD 27189	CLAP HANDS, HERE COMES ROSIE! (LP, also stereo SF 5075)	12
61	MGM C 838	SWINGS SOFTLY (LP)	12
63	RCA SF 7554	COUNTRY HITS FROM THE HEART (LP)	12

ROSEMARY CLOONEY & MARLENE DIETRICH

53	Columbia SCM 5010	Too Old To Cut The Mustard/Good For Nothin'	18

(see also Marlene Dietrich, Betty Clooney, Bob Hope & Rosemary Clooney)

CLOSE LOBSTERS

89	Caff CAFF 4	Just Too Bloody Stupid/All The Little Boys And Girls (p/s)	12

CLOUD

75	Kingsway DOVE 16	FREE TO FLY (LP)	20
77	Kingsway DOVE 44	WATERED GARDEN (LP, gatefold sleeve)	30
70s	private pressing	THE RESTING PLACE (LP)	25
85	Songs Of Fellow. SFR103	THE PROMISE (LP)	15

CLAUDE CLOUD

55	MGM MGM 820	Cloudburst/One Bone (78, as Claude Cloud & Thunderclaps)	20
57	MGM MGM 946	The Beat/Around The Horn (as Claude Cloud & His Orchestra)	10
55	MGM MGM-EP 517	LET'S GO CATSTATIC NO. 1 (EP, as Claude Cloud & Thunderclaps)	30
56	MGM MGM-D 142	ROCK 'N' ROLL (10" LP)	75

(see also Sonny Thompson, Sam 'The Man' Taylor)

CLOUDS

69	Island WIP 6055	Heritage/Make No Bones About It	10
69	Island WIP 6067	Scrapbook/Carpenter	10
69	Island ILPS 9100	THE CLOUDS SCRAPBOOK (LP, pink label or 'pink rim palm tree')	25/15
71	Chrysalis ILPS 9151	WATERCOLOUR DAYS (LP, gatefold sleeve, 'pink rim palm tree' label)	18

CLOUDS

86	Sha La La Ba Ba Ba 001	Throwaway/CLOUDS: Jenny Nowhere (p/s, flexi free with various fanzines)	8/6
88	Subway Org. SUBWAY 12	Tranquil/Get Out Of My Dream (p/s)	5
88	Subway Org. SUBWAY 12T	Tranquil/Get Out Of My Dream/Village Green (12", p/s)	8

(see also Boy Hairdressers, Teenage Fanclub)

CLOUT

90	Mooncrest JWL 1000	We'll Bring The House Down/Jim Jam (p/s)	7

(see also Slade)

CLOVEN HOOF

82	Elemental EM 001	OPENING RITUAL (12" EP)	45
84	Neat NEAT 1013	CLOVEN HOOF (LP)	12
88	Heavy Metal HMRLP 113	DOMINATOR (LP)	12

CLOVER

70	Liberty LBF 15341	Wade In The Water/Stealin'	8
76	Vertigo 6059 157	Chicken Funk/Show Me Your Love	5
77	Vertigo 6059 164	I Lie Awake And Dream Of You/Take Another Look	5
77	Vertigo 6059 171	Love Love/Leavin' Is	5
77	Vertigo 6059 175	Chain Gang/Streets Of London	5
77	Vertigo 6059 188	Oh Senorita/Ain't Nobody	5
77	Vertigo LYN 4277	There Is No Substitute For Real Magic (flexidisc, promo only)	7
69	Liberty LBS 83340	CLOVER (LP)	20
71	Liberty LBS 83487	FORTY-NINER (LP)	18
77	Vertigo 6360 145	UNAVAILABLE (LP)	12
77	Vertigo 6360 155	LOVE ON THE WIRE (LP)	12
	(see also Huey Lewis & News)		

CLOVERLEAFS

56	MGM MGM 933	Step Right Up And Say Howdy/With Plenty Of Money And You (Gold Digger's Lullaby)	7
	(see also Art Mooney)		

CLOVERS

56	London HLE 8229	Nip Sip/If I Could Be Loved By You (gold or silver label lettering)	800/400
56	London HLE 8229	Nip Sip/If I Could Be Loved By You (78)	75
56	London HLE 8314	Love, Love, Love/Hey, Doll Baby	550
56	London HLE 8314	Love, Love, Love/Hey, Doll Baby (78)	75
56	London HLE 8334	From The Bottom Of My Heart/Your Tender Lips	550
56	London HLE 8334	From The Bottom Of My Heart/Your Tender Lips (78)	75
58	London HL 7048	Wishing For Your Love/All About You (export issue)	220
58	London HL 7048	Wishing For Your Love/All About You (78, export issue)	60
58	HMV POP 542	In The Good Old Summertime/Idaho	25
58	HMV POP 542	In The Good Old Summertime/Idaho (78)	60
59	London HLT 8949	Love Potion No. 9/Stay Awhile (triangular or round centre)	45/25
59	London HLT 8949	Love Potion No. 9/Stay Awhile (78)	110
60	London HLT 9122	Lovey/One Mint Julep	35
60	London HLT 9154	Easy Lovin'/I'm Confessin' (That I Love You)	25
61	HMV POP 883	Honey Dripper/Have Gun	18
68	Atlantic 584 160	Your Cash Ain't Nothin' But Trash/I've Got My Eyes On You	10
69	Atlantic 587 162	LOVE BUG (LP)	40

CLUB QUINTET

60	Top Rank JAR 362	Caravelle (Secret Serenade)/Bluer Than Blue	5

CLUES

81	Clues CLU 001	NO VACANCIES (EP)	10

CLUTHA (FOLK GROUP)

71	Argo ZFB 18	SCOTIA! (LP, as Clutha Folk Group)	12
74	Topic 12TS 242	SCOTS BALLADS, SONGS AND DANCE TUNES (LP, as Clutha)	12

JEREMY CLYDE

65	CBS 201823	I Love My Love/Anytime	5
	(see also Chad & Jeremy)		

CLYDE VALLEY STOMPERS

56	Beltona BL 2648	Uist Tramping Song/Keep Right On To The End Of The Road (78)	8
56	Beltona BL 2649	I Love A Lassie/Old Rustic Bridge By The Mill (78)	8
56	Beltona BL 2650	Old Time Religion/Pearly Gates (78)	8
57	Decca FJ 10897	Bill Bailey Won't You Please Come Home (with Mary McGowan)/ Milenberg Joys	5
57	Decca FJ 10897	Bill Bailey Won't You Please Come Home (with Mary McGowan)/ Milenberg Joys (78)	8
62	Parlophone R 4928	Peter And The Wolf/Loch Lomond	6
60	Pye NJL 23	HAVE TARTAN — WILL TRAD (LP)	25
	(see also Ian Menzies)		

C.M.J.

68	Impression IMP 102	I Can't Do It All By Myself/Nothing At All	30
71	Mother MOT 3	La La La/Step Around It	10
65	Impression EPIM 501	THE C.M.J. TRIO (EP)	75
69	Impression IMPL 1001	C.M.J. LIVE AT THE BANKHOUSE (LP, private pressing)	100

C.M.U. (Contemporary Music Unit)

72	Transatlantic BIG 508	Heart Of The Sun/Doctor Am I Normal?	8
71	Transatlantic TRA 237	OPEN SPACES (LP, gatefold sleeve)	45
72	Transatlantic TRA 259	SPACE CABARET (LP)	30

CNN

90s	On ON 4 01	3-track white label (mail order only, in printed PVC cover)	8

COACHMEN

59	Vogue V 9154	Those Brown Eyes/Bald Mountain	8
59	Vogue V 9154	Those Brown Eyes/Bald Mountain (78)	30
61	Vogue VAE 170149	HERE COME THE COACHMEN (EP)	10
60	Vogue VA 16062	HERE COME THE COACHMEN (LP)	15

COACHMEN

66	Columbia DB 8057	Gabrielle/Seasons In The Sun	6

COAL PORTERS

92	Bucketfull/Brains BOB 32	Watching Bluegrass Burn/R.E.M.: Academy Fight Song (live) (p/s, vinyl or flexi, free with *Bucketfull Of Brains* magazine, 39/40)	12/5
	(see also Long Ryders, Spinning Whighats)		

COASTERS

COASTERS

57	London HLE 8450	Searchin'/Young Blood	40
57	London HL 7021	Searchin'/Young Blood	
		(export issue)	18
57	London HLE 8450	Searchin'/Young Blood (78)	18
58	London HLE 8665	Yakety Yak/Zing! Went The Strings Of My Heart	12
58	London HLE 8665	Yakety Yak/Zing! Went The Strings Of My Heart (78)	20
58	London HLE 8729	The Shadow Knows/Sorry But I'm Gonna Have To Pass	50
58	London HLE 8729	The Shadow Knows/Sorry But I'm Gonna Have To Pass (78)	50
59	London HLE 8819	Charlie Brown/Three Cool Cats	10
59	London HL 7073	Charlie Brown/Three Cool Cats (export issue)	12
59	London HLE 8819	Charlie Brown/Three Cool Cats (78)	35
59	London HLE 8882	Along Came Jones/That Is Rock And Roll (silver top label)	12
59	London HLE 8882	Along Came Jones/That Is Rock And Roll (78)	45
59	London HLE 8938	Poison Ivy/I'm A Hog For You	15

(The above 45s were originally issued with triangular centres,
later round centre copies are worth half to two-thirds these values.)

59	London HLE 8938	Poison Ivy/I'm A Hog For You (78)	70
60	London HLE 9020	What About Us/Run Red Run	10
60	London HLE 9020	What About Us/Run Red Run (78)	90
60	London HLK 9111	Besame Mucho (Parts 1 & 2)	10
60	London HLK 9111	Besame Mucho (Parts 1 & 2) (78)	120
60	London HLK 9151	Wake Me, Shake Me/Stewball	10
60	London HLK 9208	Shoppin' For Clothes/The Snake And The Bookworm	10
61	London HLK 9293	Wait A Minute/Thumbin' A Ride	8
61	London HLK 9349	Little Egypt/Keep On Rolling	7
61	London HLK 9413	Girls! Girls! Girls! (Parts 1 & 2)	7
62	London HLK 9493	(Ain't That) Just Like Me/Bad Blood	7
64	London HLK 9863	T'Ain't Nothin' To Me/Speedo's Back In Town	7
66	Atlantic 584 033	She's A Yum Yum/Saturday Night Fish Fry	7
67	Atlantic 584 087	Searchin'/Yakety Yak	6
67	CBS 2749	Soul Pad/Down Home Girl	10
68	Direction 58-3701	She Can/Everybody's Woman	6
71	Parlophone R 5931	Love Potion No. 9/D.W. Washburn	6
72	Stateside SS 2201	Cool Jerk/Talkin' 'Bout A Woman (withdrawn)	12
74	London HLZ 10437	Love Potion No. 9/D.W. Washburn (reissue)	5
59	London REE 1203	THE COASTERS (EP)	75
60	London HA-E 2237	GREATEST HITS (LP)	60
63	London HA-K 8033	COASTIN' ALONG WITH THE COASTERS (LP)	60
66	Atlantic 588 134	COASTIN' ALONG WITH THE COASTERS (LP, reissue)	25
67	Atlantic 590 015	ALL TIME GREATEST HITS (LP)	25
71	Joy JOYS 189	HUNGRY (LP)	18
74	London SHZ 8460	ON BROADWAY (LP)	15

COAST ROAD DRIVE

74	Deram SML 1113	DELICIOUS AND REFRESHING (LP)	25

ODIA COATES

75	United Artists UP 35779	Showdown/Leave Me In The Morning	5

C.O.B. (Clive's Original Band)

72	Polydor 2058 260	Blue Morning/Bones	20
71	CBS 69010	SPIRIT OF LOVE (LP, gatefold sleeve)	70
72	Polydor Folk Mill 2383 161	MOYSHE McSTIFF & THE TARTAN LANCERS OF THE SACRED HEART (LP, gatefold sleeve)	200

(see also Famous Jug Band, Incredible String Band)

COBBLERS LAST

79	Banshee BAN 1012	BOOT IN THE DOOR (LP, with insert)	100

COBBS

69	Amalgamated AMG 845	Hot Buttered Corn/COUNT MACHUKI: It Is I	10
69	Amalgamated AMG 849	Space Daughter/LLOYD & DEVON: Reggae Baby	10

JUNIE COBB'S HOMETOWN BAND

59	Collector JDL 38	Chicago Buzz/East Coast Trot	5

BILLY COBHAM

73	Atlantic K 40406	SPECTRUM (LP, gatefold sleeve)	12
74	Atlantic K 50098	TOTAL ECLIPSE (LP)	12
74	Atlantic K 50037	CROSSWINDS (LP)	12
75	Atlantic K 50147	SHABAZZ (LP)	12
75	Atlantic K 50185	A FUNKY SIDE OF THINGS (LP)	12

COBRA

78	Rip Off RIP 3	Graveyard Boogie/Looking For A Lady (p/s)	60

(see also Speed)

COCHISE

70	United Artists UP 35134	Watch This Space/59th St. Bridge Song	5
70	Liberty LBS 15425	Love's Made A Fool Of You/Words Of A Dying Man	5
71	Liberty LBF 15460	Why I Sing The Blues/Jed Colider	5
70	United Artists UAS 29117	COCHISE (LP, gatefold sleeve, burgundy label)	15
70	Liberty LBS 83428	SWALLOW TALES (LP, blue label)	15
72	United Artists UAS 29286	SO FAR (LP)	15

(see also B.J. Cole, Mick Grabham)

DIB COCHRAN & EARWIGS

70	Bell BLL 1121	Oh Baby/Universal Love	220

(see also Marc Bolan, Tyrannosaurus Rex, Tony Visconti, Rick Wakeman)

EDDIE COCHRAN

78s

57	London HLU 8386	20 Flight Rock/Dark Lonely Street (78) 70
57	London HLU 8433	Sittin' In The Balcony/Completely Sweet (78) 75
58	London HLU 8702	Summertime Blues/Love Again (78) 80
59	London HLU 8792	C'mon Everybody/Don't Ever Let Me Go (78) 80
59	London HLU 8880	Teenage Heaven/I Remember (78) 120
59	London HLU 8944	Somethin' Else/Boll Weevil Song (78) 135
60	London HLW 9022	Hallelujah, I Love Her So/Little Angel (78) 300
60	London HLG 9115	Three Steps To Heaven/Cut Across Shorty (78) 500
95	Cruisin' The 50s CASS 001	Three Steps To Heaven/Cut Across Shorty (78, reissue, 300 only) 50
96	Cruisin' The 50s CASB 004	Week-End/Cherished Memories (78, reissue, 400 only) 30

SINGLES

57	London HLU 8386	20 Flight Rock/Dark Lonely Street (triangular centre; also silver-top label with triangular centre; later round centre) 150/70/40
57	London HLU 8433	Sittin' In The Balcony/Completely Sweet 350
58	London HLU 8702	Summertime Blues/Love Again 25
59	London HLU 8792	C'mon Everybody/Don't Ever Let Me Go 25
59	London HLU 8880	Teenage Heaven/I Remember 30
59	London HL 7082	Teenage Heaven/Boll Weevil Song (export issue) 75
59	London HLU 8944	Somethin' Else/Boll Weevil Song 45
60	London HLW 9022	Hallelujah, I Love Her So/Little Angel (triangular centre, later round) 50/12

(The above singles were originally issued with triangular centres, later round centre copies are worth half these values unless stated.)

60	London HLG 9115	Three Steps To Heaven/Cut Across Shorty 10
60	London HLG 9196	Sweetie Pie/Lonely 12
61	London HLG 9362	Weekend/Cherished Memories 10
61	London HLG 9460	Jeannie, Jeannie, Jeannie/Pocketful Of Hearts 20
61	London HLG 9464	Pretty Girl/Teresa 25
61	London HLG 9467	Undying Love/Stockin's 'N' Shoes 25
62	Liberty LIB 10049	Never/Think Of Me 15
63	Liberty LIB 10088	My Way/Rock And Roll Blues 12
63	Liberty LIB 10108	Drive-In Show/I Almost Lost My Mind 20
64	Liberty LIB 10151	Skinny Jim/Nervous Breakdown 40
66	Liberty LIB 10233	C'mon Everybody/Summertime Blues 25
66	Liberty LIB 10249	Three Stars/Somethin' Else 50
67	Liberty LIB 10276	Three Steps To Heaven/Eddie's Blues 40
68	Liberty LBF 15071	Summertime Blues/Let's Get Together 12
68	Liberty LBF 15109	Somethin' Else/Milk Cow Blues 12
70	Liberty LBF 15366	C'mon Everybody/Mean When I'm Mad 12
72	United Artists UP 35361	Somethin' Else/Three Steps To Heaven 5
72	United Artists UP 35408	Summertime Blues/Cotton Picker 5
79	Rockstar RSR-SP 3001	What'd I Say/Milk Cow Blues (p/s) 5
79	Rockstar RSR-SP 3002	Skinny Jim/Half Loved (p/s) 5
80	United Artists FREE 16	"20TH ANNIVERSARY ALBUM" SAMPLER (no p/s) 8

EPs

59	London REU 1214	C'MON EVERYBODY (EP, orange sleeve, triangular or round centre) 90/75
59	London REU 1214	C'MON EVERYBODY (EP, yellow sleeve, silver-top label, round centre) 80
60	London REU 1239	SOMETHIN' ELSE (EP) 80
60	London REG 1262	EDDIE'S HITS (EP) 80
61	London REG 1301	CHERISHED MEMORIES OF EDDIE COCHRAN (EP) 80
62	Liberty LEP 2052	NEVER TO BE FORGOTTEN (EP) 45
63	Liberty LEP 2090	CHERISHED MEMORIES (VOL.1) (EP) 45
63	Liberty LEP 2111	C'MON EVERYBODY (EP, reissue) 40
63	Liberty LEP 2122	SOMETHIN' ELSE (EP, reissue) 40
63	Liberty LEP 2123	CHERISHED MEMORIES OF EDDIE COCHRAN (EP, reissue) 40
63	Liberty LEP 2124	EDDIE'S HITS (EP, reissue) 40
64	Liberty LEP 2165	C'MON AGAIN (EP) 60
64	Liberty LEP 2180	STOCKIN'S AND SHOES (EP) 50

LPs

58	London HA-U 2093	SINGIN' TO MY BABY (LP, early initially with laminated rear sleeve) 150/110
60	London HA-G 2267	THE EDDIE COCHRAN MEMORIAL ALBUM (LP) 70
62	Liberty LBY 1109	CHERISHED MEMORIES (LP) 40
63	Liberty LBY 1127	THE EDDIE COCHRAN MEMORIAL ALBUM (LP, reissue) 35
63	Liberty LBY 1158	SINGIN' TO MY BABY (LP, reissue) 40
64	Liberty LBY 1205	MY WAY (LP) 45
68	Liberty LBL/LBS 83009	THE EDDIE COCHRAN MEMORIAL ALBUM (LP, 2nd reissue) 15
68	Liberty LBL/LBS 83072E	CHERISHED MEMORIES (LP, reissue) 18
68	Liberty LBL 83104	MY WAY (LP, reissue in different sleeve) 18
68	Liberty LBL/LBS 83152	SINGIN' TO MY BABY (LP, 2nd reissue in different sleeve) 18
70	Liberty LBS 83337	THE VERY BEST OF EDDIE COCHRAN (LP) 15
71	United Artists UAS 29163	THE LEGENDARY EDDIE COCHRAN (LP) 12
72	United Artists UAD 60017/18	THE LEGENDARY MASTER SERIES (2-LP, with booklet) 25
72	United Artists UAS 29380	ON THE AIR (LP) 15
79	United Artists UAK 30244	THE SINGLES ALBUM (LP, with bonus 7": "Pretty Girl"/"Think Of Me" & poster) 15
79	Charly CR 30168	A LEGEND IN OUR TIME (LP) 12
80	United Artists UP ECSP 20	20TH ANNIVERSARY ALBUM (4-LP, box set) 45
88	Liberty ECB 1	THE EDDIE COCHRAN BOX SET (6-LP box set with booklet) 40

MINT VALUE £

HANK COCHRAN
68	Monument LMO 5020	HEART OF HANK (LP)	12

JACKIE LEE COCHRAN
57	Brunswick 05669	Ruby Pearl (with Jimmy Pruett)/Mama Don't You Think I Know	1,650
57	Brunswick 05669	Ruby Pearl (with Jimmy Pruett)/Mama Don't You Think I Know (78)	275

BRUCE COCKBURN
71	True North WTN 003	HIGH WINDS WHITE SKY (LP)	15
71	True North TNX 7	SUNWHEEL DANCE (LP)	15
72	CBS 65187	SUNWHEEL DANCE (LP, reissue)	12
81	Millennium BXL 17761	INNER CITY FRONT (LP)	12

JOE COCKER
64	Decca F 11974	I'll Cry Instead/Precious Words	55
68	Regal Zonophone RZ 3006	Marjorine/New Age Of The Lily	7
68	Regal Zonophone RZ 3013	With A Little Help From My Friends/Something's Coming On	6
69	Regal Zonophone RZ 3024	Delta Lady/She's So Good To Me	6
70	Regal Zonophone RZ 3027	The Letter/Space Captain	6
70	Fly BUG 3	Cry Me A River/Give Peace A Chance (p/s)	7
71	Fly BUG 9	High Time We Went/Black-Eyed Blues	5
72	Magni Fly ECHO 103	With A Little Help From My Friends/Delta Lady/The Letter (p/s)	7
72	Cube BUG 25	Woman To Woman/Midnight Rider (with Chris Stanton Band)	5
83	Island WIP 6818	Ruby Lee/Talking Back To The Night (export issue)	7
60s	Oak	JOE COCKER (EP, existence unconfirmed)	500+
67	Action ACT 002 EP	RAG GOES MAD AT THE MOJO (33rpm EP, 2 tracks by Joe Cocker's Blues Band, in conjunction with Sheffield University rag magazine *Twikker*)	75
69	Regal Zono. SLRZ 1006	WITH A LITTLE HELP FROM MY FRIENDS (LP)	25
69	Regal Zono. SLRZ 1011	JOE COCKER! (LP)	20
71	Fly HIFLY 3	COCKER HAPPY (LP)	12
74	Fly HIFLY 18	I CAN STAND A LITTLE RAIN (LP)	12

(see also Grease Band, Made In Sheffield)

COCKNEY REBEL
(see under Steve Harley/Cockney Rebel)

COCKNEY 'N' WESTERNS
80	Beggars Banquet BEG 39	She's No Angel/Had A Real Good Time (p/s)	5

(see also Boys, Rowdies)

COCKNEY REJECTS
79	Small Wonder SW 19	Flares'N'Slippers/Police Star/I Wanna Be A Star (p/s)	8
79	EMI EMI 5008	I'm Not A Fool/East End (p/s)	5
80	EMI EMI 5035	Bad Man!/The New Song (p/s)	6
80	Zonophone Z 2	The Greatest Cockney Rip-Off/Hate Of The City (p/s, yellow vinyl)	6
80	Zonophone Z 4	I'm Forever Blowing Bubbles/West Side Boys (p/s)	6
80	Zonophone Z 6	We Can Do Anything/15 Nights (p/s)	5
80	Zonophone Z 10	We Are The Firm/War On The Terraces (p/s)	5
81	Zonophone Z 20	Easy Life/Motorhead/Hang 'Em High (p/s)	6
81	Zonophone Z 21	On The Streets Again/London (p/s)	5
82	A.K.A. AKS 102	Till The End Of The Day/Rock'n'Roll Dream (p/s)	5
80	Zonophone ZONO 101	GREATEST HITS VOLUME 1 (LP)	15
80	Zonophone ZONO 102	GREATEST HITS VOLUME 2 (LP, with inner sleeve & poster)	15
81	Zonophone ZEM 101	GREATEST HITS VOLUME 3 (LIVE AND LOUD) (LP)	15
81	Zonophone ZONO 105	THE POWER AND THE GLORY (LP)	12

COCKNEYS
64	Philips BF 1303	After Tomorrow/I'll Cry Each Night	12
64	Philips BF 1338	After Tomorrow/I'll Cry Each Night (reissue)	12
64	Philips BF 1360	I Know You're Gonna Be Mine/Oh No You Won't	12

COCK SPARRER
77	Decca FR 13710	Runnin' Riot/Sister Suzie (no p/s; demos in p/s £100)	20
77	Decca FR 13732	We Love You/Chip On My Shoulder (no p/s)	15
77	Decca LFR 13732	We Love You/Chip On My Shoulder (12" p/s, with photo insert, 7,500 only)	18
82	Carrere CAR 255	England Belongs To Me/Argy Bargy (p/s)	40
83	Razor RAZ 9	SHOCK TROOPS (LP)	20
84	Syndicate SYNLP 7	RUNNIN' RIOT IN 84 (LP)	18
86	Razor RAZ 26	TRUE GRIT (LP)	15
87	Link LINKLP 05	LIVE AND LOUD (LP)	12
88	Link LINKLP 032	RUNNIN' RIOT IN 84 (LP)	12

(see also Little Roosters, Guttersnipes)

COCKTAIL CABINET
67	Page One POF 046	Puppet On A String/Breathalyser	25

COCTEAU TWINS
83	4AD AD 303	Peppermint Pig/Laugh Lines (p/s)	18
84	4AD AD 314	Sugar Hiccup (1-sided, promo only)	15
84	4AD BAD 405	Pearly-Dewdrop's Drops/The Spangle Maker/Pepper-Tree (12", embossed p/s)	8
88	4AD CAD 807	BLUE BELL KNOLL (LP, tri-foldout sleeve)	12
87	4AD CADT 807	BLUE BELL KNOLL (DAT, 500 only)	20

(see also This Mortal Coil, Felt)

C.O.D.s
66	Stateside SS 489	Michael (The Lover)/Cry No More	20

JAMIE COE
59	Parlophone R 4600	Summertime Symphony/There's Gonna Be A Day	130
60	Parlophone R 4621	School Day Blues/I'll Go On Loving You	60
61	HMV POP 991	How Low Is Low/Little Dear Little Darling	15
63	London HLX 9713	The Fool/I've Got That Feeling Again	15

PETER & CHRIS COE

72	Trailer LER 2077	OPEN THE DOOR AND LET US IN (LP)	22
76	Trailer LER 2098	OUT OF SEASON, OUT OF RHYME (LP)	18
79	Highway SHY 7007	GAME OF ALL FOURS (LP)	15
	(see also Bandoggs)		

TONY COE (QUINTET)

| 61 | Philips B 10784L | SWINGIN' TILL THE GIRLS COME HOME (LP) | 125 |
| 67 | Columbia SCX 6170 | TONY'S BASEMENT (LP) | 125 |

TONY COE & BRIAN LEMON TRIO

| 68 | '77' SEU 12/41 | TONY COE AND BRIAN LEMON TRIO (LP) | 75 |
| | (see also Robert Farnon & Tony Coe) | | |

JACK & CHARLIE COEN

| 77 | Topic 12TS 337 | THE BRANCH LINE (LP) | 20 |

COFFEE BAR SKIFFLERS

| 58 | Embassy WEP 1008 | SKIFFLE SESSION (EP) | 10 |
| | (see also Chas McDevitt Skiffle Group) | | |

COFFEE SET

| 69 | Mercury MF 1076 | Dicky Boy/Georgia On My Mind | 5 |
| 69 | Mercury MF 1113 | Happy Birthday/Our Anniversary | 5 |

DENNIS COFFEY

72	A&M AMS 7010	Getting It On/Ride Sally Ride	6
75	Sussex SXX 6	Getting It On '75/Chicano	5
77	Atlantic K 10991	Free Spirit/Our Love Goes	5
79	Atlantic LV 6	Give Me That Funk/Calling Planet Earth	5
70	A&M AMLS 68035	EVOLUTION (LP)	15
71	A&M AMLS 68072	GOIN' FOR MYSELF (LP)	15
74	Sussex LPSX 9	INSTANT COFFEY (LP)	15
77	Westbound K 50371	BACK HOME (LP)	12

ALMA COGAN

78s

52	HMV B 10280	To Be Worthy Of You/Would You? (78)	10
52	HMV B 10280	Would You/To Be Worthy Of You (78)	15
52	HMV B 10307	To Be Loved By You/The Homing Waltz (with Larry Day) (78)	12
52	HMV B 10319	Pretty Bride (Sew, Sew, Sew, Sew)/Waltz Of Paree (Sous Le Ciel De Paris) (78)	12
52	HMV B 10338	Blue Tango/Half As Much (78)	10
52	HMV B 10344	I Went To Your Wedding/You Belong To Me (78)	10
52	HMV B 10370	Take Me In Your Arms And Hold Me/Wyoming Lullaby (78)	10
53	HMV B 10449	Till I Waltz Again With You/Happy Valley Sweetheart (78)	10
53	HMV B 10460	If I Had A Penny/Hold Me, Thrill Me, Kiss Me (78)	8
53	HMV B 10464	On The First Warm Day (with Les Howerd)/LES HOWERD: The Windsor Waltz (78)	8
53	HMV B 10505	Till They've All Gone Home/Hug Me A Hug (78, with Les Howerd)	8
53	HMV B 10530	If I Had A Golden Umbrella/Mystery Street (78)	8
53	HMV B 10590	My Love, My Love/Wasted Tears (78)	10
54	HMV B 10615	Ricochet (Rick-O-Shay)/The Moon Is Blue (78)	8
54	HMV B 10743	Skinnie Minnie (Fishtail)/What Am I Going To Do, Ma (The Doo-Ma Song) (78)	10
54	HMV B 10761	This Ole House/Skokiaan (78)	10
54	HMV B 10802	(Don't Let The) Kiddygeddin/Mrs. Santa Claus (78)	10
55	HMV B 10832	Mambo Italiano/The Naughty Lady Of Shady Lane (78)	8
55	HMV B 10848	Tweedlee-Dee/More Than Ever Now (78)	10
56	HMV POP 223	Why Do Fools Fall In Love?/(The Same Thing Happen With) The Birds And The Bees? (78)	10
57	HMV POP 317	Whatever Lola Wants (Lola Gets)/Lucky Lips (78)	10
57	HMV POP 367	Fabulous/Summer Love (78)	10
58	HMV POP 450	Sugartime/Gettin' Ready For Freddy (78)	10
58	HMV POP 482	Stairway Of Love/Comes Love (78)	10
58	HMV POP 500	Sorry, Sorry, Sorry/Fly Away Lovers (78)	10
58	HMV POP 531	There's Never Been A Night/If This Isn't Love (78)	10
59	HMV POP 573	Last Night On The Back Porch/Mama Says (78)	12
59	HMV POP 670	We Got Love/I Don't Mind Being All Alone (78)	25

SINGLES

53	HMV 7M 166	Over And Over Again/Isn't Life Wonderful (with Les Howerd)	25
53	HMV 7M 106	I Went To Your Wedding/You Belong To Me	30
53	HMV 7M 107	To Be Loved By You/The Homing Waltz (B-side with Larry Day)	30
54	HMV 7M 173	Ricochet (Rick-O-Shay)/The Moon Is Blue	30
54	HMV 7M 188	Bell Bottom Blues/Love Me Again	40
54	HMV 7M 196	Make Love To Me/Said The Little Moment	25
54	HMV 7M 219	The Little Shoemaker/Chiqui-Chaqui (Chick-ee Chock-ee)	30
54	HMV 7M 228	Little Things Mean A Lot/Canoodlin' Rag	35
54	HMV 7M 239	Skinnie Minnie (Fishtail)/What Am I Going To Do, Ma (The Doo-Ma Song)	45
54	HMV 7M 269	This Ole House/Skokiaan	35
54	HMV 7M 271	I Can't Tell A Waltz From A Tango/Christmas Cards	25
55	HMV 7M 286	Paper Kisses/Softly, Softly	25
55	HMV 7M 293	Chee-Chee-Oo-Chee (Sang The Little Bird)/Tika Tika Tok	25
55	HMV 7M 301	Tweedlee-Dee/More Than Ever Now	25
55	HMV 7M 316	Got'n Idea/Give A Fool A Chance	25
55	HMV 7M 337	Never Do A Tango With An Eskimo/Twenty Tiny Fingers	30
56	HMV 7M 367	Love And Marriage/Sycamore Tree	25
56	HMV 7M 415	Why Do Fools Fall In Love?/(The Same Thing Happen With) The Birds And The Bees?	40
56	HMV POP 239	Mama Teach Me To Dance/I'm In Love Again	20

Alma COGAN

56	HMV POP 261	In The Middle Of The House/Two Innocent Hearts	30
57	HMV POP 284	You, Me And Us/Three Brothers	20
57	HMV POP 317	Whatever Lola Wants (Lola Gets)/Lucky Lips	30
57	HMV POP 336	Chantez, Chantez/Funny, Funny, Funny	20
57	HMV POP 367	Fabulous/Summer Love	20
57	HMV POP 392	That's Happiness/What You've Done To Me	15
57	HMV POP 415	Party Time/Please Mister Brown (Mister Jones, Mister Smith)	15
58	HMV POP 433	The Story Of My Life/Love Is	15
58	HMV POP 450	Sugartime/Gettin' Ready For Freddy	15
58	HMV POP 482	Stairway Of Love/Comes Love	12
58	HMV POP 500	Sorry, Sorry, Sorry/Fly Away Lovers	7
58	HMV POP 531	There's Never Been A Night/If This Isn't Love	8
59	HMV POP 573	Last Night On The Back Porch/Mama Says	8
59	HMV POP 608	Pink Shoelaces/The Universe	8
59	HMV POP 670	We Got Love/I Don't Mind Being All Alone	6
60	HMV POP 728	O Dio Mio/Dream Talk	6
60	HMV POP 760	The Train Of Love/The 'I Love You' Bit	8
60	HMV POP 815	Must Be Santa/Just Couldn't Resist Her With Her Pocket Transistor	8
61	Columbia DB 4607	Cowboy Jimmy Joe/Don't Read This Letter	6
61	Columbia DB 4679	With You In Mind/Ja-Da	6
61	Columbia DB 4749	All Alone/Keep Me In Your Heart	6
62	Columbia DB 4794	She's Got You/In The Shade Of The Old Apple Tree	6
62	Columbia DB 4912	Goodbye Joe/I Can't Give You Anything But Love	6
63	Columbia DB 4965	Tell Him/Fly Me To The Moon (Bossa Nova)	6
63	Columbia DB 7059	Hold Out Your Hand You Naughty Boy/Just Once More	6
64	Columbia DB 7233	The Tennessee Waltz/I Love You Too Much	10
64	Columbia DB 7390	It's You/I Knew Right Away	7
65	Columbia DB 7619	Love Is A Word/Now That I've Found You (unissued)	
65	Columbia DB 7652	Snakes And Snails (And Puppy Dog Tails)/	
		How Many Days, How Many Nights	8
65	Columbia DB 7757	Let Her Go/Yesterday (unissued)	
65	Columbia DB 7786	Eight Days A Week/Help!	7
66	Columbia DB 8088	Now That I've Found You/More	8
80	HMV POP 2015	Dreamboat/Twenty Tiny Fingers	6

EPs

55	HMV 7EG 8122	THE GIRL WITH A LAUGH IN HER VOICE (EP)	22
55	HMV 7EG 8151	THE GIRL WITH A LAUGH IN HER VOICE NO. 2 (EP)	20
56	HMV 7EG 8169	THE GIRL WITH A LAUGH IN HER VOICE NO. 3 (EP)	20
57	HMV 7EG 8437	SHE LOVES TO SING (EP)	30

LPs

58	HMV CLP 1152	I LOVE TO SING (LP)	60
61	HMV CLP 1459	OLIVER! (LP, with others, also stereo CSD 1370)	35/50
61	Columbia 33SX 1345	ALMA SINGS WITH YOU IN MIND (LP, also stereo SCX 3391)	50/80
62	Columbia 33SX 1469	HOW ABOUT LOVE! (LP, also stereo SCX 3459)	45/75
67	Columbia SX 6130	ALMA (LP)	40
70	M. For Pleasure MFP 1377	THE GIRL WITH THE LAUGH IN HER VOICE (LP)	12
77	One-Up OU 2168	THE ALMA COGAN COLLECTION (LP)	12
78	One-Up OU 2213	THE ALMA COGAN SECOND COLLECTION (LP)	12

(see also Ronnie Hilton, Angela & Fans, Billy Cotton)

ALMA COGAN & RONNIE HILTON

57	HMV 7EG 8352	THE HITS FROM 'MY FAIR LADY' (EP, 1 side each)	10

(see also Ronnie Hilton)

ALMA COGAN & FRANKIE VAUGHAN

54	HMV 7M 226	Do, Do, Do, Do, Do, Do, Do It Again/Jilted	25
54	HMV B 10712	Do, Do, Do, Do, Do, Do, Do It Again/Jilted (78)	10

(see also Frankie Vaughan)

DON COGAN

58	MGM MGM 984	The Fountain Of Love/I'm Takin' Over	7
58	MGM MGM 984	The Fountain Of Love/I'm Takin' Over (78)	8

SHAYE COGAN

58	Columbia DB 4055	Billy Be Sure/Doodle Doodle Doo	10
60	MGM MGM 1063	Mean To Me/They Said It Couldn't Be Done	30

(see also Buddy Morrow)

ALAN COHEN BAND

72	Argo ZDA 159	BLACK, BROWN AND BEIGE (LP)	50

LEONARD COHEN

68	CBS 3337	Suzanne/So Long, Marianne	7
69	CBS 4245	Bird On The Wire/Seems So Long Ago, Nancy	8
71	CBS 7292	Joan Of Arc/Diamonds In The Mine	7
73	CBS 8353	Suzanne/Bird On The Wire (p/s, 'Hall Of Fame Hits' series)	5
74	CBS 2494	Bird On The Wire (live)/Tonight Will Be Fine (live)	7
74	CBS 2699	Lover Lover Lover/Who By Fire	6
76	CBS 4306	Suzanne/Take This Longing	6
77	CBS 5882	Memories/Don't Go Home With Your Hard-On	6
78	CBS 6095	True Love Leaves No Traces/I Left A Woman Waiting	6
85	CBS 6052	Dance Me To The End Of Love/The Law	5
72	CBS EP 9162	McCABE AND MRS MILLER (EP, p/s)	10
68	CBS (S)BPG 63241	SONGS OF LEONARD COHEN (LP, orange label,	
		some with stickered sleeve; mono/stereo)	20/15
68	CBS 63241	SONGS OF LEONARD COHEN (LP, orange label, re-pressing w/out prefix)	15/12
69	CBS 63587	SONGS FROM A ROOM (LP, orange label)	12
71	CBS 69004	SONGS OF LOVE AND HATE (LP, orange label with booklet)	12

COIL
79	North'ton Wood H. HAV 1	Motor Industry/Alcoholic Stork (p/s)	10

COIL
85	F & F/K.422 FFK 512	Panic/Tainted Love/Aqua Regis (12", red or black vinyl, 'hair'-textured p/s)	18/12
86	Force & Form/K.422 ROTA 121	The Anal Staircase/Blood From The Air/Ravenous (12", p/s, some on clear vinyl)	18/12
87	Solar Lodge 001	HELLRAISER (10" EP, coloured vinyl [clear or pink, 500 each], or black)	20/7
90	Shock SX 002	Wrong Eye/Scope (pink p/s, signed & lettered A-Z, 26 only)	25
90	Shock SX 002	Wrong Eye/Scope (974 w/ no'd white p/s; or 1,000 w/ unno'd yellow p/s)	12/10
90	Shock SX 002	Wrong Eye/Scope (green p/s, 300 only, some with gold/black sticker)	20
92	Clawfist	Airborne Bells/Is Suicide A Solution (p/s, 1,250 only)	20
94	Loci S1	Themes From Blue (p/s, 23 on yellow vinyl, 1,000 on blue vinyl)	50/20
94	Eskaton 001	Nasa Arab/First Dark Ride (12", stickered plain black sleeve, 2,500 only)	15
95	Eskaton 003	PHILM (10" EP, with poster, 2,000 only, 50 on clear vinyl in handmade p/s)	45/12
86	Threshold ROTA 1	HORSE ROTORVATOR (LP, with A5 card insert & stickers)	15
87	Threshold House LOCI 1	GOLD IS THE METAL (LP, red vinyl; with bonus 7": "The Wheel"/ "The Wheal", unfinished proof sleeve without writing, 25 only)	150
87	Threshold House LOCI 1	GOLD IS THE METAL (LP, red [150 only] or clear vinyl [500 only], with inner sleeve; with bonus 7": "The Wheel"/"The Wheal")	40/25
87	Threshold House LOCI 1	GOLD IS THE METAL (LP, box set with 7", "The Wheel"/"The Wheal", poster & booklet in black linen folder, embossed sleeve, autographed, 55 only)	300
87	Threshold House LOCI CD1	GOLD IS THE METAL (CD, 1,000 only)	15
90	Normal NORMAL 77	GOLD IS THE METAL (LP, black vinyl re-pressing with 7": "The Wheel"/"Keel Hauler")	18
93	Loci CD 4b	STOLEN AND CONTAMINATED SONGS (CD, 1st edit with different artwork)	20
90s	Loci CD 6	ANGELIC CONVERSATION (CD, gold disc, 1,000 only)	18
95	Eskaton 007	WORSHIP THE GLITCH (2 x 10" LP, as Coil Vs. Elph, with insert, 2,000 only, 50 with white optical plastic cover)	45/20
95	Eskaton 006	WORSHIP THE GLITCH (CD, as Coil Vs. Elph, 500 only in black optical plastic)	20
(see also Psychic TV, Throbbing Gristle, Current 93)			

COINS
69	Toast TT 513	Love Power/You Can't Get Away From It	5
69	Toast TT 515	Don't You Know It's Just A Game (actually by Miss White & Mr. Green)/ Crying Over You	5

ALVADEAN COKER
55	London HLU 8191	Do Dee Oodle De Do I'm In Love/We're Gonna Bop	325
55	London HLU 8191	Do Dee Oodle De Do I'm In Love/We're Gonna Bop (78)	60

SANDY COKER & HIS BAND
54	London HL 8109	Meadowlark Melody/Toss Over	60
54	London HL 8109	Meadowlark Melody/Toss Over (78)	15

COLA BOY
91	COLA 1	7 Ways 2 Love (12", stamped white label promo, with Sarah Cracknell)	10
(see also Sarah Cracknell)			

RIC COLBECK QUARTET
70	Fontana 6383 001	THE SUN IS COMING UP (LP)	25

MARION COLBY
58	Capitol CL 14959	A Man Could Be A Wonderful Thing/He Like It! She Like	5

COLD BLOOD
70	Atlantic 584 319	You Got Me Hummin'/If You Will	5
70	Atlantic 588 218	COLD BLOOD (LP, plum/red label)	18
71	Atlantic 2400 102	SISYPHUS (LP, gatefold sleeve, plum/red label)	18
74	Warner Bros K 56047	LYDIA (LP)	15

BEN COLDER
64	MGM MGM-EP 791	MAKE THE WORLD GO BY (EP)	15
(see also Sheb Wooley)			

B.J. COLE
73	United Artists UAS 29418	NEW HOVERING DOG (LP)	10
(see also Cochise)			

BOBBY COLE
68	CBS 3626	Mister Bo Jangles/Bus 22 To Jerusalem	5

BUDDY COLE & WOOD SISTERS
55	Philips PB 464	Plantation Boogie/Foolishly (78)	8

CINDY COLE
65	Columbia DB 7519	A Love Like Yours/He's Sure The Boy I Love	8
66	Columbia DB 7973	Just Being Your Baby (Turns Me On)/Lonely City Blue Boy	10
(see also Jeannie & Big Guys)			

CLAY COLE
62	London HLP 9499	Twist Around The Clock/Don't Twist	7

COZY COLE
58	London HL 8750	Topsy (Parts 1 & 2)	10
58	London HL 7065	Topsy (Parts 1 & 2) (export issue)	8
58	London HL 8750	Topsy (Parts 1 & 2) (78)	12
59	Mercury AMT 1015	St. Louis Blues/Father Co-operates	7
59	Mercury AMT 1015	St. Louis Blues/Father Co-operates (78)	30
59	London HL 8843	Turvy (Parts 1 & 2)	10
59	London HL 8843	Turvy (Parts 1 & 2) (78)	30
62	Coral Q 72457	Big Noise From Winnetka (Parts 1 & 2)	6
57	MGM MGM-EP 622	COZY COLE ALL STARS (EP)	12

MINT VALUE £

DON COLE & ALLEYNE
65	Fontana TF 522	Gotta Find My Baby/Something's Gotta Hold Of Me	6

JERRY COLE
65	Capitol CL 15397	Every Window In The City/Come On Over To My Place	8

KEITH COLE
71	Big BG 315	Musical Attack/RUPIE EDWARDS ALLSTARS: Shack Attack	6
71	Big BG 316	Music Alone Version 3/RUPIE EDWARDS ALLSTARS: Behold Another Version	6

KING COLE TRIO/QUINTET
(see under Nat 'King' Cole)

LLOYD COLE & COMMOTIONS
84	Welcome To L. Vegas LC 1	Are You Ready To Be Heartbroken?/Down At The Mission (p/s, withdrawn)	30

NAT COLE
70	Jackpot JP 717	Pack Of Cards/RITA & NAT COLE: Spread Joy	6
70	Jackpot JP 718	Love Making/SONNY BINNS & RITA: My Love	6
70	Jackpot JP 722	Sugar Sugar/SONNY BINNS & RITA: Sign Off.	6
70	Explosion EX 2022	In The Summertime/Apollo Moon Walk	6
70	Creole CR 1002	Me And My Life/Instrumental	5

(see also Rita Alston)

NATALIE COLE
75	Capitol E-ST 11429	INSEPARABLE (LP)	12

(NAT) 'KING' COLE
78s
50	Melodisc 8011	Heads/It Had To Be You (as King Cole Quintet) (78)	15
50	Melodisc 8012	Pro-Sky/I Can't Give You Anything But Love (as King Cole Quintet) (78)	15
54	Vogue V 2214	Nat's Kicks (Parts 1 & 2) (as Nat 'King' Cole Quintet) (78)	12
54	Capitol CL 14172	I Am In Love/There Goes My Heart (78)	10
55	Capitol CL 14215	Long Long Ago/Open Up The Doghouse (with Dean Martin) (78)	20
58	Capitol CL 14820	Angel Smile/Back In My Arms (78)	10
58	Capitol CL 14853	With You On My Mind/The Song Of Raintree County (78)	10
58	Capitol CL 14898	Come Closer To Me/Nothing In The World (78)	10
58	Capitol CL 14937	Non Dimenticar (Don't Forget)/Bend A Little My Way (78)	10
59	Capitol CL 14987	Madrid/Give Me Your Love (78)	10
59	Capitol CL 15017	You Made Me Love You/I Must Be Dreaming (78)	15
59	Capitol CL 15056	Midnight Flyer/Sweet Bird Of Truth (78)	15
59	Capitol CL 15087	Buon Natale/The Happiest Little Christmas Tree (78)	25

SINGLES
54	Capitol CL 14149	Smile (Theme From 'Modern Times')/Make Her Mine	18
54	Capitol CL 14155	Unbelievable/Hajji Baba (Persian Lament)	15
54	Capitol CL 14172	I Am In Love/There Goes My Heart	15
54	Capitol CL 14203	If I Give My Heart To You/Hold My Hand	15
54	Capitol CL 14207	Papa Loves Mambo/Teach Me Tonight	18
55	Capitol CL 14215	Long Long Ago/Open Up The Doghouse (with Dean Martin)	18
55	Capitol CL 14235	A Blossom Fell/Alone Too Long	18
55	Capitol CL 14251	The Sand And The Sea/Darling, Je Vous Aime Beaucoup	15
55	Capitol CL 14295	If I May (with Four Knights)/I Envy	15
55	Capitol CL 14317	Annabelle/I'd Rather Have The Blues ('Kiss Me Deadly' Theme)	15
55	Capitol CL 14327	My One Sin/Don't Hurt The Girl	18
55	Capitol CL 14364	Love Is A Many-Splendored Thing/Autumn Leaves	15
55	Capitol CL 14378	Someone You Love/Forgive My Heart	15

(The above 45s were originally issued with triangular centres. Later round centre copies are worth around half these values.)

56	Capitol CL 14513	Dreams Can Tell A Lie/Ask Me.	12
56	Capitol CL 14529	Nothing Ever Changes (My Love For You)/I'm Gonna Laugh You Out Of My Life.	7
56	Capitol CL 14573	Too Young To Go Steady/Never Let Me Go	10
56	Capitol CL 14621	Love Me As Though There Were No Tomorrow/That's All There Is To That (as Nat 'King' Cole & Four Knights).	10
56	Capitol CL 14632	My Dream Sonata/I Just Found Out About Love	6
56	Capitol CL 14661	To The Ends Of The Earth/Toyland	6
57	Capitol CL 14678	Night Lights/Dame Crazy	6
57	Capitol CL 14688	You Are My First Love/Ballerina	6
57	Capitol CL 14709	When I Fall In Love/Calypso Blues	8
57	Capitol CL 14733	When Rock And Roll Came To Trinidad/It's All In The Game	10
57	Capitol CL 14765	My Personal Possession (as Nat 'King' Cole & Four Knights)/Send For Me	8
57	Capitol CL 14787	Stardust/Love Letters.	7
58	Capitol CL 14820	Angel Smile/Back In My Arms	6
58	Capitol CL 14853	With You On My Mind/The Song Of Raintree County	5
58	Capitol CL 14882	Looking Back/Just For The Fun Of It.	5
58	Capitol CL 14898	Come Closer To Me/Nothing In The World.	5
58	Capitol CL 14937	Non Dimenticar (Don't Forget)/Bend A Little My Way.	5
59	Capitol CL 14987	Madrid/Give Me Your Love	5
59	Capitol CL 15017	You Made Me Love You/I Must Be Dreaming.	5
59	Capitol CL 15056	Midnight Flyer/Sweet Bird Of Truth	5
59	Capitol CL 15087	Buon Natale/The Happiest Little Christmas Tree	5
59	Capitol CL 15111	Time And The River/Whatcha' Gonna Do	5
60	Capitol CL 15129	That's You/Is It Better To Have Loved And Lost	5
60	Capitol CL 15144	My Love/Steady (with Stan Kenton)	5
60	Capitol CL 15163	Just As Much As Ever/I Wish I Knew The Way To Your Heart	5

EPs
55	Capitol EAP 1-514	TENTH ANNIVERSARY ALBUM PART 1 (EP)	10
55	Capitol EAP 2-514	TENTH ANNIVERSARY ALBUM PART 2 (EP)	10
55	Capitol EAP 3-514	TENTH ANNIVERSARY ALBUM PART 3 (EP)	10
55	Capitol EAP 4-514	TENTH ANNIVERSARY ALBUM PART 4 (EP)	10
55	Capitol EAP 1-633	MOODS IN SONG (EP)	10

MINT VALUE £

56	Capitol EAP 1010	LOVE IS A MANY-SPLENDORED THING (EP)	10
56	Capitol EAP 1036	THE CHRISTMAS SONG (EP)	10
56	Capitol EAP 1040	STRIP FOR ACTION (EP)	10
57	Capitol EAP 1-801	NIGHT LIGHTS (EP)	8
57	Capitol EAP 1-813	AROUND THE WORLD (EP, with Nelson Riddle)	8
58	Capitol EAP 1-824	LOVE IS THE THING PART 1 (EP)	8
58	Capitol EAP 2-824	LOVE IS THE THING PART 2 (EP)	8
58	Capitol EAP 3-824	LOVE IS THE THING PART 3 (EP)	8
58	Capitol EAP 1-960	LOOKING BACK (EP)	8
58	Capitol EAP 1-993	ST. LOUIS BLUES PART 1 (EP)	10
58	Capitol EAP 2-993	ST. LOUIS BLUES PART 2 (EP)	10
58	Capitol EAP 3-993	ST. LOUIS BLUES PART 3 (EP)	10
58	Capitol EAP 1-782	AFTER MIDNIGHT PART 1 (EP)	8
58	Capitol EAP 2-782	AFTER MIDNIGHT PART 2 (EP)	8
58	Capitol EAP 3-782	AFTER MIDNIGHT PART 3 (EP)	8
58	Capitol EAP 4-782	AFTER MIDNIGHT PART 4 (EP)	8

LPs

53	Capitol LC 6569	CAPITOL PRESENTS NAT KING COLE (10" LP)	30
53	Capitol LC 6587	CAPITOL PRESENTS NAT KING COLE AND HIS TRIO VOLUME 1 (10" LP)	25
53	Capitol LC 6593	CAPITOL PRESENTS NAT KING COLE AT THE PIANO (10" LP)	25
53	Capitol LC 6594	CAPITOL PRESENTS NAT KING COLE AND HIS TRIO VOLUME 2 (10" LP)	25
53	Capitol LC 6627	NAT KING COLE SINGS FOR TWO IN LOVE (10" LP)	25
54	Capitol LCT 6003	NAT KING COLE TENTH ANNIVERSARY ALBUM (LP)	22
56	Capitol LC 6818	BALLADS OF THE DAY (10" LP)	20
56	Capitol LC 6830	THE PIANO STYLE OF NAT KING COLE (10" LP)	20
56	Brunswick LAT 8123	IN THE BEGINNING (LP, as King Cole Trio)	22
57	Capitol (S)LCT 6129	LOVE IS THE THING (LP)	15
57	Capitol LCT 6133	AFTER MIDNIGHT (LP, as Nat King Cole & His Trio)	15
57	Capitol LCT 6142	THIS IS NAT KING COLE (LP)	15
58	Capitol (S)LCT 6149	JUST ONE OF THOSE THINGS (LP)	15
58	Capitol (S)LCT 6156	ST LOUIS BLUES — SONGS OF W.C. HANDY (LP)	18
58	Capitol LCT 6166	COLE ESPANOL (LP)	12
59	Capitol LCT 6167	EVERY TIME I FEEL THE SPIRIT (LP)	12
59	Capitol (S)LCT 6173	THE VERY THOUGHT OF YOU (LP, mono/stereo)	12/15
59	Capitol (S)LCT 6176	WELCOME TO THE CLUB (LP, mono/stereo)	12/15
59	Capitol (S)LCT 6182	TO WHOM IT MAY CONCERN (LP, mono/stereo)	12/15
60	Capitol (S)W 1220	A MIS AMIGOS (LP, mono/stereo)	12/15
60	Capitol (S)W 1444	THE MAGIC OF CHRISTMAS (LP, mono/stereo)	12/15
61	Capitol (S)W 1392	WILD IS LOVE (LP, mono/stereo)	12/15
61	Capitol (S)W 1331	TELL ME ALL ABOUT YOURSELF (LP, mono/stereo)	12/15
61	Capitol (S)W 1574	THE TOUCH OF YOUR LIPS (LP, mono/stereo)	12/15
65	Capitol (S)W 340	CAT BALLOU AND OTHER MOTION PICTURE SONGS (LP)	15
66	Capitol (S)T 2434	AT THE SANDS (LP)	12
66	Capitol T 2529	THE VINTAGE YEARS (LP)	12

(see also Dean Martin, Four Knights)

(NAT) 'KING' COLE and GLORIA WOOD

| 53 | Capitol CL 13919 | Red Canary/Hello Sunshine (78) | 10 |

PATSY COLE

| 66 | Island WI 271 | Disappointed Bride/EARL BOSTIC: Honeymoon Night | 12 |

ROCKY COLE

| 61 | Oriole CB 1635 | Heaven And Earth/Huey's Song | 5 |

STRANGER COLE

63	R&B JB 133	Out Of Many/Nothing Tried	15
63	Island WI 110	Stranger At The Door/Conqueror	18
63	Island WI 114	Last Love/STRANGER & KEN: Hush Baby	18
63	Island WI 126	We Are Rolling/Millie Maw	18
64	Island WI 137	Goodbye Peggy (actually plays "Goodbye Peggy Darling" by Roy Panton)/BABA BROOKS: Portrait Of My Love	18
64	R&B JB 129	Morning Star/Beat Up Your Gum	12
64	Island WI 133	Til My Dying Days/STRANGER & PATSY: I Need You	18
64	Black Swan WI 413	Uno Dos Tres (act. with Ken Boothe)/Look (B-side actually by unknown artist)	18
64	Black Swan WI 415	Summer Day/Loving You Always (both actually by Dottie & Bonnie)	18
64	Black Swan WI 435	Little Boy Blue/ERIC MORRIS: Words Of Wisdom	18
65	Ska Beat JB 192	Pussy Cat/MAYTALS: Sweet Sweet Jenny	15
65	Island WI 169	Koo Koo Doo (with Owen & Leon)/GLORIA & DREAMLETTS: Stay Where You Are	18
65	Island WI 177	Run Joe (with Baba Brooks)/Make Believe	18
65	Blue Beat BB 322	When The Party Is Over/BUSTER'S ALLSTARS: Happy Independence '65	15
65	Blue Beat BB 333	Matilda (actually with Prince Buster)/BUSTER'S ALL STARS: When The Party Is Over	15
66	Doctor Bird DB 1025	We Shall Overcome/Do You Really Love Me (as Stranger Cole & Seraphines)	15
66	Doctor Bird DB 1040	Drop The Ratchet/Oh Yee Mahee (as Stranger Cole & Conquerors)	15

Stranger COLE

67	Doctor Bird DB 1066	You Took My Love (actually by Patsy Todd)/FUGITIVES: Living Soul	15
68	Island WI 3154	Jeboza Macoo/Now I Know (B-side actually with Gladdy Anderson)	40
68	Amalgamated AMG 801	Just Like A River (as Stranger Cole & Gladdy)/LEADERS: Hope Someday	12
69	Amalgamated AMG 838	What Mama Na Want She Get/We Two	12
69	Duke DU 27	Glad You're Living/Help Wanted	7
69	Unity UN 501	Last Flight To Reggae City (w/ Tommy McCook)/JUNIOR SMITH: Watch Dem Go	6
69	Unity UN 514	When I Get My Freedom/Life Can Be Beautiful	5
69	Escort ES 810	Pretty Cottage/To Me	8
69	Escort ES 819	Leana Leana/Na Na Na	6
69	Escort ES 826	Loneliness/Remember	6
70	Escort ES 830	Little Things/Till The Well Runs Dry	5
70	Escort ES 831	Everything With You/Picture On The Wall	5
70	Escort ES 832	Pussy/Let Me In	5
70	Pama PM 790	Come Dance With Me/Dance With Me	6
71	Camel CA 72	Crying Every Night/DENNIS ALCAPONE & DELROY WILSON: It Must Come	8
71	Escort ERT 849	Tomorrow/SONNY BURKE: Chicken Thief	6
72	Tropical AL 0011	Mail Man (with Charlie Ace)/Mail Man (Version)	6
72	Jackpot JP 791	My Confession/LASCELS & HORTENSE: The Might Organ	5
72	Pama PM 848	The House Where Bombo Lives/Our High School Dance	5

(see also Stranger, Stranger & Gladys, Stranger & Patsy, Stranger & Ken, Rob Walker, Charmers, Lloyd Clarke, Don Drummond, Tommy McCook, Ernest Wilson, Delroy Wilson, Lester Sterling, Baba Brooks, Roland Alphonso)

BOBBY COLEMAN
| 66 | Pye International 7N 25365 | (Baby) You Don't Have To Tell Me/Pleasure Girl | 50 |

FITZROY COLEMAN
| 61 | Starlite ST45 064 | Lucilla/Caribbean Sunset | 8 |

LONNIE COLEMAN & JESSE ROBERTSON
| 56 | London HLU 8335 | Dolores Diane/Oh Honey, Why Don'tcha | 40 |
| 56 | London HLU 8335 | Dolores Diane/Oh Honey, Why Don'tcha (78) | 12 |

MICHAEL COLEMAN
| 63 | Ace Of Hearts AH 56 | IRISH JIGS AND REELS (LP) | 12 |

ORNETTE COLEMAN
60	Contemporary LAC 12228	TOMORROW IS THE QUESTION (LP)	20
61	London Jazz LTZ-K 15199	CHANGE OF THE CENTURY	
		(LP, also stereo SAH-K 5099)	18
61	London Jazz LTZ-K 15228	THIS IS OUR MUSIC	
		(LP, also stereo SAH-K 6181)	18
62	London Jazz LTZ-K 15241	THE ORNETTE COLEMAN QUARTET	
		(LP, also stereo SAH-K 6235)	18
67	CBS 66023	CHAPPAQUA SUITE (2-LP)	18
68	Polydor 623 246/7	AN EVENING WITH ORNETTE COLEMAN (2-LP)	15
68	Atlantic 588 121	ORNETTE ON TENOR (LP)	12
69	Impulse MIPL/SIPL 518	ORNETTE AT 12 (LP)	12
69	Fontana SFJL 923	TOWN HALL 1962 (LP)	12
70	RCA RD/SF 7944	THE MUSIC OF ORNETTE COLEMAN	
		(LP, with Philadelphia Woodwind Quintet)	12
71	Atlantic 2400 109	THE ART OF THE IMPROVISERS (LP)	12
72	Atlantic K 40278	TWINS (LP)	12
72	Polydor 2383 090	ORNETTE COLEMAN IN EUROPE VOLUME 1 (LP)	12
72	Polydor 2383 091	ORNETTE COLEMAN IN EUROPE VOLUME 2 (LP)	12
72	CBS 64774	SCIENCE FICTION (LP)	12
72	CBS 65147	SKIES OF AMERICA (LP)	12

ROGER COLEMAN
| 60 | Top Rank JAR 311 | Nobody's Fool/Endlessly | 6 |

COLENSO PARADE
| 84 | Goliath SLING 01 | Standing Up/Smoky Fingered Reminder (p/s) | 5 |

(see also Levitation, House Of Love)

COLLAGE
| 73 | Studio Two TWO 410 | MISTY (LP) | 25 |

(see also Brian Bennett)

COLETTE & BANDITS
| 65 | Stateside SS 416 | A Ladies Man/Lost Love | 6 |

COLLECTIVE HORIZONTAL
| 79 | Dolmen DO 1 | COLLECTIVE HORIZONTAL EP | |
| | | (gatefold p/s, stickered white labels) | 5 |

COLLECTORS (Canada)
| 70 | London HLU 10304 | I Must Have Been Blind/The Beginning | 5 |
| 69 | Warner Bros WS 1774 | GRASS AND WILD STRAWBERRIES (LP) | 20 |

(see also Chilliwack, Electric Prunes)

COLLECTORS (U.K.)
| 80 | Central Collection COL 1 | Different World/Talking Hands (p/s) | 6 |

COLLEGE BOYS (Jamaica)
| 64 | Blue Beat BB 202 | Love Is A Treasure/Someone Will Be There | 15 |

COLLEGE BOYS (U.K.)
| 64 | Columbia DB 7306 | I Just Don't Understand/I'm Gonna Cry | 15 |
| 67 | Pye 7N 17294 | Good Times/San Antonio Rose | 5 |

BUDDY COLLETTE & HERBIE MANN GROUP
| 59 | Top Rank 25/015 | PORGY AND BESS (10" LP) | 12 |

(see also Herbie Mann)

MINT VALUE £

GRAHAM COLLIER SEXTET/SEPTET

67	Deram DML/SML 1005	DEEP DARK BLUE CENTRE (LP)	60
69	Fontana SFJL 922	DOWN ANOTHER ROAD (LP)	45
70	Fontana 6309 006	SONGS FOR MY FATHER (LP, as Graham Collier Music feat. Harry Beckett)	60
71	Philips 6308 051	MOSAICS (LP, live, as Graham Collier Music featuring Harry Beckett)	45
72	Saydisc SDL 244	PORTRAITS (LP)	30

(see also Harry Beckett)

MITTY COLLIER

64	Pye International 7N 25275	I Had A Talk With My Man/Free Girl	20

AL 'JAZZBO' COLLINS

53	Capitol CL 13995	Jack & The Beanstalk/Snow White & The Seven Dwarfs (78)	8
54	Capitol CL 14080	The Discovery Of America/The Invention Of The Airplane (78)	8
56	Vogue Coral Q 72160	Max/Sam	5
56	Vogue Coral Q 72160	Max/Sam (78)	8

ALBERT COLLINS

69	Liberty LBS 83238	LOVE CAN BE FOUND ANYWHERE (LP)	25
73	Tumbleweed TW 3501	THERE'S GOTTA BE A CHANGE (LP)	20

ANSEL(L) COLLINS

69	Trojan TR 699	Night Of Love/DERRICK MORGAN: Copy Cat	7
69	Trojan TR 7712	Cotton Dandy/CARL DAWKINS: Don't Get Weary	6
70	Trojan TR 7729	Moon Dust/Fat Cat	6
70	Trojan TR 7730	Monkey (Version I)/(Version II) (plays "High Voltage"/"High Voltage Version"; B-side actually by Beverley All Stars)	6
70	J-Dan JDN 4401	Cock Robin/KING DENNIS: Seven Zero	7
70	Techniques TE 907	Top Secret/Crazy Rhythm (both actually by Winston Wright)	7
71	Techniques TE 913	Nuclear Weapon/TECHNIQUES ALL STARS: La, La, La	7

(see also Dave & Ansell Collins, Conquerors, Lloyd Young, Prince Buster, Les Foster, Ethiopians, Eternals, Pam Brooks, Dennis Alcapone, Rad Bryan)

BOOTSY COLLINS

(see under Bootsy's Rubber Band)

DAVE & ANSELL COLLINS

70	Techniques TE 901	Double Barrel/Double Barrel (Version 2)	5
71	Techniques TE 914	Monkey Spanner (Parts 1 & 2)	5
72	Techniques TE 915	Karate/Doing Your Own Thing	6
72	Rhino RNO 106	Keep On Trying/Give Me Some Light	5
73	Rhino RNO 111	Hot Line/Sunshine Rock (label credits 'Dave Collins')	5
71	Trojan TBL 162	DOUBLE BARREL (LP)	15

(see also Ansel Collins, Les Foster & Ansell Collins, Dave Barker)

DONIE COLLINS SHOWBAND

68	Pye 7N 17682	Get Down With It/I Can't Help Myself (Sugar Pie Honey Bunch)	8

DOROTHY COLLINS

51	MGM MGM 354	Me And My Imagination/I'm Playing With Fire (78)	10
52	Brunswick 05010	So Madly In Love (with Gordon Jenkins Orchestra)/GORDON JENKINS, ORCHESTRA & CHORUS: Just Say The Word (78)	10
53	Brunswick 05042	Jump Back Honey/I Will Still Love You (with Snooky Lanson) (78)	12
53	Brunswick 05051	If'n/Puppy Love (with Raymond Scott Orchestra) (78)	10
55	Vogue Coral Q 72111	My Boy — Flat Top/In Love	30
55	Vogue Coral Q 72111	My Boy — Flat Top/In Love (78)	15
56	Vogue Coral Q 72116	Moments To Remember/Love And Marriage	12
56	Vogue Coral Q 72116	Moments To Remember/Love And Marriage (78)	10
56	Vogue Coral Q 72137	Seven Days/Manuello	18
56	Vogue Coral Q 72137	Seven Days/Manuello (78)	12
56	Vogue Coral Q 72173	Treasure Of Love/He's Got Me, Hook, Line And Sinker	18
56	Vogue Coral Q 72173	Treasure Of Love/He's Got Me, Hook, Line And Sinker (78)	15
56	Vogue Coral Q 72193	Love Me As Though There Were No Tomorrow/Rock And Roll Train	30
56	Vogue Coral Q 72193	Love Me As Though There Were No Tomorrow/Rock And Roll Train (78)	18
56	Vogue Coral Q 72198	The Italian Theme/Cool It, Baby	30
56	Vogue Coral Q 72198	The Italian Theme/Cool It, Baby (78)	18
56	Vogue Coral Q 72208	The Twelve Gifts Of Christmas/Mr. Santa	15
57	Vogue Coral Q 72232	Baby Can Rock/Would You Ever	18
57	Vogue Coral Q 72232	Baby Can Rock/Would You Ever (78)	18
57	Vogue Coral Q 72252	Mr. Wonderful/I Miss You Already	10
57	Vogue Coral Q 72262	Four Walls/Big Dreams	8
57	Vogue Coral Q 72262	Four Walls/Big Dreams (78)	10
57	Vogue Coral Q 72287	Soft Sands/Sing It, Children, Sing It	8
59	Top Rank JAR 259	Baciare, Baciare/Everything I Have Is Yours	6
60	Top Rank JAR 401	Banjo Boy/Tintarella Di Luna	6
60	Top Rank JAR 523	Unlock Those Chains/I'll Be Yours, You'll be Mine	6
55	London REP 1025	DOROTHY COLLINS SINGS (EP)	25
57	Coral LVA 9058	AT HOME WITH DOROTHY AND RAYMOND (LP)	22

EDWYN COLLINS

87	Creation CRE 047T	Don't Shilly Shally/If Ever You're Ready (12", unreleased, white label test pressings only)	35
87	Elevation ACID 6	My Beloved Girl/Clouds (Fogging Up My Mind) (p/s)	5
87	Elevation ACIDB 6	My Beloved Girl/50 Shades Of Blue (Acoustic Version)/Clouds (Fogging Up My Mind)/What's The Big Idea? (box set with 3 postcards)	8
87	Elevation ACID 6T	My Beloved Girl (Extended Version)/Clouds (Fogging Up My Mind) (Cumulonimbus Version)/My Beloved Girl (12", p/s)	8

MINT VALUE £

JUDY COLLINS   *LYN COLLINS*

89	Demon D 1064T	Coffee Table Song/Judas In Blue Jeans/Out There (12", p/s)	8
89	Demon D 1065	50 Shades Of Blue/If Ever You're Ready (p/s)	5
89	Demon D 1065T	50 Shades Of Blue (Extended)/Kindred Spirit/Just Call Her Name/ Ain't That Always The Way (12", p/s)	8
89	Demon D 1065CD	50 Shades Of Blue/Judas In Blue Jeans/Kindred Spirit/Just Call Her Name (CD)	8
97	Setanta SET 045	Adidas World/High Fashion (p/s, glitter vinyl)	8

(see also Orange Juice, Paul Quinn & Edwyn Collins)

GLENDA COLLINS
60	Decca F 11280	Take A Chance/Crazy Guy	12
61	Decca F 11321	Oh How I Miss You Tonight/Age For Love	15
61	Decca F 11417	Head Over Heels In Love/Find Another Fool	10
63	HMV POP 1163	I Lost My Heart In The Fairground/I Feel So Good	60
63	HMV POP 1233	If You Gotta Pick A Baby/In The First Place	25
64	HMV POP 1283	Baby It Hurts/Nice Wasn't It	50
64	HMV POP 1323	Lollipop/Everybody's Got To Fall In Love	45
65	HMV POP 1439	Johnny Loves Me/Paradise for Two	50
65	HMV POP 1475	Thou Shall Not Steal/Been Invited To A Party	35
66	Pye 7N 17044	Something I've Got To Tell You/My Heart Didn't Lie	55
66	Pye 7N 17150	It's Hard To Believe It/Don't Let It Rain On Sunday	70
90	Document CSAP LP 108	BEEN INVITED TO A PARTY (LP)	18
90	Document CSAP CD 108	BEEN INVITED TO A PARTY (LP)	18

JUDY COLLINS
66	London HLZ 10029	I'll Keep It With Mine/Thirsty Boots	7
67	Elektra EKSN 45011	In My Life/Hard Lovin' Loser	6
69	Elektra EKSN 45053	Some Day Soon/My Father	6
69	Elektra EKSN 45073	Chelsea Morning/Pretty Polly	6
69	Elektra EKSN 45077	Turn, Turn, Turn/Mr. Tambourine Man	6
65	Elektra EKL 209	MAID OF CONSTANT SORROW (LP)	25
68	Elektra EKL 4012	WILD FLOWERS (LP, orange label, also stereo EKS 74012)	15
69	Elektra EKL 4033	WHO KNOWS WHERE THE TIME GOES (LP, gatefold sleeve, orange label; also stereo EKS 74033)	15

LYN COLLINS
64	Sabre SA 0002	What Am I Gonna Do Without You?/When A Girl Meets A Bad, Bad Boy	10
74	Polydor 2066 490	Rock Me Again And Again And Again/Wide Awake In A Dream	6
74	Mojo 2093 029	Think (About It)/Me And My Baby Got Our Own Thing Going	6
88	Urban URBX 15	Rock Me Again And Again And Again (12")	7
72	Polydor 2918 006	THINK (ABOUT IT) (LP)	30
88	Urban URBLP 7	LYN COLLINS (THE FEMALE PREACHER) (LP)	12

(see also James Brown)

PETER COLLINS
| 70 | Decca F 13048 | Get In A Boat/Girl By The Sea | 5 |
| 70 | Decca Nova SDN 21 | PETER COLLINS (LP) | 15 |

PHIL COLLINS
81	Virgin VSK 102	In The Air Tonight/The Roof Is Leaking (12-page cartoon booklet p/s)	8
81	Virgin VS 423	If Leaving Me Is Easy/Drawing Board: In The Air Tonight-I Missed Again-If Leaving Me Is Easy (demo versions) (poster p/s)	5
82	Virgin VSY 531	You Can't Hurry Love/I Cannot Believe It's True (picture disc)	5
83	Virgin VS 572-12	Don't Let Him Steal Your Heart Away/And So To F . . . (live) (12", p/s)	8
84	Virgin VSY 674	Against All Odds/Making A Big Mistake (picture disc)	6
85	Virgin VSY 736-12	Sussudio (Extended)/Sussudio/The Man With The Horn (12", picture disc)	8
85	Virgin VSS 755	One More Night/I Like The Way (shaped picture disc with plinth)	8
85	Virgin VS 777	Take Me Home/We Said Hello, Goodbye (p/s, 'luggage' picture label)	6
85	Virgin VS 777/VS 674	Take Me Home/We Said Hello, Goodbye//Against All Odds/Making A Big Mistake (double pack, gatefold PVC sleeve)	8

85	Virgin VS 777-12	Take Me Home (Extended)/Take Me Home/We Said Hello, Goodbye (12", gatefold p/s with fold-out map)	8
87	Bold Reprieve BRM 007P	Deep Green (1-sided, promo only)	25
87	Bold Reprieve BRM 007T	Deep Green/Old Man Of The Ocean/Save A Place For Me (12", p/s)	8
88	Virgin VSCD 1141	Two Hearts/The Robbery (Full Length Version) (3" CD, heart-shaped box)	8
88	Virgin CDT 1	You Can't Hurry Love/Oddball (3" CD)	8
88	Virgin CDEP 4	12"ERS (CD EP, gatefold card sleeve)	8
89	Virgin VSCD 1234	Another Day In Paradise/Saturday Night And Sunday Morning/Heat On The Street (3" CD)	8
89	Virgin VSTX 1240	I Wish It Would Rain Down/Homeless/You've Been In Love Just That Little Bit Too Long (12", p/s, with lyric sheet)	8
89	Virgin VSCD 1240	I Wish It Would Rain Down/Homeless/You've Been In Love Just That Little Bit Too Long (3" CD)	8
90	Virgin VSP 1251	Something Happened On The Way To Heaven/Rain Down (Demo) (booklet p/s)	5
90	Virgin VSCDX 1277	That's Just The Way It Is/Broadway Chorus/In The Air Tonight (CD, 3-D p/s)	8
90	Virgin VSCDX 1300	Hang In Long Enough/That's How I Feel/Hang In Long Enough (Dub Mix) (CD, picture disc, numbered)	8
90	Virgin VSCDX 1305	Do You Remember? (live)/Doesn't Anybody Stay Together Anymore (live)/The Roof Is Leaking (live) (CD, picture disc, 'carousel' pack)	15

(see also Genesis, Flaming Youth, Brand X, Peter Banks)

PHIL COLLINS & MARILYN MARTIN
85	Virgin VSS 818	Separate Lives/Only You Know And I Know (white vinyl & poster in wallet)	6
85	Virgin VSSD 818	Separate Lives/Only You Know And I Know (2 interlocking picture discs)	8

(see also Brand X, Peter Banks, Genesis, Flaming Youth, Marilyn Martin)

RODGER COLLINS
67	Vocalion VF 9285	She's Looking Good/I'm Serving Time	10

SHIRLEY COLLINS
60	Collector JEI 1508	SINGS IRISH (EP)	60
60	Collector JEB 3	THE FOGGY DEW (EP)	60
60	Collector JEB 5	ENGLISH SONGS (EP)	60
64	Collector JEB 9	ENGLISH SONGS VOL. 2 (EP, with Robin Hall)	60
63	Topic TOP 95	HEROES IN LOVE (EP)	60
59	Folkways FG 3564	FALSE TRUE LOVERS (LP)	100
60	Argo RG 150	SWEET ENGLAND (LP)	100
64	Decca LK 4652	FOLK ROOTS, NEW ROUTES (LP, with Davy Graham)	100
67	Topic 12T 170	THE SWEET PRIMROSES (LP, originally with blue label)	35/20
68	Polydor 583 025	THE POWER OF THE TRUE LOVE KNOT (LP, with Incredible String Band)	60
71	Pegasus PEG 7	NO ROSES (LP, gatefold sleeve, with Albion Country Band)	30
74	Mooncrest CREST 11	NO ROSES (LP, reissue in different sleeve)	12
74	Topic 12T 238	ADIEU TO OLD ENGLAND (LP, originally with blue label)	30/18
75	Deram SML 1117	A FAVOURITE GARLAND (LP)	30
76	Harvest SHSM 2008	AMARANTH (LP)	20
78	Topic 12T 380	FOR AS MANY AS WILL (LP)	15
81	Righteous GDC 001	FOLK ROOTS, NEW ROUTES (LP, with Davy Graham, reissue)	12
83	Hannibal HNBL 1327	THE POWER OF THE TRUE LOVE KNOT (LP, reissue)	12

SHIRLEY & DOLLY COLLINS
69	Harvest SHVL 754	ANTHEMS IN EDEN (LP, gatefold sleeve)	40
70	Harvest SHVL 771	LOVE, DEATH AND THE LADY (LP, gatefold sleeve)	60
76	Harvest SHSM 2008	ANTHEMS IN EDEN (LP, gatefold sleeve, reissue)	15

(see also Davy Graham, Albion Country Band, Conundrum)

SIR COLLINS
(see under 'S')

TERRY COLLINS
74	Warner Bros K 16426	I L.O.V.E. Y.O.U./Action Speaks Louder Than Words	6

TOMMY COLLINS
58	Capitol CL 14838	Think It Over Boys/All Of The Monkeys Ain't In The Zoo	8
58	Capitol CL 14838	Think It Over Boys/All Of The Monkeys Ain't In The Zoo (78)	25
58	Capitol CL 14894	Let Down/It Tickles	7
59	Capitol CL 15076	Little June/A Hundred Years From Now	8
60	Capitol CL 15118	Wreck Of The Old '97/You Belong In My Arms	6
57	Capitol T 776	WORDS AND MUSIC COUNTRY STYLE (LP)	20
59	Capitol T 1196	THIS IS TOMMY COLLINS (LP)	20

COLLINS BAND & BOB STACKIE
68	Collins Downbeat CRC 0017	Bob Stackie In Soho/LORD CHARLES & HIS BAND: Jamaican Bits And Pieces	35

(see also Sir Collins)

JOE COLMAN
90	Blast First FU10	INFERNAL MACHINE (LP, picture disc, 1,000 only)	20

COLONEL
75	Ring O' 2017 104	Cokey Cokey/Away In A Manger (company sleeve)	10

COLONEL
80	Virgin VS 380	Too Many Cooks (In The Kitchen)/I Need Protection (p/s)	15

(see also XTC, Mr. Partridge)

JERRY COLONNA

54	Brunswick 05243	Ebb Tide/The Velvet Glove	15
54	Brunswick 05342	It Might As Well Be Spring/Ja-Da.	12
55	Parlophone MSP 6165	Let Me Go, Lover/I Want To Love You, Cara Mia	10
55	London HL 8143	Chicago Style/Baffi	20
55	London HL 8143	Chicago Style/Baffi (78)	10
56	HMV 7M 369	The Shifting, Whispering Sands/Waltz Me Around	8
59	London HA-U 2190	LET'S ALL SING (LP).	25
65	Ace Of Hearts AH 102	JERRY COLONNA AND GROUCHO MARX (LP)	15

COLORADOS

64	Oriole CB 1972	Lips Are Redder On You/Who You Gonna Hurt?	12

COLORS OUT OF TIME

81	Monsters In Orbit TVEYE 1	Rock Section/Mambo Girls/Dancing With You (hand-made p/s)	6
82	Monsters In Orbit TVEYE 5	She Spins/The Ocean (p/s)	5

COLOSSEUM

69	Fontana TF 1029	Walking In The Park/Those About To Die	8
69	Fontana STL 5510	THOSE WHO ARE ABOUT TO DIE SALUTE YOU (LP, gatefold sleeve).	20
69	Vertigo VO 1	VALENTYNE SUITE (LP, gatefold sleeve, spiral label & inner bag)	20
70	Vertigo 6360 017	DAUGHTER OF TIME (LP, gatefold sleeve, some with spiral label & bag).	25/20
72	Bronze HELP 4	VALENTYNE SUITE (LP, gatefold sleeve, reissue)	12

(see also Dick Heckstall-Smith, Chris Farlowe, Greenslade, John Mayall, Howard Riley Trio, Tempest, Mogul Thrash)

COLOURBOX

82	4AD AD 215	Breakdown/Tarantula (p/s).	7
82	4AD BAD 215	Breakdown/Tarantula (12", p/s)	10
83	4AD AD 314	Breakdown (Second Version)/Tarantula (Second Version) (different p/s)	6
83	4AD BAD 314	Breakdown (Second Version)/Tarantula (Second Version) (12", different p/s)	8
84	4AD 403	Say You/Fast Dump (p/s)	5
84	4AD 406	Punch/Keep On Pushing (p/s)	5
85	4AD 507	The Moon Is Blue/You Keep Me Hanging On (p/s)	5
86	4AD 604	Baby I Love You So/Looks Like We're Shy One Horse (p/s)	5
86	4AD 605	The Official Colourbox World Cup Theme/Philip Glass (p/s)	5
85	4AD CAD 508	COLOURBOX (LP, stickered sleeve, 10,000 only, with bonus LP MAD 509).	20

(see also M/A/R/R/S)

COLOURED RAISINS

70	Trojan TR 7700	One Way Love/No More Heartaches	5

COLOURFIELD

84	Chrysalis COLF D2	Thinking Of You/Wild Flames//Little Things/Thinking Of You (double pack).	6
85	Chrysalis COLF D4	Castles In The Air/Your Love Was Smashing//I Can't Get Enough Of You Baby/Castles In The Air (Instrumental Mix) (double pack, gatefold p/s)	6
87	Chrysalis CCD 1546	DECEPTION (CD).	25
89	Chrysalis CHR 1480	VIRGINS AND PHILISTINES (CD).	60

(see also Specials, Fun Boy Three, Terry Hall)

COLOURFUL SEASONS

68	MGM MGM 1433	Out Of The Blue/It's Gonna Break My Heart	5

COLOURS

68	Dot DOT 113	Love Heals/Bad Day At Black Rock Baby	5

COLO(U)RS OF LOVE

68	Page One POF 060	I'm A Train/Up On A Cotton Cloud.	6
68	Page One POF 086	Just Another Fly/Twenty Ten	6
69	Page One POF 124	Mother Of Convention/Music Mother Made.	6

(see also Elaine Paige)

CHRISTOPHER COLT

68	Decca F 12726	Virgin Sunrise/Girl In The Mirror	20

TONY COLTON('S BIG BOSS BAND)

64	Decca F 11879	Lose My Mind/So Used To Loving You (solo)	12
65	Pye 7N 15886	I Stand Accused/Further On Down The Track (with Big Boss Band)	90
66	Pye 7N 17046	You're Wrong There Baby/Have You Lost Your Mind	25
66	Pye 7N 17117	I've Laid Some Down In My Time/Run Pony Rider	30
68	Columbia DB 8385	In The World Of Marnie Dreaming/Who Is She? (solo)	12

(see also Poet & One Man Band, Head Hands & Feet, Real McCoy, Peter B's)

JOHN COLTRANE

60	Esquire EP 229	SOUL OF 'TRANE (EP).	10
61	Esquire EP 239	BASS BLUES (EP).	10
64	Fontana 469 203TE	WHILE MY LADY SLEEPS (EP)	10
58	Esquire 32-079	THE FIRST TRANE (LP)	18
58	Esquire 32-089	SOUL TRANE (LP)	18
59	Esquire 32-091	TRANEING IN (LP)	18
60	London Jazz LTZ-K 15197	GIANT STEPS (LP).	18
61	Esquire 32-129	LUSH LIFE (LP)	18
61	London Jazz LTZ-K 15219	COLTRANE JAZZ (LP, also stereo SAH-K 6162).	18
62	London Jazz LTZ-K 15232	BAGS AND TRANE (LP, also stereo SAH-K 6192).	18
62	Columbia 33SX 1399	THE BIRDLAND STORY VOL. 1: ECHOES OF AN ERA (LP)	15
62	London Jazz LTZ-K 15239	OLE COLTRANE (LP, also stereo SAH-K 6223).	18
62	HMV CLP 1548	AFRICA/BRASS (LP, also stereo CSD 1431).	15
62	Storyville SLP 28	JOHN COLTRANE & DAVE CHAMBERS (LP)	15
62	HMV CLP 1590	LIVE AT THE VILLAGE VANGUARD (LP, also stereo CSD 1456).	15

63	United Artists (S)ULP 1018	COLTRANE TIME (LP)	15
63	London HA-K/SH-K 8017	COLTRANE PLAYS THE BLUES (LP, as John Coltrane Group)	18
63	Esquire 32-179	STANDARD COLTRANE (LP)	18
63	HMV CLP 1629	COLTRANE (LP, also stereo CSD 1483)	15
63	HMV CLP 1647	BALLADS (LP, also stereo CSD 1496)	15
63	HMV CLP 1657	DUKE ELLINGTON & JOHN COLTRANE (LP, also stereo CSD 1502)	15
64	HMV CLP 1695	IMPRESSIONS (LP, also stereo CSD 1509)	15
64	HMV CLP 1700	JOHN COLTRANE WITH JOHNNY HARTMAN (LP)	15
64	Realm RM 157	ON WEST 42ND STREET (LP)	12
64	Realm RM 181	TRANE RIDE (LP)	12
64	HMV CLP 1741	LIVE AT BIRDLAND (LP, also stereo CSD 1544)	15
65	HMV CLP 1799	CRESCENT (LP, also stereo CSD 1567)	15
65	Stateside SL 10124	BLACK PEARLS (LP)	15
65	HMV CLP 1869	A LOVE SUPREME (LP, also stereo CSD 1605)	15
65	Atlantic ATL/SAL 5022	MY FAVOURITE THINGS (LP)	15
65	Realm RM 52226	TANGANYIKA STRUT (LP)	12
65	HMV CLP 1897	COLTRANE PLAYS (LP, also stereo CSD 1619)	15
66	Stateside SL 10162	BAHIA (LP)	15
66	HMV CLP/CSD 3543	ASCENSION (LP, as John Coltrane Orchestra)	15
66	HMV CLP/CSD 3551	NEW THING AT NEWPORT (LP, with Archie Shepp)	15
66	Atlantic 587/588 004	THE AVANT-GARDE (LP, with Don Cherry)	15
66	HMV CLP/CSD 3575	MEDITATIONS (LP)	15
67	Atlantic 587/588 039	COLTRANE'S SOUND (LP)	15
67	HMV CLP/CSD 3599	COLTRANE LIVE AT THE VILLAGE VANGUARD AGAIN! (LP)	15
67	Atlantic ATL 1311	GIANT STEPS (LP, reissue)	12
67	Atlantic ATL/SAL 1354	COLTRANE JAZZ (LP, reissue)	12
67	HMV CLP/CSD 3617	OM (LP, withdrawn)	25
67	HMV CLP/CSD 3617	KULU SE MAMA (LP)	15
68	Transatlantic PR 7280	DAKAR (LP)	15
68	Transatlantic PR 7378	LAST TRANE (LP)	15
68	Impulse MIPL/SIPL 502	EXPRESSION (LP)	15
69	Atlantic 588 139	THREE LITTLE WORDS (LP)	15
69	Atlantic 588 146	MY FAVOURITE THINGS (LP, reissue)	12
69	Impulse MIPL/SIPL 515	COSMIC MUSIC (LP, by Alice & John Coltrane)	15
69	Atlantic 588 168	GIANT STEPS (LP, reissue)	12
69	Realm 52157	ON WEST 42ND STREET (LP, reissue)	12
70	Impulse SIPL 522	SELFLESSNESS (LP)	15
71	Probe SPB 1025	AFRO BLUE (LP)	12
72	Prestige PR 24003	JOHN COLTRANE (2-LP)	15
73	CBS PR 24014	MORE LASTING THAN BRONZE (2-LP)	15
74	Atlantic K 60052	THE ART OF JOHN COLTRANE: THE ATLANTIC YEARS (2-LP)	15
74	CBS PR 24037	BLACK PEARLS (2-LP)	15

(see also Miles Davis, Thelonious Monk, Cannonball Adderley, Don Cherry, Archie Shepp)

COLTS

| 65 | Pye 7N 15955 | San Miguel/Where Has Our Love Gone? | 6 |

COLUMBIA BOYS

| 68 | Pye 7N 17513 | Baby Come Back/Born To Lose | 6 |
| 69 | Pye 7N 17763 | That's My Pa/She Thinks I Still Care | 5 |

COLUMBUS

| 70 | Deram DM 294 | Ev'rybody Loves The U.S. Marshall/Tired | 6 |

KEN COLYER('S JAZZMEN)

55	Decca F 10504	Early Hours/Cataract Rag	10
55	Decca F 10519	If I Ever Cease To Love/The Entertainer	10
55	Decca F 10565	It Looks Like A Big Time Tonight/Red Wing	10
56	Tempo A 117	Just A Closer Walk With Thee/Sheik Of Araby	10
56	Tempo A 120	If I Ever Cease To Love You/Isle Of Capri	10
56	Tempo A 126	My Bucket's Got A Hole In It/Wabash Blues	10
56	Tempo A 136	Maryland, My Maryland/The World Is Waiting For The Sunrise	10
56	Decca FJ 10755	All The Girls Go Crazy About The Way I Walk/Dippermouth Blues	10
61	Columbia DB 4676	The Happy Wanderer/Maryland, My Maryland	6
55	Decca DFE 6268	AND BACK TO NEW ORLEANS VOL. 1 (EP)	35
55	Decca DFE 6299	AND BACK TO NEW ORLEANS VOL. 2 (EP)	25
55	Vogue EPV 1202	KEN COLYER IN NEW ORLEANS (EP)	10
55	Tempo EXA 26	KEN COLYER JAZZMEN (EP)	10
56	Melodisc EPM7 59	KEN COLYER JAZZMEN AND THE CRANE RIVER JAZZ BAND (EP)	18
56	Vogue EPV 1102	KEN COLYER IN NEW ORLEANS (EP)	10
56	Tempo EXA 31	KEN COLYER JAZZMEN (EP)	10
57	Tempo EXA 53	KEN COLYER IN NEW ORLEANS (EP)	10
58	Decca DFE 6435	KEN COLYER AND HIS OMEGA BRASS (EP)	8
58	Decca DFE 6466	THEY ALL PLAYED RAGTIME (EP)	18
59	Esquire EP 233	RUM AND COCA COLA (EP, with Christie Brothers Stompers)	10
60	Storyville SEP 301	KEN COLYER JAZZMEN (EP)	20
60	Storyville SEP 305	KEN COLYER'S JAZZMEN (EP)	12

Ken COLYER

60	Storyville SEP 309	KEN COLYER'S JAZZMEN (EP)	10
60	Decca DFE 6645	WALKING THE BLUES	
		(EP, also stereo STO 143)	18/20
60	Columbia SEG 8038	THIS IS JAZZ (EP)	12
61	Storyville SEP 392	TRAD JAZZ SCENE IN EUROPE VOL. 2 (EP)	12
61	Storyville SEP 412	WILDCAT BLUES (EP)	12
61	Columbia SEG 8104	THIS IS JAZZ VOL. 1 NO. 2 (EP)	15
61	Esquire EP 243	STOMPING (EP)	10
62	Columbia SEG 8145	THIS IS JAZZ VOL. 2 (EP)	10
62	Columbia SEG 8180	TOO BUSY (EP)	18
60s	Melodisc EPM7 105	KEN COLYER (EP)	18
66	K.C. KCS 11EP	GREEN CORN (EP)	10
54	Decca LF 1152	NEW ORLEANS TO LONDON (10" LP)	45
54	Decca LF 1196	BACK TO THE DELTA	
		(10" LP, as Ken Colyer's Jazzmen & Skiffle Group)	35
55	Vogue LDE 161	KEN COLYER IN NEW ORLEANS (10" LP)	25
56	Tempo LAP 11	KEN COLYER'S JAZZMEN (10" LP)	35
57	Decca LK 4178	CLUB SESSION (LP)	15
58	Decca LF 1301	IN GLORY LAND (10" LP, as Ken Colyer & His Omega Brass Band)	25
59	Decca LF 1319	COLYER IN HAMBURG (10" LP)	20
59	Decca LK 4294	PLAYS STANDARDS (LP)	15
60	Columbia 33SX 1220	THIS IS JAZZ (LP)	25
61	Columbia 33SX 1297	THIS IS JAZZ VOL. 2 (LP, also stereo SCX 3360)	22
61	Columbia 33SX 1363	THIS IS THE BLUES VOL. 1 (LP)	60
63	Society SOC 914	COLYER'S PLEASURE (LP)	18
64	77 LEU 12/10	THE REAL KEN COLYER (LP)	25
65	K.C. KCS 1001	WANDERING (LP)	20
70	Joy JOYS 164	WATCH THAT DIRTY TONE (LP)	15
70	Joy JOYS 170	AT THE THAMES HOTEL (LP)	12

KEN COLYER'S SKIFFLE GROUP

55	Decca F 10631	Down By The Riverside/Take This Hammer	15
55	Decca F 10631	Down By The Riverside/Take This Hammer (78)	12
56	Decca FJ 10711	Streamline Train/Go Down Old Hannah	12
56	Decca FJ 10711	Streamline Train/Go Down Old Hannah (78)	12
56	Decca FJ 10751	Down Bound Train/Mule Skinner	12
56	Decca FJ 10751	Down Bound Train/Mule Skinner (78)	10
56	Decca FJ 10772	Old Riley/Stack O'Lee Blues	10
56	Decca FJ 10772	Old Riley/Stack O'Lee Blues (78)	10
57	Decca FJ 10889	The Grey Goose/I Can't Sleep	10
57	Decca FJ 10889	The Grey Goose/I Can't Sleep (78)	10
57	Decca FJ 10926	Sporting Life/House Rent Stomp	10
57	Decca FJ 10926	Sporting Life/House Rent Stomp (78)	12
57	Decca FJ 10972	Ella Speed/Go Down Sunshine	10
57	Decca FJ 10972	Ella Speed/Go Down Sunshine (78)	15
55	Decca DFE 6286	KEN COLYER'S SKIFFLE GROUP (EP, various coloured sleeves)	18
58	Decca DFE 6444	KEN COLYER'S SKIFFLE GROUP NO. 2 (EP)	18
60	Decca DFE 6563	KEN COLYER'S SKIFFLE GROUP IN HAMBURG (EP)	20
	(see also Crane Skiffle Group)		

COMBAT 84

82	Victory VIC 1	ORDERS OF THE DAY (EP, wraparound p/s)	20
83	Victory VIC 2	Rapist/The Right To Choose/Barry Prudom (p/s)	20

COMBINATIONS

72	Punch PH 99	1 2 3 A B C/Zee	5

COMBINE HARVESTER

70	Folk Heritage FHR 009	COMBINE HARVESTER (LP)	15

COME

79	Come Org. WDC 88001	Come Sunday/Shaved Slits	15
79	Come Org. WDC 88203	PRESENT RAMPTON (LP)	50
81	Come Org. WDC 881012	I'M JACK (LP, orange vinyl with insert)	40
	(see also Whitehouse, New Order)		

COMEDY OF ERRORS

86	private pressing	MINI ALBUM (LP)	12

COMET GAIN

98	Mei Mei MEI001	Jack Nance Hair/We Are All Rotten/Record Prayer (p/s)	5
99	Piao PIAO 17	Orwell Liberty Dance/Young Lions Devour/Hands Fit (p/s)	5

COMIC ROMANCE

78	Do It DUN 3	Cry Myself To Sleep/Cowboys And Indians (p/s)	5
79	WEA K 17418	Cry Myself To Sleep/Cowboys And Indians (reissue, p/s)	5
	(see also M, Robin Scott)		

RORY COMMADORE

(see under Tindersticks)

COMMANCHES

64	Pye 7N 15609	Tomorrow/Missed Your Loving	8
	(see also Bobby Allen)		

COMMANDERS

55	Brunswick 05366	The Elephants' Tango/Commanders Overture	6
55	Brunswick 05433	The Cat From Coos Bay/Camptown Boogie	7
55	Brunswick 05467	The Monster/Cornball No. 1	7
	(see also Louis Armstrong)		

COMMANDOS
76   Polydor 2058 781   The Bump/Drop In Sometime 5
(see also Lene Lovich)

COMMERCIALS
81   Fast Product COM 1   Sixteen Again And Again/The Heroine Dies/Simon (p/s) 8

COMMITTED
79   Ace ACE 006   Crash Victim/British Crimes/Fast Lane/Advertising 40

COMMITTEE
68   Liberty LBF 15154   Hard Way/Hey You 5

COMMITTEE
69   Pye 7N 17826   Sleep Tight Honey/Memories Of Melinda 5

COMMODORES
55   London HLD 8209   Riding On A Train/Uranium 1,000
55   London HLD 8209   Riding On A Train/Uranium 100
56   London HLD 8251   Speedo/Whole Lotta Shakin' Goin' On. 900
56   London HLD 8251   Speedo/Whole Lotta Shakin' Goin' On (78) 125

COMMODORES
69   Atlantic 584 273   Keep On Dancing/Rise Up 6
74   Tamla Motown TMG 924   The Zoo (The Human Zoo)/I'm Looking For A Love 5
75   Tamla Motown TMG 944   I Feel Sanctified/Determination 5
75   Tamla Motown TMG 952   Slippery When Wet/The Bump 5
(see also Lionel Richie)

COMMON ROUND
70s Galliard GAL 4015   FOUR PENCE A DAY (LP) 15

COMMUNARDS
86   London LONXR 103   Don't Leave Me This Way (Gotham City Mix)/Don't Leave Me This Way/
                               Sanctified/Don't Leave Me This Way (12", p/s) 8
86   London LONXRR 103   Don't Leave Me This Way (Son Of Gotham City Mix)/Sanctified
                               (Son Of Gotham City Remix) (12", p/s) 8

(see also Bronski Beat, Jimmy Somerville)

PERRY COMO
78s
51   HMV B 10020   Did Anyone Tell You Mrs. Murphy/Watchin' The Trains Go By (78) 10
51   HMV B 10042   If/Zing Zing — Zoom Zoom (78). 10
51   HMV B 10159   Cara Cara, Bella Bella/With All My Heart And Soul (with Tanner Sisters) (78).... 10
52   HMV B 10188   Rollin' Stone/Let's Go To Church (with Tanner Sisters) (78) ...'...... 10
52   HMV B 10266   Noodlin' Rag/Play Me A Hurtin' Tune (with Fontane Sisters) (78). 10
52   HMV B 10329   Maybe/Watermelon Weather (with Eddie Fisher) (78) 10
53   HMV B 10400   Don't Let The Stars Get In Your Eyes/To Know You (Is To Love You)
                               (B-side with Fontane Sisters) (78) 10
56   HMV POP 191   Juke Box Baby/The Things I Didn't Do (78). 12
56   HMV POP 271   Moonlight Love/Chincherinchee (78). 10
57   HMV POP 369   Silk Stockings/Childhood Is A Meadow (78) 10
57   HMV POP 394   As Time Goes By/All At Once You Love Her (78) 10
58   RCA RCA 1055   Kewpie Doll/Dance Only With Me (78) 10
58   RCA RCA 1086   Love Makes The World Go Round/Mandolins In The Moonlight (78) 6
59   RCA RCA 1111   Tomboy/Kiss Me And Kiss Me And Kiss Me (78) 10
59   RCA RCA 1156   A Still Small Voice/No Well On Earth (78) 12
60   RCA RCA 1170   Delaware/I Know What God Is (78) 30

SINGLES
53   HMV 7M 102   The Ruby And The Pearl/My Love And Devotion 15
53   HMV 7M 110   Some Enchanted Evening/Bali Ha'i. 18
53   HMV 7M 118   Don't Let The Stars Get In Your Eyes/To Know You (Is To Love You)
                               (B-side with Fontane Sisters) 30
53   HMV 7M 124   Wild Horses/Please Believe Me 18
53   HMV 7M 138   My Lady Loves To Dance/A Bushel And A Peck (B-side with Betty Hutton) 18
53   HMV 7M 149   My One And Only Heart/Say You're Mine Again 18
53   HMV 7M 155   Hello, Young Lovers/We Kiss In A Shadow 15
53   HMV 7M 163   Pa-Paya Mama/Why Did You Leave Me? 15
54   HMV 7M 175   You Alone/Surprising. 15
54   HMV 7M 200   Idle Gossip/Look Out The Window 25
54   HMV 7M 215   Wanted/Give Me Your Hand 18
54   HMV 7M 241   Hit And Run Affair/If You Were Only Mine 15
54   HMV 7M 263   There Never Was A Night So Beautiful/Papa Loves Mambo. 18
54   HMV 7M 278   Frosty The Snowman/The Twelve Days Of Christmas. 15
55   HMV 7M 296   Ko Ko Mo (I Love You So)/You'll Always Be My Lifetime Love 15
55   HMV 7M 305   Door Of Dreams/Nobody 12
55   HMV 7M 326   There's No Place Like Home For The Holidays/Tina Marie. 15
56   HMV 7M 366   Fooled/The Rose Tattoo. 12
56   HMV 7M 404   Hot Diggity (Dog Ziggity Boom)/My Funny Valentine 15
56   HMV 7MC 39   Hot Diggity (Dog Ziggity Boom)/Juke Box Baby (export issue) 60
56   HMV POP 240   Glendora/More 15
56   HMV 7MC 49   Glendora/More (export issue) 18
56   HMV POP 271   Moonlight Love/Chincherinchee 10
57   HMV POP 304   Somebody Up There Likes Me/Dream Along With Me
                               (I'm On My Way To A Star) 10
57   HMV 7MC 51   Somebody Up There Likes Me/Dream Along With Me
                               (I'm On My Way To A Star) (export issue) 12
57   HMV POP 328   Round And Round/My House Is Your House. 12
57   RCA RCA 1001   The Girl With The Golden Braids/My Little Baby. 6

MINT VALUE £

57	HMV POP 369	Silk Stockings/Childhood Is A Meadow	7
57	HMV POP 394	As Time Goes By/All At Once You Love Her	7
57	RCA RCA 1016	Marching Along To The Blues/Dancin'.	5
57	RCA RCA 1027	Just Born (To Be Your Baby)/Ivy Rose	5
58	RCA RCA 1036	Magic Moments/Catch A Falling Star	6
58	RCA RCA 1055	Kewpie Doll/Dance Only With Me.	10
58	RCA RCA 1062	I May Never Pass This Way Again/Prayer For Peace.	5

EPs

54	HMV 7EG 8013	PERRY COMO (EP)	8
56	HMV 7EG 8171	SO SMOOTH (EP).	8
56	HMV 7EG 8192	COMO SWINGS (EP)	10
57	HMV 7EG 8244	WITH A SONG IN MY HEART (EP).	10

LPs

54	HMV DLP 1026	PERRY COMO SINGS (10" LP).	25
57	RCA RD 27035	WE GET LETTERS (LP)	15
57	RCA RD 27070	WE GET LETTERS VOL. 2 (LP)	18
57	RCA RD 27078/SF 5011	DEAR PERRY (LP, mono/stereo).	15/18
57	RCA RD 27082	SINGS MERRY CHRISTMAS MUSIC (LP).	15
58	RCA RD 27100	COMO'S GOLDEN RECORDS (LP)	15
58	RCA RD 27106/SF 5021	WHEN YOU COME TO THE END OF THE DAY (LP, mono/stereo)	15/18
58	RCA RD 27139/SF 5045	SINGS THE SONGS OF CHRISTMAS (LP, mono/stereo)	15/18
59	RCA RD 27154/SF 5053	COMO SWINGS (LP, mono/stereo)	15/18
60	RCA RD 27206/SF 5089	FOR THE YOUNG AT HEART (LP, mono/stereo)	15/18
61	RCA RD 27232	SING TO ME, MR. C (LP).	15
63	RCA Victor RD 7582	THE SONGS I LOVE (LP).	15
66	RCA Victor RD 7802	LIGHTLY LATIN (LP).	15
66	RCA Victor RD 7836	IN ITALY (LP).	15

(see also Fontane Sisters, Betty Hutton)

LES COMPAGNONS DE LA CHANSON

53	Columbia SCM 5005	The Three Bells (The Jimmy Brown Song)/Ave Maria.	15
53	Columbia SCM 5056	The Galley Slave/Dreams Never Grow Old	12
59	Columbia DB 4358	The Three Bells (The Jimmy Brown Song)/Ave Maria (reissue)	5
60	Columbia DB 4454	Down By The Riverside/Margoton	5

COMPANY

| 79 | United Artists BP 326 | We Wish You Well/Right Time For Love (no p/s) | 25 |

(see also Whitesnake)

COMPLEX

| 70 | CLPM 001 | COMPLEX (LP, private pressing, 99 copies only) | 750 |
| 71 | Deroy | THE WAY WE FEEL (LP, private pressing, 99 copies only) | 450 |

(see also Mitchell-Coe Mysteries, Monsoon, Misfits)

COMPROMISE

| 66 | CBS 202050 | You Will Think Of Me/Love Minus Zero | 6 |

COMSAT ANGELS

| 79 | Junta JUNTA 1 | Red Planet/I Get Excited/Specimen No. 2 (p/s, later reissued on red vinyl). | 6/8 |
| 81 | Polydor POSP 359 | Do The Empty House/Now I Know/Red Planet Revisited (double pack). | 4 |

BOBBY COMSTOCK (& COUNTS)

59	Top Rank JAR 223	The Tennessee Waltz/Sweet Talk	7
60	London HLE 9080	Jambalaya/Let's Talk It Over (as Bobby Comstock & Counts)	15
63	Stateside SS 163	Let's Stomp/I Want To Do It	12
63	Stateside SS 221	Susie Baby/Take A Walk.	7
65	United Artists UP 1086	I'm A Man/I'll Make You Glad	15

COMUS

71	Dawn DNX 2506	Diana/In The Lost Queen's Eyes/Winter Is A Coloured Bird (p/s).	15
71	Dawn DNLS 3019	FIRST UTTERANCE (LP, gatefold sleeve with lyric sheet)	100
74	Virgin V 2018	TO KEEP FROM CRYING (LP)	18

(see also Gong, Henry Cow, Esperanto Rock Orchestra)

CON-CHORDS

| 65 | Polydor BM 56059 | You Can't Take It Away/Let Me Walk With You | 8 |

CONCORDE

| 70 | Attack ATT 8020 | Let Me Out/I Belong To You | 8 |

CONCORDS

| 66 | Emblem JDR 303 | SOUL PURPOSE (LP). | 15 |

CONCORDS

| 69 | Blue Cat BS 170 | Buttoo/I Need Your Loving | 10 |

CONCRETE

| 70s | Concrete Prod. CON 001 | GHOULISH PRACTICES (EP, poster p/s, stamped labels) | 5 |

(see also 400 Blows)

CONDEMNED 84

86	RFB SIN 2	Oi Ain't Dead!/Under Her Thumb/Follow The Leader/The Nutter (12", p/s, blue vinyl)	25
87	RFB SIN 3	IN SEARCH OF THE NEW BREED (12" EP).	15
88	Oi! OIR 003	BATTLE SCARRED (LP).	15

EDDIE CONDON

60	Philips JAZ 115	Heebies Jeebies/What-cha-call-'em Blues (as Eddie Condon & All-Stars)	5
62	Stateside SL 10005	JAM SESSIONS AT COMMODORE (LP, as Eddie Condon & Group)	12
62	Stateside SL 10010	CONDON A LA CARTE (LP).	12

JEFF CONDON
63	MGM MGM 1221	(Walkin' In) Freddy's Footsteps/Never You Mind	6

HOWIE G. CONDOR
65	Fontana TF 613	Big Noise From Winnetka/The Fix	8

CONEY ISLAND KIDS
55	London HLJ 8207	Baby, Baby You/Moonlight Beach	30
55	London HLJ 8207	Baby, Baby You/Moonlight Beach (78)	12

CONFLICT
82	Crass 221984/1	THE HOUSE THAT MAN BUILT (EP, foldout poster p/s)	8
82	Xntrix XN 2001	LIVE AT THE CENTRE IBERICO (EP, with insert)	8
83	Corp. Christi CHRIST IT'S 4	A Nation Of Animal Lovers/Liberate (poster p/s)	8
85	Mortarhate MORT 15	The Battle Continues (both sides) (p/s, different colours, with insert)	5
88	FUND 1	FROM PROTEST TO RESISTANCE (LP, mail order, w/l, stickered plain sleeve)	12

ARTHUR CONLEY
67	Atlantic 584 083	Sweet Soul Music/Let's Go Steady	6
67	Atlantic 584 121	Shake, Rattle And Roll/You Don't Have To See Me	6
67	Atlantic 584 143	Whole Lotta Woman/Love Comes And Goes	6
68	Atlantic 584 175	Funky Street/Put Our Love Together	6
68	Atlantic 584 197	People Sure Act Funny/Burning Fire	6
68	Atlantic 584 224	Aunt Dora's Love Soul Shack/Is That You Love	6
69	Atco 226 004	Star Revue/Love Sure Is A Powerful Thing	6
70	Atco 226 011	They Call The Wind Maria/Hurt	5
70	Atlantic 2091 025	All Day Singing/God Bless	5
71	Atlantic 2091 106	Sweet Soul Music/Shake, Rattle And Roll	5
71	Atlantic 2091 120	I'm Living Good/I'm So Glad You're Here	5
72	Capricorn K 17506	Rita/More Sweet Soul Music	5
67	Atlantic 587 069	SWEET SOUL MUSIC (LP)	25
68	Atlantic 587 084	SHAKE, RATTLE AND ROLL (LP)	20
68	Atlantic 587/588 128	SOUL DIRECTION (LP)	20
69	Atco 228 019	MORE SWEET SOUL (LP)	15

(see also Soul Clan)

FRANK CONN COMPANY
60	MGM MGM 1055	My Bonnie/Swanee River	5

BRIAN CONNELL & ROUND SOUND
66	Mercury MF 956	Just My Kind Of Loving/Something You've Got	8
66	Mercury MF 991	The Same Thing's Happened To Me/Mister Porter	8
68	Philips BF 1661	What Kind Of Girl/Just Another Wedding Day	8
68	Philips BF 1718	I Know/Mister Travel Company	8

RAY CONNIFF & ROCKIN' RHYTHM BOYS
55	Vogue Coral QW 5001	Piggy Bank Boogie/Short Stuff	15
55	Vogue Coral QW 5001	Piggy Bank Boogie/Short Stuff (78)	10
68	CBS (S)BPG 63276	HOW TO SAVE A MARRIAGE AND RUIN YOUR LIFE (LP, soundtrack)	18

BILLY CONNOLLY
85	Stiff DBUY 218	Super Gran (1-sided shaped picture disc)	5
85	Audiotrax ATX 10	Freedom (with Chris Tummings & Singing Rebels Band)/	
		JIMMY HELMS: Celebration (some in p/s)	20/8
72	Transatlantic TRA 258	LIVE! (LP)	12
76	Transatlantic GAR 1	THE CONNOLLY GOLDEN GIFT BOX (2-LP box set: "Live!" & "Solo Concert")	15

(see also Humblebums; George Harrison, Ringo Starr & Eric Clapton appear on "Freedom")

BRIAN CONNOLLY
82	Carrere CAR 231	Hypnotised/Fade Away (p/s)	15

(see also Sweet)

KIEV CONNOLLY & MISSING PASSENGERS
89	Sulan SUS 1080	The Real Me/Haze On Mizan Head (p/s, export issue for Ireland)	6

CHRIS CONNOR
59	London HLE 8869	Hallelujah I Love Him So/I Won't Cry Anymore	10
59	London HLE 8869	Hallelujah I Love Him So/I Won't Cry Anymore (78)	20
60	London HLK 9124	I Only Want Some/That's My Desire	8
56	London EZ-N 19010	CHRIS CONNOR SINGS LULLABYS OF BIRDLAND (EP, with Ellis Larkin Trio)	12
57	London RE-N 1093	LONDON'S GIRL FRIENDS — NO. 2 (EP)	15
56	London HA-K 2030	PRESENTING CHRIS CONNOR (LP, also stereo SAH-K 6032)	22
56	London LZ-N 14007	SINGS LULLABYS FOR LOVERS (10" LP)	15
57	London HB-N 1074	CHRIS (10" LP)	25
57	London HA-K 2066	HE LOVES ME, HE LOVES ME NOT (LP)	18
60	London LZ-N 14036	THIS IS CHRIS (10" LP)	20
60	London LTZ-K 15142	A JAZZ DATE WITH (LP)	20
60	London LTZ-K 15151	CHRIS CRAFT (LP)	18
60	London Jazz LTZ-K 15183	THE BALLAD OF THE SAD CAFÉ (LP)	18
60	London Jazz LTZ-K 15185	WITCHCRAFT (LP)	18
60	London Jazz LTZ-K 15195	CHRIS IN PERSON (LP, also stereo SAH-K 6088)	18
61	London SAH-K 6190	DOUPLE EXPOSURE (LP, with Maynard Ferguson)	12

EDRIC CONNOR
57	Oriole CB 1362	Manchester United Calypso/Yorumba Highlife (78)	10

KENNETH CONNOR
59	Top Rank JAR 138	Rail Road Rock/Ramona	6
59	Top Rank JAR 138	Rail Road Rock/Ramona (78)	12

CAROL CONNORS
62	London HLN 9619	Big Big Love/Two Rivers	10

(see also Teddy Bears)

CONNY
61	Columbia DB 4714	No One Can Tell Me I'm Too Young/Lovable	15
62	Columbia DB 4845	Gino/Midi-Midinette	15

CONQUERORS
67	Doctor Bird DB 1119	Won't You Come Home Now?/Oh That Day	18
67	Treasure Isle TI 7035	Lonely Street/I Fell In Love	20
69	Amalgamated AMG 832	Secret Weapon (actually by Ansell Collins)/Jumpy Jumpy Girl	12
69	High Note HS 016	If You Can't Beat Them/Anywhere You Want To Go	8
69	High Note HS 025	National Dish/Mr D.J.	8

(see also Stranger Cole & Conquerors, Baba Brooks)

JESS CONRAD
60	Decca F 11236	Cherry Pie/There's Gonna Be A Day	7
60	Decca F 11259	Unless You Meant It/Out Of Luck	6
61	Decca F 11315	Mystery Girl/The Big White House	6
61	Decca F 11348	This Pullover/Why Am I Living?	6
61	Decca F 11375	Oh You Beautiful Doll/I See You	6
61	Decca F 11394	Walkaway/Every Breath I Take	6
61	Decca F 11412	Twist My Wrist/Hey Little Girl (some in p/s)	12/6
62	Decca F 11511	Pretty Jenny/You Can Do It If You Try	6
63	Decca F 11620	It's About Time/As You Like It	5
63	Columbia DB 4969	Take Your Time/I Know You	5
64	Columbia DB 7223	Pussycat/Tempted	6
65	Columbia DB 7561	Things I'd Like To Say/Don't Turn Around	6
65	Pye 7N 15849	Hurt Me/It Can Happen To You	25
69	President PT 269	Other Side Of Life/See The Tinker Ride	5
70	President PT 292	Crystal Ball Dream/Pussycat	5
71	President PT 357	Here She Comes Again/My Idea	5
60	Decca DFE 6666	JESS CONRAD (EP)	18
62	Decca DFE 6702	TWIST MY WRIST (EP)	15
63	Decca DFE 8524	THE HUMAN JUNGLE (EP)	15
78	SRT	AN EVENING WITH JESS CONRAD (EP)	8
61	Decca LK 4390	JESS FOR YOU (LP)	35

(see also Guvners)

TONI CONRAD & FAUST
72	Caroline C 1501	OUTSIDE THE DREAM SYNDICATE (LP)	12

(see also Faust)

CONSCIOUS MINDS
71	Big BG 318	Jamaican Boy/Brainwash	8
71	Ackee ACK 141	Paul, Marcus And Norman/Version	6
71	Punch PH 97	Paul, Marcus And Norman/Version (reissue)	5
71	Escort ERT 857	Peace Treaty/Brainwash	6

(see also Ken Boothe, Jamaicans, B.B.Seaton, Charmers)

CONSORTIUM
68	Pye 7N 17635	All The Love In The World/Spending My Life Saying Goodbye	6
69	Pye 7N 17725	When The Day Breaks/Day The Train Never Came	5
69	Pye 7N 17797	Beggar Man/Cynthia Serenity	5
69	Pye 7N 17841	I Don't Want Her Anymore/The House Upon The Hill	5
70	Trend TNT 52	Melanie Cries Alone/Copper Coloured Years	5

EDDIE CONSTANTINE
58	Felsted SD 80058	Time Train/Never Never Before	5
59	Felsted SD 80060	Love Isn't Love/Portrait	5
56	Felsted ESD 3017	AN AMERICAN IN PARIS (EP)	8
58	Felsted ESD 3078	EDDIE CONSTANTINE (EP)	8

CONSUMATES
68	Coxsone CS 7054	What Is It/ROLAND ALPHONSO: Musical Happiness	20

CONTACT
79	Object Music OM 11	FUTURE/PAST (EP)	5

(see also Passage)

CONTINENTALS
62	Island WI 010	Going Crazy/Give Me All Your Love	15

CONTINUUM
70	RCA Victor SF 8157	CONTINUUM (LP)	15
71	RCA Victor SF 8196	AUTUMN GRASS (LP, gatefold sleeve)	22

CONTOURS
62	Oriole CB 1763	Do You Love Me/Move Mister Man	18
63	Oriole CB 1799	Shake Sherry/You Better Get In Line	30
63	Oriole CB 1831	Don't Let Him Be Your Baby/It Must Be Love	40
64	Stateside SS 299	Can You Do It/I'll Stand By You	30
65	Stateside SS 381	Can You Jerk Like Me/That Day She Needed Me	25
65	Tamla Motown TMG 531	First I Look At The Purse/Searching For A Girl	35
66	Tamla Motown TMG 564	Determination/Just A Little Misunderstanding	40
67	Tamla Motown TMG 605	It's So Hard Being A Loser/Your Love Grows More Precious Every Day	18
70	Tamla Motown TMG 723	Just A Little Misunderstanding/First I Look At The Purse	6
65	Tamla Motown TME 2002	THE CONTOURS (EP)	70
63	Oriole PS 40043	DO YOU LOVE ME (LP)	125
74	M. For Pleasure MFP 50054	BABY HIT AND RUN (LP)	12

CONTRABAND
74	Transatlantic BIG 518	Lady For Today/On The Road	5
74	Transatlantic TRA 278	CONTRABAND (LP, with lyric insert)	20

(see also Mae McKenna)

CONTRAST
69   Orange OAS 202   Hey That's No Way To Say Goodbye/We Can Make It If We Try 5

CONTRASTS featuring BOB MORRISON
64   Parlophone R 5190   Call Me/Come On Let's Go. 5
68   Monument MON 1018   What A Day/Lonely Child. 6
(see also Bill Forbes)

CONTROLLED BLEEDING
86   Sterile SR 11   HEADCRACK (LP) 25

CONUNDRUM & RICHARD HARVEY
78   Streetsong No. 1   Black Birds Of Brittany/SHIRLEY COLLINS & ANNIE POWER:
                              The Mariners Farewell
                              (poster p/s) 15
(see also Bert Jansch, Shirley Collins)

CONVAIRS
66   HMV POP 1549   Tomorrow Is A Long Time/Midnight Mary 8

BERT CONVY & THUNDERBIRDS
55   London HLB 8190   C'mon Back/Hoo Bop De Bow 135
55   London HLB 8190   C'mon Back/Hoo Bop De Bow (78) 35
56   Capitol CL 14601   Heaven On Earth/CHEERS: Que Pasa Muchacha 20
56   Capitol CL 14601   Heaven On Earth/CHEERS: Que Pasa Muchacha (78) 18
(see also Cheers, Thunderbirds)

CONNIE CONWAY
60   London HA-W 2214   CONNIE CONWAY (LP). 18

MIKE CONWAY
68   Plexium PXM 1   Reign Of King Sadness/I'm Gonna Get Me A Women. 5

RUSS CONWAY
57   Columbia DB 3920   Roll The Carpet Up/The Westminster Waltz 10
57   Columbia DB 3971   Soho Fair/The Spotlight Waltz 10
57   Columbia DB 3999   Late Extra/The Red Cat 10
60   Columbia DB 4418   Royal Event/Rule Britannia! (78) 12
61   Columbia DB 4564   Pepe/Matador From Trinidad
                              (with John Barry Orchestra) 6
(see also John Barry, Billy Cotton, Ronnie Harris, Olivers)

STEVE CONWAY
55   Columbia SEG 7573   MEMORIES OF STEVE CONWAY
                              (EP, company sleeve) 8
56   Columbia SEG 7649   MORE MEMORIES OF STEVE CONWAY (EP) 10

JIMMY CONWELL
72   Jay Boy BOY 64   Cigarette Ashes/Second Hand Happiness 5

COO-COO RACHAS
59   Capitol CL 15024   Chili Beans/Track Down 6

RY COODER
71   Reprise RS 23497   How Can A Poor Man Stand Such Times And Live/Goin' To Brownsville 5
82   Warners K 17952F/SAM 149 Gypsy Woman/Alimony//Teardrops Will Fall/It's All Over Now
                              (double pack) 5
71   Reprise RSLP 6402   RY COODER (LP) 15
72   Reprise K 44142   INTO THE PURPLE VALLEY
                              (LP, with lyric sheet). 12
(see also Don Everly)

ENGLAND COOK
72   Explosion EX 2063   Samba Girl/NOW GENERATION: Samba (Version) 5

LAWRENCE "PIANO ROLL" COOK
52   London L 1140   Too Much Mustard/Freddie (78). 10
52   London L 1150   Mason Dixon Boogie/Cookin' The Boogie (78) 10

LITTLE JOE COOK (U.K.)
65   Sue WI 385   Stormy Monday Blues (Parts 1 & 2) 30
(see also Chris Farlowe, Beazers)

LITTLE JOE COOK (U.S.)
68   Sonet SON 2002   Don't You Have Feelings?/Hold On To Your Money 10
74   Sonet SON 2041   Hold On To Your Money/Don't You Have Feelings?
                              (reissue, sides reversed) 5

PETER COOK
65   Pye 7N 15847   Georgia/There And Bach Again. 30
(see also Peter London)

PETER COOK
65   Decca F 12182   The Ballad Of Spotty Muldoon/Lovely Lady Of The Roses. 12
61   Parlophone PMC 1145   BEYOND THE FRINGE
                              (LP, with other artists) 20
63   Parlophone PMC 1190   BRIDGE ON THE RIVER WYE
                              (LP, with other artists; also stereo PCS 3036) 18/20
63   Parlophone PMC 1198   PETER COOK PRESENTS THE ESTABLISHMENT
                              (LP, with other artists) 18
65   Decca LK 4722   PETER COOK PRESENTS MISTY MR. WISTY (LP) 18
65   Transatlantic TRA 131   PRIVATE EYE'S BLUE RECORD
                              (LP, with other artists) 20

PETER COOK & DUDLEY MOORE

62	Parlophone R 4969	Excerpts From "Beyond The Fringe": Sitting On The Bench/The End Of The World (with Alan Bennett & Jonathan Miller)	12
65	Decca F 12158	Goodbyeee (& Dudley Moore Trio)/DUDLEY MOORE TRIO: Not Only But Also	8
66	Decca F 12380	Isn't She A Sweetie/Bo Dudley	10
67	Decca F 12551	The L.S. Bumble Bee/The Bee Side	15
67	Decca F 12710	Bedazzled/Love Me	18
65	Parlophone GEP 8940	PETER COOK AND DUDLEY MOORE (EP)	12
65	Decca DFE 8644	BY APPOINTMENT (EP)	12
65	Decca LK 4703	NOT ONLY PETER COOK BUT ALSO DUDLEY MOORE (LP)	18
66	Decca LK 4785	ONCE MOORE WITH COOK (LP)	18
68	Decca LK/SKL 4923	BEDAZZLED (LP, soundtrack)	100
71	Decca LK 5080	NOT ONLY BUT ALSO (LP)	15

(see also Dudley Moore Trio)

PAUL COOKE

71	Ackee ACK 129	That Girl Was Mine/No Harm	5

ROGER (JAMES) COOKE

68	NEMS 56 3719	If I Didn't Have You/I Know It's You	6
69	Columbia DB 8510	Not That It Matters Anymore/Paper Chase	5
69	Columbia DB 8556	Stop/Someday	5
69	Columbia DB 8596	Smiling Through My Tears/Ain't That A Wonderful Thing (with Eve Graham)	5
71	Columbia DB 8761	If You Would Stay/Mama Packed A Picnic Tea	5
71	Columbia DB 8806	People I Gotta Dream/Today I Killed A Man I Didn't Know	5
70	Columbia SCX 6388	STUDY (LP)	15
72	Regal Zono. SRZA 8508	MEANWHILE ... BACK AT THE WORLD (LP, gatefold sleeve)	15
73	Regal Zono. SLRZ 1035	MINSTREL IN FLIGHT (LP)	15

(see also David & Jonathan, Blue Mink)

SAM COOKE

57	London HLU 8506	You Send Me/Summertime	30
57	London HLU 8506	You Send Me/Summertime (78)	30
58	London HLU 8615	That's All I Need To Know/I Don't Want To Cry	35
58	London HLU 8615	That's All I Need To Know/I Don't Want To Cry (78)	40
58	HMV POP 568	Love You Most Of All/Win Your Love For Me	30
58	HMV POP 568	Love You Most Of All/Win Your Love For Me (78)	50
59	HMV POP 610	Everybody Likes To Cha Cha Cha/The Little Things You Do	30
59	HMV POP 610	Everybody Likes To Cha Cha Cha/The Little Things You Do (78)	60
59	HMV POP 642	Only Sixteen/Let's Go Steady Again	10
59	HMV POP 642	Only Sixteen/Let's Go Steady Again (78)	75
59	HMV POP 675	There, I've Said It Again/One Hour Ahead Of The Posse	25
60	London HLU 9046	Happy In Love/I Need You Now	25
60	RCA RCA 1184	Teenage Sonata/If You Were The Only Girl	10
60	HMV POP 754	Wonderful World/Along The Navajo Trail	20
60	RCA RCA 1202	Chain Gang/I Fall In Love Everyday	7
61	RCA RCA 1221	Sad Mood/Love Me	10
61	RCA RCA 1230	That's It, I Quit, I'm Movin' On/What Do You Say	8
61	RCA RCA 1242	Cupid/Farewell, My Darling	7
61	RCA RCA 1260	Feel It/It's Alright	7
62	RCA RCA 1277	Twisting The Night Away/One More Time	5
62	RCA RCA 1296	Bring It On Home To Me/Having A Party	8
62	RCA RCA 1310	Nothing Can Change This Love/Somebody Have Mercy	7
63	RCA RCA 1327	Send Me Some Loving/Baby Baby Baby	8
63	RCA RCA 1341	Another Saturday Night/Love Will Find A Way	7
63	RCA RCA 1361	Frankie And Johnny/Cool Train	7
63	RCA RCA 1367	Little Red Rooster/Shake Rattle And Roll	10
64	RCA RCA 1386	Good News/Basin Street Blues	6
64	RCA RCA 1405	Good Times/Tennessee Waltz	8
64	RCA RCA 1420	Cousin Of Mine/That's Where It's At	10
65	RCA RCA 1436	Shake/A Change Is Gonna Come	8
65	RCA RCA 1452	It's Got The Whole World Shakin'/Ease My Troublin' Mind	8
65	RCA RCA 1476	Sugar Dumpling/Bridge Of Tears	10
68	RCA RCA 1701	Another Saturday Night/DUANE EDDY: Dance With The Guitar Man (w/drawn)	12
69	RCA RCA 1817	Cupid/Farewell, My Darling (reissue)	5
63	RCA RCX 7117	HEART AND SOUL (EP)	30
64	RCA RCX 7128	SWING SWEETLY (EP)	35
58	HMV CLP 1261	SAM COOKE (LP, with Bumps Blackwell Orchestra)	90
59	HMV CLP 1273	ENCORE (LP)	75
61	RCA RD 27190	COOKE'S TOUR (LP, also stereo SF 5076)	35/45
61	RCA RD 27215	HITS OF THE FIFTIES (LP, also stereo SF 5098)	35/45
61	RCA RD 27222	SWING LOW (LP)	40
62	RCA RD 27245	MY KIND OF BLUES (LP, also stereo SF 5120)	40/45
62	RCA RD 27263	TWISTIN' THE NIGHT AWAY (LP, also stereo SF 5133)	30/35
63	RCA RD/SF 7539	MR. SOUL (LP, mono/stereo)	35/40
63	RCA RD/SF 7583	NIGHT BEAT (LP)	40/45
64	RCA RD/SF 7635	AIN'T THAT GOOD NEWS (LP, mono/stereo)	30/35
65	RCA RD/SF 7674	AT THE COPA (LP, mono/stereo)	30/35
65	RCA RD/SF 7730	SHAKE (LP, mono/stereo)	35/40
65	London HA-U 8232	THE SOUL STIRRERS FEATURING SAM COOKE (LP)	45
66	RCA RD/SF 7764	TRY A LITTLE LOVE (LP)	35
66	Immediate IMLP 002	THE WONDERFUL WORLD OF SAM COOKE (LP)	40
69	RCA Intl. INTS 1005	THE ONE AND ONLY SAM COOKE (LP)	12
70	RCA Intl. INTS 1080	THE LATE AND GREAT SAM COOKE (LP)	12
74	BBC	SAM COOKE AND OTHERS (LP, for radio use)	80

COOKIES

62	London HLU 9634	Chains/Stranger In My Arms	15
63	London HLU 9704	Don't Say Nothin' Bad About My Baby/Softly In The Night	15
63	Colpix PX 11012	Will Power/I Want A Boy For My Birthday	15
64	Colpix PX 11020	Girls Grow Up Faster Than Boys/Only To Other People	15

(see also Earl-Jean, Cinderellas, Dorothy Jones)

COOL

69	DeWolfe DW/LP 3136	POP SOUNDS (LP, music library only)	25

(see also Elastic Band)

JOE COOL & KILLERS

77	Ariola ARO 165	I Just Don't Care/My Way	5

OLIVER COOL

60	Columbia DB 4552	Oliver Cool/I Like Girls	7
61	Columbia DB 4616	Give Me The Summertime/I Said Yeah	6

COOL BREEZE

71	Patheway PAT 103	People Ask What Love Is/There'll Be No More Sad Tomorrows	18
72	Decca F 13324	Summertime Sunshine/Sing Out Your Love	5
75	Bus Stop BUS 1023	Do It Some More/Citizen Jones	5

COOL CATS

68	Jolly JY 007	What Kind Of Man/HELMSLEY MORRIS: Little Things	25
69	Jolly JY 009	Hold Your Love/ALVA LEWIS: Hang My Head And Cry	12

COOLERS

73	Bread BR 1112	The Youth Of Today/TYRONE TAYLOR: Close Observation	5

EDDIE COOLEY & DIMPLES

57	Columbia DB 3873	Priscilla/Got A Little Woman	200
57	Columbia DB 3873	Priscilla/Got A Little Woman (78)	75

SPADE COOLEY & HIS FIDDLIN' FRIENDS

51	Brunswick 04812	Horse Hair Boogie/Down Yonder (78)	10

RITA COOLIDGE

83	A&M AM 007	All Time High/All Time High (Extended Instrumental) (p/s)	6
83	Scanlite BOND 1	All Time High/All Time High (Extended Instrumental) (p/s)	12

COOL COMFORT

80	Ellie Jay EJSO 9479	COOL COMFORT (LP)	12

COOL MEN

58	Parlophone GEP 8739	COOL FOR CATS NO. 1 (EP)	15
58	Parlophone GEP 8752	COOL FOR CATS NO. 2 (EP)	15

COOL STICKY

68	Amalgamated AMG 825	Train To Soulsville/ERIC MONTY MORRIS: Cinderella (actually by Errol Dunkley)	12

CHRIS COOMBES & others

65	Holyground HG 110	WHERE IT'S AT (EP, 99 only)	30

ALICE COOPER

71	Straight W 7209	Eighteen/Body	50
71	Warner Bros K 16127	Under My Wheels/Desperado	7
72	Warner Bros K 16154	Be My Lover/You Drive Me Nervous	7
72	Warner Bros K 16188	School's Out/Gutter Cat (p/s)	8
72	Warner Bros K 16214	Elected/Luney Tune (p/s)	10
72	Warner Bros K 16248	Hello Hurray/Generation Landslide	6
73	Warner Bros/ Lyntone LYN 2585/6	Slick Black Limousine/Extracts From: Unfinished Sweet/Elected/No More Mr Nice Guy/Billion Dollar Babies/I Love The Dead (33rpm flexi free with *NME*)	12/6
73	Warner Bros K 16262	No More Mr. Nice Guy/Raped And Freezin'	5
74	Warner Bros K 16345	Teenage Lament '74/Hard Hearted Alice	5
74	Warner Bros K 16127	Under My Wheels/Desperado (reissue)	5
74	Warner Bros K 16409	School's Out/No More Mr. Nice Guy/Elected/Billion Dollar Babies (maxi-45)	6
74	Chrysalis CHS 2069	I'm Flash/ELKIE BROOKS: Sacrifice (p/s, promo only)	35
75	Anchor ANC 1012	Department Of Youth/Cold Ethyl (p/s)	6
75	Anchor ANC 1018	Only Women Bleed/Devil's Food	5
75	Anchor ANC 1025	Welcome To My Nightmare/Black Widow	5
75	Anchor ANE 7001	Welcome To My Nightmare/Department Of Youth/Black Widow/ Only Women Bleed (EP, p/s)	6
75	Anchor ANE 12001	Welcome To My Nightmare/Department Of Youth/Black Widow/ Only Women Bleed (12" EP, p/s)	10
76	Warner Bros K 16792	I Never Cry/Got To Hell (p/s)	10
77	Warner Bros K 16935	(No More) Love At Your Convenience/It's Hot Tonight (p/s, gothic type on label)	6
77	Anchor ANE 12001	Welcome To My Nightmare/Department Of Youth/Black Widow/ Only Women Bleed (12", p/s, reissue)	10
79	Warner Bros K 17287	School's Out/Elected (p/s, reissue)	5
80	Warner Bros K 17598	Clones (We're All)/Model Citizen (p/s)	7
82	Warner Bros K 17924	Seven And Seven Is (live)/Generation Landslide '81 (gatefold p/s)	5
82	Warner Bros K 17940	For Britain Only/Under My Wheels (live) (p/s)	8

Alice COOPER

82	Warner Bros K 17940M	For Britain Only/Under My Wheels (live) (picture disc, unreleased)	
82	Warner Bros K 17940T	For Britain Only/Under My Wheels (live)/Who Do You Think We Are? (live)/	
		Model Citizen (live) (12", p/s)	12
83	Warner Bros ALICE 1T	I Love America/Fresh Blood/Pass The Gun Around (12", p/s)	12
86	MCA MCA 1090	He's Back (The Man Behind The Mask)/Billion Dollar Babies	
		(poster p/s)	6
87	MCA MCA 1113	Teenage Frankenstein/School's Out (live) (poster p/s)	5
89	Epic ALICEG/R/B 3	Bed Of Nails/I'm Your Gun (p/s, green, red or blue vinyl)	5
89	Epic ALICE 3	Bed Of Nails/I'm Your Gun (p/s, with poster)	8
89	Epic ALICEP 3	Bed Of Nails/I'm Your Gun/Go To Hell (live) (12", picture disc)	8
89	Epic ALICEC 3	Bed Of Nails/I'm Your Gun/Go To Hell (live)/Only Women Bleed (live)	
		(CD, card sleeve)	10
89	Epic 655 061-2	Poison/Trash/Ballad Of Dwight Fry (live)/I Got A Line On You	
		(CD, 'bottle' pack)	12
89	Epic ALICER/Y 4	House Of Fire/This Maniac's In Love With You	
		(p/s, red or yellow vinyl)	5
89	Epic ALICEX 4	House Of Fire/Poison (live) (p/s)	5
89	Epic ALICEP 4	House Of Fire/This Maniac's In Love With You	
		(shaped picture disc)	6
89	Epic ALICEQ 4	House Of Fire/Poison (live)/Spark In The Dark (live)/Under My Wheels (live)	
		(12", with tour poster)	8
89	Epic ALICEC 4	House Of Fire/This Maniac's In Love With You/Billion Dollar Babies (live)/	
		Under My Wheels (live) (CD, card sleeve)	8
91	Epic 657 438-9	Love's A Loaded Gun/Fire/Eighteen (live)	
		(CD, gun-shaped p/s)	12
69	Straight STS 1051	PRETTIES FOR YOU	
		(LP, purple label, gatefold sleeve)	25
69	Straight STS 1061	EASY ACTION	
		(LP, purple label, gatefold sleeve)	25
71	Straight STS 1065	LOVE IT TO DEATH	
		(LP, purple label, gatefold sleeve)	25
71	Warner Bros K 56005	KILLER (LP, green label, gatefold sleeve with perforated foldout calendar)	15
72	Warner Bros K 56007	SCHOOL'S OUT	
		(LP, green label, 'desktop' gatefold sleeve, with 'paper panties' inner)	18
73	Warner Bros K 56013	BILLION DOLLAR BABIES (LP, green label, gatefold embossed sleeve with	
		attached perforated cards, with $ billion note & inner sleeve)	18
73	Warner Bros K 46177	LOVE IT TO DEATH	
		(LP, reissue, green label, gatefold sleeve)	15
73	Warner Bros K 66021	SCHOOL DAYS	
		(2-LP, gatefold sleeve, reissue of STS 1051 & 1061)	15
74	Warner Bros K 56018	MUSCLE OF LOVE	
		(LP, 'cardboard box' sleeve, with insert & inner sleeve)	12
78	Warner Bros K 56577	FROM THE INSIDE (LP, foldout sleeve)	12

(see also Billion Dollar Babies)

GARNELL COOPER & KINFOLKS
| 63 | London HL 9757 | Green Monkey/Long Distance | 12 |

HENRY COOPER
| 76 | DJM DJS 10734 | Knock Me Down With A Feather/Knocked Out For Your Love | 5 |

JIMMY COOPER
| 78 | Forest Tracks FTS 3009 | DULCIMER PLAYER (LP) | 10 |

LES COOPER & SOUL ROCKERS
| 62 | Stateside SS 142 | Wiggle Wobble/Dig Yourself | 10 |

MIKE COOPER
70	Dawn DNX 2501	Your Lovely Ways (Parts 1 & 2)/Watching You Fall (Parts 1 & 2) (p/s)	6
71	Dawn DNX 2511	Too Late Now/The Ballad Of Fulton Allen/Good Times (p/s)	6
72	Dawn DNS 1022	Time In Hand/Schaabisch Hall	5
60s	Saydisc SD 137	UP THE COUNTRY BLUES (EP)	60
68	Matchbox SDM 159	THE INVERTED WORLD (LP, with Ian A. Anderson)	75
69	Pye NSPL 18281	OH REALLY!? (LP)	20
70	Dawn DNLS 3005	DO I KNOW YOU? (LP)	12
70	Dawn DNLS 3011	TROUT STEEL (LP, some with poster insert)	15/12
71	Dawn DNLS 3026	PLACES I KNOW (LP, with insert)	12
72	Dawn DNLS 3031	THE MACHINE GUN COMPANY (LP)	12
74	Fresh Air 6370 500	LIFE AND DEATH IN PARADISE (LP)	12

(see also Ian A. Anderson, Heron)

TOMMY COOPER
| 61 | Palette PG 9019 | Don't Jump Off The Roof Dad/How Come There's No Dog Day? | 15 |

COOPERETTES
| 75 | Brunswick BR 22 | Shing-A-Ling/Don't Trust Him | 6 |

COWBOY COPAS
51	Vogue V 9001	The Feudin' Boogie (with Grandpa Jones)/Strange Little Girl (78)	12
53	Parlophone R 3708	It's No Sin To Love You/I've Grown So Used To You (78)	10
53	Parlophone R 3756	Doll Of Clay/If Wishes Were Horses (78)	10
54	Parlophone CMSP 10	I Can't Go On/A Wreath On The Door Of My Heart (export issue)	25
54	Parlophone MSP 6079	Tennessee Senorita/If You Will Let Me Be Your Love	20
54	Parlophone R 3812	Tennessee Senorita/If You Will Let Me Be Your Love (78)	10
54	Parlophone DP 384	Look What I Got/Will You Forget (78, export issue)	20
54	Parlophone MSP 6109	A Heartbreak Ago/The Blue Waltz	20
54	Parlophone R 3880	A Heartbreak Ago/The Blue Waltz (78)	10
55	Parlophone MSP 6164	I'll Waltz With You In My Dreams/Return To Sender	20
55	Parlophone R 4005	I'll Waltz With You In My Dreams/Return To Sender (78)	12
60	Melodisc M 1566	Alabam/I Can	10

MINT VALUE £

55	Parlophone GEP 8527	FAVOURITE COWBOY SONGS (EP)	15
56	Parlophone GEP 8575	WESTERN STYLE (EP)	15
62	Top Rank JKP 3014	COUNTRY MUSIC (EP)	15
63	Stateside SE 1003	COUNTRY HITS (EP)	15
64	London R-ED 1418	THE UNFORGETTABLE COWBOY COPAS VOLUME 1 (EP)	15
64	London R-ED 1419	THE UNFORGETTABLE COWBOY COPAS VOLUME 2 (EP)	15
64	London R-ED 1420	THE UNFORGETTABLE COWBOY COPAS VOLUME 3 (EP)	15
61	Melodisc MLP 12-119	COWBOY COPAS (LP)	22
63	Stateside SL 10035	SONGS THAT MADE HIM FAMOUS (LP)	15
63	London HA-B 8088	COUNTRY ENTERTAINER NO. 1 (LP)	18
64	London HA-B 8180	STARS OF THE GRAND OLE OPRY — COWBOY COPAS (LP)	18
64	Ember CW 105	OPRY STAR SPOTLIGHT ON COWBOY COPAS (LP)	12

(see also Johnny Bond)

JULIAN COPE

83	Mercury COPE 1	Sunshine Playroom/Hey High Class Butcher (p/s)	5
83	Mercury COPE 112	Sunshine Playroom/Wreck My Car/Hey High Class Butcher/Eat The Poor (12", p/s)	10
83	Mercury MER 155	The Greatness And Perfection Of Love/24A Velocity Crescent (p/s)	5
84	Mercury MERX 155	The Greatness And Perfection Of Love/24A Velocity Crescent/Pussyface (12", p/s)	10
84	Mercury MADOX 004	Head Hang Low/Elegant Chaos/Strasbourg/Lunatic And Fire Pistol (excerpts), (tracks by Spirit) (flexidisc sampler, printed plain sleeve)	10
85	Mercury MER 1822	Sunspots/I Went On A Chourney//Mik Mak Mok/Land Of Fear (double pack)	8
86	Island ISBN 290	World Shut Your Mouth/World Shut Your Mouth (Trouble Funk Remix)// Umpteenth Unnatural Blues/Levitation (double pack box set with biography, photos & stickers)	10
86	Island CIS 290	Interview/World Shut Your Mouth/I've Got Levitation/Umpteenth Unnatural Blues/ Non-Alignment Pact (cassette, marked promo but available commercially)	5
87	Antar 4503	Interview/Christmas Mourning/Transmitting (fan club box set, with card, biography, membership card, letter, photos & stickers)	8
91	Island JC 1	Safesurfer/If You Love Me At All (33rpm, sold at gigs, stickered white sleeve)	15
94	K.A.K. (no cat. no.)	Paranormal In The West Country (Original Version)/(String Quartet Version)/ (Acoustic Version)/(Krankenhausmusik Version) (mail-order only via special offer with "Queen Elizabeth" LP)	15
87	Island ILPS 9861	SAINT JULIAN (LP, with free 12" interview LP [JCCLP 1])	22
89	Copeco JULP 89	SKELLINGTON (LP)	15
89	Copeco JUCD 89	SKELLINGTON (CD)	18
90	Mofo MOFOCOLP 90	DROOLIAN (LP)	15
90	Mofo MOFOCOCD 90	DROOLIAN (CD)	18
92	K.A.K. Ma-Gog 1	RITE (CD, as Julian Cope & Donald Ross Skinner, mail-order only)	22

(see also Teardrop Explodes, Rabbi Joseph Gordan)

KEN COPE & BREAKAWAYS

| 63 | Pye 7N 15524 | Hands Off, Stop Muckin' About/Why Am I So Shy | 5 |

(see also Breakaways)

SUZY COPE

61	HMV POP 941	Teenage Fool/Juvenile Delinquent	10
62	HMV POP 1047	Not Never Not Now/Kisses And Tears	8
63	HMV POP 1167	Biggity Big/Doing What You Know Is Wrong	8
65	CBS 201792	You Can't Say I Never Told You/And Now I Don't Want You	10

AL(L)AN COPELAND

57	Vogue Coral Q 72237	Feeling Happy/You Don't Know	12
57	Vogue Coral Q 72277	How Will I Know?/Will You Still Be Mine	7
59	Pye International 7N 25007	Flip Flop/Lot's More Love (as Allan Copeland)	15
59	Pye International N 25007	Flip Flop/Lot's More Love (78, as Allan Copeland)	25

JOHNNY COPELAND

| 72 | Atlantic K 10242 | Sufferin' City/It's My Own Tears That's Being Wasted | 6 |

KEN COPELAND

| 57 | London HLP 8423 | Pledge Of Love/MINTS: Night Air | 250 |
| 57 | London HLP 8423 | Pledge Of Love/MINTS: Night Air (78) | 75 |

COPPERFIELD

| 69 | Instant IN 004 | Any Old Time/I'm No Good For Her | 10 |
| 69 | Parlophone R 5818 | I'll Hold Out My Hand/Far Away Love | 5 |

(see also Quartz)

COPS 'N ROBBERS

64	Decca F 12019	St. James Infirmary/There's Gotta Be A Reason	40
65	Pye 7N 15870	I Could Have Danced All Night/Just Keep Right On	20
65	Pye 7N 15928	It's All Over Now Baby Blue/I've Found Out	20

(see also Fairies)

COPY CATS

| 69 | Bullet BU 419 | Copy Cat (with Derrick Morgan)/BUNNY LEE ALL STARRS: Hot Lead | 6 |

CORBAN

| 78 | Acorn AC 002 | A BREAK IN THE CLOUDS (LP, with insert) | 15 |

HARRY H. CORBETT

62	Pye 7N 15468	Junk Shop/The Isle Of Clerkenwell	7
63	Pye 7N 15552	Like The Big Guys Do/The Green Eye	7
63	Pye 7N 15584	The Table And The Chair/Things We Never Had	7
67	Decca F 12714	Flower Power Fred/(I'm) Saving All My Love (with Unidentified Flower Objects)	10
71	Columbia DB 8840	Harry You Love Her/It's The End Of A Beautiful Night	5

(see also Wilfred Brambell, Wilfred Brambell & Harry H. Corbett, Faraway Folk)

MINT VALUE £

MIKE CORBETT & JAY HIRSH
71	Atlantic 2091 26	Gypsy Child/Butterfly Day (Mike Corbett solo)	5
71	Atlantic 2400 141	MIKE CORBETT & JAY HIRSH (LP, gatefold sleeve)	20
71	Atlantic K 40242	MIKE CORBETT & JAY HIRSH (LP, gatefold sleeve, reissue)	12

(see also Mr. Flood's Party)

RONNIE CORBETT
68	Columbia DB 8512	Big Man/Fancy You Fancying Me	6
70	Philips 6006 070	It's All Going Up, Up, Up/Put On A Happy Face	5

CORBY & CHAMPAGNE
66	Pye 7N 17203	Time Marches On/I'll Be Back	5

KEVIN CORCORAN (& JEROME COURTLAND)
58	Pye 7N 15145	Old Yeller (with Jerome Courtland)/How Much Is That Doggie In The Window	6

JASON CORD
69	Chapter One CH 102	I've Got My Eyes On You/I Can't Take No More Of Your Lies	5
69	Chapter One CH 110	Why Shouldn't I/Spring Never Came Twice	5

FRANK CORDELL & HIS ORCHESTRA
56	HMV 7M 397	Port-Au-Prince/"Double Cross" TV Theme	6
56	HMV 7M 419	Sadie's Shawl/Flamenco Love	5
59	HMV POP 576	Granada/Lovely Is The Evening (78)	10
61	HMV POP 824	The Black Bear/Darling Charlie	8
61	HMV POP 852	Theme From 'The Rebel'/Ou La La	6
63	HMV CSD 1475	HERE THIS! (LP)	12

PHIL CORDELL
69	Warner Bros WB 8001	Pumping The Water/Red Lady	5

(see also Thursday's Children)

CORDES
65	Cavern Sound IMSTL 1	Give Her Time/She's Leaving	45

LOUISE CORDET
62	Decca F 11476	I'm Just A Baby/In A Matter Of Moments	6
62	Decca F 11524	Sweet Enough/Someone Else's Fool	7
63	Decca F 11673	Around And Around/Which Way The Wind Blows	7
64	Decca F 11824	Don't Let The Sun Catch You Crying/Loving Baby	8
64	Decca F 11875	Don't Make Me Over/Two Lovers	10
62	Decca DFE 8515	THE SWEET BEAT OF LOUISE CORDET (EP)	40

CORDUROYS
66	Planet PLF 122	Tick Tock/Too Much Of A Woman	30

CHICK COREA (& RETURN TO FOREVER)
72	ECM ECM 1009	ARC (LP, with others)	12
72	ECM ECM 1014	PIANO IMPROVISATIONS VOL. 1 (LP)	12
72	ECM ECM 1018/9	PARIS CONCERT FEBRUARY 1971 (2-LP, as Corea & Braxton & Holland)	15
73	Polydor 2310 247	LIGHT AS A FEATHER (LP, with Flora Purim)	12
73	ECM ECM 1020	PIANO IMPROVISATIONS VOL. 2 (LP)	12
74	ECM ECM 1022	RETURN TO FOREVER (LP)	12
74	Atlantic K 60081	INNER SPACE (2-LP)	18
74	People PLEO 9	SUNDANCE (LP)	18
74	Epic EPC 65558	ROUND TRIP (LP, with S. Watanabe)	12

(see also Return To Forever)

PADDY COREA
72	Explosion EX 2066	Soul And Inspiration/STAGS: You Must Be Trying My Faith	5

CORKSCREW
79	Highway SHY 7005	FOR OPENERS (LP)	25

CORNBREAD & JERRY
61	London HLG 9352	L'il Ole Me/Loco Moto	8

DON CORNEL & ETERNALS
70	Moodisc MU 3506	Christmas Joy/WINSTON & RUPERT: Musically Beat	6

CORNELIUS BROTHERS & SISTER ROSE
72	United Artists UP 35378	Too Late To Turn Back Now/Lift Your Love Higher	12

DON CORNELL
51	HMV JO 212	I Need You So/It Couldn't Happen To A Sweeter Girl (78)	10
54	Vogue Coral Q 2013	Hold My Hand/I'm Blessed	35
54	Vogue Coral Q 2037	S'Posin'/I Was Lucky	15
55	Vogue Coral Q 72058	No Man Is An Island/All At Once	12
55	Vogue Coral Q 72070	Give Me Your Love/When You Are In Love	12
55	Vogue Coral Q 72071	Athena/Size 12	12
55	Vogue Coral Q 72073	Stranger In Paradise/The Devil's In Your Eyes	30
55	Vogue Coral Q 72080	Unchained Melody/Most Of All	15
55	Vogue Coral Q 72080	Unchained Melody/Most Of All (78)	10
55	Vogue Coral Q 72104	Love Is A Many Splendored Thing/The Bible Tells Me So	18
56	Vogue Coral Q 72132	There Once Was A Beautiful/Make A Wish	12
56	Vogue Coral Q 72144	Teenage Meeting (Gonna Rock It Right)/I Still Have A Prayer	25
56	Vogue Coral Q 72144	Teenage Meeting (Gonna Rock It Right)/I Still Have A Prayer (78)	12
56	Vogue Coral Q 72152	Rock Island Line/Na-Ne Na-Na	18
56	Vogue Coral Q 72152	Rock Island Line/Na-Ne Na-Na (78)	12
56	Vogue Coral Q 72164	But Love Me (Love But Me)/Fort Knox	12
56	Vogue Coral Q 72203	All Of You/Heaven Only Knows	10

MINT VALUE £

57	Vogue Coral Q 72218	See-Saw/From The Bottom Of My Heart	15
57	Vogue Coral Q 72234	Let's Be Friends/Afternoon In Madrid	10
57	Vogue Coral Q 72257	Sittin' In The Balcony/Let's Get Lost	22
57	Vogue Coral Q 72257	Sittin' In The Balcony/Let's Get Lost (78)	18
57	Vogue Coral Q 72276	Mama Guitar/A Face In The Crowd	18
57	Vogue Coral Q 72276	Mama Guitar/A Face In The Crowd (78)	18
57	Vogue Coral Q 72291	There's Only You/Non Dimenticar	8
58	Coral Q 72308	Before It's Time To Say Goodnight/Mailman, Bring Me No More Blues	15
58	Coral Q 72308	Before It's Time To Say Goodnight/Mailman, Bring Me No More Blues (78)	18
58	Coral Q 72313	I've Got Bells On My Heart/Keep God In The Home	8
58	Coral Q 72313	I've Got Bells On My Heart/Keep God In The Home (78)	18
59	Pye International 7N 25041	Sempe Amore/Forever Couldn't Be Long Enough	8
59	Pye International N 25041	Sempe Amore/Forever Couldn't Be Long Enough (78)	15
59	London HLD 8937	This Earth Of Mine/The Gang That Sang "Heart Of My Heart"	8
59	London HLD 8937	This Earth Of Mine/The Gang That Sang "Heart Of My Heart" (78)	30
54	Vogue Coral LVC 10004	DON CORNELL FOR YOU (10" LP)	30
56	Coral LVA 9037	LET'S GET LOST (LP)	30

JERRY CORNELL
| 55 | London HL 8157 | Please Don't Talk About Me When I'm Gone/St. Louis Blues | 40 |

LYN CORNELL
60	Decca F 11227	Like Love/Demon Lover	7
60	Decca F 11260	Teaser/What A Feeling	7
60	Decca F 11277	Never On Sunday/Swain Kelly	6
60	Decca F 11301	The Angel And The Stranger/Xmas Stocking	7
61	Decca F 11326	The Sweet Life (La Dolce Vita)/When Is Someday	5
61	Decca F 11374	Surely In Love/Adios My Love	5
62	Decca F 11430	African Waltz/Moanin'	6
62	Decca F 11469	I Sold My Heart To The Junkman/Step Up And Rescue Me	8
63	Decca F 11775	Sally Go Round The Roses/You Can Kiss Me If You Like	7

CORNFLAKES
| 62 | Fontana 267 227TF | Oh, Listen To The Band/Moonstruck | 6 |

ARNOLD CORNS
71	B&C CB 149	Moonage Daydream/Hang Onto Yourself (as 'The Arnold Corns')	50
72	B&C CB 189	Hang Onto Yourself/Man In The Middle	30
74	Mooncrest MOON 25	Hang Onto Yourself/Man In The Middle (reissue)	18

(see also David Bowie)

HUGH CORNWELL & ROBERT WILLIAMS
79	United Artists BP 320	White Room/Losers In A Lost Land (Instrumental) (p/s)	6
85	Portrait A 6509	One In A Million/Siren Song (p/s)	5
79	United Artists UAG 30251	NOSFERATU (LP, with inner sleeve)	12

(see also Stranglers, Ouida & Numbers)

CORONADOS
| 64 | London HL 9895 | Love Me With All Your Heart/Querida | 7 |
| 67 | Stateside SS 2043 | Johnny B. Goode/Shook Me Down | 6 |

CORONATION ST. CAST
| 67 | Granada GTVR 1 | SINGALONG AT THE ROVER'S RETURN (EP) | 6 |

CORONETS
54	Columbia SCM 5117	Do, Do, Do, Do, Do, Do, Do It Again/I Ain't Gonna Do It No More	12
56	Columbia SCM 5235	Lizzie Borden/My Believing Heart	7
56	Columbia SCM 5261	There's No Song Like An Old Song/The Magic Touch	12
56	Columbia DB 3827	Someone To Love/The Rocking Horse Cowboy	7
56	Columbia SEG 7603	RHYTHM AND BLUES (EP, as Coronets with Eric Jupp Orchestra)	15
56	Columbia SEG 7621	THE PERFECT COMBINATION (EP, as Coronets with Eric Jupp Orchestra)	10
56	Columbia SEG 7714	SONG SHOW (EP)	10

(see also Chris Sandford & Coronets, Tony Brent, Ronnie Harris, Benny Hill, Eric Jupp, Lee Lawrence)

CORONETS
| 68 | Stresa BEV SP 1104/1105 | I Wonder Why/You're Leaving Tomorrow | 35 |

CORPORATION (U.S.)
| 69 | Capitol E-T/E-ST 175 | THE CORPORATION (LP) | 20 |

CORPORATION (Jamaica)
| 70 | Grape GR 3022 | Sweet Musille/Walking Thru' Jerusalem | 8 |

(see also Claudette & Corporation, Billy Jack)

CARMELLA CORREN
| 58 | Oriole CB 1469 | The History Of Love/Te-Amo-A-Ti (78) | 8 |

CORRIDOR ONE
| 81 | Hip HIP 1 | Working On The Papers/Jenny (p/s) | 6 |

CORRIE FOLK TRIO/CORRIES
63	Waverley SLP 530	Love Is Teasing/O, Waly Waly (p/s)	8
63	Waverley ELP 129	CORRIE FOLK TRIO (EP)	20
63	Waverley ELP 131	YON FOLK SONGS IS FOR THE BURDS (EP)	20
63	Waverley ELP 132	MORE FOLK SONGS FOR THE BURDS (EP)	15
65	Waverley ZLP 2042	CORRIE FOLK TRIO WITH PADDIE BELL (LP, also stereo SZLP 2043)	20
65	Waverley ZLP 2050	THE PROMISE OF THE DAY (LP)	20

MINT VALUE £

65	MFP MFP 50154	THE PROMISE OF THE DAY (LP)	12
66	Fontana STL 5337	THOSE WILD CORRIES (LP)	15
67	Fontana STL 5401	BONNET, BELT & SWORD (LP)	15
68	Fontana STL 5465	KISHMUL'S GALLEY (LP)	15
69	Fontana STL 5484	IN CONCERT (LP)	15
70	Talisman STAL 5005	IN RETROSPECT (LP, with Paddie Bell)	15
70	Columbia SCX 6442	STRINGS AND THINGS (LP)	15
71	Columbia SCX 6467	LIVE AT THE ROYAL LYCEUM THEATRE, EDINBURGH (LP)	15
72	Columbia SCX 6511	SOUND THE PIBROCH (LP)	12
75	Philips 6382 083	CAM YE BY ATHOLL (LP)	12

CORRS

95	Atlantic A 5727CD	Runaway/Leave Me Alone (CD)	8
96	Atlantic A 5662 CD	Love To Love You (radio edit)/Rainy Day/Carraroe Jig (CD, includes 6 cards)	10
97	Atlantic A 5661 CD	Love To Love You (radio edit)/Rainy Day/Carraroe Jig/Runaway (LP version) (CD)	8
97	Atlantic AT 0018 CDX	I Never Loved You Anyway (Radio Edit)/What I Know/ I Never Loved You Anyway (Acoustic) (CD, includes 3 cards)	8
98	Atlantic 80917 2	TALK ON CORNERS (CD, with 4 prints & cassette)	15

Promos

| 97 | East West 19417 | 6 SONGS FROM THE ALBUM "TALK ON CORNERS" (CD, unmixed versions) | 20 |
| 98 | Atlantic SAM 3233 | DREAMS (remixes) (12", p/s) | 20 |

CORSAIRS (U.S.)

| 62 | Pye International 7N 25142 | I'll Take You Home/Sitting On Your Doorstep (with Jay 'Bird' Uzzel) | 7 |

CORSAIRS (U.K.)

| 67 | CBS 202624 | Pay You Back With Interest/I'm Gonna Shut You Down | 10 |

CORSAIRS (Jamaica)

| 70 | Unity UN 558 | Goodnight My Love/Lover Girl | 6 |

BOB CORT (SKIFFLE GROUP)

57	Decca FJ 10831	It Takes A Worried Man To Sing A Worried Blues/Don't You Rock Me Daddy-O	15
57	Decca FJ 10831	It Takes A Worried Man To Sing A Worried Blues/ Don't You Rock Me Daddy-O (78)	10
57	Decca F 10892	Six-Five Special/Roll Jen Jenkins	15
57	Decca F 10892	Six-Five Special/Roll Jen Jenkins (78)	10
57	Decca F 10899	Maggie May/Jessamine (with Liz Winters)	8
57	Decca F 10899	Maggie May/Jessamine (with Liz Winters) (78)	10
57	Decca F 10905	Schoolday (Ring! Ring! Goes The Bell)/Ain't It A Shame (To Sing Skiffle On Sunday)	15
57	Decca F 10905	Schoolday (Ring! Ring! Goes The Bell)/Ain't It A Shame (To Sing Skiffle On Sunday) (78)	12
57	Decca F 10951	'Bob Cort Skiffle Party' Medley (Parts 1 & 2)	10
57	Decca F 10951	'Bob Cort Skiffle Party' Medley (Parts 1 & 2) (78)	12
58	Decca F 10989	The Ark (Noah Found Grace In The Eyes Of God)/Yes! Suh!	10
58	Decca F 10989	The Ark (Noah Found Grace In The Eyes Of God)/Yes! Suh! (78)	10
59	Decca F 11109	Foggy Foggy Dew/On Top Of Old Smokey (solo)	6
59	Decca F 11109	Foggy Foggy Dew/On Top Of Old Smokey (solo) (78)	12
59	Decca F 11145	Waterloo/Battle Of New Orleans (solo)	8
59	Decca F 11145	Waterloo/Battle Of New Orleans (solo) (78)	15
59	Decca F 11160	Kissin' Time/I'm Gonna Get Married (solo)	8
59	Decca F 11160	Kissin' Time/I'm Gonna Get Married (solo) (78)	18
60	Decca F 11197	El Paso/A Handful Of Gold (solo)	7
60	Decca F 11256	Mule Skinner Blues/The Ballad Of Walter Williams (solo)	7
60	Decca F 11256	Mule Skinner Blues/The Ballad Of Walter Williams (solo) (78)	25
60	Decca F 11285	The Ballad Of The Alamo/Five Brothers (solo)	6
59	Decca DFE 6630	BARRACK ROOM BALLADS (EP)	10
61	Decca DFE 6686	BOB CORT'S GENTLEFOLK (EP, as Bob Cort's Gentlefolk)	8
57	Decca LK 4222	AIN'T IT A SHAME (LP)	30
59	Decca LK 4301	ESKIMO NELL (LP)	25
65	Ace Of Clubs ACL 1197	YES! SUH! (LP, reissue of LK 4222 with different sleeve & title)	15

(see also Liz Winters & Bob Cort)

DAVE 'BABY' CORTEZ

59	London HLU 8852	The Happy Organ/Love Me As I Love You	12
59	London HLU 8852	The Happy Organ/Love Me As I Love You (78)	30
59	London HLU 8919	The Whistling Organ/I'm Happy	12
59	London HLU 8919	The Whistling Organ/I'm Happy (78)	40
60	Columbia DB 4404	Piano Shuffle/Dave's Special	8
60	London HLU 9126	Deep In The Heart Of Texas/You're Just Right	12
62	Pye International 7N 25159	Rinky Dink/Getting Right	15
66	Roulette RK 7001	Countdown/Summertime	6
60	London RE-U 1233	DAVE 'BABY' CORTEZ (EP)	35
64	London HA-U 8142	THE GOLDEN HITS OF DAVE 'BABY' CORTEZ (LP)	35

CORTINAS

| 68 | Polydor 56255 | Phoebe's Flower Shop/Too Much In Love | 12 |

(see also Octopus)

CORTINAS

77	Step Forward SF 1	Fascist Dictator/Television Families (p/s)	7
78	Step Forward SF 6	Defiant Pose/Independence (p/s)	6
78	Step Forward SF 6	Defiant Pose/Independence (12", pink die-cut sleeve)	8
78	CBS 82831	TRUE ROMANCES (LP, with photo insert)	12

LARRY CORYELL

69	Vanguard SVRL 19051	LADY CORYELL (LP)	18
69	Vanguard SVRL 19059	CORYELL (LP)	18
71	Vanguard 6359 005	SPACES (LP)	18
72	Vanguard VSD 6558	SPACES (LP, reissue)	12
72	Vanguard VSD 6573	AT THE VILLAGE GATE (LP)	12
72	Vanguard 6369 407	BAREFOOT BOY (LP)	15
72	Vanguard 6369 411	FAIRYLAND (LP)	15
73	Vanguard VSD 79319	OFFERING (LP)	12
73	Vanguard VSD 79329	THE REAL GREAT ESCAPE (LP)	12
74	Vanguard VSD 79342	INTRODUCING 11TH HOUSE (LP)	12
74	Vanguard VSD 79345	SPACES (LP, reissue)	12
75	Vanguard VSD 79353	THE RESTFUL MIND (LP)	12

(see also Jazz Composers Orchestra, Alphonse Mouzon & Larry Coryell)

BILL COSBY

67	Warner Bros WB 7072	Little Ole Man (Uptight! Everything's Alright)/Don'cha Know (some in p/s)	10/6
65	Warner Bros W(S) 1567	I STARTED OUT AS A CHILD (LP)	12
66	Warner W(S) 1634	WONDERFULNESS (LP)	12
68	Warner W(S) 1770	IT'S TRUE, IT'S TRUE (LP)	12

COSEY FANNI TUTTI

82	Flowmotion	TIME TO TELL (C-30 cassette, some with 24-page magazine)	15/10

(see also Chris & Cosey, CTI)

COSMIC BABY/VANGELIS

94	East West SAM 1484	A TRIBUTE TO BLADERUNNER (12", double pack, promo only)	25

(see also Vangelis)

COSMIC EYE

72	Regal Zono. SLRZ 1030	DREAM SEQUENCE (LP)	135

COSMIC JOURNEY PROJECT

91	CJP 1	BASE PROBE (12" EP)	10

(see also Eat Static)

COSMO

63	Blue Beat BB 175	Gypsy Woman/Do Unto Others	12
64	Blue Beat BB 244	One God/BUSTER'S ALL STARS: Prince Royal (actually "Reincarnation")	15
64	Blue Beat BB 269	Rice And Badgee/BUSTER'S ALL STARS: The Tickler	15

(see also Cosmo & Dennis, Denzil Dennis)

FRANK COSMO

63	Island WI 058	Revenge/Laughin' At You (B-side actually with Bobby Aitken)	18
63	Island WI 073	Dear Dreams/Go Go Go	12
63	Island WI 100	Merry Christmas/Greetings From Beverley's	15
63	R&B JB 119	I Love You/DON DRUMMOND: Close Of Play	15
64	Island WI 135	Better Get Right/Ameletia	15
64	Black Swan WI 446	Alone/Beautiful Book	18

(see also Two Kings)

COSMO & DENNIS (alias Denzil)

62	Blue Beat BB 145	Bed Of Roses/Tonight And Evermore (as Cosmo & Denzil)	15
65	Blue Beat BB 296	Sweet Rosemarie/Lollipop I'm In Love	15
65	Blue Beat BB 312	Come On Come On/I Don't Want You	12

(see also Cosmo)

DON COSTA, HIS ORCHESTRA & CHORUS

55	London HLF 8186	Love Is A Many Splendoured Thing/Safe In The Harbour	30
55	London HLF 8186	Love Is A Many Splendoured Thing/Safe In The Harbour (78)	7
59	London HLT 8992	I Walk The Line/Cat Walk	10
59	London HLT 8992	I Walk The Line/Cat Walk (78)	45
60	London HLT 9137	Theme From "The Unforgiven"/Streets Of Paris	7
60	London HLT 7103	Theme From "The Unforgiven"/FERRANTE & TEICHER: Theme From "The Apartment" (export issue)	12
60	London HLT 9195	Never On Sunday/The Sound Of Love	6
61	London HLT 9320	The Misfits/Chi Chi	7

SAM COSTA

61	Palette PG 9026	I'm Changing My Hat To A Bowler/Oh Dear	5

JACK COSTANZO

61	London HLG 9401	Theme From Route 66/Naked City Theme	7

JACK COSTANZO & TUBBY HAYES

62	Fontana TFL 5190/ STFL 598	COSTANZO PLUS TUBBS — EQUATION IN RHYTHM (LP, mono/stereo)	40/45

(see also Tubby Hayes)

CELIA COSTELLO

75	Leader LEE 4054	CELIA COSTELLO (LP, with insert)	20

DANNY COSTELLO

57	Oriole CB 1393	Like A Brook Gets Lost In A River/That's Where I Shine	6

DAY COSTELLO

71	Spark SRL 1042	The Long And Winding Road/Free (Unlimited Horizons)	8

(see also Ross McManus)

Elvis COSTELLO

ELVIS COSTELLO & THE ATTRACTIONS

ELVIS COSTELLO (& ATTRACTIONS)

77	Stiff BUY 11	Less Than Zero/Radio Sweetheart (p/s)	5
77	Stiff BUY 14	Alison/Welcome To The Working Week (p/s)	5
77	Stiff BUY 14	Alison/Welcome To The Working Week (p/s, A-side mispress on white vinyl)	300
77	Stiff BUY 15	Red Shoes/Mystery Dance (art sleeve, press-out centre)	5
77	Stiff BUY 15	Red Shoes/Mystery Dance (p/s, mispress, plays "Dream Tobacco" by Max Wall)	8

(The above singles were later re-pressed with 'Made In England' on label; these are worth £3 each.)

78	Radar ADA 10	Pump It Up/Big Tears (p/s)	5
78	Radar ADA 24	Radio Radio/Tiny Steps (12", promo-only, 500 pressed)	15
78	Radar RG 1	Talking In The Dark/Wednesday Week (p/s, gig freebie)	8
80	2-Tone CHS TT 7	I Can't Stand Up For Falling Down/Girls Talk (unreleased, later a gig freebie, more common issue has XX1 in run-off groove, 13,000 pressed)	20/12
80	Stiff GRAB 3	STIFF SINGLES FOUR PACK (BUY 11, 14, 15 & 20 in clear plastic wallet)	12
81	F-Beat XX 17	A Good Year For The Roses/Your Angel Steps Out Of Heaven (withdrawn p/s)	20
93	Demon ECPROMO 1	TWO AND A HALF YEARS IN 31 MINUTES (CD, fold-out digipak, promo only)	10
94	Demon ECPROMO 2	HIGHLIGHTS FROM ALMOST BLUE AND IMPERIAL BEDROOM (CD, fold-out digipak, promo only)	10
95	Demon ECPROMO 3	SELECTIONS FROM THE KING OF AMERICA (CD, fold-out digipak, promo only)	10
77	Stiff SEEZ 3	MY AIM IS TRUE (LP, with insert, various coloured rear sleeves)	12
78	Radar RAD 3	THIS YEAR'S MODEL (LP, with free 7" "Stranger In The House"/"Neat Neat Neat" (live) [die-cut company sleeve, SAM 83], 50,000 pressed; 1st 5,000 shrinkwrapped & stickered)	12
79	Radar RAD 15	ARMED FORCES (LP, foldout stickered sleeve with free EP "Live At Hollywood High" [p/s, SAM 90] & postcards)	12
79	Radar RAD 15	ARMED FORCES (LP, mispress, plays "[What's So Funny 'Bout] Peace, Love & Understanding" instead of "Two Little Hitlers"; sticker on insert)	15
86	IMP FIEND CD 21	ARMED FORCES (CD, with 'Peace, Love & Understanding')	18
94	Warner Bros PRO-CD 6955	BRUTAL YOUTH WORDS AND MUSIC PROGRAMME (CD, promo only)	18

(see also Nick Lowe, George Jones, Coward Brothers, Attractions)

BILLY COTTON (& HIS ORCHESTRA/BAND)

54	Decca F 10299	Friends And Neighbours/The Kid's Last Fight	18
54	Decca F 10377	This Ole House/Somebody Goofed	8
55	Decca F 10630	The Dam Busters March/Bring Your Smile Along	6
65	Walt Disney/S. County DIS 2	Never Smile At A Crocodile/Second Star To The Right	6
67	Philips BF 1551	Thunderbirds Theme/Zero X (as Billy Cotton Band)	10
53	Decca LF 1124	SOLDIERS OF THE QUEEN (10" LP)	18
54	Decca LF 1185	WAKEY, WAKEY! (10" LP)	18
61	Columbia 33SX 1383	WAKEY, WAKEY! (LP, Billy Cotton Bandshow with Alma Cogan & Russ Conway)	20

(see also Alma Cogan, Russ Conway)

MINT VALUE £

JAMES COTTON (BLUES BAND)
78	Buddah BDS 471	Rock'n'Roll Music/Help Me 5
68	Vanguard SVRL 19035	CUT YOU LOOSE! (LP, as James Cotton Blues Band) 20

JIMMY COTTON
62	Columbia SEG 8141	CHRIS BARBER PRESENTS JIMMY COTTON (EP)........................... 20
62	Columbia SEG 8189	CHRIS BARBER PRESENTS JIMMY COTTON NO. 2 (EP)................... 20

(see also James Cotton Blues Band, Alexis Korner)

JOSIE COTTON
81	Bomp BOMP 1	Johnny, Are You Queer?/(Let's Do) The Blackout (p/s) 5

MIKE COTTON (SOUND)
62	Columbia DB 4910	The Tinker/Zulu Warrior 8
63	Columbia DB 7029	Swing That Hammer/Heartaches (as Mike Cotton Jazzmen) 8
63	Columbia DB 7134	Midnite Flyer/One Mint Julep (as Mike Cotton Band)..................... 8
64	Columbia DB 7267	I Don't Wanna Know/This Little Pig... 30
64	Columbia DB 7382	Round And Round/Beau Dudley 40
65	Columbia DB 7623	Make Up Your Mind/I've Got My Eye On You 25
66	Polydor BM 56096	Harlem Shuffle/Like That 15
62	Columbia SEG 8144	COTTON PICKING (EP) 30
63	Columbia SEG 8190	THE WILD AND THE WILLING (EP) 30
64	Columbia 33SX 1647	MIKE COTTON SOUND (LP)... 425

(see also Lucas & Mike Cotton Sound, Satisfaction)

JOHN(NY) COUGAR
78	Riva RIVA 14	I Need A Lover/Born Reckless (as Johnny Cougar, p/s).................... 7
78	Riva RIVA 16	Factory/Alley Of The Angels (as Johnny Cougar, p/s) 10
79	Riva RIVA 20	Miami/Do You Think That's Fair (p/s) 5
79	Riva RIVA 20P	Miami/Do You Think That's Fair (picture disc) 5
79	Riva RIVA 21	Taxi Dancer/Small Paradise (p/s).. 5
80	Riva RIVA 25	This Time/Don't Misunderstand Me (as Johnny Cougar) (p/s) 5
81	Riva RIVA 30	Hot Night In A Cold Town/Tonight (p/s)...................................... 5
81	Riva RIVA 31	Ain't Even Done With The Night/To M.G. Wherever She May Be (p/s) ... 5
82	Riva RIVA 36	Hurts So Good/Close Enough (p/s).. 5
83	Riva JCM 38P	Hand To Hold On To/Hurts So Good (picture disc)......................... 5

(see also John Cougar Mellencamp)

COUGARS
63	Parlophone R 4989	Saturday Night At The Duckpond/See You In Dreamland 10
63	Parlophone R 5038	Red Square/Fly-By-Nite 10
64	Parlophone R 5115	Caviare And Chips/While The City Sleeps................................. 15
63	Parlophone GEP 8886	SATURDAY NIGHT WITH THE COUGARS (EP) 30

CATHAL COUGHLAN
89	Caff CAFF 1	I'm, Long Me Measaim/EAST VILLAGE: Freeze Out
		(no p/s, flexi with fanzines) 10/8

(see also Microdisney)

ROGER COULAM QUARTET
67	CBS 52399	ORGAN IN ORBIT (LP) 15
70	Fontana 16009	BLOW HOT, BLOW COLD (LP)... 15

DENIS COULDRY (& SMILE)
68	Decca F 12734	James In The Basement (solo)/DENIS COULDRY & NEXT COLLECTION:
		I Am Nearly There. 7
68	Decca F 12786	Penny For The Wind/Tea And Toast, Mr. Watson?
		(as Denis Couldry & Smile) 7

(see also Felius Andromeda)

DENNIS COULSON
73	Elektra K 42148	DENNIS COULSON (LP, gatefold sleeve)................................... 12

COULSON, DEAN, McGUINNESS, FLINT
72	DJM DJS 267	Lay Down Your Weary Tune/Tiny Montgomery/I Wanna Be Your Lover. ... 5
72	DJM DJLPS 424	LO AND BEHOLD (LP, gatefold sleeve)................................... 18

(see also Manfred Mann, McGuinness Flint, Dennis Coulson, Lyle McGuinness Band)

PHIL COULTER ORCHESTRA
68	Pye 7N 17511	Congratulations/Gold Rush... 20

COUNCIL COLLECTIVE
84	Polydor MINEX 1	Soul Deep (Club Mix)/Soul Deep
		(12", stickered black die-cut sleeve) 8

(see also Style Council, Jimmy Ruffin)

COUNT
74	Purple PUR 122	Gazaroody/The So, So Long 8

(COUNT) BISHOPS
76	Chiswick SW 1	SPEEDBALL (EP, 1st 1,000 in glossy p/s).................................... 8
76	Chiswick S 5	Train Train/Taking It Easy (p/s).. 5
77	Chiswick S 12	Baby You're Wrong/Stay Free (p/s) 5
78	Chiswick NS 33	I Take What I Want/No Lies (p/s, as Bishops) 5
78	Chiswick NS 35	Mr Jones/Human Bean/Route 66/Too Much Too Soon (unissued,
		test pressings only, as Bishops).. 18
78	Chiswick NS 37	I Want Candy/See That Woman (p/s, as Bishops) 5
78	Chiswick NS 376	I Want Candy/See That Woman (6", p/s)..................................... 6
78	Chiswick NS 3710	I Want Candy/See That Woman (10", p/s).................................... 8
78	Chiswick CHIS 1016	I Want Candy/See That Woman (6", p/s, reissue)........................... 5
79	Chiswick CHIS 111	Mr Jones/Human Bean/Route 66/Too Much Too Soon (p/s, as Bishops) ... 5
77	Chiswick WIK 1	THE COUNT BISHOPS (LP) 12
78	Chiswick CH 7	LIVE AT THE ROUNDHOUSE (10" mini-LP)................................. 12

(see also Cannibals)

MINT VALUE £

COUNT BUSTY & RUDIES
68 Melody MRC 003   You Like It/The Reggay 8

COUNT DOWNE & ZEROS
64 Ember EMB S 189   Hello My Angel/Don't Shed A Tear. 30
(see also Peter & Headlines)

COUNTDOWNS
63 United Artists UP 1024   Mouse On The Moon/The Big Safari 7
(see also John Barry)

COUNT FIVE
66 Pye International 7N 25393   Psychotic Reaction/They're Gonna Get You 25

COUNT OSSIE & HIS MYSTIC REVELATION
71 Ashanti ASH 404   Rasta Reggae/Samia 6
71 Moodisc MU 3515   Whispering Drums/SLIM SMITH & UNIQUES: Give Me Some More Loving 6
71 Moodisc HM 105   Whispering Drums/SLIM SMITH & UNIQUES: Give Me Some More Loving 6
74 Ashanti NTI 1301   GROUNATION (3-LP, with Mystic Revelation Of Rastafari) 25
(see also Jackie Estick, Gaylads, Soul Defenders)

COUNT PRINCE
(see under Count Prince Miller)

COUNTRY BOY
64 Blue Beat BB 236   I'm A Lonely Boy (actually by Shenley Duffas)/EDWARD'S ALL STARS:
He's Gone Ska 15

COUNTRY FUNK
70 Polydor 248 2018   COUNTRY FUNK (LP). 20

COUNTRY GAZETTE
72 United Artists UAG 29404   TRAITOR IN OUR MIDST (LP) 12
73 United Artists UAS 29491   DON'T GIVE UP YOUR DAY JOB (LP) 12
(see also Flying Burrito Brothers)

COUNTRY GENTLEMEN
63 Decca F 11766   Greensleeves/Baby Jean 30
(see also High Society, Peter Cowap)

COUNTRY HAMS
74 EMI EMI 2220   Walking In The Park With Eloise/Bridge On The River Suite
(p/s, red & brown label) 45
82 EMI EMI 2220   Walking In The Park With Eloise/Bridge On The River Suite
(p/s, reissue, beige label). 12
(see also Paul McCartney/Wings, Chet Atkins, Floyd Cramer)

COUNTRY JOE & THE FISH
67 Fontana TF 882   Not So Sweet Martha Lorraine/Love 10
69 Vanguard VA 3   Here I Go Again/It's So Nice To Have Love 6
70 Vanguard 6076 250   I-Feel-Like-I'm-Fixin'-To-Die Rag/Maria 6
67 Fontana TFL 6081   ELECTRIC MUSIC FOR THE MIND AND BODY (LP) 35
68 Fontana TFL 6086   I-FEEL-LIKE-I'M-FIXIN'-TO-DIE (LP). 30
68 Vanguard SVRL 19006   TOGETHER (LP) 18
69 Vanguard SVRL 19026   ELECTRIC MUSIC FOR THE MIND AND BODY (LP, reissue) 15
69 Vanguard SVRL 19029   I-FEEL-LIKE-I'M-FIXIN'-TO-DIE (LP, reissue) 15
69 Vanguard SVRL 19048   HERE WE ARE AGAIN (LP) 18
70 Vanguard SVRL 19058   THE BEST OF COUNTRY JOE AND THE FISH (LP). 15
70 Vanguard 6359 002   C.J. FISH (LP) 18
72 Vanguard VSD 79244   ELECTRIC MUSIC FOR THE MIND AND BODY
(LP, 2nd reissue). 12
72 Vanguard VSD 79266   I-FEEL-LIKE-I'M-FIXIN'-TO-DIE (LP, 2nd reissue) 12
72 Vanguard VSD 79277   TOGETHER (LP, reissue) 12
73 Vanguard VSD 27/28   THE LIFE AND TIMES OF
(2-LP, gatefold sleeve, quadrophonic/stereo) 20/15
80 Piccadilly PIC 3009   THE EARLY YEARS (LP, private pressing, withdrawn) 50
(see also Country Joe McDonald)

COUNTRY JUG
72 Decca F 13270   I'm Sorry/Do You Wanna?/Flying 20
(see also Ray Dorset)

COUNTRYMEN
62 Piccadilly 7N 35029   I Know Where I'm Going/Swamp Legend 5
62 Piccadilly 7N 34012   I KNOW WHERE I'M GOING (EP) 10
62 Piccadilly NPL 38003   A FLYING VISIT BY THE COUNTRYMEN (LP) 12

COUNTRYMEN
69 Jayboy BOY 3   After All/White Rose Of Athens. 5

COUNTRY WASHBURNE
50 Capitol CL 13300   Chug-A-Lug/BETSY GAY: Whoa Sailor (78). 8

COUNTS
72 Janus 6146 013   (Why Not) Start All Over Again/Thinking Single 5

COUNT VICTORS
62 Coral Q 72456   Peepin' 'N' Hidin'/Don't Laugh At Me ('Cos I'm A Fool) 12
63 Coral Q 72462   Road Runner/Lorie. 15

WAYNE/JAYNE COUNTY (& ELECTRIC CHAIRS)
77 Illegal IL 002   Stuck On You/Paranoia Paradise/The Last Time (p/s) 5
77 Sweet F.A. WC 1   Fuck Off/On The Crest (p/s) 6
78 Safari SAFE 1   Eddie And Sheena/Rock And Roll Cleopatra
(p/s, some with cartoon insert) 5
78 Safari SAFE 6   I Had Too Much To Dream Last Night/Fuck Off (unissued)

MINT VALUE £

78	Safari WC 2	BLATANTLY OFFENZIVE (EP, gold or silver vinyl)	5
78	Safari SAFE 9	Trying To Get On The Radio/Evil Minded Momma (p/s)	5
79	Illegal IL 005	Thunder When She Walks/What You Got (p/s)	5
78	Safari SAFE 13	Berlin/Waiting For The Marines (p/s)	5
78	Safari SAFELS 13	Berlin (Long Version)/Waiting For The Marines/Midnight Pal (12", p/s, pink vinyl)	8
79	Safari SAFE 18	So Many Ways/J'Attends Les Marines (p/s, as Electric Chairs)	5
83	Safari WCP 3	Fuck Off/Toilet Love (picture disc)	5
78	Safari GOOD 1	STORM THE GATES OF HEAVEN (LP, multicoloured or grey marbled vinyl)	12

(see also Mystere Five's)

DIANA COUPLAND
59	HMV POP 690	Love Him/I Am Loved	6

COURIERS
66	Ember EMB S 218	Take Away/Done Me Wrong (some with p/s)	65/35

(see also William E. Kimber)

COURIERS
69	Ash ALP 201	PACK UP YOUR SORROWS (LP)	25

TOM COURTENAY
63	Decca F 11729	Mrs. Brown You've Got A Lovely Daughter/Knocking On The Door	7

COURT MARTIAL
82	Riot City RIOT 5	GOTTA GET OUT (EP)	5
82	Riot City RIOT 11	NO SOLUTION (EP)	5

BILL COURTNEY
59	RCA RCA 1142	Judy Is/Without Her Love	7
59	RCA RCA 1142	Judy Is/Without Her Love (78)	10
60	Columbia DB 4512	Petticoats Fly/Blanket On The Beach	6

DEAN COURTNEY
75	RCA RCA 2534	I'll Always Need You/Tammy	5

COURTYARD MUSIC GROUP
74	Deroy	JUST OUR WAY OF SAYING HELLO (LP, private pressing)	250

COUSIN EMMY & HER KINFOLK
56	Brunswick OE 9258	KENTUCKY MOUNTAIN BALLADS VOL. 1 (EP)	15
56	Brunswick OE 9259	KENTUCKY MOUNTAIN BALLADS VOL. 2 (EP)	15

COUSINS (Belgium)
61	Palette PG 9011	Kili Watch/Feugo	10
61	Palette PG 9017	Bouddha/Kana Kapila	10
62	Palette PG 9035	Anda/Danseuse	10

COUSINS (U.K.)
64	Decca F 11924	Yes Sir That's My Baby/Two Lovely Black Eyes	6

DAVE COUSINS
72	A&M AMS 7032	Going Home/Ways And Means	6
72	A&M AMLS 68118	TWO WEEKS LAST SUMMER (LP)	18
79	Old School SLURP 1	OLD SCHOOL SONGS (LP, private pressing with Brian Willoughby)	25
80	Passport PVC 8901	OLD SCHOOL SONGS (LP, reissue with different sleeve)	15
94	Road Goes On Forever	THE BRIDGE (advance cassettes only for cancelled LP)	12

(see also The Strawbs)

DON COVAY (& GOODTIMERS)
61	Pye International 7N 25075	Pony Time/Love Boat	10
61	Philips PB 1140	Shake Wid The Shake/Every Which Way	25
62	Cameo Parkway C 239	The Popeye Waddle/One Little Boy Had Money	20
64	Atlantic AT 4006	Mercy, Mercy/Can't Stay Away	8
65	Atlantic AT 4016	Take This Hurt Off Me/Please Don't Let Me Know	8
65	Atlantic AT 4056	See Saw/I Never Get Enough Of Your Love	7
66	Atlantic AT 4078	Sookie Sookie/Watching The Late Late Show	8
66	Atlantic 584 025	You Put Something In Me/Iron Out The Rough Spots	6
66	Atlantic 584 059	See Saw/Somebody's Got To Love You	6
67	Atlantic 584 082	Shingaling '67/I Was There	7
67	Atlantic 584 094	Sookie Sookie/Mercy Mercy	6
67	Atlantic 584 114	40 Days — 40 Nights/The Usual Place	8
70	Atlantic 2091 018	Everything I Do Goin' Be Funky/Key To The Highway	5
71	Atlantic 2091 104	See Saw/Mercy, Mercy	5
72	Atlantic K 10600	You Put Me On The Critical List/40 Days & 40 Nights	5
65	Atlantic ATL 5025	MERCY! (LP, plum label)	65
65	Atlantic 587 062	SEE-SAW (LP)	25
69	Atlantic K 50225	HOUSE OF BLUE LIGHT (LP)	18
73	Mercury 6338 211	SUPERDUDE (LP)	12
75	Mercury 9100 010	HOT BLOOD (LP)	12

(see also Soul Clan)

DAVID COVERDALE
77	Purple PUR 133	Hole In The Sky/Blindman (no p/s)	12
78	Purple PUR 136	Breakdown/Only My Soul (no p/s)	12
90	Epic 656 292 7	Last Note Of Freedom/HANS ZIMMER: Car Building (poster p/s)	10
90	Epic 656 292 6	Last Note Of Freedom/HANS ZIMMER: Car Building (12", p/s)	8
93	EMI EMPD 279	Take A Look At Yourself (with Jimmy Page)/Waiting On You (p/disc in no'd p/s)	6
77	Purple TPS 3509	DAVID COVERDALE'S WHITESNAKE (LP)	12
78	Purple TPS 3513	NORTHWINDS (LP, with inner sleeve)	12

(see also Whitesnake, Deep Purple, Wizard's Convention, Roger Glover, Jimmy Page)

MINT VALUE £

JULIAN COVEY & MACHINE
67	Island WIP 6009	A Little Bit Hurt/Sweet Bacon	30
67	Island WIP 6442	A Little Bit Hurt/Sweet Bacon (reissue)	8

JULIE COVINGTON
70	Columbia DB 8649	The Magic Wasn't There/The Way Things Ought To Be	12
70	Columbia DB 8705	Tonight Your Love Is Over/If I Had My Time Again	12
72	RCA RCA 2181	Day By Day/With Me It Goes Deeper	5
71	Columbia SCX 6466	THE BEAUTIFUL CHANGES (LP)	125

(see also Rock Follies)

PETER COWAP
70	Pye 7N 17976	Crickets/Wicked Melinda	5
71	Pye 7N 45042	The Man With The Golden Gun/Tampa, Florida	5
71	Pye 7N 45071	Safari/Oh Soloman	5

(see also 10cc, Country Gentlemen)

COWBOY
71	Atlantic 2466 022	REACH FOR THE SKY (LP)	12
72	Atlantic K 40312	5'LL GETCHA TEN (LP, with insert)	12

COWBOY CHURCH SUNDAY SCHOOL
55	Brunswick 05371	Open Up Your Heart/The Lord Is Counting On You	7
55	Brunswick 05455	Go On By/The Little Black Sheep	6
56	Brunswick 05533	These Bad Bad Kids/A Handful Of Shame	6
56	Brunswick 05598	It Is No Secret/Don't Send Those Kids To Sunday School	6

COWSILLS
67	MGM MGM 1353	The Rain, The Park And Other Things/River Blue	12
68	MGM MGM 1383	We Can Fly/A Time For Remembrance	6
68	MGM MGM 1400	In Need Of A Friend/Mr. Flynn	6
68	MGM MGM 1424	Indian Lake/Newspaper Blanket	6
68	MGM MGM 1441	Poor Baby/Meet Me At The Wishing Well	5
69	MGM MGM 1469	Hair/What Is Happy	5
69	MGM MGM 1484	The Prophecy Of Daniel And John The Divine/Gotta Get Away From It All	5
69	MGM MGM 1490	Love American Style/Silver Threads And Golden Needles	5
71	London HLU 10329	On My Side/There Is A Child	5
67	MGM C/CS 8059	THE COWSILLS (LP)	20
68	MGM CS 8077	WE CAN FLY (LP)	18
68	MGM CS 8095	CAPTAIN SAD AND HIS SHIP OF FOOLS (LP)	18
68	Fontana SFL 13055	THE COWSILLS AND THE LINCOLN PARK ZOO (LP)	18
71	London SH-U 8421	ON MY SIDE (LP)	12

BILLY COX
71	Pye Intl. NSPL 25158	NITRO FUNCTION (LP)	25

(see also Jimi Hendrix)

HARRY COX
65	EFDSS LP 1004	ENGLISH FOLK SINGER (LP)	20

IDA COX
52	Jazz Collector L 22	Graveyard Dream Blues/Weary Way Blues (78)	8
50s	Jazz Collector	Mama Do Shee Blues/Worried Mama Blues (78)	8
59	Fontana TFE 17136	IDA COX (EP)	18
54	London AL 3517	SINGS THE BLUES (10" LP)	40
60s	Riverside RLP 374	BLUES FOR RAMPART STREET (LP)	25
74	Fountain FB 301	IDA COX VOLUME 1 (LP)	15
75	Fountain FB 304	VOLUME 2: 1923-1924 (LP)	15
75	Gannet GEN 5371-5376	PARAMOUNT RECORDINGS (6-LP box set)	40

IDA COX/MA RAINEY
60	Jazz Collector JEL 12	THE FEMALE BLUES (EP)	18

(see also Ma Rainey)

IDA COX/ETHEL WATERS
50s	Poydras 104	IDA COX AND ETHEL WATERS (EP)	30

MICHAEL COX
59	Decca F 11166	Boy Meets Girl/Teenage Love	18
59	Decca F 11166	Boy Meets Girl/Teenage Love (78)	30
59	Decca F 11182	Too Hot To Handle/Serious	18
59	Decca F 11182	Too Hot To Handle/Serious (78)	30
60	Triumph RGM 1011	Angela Jones/Don't Want To Know	12
60	Ember EMB S 103	Angela Jones/Don't Want To Know (export issue)	55
60	HMV POP 789	Along Came Caroline/Lonely Road	18
61	HMV POP 830	Teenage Love/Linda	15
61	HMV POP 905	Sweet Little Sixteen/Cover Girl	15
62	HMV POP 972	Young Only Once/Honey Cause I Love You	22
62	HMV POP 1065	Stand Up/In April	22
63	HMV POP 1137	Don't You Break My Heart/Hark Is That A Cannon I Hear	22
63	HMV POP 1220	Gee What A Party/See That Again	22
64	HMV POP 1293	Rave On/Just Say Hello	25
65	HMV POP 1417	Gypsy/It Ain't Right	22
66	Parlophone R 5436	I Hate Getting Up In The Morning/Love 'Em And Leave 'Em	7
67	Parlophone R 5580	I'll Always Love You/You Never Can Tell (Till You Try)	6

SONNY COX
70	Pama PM 815	Choking Kind/Chocolate Candy	5

WALLY COX
61	Vogue V 9175	I Can't Help It/The Heebie Jeebies	18
74	Pye Disco Demand DDS 105	This Man/I've Had Enough	8

LOL COXHILL

78	Chiltern Sound CS 100	MURDER IN THE AIR (12" EP)	35
71	Dandelion DSD 8008	EAR OF THE BEHOLDER (2-LP, gatefold sleeve, also with cat. no. 69001)	60
72	Mushroom 150 MR 23	TOVERBAL SWEET (LP)	60
73	Caroline C 1503	COXHILL MILLER (LP, with Stephen Miller)	25
74	Caroline C 1507	THE STORY SO FAR ... OH REALLY? (LP, with Stephen Miller)	30
75	Caroline C 1514	LOL COXHILL & WELFARE STATE (LP)	18
75	Caroline C 1515	FLEAS IN THE CUSTARD (LP)	30
76	Ogun OG 510	DIVERSE (LP)	15
78	Ogun OG 525	THE JOY OF PARANOIA (LP)	15
78	Ictus 0008	MOOT (LP)	30
78	Ictus 0011	LID (LP)	12
79	Random Radar RRR 005	DIGWELL DUETS (LP)	12
80	Pipe PIPE 1	SLOW MUSIC (LP)	25

(see also Stephen Miller & Lol Coxhill, Kevin Ayers, Steve York's Camelo Pardalis)

COXHILL BEDFORD DUO

71	Polydor 2001 253	Pretty Little Girl (Parts 1 & 2)	5
72	Dandelion 2058 214	Mood/WILL DANDY & DANDYLETTES: Sonny Boy/Oh Mein Papa	5

(see also David Bedford, Lol Coxhill)

KEVIN COYNE

72	Dandelion 2001 357	Cheat Me/Flowering Cherry	6
76	Virgin VS 136	Don't Make Waves/Mona Where's My Trousers (p/s)	5
79	Virgin VS 255	I'll Go Too/Having A party (p/s, green vinyl)	5
80	Virgin VGD 3504	SANITY STOMP (EP, double pack)	8
82	Cherry Red CHERRY 49	So Strange/Father Dear Father (p/s)	5
72	Dandelion 2310 228	CASE HISTORY (LP)	40
73	Virgin VD 2501	MARJORY RAZORBLADE (2-LP)	20
75	Virgin V 2012	BLAME IT ON THE NIGHT (LP)	12
75	Virgin V 2033	MATCHING HEAD AND FEET (LP, with lyric sheet)	12
76	Virgin V 2047	HEARTBURN (LP, with inner sleeve)	12
82	Butt BUTBOX 1	THE DANDELION YEARS (3-LP box set, with insert)	20

(see also Clague, Coyne-Clague, Siren, Gordon Smith)

COYNE-CLAGUE

69	Dandelion S 4494	The Stride/I Wonder Where	6

(see Clague, Kevin Coyne)

CRABBY APPLETON

70	Elektra 2101 006	Go Back/Try	5
71	Elektra EK 45716	Grabon/Can't Live My Life	5
70	Elektra EKS 74067	CRABBY APPLETON (LP)	15
71	Elektra EKS 74106	ROTTEN TO THE CORE (LP)	15

(see also Michael Fennelly)

CRACK

80	JSO EAT 4	Making The Effort/Easy Street	8

CRACK

81	Bridgehouse BHS 8	Silly Fellow/Fairy Story (p/s)	5

CRACK

82	RCA RCA 214	Don't You Ever Let Me Down/I Can't Take It (die-cut 'Battle of the Bands' sleeve)	30
82	RCA RCA 255	Going Out/The Troops Have Landed (p/s)	15
83	RCA CRACK 1	All Or Nothing/I Caught You Out (p/s)	12

CRACKED MIRROR

83	CMLP 001	CRACKED MIRROR (LP, private pressing, 200 only)	75

CRACKERS

69	Fontana TF 995	Honey Do/It Happens All The Time	8

(see also Merseys)

CRACK THE SKY

76	Lifesong ELS 45016	We Want Mine/Invaders From Mars	8
75	Lifesong LSLP 6000	CRACK THE SKY (LP)	12
76	Lifesong LSLP 6005	ANIMAL NOTES (LP, with inner sleeve)	15

SARAH CRACKNELL

87	3 Bears TED 001	Love Is All You Need/Coastal Town (p/s)	10
97	Gut CDGUT 7	Goldie (Radio Edit)/(Original Version)/Empire State High/ Aussie Soap Girl (CD, slimline jewel case, withdrawn)	20

(see also St. Etienne, 50 Year Void, Cola Boy, Lovecut D.B.)

(BILLY) 'CRASH' CRADDOCK

59	Philips PB 966	Boom Boom Baby/Don't Destroy Me (as 'Crash' Craddock)	18
59	Philips PB 966	Boom Boom Baby/Don't Destroy Me (78)	90
60	Philips PB 1006	Since She Turned Seventeen/I Want That (as 'Crash' Craddock)	18
60	Philips PB 1092	Good Time Billy (Is A Happiness Fool)/Heavenly Love	15
61	Mercury AMT 1146	How Lonely He Must Be/Truly True	10

CRAFT

84	Shanghai HAI 106	CRAFT (LP, with insert)	12

CRAIG

65	King KG 1022	Ain't That A Shame/International Blues	12

CRAIG

66	Fontana TF 665	A Little Bit Of Soap/Ready Steady Let's Go	45
66	Fontana TF 715	I Must Be Mad/Suspense	200

(see also Galliard)

MINT VALUE £

PAUL CRAIG
66	CBS 202406	Midnight Girl/Autumn	8

WENDY CRAIG
68	Philips BF 1704	Hushabye Mountain/Windows Of The World	5

DON CRAINE'S NEW DOWNLINERS SECT
67	Pye 7N 17261	I Can't Get Away From You/Roses	125

(see also Downliners Sect)

BEN CRAMER
73	Philips 6000 097	The Old Street Musicians/Sylvia Come Dance With Me	5

FLOYD CRAMER
54	London HL 8012	Fancy Pants/Five Foot Two Eyes Of Blue	40
54	London HL 8012	Fancy Pants/Five Foot Two Eyes Of Blue (78)	8
54	London HL 8062	Jolly Cholly/Oh! Suzanna	50
54	London HL 8062	Jolly Cholly/Oh! Suzanna (78)	8
55	London HLU 8195	Rag-A-Tag/Aunt Dinah's Quiltin' Party	30
55	London HLU 8195	Rag-A-Tag/Aunt Dinah's Quiltin' Party (78)	10
58	RCA RCA 1050	Flip Flop And Bop/Sophisticated Swing	20
58	RCA RCA 1050	Flip Flop And Bop/Sophisticated Swing (78)	12
60	RCA RCA 1211	Last Date/Sweetie Baby	7
61	RCA RCA 1231	On The Rebound/Mood Indigo	6
61	RCA RCA 1241	San Antonio Rose/I Can Just Imagine	5
61	RCA RCA 1259	Hang On/Your Last Goodbye	6
62	RCA RCA 1275	Chattanooga Choo Choo/Let's Go	6
62	RCA RCA 1284	Lovesick Blues/First Hurt	6
62	RCA RCA 1301	Hot Pepper/For Those That Cry	5
62	RCA RCA 1311	Swing Low/Losers Weepers	5
55	London REP 1023	PIANO HAYRIDE (EP, with Louisiana Hayride Band)	35
63	RCA RCX 7120	THAT HANDSOME PIANO (EP)	15
61	RCA RD 27221/SF 5103	ON THE REBOUND (LP, mono/stereo)	12/15
62	RCA RD 27250/SF 5124	AMERICA'S BIGGEST SELLING PIANIST (LP, mono/stereo)	12/15
62	RCA RD 27260/SF 5130	GETS ORGAN-IZED (LP)	12
62	RCA RD/SF 7518	I REMEMBER HANK WILLIAMS (LP)	12
63	RCA RD/SF 7540	SWING ALONG WITH FLOYD CRAMER (LP)	12
63	RCA RD/SF 7575	COMING ON (LP)	12
64	RCA RD/SF 7622	COUNTRY PIANO — CITY STRINGS (LP)	12
64	RCA RD/SF 7646	AT THE CONSOLE (LP)	12
65	RCA RD 7665	THE BEST OF FLOYD CRAMER (LP)	12
65	RCA RD/SF 7748	CLASS OF '65 (LP)	12

(see also Country Hams)

CRAMP
78	Rip Off RIP 7	She Doesn't Love Me/Suzy Lie Down (p/s)	8

CRAMPS
79	Illegal ILS 12013	GRAVEST HITS (12" EP, blue or black vinyl)	20/8
80	Illegal ILS 0017	Fever/Garbage Man (withdrawn 1st 'full band' p/s; re-pressed in different p/s with 4 separate shots)	20/15
80	Illegal ILS 021	Drug Train/Love Me/I Can't Hardly Stand It (p/s)	12
81	IRS PFS 1003	Goo Goo Muck/She Said (p/s, yellow vinyl)	12
81	IRS PFSX 1008	The Crusher/Save It/New Kind Of Kick (12", p/s)	12
85	Big Beat NS 110	Can Your Pussy Do The Dog?/Blue Moon Baby (p/s, orange see-through vinyl)	5
86	Big Beat NS 115	What's Inside A Girl/Give Me A Woman (p/s, purple vinyl)	8
86	Big Beat NS 115	What's Inside A Girl/Get Off The Road/Give Me A Woman (12", p/s, white vinyl)	10
89	Enigma ENV 17	Bikini Girls With Machine Guns/Jackyard Backoff (p/s)	5
89	Enigma ENVPD 17	Bikini Girls With Machine Guns/Jackyard Backoff (picture disc)	8
89	Enigma ENV 19	All Women Are Bad/Teenage Rage (p/s)	6
89	Enigma ENV 19	All Women Are Bad/King Of The Drapes/Teenage Rage/High School Hellcats (12", pic disc)	10
90	Enigma ENV 22	Creature From The Black Leather Lagoon/Jailhouse Rock (p/s)	6
90	Enigma 12ENV 22	Creature From The Black Leather Lagoon/Jailhouse Rock/Beat Out My Love (12", p/s)	8
91	Big Beat NS 135	Eyeball In My Martini/Wilder Wilder Faster Faster (p/s)	6
91	Big Beat NST 135	Eyeball In My Martini/I Wanna Get In Your Pants/Wilder Wilder Faster Faster (12", p/s)	8
94	Creation CRE 180	Ultra Twist/Confessions Of A Psycho Cat (p/s)	5
94	Creation CRE 180T	Ultra Twist/Confessions Of A Psycho Cat/No Club Lone Wolf (p/s)	8
95	Creation CRE 196	Naked Girl Falling Down The Stairs/Let's Get Fucked Up (p/s, red vinyl)	6
80	Illegal ILP 005	SONGS THE LORD TAUGHT US (LP, white label with "Drug Train" in place of "T.V. Set")	100
80	Illegal ILP 005	SONGS THE LORD TAUGHT US (LP, with "T.V. Set")	15
81	IRS SP 70016	PSYCHEDELIC JUNGLE (LP)	15
83	Illegal ILP 012	OFF THE BONE (LP, white label, with different mix of "Drug Train", around 50 copies pressed, unreleased)	100+
83	Illegal ILP 012	OFF THE BONE (LP, with 3-D sleeve & glasses)	15
83	Illegal ILP 012	OFF THE BONE (LP, picture disc with extra track)	15
84	Big Beat NED 6	SMELL OF FEMALE (LP, red see-through vinyl)	15
84	Big Beat BEDP 6	SMELL OF FEMALE (LP, picture disc)	20
86	Big Beat WIKA 46	A DATE WITH ELVIS (LP, with poster)	12
86	Big Beat WIKA 46	A DATE WITH ELVIS (LP, blue vinyl)	20
91	Big Beat WIKPD 101	LOOK MOM NO HEAD (LP, picture disc)	15
91	Windsong WINDSONG 4	LUX (3 x 12" box set, with poster, T-shirt & book, numbered, withdrawn)	50

CRANBERRIES
91	Xeric XER 014	Uncertain/Nothing Left At All (p/s)	15
91	Xeric XER 014T	Uncertain/Nothing Left At All/Pathetic Senses/Them (12", p/s)	25
91	Xeric XER 014CD	Uncertain/Nothing Left At All/Pathetic Senses/Them (CD)	35
96	Island CRAN 1	EVERYBODY ELSE IS DOING IT SO WHY CAN'T WE (2-CD, tri-fold digipak, with "Linger" promo single, promo only)	20

TONY CRANE
65	Polydor BM 56008	Ideal Love/Little You	7
66	CBS 202022	Even The Bravest/I Still Remember	8
67	Pye 7N 17337	Anonymous Mr Brown/In This World	10
68	Pye 7N 17517	Scratchin' Ma Head/Patterns In The Sky	10

(see also Bob Miller)

CRANE/FARLOWE
73	Dawn DNS 1034	Can't Find A Reason/Moods	6

(see also Atomic Rooster, Crazy World Of Arthur Brown, Chris Farlowe, Katmandu)

CRANE RIVER JAZZ BAND
51	Delta D 5	Kentucky Home/Moose March (78)	8
51	Delta D 6	If I Ever Cease To Love/Gipsy Lament (78)	8
51	Esquire 12-013	Eh, La Bas!/CHRIS BARBER'S JAZZ BAND: Oh, Didn't He Ramble (78)	15
51	Melodisc 1027	Eh, La-Bas!/Just A Closer Walk With Thee (78)	8
51	Melodisc 1030	Dauphin St. Blues/Just A Little While To Stay Here (78)	8
51	Melodisc 1165	Down By The River/Blanche Touquatouz (78)	8
52	Melodisc 1202	Sheik Of Araby/Sobbin' Blues (78)	8
52	Parlophone R 3567	Slow Drag Blues/'Tain't Nobody's Bizness If I Do (78)	8
53	Parlophone MSP 6008	Lily Of The Valley/Till We Meet Again	15
57	77 LP/4	ORIGINAL CRANE RIVER JAZZ BAND (LP)	75
57	77 LP/5	ORIGINAL CRANE RIVER JAZZ BAND (LP)	60
57	77 LP/17	ORIGINAL CRANE RIVER JAZZ BAND (LP)	60
57	77 LP/18	ORIGINAL CRANE RIVER JAZZ BAND (LP)	75

(see also Ken Colyer)

CRANES
87	Biteback	FUSE (cassette LP)	25

CRANES SKIFFLE GROUP
57	Embassy WB 223	The Banana Boat Song/Don't You Rock Me Daddy-O (78)	8
57	Embassy WB 238	Freight Train/Cumberland Gap (78)	8

(see also Ken Colyer, Chas McDevitt)

CRASH
82	Crash EJSP 9819	FIGHT FOR YOUR LIFE (EP, no p/s)	10

CRASH
86	Remorse LOST 2	Don't Look Now (Now!)/International Velvet/Don't Look Now (Acoustic) (12", p/s)	8
86	Remorse LOST 4	Almost/My Machine/On And On (Version) (12", p/s)	8
87	Remorse REMLP 2	I FEEL FINE (LP)	12

(see also Ultra Vivid Scene)

CRASHERS
69	Amalgamated AMG 834	Hurry Come Up/Off Track	6

CRASS
78	Small Wonder WEENY 2	THE FEEDING OF THE 5000 (12" EP, with 4-page insert & poster)	10
78	Crass 621984	THE FEEDING OF THE 5000 (12" EP, reissue with "Reality Asylum")	8
79	Crass 521984/1	Reality Asylum/Shaved Women (brown cardboard gatefold p/s; later in white newspaper foldout sleeve)	10/5
80	Crass/Xntrix 421984/1	Bloody Revolutions/POISON GIRLS: Persons Unknown (foldout p/s)	10/5
80	Crass 421984/5	Nagasaki Nightmare/Big A Little A (foldout p/s, some with patch)	6/5
81	Crass 421984/6	Rival Tribal Rebel Revel/Bully Boys Out Fighting (flexidisc with *Toxic Graffiti* fanzine)	10/5
81	Crass 421984/6	Rival Tribal Rebel Revel/Bully Boys Out Fighting (hard vinyl promo, p/s)	25
81	Crass COLD TURKEY 1	Merry Crassmass/Merry Crassmass — Have Fun (p/s)	5
82	Crass 221984/6	How Does It Feel (To Be The Mother Of 1000 Dead?)/The Immortal Death/Don't Tell Me You Care (foldout p/s)	8
83	Crass 121984/3	Sheep Farming In The Falklands/Gotcha! (live) (foldout p/s with lyric insert)	5
83	(no label)	Gotcha! (clear flexidisc)	8
83	Crass 121984/4	Who Dunnit? (Parts 1 & 2) (p/s, brown vinyl)	5
82	Crass BOLLOX 2U2	CHRIST THE ALBUM (3-LP, box set with booklet)	20

(see also Joy De Vivre, Eve Libertine, Poison Girls)

CRAVATS
78	The Cravats CH 004	Gordon/Situations (p/s)	10
79	Small Wonder SMALL 15	The End/Burning Bridges/I Hate The Universe (p/s)	5
80	Small Wonder SMALL 24	Precinct/Who's In Here With Me? (p/s, some with free flexidisc ["Fireman"/A FLUX IN 3D: Divide])	8/5
80	Small Wonder SMALL 25	You're Driving Me Mad/I Am The Dregs (p/s)	5
81	Small Wonder SMALL 26	Off The Beach/And The Sun Shone On (p/s)	5
82	Crass 221984/2	RUB ME OUT (EP, 21" x 14" poster p/s)	5
80s	Lyntone	D.C.L. (Laboratory Series No. 1) (flexidisc)	5
85	Reflex 12 RE 10	THE LAND OF THE GIANTS (12" EP)	10
80	Small Wonder CRAVAT 1	THE CRAVATS IN TOYTOWN (LP, with inner sleeve)	15

(see also Very Things)

CAROLYN CRAWFORD
65	Stateside SS 384	When Someone's Good To You/My Heart	100

JAMES 'SUGARBOY' CRAWFORD
73	Chess 6145 024	Jock-o-mo (Iko Iko)/BOBBY CHARLES: See You Later, Alligator	5

JIMMY CRAWFORD

60	Columbia DB 4525	Long Stringy Baby/Unkind	25
61	Columbia DB 4633	Love Or Money/Does My Heartache Show	7
61	Columbia DB 4717	I Love How You Love Me/Our Last Embrace	6
62	Columbia DB 4841	I Shoulda Listened To Mama/A Boy Without A Girl	8
62	Columbia DB 4895	Thank You/There'll Be No Goodbyes	8
63	Columbia DB 4957	Another Of Your Toys/Young And Afraid	6
63	Columbia DB 7175	Don't Worry About Bobby/Take This Rose	7

JOHNNY CRAWFORD

62	Pye International 7N 25145	Cindy's Birthday/Patti Ann	7
62	London HL 9605	Your Nose Is Gonna Grow/Something Special	6
62	London HL 9638	Rumors/No One Really Loves A Clown	6
63	London HL 9669	Proud/Lonesome Town	6
64	London HL 9836	Judy Loves Me/Living In The Past	7
62	London RE 1343	JOHNNY CRAWFORD (EP)	20
64	London RE 1416	WHEN I FALL IN LOVE (EP)	25
63	London HA 8060	RUMORS (LP)	35
64	London HA 8197	JOHNNY CRAWFORD — HIS GREATEST HITS (LP)	30

MICHAEL CRAWFORD

65	United Artists UP 1095	The Knack/Oh That Girl	7

RANDY CRAWFORD

89	Warner Bros 2865	Knocking On Heaven's Door (with Eric Clapton & David Sambora)	7
89	Warner Bros 2865T	Knocking On Heaven's Door (with Eric Clapton & David Sambora) (12", p/s)	8
89	Warner Bros 2865CD	Knocking On Heaven's Door (with Eric Clapton & David Sambora) (3" CD)	12

ROSETTA CRAWFORD

51	Vocalion V 1002	Stop It Joe/My Man Jumped Salty On Me (78)	10

CRAWFORD BROTHERS

57	Vogue V 9077	Midnight Mover Groover/Midnight Happenings	225
57	Vogue V 9077	Midnight Mover Groover/Midnight Happenings (78)	60
59	Vogue V 9140	It Feels Good/I Ain't Guilty (triangular or round centre)	225/125
59	Vogue V 9140	It Feels Good/I Ain't Guilty (78)	90

CRAWLER

77	Epic EPC 82083	CRAWLER (LP)	12
78	Epic EPC 82965	SNAKE RATTLE AND ROLL (LP)	12
	(see also Back Street Crawler)		

CRAYS

65	Polydor BM 56033	Nancy's Minuet/Don't Pity Me	5

PEE WEE CRAYTON

78	Vanguard VSD 6566	THINGS I USED TO DO (LP)	15

CRAZE

79	Cobra COB 3	Motions/Spartans (p/s)	6
80	Harvest HAR 5200	Motions/Spartans (reissue in different p/s)	5
80	Harvest HAR 5205	Lucy/Stop Living In The Past (p/s)	6
	(see also Skunks, Hard Corps)		

CRAZY ELEPHANT

69	Major Minor MM 609	Gimme Gimme Good Lovin'/Dark Part Of My Mind	5
69	Major Minor MM 623	Sunshine Red Wine/Pam	5
70	Major Minor MM 672	There's A Better Day Coming/Space Buggy	5
69	Major Minor SMLP 62	CRAZY ELEPHANT (LP)	15

CRAZY FEELINGS

67	Polydor NH 56723	Please Lie/Time Is Running Out	5

CRAZY HORSE

71	Reprise RS 23503	Dance Dance Dance/Look At All The Things	5
72	Reprise K 14159	All Alone Now/One Thing I Love	5
73	Epic EPC 1121	We Ride/Outside Looking In	5
72	Reprise RSLP 6438	CRAZY HORSE (LP)	15
72	Reprise K 44171	LOOSE (LP, gatefold sleeve)	12
73	Epic EPC 65223	AT CROOKED CREEK (LP, gatefold cut-out sleeve)	12
79	RCA PL 13054	CRAZY MOON (LP, with lyric inner sleeve)	12
88	Rough Trade	LEFT FOR DEAD (LP, cancelled, promos only)	12
	(see also Neil Young, Nils Lofgren, Jack Nitzsche)		

CRAZY ROCKERS

64	King KG 1001	Third Man Theme/Mama Papa	6

PAPA JOHN CREACH

71	Grunt FTR 1003	PAPA JOHN CREACH (LP)	12
73	Grunt FTR 1009	FILTHY (LP)	12
	(see also Jefferson Airplane)		

CREAM

66	Reaction 591 007	Wrapping Paper/Cat's Squirrel	12
66	Reaction 591 011	I Feel Free/N.S.U.	10
67	Reaction 591 015	Strange Brew/Tales Of Brave Ulysses	10
68	Polydor 56258	Anyone For Tennis (The Savage Seven Theme)/Pressed Rat And Warthog	8
68	Polydor 56286	Sunshine Of Your Love/SWLABR	6
68	Polydor 56300	White Room/Those Were The Days	6
69	Polydor 56315	Strange Brew/Wrapping Paper (unissued)	
69	Polydor 56315	Badge/What A Bringdown	6
71	Polydor 2058 120	I Feel Free/Wrapping Paper	5
72	Polydor 2058 285	Badge/What A Bringdown (reissue)	5

MINT VALUE £

66	Reaction 593/594 001	FRESH CREAM	
		(LP, mono/stereo)	45/30
67	Reaction 593/594 003	DISRAELI GEARS	
		(LP, sleeve laminated on front & back, mono/stereo)	45/30
68	Reaction 593/594 003	DISRAELI GEARS	
		(LP, sleeve laminated on front only, mono/stereo)	35/25
68	Polydor 582/583 031/2	WHEELS OF FIRE	
		(2-LP, gatefold sleeve, mono/stereo; set no. 2612 001)	45/35
68	Polydor 582/583 033	WHEELS OF FIRE — IN THE STUDIO	
		(LP, mono/stereo)	25/18
68	Polydor 582/583 040	WHEELS OF FIRE — LIVE AT THE FILLMORE	
		(LP, mono/stereo)	25/18
69	Polydor 583 053	GOODBYE (LP, gatefold sleeve)	18
69	Polydor 583 060	THE BEST OF CREAM (LP)	12
70	Polydor 2383 016	LIVE CREAM (LP)	12
71	Polydor 2855 002	CREAM ON TOP	
		(LP, mail-order compilation)	35
72	Polydor 2383 119	LIVE CREAM VOL.2 (LP)	12
75	Polydor 2384 067	CREAM (LP, reissue of "Fresh Cream" with 2 extra tracks)	12
75	RSO 2394 179	GOODBYE (LP, gatefold sleeve, reissue)	12
80	RSO 2658 142	CREAM (7-LP set including "Fresh Cream", "Disraeli Gears", "Wheels Of Fire", "Goodbye", "Live Cream" & "Live Cream Vol. 2")	45
92	UFO CR 1	CREAM IN GEAR	
		(96-page book packaged with "Disraeli Gears" CD)	20

(see also Eric Clapton, Jack Bruce, Ginger Baker, Blind Faith)

CREAMERS
89	Fierce FRIGHT 045	Sunday Head/Think I'm Gonna Be Sick (p/s)	10

JOAN CREARY
71	Fab FAB 181	Your Best Friend/Version	6

CREATION (U.K.)
66	Planet PLF 116	Making Time/Try And Stop Me (some in Planet sleeves)	25/18
66	Planet PLF 119	Painter Man/Biff Bang Pow (some in Planet sleeves)	25/18
67	Polydor 56177	If I Stay Too Long/Nightmares	30
67	Polydor 56207	Life Is Just Beginning/Through My Eyes	30
68	Polydor 56230	How Does It Feel To Feel/Tom Tom	30
68	Polydor 56246	Midway Down/The Girls Are Naked	30
73	Charisma CB 213	Making Time/Painter Man	8
77	Raw RAW 4	Making Time/Painter Man (reissue, p/s)	10
84	Edsel E 5006	Making Time/Uncle Bert (p/s)	10
87	Jet JET 7047	A Spirit Called Love/Making Time (p/s)	5
87	Jet JET 12047	A Spirit Called Love/Making Time/Mumbo Jumbo (12", p/s)	8
73	Charisma Perspective CS 8	THE CREATION '66-67 (LP)	35
82	Edsel ED 106	HOW DOES IT FEEL TO FEEL (LP, with foldout insert)	15

(see also Mark Four, Birds, Ashton Gardner & Dyke, Kennedy Express, Eddy Phillips, Smiley, Spectrum)

CREATION (U.S.)
72	Stateside SS 2205	I Got The Fever/Soul Control	8

(see also Prophets)

CREATIONS
67	Rio R 133	Meet Me At Eight/Searching	10
68	Amalgamated AMG 818	Holding Out/Get On Up	10
69	Punch PH 2	Mix Up Girl/Qua Kue Shut	6

(see also Little Roys)

CREATIVE SOURCE
74	Sussex SXX 1	Who Is He And What Is He To You/Who Is He And What Is He To You (Version)	5
76	Polydor 6006 680	Don't Be Afraid (Take My Love)/Pass The Feelings On	5
74	Sussex LPSX 6	CREATIVE SOURCE (LP)	15
74	Sussex LPSX 7	MIGRATION (LP)	12
76	Polydor 2391 196	PASS THE FEELIN' ON (LP)	12

CREATOR & NORMA
63	Island WI 105	We Will Be Lovers/Come On Pretty Baby	15

CREATURES
66	CBS 202048	Turn Out The Light/It Must Be Love	7
66	CBS 202350	String Along/Night Is Warm	7
67	CBS 2666	Looking At Tomorrow/Someone Needs You	7

CREATURES
81	Polydor POSPG 354	WILD THINGS	
		(double pack EP, gatefold p/s; picture labels)	10
89	Wonderland SHET 17	Standing There (La Frontera Mix)/Divided/Solar Choir	
		(10", p/s)	8
90	Wonderland SHEB 18	Fury Eyes/Abstinence (box set with 4 photos)	5
98	Sioux 1V	Sad Cunt/Sad Cunt (Chix'n'Dix mix) (p/s)	10
98	Sioux 2	ERASER CUT (10" EP, p/s)	8

(see also Siouxsie & Banshees)

CREEDENCE CLEARWATER REVIVAL
69	Liberty LBF 15223	Proud Mary/I Put A Spell On You (withdrawn)	20
69	Liberty LBF 15223	Proud Mary/Born On The Bayou	6
69	Liberty LBF 15230	Bad Moon Rising/Lodi	6
69	Liberty LBF 15250	Green River/Commotion	6
70	Liberty LBF 15283	Down On The Corner/Fortunate Son	6
70	Liberty LBF 15310	Travellin' Band/Who'll Stop The Rain	6
70	Liberty LBF 15354	Up Around The Bend/Run Through The Jungle (initially in p/s)	10/5
70	Liberty LBF 15384	Long As I Can See The Light/Lookin' Out My Back Door (initially in p/s)	10/5

MINT VALUE £

71	Liberty LBF 15440	Have You Ever Seen The Rain/Hey Tonight	5
71	United Artists UP 35210	Hey Tonight/Have You Ever Seen The Rain (reissue)	6
71	United Artists UP 35261	Sweet Hitch-Hiker/Door To Door	6
72	Fantasy F 676	Someday Never Comes/Tearin' Up The Country	5
72	Fantasy FTC 101	Born On The Bayou/I Put A Spell On You	5
73	Fantasy FTC 104	It Came Out Of The Sky/Side O' The Road	5
78	Fantasy FTC 164	Who'll Stop The Rain/Proud Mary/Hey Tonight (p/s)	5
79	Fantasy FTC 178	I Heard It Through The Grapevine/Rockin' All Over The World (p/s)	5
79	Fantasy 12 FTC 178	I Heard It Through The Grapevine/Keep On Chooglin' (Full Length) (12")	8
69	Liberty LBS 83259	CREEDENCE CLEARWATER REVIVAL (LP)	18
69	Liberty LBS 83261	BAYOU COUNTRY (LP)	18
69	Liberty LBS 83273	GREEN RIVER (LP)	18
70	Liberty LBS 83338	WILLY AND THE POORBOYS (LP)	18
70	Liberty LBS 83388	COSMO'S FACTORY (LP)	18
71	Liberty LBG 83400	PENDULUM (LP, gatefold sleeve)	15
72	Fantasy FAN 9404	MARDI GRAS (LP)	12
73	Fantasy FT 506	CREEDENCE CLEARWATER REVIVAL (LP)	12

(see also Golliwogs, John Fogerty, Tom Fogerty, Blue Ridge Rangers)

CREEPERS
66	Blue Beat BB 366	Beat Of My Soul/LLOYD ADAMS: I Wish Your Picture Was You	12

CREME CARAMEL
69	Pye International 7N 25495	My Idea/Excursion	5

CRESCENDOS
58	London HLU 8563	Oh Julie/My Little Girl	45
58	London HLU 8563	Oh Julie/My Little Girl (78)	35

CRESCENTS
58	Columbia DB 4093	Wrong/Baby, Baby, Baby	70
58	Columbia DB 4093	Wrong/Baby, Baby, Baby (78)	25

CRESCENTS
64	London HLN 9851	Pink Dominos/Breakout	10

CRESSIDA
70	Vertigo VO 7	CRESSIDA (LP, gatefold sleeve, spiral label)	70
71	Vertigo 6360 025	ASYLUM (LP, gatefold sleeve, spiral label)	90

CRESTAS
65	Fontana TF 551	To Be Loved/When I Fall In Love	20

CRESTERS
64	HMV POP 1249	I Just Don't Understand/I Want You	10
64	HMV POP 1296	Put Your Arms Around Me/Do It With Me	10

(see also Mike Sagar & Cresters, Richard Harding)

CRESTS
59	London HL 8794	Sixteen Candles/Beside You	50
59	London HL 8794	Sixteen Candles/Beside You (78)	70
59	Top Rank JAR 150	Flower Of Love/Molly Mae	15
59	Top Rank JAR 150	Flower Of Love/Molly Mae (78)	60
59	Top Rank JAR 168	Six Nights A Week/I Do	18
59	Top Rank JAR 168	Six Nights A Week/I Do (78)	75
59	London HL 8954	The Angels Listened In/I Thank The Moon	35
59	London HL 8954	The Angels Listened In/I Thank The Moon (78)	80
60	Top Rank JAR 302	A Year Ago Tonight/Paper Crown	20
60	Top Rank JAR 372	Step By Step/Gee (But I'd Give The World)	20
60	HMV POP 768	Always You/Trouble In Paradise	25
60	HMV POP 808	Isn't It Amazing/Molly Mae	18
61	HMV POP 848	Model Girl/We've Got To Tell Them	18
62	HMV POP 976	Little Miracles/Baby I Gotta Know	18
63	London HLU 9671	Guilty/Number One With Me	15

(see also Johnny Maestro)

CREW
69	Plexium PXM 12	Marty/Danger Signs	6
70	Decca F 13000	Cecilia/1970	6

CREW-CUTS
53	Mercury MB 3135	Crazy 'Bout You Baby/Angela Mia (78)	10
54	Mercury MB 3140	Sh-Boom/I Spoke Too Soon (78)	10
54	Mercury MB 3159	Oop-Shoop/Do Me Good, Baby (78)	12
54	Mercury MB 3177	Twinkle Toes/Dance Mr. Snowman Dance (78)	8
54	Mercury MB 3185	Barking Dog/All I Wanna Do (78)	12
55	Mercury MB 3202	Earth Angel/Ko Ko Mo (78)	8
55	Mercury MB 3222	Unchained Melody/Two Hearts, Two Kisses (78)	10
55	Mercury MB 3228	Don't Be Angry/Chop Chop Boom (78)	14
56	Mercury MT 100	Angels In The Sky/Seven Days (78)	10
56	Mercury 7MT 2	Angels In The Sky/Seven Days (export issue)	25
56	Mercury MT 108	A Story Untold/Honey Hair, Sugar Lips, Eyes Of Blue (78)	12
56	Mercury MT 127	Rebel In Town/Bei Mir Bist Du Shoen (78)	14
57	Mercury MT 140	Young Love/Little By Little (78)	15
57	Mercury MT 161	Susie-Q/Such A Shame (78)	20
57	Mercury MT 178	I Sit In My Window/Hey, You Face (78)	15
58	RCA RCA 1075	Hey, Stella!/Forever, My Darling	30
58	RCA RCA 1075	Hey, Stella!/Forever, My Darling (78)	30
78	Philips 6168 032	Sh-Boom (Life Could Be A Dream)/Angels In The Skiy	5
56	Mercury MEP 9002	PRESENTING THE CREW-CUTS (EP)	45
56	Mercury MPT 7501	THE CREW-CUTS ON PARADE (10" LP)	70

BOB CREWE (GENERATION)

60	London HLI 9077	Water Boy/Voglio Cantare (solo) 5
64	Stateside SS 356	Maggie Maggie May/We Almost Made It 6
67	Stateside SS 582	Music To Watch Girls By/Girls On The Rocks 10
67	Stateside SS 2032	You Only Live Twice/A Lover's Concerto 5
67	Stateside SL 10210	MUSIC TO WATCH GIRLS BY (LP) 18
68	Stateside S(S)L 10260	BARBARELLA (LP, soundtrack) 60

CREWSY FIXERS

| 80s | Big Mix ACE 22 | CAST IRON ARM (EP, gatefold p/s) .... 6 |

BERNARD CRIBBINS

60	Parlophone R 4712	Folk Song/My Kind Of Someone (B-side with Joyce Blair) 6
62	Parlophone R 4869	The Hole In The Ground/Winkle Picker Shoes 5
62	Parlophone R 4923	Right Said Fred/Quietly Bonkers 5
62	Parlophone R 4961	Gossip Calypso/One Man Band 5
67	Parlophone R 5603	When I'm Sixty-Four/Oh My Word 8
62	Parlophone GEP 8859	THE HOLE IN THE GROUND (EP) 12
62	Parlophone PMC 1186	A COMBINATION OF CRIBBINS (LP) 18

CRICKETS featuring Buddy Holly

78s

57	Vogue Coral Q 72279	That'll Be The Day/I'm Lookin' For Someone To Love (78) 18
57	Coral Q 72298	Oh Boy!/Not Fade Away (78) 18
58	Coral Q 72279	That'll Be The Day/I'm Lookin' For Someone To Love (78) 18
58	Coral Q 72307	Maybe Baby/Tell Me How (78) 25
58	Coral Q 72329	Think It Over/Fool's Paradise (78) 35
58	Coral Q 72343	It's So Easy/Lonesome Tears (78) 40

SINGLES

57	Vogue Coral Q 72279	That'll Be The Day/I'm Lookin' For Someone To Love 18
57	Coral Q 72298	Oh Boy!/Not Fade Away 12
58	Coral Q 72279	That'll Be The Day/I'm Lookin' For Someone To Love (2nd issue) . 15
58	Coral Q 72307	Maybe Baby/Tell Me How 12
58	Coral Q 72329	Think It Over/Fool's Paradise 12
58	Coral Q 72343	It's So Easy/Lonesome Tears 12

(All the above 45s were originally issued with triangular centres; later round centre copies are worth around half these values.)

68	Decca AD 1012	Oh, Boy/That'll Be The Day (export issue) 30
68	MCA MU 1017	Oh, Boy/That'll Be The Day (as Crickets featuring Buddy Holly) . 7
81	PBF 0005	That'll Be The Day (1-sided flexidisc, available via 7UP DJ Rock'n'Roll Show) 5

EPs

58	Coral FEP 2003	THE SOUND OF THE CRICKETS (EP, triangular or round centre) .. 30/20
59	Coral FEP 2014	IT'S SO EASY (EP, triangular or round centre) 30/20
60	Coral FEP 2060	FOUR MORE BY THE CRICKETS (EP) 30
60	Coral FEP 2062	THAT'LL BE THE DAY (EP) 30

LP

| 58 | Vogue Coral LVA 9081 | THE CHIRPING CRICKETS (LP, Vogue-Coral labels & Coral sleeve) .... 70 |
| 58 | Coral LVA 9081 | THE CHIRPING CRICKETS (LP, re-pressing with Coral labels & sleeve) .... 40 |

(see also Buddy Holly)

CRICKETS

78s

59	Coral Q 72365	Love's Made A Fool Of You/Someone, Someone (78) 60
59	Coral Q 72382	When You Ask About Love/Deborah (78) 80
60	Coral Q 72395	More Than I Can Say/Baby My Heart (78, existence unconfirmed) .. 100+

SINGLES

59	Coral Q 72365	Love's Made A Fool Of You/Someone, Someone 12
59	Coral Q 72382	When You Ask About Love/Deborah 12
60	Coral Q 72395	More Than I Can Say/Baby My Heart 12
61	Coral Q 72417	Peggy Sue Got Married/Don'tcha Know 12
61	Coral Q 72440	I Fought The Law/A Sweet Love 12
61	London HLG 9486	He's Old Enough To Know Better/I'm Feeling Better 10
62	Liberty LIB 55441	Don't Ever Change/I Am Not A Bad Guy 6
62	Liberty LIB 55495	Little Hollywood Girl/Parisian Girl 10
63	Liberty LIB 10067	My Little Girl/Teardrops Fall Like Rain 7
63	Liberty LIB 10092	Don't Try To Change Me/Lost And Alone 10
63	Liberty LIB 10113	Right Or Wrong/You Can't Be In Between 7
64	Liberty LIB 10145	Lonely Avenue/Playboy 7
64	Liberty LIB 55696	(They Call Her) La Bamba/All Over You 7
64	Liberty LIB 10174	I Think I've Caught The Blues/We Gotta Get Together 7
65	Liberty LIB 10196	Now Hear This/Everybody's Got A Little Problem 8
66	Liberty LIB 55603	April Avenue/Don't Say You Love Me 10
68	Liberty LBF 15089	My Little Girl/Lonely Avenue 7
72	United Artists UP 35457	Don't Ever Change/Playboy 7
73	Philips 6006 269	My Rockin' Days/Lovesick Blues 6
73	Philips 6006 294	Hayride/Wasn't It Nice In New York City (some in p/s) 20/10
74	Mercury 6008 006	Ooh Las Vegas/Rhyme And Time 6
79	Rollercoaster RRC 2001	Cruise In It/Rock Around With Ollie Vee (2,000 only with 'single photo' p/s) 5
87	Rollercoaster RRC 2007	Forever In Mind/The Weekend/Your M-M-Memory/Three-Piece (tri-centre in overprinted p/s) 5
88	MPL/CBS TSH 1	T-Shirt/Hollywould (p/s) 8
88	MPL/CBS TSHT 1	T-Shirt/Hollywould (12", p/s) 12
88	MPL/CBS CDTSHT 1	T-Shirt/Hollywould (CD) 15

EPs

60	Coral FEP 2053	THE CRICKETS (EP, initially triangular centre, later round centre)	50/35
61	Coral FEP 2064	THE CRICKETS DON'T EVER CHANGE (EP)	30
63	Liberty (S)LEP 2094	STRAIGHT NO STRINGS (EP, mono/stereo)	25/40
64	Liberty LEP 2173	COME ON (EP)	25
77	Rollercoaster RRCEP 0001	MILLION DOLLAR MOVIE (EP, shared with Sonny Curtis; test pressings only)	12

LPs

61	Coral LVA 9142	IN STYLE WITH THE CRICKETS (LP)	45
62	Liberty (S)LBY 1120	SOMETHING OLD, SOMETHING NEW, SOMETHING BLUE, SOMETHING ELSE! (LP, mono/stereo)	30/40
65	Liberty LBY 1258	THE CRICKETS — A COLLECTION (LP)	30
71	CBS 64301	ROCKIN' FIFTIES, ROCK 'N' ROLL (LP)	18
71	Sunset SLS 50207	ROCK REFLECTIONS (LP)	12
73	Philips 6308 149	BUBBLEGUM, POP, BALLADS & BOOGIES (LP)	18
74	Mercury 6310 007	A LONG WAY FROM LUBBOCK (LP)	18
75	MCA MCFM 2710	BACK IN STYLE (LP)	15
88	Rollercoaster ROLL 2014	THREE PIECE (LP)	12

(see also Buddy Holly, Jerry Allison & Crickets, Ivan, Sonny Curtis, Earl Sinks, Sinx Mitchell, David Box)

CRICKETS & BOBBY VEE

63	Liberty LEP 2084	JUST FOR FUN (EP)	18
63	Liberty (S)LEP 2116	BOBBY VEE MEETS THE CRICKETS (EP, mono/stereo)	25/40
63	Liberty LEP 2149	BOBBY VEE MEETS THE CRICKETS VOL. 2 (EP)	25
62	Liberty (S)LBY 1086	BOBBY VEE MEETS THE CRICKETS (LP, mono/stereo)	25/35

(see also Bobby Vee)

CRIME

80	Punk Products PP 1	Generation Gap/Johnny Come Home (p/s)	20

CRIMINAL CLASS

82	Inferno HELL 7	Fighting The System/Soldier (p/s)	12

CRISIS

79	Peckham Action NOTH 1	No Town Hall (Southwark)/Holocaust/P.C. One Nine Eight Four (p/s)	18
79	Ardkor CRI 002	UK '79/White Youth (p/s)	10
80	Ardkor CRI 003	HYMNS OF FAITH (12" EP)	25
81	Ardkor CRI 004	Alienation/Brückwood/Hospital (p/s, with insert)	15
82	Crisis NOTH 1/CRI 002	HOLOCAUST UK (12" EP)	20

(see also Death In June, Current 93, Theatre Of Hate)

CRISIS

70s	private pressing	ANOTHER FINE MESS (LP)	45

CRISPY AMBULANCE

79	Aural Assault AAR 001	From The Cradle To The Grave/4 Minutes From The Frontline (glossy or matt p/s)	10/8
81	Factory FAC 32	Unsightly And Serene: Not What I Expected/Deaf (10", p/s)	8
83	CBST 7	THE BLUE AND YELLOW OF THE YACHT CLUB (cassette)	8
83	CBST 8	OPEN GATES OF FIRE (cassette)	8
89	Temps Moderne LTMV:X	FIN (LP)	12

(see also Ram Ram Kino)

GARY CRISS

62	Stateside SS 104	Our Favourite Melodies/Welcome Home To My Heart	10
62	Stateside SS 123	My Little Heavenly Angel/The Girl That I Told You About	7
63	Stateside SS 164	Long Lonely Nights/I Still Miss You So	7
63	Stateside SS 265	Sweet, Warm And Soft/Little Joe	7
65	Stateside SS 427	Hands Off Buddy/If This Is Goodbye	7

PETER CRISS

79	Casablanca CAN 139	You Matter To Me/Hooked On Rock And Roll (p/s, green vinyl with mask)	20
79	Casablanca CAN 139	You Matter To Me/Hooked On Rock And Roll (p/s, black vinyl)	15
80	Mercury 6302 065	OUT OF CONTROL (LP)	15

(see also Kiss)

LINDA CRISTAL

59	Coral Q 72350	Strictly For Pleasure (A Perfect Romance)/It's Better In Spanish	6
59	Coral Q 72350	Strictly For Pleasure (A Perfect Romance)/It's Better In Spanish (78)	8

CRISTINA

80	Island/Ze WIP 6560	Is That All There Is/Jungle Love (withdrawn)	6
80	Island/Ze WIP 6560T	Is That All There Is/Jungle Love (12", withdrawn)	10

BOBBY CRISTO & REBELS

64	Decca F 11913	The Other Side Of The Track/I've Got You Out Of My Mind	30

MARY CRISTY

76	Polydor 2056 513	Thank You For Rushing Into My Life/We Can't Hide This Time	10

CRITICS & NYAH SHUFFLE

70	Joe JRS 1	Behold/SEXY FRANKIE: Tea, Patty, Sex And Ganja	7

CRITICS GROUP

66	Argo ZDA 46	A MERRY PROGRESS TO LONDON (LP, with insert)	18
68	Argo ZDA 82	THE FEMALE FROLIC (LP, with insert)	18
68	Argo DA 86	WATERLOO PETERLOO (LP, with insert)	15
72	Argo ZFB 61	SWEET THAMES FLOW SOFTLY (LP)	12

CRITTERS
66	London HLR 10047	Younger Girl/Gone For Awhile	10
66	London HLR 10071	Mr. Dieingly Sad/It Just Won't Be That Way	10
66	London HLR 10101	Bad Misunderstanding/Forever Or No More	8
67	London HLR 10119	Marryin' Kind Of Love/New York Bound	7
67	London HLR 10149	Don't Let The Rain Fall Down On Me/Walk Like A Man Again	8
67	London HA-R 8302	THE CRITTERS (LP)	30

JIM CROCE
72	Vertigo 6073 251	Operator/Rapid Roy	5
72	Vertigo 6360 700	YOU DON'T MESS AROUND WITH JIM (LP, gatefold sleeve, spiral label)	18

CROCHETED DOUGHNUT RING
67	Polydor 56204	Two Little Ladies (Azalea And Rhododendron)/Nice	30
67	Deram DM 169	Havana Anna/Happy Castle	30
68	Deram DM 180	Maxine's Parlour/Get Out Your Rock And Roll Shoes	18

(see also Force Five, Doughnut Ring, Fingers, Daddy Lindberg)

CROCODILE RIDE
80s	Thunderball Surfacer 002	Ex-Hipster/Satellite/14 ICED BEARS: Falling Backwards/World I Love (Speed Mix) (1,000 only, numbered & stickered mailer)	8

CROFTERS
69	Say Disc SD 113	PILL FERRY (EP)	10
69	Beltona SBE 103	CROFTERS (LP)	12

TONY CROMBIE
54	Decca F 10424	Stop It All/All Of Me (& His Orchestra)	8
55	Decca F 10454	Perdido/Love You Madly (& His Orchestra)	12
55	Decca F 10547	Early One Morning/Flying Home (& His Orchestra)	8
55	Decca F 10592	Flying Hickory/String Of Pearls (& His Orchestra)	10
55	Decca F 10637	I Want You To Be My Baby (with Annie Ross)/Three Little Words	10
55	Decca F 10637	I Want You To Be My Baby (with Annie Ross)/Three Little Words (78)	8
56	Columbia DB 3822	Teach You To Rock/Short'nin' Bread Rock (as Tony Crombie & Rockets)	35
56	Columbia DB 3822	Teach You To Rock/Short'nin' Bread Rock (78)	10
56	Columbia DB 3859	Sham Rock/Let's You And I Rock (as Tony Crombie & Rockets)	30
56	Columbia DB 3859	Sham Rock/Let's You And I Rock (78)	10
57	Columbia DB 3880	Rock, Rock, Rock/The Big Beat (as Tony Crombie & Rockets) (78)	12
57	Columbia DB 3881	Lonesome Train (On A Lonesome Track)/We're Gonna Rock Tonight (78, as Tony Crombie & Rockets)	15
57	Columbia DB 3921	London Rock/Brighton Rock (as Tony Crombie & Rockets)	30
57	Columbia DB 3921	London Rock/Brighton Rock (78)	15
57	Columbia DB 4000	Sweet Beat/Sweet Georgia Brown (as Tony Crombie & His Sweet Beat)	10
57	Columbia DB 4000	Sweet Beat/Sweet Georgia Brown (78)	12
58	Columbia DB 4076	Dumplin's/Tw'on Special	8
58	Columbia DB 4076	Dumplin's/Tw'on Special (78).	12
58	Columbia DB 4145	Unguaua/Piakukaungchung (as Tony Crombie Men)	7
58	Columbia DB 4145	Unguaua/Piakukaungchung (as Tony Crombie Men) (78)	8
58	Columbia DB 4189	Rock-Cha-Cha/The Gigglin' Gurgleburp (as Tony Crombie Men)	6
58	Columbia DB 4189	Rock-Cha-Cha/The Gigglin' Gurgleburp (as Tony Crombie Men) (78)	12
59	Columbia DB 4253	Champagne Cha Cha/Shepherd's Cha Cha (as Tony Crombie Men)	5
59	Columbia DB 4253	Champagne Cha Cha/Shepherd's Cha Cha(as Tony Crombie Men) (78)	14
59	Top Rank JAR 182	"Man From Interpol" Theme/Interpol Cha Cha Cha & Chase (as Tony Crombie Orchestra)	5
59	Top Rank JAR 182	"Man From Interpol" Theme/Interpol Cha Cha Cha & Chase (78, as Tony Crombie Orchestra)	20
62	Ember JBS 706	Gutbucket/Just Like Old Times	6
56	Decca DFE 6247	PRESENTING TONY CROMBIE NO. 1 (EP)	12
56	Decca DFE 6281	PRESENTING TONY CROMBIE NO. 2 (EP)	12
57	Columbia SEG 7676	ROCK ROCK ROCK (EP)	60
57	Columbia SEG 7686	LET'S YOU AND I ROCK (EP)	60
61	Decca DFE 6670	FOUR FAVOURITE FILM THEMES (EP)	8
56	Columbia 33S 1117	TONY CROMBIE & HIS SWEETBEAT (10" LP)	25
57	Columbia 33S 1108	ROCKIN' WITH TONY CROMBIE & ROCKETS (10" LP)	120
58	Columbia SCX 3262	ATMOSPHERE (LP)	20
59	Top Rank 35/043	MAN FROM INTERPOL (LP, TV series music, by Tony Crombie & Band)	20
60	Top Rank BUY 027	DRUMS! DRUMS! DRUMS! (LP, as Tony Crombie & His Band)	40
61	Tempo TAP 30	JAZZ INC. (LP)	45
61	Decca SKL 4114	SWEET WIDE AND BLUE (LP)	30
61	Decca LK 4385	TWELVE FAVOURITE FILM THEMES (LP, also stereo SKL 4127)	40
61	Ember EMB 3336	WHOLE LOTTA TONY (LP)	50

(see also Annie Ross, Ray Ellington, London Jazz Quartet)

BILL CROMPTON
58	Fontana H 152	A Hoot An' A Holler/The Popocatepetl Beetle	8
58	Fontana H 152	A Hoot An' A Holler/The Popocatepetl Beetle (78)	10
59	Fontana H 178	Out Of Sight, Out Of Mind/My Lover	7
59	Fontana H 178	Out Of Sight, Out Of Mind/My Lover (78)	10

CROMWELL
75	Cromwell WELL 006	First Day	20
75	Cromwell WELL 005	AT THE GALLOP (LP, private pressing)	150

(see also Establishment)

LINK CROMWELL (Lenny Kaye)
66	London HLB 10040	Crazy Like A Fox/Shock Me	15

(see also Patti Smith Group)

MINT VALUE £

ANDREW CRONSHAW
77	Trailer LREP 1	CLOUD VALLEY (EP)	8
74	Xtra XTRA 1139	A IS FOR ANDREW, Z IS FOR ZITHER (LP)	15

CROOKED OAK
76	Folkland FL 0102	FROM LITTLE ACORNS GROW (LP, 500 only)	80
79	Eron ERON 019	THE FOOT O'WOR STAIRS (LP)	25

CROOKS
79	Blue Print BLU 2002	Modern Boys/The Beat Goes On (die-cut p/s)	6
80	Blue Print BLU 2006	All The Time In The World/Bangin' My Head (p/s)	8
80	Blue Print BLUP 5002	JUST RELEASED (LP)	12

DAVID CROOKS
70	Jackpot JP 759	I Won't Hold It Against You (actually by Dave Barker)/BOBBY JAMES: King Of Hearts	5

(see also Dave Barker)

STEVE CROPPER
70	Stax STAX 147	Funky Broadway/Crop Dustin'	8
69	Stax SXATS 1008	WITH A LITTLE HELP FROM MY FRIENDS (LP)	15

STEVE CROPPER & ALBERT KING
69	Stax SXATS 1020	JAMMED TOGETHER (LP, with Pop Staples)	12

(see also Booker T. & M.G.'s, Albert King)

BING CROSBY
78s
51	Brunswick 04744	A Couple Of Song And Dance Men/Everybody Step (78, with Fred Astaire)	8
51	Brunswick 04781	Gone Fishin' (with Louis Armstrong)/LOUIS ARMSTRONG & GARY CROSBY: Moonlight Bay (78)	8
52	Brunswick 05034	Hoots Mon/Chicago Style (78, with Bob Hope)	8
58	Philips PB 817	Straight Down The Middle/Tomorrow's My Lucky Day (78)	8
58	Brunswick 05770	Gigi/The Next Time It Happens (78)	8
59	Brunswick 05790	Rain/Church Bells (78)	10
59	Philips PB 921	Say One For Me/I Couldn't Care Less (78)	10

SINGLES
54	Brunswick 03384	White Christmas/Let's Start The New Year Right	10
54	Brunswick 03929	Silent Night, Holy Night/Adeste Fideles	10
54	Brunswick 05224	What A Little Moonlight Can Do/Down By The Riverside (with Gary Crosby)	7
54	Brunswick 05244	Changing Partners/Y'All Come	15
54	Brunswick 05269	Secret Love/My Love, My Love	10
54	Brunswick 05277	Young At Heart/I Get So Lonely	7
54	Brunswick 05304	If There's Anybody Here (From Out Of Town)/Back In The Old Routine (with Donald O'Connor)	6
54	Brunswick 05315	Cornbelt Symphony/The Call Of The South (with Gary Crosby)	6
54	Brunswick 05339	Count Your Blessings Instead Of Sheep/What Can You Do With A General	10
54	Brunswick 05354	White Christmas/Snow (with Danny Kaye, Peggy Lee & Trudy Stevens)	7
55	Brunswick 05377	The Song From "Desiree" (We Meet Again)/I Love Paris	5
55	Brunswick 05385	Tobermory Bay/The River (Sciummo)	5
55	Brunswick 05403	Dissertation On The State Of Bliss (with Patty Andrews)/It's Mine, It's Yours	6
55	Brunswick 05404	The Search Is Through/The Land Around Us	5
55	Brunswick 05410	Stranger In Paradise/Who Gave You The Roses	5
55	Brunswick 05419	Ohio/A Quiet Girl	5
55	Brunswick 05430	Jim, Johnny And Jonas/Nobody	5
55	Brunswick 05451	All She'd Say Was "Umh"/She Is The Sunshine Of Virginia	5
55	Brunswick 05486	Angel Bells/There's Music In You	5
55	Brunswick 05501	Let's Harmonize/Sleigh Bell Serenade	5
56	Brunswick 05511	Farewell/Early American	5
56	Brunswick 05543	In A Little Spanish Town/Ol' Man River	6
56	Brunswick 05558	No Other Love/Sleepy Time Gal	5
56	Brunswick 05585	Honeysuckle Rose/Swanee	5
56	Brunswick 05620	Christmas Is A-Comin'/Is Christmas Only A Tree	5
56	Capitol CL 14645	True Love (with Grace Kelly)/Well, Did You Evah? (with Frank Sinatra)	6
57	Brunswick 05674	Around The World/VICTOR YOUNG ORCHESTRA: Around The World	6
57	Capitol CL 14761	Man On Fire/Seven Nights A Week	5
57	London HLR 8504	Never Be Afraid/I Love You Whoever You Are	6
57	London HLR 8513	How Lovely Is Christmas/My Own Individual Star	6
57	Brunswick 05726	Chicago/Alabamy Bound	5
58	Philips PB 817	Straight Down The Middle/Tomorrow's My Lucky Day	12
58	Brunswick 05760	Love In A Home/In The Good Old Summer Time	5
58	Brunswick 05764	It's Beginning To Look Like Christmas/I Heard The Bells	5
58	Brunswick 05770	Gigi/The Next Time It Happens	5
59	Brunswick 05790	Rain/Church Bells	5
59	Philips PB 921	Say One For Me/I Couldn't Care Less	5
59	Gala GSP 801	My Own Individual Star/Never Be Afraid	5
60	Brunswick 05840	Happy Birthday & Auld Lang Syne/Home Sweet Home	5
60	MGM MGM 1098	The Second Time Around/Incurably Romantic	5
62	Decca F 21452	Let's Not Be Sensible (with Joan Collins)/Team Work (with Bob Hope)	5
65	Brunswick 05928	Where The Blue Of The Night/Goodnight Sweetheart	5
68	MCA MU 1010	Around The World/VICTOR YOUNG ORCHESTRA: Around The World	5

EPs

54	Brunswick OE 9003	BING SINGS HITS (EP)	8
55	Brunswick OE 9027	GARY CROSBY AND FRIEND (EP, with Gary Crosby)	8
55	Brunswick OE 9069	MERRY CHRISTMAS VOL. 1 (EP)	8
55	Brunswick OE 9070	MERRY CHRISTMAS VOL. 2 (EP)	8
56	Brunswick OE 9292	SONGS I WISH I HAD SUNG VOL. 2 (EP)	8
58	Philips BBE 12142	BING (EP)	8
58	Brunswick OE 9353	TO BALI AND MOROCCO (EP, with Bob Hope)	8
58	Brunswick OE 9359	BING AND THE DIXIELAND BANDS (EP, 1 track with Conee Boswell)	8
59	Brunswick OE 9421	THEY SOLD A MILLION NO. 5 (EP, with Andrews Sisters)	8
59	Brunswick OE 9422	THEY SOLD A MILLION NO. 6 (EP)	8
59	Brunswick OE 9423	THEY SOLD A MILLION NO. 7 (EP, 1 track with Gary Crosby)	8
59	Brunswick OE 9424	THEY SOLD A MILLION NO. 8 (EP)	8
59	Brunswick OE 9430	THEY SOLD A MILLION NO. 14 (EP)	8
59	Columbia SEG 7522	TRY A LITTLE TENDERNESS (EP)	8
59	Fontana TFE 17178	PLEASE (EP)	8
59	Fontana TFE 17179	REMEMBER (EP)	8
59	RCA SRC 7013	GOING PLACES (EP, stereo, with Rosemary Clooney)	8
61	MGM MGM-ES 3515	BING AND SATCHMO (EP, stereo, with Louis Armstrong)	8

LPs

51	Brunswick LA 8513	SINGS COLE PORTER SONGS (10" LP)	15
51	Brunswick LA 8514	STARDUST (10" LP)	15
51	Brunswick LA 8529	EL BINGO — A SELECTION OF LATIN AMERICAN FAVOURITES (10" LP)	15
52	Brunswick LA 8505	SINGS JEROME KERN SONGS (10" LP)	15
54	Columbia 33S 1036	CROSBY CLASSICS (10" LP)	15
56	Brunswick LAT 8106	SHILLELAGHS AND SHAMROCKS (LP)	12
52	Brunswick LA 8558	BING AND CONNIE (10" LP, with Connie Boswell)	12
53	Brunswick LA 8571	STEPHEN FOSTER SONGS (10" LP)	12
53	Brunswick LA 8579	BING CROSBY AND THE DIXIELAND BANDS (10" LP)	12
53	Brunswick LA 8584	THE QUIET MAN (10" LP)	12
53	Brunswick LA 8585	AULD LANG SYNE (10" LP)	12
53	Brunswick LA 8592	HOLIDAY INN (10" LP, with Fred Astaire)	12
53	Brunswick LA 8595	BLUE OF THE NIGHT (10" LP)	12
53	Brunswick LA 8600	BING CROSBY SINGS VICTOR HERBERT SONGS (10" LP)	12
53	Brunswick LA 8602	BLUE SKIES (10" LP, with Fred Astaire)	12
53	Brunswick LA 8606	WHEN IRISH EYES ARE SMILING (10" LP)	12
53	Brunswick LA 8620	DOWN MEMORY LANE (10" LP)	12
53	Brunswick LA 8624	DOWN MEMORY LANE VOL. 2 (10" LP)	12
54	Brunswick LA 8645	LE BING — SINGS HITS OF PARIS (10" LP)	12
54	Brunswick LA 8656	'WAY BACK HOME (10" LP)	12
54	Brunswick LA 8666	GEORGE GERSHWIN SONGS (10" LP)	12
54	Brunswick LA 8673	SOME FINE OLD CHESTNUTS (10" LP)	12
54	Brunswick LA 8674	BING SINGS THE HITS (10" LP)	12
54	Brunswick LA 8675	SONG HITS FROM BROADWAY SHOWS (10" LP)	12
54	Brunswick LA 8684	YOURS IS MY HEART ALONE (10" LP)	12
54	Brunswick LA 8686	MERRY CHRISTMAS (10" LP)	12
54	Brunswick LA 8687	CROSBY COLLECTOR'S CLASSICS VOL. 1 (10" LP)	12
54	Brunswick LAT 8051-8055	BING — A MUSICAL AUTOBIOGRAPHY (5-LP box set)	30
55	Brunswick LA 8714	COUNTRY GIRL/LITTLE BOY LOST (10" LP)	12
55	Brunswick LA 8723	CROSBY COLLECTOR'S CLASSICS VOL. 2 (10" LP)	12
55	Brunswick LA 8724	COUNTRY STYLE (10" LP)	12
55	Brunswick LA 8726	CROSBY COLLECTOR'S CLASSICS VOL. 3 (10" LP)	12
55	Brunswick LA 8727	CROSBY COLLECTOR'S CLASSICS VOL. 4 (10" LP)	12
55	Brunswick LA 8730	FAVOURITE HAWAIIAN SONGS (10" LP)	12
55	Brunswick	FAVOURITE HAWAIIAN SONGS VOL. 2 (10" LP)	12
55	Brunswick LA 8741	BING THE EARLY THIRTIES VOL. 2 (10" LP)	12
56	Brunswick LAT 8138	SONGS I WISH I'D SUNG (LP)	12
56	Brunswick LAT 8152	HOME ON THE RANGE (LP)	12
56	HMV CLP 1088	BING SINGS WHILST BREGMAN SWINGS (LP)	12
57	Brunswick LAT 8154	HIGH TOR (LP, with Julie Andrews)	12
57	Brunswick LAT 8216	A CHRISTMAS SINGS WITH BING (LP)	12
57	Brunswick LAT 8217	NEW TRICKS (LP)	12
58	Brunswick LAT 8228	BING AND THE DIXIELAND BANDS (LP)	12
58	Brunswick LAT 8253	TWILIGHT ON THE TRAIL (LP)	12
58	Fontana TFR 6000	DER BINGLE (10" LP)	15
59	Brunswick LAT 8278	WHEN IRISH EYES ARE SMILING (LP)	12
59	Brunswick LAT 8281	BING CROSBY SINGS (LP)	12
59	Philips BBL 7335	SAY ONE FOR ME (LP, soundtrack, with Debbie Reynolds)	12
57	RCA RD 27032	BING WITH A BEAT (LP, with Bob Scobey's Frisco Jazz Band)	12
61	MGM C 844	BING AND SATCHMO (LP, with Louis Armstrong)	12
62	Brunswick BING 1-15	BING'S HOLLYWOOD (15 LPs)	each 12
65	Reprise R 6106	RETURN TO PARADISE ISLAND (LP)	12

(see also Gary Crosby, Louis Armstrong, Bob Hope, Fred Astaire, Peggy Lee)

BOB CROSBY & HIS BOBCATS

59	London HLD 8828	Petite Fleur/Such A Long Night	8
59	London HLD 8828	Petite Fleur/Such A Long Night (78)	20
60	London HLD 9228	The Dark At The Top Of The Stairs/Night Theme	7
60	London HA-D 2293	BOB CROSBY'S GREAT HITS (LP, also stereo SAH-D 6105)	15/18

(see also Modernaires)

DAVID CROSBY

93	Atlantic A 7360	Hero/Coverage/Fare Thee Well (CD)	8
71	Atlantic 2401 005	IF I COULD ONLY REMEMBER MY NAME (LP, gatefold sleeve, red/plum label)	15

(see also Byrds, Crosby [Stills] Nash [& Young])

GARY CROSBY

54	Brunswick 05340	Mambo In The Moonlight/Got My Eyes On You	8
55	Brunswick 05365	Palsy Walsy/Loop-De-Loop Mambo (with Cheer Leaders)	8
55	Brunswick 05378	Ready, Willing And Able/There's A Small Hotel	12
55	Brunswick 05400	Ko Ko Mo (I Love You So)/Struttin' With Some Barbecue (w/ Louis Armstrong)	8
55	Brunswick 05400	Ko Ko Mo (I Love You So)/Struttin' With Some Barbecue (78, with Louis Armstrong)	8
55	Brunswick 05446	Ayuh Ayuh/Mississippi Pecan Pie	10
55	Brunswick 05496	Truly/Give Me A Band And My Baby (B-side with Paris Sisters)	8
56	Brunswick 05546	Yaller Yaller Gold/Get A Load O' Me	6
56	Brunswick 05546	Yaller Yaller Gold/Get A Load O' Me (78)	5
56	Brunswick 05574	Easy Street/Lazybones (with Louis Armstrong)	6
56	Brunswick 05574	Easy Street/Lazybones (78, with Louis Armstrong)	8
56	Brunswick 05633	Yaller Yaller Gold/Noah Found Grace In The Eyes Of God (with Dreamers)	5
58	HMV POP 550	Judy, Judy/Cheatin' On Me	15
58	HMV POP 550	Judy, Judy/Cheatin' On Me (78)	15
59	HMV POP 648	The Happy Bachelor/This Little Girl Of Mine	6
57	Vogue VA 160118	GARY CROSBY (LP)	15

(see also Bing Crosby, Louis Armstrong)

PHIL CROSBY

63	Reprise R 20220	Where The Blue Of The Night/Little By Little	6

CROSBY & NASH

72	Atlantic K 10192	Southbound Train/Whole Cloth	6
72	Atlantic K 50011	GRAHAM NASH & DAVID CROSBY (LP, foldout sleeve)	15

CROSBY, STILLS & NASH

69	Atlantic 584 283	Marrakesh Express/Helplessly Hoping	7
69	Atlantic 584 304	Suite: Judy Blue Eyes/Long Time Gone	6
69	Atlantic 588 189	CROSBY, STILLS & NASH (LP, gatefold sleeve, with lyric sheet)	18
69	Atlantic K 40033	CROSBY, STILLS & NASH (LP, reissue, gatefold sleeve, with lyric sheet)	12

CROSBY, STILLS, NASH & YOUNG

70	Atlantic 2091 002	Teach Your Children/Country Girl	7
70	Atlantic 2091 010	Woodstock/Helpless	7
70	Atlantic 2091 023	Ohio/Find The Cost Of Freedom	7
70	Atlantic 2091 039	Our House/Deja Vu	7
88	Atlantic A 9003TX	American Dream/Compass/Soldiers Of Peace/Ohio (12", p/s)	8
70	Atlantic 2401 001	DÉJA VU (LP, gatefold sleeve, pasted-on photo on front, plum/red label)	20
71	Atlantic 2657 007	FOUR WAY STREET (2-LP, gatefold sleeve with lyric sheet)	20

(see also David Crosby, Stephen Stills [Manassas], Graham Nash, Neil Young)

CROSS

87	Virgin VS 1007	Cowboys And Indians (4.20)/Love Lies Bleeding (She's A Wicked Wily Waitress) (p/s)	10
87	Virgin VSTC 1007	Cowboys And Indians (Full Length Version)/Love Lies Bleeding (She's A Wicked Wily Waitress) (cassette)	15
87	Virgin VST 1007	Cowboys And Indians (Full Length Version 5.53)/Love Lies Bleeding (She's A Wicked Wily Waitress) (12", p/s)	20
87	Virgin CDEP 10	Cowboys And Indians (4.20)/Cowboys And Indians (Full Length Version 6.12)/ Love Lies Bleeding (She's A Wicked Wily Waitress) (CD, promo only)	75
88	Virgin VS 1026	Shove It! (7" Version)/Rough Justice (p/s)	10
88	Virgin VST 1026	Shove It! (Extended Mix)/Shove It! (Metropolix)/Rough Justice (12", p/s)	22
88	Virgin CDEP 20	Shove It! (7" Version)/Rough Justice/Cowboys And Indians (4.20)/ Shove It! (Extended Mix) (CD)	40
88	Virgin VS 1062	Heaven For Everyone/Love On A Tightrope (Like An Animal) (p/s)	10
88	Virgin VST 1062	Heaven For Everyone/Love On A Tightrope (Like An Animal)/Contact (12", p/s)	20
88	Virgin VS 1100	Manipulator/Stand Up For Love (p/s)	15
88	Virgin VST 1100	Manipulator (Extended)/Stand Up For Love/Manipulator (7" Version) (12", p/s)	30
88	Virgin VVCS 7	Love On The Tightrope (Like An Animal)/(tracks by Phil Collins, China Crisis & Donny Osmond) (3" CD sampler, gatefold sleeve)	10
90	Parlophone R 6251	Power To Love (3.28)/Passion For Trash (p/s)	10
90	Parlophone 12R 6251	Power To Love (Extended Version)/Passion For Trash/ Power To Love (7" Version) (12", p/s)	18
90	Parlophone CDR 6251	Power To Love (Extended Version)/Passion For Trash/ Power To Love (7" Version) (CD)	30
87	Virgin V 2477	SHOVE IT! (LP, 8 tracks, with inner sleeve)	12
90	Parlophone PCS 7342	MAD, BAD AND DANGEROUS TO KNOW (LP)	20
90	Parlophone CDPCS 7342	MAD, BAD AND DANGEROUS TO KNOW (CD)	75
90	(no label)	OFFICIAL BOOTLEG (fan club-only cassette, featuring Brian May)	20
91	(no label)	LIVE IN GERMANY (fan club-only cassette)	15

(see also Roger Taylor, Queen)

JIMMIE CROSS

66	Red Bird RB 10042	Super Duper Man/Hey Little Girl	18
78	Wanted Cult 101	I Want My Baby Back/Play The Other Side (p/s)	5

(Keith) CROSS & (Peter) ROSS

71	Decca F 13224	Can You Believe It?/Blind Willie Johnson	6
72	Decca F 13316	Peace In The End/Prophets Guiders	6
72	Decca SKL 5129	BORED CIVILIANS (LP)	40

(see also T2)

CROSSBEATS

60s	Pilgrim PSR 7001	If Only/He Wants To Know	5
60s	Pilgrim PSR 7002	I Know/He Waits	5
67	Pilgrim PSR 7003	Step Aside/Forgive Me (art sleeve)	8
60s	Pilgrim PSR 7004	Busy Man/Change (p/s)	6
60s	Pilgrim KLP 12	CRAZY MIXED UP GENERATION (LP)	20

ANDRAE CROUCH
70s	Light LS 7014	JUST ANDRAE (LP)	20
70s	Light LS 7018	DISCIPLES LIVE AT CARNEGIE HALL (LP)	20
70s	Light LS 7019	KEEP ON SWINGIN' (LP)	20
70s	Light LS 7025	TAKE ME BACK (LP)	20
70s	Myrrh MYR 1188	NO TIME TO LOSE (LP)	20

CROW
70	Stateside SS 2159	Evil Woman, Don't Play Your Games With Me/Gonna Leave A Mark	5
70	Stateside SS 2171	Slow Down/Cottage Cheese	5
70	Stateside SS 2180	Don't Try To Lay No Boogie Woogie On The King Of Rock And Roll/Satisfied	5
70	Stateside SSL 10301	CROW MUSIC (LP)	15
70	Stateside SSL 10310	CROW BY CROW (LP)	15

SHERYL CROW
93	A&M 580 380-7	Run, Baby, Run/All By Myself (p/s)	7
93	A&M 580 380-4	Run, Baby, Run/All By Myself (cassette)	5
93	A&M 580 381-2	Run, Baby, Run/All By Myself/The Na-Na Song/Reach Around Jerk (CD)	15
94	A&M 580 462-7	What Can I Do For You (Radio Edit)/Volvo Cowgirl 99 (p/s)	6
94	A&M 580 462-4	What Can I Do For You (Radio Edit)/Volvo Cowgirl 99 (cassette)	5
94	A&M 580 462-7	What Can I Do For You (Radio Edit)/What Can I Do For You (LP Version)/ Volvo Cowgirl 99/I Shall Believe (CD)	10
94	A&M 580 568-7	Run, Baby, Run/Leaving Las Vegas (Acoustic Version) (p/s)	6
94	A&M 580 569-2	Run, Baby, Run/Leaving Las Vegas (Acoustic Version)/ All By Myself/Reach Around Jerk (CD)	10
94	A&M 581 147-2	Run, Baby, Run/Can't Cry Anymore/Reach Around Jerk/I Shall Believe (CD, 'The Nashville Sessions', box set with poster & no'd 'obi')	15
94	A&M 580 644-7	Leaving Las Vegas/Leaving Las Vegas (Live In Nashville) (p/s, with postcard)	5
94	A&M 580 645-2	Leaving Las Vegas/I Shall Believe (Live In Nashville)/What Can I Do For You (Live At Borderline) (CD, stickered digipak with space for 2nd CD)	10
96	A&M 581 902-7	If It Makes You Happy (Edit)/All I Wanna Do (jukebox issue, no p/s)	7
96	A&M SCJB 2	Strong Enough/All I Wanna Do (Remix) (jukebox issue, no p/s)	7
96	A&M 580 918-7	Strong Enough/No One Said It Would Be Easy (p/s)	5
95	A&M 540 368-2/ 540 126-2-18	TUESDAY NIGHT MUSIC CLUB (CD, 2nd issue, with patchwork/montage cover and bonus 6-track CD "Sheryl Crow Live" [540 367-2])	25

CROWBAR
72	Paramount PARA 2037	Hey Baby/Dream	5
71	Paramount SPFL 272	BAD MANORS (LP)	12
72	Paramount SPFL 283	HEAVY DUTY (LP, with insert)	12
72	Paramount SPFA 7002	LARGER THAN LIFE (LP, gatefold sleeve)	12

CROWBAR
84	Skinhead SKIN 1	Hippie Punks/White Riot (p/s)	30

CROWD
79	SRT SRTS/79/CUS 377	Ronnie (Is A Headbanger)/A Little Of What I Fancy/Let's Fly Together (p/s)	6

CROWDED HOUSE
86	Capitol CL 416	World Where You Live/That's What I Call Love (p/s)	7
86	Capitol TCCL 416	World Where You Live (Extended)/Something So Strong/ Don't Dream It's Over/That's What I Call Love (cassette)	5
87	Capitol 12 CL 416	World Where You Live (Extended)/Can't Carry On/ That's What I Call Love (12", p/s)	10
87	Capitol CDCL 416	World Where You Live (Extended Version)/Something So Strong/ Don't Dream It's Over/That's What I Call Love (CD, card sleeve)	25
87	Capitol CL 438	Don't Dream It's Over/That's What I Call Love (p/s)	5
87	Capitol 12 CL 438	Don't Dream It's Over (Extended)/(7")/That's What I Call Love (12", p/s)	12
87	Capitol CL 456	Something So Strong/I Walk Away (p/s)	6
87	Capitol 12 CL 456	Something So Strong/Something So Strong (live)/I Walk Away/ Don't Dream It's Over (live) (12", p/s)	12
88	Capitol CL 498	Better Be Home Soon/Kill Eye (p/s)	6
88	Capitol 12CL 498	Better Be Home Soon/Don't Dream It's Over (live)/Kill Eye (12", p/s)	10
88	Capitol CDCL 498	Better Be Home Soon/Kill Eye/Don't Dream It's Over (live)/ Better Be Home Soon (CD)	30
88	Capitol CL 509	Sister Madly/Mansion In The Slums (p/s)	5
88	Capitol 12CL 509	Sister Madly/Mansion In The Slums/Something So Strong (live) (12", p/s)	10
88	Capitol CDCL 509	Sister Madly/Mansion In The Slums/Something So Strong (live) (CD)	30
91	Capitol CDCL 618	Chocolate Cake/As Sure As I Am/Anyone Can Tell (CD)	10
91	Capitol CDCL 626	Fall At Your Feet/Don't Dream It's Over/Sister Madly/ Better Be Home Soon (CD)	12
91	Capitol CDCLX 626	Fall At Your Feet/Six Months In A Leaky Boat (live)/Now We're Getting Somewhere (live)/Something So Strong (Album Version) (CD, PVC sleeve)	12
92	Capitol CDCL 643	Weather With You (Single Edit)/Mr. Tambourine Man (live)/Eight Miles High (live)/So You Want To Be A Rock'n'Roll Star (live) (CD, in wallet)	12
92	Capitol CDCLS 643	Weather With You (single edit)/Fall At Your Feet (live)/When You Come (live)/ Walking On The Spot (live) (CD, slip cover)	7
92	Capitol CDCL 655	Four Seasons In One Day (LP)/Dr. Livingstone/Recurring Dream/ Anyone Can Tell (CD, in collector's box)	18
92	Capitol CDCLS 655	Four Seasons In One Day (LP)/Weather With You (live)/Italian Plastic (live)/ Message To My Girl (live) (CD)	8
91	Capitol CDP 793 559-2	WOODFACE (CD, foldout pack)	20
92	Capitol CH 1/2	LIVE AT THE TOWN AND COUNTRY CLUB, LONDON, NOVEMBER 9 1991 (2-CD, in PVC gatefold wallet & inserts, promo only)	120
92	Capitol CH 1/2	LIVE AT THE TOWN AND COUNTRY CLUB, LONDON, NOVEMBER 9 1991 (2-CD, in 5" x 5" black box with sampler cassette, promo only)	135
96	EMI FINNTERVIEW 2	THE FINAL INTERVIEW...? (CD, promo only)	28

(see also Split Enz, Tim Finn)

CROWDY CRAWN
(see under Brenda Wootton)

CROWFOOT
70	Paramount PARA 3008	California Rock 'N' Roll/Maybe I Can Learn To Live	5
70	Paramount SPFL 265	CROWFOOT (LP)	12

CROWNS
68	Pama PM 725	I Know, It's Alright/I Surrender	5
68	Pama PM 736	Jerking The Dog/Keep Me Going	5
68	Pama PM 745	She Ain't Gonna Do Right/I Need Your Loving	5
68	Pama PM 759	Since You Been Gone/Call Me	5
68	Pama PMLP 6	MADE OF GOLD (LP)	15

CROWS
54	Columbia SCM 5119	Gee/I Love You So	2000
54	Columbia DB 3478	Gee/I Love You So (78)	120

LESLIE CROWTHER
70	Pye 7N 45020	Santa Claus/Hypochondriac	5

TREVOR CROZIER'S BROKEN CONSORT
72	Argo AFB 60	PARCEL OF OLD CRAMS (LP)	15

CRUCIFIXION
80	Miramar MIR 4	The Fox/Death Sentence (no p/s)	80
82	Neat NEAT 19	Take It Or Leave It/On The Run (p/s)	7
84	Neat NEAT 37	Green Eyes/Moon Rising/Jailbait (p/s)	5
84	Neat NEAT 3712	Green Eyes/Jailbait/Moon Rising (12", p/s, some on purple vinyl)	20/8

ARTHUR 'BIG BOY' CRUDUP
64	RCA RCA 1401	My Baby Left Me/I Don't Know It	25
64	RCA RCX 7161	RHYTHM AND BLUES VOL. 4 (EP)	18
69	Blue Horizon 7-63855	MEAN OLE FRISCO (LP)	70
70	Delmark DS 614	LOOK ON YONDERS WALL (LP)	18
71	Delmark DS 621	CRUDUP'S MOOD (LP)	18
72	RCA RD 8224	THE FATHER OF ROCK 'N' ROLL (LP)	18
74	United Artists UAS 29092	ROEBUCK MAN (LP)	15

CRUISERS
65	Decca F 12098	It Ain't Me Babe/Baby What You Want Me To Do	18

(see also Dave Berry, Godley & Creme)

SIMON CRUM
58	Capitol CL 14965	Country Music Is Here To Stay/Stand Up, Sit Down, Shut Your Mouth	25
59	Capitol CL 15077	I Fell Out Of Love With Love/Morgan Poisoned The Water Hole	12
61	Capitol CL 15183	Enormity In Motion/Cuzz Yore So Sweet	15

(see also Ferlin Husky)

CRUSADERS
73	Blue Thumb WIP 6143	Put It Where You Want It/Mosadi Woman	5
75	ABC ABC 4051	Stomp And Buck Dance/Ballad For Joe (Louis)	5
75	ABC ABC 4088	Creole/I Felt The Love	5
75	ABC ABC 4122	Keep That Same Old Feeling/Till The Sun Shines	5
71	Rare Earth SRE 3001	OLD SOCKS NEW SHOES (LP)	15
72	Blue Thumb ILPS 9218	CRUSADERS (2-LP)	15
73	Mowest MWS 7004	HOLLYWOOD (LP)	20
75	ABC ABCD 607	SOUTHERN COMFORT (2-LP)	15
75	ABC ABCL 5144	CHAIN REACTION (LP, gatefold sleeve)	12
76	ABC ABCL 5164	THOSE SOUTHERN KNIGHTS (LP, gatefold sleeve)	12

(see also Jazz Crusaders)

CRUX/CRASH
82	No Future OI 18	KEEP ON RUNNING (12" EP)	18

CRY
87	Flowerpot CFP 001	Party After Dark (no p/s)	20
87	Flowerpot CFP 002	Give Her An Ice Cream (no p/s)	20

CRYAN' SHAMES (U.S.)
(see under Shames)

CRYER
80	Happy Face MM 124	The Single/Hesitate (p/s, with 2 inserts)	65

BARRY CRYER
58	Fontana H 139	The Purple People Eater/Hey! Eula	8
58	Fontana H 139	The Purple People Eater/Hey! Eula (78)	10
58	Fontana H 151	Nothin' Shakin'/Seven Daughters	10
58	Fontana H 151	Nothin' Shakin'/Seven Daughters (78)	12
59	Fontana H 177	Angelina/Kissin'	10
59	Fontana H 177	Angelina/Kissin' (78)	15

CRYIN' SHAMES (U.K.)
66	Decca F 12340	Please Stay/What's News Pussycat	18
66	Decca F 12425	Nobody Waved Goodbye/You	25

(see also Paul & Ritchie & Cryin' Shames, Gary Walker & Rain)

CRYING SHAMES
80	Logo GO 385	That's Rock'n'Roll/Too Late (p/s)	20

CRYSTALITES

69	Big Shot BI 510	Biafra/Drop Pan	6
69	Nu Beat NB 036	Splash Down/Finders Keepers	10
69	Songbird SB 1015	Musical Madness Parts 1 & 2	8
69	Songbird SB 1016	The Bad Parts 1 & 2	8
69	Explosion EX 2002	Doctor Who (Parts 1 & 2)	8
69	Explosion EX 2003	Barefoot Brigade/Slippery	6
69	Explosion EX 2005	Bombshell/Bag-A-Wire (B-side actually by Bobby Ellis & Crystalites)	6
69	Explosion EX 2006	A Fistful Of Dollars/The Emperor (B-side actually by Bobby Ellis & Crystalites)	6
70	Explosion EX 2010	The Bad/The Bad Version	6
70	Bullet BU 424	A Fistful Of Dollars/BOBBY ELLIS: Crystal	6
70	Songbird SB 1017	The Undertaker/Stop That Man (B-side actually "Easy Ride" by Ike Bennett & Crystalites)	7
70	Songbird SB 1020	Lady Madonna/Ghost Rider	7
70	Songbird SB 1024	Isies/Isies (Version 2)	7
70	Songbird SB 1025	Stranger In Town/Stranger In Town (Version 2)	7
70	Songbird SB 1030	Sic Him Rover/Drop Pon	7
70	Songbird SB 1034	Overtaker (Version I)/Overtaker (Version II)	8
70	Songbird SB 1035	Undertaker's Burial/Ghost Rider	5
71	Songbird SB 1057	Earthly Sounds/Version	5
73	Grape GR 3050	Blacula/Version	7

(see also Chosen Few, Scotty, Ramon & Crystalites, Kingstonians, Bongo Herman, Denzil Laing, Derrick Harriot, Ethiopians, Dennis Brown, Glen Brown, Big Youth)

CRYSTAL MANSION

69	Capitol CL 15577	The Thought Of Loving You/Hallelujah	5
70	Polydor 2058 070	Carolina On My Mind/If I Live	5

CRYSTALS

62	Parlophone R 4867	There's No Other Like My Baby/Oh Yeah Maybe Baby	100
62	London HLU 9611	He's A Rebel/I Love You Eddie	12
63	London HLU 9661	He's Sure The Boy I Love/Walking Along (La-La-La)	15
63	London HLU 9732	Da Doo Ron Ron/Git It	6
63	London HLU 9773	Then He Kissed Me/Brother Julius	6
64	London HLU 9837	Little Boy/Uptown (withdrawn)	45
64	London HLU 9852	I Wonder/Little Boy	15
64	London HLU 9909	All Grown Up/PHIL SPECTOR GROUP: Irving (Jaggered Sixteenths)	15
65	United Artists UP 1110	My Place/You Can't Tie A Girl Down	25
69	London HLU 10239	Da Doo Ron Ron/He's A Rebel	5
74	Warners/Spector K 19010	Da Doo Ron Ron/Then Kissed Me (blue vinyl)	15
76	Phil Spector Intl. 2010 020	All Grown Up/The Twist	6
63	London RE-U 1381	DA DOO RON RON (EP)	70
63	London HA-U 8120	HE'S A REBEL (LP)	100

(see also Darlene Love, Bob B. Soxx & Blue Jeans, Phil Spector)

CRY WOLF

89	Jak OSGW 101	FIRST TWELVE INCHES EP (12", p/s)	8

C.S.A.

96	Squariel Records SQ003	Don't/Till I Waltz Again With You (p/s)	6

JOE CUBA SEXTET

66	Pye International 7N 25401	Bang! Bang!/Push, Push, Push	10

CUBAN HEELS

78	Housewives' Choice JY 1/2	Downtown/Do The Smoke Walk (p/s)	6
80	Greville GR 1	Little Girl/Fast Living Friend (p/s)	4
81	Virgin VS 440	Walk On Water/Hard Times (p/s, with bonus flexidisc)	4

CUBY & BLIZZARDS

68	Philips BF 1638	Distant Smile/Don't Know Which Way To Go	10
68	Philips BF 1719	Windows Of My Eyes/Checkin' Up On My Baby	7
69	Philips BF 1827	Apple Knocker's Flophouse/Go Down Sunshine	10
69	Philips (S)BL 7874	DESOLATION (LP)	40
69	Philips SBL 7918	APPLE KNOCKERS FLOPHOUSE (LP)	30

'CUDDLY' DUDLEY (Heslop)

59	HMV POP 586	Lots More Love/Later	12
59	HMV POP 586	Lots More Love/Later (78)	45
60	HMV POP 725	Too Pooped To Pop/Miss In-Between	12
61	Ember EMB S 136	Sitting On A Train/One Thing I Like	8
62	Piccadilly 7N 35090	Monkey Party/The Ferryboat Ride (as Cudley Dudley)	8
64	Oriole International ICB 9	Blarney Blues/Peace On Earth	10
64	Oriole International ICB 10	Way Of Life/When Will You Say You'll Be Mine	10

CUES

56	Capitol CL 14501	Burn That Candle/O My Darlin'	225
56	Capitol CL 14501	Burn That Candle/O My Darlin' (78)	25
56	Capitol CL 14651	Crackerjack/The Girl I Love (featuring Jimmy Breedlove)	200
56	Capitol CL 14651	Crackerjack/The Girl I Love (78)	25
57	Capitol CL 14682	Prince Or Pauper/Why	165
57	Capitol CL 14682	Prince Or Pauper/Why (78)	18

(see also Jimmy Breedlove)

CUFF-LINKS

69	MCA MU 1101	Tracy/Where Do You Go?	5
70	MCA MU 1128	Robin's World/Lay A Little Love On Me	5
70	MCA MUP(S) 398	TRACY (LP)	15

MINT VALUE £

XAVIER CUGAT

54	Columbia SCMC 2	Spanish Dance/The Bells Of San Raquel (export issue)	6
54	Columbia SCMC 4	Yo Ta Namora/Anna Boroco Tinde (export issue)	6
54	HMV 7MC 35	MI Espanan/Society Conga (export issue)	6
63	Mercury AMT 1202	Watermelon Man/Swinging Shepherd Blues	5
65	Brunswick STA 8647	DANCE PARTY (LP)	12

CULPEPPER'S ORCHARD

72	Polydor 2480 123	SECOND SIGHT (LP)	70

CULT

84	Beggars Banquet BEG 115P	Go West/Sea And Sky (foldout poster p/s)	5
87	Beggars Banquet BEG 188CD	Lil' Devil/Zap City/She Sells Sanctuary (live)/Phoenix (live)/Love Removal Machine (CD, gatefold card sleeve)	8
87	RM Flexidisc 3	Wild Flower (Unavailable Mix)/Interview (flexidisc, gatefold p/s, free with *Record Mirror* magazine)	7/5
89	B. Banquet BEG 228CD	Fire Woman/Automatic Blues/Messin' Up The Blues (3" CD, 7" x 5" gatefold plastic wallet)	8
84	B. Banquet BEGA 57	DREAMTIME (white label test pressing, with unique version of "Go West")	30
91	Beggars Banquet CBOX 1	SINGLES COLLECTION (10-CD box set, picture discs with booklet)	30

(see also Southern Death Cult, Death Cult, Lonesome No More, Theatre Of Hate, Studio Sweethearts)

CULT FIGURES

79	Rather GEAR 4/RT 020	Zip Nolan (Highway Patrolman)/P.W.T. (Playing With Toys)/Zip Dub (gatefold p/s)	8
81	Rather GEAR EIGHT	In Love: I Remember/Laura Kate/Almost A Love Song (p/s)	5

(see also Swell Maps)

CULT HERO

79	Fiction FICS 006	I'm A Cult Hero/I Dig You (p/s, 2,000 only)	40

(see also Cure)

CULT MANIAX

82	Elephant Rock	Blitz/Lucy Looe (p/s)	6
82	Next Wave NXT 2/BAK 1	Frenzie/The Russians Are Coming/Black Horse/Death March (p/s)	6
80s	Anti-Hype DL 001	Frontier/I Always Lose My Temper/It'll Take Time (p/s)	5
80s	Elephant Rock	American Dream/Dark Pig (p/s)	6
84	Xcentric Noise SIXTH 1	FULL OF SPUNX (EP, wraparound p/s with poster)	5
84	Xcentric Noise EIGHTH 1	The Amazing Adventures Of Johnny The Duck And The Bath Time Blues/Freedom/Maniax (p/s, with lyric insert)	5
84	Xcentric Noise EIGHTH 1T	The Amazing Adventures Of Johnny The Duck And The Bath Time Blues/Blue Baby/Village Ritual/Freedom/Maniax (12", p/s)	8
85	Xcentric Noise TENTH 1	WHERE DO WE ALL GO (12" EP)	8

CULTURE CLUB

82	Virgin VS 496	White Boy/Love Twist (p/s)	5
82	Virgin VS 496-12	White Boy/Love Twist (12", p/s)	12
82	Virgin VS 509	I'm Afraid Of Me/Murder Rap Trap (p/s)	5
82	Virgin VS 509-12	I'm Afraid Of Me/Murder Rap Trap (12", p/s)	12
82	Virgin VSY 518	Do You Really Want To Hurt Me/Do You Really Want To Hurt Me (Dub Version) (picture disc)	6
82	Virgin (no cat. no.)	I'll Tumble 4 Ya/BLUE RONDO: Change (blue 1-sided flexi with *Noise* mag)	15/5
82	Virgin VSY 558	Time (Clock Of The Heart)/White Boys Can't Control It (picture disc)	6
83	Virgin VSY 571	Church Of The Poison Mind/Man Shake	6
83	Virgin VSY 612	Karma Chameleon/That's The Way (picture disc)	6
83	Virgin VSY 641	Victims/Colour By Numbers (picture disc)	5
84	Virgin VSY 657	It's A Miracle/Love Twist (picture disc)	6
84	Virgin VS 694	The War Song/La Cancion De Guerra (red vinyl)	6
84	Virgin VSY 694	The War Song/La Cancion De Guerra (picture disc, withdrawn)	75
84	Virgin VSY 730	The Medal Song/Don't Go Down That Street (picture disc)	5
84	Virgin VSY 730-12	The Medal Song/Don't Go Down That Street (12", p/s, with poster)	8
86	Virgin VSX 845	Move Away/Sexuality (5", picture disc, 33rpm, with booklet & gatefold p/s)	6
85	Virgin VS 861	God Thank You Woman/From Luxury To Heartache (poster p/s)	5
86	Virgin VSY 861	God Thank You Woman/From Luxury To Heartache (picture disc)	20
82	Virgin VP 2232	KISSING TO BE CLEVER (LP, picture disc, with insert)	15
83	Virgin VP 2285	COLOUR BY NUMBERS (LP, picture disc)	15
84	Virgin VP 2330	WAKING UP WITH THE HOUSE ON FIRE (LP, picture disc, with insert)	15
84	Virgin CDV 2330	WAKING UP WITH THE HOUSE ON FIRE (CD)	18
86	Virgin CDV 2380	FROM LUXURY TO HEARTACHE (CD)	18
87	Virgin CDV 2232	KISSING TO BE CLEVER (CD)	18

(see also Boy George, Jesus Loves You, JLY Posse, Edge)

CULVER STREET PLAYGROUND

68	President PT 145	Alley Pond Park/A Decent Sort Of Guy	8

CUMBERLAND THREE

60	Columbia DB 4460	Johnny Reb/Come Along Julie	5
64	Parlophone R 5113	The Cumberland Crew/Chilly Winds	5
61	Columbia 33SX 1302	FOLK SCENE, U.S.A. (LP, also stereo SCX 3364)	15
61	Columbia 33SX 1318	CIVIL WAR ALMANAC — YANKEES (LP)	15
61	Columbia 33SX 1325	CIVIL WAR ALMANAC — REBELS (LP)	15
64	Parlophone PMC 1233	INTRODUCING (LP)	12

(see also John Stewart)

BARBARA CUMMINGS

67	London HLU 10110	She's The Woman/There's Something Funny Going On	5

DAVID CUNNINGHAM

80	Piano PIANO 001	GREY SCALE (LP)	10

H. CUNNINGHAM

71	Tropical AL 004	Ethiopian Son/TROPICAL ALLSTARS: Version 2	5

LARRY CUNNINGHAM & MIGHTY AVONS

64	King KG 1016	Tribute To Jim Reeves/Take My Hand Precious Lord	5
66	King KGL 4000	TWO SIDES OF LARRY (LP)	12

RUPERT CUNNINGHAM

70	Duke DU 98	Funky/Sugar Cane	5

CUPIDS

58	Vogue V 9102	Now You Tell Me/Lillie Mae	750
58	Vogue V 9102	Now You Tell Me/Lillie Mae (78)	80

CUPID'S INSPIRATION

68	NEMS 56-3500	Yesterday Has Gone/Dream	6
68	NEMS 56-3702	My World/Everything Is Meant To Be	6
69	Bell BLL 1069	The Sad Thing/Look At Me	6
70	CBS 4722	Without Your Love/Different Guy	5
70	CBS 4994	Are You Growing Tired Of My Love/Sunshine	5
69	NEMS 6-63553	YESTERDAY HAS GONE (LP, as Cupid's Inspiration Featuring T. Rice-Milton)	18

(see also Gordon Haskell, Paper Blitz Tissue)

CUPOL

80	4AD BAD 9	Like This For Ages/Kluba Cupol (12", p/s, 45/33rpm)	12

(see also Wire)

CUPPA T

67	Deram DM 144	Miss Pinkerton/Brand New World	12
68	Deram DM 185	Streatham Hippodrome/One Man Band	12

(see also Overlanders)

CUPS

68	Polydor 56777	Good As Gold/Life And Times	10

(see also Gallagher & Lyle)

MIKE CURB CONGREGATION

70	Polydor 2058 075	Burning Bridges/Sweet Gingerbread Man	6

CURE

SINGLES

78	Small Wonder SMALL 11	Killing An Arab/10.15 Saturday Night (p/s, 15,000 only, beware of counterfeits)	18
79	Fiction FICS 001	Killing An Arab/10.15 Saturday Night (p/s, reissue)	8
79	Fiction FICS 002	Boys Don't Cry/Plastic Passion ('soldier' p/s)	12
79	Fiction FICS 005	Jumping Someone Else's Train/I'm Cold (p/s)	20
80	Fiction FICS 010	A Forest/Another Journey By Train (p/s or 'radiophonic' die-cut sleeve)	10/5
80	Fiction FICSX 010	A Forest (Extended Version)/Another Journey By Train (12", p/s)	20
81	Fiction FICS 012	Primary/Descent (p/s)	10
81	Fiction FICSX 012	Primary (Extended)/Descent (12", p/s)	20
81	Fiction FICS 014	Charlotte Sometimes/Splintered In Her Head (p/s)	6
81	Fiction FICSX 014	Charlotte Sometimes/Splintered In Her Head/Faith (live) (12", p/s)	15
82	Fiction FICS 015	The Hanging Garden/Killing An Arab (live) (p/s)	8
82	Fiction FICG 015	The Hanging Garden/100 Years//A Forest/Killing An Arab (double pack, gatefold p/s, 5,000 only)	15
82	Lyntone LYN 12011	Lament (1-sided flexidisc, red or green vinyl)	30/8
82	Lyntone LYN 12011	Lament (1-sided flexidisc, red or green vinyl, with Flexipop issue 22)	35/12
82	Fiction FICSX 017	Let's Go To Bed (Extended)/Just One Kiss (Extended) (12", p/s)	8
83	Fiction FICS 018	The Walk/The Dream (paper labels, poster p/s)	12
83	Fiction FICS 018	The Walk/The Dream (plastic labels, standard p/s)	8
83	Fiction FICSP 018	The Walk/The Dream (picture disc)	30
83	Fiction FICSX 018	Upstairs Room/The Dream/The Walk/Lament//Let's Go To Bed (Extended)/Just One Kiss (Extended) (12" double pack, shrinkwrapped with sticker)	20
83	Fiction FICSP 019	The Lovecats/Speak My Language (picture disc, PVC sleeve)	25
84	Fiction FIXSP 020	The Caterpillar/Happy The Man (picture disc, printed PVC sleeve)	25
85	Fiction FICSX 22	In Between Days/The Exploding Boy/A Few Hours After This (12", p/s)	8
85	Fiction 080182-2	In Between Days/The Exploding Boy/A Few Hours After This//Six Different Ways (live)/Push (live) (CD Video)	35
85	Fiction FICSG 23	Close To Me (Remix)/A Man Inside My Mouth (poster p/s; some copies with blue & white 'Head On The Door' sticker)	8
85	Fiction FICST 23	HALF AN OCTOPUS: Close To Me (Remix)/A Man Inside My Mouth/New Day/Stop Dead (10" EP, p/s)	15
85	Fiction FICSX 23	Close To You (Extended Remix)/A Man Inside My Mouth/Stop Dead (12", p/s)	8

MINT VALUE £

THE CURE

85	Fiction 080180-2	Close To Me (12" Remix)/A Man Inside My Mouth/Stop Dead/New Day (CD Video)	35
86	Fiction FICSX 24	Boys Don't Cry (New Voice Club Mix)/Pill Box Tales/Do The Hansa (12", p/s)	8
87	Fiction FICSG 25	Why Can't I Be You?/A Japanese Dream//Six Different Ways (live)/Push (live) (numbered double pack, gatefold p/s)	10
87	Fiction FICS 26	Catch/Breathe (p/s, in carrier bag)	6
87	Fiction FICSP 26	Catch/Breathe (clear vinyl, printed PVC sleeve)	15
87	Fiction FICSE 26	Catch/Breath/Kyoto Song (live)/A Night Like This (live) (12")	8
87	Fiction 080186-2	Catch/Breathe/A Chain Of Flowers/Icing Sugar (Remix) (CD Video)	35
87	Fiction FICS 27	Just Like Heaven/Snow In Summer (p/s, numbered, white vinyl)	10
87	Fiction FICS 27	Just Like Heaven/Snow In Summer (p/s, mispress, A-side plays both sides)	15
87	Fiction FICSP 27	Just Like Heaven/Snow In Summer (picture disc in custom PVC sleeve)	15
87	Fiction FIXCD 27	Just Like Heaven (Remix)/Snow In Summer/Sugar Girl (CD, card sleeve)	20
88	Fiction FIXCD 28	Hot Hot Hot!!! (Extended Remix)/Hot Hot Hot!!! (Remix)/Hey You!!! (Extended Remix) (CD, card sleeve with insert for *10 Imaginary Years* book)	20
89	Fiction FICSG 29	Lullaby (Remix)/Babble (gatefold p/s, numbered with sticker)	6
89	Fiction FICSP 29	Lullaby (Remix)/Babble (clear vinyl, numbered printed 'spider web' PVC sleeve)	12
89	Fiction FICVX 29	Lullaby (Remix)/Babble/Out Of Mind (12", pink vinyl, numbered with stickers)	15
89	Fiction FICCD 29	Lullaby (Remix)/Babble/Out Of Mind/Lullaby (Extended Remix) (3" CD, gatefold p/s)	15
89	Fiction FICSG 30	Lovesong/2 Late ('The Love Box' set with linen print)	10
89	Fiction FICCD 30	Lovesong (7" Mix)/2 Late/Fear Of Ghosts/Lovesong (Extended Mix) (CD)	10
90	Fiction FICPA 34	Pictures Of You (Remix)/Last Dance (live) (p/s, green vinyl, no'd sticker)	6
90	Fiction FICPA 34	Pictures Of You (Remix)/Last Dance (live) (p/s, green vinyl, mispress, plays "Last Dance" both sides)	20
90	Fiction FICPB 34	Pictures Of You (Remix)/Prayers For Rain (p/s, purple vinyl, numbered sticker)	8
90	Fiction FIXPA 34	Pictures Of You (Extended Remix)/Last Dance (live)/Fascination Street (live) (12", p/s, green vinyl, numbered sticker)	8
90	Fiction FIXPB 34	Pictures Of You (Strange Mix)/Prayers For Rain (live)/Disintegration (live) (12", p/s, purple vinyl, numbered sticker)	12
90	Fiction FICCDA 34	Pictures Of You (Remix)/Last Dance (live)/Fascination Street (live) (CD)	8
90	Fiction FICCDB 34	Pictures Of You (Strange Mix)/Prayers For Rain (live)/Disintegration (live) (CD)	10
90	Fiction FICDP 35	Never Enough (Big Mix)/Harold & Joe/Let's Go To Bed (Milk Mix) (CD, with window sticker, numbered slimline jewel case)	10
90	Fiction 080184-2	Why Can't I Be You? (12" Remix)/A Japanese Dream (5.40 Remix)/Hey You!!! (CD Video)	35
91	Fiction FICDR 36	Close To Me (Closer Mix)/Just Like Heaven (Dizzy Mix)/Why Can't I Be You (12" remix) (CD, with poster, shrinkwrapped with card insert & numbered sticker)	10
92	Fiction FICCD 39	High/This Twilight Garden/Play/High (Higher Mix) (CD, box set)	8
92	Fiction FICPA 42	Friday I'm In Love/Halo/Scared Of You/Friday I'm In Love (Strangelove Mix) (12", p/s, numerous different coloured or marbled vinyls)	8
96	Fiction FICDD 53	Gone! (Radio Mix)/(Critter Mix)/(Ultraliving Mix)/(Spacer Mix) (CD, 3-CD inlay)	10

PROMOS

79	Fiction CUR 1	Grinding Halt/Meat Hook (12", stickered sleeve)	50
81	Fiction FICS 12	Primary (1-sided, no p/s)	20
82	Lyntone LYN 12011	Lament (hard vinyl test pressing)	80
82	Fiction CURE 1	One Hundred Years/The Hanging Garden (12", p/s, promo/gig freebie)	50
88	Fiction FICSDJ 28	Hot Hot Hot!!! (Remix)/Hey You!!! (Remix) (die-cut title p/s)	10
84	Fiction KAREN 1	THE TOP (12", 1-sided, 3-track sampler)	65
94	Fiction FICCS 50	LOST WISHES (cassette, 4-track, mail order only)	45
96	Fiction FICSTX 53	Gone! (Ultraliving Mix) (12", same track both sides, with 'DJ' insert)	10
97	Fiction FICSX 54	Wrong Number (Single Mix)/(ISDN Mix)/(Digital Exchange Mix)/ (Dub Analogue Exchange Mix)/(Crossed Line Mix)/(Engaged Mix)/ (P2P Mix) (12", double pack, p/s, promo only)	20
89	Fiction DISIN 1	DISINTEGRATION (CD, 4-track sampler)	15
89	Fiction CIFCD 3	STRANGER THAN FICTION (CD, 6-track sampler, 1000 only)	100
90	Fiction CUREPROCD 1	MIXED UP (CD, 4-track sampler)	10
90	Fiction CUREPROCD 3	THE CURE — AN INTERVIEW (CD)	18
92	Fiction CURE 1	CLASSIC CURE: Love Cats/Close To Me (Closer Mix)/Lovesong/ Charlotte Sometimes/Lullaby/Why Can't I Be You/A Forest (CD, sampler, inlay)	18
93	Fiction SHOWPRO 1	SHOWPRO: Just Like Heaven/Doing The Unstuck (CD, 2-track sampler)	15
93	Fiction PARISPRO 01	PARISPRO: Catch/Play For Today (CD, 2-track sampler)	20
97	Fixtion FIXCD.COM 1	FIVE SWING LIVE (CD, 5-track sampler, available via the internet, 5,000 only)	25

LPs

79	Fiction FIX 1	THREE IMAGINARY BOYS (LP, with inner sleeve, postcard & badge)	20
80	Fiction FIX 004	17 SECONDS (LP, with inner sleeve & textured cover)	12
80	Fiction FIXC 6	FAITH/CARNAGE VISORS (original double-play cassette, b&w cover, paper labels)	10
84	Fiction FIXS 9	THE TOP (LP, with badge & poster, green inner sleeve)	15
84	Fiction FIXS 9	THE TOP (LP, with promo plastic snake & top)	30
86	Fiction 815 011-2	BOYS DON'T CRY (CD, original non-picture disc, with "Object" & "World War" & without "So What")	25
87	Fiction FIXH 13/FIXHA 13	KISS ME, KISS ME, KISS ME (LP, with bonus orange vinyl 6-track 12" [FIXHA 13], in custom PVC sleeve)	40
89	Fiction FIXHP 14	DISINTEGRATION (LP, picture disc, printed PVC sleeve)	20
90	Fiction FIXCD 17	ENTREAT (CD, exclusive to HMV, card p/s, yellow photo)	20
92	Fiction 513 600-0	LIMITED EDITION CD BOX (15 x CD hinged box set, 2,500 only)	175

(see also Cult Hero, Siouxsie & Banshees, Glove, Fools Dance, Tim Pope, Lockjaw, Obtainers)

MARTIN CURE & PEEPS

| 67 | Philips BF 1605 | It's All Over Now/I Can Make The Rain Fall Up | 30 |

(see also Peeps, Rainbows)

JOHNNY CURIOUS & STRANGERS

| 78 | Illegal IL 009 | In Tune/Road To Cheltenham/Pissheadsville/Jennifer (p/s) | 10 |
| 79 | Bugle BLAST 2 | Someone Else's Home/Backwards In The Night (p/s) | 12 |

CURIOSITY SHOPPE

| 68 | Deram DM 220 | Baby I Need You/So Sad | 30 |

CURRANT KRAZE

| 70 | Deram DM 292 | Lady Pearl/Breaking The Heart Of A Good Man | 8 |

CURRENT 93

83	L.a.y.l.a.h. L.A.Y. 1	Lashtal/Salt/Caresse (12", white p/s [reissued in 1988 with dark p/s and "1988" on label])	25/20
85	L.a.y.l.a.h. L.A.Y. 14	NIGHTMARE CULTURE (12" EP, with Sickness Of Snakes [i.e. Coil feat. Boyd Rice]; matt black & red sleeve)	25
87	L.a.y.l.a.h. L.A.Y. 18	HAPPY BIRTHDAY PIGFACE CHRISTUS (12" EP)	25
87	Maldoror MAL 108	Crowleymass/Christmassacre/Crowleymass (Mix Mix Mix) (12", p/s)	30
88	Yangki 002	Faith's Favourites (with Nurse With Wound)/Ballad Of The Pale Girl (12", laminated p/s)	30
88	Maldoror MAL 088	Red Face Of God/The Breath And The Pain Of God (12", p/s, with insert, 666 only)	40
89	Yangki 003	DEATH OF THE CORN (12" EP, with Sol Invictus; 'art' sleeve)	20
90	Harbinger 001	No Hiding From The Blackbird/NURSE WITH WOUND: Burial Of The Stoned Sardine (p/s, remixed reissue of giveaway 7")	15
90	Shock SX 003	She Is Dead And All Fall Down/God Has Three Faces And Wood Has No Name (folded sleeve in bag, 1,000 only, 26 signed/lettered)	50/25
90	Cerne 004	This Ain't The Summer Of Love (live) (with Sol Invictus, gig freebie, printed labels, 93 copies with ticket)	35/20

CURRENT 93

92	Durtro DURTRO 004	LOONEY RUNES	
		(12", live EP, 2,000 only, with poster)	25
94	Ptolemaic Terrascope POT6	Broken Birds Fly/(other artists)	
		(free with *Ptolemaic Terrascope* mag)	12/10
94	Durtro DURTRO 022	THE FIRE OF THE MIND	
		(CD EP, free with book 'Simply Being')	60
95	Durtro DURTRO 025	Tamlin/How The Great Satanic Glory Faded	
		(12", numbered with insert, 2,000 only)	30
95	Durtro DURTRO 025	Tamlin/How The Great Satanic Glory Faded	
		(CD, numbered, 3,000 only)	20
95	Durtro DURTRO 028	Where The Long Shadows Fall	
		(12", 1-sided clear vinyl with insert, 2,000 only)	20
96	Durtro DURTRO 033	The Seven Seals/(various artists) (CD, mail order)	20
86	Maldoror UDO 22M	IN MENSTRUAL NIGHT	
		(LP, 25 with handmade inserts & cover)	150/25
86	United Dairies UD 022	IN MENSTRUAL NIGHT	
		(LP, picture disc)	40
87	L.a.y.l.a.h. L.A.Y. 20	SWASTIKAS FOR NODDY	
		(LP, with insert)	30
88	Maldoror MAL 666	CHRIST AND THE PALE QUEEN	
		(3-sided LP, with inserts, 93 copies only)	120
88	Maldoror MAL 777	IMPERIUM	
		(LP, black label, with insert, later copies have white label)	35/20
89	Maldoror MAL 093	DAWN (LP)	50
89	Durtro DURTRO 001	LIVE AT BAR MALDOROR	
		(LP, white label, 1,000 only)	70/60
80s	Maldoror MAL 123	NATURE UNVEILED (LP, some with insert & free 7": "No Hiding From The Blackbird/NURSE WITH WOUND: Burial Of The Sardine")	35/22
90	United Dairies UD 029	EARTH COVERS EARTH (mini-LP)	40
90	Cerne 00123	THE CERNE BOX SET (3-LP set, includes "Horse"; other LPs by Sol Invictus & Nurse With Wound, 2,000 only)	75
90	NER BADVC 693	1888 (LP, split with Death In June, 500 each on clear & red vinyl; also on black vinyl)	40/30
92	Durtro DURTRO 006	ISLAND (LP, with insert, 2,000 only)	25
92	Durtro DURTRO 011	THUNDER PERFECT MIND (2-LP, with insert)	30
94	Durtro DURTRO 018	OF RUINE, OR SOME BLAZING STARRE	
		(LP, blue vinyl w/insert, 2,000 only)	25
94	Durtrohoho 019	LUCIFER OVER LONDON	
		(LP, red vinyl with insert, 2,000 only)	22
96	Durtro DURTRO 026	ALL THE PRETTY LITTLE HORSES	
		(LP, clear vinyl with insert, 2,000 only)	15
96	United Dairies UD OR 4	WHEN THE MAY RAIN COMES (CD, mail order, free with 'Ultrasonic Seraphim' [2-CD by SAND])	18

(see also Nurse With Wound, 23 Skidoo, Psychic TV, Crisis, Death In June, Sol Invictus)

CHERIE CURRIE
78	Mercury 6167 640	Call Me At Midnight/Young And Wild	7

CHERIE & MARIE CURRIE
80	Capitol CL 16119	Messin' With The Boys/Since You've Been Gone	10

(see also Runaways)

CLIFFORD CURRY
69	Action ACT 4549	She Shot A Hole In My Soul/We're Gonna Hate Ourselves In The Morning	7
69	Pama PM 793	You Turn Out The Light/Good Humour Man	5
69	Pama PM 797	I Can't Get A Hold Of Myself/Ain't No Danger	12

TIM CURRY
74	UK UK 67	Sweet Transvestite/Time Warp	5

CURTAINS
95	Detour DR 025	In My Street/Family Affair (p/s, 100 on blue vinyl)	8/5

DAN CURTIN
94	Peacefrog PF 018X	PARALLEL EP	
		(12", sampler, plain sleeve)	10
94	Peacefrog PF 018	THE SILICON DAWN (2-LP)	18
94	Peacefrog PF 018CD	THE SILICON DAWN CD (CD)	15
95	Peacefrog PF 023	PURVEYORS OF FINE FUNK — HEIGHTS TRAX VOL 1 EP	
		(12", plain sleeve)	15
95	Peacefrog PF 024	DREAMS NOT OF TODAY EP	
		(12", plain sleeve)	10
95	Peacefrog PF 032	PURVEYORS OF FINE FUNK — HEIGHTS TRAX VOL 2 EP	
		(12", plain sleeve)	10
95	Peacefrog PF 038	WEB OF LIFE (2-LP)	15
96	Peacefrog PF 058	PURVEYORS OF FINE FUNK VOL 3 EP	
		(12", plain sleeve)	10
97	Peacefrog PF 064	PURVEYORS OF FINE FUNK VOL 4 EP	
		(12", plain sleeve)	8

ALLEN CURTIS
64	Hickory 45-1226	Fireball Mail/The Hole He Said He'd Dig For Me	6

CHRIS CURTIS
66	Pye 7N 17132	Aggravation/Have I Done Something Wrong	35

(see also Searchers)

DENNY CURTIS
68	Plexium PXM 2	Crying Over You/You Don't Love Me No More	5
69	Plexium PXM 6	Message/You Gotta Be Mine	5

JOHNNY CURTIS

66	Parlophone R 5529	Our Love's Disintegrating/((I'd Be) A Legend In My Time	25
67	Parlophone R 5582	Jack And The Beanstalk/Go On Back	15
68	Major Minor MM 564	Pickin' Up Pebbles/Gentle On My Mind	5

KING CURTIS
(see under 'K')

LEE CURTIS (& ALL STARS)

63	Decca F 11622	Little Girl/Just One More Dance (solo)	12
63	Decca F 11690	Let's Stomp/Poor Unlucky Me	15
64	Decca F 11830	What About Me/I've Got My Eyes On You	12
64	Philips BF 1385	Ecstasy/A Shot Of Rhythm And Blues	12

(see also Pete Best Four)

MAC CURTIS

57	Parlophone R 4279	The Low Road/You Ain't Treatin' Me Right	1,350
57	Parlophone R 4279	The Low Road/You Ain't Treatin' Me Right (78)	200
74	Polydor 2310 293	ROCKABILLY KINGS (LP, with Charlie Feathers)	18

SONNY CURTIS

60	Coral Q 72400	The Red Headed Stranger/Talk About My Baby	25
64	Colpix PX 11024	A Beatle I Want To Be/So Used To Loving You	15
64	Liberty LIB 55710	Bo Diddley Bach/I Pledged My Love To You	15
85	Songworks S1	I Think I'm In Love/A Whole Lot Less To Me Than Meets The Eye	5
85	Songworks S2	Heart Of Gold/Why Did You Say 'I Do' To Me	5

(see also Crickets)

DAVE CURTISS & TREMORS

63	Philips BF 1257	You Don't Love Me/Sweet Girl Of Mine	6
63	Philips BF 1285	What Kind Of Girl Are You?/Dreamer's Funfair	6
64	Philips BF 1330	Summertime Blues/I'm A Hog For You Baby	6

ROCKY CURTISS & HARMONY FLAMES

| 59 | Fontana TFE 17172 | U.S.A. HIT PARADE (EP) | 30 |

CURTISS MALDOON

| 72 | Purple PUR 106 | One Way Ticket/Next Time | 7 |

BOBBY CURTOLA (& MARTELLS)

61	Columbia DB 4672	Don't You Sweetheart Me/My Heart's Tongue-Tied (solo)	10
62	London HL 9577	Fortune Teller/Johnny Take Your Time (solo)	7
62	London HL 9639	Aladdin/I Don't Want To Go On Without You (solo)	7
63	Decca F 11670	Gypsy Heart/I'm Sorry	6
63	Decca F 11725	Three Rows Over/Indian Giver	6

CURVE

91	Anxious ANXP 27	Blindfold/Ten Little Girls (picture disc)	6
93	Anxious	FALLING FREE — APHEX TWIN REMIX	
		(12", 1-sided promo only, 500 only)	60
93	Anxious ANXCDS 42	BLACKERTHREETRACKERTWO EP	
		(CD, with Future Sound Of London mix)	8

CURVED AIR

71	Warner Bros WB 8023	It Happened Today/What Happens When You Blow Yourself Up	8
71	Warner Bros WB 8029	Back Street Luv/Everdance	6
72	Warner Bros K 16164	Sarah's Concern/Phantasmagoria	6
75	Deram DM 426	Back Street Luv (live)/It Happened Today (live)	5
76	BTM SBT 103	Desiree/Kids To Blame	5
76	BTM SBT 106	Baby Please Don't Go/Broken Lady	5
84	Pearl Key PK 07350	Renegade/We're Only Human (p/s)	10
70	Warner Bros K 56004	AIR CONDITIONING	
		(LP, picture disc, some with booklet, 10,000 only)	35/25
70	Warner Bros WSX 3012	AIR CONDITIONING (LP, green label)	18
70	Warner Bros K 56004	AIR CONDITIONING (LP, green label)	12
71	Warner Bros K 46090	SECOND ALBUM	
		(LP, die-cut 'leaves' fold-out sleeve, green label)	15
72	Warner Bros K 46158	PHANTASMAGORIA (LP, green label, with inner lyric card)	18
73	Warner Bros K 46224	AIR CUT (LP, green label, gatefold sleeve)	18
76	Warner Bros K 46224	AIR CUT (LP, 'Burbank' label, gatefold sleeve)	12
75	Deram SML 1119	CURVED AIR LIVE (LP)	12

(see also Kirby, Sonja Kristina, Klark Kent, [Darryl Way's] Wolf, Trace)

JOHN CUSHING

| 69 | Carnaby CNS 4002 | She's Independent/Tell Me Now | 5 |

ADGE CUTLER & WURZELS

67	Columbia SX 6126	ADGE CUTLER AND THE WURZELS (LP)	12
67	Columbia SX 6165	ADGE CUTLER'S FAMILY ALBUM (LP)	12
68	Columbia S(C)X 6263	CUTLER OF THE WEST (LP)	12
69	Columbia S(C)X 6367	CARRY ON CUTLER (LP)	12

IVOR CUTLER TRIO

67	Parlophone R 5624	I Had A Little Boat/A Great Grey Grasshopper	6
59	Fontana TFE 17144	OF Y'HUP (EP)	15
61	Decca DFE 6677	GET AWAY FROM THE WALL (EP)	15
61	Decca LK 4405	WHO TORE YOUR TROUSERS? (LP)	35
67	Parlophone PCS 7040	LUDO (LP)	35
74	Virgin V 2021	DANDRUFF (LP)	12
75	Virgin V 3027	VELVET DONKEY (LP)	12
76	Virgin V 2065	JAMMY SMEARS (LP)	12
78	Harvest SHSP 4084	LIFE IN A SCOTCH SITTING ROOM VOL. 2 (LP)	12

MINT VALUE £

T. TOMMY CUTRER (& GINNY WRIGHT)
54	London HL 8093	Mexico Gal/Wonderful World (B-side with Ginny Wright)	40
54	London HL 8093	Mexico Gal/Wonderful World (78, B-side with Ginny Wright)	18

(see also Ginny Wright)

CUTTERS
59	Decca F 11110	I've Had It/Rockaroo	12
59	Decca F 11110	I've Had It/Rockaroo (78)	20

(see also Neville Taylor & Cutters)

CYANIDE
78	Pye 7N 46048	I'm A Boy/Do It (p/s)	35
78	Pye 7N 46094	Mac The Flash/Hate The State (p/s)	30
79	Pinnacle PIN 23	Fireball/Your Old Man (p/s)	30
78	Pye NSPL 18554	CYANIDE (LP)	30

CYAN THREE
66	Decca F 12371	Since I Lost My Baby/Face Of A Loser	15

CYBERMEN
78	Rockaway AERE 101	THE CYBERMEN (EP, available in 2 different sleeves)	40
79	Rockaway LUV 002	You're To Blame/It's You I Want (with inserts)	30

CYBERMEN
95	Detour DR 022	Word/One Spy Too Many (p/s, 1,000 only, 100 on red vinyl)	8/5

CYCLONES
64	Oriole CB 1898	Nobody/Little Egypt	35

CYCLONES
71	Banana BA 338	My Sweet Lord/DENNIS BROWN: Silky (B-side actually by Monty Alexander & Cyclones)	8

CYLOB
95	Rephlex CAT 015	INDUSTRIAL FOLKSONGS (12", initially in polystyrene sleeve)	12

CYMANDE
73	Alaska ALA 4	The Message/Zion I	10
73	Alaska ALA 10	Bras/Ras Tafarian Folk Song	10
74	Contempo CS 2019	Brothers On The Slide/Pon De Dungle	10
73	Alaska ALKA 100	CYMANDE (LP)	20
74	Contempo CLP 508	PROMISED HEIGHT (LP)	25

JOHNNY CYMBAL
60	MGM MGM 1106	It'll Be Me/Always, Always	15
63	London HLR 9682	Mr Bass Man/Sacred Lovers Vow	8
63	London HLR 9731	Teenage Heaven/Cinderella Baby	15
63	London HLR 9762	Dum Dum Dee Dum/Surfing At Tijuana	10
64	London HLR 9911	Mitsou/Robinson Crusoe On Mars	15
65	United Artists UP 1093	Go V.W. Go/Sorrow And Pain	18
63	London RER 1375	MISTER BASS MAN (EP)	45
64	London RER 1406	CYMBAL SMASHES (EP)	45

(see also Derek)

CYMBALINE
65	Pye 7N 15916	Please Little Girl/Coming Home Baby	25
65	Mercury MF 918	Top Girl/Can You Hear Me?	18
66	Mercury MF 961	I Don't Want It/Where Did Love Go Wrong	6
66	Mercury MF 975	Peanuts And Chewy Macs/Found My Girl	6
67	Philips BF 1624	Matrimonial Fears/You Will Never Love Me	30
68	Philips BF 1681	Down By The Seaside/Fire	10
69	Philips BF 1749	Turn Around/Come Back Baby	6

CYMERONS
64	Decca F 11976	I'll Be There/Making Love To Another	12
66	Polydor 56098	Everyday (Will Change)/I Can See You	6

CYNTHIA & ARCHIE
64	R&B JB 168	Every Beat/DELROY WILSON: Sammy Dead	15

CYRKLE
66	CBS 202064	Red Rubber Ball/How Can I Leave Her	6
66	CBS 202246	Turn Down Day/Big Little Woman	6
67	CBS 202516	Bony Maronie/Please Don't Ever Leave Me	6
67	CBS 202577	I Wish You Could Be There/The Visit (She Was Here)	6
67	CBS 2790	We Had A Good Thing Goin'/Two Rooms	6
67	CBS 2917	Penny Arcade/Words	6
67	CBS 62977	NEON (LP)	18

CZAR
70	Philips 6006 071	Oh Lord I'm Getting Heavy/Why Don't We Be A Rock'n'Roll Band	20
70	Fontana 6309 009	CZAR (LP)	125

(see also Hungry Wolf)

HOLGER CZUKAY
(see under Jah Wobble, Can)

KIM D
65 Pye 7N 15953   The Real Thing/Come On Baby 10
(see also Kim Davis)

TONY D & SHAKEOUTS
64 Piccadilly 7N 35168   Is It True/Never Let Her Go 10

DA BAND
78 Rip Off RIP 2   I Like It/Pirate's Lullaby (p/s) 20

DA BIZ
80 Small Operations SO 002   On The Beach/This Is No Audition (p/s) 5

MIKE D'ABO
69 Immediate IM 075   See The Little People — Gulliver's Travels/Anthology Of Gulliver's
    Travels Part 2 (withdrawn) 15
70 Uni UNS 525   Let It Roar/California Line 6
70 Bell BLL 1134   Miss Me In The Morning/Arabella, Cinderella 5
72 A&M AMS 7016   Belinda/Little Miss Understood 5
74 A&M AMS 7121   Fuel To Burn/Hold On Darlin' 5
70 Uni UNLS 114   D'ABO (LP, gatefold sleeve) 15
72 A&M AMLH 68097   DOWN AT RACHEL'S PLACE (LP, with inner sleeve) 12
74 A&M AMLH 63634   BROKEN RAINBOWS (LP) 12
(see also Manfred Mann, Band Of Angels, Gulliver's Travels, Smith & D'Abo)

PAULINO DA COSTA
82 Pablo Jazz 231 2102   HAPPY PEOPLE (LP) 10

TERRY DACTYL & DINOSAURS
73 UK UK 39   She Left I Died/Too Self-Centred 5
(see also Brett Marvin & Thunderbolts)

DADA
71 Atco 2400 030   DADA (LP) 20
(see also Robert Palmer, Elkie Brooks, Paul Korda, Vinegar Joe)

DADDY LONGLEGS
70 Warner Bros WB 8012   High Again/To The Rescue (Wet Putso) 5
70 Warner Bros WS 3004   DADDY LONGLEGS (LP) 18
71 Vertigo 6360 038   OAKDOWN FARM (LP, gatefold sleeve, spiral label) 20
72 Polydor 2371 261   THREE MUSICIANS (LP) 15
73 Polydor 2371 323   SHIFTING SANDS (LP) 15
(see also Daylight)

DADDY-O'S
58 Oriole CB 1454   Got A Match?/Have A Cigar 12
58 Oriole CB 1454   Got A Match?/Have A Cigar (78) 10

DADDY'S ACT
67 Columbia DB 8242   Eight Days A Week/Gonna Get You 12

DAD'S ARMY PLATOON
71 Columbia DB 8766   Dad's Army March/What Did You Do In The War? 4

D.A.F. (Deutsche Amerikanische Freundschaft)
81 Virgin VS 418   Der Mussolini/Der Räuber Und Der Prinz (no p/s, possibly promo only) 5
81 Virgin VS 418-12   Der Mussolini/Der Räuber Und Der Prinz (12", p/s, original issue) 8

CALVIN DAFOS
66 Blue Beat BB 347   Brown Sugar/I'm Gone 15
69 Doctor Bird DB 1174   Lash Them/C.D.s: Medicine Master 10

DAFT PUNK
94 Soma 014   ALIVE/THE NEW WAVE (12" EP, company sleeve) 15
95 Soma 025   DA FUNK (12" EP, company sleeve) 12

DAGABAND
80 Rutland RX 100   Test Flight/Images (p/s) 20
83 MHM A-M 094   Second Time Around/Reds Under The Beds/I Can See For Miles (p/s) 25

DAGGERMEN
86 Empire UPW 258J   INTRODUCING THE DAGGERMEN (EP, die-cut company sleeve) 10
86 Own Up DAG 001   DAGGERS IN MY MIND (LP) 12
(see also James Taylor Quartet)

DAG NASTY
86 Dischord 19   CAN I SAY (LP) 12

ETIENNE DAHO
89 Virgin VS 1180   Stay With Me/Bleu Comme Toi (p/s) 15

DAILY FLASH
84 Psycho PSYCHO 32   I FLASH DAILY (LP) 15

TONY DAINES
63 Fontana TF 433   Chapel In The Moonlight/Echo Of Footsteps 7
64 Fontana TF 472   Too Late/I Told You So 6

MINT VALUE £

DAISY CLAN
69	MCA MU 1057	Bonnie Bonnie Bonnie/Friends	5
70	Major Minor MM 671	Mister Walkie Talkie Man/Lions In The Tree	5
70	Pye International 7N 25532	Love Needs Love/Glory Be	5
71	Decca F 23168	San Francisco China Town/Ridin' A Rainbow	5

DAISY HILL PUPPY FARM
88	Lakeland LKND 006	Rocket Boy/Heartbreak Soup/Speedball/Heart Of Glam (p/s)	5

DAISY PLANET
60s	Oak (no cat. no.)	DAISY PLANET (EP, no p/s)	50

DAKOTA JIM
66	Blue Beat BB 358	Only Soul Can Tell (actually by Slim Smith)/DAKOTA'S ALLSTARS: Call Me Master (actually by Prince Buster All Stars)	25

(see also Slim Smith)

DAKOTAS
63	Parlophone R 5044	The Cruel Sea/The Millionaire	7
63	Parlophone R 5064	Magic Carpet/Humdinger	8
64	Parlophone R 5203	Oyeh/My Girl Josephine	20
67	Page One POF 018	I'm 'N 'Ardworkin' Barrow Boy/Seven Pounds Of Potatoes	20
68	Philips BF 1645	I Can't Break The News To Myself/The Spider And The Fly	55
63	Parlophone GEP 8888	MEET THE DAKOTAS (EP)	40

(see also Billy J. Kramer & Dakotas)

MICHAEL D'ALBUQUERQUE
74	RCA SF 8383	WE MAY BE CATTLE BUT WE ALL HAVE NAMES (LP, with lyric sheet)	15
76	Warner Bros K 56276	STALKING THE SLEEPER (LP)	12

(see also E.L.O., Michael Albuquerque)

DALE & GRACE
63	London HL 9807	I'm Leaving It Up To You/That's What I Like About You	10
64	London HL 9857	Stop And Think It Over/Bad Luck	8
69	London HL 10249	I'm Leaving It Up To You/Love Is Strange	7
64	London RE 1428	DALE AND GRACE NO. 1 (EP)	30
64	London RE 1429	DALE AND GRACE NO. 2 (EP)	30
64	London RE 1430	DALE AND GRACE NO. 3 (EP)	30

ALAN DALE
55	Vogue Coral Q 72072	Cherry Pink And Apple Blossom White/I'm Sincere	12
55	Vogue Coral Q 72089	Sweet And Gentle/You Still Mean The Same To Me	15
55	Vogue Coral Q 72105	Rockin' The Cha-Cha/Wham! (There I Go In Love Again)	12
55	Vogue Coral Q 72105	Rockin' The Cha-Cha/Wham! (There I Go In Love Again) (78)	12
56	Vogue Coral Q 72121	Robin Hood/Lisbon Antigua	18
56	Vogue Coral Q 72121	Robin Hood/Lisbon Antigua (78)	10
56	Vogue Coral Q 72156	Dance On/Mr. Moon	7
56	Vogue Coral Q 72156	Dance On/Mr. Moon (78)	7
56	Vogue Coral Q 72166	The Birds And The Bees/I Promise	7
56	Vogue Coral Q 72191	Be My Guest/Pardners (with Buddy Hackett)	6
56	Vogue Coral Q 72194	The Test Of Time/I Cry More	8
56	Vogue Coral Q 72194	The Test Of Time/I Cry More (78)	10
57	Vogue Coral Q 72225	Don't Knock The Rock/Your Love Is My Love	18
57	Vogue Coral Q 72225	Don't Knock The Rock/Your Love Is My Love (78)	10
57	Vogue Coral Q 72231	The Girl Can't Help It/Lonesome Road	18
57	Vogue Coral Q 72231	The Girl Can't Help It/Lonesome Road (78)	12
58	MGM MGM 986	Volare/Weeping Willow In The Wind	6
58	MGM MGM 986	Volare/Weeping Willow In The Wind (78)	7

(see also Johnny Desmond)

DICK DALE & HIS DELTONES
63	Capitol CL 15296	Peppermint Man/Surf Beat	15
63	Capitol CL 15320	The Scavenger/Wild Ideas	15
88	Pulch Wave PSC 666	Pick And Play/The Wedge (p/s)	5
88	Pulch Wave PSCT 666	Pick And Play/Hava Nagila/The Wedge/King Of The Surf Guitar (12", p/s)	7
63	Capitol T 1886	SURFERS' CHOICE (LP)	50
63	Capitol T/ST 1930	KING OF THE SURF GUITAR (LP, mono/stereo)	50/60

GLEN DALE
66	Decca F 12475	Good Day Sunshine/Make Me Belong To You	8
68	Page One POF 059	I've Got You On My Mind/Now I See You	6
68	Page One POF 105	I've Got Something Too/Something's Gotten Hold Of My Heart	6

(see also Fortunes)

JIM DALE
57	Parlophone R 4329	Piccadilly Line/I Didn't Mean It	10
57	Parlophone R 4329	Piccadilly Line/I Didn't Mean It (78)	7
57	Parlophone R 4343	Be My Girl/You Shouldn't Do That	8
57	Parlophone R 4356	All Shook Up/Wandering Eyes (with Vipers & King Brothers)	12
57	Parlophone R 4356	All Shook Up/Wandering Eyes (with Vipers & King Brothers) (78)	5
57	Parlophone R 4376	Just Born (To Be Your Baby)/Crazy Dream	6
58	Parlophone R 4402	Sugartime/Don't Let Go	6
58	Parlophone R 4402	Sugartime/Don't Let Go (78)	6
58	Parlophone R 4424	Tread Softly Stranger/Jane Belinda	6
59	Parlophone R 4522	Gotta Find A Girl/The Legend Of Nellie D.	6
59	Parlophone R 4522	Gotta Find A Girl/The Legend Of Nellie D. (78)	7
60	Academy AD 001	Somewhere There's A Someone/If You Come Back	6
62	Piccadilly 7N 35039	One Boy, One Girl/My Resistance is Low	5
62	Piccadilly 7N 35100	Start All Over Again/It's For Them	5
57	Parlophone GEP 8656	JIM DALE (EP)	30
58	Parlophone PMD 1055	JIM (10" LP)	60

PAUL DALE BAND

82	KA KA 6/PAUL 1	Alright On The Night/Hold On (p/s, some on clear vinyl)	6/5

(see also Marseille)

SYD DALE ORCHESTRA

65	Decca F 22300	C'mon In/Disc A Go Go	6
66	Decca F 22370	It Started With Eve/Hell Raisers	5

DALEK I LOVE YOU

80	Back Door CLOSE 1	Dalek I Love You/Eight Track (p/s, original version)	6

DALEK O.K.

80	Experimental Prod. EXPS 1	This Life/Rejected/Man Of The World (p/s)	6

DALEKS

(see under Century 21)

DALE SISTERS

60	HMV POP 781	The Kiss/Billy Boy, Billy Boy	8
61	Ember EMB S 140	My Sunday Baby/All My Life	10
62	Ember EMB S 151	Secrets/Road To Love	7

DÄLEX

81	Dodgy DODGY 1	Juvenile/Action Man Touched (p/s)	6

BASIL DALEY

68	Studio One SO 2054	Hold Me Baby/HEPTONES: I Got A Feeling	15

JIMMY DALEY & DING-A-LINGS

57	Brunswick 05648	Rock, Pretty Baby/Can I Steal A Little Love	100
57	Brunswick 05648	Rock, Pretty Baby/Can I Steal A Little Love (78)	20

SALVADOR DALI

62	Decca SET 230	DALI IN VENICE (LP, gatefold sleeve with booklet)	75

DALI'S CAR

84	Paradox DOXY 1	The Judgement Is The Mirror/High Places (picture disc)	5

(see also Bauhaus, Peter Murphy, Japan, Mick Karn)

DALLAS BOYS

67	Major Minor MM 534	He Won't Love You (Like I Do)/What Do You Know About Losin'	5

(see also Five Dallas Boys)

TONY DALLI

59	Columbia SEG 7897	SONGS FROM THE SHOWS (EP)	8
64	Decca LK 4641	THE VOICE OF TONY DALLI (LP)	12

DALLIONS

62	Oriole CB 1794	Teardrops In The Rain/Loop De Loop	6

MIKI DALLON

65	RCA RCA 1438	Do You Call That Love?/Apple Pie	30
65	RCA RCA 1478	I Care About You/I'll Give You Love	45
66	Strike JH 306	Cheat And Lie/(I'm Gonna Find A) Cave	10
66	Strike JH 318	What Will Your Mama Say Now?/Two At A Time	6

(see also Neil Christian & Crusaders)

KATHY DALTON

73	Discreet K 59202	AMAZING (LP)	12

MIKE DALTON

61	Bi-Tapes RRE 1114	GOT WHAT IT TAKES (EP, reel-to-reel tape)	7
61	Bi-Tapes RRA 104	GOT WHAT IT TAKES (reel-to-reel tape)	10
61	Bi-Tapes RRB 107	LIVING NOW (reel-to-reel tape)	10

DALTONS

67	Fab FAB 30	Never Kiss You Again/RIGHTEOUS FLAMES: When A Girl Loves A Boy	10

(see also Prince Buster)

ROGER DALTREY

73	Track 2094 110	Giving It All Away/The Way Of The World	5
73	Ode ODS 66302	I'm Free/Overture (p/s)	6
73	Track 2094 014	Thinking/There Is Love	5
73	Track 2094 016	It's A Hard Life/One Man Band	6
75	Polydor 2001 561	Listening To You/Listening To You (Overture)	5
75	Polydor 2058 593	Get Your Love/The World Over	5
75	Polydor 2058 628	Walking The Dog/Proud	5
75	A&M AMS 7206	Orpheus Song/Love's Dream	5
75	Lyntone LYN 3176/7	Wagner's Dream/Love's Theme/RICK WAKEMAN: Count Your Blessings (flexidisc with 19 magazine)	10/6
77	Polydor 2058 948	Say It Ain't So Joe/Satin And Lace (withdrawn, existence unconfirmed)	15+
78	Polydor 2058 986	Say It Ain't So Joe/The Prisoner	5
80	Polydor POSP 181	Without Your Love/Say It Ain't So Joe (p/s, without extra track "Free Me")	5
86	10 TENG 81	Under A Raging Moon/Move Better In The Night (gatefold p/s)	5
86	10 TEND 81	Under A Raging Moon/Move Better In The Night//Behind Blue Eyes/5:15 (double pack, gatefold p/s)	8
86	10 TENG 8110	Under A Raging Moon (6.43)/Move Better In The Night/Under A Raging Moon/5:15 (10" double pack, gatefold p/s)	10
86	10 TENG 8112	Under A Raging Moon (6.43)/Move Better In The Night/Under A Raging Moon (4.30) (12", gatefold p/s)	8
86	10 TEND 103	The Pride You Hide/Don't Talk To Strangers//Pictures Of Lily/Break Out (double pack)	8
75	Polydor ACB 199	RIDE A ROCK HORSE (LP, Record Club edition)	12
80	Polydor POLD 5034	McVICAR (LP, soundtrack, some on clear vinyl)	15/12

(see also Who, High Numbers, McEnroe & Cash)

MINT VALUE £

TONI DALY
66	Columbia DB 8043	Like The Big Man Said/You Can't Get No Water	7

(see also Antoinette)

DALYS
65	Fontana TF 546	Me Japanese Boy/Never Kind Of Love	6
65	Fontana TF 637	She's My Girl/When Love Has Gone	6
66	Strike JH 317	Don't Go Breaking My Heart/Little Stranger	7
67	Fontana TF 809	Sweet Maria/Leaving Time	6
67	Fontana TF 841	A Fistful Of Dollars/Man With No Name	7
68	Fontana TF 907	Let Me Go Lover/A Place In The Sun	6
69	Fontana TF 988	Early Morning Rain/Chanson D'Amour	6

DAMASCUS
80s	private pressing	OPEN YOUR EYES (12" EP, later with different back sleeve & insert)	each 65

(see also Thin End Of The Wedge)

TADD DAMERON ORCHESTRA
54	Capitol CL 14201	Focus/John's Delight	6
62	Capitol EAP1 20388	TADD'S DELIGHT (EP)	8

(see also Clifford Brown)

DAMIAN
86	Sedition EDITL 3311	The Time Warp/Dancin' (12", p/s)	7

DAMITA JO
54	HMV 7MC 2	I'd Do It Again/Do I, Do I, Do I (B-side with Steve Gibson) (export issue)	15
54	HMV JO 390	I'd Do It Again/Do I, Do I, Do I (B-side with Steve Gibson) (78, export issue)	10
60	Mercury AMT 1085	Widow Walk/Dearest Darling	6
60	Mercury AMT 1116	I'll Save The Last Dance For You/Forgive	7
60	Mercury AMT 1133	Keep Your Hands Off Him/Hush, Somebody's Calling My Name	6
61	Mercury AMT 1141	Do What You Want/Sweet Georgia Brown	5
61	Mercury AMT 1155	I'll Be There/Love Laid Its Hands On Me	5
61	Mercury ZEP 10118	I'LL SAVE THE LAST DANCE FOR YOU (EP)	15
61	Mercury MMC 14089	I'LL SAVE THE LAST DANCE FOR YOU (LP, also stereo [CMS 18059])	20
66	Columbia S(C)X 6094	MIDNIGHT SESSION (LP)	15

DAMNED
74	Youngblood YB 1067	Morning Bird/Theta	5

DAMNED
76	Stiff BUY 6	New Rose/Help! (first pressing with push-out centre & 'Delga' credit on p/s)	15
76	Stiff BUY 6	New Rose/Help! (p/s, later issues)	5
77	Stiff BUY 10	Neat Neat Neat/Stab Yor Back/Singalongascabies (glossy p/s, first pressing with solid centre & gothic lettering; later push-out centres)	15/6
77	Stiff DAMNED 1	Stretcher Case Baby/Sick Of Being Sick (p/s, *NME* competition & gig freebie)	40
77	Stiff BUY 18	Problem Child/You Take My Money (p/s, originally with press-out centre)	7/5
77	Stiff BUY 24	Don't Cry Wolf/One Way Love (20,000 on pink vinyl, no p/s; later black vinyl)	7/5
77	Stiff BUY 24	Don't Cry Wolf/One Way Love (Dave Vanian-designed p/s, existence uncomfirmed)	
78	Dodgy Demo Co. SGS 105	Love Song/Burglar (mail order issue/gig freebie, plain sleeve, stickered labels)	18
79	Chiswick CHIS 112	Love Song/Noise Noise Noise/Suicide (red vinyl, 4 different sleeves)	each 6
79	Chiswick CHIS 112	Love Song/Noise Noise Noise/Suicide (4 different sleeves)	each 5
79	Chiswick CHIS 116	Smash It Up/Burglar (p/s)	5
79	Chiswick CHIS 120	I Just Can't Be Happy Today/Ballroom Blitz/The Turkey Song (p/s)	6
80	Chiswick CHIS 130	White Rabbit/Rabid (Over You)/Seagulls (unissued in U.K., Europe-only, 2 x 1-sided white-label test pressings exist, hand-written labels)	400+
80	Chiswick CHIS 135	The History Of The World Part 1/I Believe The Impossible/Sugar And Spite (p/s)	5
80	Chiswick CHIS 12 135	The History Of The World Part 1/I Believe The Impossible/Sugar And Spite (12", p/s)	8
80	Chiswick CHIS 139	There Ain't No Sanity Clause/Hit Or Miss/Looking At You (live) (p/s)	5
81	NEMS TRY 1	FRIDAY THE 13TH (EP, p/s)	5
81	NEMS TRY 1	FRIDAY THE 13TH (12" EP)	8
81	Stiff GRAB 2	FOUR PACK (4 x 7" [BUY 6, 10, 18 & 24], in a plastic wallet)	25
82	Big Beat NS 75	Love Song/Noise Noise Noise/Suicide (3 different sleeves, blue vinyl)	5
82	Big Beat NS 76	Smash It Up/Burglar (p/s, red vinyl)	5
82	Big Beat NS 77	Wait For The Blackout/CAPTAIN SENSIBLE & SOFTIES: Jet Boy, Jet Girl (p/s, red/black 'Damned' labels)	5
82	Big Beat NSP 77	Wait For The Blackout/CAPTAIN SENSIBLE & SOFTIES: Jet Boy, Jet Girl (picture disc)	5
82	Bronze BRO 149	Lovely Money/Lovely Money (Disco Mix)/I Think I'm Wonderful (p/s)	5
82	Bronze BROP 149	Lovely Money/Lovely Money (Disco Mix)/I Think I'm Wonderful (picture disc)	7
82	Bronze BRO 156	Dozen Girls/Take That/Mine's A Large One, Landlord/Torture Me (p/s)	6
82	Big Beat NS 80	Lively Arts/Teenage Dream (p/s, some on green vinyl)	8/5
82	Bronze BRO 159	Generals/Disguise/Citadel Zombies (p/s)	8
83	Big Beat NS 85	White Rabbit/Rabid (Over You)/Seagulls (p/s)	5
84	Plus One DAMNED 1P	Thanks For The Night (picture disc)	5
84	Plus One DAMNED 1	Thanks For The Night/Nasty (p/s, 1,000 each on red, white & blue vinyl)	each 6
84	Plus One DAMNED 1T	Thanks For The Night/Nasty/Do The Blitz (12", no'd p/s, multicoloured vinyl)	10
84	Plus One DAMNED 1T	Thanks For The Night/Nasty ('woman'-shaped pic disc w/ plinth, 1,000 only)	15
85	MCA GRIM 1	Grimly Fiendish/Edward The Bear (autographed gatefold p/s, 1,000 only)	8
85	MCA GRIMP 1	Grimly Fiendish/Edward The Bear (picture disc)	5
85	MCA GRIMT 1	Grimly Fiendish (Spic'n'Span Mix)/Edward The Bear (12", autographed p/s)	10
85	MCA GRIM 2/GRIMY 2	Edition Premier: The Shadow Of Love/Nightshift/Let There Be Rats/Wiped Out (double pack)	5
85	MCA GRIM 3	Is It A Dream (Wild West End Mix)/Street Of Dreams (live) (p/s, with 5 badges)	5

86	MCA GRIMT 4	Eloise/Temptation/Beat Girl (12", p/s, 2,000 on blue vinyl) 8
86	Stiff BUY 6/BUYDJ 6A	New Rose/Help!/I'm So Bored (1-sided) (double pack, stickered PVC sleeve with insert, 1st disc on white vinyl, 2nd disc actually plays "I Fall" [live]) 8
86	Stiff BUY 6	New Rose/Help! (reissue, red vinyl, PVC sleeve, with card insert) 6
91	Deltic DELT 7T	Fun Factory/CAPTAIN SENSIBLE: Freedom/Pasties/A Riot On Eastbourne Pier (12" p/s, blue vinyl, mail-order only, 2000 only) 8
77	Stiff SEEZ 1	DAMNED DAMNED DAMNED (LP) 12
77	Stiff SEEZ 1	DAMNED DAMNED DAMNED (LP, 2,000 with Eddie & Hot Rods photograph on rear sleeve; some shrinkwrapped with title sticker) 50/35
79	Chiswick CWK 3011	MACHINE GUN ETIQUETTE (LP, with inner sleeve) 12
81	Ace DAM 1	THE BEST OF THE DAMNED (LP, red or blue vinyl) 12
82	Ace DAM 2	MACHINE GUN ETIQUETTE (LP, reissue, blue or white/clear vinyl with inner) . . . 12
82	Ace DAM 3	THE BLACK ALBUM (LP, single reissue, 12,000 with lyrics & poster) 12
82	Big Beat NED 1	LIVE SHEPPERTON 1980 (LP, with 'Collectors Catalogue', 5,000 only) 12
83	Stiff MAIL 2	DAMNED DAMNED DAMNED/MUSIC FOR PLEASURE (2-LP, reissue, gatefold sleeve, mail-order, 5000 only) 20
83	Damned DAMU 2	LIVE IN NEWCASTLE (LP, 5,000 by mail-order only) 15
83	Damned PDAMU 2	LIVE IN NEWCASTLE (LP, picture disc, 5,000 only) 15
86	Stiff GET 4	THE CAPTAIN'S BIRTHDAY PARTY — LIVE AT THE ROUNDHOUSE (mini-LP, 45rpm, blue vinyl, stickered plain white sleeve) 12
86	Stiff MAIL 2	DAMNED, DAMNED, DAMNED/MUSIC FOR PLEASURE (2-LP, reissue, yellow vinyl, 4000 by mail-order only) 18
86	Dojo DOJOPD 46	STRAWBERRIES (LP, reissue picture disc) 12
87	Demon PFIEND 91	DAMNED DAMNED DAMNED (LP, reissue picture disc) 12
87	Demon FIEND 108	MUSIC FOR PLEASURE (LP, reissue, orange vinyl) 12
89	Essential ESCLP 008	FINAL DAMNATION (LP, green vinyl, with poster) 12
92	Reviever RRLP 159	LIVE AT THE LYCEUM (LP, clear vinyl) 12

(see also Captain Sensible, Brian James, Rat Scabies, Rat & Whale, Edge, Magic Michael, Naz Nomad & Nightmares, Auntiepus, Disco Brothers, Phantom Chords, Tank, Eddie & Hot Rods, U.F.O., Tanz Der Youth)

KENNY DAMON

65	Mercury MF 907	While I Live/Fountain In Capri 6
66	Mercury MF 936	World Of No Return/You Are Everything That's Beautiful. 6
68	Mercury MF 1014	Turn Her Away/Till Then My Love 6

(see also Kenny Roberts)

RUSS DAMON

64	Stateside SS 258	Hip Huggers/Heaven Sent 8

STUART DAMON

71	Reflection	STUART 'CHAMPION' DAMON (LP) 20

DAMON & NAOMI

97	Earworm WORM 3	The Navigator/Awake In A Muddle (p/s) 5

(see also Galaxie 500)

VIC DAMONE

57	MGM MGM 949	And This Is My Beloved (with Howard Keel)/Night Of My Nights 6
57	MGM MGM 950	Stranger In Paradise (with Ann Blyth)/ANN BLYTH: Baubles, Bangles And Pearls 6
58	Philips PB 819	On The Street Where You Live/Arriverderci Roma. 5
58	Philips PB 837	Only Man On The Island/When My Love Smiles 5
58	Philips PB 866	Ooooh, My Love/Forever New (78) 7
59	Philips PB 889	Separate Tables/Gigi (78) 7
54	Mercury EP1 3121	WALKING MY BABY BACK HOME (EP) 12
57	Philips BBE 12099	VIC DAMONE (EP) 8
58	Philips BBE 12197	DAMONE FAVOURITES (EP) 8
58	Philips BBE 12222	VIC DAMONE (EP) 8
58	Mercury MEP 9534	THE VOICE OF VIC DAMONE (EP) 8
59	Mercury ZEP 10022	YOURS FOR A SONG (EP). 8
59	Philips BBE 12245	DO I LOVE YOU (EP). 8
61	Philips BBE 12502	ON THE SWINGERS SIDE (EP) 8
62	Capitol EAP1 1646	LINGER AWHILE (EP) 8
57	Mercury MPT 7514	ALL-TIME SONG HITS (10" LP) 20
57	Philips BBL 7144	THAT TOWERING FEELING! (LP) 15
58	Philips BBL 7259	CLOSER THAN A KISS (LP) 15
60	Philips BBL 7347	THIS GAME OF LOVE (LP) 12
62	Capitol (S)T 1646	LINGER AWHILE (LP). 12
62	Capitol (S)T 1691	STRANGE ENCHANTMENT (LP) 12
62	Capitol (S)T 1748	THE LIVELY ONES (LP) 12
63	Capitol (S)T 1811	MY BABY LOVES TO SWING (LP) 12
63	Capitol (S)T 1944	THE LIVELIEST (LP). 12
64	Capitol (S)T 2133	ON THE STREET WHERE YOU LIVE (LP). 12

(see also Howard Keel, Easy Riders)

DANA

70	Decca F 13004	All Kinds Of Everything/Channel Breeze (export issue). 5
70	Decca F 13073	I Will Follow You/With A Little Love (export issue) 5

VIC DANA

62	Liberty LIB 51	I Will/Proud 8
62	Liberty LIB 58	(A Girl Need) To Love And Be Loved/Time Can Change. 5
62	Liberty LIB 64	Very Good Year For Girls/Looking For Me. 5
63	Liberty LIB 10190	Red Roses For A Blue Lady/My World 5
63	Liberty LIB 73	Danger/Heart, Hand And Teardrop. 5
64	Liberty LIB 92	Warm And Tender/Shangri-La 5
65	Liberty LIB 309	Moonlight And Roses/What'll I Do. 5
65	Liberty LIB 313	Crystal Chandelier/What Now My Love (Et Maintenant). 5
66	Liberty LIB 309	I Love You Drops/Sunny Skies. 5
66	Liberty LIB 322	Million And One/My Baby Wouldn't Leave Me. 5

MINT VALUE £

DANCE CHAPTER
80	4AD AD 18	Anonymity/New Dance (p/s, some with card insert)	8/6
81	4AD BAD 115	CHAPTER II (12" EP, most with mismatched A&B-side labels)	10
85	Pleasantly Surprised PS 10	WHEN THE SPIRIT MOVES THEM (cassette, in bag with inserts)	15

DANCER, PRANCER & NERVOUS
59	Capitol CL 15097	The Happy Reindeer/Dancer's Waltz (p/s)	6
	(see also Singing Reindeer)		

DANCING DID
79	Fruit & Veg F&V 1	Dancing Did/Lorry Pirates (p/s)	8
80	Fruit & Veg F&V 2	The Haunted Tearooms/Squashed Things On The Road (p/s)	5

DANDELION WINE
93	Marineville	Daytime/High And Low (p/s)	5
	(see also Red Chair Fadeaway)		

DANDO SHAFT
70	Youngblood YB 1012	Cold Wind/Cat Song	8
72	RCA RCA 2246	Sun Clog Dance/This Gift	8
70	Youngblood SSYB 6	AN EVENING WITH DANDO SHAFT (LP)	45
71	RCA Neon NE 5	DANDO SHAFT (LP, gatefold sleeve)	45
72	RCA Victor SF 8256	LANTALOON (LP, initially with poster)	70/40
77	Rubber RUB 034	KINGDOM (LP)	25
	(see also Hedgehog Pie)		

DANDY (& SUPERBOYS)
64	Dice CC 21	Rudie Don't Go/It's Just Got To Be	12
65	Dice CC 24	You Got To Pray/I Got To Have You (as Dandy & Barbara)	12
65	Blue Beat BB 308	To Love You/I'm Looking For Love	12
65	Blue Beat BB 319	Hey Boy Hey Girl/So Long Baby (as Dandy & Del)	12
65	Blue Beat BB 327	My Baby/I'm Gonna Stop Loving You	12
65	Blue Beat BB 336	I Found Love/You've Got Something Nice	12
66	Dice CC 29	The Operation/A Little More Ska	12
66	Ska Beat JB 247	The Fight/Do You Know	12
67	Ska Beat JB 269	One Scotch One Bourbon One Beer/Maximum Pressure	12
67	Ska Beat JB 273	Rudie A Message To You/Til Death Do Us Part	12
67	Ska Beat JB 279	You're No Hustler/No No	12
67	Giant GN 3	My Time Now/East Of Suez (with Superboys)	12
67	Giant GN 5	Puppet On A String/Have Your Fun (with Superboys)	8
67	Giant GN 7	We Are Still Rude/Let's Do Rocksteady (with Superboys)	8
67	Giant GN 10	Somewhere My Love/My Kind Of Love (with Superboys)	8
67	Giant GN 15	There Is A Mountain/This Music Got Soul (with Superboys)	18
68	Giant GN 20	Charlie Brown/Groovin' At The Cue (as Dandy & Charlie Griffiths)	8
68	Giant GN 27	Sweet Ride/Up The Hill (with Superboys)	8
68	Giant GN 30	Tears On My Pillow/Mad Them (with Superboys)	8
68	Giant GN 36	I'm Back With A Bang Bang/Jungle Walk (with Superboys)	8
68	Trojan TR 618	The Toast/Kicks Out	8
68	Trojan TR 629	Sentence (as Dandy & Lee)/LEE PERRY: You Crummy	8
69	Columbia Blue Beat DB 112	Play It Cool/Rude With Me	8
68	Downtown DT 401	Move Your Mule/Reggae Me This	6
69	Downtown DT 402	Come Back Girl/Shake Me Wake Me	6
69	Downtown DT 404	Tell Me Darling/Cool Hand Luke	6
69	Downtown DT 406	Doctor Sure Shot/Put On Your Dancing Shoes	6
69	Downtown DT 410	Reggae In Your Jeggae/DREAMERS: Reggae Shuffle	6
69	Downtown DT 411	You Don't Care/Tryer (both sides with Audrey)	6
69	Downtown DT 415	Rocksteady Gone/Walking Down	6
69	Downtown DT 416	I'm Your Puppet/Water Boy	6
69	Downtown DT 421	Games People Play/AUDREY: One Fine Day	6
69	Downtown DT 429	People Get Ready/RUDIES: Near East	6
69	Downtown DT 434	Be Natural, Be Proud/Who Do You Want To Run To	6
69	Downtown DT 437	Come On Home/Love Is All You Need	6
69	Downtown DT 442	Everybody Loves A Winner/Try Me One More Time	6
69	Downtown DT 445	Let's Come Together (with Israelites)/JAKE WADE: Music Fever	6
69	Downtown DT 453	Won't You Come Home/Baby Make It Soon	6
70	Downtown DT 456	Raining In My Heart/First Note	6
70	Downtown DT 458	Build Your Love (On Solid Foundation)/Let's Talk It Over	6
70	Downtown DT 462	Morning Side Of The Mountain (as Dandy & Audrey)/AUDREY: Show Me Baby	6
70	Downtown DT 468	How Glad I Am/I'm So Glad (as Dandy & Audrey)	6
70	Trojan TR 7800	Take A Letter Maria/You're Coming Back	5
71	Downtown DT 483	Could It Be True/Your Eyes Are Dreaming (as Dandy & Jackie)	5
71	Downtown DT 484	Daddy's Home/Everyman	5
71	Trojan TR 7816	Same Old Fashioned Way/Out Of Many, One People	5
72	Trojan TR 7857	What Do You Want To Make Those Eyes At Me For/Talking About Sally	5
67	Giant GNL 1000	ROCKSTEADY WITH DANDY (LP)	50
68	Trojan TRL 2	DANDY RETURNS (LP)	25
69	Trojan TRL 17	I NEED YOU (LP, with Audrey)	18
70	Trojan TTL 26	YOUR MUSICAL DOCTOR (LP)	18
70	Trojan TBL 118	MORNINGSIDE OF THE MOUNTAIN (LP, with Audrey)	18
	(see also Bobby Thompson, Sugar & Dandy, Rub A Dubs, Don Martin, Boy Friday, Audrey, Little Sal with Dandy & Superboys)		

CHRIS DANE
55	London HLA 8165	Cynthia's In Love/My Ideal	25
55	London HLA 8165	Cynthia's In Love/My Ideal (78)	8

JERRY DANE
60	Decca F 11234	You're My Only Girl/Nothing But The Truth	7
60	Decca F 11284	Let's/Awhile In Love	8
63	Windsor WPS 127	Everybody Go Wild/Watcha Want (p/s)	15/8

PATRICK DANE
65	Columbia DB 7466	In My Baby's Eyes/The Only One (with Quiet Five)	5
65	Columbia DB 7749	Go Out And Get Somebody/Go On Your Way (with Club '69)	5
68	MGM MGM 1403	When You Lose The One You Love/Home (as Patrick Dane & Mark 7)	5

(see also Quiet Five)

SHELLEY DANE
60	Pye International 7N 25064	Hannah Lee/This Is The Time In My Life	8

CAL DANGER
62	Fontana 267 225 TF	Restless/Teenage Girlie Blues	50

A.P. DANGERFIELD
68	Fontana TF 935	Conversations (In A Station Light Refreshment Bar)/Further Conversations	18

KEITH DANGERFIELD
68	Plexium P 1237	No Life Child/She's A Witch	165

TONY DANGERFIELD & THRILLS
64	Pye 7N 15695	I've Seen Such Things/She's Too Way Out	45

(see also Savages, Circles)

DANI
74	Pye International 7N 25667	La Vie A 25 Ans/Pour Que Ça Dure (p/s)	6
74	Pye International 7N 25667	That Old Familiar Feeling/Pour Que Ça Dure	12

DANIEL IN THE LION'S DEN
70	Trojan TR 7797	Dancing In The Sun/LION'S DEN: Chick A Bow	5

DANIELLE
66	Philips BF 1532	I'm Gonna Marry The Boy/Magic Carpet Of Love	8
67	Philips BF 1574	Oh Mama/Come A Little Closer	7

BILLY DANIELS
51	London L 1003	That Old Black Magic/Love Is A Lovely Thing (78)	7
51	London L 1004	Home/Diane (78)	6
51	London L 1134	Charmaine/Trees (78)	10
56	Vogue V 2386	I Live For You/Medley: Easy To Love, etc.	6
56	Oriole CB 1087	I Get A Kick Out Of You/Too Marvelous For Words	6
56	Oriole CB 1095	That Old Black Magic/I Concentrate On You	6
60	Vogue V 9172	That Old Black Magic/My Yiddishe Mamma	12
56	Mercury MEP 9001	BILLY DANIELS (EP)	12
58	HMV 7EG 8485	BEST OF BILLY DANIELS (EP)	8
60	Mercury ZEP 10066	THAT OLD BLACK MAGIC (EP)	10
53	Oriole/Mercury MG 10003	TORCH HOUR (10" LP, Oriole label with stickered U.S. Mercury sleeve)	25
54	Mercury MG 25103	TORCH HOUR (10" LP, reissue)	20
54	Mercury MG 25163	SONGS AT MIDNIGHT (10" LP)	25
56	Mercury MPT 7006	TORCH HOUR (10" LP, 2nd reissue)	15
56	Mercury MPT 7505	SONGS AT MIDNIGHT (10" LP, reissue)	18
56	Vogue LAE 12021	AT THE CRESCENDO (LP)	15
58	HMV DLP 1174	YOU GO TO MY HEAD (10" LP)	15
58	HMV CLP 1200	THE MASCULINE TOUCH (LP)	15

JOE DANIELS' JAZZ GROUP
54	Parlophone MSP 6111	I Wish I Could Shimmy Like My Sister Kate/Susie	7
54	Parlophone MSP 6129	Little Brown Jug/Mountain Wine	7
54	Parlophone MSP 6143	Crazy Rhythm/The Champagne Touch	7
56	Parlophone R 4236	"Dixieland Party (No. 2)" Medley (both sides)	6
57	Parlophone R 4273	When The Saints Go Marching In/Spanish Shawl (solo)	6
57	Parlophone R 4324	Avalon/New Orleans Parade	6
57	Parlophone R 4330	Oi! Oi! Oi!/Bottle Beatin' Blues	6
57	Parlophone R 4378	"Juke Box Jazz" Medley (both sides)	6

JULIUS DANIELS
65	RCA RCX 7175	R.C.A. VICTOR RACE SERIES VOL. 4 (EP)	15

MAXINE DANIELS
57	Oriole CB 1366	Coffee-Bar Calypso/Cha-Cha Calypso	8
57	Oriole CB 1366	Coffee-Bar Calypso/Cha-Cha Calypso (78)	7
57	Oriole CB 1372	Why Should I Care/London Is A Village (78)	7
58	Oriole CB 1402	I Never Realised/Moonlight Serenade	8
58	Oriole CB 1402	I Never Realised/Moonlight Serenade (78)	7
58	Oriole CB 1440	You Brought A New Kind Of Love To Me/Somebody Else Is Taking My Place	8
58	Oriole CB 1440	You Brought A New Kind Of Love To Me/Somebody Else Is Taking My Place (78)	7
58	Oriole CB 1449	When It's Springtime In The Rockies/My Summer Heart	8
58	Oriole CB 1449	When It's Springtime In The Rockies/My Summer Heart (78)	7
58	Oriole CB 1462	Passionate Summer/Lola's Heart	8
58	Oriole CB 1462	Passionate Summer/Lola's Heart (78)	7

MIKE DANIELS & HIS BAND
57	Parlophone R 4285	Hiawatha/Don't You Think I Love You	5
57	Columbia 33SX 1256	MIKE ON MIKE (LP)	45

REV R.A. DANIELS
51	Capitol CL 13530	He's The Lily Of The Valley/I Shall Wear A Crown (78)	40

ROLY "YO YO" DANIELS
60s	Stardisc SD 101	Yo Yo Boy/The Teacher (p/s)	12
61	Parlophone R 4759	Late Last Evening/Bella Bella Marie	5
62	Decca F 11501	Yo Yo Boy/The Teacher (reissue)	6

SAM DANIELS
63	Sway SW 003	Tell Me Baby/ERNIE FAULKENER: Beautiful Girl (both with Planets)	8

JOHNNY DANKWORTH ORCHESTRA
53	Parlophone MSP 6026	Honeysuckle Rose (with Cleo Laine)/Swingin'	7
53	Parlophone MSP 6032	Moon Flowers/Two Ticks	7
53	Parlophone MSP 6037	I Get A Kick Out Of You (with Frank Holder)/Easy Living (with Cleo Laine)	7
54	Parlophone MSP 6067	S' Wonderful/Younger Every Day	7
54	Parlophone MSP 6077	The Slider/It's The Talk Of The Town	7
54	Parlophone MSP 6083	The Jerky Thing/My Buddy	7
54	Parlophone MSP 6092	Runnin' Wild/Oo-Be-Doop	8
54	Parlophone MSP 6113	Perdido/Four Of A Kind	7
54	Parlophone MSP 6139	Bugle Call Rag/You Go To My Head	7
55	Capitol CL 14285	Singin' In The Rain/Non-Stop London	7
56	Parlophone MSP 6255	Experiments With Mice/Applecake	12
57	Parlophone R 4274	All Clare/Melbourne Marathon	6
57	Parlophone R 4294	Duke's Joke/Coquette	6
57	Parlophone R 4321	Big Jazz Story/Firth Of Fourths	6
58	Parlophone R 4456	The Colonel's Tune/Jim And Andy's	6
59	Top Rank JAR 209	We Are The Lambeth Boys/Duet For 16	6
59	Top Rank JAR 209	We Are The Lambeth Boys/Duet For 16 (78)	12
61	Columbia DB 4590	African Waltz/Moanin'	5
61	Columbia DB 4695	The Avengers/Chano	15
63	Fontana TF 422	The Avengers/Off The Cuff	15
64	Fontana TF 512	Beefeaters/Down A Tone	25
65	Fontana TF 643	Sands Of The Kalahari/Night Thoughts	6
66	Fontana TF 700	Modesty Blaise Theme/The Frost Report	7
67	Fontana TF 805	(Ain't That) Just Like A Woman/Accident	6
78	BBC RESL 63	Telford's Change/Serenade For Sylvia (p/s)	8
61	Columbia SEG 8137	AFRICAN WALTZ (EP)	12
58	Parlophone GEP 8653	DANKWORTH WORKSHOP NO. 1 (EP)	25
58	Parlophone GEP 8697	DANKWORTH WORKSHOP NO. 2 — EXPERIMENTS WITH DANKWORTH (EP)	12
60	Columbia SEG 8037	THE CRIMINALS (EP, soundtrack; also stereo ESG 7825)	12/15
56	Parlophone PMD 1042	JOURNEY INTO JAZZ (LP)	40
58	Parlophone PMC 1076	THE VINTAGE YEARS (LP)	30
59	Parlophone PMD 1042	JOURNEY INTO JAZZ (10" LP)	30
59	Parlophone PMC 1043	FIVE STEPS TO DANKWORTH (LP)	30
60	Top Rank 25/019	LONDON TO NEWPORT (LP)	70
61	Columbia 33SX 1280	JAZZ ROUTES (LP, also stereo SCX 3347)	50
63	Columbia 33SX 1572	CURTAIN UP (LP)	35
64	Fontana TL/STL 5203	WHAT THE DICKENS! (LP)	60
65	Fontana TL 5229	THE ZODIAC VARIATIONS (LP)	130
67	Stateside S(S)L 10213	FATHOM (LP, soundtrack)	25
68	Fontana TL 5445	THE $1,000,000 COLLECTION (LP)	35
70s	Philips 6308 122	FULL CIRCLE (LP)	50
70s	Philips 6308 169	LIFELINE (LP)	20
70s	Encore ENC 165	FROM 7 ON (LP)	30
80s	Sepia RRT 1007	FAIR OAK FUSIONS (LP)	25
80s	Sepia RSR 1008	PRELUDE TO A KISS (LP)	40

(see also Cleo Laine, Philip Green, Tony Mansell, Kenny Wheeler & Johnny Dankworth, Frank Holder, Pinewood Studio Orchestra)

DANLEERS
58	Mercury AMT 1003	One Summer Night/Wheelin' And A-Dealin'	200
58	Mercury AMT 1003	One Summer Night/Wheelin' And A-Dealin' (78)	60

DANNY & DRESSMAKERS
80s	Fuck Off FEP 002	WEIRD NOISE EP	5
80s	Weird Noise WEIRD 003	39 GOLDEN GRATES (C-90 cassette)	12

(see also World Dominations Enterprises)

DANNY & THE JUNIORS
58	HMV POP 436	At The Hop/Sometimes (When I'm All Alone)	15
58	HMV POP 436	At The Hop/Sometimes (When I'm All Alone) (78)	15
58	HMV POP 467	Rock And Roll Is Here To Stay/School Boy Romance	35
58	HMV POP 467	Rock And Roll Is Here To Stay/School Boy Romance (78)	25
58	HMV POP 504	Dottie/In The Meantime	18
58	HMV POP 504	Dottie/In The Meantime (78)	20
60	Top Rank JAR 510	Twistin' U.S.A./Thousand Miles Away	10
61	Top Rank JAR 552	Pony Express/Daydreamer	10
61	Top Rank JAR 587	Back To The Hop/The Charleston Fish	10
62	Top Rank JAR 604	Twistin' All Night Long/Twistin' England (with Freddy Cannon)	10
63	London HL 9666	Oo-La-La-Limbo/Now And Then	8
68	Stateside SS 2117	At The Hop/LLOYD PRICE: (You've Got) Personality	6

C. DANOVAN
73	Randy's RAN 529	Sweet Caroline/IMPACT ALL STARS: Caroline (Version)	4

DANSE SOCIETY
81	Society SOC 3-81	The Clock/Continent (brown, black & white foldout p/s)	12
81	Society SOC 3-81	The Clock/Continent (re-pressing, black & white foldout p/s)	5
81	Pax PAX 2	There Is No Shame In Death/Dolphins/These Frayed Edges (12", p/s, blue or black vinyl)	20/6
82	Pax SOC 5	Woman's Own/We're So Happy (p/s)	10
82	Pax PAX 5	Woman's Own/Continent/We're So Happy/Belief (12", with spined p/s)	12

DANSETTE DAMAGE
78	Shoestring LACE 001	New Musical Express/The Only Sound (p/s)	80
79	Pinnacle PIN 30	2001³/₄ Approximately/Must Be Love (p/s)	8
94	Shoestring BLOO 2LP	SOLD AS SEEN (LP, gatefold sleeve)	15

DANTALIAN'S CHARIOT
67	Columbia DB 8260	The Madman Running Through The Fields/The Sun Came Bursting Through My Cloud	75
95	Tenth Planet TP 015	CHARIOT RISING (LP, numbered, 1,000 only)	20

(see also Zoot Money's Big Roll Band)

DANTE
61	Brunswick 05857	Bye Bye Baby/That's Why	7

DANTE & EVERGREENS
60	Top Rank JAR 402	Alley-Oop/The Right Time	20

RONNIE DANTE
64	Stateside SS 351	Don't Stand Up In A Canoe/If You Love Me Laurie	6

TROY DANTE (& INFERNOS)
63	Decca F 11639	Golden Earrings/Milord	6
63	Decca F 11746	It's Alright/Tell Me (as Troy Dante & Infernos)	6
64	Fontana TF 445	Tell Me When/It Had To Be (as Troy Dante & Infernos)	6
64	Fontana TF 477	This Little Girl/Loving Eyes (as Troy Dante & Infernos)	12
64	Fontana TF 498	Baby/Tell Me Now.	6
65	Fontana TF 541	I Wish I Knew/Sad Tears	6
66	Polydor NH 56110	I'll Never Know/Security.	5
68	Columbia DB 8381	My Friend The Scarecrow/Emma May Kingston	5

STEVE DARBISHIRE
65	Decca F 12261	That's The Reason Why/She's Got Quality	5
66	Decca F 12343	I Do Know/Don't Put The Phone Down	5
66	Decca F 12414	Yum Yum/Kiss Away.	5
66	Decca F 12512	Trains Trains/Alma Jones.	5
67	Decca F 12553	Holiday In Waikiki/Just A Little Lovin' Changes Things	5

JOE DARENSBOURG & HIS DIXIE FLYERS
58	Vogue V 2409	Yellow Dog Blues/Careless Love.	6
58	Vogue LAE 12149	JOE DARENSBOURG & HIS DIXIE FLYERS (LP).	15

BOBBY DARIN
78s
56	Brunswick 05561	Rock Island Line/Timber (as Bobby Darin & Jaybirds) (78)	45
58	London HLE 8666	Splish Splash/Judy Don't Be Moody (78)	25
58	London HLE 8679	Early In The Morning/Now We're One (78).	40
58	London HLE 8737	Queen Of The Hop/Lost Love (78)	40
59	London HLE 8793	Mighty Mighty Man/You're Mine (as Bobby Darin with Rinky Dinks) (78)	45
59	London HLE 8815	Plain Jane/While I'm Gone (78)	45
59	London HLE 8867	Dream Lover/Bullmoose (78)	30
59	London HLK 8939	Mack The Knife/Was There A Call For Me (78).	30
60	London HLK 9034	La Mer (Beyond The Sea)/That's The Way Love Is (78)	30
60	London HLK 9086	Clementine/Down With Love (78).	40
60	London HLK 9142	Bill Bailey Won't You Please Come Home/Tall Story (78)	50

SINGLES
56	Brunswick 05561	Rock Island Line/Timber (as Bobby Darin & Jaybirds)	130
58	London HLE 8666	Splish Splash/Judy Don't Be Moody.	30
58	London HLE 8679	Early In The Morning/Now We're One (as Rinky-Dinks featuring Bobby Darin)	40
58	London HLE 8737	Queen Of The Hop/Lost Love	25
58	London HL 7060	Queen Of The Hop/Lost Love (export issue).	15
59	London HLE 8793	Mighty Mighty Man/You're Mine (as Bobby Darin with Rinky Dinks)	30
59	London HLE 8815	Plain Jane/While I'm Gone.	25
59	London HL 7078	Plain Jane/Dream Lover (export issue)	20
59	London HLE 8867	Dream Lover/Bullmoose	5
59	London HLK 8939	Mack The Knife/Was There A Call For Me	6
60	London HLK 9034	La Mer (Beyond The Sea)/That's The Way Love Is.	5

(The above 45s were originally issued with triangular centres, later round centre pressings are worth around two-thirds these values.)

60	London HLK 9086	Clementine/Down With Love	6
60	London HLK 9142	Bill Bailey Won't You Please Come Home/Tall Story.	6
60	Brunswick 05831	Hear Them Bells/The Greatest Builder	12
60	London HLK 9197	Beachcomber/Autumn Blues (credited to 'Bobby Darin At The Piano').	7
60	Lonson HLK 9215	Somebody To Love/I'll Be There	6
61	London HLK 9303	Lazy River/Oo-Ee-Train	6
61	London HLK 9375	Nature Boy/Look For My True Love	6
61	London HLK 9407	Theme From "Come September"/Walk Bach To Me (with Orchestra).	10
61	London HLK 9429	You Must Have Been A Beautiful Baby/Sorrow Tomorrow	6
61	London HLK 9474	Multiplication (From "Come September")/Irresistible You	5
62	London HLK 9540	What'd I Say/Ain't That Love	5
62	London HLK 9575	Things/Jailer Bring Me Water.	5
62	Capitol CL 15272	If A Man Answers/A True, True Love	5
62	London HLK 9624	Baby Face/You Know How.	5
63	London HLK 9663	I've Found A New Baby/Keep A-Walkin'	7
63	Capitol CL 15286	You're The Reason I'm Living/Now You're Gone	6
63	Capitol CL 15306	Eighteen Yellow Roses/Not For Me	7
63	Capitol CL 15328	Be Mad Little Girl/Since You've Been Gone	8
64	Capitol CL 15338	I Wonder Who's Kissing Her Now/As Long As I'm Singing	6
64	Atlantic AT 4002	Milord/Golden Earrings	7
64	Capitol CL 15360	The Things In This House/Wait By The Water	6
65	Capitol CL 15401	When I Get Home/Lonely Road	6
65	Capitol CL 15414	Gyp The Cat/That Funny Feeling	6
65	Atlantic AT 4046	We Didn't Ask To Be Brought Here/Funny What Love Can Do	7

Bobby DARIN

66	Atlantic 584 014	Mame/Walking In The Shadow Of Love	6
66	Atlantic 584 051	If I Were A Carpenter/Rainin'	5
67	Atlantic 584 063	The Girl That Stood Beside Me/Reason To Believe	6
67	Atlantic 584 079	Lovin' You/Amy	6
67	Atlantic 584 105	The Lady Came From Baltimore/I Am	6
67	Atlantic 584 147	At The Crossroads/She Knows	5
68	Bell BLL 1040	Change/Long Line Rider	5
69	Bell BLL 1090	Sugar-Man/Jive	5
70	Major Minor MM 697	Maybe We Can Get It Together/RX-Pyro (Prescription: Fire) (as Bob Darin)	5
72	Atlantic K 10238	Splish Splash/Clementine/Dream Lover/Mack The Knife (p/s)	5
74	Mowest MW 3014	Blue Monday/Moritat: Mack The Knife	6

EPs

59	London REE 1173	BOBBY DARIN (EP)	50
59	London REE 1225	BOBBY DARIN NO. 2 (EP)	40
60	London REK 1243	THAT'S ALL (EP)	25
61	London REK 1286	FOR TEENAGERS ONLY (EP)	30
61	London REK 1290	UP A LAZY RIVER (EP)	20
61	London REK 1310	TWO OF A KIND (EP, with Johnny Mercer)	25
61	London REK 1321	THE 25TH DAY OF DECEMBER (EP)	35
61	London REK 1334	LOVE SWINGS (EP)	22
62	London REK 1338	TWIST WITH BOBBY DARIN (EP)	20
62	London REK 1342	THINGS! (EP)	20
65	Atlantic AET 6013	MILORD (EP)	20

LPs

58	London HA-E 2140	BOBBY DARIN (LP)	75
59	London HA-E 2172	THAT'S ALL (LP)	30
59	London HA-K 2235	THIS IS DARIN (LP, also stereo SAH-K 6067)	25/30
60	London HA-K 2291	DARIN AT THE COPA (LP, also stereo SAH-K 6103)	25/30
60	London HA-K 2311	FOR TEENAGERS ONLY (LP)	40
61	London HA-K 2363	TWO OF A KIND (LP, with Johnny Mercer; also stereo SAH-K 6164)	25/35
61	London HA-K 2372	THE BOBBY DARIN STORY (LP)	30
61	London HA-K 2394	LOVE SWINGS (LP, also stereo SAH-K 6194)	25/35
62	London HA-K 2456	DARIN SINGS RAY CHARLES (LP, also stereo SAH-K 6243)	25/35
62	Capitol T 1791	OH! LOOK AT ME NOW (LP)	20
62	Capitol W 8030	THINGS AND OTHER THINGS (LP)	25
63	London HA-K/SH-K 8102	IT'S YOU OR NO-ONE (LP, mono/stereo)	25/35
63	Capitol T 1826	EARTHY (LP)	25
63	Capitol T 1866	YOU'RE THE REASON I'M LIVING (LP)	25
63	Capitol (S)T 1942	EIGHTEEN YELLOW ROSES & 11 OTHER HITS (LP, mono/stereo)	25/30
64	Capitol (S)T 2007	GOLDEN FOLK HITS (LP, mono/stereo)	30/35
65	Capitol T 2194	FROM HELLO DOLLY TO GOODBYE CHARLIE (LP)	18
65	Atlantic ATL 5014	BOBBY DARIN WINNERS (LP)	30
65	Capitol T 2322	I WANNA BE AROUND (LP)	30
66	Capitol T 2571	THE BEST OF BOBBY DARIN (LP)	20
66	Atlantic 587/588 014	SINGS THE SHADOW OF YOUR SMILE (LP)	20
66	Atlantic 587/588 020	IN A BROADWAY BAG (MAME) (LP)	18
66	Atlantic 587/588 051	IF I WERE A CARPENTER (LP)	18
67	Atlantic 587 065	THE BOBBY DARIN STORY (LP)	18
67	Atlantic 587 073	SOMETHING SPECIAL (LP)	50
67	Atlantic 587 076	INSIDE OUT (LP)	18
67	Atlantic 587 089	SINGS DR. DOOLITTLE (LP)	15
69	Bell MBLL/SBLL 112	BORN WALDEN ROBERT CASSOTTO (LP)	15
69	Bell SBLL 128	COMMITMENT (LP)	18
	(see also Rinky Dinks)		

DARK

72	SIS 0102	DARK ROUND THE EDGES (LP, private pressing, 12 copies with colour gatefold sleeve & booklet)	1,800
72	SIS 0102	DARK ROUND THE EDGES (LP, private pressing, 8 copies with black & white gatefold sleeve)	1,300
72	SIS 0102	DARK ROUND THE EDGES (LP, private pressing, 40 copies with single black & white sleeve)	1,000
90	Swank	DARK ROUND THE EDGES (LP, reissue, U.K. pressing marketed in U.S.)	50
91	Swank/Darkside 001	DARK ROUND THE EDGES (LP, as above, with different insert, 225 only)	30
92	Kissing Spell KSCD 9204	DARK ROUND THE EDGES (CD, with 8-page booklet, 1,500 only)	20
95	Acme AC 8009LP	ARTEFACTS FROM THE BLACK MUSEUM (LP, 500 only, with insert)	15

DARK

81	Fresh FRESH 2	My Friends/John Wayne (p/s)	5
81	Fresh FRESH 13	Hawaii Five O/Don't Look Now (p/s)	5
81	Fresh FRESH 24	Einstein's Brain/Shattered Glass (p/s)	6
81	Fresh FRESH 35	In The Wires/Shattered Glass (p/s)	5
82	Fresh FRESH 46	The Masque/War Zone (p/s)	5
82	Fresh FRESH LP 9	CHEMICAL WARFARE (LP, with inner sleeve)	12
82	Fall Out FALL LIVE 005	THE LIVING END (mini-LP)	15

DARKER SHADE OF BLACK

71	Jackpot JP 758	War/JEFF BARNES: People's Version	6

DARKSIDE

90	Situation 2 SITU 29P	ALL THAT NOISE (LP, picture disc)	12
91	Acid Ray DARK 2	PSYCHEDELIZE SUBURBIA (LP, mail-order only, with poster)	12
93	Situation 2 SITU 34P	MELOMANIA (LP, picture disc, die-cut sleeve)	12
	(see also Spacemen 3)		

DARK STAR

81	Avatar AAA 105	Lady Of Mars/Rock 'N' Romancin' (company sleeve)	10
81	private pressing	Lady Of Mars/Rock 'N' Romancin' (12")	75
81	Avatar AALP 5003	DARK STAR (LP, some with patch)	22/18

DARLETTES
70	President PT 317	Lost/Sweet Kind Of Loneliness	8

DARLING BUDS
87	Darling Buds DAR 1	If I Said/Just To Be Seen (p/s, some with insert, 2,000 only)	15/10
88	Bonk On 001	Spin/BUBBLEGUM SPLASH track (flexidisc free with *So Naive* fanzine)	10/6
88	Native NTV 33L	It's All Up To You/Think Of Me/Spin (numbered gatefold p/s)	5
89	Flexi FLX 448	Valentine (live)/That's The Reason (live) (fan club flexidisc)	7
90	Native NTV 54	Shame On You/Valentine//It's All Up To You/Spin//Think Of Me/ That's The Reason (triple-pack in envelope sleeve)	6

BILL DARNEL
55	London HLU 8204	My Little Mother/Bring Me A Bluebird (with Frank Weir & His Orchestra)	35
55	London HLU 8204	My Little Mother/Bring Me A Bluebird (with Frank Weir & His Orchestra) (78)	8
56	London HLU 8234	The Last Frontier/Rock-A-Boogie Baby	40
56	London HLU 8234	The Last Frontier/Rock-A-Boogie Baby (78)	12
56	London HLU 8267	Guilty Lips/Ain't Misbehavin'.	30
56	London HLU 8267	Guilty Lips/Ain't Misbehavin' (78)	7
56	London HLU 8292	Tell Me More/Satin Doll	30
56	London HLU 8292	Tell Me More/Satin Doll (78)	7

(see also Frank Weir & His Orchestra)

GLENN DARRELL
54	London HL 8023	Write And Tell Me Why/Don't Let Me Down (78)	7

GUY DARRELL (& MIDNIGHTERS)
63	Oriole CB 1932	Go Home Girl/You Won't Come Home (as Guy Darrell & Midnighters)	10
64	Oriole CB 1964	Sorry/Sweet Dreams (as Guy Darrell & Midnighters)	10
65	CBS 201806	Stupidity/One Of These Days.	7
66	CBS 202033	Somewhere They Can't Find Me/It Takes A Lot To Laugh	7
66	CBS 202082	I've Been Hurt/Blessed	15
66	CBS 202296	Big Louie/My Way Of Thinking.	6
67	CBS 202510	Hard Lovin'/I've Never Had A Love Like That	6
67	CBS 202642	Crystal Ball/Didn't I	6
67	Piccadilly 7N 35406	Evil Woman/What You Do About That	18
67	Pye 7N 17435	Cupid/What's Happened To Our Love	6
68	Pye 7N 17586	Skyline Pigeon/Everything	6
69	Page One POF 120	Turn To Me/What's Her Name.	5
69	Page One POF 141	Birds Of A Feather/Keep The Rain From My Door	5
69	Page One POF 155	How Are You/Turtle Turquoise And The Hare (as Guy Darrell Syndicate).	5
73	Santa Ponsa PNS 4	I've Been Hurt/Blessed (reissue).	5
72	CBS 53364	GUY DARRELL (LP).	20

JOHNNY DARRELL
69	United Artists UP 35012	Why You Been Gone So Long?/You're Always The One	4

JAMES DARREN
59	Pye International 7N 25019	Gidget/There's No Such Thing (as Jimmy Darren)	12
59	Pye International N 25019	Gidget/There's No Such Thing (as Jimmy Darren) (78).	10
59	Pye International 7N 25034	Angel Face/I Don't Wanna Lose You (as Jimmy Darren).	10
59	Pye International N 25034	Angel Face/I Don't Wanna Lose You (as Jimmy Darren) (78)	15
60	Pye International 7N 25059	Because They're Young/Let There Be Love	6
61	Pye International 7N 25116	Goodbye Cruel World/Valerie	6
62	Pye International 7N 25125	Her Royal Majesty/If I Could Only Tell You.	6
62	Pye International 7N 25138	Conscience/Dream Big	6
62	Pye International 7N 25155	Mary's Little Lamb/The Life Of The Party	6
62	Pye International 7N 25168	Too Young To Go Steady/Hail To The Conquering Hero	6
63	Pye International 7N 25170	Pin A Medal On Joey/I'll Be Loving You	6
63	Colpix PX 708	Backstage/Gegetta.	5
65	Warner Bros WB 5648	Because You're Mine/Millions Of Roses	6
66	Warner Bros WB 5689	Tom Hawk/I Want To Be Lonely	6
67	Warner Bros WB 5874	All/Misty Morning Eyes	6
59	Pye Intl. NEP 44004	P.S. I LOVE YOU (EP)	15
62	Pye Intl. NEP 44008	JAMES DARREN HIT PARADE (EP).	18
63	Pye Intl. NPL 28021	LOVE AMONG THE YOUNG (LP)	25

JEANNIE DARREN & SECOND CITY SOUND
69	Major Minor MM 611	River Deep, Mountain High/Julie	4

JENNY DARREN
73	Decca F 13452	Be My Baby/How Soon Hello Becomes Goodbye	4

MAXINE DARREN
65	Pye 7N 15796	How Can I Hide It From My Heart/Don't You Know	10

CHRIS DARROW
73	United Artists UAG 29453	CHRIS DARROW (LP).	18
74	United Artists UAG 29634	UNDER MY OWN DISGUISE (LP).	18

(see also Kaleidoscope)

DARTELLS
63	London HLD 9719	Dartell Stomp/Hot Pastrami	12

BARRY DARVELL
60	London HL 9191	Geronimo Stomp/How Will It End?	70

DARWIN'S THEORY
67	Major Minor MM 503	Daytime/Hosanna	40

NITAE DASGUPTA
72	Mushroom 100 MR 22	SONGS OF INDIA (LP)	40

DAS PSYCH-OH RANGERS

| 86 | ZTT ZTAS 24 | Homage To The Blessed/The Essential Art Of Communication/He He Radical/Medeq Terrorists (p/s) | 5 |
| 86 | ZTT 12 ZTAS 24 | The Essential Art Of Communication (Extra Extra)/Homage To The Blessed/He He Radical (Episode 2)/Medeq Terrorists (Living) (12", p/s) | 7 |

DAS SCHNITZ
| 79 | Ellie Jay EJSP 9249 | 4 AM (EP) | 200 |

DATE WITH SOUL
| 67 | Stateside SS 2062 | Yes Sir, That's My Baby/PRISCILLA: He Noticed Me | 30 |

(see also Jack Nitzsche, Brian Wilson, Sonny & Cher, Darlene Love/Blossoms, Jackie De Shannon, Paris Sisters)

DAUGHTERS OF ALBION
| 69 | Fontana STL 5486 | DAUGHTERS OF ALBION (LP) | 15 |

CLAUDE DAUPHIN
| 59 | Top Rank JAR 195 | From The French/JOE PARADISE TRIO: From The French | 5 |

DAVE DAVANI & D MEN
| 63 | Columbia DB 7125 | Don't Fool Around/She's The Best For Me | 10 |
| 64 | Decca F 11896 | Midnight Special/Sho' Know A Lot About Love | 12 |

DAVE DAVANI (FOUR)
65	Parlophone R 5329	Top Of The Pops/Workin' Out	12
66	Parlophone R 5490	Tossin' And Turnin'/Jupe	25
66	Parlophone R 5525	One Track Mind/On The Cooler Side	15
72	Philips 6006 195	King Kong Blues/Come Back Baby (solo)	8
65	Parlophone PMC 1258	FUSED (LP)	40

DAVE & DIAMONDS
| 65 | Columbia DB 7692 | I Walk The Lonely Night/You Do Love (some in p/s) | 35/10 |

(see also Dave Russell)

DAVE & DON
| 67 | Polydor 56212 | What A Feeling/That's My Way | 5 |

BOB DAVENPORT (& RAKES)
60	Collector JEB 4	GEORDIE SONGS (EP)	15
62	Topic TOP 83	WOR GEORDIE (EP, with Rakes)	15
66	Columbia SX 1786	BOB DAVENPORT AND THE RAKES (LP, with Rakes)	20
71	Leader LER 3008	BOB DAVENPORT (LP)	12
75	Topic 12TS 274	DOWN THE LONG ROAD (LP, originally with blue label)	15/12
77	Topic 12TS 318	POSTCARDS HOME (LP)	12
77	Topic 12TS 350	BOB DAVENPORT AND THE RAKES 1977 (LP, with Rakes)	12

ALAN DAVEY
| 87 | Hawkfan HWFB 3/4 | THE ELF EP (double pack, 2 x 7" with insert in wraparound p/s in poly bag) | 10 |

(see also Hawkwind)

(Shaun) DAVEY & (James) MORRIS
| 73 | York FYK 417 | DAVEY AND MORRIS (LP, with insert) | 100 |

(see also Strawbs)

DAVID
| 69 | Philips BF 1776 | Please Mister Postman/Light Of Your Mind | 40 |
| 70 | Fontana TF 1081 | I'm Going Back/Selppin | 5 |

ALAN DAVID
64	Decca F 11956	I Want So Much To Know You/I Can't Go Wrong	5
65	Decca F 12130	Crazy 'Bout My Baby/A Thousand Years Too Late	5
67	Polydor BM 56201	Flower Power/Completely Free	5
65	Decca LK 4674	ALAN DAVID (LP)	15

ANNE MARIE DAVID
| 73 | Epic EPC 1446 | Wonderful Dream/Tu Te Reconnaitres | 5 |
| 79 | Chrysalis CHS 2327 | Je Suis L'Enfant Soleil/Just Like Loving You (p/s) | 5 |

DAVID & EMBERS
| 63 | Decca F 11717 | What Is This/Teddy Bear Special | 6 |

(see also Embers)

DAVID & GIANTS
| 77 | Capitol CL 15915 | Ten Miles High/Super Love | 6 |

DAVID & JONATHAN
65	Columbia DB 7717	Laughing Fit To Cry/Remember What You Said	6
66	Columbia DB 7800	Michelle/How Bitter The Taste Of Love	6
66	Columbia DB 7873	Speak Her Name/Take It While You Can	6
66	Columbia DB 7950	Lovers Of The World Unite/Oh My Word	5
66	Columbia DB 8035	Ten Storeys High/Looking For My Life	7
66	Columbia DB 8167	Gilly Gilly Ossenfeffer Katzenellenbogen By The Sea/Scarlet Ribbons For Her Hair	6
67	Columbia DB 8208	She's Leaving Home/One Born Every Minute	5
67	Columbia DB 8287	Softly Whispering I Love You/Such A Peaceful Day	5
68	Columbia DB 8428	You Ought To Meet My Baby/I've Got That Girl On My Mind	5
67	Columbia S(C)X 6031	DAVID AND JONATHAN (LP)	18

(see also Roger Cook, Edison Lighthouse, White Plains)

DAVID & ROZAA
| 70 | Philips 6006 040 | Time Of Our Life/We Can Reach An Understanding | 12 |
| 71 | Philips 6006 094 | The Spark That Lights The Flame/Two Can Share | 12 |

(see also David Essex)

DIANNE DAVIDSON
72	Janus 6146 019	Sympathy/All I Wanted	6
72	Janus 6146 021	Ain't Gonna Be Treated This Way/All I Wanted (All The Time)	5
72	Janus 6310 209	BACKWOODS WOMAN (LP)	12

FRANKIE DAVIDSON & HI MARKS
61	Starlite ST45 5037	You're Driving Me Crazy/I Care For You (B-side with Unicords)	18
61	London HL 9309	Detour/Just For Today	7
68	Decca F 22780	Hector The Trash Collector/Somebody Come And Take My Wife	5

TOMMY DAVIDSON
56	London HLU 8219	Half Past Kissing Time/I Don't Know Yet But I'm Learning	75
56	London HLU 8219	Half Past Kissing Time/I Don't Know Yet But I'm Learning (78)	18

HUTCH DAVIE
58	London HLE 8667	At The Woodchopper's Ball/Honky Tonk Train Blues (& His Honky Tonkers)	12
58	London HLE 8667	At The Woodchopper's Ball/Honky Tonk Train Blues (78)	10
60	London HLE 9076	Sweet Georgia Brown/Heartaches	8
62	Pye International 7N 25149	But I Do/Time Was (& Orchestra)	5
60	London HA-E 2216	MUCH HUTCH (LP)	18

ALUN DAVIES
65	Parlophone R 5384	Girls Were Made To Love And Kiss/Rose Marie	6
68	Mercury MF 1043	One Day Soon/Pretend You Don't See Her	5
72	CBS 65108	DAYDO (LP)	15
	(see also Cat Stevens)		

BOB DAVIES
63	London HLU 9767	Rock'N'Roll Show/With You Tonight	25

CYRIL DAVIES (R&B ALLSTARS)
63	Pye International 7N 25194	Country Line Special/Chicago Calling	25
63	Pye International 7N 25221	Preachin' The Blues/Sweet Mary	25
69	7N 17663	Country Line Special/Sweet Mary	15
64	Pye Intl. NEP 44025	THE SOUND OF CYRIL DAVIES (EP)	60
57	'77' LP 2	THE LEGENDARY CYRIL DAVIES (10" LP, 99 only, with Alexis Korner)	300
70	Folklore F-LEAT 9	THE LEGENDARY CYRIL DAVIES (LP, reissue, with 4 extra tracks)	75
	(see also Alexis Korner, Beryl Bryden)		

DAVE DAVIES
67	Pye 7N 17356	Death Of A Clown/Love Me Till The Sun Shines	6
67	Pye 7N 17429	Susannah's Still Alive/Funny Face	8
68	Pye 7N 17514	Lincoln County/There's No Life Without Love	15
69	Pye 7N 17678	Hold My Hand/Creeping Jean	15
68	Pye NEP 24289	DAVE DAVIES HITS (EP)	225
	(see also Kinks)		

FREDDY DAVIES
67	Major Minor MM 536	Sentimental Songs/Cynthia Crisp	4

IRVING DAVIES & METHOD MEN
62	Decca F 11456	The Method/ABC The Method	6

JACKIE DAVIES & HIS QUARTET
57	Pye Nixa N 15115	Land Of Make Believe/Over The Rainbow (78)	70
	(see also Chico Arnez)		

MARION DAVIES
69	Columbia DB 8589	Walk Out Of My Mind/This Is My Lonely Life	5
	(see also Ladybirds)		

MIAR DAVIES
64	Decca F 11805	Ten Good Reasons/I Won't Remember You	7
64	Decca F 11894	I Hear You Knocking/Navy Blue	7

NICOLA DAVIES
68	SNB 55-3627	Infatuation/My Boy	4

RAY DAVIES & BUTTON DOWN BRASS
68	Philips 6308 065	16 STARTRACKS (LP)	12
70	Fontana 6309 010	THIS IS THE BUTTON DOWN BRASS (LP)	12
72	Pye QUAD 1004	WHY CAN'T WE ALL GET TOGETHER (LP, quadrophonic)	12
73	Pye NSPL 41021	I BELIEVE IN MUSIC (LP)	20
74	Philips 6382 103	THEMES FROM THE EXORCIST AND OTHER GREAT FILMS (LP)	15
75	Philips 6382 111	FLASHPOINT (LP)	18
76	DJM DJSLP 22046	FUNK IN HELL (LP)	25

RAY DAVIES
86	Virgin VS 865-12	Quiet Life/Voices In The Dark/GIL EVANS: Va Va Voom (12", p/s)	8
	(see also Kinks)		

RON DAVIES
70	A&M AMLS 933	SILENT SONG THROUGH THE LAND (LP)	10

RUPERT DAVIES
63	Parlophone R 5067	October Dreams/Smoking My Pipe (La Pipa)	7

BARRINGTON DAVIS
72	Montague MONS 2	TRACKS OF MIND (LP, with lyric insert)	40

BETTE DAVIS & DEBBIE BURTON
63	London HLU 9711	Whatever Happened To Baby Jane?/I've Written A Letter To Daddy	8
76	EMI EMA 778	MISS BETTE DAVIS (LP)	20

MINT VALUE £

BETTY DAVIS
75	Island USA 2011	Shut Off The Light/He Was A Big Freak.	5
75	Island ILPS 9329	NASTY GIRL (LP)	20

BILLIE DAVIS
63	Decca F 11572	Tell Him/I'm Thankful	6
63	Decca F 11658	He's The One/V.I.P.	7
63	Columbia DB 7115	Bedtime Stories/You And I.	10
64	Columbia DB 7195	That Boy John/Say Nothin' Don't Tell	7
64	Columbia DB 7246	School Is Over/Give Me Love	7
64	Columbia DB 7346	Whatcha Gonna Do/Everybody Knows (as Billie Davis & Le Roys)	7
65	Piccadilly 7N 35227	Last One To Be Loved/You Don't Know.	6
65	Piccadilly 7N 35266	No Other Baby/Hands Off	7
66	Piccadilly 7N 35308	Heart And Soul/Don't Take All Night	10
66	Piccadilly 7N 35350	Just Walk In My Shoes/Ev'ry Day	15
67	Decca F 12620	Wasn't It You?/Until It's Time For You To Go	7
67	Decca F 12696	Angel Of The Morning/Darling Be Home Soon	6
68	Decca F 12823	I Want You To Be My Baby/Suffer.	6
69	Decca F 12870	I'll Come Home/Make The Feeling Go Away	6
69	Decca F 12923	I Can Remember/Nobody's Home To Go Home To	12
69	Decca F 12977	Nights In White Satin/It's Over.	5
70	Decca F 13049	Venid Con Migo/Love (Spanish export issue)	7
70	Decca F 13085	There Must Be A Reason/Love	5
72	Regal Zonophone RZ 3050	I Tried/Touch My Love	5
78	Magnet MAG 124	Run Joey Run/East Come Easy Go.	5
70	Decca LK/SKL 5029	BILLIE DAVIS (LP, mono/stereo)	30/25

(see also Keith & Billie, Le Roys, Mike Sarne)

BLIND GARY DAVIS/REVEREND GARY DAVIS
63	'77' LA 12-14	PURE RELIGION AND BAD COMPANY (LP)	25
60s	Fontana 688 303 ZL	HARLEM STREET SINGER (LP).	18
64	XTRA XTRA 1009	REV. GARY DAVIS/SHORT STUFF MACON (LP, 1 side each).	15
66	Xtra XTRA 5014	SAY NO TO THE DEVIL (LP).	25
60s	Xtra XTRA 5042	A LITTLE MORE FAITH (LP).	25
69	Fontana SFJL 914	BRING YOUR MONEY HONEY (LP)	18
71	Transatlantic TRA 244	RAGTIME GUITAR (LP).	12
72	Transatlantic TRA 249	CHILDREN OF ZION (LP)	15
74	Kicking Mule SNKD 1	LO I BE WITH YOU ALWAYS (2-LP)	15

BLIND JOHNNY DAVIS
52	MGM MGM 463	Your Love Belongs To Me/Magic Carpet	15

BOBBY DAVIS (U.S.)
61	Starlite ST45 056	I Was Wrong/Hype You Into Selling Your Head	30

BOBBY DAVIS (Jamaica)
71	Banana BA 344	Return Your Love/RILEY'S ALLSTARS: Version	7

(see also Barbara Dunkley)

BONNIE DAVIS
55	Brunswick 05507	Pepper-Hot Baby/For Always, Darling	40
55	Brunswick 05507	Pepper-Hot Baby/For Always, Darling (78)	8

CLIFFORD DAVIS
69	Reprise RS 27003	Before The Beginning/Man Of The World.	10
70	Reprise RS 27008	Come On Down And Follow Me/Homework	7
70s	Reprise K 14282	Before The Beginning/Man Of The World (reissue)	7

DANNY DAVIS (U.K.)
60	Parlophone R 4657	Love Me/You're My Only Girl	6
60	Parlophone R 4796	Talking In My Sleep/Lullaby Of Love	6
61	Pye 7N 15391	Tell All The World/Rumours	6
62	Pye 7N 15427	Rome Wasn't Built In A Day/Tell Me	8
62	Pye 7N 15470	Patches/September In The Rain.	6

(see also Marauders)

DANNY DAVIS ORCHESTRA (U.S.)
58	London HL 8766	Trumpet Cha-Cha-Cha/Lonesome Trumpet	5
58	London HL 8766	Trumpet Cha-Cha-Cha/Lonesome Trumpet (78)	6
65	MGM MGM 1277	Main Theme From "The Saint"/Little Bandits Of Juarez	10
64	London HAR 8204	THEY'RE PLAYING OUR SONG (LP, with Ruby & Romantics)	25

(see also Ruby & Romantics, Byron Lee)

EDDIE ('LOCKJAW') DAVIS
56	Parlophone GEP 8587	EDDIE 'LOCKJAW' DAVIS TRIO (EP)	8
57	Parlophone GEP 8678	LOCKJAW (EP).	8
58	Parlophone GEP 8685	EDDIE 'LOCKJAW' DAVIS TRIO (EP)	8
59	Esquire EP 217	EDDIE 'LOCKJAW' DAVIS (EP).	10
61	Esquire EP 237	EDDIE 'LOCKJAW' DAVIS QUARTET (EP)	10
60	Esquire 32-104	THE EDDIE 'LOCKJAW' DAVIS COOK BOOK (LP)	18
60	Esquire 32-117	VERY SAXY (LP, with Coleman Hawkins, Arnett Cobb & Bobby Tate)	18
61	Esquire 32-128	JAWS IN ORBIT (LP)	18
64	Stateside SL 10102	THE FIRST SET — LIVE AT MINTONS (LP, with Johnny Griffin)	15

(see also Coleman Hawkins, Johnny Griffin)

EDWARD H. DAVIS
74	Sain SAIN 1016M	HEN FFORDD GYMREIG O FYW (LP)	20
76	Sain SAIN 1053M	SNEB YN BECSO DAM (LP).	15

JESSE (ED) DAVIS

71	Atlantic 2091 076	Every Night Is Saturday Night/Washita Love Child (as Jesse Davis)	6
71	Atco 2400 106	JESSE 'ED' DAVIS (LP)	15
72	Atlantic K 40329	ULULU (LP)	15
73	CBS 65649	KEEP ON COMING (LP)	12

KIM DAVIS

66	Decca F 12387	Don't Take Your Lovin' Away/Feelin' Blue	15
67	CBS 202568	Tell It Like It Is/Losing Kind	8
68	CBS 3260	Until It's Time For You To Go/I Hold No Grudge	5
69	CBS 4210	Are You Ready For Love/Taste Of Excitement	5

(see also Kim D, Kim & Kinetics)

LARRY DAVIS/FENTON ROBINSON

72	Python PLP 24	LARRY DAVIS AND FENTON ROBINSON (LP, 99 copies only)	40

MAXWELL DAVIS

66	Ember FA 2040	BATMAN THEME AND OTHER BAT SONGS (LP)	35

MAXWELL STREET JIMMY DAVIS

66	Bounty BY 6009	MAXWELL STREET JIMMY DAVIS (LP)	25

MELVIN DAVIS

69	Action ACT 4531	Save It/This Love Was Meant To Be	12

MILES DAVIS

SINGLES

50	Capitol CL 13249	Budo/Move (78)	6
50	Capitol CL 13255	Boplicity/Israel (78)	6
50	Capitol CL 13429	Venus De Milo/Darn That Dream (78)	6
60	Philips JAZ 100	Budo/Tadd's Delight (p/s)	
70	CBS 5104	Miles Runs The Voodoo Down/Spanish Key	5

EPs

54	Capitol EAP1 459	MILES DAVIS ORCHESTRA (EP)	8
54	Capitol EAP2 459	MILES DAVIS ORCHESTRA (EP)	8
55	Vogue EPV 1075	MILES DAVIS SEXTET (EP)	8
57	Vogue EPV 1191	MILES DAVIS (EP)	8
57	Esquire EP 12	MILES DAVIS QUARTET (EP)	8
58	Esquire EP 132	MILES DAVIS QUARTET (EP)	8
58	Esquire EP 152	MILES DAVIS (EP)	8
58	Esquire EP 172	MILES DAVIS QUARTET (EP)	8
59	Philips BBE 12266	MILES DAVIS (EP)	8
59	Esquire EP 212	MILES DAVIS NEW QUARTET (EP)	8
59	Esquire EP 222	MILES THEME (EP)	8
59	Fontana TFE 17119	MILES DAVIS (EP)	8
59	Fontana TFE 17195	MORE MILES (EP)	8
59	Fontana TFE 17197	STRAIGHT NO CHASER (EP)	8
60	Fontana TFE 17223	MILES DAVIS NO. 2 (EP)	8
60	Fontana TFE 17225	MILES DAVIS NO. 3 (EP)	8
60	Fontana TFE 17247	PORGY AND BESS (EP)	8
60	Esquire EP 232	BLUE MILES (EP)	8
60	Philips BBE 12351	MILES DAVIS (EP)	8
61	Philips BBE 12418	DAVIS CUP (EP)	8
61	Esquire EP 242	BLUE CHANGES (EP, with Milt Jackson)	8
61	Fontana TFE 17359	MILES DAVIS QT. (EP, with Cannonball Adderley/John Coltrane Group)	8

LPs

55	Esquire 20-041	MILES DAVIS QUINTET (10" LP)	25
53	Esquire 20-017	MILES DAVIS PLAYS (10" LP)	25
53	Esquire 20-021	MILES DAVIS ALL STARS (10" LP)	25
54	Esquire 20-052	MILES DAVIS ALL STARS (A HIFI MODERN JAZZ JAM SESSION) (10" LP)	25
54	Vogue LDE 064	MILES DAVIS AND HIS ORCHESTRA (10" LP)	25
54	Esquire 20-056	MILES DAVIS ALL STARS (A SECOND HIFI MODERN JAZZ JAM SESSION) (10" LP)	25
54	Capitol LC 6683	CLASSICS IN JAZZ (10" LP)	25
55	Esquire 20-062	MILES DAVIS ALL STARS SEXTET (10" LP)	25
55	Esquire 20-072	MILES DAVIS QUINTET (10" LP)	25
56	Philips BBL 7140	'ROUND ABOUT MIDNIGHT (LP)	18
57	Fontana TFL 5007	MILES AHEAD (LP)	20
58	Fontana TFL 5035	MILESTONES (LP)	20
58	Esquire 32-068	RELAXIN' WITH THE MILES DAVIS QUARTET (LP)	25
59	Fontana TFL 5056	PORGY AND BESS (LP)	20
59	Esquire 32-012	THE MUSINGS OF MILES (LP)	25
60	Fontana TFL 5081	JAZZ TRACK — "L'ANSCENSEUR POUR L'ECHAFAUD" (LP)	20
60	Fontana TFL 5089	THE "MOST" OF MILES (LP)	15
60	Fontana STFL 513	A KIND OF BLUE (LP)	20
60	Esquire 32-098	WALKIN' (LP)	18
60	Esquire 32-100	MILES DAVIS AND THE MODERN JAZZ GIANTS VOL. 2 (LP)	18
60	Esquire 32-108	WORKIN' WITH THE MILES DAVIS QUINTET (LP)	18
61	Font. TFL 5100/STFL 531	SKETCHES OF SPAIN (LP)	18
61	Esquire 32-118	EARLY MILES (LP)	20
61	Esquire 32-138	STEAMIN' WITH THE MILES DAVIS QUINTET (LP)	18
61	Fontana TFL 5163	FRIDAY NIGHT AT THE BLACKHAWK, SAN FRANCISCO (VOL. 1) (with Cannonball Adderley & John Coltrane; also stereo STFL 580)	18
61	Fontana TFL 5164	SATURDAY NIGHT AT THE BLACKHAWK, SAN FRANCISCO (VOL. 2) (with Cannonball Adderley & John Coltrane; also stereo STFL 581)	18
62	Fontana TFL 5172	SOMEDAY MY PRINCE WILL COME (LP, also stereo STFL 587)	18
62	CBS (S)BPG 62081	AT THE CARNEGIE HALL, MAY 19TH 1961 (LP)	15
64	CBS (S)BPG 62170	SEVEN STEPS TO HEAVEN (LP)	15

Miles DAVIS

64	CBS (S)BPG 62327	SKETCHES OF SPAIN (LP, reissue)	12
64	CBS (S)BPG 62213	QUIET NIGHTS (LP)	15
64	CBS (S)BPG 62306	FRIDAY NIGHT AT THE BLACKHAWK (LP, reissue)	12
64	CBS (S)BPG 62307	SATURDAY NIGHT AT THE BLACKHAWK (LP, reissue)	12
64	Vocalion LAEF 584	BLUE MOODS (LP)	15
64	CBS (S)BPG 62389	MILES AND MONK AT NEWPORT LP, with Thelonious Monk)	15
64	CBS (S)BPG 62390	DAVIS IN EUROPE (LP)	15
65	Stateside SL 10111	MILES DAVIS AND JOHN COLTRANE PLAY RICHARD ROGERS (LP, with John Coltrane)	12
65	Pacific Jazz 688 204 ZL	DAVIS AND COLTRANE PLAY RICHARD RODGERS (LP, with John Coltrane)	15
65	CBS (S)BPG 62510	MY FUNNY VALENTINE (LP)	12
66	CBS (S)BPG 62066	A KIND OF BLUE (LP, reissue)	12
66	CBS (S)BPG 62104	SOMEDAY MY PRINCE WILL COME (LP, reissue)	12
66	CBS (S)BPG 62108	PORGY AND BESS (LP, reissue)	12
66	CBS (S)BPG 62577	E.S.P. (LP)	12
66	Stateside SL 10168	MILES DAVIS PLAYS FOR LOVERS (LP)	10
66	Capitol T 1974	THE BIRTH OF THE COOL (LP)	12
66	CBS (S)BPG 62655	"FOUR" AND MORE (LP)	12
66	CBS (S)BPG 62496	MILES AHEAD (LP, reissue)	12
67	CBS (S)BPG 62933	MILES SMILES (LP, as Miles Davis Quintet)	12
67	Transatlantic PR 7150	MODERN JAZZ GIANTS (LP)	12
67	CBS (S)BPG 62308	MILESTONES (LP, reissue)	12
68	CBS (S)BPG 63097	THE SORCERER (LP)	12
68	Transatlantic PR 7322	DAVIS AND COLTRANE PLAY RICHARD RODGERS (LP, reissue)	12
66	CBS 62323	'ROUND ABOUT MIDNIGHT (LP, reissue)	12
66	CBS 62390	MILES AT ANTIBES (LP)	12
67	CBS 62637	FACETS (LP)	12
67	CBS 62976	MILES IN BERLIN (LP)	12
68	CBS 63248	NEFERTITI (LP)	12
68	CBS 63352	MILES IN THE SKY (LP)	12
68	CBS 63417	MILES AT NEWPORT (LP)	12
69	CBS 63551	FILLES DE KILIMANJARO (LP)	12
69	CBS 63620	GREATEST HITS (LP)	12
70	CBS 63630	IN A SILENT WAY (LP)	12
70	CBS 66236	BITCHES BREW (2-LP)	15
71	CBS 66257	MILES DAVIS AT FILLMORE (2-LP)	15
72	CBS 64575	LIVE-EVIL (2-LP)	15
72	Prestige PR 24001	MILES DAVIS (2-LP)	15
72	Prestige PR 24012	TALLEST TREES (2-LP)	15
73	CBS CQ 30997/Q 66236	BITCHES BREW (2-LP, quadrophonic)	20
73	CBS GQ 30954/Q 67219	LIVE-EVIL (2-LP, quadrophonic)	20
74	Prestige PR 24034	WORKIN' & STEAMIN' (2-LP)	15
70s	Xtra XTRA 5004	EZZ THETIC (LP)	12

MILES DAVIS/ART BLAKEY

66	Fontana FJL 135	L'ASCENSEUR POUR L'ECHAFAUD/LA FEMME DISPARAISSANTE (LP, soundtrack, 1 side each)	45

(see also Art Blakey, Thelonius Monk, Dizzy Gillespie, Milt Jackson, Cannonball Adderley, Charlie Parker)

MILES DAVIS & JOHN COLTRANE
(see under Miles Davis, John Coltrane)

SAMMY DAVIS (Jnr.)

50	Capitol CL 13269	The Way You Look Tonight/Can't You See I've Got The Blues (78)	7
54	Brunswick 05326	Because Of You (Parts 1 & 2)	8
55	Brunswick 05383	The Birth Of The Blues/Love (Your Magic Spell Is Everywhere)	10
55	Brunswick 05389	Six Bridges To Cross/Glad To Be Unhappy	8
55	Brunswick 05409	And This Is My Beloved/The Red Grapes	7
55	Brunswick 05428	Love Me Or Leave Me/Something's Gotta Give	15
55	Brunswick 05450	That Old Black Magic/Give A Fool A Chance	12
55	Brunswick 05469	Hey There/My Funny Valentine	12
55	Brunswick 05478	Backtrack/It's Bigger Than You And Me	6
56	Brunswick 05518	In A Persian Market/The Man With The Golden Arm	8
56	Capitol CL 14562	Azure/Dedicated To You	6
56	Brunswick 05583	Adelaide/I'll Know	6
56	Brunswick 05594	Earthbound/Five	6
56	Brunswick 05611	Frankie And Johnny/Circus	6
56	Brunswick 05617	You're Sensational/Don't Let Her Go	6
56	Brunswick 05629	All Of You/Just One Of Those Things	12
57	Brunswick 05637	The Golden Key/All About Love	6
57	Brunswick 05647	Dangerous/The World Is Mine Tonight	6
57	Brunswick 05668	Too Close For Comfort/Jacques D'Iraque	6
57	Brunswick 05694	Goodbye, So Long, I'm Gone/French Fried Potatoes And Ketchup	6
57	Brunswick 05717	Mad Ball/The Nearness Of You	6
57	Brunswick 05724	Long Before I Knew You/Never Like This	6
58	Brunswick 05732	I'm Comin' Home/Hallelujah, I Love Her	6
58	Brunswick 05763	Song And Dance Man/I Ain't Gonna Change (The Way I Am) (78)	7
59	Brunswick 05778	That's Anna/I Never Got Out Of Paris (78)	10
60	Brunswick 05830	Happy To Make Your Acquaintance/Baby, It's Cold Outside (with Carmen McRae)	6
64	Reprise R 20227	The Shelter Of Your Arms/Falling In Love With You	6
64	Reprise R 20289	Not For Me/Bang Bang	8
69	MCA MK 5016	Rhythm Of Life/Pompeii Club/Rich Man's Frug	15
50	Brunswick OE 9445	BOY MEETS GIRL (EP, with Carmen McRae)	8
56	Capitol EAP1 555	SAMMY DAVIS JNR. (EP)	8

SPENCER DAVIS GROUP

56	Brunswick LAT 8088	JUST FOR LOVERS (LP)	15
56	Brunswick LAT 8153	STARRING SAMMY DAVIS (LP)	15
57	Brunswick LAT 8157	HE'S LOOKING AT YOU (LP)	12
57	Brunswick LAT 8215	SAMMY SWINGS (LP)	12
58	Brunswick LAT 8248	IT'S ALL OVER BUT THE SWINGIN' (LP)	12
59	Brunswick LAT 8296	SAMMY AT THE TOWN HALL, NEW YORK (LP, also stereo STA 3012)	12/15
59	Brunswick LAT 8308	PORGY AND BESS (LP, with Carmen McRae, also stereo STA 3017)	12/15
60	Brunswick LAT 8330	SAMMY AWARDS (LP)	12
60	Brunswick LAT 8352	I GOTTA RIGHT TO SWING (LP)	12
70	Tamla Motown STML 11160	SOMETHING FOR EVERYONE (LP)	20
77	20th Century BT 426	THE SONG AND DANCE MAN (LP)	12

(see also Dean Martin)

SILKIE DAVIS

| 70 | Torpedo TOR 2 | Conversations/TWINKLE: Peace & Tranquility | 5 |
| 70 | Torpedo TOR 12 | When I Was A Little Girl/I'm So Lonely | 5 |

SKEETER DAVIS

60	RCA Victor RCA 1201	No Never/(I Can't Help You) I'm Falling Too	8
61	RCA Victor RCA 1222	My Last Date With You/Someone I'd Like To Forget	6
63	RCA Victor RCA 1328	The End Of The World/Somebody Loves You	6
63	RCA Victor RCA 1345	I'm Saving My Love/Somebody Else On Your Mind	5
63	RCA Victor RCA 1363	I Can't Stay Mad At You/It Was Only My Heart	6
64	RCA Victor RCA 1384	He Says The Same Things To Me/How Much	5
64	RCA Victor RCA 1398	Now You're Gone/Gonna Get Along Without You Now	5
65	RCA Victor RCA 1474	Sun Glasses/He Loved Me Too Little	6
64	RCA Victor RCX 7153	SILVER THREADS AND GOLDEN NEEDLES (EP)	15
63	RCA Victor RD/SF 7563	THE END OF THE WORLD (LP, mono/stereo)	20/25
63	RCA Victor RD/SF 7604	CLOUDY, WITH OCCASIONAL TEARS (LP, mono/stereo)	18/22
64	RCA Camden CDN 5119	I FORGOT MORE THAN YOU'LL EVER KNOW (LP)	12
64	RCA Victor RD 7676	LET ME GET CLOSE TO YOU (LP)	18
69	RCA Victor SF 8068	MARY FRANCES (LP)	15

SKEETER DAVIS & BOBBY BARE

| 65 | RCA RD 7711 | TUNES FOR TWO (LP) | 18 |

(see also Bobby Bare)

SMILEY DAVIS

| 53 | London L 1189 | Big Mamou/Play Girl (78, actually by Smiley Lewis) | 100 |

SPENCER DAVIS (GROUP)

64	Fontana TF 471	Dimples/Sittin' And Thinkin'	20
64	Fontana TF 499	I Can't Stand It/Midnight Train	12
65	Fontana TF 530	Every Little Bit Hurts/It Hurts Me So	10
65	Fontana TF 571	Strong Love/This Hammer	10
65	Fontana TF 632	Keep On Running/High Time Baby	6
66	Fontana TF 679	Somebody Help Me/Stevie's Blues	6
66	Fontana TF 739	When I Come Home/Trampoline	6
66	Fontana TF 762	Gimme Some Loving/Blues In F	6
67	Fontana TF 785	I'm A Man/I Can't Get Enough Of It	10
67	Fontana TF 854	Time Seller/Don't Want You No More	8
67	United Artists UP 1203	Mr. Second Class/Sanity Inspector	6
68	United Artists UP 2213	After Tea/Moonshine	6
68	United Artists UP 2226	Short Change/Picture Of Heaven	6
73	Vertigo 6059 087	Livin' In A Back Street/Sure Need A Helping Hand	5

Spencer DAVIS (GROUP)

91	Island 12 IS 487	Keep On Running/Somebody Help Me/High Baby/This Hammer (12", p/s)	7
65	Fontana TE 17444	YOU PUT THE HURT ON ME (EP)	25
65	Fontana TE 17450	EVERY LITTLE BIT HURTS (EP)	15
66	Fontana TE 17463	SITTIN' AND THINKIN' (EP)	25
78	Island IEP 10	THE SPENCER DAVIS GROUP (EP)	5
65	Fontana TL 5242	THEIR FIRST LP (LP)	30
66	Fontana TL 5295	THE SECOND ALBUM (LP)	35
66	Fontana TL 5359	AUTUMN '66 (LP)	30
67	Fontana TL 5443	THE BEST OF THE SPENCER DAVIS GROUP (LP, unissued)	
67	United Artists (S)ULP 1186	HERE WE GO ROUND THE MULBERRY BUSH (LP, soundtrack, with Traffic, mono/stereo)	35/30
68	United Artists (S)ULP 1192	WITH THEIR NEW FACE ON (LP, mono/stereo)	30/25
68	Wing WL 1165	EVERY LITTLE BIT HURTS (LP, reissue of "Their First LP")	15
68	Island ILP 970/ILPS 9070	THE BEST OF THE SPENCER DAVIS GROUP FEATURING STEVIE WINWOOD (LP, plain pink label, flipback sleeve; sleeve lists "Please Do Something" but plays "Together Till The End Of Time"; mono/stereo)	20/15
69	CBS 63842	LETTERS FROM EDITH (LP, unissued, 50 white label test pressings only)	200+
71	United Artists UAS 29177	IT'S BEEN SO LONG (LP, solo with Peter Jameson, 'envelope' cover)	12
72	United Artists UAS 29361	MOUSETRAP (LP, solo)	12
73	Vertigo 6360 088	GLUGGO (LP, gatefold sleeve)	12
74	Vertigo 6360 105	LIVIN' IN A BACK STREET (LP)	12
88	Island ILPS/CID 9919	STEVIE WINWOOD: THE SPENCER DAVIS GROUP YEARS (LP & CD, unissued)	

(see also Stevie Winwood, Traffic, Anglos, Blind Faith, Ray Fenwick, Pete York, Hardin & York, Murgatroyd Band, Mirage, Portobello Explosion, Shotgun Express)

STEVE DAVIS

68	Fontana TF 922	Takes Time To Know Her/She Said Yeah	40

TYRONE DAVIS

68	Stateside SS 2092	What If A Man/Bet You Win	12
69	Atlantic 584 253	Can I Change My Mind/A Woman Needs To Be Loved	10
69	Atlantic 584 265	Is It Something You've Got?/Undying Love	10
69	Atlantic 584 288	All The Waiting Is Not In Vain/Need Your Lovin' Everyday	10
70	Atlantic 2091 003	Turn Back The Hands Of Time/I Keep Coming Back	10
71	Atlantic 2091 078	Could I Forget You/Just My Way Of Loving You	10
71	Atlantic 2091 131	One Way Ticket/We Got A Love	10
72	Atlantic K 10207	Can I Change My Mind/Turn Back The Hands Of Time/One Way Ticket	8
73	Brunswick BR 4	Without You In My Life/How Could I Forget You	10
73	Brunswick BR 6	There It Is/You Wouldn't Believe	10
74	Brunswick BR 10	I Wish It Was Me/You Don't Have To Beg To Stay	10
76	Brunswick BR 31	Turning Point/Don't Let It Be Too Late	10
77	Brunswick BR 40	Ever Lovin' Girl/Forever	10
70	Atlantic 588 209	CAN I CHANGE MY MIND (LP)	20
71	Atlantic 2465 021	TURN BACK THE HANDS OF TIME (LP)	15
73	Brunswick BRLS 3002	I HAD IT ALL THE TIME (LP)	15
73	Brunswick BRLS 3005	GREATEST HITS (LP)	15

WALTER DAVIS

64	RCA RCX 7169	R.C.A. VICTOR RACE SERIES VOL. 3 (EP)	15
70	RCA Intl. INTS 1085	THINK YOU NEED A SHOT (LP)	18

WARREN DAVIS MONDAY BAND

67	Columbia DB 8190	Wait For Me/I Don't Wanna Hurt You	15
67	Columbia DB 8270	Love Is A Hurtin' Thing/Without Fear	10

(see also Boardwalkers)

DAVIS SISTERS

53	HMV B 10582	Rock-A-Bye Boogie/I Forgot More Than You'll Ever Know (78)	25

BRIAN DAVISON

70	Charisma CAS 1021	BRIAN DAVISON'S EVERY WHICH WAY (LP, pink label)	12

(see also Habits, Nice, Every Which Way)

WILD BILL DAVISON

55	Melodisc MLP 501	WILD BILL DAVISON (LP)	15

TIM DAWE

69	Straight ST(S) 1058	PENROD (LP)	20

CARL DAWKINS

67	Rio R 136	All Of A Sudden/Running Shoes	12
67	Rio R 137	Baby I Love You/Hard Time	12
68	Blue Cat BS 114	I Love The Way You Are/DERMOTT LYNCH: I Can't Stand It	12
68	Duke DU 3	I'll Make It Up/J.J. ALL STARS: One Dollar Of Music	8
69	Nu Beat NB 030	Rodney's History/DYNAMITES: Tribute To Drumbage	8
70	Duke DU 93	Get Together/FAMILY MAN: Instalment Plan	8
70	Duke DU 95	This Land/J.J. ALL STARS: Land Version	8
70	Trojan TR 7765	Satisfaction/Things A Get Bad To Worse	6
71	Big Shot BI 570	Perseverence/J.J. ALL STARS: Perseverance (Version)	12
71	Explosion EX 2051	I Feel Good/J.J. ALL STARS: I Feel Good Version Two	5
71	Explosion EX 2059	Make It Great/STONE: What A Day	5
71	New Beat NB 086	Walk A Little Prouder/YOUTH PROFESSIONALS: Walk (Version)	5
72	Duke DU 133	My Whole World/Men A Broken Heart	5

(see also Rass Dawkins, Untouchables, Winston Wright, Ansell Collins, Roland Alphonso, West Indians)

HORRELL DAWKINS

66	Ska Beat JB 240	Cling To Me/Butterfly	15

JIMMY DAWKINS

73	Mojo 2027 011	The Things I Used To Do/Put It On The Hawg	6
71	Delmark DS 623	FAST FINGERS (LP)	15
78	Sonet SNTF 758	TRANSATLANTIC 770 (LP)	12

RASS DAWKINS & WAILERS
71	Upsetter US 368	Picture On The Wall/UPSETTERS: Picture Version	25

(see also Bob Marley/Wailers, Carl Dawkins)

JULIE DAWN
53	Columbia SCM 5035	Wild Horses/A Whistling Kettle And A Dancing Cat	12

(see also Tony Brent & Julie Dawn, Cyril Stapleton)

DAWN & DEEJAYS
65	RCA RCA 1470	These Are The Things About You/I Will Think Of You	6

DAWNBREAKERS
65	Decca F 12110	Let's Live/Lovin' For You	6

DAWN CHORUS
69	MCA MK 5004	A Night To Be Remembered/Crying All Night	5

(see also Carter-Lewis)

DAWN OF THE REPLICANTS
97	dumb/SULK trigg-er DST 71	SO FAR SO SPITFIRE EP (no p/s, 1,000 only, hand-stencilled label)	5
97	East West SAM 3152	Skullcrusher (p/s, 1-sided 10" promo, credited to "Let's Get The Replicants")	8

DAWN TRADER
80	AFE 1980	NO ONE GONNA BETTER ME (EP, private pressing)	100

DAWNWATCHER
80	Dawnwatcher DWS 001	Spellbound (no p/s)	150
82	Dawnwatcher DWS 002	Backlash (p/s)	30

DAWNWIND
76	Amron ARN 5003	LOOKING BACK ON THE FUTURE (LP, private pressing)	125

DONNA DAWSON
73	Trojan TR 7892	You Can't Buy Me Love/First Cut Is The Deepest	5

LES DAWSON SYNDICATE
62	Melodisc MEL 1586	Last Chicken In The Shop/Oh Yeah	8

(see also Johnny Stevens, Owne Gray)

LESLEY DAWSON
66	Mercury MF 924	Pastel Shades Of Love/The Time Has Come	5
67	Mercury MF 946	Just Say Goodbye/Just A Passing Phase	6
67	Mercury MF 965	Run For Shelter/I'll Climb On A Rainbow	12

DANIELLE DAX
85	Awesome AOR 3	Bad Miss 'M'/Yummer Yummer Man (p/s)	5
83	Initial IRC 009	POP-EYES (LP, with 'Meat Harvest' cover & lyric sheet)	35

(see also Lemon Kittens)

DAY
94	Detour DR 019	Another Country/Gospel (p/s, 1,000 only, 100 on green vinyl)	8/5

BING DAY
59	Mercury AMT 1047	I Can't Help It/Mama's Place	70

BOBBY DAY (& SATELLITES)
57	HMV POP 425	Little Bitty Pretty One/When The Swallows Come Back To Capistrano (as Bobby Day & Satellites)	165
57	HMV POP 425	Little Bitty Pretty One/When The Swallows Come Back To Capistrano (78)	45
58	London HL 8726	Rockin' Robin/Over And Over	18
58	London HL 8726	Rockin' Robin/Over And Over (78)	35
59	London HL 8800	The Bluebird, The Buzzard And The Oriole/Alone Too Long	35
59	London HL 8800	The Bluebird, The Buzzard And The Oriole/Alone Too Long (78)	50
59	London HL 8964	Love Is A One Time Affair/Ain't Gonna Cry No More	18
59	London HL 8964	Love Is A One Time Affair/Ain't Gonna Cry No More (78)	70
60	London HLY 9044	My Blue Heaven/I Don't Want To	18
61	Top Rank JAR 538	Over And Over/Gee Whiz	12
65	Sue WI 388	Rockin' Robin/Over And Over (reissue)	18

DORIS DAY
78s
50	Columbia DB 2629	Canadian Capers (Cuttin' Capers)/The Seine (78)	7
50	Columbia DB 2643	It's Better To Conceal Than Reveal (with Dinah Shore)/I'll Never Slip Around Again (78)	7
50	Columbia DB 2652	It's A Great Feeling/At The Cafe Rendezvous (78)	7
50	Columbia DB 2656	Quicksilver/There's A Bluebird On Your Windowsill (78)	7
50	Columbia DB 2663	You're My Thrill/Blame My Absent-Minded Heart (78)	7
50	Columbia DB 2689	I Said My Pyjamas/Enjoy Yourself (78)	7
50	Columbia DB 2690	I Don't Wanna Be Kissed By Anyone But You/Festival Of Roses (78)	7
50	Columbia DB 2727	You Go To My Head/I Didn't Slip, I Wasn't Pushed, I Fell (78)	7
50	Columbia DB 2750	Crazy Rhythm/Orange Coloured Sky (78)	7
50	Columbia DB 2769	I Only Have Eyes For You/The Comb And Paper Polka (78)	7
50	Columbia DB 2770	Christmas Story/Silver Bells (78)	7
51	Columbia DB 2815	Tea For Two/I Want To Be Happy (78)	7
52	Columbia DB 3123	Sugarbush (with Frankie Laine)/How It Lies, How It Lies, How It Lies! (78)	7
52	Columbia DB 3157	My Love And Devotion/When I Fall In Love (78)	7
59	Philips PB 910	Love Me In The Daytime/He's So Married (78)	8
59	Philips PB 923	Be Prepared/It Happened To Jane (78)	10
59	Philips PB 949	The Tunnel Of Love/Run Away, Skidaddle, Skidoo (78)	12
59	Philips PB 958	Possess Me/Roly Poly (78)	12

Doris DAY

SINGLES

53	Columbia SCM 5038	April In Paris/Your Mother And Mine (with Four Lads)	15
53	Columbia SCM 5039	That's What Makes Paris Paree/I Know A Place	12
53	Columbia SCM 5044	A Bushel And A Peck/If I Were A Bell	18
53	Columbia SCM 5045	The Second Star To The Right (with Four Lads)/	
		I'm Gonna Ring The Bell Tonight	12
53	Columbia SCM 5059	The Cherries/Papa, Won't You Dance With Me?	12
53	Columbia SCM 5062	Mister Tap-Toe/Why Should We Both Be Lonely?	12
53	Columbia SCM 5067	We Kiss In A Shadow/Something Wonderful	12
53	Columbia SCM 5075	That's The Way He Does It/Cuddle Up A Little Closer	15
54	Columbia SCM 5087	A Load Of Hay/It Had To Be You	15
55	Columbia SCM 5171	Just One Of Those Things/Sometimes I'm Happy	15
57	Philips JK 1020	Twelve O'Clock Tonight/Today Will Be Yesterday Tomorrow! (jukebox issue)	15
57	Philips JK 1031	The Party's Over/Rickety-Rackety Rendezvous (jukebox issue)	15
58	Philips PB 799	A Very Precious Love/Teacher's Pet	5
58	Philips PB 843	Everybody Loves A Lover/Instant Love	5
58	Philips PB 863	Love In A Home/Blues In The Night	5
59	Philips PB 910	Love Me In The Daytime/He's So Married	5
59	Philips PB 923	Be Prepared/It Happened To Jane	5
59	Philips PB 949	The Tunnel Of Love/Run Away, Skidaddle, Skidoo	5
59	Philips PB 958	Possess Me/Roly Poly	5
64	CBS AAG 183	Move Over Darling/Twinkle Lullaby	5
64	CBS AAG 219	Oowee Baby/The Rainbow's End	10
64	CBS AAG 231	Send Me No Flowers/Love Him	5
65	CBS 201808	Catch The Bouquet/Summer Has Gone	5
65	CBS 201898	Do Not Disturb/Au Revoir Is Goodbye With A Smile	5
66	CBS 202229	Glass Bottomed Boat/Soft As The Starlight	5

EPs

54	Columbia SEG 7507	CANADIAN CAPERS (EP, company sleeve)	12
54	Columbia SEG 7515	WE KISS IN A SHADOW (EP, company sleeve)	12
54	Columbia SEG 7531	NOBODY'S SWEETHEART (EP, company sleeve)	12
54	Columbia SEG 7546	SOMETIMES I'M HAPPY (EP, company sleeve)	12
55	Columbia SEG 7572	VOCAL GEMS FROM THE FILM "YOUNG MAN OF MUSIC" (EP)	12
55	Philips BBE 12007	DORIS DAY (EP)	15
55	Philips BBE 12011	I'LL NEVER STOP LOVING YOU (EP)	15
56	Philips BBE 12089	DORIS DAY NO. 2 (EP)	15
57	Philips BBE 12151	DAY DREAMS (EP)	15
58	Philips BBE 12167	DORIS (EP)	15
58	Philips BBE 12187	THE SONG IS YOU (EP)	15
58	Philips BBE 12213	DREAM A LITTLE DREAM OF ME (EP)	15
59	Philips BBE 12298	LET'S FLY AWAY (EP, also stereo SBBE 9006)	15/18
59	Philips BBE 12339	PILLOW TALK (EP)	12
60	Philips BBE 12388	YOU CAN'T HAVE EVERYTHING (EP, also stereo SBBE 9021)	15/18
61	Philips SBBE 9034	SHOW TIME NO. 1 (EP, stereo)	15
62	CBS AGG 20009	I HAVE DREAMED (EP)	12
62	CBS AGG 20018	DUET (EP, with André Previn Trio)	10
63	CBS AGG 20029	DUET NO. 2 (EP, with André Previn Trio)	10
64	CBS AGG 20048	MOVE OVER DARLING (EP)	10

LPs

54	Columbia 33S 1038	LULLABY OF BROADWAY (10" LP, 2 different sleeve designs)	each 30
54	Philips BBR 8026	THE VOICE OF YOUR CHOICE (10" LP)	20
55	Philips BBR 8040	YOUNG AT HEART (10" LP, with Frank Sinatra)	25
55	Philips BBL 7047	LOVE ME OR LEAVE ME (LP)	30
56	Philips BBR 8094	DORIS DAY FAVOURITES (10" LP)	20
56	Philips BBR 8104	CALAMITY JANE (10" LP, with Howard Keel)	20
57	Philips BBL 7120	DAY DREAMS (LP)	25
57	Philips BBL 7137	DORIS AND FRANK (LP, 6 tracks each by Doris Day & Frank Sinatra)	25
57	Philips BBL 7142	DAY BY DAY (LP)	30
58	Philips BBL 7175	DAY IN HOLLYWOOD (LP)	22
58	Philips BBL 7197	THE PYJAMA GAME (LP with other artists, 5 tracks by Doris Day)	15
58	Philips BBL 7211	DAY BY NIGHT (LP)	30
58	Philips BBL 7247	HOORAY FOR HOLLYWOOD VOL. 1 (LP)	25
58	Philips BBL 7248	HOORAY FOR HOLLYWOOD VOL. 2 (LP)	20
59	Philips BBL 7296	CUTTIN' CAPERS (LP, also stereo SBBL 540)	18/22
59	Philips BBL 7297	SHOWCASE OF HITS (LP)	15
59	Philips SBBL 519	HOORAY FOR HOLLYWOOD (LP, stereo reissue)	22
59	Philips SBBL 548	DAY BY NIGHT (LP, stereo reissue)	22
60	Philips BBL 7377	WHAT EVERY GIRL SHOULD KNOW (LP, also stereo SBBL 563)	15/18
60	Philips SBBL 537	IN THE STILL OF THE NIGHT (LP)	20
60	Philips BBL 7392	SHOW TIME (LP, also stereo SBBL 577)	15/18
61	Philips BBL 7471	BRIGHT AND SHINY (LP, also stereo SBBL 619)	25/30
61	Philips BBL 7496	I HAVE DREAMED (LP, also stereo SBBL 643)	25/30
62	CBS (S)BPG 62053	BRIGHT AND SHINY (LP, reissue, mono/stereo)	12/15
62	CBS (S)BPG 62057	I HAVE DREAMED (LP, reissue, mono/stereo)	12/15
62	CBS (S)BPG 62010	DUET (LP, with André Previn Trio, mono/stereo)	14/16
63	CBS (S)BPG 62101	YOU'LL NEVER WALK ALONE (LP, mono/stereo)	25/30
63	CBS (S)BPG 62129	ANNIE GET YOUR GUN (LP, with Robert Goulet, mono/stereo)	14/16
64	CBS (S)BPG 62226	LOVE HIM (LP, mono/stereo)	25/30
65	CBS (S)BPG 62419	GREATEST HITS (LP)	12
65	CBS (S)BPG 62461	WITH A SMILE AND A SONG (LP)	25
65	CBS (S)BPG 62502	LATIN FOR LOVERS (LP)	18
66	CBS (S)BPG 62562	SENTIMENTAL JOURNEY (LP)	15
66	CBS BPG 62785	SINGS HER GREAT MOVIE HITS (LP)	15
66	CBS (S)BPG 62712	THE DORIS DAY CHRISTMAS ALBUM (LP)	15
66	CBS BPG 63032	SINGS SONGS FROM "CALAMITY JANE" & "THE PYJAMA GAME" (LP, with Howard Keel)	12

(see also Four Lads, Frank Sinatra, Frankie Laine, Howard Keel)

DORIS DAY & JOHNNIE RAY
53   Columbia SCM 5033   Ma Says, Pa Says/A Full Time Job. 18
(see also Johnnie Ray)

JACKIE DAY
67   Sue WI 4040   Before It's Too Late/Without A Love 90

JILL DAY
55   Parlophone MSP 6169   Sincerely/Chee-Chee-Oo Chee (Sang The Little Bird). 12
55   Parlophone MSP 6177   Promises/Whistlin' Willie 10
56   HMV 7M 362   I Hear You Knocking/Far Away From Everybody. 15
56   HMV 7M 391   A Tear Fell/Holiday Affair 10
56   HMV POP 254   Happiness Street (Corner Sunshine Square)/Somewhere In The Great Beyond . . . 7
57   HMV POP 288   I Dreamed/Give Her My Love When You See Her 7
57   HMV POP 320   Mangos/Cinco Robles (Five Oaks) 8

KENNY DAY
60   Top Rank JAR 339   Teenage Sonata/My Love Doesn't Love Me At All (some with p/s). 8/5
61   Top Rank JAR 400   Why Don't We Do This More Often/The Sheik Of Morocco
                             (some with p/s) 8/5

MURIEL DAY
69   CBS 4115   The Wages Of Love/Thinking Of You. 8
69   Page One POF 151   Optimistic Fool/Nine Times Out Of Ten 20
84   Soul Stop SS 3001   Nine Times Out Of Ten/JIMBO: Do The Skunk. 5

TANYA DAY & NU-NOTES
64   Polydor NH 52331   His Lips Get In The Way/I Get So Lonely. 6

TERRY DAY
62   CBS AAG 104   That's All I Want/I Waited Too Long 8
(see also Rip-Chords, Rogues)

DAY BROTHERS
60   Oriole CB 1575   Angel/Just One More Kiss. 10

JOHNNY DAYE
69   Stax STAX 111   Stay Baby Stay/I Love Love 5

DAYLIGHT
71   RCA RCA 2106   Lady Of St. Clare/Wednesday People 7
71   RCA SF 8194   DAYLIGHT (LP). 35
(see also Daddy Longlegs)

DAYLIGHTERS
64   Sue WI 343   Oh Mom! (Teach Me How To Uncle Willie)/Hard-Headed Girl 25

DAY OF THE PHOENIX
70   Greenwich GLSPR 1002   WIDE OPEN N-WAY (LP) 25
72   Chapter One CNSR 812   THE NEIGHBOUR'S SON (LP) 35

DAYSHIFT
79   WOT WOT 1   Living In The UK/Cedric Wazza, Superstar/Yeah Oh Yeah Oh!
                             (die-cut stamped p/s) 6

DAYTRIPPERS
71   Trojan TR 7839   The Birds And The Bees/My Family. 4

DAYTON
83   Capitol 12 CL 318   The Sound Of Music/Eyes On You/Love You Anyway (12", p/s) 8
83   Capitol EST 712 2971   FEEL THE MUSIC (LP) 20

DAZZLING ALL NIGHT ROCK SHOW
73   Magnet MAG 4   20 Fantastic Bands/Version. 5

DBX
93   Peacefrog PF 015   ALIEN EP (12", plain sleeve) 10
94   Peacefrog PF 022   Losing Control/Beat Phreak/Live Wire/Spock's Brain
                             (12", plain sleeve). 20
95   Peacefrog PR 025   LOSING CONTROL REMIXES (12", plain sleeve) 12

D.C. 10's
80   Certain Euphoria ACE 451 Bermuda/I Can See Through Walls 8

BOBBY DEACON
60   Pye 7N 15270   Fool Was I/Where's My Love 12
60   Pye 7N 15299   I Love You So/Your Kisses Are Fine 10

GEORGE DEACON & MARION ROSS
73   Xtra XTRA 1130   SWEET WILLIAM'S GHOST (LP, with lyric insert). 80

DEACON BLUE
87   CBS DEAC 1   Dignity/Riches (p/s, with cassette of "Raintown" LP excerpts
                             [XPC 4011], shrink-wrapped) 5
88   CBS CD DEAC 5   When Will You (Make My Telephone Ring) (Remix)/That Brilliant Feeling No. 2/
                             Punch And Judy Man/Disney World
                             (CD, card sleeve) 10
88   CBS CP DEAC 5   When Will You (Make My Telephone Ring)/That Brilliant Feeling No. 2/
                             Punch And Judy Man/Disney World
                             (CD, picture disc) 8
88   CBS 450 549-0   RAINTOWN (LP, with bonus LP "Riches" [XPR 1361] & sticker). 30
88   CBS XPR 1361   RICHES (LP, white embossed sleeve, available separately via fan club). 15
(see also Ricky Ross)

DEADBEATS
80   Red Rhino RED 3   Choose You/Julie's New Boyfriend (p/s) 6

MINT VALUE £

DEAD BOYS

77	Sire SRE 1004	Sonic Reducer/Down In Flames (no p/s)	12
77	Sire 6078 609	Sonic Reducer/Little Girl/Down In Flames (12", p/s)	15
78	Sire SRE 1029	Tell Me/Not Anymore/Ain't Nothin' To Do (p/s)	12
77	Sire 9103 329	YOUNG, LOUD & SNOTTY (LP)	25
78	Sire SRK 6054	WE HAVE COME FOR YOUR CHILDREN (LP)	15
87	Line LILP 400200	NIGHT OF THE LIVING DEAD BOYS (LP)	15

(see also Stiv Bators, Lords Of The New Church, Wanderers)

DEAD CAN DANCE

93	4AD DCD 1	The Host Of Seraphim/Yulunga (Spirit Dance) (CD, digipak, promo only)	15

DEAD KENNEDYS

80	Fast Products FAST 12	California Uber Alles/Man With The Dogs (p/s, moulded or paper labels)	8
81	Statik STAT EP 2	IN GOD WE TRUST (12" EP, with insert)	8
81	Cherry Red CHERRY 13	Holiday In Cambodia/Police Truck ('digger' p/s)	5
81	Cherry Red CHERRY 13	Holiday In Cambodia/Police Truck ('burning man' p/s, with lyric sheet)	6
81	Cherry CHERRY 16	Kill The Poor/In-Sight (p/s, with badge)	5
81	Cherry CHERRY 24	Too Drunk To Fuck/The Prey (p/s, with lyric sheet)	6
82	Statik STAT 24	Nazi Punks Fuck Off/Moral Majority (p/s)	5
81	Cherry Red B RED 10	FRESH FRUIT FOR ROTTING VEGETABLES (LP, with insert)	12
87	Alternative Tent. VIRUS 57	GIVE ME CONVENIENCE... (LP, with "Buzzbomb From Pasadena" flexidisc)	25

(see also East Bay Ray, Lard)

DEADLY TOYS

79	Bonhard/Hunt DT 1	Nice Weather/Roll On Doomsday/I'm Logical/Deadly Mess Around (EP, some in hand made gatefold sleeve)	50

DEAD MAN'S SHADOW

80	Hog HOG 1	Neighbours/Poxy Politics/War Ploys/Morons (p/s)	5
81	Subversive ANARCHO 1	HEATHROW TOUCHDOWN (EP, 1 side by Action Pact)	6
82	Rondelet ROUND 16	BOMB SCARE (EP)	6
82	Rondelet ROUND 27	Flower In The Gun/The Last Cowboy (p/s)	6
83	Expulsion OUT 4	Toleration Street/In My Dreams (p/s)	5
83	Criminal Damage CRI 106	Another Year/One Man's Crusade (p/s)	5
84	Criminal Damage CRILP 110	TO MOHAMMED ... A MOUNTAIN (LP)	10

DEAD OR ALIVE

80	Inevitable INEV 005	I'm Falling/Flowers (foldout p/s)	18
81	Inevitable INEV 008	Number Eleven/Name Game (live) (p/s)	10
82	Black Eyes BE 1	It's Been Hours Now/Whirlpool/Nowhere To Nowhere/It's Been Hours Now (Alternative Mix) (12", p/s)	18
82	Black Eyes BE 2	The Stranger/Some Of That (p/s)	10
83	Epic A 3399	Misty Circles/Misty Circles (Instrumental) (p/s)	12
83	Epic TA 3399	Misty Circles (Dance Mix)/Misty Circles (Dub Mix)/Selfish Side (12", p/s)	20
83	Epic A 3676	What I Want/The Stranger (Remix) (white 'floppy hat' p/s, withdrawn)	50
83	Epic A 3676	What I Want/The Stranger (black p/s)	10
83	Epic TA 3676	What I Want (Dance Mix)/The Stranger (12", p/s, some with poster)	25/12
84	Epic A 4069	I'd Do Anything/Anything (Dub) (p/s)	6
84	Epic QA 4069	I'd Do Anything/Anything (Dub)/Give It To Me (10", p/s)	18
84	Epic TA 4069	I'd Do Anything/Misty Circles/What I Want/Give It To Me (12", p/s)	20
84	Epic WA 4271	That's The Way (I Like It)/Keep That Body Strong (That's The Way) (picture disc)	10
84	Epic TA 4271	That's The Way (I Like It) (Extended Version)/Keep That Body Strong (That's The Way) (12", p/s)	15
84	Epic A 4510	What I Want (Remix)/The Stranger (p/s)	10
84	Epic A 4510	What I Want (Remix)/The Stranger (poster p/s)	20
84	Epic TA 4510	What I Want (Dance Mix)/The Stranger (12", p/s, some with poster)	18/12
84	Epic XPR 1257	MIGHTY MIX: Wish You Were Here/What I Want/Do It/Misty Circles/Absolutely Nothing/Sit On It/You Make Me Wanna/That's The Way (I Like It) (12", white label, promo only)	60
84	Epic	You Spin Me Round (Big Ben Mix) (1-sided, stickered p/s, promo only)	85
84	Epic DA 4861	You Spin Me Round (Like A Record)/Misty Circles//Mighty Mix Part 1/Part 1 (Continued) (double pack)	10
84	Epic TX 4861/TA 4510	You Spin Me Round (Like A Record) (Murder Mix)/Misty Circles (Extended Mix)//What I Want (Dance Mix)/The Stranger (12", p/s, double pack, shrinkwrapped)	40
85	Epic A 6086	Lover Come Back To Me/Far Too Hard (blue p/s, withdrawn)	150
85	Epic WA 6086	Lover Come Back To Me/Far Too Hard (fan-shaped picture disc with plinth)	15
85	Epic QTA 6086	Lover Come Back To Me (Extended Remix)/Far Too Hard (12", poster p/s)	20
85	Epic GA 6360	In Too Deep/I'd Do Anything (gatefold p/s)	5
85	Epic QTA 6360	In Too Deep (Off Yer Mong Mix)/I'd Do Anything (12" Version)/I'd Do Anything (12" Version) (12", p/s with poster)	15
85	Epic DA 6571	My Heart Goes Bang (Get Me To The Doctor)/Big Daddy Of The Rhythm (live)//Cake And Eat It (live)/In Too Deep (live) (double pack, gatefold p/s)	5
85	Epic QTA 6571	My Heart Goes Bang (American Wipeout Mix)/Big Daddy Of The Rhythm (live)/My Heart Goes Bang (Instrumental) (12", p/s)	12
86	Epic 6500 750	Brand New Lover (Up Ducky Mix)/Cake And Eat It (live)/In Too Deep (live) (12", poster p/s)	10
87	Epic BURNSG 1	Something In My House/D.J. Hit That Button (gatefold pop-up p/s)	5
87	Epic BURNSD 1/6500 757	Something In My House/D.J. Hit That Button//Brand New Lover/In Too Deep (live) (double pack, shrinkwrapped)	6
87	Epic BURNSQ 1	Something In My House (U.S. Wipe-Out Mix Pt 2)/Something In My House (House Instrumental)/DJ Hit That Button (12", p/s)	8

87	Epic XPR 1328	CLEAN AND DIRTY: Something In My House (Mortevicar Mix)/Something In My House (Naughty XXX Mix) (12", white label, plain white sleeve)	125
87	Epic BURNSG 3	I'll Save You All My Kisses/Lover Come Back To Me (gatefold p/s, with 'censored' sticker)	5
87	Epic BURNSQ 3	I'll Save You All My Kisses (The Long Wet Sloppy Kiss Mix)/Lover Come Back To Me/Whirlpool/Nowhere To Nowhere (12", p/s)	10
88	Epic BURNSP 4	Turn Around And Count 2 Ten/Something In My House (Instru-Mental) (poster p/s)	10
88	Epic BURNSQ 4	Turn Around And Count 2 Ten (I Had A Disco Dream Mix)/Something In My House (Instru-Mental)/Then There Was You/Come Inside (12", p/s)	50
88	Epic BURNSC 4	Turn Around And Count 2 Ten/Something In My House (Instru-Mental)/Turn Around And Count 2 Ten (I Love BPM Mix)/(Instru-Mental) (CD, picture disc)	35
89	Epic BURNSQ 5	Come Home With Me Baby (Deadhouse Dub 12")/Come Home With Me Baby (Deadhouse Dub 7" Edit)/Come Home With Me Baby (7" Version) (12", p/s)	8
89	Epic BURNSC 5	Come Home With Me Baby (Remix)/Come Home With Me Baby (12" Version)/(Deadhouse Dub 12") (CD)	15

(see also Nightmares In Wax, Sisters Of Mercy, Pauline Murray & Invisible Girls, International Chrysis, Mission)

DEAD SEA FRUIT

67	Camp 602 001	Kensington High Street/Put Another Record On	8
68	Camp 602 004	Love At The Hippiedrome/My Naughty Bluebell	8
67	Camp 603 001	DEAD SEA FRUIT (LP)	40

DEAD WRETCHED

82	Inferno HELL 2	NO HOPE FOR ANYONE (EP)	5
82	Inferno HELL 5	Convicted/Infiltrator (p/s)	5

DEAF SCHOOL

77	Warner Bros K 16870	Taxi/Last Night (p/s)	8
76	Warner Bros K 56280	SECOND HONEYMOON (LP, some with innersleeve)	15/12

BILL DEAL & RHONDELLS

69	MGM MGM 1466	May I/Day By Day My Love Grows Stronger	5
69	MGM MGM 1479	I've Been Hurt/I've Got My Needs	8
69	MGM MGM 1488	What Kind Of Fool Do You Think I Am/Are You Ready For This	5

DEALER

83	Windrush WR 1030	Better Things To Do (p/s)	60
86	Ebony EBON 42	FIRST STRIKE (LP)	15

ALAN DEAN

55	MGM SP 1116	The Song From "Desiree"/Tonight, My Love	5
55	MGM SP 1139	Remember Me, Wherever You Go/Love Is All That Matters	5
56	MGM SP 1173	Without You/Take A Bow	5
57	Columbia DB 3932	Rock 'n' Roll Tarantella/Life Is But A Dream	12
57	Columbia DB 3932	Rock 'n' Roll Tarantella/Life Is But A Dream (78)	6

ALAN DEAN & HIS PROBLEMS

64	Decca F 11947	The Time It Takes/Dizzy Heights	15
65	Pye 7N 15749	Thunder And Rain/As Time Goes By	50

LITTLE BILLY DEAN

67	Strike JH 325	That's Always Like You/Tic Toc	20

BOBBY DEAN

65	Parlophone R 5254	More And More/Saint James' Infirmiary	6

DEREK DEAN & FRESHMEN

66	Pye 7N 17037	So This Is Love/King Cole Yenka	5

(see also Derek & Freshmen)

ELTON DEAN

71	CBS 64539	ELTON DEAN (LP)	40
77	Ogun OG 610	THE CHEQUE IS IN THE MAIL (LP, with Joe Gallivan & Kenny Wheeler)	15

(see also Bluesology, Soft Machine, Centipede, Ninesense, Julie Tippetts, Hugh Hopper, Mike Hugg, Reg King, Keith Tippett)

EMIL DEAN

68	Island WIP 6033	This Is Our Anniversary/Lonely Boy	5

(see also Nirvana [UK])

JIMMY DEAN

57	Philips PB 747	Deep Blue Sea/Love Me So I'll Know (78)	7
58	Philips PB 813	Makin' My Mind Up/Starlight Starbright (78)	7
59	Philips PB 940	Weekend Blues/Sing Along	8
59	Philips PB 940	Weekend Blues/Sing Along (78)	10
60	Philips PB 984	There's Still Time, Brother/Thanks For The Dream	6
61	Philips PB 1187	Big Bad John/I Won't Go Hunting With You Jake	5
61	Philips PB 1210	To A Sleeping Beauty/The Cajun Queen	5
62	Philips PB 1223	Smoke Smoke (Smoke) That Cigarette/Dear Ivan	7
62	CBS AAG 107	Steel Men/Little Bitty Big John	5
62	CBS AAG 122	Little Black Book/Please Pass The Biscuits	6
61	Philips BBE 12501	JIMMY DEAN (EP)	15
66	CBS EP 6075	THE BEST OF JIMMY DEAN (EP)	12
63	CBS	PORTRAIT OF JIMMY DEAN (LP)	15
65	Fontana FJL 303	GOLDEN FAVOURITES (LP)	12

MINT VALUE £

NORA DEAN

69	Upsetter US 322	The Same Thing You Gave To Daddy/	
		UPSETTER PILGRIMS: A Testimony	8
70	Trojan TR 7735	Barbwire/BARONS: Calypso Mama	6
71	Randy's RAN 508	Want Man/RANDY'S ALL STARS: Man	7
71	High Note HS 050	I Must Get A Man/The Valet	7
71	Bullet BU 472	Peace Begins Within/SLICKERS: Go Back Home	6
71	Gas GAS 165	Greedy Boy/KEITH: Please Stay	
		(B-side actually by Slim Smith)	6
72	Big Shot BI 611	Night Food Reggae/PROPHETS: Jaco.	5
73	Bread BR 1117	Mama/Man A Walk And Talk	5

(see also Hugh Roy)

PAUL DEAN (& SOUL SAVAGES)

64	Polydor NH 59102	She Can Build A Mountain/A Day Gone By (probably unreleased)	
65	Decca F 12136	You Don't Own Me/Hole In The Head (as Paul Dean & Thoughts)	15
66	Reaction 591 002	She Can Build A Mountain/A Day Gone By (as Paul Dean & Soul Savages)	10

(see also Paul Nicholas, Oscar, Ivor Bird, Thoughts)

PAULA DEAN & NYAH SHUFFLE

70	Joe's JRS 2	Since I Met You Baby/Jug Head	7

ROGER DEAN'S LYSIS

77	Mosaic GCM 762	LYSIS LIVE (LP)	12
77	Mosaic GCM 774	CYCLE (LP)	12

TERRI DEAN

59	Top Rank JAR 141	I'm Confessin' (That I Love You)/I Blew Out The Flame.	7
59	Top Rank JAR 141	I'm Confessin' (That I Love You)/I Blew Out The Flame (78)	12
59	Top Rank JAR 179	Adonis/You Treat Me Like A Boy	6
59	Top Rank JAR 179	Adonis/You Treat Me Like A Boy (78)	12

DEAN & JEAN

64	Stateside SS 249	Tra La La La Suzy/I Love The Summertime	15
64	Stateside SS 283	Hey Jean Hey Dean/Please Don't Tell Me How	12
64	Stateside SS 313	Thread Your Needle/I Wanna Be Loved	15

(see also Brenda Lee Jones)

DEAN & MARK

64	Hickory 45-1227	With Tears In My Eyes/Kissin' Games	8
64	Hickory 45-1249	When I Stop Dreaming/There Oughta Be A Law	8
65	Hickory 45-1294	Just A Step Away/Fallen Star	8

(see also Newbeats, Larry Henley)

JASON DEANE

66	King KG 1049	Make Believe/Don't Ever Want To See You No More	20
67	King KG 1060	Down In The Street/Ain't Got No Love	30

(see also Jason Dene)

PETER DE ANGELIS ORCHESTRA & CHORUS

58	London HL 8743	The Happy Mandolin/Holiday In Naples	6
58	London HL 8743	The Happy Mandolin/Holiday In Naples (78)	8

DEANO

65	Columbia DB 7728	Just A Child In This World/Little Miss With-It	5
66	Columbia DB 7898	Starlight, Starbright/I'm So Happy	6
66	Columbia DB 7965	Please Don't Talk To The Lifeguard/When You Wish Upon A Star	5
67	Columbia DB 8233	What's The Matter With The Matador?/Baby, Let Me Be Your Baby	6
65	Columbia SEG 8470	DEANO (EP)	12

BLOSSOM DEARIE

66	Fontana TF 719	I'm Hip/Wallflower Lonely, Cornflower Blue	6
67	Fontana TF 788	Sweet Georgie Fame/One Note Samba	15
67	Fontana TF 886	Once I Loved/Sunny.	5
68	Fontana TF 986	Hey John/59th Street Bridge Song	5
67	Fontana TL 5399	SWEET BLOSSOM DEARIE (LP)	45
67	Fontana TL 5352	BLOSSOM TIME AT RONNIE'S (LP)	70
67	Fontana STL 5454	SOON IT'S GONNA RAIN (LP)	45
70	Fontana 6309 015	THAT'S THE WAY I WANT IT TO BE (LP)	60

DEARLY BELOVED

66	CBS 202398	Peep Peep Pop Pop/It Is Better	10

DEAR MR. TIME

70	Square SQ 3	Prayer For Her/Light Up A Light	10
71	Square SQA 101	GRANDFATHER (LP)	70

DEATH ADDICT

83	Stench STN 1	Killing Time/Dead And Buried (p/s)	12

DEATH CULT

83	Situation 2 SIT 29	God's Zoo/God's Zoo (These Times) (p/s)	5

(see also Southern Death Cult, Cult)

DEATH IN JUNE

84	New European SA 29634	Heaven Street/We Drive East/In The Night Time (12", 2,000 with brown/gold embossed/textured sleeve, later 2,000 with blue/white sleeve)	80/60
84	New European SA 30634	State Laughter/Holy Water (p/s)	60
84	New European BADVC 6	She Said Destroy/The Calling (p/s)	35
84	New European 12BADVC 6	The Calling/She Said Destroy/Doubt To Nothing (12", p/s with insert)	50
85	New European BADVC 69	Born Again/The Calling (Mk II)/Carousel (Bolt Mix) (12", p/s)	30
85	New European BADVC 73	...And Murder Love/A.M.L. (Instrumental) (p/s)	30

85	New European 12BADVC73	Come Before Christ And Murder Love/Torture By Roses (12", p/s)	35
87	New European BADVC 10	To Drown A Rose/Zimmerit/Europa/The Gates Of Heaven (10", p/s)	20
88	Cenaz CENAZ 09	Born Again/The Calling (Mk II)/Carousel (Remix) (12" picture disc, 1st pressing with silver print & rim, 970 only; 2nd pressing bronze)	25/20
94	Twilight Command NERO I	SUNDOGS (Rose Clouds Of Holocaust/13 Years Of Carrion) (p/s with sticker)	7
92	New European BADVC 8	CATHEDRAL OF TEARS (12" EP, picture disc with sticker)	25
93	New European BADVC 63	PARADISE RISING (12" EP)	20
96	Twil. Command NERO XIII	Kapo!/Occidental Martyr (p/s)	20
85	New European BADVC 3	THE GUILTY HAVE NO PRIDE (LP)	30
80s	Leprosy UBADVC 4	BURIAL (LP, 'quilted' sleeve, brown, pink, white & other coloured vinyl)	40
90s	Leprosy UBADVC 4	BURIAL (LP, textured sleeve, various coloured vinyls)	35
92	Leprosy UBADVC 4	BURIAL (LP, standard sleeve, green vinyl)	30
85	New European BADVC 13	NADA (LP, blue or brown sleeve; also picture disc)	40/25/15
86	New European BADVC 726	LESSON ONE: MISANTHROPY (LP, embossed sleeve with insert)	25
87	New European BADVC 11	BROWN BOOK (LP, textured sleeve with inner & insert; export copies had extra inserts & postcards)	35/25
88	New European BADVC 8	THE WORLD THAT SUMMER (2-LP, gatefold textured sleeve)	40
88	New European BADVC 88	WALL OF SACRIFICE (LP, red sleeve or green/yellow sleeve)	70/50
89	New European BADVC 93	93 DEAD SUN WHEELS (mini-LP, with Current 93)	25
92	Leprosy LEPER 2	NIGHT AND FOG (LP, red vinyl, 1,000 only)	40
93	New European BADVC 36	BUT WHAT ENDS WHEN THE SYMBOLS SHATTER (LP, with inner & insert, 500 on purple vinyl, 3,000 on black vinyl)	40/25
93	New Euro'n BADVCCD 36	BUT WHAT ENDS WHEN THE SYMBOLS SHATTER (CD, gold disc digipak, 5,000 only)	25
93	New Euro'n BADVCCD 96	SOMETHING IS COMING (2-CD, digipak, 5,000 only)	30
94	New European BADVC 38	ROSE CLOUDS OF HOLOCAUST (LP, with insert & inner)	12
94	New Euro'n BADVCCD 38	ROSE CLOUDS OF HOLOCAUST (CD, digipak, 5,000 only)	20
95	New European BADVC 39	BLACK WHOLE OF LOVE (box set with 12", 10", 7" & CDs with inserts)	30
96	New European BADVC 96	SOMETHING IS COMING (2-LP, textured sleeve with insert)	20

(see also Crisis, Current 93, Boyd Rice & Friends, Sol Invictus)

DEATH SENTENCE
| 82 | Beat The System DEATH 1 | DEATH & PURE DESTRUCTION (EP) | 6 |

DEBONAIRES (U.K.)
| 66 | Pye 7N 17151 | A Love Of Our Own/The Night Meets The Dawn | 5 |
| 66 | Pye 7N 17204 | Crying Behind Your Smile/Forever More | 5 |

DEBONAIRES (U.S.)
| 70 | Track 604 035 | I'm In Love Again/Headache In My Heart | 15 |

DEBONAIRS
| 63 | Parlophone R 5054 | That's Right/When True Love Comes Your Way | 4 |

DEBS
| 65 | Mercury MF 888 | Sloopy's Gonna Hang On/Under A Street Light | 6 |

DEB-TONES
| 59 | RCA RCA 1137 | Knock, Knock — Who's There?/I'm In Love Again | 20 |
| 59 | RCA RCA 1137 | Knock, Knock — Who's There?/I'm In Love Again (78) | 15 |

DEBUTANTES
| 80 | Rok ROK XVII/XVIII | Man In The Street/INNOCENT BYSTANDERS: Where Is Johnny (co. sleeve) | 6 |

DECAMERON
73	Vertigo 6360 097	SAY HELLO TO THE BAND (LP)	12
74	Mooncrest CREST 19	MAMMOTH SPECIAL (LP, with lyric insert)	12
75	Transatlantic TRA 304	THIRD LIGHT (LP)	12
75	Mooncrest CREST 28	BEYOND THE LIGHT (LP)	12
76	Transatlantic TRA 325	TOMORROW'S PANTOMIME (LP)	12

VINNI DE CAMPO
| 50 | London L 960 | Bring Back The Thrill/Faithfull (78) | 7 |

YVONNE DE CARLO
| 55 | Capitol CL 14380 | Take It Or Leave It/Three Little Stars | 7 |

PAULO DE CARVALHO
| 74 | Pye International 7N 25647 | (And Then) After Love/E Depois Do Adeus (p/s) | 10 |

DE CASTRO SISTERS
54	London HL 8104	Teach Me Tonight/It's Love	35
54	London HL 8104	Teach Me Tonight/It's Love (78)	8
55	London HL 8137	Boom Boom Boomerang/Let Your Love Walk In	35
55	London HL 8137	Boom Boom Boomerang/Let Your Love Walk In (78)	12
55	London HL 8158	I'm Bewildered/To Say You're Mine	35
55	London HL 8158	I'm Bewildered/To Say You're Mine (78)	12
55	London HLU 8189	If I Ever Fall In Love/Cuckoo In The Clock	30
55	London HLU 8189	If I Ever Fall In Love/Cuckoo In The Clock (78)	10
55	London HLU 8212	Christmas Is A-Comin'/Snowbound For Christmas	30
55	London HLU 8212	Christmas Is A-Comin'/Snowbound For Christmas (78)	8
56	London HLU 8228	Give Me Time/Too Late Now	30
56	London HLU 8228	Give Me Time/Too Late Now (78)	15
56	London HLU 8296	No One To Blame But You/Cowboys Don't Cry	30
56	London HLU 8296	No One To Blame But You/Cowboys Don't Cry (78)	15
58	HMV POP 527	Who Are They To Say?/When You Look At Me	8
58	HMV POP 527	Who Are They To Say?/When You Look At Me (78)	18
59	HMV POP 583	The Things I Tell My Pillow/Teach Me Tonight Cha Cha	8
59	HMV POP 583	The Things I Tell My Pillow/Teach Me Tonight Cha Cha (78)	20
61	Capitol CL 15199	Red Sails In The Sunset/Bells	6

MINT VALUE £

DIANA DECKER

54	Columbia SCM 5083	Oh, My Papa/Crystal Ball	12
54	Columbia SCM 5096	The Happy Wanderer/Till We Two Are One	8
54	Columbia SCM 5120	Jilted/The Man With The Banjo	10
54	Columbia SCM 5123	Kitty In The Basket/Never Never Land	8
54	Columbia SCM 5130	Mama Mia/Percy The Penguin	10
54	Columbia SCM 5145	Sisters/Abracadabra	12
55	Columbia SCM 5166	Open The Window Of Your Heart/The Violin Song	8
55	Columbia SCM 5173	Apples, Peaches And Cherries/Paper Valentine	8
56	Columbia SCM 5246	Rock-A-Boogie Baby/Willie Can	18
56	Columbia DB 3739	Rock-A-Boogie Baby/Willie Can (78)	8

(see also Ray Burns, Ruby Murray)

DECORATORS

81	New Hormones/Red RS 9	Pendulum And Swing/Rendezvous/Strange One (p/s)	4
81	New Hormones ORG 5	Twilight View/Reflections (p/s)	4

DE COURCY'S

65	Egmont EGM 9220	SALUTE TO THE SHADOWS (LP)	12

DE DANAAN

82	Cara CARA 1	Hey Jude/St. Jude's Hornpipe/Trip To Taum Reel/Teetotaller	5
75	Polydor 2904 005	DE DANAAN (LP)	15
77	Decca SKL-R 5287	DE DANAAN — SELECTED JIGS AND REELS (LP)	20
80	Decca SKL 5318	BANKS OF THE NILE (LP)	12

DEDICATED MEN'S JUG BAND

65	Piccadilly 7N 35245	Boodle-Am-Shake/Come On Boys	6
66	Piccadilly 7N 35283	Don't Come Knocking/Out Time Blues	6

DEDRINGER

80	DinDisc DIN 10	Sunday Drivers/We Don't Mind (p/s)	5
80	DinDisc DIN 11	Innocent 'Till Proven Guilty/Maxine//Took A Long Time/ We Don't Mind (double pack)	6
81	DinDisc DIN 12	Direct Line/She's Not Ready (p/s)	5
82	Neat NEAT 18	Hot Lady/Hot Licks And Rock'N'Roll (p/s)	5
81	DinDisc DID 7	DIRECT LINE (LP)	12
83	Neat NEAT 1009	SECOND RISING (LP, with inner sleeve)	12

DAVE DEE

70	Fontana TF 1074	My Woman's Man/Gotta Make You Part Of Me	5
70	Fontana 6007 021	Annabella/Kelly	5
70	Philips 6006 061	Everything About Her/If I Believed In Tomorrow	5
71	Philips 6006 100	Wedding Bells/Sweden	5
71	Philips 6006 154	Hold On/Mary Morning, Mary Evening	5
71	Philips 6006 180	Swingy/Don't You Ever Change Your Mind	5

(see also Dave Dee, Dozy, Beaky, Mick & Tich)

DAVE DEE, DOZY, BEAKY, MICK & TICH

65	Fontana TF 531	No Time/Is It Love	20
65	Fontana TF 586	All I Want/It Seems A Pity	18
65	Fontana TF 630	You Make It Move/I Can't Stop	7
66	Fontana TF 671	Hold Tight!/You Know What I Want	6
66	Fontana TF 711	Hideaway/Here's A Heart	6
66	Fontana TF 746	Bend It/She's So Good	6
66	Fontana TF 775	Save Me/Shame	6
67	Fontana TF 798	Touch Me Touch Me/Marina	6
67	Fontana TF 830	Okay!/He's A Raver	6
67	Fontana TF 873	Zabadak!/The Sun Goes Down	6
68	Fontana TF 903	The Legend Of Xanadu/Please	5
74	Antic K 11510	She's My Lady/Babeigh	5
67	Fontana TE 17488	LOOS OF ENGLAND (EP)	12
67	Philips MCF 5005	THE HITS OF MANFRED MANN AND DDDBM&T (cassette EP)	10
66	Fontana TL 5350	DAVE DEE, DOZY, BEAKY, MICK & TICH (LP)	18
66	Fontana (S)TL 5388	IF MUSIC BE THE FOOD OF LOVE PREPARE FOR INDIGESTION (LP)	20
67	Fontana (S)TL 5441	GOLDEN HITS OF DAVE DEE, DOZY, BEAKY, MICK & TICH (LP)	15
68	Fontana (S)TL 5471	IF NO-ONE SANG (LP)	18
69	Fontana SFL 13002	DDDBM&T (LP)	15
70	Fontana SFL 13173	TOGETHER (LP)	15

(see also Dozy Beaky Mick & Tich [D,B,M & T], Dave Dee)

JEANNIE DEE

69	Beacon BEA 115	Come Into My Arms/Sun Shine On Me	5
69	Beacon BEA 142	Don't Go Home My Little Darling/Come See About Me	8

JOEY DEE & STARLI(GH)TERS

61	Columbia DB 4758	Peppermint Twist (Parts 1 & 2)	6
62	Columbia DB 4803	Hey, Let's Twist/Roly Poly	6
62	Columbia DB 4842	Shout (Parts 1 & 2)	6
62	Columbia DB 4862	Ya Ya/Fanny Mae	6
62	Columbia DB 4905	What Kind Of Love Is This?/Wing Ding	6
63	Columbia DB 4955	I Lost My Baby/Keep Your Mind On What You're Doin'	6
63	Columbia DB 7005	Baby You're Driving Me Crazy/Help Me Pick Up The Pieces	6
63	Columbia DB 7055	Hot Pastrami With Mashed Potatoes (Parts 1 & 2)	6
63	Columbia DB 7102	Dance, Dance, Dance/Let's Have A Party (features Ronettes uncredited)	7
63	Columbia DB 7277	Down By The Riverside/Getting Nearer (features Ronettes uncredited)	7
61	Columbia 33SX 1406	DOIN' THE TWIST LIVE AT THE PEPPERMINT LOUNGE (LP)	25
62	Columbia 33SX 1461	BACK AT THE PEPPERMINT LOUNGE (LP)	25
62	Columbia 33SX 1502	ALL THE WORLD IS TWISTIN' (LP)	25
63	Columbia 33SX 1532	JOEY DEE (LP)	25
63	Columbia 33SX 1607	DANCE DANCE DANCE (LP, with Starlighters, also with Ronettes uncredited)	25

(see also Young Rascals)

JOHNNIE DEE
65	Columbia DB 7612	Frankie's Angel/Everything's Upside Down	6

JOHNNY DEE
57	Oriole CB 1367	Sittin' In The Balcony/A-Plus Love	120
57	Oriole CB 1367	Sittin' In The Balcony/A-Plus Love (78)	35

(see also John D. Loudermilk)

KIKI DEE
63	Fontana TF 394	Early Night/Lucky High Heels	10
63	Fontana TF 414	I Was Only Kidding/Don't Put Your Heart In His Hand	7
64	Fontana TF 443	Miracles/That's Right, Walk On By	12
64	Fontana TF 490	(You Don't Know) How Glad I Am/Baby I Don't Care	8
65	Fontana TF 596	Runnin' Out Of Fools/There He Goes	7
66	Fontana TF 669	Why Don't I Run Away From You?/Small Town	10
67	Fontana TF 792	I'm Going Out (The Same Way I Came In)/We've Got Everything Going For Us	7
67	Fontana TF 833	I/Stop And Think	6
67	Fontana TF 870	Excuse Me/Patterns	6
68	Fontana TF 926	Can't Take My Eyes Off You/Hungry Heart	6
68	Fontana TF 983	Now The Flowers Cry/On A Magic Carpet Ride	50
70	Tamla Motown TMG 739	The Day Will Come Between Sunday And Monday/My Whole World Ended (The Moment You Left Me)	10
73	Rocket PIG 2	Lonnie And Josie/The Last Good Man In My Life	7
74	Philips 6006 352	Excuse Me/Patterns (reissue)	5
74	Rocket PIG 10	Hard Luck Story/Everyone Should Have Their Way	5
76	Rocket ROKN 512	Don't Go Breaking My Heart/Snow Queen (with Elton John, p/s)	5
76	Rocket ROKN 515	Loving And Free/Amoureuse/I've Got The Music In Me (p/s)	5
77	Rocket ROKN 520	First Thing In The Morning/The Man Who Loved To Dance	5
77	Rocket ROKN 526	Chicago/ELTON JOHN: Bite Your Lip (Get Up And Dance)	5
77	Rocket RU 1	Chicago/ELTON JOHN: Bite Your Lip (Get Up And Dance) (12", printed sleeve)	8
81	Rocket XPRESS 49	Don't Go Breaking My Heart/Snow Queen (with Elton John, reissue)	5
81	Ariola ARO 269	Loving You Is Sweeter Than Ever (with Elton John)/Twenty Four Hours (p/s)	8
65	Fontana TE 17443	KIKI DEE (EP)	30
66	Fontana TE 17470	KIKI DEE IN CLOVER (EP)	25
68	Fontana (S)TL 5455	I'M KIKI DEE (LP)	30
70	Tamla Motown STML 11158	GREAT EXPECTATIONS (LP)	45
73	Rocket PIGL 5	LOVING AND FREE (LP)	12
73	Philips Intl. 6382 079	PATTERNS (LP)	15
74	Rocket PIGL 10	I'VE GOT THE MUSIC IN ME (LP)	12
80	Ariola ARL 5050	PERFECT TIMING (LP)	12

(see also Elton John)

LENNY DEE
55	Brunswick 05440	Plantation Boogie/Birth Of The Blues	7

RICKY DEE & EMBERS
62	Stateside SS 136	Workout/JOHN MOBLEY: Tunnel Of Love	10

SANDRA DEE
61	Brunswick 05858	Tammy Tell Me True/Let's Fall In Love	7

SIMON DEE
69	Chapter One CH 105	Julie/Whatever Happened To Us?	6

TAMMI DEE
71	Downtown DT 479	Val/MUSIC DOCTORS: Bank Raid	6

TOMMY DEE
59	Melodisc 1516	Three Stars/TEEN JONES (TONES): I'll Never Change (tri or round centre)	70/45
59	Melodisc 1516	Three Stars/TEEN JONES (TONES): I'll Never Change (78)	65

DEE & DYNAMITES
60	Philips PB 1081	Blaze Away/South Bound Gasser	10

MAURICE DEEBANK
84	Cherry Red MRED 61	INNER THOUGHT ZONE (LP)	10

(see also Felt)

DEEJAYS
65	Polydor BM 56034	Dimples/Coming On Strong	45
65	Polydor BM 56501	Blackeyed Woman/I Just Can't Go To Sleep	100

ANTHONY DEELEY
68	Pama PM 728	Anytime Man/Don't Change Your Mind About Me	6

ANGELA DEEN
64	Fontana TF 491	There's So Much About My Baby That I Love/Gotta Hand It To The Boy	7

CAROL DEENE
61	HMV POP 922	Sad Movies/Don't Forget	7
62	HMV POP 973	Norman/On The Outside Looking In	6
62	HMV POP 1027	Johnny Get Angry/Somebody's Smiling	6
62	HMV POP 1058	Some People/Kissin'	6
62	HMV POP 1086	James/It Happened Last Night	7
63	HMV POP 1123	Let Me Do It My Way/Growin' Up	7
63	HMV POP 1200	Oh Oh Oh Willie/I Want To Stay Here	7
64	HMV POP 1275	Who's Been Sleeping In My Bed?/Love Is Wonderful	7
64	HMV POP 1337	Very First Kiss/Hard To Say Goodnight	7
65	HMV POP 1405	Most People Do/I Can't Forget Someone Like You	7
65	Columbia DB 7743	He Just Don't Know/Up In The Penthouse	7
66	Columbia DB 7890	Dancing In Your Eyes/Please Don't Be Unfaithful Again	7
67	Columbia DB 8107	Love Not Have I/Time	6
68	CBS 3206	When He Wants A Woman/I'm Not Crying	6
69	Conquest CXT 102	One More Chance/Invisible Tears	7
70	World Records ST 1031	A LOVE AFFAIR (LP)	25

MINT VALUE £

DEEP END
| 78 | private pressing | BEGGED AND BORROWED (LP, listed as CPLP 016) | 15 |

DEEP FEELING
70	Page One POF 165	Do You Love Me/Move On	5
70	Page One POF 177	Skyline Pigeon/We've Thrown It All Away	6
70	DJM DJS 231	Do You Wanna Dance/The Day My Lady Cried	5
72	DJM DJS 237	Sweat, Dust And Red Wine/Turn Around	5
72	DJM DJS 257	Country Heir/We've Thrown It All Away	5
74	Santa Ponsa PNS 12	Let's Spend The Night Together/Avalon	5
71	DJM DJLPS 419	DEEP FEELING (LP)	25

DEEP FREEZE
| 70s | Guardian GRL 43 | Keeping You In Furs/Don't Look Back | 4 |

DEEP FREEZE MICE
80s	Cordelia ERICAT 002	THESE FLOORS ARE SMOOTH (EP)	10
80s	Cordelia ERICAT 004	HANG ON CONSTANCE LET ME HEAR THE NEWS (EP)	8
80s	Cordelia ERICAT 013	RAIN IS WHEN THE EARTH IS TELEVISION (EP)	7
80s	Cordelia ERICAT 016	NEURON MUSIC (12" EP)	8
79	Mole Embalming MOLE 1	MY GERANIUMS ARE BULLETPROOF (LP, 1st 200 with paste-on sleeve, 8-page booklet & various A4 inserts)	60/30
81	Mole Embalming MOLE 2	TEENAGE HEAD IN MY REFRIGERATOR (LP)	30
81	Mole Embalming MOLE C2	HEGEL'S BRAIN (cassette)	12
81	Inedible MOLE 3	GATES OF LUNCH (LP)	15
83	Mole Embalming MOLE 4	SAW A RANCH BURNING LAST NIGHT (LP)	15
80s	Cordelia ERICAT 001	I LOVE YOU LITTLE BO BO WITH YOUR DELICATE GOLDEN LIONS (2-LP)	15

DEEP PURPLE
68	Parlophone R 5708	Hush/One More Rainy Day (some in promo-only p/s)	250/25
68	Parlophone R 5745	Kentucky Woman/Wring That Neck (withdrawn)	50
69	Parlophone R 5763	Emmaretta/Wring That Neck	25
69	Harvest HAR 5006	Hallelujah (I Am The Preacher)/April Part 1 (some in promo-only p/s)	250/15
70	Harvest HAR 5020	Black Night/Speed King	5
71	Harvest HAR 5033	Strange Kind Of Woman/I'm Alone	5
71	Harvest HAR 5045	Fireball/Demon's Eye	5
72	Purple PUR 102	Never Before/When A Blind Man Cries	6
74	Purple PUR 117	Might Just Take Your Life/Coronarias Redig	7
76	Purple PUR 130	You Keep On Moving/Love Child	7
77	Purple PUR 132	Smoke On The Water/Woman From Tokyo/Child In Time (10,000 with p/s)	7
77	Purple PUR 135	NEW LIVE AND RARE VOL. 1 (EP, 15,000 on purple vinyl)	8
78	Purple PUR 137	NEW LIVE AND RARE VOL. 2 (EP)	7
80	Harvest SHEP 101	NEW LIVE AND RARE VOL. 3 (EP)	7
85	Polydor POSPP 719	Perfect Strangers (edit)/Son Of Alerik (edit) (picture disc)	7
87	Polydor POSPP 843	Call Of The Wild/Strange Ways (12", picture disc)	10
88	Polydor PZCD 4	Hush ('88 Re-recording)Dead Or Alive/Bad Attitude (CD)	12
88	Polydor 080 088-2	Bad Attitude/Black And White/Unwritten Law/Strangeways (CD Video)	25
68	Parlophone PMC/PCS 7055	SHADES OF DEEP PURPLE (LP, yellow/black label, mono/stereo)	85/50
69	Parlophone PCS 7055	SHADES OF DEEP PURPLE (LP, stereo repressing, white/black label)	18
69	Harvest SHVL 751	THE BOOK OF TALIESYN (LP)	18
69	Harvest SHVL 759	DEEP PURPLE (LP, laminated gatefold sleeve)	18
70	Harvest SHVL 767	CONCERTO FOR GROUP AND ORCHESTRA (LP, laminated gatefold sleeve)	12
70	Harvest SHVL 777	IN ROCK (LP, laminated gatefold sleeve)	12
71	Harvest SHVL 793	FIREBALL (LP, textured gatefold sleeve, with insert)	15
72	Purple TPSA 7504	MACHINE HEAD (LP, laminated gatefold sleeve, with insert)	12
73	Purple TPSA 7508	WHO DO WE THINK WE ARE (LP, laminated gatefold sleeve, with insert)	12
74	Purple Q4TPS 7504	MACHINE HEAD (LP, laminated gatefold sleeve, quadrophonic)	35
74	Purple TPS 3505	BURN (LP)	10
74	Purple TPS 3508	STORMBRINGER (LP)	10
75	Purple TPSA 7515	COME TASTE THE BAND (LP, gatefold sleeve with inner)	12
78	Harvest SHSM 2026	THE SINGLES A's AND B's (LP, purple vinyl)	20
79	Purple TPS 3514	THE MARK 2 PURPLE SINGLES (LP, purple vinyl)	12
80	Harvest SHSM 2016	SHADES OF DEEP PURPLE (LP, 'dismembered doll-limb' sleeve, withdrawn)	75
84	Polydor POLHP 16	PERFECT STRANGERS (LP, picture disc, with extra track & die-cut sleeve)	15
85	EMI EJ 26 0343 0	IN ROCK (LP, picture disc with poster)	15
85	EMI EJ 34 0344 0	FIREBALL (LP, picture disc with poster)	15
85	EMI EG 26 0345 0	MACHINE HEAD (LP, picture disc with poster)	15
85	EMI PUR 1	DEEP PURPLE — ANTHOLOGY (2-LP, blue vinyl)	25
87	Polydor 831 318-2	HOUSE OF BLUE LIGHT (CD)	20
93	BMG 74321 15420-1	THE BATTLE RAGES ON (LP, with inner sleeve)	20
97	EMI DEEPP 3	MACHINE HEAD (2-LP, 'EMI 100' remixed anniversary edition, purple vinyl, gatefold sleeve, with insert)	15
97	EMI LPCENT 25	SHADES OF DEEP PURPLE (LP, 'EMI 100', 180gm vinyl edition, yellow/black label)	15

(see also Ritchie Blackmore, Rainbow, Gillan, [David Coverdale's] Whitesnake, Tommy Bolin, [Sheila Carter &] Episode Six, Jon Lord, Roger Glover, Green Bullfrog, Wizard's Convention, Elf, Maze, M.I. Five, Warhorse, Captain Beyond, John Lawton, Hell Preachers Inc., Glen Hughes, Trapeze, Leading Figures, Paice Ashton & Lord, Silverhead, Pete York Percussion Band)

DEEP RIVER BOYS

52	HMV B 10381	Trying/Tennessee Newsboy (78)	7
53	HMV B 10542	The Biggest Fool/Oo-Shoo-Be-Do-Be (78)	8
54	HMV 7M 174	Sweet Mama Tree Top Tall/A Kiss And Cuddle Polka	18
54	HMV B 10625	Sweet Mama Tree Top Tall/A Kiss And Cuddle Polka (78)	8
54	HMV 7M 280	Shake, Rattle And Roll/St. Louis Blues	20
54	HMV B 10790	Shake, Rattle And Roll/St. Louis Blues (78)	7
54	HMV B 10633	Lucky Black Cat/My Castle On The Nile (78)	7
55	HMV B 10902	Smack Dab In The Middle/I Wonder (78)	7
55	HMV POP 113	Rock Around The Clock/Adam Never Had A Mommy (78)	7
56	HMV 7M 361	Rock-A-Beatin' Boogie/Just A Little Bit More!	25
56	HMV POP 157	Rock-A-Beatin' Boogie/Just A Little Bit More! (78)	7
56	HMV POP 263	That's Right/Honey Honey	15
56	HMV POP 263	That's Right/Honey Honey (78)	7
57	HMV POP 395	Whole Lotta Shakin' Goin' On/There's A Goldmine In The Sky	20
57	HMV POP 395	Whole Lotta Shakin' Goin' On/There's A Goldmine In The Sky (78)	8
58	HMV POP 449	Not Too Old To Rock And Roll/Slow Train To Nowhere	18
58	HMV POP 449	Not Too Old To Rock And Roll/Slow Train To Nowhere (78)	12
58	HMV POP 537	Itchy Twitchy Feeling/I Shall Not Be Moved.	15
58	HMV POP 537	Itchy Twitchy Feeling/I Shall Not Be Moved (78)	12
59	Top Rank JAR 172	Nola/Kissin'	6
59	Top Rank JAR 172	Nola/Kissin' (78)	12
59	Top Rank JAR 174	I Don't Know Why (I Just Do)/Timbers Gotta Roll (with Harry Douglass)	6
59	Top Rank JAR 174	I Don't Know Why (I Just Do)/Timbers Gotta Roll (with Harry Douglass) (78)	10
60	Top Rank JAR 352	Go Galloway, Go/Dum Dum De Dum (with Harry Douglass).	5
62	HMV POP 1081	Settle Down/Ashes Of Roses.	8
55	Nixa 45EP 113	GO ON BOARD LITTLE CHILDREN (EP)	8
55	Nixa 45EP 114	SWING LOW SWEET CHARIOT (EP)	8
55	Nixa 45EP 130	WALK TOGETHER CHILDREN (EP)	8
55	Nixa 45EP 131	EZEKIEL SAW THE WHEEL (EP)	8
55	HMV 7EG 8133	DEEP RIVER BOYS (EP)	8
57	HMV 7EG 8321	ROMANCE A LA MODE (EP)	8
57	HMV 7EG 8445	NEGRO SPIRITUALS (EP)	8
54	Nixa XLTY 135	SPIRITUALS SUNG BY THE DEEP RIVER BOYS (10" LP)	18
54	Nixa XLTY 138	SPIRITUALS SUNG BY THE DEEP RIVER BOYS (10" LP).	18
60	Top Rank 35/108	THE BLUE DEEPS (LP)	15

(see also Fats Waller, Harry Douglass & Deep River Boys)

DEEP SET

68	Pye 7N 17594	That's The Way Life Goes/Hello Amy	6
69	Major Minor MM 607	I Started A Joke/Spicks And Specks	8

DEEP SIX

66	Liberty LIB 55882	Counting/When Morning Breaks	6

DEEP SWITCH

86	SWITCH 1	NINE INCHES OF GOD (LP, private pressing)	30

DEEP TIMBRE

72	Westwood WR 5006	DEEP TIMBRE (LP)	45

SAM DEES

69	Major Minor MM 655	If It's All Wrong (It's All Right)/Don't Keep Me Hangin' On	15
75	Atlantic K 10676	Fragile, Handle With Care/Save The Love At Any Cost	20
75	Atlantic K 50142	THE SHOW MUST GO ON (LP)	30

SAM DEES & BETTYE SWANN

76	Atlantic K 10719	Storybook Children/Just As Sure	10

(see also Bettye Swann)

DEE SET

68	Blue Cat BS 146	I Know A Place/ROY BENNETT: I Dangerous	10

DEFECTS

81	Casualty CR 001	Dance Till You Drop/Guilty Conscience/Brutality (p/s)	5
82	WXYZ ABCD 3	Survival/Brutality (p/s)	6
82	Lyntone LYN 12647	Dance/ANTI NOWHERE LEAGUE: World War III/METEORS: Mutant Rock (Instrumental) (red vinyl flexidisc free with *Flexipop* magazine, issue 26)	8/5
83	I.D. EYE 2	Suspicious Minds/Song For Mark Walker/Know 'Bout You (p/s)	5
82	WXYZ LMNOP 2	DEFECTIVE BREAKDOWN (LP)	15

DEFENDANTS

80s	Edible EAT 001	Headmaster/Such A Spiv (stickered insert cover & stickered labels)	15

DEFENDERS

68	Doctor Bird DB 1104	Set Them Free/Don't Blame The Children (actually by Lee Perry & Sensations).	15

(see also Lee Perry)

DEF LEPPARD

79	Bludgeon Riffola SRT/CUS/232	THE DEF LEPPARD EP: Ride Into The Sun/Getcha Rocks Off/The Overture (red label, p/s with lyric insert, 150 only)	300
79	Bludgeon Riffola SRT/CUS/232	THE DEF LEPPARD EP: Ride Into The Sun/Getcha Rocks Off/The Overture (red label, with/without p/s, 850 only)	250/60
79	Bludgeon Riffola MSB 001	Ride Into The Sun/Getcha Rocks Off/The Overture (reissue, yellow label, 15,000 pressed, no p/s)	18
79	Phonogram 6059 240	Getcha Rocks Off/Ride Into The Sun/The Overture (2nd reissue, no p/s)	10
79	Phonogram 6059 240	Getcha Rocks Off/Ride Into The Sun/The Overture (mispressing, both sides play "The Overture")	40
79	Phonogram 6059 247	Wasted/Hello America (p/s)	10
80	Phonogram LEPP 1	Hello America/Good Morning Freedom (p/s).	12
81	Phonogram LEPP 2	Let It Go/Switch 625 (p/s, 10,000 shrinkwrapped with patch)	15/10
82	Phonogram LEPP 3	Bringin' On The Heartbreak/Me And My Wine (p/s)	35
82	Phonogram LEPP 312	Bringin' On The Heartbreak/Me And My Wine/You Got Me Runnin' (12", p/s)	20

DEF LEPPARD

83	Phonogram VER 5	Photograph/Bringin' On The Heartbreak (p/s)	10
83	Phonogram VERP 5	Photograph/Bringin' On The Heartbreak (camera-shaped fold-out/pop-up sleeve, 500 only)	25
83	Phonogram VERX 5	Photograph/Bringin' On The Heartbreak/Mirror, Mirror (12", p/s)	20
83	Phonogram VER 6	Rock Of Ages/Action! Not Words (p/s)	7
83	Phonogram VERP 6	Rock Of Ages/Action! Not Words (guitar-shaped picture disc)	35
83	Phonogram VERQ 6	Rock Of Ages/Action! Not Words (foldout 'rock box' cube sleeve, 500 only)	40
83	Phonogram VERX 6	Rock Of Ages/Action! Not Words (12", p/s)	18
83	Phonogram VERDJ 8	Too Late/Foolin' (p/s, DJ-only promo with rear band photo in football kit)	150
83	Phonogram VER 8	Too Late For Love/Foolin' (p/s)	12
83	Phonogram VERX 8	Too Late For Love/Foolin'/High And Dry (12", p/s)	20
84	Phonogram VER 9	Photograph/Bringin' On The Heartbreak (reissue, 'wallet' p/s)	10
84	Phonogram VERG 9	Photograph/Bringin' On The Heartbreak (g/fold printed 'wallet' p/s, 500 only)	40
84	Phonogram VERX 9	Photograph/Bringin' On The Heartbreak/Mirror, Mirror (12", p/s)	20
87	Phonogram LEPX 1	Animal/Animal (Extended Mix)/Tear It Down (12", p/s, black vinyl)	8
87	Phonogram LEPC 1	Animal/Animal (Extended Mix)/Tear It Down (12", p/s, red vinyl)	20
87	Phonogram LEPCD 1	Animal/Women/Animal (Extended Mix)/Tear It Down (CD, no'd, 1,000 only)	30
87	Phonogram LEPS 2	Pour Some Sugar On Me/I Wanna Be Your Hero (tri-shaped picture disc in silver 12" foldout p/s with tour dates)	15
87	Phonogram LEPMC 2	Pour Some Sugar On Me/I Wanna Be Your Hero (cassette)	7
87	Phonogram LEPX 2	Pour Some Sugar On Me (Extended Version)/Pour Some Sugar On Me/I Wanna Be Your Hero (12", p/s)	8
87	Phonogram LEPPX 2	Pour Some Sugar On Me (Extended Version)/Pour Some Sugar On Me (Extended)/I Wanna Be Your Hero (12", picture disc, unissued)	
87	Phonogram LEPMC 333	Hysteria/Ride Into The Sun (1987 Version) (cassette)	8
87	Phonogram LEPS 3	Hysteria/Ride Into The Sun (1987 Version) (p/s, shrinkwrapped with patch)	10
87	Phonogram LEPX 3	Hysteria/Ride Into The Sun (1987 Version)/Love And Affection (live) (12", p/s)	8
87	Phonogram LEPX 313	Hysteria/Ride Into The Sun (1987 Version)/Love And Affection (live) (12", envelope box sleeve with poster & international discography, 5,000 only)	15
87	Phonogram LEPCD 3	Hysteria/Ride Into The Sun (1987 Version)/Love And Affection (live)/I Wanna Be Your Hero (CD, 5,000 only with titles not numbered)	15
88	Phonogram LEPP 4	Armageddon It! (The Atomic Mix)/Ring Of Fire (poster p/s)	7
88	Phonogram LEPX 4	Armageddon It!/Armageddon It! (The Atomic Mix)/Ring Of Fire (12", p/s)	8
88	Phonogram LEPXB 4	Armageddon It!/Armageddon It! (The Atomic Mix)/Ring Of Fire (12", numbered box set with poster, enamel badge & 5 postcards, 5,000 only)	18
88	Phonogram LEPCD 4	Armageddon It! (The Atomic Mix)/Ring Of Fire/Animal/Pour Some Sugar On Me (CD, picture disc)	15
88	Phonogram LEPG 5	Love Bites/Billy's Got A Gun (live) (no'd gatefold p/s with 8-page lyric book)	8
88	Phonogram LEPX 5	Love Bites/Billy's Got A Gun (live)/Excitable (Orgasmic Mix) (12", p/s)	8
88	Phonogram LEPXB 5	Love Bites/Billy's Got A Gun (live)/Excitable (Orgasmic Mix) (12", box set with 4 cardboard inserts, 5,000 only)	18
88	Phonogram LEPCD 5	Love Bites/Rocket (The Lunar Mix)/Billy's Got A Gun (live) (CD, card sleeve)	15
89	Phonogram LEPC 6	Rocket/Release Me (foldout 'Brit' pack, envelope sleeve with 3 inserts)	8
89	Phonogram LEPXP 6	Rocket (The Lunar Mix)/(Radio Edit)/Release Me (12", picture disc, some numbered)	15/10
89	Phonogram LEPX 6	Rocket (The Lunar Mix)/Release Me/Rock Of Ages (live) (12", p/s)	8
89	Phonogram LEPXC 6	Rocket (The Lunar Mix)/Release Me/Rock Of Ages (live) (12", calendar pack)	20
89	Phonogram LEPCD 6	Rocket (The Lunar Mix)/Rock Of Ages (live)/Release Me (CD)	15
92	Phonogram DEFXP 7	Let's Get Rocked/Only After Dark/Too Late For Love (live) (12", picture disc, with insert)	10
92	Phonogram DEFCD 7	Let's Get Rocked/Only After Dark/Women (live) (CD, picture disc, in box with space for 4 CDs)	20
92	Phonogram LEPXP 7	Make Love Like A Man/Miss You In A Heartbeat/Two Steps Behind (Acoustic Version) (12", picture disc)	8
92	Phonogram LEPXP 8	Have You Ever Needed Someone So Bad/From The Inside/You Can't Always Get What You Want (12", picture disc)	8
93	Phonogram LEP 9	Heaven Is/She's Too Tough (p/s, with etched autographs on 1 side)	5
93	Phonogram LEPX 9	Heaven Is/She's Too Tough/Let's Get Rocked (live) (12", picture disc)	8
93	Phonogram LEPCB 10	Tonight/Pour Some Sugar On Me (live)/Tonight (Demo) (CD)	8
93	Phonogram LEPCD 9	Heaven Is/She's Too Tough/Elected (live)/Let's Get Rocked (live) (CD)	8
93	Phonogram LEPX 11	Tonight/Now I'm Here (live)/Hysteria (12", picture disc)	10
93	Phonogram LEPTN 12	Two Steps Behind/Tonight/SMC (CD, in embossed metal tin)	8
94	Phonogram LEPCX 13	Action/Two Steps Behind (Joe's Demo)/Love Bites (live) (CD, digipak)	8
94	Phonogram LEPCB 13	Action/Two Steps Behind (Joe's Demo)/Love Bites (live) (CD, video cassette box pack)	8
88	Bludgeon Riffola 080 458-2	Love Bites/Rocket (Lunar Mix)/Billy's Got A Gun (live)/Love Bites (Video) (CD Video)	30
89	Bludgeon Riffola 080 034-2	Rock Of Ages/Stagefright/Billy's Got A Gun/Too Late For Love/Rock Of Ages (live) (CD Video)	30
89	Bludgeon Riffola 080 626-2	Animal (Extended Version)/Animal/Tear It Down/Animal (Video) (CD Video)	30
90	Bludgeon Riffola 080 990-2	Rocket (Radio Edit)/Release Me/Rock Of Ages/Rocket (Video) (CD Video)	30
87	Phonogram HYSPD 1	HYSTERIA (LP, picture disc)	15
89	Phonogram 836 606-2	THE FOUR ALBUMS (4-CD box set, with booklet)	50
92	Phonogram 510 978-1	ADRENALIZE (LP, picture disc, 5,000 only, numbered, die-cut sleeve)	12
94	Phonogram (no cat. no.)	ADRENALIZE — MAHOGANY BOX SET (CD, picture disc, with interview picture CD, 3 booklets, signed/no'd certificate, signed photo & plectrum, 1,000 only)	200
95	Mercury DLINT 3	1980-1995 VAULT — AN INTERVIEW WITH JOE ELLIOT & RICK SAVAGE (CD, promo only)	30

(see also Lucy, Gogmagog, Girl)

ZION DE GALLIER

68	Parlophone R 5686	Me/Winter Will Be Cold	12
68	Parlophone R 5710	Dream Dream Dream/Geraldine	15
	(see also Mark Wirtz)		

GLORIA DE HAVEN

55	Brunswick 05369	So This Is Paris/The Two Of Us	6
55	Brunswick 05457	Red Hot Pepper Pot/Won't You Save Me?	8
59	Oriole CB 1524	Dearly Beloved/Life	6
59	Oriole CB 1524	Dearly Beloved/Life (78)	12

DE-HEMS

72	President PT 388	Don't Cross That Line/Lover Let Me Go	8

DE JOHN SISTERS

56	Philips PB 524	Hotta Chocolotta/I'm Learnin' The Charleston (78)	7
57	Mercury MT 174	What Am I/Where Would I Be	7
57	Mercury MT 174	What Am I/Where Would I Be (78)	7
60	London HLT 9127	Yes Indeed/Be Anything (But Be Mine)	7

DEK & JERRY

66	Philips BF 1494	What's The Matter With Me?/Don't Waste Your Time	8

DESMOND DEKKER (& ACES)

63	Island WI 054	Honour Your Mother And Father (as Desmond Decker & Beverley's Allstars)/Maddie ('63) (with Beverley's Allstars)	15
63	Island WI 111	Parents/Labour For Learning (solo)	18
64	Island WI 158	Jeserine/King Of Ska (as Desmond Dekkar & His Cherry Pies)	18
64	Black Swan WI 455	Dracula (as Desmond Dekkar)/DON DRUMMOND: Spitfire	20
65	Island WI 181	Get Up Adine (as Desmond Dekkar, actually with Four Aces)/Be Mine Forever (as Patsy & Desmond; song is actually "Down Down Down" by Clive & Naomi)	18
65	Island WI 202	This Woman (as Desmond Dekkar & Four Aces)/LEE PERRY & UPSETTERS: Si Senora (B-side actually by Ossie & Upsetters)	18
67	Pyramid PYR 6003	Wise Man/ROLAND ALPHONSO: Middle East	10
67	Pyramid PYR 6004	007 (Shanty Town)/ROLAND ALPHONSO: El Torro	5
67	Pyramid PYR 6006	It's A Shame/ROLAND ALPHONSO: On The Move	10
67	Pyramid PYR 6008	Rudy Got Soul/ROLAND ALPHONSO: The Cat	10
67	Pyramid PYR 6011	Rude Boy Train/ROLAND ALPHONSO: Nothing For Nothing	10
67	Pyramid PYR 6012	Mother's Young Girl/SOUL BROTHERS: Confucious	20
67	Pyramid PYR 6017	Unity/Sweet Music	10
67	Pyramid PYR 6020	Sabotage/Pretty Africa	10
67	Pyramid PYR 6020	Sabotage/It Pays	10
67	Pyramid PYR 6026	It Pays/Young Generation	10
67	Pyramid PYR 6031	Beautiful And Dangerous/I've Got The Blues	10
68	Pyramid PYR 6035	Bongo Gal/Shing A Ling	10
68	Pyramid PYR 6037	To Sir, With Love/Fu Manchu	12
68	Pyramid PYR 6044	Mother Pepper/Don't Blame Me	10
68	Pyramid PYR 6047	Hey Grandma/Young Generation	10
68	Pyramid PYR 6051	Music Like Dirt (Intensified)/Coconut Water	10
68	Pyramid PYR 6054	It Mek/Writing On The Wall	8
68	Pyramid PYR 6058	Israelites/BEVERLEY'S ALLSTARS: The Man	5
68	Pyramid PYR 6059	Christmas Day/I've Got The Blues	8
69	Pyramid PYR 6068	It Mek/Problems	5
69	J.J. PYR 6058	Israelites/BEVERLEY'S ALLSTARS: The Man (reissue, mis-labelled copy)	5
70	Trojan TR 7777	You Can Get It If You Really Want/Perseverance	5
70	Trojan TR 7802	The Song We Used To Sing/Get Up Little Suzie	5
71	Trojan TR 7847	Lightning Stick/Troubles And Miseries	5
72	Trojan TR 7876	It Gotta Be So/The First Time For A Long Time	5
73	Rhino RNO 115	Sing A Little Song/I'm A Busted Lad	5
67	Doctor Bird DLM 5007	007 SHANTY TOWN (LP)	100
69	Doctor Bird DLM 5013	THE ISRAELITES (LP, solo)	75
69	Trojan TTL 4	THIS IS DESMOND DEKKAR (LP, label credits Dekker)	15
70	Trojan TBL 146	YOU CAN GET IT IF YOU REALLY WANT (LP)	18
73	Trojan TRLD 401	DOUBLE DEKKER (2-LP)	18
	(see also Al Barry, Skatalites, Maytals)		

GEORGE DEKKER

71	Trojan TR 7879	Time Hard/SYDNEY, GEORGE & JACKIE: Fall In Love	4

DEL AMITRI

82	Lyntone LYN 1548	What She Calls It (flexi, free with Stand & Deliver)	10
83	No Strings NOSP 1	Sense Sickness/The Difference Is (p/s)	30
85	Chrysalis CHS 2859	Sticks And Stones Girl/This King Is Poor (p/s)	7
85	Chrysalis CHS 12 2859	Sticks And Stones Girl/This King Is Poor/The Difference Is (12", p/s)	10
85	Chrysalis CHS 2925	Hammering Heart/Lines Running North (p/s)	6
85	Chrysalis CHS 12 2925	Hammering Heart/Lines Running North/Brown Eyed Girl (12", p/s)	10
86	Record Mirror	Out In The Wind (flexi, p/s, free with Record Mirror)	10
89	A&M CDEE 527	Stone Cold Sober/The Return Of Maggie Brown/Talk It To Death (3" CD)	10
89	A&M CDEE 515	Kiss This Thing Goodbye/No Holding On/Slowly, It's Coming Back (3" CD)	10
80s	Fan Club	Charlie's Bar (flexi, 1-track)	20
90	A&M AMCD 551	Kiss This Thing Goodbye/No Holding On/Slowly, It's Coming Back (3" CD, reissue)	10
90	A&M AMCDW 551	Kiss This Thing Goodbye/No Holding On/Slowly, It's Coming Back (3" CD, numberedd gatefold sleeve with lyric insert, reissue)	10
90	A&M 390 501-2	Nothing Ever Happens/So Many Souls To Change/Don't I Look Like The Kind Of Guy You Used To Hate?/Evidence (CD)	10

MINT VALUE £

97	A&M 582 365-2	Medicine/Driving With The Brakes On (Live)/Move Away Jimmy Blue (live)/ The Ones That You Love... (live) (CD, slimline jewel case, withdrawn)	15
97	A&M 582 367-2	Medicine/Roll To Me (Live At Leeds)/Here & Now (Live At Leeds)/ Hatful Of Rain (Live At Leeds) (CD, slimline jewel case, withdrawn)	15
97	A&M 582 369-2	Medicine/Some Other Sucker's Parade (Live At Leeds)/Always The Last To Know (Live At Leeds)/Stone Cold Sober (Live At Leeds) (CD, slimline jewel case, withdrawn)	15
97	A&M 582 4332	Some Other Sucker's Parade/Driving With The Brakes On (Live At Leeds)/ Move Away Jimmy Blue (Live At Leeds)/The Ones That You Love Lead You Nowhere (Live At Leeds) (CD, with postcards)	15
97	A&M 582 4352	Some Other Sucker's Parade (Version)/Roll To Me (Live At Leeds)/ Here & Now (Live At Leeds)/Hatful Of Rain (Live At Leeds) (CD)	15
85	Chrysalis CHR 1499	DEL AMITRI (LP, original issue)	12

DELACARDOS
61	HMV POP 890	Hold Back The Tears/Mister Dillon	35

DE LAINE SISTERS
62	Piccadilly 7N 35070	It Might As Well Rain Until September/Puppet On A String	7

(see also Ladybirds, Breakaways)

ERIC DELANEY BAND
56	Pye N 15069	Rockin' The Tymps/Ain't She Sweet (78)	7
56	Pye N 15079	Rock 'N' Roll King Cole/Time For Chimes (78)	8
57	Pye 7N 15113	Fanfare Jump/Jingle Bells	5
60	Parlophone R 4646	Bass Drum Boogie/Let's Get Organised	4
62	Parlophone R 4925	Manhattan Spiritual/Down Home	7
50s	Pye	HI-FI DELANEY (10" LP)	20

ERIC DELANEY'S BIG BEAT SIX
65	Pye 7N 15782	The Big Beat/Big Noise From Winnetka	6

DELANEY & BONNIE (& FRIENDS)
69	Elektra EKSN 45066	Get Ourselves Together/Soldiers Of The Cross (withdrawn)	15
69	Atlantic 584 308	Comin' Home/Groupie (Superstar) (featuring Eric Clapton; with large centre hole)	5
70	Elektra EKSN 45078	Someday/Dirty Old Man	5
70	Atlantic 2091 016	Free The People/Soul Shake	5
71	Atlantic 2091 065	Miss Ann/Let Me Be Your Man	5
71	Atlantic 2091 115	Never Ending Song Of Love/Don't Deceive Me	5
69	Apple SAPCOR 7	THE ORIGINAL DELANEY & BONNIE (LP, unreleased, no sleeve)	600
69	Elektra EKS 74039	THE ORIGINAL DELANEY & BONNIE — ACCEPT NO SUBSTITUTE (LP, commercial release of above LP)	15
69	Stax SXATS 1029	HOME (LP)	15
70	Atlantic 2400 013	ON TOUR WITH ERIC CLAPTON (LP)	15
71	Atco 2400 029	TO BONNIE FROM DELANEY (LP)	12
71	London ZGL 113	GENESIS (LP)	12
71	Atlantic 2400 119	MOTEL SHOT (LP)	12
72	CBS 64959	TOGETHER (LP)	12
74	Stax 2362 001	HOME (LP, reissue)	12

(see also Eric Clapton, Delaney Bramlett, King Curtis with Delaney & Friends, Shindogs)

DEL-CAPRIS
79	Grapevine GRP 112	Hey Little Way Out Girl (actually by Construction)/ EULA COOPER: Beggars Can't Be Choosey (p/s)	7

DELFONICS
68	Bell BLL 1005	La La Means I Love You/Can't Get Over Losing You	7
68	Bell BLL 1028	Break Your Promises/Alfie	5
69	Bell BLL 1042	Ready Or Not Here I Come/Somebody Loves Me	5
71	Mojo 2092 007	He Don't Really Love You/Without You	5
68	Bell SBLL 106	LA-LA MEANS I LOVE YOU (LP)	15
69	Bell SBLL 121	THE SOUND OF SEXY SOUL (LP)	15
71	Bell SBLL 137	THE DELFONICS (LP)	12
74	Bell BELLS 245	ALIVE AND KICKING (LP)	12

TERESA DEL FUEGO
81	Satril HH 155	Don't Hang Up/Wonder Wonder (no p/s)	8

(see also Swing Out Sister)

DELGADOS
95	Chemikal Underground CHEM 001	Monica Webster/Brand New Car (p/s)	6
95	Radar SCAN 07	THE LAZARWALKER EP (p/s)	10
96	Chemikal Underground CHEM 004	Cinecentre/Thirteen Gliding Prices/Mule Emulator (p/s)	5
96	Chemikal Underground CHEM 006	Under Canvas/Een Telf/Bear Cub/Strathcona (p/s)	5
96	Chemikal Underground CHEM 008	Sucrose/Chalk/Eurosprint/The Dirge (p/s)	5
96	Boa HISS 4	Liquidation Girl/VAN IMPE: Piranha (hand-painted brown paper bag p/s, 500 only)	15

DELICATES
59	London HLT 8953	Ronnie Is My Lover/Black And White Thunderbird	100
59	London HLT 8953	Ronnie Is My Lover/Black And White Thunderbird (78)	60
60	London HLT 9176	Too Young To Date/The Kiss	45

DELICATESSAN
67	Vocalion VN 9286	The Red Baron's Revenge/The Dog Fight (Der Hundkampf)	6

DELIGHT'S ORCHESTRA
69	Atco 226 005	Do Your Thing/King Of The Horse	4

DELITES
80	Grapevine GRP 127	Lover/Tell Me Why	5

JOHNNY DE LITTLE
61	Columbia DB 4578	Not Guilty/They	7
62	Columbia DB 4907	Lover/You Made Me Love You	7
63	Columbia DB 7023	Days Of Wine And Roses/Ride On	7
63	Columbia DB 7044	The Wind And The Rain/Unchained Melody	8
65	CBS 201790	The Knack/What To Do With Laurie	8

(see also John Barry)

DENNIS D'ELL
67	CBS 202605	It Breaks My Heart In Two/Better Use Your Head (withdrawn; demos £150)	225
67	Decca F 12647	A Woman Called Sorrow/The Night Has A Thousand Eyes (as Denny D'Ell)	6
76	Polydor 2058 715	Home Is Home/Morning Without You (as Denis D'Ell)	5

(see also Honeycombs)

JIMMY DELL
58	RCA RCA 1066	Teeny Weeny/BARRY DE VORZON: Barbara Jean	70
58	RCA RCA 1066	Teeny Weeny/BARRY DE VORZON: Barbara Jean (78)	50

PETE DELLO & FRIENDS
71	Nepentha 6437 001	INTO YOUR EARS (LP, gatefold sleeve)	90

(see also Honeybus, Lace, Red Herring, Leah, John Killigrew, Magic Valley, Grant Tracy & Sunsets, Sunsets)

DELLS
63	Pye International 7N 25178	The (Bossa Nova) Bird/Eternally	15
67	Chess CRS 8066	O-O I Love You/There Is	7
68	Chess CRS 8071	Wear It On Our Face/Please Don't Change Me Now	10
68	Chess CRS 8079	Stay In My Corner/Love Is So Simple	8
68	President PT 223	It's Not Unusual/Stay In My Corner	5
68	Chess CRS 8084	Always Together/I Want My Momma	5
69	Chess CRS 8099	I Can Sing A Rainbow/Love Is Blue-Hallelujah Baby	5
69	Chess CRS 8102	Oh What A Night/Believe Me	6
69	President PT 270	Oh What A Night/Moving On	6
69	Chess CRS 8105	On The Dock Of The Bay/When I'm In Your Arms	6
72	Chess 6145 008	It's All Up To You/Oh, My Dear	6
73	Chess 6145 022	Give Your Baby A Standing Ovation/Run For Cover	6
79	20th Century TC 2463	All About The Paper/I Touched A Dream (12")	8
68	Chess CRLS 4554	GREATEST HITS (LP)	18
69	Chess CRLS 4555	LOVE IS BLUE/OH, WHAT A NIGHT (LP)	18
71	Joy JOYS 186	OH WHAT A NIGHT (LP)	12
73	Chess 6467 303	THE BEST OF THE DELLS (LP)	12
75	Chess 9109 100	THE MIGHTY MIGHTY DELLS (LP)	12

DELKOM
91	Wau! MWS 034R	Superjack — Orbital Infusion 2000/Neutron 9000 Mix (12", 500 only)	12

ELAINE DELMAR
59	Fontana H 227	I Loves You Porgy/Porgy (78)	7
70	CBS 5329	Hurt So Bad/The Train	5

DELMONAS
84	Big Beat SW 101	Comin' Home Baby/Woa Now/He Tells Me He Loves Me (p/s)	5
84	Big Beat SW 102	Hello We Love You/I'm The One For You/Peter Gunn Locomotion (p/s)	5

DELMONTES
81	Rational RATE 1	Tous Les Soirs/Ga Ga/Infectious Smile (with insert in bag or normal p/s)	5/6
81	Rational RATE 3	Don't Cry Your Tears/So It's Not To Be (gatefold p/s in bag, yellow or blue p/s)	5

DELMORE BROTHERS
58	Parlophone GEP 8728	COUNTRY AND WESTERN (EP)	25

AL DE LORY
65	London HLU 9999	Yesterday/Traffic Jam	15
70	Capitol CL 15644	Song From M*A*S*H/Feeling Of Love	5

DELROY & SPORTY
71	Banana BA 322	Lovers Version/DUDLEY SIBLEY: Having A Party	10

DELROY & TENNORS
71	Camel CA 62	Donkey Shank/MURPHY'S ALL STARS: Donkey Track	8

DELTA CATS
69	Bamboo BAM 3	I Can't Re-Live (song actually "I Can't Believe")/I've Been Hurt	8

(see also Thrillers)

DELTA KINGS
61	London RE-R 1318	AT SUNDOWN (EP)	10
61	London Jazz LTZ-R 15204	AT SUNDOWN (LP, also stereo SAH-R 6118)	15/18

DELTA RHYTHM BOYS
51	London L 1145	Blow Out The Candle/All The Things You Are (78)	10
54	Brunswick 05353	Mood Indigo/Have A Hope, Have A Wish, Have A Prayer	8
52	Esquire 15-001	DELTA RHYTHM BOYS WITH THE METRONOME ALLSTARS (10" LP)	18

DELTAS
64	Blue Beat BB 265	Georgia/The Party	15
65	Blue Beat BB 275	The Visitor/SKATALITES: Hanging The Beam	20

DELTA SKIFFLE GROUP

DELTA SKIFFLE GROUP
57	Esquire 10-504	Skip To My Lou/John Brown's Body (78)	12
57	Esquire 10-507	K.C. Moan/Pick A Bale Of Cotton (78)	12
58	Esquire 10-517	Ain't You Glad?/Open Up Them Pearly Gates (78)	15
58	Esquire EP 162	DELTA SKIFFLE GROUP (EP)	45

DEL-TONES
59	Top Rank JAR 171	Rockin' Blues/Moonlight Party	50
59	Top Rank JAR 171	Rockin' Blues/Moonlight Party (78)	45
70	Columbia DB 8719	Gimme Some Lovin'/Have A Little Talk With Myself	5

(see also Beau-Marks)

DELTONES
71	Green Door GD 4010	Chopsticks/DES BRYAN: Belmont Street	6
72	Trojan TRM 9001	Chopsticks/I Got It/Put It On	5

MILTON DE LUGG ORCHESTRA
65	Columbia DB 7474	The Addams Family Theme/The Alfred Hitchcock Theme	10
66	Columbia DB 7762	The Munsters Theme/The Addams Family Theme	12

(see also Beau-Marks)

DELUSION
80s	Wizzo WIZZO 2	Pessimists Paradise/Desert Island (gatefold p/s)	8

DEL(L)-VIKINGS
57	London HLD 8405	Come Go With Me/How Can I Find A True Love (gold or silver label lettering)	125/50
57	London HLD 8405	Come Go With Me/How Can I Find A True Love (78)	15
57	London HLD 8464	Whispering Bells/Little Billy Boy	40
57	London HLD 8464	Whispering Bells/Little Billy Boy (78)	15
57	Mercury MT 169	Cool Shake/Jitterbug Mary (78)	30
58	Mercury 7MT 199	The Voodoo Man/Can't Wait	50
58	Mercury MT 199	The Voodoo Man/Can't Wait (78)	30
59	Mercury AMT 1027	Flat Tyre/How Could You	45
59	Mercury AMT 1027	Flat Tyre/How Could You (78)	40
62	HMV POP 1072	Confession Of Love/Kilimanjaro	10
63	HMV POP 1145	An Angel Up In Heaven/The Fishing Chant	10
71	Contour 2870 388	COME GO WITH ME (LP)	12

(see also Chuck Jackson)

LEO DE LYON
54	MGM SP 1087	The Band Played On/Say It Isn't So	5
60	Oriole CB 1561	Rich In Love/The Blue Train	5
60	Oriole MG 20053	LEO DE LYON (LP)	12

JULIE DE MARCO
64	HMV POP 1255	And This Is My Beloved/Bless This House	5

RALPH DE MARCO
59	London HLL 9010	Old Shep/More Than Riches	7
59	London HLL 9010	Old Shep/More Than Riches (78)	35

DEMENSIONS
60	Top Rank JAR 505	Over The Rainbow/Nursery Rhyme Rock	40
61	Coral Q 72437	Count Your Blessings Instead Of Sheep/Again	12

DEMENTED ARE GO
85	I.D. EYET 8	Holly Hack Jack/Rubber Buccaneer/Don't Go In The Woods (12", p/s)	10
86	I.D. NOSE 9	IN SICKNESS AND IN HEALTH (LP)	12

(ROD) DEMICK & (HERBIE) ARMSTRONG
70	Decca F 13056	We're On The Right Track/Dreaming (as Demick-Armstrong)	6
71	Mam MAM 10	If I Ever Get To You/Girl	5
71	Mam MAM-AS 1001	LITTLE WILLY RAMBLE (LP)	12
72	A&M AMLH 68908	LOOKIN' THROUGH (LP)	12

(see also Wheels, James Brothers, Yellow Dog, Fox)

DEMOB
81	Round Ear ROUND 1	Anti Police/Teenage Adolescence (foldout p/s, later standard p/s)	12/7
81	Round Ear EAR 3	No Room For You/Think Straight/New Breed (p/s)	15

DEMON
81	Clay CLAY 4	Liar/Wild Woman (p/s, red vinyl)	8
82	Carrere CAR 226	One Helluva Night/Into The Nightmare (picture disc)	5
83	Clay CLAY 25	The Plague/The Only Sane Man (p/s)	5
84	Clay CLAY 41	Wonderland/Blackheath (p/s)	5
84	Clay 12CLAY 41	Wonderland/Blackheath/Nowhere To Run (12", p/s)	8
88	Clay CLAY 48D	Tonight (The Hero Is Back)/Hurricane//Night Of The Demon/Don't Break The Circle (double pack)	5
83	Clay CLAYLP 6P	THE PLAGUE (LP, picture disc)	12

DEMON FUZZ
70	Dawn DNX 2504	I Put A Spell On You/Message To Mankind/Fuzz Oriental Blues (some in p/s)	8/5
70	Dawn DNLS 3013	AFREAKA! (LP)	20

DEMON PACT
81	Slime PACT 1	Eaten Alive/Raiders (p/s)	50
81	Slime PACT 2	Escape/Demon Pact (unreleased, labels only)	

DEMON PREACHER
78	Illegal SRTS/CUS/78110	Royal Northern (N7)/Laughing At Me/Steal Your Love/Dead End Kidz (numbered p/s)	15
78	Small Wonder SMALL TEN	Little Miss Perfect/Perfect Dub (p/s)	10

(see also Demons, Alien Sex Fiend, Fenzyx)

DEMONS (Jamaica)
69	Big Shot BI 523	You Belong To My Heart/Bless You	7

DEMONS (U.K.)
80	Crypt Music DEM 1	Action By Example/I Wish I Was A Dog (p/s)	10

(see also Alien Sex Fiend, Demon Preacher)

TOMMY DEMPSEY & JOHN SWIFT
76	Trailer LER 2096	GREEN GROW THE LAUREL (LP)	10

JASON DENE
66	Parlophone R 5485	Opportunity/It's Me	5

(see also Jason Deane)

TERRY DENE
57	Decca F 10895	A White Sport Coat/The Man In The Phone Booth	30
57	Decca F 10895	A White Sport Coat/The Man In The Phone Booth (78)	8
57	Decca F 10914	Start Movin'/Green Corn	22
57	Decca F 10914	Start Movin'/Green Corn (78)	6
57	Decca F 10938	Come And Get It/Teenage Dream	18
57	Decca F 10938	Come And Get It/Teenage Dream (78)	7
57	Decca F 10964	Lucky Lucky Bobby/Baby, She's Gone	18
57	Decca F 10964	Lucky Lucky Bobby/Baby, She's Gone (78)	8
58	Decca F 10977	The Golden Age/C'Min And Be Loved	18
58	Decca F 10977	The Golden Age/C'Min And Be Loved (78)	7
58	Decca F 11016	Stairway Of Love/Lover, Lover!	12
58	Decca F 11016	Stairway Of Love/Lover, Lover! (78)	8
58	Decca F 11037	Seven Steps To Love/Can I Walk You Home	12
58	Decca F 11037	Seven Steps To Love/Can I Walk You Home (78)	8
58	Decca F 11076	Who Baby Who/Pretty Little Pearly	15
58	Decca F 11076	Who Baby Who/Pretty Little Pearly (78)	10
59	Decca F 11100	I've Got A Good Thing Going/Bimbombey	10
59	Decca F 11100	I've Got A Good Thing Going/Bimbombey (78)	12
59	Decca F 11136	There's No Fool Like A Young Fool/I've Come Of Age	10
59	Decca F 11136	There's No Fool Like A Young Fool/I've Come Of Age (78)	15
59	Decca F 11154	Thank You Pretty Baby/A Boy Without A Girl	15
59	Decca F 11154	Thank You Pretty Baby/A Boy Without A Girl (78)	18
60	Oriole CB 1562	Geraldine/Love Me Or Leave Me	18
61	Oriole CB 1594	Like A Baby/Next Stop Paradise	15
63	Aral PS 107	The Feminine Look/Fever (initially in p/s)	10/5
82	Logo GO 412	Paralysed/Lorna/The Girl In The Long Black Dress	5
57	Decca DFE 6427	THE GOLDEN DISC (EP)	35
58	Decca DFE 6459	TERRY DENE NO. 1 (EP)	50
58	Decca DFE 6507	TERRY DENE NO. 2 (EP)	35
66	Herald ELR 107	TERRY DENE NOW (EP)	18
72	Pilgrim JLPS 175	IF THAT ISN'T LOVE (LP)	15
73	Pilgrim JLPS 188	CALL TO THE WIND (LP)	15
74	Decca SPA 368	I THOUGHT TERRY DENE WAS DEAD (LP)	15

DENE BOYS
57	HMV POP 374	Bye Bye Love/Love Is The Thing	12
57	HMV POP 374	Bye Bye Love/Love Is The Thing (78)	7
58	HMV POP 455	Skylark/I Walk Down The Street	6
58	HMV POP 455	Skylark/I Walk Down The Street (78)	8

DENE FOUR
59	HMV POP 666	Hush-a-bye/Something New	15

(see also Dene Boys)

DENIGH
80	Ace ACE 16	No Way (no p/s)	80

DENIMS
65	CBS 201807	I'm Your Man/Ya Ya	45

CLAUDE DENJEAN
71	Decca PFS 4212	MOOG! (LP)	12

ROGER DENISON
66	Parlophone R 5545	I'm On An Island/I'm Running Out Of Time	10
67	Parlophone R 5566	She Wanders Through My Mind/This Just Doesn't Seem To Be My Day	7

WADE DENNING & PORT WASHINGTONS
67	MGM MGM 1339	Tarzan's March/Batman	10

D.D. (Denzil) DENNIS
70	Crab CRAB 60	Having A Party/Man With Ambition	5
70	Pama Supreme PS 301	My Way/Happy Days	5
71	Punch PH 93	Christmas Message/Cool It Girl	5
71	Pama Supreme PS 330	I'm A Believer/I'll Make The Way Easy	5
74	Pama Supreme PS 391	Women And Money/UPSETTERS: Ten Cent Skank	6

(see also Denzil Dennis)

DENZIL DENNIS
63	Blue Beat BB 181	Seven Nights In Rome/Love Is For Fools	12
68	Trojan TR 614	Donkey Train/Down By The Riverside	8
68	Trojan TR 615	Me Nah Worry/Hush Don't You Cry	8
68	Jolly JY 011	Oh Carol/Where Has My Little Girl Gone	6
70	Pama Supreme PS 304	Painful Situation/Nothing Has Changed	5
71	Pama Supreme PS 350	South Of The Border/GRAHAM: Long Island	18
72	Pama Supreme PS 375	Mama We're All Crazy Now/ROY SHIRLEY: A Lady's A Man's Best Friend	5
72	Duke DU 142	I Forgot To Be Your Lover/I've Got To Settle Down	5
73	Grape GR 3059	People Got To Be Friends/Ups And Downs (actually by Pat Rhoden)	5

(see also D.D. Dennis, Cosmo & Dennis, Denzil & Pat, Denzil & Jennifer, Les & Silkie)

MINT VALUE £

JACKIE DENNIS

58	Decca F 10992	La Dee Dah/You're The Greatest	7
58	Decca F 10992	La Dee Dah/You're The Greatest (78)	7
58	Decca F 11011	Miss Valerie/My Dream	12
58	Decca F 11011	Miss Valerie/My Dream (78)	8
58	Decca F 11033	The Purple People Eater/You-Oo	12
58	Decca F 11033	The Purple People Eater/You-Oo (78)	6
58	Decca F 11060	More Than Ever (Coma Prima)/Linton Addie	7
58	Decca F 11060	More Than Ever (Coma Prima)/Linton Addie (78)	8
58	Decca F 11090	Gingerbread/Lucky Ladybug	8
58	Decca F 11090	Gingerbread/Lucky Ladybug (78)	8
59	Top Rank JAR 129	Summer Snow/Night Bird	5
59	Top Rank JAR 129	Summer Snow/Night Bird (78)	7
58	Decca DFE 6513	JACKIE DENNIS NO. 1 (EP)	35

DENNIS & LIZZY

70	Camel CA 56	Everybody Bawlin'/Mr Brown	8
73	Pyramid PYR 7002	Ba-Ba-Ri-Ba-Shank/TOMMY McCOOK ALL STARS: Buck And The Preacher	8

(see also Dennis Alcapone, Lizzy & Dennis)

DENNISONS

63	Decca F 11691	(Come On) Be My Girl/Little Latin Lupe Lu	15
64	Decca F 11880	Walkin' The Dog/You Don't Know What Love Is	18
64	Decca F 11990	Nobody Like My Babe/Lucy (You Sure Did It This Time)	15

DENNY & WILSON

72	Hillcrest HCT 6	Hey Hey Girl/CARLTON ALPHONSO: Girl I Love You	6

MARTIN DENNY (& HIS ORCHESTRA)

59	London HLU 8860	Quiet Village/Llama Serenade	6
59	London SLW 4004	Quiet Village/Llama Serenade (stereo export issue)	30
59	London HLU 8860	Quiet Village/Llama Serenade (78)	8
59	London HLU 8976	The Enchanted Sea/Martinique	5
59	London HLU 8976	The Enchanted Sea/Martinique (78)	10
62	Liberty LIB 55470	A Taste Of Honey/The Brighter Side	5
60	London REU 1241	THE EXOTIC SOUNDS OF MARTIN DENNY (EP)	20
58	London HB-U 1079	EXOTICA (10" LP, mono only)	30
58	London SAH-U 6004	FORBIDDEN ISLAND (LP, stereo only)	30
59	London HA-U 2196	AFRO-DESIA (LP, also stereo SAH-U 6048)	30/20
60	London HA-U 2208	QUIET VILLAGE (LP, also stereo SAH-U 6055)	20/25
60	London SAH-W 6062	EXOTICA (12" LP, stereo reissue with extra tracks "Busy Port" & "Waipio")	25
60	London HA-G 2253	EXOTICA — VOL. 2 (LP, also stereo SAH-G 6076)	20/25
60	London HA-W 2264	EXOTICA — VOL. 3 (LP, also stereo SAH-W 6069)	20/25
60	London HA-G 2281	THE ENCHANTED SEA (LP, also stereo SAH-G 6098)	20/25
61	London HA-G 2317	THE SILVER SCREEN (LP, also stereo SAH-G 6122)	15/18
61	London HA-G 2387	EXOTIC PERCUSSION (LP, also stereo SAH-G 6187)	15/18
62	London HA-G 2417	ROMANTICA (LP, also stereo SAH-G 6215)	15/18
64	Liberty LBY 1241	HAWAII TATTOO (LP)	18
65	Liberty (S)LBY 1221	LATIN VILLAGE (LP)	12
65	Liberty (S)LBY 1267	SPANISH VILLAGE (LP)	12
66	Liberty (S)LBY 1276	20 GOLDEN HAWAIIAN HITS (LP)	12
66	Liberty (S)LBY 1301	MARTIN DENNY PLAYS (LP)	12
66	Liberty (S)LBY 1354	HAWAII TOUCH (LP)	15
68	Sunset SLS 50002	SAYONARA (LP)	12

SANDY DENNY

72	Island WIP 6141	Here In Silence/Man Of Iron (soundtrack from *Pass Of Arms* film, some in p/s)	40/25
72	Island WIP 6142	Listen Listen/Tomorrow Is A Long Time	6
73	Island WIP 6176	Whispering Grass/Friends (some in p/s)	10/6
74	Island WIP 6195	Like An Old Fashioned Waltz (unissued)	
76	Mooncrest MOON 54	Make Me A Pallet On Your Floor/This Train	6
77	Island WIP 6391	Candle In The Wind/Still Waters Run Deep (unissued, promo only)	30
67	Saga EROS 8041	SANDY AND JOHNNY (LP, with Johnny Silvo)	30
70	Saga EROS 8153	SANDY DENNY (LP)	35
71	Island ILPS 9165	THE NORTH STAR GRASSMAN AND THE RAVENS (LP, gatefold sleeve, 'pink rim palm tree' label)	18
72	Island ILPS 9207	SANDY (LP, gatefold sleeve, originally with 'pink rim palm tree' label)	20/12
73	Island ILPS 9258	LIKE AN OLD FASHIONED WALTZ (LP, gatefold sleeve, 'pink rim palm tree' label)	15
73	Hallmark SHM 813	ALL OUR OWN WORK (LP, with Strawbs)	15
77	Island ILPS 9433	RENDEZVOUS (LP, with insert)	12
78	Mooncrest CREST 28	THE ORIGINAL SANDY DENNY (LP)	20
85	Island SDSP 100	WHO KNOWS WHERE THE TIME GOES? (4-LP box set)	30

(see also Fairport Convention, Bunch, Strawbs, Fotheringay, Alex Campbell, Trevor Lucas, Richard Thompson)

SUSAN DENNY

65	Melodisc MEL 1596	Don't Touch Me/Johnny	10

DENTISTS

85	Spruck SP 003	Strawberries Are Growing In My Garden (And It's Wintertime)/Burning The Thoughts From My Skin/Doreen (p/s)	10
85	Spruck SP 004	YOU AND YOUR BLOODY ORANGES (12" EP, p/s)	10
86	Tambourine SP 006	DOWN AND OUT IN PARIS AND CHATHAM (12" EP, brown/white or group p/s)	8
87	Tambourine URINE 3	Writhing On The Shagpile/Just Like Oliver Reed/A Strange Way To Go About Things/Calm You Down/The Turquoise Castle (12", p/s)	8
85	Spruck SPR 001	SOME PEOPLE ARE ON THE PITCH THEY THINK IT'S ALL OVER IT IS NOW (LP)	15

MICKEY DENTON
61   London HLX 9398   The Steady Kind/Now You Can't Give Them Away 8

KARL DENVER
61	Decca F 11360	Marcheta/Joe Sweeney	5
61	Decca F 11395	Mexicali Rose/Bonny Scotland	5
62	Decca F 11420	Wimoweh/Gypsy Davy	5
62	Decca F 11431	Never Goodbye/Highland Fling	5
62	Decca F 11470	A Little Love, A Little Kiss/Lonely Sailor.	5
62	Decca F 11505	Blue Weekend/My Mother's Eyes.	5
62	Decca F 11553	Dry Tears/Pastures Of Plenty.	5
63	Decca F 11608	Can You Forgive Me/Love From A Heart Of Gold	5
63	Decca F 11674	Indian Love Call/My Melancholy Baby.	5
63	Decca F 11720	Still/My Canary Has Circles Under His Eyes.	5
64	Decca F 11828	My World Of Blue/The Green Grass Grows All Round	5
64	Decca F 11905	Love Me With All Your Heart/Am I That Easy To Forget?	6
64	Decca F 12025	Sally/Swanee River	5
65	Mercury MF 878	Cry A Little Sometimes/Today Will Be Yesterday Tomorrow.	8
65	Mercury MF 904	Marta/I'll Never Forget To Remember	8
65	Mercury MF 926	The Tips Of My Fingers/I'm Alone Because I Love You	8
68	Page One POF 063	You've Still Got A Place In My Heart/	
		I Still Miss Someone (as Karl Denver Trio).	5
62	Decca DFE 8501	BY A SLEEPY LAGOON (EP).	12
62	Decca DFE 8504	KARL DENVER HITS (EP)	12
61	Ace Of Clubs ACL 1098	WIMOWEH (LP).	15
62	Ace Of Clubs ACL 1131	KARL DENVER (LP).	18
63	Decca LK 4540	LIVE AT THE YEW TREE (LP)	25
64	Decca LK 4596	WITH LOVE (LP).	25

NIGEL DENVER
66	Decca LK 4728	MOVIN' ON (LP, featuring Martin Carthy).	40
67	Major Minor MMLP 1	SCOTTISH REPUBLICAN SONGS (LP)	20
68	Decca SKL 4943	FOLK OLD AND NEW (LP).	20

DENZIL & JENNIFER
70   Escort ES 824   Young, Gifted And Black/OWEN GRAY: I Am Satisfied. 5

DENZIL (Dennis) & PAT (Rhoden)
69   Downtown DT 403   Dream/Sincerely. 5

DEODATO
73	CTI CTS 4000	Also Sprach Zarathustra/Spirit Of Summer	5
73	CTI CTS 4003	Do It Again/Branches	
		(as Deodato-Airto)	5
73	CTI CTL 10	PRELUDE (LP)	12
73	CTI CTL 17	DEODATO 2 (LP).	12
74	CTI CTL 21	IN CONCERT (LP, with Airto)	12
74	MCA MCG 3518	WHIRLWINDS (LP)	12
75	MCA MCF 2587	ARTISTRY (LP).	10
75	MCA MCF 2728	FIRST CUCKOO (LP)	10

(see also Airto)

WILBUR DE PARIS' NEW ORLEANS BAND
59	London HLE 8816	Petite Fleur/Over And Over Again.	5
59	London HLE 8816	Petite Fleur/Over And Over Again (78)	8
60	London Jazz LTZK 15192	THAT'S A-PLENTY (LP, also stereo SAHK 6079).	12
61	London Jazz LTZK 15201	THE WILD JAZZ AGE (LP, also stereo SAHK 6115).	12

DEPECHE MODE
81	Lyntone LYN 10209	Sometimes I Wish I Was Dead/FAD GADGET: King Of The Flies	
		(red flexidisc free with *Flexipop* magazine, issue 11)	25/15
81	Mute MUTE 013	Dreaming Of Me/Ice Machine (p/s)	5
83	Mute L12BONG 2	Get The Balance Right/My Secret Garden (live)/See You (live)/	
		Satellite (live) (12", numbered p/s)	12
83	Mute L12BONG 3	Everything Counts/Boys Say Go (live)/New Life (live)/Nothing To Fear (live)/	
		The Meaning Of Love (live) (12", numbered p/s).	12
83	Mute L12BONG 4	Love In Itself (2)/Just Can't Get Enough (live)/Photograph Of You (live)/	
		Shout (live)/Photographic (live) (12", numbered p/s)	12
84	Mute L12BONG 5	People Are People (On-U-Sound Remix)/In Your Memory/	
		People Are People (12", numbered in die-cut p/s)	12
84	Mute L12BONG 6	Master And Servant (On-U-Sound Science Fiction Dancehall Classic)/	
		Are People People?/(Set Me Free) Remotivate Me (12", numbered p/s).	12
84	Mute 7BONG 7E	Blasphemous Rumours/Somebody/Told You So (live)/	
		Everything Counts (live) (EP, p/s)	5
85	Mute L12 BONG 8	Edit The Shake/Master And Servant (live)/Flexible (Pre-Deportation Mix)/	
		Something To Do (Metal Mix) (12", p/s).	10
85	Mute 7BONG 9	It's Called A Heart/Fly On The Windscreen (p/s, sealed with poster)	5
85	Mute D12BONG 9	It's Called A Heart (Mixes)/Fly On The Windscreen (Mixes) (12", p/s, dbl-pack). . .	10
86	Mute CBONG 11	A Question Of Lust (Flood Mix)/If You Want (live)/Shame (live)/	
		Blasphemous Rumours (live) (cassette in 7" pack with book & badge)	10
86	Mute L12BONG 12	A Question Of Time (Remix)/Black Celebration (Black Tulip Mix)/More Than A	
		Party (Live Remix) (12", p/s)	10
87	Mute L12 BONG 13	Strangelove (Blind Mix)/PIMPF/Strangelove (Pain Mix)/	
		Agent Orange (12", p/s)	10
87	Mute DANCE BONG 13	Strangelove (Fresh Ground Mix)/(Blind Mix) (12", promo-only remix)	30
87	Mute CDBONG 13	Strangelove (Maxi-Mix)/Strangelove (Midi-Mix)/Strangelove (LP Mix)/	
		PIMPF/Agent Orange (CD, card p/s)	8
87	Mute L12BONG 14	Never Let Me Down Again (Tsangarides Mix)/Pleasure Little Treasure	
		(Join Mix)/To Have And To Hold (Spanish Taster) (12", p/s)	10

MINT VALUE £

DEPECHE MODE

87	Mute CBONG 14	Never Let Me Down Again (Split Mix)/(Aggro Mix)/Pleasure Little Treasure (Glitter Mix) (cassette with 'overlay') 5
87	Mute CDBONG 14	Never Let Me Down Again (Split Mix)/Pleasure, Little Treasure (Join Mix)/ To Have And To Hold (Spanish Taster)/Never Let Me Down Again (Aggro Mix) (CD in pouch) 12
88	Mute L12BONG 15	Behind The Wheel (Beatmasters Remix)/Route 66 (Casuality Mix) (12", p/s) 10
88	Mute CBONG 15	Behind The Wheel (Beatmasters Remix)/Route 66 (Casuality Mix) (cassette with 'overlay') 5
89	Mute 10BONG 16	Everything Counts (Absolute Mix)/(1983 12" Mix)/Nothing (US 7" Mix) (10", envelope p/s, with 2 postcards & window sticker) 15
89	Mute L12BONG 16	Everything Counts (Tim Simenon & M. Saunders Remix)/Nothing (Justin Strauss Remix)/Strangelove (Tim Simenon & M. Saunders Remix) (12", p/s) 10
89	Mute LCDBONG 16	Everything Counts (Tim Simenon & M. Saunders Remix)/Nothing (Justin Strauss Remix)/Strangelove (Tim Simenon & M. Saunders Remix) (3" CD, 'filofax page' p/s) 20
89	Mute GBONG 17	Personal Jesus/(Acoustic)/Dangerous (Hazchemix) (gatefold p/s with photos) 7
89	Mute L12BONG 17	Personal Jesus (Mixes)/Dangerous (Hazchemix) (12", p/s) 10
89	Mute LCDBONG 17	Personal Jesus (Pump Mix)/Personal Jesus (Telephone Stomp Mix)/ Dangerous (Hazchemix) (3" CD) 15
90	Mute XL12BONG 18	Enjoy The Silence (The Quad: Final Mix) (12", 1-side etched, p/s) 10
90	Mute LCDBONG 18	Enjoy The Silence (Bassline): Bassline/Harmonium/Ricki Tick Tick Mix/ Memphesto (CD) 10
90	Mute XLCDBONG 18	Enjoy The Silence (The Quad: Final Mix) (3" CD, 1-track) 25
90	Mute L12BONG 19	Policy Of Truth (Trancentral Mix)/Policy Of Truth (Pavlov's Dub)/ Kaleid (remix) (12", gatefold p/s) 8
90	Mute L12BONG 20	World In My Eyes (Dub In My Eyes)/(Mode To Joy)/Happiest Girl (The Pulsating Orbital Mix) (12", p/s with inner, in sealed blue PVC pack) 10
90	Mute LCDBONG 20	World In My Eyes (Dub In My Eyes)/World In My Eyes (Mode To Joy)/ Happiest Girl (The Pulsating Orbital Vocal Mix)/Sea Of Sin (Sensoria)/ World In My Eyes (Mayhem Mode)/Happiest Girl (Jack Mix) (CD) 25
91	Mute DMBX 1	1 (6-CD single box set, with booklet) 25
91	Mute DMBX 2	2 (6-CD single box set, with booklet) 25
91	Mute DMBX 3	3 (6-CD single box set, with booklet) 25
94	Mute XLCDBONG 24	In Your Room (Mixes)/Higher Love (Adrenaline Mix) (CD) 10
97	Mute BONG 26	It's No Good (Club 69 Future Mix)/It's No Good (Club 69 Future Dub)/ It's No Good (Club 69 Funk Dub) (12", promo only) 70
87	Mute STUMM 47	MUSIC FOR THE MASSES (LP, clear vinyl) 20
87	Mute STUMM 47	MUSIC FOR THE MASSES (LP, with bonus 12" "Strangelove (Maximix)"/ "Never Let Me Down Again (Split Mix)" [HMV 1]) 30
88	Mute CDSTUMM 5	SPEAK AND SPELL (CD) 15
89	Mute CD TUMM 100	101 (2-CD, tri-fold card sleeve, with booklet in slip case) 20
89	Mute (no cat. no.)	B-SIDES (4-LP set, plain white box, unreleased, test pressings only) 1,000
90	Mute PSTUMM 64	VIOLATOR (12", 4-track sampler, promo only) 18
93	Mute LCDSTUMM 106	SONGS OF FAITH AND DEVOTION LIVE (CD, in slipcase with photo-book) 20
98	Mute MUTEL 5	SINGLES 86-98 (3 x 12" box set, numbered) 15

(see also Vince Clarke & Paul Quinn)

DEPRAVED
86 Children Of Rev. GURT 6 COME ON DOWN (LP, with lyric inner) 12

DEPRESSIONS
77 Barn 2014 112 Living On Dreams/Family Planning (p/s) 5
78 Barn 2014 119 Messing With Your Heart/Street Kid (p/s) 5
78 Barn 2014 122 Get Out Of This Town/Basement Daze (p/s) 5
78 Barn 2314 105 THE DEPRESSIONS (LP) 12
(see also DP's)

DEPUTIES
66 Strike JH 305 Given Half A Chance/Where Do People Go 8

DEPUTY DAWG
96 Peacefrog P F053 GUN SLINGER EP (12", plain sleeve) 10
(see also Luke Slater)

DEREK
68 London HLZ 10230 Cinnamon/This Is My Story 7
(see also Johnny Cymbal)

DEREK & CYNDI
74 Philadelphia Intl. PIR 2662 You Bring Out The Best In Me/I'll Do For You The Impossible 4

DEREK & THE DOMINOES
70 Polydor 2058 057 Tell The Truth/Roll It Over (withdrawn) 80
71 Polydor 2058 130 Layla/Bell Bottom Blues (original, red paper label) 5
74 RSO 2090 104 Why Does Love Got To Be Sad?/Presence Of The Lord 5
82 RSO RSO 87 Layla/ERIC CLAPTON: Wonderful Tonight (p/s) 5
71 Polydor 2625 005 LAYLA AND OTHER ASSORTED LOVE SONGS (2-LP) 18
(see also Eric Clapton, Bobby Whitlock)

DEREK & FRESHMEN
65 Oriole CB 305 Gone Away/I Stand Alone 10
(see also Derek Dean & Freshmen)

FRANK DE ROSA & HIS ORCHESTRA
58 London HLD 8576 Big Guitar/Irish Rock 25
58 London HLD 8576 Big Guitar/Irish Rock (78) 10

DERRICK (Morgan) & JENNIFER
70 Crab CRAB 47 Need To Belong/Let's Have Some Fun 6
70 Crab CRAB 54 Rocking Good Way/Wipe These Tears 6
(see also Derrick Morgan)

DERRICK (Morgan) & LLOYDS (Clarke)
62 Blue Beat BB 135 Love And Leave Me (actually by Lloyd Clarke)/Merry Twist
(actually "Whistle Stop Tour" by Roy Richards) 15
(see also Derrick Morgan, Lloyd Clarke)

DERRICK (Morgan) & NAOMI (Campbell)
65 Island WI 193 Two Of A Kind/I Want A Lover (credited to Derrick Morgan) 18
65 Ska Beat JB 185 Heart Of Stone/DERRICK MORGAN: Let Me Go 15
65 Ska Beat JB 188 I Wish I Were An Apple/DERRICK MORGAN: Around The Corner 15
(see also Derrick Morgan, Naomi, Don Drummond)

DERRICK (Morgan) & PATSY (Todd)
61 Blue Beat BB 57 Feel So Fine/ROLAND ALPHONSO & GROUP: Mean To Me 15
61 Blue Beat BB 65 Baby Please Don't Leave Me/Let The Good Times Roll 12
62 Blue Beat BB 97 Love Not To Brag/DRUMBAGO'S ALL STARS: Duck Soup 15
62 Blue Beat BB 100 In My Heart (actually by Derrick Morgan)/BELL'S GROUP: Kingston 13 15
62 Blue Beat BB 106 Oh Shirley/BASIL GABIDON'S GROUP: Sam The Fisherman
(B-side actually by Roland Alphonso) 15
62 Blue Beat BB 121 Crying In The Chapel/Come Back My Love 15
62 Blue Beat BB 123 Oh My Love/Let's Go To The Party 15
62 Island WI 018 Housewife's Choice/Gypsy Woman 15
63 Blue Beat BB 152 Little Brown Jug/Mow Sen Wa (with Lloyd Clarke) 15
63 Blue Beat BB 160 Trying To Make You Mine (actually "Baby Please Don't Leave Me" by
Derrick Morgan)/Hold Me 15
63 Island WI 055 Sea Wave/Look Before You Leap 15
64 Blue Beat BB 207 Lover Boy/The Moon 15
64 Blue Beat BB 224 Steal Away/Money 15
64 Blue Beat BB 247 Troubles/Right (B-side actually "Baby Face") 15
65 Blue Beat BB 291 You I Love/Let Me Hold Your hand (song actually "Steal Away") 15
65 Blue Beat BB 318 Eternity/Want My Baby 12
65 Island WI 224 The National Dance/DESMOND DEKKAR & FOUR ACES: Mount Zion 18
66 Island WI 288 I Found A Queen/It's True My Darling 12
68 Nu Beat NB 008 Hey Boy, Hey Girl/Music Is The Food Of Life 8
(see also Derrick Morgan, Patsy Todd)

DERRICK (Morgan) & PAULETT
69 Nu Beat NB 027 I'll Do It/Give You My Love 8
(see also Derrick Morgan, Paulette)

DERRICK (Morgan) & PAULINE (Morgan)
68 Pyramid PYR 6027 You Never Miss Your Water/DERRICK MORGAN: Got You On My Mind 10
68 Pyramid/J.J. PYR 6063 Don't Say/DERRICK MORGAN: Johnny Pram Pram 10
(see also Derrick Morgan, Patsy Todd, Basil Gabbidon)

DERRICK & SOUNDS
68 Pye 7N 17601 Power Of Love/I'll Take You Home 5
69 Pye 7N 17709 My Sly Sadie/I Can't Lose That Girl 5
69 Pye 7N 17801 Morning Papers And Margarine/Winter Of Your Love 5

MINT VALUE £

DERRINGERS
| 61 | Capitol CL 15189 | (If You Cry) True Love, True Love/Sheree | 6 |

GLEN DERRY ORCHESTRA
| 61 | Oriole CB 1609 | Blue Sax/Beatnik | 6 |

HENRI DES
| 70 | United Artists UP 35109 | Return/Retour | 15 |

DES & DAVE
| 66 | Columbia DB 7957 | That's Us/Gotta Little Gal | 5 |

DES (Bryan) ALLSTARS
70	Grape GR 3014	Night Food Reggae/Walk With Des	7
70	Grape GR 3015	If I Had A Hammer/Hammer Reggae	7
70	Grape GR 3016	Henry The Great/Black Scorcher	7

SUGAR PIE DE SANTO
64	Pye International 7N 25249	Soulful Dress/Use What You Got	15
64	Pye International 7N 25267	I Don't Wanna Fuss/I Love You So Much	15
66	Chess CRS 8034	There's Gonna Be Trouble/In The Basement (B-side with Etta James)	15
69	Chess CRS 8093	Soulful Dress/There's Gonna Be Trouble	7

(see also Etta James & Sugar Pie De Santo)

MICHAEL DES BARRES
| 74 | Purple PUR 123 | Leon/New Moon Tonight | 8 |

(see also Silverhead, Detective, Phoenix)

DESCENDANTS
| 67 | CBS 202545 | Garden Of Eden/Lela | 50 |

DESECRATION
| 88 | TPC | WHO'S IN CONTROL (EP, pink, green or black vinyl, with flexi) | 8 |

DESECTORS
| 70 | GAS GAS 137 | King Kong/Please Stay | 5 |

DESERT WOLVES
87	Ugly Man UGLY 6T	Love Shattered Lives/Stopped In My Tracks/Desolation/Sunday Morning (12", p/s)	8
88	Ugly Man UGLY 9	Speak To Me Rochelle/Besotted (p/s)	5
88	Ugly Man UGLY 9T	Speak To Me Rochelle/Mexico/Besotted/La Petite Rochelle (12", p/s)	8

JACKIE DE SHANNON
62	Liberty LIB 55497	You Won't Forget Me/I Don't Think So Much	6
63	Liberty LIB 55563	Needles And Pins/Did He Call Today Mama?	10
64	Liberty LIB 55645	When You Walk In The Room/Till You Say You'll Be Mine	10
64	Liberty LIB 10165	Dancing Silhouettes/Hold Your Head High	8
64	Liberty LIB 10175	Don't Turn Your Back On Me/Be Good Baby	8
65	Liberty LIB 10192	She Don't Understand Him Like I Do/The Prince	6
65	Liberty LIB 10202	What The World Needs Now Is Love/It's Love Baby	6
65	Liberty LIB 12019	A Lifetime Of Loneliness/I Remember The Boy	8
66	Liberty LIB 66171	Come And Get Me/Splendour In The Grass	6
66	Liberty LIB 66202	I Can Make It With You/To Be Myself	6
66	Liberty LIB 66224	Come On Down/Find Me Love	12
68	Liberty LBF 15133	The Weight/Effervescent Blue	6
69	Liberty LBF 15238	Put A Little Love In Your Heart/Always Together	6
70	Liberty LBF 15281	Love Will Find A Way/I Let Go Completely	6
70	Liberty LBF 15324	What The World Needs Now/Keep Me In Mind	6
72	Atlantic K 10184	Vanilla Olay/I Wanna Roo You	5
72	Atlantic K 10241	Only Love Can Break Your Heart/Would You Like To Learn To Dance	5
65	Liberty LEP 2233	JACKIE (EP)	25
64	Liberty LBY 1182	THIS IS JACKIE DE SHANNON (LP)	15
65	Liberty LBY 1245	DON'T TURN YOUR BACK ON ME (LP)	18
65	Liberty LBY 3063	THIS IS JACKIE DE SHANNON (LP)	18
66	Liberty (S)BLY 3085	ARE YOU READY FOR THIS? (LP)	18
68	Liberty LBS 83117E	GREAT PERFORMANCES (LP)	18
69	Liberty LBS 83148E	ME ABOUT YOU (LP)	18
70	Liberty LBS 83304	PUT A LITTLE LOVE IN YOUR HEART (LP)	18
72	Atlantic K 40396	JACKIE (LP)	12

(see also Date With Soul)

DESIGN
70	CBS 5112	Willow Stream/Coloured Mile	5
71	Epic EPC 7119	Jet Song/Minstrel's Theme	5
72	Regal Zonophone RZ 3044	Colour All The World/Lazy Song	5
72	Regal Zonophone RZ 3060	Mayday/Yellow Bird	5
73	Regal Zonophone RZ 3082	One Sunny Day/End Of The Party	5
71	Epic EPC 64322	DESIGN (LP)	12
71	Epic EPC 64653	TOMORROW IS SO FAR AWAY (LP, with insert)	25
73	Regal Zono. SLRZ 1037	DAY OF THE FOX (LP)	18

DESIRELESS
| 88 | CBS CD DESI 2 | Voyage Voyage (Britmix)/Voyage Voyage (Euro Remix)/Destin Fragile (Instrumental) (CD) | 10 |
| 88 | CBS CD DESI 3 | John/Qui Peut Savoir (CD) | 8 |

ANDY DESMOND
75	Konk KOS 2	So It Goes/She Can Move Mountains	5
75	Konk KOS 4	Beware/Only Child	5
75	Konk KONK 103	LIVING ON A SHOESTRING (LP)	12

(see also Gothic Horizon)

JOHNNY DESMOND

Year	Label	Title	Value
53	MGM SP 1042	A Bushel And A Peck/ART LUND: If I Were A Bell	8
54	Vogue Coral Q 2019	The High And The Mighty/Got No Time	6
55	Vogue Coral Q 72055	Don't/There's No Happiness For Me (with Alan Dale & Buddy Greco)	6
55	Vogue Coral Q 72076	Play Me Hearts And Flowers/I'm So Ashamed	7
55	Vogue Coral Q 72090	Togetherness/A Straw Hat And A Cane	6
55	Vogue Coral Q 72099	Yellow Rose Of Texas/You're In Love With Someone	7
55	Vogue Coral Q 72110	Land Of The Pharaohs/This Too Shall Pass	6
56	Vogue Coral Q 72115	Sixteen Tons/Ballo Italiano	7
56	Vogue Coral Q 72153	Without You/I'll Cry Tomorrow	6
56	Vogue Coral Q 72170	A Little Love Can Go A Long Way/Please Don't Forget Me	6
56	Vogue Coral Q 72190	"The Proud Ones" Theme/I Only Know I Love You	6
56	Vogue Coral Q 72207	A Girl Named Mary/"Run For The Sun" Theme	6
57	Vogue Coral Q 72235	Where The River Meets The Sea/18th Century Music Box (B-side with Jimmy Saunders)	7
57	Vogue Coral Q 72246	That's Where I Shine/I Just Want You To Want Me	6
57	Vogue Coral Q 72261	A White Sports Coat (And A Pink Carnation)/Just Lookin'	7
57	Vogue Coral Q 72261	A White Sports Coat (And A Pink Carnation)/Just Lookin' (78)	8
57	Vogue Coral Q 72269	Shenandoah Rose/Consideration	6
58	MGM MGM 994	Hot Cha Cha/I'll Close My Eyes	5
59	Philips PB 890	Willingly/Apple (When Ya Gonna Fall From The Tree?)	5
60	Coral Q 72398	The Most Happy Fella/LANCERS: Joey, Joey, Joey	5
60	Philips PB 1044	Hawk/Playing The Field	5
62	Top Rank JAR 612	Twistin' Rose Of Texas/ Hello Honey	5

LORRAE DESMOND (& REBELS)

Year	Label	Title	Value
54	Decca F 10375	Hold My Hand/On The Waterfront	12
54	Decca F 10375	Hold My Hand/On The Waterfront (78)	7
54	Decca F 10398	Far Away (My Love Is Far Away)/No One But You	12
54	Decca F 10398	Far Away (My Love Is Far Away)/No One But You (78)	7
54	Decca F 10404	I Can't Tell A Waltz From A Tango/For Better, For Worse (with Johnston Brothers)	12
54	Decca F 10404	I Can't Tell A Waltz From A Tango/For Better, For Worse (78)	7
55	Decca F 10461	A Boy On Saturday Night/Why — Oh Why?	12
55	Decca F 10461	A Boy On Saturday Night/Why — Oh Why? (78)	7
55	Decca F 10510	Don't/Where Will The Baby's Dimple Be?	12
55	Decca F 10510	Don't/Where Will The Baby's Dimple Be? (78)	7
55	Decca F 10533	Stowaway/Heartbroken (B-side with Johnston Brothers)	10
55	Decca F 10533	Stowaway/Heartbroken (B-side with Johnston Brothers) (78)	7
55	Decca F 10612	You Should Know/Wake The Town And Tell The People	10
55	Decca F 10612	You Should Know/Wake The Town And Tell The People (78)	7
56	Parlophone R 4239	Written On The Wind/A House With Love In It	8
56	Parlophone R 4239	Written On The Wind/A House With Love In It (78)	7
57	Parlophone R 4287	You Won't Be Around/Play The Music (as Lorrae Desmond & Rebels)	8
57	Parlophone R 4287	You Won't Be Around/Play The Music (as Lorrae Desmond & Rebels) (78)	7
57	Parlophone R 4320	Kansas City Special/Preacher, Preacher (as Lorrae Desmond & Rebels)	8
57	Parlophone R 4320	Kansas City Special/Preacher, Preacher (78)	7
57	Parlophone R 4361	Ding-Dong Rock-a-billy Weddin'/Cabin Boy (as Lorrae Desmond & Rebels)	18
57	Parlophone R 4361	Ding-Dong Rock-a-billy Weddin'/Cabin Boy (78)	8
58	Parlophone R 4400	Two Ships/Little David	7
58	Parlophone R 4400	Two Ships/Little David (78)	7
58	Parlophone R 4430	Down By The River/The Secret Of Happiness	7
58	Parlophone R 4430	Down By The River/The Secret Of Happiness (78)	7
58	Parlophone R 4463	Soda Pop Hop/Blue, Blue Day	10
58	Parlophone R 4463	Soda Pop Hop/Blue, Blue Day (78)	8
59	Parlophone R 4534	Tall Paul/Wait For It	12
59	Parlophone R 4534	Tall Paul/Wait For It (78)	25
60	Parlophone R 4670	Tell Me Again/Get Your Daddie's Car Tonight	6

MIKE DESMOND

Year	Label	Title	Value
57	Columbia DB 3954	Young And In Love/Two Loves (as Michael Desmond)	6
57	Columbia DB 4018	Chances Are/If You're Not Completely Satisfied (as Michael Desmond)	6
59	Top Rank JAR 225	If I Were The Sky/Tua	5
60	Top Rank JAR 298	The Happy Muleteer/Oh, So Wunderbar	5

PAUL DESMOND

Year	Label	Title	Value
61	Warner Bros WM 4020	PAUL DESMOND & FRIENDS (LP, also stereo WS 8020)	12
62	RCA Victor RD 7525	TWO OF A MIND (LP, with Gerry Mulligan)	12
	(see also Gerry Mulligan, Dave Brubeck)		

DESOLATION ANGELS

Year	Label	Title	Value
84	AM AM 266	Valhalla (p/s)	15
85	Thameside TRR 111	DESOLATION ANGELS (LP)	30

DESPERATE BICYCLES

Year	Label	Title	Value
77	Refill RR 1	Smokescreen/Handlebars (p/s, same tracks both sides)	8
77	Refill RR 2	The Medium Was Tedium/Don't Back The Front (p/s, same tracks both sides)	8
78	Refill RR 3	NEW CROSS NEW CROSS (EP)	7
78	Refill RR 4	Occupied Territory/Skill (p/s)	7
78	Refill RR 7	Grief Is Very Private/Obstructive/Conundrum (p/s)	8
80	Refill RR 6	REMORSE CODE (LP)	15

DESSIE & JOHN

Year	Label	Title	Value
69	Downtown DT 440	Boss Sound/Everything Is Alright	6

JIMMY DESTRI

Year	Label	Title	Value
82	Chrysalis CHR 1368	HEART ON A WALL (LP)	12
	(see also Blondie)		

MINT VALUE £

DESTROY ALL MONSTERS

79	Cherry Red CHERRY 3	Bored/You're Gonna Die (p/s, red vinyl)	5
79	Cherry Red CHERRY 7	Meet The Creeper/November 22nd 1963 (p/s)	5
79	Cherry Red CHERRY 9	Nobody Knows/What Do I Get? (p/s)	5

(see also MC5)

DESTROYER

81	Clean Kill SJP 829	Evil Place (no p/s)	50

DESTROYERS

70	Amalgamated AMG 856	Niney Special/Danger Zone	12
70	Pressure Beat PR 5505	Pressure Tonic/Machuki's Cooking (B-side actually with Count Machuki)	12

(see also Soul Brothers, Nicky Thomas)

DESTRUCTORS (V)

82	Carnage BOOK 2	Meaningless Names/AK 47/Police State/Dachau/Death Squad (p/s)	5
82	Carnage Benelux KILL 2	Religion/Soldier Boy/Agent Orange/Corpse Gas (p/s)	5
82	Illuminated ILL 14	JAILBAIT (EP)	7
83	Illuminated ILL 19	FORCES OF LAW (EP)	5
83	Criminal Damage 12104	CRY HAVOC AND UNLEASH THE DOGS OF WAR (12" EP)	8
84	Criminal Damage CRI 108	TV EYE (EP, as Destructors V)	5
80s		EXORCISE THE DEMONS OF YOUTH (EP, with insert)	12
80s		SENSELESS VIOLENCE (EP)	8

(see also Blanks)

STEPHANIE DE SYKES

75	Bradley BRADL 1009	STEPHANIE DE SYKES (LP)	12

DETAILS

80	Energy NRG 2	Keep On Running/Run'ins (p/s)	5
80	Energy NRG 002	Keep On Running/Run'ins (12", stickered plain sleeve, promo only)	8
82	Energy NRG 6	The London Marathon (Keep On Running)/Run'ins (Version) (reissue, p/s)	5

DETECTIVE

78	Swansong SS 8504	IT TAKES ONE TO KNOW ONE (LP, with inner sleeve)	12

(see also Michael Des Barres)

DETERGENTS

65	Columbia DB 7513	Leader Of The Laundromat/Ulcers	15
65	Columbia DB 7591	I Don't Know/The Blue Kangaroo	8

DETONATORS

78	Local LR 1	Need Love Tonight/Great Big Ghetto/Shoob Shooby Do/ Give Me A Helping Hand (p/s)	6
70s	Big Blast	THE DANCE (EP)	5

DETOURS

68	CBS 3213	Run To Me Baby/Hangin' On	25
68	CBS 3401	Whole Lotta Lovin'/Pieces Of You	35

(see also Gene Latter)

DETROIT with MITCH RYDER

72	Paramount PARA 3022	It Ain't Easy/Long Neck Goose	5
72	Paramount SPFL 277	DETROIT (LP)	20

(see also Mitch Ryder)

DETROIT EMERALDS

71	Pye International 7N 25544	Do Me Right/Just Now And Then	6
71	Janus 6146 004	Wear This Ring/I Bet You Get The One	5
72	Janus 6146 007	You Want It, You Got It/Till You Decide To Come Home	5
72	Janus 6146 015	Do Me Right/Baby Let Me Take You In My Arms	10
72	Janus 6146 020	Feel The Need In Me/And I Love Her	8
73	Westbound 6146 103	You Want It, You Got It/Whatcha Gonna Wear Tomorrow	5
73	Westbound 6146 104	I Think Of You/So Long	5
71	Janus 6310 204	DO ME RIGHT (LP)	20
72	Janus 6310 207	YOU WANT IT, YOU GOT IT (LP)	20
73	Janus 6309 101	ABE, JAMES AND IVORY (LP)	12

DETROITS

70	Fontana 6438 006	'TIS US OURSELVES (LP)	12

DETROIT SPINNERS

65	Tamla Motown TMG 514	Sweet Thing/How Can I? (demos credited to either 'Spinners' or 'Detroit Spinners')	100/50
65	Tamla Motown TMG 514	Sweet Thing/How Can I? (stock copies credited to 'Spinners')	165
65	Tamla Motown TMG 523	I'll Always Love You/Tomorrow May Never Come (as 'Spinners' or 'Detroit Spinners')	50/40
67	Tamla Motown TMG 627	For All We Know/I'll Always Love You (1st pressing with tall, narrow print)	18/12
70	Tamla Motown TMG 755	It's A Shame/Together We Can Make Such Sweet Music (unissued)	
70	Tamla Motown TMG 755	It's A Shame/Sweet Thing (as Motown Spinners)	10
71	Tamla Motown TMG 766	Together We Can Make Such Sweet Music/Truly Yours (as Motown Spinners)	5
72	Atlantic K 10243	I'll Be Around/How Can I Let You Get Away	5
74	Atlantic K 10416	Mighty Love (Parts 1 & 2)	5
74	Atlantic K 10480	I'm Coming Home/He'll Never Love You Like I Do	5
80	Atlantic K 11558	Split Decision/Now That You're Mine Again	8
80	Atlantic K 11558	Split Decision/Now That You're Mine Again (12")	25
68	T. Motown (S)TML 11060	THE DETROIT SPINNERS (LP)	40
71	T. Motown STML 11182	SECOND TIME AROUND (LP, as Motown Spinners)	15

(see also Spinners, G.C. Cameron)

DEUCE COUP

67	Mercury MF 1013	A Clown In One Town/Angela (some in p/s)	8/5

DEUCE OF HEARTS

66	CBS 202345	Closer Together/The Times They Are A Changin'	6

JIMMY DEUCHAR

58	Tempo A 167	Bewitched/My Funny Valentine (as Jimmy Deuchar & His Pals)	6
58	Tempo A 167	Bewitched/My Funny Valentine (78, as Jimmy Deuchar & His Pals)	8
55	Tempo EXA 18	JIMMY DEUCHAR ENSEMBLE (EP)	10
56	Esquire EP 93	JIMMY DEUCHAR QUARTET (EP)	25
56	Esquire EP 103	JIMMY DEUCHAR QUARTET (EP)	25
58	Tempo EXA 79	OPUS DE FUNK (EP, as Jimmy Deuchar Sextet)	8
58	Tempo EXA 81	SWINGIN' IN STUDIO TWO (EP)	35
59	Tempo EXA 88	WAIL (EP, with Victor Feldman Quintet)	8
54	Esquire 20-059	DIG DEUCHAR, DON'T DANCE (LP)	120
55	Tempo LAP 2	JIMMY DEUCHAR ENSEMBLE (10" LP)	125
56	Tempo TAP 4	TOP TRUMPETS (LP)	375
56	Vogue LDE	SHOWCASE (LP)	65
58	Tempo TAP 20	PAL JIMMY (LP)	575

BIG PETE DEUCHAR/DEUKER

| 63 | Fontana 267 278 TF | Google Eye/There's A Hand Leading Me (as Big Pete Deuchar) | 7 |
| 65 | Columbia DB 7763 | Goin' In Training/I Saw Your Face In The Moon | 6 |

DAVID DEVANT & HIS SPIRIT WIFE

| 95 | Humbug HUM 4 | Pimlico/This Is For Real/Magic Life/David's Coming Back (CD) | 8 |

DEVASTATING AFFAIR

| 73 | Mowest MW 3020 | That's How It Was/It's So Sad | 5 |

DEVIANTS

68	Stable STA 5601	You Got To Hold On/Let's Loot The Supermarket	20
67	Underground Imp. IMP 1	PTOOFF! (LP, foldout sleeve, private pressing via IT magazine)	75
68	Stable SLP 007	DISPOSABLE (LP, gatefold sleeve)	50
69	Transatlantic TRA 204	THE DEVIANTS THREE (LP, some with booklet)	40/30
69	Decca LK-R/SKL-R 4993	PTOOFF! (LP, reissue)	35
78	Logo MOGO 4001	THE DEVIANTS (LP, reissue, with insert)	12
83	Psycho PSYCHO 16	PTOOFF! (LP, 2nd reissue in original sleeve)	20
84	Psycho PSYCHO 25	HUMAN GARBAGE (LIVE AT DINGWALLS '84) (LP)	15

(see also Mick Farren, Pink Fairies, Larry Wallis)

DEVIL'S HOLE GANG

| 70s | Slow Burning Fuse SSSS 1 | Free The People/Isn't It/Something To Look Forward To (p/s, with insert) | 7 |

JOHNNY DEVLIN (& DETOURS)

64	Pye 7N 15598	Sometimes/If You Want Someone (as Johnny Devlin & Detours)	7
66	CBS 202085	Hung On You/Prove It	7
66	CBS 202339	My Strength; Heart Of Soul/I Can't Get You Off My Mind	7
67	CBS 202452	Tender Lovin' Care/Five O'Clock World	7
67	CBS 2751	Hurtin'/You Gotta Tell Me	6

DEVO

78	Stiff DEV 1	Jocko Homo/Mongoloid (foldout p/s)	5
78	Stiff DEV 2/BOY 1	(I Can't Get No) Satisfaction/Sloppy (I Saw My Baby Getting) (p/s)	5
78	Stiff BOY 1	(I Can't Get No) Satisfaction/Sloppy (I Saw My Baby Getting) (12", stickered p/s)	8
78	Stiff BOY 2	Be Stiff/Social Fools (clear or lemon yellow vinyl, company sleeve)	5
78	Stiff BOY 2	Be Stiff/Social Fools (black vinyl, p/s)	5
78	Stiff ODD 1	BE STIFF (12" EP, white label)	8
78	Virgin VS 223	Come Back Jonee/Social Fools (p/s, grey vinyl with sticker)	5
79	Elevator NICE 1	Mechanical Man/Blockhead/Blackout/Auto-Modern (official bootleg, no'd p/s)	6
81	Virgin VS 450	Through Being Cool/Race Of Doom (poster p/s)	5
85	Warner Bros W 9119F	Shout/C'mon/Jocko Homo/Mongoloid (double pack)	5
78	Virgin V 2106	Q: ARE WE NOT MEN? (LP, various colour vinyls)	12
78	Virgin VP 2106	Q: ARE WE NOT MEN? (LP, picture disc, with 'Flimsy Wrap' 33rpm 1-sided flexidisc [VDJ 27/Lyntone LYN 6260])	12

DEVON (Russell) & TARTANS

| 68 | Nu Beat NB 021 | Let's Have Some Fun/Making Love | 6 |

(see also Tartans)

DEVON (Russell) & SEDRIC (Myton)

| 69 | Blue Cat BS 158 | What A Sin Thing/Short Up Dress | 10 |

DEVONNES

| 75 | UK USA 5 | I'm Gonna Pick Up My Toys/Limits | 5 |

DEVORAH

| 98 | Klone KLONE 50 | Bitter Sweet Symphony/The Drugs Don't Work/Paradise (12", withdrawn) | 15 |

BARRY DE VORZON

58	RCA RCA 1066	Barbara Jean/JIMMY DELL: Teeny Weeny	70
58	RCA RCA 1066	Barbara Jean/JIMMY DELL: Teeny Weeny (78)	50
60	Philips PB 993	Betty Betty (Go Steady With Me)/Across The Street From	12

(see also Barry & Tamerlanes)

DEVOTED

| 68 | Page One POF 076 | I Love George Best/United (initially in p/s) | 10/5 |

DEVOTIONS

| 64 | Columbia DB 7256 | Rip Van Winkle/I Love You For Sentimental Reasons | 40 |

JANINE DE WAYLENE & HER MARTENOT

| 60 | Top Rank JAR 363 | Faces In The Dark/Martenot Theme/Farewell Christina | 5 |

DEWDROPS

| 67 | Blue Beat BB 381 | Somebody's Knocking/By And By | 12 |

KEITH DEWHURST & ALBION BAND

80	Charisma CDS 4020	LARK RISE TO CANDLEFORD (A COUNTRY TAPESTRY) (LP, soundtrack)	10

(see also Albion Band)

FAY DEWITT

54	London HL 8021	Misirlou/Snap Snap Snap Your Fingers (78)	8

DANNY DEXTER

63	London HLU 9690	Sweet Mama/Go On	12

EDDIE DEXTER & HIS BAND

55	Capitol CL 14371	Moonlight/The Verse Of Stardust	6

RAY DEXTER & LAYABOUTS

62	Decca F 11538	The Coalman's Lament/Lonely Weekend	20

DEXY'S MIDNIGHT RUNNERS

89	Mercury 080 628-2	Come On Eileen/The Celtic Soul Brothers/Jackie Wilson Said (I'm In Heaven When You Smile)/Liars A To E (CD Video)	8

(see also Killjoys, Kevin Rowland)

TRACEY DEY

64	Stateside SS 287	Go Away/Gonna Get Along Without You Now	10

BARRY D'FANO

62	Palette PG 9038	Message Of Love/The Kiss That Broke My Heart	7

DHARMA BLUES BAND

69	Major Minor SMPC 5017	DHARMA BLUES (LP)	45

DIALS (Jamaica)

69	Duke DU 48	Bye Bye Love/It's Love	6
69	Duke DU 49	Love Is A Treasure/DIAMONDS: I Want To Be	6

DIALS (U.K.)

79	Wessex WEX 266	Maxine/Hey Denise (p/s)	5

BRIAN DIAMOND & THE CUTTERS

63	Decca F 11724	Jealousy Will Get You Nowhere/Brady Brady	12
64	Fontana TF 452	Shake, Shout And Go/Whatcha Gonna Do Now Pretty Baby	12
65	Pye 7N 15779	Big Bad Wolf/See If I Care	10
65	Pye 7N 15952	Bone Idol/Sands Of Time	10

(GREGG DIAMOND'S) BIONIC BOOGIE

79	Polydor PB 50	Chains/Hot Butterfly	5
79	Polydor POSPX 50	Chains/Hot Butterfly (12")	10
88	Urban URBX 16	Hot Butterfly/Mess Up The Boogie/When The Shit Hits The Fan (12", p/s)	8
79	Polydor 2391 322	BIONIC BOOGIE (LP)	12

JERRY DIAMOND

57	London HLE 8496	Sunburned Lips/Don't Trust Love	30
57	London HLE 8496	Sunburned Lips/Don't Trust Love (78)	18

LEE DIAMOND (& CHEROKEES)

61	Fontana H 310	I'll Step Down/Josephine (as Lee Diamond & Cherokees)	12
61	Fontana H 345	Stop Your Crying/You'll Want Me	12

(see also Cherokees)

NEIL DIAMOND

66	London HLZ 10049	Solitary Man/Do It	8
66	London HLZ 10072	Cherry, Cherry/I'll Come Running	7
66	London HLZ 10092	I Got The Feelin' (Oh No No)/The Boat That I Row	7
67	London HLZ 10111	You Got To Me/Someday Baby	7
67	London HLZ 10126	Girl, You'll Be A Woman Soon/You'll Forget	7
67	London HLZ 10151	Thank The Lord For The Night Time/The Long Way Home	7
67	London HLZ 10161	Kentucky Woman/The Time Is Now	6
68	London HLZ 10177	New Orleans/Hanky Panky	6
68	London HLZ 10187	Red Red Wine/Red Rubber Ball	6
68	Uni UN 503	Brooklyn Roads/Holiday Inn Blues	5
68	MCA MU 1033	Two-Bit Manchild/Broad Old Woman	5
69	MCA MU 1070	Brother Love's Travelling Salvation Show/A Modern Day Version Of Love	5
69	MCA MU 1087	Sweet Caroline (Good Times Never Seemed So Good)/Dig In	5
69	Uni UN 512	Holy Holy/Hurtin' You Don't Come Easy	5
70	Uni UN 522	Soolaimon (African Trilogy II)/And The Grass Won't Pay No Mind	5
71	President PT 335	Kentucky Woman/Cherry, Cherry/I Thank The Lord For The Night Time (p/s)	7
71	Uni UN 536	Stones/Crunchy Granola Suite	5
87	CBS 651 201-7	I Dreamed A Dream/Sweet Caroline (box set with calendar)	6
66	London HA-Z 8307	THE FEEL OF NEIL DIAMOND (LP)	40
68	MCA MUPS 365	VELVET GLOVES AND SPIT (LP)	18
69	MCA MUPS 382	BROTHER LOVE'S TRAVELLING SALVATION SHOW (LP)	18
69	Uni UNLS 106	VELVET GLOVES AND SPIT (LP, reissue)	12
69	Uni UNLS 107	BROTHER LOVE'S TRAVELLING SALVATION SHOW (LP, reissue)	12
70	Uni UNLS 110	TOUCHING ME, TOUCHING YOU (LP)	12
70	Uni UNLS 116	GOLD (LP)	12
71	Uni UNLS 117	TAP ROOT MANUSCRIPT (LP)	12
71	Uni UNLS 121	STONES (LP)	12
74	CBS Q 69067	SERENADE (LP, quadrophonic)	15
76	CBS Q 86004	BEAUTIFUL NOISE (LP, quadrophonic)	15
81	World Records ALBUM 91	THE BEST OF NEIL DIAMOND (4-LP box set, mail-order only)	25
96	Sony Publishing XPCD 708	THE NEIL DIAMOND SONG BOOK (CD, promo only)	25

DIAMOND BOYS

62	Parlophone GIB 102	Fool In Love/New Orleans (export issue)	30
63	RCA RCA 1351	Hey Little Girl/What'd I Say	7

(see also Albert Ammons)

DIAMOND HEAD

80	Happy Face MMDH 120	Shoot Out The Lights/Helpless (p/s)	15
80	Media SCREEN 1	Sweet And Innocent/Streets Of Gold (p/s)	15
81	DHM DHM 004	Play It Loud/Waited Too Long (p/s)	7
81	DHM DHM 005	DIAMOND LIGHTS EP (Diamond Lights/ We Won't Be Back/I Don't Got/It's Electric) (12", p/s)	20
82	MCA DHM 101	FOUR CUTS (EP, p/s)	7
82	MCA DHMT 101	FOUR CUTS (12" EP, with insert)	10
82	MCA DHM 102/MSAM 23	In The Heat Of The Night/Play It Loud (live)//Sweet And Innocent (live)/ (Interview With Tommy Vance) (double pack, gatefold p/s)	6
82	MCA DHMT 102	In The Heat Of The Night (Full Length Version)/Play It Loud (live) (12", p/s)	10
83	MCA DHM 103	Making Music/(Andy Peebles Interview) (p/s)	6
83	MCA DHMT 103	Making Music/(Andy Peebles Interview) (12", p/s)	10
83	MCA DHM 104	Out Of Phase/The Kingmaker (p/s)	5
83	MCA DHMP 104	Out Of Phase/The Kingmaker (picture disc)	6
83	MCA DHMT 104	Out Of Phase/The Kingmaker/Sucking My Love (live) (12", p/s)	20
92	Bronze	Wild In The Streets (12", p/s, 1 side etched)	8
80	DHM MMDHLP 105	LIGHTNING TO THE NATIONS (LP, plain or printed white labels, plain white sleeve, sold at gigs, a few signed in blue ink & available via *Sounds*)	60/50
81	MCA DH 1001	LIVING ON BORROWED TIME (LP, gatefold sleeve with inner sleeve, some with poster & fan club insert)	22/15
83	MCA DH 1002	CANTERBURY (LP)	12
86	Metal Masters METALP 110	BEHOLD THE BEGINNING (LP, remixed reissue of 1st LP)	12
87	FM WKFMLP 92	AM I EVIL (LP, with inner sleeve)	20

DIAMONDS (U.S.)

55	Vogue Coral Q 72109	Black Denim Trousers And Motorcycle Boots/Nip Sip	50
55	Vogue Coral Q 72109	Black Denim Trousers And Motorcycle Boots/Nip Sip (78)	25
55	Mercury MT 121	Love, Love, Love/Ev'ry Night About This Time (78)	20
57	Mercury MT 148	Little Darlin'/Faithful And True (78)	7
57	Mercury MT 167	Don't Say Goodbye/Words Of Love (78)	15
57	Mercury MT 179	Oh, How I Wish/Zip Zip (78)	15
58	Mercury 7MT 187	Silhouettes/Honey Bird	30
58	Mercury MT 187	Silhouettes/Honey Bird (78)	15
58	Mercury 7MT 195	The Stroll/Land Of Beauty	25
58	Mercury MT 195	The Stroll/Land Of Beauty (78)	15
58	Mercury 7MT 207	Don't Let Me Down/High Sign	30
58	Mercury MT 207	Don't Let Me Down/High Sign (78)	18
58	Mercury 7MT 208	Straight Skirts/Patsy	30
58	Mercury MT 208	Straight Skirts/Patsy (78)	25
58	Mercury 7MT 233	Where Mary Go?/Kathy-O	8
58	Mercury MT 233	Where Mary Go?/Kathy-O (78)	20
58	Mercury AMT 1004	Eternal Lovers/Walking Along	12
58	Mercury AMT 1004	Eternal Lovers/Walking Along (78)	15
59	Mercury AMT 1024	She Say (Oom Dooby Doom)/From The Bottom Of My Heart	12
59	Mercury AMT 1024	She Say (Oom Dooby Doom)/From The Bottom Of My Heart (78)	30
60	Mercury AMT 1086	Tell The Truth/Real True Love	15
61	Mercury AMT 1156	One Summer Night/It's A Doggone Shame	15
57	Mercury MEP 9515	PRESENTING THE DIAMONDS (EP)	25
57	Mercury MEP 9523	THE DIAMONDS VOL. 1 (EP)	35
58	Mercury MEP 9527	THE DIAMONDS VOL. 2 (EP)	35
58	Mercury MEP 9530	THE DIAMONDS VOL. 3 (EP)	35
59	Mercury ZEP 10003	DIG THE DIAMONDS (EP)	35
59	Mercury ZEP 10020	THE DIAMONDS MEET PETE RUGOLO (EP)	20
59	Mercury ZEP 10026	DIAMONDS ARE TRUMPS (EP)	35
60	Mercury ZEP 10053	STAR STUDDED DIAMONDS (EP)	30
61	Mercury ZEP 10097	PETE RUGOLO LEADS THE DIAMONDS (EP, also stereo SEZ 10912)	25/30
57	Mercury MPT 7526	THE DIAMONDS (10" LP)	125
58	Mercury	THE DIAMONDS (LP, existence unconfirmed)	50+
59	Mercury	THE DIAMONDS MEET PETE RUGOLO (LP, existence unconfirmed)	25+
60	Mercury MMC 14039	SONGS FROM THE OLD WEST (LP)	20

(see also Pete Rugolo)

DIAMONDS (U.K.)

63	Philips BF 1264	The Lost City/Chasey Chasey	10

DIAMONDS (Jamaica)

72	Songbird SB 1079	Mash Up/DYNAMITES: Mash Up (Version)	6

(see also Dymonds, Sir Collins Band)

DIAMOND TWINS

66	HMV POP 1508	Crying The Night Away/Start The World Spinning Again	6

(see also Sonia Kent)

DIANE & JAVELINS

66	Columbia DB 7819	Heart And Soul/Who's The Girl	40

(PAUL) DI'ANNO

84	FM VHF 1	Heart User/Road Rat (p/s)	8
84	FM WKFM LP1	DI'ANNO (LP, blue vinyl)	15
84	FM WKFM PD1	DI'ANNO (LP, picture disc)	18

(see also Gogmagog, Iron Maiden)

DIATONES

61	Starlite ST45 057	Ruby Has Gone/Oh Baby Come Dance With Me	10

MINT VALUE £

DANNY DIAZ & CHECKMATES
69	Pye 7N 17690	Solomon Grundy/Goodbye Baby	5

MANU DIBANGO
73	London HL 10423	Soul Makossa/Lily	5
73	London SH 8451	O BOSO (LP)	20
75	Creole CRLP 503	MAKOSSA MUSIC (LP)	12
78	Decca SKL-R 5296	AFROVISION (LP)	12
79	Decca SKL-R 5303	MANU '76 (LP)	12

LLOYD DICE
70	Joe JRS 5	Trial Of Pama Dice/JOE: Jughead Returns	8

(see also Trevor Lloyd)

DICE THE BOSS
69	Duke/Joe DU 51	Gun The Man Down/JOE MANSANO: The Thief	8
69	Duke/Joe DU 52	But Officer/JOE'S ALL STARS: Reggae On The Shore	7
70	Duke/Joe DU 57	Your Boss D.J./TITO SIMON: Read The News	7
70	Joe's JRS 17	The Informer/Cool It	5
70	Explosion EX 2017	Funky Monkey/JOE'S ALL STARS: Funky Monkey Version	7
70	Explosion EX 2020	Funky Duck/Dunkier Than Duck	6

(see also Pama Dice, Joe The Boss)

PAMA DICE
69	Jackpot JP 715	Honky Tonk Popcorn/Bongo Man	6
69	Jackpot JP 716	Sin, Sun And Sex/Reggae Popcorn	6

(see also Dice The Boss, Joe The Boss)

DICK & DEE DEE
61	London HLG 9408	The Mountains High/I Want Someone	8
62	London HLG 9483	Goodbye To Love/Swing Low	8
62	Liberty LIB 55412	Tell Me/Will You Always Love Me	6
63	Warner Bros WB 96	Young And In Love/Say To Me	6
63	Warner Bros WB 111	Where Did The Good Times Go/Guess Our Love Must Show	6
63	Warner Bros WB 119	Turn Around/Don't Leave Me	6
64	Warner Bros WB 126	All My Trails/Don't Twice, It's All Right	7
64	Warner Bros WB 138	Remember When/You Were Mine	7
64	Warner Bros WB 145	Thou Shalt Not Steal/Just 'Round The River Bend	6
65	Warner Bros WB 156	Be My Baby/Room 404	7
65	Warner Bros WB 5671	Use What You've Got/P.S. 1402	6
63	Warner Bros WM/WS 8132	YOUNG AND IN LOVE (LP, mono/stereo)	30/35
63	Warner Bros WM/WS 8150	TURN AROUND (LP, mono/stereo)	25/30

DOLES DICKEN'S BAND
58	London HLD 8639	Piakukaungchung (Pie-ah-coo-ka-ung-chung)/Our Melody	6

DICKENS
80	Hawkmoon ROCK 101	STANDING OUT (LP, private pressing)	12

(see also Ice)

CHARLES DICKENS
65	Pye 7N 15887	That's The Way Love Goes/In The City	7
65	Pye 7N 15938	I Stand Alone/Hey Little Girl	7
66	Immediate IM 025	So Much In Love/Our Soul Brothers	15

(see also Habits)

LITTLE JIMMY DICKENS
54	Columbia DC 670	Then I Had To Turn Around/Hot Diggity Dog	
		(78, export issue)	10
65	CBS 201969	May The Bird Of Paradise Fly Up Your Nose/My Eyes Are Jealous	6

DICKIES
78	A&M AMS 7368	Paranoid/I'm OK, You're OK (p/s, clear, black or milky vinyl)	5/6/7
78	A&M AMS 7373	Eve Of Destruction/Doggie Do (p/s, pink or black vinyl)	5
78	A&M AMS 7391	Give It Back/You Drive Me Ape (p/s, white or black vinyl)	5
78	A&M AMS 7403	Silent Night/The Sounds Of Silence (p/s, white or black vinyl)	6/5
78	A&M AMS	Paranoid/I'm OK, You're OK (10", p/s, white vinyl)	15
79	A&M AMS 7431	Banana Splits/Hideous/Got It At The Store	
		(p/s, opaque or translucent yellow vinyl; also black vinyl)	5/7/6
79	A&M AMS 7469	Nights In White Satin/Waterslide (p/s, white vinyl)	5
79	A&M AMS 7491	Manny, Moe And Jack/She Loves Me Not (p/s, black vinyl only)	5
80	A&M AMS 7504	Fan Mail/Tricia Toyota (I'm Stuck In A Pagoda)	
		(opaque or translucent red vinyl, poster p/s)	6
80	A&M AMS 7544	Gigantor/Bowling With Bedrock Barney	
		(yellow vinyl, p/s with full colour or b&w reverse)	8
90	Overground OVER 12	Just Say Yes/Ayatollah You So (p/s with lyric sheet,	
		mauve, blue or white vinyl, 2,000 of each colour)	6
90	Overground OVER 12	Just Say Yes/Ayatollah You So	
		(black vinyl test pressing, 50 only)	15
90	Overground OVER 017	Roadkill (flexidisc available on 'Just Say Yes' European Tour,	
		no p/s, 5000 only)	5
95	Plastic Head HOLE 008	Make It So/Oh Baby (p/s, black vinyl, 1,000 only)	8
79	A&M AMLE 64742	THE INCREDIBLE SHRINKING DICKIES	
		(LP, black or yellow vinyl)	each 12
79	A&M AMLE 64742	THE INCREDIBLE SHRINKING DICKIES	
		(LP, blue or orange vinyl,	
		with black or red-and-black on sleeve)	15
79	A&M AMLH 68510	DAWN OF THE DICKIES	
		(LP, black or blue vinyl)	12

(see also Chuck Wagon)

BRUCE DICKINSON

90	EMI EM 138	Tattooed Millionaire/Ballad Of Mutt (paper label, glossy p/s)	5
90	EMI EMPD 138	Tattooed Millionaire/Ballad Of Mutt (shaped picture disc)	10
90	EMI EMCD 138	Tattooed Millionaire/Ballad Of Mutt/Wind Of Change (CD)	8
90	EMI EMPD 142	All The Young Dudes/Darkness Be My Friend (shaped picture disc with plinth)	10
90	EMI EMCD 142	All The Young Dudes/Darkness Be My Friend/Sin City (CD picture disc)	10
90	EMI EMPD 151	Dive! Dive! Dive!/Riding With The Angels (live)/Sin City (live)/Black Night (live) (12", picture disc)	10
90	EMI EMCD 151	Dive! Dive! Dive!/Riding With The Angels (live)/Sin City (live)/Black Night (live) (CD)	8
94	EMI EM 341	Shoot All The Clowns/Over And Out (p/s, clear vinyl with insert)	4

(see also Iron Maiden, Samson, Xero, Rock Aid Armenia)

VIC DICKINSON & JOE THOMAS GROUPS

60	London Jazz LTZ-K 15182	MAINSTREAM (LP, also stereo SAH-K 6066)	10

BARBARA DICKSON

74	RSO 2090 144	Here Comes The Sun/The Long And Winding Road	5
69	Trailer LER 3002	THE FATE O'CHARLIE (LP)	45
70	Decca SKL 5041	THRO' RECENT YEARS (LP, with Archie Fisher)	35
71	Decca SKL 5058	DO RIGHT WOMAN (LP)	45
72	Decca SKL 5116	FROM THE BEGGAR'S MANTLE FRINGED WITH GOLD (LP)	40
74	RSO 2394 141	JOHN, PAUL, GEORGE, RINGO AND BERT (LP, with London Cast)	12

DICTATORS with TONY & HOWARD

63	Oriole CB 1934	So Long Little Girl/Say Little Girl	10

(see also Tony & Howard)

DICTATORS

77	Asylum K 13091	Search And Destroy/Sleepin' With The TV On	5
77	Asylum K 13091T	Search And Destroy/Sleepin' With The TV On (12", p/s)	10
77	Asylum K 53061	MANIFEST DESTINY (LP)	12

BO DIDDLEY

59	London HLM 8913	The Great Grandfather/Crackin' Up	45
59	London HLM 8913	The Great Grandfather/Crackin' Up (78)	60
59	London HLM 8975	Say Man/The Clock Strikes Twelve	40
59	London HLM 8975	Say Man/The Clock Strikes Twelve (78)	60
60	London HLM 9035	Say Man, Back Again/She's Alright	40
60	London HLM 9112	Road Runner/My Story	50
62	Pye Intl. 7N 25165	You Can't Judge A Book By The Cover/I Can Tell	15
63	Pye Intl. 7N 25193	Who Do You Love?/The Twister	12
63	Pye Intl. 7N 25210	Bo Diddley/Detour	12
63	Pye Intl. 7N 25216	You Can't Judge A Book By The Cover/I Can Tell (reissue)	10
63	Pye Intl. 7N 25217	Pretty Thing/Road Runner	12
63	Pye Intl. 7N 25227	Bo Diddley Is A Lover/Doin' The Jaguar	10
64	Pye Intl. 7N 25235	Memphis/Monkey Diddle	10
64	Pye Intl. 7N 25243	Mona/Gimme Gimme	12
64	Pye Intl. 7N 25258	Mama Keep Your Big Mouth Shut/Jo-Ann	10
65	Chess CRS 8000	Hey Good Lookin'/You Ain't Bad (As You Claim To Be)	8
65	Chess CRS 8014	Somebody Beat Me/Mush Mouth Millie	8
65	Chess CRS 8021	Let The Kids Dance/Let Me Pass	8
66	Chess CRS 8026	500% More Man/Stop My Monkey	8
66	Chess CRS 8036	We're Gonna Get Married/Easy	8
67	Chess CRS 8053	Ooh Baby/Back To School	7
67	Chess CRS 8057	Wrecking My Love Life/Boo-Ga-Loo Before You Go	7
68	Chess CRS 8078	Another Sugar Daddy/I'm High Again	7
69	Chess CRS 8088	Bo Diddley 1969/Soul Train	7
72	Chess 6145 002	I Said Shut Up Woman/I Love You More Than You'll Ever Know	5
56	London RE-U 1054	RHYTHM AND BLUES WITH BO DIDDLEY (EP, gold label lettering)	175
63	Pye Intl. NEP 44014	HEY! BO DIDDLEY (EP)	18
64	Pye Intl. NEP 44019	THE STORY OF BO DIDDLEY (EP)	18
64	Pye Intl. NEP 44031	BO DIDDLEY IS A LUMBERJACK (EP)	18
64	Pye Intl. NEP 44036	DIDDLING (EP)	18
65	Chess CRE 6008	I'M A MAN (EP)	18
66	Chess CRE 6023	ROOSTER STEW (EP)	18
59	London HA-M 2230	GO BO DIDDLEY (LP)	175
62	Pye Jazz NJL 33	BO DIDDLEY IS A GUNSLINGER (LP)	35
63	Pye Intl. NPL 28025	HEY! BO DIDDLEY (LP)	22
63	Pye Intl. NPL 28026	BO DIDDLEY (LP)	22
63	Pye Intl. NPL 28029	BO DIDDLEY RIDES AGAIN (LP)	22
63	Pye Intl. NPL 28032	BO DIDDLEY'S BEACH PARTY (LP)	20
64	Pye Intl. NPL 28034	BO DIDDLEY IN THE SPOTLIGHT (LP)	30
64	Pye Intl. NPL 28049	16 ALL-TIME HITS (LP)	22
64	Chess CRL 4002	HEY GOOD LOOKIN' (LP)	22
65	Chess CRL 4507	LET ME PASS (LP)	22
66	Golden Guinea GG 0358	HEY! BO DIDDLEY (LP, reissue)	12
67	Chess CRL 4525	THE ORIGINATOR (LP)	22
68	Chess CRL 4529	SUPER BLUES (LP, with Muddy Waters & Little Walter)	30
68	Chess CRL 4537	THE SUPER SUPER BLUES BAND (LP, with Muddy Waters & Howlin' Wolf)	40
71	Chess 6310 107	ANOTHER DIMENSION (LP)	12
73	Checker 6467 304	GOT ANOTHER BAG OF TRICKS (LP)	12
73	Chess 6499 476	THE LONDON SESSIONS (LP)	15

(see also Chuck Berry & Bo Diddley)

MINT VALUE £

DIDDY MEN
65	Columbia DB 7782	The Song Of The Diddy Men/Hello Doddy	5

DIE ELECTRIC EELS
79	Rough Trade RT 008	Agitated/Cyclotron (p/s)	10

DIESEL M
94	Choci's Chewns CCB 001	M FOR MULTIPLE	
		(12", blue vinyl, 666 only)	25
95	Choci's Chewns DDL 001	M FOR MANGOES	
		(12", red vinyl, 666 only)	25

(see also µ-Ziq)

MARLENE DIETRICH
52	Columbia DB 3160	Too Old To Cut The Mustard/Good For Nothin'	
		(with Rosemary Clooney) (78)	10
53	Philips PB 164	Dot's Nice — Donna Fights/It's The Same	
		(with Rosemary Clooney) (78)	8
54	Philips PB 314	Besides/Land, Sea And Air (with Rosemary Clooney) (78)	8
55	Philips PB 472	I Am A Camera Theme/Peter (78)	8
57	London HLD 8492	Near You/Another Spring, Another Love	7
57	London HLD 8492	Near You/Another Spring, Another Love (78)	10
63	HMV POP 1196	Lili Marlene/Sag Mir Wo Die Blumen Sind?	5
65	HMV POP 1379	Where Have All The Flowers Gone?/Blowin' In The Wind	5
65	Pye 7N 15770	Go Away From My Window/Shir Hatan	5
57	HMV 7EG 8257	MARLENE DIETRICH IN 'THE BLUE ANGEL' (EP)	10
58	London RED 1146	MARLENE DIETRICH (EP)	12
64	HMV 7EG 8844	RETURNS TO GERMANY (EP)	8
53	Brunswick LA 8591	SOUVENIR ALBUM (10" LP)	20
54	Philips BBR 8006	AT THE CAFÉ DE PARIS (10" LP, introduced by Noel Coward)	18
59	Philips BBL 7322	LILI MARLENE (LP)	15
60	Philips BBL 7386	DIETRICH IN RIO (LP, also stereo SBBL 571)	15/18
63	HMV CLP 1659	RETURNS TO GERMANY (LP)	15
60s	Philips	other LPs	15

(see also Rosemary Clooney)

DIF JUZ
81	4AD BAD 109	HU/RE/MI/CS (12" EP)	15
81	4AD BAD 116	VIBRATING AIR: Heset/Diselt/Gunet/Soarn (12" EP)	12
83	Red Flame RFM 24	WHO SAYS SO (LP)	12
85	Pleasantly Surprised PS 9	TIME CLOCK TURNS BACK	
		(cassette, with inserts)	15

DIGA RHYTHM BAND
76	United Artists UAG 29975	DIGA RHYTHM BAND (LP)	20

(see also Grateful Dead, Mickey Hart, Jerry Garcia)

STEVE DIGGLE
80	Faulty Products FEP 7000	Fifty Years Of Comparative Wealth/Shut Out The Light/	
		Here Comes The Fire Brigade (unreleased)	
81	Liberty BP 389	Fifty Years Of Comparative Wealth/Shut Out The Light/	
		Here Comes The Fire Brigade (p/s)	6

(see also Buzzcocks, Flag Of Convenience)

COBY DIJON
59	Fontana H 173	Locked In The Arms Of Love/I Go (78)	6

MOSES & JOSHUA (DILLARD)
67	Stateside SS 2059	My Elusive Dreams/What's Better Than Love	
		(as Moses & Joshua Dillard)	12
68	Bell BELL 1018	Get Out Of My Heart/They Don't Want Us Together	
		(as Moses & Joshua)	7
72	Mojo 2092 054	My Elusive Dreams/Get Out Of My Heart	5

DILLARD & CLARK
69	A&M AMS 764	Radio Song/Why Not Your Baby	6
69	A&M AMLS 939	THE FANTASTIC EXPEDITION OF DILLARD & CLARK (LP)	15
69	A&M AMLS 966	THROUGH THE MORNING (LP)	15

(see also Gene Clark, Byrds, Dillards)

DILLARDS
65	Capitol CL 15420	Nobody Knows/Ebo Walker	6
69	Elektra EKSN 45048	Reason To Believe/Nobody Knows	6
69	Elektra EKSN 45062	She Sang Hymns Out Of Tune/Single Saddle	5
69	Elektra EKSN 45081	Rainmaker/West Montana Hanna	6
68	Elektra EKS 74035	WHEATSHEAF SUITE (LP)	12
69	Polydor 236 559	BACK PORCH BLUE GRASS (LP)	12
70	Elektra EKS 74054	COPPERFIELDS (LP)	12
72	United Artists UAG 29366	ROOTS AND BRANCHES (LP)	12
73	United Artists UAS 29516	TRIBUTE TO THE AMERICAN DUCK (LP)	12

(see also Dillard & Clark)

DILLINGER
73	Duke DU 149	Headquarters (as Dellenger)/CHENLEY DUFFAS: Black Girl In My Bed	12
73	Downtown DT 512	Tighten Up Skank/Middle East Rock	15
79	Island ISL 976	Cokane In My Brain/Power	6

(see also David Isaacs)

TODD DILLINGHAM
95	Woronzow WOO 25	SGT. KIPPER (2-LP)	15

PHYLLIS DILLON

66	Doctor Bird DB 1061	Don't Stay Away (as Phillis Dillon)/TOMMY McCOOK & SUPERSONICS: What Now	25
67	Trojan TR 006	This Is A Lovely Way/Thing Of The Past (as Phyllis Dellon)	15
67	Treasure Isle TI 7003	This Is A Lovely Way/Thing Of The Past	15
67	Treasure Isle TI 7015	Perfidia/It's Rocking Time	15
68	Treasure Isle TI 7041	I Wear This Ring/Don't Touch Me Tomato	12
69	Trojan TR 651	Love Is All I Had/Boys And Girls Reggae (as Phillis Dylon)	10
69	Trojan TR 671	The Right Track/TOMMY McCOOK & SUPERSONICS: Moonshot	10
69	Trojan TR 686	Lipstick On Your Collar (as Phillis Dillon)/TOMMY McCOOK & SUPERSONICS: Tribute To Rameses	8
70	Duke Reid DR 2508	This Is Me/Skabuvie (act. "If Your Name Is Andy"/"Ska Vovi" by Dorothy Reid)	8
70	Duke DU 76	Walk Through This World/The Rooster	8
71	Treasure Isle TI 7058	One Life To Live, One Love To Give/TOMMY McCOOK: My Best Dress	10
71	Treasure Isle TI 7070	Midnight Confession/TOMMY McCOOK & SOUL SYNDICATE: Version	10
72	Sioux SI 009	In The Ghetto/NYAH EARTH: Knight Of The Long Knives	12
72	Trojan TRL 41	ONE LIFE TO GIVE (LP)	25

DIMENSIONALS

53	London L 1217	Sleepy Time Gal/DON BAKER/DIMENSIONALS: Drinkin' Pop-Sodee Odee (78)	25

DIMENSIONS

65	Parlophone R 5294	Tears On My Pillow/You Don't Have To Whisper	18

DIMPLES

66	Decca F 12537	The Love Of A Lifetime/My Heart Is Tied To You	25

(see also Gospel Garden, Amazing Blondel)

DIMPLES & EDDIE with RICO's COMBO

62	Planetone RC 3	Fleet Street/Good Bye World	15

DINAH ROD & DRAINS

83	Secret SHH 146	Somebody's In My Drain/Somebodies (p/s)	5
83	Secret SHH 146-12	Somebody's In My Drain/Somebodies (Parts I, II, III) (12", p/s)	8

DINGER

85	Face Value FVRA 221	Air Of Mystery/I Love To Love (no p/s)	35

(see also Erasure)

DINGLE BROTHERS

71	Dynamic DYN 418	You Don't Know/CABLES: Rich Man, Poor Man	6

BOB DINI

53	London L 1213	Too Long/Remember Me (78)	8
54	London HL 8019	Good-bye My Love/Sometime (78)	8

MARK DINNING

60	MGM MGM 1053	Teen Angel/Bye Now Baby	10
60	MGM MGM 1069	You Win Again/A Star Is Born (A Love Is Dead)	7
60	MGM MGM 1101	The Lovin' Touch/Come Back To Me (My Love)	7
61	MGM MGM 1125	Top Forty, News, Weather And Sport/Suddenly	7
62	MGM MGM 1148	In A Matter Of Moments/What Will My Mary Say	7
62	MGM MGM 1155	All Of This For Sally/The Pickup	7
65	Hickory 45-1293	Dial Al 1-4883/I'm Glad We Fell In Love	7

DINNING SISTERS

55	Polygon P 1161	Goofus/Mama (He Treats Your Daughter Mean) (78)	10
55	London HLF 8179	Drifting And Dreaming/Truly	40
55	London HLF 8179	Drifting And Dreaming/Truly (78)	15
56	London HLF 8218	Hold Me Tight/Uncle Joe	40
56	London HLF 8218	Hold Me Tight/Uncle Joe (78)	10

(see also 'Tennessee' Ernie Ford)

KENNY DINO

61	HMV POP 960	Your Ma Said You Cried In Your Sleep Last Night/Dream A Girl	6

DINO, DESI & BILLY

65	Reprise R 20367	I'm A Fool/So Many Ways	6
66	Reprise R 23047	Not The Loving Kind/Chimes Of Freedom	6

DINOSAUR

79	Sire SRE 1034	Kiss Me Again/Kiss Me Again (Version) (company sleeve)	5
79	Sire SRE 1034	Kiss Me Again/Kiss Me Again (Version) (12", company sleeve)	8

(see also David Byrne, Talking Heads)

DINOSAUR JR

88	Blast First BFFP 30	Freak Scene/Keep The Glove (p/s)	5
88	Blast First BFFP 30	Freak Scene (censored)/Keep The Glove (plain white labels, no p/s, promo only)	10
89	The Catalogue CAT 069/2	Just Like Heaven/LUNACHICKS: Get Off The Road (33rpm square flexidisc free with *The Catalogue* magazine)	6/5
89	Blast First BFFP 47CD	Just Like Heaven/Throw Down/Chunks (A Last Rites Tune)/Freak Scene (Uncensored Version)/Keep The Glove (CD, picture disc)	8

DIO

MINT VALUE £

75	Purple PUR 128	Sitting In A Dream (as Ronnie Dio featuring Roger Glover & Guests)/	
		JOHN LAWTON: Little Chalk Blue	10
83	Vertigo DIOP 2	Rainbow In The Dark/Stand Up And Shout (live) (picture disc)	7
84	Vertigo DIOP 4	Mystery/Eat Your Heart Out (live) (picture disc)	6
85	Vertigo DIOD 5	Rock'n'Roll Children/Sacred Heart (gatefold p/s)	5
85	Vertigo DIOW 512	Rock'n'Roll Children/We Rock (live)/The Last In Line (live)	
		(12", white vinyl, stickered PVC sleeve)	8
85	Vertigo DIOFP 6	Hungry For Heaven/King Of Rock And Roll (p/s, with poster & sticker)	5
85	Vertigo DIOP 6	Hungry For Heaven/King Of Rock And Roll (dragon-shaped picture disc)	8
85	Vertigo DIOW 612	Hungry For Heaven/The Message (12", white vinyl)	8
86	Vertigo DIOEP 7	THE DIO EP (double pack)	5
86	Vertigo DIOP 710	THE DIO EP (10", shaped picture disc)	8
86	Vertigo DIO 712	THE DIO EP (12", p/s with family tree)	8
87	Vertigo DIOP 912	Hey Angel/Why Are They Watching Me?/Rock'n'Roll Children/Mystery	
		(12", picture disc with insert)	8
86	Vertigo VERB 40	INTERMISSION (mini-LP with postcards & discography, stickered sleeve).....	12

(see also Elf, Rainbow, Roger Glover, Black Sabbath, John Lawton)

DION (& BELMONTS)

78s

58	London HL 8646	I Wonder Why/Teen Angel (as Dion & Belmonts) (78)......................	50
58	London HL 8718	I Can't Go On (Rosalie)/No One Knows (as Dion & Belmonts) (78)	50
59	London HL 8799	Don't Pity Me/Just You (as Dion & Belmonts) (78)	50
59	London HLU 8874	A Teenager In Love/I've Cried Before (as Dion & Belmonts) (78)...........	60
59	Pye International 7N 25038	A Lover's Prayer/Every Little Thing I Do (as Dion & Belmonts) (78)	75
60	London HLU 9030	Where Or When/That's My Desire (as Dion & Belmonts) (78)...............	80

SINGLES

58	London HL 8646	I Wonder Why/Teen Angel (as Dion & Belmonts)	50
58	London HL 8718	I Can't Go On (Rosalie)/No One Knows (as Dion & Belmonts)...............	45
59	London HL 8799	Don't Pity Me/Just You (as Dion & Belmonts)	35
59	London HL 8874	A Teenager In Love/I've Cried Before (mispressing as Dion & Delmonts)	35
59	London HLU 8874	A Teenager In Love/I've Cried Before (as Dion & Belmonts)	30

(The above 45s were originally issued with triangular centres, round-centre re-pressings are worth two-thirds these values.)

59	Pye International 7N 25038	A Lover's Prayer/Every Little Thing I Do (as Dion & Belmonts)	25
60	London HLU 9030	Where Or When/That's My Desire (as Dion & Belmonts)	15
60	Top Rank JAR 368	When You Wish Upon A Star/My Private Joy (as Dion & Belmonts)..........	15
60	Top Rank JAR 503	In The Still Of The Night/Swinging On A Star (as Dion & Belmonts)	15
61	Top Rank JAR 521	Lonely Teenager/Little Miss Blue..	12
61	Top Rank JAR 545	Havin' Fun/North-East End Of The Corner.	10
61	Top Rank JAR 586	Runaround Sue/Runaway Girl	8
62	HMV POP 971	The Wanderer/The Majestic	8
62	HMV POP 1020	Lovers Who Wander/(I Was) Born To Cry	8
62	Stateside SS 115	Little Diane/Lost For Sure	6
62	Stateside SS 139	Love Came To Me/Little Girl.	7
63	CBS AAG 133	Ruby Baby/He'll Only Hurt You	10
63	Stateside SS 161	Sandy/Faith	12
63	CBS AAG 145	This Little Girl/The Loneliest Man In The World	8
63	Stateside SS 209	Come Go With Me/King Without A Queen.................................	10
63	CBS AAG 161	Be Careful Of Stones That You Throw/I Can't Believe	
		(That You Don't Love Me Anymore)	8
63	CBS AAG 169	Donna, The Prima Donna/You're Mine	6
63	CBS AAG 177	Drip Drop/No One's Waiting For Me.....................................	8
64	CBS AAG 188	I'm Your Hoochie Coochie Man/The Road I'm On (Gloria)	10
64	CBS AAG 224	Johnnie B. Goode/Chicago Blues..	10
65	CBS 201728	Sweet, Sweet Baby/Unloved, Unwanted Me (as Dion Di Mucci).............	8
65	CBS 201780	Spoonful/Kickin' Child	8
66	HMV POP 1565	Berimbau/My Girl The Month Of May (as Dion & Belmonts)................	8
67	HMV POP 1586	Movin' Man/For Bobbie (as Dion & Belmonts)	8
68	London HLP 10229	Abraham, Martin And John/Daddy Rollin'.	7
69	London HLP 10277	Both Sides Now/You Better Watch Yourself (Sonny Boy)	7
70	Warner Bros WB 7356	If We Only Have Love/Natural Man	5
70	Warner Bros WB 7401	Your Own Back Yard/Sit Down, Old Friend	6
71	Warner Bros WB 6120	Close To It All/Windows	5
71	Warner Bros K 16100	Peaceful Place/Sunniland	5
72	Warner Bros K 16132	Sanctuary/Brand New Morning	5
75	Phil Spector Intl. 2010 012	Born To Be With You/Good Lovin' Man	5

EPs

62	HMV 7EG 8749	SWINGALONG WITH DION (EP).	75
63	Stateside SE 1006	DION'S HITS (EP)	50

LPs

59	London HA-U 2194	PRESENTING DION AND THE BELMONTS (LP, as Dion & Belmonts)	275
60	Top Rank 25-027	THE TOPPERMOST — VOL. 1 (LP, as Dion & Belmonts, with others)	65
61	HMV CLP 1539	RUNAROUND SUE (LP)	60
63	Stateside SL 10034	LOVERS WHO WANDER (LP)	60
63	CBS (S) BPG 62137	RUBY BABY (LP, mono/stereo)...	22/25
64	CBS (S) BPG 62203	DONNA THE PRIMA DONNA (LP, mono/stereo)	22/25
67	HMV CLP 3618	TOGETHER AGAIN (LP, as Dion & Belmonts, also stereo CSD 3618)	30
69	B&C CAS 1002	TOGETHER AGAIN (LP, reissue)	12
70	London HA-P/SH-P 8390	DION (LP)	15
70	Warner Brothers WS 1826	SIT DOWN OLD FRIEND (LP)..	15
71	Warner Brothers WS 1872	YOU'RE NOT ALONE (LP)	15
72	Warner Brothers K 46122	SANCTUARY (LP)	15
72	Warner Brothers K 46199	SUITE FOR LATE SUMMER (LP)	15
73	Warner Brothers K 46208	REUNION — LIVE AT MADISON SQUARE GARDEN, 1972 (LP, with Belmonts)...	12
75	Phil Spector Intl. 2307 002	BORN TO BE WITH YOU (LP)	12

(see also Belmonts)

DION (Cameron) & THREE TOPS

| 67 | Doctor Bird DB 1101 | Miserable Friday/This World Has A Feeling........................... | 15 |
| 72 | Big BG 331 | Three Tops Time/UNDERGROUND PEOPLE: Tops (Version) .... | 5 |

(see also Three Tops)

CELINE DION

91	Epic 656 326-7	Where Does My Heart Beat Now?/I Feel Too Much (p/s)...............	6
91	Epic 656 326-6	Where Does My Heart Beat Now?/I'm Loving Every Moment With You/ I Feel Too Much (12", p/s)..	8
91	Epic 656 326-2/5	Where Does My Heart Beat Now?/I'm Loving Every Moment With You/ I Feel Too Much (CD, card sleeve or jewel case) .... each	15
91	Epic 657 333-7	The Last To Know/Unison (p/s)	5
91	Epic 657 333-0	The Last To Know/Unison (poster p/s)	8
91	Epic 657 333-2	The Last To Know/Unison/If We Could Start Over (CD)	12
92	Epic 657 660-7	Beauty And The Beast (duet with Peabo Bryson)/ The Beast Lets Belle Go (Instrumental) (p/s).....................	5
92	Epic 657 660-2	Beauty And The Beast (duet with Peabo Bryson)/ The Beast Lets Belle Go (Instrumental) (CD).....................	8
92	Epic 657 660-5	Beauty And The Beast (duet with Peabo Bryson)/The Beast Lets Belle Go (Instrumental) (CD, textured blue digipak)	15
92	Epic 658 192-7	If You Asked Me To/Love You Blind (p/s)	5
92	Epic 658 192-2	If You Asked Me To/Where Does My Heart Beat Now/Love You Blind (CD)	10
92	Epic 658 778-7	Love Can Move Mountains (Remix)/Beauty And The Beast (duet with Peabo Bryson) (p/s)	5
92	Epic 658 778-2	Love Can Move Mountains (Remix)/Love Can Move Mountains (Club Mix)/ Cry Just A Little/Beauty And The Beast (duet with Peabo Bryson) (CD)........	15
94	Epic 659 799-7	The Power Of Love (Radio Edit)/No Living Without Loving You (p/s)........	5
94	Epic 660 292-7	Misled/Real Emotion (p/s)	5
94	Epic 660 292-2	Misled/Love Can Move Mountains (Album Version)/ Real Emotion/Misled (Remix) (CD)	8
96	Epic 01 662979 00	Falling Into You (jukebox issue, white label, promo only)..............	8
97	Epic 01 663711 00	It's All Coming Back To Me Now/Think Twice (jukebox issue, white label, promo only).........................	8
91	Epic 467 203-1	UNISON (LP)..	15
92	Epic 471 508-1	CELINE DION (LP, some with bonus track "Where Does My Heart Beat Now")..............................	15
92	Epic 471 508-2	CELINE DION (CD)...	18

DIPLOMATS

67	Caltone TONE 108	Meet Me At The Corner/Do It To Me Baby (by Lloyd & Groovers)........	12
68	Caltone TONE 109	Going Alone/My Heart My Soul (by Lloyd & Groovers)	12
68	Caltone TONE 112	Strong Man/Listen To The Music (by Lloyd & Groovers)................	12

DIPLOMATS

| 68 | Direction 58-3899 | I Can Give You Love/I'm So Glad I Found You....................... | 5 |

(see also Sam, Erv & Tom)

DIPLOMATS

| 82 | Exchange EX 1 | Memories Of You/I'll Keep Holding On (p/s) .... | 7 |

(see also Scene)

DIRECT HITS

82	Whaam! WHAAM 007	Modesty Blaise/Sunny Honey Girl (p/s)............................	15
85	Direct POP 001	Christopher Cooper/She Really Didn't Care (p/s)...................	7
84	Whaam! BIG 7	BLOW UP (LP)	35

(see also Exits)

DIRECTION

| 93 | Detour DR 003 | Yesterday/The Kids Wanna New Direction (p/s, 1,000 only) .... | 6 |

DIRECTIONS

| 79 | Tortch TOR 004 | Three Bands Tonite/On The Train (p/s).......................... | 75 |

(see also Big Sound Authority)

DIRE STRAITS

82	Vertigo DSTR 101	Private Investigations/Badges Posters Stickers T-Shirts (10", p/s)	7
84	Vertigo DSTR 610	Love Over Gold (live)/Solid Rock (live) (10", p/s)	7
85	Vertigo DSTR 910	So Far Away/Walk Of Life (10", p/s).............................	7
85	Vertigo DSTR 1010	Money For Nothing/Love Over Gold (live) (10", p/s).................	7
85	Vertigo DSPIC 10	Money For Nothing/Love Over Gold (live) (shaped picture disc with plinth).............................	8
85	Vertigo DSPIC 11	Brothers In Arms/Going Home — Theme From 'Local Hero' (Live Version) (oblong picture disc in stickered PVC sleeve)	12
85	Vertigo DSTR 1110	Brothers In Arms/Going Home — Theme From 'Local Hero' (Live Version) (10", p/s)	7
85	Vertigo 884 285-2	Brothers In Arms (short)/Going Home (live)/Brothers In Arms (long)/ Why Worry (CD, promo only)	50
88	Vertigo DSCD 15	Sultans Of Swing/Portobello Belle (live)/Romeo And Juliet/ Money For Nothing (CD, card sleeve)	10
88	Vertigo 080 130-2	Money For Nothing (Full Length Version)/One World/So Far Away (CD Video)	20
88	Vertigo 080 134-2	Walk Of Life/Why Worry (LP Version)/Ride Across The River (CD Video)........	20
89	Vertigo 080 128-2	Sultans Of Swing/Wild West End/Down The Waterline (CD Video)	20
89	Vertigo 080 132-2	Brothers In Arms (Full Length Version)/Your Latest Trick/ Ride Across The River (CD Video)..............................	20
89	Vertigo 080 136-2	Twisting By The Pool/Two Young Lovers/If I Had You/ Twisting By The Pool (live) (CD Video)	20
82	Vertigo HS 6359 034	MAKING MOVIES (LP, half-speed master recording)	15
82	Vertigo HS 9102 021	DIRE STRAITS (LP, half-speed master recording)...................	15

(see also Mark Knopfler, David Knopfler)

DIRK & STIG
78	Ring O' 2017 109/DIB 1	Ging Gang Goolie/Mr. Sheene (unissued)	
79	EMI EMI 2852	Ging Gang Goolie/Mr. Sheene (p/s, black or khaki vinyl)	18/10

(see also Rutles, Neil Innes)

DIRTY BLUES BAND
68	Stateside S(S)L 10234	DIRTY BLUES BAND (LP)	25
69	Stateside S(S)L 10268	STONE DIRT (LP)	18

(see also Baconfat)

DIRTY DOG
78	Lightning GIL 511	Let Go Of My Hand/Shouldn't Do It/Gonna Quit/Guitar In My Hand (p/s)	15

DIRTY HARRY
73	Unity UN 573	Big Haire/YOUNG DOUG: Skank In Skank	5

DIRTY STRANGERS
89	Thrill TH 3	Bathing Belles/Oh Yeah/Hands Up (p/s, featuring Keith Richards)	8

DISCHARGE
80	Clay CLAY 1	Realities Of War/They Declare It/But After The Gig/Society's Victim (p/s)	7
80	Clay CLAY 3	Fight Back/War's No Fairy Tale/Always Restrictions/You Take Part In Creating This System/Religion Instigates (p/s)	6
80	Clay CLAY 5	Decontrol/It's No TV Sketch/Tomorrow Belongs To Us (p/s)	6
81	Clay CLAY 6	Never Again/Death Dealers/Two Monstrous Nuclear Stock-Piles (p/s)	6
81	Clay PLATE 2	WHY (12" EP)	10
82	Clay CLAY 14	State Violence, State Control/Doomsday (p/s)	12
83	Clay CLAY 29	Price Of Silence/Born To Die In The Gutter (p/s)	7
84	Clay CLAY 34	The More I See/Protest And Survive (p/s)	5
84	Clay 12CLAY 34	The More I See (Extended Version)/Protest And Survive (12", p/s)	8
85	Clay CLAY 43	Ignorance/No Compromise (p/s)	6
85	Clay 12CLAY 43	Ignorance (Extended)/No Compromise/Ignorance (12", p/s)	8
82	Clay CLAYLP 3	HEAR NOTHING, SEE NOTHING, SAY NOTHING (LP)	18
84	Clay CLAYLP 12	NEVER AGAIN (LP, red vinyl)	18

DISCIPLE
69	Parlophone R 5760	Cherie Alamayonaika/Caucasoid Junkie	5

DISCO BIPEDS
79	Bun	Disco Bipeds/Bathroom Technology (p/s)	5

DISCO BROTHERS
76	United Artists UP 36057	Let's Go To The Disco/Everybody Dance	6
76	United Artists	THE DISCO BROTHERS/THE TARTAN HORDE (EP, p/s)	8

(see also Nick Lowe, Tartan Horde, Roogalator, Damned, Brinsley Schwartz)

DISCO STUDENTS
79	Yeah Yeah Yeah UHHUH 1	South Africa House/Kafkaesque (no p/s)	15
80	Yeah Yeah Yeah UHHUH 2	A Boy With A Penchant For Open-Necked Shirts (no p/s)	15

DISCO 2000
87	KLF Comms. D 2001	I Gotta CD (7" Edit) (unissued, white labels only)	18
87	KLF Comms. D 2000	I Gotta CD/I Love Disco 2000 (12", p/s)	12

(see also J.A.M.s, KLF, Timelords, Bill Drummond, Space)

DISCO ZOMBIES
79	South Circular SGS 106	Drums Over London/Heartbeats Love (black, white & pink or black, white & green handmade wraparound p/s)	25/20
79	Uptown/Wizzo WIZZO 1	THE INVISIBLE (EP)	15
81	Dining Out TUX 2	Here Come The Buts/Mary Millington (p/s)	10

(see also Steppes, Fifty Fantastics)

DISCS
65	Columbia DB 7477	Not Meant To Be/Come Back To Me	6

BABA DISE
69	Gas GAS 118	Wanted/SENSATIONS: I'll Always Love You	6

DISKORD DATKORD
88	Soho Girl 12 SG 002	Identity (House Wife Mix)/Identity (Play List Mix)/D.D. & E.O.F.K. (12", p/s)	8

(see also Specimen)

DISORDER
80	Durham B. Centre BOOK 1	Reality Crisis/1984 (p/s)	15

DISORDER
81	Disorder ORDER 1	Complete Disorder/Insane Youth/Today's World/Violent Crime (p/s)	6
81	Disorder ORDER 2	Distortion To Deafness/More Than Fights/Daily Life/You've Got To Be Someone (p/s)	5
82	Disorder 12ORDER 3	PERDITION (12" EP)	8
83	Disorder ORDER 4	MENTAL DISORDER (EP)	6
84	Disorder 12 ORDER 5	THE SINGLES COLLECTION (12" EP)	10
84	Disorder AARGH 1	UNDER THE SCALPEL BLADE (LP)	10

DISRUPTORS
82	Radical RC 1	Young Offender/UK Soldier/No Place For You (p/s)	6
82	Radical RC 2	Shelters For The Rich/Animal Farm/Self Rule (p/s)	6
84	Radical RC 6	Bomb Heaven/Die With Mother/Poem (p/s)	5
85	Radical RC 8	ALIVE IN THE ELECTRIC CHAIR (EP)	5
85	Radical RC 128	ALIVE IN THE ELECTRIC CHAIR (12" EP)	8

TOM DISSIVELT
65	Philips BL 7681	FANTASY IN ORBIT (LP)	15

DISTANT COUSINS
| 66 | CBS 202352 | She Ain't Loving You/Here Today, Gone Tomorrow | 15 |
| 67 | CBS 2800 | Mister Sebastian/Empty House | 6 |

DISTRACTIONS
| 79 | TJM TJM 2 | YOU'RE NOT GOING OUT DRESSED LIKE THAT (12" EP) | 12 |
| 79 | Factory FAC 12 | Time Goes By So Slow/Pillow Fight (p/s) | 5 |

DISTRIBUTORS
| 80 | Tap TAP 1 | TV Me/Wireless (foldover p/s) | 6 |
| 81 | Red Rhino RED 9 | Hold/Get Rid Of These Things/Wages For Lovers (12", p/s) | 8 |

DIVERSIONS
75	Gull GULS 18	Fattie Bum-Bum/Jamaica	5
76	Gull GULS 28	But Is It Funky/To Make Us Happy	5
76	Polydor 2058 794	Raincheck/Disco Limbo	5

(see also Lene Lovich)

DIVINE COMEDY
91	Setanta SET 008	Timewatch/Jerusalem/The Rise And Fall (12", p/s)	20
92	Setanta SET 011	Europop: New Wave/Intifada/Monitor/Timewatch/Jerusalem/The Rise And Fall (12", p/s)	25
92	Setanta SET 011CD	Europop: New Wave/Intifada/Monitor/Timewatch/Jerusalem/The Rise And Fall (CD)	50
93	Setanta CAO 008	Lucy/The Pop Singer's Fear Of The Pollen Count/I Was Born Yesterday (mail order, p/s)	15
93	Setanta CAO 009	Your Daddy's Car (Demo)/THE GLEE CLUB: Free To Believe (33 rpm clear vinyl flexi)	15
93	Setanta DC 001	Indulgence No. 1: Hate My Way/Untitled Melody/Europe By Train (picture disc)	20
94	Setanta DC 002	Indulgence No. 2: A Drinking Song/When The Lights Go Out All Over Europe/Tonight We Fly (handfinished wraparound p/s, stamped labels)	15
98	TC 12TC BJD 001	I've Been To A Marvellous Party (Mixes) (12", p/s, double pack promo)	20
90	Setanta SETLPM 002	FANFARE FOR THE COMIC MUSE (LP, with inner sleeve)	50
90	Setanta SETCD 002	FANFARE FOR THE COMIC MUSE (CD)	75
93	Setanta SETCD 011	LIBERATION (CD)	15
94	Setanta SETCD 013	PROMENADE (CD, with bonus 4-track live CD)	50
97	Setanta SETCDL 036	A SHORT ALBUM ABOUT LOVE (numbered boxed digipak, with 3 postcards)	20
98	MPO IRL 01	OH YEAH (CD, 'Heineken Rock Awards' issue free with *Hot Press* magazine, with Ash & other artists)	20
98	Setanta SET CDL 057	FIN DE SIÈCLE (CD, gatefold digipak with lyric booklet)	15

JOE DIXIE & HIS BAND
| 60 | Qualiton Offbeat PSP 7126 | Prego, Prego | 6 |

DIXIE BELLES
63	London HLU 9797	Down At Papa Joe's/Rock, Rock, Rock	7
64	London HLU 9842	Southtown, U.S.A./Why Don't You Set Me Free?	6
64	London REU 1434	THE DIXIE BELLES (EP)	15
64	London HA-U/SH-U 8152	DOWN AT PAPA JOE'S (LP, with Cornbread & Jerry)	22

DIXIE CUPS
64	Pye International 7N 25245	Chapel Of Love/Ain't That Nice	10
64	Red Bird RB 10006	People Say/Girls Can Tell (some copies on Pye label)	10/8
64	Red Bird RB 10012	You Should Have Seen The Way He Looked At Me/No True Love	8
64	Red Bird RB 10017	Little Bell/Another Boy Like Mine	7
65	Red Bird RB 10024	Iko Iko/Gee Baby Gee	7
65	Red Bird RB 10032	Gee The Moon Is Shining Bright/I'm Gonna Get You Yet	15
65	HMV POP 1453	Two Way Poc A Way/That's Where It's At	8
66	HMV POP 1524	What Kind Of Fool/Danny Boy	10
66	HMV POP 1557	Love Ain't So Bad (After All)/Daddy Said No	7
71	Buddah 2011 079	Chapel Of Love/People Say	5
65	Red Bird RB 20100	CHAPEL OF LOVE (LP)	50
66	HMV CLP 1916	RIDING HIGH (LP)	35

DIXIE DRIFTER
| 65 | Columbia DB 7710 | Soul Heaven/Three Chairs Theme | 15 |

DIXIE FOUR
| 60s | Rarities RA 3 | THE DIXIE FOUR (EP) | 20 |

DIXIE HUMMINGBIRDS
| 64 | Vogue V 2422 | Have A Talk With Jesus/In The Morning | 12 |

DIXIELANDERS
| 63 | Vocalion V 9209 | Cyclone/Mardyke | 25 |

DIXIELAND JUG BLOWERS
54	HMV 7M 223	Memphis Shake/Boodle-Am-Shake	10
54	HMV B 10707	Memphis Shake/Boodle-Am-Shake (78)	8
54	HMV 7M 233	Hen Party Blues/Carpet Alley Breakdown	10
54	HMV B 10727	Hen Party Blues/Carpet Alley Breakdown (78)	8

(see also Johnny Dodds)

MINT VALUE £

ERROL DIXON

60	Blue Beat BB 27	Midnight Track/Anytime Anywhere	12
61	Blue Beat BB 46	Mama Shut Your Door/Too Much Whisky.	12
62	Blue Beat BB 86	Bad Bad Woman/Early This Morning	15
62	Island WI 017	Morning Train/Lonely Heart	15
63	Island WI 069	I Love You/Tell Me More	15
63	Carnival CV 7001	Oo Wee Baby/Twisting And Shaking	12
63	Carnival CV 7004	Mean And Evil Woman/Tutti Frutti	10
64	Oriole CB 1945	Rocks In My Pillow/Give Me More Time (as Errol Dixon & Bluebeaters)	20
66	Blue Beat BB 337	Gloria/Heavy Shuffle	12
66	Blue Beat BB 344	You're No Good/Midnight Bus	12
66	Rainbow RAI 104	I Need Someone To Love/I Want (as Errol Dixon & Goodtime Band)	12
66	Fab EP 1	I Need Someone To Love/I Want (reissue)	10
67	Ska Beat JB 271	Midnight Party/It Makes No Difference	12
67	Direct DS 5002	I Don't Want/The Hoop	12
67	Decca F 12613	Six Questions/Not Again	12
67	Decca F 12717	True Love Never Runs Smooth/What Ya Gonna Do (B-side with Judy Kay)	12
68	Decca F 12826	Back To The Chicken Shack (as Big City Blues Of Errol Dixon)/ I Done Found Out	15
69	Doctor Bird DB 1197	Why Hurt Yourself/She Started To Scream	12
70	Gas GAS 148	Something On Your Mind/I Need Love	7
65	Decca DFE 8626	SINGS FATS (EP, with Honeydrippers)	50
68	Decca LK/SKL 4962	BLUES IN THE POT (LP, with Chicken Shack)	60
70	Transatlantic TRA 225	THAT'S HOW YOU GOT KILLED BEFORE (LP)	20

(see also Chicken Shack)

HUGH DIXON

64	London HA-U 8188	FRANTIC GUITARS (LP)	15

JEFF DIXON

67	Coxsone CS 7015	The Rock/HAMBOYS: Harder On The Rock	18
68	Studio One SO 2051	Tickle Me/ENFORCERS: Forgive Me	18

TEX DIXON

70	Ackee ACK 111	Funky Trombone/Crying Horn	6
70	Ackee ACK 112	My Ring/Here I Am	6

WILLIE DIXON & ALLSTARS

56	London HLU 8297	Walking The Blues/Crazy For My Baby	2,000
56	London HLU 8297	Walking The Blues/Crazy For My Baby (78)	200
64	Pye International 7N 25270	Crazy For My Baby/Walkin' The Blues (reissue)	20
74	London HA-O 8465	CATALYST (LP, unreleased)	

DIXXY SISTERS

54	Columbia SCM 5105	Spin The Bottle Polka/The Game Of Broken Hearts	10

D.J. SHADOW

93	Mo Wax MW 014	In/Flux/Hindsight (12", p/s)	12
94	Mo Wax MW 024	Lost And Found/DJ KRUSH: Kemur (12", p/s)	12
94	Mo Wax MW 027	What Does Your Soul Look Like (parts 1-4) (p/s)	10
96	Mo Wax MW 057	Midnight In A Perfect World (remixes)/Mutual Slump (p/s)	12
96	Mo Wax MW 058	Stem/Red Bus Needs To Leave (p/s)	10
97	Mo Wax MW 063s	High Noon/Organ Donor (p/s)	10
97	Mo Wax MW 063	High Noon/Devil's Advocate/Organ Donor (p/s)	8
98	Mo Wax MW 059	ENDTRODUCING ... D.J. SHADOW (LP)	15

D'JURANN JURANN

74	Dawn DNS 1068	Streakin'/Oh! Janine	10

(see also Paul King, King Earl Boogie Band, Mungo Jerry)

D-MOB

89	FX 117	C'mon And Get My Love (Dance Hall Mix)/C'mon And Get My Love (Spaghetti Western Remix) (12", p/s)	8
90	FX 132	That's The Way Of The World (Essential Beat Mix)/(Instrumental)/ (Acappella Mix)/(D Beats Mix) (12", p/s)	8

JED(RZEZ) DMOCHOWSKI

83	Whaam! WHAAM 009	Sha-La-La-La (Dance With Me)/Ruined City (with or without 'Jed' on p/s)	8/10
82	Whaam! WHAAM 84	STALLIONS OF MY HEART (LP)	12

(see also V.I.P.'s)

DNA

90	Raw Bass 12 RBASS 006	LA SERENISSIMA (12" EP)	10

DNV

79	New Pleasures Z2	Mafia/Death In Venice/Goodbye 70s (foldout p/s)	20

(see also Another Pretty Face, Funhouse, Waterboys, TV21)

D.O.A.

93	Alt. Tentacles VIRUS 120	It's Not Unusual/Dead Men Tell No Tales (yellow vinyl)	5
81	Alt. Tentacles VIRUS 4	POSITIVELY D.O.A. (EP)	7
83	Alt. Tentacles VIRUS 31	BLOODIED BUT UNBOWED — THE DAMAGE TO DATE 1978-84 (12" EP)	8
84	Alt. Tentacles VIRUS 24	WAR ON 45 (12" EP)	8
85	Alt. Tentacles VIRUS 42	DON'T TURN YOUR BACK (ON DESPERATE TIMES) (LP)	12
85	Alt. Tentacles VIRUS 44	LET'S WRECK THE PARTY (LP, with insert & small 'spy' logo)	12

J.R. "BOB" DOBBS

97	Stang JHVH-1	Gimme Some Slack/CONNIE DOBBS: Dagon — Fish God (p/s)	8

CARL DOBKINS JNR.

59	Brunswick 05804	My Heart Is An Open Book/My Pledge To You	8
59	Brunswick 05804	My Heart Is An Open Book/My Pledge To You (78)	8
59	Brunswick 05811	If You Don't Want My Lovin'/Love Is Everything	20
59	Brunswick 05811	If You Don't Want My Lovin'/Love Is Everything (78)	15
60	Brunswick 05817	Lucky Devil/(There's A Little Song A-Singing) In My Heart	8
60	Brunswick 05832	Exclusively Yours/One Little Girl	6
60	Brunswick LAT 8329	CARL DOBKINS JNR. (LP)	45

BOBBY DOBSON

| 69 | Punch PH 4 | Strange/Your New Love | 6 |

(see also Dobby Dobson)

BONNIE DOBSON

69	RCA RCA 1901	I'm Your Woman/I Got Stung	5
70	RCA SF 8079	BONNIE DOBSON (LP)	12
72	Argo ZFB 79	BONNIE DOBSON (LP)	40
76	Polydor 2383 400	MORNING DEW (LP)	15

DOBBY DOBSON (& DELTAS)

65	King KG 1008	Cry A Little Cry/Diamonds And Pearls (as Dobby Dobson & Deltas)	10
67	Trojan TR 011	Loving Pauper/TOMMY McCOOK & SUPERSONICS: Sir Don.	15
68	Studio One SO 2068	Walking In The Footsteps/SOUL VENDORS: Studio Rock	18
68	Coxsone CS 7058	Seems To Me I'm Losing You/GAYLADS: Red Rose	22
69	Blue Cat BS 171	Strange/Your New Love	10
69	Punch PH 12	The Masquerade Is Over/Love For Ambition	6
70	Success RE 906	Crazy/RUPIE EDWARDS ALL STARS: Your New Love	6
70	Big BG 303	That Wonderful Sound/I Wasn't Born Yesterday	6
70	Big BG 310	Halfway To Paradise/Utopia	5
71	Dynamic DYN 426	Carry That Weight/More Weight	5
69	Pama SECO 33	STRANGE (LP)	25
70	Trojan TBL 145	THAT WONDERFUL SOUND (LP)	25

(see also Bobby Dobson, Chuck & Dobby, Bruce Bennett, Ernest Wilson & Freddy)

LYN DOBSON

| 74 | Fresh Air 6370 501 | JAM SANDWICH (LP) | 12 |

(see also Manfred Mann, Soft Machine, Miller Anderson)

ROY DOCKER

68	Domain D3	Mellow Moonlight/MUSIC THROUGH SIX: Riff Raff	6
69	Pama PM 750	When/Go	6
69	Pama PM 756	I'm An Outcast/Everyday Will Be A Holiday	6

DOCTOR & MEDICS

| 82 | Whaam! WHAAM 6 | The Druids Are Here/The Goats Are Trying To Kill Me (p/s) | 15 |
| 84 | white label | LIVE AT ALICE IN WONDERLAND (EP, sold at gigs) | 6 |

DOCTOR BROWN

| 95 | Magic Gnome | ANOTHER REALM (LP, 500 only) | 15 |

DR. CALCULUS

84	10 TEN 32	Programme 7/Killed By Poetry (p/s)	5
84	10 TEN 3212	Programme 7/Killed By Poetry/Programme 7 (Extended Version) (12", p/s)	8
86	10 TEN 131	Perfume From Spain/Straight Stereo (p/s)	5
86	10 TENT 131	Perfume From Spain/Straight Stereo (12", p/s)	8
86	10 DIX 45	DESIGNER BEATNIK (LP)	12
86	10 DIXCD 45	DESIGNER BEATNIK (CD)	50

(see also Stephen 'Tin Tin' Duffy)

DOCTOR DARK

| 76 | Target TGT 102 | Red Hot Passion/Instrumental | 6 |

(see also Snivelling Shits)

DOCTOR FATHER

| 70 | Pye 7N 17977 | Umbopo/Roll On | 6 |

(see also 10cc, Godley & Creme, Hotlegs)

DR. FEELGOOD & THE INTERNS (U.S.)

62	Columbia DB 4838	Dr. Feelgood/Mister Moonlight	15
64	Columbia DB 7228	The Doctor's Doogie/Blang Dong	12
66	CBS 202099	Don't Tell Me No Dirty/Where Did You Go	15
68	Capitol CL 15569	Sugar Bee/You're So Used To It	15
64	Columbia SEG 8310	DR. FEELGOOD AND THE INTERNS (EP)	60

(see also Piano Red)

DR. FEELGOOD (U.K.)

74	United Artists UP 35760	Roxette/(Get Your Kicks On) Route 66 (no p/s)	5
75	United Artists UP 35815	She Does It Right/I Don't Mind (no p/s)	5
75	United Artists UP 35857	Back In The Night/I'm A Man	5
77	United Artists UP 36304	She's A Windup/Hi-Rise (p/s)	5
77	United Artists UP 36332	Baby Jane/Looking Back	7
79	United Artists UP 36468	Milk And Alcohol/Every Kind Of Vice (p/s, brown or white vinyl)	5
79	United Artists X/Y/ZUP 36506	As Long As The Price Is Right/Down At The (Other) Doctors (p/s, either black, blue, brown or violet vinyl, 3 different p/s designs)	each 5
86	Stiff BUY 253	Don't Wait Up/Something Good (shrink-wrapped with bonus 45: "Back In The Night"/"Milk And Alcohol" [FBUY 56]) (p/s)	6
75	United Artists UAS 29727	DOWN BY THE JETTY (LP, mono only)	12
75	United Artists UAS 29880	MALPRACTICE (LP)	12
76	United Artists UAS 29990	STUPIDITY (LP initially with stickered covers & bonus 7": "Riot In Cell Block No. 9"/"Johnny B. Goode" [FEEL 1])	12
79	United Artists UAK 30239	AS IT HAPPENS (LP, with inner sleeve & bonus 7" "Encore EP": "Riot In Cell Block No. 9"/"The Blues Had A Baby And They Named It Rock'N'Roll"/"Lights Out"/"Great Balls Of Fire" [p/s, FEEL 2], with inner sleeve)	12

(see also Wilko Johnson, Lew Lewis, Oil City Sheiks)

MINT VALUE £

DR. HOOK
73	CBS 1037	The Cover Of "Rolling Stone"/Queen Of The Silver Dollar	5
73	CBS 1037	The Cover Of "Radio Times" (1-sided, promo only, by Dr. Hook & Friends)	75
78	Capitol CL 15958	Makin' Love And Music/I Wanna Make That Woman Tremble (promo only)	5
78	Capitol CL 15992	The Radio/Only Sixteen/I'm A Lamb (p/s)	8
81	Mercury MER 58	SOS For Love/99 And Me (p/s)	5
82	Mercury MER 93	Baby Makes Her Blue Jeans Talk/The Turn On (p/s)	5
82	Mercury MER 104	Loveline/Chained To Your Memory (p/s)	5
82	Mercury MER 124	Rings/Crazy Rosie (p/s)	5
78	Capitol PSLP 314	FOR YOU FROM DR. HOOK (EP, promo only)	10
71	CBS 64754	DR. HOOK AND THE MEDICINE SHOW (LP, plain orange label)	15
71	CBS 65132	SLOPPY SECONDS (LP, plain orange label)	15
71	CBS 65560	BELLY UP (LP, plain orange label)	12

DR. JOHN (The Night Tripper)
70	Atco 2091 019	Wash Mama Wash/Mama Roux	6
72	Atlantic K 10158	Iko Iko/Huey Smith Medley	5
72	Atlantic K 10214	Wang Dang Doodle/Big Chief	5
73	Atlantic K 10291	Right Place, Wrong Time/I Been Hoodooed	10
73	Atlantic K 10329	Such A Night/Life	8
68	Atlantic 587/588 147	GRIS GRIS (LP, plum label, mono/stereo)	30
69	Atco 228 018	BABYLON (LP, plum label)	18
70	Atco 2400 015	REMEDIES (LP, plum label)	18
71	Atlantic 2400 161	THE SUN, MOON AND HERBS (LP, plum label, gatefold sleeve with insert)	25
72	Atlantic K 40384	GUMBO (LP, green & orange label, gatefold sleeve)	15
72	Atlantic K 40168	GRIS GRIS (LP, reissue, green & orange label)	15
72	Atlantic K 40250	THE SUN, MOON AND HERBS (LP, reissue, green & orange label, gatefold sleeve with insert)	15
73	Atco K 50017	IN THE RIGHT PLACE (LP, U.K. disc in U.S. stickered 3-way gatefold sleeve)	20
73	CBS 65659	TRIUMVIRATE (LP, with John Hammond & Mike Bloomfield)	12
74	Atlantic K 50035	DESITIVELY BONNAROO (LP)	15
75	United Artists UAG 29902	HOLLYWOOD BE THY NAME (LP, with inner sleeve)	15
75	DJM DJSLM 2019	CUT ME WHILE I'M HOT (ANYTIME, ANYPLACE) (LP)	12

DR. K'S BLUES BAND
68	Spark SRLP 101	DR. K'S BLUES BAND (LP)	50

DR. MARIGOLD'S PRESCRIPTION
68	Pye 7N 17493	My Old Man's A Groovy Old Man/People Get Ready	5
69	Pye 7N 17832	You've Got To Build Your Love/My Picture Of Love	5
70	Bell BLL 1096	Breaking The Heart Of A Good Man/Night Hurries On By	5
70	Bell BLL 1126	Sing Along, Sing Along, Sing Along/Father Jim	5
71	Bell BLL 1149	Muddy Water/Come With Me	5
69	Marble Arch MALS 1222	PICTURES OF LIFE (LP)	12
73	Pye/Santa Ponsa PNL 501	HELLO GIRL (LP, as Dr. Marigold's)	12

DOCTOR ROCKIT
96	Clear CLR 411	READY TO ROCKIT EP (2 x 10", p/s)	10
96	Clear CLR 416	D FOR DOKTOR EP (12", p/s)	8

DOCTORS OF MADNESS
76	Polydor 2383 378	LATE NIGHT MOVIES (LP)	12
76	Polydor 2383 403	FIGMENTS OF EMANCIPATION (LP, with inner sleeve)	12

DR. STRANGELY STRANGE
69	Island ILPS 9106	KIP OF THE SERENES (LP, pink label, later 'palm-tree' with remix)	80/90
70	Vertigo 6360 009	HEAVY PETTING (LP, gatefold sleeve, spiral label; beware of counterfeits)	70
	(see also Sweeney's Men, Gary Moore)		

DR. TECHNICAL & MACHINES
83	Hawkfan HWFB 1	Zones/Processed (1-sided with insert, mail-order issue, no p/s)	12
	(see also Dave Brock, Hawkwind)		

DR. WEST'S MEDICINE SHOW & JUNK BAND
67	CBS 202492	The Eggplant That Ate Chicago/You Can't Fight City Hall Blues	6
67	CBS 202658	Gondoliers, Shakespeares, Overseers/Daddy I Know	6
68	Page One POF 061	Bullets La Verne/Jigsaw	25
70	Page One POF 176	Gondoliers, Shakespeares, Overseers/Daddy I Know (reissue)	5
69	Page One POLS 017	THE EGGPLANT THAT ATE CHICAGO (LP)	25
	(see also Norman Greenbaum)		

DR. WHO
76	Argo ZSW 564	DR. WHO AND THE PESCATONS (LP, spoken word, read by Tom Baker & Elizabeth Sladen)	12
79	BBC REC 364	GENESIS OF THE DALEKS (LP, spoken word)	12
81	RNIB	TALKING BOOK (reel-to-reel tape, read by Gabriel Wolf)	20
82	BBC 2LP-22001	DOCTOR WHO COLLECTOR'S EDITION (2-LP, includes "Genesis Of The Daleks" [BBC 22364], "Sound Effects" [BBC 22316], & bonus 7" "Doctor Who"/"The Astronauts" [RESL 451], with poster)	30
	(see also BBC Radiophonic Workshop, Century 21, Jon Pertwee)		

DR. Z
70	Fontana 6007 023	Lady Ladybird/People In The Street	25
71	Vertigo 6360 048	THREE PARTS TO MY SOUL (LP, gatefold sleeve, spiral label)	150

PAT DODD
59	Pye International 7N 25030	Stag Party/Odds'n'Dodds	6
59	Pye International N 25030	Stag Party/Odds'n'Dodds (78)	12

DODD'S ALLSTARS
69	Coxsone CS 7096	Mother Aitken (actually by Lord Power)/What A Love (actually by Denzil Laing)	18

JOHNNY DODDS

51	HMV B 10082	Bucktown Stomp/Weary City Stomp (78)	8
52	HMV B 10223	Blue Washboard Stomp/Bull Fiddle Blues (78)	6
52	Vocalion V 1003	After You've Gone/Come On And Stomp Stomp Stomp (78)	10
52	Vocalion V 1008	Weary Blues/New Orleans Stomp (78)	10
52	Vocalion V 1022	When Erastus Plays His Old Kazoo/Joe Turner Blues (78)	10
53	Vocalion V 1025	San/New St. Louis Blues (78, mispressing)	30
53	Vocalion V 1025	Oh! Lizzie (A Lover's Lament)/Clarinet Wobble (78)	10
53	HMV B 10419	Too Tight/Goober Dance (78)	5
53	London AL 3505	JOHNNY DODDS VOLUME 1 (10" LP)	15
54	London AL 3513	JOHNNY DODDS VOLUME 2 (10" LP)	15
55	Vogue Coral LRA 10025	JOHNNY DODDS VOL. 1 (10" LP)	25
55	HMV DLP 1073	JOHNNY DODDS WASHBOARD BAND (10" LP)	15
56	London AL 3555	JOHNNY DODDS VOLUME 3 (10" LP)	18
57	London AL 3560	JOHNNY DODDS VOLUME 4 (10" LP)	18

(see also Dixieland Jugblowers)

MALCOLM DODDS

59	Brunswick 05774	This Is Real (This Is Love)/I'll Always Be With You	6
59	Brunswick 05774	This Is Real (This Is Love)/I'll Always Be With You (78)	8
59	Brunswick 05796	Tremble/Deep Inside	6
59	Brunswick 05796	Tremble/Deep Inside (78)	8

NELLA DODDS

65	Pye 7N 25281	Come See About Me/You Don't Love Me Anymore	20
65	Pye 7N 25291	Finders Keepers, Losers Weepers/A Girl's Life	18

DODGERS

60	Downbeat CHA 2	Let's Make A Whole Lot Of Love/You Make Me Happy	20

DODGERS

76	Island WIP 6292	Don't Let Me Be Wrong/Get To You	5
76	Island WIP 6342	Just Wanna Love You/Don't Know What You're Doing	5
76	Island WIP 6361	Down/Don't Know What You're Doing	5
78	Polydor 2059 028	Love On The Rebound/Come Out Fighting (p/s)	5
78	Polydor 2059 046	Don't Let Me Be Wrong/Come Out Fighting (p/s)	5
78	Polydor 2059 074	Anytime/Little Darlin'	5
78	Polydor 2383 513	LOVE ON THE REBOUND (LP)	12

(see also Badfinger, Indian Summer)

DODGY

91	Bostin BTN 001	Summer Fayre/St. Lucia (p/s)	7
91	Bostin BTN 002	Easy Way/Seems Like A Bad Day (p/s)	7
92	Bostin BTN 003	THE BLACK AND WHITE SINGLE (Black Side: Worth The Blood/White Side: The Elephant) (p/s)	5
92	Bostin BTN 003CDS	THE BLACK AND WHITE SINGLE (Black Side: Worth The Blood/White Side: The Elephant/Worth The Blood (Full Version)/Introducing The D Club: See The Way) (CD)	8

DODO RESURRECTION

72	Elegiac SNT 7926	NOSTRADAMUS (LP, private pressing, with fold-out 'treatise' insert)	2,500
95	Spam Lanza BA-F-ST 01	BAPHOMET! (LP, private re-pressing of 'Nostradamus' with free 7" [Five-Fingered Fury/Caput LVIII/Melek Taus, The Peacock Angel], 100 only)	800

(see also Underwater Hairdressers)

DODO'S

67	Polydor BM 56153	I Made Up My Mind/Can't Make It Out	8

ERNIE K-DOE

(see under 'K')

DOG FACED HERMANS

87	Demon Radge RADGE 1	UNBEND (EP)	5
88	Calculus KIT 003	Miss O'Grady/Bella Ciao (p/s, with inserts)	5

DOGFEET

71	Reflection HRS 7	Sad Story/On The Road	25
71	Reflection HRS 12	Since I Went Away/Evil Woman	25
70	Reflection REFL 8	DOGFEET (LP)	300
94	Kissing Spell CA 36001	DOGFEET (LP, reissue)	15

TYMON DOGG

81	Ghost Dance GHO 1	Lose This Skin (featuring the Clash)/Indestructable (p/s)	6

(see also Timon, Clash)

DOGGEREL BANK

73	Charisma CB 220	Tiny Seed Of Love/Down On The Farm	5
73	Charisma CAS 1079	SILVER FACES (LP)	12
75	Charisma CAS 1102	MISTER SKILLCORN DANCES (LP)	18

BILL DOGGETT

55	Parlophone DP 411	Gumbo/Tara's Theme (78, export issue)	20
55	Parlophone DP 432	Christmas Song/Winter Wonderland (78, export issue)	20
56	Parlophone CMSP 39	Honky Tonk (Parts 1 & 2) (gold label lettering, export issue)	12
56	Parlophone R 4231	Honky Tonk (Parts 1 & 2) (gold label lettering, later silver)	15/10
56	Parlophone R 4231	Honky Tonk (Parts 1 & 2) (78)	8
57	Parlophone R 4265	Slow Walk/Peacock Alley	12
57	Parlophone R 4265	Slow Walk/Peacock Alley (78)	8
57	Parlophone R 4306	Ram-Bunk-Shush/Blue Largo	10
57	Parlophone R 4306	Ram-Bunk-Shush/Blue Largo (78)	8
57	Parlophone R 4379	Hot Ginger/Soft	15
57	Parlophone R 4379	Hot Ginger/Soft (78)	12
58	Parlophone R 4413	Leaps And Bounds (Parts 1 & 2)	10

MINT VALUE £

58	Parlophone R 4413	Leaps And Bounds (Parts 1 & 2) (78)	12
60	Parlophone R 4629	Smokie/Evening Dreams	8
61	Warner Bros WB 32	The Hully Gully Twist/Jackrabbit	5
61	Warner Bros WB 46	You Can't Sit Down (Parts 1 & 2)	8
57	Parlophone GEP 8644	HONKY TONK (EP)	12
57	Parlophone GEP 8674	PLAYS DUKE ELLINGTON (EP)	10
58	Parlophone GEP 8711	BILL DOGGETT (EP)	12
58	Parlophone GEP 8727	RAINBOW RIOT (EP)	10
59	Parlophone GEP 8771	A JOLLY CHRISTMAS (EP)	12
58	Parlophone PMD 1067	DAME DREAMING (10" LP)	30
59	Parlophone PMD 1073	DANCE AWHILE WITH DOGGETT (10" LP)	30
60	Parlophone PMC 1124	ON TOUR (LP)	18
60	Parlophone PMC 1118	DOGGETT'S BIG CITY DANCE PARTY (LP)	20
61	Warner Bros WM 402	3046 PEOPLE DANCED 'TIL 4 A.M. (LP, live, as Bill Doggett & His Combo)	15
62	Parlophone PMC 1165	BACK WITH MORE BILL DOGGETT (LP)	20
62	Warner Bros WM 4056	THE BAND WITH THE BEAT (LP, with His Combo, also stereo WS 8056)	12/15
65	HMV CLP 1884	WOW (LP)	15

(see also Ella Fitzgerald, Earl Bostic)

DOGROSE
73	Satril SAT 6	All For The Love Of City Lights/Each Other	5
72	Satril SATL 4002	ALL FOR THE LOVE OF DOGROSE (LP)	20

DOG SOLDIER
75	United Artists UAS 29769	DOG SOLDIER (LP)	12

DOG THAT BIT PEOPLE
71	Parlophone R 5880	Lovely Lady/Merry-Go-Round	18
71	Parlophone PCS 7125	THE DOG THAT BIT PEOPLE (LP)	200

(see also Locomotive)

DOGWATCH
79	Bridgehouse BHLP 002	PENFRIEND (LP, with insert)	20

NED DOHENY
81	CBS 9481	To Prove My Love/On The Swing Shift (p/s)	8
81	CBS 13-9481	To Prove My Love/On The Swing Shift (12", p/s)	10

DOKKEN
82	Carrere CAR 229	We're Illegal/Paris Is Burning (p/s)	5
82	Carrere CAL 136	BREAKIN' THE CHAINS (LP)	12

JOE DOLAN
67	Piccadilly 7N 35368	House With The Whitewashed Gable/Work Day Blues	6
67	Pye 7N 17354	Tar And Cement/Time Of My Life	7

RAMBLIN' JIMMY DOLAN
53	Capitol CL 13982	The Wheel That Does The Squeakin'/Playin' Dominoes And Shootin' Dice (78)	10

THOMAS DOLBY
81	Armageddon AS 007	Urges/Leipzig (p/s)	5
81	Venice In Peril 12R 6051	Europa And The Pirate Twins/Therapy-Growth (12", p/s)	8
82	Statik TAK 4	Urges/Leipzig (p/s, reissue)	5
81	Venice In Peril VIPS 101	Airwaves/Wreck Of The Fairchild (p/s)	5
82	Venice In Peril 12VIPS 103	Windpower/Flying North (12", p/s)	8
82	Venice In Peril 12VIPS 104	She Blinded Me With Science/One Of Our Submarines (12", p/s)	8
88	EMI Manhattan CDMT 38	Airhead (7" Edit)/Budapest By Blimp/Hyperactive (7" Version)/Airhead (Extended Version) (CD)	8
88	EMI Manhattan CDMT 59	Hot Sauce (7" Remix)/(Extended Version)/Salsa Picante (7" Version)/Get Out Of My Mix (CD)	8
89	EMI USA CDMT 71	My Brain Is Like A Sieve/My Brain Is Like A Sieve (Instrumental)/Ravivar Fiore (CD)	8

(see also Low Noise, Dolby's Cube)

DOLBY'S CUBE
85	Parlophone 12RA 6100	May The Cube Be With You (Cubular Dub Mix)/Googoo Plexus/Cube Creature Caviar (12", p/s, with George Clinton)	8

(see also Thomas Dolby)

DOLE
78	Ultimate ULT 402	New Wave Love/Hungry Men No Longer Steal Sheep But Are There Hanging Judges? (die-cut p/s)	20

MICKY DOLENZ
67	London HLH 10117	Don't Do It/FINDERS KEEPERS: (We Wear) Lavender Blue	12
67	London HLH 10152	Huff Puff/OBVIOUS: Fate	12
73	MGM 2006 265	Daybreak/Love War	10
74	MGM 2006 392	Ooh She's Young/Love War	10
79	Chrysalis CHS 2297	Love Light/Alicia (p/s)	6
83	A&M BUGSY 1	Tomorrow/BUGSY MALONE GANG: Fat Sam's Grand Slam (with poster)	10

(see also Monkees)

ANDY DOLL
62	Starlite ST45 068	Wild Desire/Wyat	10
63	Starlite STLP II	ON STAGE (LP, by Andy Doll Band & Guests)	20

LINDA DOLL & SUNDOWNERS
64	Piccadilly 7N 35166	Bonie Maronie/He Don't Want Your Love Anymore	8

DOLLIES
65	CBS 201788	You Touch Me Baby/I Can't Go On	7

THOMAS DOLBY *FATS DOMINO*

DOLPHIN
77	Private Stock PVLP 1055	GOODBYE (LP)	12
80	Gale GALELP 02	MOLECULES (LP)	12

ERIC DOLPHIN QUINTET
61	Esquire 32-123	THE ERIC DOLPHIN QUINTET (LP)	12

DOLPHINS
65	Stateside SS 375	Hey Da Da Dow/I Don't Want To Go On Without You	8

ERIC DOLPHY
69	Transatlantic PR 7311	OUTWARD BOUND (LP)	12

ERIC DOLPHY & BOOKER LITTLE
66	Stateside SL 10160	ERIC DOLPHY AND BOOKER LITTLE MEMORIAL ALBUM (LP)	15

BILLY DOLTON
61	Parlophone R 4733	Winkie Doll/Girls	7

DOME
81	Dome DOME 3	Jasz (1-sided flexidisc)	6
80	4AD CAD 16	3R4 (mini-LP)	12
80	Dome DOME 1	DOME ONE (LP)	15
80	Dome DOME 2	DOME 2 (LP)	12
81	Dome DOME 3	DOME 3 (LP)	12

(see also Wire, Gilbert & Lewis, A.C. Marias A.C.)

FATS DOMINO
78s
54	London HL 8007	Rose Mary/You Said You Love Me (78)	60
54	London HL 8063	Little School Girl/You Done Me Wrong (78)	50
54	London HL 8096	Don't Leave Me This Way/Something's Wrong (78)	45
55	London HL 8124	Love Me/Don't You Hear Me Calling You (78)	40
55	London HL 8133	Thinking Of You/I Know (78)	25
55	London HLU 8173	Ain't That A Shame/La La (78)	10
56	London HLU 8256	Bo Weevil/Don't Blame It On Me (78)	20
56	London HLU 8280	I'm In Love Again/My Blue Heaven (78)	10
56	London HLU 8309	When My Dream Boat Comes Home/So Long (78)	10
56	London HLU 8330	Blueberry Hill/I Can't Go On (Rosalie) (78)	10
57	London HLU 8356	Honey Chile/Don't You Know (78)	10
57	London HLP 8377	Blue Monday/What's The Reason I'm Not Pleasing You (78)	8
57	London HLP 8407	I'm Walkin'/I'm In The Mood For Love (78)	10
57	London HLP 8449	The Valley Of Tears/It's You I Love (78)	10
57	London HLP 8471	What Will I Tell My Heart/When I See You (78)	12
57	London HLP 8519	Wait And See/I Still Love You (78)	10
58	London HLP 8575	The Big Beat (from the film)/I Want You To Know (78)	12
58	London HLP 8628	Sick And Tired/No, No (78)	15
58	London HLP 8663	Little Mary/The Prisoner's Song (78)	15
58	London HLP 8727	Young School Girl/It Must Be Love (78)	20
58	London HLP 8759	Whole Lotta Loving/Coquette (78)	20
59	London HLP 8822	When The Saints Go Marching In/Telling Lies (78)	25
59	London HLP 8865	Margie/I'm Ready (78)	30
59	London HLP 8942	I Want To Walk You Home/I'm Gonna Be A Wheel Some Day (78)	40
59	London HLP 9005	Be My Guest/I've Been Around (78)	50
60	London HLP 9073	Country Boy/If You Need Me (78)	60
60	London HLP 9163	Walking To New Orleans/Don't Come Knockin' (78)	100

Fats DOMINO

SINGLES

55	London HL 8124	Love Me/Don't You Hear Me Calling You	150
55	London HL 8133	Thinking Of You/I Know	125
55	London HLU 8173	Ain't That A Shame/La La	50
56	London HLU 8256	Bo Weevil/Don't Blame It On Me	100
56	London HLU 8280	I'm In Love Again/My Blue Heaven	70
56	London HLU 8309	When My Dream Boat Comes Home/So Long	50
56	London HLU 8330	Blueberry Hill/I Can't Go On (Rosalie)	50
57	London HL 8356	Honey Chile/Don't You Know	50
57	London HLP 8377	Blue Monday/What's The Reason I'm Not Pleasing You	40

(The above 45s were originally issued with triangular centres & gold lettering labels; later silver-label re-pressings are worth around half these values.)

57	London HLP 8407	I'm Walkin'/I'm In The Mood For Love	20
57	London HLP 8449	The Valley Of Tears/It's You I Love	20
57	London HLP 8471	What Will I Tell My Heart/When I See You	20
57	London HLP 8519	Wait And See/I Still Love You	18
58	London HLP 8575	The Big Beat (From The Film)/I Want You To Know	15
58	London HLP 8628	Sick And Tired/No, No	15
58	London HLP 8663	Little Mary/The Prisoner's Song	18
58	London HLP 8727	Young School Girl/It Must Be Love	20
58	London HLP 8759	Whole Lotta Loving/Coquette	18
59	London HLP 8822	When The Saints Go Marching In/Telling Lies	12

(HLP 8407 through to 8822 45s were issued with triangular centres & silver lettering on all-black labels; later copies are worth around half these values.)

59	London HLP 8865	Margie/I'm Ready (triangular centre & silver-top label, later round centre)	10/6
59	London HLP 8942	I Want To Walk You Home/I'm Gonna Be A Wheel Some Day (tri or round)	12/8
59	London HLP 9005	Be My Guest/I've Been Around (triangular or round centre)	30/8

(All subsequent London 45s were issued with round centres & silver-top labels.)

60	London HLP 9073	Country Boy/If You Need Me	10
60	London HLP 9133	Tell Me That You Love Me/Before I Grow Too Old	15
60	London HLP 9163	Walking To New Orleans/Don't Come Knockin'.	10
60	London HLP 9198	Three Nights A Week/Put Your Arms Around Me, Honey	10
60	London HLP 9244	My Girl Josephine/Natural Born Lover	8
61	London HLP 9301	What A Price/Ain't That Just Like A Woman	12
61	London HLP 9327	Fell In Love On Monday/Shu-Rah	12
61	London HLP 9374	It Keeps Rainin'/I Just Cry	20
61	London HLP 9415	Let The Four Winds Blow/Good Hearted Man	10
61	London HLP 9456	What A Party/Rockin' Bicycle	10
62	London HLP 9520	Jambalaya/You Win Again	8
62	London HLP 9557	My Real Name/My Heart Is Bleeding	12
62	London HLP 9590	Dance With Mr. Domino/Nothing New (Same Old Thing)	12
62	London HLP 9616	Did You Ever See A Dream Walking/Stop The Clock	12
63	London HLP 9738	You Always Hurt The One You Love/Trouble Blues	10
63	HMV POP 1164	There Goes My Heart Again/Can't Go On Without You	10
63	HMV POP 1197	When I'm Walkin'/I've Got A Right To Cry	8
63	HMV POP 1219	Red Sails In The Sunset/Song For Rosemary	6
63	HMV POP 1265	Just A Lonely Man/Who Cares	7
64	HMV POP 1281	I Don't Want To Set The World On Fire/Lazy Lady	6
64	HMV POP 1303	If You Don't Know What Love Is/Something You Got Baby	20
64	HMV POP 1324	Mary Oh Mary/Packin' Up.	6
64	HMV POP 1370	Kansas City/Heartbreak Hill	7
65	Mercury MF 869	(I Left My Heart) In San Francisco/I Done Got Over It	10
65	Mercury MF 873	What's That You Got?/It's Never Too Late	7
65	HMV POP 1421	Why Don't You Do Right?/Wigs	7
67	HMV POP 1582	I'm Livin' Right/I Don't Want To Set The World On Fire	7
67	Liberty LBF 12055	It Keeps Rainin'/Blue Monday	
68	Liberty LBF 15098	Walking To New Orleans/Blueberry Hill	5
68	Reprise RS 20696	Honest Mamas Love Their Papas Better/ One For The Highway (withdrawn)	10
68	Reprise RS 20763	Lady Madonna/One For The Highway	10
69	Reprise RS 20810	Everybody's Got Something To Hide Except Me And My Monkey/ So Swell When You're Well	6
69	Liberty LBF 15274	I'm Ready/The Fat Man	10
69	Mercury MF 1104	What's That You Got?/Jambalaya (On The Bayou)	8
78	Sonet SON 2168	Sleeping On The Job/After Hours	5

EXPORT SINGLES

57	London HL 7028	Wait And See/I Still Love You	25
58	London HL 7040	Sick And Tired/No, No	25
58	London HL 7054	The Big Beat (From The Film)/Little Mary	25

EPs

55	London RE-P 1022	BLUES FOR LOVE (EP, 1st pressing with gold lettering label, later silver)	70/45
56	London RE-U 1062	BLUES FOR LOVE VOL. 2 (EP, 1st pressing with gold label, later silver)	60/40
57	London RE-U 1073	FATS (EP, export issue, plain sleeve)	125
57	London RE-P 1079	HERE COMES FATS VOL. 1 (EP)	35
58	London RE-P 1080	HERE COMES FATS VOL. 2 (EP)	35
58	London RE-P 1115	CARRY ON ROCKIN' PART 1 (EP)	35
58	London RE-P 1116	CARRY ON ROCKIN' PART 2 (EP)	35
58	London RE-P 1117	BLUES FOR LOVE VOL. 3 (EP)	40
58	London RE-P 1121	BLUES FOR LOVE VOL. 4 (EP)	35
58	London RE-P 1138	HERE COMES FATS VOL. 3 (EP)	35
59	London RE-P 1206	THE ROCKIN' MR. D VOL. 1 (EP)	35
59	London RE-P 1207	THE ROCKIN' MR. D VOL. 2 (EP)	35

(The above EPs were originally issued with triangular centres; round-centre re-pressings are worth two-thirds these values.)

MINT VALUE £

60	London RE-P 1261	BE MY GUEST (EP)	30
60	London RE-P 1265	THE ROCKIN' MR. D VOL. 3 (EP)	30
62	London RE-P 1340	WHAT A PARTY (EP)	30
64	HMV 7EG 8862	RED SAILS IN THE SUNSET (EP)	25
65	Liberty LEP 4026	MY BLUE HEAVEN (EP)	25
66	Liberty LEP 4045	ROLLIN' (EP)	25

LPs

56	London HA-U 2028	FATS' ROCK AND ROLLIN' (LP)	80
56	London HA-P 2041	CARRY ON ROCKIN' (LP)	80
57	London HA-P 2052	HERE STANDS FATS DOMINO (LP)	80
56	London HA-P 2073	THIS IS FATS DOMINO (LP)	50
58	London HA-P 2087	THIS IS FATS (LP)	50
58	London HA-P 2135	THE FABULOUS "MR. D" (LP)	50
59	London HA-P 2223	LET'S PLAY FATS DOMINO (LP)	50
60	London HA-P 2312	A LOT OF DOMINOES! (LP)	50
61	London HA-P 2364	I MISS YOU SO (LP)	50
61	London HA-P 2420	LET THE FOUR WINDS BLOW (LP)	50
61	London HA-P 2426	WHAT A PARTY (LP)	50
62	London HA-P 2447	TWISTIN' THE STOMP (LP)	55
63	London HA-P 8039	JUST DOMINO (LP)	55
63	London HA-P 8084	WALKING TO NEW ORLEANS (LP)	55
63	HMV CLP 1690	HERE COMES FATS DOMINO (LP, also stereo CSD 1520)	30/35
63	HMV CLP 1740	FATS ON FIRE (LP, also stereo CSD 1543)	30/35
65	Liberty LBY 3033	MILLION SELLERS BY FATS VOL. 1 (LP)	18
65	Liberty LBY 3046	MILLION SELLERS BY FATS VOL. 2 (LP)	18
65	HMV CLP 1821	GETAWAY WITH FATS DOMINO (LP, also stereo CSD 1580)	20/25
65	Mercury (S)MCL 20070	DOMINO '65 (LP, mono/stereo)	15
67	Liberty LBL 83023	MILLION SELLERS BY FATS VOL. 1 (LP, reissue)	12
67	Liberty LBL 83024	MILLION SELLERS BY FATS VOL. 2 (LP, reissue)	12
68	Liberty LBL 83101	MILLION SELLERS BY FATS VOL. 3 (LP)	15
68	Stateside (S)SL 10240	FANTASTIC FATS (LP)	12
68	Liberty LBL/LBS 83142E	FAT SOUND (LP)	12
70	Liberty LBL/LBS 83174E	RARE DOMINO'S (LP)	12
70	Liberty LBS 83331E	VERY BEST OF FATS DOMINO (LP)	12
71	United Artists UAS 29152	RARE DOMINOS VOL. II (LP)	12

DOMINOES (U.S.)

51	Vogue V 9012	Sixty Minute Man/I Can't Escape From You (78)	45
52	Vogue V 2135	Have Mercy, Baby/That's What You're Doing To Me (78)	40
56	Vogue EPV 1113	RHYTHM AND BLUES (EP, 2 tracks by Swallows)	275

(see also Billy Ward & Dominoes, Clyde McPhatter, Jackie Wilson)

DOMINOES (U.K.)

| 58 | Reading Rag LYN 545 | Bye Bye Johnny/Yakety Yak | 10 |

DOMINOES (Jamaica)

| 68 | Melody MRC 002 | A Tribute (actually by Ann Reid)/Hooray (actually by Uniques) | 8 |

JERRY DONAHUE

| 86 | Musicmaker MML 880011 | TELECASTING (LP) | 12 |

(see also Fairport Convention, Fotheringay, Mick Greenwood)

SAM DONAHUE & HIS ORCHESTRA

| 55 | Capitol CL 14349 | Saxaboogie/September In The Rain | 15 |

TROY DONAHUE

| 63 | Warner Bros WB 111 | Live Young/Somebody Loves Me | 6 |

MIKE DONALD

| 71 | Folk Heritage FHR 021 | YORKSHIRE SONGS OF THE BROAD ACRES (LP) | 25 |

ERIC DONALDSON

71	Dynamic DYN 420	Cherry Oh Baby/LLOYD CHARMERS: Sir Charmers Special	8
71	Dynamic DYN 423	Love Of The Common People/DRAGONAIRES: The Dragon's Net	12
71	Dynamic DYN 425	Just Can't (Happen This Way)/Just Can't (Happen This Way) Version	6
72	Dynamic DYN 431	I'm Indebted/I'm Indebted (Version)	6
72	Dynamic DYN 439	Miserable Woman/The Lion Sleeps	6
72	Dynamic DYN 445	Blue Boot/Blue Boot (Version)	10
72	Dynamic DYN 452	Little Did You Know/Little Did You Know (Version)	5
73	Dragon DRA 1017	What A Festival/I ROY & ERIC: Festival Version	5
73	Dragon DRA 1018	The Way You Do The Things You Do/Version	5
73	Dragon DRA 1020	Watch What You're Doing To Me/You Must Believe Me	5
73	Dragon DRA 1027	A Weh We A Go Go/SOUL DEFENDERS: Version	5
72	Trojan TRL 42	ERIC DONALDSON (LP)	20

(see also Prunes, Satchmo)

JAMES DONALDSON BAND

| 76 | Look LKLP 7-6060 | JUSTIFIED (LP) | 10 |

DON & DEWEY

64	London HL 9897	Get Your Hat/Annie Lee	18
66	Cameo Parkway CP 750	Soul Motion/Stretchin' Out	22
67	Sue WI 4032	Soul Motion/Stretchin' Out (reissue)	22
71	Sonet SNTF 5006	DON AND DEWEY (LP)	12

(see also Don 'Sugarcane' Harris, Dewey Terry)

DON & GOODTIMES

| 67 | Columbia DB 8199 | I Could Be So Good To You/And It's So Good | 4 |
| 67 | Columbia DB 8266 | Happy And Me/If You Love Her, Cherish Her And Such | 4 |

DON & JUAN

| 62 | London HLX 9529 | What's Your Name?/Chicken Necks | 25 |

DON & PETE
66	Columbia DB 7881	And I'm Crying Again/Time Will Tell	4

DONAYS
62	Oriole CB 1770	Devil In His Heart/Bad Boy	130

DON, DICK & JIMMY
54	Columbia SCM 5110	Brand Me With Your Kisses/Angela Mia	15
55	London HL 8117	You Can't Have Your Cake And Eat It Too/That's What I Like	20
55	London HL 8117	You Can't Have Your Cake And Eat It Too/That's What I Like (78)	8
55	London HL 8144	Make Yourself Comfortable/(Whatever Happened To) Piano Players (That Played Like This)	20
55	London HL 8144	Make Yourself Comfortable/(Whatever Happened To) Piano Players (That Played Like This) (78)	8
56	HMV POP 280	That's The Way I Feel/Two Voices In The Night	8
55	London RE-U 1043	DON, DICK AND JIMMY (EP)	30

DOROTHY DONEGAN
56	MGM MGM-EP 532	DOROTHY DONEGAN TRIO (EP)	8

LONNIE DONEGAN
78s
55	Decca F 10647	Rock Island Line/John Henry (78, as Lonnie Donegan Skiffle Group)	8
56	Decca FJ 10695	Diggin' My Potatoes/Bury My Body (78, Lonnie Donegan Skiffle Group)	8
56	Oriole CB 1329	The Passing Stranger/TOMMY REILLY: The Intimate Stranger (78)	12
56	Columbia DB 3850	On A Christmas Day/Take My Hand, Precious Lord (78)	10
56	Pye N 15036	Lost John/Stewball (78, vinyl pressing)	8
56	Pye N 15071	Bring A Little Water Sylvie/Dead Or Alive (78, vinyl pressing)	8
57	Pye N 15080	Don't You Rock Me Daddy-O/I'm Alabamy Bound (78, shellac or vinyl)	each 8
57	Pye N 15087	Cumberland Gap/Love Is Strange (78, shellac or vinyl pressing)	each 8
57	Pye N 15108	My Dixie Darling/I'm Just A Rollin' Stone (78, shellac pressing)	8
57	Pye Nixa N 15116	Jack O' Diamonds/Ham 'N' Eggs (78, shellac or vinyl pressing)	8
58	Pye Nixa N 15129	The Grand Coolie Dam/Nobody Loves Like An Irishman (78, vinyl pressing)	8
58	Pye Jazz NJS 2006	Midnight Special/When The Sun Goes Down (78)	8
58	Pye Nixa N 15148	Sally, Don't You Grieve/Betty, Betty, Betty (78)	8
58	Pye Nixa N 15158	Lonesome Traveller/Times Are Getting Hard Boys (78)	8
58	Pye Nixa N 15165	Lonnie's Skiffle Party (Parts 1 & 2) (78)	8
58	Pye Nixa N 15172	Tom Dooley/Rock O' My Soul (78)	8
59	Pye Nixa N 15181	Does Your Chewing Gum Lose Its Flavour/Aunt Rhody (78)	8
59	Pye Nixa N 15198	Fort Worth Jail/Whoa Buck (78)	8
59	Pye Nixa N 15206	Battle Of New Orleans/Darling Corey (78)	8
59	Pye N 15219	Kevin Barry/My Laggan Love (78, Irish-only issue)	12
59	Pye N 15223	Sal's Got A Sugar Lip/Chesapeake Bay (78)	8
59	Pye N 15237	San Miguel/Talking Guitar Blues (78)	12
60	Pye N 15256	My Old Man's A Dustman/The Golden Vanity (78)	15
60	Pye N 15267	I Wanna Go Home (The Wreck Of The John B)/Jimmy Brown The Newsboy (78)	20
60	Pye 7N 15275	Lorelei/In All My Wildest Dreams (78)	30

SINGLES
55	Decca F 10647	Rock Island Line/John Henry (as Lonnie Donegan Skiffle Group) (tri-centre)	18
56	Decca FJ 10695	Diggin' My Potatoes/Bury My Body (as Lonnie Donegan Skiffle Group) (tri-centre)	18
56	Columbia DB 3850	On A Christmas Day/Take My Hand, Precious Lord (as Lonnie Donegan with Chris Barber's Jazz Band)	25
57	Pye Nixa 7N 15116	Jack O' Diamonds/Ham 'N' Eggs	6
58	Pye Nixa 7N 15129	The Grand Coolie Dam/Nobody Loves Like An Irishman	10
58	Pye Jazz 7NJ 2006	Midnight Special/When The Sun Goes Down	15
58	Pye Nixa 7N 15148	Sally, Don't You Grieve/Betty, Betty, Betty	6
58	Pye Nixa 7N 15158	Lonesome Traveller/Times Are Getting Hard Boys	6
58	Pye Nixa 7N 15165	Lonnie's Skiffle Party (Parts 1 & 2)	6
58	Pye Nixa 7N 15172	Tom Dooley/Rock O' My Soul	5
59	Pye Nixa 7N 15181	Does Your Chewing Gum Lose Its Flavour/Aunt Rhody	6
59	Pye Nixa 7N 15198	Fort Worth Jail/Whoa Buck	6
59	Pye Nixa 7N 15206	Battle Of New Orleans/Darling Corey	5
59	Pye 7N 15219	Kevin Barry/My Laggan Love (Irish-only issue)	25
59	Pye 7N 15223	Sal's Got A Sugar Lip/Chesapeake Bay	5
59	Pye 7N 15237	San Miguel/Talking Guitar Blues	6
60	Pye 7N 15256	My Old Man's A Dustman/The Golden Vanity	5
60	Pye 7N 15267	I Wanna Go Home (The Wreck Of The John B)/Jimmy Brown The Newsboy	5
60	Pye 7N 15275	Lorelei/In All My Wildest Dreams	5
60	Pye 7N 15312	Lively/Black Cat (Cross My Path Today)	5
60	Pye 7N 15315	Virgin Mary/Beyond The Sunset	5
61	Pye 7N 15330	(Bury Me) Beneath The Willow/Leave My Woman Alone	5
61	Pye 7N 15354	Have A Drink On Me/Seven Daffodils	5
61	Pye 7N 15371	Michael Row The Boat/Lumbered	5
61	Pye 7N 15410	The Comancheros/Ramblin' Round	5
62	Pye 7N 3109	The Comancheros/So Long (Medley) (export issue, 'sombrero' or 'chair' p/s)	15/12
62	Pye 7N 15424	The Party's Over/Over The Rainbow	5
62	Pye 7N 15446	I'll Never Fall In Love Again/Keep On The Sunny Side	5
62	Pye 7N 15455	Pick A Bale Of Cotton/Steal Away (some in p/s)	15/5

MINT VALUE £

62	Pye 7N 15493	The Market Song/Tit-bits (with Max Miller & Lonnie Donegan Group)	6
63	Pye 7N 15514	Losing My Hair/Trumpet Sounds	5
63	Pye 7N 15530	It Was A Very Good Year/Rise Up	5
63	Pye 7N 15564	Lemon Tree/I've Gotta Girl So Far	5
63	Pye 7N 15579	500 Miles Away From Home/This Train	5
64	Pye 7N 15669	Beans In My Ears/It's A Long Road To Travel	5
64	Pye 7N 15679	Fisherman's Luck/There's A Big Wheel	5
65	Pye 7N 15803	Get Out Of My Life/Won't You Tell Me	5
65	Pye 7N 15893	Louisiana Man/Bound For Zion	5
66	Pye 7N 15993	World Cup Willie/Where In This World Are We Going	5
66	Pye 7N 17109	I Wanna Go Home/Black Cat (Cross My Path Today)	5
67	Pye 7N 17232	Aunt Maggie's Remedy/(Ah) My Sweet Marie	6
68	Columbia DB 8371	Toys/Relax Your Mind	7
69	Decca F 12984	My Lovely Juanita/Who Knows Where The Time Goes	7

EPs

56	Decca DFE 6345	THE LONNIE DONEGAN SKIFFLE GROUP (EP, tri-centre, later round)	18/12
56	Jazz Today JTE 107	BACKSTAIRS SESSION (EP)	25
56	Pye Nixa Jazz NJE 1014	BACKSTAIRS SESSION (EP, reissue)	15
56	Pye Nixa Jazz NJE 1017	SKIFFLE SESSION (EP)	10
57	Pye Nixa NEP 24031	HIT PARADE (EP)	12
57	Pye Nixa NEP 24040	HIT PARADE VOL. 2 (EP)	12
58	Pye Nixa NEP 24067	HIT PARADE VOL. 3 (EP)	12
58	Pye Nixa NEP 24075	DONEGAN ON STAGE (EP)	15
58	Pye Nixa NEP 24081	HIT PARADE VOL. 4 (EP)	12
59	Pye Nixa NEP 24104	HIT PARADE VOL. 5 (EP)	12
59	Pye Nixa NEP 24107	RELAX WITH LONNIE (EP)	15
59	Pye Nixa NEP 24114	HIT PARADE VOL. 6 (EP)	12
60	Pye Nixa NEP 24127	YANKEE DOODLE DONEGAN (EP)	12
61	Pye Nixa NEP 24134	HIT PARADE VOL. 7 (EP)	15
61	Pye Nixa NEP 24149	HIT PARADE VOL. 8 (EP)	15

LPs

56	Pye Nixa NPT 19012	LONNIE DONEGAN SHOWCASE (10" LP)	20
57	Pye Nixa NPT 19027	LONNIE (10" LP, also stereo NSPT 84000)	22/50
58	Pye NPL 18034	TOPS WITH LONNIE (LP)	18
59	Pye NPL 18043	LONNIE RIDES AGAIN (LP)	18
61	Pye NPL 18063	MORE TOPS WITH LONNIE (LP)	18
62	Pye NPL 18073	SING HALLELUJAH (LP)	25
62	Golden Guinea GGL 0135	GOLDEN AGE OF DONEGAN (LP)	25
63	Golden Guinea GGL 0170	GOLDEN AGE OF DONEGAN VOL. 2 (LP)	12
65	Pye NPL 18126	THE LONNIE DONEGAN FOLK ALBUM (LP)	25
67	Golden Guinea GGL 0382	THE LONNIE DONEGAN FOLK ALBUM (LP, reissue)	12
70	Decca SKL 5068	LONNIEPOPS — LONNIE DONEGAN TODAY (LP)	15
78	Chrysalis CHR 1158	PUTTIN' ON THE STYLE (LP)	12

(see also Monty Sunshine, Chris Barber, Max Miller)

TANYA DONELLY

| 96 | 4AD TANYA 1 | Bum/Human (12", plain grey die-cut sleeve, promo only) | 8 |

(see also Throwing Muses, Belly)

DONKEYS

80	Rhesus GO APE 102	What I Want/Four Letters (yellow or orange label, p/s)	8
80	Rhesus GO APE 3	No Way/You Jane (p/s)	8
80	Rhesus GO APE 105	Don't Go/Living Legends (p/s)	8
80	Back Door DOOR 006	No Way/You Jane (reissue, p/s)	7
80	Deram DM-R 431	What I Want/Four Letters (reissue, p/s)	5
81	MCA MCA 682	Don't Go/Living Legends (reissue, p/s)	5
81	MCA MCA 721	Let's Float/Watched By Everyone (p/s)	7
81	MCA MCA 737	Listen To Your Radio/Watched By Everyone (as Donkees) (p/s)	7

JIMMY DONLEY

57	Brunswick 05715	South Of The Border/The Trail Of The Lonesome Pine	12
57	Brunswick 05715	South Of The Border/The Trail Of The Lonesome Pine (78)	6
59	Brunswick 05807	The Shape You Left Me In/What Must I Do (triangular centre)	100
59	Brunswick 05807	The Shape You Left Me In/What Must I Do (78)	50

DONNA & FREEDOM SINGERS

| 70 | Bamboo BAM 53 | Oh Me Oh My (actually by Jerry Jones)/JACKIE MITTOO: Gold Mine | 10 |

RAL DONNER

61	Parlophone R 4820	You Don't Know What You've Got/So Close To Heaven	10
61	Parlophone R 4859	Please Don't Go/I Didn't Figure On Him	12
62	Parlophone R 4889	I Don't Need You/She's Everything (I Wanted You To Be)	15
62	Stateside SS 109	Bells Of Love/Loveless Life	15
63	Reprise R 20141	I Got Burned/A Tear In My Eye	25

DONNIE & DREAMERS

| 61 | Top Rank JAR 571 | Count Every Star/Dorothy | 25 |

DONOVAN

65	Pye 7N 15801	Catch The Wind/Why Do You Treat Me Like You Do	5
65	Pye 7N 15866	Colours/To Sing For You	5
65	Pye 7N 15984	Turquoise/Hey Gyp (Dig The Slowness)	7
66	Pye 7N 17067	Josie/Little Tin Soldier	6
66	Pye 7N 17088	Remember The Alamo/The Ballad Of A Crystal Man	15
66	Pye 7N 17241	Sunshine Superman/The Trip	5
67	Pye 7N 17267	Mellow Yellow/Preachin' Love	5
67	Pye 7N 17403	There Is A Mountain/Sand And Foam	5
68	Pye 7N 17457	Jennifer Juniper/Poor Cow	5
68	Pye 7N 17537	Hurdy Gurdy Man/Teen Angel	5
68	Pye 7N 17660	To Susan On The West Coast Waiting/Atlantis (unreleased)	
68	Pye 7N 17660	Atlantis/I Love My Shirt	6
69	Pye 7N 17778	Goo Goo Barabajagal (Love Is Hot)/Bed With Me (with Jeff Beck Group)	12
69	Pye 7N 17778	Barabajagal/Trudi (shortened A-side title & retitled B-side)	8
70	Dawn DNS 1006	Ricki Ticki Tavi/Roots Of Oak (as Donovan with Open Road)	6
70	Dawn DNS 1006	Riki Tiki Tavi (shortened spelling of A-side)/Roots Of Oak (with Open Road)	5
70	Dawn DNS 1007	Celia Of The Seals (with Danny Thompson)/Mr. Wind	6
71	Pye PMM 104	There Is A Mountain/Jennifer Juniper/Sunshine Superman/Mellow Yellow	5
72	private pressing	The Music Makers (one-sided, paper sleeve, 50 only)	50
73	Epic EPC 1644	Maria Magenta/Intergalactic Laxative (p/s)	8
73	Epic EPC 1960	Sailing Homeward/Lazy Daze (p/s)	6
74	Epic EPC 1960	Sailing Homeward/Yellow Star (p/s, reissue with different B-side; some copies list both Donovan & Andrew Oldham as producers)	each 6
75	Epic EPC 2661	Rock'n'Roll With Me/Divine Daze Of Deathless Delight (some in p/s)	30/6
77	Rak RAK 265	The Light/The International Man (some in p/s)	8/5
81	Luggage 7-LUG 03	Lay Down Lassie/Love Is Only Feeling (p/s)	5
65	Pye NEP 24219	THE UNIVERSAL SOLDIER (EP, some incorrectly list 'Summer 1955' instead of 'Summer 1965' as date on rear sleeve)	each 12
65	Pye NEP 24229	COLOURS (EP)	18
66	Pye NEP 24239	DONOVAN VOL. 1 (EP)	15
68	Pye NEP 24287	CATCH THE WIND (EP)	15
68	Pye NEP 24299	HURDY GURDY DONOVAN (EP)	18
65	Pye NPL 18117	WHAT'S BIN DID AND WHAT'S BIN HID (LP, some with misprinted Side 2 label)	22
65	Pye NPL 18128	FAIRYTALE (LP, some copies with blank rear sleeve)	20
66	World Records ST 951	DONOVAN (LP)	15
67	Pye NPL 18181	SUNSHINE SUPERMAN (LP)	25
68	Pye N(S)PL 20000	A GIFT FROM A FLOWER TO A GARDEN (2-LP, black or navy blue box set, separate halves or with taped hinge; with 12 inserts in folder, mono/stereo)	50/40
68	Pye N(S)PL 18237	DONOVAN IN CONCERT (LP, mono/stereo)	18/15
69	Pye N(S)PL 18283	DONOVAN'S GREATEST HITS (LP, gatefold sleeve with booklet, mono/stereo)	15/12
68	Marble Arch MAL 795	WHAT'S BIN DID AND WHAT'S BIN HID (LP, reissue)	12
69	Marble Arch MAL 867	FAIRYTALE (LP, reissue)	12
70	Dawn DNLS 3009	OPEN ROAD (LP, gatefold sleeve)	18
71	Dawn DNLD 4001	H.M.S. DONOVAN (2-LP, gatefold sleeve, some with foldout poster)	50/18
73	Pye 11PP 102	FOUR SHADES ("H.M.S. Donovan"/"Greatest Hits"/"Open Road") (4-LP box set)	45
73	Epic EPC 65490	COSMIC WHEELS (LP, gatefold sleeve with inner sleeve & poster)	12
90	Permanent PERMLP 2	DONOVAN RISING (LP, 500 only)	12
95	Fiona CD 031	LOUDEST WHISPER (CD, Ireland only)	15
97	American Recordings 74321 39743 2	SUTRAS (CD)	15

(see also Jeff Beck, Open Road)

JASON DONOVAN

88	PWL PWLCD 17	Nothing Can Divide Us (7" Version)/(Dub Mix)/(Instrumental) (CD)	15
89	PWL PWCD 32	Too Many Broken Hearts/(Instrumental)/Wrap My Arms Around You (CD)	15
89	PWL PWCD 39	Sealed With A Kiss/Just Call Me Up/Too Many Broken Hearts (Techno Remix) (CD)	8
89	PWL PWCD 43	Every Day (I Love You More) (7" Version)/(Extended)/ I Guess She Never Loved Me (CD)	10
93	Polydor PZCD 295	Angel (Forever In Your Debt)/Shout About/Symptoms Of A Real Love (7" Mix)/ Symptoms Of A Real Love (12" Mix) (CD, withdrawn)	10

DONTELLS

65	Fontana TF 566	In Your Heart/Nothing But Nothing	35
74	President PT 373	In Your Heart/Nothing But Nothing (reissue)	6

DICKY DOO & DON'TS

58	London HLU 8589	Click Click/Did You Cry	30
58	London HLU 8589	Click Click/Did You Cry (78)	25
58	London HLU 8754	Leave Me Alone/Wild, Wild Party (with Orchestra)	35
58	London HLU 8754	Leave Me Alone/Wild, Wild Party (with Orchestra) (78)	30
60	Top Rank JAR 318	Wabash Cannonball/WEST TEXAS MARCHING BAND: The Drums Of Richard A Doo	6

DOOF

80	Doof	EXIST (10" mini-LP, with booklet)	8

(see also Exhibit A)

ACE DOOLEY

53	London L 1208	Counterfeit Dollar (with Dick James)/Louisville Lou (with Les Heldon) (78)	8

DOOLEY SISTERS
| 55 | London HL 8128 | Ko Ko Mo (I Love You So)/Heart Throb | 35 |
| 55 | London HL 8128 | Ko Ko Mo (I Love You So)/Heart Throb (78) | 12 |

JOHN DOONAN
| 72 | Leader LEA 2043 | FLUTE FOR THE FEIS (LP) | 12 |

DOOR & THE WINDOW
79	NB Records NB 3	He Feels Like A Doris/I Like Sound/Innocent/Dig/Production Line (white label with stickers & insert p/s in poly bag)	5
80	NB Records NB 5	DETAILED TWANG (LP, blank labels)	12
80	NB Records NB 9	MUSIC AND MOVEMENT (live cassette)	12

(see also Alternative TV)

DOORS
SINGLES
67	Elektra EKSN 45009	Break On Through (To The Other Side)/End Of The Night	25
67	Elektra EKSN 45012	Alabama Song (Whisky Bar)/Take It As It Comes	15
67	Elektra EKSN 45014	Light My Fire/The Crystal Ship	15
67	Elektra EKSN 45017	People Are Strange/Unhappy Girl	15
67	Elektra EKSN 45022	Love Me Two Times/Moonlight Drive	10
68	Elektra EKSN 45030	We Could Be So Good Together/The Unknown Soldier	10
68	Elektra EKSN 45037	Hello, I Love You/Love Street	7
69	Elektra EKSN 45050	Touch Me/Wild Child	8
69	Elektra EKSN 45059	Wishful Sinful/Who Scared You?	8
69	Elektra EKSN 45065	Tell All The People/Easy Ride	8
70	Elektra 2101 004	You Make Me Real/The Spy	7
70	Elektra 2101 008	Roadhouse Blues/Blue Sunday	7
71	Elektra EK 45726	Love Her Madly/(You Need Meat) Don't Go No Further	6
71	Elektra K 12001	Light My Fire/The Crystal Ship (reissue)	5
71	Elektra K 12004	We Could Be So Good Together/The Unknown Soldier (reissue)	5
71	Elektra K 12021	Riders On The Storm/The Changeling	5
72	Elektra K 12036	Tightrope Ride/Variety Is The Spice Of Life	5
72	Elektra K 12048	Ship W/ Sails/In The Eye Of The Sun	5
72	Elektra K 12059	Get Up And Dance/Tree Trunks	5
79	Elektra K 12215/SAM 94	Love Me Two Times/Hello, I Love You//Ghost Song/Roadhouse Blues (double pack)	8
83	Elektra E 9974T	Gloria/Love Me Two Times (12", p/s with poster)	10
89	Elektra 969 344-2	Riders On The Storm/The End (3" CD, card sleeve)	8
91	Elektra EKR 125TW	Light My Fire/People Are Strange/Soul Kitchen (12", p/s, with poster)	8
92	Final Vinyl FV 1/2	INTERVIEW TAPES (2 x 7" box set, with 7 inserts, numbered, 500 only)	10

ORIGINAL LPs
67	Elektra EKL 4007	THE DOORS (LP, orange label, also stereo EKS 74007)	40/30
68	Elektra EKL 4014	STRANGE DAYS (LP, textured orange label, inner sleeve, also stereo EKS 74014)	40/30
68	Elektra EKL 4024	WAITING FOR THE SUN (LP, orange label, gatefold sleeve with insert, also stereo EKS 74024)	40/30
69	Elektra EKS 75005	THE SOFT PARADE (LP, orange label, gatefold sleeve, with lyric sheet)	25
70	Elektra EKS 75007	MORRISON HOTEL (LP, orange label, gatefold sleeve)	20
70	Elektra 2665 002	ABSOLUTELY LIVE (2-LP, orange label, gatefold sleeve)	20
71	Elektra EKS 74079	13 (LP, 'butterfly' label, compilation)	15
71	Elektra K 42090	L.A. WOMAN (LP, 'butterfly' label, round-cornered, die-cut PVC 'window' sleeve & yellow inner sleeve)	15
71	Elektra K 42104	OTHER VOICES (LP, 'butterfly' label, gatefold sleeve)	15
72	Elektra K 62009	WEIRD SCENES INSIDE THE GOLDMINE (2-LP, 'butterfly' label, gatefold sleeve)	20
72	Elektra K 62116	FULL CIRCLE (LP, 'butterfly label', gatefold sleeve)	12

REISSUE LPs
70	Elektra EKS 74024	WAITING FOR THE SUN (LP, 'butterfly' label, gatefold sleeve)	15
71	Elektra K 42062	13 (LP)	12
71	Elektra K 42012	THE DOORS (LP, 'butterfly' label)	15
71	Elektra K 42016	STRANGE DAYS (LP, 'butterfly' label)	15
71	Elektra K 42041	WAITING FOR THE SUN (LP, 'butterfly' label, single sleeve, 2nd reissue)	12
71	Elektra K 42079	THE SOFT PARADE (LP, 'butterfy' label, gatefold sleeve, with lyric sheet)	15
72	Elektra K 42080	MORRISON HOTEL (LP, 'butterlfly' label, gatefold sleeve)	15
72	Elektra K 75011	L.A. WOMAN (LP, 'butterfly' label, standard sleeve)	12
74	Elektra K 42090	L.A. WOMAN (LP, 'butterfly' label, standard sleeve)	12
74	Elektra K2 42143	THE BEST OF THE DOORS (LP, quadrophonic)	15
78	Elektra K 52111	AN AMERICAN PRAYER (LP, 'butterfly' label, gatefold sleeve, with 8-page booklet)	22

CDs
85	Elektra 960 345-2	THE BEST OF THE DOORS (2-CD)	20
87	Elektra K 262005	ABSOLUTELY LIVE (2-CD, withdrawn)	25
87	Elektra 960 269-2	ALIVE, SHE CRIED (CD)	15
87	Elektra 960 741-2	LIVE AT THE HOLLYWOOD BOWL (CD)	15
88	HMV C 8816	L.A. WOMAN (CD, HMV box set, 2,500 only, numbered with booklet)	15
91	Elektra 7559 61082-2	IN CONCERT (2-CD)	20
98	Elektra 7559 62295-2	THE DOORS BOX SET VOL. I (2-CD, with booklet)	25
98	Elektra 7559 62296-2	THE DOORS BOX SET VOL. II (2-CD, with booklet)	25

(see also Ray Manzarek)

MINT VALUE £

DOORS OF PERCEPTION
91	Lizard Nation LN 002	ACID DREAMS (12" EP, includes Jim Morrison sample, withdrawn)	8
91	Lizard Nation LN 001	SO JOIN MR. DREAMS (LP, with inner sleeve, some with booklet, 850 only)	15/12
92	Lizard Nation LN 005	LORDS SO STRANGE R. (LP, test pressings only)	12

DORA
86	CBS A 7208	You're Hurting Me/This Will Be The Last Time (p/s)	5
87	CBS 651572 7	I'll Come Back/Voltarei (withdrawn, promo copies may exist)	6+

FELIX DORAN
76	Topic 12TS 288	THE LAST OF THE TRAVELLING PIPERS (LP)	10

MIKE DORANE & CIMARONS
71	Ackee ACK 144	Penguin Funk/Ad-Lib	5

CHARLIE DORE
79	Island ILPS 9559	WHERE TO NOW (LP)	10

DOREEN (Campbell) & ALL STARS
67	Rainbow RAI 114	Rude Girls/Please Stay	8

DOREEN (Shaeffer) & JACKIE (Opel)
65	Ska Beat JB 208	Welcome Home/You And I	15

(see also Jackie & Doreen)

DORIAN
70	Ember EMB S 285	Psychedelic Lipstick/Help For My Waiting	5

DORIS
81	ABCD ABCD 1	Sitting Here Waiting (no p/s)	15
82	ABCD ABCD 3	GYPSY LADY (LP, actually credited to A Band Called Doris)	150

DORIS
98	EMI/Mr. Bongo MRBLP 010	DID YOU GIVE THE WORLD SOME LOVE TODAY, BABY? (LP, reissue of Swedish 60s LP)	10

HAROLD DORMAN
60	Top Rank JAR 357	Mountain Of Love/To Be With You	12
61	London HLS 9386	There They Go/I'll Stick By You	20

DOROTHY
80	Industrial IR 0014	I Confess/Softness (p/s)	12

RALPH DORPER
83	Operation Twilight OPT 18	THE ERASERHEAD EP (12")	10

(see also Propaganda)

DIANA DORS
53	HMV B 10613	I Feel So Mmm.../A Kiss And A Cuddle (78)	18
60	Pye 7N 15242	April Heart/Point Of No Return	6
60	Pye N 15242	April Heart/Point Of No Return (78)	20
64	Fontana TF 506	So Little Time/It's Too Late	10
66	Polydor BM 56111	Security/Gary	8
77	EMI EMI 2705	Passing By/It's A Small World	5
82	Nomis NOM 1	Where Did They Go/It's You Again (with Gary Dors)	6
60	Pye NPL 18044	SWINGIN' DORS (LP, foldout sleeve, red vinyl)	60

RAY DORSET (WITH MUNGO JERRY)
72	Dawn DNS 1018	Cold Blue Excursion/I Need It (solo)	10
77	Polydor 2230 103	MUNGO BOX (EP, as Ray Dorset & Mungo Jerry, p/s)	8
79	Polydor 2059 127	Dancin' In The Street/Rockin' On The Road (as Ray Dorset & Mungo Jerry, p/s)	8
79	Satellite RAY 001	Forgotten Land/New Way Of Life (solo, unreleased; 100 promos only)	10
81	Stagecoach TRI 101	Knocking On Heaven's Door/Hazel Eyes (as Ray Dorset with Mungo Jerry)	8
87	Pier 7 KS 1152	Come On You Latics/Blaze Away (as Ray Dorset & Fabulous Lactics)	5
72	Dawn DNLS 3033	COLD BLUE EXCURSION (LP, solo; gatefold sleeve with lyric inner)	15
72	Boulevard 4078	RAY DORSET'S BEST (LP, actually featuring 4 tracks by Good Earth & 6 tracks by Macon Jug)	12
78	Polydor 2383 485	RAY DORSET & MUNGO JERRY (LP)	12

(see also Mungo Jerry, Good Earth, County Jug, Macon Jug, Katmandu, Insiders, Panache, Made In England)

DORSETS
65	Sue WI 391	Pork Chops/Cool It	25

GERRY DORSEY
59	Decca F 11108	Mister Music Man/Crazy Bells	7
59	Decca F 11108	Mister Music Man/Crazy Bells (78)	12
59	Parlophone R 4595	I'll Never Fall In Love Again/Every Day Is A Wonderful Day	7
61	Parlophone R 4739	Big Wheel/The Sentimental Joker	6
64	Pye 7N 15622	Baby i Do/Take Your Time	6
65	Hickory 45-1337	Baby Turn Around/Things I Wanna Do	12

(see also Engelbert Humperdinck)

JACK DORSEY ORCHESTRA
65	Polydor 56020	Dance Of The Daleks/Likely Lads	12
68	Pye 7N 17501	Soul Coaxing/Elizabeth's Waltz	6

JIMMY DORSEY ORCHESTRA
57	HMV POP 324	So Rare/Sophisticated Swing	8
57	HMV POP 324	So Rare/Sophisticated Swing (78)	5
57	HMV POP 383	Jay-Dee's Boogie Woogie/June Night	18
57	HMV POP 383	Jay-Dee's Boogie Woogie/June Night (78)	6
54	Columbia 33S 1026	DIXIE BY DORSEY (10" LP)	12

LEE DORSEY

62	Top Rank JAR 606	Do-Re-Mi/People Gonna Talk	15
65	Sue WI 367	Do-Re-Mi/Ya Ya	18
65	Stateside SS 441	Ride Your Pony/The Kitty Cat Song	8
65	Stateside SS 465	Work Work Work/Can You Hear Me	8
66	Sue WI 399	Messed Around/When I Meet My Baby	18
66	Stateside SS 485	Get Out Of My Life, Woman/So Long	10
66	Stateside SS 506	Confusion/Neighbour's Daughter	7
66	Stateside SS 528	Working In A Coalmine/Mexico	5
66	Stateside SS 552	Holy Cow/Operation Heartache	5
67	Stateside SS 593	Rain Rain Go Away/Gotta Find A Job	6
67	Stateside SS 2017	My Old Car/Why Wait Until Tomorrow	5
67	Stateside SS 2055	Go-Go Girl/I Can Hear You Callin'	5
68	President PT 226	Ya Ya/Give Me You	5
68	Bell BLL 1006	Can You Hear Me/Cynthia	5
69	Bell BLL 1051	I'm Gonna Sit Right Down And Write Myself A Letter/Little Baby	5
69	Bell BLL 1060	Ride Your Pony/Get Out Of My Life, Woman	5
69	Bell BLL 1074	Everything I Do Gonh Be Funky/There Should Be A Book	10
71	Mojo 2066 063	Occapella/Yes We Can Part 1	5
72	Mojo 2093 009	Freedom For The Stallion/If She Won't (Find Someone Who Will)	5
66	Stateside SE 1038	RIDE YOUR PONY (EP)	25
66	Stateside SE 1043	YOU'RE BREAKING ME UP (EP)	25
65	Sue ILP 924	THE BEST OF LEE DORSEY (LP)	50
66	Stateside S(S)L 10177	LEE DORSEY — RIDE YOUR PONY (LP)	25
66	Stateside S(S)L 10192	THE NEW LEE DORSEY (LP)	25
71	Polydor 2489 006	YES WE CAN (LP)	15

LEE DORSEY & BETTY HARRIS

69	Buffalo BFS 1002	Love Lots Of Lovin'/Take Care Of Your Love	6
	(see also Betty Harris)		

TOMMY DORSEY ORCHESTRA

58	Brunswick 05757	Tea For Two Cha Cha/My Baby Just Cares For Me (as Tommy Dorsey Orchestra featuring Warren Covington)	5
58	Brunswick 05769	I Want To Be Happy — Cha Cha/Spooky Takes A Holiday (as Tommy Dorsey Orchestra featuring Warren Covington)	6
58	Brunswick 05769	I Want To Be Happy — Cha Cha/Spooky Takes A Holiday (as Tommy Dorsey Orchestra featuring Warren Covington) (78)	8
59	Top Rank TR 5010	Swing High/The Minor Goes Muggin'	5
54	HMV 7EG 8004	TOMMY DORSEY AND HIS ORCHESTRA (EP, 2 tracks with Frank Sinatra, no p/s)	10
54	Brunswick OE 9012	TOMMY DORSEY AND HIS ORCHESTRA (EP)	8
58	RCA RCX 1002	TOMMY DORSEY NO. 1 (EP)	8
53	Brunswick LA 8610	TOMMY DORSEY (10" LP)	12
54	Brunswick LA 8640	TENDERLY (10" LP)	12
54	Brunswick LA 8669	ECSTASY (10" LP)	12
58	RCA RD 27069	FRANKIE AND TOMMY (LP, with Frank Sinatra)	20
	(see also Frank Sinatra, Jo Stafford)		

DORSEY BROTHERS

58	Brunswick LAT 8256	DIXIELAND JAZZ 1934-5 (LP)	12

D.O.S.E.

95	Colosseum TOGA 001TJX	Plug Myself In (p/s, with Mark E. Smith, numbered, 1-sided, 500 only)	5
	(see also Fall)		

DOSSERS

83	Secret SHH 148-12	THE DOSSERS EP (12", company sleeve)	8

JOHNNY DOT & DASHERS

62	Salvo SLO 1805	I Love An Angel/Just For You (99 copies only)	18

DOTTY & BONNIE

64	Rio R 43	I'm So Glad/DOUGLAS BROTHERS: Got You On My Mind	15
64	Island WI 143	Your Kisses/Why Worry	20
64	Island WI 148	Dearest/Tears Are Falling	20
65	Ska Beat JB 183	Foul Play/ROLAND ALPHONSO & GROUP: Yard Broom	20
67	Ska Beat JB 274	I'll Know/Love Is Great	15
	(see also Bonnie Frankson, Eric Morris, Don Drummond, Skatalites, Baba Brooks)		

DOUBLE FEATURE

67	Deram DM 115	Baby Get Your Head Screwed On/Come On Baby	25
67	Deram DM 165	Handbags And Gladrags/Just Another Lonely Night	12

DOUBLES with GAY BLADES

59	HMV POP 613	Hey Girl!/Little Joe	90

SUZANNE DOUCET

68	Liberty LBF 15150	Swan Song/Cry My Heart	8

DOUGHNUT RING

68	Deram DM 215	Dance Around Julie/The Bandit	20
	(see also Crocheted Doughnut Ring)		

JOHNNY DOUGHTY

77	Topic 12TS 324	ROUND RYE BAY FOR MORE (LP, with insert)	15

CARL DOUGLAS (& BIG STAMPEDE)

66	Go AJ 11401	Crazy Feeling/PETER PERRY SOUL BAND: Keep It To Myself	12
67	Go AJ 11408	Let The Birds Sing/Something For Nothing	15
67	United Artists UP 1206	Nobody Cries/Serving A Sentence Of Life (solo)	80
68	United Artists UP 2227	Sell My Soul To The Devil/Good Hard Worker	10
71	CBS 7101	Do You Need My Love/Lean On Me	5
72	Blue Mountain BM 1007	Somebody Stop This Madness/Ain't No Use (as Karl Douglas)	5

CHIC DOUGLAS

58	Fontana H 121	I'm Not Afraid Anymore/Jo-Ann	6

CRAIG DOUGLAS

58	Decca F 11055	Nothin' Shakin'/Sitting In A Tree House	15
58	Decca F 11055	Nothin' Shakin'/Sitting In A Tree House (78)	12
58	Decca F 11075	Go Chase A Moonbeam/Are You Really Mine	12
58	Decca F 11075	Go Chase A Moonbeam/Are You Really Mine (78)	8
59	Top Rank JAR 110	Come Softly To Me/Golden Girl	6
59	Top Rank JAR 110	Come Softly To Me/Golden Girl (78)	12
59	Top Rank JAR 133	Teenager In Love/The 39 Steps	6
59	Top Rank JAR 133	Teenager In Love/The 39 Steps (78)	15
59	Top Rank JAR 159	Only Sixteen/My First Love Affair	6
59	Top Rank JAR 159	Only Sixteen/My First Love Affair (78)	10
59	Top Rank JAR 204	The Riddle Of Love/Wish It Were Me	5
59	Top Rank TR 5004	Battle Of New Orleans/Dream Lover/SHEILA BUXTON: Personality/ Where Were You On Our Wedding Day/BERT WEEDON: I Need Your Love Tonight ('King-Size' 7", special sleeve)	15
60	Top Rank JAR 268	Pretty Blue Eyes/Sandy	5
60	Top Rank JAR 340	Heart Of A Teenage Girl/New Boy	5
60	Top Rank JAR 406	Oh, What A Day/Why, Why, Why	5
60	Top Rank JAR 515	Where's The Girl (I Never Met)/My Hour Of Love	5
61	Top Rank JAR 543	The Girl Next Door/Hey Mister Conscience	5
61	Top Rank JAR 555	A Hundred Pounds Of Clay/Hello Spring	10
61	Top Rank JAR 556	A Hundred Pounds Of Clay (censored version)/Hello Spring (some in p/s)	18/6
61	Top Rank JAR 569	Time/After All	5
61	Top Rank JAR 589	No Greater Love/We'll Have A Lot To Tell	5
62	Top Rank JAR 603	A Change Of Heart/Another You	6
62	Top Rank JAR 610	When My Little Girl Is Smiling/Ring A Ding	6
62	Columbia DB 4854	Our Favourite Melodies/Rainbows	6
62	Decca F 11523	Oh Lonesome Me/Please Don't Take My Heart	5
63	Decca F 11575	Town Crier/I'd Be Smiling Now	5
63	Decca F 11665	Danke Shoen/Teenage Mona Lisa	5
63	Decca F 11722	I'm So Glad I Found Her/Love Her While She's Young	5
63	Decca F 11763	Counting Up The Kisses/From Russia With Love	5
64	Fontana TF 458	Silly Boy/Love Leave Me Alone	7
64	Fontana TF 475	Come Closer/She's Smiling At Me (as Craig Douglas & Tridents)	10
65	Fontana TF 525	Across The Street/Party Girl	7
65	Fontana TF 580	Around The Corner/Find The Girl	7
66	Fontana TF 690	I'm On The Outside Looking In/Knock On Any Door	6
69	Pye 7N 17746	How Do You Feel About That/Then	5
69	Pye 7N 17863	Raindrops Keep Falling On My Head/Don't Mind If I Cry	5
71	Crystal CR 7011	All Kinds Of People/Evenin' Rain	5
76	Cube BUG 72	Who's Sorry Now/Both Sides Now	5
77	Cube BUG 76	Turn Away/Baby Blue	5
59	Top Rank JKR 8033	CRAIG SINGS FOR 'ROXY' (EP)	20
60	Decca DFE 6633	CRAIG (EP)	20
62	Decca DFE 8509	CUDDLE UP WITH CRAIG (EP)	18
63	Columbia SEG 8219	CRAIG MOVIE SONGS (EP)	25
60	Top Rank BUY 049	CRAIG DOUGLAS (LP)	45
61	Top Rank 35-103	BANDWAGON BALL (LP)	35
62	Columbia 33SX 1468	OUR FAVOURITE MELODIES (LP)	75
81	Jackson JKS 5	OH LONESOME ME (LP)	12

(see also Bert Weedon)

DONNA DOUGLAS

58	Fontana H 158	The Shepherd/I'm Dancing With Tears In My Eyes	7
59	Fontana H 223	Six Boys And Seven Girls/Into Each Life Some Rain Must Fall	6
59	Fontana H 223	Six Boys And Seven Girls/Into Each Life Some Rain Must Fall (78)	8
61	Piccadilly 7N 35014	Tammy Tell Me True/Memory Lane	6
62	Piccadilly 7N 35031	The Message In A Bottle/If This Is Love	6
62	Piccadilly 7N 35042	Matelot/All The Other Girls	6
63	Piccadilly 7N 35111	It's A Pity To Say Goodnight/Do I Know	6
63	Piccadilly 7N 35135	He's So Near/Turn Around	6
64	Pye 7N 15654	Blue Star/Java Jones	6

JOHNNY DOUGLAS (& HIS ORCHESTRA/COMBO)

54	Decca F 10276	Ballet Of The Bells/Solfeggio (as Johnny Douglas & His Orchestra)	5
63	Speyside SK 1501	Ski Jump/Clementine (as Johnny Douglas Combo)	5
65	RCA 1444	Crack The World/Time	10

KIRK DOUGLAS & MELLOMEN

55	Brunswick 05408	A Whale Of A Tale/And The Moon Grew Brighter And Brighter	10

LEW DOUGLAS & HIS ORCHESTRA

54	MGM SP 1093	Caesar's Boogie/Turn Around Boy	10

MARK DOUGLAS

62	Ember EMB S 166	It Matters Not/Upside Down	55

NORMA DOUGLAS
57	London HLZ 8475	Be It Resolved/Joe He Gone	20
57	London HLZ 8475	Be It Resolved/Joe He Gone (78)	10

DOUGLAS BROTHERS
66	Rio R 57	Valley Of Tears/CHARMERS: Where Do I Turn	10
66	Rio R 63	Down And Out/RONALD WILSON: Lonely Man	10

(see also Dotty & Bonnie)

HARRY DOUGLASS & DEEP RIVER BOYS
60	Top Rank JAR 352	Dum Dum De Dum/Go Galloway, Go	4

(see also Deep River Boys)

RONNIE DOVE
64	Stateside SS 314	Sweeter Than Sugar/I Believed In You	5
65	Stateside SS 412	One Kiss For Old Times' Sake/Bluebird	6
68	Stateside SS 2119	Mountain Of Love/Never Gonna Cry (The Way I'll Cry Tonight)	6
65	Stateside SL 10149	RONNIE DOVE (LP)	25

DOVELLS
61	Columbia DB 4718	The Bristol Stomp/Out In The Cold Again	15
62	Columbia DB 4810	Do The New Continental/Mopitty Mope Stomp	15
62	Columbia DB 4877	Bristol Twistin' Annie/The Actor	15
62	Cameo Parkway P 845	Hully Gully Baby/Your Last Chance	7
63	Cameo Parkway P 861	You Can't Run Away From Yourself/Save Me Baby	7
63	Cameo Parkway P 867	You Can't Sit Down/Stompin' Everywhere	10
63	Cameo Parkway P 882	Betty In Bermudas/Dance The Froog	8
63	Cameo Parkway P 901	Be My Girl/Dragster On The Prowl	12

(see also Len Barry)

BRENT DOWE
71	Summit SUM 8521	Knock Three Times/GAYLADS: This Time I Won't Hurt You	6
71	Summit SUM 8525	Put Your Hand In The Hand/Miracle (B-side actually "It Took A Miracle Version" by Beverley's All Stars)	6
71	Summit SUM 8530	Freedom Train/BEVERLEY'S ALL STARS: Freedom Train (Version)	6
73	Green Door GD 4061	Reggae Makossa/No Nola (B-side actually by Melodians)	6

(see also Melodians)

JOE DOWELL
61	Mercury AMT 1161	The Bridge Of Love/Just My Love	6
62	Mercury AMT 1180	Little Red Rented Rowboat/The One I Left For You	6
60s	Wing	WOODEN HEART (LP)	15

DOWLANDS
62	Oriole CB 1748	Little Sue/Julie (as Dowlands & Soundtracks)	40
62	Oriole CB 1781	Big Big Fella/Don't Ever Change	125
63	Oriole CB 1815	Break Ups/A Love Like Ours	40
63	Oriole CB 1892	Lonely Johnny (song actually titled "Lucky Johnny")/Do You Have To Have Me Blue?	500
64	Oriole CB 1897	All My Loving/Hey Sally (as Dowlands & Soundtracks)	12
64	Oriole CB 1926	I Walk The Line/Happy Endings	35
64	Oriole CB 1947	Wishing And Hoping/You Will Regret It	75
65	Columbia DB 7547	Don't Make Me Over/Someone Must Be Feeling Sad	35

DOWNBEATS
61	Starlite ST45 051	Thinkin' Of You/Midnight Love	18

BRUCE DOWNER
71	Summit SUM 8524	Free The People (actually by Bruce Ruffin)/BEVERLEY'S ALL STARS: Free The People (Version)	5

BOB DOWNES
70	Vertigo 6059 011	No Time Like The Present/Keep Off The Grass	5
70	Philips SBL 7922	BOB DOWNES' OPEN MUSIC (LP)	70
70	Vertigo 6360 005	ELECTRIC CITY (LP, gatefold sleeve, spiral label)	18
70	M. For Pleasure MFP 1412	DEEP DOWN HEAVY (LP)	12
73	Ophenian BDOM 001	DIVERSIONS (LP)	15
74	Ophenian BDOM 002	EPISODES AT 4AM (LP, with insert)	15
75	Ophenian BDOM 003	HELLS ANGELS (LP)	15

DEIRDRE DOWNES & BROADSIDERS
69	Pye 7N 17781	Lady Mary/Did He Mention My Name	5

DOWN HOME
70s	Lismor Folk LIFL 7011	FIDDLE MUSIC VOLUME ONE (LP)	15

BIG AL DOWNING
64	Sue WI 341	Yes I'm Loving You/Please Come Home	25

DOWNLINERS SECT
64	Columbia DB 7300	Baby What's Wrong/Be A Sect Maniac	20
64	Columbia DB 7347	Little Egypt/Sect Appeal	20
64	Columbia DB 7415	Find Out What's Happening/Insecticide	20
65	Columbia DB 7509	Wreck Of The Old '97/Leader Of The Sect	20
65	Columbia DB 7597	I Got Mine/Waiting In Heaven Somewhere	20
65	Columbia DB 7712	Bad Storm Coming/Lonely And Blue	20
66	Columbia DB 7817	All Night Worker/He Was A Square	20

MINT VALUE £

66	Columbia DB 7939	Glendora/I'll Find Out	30
66	Columbia DB 8008	The Cost Of Living/Everything I've Got To Give	25
76	Charly CYS 1020	Little Egypt/Sect Appeal (p/s)	5
77	Raw RAW 10	Showbiz/Killing Me (p/s)	5
64	Contrast Sound RBCSP 1	NITE IN GREAT NEWPORT STREET (EP)	275
65	Columbia SEG 8438	THE SECT SING SICK SONGS (EP)	100
78	Charly CEP 119	DOWNLINERS SECT (EP, reissue of "The Sect Sing Sick Songs")	10
64	Columbia 33SX 1658	THE SECT (LP)	70
65	Columbia 33SX 1745	THE COUNTRY SECT (LP)	60
66	Columbia S(C)X 6028	THE ROCK SECT'S IN (LP, mono/stereo)	70/80

(see also Don Crane's Downliners Sect)

DOWN TO EARTH
71	Downtown DT 485	Under The Boardwalk/Under The Boardwalk (Version) (B-side actually "Double Barrel Version")	5

DOWNTOWN ALL STARS
69	Downtown DT 426	Everybody Feel Good/RUDIES: Downtown Jump	6

LAMONT DOZIER
74	Probe PRO 618	Trying To Hold On To My Woman/We Don't Want Nobody To Come	5
74	Anchor ABC 4003	Fish Ain't Bitin'/Breaking Out All Over	5
75	Anchor ABC 4056	All Cried Out/Rose	5
77	Warner Bros K 16942	Going Back To My Roots/Going Back To My Roots (Version)	5
81	CBS A 1235	To Cool Me Out/Starting Over	5
74	ABC ABCL 5042	OUT HERE ON MY OWN (LP)	12
75	ABC ABCL 5096	BLACK BACH (LP)	12
77	Warner Bros K 56396	PEDDLIN' MUSIC ON THE SIDE (LP)	15

(see also Holland & Dozier)

DOZY, BEAKY, MICK & TICH (D.B.M.&T.)
69	Fontana TF 1061	Tonight Today/Bad News	6
70	Fontana 6007 022	Mr. President/Frisco Annie (as D.B.M.&T)	5
70	Philips 6006 066	Festival/Leader Of A Rock'N'Roll Band	5
71	Philips 6006 114	I Want To Be There/For The Use Of Your Son (as D.B.M.&T)	5
72	Philips 6006 198	They Won't Sing My Song/Soukie	5
70	Philips 6308 029	FRESH EAR (LP, gatefold sleeve, credited to D.B.M.&T)	12

(see also Dave Dee Dozy Beaky Mick & Tich)

DP's
78	Barn 2014 126	If You Know What I Mean/Running Away (p/s)	4
78	Barn 2014 129	Television Romeo/Innocent Man (p/s)	4
78	Barn 2314 107	IF YOU KNOW WHAT I MEAN (LP)	10

(see also Depressions)

DRAGON
76	Acorn CF 268	DRAGON (LP, gatefold sleeve)	25

DRAGONFLY
74	Retreat RTS 257	Gondola/Almost Abandoned (demo)	15
75	Retreat RTS 261	Driving Around The World/Since I Left My Home	8
74	Retreat RTL 6002	ALMOST ABANDONED (LP)	15

DRAGONFLY
80s	Dragonfly DF 001	SILENT NIGHTS EP (p/s, private pressing)	200

DRAGONSFIRE
82	Belltree BTR 001	RISING PHOENIX (LP, with insert)	25

(see also Spinning Wheel)

DRAG RACING UNDERGROUND
89	Snakeskin SS 003	Broadcast Booth/Hellfire (p/s, numbered, 300 only)	8

DRAG SET
66	Go AJ 11405	Get Out Of My Way/Day And Night	140

(see also Open Mind)

DRAGSTER
81	Heavy Metal HEAVY 4	Ambition/Won't Bring You Back (p/s)	10

DRAGSTERS
86	Union City SNICK 1	Where Is The Hamburger Relish?/I Wanna Be An Albino/It Takes A Worried Girl (p/s)	4
87	Union City SNICK 2	I'm Not An American/Land Of The Giants (p/s)	4

CHARLIE DRAKE
58	Parlophone R 4461	Splish Splash/Hello, My Darlings	6
58	Parlophone R 4461	Splish Splash/Hello, My Darlings (78)	7
58	Parlophone R 4478	Volare/Itchy Twitchy Feeling	6
58	Parlophone R 4478	Volare/Itchy Twitchy Feeling (78)	8
58	Parlophone R 4496	Tom Thumb's Tune/Goggle Eye Ghee	5
58	Parlophone R 4496	Tom Thumb's Tune/Goggle Eye Ghee (78)	8
59	Parlophone R 4552	Sea Cruise/Starkle, Starkle Little Twink	6
59	Parlophone R 4552	Sea Cruise/Starkle, Starkle Little Twink (78)	15
60	Parlophone R 4675	Naughty/Old Mr. Shadow	5
60	Parlophone R 4701	Mr. Custer/Glow Worm	5
61	Parlophone R 4824	My Boomerang Won't Come Back/She's My Girl	5

MINT VALUE £

62	Parlophone R 4875	Tanglefoot/Drake's Progress	5
62	Parlophone R 4918	I Bent My Assigai/Sweet Freddy Green	5
63	Parlophone R 5057	I've Lost The End Of My Yodel/I Can Can't I	5
64	Parlophone R 5143	I'm Too Heavy For The Light Brigade/The Reluctant Tight-Rope Walker	5
64	Parlophone R 5209	Charles Drake 007/Bumpanology (Bump Head Blues)	5
71	Columbia DB 8829	Puckwudgie/Toffee And Tears	5
75	Charisma CB 270	You Never Know/I'm Big Enough For Me (produced by Peter Gabriel)	8
58	Parlophone GEP 8720	HELLO MY DARLINGS (EP)	12
60	Parlophone GEP 8812	NAUGHTY CHARLIE DRAKE (EP)	12
64	Parlophone GEP 8903	HITS FROM THE MAN IN THE MOON (EP)	12
60s	Music F. Pleasure MFP 1310	HELLO MY DARLINGS (LP)	12

NICK DRAKE

79	Island RSS 7	Introduction/Hazy Jane II/Time Has Told Me/Fruit Tree/Rider On The Wheel ("Fruit Tree" sampler, 1-sided promo only)	175
69	Island ILPS 9105	FIVE LEAVES LEFT (LP, 1st pressing, pink label, black 'circle' logo, g/fold sleeve)	80
69	Island ILPS 9105	FIVE LEAVES LEFT (LP, gatefold sleeve, 2nd pressing, 'pink rim label, 'palm tree' logo)	25
70	Island ILPS 9134	BRYTER LAYTER (LP, 'pink rim label, 'palm tree' logo)	30
72	Island ILPS 9184	PINK MOON (LP, 'pink rim label, 'palm tree' logo, gatefold sleeve)	30
79	Island NDSP 100	FRUIT TREE (3-LP, box set with booklet)	40
85	Island ILPS 9826	HEAVEN IN A WILD FLOWER (THE BEST OF NICK DRAKE) (LP)	15
86	Hannibal HNBX 5302	FRUIT TREE (4-LP, expanded reissue with booklet)	50
87	Hannibal HNBL 1318	TIME OF NO REPLY (LP)	12
89	Island ILPS 9105	FIVE LEAVES LEFT (LP, reissue, 'blue with white palm tree' label)	12
89	Island ILPS 9134	BRYTER LAYTER (LP, reissue, 'blue with white palm tree' label)	12
89	Island ILPS 9184	PINK MOON (LP, reissue, 'blue with white palm tree' label)	12
91	Hannibal HNCD 5402	FRUIT TREE (4-CD, with booklet in 12" x 12" box)	45

DRAMATICS

72	Stax 2025 053	Whatcha See Is Whatcha Get/Thankful For Your Love	7
72	Stax 2025 101	In The Rain/Get Up And Get Down	5
73	Stax 2025 117	Toast To A Fool/Your Love Was Strange	10
73	Stax 2025 181	Hey You, Get Off My Mountain/Devil Is Dope	5
76	ABC ABC 4101	You're Fooling You/I'll Make It So Good	5
72	Stax 2362 025	WHATCHA SEE IS WHATCHA GET (LP)	15
74	Stax STX 1021	A DRAMATIC EXPERIENCE (LP)	12
75	ABC ABCL 5121	DRAMATIC JACKPOT (LP, gatefold sleeve)	12
75	ABC ABCL 5150	DRAMA V (LP, gatefold sleeve)	12

DRAMATIS

82	Rocket XPRES 79-12	The Shame (Dance Party Mix 1)/Only Find Rewind (12", p/s, with poster)	8

(see also Gary Numan, Paul Gardiner)

BARRY DRANSFIELD

72	Polydor Folk Mill 2383 160	BARRY DRANSFIELD (LP)	200

(see also Robin & Barry Dransfield, Dransfields)

ROBIN DRANSFIELD

80	Topic 12TS 414	TIDEWAVE (LP)	15

(see also Robin & Barry Dransfield, Dransfields)

ROBIN & BARRY DRANSFIELD

70	Trailer LER 2011	THE ROUT OF THE BLUES (LP)	25
71	Trailer LER 2026	LORD OF ALL I BEHOLD (LP)	25

(see also Robin Dransfield, Barry Dransfield, Dransfields)

DRANSFIELDS

76	Transatlantic TRA 322	THE FIDDLER'S DREAM (LP)	20
77	Free Reed 018	POPULAR TO CONTRARY BELIEF (LP)	15
78	Transatlantic TRA 386	BOWIN' AND SCRAPIN' (LP)	15

(see also Robin & Barry Dransfield, Robin Dransfield, Barry Dransfield)

RUSTY DRAPER

53	Oriole CB 1165	No Help Wanted/Angry (78)	7
53	Oriole CB 1195	Big Mamou/Why Why Why (78)	7
53	Oriole CB 1214	Gambler's Guitar/Free Home Demonstration (78)	7
53	Oriole CB 1220	I Love To Jump/Lighthouse (78)	7
54	Oriole CB 1245	Lonesome Song/Native Dancer (78)	7
54	Oriole CB 1277	The Train With The Rhumba Beat/Melancholy Baby (78)	7
54	Oriole CB 1287	Knock On Wood/It Ain't My Baby (78)	7
54	Mercury MB 3021	No Help Wanted/Angry (78, reissue)	7
54	Mercury MB 3045	Big Mamou/Why Why Why (78, reissue)	7
54	Mercury MB 3054	Gambler's Guitar/Free Home Demonstration (78)	7
54	Mercury MB 3058	I Love To Jump/Lighthouse (78, reissue)	7
54	Mercury MB 3080	Lonesome Song/Native Dancer (78, reissue)	7
54	Mercury MB 3106	The Train With The Rhumba Beat/Melancholy Baby (78, reissue)	7
54	Mercury MB 3116	Knock On Wood/It Ain't My Baby (78, reissue)	7
54	Mercury MB 3165	Muskrat Rumble/The Magic Circle (78)	7
55	Mercury MB 3198	Lookin' Back To See/Shame On You (78)	7
56	Mercury MT 101	Are You Satisfied?/Wabash Cannonball (78)	7
56	Mercury MT 113	Rock And Roll Ruby/House Of Cards (78)	12
56	Mercury MT 128	In The Middle Of The House/Pink Cadillac (78)	10
57	Mercury MT 137	Giant (from the film)/Tiger Lilly (with Jack Halloran Singers) (78)	7

MINT VALUE £

57	Mercury MT 147	Let's Go Calypso/Should I Never Love Again (78)	7
57	Mercury MT 155	Freight Train/Seven Come Eleven (with Dick Noel Singers) (78)	7
58	Mercury MT 194	Buzz Buzz Buzz/I Get The Blues When It Rains (78)	10
58	Mercury 7MT 211	Gamblin' Gal/That's My Doll	10
58	Mercury MT 211	Gamblin' Gal/That's My Doll (78)	8
58	Mercury 7MT 229	Chicken-Pickin' Hawk/June, July And August	10
58	Mercury MT 229	Chicken-Pickin' Hawk/June, July And August (78)	8
59	Mercury AMT 1019	Shoppin' Around/With This Ring	15
59	Mercury AMT 1019	Shoppin' Around/With This Ring (78)	25
59	Mercury AMT 1034	The Sun Will Always Shine/Hey Li Lee Li Lee Li	7
60	Mercury AMT 1101	Mule Skinner Blues/Please Help Me, I'm Falling	8
60	Mercury AMT 1110	Luck Of The Irish/It's A Little More Like Heaven	5
61	Mercury AMT 1127	Jealous Heart/Ten Thousand Years Ago	5
63	London HLU 9786	Night Life/That's Why I Love You Like I Do	12
65	London HLU 9989	Folsom Prison Blues/You Can't Be True, Dear	8
56	Mercury MEP 9506	PRESENTING RUSTY DRAPER (EP)	22
59	Mercury ZEP 10016	RUSTY DRAPER (EP)	18
60	Mercury ZEP 10059	RUSTY IN GAMBLING MOOD (EP)	18
60	Mercury ZEP 10095	MULE SKINNER BLUES (EP)	18
64	London RE-U 1431	RUSTY DRAPER NO. 1 (EP)	20
64	London RE-U 1432	RUSTY DRAPER NO. 2 (EP)	20
60	Mercury MMC 14040	HITS THAT SOLD A MILLION (LP)	30

DREAMERS
68	Columbia DB 8340	The Maybe Song/The Long Road	7

(see also Freddie & Dreamers)

DREAMERS
69	Downtown DT 407	Sweet Chariot/Let's Go Downtown	6
69	Downtown DT 408	I Second That Emotion/Dear Love	6

DREAMLETS
65	Ska Beat JB 182	Really Now/SKATALITES: Street Corner	20

DREAMLOVERS
61	Columbia DB 4711	When We Get Married/Just Because	100

(see also Chubby Checker)

DREAM MERCHANTS
67	Decca F 12617	Rattler/I'll Be With You In Apple Blossom Time	6

DREAM POLICE
70	Decca F 12998	I'll Be Home (In A Day Or So)/Living Is Easy	8
70	Decca F 13078	Our Song/Much Too Much	5
70	Decca F 13105	I've Got No Choice/What's The Cure For Happiness?	5

(see also Average White Band)

DREAMS
68	United Artists UP 2249	I Will See You There/A Boy Needs A Girl	5
69	CBS 4247	Baby I'm Your Man/Softly, Softly	5
69	Dolphin 4432	Casatschok/Don't You Ask Me	5
70	CBS 64203	DREAMS (LP)	15
72	CBS 64597	IMAGINE MY SURPRISE (LP)	15

DREAM SYNDICATE
88	Bucketfull Of Brains BOB 21	Blind Willie McTell/BEVIS FROND: High In A Flat (free with *Bucketfull Of Brains* issue 27, 33rpm, yellow die-cut sleeve)	15/12

DREAM THEATER
93	East West	Another Day/Status Seeker (live) (cassette)	12
94	East West A 5835	Lie/Space-Dye Vest/To Live Forever/Another Day (live) (p/s)	8
94	East West A 5835 T	Lie/Take The Time (Demo)/Space-Dye Vest (12", p/s)	20
94	East West A 5835 CD	Lie/Space-Dye Vest/To Live Forever/Another Day (live) (CD)	8
89	MCA MCF 3445	WHEN DREAM AND DAY UNITE (LP)	12
92	Atco 7567 92148 1	IMAGES AND WORDS (LP)	15

DREAMTIMERS
61	London HLU 9368	The Dancin' Lady/An Invitation	15

DREAM WEAVERS
56	Brunswick 05515	It's Almost Tomorrow/You've Got Me Wondering (gold label lettering, later silver)	30/20
56	Brunswick 05568	A Little Love Can Go A Long, Long Way/Into The Night (featuring Wade Buff)	18
56	Brunswick 05607	You're Mine/Is There Somebody Else? (featuring Wade Buff)	10

DREGS
79	Disturbing DRO 1	THE DREGS EP (p/s, numbered, stamped sleeve, 150 only)	50

LEN DRESSLAR
56	Mercury 7MT 3	Chain Gang/These Hands (export issue)	10

JOHN DREVAR('S EXPRESSION)
67	MGM MGM 1367	The Closer She Gets/When I Come Home	50
68	Polydor BM 56290	What Greater Love/I've Decided (solo)	6

ALAN DREW
63	Columbia DB 7090	Here Comes The Rain/Always The Lonely One	5

PATTI DREW
68	Capitol CL 15557	Workin' On A Groovy Thing/Without A Doubt	7
68	Capitol CL 15575	Hard To Handle/Just Can't Forget About You	5

DREXCIYA
93	Rephlex CAT 017	3 — MOLECULAR ENHANCEMENT (12", 4-track)	8
95	Warp WAP 57	THE JOURNEY HOME (12", company sleeve)	8

DRIFTERS (U.S.)

78s

56	London HLE 8344	Soldier Of Fortune/I Gotta Get Myself A Woman (78)	100
58	London HLE 8686	Moonlight Bay/Drip-Drop (78)	50
59	London HLE 8892	There Goes My Baby/Oh, My Love (78)	80
59	London HLE 8988	Dance With Me/True Love, True Love (78)	80
60	London HLE 9081	This Magic Moment/Baltimore (78)	100

SINGLES

56	London HLE 8344	Soldier Of Fortune/I Gotta Get Myself A Woman	1,200
58	London HLE 8686	Moonlight Bay/Drip-Drop	125
59	London HLE 8892	There Goes My Baby/Oh, My Love	18
59	London HLE 8988	Dance With Me/True Love, True Love	15
60	London HLE 9081	This Magic Moment/Baltimore	10
60	London HLK 9145	Lonely Winds/Hey Senorita	10
60	London HLK 9201	Save The Last Dance For Me/Nobody But Me	5
61	London HLK 7114	Save The Last Dance For Me/This Magic Moment (export issue)	15
61	London HLK 7115	I Count The Tears/Dance With Me (export issue)	15
61	London HLK 9287	I Count The Tears/Sadie My Lady	6
61	London HLK 9326	Some Kind Of Wonderful/Honey Bee	10
61	London HLK 9382	Please Stay/No Sweet Lovin'	8
61	London HLK 9427	Sweets For My Sweet/Loneliness Or Happiness	8
62	London HLK 9500	Room Full Of Tears/Somebody New Dancin' With You	8
62	London HLK 9522	When My Little Girl Is Smiling/Mexican Divorce	7
62	London HLK 9554	Stranger On The Shore/What To Do	7
62	London HLK 9626	Up On The Roof/Another Night With The Boys	7
63	London HLK 9699	On Broadway/Let The Music Play	8
63	London HLK 9750	Rat Race/If You Don't Come Back	8
63	London HLK 9785	I'll Take You Home/I Feel Good All Over	7
64	London HLK 9848	Vaya Con Dios/In The Land Of Make Believe	7
64	London HLK 9886	One Way Love/Didn't It	7
64	Atlantic AT 4001	Under The Boardwalk/I Don't Want To Go On Without You	7
64	Atlantic AT 4008	I've Got Sand In My Shoes/He's Just A Playboy	8
64	Atlantic AT 4012	Saturday Night At The Movies/Spanish Lace	6
65	Atlantic AT 4019	At The Club/Answer The Phone	8
65	Atlantic AT 4023	Come On Over To My Place/Chains Of Love	7
65	Atlantic AT 4034	Follow Me/The Outside World	12
65	Atlantic AT 4040	I'll Take You Where The Music's Playing/Far From The Maddening Crowd	7
66	Atlantic AT 4062	We Gotta Sing/Nylon Stockings	12
66	Atlantic AT 4084	Memories Are Made Of This/My Island In The Sun	7
66	Atlantic 584 020	Up In The Streets Of Harlem/You Can't Love 'Em All	6
67	Atlantic 584 065	Baby What I Mean/Aretha	8
68	Atlantic 584 152	I'll Take You Where The Music's Playing/On Broadway	5
68	Atlantic 584 195	Still Burning In My Heart/I Need You Now	6
69	Atlantic 584 246	Saturday Night At The Movies/Under The Boardwalk	5
71	Atlantic 2091 064	A Rose By Any Other Name/Be My Lady	5
76	Atlantic K 10700	You Gotta Pay Your Dues/Black Silk	5

EPs

61	London RE-K 1282	THE DRIFTERS' GREATEST HITS (EP)	35
63	London RE-K 1355	THE DRIFTERS (EP)	35
63	London RE-K 1385	DRIFTIN' (EP)	35
64	Atlantic AET 6003	DRIFTIN' VOL. 2 (EP)	25
65	Atlantic AET 6012	TONIGHT (EP)	25

LPs

60	London HA-K 2318	THE DRIFTERS' GREATEST HITS (LP)	45
62	London HA-K 2450	SAVE THE LAST DANCE FOR ME (LP)	50
65	Atlantic ATL 5015	OUR BIGGEST HITS (LP)	25
65	Atlantic ATL/STL 5023	THE GOOD LIFE WITH THE DRIFTERS (LP, mono/stereo)	30/35
66	Atlantic ATL/STL 5039	I'LL TAKE YOU WHERE THE MUSIC'S PLAYING (LP, mono/stereo)	30/35
67	Atlantic 587 038	BIGGEST HITS (LP)	15
67	Atlantic 587 061	I'LL TAKE YOU WHERE THE MUSIC'S PLAYING (LP, reissue)	15
67	Atlantic 590 010	SOUVENIRS (LP)	18
67	Atlantic 587 063	SAVE THE LAST DANCE FOR ME (LP, reissue)	18
68	Atlantic 587/588 103	THE DRIFTERS' GOLDEN HITS (LP)	12
68	Atlantic 587 123	ROCKIN' AND DRIFTIN' (LP)	25
68	Atlantic 587 144	GOOD GRAVY (LP, as Clyde McPhatter & Drifters)	30
69	Atlantic 587/588 160	UP ON THE ROOF (LP)	15

(see also Clyde McPhatter, Ben E. King, Bobby Hendricks)

DRIFTERS (U.K.)

59	Columbia DB 4263	Feelin' Fine/Don't Be A Fool (With Love)	70
59	Columbia DB 4263	Feelin' Fine/Don't Be A Fool (With Love) (78)	90
59	Columbia DB 4325	Driftin'/Jet Black	40

(see also Shadows, Cliff Richard)

DRIFTING SLIM

| 66 | Blue Horizon 45-1005 | Good Morning Baby/My Sweet Woman (99 copies only) | 70 |

DRIFTWOOD

70	Decca F 13084	Shylock Bay/The Wind Cries Above You	5
71	Decca F 13139	Say The Right Things/Still I'll Stay With You	5
70	Decca SKL 5069	DRIFTWOOD (LP)	30

(see also Neil Harrison)

JIMMY DRIFTWOOD

60	RCA RCX 191	COUNTRY GUITAR VOL. 13 (EP)	8
60	RCA RCX 193	TALL TALES IN SONG VOL. 1 (EP)	10
60	RCA RCX 195	TALL TALES IN SONG VOL. 2 (EP)	10
60	RCA RCX 198	TALL TALES IN SONG VOL. 3 (EP)	10
61	RCA RD 27226	SONGS OF BILLY YANK AND JOHNNY REB (LP)	12

JULIE DRISCOLL

63	Columbia DB 7118	Take Me By The Hand/Stay Away From Me	25
65	Parlophone R 5296	Don't Do It No More/I Know You	22
66	Parlophone R 5444	I Didn't Want To Have To Do It/Don't Do It No More.	12
67	Parlophone R 5588	I Know You Love Me Not/If You Should Ever Leave Me.	12
67	Marmalade 598 005	Save Me (Parts 1 & 2).	10
71	Polydor 2480 074	JULIE DRISCOLL — 1969 (LP).	22
72	Polydor 2383 077	JULIE DRISCOLL — 1969 (LP, reissue)	12

JULIE DRISCOLL, BRIAN AUGER & TRINITY

68	Marmalade 598 006	This Wheel's On Fire/A Kind Of Love In	7
68	Marmalade 598 011	Road To Cairo/Shadows Of You	6
69	Marmalade 598 018	Take Me To The Water/Indian Rope Man	10
67	Marmalade 607/608 002	OPEN (LP, mono/stereo)	30/25
68	M. For Pleasure MFP 1265	JOOLS/BRIAN (LP, tracks shared by Julie Driscoll & Brian Auger)	15
69	Marmalade 608 005/6	STREET NOISE (2-LP)	30
69	Marmalade 608 014	STREET NOISE PART 1 (LP)	15
69	Marmalade 608 015	STREET NOISE PART 2 (LP)	15

(see also Brian Auger & Trinity, Working Week, Julie Tippetts, B.B. Blunder)

DRIVE

78	NRG NE 467	Jerkin'/Push'N'Shove	25

DRIVE

90	First Strike FST 007	No Girls/Peephole (hand-made numbered gatefold p/s with insert)	12
90	First Strike FST 007	No Girls/Peephole/Vegan In Furs/Process White (12", p/s).	8
92	First Strike FST 020L	This Ain't No Picnic/My World (p/s, white vinyl in bag, numbered, 120 only)	6

DRIVE

93	Ninja Tune DRIVE 1	Curfew (Beatmasters 12" Mix)/(Rebel Funk Mix)/(Beatmasters Instrumental) (12", p/s)	30
93	Ninja Tune DRIVE CD 1	Curfew (Rebel Radio Mix)/(Beatmasters 12" Mix)/(Rebel Funk Mix) (Beatmasters Instrumental) (CD)	50

(see also All Saints)

DRIVERS

83	Greyhound GRK 701	Talk All Night/Sister (p/s)	6
84	Nouveau NMS 5	Things/Stolen Treasure (p/s)	6
83	Greyhound GRK 3301	SHORT CUTS (LP)	12

(see also Nick Van Eede)

D-ROK

91	Warhammer DROK 08722	Get Out Of My Way (D-Mix)/Renegade/Get Out Of My Way (Airnix) (12", p/s)	10
91	Warhammer DROK 08724	Get Out Of My Way (D-Mix)/Renegade/Get Out Of My Way (Airnix) (CD)	10
91	Warhammer DROK 08710	OBLIVION (LP)	12

(see also Brian May)

FRANK D'RONE

60	Mercury AMT 1123	Strawberry Blonde (The Band Rocked On)/Time Hurries By	8
59	Mercury ZEP 10083	BLUE SERENADE (EP)	10
59	Mercury ZEP 10116	THE BAND ROCKED ON (EP)	25
60	Mercury MMC 14053	AFTER THE BALL (LP)	25

DRONES

77	Ohms GOOD MIX 1	TEMPTATIONS OF A WHITE COLLAR WORKER (EP, different coloured sleeves, some with writing on inner sleeve)	10
77	Valer VRS 1	Bone Idle/I Just Wanna Be Myself (gatefold p/s, made in France or England)	12/6
77	Fifth Avenue CAS 107	Bone Idle/I Just Wanna Be Myself (cassette, flip-open 'cigarette box' sleeve)	30
77	Valer VRSP 1	Be My Baby/Lift Off The Bans (12", white label, unreleased)	50
77	Valer	Be My Baby (Take Two)/The Clique (white label, unreleased)	15
80	Fabulous JC 4	Can't See/Fooled Today (p/s)	7
77	Valer VRLP 1	FURTHER TEMPTATIONS (LP)	30

DRUG ADDIX

78	Chiswick SW 39	MAKE A RECORD (EP)	10

(see also Kirsty MacColl)

DRUG SQUAD

80	Bathroom Floor BFR 001	Operation Julie/Switchcleaner (p/s).	5

DRUGSTORE

93	Honey	Alive (yellow vinyl flexidisc)	12
93	Honey HON 1	Alive/Gravity (p/s, 500 only)	10

DRUID

75	EMI EMC 3081	TOWARDS THE SUN (LP, with inner sleeve)	12
76	EMI EMC 3128	FLUID DRUID (LP, with inner sleeve)	12

DRUID CHASE

67	CBS 3053	Take Me In Your Garden/I Wanna Get My Hands On You	15

DRUIDS

63	Parlophone R 5097	Long Tall Texan/Love So Blue	12
64	Parlophone R 5134	See What You've Done/It's Just A Little Bit Too Late	15

DRUIDS

71	Argo ZFB 22	BURNT OFFERING (LP)	75
73	Argo ZFB 39	PASTIME WITH GOOD COMPANY (LP)	75

(see also Giles Farnaby's Dream Band)

DRUMBAGO

63	Island WI 085	I Am Drunk (actually by Raymond Harper & Drumbago's Group)/Sea Breeze	
		(actually by Sammy & Drumbago's Group)	18
68	Blue Cat BS 145	Reggae Jeggae (with Blenders)/TYRONE TAYLOR: Delilah	12
69	Trojan TR 638	Dulcemania (with Dynamites)/CLANCY ECCLES: China Man	7

(see also Derrick Patsy, Dennis Walks)

BILL DRUMMOND

87	Creation CRE 039T	King Of Joy/The Manager (12", p/s)	15

(see also Big In Japan, Lori & Chameleons, J.A.M.s, KLF, Disco 2000, Timelords)

DON DRUMMOND

62	Island WI 021	Schooling The Duke/Bitter Rose (as Don Drummond Orchestra; B-side is	
		actually by Shenley Duffas)	20
63	Black Swan WI 406	Scrap Iron/DRAGONAIRE: Prevention	20
63	Blue Beat BB 179	Reload/Far East	15
63	Island WI 094	Scandal/My Ideal (B-side actually by W. Sparks)	18
63	R&B JB 103	Royal Flush/MAYTALS: Matthew Mark	15
63	R&B JB 105	The Shock/TONETTES: Tell Me You're Mine	12
64	Ska Beat JB 178	Silver Dollar/TOMMY McCOOK: My Business	15
64	Island WI 149	Eastern Standard Time/DOTTY & BONNIE: Sun Rises	18
64	Island WI 153	Musical Storeroom/STRANGER COLE: He Who Feels	18
64	Island WI 162	Garden Of Love/STRANGER COLE: Cherry May	25
65	Island WI 192	Stampede (with Drumbago)/JUSTIN HINDS & DOMINOES: Come Bail Me	18
65	Island WI 204	Coolie Baby/LORD ANTICS: You May Stray	18
65	Island WI 208	Man In The Street/RITA & BENNY: You Are My Only Love	18
65	Island WI 242	University Goes Ska/DERRICK & NAOMI: Pain In My Heart	25
69	Studio One SO 2078	Heavenless/GLEN BROWN & DAVE BARKER: Lady Lovelight	30
69	Trojan TR 678	Memory Of Don/JOHN HOLT: Darling I Love You	10
69	Studio One SO 9008	THE BEST OF DON DRUMMOND (LP)	100
69	Trojan TTL 23	MEMORIAL ALBUM (LP)	25

(see also Joe White, Rhythm Aces, Roy & Millie, Movers, Desmond Dekker, Shirley Duffas, Hi-Tones, Duke Reid, Soul Brothers, Baba Brooks, Bonnie & Skitto, Eric Morris, Pioneers, Stranger & Patsy, Techniques, Winston Wright)

DON DRUMMOND JUNIOR

67	Caltone TONE 104	Sir Pratt Special/HEMSLEY MORRIS: Love Is Strange	18
68	Caltone TONE 124	Dirty Dozen/PHIL PRATT: Reach Out	25
70	Jackpot JP 710	Memory Of Don Drummond/TOBIES: Resting	8

(see also Vincent Gordon)

K. DRUMMOND

73	Jackpot JP 810	Your Pretty Face/Your Pretty Face (Version)	5

(see also Cables)

DRUNKS WITH GUNS

90	Shock SX 005	Drunks Theme/Punched In The Head/	
		Cowboy (Instrumental) (p/s, numbered, 1,000 only)	5

ROY DRUSKY

59	Brunswick 05785	Wait 'N' See/Just About That Time	8
59	Brunswick 05785	Wait 'N' See/Just About That Time (78)	7
61	Brunswick 05856	Three Hearts In A Tangle/I'd Rather Loan You Out	6

DRY ICE

69	B&C CB 115	Running To The Convent/Nowhere To Go	12

(see also Pluto)

DRY RIB

79	Clockwork COR 001	THE DRY SEASON (EP, 33rpm, photocopied foldover p/s,	
		screen-printed labels)	30

(see also Television Personalities, Times, L'Orange Mechanik)

AMANCIO D'SILVA

69	Columbia S(C)X 6322	INTEGRATION (LP)	30
71	Columbia SCX 6465	REFLECTIONS (LP)	25

(see also Cosmic Eye)

D-TRAIN

82	Prelude EPCA 12-2016	You're The One For Me/You're The One For Me (Version) (12", p/s)	8

DUALS

61	London HL 9450	Stick Shift/Cruising	25

DUBLINERS

60s	Transatlantic TRAEP 136	MAINLY BLARNEY (EP)	8
66	Transatlantic TRA 139	FINNEGAN WAKES (LP)	18
68	Major Minor GOL 200	THE DUBLINERS (LP)	12
68	Major Minor SMLP 34	AT IT AGAIN (LP)	12
69	Columbia SCX 6380	AT HOME WITH THE DUBLINERS (LP)	15
70	Columbia SCX 6423	REVOLUTION (LP)	12
73	Polydor 2383 235	PLAIN AND SIMPLE (LP, gatefold sleeve)	12

DUBS

57	London HLU 8526	Could This Be Magic/Such Lovin'	225
57	London HLU 8526	Could This Be Magic/Such Lovin' (78)	50
58	London HL 8684	Gonna Make A Change/Beside My Love	325
58	London HL 8684	Gonna Make A Change/Beside My Love (78)	75

MINT VALUE £

JOHN DU CANN

77	Arista ARIST 128	Throw Him In Jail/Street Stutter	5
77	Arista ARIST 145	Where's The Show/Hang Around	5
79	Vertigo 6059 241	Don't Be A Dummy/If I'm Makin' (p/s)	8
77	Arista SPARTY 1027	THE WORLD'S NOT BIG ENOUGH (LP, unreleased)	

(see also Attack, Andromeda, Five Day Week Straw People, Atomic Rooster, Hard Stuff, Status Quo)

DUCHESS

| 53 | London L 1172 | Ragging The Scale/Kitten On The Keys (78) | 6 |

DUCKS DELUXE

73	RCA RCA 2438	Coast To Coast/Bring Back That Packard Car	6
74	RCA LPBO 5019	Fireball/Saratoga Suzie	5
74	RCA RCA 2477	Love's Melody/Two Time Twister	5
75	RCA RCA 2531	I Fought The Law/Cherry Pie	5
74	RCA LPL1 5008	DUCKS DELUXE (LP)	12
74	RCA SF 8402	TAXI TO THE TERMINAL ZONE (LP)	12
82	Blue Moon BMLP 001	LAST NIGHT OF A PUB ROCK BAND (2-LP)	15

(see also Motors, Tyla Gang, Brinsley Schwarz, Nick Garvey)

DUDLEY

| 60 | Vogue V 9171 | Lone Prairie Rock/El Pizza | 15 |

DAVE DUDLEY

63	United Artists UP 1029	Six Days On The Road/I Feel A Cry Coming On	7
67	Mercury MF 1003	Trucker's Prayer/Don't Come Cryin' To Me	6
68	Mercury MF 1037	There Ain't No Easy Run/Why Can't I Be With You? (It's A Shame)	5
70	Mercury MF 1134	George (And The North Wind)/It's Not A Very Pleasant Day Today	5

ROBERTA DUDLEY

| 50 | Tempo R 22 | Krooked Blues/When You're Alone (78) | 15 |
| 51 | Poydras 3 | Krooked Blues/When You're Alone (78, reissue) | 8 |

(see also Kid Ory)

DU-ETTES

| 72 | President PT 382 | Every Beat Of My Heart/Sugar Daddy | 4 |
| 72 | President PT 398 | Please Forgive Me/Lonely Days | 4 |

SHENLEY DUFFAS

62	Island WI 036	Give To Get/What You Gonna Do (as S. Duffas; B-side actually with Millie Small)	18
63	Island WI 063	Fret Man Fret/Doreen	18
63	Island WI 093	What A Disaster/I Am Rich	18
63	Island WI 115	Know The Lord/TOMMY McCOOK: Ska Ba	18
63	Island WI 125	Easy Squeal/Things Ain't Going Right	18
63	R&B JB 134	No More Wedding Bells/Let Them Fret	10
64	R&B JB 146	Big Mouth/FRANKIE ANDERSON: Peanut Vendor	12
64	R&B JB 152	Christopher Columbus/CARL BRYAN ORCHESTRA: Barber Chair	12
64	R&B JB 154	Mother-In-Law/DON DRUMMOND & GROUP: Festival	12
64	Black Swan WI 440	Digging A Ditch/He's Coming Down	18
64	Black Swan WI 443	Gather Them In/Crucifixion	18
64	Rio R 41	I Will Be Glad/Heariso (as Shandly Duffus)	12
65	Island WI 182	La La La/UPCOMING WILLOWS: Jonestown Special	18
65	Island WI 184	You Are Mine/UPCOMING WILLOWS: Red China	18
65	Island WI 186	Rukumbine/One Morning	18
72	Upsetter US 380	Bet You Don't Know/UPSETTERS: Ring Of Fire	12
72	Dynamic DYN 451	Peace (with Soul Avengers)/UPSETTERS: Peace — Version	5
72	Grape GR 3031	Sincerely/Sincerely — Version (with Upsetters)	6

(see also Chenley Duffus, Billy Dyce)

CHENLEY DUFFUS

| 72 | Pama PM 859 | At The End/Good Night My Love | 15 |

(see also Shenley Duffas)

DUFFY

| 73 | Chapter One SCHR 184 | The Joker/Running Away | 12 |
| 70 | Chapter One CHSR 814 | SCRUFFY DUFFY (LP) | 80 |

STEPHEN 'TIN TIN' DUFFY

82	WEA TIN 1	Kiss Me/Love's Duet (p/s)	7
82	WEA TIN 1T	Kiss Me (Dub Version)/Love's Duet (Dub Version) (12", p/s)	10
84	10 TEN 28-12	She Makes Me Quiver (Version)/(Dub)/(7" Mix) (12", p/s)	8
85	10 TIN 2	Kiss Me (1985)/In This Twilight (p/s, with inner sleeve)	5
85	10 TINP 2	Kiss Me (1985)/In This Twilight (picture disc)	5
85	10 TING 2	Kiss Me (1985)/In This Twilight//Kiss Me (1983)/Holes In My Shoes (double pack, gatefold p/s)	6
85	10 TIN 2-12	Kiss Me (1985)/In This Twilight (12", gatefold p/s with 8-page portfolio)	8
85	10 TING 2-12	Kiss Me (1985)/In This Twilight//Kiss Me (1983)/Holes In My Shoes (12", double pack)	8
85	10 TING 3	Icing On The Cake/Broken Home/Hold It/She Makes Me Quiver (double pack, gatefold p/s)	5
85	10 TING 3-12	Icing On The Cake (7.10)/Icing On The Cake (3.50)/Broken Home//Hold It/She Makes Me Quiver (12", double pack, gatefold p/s)	8
85	10 TING 3-13	Icing On The Cake/Broken Home/Icing On The Cake (Remix) (12", pink p/s)	18
85	10 TIND 4	Unkiss That Kiss/Done For/"Love's Duet"/Holes In My Shoes (Carry On Version) (double pack, gatefold p/s)	5

85	10	She Loves Me/She Loves It (p/s, withdrawn)	100
85	10	Baby Impossible (p/s, withdrawn)	100
86	10 TENP 91	I Love You (Aversion)/I Love You/Love Is Driving Me Insane (gatefold p/s with poster, withdrawn)	6
86	10 TIN 91-12	I Love You/Love Is Driving Me Insane/I Love You (The Inervision)/Wednesday Jones/Icing On The Kake/Kiss Me (12", p/s)	15
86	10 TIND 5-10	I Love You (Inversion)/Wednesday Jones (Dixie)//Icing On The Cake/Kiss Me (10", double pack, gatefold p/s)	6
86	10 DIXCD 29	BECAUSE WE LOVE YOU (CD)	30

(see also Hawks, Tin Tin, Dr. Calculus, Lilac Time)

DUFFY'S NUCLEUS
67	Decca F 22547	Hound Dog/Mary Open The Door	30

(see also Duffy Power, Pentangle)

BILLY DUKE
62	Ember EMB S 153	Walking Cane/Amen	7
62	Ember EMB S 160	Ain't She Pretty/Timbuctu	7
64	London HLU 9907	While The Bloom Is On The Rose/I'm The Lonesomest Guy In Town	7
65	London HLU 9960	Sugar'N'Spice/Prisoner Of Love	8

DENVER DUKE & JEFFREY NULL BLUEGRASS BOYS
63	Starlite STEP 33	DENVER DUKE & JEFFREY NULL BLUEGRASS BOYS (EP)	15

DON DUKE
60	Embassy WB 402	Please Don't Tease/Made You (78)	12
60	Embassy WB 405	When Will I Be Loved/Look For A Star (78)	12
60	Embassy WB 414	Only The Lonely/Chain Gang (78)	15
60	Embassy WB 416	So Sad (To See Good Love Go Bad)/Please Help Me I'm Falling (78)	12
60	Embassy WB 418	Dreamin'/Let's Think About Living (78)	15

(see also Dick Jordan, Bud Ashton)

DORIS DUKE
71	Mojo 2092 005	To The Other Woman/I Don't Care Anymore	5
71	Mojo 2092 017	If She's Your Wife Who Am I?/It Sure Was Fun	5
73	Mainstream MSS 302	Business Deal/Nobody But You	6
76	Contempo CX15	Woman Of The Ghetto/TAMIKO JONES: Let It Flow	12
71	Mojo 2916 001	I'M A LOSER (LP)	20
71	Mojo 2916 006	A LEGEND IN HER OWN TIME (LP)	20
75	Contempo CRM 111	A LEGEND IN HER OWN TIME (LP, reissue)	12
75	Contempo CLP 519	WOMAN (LP)	15

GEORGE DUKE
71	Sunset SLS 50232	LIVE IN LOS ANGELES (LP)	12
74	BASF BAP 5064	THE AURA WILL PREVAIL (LP)	12
75	BASF BAP 5071	I LOVE THE BLUES, SHE HEARD MY CRY (LP)	12
80	Epic EPC 84311	A BRAZILIAN LOVE AFFAIR (LP)	10

PATTY DUKE
65	United Artists UP 1103	Don't Just Stand There/Everything But Love	7
65	United Artists UP 1116	Say Something Funny/Funny Little Butterflies	7

DUKE ALL STARS
68	Blue Cat BS 111	Letter To Mummy And Daddy (Parts 1 & 2)	10

DUKE & DUCHESS
55	London HLU 8206	Borrowed Sunshine/Get Ready For Love (with Sir Hubert Pimm)	25
55	London HLU 8206	Borrowed Sunshine/Get Ready For Love (with Sir Hubert Pimm) (78)	7

(see also Sir Hubert Pimm)

DUKE'S NOBLEMEN
68	Philips BF 1691	City Of Windows/Thank You For Your Loving	5

AGGIE DUKES
57	Vogue V 9090	John John/Well Of Loneliness	450
57	Vogue V 9090	John John/Well Of Loneliness (78)	90

DUKES OF DIXIELAND
62	CBS BPG 62014	BREAKIN' IT UP ON BROADWAY (LP)	12

DUKES OF IRON
54	Melodisc 1316	Last Train To San Fernando/Big Bamboo (78)	5

DUKES OF STRATOSPHEAR
85	Virgin VS 763	The Mole From The Ministry/My Love Explodes (no p/s)	6
87	Virgin VSY 982	You're A Good Man Albert Brown/Vanishing Girl (p/s, 5,000 on multi-coloured vinyl)	7
87	Virgin VP 2440	PSONIC PSUNSPOT (LP, gatefold sleeve, 5,000 on multi-coloured vinyl)	15

(see also XTC, Mr. Partridge)

DULCIMER
71	Nepentha 6437 003	AND I TURNED AS I HAD TURNED AS A BOY (LP, gatefold sleeve)	50
80	Happy Face MMLP 1021	A LAND FIT FOR HEROES (LP, private pressing)	15

LIZA DULITTLE
68	Pye 7N 17590	I've Got To Get A Grip Of Myself/Did You Hear A Heart Break Last Night?	6

(see also Margo & Marvettes)

DUM
74	RAK RAK 179	In The Mood/Watching The Clock	6

(see also Mud)

MINT VALUE £

DUMB ANGELS
88	Fierce FRIGHT 033	Love And Mercy/Love And Mercy (p/s, numbered)	20

(see also Pooh Sticks)

DUMBELLES
80	Polydor POSP 209/EGO 3	Giddy Up/A Christmas Dream (no p/s)	10

(see also Roxy Music)

JOHN DUMMER (BLUES BAND)
68	Mercury MF 1040	Travelling Man/40 Days (as John Dummer Blues Band)	12
69	Mercury MF 1119	Try Me One More Time/Riding At Midnight (as John Dummer Blues Band)	10
70	Fontana 6007 027	Happy/Nightingale (unissued in U.K.; France-only)	
70	Philips 6006 111	Nine By Nine/Going In The Out (credited to either Famous Music Band or John Dummer Band)	8
71	Philips 6006 176	Medicine Weasel/The Endgame (with Nick Pickett)	5
73	Vertigo 6059 074	Ooblee-Dooblee Jubilee/The Monkey Speaks His Mind (as John Dummer Oobleedooblee Band)	5
69	Mercury SMCL 20136	CABAL (LP)	70
69	Mercury SMCL 20167	JOHN DUMMER BAND (LP)	100
70	Philips 6309 008	FAMOUS MUSIC BAND (LP)	45
72	Philips 6382 039	THIS IS THE JOHN DUMMER BLUES BAND (LP)	30
73	Philips 6382 040	VOLUME II — TRY ME ONE MORE TIME (LP)	30
72	Vertigo 6360 055	BLUE (LP, gatefold sleeve, spiral label)	70
73	Vertigo 6360 083	OOBLEEDOOBLEE JUBILEE (LP, as John Dummer Oobleedooblee Band, spiral label)	30

(see also Nick Pickett, Dave Kelly, Famous Music Band, Tony McPhee)

DUMMIES
79	Cheapskate FWL 001	When The Lights Are Out/She's The Only Woman (no p/s)	8
80	Pye 7P 163	When The Lights Are Out/She's The Only Woman (no p/s, reissue)	8
80	Cheapskate CHEAP 003	Didn't You Used To Use To Be You?/Miles Out To Sea (p/s)	10
81	Cheapskate CHEAP 014	Maybe Tonite/When I'm Dancin' I Ain't Fightin' (p/s)	12

(see also China Dolls, Slade)

DUMPY'S RUSTY NUTS
81	Cool King CNK 006	Just For Kicks/Ride With Me (p/s, reissued as Dumpy's Rusty Bolts)	8/5
82	Cool King CK 008	Boxhill Or Bust/It's Got To Be Blues (p/s, initially with free patch)	6/5
90	A Side DRN 21	Run Run Run/Rock City (withdrawn, promos more common)	5
84	Landslide LDLP 101	SOMEWHERE IN ENGLAND (LP)	12

DUNAMIS
79	Daybreak DB 2602	I CAN FLY (LP)	15

AYNSLEY DUNBAR (RETALIATION)
67	Blue Horizon 3109	Warning/Cobwebs (some in p/s)	40/18
68	Liberty LBF 15132	Watch 'N' Chain/Roamin' And Ramblin'	10
68	Liberty LBL/LBS 83154	AYNSLEY DUNBAR RETALIATION (LP, mono/stereo)	35
68	Liberty LBL/LBS 83177	DR. DUNBAR'S PRESCRIPTION (LP, mono/stereo)	35
69	Liberty LBS 83223	RETALIATION (LP)	35
70	Liberty LBS 83316	REMAINS TO BE HEARD (LP)	30
71	Warner Bros WS 3010	BLUE WHALE (LP)	18
71	Warner Bros K 46062	BLUE WHALE (LP, reissue)	15

(see also John Mayall & Bluesbreakers, Heavy Jelly, Annette & Victor Brox, Excheckers)

SCOTT DUNBAR
71	Ahura Mazda AMS SDS 1	FROM LAKE MARY (LP)	25

JOHNNY DUNCAN (& BLUE GRASS BOYS)
57	Columbia DB 3925	Kaw-Liga/Ella Speed (gold label lettering, later silver)	20/15
57	Columbia DB 3925	Kaw-Liga/Ella Speed (78)	12
57	Columbia DB 3959	Last Train To San Fernando/Rock-A-Billy Baby (gold label lettering, later silver)	15/7
57	Columbia DB 3959	Last Train To San Fernando/Rock-A-Billy Baby (78)	5
57	Columbia DB 3996	Blue, Blue Heartache/Jig Along Home	8
57	Columbia DB 3996	Blue, Blue Heartache/Jig Along Home (78)	5
57	Columbia DB 4029	Footprints In The Snow/Get Along Home, Cindy	8
57	Columbia DB 4029	Footprints In The Snow/Get Along Home, Cindy (78)	7
58	Columbia DB 4074	Goodnight Irene/If You Love Me Baby	15
58	Columbia DB 4074	Goodnight Irene/If You Love Me Baby (78)	7
58	Columbia DB 4118	Itching For My Baby/I Heard The Bluebirds Sing	12
58	Columbia DB 4118	Itching For My Baby/I Heard The Bluebirds Sing (78)	8
58	Columbia DB 4167	All Of The Monkeys Ain't In The Zoo/More And More	8
58	Columbia DB 4167	All Of The Monkeys Ain't In The Zoo/More And More (78)	7
58	Columbia DB 4179	My Lucky Love/Geisha Girl	7
58	Columbia DB 4179	My Lucky Love/Geisha Girl (78)	8
59	Columbia DB 4282	Rosalie/This Train	8
59	Columbia DB 4282	Rosalie/This Train (78)	10
59	Columbia DB 4311	Kansas City/That's All Right Darlin'	10
59	Columbia DB 4311	Kansas City/That's All Right Darlin' (78)	12
60	Columbia DB 4415	Any Time/Yellow, Yellow Moon (solo)	6
61	Pye 7N 15358	Tobacco Road/Sleepy-Eyed John (solo)	8
61	Pye 7N 15380	The Legend Of Gunga Din/Hannah (solo)	8
62	Pye 7N 15420	A Long Time Gone/Waitin' For The Sandman (solo)	8
63	Columbia DB 7164	The Ballad Of Jed Clampett/Will You Be Mine? (as Johnny Duncan & Kingpins)	8

MINT VALUE £

64	Columbia DB 7334	Dang Me/Which Way Did He Go? (solo)	6
66	Columbia DB 7833	My Little Baby/I Thank My Lucky Stars (solo)	5
57	Columbia SEG 7708	JOHNNY DUNCAN AND HIS BLUE GRASS BOYS (EP)	20
57	Columbia SEG 7773	JOHNNY DUNCAN AND HIS BLUE GRASS BOYS NO. 2 (EP)	20
58	Columbia SEG 7753	FOOTPRINTS IN THE SNOW (EP)	20
58	Columbia SEG 7850	TENNESSEE SING SONG (EP)	18
57	Columbia 33S 1122	TENNESSEE SONG BAG (10" LP)	40
58	Columbia 33S 1129	JOHNNY DUNCAN SALUTES HANK WILLIAMS (10" LP)	40
61	Columbia 33SX 1328	BEYOND THE SUNSET (LP)	30
68	M. For Pleasure MFP 1032	BEYOND THE SUNSET (LP, reissue)	12

(see also Chris Barber's Skiffle Group)

LESLEY DUNCAN (& JOKERS)
63	Parlophone R 5034	I Want A Steady Guy/Movin' Away (as Lesley Duncan & Jokers)	5
64	Parlophone R 5106	Tell Me/You Kissed Me Boy	5
64	Mercury MF 830	When My Baby Cries/Did It Hurt?	6
65	Mercury MF 847	Just For The Boy/See That Guy	7
65	Mercury MF 876	Run To Love/Only The Lonely And Me	5
65	Mercury MF 939	Hey Boy/I Go To Sleep	8
68	RCA 1746	Lullaby/I Love You, I Love You	5
69	RCA RCA 1783	A Road To Nowhere/Love Song	5
69	CBS 4585	Sing Children Sing/Exactly Who You Are	5
79	CBS 8061	Sing Children Sing/Rainbow Games (p/s, with Kate Bush)	20
82	Korova KOW 22	Masters Of War/Another Light Goes Out (p/s)	5
71	CBS 64202	SING CHILDREN SING (LP)	12
72	CBS 64807	EARTH MOTHER (LP)	12
74	GM GML 1007	EVERYTHING CHANGES (LP)	12

(see also Mitchell/Coe Mysteries)

TOMMY DUNCAN
66	Sue WI 4002	Dance, Dance, Dance/Let's Try It Over Again	25

TOMMY DUNCAN & HIS WESTERN ALL STARS
50	Capitol CL 13261	Gamblin' Polka Dot Blues/Chattanooga Shoe Shine Boy (78)	10

BARBARA DUNKLEY
71	Banana BA 342	We'll Cry Together/BOBBY DAVIS: Got To Get Away	4

DELROY DUNKLEY
70	Hot Rod HR 109	I Wish You Well/TONY & DELROY: Impossible Love	7

ERROL(L) DUNKLEY
67	Rio R 109	Love Me Forever/VIETNAM ALLSTARS: The Toughest	40
67	Rio R 131	You're Gonna Need Me/Seek And You'll Find	25
68	Island WI 3150	Once More/I'm Not Your Man	18
68	Amalgamated AMG 800	Please Stop Your Lying/Feel So Fine (B-side act. by Tommy McCook & Band)	25
68	Amalgamated AMG 805	I'm Going Home/I'm Not Your Man	25
68	Amalgamated AMG 807	The Scorcher/Do It Right Tonight	30
68	Amalgamated AMG 820	Love Brother/I Spy	10
69	Fab FAB 117	I'll Take You In My Arms/KING CANNON: Daphney Reggae	8
70	Unity UN 554	My Special Prayer/Never Hurt The One You Love	7
70	Banana BA 302	Satisfaction/CECIL LOCKE: Sing Out Loud	8
71	Big BG 324	Deep Meditation/RUPIE EDWARDS ALL STARS: Meditation Version	18
71	Big BG 327	Three In One/RUPIE EDWARDS ALL STARS: One In Three	6
71	Nu Beat NB 091	Three In One/RUPIE EDWARDS ALL STARS: One In Three	6
71	Explosion EX 2053	O Lord/KEITH with IMPACT ALL STARS: Raindrops (B-side actually "My Baby" by Lloyd Charmers)	6
72	Camel CA 87	Black Cinderella/PHIL PRATT ALLSTARS: Our Anniversary (B-side actually Tropic Shadows)	6
73	Grape GR 3039	Why Did You Do It/One Love	12
73	Count Shelley CS 3039	Girl You Cried/Where Must I Go	5
70s	Attack AT 1003	YOU NEVER KNOW (LP)	15
73	Attack ATLP 1003	DARLING OOH (LP)	12

(see also Errol & His Group, Gaynor & Erroll], Mister Versatile, Don Lee, Ken Parker, Bongo Herman)

BLIND WILLIE DUNN'S GIN BOTTLE FOUR with KING OLIVER
54	Columbia SCM 5100	Jet Black Blues/Blue Blood Blues	18
54	Columbia DB 3440	Jet Black Blues/Blue Blood Blues (78)	18

(see also Eddie Lang & Lonnie Johnson)

GEORGE DUNN
73	Leader LEE 4042	GEORGE DUNN (LP, with insert)	15

CATHAL DUNNE
79	Epic SEPC 7190	Happy Man/Sweet Woman Of Mine (p/s)	4

TONY DUNNING (& TREMELOS)
60	Palette PG 9006	Seventeen Tomorrow/Be My Girl	8
61	Palette PG 9018	Pretend/Don't Bother To Call	8
61	Palette PG 9027	Under Moscow Skies/Sixteen Candles	8

SEAN DUNPHY
67	Pye 7N 17291	If I Could Choose/Yellow Bandana	5

Champion Jack DUPREE

CHAMPION JACK DUPREE

51	Jazz Parade B 16	Fisherman's Blues/County Jail Special (78)	30
62	Storyville A 45051	Whiskey Head Woman/Shirley May	18
67	Decca F 12611	Barrelhouse Woman/Under Your Hood	18
67	Blue Horizon 45-1007	Get Your Head Happy/Easy Is The Way (with T.S. McPhee)	100
68	Blue Horizon 57-3140	I Haven't Done No-One No Harm/How Am I Doing It (with Stan Webb)	18
69	Blue Horizon 57-3152	Ba'la Fouche/Kansas City	18
69	Blue Horizon 57-3158	I Want To Be A Hippy/Goin' Back To Louisiana	18
61	Storyville SEP 381	BLUES ANTHOLOGY VOL. 1 (EP)	20
64	RCA RCX 7137	RHYTHM AND BLUES VOL. 1 (EP)	22
64	Decca DFE 8586	LONDON SPECIAL (EP, with Keith Smith Climax Band)	50
65	Ember EMB 4564	JACK DUPREE (EP)	20
60s	XX MIN 716	CHAMPION JACK DUPREE (EP)	20
59	London Jazz LTZ-K 15171	BLUES FROM THE GUTTER (LP)	70
61	London Jazz LTZ-K 15217	CHAMPION JACK'S NATURAL AND SOULFUL BLUES (LP, also stereo SAH-K 6151)	60/75
65	Storyville SLP 145	TROUBLE TROUBLE (LP)	25
65	Xtra XTRA 1028	CABBAGE GREENS (LP)	20
65	Storyville SLP 161	PORTRAITS IN BLUES (LP)	25
66	Decca LK/SKL 4747	FROM NEW ORLEANS TO CHICAGO (LP)	80
67	Storyville 670 194	CHAMPION JACK DUPREE (LP)	30
67	Decca SKL 4871	CHAMPION JACK DUPREE AND HIS BIG BLUES BAND (LP)	80
68	Blue Horizon 7-63206	WHEN YOU FEEL THE FEELING YOU WAS FEELING (LP)	70
69	Blue Horizon 7-63214	SCOOBYDOOBYDOO (LP)	70
70	Sonet SNTF 614	THE INCREDIBLE CHAMPION JACK DUPREE (LP)	12
72	Sonet SNTF 626	LEGACY OF THE BLUES (LP)	12
75	Atlantic K 40526	BLUES FROM THE GUTTER (LP)	12

(see also T.S. McPhee)

CHAMPION JACK DUPREE/JIMMY RUSHING

64	Ember CJS 800	TWO SHADES OF BLUE (LP)	30

(see also Jimmy Rushing)

CHAMPION JACK DUPREE & KING CURTIS

73	Atlantic K 40434	BLUES FROM MONTREUX (LP)	12

(see also King Curtis)

SIMON DUPREE & BIG SOUND

66	Parlophone R 5542	I See The Light/It Is Finished	8
67	Parlophone R 5574	Reservations/You Need A Man	10
67	Parlophone R 5594	Day Time, Night Time/I've Seen It All Before	7
67	Parlophone R 5646	Kites/Like The Sun Like The Fire (with Jacqui Chan)	5
68	Parlophone R 5670	For Whom The Bell Tolls/Sleep	5
68	Parlophone R 5697	Part Of My Past/This Story Never Ends	7
68	Parlophone R 5727	Thinking About My Life/Velvet And Lace	6
69	Parlophone R 5757	Broken Hearted Pirates/She Gave Me The Sun	6
69	Parlophone R 5816	The Eagle Flies Tonight/Give It All Back	6
67	Parlophone PMC/PCS 7029	WITHOUT RESERVATIONS (LP, yellow & black label)	35
69	Parlophone PCS 7029	WITHOUT RESERVATIONS (LP, re-pressing, silver & black label)	18

(see also Moles, Gentle Giant, Jacqui Chan)

DUPREES

62	HMV POP 1073	You Belong To Me/Take Me As I Am	25
62	Stateside SS 143	My Own True Love/Ginny	15
63	London HLU 9678	I'd Rather Be Here In Your Arms/I Wish I Could Believe You	18
63	London HLU 9709	Gone With The Wind/Let's Make Love Again	15
63	London HLU 9774	Why Don't You Believe Me?/My Dearest One	15
63	London HLU 9813	Have You Heard?/Love Eyes	15
64	London HLU 9843	It's No Sin/The Sand And The Sea	15
65	CBS 201803	Around The Corner/They Said It Couldn't Be Done	8
66	CBS 202028	She Waits For Him/Norma Jean	8
68	MGM MGM 460	My Special Angel/Ring Of Love	7
70	Polydor 2058 077	Check Yourself/The Sky's The Limit	6

DURAN DURAN

81	EMI EMI 5137	Planet Earth/Late Bar (glossy p/s)	5
81	EMI 12EMI 5137	Planet Earth (Night Version)/Planet Earth/Late Bar (12", p/s)	8
81	EMI EMI 5168	Careless Memories/Khanada (p/s)	5
81	EMI 12EMI 5168	Careless Memories/Fame/Khanada (12", p/s)	10
81	EMI 12EMI 5206	Girls On Film (Night Version)/Girls On Film/Faster Than Light (12", p/s)	8
81	EMI EMI 5254	My Own Way/Like An Angel (p/s)	6
81	EMI 12EMI 5254	My Own Way (Night Version)/Like An Angel/My Own Way (Short Version) (12", p/s)	8
82	EMI 12EMI 5327	Save A Prayer/Hold Back The Rain (12" remix) (12", p/s)	8
82	EMI 12EMI 5346	Rio (Part 1)/Rio (Part 2)/My Own Way (12", p/s)	8
83	Flexi (no cat. no.)	The Smash Hits Interview (flexidisc free with *Smash Hits*)	12/5
84	EMI DURANP 2	The Reflex/Make Me Smile (poster p/s)	6
84	EMI 12 DURANP 2	The Reflex (Dance Mix)/Make Me Smile/The Reflex (12", picture disc)	12
84	EMI DURAN (A-E) 3	The Wild Boys/Cracks In The Pavement (Live) (5 different p/s)	each 6
85	Parlophone DURANG 007	A View To A Kill/A View To A Kill (That Fatal Kiss) (white vinyl, gatefold p/s)	5
86	Parlophone TCDDNX 45	Notorious (Latin Rascals Mix)/Winter Marches On/Notorious (cassette)	5
86	Parlophone 12 DDNX 45	Notorious (Latin Rascals Mix)/Winter Marches On/Notorious (12", p/s)	15
87	Parlophone TRADE 1	Skin Trade/We Need You ('bum' p/s)	25

DURAN DURAN

(see also Simon Le Bon, Arcadia, Power Station)

JIMMY DURANTE

55	Brunswick 05395	Pupalina (My Little Doll)/Little People	7
55	Brunswick 05445	It's Bigger Than Both Of Us (w/ Patty Andrews)/When The Circus Leaves Town	6
55	Brunswick 05495	Swingin' With Rhythm And Blues (with Peter Lawford)/	
		I Love You, I Do (with Eddie Jackson)	7
60	Brunswick 05829	Shine On Harvest Moon/The Best Things In Life Are Free	5
63	Warner Bros WB 112	September Song/Young At Heart	6
64	Warner Bros WB 149	Old Man Time/I Came Here To Swim	5
54	MGM EPC 2	JIMMY DURANTE	
		(EP, export issue)	15
57	MGM MGM-EP 508	JIMMY DURANTE (EP)	12
57	MGM MGM-EP 597	SCHNOZZLES (EP)	10
52	MGM MGM-D 102	IN PERSON (10" LP)	20
53	Brunswick LA 8582	JIMMY DURANTE SINGS (10" LP)	20
57	Brunswick LAT 8216	CLUB DURANTE (LP)	15

(see also Ethel Merman, Groucho Marx)

ALLISON DURBIN

69	Decca LK-R/SKL-R 4996	I HAVE LOVED ME A MAN (LP)	30

JUDITH DURHAM

67	Columbia DB 8207	The Olive Tree/The Non Performing Lion Quickstep	5
67	Columbia DB 8290	Again And Again/Memories	8
70	A&M AMS 777	The Light Is Dark Enough/Wanderlove	5
69	Columbia S(C)X 6374	FOR CHRISTMAS WITH LOVE (LP)	15
70	A&M AMLS 967	GIFT OF SONG (LP)	15
71	A&M AMLS 2011	CLIMB EV'RY MOUNTAIN (LP)	15

(see also Seekers, Keith Potger)

KENNY DURHAM

58	London LTZU 15133	JAZZ CONTRASTS (LP, with Sonny Rollins)	20

TERRY DURHAM

69	Deram DML/SML 1042	CRYSTAL TELEPHONE (LP, with insert)	15

(see also Storyteller)

DURUTTI COLUMN

82	Factory FAC 64	I Get Along Without You Very Well/Prayer (p/s)	5
80	Factory FACT 14	THE RETURN OF THE DURUTTI COLUMN (LP, with sandpaper sleeve,	
		some with Martin Hannett's "Testcard" flexidisc [FACT 14C])	20/15
83	Factory FACT 74	ANOTHER SETTING	
		(LP, with perfumed cut-out insert)	12
83	VU VINI 1	LIVE AT THE VENUE LONDON (LP)	12
88	Factory FACT 244	VINI REILLY (LP, with free p/s 7" "I Know Very Well How I Got My Note Wrong"	
		[FAC 244++] by Vincent Gerard & Steven Patrick)	18
88	Factory FACD 244	VINI REILLY (CD, with 3" CD "I Know Very Well How I Got My Note Wrong"	
		[FAC CD 244++] by Vincent Gerard & Steven Patrick)	20

(see also Nosebleeds, Gammer & His Familiars, Morrissey)

IAN DURY (& THE BLOCKHEADS)

77	Stiff BUY 17	Sex And Drugs And Rock And Roll/Razzle In My Pocket	
		(p/s, orange vinyl)	8
78	Stiff FREEBIE 1	Sex And Drugs And Rock And Roll/England's Glory/Two Steep Hills	
		(p/s, free at NME party/competition)	8

(see also Kilburn & The High Roads, Greatest Show On Earth, Loving Awareness)

ANDREW DURYER

75	Real RR 2003	BALLADS OF A WANDERER (LP)	25

JEAN DUSHON

65	Chess CRL 4000	MAKE WAY FOR JEAN DUSHON (LP)	25

DUSK

71	Bell BLL 1167	I Hear Those Church Bells Ringing/I Cannot See To See You	6

PAT DUSKY AND MARINES

67	Stardust STP 1	I Fall To Pieces/This Can Be The Night	6

DON DUSSAN

68	Pye 7N 17633	Let Her Dance/Westmeath Bachelor (with The Savoys)	6

DÜSSELDORF

78	Radar ADA 5	La Dusseldorf/Silver Cloud	
		(unissued, white label promo only)	25

DUST BROTHERS

93	Dust Brothers DB's 333	Song To The Siren	
		(12", no p/s, 500 only)	75
93	Junior Boys Own JBO 10	Song To The Siren/Song To The Siren	
		(Sabres Of Paradise Mixes) (12", p/s)	25
94	Boys Own COLLECT 004	14TH CENTURY SKY EP (12", no p/s)	20
94	Junior Boys Own JBO 20	MY MERCURY MOUTH EP (12", JBO sleeve)	15

(see also Chemical Brothers)

SLIM DUSTY

58	Columbia DB 4212	A Pub With No Beer/Once When I Was Mustering	
		(with His Country Rockers)	10
58	Columbia DB 4212	A Pub With No Beer/Once When I Was Mustering	
		(78, with His Country Rockers)	8
59	Columbia DB 4294	The Answer To A Pub With No Beer/Winter Winds	
		(with His Bushlanders)	6
60	Columbia SEG 8009	SLIM DUSTY AND HIS COUNTRY ROCKERS (EP)	12
63	Decca LK 4551	SLIM DUSTY SINGSONG (LP)	18

JACQUES DUTRONC

66	Vogue VRS 7015	Et Moi, Et Moi, Et Moi/Mini-Mini-Mini	10
66	Vogue VRS 7021	Les Cactus/L'Espace D'Une Felle	6
66	Vogue VRS 7024	J'Aime Les Filles/L'Idole	6
67	Vogue VRS 7027	Le Plus Difficile/Les Rois De La Reforme	6
67	Vogue VRL 3029	JACQUES DUTRONC (LP)	15

JOSE DUVAL

57	London HLR 8458	Message Of Love/That's What You Mean To Me	18
57	London HLR 8458	Message Of Love/That's What You Mean To Me (78)	7

MARK DWAYNE

62	Oriole CB 1712	Remember Me Huh/Poorest Boy In Town	8
62	Oriole CB 1744	Today's Teardrops/Little Bitty Heart	8

DYAKS

78	Bonaparte BONE 2	Gutter Kids/It's A Game (p/s)	5

BILLY DYCE

72	G.G. GG 4532	Be My Guest/HUGH ROY: Way Down South	6
72	G.G. GG 4534	Take Warning/TYPHOON ALL STARS: Warning (Version)	7
72	G.G. GG 4537	Time Is Still Here/G.G. ALL STARS: Time — Version	6
72	Pama PM 835	Be My Guest/HUGH ROY: Way Down South	6
73	Pama PM 874	Woman Smarter/SHENLEY DUFFAS: Standing On The Hill	5
73	Bread BR 1115	You Need Love (with Millions)/G.G. ALL STARS: Love — Dub	5

DYKE & BLAZERS

67	Pye International 7N 25413	Funky Broadway (Parts 1 & 2)	12

BOB DYLAN

SINGLES

65	CBS 201751	The Times They Are A-Changin'/Honey, Just Allow Me One More Chance	12
65	CBS 201753	Subterranean Homesick Blues/She Belongs To Me	12
65	CBS 201781	Maggie's Farm/On The Road Again	10
65	CBS 201811	Like A Rolling Stone/Gates Of Eden	7
65	CBS 201811	Like A Rolling Stone (Parts 1 & 2) (demo only)	70
65	CBS 201824	Positively 4th Street/From A Buick 6	7
66	CBS 201900	Can You Please Crawl Out Your Window/Highway 61 Revisited	8
66	CBS 202053	One Of Us Must Know (Sooner Or Later)/Queen Jane Approximately	15
66	CBS 202307	Rainy Day Women Nos. 12 & 35/Pledging My Time	5
66	CBS 202258	I Want You/Just Like Tom Thumb's Blues (live)	10

(Some of the above singles were issued with four-figure catalogue numbers, e.g. CBS 1811, which are worth £4-£7 each.)

66	CBS 2700	Leopard-Skin Pill-Box Hat/Most Likely You Go Your Way And I'll Go Mine (p/s)	50
66	CBS 2700	Leopard-Skin Pill-Box Hat/Most Likely You Go Your Way And I'll Go Mine	8
66	CBS 2476	Mixed Up Confusion/Corrine Corrina (unissued in U.K.)	
69	CBS 4219	I Threw It All Away/The Drifter's Escape	5
70	CBS 5122	Wigwam/Copper Kettle (The Pale Moonlight)	6
71	CBS 7329	Watching The River Flow/Spanish Is The Loving Tongue	6
71	CBS 7688	George Jackson (Acoustic)/George Jackson (Big Band Version)	8
73	CBS 1158	Just Like A Woman/I Want You (p/s, 'Hall Of Fame Hits' series)	6
74	CBS 2006	A Fool Such As I/Lily Of The West	6
74	Island WIP 6168	On A Night Like This/Forever Young	6
75	CBS 3160	Tangled Up In Blue/If You See Her, Say Hello	6
75	CBS 3665	Million Dollar Bash/Tears Of Rage	6
76	CBS 3878	Hurricane (Part 1)/(Full Version) (some list 'Pt 1'/'Pt 2'; with/without p/s)	8/5
76	CBS 3945	Lay Lady Lay/I Threw It All Away (p/s)	5
76	CBS 4113	Mozambique/Oh Sister	5
76	CBS 4859	Stuck Inside Of Mobile With The Memphis Blues Again/Rita May (p/s;demos have "Rita May" as A-side, p/s)	12/8
78	CBS 12-6499	Baby Stop Crying/New Pony (12", p/s)	8
78	CBS 12-6718	Is Your Love In Vain?/We Better Talk This Over (12", p/s)	8
78	CBS 6935	Changing Of The Guard/Sènor	5
81	CBS A 1406	Heart Of Mine/Let It Be Me	5
83	CBS A 3916	Union Sundown/Angels Flying Too Close To The Ground (p/s)	5
84	CBS A 4055	Jokerman/Licence To Kill (p/s, embossed or standard label)	5
84	CBS A 4055	Jokerman (Special Faded Radio Version)/Licence To Kill (p/s, promo only)	12
85	CBS GA 5020	Highway 61 Revisited (live)/It Ain't Me Babe (live) (gatefold p/s)	8
85	CBA TA 6469	When The Night Comes Falling Down (Full Length Version)/Dark Eyes (12", p/s)	8
86	MCA 23633	Band Of The Hand/("Theme From Joe's Death" by M. Rubini) (12", p/s)	8
87	CBS 651 148-6	The Usual/Got My Mind Made Up/They Killed Him (12", p/s; mispressing, 3rd track plays either "Drifting Too Far From Shore" or "Precious Memories")	8
89	CBS 655 358-2	Everything Is Broken/Where Teardrops Fall/Dead Man Dead Man/ Ugliest Girl In The World (CD, card sleeve)	8
89	CBS 655 358-3	Everything Is Broken/Where Teardrops Fall/Dead Man Dead Man/ Ugliest Girl In The World (3" CD, gatefold sleeve)	8

Bob DYLAN

| 90 | CBS 655 643-2 | Political World/Ring Them Bells/Silvio/All Along The Watchtower (live) (CD) . . . . . 8 |
| 90 | CBS 655 643-5 | Political World/Caribbean Wind/You're A Big Girl Now/It's All Over Now, Baby Blue (live 17/5/66) (CD, picture disc, no front inlay) . . . . 8 |

EPs
65	CBS EP 6051	DYLAN (EP) 25
66	CBS EP 6070	ONE TOO MANY MORNINGS (EP) 30
66	CBS EP 6078	MR TAMBOURINE MAN (EP) 30

ORIGINAL LPs
62	CBS (S)BPG 62022	BOB DYLAN (LP, mono/stereo) 25
63	CBS (S)BPG 62193	THE FREEWHEELIN' BOB DYLAN (LP, mono/stereo) 25
63	CBS (S)BPG 62251	THE TIMES THEY ARE A-CHANGIN' (LP, mono/stereo) 25
64	CBS (S)BPG 62429	ANOTHER SIDE OF BOB DYLAN (LP, mono/stereo) 25
65	CBS (S)BPG 62515	BRINGING IT ALL BACK HOME (LP, mono/stereo) 25
65	CBS (S)BPG 62572	HIGHWAY 61 REVISITED (LP, mono/stereo) 25
66	CBS (S)BPG 66012	BLONDE ON BLONDE (2-LP, 8 or 9 photos on inside gatefold sleeve, mono/stereo) 40/30
67	CBS BPG 62847	BOB DYLAN'S GREATEST HITS (LP, mono) 15
68	CBS (S)BGP 63252	JOHN WESLEY HARDING (LP, mono/stereo) 20/15

(The above LPs were originally issued with rough textured labels & flipback sleeves, without 'CBS Records' credit on rear sleeve & with inner sleeves advertising other CBS LPs.)

69	CBS (M/S) 63601	NASHVILLE SKYLINE (LP, mono/stereo) 20/12
74	Island ILPS 9261	PLANET WAVES (LP, 'pink rim palm tree' label, with inner sleeve) 12
75	CBS 69097	BLOOD ON THE TRACKS (LP, orange label, red inner with painting or liner notes on rear sleeve) . . . . each 12/15

REISSUE LPs
| 69 | CBS SDDP 66012 | BLONDE ON BLONDE (2-LP, with 8 or 9 photos on inside gatefold sleeve) . . . . 20 |
| 70s | CBS SDDP 66012 | BLONDE ON BLONDE (2-LP, with 12 or 15 photos on inside gatefold sleeve) . . . . 15 |

(The above stereo reissues have smooth orange labels, with 'CBS Records' credit on rear sleeve & with ad. inner sleeves.)

| 70s | CBS Q 63601 | NASHVILLE SKYLINE (LP, reissue, quadrophonic) . . . . 15 |
| 76 | CBS Q 86003 | DESIRE (LP, quadrophonic) . . . . 15 |

PROMOS
| 88 | CBS SAMPCD 1224 | FOREVER YOUNG (CD, 18 tracks) . . . . 40 |
| 90 | CBS XPCD 116 | FOREVER YOUNG (CD, 13 tracks) . . . . 40 |

(see also Dick Farina, Band, George Harrison, Traveling Wilburys, Doug Sahm, Earl Scruggs)

DYMONDS
| 71 | Big BG 326 | Girl You Are Too Young/RUPIE EDWARDS ALL STARS: Version . . . . 6 |

DYNAMIC CORVETTES
| 75 | Contempo CS 2059 | Funky Music Is The Thing (Parts 1 & 2) . . . . 6 |

DYNAMIC GANG (Bob Andy & Marcia Griffiths)
| 71 | Moodisc MU 3511 | I'll Never Believe In You/LLOYD WILLIS: Black Attack . . . . 6 |

DYNAMICS (U.S.)
63	London HLX 9809	Misery/I'm The Man 30
64	King KG 1007	So In Love With Me/Say You Will 12
69	Atlantic 584 270	Ice Cream Song/The Love That I Need 7

DYNAMICS (Jamaica)
| 68 | Blue Cat BS 104 | My Friends/NEVILLE IRONS: Soul Glide . . . . 10 |
| 69 | Punch PH 1 | The Burner/Juckie Juckie (B-side actually by Tommy McCook & Carl Bryan) . . . . 8 |

DYNAMITES
69	Duke DU 30	John Public/CLANCY ECCLES: Fire Corner (B-side actually by King Stitt) 7
69	Duke DU 31	I Don't Care (actually by Dingle Brothers)/CLANCY ECCLES: Shoo-Be-Do 7
69	Clandisc CLA 200	Mr. Midnight (Skokiaan)/KING STITT: Who Yeah 7
70	Clandisc CLA 212	Black Beret/BARRY & AFFECTIONS: Love Me Tender 8
70	Clandisc CLA 219	Sha La La La/Pop It Up 8
71	Clandisc CLA 237	Hello Mother/FABULOUS FLAMES: Hi-De-Ho 6
69	Trojan/Clandisc TTL 21	FIRE CORNER (LP, with King Stitt) 25

(see also Clancy Eccles & Dynamites, Baba Brooks, Dennis Alcapone, Diamonds, Joe Higgs, Silvertones, Carl Dawkins, Chris Leon, Hopeton Lewis, Melodians, Cynthia Richards, Soul Twins, Stranger & Gladys, Carey & Lloyd)

DYNATONES
59	Top Rank JAR 149	Steel Guitar Rag/The Girl I'm Searching For 8
59	Top Rank JAR 149	Steel Guitar Rag/The Girl I'm Searching For (78) 15
66	Pye International 7N 25389	The Fife Piper/And I Always Will 50

ALAN DYSON
| 68 | Pye NPL 18218 | THE STILL SMALL VOICE OF ALAN DYSON (LP) . . . . 12 |

VINCE EAGER (& VAGABONDS)
58	Decca F 11023	Tread Softly Stranger & Yea Yea (as Vince Eager & Vagabonds; unissued, 2 x 1-sided demos only)............................... each 20
58	Parlophone R 4482	Five Days, Five Days/No More................................ 20
58	Parlophone R 4482	Five Days, Five Days/No More (78)........................... 20
59	Parlophone R 4531	When's Your Birthday, Baby?/The Railroad Song............. 15
59	Parlophone R 4531	When's Your Birthday, Baby?/The Railroad Song (78)........ 25
59	Parlophone R 4550	This Should Go On Forever/No Other Arms, No Other Lips.... 15
59	Top Rank JAR 191	Makin' Love/Primrose Lane.................................. 6
59	Top Rank JAR 191	Makin' Love/Primrose Lane (78)............................ 60
60	Top Rank JAR 275	Why/El Paso... 6
60	Top Rank JAR 307	No Love Have I/Lonely Blue Boy............................ 8
61	Top Rank JAR 539	(I Wanna) Love My Life Away/I Know What I Want........... 5
61	Top Rank JAR 593	The World's Loneliest Man/Created In A Dream.............. 5
63	Piccadilly 7N 35110	Any Time Is The Right Time/Heavenly..................... 5
63	Piccadilly 7N 35157	I Shall Not Be Moved/It's Only Make Believe............. 5
58	Decca DFE 6504	VINCE EAGER AND THE VAGABONDS NO. 1 (EP)............... 80
71	Avenue AVE 093	VINCE EAGER PAYS TRIBUTE TO ELVIS PRESLEY (LP).......... 15

EAGLE
70	Pye International 7N 25530	Kickin' It Back To You/Come In, It's All For Free........ 6
69	Pye Intl. NSPL 28138	COME UNDER NANCY'S TENT (LP)............................ 25

EAGLES (U.K.)
62	Pye 7N 15451	Bristol Express/Johnny's Tune.............................. 7
62	Pye 7N 15473	Exodus: The Main Theme/March Of The Eagles................ 7
62	Pye 7N 15503	The Desperados/Special Agent............................. 7
63	Pye 7N 15550	Come On Baby (To The Floral Dance)/Theme From Station Six Sahara.. 7
63	Pye 7N 15571	Eagles Nest/Poinciana (unreleased)
64	Pye 7N 15613	Andorra/Moonstruck....................................... 7
64	Pye 7N 15650	Write Me A Letter/Wishin' And Hopin'..................... 12
62	Pye NEP 24166	NEW SOUND T.V. THEMES (EP).............................. 18
63	Pye NPL 18084	SMASH HITS (LP).. 40
	(see also Valerie Mountain)	

EAGLES (Jamaica)
69	Songbird SB 1006	Rudam Bam/Prodigal Boy (B-side actually "Any Little Bit" by Crystals)................ 6
72	Duke Reid DR 2522	Your Enemies Can't Hurt You/Version...................... 6
73	Techniques TE 927	Rub It Down/TOMMY McCOOK ALL STARS: Rub It Down — Version........... 5
	(see also Jamaican Eagles, Roy Richards)	

EAGLES (U.S.)
72	Asylum AYM 505	Take It Easy/Get You In The Mood (promo only p/s)......... 8
88	Elektra EKR 10CD	Hotel California/Pretty Maids All In A Row/Hotel California (live) (3" CD).. 8
89	Asylum 969 341-2	Take It Easy/One Of These Nights/Desperado/Lyin' Eyes (edit) (3" CD, card sleeve)..................................... 8
75	Asylum K 53003	DESERADO (LP, audiophile pressing, mail-order via *Hi-Fi Today* mag)....... 12
	(see also Joe Walsh)	

SNOOKS EAGLIN
60s	Storyville A 45056	Country Boy/Alberta....................................... 12
60s	Storyville SEP 386	BLUES ANTHOLOGY VOL. 6 (EP)............................. 15
61	Heritage HLP 1002	SNOOKS EAGLIN (LP)...................................... 30
63	Storyville SLP 119	NEW ORLEANS STREET SINGER (LP)......................... 15
64	Storyville SLP 140	VOL. 2 — BLUES FROM NEW ORLEANS (LP).................. 15
70s	Storyville 670 146	PORTRAITS IN BLUES VOLUME 1 (LP)....................... 18

JIM EANES
59	Melodisc 1530	Christmas Doll/It Won't Seem Like Christmas.............. 12

EARCANDY
93	Poor Person Prod. PPPR 1	SPACE IS JUST A PLACE (LP, handmade sleeve, 500 only).......................... 15
94	Poor Person Prod. PPPR 2	TIME IS JUST A STATE OF MIND (LP, handmade sleeve)..... 15
95	Poor Person Prod. PPPR 5	SOUND IS JUST THE WAY YOU EAR IT (LP, handmade sleeve with insert, numbered, 600 only)......................... 15
95	Poor Person Prod. PPPR 8	TASTING 1,2,3, TASTING (LP, handmade sleeve & insert, numbered, 500 only)............... 15

ROBERT EARL
58	Philips PB 805	I May Never Pass This Way Again/Someone.................. 5
58	Philips PB 867	More Than Ever (Come Prima)/No One But You (In My Heart).. 5
59	Philips PB 891	The Wonderful Secret Of Love/The Boulevard Of Broken Dreams.. 5
59	Philips PB 960	The Test Of Time/The Key (78)............................ 8
58	Philips BBE 12032	ROBERT EARL (EP).. 10
59	Philips BBE 12240	THE WONDERFUL SECRET OF LOVE (EP)...................... 10
60	Philips BBL 7394	SHOWCASE (LP)... 15

EARL & DEAN
66	Strike JH 323	Slowly Goin' Out Of My Head/Little Buddy................. 5

MINT VALUE £

CHARLES EARLAND
76	Mercury 6167 360	Intergalactic Love Song/From My Heart To Yours	5
76	Mercury 6167 414	We All Live In The Jungle/Intergalactic Love Song	5
78	Mercury 6167 703	Let The Music Play/Broken Heart	5
78	Mercury 9199 831	Let The Music Play/Broken Heart (12")	10
70s	Prestige PR 10041	INTENSITY (LP)	12
76	Mercury SRM 11049	ODYSSEY (LP)	12

KENNETH EARLE
60	Decca F 11205	The New Frankie And Johnny/40-30-40	6
60	Decca F 11224	Standing On The Corner/Put Your Arms Around Me, Honey	6

EARL-JEAN
64	Colpix PX 729	I'm Into Somethin' Good/We Love And Learn	18
64	Colpix PX 748	Randy/They're Jealous Of Me	15

(see also Cookies)

EARLS
63	Stateside SS 153	Remember Then/Let's Waddle	30
63	London HL 9702	Never/I Keep-A Tellin' You	35
71	Atlantic 2091 129	Remember Then/I Believe	5

EARLS OF SUAVE
92	Camden Town GNAR 002	A Cheat/Who Will The Next Fool Be (p/s)	6
94	Vinyl Japan PAD 16	In My Dreams/Somebody Buy Me A Drink (p/s)	6

EARTH
69	CBS 4671	Resurrection City/Comical Man	25
69	Decca F 22908	Stranger Of Fortune/Everybody Sing The Song	10

EARTH & FIRE
70	Polydor 56790	Seasons/Paradise	10
71	Nepentha 6129 001	Invitation/Wild And Exciting	10
72	Polydor 2001 356	Memories/From The End To The Beginning	5
73	Polydor 2001 435	Maybe Tomorrow/Theme From Atlantis	5
74	Polydor 2121 235	Love Of Life/Tuffy The Cat	5
71	Nepentha 6437 004	EARTH AND FIRE (LP, gatefold sleeve)	175
73	Polydor 2310 262	ATLANTIS (LP)	15
75	Polydor 2925 033	TO THE WORLD A FUTURE (LP)	12

EARTH BAND
(see under Manfred Mann's Earth Band)

EARTH BOYS
59	Capitol CL 14979	Barbara Ann/Space Girl	12

EARTHLINGS
65	Parlophone R 5242	Landing Of The Daleks/March Of The Robots	35

EARTH OPERA
68	Elektra EKSN 45035	Close Your Eyes And Shut The Door/Dreamless	6
69	Elektra EKSN 45049	American Eagle Tragedy/When You Were Full Of Wonder	5
69	Elektra EKSN 45061	Alfie Finney/Home To You	5
68	Elektra EKS 74016	EARTH OPERA (LP, gatefold sleeve)	25
69	Elektra EKS 74038	GREAT AMERICAN EAGLE TRAGEDY (LP)	15

(see also Rowan Brothers)

EARTHQUAKE
74	Cloud One HIT 4	Friday On My Mind/Madness	5
75	United Artists UP 35787	Tall Order For A Short Guy/Mr Security	5
75	United Artists UAS 29853	LIVE (LP)	12

EARTHQUAKERS
67	Stateside SS 2050	Whistling In The Sunshine/Dreaming In The Moonlight	6

EARTHQUAKES
69	Duke DU 54	Pair Of Wings/I Can't Stop Loving You	7
69	Duke DU 56	Earthquake/Simmering	7

(see also Sir Collins & Earthquakes)

EARTH, WIND & FIRE
71	Warner Bros WB 6125	Help Somebody/Love Is Life	6
73	CBS 1792	Evil/Clover	5
74	CBS 2033	Keep Your Head To The Sky/Build Your Nest	5
74	CBS 2284	Mighty Mighty/Drum Song	5
74	CBS 2782	Kalimba Story/The Nine Chee Bit	5
71	Warner Bros WS 1905	EARTH, WIND & FIRE (LP, with insert)	30
73	CBS 65208	LAST DAYS AND TIME (LP)	15
73	CBS Q 65604	HEAD TO THE SKY (LP, quadrophonic)	15
73	CBS 65604	HEAD TO THE SKY (LP)	12
74	CBS 65844	OPEN OUR EYES (LP, with inner sleeve)	12
75	CBS 80575	THAT'S THE WAY OF THE WORLD (LP, gatefold sleeve with inner)	12

TIM EASLEY
68	Bell BLL 1036	Susie Q (Parts 1 & 2)	7

EAST BAY RAY
84	Alt. Tentacles VIRUS 34	Trouble In Town/Poisonheart (p/s)	4

(see also Dead Kennedys)

EASTER & TOTEM
84	Smoking Beagle/Lyntone LYN 11873/4	HIP REPLACEMENT (LP)	12

EASTERHOUSE
85	Easterhouse EIREX 1	IN OUR OWN HANDS	
		(12" EP, some with stickered w/l & hand-stencilled p/s)	10/8
88	Easterhouse EAST 1	Come Out Fighting (4.26)/Come Out Fighting (4.25)	
		(12", gatefold folder with photos & inserts)	8
86	Rough Trade ROUGH 94	CONTENDERS (LP, with bonus 7" "Get Back To Russia" [RDJ 94])	12

EAST MAIN ST. EXPLOSION
69	Fontana TF 1039	Hop, Skip And Jump/Little Jackie Horner	4

EAST OF EDEN
68	Atlantic 584 198	King Of Siam/Ballad Of Harvey Kaye	20
69	Deram DM 242	Northern Hemisphere/Communion	12
70	Deram DM 297	Jig-A-Jig/Marcus Junior	8
71	Deram DM 338	Ramadhan/In The Snow For A Blow/Better Git It In Your Soul/	
		Have To Whack It Up A Bit	10
72	Harvest HAR 5055	Boogie Woogie 'Flu/Last Dance Of The Clown (p/s)	8
73	United Artists UP 35567	Sin City Girls/All Our Yesterdays	8
69	Deram DML/SML 1038	MERCATOR PROJECTED (LP, mono/stereo)	30/25
70	Deram SML 1050	SNAFU (LP)	18
71	Decca SPA 157	WORLD OF EAST OF EDEN (LP)	12
71	Harvest SHVL 792	EAST OF EDEN (LP)	20
71	Harvest SHVL 796	NEW LEAF (LP)	20

BUGSY EASTWOOD
68	President PT 209	Blackbird Charlie/My Sun	4
(see also Exception)			

CLINT EASTWOOD
62	Cameo Parkway C 240	Rowdy/Cowboy Wedding Song (some in p/s)	15/8

EASYBEATS
66	United Artists UP 1144	Come And See Her/Make You Feel Alright (Women)	15
66	United Artists UP 1157	Friday On My Mind/Made My Bed, Gonna Lie In It	6
66	United Artists UP 1175	Who'll Be The One?/Saturday Night	8
67	United Artists UP 1183	Heaven And Hell/Pretty Girl	8
67	United Artists UP 1201	The Music Goes Round My Head/Come In, You'll Get Pneumonia	8
68	United Artists UP 2209	Hello, How Are You?/Falling Off The Edge Of The World	6
68	United Artists UP 2219	The Land Of Make-Believe/We All Live Happily	7
68	United Artists UP 2243	Good Times/Lay Me Down And Die	7
69	Polydor 56335	St. Louis/Can't Find Love	7
70	Polydor 2001 028	(Who Are My) Friends?/Rock'n'Roll Boogie	8
67	United Artists (S)ULP 1167	GOOD FRIDAY (LP)	80
68	United Artists (S)ULP 1193	VIGIL (LP)	45
70	Polydor Special 2482 010	FRIENDS (LP)	45
70s	Hallmark HM 609	EASYBEATS (LP, reissue of "Good Friday")	12
(see also Paintbox, Haffy's Whisky Sour, Harry Vanda, Grapefruit)			

EASY RIDERS
58	Philips PB 823	Salute To Windjammer/Kari Waits For Me	5
58	Philips PB 823	Salute To Windjammer/Kari Waits For Me (78)	10
60	London HLR 9204	Young In Love/Saturday's Child	7
60	London HA-R 2323	REMEMBER THE ALAMO (LP, also stereo SAH-R 6126)	16/18
(see also Terry Gilkyson & Easy Riders, Vic Damone, Frankie Laine)			

EASY STREET
70s	Muscle Music AP 591	Person To Person/Easy Come Easy Go (no p/s)	30
77	Polydor 2383 444	UNDER THE GLASS (LP)	15

EATER
77	The Label TLR 001	Outside View/You (p/s)	6
77	The Label TLR 003	Thinkin' Of The USA/Space Dreamin'/Michael's Monetary System (p/s)	6
77	The Label TLR 004	Lock It Up/Jeepster (p/s)	6
77	The Label TLR 004/12	Lock It Up/Jeepster (12", p/s)	8
78	The Label TLR 007	GET YOUR YO-YO'S OUT (EP, white vinyl; blue, green or red p/s)	8
78	The Label TLR 007	GET YOUR YO-YO'S OUT (12" EP, white vinyl; blue, green or red p/s)	8
78	The Label TLR 009	What She Wants She Needs/Reaching For The Sky (p/s)	6
78	The Label TLRLP 001	THE ALBUM (LP, with inner sleeve)	30
85	De Lorean EAT 1	THE HISTORY OF EATER (LP, 1,000 each on red, white & blue vinyl,	
		with bonus 7" [EAT FREEBIE 1, no p/s])	12
85	De Lorean EAT 1	THE HISTORY OF EATER (LP, green vinyl)	10
(see also Andy Blade)			

EATHOPIANS
69	Nu Beat NB 038	Buss Your Mouth (actually "Contention" by Ethiopians)/REGGAE BOYS:	
		Rough Way Ahead (B-side actually by Keith Blake & Hi-Tals)	8
(see also Ethiopians)			

KOOKIE EATON
68	Condor PS 1002	Cream Machine/Joke B-Side	5

EAT STATIC
92	Static Music AR 1	INANNA (12", p/s)	10
92	HAB 1	MONKEY MAN (12", p/s)	10
92	Alien ARO 2	ALMOST HUMAN EP (12")	10
(see also Ozric Tentacles, Cosmic Journey Project)			

EAZIE RYDER
78	Graduate GRAD 1	Motorbikin' (p/s)	40

EBONIES
68	Philips BF 1648	Never Gonna Break Your Heart Again/Shoeshine Boy	8

MINT VALUE £

EBONYS
71 CBS 7384   You're The Reason Why/Sexy Ways.................................... 5

EBONY SISTERS
69 Bullet BU 401   Let Me Tell You Boy/RHYTHM RULERS: Mannix
                       (B-side actually by Rhythm Rulers)................................. 6
70 Bullet BU 420   Each Time/BUNNY LEE ALLSTARS: Boss Walk 5
    (see also Sister)

KATJA EBSTEIN
70 Liberty LBF 15317 No More Love For Me/Without Love 12

ECCENTRICS
65 Pye 7N 15850   What You Got/Fe Fi Fo Fum.. 30

CLANCY ECCLES (& DYNAMITES)
61 Blue Beat BB 34   River Jordan/I Live And I Love
                       (with Hersan & His City Slickers)................................. 18
61 Blue Beat BB 67   Freedom/More Proof 20
63 Island WI 044   Judgement/Baby Please (B-side actually with Paulette)........... 18
63 Island WI 098   Glory Hallelujah/Hot Rod (B-side actually by Roland Alphonso)... 18
65 Ska Beat JB 194   Sammy No Dead/Roam Jerusalem 15
65 Ska Beat JB 198   Miss Ida/KING ROCKY: What Is Katty 15
67 Doctor Bird DB 1156 Feel The Rhythm/Easy Snapping
                       (B-side actually by Theo Beckford).............................. 15
67 Pama PM 701   What Will Your Mama Say/Darling Don't Do That 10
68 Pama PM 712   The Fight/Great 18
68 Nu Beat NB 006   Festival '68/I Really Love You 8
69 Trojan TR 639   Sweet Africa/Let Us Be Lovers 8
69 Trojan TR 647   Bangarang Crash/DYNAMITES: Rahthid 8
69 Trojan TR 648   Constantinople/Deacon Sun 8
69 Trojan TR 649   Demonstration/VAL BENNETT: My Girl 8
69 Trojan TR 658   Fattie Fattie/SILVERSTARS: Last Call 8
69 Duke DU 9   Auntie Lulu/SLICKERS: Bag A Boo................................ 7
69 Duke DU 31   Shoo-Be-Do/DYNAMITES: I Don't Care
                       (B-side actually by Dingle Brothers)........................... 7
69 Clandisc CLA 201   The World Needs Loving/DYNAMITES: Dollar Train
                       (B-side actually by Clancy Eccles)............................. 8
69 Clandisc CLA 206   Dance Beat/KING STITT: The Ugly One............................ 8
70 Clandisc CLA 209   Open Up/HIGGS & WILSON: Agane (B-side actually "Again")........ 8
70 Clandisc CLA 211   Promises/Real Sweet (both sides with Dynamites)................ 8
70 Clandisc CLA 212   Black Beret (with Dynamites)/BARRY & AFFECTIONS: Love Me Tender... 8
70 Clandisc CLA 213   Phantom/Skank Me (both sides with Dynamites)
                       (B-side actually by Barry & Affections)........................ 8
70 Clandisc CLA 214   Africa/Africa Part Two (both sides with Dynamites)............. 8
70 Clandisc CLA 221   Unite Tonight/Uncle Joe.. 5
70 Clandisc CLA 227   Credit Squeeze/DYNAMITES: Credit Squeeze....................... 5
71 Clandisc CLA 231   Sweet Jamaica/DYNAMITES: Going Up West 5
71 Clandisc CLA 232   Rod Of Correction/Rod Of Correction Version 5
71 Clandisc CLA 235   John Crow Skank/KING STITT: Merry Rhythm 5
71 Clandisc CLA 236   Power For The People/DYNAMITES: Power For The People — Version . 5
71 Pama Supreme PS 332 What Will Your Mama Say/TIGER: United We Stand 5
72 Clandisc CLA 239   Hallelujah, Free At Last/DYNAMITES: Sha-La-La 5
69 Trojan TTL 72   FREEDOM (LP).. 25
    (see also Dynamites, Drumbago, Marlene Webber, Westmorelites)

JIMMY ECHO
65 Columbia DB 7629   After Tonight/Practise What You Preach 5

ECHO & BUNNYMEN
79 Zoo CAGE 004   The Pictures On My Wall/Read It In Books (p/s, original issue with yellow or
                       grey labels, with "The Revenge Of Voodoo Billy" scratched in B-side run-off).... 6
80 Korova KOW 1   Rescue/Simple Stuff
                       (2 different p/s designs) .... each 5
80 Korova KOW 1T   Rescue/Simple Stuff/Pride (12", p/s)........................... 8
80 Korova KOW 11   The Puppet/Do It Clean (p/s) 5
81 Korova KOW 15   A Promise/Broke My Neck (p/s)................................. 5
81 Korova KOW 15T   A Promise/Broke My Neck (Long Version) (12", p/s).............. 8
83 Korova KOW 26   The Cutter/Way Out And Up We Go/Zimbo
                       (12", with bonus Peel Session cassette [KOW 26C])............. 10
83 Korova KOW 26T   The Cutter/Way Out And Up We Go/Zimbo (live) (12", with poster).... 8
84 Korova KOW 35F/   Seven Seas/All You Need Is Love//The Killing Moon/Stars Are Stars/
    SAM 202   Villiers Terrace (numbered double pack, gatefold p/s) 6
88 Korova KOW 43P   Bring On The Dancing Horses/Over Your Shoulder
                       ('cow'-shaped picture disc in stickered PVC sleeve) 8
88 Korowa KOW 43F/SAM 269 Bring On The Dancing Horses/Over Your Shoulder/Villiers Terrace/Monkeys
                       (double pack)... 6
87 WEA YZ 134   The Game/Lost And Found (unreleased alternate p/s without title, promo only).. 5
87 WEA YZ 144B   Lips Like Sugar/Rollercoaster (box set with 3 postcards)....... 6
91 Imaginary FREE 001 Foggy Notion/MOCK TURTLES: Pale Blue Eyes (no p/s, promo only).... 5
81 Korova KODE 1   CROCODILES (LP, with bonus 7", "Do It Clean"/"Read It In Books"
                       [SAM 128] & inner sleeve) 12
83 Korova KODE 6   PORCUPINE (LP, with bonus Peel Session cassette [KOW 26C]) 15
85 Korova KODE 13   SONGS TO LEARN AND SING (LP, with lyric booklet & 7": "The Pictures
                       On My Wall"/"Read It In Books" [p/s, yellow/blue labels, CAGE 004],
                       no "Voodoo Billy" run-off groove message; some signed) 40/12
85 Korova KODE 13P   SONGS TO LEARN AND SING
                       (LP, picture disc) 12
    (see also Ian McCulloch, Will Sergeant)

ECHO BASE

84	DEP International DEP 14	Out Of My Reach/Splash Down (p/s)	12
85	DEP International DEP 19	Puppet At The Go Go/Genius + Soul = Jazz (p/s)	12
85	DEP International LPDEP 9	BUY ME (LP)	12

(see also Ocean Colour Scene)

ECHOBELLY

93	Pandemonium	BELLYACHE (CD EP, 1st issue with tri-foldout sleeve)	8
94	Rhythm King FAUV 1	Insomniac/Talent (p/s)	5

ECHOES (U.S.)

60	Top Rank JAR 399	Born To Be With You/My Guiding Light	15
61	Top Rank JAR 553	Baby Blue/Boomerang	15

ECHOES (U.K.)

62	Fontana 267254 TF	Cloak And Dagger/Sounds Like Winter	7
62	Fontana TF 392	The Happy Whistler/Sticks And Stones	5
63	Fontana TF 415	The Jog/Marching Thru'	6
64	Fontana TF 439	My Little Girl/More	6
64	Philips BF 1370	Don't You Believe Them/I'll Get Over You	5
66	Philips BF 1480	Got To Run/Thanks A Lot	6
68	Philips BF 1687	Searchin' For You Baby/Listen To Me Baby	12

ECHOES & CELESTIALS (Jamaica)

61	Hornet H 1004	Are You Mine/I'll Love You Forever	12
62	Blue Beat BB 89	Are You Mine/I'll Love You Forever (reissue)	15

BILLY ECKSTINE

51	Vogue V 9005	I Stay In The Mood For You/I Want To Talk About You (78)	6
53	MGM SP 1011	Kiss Of Fire/I Apologise	12
53	MGM SP 1020	Come To The Mardi Gras/Be Fair	6
53	MGM SP 1040	Coquette/A Fool In Love	5
53	MGM SP 1055	I've Never Been In Love Before/I'll Know	5
53	MGM SP 1060	St. Louis Blues (Parts 1 & 2) (as Billy Eckstine & Metronome All Stars)	5
54	MGM SP 1082	Tenderly/Fortune Telling Cards	7
54	MGM SP 1084	Rendezvous/Don't Get Around Much Anymore	5
54	MGM SP 1095	Seabreeze/Sophisticated Lady	5
54	MGM SP 1101	No One But You/I Let A Song Go Out Of My Heart	12
54	MGM SP 1107	Beloved/Olay Olay (The Bullfighter's Song)	5
55	MGM SP 1117	Mood Indigo/Do Nothin' Till You Hear From Me	5
55	MGM SP 1124	What More Is There To Say?/Prelude To A Kiss	5
55	MGM SP 1136	Love Me Or Leave Me/The Life Of The Party	7
55	MGM SP 1140	More Than You Know/La De Do De Do (Honey Bug Song)	5
56	MGM SP 1153	Farewell To Romance/Lost In Loveliness	5
56	MGM SP 1167	Good-bye/You've Got Me Crying Again	5
56	MGM SP 1170	The Show Must Go On/You'll Get Yours	5
56	MGM MGM 925	Solitude/I Got It Bad (And That Ain't Good)	5
57	MGM MGM 948	A Man Doesn't Know/My Fickle Heart	5
57	HMV POP 341	Pretty, Pretty/Blue Illusion	5
57	MGM MGM 970	Bring Back The Thrill/Over The Rainbow	5
58	Mercury 7MT 191	Boulevard Of Broken Dreams/If I Can Help Somebody	5
58	Mercury 7MT 224	Vertigo/In The Rain	5
58	Mercury MT 224	Vertigo/In The Rain (78, vinyl pressing)	10
58	Mercury AMT 1008	Prisoner Of Love/Funny	5
58	Mercury AMT 1008	Prisoner Of Love/Funny (78)	10
59	Mercury AMT 1018	Gigi/Trust In Me	6
59	Mercury AMT 1018	Gigi/Trust In Me (78)	10
59	Columbia DB 4334	I Want A Little Girl/Lonesome Lover Blues (with Count Basie Orchestra)	5
59	Columbia DB 4334	I Want A Little Girl/Lonesome Lover Blues (78, with Count Basie Orchestra)	10
60	Columbia DB 4407	Anything You Wanna Do (I Wanna Do With You)/Like Wow	5
62	Ember JBS 703	Good Jelly Blues/If That's The Way You Feel	5
65	Tamla Motown TMG 533	Had You Been Around/Down To Earth	50
69	Mercury MF 1103	I Apologise/My Foolish Heart (p/s)	5
69	Mercury MF 1106	Gigi/Coquette (p/s)	5
54	MGM EPC 6	BILLY ECKSTINE (EP, export issue)	10
55	MGM MGM-EP 511	BILLY ECKSTINE (EP)	10
55	MGM MGM-EP 523	THE CASHMERE VOICE (EP)	10
57	MGM MGM-EP 598	FOUR GREAT STANDARDS (EP)	10
57	Parlophone GEP 8672	A DATE WITH RHYTHM (EP, with His All Star Band)	10
57	Mercury ZEP 10005	THE BEST OF MISTER B. NO. 1 (EP)	10
57	Mercury ZEP 10110	BOULEVARD OF BROKEN DREAMS (EP)	10
60	Emarcy JAZZYEP 9509	THE BEST OF MISTER B. NO. 2 (EP)	10
61	Columbia SEG 8042	BASIE-ECKSTINE INCORPORATED (EP; also stereo ESG 7827)	10/12
54	MGM MGM-D 126	TENDERLY (10" LP)	18
56	MGM MGM-D 138	THAT OLD FEELING (10" LP)	18
58	MGM MGM-D 151	A WEAVER OF DREAMS (10" LP)	18
59	Mercury MMB 12002	BILLY ECKSTINE'S IMAGINATION (LP)	15
60	Mercury MMC 14043	BILLY'S BEST (LP)	15
60	Columbia 33SX 1249	ONCE MORE WITH FEELING (LP, also stereo SCX 3322)	15
61	Columbia 33SX 1327	NO COVER, NO MINIMUM (LP, also stereo SCX 3381)	15
62	Ember EMB 3338	MR. B (LP)	12
62	Mercury MMC 14100	AT BASIN STREET EAST (LP, also stereo CMS 18066)	12/15
64	Mercury 20012 MCL	NOW SINGING 12 GREAT MOVIES (LP)	15
66	T. Motown (S)TML 11025	THE PRIME OF MY LIFE (LP, mono/stereo)	45/55
67	T. Motown (S)TML 11046	MY WAY (LP, mono/stereo)	35/40
68	Fontana SFL 13039	AT BASIN STREET EAST (LP, reissue)	12
69	T. Motown (S)TML 11101	GENTLE ON MY MIND (LP)	30
71	Stax 2362 013	STORMY (LP)	12
72	Stax 2325 084	SENIOR SOUL (LP)	12

(see also Sarah Vaughan & Billy Eckstine)

MINT VALUE £

ECLECTION

68	Elektra EKSN 45033	Nevertheless/Mark Time	8
68	Elektra EKSN 45040	Another Time, Another Place/Betty Brown	8
68	Elektra EKSN 45042	Please/Saint George And The Dragon	8
68	Elektra EKSN 45046	Please (Mark II)/In The Early Days	7
76	Elektra K 12196	Nevertheless/Please	5
68	Elektra EKL 4023	ECLECTION (LP, gatefold sleeve, also stereo EKS 74023)	45

(see also Fotheringay, Dorris Henderson, Trevor Lucas, Mogul Thrash)

ECSTASY CLUB

| 88 | Hardware HWR 001 | JESUS LOVES THE ACID (EP) | 8 |

ECSTASY, PASSION & PAIN

| 74 | Pye International 7N 25669 | Ask Me/I'll Take The Blame | 8 |
| 74 | Pye Intl. NSPL 28204 | ECSTASY, PASSION & PAIN (LP) | 15 |

ECTOMORPH

| 90s | Woronzow WOO 15 | THE FURIOUS SLEEPER (LP, with poster & inserts, 500 only) | 20 |

JASON EDDIE & CENTREMEN

65	Parlophone R 5388	Whatcha Gonna Do Baby/Come On Baby (as Jason Eddie & Centremen)	100
66	Parlophone R 5473	Singing The Blues/True To You (as Jason Eddie & Centremen)	100
69	Tangerine DP 0010	Heart And Soul/Playing The Clown (solo)	7

EDDIE & CRAZY JETS

| 64 | King KG 1000 | Come On Let's Slop/Down By The Riverside | 4 |

EDDIE & HOT RODS

76	Island WIP 6270DJ	Writing On The Wall/Cruisin' (In The Lincoln) (promos in generic title p/s)	15
76	Island WIP 6270	Writing On The Wall/Cruisin' (In The Lincoln) (some in black & white p/s)	15/5
76	Island WIP 6306	Wooly Bully/Horseplay (Weary Of The Schmaltz) (p/s)	8
76	Island IEP 2	LIVE AT THE MARQUEE (EP, p/s)	6
76	Island WIP 6354	Teenage Depression/Shake	6
77	Island WIP 6388	I Might Be Lying/Ignore Them	6
77	Island WIP 6401	Do Anything You Wanna Do/Schoolgirl (p/s)	6
77	Island 12WIP 6401	Do Anything You Wanna Do/Schoolgirl (12", white stickered sleeve)	8
77	Island IEP 5	AT THE SPEED OF SOUND (EP, p/s)	5
77	Island IEP 5	AT THE SPEED OF SOUND (12", plain sleeve)	8
77	Island WIP 6411	Quit This Town/Distortion May Be Expected (p/s)	5
77	Island WIP 6438	Life On The Line/Do Anything You Wanna Do (live) (p/s)	5
77	Island 12WIP 6438	Life On The Line/Do Anything You Wanna Do (live)/(I Don't Know) What's Really Going On (live)/Why Can't It Be (live) (12", p/s)	8
76	Island ILPS 9457	TEENAGE DEPRESSION (LP, with poster)	15

(see also Rods, Rob Tyner & Hot Rods, Lew Lewis)

EDDIE & JERRY

| 72 | Hillcrest HCT 4 | Hail Rasta Man Hail/UPSETTERS: Scorcher | 5 |

EDDIE'S CROWD

| 66 | CBS 202078 | Baby Don't Look Down/Take It Easy Baby | 30 |

EDDIE WEST

| 67 | Columbia DB 8174 | All The Children Sleep/Desolation | 4 |

DUANE EDDY (& REBELS)

78s

58	London HL 8669	Rebel-Rouser/Stalkin' (78)	30
58	London HL 8723	Ramrod/The Walker (78)	40
58	London HL 8764	Cannonball/Mason-Dixon Lion (78)	40
59	London HLW 8821	The Lonely One/Detour (78)	60
59	London HLW 8879	Peter Gunn/Yep! (78)	50
59	London HLW 8929	Forty Miles Of Bad Road/The Quiet Three (78)	60
59	London HLW 9007	Some Kind-A Earthquake/First Love, First Tears (78)	80
60	London HLW 9050	Bonnie Came Back/Movin' 'N' Groovin' (78)	50
60	London HLW 9104	Shazam!/The Secret Seven (78)	100
60	London HLW 9162	Because They're Young/Rebel Walk (78)	120

SINGLES

58	London HL 8669	Rebel-Rouser/Stalkin' (initially with triangular centre, later round centre)	12/6
58	London HL 8723	Ramrod/The Walker (as Duane Eddy & Rebels, tri-centre or round centre)	10/5
58	London HL 8764	Cannonball/Mason-Dixon Lion (as Duane Eddy & Rebels, tri or round centre)	10/5
59	London HLW 8821	The Lonely One/Detour (triangular centre or round centre)	10/5
59	London HLW 8879	Peter Gunn/Yep!	6
59	London HLW 8929	Forty Miles Of Bad Road/The Quiet Three	6
59	London HLW 9007	Some Kind-A Earthquake/First Love, First Tears	6
60	London HLW 9050	Bonnie Came Back/Movin' 'N' Groovin'	6
60	London HLW 9104	Shazam!/The Secret Seven	6
60	London HLW 9162	Because They're Young/Rebel Walk	6
60	London HLW 9225	Kommotion/Theme For Moon Children	6
61	London HLW 9257	Pepe/Lost Friend	5
61	London HLW 9324	Theme From Dixie/The Battle	6
61	London HLW 9370	Ring Of Fire/Gidget Goes Hawaiian	6
61	London HLW 9406	Drivin' Home/My Blue Heaven	6
61	London HLW 9477	The Avenger/Londonderry Air	7
61	Parlophone R 4826	Caravan (Parts 1 & 2) (actually by Al Casey)	8
62	RCA RCA 1288	Deep In The Heart Of Texas/Saints And Sinners	6
62	RCA RCA 1300	The Ballad Of Paladin/Wild Westerner	5
62	RCA RCA 1316	(Dance With Me) Guitar Man/Stretchin' Out (with Rebelettes)	5
63	RCA RCA 1329	Boss Guitar/Desert Rat (with Rebelettes)	6
63	RCA RCA 1344	Lonely Boy, Lonely Guitar/Joshin'	6

63	RCA RCA 1357	You're Baby's Gone Surfin'/Shuckin'.......................... 7
63	RCA RCA 1369	My Baby Plays The Same Old Song On His Guitar All Night Long/
		Guitar'd And Feather'd.. 7
64	RCA RCA 1389	The Son Of Rebel Rouser/The Story Of Three Loves 7
64	RCA RCA 1425	Guitar Star/The Iguana.. 7
65	Colpix PX 779	Trash/South Phoenix.. 10
65	Colpix PX 788	The House Of The Rising Sun/Don't Think Twice, It's All Right 10
66	Reprise RS 20504	Daydream/This Guitar Was Made For Twangin'................. 12
67	Reprise RS 20557	Monsoon/Roarin' 12
68	Reprise RS 20690	Niki Hoeky/Velvet Nights (Theme From "Elvira Madigan") 12
68	RCA RCA 1701	Dance With The Guitar Man/SAM COOKE: Another Saturday Night
		(withdrawn)... 12
68	London HLW 10191	Peter Gunn/Rebel-Rouser 5
69	CBS 3962	Break My Mind/Loving Bird 12
75	Target 101	Love Confusion/Love Is A Warm Emotion..................... 8
87	Capitol CL 463	Rockestra Theme/Blue City (p/s)............................. 5
87	Capitol 12 CL 463	Rockestra Theme/Rockestra Theme (Version)/Blue City
		(12", p/s)... 8

EXPORT SINGLES

58	London HL 7057	Ramrod/The Walker (as Duane Eddy & Rebels) 12
59	London HL 7072	The Lonely One/Detour 12
59	London HL 7076	Yep!/Three-30-Blues... 20
59	London SLW 4001	Peter Gunn/Yep! (stereo) 75
59	London HL 7080	Forty Miles Of Bad Road/The Quiet Three.................... 12
60	London HL 7090	Bonnie Come Back/Lost Island 20
60	London HL 7096	Because They're Young/Rebel Walk.......................... 10

EPs

58	London RE 1175	REBEL ROUSER (EP, as Douane Eddy) 18
59	London RE-W 1216	THE LONELY ONE (EP) 15
59	London RE-W 1217	YEP! (EP) 15
60	London RE-W 1252	BECAUSE THEY'RE YOUNG (EP)............................. 15
60	London RE-W 1257	TWANGY (EP)... 15
61	London RE-W 1287	PEPE (EP).. 15
61	London RE-W 1303	DUANE EDDY PLAYS MOVIE THEMES (EP)..................... 15
61	London RE-W 1341	TWANGY NO. 2 (EP)... 18
63	RCA RCX 7115	A COUNTRY TWANG (EP) 20
63	RCA RCX 7129	MR. TWANG (EP) 25
64	RCA RCX 7146	TWANGIN' UP A SMALL STORM (EP) 30
65	Colpix PXE 304	COTTONMOUTH (EP).. 40

LPs

58	London HA-W 2160	HAVE 'TWANGY' GUITAR, WILL TRAVEL (LP)..................... 30
59	London HA-W 2191	ESPECIALLY FOR YOU (LP, also stereo SAH-W 6045 with different
		version of "Tuxedo Junction")................................ 22/30
60	London HA-W 2236	THE "TWANG'S" THE "THANG!" (LP, also stereo SAH-W 6068)...... 22/30
60	London HA-W 2285	SONGS OF OUR HERITAGE (LP, gatefold sleeve,
		also stereo SAH-W 6119) 22/30
61	London HA-W 2325	A MILLION DOLLARS' WORTH OF TWANG (LP).................. 22
61	London HA-W 2373	GIRLS, GIRLS, GIRLS (LP, also stereo SAH-W 6173)............ 22/30
62	London HA-W 2435	A MILLION DOLLARS' WORTH OF TWANG VOL. 2 (LP) 25
62	RCA RD 27264/SF 5134	TWISTIN' AND TWANGIN' (LP, mono/stereo) 22/25
62	RCA RD/SF 7510	TWANGY GUITAR — SILKY STRINGS (LP, mono/stereo)......... 15/22
63	RCA RD/SF 7545	DANCE WITH THE GUITAR MAN (LP, mono/stereo)............. 18/22
63	RCA RD/SF 7560	TWANG A COUNTRY SONG (LP, mono/stereo) 18/22
63	RCA RD/SF 7568	TWANGIN' UP A STORM (LP, mono/stereo) 18/22
64	RCA RD/SF 7621	LONELY GUITAR (LP, mono/stereo) 22/25
64	RCA RD/SF 7656	WATER SKIING (LP, mono/stereo) 25/30
65	RCA RD/SF 7689	TWANGIN' THE GOLDEN HITS (LP, mono/stereo)............... 18/20
65	RCA RD/SF 7754	TWANGSVILLE (LP, mono/stereo)............................. 22/30
65	Colpix PXL 490	DUANE A-GO-GO-GO (LP)..................................... 18
66	Colpix PXL 494	DUANE EDDY DOES BOB DYLAN (LP) 18
67	Reprise R(S)LP 6218	THE BIGGEST TWANG OF THEM ALL (LP, mono/stereo)........ 15/18
67	Reprise RLP 6240	THE ROARIN' TWANGIES (LP, mono only) 30
67	G. Guinea GG(S)L 10337	DUANE DOES BOB DYLAN
		(LP, reissue, mono/stereo) 15/22
70	Valiant VS 108	THE BIGGEST TWANG OF THEM ALL (LP) 12
70	London ZGW 105	MOVIN' 'N' GROOVIN' (LP).................................... 12
75	GTO GTLP 002	GUITAR MAN (LP) 12
84	Magnum Force MFM 023	REBEL ROUSIN' (LP, Duane Eddy Convention anniversary issue,
		with overprinted labels, 200 only) 12

(see also Lee Hazlewood, Art Of Noise)

PEARL EDDY

| 54 | HMV 7M 262 | Devil Lips/That's What A Heart Is For .... 10 |

EDDY & TEDDY

| 61 | London HLU 9367 | Bye Bye Butterfly/Star Crossed Lovers....................... 10 |

EDDYSONS

| 68 | Olga OLE 010 | Ups And Downs/Sweet Memories .... 6 |

DAVID EDE BAND

60	Pye 7N 15280	Easy Go/The Blue Bird (as David Ede & Rabin Rock) 7
61	Pye 7N 15329	Obsession/Bootnik 7
61	Pye 7N 15370	Last Night/Ding Dong John (as David Ede & Go Man Go Men)...... 7
61	Pye 7N 15399	Twelfth Street Rag/No Hats On Ilkley 7
62	Pye 7N 15417	Twistin' Those Meeces To Pieces/Twistin' The Trad............ 7

(see also Oscar Rabin)

MINT VALUE £

TONI EDEN
60	Columbia DB 4409	Teen Street/No One Understands (My Johnny)	15
60	Columbia DB 4458	Grown Up Dreams/Whad'ya Gonna Do	12
60	Columbia DB 4527	Will I Ever/The Waitin' Game	10
61	Decca F 11342	Send Me/Interesting Facts	6

EDEN'S CHILDREN
68	Stateside (S)SL 10235	EDEN'S CHILDREN (LP)	35

EDEN STREET SKIFFLE GROUP
57	Headquarter & General Stores (no cat. no.)	SKIFFLE ALBUM NO. 1 (10 x 7" 78rpm clear flexidiscs in p/s)	120

EDGE
78	Albion ION 4	Macho Man/I'm Cold (p/s)	5
79	Hurricane FIRE 3	Downhill/American Express (p/s, white vinyl)	6

(see also Damned, Culture Club)

THE EDGE with SINÉAD O'CONNOR
86	Virgin VS 897	Heroine (Theme From "Captive")/Heroine (Mix II) (p/s)	5
86	Virgin VS 897-12	Heroine (Theme From "Captive")/Heroine (Mix II) (12", p/s)	10
86	Virgin V 2401	CAPTIVE (LP, soundtrack)	12

(see also U2, Sinéad O'Connor, Jah Wobble)

EDISON LIGHTHOUSE
71	Bell BLL 1153	What's Happening/Take A Little Time	5
72	Bell BLL 1206	Find Mr. Zebedee?/Reconsider, My Belinda	5

(see also Flowerpot Men, White Plains, David & Jonathan, First Class)

HARRY 'SWEETS' EDISON SEXTET
60	HMV POP 720	Hollering At The Watkins/K.M. Blues	5

LADA EDMUND JR
75	MCA MU 172	The Larue/Soul Au Go-Go	5

DAVE EDMUNDS (& ROCKPILE)
71	Regal Zonophone RZ 3032	I'm-A Comin' Home/Country Roll	10
71	Regal Zonophone RZ 3037	Blue Monday/I'll Get Along	10
72	Regal Zonophone RZ 3059	Down, Down, Down/It Ain't Easy	10
73	Rockfield ROC 1	Baby I Love You/Maybe	5
73	Rockfield ROC 2	Born To Be With You/Pick Axe Rag (with Mickie Gee)	6
74	Rockfield ROC 4	Need A Shot Of Rhythm And Blues/Let It Be Me	6
75	Rockfield ROC 6	I Ain't Never/Some Other Guy	6
76	Swan Song SSK 19408	Here Comes The Weekend/As Lovers Do	5
76	Swan Song SSK 19409	Where Or When/New York's A Lonely Town	5
77	Swan Song SSK 19410	Ju Ju Man/What Did I Do Last Night?	5
77	Swan Song SSK 19411	I Knew The Bride/Back To Schooldays	5
78	Swan Song SSK 19413	Deborah/What Looks Best On You	5
79	Swan Song SSK 19418	Girls Talk/Bad Is Bad (p/s, clear vinyl)	5
90	Capitol 10CL 568	King Of Love/Stay With Me Tonight (45rpm)/King Of Love (78 rpm) (10", p/s)	10
90	Capitol 12CL 568	King Of Love/Stay With Me Tonight/Every Time I See Her (12", p/s)	8
71	Regal Zono. SRZA 8503	ROCKPILE COLLECTION (LP, unreleased)	
72	Regal Zono. SLRZ 1026	ROCKPILE (LP)	25
75	Rockfield RRL 101	SUBTLE AS A FLYING MALLET (LP)	15
82	Arista SPART 1184	DE 7TH (LP, with bonus EP "Live At The Venue" [JUKE 1])	12

(see also Image, Human Beans, Love Sculpture, Rockpile, Andy Fairweather-Low)

EDOUARD
66	CBS 202200	My Name Is Edouard/N'aie Pas Peur Antoinette (p/s)	6

EDSELS
61	Pye International 7N 25086	Rama Lama Ding Dong/Bells	85

IAN EDWARD & ZODIACS
(see under Ian & Zodiacs)

(KING) EDWARDS GROUP
63	Island WI 040	Dear Hearts/Oh Mary (B-side actually by Ransford Barnett)	15
63	Island WI 047	Russian Roulette (actually by King Edwards All Stars)/You're Mine (actually by Douglas Brothers)	15
63	Island WI 082	He Gave You To Me/Kings Priests And Prophets (both actually by Schoolboys)	15
63	Island WI 087	Hey Girl/Skies Are Grey (both actually by Ransford Barnett)	15

ADINA EDWARDS
72	Dynamic DYN 454	Talk About Love/Don't Forget To Remember	5

BOBBY EDWARDS
61	Top Rank JAR 584	You're The Reason/I'm A Fool Loving You	10

BRENT EDWARDS
63	Pye International 7N 25197	Pride/Over The Weekend	8

CHUCK EDWARDS
68	Soul City SC 104	Downtown Soulville/I Need You	10

DENNIS EDWARDS
84	Gordy TMG 1334	Don't Look Any Further/I Thought I Could Handle It	5
84	Gordy TMGT 1334	Don't Look Any Further/I Thought I Could Handle It (12")	8

GARY EDWARDS (COMBO)
62	Oriole CB 1700	Twist Or Bust/The Franz Liszt Twist (as Gary Edwards Combo)	10
62	Oriole CB 1717	The Method/Twistful Thinkin'	7
62	Oriole CB 1733	Africa/One Fifteen A.M.	10
62	Oriole CB 1759	Hopscotch/Theme For A Broken Dream	18

(WILFRED) JACKIE EDWARDS

60	Starlite ST45 016	We're Gonna Love/Your Eyes Are Dreaming (as Wilfred Edwards & Caribs)	12
60	Starlite ST45 026	I Know/Tell Me Darling (as Wilfred Edwards)	12
61	Starlite ST45 046	Whenever There's Moonlight/Heaven Just Knows (as Wilfred Edwards)	12
61	Starlite ST45 062	More Than Words Can Say/I Love You No More (as Wilfred Edwards)	12
62	Starlite ST45 076	Little Bitty Girl/Never Go Away (as Wilfred Edwards)	12
62	Island WI 008	All My Days/Hear Me Cry (as Wilfred Jackie Edwards)	12
62	Island WI 019	One More Week/Tears Like Rain (as Wilfred Edwards)	12
62	Decca F 11547	Lonely Game/Suddenly	8
63	Black Swan WI 404	Why Make Believe/Do You Want Me (as Wilfred Jackie Edwards & Velvetts)	15
64	Black Swan WI 416	The Things You Do/Little Smile (as Wilfred Jackie Edwards)	15
64	Fontana TF 465	Sea Cruise/Little Princess	15
64	Sue WI 329	Stagger Lee/Pretty Girl	25
65	Aladdin WI 601	He'll Have To Go/Gotta Learn To Love Again	12
65	Aladdin WI 605	Hush/I Am In Love With You No More	12
65	Aladdin WI 611	The Same One/I Don't Know	12
65	Island WI 255	White Christmas/My Love And I	10
66	Island WI 270	Sometimes/Come On Home	18
66	Island WI 274	L-O-V-E/What's Your Name	10
66	Island WI 287	Think Twice/Oh Mary	10
66	Island WI 3006	I Feel So Bad/I Don't Want To Be Made A Fool Of	90
66	Island WI 3018	Royal Telephone/It's No Secret	8
67	Island WI 3030	Only A Fool Breaks His Own Heart/The End	8
67	Island WIP 6008	Come Back Girl/Tell Him You Lied	5
68	Island WIP 6026	Julie On My Mind/If This Is Heaven	5
68	Island WI 3157	You're My Girl/Heaven Only Knows	10
69	Direction 58-4096	Why Must I Be Alone/I'm Gonna Make You Cry	5
69	Direction 58-4402	Too Experienced/Someone To Love	5
69	Direction 58-4630	Oh Manio/Here We Go Again	5
70	CBS 5147	Tell Me Why Say Goodbye/Walter Walter	5
71	Horse HOSS 1	I Must Go Back/Baby I Want To Be Near You (some in p/s)	8/5
71	Trojan TR 7833	In Paradise/Take Me As I Am (with Julie Anne)	5
71	Bread BR 1107	Johnny Gunman (Parts 1 & 2)	5
76	Island WIP 6285	Come On Home/I Feel So Bad	5
66	St. Mary's IEP 701	SACRED HYMNS VOL. 1 (EP, some in p/s)	40/20
66	St. Mary's IEP 702	SACRED HYMNS VOL. 2 (EP, with St. Mary's label, some in p/s)	40/20
66	St. Mary's IEP 702	SACRED HYMNS VOL. 2 (EP, with red-and-white Island label; some in p/s)	40/20
66	Island IEP 708	HUSH! (EP)	40
64	Island ILP 906	THE MOST OF WILFRED JACKIE EDWARDS (LP)	50
64	Island ILP 912	STAND UP FOR JESUS (LP)	40
66	Island ILP 931	COME ON HOME (LP)	50
66	Island ILP 936	THE BEST OF JACKIE EDWARDS (LP)	50
66	Island ILP 940	BY DEMAND (LP)	50
67	Island ILP(S) 960	PREMATURE GOLDEN SANDS (LP)	35
69	Island IWP 4	PUT YOUR TEARS AWAY (LP)	35
69	Direction 8-63977	LET IT BE ME (LP)	18
70	Trojan TTL 40	THE MOST OF WILFRED JACKIE EDWARDS (LP, as Wilfred Jackie Edwards)	18
70	Trojan TTL 45	COME ON HOME (LP)	18
70	Trojan TTL 46	BY DEMAND (LP)	18
70	Trojan TTL 57	PREMATURE GOLDEN SANDS (LP, reissue)	18
70	Trojan TBL 156	PREMATURE GOLDEN SANDS (LP, 2nd reissue)	15

(see also Wilfred & Millicent, Wilfred & Millie, Jackie & Millie)

JACKIE EDWARDS & JIMMY CLIFF

68	Island WIP 6036	Set Me Free/Here I Come	6
68	Island WIP 6042	You're My Girl/Heaven Only Knows	6

(see also Jackie & Millie, Millie, Jimmy Cliff, Wilfred & Millie)

JIMMY EDWARDS (U.S.)

58	Mercury 7MT 193	Love Bug Crawl/Honey Lovin'	450
58	Mercury MT 193	Love Bug Crawl/Honey Lovin' (78)	90

JIMMY EDWARDS (U.K.)

60	Fontana H 260	I've Never Seen A Straight Banana/Rhymes	6
60	Fontana TFE 17296	JIMMY EDWARDS SINGS "PA GLUM" (EP)	20

JIMMY EDWARDS (& PROFILE)

79	Warner Bros K 17415	Nora's Diary/Call Me A Fraud (features Sham 69) (p/s)	5
79	Warner Bros K 17464	Twentieth Century Time/Seven Hail Marys (features Pretenders) (p/s)	5
80	Polydor 2059 240	Toys/Hard Heart (p/s)	5
80	Polydor 2059 256	Cabaret/Drag It Back (p/s, solo)	5
81	Polydor POSP 240	In The City/Five Minute Girl (p/s, solo)	5

(see also Time U.K., Pretenders, Sham 69)

JONATHAN & DARLENE EDWARDS

58	Philips PB 789	It's Magic (as Jonathan Edwards)/It Might As Well Be Spring (78)	8
57	Philips BBE 12155	THE PIANO ARTISTRY OF JONATHAN EDWARDS (EP)	8
58	Philips BBE 12179	THE PIANO ARTISTRY OF JONATHAN EDWARDS NO. 2 (EP)	8
60	Philips BBL 7412	JONATHAN & DARLENE EDWARDS IN PARIS (LP, also stereo SBBL 590)	12/15
64	RCA Victor RD/SF 7698	SING ALONG WITH JONATHAN AND DARLENE EDWARDS (LP)	12

(see also Gordon MacRae, Jo Stafford)

MILL EDWARDS

73	Action ACT 4617	I Found Myself/Don't Forget About Me	4

MINT VALUE £

PAUL EDWARDS
76	Cottage COT 301	LONGSTONE FARM (LP)	15

R. EDWARDS & SOCIAL EAGLES
73	Dip DL 5014	One Sunday Morning/Version Sunday Morning (with Allstars)	5
73	Dip DL 5014	One Sunday Morning/AFRICAN BROTHERS: Mysterious Nature (2nd issue, different B-side)	6

RUPIE EDWARDS (ALL STARS)
62	Blue Beat BB 90	Guilty Convict/Just Because (as Rupert Edwards & Smithie's Sextet)................................	15
68	Doctor Bird DB 1163	I Can't Forget/I'm Writing Again	15
69	Crab CRAB 35	Long Lost Love/Uncertain Love	7
70	Crab CRAB 41	Sharp Pan Ya Machete/Redemption.................................	7
70	Explosion EX 2030	Full Moon/Baby	5
70	Explosion EX 2031	Love At First Sight/I Need Your Care...............................	5
71	Bullet BU 494	I'm Gonna Live Some Life/RUPIE EDWARDS ALLSTARS: Rock 'In'	5
71	Nu Beat NB 082	Black Man/Tell The People	5
71	Nu Beat NB 091	One In Three/ERROLL DUNKLEY: Three In One	6
71	Big BG 320	Soulful Stew/Soulful Stew — Version Two (as Rupie Edwards Allstars)	8
71	Big BG 324	Deep Meditation (version)/ERROLL DUNKLEY: Deep Meditation............	18
71	Big BG 327	One In Three/ERROLL DUNKLEY: Three In One	6
72	Big BG 333	Press Along/Press Along — Version (as Rupie Edwards Allstars)	6
72	Big BG 335	Jimmy As Job Card (actually titled "Jimmy Has A Job Card")/ Riot (as Rupie Edwards Allstars)...............................	10
72	Big BG 337	Christmas Parade (actually by Rupie Edwards Allstars)/ UNDERGROUND PEOPLE: Santa	5

(see also R. Edwards & Social Eagles, Gaylads, Heptones, Ethiopians, Dymonds, Dobby Dobson, Keith Cole, Country Boy, Keith Cole, Laurel Aitken, Dennis Alcapone, Gregory Isaacs, Itals, Hugh Roy, Kingstonians, Little George, Mediators, Max Romeo, I Roy, B.B. Seaton, Soul Kings, Joe White)

SAMUEL EDWARDS
69	Blue Cat BS 159	Want It Want It/SPARKERS: Israel	12

TOM EDWARDS
57	Vogue Coral Q 72236	What Is A Teen Age Girl?/What Is A Teen Age Boy?	6

TOMMY EDWARDS
52	MGM MGM 466	It's All In The Game/My Concerto (78).............................	8
52	MGM MGM 540	Easy To Say/Greatest Sinner Of Them All (78)	8
52	MGM MGM 567	Piano Bass And Drums/Sinner Or Saint (78)	8
53	MGM MGM 598	A Fool Such As I/Take These Chains From My Heart (78)	10
53	MGM SP 1030	(Now And Then, There's) A Fool Such As I/Take These Chains From My Heart	12
53	MGM MGM 598	(Now And Then, There's) A Fool Such As I/Take These Chains From My Heart (78)	7
56	MGM SP 1168	Baby, Let Me Take You Dreaming/MARION SISTERS: Life Could Not Be Better	12
56	MGM MGM 894	Baby, Let Me Take You Dreaming/MARION SISTERS: Life Could Not Better Be (78)...................................	8
58	MGM MGM 989	It's All In The Game/Please Love Me Forever	5
58	MGM MGM 995	Mr. Music Man/Love Is All We Need	5
58	MGM MGM 995	Mr. Music Man/Love Is All We Need (78)............................	8
59	MGM MGM 1006	Please, Mr. Sun/The Morning Side Of The Mountain...................	6
59	MGM MGM 1006	Please, Mr. Sun/The Morning Side Of The Mountain (78)	10
59	MGM MGM 1020	My Melancholy Baby/It's Only The Good Times	5
59	MGM MGM 1020	My Melancholy Baby/It's Only The Good Times (78)...................	15
59	MGM MGM 1032	I've Been There/I Looked At Heaven	5
59	MGM MGM 1045	(New In) The Ways Of Love/Honestly And Truly	5
60	MGM MGM 1065	Don't Fence Me In/I'm Building Castles Again	5
60	MGM MGM 1080	I Really Don't Want To Know/Unloved	5
60	MGM MGM 1097	Blue Heartaches/It's Not The End Of Everything	5
60	MGM MGM 1113	As You Desire Me/Suzie Wong	5
61	MGM MGM 1130	The Golden Chain/That's The Way With Love	5
62	MGM MGM 1156	The Tables Are Turning/I'll Cry You Out Of My Heart..................	5
59	MGM MGM-EP 707	I'VE BEEN THERE (EP)..	30
60	MGM MGM-EP 712	THE WAYS OF LOVE (EP).	30
59	MGM MGM-C 774	IT'S ALL IN THE GAME (LP).......................................	40
59	MGM MGM-C 791	FOR YOUNG LOVERS (LP).	35
60	MGM MGM-C 824	YOU STARTED ME DREAMING (LP)	35

TYRONE EDWARDS
74	Invictus S INV 2542	Can't Get Enough Of You/You Took Me From A World Outside	5

VINCE EDWARDS (U.S.)
58	Capitol CL 14825	Widget/Lollipop	5
64	Colpix PX 771	No Not Much/See That Girl (p/s)	6
62	Brunswick OE 9498	VINCE EDWARDS SINGS (EP).....................................	7
62	Brunswick LAT 8515	VINCE EDWARDS SINGS (LP)	12
60s	United Artists	BEN CASEY (LP)	12

VINCE EDWARDS (U.K.)
66	United Artists UP 1166	I Like It/Skip To Ma Loo	5
67	United Artists UP 1179	I Can't Turn Back Time/The Lively One	8
68	United Artists UP 2230	County Durham Dream/It's The Same Old Song.......................	6
68	United Artists UP 2236	Aquarius/Hair...	5

WILFRED EDWARDS
(see under Jackie Edwards)

EDWARDS HAND
71	RCA SF 8154	STRANDED (LP)	18
73	Regal Zono. SRZA 8513	RAINSHINE (LP, unissued, demos only)	100+

(see also Piccadilly Line)

EDWICK RUMBOLD
66	CBS 202393	Specially When/Come Back	50
67	Parlophone R 5622	Shades Of Grey/Boggle Woggle	50

E.F. BAND
80	Rok ROK XI/XII	Another Day Gone/SYNCHROMESH: October Friday (die-cut co. sleeve)	40
80	Aerco/EF Band EF 1	Night Angel/Another Day Gone (some with p/s)	20/7
80	Redball RR 026	Self Made Suicide/Sister Syne (wraparound p/s)	30
80	Redball RR 036	The Devil's Eye/Comprende (some with wraparound p/s)	30/7
83	Bullet CULP 2	DEEP CUT (LP)	15

WALTER EGAN
77	United Artists UP 36245	Only The Lucky/I'd Rather Have Fun	4

(see also Buckingham-Nicks)

WILLIE EGANS
60s	XX MIN 714	WILLIE EGANS (EP)	15
70s	Flyright LP 6000	ROCKS, BOOGIES AND ROLLS (LP)	12

JULIE EGE
71	CBS 5431	Love/In One Of Your Weaker Moments	7

JOSEPH EGER
70	Charisma CAS 1008	CLASSICAL HEADS (LP)	15

EGG
69	Deram DM 269	Seven Is A Jolly Good Time/You Are All Princes	15
70	Deram Nova (S)DN 14	EGG (LP)	30
71	Deram SML 1074	THE POLITE FORCE (LP)	25
74	Caroline C 1510	THE CIVIL SURFACE (LP)	20

(see also Hatfield & The North, Arzachel, Bunch Of Fives, Khan)

EGGY
69	Spark SRL 1024	Hookey/You're Still Mine	15

EGYPT
88	HTD 7HTD 1	Crazy Horses /Got No Fear (p/s)	10
88	HTD HTD LP 1	EGYPT (LP, with inner)	15

EIFFEL TOWER
69	Chappell LPC 1032	THE EIFFEL TOWER (LP, library edition)	50

801
76	Island ILPS 9444	801 LIVE (LP)	10

(see also Phil Manzanera, Roxy Music)

8-EYED SPY
82	Fetish FE 19	Diddy Wah Diddy/Dead You Me B Side (p/s)	10
81	Fetish FR 2003	8-EYED SPY (LP)	15

(see also Lydia Lunch)

EIGHTH DAY
71	Invictus INV 514	She's Not Just Another Woman/I Can't Fool Myself	4
72	Invictus INV 521	Eeny Meeny Miny Mo/Rocks In My Head	4

EIGHTH WONDER
85	CBS QTX 6594	Stay With Me/Loser In Love/Open Your Mind (12", poster p/s)	8
87	CBS PHONE P1	When The Phone Stops Ringing (Single Version)/Let Me In (picture disc)	5
88	CBS SCARE Y1	I'm Not Scared/I'm Not Scared (Disco Mix)/J'ai Pas Peur (10", p/s, with PSB)	18
88	CBS SCAREC 1	I'm Not Scared (Disco Mix)/I'm Not Scared/J'ai Pas Peur (CD, with PSB)	25

(see also Pet Shop Boys, Rock Aid Armenia)

EIGHTIES LADIES
86	Music Of Life MOLIF 6	Turned On To You/Turned On To You (Alternative Mix) (12", p/s)	15

(see also Roy Ayers)

808 STATE
88	Creed STATE 003	Let Yourself Go (303 Mix)/Let Yourself Go (D50 Mix)/Deepville (12", plain stickered sleeve)	10
89	ZTT ZANG 1TX	Pacific — 909 (Mellow Birds Mega Edit)/Bonus Bird Beats/Cobra Bora (12", plain stickered sleeve)	12
89	ZTT ZANG 1CD	Pacific 202/Pacific State Origin/Pacific 303/Cobra Bora Shortcut (3" CD)	12
89	ZTT ZANG 2CD	THE EXTENDED PLEASURES OF DANCE EP (CD, withdrawn)	40
91	ZTT ZANG 19CD	Ooops!/Ski Family/808091 (live) (CD, featuring Björk)	10
93	ZTT SAM 933	10 X 10 (Vox Mix)/10 X 10 (Beats Version) (12", promo only)	10
88	Creed STATE 002	NEWBUILD (LP)	18
89	Creed STATE 003	QUADRASTATE (LP)	10
94	FCL 001	STATE TO STATE (CD, fan club issue)	15

(see also Hit Squad, Biting Tongues)

EINSTÜRZENDE NEUBAUTEN
85	Some Bizzare BART 12	Yü-Gung/Seelebrennt/Sand (12", p/s)	8
85	Some Bizzare BART 451	Das Schaben/Das Schaben (LP freebie, no p/s)	8

EIRE APPARENT
67	Track 604 019	Follow Me/Here I Go Again	30
69	Buddah 201 039	Rock'N'Roll Band/Yes I Need Someone	25
72	Buddah 2011 117	Rock'N'Roll Band/Yes I Need Someone (reissue)	8
69	Buddah 203 021	SUN RISE (LP, featuring Jimi Hendrix)	40

(see also Ernie Graham, Henry McCulloch)

EJECTED
82	Riot City RIOT 14	HAVE YOU GOT 10p? (EP)	7
82	Riot City RIOT 19	NOISE FOR THE BOYS (EP)	7
83	Riot City RIOT 28	PRESS THE BUTTON (EP)	6
82	Riot City CITY 003	A TOUCH OF CLASS (LP)	12
83	Riot City CITY 007	THE SPIRIT OF REBELLION (LP)	12

BRITT EKLAND
79	Jet JET 161	Do It To Me (Once More With Feeling)/Private Party (gatefold p/s)	5
79	Jet JETP 161	Do It To Me (Once More With Feeling)/Private Party (picture disc)	10
79	Jet JET 12161	Do It To Me (Once More With Feeling)/Private Party (12", foldout p/s)	8

(see also Britt)

EKSEN TRICK BRICK BAND
78	Aerco AERL 17	SKY STORY (LP, with insert)	30

EKSEPTION
70	Philips 318 992 BF	Air/Dharma For One	5
72	Philips 6012 219	Ava Maria/Dharma For One	5
69	Philips 6314 001	BEGGAR JULIAN'S TIME TRIP (LP)	15
70	Philips 6314 005	EKSEPTION (LP)	18
71	Philips 6423 005	EKSEPTION III (LP)	15
72	Philips 6423 019	00.04 (LP)	15
72	Philips 6423 042	V (LP)	15
74	Philips 6423 079	CLASSICS IN POP (LP)	12
75	Philips 6423 082	MIND MIRROR (LP)	12
75	Philips 6314 044	EKSEPTIONAL CLASSICS (LP)	12

MARGARET ELAINA
73	Bullet BU 522	Ben/RICHIE & NOW GENERATION: Laughing Stock Version	5

ELAINE
63	Columbia DB 7091	I Never Wonder Where My Baby Goes/Look But Don't Touch	8

ELASTICA
93	Deceptive BLUFF 003	Stutter/Pussycat (numbered die-cut sleeve, 1,500 only)	20
94	Deceptive BLUFF 004	Line Up/Vaseline (numbered die-cut sleeve, 1,500 only)	8
94	Deceptive BLUFF 010	Connection/See That Animal (numbered die-cut sleeve, 3,000 only)	6
94	Deceptive BLUFF 010T	Connection/See That Animal/Blue (Donna's 4 Track Demo)/Spastica (12", p/s)	8
95	Deceptive BLUFF 011	Waking Up/Gloria (numbered die-cut sleeve, 5,000 only)	5
95	Deceptive BLUFF 014LP	ELASTICA (LP, with flexidisc & booklet, no'd & stickered sleeve, 5,000 only)	12

(see also Suede)

ELASTIC BAND
68	Decca F 12763	Think Of You Baby/It's Been A Long Time Baby	15
68	Decca F 12815	Do Unto Others (From "Mr. Rose" T.V. Series)/8½ Hours Of Paradise	15
69	Decca Nova (S)DN 6	EXPANSIONS ON LIFE (LP, mono/stereo)	40/35

(see also Mayfield's Mule, Sweet, Andy Scott, Love Affair, Northwind)

ELASTICK BAND
67	Stateside SS 2056	Spazz/Papier Mache (unissued, demos only)	250

ELASTIC OZ BAND
(see under Bill Elliott)

DONNIE ELBERT
58	Parlophone R 4403	Let's Do The Stroll/Wild Child	100
58	Parlophone R 4403	Let's Do The Stroll/Wild Child (78)	75
65	Sue WI 377	A Little Piece Of Leather/Do Wat'cha Wanna	20
65	Sue WI 396	You Can Push It (Or Pull It)/Lily Lou	20
67	CBS 2807	Get Ready/Along Came Pride	6
68	Polydor BM 56234	In Between The Heartaches/Too Far Gone	12
68	Polydor BM 56265	This Old Heart Of Mine (Is Weak For You)/Run Little Girl	7
68	New Wave NW 001	Baby Please Come Home/Without You	6
69	Deram DM 235	Without You/Baby Please Come Home (reissue)	5
69	R&B UP 2000	Without You/(different B-side) (white label test pressing only)	7
72	Epic EPC 7943	Get Ready/Alone Came Pride	5
72	Mojo 2092 040	This Old Heart Of Mine (Is Weak For You)/Good To Me	5
72	Jay Boy BOY 70	Half As Old/Baby Let Me Love You Tonite	6
97	Joe Boy JBV 1	So Soon/Can't Get Over Losing You (p/s with numbered certificate, 300 only)	18
69	Polydor 236 560	TRIBUTE TO A KING (LP)	15
73	Ember EMB 3421	THE ROOTS OF DONNIE ELBERT (LP)	15

ELCORT
66	Parlophone R 5447	Tammy/Searchin'	10

ERIC ELDER
70	Philips 6006 081	San Tokay/Sunflower	4

ELDORADOS (Rhodesia)
63	Decca DFE 8543	THE ELDORADOS (EP)	90

ELDORADOS (Jamaica)
70	Bullet BU 428	Savage Colt/The Clea Hog	5

ELDORADOS (U.S.)
72	Mojo 2092 050	Loose Booty (Parts 1 & 2)	4

ROY ELDRIDGE & CLAUDE BOLLING
56	Vogue V 2373	Wild Man Blues/Fireworks	8

ELECAMPANE
75	Dame Jane ODJ 1	WHEN GOD'S ON THE WATER (LP, private pressing with insert)	80
78	Dame Jane ODJ 2	FURTHER ADVENTURES OF MR PUNCH (LP, private pressing with booklet)	30
87	Dame Jane ODJ 3	SWINGS AND ROUNDABOUTS (private cassette)	10

ELECTRIC BANANA
67	De Wolfe DW/LP 3040	ELECTRIC BANANA (LP, 10", original issue, tricolour label)	70
67	De Wolfe DWLP 3040	ELECTRIC BANANA (LP, second issue, with other artists)	25
68	De Wolfe DWLP 3069	MORE ELECTRIC BANANA (LP)	60
69	De Wolfe DWLP 3123	EVEN MORE ELECTRIC BANANA (LP)	40
73	De Wolfe DWLP 3284	HOT LICKS (LP)	35
76	De Wolfe DWLP 3381	THE RETURN OF THE ELECTRIC BANANA (LP)	30
79	Butt NOTT 001	THE SEVENTIES (LP)	18
80	Butt NOTT 003	THE SIXTIES (LP)	18
97	Tenth Planet TP 031	THE ELECTRIC BANANA BLOWS YOUR MIND (LP, numbered, 1,000 only)	15

(see also Pretty Things, Zac Zolar & Electric Banana)

ELECTRIC CHAIRS
(see under Wayne/Jayne County)

ELECTRIC CRAYONS
89	Emergency MIV 3	Hip Shake Junkie/Happy To Be Hated (p/s)	12

(see also Charlatans)

ELECTRIC EELS (U.S.)
(see under Die Electric Eels)

ELECTRIC FLAG
68	CBS 3584	Groovin' Is Easy/Over-Lovin' You	7
69	CBS 4066	Sunny/Soul Searchin'	7
68	CBS 62394	A LONG TIME COMIN' (LP)	15
69	CBS 63462	THE ELECTRIC FLAG — AN AMERICAN MUSIC BAND (LP)	18
71	CBS 64337	THE BEST OF ELECTRIC FLAG (LP)	12
75	Atlantic K 50090	THE BAND KEPT PLAYING (LP)	12

(see also Mike Bloomfield, Buddy Miles, Barry Goldberg)

ELECTRIC GUITARS
81	Fried Egg EGG 12	Health/The Continental Shelf (p/s, with insert)	4

ELECTRICIANS
67	Columbia DB 8228	Champion House Theme/DON HARPER & ELECTRICIANS: Shin Bone	5

(see also Don Harper)

ELECTRIC INDIAN
69	United Artists UP 35039	Keem-O-Sabe/Broad Street	5

(see also Len Barry)

ELECTRIC JOHNNY
61	London HLU 9384	Black-Eyes Rock/Johnny On His Strings	30

ELECTRIC LIGHT ORCHESTRA (E.L.O.)
SINGLES
72	Harvest HAR 5053	10538 Overture/1st Movement (Jumping Biz)	5
72	Harvest HAR 5063	Roll Over Beethoven/Manhattan Rumble (49th Street Massacre) (with withdrawn B-side)	12
72	Harvest HAR 5063	Roll Over Beethoven/Queen Of The Hours	5
73	Harvest HAR 5077	Showdown/In Old England Town (Boogie #2) (Instrumental)	8
74	Warner Brothers K 16349	Ma-Ma-Ma Belle/Oh No Not Susan	5
75	Warner Bros K 16510	Can't Get It Out Of My Head/Illusions In G Major	6
75	Jet JET 764	Evil Woman/10538 Overture (live)	5
76	Jet JET 769	Night Rider/Daybreaker (live)	6
76	Jet JET 779	Strange Magic/Showdown (live)	5
76	Jet UP 36184	Livin' Thing/Fire On High (blue vinyl, no p/s)	12
77	Jet UP 36209	Rockaria!/Poker (p/s)	5
77	Jet UP 36254	Telephone Line/Poor Boy (The Greenwood)/King Of The Universe	5
77	Harvest HAR 5121	Showdown/Roll Over Beethoven (p/s)	5
77	Harvest HAR 12-5121	Showdown/Roll Over Beethoven (12", p/s)	10
77	Harvest PSLP 213	Showdown/Roll Over Beethoven (12", promo-only art sleeve)	12
77	Jet UP 36313	Turn To Stone/Mr. Kingdom (p/s)	5
78	Jet UP 36342	Mr. Blue Sky/One Summer Dream (p/s, some on blue vinyl)	6/5
78	Jet SJET 100	Rockaria!/Poker (reissue, no p/s)	5
78	Jet SJET 101	Telephone Line/Call Boy (reissue, no p/s)	5
78	Jet SJET 103	Turn To Stone/Mr. Kingdom (reissue, no p/s)	5
78	Jet SJET 104	Mr. Blue Sky/One Summer Dream (reissue, no p/s)	5
78	Jet SJET 109	Wild West Hero/Eldorado (p/s)	5
78	Jet SJET 12-109	Wild West Hero/Eldorado (12", yellow vinyl, die-cut company sleeve, 'Jet' or picture labels)	12/10
78	Jet SJET 121	Sweet Talkin' Woman/Bluebird Is Dead (mauve or black vinyl, p/s)	6/5
78	Jet SJET 12-121	Sweet Talkin' Woman/Bluebird Is Dead (12", mauve vinyl, p/s)	12
78	Jet ELO 1	THE ELO EP (p/s)	6
79	Jet SJET 144	Shine A Little Love/Jungle (white or black vinyl, p/s)	7/5
79	Jet SJET 12-144	Shine A Little Love/Jungle (12", black vinyl, company sleeve)	20
79	Jet SJET 12-144	Shine A Little Love/Jungle (12", white vinyl, company sleeve)	7
79	Harvest HAR 5179	Roll Over Beethoven/Showdown (p/s)	5
79	Harvest 12HAR 5179	Roll Over Beethoven/Showdown (12", p/s)	8
79	Jet SJET 150	The Diary Of Horace Wimp/Down Home Town (p/s)	6
79	Jet JET 153	Don't Bring Me Down/Dreaming Of 4000 (p/s)	5
79	Jet SJET 153	Don't Bring Me Down/Dreaming Of 4000 (with different prefix, no p/s)	5
79	Jet SJET 12-153	Don't Bring Me Down/Dreaming Of 4000 (12", p/s)	7
79	Jet JET 166	Confusion/Last Train To London (p/s, some with sticker)	7/5

ELECTRIC LIGHT ORCHESTRA

80	Jet SJET 179	I'm Alive/Drum Drums (p/s)	5
80	Jet JET 185	Xanadu/Fool Country	
		(gatefold p/s, red or Jet label, with Olivia Newton-John)	8
80	Jet JET 10-185	Xanadu/Fool Country	
		(10", pink vinyl, die-cut p/s, with Olivia Newton-John)	15
80	Jet JET 195	All Over The World/Midnight Blue (p/s)	5
80	Jet JET 10-195	All Over The World/Midnight Blue (10", blue vinyl, die-cut p/s)	15
80	Jet JET 7004	Don't Walk Away/Across The Border (p/s)	6
81	Jet ELO 2	Mr Blue Sky/Across The Border/Telephone Line/Don't Bring Me Down	
		(withdrawn, some in p/s)	35/30
81	Jet JET 7011	Hold On Tight/When Time Stood Still (p/s)	7
81	Jet JET 7015	Twilight/Julie Don't Live Here Any more (p/s)	5
81	Jet JET 7018	Ticket To The Moon/Here Is The News (p/s)	7
81	Jet JET 12-7018	Ticket To The Moon/Here Is The News (12", picture disc)	15
82	Jet JET 7021	The Way Life's Meant To Be/Wishing	
		(p/s, B-side without black text)	5
83	Jet JET A3500	Rock'n'Roll Is King/After All (p/s, silver or Jet labels)	6/5
83	Jet JET TA 3500	Rock'n'Roll Is King/After All/Time After Time (12", p/s)	8
83	Jet A 3720	Secret Messages/Buildings Have Eyes (p/s, silver or Jet labels)	6/5
83	Jet JET 7038	Secret Messages/Buildings Have Eyes	
		(p/s, U.K. export to Holland)	5
83	Jet PA 3720	Secret Messages/Buildings Have Eyes	
		(picture disc, stickered PVC sleeve)	10
83	Jet A 3869	Four Little Diamonds/Letter From Spain (p/s)	5
83	Jet TA 3869	Four Little Diamonds/Letter From Spain/The Bouncer (12", p/s)	12
84	Old Gold/Harvest G 45 22	10538 Overture/Roll Over Beethoven (p/s)	5
86	Epic EPC A 6844	Calling America/Caught In The Trap (p/s)	5
86	Epic QTA 6844	Calling America/Caught In The Trap/Destination Unknown (12", p/s)	10
86	Epic EPC A 7090	So Serious/Matter Of Fact (p/s)	5
86	Epic QTA 7090	So Serious/Matter Of Fact/Matter Of Fact (Alternate Lyrics) (12", p/s)	10
86	Epic EPCA 7317	Getting To The Point/Secret Lives (p/s)	6
86	Epic QTA 7317	Getting To The Point/Secret Lives/E.L.O. Megamix (12", p/s)	12

LPs

71	Harvest SHVL 797	ELECTRIC LIGHT ORCHESTRA (LP, gatefold sleeve,	
		with inner sleeve & lyric insert)	12
73	Harvest Q4SHVL 797	ELECTRIC LIGHT ORCHESTRA (LP, quadrophonic, promo only)	75
73	Harvest SHVL 806	ELECTRIC LIGHT ORCHESTRA II (LP, gatefold sleeve)	12
73	Warner Bros K 56021	ON THE THIRD DAY (LP, cut-out gatefold sleeve)	12
76	Jet JETLP 19	OLE ELO (LP, withdrawn)	15
77	Jet UAG 30091	ON THE THIRD DAY (LP, new mix, new sleeve & inner sleeve)	15
78	Jet JETBX 1	THREE LIGHT YEARS (3-LP, boxed set of "On The Third Day", "Eldorado"	
		& "Face The Music", with booklet & inserts)	15
78	Jet JETLP 200	A NEW WORLD RECORD (LP, red vinyl, with inner sleeve)	12
78	Jet JETLP 201	FACE THE MUSIC (LP, green vinyl, with inner sleeve)	12
78	Jet JETLP 202	ON THE THIRD DAY (LP, clear vinyl, with inner sleeve)	12
78	Jet JETLP 203	ELDORADO (LP, yellow vinyl, with inner sleeve)	12
78	Jet JETDP 400	OUT OF THE BLUE (2-LP, clear or dark blue vinyl, with inner sleeves,	
		with cut-out spaceship, poster & insert)	15
82	Jet JETBX 2	FOUR LIGHT YEARS (4-LP, box set of "A New World Record",	
		"Out Of The Blue" [2-LP] & "Discovery", with booklet & insert)	20
85	Epic EP 32700	THE NIGHT THE LIGHT WENT ON (IN LONG BEACH) (LP)	15

(see also Idle Race, Jeff Lynne, Move, Roy Wood, Michael D'Albuquerque, Louis Clark, Wilson Gale & Co., Tandy-Morgan)

ELECTRIC PRUNES

66	Reprise RS 20532	I Had Too Much To Dream (Last Night)/Luvin'	15
67	Reprise RS 20564	Get Me To The World On Time/Are You Lovin' Me More (But Enjoying It Less)	15
67	Reprise RS 20607	The Great Banana Hoax/Wind-Up Toys	15
67	Reprise RS 23212	A Long Day's Flight/The King Is In His Counting House	15
68	Reprise RS 20652	Everybody Knows You're Not In Love/You Never Had It Better	25
73	Elektra K 12102	I Had Too Much To Dream (Last Night)/KNICKERBOCKERS: Lies	5
79	Radar ADA 16	I Had Too Much To Dream (Last Night)/Luvin' (p/s)	8
67	Reprise R(S)LP 6248	THE ELECTRIC PRUNES (LP, mono/stereo)	50
68	Reprise R(S)LP 6275	MASS IN F MINOR (LP, mono/stereo)	35
68	Reprise RSLP 6316	RELEASE OF AN OATH (LP)	35
73	Reprise K 34003	MASS IN F MINOR (LP, reissue)	12
97	Heartbeat HB 67	STOCKHOLM '67 (LP, gatefold sleeve with booklet)	20

ELECTRIC TOILET

83	Psycho PSYCHO 8	IN THE HANDS OF KARMA (LP, reissue of U.S. LP)	15

ELECTRIX

79	ELX 001	HOLLAND (EP)	6

ELECTRONIC

89	Factory FAC 257	Getting Away With It (white label test pressing, no p/s)	15
89	Factory FAC 257	Getting Away With It (Full Length Version)/Getting Away With It (Inst.) (12", p/s)	10
89	Factory FACD 257	Getting Away With It (Full Length Version)/Getting Away With It (Instrumental)	
		Getting Away With It (Extended Version) (CD)	10
91	Factory FACD 287	Get The Message (7" Mix)/The Message (12" Mix)/Free Will (CD)	10
93	Parlophone 10RD 6311	Disappointed (7" Mix)/Disappointed (12" Remix) (10", promo only)	12
93	Parlophone CDR 6311	Disappointed (7" Mix)/Disappointed (12" Remix)/Disappointed	
		(Original Mix)/Idiot Country Two (CD, card p/s)	8
96	Parlophone no cat. no.	Forbidden City (1-track promo CD, special sleeve)	10

(see also New Order, Smiths, Pet Shop Boys)

ELECTROSCOPE

97	Wurlitzer Jukebox WJ 19	THE VANISHING PULSAR PLANET EP (p/s)	5
97	Wurlitzer Jukebox WJ 23	SOMMERSO EP (p/s)	5

ELECTRIC LIGHT ORCHESTRA

MINT VALUE £

ELGINS
66	Tamla Motown TMG 551	Put Yourself In My Place/Darling Baby	40
66	Tamla Motown TMG 583	Heaven Must Have Sent You/Stay In My Lonely Arms	20
67	Tamla Motown TMG 615	It's Been A Long Long Time/I Understand My Man	20
68	Tamla Motown TMG 642	Put Yourself In My Place/Darling Baby (reissue)	12
71	Tamla Motown TMG 771	Heaven Must Have Sent You/Stay In My Lonely Arms (reissue)	6
71	Tamla Motown TMG 787	Put Yourself In My Place/It's Gonna Be Hard Times	6
68	T. Motown (S)TML 11081	DARLING BABY (LP)	65

ELIAS & HIS ZIG-ZAG JIVE FLUTES
58	Columbia DB 4109	Tom Hark/Ry-Ry	7
58	Columbia DB 4146	Zeph Boogie/Vucka' Magcwabeni (Back From The Dead)	6
58	Columbia DB 4146	Zeph Boogie/Vucka' Magcwabeni (Back From The Dead) (78)	10

ELIAS HULK
70	Youngblood SSYB 8	UNCHAINED (LP)	225

ELIGIBLES
59	Capitol CL 15067	Faker, Faker/24 Hours (Till My Date With You)	8
59	Capitol CL 15098	The Little Engine/My First Christmas With You	8
60	Capitol CL 15203	Young Is My Lover/East Of West Berlin	7
60	Capitol (S)T 1310	ALONG THE TRAIL (LP)	15
61	Capitol (S)T 1411	LOVE IS A GAMBLE (LP)	15

ELIJAH
71	Ackee ACK 121	Selassie High/Mount Zion	6

ELIMINATORS
66	Pye NPL 18160	GUITARS AND PERCUSSION (LP)	18

ELIXIR
85	Elixir ELIXIR 1	Treachery (Ride Like The Wind)/Winds Of Time (folded p/s with insert)	80
86	Elixir ELIXIR 2	THE SON OF ODIN (LP, private pressing with insert)	50
90	Sonic SONICLP 9	LETHAL POTION (LP)	12

ELIZABETH
73	Paramount PARA 3032	Stop Killing Me With Kindness/Oh Bird	5
68	Vanguard SVRL 19010	ELIZABETH (LP)	30

ELKI & OWEN & RIM RAM BAND
69	Revolution REV 004	Groovie Kinda Love	6

(see also Elkie Brooks, Owen Gray)

JIMMY ELLEDGE
62	RCA RCA 1274	Swanee River Rocket/Funny How Time Slips Away	10
65	Hickory 45-1363	Pink Dally Rue/Legend In My Time	6
64	RCA RCX 7132	FUNNY HOW TIME SLIPS AWAY (EP)	30

ELLI
67	Parlophone R 5575	Never Mind/I'll Be Looking Out For You	4

YVONNE ELLIMAN
71	MCA MK 5063	I Don't Know How To Love Him/Jesus Christ Superstar Overture	5
73	Purple PUR 114	I Can't Explain/Hawaii	15

DUKE ELLINGTON & HIS (FAMOUS) ORCHESTRA
78s
51	Columbia DC 602	Vip's Boogie/Jam With Sam (78, export issue)	8
52	Vogue V 2080	Caravan/Indian Summer (78)	10
52	Vogue V 2087	She/The Happening (78)	10
59	Philips PB 946	Anatomy Of A Murder/Flirtibird (78)	20

SINGLES
53	HMV 7M 156	Otto Make That Riff Staccato/Time's A-Wastin'	7
54	HMV 7MC 1	Flamingo/Jump For Joy (export issue)	6
54	HMV 7MC 9	In A Sentimental Mood/I Let A Song Go Out Of My Heart (export issue)	6
54	HMV 7M 170	The Flaming Sword/BARNEY BIGARD ORCHESTRA: A Lull At Dawn	7
54	Capitol CL 14186	Smile/If I Give My Heart To You	7
55	Capitol CL 14229	Twelfth Street Rag (Mambo)/Chile Bowl	7
55	Capitol CL 14260	Tyrolean Tango/All Day Long	6
55	Columbia SCM 5182	Brown Betty/Ting-A-Ling	7
59	Philips PB 946	Anatomy Of A Murder/Flirtibird	5
59	Philips PB 243	Skin Deep (Parts 1 & 2) (with Louis Bellson)	12
60	Philips JAZ 101	Malletoba Skank/All Of Me (p/s)	5
60	Philips JAZ 117	Duke's Place/Jones (p/s)	5

EPs
54	Capitol EAP1 477	THE DUKE PLAYS ELLINGTON (EP)	8
54	Capitol EAP2 477	THE DUKE PLAYS ELLINGTON PT. 2 (EP)	8
54	HMV 7EG 8033	DUKE ELLINGTON AND HIS ORCHESTRA (EP)	8
55	HMV 7EG 8158	DUKE ELLINGTON AND AL HIBBLER (EP)	8
55	Capitol EAP1 521	ELLINGTON '55 (EP)	8
55	Capitol EAP2 521	ELLINGTON '55 (EP)	8
55	Capitol EAP3 521	ELLINGTON '55 (EP)	8
55	Vogue EPV 1051	DUKE ELLINGTON — BILLY STRAYHORN (EP)	8
55	Vogue EPV 1060	DUKE ELLINGTON AND THE CORONETS (EP)	8
55	Philips BBE 12002	DUKE ELLINGTON — BETTY ROCHE (EP)	8
56	Capitol EAP2 637	DANCE TO THE DUKE NO. 2 (EP)	8
56	Capitol EAP3 637	DANCE TO THE DUKE NO. 3 (EP)	8
56	HMV 7EG 8189	DUKE ELLINGTON AND JIMMY BLANTON (EP)	8
57	HMV 7EG 8209	DUKE ELLINGTON PRESENTS IVIE ANDERSON (EP)	8

57	Capitol EAP 1004	DANCE TO THE DUKE (EP)	8
57	Decca DFE 6376	THE DUKE IN LONDON (EP)	8
58	RCA RCX 1006	DUKE ELLINGTON (EP)	8
59	RCA RCX 1022	CARAVAN (EP)	8
59	Fontana TFE 17117	HARLEM TWIST (EP, with Lonnie Johnson Harlem Footwarmers & Chicago Footwarmers)	8
61	Capitol EAP1 20114	ULTRA DELUXE (EP)	8

LPs

53	HMV DLP 1007	ELLINGTON'S GREATEST (10" LP)	18
53	Vogue LDE 035	DUKE ELLINGTON AND THE CORONETS (10" LP)	18
53	Capitol LC 6616	PREMIERED BY ELLINGTON (10" LP)	18
54	Capitol LC 6670	THE DUKE PLAYS ELLINGTON (10" LP)	18
54	HMV DLP 1025	GREAT ELLINGTON SOLOISTS (10" LP)	15
54	HMV DLP 1034	ELLINGTON HIGHLIGHTS, 1940 (10" LP)	18
54	Columbia 33S 1044	JAZZ COCKTAIL (10" LP)	15
54	Capitol LCT 6008	ELLINGTON '55 (LP)	15
54	Philips BBL 7003	ELLINGTON UPTOWN (LP)	15
55	HMV DLP 1070	PERFUME SUITE/BLACK BROWN AND BEIGE (10" LP)	18
55	HMV DLP 1094	SATURDAY NIGHT FUNCTION (10" LP)	15
55	Vogue Coral LRA 10027	DUKE ELLINGTON AND HIS ORCHESTRA VOL. 1 (10" LP)	18
55	Vogue Coral LRA 10028	DUKE ELLINGTON AND HIS ORCHESTRA VOL. 2 (10" LP)	18
55	Philips BBR 8044	MOOD ELLINGTON (10" LP)	18
56	London AL 3551	THE DUKE — 1926 (10" LP)	18
56	London Jazz LTZ-N 15029	HISTORICALLY SPEAKING — THE DUKE (LP)	15
56	Capitol T 679	ELLINGTON SHOWCASE (LP)	15
57	Philips BBL 7133	AT NEWPORT (LP)	15
58	HMV DLP 1172	A BLUES SERENADE (10" LP)	18
60	Philips SBBL 514	ANATOMY OF A MURDER (LP, soundtrack)	15
60	Philips SBBL 543	AT THE BALL MASQUE (LP)	12
60	Philips BBL 7355	FESTIVAL SESSION (LP, also stereo SBBL 556)	12
60	Philips BBL 7381	BLUES IN ORBIT (LP, also stereo SBBL 567)	12
61	Philips BBL 7418	THE NUTCRACKER SUITE (LP, also stereo SBBL 594)	12
61	Philips BBL 7443	ELLINGTON UPTOWN (LP)	12
61	HMV CLP 1374	SIDE BY SIDE (LP, with Johnny Hodges)	12
61	Parlophone PMC 1136	DUKE ELLINGTON PRESENTS... (LP)	12

MARC ELLINGTON

68	Philips BF 1665	I Shall Be Released/Mrs. Whittle	6
69	Philips BF 1742	Did You Give The World Some Love Today Baby/Bless The Executioner	5
69	Philips BF 1779	Four In The Morning/Peggy Day	5
71	Charisma CB 161	Alligator Man/Song For A Friend	5
69	Philips (S)BL 7883	MARC ELLINGTON (LP)	15
71	Charisma CAS 1033	RAINS, REINS OF CHANGES (LP, with lyric insert)	20
72	Philips 6308 120	A QUESTION OF ROADS (LP)	18
72	Xtra XTRA 1154	MARC TIME (LP, with Fairport Convention)	25
73	Philips 6308 143	RESTORATION (LP)	15

(see also Fairport Convention, Matthews Southern Comfort)

RAY ELLINGTON QUARTET

53	Columbia SCM 5050	The Little Red Monkey/Kaw-Liga	7
54	Columbia SCM 5088	All's Going Well (My Lady Montmorency) (with Marion Ryan)/ Ol' Man River	7
54	Columbia SCM 5104	Rub-A-Dub-Dub/The Owl Song	7
54	Columbia SCM 5147	A.B.C. Boogie/Christmas Cards	18
55	Columbia SCM 5177	Ko Ko Mo (I Love You So)/Woodpecker	15
55	Columbia SCM 5187	Play It Boy, Play/The Irish Were Egyptians Long Ago	7
55	Columbia SCM 5199	Cloudburst/Pet	7
56	Columbia SCM 5250	Hold Him Tight/Who's Got The Money?	7
56	Columbia SCM 5274	Keep The Coffee Hot/Lucky 13	7
56	Columbia DB 3821	Stranded In The Jungle/Left Hand Boogie	18
56	Columbia DB 3821	Stranded In The Jungle/Left Hand Boogie (78)	12
56	Columbia DB 3838	Giddy-Up-A Ding Dong/The Green Door	18
56	Columbia DB 3838	Giddy-Up-A Ding Dong/The Green Door (78)	10
57	Columbia DB 3905	Marianne/That Rock 'N' Rollin' Man	18
57	Columbia DB 3905	Marianne/That Rock 'N' Rollin' Man (78)	10
57	Columbia DB 4013	Don't Burn Me Up/Swaller-Tail Coat	18
57	Columbia DB 4013	Don't Burn Me Up/Swaller-Tail Coat (78)	10
58	Columbia DB 4057	Living Doll/Long Black Nylons (solo)	18
58	Columbia DB 4057	Living Doll/Long Black Nylons (solo) (78)	10
58	Pye Nixa 7N 15159	The Sultan Of Bezaaz/You Gotta Love Somebody	5
58	Pye Nixa 7N 15159	The Sultan Of Bezaaz/You Gotta Love Somebody (78)	10
59	Pye Nixa 7N 15189	Chip Off The Old Block/Charlie Brown	5
59	Pye Nixa N 15189	Chip Off The Old Block/Charlie Brown (78)	18
59	Oriole CB 1512	Carina/I Was A Little Too Lonely	5
59	Oriole CB 1512	Carina/I Was A Little Too Lonely (78)	12
60	Ember EMB S 102	The Madison/Jump Over (with Tony Crombie Orchestra) (p/s with insert)	10
60	Ember EMB S 114	Très Jolie/Dracula's Three Daughters	6
63	Ember EMB S 172	Too Old To Cut The Mustard/She Lied	5
64	Ember EMB S 188	Rhythm Of The World/If You Can't Say Something Nice	5

(see also Tony Crombie, Marion Ryan)

ELLINGTONS

| 79 | Grapevine GRP 114 | (I'm Not) Destined To Become A Loser/MILLIONAIRES: You've Got To Love Your Baby | 7 |

DEREK & DOROTHY ELLIOT

| 72 | Trailer LER 2023 | DEREK & DOROTHY ELLIOT (LP) | 15 |
| 76 | Tradition TSR 025 | YORKSHIRE RELISH (LP) | 12 |

MINT VALUE £

MAMA CASS (ELLIOT)
68	RCA Victor RCA 1726	Dream A Little Dream Of Me/Midnight Voyage (as Mama Cass)	6
68	Stateside SS 8002	California Earthquake/Talkin' To Your Toothbrush	5
69	Stateside SS 8014	I Can Dream Can't I?/Move A Little Closer Baby	5
69	Stateside SS 8021	It's Getting Better/Who's To Blame? (as Mama Cass)	6
69	Stateside SS 8031	Make Your Own Kind Of Music/Lady Love	6
70	Stateside SS 8039	New World Coming/Blow Me A Kiss	5
70	Stateside SS 8057	A Song That Never Comes/I Can Dream, Can't I?	5
71	Probe PRO 512	Good Times Are Comin'/Welcome To The World	5
71	Probe PRO 519	Easy Come, Easy Go/Ain't Nobody Else Like You	5
68	Stateside S(S)L 5004	DREAM A LITTLE DREAM (LP)	15
69	Stateside S(S)L 5014	BUBBLEGUM, LEMONADE AND SOMETHING FOR MAMA (LP)	15

(see also Mamas & Papas, Big Three, Dave Mason & Cass Elliot, Mugwumps)

BERN ELLIOTT (& FENMEN)
63	Decca F 11770	Money/Nobody But Me	6
64	Decca F 11852	New Orleans/Everybody Needs A Little Love	7
64	Decca F 11970	Good Times/What Do You Want With My Baby (as Bern Elliott & Klan)	7
65	Decca F 12051	Guess Who/Make It Easy On Yourself (solo)	8
65	Decca F 12171	Lipstick Traces/Voodoo Woman (solo)	7
64	Decca DFE 8561	BERN ELLIOTT AND THE FENMEN (EP)	25

(see also Fenmen)

BILL ELLIOTT & ELASTIC OZ BAND
71	Apple APPLE 36	God Save Us/Do The Oz (initially with p/s)	30/15

(see also Splinter, John Lennon/Yoko Ono)

JACK ELLIOTT
69	Leader LEA 4001	JACK ELLIOTT OF BIRTLEY (LP, with booklet)	15

(see also Elliotts Of Birtley)

MARI ELLIOTT
76	GTO GT 58	Silly Billy/Half Past One	15

(see also Poly Styrene, X Ray Spex)

MIKE ELLIOTT
72	Ackee ACK 151	Milk And Honey/Burst A Shirt	12

PETER ELLIOTT
57	Parlophone R 4355	To The Aisle/All At Once (You Love Her)	8
58	Parlophone R 4457	Devotion/No Fool Like An Old Fool	6
58	Parlophone R 4457	Devotion/No Fool Like An Old Fool (78)	8
59	Parlophone R 4514	Call Me/Flamingo	5
59	Parlophone R 4514	Call Me/Flamingo (78)	8
59	Parlophone R 4529	The Young Have No Time/Over And Over	5
59	Parlophone R 4529	The Young Have No Time/Over And Over (78)	10
61	Top Rank JAR 390	Waiting For Robert E. Lee/Toot Toot Tootsie	5
66	Strike JH 311	Thinking/Song Is Love	5
60s	Honey Hit TB 123	The Devil's Workshop/Three Little Peggies (p/s)	5

(RAMBLIN') JACK ELLIOTT
54	Topic TRC 98	Talking Miner Blues/Pretty Boy Floyd (78)	20
65	Fontana TF 575	More Pretty Girls/Roll On Buddy (as Ramblin' Jack Elliott)	5
65	Columbia DB 7593	Rusty Jigs And Sandy Sam/Rocky Mountain Belle (as Ramblin' Jack Elliott)	5
63	Collector JEA 5	RAMBLING JACK ELLIOTT (EP)	20
64	Collector JEA 6	BLUES AND COUNTRY (EP)	20
55	Topic T 5	WOODY GUTHRIE'S BLUES (8" mini-LP)	25
57	Topic 10T 15	JACK TAKES THE FLOOR (10" LP)	25
59	Encore ENC 194	IN LONDON (LP)	20
60	Columbia 33SX 1291	RAMBLIN' JACK ELLIOTT SINGS WOODY GUTHRIE & JIMMIE RODGERS (LP)	20
65	Fontana TFL 6044	JACK ELLIOTT (LP)	15
65	Stateside SL 10143	JACK ELLIOTT COUNTRY STYLE (LP)	15
66	Stateside SL 10167	SINGS THE SONGS OF WOODY GUTHRIE (LP)	15
70	Reprise RSLP 6387	BILL DURHAM SACKS AND RAILROAD SACKS (LP)	15

SHAWN ELLIOTT
62	Stateside SS 124	Goodbye My Lover/Ain't That A Shame	6
63	Stateside SS 174	Sincerely And Tenderly/Why Don't You Love Me Anymore	6
64	Rio R 51	Shame And Scandal In The Family/My Girl	8
64	Columbia DB 7418	My Girl/Shame And Scandal In The Family (reissue)	7

ELLIOTTS OF BIRTLEY
69	Xtra XTRA 1091	A MUSICAL PORTRAIT OF A DURHAM MINING FAMILY (LP)	15

(see also Jack Elliott)

ELLIOTT'S SUNSHINE
68	Philips BF 1649	Is It Too Late/'Cause I'm Lonely	6

ELLIS/ELLIS GROUP
(see under Steve Ellis)

ALTON ELLIS (& FLAMES)
65	Island WI 239	Dance Crasher (with Flames)/BABA BROOKS: Vitamin A	20
65	Island WI 241	You Are Not To Blame/BABA BROOKS: Teenage Ska	18
66	Doctor Bird DB 1044	Blessings Of Love/Nothing Sweeter (as Alton & Flames)	18
66	Doctor Bird DB 1049	The Preacher (as Alton & Flames)/LYNN TAITT & COMETS: Tender Loving Care	15
66	Doctor Bird DB 1055	Shake It (with Flames)/SILVERTONES: Whoo Baby	18
66	Doctor Bird DB 1059	Girl I've Got A Date (with Flames)/LYN TAITT & TOMMY McCOOK: The Yellow Basket	18
67	Island WI 3046	Cry Tough (with Flames)/TOMMY McCOOK & SUPERSONICS: Mr Solo	20

67	Treasure Isle TI 7004	Rocksteady (with Flames)/TOMMY McCOOK & SUPERSONICS:	
		Wall Street Shuffle	18
67	Treasure Isle TI 7010	Duke Of Earl/All My Tears (with Flames)	18
67	Treasure Isle TI 7016	Ain't That Loving You (with Flames)/TOMMY McCOOK & SUPERSONICS:	
		Tommy's Rocksteady	18
67	Treasure Isle TI 7030	Oowee Baby/How Can I (with Flames)	18
67	Treasure Isle TI 7044	Willow Tree/I Can't Stop Now	18
67	Trojan TR 004	Ain't That Loving You (with Flames)/TOMMY McCOOK & SUPERSONICS:	
		Comet Rocksteady	18
67	Trojan TR 009	Wise Birds Follow Spring/TOMMY McCOOK & SUPERSONICS: Soul Rock	18
67	Studio One SO 2028	I Am Just A Guy/SOUL VENDORS: Just A Little Bit Of Soul	18
67	Studio One SO 2033	Only Sixteen/Baby (both actually by Heptones)	18
68	Studio One SO 2037	Live And Learn/HEPTONES: Cry Baby Cry	18
68	Trojan TR 630	I Can't Stand It/Trying To Reach My Goal	12
68	Trojan TR 642	Breaking Up/Party Time	12
68	Nu Beat NB 010	I Can't Stand It/Tonight	8
68	Nu Beat NB 013	Bye Bye Love/MONTY MORRIS: My Lonely Days	8
68	Nu Beat NB 014	La La Means I Love You/Give Me Your Love	8
68	Pama PM 707	The Message/Some Talk	8
68	Pama PM 717	My Time Is The Right Time/JOHNNY MOORE: Tribute To Sir Alex	8
68	Coxsone CS 7071	A Fool/SOUL VENDORS: West Of The Sun	20
69	Studio One SO 2084	Change Of Plans/CABLES: He'll Break Your Heart	
		(B-side act. by Mad Lads)	15
69	Gas GAS 105	Diana/Some Talk	7
69	Bamboo BAM 2	Better Example/DUKE MORGAN: Lick Olt Back	8
69	Duke DU 14	Diana/Personality	8
70	Duke DU 72	Remember That Sunday/TOMMY McCOOK & SUPERSONICS: Last Lick	7
70	Gas GAS 151	Suzie/Life Is Down In Denver	
		(some copies credit Alton Ellis & Flames)	6
70	Gas GAS 161	Deliver Us/NEVILLE HINDS: Originator	6
70	Duke Reid DR 2501	What Does It Take To Win Your Love/TOMMY McCOOK: Reggae Meringue	10
70	Duke Reid DR 2512	You Made Me So Very Happy/TOMMY McCOOK & SUPERSONICS: Continental	8
70	Bamboo BAM 29	Tumbling Tears/SOUND DIMENSION: Today Version	8
70	Techniques TE 903	It's Your Thing/TECHNIQUES ALL STARS: Get Left	7
70	Techniques TE 905	I'll Be Waiting/TECHNIQUES ALL STARS: I'll Be Waiting Version	7
71	Banana BA 318	Sunday Coming/CARL BRYAN: Sunday Version	8
71	Banana BA 330	Bam Bye/Keep On Yearning	8
71	Banana BA 347	Hey World/Harder And Harder	8
71	Gas GAS 164	Back To Africa/NEVILLE HINDS: Originator	6
71	Fab FAB 165	Good Good Loving/Since I Fell For You	20
71	Bullet BU 466	Black Man's Pride/LEROY PALMER: Groove With It	12
71	Bullet BU 485	Don't Care/True Born African	6
71	Smash SMA 2319	A Little Loving/DELROY WILSON & ALTON ELLIS: Loving Version	7
71	Smash SMA 2320	I'll Be There/ITALS: Rude Boy Train	7
71	Big Shot BI 589	Be True/Be True — Version	5
72	Big Shot BI 602	I'm Trying/Luna's Mood	5
72	Spur SP 3	All That We Need Is Love/KEITH HUDSON: Better Love	25
72	Grape GR 3029	Big Bad Boy/HUDSON'S ALLSTARS: Big Bad Version	6
72	Ackee ACK 145	Oppression/Oppression Version	
		(both with Zoot Simms)	20
72	Ackee ACK 148	Let's Stay Together/Version	12
72	Ackee ACK 502	Too Late To Turn Back Now/IMPACT ALLSTARS: Version	10
72	Jackpot JP 796	Play It Cool/AGGROVATORS: King Of The Zozas	6
72	Camel CA 94	Wonderful World/FAB DIMENSION: Wonderful Version	6
72	Pama PM 840	Girl I've Got A Date/Eat Bread	5
72	Pama Supreme PS 347	Moon River/I Can't Find Out	5
72	Pama Supreme PS 361	Working On A Groovy Thing/HARLESDEN SKANKERS: Version	6
73	Ackee ACK 511	Alton's Official Daughter/Aquarius Dub	
		(both with Herman)	12
73	Harry J. HJ 6653	Deliver Us To Africa/Nyah Medley	5
73	Pyramid PYR 7003	Truly/LLOYD COXSONE SIX: Cruising	5
67	Coxsone CSL 8008	SINGS ROCK AND SOUL (LP)	90
71	Bamboo BDLPS 214	SUNDAY COMING (LP)	50
73	Count Shelly SSLO 02	ALTON ELLIS'S GREATEST HITS (LP)	30

(see also Alton & Eddy, Hortense Ellis, Hortense & Alton, Flames [Jamaica], Righteous Flames, Tony Gordon)

BOBBY ELLIS

| 68 | Island WI 3136 | Dollar A Head (with Crystalites)/RUDY MILLS: I'm Trapped | 15 |
| 74 | Dragon DRA 1033 | Up Park Camp/Verse 4 | 5 |

(see also Jerry Lewis, Derrick Harriot, Rudy Mills, Crystalites, Keith & Tex, Eric Morris, Roy Richards, Soul Vendors)

DAVE ELLIS

| 73 | Sonet SNTF 646 | THE DAVE ELLIS ALBUM (LP, with Gordon Giltrap) | 12 |

(see also Gordon Giltrap)

DON ELLIS (ORCHESTRA)

69	CBS 4518	Eli's Comin'/House In The Country	5
67	Fontana (S)TL 5426	'LIVE' AT MONTEREY (LP)	12
68	Liberty LBL/LBS 83060	THE DON ELLIS ORCHESTRA LIVE (LP)	12
68	CBS 63230	ELECTRIC BATH (LP)	12
68	CBS 63356	SHOCK TREATMENT (LP)	12
69	CBS 63503	AUTUMN (LP)	12
69	CBS 63680	THE NEW DON ELLIS BAND GOES UNDERGROUND (LP)	12
71	CBS 66261	DON ELLIS AT FILLMORE (2-LP)	18
72	CBS GQ 30927	TEARS OF JOY (LP, quadrophonic)	12

HERB ELLIS-JIMMY GIUFFRE ALL STARS

| 60 | HMV POP 721 | Goose Grease/My Old Flame | 4 |

MINT VALUE £

HORTENSE ELLIS
63	R&B JB 101	I'll Come Softly/I'm In Love (with Alton Ellis)	12
65	Blue Beat BB 295	I've Been A Fool/Hold Me Tenderly	15
67	Fab FAB 20	Somebody Help Me (with Buster's All Stars)/ PRINCE BUSTER & ALL STARS: Rock & Shake	10
70	Bullet BU 427	Last Date/PAT SATCHMO: Cherry Pink	6
70	Gas GAS 160	To The Other Man/MUSIC BLENDERS: Raindrops	6
70	Techniques TE 908	To The Other Man/TECHNIQUES ALL STARS: To The Other Man Version	6
72	Green Door GD 4035	Bringing In The Sheaves (with Stranger Cole)/Version	5

(see also Hortense & Alton, Hortense & Delroy, Hortense & Jackie, Alton Ellis, Duke Reid, Three Tops, Jackie Opal)

JOHN ELLIS
80	Rat Race RAT 6	Hit Man/Hollow Graham (p/s)	5

(see also Vibrators, Snivelling Shits)

JO-JO ELLIS
72	Fury FY 302	The Fly/Perdona Mia	18

LARRY ELLIS
58	Felsted AF 110	Buzz Goes The Bee/Nothing You Can Do	12
58	Felsted AF 110	Buzz Goes The Bee/Nothing You Can Do (78)	25

MATTHEW ELLIS
71	Regal Zonophone RZ 3033	Avalon/You Are	5
71	Regal Zonophone RZ 3039	Birthday Song/Salvation	5
72	Regal Zonophone RZ 3045	Palace Of Plenty/Two By Two	5
71	Regal Zono. SRZA 8501	MATTHEW ELLIS (LP)	5
72	Regal Zono. SRZA 8505	AM I...? (LP)	25

(see also Procol Harum, Chris Spedding)

SHIRLEY ELLIS
63	London HLR 9824	The Nitty Gritty/Give Me A List	6
65	London HLR 9946	The Name Game/Whisper To Me Wind	6
65	London HLR 9961	The Clapping Song/This Is Beautiful	6
65	London HLR 9973	The Puzzle Song/I See It, I Like It, I Want It	6
66	London HLR 10021	Ever See A Diver Kiss His Wife While The Bubbles Bounce About Above The Water?/Stardust	6
67	CBS 202606	Soul Time/Waitin'	15
67	CBS 2817	Sugar Let's Shing-A-Ling/How Lonely Is Lonely	8
71	CBS 7463	Soul Time/Waitin' (reissue)	5
77	CBS 4901	Soul Time/Waitin' (2nd reissue, coloured vinyl)	5
67	CBS (S)BPG 63044	SOUL TIME WITH SHIRLEY ELLIS (LP)	35

STEVE ELLIS
70	CBS 4992	Loot/More More More	6
70	CBS 5199	Evie/Fat Crow	5
71	CBS 7037	Take Your Love/Jingle Jangle Jasmine	5
71	CBS 7411	Hold On/Goody Goody Dancing Shoes	5
72	Epic EPC 8318	Good To Be Alive/Morning Paper (as Ellis)	5
73	Epic SEPC 1627	Open Road/Leaving In The Morning (as Ellis)	5
73	Epic EPC 1803	Loud And Lazy Love Song/Goodbye Boredom (as Ellis Group)	5
74	Epic SEPC 1052	El Doomo/Your Game (as Ellis Group)	5
88	Ocean OCN 2	Hot Lips/Little One (withdrawn, no p/s)	6
72	Epic EPC 64878	RIDING ON THE CREST OF A SLUMP (LP, as Ellis Group)	15
73	Epic EPC 65650	WHY NOT? (LP, as Ellis Group)	12

(see also Love Affair, Widowmaker, Zoot Money, Peter Bardens)

ANDY ELLISON
68	Track 604 018	It's Been A Long Time/JOHN'S CHILDREN: Arthur Green	50
68	CBS 3357	Fool From Upper Eden/Another Lucky Lie	50
68	S.N.B. 55-3308	You Can't Do That/Casbah	60
68	S.N.B. 55-3308	You Can't Do That/Cornflake Zoo (second issue, different B-side)	60

(see also John's Children, Jet, Radio Stars)

LORRAINE ELLISON
66	Warner Bros WB 5850	Stay With Me/I Got My Baby Back (re-pressed in 1969)	each 7
68	Warner Bros WB 2094	Try (Just A Little Bit Harder)/In My Tomorrow	5
70	Warner Bros WB 7394	You've Really Got A Hold On Me/You Don't Know Anything About Love	5
71	Mercury 6052 073	Call Me Anytime You Need Some Lovin'/Please Don't Teach Me To Love You	8
70	Warner Bros WS 1821	STAY WITH ME (LP)	20

ELMER HOCKETT'S HURDY GURDY
68	Parlophone R 5716	Fantastic Fair/MOOD MOSAIC: The Yellow Spotted Capricorn	6

(see also Mood Mosaic, Mark Wirtz)

ELOY
83	Heavy Metal HMINT 1	Fools/Heartbeat (p/s)	5
83	Heavy Metal HMPD 1	Fools/Heartbeat (picture disc)	8
82	Heavy Metal HMILP 1	PLANETS (LP, clear vinyl with inner sleeve)	12
82	Heavy Metal HMIPD 1	PLANETS (LP, picture disc)	18
82	Heavy Metal HMILP 3	TIME TO TURN (LP, clear vinyl with inner sleeve)	12
82	Heavy Metal HMIPD 3	TIME TO TURN (LP, picture disc)	18
83	Heavy Metal HMIPD 12	PERFORMANCE (LP, picture disc)	12
84	Heavy Metal HMIPD 21	METROMANIA (LP, picture disc)	18
84	Heavy Metal HMICD 21	METROMANIA (CD)	20
85	IMS MILCH 014	CODENAME WILDGEESE (LP, soundtrack)	12
89	FM Revolver REV PD120	RA (LP, picture disc)	15

EL PAS(S)O
71	Big Shot BI 572	Out De Light, Baby/Mosquito I (both actually by Dennis Alcapone)	8
71	Punch PH 61	Mosquito One/Out De Light (reissue)	8

(see also Dennis Alcapone)

JEFF ELROY & BOYS BLUE
66   Philips BF 1533   Honey Machine/Three Woman 15
(see also Boys Blue)

ELTI-FITS
70s Worthing Street WSEF 1   GOING STRAIGHT (EP, foldover p/s) 5

ELVES
70   MCA MU 1114   Amber Velvet/West Virginia 6

CAROL ELVIN
63   Columbia DB 7095   'Cos I Know/C'mon Over 6
65   Parlophone R 5228   Don't Leave Me/'Cos I Love You 6

LEE & JAY ELVIN
59   Fontana H 191   So The Story Goes/When You See Her 15
59   Fontana H 191   So The Story Goes/When You See Her (78) 10
(see also Jerry Lordan)

EMANON
77   Clubland SJP 777   Raging Pain/Rip A Bough (stamped sleeve) 30

BOBBIE EMBER
65   Polydor BM 56062   Why Can't You Bring Me Home/When Love Isn't There 6

EMBERS
63   Decca F 11625   Chelsea Boots/Samantha. 15
(see also David & Embers, Three's A Crowd)

EMBRACE
96   Fierce Panda NING 29 All You Good Good People/My Weakness Is None Of Your Business
                         (p/s, 1,300 only) 40

EMBRYO
80   Rampant RAM 001   I'm Different/You Know He Did (p/s) 5
(see also Jump Squad)

EMERALDS (U.S.)
64   London HL 9839   Donkey Kick Back/Sittin' Bull 7

EMERALDS (U.K.)
65   Decca F 12096   Don't Listen To Your Friends/Say You're Mine 5
65   Decca F 12304   King Lonely The Blue/Someone Else's Fool 30

EMERGENCY
83   Riot City RIOT 21   POINTS OF VIEW (EP) 5

EMERSON
83   Neat NEAT 34   Something Special/Stars In Hollywood (p/s) 6

KEITH EMERSON
76   Manticore K 13513   Honky Tonk Train Blues/Barrel House Shake Down (p/s) 6
80   Atlantic K 11612   Taxi Ride (Rome)/Mater Tenebrarum (p/s) 6
81   MCA MCA 697   I'm A Man/Nighthawks Main Title Theme (p/s) 7
80   Atlantic K 50753   INFERNO (LP, soundtrack) 12
81   MCA MCF 3107   NIGHTHAWKS (LP, soundtrack) 12
(see also Emerson Lake & Palmer, Nice, V.I.P.'s, Rock Aid Armenia)

EMERSON, LAKE & PALMER
73   Lyntone/Manticore   Brain Salad Surgery/(excerpts from "Brain Salad Surgery" LP)
     LYN 2762   (flexidisc in gatefold p/s free with *NME*) 15/7
74   Manticore K 13503   Jerusalem/When The Apple Blossoms Bloom In The WIndmills
                         Of Your Mind, I'll Be Your Valentine (some with p/s) 10/6
77   Atlantic K 10946   Fanfare For The Common Man/Brain Salad Surgery (p/s) 6
77   Atlantic K 10946T   Fanfare For The Common Man (Album Version)/Brain Salad Surgery (12", p/s) . . 15
70   Island ILPS 9123   EMERSON, LAKE AND PALMER (LP, pink label, later 'pink rim palm tree') . . . 20/15
71   Island ILSP 9155   TARKUS (LP, gatefold sleeve) 12
71   Island HELP 1   PICTURES AT AN EXHIBITION (LP, gatefold sleeve). 12
72   Island ILPS 9186   TRILOGY (LP, gatefold sleeve). 12
73   Manticore K 53501   BRAIN SALAD SURGERY (LP, gatefold sleeve with poster). 12
(see also Emerson Lake & Powell, Nice, Keith Emerson, Greg Lake, Shame, Asia, King Crimson, Stray Dog)

EMERSON, LAKE & POWELL
86   Polydor POSP 804   Touch And Go/Learning To Fly (p/s) 5
86   Polydor POSPX 804   Touch And Go/Learning To Fly/The Locomotion (12", p/s) 10
(see also Emerson Lake & Palmer, Cozy Powell)

DICK EMERY
62   Philips 326559 BF   A Cockney Christmas/(All I Want For Christmas Is) My Two Front Teeth. 6
63   Philips BF 1272   I (Who Have Nothing)/Walk With Me, My Angel. 6
69   Pye 7N 17644   If You Love Her/Day After Day 6
70   Pye 7N 17888   With Ageing/Wonderful World Of Love 5
72   Pye 7N 45202   You Are Awful/Dance Dance 5
73   Pye 7N 45288   You're Just As Lovely Today/Our Young Idea 5
69   Pye NSPL 18277   DICK EMERY SINGS (LP) 15

EMILY
87   Sha La La 007   The Old Stone Bridge/REMEMBER FUN: Hey Hey Hate (flexidisc, p/s) 7
87   Big Fun BIG FUN 001 The Old Stone Bridge/What The Fool Said (flexidisc) 7
88   Esurient PACE 5   Stumble/Boxing Day Blues/Rachel (p/s, with insert) 5

EMJAYS
59   Top Rank JAR 145   All My Love All My Life/Cross My Heart 35
59   Top Rank JAR 145   All My Love All My Life/Cross My Heart (78). 40

EMMET SPICELAND
68	Page One POF 089	Lowlands Low/Bunclody	5
69	Page One POF 143	So Long Marianne/In Search Of Franklin	5
68	Page One POLS 011	THE FIRST (LP)	55
77	Hawk HALP 166	THE EMMET SPICELAND ALBUM (LP, reissue of above LP)	45

EMMETT
| 65 | Columbia DB 7582 | Baby Ain't No Lie/Hard Travelling | 6 |
| 65 | Columbia DB 7695 | Nancy/Kilkenny Mountains | 5 |

FRED EMNEY
| 60s | Decca DFE 6554 | FRED EMNEY (EP) | 12 |

EMOTIONS (U.S.)
62	London HLR 9640	Echo/Come Dance Baby	30
63	London HLR 9701	L-O-V-E/A Million Reasons	30
63	Stateside SS 237	A Story Untold/One Life One Love One You	18

EMOTIONS (U.K.)
| 65 | Polydor BM 56025 | Lonely Man/Line Shooter | 4 |

EMOTIONS (Jamaica)
66	Ska Beat JB 263	Rude Boy Confession/Heartbreaking Gypsy	15
67	Caltone TONE 100	A Rainbow/TONY & DOREEN: Just You And I	10
68	Caltone TONE 118	Soulful Music/No Use To Cry	10
68	Caltone TONE 129	Careless Hands/TOMMY McCOOK & SUPERSONICS: Caltone Special	12
69	High Note HS 018	The Storm/Easy Squeeze	8
69	High Note HS 026	Rum Bay/PATSY: Find Someone	6
70	Supreme SUP 209	Halleluiah/MATADOR ALLSTARS: Boat Of Joy	5

(see also Romeo & Emotions, Horace Faith)

EMOTIONS (U.K.)
| 69 | Downtown DT 446 | Give Me Love/HORACE FAITH: Daddy's Home | 6 |

EMOTIONS (U.S.)
69	Stax STAX 123	So I Can Love You/Got To Be The Man	5
69	Stax STAX 134	I Like It/Best Part Of A Love Affair	10
69	Deep Soul DS 9104	Somebody New/Brushfire	15
75	Stax STXS 2020	Baby I'm Through/I Wanna Come Back	5
70	Stax SXATS 1030	SO I CAN LOVE YOU (LP)	18
77	CBS 81639	FLOWERS (LP)	12
77	CBS 82065	REJOICE (LP)	12

EMPEROR
| 77 | Private Stock | EMPEROR (LP) | 10 |

EMPERORS
| 66 | Stateside SS 565 | Karate/I've Got To Have Her | 10 |
| 69 | Pama PM 786 | Karate/I've Got To Have Her (reissue) | 7 |

EMPIRE
| 81 | Dinosaur DE 004 | Hot Seat/All These Things (p/s) | 5 |
| 80 | White Line DE 001 | EXPENSIVE SOUND (LP) | 12 |

(see also Generation X)

EMPYRE
| 86 | EMP | Worlds Apart/Sword Play (p/s) | 5 |

ENCHANTED FOREST
| 68 | Stateside SS 2080 | You're Never Gonna Get My Lovin'/Suzanne | 7 |

ENCHANTERS
| 67 | Warner Bros WB 2054 | We Got Love/I've Lost All Communications | 8 |

END
65	Philips BF 1444	I Can't Get Any Joy/Hey Little Girl	15
68	Decca F 22750	Shades Of Orange/Loving, Sacred Loving	25
69	Decca LK-R/SKL-R 5015	INTROSPECTION (LP)	80
96	Tenth Planet TP 025	IN THE BEGINNING ... THE END (LP, gatefold sleeve, numbered, 1,000 only)	15
97	Tenth Planet TP 033	RETROSPECTION (LP, numbered, 1,000 only)	15

(see also Tucky Buzzard, Bill Wyman, Innocents, Bobby Angelo, Tuxedo)

ENDEVERS
68	Decca F 12817	Remember When We Were Young/Taking Care Of Myself	5
68	Decca F 12859	She's My Girl/She's That Kind Of Girl	5
69	Decca F 12939	Sunny And Me/I Really Hope You Do	5

SERGIO ENDRIGO
| 68 | Pye International 7N 25502 | Marianne/Il Dolce Paese | 10 |

MELVIN ENDSLEY
57	RCA RCA 1004	I Like Your Kind Of Love/Is It True?	35
57	RCA RCA 1004	I Like Your Kind Of Love/Is It True? (78)	30
58	RCA RCA 1051	I Got A Feelin'/There's Bound To Be	30
58	RCA RCA 1051	I Got A Feelin'/There's Bound To Be (78)	25

ENEMY
81	Tin Tin NM 1	50,000 Dead/Society's Fool/Neutral Ground (p/s)	8
82	Fallout FALL 001	Fallen Hero/Tomorrow's Warning/Prisoner Of War (p/s, with inner)	7
82	Fallout FALL 004	Punks Alive/Piccadilly Sidetracks/Twist And Turn (p/s, orange vinyl)	7
83	Fallout FALL 014	Last Rites/Why Not (p/s)	5
84	Rot ASS 9	Last But Not Least/Images (live) (p/s)	6

ENERGY
81	GRN 1	CONQUER THE WORLD (EP, no p/s)	100
80s	BIPS BECK 927	ENERGISED (EP)	80

ENERGY IQ
80	Optimistic OPT 008	THROUGH THE PLUGHOLE (EP)	8

SCOTT ENGEL
58	Vogue V 9125	Blue Bell/Paper Doll	350
58	Vogue V 9125	Blue Bell/Paper Doll (78)	125
59	Vogue V 9145	The Livin' End/Good For Nothin' (with Count Dracula & Boys)	450
59	Vogue V 9145	The Livin' End/Good For Nothin' (with Count Dracula & Boys) (78)	140
59	Vogue V 9150	Charlie Bop/All I Do Is Dream Of You	350
59	Vogue V 9150	Charlie Bop/All I Do Is Dream Of You (78)	165
66	Liberty LEP 2261	SCOTT ENGEL (EP)	40

(see also Scott Walker, Walker Brothers)

SCOTT ENGEL & JOHN STEWART
66	Capitol CL 15440	I Only Came To Dance With You/Greens	18

(see also Scott Walker, Walker Brothers)

ENGLAND
76	Deroy DER 1356	ENGLAND (LP, private pressing)	250

ENGLAND
77	Arista ARIST 88	Pariffinalea/Nanagram	6
77	Arista ARTY 153	GARDEN SHED (LP, allegedly some with booklet)	100+/40

ENGLAND'S GLORY
73	Venus VEN 105	ENGLAND'S GLORY (LP, private pressing, pink label, 25 copies only; beware of white label counterfeits)	250
87	Five Hours Back TOCK 4	ENGLAND'S GLORY (LP, stickered sleeve)	12

(see also Only Ones)

ENGLAND SISTERS
60	HMV POP 710	Heartbeat/Little Child	40

ENGLISH
81	Albion ION 1008	Hooray For The English/When You Fly (p/s)	5

BARBARA JEAN ENGLISH
74	Contempo CS 2031	Breaking Up A Happy Home/Guess Who	5
75	Contempo CS 2062	I'm Living In A Lie/Key In The Mailbox	5

ERROL(L) ENGLISH
70	Big Shot BI 547	I Don't Want To Love You/Love Is Pure	6
70	Big Shot BI 548	Once In My Life/Rabbit In A Cottage	6
70	Torpedo TOR 8	Open The Door To Your Heart/That Will Do	6
70	Torpedo TOR 9	Where You Lead Me/Hitchin' A Ride	6
70	Torpedo TOR 16	Sad Girl/Welcome Me Back Home	6
70	Torpedo TOR 22	Sha La La La Lee/BOVVER BOYS: A.G.G.R.O.	12
71	Duke DU 99	Sometimes (with Champions)/Sugar Cane	6

(see also Junior English, Errol & Champions)

JUNIOR ENGLISH
69	Camel CA 35	Nobody Knows (with Tony Sexton)/Somewhere	6
71	Pama PM 828	Jesamine/SYDNEY ALL STARS: The Flash	6
72	Pama PM 841	Miss Playgirl/Once In My Life	5
72	Pama PM 866	I Don't Want To Die/Land Of Sea And Sand	5
72	Pama PM 869	Daniel/Perfidia	5
72	Banana BA 368	Anniversary/Girls Like You	6
73	Pama Supreme PS 381	Garden Party/Version	5

(see also Errol English)

MR JOE ENGLISH
69	Fontana TF 1034	Lay Lady Lay/Two Minute Silence	4

SCOTT ENGLISH
71	Horse HOSS 7	Brandy/Lead Me Back	4
72	Blue Mountain BM 1004	Waterfall Woman/Denver's Calling	4

ENGLISH ROSE
70	Polydor 2058 040	Yesterday's Hero/To Jackie	6

(see also Neat Change, Love Affair)

ENGLISH SUBTITLES
79	Small Wonder SMALL 22	Time Tunnel/Sweat/Reconstruction (p/s)	5
82	Glass 007/10 SEC 21	Tannoy/Cars On Fire (folded p/s in bag with insert)	6
82	Glass GLASS LP 013	ORIGINAL DIALOGUE (LP, with inner sleeve)	12

ENID

SINGLES
76	Buk BUK 3002	The Lovers/In The Region Of The Summer Stars	15
77	EMI International INT 534	Jubilee/Omega (p/s)	5
77	EMI International INT 540	Golden Earrings/Omega (p/s)	12
79	Pye 7P 106	Dambusters March — Land Of Hope And Glory/ The Skye Boat Song (p/s, blue vinyl)	10
80	Pye 7P 187	Fool/Tito (p/s)	10
80	EMI EMI 5109	Golden Earrings/665 The Great Bean (p/s)	10
81	Bronze BRO 127	When You Wish Upon A Star/Jessica (p/s)	6
81	Bronze BRO 134	Heigh Ho/Twinkle Twinkle Little Star (p/s)	8
82	Rak RAK 349	And Then There Were None/Letter From America (p/s)	7
84	EMI 12EMI 5505	And Then There Were None/Letter From America/Raindown (12", p/s)	10
86	Sedition EDIT 3314	Itchycoo Park/Sheets Of Blue (p/s)	5

ENID

86	Sedition EDITL 3314	Itchycoo Park/Sheets Of Blue (12", p/s) 10
90	Enid ENID 7999	Salome/Salomee (p/s) 5
90	Enid ENID 6999	Salome/Salomee (12", p/s)... 8

LPs

76	Buk BULP 2014	IN THE REGION OF THE SUMMER STARS (LP, 1st issue, white label, with insert, without mention of "Enid" on front cover; distributed by Decca) 20
77	Buk BULP 2014	IN THE REGION OF THE SUMMER STARS (LP, 2nd issue, black label, with "Enid" on front cover) 15
77	Honeybee INS 3005	IN THE REGION OF THE SUMMER STARS (LP, 3rd issue, brown label, some with poster)... 15/12
77	Honeybee INS 3012	AERIE FAIRIE NONSENSE (LP)... 12
79	Pye NSPH 18593	TOUCH ME (LP, with insert)... 12
79	Pye NH 116	SIX PIECES (LP, with insert, 2,000 only) 15
84	The Enid ENID 1	LIVE AT HAMMERSMITH VOL. I (LP, 5,500 only) 15
84	The Enid ENID 2	LIVE AT HAMMERSMITH VOL. II (LP, 2,000 only).......................... 15
84	The Enid ENID 3	SOMETHING WICKED THIS WAY COMES (LP) 12
84	The Enid ENID 4	SIX PIECES (LP, 'enhanced' version, 3,500 only) 15
84	The Enid ENID 5	TOUCH ME (LP, 'enhanced' version, 4,000 only)......................... 15
84	The Enid ENID 6	AERIE FAERIE NONSENSE (LP, remixed/re-recorded version) 12
84	The Enid ENID 7	IN THE REGION OF THE SUMMER STARS (LP, remastered & re-recorded version) 12
84	The Enid ENID 8	THE SPELL (2-LP, 45rpm, gatefold sleeve) 15
84	The Stand LE 1	"THE LIVERPOOL ALBUM" (LP, untitled mini-album, sold at gigs, 800 only) 30
84	The Stand THE STAND 1	THE STAND (LP, fan club issue, 5,000 only, some autographed) .... 40+/30
85	The Stand THE STAND 2	THE STAND 1985-1986 (LP, fan club issue, 2,000 only, some autographed)... 25+/20
85	The Enid ENID 9	FAND (LP, re-recorded version of "Fand" track, 3,000 only) 15
86	The Enid ENID 10	SALOME (LP).. 12
87	Dojo DOJOC 24	LOVERS AND FOOLS (2-LP) 15

(Cassette copies of the above Enid-label albums with Lodge Recording Studios inlays are worth £15 each; copies with typewritten & colour-cover inlays are worth £10 each.)

CASSETTES

77	Honeybee TC-INS 3012	AERIE FAIRIE NONSENSE (1,000 only)................................... 12
79	Pye ZCNH 116	SIX PIECES (500 only) 10
87	Dojo DOJOC 24	LOVERS AND FOOLS... 20
86	The Enid (no cat. no.)	INNER PIECES 10
86	The Enid (no cat. no.)	INNER VISIONS 10
86	The Enid (no cat. no.)	AT HAMMERSMITH 17TH OCTOBER 1986 (cassette, official bootleg, typed inlay).. 12
87	The Enid (no cat. no.)	AT HAMMERSMITH 30TH OCTOBER 1987 (cassette, official bootleg, typed inlay).. 12
87	The Enid (no cat. no.)	THE STAND MEMBERS ONE OF ANOTHER (cassette, typed inlay)............ 10
80s	The Enid (no cat. no.)	THE HISTORY OF THE ENID (double cassette, fan club only) 15
80s	The Stand HAM 1	AT HAMMERSMITH 17TH OCTOBER 1986 (cassette, reissue, typed inlay) 10
80s	The Stand HAM 2	AT HAMMERSMITH 30TH OCTOBER 1987 (cassette, reissue, typed inlay) 10
80s	The Enid (no cat. no.)	INTRODUCING THE ENID (cassette, 5-track sampler, typed inlay)............. 8

(see also Robert John Godfrey, Godfrey & Stewart, William Arkle, Glen Baker, Kim Wilde)

ETHEL ENNIS

64	RCA SF 7654	ONCE AGAIN (LP) 12

RAY ENNIS & BLUE JEANS

68	Columbia DB 8431	What Have They Done To Hazel?/Now That You've Got Me (You Don't Seem To Want Me) 20

(see also Swinging Blue Jeans, Blue Jeans)

SEAMUS ENNIS

68	Ember FA 2054	THE BONNY BUNCH OF ROSES (LP, reissue) 15
70	Leader LEA 2003	SEAMUS ENNIS (LP) 15
74	Topic 12TS 250	THE WANDERING MINSTREL (LP).. 12
76	Free Reed FROO 1/2	FORTY YEARS OF IRISH PIPING (2-LP with insert) 20

BRIAN ENO

74	Island WIP 6178	Seven Deadly Finns/Later On 8
75	Island WIP 6233	The Lion Sleeps Tonight (Wimoweh)/I'll Come Running..................... 8
78	Polydor 2001 762	The King's Lead Hat/R.A.F. (B-side with Snatch) 5
89	Virgin CDT 41	Another Green World/Dover Beach/Deep Blue Day (3" CD, g/fold card sleeve).... 7
74	Island ILPS 9268	HERE COME THE WARM JETS (LP) 12
74	Island ILPS 9309	TAKING TIGER MOUNTAIN (BY STRATEGY) (LP).......................... 12
75	Island ILPS 9351	ANOTHER GREEN WORLD (LP) 12
75	Island HELP 22	EVENING STAR (LP, as Fripp & Eno)...................................... 12
75	Obscure OBS 3	DISCREET MUSIC (LP)... 12
76	Island ILPS 9444	801 LIVE (LP) 12
76	Editions EG EGM 1	MUSIC FOR FILMS (LP, private pressing) 150
77	Polydor 2302 071	BEFORE AND AFTER SCIENCE (LP, with 4 Peter Schmidt prints)............. 15
83	EG EGBS 002	WORKING BACKWARDS 1983-1973 (9-LP box set with "Music For Films, Vol. 2" LP & "Rarities" 12")........................... 40

(see also Eno Moebius Roebius, Ayers Cale Nico & Eno, Roxy Music, Passengers, Robert Fripp, Lady June, David Toop, Gavin Bryars, Toto)

BRIAN ENO & DAVID BYRNE

81	EG EGO 1	The Jezebel Spirit/Regiment (p/s)... 4

(see also David Byrne, Talking Heads)

ENO, MOEBIUS, ROEBIUS

76	Sky SKY 120	AFTER THE HEAT (LP)... 10

(see also Brian Eno)

ENORMOUS ROOM
86	Sharp CAL 5	100 Different Words/Sylvia's Children/Melanie And Martin/ You Wrote A Book (12", p/s)	8
86	Medium Cool MC 001	I Don't Need You/Melanie And Martin (flexidisc, p/s)	6

ENOS & SHEILA
68	Blue Cat BS 138	Tonight You're Mine/UNTOUCHABLES: Your Love	15

(see also Enos McLeod)

ENOUGH'S ENOUGH
68	Tattoo TT 101	Please Remember/Look Around You Baby	150

ENTICERS
72	Atlantic 2091 136	Calling For Your Love/Storyteller	10

JOHN ENTWISTLE('S OX)
71	Track 2094 008	I Believe In Everything/My Size	8
75	Decca FR 13567	Mad Dog/Cell No.7 (as John Entwistle's Ox)	8
81	WEA K 79249P	Too Late The Hero/I'm Coming Back (picture disc, some autographed)	8/5
71	Track 2406 005	SMASH YOUR HEAD AGAINST THE WALL (LP)	18
72	Track 2406 104	WHISTLE RYMES (LP)	18
75	Decca TXS 114	MAD DOG (LP, as John Entwistle's Ox)	15

(see also Who, Rigor Mortis)

ENVOYS
67	Pilgrim 3048	ENVOYS (EP)	8

ENYA
87	BBC RESL 201	I Want Tomorrow/The Celts Theme (p/s)	10
87	BBC CDRSL 201	I Want Tomorrow/The Celts Theme/To Go Beyond I/To Go Beyond II (CD)	45
88	WEA YZ 312 CD	Orinoco Flow/Smaotin.../Out Of The Blue (3" CD)	15
88	WEA YZ 356 CD	Evening Falls/Oiche Chiun (Silent Night)/Morning Glory (3" CD)	15
89	WEA YZ 368 CD	Storms In Africa (Part II)/Storms In Africa (Part I) (3" CD, card sleeve)	15
89	WEA YZ 368 CDX	Storms In Africa (Part II)/The Celts/Aldebaran/Storms In Africa (Part I) (5" CD, picture disc)	20
91	WEA YZ 580 CD	Exile/On Your Shore/Watermark/River (CD, slimline jewel case)	12
91	WEA YZ 604 CDX	Caribbean Blue/Orinoco Flow/As Baile/Oriel Window (CD, digipak)	10
91	WEA YZ 635 T	How Can I Keep From Singing/O'che Chi'n (Silent Night) (12", metallic p/s)	8
91	WEA YZ 635 CD	How Can I Keep From Singing/O'che Chi'n (Silent Night)/'S Fagain Mo Bhaile (CD, slimline jewel case)	8
92	WEA YZ 640 CDX	Book Of Days/Watermark/On Your Shore/Exile (CD, box set with 4 prints)	15
92	WEA YZ 705 CDX	The Celts/O'che Chi'n (Silent Night)/Storms In Africa (Pt. II)/ Eclipse (CD, with 4 prints)	12
87	BBC REB 605	ENYA (LP)	25
87	BBC BBCCD 605	ENYA (CD)	50
93	WEA 2292-43875-8	WATERMARK (mini-disc)	25

EPICS (U.K.)
65	Pye 7N 15829	There's Just No Pleasing You/My Little Girl	6
66	Pye 7N 17053	Just How Wrong Can You Be/Blue Turns To Grey	7
68	CBS 3564	Travelling Circus/Henry Long	7

(see also Acid Gallery, Christie, T. Rex)

EPICS (Jamaica)
70	Bamboo BAM 37	Your Love/Driving Me Crazy	5

EPILEPTICS
80	Stortbeat/Mirror BEAT 8	1970'S EP (black & white p/s, stencilled white labels)	12
81	Spiderleg SDL 1	1970'S EP (re-recorded, printed labels, folded different print b&w p/s)	8
81	Spiderleg SDL 2	LAST BUS TO DEBDEN (EP, hand-written labels & photocopied p/s)	10
81	Spiderleg SDL 2	LAST BUS TO DEBDEN (EP, with printed labels in printed card gatefold p/s)	7

(see also Licks, Flux Of Pink Indians)

EPISODE
68	MGM MGM 1409	Little One/Wide Smiles	35

(see also Episode Six)

EPISODE SIX
66	Pye 7N 17018	Put Yourself In My Place/That's All I Want	20
66	Pye 7N 17110	I Hear Trumpets Blow/True Love Is Funny That Way	20
66	Pye 7N 17147	Here, There And Everywhere/Mighty Morris Ten	20
67	Pye 7N 17244	Love, Hate, Revenge/Baby Baby Baby	18
67	Pye 7N 17330	Morning Dew/Sunshine Girl	18
67	Pye 7N 17376	I Can See Through You/When I Fall In Love	18
68	Chapter One CH 103	Lucky Sunday/Mr. Universe	18
69	Chapter One CH 104	Mozart Versus The Rest/Jak D'Or	18

(see also Episode, Sheila Carter & Episode Six, Neo Maya, Roger Glover, Jon Lord, Gillan, Deep Purple, Quatermass)

MINNIE EPPERSON
68	Action ACT 4503	Grab Your Clothes (And Get On Out)/No Love At All	10

PRESTON EPPS
59	Top Rank JAR 140	Bongo Rock/Bongo Party	12
59	Top Rank JAR 140	Bongo Rock/Bongo Party (78)	25
59	Top Rank JAR 180	Bongos In Pastel/Doin' The Cha Cha Cha	6
59	Top Rank JAR 180	Bongos In Pastel/Doin' The Cha Cha Cha (78)	12
60	Top Rank JAR 345	Bongo Boogie/Flamenco Boogie	10
60	Top Rank JAR 413	Bongo Bongo Bongo/Hully Gully Bongo	8
60	Top Rank JAR 522	Bongola/Blue Bongo	6
70	President PT 294	Bongo Rock/SANDY NELSON: Teen Beat	6

EQUALS

67	President PT 117	I Won't Be There/Fire	6
67	President PT 135	Baby, Come Back/Hold Me Closer	5
67	President PT 158	Give Love A Try/Another Sad And Lonely Night	5
68	President PT 180	I Get So Excited/Skies Above	5
68	President PT 200	Laurel And Hardy/The Guy Who Made Her A Star	5
68	President PT 222	Softly Softly/Lonely Rita	5
69	President PT 240	Michael And The Slipper Tree/Honey Gum	8
69	President PT 260	Viva Bobby Joe/I Can't Let You Go	8
69	President PT 275	Rub A Dub Dub/After The Lights Go Down Low	8
70	President PT 303	I Can See But You Don't Know/Gigolo Sam	15
70	President PT 325	Black Skin Blue Eyed Boys/Happy Birthday Girl	5
70	President PT 345	Help Me Simone/Love Potion	5
73	President PT 414	Diversion/Here Today Gone Tomorrow	5
75	President PT 436	Georgetown Girl/We've Got It All Worked Out	5
76	Mercury 6007 104	Kaiwana Sunshine Girl/Soul Mother	5
76	Mercury 6007 106	Funky Like A Train/If You Didn't Miss Me	12
76	Mercury 6007 107	Funky Like A Train/If You Didn't Miss Me (12")	20
77	Mercury 6007 139	Irma La Douce/Ar'e Harry	5
77	President PT 464	Beautiful Clown/Daily Love	5
78	Ice GUY 5	Red Dog/Something Beautiful	5
88	Club JAB 58	Funky Like A Train/Born Ya!/Funky Like A Train (extended) (reissue)	7
88	Club JABX 58	Funky Like A Train/Born Ya!/Funky Like A Train (extended) (12", reissue)	12
68	President PTE 1	BABY COME BACK (EP)	15
68	President PTE 2	THE EQUALS (EP)	15
67	President PTL 1006	UNEQUALLED EQUALS (LP)	15
68	President PTL 1015	EQUALS EXPLOSION (LP)	15
68	President PTL(S)1020	SENSATIONAL EQUALS (LP)	15
68	President PTL(S) 1025	SUPREME (LP)	15
69	President PTLS 1030	THE EQUALS STRIKE AGAIN (LP)	15
69	President PTLS 1050	BEST OF THE EQUALS (LP)	15
70	President PTLS 1038	AT THE TOP (LP)	15
76	Mercury 9109 601	BORN YA! (LP)	25
78	Ice ICEL 1002	MYSTIC SISTER (LP)	25

(see also Little Grants & Eddie, Pyramids, Hickory, Little Brother Grant, Zappata Schmitt, Seven Letters/Syramip, Thirty-Second Turn-Off)

EQUATIONS

69	Fontana TF 1035	Waiting On The Shores Of Nowhere/You Stood Beside Me	4

EQUINOX

73	Boulevard BLVD 4118	HARD ROCK (LP)	18

EQUIPE 84

67	Major Minor MM 517	Auschwitz/Twenty Ninth Of September	15

ERASURE

SINGLES

85	Mute L12MUTE 40	Who Needs Love (Like That) (Mexican Mix)/Push Me Shove Me (Tacos Mix) (12", p/s)	35
85	Mute L12MUTE 42	Heavenly Action (Yellow Brick Mix)/Don't Say No (Ruby Red Mix) (12", p/s, L12 cat. no. must be listed on sleeve & label)	70
85	Mute DMUTE 42	Heavenly Action/Don't Say No (Ruby Red Mix)//Who Needs Love (Like That) (Mexican Mix)/Push Me Shove Me (Tacos Mix) (12", shrinkwrapped double pack)	45
86	Mute MUTE 45	Oh L'Amour/March On Down The Line ('Thomas The Tank Engine' p/s, withdrawn)	5
86	Mute 12MUTE 45	Oh L'Amour/March On Down The Line/Gimme! Gimme! Gimme! (12", 'Thomas The Tank Engine' p/s, withdrawn)	18
86	Mute L12MUTE 45	Oh L'Amour (Funky Sisters Mix)/March On Down The Line/Gimme! Gimme! Gimme! (Remix) (12", p/s)	15
86	Mute DMUTE 51	Sometimes/Sexuality//Who Needs Love (Like That)/Push Me Shove Me (double pack, with insert, shrinkwrapped with sticker)	10
86	Mute DMUTE 51	Sometimes/Sexuality//Oh L'Amour/March On Down The Line (double pack, with insert, shrinkwrapped with sticker)	10
86	Mute L12MUTE 51	Sometimes (Shiver Mix)/Sexuality (Private Mix)/Senseless (CD Mix) (12", p/s)	8
87	Mute CDMUTE 56	It Doesn't Have To Be/Sometimes/Oh L'Amour/Heavenly Action/Who Needs Love (Like That)/Gimme! Gimme! Gimme!/In The Hall Of The Mountain King (CD, 7"-sized 'tray' p/s)	12
88	Mute PMUTE 85	A Little Respect/Like Zsa Zsa Zsa Gabor (p/s, mailing pack with 3 postcards)	5
88	Mute LCDMUTE 93	Crackers International: Stop! (Mark Saunders Remix)/Knocking On Your Door (Mark Saunders Remix)/God Rest Ye Merry Gentlemen (3" CD, Xmas pack with card & gift label, 6" x 3" sleeve; later in 3" pouch)	25/8
90	Mute XL12MUTE 99	Supernature (Mark Saunders Remix)/You Surround Me (Gareth Jones Remix)/Supernature (Daniel Miller & Phil Legg Remix) (12", envelope p/s)	12
90	Mute XL12MUTE 109	Blue Savannah (Der Deutsche Mix II)/Blue Savannah (Der Deutsche Mix I) (12", 1-sided, numbered envelope p/s)	12
90	Mute LCDMUTE 109	Blue Savannah (Der Deutsche Mix I & II)/Runaround On The Underground (CD, silver/blue embossed sleeve)	8
94	Mute MUTE 166	I Love Saturday/Dodo/Because You're So Sweet (unreleased, p/s only)	50

LPs

86	Mute STUMM 25	WONDERLAND (LP, stickered sleeve, with 12" "Oh L'Amour" [12 MUTE 45])	12
89	Mute STUMM 75	WILD! (LP, with bonus 12" "Blue Savannah" [XL12 MUTE 109])	12

PROMOS

86	Mute P12MUTE 45	Oh L'Amour/March On Down The Line/Gimme! Gimme! Gimme! (12", plain white sleeve, dark blue vinyl)	25
90	Mute ERAS 1	Push Me Shove Me (Moonbeam Mix)/(Catatonic Mix)/Senseless (Avalon Mix) (12", p/s)	25
90	Mute ERAS 2	ERAS 2: Who Needs Love Like That (Winnie Cooper Mix)/ Ship Of Fools (Orbital South Seas Isles Of Holy Beats Mix) (12", die-cut title sleeve)	20
90	Mute ERAS 3	Sometimes (Danny Rampling Mix) (12", die-cut title sleeve)	25
91	Mute P12MUTE 125	Chorus (Youth's Agreessive Dance Mix)/(Pure Dance Mix)/Snappy (Martyn Phillips Mix)/Snappy (Justin Robertson Mix) (12", green label, no p/s)	15
90s	Mute P12MUTE 195	Don't Say Your Love Is Killing Me (Tall Paul Mix)/(John Pleased Wimmin Flashback Vox) Oh L'Amour (Tin Tin Out Remix)/(Matt Darey Mix) (12", white label test pressing with press release & release sheet, 10 copies only)	80
92	Mute ERAS 4	ABBA-ESQUE EP: Voulez Vous (Brain Stem Death Dest Mix)/Lay All Your Love On Me (No Panties Mix)/Take A Chance On Me (Take A Trance On Me)/ SOS (Perimeter Mix) (12")	30
94	Mute PL12 MUTE 166	Ghost (12", 1-sided)	18
97	Mute P12 MUTE 208	Rain (Blue Amazon Twisted Circles Mix)/In My Arms (Dekkard Dub)/ Sometimes (John "00" Flemings Full Vocal Club Mix)/Sometimes (John "00" Flemings Give It Some Welly Dub Mix) (12", p/s)	12
97	Mute PL12 MUTE 208	Rain (John Of The Pleased Wimmin Vocal Mix)/(John Of The Pleased Wimmin Dub)/Sometimes (John "00" Flemings Full Vocal Club Mix)/ In My Arms (BBE Mix) (12", p/s)	12
92	Mute ERAS 5	POP (CD, 19-track compilation, without "Take A Chance On Me" & "Who Needs Love Like That [Hamburg Mix]", numbered, promo only)	50
92	Mute ERAS INT 1	POP (CD, interview disc)	60
96	Mute ERAS SAY 1	I SAY I SAY I SAY I SAY (CD, interview disc)	60
96	Mute ERAS SAY 2	ERASURE (CD, interview disc)	60
96	Mute ERAS SAY 3	COWBOY (CD, interview disc)	60

(see also Depeche Mode, Vince Clarke & Paul Quinn, Yazoo, Dinger)

ERAZERHEAD

81	Test Pressing TP 4	Ape Man/Wipeout/Rock And Roll Zombie (p/s)	5
82	Flicknife FLS 208	Shell Shock/She Can Dance (p/s)	5
82	Flicknife FLS 210	Teenager In Love/All For Me (p/s)	5

EREHWON

81	Harvest HAR 5213	Tiny Goddess/The Hero (p/s)	5

(see also Patrick Campbell-Lyons)

ERIC (Sykes) & HATTIE (Jacques)

63	Decca LK 4507	ERIC, HATTIE AND THINGS (LP)	15

(see also Eric Sykes & Hattie Jacques)

ERIC HYSTERIC & ESOTERICS

80	Wasted Vinyl WASTE 1	Tropical Vision/Dance And Sing (p/s)	5

ROKY ERICKSON (& ALIENS)

77	Virgin VS 180	Bermuda/The Interpreter (p/s)	10
80	CBS 8888	Creature With The Atom Brain/The Wind And More (with Aliens)	8
80	CBS 9055	Mine Mine Mind/Bloody Hammer (Acoustic Version) (p/s, with Aliens)	8
87	B'full Of Brains BOB 13	Don't Shake Me Lucifer (live) (flexidisc free with *Bucketfull Of Brains* mag)	6/5
87	Five Hours Back TOCK 7P	CASTING THE RUNES (LP, picture disc)	18

(see also 13th Floor Elevators)

ERROL (English) & CHAMPIONS

70	Jackpot JP 732	Lonely Boy/Da Boo	6
70	Jackpot JP 738	Lonely Boy/TONY & CHAMPIONS: All Of My Life	6

(see also Errol English)

ERROL (Dunkley) & HIS GROUP

65	Blue Beat BB 284	Gypsy/Miss May (actually by Errol Dunkley & Roy Shirley)	15

(see also Errol Dunkley)

ERROL (Dunkley) & U ROY

72	Punch PH 105	Darling Ooh Wee/GOD SONS: Merry Up Version	8

ERSATZ

81	Raw RAW 35	Motorbody Love/One Good Reason/Gimme A Chance (poster p/s)	6
80s	Leisure Sounds SRS 32	Smile In Shadow/House Of Cards (p/s)	6

NORMAN ERSKINE

57	Capitol CL 14784	Till We Meet Again/What's To Become Of Me	5

BLUEGRASS ERWIN

59	Top Rank JAR 252	I Won't Cry Alone/I Can't Love You	6

ESCALATORS

83	Big Beat NS 86	Something's Missing/The Edge (p/s)	10
83	Big Beat NS 87	The Munsters Theme/Monday (p/s)	6

ESCALATORS

85	Rococco COCO 1	Beach Boys/Ford Escort (p/s, with free single)	6

ESCORTS (U.S.)

63	Coral Q 72458	Submarine Race Watching/Somewhere	10

MINT VALUE £

ESCORTS (U.K.)

64	Fontana TF 453	Dizzy Miss Lizzy/All I Want Is You	18
64	Fontana TF 474	The One To Cry/Tell Me Baby	18
64	Fontana TF 516	I Don't Want To Go On Without You/Don't Forget To Write	15
65	Fontana TF 570	C'Mon Home Baby/You'll Get No Lovin' That Way	18
66	Fontana TF 651	Let It Be Me/Mad Mad World	18
66	Columbia DB 8061	From Head To Toe/Night Time	25

(see also Big Three, Paddy Klaus & Gibson, Swinging Blue Jeans, Terry Sylvester)

ESCORTS (Jamaica)

| 70 | Big Shot BI 535 | I'm So Afraid/Mother Nature | 6 |
| 74 | Fab FAB 245 | Sixpense/Loving Feeling | 6 |

(see also Sensations)

ESCORTS (U.S.)

| 75 | Contempo CLP 521 | ALL WE NEED IS ANOTHER CHANCE (LP) | 10 |

ESCORTS & KAY JUSTICE

| 54 | Columbia SCM 5132 | If You Took Your Love From Me/Yes, Indeed | 8 |

ESCOURTS

| 76 | Alaska ALA 1014 | Disrespect Can Wreck/Bam A Lam A Boogie | 8 |

ESKA

95	Modern Ind. MIR 003	Trucking And Paving/False Start/These Are The Dry Years (p/s, 500 only)	4
95	F. & Jetsam SHAG 7002	In The Bottle/POISON SISTERS: Aristotle (p/s)	4
96	Love Train PUBE 010	III Spike/Let's Fence! (p/s)	4
96	Love Train PUBE 015	Running On Sum Six Due/Nova Scotia (p/s)	4

ESPERANTO ROCK ORCHESTRA

73	A&M AMLH 68175	ESPERANTO ROCK ORCHESTRA (LP)	10
74	A&M AMLH 63624	DANSE MACABRE (LP, with Keith Christmas)	10
75	A&M AMLH 68294	LAST TANGO (LP)	10

(see also Keith Christmas, Comus)

ESPRIT DE CORPS

| 73 | Jam JAM 24 | If (Would It Turn Out Wrong)/Picture On The Wall | 15 |
| 73 | Jam JAM 32 | Lonely/Do You Remember Me | 10 |

(see also Mike Read, David Ballantyne, Just Plain Smith, Just Plain Jones, Trainspotters)

ESPRIT DE CORPS

| 80s | Come 0001 | Anxiety/The Tea Cup Song (hand-made silk-screened sleeve) | 6 |

ESQUERITA

| 58 | Capitol CL 14938 | Rockin' The Joint/Esquerita And The Voola | 90 |
| 72 | Specialty SPE 6603 | WILDCAT SHAKEOUT (LP) | 30 |

ESQUIRES

67	Stateside SS 2048	Get On Up/Listen To Me	10
68	Stateside SS 2077	And Get Away/Everybody's Laughing	8
73	Action ACT 4618	My Sweet Baby/Henry Ralph	6
68	London HA-Q/SH-Q 8356	GET ON UP AND GET AWAY (LP)	15

ESSENTIAL LOGIC

| 78 | Cells SELL ONE | Aerosol Burns/World Friction (p/s) | 5 |

(see also X-Ray Spex)

ESSEX

63	Columbia DB 7077	Easier Said Than Done/Are You Going My Way	10
63	Columbia DB 7122	A Walkin' Miracle/What I Don't Know Won't Hurt Me (with Anita Humes)	10
63	Columbia DB 7178	She's Got Everything/Out Of Sight, Out Of Mind	8
63	Columbia 33SX 1593	EASIER SAID THAN DONE (LP)	30
64	Columbia 33SX 1613	A WALKIN' MIRACLE (LP)	30

DAVID ESSEX

65	Fontana TF 559	And The Tears Came Tumbling Down/You Can't Stop Me Loving You	35
65	Fontana TF 620	Can't Nobody Love You/Baby I Don't Mind	35
66	Fontana TF 680	This Little Girl Of Mine/Brokenhearted	35
66	Fontana TF 733	Thigh High/De Boom Lay Boom	30
68	Uni UN 502	Love Story/High Than High	15
68	Pye 7N 17621	Just For Tonight/Goodbye	15
69	Decca F 12935	That Takes Me Back/Lost Without Linda	25
69	Decca F 12967	The Day The Earth Stood Still/Is It So Strange?	25
73	CBS 1693	Rock On/On And On (p/s)	5
73	CBS 1902	Lamplight/We All Insane (p/s)	5
74	CBS 2176	America/Dance Little Girl (p/s)	6
74	CBS 2492	Gonna Make You A Star/Window (p/s)	5
74	CBS 2828	Stardust/Miss Sweetness (p/s)	5
75	CBS 3425	Rollin' Stone/Coconut Ice (p/s)	5
75	CBS 3572	Hold Me Close/Good Old Rock & Roll (p/s)	5
75	CBS 3676	If I Could/Funfair (p/s)	5
75	Sound For Industry SFI 200	Hello It's Me (fan club flexidisc)	15
76	CBS 4050	City Lights/St. Amie (p/s)	6
76	CBS 4486	Coming Home/Good Lovin' (p/s, some copies b/w "Won't Get Burned Again")	6
78	CBS 6063	Stay With Me Baby/Lend Me Your Comb (p/s)	5
78	CBS 6705	Brave New World/Street Fight (p/s)	5
79	Mercury 6007 202	Imperial Wizard/Midnight Train (p/s, blue vinyl)	5
79	Mercury 6007 220	20 Flights Up/Are You Still My True Love (p/s)	5
79	Vertigo 6059 233	M.O.D./M.O.D. (2) (as M.O.D., songwriting credited to D. Cook, p/s, some allegedly mispressed on 2-Tone label)	75+/7
80	United Artists UP 605	World/I Who Am I (p/s)	6
80	Mercury BIKE 1	Silver Dream Machine (Part 1)/(Part 2) (p/s)	5

MINT VALUE £

80	Mercury HOT 1	Hot Love/Rock And Roll Me (p/s) 5
80	Mercury BIKE 2	The Race/Suzuki Warlord (p/s)...................................... 5
80	Mercury MER 47	On My Bike/Swim Against The Flow (p/s) 6
80	Mercury MER 55	Heart On My Sleeve/I Don't Want To Go To The Disco (p/s) 5
81	Mercury MER 72	Be-Bop-A-Lula/Secret Lover (p/s) 5
81	Mercury MER 77	Sunshine Girl/Don't Leave Me This Way (p/s) 5
81	Mercury MER 82	The Magician/Life Support System (p/s) 5
82	Mercury MER 100	Sweethearts/Hold On Me (p/s) 5
82	Mercury MER 118	No Substitutes/She's My World (p/s)............................... 5
83	Mercury ESSEP 1	The Smile/Slave (picture disc)..................................... 7
83	Mercury ESSEX 12	The Smile/Slave (12", p/s) 8
83	Mercury ESSEX 22	You're In My Heart/Come On Little Darlin'//A Winter's Tale/Verity (double pack gatefold p/s, some with inner picture sleeve) 8/6
87	Arista RISCD 11	Myfanwy (Long Version)/Myfanwy/Myfanwy (Love Theme) (CD, card sleeve) 10
89	CBS 654 948-0	Rock On (Shep Pettibone Remix)/The Zone (poster p/s) 5
89	CBS 654 948-2	Rock On (Shep Pettibone Remix)/Rock On (Dub Mix)/Rock On (7" Version)/ The Zone (CD, card sleeve) 8
89	Lamplight CDLAMP 6	The Sun Ain't Gonna (Anymore) (Extended)/(7" Version)/ Heart Beats Like A Drum/Heaven Knows (CD) 8
79	Mercury 9109 616	IMPERIAL WIZARD (LP, blue vinyl) 12
	(see also David & Rozaa, Us)	

ESSJAY
| 71 | DJM DJS 254 | Twins Of Evil/Fastback... 8 |

NEVILLE ESSON
| 61 | Blue Beat BB 37 | Lover's Jive/Wicked And Dreadful (with Clue J. & His Blues Busters) .... 15 |

ESTABLISHMENT
| 81 | Foetain | BAD CATHOLICS (LP) .... 30 |
| | (see also Cromwell) | |

GLORIA ESTEFAN & MIAMI SOUND MACHINE
84	Epic A 4800	Prisoner Of Love/Toda Tuya (Toda Dia Eva Dia De Indio) (p/s)......... 5
84	Epic TX 4800	Prisoner Of Love/Toda Tuya (Toda Dia Eva Dia De Indio)/ Prisoner Of Love (instrumental) (12", p/s) 8
85	Epic A 6537	Bad Boy (Club Mix)/Movies (p/s).................................. 5
85	Epic QTA 6537	Bad Boy (Club Mix)/Bad Boy (Rubber-Club-Dub-Mix)/Movies (12", p/s) 8
85	Epic TA 6361	Conga! (Dance Mix)/Conga! (Instrumental)/Mucho Money (12", p/s).. 8
86	Epic A 6956	Falling In Love (Uh-Oh)/Surrender Paradise (p/s)................... 5
86	Epic 650251 7	Falling In Love (Uh-Oh) (Remix)/Surrender Paradise (p/s) 5
86	Epic TA 6956	Falling In Love (Uh-Oh)/Conga! (The Stronga-Conga Remix)/ Surrender Paradise (p/s) 8
87	Epic 650805 7	Rhythm Is Gonna Get You/Give It Up ('red dress' p/s) 5
87	Epic 650805 8	Rhythm Is Gonna Get You/Rhythm Is Gonna Get You (Dub Mix)/Give It Up (12", 'red dress' p/s)... 8
87	Epic 651125 7	Betcha Say That/Love Toy (p/s) 5
87	Epic 651125 8	Betcha Say That/Betcha Say That (Dub)/Love Toy (12", p/s)......... 8
87	Epic 651125 9	Betcha Say That/Love Toy/The Megamix (Rhythm Is Gonna Get You/ Conga/Dr. Beat/Betcha Say That/Bad Boy) (12", p/s) 10
88	Epic 650805 7	Rhythm Is Gonna Get You/Give It Up (reissue, 'Stakeout' p/s)......... 8
88	Epic 650805 8	Rhythm Is Gonna Get You/Rhythm Is Gonna Get You (Dub Mix)/ Give It Up (12", reissue, white 'Stakeout' p/s)...................... 8
88	Epic 650805 9	Rhythm Is Gonna Get You (7.09)/Rhythm Is Gonna Get You (live)/ Give It Up (12", reissue, black 'Stakeout' p/s)...................... 15
88	Epic 651444 0	Can't Stay Away From You/Let It Loose (poster p/s)................ 20
88	Epic 651444 7	Can't Stay Away From You/Let It Loose ('dreamy' p/s)............... 5
88	Epic 651444 8	Can't Stay Away From You/Let It Loose/Primitive Love (12", 'dreamy' p/s) 8
88	Epic 651444 9	Can't Stay Away From You/Let It Loose/Bad Boy (Remix) (12", 'dreamy' p/s) 10
88	Epic 651444 2	Can't Stay Away From You/Rhythm Is Gonna Get You/Surrender (Remix) (3" CD with adaptor in 5" p/s) 10
88	Epic 651444 2	Can't Stay Away From You/Rhythm Is Gonna Get You/Surrender (Remix) (5" CD) 8
88	Epic 651673 9	Anything For You (English)/Words Get In The Way/The Megamix (Rhythm Is Gonna Get You/Conga/Dr. Beat/Betcha Say That/Bad Boy) (12", p/s)... 8
88	Epic 651673 2	Anything For You (English Version)/Anything For You (Spanish Version)/ The Megamix: Rhythm Is Gonna Get You/Conga!/Dr. Beat/Betcha Say That/ Bad Boy (CD, card sleeve).. 8
88	Epic 652958 0	1-2-3/Surrender (poster p/s)...................................... 8
88	Epic 652958 1	1-2-3 (The Dancing By Numbers Mix)/Anything For You (English/Spanish Version)/Surrender (Remixed By Humberto Gatica) (12", p/s) 8
88	Epic 652958 2	1-2-3 (Extended Version)/1-2-3 (Dub Mix)/Surrender/ Primitive Love (CD, card sleeve) 8
88	Epic 654534 7	Rhythm Is Gonna Get You/Give It Up (reissue, badge shrinkwrapped to p/s) 10
88	Epic 654514 0	Rhythm Is Gonna Get You/Give It Up (calendar gatefold p/s)... 8
88	Epic 654514 9	Rhythm Is Gonna Get You/Give It Up (poster p/s).. 8
88	Epic 654514 8	Rhythm Is Gonna Get You/Rhythm Is Gonna Get You (live)/Give It Up (12", p/s)... 8
88	Epic 654514 2	Rhythm Is Gonna Get You (Special Version)/Conga! (Dance Mix)/Give It Up (CD, card sleeve) 8
89	Epic 654854 3	SOLID GOLD: Can't Stay Away From You/Dr. Beat/Conga! (3" CD, gatefold card sleeve).. 8
87	Epic 450910 1	LET IT LOOSE (LP) 15
84	Epic EPC 26167	EYES OF INNOCENCE (CD)...................................... 25
85	Epic EPC 26491	PRIMITIVE LOVE (CD) 25
87	Epic EPC 450910 2	LET IT LOOSE (CD) 25
	(see also Gloria Estefan, Miami Sound Machine)	

GLORIA ESTEFAN

89	Epic 653195 0	Can't Stay Away From You/Let It Loose (reissue, poster p/s)	7
89	Epic 653195 7	Can't Stay Away From You/Let It Loose (shaped picture disc)	10
89	Epic 653195 2	Can't Stay Away From You/Let It Loose/Primitive (CD, card sleeve)	8
89	Epic 655054 9	Don't Wanna Lose You/Words Get In The Way (live) (poster p/s)	7
89	Epic 655054 1	THE BALLADS TWELVE INCH: Don't Wanna Lose You/Anything For You/ Can't Stay Away From You/Words Get In The Way (12" p/s)	8
89	Epic 655054 3	Don't Wanna Lose You/Si Voy A Perderte/Words Get In The Way (live) (3" CD)	8
89	Epic 655287 8	Oye Mi Canto (Hear My Voice) (English Version) (Def 12" Mix (8.18)/ Oye Mi Canto (Hear My Voice) (English Version) (Def Dub Mix) (5.12)/ Oye Mi Canto (Hear My Voice) (English Version) (House Mix) (4.33) (12", p/s)	8
89	Epic 655287 5	Oye Mi Canto (Spanish Version) (Edit)/Anything For You (Spanish Version)/ Words Get In The Way (Spanish Version)/Si Voy A Perderte (Don't Wanna Lose You) (Spanish Version) (CD, picture disc)	20
89	Epic 655450 0	Get On Your Feet/1-2-3 (live) ('Tour Souvenir' issue with 4 postcards)	7
89	Epic 655450 5	Get On Your Feet (Pop Vocal)/Get On Your Feet (Special Mix)/1-2-3 (live) (12", calendar gatefold p/s)	8
89	Epic 655450 8	Get On Your Feet (House Vocal) (6.50)/Get On Your Feet (House Techno Dub) (5.30)/Get On Your Feet (Deep Bass Vocal) (5.29) (12", p/s)	12
89	Epic 655450 2	Get On Your Feet (7" Version)/Get On Your Feet (Pop Vocal)/ 1-2-3 (live)/Don't Wanna Lose You (Portuguese) (CD, card sleeve)	8
90	Epic 655728 7	Here We Are/Don't Let The Sun Go Down On Me (envelope pack, with print)	8
90	Epic 655982 0	Cuts Both Ways/You Made A Fool Of Me (poster p/s)	6
91	Epic 656574 0	Coming Out Of The Dark/Desde La Oscuridad (Spanish Version) (frame pack with 2 prints)	5
91	Epic 656773 0	Seal Our Fate/Seal Our Fate (Remix Edit) (foldout tour souvenir pack with 2 prints, postcards & poster)	5
91	Epic 656968 0	Remember Me With Love/Your Love Is Bad For Me (pull-out portrait pack with 4 photos & lyrics)	5

(see also Gloria Estefan & Miami Sound Machine)

'SLEEPY' JOHN ESTES

66	Delmark DJB 3	SLEEPY JOHN'S GOT THE BLUES (EP)	20
63	Esquire 32-195	THE LEGEND OF SLEEPY JOHN ESTES (LP)	40
63	'77' LA 12-27	TENNESSEE JUG BUSTERS — BROKE AND HUNGRY (LP)	25
65	Storyville SLP 172	PORTRAITS IN BLUES VOLUME 10 (LP)	20
72	Delmark DS 619	ELECTRIC SLEEP (LP)	12

JOHN ESTES/FURRY LEWIS/WILL SHADE

71	Revival RVS 1008	OLD ORIGINAL TENNESSEE BLUES (LP)	15

JACKIE ESTICK

61	Blue Beat BB 64	Boss Girl/COUNT OSSIE & GROUP: Cassavubu	18
63	Island WI 042	Since You've Been Gone/Daisy I Love You	18
66	Ska Beat JB 256	The Ska/Daisy I Love You	15

DEON ESTUS

89	Mika MIKAG 2	Heaven Help Me/It's A Party/Love Can't Wait (poster p/s)	5
89	Mika MIKCD 2	Heaven Help Me/It's A Party/Love Can't Wait/Me Or The Rumours (Instrumental) (CD, card p/s)	12

(see also George Michael)

ETCETERAS

64	Oriole CB 1950	Where Is My Love/Bengawan Solo	10
64	Oriole CB 1973	Little Lady/Now I Know	15

ETERNAL

93	EMI EM 283	Stay/Don't Say Goodbye (p/s)	6
93	EMI CDEM 283	Stay (7" Mix)/Stay (12" Mix)/Stay (Original Mix)/Don't Say Goodbye (CD)	8
94	EMI EMLH 353	Oh Baby I.../Sweet Funky Thing (jukebox issue, no p/s)	6
94	EMI CDEM 353	Oh Baby I... (Nigel Lowis Remix)/Sweet Funky Thing (Puff The Blunted Dragon Mix)/Sweet Funky Thing (K&T Atlanta Remix)/Decisions (CD)	8
94	EMI EM 364	Crazy/Something So Strong/Amazing Grace/His Eye's On The Sparrow (p/s, unreleased, 25 copies pressed)	25+
95	EMI EMLH 396	Power Of A Woman (jukebox issue, no p/s)	6
95	EMI 12EMDJX 396	Power Of A Woman (Fathers Of Sound Vocal Mix)/(Bottom Dollar Vocal Mix)/ Fathers Of Sound Dub Mix)/(Bottom Dollar Dub Mix)/(Boot & Mac Mix) (12", double pack, promo only)	12
96	EMI EMLH 408	I Am Blessed/Faith In Love (jukebox issue, no p/s)	6
96	EMI 12EMDJD 419	GOOD THING — THE HOUSE MIXES: Frankie Knuckles Vocal Club Mix/ Frankie Knuckles Vocal Dub Mix/Bottom Dollar Vocal Mix/Bottom Dollar Dub Mix/Argonauts Club Mix (12", double pack, p/s, promo only)	12
96	EMI EMLH 439	Someday (jukebox issue, no p/s)	6
96	EMI CDEMDDJ 1090	Power Of A Woman/And I Am Blessed/Good Thing/Telling You Now (CD, sampler, promo only)	10
97	EMI EMLH 465	Don't You Love Me/Someday (jukebox issue, no p/s)	6
97	EMI 12EMDJX 465	Don't You Love Me (Eternal's Rap)/(Ronnie Size Mix) (12", p/s, promo only)	7
97	EMI 12EMDJ 465	Don't You Love Me (Trade Mix)/(S&T Mix)//(Mark's Dream House Vocal)/ (Mark's Dream House Dub) (12", double pack, p/s, promo only)	12

97	EMI 12EMDJ 493	Angel Of Mine (Blacksmith's Eternal Meets D&D Mix)/Angel Of Mine (Ignorants Club Mix)/Dreams (12", p/s, promo only)	10
97	EMI 12EMDJ 472	I Wanna Be The Only One (SPS Cained Extended Club Mix)/ (SPS Cained Mix) (12", orange title p/s, promo only)	10
97	EMI 12EMDJX 472	I Wanna Be The Only One (Blacksmith's Eternal Mix Tape)/(Blacksmith's R&B Rub Mix)/(Bosskat Main Mix) (12", white title p/s, promo only)	10
97	EMI 12EMDJD 472	I Wanna Be The Only One (Black Box Lelewel Till The End Mix)/ (Paul Gotel Dark Skies Mix)/(Black Box Lelewel Scuba Dub Mix)/ (Paul Gotel Full Tilt Mix) (12", double pack, burgandy title p/s, promo only)	12
97	EMI CDEMDJX 472	I Wanna Be The Only One (Blacksmith's Eternal Mix Tape)/(Blacksmith's R&B Rub Mix)/(Boxx Cat Mean Mix)/(Boss Cat Beatless Mix) (CD, promo only)	8
97	EMI 12DJ HITS 001	THE MEGAMIX (ETERNAL VERSUS DMC) (12", 1-sided, etched B-side, promo only)	12
97	EMI CDDJ HITS 001	THE MEGAMIX (ETERNAL VERSUS DMC) (CD, 1-track, promo only)	12
99	EMI (no cat. no.)	ETERNAL (box set, CD in digipak, video, photos and biography, promo only)	30

(see also Louise)

ETERNALS (U.S.)

| 59 | London HL 8995 | Rockin' In The Jungle/Rock 'N' Roll Cha-Cha (triangular or round centre) | 100/60 |
| 59 | London HL 8995 | Rockin' In The Jungle/Rock 'N' Roll Cha-Cha (78) | 60 |

ETERNALS (Jamaica)

69	Coxsone CS 7091	Queen Of The Minstrels/Stars	18
70	Moodisc MU 3506	Christmas Joy/WINSTON & RUPERT: Musically Beat	6
71	Moodisc MU 3507	Push Me In The Corner/MUDIE'S ALL STARS: Mudie's Madness (B-side actually by Ansell Collins)	10
71	Moodisc MU 3508	Keep On Dancing/HAZEL WRIGHT: My Jealous Eyes	8

(see also Don Cornel & Eternals)

ETERNAL SCREAM

| 82 | Eternal ERO 1 | Hypocrite/Action In My Life (p/s) | 4 |

ETERNAL TRIANGLE

| 69 | Decca F 12954 | Turn To Me/Windows | 5 |
| 69 | Decca F 12979 | I Guess The Lord Must Be In New York City/Perfumed Candle | 5 |

ETHEL THE FROG

80	Best SRTSFMR 014	Eleanor Rigby/Fight Back	120
80	EMI EMI 5041	Eleanor Rigby/Fight Back (reissue)	15
80	EMI EMC 3329	ETHEL THE FROG (LP, with Terry Hopkinson & Doug Sheppard)	20

MELISSA ETHERIDGE

88	Island CID 376	Don't You Need (Extended)/Similar Features/Precocious Pain/	
88	Island CID 393	Bring Me Some Water/Occasionally/I Want You (CD)	8
89	Island CID 431	No Souvenirs/No Souvenirs (live)/Brave And Crazy Life (CD)	8
96	Island CID 642	Nowhere To Go (Remix)/Bring Me Some Water/Nowhere To Go (live)/ Like The Way I Do (live) (CD, withdrawn)	8

ETHIOPIANS

66	Ska Beat JB 260	Live Good (credited to the Etheopians)/SOUL BROTHERS: Soho	25
66	Island WI 3015	I Am Free/SOUL BROTHERS: Shanty Town	18
67	Rio R 110	Owe Me No Pay Me/SHARKS: I Wouldn't Baby	12
67	Rio R 114	I'm Gonna Take Over Now/JACKIE MITTOO: Home Made	20
67	Rio R 123	What To Do/JACKIE MITTOO: Got My Bugaloo	18
67	Rio R 126	Dun Dead A'Ready/Stay In My Lonely Arms	20
67	Rio R 130	Train To Skaville/You Are The Girl (B-side actually by Gladiators)	15
67	Doctor Bird DB 1092	I Need You/Do It Sweet	18
67	Doctor Bird DB 1096	The Whip/Cool It, Amigo	15
67	Doctor Bird DB 1103	Stay Loose, Mama/The World Goes Ska	18
68	Doctor Bird DB 1141	Come On Now/Sh'Boom	18
68	Doctor Bird DB 1147	Engine 54/Give Me Your Love	40
68	Doctor Bird DB 1148	Train To Glory/You Got The Dough	18
68	Doctor Bird DB 1169	Everything Crash/I'm Not Losing You	15
68	Crab CRAB 2	Fire A Muss Tail/Blacker Black (B-side actually by Count Ossie)	10
68	Crab CRAB 5	Reggie Hit The Town/Ding Dong Bell	10
69	Crab CRAB 7	I Am A King/What A Big Surprise	10
69	Doctor Bird DB 1172	Not Me/Cut Down	10
69	Doctor Bird DB 1185	Hong Kong Flu/Clap Your Hands	12
69	Doctor Bird DB 1186	What A Fire/You	12
69	Doctor Bird DB 1199	Everyday Talking/Sharing You	12
69	Trojan TR 666	Woman Capture Man/One	7
69	Trojan TR 697	Well Red/J.J. ALLSTARS: R.F.K.	7
69	Nu Beat NB 031	My Testimony/J.J. ALL STARS: One Dollar Of Soul	8
69	Duke DU 35	My Girl/ANSELL COLLINS: Bigger Boss	8
70	Duke DU 61	Mek You Go On So/WINSTON WRIGHT & J.J. ALL STARS: Neck Tie	8
70	Duke Reid DR 2507	Mother's Tender Care/TOMMY McCOOK: Soldier Man	5
70	Bamboo BAM 26	Walkie Talkie/SOUND DIMENSION: Moan And Groan	8
70	Bamboo BAM 38	You'll Want To Come Back/JACKIE MITTOO: Baby Why (Instrumental) (B-side actually by Sound Dimension)	8
70	J.J. JJ 3302	Wreck It Up/Don't Go	8
70	J.J. JJ 3303	Hong Kong Flu/Everything Crash	6
70	Gas GAS 142	Satan Girl/MATADORS: The Pum	6
70	High Note HS 042	Praise For I (actually "Praise Fari")/GAYTONES: Charrie Part II.	8
70	Songbird SB 1040	No Baptism/CRYSTALITES: No Baptism (Version Two)	7
70	Songbird SB 1047	Good Ambition/CRYSTALITES: Ambition Version	6
71	Randy's RAN 509	Mi Want Girl/RANDY'S ALL STARS: Girl — Version	7
71	Randy's RAN 510	True Man, Free Man/RANDY'S ALL STARS: Truthful — Version	7
71	Randy's RAN 512	Mr. Tom/Sad News	7
71	Fab FAB 180	Monkey Money/Version	8

71	Treasure Isle TI 7067	Pirate/TOMMY McCOOK & SOUL SYNDICATE: Depth Charge	8
71	Songbird SB 1059	What A Pain/CRYSTALITES: Pain Version	6
71	Songbird SB 1062	Lot's Wife/DERRICK HARRIOTT: Slave	6
71	Songbird SB 1064	Best Of Five (Parts 1 & 2)	6
71	Big Shot BI 569	He's Not A Rebel/J.J. ALL STARS: He's Not A Rebel — Version	15
71	Big Shot BI 574	The Selah/Don't Let Me Go	6
71	Duke DU 102	Drop Him/J.J. ALL STARS: Drop Him Version	6
71	Duke DU 108	Rim Bim Bam/RANDY'S ALL STARS: Rim Bim Bam Version	7
71	Explosion EX 2050	Starvation/TROJAN ALL STARS: Starvation Version	6
71	G.G. GG 4519	Love Bug/Sound Of Our Forefathers	7
71	Supreme SUP 221	Love Bug/Sound Of Our Forefathers	6
71	Supreme SUP 226	Starvation/MAXIE & GLEN: Jordan River	6
71	Big BG 330	Solid As A Rock/RUPIE EDWARDS ALL STARS: Solid As A Rock Version	6
71	Punch PH 96	Solid As A Rock/RUPIE EDWARDS ALL STARS: Solid As A Rock Version	5
72	G.G. GG 4533	Israel Want To be Free/TYPHOON ALL STARS: Israel (Version)	6
72	Prince Buster PB 38	You Are For Me/Playboy	6
72	Techniques TE 919	Promises/TIVOLIS: Promises — Version	6
73	Harry J. HJ 6646	The Word Is Love/The Word Is Love — Version	5
74	Harry J. HJ 6663	Buy You A Ring/Pray Muma	5
75	Dragon DRA 1032	Knowledge Is Power/Power Version	5
68	Doctor Bird DLM 5011	THE ETHIOPIANS GO ROCK STEADY/ENGINE 54 (LP)	125
69	Trojan TTL 10	REGGAE POWER (LP)	20
70	Trojan TBL 112	WOMAN CAPTURE MAN (LP)	35

(see Eathopians, Soul Brothers, Soul Vendors, Hamliins)

ETIVES
81	Ayrespin AYRC 106	A BREATH OF FRESH AIR (cassette)	20
84	Ayrespin AYRC 015	AN GAOL A THUG MI OG (MY LOVE OF EARLY DAYS) (LP)	20
84	Ayrespin AYRC 015	AN GAOL A THUG MI OG (MY LOVE OF EARLY DAYS) (cassette)	12

(see also Capercaillie)

ETTA (James) & HARVEY (Fuqua)
60	London HLM 9180	If I Can't Have You/My Heart Cries	40

(see also Etta James, Moonglows, Harvey & Moonglows)

JACK EUBANK'S ORCHESTRA
61	London HLU 9312	What'd I Say/Chiricahua	7
62	London HLU 9501	Searchin'/Take A Message To Mary	7

EUGENE & BURST
71	Supreme SUP 225	Let It Fall/DENZIL & BURST: Can't Change	4

EUREKA BRASS BAND OF NEW ORLEANS
59	Melodisc MLP 12-110	MUSIC OF NEW ORLEANS (LP)	12
64	London HA-K/SH-K 8162	JAZZ AT PRESERVATION HALL VOL. 1 (LP)	12

EUREKA STOCKADE
70	Decca F 22996	Sing No Love Songs/Jump Down Turn Around	5

EUROPEANS
79	Heartbeat PULSE 2	Europeans/Voices (p/s)	5

EUROPEANS
82	A&M AMS 8245	Animal Song/Someone's Changing (p/s)	5
83	A&M AM 113	Aeious/Voice On The Telephone (p/s)	5
83	A&M AM 138	Recognition/New Industry (p/s)	7
83	A&M AM 158	American People/Going To Work (p/s)	5
83	A&M AMX 158	American People/Going To Work/Someone's Changing/New Industy (12", p/s)	8
84	A&M AM 184	Typical/Falling (p/s)	5
84	A&M AM 201	Listen/Climb The Wall (p/s)	5
84	A&M AMX 201	Listen/Climb The Wall (12", p/s)	8
83	A&M AMLX 68558	VOCABULARY (LP)	12
84	A&M SCOT 1	LIVE (LP)	12
84	A&M AMA 5034	RECURRING DREAMS (LP)	12

(see also Marillion)

EURYTHMICS
81	RCA RCA 68	Never Gonna Cry Again/Le Sinistre (p/s)	8
81	RCA RCAT 68	Never Gonna Cry Again (Extended)/Le Sinistre (Extended) (12", p/s)	25
81	RCA RCA 115	Belinda/Heartbeat, Heartbeat (p/s)	15
82	RCA RCA 199	This Is The House/Home Is Where The Heart Is (p/s)	15
82	RCA RCAT 199	This Is The House/Your Time Will Come (live)/Never Gonna Cry Again/ 4/4 In Leather (live)/Take Me To Your Heart (live) (12", p/s)	35
82	RCA RCA 230	The Walk/Step On The Beast/The Walk (Part 2) (p/s)	12
82	RCA RCAT 230	The Walk/Invisible Hands/Dr Trash/The Walk (Part 2) (12", printed die-cut sl.)	35
82	RCA DA 1	Love Is A Stranger/Monkey, Monkey (with reverse print on rear of p/s)	5
82	RCA DAP 1	Love Is A Stranger/Monkey, Monkey (picture disc)	5
82	RCA DAT 1	Love Is A Stranger/Let's Just Close Our Eyes/Monkey, Monkey (12", blue p/s)	8
83	RCA DAP 2	Sweet Dreams (Are Made Of This)/I Could Give You (A Mirror) (picture disc)	6
83	RCA DAT 2	Sweet Dreams (Are Made Of This)/I Could Give You (A Mirror)/ Baby's Gone Blue (12", p/s)	8
83	RCA DAP 3	Who's That Girl?/You Take Some Lentils … And You Take Some Rice (picture disc)	7
83	RCA DAT 3	Who's That Girl?/You Take Some Lentils … And You Take Some Rice/ ABC (Freeform) (12", p/s)	8
83	RCA DA 4/EUC 001	Right By Your Side/Right By Your Side (Party Mix) (stickered p/s)	5
83	RCA EUC 001	INTRO SPEECH: "Intro Speech"/"Step On The Beast"/ "Invisible Hands"/"Angel (Dub)"/"Satellite Of Love")	30
83	RCA DAP 4	Right By Your Side/Right By Your Side (Party Mix) (picture disc)	6
83	RCA DAT 4	Right By Your Side/Right By Your Side (Special Mix)/ Pluse Something Else (12", p/s)	8
84	RCA DAP 5	Here Comes The Rain Again/Paint A Rumour (picture disc)	5

84	RCA DAT 5	Here Comes The Rain Again/This City Never Sleeps (live)/ Paint A Rumour (Long Version) (12", p/s)	8
84	Virgin VSY 728-12	Sexcrime (1984) (Extended Mix)/Sexcrime (1984) (Single Version)/ I Did It Just The Same (12" picture disc)	10
85	Virgin VSY 734	Julia/Ministry Of Love (picture disc in pop-up p/s)	8
85	Virgin VSY 734-12	Julia (Extended Version)/Ministry Of Love (12", picture disc, unissued)	
85	RCA PB 40101	Would I Lie To You?/Here Comes That Sinking Feeling (p/s, red, blue, or yellow vinyl)	each 5
85	RCA PT 40102	Would I Lie To You? (E.T. Mix)/Would I Lie To You? (Extended Remix)/Here Comes That Sinking Feeling (12", p/s, red, blue or yellow vinyl)	each 8
85	RCA PT 40248R	There Must Be An Angel (Playing With My Heart) (Special Dance Mix)/ Grown Up Girls (12", p/s)	8
85	RCA PB 40375	It's Alright (Baby's Coming Back)/Conditioned Soul ('video still' p/s)	5
85	RCA PB 40375/PB 40101	It's Alright (Baby's Coming Back)/Conditioned Soul//Would I Lie To You?/ Here Comes That Sinking Feeling (double pack, with free coloured vinyl 7")	12
85	RCA PB 40376/PB 40102	It's Alright (Baby's Coming Back)/Conditioned Soul/Tous Les Garçons Et Les Filles//Would I Lie To You? (E.T. Mix)/Would I Lie To You? (Extended Remix)/ Here Comes That Sinking Feeling (12", double pack, gatefold PVC sleeve; 2nd on coloured vinyl)	12
85	RCA BYTI 100	I Love You Like A Ball And Chain (mono)/I Love You Like A Ball And Chain (stereo) (promo only)	8
86	RCA DA 8	Thorn In My Side/In This Town (p/s, with shrinkwrapped enamel badge)	8
86	RCA DA 9P	The Miracle Of Love/When Tomorrow Comes (live) (shaped picture disc)	10
87	RCA DA 11P	Beethoven (I Love To Listen To)/Heaven (poster p/s)	5
87	RCA DA 11CD	Beethoven (I Love To Listen To)/Heaven/Beethoven (I Love To Listen To) (Dance Mix) (CD, card sleeve)	8
87	RCA DAT 14P	Shame (Dance Mix)/I've Got A Lover (Back In Japan)/Shame (12", p/s & print)	8
87	RCA DA 14CD	Shame (Dance Mix)/I've Got A Lover (Back In Japan)/There Must Be An Angel (Playing With My Heart) (live) (CD)	10
88	RCA DA 15R	I Need A Man (live)/I Need A Man/I Need You (numbered gatefold p/s)	5
88	RCA DA 15X	I Need A Man/I Need You/There Must Be An Angel (Playing With My Heart) (live)/ Missionary Man (live) (10", p/s)	8
88	RCA DA 15CD	I Need A Man/Missionary Man (Live Version)/I Need You/I Need A Man (Macho Mix) (CD, picture disc in numbered metal tin)	8
88	RCA DA 16CD	You Have Placed A Chill In My Heart (Remix)/Do You Want To Break Up? (Dance Mix)/Here Comes The Rain Again (Live Version)/You Have Placed A Chill In My Heart (Acoustic Version) (CD, numbered black metal tin)	8
88	Virgin CDT 22	Sexcrime (1984) (Extended 12" Remix)/Julia (Extended 12" Remix)/I Did It Just The Same (3" CD, gatefold card sleeve)	10
88	Virgin CDF 22	Sexcrime (1984) (Extended 12" Remix)/Julia (Extended 12" Remix)/I Did It Just The Same (5" CD)	8
89	RCA DACD 17	Revival (E.T. Mix)/Precious/Revival (Extended Dance Mix) (CD)	8
89	RCA DACD 20	Don't Ask Me Why/Rich Girl/When The Day Goes Down (Acoustic Version)/ Don't Ask Me Why (Acoustic Version) (CD, numbered 7" box with poster)	12
90	RCA DACD 24	The King And Queen Of America/There Must Be An Angel (Playing With My Heart) (live)/I Love You Like A Ball And Chain (live)/See No Evil (CD, in numbered wood box)	12
90	RCA DAT 25	Angel (Remix)/Sweet Dreams (Are Made Of This) (Nightmare Mix) (12", p/s)	10
83	Lyntone LYN 13916	A CHRISTMAS MESSAGE (fan club flexidisc, no p/s)	10
84	Lyntone LYN 15292	A YULETIDE MESSAGE TO ALL OUR PALS (fan club flexidisc, no p/s)	10
87	Lyntone (no cat. no.)	DAVE AND ANNIE'S CHRISTMAS MESSAGE '87 (fan club flexidisc, no p/s)	10
89	Flexi FLX 880	DAVE AND ANNIE'S CHRISTMAS MESSAGE '89 (fan club flexidisc, foldout p/s)	10
90	Flexi FLX 1000	DAVE AND ANNIE'S CHRISTMAS MESSAGE '90 (fan club flexidisc, foldout p/s)	10
83	RCA RCALP 6063	SWEET DREAMS (LP, picture disc)	12
83	RCA PL 70109	TOUCH (LP, picture disc)	12
00	Parlophone (no cat. no.)	PEACE (CD, promo, with book)	75

(see also David A. Stewart, Annie Lennox & Al Green, Catch, Tourists, Chris & Cosey, Longdancer, Stewart & Harrison)

JOHN EVAN BAND
90	A New Day NRS/CD 1	THE JOHN EVAN BAND LIVE '66 (CD, 500 only)	75

(see also Jethro Tull)

BARBARA EVANS
59	RCA RCA 1122	Souvenirs/Pray For Me, Mother (78)	20
59	RCA RCA 1122	Souvenirs/Pray For Me, Mother (triangular centre)	20
61	Mercury AMT 1151	Charlie Wasn't There/Nothing You Can Do	5

CHRISTINE EVANS
65	Philips BF 1406	Growing Pains/Someone In Love	6
66	Philips BF 1496	Somewhere There's Love/Right Or Wrong	10
67	Melodisc MEL 1620	I'm Gonna Tell Tony/Someone In Love	6

DAVE EVANS
71	Village Thing VTS 6	THE WORDS IN BETWEEN (LP)	12
72	Village Thing VTS 14	ELEPHANTASIA (LP)	12
74	Kicking Mule SNKF 107	SAD PIG DANCE (LP, with booklet)	12

GIL EVANS ORCHESTRA
60	Vogue EPV 1266	GREAT JAZZ STANDARDS (EP)	10
60	Vogue LAE 12234	GREAT JAZZ STANDARDS (LP)	15
75	RCA LSA 3192	PLAYS THE MUSIC OF JIMI HENDRIX (LP)	15

JOHN EVANS
62	Palette PG 9040	Melodie Pour Madame/Cry Me A River	7

LARRY EVANS
56	London HLU 8269	Crazy 'Bout My Baby/Henpecked	550
56	London HLU 8269	Crazy 'Bout My Baby/Henpecked (78)	100

MINT VALUE £

MAUREEN EVANS

78s

58	Embassy WB 300	Carolina Moon/Stupid Cupid (78)	8
58	Embassy WB 303	Fever/Born Too Late (78)	8
58	Embassy WB 309	The Hula Hoop Song/Hoopa Hoola (78)	8
58	Embassy WB 313	I'll Get By/Someday (You'll Want Me To Want You) (78)	8
58	Embassy WB 316	You Always Hurt The One You Love/The Day The Rains Came (78)	8
58	Embassy WB 319	To Know Him Is To Love Him/Kiss Me, Honey Honey, Kiss Me (78)	8
59	Embassy WB 344	Goodbye Jimmy, Goodbye/May You Always (78)	8
59	Embassy WB 348	Lipstick On Your Collar/What A Diff'rence A Day Made (78)	12
59	Embassy WB 356	Broken-Hearted Melody/Plenty Good Lovin' (78)	8
59	Embassy WB 371	Among My Souvenirs/Happy Anniversary (78)	12
59	Oriole CB 1517	Don't Want The Moonlight/The Years Between (78)	10
60	Oriole CB 1533	The Big Hurt/I Can't Begin To Tell You (78)	15
60	Oriole CB 1540	Love, Kisses And Heartaches/We Just Couldn't Say Goodbye (78)	15
60	Oriole CB 1550	Paper Roses/Please Understand (78)	25

SINGLES

58	Embassy WB 300	Carolina Moon/Stupid Cupid	6
58	Embassy WB 303	Fever/Born Too Late	6
58	Embassy WB 309	The Hula Hoop Song/Hoopa Hoola	6
58	Embassy WB 313	I'll Get By/Someday (You'll Want Me To Want You)	6
58	Embassy WB 316	You Always Hurt The One You Love/The Day The Rains Came	6
58	Embassy WB 319	To Know Him Is To Love Him/Kiss Me, Honey Honey, Kiss Me	6
59	Embassy WB 344	Goodbye Jimmy, Goodbye/May You Always	6
59	Embassy WB 348	Lipstick On Your Collar/What A Diff'rence A Day Made	6
59	Embassy WB 356	Broken-Hearted Melody/Plenty Good Lovin'	6
59	Embassy WB 371	Among My Souvenirs/Happy Anniversary	6
59	Oriole CB 1517	Don't Want The Moonlight/The Years Between	5
60	Oriole CB 1533	The Big Hurt/I Can't Begin To Tell You	5
60	Oriole CB 1540	Love, Kisses And Heartaches/We Just Couldn't Say Goodbye	5
60	Oriole CB 1550	Paper Roses/Please Understand	5
61	Oriole CB 1563	Mama Wouldn't Like It/My Little Corner Of The World	5
61	Oriole CB 1578	As Long As He Needs Me/Where Is Love?	5
61	Oriole CB 1581	Till/Why Don't You Believe Me	5
61	Oriole CB 1613	My Foolish Heart/Oh Gypsy Oh Gypsy	5
62	Oriole CB 1743	Never In A Million Years/We Had Words	5
62	Oriole CB 1760	Like I Do/Starlight Starbright	5
63	Oriole CB 1804	Pick The Petals/Melancholy Me	5
63	Oriole CB 1806	Tomorrow Is Another Day/Acapulco Mexico	5
63	Oriole CB 1851	What A Difference A Day Made/Oh What A Guy	5
63	Oriole CB 1875	Like You Used To Do/As You Love Her	5
64	Oriole CB 1906	I Love How You Love Me/John John	5
64	Oriole CB 1939	He Knows I Love Him Too Much/Don't Believe Him	5
64	Oriole CB 1969	Get Away/I've Often Wondered	5
65	CBS 201733	All The Angels Sing/Speak Sugar Speak	6
65	CBS 201752	Never Let Him Go/Poco Sole	6
67	CBS 202621	Somewhere There's Love/It Takes A Little Time	8
68	CBS 3222	I Almost Called Your Name/Searching For Home	6
63	Oriole EP 7076	MELANCHOLY ME (EP)	40
63	Oriole PS 40046	LIKE I DO (LP)	40

(see also Matt Bryant & Linda Joyce)

PAUL EVANS (& CURLS)

59	London HLL 8968	Seven Little Girls Sitting In The Back Seat/Worshipping An Idol (with Curls)	10
59	London HLL 8968	Seven Little Girls Sitting In The Back Seat/Worshipping An Idol (78)	50
60	London HLL 9045	Midnite Special/Since I Met You, Baby	12
60	London HLL 9129	Happy-Go-Lucky Me/Fish In The Ocean	8
60	London HLL 9183	Brigade Of Broken Hearts/Twins	8
60	London HLL 9239	Hushabye Little Guitar/Blind Boy	12
62	London HLR 9636	The Bell That Couldn't Jingle/Gilding The Lily	6
63	London HLR 9770	Even Tan/Ten Thousand Years	10
63	London RE-R 1349	PAUL EVANS (EP)	75
60	London HA-L 2248	PAUL EVANS SINGS THE FABULOUS TEENS (LP)	75

RUSSELL EVANS & NITEHAWKS

66	Atlantic 584 010	Send Me Some Cornbread/The Bold	8

EVEN DOZEN JUG BAND

66	Bounty BY 6023	THE EVEN DOZEN JUG BAND (LP)	15

(see also Lovin' Spoonful, John Sebastian)

DAME EDNA EVERAGE

78	Charisma CB 329	Every Mother Wants A Boy Like Elton/S&M Lady	5
79	Charisma CB 336	Disco Matilda/EVERAGE WHITE BAND: Disco Matilda	5

BETTY EVERETT

64	Stateside SS 259	You're No Good/Chained To Your Love	12
64	Stateside SS 280	It's In His Kiss (The Shoop Shoop Song)/Hands Off	10
64	Stateside SS 321	I Can't Hear You/Can I Get To Know You	12
64	Fontana TF 520	Getting Mighty Crowded/Chained To A Memory	10
64	King KG 1002	Happy I Long To Be/Your Loving Arms	8
65	Sue WI 352	I've Got A Claim On You/Your Love Is Important To Me	25
68	President PT 215	It's In His Kiss (The Shoop Shoop Song)/Getting Mighty Crowded	5
69	President PT 251	You're No Good/Hands Off	5
69	MCA Soul Bag BAG 3	I Can't Say No To You/Better Tomorrow Than Today	6
69	MCA MU 1055	There'll Come A Time/Take Me	5
70	Uni UN 517	Sugar/Hold On	6
71	Liberty LBF 15428	I Got To Tell Somebody/Why Are You Leaving Me	5
72	President PT 372	Trouble Over The Weekend/The Shoe Doesn't Fit	6
65	Fontana TL 5236	IT'S IN HIS KISS (LP)	45
68	Joy JOYS 106	IT'S IN HIS KISS (LP, reissue)	15
69	Uni UNLS 109	THERE'LL COME A TIME (LP)	18

BETTY EVERETT & JERRY BUTLER

64	Stateside SS 339	Let It Be Me/Ain't That Lovin' You Baby	8
65	Fontana TF 528	Smile/Love Is Strange	8
68	President PT 214	Let It Be Me/Smile	5
69	President PT 252	Our Day Will Come/Just Be True	5
65	Fontana TL 5237	DELICIOUS TOGETHER (LP)	30
68	Joy JOYS 123	DELICIOUS TOGETHER (LP, reissue)	15

(see also Jerry Butler)

KENNY EVERETT

68	MGM MGM 1421	It's Been So Long/Without Her	6
69	Deram DM 245	Nice Time/And Now For A Little Train Number	6
78	Yuk NE 1023	20 WORST SONGS EVER RECORDED (LP, 'puke' coloured vinyl)	12

(see also Kenny & Cash)

VINCE EVERETT

65	Fontana TF 606	Bless You/'Til I Lost You	6
67	Fontana TF 818	Endlessly/Who's That Girl?	6
68	Fontana TF 915	Every Now And Then/Barbarella	15

EVERGREEN BLUES

67	Mercury MF 1012	Midnight Confessions/(Yes) That's My Baby	6
68	Mercury MF 1025	Laura (Keep Hangin' On)/Yesterday's Coming	6
68	Mercury 20122 SMCL	7 DO ELEVEN (LP)	12

EVERGREEN BLUESHOES

69	London HA-U/SH-U 8399	THE BALLAD OF THE EVERGREEN BLUESHOES (LP)	15

(see also Skip Battin, Byrds)

EVERLY BROTHERS

78s

57	London HLA 8440	Bye Bye, Love/I Wonder If I Care As Much (78)	10
57	London HLA 8498	Wake Up Little Susie/Maybe Tomorrow (78)	10
58	London HLA 8554	Should We Tell Him/This Little Girl Of Mine (78)	20
58	London HLA 8618	All I Have To Do Is Dream/Claudette (78)	12
58	London HLA 8685	Bird Dog/Devoted To You (78)	20
58	London HLA 8781	Problems/Love Of My Life (78)	30
59	London HLA 8863	Poor Jenny/Take A Message To Mary (78)	40
59	London HLA 8934	('Til) I Kissed You/Oh, What A Feeling (78)	60
60	London HLA 9039	Let It Be Me/Since You Broke My Heart (78)	80
60	Warner Bros WB 1	Cathy's Clown/Always It's You (78)	200
60	London HLA 9157	When Will I Be Loved/Be-Bop-A-Lula (78)	150
60	Warner Bros WB 19	Lucille/So Sad (To Watch Good Love Go Bad) (78)	250

SINGLES

57	London HLA 8440	Bye Bye, Love/I Wonder If I Care As Much	20/8
57	London HLA 8498	Wake Up Little Susie/Maybe Tomorrow	15/8
58	London HLA 8554	Should We Tell Him/This Little Girl Of Mine	20/8
58	London HLA 8618	All I Have To Do Is Dream/Claudette	8/5
58	London HLA 8685	Bird Dog/Devoted To You	8/5
58	London HLA 8781	Problems/Love Of My Life	8/5
59	London HLA 8863	Poor Jenny/Take A Message To Mary	10/6
59	London HLA 8934	('Til) I Kissed You/Oh, What A Feeling	10/6
60	London HLA 9039	Let It Be Me/Since You Broke My Heart	15/6

(Where two prices are listed above, the first refers to original triangular centres, the second to later round centres.)

60	Warner Bros WB 1	Cathy's Clown/Always It's You	5
60	London HLA 9157	When Will I Be Loved/Be-Bop-A-Lula	8
60	Warner Bros WB 19	Lucille/So Sad (To Watch Good Love Go Bad)	8
60	London HLA 9250	Like Strangers/Leave My Woman Alone	8
61	Warner Bros WB 33	Walk Right Back/Ebony Eyes	5
61	Warner Bros WB 42	Temptation/Stick With Me Baby	5
61	Warner Bros WB 50	Muskrat/Don't Blame Me	5
62	Warner Bros WB 56	Crying In The Rain/I'm Not Angry	5
62	Warner Bros WB 67	How Can I Meet Her?/That's Old Fashioned	6
62	Warner Bros WB 79	No One Can Make My Sunshine Smile/Don't Ask Me To Be Friends	6
63	Warner Bros WB 94	So It Will Always Be/Nancy's Minuet	6
63	Warner Bros WB 99	It's Been Nice/I'm Afraid	6
63	Warner Bros WB 109	The Girl Sang The Blues/Love Her	6
64	Warner Bros WB 129	Ain't That Lovin' You Baby/Hello Amy	7
64	Warner Bros WB 135	The Ferris Wheel/Don't Forget To Cry	5
64	Warner Bros WB 143	You're The One I Love/Ring Around My Rosie (withdrawn)	15
64	Warner Bros WB 146	Gone, Gone, Gone/Torture	8
65	Warner Bros WB 154	You're My Girl/Don't Let The Whole World Know	6
65	Warner Bros WB 158	That'll Be The Day/Give Me A Sweetheart	10
65	Warner Bros WB 161	The Price Of Love/It Only Costs A Dime	5
65	Warner Bros WB 5628	The Price Of Love/It Only Costs A Dime (reissue)	6
65	Warner Bros WB 5639	I'll Never Get Over You/Follow Me	6
65	Warner Bros WB 5649	Love Is Strange/Man With Money	5
66	Warner Bros WB 5682	It's All Over/I Used To Love You (unissued)	
66	Warner Bros WB 5743	(You Got) The Power Of Love/Leave My Girl Alone	10
66	Warner Bros WB 5754	I've Been Wrong Before/Hard Hard Year	12
67	Warner Bros WB 7520	Bowling Green/I Don't Want To Love You	12
67	Warner Bros WB 7062	Mary Jane/Talking To The Flowers	12
67	Warner Bros WB 7088	Love Of The Common People/A Voice Within	12
68	Warner Bros WB 7192	It's My Time/Empty Boxes	10
68	Warner Bros WB 7226	Milk Train/Lord Of The Manor	12
69	Warner Bros WB 6056	Cathy's Clown/Walk Right Back	6
70	Warner Bros WB 6074	Good Golly, Miss Molly/Oh, Boy!	12
70	Warner Bros WB 7425	Yves/Human Race	12
72	RCA Victor RCA 2232	Ridin' High/Stories We Could Tell	10

MINT VALUE £

EVERLY BROTHERS

73	RCA Victor RCA 2286	Not Fade Away/Lay It Down	6
77	Warner Bros K 17004	Silent Treatment/Dancing On My Feet	5
79	Old Gold OG 9018	Bird Dog/Devoted To You (picture disc)	5
80	Old Gold SET 1	THE EVERLY BROTHERS SINGLES SET (15 x p/s 7", box set with book)	30

EPs

58	London RE-A 1113	THE EVERLY BROTHERS (EP)	25
58	London RE-A 1148	THE EVERLY BROTHERS — NO. 2 (EP)	25
58	London RE-A 1149	THE EVERLY BROTHERS — NO. 3 (EP)	30
59	London RE-A 1174	THE EVERLY BROTHERS — NO. 4 (EP)	30
59	London RE-A 1195	SONGS OUR DADDY TAUGHT US PART 1 (EP)	35
59	London RE-A 1196	SONGS OUR DADDY TAUGHT US PART 2 (EP)	35
59	London RE-A 1197	SONGS OUR DADDY TAUGHT US PART 3 (EP)	35
60	London RE-A 1229	THE EVERLY BROTHERS — NO. 5 (EP)	30

(Prices for the above EPs refer to original triangular centre labels, round-centre editions are worth two-thirds these values.)

61	Warners W(S)EP 6034	ESPECIALLY FOR YOU (EP, mono/stereo)	25/45
61	London RE-A 1311	THE EVERLY BROTHERS — NO. 6 (EP)	35
62	Warners W(S)EP 6049	FOREVERLY YOURS (EP, mono/stereo)	25/50
62	Warners W(S)EP 6056	IT'S EVERLY TIME (EP, mono/stereo)	25/50
63	Warners W(S)EP 6107	A DATE WITH THE EVERLY BROTHERS VOL. 1 (EP, mono/stereo)	35/60
63	Warners W(S)EP 6109	A DATE WITH THE EVERLY BROTHERS VOL. 2 (EP, mono/stereo)	35/60
63	Warners W(S)EP 6111	INSTANT PARTY VOL. 1 (EP, mono/stereo)	35/60
63	Warners W(S)EP 6113	INSTANT PARTY VOL. 2 (EP, mono/stereo)	35/60
63	Warners W(S)EP 6115	BOTH SIDES OF AN EVENING — FOR DANCING VOL. 1 (EP, mono/stereo)	35/60
64	Warners W(S)EP 6117	BOTH SIDES OF AN EVENING — FOR DREAMING VOL. 2 (EP, mono/st.)	35/60
64	Warners WEP 6128	THE EVERLY BROTHERS SING GREAT COUNTRY HITS VOL. 1 (EP)	35
64	Warners WEP 6131	THE EVERLY BROTHERS SING GREAT COUNTRY HITS VOL. 2 (EP)	35
64	Warners WEP 6132	THE EVERLY BROTHERS SING GREAT COUNTRY HITS VOL. 3 (EP)	35
65	Warner Bros WEP 6138	BOTH SIDES OF AN EVENING — FOR FUN VOL. 3 (EP)	35
65	Warner Bros WEP 604	THE PRICE OF LOVE (EP)	25
65	Warner Bros WEP 608	ROCK'N'SOUL VOL. 1 (EP)	25
65	Warner Bros WEP 609	ROCK'N'SOUL VOL. 2 (EP)	25
66	Warner Bros WEP 610	LOVE IS STRANGE (EP)	35
66	Warner Bros WEP 612	PEOPLE GET READY (EP)	30
66	Warner Bros WEP 618	WHAT AM I LIVING FOR? (EP)	40
67	Warner Bros WEP 622	LEAVE MY GIRL ALONE (EP)	40
67	Warner Bros WEP 623	SOMEBODY HELP ME (EP)	30
72	Warner Bros K 16209	CRYING IN THE RAIN (EP)	10
74	Warner Bros K 16407	WAKE UP LITTLE SUSIE (EP)	10

LPs

58	London HA-A 2081	THE EVERLY BROTHERS (LP)	50
58	London HA-A 2150	SONGS OUR DADDY TAUGHT US (LP)	50
60	Warner Bros WM 4012	IT'S EVERLY TIME (LP, also stereo WS 8012)	25/35
60	London HA-A 2266	THE FABULOUS STYLE OF THE EVERLY BROTHERS (LP)	30
60	Warner Bros WM 4028	A DATE WITH THE EVERLY BROTHERS (LP, also stereo WS 8028)	25/35
61	Warner Bros WM 4052	BOTH SIDES OF AN EVENING (LP, also stereo WS 8052)	25/35
62	Warner Bros WM 4061	INSTANT PARTY (LP, also stereo WS 8061)	25/35
62	Warner Bros WM/WS 8108	THE GOLDEN HITS OF THE EVERLY BROTHERS (LP, mono/stereo)	15/18
62	Warner Bros WM/WS 8116	CHRISTMAS WITH THE EVERLY BROTHERS AND THE BOYS TOWN CHOIR (LP, mono/stereo)	30/40
63	Warner Bros WM/WS 8138	SING GREAT COUNTRY HITS (LP, mono/stereo)	25/30
64	Warner Bros WM/WS 8163	THE VERY BEST OF THE EVERLY BROTHERS (LP, mono/stereo)	12/15

MINT VALUE £

65	Warner Bros WM/WS 8169	GONE GONE GONE (LP, mono/stereo)	25/30
65	Warner Bros WM/WS 8171	ROCK 'N' SOUL (LP, mono/stereo)	25/35
65	Warner Bros W(S) 1471	THE GOLDEN HITS OF THE EVERLY BROTHERS (LP, reissue, m/s)	12/15
65	Warner Bros W(S) 1554	THE VERY BEST OF THE EVERLY BROTHERS (LP, reissue, m/s)	12/15
65	Warner Bros W(S) 1578	ROCK 'N' SOUL (LP, reissue)	20/25
65	Warner Bros W(S) 1605	BEAT 'N' SOUL (LP)	25
65	Warner Bros W(S) 1620	IN OUR IMAGE (LP, mono/stereo)	25/35
67	Warner Bros W(S) 1646	TWO YANKS IN ENGLAND (LP, mono/stereo)	25/35
67	Warner Bros W(S) 1676	THE HIT SOUND OF THE EVERLY BROTHERS (LP, mono/stereo)	25/35
67	Warner Bros W(S) 1708	THE EVERLY BROTHERS SING (LP, mono/stereo)	25/35
68	Warner Bros W(S) 1752	ROOTS (LP)	20
70	Warner Bros WS 1858	THE EVERLY BROTHERS SHOW (2-LP)	18
70	Valiant VS 109	GONE GONE GONE (LP, reissue)	12
71	CBS 66259	END OF AN ERA (2-LP)	15
71	Warner Bros K 46128	ROOTS (LP, reissue)	12
72	RCA Victor SF 8270	STORIES WE COULD TELL (LP)	15
73	RCA Victor SF 8332	PASS THE CHICKEN AND LISTEN (LP)	15
77	Warner Bros K 56415	THE NEW ALBUM (LP)	12
80	Marks & Spencer IMP 111	THE VERY BEST OF THE EVERLY BROTHERS (LP)	40
90	Knight EVYLP 47004	PERFECT HARMONY (multi-LP, box set)	20

(see also Don Everly, Phil Everly)

DON EVERLY

74	Ode ODS 66046	Warmin' Up The Band/Evelyn Swing	5
76	DJM DJS 10692	Yesterday Just Passed Away Again/Never Like This	5
77	DJM DJS 10760	So Sad/Love At Last Sight (p/s)	6
77	DJM DJS 10842	Brother Juke Box/Oh What A Feeling	5
71	A&M AMLS 2007	DON EVERLY (LP, with Ry Cooder)	18
74	Ode ODE 77023	SUNSET TOWERS (LP, with Heads, Hands & Feet)	18

PHIL EVERLY

73	RCA RCA 2409	The Air That I Breathe/God Bless Older Ladies	6
74	Pye 7N 45398	Invisible Man/It's True	5
74	Pye 7N 45415	Sweet Music/Goodbye Line	5
75	Pye 7N 45544	Better Than Now/You And I Are A Song	5
83	Capitol CL 2276	She Means Nothing To Me (with Cliff Richard)/A Man And A Woman (p/s)	5
73	RCA SF 8370	STAR SPANGLED SPRINGER (LP)	20
74	Pye NSPL 18448	THERE'S NOTHING TOO GOOD FOR MY BABY (LP)	18
75	Pye NSPL 18473	MYSTIC LINE (LP)	15

(see also Cliff Richard)

EVERREADY'S

| 80 | Taaga TAG 3 | Don't Do It Again/Martian Girl (gatefold p/s) | 15 |

LENNY EVERSONG

| 57 | Vogue Coral Q 72255 | Jezebel/Jealousy | 7 |
| 57 | Vogue Coral Q 72255 | Jezebel/Jealousy (78) | 8 |

EVERYBODY'S CHILDREN

| 70 | Fontana TF 1070 | Time Is Now/Abide With Me | 5 |

EVERY MOTHER'S SON

67	MGM MGM 1341	Come And Take A Ride In My Boat/I Believe In You	15
67	MGM MGM 1350	Put Your Mind At Ease/Proper Four Leaf Clover	8
67	MGM MGM 1372	Pony With The Golden Mane/Dolls In The Clock	8
67	MGM C(S) 8044	EVERY MOTHER'S SON (LP)	22
68	MGM C(S) 8061	EVERY MOTHER'S SON'S BACK (LP)	22

EVERYONE

| 71 | Charisma CB 146 | Trouble At The Mill/Radio Lady | 4 |
| 71 | Charisma CAS 1028 | EVERYONE (LP) | 10 |

(see also Andy Roberts)

EVERYONE INVOLVED

| 72 | Arcturus ARC 3 | The Circus Keeps On Turning/Motor Car Madness | 30 |
| 72 | Arcturus ARC 4 | EITHER OR (LP, private pressing, embossed plain white sleeve with inserts) | 300 |

EVERYTHING BUT THE GIRL

82	Cherry Red CHERRY 37	Night And Day/Feeling Dizzy/On My Mind (yellow or white p/s)	6/5
83	Cherry Red 12CHERRY 37	Night And Day/Feeling Dizzy/On My Mind (12", p/s)	8
89	Cherry Red CDCHERRY 37	Night And Day/Feeling Dizzy/On My Mind (CD)	8
84	Blanco Y Negro NEG 1	Each And Every One/Laugh You Out The House/Never Could Have Been Worse (12", p/s)	8
84	Blanco Y Negro NEG 3T	Mine/Easy As Sin/Gun Cupboard Love (p/s)	5
84	Blanco Y Negro NEG 6T	Native Land/Riverbed Dry/Don't You Go (12", p/s)	8
84	Blanco Y Negro NEG 6T	Native Land/Riverbed Dry/Easy As Sin/Gun Cupboard Love/Don't You Go (12", stickered p/s)	10
85	Blanco Y Negro NEG 7T	When All's Well/Heaven Help Me/Kid (12", p/s)	8
85	Blanco Y Negro NEG 15T	Angel/Pigeons In The Attic Room/Charmless, Callous Ways/Easy As Sin (Version) (12", p/s)	8
86	Blanco Y Negro NEG 23F	Don't Leave Me Behind/Alfie//Come On Home (Acoustic)/Always On My Mind (live) (double pack, gatefold p/s)	5
88	Blanco Y Negro NEG 30CD	These Early Days/Those Early Days (Demo)/Dyed In The Grain/Another Day Another Dollar (3" CD)	12
88	Blanco Y Negro NEG 33CD	I Always Was Your Girl/Hang Out The Flags/Home From Home/Almost Blue (3" CD)	12
88	Blanco Y Negro NEG 34CD	I Don't Want To Talk About It/Oxford Street/I Don't Want To Talk About It (Instrumental)/Come On Home (3" CD)	8
88	Blanco Y Negro NEG 37CD	Love Is Here Where I Live/Living On Honeycomb/How About Me?/Each And Every One (3" CD)	8

88	Blanco Y Negro NEG 39CD	These Early Days (Dave Bascombe Remix)/Dyed In The Grain/ No Place Like Home/Another Day, Another Dollar (3" CD)	8
90	Blanco Y Negro NEG 40CD	Driving (Radio Edit)/Me And Bobby D/Downtown Train/ Driving (Full Version) (CD)	8
90	Blanco Y Negro NEG 44CD	Take Me/Take Me (Hamblin Remix)/Driving (Acoustic Version)/ Take Me (Love Mix) (CD)	8
91	Blanco Y Negro NEG 51CD	Old Friends/Apron Strings (live)/Politics Aside (Instrumental)/ Back To The Old House (live) (CD)	8
91	Blanco Y Negro NEG 53CD	Twin Cities (Wildwood Mix)/Meet Me In The Morning (live)/ Twin Cities (The Green Plains A Cappella Mix)/Mine (CD)	8
96	Blanco Y Negro SAM 1936	Driving (Masters At Work Extended 12")(Masters At Work Dub)/ (Acapella) (T's Master Mix)(T's Frozen Sun Mix)/(Underdog Vocal Mix)/ (Underdog Instrumental Mix) (12", double pack, stickered title p/s)	8
97	Virgin VSTXDJ 1589	Wrong (Mood II Swing Dub)/(Deep Dish Remix) (12", stickered sleeve)	8
97	Virgin VSTDJ 1589	Wrong (Todd Terry Remix)/(Everything But The Drums)/(Deep Dish Remix)/ (Tee's Beats)/(EBTG Original Mix)/(Deep Dish Dub) (12", double pack, stickered sleeve)	10

(see also Ben Watt, Marine Girls, Tracey Thorn)

EVERYTHING IS EVERYTHING
| 69 | Vanguard VA 1 | Oooh Baby/Witchi Tai To | 5 |
| 68 | Vanguard SVRL 19036 | EVERYTHING IS EVERYTHING (LP) | 15 |

EVERY WHICH WAY
| 70 | Charisma BD 1 | Go Placidly | 5 |

(see also Brian Davison, Griffin, Heavy Jelly, Skip Bifferty, Graham Bell, Bell & Arc)

EWAN (McDermott) & DENVER
| 67 | Giant GN 17 | I Want You So Bad/ERIC McDERMOTT: I'm Gonna Love You | 8 |

EWAN (McDermott) & JERRY (McCarthy)
67	Blue Beat BB 385	Oh Babe/Dance With Me (with Carib Beats)	12
67	Giant GN 5	The Right Track/We Got To Be One	8
67	Giant GN 10	Rock Steady Train/My Baby Is Gone	8
67	Giant GN 14	Tennessee Waltz/You've Got Something	8

DON EWELL
| 57 | Tempo TAP 7 | PIANO SOLOS OF KING OLIVER CREOLE JAZZ BAND (LP) | 15 |

(see also Mama Yancey/Don Ewell)

EX
| 86 | Ron Johnson ZRON 11 | '1936' THE SPANISH REVOLUTION (double pack with book) | 7 |

EX/ALERTA
| 84 | CNT CNT 017 | THE RED DANCE PACKAGE (12", split EP) | 8 |

EXCALIBUR
| 88 | Clay PLATE 1 | HOT FOR LOVE (12" EP) | 8 |
| 85 | Conquest QUEST 5 | THE BITTER END (mini-LP) | 12 |

EXCEL
| 79 | ARSS XL1 | If It Rains/Rolling Home/She's One Of The Boys/Rock Show (EP, p/s) | 20 |
| 80 | Polydor POSP 110 | What Went Wrong?/Junita (p/s) | 8 |

EXCELS
| 67 | Atlantic 584 133 | California On My Mind/The Arrival Of Mary | 6 |

EXCELSIOR SPRING
| 69 | Instant IN 002 | Happy Miranda/It | 12 |

EXCEPTION(S)
67	CBS 202632	The Eagle Flies On Friday/Girl Trouble	15
67	CBS 2830	Gaberdine Saturday Night Street Walker/Sunday Night At The Prince Rupert	15
68	President PT 181	Rub It Down/It's Snowing In The Desert	5
68	President PT 205	Helicopter/Back Room	5
68	President PT 218	Tailor Made Babe/Turn Over The Soil	5
69	President PT 236	Jack Rabbit/Keep The Motor Running	5
69	President PT 271	Pendulum/Don't Torture Your Mind	5
69	President PTLS 1026	THE EXCEPTIONAL EXCEPTION (LP)	18

(see also Bugsy Eastwood, Fotheringay, Fairport Convention)

EXCEPTIONS
| 65 | Decca F 12100 | What More Do You Want?/Soldier Boy | 12 |

(see also Orchids)

EXCHECKERS
| 64 | Decca F 11871 | All The World Is Mine/It's All Over | 12 |

(see also Aynsley Dunbar Retaliation)

EXCITERS
63	United Artists UP 1011	Tell Him/Hard Way To Go	8
64	United Artists UP 1014	Do Wah Diddy Diddy/If Love Came Your Way	12
64	United Artists UP 1017	He's Got The Power/Drama Of Love	8
64	United Artists UP 1026	Get Him/It's So Exciting	8
65	Columbia DB 7479	I Want You To Be My Boy/Tonight, Tonight	7
65	Columbia DB 7544	Just Not Ready/Are You Satisfied	8
65	Columbia DB 7606	Run Mascara/My Father	10
66	London HLZ 10018	A Little Bit Of Soap/I'm Gonna Get Him Someday	8
66	London HLZ 10038	You Better Come Home/Weddings Make Me Cry	15
69	United Artists UP 2274	Do Wah Diddy Diddy/Hard Way To Go	6
71	Jay Boy BOY 38	Soul Motion/You Know It Ain't Right	5
65	United Artists UEP 1005	DO WAH DIDDY DIDDY (EP)	75
64	United Artists ULP 1032	THE EXCITERS (LP)	75

EXCURSION
69	Gemini GMX 5029	NIGHT TRAIN (LP)	12

EXECUTIVE(S)
64	Columbia DB 7323	March Of The Mods/Why, Why, Why	7
64	Columbia DB 7393	Strictly For The Beat/No Room For Squares	6
65	Columbia DB 7573	It's Been So Long/You're For Me (as Executives)	6
65	Columbia DB 7770	Return Of The Mods/How Sad	8
66	Columbia DB 7919	Lock Your Door/In My Arms (as Executives)	6

EXECUTIVE(S)
67	CBS 202652	Smokey Atmosphere/Sensation	7
67	CBS 3067	Ginza Strip/I'll Always Love You	7
68	CBS 3431	Tracy Took A Trip/Gardena Dreamer (as Executive,	
		some with promo only p/s)	25/10
69	CBS 4013	I Ain't Got Nobody/To Kingdom Come (as Executive)	7

EXECUTIVES
80	Attrix RB 05	Shy Little Girl/Never Go Home/JOHNNIE & LUBES: I Got Rabies/	
		Terror In The Parking Lot (p/s)	5

EXECUTIVE SLACKS
80s	Fundamental DEITY 9	Say It Isn't So/Rock & Roll (no p/s, promo only)	5

EXHIBIT A
80	Irrelevant Wombat DAMP 1	NO ELEPHANTS THIS SIDE OF THE WATFORD GAP	
		(EP, with insert)	5
80	Irrelevant Wombat DAMP 2	DISTANCE (EP)	5
	(see also Doof)		

EXILE
77	Boring BO 1	DON'T TAX ME (EP, p/s)	35
78	Charly CYS 1033	The Real People/Tomorrow Today/Disaster Movie (p/s)	20

EXILES
66	Topic 12T 143	FREEDOM, COME ALL YE (LP)	15
67	Topic 12T 164	THE HALE AND THE HANGED (LP)	15

EXITS
78	Way Out WOO 1	YODELLING (EP, numbered, gatefold p/s, hand-stamped labels)	60

EXITS
78	Red Lightning GIL 519	The Fashion Plague/Cheam (p/s, labels on wrong sides)	20
	(see also Direct Hits)		

EXIT STANCE
84	Exit Stance ES 2	Esthetics/Conspiracy Of Silence (p/s)	5
80s	Fight Back FIGHT 4	Crimes Against Humanity (p/s)	6

EXODUS
71	Duke DU 103	Pharaoh's Walk/Little Caesar	6
72	Sioux SI 001	Pharaoh's Walk No. 9/SAMMY JONES: Worried Over You	5
72	Sioux SI 010	Julia Sees Me/LLOYD THE MATADOR: The Train (Engine 54)	8

EXODUS
88	Music For Nations MFN 90P	FABULOUS DISASTER (LP, picture disc)	10

EXORDIUM
70s	Face To Face FTF 1001	TROUBLE WITH ADAM (LP, private pressing)	25

EXOTICS
64	Decca F 11850	Cross My Heart/Ooh La La	6

EXOTICS
68	Columbia DB 8418	Don't Lead Me On/You Can Try	6

EXPELAIRES
79	Zoo CAGE 007	To See You/Frequency (p/s)	5
80	Rockburgh ROCS 222	Sympathy (Don't Be Taken In)/Kicks (p/s)	5
	(see also Mission)		

EXPELLED
82	Riot City RIOT 8	Dreaming/No Life, No Future/What Justice (p/s)	6
82	Riot City RIOT 17	Government Policy/Make It Alone (p/s)	6
84	Riot City 12RIOT 33	THE SINGLES (12" EP)	8

EXPERIMENTS WITH ICE
81	United Dairies EX 001	EXPERIMENTS WITH ICE (LP)	20

EXPLICIT CORPSE
81	Gistol	That Day Before.../I Gotta Gistol	
		(stickered white labels, plastic gatefold p/s)	5

EXPLODING SEAGULLS
81	Fried Egg EGG 8	Johnny Runs For Paregoric/Take Me To The Cinema (p/s)	5
	(see also Blue Aeroplanes)		

EXPLOITED
81	Exploited EXP 001	Army Life/Fuck The Mods/Crashed Out (p/s)	6
81	Exploited EXP 002	Exploited Barmy Army/I Believe In Anarchy/What You Gonna Do?	
		(p/s)	6
81	Exploited EXP 003	EXTRACTS FROM EDINBURGH NITE CLUB (EP)	6
81	Secret SHH 110	Dogs Of War/Blown To Bits (live) (p/s)	5
81	Secret SHH 112	Army Life/Fuck The Mods/Crashed Out (p/s, reissue)	5
81	Secret SHH 113	Exploited Barmy Army/I Believe In Anarchy/What You Gonna Do?	
		(p/s, reissue)	5

EXPLOITED

SHELLEY FABARES
62	Pye International 7N 25132	Johnny Angel/Where's It Gonna Get Me? (blue label, later yellow label)	10/8
62	Pye International 7N 25133	She Can't Find Her Keys/Very Unlikely (with Paul Peterson)	7
62	Pye International 7N 25151	Johnny Loves Me/I'm Growing Up	8
62	Pye International 7N 25166	The Things We Did Last Summer/Breaking Up Is Hard To Do	7
63	Pye International 7N 25184	Telephone (Won't You Ring)/Big Star	7
63	Pye International 7N 25207	Ronnie, Call Me When You Get A Chance/I Left A Note To Say Goodbye	7
65	Fontana TF 592	My Prayer/Pretty Please	10

(see also Paul Peterson & Shelley Fabares)

FABIAN
59	HMV POP 587	I'm A Man/Hypnotized	25
59	HMV POP 587	I'm A Man/Hypnotized (78)	75
59	HMV POP 612	Turn Me Loose/Stop Thief!	20
59	HMV POP 643	Tiger/Mighty Cold (To A Warm, Warm Heart)	15
59	HMV POP 659	Got The Feeling/Come On And Get Me	12
60	HMV POP 695	Hound Dog Man/This Friendly World	12
60	HMV POP 724	String Along/About This Thing Called Love	6
60	HMV POP 778	I'm Gonna Sit Right Down And Write Myself A Letter/Strollin' In The Springtime	6
60	HMV POP 800	Tomorrow/King Of Love	6
60	HMV POP 810	Kissin' And Twistin'/Long Before	6
61	HMV POP 829	You Know You Belong To Somebody Else/Hold On	6
61	HMV POP 869	Grapevine/David And Goliath	6
61	HMV POP 934	You're Only Young Once/The Love That I'm Giving To You	6
59	HMV CLP 1301	HOLD THAT TIGER (LP)	50
60	HMV CLP 1345	THE FABULOUS FABIAN (LP)	45
61	HMV CLP 1433	YOUNG AND WONDERFUL (LP, also stereo CSD 1352)	40/50

FABIONS
69	Bullet BU 410	V. Rocket/Smile (B-side actually "My Baby" by Tennors)	6

FABLE
70	Penny Farthing PEN 725	Minstrel Song/She Said Yes	5
71	Penny Farthing PEN 751	With A Boy Like You/She Said Yes	5
74	Magnet MAG 5002	FABLE (LP)	12

FABULOUS COUNTS
71	Mojo 2092 021	Get Down People/Lunar Funk	8

FABULOUS DIALS
63	Pye International 7N 25200	Bossa Nova Stomp/Forget Me Not	20

FABULOUS FIVE INC.
72	Harry J. HJ 6640	Come Back And Stay/PETER ASHBOURNE AFFAIR: Version	5
74	Ashanti ASH 417	Samba Pa Ti/Oh Dad	5

FABULOUS FLAMES
70	Clandisc CLA 224	Holly Holy/LORD CREATOR: Kingston Town	7
71	Trojan TR 7822	Growing Up/Lovitis	5

(see also Dynamites)

FABULOUS IMPACT
90	Kent 6T 6	Baby Baby, I Want You/HAMPTONS: No No No No No No No Not My Girl (100 Club 6Ts allnighter anniversary disc)	15

FABULOUS SHADES
71	Tropical AL 005	Lonely Man/Version 2	5

FABULOUS SWINGTONES
58	HMV POP 471	Geraldine/You Know Baby	325
58	HMV POP 471	Geraldine/You Know Baby (78)	60

FABULOUS TALBOT BROTHERS
50s	Melodisc M 1507	Bloodshot Blues/Ooh La La (flexidisc free with *NME*)	10
50s	Melodisc M 1507	Bloodshot Blues/She's Got Freckles (78)	10

FACELLS
60s	Kalypso AB 116	So Fine/If You Love Me (I Won't Care)	5

FACES
70	Warner Bros WB 8005	Flying/Three-Button Hand-Me-Down	7
70	Warner Bros WB 8014	Wicked Messenger/Nobody Knows (unissued)	
70	Warner Bros WB 8018	Had Me A Real Good Time/Rear Wheel Skid	8
73	Warner Bros K 16247	Cindy Incidentally/Skewiff (Mend The Fuse) (with lyric insert, no p/s)	6
73	Warner Bros K 16281	Borstal Boys (withdrawn, any pressed?)	10+
73	Sound For Industry SFI 139	Dishevelment Blues/Ooh La La (flexidisc free with *NME*)	12/6
70	Warner Bros WS 3000	FIRST STEP (LP, orange label, gatefold sleeve)	22
71	Warner Bros WS 3011	LONG PLAYER (LP, blue & silver label, stitched die-cut '78rpm' style sleeve)	15
71	Warner Bros K 46053	FIRST STEP (LP, reissue, green label, gatefold sleeve)	18
71	Warner Bros K 56006	A NOD IS AS GOOD AS A WINK ... TO A BLIND HORSE (LP, green label, some with poster)	20/12

FACES

72	Warner Bros K 46064	LONG PLAYER (LP, reissue, blue & silver label, stitched die-cut '78rpm'-style sleeve)	15
73	Warner Bros K 56011	OOH-LA-LA (LP, green label, 'Faces' sleeve with lyric poster)	15
73	Warner Bros K 56172	SNAKES AND LADDERS: BEST OF (LP)	12
74	Warner Bros K 46053	FIRST STEP (LP, 2nd reissue, 'Burbank' label, gatefold sleeve)	12
74	Warner Bros K 56006	A NOD IS AS GOOD AS A WINK ... TO A BLIND HORSE (LP, reissue, 'Burbank' label)	12
74	Warner Bros K 56011	OOH-LA-LA (LP, 'Burbank' label, 'Faces' sleeve, some with lyric poster)	15/12
75	Warner Bros K 66027	TWO ORIGINALS OF ... (2-LP, reissue of "First Steps" & "Long Player", gatefold sleeve)	18

(see also Small Faces, Rod Stewart, Ronnie Lane & Slim Chance, Ron Wood, Jeff Beck Group, Kenney Jones)

FACTORY
68	MGM MGM 1444	Path Through The Forest/Gone	170
69	CBS 4540	Try A Little Sunshine/Red Chalk Hill	170

(see also Peter & Wolves, Norman Conquest, John Pantry)

FACTORY
70	Oak RGJ 718	Time Machine/Castle On The Hill (99 copies only)	190

(see also Velvet Hush)

FACTORY
82	Future Earth FER 011	You Are The Music/History Of The World (silver die-cut sleeve)	12

FACTOTUMS
65	Immediate IM 009	In My Lonely Room/Run In The Green And Tangerine Flaked Forest	20
65	Immediate IM 022	You're So Good To Me/Can't Go Home Anymore My Love	20
66	Piccadilly 7N 35333	Here Today/In My Room	12
66	Piccadilly 7N 35355	I Can't Give You Anything But Love/Absolutely Sweet Marie	12
67	Pye 7N 17402	Cloudy/Easy Said, Easy Done	10
69	CBS 4140	Mr And Mrs Regards/Driftwood	8

FADERS
70s	Rip Off RIP 8	Cheatin'/Library Book (p/s)	5

FAD GADGET
81	Lyntone LYN 10209	King Of The Flies/DEPECHE MODE: Sometimes I Wish I Was Dead (red vinyl flexidisc free with *Flexipop* magazine, issue 11)	25/15

FADING COLOURS
66	Ember EMB S 229	(Just Like) Romeo And Juliet/Billy Christian	15
67	Ember EMB S 237	Be With Me/You're No Use	6

(see also Orange Seaweed)

FAERIE SYMPHONY
77	Decca F 13735	Dance Of The Theena Shee (Daoine Sidhe)/The Unseelie Court	5

(see also Tom Newman)

DONALD FAGEN
88	Warner Bros W 7972CD	Century's End (Single Version)/Shanghai Confidential/The Night Fly/The Goodbye Look (3" CD, with adaptor, 5" case)	8

(see also Steely Dan)

BRIAN FAHEY (& HIS ORCHESTRA)
59	Parlophone R 4655	Street Of A Thousand Bongos/Waltz For Beatniks	5
60	Parlophone R 4686	At The Sign Of The Swingin' Cymbal/The Clanger	12
62	Parlophone R 4909	At The Sign Of The Swingin' Cymbal/The Clanger (reissue, as Brian Faye & His Orchestra)	6
65	Parlophone R 5262	Gidian's Way/Love Theme From "In Harm's Way"	10
65	United Artists UP 1115	Twang/You Can't Catch Me	6
67	Parlophone R 5615	The Plank/Stay On The Island	6
68	Columbia DB 8447	Late Night Extra/Oh The Pity Of It All	10
69	Major Minor MM 656	Open House/Countdown	12
67	Studio Two TWO 175	TIME FOR TV (LP)	18

JOHN FAHEY
67	Transatlantic TRA 173	THE TRANSFIGURATION OF BLIND JOE DEATH (LP, some with booklet)	20/15
68	Vanguard SVRL 19033	YELLOW PRINCESS (LP)	15
68	Vanguard SVRL 19055	REQUIA (LP)	15
69	Takoma SNTF 607	BLIND JOE DEATH (LP)	12
69	Takoma SNTF 608	DEATH CHANTS, WALTZES & MILITARY BREAKDOWNS (LP)	12
72	Reprise K 44213	OF RIVERS AND RELIGION (LP)	12
73	Reprise K 44246	AFTER THE BALL (LP)	12
74	Takoma SNTF 675	JOHN FAHEY, PETER LANG AND LEO KOTTKE (LP)	12

(see also Leo Kottke)

JAD FAIR
80	Armageddon AEP 003	THE ZOMBIES OF MORA-TAU (EP, die-cut p/s with insert)	15

(see also Half Japanese)

YVONNE FAIR
74	Tamla Motown TMG 913	Funky Music Sho Nuff Turns Me On/Let Your Hair Down	5
75	Tamla Motown TMG 1013	It Should Have Been Me/You Can't Judge A Book By It's Cover	5
75	Tamla Motown STML 12008	THE BITCH IS BLACK (LP)	12

WERLY FAIRBURN & DELTA BOYS
56	London HLC 8349	I'm A Fool About Your Love/All The Time	1,000
56	London HLC 8349	I'm A Fool About Your Love/All The Time (78)	100

JOHNNY FAIRE
58	London HLU 8569	Bertha Lou/Till The Law Says Stop	450
58	London HLU 8569	Bertha Lou/Till The Law Says Stop (78)	90

442   Rare Record Price Guide 2002

MINT VALUE £

FAIRFIELD PARLOUR

70	Vertigo 6059 003	Bordeaux Rosé/Chalk On The Wall	15
70	Vertigo 6059 008	Just Another Day/Caraminda/I Am All The Animals/Song For You	15
76	Prism PRI 1	Bordeaux Rosé/Baby Stay For Tonight	8
90s	Bucketfull Of Brains	Nursey Nursey (free with *Bucketfull Of Brains*, issue 29)	5
70	Vertigo 6360 001	FROM HOME TO HOME (LP, gatefold sleeve, spiral label)	60
90s	U.F.O. no cat. number	FROM HOME TO HOME (LP, reissue)	15

(see also Kaleidoscope [U.K.], I Luv Wight)

FAIRIES

64	Decca F 11943	Don't Think Twice, It's Alright/Anytime At All	75
65	HMV POP 1404	Get Yourself Home/I'll Dance	140
65	HMV POP 1445	Don't Mind/Baby Don't	75

(see also Twink, Cops 'N Robbers)

FAIRPORT CONVENTION
SINGLES

67	Track 604 020	If I Had A Ribbon Bow/If (Stomp)	35
68	Island WIP 6047	Meet On The Ledge/Throwaway Street Puzzle	12
69	Island WIP 6064	Si Tu Dois Partir/Genesis Hall	6
70	Island WIP 6089	Now Be Thankful/Sir B. McKenzie's Daughter's Lament	10
70	Polydor 2058 014	If (Stomp)/Chelsea Morning	12
71	Island WIP 6128	John Lee/The Time Is Near (some in p/s)	12/6
73	Island WIP 6155	Rosie/Knights Of The Road	5
75	Island WIP 6241	White Dress/Tears (some in p/s)	12/6
78	Hawk HASP 423	Jam's O'Donnell's Jig/The Last Waltz (Irish-only)	20
79	Simons PMW 1	Rubber Band/The Bonny Black Hare	12
86	Sunrise Bong 1	Quazi B Goode/MIKE SILVER: Where Would You Rather Be Tonight	10
87	Island IF 324	Meet On The Ledge (Re-recorded)/Sigh Bheg Sigh Mhor (live)	5
87	Island 12IF 324	Meet On The Ledge (Re-recorded)/John Barleycorn (live)/ Sigh Bheg Sigh Mhor (live) (12", p/s, some with poster)	10/8

POLYDOR LP
| 68 | Polydor 582/583 035 | FAIRPORT CONVENTION (LP, mono/stereo) | 80/70 |

ISLAND LPs
69	Island ILPS 9092	WHAT WE DID ON OUR HOLIDAYS (LP, 1st pressing, pink label with black 'circle' logo; 2nd pressing, pink label with black 'block' logo)	35/30
69	Island ILPS 9092	WHAT WE DID ON OUR HOLIDAYS (LP, 3rd pressing, pink label with 'i' logo)	20
69	Island ILPS 9092	WHAT WE DID ON OUR HOLIDAYS (LP, 4th pressing, pink rim label with 'palm tree' logo)	15
69	Island ILPS 9102	UNHALFBRICKING (LP, 1st pressing, pink label with black 'circle' logo)	35
69	Island ILPS 9102	UNHALFBRICKING (LP, 2nd pressing, pink label with black 'block' logo)	25
69	Island ILPS 9102	UNHALFBRICKING (LP, 3rd pressing, pink label with 'i' logo)	20
70	Island ILPS 9102	UNHALFBRICKING (LP, 4th pressing, pink rim label with 'palm tree' logo)	15
69	Island ILPS 9115	LIEGE AND LIEF (LP, gatefold sleeve, 1st pressing, pink label with 'i' logo)	20
70	Island ILPS 9115	LIEGE AND LIEF (LP, gatefold sleeve, 2nd pressing, pink rim label with 'palm tree' logo)	15
70	Island ILPS 9130	FULL HOUSE (LP, white label test pressing, with "Poor Will & The Jolly Hangman")	225+
70	Island ILPS 9130	FULL HOUSE (LP, 1st pressing, gatefold sleeve lists "Poor Will & The Jolly Hangman")	20
70	Island ILPS 9130	FULL HOUSE (LP, 2nd pressing, gatefold sleeve without reference to "Poor Will & The Jolly Hangman")	18
70	Island ILPS 9130	FULL HOUSE (LP, gatefold sleeve, 3rd pressing, pink rim label with 'palm tree' logo)	15
71	Island ILPS 9162	ANGEL DELIGHT (LP, gatefold sleeve with 'stuck-on' photos, pink rim label)	12
71	Island ILPS 9176	BABBACOMBE LEE (LP, gatefold sleeve, with innersleeve and booklet, some with sticker)	35/18
72	Island ICD 4	THE HISTORY OF FAIRPORT CONVENTION (2-LP, with 12-page booklet & blue ribbons; later with book & green, red or light blue ribbons)	20/18
73	Island ILPS 9208	ROSIE (LP)	12
73	Island ILPS 9246	FAIRPORT NINE (LP, gatefold sleeve)	12
74	Island ILPS 9285	LIVE CONVENTION (LP, with insert)	12
75	Island ILPS 9313	RISING FOR THE MOON (LP, with insert, 'palm tree' label)	12
75	Island ISS 2	FAIRPORT TOUR SAMPLER (LP, free in *NME* competition, 500 only)	140
76	Island ILPS 9389	GOTTLE O' GEER (LP)	15
76	Island HELP 28	LIVE AT THE L.A. TROUBADOR 1974 (LP)	25

OTHER LPs
77	Vertigo 9102 015	BONNY BUNCH OF ROSES (LP, gatefold sleeve)	18
78	Vertigo 9102 022	TIPPLER'S TALES (LP, with lyric insert)	15
79	Woodworm BEAR 22	FAREWELL FAREWELL (LP, gatefold sleeve)	25
79	Simons GAMA 1	FAREWELL FAREWELL (LP, reissue, gatefold sleeve)	20
82	Woodworm WR 001	MOAT ON THE LEDGE — LIVE 1981 (LP)	12
82	Woodworm (no cat. no.)	AIRING CUPBOARD TAPES (cassette)	12
83	Woodworm WRC 1	AT 2 (AIRING CUPBOARD TAPES 2) (cassette)	20
84	Woodworm (no cat. no.)	THE BOOT (2-cassette in video box, 1,000 only)	25
87	Woodworm (no cat. no.)	THE OTHER BOOT (2-cassette in video box, 1,000 only)	25
88	Woodworm (no cat. no.)	THE THIRD LEG (2-cassette in video box, 1,000 only)	25
88	Woodworm WR 011	BONNY BUNCH OF ROSES (LP, reissue)	12
89	BGO BGOCD 72	TIPPLER'S TALES (CD)	20
92	Vertigo 512882	BONNY BUNCH OF ROSES / TIPPLERS TALES (CD)	30

(see also Richard Thompson, Ian Matthews, Dave Swarbrick, Sandy Denny, Ashley Hutchings, Trevor Lucas, Jerry Donahue, Albion Band, Bunch, Fotheringay, Vashti Bunyan, Trader Horne, Thieves, Pyramid, Allan Taylor, Krysia, Marc Ellington, Brian Maxine, Steeleye Span, Vikki Clayton)

MINT VALUE £

FAIR WARNING
87	Areba ERA 2	ROCKING AT THE SPEED OF LIGHT EP (12", p/s)	20

FAIRWAYS (featuring Gary Street)
69	Mercury MF 1116	Yoko Ono/I Don't Care	10

FAIR WEATHER
70	RCA RCA 1977	Natural Sinner/Haven't I Tried?	7
70	RCA RCA 2040	Road To Freedom/Tutti Frutti	8
71	RCA Neon NE 1000	Lay It On Me/Looking For The Red Label Pt 2	8
71	RCA Neon NE 1	BEGINNING FROM AN END (LP)	30

(see also Andy Fairweather-Low, Amen Corner, Wynder K. Frog)

AL FAIRWEATHER
57	Columbia SEG 7653	AL FAIRWEATHER'S JAZZ BAND (EP)	8
58	Tempo EXA 63	AL FAIRWEATHER'S JAZZMEN	
		(EP, with Henrick Johansen)	10
60s	Columbia SEG 8157	STUDY IN BROWN	
		(EP, with Sandy Brown)	20
60s	Columbia SEG 8181	GROOVER WAILIN'	
		(EP, with Sandy Brown)	15
58	Nixa NJT 511	FAIRWEATHER FRIENDS (LP)	40
60	Columbia 33SX 1159	AL AND SANDY (LP)	25
60	Columbia 33SX 1221	AL'S PALS (LP)	35
61	Columbia 33SX 1306	DOCTOR McJAZZ	
		(LP, also stereo SCX 3367, with Sandy Brown)	50/60
63	Columbia 33SX 1509	THE INCREDIBLE McJAZZ	
		(LP, with Sandy Brown's All Stars)	60

(see also Sandy Brown)

ANDY FAIRWEATHER-LOW
76	A&M AMLH 64602	BE BOP'N'HOLLA (LP, blue vinyl)	12

(see also Amen Corner, Fair Weather, Gary Pickford-Hopkins & Friends, Dave Edmunds & Rockpile)

FAIRY'S MOKE
75	Deroy 1175	FAIRY'S MOKE (LP, private pressing, actually various artists LP)	50

(see also Baby Sunshine)

FAIRYTALE
67	Decca F 12644	Guess I Was Dreaming/Run And Hide	60
67	Decca F 12665	Lovely People/Listen To Mary Cry	60

ADAM FAITH (& ROULETTES)
78s
58	HMV POP 438	(Got A) Heartsick Feeling/Brother Heartache And Sister Tears (78)	60
58	HMV POP 557	High School Confidential/Country Music Holiday (78)	70
59	Top Rank JAR 126	Ah, Poor Little Baby!/Runk Bunk (78)	75
59	Parlophone R 4591	What Do You Want?/From Now Until Forever (78)	25
60	Parlophone R 4623	Poor Me/The Reason (78)	30

SINGLES
58	HMV POP 438	(Got A) Heartsick Feeling/Brother Heartache And Sister Tears	90
58	HMV POP 557	High School Confidential/Country Music Holiday	70
59	Top Rank JAR 126	Ah, Poor Little Baby!/Runk Bunk	20
59	Parlophone R 4591	What Do You Want?/From Now Until Forever	5
60	Parlophone R 4623	Poor Me/The Reason	5
60	Parlophone R 4643	Someone Else's Baby/Big Time	5
60	Parlophone R 4665	Johnny Comes Marching Home/Made You	5
60	Parlophone R 4689	How About That?/With Open Arms	5
60	Parlophone R 4708	Lonely Pup (In A Christmas Shop)/Green Finger	5
61	Parlophone R 4735	Who Am I?/This Is It!	5
61	Parlophone R 4766	Easy Going Me/Wondering	5
61	Parlophone R 4807	Don't You Know It/My Last Wish	5
61	Parlophone R 4837	The Time Has Come/Help Each Other Romance	5
62	Parlophone R 4864	Lonesome/Watch Your Step	6
62	Parlophone R 4896	As You Like It/Face To Face	5
62	Parlophone R 4930	Don't That Beat All/Mix Me A Person	5
62	Parlophone R 4964	Baby Take A Bow/Knocking On Wood	6
63	Parlophone R 4990	What Now/What Have I Got	6
63	Parlophone R 5039	Walkin' Tall/Just Mention My Name	6
63	Parlophone R 5061	The First Time/So Long Baby	5
63	Parlophone R 5091	We Are In Love/Made For Me	
		(with Roulettes)	5
64	Parlophone R 5109	If He Tells You/Talk To Me	6
64	Parlophone R 5138	I Love Being In Love With You/It's Alright	
		(with Roulettes)	6
64	Parlophone R 5174	I Just Don't Know/Only One Such As You	5
64	Parlophone R 5201	A Message To Martha (Kentucky Bluebird)/It Sounds Good To Me	5
65	Parlophone R 5235	Stop Feeling Sorry For Yourself/I've Gotta See My Baby	6
65	Parlophone R 5260	Hand Me Down Things/Talk About Love	7
65	Parlophone R 5289	Someone's Taken Maria Away/I Can't Think Of Anyone Else	
		(with Roulettes)	6
65	Parlophone R 5349	I Don't Need That Kind Of Lovin'/I'm Used To Losing You	7
66	Parlophone R 5398	Idle Gossip/If You Ever Need Me	7
66	Parlophone R 5412	To Make A Big Man Cry/Here's Another Day	7
66	Parlophone R 5516	Cheryl's Goin' Home/Funny Kind Of Love	8
67	Parlophone R 5556	What More Can Anyone Do/You've Got A Way With Me	12
67	Parlophone R 5635	Cowman Milk Your Cow/Daddy, What'll Happen To Me	12
67	Parlophone R 5649	To Hell With Love/Close The Door	8
68	Parlophone R 5673	You Make My Life Worth While/Hey Little Lovin' Girl	8

EPs

60	Parlophone GEP 8811	ADAM'S HIT PARADE (EP).	12
60	Parlophone GEP 8824	ADAM NO. 1 (EP, also stereo SGE 2014).	12/20
60	Parlophone GEP 8826	ADAM NO. 2 (EP, also stereo SGE 2015).	12/20
60	Parlophone GEP 8831	ADAM NO. 3 (EP, also stereo SGE 2018).	12/20
61	Parlophone GEP 8841	ADAM'S HIT PARADE VOL. 2 (EP)	12
62	Parlophone GEP 8851	ADAM FAITH NO. 1 (EP).	15
62	Parlophone GEP 8852	ADAM FAITH NO. 2 (EP).	15
62	Parlophone GEP 8854	ADAM FAITH NO. 3 (EP, with John Barry)	15
62	Columbia SEG 8138	BEAT GIRL (EP, 2 Faith tracks, with John Barry Orchestra)	35
62	Parlophone GEP 8862	ADAM'S HIT PARADE VOL. 3 (EP)	15
63	Parlophone GEP 8877	ADAM'S LATEST HITS (EP)	15
64	Parlophone GEP 8893	TOP OF THE POPS (EP, with Roulettes)	18
64	Parlophone GEP 8904	FOR YOU — ADAM (EP).	15
65	Parlophone GEP 8929	A MESSAGE TO MARTHA — FROM ADAM (EP)	15
65	Parlophone GEP 8939	SONGS AND THINGS (EP)	18

LPs

60	Columbia 33SX 1225	BEAT GIRL (LP, soundtrack, with John Barry Orchestra)	40
60	Parlophone PMC 1128	ADAM (LP, also stereo PCS 3010)	18/22
61	Parlophone PMC 1162	ADAM FAITH (LP, also stereo PCS 3025)	18/22
62	Parlophone PMC 1192	FROM ADAM WITH LOVE (LP, also stereo PCS 3038)	15/20
63	Parlophone PMC 1213	FOR YOU — ADAM (LP, also stereo)	18/25
64	Parlophone PMC 1228	ON THE MOVE (LP, with Roulettes)	35
65	Parlophone PMC 1249	FAITH ALIVE! (LP, with Roulettes)	75
60	EMI Regal (S)REG 1033	ADAM (LP, mono/stereo export issue in different sleeve).	18/22

(see also Roulettes, John Barry)

AUSTIN FAITH

71	Dynamic DYN 407	634 5789/DYNAMIC BOYS: Warm And Tender Love	6

(see also Austin Faithful)

HORACE FAITH

69	B&C CB 104	Spinning Wheel/Like I Used To Do.	5
69	Downtown DT 446	Daddy's Home/EMOTIONS: Give Me A Love	5
70	Trojan TR 7766	Susie Is Sorrow/DERRICK PEPPER: Don't Go	5
70	Trojan TR 7790	Black Pearl/Help Me Help Myself.	5
70	A&M AMS 817	Shame And Scandal In The Family/REGGAE STRINGS: Reggae Strings.	5

PERCY FAITH ORCHESTRA

60	Philips PB 989	Theme From 'A Summer Place'/Go-Go-Po-Go	5
64	CBS AAG 226	The Virginian/Judy .	5
66	CBS 62663	THEMES FOR THE IN CROWD (LP)	12

AUSTIN FAITHFUL

68	Blue Cat BS 140	Uncle Joe/Can't Understand	12
68	Pyramid PYR 6016	I'm In A Rocking Mood/ROLAND ALPHONSO: Stream Of Life.	10
69	Pyramid PYR 6028	Eternal Love/ROLAND ALPHONSO: Goodnight My Love.	10
69	Pyramid PYR 6042	Ain't That Peculiar?/Miss Anti-Social	20

(see also Austin Faith)

MARIANNE FAITHFULL

64	Decca F 11923	As Tears Go By/Greensleeves.	5
64	Decca F 12007	Blowin' In The Wind/The House Of The Rising Sun.	8
65	Decca F 12075	Come And Stay With Me/What Have I Done Wrong?	6
65	Decca F 12162	This Little Bird/Morning Sun	5
65	Decca F 12193	Summer Nights/The Sha La La Song	5
65	Decca F 12268	Yesterday/Oh Look Around You.	5
66	Decca F 12408	Tomorrow's Calling/That's Right Baby	6
66	Decca F 12443	Counting/I'd Like To Dial Your Number	7
66	Decca F 22524	Is This What I Get For Loving You?/Tomorrow's Calling	7
69	Decca F 12889	Something Better/Sister Morphine (withdrawn)	35
75	NEMS NES 004	Dreamin' My Dreams/Lady Madalene	5
76	NEMS NES 013	All I Wanna Do In Life/Wrong Road Again.	5
77	NEMS NES 014	Wrong Road Again/The Way You Want Me To Be	5
78	NEMS NES 117	The Way You Want Me To Be/That Was The Day (Nashville)	5
79	Island WIP 6491	The Ballad Of Lucy Jordan/Brain Drain	5
80	Island 12WIP 6542	Broken English/Why D'Ya Do It? (12", p/s)	8
80	Decca F 13890	As Tears Go By/Come And Stay With Me/This Little Bird/Summer Nights (p/s)	5
65	Decca DFE 8624	MARIANNE FAITHFULL (EP)	25
65	Decca LK 4688	COME MY WAY (LP)	35
65	Decca LK 4689	MARIANNE FAITHFULL (LP)	40
66	Decca LK 4778	NORTH COUNTRY MAID (LP)	45
67	Decca LK/SKL 4854	LOVEINAMIST (LP).	50
69	Decca SPA 17	THE WORLD OF MARIANNE FAITHFULL (LP).	12
76	NEMS NEL 6007	DREAMIN' MY DREAMS (LP)	12

FAITH, HOPE & CHARITY

70	Crewe CRW 3	So Much Love/Life Won't Be The Same Without You.	6
70	Crewe CRW 3	So Much Love/Let's Try It Over	5

MINT VALUE £

FAITH NO MORE

88	Slash LASH 17	We Care A Lot/Spirit (p/s)	8
88	Slash LASHX 17	We Care A Lot/Spirit/Chinese Arithmetic (Radio Mix) (12", p/s)	12
88	Slash LASH 18	Anne's Song (Remix)/Greed (p/s)	6
88	Slash LASHP 18	Anne's Song (Remix)/Greed (picture disc)	10
88	Slash LASHX 18	Anne's Song (Remix)/Greed (12", p/s)	12
89	Kerrang! FIEND 3	Sweet Emotion/(Balaam & The Angel track) (flexidisc with *Kerrang!* mag)	10/6
90	Slash LASPD 21	Epic/War Pigs (live) (shaped picture disc)	8
90	Slash LASCD 21	Epic/War Pigs (live)/Surprise You're Dead (live)/Chinese Arithmetic (live) (CD, card sleeve)	10
90	Slash LASCD 24	From Out Of Nowhere/Woodpecker From Mars (live)/The Real Thing (live)/ Epic (live) (CD, card sleeve)	8
90	Slash LASPD 26	Epic/Falling To Pieces (live) (shaped picture disc, 12" insert in PVC sleeve)	6
90	Slash LASPD 26	Epic/Falling To Pieces (live)/Epic (live)/As The Worm Turns (live) (CD)	8
90	London/Slash 850 228	KING FOR A DAY, FOOL FOR A LIFETIME (7x7" box set)	25
89	Slash 828 217-1	THE REAL THING (LP, picture disc)	12

FAKES

79	Deep Cuts DEEP TWO	Production/Look-Out (p/s)	5

TAV FALCO'S PANTHER BURNS
(see under Panther Burns)

EDDIE FALCON

60	Columbia DB 4420	The Young Have No Time To Lose/My Thanks To You	6
61	Columbia DB 4646	Linda Rose/If Ever I Should Fall In Love	5

FALCONS (U.S.)

59	London HLT 8876	You're So Fine/Goddess Of Angels	90
59	London HLT 8876	You're So Fine/Goddess Of Angels (78)	90
62	London HLK 9565	I Found A Love/Swim (some labels credit B-side as "Swin")	40

(see also Wilson Pickett, Eddie Floyd)

FALCONS (U.K.)

64	Philips BF 1297	Stampede/Kazutzka	10

FALL

78	Step Forward SF 7	BINGO-MASTERS' BREAKOUT! (EP)	10
78	Step Forward SF 9	It's The New Thing/Various Times (p/s)	7
79	Step Forward SF 11	Rowche Rumble/In My Area (p/s)	7
80	Step Forward SF 13	Fiery Jack/Second Dark Age/Psykick Dancehall #2 (b&w or yellow p/s)	10/8
80	Rough Trade RT 048	How I Wrote Elastic Man/City Hobgoblins (p/s)	6
80	Rough Trade RT 056	Totally Wired/Putta Block (p/s)	6
81	Rough Trade RT 071	SLATES (10" EP, 33rpm)	10
81	Kamera ERA 001	Lie Dream Of A Casino Soul/Fantastic Life (p/s)	6
82	Kamera ERA 004	Look, Know/I'm Into C.B. (p/s)	6
82	Rough Trade RT 133	The Man Whose Head Expanded/Ludd Gang (p/s)	6
82	Kamera ERA 014	Marquis Cha Cha/Papal Visit (p/s, B-side plays "Room To Live", withdrawn)	22
83	Rough Trade RT 143	Kicker Conspiracy/Wings//Container Drivers/New Puritan (g/fold double pack)	10
84	Beggars Banquet BEG 116T	C.R.E.E.P./(Extended Version)/Pat-Trip Dispenser (12", p/s, green vinyl)	8
84	B. Banquet BEG 116TP	C.R.E.E.P./(Extended Version)/Pat-Trip Dispenser (12", p/s, with art print)	8
84	Beggars Banquet BEG 120E	CALL FOR ESCAPE ROUTE (7"/12" double pack EP)	8
87	Beggars Banquet BEG 187H	There's A Ghost In My House/Haf Found Bormann (hologram p/s)	5
87	Beggars Banquet BEG 200P	Hit The North (Parts 1 & 2) (picture disc, printed PVC sleeve)	5
87	Beggars Banquet BEG 206B	Victoria/Tuff Life Boogie (box set with inserts & badge)	5
88	Beggars Banquet FALL 2B	Jerusalem (Remix)/Acid Priest 2088 (Remix)//Big New Prinz (Remix)/ Wrong Place Right Time No. 2 (Remix) (double pack box set, with postcard)	5
88	Beggars Banquet FALL 2CD	Jerusalem (Remix)/Acid Priest 2088 (Remix)//Big New Prinz (Remix)/ Wrong Place, Right Time No. 2 (Remix) (3" CD, double pack, gatefold wallet, 4,000 only)	10
90	Cog Sinister SINCD 4	Telephone Thing/British People In Hot Weather/Telephone Dub (CD)	8
90	Cog Sinister SINR 5	Popcorn Double Feature/Zandra (p/s)	6
90	Cog Sinister SINCD 5	Popcorn Double Feature/Arms Control Poseur/Butterflies/Brains (CD)	8
90	Cog Sinister SINDJ 6	White Lightning (stickered sleeve)	5
79	Step Forward SFLP 1	LIVE AT THE WITCH TRIALS (LP)	12
79	Step Forward SFLP 4	DRAGNET (LP, with insert)	12
80	Rough Trade ROUGH 10	TOTALE'S TURNS (IT'S NOW OR NEVER) (LP)	12
80	Rough Trade ROUGH 18	GROTESQUE (AFTER THE GRAMME) (LP)	12
81	Step Forward SFLP 6	THE EARLY YEARS 1977-79 (LP)	12
82	Chaos LIVE 006	LIVE AT ACKLAM HALL (cassette)	12
87	Cog Sinister CDCOG 1	PALACE OF SWORDS REVERSED (CD)	18

(see also D.O.S.E.)

FALLEN ANGELS (U.S.)

67	London HL 10166	I Don't Want To Fall/Most Children Do	5
68	London HA-Z/SH-Z 8359	THE FALLEN ANGELS (LP)	20

FALLEN ANGELS (U.K.)

84	Fallout FALL 022	Amphetamine Blues/He's A Rebel	6
84	Fallout FALL 12 027	INNER PLANET LOVE (mini-LP)	12
84	Fallout FALL LP 23	FALLEN ANGELS (LP)	12
84	Fallout FALL CLP 23	FALLEN ANGELS (cassette with extra track)	12

(see also Knox, Hanoi Rocks, Troops Of Tomorrow)

JOHNNY FALLIN

59	Capitol CL 15043	Party Kiss/The Creation Of Love	25
59	Capitol CL 15091	Wild Streak/If I Could Write A Love Song	35

FALLING LEAVES

65	Parlophone R 5233	She Loves To Be Loved/Not Guilty	45
66	Decca F 12420	Beggar's Parade/Tomorrow Night	20

FALLOUT

83	Mouth Too Small To F. F2	SALAMI TACTICS (EP)	5
84	I FLP 2	BUTCHERY	
		(10" EP, with lyric inner).	8

FALSE IDOLS

78	Old Knew Wave BOG 005	Broken Judy/Marbled Hands/H-Brain	
		(tri-fold p/s).	5
78	Old Knew Wave BOG 007	Ego Wino/Good Night	
		(p/s, pink vinyl).	5

AGNETHA FALTSKOG

82	Epic EPC A 2824	Never Again/Just For The Fun (p/s, with Tomas Ledin)	12
83	Epic EPC A 3436	The Heat Is On/Man (p/s)	8
83	Epic EPC WA 3436	The Heat Is On/Man (picture disc).	30
83	Epic EPC A 3622	Wrap Your Arms Around Me/Take Good Care Of The Children (p/s)	8
83	Epic EPC TA 3622	Wrap Your Arms Around Me/The Heat Is On/	
		Take Good Care Of The Children (Extended) (12", p/s).	15
83	Epic EPC A 3812	Can't Shake Loose/To Love (p/s).	8
83	Epic EPC A 3812	Can't Shake Loose/To Love (poster p/s)	15
83	Epic EPC WA 3812	Can't Shake Loose/To Love (picture disc)	25
85	Epic EPC A 6133	I Won't Let You Go/You're There (p/s)	8
85	Epic EPC TA 6133	I Won't Let You Go (Extended)/You're There (12", p/s)	15
86	Sonet SON 2317	The Way You Are/Fly Like The Eagle	
		(p/s, with Ola Hanansson)	10
88	WEA YZ 170	The Last Time/Are You Gonna Throw It All Away (p/s)	8
88	WEA YZ 170T	The Last Time (Extended Remix)/The Last Time/	
		Are You Gonna Throw It All Away (12", p/s).	15
88	WEA YZ 177	I Wasn't The One (Who Said Goodbye)/If You Need Somebody Tonight	
		(p/s, with Peter Cetera)	8
88	WEA YZ 177T	I Wasn't The One (Who Said Goodbye) (Extended Version)/(Yo No Fui [Quien	
		Dijo Adios])/If You Need Somebody Tonight	
		(12", p/s, with Peter Cetera).	15
88	WEA YZ 300	Let It Shine/Maybe It Was Magic (p/s)	8
88	WEA YZ 300T	Let It Shine (Extended)/('Bright' Mix)/Maybe It Was Magic	
		(12", p/s).	15
98	Polydor POLPROCD 2	The Queen Of Hearts (Nar Du Tar Mej I Din Fam)	
		(CD, promo only)	40
74	Embassy EMB 31094	AGNETHA (LP).	70
	(see also Abba)		

GEORGIE FAME (& BLUE FLAMES)

SINGLES

64	Columbia DB 7193	Do The Dog/Shop Around	15
64	Columbia DB 7255	Green Onions/Do-Re-Mi.	15
64	Columbia DB 7328	Bend A Little/I'm In Love With You (solo)	8
64	Columbia DB 7428	Yeh Yeh/Preach And Teach	
		(some copies list "Yeah, Yeah" on label) . . . . each 5
64	Columbia DB 7428	Yeh Yeh/Preach And Teach	
		(99 promo copies only with p/s)	65
65	Columbia DB 7494	In The Meantime/Telegram	8
65	Columbia DB 7633	Like We Used To Be/It Ain't Right	7
65	Columbia DB 7727	Something/Outrage	7
66	Columbia DB 7946	Getaway/El Bandido.	7
	(All the above singles credited to Georgie Fame & Blue Flames unless stated; the singles listed below were solo.)		
66	Columbia DB 8015	Sunny/Don't Make Promises	6
66	Columbia DB 8096	Sitting In The Park/Many Happy Returns.	6
67	CBS 202587	Because I Love You/Bidin' My Time (p/s).	7
67	CBS 2945	Try My World/No Thanks (p/s)	7
67	CBS 3124	The Ballad Of Bonnie And Clyde/Beware Of The Dog (p/s)	7
69	CBS 4295	Peaceful/Hideaway (with John Barry)	6
69	CBS 4659	Seventh Son/Fully Booked	5
70	CBS 5035	Somebody Stole My Thunder/Entertaining Mr. Sloane	18
70	CBS 5131	Fire And Rain/Someday Man	5

EPs

64	Columbia SEG 8334	RHYTHM AND BLUEBEAT (EP).	25
64	Columbia SEG 8382	RHYTHM AND BLUES AT THE FLAMINGO (EP)	20
64	Columbia SEG 8393	FAME AT LAST (EP).	18
65	Columbia SEG 8406	FATS FOR FAME (EP).	20
65	Columbia SEG 8454	MOVE IT ON OVER (EP).	20
66	Columbia SEG 8518	GETAWAY (EP)	18
67	CBS EP 6363	KNOCK ON WOOD (EP)	15

LPs

64	Columbia 33SX 1599	RHYTHM AND BLUES AT THE FLAMINGO (LP)	50
64	Columbia 33SX 1638	FAME AT LAST (LP)	20
66	Columbia SX 6043	SWEET THINGS (LP)	20
66	Columbia SX 6076	SOUND VENTURE (LP).	25
67	Columbia SX 6120	HALL OF FAME (LP).	25
67	CBS (S)BPG 63018	TWO FACES OF FAME (LP)	25
68	CBS (S) 63293	THE THIRD FACE OF FAME (LP, mono/stereo). 18/15
69	CBS (S) 63650	GEORGIE DOES HIS OWN THING WITH STRINGS	
		(LP, mono/stereo) 18/15
69	CBS S 63786	SEVENTH SON (LP)	15
71	CBS S 64350	GOING HOME (LP)	12
72	Reprise K 44183	ALL ME OWN WORK (LP)	18
74	Island ILPS 9293	GEORGIE FAME (LP)	30
	(see also Blue Flames, Jimmy Nicol, Perry Ford & Sapphires)		

FAMILY

67	Liberty LBF 15031	Scene Thru The Eye Of A Lens/Gypsy Woman (mispress, B-side plays "Let Me Be Good To You" by Otis Redding)	100
67	Liberty LBF 15031	Scene Thru The Eye Of A Lens/Gypsy Woman	100
68	Reprise RS 23270	Me My Friend/Hey Mr. Policeman	12
68	Reprise RS 23315	Second Generation Woman/Home Town	12
69	Reprise RS 27001	No Mule's Fool/Good Friend Of Mine (initially in p/s)	15/5
70	Reprise RS 27005	Today/Song For Lots (initially in p/s)	15/5
70	Reprise RS 27009	The Weaver's Answer/Strange Band/Hung Up Down (initially in p/s)	8/5
71	Reprise K 14090	In My Own Time/Seasons (initially in p/s)	8/5
71	Reprise SAM 1	Larf And Sing/Children (promo only)	15
72	Reprise K 14196	Burlesque/The Rockin' R's	7
72	Reprise K 14218	My Friend The Sun/Glove	7
73	Raft RA 18501	Boom Bang/Stop This Car	7
73	Raft RA 18503	Sweet Desiree/Drink To You	7
68	Reprise R(S)LP 6312	MUSIC IN A DOLL'S HOUSE (LP, with insert, mono/stereo)	80/30
69	Reprise RLP 6340	FAMILY ENTERTAINMENT (LP, mono, some with poster)	40/25
69	Reprise RSLP 6340	FAMILY ENTERTAINMENT (LP, stereo, some with poster)	25/18

(The above LPs were originally issued with 'steamboat' label designs, later pressings with same cat. no. are worth £2 less.)

70	Reprise RSLP 9001	A SONG FOR ME (LP, with lyric sheet)	15
70	Reprise RSX 9005	ANYWAY (LP, custom polythene sleeve)	15
71	Reprise RMP 9007	OLD SONGS NEW SONGS (LP)	15
71	Reprise K 54003	FEARLESS (LP)	12
72	Reprise K 54006	BANDSTAND (LP, 'window' sleeve)	15
73	Raft RA 58501	IT'S ONLY A MOVIE (LP)	12

(see also Roger Chapman, Farinas, Stud, Mogul Thrash, Hellions, Ashton Gardner & Dyke, Revolution, Streetwalkers)

FAMILY AFFAIR

60s	Saga	FAMILY AFFAIR (LP)	12

FAMILY AFFAIR

76	Pye 7N 45609	Call Me/Love Hustle	5

(see also Jackie Trent)

FAMILY CAT

89	Bad Girl BGRIFC 01	Tom Verlaine (Demo Version) (gig freebie flexidisc, hand-sprayed p/s & insert)	5
89	Bad Girl BGRLT 01	Tom Verlaine/Gabriel's Wings/Octopus (p/s)	5
91	Bad Girl BGRLT 009T	Color Me Grey/I Must Have Been Blind/Great Ugly Place (12", p/s)	8
92	Dedicated DEDLP 007	FURTHEST FROM THE SUN (LP, with bonus 7" "Kolumbus"/"Montague Terrace" [DEDLP 007S])	12
92	Dedicated DEDCD 007	FURTHEST FROM THE SUN (CD)	15

(see also P.J. Harvey)

FAMILY CIRCLE

69	Attack AT 8001	Phoenix Reggae/BIG L: Music Box	8

FAMILY DOGG

67	MGM MGM 1360	Family Dogg/The Storm	8
68	Fontana TF 921	I Wear A Silly Grin/Couldn't Help It	5
68	Fontana TF 968	Brown-Eyed Girl/Let It Rain	6
69	Bell BLL 1055	A Way Of Life/Throw It Away	5
69	Bell BLL 1077	Arizona/The House In The Heather	5
70	Bell BLL 1100	When Tomorrow Comes Today/This Unhappy Heart Of Mine	5
71	Bell BLL 1139	Coat Of Many Colours/Jesus Loves You	5
69	Bell SBLL 122	A WAY OF LIFE (LP, with members of Led Zeppelin)	18
72	Polydor 2318 061	THE VIEW FROM ROWLAND'S HEAD (LP)	12

(see also Steve Rowland, Albert Hammond, Christine Holmes)

FAMILY FODDER

79	Parole/Fresh PURL 4	Playing Golf/My Baby Takes Valium (p/s)	5

FAMILY MAN (Aston Barrett)

70	Escort ERT 834	Midnight Sunshine/GREGORY & STICKY: You Are My Sunshine	6
72	Downtown DT 491	Herb Tree/STUDIO SOUND: Holy Poly (reissue)	6

(see also Hippy Boys, Upsetters, Bob Marley & Wailers, Carl Dawkins)

FAMILY PLANN

75	President PT 441	Sexy Summer/Can You Get Into The Music	5

FAMOUS ECCLES & MISS FREDA THING

56	Parlophone R 4251	My September Love/JIM MORIARTY: You Gotta Go Oww!	10
56	Parlophone R 4251	My September Love/JIM MORIARTY: You Gotta Go Oww! (78)	8

(see also Spike Milligan, Goons)

FAMOUS JUG BAND

69	Liberty LBF 15224	The Only Friend I Own/A Leaf Must Fall	6
69	Liberty LBS 83263	SUNSHINE POSSIBILITIES (LP)	30
70	Liberty LBS 83355	CHAMELEON (LP)	20

(see also Incredible String Band, C.O.B.)

FAMOUS MUSIC BAND

69	Philips 6006 111	Nine By Nine/Going In The Out (with John Dummer)	8

(see also John Dummer)

FAMOUS WARD SINGERS

54	London HL 8065	I Know It Was The Lord/Conclusion (78)	10

FANATICS

89	Chapter 22 12 CHAP 38	SUBURBAN LOVE SONGS (12" EP)	25

(see also Ocean Colour Scene)

FAN-CLUB
78   M&S SJP 791B   Avenue/Night Caller (photocopied wraparound p/s) 15
(see also Transvision Vamp)

FANCY
73   Atlantic K 10383   Wild Thing/Fancy (some with p/s)................................. 8/5
76   Arista ARIST 32   Music Maker/Bluebird 8
74   Antic K 51502   WILD THING (LP) 12
75   Arista ARTY 102   SOMETHING TO REMEMBER (LP).............................. 12
(see also Ray Fenwick, Judas Priest)

FANDANGO
(see Nic Simper's Fandango, under 'S')

FANNY
70   Reprise RSLP 6416   FANNY (LP).. 12
72   Reprise K 44144   CHARITY BALL (LP)... 12

FANTASIA
67   Stateside SS 2031   Gotta Get Away/She Needs My Love.......................... 5

FANTASTIC BAGGYS
76   United Artists UP 36142   Summer Means Fun/JAN & DEAN: Surf City/Sidewalk Surfin'............... 6
(see also Jan & Dean, Bruce Johnston)

FANTASTIC FOUR
68   Tamla Motown TMG 678   I Love You Madly/I Love You Madly (Instrumental) 15
69   T. Motown (S)TML 11105   THE FANTASTIC FOUR (LP)................................... 25

FANTASTIC JOHNNY C
(see under 'C')

FANTASTICS
68   MGM MGM 1434   Baby Make Your Own Sweet Music/Who Could Be Lovin' You 12
68   MGM MGM 1434DJ   Baby Make Your Own Sweet Music/Who Could Be Lovin' You (promo) 22
69   Deram DM 264   Face To Face With Heartache/This Must Be My Rainy Day.................. 5
70   Deram DM 283   Waiting Round For Heartaches/Ask The Lonely 5
71   Deram DM 334   For Old Times Sake/Exodus Main Theme 5
71   Mojo 2027 004   Baby Make Your Own Sweet Music/Who Could Be Lovin' You? (reissue) 5
(see also Velours)

FANTASY
73   Polydor 2058 405   Politely Insane/I Was Once Aware 25
73   Polydor 2383 246   PAINT A PICTURE (LP, gatefold sleeve) 175

BARRY FANTONI
66   Fontana TF 707   Little Man In A Little Box/Fat Man 20
67   Columbia DB 8238   Nothing Today/The Spanish Lady Tango 5

FAPARDOKLY
83   Psycho PSYCHO 5   FAPARDOKLY (LP, 300 only) 15
(see also Mu)

FARAWAY FOLK
70s   Tabitha TAB 3   Shadow Of A Pie/Folsom Prison Blues/Rent A Man/Soulful Shade Of Blue 8
70s   RA EP 7001   INTRODUCING THE FARAWAY FOLK (EP) 25
70s   RA LP 6006ST   LIVE AT THE BOLTON (LP)..................................... 40
72   RA LP 6012ST   TIME AND TIDE (LP)... 60
70s   RA LP 6019   ON THE RADIO (LP)... 25
70s   RA LP 6022   ONLY AUTHORISED EMPLOYEES TO BREAK BOTTLES
                (LP, with Harry H. Corbett)................................... 30
75   RA LP 6029   SEASONAL MAN (LP, gatefold sleeve with insert) 100
80s   RA   BATTLE OF THE DRAGONS (cassette) 15
(see also Harry H. Corbett)

FAR CRY
69   Vanguard SVRL 19041   THE FAR CRY (LP)... 25

DON FARDON
67   Pye International 7N 25437   (The Lament Of The Cherokee) Indian Reservation/Dreamin' Room 7
68   Pye International 7N 25475   (The Lament Of The Cherokee) Indian Reservation/Dreamin' Room (reissue)..... 5
69   Pye International 7N 25483   We Can Make It Together/Coming On Strong 5
69   Pye International 7N 25486   Good Lovin'/Ruby's Pictures On My Wall 5
69   Young Blood YB 1007   It's Been Nice Loving You/Let The Love Live 7
70   Young Blood YB 1010   Belfast Boy/Echoes Of The Cheers 5
71   Young Blood YB 1013   Delta Queen/Hometown Baby 5
71   Young Blood YB 1021   Girl/Sandiago 5
71   Young Blood YB 1027   Follow Your Drum/Get Away John 5
70   Young Blood SYB 4   I'VE PAID MY DUES! (LP)...................................... 12
70   Young Blood SSYB 13   RELEASED (LP).. 12
(see also Sorrows)

FAR EAST FAMILY BAND
75   Vertigo 6370 850   NIPPONJIN (LP)... 18

DICK FARINA & ERIC VON SCHMIDT
63   Folklore F-LEUT/7   DICK FARINA & ERIC VON SCHMIDT (LP, featuring 'Blind Boy Grunt')........ 50
(see also Bob Dylan, Richard & Mimi Farina)

RICHARD & MIMI FARINA
65   Fontana STFL 6060   CELEBRATIONS FOR A GREY DAY (LP)......................... 15
65   Fontana STFL 6075   REFLECTIONS IN A CRYSTAL WIND (LP)........................ 15
73   Vanguard VSD 21/22   THE BEST OF RICHARD & MIMI FARINA (2-LP).................. 15
(see also Dick Farina & Eric Von Schmidt)

MINT VALUE £

FARINAS

64	Victor Buckland Sound Studio	Bye Bye Johnny/All You Gotta Do/Twist And Shout (as James King & Farinas)	500
64	Fontana TF 493	You'd Better Stop/I Like It Like That	50

(see also Family, Roger Chapman)

TERRY FARLAN

71	Hallmark HM 637	SINGS BUDDY HOLLY'S GREATEST HITS (LP)	12

CHRIS FARLOWE (& THUNDERBIRDS)

62	Decca F 11536	Air Travel/Why Did You Break My Heart?	30
63	Columbia DB 7120	I Remember/Push Push (as Chris Farlowe & Thunderbirds)	15
64	Columbia DB 7237	Girl Trouble/Itty Bitty Pieces (as Chris Farlowe & Thunderbirds)	15
64	Columbia DB 7311	Just A Dream/What You Gonna Do? (as Chris Farlow & Thunderbirds)	15
64	Columbia DB 7379	Hey, Hey, Hey/Hound Dog (as Chris Farlow & Thunderbirds)	15
65	Columbia DB 7614	Buzz With The Fuzz/You're The One (withdrawn, as Chris Farlow & Thunderbirds, demos more common £100)	140
65	Immediate IM 016	The Fool/Treat Her Good	10
66	Immediate IM 023	Don't Just Look At Me/Think	12
66	Immediate IM 035	Out Of Time/Baby Make It Soon	6
66	Columbia DB 7983	Just A Dream/Hey, Hey, Hey, Hey	12
66	Immediate IM 038	Ride On Baby/Headlines	6
67	Immediate IM 041	My Way Of Giving/You're So Good To Me	12
67	Immediate IM 049	Yesterday's Papers/Life Is But Nothing	6
67	Immediate IM 056	Moanin'/What Have I Been Doin'?	6
67	Immediate IM 065	Handbags And Gladrags/Everyone Makes A Mistake	6
68	Immediate IM 066	The Last Goodbye/Paperman Fly In The Sky (B-side with Thunderbirds)	10
68	Immediate IM 071	Paint It Black/I Just Need Your Lovin'	10
69	Immediate IM 074	Dawn/April Was The Month	8
69	Immediate IM 078	Out Of Time/Ride On Baby	5
70	Polydor 2066 017	Black Sheep/Fifty Years	5
70	Polydor 2066 046	Put Out The Light/Questions (as Chris Farlowe & Hill)	5
75	Polydor 2066 650	We Can Work It Out/Only Women Bleed	5
75	Polydor 2058 650	We Can Work It Out (as Chris Farlowe Band, 1-sided gold flexidisc)	6
75	Virgin SV 102	Out Of Time/Handbags And Gladrags//Yesterday's Papers/ Ride On Baby (double pack)	5
78	Beeb BEEB 022	Gangsters (as Chris Farlowe & Dave Greenslade)/ DAVE GREENSLADE'S GANGSTERS: Sarah Gant Theme	6
65	Decca DFE 8665	CHRIS FARLOWE (EP)	60
65	Immediate IMEP 001	FARLOWE IN THE MIDNIGHT HOUR (EP)	40
66	Immediate IMEP 004	CHRIS FARLOWE HITS (EP)	30
66	Island IEP 709	STORMY MONDAY (EP)	75
66	Columbia SX 6034	CHRIS FARLOWE AND THE THUNDERBIRDS (LP)	85
66	Immediate IMLP 005	14 THINGS TO THINK ABOUT (LP)	40
66	Immediate IMLP 006	THE ART OF CHRIS FARLOWE (LP)	45
67	MFP MFP 1186	STORMY MONDAY (LP, reissue of SX 6034 in different sleeve)	12
67	EMI Regal REG 2025	CHRIS FARLOWE (LP, export issue)	25
68	Immediate IMLP/IMCP 010	THE BEST OF CHRIS FARLOWE VOLUME ONE (LP)	22
69	Immediate IMLP 021	THE LAST GOODBYE (LP)	50
70	Polydor 2425 029	FROM HERE TO MAMA ROSA (LP, as Chris Farlowe & Hill)	15
75	Polydor 2469 259	THE CHRIS FARLOWE BAND LIVE (LP)	12

(see also Thunderbirds, Beazers, Little Joe Cook, Crane/Farlowe, Atomic Rooster, Colosseum, Dave Greenslade, Spectrum)

ART FARMER

56	Vogue EPV 1045	ART FARMER (EP, as Art Farmer New Jazz All Stars)	7
54	Esquire 20-033	ART FARMER SEXTET — WORK OF ART (10" LP)	15
56	Esquire 32-072	TWO TRUMPETS (LP, with Donald Byrd)	12
59	London SAH-T 6028	MODERN ART (LP)	12
60	London Jazz LTZ-T 15184	BRASS SHOUT (LP)	12
60	London Jazz LTZ-T 15198	THE AZTEC SUITE (LP)	12
61	Esquire 32-120	EARTHY (LP)	12
64	London HA-K/SH-K 8135	INTERACTION (LP, as Art Farmer Quartet featuring Jim Hall)	12

(see also Clifford Brown, Benny Golson, Donald Byrd)

JULES FARMER

59	London HLP 8967	Love Me Now/Part Of Me (Is Still With You)	10
59	London HLP 8967	Love Me Now/Part Of Me (Is Still With You) (78)	30

MYLENE FARMER

89	Polydor 080 360-2	Ainsi Soit Je. . . (Maxi Remix)/Ainsi Soit Je. . . (Lamentations)/ Ainsi Soit Je. . . (Classic Bonus Beats) (CD Video, export only)	45

FARMLIFE

82	Dining Out TUX 19	Susie's Party/Simple Men	6
83	Whaam! WHAAM 13	Big Country 1 & 2 (unreleased; Echantillan test pressings only)	40

(see also Bomb Party)

GILES FARNABY'S DREAM BAND

73	Argo AFW 112	Newcastle Brown/29th Of May	8
73	Argo ZDA 158	GILES FARNABY'S DREAM BAND (LP)	60

(see also Druids)

ROBERT FARNON ORCHESTRA

55	Decca LK 4119	CANADIAN IMPRESSIONS (LP)	20
60	Delyse ECB 3157/DS 6057	CAPTAIN HORATIO HORNBLOWER (LP, soundtrack, mono/stereo)	60/75
65	Philips BL 7659	PORTRAIT OF JOHNNY MATHIS (LP)	12
65	Philips BL 7672	SINATRA (LP)	12

ROBERT FARNON & TONY COE
70 Chapter One CHS 804   POP MAKES PROGRESS (LP).. 30
(see also Tony Coe)

FARON'S FLAMINGOS
63 Oriole CB 1834   Do You Love Me?/See If She Cares 12
63 Oriole CB 1867   Shake Sherry/Give Me Time... 15
(see also Big Three, Mojos)

WAYNE FARO'S SCHMALTZ BAND
69 Deram DM 222   There's Still Time/Give It Time 8

GARY FARR (& THE T-BONES)
65 Columbia DB 7608   Give All She's Got/Don't Stop And Stare
                         (as Gary Farr & T-Bones)... 40
68 Marmalade 598 007   Everyday/Green (with Kevin Westlake) 7
69 Marmalade 598 017   Hey Daddy/The Vicar And The Pope 10
71 CBS 5430   Revolution Of The Seasons/Old Man Boulder.............................. 6
65 Columbia SEG 8414   DEM BONES, DEM BONES, DEM T-BONES (EP).......................... 100
69 Marmalade 608 013   TAKE SOMETHING WITH YOU (LP) 40
71 CBS 64138   STRANGE FRUIT
                   (LP, with Richard Thompson & Mighty Baby) 30
(see also T-Bones, Richard Thompson, Mighty Baby, Meic Stevens, Kevin Westlake & Gary Farr)

MARY ANN FARRAR & SATIN SOUL
76 Brunswick BR 38   Stoned Out Of My Mind/Living In The Footsteps Of Another Girl 5

ALRIC 'PRETENDER' FARRELL
51 Sagomes SG 131   My Girl Join Baptist — Calypso/Ham From Customs — Calypso (78).......... 10

BILLY FARRELL
53 MGM MGM 607   Kaw-Liga/You Can't Stop Me From Dreaming (78) 8
55 Mercury MB 3206   It May Sound Silly/Rock Love (78).................................... 8
58 Philips PB 828   Yeah Yeah/Someday (You'll Want Me To Want You) 7
58 Philips PB 828   Yeah Yeah/Someday (You'll Want Me To Want You) (78)................... 12

DO & DENA FARRELL
57 HMV POP 427   Young Magic/New Love Tonight....................................... 10
57 HMV POP 427   Young Magic/New Love Tonight (78).................................. 10

MICK FARREN
78 Stiff LAST 4   ALL SCREWED UP (EP, as Mick Farren & Deviants) 5
78 Logo GO 321   Half Price Drinks/I Don't Want To Go This Way 6
79 Logo GO 345   Broken Statue/It's All In The Picture 5
70 Transatlantic TRA 212   MONA (THE CARNIVOROUS CIRCUS) (LP)........................... 50
78 Logo LOGO 2010   VAMPIRES STOLE MY LUNCH MONEY
                       (LP, with lyric insert) 20
84 Psycho PSYCHO 20   MONA (THE CARNIVOROUS CIRCUS) (LP, reissue)..................... 15
(see also Deviants, Twink)

MIA FARROW
68 Dot DOT 116   Lullaby From Rosemary's Baby (Parts 1 & 2)........................... 6

FASCINATIONS
67 Stateside SS 594   Girls Are Out To Get You/You'll Be Sorry............................. 50
68 Sue WI 4049   Girls Are Out To Get You/You'll Be Sorry (reissue) 25
71 Mojo 2092 004   Girls Are Out To Get You/You'll Be Sorry (2nd reissue) 10
71 Mojo 2092 018   I'm So Lucky He Loves Me/Say It Isn't So............................ 5

FASCINATORS
58 Capitol CL 14942   Chapel Bells/I Wonder Who 200
59 Capitol CL 15062   Oh, Rose Marie/Fried Chicken And Macaroni 70

FASHIONS
68 Stateside SS 2115   I.O.U. (A Lifetime Of Love)/When Love Slips Away..................... 10
69 Evolution E 2444   I.O.U. (A Lifetime Of Love)/He Gives Me Love......................... 6

FAST BREEDERS & RADIO ACTORS
78 Nuke NUKE 235   Nuclear Waste/Digital Love (some in p/s & insert)................... 20/10
(see also Radio Actors)

FAST CARS
79 Streets Ahead SA 3   The Kids Just Wanna Dance/You're So Funny (p/s) 50

FAST EDDIE
82 Well Suspect BLAM 001   My Babe/Help Me/Sweet Sensations (p/s)........................... 8

FAST SET
80 Axis AXIS 1   Junction One/Children Of The Revolution (p/s) 15

FAT
71 RCA LSA 3009   FAT (LP) 15

FATAL CHARM
79 Company CR 005   Paris/Glitterbit/Out Of My Head..................................... 8
81 D.D. FATAL 1   Christine/Paris (p/s) 10

FATAL MICROBES
79 Small Wonder SMALL 20   Violence Grows/Beautiful Pictures/Cry Baby (p/s) 5
(see also Pete Fender, Honey Bane)

FATAL MICROBES/POISON GIRLS
79 Small Wonder WEENY 3   FATAL MICROBES MEET THE POISON GIRLS
                            (12" EP, with insert) 8
(see also Poison Girls)

FATBACK BAND

FATBACK BAND
75	Polydor 2066 494	Keep On Steppin'/Breakin' Up Is Hard To Do	5
75	Polydor 2066 524	Wicky Wacky/Can't Fight The Flame	5
75	Polydor 2066 590	Yum, Yum (Gimme Some)/Trompin'	5
75	Polydor 2066 637	(Are You Ready) Do The Bus Stop/Got To Learn How To Dance	5
76	Polydor 2066 682	Par-r-rty Time/Put Your Love In My Tender Care	5
75	Polydor 2391 143	KEEP ON STEPPIN' (LP)	12
75	Polydor 2391 184	YUM, YUM (LP)	12

FAT CITY
69	Probe SPB 1008	REINCARNATION (LP)	15

FATHER'S ANGELS
68	MGM MGM 1459	Don't Knock It/Bok To Bach	80
75	Black Magic BM 103	Bok To Bach/Disco Trucking	6

FAT MATTRESS
69	Polydor 56352	Naturally/Iridescent Butterfly	6
69	Polydor 56367	Magic Lanterns/Bright New Way	8
70	Polydor 2058 053	Highway/Black Sheep Of The Family	8
69	Polydor 582/583 056	FAT MATTRESS (LP, open-out sleeve)	18
70	Polydor 2383 025	FAT MATTRESS II (LP)	15

(see also Noel Redding Band, Jimi Hendrix Experience, Flowerpot Men)

FATS & CHESSMEN
62	Pye International 7N 25122	Big Ben Twist/Old Macdonald Had A Twist	7
61	Golden Guinea GGL 0117	LET'S TWIST (LP)	12
62	Golden Guinea GGL 0125	LET'S TWIST TO THE OLDIES (LP)	12

ERIC FATTER
69	Camel CA 20	Since You've Been Gone (actually Eric Fratter)/ WINSTON HINES: Cool Down (B-side actually by Winston Hinds)	6

(see also Eric Fratter, Afrotones)

ERNIE FAULKNER
63	Sway SW 003	Beautiful Girl/SAM DANIELS: Tell Me Baby (both with Planets)	8

FAUST
72	Faust/Polydor 2001 299	So Far/It's A Bit Of Pain	8
80	Recommended RRI 15	EXTRACTS FROM FAUST PARTY 3 (EP)	8
72	Polydor 2310 142	FAUST (LP, initially on clear vinyl in printed PVC sleeve)	25/12
73	Polydor 2310 196	FAUST SO FAR (LP, with 10 prints in wallet)	20
73	Virgin V 2004	FAUST 4 (LP)	12
79	Recommended RRA 1	FAUST ONE (LP, reissue of "Faust")	12
79	Recommended R.R. TWO	FAUST SO FAR (LP, reissue, with 10 insert prints, numbered, 600 only)	20
80	Recommended RRA 6	THE FAUST TAPES (LP, plastic bag cover)	15

(see also Toni Conrad & Faust)

FAVOURITES
80	4 Play FOUR 002	S.O.S./Favourite Shoes (p/s)	6
80	4 Play FOUR 003	Angelica/Cold (p/s)	5

FAVOURITE SONS
65	Mercury MF 911	That Driving Beat/Walkin' Walkin' Walkin'	75

WALLY FAWKES (& HIS TROGLODYTES)
57	Decca FJ 10855	Petite Fleur/Baby Brown (with Sandy Brown Quintet)	10
57	Decca FJ 10855	Petite Fleur/Baby Brown (78, with Sandy Brown Quintet)	5
57	Decca FJ 10936	Sent For You Yesterday And Here You Came Today/Why Can't You Behave	5
58	Decca F 11002	The Pilot Fish And The Whale/Pale Blues	5
56	Decca DFE 6192	TAKIN' IT EASY -- VOL 1 (EP, with Bruce Turner)	10
56	Decca DFE 6193	TAKIN' IT EASY -- VOL 2 (EP, with Bruce Turner)	15
57	Decca DEF 6407	AND HIS TROGLODYTES (EP)	10
60	Decca DFE 6600	FLOOK DIGS JAZZ (EP)	18
61	Decca STO 136	A NIGHT AT THE SIX BELLS (EP)	25
56	Decca LF 1214	TAKIN' IT EASY (LP, with Bruce Turner)	15
58	Decca LF 312	FAWKES ON HOLIDAY (LP)	18

(see also Sandy Brown)

BILL FAY
67	Deram DM 143	Some Good Advice/Screams In The Ears	40
70	Deram Nova SDN 12	BILL FAY (LP)	25
71	Deram SML 1079	TIME OF THE LAST PERSECUTION (LP)	65

BRIAN FAYE & ORCHESTRA
(see under Brian Fahey)

FRANCIS FAYE
61	Vogue V 9186	I Wish I Could Shimmy Like My Sister Kate/Night And Day	12
61	HMV POP 898	Frenesi/Miserlou	6
65	Stateside SL 10129	YOU GOTTA GO! GO! GO! (LP)	12

LITTLE RITA FAYE
53	MGM MGM 671	Rock City Boogie/Wait A Little Longer (78)	15
53	MGM MGM 697	I Fell Out Of The Christmas Tree/I'm A Problem Child (78)	12

F.B.I. (FOLK BLUES INC.)
66	Eyemark EMS 1006	Don't Hide/When The Ship Comes In	15
73	A&M AMS 7050	I Wonder What She's Doing Tonight/Boogaloo Boo-Boo	10
76	Good Earth GD 6	F.B.I./The Time Is Right To Leave The City	10
77	Good Earth GDS 802	F.B.I. (LP)	75

FEARN'S BRASS FOUNDRY
68	Decca F 12721	Don't Change It/John White	12
68	Decca F 12835	Now I Taste The Tears/Love, Sink And Drown	8

FEAR OF FALLING
83	Excellent XL 7	Like A Lion/You My Prodigal Son (p/s)	20

CHARLIE FEATHERS/MAC CURTIS
74	Polydor 2310 293	ROCKABILLY KINGS (LP, withdrawn)	15

(see also Mac Curtis)

FEATURES
70s	Progress PR 01	Drab City/Job Satisfaction	5

FEDERALMEN
70	London HLU 10303	Soul Serenade/Scorcher	5

FEDERALS (U.K.)
63	Parlophone R 4988	Brazil/In A Persian Market	10
63	Parlophone R 5013	Boot Hill/Keep On Dancing With Me	10
64	Parlophone R 5100	The Climb/Dance With A Dolly	10
64	Parlophone R 5139	Marlena/Please Believe Me	10
64	Parlophone R 5193	Twilight Time/Lost And Alone	10
65	Parlophone R 5320	Bucket Full Of Love/Leah	12

(see also Winston's Fumbs, Yes)

FEDERALS (Jamaica)
67	Island WI 3126	Penny For Your Song/I've Passed This Way Before	15
68	Island WI 3152	Shocking Love/By The River	15
69	High Note HS 024	Wailing Festival/Me And My Baby (B-side actually "By The River")	8
70	Camel CA 40	In This World/You Better Call On Me (B-side actually "Shocking Love")	6

FEDERATION
76	20th Century BTC 1023	25 Minutes To Love/Hooked On Love	5

FEEDER
96	Echo ECS 13	TWO COLOURS: Pictures Of Rain/Chicken On A Bone (p/s, clear vinyl)	25
96	Echo ECS 13	TWO COLOURS: Pictures Of Rain/Chicken On A Bone (CD, 1,000 only)	30
96	Echo ECHLP 9	SWIM (LP)	20

FEELIES
79	Stiff (no cat. no.)	Facé La/The Boy With Perpetual Nervousness/ Everybody's Got Something To Hide (Except Me And My Monkey) (flexidisc, promo only, free with *Be Stiff* fanzine issue 6, 5,000 only)	6/4

FELDER'S ORIOLES
65	Piccadilly 7N 35247	Down Home Girl/Misty	15
65	Piccadilly 7N 35269	Sweet Tasting Wine/Turn On Your Lovelight	15
66	Piccadilly 7N 35311	I Know You Don't Love Me No More/Only Three Can Pay	15
66	Piccadilly 7N 35332	Back Street/Something You Got	15

(see also V.I.P.s, Mike Patto)

MARTY FELDMAN
68	Pye 7N 17643	Funny He Never Married/Travel Agency (with Tim Brooke-Taylor)	6
68	Decca F 12857	A Joyous Time Of Year/B Side	6
68	Pye NPL 18258	MARTY (LP)	18
69	Decca LK/SKL 4983	I FEEL A SONG GOING OFF (LP)	18

VICTOR FELDMAN BIG BAND/QUARTET
55	Tempo A 127	Elegy/Maenya (78)	7
56	Tempo A 142	Big Top/Cabaletto	5
57	Tempo A 154	Jackpot/You Are My Heart's Desire	5
55	Tempo EXA 29	BIG BAND (EP)	50
57	Tempo EXA 57	VICTOR FELDMAN IN LONDON –THE QUARTET VOLUME 1 (EP)	60
57	Tempo EXA 67	VICTOR FELDMAN IN LONDON VOLUME 2 (EP)	15
58	Tempo EXA 85	MUTUAL ADMIRATION (EP, with Dizzy Reece)	15
50s	Esquire EP 43	MODERN JAZZ QUARTET (EP)	40
50s	Esquire EP 54	MODERN JAZZ QUARTET (EP)	20
50s	Esquire EP 64	MODERN JAZZ QUINTET/SEXTET (EP)	25
50s	Esquire EP 84	MODERN JAZZ QUARTET/SEXTET (EP)	20
50s	Esquire EP 104	MODERN JAZZ QUARTET (EP)	40
50s	Esquire EP 114	VIC FELDMAN ENCORE (EP)	15
50s	Esquire 20 - 046	MULTIPLE TALENTS (LP)	30
50s	Esquire 20 - 064	EXPERIMENT IN TIME (LP)	40
55	Tempo LAP 5	VICTOR FELDMAN'S SEXTET (10" LP)	200
56	Tempo LAP 6	VICTOR FELDMAN MODERN JAZZ QUARTET (10" LP)	120
57	Tempo TAP 8	VICTOR FELDMAN IN LONDON VOL. 1 (LP)	175
57	Tempo TAP 12	VICTOR FELDMAN IN LONDON VOL. 2 (LP)	100
58	Tempo TAP 19	TRANSATLANTIC ALLIANCE (LP)	350
59	Contemporary LAC 12172	THE ARRIVAL OF VICTOR FELDMAN (LP)	15

(see also Dizzy Reece)

VICTOR FELDMAN, TERRY GIBBS & LARRY BUNKER
60	Top Rank 30/007	VIBES TO THE POWER OF THREE (LP)	15

JOSE FELICIANO
68	RCA RCA 1715	(Baby Will You) Light My Fire/California Dreamin'	5
68	RCA RCA 1769	Hi Heel Sneakers/Hitchcock Railway	5
69	RCA RCA 1871	And The Sun Will Shine/Rain	5

FELIUS ANDROMEDA
67	Decca F 12694	Meditations/Cheadle Heath Delusions	40

(see also Denis Couldry)

Julie FELIX

JULIE FELIX
64	Decca LK 4626	JULIE FELIX (LP)	12
65	Decca LK 4683	SINGS DYLAN AND GUTHRIE (LP)	12
65	Decca LK 4724	SECOND ALBUM (LP)	12
66	Decca LK 4820	THIRD ALBUM (LP)	12

MIKE FELIX
66	Pye 7N 17058	You Belong To Me/Booga Dee	5
67	Decca F 12701	Blueberry Hill/I Don't Think You Want Me Anymore	5

FELIX & HIS GUITAR
59	London HLU 8875	Chili Beans/Puerto Rican Riot	10
59	London HLU 8875	Chili Beans/Puerto Rican Riot (78)	20

RAY FELL
70	Columbia DB 8734	Today I Killed A Man I Didn't Know/Roots Of Our Past	5

FELT
79	Shanghai S79/CUS 321	Index/Break It (p/s, early copies have notes on rear sleeve)	50/40
81	Cherry Red CHERRY 26	Something Sends Me To Sleep/Red Indians/Something Sends Me To Sleep (Version)/Red Indians (p/s)	12
82	Cherry Red CHERRY 45	My Face Is On Fire/Trails Of Colour Dissolve (p/s)	8
83	Cherry Red CHERRY 59	Penelope Tree/A Preacher In New England (p/s)	6
83	Cherry Red 12CHERRY 59	Penelope Tree/A Preacher In New England/Now Summer's Spread Its Wings Again (12", p/s)	8
84	Cherry Red CHERRY 78	Mexican Bandits/The World Is As Soft As Lace (p/s)	5
84	Cherry Red CHERRY 81	Sunlight Bathed The Golden Glow/Fortune (p/s)	6
84	Cherry Red 12CHERRY 81	Sunlight Bathed The Golden Glow/Fortune/Sunlight Strings (12", p/s)	8
85	Cherry Red 12CHERRY 89	Primitive Painters/Cathedral (12", p/s, with Liz Frazer)	8
86	Creation CRE 027	Ballad Of The Band/I Didn't Mean To Hurt You (p/s)	5
86	Creation CRE 032	Rain Of Crystal Spires/I Will Die With My Head In Flames (p/s)	5
88	Cherry Red CDCHERRY 89	Primitive Painters/Cathedral (reissue, picture CD)	8
88	Creation CRE 060	Space Blues/Tuesday's Secret (company die-cut sleeve)	5
89	él GPO F44	Get Out Of My Mirror (flexidisc)	5
89	él GPO 44	Get Out Of My Mirror (hard vinyl test pressing, 200 only)	15

(see also Versatile Newts, Maurice Deebank, Cocteau Twins)

FEMININE TOUCH featuring DUKE DURRELL
76	Paladin PAL 11	You Make Me Come Alive/You Make Me Come Alive (Instrumental)	5

JAYMES FENDA & VULCANS
64	Parlophone R 5210	Mistletoe Love/The Only Girl	10

JAN FENDER
71	Prince Buster PB 5	Sea Of Love/PRINCE BUSTER: Heaven Help Us All	8
71	Fab FAB 164	Sweet P/CLIFF & ORGANIZERS: Mr Brown	8
71	Fab FAB 166	Holly Holy Version/Old Kentrone Version (as Jal Fender)	8

PETE FENDER
81	Xntrix 2002	FOUR FORMULAS (EP, some in 8" silk-screened book p/s)	10/5

(see also Fatal Microbes, Omega Tribe)

FENDER BENDERS
79	Sticky SL 001	Big Green Thing/Hillman Hunter Paranoia (textured p/s, various colours)	6

FENDERMEN
60	Top Rank JAR 395	Mule Skinner Blues/Torture	10
60	Top Rank JAR 513	Don't You Just Know It/Beach Party	12

FENMEN
64	Decca F 11955	Rag Doll/Be My Girl	12
65	Decca F 12269	I've Got Everthing You Need Babe/Every Little Day Now	8
66	CBS 202075	California Dreamin'/Is This Your Way?	8
66	CBS 202236	Rejected/Girl Don't Bring Me Down	20

(see also Bern Elliott & Fenmen, Pretty Things, Zac Zolar & Electric Banana)

MICHAEL FENNELLY
74	Epic EPC 80230	LANE CHANGER (LP)	10

(see also Crabby Appleton)

PETER FENTON
66	Fontana TF 748	Marble Breaks, Iron Bends/Small Town	8

SHANE FENTON (& FENTONES)
61	Parlophone R 4827	I'm A Moody Guy/Five Foot Two, Eyes Of Blue	7
62	Parlophone R 4866	Walk Away/Fallen Leaves On The Ground	8
62	Parlophone R 4883	Why Little Girl/It's All Over Now	8
62	Parlophone R 4921	It's Gonna Take Magic/Cindy's Birthday	7
62	Parlophone R 4951	Too Young For Sad Memories/You're Telling Me	7
63	Parlophone R 4982	I Ain't Got Nobody/Hey Miss Ruby	6
63	Parlophone R 5020	A Fool's Paradise/You Need Love (solo)	7
63	Parlophone R 5047	Don't Do That/I'll Know (solo)	8
64	Parlophone R 5131	Hey, Lulu/I Do, Do You?	7
72	Fury FY 305	Eastern Seaboard/Blind Fool	15
74	Contour 2870 409	GOOD ROCKIN' TONIGHT (LP)	12

(see also Alvin Stardust, Fentones)

FENTONES
62	Parlophone R 4899	The Mexican/Lover's Guitar	10
62	Parlophone R 4937	The Breeze And I/Just For Jerry	8

(see also Shane Fenton)

FENWAYS
65	Liberty LIB 66082	Walk/Whip And Jerk	10

454   Rare Record Price Guide 2002

RAY FENWICK
78	Mercury 6007 176	Queen Of The Night/I Wanna Boogie	6
71	Decca SKL 5090	KEEP AMERICA BEAUTIFUL, GET A HAIRCUT (LP)	30

(see also Spencer Davis Group, After Tea, Fancy, Ian Gillan Band, Wizard's Convention, Murgatroyd Band, Marlon, Forcefield)

FERDIA
78	Polydor 2904 012	A SIGH FOR OLD TIMES (LP)	15

FERDINAND & DILL
70	Pama PM 805	Take Back Your Nicklet/Blueberry Hill	6

DOTTIE FERGUSON
57	Mercury MT 182	Happy Happy Birthday Baby/Darling, It's Wonderful (78)	12

H-BOMB FERGUSON
54	Esquire 10-372	Feel Like I Do/My Love (78)	35

HELENA FERGUSON
67	London HLZ 10164	Where Is The Party?/My Terms	25

JESSIE LEE FERGUSON & OUTER LIMITS
69	Pye International 7N 25492	New Shoes/Puttin' It On, Puttin' It Off	6

JOHNNY FERGUSON
60	MGM MGM 1059	Angela Jones/Blue Serge And White Lace	6
61	MGM MGM 1119	No One Can Love You/The Valley Of Love	6

MAYNARD FERGUSON ORCHESTRA
60	Mercury MMC 14050	THE BOY WITH LOTS OF BRASS (LP, also stereo CMS 18034)	12
60	Columbia 33SX 1270	JAZZ FOR DANCING (LP, also stereo SCX 3338)	12
61	Columbia 33SX 1301	NEWPORT SUITE (LP, also stereo SCX 3368)	12
72	CBS 65027	M.F. HORN 2 (LP)	12

ALEX FERGUSSON
80	Red RS 003	Stay With Me Tonight/Brushing Your Hair (p/s)	5
94	own label	ALEX FERGUSSON (LP, white label, plain cover with postcard, 500 only)	12

(see also ATV)

FERKO STRING BAND
55	London HL 8140	Alabama Jubilee/Sing A Little Melody	20
55	London HL 8140	Alabama Jubilee/Sing A Little Melody (78)	8
55	London HLF 8183	Ma (She's Making Eyes At Me)/You Are My Sunshine	18
55	London HLF 8183	Ma (She's Making Eyes At Me)/You Are My Sunshine (78)	8
55	London HLF 8215	Happy Days Are Here Again/Deep In The Heart Of Texas	18
55	London HLF 8215	Happy Days Are Here Again/Deep In The Heart Of Texas (78)	10
58	London HL 7052	Happy Days Are Here Again/Alabama Jubilee (export issue)	12
56	London RE-F 1041	PHILADELPHIA MUMMERS PARADE VOL. 1 (EP)	12
56	London RE-F 1052	PHILADELPHIA MUMMERS PARADE VOL. 2 (EP)	12
57	London HB-C 1064	THE FERKO STRING BAND VOL. 1 (10" LP)	20

FERMENA
71	Pama PM 839	Come What May/Version (B-side with Ranny)	5
73	Pama PM 879	Wonderful Dreams/Version	5

PHIL FERNANDO
58	Pye Nixa 7N 15142	Blonde Bombshell/Make Ready for Love	7
58	Pye Nixa N 15142	Blonde Bombshell/Make Ready for Love (78)	8
62	Palette PG 9029	Do The High Life/High Life Girl	6

ANDY FERNBACH
69	Liberty LBL/LBS 83233	IF YOU MISS YOUR CONNEXION (LP)	80

(see also Groundhogs)

MAJA FERNICK
72	Philips 6006 196	Give Me Your Love Again/Flowers In The City	8

FERRANTE & TEICHER
60	London HLT 9164	Theme From "The Apartment"/Lonely Room	6
60	London HLT 7103	Theme From "The Apartment"/DON COSTA & HIS ORCHESTRA: Theme From "The Unforgiven" (export issue)	8
61	London HLT 9298	Theme From "Exodus"/Twilight	6
61	London HLT 7105	Theme From "Exodus"/Twilight (export issue)	6
61	HMV POP 881	Theme From "Exodus"/Twilight (reissue)	5
65	United Artists UP 1097	The Knack/Country Boy	7
61	HMV/Utd. Artists 7EG 8700	EXODUS (EP)	8

DIANE FERRAZ & NICKY SCOTT
66	Columbia DB 7824	Me And You/Don't Pretend	6
66	Columbia DB 7897	You've Got To Learn/Like You As You Are	6
66	Columbia DB 7963	Sh-Boom, Sh-Boom/Allah Mobish	6

(see also Nicky Scott)

JOE FERRER & HIS DEVILS BOYS
61	Oriole CB 1629	Rockin' Crickets/Blue Guitar	12

EUGENE FERRIS
66	Planet PLF 112	There Was A Smile In Your Eyes/Soft Moonlight (with/without company sleeve)	15/10

GEORGE FERRIS
71	Ackee ACK 117	With Every Dream/Diana	6

FERRIS WHEEL

67	Pye 7N 17387	I Can't Break The Habit/Number One Guy	7
68	Pye 7N 17538	Let It Be Me/You Look At Me	6
68	Pye 7N 17631	The Na Na Song/Three Cool Cats	6
69	Polydor 56366	Can't Stop Now/I Know You Well	5
67	Pye NPL 18203	CAN'T BREAK THE HABIT (LP)	20
70	Polydor 583 066	FERRIS WHEEL (LP)	12

(see also Linda Lewis, West Five)

BRYAN FERRY

73	Island WIP 6170	A Hard Rain's Gonna Fall/2 HB (some in promo only p/s)	50/5
74	Island WIP 6196	The 'In' Crowd/Chance Meeting (initially in p/s)	8/5
74	Island WIP 6205	Smoke Gets In Your Eyes/Another Time, Another Place	5
75	Island WIP 6234	You Go To My Head/Re-Make, Re-Model (no p/s)	5
75	Island WIP 6234	You Go To My Head/Re-Make, Re-Model (DJ copies in generic promo p/s)	20
76	Island WIP 6307	Let's Stick Together/Sea Breezes	5
76	Island IEP 1	EXTENDED PLAY (EP, p/s)	7
78	Polydor PPSP 10	Hold On I'm Coming/Take Me To The River (12", unissued, promo only, numbered stamped p/s)	20
85	E.G. FERPX 2	Don't Stop The Dance (Special 12" Remix)/Slave To Love (Special 12" Remix)/Nocturne (12", picture disc, printed PVC sleeve)	10
85	E.G. FEREP 3	Windswept/Crazy Love/Feel The Need/Broken Wings (p/s)	5
88	Virgin CDT 10/EGOCD 41	Let's Stick Together/Shame Shame Shame/Chance Meeting/Sea Breezes (3" CD, card sleeve)	10
88	Virgin CDEP 8	The Right Stuff (4.25)/(6.40)/(Dub Mix) (CD, gatefold sleeve)	10
88	Virgin CDEP 19	Kiss And Tell/Kiss And Tell (Dub Mix)/Zamba/Kiss And Tell (Dance Mix) (CD)	8
88	Virgin VSCD 1066	Limbo (Latin Mix)/Bête Noire (Instrumental)/Limbo (Brooklyn Dub Mix) (CD in 6" x 5" cardboard box)	10
88	E.G. EGOCD 44	Let's Stick Together (Westside '88 Mix)/Trash/Sign Of The Times/Casanova (CD)	10
89	E.G. EGOCD 46	The Price Of Love (The R&B '89 Remix)/Don't Stop The Dance (Special 12" Remix)/Slave To Love (12" Remix)/Loner (3" CD, card sleeve)	10
89	E.G. EGOCD 48	He'll Have To Go/Take Me To The River/Broken Wings/Carrickfergus (3" CD, card sleeve)	10
73	Island ILPS 9239	THESE FOOLISH THINGS (LP, unissued gatefold sleeve)	500
76	Island ILPS 9367	LET'S STICK TOGETHER (LP, original issue)	12
78	Polydor POLD 5003	THE BRIDE STRIPPED BARE (LP, original with A//3 P matrix, includes 'Broken Wings', white label test pressings only, some in different proof sleeve)	400/200

(see also Roxy Music)

CATHERINE FERRY

76	Barclay BAR 42	One, Two, Three/1, 2, 3	12

FERRY AID

87	Sun AID T1	Let It Be/Let It Be (Mega Message Mix) (12", p/s, mail-order only)	10

FEVER TREE

68	MCA MU 1043	San Francisco Girls/Come With Me	8
68	Uni UNLS 102	FEVER TREE (LP)	20
68	MCA MUPS 347	ANOTHER TIME, ANOTHER PLACE (LP)	25

FICKLE FINGER

69	Page One POF 150	Fickle Lizzie-Anne/Cellophane Mary Jane	10

(see also Matchmakers, Mark Wirtz)

FICKLE PICKLE

70	Fontana TF 1069	Millionaire/Sam And Sadie	8
70	Philips 6006 038	Maybe I'm Amazed/Sitting On A Goldmine	5

EDDIE FICTION

79	Absurd ABSURD 2	U.F.O. (Pt. 2)/U.F.O. (Pt. 1) (p/s)	5

FIDDLER'S DRAM

80	Dingles DIN 304	TO SEE THE PLAY (LP)	12
80	Dingles DID 711	FIDDLER'S DRAM (LP)	10

FI-DELS

72	Jay Boy BOY 69	Try A Little Harder/You Never Do Right	6
70s	DJM DJS 689	Try A Little Harder/KEYMAN STRINGS: Instrumental Version	5

KEITH FIELD

68	Polydor 56278	The Day That War Broke Out/Stop Thief	10

ALAN FIELDING

58	Fontana H 124	Just Remember/Don't Say Goodbye	5
60	Decca F 11261	I'll Never Understand/I Love Suzie Brown	5
61	Decca F 11487	Scatter Brain/I've Got To Learn To Forget	5
62	Decca F 11404	How Many Nights, How Many Days/Building Castles In The Air	6
62	Decca F 11518	Too Late To Worry Too Blue To Cry/You Reap Just What You Sow	6

FENELLA FIELDING

66	Columbia DB 8056	Big Bad Mouse/Later	5

JERRY FIELDING & HIS ORCHESTRA

54	London HL 8017	When I Grow Too Old To Dream/Button Up Your Overcoat	30
54	London HL 8017	When I Grow Too Old To Dream/Button Up Your Overcoat (78)	7
55	London HL 7001	Faintly Reminiscent/Blues Serenade (export issue)	12
55	London HL 7002	Pea-nut Vendor/Can't Help Lovin' Dat Man (export issue)	12
55	London HL 7003	Tea For Two/Here In My Arms (export issue)	12
55	London HL 7004	I'm In Love/Blue Prelude (export issue)	12
55	Brunswick 05399	The Gypsy In My Soul/The Glory Of Love	10
55	London RE-P 1026	DANCE DATE VOL. 1 (EP)	12
54	London H-APB 1022	FAINTLY REMINISCENT (10" LP)	15
54	London H-APB 1027	PLAYS A DANCE CONCERT (10" LP)	15

FIELD MICE

88	Sarah SARAH 012	Emma's House/When You Sleep/Fabulous Friend/The Last Letter (p/s)	6
89	Caff CAFF 2	I Can See Myself Alone Forever/Everything About You (foldaround p/s in poly bag with insert)	18

FIELDS

69	Uni UNLS 104	FIELDS (LP)	25

FIELDS

71	CBS 7555	Friends Of Mine/Three Minstrels	5
71	CBS 69009	FIELDS (LP, with/without poster)	40/25
	(see also Rare Bird)		

BILLY FIELDS

55	MGM SP 1126	Sincerely/Thrilled	5
59	Mercury AMT 1067	The Greatest Love In The World/No Other Love	5

ERNIE FIELDS & HIS ORCHESTRA

59	London HL 8985	In The Mood/Christopher Columbus	6
59	London HL 8985	In The Mood/Christopher Columbus (78)	22
60	London HL 9100	Chattanooga Choo Choo/Workin' Out	8
60	London HL 9227	Raunchy/My Prayer	7
60	London RE 1260	SAXY (EP)	40
60	London HA 2263	IN THE MOOD (LP)	35

GRACIE FIELDS

55	Decca F 10614	Twenty/Summertime In Venice	5
56	Decca F 10824	A Letter To A Soldier/The Sweetest Prayer In All The World	5
57	Columbia DB 3953	Around The World/Far Away	5
52	Decca LF 1080	NOW IS THE HOUR (10" LP)	15
53	Decca LF 1140	GRACIE FIELDS (10" LP)	15
57	Conquest CL 1001	OUR GRACIE (LP)	12

IRVING FIELDS TRIO & ORCHESTRA

54	Parlophone CMSP 9	Mr. Piano Player/Cuban Carnival (export issue)	10
58	Oriole CB 1436	Ragtime Rock/Syncopated Sadie	5
58	Oriole CB 1436	Ragtime Rock/Syncopated Sadie (78)	8

KANSAS FIELDS & MILTON SEALEY

56	Ducretet DEP 95017	KANSAS FIELDS & MILTON SEALEY (EP)	10

FIELDS OF THE NEPHILIM

84	Tower N1	BURNING THE FIELDS (12" EP, red/black p/s)	80
85	Tower N1/Jung. JUNG 28T	BURNING THE FIELDS (12" EP, green p/s with insert & band photo label)	15
85	Tower N1/Jung. JUNG 28T	BURNING THE FIELDS (12" EP, green & other coloured vinyl export issue)	10
86	Situation 2 SIT 42	Power/Secrets (7", white label promos only, stickered plain sleeve)	40
87	Situation 2 SIT 46	Preacher Man/Laura II (p/s, some with Beggars Banquet sticker)	20/18
87	Situation 2 SIT 48	Blue Water/In Every Dream Home A Heartache (p/s)	12
87	Situation 2 SIT 48T	Blue Water (Electrostatic)/In Every Dream Home A Heartache (live)/ Blue Water (Hot Wire) (12", p/s, some with magazine)	15/8
87	House Of Dolls HOD 15	Dawnrazor (on free EP with House Of Dolls magazine, issue 15)	8/6
88	Situation 2 SIT 52TR	Moonchild (Second Seal)/Shiva/Power/Vet For The Insane (12", p/s)	8
89	Situation 2 SIT 57	Psychonaut/Celebrate (Second Seal) (blue/green p/s)	5
90	Beggars Banquet BEG 250	Sumerland/Phobia (live) (no p/s)	5
88	Situation 2 SITU 22L	THE NEPHILIM (LP, 2 x 45rpm 12", gatefold sleeve, numbered)	12

FIESTAS

59	London HL 8870	So Fine/Last Night I Dreamed	25
59	London HL 8870	So Fine/Last Night I Dreamed (78)	50
71	Atlantic 2091 121	So Fine/Broken Heart	5

FIFTEENTH

86	Tanz TANZ 3	ANDELAIN (12" EP)	10

FIFTH AVENUE

65	Immediate IM 002	The Bells Of Rhymney/Just Like Anyone Would Do	20
	(see also Denny Gerrard, Warm Sounds)		

FIFTH COLUMN

66	Columbia DB 8068	Benjamin Day/There's Nobody There	15
	(see also Gerry Rafferty)		

MINT VALUE £

5TH DIMENSION

5TH DIMENSION

67	Liberty LIB 12051	Go Where You Wanna Go/Too Poor To Die	12
67	Liberty LIB 12056	Another Day, Another Heartache/Rosecrans Blvd	5
67	Liberty LBF 15014	Up Up And Away/Pattern People	6
68	Liberty LBF 15052	Carpet Man/Magic Garden	5
68	Liberty LBF 15081	Ticket To Ride/Orange Air	5
69	Liberty LBF 15193	Aquarius-Let The Sun Shine In/Don'tcha Hear Me Callin' To Ya	8
69	Liberty LBF 15288	Wedding Bell Blues/Let It Be Me	5
70	Liberty LBF 15356	I'll Be Lovin' You Forever/Train Keep On Movin'	15
76	ABC ABC 4118	Love Hangover/Will You Be There	10
68	Liberty LBL/LBS 83098E	MAGIC GARDEN (LP)	12
68	Liberty LBL/LBS 83155E	STONED SOUL PICNIC (LP)	15
69	Liberty LBS 83205	AGE OF AQUARIUS (LP)	12
70	Liberty LBS 83228	THE FANTASTIC 5TH DIMENSION (LP)	12
71	Bell SBLL 144	LOVE'S LINES, ANGLES AND RHYMES (LP)	12

FIFTH ESTATE

67	Stateside SS 2034	Ding Dong The Witch Is Dead/Rub A Dub	6
67	Stateside SS 2068	Heigh Ho/It's Waiting There For You	6
68	Stateside SS 2105	Do Drop In/That's Love	6
69	Stateside SS 2125	Coney Island Sally/Tomorrow Is My Turn	6

FIFTY FANTASTICS

79	South Circular SGS 108	God's Got Religion/STEPPES: The Beat Drill (white label)	10
80	Dining Out TUX 5	God's Got Religion/The Beat Drill (reissue, foldout p/s, handdone labels)	8

(see also Steppes, Disco Zombies)

FIFTY FOOT HOSE

69	Mercury SLML 4030	CAULDRON (LP)	75

50 YEAR VOID

92	BLADE 1	Blade's Love Machine (1-sided 12", white label promo, 100 only)	30+

(see also St. Etienne, Sarah Cracknell)

FIGGY DUFF

85	Celtic CM 023	AFTER THE TEMPEST (LP, with insert)	20

PAULINE FILBY

60s	Church Miss. Soc. LIV/SP/81	I'm Hungry/NADIA CATTOUSE: The Larder	15
68	Herald ELR 1081	MY WORLD BY PAULINE FILBY (EP)	30
69	Herald LLR 567	SHOW ME A RAINBOW (LP)	75

(see also Narnia, Accolade, Gordon Giltrap)

FILE UNDER POP

79	Rough Trade RT 011	Heathrow/Corrugate/Heathrow SLB (p/s)	6

(see also AK Process)

FILTHY PHIL & FAST EDDIE

89	Receiver RRLP 124	NAUGHTY OLD SANTA'S CHRISTMAS CLASSICS (LP)	15

(see also Motörhead)

FILTHY RICH

87	JM TR 102	She's 17 (p/s)	25

(see also Trident)

FINAL CONFLICT
86	Futuresound FS 001	CHANNEL 8 (cassette)	8
86	Futuresound FS 001	EP (EP)	10
86	Futuresound FS 002	THE TIME HAS ARRIVED (EP, with 22-page booklet)	10
89	Futuresound VFS 001	My England/Across The Room (stickered white sleeve)	20

FINAL PROGRAM
81	Program FINAL 001	PROTECT AND SURVIVE (EP)	6

FINAL TOUCH
70s	Myrrh MYR 1188	LOVE SONG (LP)	20

FINCH
78	Rockburgh ROC 103	GALLEONS OF PASSION (LP)	15

FINDERS KEEPERS (U.S.)
67	London HLH 10117	Lavender Blue/MICKEY DOLENZ: Don't Do It	12

FINDERS KEEPERS (U.K.)
66	CBS 202249	Light/Power Of Love (withdrawn, promos may exist)	60+
66	CBS 202249	Light/Come On Now	10
67	Fontana TF 892	On The Beach/Friday Kind Of Monday	20
68	Fontana TF 938	Sadie (The Cleaning Lady)/Without Her	10

(see also Trapeze, Glenn Hughes, News)

FINGERS
66	Columbia DB 8026	I'll Take You Where The Music's Playing/My Way Of Thinking	7
67	Columbia DB 8112	All Kinds Of People/Circus With A Female Clown	20

(see also Crocheted Doughnut Ring, Legend)

FINI TRIBE (101)
84	Finiflex LT 1001	CURLING & STRETCHING EP (12", p/s, original issue)	10
88	Finiflex FT 002	DESTIMONY EP (12", p/s)	10
91	Finiflex/One Little Indian 54 TP 7	101: Sonic Shuffle (Edit)/101: 303 (3D Bass Edit) (promo only, plain stickered sleeve)	5
92	O. L. Indian 74TP12 F/J/Y	FOREVERGREEN (3 x 12" set)	10
89	O. L. Indian TPLP 21 CD	NOISE, LUST AND FUN (CD)	15
89	O. L. Indian TPLP 24 CD	GROSSING 10K (CD)	15

FINK BROTHERS
85	Zarjazz JAZZ 2	Mutants In Mega-City One/Mutant Blues (p/s)	4
85	Zarjazz JAZZ S2	Mutants In Mega-City One/Mutant Blues (square picture disc)	5
85	Zarjazz JAZZ 2-12	Mutants In Mega-City One (Mutie Mix)/Mutant Blues (12", p/s)	7

(see also Madness)

LEE FINN & RHYTHM MEN
63	Starlite ST45 103	High Class Feelin'/Pour Me A Glass Of Wine	250

MICKEY FINN & BLUE MEN
(see under 'M')

SIMON FINN
70	Mushroom 100 MR 2	PASS THE DISTANCE (LP, with lyric insert)	75

TIM FINN
83	Epic A 3932	Fraction Too Much Friction/Below The Belt (p/s)	5
86	Virgin VS 849-12	No Thunder No Fire No Rain (Extended Version)/ No Thunder No Fire No Rain/Searching The Streets (12", p/s)	8
86	Virgin VS 866-12	Carve You In Marble/Hole In My Heart (12", p/s)	8
89	Capitol CDCL 542	How'm I Gonna Sleep?/Cruel Black Crow (live)/ Six Months In A Leaky Boat (live) (CD)	8
94	Capitol	LIVE AT THE BORDERLINE (CD, promo only)	25

(see also Split Enz, Crowded House)

LARRY FINNEGAN
62	HMV POP 1022	Dear One/Candy Lips	10
62	London HLU 9613	Pretty Suzy Sunshine/It's Walkin' Talkin' Time	12
65	Ember EMB S 207	The Other Ringo (A Tribute To Ringo Starr)/When My Love Passes By (p/s)	12/7

MIKE FINNIGAN
78	CBS 6656	Just One Minute More/Blood Is Thicker Than Water	8

FINN MACCUILL
77	private pressing	SINK YE SWIM YE (LP)	80

ELISA FIORILLO
88	Chrysalis ELISAP 1	How Can I Forget You?/How Can I Forget You? (Version) (picture disc)	5

FIRE
68	Decca F 12753	Father's Name Is Dad/Treacle Toffee World	120
68	Decca F 12856	Round The Gum Tree/Toothie Ruthie	15
70	Pye NSPL 18343	THE MAGIC SHOEMAKER (LP)	200
97	Tenth Planet TP 029	UNDERGROUND AND OVERHEAD: THE ALTERNATE FIRE (LP, gatefold sleeve, numbered, 1,000 only)	12

(see also Strawbs, Paul Brett's Sage)

MINT VALUE £

FIREBALLS

59	Top Rank JAR 218	Torquay/Cry Baby	12
60	Top Rank JAR 276	Bulldog/Nearly Sunrise	12
60	Top Rank JAR 354	Foot-Patter/Kissin'	10
60	Top Rank JAR 507	Vaquero (Cowboy)/Chief Whoopin'-Koff	10
61	Pye International 7N 25092	Quite A Party/Gunshot	7
62	Stateside SS 106	Rik-A-Tik/Yacky Doo	7
63	Stateside SS 151	Carioca/Find Me A Golden Street	7
65	Stateside SS 417	Baby What's Wrong/Yummie Yama Papa	7
67	Stateside SS 2095	Bottle Of Wine/Ain't That Rain	6
68	Stateside SS 2106	Goin' Away/Groovy Motions	6
69	Stateside SS 2134	Come On, React!/Woman Help Me	6
69	London HLZ 10260	Long Green/Light In The Window	5
61	Top Rank 35/105	VAQUERO (LP)	50
68	Stateside S(S)L 10237	BOTTLE OF WINE (LP)	25
69	London HA/SH 8396	COME ON, REACT! (LP)	15

(see also Jimmy Gilmer, Buddy Holly)

FIREBALL XL5
(see under Century 21)

FIRECLOWN
83	Fireclown FC 1001	INVASION EP (Magic/Poor Man/Invasion) (10", no p/s)	15

FIRE ENGINES
80	Codex Comms. CDX 01	Get Up And Use Me/Everything's Roses (p/s)	6
81	Pop:Aural POP 010	Candy Skin/Meat Whiplash (foldout p/s in poly bag)	6
81	Pop:Aural POP 013	Big Gold Dream/Sympathetic Anaesthetic (p/s)	5
81	Pop:Aural POP 01312	Big Gold Dream/Sympathetic Anaesthetic/New Thing In Cartons (12", non-gatefold p/s; gatefold p/s £5)	7
81	Accessory ACC 001	LUBRICATE YOUR LIVING ROOM (LP, in plastic bag)	12

FIRE EXIT
79	Time Bomb Explosion 1	Timewall/Talkin' About Myself (p/s, stamped labels)	8

FIREFLIES
59	Top Rank JAR 198	You Were Mine/Stella Got A Fella	12
59	Top Rank JAR 198	You Were Mine/Stella Got A Fella (78)	40
60	London HLU 9057	I Can't Say Goodbye/What Did I Do Wrong	15

FIREHOUSE FIVE PLUS TWO
56	Good Time Jazz GV 2192	Runnin' Wild/Lonesome Railroad Blues	5
50s	Good Time Jazz LDG 036	GOES SOUTH VOL. 1 (10" LP)	12
50s	Good Time Jazz LDG 079	GOES SOUTH VOL. 2 (10" LP)	12
50s	Good Time Jazz LDG 094	GOES SOUTH VOL. 3 (10" LP)	12
50s	Good Time Jazz LDG 169	GOES SOUTH VOL. 4 (10" LP)	12
50s	Good Time Jazz LDG 183	FIREHOUSE FIVE (10" LP)	12
50s	Good Time Jazz LAG 12079	THE FIREHOUSE FIVE PLUS TWO (LP)	12
50s	Good Time Jazz LAG 12089	THE FIREHOUSE FIVE PLUS TWO VOL. 2 (LP)	12

FIRE ISLAND
92	Boys Own BOIX 11	In Your Bones/Fire Island (12", 4-track)	15

FIREMAN
99	Hydra HYPRO 12 008	Fluid (12", p/s, promo only)	50
99	Hydra HYPRO CD 008	Fluid (CD, promo only)	25
93	Parlophone FIRE 1	STRAWBERRIES OCEANS SHIPS FOREST (2-LP, clear vinyl, numbered white sleeve, with inners, promo only)	50
93	Parlophone PCSD 145	STRAWBERRIES OCEANS SHIPS FOREST (2-LP, clear vinyl, red sleeve, with inners)	25
93	Parlophone PCSD 145	STRAWBERRIES OCEANS SHIPS FOREST (CD)	20
98	Hydra 4970551	RUSHES (LP)	20

(see also Paul McCartney, Youth)

FIRE SESSION
70	Revolution REV 10	Souvenir/Bad Girl	5
70	Revolution REV 13	Sleeping Reggae/CAROLS: Everyday I Have To Cry Some	5
70	Revolution REV 14	Death Of The Ugly One/Big Feet	5

FIRESIGN THEATRE
68	CBS 65129	WAITING FOR THE ELECTRICIAN OR SOMEONE LIKE HIM (LP)	15
68	CBS 65130	HOW TO BE IN TWO PLACES AT ONCE WHEN YOU'RE NOT ANYWHERE AT ALL? (LP)	15
72	CBS CQ 30737	FIRESIGN THEATRE (LP, quadrophonic)	15

FIRESTONES
62	Decca F 11436	Party Twist (Medley) (Parts 1 & 2)	5

FIRING SQUAD
64	Parlophone R 5152	A Little Bit More/Bull Moose	20

FIRKIN THE FOX
84	Woodworm WR 005	BEHIND BARS (LP)	25

FIRM
85	Atlantic A 9586P	Radioactive/Together (shaped picture disc)	10
85	Atlantic AT 9586	Radioactive/Together/City Sirens/Live In Peace (12", p/s)	10
86	Atlantic A 9458	All The King's Horses/Fortune Hunter (p/s)	5
85	Atlantic 781 239-2	THE FIRM (CD)	18
86	Atlantic 781 628-2	THE FIRM MEAN BUSINESS (CD)	18

(see also Jimmy Page, Bad Company, Rock Aid Armenia)

FIRST AID
77   Decca TXS 117   NOSTRADAMUS (LP) 20

FIRST CHOICE
73   Pye International 7N 25613   This Is The House Where Love Died/One Step Away (unissued, demos may exist)
74   Bell BLL 1376   The Player (Parts 1 & 2) 5
73   Bell BELLS 229   ARMED AND EXTREMELY DANGEROUS (LP) 12

FIRST CHURCH OF NAPOLEON SOLO
84   Off Beaten Track Offbeat 2   Debbydid/Game Of Bagatelle
                                         (hand-painted, stickered p/s) 5

FIRST CLASS
74   UK UKAL 1008   THE FIRST CLASS (LP) 12
76   UK UKAL 1022   S.S.T. (LP) 12
     (see also White Plains, Edison Lighthouse, Brotherhood Of Man, Carter-Lewis & Southerners, Ivy League)

FIRST EDITION
68   Reprise RS 20655   Just Dropped In (To See What Condition My Condition Was In)/
                                         Shadow In The Corner Of Your Mind 5
68   Reprise RS 20693   Charlie The Fer'de Lance/Look Around I'll Be There. 5
69   Reprise RS 20799   But You Know I Love You/Homemade Lies 5
68   Reprise RSLP 6276   THE FIRST EDITION (LP) 12
     (see also Kenny Rogers)

FIRST GEAR
64   Pye 7N 15703   A Certain Girl/Leave My Kitten Alone 125
65   Pye 7N 15763   The 'In' Crowd/Gotta Make Their Future Bright. 30

FIRST GENERATION
70   High Note HS 045   When/Chapter 6
     (see also Dave Barker)

FIRST IMPRESSION
67   Saga SOC 1045   BEAT CLUB (LP) 15

FIRST IMPRESSION/GOOD EARTH
68   Saga FID 2117   SWINGING LONDON (LP) 15
     (see also Good Earth, Mungo Jerry)

FIRST IMPRESSIONS
65   Pye 7N 15797   I'm Coming Home/Looking For Her. 10
     (see also Legends)

FIRST OFFENCE
88   Metal Other OTH 11   FIRST OFFENCE (LP, with insert) 12

FIRST STEPS
80   English Rose ER I   The Beat Is Back/She Ain't In Love/Let's Go Cuboids
                                         (p/s, with insert) 20
81   English Rose ER III   Anywhere Else But Here/Airplay/I Got The News (p/s) 20

CLARE FISCHER
62   Fontana 688124 ZL   FIRST TIME OUT (LP). 20

WILD MAN FISCHER
69   Reprise RSLP 6332   AN EVENING WITH WILD MAN FISCHER
                                         (gatefold sleeve). 30

     (see also Frank Zappa)

FISCHERMAN'S FRIEND
91   EG OP 51   MONEY (12", with "Orb Clubmix", 500 only) 12

FISH
89   EMI 12EMPD 109   State Of Mind/The Voyeur (I Like To Watch)/State Of Mind
                                         (Presidential Mix) (12", picture disc) 10
89   EMI CDEM 109   State Of Mind (Album Version)/The Voyeur (I Like To Watch)/
                                         State Of Mind (Presidential Mix) (CD) 12
90   EMI CDEM 125   Big Wedge/Jack And Jill/Faith Healer (live) (CD) 8
90   EMI EMPD 135   A Gentleman's Excuse Me/Whiplash (shaped picture disc). 8
90   EMI 12EMPD 135   A Gentleman's Excuse Me/Whiplash/A Gentleman's Excuse Me
                                         (Demo Version) (12", picture disc) 10
90   EMI CDEM 135   A Gentleman's Excuse Me/Whiplash/A Gentleman's Excuse Me
                                         (Demo Version) (CD) 8
91   Polydor FISHS 1   Internal Exile/Carnival Man (12" picture disc, numbered die cut sleeve). .. 12
91   Polydor FISHS 2   Credo/Credo (7" Mix)/Poet's Moon
                                         (12", box set with poster & numbered seal) 12
91   Polydor FISHCD 2   Credo/Credo (7" Mix)/Poet's Moon
                                         (CD, picture disc, signed numbered digipak) 20
91   Polydor FISHP 3   Something In The Air/Dear Friend (picture disc). 5
90   EMI EMDPD 1015   VIGIL IN A WILDERNESS OF MIRRORS (LP, picture disc) 18
94   Dick Bros DDICK 4   SUITS (LP, picture disc). 15
     (see also Marillion, Tony Banks)

ARCHIE FISHER
68   Xtra XTRA 1070   ARCHIE FISHER (LP). 20
70   Decca SKL 5057   ORFEO (LP) 25
     (see also Barbara Dickson)

CHIP FISHER
59   Parlophone R 4604   Poor Me/No One. 15
59   RCA RCX 143   AT THE SUGAR BOWL (EP) 60

MINT VALUE £

EDDIE FISHER

53	HMV 7M 101	I'm Yours/That's The Chance You Take	15
53	HMV 7M 115	Everything I Have Is Yours/You'll Never Know	20
53	HMV 7M 116	Trust In Me/Forgive Me	12
53	HMV 7M 117	Outside Of Heaven/Lady Of Spain	25
53	HMV 7M 125	Even Now/If It Were Up To Me	12
53	HMV 7M 126	Downhearted/Am I Wasting My Time On You	20
53	HMV 7M 133	I'm Walking Behind You (with Sally Sweetland)/Hold Me	25
53	HMV 7M 146	Just Another Polka/When I Was Young (Yes, Very Young)	10
53	HMV 7M 159	Wish You Were Here/A Fool Was I	15
53	HMV 7M 168	Many Times/With These Hands	10
54	HMV 7M 172	Oh My Papa/(I Never Missed You) Until You Said "Goodbye"	12
54	HMV 7M 185	How Deep Is The Ocean?/That Old Feeling	8
54	HMV 7M 201	April Showers/Just To Be With You	8
54	HMV 7M 212	I'm In The Mood For Love/A Girl, A Girl	10
54	HMV 7M 235	May I Sing To You?/My Friend	10
54	HMV 7M 242	How Do You Speak To An Angel?/My Arms, My Heart, My Love	10
54	HMV 7M 251	I Need You Now/Heaven Was Never Like This	12
54	HMV 7M 257	They Say It's Wonderful/Green Years	8
54	HMV 7M 266	Count Your Blessings Instead Of Sheep/White Christmas	12
55	HMV 7M 294	(I'm Always Hearing) Wedding Bells/A Man Chases A Girl	12
55	HMV 7M 353	Magic Fingers/My One And Only Love	8
56	HMV 7M 374	Dungaree Doll/If It Hadn't Been For You	15
56	HMV POP 171	Dungaree Doll/If It Hadn't Been For You (78)	8
56	HMV 7M 402	Without You/No Other One	8
56	HMV 7M 421	Sweet Heartaches/What Is This Thing Called Love?	8
56	HMV POP 273	Cindy, Oh Cindy/Fanny	15
57	HMV POP 296	Some Day Soon/All About Love	6
57	HMV POP 342	Tonight My Heart She Is Crying/Blues For Me	6
57	RCA RCA 1009	A Second Chance/Slow Burning Love	5
58	RCA RCA 1030	Sayonara/That's The Way It Goes	6
58	RCA RCA 1061	Kari Waits For Me/I Don't Hurt Anymore	6
58	RCA RCA 1061	Kari Waits For Me/I Don't Hurt Anymore (78)	8
59	RCA RCA 1147	The Last Mile Home/I'd Sail A Thousand Seas	5
61	London HL 9469	Tonight/Breezin' Along With The Breeze	5
54	HMV 7EG 8026	NIGHT AND DAY (EP)	10
54	HMV 7EG 8046	APRIL SHOWERS (EP)	10
55	HMV 7EG 8146	HOW DEEP IS THE OCEAN (EP)	10
55	HMV 7EG 8156	EDDIE FISHER SINGS NO. 3 — TAKE MY LOVE (EP)	10
56	HMV 7EG 8207	BUNDLE OF JOY (EP, with Debbie Reynolds)	8
54	HMV DLP 1040	TIME FOR ROMANCE (10" LP)	20
55	HMV DLP 1074	MY SERENADE IS YOU (10" LP)	20
56	HMV CLP 1095	SINGS ACADEMY AWARD WINNING SONGS (LP)	15
59	RCA Camden CDN 123	HEART! (LP)	12

FAYE FISHER

65	Columbia DB 7575	Our Love/I Just Don't Know What To Say	5
65	Columbia DB 7732	Oh Heartache You're Bothering Me/It's You	5

MATTHEW FISHER

73	RCA APL1 0195	JOURNEY'S END (LP)	12

(see also Procol Harum, Green Bullfrog)

RAY FISHER

72	Trailer LER 2038	THE BONNY BIRDY	
		(LP, red label, later yellow)	20/15

SONNY FISHER

77	Ace NST 59	Rockin' Daddy/I Can't Lose (78)	20

TONI FISHER

60	Top Rank JAR 261	The Big Hurt/Memphis Belle	7
60	Top Rank JAR 341	How Deep Is The Ocean/Blue, Blue, Blue	6
62	London HLX 9564	West Of The Wall/What Did I Do	7

FISHER BROTHERS

64	London HLN 9928	Big Round Wheel/By The Time You Read This Letter	7

FISHER FAMILY

60s	Topic TOP 67	FAR OVER THE FORTH (EP)	8
66	Topic 12T 137	THE FISHER FAMILY (LP)	15

FISHERFOLK

70s	Celebration CR 1030	WILLING TO ROW (LP)	15

FIST

80	Neat NEAT 04	Name Rank And Serial Number/You'll Never Get Me In One Of Those	
		(p/s, some with poster insert)	8/6
80	MCA MCA 615	Name Rank And Serial Number/You'll Never Get Me (In One Of Those)	
		(p/s, reissue, some with poster insert)	18/15
80	MCA MCA 640	Forever Amber/Brain Damage (p/s)	12
81	MCA MCA 663	Collision Course/Law Of The Jungle (some in p/s)	70/12
82	Neat NEAT 021	The Wanderer/Too Hot (p/s)	7
80	MCA MCF 3082	TURN THE HELL ON (LP)	18
85	Neat NEAT 1003	BACK WITH A VENGEANCE	
		(LP, some on yellow vinyl)	35/18

JOHN FITCH & ASSOCIATES

71	Beacon BEA 117	Romantic Altitude/Stoned Out Of It	15

FITS

81	Beat The System FIT 1	YOU SAID WE'D NEVER MAKE IT (EP, wraparound p/s)	8
82	Rondelet ROUND 13	Think For Yourself: Burial/Straps (p/s)	4
82	Rondelet ROUND 30	THE LAST LAUGH (EP)	4
83	Corpus Christi ITS 9	Tears Of A Nation/Bravado/Breaking Point (p/s)	6
84	Trapper FIT 1	Action/Achilles Heel (p/s)	7
85	Trapper FIT 2	Fact Or Fiction/Give Away (p/s)	5
82	Rondelet ABOUT 6	NOTHING AND NOWHERE (LP)	12
85	Trapper FIT 3	FACT OR FICTION (mini-LP)	10

FITZ & COOLERS

68	Nu Beat NB 003	Cover Me/Darling	8

ELLA FITZGERALD

78s

50	Brunswick 04617	Ain't Nobody's Business If I Do/I'll Never Be Free (with Louis Jordan) (78)	8
57	HMV POP 373	Ev'ry Time We Say Goodbye/Manhattan (78)	8
58	HMV POP 486	The Swingin' Shepherd Blues/Midnight Sun (78)	8
57	HMV POP 380	Goody Goody/A Tisket, A Tasket (78)	8
58	HMV POP 499	Beale Street Blues/St. Louis Blues (78)	8
58	HMV POP 518	Your Red Wagon/Trav'lin Light (78)	8
59	Brunswick 05783	My Happiness/A Satisfied Mind (78)	10

SINGLES

54	Brunswick 05324	Who's Afraid (Not I, Not I, Not I)/I Wished On The Moon (with Gordon Jenkins)	7
55	Brunswick 05392	Lullaby Of Birdland/Later	7
55	Brunswick 05427	Moanin' Low/Take A Chance On Love	7
55	Brunswick 05468	Lover, Come Back To Me/Old Devil Moon	7
55	Brunswick 05473	Pete Kelly's Blues/Hard Hearted Hannah	7
55	Brunswick 05477	Soldier Boy/Air Mail Special (with Bill Doggett)	7
56	Brunswick 05514	My One And Only Love/(Love Is) The Tender Trap	7
56	Brunswick 05539	Ella's Contribution To The Blues/Early Autumn	6
56	Brunswick 05584	You'll Never Know/But Not Like Mine	7
56	HMV POP 266	The Silent Treatment/The Sun Forgot To Shine This Morning	6
57	HMV POP 290	A Beautiful Friendship/Too Young For The Blues	6
57	HMV POP 316	Hotta Chocolatta/Stay There	6
57	HMV POP 348	Johnny One Note/To Keep My Love Alive	6
57	HMV POP 373	Ev'ry Time We Say Goodbye/Manhattan	6
57	HMV POP 380	Goody Goody/A Tisket, A Tasket	6
58	HMV POP 486	The Swingin' Shepherd Blues/Midnight Sun	6
58	HMV POP 499	Beale Street Blues/St. Louis Blues	5
58	HMV POP 518	Your Red Wagon/Trav'lin Light	5
59	Brunswick 05783	My Happiness/A Satisfied Mind	5
59	HMV POP 657	But Not For Me/You Make Me Feel So Young	6
59	HMV POP 686	The Christmas Song/You Make Me Feel So Young	6
60	HMV POP 701	Like Young/Beat Me Daddy Eight To The Bar	6
60	HMV POP 719	It's All Right With Me/Don'cha Go Way Mad (with Oscar Peterson)	5
60	HMV POP 736	Mack The Knife/Lorelei	6
60	HMV POP 782	How High The Moon (Parts 1 & 2)	6
60	HMV POP 809	Good Morning Blues/Jingle Blues	5
60	HMV POP 817	We Three Kings Of Orient Are/White Christmas	6
61	HMV POP 849	The Lady Is A Tramp/Misty	5
64	Verve VS 502	Desafinado/Stardust	5
65	Verve VS 519	Can't Buy Me Love/Sweetest Sound	5
65	Verve VS 524	Why Was I Born/All The Things You Are	5
66	Stateside SS 569	These Boots Were Made for Walkin'/Stardust	5
69	Reprise RS 20850	Get Ready/Open Your Window	8
69	Polydor 56767	Hey Jude/Sunshine Of Your Love	5
71	Reprise RS 23507	I Heard It Through The Grapevine/Days Of Wine & Roses	5

LPs

53	Brunswick LA 8581	SOUVENIR ALBUM (10" LP)	20
54	Brunswick LA 8648	ELLA SINGS GERSHWIN (10" LP)	20
55	Brunswick LAT 8056	ELLA — SONGS IN A MELLOW MOOD (LP)	15
56	Brunswick LAT 8091	SWEET AND HOT (LP)	15
56	Brunswick LAT 8115	LULLABIES OF BIRDLAND (LP)	15
56	HMV CLP 1083	THE COLE PORTER SONGBOOK VOLUME 1 (LP)	15
56	HMV CLP 1084	THE COLE PORTER SONGBOOK VOLUME 2 (LP)	15
57	Brunswick LAT 8223	ELLA AND HER FELLAS (LP)	15
57	HMV CLP 1116	THE RODGERS AND HART SONGBOOK VOLUME 1 (LP)	15
57	HMV CLP 1117	THE RODGERS AND HART SONGBOOK VOLUME 2 (LP)	15
58	HMV CLP 1166	LIKE SOMEONE IN LOVE (LP)	12
58	HMV CLP 1183	THE IRVING BERLIN SONGBOOK VOLUME ONE (LP)	12
58	HMV CLP 1184	THE IRVING BERLIN SONGBOOK VOLUME TWO (LP)	12
58	HMV CLP 1213/1214	THE DUKE ELLINGTON SONGBOOK NUMBER ONE (2-LP)	18
58	HMV CLP 1227/1228	THE DUKE ELLINGTON SONGBOOK NUMBER TWO (2-LP)	18
59	HMV CLP 1267	ELLA SWINGS LIGHTLY (LP)	12
59	HMV CLP 1338	SINGS GERSHWIN VOL. 1 (LP)	12
59	HMV CLP 1339	SINGS GERSHWIN VOL. 2 (LP)	12
60	HMV CLP 1347	SINGS GERSHWIN VOL. 3 (LP, also stereo CSD 1299)	12/15
60	HMV CLP 1348	SINGS GERSHWIN VOL. 4 (LP, also stereo CSD 1300)	12/15
60	HMV CLP 1353	SINGS GERSHWIN VOL. 5 (LP, also stereo CSD 1304)	12/15
60	HMV CSD 1287	SWEET SONGS FOR SWINGERS (LP)	12
60	HMV CLP 1391	ELLA IN BERLIN — MACK THE KNIFE (LP)	12
60	HMV CLP 1396	SONGS FROM THE FILM "LET NO MAN WRITE MY EPITAPH" (LP)	12
60	HMV CLP 1397	ELLA WISHES YOU A SWINGING CHRISTMAS (LP)	12
61	HMV CLP 1383	HELLO LOVE! (LP, also stereo CSD 1315)	12/15
63	Verve VLP 9020	RHYTHM IS MY BUSINESS (LP)	12
65	Verve VLP 9083	ELLA AT JUAN-LES-PINS (LP)	12

(see also Oscar Peterson, Count Basie, Ink Spots)

ELLA FITZGERALD & LOUIS ARMSTRONG

53	Brunswick 05112	Who Walks In When I Walk Out/Would You Like To Take A Walk (78)	8
56	HMV CLP 1098	ELLA AND LOUIS (LP)	12
57	HMV CLP 1146	ELLA AND LOUIS AGAIN NO. 1 (LP)	12
57	HMV CLP 1147	ELLA AND LOUIS AGAIN NO. 2 (LP)	12
59	HMV CLP 1245	PORGY AND BESS (LP)	12
59	HMV CLP 1246	PORGY AND BESS (LP)	12

(see also Louis Armstrong)

ELLA FITZGERALD/BILLIE HOLIDAY

58	Columbia Clef 33CX 10100	AT NEWPORT (LP)	12

G.F. FITZGERALD

70	Uni UNLS 115	MOUSEPROOF (LP, with insert)	50

(see also Sam Gopal)

PATRICK FITZGERALD

77	Small Wonder SMALL 4	SAFETY PIN STUCK IN MY HEART (EP, with lyrics)	5
78	Small Wonder SMALL 6	Buy Me, Sell Me/The Little Dippers/Trendy/The Backstreet Boys (p/s)	5
78	Small Wonder WEENY ONE	THE PARANOID WARD/THE BEDROOM TAPES (EP, mono/stereo, 33rpm)	5
78	Small Wonder WEENY ONE	THE PARANOID WARD/THE BEDROOM TAPES (12" EP)	8
79	Polydor 2383 533	GRUBBY STORIES (LP)	12

MAGGIE FITZGIBBON

59	Pye International N 25047	Kookaburra/The Right Kind Of Man (78)	12

FITZROY (Sterling) & HARRY

70	Bullet BU 439	Freedom Street/Freedom Street Version	6
70	Escort ERT 827	Pop A Top Train/Doing The Moonwalk	6

FIVE AMERICANS

66	Pye International 7N 25354	I See The Light/The Outcasts	15
66	Pye International 7N 25373	Evol — Not Love/Don't Blame Me	25
67	Stateside SS 2012	Western Union/Now That It's All Over	6
67	Stateside SS 2036	Sound Of Love/Sympathy	6
68	Stateside SS 2097	7.30 Guided Tour/See-Saw Man	6

5 A.M. EVENT

66	Pye 7N 17154	Hungry/I Wash My Hands (In Muddy Water)	140

FIVE & A PENNY

68	Polydor 56282	You Don't Know Where Your Interest Lies/Mary Go Round	20

FIVE BLIND BOYS

64	Vocalion EPVP 1276	NEGRO SPIRITUALS (EP, 2 tracks by Spirits Of Memphis)	18
64	Vocalion EPVP 1282	FIVE BLIND BOYS (EP)	18

FIVE BLOBS

58	Philips PB 881	The Blob/Saturday Night In Tijuana	15
58	Philips PB 881	The Blob/Saturday Night In Tijuana (78)	18

FIVE BY FIVE

68	Pye International 7N 25477	Fire/Hang Up	25

FIVE CARD STUD

67	Philips BF 1567	Beg Me/Once	10

FIVE CHESTERNUTS

58	Columbia DB 4165	Jean Dorothy/Teenage Love	165
58	Columbia DB 4165	Jean Dorothy/Teenage Love (78)	120

(see also Shadows, Pete Chester)

FIVE COUNTS

62	Oriole CB 1769	Watermelon Walk/Spanish Nights	10

FIVE CRESTAS

66	Excel ES SP 288/289	How Sweet It Is (To Be Loved By You)/You Used To Love Me (private pressing)	60

FIVE DALLAS BOYS

57	Columbia DB 4005	Shangri-La/By The Fireside	6
57	Columbia DB 4041	I Never Had The Blues/All The Way	6
58	Columbia DB 4102	26 Miles (Santa Catalina)/Sail Along, Silv'ry Moon	6
58	Columbia DB 4154	Big Man/Lonesome Traveller	6
58	Columbia DB 4154	Big Man/Lonesome Traveller (78)	8
58	Columbia DB 4231	Fatty Patty/Do You Wanna Jump Children?	8
58	Columbia DB 4231	Fatty Patty/Do You Wanna Jump Children? (78)	12
59	Columbia DB 4244	Gigi/The Mocking Bird	5
59	Columbia DB 4244	Gigi/The Mocking Bird (78)	8
59	Columbia DB 4313	Morning Papers/I'm Aware	5
60	Columbia DB 4445	Boston Tea Party/Ramona	5
61	Columbia DB 4599	One Finger, One Thumb/Nice To Know You Care	5
60	Columbia SEG 8035	THE FIVE DALLAS BOYS (EP)	10

(see also Dallas Boys)

FIVE DAY RAIN

70	private pressing	FIVE DAY RAIN (LP, no sleeve, 15 copies only)	750
93	private pressing	FIVE DAY RAIN (LP, re-pressing in signed, numbered sleeve, signed note in run-out groove & letter of authenticity, 25 only)	75
94	Background HBG 123	FIVE DAY RAIN (LP, reissue)	12

(see also Scots Of St. James, Hopscotch, One Way Ticket, Glencoe)

FIVE DAY WEEK STRAW PEOPLE

68	Saga FID 2123	FIVE DAY WEEK STRAW PEOPLE (LP)	75

(see also Attack, Andromeda, John Du Cann)

FIVE DE MARCO SISTERS
53	MGM SP 1043	Bouillabasse/I'm Never Satisfied	10
54	Brunswick 05349	Love Me/Just A Girl That Men Forget	12
55	Brunswick 05425	Dreamboat/Two Hearts, Two Kisses (Make One Love)	12
55	Brunswick 05474	The Hot Barcarolle/Sailor Boys Have Talk To Me In English	10
56	Brunswick 05526	Romance Me/This Love Of Mine	10

FIVE DU-TONES
63	Stateside SS 206	Shake A Tail Feather/Divorce Court	18
68	President PT 134	Shake A Tail Feather/Divorce Court (reissue)	6

FIVE EMPREES
65	Stateside SS 470	Little Miss Sad/Hey Lover	7

FIVE FLEETS
58	Felsted AF 103	Oh What A Feeling/I Been Cryin'	275
58	Felsted AF 103	Oh What A Feeling/I Been Cryin' (78)	90

FIVE GO DOWN TO THE SEA
83	Kabuki KAFIVE 5	KNOT A FISH (EP)	6
84	Abstract 12 ABS 027	THE GLEE CLUB (12" EP)	8
85	Creation CRE 021T	Singing In Braille/Aunt Nelly/Silk Brain Worm/Women (12", p/s)	8

FIVE GUYS NAMED MOE
89	No Moe MOE 001	Fairvan/Eyes Like Thunder/Beneath The Willow (12", p/s)	8

FIVE HAND REEL
76	Rubber RUB 019	FIVE HAND REEL (LP, with lyric insert)	10

FIVE KEYS
54	Capitol CL 14184	Ling, Ting, Tong/I'm Alone (78)	100
55	Capitol CL 14313	The Verdict/Make Me Um Pow Pow (triangular centre)	600
55	Capitol CL 14313	The Verdict/Make Me Um Pow Pow (78)	80
55	Capitol CL 14325	Doggone It, You Did It/(Close Your Eyes) Take A Deep Breath (tri centre)	500
55	Capitol CL 14325	Doggone It, You Did It/(Close Your Eyes) Take A Deep Breath (78)	70
56	Capitol CL 14545	Gee Whittakers!/'Cause You're My Lover	250
56	Capitol CL 14545	Gee Whittakers!/'Cause You're My Lover (78)	45
56	Capitol CL 14582	She's The Most/I Dreamt I Dwelt In Heaven	250
56	Capitol CL 14582	She's The Most/I Dreamt I Dwelt In Heaven (78)	45
56	Capitol CL 14639	That's Right/Out Of Sight, Out Of Mind	150
56	Capitol CL 14639	That's Right/Out Of Sight, Out Of Mind (78)	35
57	Capitol CL 14686	The Wisdom Of A Fool/Now Don't That Prove I Love You?	150
57	Capitol CL 14686	The Wisdom Of A Fool/Now Don't That Prove I Love You? (78)	20
57	Capitol CL 14736	Four Walls/Let There Be You	75
57	Capitol CL 14736	Four Walls/Let There Be You (78)	25
57	Capitol CL 14756	The Blues Don't Care/This I Promise You	90
57	Capitol CL 14756	The Blues Don't Care/This I Promise You (78)	40
58	Capitol CL 14829	From Me To You/Whippety Whirl	120
58	Capitol CL 14829	From Me To You/Whippety Whirl (78)	50
58	Capitol CL 14967	One Great Love/Really-O Truly-O	120
57	Capitol T 828	THE FIVE KEYS ON STAGE! (LP)	150

FIVE MILES OUT
73	Action ACT 4614	Super Sweet Girl Of Mine/Set Your Mind Free	5

FIVE OF DIAMONDS
65	Oak RGJ 150 FD	FIVE OF DIAMONDS (EP)	350

FIVE OR SIX
81	Cherry Red CHERRY 19	Another Reason/The Trial (p/s)	5
81	Cherry Red 12CHERRY 23	POLAR EXPOSURE (12" EP)	8
82	Cherry Red 12CHERRY 43	FOUR FROM FIVE OR SIX (12" EP)	8
82	Cherry Red FRIZBEE 2	A THRIVING AND HAPPY LAND (LP)	12

FIVEPENNY PIECE
69	Columbia DB 8558	Hang The Flag Out Mrs Jones/Little Boy Little Girl	5
72	Columbia SCX 6488	FIVEPENNY PIECE (LP)	12
73	Columbia SCX 6536	MAKIN' TRACKS (LP)	12

FIVE ROYALES
60	Ember EMB S 124	Dedicated To The One I Love/Miracle Of Love	80

FIVE SATINS
57	London HL 8501	To The Aisle/Wish I Had My Baby	800
57	London HL 8501	To The Aisle/Wish I Had My Baby (78)	100
59	Top Rank JAR 199	Wonderful Girl/Weeping Willow	30
59	Top Rank JAR 239	Shadows/Toni My Love	30
60	MGM MGM 1087	Your Memory/I Didn't Know	60

FIVE'S COMPANY
66	Pye 7N 17118	Sunday For Seven Days/The Big Kill	8
66	Pye 7N 17162	Some Girls/Big Deal	5
66	Pye 7N 17199	Session Man/Dejection	15
69	Saga FID 2151	THE BALLAD OF FRED THE PIXIE (LP)	20

(see also Brunning Hall Sunflower Blues Band)

FIVE SMITH BROTHERS
54	Decca F 10403	A.B.C. Boogie/Veni-Vidi-Vici (with Dennis Wilson Quartet)	12
55	Decca F 10507	Paper Valentine/You're As Sweet Today (As Yesterday)	10
55	Decca F 10527	Don't Worry/I'm In Favour Of Friendship	10
56	Decca F 10698	You Took My Heart (My Only Heart)/The Grass Is Green	7

(see also Smith Brothers)

MINT VALUE £

FIVE STAIRSTEPS (& CUBIE)
68	Pye International 7N 25448	A Million To One/Something's Missing (with Cubie)	10
69	Buddah 201 026	Stay Close To Me/I Made A Mistake (with Cubie)	8
69	Buddah 201 070	We Must Be In Love/Little Young Lovers (with Cubie)	10
70	Buddah 201 083	Dear Prudence/O-o-h Child	10
70	Buddah 2011 036	O-o-h Child/Who Do You Belong To?	10
70	Buddah 2011 053	Because I Love You/America — Standing	5

(see also Stairsteps)

FIVE STEPS BEYOND
67	CBS 202490	Not So Young Today/Meanwhile Back In My Heart	10
95	Tenth Planet TP 019	FAINT HEARTS AND FAIR MAIDS (LP, 600 only)	12
96	Tenth Planet TP 021	SMILE (LP, with A4 booklet, 600 only)	12

FIVE THIRTY/5:30
85	Other 12 OTH 2	Catcher In The Rye/Weight Of The World/Mood Suite/	
		Suburban Town (12", p/s, as Five Thirty)	20
85	East West WX 530	BED (LP, as 5:30)	15

FIVE TOWNS
67	Direction 58-3115	It Isn't What You've Got/Advice	6

FIX
81	101 CLUB 101	Lost Planes/I've Been Here Before (p/s)	5

(see also Fixx)

FIXX
82	MCA FIXX 2	Stand Or Fall/The Strain (picture disc)	5
82	MCA FIXX 3	Red Skies/Is It By Instinct (picture disc)	5
83	MCA FIXXD 5	One Thing Leads To Another/Opinions//Red Skies/Stand Or Fall (double pack)	6

(see also Fix)

FIZZBOMBS
87	Narodnik NRK 003	Sign On The Line/The Lines That (p/s)	8
87	Wild Rumpus SHEP 001	You Worry Me/JESSE GARON & DESPERADOS: Hank Williams Is Dead	
		(p/s, flexidisc)	6
88	Calculus KIT 002	THE SURFIN' WINTER EP (p/s)	5
88	Calculus KIT 002T	THE SURFIN' WINTER EP (12", p/s)	8

ROBERTA FLACK
69	Atlantic 584 294	Compared To What/Hey, That's No Way To Say Goodbye	5
73	Atlantic K 10282	Killing Me Softly With His Song/Just Like A Woman	5
69	Atlantic 588 204	FIRST TAKE (LP, with Donny Hathaway)	15
71	Atlantic K 40040	FIRST TAKE (LP, reissue)	12
71	Atlantic K 40097	CHAPTER TWO (LP)	12
72	Atlantic K 40297	QUIET FIRE (LP)	12
73	Atlantic K 50021	KILLING ME SOFTLY (LP)	12
75	Atlantic K 50049	FEEL LIKE MAKIN' LOVE (LP)	12

(see also Donny Hathaway)

FLAG OF CONVENIENCE
82	Sire SIR 4057	Life On The Telephone/The Other Man's Sin (no p/s)	5

(see also Steve Diggle, Buzzcocks)

FLAIRS
57	Oriole CB 1392	Swing Pretty Mama/I'd Climb The Hills And Mountains	450
57	Oriole CB 1392	Swing Pretty Mama/I'd Climb The Hills And Mountains (78)	85

LES FLAMBEAUX
65	HMV POP 1456	Cachita/Greensleeves	5
71	Mushroom 100 MR 13	LES FLAMBEAUX (LP, 2 different sleeve designs)	15

FLAME
70	Stateside SS 2183	See The Light/Get Your Mind Made Up	6
71	Stateside SSL 10312	THE FLAME (LP)	15

(see also Flames [South Africa], Beach Boys)

FLAME
77	RCA PC 12160	QUEEN OF THE NEIGHBOURHOOD (LP)	12

(see also Aerosmith)

FLAME 'N' KING & BOLD ONES
79	Grapevine GRP 123	Ho Happy Day/Ain't Nobody Jivin'	5

FLAMES (Jamaica)
64	Island WI 130	He's The Greatest/Someone Going To Bawl (both actually by Maytals)	18
64	Island WI 136	Little Flea/Good Idea (both actually by Maytals)	18
64	Island WI 138	When I Get Home/Neither Silver Nor Gold (both actually by Maytals)	18
64	Island WI 139	Broadway Jungle/Beat Lied (both actually by Maytals)	18

(see also Maytals, Vikings)

FLAMES (Jamaica)
64	Blue Beat BB 205	Helena Darling/My Darling (both actually by Plamers)	15

FLAMES (Jamaica)
68	Nu Beat NB 020	Mini Really Fit Dem/Soul Train (both actually by Alton Ellis & Flames)	8
73	Ackee ACK 528	Feeling Good/Zig Zag	5

(see also Alton Ellis & Flames, Righteous Flames, Larry Marshall)

FLAMES (South Africa)
68	Flame FAN 101/1	Streamliner/Follow The Sun (p/s)	15
68	Page One FOR(S) 009	BURNING SOUL (LP)	25

(see also Flame, Beach Boys)

FLAMING EMERALDS
78	Grapevine GRP 104	Have Some Everybody/Have Some Everybody (Instrumental)	6

JOHNNY FLAMINGO
57	Vogue V 9089	My Teen-Age Girl/When I Lost You	100
57	Vogue V 9089	My Teen-Age Girl/When I Lost You (78)	35
58	Vogue V 9100	So Long/Make Me A Present Of You	75
58	Vogue V 9100	So Long/Make Me A Present Of You (78)	45

FLAMINGOS
57	London HLN 8373	Would I Be Crying?/Just For A Kick	550
57	London HLN 8373	Would I Be Crying?/Just For A Kick (78)	80
57	Brunswick 05696	The Ladder Of Love/Let's Make Up	500
57	Brunswick 05696	The Ladder Of Love/Let's Make Up (78)	80
59	Top Rank JAR 213	Love Walked In/Yours	25
60	Top Rank JAR 263	I Only Have Eyes For You/I Was Such A Fool	100
60	Top Rank JAR 367	Nobody Loves Me Like You/You, Me And The Sea	25
60	Top Rank JAR 519	Mio Amore/At Night	20
66	Philips BF 1483	Boogaloo Party/Nearness Of You	10
69	Philips BF 1786	Boogaloo Party/Nearness Of You (reissue, some in p/s)	10/5
69	Philips SBL 7906	HITS NOW AND THEN (LP)	12

FLAMIN' GROOVIES
71	Kama Sutra 2013 031	Teenage Head/Evil-Hearted Ada	10
72	Kama Sutra 2013 042	Gonna Rock Tonite/Keep A-Knockin'/SHA NA NA: Rock'n'Roll Is Here To Stay/At The Hop/Duke Of Earl	6
72	United Artists UP 35392	Slow Death/Talahassie Lassie (some in promo only p/s)	25/7
72	United Artists UP 35464	Married Woman/Get A Shot Of Rhythm And Blues	8
76	Sire 6198 086	Don't You Lie To Me/She Said Yeah/Shake Some Action (p/s)	5
76	Sire 6078 602	Shake Some Action/Teenage Confidential (p/s, 2 different versions of A-side)	8
76	Kama Sutra KSS 707	Teenage Head/Headin' For The Texas Border	6
78	Sire 6078 619	Feel A Whole Lot Better/Paint It Black/Shake Some Action (p/s)	7
78	Sire 6078 619	Feel A Whole Lot Better/Paint It Black/Shake Some Action (12", p/s)	8
78	Sire SIR 4002	Move It/When I Heard Your Name	6
79	Sire SIR 4018	Absolutely Sweet Marie/Werewolves Of London/Next One Crying (p/s)	6
76	United Artists REM 406	SLOW DEATH (EP)	8
71	Kama Sutra 2683 003	FLAMIN' GROOVIES (2-LP)	15
77	Sire 9103 251	SHAKE SOME ACTION (LP)	12
78	Sire 9103 333	THE FLAMIN' GROOVIES NOW! (LP)	12

(see also Mike Wilhelm)

FLAMING YOUTH
69	Fontana TF 1057	Guide Me Orion/From Now On (Immortal Invisible)	18
70	Fontana 6001 002	Every Man, Woman And Child/Drifting	12
70	Fontana 6001 003	From Now On/Space Child	12
69	Fontana STL 5533	ARK II (LP, with plastic window sleeve)	40

(see also Genesis, Phil Collins, Jackson Heights)

FLAMMA-SHERMAN
68	SNB 55-3488	No Need To Explain/Bassa Love	5
68	SNB 55-3769	Love Is In The Air/Super Day	5
69	SNB 55-4142	Move Me/Where Is He	15

BUD FLANAGAN
59	Columbia DB 4265	Strollin'/Home Is Where Your Heart Is	5
59	Columbia DB 4265	Strollin'/Home Is Where Your Heart Is (78)	10
69	Pye 7N 17854	Who Do You Think You're Kidding, Mr Hitler (Dad's Army Theme)/BERNARD BEDFORD & CHORUS: It Ain't Gonna Rain No Mo!	7
75	Pye 7N 45530	Who Do You Think You're Kidding, Mr Hitler (Dad's Army Theme)/BERNARD BEDFORD & CHORUS: It Ain't Gonna Rain No Mo! (reissue)	5
50s	Columbia SEG 7876	BUD (EP)	8

FLANAGAN & ALLEN
53	Columbia SEG 7709	TOGETHER AGAIN (EP)	10
53	Columbia 33S 1010	FLANAGAN AND ALLEN (10" LP)	12
53	Decca LF 1125	FAVOURITES (10" LP)	12

FLANAGAN BROTHERS
58	Vogue Coral Q 72342	Salton City/Early One Evening	12
58	Vogue Coral Q 72342	Salton City/Early One Evening (78)	15

MICHAEL FLANDERS (& DONALD SWANN)
57	Parlophone R 4354	A Gnu/Misalliance	5
59	Parlophone R 4528	The Little Drummer Boy/DONALD SWANN: The Youth Of The Heart	5
59	Parlophone R 4528	The Little Drummer Boy/DONALD SWANN: The Youth Of The Heart (78)	8
57	Parlophone PMC 1033	AT THE DROP OF A HAT (LP, also stereo PCS 3001)	12
61	Parlophone PMC 1164	BESTIARY OF FLANDERS AND SWANN (LP)	12
64	Parlophone PMC 1216	AT THE DROP OF ANOTHER HAT (LP)	12

TOMMY FLANDERS
69	Verve SVLP 6020	MOONSTONE (LP)	15

(see also Blues Project)

FLARES
61	London HLU 9441	Foot Stompin'/Hotcha Cha-Cha Brown	20
63	London HA-U 8034	FOOT STOMPIN' HITS (LP)	50

MINT VALUE £

FLASH

72	Sovereign SOV 105	Small Beginnings/Morning Haze	7
73	Sovereign SOV 116	Watch Your Step/Lifetime	7
72	Sovereign SVNA 7251	FLASH (LP)	15
72	Sovereign SVNA 7255	FLASH IN THE CAN (LP, some in unissued 'band in studio' proof sleeve)	25/15
73	Sovereign SVNA 7260	OUT OF OUR HANDS (LP)	15

(see also Peter Banks, Yes)

FLASH & BOARD OF DIRECTORS

68	Bell BLL 1007	Busy Signal/Love Ain't Easy	6

FLASHPOINT

87	private pressing FP 01	NO POINT OF REFERENCE (LP)	30

FLAT EARTH SOCIETY

83	Psycho PSYCHO 17	WALEECO (LP)	15

FLATMATES

86	Subway Organisation SUBWAY 6	I Could Be In Heaven/Tell Me Why/So In Love With You (foldaround p/s with insert in poly bag)	6
88	Subway Org. SUBWAY 17T	Shimmer/On My Mind/If Not For You/Bad (12", p/s, with 'flat sharing guide')	8

(Lester) FLATT & (Earl) SCRUGGS

65	CBS 201793	Ballad Of Jed Clampett/Gonna Give Myself A Ball	7
67	CBS 3038	Foggy Mountain Breakdown/California Uptight Band	5
67	Mercury MF 1007	Foggy Mountain Breakdown/My Cabin In Caroline	5
61	Mercury ZEP 10106	C & W TRAIL BLAZERS NO. 4 (EP)	15
64	Mercury 10010 MCE	COUNTRY AND WESTERN ACES (EP)	15
63	CBS BPG 62095	FOLK SONGS OF OUR LAND (LP)	12
63	CBS BPG 62259	AT CARNEGIE HALL (LP)	12
60s	Philips BBL 7516	SONGS OF THE FAMOUS CARTER FAMILY (LP)	12

LINDA FLAVELL

66	Decca F 12312	And The Trouble With Me Is You/Over And Over	7

FLAVOUR

68	Direction 58-3597	Sally Had A Party/Shop Around	6

LOS FLECHAZOS

94	Detour Records DRO 13	Try It/You Drove Me Crazy (p/s, 1,000 only, 100 red vinyl)	8/5

GREGORY FLECKNER QUINTET

96	Clear CLR 418	Oi, That's My Bird (12", with Plaid & Dr Rockit mixes, p/s)	8

(FABULOUS) FLEE-REKKERS/FLEE-RAKKERS

60	Triumph RGM 1008	Green Jeans/You Are My Sunshine (as Fabulous Flee-Rakkers)	30
60	Top Rank JAR 431	Green Jeans/You Are My Sunshine (reissue, as Fabulous Flea Rakkers)	50
60	Pye 7N 15288	Sunday Date/Shiftless Sam	10
60	Pye 7N 15326	Blue Tango/Bitter Rice	10
61	Piccadilly 7N 35006	Lone Rider/Miller Like Wow	15
62	Piccadilly 7N 35048	Stage To Cimarron/Twistin' The Chestnuts	15
62	Piccadilly 7N 35081	Sunburst/Black Buffalo	15
63	Piccadilly 7N 35109	Fireball/Fandango	15
61	Pye NEP 24141	THE FABULOUS FLEE-REKKERS (EP)	50

(see also Ricky Wayne & Fabulous Flee-Rakkers)

(PETER GREEN'S) FLEETWOOD MAC

SINGLES

67	Blue Horizon 57-3051	I Believe My Time Ain't Long/Rambling Pony (as Peter Green's Fleetwood Mac, initially with p/s)	65/12
68	Blue Horizon 57-3138	Black Magic Woman/The Sun Is Shining	12
68	Blue Horizon 57-3139	Need Your Love So Bad/Stop Messin' Around	8
68	Blue Horizon 57-3145	Albatross/Jigsaw Puzzle Blues	6
69	Immediate IM 080	Man Of The World/EARL VINCE & VALIANTS: Somebody's Gonna Get Their Head Kicked In Tonight	6
69	Blue Horizon 57-3157	Need Your Love So Bad/Black Magic Woman (unissued)	
69	Blue Horizon 57-3157	Black Magic Woman/No Place To Go (unissued)	
69	Blue Horizon 57-3157	Need Your Love So Bad/No Place To Go	8
69	CBS 3051	I Believe My Time Ain't Long/Rambling Pony (reissue)	5
69	Reprise RS 27000	Oh Well (Parts 1 & 2)	6
70	Reprise RS 27007	The Green Manalishi (With The Two-Prong Crown)/ World In Harmony (initially with p/s)	25/7
71	Reprise RS 27010	Dragonfly/The Purple Dancer	5
71	CBS/Blue Horizon 3145	Albatross/Jigsaw Puzzle Blues (reissue)	5
72	Reprise K 14194	Spare Me A Little Of Your Love/Sunny Side Of Heaven	5
73	Reprise K 14280	Did You Ever Love Me?/The Derelict	5
73	CBS 1722	Black Magic Woman/Stop Messin' Around	5
73	CBS 8306	Albatross/Need Your Love So Bad (p/s, 'Hall Of Fame Hits' reissue)	5
74	Reprise K 14315	For Your Love/Hypnotised	5
75	Reprise K 14388	Heroes Are Hard To Find/Born Enchanter	5
75	DJM DJS 10620	Man Of The World/DANNY KIRWAN: Second Chapter	5
75	Reprise K 14403	Warm Ways/Blue Letter (initially with p/s)	12/5
76	Reprise K 14413	Over My Head (Edit)/I'm So Afraid	5
76	Reprise K 14430	Rhiannon/Sugar Daddy (initially with p/s)	12/5
76	Reprise K 14447	Say You Love Me/Monday Morning	5
77	Warner Bros K 16872	Go Your Own Way/Silver Springs (p/s)	20
77	Warner Bros K 16930	Don't Stop/Gold Dust Women	5
77	Warner Bros K 16969	Dreams/Songbird	5
77	Warner Bros K 17013	You Make Loving Fun/Never Going Back Again	5
79	Warner Bros K 17468	Tusk/Never Make Me Cry ('dog' or 'plain' p/s)	each 5

MINT VALUE £

79	Warner Bros K 17533	Sara/That's Enough For Me (p/s)	6
80	Warner Bros K 17577	Not That Funny/Save Me A Place (p/s)	5
80	Warner Bros K 17614	Think About Me/Honey Hi (p/s)	5
81	Warner Bros K 17746	The Farmer's Daughter/Dreams (live) (p/s)	7
82	Warner Bros K 17965	Hold Me/Eyes Of The World (p/s)	5
82	Warner Bros K 17997	Gypsy (Edit)/Cool Water (p/s)	5
82	Warner Bros FLEET 1P	Oh Diane/Rhiannon/The Chain (picture disc)	10
83	Warner Bros W 9848	Can't Go Back/That's Alright (p/s)	5
83	Warner Bros W 9848T	Can't Go Back/Rhiannon/Tusk/Over And Over (12", p/s)	10
87	Warner Bros W 8398	Big Love/You And I Part 1//The Chain/Go Your Own Way (gatefold double pack)	6
87	Warner Bros W 8398TP	Big Love (Extended)/You And I Part 1 (12", picture disc)	10
87	Warner Bros W 8317TP	Seven Wonders (Extended Remix)/Book Of Miracles (Instrumental)/Seven Wonders (Dub) (12", picture disc)	10
87	Warner Bros W 8291	Little Lies/Ricky (picture disc)	5
87	Warner Bros W 8291TP	Little Lies (Extended)/Little Lies (Dub)/Ricky (12", picture disc)	10
88	Warner Bros W 8143CD	Everywhere/When I See You Again/Rhiannon/Say You Love Me (3" CD with adaptor, 5" case)	8
88	Warner Bros W 8114B	Family Man/Down Endless Street (box set, with 2 colour prints)	8
88	Warner Bros W 8114T	Family Man (Extended Vocal Mix)/Family Party Bonus Beats/You And I Part II (12", p/s)	8
88	Warner Bros W 7860CD	Isn't It Midnight?/Mystified/Say You Love Me/Gypsy (3" CD w/ adaptor, 5" case)	8
88	Warner Bros W 7644CD	As Long As You Follow/Oh Well (live)/Gold Dust Woman (3" CD with adaptor, 5" case)	8
89	Warner Bros W 7528CD	Hold Me/No Questions Asked/I Loved Another Woman (live) (3" CD, gatefold p/s)	8
89	CBS 654 613-6	Albatross/Man Of The World/Black Magic Woman/Love That Burns (12", p/s)	8
89	CBS 654 613-3	Albatross/Black Magic Woman/Love That Burns (CD)	8
89	CBS 655 171-3	Solid Gold: Albatross/Black Magic Woman/Need Your Love So Bad/I'd Rather Go Blind (3" CD, gatefold card sleeve, as Fleetwood Mac & Christine Perfect)	8
90	Warner Bros W 9866CDX	Save Me/Another Woman (live)/Everywhere (live) (CD, foldout sleeve)	8
90	Warner Bros W 9739CDX	In The Back Of My Mind (edit)/Lizard People/Little Lies (live)/The Chain (live) (CD, foldout sleeve)	8

LPs

68	Blue Horizon 7-63200	PETER GREEN'S FLEETWOOD MAC (LP, mono/stereo)	40/30
68	Blue Horizon 7-63205	MR. WONDERFUL (LP, gatefold sleeve)	25
69	Blue Horizon 7-63215	THE PIOUS BIRD OF GOOD OMEN (LP)	25
69	Reprise RSLP 9000	THEN PLAY ON (LP, gatefold sleeve)	15
70	Reprise RSLP 9004	KILN HOUSE (LP, gatefold sleeve, some with insert)	15/12
71	CBS Blue Horizon 63875	THE ORIGINAL FLEETWOOD MAC (LP)	15
71	CBS 69011	GREATEST HITS (LP, plain orange label)	12
77	Reprise K 54043	FLEETWOOD MAC (LP, white vinyl with lyric sheet)	18
77	Warner Bros K 56344	RUMOURS (LP, white vinyl with lyric sheet)	18
90	Warner Bros 7599-26206-2	BEHIND THE MASK (LP, picture disc, box set, with print & graphics software)	20

(see also Mick Fleetwood's Zoo, Peter Green, Stevie Nicks, Buckingham-Nicks, Jeremy Spencer, Christine Perfect, Danny Kirwan, John Mayall, Otis Spann, Eddie Boyd, Duster Bennett, Chicken Shack, Shotgun Express, Bo Street Runners, Cheynes, Tramp, Brunning Hall Sunflower Blues Band)

FLEETWOODS

59	London HLU 8841	Come Softly To Me/I Care So Much	10
59	London HLU 8841	Come Softly To Me/I Care So Much (78)	20
59	London HLU 4003	Come Softly To Me/I Care So Much (stereo export issue)	40
59	London HLU 8895	Graduation's Here/Oh Lord Let It Be Me	12
59	London HLU 8895	Graduation's Here/Oh Lord Let It Be Me (78)	35
59	Top Rank JAR 202	Mr. Blue/You Mean Everything To Me	10
59	Top Rank JAR 202	Mr. Blue/You Mean Everything To Me (78)	50
60	Top Rank JAR 294	Outside My Window/Magic Star (some in p/s)	15/7
60	Top Rank JAR 383	Runaround/Truly Do	8
61	London HLG 9341	Tragedy/Little Miss Sad One	10
61	London HLG 9426	He's The Great Imposter/Poor Little Girl	10
62	Liberty LIB 62	They Tell Me It's Summer/Lovers By Night Strangers By Day	8
63	Liberty LIB 75	Goodnight My Love Pleasant Dreams/Jimmy Beware	8
64	Liberty LIB 93	Ruby Red Baby Blue/Lonesome Town	10
65	Liberty LIB 10191	Almost There/Before And After (Losing You)	10
60	Top Rank BUY 028	MR BLUE (LP, with 3 tracks by other artists)	30
61	London HA-G 2388	SOFTLY (LP, also stereo SAH-G 6188)	50/60
61	London HA-G 2419	DEEP IN A DREAM (LP)	50

MICK FLEETWOOD'S ZOO

81	RCA RCA 118	You Weren't In Love/O-Niamali (p/s)	5
83	RCA RCA 360	I Want You Back/Put Me Right (p/s)	8

(see also Fleetwood Mac)

HELEN FLEMING

66	Blue Beat BB 341	Eve's Ten Commandments/Don't Take Your Love Away	8

JOY FLEMING

75	Antic K 11518	A Bridge Of Love/Divorcee	5

WADE FLEMONS

59	Top Rank JAR 206	Slow Motion/Walkin' By The River	8
60	Top Rank JAR 327	What's Happening?/Goodnight, It's Time To Go	8
60	Top Rank JAR 371	Easy Lovin'/Woops Now	8

FLESHEATERS

81	Initial IRC 007	A MINUTE TO PRAY, A SECOND TO DIE (LP)	18

MINT VALUE £

FLESH VOLCANO
87   Some Bizzare SLUT 1   Slut/The Universal Cesspool/Bruisin' Chain (12", p/s) 15
(see also Marc Almond, Foetus)

DARROW FLETCHER
66   London HLU 10024   The Pain Gets A Little Deeper/My Judgement Day 50

DON FLETCHER
66   Vocalion VP 9271   Two Wrongs Don't Make A Right/I'm So Glad 12

GUY FLETCHER
69   Pye 7N 17765   Magic Woman/All Fall Down 5

SAM FLETCHER
59   MGM MGM 1024   Time Has A Way/No Such Luck 5
60   RCA RCA 1255   Tall Hope/You're So Far Away From Home 6

FLEUR-DE-LYS
65   Immediate IM 020   Moondreams/Wait For Me 140
66   Immediate IM 032   Circles/So Come On 190
66   Polydor 56124   Mud In Your Eye/I've Been Trying 175
67   Polydor 56200   I Can See A Light/Prodigal Son 50
68   Polydor 56251   The Gong With The Luminous Nose/Hammer Head 60
68   Atlantic 584 193   Stop Crossing The Bridge/Brick By Brick (Stone By Stone) 30
69   Atlantic 584 243   You're Just A Liar/One Girl City 60
(see also John Bromley, Terry Durham, Tony & Tandy, Sharon Tandy, Rupert's People, Shyster, Quotations, Bryn Haworth, Chocolate Frog, Gordon Haskell, Waygood Ellis)

VIC FLICK SOUND
70   Chapter One CH 136   Hang On/Wonderful World 12
71   Chapter One CH 155   Quest For Love/Clarice 5

FLIES
66   Decca F 12533   I'm Not Your Stepping Stone/Talk To Me 60
67   Decca F 12594   House Of Love/It Had To Be You 45
68   RCA RCA 1757   The Magic Train/Gently As You Feel 25
(see also Bulldog Breed, T2)

SHELBY FLINT
61   Warner Bros WB 30   Angel On My Shoulder/Somebody 7
66   London HLT 10068   Cast Your Fate To The Wind/The Lilly 10

FLINTLOCKS
66   Decca F 12412   What Goes On?/I Walked Right Into A Heaven 5

FLINTSTONES
64   HMV POP 1266   Safari/Work Out 15

BUNNY FLIP
72   Pressure Beat PB 5510   Shanky Dog (actually "Skanky Dog" by Winston Scotland)/
                              JOE GIBBS & NOW GENERATION: Boney Dog 8

(see also Winston Scotland)

FLIP & DATELINERS
64   HMV POP 1359   My Johnny Doesn't Come Around Anymore/Please Listen To Me 45
(see also Vivienne Chering)

FLIPPER
81   Alt. Tentacles VIRUS 8   Ha Ha Ha/Love Canal (p/s, with insert) 6

FLIPS
62   London HLU 9490   Rockin' Twist/Oh, You Beautiful Doll — Twist 12

FLIRTATIONS
68   Deram DM 195   Someone Out There/How Can You Tell Me? 5
68   Deram DM 195DJ   Someone Out There/How Can You Tell Me? 12
68   Deram DM 216   Nothing But A Heartache/Christmas Time Is Here Again 15
69   Deram DM 252   What's Good About Goodbye My Love?/Once I Had A Love 5
70   Deram DM 281   Keep On Searchin'/Moma I'm Coming Home 5
70   Deram DM 295   Can't Stop Loving You/Everybody Needs Somebody 5
71   Deram DM 329   Give Me Love/This Must Be The End Of The Line 5
72   Deram DM 351   Need Your Lovin'/I Wanna Be There 6
71   Polydor 2058 167   Little Darlin'/Take Me In Your Arms And Love Me 15
72   Polydor 2058 249   Love A Little Longer/Hold On To Me Babe 5
74   Polydor 2058 295   Dirty Work/No Such Thing As A Miracle 5
73   Mojo 2092 058   Why Didn't I Think Of That?/Oh Mia Bamba 5
78   Casino Classics CC 1   Little Darling (I Need You)/LENNY GAMBLE: I'll Do Anything For You 5
98   London Traffic TRAF 1   Nothing But A Heartache (1-sided, reissue promo, 500 only) 8
69   Deram DML/SML 1046   SOUNDS LIKE THE FLIRTATIONS (LP) 15
(see also Pearly Gates, Gypsies)

FLO & EDDIE
73   Reprise K 14261   Afterglow/Carlos And De Bull 5
72   Reprise K 44201   THE PHLORESCENT LEECH AND EDDIE (LP) 12
73   Reprise K 44234   FLO AND EDDIE (LP) 12
(see also Turtles, Frank Zappa/Mothers Of Invention)

FLOATING BRIDGE
69   Liberty LBS 83271   FLOATING BRIDGE (LP) 25

FLOCK
70   CBS 4932   Tired Of Waiting For You/Store Bought — Store Thought 5
69   CBS 63733   THE FLOCK (LP, orange label) 15
70   CBS 64055   DINOSAUR SWAMPS (LP, orange label, gatefold sleeve) 12

FLOCK OF SEAGULLS
(see under A Flock Of Seagulls)

DICK FLOOD
59	Felsted AF 125	The Three Bells/Far Away	6
59	Felsted AF 125	The Three Bells/Far Away (78)	15

FLORIBUNDA ROSE
67	Piccadilly 7N 35408	One Way Street/Linda Loves Linda	15

(see also Scrugg, John T. Kongos)

FLOWERED UP
90	Heavenly 10 HVN 3	It's On — Feel Pain (10", p/s, 1 side etched)	6
90	The Catalogue CAT 084	It's On (The Posh Facker Mix)/SAINT ETIENNE: Only Love Can Break Your Heart (remixed by Flowered Up) (square flexidisc with *The Catalogue* mag)	7/5
92	Heavenly HVN 16	Weekender (12.53) (12", 1-sided, p/s)	10
92	Heavenly HVN 16X	Weatherall's Weekender (Andy Weatherall Remix) (12", p/s)	15
92	Heavenly HVN 16CD	Weekender (12.53) (CD, 1-track)	15

FLOWERPOT MEN
67	Deram DM 142	Let's Go To San Francisco (Parts 1 & 2)	5
68	Page One POF 065	Mighty Quinn/Voices From The Sky	6
67	Deram DM 160	A Walk In The Sky/Am I Losing You?	7
68	Deram DM 183	A Man Without A Woman/You Can Never Be Wrong	7
69	Deram DM 248	In A Moment Of Madness/Young Birds Fly	6

(see also Ivy League, Friends, Carter-Lewis & Southerners, Edison Lighthouse, Fat Mattress, Gordon Haskell, Kestrels, One & One)

LLOYD FLOWERS & RECO'S RHYTHM GROUP
62	Blue Beat BB 88	I'm Going Home/Lover's Town	15

PHIL FLOWER(S)
69	A&M AMS 766	Like A Rolling Stone/Keep On Sockin' It Children	10
70	A&M AMS 784	Every Day I Have To Cry/If It Feels Good Do It (miscredited as Phil Flower)	20

(Lloyd) FLOWERS & ALVIN (Ranglin)
72	Explosion EX 2067	Howdy And Tenky/SHORTY PERRY: Sprinkle Some Water	5
72	Grape GR 3028	In De Pum Pum/MAYTONES: If Loving You Was Wrong	6
72	Bullet BU 512	Howdy And Tenky/SHORTY PERRY: Sprinkle Some Water	5
73	Duke DU 150	Rastaman Going Back Home/LITTLE YOUTH: Barble Dove Skank	5

FLOWER TRAVELLING BAND
71	Atlantic 2091 128	Satori (Enlightment) (Parts 1 & 2)	20

BOBBY FLOYD
72	Pama PM 860	Sound Doctor/YOUNG DILLINGER: Doctor Skank	12

EDDIE FLOYD
66	Atlantic 584 041	Knock On Wood/Got To Make A Comeback	6
67	Stax 601 001	Raise Your Hand/I've Just Been Feeling Bad (dark or light blue label)	8/5
67	London HL 10129	Set My Soul On Fire/Will I Be The One?	8
67	Speciality SPE 1001	Never Get Enough Of Your Love/Bye Bye Baby	10
67	Stax 601 016	Things Get Better/Good Love, Bad Love	7
67	Stax 601 024	On A Saturday Night/Under My Nose	7
68	Stax 601 035	Big Bird/Holding On With Both Hands	10
68	Stax STAX 104	I've Never Found A Girl (To Love Me Like You Do)/I'm Just The Kind of Fool	10
69	Stax STAX 108	Bring It On Home To Me/Sweet Things You Do	5
69	Stax STAX 116	I've Got To Have Your Love/Girl I Love You	5
69	Stax STAX 125	Don't Tell Your Mama/Consider Me	5
70	Stax STAX 153	My Girl/Laurie	5
72	Polydor 2025 098	Yum Yum Yum/I Want Some/Tears Of Joy	5
74	Stax STXS 2005	Soul Street/The Highway Man	5
81	I-Spy SEE 9	The Beat Song/London ('I-Spy' sleeve)	5
67	Stax 589 006	KNOCK ON WOOD (LP)	20
68	Stax (S)XATS 1003	I'VE NEVER FOUND A GIRL (LP)	20
69	Atco 228 014	KNOCK ON WOOD (LP, reissue)	15
69	Stax SXATS 1023	YOU'VE GOT TO HAVE EDDIE (LP)	15
71	Stax 2363 010	YOU'VE GOT TO HAVE EDDIE (LP, reissue)	12
74	Stax STX 1002	SOUL STREET (LP)	12

(see also Falcons, Primettes/Eddie Floyd)

FLUKE
89	Fluke FLUKE 001T	Thumper!/Cool Hand Flute (12", stamped white label with stickered sleeve)	7
90	Creation CRE 090T	PHILLY (12")	10

FLUX (OF PINK INDIANS)
81	Crass 321984/2	NEU SMELL (EP, foldout poster sleeve)	6
85	Spiderleg SDL 16	TAKING A LIBERTY (EP, as Flux, with booklet sleeve)	6
83	Spiderleg SDL 8	STRIVE TO SURVIVE CAUSING THE LEAST SUFFERING POSSIBLE (LP, with booklet)	12

(see also Epileptics, Licks)

FLYER
79	Redball RR 004	FLYER (EP)	4

MINT VALUE £

FLYING BURRITO BROTHERS

69	A&M AMS 756	The Train Song/Hot Burrito No. 1	8
70	A&M AMS 794	Older Guys/Down In The Churchyard	5
70	A&M AMS 816	Tried So Hard/Lazy Days	6
72	A&M AMS 871	White Line Fever/Colorado	5
69	A&M AML(S) 931	THE GILDED PALACE OF SIN (LP)	15
70	A&M AMLS 983	BURRITO DELUXE (LP)	15
71	A&M AMLS 64295	THE FLYING BURRITO BROTHERS (LP)	12
72	A&M AMLS 64343	LAST OF THE RED-HOT BURRITOS (LP)	12
73	Bumble GEXD 301	LIVE IN AMSTERDAM (2-LP)	15

(see also Byrds, Gram Parsons, Gene Parsons, Stephen Stills & Manassas, Rick Roberts, Country Gazette, Skip Battin)

FLYING CIRCUS

71	Harvest SHSP 4010	PREPARED IN PEACE (LP)	12

FLYING MACHINE

69	Pye 7N 17722	Smile A Little Smile For Me/Maybe We've Been Loving Too Long	6
69	Pye 7N 17722	Baby Make It Soon/Smile A Little Smile For Me	5
69	Pye 7N 17811	Send My Baby Home Again/Look At Me, Look At Me	5
70	Pye 7N 17914	Hanging On The Edge Of Sadness/Flying Machine	7
70	Pye 7N 45001	The Devil Has Possession Of Your Mind/Hey Little Girl	5
70	Pye 7N 45093	Yes I Understand/Pages Of Your Life	5
70	Pye NSPL 18328	DOWN TO EARTH WITH THE FLYING MACHINE (LP)	18

(see also Pinkertons, Pinkerton's Assorted Colours, Tony Newman)

FLYING SAUCER ATTACK

92	Heartbeat FSA 6	Soaring High/Standing Stone (p/s, 500 only, 1st few with autographed postcards; later with various different designs)	30/35
93	Heartbeat FSA 61	Wish/Oceans (p/s, 700 only)	20
94	Domino RUG 23	Land Beyond The Sun/Everywhere Was Everything (p/s, hand-painted rear sleeve, 500 only)	12
95	Planet PUNK 008	Beach Red Lullaby/Second Hour (p/s, 1,300 only)	8
96	Enraptured RAPT 4505	At Night/JESSAMINE: From Hereto And Now Otherwise (500 on clear vinyl, 2500 black)	8/5
98	Earworm WORMSC 1	Land Beyond The Sun (2 -Track Version)/Instrumental For Silence (green vinyl, 500 only)	8
94	Heartbeat FSA 62	FLYING SAUCER ATTACK (LP, 1,000 only)	25

FLYING SAUCERS

76	Alaska ALA 2001	Fabulous/Fish On My Line	4
76	Alaska ALA 2003	Keep On Comin'/Shadow Walk	4
78	Alaska ALA 2014	Texas Calls You Home/Pretty Baby (p/s)	4
76	Nevis NEV LP 114	PLANET OF THE DRAPES (LP)	10
78	Alaska LP 101	KEEP ON COMING (LP)	10

ERROL FLYNN

55	Philips PB 380	Lily Of Laguna/We'll Gather Lilacs (B-side with Patrice Wymore) (78)	12

STEVE FLYNN

67	Parlophone R 5625	Mr Rainbow/Let's Live For Tomorrow	20
68	Parlophone R 5689	Your Life And My Life/Come Tomorrow	6

(see also Mark Wirtz)

FLY ON THE WALL

79	Next Wave NEXT 1	DEVON DUMB (EP, numbered)	20

FLYS

77	Zama ZA 10 EP	BUNCH OF FIVE (33rpm EP, die-cut p/s)	15
78	EMI EMI 2747	Love And A Molotov Cocktail/Can I Crash Here?/Civilisation (p/s)	6
78	EMI EMI 2795	Fun City/E.C. 4 (p/s)	6
78	EMI EMIY 2867	Waikiki Beach Refugees/We Don't Mind The Rave (p/s, yellow vinyl)	6
79	EMI EMI 2907	Oh Beverley/Don't Moonlight On Me (p/s)	6
79	EMI EMI 2936	Name Dropping/Fly V Fly (p/s, some on coloured vinyl)	6
79	EMI EMI 2979	Living In The Sticks/We Are The Lucky Ones (p/s)	6
79	Parlophone R 6030	16 Down/Night Creatures/Lois Lane/Today Belongs To Me (p/s)	6
80	Parlophone R 6036	What Will Mother Say?/Undercover Agent Zero (p/s)	6
80	Parlophone R 6063	FOUR FROM THE SQUARE (EP, p/s)	6

FLYTE REACTION

91	Woronzow W0014	SONGS IN A CIRCLE (LP)	15
92	Splendid SPLEN 001	STRAWBERRY LIP SALVATION (LP)	12
93	Splendid SPLEN 002	SPECTRAL FOOTWEAR (LP)	12
95	Splendid SPLEN 003	CREATE A SMILE (LP)	12

FOCAL POINT

68	Deram DM 186	Love You Forever/Sycamore Sid	25

FOCUS

71	Polydor 2001 134	House Of The King/Black Beauty	6
71	Blue Horizon 2094 006	Hocus Pocus/Janis	12
72	Blue Horizon 2096 008	Tommy/Focus II	12
76	Polydor 2001 640	House Of The King/O Avendrood	5
71	Polydor 2344 003	IN AND OUT OF FOCUS (LP, gatefold sleeve)	12
72	Blue Horizon 2096 002	MOVING WAVES (LP, with poster)	15
72	Polydor 2659 016	FOCUS III (2-LP, gatefold sleeve)	15
73	Polydor 2443 118	LIVE AT THE RAINBOW (LP, gatefold sleeve)	12

(see also Jan Akkerman, Thijs Van Leer, Brainbox, Robin Lent)

FOCUS THREE

67	Columbia DB 8279	10,000 Years Behind My Mind/The Sunkeeper	40

FOETUS ART TERRORISM
84	Self Immolation FAT 1122	Calamity Crush/Catastrophe Crunch (12", p/s) 8

(see also You've Got Foetus On Your Breath, Philip & His Foetus Vibrations, Scraping Foetus Off The Wheel, Flesh Volcano)

FOETUS CORRUPTUS
91	Rifle RIFLE 1	RIFE (2-LP, stickered black sleeve) 20

(see also You've Got Foetus On Your Breath, Philip & His Foetus Vibrations, Scraping Foetus Off The Wheel, Flesh Volcano)

FOETUS ÜBER FRISCO
82	Self Immolation WOMB 125/SUSC 12	Custom Built For Capitalism/1.0.4.5./Birthday (12", p/s) 30
85	Self Imm. WOMB UNC 7.12	Finely Honed Machine/Sick Minutes (12", p/s) 8

(see also You've Got Foetus On Your Breath, Philip & His Foetus Vibrations, Scraping Foetus Off The Wheel, Flesh Volcano)

FOETUS UNDER GLASS
85	Self Imm. WOMB S201	Spite Your Face/OKFM (p/s) 25

(see also You've Got Foetus On Your Breath, Philip & His Foetus Vibrations, Scraping Foetus Off The Wheel, Flesh Volcano)

FOGCUTTERS
64	Liberty LIB 55793	Cry Cry Cry/You Say 10

JOHN FOGERTY
74	Fantasy FTC 111	Comin' Down The Road/Ricochet 5
75	Fantasy FTC 119	Rockin' All Over The World/The Wall 5
75	Fantasy FTC 120	Almost Saturday Night/Sea Cruise 5
76	Fantasy FTC 133	You Got The Magic/Evil Thing 5
75	Fantasy FT 526	JOHN FOGERTY (LP) 12

(see also Creedence Clearwater Revival, Blue Ridge Rangers)

TOM FOGERTY
71	United Artists UP 35264	Goodbye Media Man (Parts 1 & 2) 5
72	Fantasy F 680	Cast The First Stone/Lady Of Fatima 5
73	Fantasy FTC 109	Joyful Resurrection/Heartbeat 5
72	Fantasy FAN 9407	TOM FOGERTY (LP) 12

(see also Creedence Clearwater Revival, Ruby)

FOGGY
72	York SYK 534	How Come The Sun/Take Your Time 5
73	York SYK 542	Kitty Starr/She's Far Away (p/s) 7
72	York FYK 411	SIMPLE GIFTS (LP, with insert, featuring Strawbs) 50
75	Canon CNN 5759	PATCHWORK (LP) 35

(see also Strawbs, Foggy Dew-O)

FOGGY DEW-O
68	Decca F 12776	Reflections/Grandfather's Clock 7
71	York SYK 503	Me And Bobby McGee/Feelin' Groovy 5
68	Decca LK/SKL 4940	THE FOGGY DEW-O (LP) 30
68	Decca Eclipse ECS 2118	THE FOGGY DEW-O (LP) 15
70	Decca LK/SKL 5035	BORN TO TAKE THE HIGHWAY (LP) 20

(see also Strawbs, Foggy)

FOGHAT
72	Bearsville K 15501	What A Shame/Hole To Hide In 5
74	Bearsville K 15511	Long Way To Go/Ride Ride Ride 5
74	Bearsville K 15517	Step Outside (Edit)/Mabellene 5
76	Bearsville K 15522	Slow Ride (Edit)/Save Your Loving (For Me) 5
77	Bearsville K 15537	I Just Want To Make Love To You (Live Edit)/Fool For The City (Live Edit) 5
79	Bearsville WIP 6582	Third Time Lucky/Somebody's Been Sleeping In My Bed 5
72	Bearsville K 45503	FOGHAT (LP) 15
73	Bearsville K 45514	FOGHAT — ROCK'N'ROLL (LP) 12
74	Bearsville K 55500	ENERGISED (LP) 12

(see also Black Cat Bones, Savoy Brown, Warren Philips & The Rockets)

ELLEN FOLEY (& CLASH)
81	Epic EPC A 9522	The Shuttered Palace/Beautiful Waste Of Time (p/s) 6
81	Epic EPC A 1160	Torchlight/Game Of A Man (p/s) 5
81	Epic SEPC 84809	SPIRIT OF ST. LOUIS
		(LP, with inner sleeve) 12

(see also Clash)

RED FOLEY
50	Brunswick 04467	Sugarfoot Rag-Square Dance/Chattanoochie Shoe Shine Boy (78) 8
51	Brunswick 04481	I'm Throwing Rice At The Girl I Love/Tennessee Polka (78) 8
51	Brunswick 04538	Birmingham Bounce/Choc'late Ice Cream Cone (78) 10
51	Brunswick 04548	M-i-s-s-i-s-s-i-p-p-i/Remember Me (78) 8
51	Brunswick 04565	I Gotta Have My Baby Back/Have I Told You Lately That I Love You (78) 8
51	Brunswick 04593	Cincinnati Dancing Pig/Somebody's Cryin' (78) 8
51	Brunswick 04644	My Heart Cries For You/Tater Pie (78, with Evelyn Knight) 8
51	Brunswick 04679	Hot Rod Race/The Chicken Song
		(B-side with Ernest Tubb) (78) 10
52	Brunswick 04820	Rudolph The Red-Nosed Reindeer/Frosty The Snowman
		(with Little Foleys) (78) 8
52	Brunswick 04852	Alabama Jubilee/Let's Go To Church Next Sunday Morning (78) 8
52	Brunswick 04895	I'm In Love With With Molly/Too Old To Cut The Mustard
		(78, with Ernest Tubb) 8
52	Brunswick 04962	Hang Your Head In Shame/I Want To Be With You Always (78) 8

53	Brunswick 05076	Hot Toddy/ROBERTA LEE & HARDROCK GUNTER:	
		Sixty Minute Man (78)	12
53	Brunswick 05131	No Help Wanted/Don't Be Ashamed Of Your Age	
		(78, with Ernest Tubb)	8
54	Brunswick 05307	Pin Ball Boogie/Jilted (78)	10
54	Brunswick 05321	Skinnie Minnie (Fishtail)/Thank You For Calling	12
54	Brunswick 05321	Skinnie Minnie (Fishtail)/Thank You For Calling (78)	8
55	Brunswick 05363	Hearts Of Stone/RED FOLEY & BETTY FOLEY: Never	15
55	Brunswick 05363	Hearts Of Stone/RED FOLEY & BETTY FOLEY: Never (78)	8
60	Brunswick LAT 8343	SING ALONG WITH RED FOLEY	
		(LP, also stereo STA 3034)	18/22

(see also Roberta Lee)

RED FOLEY & BETTY FOLEY

55	Brunswick 05508	Croce Di Oro (Cross Of Gold)/RED FOLEY: The Night Watch	15
55	Brunswick 05508	Croce Di Oro (Cross Of Gold)/RED FOLEY: The Night Watch (78)	8

RED FOLEY & ERNEST TUBB

55	Brunswick OE 9148	COUNTRY DOUBLE DATE	
		(EP, with Minnie Pearl)	18
57	Brunswick LAT 8206	RED AND ERNIE (LP)	20

(see also Ernest Tubb)

SIMON FOLEY

77	Look LKLP 6324	TO STRIVE WITH PRINCES (LP, with booklet)	20

FOLKAL POINT

72	Midas MR 003	FOLKAL POINT (LP)	400

CALVIN FOLKES

63	Rio R 5	Someone/Kentucky Home	10
63	Rio R 8	You'll Never Know/Is It Time?	10
64	Port-O-Jam PJ 4117	My Bonnie/What A Day	10
64	Port-O-Jam PJ 4118	Hello Everybody/IRVING SIX: King's Boogie	10

FOLK(S) BROTHERS

61	Blue Beat BB 30	Carolina/I Met A Man	
		(original, blue label, as Folks Brothers)	10
60s	Fab BB 30	Carolina (as Folks Brothers)/ERIC 'HUMPTY DUMPTY' MORRIS:	
		Humpty Dumpty	6
70s	Blue Beat BB 30	Carolina/I Met A Man (reissue, white label, as Folk Brothers)	6

FOLKLANDERS

60s	Urban PB 001	TWO LITTLE FISHES (EP)	8

FOLKLORE

75	Homespun HPL 104	FIRST OF FOLKLORE	
		(LP, Ireland-only)	40

FOLK SONG CLUB

65	white label (no cat. no.)	IMPERIAL COLLEGE	
		(LP, private pressing)	200

FOLKWAYS

72	Folk Heritage	NO OTHER NAME (LP)	12

EDDIE FONTAINE

55	HMV 7M 304	Rock Love/All My Love Belongs To You (with Neal Hefti & Excels)	325
55	HMV B 10852	Rock Love/All My Love Belongs To You (with Neal Hefti & Excels) (78)	60
56	Brunswick 05624	Cool It, Baby/Into Each Life Some Rain Must Fall	165
56	Brunswick 05624	Cool It, Baby/Into Each Life Some Rain Must Fall (78)	45
58	London HLM 8711	Nothin' Shakin' (But The Leaves On The Trees)/Don't Ya Know	25
58	London HLM 8711	Nothin' Shakin' (But The Leaves On The Trees)/Don't Ya Know (78)	45

ARLENE FONTANA

59	Pye International 7N 25010	I'm In Love/Easy	8
59	Pye International N 25010	I'm In Love/Easy (78)	10

WAYNE FONTANA & MINDBENDERS

63	Fontana TF 404	Hello! Josephine/Road Runner	12
63	Fontana TF 418	For You, For You/Love Potion No.9	8
64	Fontana TF 436	Little Darlin'/Come Dance With Me	10
64	Fontana TF 451	Stop Look And Listen/Duke Of Earl	7
64	Fontana TF 497	Um, Um, Um, Um, Um/First Taste Of Love	5
65	Fontana TF 535	The Game Of Love/Since You've Been Gone	5
65	Fontana TF 579	It's Just A Little Bit Too Late/Long Time Comin'	7
65	Fontana TF 611	She Needs Love/Like I Did	6
69	Fontana H 1022	Um, Um, Um, Um, Um, Um/The Game Of Love	
		(p/s)	5
64	Fontana TE 17421	ROAD RUNNER (EP)	40
64	Fontana TE 17435	UM, UM, UM, UM, UM, UM (EP)	20
65	Fontana TE 17449	THE GAME OF LOVE (EP)	20
65	Fontana TE 17453	WALKING ON AIR (EP)	45
64	Fontana TL 5230	WAYNE FONTANA AND THE MINDBENDERS (LP)	40
65	Fontana TL 5257	ERIC, RICK, WAYNE, BOB — IT'S WAYNE FONTANA	
		AND THE MINDBENDERS (LP)	40
67	Wing WL 1166	WAYNE FONTANA AND THE MINDBENDERS	
		(LP, reissue)	18
69	Fontana SFL 13106	WAYNE FONTANA AND THE MINDBENDERS	
		(LP, 2nd reissue)	12

(see also Wayne Fontana, Mindbenders)

WAYNE FONTANA

65	Fontana TF 642	It Was Easier To Hurt Her/You Made Me What I Am Today	5
66	Fontana TF 684	Come On Home/My Eyes Break Out In Tears	5
66	Fontana TF 737	Goodbye Bluebird/The Sun's So Hot Today	5
66	Fontana TF 770	Pamela Pamela/Something Keeps Calling Me Back	5
67	Fontana TF 827	24 Sycamore/From A Boy To A Man	5
67	Fontana TF 866	The Impossible Years/In My World	5
67	Fontana TF 889	Gina/We All Love The Human Race	5
68	Fontana TF 911	Storybook Children/I Need To Love You	5
68	Fontana TF 933	The Words Of Bartholomew/Mind Excursion	5
68	Fontana TF 976	Never An Everyday Thing/Waiting For A Break In The Clouds	5
69	Fontana TF 1008	Dayton Ohio 1903/Say Goodbye To Yesterday	5
69	Fontana TF 1054	Charlie Cass/Linda (withdrawn issue)	15
69	Fontana TF 1054	We're Building A Love/Charlie Cass	6
69	Fontana H 1027	Come On Home/Pamela Pamela (p/s)	5
70	Philips 6006 035	Give Me Just A Little More Time/I'm In Love (withdrawn)	25
73	Warner Bros K 16269	Together/One Man Woman	5
66	Fontana (S)TL 5351	WAYNE ONE (LP)	18
69	Fontana SFL 13144	WAYNE ONE (LP, reissue)	12

(see also Mindbenders)

FONTANE SISTERS
78s

51	HMV B 10021	Tennessee Waltz/As We Are Today (78)	10
54	HMV B 10765	Please Play Our Song/Mexican Joe (78)	10
54	London HL 8099	Happy Days And Lonely Nights/If I Didn't Have You (78)	15
55	London HL 8113	Hearts Of Stone/Bless Your Heart (78)	15
55	London HL 8126	Rock Love/You're Mine (78)	15
55	London HLD 8177	Seventeen/If I Could Be With You (78)	12
55	London HLD 8211	Rolling Stone/Daddy-O (78)	12
56	London HLD 8225	Adorable/Playmates (78)	15
56	London HLD 8265	Eddie My Love/Yum Yum (78)	12
56	London HLD 8289	I'm In Love Again/You Always Hurt The One You Love (78)	15
56	London HLD 8318	Voices (with narration by Pat Boone)/Willow Weep For Me (78)	10
56	London HLD 8343	Silver Bells/Nuttin' For Christmas (78)	15
57	London HLD 8378	The Banana Boat Song/Lonesome Lover Blues (78)	10
57	London HLD 8415	Please Don't Leave Me/Still (78)	15
57	London HLD 8488	Fool Around/Which Way To Your Heart? (78)	15
58	London HLD 8621	Chanson D'Amour (Song Of Love)/Cocoanut Grove (78)	12
59	London HLD 8861	Billy Boy/Encore D'Amour (78)	15

SINGLES

54	London HL 8099	Happy Days And Lonely Nights/If I Didn't Have You	75
55	London HL 8113	Hearts Of Stone/Bless Your Heart	100
55	London HL 8126	Rock Love/You're Mine	80
55	London HLD 8177	Seventeen/If I Could Be With You	80
55	London HLD 8211	Rolling Stone/Daddy-O	70
56	London HLD 8225	Adorable/Playmates	45
56	London HLD 8265	Eddie My Love/Yum Yum	45
56	London HL 7009	Eddie My Love/Yum Yum (export issue)	30
56	London HLD 8289	I'm In Love Again/You Always Hurt The One You Love (gold lettering label, later silver)	30/20
56	London HLD 8318	Voices (with narration by Pat Boone)/Willow Weep For Me (gold lettering label, later silver)	25/15
56	London HLD 8343	Silver Bells/Nuttin' For Christmas	20
57	London HLD 8378	The Banana Boat Song/Lonesome Lover Blues (gold or silver lettering)	18/12
57	London HLD 8415	Please Don't Leave Me/Still	20
57	London HLD 8488	Fool Around/Which Way To Your Heart?	18
58	London HLD 8621	Chanson D'Amour (Song Of Love)/Cocoanut Grove	12
59	London HLD 8861	Billy Boy/Encore D'Amour	12
60	London HLD 9037	Listen To Your Heart/Please Be Kind	8
60	London HLD 9078	Theme From "A Summer Place"/Darling, It's Wonderful	8

EPs

55	London RE-D 1029	FONTANE SISTERS NO. 1 (EP)	60
55	London RE-D 1037	FONTANE SISTERS NO. 2 (EP)	50

LP

| 57 | London HA-D 2053 | THE FONTANES SING (LP) | 100 |

(see also Pat Boone, Perry Como)

SAM FONTEYN

66	Parlophone R 5519	Lost In Space/BERNARD SHARPE: Jorrocks	6

BILLY FONTEYNE

63	Oriole CB 1917	Little Child/Look Before You Leap	7

FOO FIGHTERS

95	Roswell CL 757	I'll Stick Around/How I Miss You (p/s, red vinyl)	8
95	Roswell CL 762	For All The Cows/Watershed (p/s, blue vinyl)	8
95	Roswell CL 768	Big Me/Floaty/Gas Chamber (p/s, white vinyl)	6
97	Roswell CL 792	Everlong/Drive Me Wild (p/s, blue vinyl)	5

FOOL

69	Mercury MF 1111	We Are One/Shining Light	7
69	Mercury SMCL 20138	THE FOOL (LP)	20

MINT VALUE £

FOOLS DANCE
87	L.T.T. Slaughter LTS 22	They'll Never Know/Empty Hours (p/s)	10
87	L.T.T. Slaughter LTS 22T	They'll Never Know/The Collector/Empty Hours/The Ring (12", p/s)	15
85	Top Hole Turn TURN 19	FOOLS DANCE (mini-LP)	20
86	Top Hat TH 22	FOOLS DANCE (mini-LP, reissue)	15
86	L.T.T. Slaughter LTS 18	FOOLS DANCE (mini-LP, 2nd reissue)	12

(see also Cure, Stranglers)

CHUCK FOOTE
62	London HLU 9495	You're Running Out Of Kisses/Come On Back	10

FOOT IN COLD WATER
73	Island WIP 6162	(Isn't Love Unkind) In My Life/Deep Freeze	5
74	Elektra K 52011	OR ALL AROUND US (LP)	15

FORBES
77	Power Exchange PX 253	The Beatles/Sweet Kiss Of Fire	7

BILL FORBES
58	Columbia DB 4232	My Cherie/God's Little Acre	6
58	Columbia DB 4232	My Cherie/God's Little Acre (78)	8
59	Columbia DB 4269	Once More/Believe In Me	10
59	Columbia DB 4386	Too Young/It's Not The End Of The World	6
61	Columbia DB 4566	You're Sixteen, You're Beautiful/Backward Child	7
61	Columbia DB 4619	That's It, I Quit, I'm Moving On/Big City Boy	6
61	Columbia DB 4747	Goodbye Cruel World/Next Time	6
62	Columbia DB 4855	Laughter Or Tears/Like A Good Girl Should	6
62	Columbia DB 4945	Poker Face/Marianne	6

(see also Contrasts)

FORCEFIELD
87	President PT 551	Smoke On The Water/Shine It On Me (p/s)	5
88	President PT 578	Heartache/I Lose Again (Instrumental Version) (p/s)	5

(see also Cozy Powell, Graham Bonnet, Ray Fenwick, Whitesnake)

FORCE FIVE
64	United Artists UP 1051	Don't Make My Baby Blue/Shaking Postman	10
65	United Artists UP 1089	Yeah, I'm Waiting/I Don't Want To See You Again	20
65	United Artists UP 1102	Baby Don't Care/Come Down To Earth	30
65	United Artists UP 1118	I Want You Babe/Gee Too Tiger	20
66	United Artists UP 1141	Don't Know Which Way To Turn/Baby Let Your Hair Down	30

(see also Crocheted Doughnut Ring)

FORCE WEST
65	Decca F 12223	I Can't Give What I Haven't Got/Why Won't She Stay	8
66	Columbia DB 7908	Gotta Find Another Baby/Talkin' About Our Love	10
66	Columbia DB 7963	When The Sun Comes Out (Weatherman)/Gotta Tell Somebody	8
67	Columbia DB 8174	All The Children Sleep/Desolation	10
68	CBS 3632	I'll Walk In The Rain/What's It To Be?	6
68	CBS 3798	I'll Be Moving On/Like The Tide, Like The Ocean	6
69	CBS 4385	Sherry/Mister Blue	8

CLINTON FORD
78s
58	Oriole CB 1425	Sweet Sixteen/Eleven More Months And Ten More Days (78)	10
58	Oriole CB 1427	Jesus Remember Me/In The Sweet Bye & Bye (w/ Hallelujah Skiffle Group) (78)	15
59	Oriole CB 1483	I Cried A Tear/(You Were Only) Teasin' (78)	10
59	Oriole CB 1500	Old Shep/Nellie Dean Rock (78)	15
59	Oriole CB 1516	Lovesick Blues/Give A Little, Take A Little (78)	15
59	Oriole CB 1518	Silver Threads Among The Gold/Red Indian Christmas Carol (78)	10

SINGLES
58	Oriole CB 1425	Sweet Sixteen/Eleven More Months And Ten More Days	6
59	Oriole CB 1483	I Cried A Tear/(You Were Only) Teasin'	6
59	Oriole CB 1500	Old Shep/Nellie Dean Rock	6
59	Oriole CB 1516	Lovesick Blues/Give A Little, Take A Little	5
59	Oriole CB 1518	Silver Threads Among The Gold/Red Indian Christmas Carol	5
61	Oriole CB 1551	Mustapha/Two Brothers	5
61	Oriole CB 1612	Oh By Jingo/Get Out And Get Under	5
61	Oriole CB 1623	Too Many Beautiful Girls/Everybody's Doing It	5
62	Oriole CB 1706	Fanlight Fanny/Dreamy City Lullaby	6
62	Oriole CB 1747	Under The Bamboo Tree/Who's Next In Line	5
62	Oriole CB 1768	Opening Night In Loveland/Madam Moscovitch	5
63	Oriole CB 1798	Popsy Wopsy/You Can Tell Her Anything	5
63	Oriole CB 1884	Rainbow/On Mother Kelly's Doorstep	5
64	Columbia DB 7220	Southtown U.S.A./Honey Baby	5
64	Columbia DB 7413	Oh, Johnny! Oh, Johnny! Oh!/Since I Found You	5
66	Piccadilly 7N 35343	Dandy/Why Don't Women Like Me	5
67	Piccadilly 7N 35361	Run To The Door/Best Job Yet	5
67	Piccadilly 7N 35378	This Song Is Just For You/Take Care On The Road	5
67	Piccadilly 7N 35404	Dance With A Dolly (With A Hole In Her Stocking)/Streets Of Laredo	5
67	Pye 7N 17428	Last One To Say Goodnight/Greatest Clown	5
68	Pye 7N 17521	Cathy I Love You/American Girl	5
68	Pye 7N 17572	Give A Little Take A Little/West Wind Blow Me Home	5
68	Pye 7N 17628	Sounds Of Goodbye/Try A Little Tenderness	5
69	Pye 7N 17718	Moonlight Brings Memories/Now That You've Gone	5
69	Pye 7N 17766	Cielito Lindo/Lonelyville	5
69	Pye 7N 17838	Angel In My Pocket/Lorena	5
70	Pye 7N 45079	Turn The Good Times On/The Pockets Of One Little Boy	5

EP
67	Piccadilly NEP 34057	DANDY (EP)	10

LPs
62	Oriole PS 40021	CLINTON FORD (LP, with George Chisholm Allstars)	12
63	Columbia 33SX 1560	THE MELODY MAN (LP, also stereo SCX 3496)	12/15
64	Realm RM 147	BY JINGO (LP)	12
65	Columbia 33SX 1689	LISTEN WITH US (LP, also stereo SCX 3529)	12/15
67	Pye NPL 18210	CLINTON THE CLOWN (LP)	12
67	Piccadilly N(S)PL 38028	DANDY (LP)	12
67	Piccadilly N(S)PL 38034	BIG WILLY BROKE JAIL TONIGHT (LP)	12

(see also Hallelujah Skiffle Group)

DEAN FORD (& GAYLORDS)
64	Columbia DB 7264	Twenty Miles/What's The Matter With Me?	18
64	Columbia DB 7402	Mr Heartbreak's Here Instead/I Won't	18
65	Columbia DB 7610	The Name Game/That Lonely Feeling	18
75	EMI EMC 3079	DEAN FORD (LP)	12

(see also Gaylords, Marmalade, Junior Campbell)

DEE DEE FORD
60	London HLU 9245	Good-Morning Blues/I Just Can't Believe	40

(see also Don Gardner & Dee Dee Ford)

EDDIE/EDDY FORD
72	Pressure Beat PB 5512	You Wrong Fe Trouble Joshua/KENNETH POWER: Joshua Row Us Home	6
73	Duke Reid DR 2523	Guess I This Riddle/Riddle Version (as Eddie Ford)	5

EMILE FORD (& CHECKMATES)
59	Pye 7N 15225	What Do You Want To Make Those Eyes At Me For?/Don't Tell Me Your Troubles	5
59	Pye N 15225	What Do You Want To Make Those Eyes At Me For?/	
		Don't Tell Me Your Troubles (78)	20
60	Pye 7N 15245	On A Slow Boat To China/That Lucky Old Sun	5
60	Pye N 15245	On A Slow Boat To China/That Lucky Old Sun (78)	20
60	Pye 7N 15268	You'll Never Know What You're Missin' 'Til You Try/Still	8
60	Pye 7N 15279	Red Sails In The Sunset/Afraid	5
60	Pye 7N 15282	Question/Them There Eyes (solo)	5
60	Pye 7N 15314	Counting Teardrops/White Christmas	5
61	Pye 7N 15331	A Kiss To Build A Dream On/What Am I Gonna Do	5
61	Piccadilly 7N 35003	Half Of My Heart/Gypsy Love (solo)	6
61	Piccadilly 7N 35007	Hush, Somebody's Calling My Name/After You've Gone	6
61	Piccadilly 7N 35019	The Alphabet Song/Keep A-Lovin' Me (solo)	6
62	Piccadilly 7N 35033	I Wonder Who's Kissing Her Now/Doin' The Twist (solo)	6
62	Piccadilly 7N 35078	Your Nose Is Gonna Grow/Rains Come	6
63	Piccadilly 7N 35116	Doin' What You Do To Me/Hold Me Thrill Me Kiss Me	6
69	Decca F 12959	Set Me Free/Don't Remind Me (export issue)	12
59	Pye NEP 24119	EMILE (EP)	12
60	Pye NEP 24124	EMILE FORD HIT PARADE (EP)	15
60	Pye NEP 24133	EMILE FORD HIT PARADE VOL. 2 (EP)	20
60	Pye NPL 18049	NEW TRACKS WITH EMILE (LP)	20
61	Piccadilly NPL 38001	EMILE (LP)	25

FRANKIE FORD
59	London HL 8850	Sea Cruise/Roberta (with Huey 'Piano' Smith & Clowns)	
		(black triangular centre, later silver-top triangular centre)	50/35
59	London HL 8850	Sea Cruise/Roberta (with Huey 'Piano' Smith & Clowns) (78)	80
59	Top Rank JAR 186	Alimony/Can't Tell My Heart (What To Do) (with Huey 'Piano' Smith & Clowns)	10
59	Top Rank JAR 186	Alimony/Can't Tell My Heart (What To Do) (78)	60
60	Top Rank JAR 282	Cheatin' Woman/HUEY 'PIANO' SMITH & CLOWNS:	
		Don't You Just Know Kokomo	20
60	Top Rank JAR 299	Time After Time/I Want To Be Your Man	8
60	London HL 9222	You Talk Too Much/If You've Got Troubles	20
65	Sue WI 366	Sea Cruise/Roberta (with Huey 'Piano' Smith & Clowns) (reissue)	15
65	Sue WI 369	What's Going On?/Watchdog	25
78	Chiswick NS 38	Sea Cruise/Alimony (p/s)	5

(see also Huey 'Piano' Smith)

JON FORD
68	Philips BF 1690	Two's Company, Three's A Crowd/Place In Your Heart	6
69	Philips BF 1791	I Know It's Love/Look Before You Leap	5
69	Philips BF 1817	Ice Cream Man/This Was The Time	5
70	Philips BF 1833	Yesterday When I Was Young/Running Around	5
70	Philips 6006 030	You've Got Me Where You Want Me/You're All Alone Tonight	50

LITA FORD & OZZY OSBOURNE
89	Dreamland A 49396	Close My Eyes Forever (Remix)/Under The Gun (p/s)	5
89	Dreamland PA 49396	Close My Eyes Forever (Remix)/Under The Gun/Blueberry (12", picture disc)	8
89	Dreamland PA 49396	Close My Eyes Forever (Remix)/Under The Gun/Blueberry (3" CD, g/fold p/s)	10

(see also Ozzy Osbourne, Runaways)

PERRY FORD (& SAPPHIRES)
59	Parlophone R 4573	Bye, Bye Baby, Goodbye/She Came As A Stranger	6
60	Parlophone R 4633	Crazy Over You/Garden Of Happiness	6
60	Parlophone R 4683	Don't Weep (Little Lady)/Little Grown-Up	5
62	Decca F 11497	Baby, Baby (Don't You Worry)/Prince Of Fools (with Sapphires & Small Flames)	7

(see also Ivy League, Georgie Fame)

RICKY FORD (& TENNESSEANS)
63	Parlophone R 5018	Sweet And Tender Romance/Cheat Cheat	5
64	Parlophone R 5230	You Are My Love/Long Way From Home (with Tennesseans)	5

MINT VALUE £

'TENNESSEE' ERNIE FORD

78s

51	Capitol CL 13447	The Shot Gun Boogie/My Hobby (78)	8
51	Capitol CL 13481	Tailor Made Woman/I Ain't Gonna Let It Happen No More (78)	8
51	Capitol CL 13599	Leetle Juan Pedro (with Eddie Kirk)/Feed 'Em In The Mornin' Blues (78)	10
51	Capitol CL 13604	Kissin' Bug Boogie/Woman Is A Five Letter Word (78)	8
51	Capitol CL 13623	Cool Cool Kisses/Hey Good Lookin' (with Helen O'Connell) (78)	8
52	Capitol CL 13682	Rock City Boogie/Streamlined Cannon Ball (with Dinning Sisters) (78)	8
52	Capitol CL 13797	Blackberry Boogie/Tennessee Local (78)	8
52	Capitol CL 13809	False Hearted Girl/I'm Hogtied Over You (with Ella Mae Morse) (78)	10
53	Capitol CL 13942	Don't Start Courtin' In A Hot Rod/We're A-Growin' Up (with Mollie Bee) (78)	8
53	Capitol CL 14006	Catfish Boogie/Kiss Me Big (78)	8
57	Capitol CL 14734	The Lonely Man/False Hearted Girl (78)	8
57	Capitol CL 14759	In The Middle Of An Island/Ivy League (78)	8
58	Capitol CL 14846	Down Deep/Bless Your Pea Pickin' Heart (78)	8
58	Capitol CL 14896	Love Makes The World Go 'Round/Sunday Barbecue (78)	10

SINGLES

54	Capitol CL 14005	Give Me Your Word/River Of No Return	20
54	Capitol CL 14006	Catfish Boogie/Kiss Me Big	30
55	Capitol CL 14261	His Hands/I Am A Pilgrim	10
55	Capitol CL 14273	Losing You/There Is Beauty In Everything	10
56	Capitol CL 14500	Sixteen Tons/You Don't Have To Be A Baby To Cry	18
56	Capitol CL 14506	The Ballad Of Davy Crockett/Farewell	18
56	Capitol CL 14557	That's All/Bright Lights And Blonde-Haired Women	10
56	Capitol CL 14616	Who Will Shoe Your Pretty Little Foot?/Gaily The Troubadour	5
56	Capitol CL 14657	First Born/Have You Seen Her?	5
57	Capitol CL 14691	The Watermelon Song/One Suit	5
57	Capitol CL 14734	The Lonely Man/False Hearted Girl	5
57	Capitol CL 14759	In The Middle Of An Island/Ivy League	6
58	Capitol CL 14846	Down Deep/Bless Your Pea Pickin' Heart	5
58	Capitol CL 14896	Love Makes The World Go 'Round/Sunday Barbecue	6
59	Capitol CL 14972	Glad Rags/Sleepin' At The Foot Of The Bed	5
59	Capitol CL 15010	Blackeyed Susie/Code Of The Mountains	6
59	Capitol CL 15100	Sunny Side Of Heaven/Love Is The Only Thing	5
60	Capitol CL 15148	Joshua Fit The Battle Of Jericho/O Mary, Don't You Weep	5
60	Capitol CL 15171	Little Klinker/Jingle-O-The-Brownie	5
61	Capitol CL 15190	Dark As A Dungeon/His Love	5
61	Capitol CL 15210	Little Red Rockin' Hood/I Gotta Have My Baby Back	10
65	Capitol CL 15403	Sixteen Tons/Hicktown	5
65	Capitol CL 15426	The Little Drummer Boy/Sing We Now Of Christmas	5

EPs

56	Capitol EAP 1014	SIXTEEN TONS (EP)	18
57	Capitol EAP 1-639	"TENNESSEE" ERNIE FORD (EP)	12
60	Capitol EAP1 1227	GATHER ROUND (EP)	15
61	Capitol EAP1 20067	ANTICIPATION BLUES (EP)	25

LPs

52	Capitol LC 6573	CAPITOL PRESENTS (10" LP)	40
56	Capitol LC 6825	THIS LUSTY LAND (10" LP)	20
58	Capitol T 888	OL' ROCKIN' ERN (LP)	35
60	Capitol T 1380	SIXTEEN TONS (LP)	30
61	Capitol (S)T 1473	COME TO THE FAIR (LP)	12

(see also Dinning Sisters)

'TENNESSEE' ERNIE FORD & BETTY HUTTON

54	Capitol CL 14133	This Must Be The Place/The Honeymoon's Over (green label)	15

FORD THEATRE

69	Stateside SSL 10288	TIME CHANGES (LP)	15

EDDIE 'BUSTER' FOREHAND

69	Action ACT 4519	Young Boy Blues/You Were Meant For Me	10

FOREIGNER

77	Atlantic K 10986	Cold As Ice/I Need You (ice-coloured clear vinyl, printed PVC sleeve)	5
78	Atlantic K 11167	Hot Blooded/Tramontane (red vinyl, printed PVC sleeve)	5
79	Atlantic K 11236	Blue Morning, Blue Day/I Have Waited So Long (picture disc)	5
81	Atlantic K 11665	Urgent/Girl On The Moon (printed PVC sleeve with sticker insert)	5
81	Atlantic K 11678	Juke Box Hero/I'm Gonna Win (with foldout sleeve)	5
85	Atlantic A 9596	I Want To Know What Love Is/Street Thunder ('F'-shaped picture disc)	6
85	Atlantic A 9539/SAM 247	Cold As Ice/Reaction To Action//Head Games (live)/Hot Blooded (live) (double pack)	5
88	Atlantic A 9101CD	I Don't Want To Live Without You (LP Version)/Face To Face/I Don't Want To Live Without You (7" Mix)/Urgent (LP Version) (3" CD, 5" case)	8

(see also Mick Jones, J&B, State Of Mickey & Tommy, Spooky Tooth)

FORERUNNERS

64	Solar SRP 100	Bony Maronie/Pride	40

JOHN FOREMAN

70s	Reality RY 1004	THE 'OUSES IN BETWEEN (LP)	12

FOREST

69	Harvest HAR 5007	Searching For Shadows/Mirror Of Life	12
69	Harvest SHVL 760	FOREST (LP)	50
70	Harvest SHVL 784	FULL CIRCLE (LP)	80
88	Zap! ZAP 3	FULL CIRCLE (LP, reissue)	12

JIMMY FORREST

54	Vogue V 2282	Flight 3D/Sophisticated Lady (78)	8

FOR(R)ESTERS
65	Polydor 56038	Broken Hearted Clown/Lonely Boy	7
65	Polydor 56057	How Can I Tell Her/So Shy	7
66	Polydor 56104	Early Morning Hours/World Is Mine	7
66	Columbia DB 8040	Sometimes When You're Lonely/Today Or Tomorrow (as Forresters)	6
66	Columbia DB 8086	Mr. Smith/Ship On The Sea (as Foresters)	5
67	Columbia DB 8176	Comin' Home In The Evening/Sunshine's On Its Way (as Foresters)	5

FOREVER AMBER
| 69 | Advance (no cat. no.) | THE LOVE CYCLE (LP, private pressing, 99 copies only) | 1,000 |

FOREVER MORE
70	RCA RCA 2024	Put Your Money On A Pony/Yours	5
70	RCA SF 8016	YOURS FOREVER MORE (LP)	15
71	RCA LSA 3015	WORDS ON BLACK PLASTIC (LP)	15

(see also Scots Of St. James, Hopscotch, Average White Band)

FORGEMASTERS
| 89 | WARP WAP 1 | TRACK WITH NO NAME (12", p/s) | 10 |

FORK IN THE ROAD
| 70 | Ember EMB S 311 | I Can't Turn Around/Skeleton In My Closet | 150 |

FORMAT
| 69 | CBS 4600 | Maxwell's Silver Hammer/Music Man | 5 |

(see also Fourmost)

FORMATIONS
| 68 | MGM MGM 1399 | At The Top Of The Stairs/Magic Melody | 80 |
| 71 | Mojo 2027 001 | At The Top Of The Stairs/Magic Melody (reissue) | 8 |

GEORGE FORMBY
51	HMV B 10179	Pleasure Cruise/Saving Up For Sally (78)	8
52	Decca F 9444	When I'm Cleaning Windows/Leanin' On A Lamppost (78)	8
60	Pye 7N 15269	Banjo Boy/Happy Go Lucky Me	5
55	Decca DFE 6144	GEORGE FORMBY AND HIS UKULELE GUITAR (EP)	8
56	Decca DFE 6328	GEORGE FORMBY AND HIS UKULELE GUITAR, NO. 2 (EP)	8
56	Decca DFE 6355	GEORGE FORMBY AND HIS UKULELE GUITAR, NO. 3 (EP)	8
61	Ace Of Clubs ACL 1062	GEORGE FORMBY SOUVENIR (LP)	12
63	Ace Of Clubs ACL 1145	TURNED OUT NICE AGAIN (LP)	12

FORMERLY FAT HARRY
| 71 | Harvest SHSP 4016 | FORMERLY FAT HARRY (LP) | 15 |

FORMINX
| 65 | Vocalion V 9235 | Jenka Beat/Geronimo Jenka | 25 |

(see also Aphrodite's Child, Vangelis, Demis Roussos)

FORMULA
| 65 | HMV POP 1438 | Close To Me/If Ever | 6 |

FORMULA 1
| 65 | Warner Bros WB 155 | I Just Can't Go To Sleep/Sure Know A Lot About Love | 15 |

ANDY FORRAY
68	Parlophone R 5715	Sarah Jane/Don't Care Anymore	6
68	Parlophone R 5729	The Proud One/Messin' Round With Me	6
68	Decca F 12733	Epitaph To You/Dream With Me	35
69	Fontana TF 999	Let The Sunshine In/Baby Is Coming	5

HELEN FORREST
| 56 | Capitol CL 14594 | Taking A Chance On Love/I Love You Much Too Much | 6 |

JANE FORREST
| 56 | Columbia SCM 5213 | Sincerely Yours/A Girl Can't Say | 6 |

SHARON FORRESTER
| 73 | Ashanti ASH 403 | Silly Wasn't I?/NOW-GEN: Silly Wasn't I? — Version | 8 |

THOMAS FORSTNER
| 89 | Ariola 112 298 | Song Of Love/Nur Ein Lied (p/s, withdrawn) | 5 |
| 89 | Ariola 662 298 | Song Of Love (12" Version)/Nur Ein Lied/Song Of Love (7") (CD, withdrawn) | 8 |

BRUCE FORSYTH
62	Piccadilly 7N 35086	The Oh-Be-Joyfuls/I Like People	5
64	Piccadilly 7N 35189	The Mysterious People/You've Just Found Out	5
65	Pye 7N 15879	Hush Hush Sweet Charlotte/Don't Say Goodbye	5
68	Mercury MF 1047	Star/Do, Do, Do	5
68	Pye 7N 17460	I'm Backing Britain/There's Not Enough Love In The World (p/s)	6
69	Decca F 12940	When You Gotta Go/By The Fireside	5
60	Parlophone GEP 8807	I'M IN CHARGE (EP)	8
60	Parlophone PMC 1132	MR ENTERTAINMENT (LP, also stereo PCS 3031)	12

FORTES MENTUM
68	Parlophone R 5684	Saga Of A Wrinkled Man/Mr. Partridge Passed Away Today	20
68	Parlophone R 5726	I Can't Go On Loving You/Humdiggle We Love You	8
69	Parlophone R 5768	Gotta Go/Marrakesh	8

(see also Angel Pavement, Pussy)

LANCE FORTUNE
60	Pye 7N 15240	Be Mine/Action (with Johnny Prendy, alias John Barry)	7
60	Pye 7N 15240	Be Mine/Action (78, with Johnny Prendy, alias John Barry)	20
60	Pye 7N 15260	All On My Own/This Love I Have For You	7
60	Pye 7N 15297	I Wonder/Will You Still Be My Girl?	8
61	Pye 7N 15347	Who's Gonna Tell Me?/Love Is The Sweetest Thing	8

MINT VALUE £

FORTUNES

63	Decca F 11718	Summertime Summertime/I Love Her Still (as Fortunes & Cliftones) (some in p/s)	30/12
64	Decca F 11809	Caroline/If You Don't Want Me Now	20
64	Decca F 11912	Come On Girl/I Like The Look Of You	8
64	Decca F 11985	Look Homeward Angel/I'll Have My Tears To Remind Me	8
65	Decca F 12173	You've Got Your Troubles/I've Got To Go	5
65	Decca F 12243	Here It Comes Again/Things I Should Have Known	5
66	Decca F 12321	This Golden Ring/Someone To Care	6
66	Decca F 12429	You Gave Me Somebody To Love/Silent Street	7
66	Decca F 12485	Is It Really Worth Your While?/Am I Losing My Touch	8
67	Decca F 12612	Our Love Has Gone/Truly Yours	8
67	United Artists UP 1188	The Idol/His Smile Was A Lie	5
68	United Artists UP 2218	Loving Cup/Hour At The Movies	5
68	United Artists UP 2239	Seasons In The Sun/Louise	5
69	Decca F 12874	Here It Comes Again/Our Love Has Gone	5
69	United Artists UP 35054	Lifetime Of Love/Sad Sad Sad (withdrawn, existence unconfirmed)	
69	United Artists UP 35054	Books And Films/Sad Sad Sad	5
71	Capitol CL 15671	Here Comes That Rainy Day Feeling Again/Bad Side Of Town	5
65	Decca LK/SKL 4736	THE FORTUNES (LP, mono/stereo)	25/50
72	Capitol ST 21891	THE FORTUNES (LP)	12

(see also Glen Dale)

45's

79	Chopper CHEAP 5	Couldn't Believe A Word/Lonesome Lane (p/s)	7
79	Stiff BUY 52	Couldn't Believe A Word/Lonesome Lane (p/s, reissue)	5

48 CHAIRS

79	Absurd ABSURD 3	Snap It Around/Psycle Sluts (p/s)	4

49 AMERICANS

80	No Bad NB 4	THE HIT ALBUM (14-track EP)	6
80	Choo Choo Train CHUG 2	TOO YOUNG TO BE IDEAL (12" EP)	8
80	Choo Choo Train CHUG 1	EL PLURIBUS UNUM (LP)	12

FORUM

67	London HLM 10120	The River Is Wide/I Fall In Love (All Over Again)	7
70	B&C CB 119	The River Is Wide/I Fall In Love (All Over Again) (reissue)	5

SHIRLEY FORWOOD

57	London HLD 8402	Two Hearts (With An Arrow Between)/Juke Box Lovers	25
57	London HLD 8402	Two Hearts (With An Arrow Between)/Juke Box Lovers (78)	6

BOBBY FOSTER

70	Bread BR 1101	Tell Me Why You Say Goodbye/YOUTH: I'll Make Him Believe In You	6

JACKIE FOSTER

63	Planetone RC 13	Oh Leona/I Fell In Love	12

JOHN FOSTER

66	Island ILP 939	JOHN FOSTER SINGS (LP)	25

LARRY FOSTER & SOUL EXPLOSION

70	Fab FAB 130	Boom Biddy Boom/Next To Me (actually by Sugar Simone)	6

(see also Sugar Simone)

LES FOSTER

70	Torpedo TOR 7	Run Like A Thief/Nobody's Fool	6

LES FOSTER & ANSELL COLLINS

73	Camel CA 102	The Man In Your Life/Version	5

(see also Dave & Ansell Collins, Sugar Simone, Lance Hannibal)

LESLIE FOSTER

69	Jolly JY 022	Muriel/Nowhere To Hide	6

VINCENT FOSTER

69	Escort ES 803	Shine Eye Gal/Who Nest (B-side actually "Who Next" by Carl Bryan)	6

FOTHERINGAY

70	Island WIP 6085	Peace In The End/Winter Winds	10
70	Island ILPS 9125	FOTHERINGAY (LP, pink label/'i' logo, gatefold sleeve)	40
70	Island ILPS 9125	FOTHERINGAY (LP, later issue, pink rim label/'palm tree' logo, g/fold sleeve)	18

(see also Sandy Denny, Trevor Lucas, Eclection, Exception[s], Fairport Convention, Jerry Donahue, Mick Greenwood)

MR FOUNDATION

(see under 'M')

FOUNDATIONS

67	Pye 7N 17366	Baby, Now That I've Found You/Come On Back To Me	5
68	Pye 7N 17417	Back On My Feet Again/I Can Take Or Leave Your Loving	5
68	Pye 7N 17503	Any Old Time (You're Lonely And Sad)/We Are Happy People	5
68	Pye 7N 17636	Build Me Up Buttercup/New Direction	5
69	Pye 7N 17702	In The Bad Bad Old Days/Give Me Love	5
69	Pye 7N 17809	Born To Live, Born To Die/Why Did You Cry	5
69	Pye 7N 17849	Baby I Couldn't See/Penny, Sir	5
70	Pye 7N 17904	Take A Girl Like You/I'm Gonna Be A Rich Man	5
70	Pye 7N 17956	I'm Gonna Be A Rich Man/Who Am I?	5
71	MCA MCA 5075	Stoney Ground/I'll Give You Love	7
70s	Summit SU 100	Where Were You When I Needed Your Love/Love Me Nice 'n Easy	5
68	Pye NEP 24297	IT'S ALL RIGHT (EP)	18
67	Pye NPL 18206	FROM THE FOUNDATIONS (LP)	15
68	Pye NPL 18227	ROCKING THE FOUNDATIONS (LP)	15
69	Pye N(S)PL 18290	DIGGING THE FOUNDATIONS (LP)	15

(see also Pluto)

FOUNDATIONS

JAMES FOUNTAIN
76	Cream CRM 5002	Seven Day Lover/Malnutrition	5

PETE FOUNTAIN
60	Coral Q 72389	Do You Know What It Means To Miss New Orleans?/A Closer Walk	5
60	Coral Q 72404	Columbus Stockade Blues/Sentimental Journey	5
60	Coral Q 72404	Columbus Stockade Blues/Sentimental Journey (78)	15
59	Tempo EXA 93	DIXIELAND ALL STARS (EP)	8
71	Xtra XTRA 1120	NEW ORLEANS ALL STARS (LP)	12

(see also Brenda Lee)

THE 4
64	Decca F 11999	It's Alright/There's Nothing Like It	8

FOUR ACES (U.S.)
54	Brunswick 05256	The Gang That Sang "Heart Of My Heart"/Heaven Can Wait	7
54	Brunswick 05308	Three Coins In The Fountain/Wedding Bells (Are Breaking Up This Gang Of Mine)	18
54	Brunswick 05322	It Shall Come To Pass/Dream	6
54	Brunswick 05348	It's A Woman's World/The Cuckoo Bird In The Pickle Tree	8
54	Brunswick 05355	Mister Sandman/(I'll Be With You) In Apple Blossom Time	20
55	Brunswick 05379	Melody Of Love/There Is A Tavern In The Town	8
55	Brunswick 05401	There Goes My Heart/Take Me In Your Arms	6
55	Brunswick 05418	Stranger In Paradise/You'll Always Be The One	15
55	Brunswick 05429	Sluefoot/I'm In The Mood For Love	6
55	Brunswick 05480	Love Is A Many Splendored Thing/Shine On Harvest Moon	15
55	Brunswick 05504	Jingle Bells/The Christmas Song (Merry Christmas To You)	7
56	Brunswick 05562	To Love Again/Charlie Was A Boxer	6
56	Brunswick 05566	The Gal With The Yaller Shoes/Of This I'm Sure	6
56	Brunswick 05573	If You Can Dream/It's The Talk Of The Town	6
56	Brunswick 05589	A Woman In Love/I Only Know I Love You	8
56	Brunswick 05601	Dreamer/Let's Fall In Love	5
56	Brunswick 05613	You Can't Run Away From It/Written On The Wind	5
56	Brunswick 05623	Friendly Persuasion (Thee I Love)/Someone To Love	7
57	Brunswick 05651	Heart/What A Difference A Day Made	6
57	Brunswick 05663	Bahama Mama/You're Mine	6
57	Brunswick 05695	Three Sheets To The Wind/Yes, Sir, That's My Baby	5
57	Brunswick 05712	Half Of My Heart/When My Sugar Walks Down The Street	5
58	Brunswick 05743	Rock And Roll Rhapsody/I Wish I May, I Wish I Might	6
58	Brunswick 05743	Rock And Roll Rhapsody/I Wish I May, I Wish I Might (78)	8
58	Brunswick 05758	Hangin' Up A Horseshoe/Two Arms, Two Lips, One Heart!	6
58	Brunswick 05758	Hangin' Up A Horseshoe/Two Arms, Two Lips, One Heart! (78)	8
58	Brunswick 05767	The World Outside/The Christmas Tree	6
58	Brunswick 05767	The World Outside/The Christmas Tree (78)	10
59	Brunswick 05773	The World Outside/The Inn Of The Sixth Happiness	5
59	Brunswick 05773	The World Outside/The Inn Of The Sixth Happiness (78)	8
59	Brunswick 05812	Waltzin' Matilda/Roses Of Rio	5
59	Brunswick 05812	Waltzin' Matilda/Roses Of Rio (78)	10
50s	Decca A 73010	I'm Yours/I Understand (export issue)	12

54	Brunswick OE 9090	PRESENTING THE FOUR ACES (EP).	10
55	Brunswick OE 9157	MOOD FOR LOVE VOL. 1 (EP)	8
55	Brunswick OE 9192	MOOD FOR LOVE VOL. 2 (EP)	8
57	Brunswick OE 9324	ACES SING FILM TITLES (EP)	10
59	Brunswick OE 9458	THE FOUR ACES (EP)	8
53	Brunswick LA 8614	JUST SQUEEZE ME (10" LP)	25
57	Brunswick LAT 8221	SHUFFLIN' ALONG (LP)	18
58	Brunswick LAT 8249	HITS FROM HOLLYWOOD (LP)	18
59	Brunswick STA 3014	THE SWINGIN' ACES (LP, stereo)	18

(see also Al Alberts)

FOUR ACES (U.K.)

60s	Anton/E.R.S. EAG 178/179	Why Do You/Fortune Teller	
		(private pressing)	250

FOUR ACES (Jamaica)

65	Island WI 178	Hoochy-Koochy-Kai-Po/River Bank Coberly Again.	15
65	Island WI 178	Hoochy-Koochy-Kai-Po/SKATALITES: Sucu Sucu (different B-side)	18
65	Island WI 179	Sweet Chariot/Peace And Love	15
65	Island WI 180	Little Girl/CLARENDONIANS: Day Will Come	15

(see also Desmond Dekker)

4 BE 2's

79	Island WIP 6530	One Of The Lads/Ummbaba (p/s).	4
79	Island 12 WIP 6530	One Of The Lads (Dub)/Ummbaba/One Of The Lads (Vocal) (12", p/s).	7
80	WEA K 18290	Frustration/I Can't Explain (p/s).	4

FOUR COINS

56	Philips PB 615	One Kiss/This I Offer You (78)	8
57	Philips PB 739	Shangri-La/First In Line (78)	8
58	Fontana H 101	My One Sin/A Broken Promise (78)	15
58	Fontana H 168	The World Outside/Be Still My Heart	7
58	Fontana H 168	The World Outside/Be Still My Heart (78)	12

4 DEGREES

65	Oak RGJ 187	4 DEGREES (LP, 1-sided, no sleeve)	400

FOUR DOLLS

57	Capitol CL 14778	Three On A Date/Proud Of You	7
57	Capitol CL 14778	Three On A Date/Proud Of You (78)	8
58	Capitol CL 14845	Whoop-A-Lala/I'm Following You.	7
58	Capitol CL 14845	Whoop-A-Lala/I'm Following You (78)	8

FOUR ESCORTS

54	HMV 7M 277	Loop De Loop Mambo/Love Me	10
54	HMV B 10795	Loop De Loop Mambo/Love Me (78)	10

FOUR ESQUIRES

55	London HL 8152	The Sphinx Won't Tell/Three Things (A Man Must Do)	35
55	London HL 8152	The Sphinx Won't Tell/Three Things (A Man Must Do) (78)	15
56	London HLA 8224	Adorable/Thunderbolt	35
56	London HLA 8224	Adorable/Thunderbolt (78).	15
57	London HL 8376	Look Homeward Angel/Santo Domingo (unreleased)	
57	London HL 8376	Look Homeward Angel/Santo Domingo (78) (unreleased)	
58	London HLO 8533	Love Me Forever/I Ain't Been Right Since You Left	15
58	London HLO 8533	Love Me Forever/I Ain't Been Right Since You Left (78)	10
58	London HLO 8579	Always And Forever/I Walk Down The Street	10
58	London HLO 8579	Always And Forever/I Walk Down The Street (78)	12
58	London HL 8746	Hideaway/Repeat After Me.	8
58	London HL 8746	Hideaway/Repeat After Me (78)	20
59	Pye Intl. 7N 25012	Non E Cosi/Land Of You And Me.	5
59	Pye Intl. N 25012	Non E Cosi/Land Of You And Me (78)	10
59	Pye Intl. 7N 25027	Act Your Age/So Ends The Night	6
59	Pye Intl. N 25027	Act Your Age/So Ends The Night (78)	15
60	Pye Intl. 7N 25049	Wouldn't It Be Wonderful/Wonderful One	6

FOUR FRESHMEN

54	Capitol CL 14196	Love Turns Winter To Spring/Mood Indigo	5
55	Capitol CL 14338	Day By Day/How Can I Tell Her	5
56	Capitol CL 14580	Love Is Just Around The Corner/Angel Eyes	
		(as Four Freshmen & Five Trombones).	5
56	Capitol CL 14580	Love Is Just Around The Corner/Angel Eyes (78).	8
56	Capitol CL 14610	Graduation Day/Lonely Night In Paris.	7
56	Capitol CL 14610	Graduation Day/Lonely Night In Paris (78)	12
56	Capitol CL 14633	You're So Far Above Me/He Who Loves And Runs Away	5
57	Capitol CL 14731	Ev'ry Time We Say Goodbye/Charmaine (78)	8
57	Capitol CL 14780	Sometimes I'm Happy/Julie Is Her Name (78)	8
57	Capitol CL 14810	Granada/How Can I Begin To Tell (78)	10
54	Capitol LC 6685	VOICES IN MODERN (10" LP)	15

FOUR GEES

67	President PT 160	Ethiopia/Rough Rider.	5

FOUR GIBSON GIRLS

58	Oriole CB 1447	No School Tomorrow/June, July And August	12
58	Oriole CB 1447	No School Tomorrow/June, July And August (78).	10
58	Oriole CB 1453	Safety Sue/VARIOUS ARTISTS: Safety Sue.	10
58	Oriole CB 1453	Safety Sue/VARIOUS ARTISTS: Safety Sue (78)	12

FOUR GRADS

57	Conquest CE 1007	THE FOUR GRADS PART 1 (EP)	8
57	Conquest CE 1017	THE FOUR GRADS PART 2 (EP)	8

FOUR GUYS
| 55 | Vogue Coral Q 72054 | Half Hearted Kisses/Mine. | 10 |
(see also Modernaires)

FOUR INSTANTS
| 66 | Society | DISCOTHEQUE (LP) | 15 |

FOUR JACKS
58	Decca F 10984	Hey! Baby/The Prayer Of Love	8
58	Decca F 10984	Hey! Baby/The Prayer Of Love (78)	8
58	Decca DFE 6460	HEY! BABY (EP)	30

FOUR JACKS & A JILL
| 68 | RCA Victor RCA 1669 | Master Jack/I Looked Back | 5 |

FOUR JONES BOYS
55	Decca F 10568	A Real Romance/When I Let You Go	6
55	Decca F 10671	Moments To Remember/Sing-ing-ing-ing	6
56	Decca F 10717	Tutti Frutti/Are You Satisfied?	12
56	Decca F 10717	Tutti Frutti/Are You Satisfied? (78)	10
56	Decca F 10789	Happiness Street (Corner Of Sunshine Square)/Someone To Love	6
56	Decca F 10829	Priscilla/It Isn't Right	6
(see also Jones Boys, Annette Klooger)

FOUR JUST MEN
| 64 | Parlophone R 5186 | That's My Baby/Things Will Never Be The Same | 60 |
(see also Just Four Men, Wimple Winch)

FOUR KENTS
| 68 | RCA RCA 1705 | The Moving Finger Writes/Searchin' | 7 |

FOUR KESTRELS
| 61 | Decca F 11333 | Sound Off/Can't Say I Do | 5 |

FOUR KINSMEN
| 67 | Decca F 22671 | It Looks Like The Daybreak/Forget About Him | 7 |
(see also Kinsmen)

FOUR KNIGHTS
54	Capitol CL 14076	I Get So Lonely/Till Then	20
54	Capitol CL 14154	Easy Street/In The Chapel In The Moonlight	15
54	Capitol CL 14204	I Don't Wanna See You Cryin'/Saw Your Eyes	12
55	Capitol CL 14244	Honey Bunch/Write Me, Baby	25
55	Capitol CL 14244	Honey Bunch/Write Me, Baby (78)	10
55	Capitol CL 14290	Inside Out/Foolishly Yours	10
56	Capitol CL 14516	Guilty/You	8
59	Coral Q 72355	Foolish Tears/O' Falling Star	10
59	Coral Q 72355	Foolish Tears/O' Falling Star (78)	15
55	Capitol EAP1 506	THE FOUR KNIGHTS (EP)	45
53	Capitol LC 6604	SPOTLIGHT SONGS (10" LP)	40
(see also Nat 'King' Cole)

FOUR LADS
55	Philips PB 440	Pledging My Love/I've Been Thinking (78)	8
57	Philips JK 1021	Golly/I Just Don't Know (jukebox issue)	10
57	Philips PB 769	The Eyes Of God/His Invisible Hand (78)	10
58	Philips PB 839	Enchanted Island/Guess What The Neighbours'll Say	5
58	Philips PB 839	Enchanted Island/Guess What The Neighbours'll Say (78)	10
59	Philips PB 894	The Girl On Page 44/The Mocking Bird	5
60	Philips PB 1000	Standing On The Corner/Sunday	6
60	Philips PB 1020	You're Nobody 'Til Somebody Loves You/Goona Goona	5
55	Philips BBE 12044	MOMENTS TO REMEMBER (EP)	10
61	London RE-R 1289	FOUR LADS FOUR HITS (EP)	12
62	London HA-R 2413	DIXIELAND DOIN'S (LP, also stereo SAH-R 6213)	12/15
(see also Johnnie Ray, Frankie Laine, Doris Day)

FOUR LEAVED CLOVER
| 65 | Oak RGJ 207 | Alright Girl/Why | 200 |

FOUR MACS
| 64 | Parlophone R 5204 | Come Back Silly Girl/Darlin' | 5 |
(see also Sands Of Time)

FOUR MATADORS
| 66 | Columbia DB 7806 | A Man's Gotta Stand Tall/Fast Cars And Money | 50 |

FOURMOST
63	Parlophone R 5056	Hello Little Girl/Just In Case	5
63	Parlophone R 5078	I'm In Love/Respectable	5
64	Parlophone R 5128	A Little Loving/Waiting For You	5
64	Parlophone R 5157	How Can I Tell Her/You Got That Way	6
64	Parlophone R 5194	Baby I Need Your Loving/That's Only What They Say	6
65	Parlophone R 5304	Everything In The Garden/He Could Never	7
65	Parlophone R 5379	Girls Girls Girls/Why Do Fools Fall In Love?	6
66	Parlophone R 5491	Here, There And Everywhere/You've Changed	8
66	Parlophone R 5528	Auntie Maggie's Remedy/Turn The Lights Down	10
68	CBS 3814	Apples, Peaches, Pumpkin Pie/He Could Never	10
69	CBS 4041	Rosetta/Just Like Before	18
69	CBS 4461	Easy Squeezy/Do I Love You?	15
72	Phoenix SNIX 126	Goodnight Sweet Dreams/Memphis	5
64	Parlophone GEP 8892	THE SOUND OF THE FOURMOST (EP)	50
64	Parlophone GEP 8917	THE FOURMOST (EP)	60
65	Parlophone PMC 1259	FIRST AND FOURMOST (LP)	75
75	Fourmost SOF 001	THE FOURMOST (LP, private pressing, signed sleeve)	12
(see also Format)

FOURMYULA

69	Columbia DB 8549	Honey Chile/Come With Me	6

FOUR PALMS

58	Vogue V 9116	Jeanie, Joanie, Shirley, Toni/Consideration	400
58	Vogue V 9116	Jeanie, Joanie, Shirley, Toni/Consideration (78)	75

FOUR PENNIES (U.S.)

63	Stateside SS 198	My Block/Dry Your Eyes	22
63	Stateside SS 244	When The Boy's Happy (The Girl's Happy Too)/Hockaday Part 1	18
	(see also Chiffons)		

FOUR PENNIES (U.K.)

63	Philips BF 1296	Do You Want Me To/Miss Bad Daddy	6
64	Philips BF 1322	Tell Me Girl/Juliet	5
64	Philips BF 1322	Juliet/Tell Me Girl (supposedly flipped after original release)	10
64	Philips BF 1349	I Found Out The Hard Way/Don't Tell Me You Love Me	5
64	Philips BF 1366	Black Girl/You Went Away	7
65	Philips BF 1398	The Way Of Love/A Place Where No-One Goes	5
65	Philips BF 1435	Until It's Time For You To Go/Till Another Day	6
66	Philips BF 1469	Trouble Is My Middle Name/Way Out Love	5
66	Philips BF 1491	Keep The Freeway Open/Square Peg	6
66	Philips BF 1519	No Sad Songs For Me/Cats	7
64	Philips BBE 12561	THE FOUR PENNIES (EP)	15
64	Philips BBE 12562	SPIN WITH THE PENNIES (EP)	18
64	Philips BBE 12570	THE SWINGING SIDE OF THE FOUR PENNIES (EP)	18
64	Philips BBE 12571	THE SMOOTH SIDE OF THE FOUR PENNIES (EP)	12
64	Philips BL 7642	TWO SIDES OF THE FOUR PENNIES (LP)	40
66	Philips BL 7734	MIXED BAG (LP)	100
67	Wing WL 1146	JULIET (LP)	25
	(see also Lionel Morton, Fritz Mike & Mo)		

FOUR + ONE

65	Parlophone R 5221	Time Is On My Side/Don't Lie To Me	60
	(see also In Crowd, Tomorrow, Keith West)		

FOUR PREPS

57	Capitol CL 14727	Falling Star/Where Wuz You	5
57	Capitol CL 14727	Falling Star/Where Wuz You (78)	8
57	Capitol CL 14747	I Cried A Million Tears/Moonstruck In Madrid	8
57	Capitol CL 14747	I Cried A Million Tears/Moonstruck In Madrid (78)	8
57	Capitol CL 14768	Again 'n' Again 'n' Again/Promise Me Baby	5
57	Capitol CL 14768	Again 'n' Again 'n' Again/Promise Me Baby (78)	8
57	Capitol CL 14783	Band Of Angels/How About That?	5
57	Capitol CL 14783	Band Of Angels/How About That? (78)	8
58	Capitol CL 14815	26 Miles (Santa Catalina)/Fools Will Be Fools	6
58	Capitol CL 14815	26 Miles (Santa Catalina)/Fools Will Be Fools (78)	8
58	Capitol CL 14873	Big Man/Stop, Baby	5
58	Capitol CL 14873	Big Man/Stop, Baby (78)	8
58	Capitol CL 14914	Lazy Summer Night/Summertime Lies	5
59	Capitol CL 14992	The Riddle Of Love/She Was Five And He Was Ten	5
59	Capitol CL 15032	Cinderella/Gidget	5
59	Capitol CL 15044	The Big Surprise/Try My Arms	5
59	Capitol CL 15065	I Ain't Never/Memories, Memories	5
60	Capitol CL 15110	Listen Honey (I'll Be Home)/Down By The Station	5
60	Capitol CL 15128	Got A Girl/(Wait Till You) Hear It From Me	5
61	Capitol CL 15182	Calcutta/Gone Are The Days	5
61	Capitol CL 15217	More Money For You And Me (Medley)/Swing Down Chariot	5
57	Capitol EAP1 862	DREAMY EYES (EP)	12
58	Capitol EAP1 1015	TWENTY SIX MILES (EP)	12
59	Capitol EAP1 1064	BIG MAN (EP)	12
59	Capitol EAP1 1139	LAZY SUMMER NIGHTS (EP)	10
61	Capitol EAP4 1647	CAMPUS ENCORES (EP)	10
59	Capitol T 1216	DANCING AND DREAMING (LP)	15
61	Capitol T 1291	DOWN BY THE STATION (LP)	15
61	Capitol T 1566	ON THE CAMPUS (LP)	15
61	Capitol (S)T 1647	CAMPUS ENCORE (LP)	15
62	Capitol (S)T 1814	CAMPUS CONFIDENTIAL (LP)	15
63	Capitol (S)T 1976	SONGS FOR A CAMPUS PARTY (LP)	15
64	Capitol (S)T 2169	HOW TO SUCCEED IN LOVE (LP)	15

4 SAXOPHONES IN 12 TONES

56	Vogue V 2355	Fantastic/Frankly Speaking	6

FOUR SEASONS

SINGLES

62	Stateside SS 122	Sherry/I've Cried Before	7
63	Stateside SS 145	Big Girls Don't Cry/Connie-O	7
63	Stateside SS 169	Walk Like A Man/Lucky Ladybug	7
63	Stateside SS 194	Ain't That A Shame/Soon (I'll Be Home Again)	7
63	Stateside SS 216	Candy Girl/Marlena	7
63	Stateside SS 241	Santa Claus Is Coming To Town/Christmas Tears	12
64	Stateside SS 262	Peanuts/Silhouettes	10
64	Philips BF 1317	Dawn (Go Away)/No Surfin' Today	6
64	Philips BF 1334	Ronnie/Born To Wander	6
64	Stateside SS 315	Alone/Long Lonely Nights	8
64	Philips BF 1347	Rag Doll/Silence Is Golden	6
64	Stateside SS 343	Since I Don't Have You/Sincerely	8
65	Philips BF 1364	Save It For Me/Funny Face	6
65	Philips BF 1372	Big Man In Town/Little Angel	6

MINT VALUE £

65	Philips BF 1395	Bye Bye Baby (Baby Goodbye)/Searching Wind	6
65	Philips BF 1411	Toy Soldier/Betrayed	6
65	Philips BF 1420	Girl Come Running/Cry Myself To Sleep	6
65	Philips BF 1439	Let's Hang On!/On Broadway Tonight	5
66	Philips BF 1474	Working My Way Back To You/Too Many Memories	5
66	Philips BF 1493	Opus 17 (Don't Worry 'Bout Me)/Beggar's Parade	6
66	Philips BF 1511	I've Got You Under My Skin/Huggin' My Pillow	7
67	Philips BF 1538	Tell It To The Rain/Show Girl	6
67	Philips BF 1556	Beggin'/Dody	6
67	Philips BF 1584	C'mon Marianne/Let's Ride Again	6
67	Philips BF 1600	Around And Around/WONDER WHO: Lonesome Road	7
67	Philips BF 1621	Watch The Flowers Grow/Raven	7
68	Philips BF 1651	Will You Love Me Tomorrow?/Silhouettes	6
68	Philips BF 1685	Saturday's Father/Goodbye Girl	6
69	Philips BF 1743	Electric Stories/Pity	10
69	Philips BF 1763	Rag Doll/Working My Way Back To You (p/s)	6
71	Philips 6051 018	Rag Doll/Let's Hang On!/I've Got You Under My Skin (maxi-single)	5
71	Warner Bros K 16107	Whatever You Say/Sleeping Man (withdrawn, 300 only)	20

EPs

64	Stateside SE 1011	THE FOUR SEASONS SING (EP)	30
68	Philips MCP 1000	HITS OF THE FOUR SEASONS	
		(cassette EP, in plastic tray, card p/s)	10

LPs

63	Stateside SL 10033	SHERRY AND 11 OTHERS (LP)	30
63	Stateside SL 10042	AIN'T THAT A SHAME (LP)	30
63	Stateside SL 10051	THE FOUR SEASONS' GREETINGS (LP)	30
64	Philips BL 7611	BORN TO WANDER (LP)	18
64	Philips BL 7621	DAWN (GO AWAY) AND 11 OTHER GREAT SONGS (LP)	18
64	Philips BL 7643	RAG DOLL (LP)	15
65	Philips BL 7663	ENTERTAIN YOU (LP)	18
65	Philips (S)BL 7687	SING BIG HITS BY BURT BACHARACH … HAL DAVID … BOB DYLAN (LP)	15
65	Philips BL 7699	WORKING MY WAY BACK TO YOU (LP)	15
66	Philips (S)BL 7719	GOLD VAULT OF HITS (LP)	12
67	Philips (S)BL 7751	SECOND VAULT OF GOLDEN HITS (LP)	12
67	Philips (S)BL 7752	LOOKIN' BACK (LP)	15
67	Philips (S)BL 7753	CHRISTMAS ALBUM (LP)	20
69	Philips (S)BL 7880	THE GENUINE IMITATION LIFE GAZETTE (LP)	12
69	Philips (S)DBL 003	EDIZIONE D'ORO (GOLD EDITION) (2-LP)	15
76	Private Stock DAPS 1001	THE FOUR SEASONS STORY (LP)	12

(see also Frankie Valli, Wonder Who)

FOUR SENSATIONS

| 52 | London L 1137 | Heaven Knows Why/Believing In You (78) | 25 |
| 52 | Melodisc P 216 | Raindrops/When Honeymoon Lane Becomes Memory Lane (78) | 8 |

FOUR SIGHTS

| 64 | Columbia DB 7227 | But I Can Tell/And I Cry | 10 |

4-SKINS

81	Clockwork Fun CF 101	One Law For Them/Brave New World (p/s)	15
81	Secret SHH 125	Yesterday's Heroes/Justice/Get Out Of My Life (p/s)	10
82	Secret SHH 141	Lowlife/Bread Or Blood (p/s)	12
82	Secret SEC 4	THE GOOD, THE BAD AND THE 4-SKINS	
		(LP, with photo inner)	15
83	Syndicate SYN 1	A FISTFUL OF … 4-SKINS (LP)	15
84	Syndicate SYN LP 5	FROM CHAOS TO 1984 (LP)	20

(see also Plastic Gangsters)

FOUR SPICES

| 57 | MGM MGM 944 | Armen's Theme (Yesterday And You)/Fire Engine Boogie | 25 |
| 57 | MGM MGM 944 | Armen's Theme (Yesterday And You)/Fire Engine Boogie (78) | 10 |

FOUR SQUARES

| 64 | Hollick & Taylor HT 1009 | FOUR SQUARES (EP) | 60 |

(see also Pink People)

FOURTEEN (14)

68	Olga OLE 002	Through My Door/Meet Mr. Edgar	8
68	Olga OLE 006	Umbrella/Drizzle (Rain)	10
68	Olga S 051	Easy To Fool/Frosty Stars On A Window Pane	8

14 ICED BEARS

86	Frank COPPOLA 1	Inside/Bluesuit/Cut (hand-printed paper bag sleeve)	12
87	Frank CAPRA 202	Like A Dolphin/Balloon Song/Train Song/Lie To Choose (12", p/s)	10
87	Penetration	Balloon Song (flexidisc)	8
87	Penetration 001	Lie To Choose/SPLENDOUR IN THE GRASS: Twist Me (flexidisc)	6
88	Sarah SARAH 005	Come Get Me/Unhappy Days/Sure To See (poster p/s)	12
89	Thunderball 7TBL 2	Mother Sleep (7", unreleased, Mayking test pressings only)	25
90s	Thunderball Surfacer 002	Falling Backwards/World I Love/CROCODILE RIDE: Ex-Hipster/Satellite	
		(Speed Mix) (numbered & stickered mailer, 1,000 only)	8

FOUR TONES

| 58 | Decca F 11074 | Voom Ba Voom/Rickshaw Boy | 12 |
| 58 | Decca F 11074 | Voom Ba Voom/Rickshaw Boy (78) | 8 |

FOUR TOPHATTERS

55	London HLA 8163	Leave-a My Gal Alone/Go Baby Go	250
55	London HLA 8163	Leave-a My Gal Alone/Go Baby Go (78)	30
55	London HLA 8198	Forty Five Men In A Telephone Booth/Wild Rosie	250
55	London HLA 8198	Forty Five Men In A Telephone Booth/Wild Rosie (78)	30

FOUR TOPS

FOUR TOPS

SINGLES

64	Stateside SS 336	Baby I Need Your Lovin'/Call On Me	25
65	Stateside SS 371	Without The One You Love (Life's Not Worthwhile)/Love Has Gone	30
65	Tamla Motown TMG 507	Ask The Lonely/Where Did You Go?	35
65	Tamla Motown TMG 515	I Can't Help Myself/Sad Souvenirs	10
65	Tamla Motown TMG 528	It's The Same Old Song/Your Love Is Amazing	15
65	Tamla Motown TMG 542	Something About You/Darling I Hum Our Song	12
66	Tamla Motown TMG 553	Shake Me, Wake Me (When It's Over)/Just As Long As You Need Me	20
66	Tamla Motown TMG 568	Loving You Is Sweeter Than Ever/I Like Everything About You	10
66	Tamla Motown TMG 579	Reach Out, I'll Be There/Until You Love Someone (small print, later large)	8/5
67	Tamla Motown TMG 589	Standing In The Shadows Of Love/Since You've Been Gone (small print, later large)	10/5
67	Tamla Motown TMG 601	Bernadette/I Got A Feeling	6
67	Tamla Motown TMG 612	Seven Rooms Of Gloom/I'll Turn To Stone	8
67	Tamla Motown TMG 623	You Keep Running Away/If You Don't Want My Love	7
67	Tamla Motown TMG 634	Walk Away Renee/Mame	6
68	Tamla Motown TMG 647	If I Were A Carpenter/Your Love Is Wonderful	6
68	Tamla Motown TMG 665	Yesterday's Dreams/For Once In My Life	6
68	Tamla Motown TMG 675	I'm In A Different World/Remember When	6
69	Tamla Motown TMG 698	What Is A Man?/Don't Bring Back Memories	7
69	Tamla Motown TMG 710	Do What You Gotta Do/Can't Seem To Get You Out Of My Mind	8
70	Tamla Motown TMG 736	It's All In The Game/Love (Is The Answer)	6
70	Tamla Motown TMG 752	Still Water (Love)/Still Water (Peace)	6
71	Tamla Motown TMG 770	Just Seven Numbers (Can Straighten Out My Life)/I Wish I Were Your Mirror	6
71	Tamla Motown TMG 785	Simple Game/You Stole My Love	5
72	Tamla Motown TMG 803	Bernadette/I Got A Feeling/It's The Same Old Song	5
72	Tamla Motown TMG 829	I'll Turn To Stone/Love Feels Like Fire	5
72	Probe PRO 575	Keeper Of The Castle/Jubilee With Soul	5
73	Probe PRO 596	Are You Man Enough/Peace Of Mind	6
75	ABC ABC 4057	Seven Lonely Nights/I Can't Hold On Much Longer	5

EPs

66	Tamla Motown TME 2012	THE FOUR TOPS (EP)	18
67	Tamla Motown TME 2018	FOUR TOP HITS (EP)	15

LPs

65	Tamla Motown TML 11010	THE FOUR TOPS (LP)	40
66	T. Motown (S)TML 11021	SECOND ALBUM (LP, mono/stereo)	25/30
66	T. Motown (S)TML 11037	FOUR TOPS ON TOP (LP, mono/stereo)	22/25
67	T. Motown (S)TML 11041	FOUR TOPS LIVE! (LP, mono/stereo)	22/25
67	T. Motown (S)TML 11056	REACH OUT (LP)	18
68	T. Motown (S)TML 11061	FOUR TOPS GREATEST HITS (LP)	15
69	T. Motown (S)TML 11087	YESTERDAY'S DREAMS (LP)	15
69	T. Motown (S)TML 11113	FOUR TOPS NOW (LP)	15
70	T. Motown (S)TML 11138	SOUL SPIN (LP, mono/stereo)	15/12
70	Tamla Motown STML 11149	STILL WATERS RUN DEEP (LP)	12
71	Tamla Motown STML 11173	CHANGING TIMES (LP)	15
71	Tamla Motown STML 11195	GREATEST HITS VOL. 2 (LP)	15
72	Tamla Motown STML 11206	NATURE PLANNED IT (LP)	12
73	Probe SPB 1064	KEEPER OF THE CASTLE (LP)	15
73	Probe SPB 1077	SHAFT IN AFRICA (LP, soundtrack, with Johnny Pate)	20
73	Probe SPBA 6277	MAIN STREET PEOPLE (LP)	12
74	Probe SPBA 6283	MEETING OF THE MINDS (LP)	12
74	ABC ABCL 5035	SHAFT IN AFRICA (LP, soundtrack, reissue)	15
74	ABC ABCL 5062	LIVE AND IN CONCERT (LP)	12
75	ABC ABCL 5132	NIGHT LIGHTS HARMONY (LP)	12

(see also Supremes & Four Tops)

FOUR TUNES

54	London L 1231	I Gambled With Love/Marie (78)	70
54	London HL 8050	Do, Do, Do, Do, Do Do It Again/My Wild Irish Rose (78)	20
55	London HL 8151	I Sold My Heart To A Junkman/The Greatest Feeling In The World	100
55	London HL 8151	I Sold My Heart To A Junkman/The Greatest Feeling In The World (78)	30
55	London HLJ 8164	Tired Of Waitin'/L'Amour, Toujours L'Amour (Love Everlasting)	40
55	London HLJ 8164	Tired Of Waitin'/L'Amour, Toujours L'Amour (Love Everlasting) (78)	25

FOUR VOICES

56	Philips PB 591	Geronimo/Lovely One (78)	8
58	Philips PB 864	Tell Me You're Mine/Tight Spot	5
58	Philips PB 864	Tell Me You're Mine/Tight Spot (78)	12

FOUR WINDS

58	London HLU 8556	Short Shorts/Five Minutes More	35
58	London HLU 8556	Short Shorts/Five Minutes More (78)	25

KIM FOWLEY

66	Parlophone R 5521	Lights/Something New And Different	15
66	CBS 202243	They're Coming To Take Me Away Ha-Haaa!!/You Get More For Your Money On The Flip Side Of This Record Talking Blues	8
66	CBS 202338	Lights (The Blind Can See)/Something New And Different (reissue)	10
66	Island WI 278	The Trip/Beautiful People	10
72	Action ACT 4606	Born To Make You Cry/Thunder Road	6
73	Capitol CL 15743	International Heroes/E.S.P. Reader	5
78	Mercury 6005 009	Control/Rubber Rainbow	5
79	Illegal ILS 012	Rubber Rainbow/In My Garage (p/s)	5
80	Island WIP 6555	1989: Waiting For The Next Ten Years/1987: Lost Like A Lizard In Snow	5
73	Capitol E-ST 11159	INTERNATIONAL HEROES (LP)	12

(see also Freaks Of Nature, Hollywood Argyles, Napoleon XIV, B. Bumble & Stingers)

FOX

68	CBS 3381	Mister Carpenter/Seek And You Find	45

(see also Top Topham, Dave Mason)

FOX

70	Fontana 6007 016	Second Hand Love/Butterfly	25
70	Fontana 6309 007	FOR FOX SAKE (LP)	60

FOX

75	GTO GTLP 006	TAILS OF ILLUSION (LP)	12
77	GTO GTLP 020	BLUE HOTEL (LP)	12

(see also Wooden Horse, Demick & Armstrong)

DON FOX

57	Decca F 10927	Be My Girl/You'll Never Go To Heaven	7
57	Decca F 10955	The Majesty Of Love/Party Time	7
58	Decca F 10983	Pretend You Don't See Her/Wasteland	7
58	Decca F 11057	She Was Only Seventeen/When You're A Long, Long Way Away	8
58	Decca F 11057	She Was Only Seventeen/When You're A Long, Long Way Away (78)	8
60	Triumph RGM 1022	T'ain't What You Do/Out There	35
61	Oriole CB 1643	Don't Fool With Love/If You Go	6
60s	Honey Hit TB 125	Three Swinging Clicks/I Found The Girl I Love In My Home Town (some in p/s)	10/5

SAMANTHA FOX

84	Lamborghini LMG 10	Aim To Win/17 And Holding (p/s)	5
84	Lamborghini LMG 10	Aim To Win/17 And Holding (12", p/s)	8
84	Lamborghini LMG 10	Aim To Win/17 And Holding (12", picture disc)	12
86	Jive FOXYP 5	Nothing's Gonna Stop Me Now/Dream City (picture disc)	5
87	Jive FOXY CD 8	True Devotion/Even In The Darkest Hours/Fox Hunt Mix featuring "I Surrender (To The Spirit Of The Night)"/Touch Me (I Want Your Body)/ Nothing's Gonna Stop Me Now (CD)	10
88	Jive FOXY CD 9	Naughty Girls (Need Love Too) (Special Extended Version)/ (Instrumental Edit)/Dream City (CD, picture disc)	10
89	Jive FOXY CD 11	I Only Wanna Be With You/Nothing's Gonna Stop Me Now/I Only Wanna Be With You (Extended Version)/Confession (CD, in circular tin)	10
89	Jive FOXY CD 12	I Wanna Have Some Fun (7" Version)/Lovin' Don't Grow On Trees/I Wanna Have Some Fun (Have Some Fun Mix)/Out Of Our Hands (CD, in tin)	10
88	Jive HIPR 39	TOUCH ME (LP, picture disc)	12

(see also David Cassidy)

BRUCE FOXTON

86	Harvest HAR 5239	Play This Game To Win/Welcome To The Hero (p/s)	5

(see also Jam)

FOXX

71	MCA MUPS 419	REVOLT OF EMILY YOUNG (LP)	12

INEZ FOXX

63	Sue WI 301	Mockingbird/He's The One You Love (actually by Inez & Charlie Foxx)	15
64	Sue WI 304	Jaybirds/Broken-Hearted Fool (actually by Inez & Charlie Foxx)	18
64	Sue WI 314	Ask Me/Hi Diddle Diddle (actually by Inez & Charlie Foxx)	18
64	Sue WI 323	Hurt By Love/Confusion (actually by Inez & Charlie Foxx)	18
71	Pye International 7N 25546	You Shouldn't Have Set My Soul On Fire/Live For Today	6
73	Stax 2025 151	You Hurt Me For The Last Time/Watch The Dog (That Brings The Bone)	6

INEZ & CHARLIE FOXX

64	Sue WI 307	Competition/Here We Go Round The Mulberry Bush (as Charlie & Inez Foxx)	18
64	Sue WI 356	La De Da I Love You/Yankee Doodle Dandy	18
65	London HLC 9971	My Momma Told Me/I Feel Alright	8
65	London HLC 10009	Hummingbird/If I Need Anyone (Let It Be You)	7
66	Stateside SS 556	Come By Here/No Stranger To Love	15
67	Stateside SS 586	Tightrope/My Special Prayer	18
67	Direction 58-2712	I Ain't Goin' For That/Undecided	6
67	Direction 58-3192	(1, 2, 3, 4, 5, 6, 7) Count The Days/A Stranger I Don't Know	6
68	Direction 58-3816	Come On In/Baby Drop Your Dime	6
69	Direction 58-4042	Baby Give It To Me/You Fixed My Heartache	6
69	London HLC 10250	Mockingbird/Hummingbird (unissued)	
69	United Artists UP 2269	Mockingbird/Hurt By Love	5
69	United Artists UP 35013	La De Da I Love You/Don't Do It No More	6
71	Pye International 7N 25561	Tightrope/Baby Take It All	6
64	Sue ILP 911	MOCKINGBIRD (LP)	60
65	London HA-C 8241	INEZ AND CHARLIE FOXX (LP, plum label, later black)	40/30
68	Direction 8-63085	COME BY HERE (LP)	18
68	Direction 8-63281	GREATEST HITS (LP)	18
69	United Artists UA(S) 29025	MOCKINGBIRD (LP)	15
71	Pye PKL 4406	GREATEST HITS (LP)	12

JOHN FOXX

80	Island Music/Smash Hits	My Face (yellow vinyl 1-sided flexidisc free with *Smash Hits* magazine)	10/5
80	Virgin VS 338	No-One Driving/Glimmer//This City/Mr. No (double pack, gatefold p/s)	6
80	Virgin VS 338	No-One Driving (2.53 DJ Version)/Glimmer//This City/Mr. No (double pack, stickered gatefold p/s, matrix no. VS 338 A5DJ)	15
80	Virgin VS 360	Burning Car/20th Century (picture disc)	5
82	Virgin VS 543	Endlessly/Ghosts On Water//Dance With Me/A Kind Of Love (double pack)	5
82	Virgin VSY 543	Endlessly/Young Man (picture disc)	5
84	Virgin VS 615	Your Dress/Woman On A Stairway//Lifting Sky/Annexe (double pack)	5
84	Virgin VSP 645	Like A Miracle/Wings And A Wind (shaped picture disc)	8
85	Virgin VS 771	The Stars On Fire/What Kind Of Girl (p/s, with bonus single)	5
87	Virgin CDV 2355	IN MYSTERIOUS WAYS (CD)	20

(see also Ultravox)

MINT VALUE £

FRABJOY & RUNCIBLE SPOON
69	Marmalade 598 019	I'm Beside Myself/Animal Song	12

(see also Godley & Creme, Doctor Father, Hotlegs, Mockingbirds, 10cc)

FRAME
66	RCA RCA 1556	My Feet Don't Fit In His Shoes/She	10
67	RCA RCA 1571	Doctor Doctor/I Can't Go On	45
70	Pye 7N 45213	Rockin' Machine/One More Time	5

FRAMES
79	Brain Booster BBC 2	False Accusations/69 (p/s)	4

PETER FRAMPTON
72	A&M AMS 7025	It's A Plain Shame/Oh For Another Day	5
75	A&M AMS 7174	Show Me The Way/Crying Clown	5
81	A&M AMS 8154	Breaking All The Rules/Night Town (p/s)	7
85	Virgin VSS 827	Lying/You Know So Well (shaped disc)	7
72	A&M AMLS 68099	WIND OF CHANGE (LP)	12
74	A&M AMLH 6369	SOMETHING'S HAPPENING (LP)	12
75	A&M AMLH 64512	FRAMPTON (LP)	12

(see also Preachers, Herd, Humble Pie, Frampton's Camel, Moon's Train)

FRAMPTON'S CAMEL
73	A&M AMS 7069	All Night Long/Don't Fade Away	5
73	A&M AMLH 68150	FRAMPTON'S CAMEL (LP, with poster)	12

(see also Peter Frampton, Parrish & Gurvitz)

PETER FRANC
73	Dawn DNS 1033	I'll Move Along/Song For Every Season	5
73	Dawn DNS 1039	Ballad Of the Superstar/Strange Kind Of Woman	5
74	Dawn DNS 1088	Flag Of Convenience/At Home With You	5
73	Dawn DNLS 3043	PROFILE (LP)	12
73	Dawn DNLS 3051	EN ROUTE (LP)	12

FRANCIS
67	Blue Beat BB 379	Warn The People (actually by Willie Francis)/SWINGERS: Simpleton (actually by Peter Tosh & Crackers)	40
72	Fab FAB 182	Rocking Machine/SOUL CLANS: Flying Rhythm	8
73	Fab FAB 251	Locks/Version	8

B. FRANCIS
65	Ska Beat JB 193	Judy Crowned/Who Crunch	12

BOBBY FRANCIS
67	Doctor Bird DB 1153	Chain Gang/Venus	12

(see also Winston Francis)

CLAIRE FRANCIS
66	Polydor 56079	I've Got My Own Thing Going/Here I Go Again	7
67	Polydor 56142	But I Don't Care/If You Don't Know	7

CONNIE FRANCIS
78s
56	MGM MGM 902	My First Real Love (with Jaybirds)/Believe In Me (Crede Mi) (78)	60
56	MGM MGM 932	My Sailor Boy/Everyone Needs Someone (78)	20
57	MGM MGM 945	Little Blue Wren/I Never Had A Sweetheart (78)	40
57	MGM MGM 962	Eighteen/Faded Orchid (78)	35
58	MGM MGM 975	Who's Sorry Now?/You Were Only Fooling (While I Was Falling In Love) (78)	8
58	MGM MGM 982	I'm Sorry I Made You Cry/Lock Up Your Heart (78)	8
58	MGM MGM 985	Carolina Moon/Stupid Cupid (78)	10
58	MGM MGM 993	I'll Get By/Fallin' (78)	10
58	MGM MGM 998	You Always Hurt The One You Love/In The Valley Of Love (78)	10
59	MGM MGM 1001	My Happiness/Happy Days And Lonely Nights (78)	15
59	MGM MGM 1012	If I Didn't Care/Toward The End Of The Day (78)	30
59	MGM MGM 1018	Lipstick On Your Collar/Frankie (78)	40
59	MGM MGM 1036	Plenty Good Lovin'/You're Gonna Miss Me (78)	40
59	MGM MGM 1046	Among My Souvenirs/Do You Love Me Like You Kiss Me? (78)	50

SINGLES
56	MGM SP 1169	My First Real Love (with Jaybirds)/Believe In Me (Crede Mi)	175
56	MGM MGM 932	My Sailor Boy/Everyone Needs Someone	75
57	MGM MGM 945	Little Blue Wren/I Never Had A Sweetheart	50
57	MGM MGM 962	Eighteen/Faded Orchid	50
58	MGM MGM 975	Who's Sorry Now?/You Were Only Fooling (While I Was Falling In Love)	5
58	MGM MGM 982	I'm Sorry I Made You Cry/Lock Up Your Heart	5
58	MGM MGM 985	Carolina Moon/Stupid Cupid	5
58	MGM MGM 993	I'll Get By/Fallin'	6
58	MGM MGM 998	You Always Hurt The One You Love/In The Valley Of Love	6
59	MGM MGM 1001	My Happiness/Happy Days And Lonely Nights	5
59	MGM MGM 1012	If I Didn't Care/Toward The End Of The Day	6
59	MGM MGM 1018	Lipstick On Your Collar/Frankie	5
59	MGM MGM 1036	Plenty Good Lovin'/You're Gonna Miss Me	6
59	MGM MGM 1046	Among My Souvenirs/Do You Love Me Like You Kiss Me?	5
60	MGM MGM 1060	Valentino/It Would Be Worth It	6
60	MGM MGM 1070	Mama/Teddy (withdrawn; demos more common, £30)	40
60	MGM MGM 1076	Mama/Robot Man	5
60	MGM MGM 1086	Everybody's Somebody's Fool/Jealous Of You	5
60	MGM MGM 1100	My Heart Has A Mind Of Its Own/Malaguena	5
60	MGM MGM 1111	Many Tears Ago/Senza Mama (With No-One)	5
61	MGM MGM 1121	Where The Boys Are/Baby Roo	5

MINT VALUE £

61	MGM MGM 1136	Breakin' In A Brand New Broken Heart/Someone Else's Boy	5
61	MGM MGM 1138	Together/Too Many Rules	5
61	MGM MGM 1145	Baby's First Christmas/I'm Falling In Love With You Tonight	5
62	MGM MGM 1151	Don't Cry On My Shoulder/Mr. Twister	7
62	MGM MGM 1157	Don't Break The Heart That Loves You/Ain't That Better Baby?	6
62	MGM MGM 1165	Vacation/It's Gonna Take Me Some Time	6
62	MGM MGM 1171	Playin' Games/I Was Such A Fool	7
62	MGM MGM 1185	I'm Gonna Be Warm This Winter/Pretty Little Baby	6
62	MGM MGM 1193	Follow The Boys/Tonight's My Night	6
63	MGM MGM 1202	If My Pillow Could Talk/Lollipop Lips	6
63	MGM MGM 1207	Drownin' My Sorrows/Look At Him	6
63	MGM MGM 1212	Your Other Love/Whatever Happened To Rosemary	6
63	MGM MGM 1220	The Summer Of His Years/My Buddy	6
63	MGM MGM 1224	Blue Winter/Souvenirs	6
63	MGM MGM 1236	Be Anything (But Be Mine)/Tommy	6
64	MGM MGM 1253	Don't Ever Leave Me/Waiting For You	6
65	MGM MGM 1265	Forget Domani/I Don't Want To Be No Better Off	12
65	MGM MGM 1271	My Child/No One Ever Sends Me Roses	5
65	MGM MGM 1282	Roundabout/Love Is Me, Love Is You	7
66	MGM MGM 1293	Jealous Heart/Can I Rely On You?	6
66	MGM MGM 1295	The Phoenix Love Theme — Senza Fine/Bossa Nova Hand Dance	6
66	MGM MGM 1305	Love Is Me, Love Is You/I'd Let You Break My Heart All Over Again	6
66	MGM MGM 1320	Somewhere My Love (Lara's Theme)/Letter From A Soldier (Dear Mama)	6
66	MGM MGM 1327	Spanish Nights And You/Games That Lovers Play	6
67	MGM MGM 1334	Another Page/Souvenir D'Italie	6
67	MGM MGM 1336	Time Alone Will Tell/Born Free	6
67	MGM MGM 1347	My Heart Cries For You/If My Friends Could See Me Now (Medley)	6
68	MGM MGM 1381	My World Is Slipping Away/Till We're Together	6
68	MGM MGM 1407	Why Say Goodbye?/Addio Mi Amore	6
68	MGM MGM 1446	Somebody Else Is Taking My Place/Brother Can You Spare A Dime?	6
69	MGM MGM 1471	The Wedding Cake/Overhill Underground	10
69	MGM MGM 1483	Who's Sorry Now?/Vacation	8
69	MGM MGM 1493	Mr. Love/Zingara	7
71	MGM 2006 052	Lipstick On Your Collar/Who's Sorry Now?/Robot Man	5
73	MGM 2006 221	Lipstick On Your Collar/Frankie	5
73	GSF GSZ 10	The Answer/Paint The Rain	5
75	MGM 1110 004	Who's Sorry Now?/Mama	5
75	MGM 1110 005	Stupid Cupid/Carolina Moon	5
78	Polydor 2066 881	Burning Bridges/Let's Go Where The Good Times Go	5
78	United Artists UP 36430	Where The Boys Are/A-Ba-Ni-Bi	5
78	United Artists UP 26463	My Mother's Eyes/Lovin' Man	5
79	Polydor POSP 75	Three Good Reasons/What's Wrong With My World?	5

EPs

56	MGM MGM-EP 658	A GIRL IN LOVE (EP)	25
58	MGM MGM-EP 677	HEARTACHES (EP)	15
58	MGM MGM-EP 686	CONNIE FRANCIS (EP)	25
59	MGM MGM-EP 697	IF I DIDN'T CARE (EP)	20
60	MGM MGM-EP 711	YOU'RE MY EVERYTHING (EP)	25
60	MGM MGM-EP 717	ROCK AND ROLL MILLION SELLERS NO. 1 (EP)	25
60	MGM MGM-EP 720	ROCK AND ROLL MILLION SELLERS NO. 2 (EP)	25
60	MGM MGM-EP 731	ROCK AND ROLL MILLION SELLERS NO. 3 (EP)	20
60	MGM MGM-EP 742	FIRST LADY OF RECORD (EP, laminated or matt rear sleeve)	18
61	MGM MGM-EP 756	WHERE THE BOYS ARE (EP)	22
61	MGM MGM-EP 759	CONNIE FRANCIS FAVOURITES (EP)	25
61	MGM MGM-EP 760	SINGS ITALIAN FAVOURITES (EP)	25
63	MGM MGM-EP 769	CONNIE'S AMERICAN HITS (EP)	25
63	MGM MGM-EP 773	HEY RING-A-DING (EP)	25
63	MGM MGM-EP 775	WHAT KIND OF FOOL AM I? (EP)	25
63	MGM MGM-EP 780	MALA FEMMENA (EP)	25
63	MGM MGM-EP 783	FROM ITALY ... WITH LOVE (EP)	25
65	MGM MGM-EP 789	SINGS FOR MAMA (EP)	25
66	MGM MGM-EP 792	JEALOUS HEART (EP)	25

LPs

58	MGM MGM-D 153	WHO'S SORRY NOW? (10" LP)	60
59	MGM MGM-C 782	MY THANKS TO YOU (LP)	25
59	MGM MGM-C 786	THE EXCITING CONNIE FRANCIS (LP)	20
59	MGM MGM-C 797	CHRISTMAS WITH CONNIE (LP)	35
60	MGM MGM-C 804	ROCK AND ROLL MILLION SELLERS NO. 1 (LP)	30
60	MGM MGM-C 812	COUNTRY AND WESTERN GOLDEN HITS (LP)	30
60	MGM MGM-C 819	FUN SONGS FOR CHILDREN (LP)	50
60	MGM MGM-C 821	SINGS ITALIAN FAVOURITES (LP, also stereo CS 6002)	18/22
60	MGM MGM-C 831	CONNIE'S GREATEST HITS (LP)	15
60	MGM MGM-C 836	SPANISH AND LATIN AMERICAN FAVOURITES (LP, also stereo CS 6012)	15/20
61	MGM MGM-C 845	SINGS JEWISH FAVOURITES (LP, also stereo CS 6021)	15/20
61	MGM MGM-C 854	MORE ITALIAN FAVOURITES (LP, also stereo CS 6029)	15/20
61	MGM MGM-C 861	AT THE COPA (LP, also stereo CS 6035)	15/20
61	MGM MGM-C 870	SONGS TO A SWINGIN' BAND (LP, also stereo CS 6044)	15/20
61	MGM MGM-C 875	SINGS 'NEVER ON SUNDAY' AND OTHER TITLE SONGS FROM MOTION PICTURES (LP, also stereo CS 6047)	15/20
61	MGM MGM-C 879	DO THE TWIST (LP)	35
62	MGM MGM-C 883	SINGS FOLK SONG FAVOURITES (LP, also stereo CS 6054)	15/20
62	MGM MGM-C 898	SINGS IRISH FAVOURITES (LP, also stereo CS 6056)	25/30
62	MGM MGM-C 916	COUNTRY MUSIC CONNIE STYLE (LP, also stereo CS 6062)	20/25
63	MGM MGM-C 930	MODERN ITALIAN HITS (LP, also stereo CS 6067)	15/20
63	MGM MGM-C 931	FOLLOW THE BOYS (LP, also stereo CS 6068)	15/20
63	MGM MGM-C 940	SINGS AWARD-WINNING MOTION PICTURE HITS (LP, stereo CS 6070)	15/20

Connie FRANCIS

64	MGM MGM-C 958	GREATEST AMERICAN WALTZES (LP, also stereo CS 6075)	15/20
64	MGM MGM-C 970	16 OF CONNIE'S BIGGEST HITS (LP)	15
65	MGM MGM-C 983	LOOKING FOR LOVE (LP, also stereo CS 6079)	18
65	MGM MGM-C 998	A NEW KIND OF CONNIE... (LP, also stereo CS 6080)	15
65	MGM MGM-C 1003	SINGS GREAT COUNTRY FAVOURITES (LP, with Hank Williams Jnr, also stereo CS 6081)	18/20
65	MGM MGM-C 1006	SINGS 'FOR MAMA' (LP, also stereo CS 6082)	18/20
65	MGM MGM-C 1012	SINGS THE ALL-TIME INTERNATIONAL HITS (LP, also stereo CS 6083)	15/18
66	MGM MGM-C(S) 8006	WHEN THE BOYS MEET THE GIRLS (LP, soundtrack, mono/stereo)	15/18
66	MGM MGM-C(S) 8009	JEALOUS HEART (LP)	18
66	MGM MGM-C(S) 8027	MOVIE GREATS OF THE SIXTIES (LP)	18
66	MGM MGM-C(S) 8036	LIVE AT THE SAHARA IN LAS VEGAS (LP)	18
66	World Record Club TP 618	MY THANKS TO YOU (LP)	12
67	MGM MGM-C 8041	THE BEST OF CONNIE FRANCIS (LP)	15
68	MGM MGM-C(S) 8050	LOVE ITALIAN STYLE (LP, mono/stereo)	15/18
68	MGM MGM-C(S) 8054	MY HEART CRIES FOR YOU (LP, mono/stereo)	15/18
68	MGM MGM-C(S) 8086	CONNIE AND CLYDE (LP)	18
69	MGM MGM-C(S) 8110	HAWAII CONNIE (LP)	35
70	MGM MGM-CS 8117	SINGS THE SONGS OF LES REED (LP)	18
73	MGM 2353 072	GREAT SONGS OF THE SIXTIES (LP)	12
74	MGM ACB 00143	SINGS GREAT COUNTRY HITS (LP, Audio Club Of Great Britain issue)	12
75	MGM ACB 00167	SINGS GREAT COUNTRY HITS VOL. 2 (LP, Audio Club Of G.B. issue)	15
76	MGM ACB 00195	THE SPECIAL MAGIC OF CONNIE FRANCIS (LP, Audio Club Of G.B. issue)	12
77	Polydor 2391 290	20 ALL TIME GREATS (LP, 2 different label designs)	each 12
78	United Artists ULP 30182	WHO'S HAPPY NOW? (LP, withdrawn sleeve with different lettering)	150
78	United Artists ULP 30182	WHO'S HAPPY NOW? (LP)	12
81	R/Digest GBCF-A-106	THE BEST OF CONNIE FRANCIS (4-LP)	30

CONNIE FRANCIS & MARVIN RAINWATER

58	MGM MGM 969	The Majesty Of Love/You My Darling You	35
58	MGM MGM 969	The Majesty Of Love/You My Darling You (78)	30

(see also Marvin Rainwater)

(KING) JOE FRANCIS

65	Blue Beat BB 323	Wicked Woman/King Joe's Ska (as King Joe Francis)	10
66	Ska Beat JB 262	Scarborough Ska/I Got A Scar (as Joe Francis & Ricky Logan & Snowballs)	10
66	Rio R 90	Have My Body (song actually "Have Mercy Baby")/Everybody's Got To Know (as King Joe Francis & Hijackers)	8
67	Rainbow RAI 114	My Granny/Pull It Out (as J. Francis & Rico's Boys)	8

JOHNNIE FRANCIS

55	Decca F 10440	Funny Thing/Give Me The Right	6

LEE FRANCIS

65	Decca F 12148	Ciao/If He Wants Me	6

(see also Vernons Girls)

NAT FRANCIS

66	Blue Beat BB 346	Mama Kiss Him Goodnight/Tra La La (with Prince Buster Junior & Sunsets)	15
66	Blue Beat BB 361	Just To Keep You (credited to B. Junior)/You Only Want My Money	12
67	Blue Beat BB 376	Seven Nights Of Love/Feeling Blue	12

RITCHIE FRANCIS

72	Pegasus PEG 11	SONGBIRD (LP)	18

(see also Eyes Of Blue, Big Sleep)

STEVE FRANCIS

64	King KG 1012	Watch Your Step/Lovey Dovey	5

WILBERT FRANCIS & VIBRATORS

66	Ska Beat JB 267	Memories Of You/CHUCK JACQUES: Now That You're Gone	15

(see also Little Willie, Vibrators [Jamaica])

WILLIE FRANCIS

69	Bullet BU 415	Motherless Children/I Am Not Afraid	6
71	Escort ERT 848	Burn Them/Poor Boy	6
71	Pama PM 829	Oh What A Mini/Version	5

(see also Martin Riley)

WINSTON FRANCIS

69	Coxsone CS 7089	Reggae And Cry/FREEDOM SINGERS: Easy Come Easy Go (B-side actually by Righteous Flames)	18
69	Studio One SO 2086	The Games People Play/ALBERT GRIFFITHS: The Kicks	18
69	Punch PH 5	Too Experienced/JACKIE MINTO: Mule Jerk (B-side actually by Jackie Mittoo)	8
69	Bamboo BAM 10	The Same Old Song/SOUND DIMENSION: Rattle On	8
70	Bamboo BAM 46	Turn Back The Hands Of Time/Soul Bowl	20
70	Bamboo BAM 48	California Dreaming/JACKIE MITTOO & SOUND DIMENSION: Soul Stew	20
72	Camel CA 99	Ten Times Sweeter Than You/Fat Boy	5
73	Fab FAB 271	Mr Fix It/Version	7
74	Ashanti ASH 415	California Dreaming/SOUND DIMENSION: Soul Food (reissue)	10
70	Bamboo BDLP 207	MR FIX IT (LP)	40
71	Bamboo BDLPS 216	CALIFORNIA DREAMING (LP)	35

(see also Bobby Francis, Jerry & Freedom Singers, Zimm & Dee Dee)

JACQUELINE FRANCOIS

59	Philips BBL 7273	THE SWEET LANGUAGE OF LOVE (LP)	12

JACKSON C. FRANK

65	Columbia DB 7795	Blues Run The Game/Can't Get Away From My Love	25
65	Columbia 33SX 1788	JACKSON C. FRANK (LP)	250
78	B&C BCLP 4	AGAIN (LP, reissue of above LP)	40

FRANK & BARBARIANS
| 62 | Oriole CB 1758 | The Bouncer/Concerto In The Stars .... 7 |

(see Frank Barber)

FRANKIE & CLASSICALS
| 67 | Philips BF 1586 | I Only Have Eyes For You/What Shall I Do? .... 100 |
| 74 | Pye Intl. DDS 101 | What Shall I Do?/Goodbye Love, Hello Sadness .... 5 |

FRANKIE & JOHNNY
| 66 | Decca F 22376 | Never Gonna Leave You/I'll Hold You............................... 100 |
| 66 | Parlophone R 5518 | Climb Ev'ry Mountain/I Wanna Make You Understand .... 8 |

(see also Maggie Bell)

FRANKIE & KNOCKOUTS
| 81 | RCA RCALP 5026 | FRANKIE & THE KNOCKOUTS (LP)................................ 10 |

FRANKIE & LARRY
| 60 | Capitol CL 15153 | Not Yet/A Fool For You .... 5 |

FRANKIE GOES TO HOLLYWOOD
SINGLES
83	ZTT P ZTAS 1	Relax (Move)/One September Monday (picture disc) 7
83	ZTT 12 ZTAS 1	Relax (Original Mix)/Ferry Across The Mersey/Relax Bonus (Again) (12", ZTT sleeve or standard p/s) 20
83	ZTT 12 ZTAS 1	Relax (Original Mix)/Ferry Across The Mersey/Relax Bonus (Again) (12", ZTT sleeve or standard p/s, some copies play at 33rpm but list 45rpm).... 18
83	ZTT 12 ZTAS 1 (matrix no.: 1A 2U)	Relax (Sex Mix [alias 8.20 "New York Mix"])/Ferry Across The Mersey/ Relax Bonus (Again) (12", p/s, 45rpm) 15
83	ZTT 12 ZTAS 1 (matrix no.: 1A 5U)	Relax (Sex Mix)/Ferry Across The Mersey/Relax Bonus (Again) (12", p/s, 45rpm, different 'U.S. chequered' p/s) 10
83	ZTT 12P ZTAS 1	Relax (Sex Mix)/Ferry Across The Mersey/Relax Bonus (Again) (12", picture disc).. 10
83	ZTT CTIS 102	Relax: The Party Trick (Acting Dumb)/The Special Act (Adapted From The Sex Mix)/The U.S. Mix (Come Dancing)/The Single (The Act)/Later On (From One September Monday)/Gerry Marsden's Ferry Across The Mersey (And Here I'll Stay) (cassette) 10
84	ZTT P ZTAS 3	Two Tribes (We Don't Want To Die)/One February Friday (picture disc) 7
84	ZTT 12 ZTAS 3	Two Tribes (Annihilation)/War (Hide Yourself)/Two Tribes (Surrender)/ One February Friday (12", p/s, with poster: 3 different poster designs) .... each 8
84	ZTT X ZTAS 3	Two Tribes (Carnage)/War (Hide Yourself)/Two Tribes/One February Friday (12", different 'fighting presidents' p/s)................................ 8
84	ZTT CTIS 103	TWO TRIBES (KEEP THE PEACE) (cassette) 7
84	ZTT WARTZ 3	War (Hidden)/Two Tribes (Carnage)/One February Friday (12", p/s)........ 8
84	ZTT WARTZ 3	War (Hidden)/Two Tribes (Carnage)/One February Friday (Only Bullets Can Stop Them Now) (12", picture disc)................... 8
84	ZTT P ZTAS 5	The Power Of Love/The World Is My Oyster (picture disc)............... 5
84	ZTT 12P ZTAS 5	The Power Of Love/Trapped And Scrapped/Holier Than Thou (12", picture disc).. 8
84	ZTT 12X ZTAS 5	The Power Of Love/The World Is My Oyster/Welcome To The Pleasuredome (Pleasurefix)/The Only Star In Heaven (Starfix) (12", g/fold p/s with 5 photos) 10
84	ZTT CTIS 105	The Power Of Love (Extended Version)/Trapped And Scrapped/Holier Than Thou (cassette, picture 'envelope' box) 10
85	ZTT ZTAS 7	Welcome To The Pleasure Dome (Altered Reel) (actually plays "Video Mix 5.05")/Happy Hi Get It On (p/s, blue label) 12
85	ZTT P ZTAS 7	Welcome To The Pleasure Dome (Alternative Reel ["Fruitiness Mix"])/ Happy Hi/Get It On (apple-shaped picture disc) 8
85	ZTT X ZTAS 7	Welcome To The Pleasure Dome (The Alternative 8.30)/Get It On/ Happy Hi Born To Run (12", p/s) 8
85	ZTT CTIS 107	Welcome To The Pleasure Dome (Soundtrack From Bernard Rose Video)/ Happy Hi (All In The Mind)/Get It On/How To Remake The World (cassette) 7
86	ZTT ZTAX 22	Rage Hard (Stamped)/(Don't Lose What's Left) Of Your Little Mind (p/s) 6
86	ZTT ZTD 22	Rage Hard/(Don't Lose What's Left) Of Your Little Mind ('pop-up fists' p/s) 5
86	ZTT 12 ZTAQ 22	Rage Hard/Suffragette City/(Don't Lose What's Left) Of Your Little Mind (extended) (12", stickered p/s with poster) 8
86	ZTT 12 ZTAX 22	Rage Hard (++ Mix)/Roadhouse Blues/(Don't Lose What's Left) Of Your Little Mind (extended) (12", p/s) 8
86	ZTT 12 ZTAX B 22	Rage Hard (++ Mix)/Roadhouse Blues/(Don't Lose What's Left) Of Your Little Mind (extended) (12", in 'action series 22' box) 10
86	ZTT ZCID 22	Rage Hard +/Rage Hard ++/Rage Hard*/(Don't Lose What's Left) Of Your Little Mind/Suffragette City/Roadhouse Blues (CD, card sleeve) 12
86	ZTT 12 ZTAX 25	Warriors (The Turn Of The Knife Mix)/(Return)/(End) (12", p/s)........ 8
86	ZTT CTIS 25	WARRIORS OF THE WASTELAND (Cassetted) (cassette EP) 5
86	ZTT ZCID 25	WARRIORS OF THE WASTELAND (Compacted) (CD EP, card sleeve) 10
87	ZTT ZTE 26	Watching The Wildlife (Die Letzen Tag Der Menscheit Mix)/ Watching The Wildlife/The Waves (12", p/s)......................... 10
87	ZTT ZTAX 26	Watching The Wildlife (Movement II)/Watching The Wildlife (Bit 3)/ Watching The Wildlife (Bit 4)/The Waves (12", p/s) 8
87	ZTT CTIS 26	Watching The Wildlife (Cassetted) (EP, cassette, includes "Condom Mix" & "Orchestral Wildlife") 6

MINT VALUE £

PROMOS

83	ZTT ZTAS 1DJ	Relax — The Last Seven Inches/One September Monday (white label, stamped label, no p/s)	8
84	ZTT XZTAS 3DJ	Two Tribes (Carnage)/Relax (U.S. Mix) (12", ZTT sleeve)	12
84	ZTT XZIP 1	Two Tribes (Hibakusha)/War (Hide Yourself)/Two Tribes/ One February Friday (12", ZTT sleeve)	20
84	ZTT ZTAS 5 DJ-A	The Power Of Love (5.28)/The World Is My Oyster (12")	20
86	ZTT 12 ZTAK 25	Warriors (The Attack Mix) (12", white label)	12
93	ZTT SAM 1231	Relax (Ollie J. Remix) (6.38)/(Trip-Ship Edit) (6.12)/(Ollie J.'s Seven Inches)/ (Jam & Spoon Hi-N-R-G Mix) (7.55)/(C Jam & Spoon Trip-O-Matic Fairy Tale Space Mix) (7.52)/(MCMXCIII) (3.45) (12", double pack, gatefold sleeve)	18
93	ZTT SAM 1275	Welcome To The Pleasuredom (Brothers In Rhythm Rollercoaster Mix) (15.15)/ (Pleasurefix — Original 12" Mix) (9.55)/(Elevatorman's Top Floor Club Mix) (6.02)/(Elevatorman's Deep Down Bass-Ment Dub) (6.00) (12", double pack, gatefold sleeve, promo sleeve)	12
94	ZTT SAM 1331	Two Tribes (The Intermission Mixes): (Legend Mix)/(Legend Instrumental)/ (Workout Mix)/(Workout Instrumental) (12", stickered title sleeve)	12
94	ZTT (no cat. no)	Two Tribes (808 State Remix) (10", 1-sided red vinyl)	18

ALBUMS

84	ZTT NEAT 1	WELCOME TO THE PLEASURE DOME (2-LP, picture discs, printed PVC gatefold sleeve)	18
84	ZTT CID 101	WELCOME TO THE PLEASURE DOME (CD, with "San José", omits "Happy Hi")	35

(see also Holly, Holly Johnson, Spitfire Boys)

ARETHA FRANKLIN

SINGLES

61	Fontana H 271	Love Is The Only Thing/Today I Sing The Blues (with Ray Bryant Combo)	15
61	Fontana H 343	Operation Heartbreak/Rock-A-Bye Your Baby With A Dixie Melody	10
65	CBS 201732	Can't You Just See Me/You Little Miss Raggedy Anne	8
67	CBS 202468	Cry Like A Baby/Swanee	7
67	CBS 3059	Take A Look/Lee Cross	7
67	Atlantic 584 084	I Never Loved A Man (The Way I Love You)/Do Right Woman – Do Right Man	6
67	Atlantic 584 115	Respect/Save Me	6
67	Atlantic 584 127	Baby I Love You/Going Down Slow	6
67	Atlantic 584 141	(You Make Me Feel Like A) Natural Woman/Never Let Me Go	6
67	Atlantic 584 157	(I Can't Get No) Satisfaction/Night Life (withdrawn B-side)	8
67	Atlantic 584 157	(I Can't Get No) Satisfaction/Chain Of Fools	6
68	Atlantic 584 172	Since You've Been Gone/Ain't No Way	8
68	Atlantic 584 186	Think/You Send Me	6
68	Atlantic 584 206	I Say A Little Prayer/See-Saw	6
69	Atlantic 584 239	Don't Let Me Lose This Dream/The House That Jack Built	5
69	Atlantic 584 252	The Weight/The Tracks Of My Tears	8
69	Atlantic 584 285	Share Your Love With Me/Pledging My Love/The Clock	5
69	Atlantic 584 306	Eleanor Rigby/It Ain't Fair	5
70	Atlantic 584 322	Call Me/Son Of A Preacher Man	8
70	Atlantic 2091 027	Don't Play That Song/The Thrill Is Gone	5
70	Atlantic 2091 042	Border Song (Holy Moses)/You And Me (unissued)	
70	Atlantic 2091 044	Oh No, Not My Baby/You And Me	5
71	Atlantic 2091 063	You're All I Need To Get By/The Border Song	5
71	Atlantic 2091 111	I Say A Little Prayer/(I Can't Get No) Satisfaction	5
71	Atlantic 2091 127	Brand New Me/Spirit In The Dark	5
71	Atlantic 2091 168	Rock Steady/Oh Me, Oh My	10
72	Atlantic K 10224	Rock Steady/All The King's Horses	7
74	Atlantic K 10399	Until You Come Back To Me/If You Don't Think	5
86	Arista ARIDP 624	Freeway Of Love/Until You Say You Love Me//Jump To It/ Zoomin' To The Freeway (double pack)	5
86	Arista ARIST 22624	Freeway Of Love (Pink Cadillac Mix)/ Until You Say You Love Me (p/s, pink vinyl)	8
86	Arista ARIST 22678	Jumpin' Jack Flash/Who's Zoomin' Who//Sweet Bitter Love/Integrity (double pack)	5
89	Arista 112 377	Through The Storm (with Elton John)/Come To Me (picture disc)	5
89	Arista 612 185	Through The Storm (with Elton John)/Come To Me/Oh Happy Day (live) (with Mavis Staples) (12", p/s)	8
89	Arista 162 185	Through The Storm (with Elton John)/Come To Me/Oh Happy Day (live) (with Mavis Staples) (3" CD, card sleeve)	8

EP

62	Fontana TE 467217	TODAY I SING THE BLUES (EP)	30

LPs

61	Fontana TFL 5173	ARETHA (LP)	40
65	CBS (S)BPG 62566	YEAH!!! — IN PERSON (LP)	20
67	CBS (S)BPG 62744	SOUL SISTER (LP)	20
67	Atlantic 587/588 066	I NEVER LOVED A MAN (LP)	20
67	CBS (S)BPG 62969	TAKE IT LIKE YOU GIVE IT (LP)	20
67	CBS 63160	LEE CROSS (LP)	20
67	Atlantic 587/588 085	ARETHA ARRIVES (LP)	15
67	CBS 64536	GREATEST HITS (LP)	15
68	Atlantic 587/588 099	LADY SOUL (LP)	18
68	CBS 63269	TAKE A LOOK AT ARETHA FRANKLIN (LP)	15
68	Atlantic 587/588 114	ARETHA NOW (LP)	18
68	CBS 63064	GREATEST HITS VOL. 2 (LP)	15

68	Atlantic 587/588 149	ARETHA IN PARIS — LIVE AT THE OLYMPIA (LP)	22
69	Atlantic 588 169	SOUL '69 (LP)	18
69	Atlantic 588 182	ARETHA'S GOLD (LP)	15
69	Chess (S)CRL 54550	SONGS OF FAITH (LP)	15
70	Atlantic 2400 004	THIS GIRL'S IN LOVE WITH YOU (LP)	15
70	Atlantic 2464 007	I SAY A LITTLE PRAYER (LP)	15
70	Atlantic 2400 021	DON'T PLAY THAT SONG (LP)	18
71	Atlantic 2400 136	LIVE AT THE FILLMORE WEST (LP, gatefold sleeve)	15
71	Atlantic 2400 188	GREATEST HITS (LP)	12
72	Atlantic K 40095	SPIRIT IN THE DARK (LP)	12
72	Atlantic K 40323	YOUNG, GIFTED AND BLACK (LP)	12
72	Atlantic K 60023	AMAZING GRACE (2-LP)	18
73	Atlantic K 40504	HEY NOW HEY (THE OTHER SIDE OF THE SKY) (LP)	12
74	Atlantic K 50031	LET ME IN YOUR LIFE (LP)	12
75	Atlantic K 50093	WITH EVERYTHING I FEEL (LP)	12
75	Atlantic K 50159	YOU (LP)	12
76	Atlantic K 56248	SPARKLE (LP, soundtrack, with Curtis Mayfield)	12

ARETHA FRANKLIN & WHITNEY HOUSTON

| 89 | Arista 662 545 | It Isn't, It Wasn't, It Ain't Never Gonna Be (Single Remix)/(Extended Remix)/(Hip Hop Remix)/ARETHA FRANKLIN: Think (1989) (CD) | 8 |

(see also Whitney Houston)

CAROLYN FRANKLIN

69	RCA Victor RCA 1851	Boxer/I Don't Want To Lose You	7
70	RCA Victor RCA 2009	All I Want To Be Is Your Woman/You Really Didn't Mean It	5
69	RCA RD/SF 8035	BABY DYNAMITE! (LP)	12
70s	Joy JOYS 180	THE FIRST TIME I CRIED (LP)	12

ERMA FRANKLIN

67	London HLZ 10170	Piece Of My Heart/Big Boss Man	12
68	London HLZ 10201	Open Up Your Soul/I Just Ain't Ready For Love	8
68	London HLZ 10220	The Right To Cry/Don't Catch The Dog's Bone	8
69	Soul City SC 118	Don't Wait Too Long/Time After Time	10
69	MCA MU 1073	Gotta Find Me A Lover (24 Hours A Day)/Change My Thoughts From You	6
71	Jay Boy BOY 36	I Just Ain't Ready For Love/The Right To Cry	5
71	Jay Boy BOY 41	Piece Of My Heart/Big Boss Man (reissue)	5
70	MCA MUP MUPS 394	SOUL SISTER (LP)	25

MARIE FRANKLIN

| 68 | MGM MGM 1455 | You Ain't Changed/Don'tcha Bet No Money | 8 |

GORDON FRANKS

62	Parlophone R 4910	Rag Trade Rag/Sid's Tune	5
62	Parlophone R 4929	Outbreak Of Murder/Johnny's Tune	7
63	Decca F 11587	Sam Benedict Theme/Sweet And Sour	5

JOHNNY FRANKS

55	Melodisc P 230	Tweedle Dee/Shake, Rattle And Roll (78)	25
56	Melodisc 1355	Rock Candy Baby/Sing-ing-ing (78)	10
58	Melodisc 1459	Good Old Country Music/Cheatin' On Me	6
58	Melodisc 1459	Good Old Country Music/Cheatin' On Me (78)	25

BONNIE (BLUE) FRANKSON

68	Jolly JY 014	Loving You/Shoo Be Do (both with Joe Nolan Band)	7
69	Jolly JY 021	London City/Dearest (both with Joe Nolan & Dynamic Heatwave)	7
69	Columbia Blue Beat DB 114	Dearest/London City	8
73	Ackee ACK 512	Getting Things Together/Version	5

(see also Dotty & Bonnie)

FRANTIC ELEVATORS

79	TJM TJM 5	Voice In The Dark/Passion/Every Day I Die (p/s)	20
80	TJM TJM 6	Hunchback Of Notre Dame/See Nothing And Everything/Don't Judge Me (unreleased; demos only)	100+
80	Eric's ERIC'S 6	You Know What You Told Me/Production Prevention (p/s)	20
81	Crackin' Up CRAK 1	Searching For The Only One/Hunchback Of Notre Dame (p/s)	20
82	No Waiting WAIT 1	Holding Back The Years/Pistols In My Brain (p/s)	25
87	TJM TJM 101	THE EARLY YEARS (mini-LP)	25
88	Receiver KNOB 2	THE EARLY YEARS (mini-LP, reissue with new sleeve & interview disc, as Mick Hucknall & Frantic Elevators)	18

(see also Simply Red)

ANDY FRASER BAND

| 75 | CBS 80731 | THE ANDY FRASER BAND (LP) | 12 |
| 75 | CBS 81027 | IN YOUR EYES (LP) | 12 |

(see also Free, Sharks)

JIMMY FRASER

| 97 | Sony NSTA1 | Of Hopes And Dreams And Tombstones/PATTI AUSTIN: Are You Ready For Love (promo, 500 only) | 8 |

JOHN FRASER

58	Pye N 15098	Bye Bye Love/Why Don't They Understand? (78)	8
58	Pye 7N 15118	Trolley Stop/Don't Take Your Love From Me	5
58	Pye N 15118	Trolley Stop/Don't Take Your Love From Me (78)	8
59	Pye 7N 15212	Bye Bye, Baby, Goodbye/Golden Age	5
59	Pye N 15212	Bye Bye, Baby, Goodbye/Golden Age (78)	10
58	Pye NEP 24068	PRESENTING JOHN FRASER (EP)	15

MINT VALUE £

NORTON FRASER
57	Columbia DC 709	Rock Around The Clock/Bongalulu (78) (export issue)	12

FRATERNITY BROTHERS
59	HMV POP 582	Passion Flower/A Nobody Like Me (B-side with Gil Fields)	5
59	HMV POP 582	Passion Flower/A Nobody Like Me (78, B-side with Gil Fields)	15

FRATERNITY OF MAN
70	Stateside SS 2166	Don't Bogart Me/Wispy Paisley Skies	5

ERIC FRATTER
69	Trojan TR 655	Since You've Been Gone/AFROTONES: Things I Love	8

(see also Eric Fatter)

FRAYS
65	Decca F 12153	Keep Me Covered/Walk On	100
65	Decca F 12229	My Girl Sloopy/For Your Precious Love	35

(see also Mike Patto)

NORMA FRAZER
65	Ska Beat JB 223	Heartaches/Everybody Loves A Lover	15
67	Coxsone CS 7017	The First Cut Is The Deepest/BUMPS OAKLEY: Rag Doll	20
67	Studio One SO 2024	Come By Here/WAILERS: I Stand Predominate	60
68	Coxsone CS 7060	Respect/Time	20

(see also Sound Dimension, Righteous Homes, Viceroys, Tommy McCook)

DALLAS FRAZIER
66	Capitol CL 15445	Elvira/That Ain't No Stuff	5
66	Capitol CL 15457	Just A Little Bit Of You/Walkin' Wonder	5
59	Capitol EAP 1035	DALLAS FRAZIER (EP)	15

FRAZIER CHORUS
87	4AD AD 708	Sloppy Heart/Typical (no p/s, promo only)	8
87	4AD BAD 708	Sloppy Heart/Typical 12", p/s)	8

FREAKS OF NATURE
66	Island WI 3017	People! Let's Freak Out/The Shadow Chasers	45

(see also Kim Fowley, Belfast Gypsies, Jackie McAuley)

STAN FREBERG
52	Capitol CL 13846	The Boogie-Woogie Banjo Man From Birmingham/The World Is Waiting (78)	8
52	Capitol CL 13830	Ba-Ba-Ball And Chain/Abe Snake For President (78)	10
53	Capitol CL 14000	Dinky Pinky parts 1&2 (78)	10
53	Capitol CL 14019	Christmas Dragnet (Parts 1 & 2) (78)	8
53	Capitol CL 14025	St. George And The Dragonet (with Daws Butler & June Foray)/ Little Blue Riding Hood (78)	8
54	Capitol CL 14187	Sh-Boom (Life Could Be A Dream)/C'est Ci Bon (as Stan Freberg & Toads)	25
54	Capitol CL 14187	Sh-Boom (Life Could Be A Dream)/C'est Ci Bon (78)	8
55	Capitol CL 14316	The Lone Psychiatrist/The Honey-Earthers (with Daws Butler)	18
55	Capitol CL 14316	The Lone Psychiatrist/The Honey-Earthers (78, with Daws Butler)	8
56	Capitol CL 14509	The Yellow Rose Of Texas/Rock Around Stephen Foster	15
56	Capitol CL 14571	The Great Pretender/The Quest For Bridey Hammerschlaugen (B-side with June Foray)	15
56	Capitol CL 14571	The Great Pretender/The Quest For Bridey Hammerschlaugen (78)	10
56	Capitol CL 14608	Heartbreak Hotel/Rock Island Line	22
56	Capitol CL 14608	Heartbreak Hotel/Rock Island Line (78)	10
57	Capitol CL 14712	Banana Boat (Day-O)/Tele-vee-shun	12
57	Capitol CL 14712	Banana Boat (Day-O)/Tele-vee-shun (78)	8
58	Capitol CL 14966	Green Chritma (with Daws Butler)/The Meaning Of Christmas (with Jud Conlon Chorale)	10
60	Capitol CL 15122	The Old Payola Roll Blues (with Jesse White)/ Sh-Boom (Life Could Be A Dream)	12
55	Capitol EAP1 496	ANY REQUESTS (EP)	12
56	Capitol EAP1 628	THE REAL SAINT GEORGE (EP)	12
61	Capitol EAP1 1101	OMAHA (EP)	10
61	Capitol EAP1 20050	THE GREAT PRETENDER (EP)	12
61	Capitol EAP1 20115	FREBERG AGAIN (EP, with Daws Butler)	10
57	Capitol T 777	A CHILD'S GARDEN OF FREBERG (LP)	25
58	Capitol LCT 6171	THE BEST OF THE STAN FREBERG SHOWS (LP)	18
61	Capitol W 1573	PRESENTS THE UNITED STATES OF AMERICA (LP)	15
64	Capitol T 2020	THE BEST OF STAN FREBERG (LP)	18

JOHN FRED & HIS PLAYBOY BAND
67	Pye International 7N 25442	Judy In Disguise (With Glasses)/When The Lights Go Out	6
68	Pye International 7N 25453	Hey Hey Bunny/No Letter Today	6
68	Pye International 7N 25462	We Played Games/Lonely Are The Lonely	5
68	Pye International 7N 25470	Little Dum Dum/Tissue Paper	5
68	CBS 3475	Shirley/High Heel Sneakers	10
69	MCA MU 1088	Silly Sarah Carter/Back In The USSR	5
67	Pye Intl. NPL 28111	AGNES ENGLISH (LP)	18

FRED BANANA COMBO
78	Warm AWMR 2004	No Destination Blues/Jerk Off All Nite Long (p/s)	5

FREDDIE & DREAMERS
63	Columbia DB 7032	If You Gotta Make A Fool Of Somebody/Feel So Blue	5
63	Columbia DB 7086	I'm Telling You Now/What Have I Done To You?	5
63	Columbia DB 7147	You Were Made For Me/Send A Letter To Me	5
64	Columbia DB 7214	Over You/Come Back When You're Ready	5
64	Columbia DB 7286	I Love You Baby/Don't Make Me Cry	5
64	Columbia DB 7322	Just For You/Don't Do That To Me	5
64	Columbia DB 7381	I Understand/I Will	5
65	Columbia DB 7526	A Little You/Things I'd Like To Say	5
65	Columbia DB 7720	Thou Shalt Not Steal/I Don't Know	6
65	Columbia DC 763	A Windmill In Old Amsterdam/A Love Like You (export issue)	12
66	Columbia DB 7857	If You've Gotta Minute Baby/When I'm Home With You	6
66	Columbia DB 7929	Playboy/Some Day	6
66	Columbia DB 8033	Turn Around/Funny Over You	6
67	Columbia DB 8137	Hello, Hello/All I Ever Want Is You	6
67	Columbia DB 8200	Brown And Porter's (Meat Exporters) Lorry/Little Brown Eyes	8
68	Columbia DB 8496	Little Big Time/FREDDIE GARRITY: You Belong To Me	8
68	Columbia DB 8517	It's Great/Gaberdine Mac	8
69	Columbia DB 8606	Get Around Downtown Girl/What To Do	8
71	Philips 6006 098	Susan's Tuba/You Hurt Me Girl	5
78	Polydor 2059 041	Here We Go/I Saw Ya	5
63	Columbia SEG 8275	IF YOU GOTTA MAKE A FOOL OF SOMEBODY (EP)	12
63	Columbia SEG 8287	SONGS FROM THE FILM "WHAT A CRAZY WORLD" (EP)	15
64	Columbia SEG 8302	YOU WERE MADE FOR ME (EP)	12
64	Columbia SEG 8323	OVER YOU (EP)	12
64	Columbia SEG 8349	FREDDIE SINGS JUST FOR YOU (EP)	12
65	Columbia SEG 8403	READY, FREDDIE, GO! (EP)	18
65	Columbia SEG 8457	FREDDIE AND THE DREAMERS (EP)	18
63	Columbia 33SX 1577	FREDDIE AND THE DREAMERS (LP)	25
64	Columbia 33SX 1663	YOU WERE MADE FOR ME (LP)	25
65	Columbia SX 1785	SING ALONG PARTY (LP)	22
66	Columbia S(C)X 6069	IN DISNEYLAND (LP, mono/stereo)	18/20
67	Columbia SX 6177	KING FREDDIE AND THE DREAMING KNIGHTS (LP)	30
67	M. For Pleasure MFP 1168	HITS WITH FREDDIE AND THE DREAMERS (LP, repackage of 33SX 1663)	12
60s	World Record Club ST 928	SING ALONG PARTY (LP, reissue)	15
71	World Record Club ST 1050	IN DISNEYLAND (LP, reissue)	12

(see also Freddie Garrity, Dreamers)

FREDDIE & DREAMERS/PETER & GORDON
64	Columbia SEG 8337	JUST FOR YOU (EP, 2 tracks each)	15

(see also Peter & Gordon)

DOTTY FREDERICK
59	Top Rank JAR 106	Ricky/Just Wait	10
59	Top Rank JAR 106	Ricky/Just Wait (78)	20

TOMMY FREDERICK & HI-NOTES
58	London HLU 8555	Prince Of Players/I'm Not Pretending	45
58	London HLU 8555	Prince Of Players/I'm Not Pretending (78)	25

BILL FREDERICKS
78	Polydor 2059 035	Almost/Wind Of Change	7

DOLORES FREDERICKS
56	Brunswick 05540	Cha Cha Joe/Whole Lotta Shakin' Goin' On	20
56	Brunswick 05540	Cha Cha Joe/Whole Lotta Shakin' Goin' On (78)	8

MARC FREDERICKS
56	London HLD 8281	Mystic Midnight/Symphony To Anne	22
56	London HLD 8281	Mystic Midnight/Symphony To Anne (78)	8

FREE (Holland)
69	Philips BF 1738	Soul Party/Down To The Bone	5
69	Philips BF 1754	Keep In Touch/Taking It Away	20

FREE (U.K.)
69	Island WIP 6054	Broad Daylight/The Worm	30
69	Island WIP 6062	I'll Be Creepin'/Sugar For Mr Morrison	30
70	Island WIP 6082	All Right Now/Mouthful Of Grass (pink label)	6
70	Island WIP 6093	The Stealer/Lying In The Sunshine	6
71	Island WIP 6100	My Brother Jake/Only My Soul	5
72	Island WIP 6129	Little Bit Of Love/Sail On	5
72	Island WIP 6146	Wishing Well/Let Me Show You	5
73	Island WIP 6160	Travellin' In Style/Easy On My Soul	5
76	Island WIP 6351	The Hunter/Worry	5
85	Island 12 IS 221	Wishing Well/Woman (live)/Walk In My Shadow (live) (12", p/s)	8
78	Island IEP 6	THE FREE EP (p/s)	5
82	Island PIEP 6	THE FREE EP (12", picture disc)	10
69	Island ILPS 9089	TONS OF SOBS (LP, gatefold sleeve, 1st pressing, pink label/ black & orange 'circle' logo)	50
69	Island ILPS 9089	TONS OF SOBS (LP, gatefold sleeve, 2nd pressing, pink label/ black 'block' logo)	30

70	Island ILPS 9089	TONS OF SOBS	
		(LP, gatefold sleeve, 3rd pressing, pink label/'i' logo)	20
71	Island ILPS 9089	TONS OF SOBS (LP, gatefold sleeve, 4th pressing, pink rim label/ 'palm tree' logo)	15
69	Island ILPS 9104	FREE	
		(LP, gatefold sleeve, 1st pressing, pink label/'i' logo)	35
70	Island ILPS 9104	FREE (LP, gatefold sleeve, 2nd pressing, pink rim label/ 'palm tree' logo)	15
70	Island ILPS 9120	FIRE AND WATER	
		(LP, 1st pressing, pink label/'i' logo)	25
70	Island ILPS 9120	FIRE AND WATER	
		(LP, 2nd pressing, pink rim label/'palm tree' logo)	15
70	Island ILPS 9138	HIGHWAY (LP)	12
71	Island ILPS 9160	LIVE	
		(LP, in envelope sleeve with inner)	15
72	Island ILPS 9192	FREE AT LAST (LP)	12
73	Island ILPS 9217	HEARTBREAKER	
		(LP, with inner sleeve)	12
74	Island ISLD 4	THE FREE STORY	
		(2-LP, with 4-page booklet, numbered)	20

(see also Paul Kossoff, Bad Company, Rabbit, Kossoff Kirke Tetsu & Rabbit, Sharks, Andy Fraser Band, Black Cat Bones, Rock Aid Armenia)

FREE AGENTS
| 80 | Groovy STP 1 | FREE AGENTS (LP, hand-made sleeve) | 20 |

(see also Pete Shelley, Eric Random)

ALAN FREED & HIS ROCK'N'ROLL BAND
57	Vogue Coral Q 72219	Teen Rock/Right Now, Right Now (with Alan Freed's Rock'n'Rollers)	100
57	Vogue Coral Q 72219	Teen Rock/Right Now, Right Now (78)	35
57	Vogue Coral Q 72230	Rock'n'Roll Boogie/Teener's Canteen (with Alan Freed's Rock'n'Rollers)	100
57	Vogue Coral Q 72230	Rock'n'Roll Boogie/Teener's Canteen (78)	35
56	Vogue Coral LVA 9033	ROCK'N'ROLL DANCE PARTY VOL. 1	
		(LP, featuring Modernaires)	50
57	Vogue Coral LVA 9066	ROCK'N'ROLL DANCE PARTY VOL. 2	
		(LP, with Jimmy Cavello)	75

(see also Jimmy Cavello)

FREE DESIGN
| 69 | Project 3 | HEAVEN/EARTH (LP) | 15 |

FREEDOM
68	Mercury MF 1033	Where Will You Be Tonight/Trying To Get A Glimpse Of You	
		(some in p/s)	35/15
69	Plexium PXM 3	Escape While You Can/Kandy Kay	12
70	Probe PRO 504	Frustrated Woman/Man Made Laws	5
71	Vertigo 6059 051	Thanks/Miss Little Louise	6
70	Probe SPBA 6252	FREEDOM (LP)	18
71	Vertigo 6360 050	THROUGH THE YEARS (LP, gatefold sleeve, spiral label)	30
72	Vertigo 6360 072	FREEDOM IS MORE THAN A WORD	
		(LP, gatefold sleeve, spiral label)	65

(see also Procol Harum, Snafu)

FREEDOM GROUP
| 72 | Randy's RAN 525 | Sing A Song Of Freedom (actually by Max Romeo)/IMPACT ALLSTARS: Song Of Freedom (Version) | 6 |

FREEDOM SINGERS (Jamaica)
| 67 | Studio One SO 2010 | Have Faith/Work Crazy | 18 |
| 70 | Bamboo BAM 21 | Give Peace A Chance/SOUND DIMENSION: In Cold Blood | 12 |

(see also Winston Francis)

FREEDOM SINGERS (U.K.)
| 70 | New Beat NB 059 | Election (with Live Stocks)/FLECE & LIVE SHOCKS: Tomorrow's World | 6 |
| 71 | New Beat NB 074 | Your Testimony/Train Coming | 5 |

FREE FERRY
| 69 | CBS 4456 | Mary, What Have You Become?/Friend | 8 |
| 70 | CBS 4647 | Haverjack Drive/Flying | 5 |

FREEFORM
| 95 | Skam SKA 3 | Fane/Recut/Rail/Siamese Telebox/The Brink/Many/Freeform Dub (12") | 25 |

ART FREEMAN
| 66 | Atlantic 584 053 | Slippin' Around/Can't Get You Out Of My Mind | 90 |

BOBBY FREEMAN
58	London HLJ 8644	Do You Want To Dance?/Big Fat Woman	20
58	London HLJ 8644	Do You Want To Dance?/Big Fat Woman (78)	20
58	London HLJ 8721	Betty Lou Got A New Pair Of Shoes/Starlight	35
58	London HLJ 8721	Betty Lou Got A New Pair Of Shoes/Starlight (78)	35
59	London HLJ 8782	Shame On You Miss Johnson/Need Your Love	30
59	London HLJ 8782	Shame On You Miss Johnson/Need Your Love (78)	35
59	London HLJ 8898	Mary Ann Thomas/Love Me	25
59	London HLJ 8898	Mary Ann Thomas/Love Me (78)	60
60	London HLJ 9031	Sinbad/Ebb Tide (The Sea)	12
60	Parlophone R 4684	(I Do The) Shimmy Shimmy/You Don't Understand Me	12
64	Pye International 7N 25260	C'mon And Swim (Parts 1 & 2)	15
64	Pye International 7N 25280	S-W-I-M/That Little Old Heartbreaker Me	18
66	Pye International 7N 25347	The Duck/Cross My Heart	12
66	Pye International 7N 25347	The Duck/The Devil (2nd issue with different B-side)	12

BUD FREEMAN
58	Fontana TFE 17082	CHICAGO STYLE (EP, as Bud Freeman & Orchestra)	8
59	Parlophone GEP 8783	THE JAZZ SCENE (EP, as Bud Freeman & Trio)	8
59	Top Rank JKR 8021	JAZZ FOR SALE VOL. 1 (EP, as Bud Freeman & Quartet)	8
54	Columbia 33S 1016	COMES JAZZ (10" LP)	12
55	Capitol LC 6706	CLASSICS IN JAZZ (10" LP)	12
60s	Fontana TL 5370	BUD FREEMAN ESQ. (LP)	40
60s	Fontana TL 5414	FREEMAN & CO (LP)	40
70s	Philips 6308 254	SONG OF THE TENOR (LP)	20

CAROL FREEMAN
67	CBS 202579	The Rolling Sea/Leaving You Now	10

ERNIE FREEMAN
57	London HLP 8523	Raunchy/Puddin'	12
57	London HLP 8523	Raunchy/Puddin' (78)	10
57	London HL 7029	Dumplin's/Beautiful Weekend (export issue)	10
58	London HLP 8558	Dumplin's/Beautiful Weekend	12
58	London HLP 8558	Dumplin's/Beautiful Weekend (78)	15
58	London HLP 8660	Indian Love Call/Summer Serenade	8
58	London HLP 8660	Indian Love Call/Summer Serenade (78)	15
60	London HLP 9041	Big River/Night Sounds	6
65	London HLP 9944	Raunchy '65/Jivin' Around	8
56	London RE-U 1059	ERNIE FREEMAN AND HIS RHYTHM GUITAR (EP)	45
59	London RE-P 1210	ERNIE FREEMAN VOL. 2 (EP)	30

(see also Sir Chauncey)

EVELYN FREEMAN EXCITING VOICES
69	London HLU 10287	I Heard The Voice/I Dreamed Last Night	5

GEORGE FREEMAN
71	Jay Boy BOY 54	I'm Like A Fish/Why Are You Doing This To Me	10

MARGARET FREEMAN
61	Starlite ST45 040	Forbidden Fruit/Mister Ting A Ling	10

PAUL FREEMAN
71	Punch PH 82	Don't Give Up/UPSETTERS: Give Up (Version)	6

R.B. FREEMAN
75	Avco/Embassy 6105 040	I'm Shaft/I'm Shaft You Ain't Shaft	5

RUSS FREEMAN & CHET BAKER QUARTET
60	Vogue EPV 1255	RUSS FREEMAN & CHET BAKER QUARTET (EP)	8

(see also Chet Baker)

FREE MOVEMENT
72	CBS 7768	The Harder I Try/Comin' Home	5

FREE 'N EASY
68	Oak RGJ 628	FREE 'N EASY (LP, private pressing [Warren Coley W.C.P. 001])	100

FREE SOULS
64	Blue Beat BB 264	I Want To Be Free/Angel	15

FREESTYLE ORCHESTRA
89	SBK 12SBKDJ 7011	Keep On Pumping It Up (12", promo only)	15

FREEWHEELERS
65	HMV POP 1406	Why Do You Treat Me Like A Fool?/Ad Lib Blues	7

FREEZE
79	A1.A.1.1.A.1	IN COLOUR (EP, p/s)	6
80	A1 A.1.1.S.1	Celebration/Cross-Over	6

ACE FREHLEY
78	Casablanca CAN 135	New York Groove/Snow Blind (p/s, blue vinyl with mask)	35
78	Casablanca CAN 135	New York Groove/Snow Blind (no p/s, black vinyl)	20
87	Atlantic A 9255T	Into The Night/Fractured Too/Breakout (12", p/s)	10

(see also Kiss)

DON FRENCH
59	London HLW 8884	Lonely Saturday Night/Goldilocks	120
59	London HLW 8884	Lonely Saturday Night/Goldilocks (78)	60
59	London HLW 8989	Little Blonde Girl/I Look Into My Heart	100
59	London HLW 8989	Little Blonde Girl/I Look Into My Heart (78)	90

RAY FRENCH
66	Pye 7N 17215	Since I Lost My Baby/Gun Me Down	8

FRENCH IMPRESSIONISTS
82	Operation Twilight OPT 20	Santa Baby/Jingle Bell Rock (p/s)	10

(see also Aztec Camera)

FRENCH REVOLUTION
69	Decca F 22898	Nine Till Five/Why?	60

FRENZ
70	Sugar SU 101	Mee Lei Moi/I Hear Music... 5

FRENZY
81	Frenzy FRENZY 1	This Is The Last Time/Gypsy Dancer (no p/s)............................. 8
81	Frenzy FRENZY 3	Without You/Thanks For Nothing (no p/s)................................ 8
84	Nervous NEP 002	Robot Riot/All Alone (p/s).. 6
84	Nervous 12 NEP 002	Robot Riot/All Alone/Cry Or Die/Torment (12", p/s, 1st 500 on blue vinyl)................................. 10/8
86	ABC EYE T7	I See Red/Who's Life/Don't Give Up (12", p/s)........................ 8
85	Nervous NERD 016	HALL OF MIRRORS (LP, orange vinyl).. 12

FRESH
70	RCA RCA 2003	Stoned In Saigon/Just A Note.. 5
70	RCA SF 8122	FRESH OUT OF BORSTAL (LP).. 12
71	RCA LSA 3027	FRESH TODAY (LP) 12

(see also Paul Korda, Brother Bung, Fruit Machine)

FRESH AIR
69	Pye 7N 17736	Running Wild/Stop, Look, Listen..................................... 80
72	Philips 6006 187	It Takes Too Long/Here Comes Summer.............................. 5
72	Columbia DB 8872	Bye Bye Jane/It's All Over... 5

FRESHIES
78	Razz RAZZXEP 1	BAISER (EP, with Chris Sievey solo tracks, 33rpm, no'd, handwritten labels).... 15
79	Razz RAZZXEP 2	STRAIGHT IN AT NO. 2 (EP, handwritten labels with inserts, 1,000 only, numbered, green or orange p/s)....................................... 10
79	Razz RAZZ 3	THE MEN FROM BANANA ISLAND WHOSE STUPID IDEAS NEVER CAUGHT ON IN THE WESTERN WORLD AS WE KNOW IT (EP, black & white photocopied p/s or numbered blue p/s)............... 6/8
79	Razz RAZZ 5	We're Like You/CHRIS SIEVEY: Hey (p/s).............................. 5
80	Absurd A9	Octopus/Sheet Music.. 5
80	Razz RAZZ 6	Yellow Spot/If It's News (p/s).. 5
80	Razz RAZZ 7	No Money/Oh Girl (p/s)... 5
80	Razz RAZZ 8	RED INDIAN MUSIC (EP, with Chris Sievey)............................ 5
80	Razz RAZZ 11	I'm In Love With The Girl On The Manchester Checkout Desk/Singalong Version (p/s, some with free lyric book)............................. 5/4
80	Razz RAZZ 12	I'm In Love With The Girl On The Manchester Checkout Desk (Radio Version)/ Singalong Version ('bleeped') (white label radio issue, 200 only)................................. 10
80	Razz RAZZ 13	One To One/House Beautiful (unreleased)
81	MCA MCAS 693	Wrap Up The Rockets And It's Gonna Get Better/Tell Her I'm Ill (cassette).. 5
81	CV CVS 1	If You Really Love ... Buy Me A Shirt/I Am A Walrus (p/s).............. 5
81	HANNA 1	Virgin Megastore/Wrap Up The Rockets/Buy Me A Shirt/Tell Her I'm Ill/ Frank Talks To Chris (Conversation) (12", white label, stickered sleeve)................................. 8
78	Razz RAZZC 1	ALL SLEEP'S SECRETS (12-track cassette).......................... 12
79	Razz RAZZCS-2	MANCHESTER PLAYS (cassette, radio sessions & interview, 1,000 only).................... 12
79	Razz RAZZCS-3	SING THE GIRLS FROM BANANA ISLAND... (16-track cassette, 1,000 only)..................................... 12
80	Razz CS-4	ROUGH AND READY (12-track cassette, 1,000 only) 12
81	Razz CS-5	LONDON PLAYS (cassette, live & radio sessions, 1,000 only)........................ 12
85	ETS 1	JOHNNY RADAR STORY (20-track cassette, some with bonus Frank Sidebottom 8-track: "Firm Favourites")..................... 15/12
85	ETS 1	JOHNNY RADAR STORY (LP, vinyl test pressing of cassette)............... 40
85	ETS 3	EARLY RAZZ (cassette)... 12
85	ETS 4	STUDIO OUT-TAKES (cassette)...................................... 12

(see also Chris Sievey, Frank Sidebottom, Going Red?)

FRESH MAGGOTS
71	RCA RCA 2150	Car Song/What Would You Do...................................... 18
71	RCA SF 8205	FRESH MAGGOTS (LP)... 160

FRESH MEAT
73	Deram DMR 384	Never Mind The Money/Candy Eyes 5

FRESHMEN
67	Pye 7N 17432	Papa Oom Mow Mow/Let's Dance 7
68	Pye 7N 17592	Go Granny Go/Look At The Sunshine................................ 7
69	Pye 7N 17689	Just To See You Smile/Indian Lake 7
69	Pye 7N 17757	She Sang Hymns Out Of Tune/Mr. Beverly's Heavy Days 7
70	CBS 4842	Halfway To Where/Time Hasn't Changed Her 5
70	CBS 5168	Banquet For The World/Time Hasn't Changed Her 5
71	CBS 7241	One Bad Thing/Everywhere There Is Love 5
72	CBS 7694	Swanee River/Take The Time It Takes 5
68	Pye N(S)PL 18263	MOVIN' ON (LP) 35
70	CBS 64099	PEACE ON EARTH (LP) 25

FRESH WINDOWS
67	Fontana TF 839	Fashion Conscious/Summer Sun Shines 50

FREUR
83	CBS WA 3141	Doot Doot/Hold Me Mother (picture disc, stickered PVC sleeve).............. 5
83	CBS A13 3141	Doot Doot (Extended Version)/Hold Me Mother (Extended) (12", textured p/s)... 8

(see also Underworld)

FRIDA

82	Epic EPC A 2603	I Know There's Something Going On/Threnody (p/s)	8
82	Epic EPC A 2863	To Turn To Stone/I Got Something (p/s)	12
83	Epic EPC A 3435	Here We'll Stay/Strangers (p/s)	8
83	Epic EPC A 3983	Time/I Am A Seeker (p/s, with B.A. Robertson)	8
84	Epic EPC A 4717	Shine/That's Tough (p/s)	8
84	Epic EPC TA 4717	Shine (6.27 Version)/That's Tough (12", p/s)	15
84	Epic EPC A 4886	Heart Of The Country/Slowly (p/s)	12
84	Epic EPC TA 4886	Heart Of The Country/Slowly/I Know There's Something Going On (Extended) (12", p/s)	20

(see also Abba)

BOY FRIDAY (& GROOVERS)

70	Downtown DT 470	Version Girl/Grumble Man	7
71	Downtown DT 471	Music So Good/Right Track (both with Groovers)	7
71	Downtown DT 472	Sounds I Remember/JOAN LONG: Reconsider Our Love	5
71	Downtown DT 473	Take A Message Ruby/Second Note	8
71	Downtown DT 476	There'll Always Be Sunshine/Sunshine Track	7
71	Downtown DT 477	Hot Pants Girl/Raunchy	6
71	Downtown DT 481	El Raunchy/Conversation (as Boy Friday & Collins)	6
71	J-Dan JDN 4416	I Don't Want No War/Third Note Swing	7
71	J-Dan JDN 4418	Situation Version/OUR BAND: Keep Tracking	7

(see also Dandy & Superboys)

CAROL FRIDAY

65	Parlophone R 5297	Gone Tomorrow/Show Me The Way	6
65	Parlophone R 5369	Everybody I Know/Wasted Days	15
67	Parlophone R 5567	Big Sister/I Look Around Me	6

FRIDAY KNIGHTS

60	Oriole CB 1579	Poor Man's Roses/Don't Open That Door	6

FRIDGE

98	Earworm WORM 37	Deadly Cube/PORTAL: Hydro-Electric (tracing paper p/s)	5

FRIDGES

80	Ink-Ink II 01	Lynn Freeze/Shower Of B's/That's Why I Took Up The Harmonica/ No Room! (p/s, with insert)	4

KINKY FRIEDMAN

74	Vanguard VSD 79333	SOLD AMERICAN (LP)	12
75	ABC ABCL 5134	KINKY FRIEDMAN (LP)	12
76	Epic EPC 81640	LASSO FROM EL PASO (LP)	12

MARTY FRIEDMAN

86	Shrapnel RR 95291	DRAGON'S KISS (LP)	12

(see also Megadeth, Cacophony)

PERRY FRIEDMAN

60	Topic TOP 56	VIVE LA CANADIENNE (EP)	8

BRIAN JOSEPH FRIEL

74	Dawn DNLS 3054	BRIAN JOSEPH FRIEL (LP)	12
75	Dawn DNLS 3064	ARRIVERDERCI ARDROSSAN (LP)	12

TERRY FRIEND & FRIENDS

77	Tramp (no cat. no.)	COME THE DAY (LP, private pressing, 100 only)	40

(see also Stonefield Tramp)

FRIEND & LOVER

68	Verve VS 1515	Reach Out Of The Darkness/Time Is On Your Side	8

FRIENDLY HOPEFULS

81	Abstract ABS 004	Tribute To The Punks Of '76/Tribute To The Punks Of '76 (Disco Dub Mix) (p/s, coloured vinyl)	4

FRIENDLY PERSUASION

74	Rare Earth RES 120	Remember (Sha La La)/I'll Always Do The Best I Can	4

FRIENDS

68	Deram DM 198	Piccolo Man/Mythological Sunday	20

(see also Flowerpot Men, Ivy League)

FRIENDS

70	United Artists UP 35146	Futz/Costa Del Sol	5

FRIENDS

74	Merlin HF 4	FRIENDS (LP, white label test pressing, 1 copy only!)	1,500

(see also Ithaca, Alice Through The Looking Glass, Agincourt, Tomorrow Come Someday, BBC Radiophonic Workshop)

FRIENDS

83	Rock Shop RSR 002	Night Walker (no p/s)	25

FRIENDS AGAIN

83	Moonboot MOON 1	Honey At The Core/Lucky Star (p/s)	10
84	Mercury FAEP 1	THE FRIENDS AGAIN EP: Lullaby No. 2 Love On Board/Wand You Wave/ Thank You For Being An Angel//Sunkissed (New Version)/ State Of Art (Remix) (double pack, stickered gatefold p/s)	6

MINT VALUE £

FRIENDSHIP
| 70 | B&C CB 133 | The World Is Going To Be A Better Place/Million Hearts . . . . | 5 |

FRIENDS O' MINE
| 72 | Westwood WRS 021 | FRIENDS O' MINE (LP, 250 copies only) . . . . | 100 |

(see also Mark Kjeldsen)

FRIJID PINK
70	Deram DM-R 288	The House Of The Rising Sun/Drivin' Blues	5
70	Deram DM 309	Sing A Song Of Freedom/End Of The Line	5
70	Deram DM 321	Heartbreak Hotel/Bye Bye Blues	6
71	Deram DM 332	Music For The People/Sloony	5
71	Deram DM 336	We're Gonna Be There (When Johnny Comes Marching Home)/Shortly Kline	5
71	Deram DM 347	Lost Son/I Love Her	6
70	Deram SML 1062	FRIJID PINK (LP)	30
70	Deram SML 1077	DEFROSTED (LP)	30

(Robert) FRIPP & (Brian) ENO
| 73 | Island HELP 16 | NO PUSSYFOOTIN' (LP) . . . . | 12 |
| 75 | Island HELP 22 | EVENING STAR (LP) . . . . | 12 |

(see also Giles Giles & Fripp, King Crimson, Brian Eno, Roxy Music, David Byrne)

JACKIE FRISCO
| 63 | Decca F 11566 | You Can't Catch Me/Sugar Baby . . . . | 8 |
| 63 | Decca F 11692 | When You Ask About Love/He's So Near . . . . | 6 |

VONNIE FRITCHIE
| 55 | London HLU 8178 | Sugar Booger Avenue/There I Stood (To Throw Old Shoes And Rice) . . . . | 40 |

FRED FRITH
| 74 | Caroline C 1508 | GUITAR SOLOS (LP) . . . . | 12 |
| 76 | Caroline C 1518 | GUITAR SOLOS 2 (LP) . . . . | 12 |

(see also Henry Cow)

FRITZ, MIKE & MO
| 65 | Philips BF 1427 | Somebody Stole The Sun/Let Me Hear Your Voice . . . . | 8 |
| 65 | Philips BF 1441 | What Colour Is A Man?/So Now You're Gone . . . . | 8 |

(see also Four Pennies)

LEFTY FRIZZELL
51	HMV MC 3412	Shine Shave Shower/Look What Thoughts Will Do (78, export issue)	20
51	HMV MC 3422	Travellin' Blues/I Want To Be With You Always (78, export issue)	20
52	Columbia FB 3632	Always Late (With Your Kisses)/Mom & Dad's Waltz (78)	20
63	CBS BPG 62188	THE ONE AND ONLY LEFTY FRIZZELL (LP)	15
66	CBS BPG 62595	THE SAD SIDE OF LOVE (LP)	15

EDGAR FROESE
| 74 | Virgin V 2016 | AQUA (LP) . . . . | 12 |

(see also Tangerine Dream)

WYNDER K. FROG
(see under 'W')

RAYMOND FROGGATT
68	Polydor 56249	Callow-La-Vita/Lost Autumn	6
68	Polydor 56274	Just A Little Bit Of Love/ABC Gold Fish	6
68	Polydor 56284	The Red Balloon/Lost Autumn	6
68	Polydor 56294	Time Goes By/Rolly	6
69	Polydor 56314	Ring Ting A Ling/Anything You Want To	6
69	Polydor 56334	Movin' Down South/It's Only Me	6
69	Polydor 56358	Lazy Jack/Hasn't The Lord Blessed You?	6
70	Polydor 2058 028	Matter Of Pride/Fisher Boy	5
71	Bell BLL 1156	Singer/Church Fête (as Froggatt)	5
72	Bell BLL 1209	Rachel/Kentucky Sue	5
72	Bell BLL 1261	Running Water/Rock'n'Roll Song	5
74	Reprise K 14328	Roadshow/Salt	5
75	Jet JET 749	Try To Get You Into My Life/This Could Last All Night	5
69	Polydor 583 044	THE VOICE AND WRITING OF RAYMOND FROGGATT (LP)	20
72	Bell BELLS 207	BLEACH (LP)	18
74	Reprise K 44257	ROGUES AND THIEVES (LP)	12

(see also Monopoly)

FROGMEN
| 61 | Oriole CB 1617 | Underwater/Mad Rush |
| | | (withdrawn) . . . . | 40 |

FROGMORTON
| 76 | Philips 6006 506 | White Swans/Uncivilised Man . . . . | 5 |
| 76 | Philips 6308 261 | AT LAST (LP) . . . . | 20 |

JANE FROMAN
54	Capitol CL 14208	The Song From "Desiree" (We Meet Again)/Mine	6
54	Capitol CL 14209	The Finger Of Suspicion Points At You/My Shining Hour	12
55	Capitol CL 14254	I Wonder/I'll Never Be The Same	12
56	Capitol CL 14658	You'll Never Walk Alone/One Little Candle	5
56	Capitol EAP1 600	JANE FROMAN (EP).	8
56	Capitol EAP1 889	SONGS AT SUNSET (EP)	8
56	Capitol EAP2 889	SONGS AT SUNSET (EP)	8
56	Capitol EAP3 889	SONGS AT SUNSET (EP)	8
52	Capitol LC 6554	WITH A SONG IN MY HEART (10" LP).	15
53	Capitol LC 6605	YOURS ALONE (10" LP).	15

FRONT
| 77 | The Label TLR 005 | System/Queen's Mafia (p/s) .... 8 |

DOM FRONTIERE & HIS ORCHESTRA
| 57 | London HLU 8385 | Jet Rink Ballad/Uno Mas .... 30 |
| 57 | London HLU 8385 | Jet Rink Ballad/Uno Mas (78) .... 10 |

FRONT LINE
| 65 | Atlantic AT 4057 | I Don't Care/Got Love .... 30 |

FROST
| 69 | Vanguard SVRL 19056 | ROCK AND ROLL MUSIC (LP) .... 20 |
| 69 | Vanguard SVRL 19052 | FROST MUSIC (LP) .... 20 |

DAVID FROST (& others)
66	Parlophone R 5441	Zookeeper/Deck Of Cards 5
66	Parlophone PMC 7005	THE FROST REPORT ON BRITAIN (LP) 15
67	Pye NPL 18199	THE FROST REPORT ON EVERYTHING (LP) 15

MAX FROST & TROOPERS
| 68 | Capitol CL 15565 | Shape Of Things To Come/Free Lovin' .... 20 |

FROST LANE
| 71 | Cutty Wren MM 1 | FROST LANE |
| | | (LP, actually various artists LP) .... 40 |

FRUGAL SOUND
66	Pye 7N 17062	Norwegian Wood/Cruel To Be Kind 6
66	Pye 7N 17129	Just Outside The Door/I'm On Your Side 5
67	RCA Victor RCA 1556	Backstreet Girl/Reason To Believe 6
67	RCA Victor RCA 1595	Abilene/Love Is A New Face 5
68	RCA Victor RCA 1659	All Strung Out/Miss Mary 5

FRUIT EATING BEARS
| 78 | DJM DJS 857 | Door In My Face/Going Through The Motions .... 25 |
| 78 | Raw RAW 9 | Chevy Heavy (p/s) .... 18 |

FRUIT GUMS
| 70 | Fab FAB 138 | Sweet Pork/Crying All Night .... 6 |

FRUIT MACHINE
69	Spark SRL 1003	Follow Me/Cuddly Toy 30
69	Spark SRL 1027	I'm Alone Today/Sunshine Of Your Love (some in title p/s) 125/75
(see also Rare Bird)		

FRUMPY
71	Philips 6003 133	Life Without Pain/Morning 5
71	Philips 6305 067	ALL WILL BE CHANGED (LP) 15
72	Philips 6305 098	FRUMP 2 (LP, black & blue vinyl) 20
(see also Atlantis)		

FRUUPP
74	Dawn DNS 1087	Prince Of Heaven/Jaunting Car 8
73	Dawn DNLS 3053	FUTURE LEGENDS (LP) 18
74	Dawn DNLS 3058	SEVEN SECRETS (LP, with lyric insert) 18
74	Dawn DNLH 2	THE PRINCE OF HEAVEN'S EYES (LP, some with book) 25/18
75	Dawn DNLS 3070	MODERN MASQUERADES (LP, with lyric insert) 18

LEO FUCHS
| 52 | HMV JO 236 | Die Zach (The Thing)/Uncle Sam Und Reb Isruel (78, export issue) .... 8 |

FUCHSIA
| 71 | Pegasus PEG 8 | FUCHSIA (LP) .... 60 |

FUD (Christian) & DEL
| 73 | Duke DU 165 | Beef Sticker/PRINCE HERON: Ten Commandments .... 6 |
| 73 | Songbird SB 1086 | Dr. Fud/FUD CHRISTIAN ALLSTARS: La-Fud-Del Skank .... 6 |

FUD CHRISTIAN ALLSTARS
| 71 | Big Shot BI 571 | Never Fall In Love (actually by Winston Heywood)/Never Fall In Love Version .... 6 |
| *(see also Linkers, Ansel Linkers)* | | |

FUGI
| 71 | Blue Horizon 2096 005 | Red Moon (Parts 1 & 2) .... 18 |

FUGITIVE
| 81 | private pressing FMR 050 | Need My Freedom (no p/s) .... 30 |

FUGITIVES (U.S.)
| 61 | Vogue V 9176 | Freeway/Fugitive .... 25 |

FUGITIVES (Jamaica)
| 67 | Doctor Bird DB 1082 | Musical Pressure/LESLIE BUTLER & FUGITIVES: Winchester Rocksteady ...... 18 |
| *(see also Jo Jo Bennett & Fugitives, Two Kings, Jo Jo Bennett, Stranger Cole)* | | |

FUGS
68	Big T BIG 115	Crystal Liaison/When The Mode Of The Music Changes 7
68	Transatlantic TRA 180	TENDERNESS JUNCTION (LP, some with poster) 25/15
68	Transatlantic TRA 181	IT CRAWLED INTO MY HAND, HONEST (LP) 15
69	Fontana (S)TL 5501	VIRGIN FUGS (LP) 20
69	Fontana (S)TL 5513	THE FUGS ... FIRST ALBUM (LP) 20
69	Fontana (S)TL 5524	FUGS II (LP) 20
69	Reprise RSLP 6359	THE BELLE OF AVENUE A (LP) 15
75	ESP-Disk ESP 2018	ROUNDERS SCORE (LP) 12

MINT VALUE £

HIROSHI FUKUMURA
80	Champagne	HUNT UP THE WIND (LP)	10

FULHAM FURIES
78	GM GMS 9050	These Boots Are Made For Walking/Under Pressure (no p/s)	35

(see also Lurkers)

BLIND BOY FULLER
57	Philips BBL 7512	BLIND BOY FULLER 1935-40 (LP)	45
68	Matchbox SDR 143	BLIND BOY FULLER ON DOWN VOLUME 1 (LP)	18
69	Matchbox SDR 168	BLIND BOY FULLER ON DOWN VOLUME 2 (LP)	18
60s	Flyright LP 105	CAROLINA BLUES (LP)	12

GIL FULLER & DIZZY GILLESPIE
66	Fontana 688 147 ZL	MAN FROM MONTEREY (LP)	12

(see also Dizzy Gillespie)

BOBBY FULLER FOUR
66	London HLU 10030	I Fought The Law/Little Annie Lou	20
66	London HLU 10041	Love's Made A Fool Of You/Don't You Ever Let Me Know	12
73	President PT 394	Another Sad And Lonely Night/Only When I Dream	5
67	President PTL 1003	MEMORIAL ALBUM (LP)	25

(see also Randy Fuller)

JERRY FULLER
59	London HLH 8982	The Tennessee Waltz/Charlene	8
59	London HLH 8982	The Tennessee Waltz/Charlene (78)	45
61	London HLN 9439	Guilty Of Loving You/First Love Never Dies	6
62	Salvo SLO 1802	Lipstick And Rouge/Mother Goose At The Bandstand (99 copies only)	15

JESSE FULLER
65	Good Time Jazz GV 2426	San Francisco Bay Blues/New Midnight Special	6
67	Good Time Jazz GV 2427	Runnin' Wild/The Monkey And The Engineer	6
67	Fontana TF 821	Going Back To My Old Used To Be/Bye And Bye	12
58	Good Time Jazz LAG 12159	JESSE FULLER (LP)	15
60	Good Time Jazz LAG 12279	LONE CAT (LP)	15
60	Topic 10T 59	WORKING ON THE RAILROAD (10" LP)	25
63	Good Time Jazz LAG 574	SAN FRANCISCO BAY BLUES (LP)	12
65	Stateside SL 10154	JESSE FULLER'S FAVOURITES (LP)	12
66	Fontana TL 5313	SESSION WITH JESSE FULLER (LP)	15
66	Topic 12T 134	MOVE ON DOWN THE LINE (LP)	25
66	Stateside SL 10166	SAN FRANCISCAN BAY BLUES (LP, reissue)	12
60s	Vocalion VRLP 574	SAN FRANCISCO BAY BLUES (LP)	15

JOHNNY FULLER
73	Speciality SON 5017	Haunted House/Swinging At The Creek	6

RANDY FULLER
67	President PT 111	It's Love, Come What May/The Things You Do	8

(see also Bobby Fuller Four)

WALTER 'GIL' FULLER
51	Vogue V 2037	The Scene Changes/Mean To Me (78)	8

FULL MOON
89	private pressing LUNAR 13	FULL MOON (LP, private pressing)	12
90	private pressing LUNAR 14	A LIVE ENCOUNTER (LP, private pressing)	15

FULL TIME MEN
86	Shigaku SHIG 1T	I Got Wheels/One More Time/Way Down South (12", p/s)	8

(see also R.E.M.)

LOWELL FULSON/FULSOM
53	London L 1199	I Love My Baby/The Blues Came Rollin' In (78)	50
65	Sue WI 375	Too Many Drivers/Key To Your Heart	18
66	Sue WI 4023	Talking Woman/Blues Around Midnight	30
66	Outasite 45-502	Stop And Think/Baby (with Leon Blue)	60
66	Polydor 56515	Black Nights/Little Angel	12
67	Fontana TF 795	Tramp/Pico	20
76	Jet JET 770	Do You Love Me?/Monday Morning	6
69	Fontana SFJL 920	SAN FRANCISCO BLUES (LP)	30
69	Polydor 2384 038	IN A HEAVY BAG (LP, as Lowell Fulsom)	15

FUMBLE
72	Sovereign SOV 110	Hullo Mary Lou/Hanging On	5
73	Sovereign SOV 118	Million Seller/Get Up	5
73	Sovereign SOV 121	Alexandra Park/Mama I Can't Tell You	5
72	Sovereign SVNA 7254	FUMBLE (LP, gatefold sleeve)	18
74	RCA SF 8403	POETRY IN LOTION (LP)	12

FUNBOY FIVE
80s	Cool Cat Daddy-O PHUN 1	Life After Death/Compulsive Eater (foldover p/s)	5

FUN BOY THREE
82	Chrysalis CHSP 2609	The Telephone Always Rings/The Alibi (2 different picture discs)	each 5
82	Chrysalis CHSP 2629	Summertime/Summer Of '82 (picture disc)	5
83	Chrysalis CHSP 2678	Tunnel Of Love/The Lunacy Legacy (picture disc)	5

(see also Terry Hall, Specials, Colourfield)

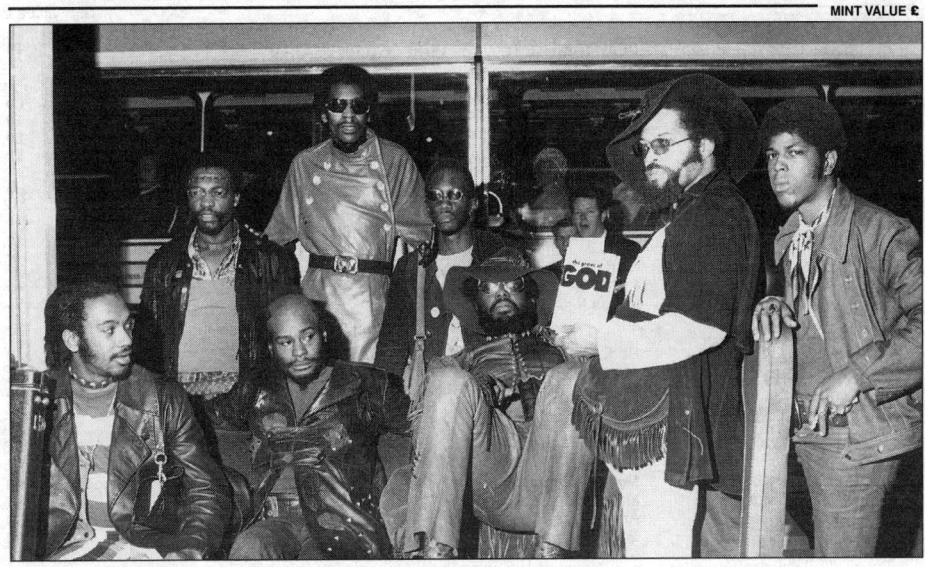

FUNKADELIC

MINT VALUE £

FUNKY JUNCTION
73	Stereo Gold Award MER 373	PLAY TRIBUTE TO DEEP PURPLE (LP)	12

FINBAR & EDDIE FUREY
72	Dawn DNS 1025	Her Father Didn't Like Me Anyway/Reynardine	5
68	Transatlantic TRA 168	FINBAR AND EDDIE FUREY (LP)	20
69	Xtra XTRA 1077	TRADITIONAL IRISH PIPE MUSIC (LP)	20
69	Transatlantic TRA 191	THE LONESOME BOATMAN (LP)	18
72	Dawn DNLS 3037	THE DAWNING OF THE DAY (LP, with lyric insert)	20

FINBAR FUREY & BOB STEWART
76	Crescent ARS 110	TOMORROW WE PART (LP)	12

FUR FUR
80s	Daark Inc. D.I. 7	FUR FUR (cassette)	12

(see also Karl Blake, Danielle Dax, Lemon Kittens, Gland Shrouds)

FURRY DICE
80	White Line WHLS 001	Rudi Don't Take Your Love To Town/K.G.B. (p/s)	6

TOMMY FURTADO
57	London HLA 8418	Sun Tan Sam/Isabella	25
57	London HLA 8418	Sun Tan Sam/Isabella (78)	7

BILLY FURY
78s
59	Decca F 11102	Maybe Tomorrow/Gonna Type A Letter (78)	100
59	Decca F 11128	Margo/Don't Knock Upon My Door (78)	150
59	Decca F 11158	Angel Face/Time Has Come (78)	200
59	Decca F 11189	My Christmas Prayer/Last Kiss (78)	300

SINGLES
59	Decca F 11102	Maybe Tomorrow/Gonna Type A Letter (triangular centre, later round)	25
59	Decca F 11128	Margo/Don't Knock Upon My Door (triangular centre, later round)	25/30
59	Decca F 11158	Angel Face/Time Has Come (triangular centre, later round)	30/20
59	Decca F 11189	My Christmas Prayer/Last Kiss (triangular centre, later round)	65/35
60	Decca F 11200	Colette/Baby How I Cried (triangular centre, later round)	40/15
60	Decca F 11237	That's Love/You Don't Know (as Billy Fury & Four Jays)	15
60	Decca F 11267	Wondrous Place/Alright, Goodbye	18
60	Decca F 11311	A Thousand Stars/Push Push	12
61	Decca F 11334	Don't Worry/Talkin' In My Sleep (with Four Kestrels)	8
61	Decca F 11349	Halfway To Paradise/Cross My Heart	6
61	Decca F 11384	Jealousy/Open Your Arms	6
61	Decca F 11409	I'd Never Find Another You/Sleepless Nights	6
62	Decca F 11437	Letter Full Of Tears/Magic Eyes	6
62	Decca F 11458	Last Night Was Made For Love/King For Tonight	6
62	Decca F 11485	Once Upon A Dream/If I Lose You	6
62	Decca F 11508	Because Of Love/Running Around	6
63	Decca F 11582	Like I've Never Been Gone/What Do You Think You're Doing?	6
63	Decca F 11655	When Will You Say I Love You?/All I Wanna Do Is Cry	6
63	Decca F 11701	In Summer/I'll Never Fall In Love Again	6
63	Decca F 11744	Somebody Else's Girl/Go Ahead And Ask Her	6
63	Decca F 11792	Do You Really Love Me Too?/What Am I Gonna Do?	6
64	Decca F 11888	I Will/Nothin' Shakin' (But The Leaves On The Trees) (some B-sides list "Nothin' Shakin' ")	each 6
64	Decca F 11939	It's Only Make Believe/Baby What Do You Want Me To Do?	6
64	Decca F 40719	Hippy Hippy Shake/Glad All Over (export-only, some with p/s)	80/50
65	Decca F 12048	I'm Lost Without You/You Better Believe It, Baby	6
65	Decca F 12178	In Thoughts Of You/Away From You	6
65	Decca F 12230	Run To My Lovin' Arms/Where Do You Run?	6
66	Decca F 12325	I'll Never Quite Get Over You/I Belong To The Wind	7
66	Decca F 12409	Don't Let A Little Pride Stand In Your Way/Didn't See The Real Thing Come Along	12
66	Decca F 12459	Give Me Your Word/She's So Far Out She's In	12
67	Parlophone R 5560	Hurtin' Is Loving/Things Are Changing	18
67	Parlophone R 5605	Loving You/I'll Go Along With It Now	12
67	Parlophone R 5634	Suzanne In The Mirror/It Just Don't Matter Now	15
67	Parlophone R 5658	Beyond The Shadow Of A Doubt/Baby Do You Love Me?	12
68	Parlophone R 5681	Silly Boy Blue/One Minute Woman	30
68	Parlophone R 5723	Phone Box/Any Morning Now	18
68	Parlophone R 5747	Lady/Certain Things	18
69	Parlophone R 5788	I Call For My Rose/Bye Bye	18
69	Parlophone R 5819	All The Way To The U.S.A./Do My Best For You	25
70	Parlophone R 5845	Why Are You Leaving?/Old Sweet Roll (Hi-De-Ho)	25
70	Parlophone R 5874	Paradise Alley/Well ... All Right	30
72	Fury FY 301	Will The Real Man Please Stand Up/At This Stage	18
74	Warner Bros WB 16402	I'll Be Your Sweetheart/Fascinating Candle Flame	8
76	NEMS NES 018	Halfway To Paradise/Turn My Back On You	10
81	Polydor POSP 355	Be Mine Tonight/No Trespassers (p/s)	6

82	Polydor POSP 488	Love Or Money/Love Sweet Love (p/s)	6
82	Polydor POSP 528	Devil Or Angel/Don't Tell Me Lies	
		('guitar' or 'microphone' p/s)	6/12
83	Polydor POSP 558	Forget Him/Your Words (p/s)	7
83	Polydor POSP 558	Let Me Go Lover/Your Words	
		(same p/s as above but diff. A-side, 500 only)	20
83	Lyntone LYN 13078/BF 1	Devil Or Angel/Lost Without You	
		(flexi free within memorial concert booklet)	15/5
83	private pressing	BILLY FURY IN INTERVIEW WITH STUART COLEMAN	
		(10", 500 white label copies only, 1st 200 numbered)	35/30

EPs

59	Decca DFE 6597	MAYBE TOMORROW	
		(EP, triangular centre, orange/red p/s)	90
59	Decca DFE 6597	MAYBE TOMORROW	
		(EP, round centre, orange/red or yellow p/s)	75/60
61	Decca DFE 6694	BILLY FURY (EP)	60
62	Decca DFE 6699	BILLY FURY NO. 2 (EP)	60
62	Decca DFE 6708	PLAY IT COOL (EP)	30
62	Decca DFE 6708	PLAY IT COOL	
		(EP, export issue, blue/green 'crouching' cover)	100+
62	Decca DFE 8505	BILLY FURY HITS (EP)	30
63	Decca DFE 8525	BILLY FURY AND THE TORNADOS (EP)	40
63	Decca DFE 8558	AM I BLUE (EP)	45
65	Decca DFE 8641	BILLY FURY AND THE GAMBLERS (EP)	90
73	Ronco MR EP 001	LONG LIVE ROCK (EP, with others, no p/s)	20
83	Decca DFE 8686	MY CHRISTMAS PRAYER (EP)	12

LPs

60	Decca LF 1329	THE SOUND OF FURY (10" LP)	80
60	Ace Of Clubs ACL 1047	BILLY FURY (LP)	30
61	Ace Of Clubs ACL 1083	HALFWAY TO PARADISE (LP)	30
63	Decca LK 4533	BILLY (LP)	40
63	Decca LK 4548/SKL 4548	WE WANT BILLY!	
		(live LP, with Tornados, mono/stereo)	40/55
65	Decca LK 4677	I'VE GOTTA HORSE (LP, soundtrack)	50
67	Ace Of Clubs ACL 1229	THE BEST OF BILLY FURY (LP)	25
71	Decca SPA 188	THE WORLD OF BILLY FURY (LP)	15
72	Decca SPA 575	THE WORLD OF BILLY FURY VOLUME 2 (LP)	15
76	Decca DPA 3033/4	THE BILLY FURY STORY (2-LP)	15
81	Decca LFT 1329	THE SOUND OF FURY	
		(10" LP, reissue)	15
83	Red Bus BUSLP 1003	THE MISSING YEARS (LP)	15

(see also Tornados, Gamblers)

FURYS

63	Stateside SS 182	Never More/Zing! Went The Strings Of My Heart	6
72	Jay Boy BOY 65	What Is Soul?/I Lost My Baby	5
72	Jay Boy BOY 68	I'm Satisfied With You/Just A Little Mixed Up	6

FURY'S TORNADOES

| 74 | Warner Bros K 16442 | Telstar '74/I Would Give You Anything | 6 |

(see also Billy Fury)

F.U.S.E.

| 93 | Warp WAP38 | TRAIN TRACS (12", some white vinyl, p/s) | 10/7 |
| 93 | Warp LP12LTD | DIMENSION INTRUSION (2-LP, white vinyl) | 15 |

FUSION

| 79 | Plastic Fantastic PFUL 1104 | COLD OUTSIDE EP (12") | 8 |
| 80 | Telephone TEL 101 | TILL I HEAR FROM YOU (LP, blue vinyl) | 20 |

(see also Nik Kershaw)

FUSION ORCHESTRA

| 73 | EMI EMI 2056 | When My Mama's Not At Home/Nuthouse Rock | 6 |
| 73 | EMI EMA 758 | A SKELETON IN ARMOUR (LP, gatefold sleeve) | 30 |

FUT

| 70 | Beacon BEA 160 | Have You Heard The Word/Futting Around | 25 |

(see also Graham Bonnet, Bee Gees, Marbles, Maurice Gibb, Steve & Stevie; this record has NO Beatles involvement)

FUTURA 2000 with The Clash

| 83 | Celluloid CYZ 104 | The Escapades Of Futura 2000/Instrumental (p/s) | 5 |
| 83 | Celluloid CYZ 104 | The Escapades Of Futura 2000/Instrumental (12", p/s) | 8 |

(see also Clash)

FUTURE HEROES

| 82 | Eagle BSB 020 | Antmania/Hold On (p/s) | 5 |

FUTURE PAST

| 91 | B12 03 | Our Paths Meet/Harmony Park/Your Hand In My Mind/Dance Intellect/ | |
| | | TV People (12", black vinyl) | 15 |

FUTURE PILOT AKA VS ALAN VEGA & REVOLUTIONARY
CORPS OF TEENAGE JESUS

| 97 | Creeping Bent BENT 029/ | Meditation Rat/Mount Vernon Arts Lab (p/s, 1,000 only) | 5 |
| | Singles Club No. 5 | | |

FUTURES

| 75 | Buddah BDS 430 | You Better Be Certain/No One Could Compare | 6 |
| 75 | Buddah BDLP 4031 | CASTLES IN THE SKY (LP) | 12 |

MINT VALUE £

FUTURE SOUND OF LONDON
SINGLES

91	Jumpin' & Pumpin' TOT 17	Papua New Guinea/Papua New Guinea (Andrew Weatherall Mix) (p/s)	6
94	Virgin PROMO 500	Slider/Snake Hips/You're Creeping Me Out/ Herd Killing/Live In New York (double pack, promo only, 500 copies)	25

12" SINGLES

91	Jumpin' & Pumpin' 12TOT 11	PULSE: Bring On The Pulse/In The Mind Of A Child/ Hardhead/Pulse State (12")	15
91	Jumpin' & Pumpin' 12TOT 16	PULSE 3: Tingler/Owl/Bite The Bullet/Calcium (12")	12
91	Jumpin' & Pumpin' 12TOT 17	Papua New Guinea (Dali Mix)/(Dumb Child Of Q Mix)/ (Qube Mix) (12", p/s)	12
92	Jumpin' & Pumpin' 12TOT 17R	Papua New Guinea (Andrew Weatherall Mix)/(Dub Mix)/(Journey To Pyramid)/ (Monsoon Mix)/(Graham Massey Mix)/(Dumb Child Of Q Mix) (12", p/s)	8
94	Virgin VST 1540P	Far Out Son Of Lung And The Ramblings Of A Madman/ Snake Hips/Smokin' Japanese Babe/Amoeba (12", white vinyl, promo only)	25
95	Virgin SEMTEX DJ 1	Semtex (Part 1)/Semtex (Part 2)/We Have Explosive/Semtex (12", stamped sleeve, promo only, 500 copies)	20
97	Virgin VSTDJ 1616	We Have Explosive Mantronix Plastik Formula (Mix #1)/(Mix #2) (12", stickered sleeve, promo only)	10
97	Virgin VSTXDJ 1616	We Have Explosive (Original Mix)/(Leon Mar Mix)/ (Oil Funk Mix)/(Part 4)/(Part 5) (12", stickered black sleeve, promo only)	8

12" EPs

91	Jumpin' & Pumpin' 12TOT 15	PRINCIPALS OF MOTION EP (12")	8
91	Jumpin' & Pumpin' 12TOT 18	SMART SYSTEMS EP (12")	10
92	Jumpin' & Pumpin' 12TOT 25	PULSE 4 (I'm Not Gonna Let You Do It/The Creator/Shrink/18 Space Virus) (12")	12
92	Union City UCRT 11	METROPOLIS EP (12")	12
93	Virgin VST 1478	CASCADE EP (12")	8

CD SINGLES

92	Jumpin' & Pumpin' CDSTOT 17	Papua New Guinea/(Andrew Weatherall Mix)/(Dub Mix)/ (Journey To Pyramid)/(Graham Mix)/ (Dumb Child Of Of Q)/(Hamish McDonald Mix) (CD)	10
93	Virgin VSCDT 1478	Cascade (Part 1)/(Part 2)/(Part 3)/ (Part 4)/(Part 5)/Short Form (CD)	8
96	Virgin VCD 1605	MY KINGDOM (CD, 5 mixes & radio edits, card slipcase, promo only)	12
96	Virgin VSCDDJ 1805	My Kingdom (Media Mix)/(Part 4) (CD, card sleeve, promo only)	10

ALBUMS

92	Jumpin'/Pumpin' LPTOT 2	ACCELERATOR (2-LP)	15
94	Virgin V 2755	ISDN (LP, embossed, fold-out black sleeve with insert)	25
94	Virgin CDV 2755	ISDN (CD, embossed black wallet)	20
97	Virgin ISDNSHOW 1	ISDN SHOW (CD, promo only, no inlay)	25

(see also Amorphous Androgynous, Art Science Technology, Humanoid, Humanoid featuring Sharon Benson, Intelligent Communications, Mental Cube, Metropolis, Pulse Systems, Semi Real, Smart Systems, Yage, Stakker)

FUZZ

71	Mojo 2092 003	I Love You For All Seasons (Parts 1 & 2)	5
71	Mojo 2092 008	Like An Open Door/Leave It All Behind	5
71	Mojo 2916 010	FUZZ (LP)	20

FUZZ FACE

68	Page One POF 065	Mighty Quinn/Voices From The Sky	5

FUZZTONES

85	ABC S 006	She's Wicked/Epitaph For A Head (p/s)	6

FUZZY DUCK

71	MAM MAM 37	Double Time Woman/Just Look Around You	15
71	MAM MAM 51	Big Brass Band/One More Hour	15
71	MAM AS 1005	FUZZY DUCK (LP, with poster)	140
90	Reflection MM 05	FUZZY DUCK (LP, reissue with booklet & single "Double Time Woman"/ "One More Hour" [MMS 01])	15

(see also Andromeda, Greatest Show On Earth)

FX

79	own label	SOUTH'S GONNA RISE AGAIN (EP)	20

FYNN McCOOL

70	RCA RCA 1956	U.S. Thumbstyle/Diamond Lil	7
70	RCA SF 8112	FYNN McCOOL (LP, gatefold sleeve)	35

(see also Shakespears, Grapefruit, Sleepy)

JOHNNY G
80   Beggars Banquet SAM 123   G BEAT (12" sampler, stickered white label, hand-made sleeve) 8

TOMMY G & CHARMS
67   London HLB 10107   I Know What I Want/I Want You So Bad 12

WINSTON G (& WICKED)
65   Parlophone R 5266   Please Don't Say/Like A Baby 25
66   Parlophone R 5330   Until You Were Gone/That Way Too (as Winston G. & Wicked) 10
66   Decca F 12444   Cloud Nine/I'll Make You Cry Tomorrow. 12
67   Decca F 12559   Mother Ferguson's Love Dust/Judge And Jury 18
67   Decca F 12623   Riding With The Milkman/Bye Bye Baby 18

B(ASIL) GABBIDON
61   Blue Beat BB 69   Warpaint Baby (miscredited to B. Cabbidon & Buster's Group)/
                         I Was Wrong (miscredited to Chuck & Dobbie with Buster's Group) 15
62   Blue Beat BB 111   Iverene/Lover Man 12
62   Blue Beat BB 124   Independence Blues/For My Love (as B. Gabbidon). 12
62   Blue Beat BB 129   Our Melody/Going Back To Ja (with Randy's All Stars) 12
62   Island WI 033   I Found My Baby (actually by Roy Braham)/No Fault Of Mine 18
63   Island WI 076   I Bet You Don't Know/3 x 7. 18
63   Island WI 089   St. Louis Woman/Get On The Ball 15
63   Blue Beat BB 155   Ena Mena/Since You Are Gone (with Prince Buster All Stars) 12
63   Blue Beat BB 161   I'll Find Love (with Prince Buster All Stars)/
                         MELLOW LARKS: What You Gonna Do? 12
65   Blue Beat BB 288   Tick Tock (actually by Theo Beckford)/The Streets Of Glory
                         (actually by Theo Beckford & Yvonne Harrison) 12

(see also Derrick Patsy & Basil, Mellow Larks, Derrick Morgan)

GABERLUNZIE
76   MWS LS 507   WIND AND WATER, TIME AND TIDE (LP) 20

GABLE HALL SCHOOL CHOIR
72   Trojan TR 7881   Reggae Christmas/Candy Man 4

PETER GABRIEL
77   Charisma CB 301   Solsbury Hill/Moribund The Burgermeister (p/s) 10
77   Charisma CB 302   Modern Love/Slowburn
                         (no p/s, 'nude' picture label, withdrawn) 40
78   Charisma CB 311   D.I.Y./Perspective (p/s, purple label, Irish-only sleeve) 10
78   Charisma CB 311   D.I.Y./Perspective (p/s, silver label, possibly Irish-only sleeve) 10
78   Charisma CB 319   D.I.Y. (Remix)/Mother Of Violence/Teddy Bear (no p/s, withdrawn) 25
78   Sound For Industry SFI 381   Solsbury Hill (live) (1-sided flexidisc, concert freebie) 8
80   Charisma CB 354   Games Without Frontiers/The Start/I Don't Remember (p/s) 5
80   Charisma CB 370   Biko/Shosholoza/Jetzt Kommt Die Flut (p/s, 33rpm) 5
80   Charisma CB 370-12   Biko/Shosholoza/Jetzt Kommt Die Flut (12", p/s) 8
82   Charisma SHOCK 1   Shock The Monkey/Soft Dog (Instrumental) (p/s) 5
82   Charisma SHOCK 1   Shock The Monkey/Shock The Monkey (Instrumental)
                         (same p/s as above) 30
82   Charisma SHOCK 122   Shock The Monkey/Soft Dog (Instrumental) (picture disc) 10
82   Charisma SHOCK 12   Shock The Monkey/Soft Dog (Instrumental) (12", p/s) 8
82   Charisma SHOCK 350   Shock The Monkey/Shock The Monkey (Instrumental)
                         (12", same p/s as above [SHOCK 12]) 20
82   Charisma CB 405   I Have The Touch/Across The River (p/s) 5
83   Charisma GAB 12   I Don't Remember (live)/Solsbury Hill (live)/Kiss Of Life (live) (12",
                         shrinkwrapped stickered double pack, with 12" white label [GAB 122],
                         "Games Without Frontiers"/"Schnappschuss (Ein Familienfoto)", no p/s) 12
86   Charisma/Virgin PGT 112   Sledgehammer (Dance Mix)/Don't Break This Rhythm/Sledgehammer
                         (Album Version)/Biko (Original 12" Mix) (cassette, silver card box). 7
87   Charisma/Virgin PGT 312   Big Time (Extended)/Curtains/No Self Control (live)/
                         Across The River (cassette, gold card box) 5
87   Charisma/Virgin GAIL 312   Big Time (Extended Version)/Curtains/No Self Control (live)/
                         Across The River/Big Time (7" Version) (CD, gatefold card p/s) 8
87   Charisma/Virgin PGSC 412   Red Rain/Ga Ga (I Go Swimming)/Walk Through Fire (cassette) 5
88   Charisma/Virgin CDT 4   Sledgehammer/Don't Break This Rhythm/
                         I Have The Touch ('85 Remix) (3" CD, card p/s). 8
88   Charisma/Virgin CDT 33   Solsbury Hill/Moribund The Burgermeister/Solsbury Hill (live) (3" CD, card p/s) . . 7
92   Virgin PGSDG 712   Digging In The Dirt/Digging In The Dirt (Instrumental)/Quiet Steam/
                         Bashi-Bazouk (12", p/s, withdrawn). 15
92   Virgin PGSDG 7   Digging In The Dirt/Digging In The Dirt (Instrumental)/Quiet Steam/
                         Bashi-Bazouk (CD, picture disc in box with lyric sheet). 8
92   Virgin PGSDX 8   Steam/Games Without Frontiers (Massive DB Mix)/Steam
                         (Oh, Oh, Let Off Steam Mix)/Games Without Frontiers (live)
                         (CD in fold-out house-shaped box) 12
92   Virgin PGSDX 9   Blood Of Eden/Mercy Street/Sledgehammer
                         (CD, foldout sleeve with booklet). 10
92   Virgin PGSDX 10   Kiss That Frog (Edit)/Across The River/Kiss That Frog (Mindbender Mix Edit)/
                         Shakin' The Tree (Bottrill Remix) (CD, digipak with postcards) 8
86   Virgin PGCDP 5   SO (CD, picture disc) 15

(see also Genesis, Youssou 'Ndour & Peter Gabriel, Colin Scot)

PETER GABRIEL & KATE BUSH
86	Charisma/Virgin PGSP 2	Don't Give Up/In Your Eyes (Special Mix) (poster p/s in stickered PVC sleeve)	15
86	Charisma/Virgin PGS 212	Don't Give Up/In Your Eyes (Special Mix)/This Is The Picture (Excellent Birds) (12", p/s)	8

(see also Kate Bush)

RUSS GABRIEL
95	Input Neuron INMD(X)1	FUTURE FUNK VOL. 1 (12", double pack, p/s)	10

GABRIEL & ANGELS
63	Stateside SS 150	That's Life That's Tough/Don't Wanna Twist No More	10

GABRIELLI BRASS
65	Polydor 56031	Angel Cake/Cat Walk	5
65	Polydor 56047	Ride Your Pony/Anyone Who Had A Heart	6
68	Polydor 56252	'Canterbury Tales' Theme/Working My Way Back To You	6

GABY & CABLES
72	Duke DU 129	Only Love Can Make You Smile/Only Love Version	6

(see also Gaby & Wilton)

GABY & WILTON
72	Camel CA 92	Only Love/CHARLEY ACE: The Ten Commandments Of Joshua	5

(see also Gaby & Cables)

GADGETS
83	Glass GLASS 026	We Had No Way Of Knowing/Acid Bath (unissued)	
83	Glass GLASS 12026	We Had No Way Of Knowing/Acid Bath (12", unissued)	
79	Final Solution FSLP 001	GADGETREE (LP, with insert, blue or beige picture on sleeve)	20
80	Final Solution FSLP 002	LOVE, CURIOSITY, FRECKLES & DOUBT (LP)	20
83	Glass GLALP 006	THE BLUE ALBUM (LP, with inner sleeve)	12
83	Glass GLAMC 006	THE BLUE ALBUM (cassette)	12

(see also The The, Matt Johnson, Colin Lloyd Tucker, Plain Characters)

MEL GADSON
60	London HLX 9105	Comin' Down With Love/I'm Gettin' Sentimental Over You	8

GAGALACTYCA
90	Holyground HG 1135/ Magic Mixture MM 3	GAGALACTYCA (LP, with booklet, actually by Lightyears Away & Thundermother, 425 only)	18

(see also Bill Nelson, David John & Mood)

MAJOR YURI GAGARIN
61	Britone MK 100	CONQUEST OF SPACE (EP)	25

GAGS
79	Look LKLP 6312	DEATH IN BUZZARD'S GULCH (LP)	30

BASIL GAIL
70	Bullet BU 454	I Wish/Black Is Black	5

SLIM GAILLARD (QUARTET/TRIO)
50	Parlophone R 3291	Jam Man/JOHNNY OTIS & MARCIE LEE: Harlem Nocturne (78)	25
51	Vogue V 2029	Voot Boogie/Queen's Boogie (78)	10
51	Vogue V 2044	Central Avenue Breakdown/Sighing Boogie (78)	10
56	Parlophone GEP 8595	SLIM GAILLARD NO. 1 (EP)	20
56	Columbia Clef SEB 10046	MUSICAL AGGREGATIONS (EP)	25
60	London RED 1251	SLIM GAILLARD RIDES AGAIN (EP)	30

(see also Meade 'Lux' Lewis & Slim Gaillard)

DONNA GAINES
71	MCA MK 5060	Sally Go Round The Roses/So Said The Man	5

(see also Donna Summer)

GAINORS
58	London HLU 8734	The Secret/Gonna Rock Tonite	125
58	London HLU 8734	The Secret/Gonna Rock Tonite (78)	50

GALACTIC FEDERATION
66	Polydor BM 56093	The March Of The Sky People/Moon Shot	25

GALACTIC SYMPOSIUM
80	Vague VOG 2	Money/In The Navy (gatefold p/s)	5

GALADRIEL
82	Pennine PPS 191	AIRBORNE (LP, with insert)	12

GALAHAD
87	private pressing G 1001	Dreaming From The Inside/The Opiate (p/s, 500 only)	15

DIAMANDA GALAS
82	Y Y 18	LITANIES DU SATAN (LP)	12

GALAXIE 500
89	Chemical Imbalance C 1005	Oblivious/tracks by other artists (free with issue 8 of *Chemical Imbalance* magazine)	8
89	Catalogue CAT 075	Victory Garden/STRAIGHTJACKET FITS: Hail (1-sided flexi free with *The Catalogue* magazine)	5
90	Caff CAFF 9	Rain/Don't Let Your Youth Go To Waste (p/s, with insert in bag)	25
90	Rough Trade G5SFI	Blue Thunder/Victory Garden/STRAITJACKET FITS: Hail (promo only, stickered sleeve)	8
89	Schemer 8905 CD	TODAY (CD, with 2 extra tracks)	15
89	Rough Trade ROUGH 146	ON FIRE (LP)	12
90	Rough Trade ROUGH 156	THIS IS OUR MUSIC (LP, with sticker and 3 postcards)	12
90	Rough Trade ROUGHCD 156	THIS IS OUR MUSIC (CD, trifold case)	15
91	Rough Trade ROUGH 146L	ON FIRE (LP, reissue with shrinkwrapped CD single)	15
96	Rykodisc RCD 10355	GALAXIE 500 (4-CD box set with booklet)	25

(see also Damon & Naomi)

GALAXIES
60	Capitol CL 15158	The Big Triangle/Until The Next Time	6

DAVID GALBRAITH
57	Columbia DB 3947	Heartbreak Is New To Me/Miracle In Milan	6
58	Columbia DB 4226	Do I Love You/Tonight	5
58	Columbia DB 4226	Do I Love You/Tonight (78)	8

EDDIE GALE
69	Blue Note BST 84294	GHETTO MUSIC (LP)	12

SANDRA GALE
63	Ember EMB S 162	Hello Heartbreak/If She's Right For You	7

SUNNY GALE
53	HMV 7M 147	Teardrops On My Pillow/Send My Baby Back To Me	12
54	HMV 7M 243	Goodnight, Well It's Time To Go/Close To Me	12
55	HMV 7M 344	C'est La Vie/Looking Glass	10
57	Brunswick 05659	Two Hearts (With An Arrow Between)/Maybe You'll Be There	7
57	Brunswick 05661	Come Go With Me/Please Go	10
58	Brunswick 05753	A Certain Smile/Just Friends	10
58	Brunswick 05753	A Certain Smile/Just Friends (78)	10
61	London HLU 9322	Please Love Me Forever/Sunny	7

GALE BROTHERS
66	Parlophone R 5535	Every Day Of My Life/All Strung Out	5

GALENS
63	London HLH 9804	Baby I Do Love You/Love Bells	10

FRANCE GALL
65	Philips BF 1408	Poupée De Cire, Poupeé De Son/Le Coeur Qui Jazze	6
88	WEA YZ 316 CD	Ella Elle L'a (CD, slimline jewel case)	15

BRIDIE GALLAGHER
59	Decca F 11131	Stay With Me/I'll Always Be With You (78)	8
60s	Emerald MLD 5	SINGS IRISH REQUESTS (LP)	15

RORY GALLAGHER
79	Chrysalis CHS 2364	Philby/Hellcat/Country Mile (p/s, coloured vinyl)	5
80	Chrysalis CHS 2453	Wayward Child/Keychain (p/s, coloured vinyl)	5
71	Polydor 2383 044	RORY GALLAGHER (LP)	25
71	Polydor 2383 076	DEUCE (LP)	20
72	Polydor 2383 112	LIVE! IN EUROPE (LP, gatefold sleeve)	20
73	Polydor 2383 189	BLUEPRINT (LP)	20
73	Polydor 2383 230	TATTOO (LP)	15
74	Polydor 2659 031	IRISH TOUR '74 (2-LP)	15
87	Capo/Demon XFIEND 98	DEFENDER (LP, with bonus 7", "Seems To Me"/"No Peace For The Wicked")	12

(see also Taste, Killing Floor, Joe O'Donnell)

GALLAGHER-LYLE
67	Polydor BM 56170	Trees/In The Crowd	8
72	Capitol ST 21906	GALLAGHER AND LYLE (LP)	12

(see also James Galt, McGuinness Flint, Cups)

GALLAHADS
55	Capitol CL 14282	Ooh-Ah/Careless	8
55	Capitol CL 14282	Ooh-Ah/Careless (78)	8

GALLANTS
64	Capitol CL 15366	Happy Beat/Rhino	5
65	Capitol CL 15408	"Man From U.N.C.L.E." Theme/Vagabond	12

GALLIARD
70	Deram DM 306	I Wrapped Her In Ribbons/The Hermit And The Knight	6
70	Deram Nova (S)DN 4	STRANGE PLEASURE (LP)	25
70	Deram SML 1075	NEW DAWN (LP)	45

(see also Craig)

GALLIARDS
60	Topic STOP 101	Black And White/Bahnuah	6

BOB GALLION
59	MGM MGM 1028	Out Of A Honky Tonk/You Take The Table And I'll Take The Chairs	8
60	MGM MGM 1057	Froggy Went A Courtin'/Hey! Joe	8
65	Hickory 45-1300	I Don't Have The Right (To Disagree)/Thank The Devil For Hideaways	5

GALLON DRUNK
88	Gallon Drunk GAL 003	Snakepit/Please Give Me Something (p/s)	15
90	Clawfist HUNKA LURVE 1	Ruby/Us And Cousin Emmy (p/s)	5
91	Clawfist HUNKA 002	Draggin' Along/Miserlou (p/s)	5
91	Clawfist HUNKA 003	The Last Gasp (Safty)/The Whirlpool (p/s)	5
91	Clawfist HUNKA 006	Some Fools Mess/May The Earth Open Here/Rolling Home (p/s)	5
91	Clawfist HUNKA 006T	Some Fools Mess/May The Earth Open Here/Rolling Home (12", p/s, purple/black vinyl)	12/8
92	Clawfist HUNKA 011	Bedlam/Look At That Woman/Solitaire (p/s)	5
92	Clawfist HUNKA 011T	Bedlam/Look At That Woman/Solitaire (12", p/s)	8
93	Clawfist HUNKA 18T	You Should Be Ashamed/Silver Wings/The Amsterdam Run (12", p/s)	8
93	Clawfist XPIG 21	Known, Not Wanted/TINDERSTICKS: We Have All The Time In The World ('singles club' release, p/s, 1,400 only)	25
96	City Slang LC 6853	Two Clear Eyes/Fade Away/My Spent Love/Mr. Slinkys (p/s)	5
93	Clawfist HUNKA LP5G	FROM THE HEART OF TOWN (LP, with 12" E.P [GLOBAL 1])	12

GALLOW GLASS CEILI BAND
60s	Top Rank RX 30314	COME TO THE CEILI (LP)	20

MINT VALUE £

FRANK GALLUP
58	HMV POP 509	Got A Match?/I Beg Your Pardon	6
58	HMV POP 509	Got A Match?/I Beg Your Pardon (78)	8

JAMES GALT
65	Pye 7N 15936	Comes The Dawn/My Own Way	8
65	Pye 7N 17021	With My Baby/A Most Unusual Feeling	25

(see also Gallagher-Lyle)

GALWAD AR HOLL FILWYR BYFFALO
80s	Anhrefn 006	CYMRU (EP)	8

ARMANDO GAMA
83	WEA 24-9801-7	Esta Balada Que Te Dou/When Love Has Gone (p/s)	7

GAMBLERS
63	Decca F 11780	You've Really Got A Hold On Me/Can I See You Tonight?	8
64	Decca F 11872	Nobody But Me/It's So Nice	12
65	Decca F 12060	Now I'm All Alone/Find Out What's Happening	15
66	Decca F 12399	Doctor Goldfoot (And His Bikini Machine)/It Seems So Long	15
67	Parlophone R 5557	Cry Me A River/Who Will Buy	18

(see also Billy Fury)

GAME
65	Pye 7N 15889	But I Do/Gotta Keep On Moving Baby	50
66	Decca F 12469	Gonna Get Me Someone/Gotta Wait	75
67	Parlophone R 5553	The Addicted Man/Help Me Mummy's Gone (withdrawn)	225
67	Parlophone R 5569	It's Shocking What They Call Me/Help Me Mummy's Gone	225

GAMMER & HIS FAMILIARS
84	Gammer GAMMER 5	Will The New Baby/All Above (12", p/s)	10
81	Gammer EJ 9699	WON'T LOOK OUT (LP)	15
81	Gammer 4/EJ 9851	ROCKET TICKET (LP)	15

(see also Durutti Column)

GANDALF THE GREY
80s	Heyoka	THE GREY WIZARD AM I (LP, reissue of U.S. LP)	25

RON WARREN GANDERTON
(see under Sound Ceremony)

LITTLE JIMMY GANDY
69	Roulette RO 510	Cool Thirteen/I'm Not Like The Others	8

GANGBUSTERS
63	Fontana TF 419	The Memory Of Your Face/When We Met	6

GANGER
96	Vesuvius POMP 004	HALF NELSON EP (12", 500 only)	8

GANG OF ANGELS
94	Shotgun CDBOR 012	Hello Goodbye/Jim Jam (CD)	8

(see also Slade)

GANG OF FOUR
80	Fast Product FAST 5	DAMAGED GOODS (EP, original with b&w labels, some with sticker)	8/5

GANGSTERS
79	Stortbeat A45/B45	Harlow Town/Record Company (p/s)	6
79	Stortbeat BEAT 3	Best Friend/Best Friend Dub (p/s)	5
80	Big Bear BB 25	Rudi The Red Nose Reindeer/White Christmas	5
80	Big Bear BB 28	Wooly Bully/We Are The Gangsters	4
80	Big Bear 12BB 28	Wooly Bully/We Are The Gangsters (12")	7
79	Stortbeat BEAT 2	GANGSTERS (LP)	15

GANIM'S ASIA MINORS
58	London HLE 8637	Daddy Lolo/Halvah	10

CECIL GANT
74	Flyright LP 4710	ROCK LITTLE BABY (LP)	15
75	Flyright LP 4714	CECIL'S BOOGIE (LP)	12
79	Magpie 1816	KILLER DILLER BOOGIE (LP)	12

CLENTT GANT
60	Starlite ST45 023	I'm Just A Lucky So-And-So/I Need You So	5

DON GANT
65	Hickory 45-1297	Early In The Morning/Don't Ya Even Cry	10

ELMER GANTRY'S (VELVET) OPERA
67	Direction 58-3083	Flames/Salisbury Plain	15
68	Direction 58-3481	Mary Jane/Dreamy	10
69	Direction 58-3924	Volcano/A Quick 'B'	6
68	Direction 8-63300	ELMER GANTRY'S VELVET OPERA (LP)	40

(see also Velvet Opera, Stretch, Strawbs, Hudson-Ford, Paul Brett's Sage)

GANTS
65	Liberty LIB 55829	Road Runner/My Baby Don't Care	20
67	Liberty LIB 55940	I Wonder/Greener Days	8

GARBAGE
SINGLES

95	Discordant CORD 001	Vow/Torn Apart (embossed metal 'G' logo sleeve, with insert, 3,000 pressed [934 issued], stickered, some sealed)	70/50
95	Discordant CORD 001	Vow/Torn Apart (plain black embossed 'G' logo sleeve, with insert in poly bag, 500 only, some sealed)	25/20
95	Mushroom SX 1138	Subhuman/#1 Crush (embossed rubber 'G' logo sleeve, with SX 1138 insert, some in white 'G' logo carrier bag, 3,000 only; some with incorrect insert [S 1138])	35/30
95	Mushroom S 1138	Subhuman/#1 Crush (embossed card 'G' logo sleeve, with insert, 2,000 pressed [1,000 issued])	20
95	Mushroom D 1138	Subhuman/#1 Crush/Vow (CD, embossed inlay, stickered case, 3,000 only)	20
95	Mushroom SX 1199	Only Happy When It Rains/Girl Can't Come/Sleep (double-grooved B-side, stickered 'hologram prismaboard' 'G' logo sleeve, with inner sleeve & insert; some in blue 'G' logo carrier bag, 5,000 only)	12
95	Mushroom SX 1199	Only Happy When It Rains/Girl Can't Come/Sleep (as above, shrinkwrapped)	12
95	Mushroom C 1199	Only Happy When It Rains/Girl Can't Come/Sleep (cassette, embossed inlay)	5
95	Mushroom SX 1237	Queer/Queer (Adrian Sherwood Remix) (p/s, in stickered 'crystal' outer 'G' logo sleeve, 5,000 only, some with 12" pink 'Garbage' carrier bag)	10
96	Mushroom SX 1271	Stupid Girl/Dog New Tricks (The Pal Mix) (jukebox issue, white label, no p/s)	8
96	Mushroom SX 1271/1237	Stupid Girl/Queer (jukebox issue, white label, stamped 'Garbage' logo, no p/s)	10
96	Mushroom SX 1271	Stupid Girl/Dog New Tricks (The Pal Mix) (stickered red 'Tak-Tile' cloth 'G' logo sleeve, some with stickered shrinkwrap, 10,000 only)	10/8
96	Mushroom SX 1271	Stupid Girl/Dog New Tricks (The Pal Mix) (stickered blue 'Tak-Tile' cloth 'G' logo sleeve, some with stickered shrinkwrap, 10,000 only)	12/10
96	Mushroom SX 1494	Milk (The Wicked Mix)/(The Tricky Remix) (embossed/hologram 'G' logo sleeve, with inner sleeve & poster, most sealed)	6/5
96	Mushroom DJMILK 1	RABBIT IN THE MOON MILK (Udder Edit)/(Got It Mix)/(Butchered Vegas Mix)/ (12", die-cut white embossed 'G' logo sleeve, day-glo yellow inner sleeve, 500 only)	18
96	Mushroom DJMILK 2	GOLDIE MILK ('Completely Trashed' Mix)/('VIP Refuge Trash Your Shit') (12", die-cut white embossed 'G' logo sleeve, day-glo orange inner sleeve, 500 only)	18
96	Mushroom DJMILK 3	MASSIVE ATTACK MILK ('D' Mix)/('Trance' Mix) (12", die-cut white embossed 'G' logo sleeve, day-glo pink inner sleeve, 500 only)	18

LP

95	Mushroom L 31450	GARBAGE (LP, as 2 x 45rpm 12", with inner sleeves)	12
95	Mushroom LX 31450	GARBAGE (LP, as 6 x 7" singles in box set with 3 inserts [now import only], most sealed)	20/15
98	Mushroom MUSH 29LP	VERSION 2.0 (LP)	12

PROMOS

95	Mushroom (no cat. no.)	Subhuman/#1 Crush/Vow (cassette, black embossed inlay)	35
95	Mushroom (no cat. no.)	Vow/Queer/Only Happy When It Rains/Fix Me Now/As Heaven Is Fine (cassette, black embossed inlay)	35
95	Mushroom TRASH 02	Vow/Subhuman/#1 Crush (CD, embossed rubber sleeve with insert, promo only)	70
96	Mushroom TRASH 09/010	Stupid Girl (Red Snapper Mix)/(Dreadzone Mix) (12", hand-stamped label, plain black die-cut sleeve, 1,000 only)	20
96	Mushroom TRASH 011	Stupid Girl Remixes (Todd Terry)/(Danny Saber) (CD, no inlay, 500 only; 125 distributed)	25
96	Mushroom MILK CDP	Milk (Wicked Mix)/(The Siren Mix)/(Album Version) (CD, hologram inlay)	20
96	Mushroom CDP (no cat no.) (no cat no.)	Milk (Garbage Wicked Mix)/(Goldie Completely Trashed Mix)/ (Massive Attack Massive Mix)/(The Tricky Mix)/ (Rabbit In The Moon Utter Mix) (CD, hologram inlay)	20
98	Mushroom TRASH 17	Push It (1-track CD, shaped card sleeve, some in re-sealable foil bag)	15/8
98	Mushroom TRASH 16	THIS IS A PROMOTIONAL ITEM: Stupid Girl/Only Happy When It Rains/ Queer/Milk (CD, card sleeve in resealable foil bag)	20
98	Mushroom TRASH 19	VERSION 2.0 (CD/CD-ROM, stickered, embossed shaped card sleeve with insert, promo only)	25

(see also Goodbye Mr. MacKenzine, Angelfish)

VIN GARBUTT

72	Trailer LER 2078	THE VALLEY OF TREES (LP, red label)	15
75	Trailer LER 2081	THE YOUNG TIN WHISTLE PEST (LP, red label)	12

DIGNO GARCIA Y SUS CARIOS

61	Palette PG 9024	Brigitte Bardot/Morena	8
66	Pye 7N 17172	Guantanamera/The Bird	5

JERRY GARCIA

71	Douglas DGL 69013	HOOTEROLL? (LP, with Howard Wales)	15
72	Warner Bros K 46139	GARCIA (LP)	12
74	Round RX 59301	GARCIA (LP)	12
76	United Artists UAG 29921	REFLECTIONS (LP)	12

(see also Grateful Dead, Diga Rhythm Band, Old & In The Way)

RUSS GARCIA ORCHESTRA

58	London	FANTASTICA! (LP)	30

GARDEN ODYSSEY (ENTERPRISE)

69	Deram DM 267	Sad And Lonely/Sky Pilot (8/M/1) (as Garden Odyssey Enterprise)	15
72	RCA RCA 2159	Joker/Have You Ever Been To Georgia (as Garden Odyssey)	5

(see also Graham Gouldman)

Paul GARDINER

PAUL GARDINER
81	Beggars Banquet BEG 61	Stormtrooper In Drag/Night Talk (p/s)	5
81	Beggars Banquet BEG 61T	Stormtrooper In Drag/Night Talk (12", unreleased, white label promos only)	350+
84	Numa NU 1	Venus In Furs/No Sense (p/s)	6
84	Numa NUM 1	Venus In Furs (Extended Mix)/No Sense/Venus In Furs (7" Mix) (12", p/s)	10

(see also Dramatis, Tubeway Army, Gary Numan)

AVA GARDNER
53	MGM SP 1005	Can't Help Lovin' Dat Man/Bill	6

BORIS GARD(I)NER (& LOVE PEOPLE)
69	High Note HS 010	Lucky Is The Boy/Bobby Sox To Stockings	20
69	Doctor Bird DB 1205	Elizabethan Reggae/Hooked On A Feeling	12
69	Duke DU 21	Never My Love/The Bold One	8
70	Treasure Isle TI 7056	Hooked On A Feeling/MESSAGE: Turn Around Twice	10
70	Big Shot BI 537	Sweet Soul Special/Memories Of Love (with Love People)	6
70	Big Shot BI 538	Darkness/Watch This Music (B-side actually "Keep Out") (with Love People)	6
70	Big Shot BI 539	Hot Shot/Watch This Music (with Love People)	6
70	Dynamic DYN 404	Commanding Wife/Band Of Gold (as Boris Gardner & Happening)	5
70	Trojan TR 7753	Dynamic Pressure/Reggae Me Dis, Reggae Me Dat	5
70	Trojan TBL 121	REGGAE HAPPENING (LP)	20

DAVE GARDNER
58	Brunswick 05740	Hop Along Rock/All By Myself (B-side with Anita Kerr Singers)	25
58	Brunswick 05740	Hop Along Rock/All By Myself (B-side with Anita Kerr Singers) (78)	7

DON GARDNER & DEE DEE FORD
62	Stateside SS 114	I Need Your Loving/Tell Me	10
62	Stateside SS 130	Don't You Worry/I'm Coming Home To Stay	12
68	Soul City SC 101	Don't You Worry/I'm Coming Home To Stay (reissue)	10

(see also Baby Washington & Don Gardner, Dee Dee Ford)

JOANNE GARDNER
70s	Polydor	JOANNE GARDNER (LP)	15

JOHNNY GARFIELD
65	Pye 7N 15758	Stranger In Paradise/Anyone Can Lose A Heart	35

(Art) GARFUNKEL
74	CBS CQ 31474/Q 69021	ANGEL CLARE (LP, quadrophonic)	12

(see also Simon & Garfunkel, Tom & Jerry)

FRANK GARI
60	London HLU 9277	I Ain't Got A Girl/Utopia	7

JUDY GARLAND
50	Brunswick 04530	You'll Never Walk Alone/Smilin' Through (78)	8
51	MGM MGM 345	Happy Harvest/If You Feel Like Singing, Sing (78)	8
51	MGM MGM 345	Friendly Star/Get Happy (78)	8
52	Brunswick 04887	Skip To My Lou/I Wish I Were In Love Again (78)	8
53	Philips PB 155	Without A Memory/Send My Baby Back To Me (78)	8
53	MGM SP 1001	A Couple Of Swells/Medley: I Love A Piano/Snooky Ookums/When The Midnight Choo Choo Leaves (with Fred Astaire)	8
55	Philips PB 366	The Man That Got Away/Here's What I'm Here For (78)	8
55	Philips PB 394	It's A New World/Gotta Have Me Go With You (78)	8
56	MGM SP 1157	Look For The Silver Lining/Who?	8
56	MGM MGM 883	Look For The Silver Lining/Who? (78)	10
57	Capitol CL 14789	Rock-a-bye Your Baby With A Dixie Melody/After You've Gone	6
57	Capitol CL 14789	Rock-a-bye Your Baby With A Dixie Melody/After You've Gone (78)	8
57	Capitol CL 14790	I Feel A Song Coming On/Just Imagine	6
57	Capitol CL 14790	I Feel A Song Coming On/Just Imagine (78)	8
57	Capitol CL 14791	By Myself/It's Lovely To Be Back In London	6
57	Capitol CL 14791	By Myself/It's Lovely To Be Back In London (78)	8
55	Philips BBE 12012	BORN IN A TRUNK — SELECTIONS FROM A STAR IS BORN (EP)	8
56	MGM MGM-EP 568	IF YOU FEEL LIKE SINGING (EP)	8
56	MGM MGM-EP 641	EASTER PARADE — EXCERPTS (EP, with Fred Astaire & Peter Lawford)	8
56	MGM MGM-EP 672	WORDS AND MUSIC — SOUNDTRACK EXCERPTS (EP, 1 track with June Allyson & Mickey Rooney)	8
59	Capitol EAP1 1036	JUDY IN LOVE (EP)	8
59	Capitol EAP2 1036	JUDY IN LOVE (EP)	8
59	Capitol EAP3 1036	JUDY IN LOVE (EP)	8
59	Capitol EAP7 1569	JUDY AT CARNEGIE HALL (EP)	8
59	Capitol EAP8 1569	JUDY AT CARNEGIE HALL (EP)	8
60	Capitol EAP1 20051	A GARLAND FOR JUDY (EP)	8
55	Brunswick LA 8725	JUDY AT THE PALACE (10" LP)	20
55	MGM MGM-D 134	BORN TO SING (10" LP)	18
55	Philips BBL 7007	A STAR IS BORN (LP, soundtrack)	15
56	Capitol LCT 6103	MISS SHOW BUSINESS (LP)	12
57	Capitol LCT 6129	JUDY (LP)	12
57	Capitol LCT 6136	ALONE (LP)	12
59	Capitol (S)T 1036	JUDY IN LOVE (LP, mono/stereo)	12/15
59	Capitol (S)T 1118	AT THE GROVE (LP, mono/stereo)	12/15
59	Capitol (S)T 1188	THE LETTER (LP, mono/stereo)	12/15
61	Capitol (S)T 1467	JUDY! THAT'S ENTERTAINMENT (LP, mono/stereo)	12/15
63	Capitol T 1999	THE HITS OF JUDY GARLAND (LP)	12
63	Ace Of Hearts AH 11	GREATEST PERFORMANCES (LP)	12

(see also Fred Astaire)

ERROL GARNER

50	Esquire 10-104	Love For Sale/Don't Worry About Me (78)	8
51	Esquire 10-136	Flamingo/I Can't Give You Anything But Love (78)	8
51	Vogue V 2069	Slamboree/Wrap Your Troubles In Dreams (78)	8
54	Columbia DC 654	Summertime/What's New (78, export issue)	8
59	Melodisc MEL 1135	Lady Be Good/Don't Blame Me (78)	8
60	Philips JAZ 103	Cheek To Cheek/The Way You Look Tonight (p/s)	6
60	Philips JAZ 105	Lullaby Of Birdland/Easy To Love (p/s)	6
56	London RE-U 1066	THE PIANO WIZARDRY OF ERROL GARNER (EP)	12
60s	Realm REP 4006	UNDECIDED (EP)	8
53	Vogue LDE 034	ERROL GARNER TRIO VOLUME ONE (10" LP)	15
54	Felsted EDL 87002	MARGIE (10" LP)	15
54	Philips BBR 8002	PLAYS FOR DANCING (10" LP)	15
55	Philips BBR 8045	SOLO FLIGHT (10" LP)	15
55	Philips BBL 7034	GONE GARNER GONEST (LP)	12
55	Columbia 33S 1050	PIANO MOODS (10" LP)	15
55	Columbia 33S 1059	PIANO GEMS (10" LP)	15
55	Oriole MG 26042	GONE WITH GARNER (10" LP)	15
55	Felsted EDL 87015	PASSPORT TO FAME (10" LP)	15
56	Philips BBL 7078	AT THE PIANO (LP)	12
56	Mercury MPL 6501	MAMBO MOVES GARNER (LP)	12
57	Philips BBL 7106	CONCERT BY THE SEA (LP)	12
57	Mercury MPL 6507	AT THE PIANO (LP)	12
58	Mercury MPL 6539	AFTERNOON OF AN ELF (LP)	12
59	Mercury MMB 12010	ERROL (LP)	12
60	Vogue LAE 12209	THE ERROL GARNER TRIO (LP)	12
69	Pye Intl. NSPL 28123	UP IN ERROL'S ROOM (LP)	12

BLIND LEROY GARNET

52	Jazz Collector L 74	Chain 'Em Down/Louisiana Glide (78)	15

COL GARNET

66	Page One POF 002	With A Girl Like You/Monday Monday	8

ALF GARNETT (& FAMILY)

67	CBS 202607	All/Among My Souvenirs	5
68	Pye NPL 18192	SEX AND OTHER THOUGHTS (LP)	15

GALE GARNETT

64	RCA RCA 1418	We'll Sing In The Sunshine/Prism Song	10
65	RCA RCA 1451	I'll Cry Alone/Where Do You Go To Go Away?	20
65	RCA RD 7726	MY KIND OF FOLK SONGS (LP)	20
66	RCA RD 7750	LOVIN' PLACE	15

LAURENT GARNIER

93	Warp WAP36	A BOUT DE SOUFFLE (12", company sleeve)	8

JESSE GARON & DESPERADOS

(see under 'J')

GARRET SINGERS

70	Argo ZFB 7	THE GARRET SINGERS (LP)	10

VERNON GARRETT

67	Stateside SS 2006	If I Could Turn Back The Hands Of Time/You And Me Together	15
67	Stateside SS 2026	Shine It On/Things Are Lookin' Better	10
68	Action ACT 4508	Shine It On/Things Are Lookin' Better (reissue)	7

DAVID GARRICK

65	Piccadilly 7N 35231	Go/When The World Was Our Own	6
65	Piccadilly 7N 35263	One Little Smile/We Must Be In Love	6
66	Piccadilly 7N 35317	Lady Jane/Let's Go Somewhere	7
66	Piccadilly 7N 35335	Dear Mrs Applebee/You're What I'm Living For	6
67	Piccadilly 7N 35371	I've Found A Love/(You Can't Hide) A Broken Heart	5
67	Piccadilly 7N 35377	A Certain Misunderstanding/I'm Looking Straight At You	5
67	Piccadilly 7N 35402	Don't Go Out In The Rain (You're Gonna Melt, Sugar)/	
		Theme For A Wishing Heart	5
67	Pye 7N 17409	Ave Maria/Please Stay	5
67	Pye 7N 17409	Ave Maria/You Don't Know (different B-side)	5
68	Pye 7N 17509	Rainbow/I'll Be Home	6
68	Pye 7N 17610	A Little Bit Of This (And A Little Bit Of That)/Flutterby Butterfly	5
69	Pye 7N 17685	Maypole Mews/Like To Get To Know You Better	5
69	Pye 7N 17820	Poor Little Me/Molly With The Hair Like Silver	5
69	Columbia DB 8680	Bake Me A Woman/House In The Heather	5
71	Columbia DB 8784	Mary In The Morning/Beautiful People	5
67	Piccadilly NEP 34056	DAVID (EP)	40
66	Piccadilly N(S)PL 38024	A BOY CALLED DAVID (LP, mono/stereo)	18/22
67	Piccadilly N(S)PL 38035	DON'T GO OUT INTO THE RAIN, SUGAR (LP)	18
68	Pye N(S)PL 18223	BLOW UP — LIVE! (LP, unreleased)	
68	Marble Arch MAL 822	A BOY CALLED DAVID (LP, reissue)	12

MICHAEL GARRICK

65	Argo EAF/ZFA 92	ANTHEM — MICHAEL GARRICK QUINTET (EP, mono/stereo)	85
66	Argo EAF 115	BEFORE NIGHT/DAY (EP)	45
63	Airborne	CASE OF JAZZ (LP)	45
64	Airborne	MOONSCAPE (LP)	350
64	Argo ZDA 26/27	POETRY AND JAZZ IN CONCERT (2-LP, with Norma Winstone)	60
65	Argo (Z)DA 33	OCTOBER WOMAN (LP, as Michael Garrick Quintet, with Joe Harriott)	60
65	Argo (Z)DA 36	PROMISES (LP, as Michael Garrick Sextet, with Ian Carr)	70

Michael GARRICK

MINT VALUE £

68	Argo (Z)DA 88	BLACK MARIGOLDS (LP, as Michael Garrick Septet)	50
68	Airborne NBP 0021	JAZZ PRAISES AT ST. PAULS (LP)	50
69	Argo ZPR 264/5	POETRY AND JAZZ IN CONCERT 250 (2-LP, as Michael Garrick Quintet)	55
70	Argo ZDA 135	HEART IS A LOTUS (LP, as Michael Garrick Sextet with Norma Winstone)	75
72	Argo ZDA 153	COLD MOUNTAIN (LP, as Michael Garrick Trio)	75
72	Argo ZDA 154	HOME STRETCH BLUES (LP, as Michael Garrick Band with Norma Winstone)	75
73	Impulse AS 49	ILLUMINATION (LP, as Michael Garrick Sextet)	25
74	Argo ZDA 163	TROPPO (LP)	45

(see also Ian Carr, Norma Winstone, Joe Harriott, Garrick's Fairground)

GARRICK'S FAIRGROUND
71	Argo AFW 105	Epiphany/Blessed Are The Peacemakers	6
72	Argo ZAGF 1	MR. SMITH'S APOCALYPSE (LP)	60

(see also Michael Garrick)

FREDDIE GARRITY
68	Columbia DB 8348	Little Red Donkey/So Many Different Ways	7
74	Bus Stop BUS 1017	Hello Kids/It's Good For You	6
74	Bus Stop BUS 1022	The Chicken Song/Pooh Pooh Pooh	6
70	Starline SRS 5019	OLIVER IN THE OVERWORLD (LP, soundtrack)	15
71	CBS 70096	OLIVER IN THE UNDERWORLD (LP, reissue soundtrack)	12

(see also Freddie & Dreamers)

ROBIN GARSIDE & PAUL GOUGH
77	Northern Sound NSR 01	SEA SONGS (LP)	15

NICK GARVEY
82	Virgin VS 504	Take A Look Over My Shoulder/The Lion And Me (p/s)	5

(see also Ducks Deluxe, Motors)

REX GARVIN & MIGHTY CRAVERS
66	Atlantic 584 028	Sock It To 'Em J.B. (Parts 1 & 2)	10
67	Atlantic 584 097	I Gotta Go Now (Up On The Floor)/Believe It Or Not	15

JOHN GARY
59	Top Rank JAR 177	Let Them Talk/Tell My Love	6
59	Top Rank JAR 177	Let Them Talk/Tell My Love (78)	10
60	Top Rank JAR 392	Little Things Mean A Lot/Ever Since I Met Lucy	6

GARY & ARIELS
64	Fontana TF 476	Say You Love Me/Town Girl	8

(see also Garry Mills)

GARY & STU
72	Carnaby 6151 003	Sweet White Dove/Good Lady Fair	8
72	Carnaby 6302 012	HARLAN FARE (LP)	25

(see also Koobas, March Hare)

GASKIN
81	Rondelet ROUND 7	I'm No Fool/Sweet Dream Maker (p/s)	15
82	Rondelet ROUND 21	Mony Mony/Queen Of Hams (p/s)	15
81	Rondelet ABOUT 4	END OF THE WORLD (LP, gatefold sleeve)	30
82	Rondelet ABOUT 8	NO WAY OUT (LP, with inner)	20

GASLIGHT
70	SDE 32732	GASLIGHT (2-LP, private pressing, gatefold sleeve with inserts, 2nd disc by Gaslight Choir)	75

GASOLINE BAND
72	Cube HIFLY 9	GASOLINE BAND (LP)	12

GASS
65	Parlophone R 5344	One Of These Days/I Don't Know Why	10
66	Parlophone R 5456	The New Breed/In The City	20
67	CBS 202647	Dream Baby (How Long Must I Dream?)/Jitterbug Sid	5
71	Polydor 2058 147	Something's Got To Change Your Ways/Mr Banana	5
70	Polydor 2383 022	JUJU (LP, featuring Peter Green)	35
71	Polydor 2383 035	CATCH MY SOUL — THE ROCK-OTHELLO (LP, cast recording featuring Gass)	15

GASS COMPANY
68	President PT 170	Everybody Needs Love/Nightmare	30

(see also Wake)

GAS WORKS
73	Regal Zonophone RZ 3075	Standing Stiff/Keep On Rolling	5
73	Regal Zonophone RZ 3080	God's Great Spaceship/Cider With Rosie	5
73	Regal Zono. SRLZ 1036	GAS WORKS (LP)	15

DAVID GATES
60	Top Rank JAR 504	The Happiest Man Alive/The Road That Leads To Love	18
73	Elektra K 42150	DAVID GATES — FIRST (LP)	12

(see also Bread)

PEARLY GATES
74	Polydor 2058 443	Johnny And The Juke-Box/They Were Good Times	5
78	Bronze BRO 61	Burnin' Love (Parts 1 & 2)	5

(see also Flirtations, Gypsies)

GATES OF EDEN
66	Pye 7N 17195	Too Much On My Mind/I'm Warning You	12
67	Pye 7N 17252	In Your Love/Snoopy Versus The Red Baron	8
67	Pye 7N 17278	1 To 7/Hey Now	15

GATEWAY SINGERS
57	Brunswick LAT 8176	PUTTIN' ON THE STYLE (LP)	12

GATHERERS
73	Duke DU 153	Words Of My Mouth/UPSETTERS: Version	30

LUCHO GATICA
54	Parlophone CMSP 16	Besame Mucho/Las Muchachas De La Plaza De Espana (export issue)	7

GATOR CREEK
71	Mercury 6052 058	Danny's Song/Take A Look	5
71	Mercury 6338 035	GATOR CREEK (LP)	12

DICK GAUGHAN
72	Trailer LER 2072	NO MORE FOREVER (LP, red label)	12

GEORGES GAVARENTZ
69	Philips SBL 7898	THEY CAME TO ROB LAS VEGAS (LP, soundtrack)	70

JIMMY GAVIN
57	London HLU 8478	I Sit In My Window/Lonely Chair	65
57	London HLU 8478	I Sit In My Window/Lonely Chair (78)	30

JOHNNY GAVOTTE
60	Parlophone R 4631	It's Not Too Late/Can't Forget	7

BETSY GAY
50	Capitol CL 13300	Country Washburne — Chug-A-Lug/Whoa Sailor (78)	8
50	Capitol CL 13315	Honky Tonkin'/DEUCE SPRIGGENS: Red Hot Mama (78)	8
51	Capitol CL 13425	Cigars, Cigarettes, Souvenirs/That Ain't In My Catalogue (78)	8

ELAINE GAY
54	Parlophone MSP 6140	Love/Instantly	7
55	Parlophone R 3997	Rock Love/Ebony Eyes (78)	8

MAC GAYDEN
73	EMI EMA 760	McGAVOCK GAYDEN (LP)	20

(see also Area Code 615)

BILLY GAYE & GAYTONES
73	Waverley SLP 501	Oh Honey Love Me/I'll Never Say Never Again	5

MARVIN GAYE
63	Oriole CBA 1803	Stubborn Kind Of Fellow/It Hurt Me Too	75
63	Oriole CBA 1846	Pride And Joy/One Of These Days	55
63	Stateside SS 243	Can I Get A Witness?/I'm Crazy 'Bout My Baby	40
64	Stateside SS 284	You're A Wonderful One/When I'm Alone I Cry	30
64	Stateside SS 326	Try It Baby/If My Heart Could Sing	30
64	Stateside SS 360	How Sweet It Is (To Be Loved By You)/Forever	30
65	Tamla Motown TMG 510	I'll Be Doggone/You've Been A Long Time Coming	35
65	Tamla Motown TMG 524	Pretty Little Baby/Now That You've Won Me	25
65	Tamla Motown TMG 539	Ain't That Peculiar?/She's Got To Be Real	18
66	Tamla Motown TMG 552	One More Heartache/When I Had Your Love	18
66	Tamla Motown TMG 563	Take This Heart Of Mine/Need Your Lovin' (Want You Back)	18
66	Tamla Motown TMG 574	Little Darlin' (I Need You)/Hey Diddle Diddle	18
67	Tamla Motown TMG 618	Your Unchanging Love/I'll Take Care Of You	15
68	Tamla Motown TMG 640	You/Change What You Can	12
68	Tamla Motown TMG 676	Chained/At Last (I Found A Love)	12
69	Tamla Motown TMG 686	I Heard It Through The Grapevine/Need Somebody	5
69	Tamla Motown TMG 705	Too Busy Thinking 'Bout My Baby/Wherever I Lay My Hat	5
69	Tamla Motown TMG 718	That's The Way Love Is/Gonna Keep On Tryin' Till I Win Your Love	6
70	Tamla Motown TMG 734	Abraham, Martin And John/How Can I Forget?	6
71	Tamla Motown TMG 775	What's Going On?/God Is Love	5
71	Tamla Motown TMG 796	Save The Children/Little Darling (I Need You)	6
72	Tamla Motown TMG 802	Mercy Mercy Me/Bad Tomorrows	5
72	Tamla Motown TMG 817	Inner City Blues/Wholly Holy	8
73	Tamla Motown TMG 846	Trouble Man/Don't Mess With Mister 'T'	10
74	Tamla Motown TMG 882	Come Get To This/Distant Lover	10
85	CBS DA 4894	Sanctified Lady/Sanctified Lady (Instrumental)//Sexual Healing/ Rockin' After Midnight (double pack)	5
66	Tamla Motown TME 2016	MARVIN GAYE (EP)	40
67	Tamla Motown TME 2019	ORIGINALS FROM MARVIN GAYE (EP)	35
64	Stateside SL 10100	MARVIN GAYE (LP)	140
65	Tamla Motown TML 11004	HOW SWEET IT IS TO BE LOVED BY YOU (LP)	60
65	Tamla Motown TML 11015	HELLO BROADWAY (LP)	65
66	T. Motown (S)TML 11022	A TRIBUTE TO THE GREAT NAT KING COLE (LP, mono/stereo)	50/60
66	T. Motown (S)TML 11033	MOODS OF MARVIN GAYE (LP, mono/stereo)	40/45
68	T. Motown (S)TML 11065	MARVIN GAYE'S GREATEST HITS (LP)	18
69	T. Motown (S)TML 11091	IN THE GROOVE (LP)	30
69	T. Motown (S)TML 11119	M.P.G. (LP)	18
69	T. Motown (S)TML 11123	MARVIN GAYE AND HIS GIRLS (LP, with T. Terrell, M. Wells & K. Weston)	20
70	T. Motown (S)TML 11136	THAT'S THE WAY LOVE IS (LP)	18
71	Tamla Motown STML 11190	WHAT'S GOING ON? (LP, initially with lyric sheet)	18/12
72	Tamla Motown STML 11201	THE HITS OF MARVIN GAYE (LP)	12
73	Tamla Motown STML 11225	TROUBLE MAN (LP, soundtrack)	18
78	Tamla Motown TMSP 6008	HERE, MY DEAR (2-LP)	20
76	Tamla Motown STML 12025	I WANT YOU (LP)	12

MARVIN GAYE & TAMMI TERRELL
67	Tamla Motown TMG 611	Ain't No Mountain High Enough/Give A Little Love	12
67	Tamla Motown TMG 625	Your Precious Love/Hold Me Oh My Darling	10
67	Tamla Motown TMG 635	If I Could Build My Whole World Around You/If This World Were Mine	8
68	Tamla Motown TMG 655	Ain't Nothin' Like The Real Thing/Little Ole Boy, Little Ole Girl	7
68	Tamla Motown TMG 668	You're All I Need To Get By/Two Can Have A Party	6

Marvin GAYE & Tammi Terrell

69	Tamla Motown TMG 681	You Ain't Livin' Till You're Lovin'/Oh How I'd Miss You	7
69	Tamla Motown TMG 697	Good Lovin' Ain't Easy To Come By/Satisfied Feelin'	6
69	Tamla Motown TMG 715	The Onion Song/I Can't Believe You Love Me (demos in p/s £35)	5
68	T. Motown (S)TML 11062	UNITED (LP)	30
68	T. Motown (S)TML 11084	YOU'RE ALL I NEED (LP)	25
70	T. Motown (S)TML 11132	EASY (LP)	18
70	T. Motown (S)TML 11153	GREATEST HITS (LP)	15

MARVIN GAYE & MARY WELLS

| 64 | Stateside SS 316 | Once Upon A Time/What's The Matter With You, Baby? | 15 |
| 64 | Stateside SL 10097 | TOGETHER (LP) | 75 |

MARVIN GAYE & KIM WESTON

64	Stateside SS 363	What Good Am I Without You?/I Want You Around	18
67	Tamla Motown TMG 590	It Takes Two/It's Got To Be A Miracle (This Thing Called Love)	
		(1st pressing with narrow print; later issues with wider print)	10/6
67	T. Motown (S)TML 11049	TAKE TWO (LP, mono/stereo)	30/35

(see also Diana Ross, Tammi Terrell, Mary Wells, Kim Weston)

GAYLADS

64	R&B JB 159	There'll Come A Day/BILLY COOKE: Iron Bar	15
64	R&B JB 165	What Is Wrong With Me?/Whap Whap	15
66	Island WI 281	Goodbye Daddy/Your Eyes	18
66	Island WI 291	You Never Leave Him/Message To My Girl	18
66	Island WI 3002	Stop Making Love/They Call Her Dawn	15
66	Doctor Bird DB 1014	Lady With The Red Dress/Dinner For Two	18
66	Doctor Bird DB 1031	You Should Never Do That/WINSTON STEWART:	
		I Don't Know Why I Love You	18
66	Rymska RA 104	You Should Never Do That/TECHNIQUES: So Many Times	18
67	Island WI 3022	Don't Say No/SONNY BURKE: You Rule My Heart	18
67	Island WI 3025	You No Good Girl/Yes Girl	18
67	Studio One SO 2002	Tears From My Eyes/Never Let Your Country Down	18
67	Studio One SO 2013	I Am Going To Cool It (actually by Little Roy)/	
		MELODIANS: Let's Join Together	18
67	Studio One SO 2017	Love Me With All Your Heart/I Don't Care	18
67	Rio R 125	Put On Your Style/SOUL BROTHERS: Soul Serenade	12
68	Blue Cat BS 110	Go Away/SOUL VENDORS: Julie On My Mind	15
68	Doctor Bird DB 1124	It's Hard To Confess/I Need Your Loving	20
68	Doctor Bird DB 1145	She Want It/Joy In The Morning	15
68	Fab FAB 62	Looking For A Girl/Aren't You The Guy	20
68	Hi Note HS 001	A B C Rocksteady/LESLIE BUTLER & COUNT OSSIE: Soul Drums	15
69	Trojan TR 688	You Had Your Chance/Wha' She Do Now	8
69	Upsetter US 323	The Same Things/I Wear My Slanders	8
70	Trojan TR 7703	There's A Fire/Last Time	6
70	Trojan TR 7738	That's What Love Will Do/This Time I Won't Hurt You	8
70	Trojan TR 7743	Young, Gifted And Black/BEVERLEY'S ALLSTARS: Moon Glow	8
70	Trojan TR 7763	Tell The Children The Truth/Something Is Wrong Somewhere	6
70	Trojan TR 7771	Soul Sister/BEVERLEY'S ALLSTARS: Soul Version	6
70	Trojan TR 7782	It's All In The Game/BEVERLEY'S ALLSTARS: Version II	6
70	Trojan TR 7799	Fire And Rain/Cold And Lonely Night	5
71	Ackee AC 141	Accept My Apologies (actually by B.B. Seaton & Ken Boothe)/	
		My Version (actually by Conscious Minds)	6
71	Big BG 319	Can't Hide The Feeling/RUPIE EDWARDS ALLSTARS: Version	6
71	Camel CA 79	Seven In One Medley (Parts 1 & 2)	6
71	Summit SUM 8514	My Jamaican Girl/BEVERLEY'S ALLSTARS: Version	5
71	Bullet BU 462	My Love/Stranger Love	5
74	Dip DL 5009	You Made A Mistake/Shower Of Blessings	5
67	Coxsone CSL 8005	ROCKSTEADY (LP)	100
67	Coxsone CSL 8006	SUNSHINE IS GOLDEN (LP)	60

(see also Gaylords, Rockstones, Delano Stewart, Ken Boothe, B.B. Seaton, Brent Dowe, Dobby Dobson, Jackie Mittoo, Heptones, Clarendonians, Soul Vendors)

JEANNE GAYLE

52	Capitol CL 13764	The Boom Song (with Cliffie Stone's Music)/It's Been So Long (78)	8
52	Capitol CL 13757	Goody, Goody/Angels Are Lighting God's Candles (78)	8
52	Capitol CL 13814	Takes Two To Tango/It Wasn't God Who Made Honky Tonk Angels	
		(78, with Cliffie Stone's Music)	8
52	Capitol CL 13847	Bim Bam Baby/Butterflies (78, with Cliffie Stone's Music)	8

VINLEY GAYLE

| 64 | Black Swan WI 453 | Go-Go/BABA BROOKS: Take Five | 18 |

GAYLET(T)S

68	Island WI 3129	Silent River Runs Deep/You're My Kind Of Man	18
68	Island WI 3141	I Like Your World/Lonely Feeling	18
68	Big Shot BI 502	If You Can't Be Good/Something About My Man	8
69	Big Shot BI 516	Son-Of-A-Preacher-Man/That's How Strong My Love Is	8
70	London HLJ 10302	Son-Of-A-Preacher-Man/I Like Your World	6

(see also Bob Andy)

GAYLORDS (U.S.)

55	Mercury MB 3226	Mambo Rock/Plantation Boogie (78)	8
58	Mercury AMT 1006	Flamingo L'Amore/I'm Longin' For Love	5
58	Mercury AMT 1006	Flamingo L'Amore/I'm Longin' For Love (78)	10
59	Mercury AMT 1023	Again/How About Me	5
59	Mercury AMT 1023	Again/How About Me (78)	18
59	Mercury AMT 1049	Sweet Than You/Homin' Pigeon	5
60	Mercury MMC 14032	THAT'S AMORE (LP)	12

GAYLORDS (Jamaica)

| 66 | Island WI 269 | Chipmunk Ska/What Is Wrong? (both actually by Gaylads) | 15 |

(see also Gaylads)

GAYLORDS (U.K.)
66   Columbia DB 7805   He's A Good Face But He's Down And Out/You Know It Too 12
(see also Dean Ford & Gaylords, Marmalade)

WILTON 'BOGEY' GAYNAIR QUARTET
61   Tempo EXA 103   BLUE BOGEY VOLUME ONE (EP) 8
59   Tempo TAP 25   BLUE BOGEY (LP) 12

GAYNOR (Junior English) & ERROL (Dunkley)
65   Blue Beat BB 286   My Queen/ROLAND ALPHONSO: Roland Plays Prince
                               (B-side actually "Hanging The Beam" by Skatalites) 20

(see also Errol Dunkley)

MEL GAYNOR
55   Decca F 10497   Just A Man/How Important Can It Be? 5
55   Decca F 10542   With You Beside Me/Oh, My Love 5
55   Decca F 10618   Bella Notte/Sweet Kentucky Rose 5
(see also Oscar Rabin)

MITZI GAYNOR
59   Top Rank JAR 258   Happy Anniversary/Play For Keeps. 5
60   Top Rank JAR 289   I Don't Regret A Thing/The Touch Of Time 5
58   HMV 7EG 8460   MITZI (EP) 8

ROSEMARY GAYNOR
55   Columbia SCM 5196   Ain't That A Shame/A Happy Song 7

PAUL GAYTEN
57   London HL 8503   Yo, Yo, Walk/TUNE WEAVERS: Happy Happy Birthday Baby. 165
57   London HL 8503   Yo, Yo, Walk/TUNE WEAVERS: Happy Happy Birthday Baby (78) 50
59   London HLM 8998   The Hunch/Hot Cross Buns 125
59   London HLM 8998   The Hunch/Hot Cross Buns (78) 120

GAYTONES (Jamaica)
70   High Note HS 037   Target (actually "Musical Fight" by Crashers)/PATSY: Find Someone
                               (song actually "True Love") 10
70   High Note HS 048   Ten To One/Another Version 6
71   High Note HS 055   Heart Of The Knights/One Toke Over The Line (B-side actually by
                               Stranger & Gladdy) 12
71   Green Door GD 4016   Jamaican Hilite (Parts 1 & 2) 5
73   Smash SMA 2330   Blackman Kingdom Come/Swing And Dine (B-side actually by Melodians) 6
(see also Righteous Flames, Max Romeo, Ethiopians, Jackie Brown, Jean & Gaytones, Huxbrown & Scotty, Charlie Ace, Delano Stewart, Teddy & Conquerors)

GAYTONES (U.S.)
73   Action ACT 4610   Soul Makossa/Soul Makossa (Version) 10

GBH
82   Clay CLAY 8   No Survivors/Self Destruct/Big Women (p/s) 8
82   Clay CLAY 11   Sick Boy/Slit Your Own Throat/Am I Dead Yet? (p/s) 8
82   Clay CLAY 16   Give Me Fire/Mantrap (p/s). 8
82   Clay CLAY 16P   Give Me Fire/Mantrap (picture disc) 10
83   Clay CLAY 22   Catch 23/Hellhole (p/s). 5
84   Clay CLAY 36   Do What You Do/Four Men (p/s). 5
82   Clay CLAYLP 4   CITY BABY ATTACKED BY RATS (LP). 20

G-CLEFS
56   Columbia DB 3851   Ka-Ding Dong/Darla, My Darlin' 375
56   Columbia DB 3851   Ka-Ding Dong/Darla, My Darlin' (78) 45
61   London HLU 9433   I Understand/Little Girl I Love You. 8
62   London HLU 9530   A Girl Has To Know/(There Never Was A Dog Like) Dad. 12
62   London HLU 9563   Make Up Your Mind/Call Me Away 12

GEDDES AXE
80   ACS ACS 1   Return Of The Gods/Wildfire/Aftermath (p/s, with insert) 20
81   Steel City AXE 1   Sharpen Your Wits/Rock 'N' Roll (p/s) 10
82   Bullet BOLT 4   Escape From New York/Day The Wells Ran Dry/Six Six Six (12", p/s) 10

ROY GEE
70   J-Dan JDN 4412   Consider Me/You Walked Away 8
70   J-Dan JDN 4413   Try To Understand/I'd Rather Go Blind 7

RON GEESIN
65   RRG 319/320   RON GEESIN (EP, handmade p/s, 100 only) 60
67   Transatlantic (S)TRA 161 A RAISE OF EYEBROWS (LP) 35
72   KPM KPM 1102   ELECTROSOUND (LP, library issue, 1,000 only) 20
73   Ron Geesin RON 28   AS HE STANDS (LP). 15
75   KPM KPM 1154   ELECTROSOUND VOL. 2 (LP, library issue, 1,000 only) 20
75   Ron Geesin RON 31   PATRUNS (LP) 15
77   Ron Geesin RON 323   RIGHT THROUGH (LP) 15
77   KPM KPM 1201   ATMOSPHERES (LP, library issue, 1,000 only) 20
(see also Bridget St. John, Pink Floyd, Original Downtown Syncopators, Amory Kane)

RON GEESIN & ROGER WATERS
70   Harvest SHSP 4008   MUSIC FROM THE BODY (LP, soundtrack; initially green labels with
                               Waters/Geesin photos; later with black labels) 18/12

(see also Roger Waters, Pink Floyd)

J. GEILS BAND
78   EMI AM 507   One Last Kiss/I Can't Believe You 5
80   EMI EA 141   Love Stinks/Till The Walls Come Tumbling Down 6
80   EMI EAP 141   Love Stinks/Till The Walls Come Tumbling Down 6
81   EMI EA 134   Freeze Frame/Rage In The Cage (picture disc) 10
72   ATCO 2400 196   THE MORNING AFTER (LP) 12

HERB GELLER QUARTET
56	London RE-U 1067	SENSATIONAL SAX OF HERB GELLER (EP)	10

GEMAGE
80	private pressing BGA 1	Story So Far (no p/s)	50

GEMINI (U.K.)
65	Columbia DB 7638	Space Walk/Goodbye Joe (demos may credit the 'Original Tornados')	35
	(see also Tornados)		

GEMINI (Portugal)
78	Philips 6031 070	Dal-Li-Dou (Falling In Love)/Dal-Li-Dou	12

GEMINI (U.K.)
81	Airship AP 345	COUNTER BALANCE (LP)	60

GENE
94	Costermonger COST 1	For The Dead/Child's Body (p/s, 1,994 numbered copies only)	30
94	Costermonger COST 2	Be My Light, Be My Guide/This Is Not My Crime (numbered p/s)	12
94	Costermonger COST 2CD	Be My Light, Be My Guide/This Is Not My Crime/I Can't Help Myself (CD)	12
94	Costermonger COST 3	Sleep Well Tonight/Sick, Sober & Sorry/Her Fifteen Years (numbered p/s)	6
94	Costermonger COST 3CD	Sleep Well Tonight/Sick, Sober & Sorry/Her Fifteen Years (CD)	7
95	Costermonger COST 4	Haunted By You/Do You Want To Hear It From Me?/How Much For Love? (numbered p/s)	5

GENE & DEBBE
67	London HLE 10165	Go With Me/Torch I Carry	6
68	London HLE 10179	Playboy/I'll Come Running	8
68	London HLE 10203	Lovin' Season/Love Will Give Us Wings	6

GENE & EUNICE
56	Vogue V 9062	I Gotta Go Home/Have You Changed Your Mind?	150
56	Vogue V 9062	I Gotta Go Home/Have You Changed Your Mind? (78)	45
57	Vogue V 9066	Move It Over, Baby/This Is My Story	125
57	Vogue V 9066	Move It Over, Baby/This Is My Story (78)	50
57	Vogue V 9071	Let's Get Together/I'm So In Love With You	125
57	Vogue V 9071	Let's Get Together/I'm So In Love With You (78)	55
57	Vogue V 9083	Doodle Doodle Doo/Don't Treat Me This Way	125
57	Vogue V 9083	Doodle Doodle Doo/Don't Treat Me This Way (78)	55
58	Vogue V 9106	I Mean Love/The Angels Gave You To Me	125
58	Vogue V 9106	I Mean Love/The Angels Gave You To Me (78)	60
58	Vogue V 9126	Strange World/The Vow	40
58	Vogue V 9126	Strange World/The Vow (78)	70

(The above 45s were originally issued with triangular centres; later issues with round centres are worth about half the values listed.)

59	Vogue V 9136	Bom Bom Lulu/Hi Diddle Diddle	50
59	Vogue V 9136	Bom Bom Lulu/Hi Diddle Diddle (78)	80
59	London HL 8956	Poco-Loco/Go-On Kokomo	35
59	London HL 8956	Poco-Loco/Go-On Kokomo (78)	100

GENE & GENTS
68	Pye 7N 17532	C'mon Everybody/Hound Dog	6

GENE & JERRY
71	Mercury 6052 050	You Just Can't Win/Sho' Is Groovin'	5
71	Mercury 6052 087	Everybody Is Waiting/Ten And Two	5
71	Mercury 6338 051	ONE AND ONE (LP)	12
	(see also Gene Chandler, Jerry Butler)		

GENE LOVES JEZEBEL
82	Situation 2 SIT 18T	Shavin' My Neck/Sun & Insanity/Machismo/Glad To Be Alive (12", p/s)	20
82	Situation 2 SIT 20T	Screaming (For Emmalene)/So Young (Heave Hard Heave Ho) (12", p/s)	8
83	Situation 2 SIT 24T	Bruises/Punch Drunk/Brando Bruises (12", p/s)	8
85	Situation 2 SIT 36T	Cow (Extended)/Weep For Her (Cow) (12", p/s, label lists "You Weaken Her [Cow]", with poster)	8
86	B. Banquet BEG 156T	Sweetest Thing/Psycho II/Sweetest Jezebel (12", p/s, with poster)	8
86	B. Banquet BEG 173TC	Desire (US Club Mix)/Heartache (UK Club Mix) (12", p/s, 5,000 only)	8
83	Situation 2 SITU 7	PROMISE (LP, 1st pressing with matrix number SITU 7B)	12
86	Beggars Banquet BEG 73	DISCOVER (LP, with bonus live LP "Glad To Be Alive")	12
88	B. Banquet BEG 14CD	IMMIGRANTS (CD)	20

GENERAL JOHNSON
(see under 'J')

GENERAL STRIKE
79	Canal CANAL 01	Part 1: My Body/Part 2: (Parts Of) My Body (p/s)	5
84	Touch	GENERAL STRIKE (cassette in PVC wallet with inserts)	6

GENERATION GAP
69	Pye 7N 17845	She's Coming Home/Reach The Top	5
70	Pye 7N 17979	Any Old Time You're Lonely And Sad/Rainbows 'N' Sorrows	5

GENERATION X
77	Generation X GX 1	Day By Day/Listen!/Youth Youth Youth/Your Generation (white label test pressing, official bootleg sold at gigs, no p/s)	30
77	Chrysalis CHS 2165	Your Generation/Day By Day (p/s)	5
77	Chrysalis CHS 2189	Wild Youth/Wild Dub (Version) (p/s)	6
77	Chrysalis CHS 2189	Wild Youth/Wild Dub (Version) (p/s, mispressing, plays "No No No", B-side matrix: CHS 2189 B/1)	25
78	Chrysalis CHS 2207	Ready Steady Go/No No No (no p/s)	5
79	Chrysalis CHS(A) 2261	King Rocker/Gimme Some Truth (pink vinyl, Tony James p/s)	5

79	Chrysalis CHS(B) 2261	King Rocker/Gimme Some Truth (red vinyl, Billy Idol p/s) 5
79	Chrysalis CHS(C) 2261	King Rocker/Gimme Some Truth (yellow vinyl, Mark Laff p/s) 6
79	Chrysalis CHS(D) 2261	King Rocker/Gimme Some Truth (orange vinyl, Bob Andrews p/s) 6
79	Chrysalis CHS 2310	Valley Of The Dolls/Shakin' All Over (p/s, streaked brown or black vinyl) 5
79	Chrysalis CHS 2330	Friday's Angels/Trying For Kicks/This Heat (p/s, pink vinyl) 5
78	Chrysalis CHR 1169	GENERATION X (LP, with 'T-shirt offer' wraparound). 15

(see also Billy Idol, Gen X, Sigue Sigue Sputnik, Empire, Westworld)

GENERATOR (featuring Gary Numan)

| 94 | JVO JVOT 001 | Are 'Friends' Electric? (Eccentric Mix)/Bring Back The Love/ Going Home (12", p/s) . . . . 8 |
| 94 | JVO JVO 001 | Are 'Friends' Electric? (Radio Mix)/Are 'Friends' Electric? (Eccentric Mix)/Bring Back The Love/Going Home (CD). . . . . 8 |

(see also Gary Numan)

GEN X

| 81 | Chrysalis CHS 2488 | Dancing With Myself/Untouchables/King Rocker/Rock On (p/s, clear vinyl) . . . . . . 5 |

(see also Generation X, Billy Idol)

GENESIS

SINGLES

68	Decca F 12735	The Silent Sun/That's Me 225
68	Decca F 12775	A Winter's Tale/One Eyed Hound 225
69	Decca F 12949	Where The Sour Turns To Sweet/In Hiding. 250
70	Charisma GS 1/2	Looking For Someone/Visions Of Angels (promo only). 450
71	Charisma CB 152	The Knife (Parts 1 & 2) (some in p/s) 300/50
72	Charisma CB 181	Happy The Man/Seven Stones (some belated copies in p/s) 300/50
73	Charisma (no cat. no.)	Twilight Alehouse (1-sided flexidisc free with *Zig Zag* & later via fan club, [black vinyl test pressings exist] with/without magazine) 35/20
74	Charisma CB 224	I Know What I Like (In Your Wardrobe)/Twilight Alehouse 5
74	Charisma CB 238	Counting Out Time/Riding The Scree 8
75	Charisma CB 251	The Carpet Crawlers/Evil Jam ("The Waiting Room" live) 20
76	Charisma CB 277	A Trick Of The Tail/Ripples (purple or silver label) 8/5
77	Charisma CB 300	Your Own Special Way/It's Yourself 6
78	Charisma CB 309	Follow You, Follow Me/Ballad Of Big (p/s). 5
78	Charisma CB 315	Many Too Many/The Day The Light Went Out/Vancouver (p/s) 8
80	Charisma CB 369	Misunderstanding/Evidence Of Autumn (p/s) 8
81	Charisma CB 39	Keep It Dark/Naminanu (p/s) 5
81	Charisma CB 391-12	Keep It Dark/Naminanu/Abacab (Long Version) (12", p/s) 8
82	Charisma CB 393	Man On The Corner/Submarine (blue label, some with p/s). 70/5
82	Charisma GEN 1	3 X 3 (Paperlate/You Might Recall/Me And Virgil) (EP, picture disc). 7
82	Lyntone LYN 11806	The Lady Lies (live) (green flexidisc free with *Flexipop* mag, issue 21) 12/7
83	Lyntone LYN 13143	Firth Of Fifth (live edit) (flexidisc, some with numbered gatefold p/s) 20/5
83	Charisma/Virgin TATA Y-1	That's All/Taking It All Too Hard (shaped picture disc). 20
84	Charisma/Virgin ALS 1	Illegal Alien/Turn It On Again (live) (shaped picture disc) 20
84	Charisma/Virgin CB 300	Your Own Special Way/It's Yourself (blue label reissue, no p/s) 6
84	Charisma/Virgin CB 356	Turn It On Again/Behind The Lines Part 2 (blue label reissue, no p/s). 6
84	Charisma/Virgin CB 369	Misunderstanding/Evidence Of Autumn (blue label reissue, no p/s) 6
86	Charisma/Virgin GENSY 1	Invisible Touch/The Last Domino (clear vinyl, foldout p/s) 6
86	Charisma/Virgin GENSY 2-12	In Too Deep (Unedited)/Do The Neurotic (Unedited) (12" picture disc in stickered sleeve) 10
86	Virgin SNEG 3-12	Land Of Confusion/Land Of Confusion (Extended)/Feeding The Fire/ Do The Neurotic (CD, gatefold p/s) 10
87	Virgin GENSG 412	Tonight, Tonight, Tonight (Edit)/In The Glow Of The Night/ Paperlate/Tonight, Tonight, Tonight (12" Remix) (12", gatefold p/s) 8
87	Virgin CDEP 1	Tonight, Tonight, Tonight (Edit)/In The Glow Of The Night/ Invisible Touch (12" Remix)/Tonight, Tonight, Tonight (CD, gatefold p/s) 40
87	Virgin DRAW 412	Tonight, Tonight, Tonight (Edit)/In The Glow Of The Night/Paperlate/ Tonight, Tonight, Tonight (12" Remix) (CD, gatefold p/s) 10
87	Virgin GENS 512	Throwing It All Away (live)/I'd Rather Be You/Invisible Touch (live) (12", p/s) 8
88	Virgin CDT 5	Mama (Long Version)/It's Gonna Get Better (Long Version) (3" CD, card p/s). 8
88	Charisma/Virgin CDT 40	SPOT THE PIGEON EP (Match Of The Day/Pigeons/Inside And Out) (3" CD, card sleeve) 10
88	Charisma/Virgin CDF 40	SPOT THE PIGEON EP (Match Of The Day/Pigeons/Inside And Out) (5" export CD, card sleeve) 8
89	Virgin VVD 359	Domino: (Part 1) In The Glow Of The Night/(Part 2) The Last Domino (3" CD free with "Invisible Touch Tour" video) 20
91	Virgin GENDG7	I Can't Dance/On The Shoreline/That's All (live)/In Too Deep (live) (CD, with limited edition history & discography booklet) 8
92	Virgin GENDG 8	Hold On My Heart/Way Of The World/Your Own Special Way (live) (CD, digipak with 4 postcards). 10
92	Virgin GENDX 9	Jesus He Knows Me (Single Mix)/Hearts On Fire/Land Of Confusion (Rehearsal Version) (CD, 'Invisible Series' box set w/ space for other CDs). 10
92	Virgin GENS 10	Invisible Touch (live)/Abacab (live) (no'd gatefold p/s) 8
92	Virgin GENDX 10	Invisible Touch (live)/Abacab (live)/The Brazilian (live) (CD, numbered box with booklet) 10
98	Virgin GENCDJ 6	CALLING ALL STATIONS (CD, 7-track sampler, promo only). 7
99	Virgin SAMPGEN 8	TURN IT ON AGAIN (CD, 3 - track sampler, promo only). 20

GENESIS

ALBUMS

69	Decca LK 4990	FROM GENESIS TO REVELATION (LP, mono, w/ lyric sheet, unboxed logo)	175
69	Decca SKL 4990	FROM GENESIS TO REVELATION (LP, stereo, w/ lyric sheet, unboxed logo)	60
70	Decca SKL 4990	FROM GENESIS TO REVELATION (LP, stereo, with lyric sheet, boxed logo)	30
70	Charisma CAS 1020	TRESPASS (LP, original pink scroll label & gatefold sleeve with lyric sheet)	20
71	Charisma CAS 1052	NURSERY CRYME (LP, original pink scroll label, gatefold sleeve)	20
72	Charisma CAS 1052	NURSERY CRYME (LP, 2nd pressing, 'tour' label, gatefold sleeve)	60
74	Decca SKL 4990	IN THE BEGINNING (LP, reissue of 1st LP, 'snake' sleeve with lyric insert)	15
75	Charisma CGS 102	GENESIS COLLECTION VOLUME ONE (2-LP, boxed set of "Trespass" & "Nursery Cryme" in original sleeves, with poster)	80
75	Charisma CGS 103	GENESIS COLLECTION VOLUME TWO (2-LP, boxed set of "Foxtrot" & "Selling England By The Pound", with poster)	80
87	Charisma/Virgin GENPCD 1	INVISIBLE TOUCH (CD, picture disc)	15
97	EMI LPCENT 17	SELLING ENGLAND BY THE POUND (LP, reissue, gatefold sleeve)	15
98	Virgin GENCDP 6	CALLING ALL STATIONS (CD, with spoken-word introductions, promo only)	15

(see also Flaming Youth, Phil Collins, Tony Banks, Mike Rutherford, Peter Gabriel, Steve Hackett, Anthony Phillips, Brand X, Quiet World)

GENEVA

96	Nude PNUD 22CD	Nature's Whore (CD, 1-track, promo-only)	15
96	Nude NUD 22S	No One Speaks/What Your Shrink Says (stickered p/s, 2,000 only)	6

GENEVEVE

66	CBS 202061	Once/Just A Whisper (some in p/s)	12/6
66	CBS 202096	Nothing In The World/Summer Days	5
67	CBS 202524	That Can't Be Bad/I Love Him, I Need Him	5

GENGHIS KHAN (Germany)

79	Ariola ARO 163	Genghis Khan/Desert Land (unissued; promos may exist)	6
79	CBS 12-7317	Genghis Khan/Desert Land (12", clear vinyl with p/s insert)	8

GENGHIS KHAN (U.K.)

83	Wabbit WAB 61/63	Love You/Lady Lady//Mongol Nation/Gone For A Drive (double pack)	40

GENOCIDE

79	Safari SAP 2	IMAGES OF DELUSION (EP)	8

GENOCIDES

82	Action TAKE 1	Is That All Right?/Born To Lose (p/s)	5

GENTILES (U.K.)

68	Pye 7N 17530	Goodbye Baby/Marlena	8

GENTILES (Jamaica)

70	High Note HS 046	Your Destiny/Lock Love Away (actually by Melodians)	8

(see also Melodians)

JOHNNY GENTLE

59	Philips PB 908	Wendy/Boys And Girls (Were Meant For Each Other)	6
59	Philips PB 908	Wendy/Boys And Girls (Were Meant For Each Other) (78)	30
59	Philips PB 945	Milk From The Coconut/I Like The Way	6
59	Philips PB 945	Milk From The Coconut/I Like The Way (78)	30
60	Philips PB 988	Darlin' Won't You Wait/This Friendly World	5
60	Philips PB 1069	After My Laughter Came Tears/Sonja	5
61	Philips PB 1142	Pick A Star/Darlin'	5
59	Philips BBE 12345	THE GENTLE TOUCH (EP)	50

(see also Darren Young)

TIM GENTLE & HIS GENTLEMEN

65	Oriole CB 1988	Without You/Someone's In The Kitchen With Dinah	12

GENTLE GIANT

73	WWA WWP 1001	In A Glass House/An Inmate's Lullaby	10
74	WWA WWS 017	The Power And The Glory/Playing The Game	10
77	Chrysalis CHS 2160	I'm Turning Around/Just The Same (live)	5
77	Chrysalis CHS 2181	Two Weeks In Spain/Free Hand	5
78	Chrysalis CHS 2245	Thank You/Spooky Boogie	5
79	Chrysalis CHS 2270	Words From The Wise/No Stranger	5
70	Vertigo 6360 020	GENTLE GIANT (LP, gatefold sleeve, spiral label, later 'spaceship' label)	25/12
71	Vertigo 6360 041	ACQUIRING THE TASTE (LP, gatefold sleeve, spiral or 'spaceship' label)	20/12
72	Vertigo 6360 070	THREE FRIENDS (LP, gatefold sleeve, spiral label, later 'spaceship' label)	20/12
72	Vertigo 6360 080	OCTOPUS (LP, gatefold sleeve, spiral label)	18
73	WWA WWA 002	IN A GLASS HOUSE (LP, silk-screen cover, with photo insert & lyric inner)	18
74	WWA WWA 010	THE POWER AND THE GLORY (LP, with insert)	18
75	Chrysalis CHR 1093	FREE HAND (LP, green label, with insert)	12
75	Vertigo 6641 334	GIANT STEPS – THE FIRST FIVE YEARS (2-LP)	15
76	Chrysalis CHR 1115	INTERVIEW (LP, green label, with lyric inner sleeve)	12
77	Chrysalis CTY 1133	LIVE (PLAYING THE FOOL) (2-LP, with 12-page booklet)	15
77	Chrysalis CHR 1152	THE MISSING PIECE (LP, with inner sleeve)	12
78	Chrysalis CHR 1186	GIANT FOR A DAY (LP, with mask insert & lyric inner sleeve)	12
80	Chrysalis CHR 1285	CIVILIAN (LP, with lyric inner sleeve)	12

(see also Simon Dupree & Big Sound)

GENTLE INFLUENCE

69	Pye 7N 17666	Never Trust In Tomorrow/Easy To Love	8
69	Pye 7N 17743	Always Be A Part Of My Living/Captain Reale	8

GENTLE PEOPLE

67	Columbia DB 8276	It's Too Late/Sea Of Heartbreak	8

GENTLE PEOPLE

95	Rephlex CAT 040R	JOURNEY (12", Aphex Twin Remix)	8

GENTLE PERSUASION
73	People PEO 103	Dynamite Explodes/Bring It On Home. 5

BILL GENTLES
69	Gas GAS 104	Long Life/SCHOOLBOYS: O Tell Me 7
70	Pama PM 801	What A Woman/Sleepy Cat 6
70	Punch PH 54	Fight The Good Fight/Fight Beat 6
71	Escort ERT 853	Bachelor Boy/SCORPIONS: Colour Rites 6
72	Bullet BU 506	Pure In Heart/Clean Hands 5

(see also Bill Jentles, Bill Jenties)

ART GENTRY
72	Mojo 2092 048	Breakthrough/Wonderful Dream 5

BOBBIE GENTRY
67	Capitol CL 15511	Ode To Billie Joe/Mississippi Delta 5
67	Capitol (S)T 2830	ODE TO BILLIE JOE (LP) 12
68	Capitol (S)T 2842	THE DELTA SWEETE (LP) 12
69	Capitol E-(S)T 155	TOUCH 'EM WITH LOVE (LP) 12

BO GENTRY & RITCHIE CORDELL
69	CBS 4299	Stone Go-Getter/Hung Up 5

GENTRYS
65	MGM MGM 1284	Keep On Dancing/Make Up Your Mind. 8
66	MGM MGM 1296	Brown Paper Sack/Spread It On Thick. 18
66	MGM MGM 1312	Everyday I Have To Cry/Don't Let It Be 7
68	Bell BLL 1012	I Can't Go Back To Denver/You Better Come Home 5

GENTS
81	Posh POSH 001	The Faker/The Pink Panther (no p/s) 6
82	Kosmic KOS 6886	Schooldays/True Stories (some with p/s) 8/5
83	Posh POSH 007	Revenge/Girl (p/s) 5
80s	Posh MEGA 1	Revenge/Over Me/The Gent (p/s). 5

GEOFFREY
78	Music Bank BECK 694	ABH (Who Wants To Listen To Punk Rock?)/Colt 45 Rock (p/s) 15

GEORDIE
72	Regal Zonophone RZ 3067	Don't Do That/Francis Was A Rocker. 10
73	EMI EMI 2008	All Because Of You/Ain't It Just Like A Woman 6
73	EMI EMI 2031	Red Eyed Lady/Can You Do It 5
73	EMI EMI 2048	Electric Lady/Geordie Stomp 5
73	EMI EMI 2100	Black Cat Woman/Geordie's Lost His Liggy 5
73	EMI EMC 3001	HOPE YOU LIKE IT (LP) 12
74	EMI EMA 764	DON'T BE FOOLED BY THE NAME (LP) 15
76	EMI EMC 3134	SAVE THE WORLD (LP) 18

(see also Influence, AC/DC)

BARBARA GEORGE
62	London HL 9513	I Know/Love 15
64	Sue WI 316	Send For Me/Bless You 25

EARL GEORGE
73	Count Shelly CS 025	Gonna Give Her All The Love/PRINCE JAZZBO: Wise Shepherd 5

LLOYD GEORGE
62	London HLP 9562	Lucy Lee/Sing Real Loud. 40

GEORGETTES
58	London HL 8548	Love Like A Fool/Oh Tonight 35
58	London HL 8548	Love Like A Fool/Oh Tonight (78) 35
60	Pye International 7N 25058	Down By The River/A Pair Of Eyes 8

GEORGIA SLIM/WALTER ROLAND
59	Jazz Collector JEL 2	THE MALE BLUES VOL. 1 (EP) 15

GEORGIA TOM
60s	Riverside RLP 8803	GEORGIA TOM AND FRIENDS (LP) 20

(see also Paramount Allstars)

GEORGIE'S VARSITY 5
61	Vogue Pop V 9189	When My Sugar Walks Down The Street/Five Foot Two, Eyes Of Blue. 6

GERALDINE FIBBERS
94	Hut HUT 49	Marmalade/Get Thee Gone (p/s) 5

GERBILS
98	Earworm WORM 14	Lucky Girl/Big White Limo (p/s, 1,000 only) 4

WESLEY GERMS
72	Upsetter US 390	Whiplash/UPSETTERS: Whiplash Version. 10

GERONIMO BLACK
72	Uni UNLS 126	GERONIMO BLACK (LP) 20
74	MCA MCF 2683	GERONIMO BLACK (LP, reissue). 12

(see also Frank Zappa/Mothers Of Invention)

DENNY GERRARD
70	Deram Nova SDN 10	SINISTER MORNING (LP, with High Tide) 40

(see also Warm Sounds, High Tide, Open Road, Fifth Avenue, High Tide)

GERRY & HOLOGRAMS
79	Absurd ABSURD 4	Gerry And The Holograms/Increased Resistance (p/s). 5
79	Absurd ABSURD 5	The Emperor's New Music (unplayable record, glued into p/s) 8

GERRY & PACEMAKERS

63	Columbia DB 4987	How Do You Do It?/Away From You	6
63	Columbia DB 7041	I Like It/It's Happened To Me	5
63	Columbia DB 7126	You'll Never Walk Alone/It's All Right	6
64	Columbia DB 7189	I'm The One/You've Got What I Like	5
64	Columbia DB 7268	Don't Let The Sun Catch You Crying/Show Me That You Care	6
64	Columbia DB 7353	It's Gonna Be Alright/It's Just Because.	6
64	Columbia DB 7437	Ferry Cross The Mersey/You You You	6
65	Columbia DB 7504	I'll Be There/Baby, You're So Good To Me	6
65	Columbia DB 7738	Walk Hand In Hand/Dreams	6
66	Columbia DB 7835	La La La/Without You	6
66	Columbia DB 8044	Girl On A Swing/A Fool To Myself	8
74	DJM DJS 298	Remember (The Days Of Rock And Roll)/There's Still Time	7
78	EMI EMI 2814	Ferry Cross The Mersey/Don't Let The Sun Catch You Crying (promo p/s)	5
63	Columbia SEG 8257	HOW DO YOU DO IT? (EP)	18
64	Columbia SEG 8295	YOU'LL NEVER WALK ALONE (EP, initially in misprinted sleeve listing "It's All Right" instead of "Jambalaya" on front)	20/18
64	Columbia SEG 8311	I'M THE ONE (EP)	18
64	Columbia SEG 8346	DON'T LET THE SUN CATCH YOU CRYING (EP)	20
64	Columbia SEG 8367	IT'S GONNA BE ALRIGHT (EP)	20
65	Columbia SEG 8388	GERRY IN CALIFORNIA (EP)	30
65	Columbia SEG 8397	HITS FROM 'FERRY CROSS THE MERSEY' (EP)	25
65	Columbia SEG 8426	RIP IT UP (EP)	35
63	Columbia 33SX 1546	HOW DO YOU LIKE IT? (LP, also stereo SCX 3492)	20/30
65	Columbia 33SX 1693	FERRY CROSS THE MERSEY (LP, soundtrack, with Cilla Black & Fourmost, also stereo SCX 3544)	25/35
67	M. For Pleasure MFP 1153	YOU'LL NEVER WALK ALONE (LP, reissue of "How Do You Like It", different sleeve)	12
65	EMI Regal REG 2018	YOU'LL NEVER WALK ALONE (LP, export issue)	25

(see also Gerry Marsden)

GEORGE GERSHWIN

60	Ember EMB 3315	GEORGE GERSHWIN (LP)	12

GERVASE

68	Decca F 12822	Pepper Grinder/Visions	10

GESCOM

94	Skam SKA 2	Dan One/Five/Cicada/Sciew Spo (12", card folder p/s)	30
95	Skam SKA 3	Snackwitch/Mag (12", printed card folder p/s)	30
95	Clear CLR 408	THE SOUNDS OF MACHINES OUR PARENTS USED (12", p/s)	35
96	Skam SKA 7	KEY NELL 1/2/3/4 (12", bubblewrap sleeve)	10

(see also Autechre)

GESTURES

65	Stateside SS 379	Run Run Run/It Seems To Me	15

GETTING THE FEAR

84	RCA RCA 432	Last Salute/We Struggle (p/s)	5
84	RCA RCAT 432	Last Salute/We Struggle (12", p/s)	8

(see also Southern Death Cult, Into A Circle)

STAN GETZ (QUARTET/QUINTET)

78s

50	Melodisc MEL 1122	Cuddles (with Terry Gibbs)/J.J. JOHNSON: Afternoon In Paris (78)	8
50	Esquire 10-198	'S Cool Boy/Standanavian (78)	8
50	Esquire 10-208	Don't Get Scared/Flamingo (78)	8
52	Vogue V 2031	Bopelbath/Pin Head (78)	8
52	Vogue V 2103	On The Alamo/For Stompers Only (78)	8

SINGLES

60	HMV POP 735	With The Wind And The Rain In Your Hair/I Hadn't Anyone Till You	5
62	Verve POP 1061	Jazz Theme From Dr. Kildare/Desafinado (with Charlie Byrd)	5

EPs

50s	Esquire EP 16	STAN GETZ QUARTET (EP)	8
50s	Esquire EP 48	STAN GETZ QUARTET (EP)	8
50s	Esquire EP 133	STAN GETZ IN RETROSPECT (EP, as Stan Getz Quartet)	8
50s	Esquire EP 134	THE BROTHERS (EP, as Stan Getz & His Four Brothers)	8
50s	Esquire EP 173	STAN GETZ QUARTET (EP)	8
50s	Esquire EP 194	DON'T GET SCARED (EP)	8
50s	Vogue EPV 1016	STAN GETZ QUARTET (EP)	10
50s	Vogue EPV 1084	THE BROTHERS — STAN GETZ VOL. 1 (EP)	8
50s	Columbia SEB 10001	THE ARTISTRY OF STAN GETZ NO. 1 (EP)	8
50s	Columbia SEB 10021	THE ARTISTRY OF STAN GETZ NO. 2 (EP)	8
50s	Columbia SEB 10034	'TIS AUTUMN (EP, as Stan Getz Quintet)	8
50s	Columbia SEB 10063	THE ARTISTRY OF STAN GETZ NO. 3 (EP)	8
50s	Columbia SEB 10076	MINOR BLUES (EP)	8
50s	Columbia SEB 10089	COOL SOUNDS (EP)	8
50s	Columbia SEB 10117	MORE COOL SOUNDS (EP, as Stan Getz Group)	8
60s	HMV 7EG 8556	STAN GETZ/OSCAR PETERSON TRIO (EP)	8
60s	HMV 7EG 8596	STAN GETZ/DIZZY GILLESPIE SEXTET (EP)	8
60s	HMV 7EG 8641	STAN GETZ/OSCAR PETERSON TRIO NO. 2 (EP)	8
60s	HMV 7EG 8689	COOL VELVET (EP, also stereo GES 5828)	8/10
60s	Verve VEP 5009	DESAFINADO (EP, with Charlie Byrd)	8
60s	Verve VEP 5014	THE GIRL FROM IPANEMA (EP, with Joao Gilberto)	8

LPs

53	Esquire 20-007	STAN GETZ PLAYS (10" LP)	25
54	Vogue LDE 089	AT STORYVILLE (10" LP)	25
55	Vogue LDE 147	STAN GETZ QUARTET (10" LP)	25
55	Columbia Clef 33CX 10000	AT THE SHRINE NO. 1 (LP, as Stan Getz Quintet)	15
55	Columbia Clef 33CX 10001	AT THE SHRINE NO. 2 (LP, as Stan Getz Quintet)	15
62	HMV CLP 1577	FOCUS (LP, also stereo CSD 1448)	12/15
63	Verve (S)VLP 9013	JAZZ SAMBA (LP, with Charlie Byrd, mono/stereo)	12/15
63	Verve VLP 9024	BIG BAND BOSSA NOVA (LP)	12
63	Verve (S)VLP 9038	JAZZ SAMBA ENCORE! (LP, with Luiz Bonfa, mono/stereo)	12/15
64	Verve VLP 9065	GETZ—GILBERTO (LP)	12
64	Verve VLP 9069	REFLECTIONS (LP)	12
64	Verve VLP 9081	GETZ AU GO GO (LP)	12
65	Verve VLP 9132	GETZ—GILBERTO NO. 2 (LP)	12
66	Verve VLP 9139	CRAZY RHYTHM (LP)	12
64	Columbia 33SX 1686	THE MODERN WORLD OF GETZ (LP)	12
65	Columbia 33SX 1707	THE GETZ AGE (LP)	12
65	MGM MGM-C(S) 8001	MICKEY ONE (LP, soundtrack, mono/stereo, with booklet)	18/20
66	Stateside SL 10161	GREATEST HITS (LP)	12
67	Verve 2317 062	THE SPECIAL MAGIC OF STAN GETZ AND BURT BACHARACH (LP)	12

(see also Dizzy Gillespie, Gil Fuller & Dizzy Gillespie, Astrud Gilberto, Johnny Smith)

GEZA X

| 82 | Alt. Tentacles VIRUS 20 | We Need More Power/I'm Not Hungarian/Mean Mr Money Man (EP) | 4 |

G-FORCE

80	Jet JET 183	Hot Gossip/Because Of Your Love (p/s)	12
80	Jet JET 194	You/Trust You Lovin' (no p/s)	7
80	Jet JET 7005	White Knuckles/Rockin' And Rollin'/I Look At You (p/s)	12
80	Jet JETLP 229	G-FORCE (LP, with inner sleeve and patch)	12
80	Jet JETPD 229	G-FORCE (LP, picture disc)	18

(see also Gary Moore, Johnny Gustafson)

G.G. ALLSTARS

70	Explosion EX 2012	Champion/MAYTONES: Funny Man	7
70	Explosion EX 2014	Barabus/This Kind Of Life	7
70	Explosion EX 2023	Man From Carolina/Gold On Your Dress (B-side actually by Slickers)	7
70	Explosion EX 2024	African Melody/Serious Love (B-side actually by Maytones)	5
70	Explosion EX 2025	Ganja Plane/Deep River	6
70	Gas GAS 153	So Alive/Mercy Mr D.J.	6
70	Escort ERT 835	African Melody/Man From Carolina	6
70	G.G. GG 4501	Music Keep On Playing (actually by Cornell Campbell)/ Music Keep On Playing Version	7
71	G.G. GG 4508	Cleanliness Version 2/MAYTONES: Cleanliness	7
71	G.G. GG 4510	Rocking On The G.G. Beat (actually by Maytones)/WINSTON WRIGHT: Rocking On The G.G. Beat Version II	8
71	G.G. GG 4511	Lonely Nights (actually by Eric Donaldson & West Indians)/ MAYTONES: Let The Version Play	6
71	G.G. GG 4513	All One Nation (actually by Maytones)/VAL BENNETT: Judgement Warrant	7
71	G.G. GG 4526	Rod Of Righteousness (actually "Stretch Forth His Hand" by Jah Huntly)/ DENNIS ALCAPONE: King Of Kings (B-side actually "King Of Glory")	6
72	G.G. GG 4530	Donkey Face Version/MAYTONES: Donkey Face	6
72	Pama PM 846	I'm Feeling Lonely Version/MAYTONES: I'm Feeling Lonely	6
73	Bullet BU 528	People Get Funny Version/MAYTONES: People Get Funny	5
70	Trojan TBL 129	MAN FROM CAROLINA (LP)	18

(see also Paulette & Gee, Billy Dyce, Maytones, Charlie Ace, Monty Morris, Starlights, Lloyd & Carey, Gladdy & Stranger,
Heptones, Shorty Perry, Barbara Jones)

G.G. RHYTHM SECTION

| 69 | Blue Cat BS 165 | T.N.T./MAYTONES: Botheration | 10 |

AMOS GHERKIN QUARTET

| 70 | Parlophone R 5872 | Blakey And Me/Theme From An Unmade Silent Movie | 5 |

(see also Hurricane Smith)

GHETTO CHILDREN

| 73 | CBS 1450 | I Just Gotta Find Somebody To Love Me/Rat-a-tat-tat | 5 |

WESS & DORI GHEZZI

| 75 | Bradleys BRAD 7515 | Fallin'/Era | 8 |

GHOST

69	Gemini GMS 007	When You're Dead/Indian Maid	18
70	Gemini GMS 014	I've Got To Get To Know You/For One Second	15
88	Bam Caruso OPRA 088	Time Is My Enemy/POETS: I Love Her Still (company sleeve, promo only)	6
70	Gemini GME 1004	WHEN YOU'RE DEAD — ONE SECOND (LP)	120
87	Bam Caruso KIRI 077	FOR ONE SECOND (LP, reissue of "When You're Dead" with extra track "I've Got To Get To Know You" & in different sleeve)	12

(see also Velvett Fogg, Shirley Kent, Virginia Tree)

GHOST DANCE

86	Karbon KAR 602T	River Of No Return/Yesterday Again/Both Ends Burning (12", p/s)	10
86	Karbon KAR 606	Heart Full Of Soul/Radar Love (promo only)	10
86	Karbon KAR 606T	Heart Full Of Soul/Radar Love (12", p/s)	8
86	Karbon KAR 604	The Grip Of Love/Where Spirits Fly (p/s)	8
86	Karbon KAR 604T	The Grip Of Love/Last Train/A Deeper Blue/ The Grip Of Love (Version) (12", p/s)	10
87	Karbon KAR 608T	A WORD TO THE WISE (12" EP)	8
86	Karbon KARXL 303	GATHERING DUST (LP)	12

(see also Skeletal Family, All About Eve, Sisters Of Mercy)

MINT VALUE £

BILL GIANT
61	MGM MGM 1135	Better Let Her Go/When I Grow Too Old To Dream	12

GIANT CRAB
68	Uni UN 509	Hot Line Conversation/E.S.P.	5

GIANTS
60s	Polydor LPHM 46426	IN GERMANY (LP, also stereo SLPHM 237626)	20/25

GIANT SAND
87	Bucketfull Of Brains BOB 14	Wishing Well/PAUL ROLAND: Madhouse (Demo) (flexidisc free with *Bucketfull Of Brains* magazine)	6/5
87	B'full Of Brains BOB 14	Wishing Well/PAUL ROLAND: Madhouse (Demo) (hard vinyl test pressing)	10

GIANT SUNFLOWER
67	CBS 2805	Big Apple/February Sunshine	8
67	CBS 3033	Mark Twain/What's So Good About Goodbye?	7

BARRY GIBB
70	Polydor 2058 030	I'll Kiss Your Memory/This Time	6
84	Polydor POSPP 695	Shine Shine/She Says ('mirror' picture disc)	5

(see also Bee Gees)

MAURICE GIBB
70	Polydor 2058 013	Railroad/I've Come Back	6

(see also Bee Gees, Fut)

ROBIN GIBB
69	Polydor 56337	Saved By The Bell/Alexandria Good Time (withdrawn)	20
69	Polydor 56337	Saved By The Bell/Mother And Jack	5
69	Polydor 56368	One Million Years/Weekend	6
70	Polydor 56371	August October/Give Me A Smile	5
84	Polydor POSPG 668	Another Long Night In New York/I Believe In Miracles (with free single)	5
69	Polydor 583 085	ROBIN'S REIGN (LP)	22

(see also Bee Gees)

DOUG GIBBONS
65	Decca F 12122	I've Got Tears To Remind Me/I Found Out	6

STEVE GIBBONS (BAND)
71	Wizard WIZ 102	Alright Now/Lay Some Lovin' Down	7
82	RCA RCA 174	Loving Me, Loving You/That Makes It Tough/No Money Down (picture disc)	5
71	Wizard SWZA 5501	SHORT STORIES (LP)	35

(see also Uglys, Magic Christians, B, L&G)

CALY GIBBS
71	Amalgamated AMG 870	Seeing Is Believing/JOE GIBBS ALLSTARS: Ghost Capturer	12

(see also Carlton Gibbs)

CARLTON GIBBS
70	Amalgamated AMG 872	Ghost Walk/Joy Stick	10

GEORGIA GIBBS
53	Oriole CB 1173	Seven Lonely Days/If You Take My Heart Away (78)	8
53	Oriole CB 1215	Thunder And Lightning/For Me, For Me (78)	5
55	Mercury MB 3196	Tweedle Dee/You're Wrong, All Wrong (78)	10
55	Mercury MB 3217	Cherry Pink & Apple Blossom White/Got Him Off My Hands (78)	8
55	Mercury MB 3223	Dance With Me Henry/Ballin' The Jack (78)	8
55	Vogue Coral Q 72088	Ballin' The Jack/I Still Feel The Same About You	8
55	Vogue Coral Q 72088	Ballin' The Jack/I Still Feel The Same About You (78)	8
56	Mercury MT 110	Kiss Me Another/Rock Right (78)	10
56	Mercury MT 118	Happiness Street/Fool Of The Year (78)	8
56	Vogue Coral Q 72182	If I Were A Bell/I'll Know	10
57	Mercury MT 133	Tra La La/Morning, Noon And Night (78)	5
57	Mercury MT 144	Silent Lips/Pretty Pretty (78)	6
57	RCA RCA 1011	Sugar Candy/I'm Walking The Floor Over You	10
57	RCA RCA 1011	Sugar Candy/I'm Walking The Floor Over You (78)	10
58	RCA RCA 1029	Great Balls Of Fire/I Miss You	20
58	RCA RCA 1029	Great Balls Of Fire/I Miss You (78)	18
58	Mercury 7MT 210	Arriverderci Roma/24 Hours A Day	12
58	Mercury MT 210	Arriverderci Roma/24 Hours A Day (78)	10
58	Columbia DB 4201	The Hula Hoop Song/Keep In Touch	6
58	Columbia DB 4201	The Hula Hoop Song/Keep In Touch (78)	10
59	Columbia DB 4259	The Hucklebuck/Better Loved You'll Never Be	8
59	Columbia DB 4259	The Hucklebuck/Better Loved You'll Never Be (78)	15
60	London HLP 9098	The Stroll That Stole My Heart/Seven Lonely Days	6
65	Stateside SS 423	Let Me Cry On Your Shoulder/Venice Blues	5
55	Mercury EP-1-3265	THE MAN THAT GOT AWAY (EP)	10
56	Mercury MEP 9505	SWEET GEORGIA GIBBS (EP)	10
57	Mercury MEP 9516	SWEET GEORGIA GIBBS VOL. 2 (EP)	15
56	Mercury MPT 7500	SINGS THE OLDIES (10" LP)	30
57	Mercury MPT 7511	HER NIBS MISS GIBBS (10" LP)	30
57	Mercury MPL 6508	SWINGING WITH HER NIBS (LP)	18

JOE GIBBS (& DESTROYERS)
70	Amalgamated AMG 855	Nevada Joe (act. by Johnny Lover)/Straight To The Head (act. by Destroyers)	12
70	Amalgamated AMG 858	Franco Nero (actually by Count Machuki & Destroyers)/Version Two (actually by Destroyers)	12
70	Amalgamated AMG 859	Rock The Clock/Version Two	12
70	Amalgamated AMG 860	Let It Be/Turn Back The Hands Of Time (both actually by Nicky Thomas)	6

70	Amalgamated AMG 865	Hijacked/Life Is Down In Denver	7
70	Amalgamated AMG 867	Movements/Caesar	12
70	Amalgamated AMG 868	Gift Of God (actually by Lizzy)/The Rapper	8
70	Pressure Beat PR 5504	News Flash/Version Two	8
73	Jackpot JP 811	Ration/Version (as Joe Gibbs All Stars)	6

(see also Lizzy, Reggae Boys, Bunny Flip, Destroyers, Dennis Brown, Caly Gibbs, Nicky Thomas)

MICHAEL GIBBS

70	Deram DML/SML 1063	MICHAEL GIBBS (LP)	50
71	Deram SML 1087	TANGLEWOOD '63 (LP)	50
72	Polydor 2683 011	JUST AHEAD (2-LP)	50
74	Polydor 2383 252	IN THE PUBLIC INTEREST (LP, with Gary Burton)	40
70s	Bronze ILPS 9353	ONLY CHROME ... WATERFALL (LP)	25

(see also Neil Ardley, Gary Burton)

TERRY GIBBS BIG BAND

61	HMV/Verve CLP 1560	THE EXCITING TERRY GIBBS BIG BAND (LP, also stereo CSD 1439)	12/15

DEBBIE GIBSON

87	Atlantic A 9322	Only In My Dreams/Only In My Dreams (Version) (original red p/s)	6
87	Atlantic A 9322T	Only In My Dreams/Only In My Dreams (Version) (12", original blue p/s, possibly unissued in U.K.)	20
87	Atlantic A 9322TP	Only In My Dreams/Only In My Dreams (Version) (12", picture disc)	20
88	Atlantic A 9091CD	Out Of The Blue/Fallen Angel/Shake Your Love/Out Of The Blue (Extended Version) (3" CD with adaptor, 5" case)	8
88	Atlantic A 9059CD	Foolish Beat (Vocal/Extended Mix)/Between The Lines/ Shake Your Love (live) (3" CD with adaptor, 5" case)	8
88	Atlantic A 9020V	Staying Together/Red Hot (window pack)	10
88	Atlantic A 9020CD	Staying Together/Red Hot/Debbie Gibson Mega Mix/Play The Field (3" CD with adaptor, 5" case)	8
89	Atlantic A 8970CD	Lost In Your Eyes/Silence Speaks (A Thousand Words) (Acoustic Mix)/ Lost In Your Eyes (Piano And Vocal Mix) (CD, gatefold card sleeve)	8
		Electric Youth (House Version) (3" CD, gatefold card sleeve)	8
89	Atlantic A 8919CDP	Electric Youth/We Could Be Together (Campfire Mix)/ Electric Youth (House Version) (CD, picture disc)	8
89	Atlantic A 8896CD	We Could Be Together (House Mix)/(House Of Trix)/(Radio Mix) (3" CD, gatefold card sleeve)	8
89	WEA WX 231X	ELECTRIC YOUTH (LP, yellow vinyl with poster)	15

DON GIBSON

56	MGM SP 1177	Sweet Dreams/The Road Of Life Alone	135
56	MGM MGM 909	Sweet Dreams/The Road Of Life Alone (78)	18
58	RCA RCA 1056	Oh Lonesome Me/I Can't Stop Lovin' You	8
58	RCA RCA 1056	Oh Lonesome Me/I Can't Stop Lovin' You (78)	12
58	RCA RCA 1073	Blue Blue Day/Too Soon	8
58	RCA RCA 1073	Blue Blue Day/Too Soon (78)	12
58	RCA RCA 1098	Give Myself A Party/Look Who's Blue	7
58	RCA RCA 1098	Give Myself A Party/Look Who's Blue (78)	12
59	RCA RCA 1110	A Stranger To Me/Who Cares?	6
59	RCA RCA 1110	A Stranger To Me/Who Cares? (78)	18
59	RCA RCA 1150	Don't Tell Me Your Troubles/Heartbreak Avenue	7
59	RCA RCA 1150	Don't Tell Me Your Troubles/Heartbreak Avenue (78)	25
59	RCA RCA 1158	Big Hearted Me/I'm Movin' On	7
59	RCA RCA 1158	Big Hearted Me/I'm Movin' On (78)	25

(The above RCA 45s were originally issued with triangular centres; later round-centre copies are worth half these values.)

60	RCA RCA 1183	Just One Time/I May Never Get To Heaven	6
60	RCA RCA 1200	Far Far Away/A Legend In My Time	6
60	RCA RCA 1217	Sweet Dreams/The Same Street	6
61	RCA RCA 1243	Sea Of Heartbreak/I Think It's Best (To Forget Me)	7
62	RCA RCA 1272	Lonesome Number One/The Same Old Trouble	6
62	RCA RCA 1297	I Can Mend Your Broken Heart/I Let Her Get Lonely	6
63	RCA RCA 1335	Head Over Heels In Love With You/It Was Worth It	7
65	RCA RCA 1456	Again/You're Going Away	7
66	RCA RCA 1524	(Yes) I'm Hurting/My Whole World Is Hurt	7
67	RCA RCA 1626	All My Love/No Doubt About It (as Don Gibson & Jordanaires)	7
68	RCA RCA 1680	Ashes Of Love/Good Morning Dear	7
60	RCA RCX 1050	BLUE AND LONESOME (EP)	15
62	RCA RCX 213	LOOK WHO'S BLUE (EP)	15
62	RCA RCX 214	THAT GIBSON BOY (EP)	15
63	RCA RCX 7122	MAY YOU NEVER BE ALONE (EP)	15
60	RCA RD 27158	THE GIBSON BOY (LP)	25
62	RCA Victor RD/SF 7506	SOME FAVOURITES OF MINE (LP)	18
63	RCA Victor RD/SF 7576	I WROTE A SONG (LP)	18
64	RCA Victor RD 7641	GOD WALKS THESE HILLS (LP)	18

GINNY GIBSON

55	MGM SP 1121	Like Ma-a-d/Once There Was A Little Girl	8
58	MGM MGM 953	Whatever Lola Wants (Lola Gets)/If Anything Should Happen	6

JODY GIBSON & MULESKINNERS

59	Parlophone R 4579	Kissin' Time/Man On My Trail	7
60	Parlophone R 4645	If You Don't Know/So You Think You've Got Troubles	7

LORNE GIBSON TRIO

62	Decca F 11519	Little Black Book/What Kind Of Love Is This?	6
63	Decca F 11684	Some Do, Some Don't (Some Will, Some Won't)/Heaven's Above	6
64	Decca F 11814	Hang Up The Phone/I Think It's Best To Forget Me	6
64	Decca F 12005	The Girl I Loved/Don't Go Near The Indians	6

Lorne GIBSON Trio

65	Decca F 12102	Red Roses For A Blue Lady/Talking To Your Picture	6
65	Decca F 12290	I'll Give You Me/As Lovers Do	6
66	Decca F 12357	A Little Lovin' Light/When Baby Says Goodbye	6
66	Decca F 12450	Jingle Jangle/Roses From A Stranger (solo)	5
69	RCA RCA 1917	Eva Magdalena/A Thing Called Love	5

STEVE GIBSON & RED CAPS
| 57 | HMV POP 417 | Silhouettes/Flamingo | 135 |
| 57 | HMV POP 417 | Silhouettes/Flamingo (78) | 15 |

WAYNE GIBSON (& DYNAMIC SOUNDS)
63	Decca F 11713	Linda Lu/Beachcomber	12
64	Decca F 11800	Come On Let's Go/Pop The Whip	12
64	Pye 7N 15680	See You Later Alligator/Kelly	7
65	Pye 7N 15798	Portland Town/Please Baby Please	7
65	Parlophone R 5357	Ding Dong The Witch Is Dead/In The Night	20
65	Columbia DB 7683	One Little Smile/Baby, Baby, Baby Pity Me	25
66	Columbia DB 7911	Under My Thumb/It Always Happens (Icey) (solo)	18
66	Columbia DB 7998	For No One/He's Got The Whole World In his Hands (solo)	7
75	Pye 7N 45455	Yesterday's Papers/Don't Waste Time Following Me (solo)	5

GIBSONS
65	CBS 202015	Any Time That You're Lonely/Born To Be Free	6
66	CBS 202063	Come Summertime/Summer Affair	6
66	Deram DM 103	Two Kinds Of Lovers/Hey Girl	6
67	Deram DM 119	The Magic Book/You Know I Need Your Lovin'	6
67	Major Minor MM 524	Night And Day/City Life	5
67	Major Minor MM 538	Lazy Summer Day/She's Not Like Any Girl	6
67	Major Minor MM 547	Only When You're Lonely/Ode To A Dolls House	6

GIDIAN (& UNIVERSALS)
66	Columbia DB 7826	Try Me Out/There Isn't Anything	15
66	Columbia DB 7916	Fight For Your Love/See If She Cares	6
66	Columbia DB 8041	Feeling/Don't Be Sentimental (as Gidian & Universals)	7
70	UPC UPC 107	That's Love/We Are The Happiest	5

(see also Universals, Chris Lamb & Universals)

GIFT
| 81 | Venus ORBIT 1 | Crashing Down/It'll End In Tears (p/s) | 20 |

GIFTED CHILDREN
| 81 | Whaam! WHAAM 001 | Painting By Numbers/Lichtenstein Girl (p/s) | 25 |

(see also Television Personalities)

GIGGETTY
75	GE 100	DAWN TO DUSK IN THE BLACK COUNTRY (LP, with insert)	50
77	Bridge GE 101	TAMBOURINE (LP)	40
80	Bridge GE 103	BLACK COUNTRY TIME (LP, also listed as Revolver REV LP1)	40

GILBERTO GIL
| 71 | Famous SFM 1001 | GILBERTO GIL (LP) | 15 |

GILBERT
67	CBS 3089	Disappear/You	12
68	CBS 3399	What Can I Do?/You	12
69	Major Minor MM 613	Mister Moody's Garden/I Wish I Could Cry	15

(see also Gilbert O'Sullivan)

HERSCHEL BURKE GILBERT
| 63 | London HLD 9655 | Dick Powell Theme/Nervous Teaser Theme | 6 |

GEORGE GILBERT
| 74 | Mime LPMS 7041 | MEDWAY FLOWS SOFTLY (LP, with insert) | 15 |

GILBERT & LEWIS
| 81 | 4AD AD 106 | Ends With The Sea/Hung Up To Dry Whilst Building An Arch (p/s) | 7 |
| 82 | Cherry Red BRED 27 | MZUI (LP, PVC cover, insert sleeve) | 12 |

(see also Wire, Dome, Cupol, A.C. Marias)

ASTRUD GILBERTO
64	Verve VS 520	Girl From Ipanema (with Stan Getz)/STAN GETZ & JOAO GILBERTO: Blowin' In The Wind	5
66	Verve VEP 5019	AND ROSES AND ROSES (EP, with Antonio Carlos Jobim)	8
66	Verve (S)VLP 9163	A CERTAIN SMILE AND A CERTAIN KIND OF SADNESS (LP)	12
69	Verve (S)VLP 9242	I HAVEN'T GOT ANYTHING BETTER TO DO (LP)	12
72	C.T.I. CTL 1	GILBERTO WITH TURRENTINE (LP, with Stanley Turrentine)	12

(see also Stan Getz, Stanley Turrentine)

GILDED CAGE
| 69 | Tepee TPR 1003 | Long Long Road (For The Broken Heart)/Baby Grumpling | 5 |

(see also She Trinity)

COSMO GILE
| 60 | Top Rank JAR 410 | Bambina D'Amsterdam/Tintarella Di Luna | 6 |

MINT VALUE £

GILES, GILES & FRIPP

68	Deram DM 188	One In A Million/Newly-Weds	50
68	Deram DM 210	Thursday Morning/Elephant Song	40
68	Deram DML/SML 1022	THE CHEERFUL INSANITY OF GILES, GILES AND FRIPP	
		(LP, mono/stereo)	35/30
70	Deram SPA 423	THE CHEERFUL INSANITY OF GILES, GILES AND FRIPP	
		(LP, stereo reissue)	25

(see also Brain, Trendsetters Ltd, League Of Gentlemen, King Crimson, Fripp & Eno, McDonald & Giles)

TOM GILFELLON

72	Trailer LER 2079	LOVING MAD TOM	
		(LP, red label)	15
76	Topic 12TS 282	IN THE MIDDLE OF THE TUNE	
		(LP, blue label)	15

GILGAMESH

75	Caroline CA 2007	GILGAMESH (LP)	18

(see also Hugh Hopper)

TERRY GILKYSON & EASY RIDERS

58	Philips JK 1007	Marianne/Goodbye Chaquita	
		(jukebox issue)	15
60	Fontana TFE 17326	STROLLING BLUES (EP)	15
60	Fontana TFE 17327	LONESOME RIDER (EP)	15
61	London RER 1333	ROLLIN' (EP)	12
53	Brunswick LA 8618	GOLDEN MINUTES OF FOLK MUSIC (10" LP)	20
61	London HA-R 2301	ROLLIN' (LP, also stereo SAH-R 6111)	15/18
61	London HA-R 2323	REMEMBER THE ALAMO	
		(LP, as Easyriders Including Terry Gilkyson)	15

(see also Easy Riders)

(IAN) GILLAN (BAND)

78	Island R 553-B	Twin Exhausted (live)/Smoke On The Water(live)/ILLUSION: Madonna Blue/Revolutionary	
		(12", promo only, as Ian Gillan Band)	20
78	Island WIP 6423	Mad Elaine/Mercury High	
		(as Ian Gillan Band, company sleeve)	8
79	Acrobat BAT 2	Vengeance/Smoke On The Water (p/s)	6
79	Acrobat BAT 1212	She Tears Me Down/Puget Sound/Vengeance/Mr. Universe	
		(12", stickered card sleeve, promo only)	15
80	Virgin VS 355	Sleeping On The Job/Higher And Higher	
		(p/s, with free patch)	5
80	Virgin VS 362	No Easy Way/Handles On Her Hips/Might As Well Go Home	
		(p/s)	5
80	Virgin VS 377	Trouble/Your Sister's On My List	
		(poster p/s)	5
80	Virgin VS 377	Trouble/Your Sister's On My List//Mr Universe (live)/Vengeance (live)/ Smoke On The Water (live)	
		(double pack, gatefold p/s)	6
81	Virgin VSK 103	Mutually Assured Destruction/The Maelstrom	
		(gatefold p/s, with booklet)	5
81	Sounds FREEBIE No. 2	I'll Rip Out Your Spine (extract)/PROFESSIONALS: Little Boys In Blue (extract)	
		(33rpm 1-sided flexi, printed die-cut sleeve, free with Sounds paper)	8/5
81	Lyntone LYN 10599	Higher And Higher/Spanish Guitar	
		(1-sided blue flexi with Flexipop magazine 13)	10/6
81	Lyntone LYN 10599	Higher And Higher/Spanish Guitar (same tracks both sides, hard vinyl test pressing, handwritten white labels)	35
82	Virgin VSY 465	Restless/On The Rocks (live)	
		(picture disc)	5
82	Virgin VSY 519	Living For The City/Purple Sky	
		(picture disc, mispressed, B-side plays "Breaking Chains", some with explanatory sticker)	5
82	Virgin VSY 519	Living For The City/Purple Sky	
		(picture disc)	7
82	Virgin VS 537	Long Gone/Figi	
		(foldout p/s)	5
82	Kerrang!	Purple Sky/GARY MOORE: Wishing Well/TELEPHONE: Squeeze	
		(flexidisc free with Kerrang! magazine)	12/5
88	Virgin VS 1088	South Africa/John (p/s, as Ian Gillan)	5
88	Virgin TVS 1088	South Africa (extended mix)/South Africa/John	
		(12", p/s, as Ian Gillan)	10
90	Teldec YZ 513	No Good Luck/Love Gun (p/s, as Ian Gillan)	5
90	Teldec YZ 513 (TW)	No Good Luck/Love Gun/Rock'N'Roll Girls	
		(12", "In Rock" or portrait p/s)	each 8
76	Polydor/Oyster 2490 136	CHILD IN TIME	
		(LP, gatefold sleeve, as Ian Gillan Band)	15
77	Island ILPS 9511DJ	IAN GILLAN BAND SAMPLER	
		(LP, 1-sided promo for "Scarabus", company sleeve)	25
78	Island ILPS 9545	LIVE AT THE BUDO-KAN	
		(LP, unissued)	
80	Virgin V 2171	GLORY ROAD	
		(LP, with bonus LP "For Gillan Fans Only" [VDJ 32], stickered, embossed sleeve & inner sleeves)	12
82	Virgin VP 2238	MAGIC	
		(LP, picture disc in die-cut sleeve with insert)	12

(see also Episode Six, Deep Purple, Ray Fenwick, Split Knee Loons, John McCoy, Johnny Gustafson, Bernie Tormé, Thunderstick, Jerusalem, Quatermass, Strapps, Colin Towns, White Spirit, Zzebra, Rock Aid Armenia)

Dana GILLESPIE

DANA GILLESPIE　　　　*DAVE GILMOUR*

DANA GILLESPIE

65	Pye 7N 15872	Donna Donna/It's No Use Saying If	10
65	Pye 7N 15962	Thank You Boy/You're A Heartbreak Man	7
67	Pye 7N 17280	Pay You Back With Interest/Adam Can You Beat That	7
68	Decca F 12847	You Just Gotta Know My Mind/He Loves Me, He Loves Me Not	8
74	RCA RCA 0211	Weren't Born A Man/All Gone	5
74	RCA RCA 2466	Andy Warhol/Dizzy Heights	10
75	RCA RCA 2489	Really Love That Man/Hold Me Gently	5
69	Decca SKL 5012	BOX OF SURPRISES (LP)	40
73	RCA APL1 0354	WEREN'T BORN A MAN (LP)	18
74	RCA APL1 0682	AIN'T GONNA PLAY NO SECOND FIDDLE (LP)	15

DIZZY GILLESPIE (QUINTET)

56	Vogue V 2116	The Champ (Parts 1 & 2)	5
60	HMV POP 705	Doddlin'/Dizzy's Blues	5
55	Vogue EPV 1022	DIZZY GILLESPIE (EP)	10
55	Vogue EPV 1049	DIZZY GILLESPIE WITH STRINGS (EP)	10
56	Vogue EPV 1078	DIZZY GILLESPIE (EP)	10
56	Vogue EPV 1094	THE CHAMP — DIZZY GILLESPIE (EP)	10
56	Vogue EPV 1157	DIZZY GILLESPIE AND HIS ORCHESTRA (EP)	10
56	Vogue EPV 1158	DIZZY GILLESPIE AND HIS ORCHESTRA (EP)	10
57	Columbia Clef SEB 10075	PILE DRIVER (EP)	8
57	Columbia Clef SEB 10096	BIRKS WORKS (EP)	8
60	HMV 7EG 8577	MELLOW SOUNDS (EP, as Dizzy Gillespie Quintet)	8
61	HMV 7EG 8646	MORE MELLOW SOUNDS (EP, as Dizzy Gillespie Quintet)	8
63	Philips 430 793BE	NEW SOUND IN JAZZ (EP)	8
64	Philips BE 12552	BE BOP (EP)	8
65	Philips BE 12583	FILM THEMES (EP)	8
66	Verve VRE 5022	ALWAYS (EP)	8
60	Esquire EP 193	DIZZY WITH STRINGS (EP, with Operatic Strings)	8
52	Esquire 20-003	OPERATIC STRINGS (10" LP)	18
53	Vogue LDE 017	DIZZY GILLESPIE PLAYS (10" LP)	18
53	Vogue LDE 033	DIZZY GILLESPIE PLAYS — JOHNNY RICHARDS CONDUCTS (10" LP)	18
54	Vogue LDE 039	PARIS CONCERT (10" LP)	18
54	Vogue LDE 076	DIZZY GILLESPIE AND ORCHESTRA (10" LP)	18
54	HMV DLP 1047	DIZZY GILLESPIE AND HIS ORCHESTRA (10" LP)	18
54	Felsted EDL 87006	DIZZY GILLESPIE'S OPERATIC STRINGS — JEALOUSY (10" LP)	18
55	Vogue LDE 135	DIZZY GILLESPIE AND HIS ORCHESTRA (10" LP)	18
55	Columbia Clef 33CX 10002	DIZZY GILLESPIE AND HIS ORCHESTRA (LP)	15
58	Columbia Clef 33CX 10144	DIZZY IN GREECE (LP)	20
59	HMV CLP 1318	HAVE TRUMPET, WILL TRAVEL (LP)	15
60	HMV CLP 1381	THE GREATEST TRUMPET OF THEM ALL (LP)	12
61	HMV CLP 1431	PORTRAIT OF DUKE ELLINGTON (LP)	12
62	HMV CLP 1484	GILLESPIANA (LP, also stereo CSD 1392)	12/15
62	Verve VLP/SVLP 9016	CARNEGIE HALL CONCERT (LP)	12
67	Fontana TL 5343	OPERATIC STRINGS (LP, reissue)	12
71	Pye PKL 4403	SOULED OUT (LP)	12
73	Mainstream MSL 1010	DIZZY GILLESPIE & MITCHELL RUFF DUO (LP)	12
70s	Pablo 231 0794	FREE RIDE (LP)	12

(see also Miles Davis, Lalo Schifrin)

DIZZY GILLESPIE & STAN GETZ

60	HMV 7EG 8596	DIZZY GILLESPIE/STAN GETZ SEXTET (EP)	8
55	Columbia Clef 33C 9009	DIZZY GILLESPIE — STAN GETZ SEXTET (LP)	12

(see also Stan Getz)

DIZZY GILLESPIE & CHARLIE PARKER

| 57 | Columbia Clef SEB 10087 | ONE MORE TIME: WITH BIRD AND DIZ (EP) | 8 |
| 61 | Vogue LAE 12252 | DIZ 'N BIRD IN CONCERT (LP) | 12 |

(see also Charlie Parker)

DIZZY GILLESPIE & ORCHESTRA/DON BYAS QUARTET

| 57 | MGM MGM-EP 579 | DIZZ AND DON (EP, 2 tracks each) | 8 |

DIZZY GILLESPIE/KAI WINDING'S BIRDLANDERS

| 58 | MGM MGM-EP 681 | TWO BY TWO (EP, 2 tracks each) | 8 |

JAZZ GILLUM

66	RCA Victor RD 7816	JAZZ GILLUM 1938-1947 (LP)	20
70	RCA Intl. INTS 1177	YOU GOT TO REAP WHAT YOU SOW (LP)	12
71	Xtra XTRA 1111	BLUES BY JAZZ GILLUM, WITH ARBEE STIDHAM AND MEMPHIS SLIM (LP)	12

JIMMY GILMER & FIREBALLS

62	London HLD 9632	I'm Gonna Go Walkin'/Born To Be With You (as Chimmy Gilmer)	10
63	London HLD 9789	Sugar Shack/My Heart Is Free	8
64	London HLD 9827	Daisy Petal Pickin'/When My Tears Have Dried	7
64	London HLD 9872	Ain't Gonna Tell Nobody/Young Am I	8
64	London BUG 9898	Look At Me/I'll Send For You	10
65	Dot DS 16666	Thunder 'N' Lightnin'/Cry Baby (unissued)	
65	Stateside SS 418	Thunder 'N' Lightnin'/What Do You Do	10
65	Stateside SS 472	She Belongs To Me/Rambler's Blues	7
68	London HL 10232	Three Squares/Baby	5
64	London HA-D/SH-D 8150	SUGAR SHACK (LP)	45
65	Dot DLP 3577	BUDDY'S BUDDY — BUDDY HOLLY SONGS BY JIMMY GILMER (LP)	35

(see also Fireballs, Jim & Monica)

DAVE GILMOUR

78	Harvest HAR 5167	There's No Way Out Of Here/Deafinitely (no p/s)	7
84	Harvest HAR 5226	Blue Light (LP Version)/Cruise (blue or red titles on p/s)	each 5
84	Harvest 12HAR 5226	Blue Light (LP Version)/Cruise (12", p/s)	10
84	Harvest HAR 5229	Love On The Air/Let's Get Metaphysical (p/s)	5
84	Harvest HARP 5229	Love On The Air/Let's Get Metaphysical (shaped picture disc)	12
84	Harvest 12HAR 5229	Love On The Air/Let's Get Metaphysical (12", p/s)	8

(see also Pink Floyd, Joker's Wild, Rock Aid Armenia)

PETER GILMORE

| 60 | HMV POP 740 | Follow That Girl/Come Away | 6 |

JAMES GILREATH

| 63 | Pye International 7N 25190 | Little Band Of Gold/I'll Walk With You | 5 |
| 63 | Pye International 7N 25213 | Lollipops, Lace And Lipstick/Mean Ole River | 6 |

GORDON GILTRAP (BAND)

73	Philips 6006 344	No Way Of Knowing/I See A Road	15
79	Cube BUG 89	The Waltons Theme/Birds Of A Feather (p/s)	5
79	Electric LWOP 29	Fear Of The Dark/Catwalk Blues/Inner Dream (12", picture disc)	8
68	Transatlantic TRA 175	GORDON GILTRAP (LP)	30
69	Transatlantic TRA 202	PORTRAIT (LP)	25
71	MCA MKPS 2020	A TESTAMENT OF TIME (LP)	20
73	Philips 6308 175	GILTRAP (LP, with lyric insert)	20
81	Themes International	THEMES (LP, by Gordon Giltrap Band, library issue)	15
82	KPM KPM 1292	SOUNDWAVES (LP, by Gordon Giltrap Band, library issue)	15
82	KPM KPM 1330	IN AT THE DEEP END (LP, by Gordon Giltrap Band, library issue)	15

(see also Accolade, Pauline Filby, Catherine Andrews, Dave Ellis)

GINA X

| 80 | Plastic Poison MRC 5014 | Do It Yourself/Be A Boy (p/s) | 4 |

GINGER ALE

| 70 | Famous FAM 102 | In The Sand/Get Off My Life Woman | 5 |

GINGER JUG BAND

| 70s | GJB 001 | GINGER JUG BAND (LP, private pressing) | 20 |

GINGER SNAPS

| 65 | RCA RCA 1483 | The Sh Down Down Song/I've Got Faith In Him | 8 |

HERMIONE GINGOLD & GILBERT HARDING

| 53 | Philips PB 104 | Oh, Grandma/Takes Two To Tango (78) | 6 |

GINGRINI

| 73 | Harry J. HJ 6647 | Zion 'lah/Zion 'lah (Version) | 5 |

GINHOUSE

| 71 | Charisma CAS 1031 | GINHOUSE (LP) | 45 |

GINKS

| 65 | Summit ATL 4176 | A TRIBUTE TO THE BEATLES (LP) | 15 |

GINO & GINA

| 58 | Mercury 7MT 230 | Pretty Baby/Love's A Carousel | 35 |
| 58 | Mercury MT 230 | Pretty Baby/Love's A Carousel (78) | 15 |

ALLEN GINSBERG

60s	Cape Goliard	Wales: A Visitation (single issued with book of same title)	25
65	Better Books (no cat. no.)	ALLEN GINSBERG READING AT BETTER BOOKS (LP)	80
65	Love Books Ltd. LB 0001	ALLEN GINSBERG, LAURENCE FERLINGHETTI, GREGORY CORSO & ANDREI VOZNESENSKY READING AT THE ARCHITECTURAL ASSOCIATION (LP)	80
68	Transatlantic TRA 192	GINSBERG'S THING (LP)	25

(see also Ginsbergs)

GINSBERGS
| 67 | Saga Psyche PSY 3002 | THE GINSBERGS AT THE ICA (LP) | 15 |

(see also Allen Ginsberg)

GIORGIO
66	Page One POF 003	Full Stop/Believe Me	5
67	Page One POF 028	How Much Longer Must I Wait/Bla Bla Diddly	5
69	MCA MCA 1094	Happy Birthday/Looky Looky	5

(see also Giorgio Moroder, Giorgio & Marco's Men)

GIORGIO & MARCO'S MEN
| 66 | Polydor 56101 | Girl Without A Heart/Run Run | 6 |
| 68 | Electratone EP 1003 | Baby I Need You/Maureen | 50 |

GIPSY LOVE
| 72 | BASF BAP 5026 | GIPSY LOVE (LP) | 20 |

CHUCK GIRARD
| 70s | Myrrh MYR 1025 | CHUCK GIRARD (LP) | 15 |
| 70s | Myrrh MYR 1065 | WRITTEN ON THE WIND (LP) | 15 |

GIRL
79	Jet JET 159	My Number/My Number (Version) (clear vinyl, PVC sleeve, some with 2 stickers)	6/5
79	Jet JET 159	My Number/My Number (Version) (black vinyl, promo only)	5
80	Jet JET 169	Do You Love Me?/Strawberries (p/s)	5
80	Jet JET 176	Hollywood Tease (Remix)/You Really Got Me/My Number (some in poster p/s)	7/5
80	Jet JET 191	Love Is A Game/Little Miss Ann (white vinyl, patch & sticker in PVC sleeve)	7
80	Jet JET 10 191	Love Is A Game/Little Miss Ann (10", white vinyl with sticker in PVC sleeve)	7
81	Jet JET 7014	Thru The Twilite/McKitty's Back (p/s)	5
81	Jet JETP 7014	Thru The Twilite/McKitty's Back (picture disc)	6
82	Jet JET 7019	Old Dogs/Passing Clouds (p/s)	5
80	Jet JETLP 224	SHEER GREED (LP, stickered sleeve with inner)	12
82	Jet JETLP 238	WASTED YOUTH (LP, with inner sleeve)	12

(see also Def Leppard, Bernie Tormé)

GIRLFRIENDS
| 63 | Colpix PX 712 | Jimmy Boy/For My Sake | 18 |

GIRLIE
69	Treasure Isle TI 7053	Boss Cocky/LOVE SHOCKS: Musical True	10
69	Bullet BU 400	Madame Straggae/LAUREL AITKEN: Stupid Married Man	6
69	Duke DU 42	African Meeting (as Girlie & Junior)/JOSH: Higher And Higher	6
70	Joe JRS 7	Small Change/Mind Your Business (as Girlie & Joe [Mansano])	7
70	Ackee ACK 124	Decimilization/Decimilization Version (as Girlie & Paul)	5

(see also Laurel Aitken & Girlie)

GIRLS AT OUR BEST
80	Records RR 001	Getting Nowhere Fast/Warm Girls (p/s)	6
81	Rough Trade RT 055	Politics/It's Fashion (p/s)	5
81	Happy Birthday UR 4	Go For Gold/I'm Beautiful Now (p/s)	5
81	Happy Birthday UR 6	Fast Boyfriends/This Train (p/s)	5
81	Happy Birthday RULP 1	PLEASURE (LP, with lyric insert, 1st 10,000 with free 'pleasure bag' with 2 postcards, sticker & stencil)	12/10

GIRLSCHOOL
79	City NIK 6	Take It All Away/It Could Be Better (p/s, red vinyl, pink p/s, b&w front photo)	7
79	City NIK 6	Take It All Away/It Could Be Better (p/s, black vinyl, orange p/s)	5
79	Mulligan LUNS 723	Take It All Away/It Could Be Better (Irish version, no p/s, red vinyl)	10
82	Bronze BRO 144	THE WILDLIFE EP: Don't Call It Love/Wildlife/Don't Stop (red vinyl, p/s)	5
81	Bronze BRON 534	HIT AND RUN (LP, red vinyl)	12

(see also Motörhead, Killjoys)

GITTE
| 64 | Columbia DB 7440 | The Heart That You Break (May Be Your Own)/Seems Just Like Old Times | 6 |

JIMMY GIUFFRE
55	Capitol LC 6699	JIMMY GIUFFRE (10" LP)	15
57	London Jazz LTZK 15059	THE JIMMY GIUFFRE CLARINET (LP)	12
58	London Jazz LTZK 15130	JIMMY GIUFFRE (LP)	12
58	London Jazz LTZK 15137	TRAV'LIN' LIGHT (LP)	12

(see also Shelly Manne)

GLADDY (Anderson) & FOLLOWERS
| 69 | Blue Cat BS 172 | Judas/The World Come To An End | 12 |

(see also Stranger & Glady)

GLADDY (Anderson) & STRANGER (Cole)
| 73 | Pama PM 872 | Dedicated To Illiteracy/G.G. ALLSTARS: Dub | 6 |

(see also Gladstone Anderson, Stranger Cole, Stranger & Gladys)

GLADIATORS
| 63 | HMV POP 1134 | Tovaritch/Bleak House | 15 |

(see also Nero & Gladiators)

GLADIATORS
68	Direction 58-3854	Girl Don't Make Me Wait/Can't Get Away From Heartbreak	7
69	Direction 58-4308	Waiting On The Shores Of Nowhere/I'll Always Love You	7
69	Direction 58-4507	As Long As I Live/Everything	5
69	Direction 58-4660	Twelfth Of Never/Lovin' My Baby Back Home	5

GLADIATORS (Jamaica)

69	Doctor Bird DB 1114	The Train Is Coming/So Fine	20
69	Studio One SO 2072	Hello Carol/RICHARD ACE: More Reggae	20
69	Bamboo BAM 7	Anywhere/SOUND DIMENSION: Baby Face	10
70	Duke DU 58	My Girl (actually by Glen Adams)/You Were To Be	8
72	Ackee ACK 149	Sonia/SOUND DIMENSION: Solas	10

GLADIATORS

| 72 | Pye 7N 45155 | Tiptoe Through The Tulips/When We All Go In The Ring (p/s) | 5 |

GLADIATORS (Jamaica)

| 70s | Rock Steady Rev. REVR 12 | Unusual Reggae/Andue | 5 |

GLADIOLAS

| 57 | London HLO 8435 | Little Darlin'/Sweetheart, Please Don't Go | 240 |
| 57 | London HLO 8435 | Little Darlin'/Sweetheart, Please Don't Go (78) | 50 |

(see also Maurice Williams & Zodiacs)

GLAND SHROUDS

80s	Daark Inc. D.I. 3	STAFF IN CONFIDENCE/TOYSHOP UNIVERSAL (cassette)	12
80s	Daark Inc. D.I. 4	ANIMAL DANCE (cassette)	12
80s	Daark Inc. D.I. 5	YOUR ANIMALS (cassette)	12
80s	Daark Inc. D.I. 6	EVERYONE WANTS TO WIN (cassette)	12
80s	Detrimental History DHSS 2	FERTIVE CHEATS (cassette)	12
80s	Detrimental History DHSS 3	A TELESCOPE IN THE SKY (cassette)	12

(see also Karl Blake, Lemon Kittens, Fur Fur)

GLASER BROTHERS

| 69 | MGM MGM-CS 8115 | NOW COUNTRY (LP) | 12 |

GLASGOW

84	Clydebank CLY 001	GLASGOW'S MILES BETTER (12" EP)	25
84	Neat NEAT 40	Stranded/Heat Of The Night (p/s)	10
88	Zero 0417	Secrets In The Dark/Meet Me Halfway (p/s)	6
88	041 0418	Under The Lights (p/s)	15
88	Sonet 0419	Will You Be Mine (p/s)	12
87	private pressing 041	041 (LP)	12

GLASS

82	Glass GLASS 1	New Colours/Sweet Entropy (p/s)	5
82	Glass GLASS 002	SIXTEEN GIGS (LP)	10
82	Glass GLASS 002	SIXTEEN GIGS (cassette in freezer bag)	10

(see also Ciaran Harte)

PHILIP GLASS

70s	Chatham Square LP 1001/2	MUSIC WITH CHANGING PARTS (2-LP)	25
70s	Chatham Square LP 1003	MUSIC IN FIFTHS/MUSIC IN A SIMILAR MOTION (LP)	15
70s	Folkways FTS 33902	TWO PAGES (LP)	12
76	Cardine LA 2010	MUSIC IN 12 (PARTS 1 & 2) (LP)	12
78	Shandar SHAN 83515	SOLO MUSIC (LP)	12

(see also Ray Manzarek)

GLASS HARP

72	MCA MUPS 431	GLASS HARP (LP)	15
72	MCA MUPS 449	SYNERGY (LP)	15
73	MCA MUPS 470	IT MAKES ME GLAD (LP)	12

GLASS HOUSE

| 70 | Invictus INV 506 | Stealing Moments From Another Woman's Life/If It Ain't Love, It Don't Matter | 5 |
| 71 | Invictus INV 510 | I Can't Be You/He's In My Life | 5 |

GLASS MENAGERIE

68	Pye 7N 17518	She's A Rainbow/But That's When I Start To Love Her	8
68	Pye 7N 17568	You Didn't Have To Be So Nice/Let's All Run To The Sun	6
68	Pye 7N 17615	Frederick Jordan/I Said Goodbye To Me	50
69	Polydor 56318	Have You Forgotten Who You Are/Do You Ever Think?	6
69	Polydor 56341	Do My Thing Myself/Watching The World Pass By	6

(see also Paladin, Toe-Fat)

GLASS OPENING

| 68 | Plexium P 1236 | Silver Bells And Cockle Shells/Does It Really Matter | 250 |

GLASS TORPEDOES

| 79 | Teen Beat TBR 1 | Someone Different/Morning, Noon & Night/Heart Surgery (p/s) | 5 |

TOM GLAZER & DO-RE-MI CHILDREN'S CHORUS

| 63 | London HLR 9742 | On Top Of Spaghetti/Battle Hymn Of The Children | 6 |
| 63 | London HLR 9817 | It's A Mad, Mad, Mad, Mad World/Dance With The Dolly | 7 |

JACKIE GLEASON (& ORCHESTRA)

55	Capitol CL 14363	Autumn Leaves/Oo! What You Do To Me (with Orchestra)	6
60	Brunswick 04775	What Is A Boy?/What Is A Girl?	7
69	MCA MU 1108	What Is A Boy?/What Is A Girl? (reissue)	5

CAPTAIN GLEASON'S GARDEN BAND

| 55 | Capitol CL 14323 | In The Good Old Summertime/The Band Played On | 6 |

(see also Jackie Gleason)

GLEN (Brown) & LLOYD (Robinson)

| 66 | Ska Beat JB 250 | Live And Let Others Die/Too Late | 15 |
| 67 | Doctor Bird DB 1099 | Feel Good Now/What You've Got (credited as Lloyd Glen) | 15 |

DARRELL GLEN

| 53 | Oriole CB 1235 | Crying In The Chapel/Hang Up That Telephone (78) | 6 |

MINT VALUE £

GLENCOE
72	Epic EPC 8383	Look Me In The Eye/Telephonia	5
72	Epic EPC 65207	GLENCOE (LP)	12
73	Epic EPC 65717	SPIRIT OF GLENCOE (LP)	12

(see also Hopscotch, Five Day Rain, Greatest Show On Earth, Loving Awareness)

DARRYL GLEN
54	HMV 7MC 23	In The Chapel In The Moonlight/Once And Only Once (export issue)	12

GERRY GLENN
64	Embassy WEP 1120	MUSIC FOR JAMES BOND (EP)	12

PADDY GLICKIN, MICK GAVIN & MICHAEL O'BRIEN
79	Topic 12TS 383	THE FLAGS OF DUBLIN (LP)	12

GLIDE
95	Ochre OCH 003	EXCERPTS FROM A SPACE AGE FREAK OUT (Part 1) (orange vinyl, p/s)	5

(see also Echo & Bunnymen)

GLITTERHOUSE
68	Stateside SS 2129	Barbarella/BOB CREWE: An Angel Is Love	8
68	Stateside SS 2129	Barbarella/Love Drags Me Down (different B-side)	8

GLOBAL COMMUNICATIONS
93	Evolution EVO 04	KEONGAKU EP (12", 4-track, plain sleeve)	25
94	Dedicated DEDLP 014L	76: 14 (2-LP, gatefold sleeve with bonus 12")	20
94	Dedicated DEDLP 014	76: 14 (2-LP, gatefold sleeve)	15
94	Dedicated DEDCD 014L	76: 14 (CD, gatefold, wraparound sleeve)	20
94	Dedicated DEDCD 014	76: 14 (CD)	15
96	Dedicated DED 21LP	REMOTION — THE GLOBAL COMMUNICATIONS REMIX ALBUM (LP)	18

(see also Mystic Institue, Link, Reload, Reload & E621, Chaos & Julia Set, Appaloosa, Jedi Knights)

GLOBAL VILLAGE TRUCKING COMPANY
76	Caroline C 1516	GLOBAL VILLAGE TRUCKING COMPANY (LP, with insert)	15

GLOBE SHOW
69	Page One POF 128	Yes Or No/Gettin' On Back	5

(see also Chris Shakespeare Globe Show)

GLOBE TROTTERS
54	Parlophone CMSP 18	At Sundown/My Gal Sal (export issue)	15
54	Parlophone GEP 8528	SATURDAY NIGHT HOP (EP)	20

GLOBETROTTERS
70	RCA RCA 2017	Gravy/Cheer Me Up	5
71	RCA SF 8158	THE GLOBETROTTERS (LP)	12

GLOOMYS
68	Columbia DB 8391	Daybreak/Queen And King	8
71	DJM DJS 240	I'm A Bum/Let Me Dream	5

GLORIA MUNDI
78	RCA PB 5068	Fight Back/Do It (p/s)	5
78	RCA PL2 5157	I INDIVIDUAL (LP, with inner sleeve)	12
79	RCA PL2 5244	THE WORD IS OUT (LP)	10

GLORIES
67	CBS 2786	I Stand Accused (Of Loving You)/Wish They Could Write A Song	10
67	Direction 58-3084	Give Me My Freedom/Security	7
68	Direction 58-3300	Sing Me A Love Song/Oh Baby That's Love	5
68	Direction 58-3646	My Sweet Sweet Baby/Stand By (I'm Comin' Home)	5

GLOVE
83	Wonderland SHE 3	Like An Animal/Mouth To Mouth (p/s, some sleeves with centre holes)	7
83	Wonderland SHEX 3	Like An Animal (Club, What Club? Mix)/Like Animal/Mouth To Mouth (12", p/s, some sleeves with centre hole)	10
83	Wonderland SHE 5	Punish Me With Kisses/The Tightrope (p/s)	8
83	Wonderland SHELP 2	BLUE SUNSHINE (LP, with inner sleeve)	12
83	Wonderland SHELP 2	BLUE SUNSHINE (LP, mispressing with double-printed sleeve)	20

(see also Cure, Siouxsie & Banshees)

ROGER GLOVER (& GUESTS)
74	Purple PUR 125	Love Is All/Old Blind Mole/Magician Moth	8
84	Safari SAF EP 1	Love Is All/Old Blind Mole/Magician Moth (p/s, reissue)	5
84	Polydor POSP 678	The Mask/So Remote (p/s, solo)	6
74	Purple TPSA 7514	THE BUTTERFLY BALL (AND THE GRASSHOPPER'S FEAST) (LP, g/fold sl.)	15
78	Polydor 2391 306	ELEMENTS (LP, solo)	12
84	Polydor POLD 5139	THE MASK (LP, solo, with insert)	12

(see also [Sheila Carter &] Episode [Six], Deep Purple, Elf, Eddie Hardin, Whitesnake, Rainbow, Glenn Hughes, John Lawton, Wizard's Convention, Marlon, Green Bullfrog, David Coverdale, Dio)

JEREMY GLUCK
86	Flicknife SHARP 037	I KNEW BUFFALO BILL (LP)	15

(see also Barracudas)

GMT
91	Mausoleum BONE 12-83102	One By One (12", p/s)	10

GNAC
98	Earworm WORM 29	The Moustache/Armchair Thriller (p/s, black vinyl)	6

GNANK
99	Gnank GNANK 01	Gnank Gnank/Oi, Gnank (p/s)	8

GNASHER
74	Purple PUR 119	Medina Road/Easy Meat	8

GNIDROLOG

| 72 | RCA SF 8261 | IN SPITE OF HARRY'S TOE-NAIL (LP) | 50 |
| 72 | RCA SF 8322 | LADY LAKE (LP, some with insert) | 90/70 |

GNOMES OF ZURICH

66	Planet PLF 121	Please Mr Sun/I'm Coming Down With The Blues (with custom 'Planet' sleeve)	30/25
67	CBS 202556	Hang On Baby/Blues For My Baby	22
67	CBS 2694	High Hopes/Pretender	22
67	RCA Victor RCA 1606	Second Fiddle/Publicity Girl	18

G-NOTES

| 58 | Oriole CB 1456 | Ronnie/I Would | 15 |
| 58 | Oriole CB 1456 | Ronnie/I Would (78) | 6 |

GOAT

| 82 | Real Kavoom ARK 1 | REAL KAVOOM (12" EP) | 8 |

GOBBLEDEGOOKS

| 64 | Decca F 12023 | Now And Again/Where Have You Been | 10 |

GO-BETWEENS

80	Postcard 80-4	I Need Two Heads/Stop Before You Say It (brown label & brown co. sleeve)	12
80	Postcard 80-4	I Need Two Heads/Stop Before You Say It (yellow label & cream co. sleeve)	15
82	Rough Trade RT 108	Hammer The Hammer/By Chance (p/s)	5
83	Rough Trade RT 124	Cattle And Cane/Heaven Says (p/s)	5
83	Rough Trade RT 114	Man O'Sand To Girl O'See/This Girl Black Girl (p/s)	5
87	Beggars Banquet BEG 183D	Right Here/When People Are Dead/A Little Romance//Don't Call Me Gone/ A Little Romance (live) (double pack)	5
88	B. Banquet BEG 218B	Streets Of Your Town/Wait Until June (box set)	5

GOBLIN

| 79 | EMI EMC 3222 | SUSPIRIA (LP, soundtrack) | 25 |

VIC GODARD (& SUBWAY SECT)

80	Oddball/MCA 585	Split Up The Money/Out Of Touch (p/s, with Subway Sect)	5
81	Rough Trade RT 068	Stop That Girl/Instrumentally Scared/Vertical Integration (p/s, w/Subway Sect)	5
81	Club Left CLUB 1	Stamp Of A Vamp/Hey Now (I'm In Love) (p/s, with Subway Sect)	5
85	El Benelux EL 4	Holiday Hymn/Nice On The Ice (p/s)	5
85	El Benelux EL 4T	Holiday Hymn/Nice On The Ice/Stop That Girl/Ice On The Volcano/ T.R.O.U.B.L.E. (12", p/s)	10
93	Postcard DUBH 937	Won't Turn Back/Won't Turn Back (Version) (p/s, 1,000 only)	5
80	Oddball/MCA MCF 3070	WHAT'S THE MATTER BOY? (LP, with Subway Sect)	12
82	London SH 8549	SONGS FOR SALE (LP, with Subway Sect)	12
85	Rough Trade ROUGH 56	A RETROSPECTIVE (LP, with Subway Sect)	12
85	MCA/El 01	HOLIDAY HYMN (LP, 10 test pressings only; abandoned issue of "T.R.O.U.B.L.E.")	30+
86	Rough Trade ROUGH 86	T.R.O.U.B.L.E. (LP)	12
93	Postcard DUBH 936	END OF THE SURREY PEOPLE (LP)	12

KEITH & DONNA GODCHAUX

| 75 | Round RX 104 | KEITH & DONNA GODCHAUX (LP) | 18 |
| | *(see also Grateful Dead)* | | |

GEOFF GODDARD

61	HMV POP 938	Girl Bride/For Eternity	40
62	HMV POP 1068	My Little Girl's Come Home/Try Once More	50
63	HMV POP 1160	Saturday Dance/Come Back To Me	40
63	HMV POP 1213	Sky Men/Walk With Me My Angel	90

HUGH GODFREY

67	Coxsone CS 7001	A Dey Pon Dem/SOUL BROTHERS: Take Ten	18
67	Studio One SO 2008	My Time/MARCIA GRIFFITHS: Hound Dog	18
67	Studio One SO 2015	Go Tell Him/MARCIA GRIFFITHS: After Laughter	18
	(see also Soul Brothers)		

RAY GODFREY

| 78 | Grapevine GRP 111 | Come And Get These Memories/I'm The Other Half Of You | 5 |

ROBERT JOHN GODFREY

74	Charisma CAS 1084	FALL OF HYPERION (LP)	30
80s	Nuage (no cat. no.)	REVERBERATIONS (cassette)	12
	(see also Enid, Godfrey & Stewart, William Arkle, Don Bradshaw)		

GODFREY & STEWART

86	The Enid ENID 11	THE SEED AND THE SOWER (LP)	15
86	The Enid ENID 11	THE SEED AND THE SOWER (cassette)	12
80s	The Stand HEARTLP	JOINED BY THE HEART (LP, fan club issue, 2,000 only)	20
86	The Enid (no cat. no.)	JOINED BY THE HEART (cassette)	12
80s	The Stand HEARTC	JOINED BY THE HEART (cassette, fan club issue)	12
	(see also Robert John Godfrey, Enid)		

GODIEGO

| 78 | Satril SATL 4009 | THE WATER MARGIN (LP) | 12 |

GODLEY & CREME

79	Mercury SAMP 017	5 O'Clock/The Flood//Lost Weekend/Honolulu (double pack sampler, promo)	12
81	Polydor POSP 322	Under Your Thumb (Short Version)/Power Behind The Throne (2,000 only with p/s)	7
85	Polydor POSP 372	Cry/Love Bombs (picture disc)	5
85	Polydor 080 101 2	Cry/Love Bombs/Cry (CD Video)	15
77	Mercury CONS 017	CONSEQUENCES (3-LP, box set with booklet)	25
81	Polydor POLD 543	ISMISM (LP, white sleeve with die-cut holes)	12
	(see also Mockingbirds, Hotlegs, 10cc, Dave Berry, Frabjoy & Runcible Spoon, Cruisers, Whirlwinds, Doctor Father)		

MINT VALUE £

GODS
67	Polydor 56168	Come On Down To My Boat Baby/Garage Man	100
68	Columbia DB 8486	Baby's Rich/Somewhere In The Street	22
69	Columbia DB 8544	Hey! Bulldog/Real Love Guaranteed	25
69	Columbia DB 8572	Maria/Long Time, Sad Time, Bad Time	25
68	Columbia S(C)X 6286	GENESIS (LP)	130
70	Columbia SCX 6372	TO SAMUEL A SON (LP)	110
76	Harvest SHSM 2011	GODS (LP)	18

(see also Uriah Heep, Shame, Toe-Fat, Mick Taylor)

GOD'S GIFT
79	Newmarket	THESE DAYS (EP)	10
81	New Hormones ORG 14	Soldiers/Anthony Perkins/No God/The Hunger Of Millions (12", p/s)	8
83	Pleasantly Surprised PS 7	FOLIE A QUATRE (cassette, in bag with inserts)	12

GOD SONS
72	Green Door GD 4024	Merry Up/Merry Up — Version	8

(see also Errol & U Roy, Carl Masters)

GOD SPEED YOU BLACK EMPEROR
99	Kranky KRANK 034	SLOW RIOT FOR NEW ZERO KANADA (CD EP)	8

GODZ
67	Fontana STL 5500	CONTACT WITH THE GODZ (LP)	20
69	Fontana STL 5512	GODZ II (LP)	20

GOGMAGOG
85	F. For Thought YUMT 109	I Will Be There/Living In A Timewarp/It's Illegal, It's Immoral, It's Unhealthy But It's Fun (12", p/s & insert)	50

(see also Iron Maiden, Di'Anno, Def Leppard, Whitesnake, Gillan, White Spirit)

GO-GO's (U.K.)
64	Oriole CB 1982	I'm Gonna Spend My Christmas With A Dalek/Big Boss Man (some in p/s)	45/30

GO-GO's (U.S.)
80	Stiff BUY 78	We Got The Beat/How Much More (p/s)	5
81	I.R.S. PFP 1007	Our Lips Are Sealed/Surfing And Spying (p/s, pink vinyl)	8
81	I.R.S. GONP 101	Automatic/Tonite (picture disc)	7
90	A&M AMP 712	Cool Jerk/We Got The Beat (picture disc)	5
90	A&M AMCD 712	Cool Jerk/We Got The Beat (CD)	8

(see also Belinda Carlisle, Jane Wiedlin)

GOING RED?
81	Razz CLEAN 1	Some Boys/Tune Kevin's Strings (p/s)	8
81	MCA MCA 673	Some Boys/Tune Kevin's Strings (reissue, p/s)	5

(see also Freshies, Chris Sievey, Jilted John)

HERBIE GOINS & NIGHT-TIMERS
66	Parlophone R 5478	No. 1 In Your Heart/Cruisin'	50
66	Parlophone R 5533	The Incredible Miss Brown/Comin' Home To You	30
67	Parlophone PMC 7026	NUMBER ONE IN YOUR HEART (LP)	100

(see also Night-Timers, Alexis Korner's Blues Incorporated)

HARRY GOLD with NORRIE PARAMOR ORCHESTRA
54	Columbia SCM 5144	Be Good To Me/Frou Frou	7

(see also Norrie Paramor)

MARTY GOLD
70	Avco Embassy 6466 001	MOOG PLAYS THE BEATLES (LP)	10

BARRY GOLDBERG (REUNION)
68	Pye International 7N 25465	Another Day/Capricorn Blues (as Barry Goldberg Reunion)	6
68	Pye Intl. NSPL 28116	BARRY GOLDBERG REUNION (LP)	15
69	Buddah 203 020	TWO JEWS BLUES (LP, with Mike Bloomfield)	12
71	Buddah 2318 038	BLASTS FROM MY PAST (LP)	12

(see also Electric Flag, Mike Bloomfield)

GOLDEBRIARS
64	Columbia DB 7384	Sea Of Tears/I've Got To Love Somebody	6

GOLDEN APPLES OF THE SUN
65	Decca F 12194	Monkey Time/Chocolate Rolls, Tea And Monopoly (unissued, test pressings only)	50
65	Immediate IM 010	Monkey Time/Chocolate Rolls, Tea And Monopoly	30

GOLDEN CRUSADERS
64	Columbia DB 7232	I'm In Love With You/Always On My Mind	12
64	Columbia DB 7357	Hey Good Lookin'/Come On, Come On	12
65	Columbia DB 7485	I Don't Care/That Broken Heart Is Mine	12

GOLDEN DAWN
88	Sarah SARAH 009	My Secret World/Spring-Heeled Jack/The Railway Track (p/s, with poster)	7

GOLDEN EARRING(S)
68	Capitol CL 15552	I've Just Lost Somebody/The Truth About Arthur (as Golden Earrings)	8
68	Capitol CL 15567	Dong Dong Di Ki Di Gi Dong/Wake Up — Breakfast (as Golden Earrings)	8
69	Major Minor MM 601	Just A Little Peace In My Heart/Remember My Friend (as Golden Earrings)	7
69	Major Minor MM 633	It's Alright But It Could Be Better/Where Will I Be (as Golden Earrings)	7
70	Major Minor MM 679	Another Forty-Five Miles/I Can't Get Hold Of Her	7
70	Polydor BM 56514	That Day/Words I Need	12
70	Polydor 2001 073	Back Home/This Is The Time Of Year	5
72	Polydor 2001 346	Buddy Joe/Avalanche	5
73	Track 2094 116	Radar Love/Just Like Vince Taylor	5
74	Track 2094 121	Instant Poetry/From Heaven, From Hell	5
74	Track 2094 126	Candy's Going Bad/She Flies On Strange Wings	5

75	Track 2094 130	Ce Soir/Lucky Number	5
76	Polydor 2001 626	Sleepwalking/Babylon (no p/s)	5
77	Polydor 2121 312	Bombay/Faded Jeans (no p/s)	5
77	Polydor 2121 335	Radar Love (live)/Just Like Vince (live) (12", p/s)	8
83	Mercury MER 122	Twilight Zone/King Dark (p/s)	5
83	Mercury MERX 122	Twilight Zone/King Dark (12", blue or yellow p/s)	8
84	Carrere CAR 321	When The Lady Smiles/Orwell's Year (p/s)	5
84	Carrere CART 321	When The Lady Smiles/Orwell's Year (12", p/s)	8
69	Major Minor SMLP 65	EIGHT MILES HIGH (LP)	25
71	Polydor 2310 135	SEVEN TEARS (LP)	15
72	Polydor 2310 210	TOGETHER (LP)	15
73	Track 2406 109	HEARING EARRING (LP, braille sleeve)	12
73	Track 2406 112	MOONTAN (LP, gatefold sleeve with insert)	12
75	Track 2406 117	SWITCH (LP)	12
76	Polydor 2430 330	TO THE HILT (LP, gatefold sleeve with insert)	12
77	Polydor 2344 059	CONTRABAND (LP, with insert)	12
77	Polydor 2625 034	LIVE (2-LP, gatefold sleeve)	15

GOLDEN FLEECE
| 67 | Decca F 12669 | Athens 6 a.m./Girl From Syracuse | 6 |

GOLDEN GATE QUARTET
51	Columbia DB 3035	Do Unto Others/JEFF ALEXANDER CHOIR: Little Bitty Baby (78)	8
53	Columbia SCM 5054	Moses Smote The Waters/Bones, Bones, Bones	5
53	Columbia DB 3310	Moses Smote The Waters/Bones, Bones, Bones (78)	10
56	Columbia SEG 7700	SINGS GREAT SPIRITUALS (EP)	8
58	Fontana TFR 6009	THAT GOLDEN CHARIOT (10" LP)	15
59	Columbia 33SX 1172	SHOUT FOR JOY! (LP)	12
50s	Columbia 33CSX 9	NEGRO SPIRITUALS (LP)	12
61	Columbia 33SX 1370	GET ON BOARD (LP)	12

GOLDEN GATE STRINGS
| 65 | Columbia DB 7634 | Mr. Tambourine Man/With God On Our Side | 8 |

GOLDEN HORDE
85	Hot Wire WAY OUT 1	DIG THAT CRAZY GRAVE (EP)	5
80s	Hot Wire HWS 855	Young And Happy/Little UFO/Fiona (p/s)	5
85	Hot Wire/I.D. NOSE 7	THE CHOCOLATE BISCUIT CONSPIRACY (LP)	12
86	Media Burn MB 6	IN REALITY (mini-LP)	10

GOLDIE (& GINGERBREADS)
65	Decca F 12070	Can't You Hear My Heartbeat/Little Boy	8
65	Decca F 12126	That's Why I Love You/Skip	6
65	Decca F 12199	Sailor Boy/Please Please	6
66	Immediate IM 026	Goin' Back/Headlines (solo)	10
66	Fontana TF 693	I Do/Think About The Good Times (solo)	10
69	Decca F 12931	Can't You Hear My Heartbeat/That's Why I Love You	5
	(see also Ten Wheel Drive)		

JOHN GOLDING
| 74 | Cottage 101S | DISCARDED VERSE (LP, 2,000 only) | 12 |

VIVIEN GOLDMAN
| 81 | Window WIN 1 | Launderette/Private Armies (gatefold p/s, with PiL) | 5 |
| | *(see also Public Image Ltd)* | | |

BOBBY GOLDSBORO
63	Stateside SS 193	The Runaround/The Letter	12
63	United Artists UP 1046	See The Funny Little Clown/Hello Loser	7
64	United Artists UP 1054	Whenever He Holds You/If She Was Mine	7
65	United Artists UP 1079	Little Things/I Just Can't Go On Pretending	10
65	United Artists UP 1091	Voodoo Woman/It Breaks My Heart	6
65	United Artists UP 1104	If You Wait For Love/If You've Got A Heart	6
66	United Artists UP 1120	Broomstick Cowboy/Ain't Got Time For Happy	6
66	United Artists UP 1128	It's Too Late/I'm Goin' Home	10
66	United Artists UP 1135	I Know You Better Than That/When Your Love Has Gone	6
66	United Artists UP 1146	Take Your Love/Longer Than Forever	10
67	United Artists UP 1156	It Hurts Me/Pity The Fool	6
67	United Artists UP 1166	No Fun At The Fair/Hold On	6
67	United Artists UP 1177	Too Many People/Goodbye To All You Women	20
68	United Artists UP 2215	Honey/Danny	5
68	United Artists UP 2223	Autumn Of My Life/She Chased Me	6
69	United Artists UP 2264	Love Arrester/Dissatisfied Man	5
69	United Artists UP 35034	Muddy Mississippi Line/Richer Man Than I	6
69	United Artists UP 35053	Letter To Emily/Tomorrow Is Forgotten	6
65	United Artists UEP 1006	LITTLE THINGS (EP)	30
66	United Artists UEP 1016	THE TALENTED BOBBY GOLDSBORO (EP)	30
66	United Artists (S)ULP 1135	IT'S TOO LATE (LP)	25
67	United Artists (S)ULP 1163	SOLID GOLDSBORO — GREATEST HITS (LP)	20
68	United Artists (S)ULP 1195	HONEY (LP, black label)	18
69	United Artists UAS 29008	TODAY (LP)	12

GOLDSMITH
| 83 | Bedlam BLM 001 | Life Is Killing Me/Music Man (p/s) | 25 |

JERRY GOLDSMITH
| | *(see under Soundtrack LPs)* | | |

GOLGOTHA
| 84 | Golgotha GOTH 002 | DANGEROUS GAMES (EP, no p/s) | 20 |

GOLIARD
| 76 | Broadside BRO 127 | FORTUNE MY FOE (LP, with booklet) | 15 |

MINT VALUE £

GOLIATH
70	CBS 5312	Port And Lemon Lady/I Heard About A Friend	6
70	CBS 64229	GOLIATH (LP)	40

GOLLIWOGS
66	Vocalion VF 9266	Brown-Eyed Girl/You Better Be Careful	35
67	Vocalion VF 9283	Fragile Child/Fight Fire	35
72	Fantasy FAN 5996	GOLLIWOGS (LP, pressed in U.S. for U.K. distribution)	12

(see also Creedence Clearwater Revival)

GOLLYWOGS
60	Parlophone R 4647	Parade Of The Jelly Babies/The Teddy Bears' Picnic	5

BENNY GOLSON
81	CBS A 1223	The New Killer Joe/Walkin' And Stalkin'	5
81	CBS 12A 1223	The New Killer Joe/Walkin' And Stalkin' (12")	8
59	Esquire 32-125	GONE WITH GOLSON (LP)	15
60	Esquire 32-105	GROOVIN' WITH GOLSON (LP)	15

BENNY GOLSON & ART FARMER
62	Pye International 7N 25120	Blues March/Serenata	5
65	Stateside SL 10150	STOCKHOLM SOJOURN (LP)	12

(see also Art Farmer)

GONADS
82	Secret SHH 131	PURE PUNK FOR NOW PEOPLE (EP)	8
82	Secret SHH 134	PEACE ARTISTS (EP)	6
83	Razor RZS 103	DELILAH (THE PUNK EPIC) (EP)	5

GONDOLIERS
58	Starlite ST45 001	Fly, Seagull, Fly/God's Green Acres	8

NAT GONELLA & HIS GEORGIA JAZZ BAND
60	Columbia DB 4465	Show Me The Way To Go Home/My Gal Sal	6
50s	Columbia 33S 1146	SALUTE TO SATCHMO (LP)	40
60s	Columbia 33SX 1380	THE NAT GONELLA STORY (LP)	40

GONG
71	Philips 6332 033	CONTINENTAL CIRCUS (LP, soundtrack)	25
73	Virgin V 2002	RADIO GNOME INVISIBLE PART 1 — THE FLYING TEAPOT (LP, originally with black & white label design)	15/12
73	Virgin V 2007	RADIO GNOME INVISIBLE PART 2 — ANGEL'S EGG (LP, gatefold sleeve, initially with b&w label; some with book)	30/12
74	Virgin VC 502	CAMEMBERT ELECTRIQUE (LP)	12
74	Virgin V 2019	YOU (LP, with lyric insert)	12
76	Virgin V 2046	SHAMAL (LP)	12
77	Virgin V 2074	GAZEUSE! (LP, with poster)	15
77	Virgin VGD 3501	LIVE ETC. (2-LP, with cut-out cover & inner sleeves)	15
78	Virgin V 2099	EXPRESSO II (LP, with inner)	12

(see also Mother Gong, Gilli Smyth & Mother Gong, Daevid Allen, Steve Hillage, Clearlight, Radio Actors, Sphynx, Tim Blake, Comus)

GONG/CAMEL/HENRY COW/GLOBAL TRUCKING COMPANY
73	Greasy Truckers GT 4997	GREASY TRUCKERS (2-LP, 1 side each; with insert)	15

(see also Camel, Henry Cow, Global Trucking Company)

GONKS
64	Decca F 11984	The Gonk Song/That's All Right, Mamma	18

(see also Twinkle)

RON GONNELLA
70s	LISMOR LILP 5017	FIDDLERS FANCY (LP)	12

PAUL GONSALVES
64	Vocalion LAE 587	BOOM JACKIE BOOM CHICK (LP)	100
70	Deram SML 1064	HUMMINGBIRD (LP)	30
73	Black Lion 2460 191	JUST A-SITTIN' AND A-ROCKIN' (LP, with Ray Nance)	12

(see also Tubby Hayes & Paul Gonsalves)

GONZALEZ
74	EMI EMI 2706	I Haven't Stopped Dancing Yet/Carnival	5
74	EMI EMC 3046	GONZALEZ (LP)	25
75	EMI EMC 3100	OUR ONLY WEAPON IS OUR MUSIC (LP)	15

BELLE GONZALEZ
72	Columbia DB 8852	Bottles/I Hate Sunday	7
65	Jupiter JEPOC 37	POETS SET IN JAZZ (EP, as Belle Gonzalez & Sextet)	15
66	Jupiter JEPOC 39	CONTEMPORARY POETS SET IN JAZZ (EP)	15
72	Columbia SCX 6484	BELLE (LP)	50

(see also Mark Wirtz)

DOUGLAS GOOD & GINNY PLENTY
68	Stateside SS 2104	Sunny And Me/Living In A World Of Make Believe	5

JACK GOOD'S FAT NOISE
60	Decca F 11233	The Fat Washerwoman/The Fat Noise	5

GOODBYE MR MACKENZIE

84	Scruples YTS 1	Death Of A Salesman/LINDY BERGMAN: Locked Inside Your Prison (no p/s, 1,000 only)	15
86	Precious Org. JEWEL 2	The Rattler/Candlestick Park (p/s)	5
86	Precious Org. JEWEL 2T	The Rattler/Candlestick Park/The End (12", p/s)	8
86	Clandestine MACK 1	Face To Face/Secrets/Good Deeds (12", p/s)	8
88	Capitol CLCD 501	Goodbye Mr MacKenzie (extended)/Green Turn Red/Knockin' On Joe (CD)	8
88	Capitol CLCD 513	Open Your Arms (extended)/Secrets/Amsterdam/Pleasure Search (CD)	8
89	Capitol CDCL 522	The Rattler/Here Comes Deacon Brodie/Calton Hall/Drunken Sailor (CD)	8
89	Capitol CLCD 538	Goodwill City (5.03)/I'm Sick Of You/What's Got Into You/Insidious Thing (CD)	8
90	Parlophone PCS 7345	HAMMER AND TONGS (LP, unreleased, white label test pressings only)	40

(see also Garbage, Angelfish)

GOOD EARTH

68	Saga FID 2112	IT'S HARD ROCK AND ALL THAT (LP)	20
70	Saga FID 8157	IN THE SUMMERTIME (LP, with tracks by Macon Jug)	12
72	Boulevard 4078	RAY DORSET'S BEST (LP, 4 tracks by Good Earth & 6 tracks by Macon Jug)	12

(see also First Impression/Good Earth, Mungo Jerry, Ray Dorset)

GOODEES

69	Stax STAX 113	Condition Red/Didn't Know Love Was So Good	8

GOOD GUYS

70	Duke DU 82	Death Rides/Destruction	6
70	Duke DU 83	Wreck It Up/Dynamic Groove	6
70	Duke DU 84	Happiness/Latissimo	7

(see also Byron Lee & Dragonaires)

PHILIP GOODHAND-TAIT (& STORMSVILLE SHAKERS)

66	Parlophone R 5448	I'm Gonna Put Some Hurt On You/It's A Lie (with Stormsville Shakers)	10
66	Parlophone R 5498	No Problem/What More Do You Want (with Stormsville Shakers)	8
66	Parlophone R 5547	You Can't Take Love/J.C. Greaseburger (solo)	10
69	Decca F 12868	Love Has Got Hold Of Me/Too Pleased To Help	6
70	DJM DJS 230	Jeannie/Run See The Sun	5
71	DJM DJS 236	Oh Rosanna/I Didn't Know Myself	5
71	DJM DJLPS 411	REHEARSAL (LP)	12
71	DJM DJLPS 416	I THINK I'LL WRITE A SONG (LP)	12
72	DJM DJLPS 425	SONGFALL (LP, gatefold sleeve)	12
73	DJM DJLPS 432	PHILIP GOODHAND-TAIT (LP)	12
75	DJM DJLPS 453	JINGLE JANGLE MAN (LP)	12

(see also Circus, Larry Williams, Love Affair)

CUBA GOODING

83	London LONX 41	Happiness Is Just Around The Bend/(Version) (12")	8

JOHNNY GOODISON

70	Deram DM 319	A Little Understanding/One Mistake	6

(see also Quotations, Johnny B. Great)

GOODLETTSVILLE FIVE

64	London HLW 9854	Eef/Baby's Gone Eefing	6

JOHN GOODLUCK

74	Tradition TSR 015	SUFFOLK MIRACLE (LP, with insert)	30

BENNY GOODMAN

53	Columbia SCM 5053	Temptation Rag/Bugle Call Rag	6
55	Capitol CL 14258	Jumpin' At The Woodside/Let's Dance	6
56	Columbia SCM 5239	King Porter Stomp/Memories Of You	6
56	HMV 7M 380	Don't Be That Way/Down South Camp Meeting	6
56	Capitol CL 14531	Goody Goody/Sometimes I'm Happy	5
56	Capitol CL 14570	Don't Be That Way/And The Angels Sing	5
60	Philips JAZ 107	Liza/Slipped Disc (p/s)	5
58	Philips BBE 12172	PEGGY WITH BENNY (EP, with Peggy Lee)	8
52	Capitol LC 6557	EASY DOES IT (10" LP)	15
52	Capitol LC 6565	AFTER HOURS (10" LP)	15
53	Capitol LC 6601	DIZZY FINGERS (10" LP)	15
53	Capitol LC 6620	THE GOODMAN TOUCH (10" LP)	15
54	Columbia 33S 1048	SESSION FOR SEXTET (10" LP)	15
54	Capitol LC 6680	CLASSICS IN JAZZ (10" LP)	15
54	Philips BBL 7000	CARNEGIE HALL JAZZ CONCERT (LP, auto-coupling)	12
54	Philips BBL 7001	CARNEGIE HALL JAZZ CONCERT (LP, auto-coupling)	12
55	Philips BBR 8064	LET'S HEAR THE MELODY (10" LP)	15
55	Philips BBL 7009	1937-1938 JAZZ CONCERT NO. 2 (LP, auto-coupling)	12
55	Philips BBL 7010	1937-1938 JAZZ CONCERT NO. 2 (LP, auto-coupling)	12
55	Philips BBL 7043	PRESENTS EDDIE SAUTER ARRANGEMENTS (LP)	12
56	Philips BBL 7073	MAKES HISTORY (LP)	12
56	Brunswick LAT 8102	THE BENNY GOODMAN STORY VOLUME ONE (LP)	12
56	Brunswick LAT 8103	THE BENNY GOODMAN STORY VOLUME TWO (LP)	12
58	Fontana TFR 6006	BENNY GOODMAN SEXTET (10" LP)	15

DAVE GOODMAN & FRIENDS

78	The Label TLR 008	Justifiable Homicide/Take Down Your Fences (p/s, 1st 15,000 on red vinyl)	6/5
78	The Label TLR 008	Justifiable Homicide/Take Down Your Fences (p/s, with 'Steve Jones & Paul Cook' credit)	50

(see also Sex Pistols)

MINT VALUE £

GOOD MISSIONARIES

80	Kif KIF'S 1	Good Missionary (Parts 1 & 2) (p/s)	5
80	Unnormality NORM 001	VIBING UP THE SENILE WORLD (The Good Missionary Part 1 [live]/ The Good Missionary Part/Kif Kif's Free Freak Out [live]) (EP, 1,000 only)	5
81	Unnormality NORM 002	DERANGED IN HASTINGS (Keep Going Backwards/Attitudes) (EP, with printed insert, PVC sleeve)	5
79	Deptford Fun City DLP 04	FIRE FROM HEAVEN (LP)	12
80	Conventional (no cat. no.)	SPONTANEOUS EMISSIONS (studio/live cassette)	12

(see also Mark Perry, Alternative TV)

GOOD RATS

69	London HLR 10237	The Hobo/The Truth Is Gone	5

GOOD SHIP LOLLIPOP

69	Ember EMB S 276	Maxwell's Silver Hammer/How Does It Feel (some in p/s)	10/6

GOOD TIME LOSERS

67	Fontana TF 791	Trafalgar Square/Where Did My Heart Go	5

GOODTIMERS

62	Fontana H 360	It's Twistin' Time/Twisting Train	5

GOOD VIBRATIONS

70	Ember EMB S 270	Call Me Lightning/Nantucket Ferry	5

ROD GOODWAY

90	Woronzow WOO 12	ETHEREAL COUNTERBALANCE (LP)	18

RON GOODWIN CONCERT ORCHESTRA

53	Parlophone MSP 6035	Limelight/The Song From Moulin Rouge	7
56	Parlophone R 4250	Rock Around The Clock/Giddy-Up-A Ding Dong (78)	7
57	Parlophone R 4297	Skiffling Strings (Swinging Sweetheart)/I'll Find You	5
61	Parlophone R 4821	Murder She Says/Double Scotch	5
64	Parlophone R 5146	633 Squadron/Love Theme From 633 Squadron	5
66	Parlophone R 5501	The Trap/Operation Crossbow	5
67	Parlophone R 5618	The Magnificent Two/Venus Waltz	5
72	Columbia DB 8938	Pathfinders March/Aces High	5
55	Parlophone GEP 8555	RON GOODWIN AND HIS CONCERT ORCHESTRA (EP)	10
54	Parlophone PMD 1014	FILM FAVOURITES (10" LP)	12
56	Parlophone PMD 1038	MUSIC TO SET YOU DREAMING (10" LP)	12
58	Parlophone PCS 3002	MUSIC FOR AN ARABIAN NIGHT (LP)	15
58	Parlophone PCS 3006	OUT OF THIS WORLD! (LP)	25
68	Stateside (S)SL 10259	DECLINE AND FALL ... OF A BIRDWATCHER (LP, soundtrack)	100
69	Paramount SPFL 255	MONTE CARLO OR BUST! (LP, soundtrack)	40
72	Studio 2 TWO 373	PLAY BURT BACHARACH (LP)	12
76	EMI EMC 3148	ESCAPE FROM THE DARK (LP, soundtrack)	25
78	Studio Two TWOSP 108	THE FIRST 25 YEARS (2-LP)	15

GOOFERS

55	Vogue Coral Q 72051	Hearts Of Stone/You're The One	50
55	Vogue Coral Q 72051	Hearts Of Stone/You're The One (78)	25
55	Vogue Coral Q 72074	Flip, Flop And Fly/My Babe	50
55	Vogue Coral Q 72074	Flip, Flop And Fly/My Babe (78)	25
55	Vogue Coral Q 72094	Goofy Drybones/Nare	25
55	Vogue Coral Q 72094	Goofy Drybones/Nare (78)	20
56	Vogue Coral Q 72124	Sick! Sick! Sick!/Twenty One	20
56	Vogue Coral Q 72124	Sick! Sick! Sick!/Twenty One (78)	35
56	Vogue Coral Q 72171	Tear Drop Motel/Tennessee Rock And Roll	30
56	Vogue Coral Q 72171	Tear Drop Motel/Tennessee Rock And Roll (78)	35
57	Vogue Coral Q 72267	Wow!/Push, Push, Push Cart	20
57	Vogue Coral Q 72267	Wow!/Push, Push, Push Cart (78)	35
57	Vogue Coral Q 72289	The Dipsy Doodle/Take This Heart	20
57	Vogue Coral Q 72289	The Dipsy Doodle/Take This Heart (78)	20

GOONS

56	Decca F 10756	I'm Walking Backwards For Christmas/Bluebottle Blues	12
56	Decca F 10756	I'm Walking Backwards For Christmas/Bluebottle Blues (78)	7
56	Decca F 10780	The Ying Tong Song/Bloodnok's Rock 'N' Roll Call	10
56	Decca F 10780	The Ying Tong Song/Bloodnok's Rock 'N' Roll Call (78)	7
57	Decca F 10885	Eeh! Ah! Oh! Ooh!/I Love You	8
57	Decca F 10885	Eeh! Ah! Oh! Ooh!/I Love You (78)	7
57	Decca F 10945	A Russian Love Song/Whistle Your Cares Away	7
57	Decca F 10945	A Russian Love Song/Whistle Your Cares Away (78)	6
70s	Lyntone	SCHOOL LEAVERS GOING TO COLLEGE (EP, flexidisc for Barclays Bank)	5
56	Decca DFE 6396	THE GOONS (EP)	10
64	Decca LF 1332	UNCHAINED MELODIES (10" LP)	20
59	Parlophone PMC 1108	BEST OF THE GOON SHOWS (LP)	15
60	Parlophone PMC 1129	BEST OF THE GOON SHOWS (NO. 2) (LP)	15
75	EMI EMC 3082	VERY BEST OF (LP)	12

(see also Peter Sellers, Spike Milligan, Harry Secombe, Michael Bentine, Famous Eccles, Eric Sykes)

SAM GOPAL

69	Stable STA 5602	Horse/Back Door Man (unissued, existence unconfirmed)	
69	Stable SLE 8001	Escalator/Gold Embrace/The Sky Is Burning/Angry Faces (LP sampler)	35
69	Stable SLE 8001	ESCALATOR (LP, gatefold sleeve)	90

(see also Hawkwind, Motörhead, Vamp, Isaac Guillory, Clark-Hutchinson, G. F. Fitzgerald)

RABBI JOSEPH GORDAN

(see under 'R')

PETE(R) GORDENO

MINT VALUE £

61	Fontana H 319	Be My Girl/Haven't Got Time (as Pete Gordeno)	8
62	Parlophone R 4862	I Got Eyes/You're Following Me	6
62	Parlophone R 4931	Down By The Riverside/The Boys Kept Hanging Around	6
65	Decca F 12088	Have You Looked Into Your Heart/Don't Come To Me	6
69	Decca F 12947	Everybody Knows/Man And Wife Time	6
68	MCA MU 1009	Shout It From The Hilltop/Born To Be Wanted	5
69	MCA MU 1058	My Girl Maria/I Appreciate	5
70	Decca PA 78	THE WORLD OF PETER GORDENO (LP)	12

GORDON
(see under Gordon Waller)

ANITA GORDON
| 55 | Brunswick 05456 | Lonesome Like Nobody Knows/His Hands | 7 |

BARRY GORDON
| 56 | MGM MGM 928 | I Can't Whistle/The Milkman's Polka | 7 |
| 56 | MGM MGM 935 | Rock Around Mother Goose/Nuttin' For Christmas | 15 |

CURTIS GORDON
| 57 | Mercury MT 163 | Sixteen/Cry, Cry (78) | 20 |

DEXTER GORDON
60s	Realm RM 191	DEXTER RIDES AGAIN (LP)	12
60s	Fontana Jazz FJL 907	MASTER SWINGERS (LP, with Wardell Gray)	15
71	Black Lion 2460 108	MONTMARTRE COLLECTION VOL. 1 (LP)	12

FLESH GORDON & NUDE HOLLYWOOD
| 74 | Paramount PARA 3049 | Superstreaker/Naked | 5 |

JOE GORDON (FOLK FOUR)
59	HMV POP 600	Gotta Travel On/Ho Ro My Nutbrown Maid	5
59	HMV POP 600	Gotta Travel On/Ho Ro My Nutbrown Maid (78)	8
59	HMV POP 634	Dream Lover/Dance To Your Daddy	5
59	HMV POP 634	Dream Lover/Dance To Your Daddy (78)	12
60	HMV POP 737	Football Crazy/By The Bright Shining Light Of The Moon	5

PHIL GORDON
55	Brunswick 05481	Get A Load Of That Crazy Walk/Strip Polka	6
56	Brunswick 05545	Down The Road Apiece/I'm Gonna Move To The Outskirts Of Town	12
56	Brunswick 05545	Down The Road Apiece/I'm Gonna Move To The Outskirts Of Town (78)	7

RONNIE GORDON
| 63 | R&B JB 127 | Shake Some Time/Comin' Home | 20 |

ROSCO(E) GORDON
60	Top Rank JAR 332	Just A Little Bit/Goin' Home (as Rosco Gordon)	22
63	Stateside SS 204	Just A Little Bit/What I Wouldn't Do	20
65	Vocalion V-P 9245	Keep On Doggin'/Bad Dream	20
65	Island WI 256	Surely I Love You/What You Do To Me	15
66	Island WI 272	No More Doggin'/Goin' Home	20

TONY GORDON
| 73 | Grape GR 3056 | Be True (actually by Alton Ellis)/Navajo Trail | 5 |
(see also Alton Ellis)

TREVOR GORDON
| 70 | Polydor 2058 045 | Spend All The Money/Daytime | 4 |
| 70 | Polydor 2343 011 | ALPHABET (LP) | 10 |
(see also Marbles)

VINCENT GORDON
69	Coxsone CS 7085	Soul Trombone/LARRY & ALVIN: Your Cheating Heart	18
69	Duke DU 37	Everybody Bawlin'/SILVERTONES: Come Look Here	8
69	Crab CRAB 16	Walking By/VICEROYS: Promises Promises	8
74	Big Shot BI 630	Come Go With Me/SKIN, FLESH & BONES: Dub Ali Dub	5
(see also Don Drummond Junior)

CHARLIE GORE
54	Parlophone CMSP 19	I'll Find Somebody/Heaven Sent You To Me (export issue)	20
54	Parlophone DP 379	I'll Find Somebody/Heaven Sent You To Me (78)	8
54	Parlophone CMSP 26	Two Of A Kind/It's A Long Walk Back To Town (export issue)	20
54	Parlophone DP 397	Two Of A Kind/It's A Long Walk Back To Town (78)	8
54	Parlophone CMSP 30	I Didn't Know/Oh! Mis'rable Love (export issue)	20
(see also Hawkshaw Hawkins, Ruby Wright)

LESLEY GORE
63	Mercury AMT 1205	It's My Party/Danny	5
63	Mercury AMT 1210	Judy's Turn To Cry/Just Let Me Cry	5
63	Mercury AMT 1213	She's A Fool/The Old Crowd	5
64	Mercury MF 803	You Don't Own Me/Run Bobby Run	6
64	Mercury MF 810	That's The Way Boys Are/That's The Way The Ball Bounces	5
64	Mercury MF 821	I Don't Wanna Be A Loser/It's Gotta Be You	5
64	Mercury MF 829	Maybe I Know/Wonder Boy	6
64	Mercury MF 837	Sometimes I Wish I Were A Boy/Hey Now	5
65	Mercury MF 846	The Look Of Love/Little Girl Go Home	5
65	Mercury MF 862	Sunshine Lollipops And Rainbows/You've Come Back	5
65	Mercury MF 872	My Town, My Guy And Me/Girl In Love	7
65	Mercury MF 889	I Won't Love You Anymore (Sorry)/No Matter What You Do	7

Lesley GORE

66	Mercury MF 902	Young Love/I Just Don't Know If I Can	5
66	Mercury MF 963	California Nights/I'm Going Out (The Same Way I Came In)	5
66	Mercury MF 984	I'm Fallin' Down/Summer And Sandy	8
68	Mercury MF 1017	Magic Colours/It's A Happening World	5
75	A&M AMS 7184	Immortality/Give It To Me, Sweet Thing	5
64	Mercury 10017 MCE	LESLEY GORE (EP)	25
63	Mercury MMC 14127	I'LL CRY IF I WANT TO (LP)	25
63	Mercury 20001 MCL	SINGS OF MIXED-UP HEARTS (LP)	22
64	Mercury 20020 MCL	BOYS BOYS BOYS (LP)	22
64	Mercury 20033 MCL	GIRL TALK (LP)	22
65	Mercury 20076 MCL	ALL ABOUT LOVE (LP)	20
67	Wing WL 1183	GIRL TALK (LP, reissue)	12

GORKY'S ZYGOTIC MYNCI

93	Ankst ANKST/GZM 040	PATIO (10" EP)	15
94	Ankst ANKST 048	Merched Yn Neud Gwallt Eu Gilydd/Bocs Angelica/	
		When You Laugh At Your Own Garden In A Blazer (p/s)	6
95	Ankst ANKST 053	Pentref Wrth Y Môr/The Game Of Eyes/Cwpwrdd Sadwrn (p/s)	6
95	Ankst ANKST 058	Gewn Ni Gorffen/12 Impressionistic Soundscapes	
		(clear vinyl, p/s, mail order only, 1,000 copies)	5

JOHN GORMAN

73	Island WIP 6151	WPC Hodges/I Remember	5
77	DJM DJF 20491	GO MAN GORMAN (LP)	12
	(see also Scaffold, Grimms)		

EYDIE GORMÉ

54	Vogue Coral Q 2014	Frenesi/Climb Up The Wall	10
54	Vogue Coral Q 2027	Tea For Two/Sure	8
55	Vogue Coral Q 72067	Give A Fool A Chance/A Girl Can't Say (unissued)	
55	Vogue Coral Q 72092	Give A Fool A Chance/A Girl Can't Say	8
55	Vogue Coral Q 72103	Soldier Boy/What Is The Secret Of Your Success?	8
56	London HL 8227	Sincerely Yours/Come Home	15
56	London HL 8227	Sincerely Yours/Come Home (78)	8
57	HMV POP 400	Kiss In Your Eyes/Your Kisses Kill Me	6
58	HMV POP 432	Love Me Forever/Until They Sail	8
58	HMV POP 493	You Need Hands/The Gentleman Is A Dope	5
58	HMV POP 513	Gotta Have Rain/To You, From Me	5
58	HMV POP 513	Gotta Have Rain/To You, From Me (78)	7
58	HMV POP 529	Dormi, Dormi, Dormi/Be Careful, It's My Heart	5
58	HMV POP 529	Dormi, Dormi, Dormi/Be Careful, It's My Heart (78)	7
59	HMV POP 577	Separate Tables/The Voice Of My Heart	5
59	HMV POP 577	Separate Tables/The Voice Of My Heart (78)	10
59	HMV POP 616	I'm Yours/Don't Take Your Love From Me	5
60	HMV POP 767	The Dance Is Over/Too Young To Know	6
62	CBS AAG 105	Yes, My Darling Daughter/Sonny Boy	5
63	CBS AAG 131	Blame It On The Bossa Nova/Guess I Should Have Loved Him More	5
63	CBS AAG 149	Don't Try To Fight It Baby/Theme From Light Fantastic	8
63	CBS AAG 170	Everybody Go Home/The Message	6
64	CBS AAG 215	I Want You To Meet My Baby/Can't Get Over (The Bossa Nova)	5
67	CBS 202470	Everybody Go Home/The Message (reissue)	5
59	HMV 7EG 8547	LOVE IS A SEASON (EP, also stereo [GES 5789])	8/10
59	HMV 7EG 8562	I'LL REMEMBER APRIL	
		(EP, also stereo [GES 5795])	8/10
59	HMV 7EG 8409	EXCITING EYDIE (EP)	8
59	HMV 7EG 8474	FINE AND DANDY (EP)	8
59	HMV 7EG 8515	WHEN YOUR LOVER (EP)	8
64	CBS AGG 20047	THE SWEETEST SOUNDS (EP)	8
58	Coral LVA 9086	EYDIE GORME'S DELIGHT (LP)	15
58	HMV CLP 1156	EYDIE GORME (LP)	15
58	HMV CLP 1170	EYDIE SWINGS THE BLUES (LP)	15
58	HMV CLP 1201	VAMPS THE ROARING 20's (LP)	15
59	HMV CLP 1250	EYDIE IN LOVE (LP)	15
59	HMV CLP 1257	GORME SINGS SHOWSTOPPERS (LP)	12
59	HMV CLP 1290	LOVE IS A SEASON (LP)	15
60	HMV CLP 1323	ON STAGE (LP)	12
60	HMV CLP 1392/CSD 1322	EYDIE IN DIXIE-LAND (LP, mono/stereo)	12/15

EYDIE GORMÉ & STEVE LAWRENCE

55	Vogue Coral Q 72044	Make Yourself Comfortable/EYDIE GORME: Chain Reaction	8
55	Vogue Coral Q 72085	Besame Mucho/Take A Deep Breath	8
61	London HLT 9290	The Facts Of Life/I'm A Girl, You're A Boy	8
63	CBS AAG 163	I Want To Stay Here/Ain't Love (some in p/s)	8/5
63	CBS AAG 178	I Can't Stop Talking About You/To The Movies We Go	5
59	Vogue Coral FEP 2017	STEVE LAWRENCE AND EYDIE GORME (EP)	12
63	CBS AGG 20035	STEVE AND EYDIE (EP)	10
60	HMV CLP 1372/CSD 1310	STEVE AND EYDIE — WE GOT US (LP)	15
61	HMV CLP 1404/CSD 1329	THE GOLDEN HITS (LP)	15
61	HMV CLP 1463	COZY (LP)	15
62	HMV CLP 1517	COME SING WITH ME (LP)	15
	(see also Steve Lawrence)		

FRANK GORSHIN

| 66 | Pye International 7N 25402 | The Riddler/Never Let Her Go (some in p/s) | 60/20 |

GO! SERVICE

| 85 | Dreamworld DREAM 3 | It Makes Me Realise/Real Life/I Just Don't Know (12", p/s) | 8 |
| | (see also Blue Train) | | |

G.O.S.H. (Great Ormond Street Hospital Charity)
87 G.O.S.H. GOSHR 1   The Wishing Well (Remix)/Wishing Well Message (p/s) 5
(see also Andy Scott)

GOSPEL CLASSICS
68 Chess CRS 8080   More Love, That's What We Need/You Need Faith 25

GOSPELFOLK
69 Emblem 7DR 324   PRODIGAL (LP) 250

GOSPEL GARDEN
68 Camp 602 006   Finders Keepers/Just A Tear 10
(see also Dimples, Amazing Blondel)

GOSPEL OAK
70 Uni UNS 527   Recollections Of Jessica/Brown Haired Girl 6
70 Uni UNLS 113   GOSPEL OAK (LP) 18

GOTHIC HORIZON
70 Argo AFW 102   The Jason Lodge Poetry Book/Wilhelmina Before Sunrise 12
71 Argo AFW 104   Marjorie/Song 10
72 Argo AFW 107   If You Can Smile/Thoughts 10
72 Argo AFW 108   Girl With Guitar/Can't Bear To Think About You 10
71 Argo ZFB 26   THE JASON LODGE POETRY BOOK (LP) 50
72 Argo ZDA 150   TOMORROW IS ANOTHER DAY (LP) 80
(see also Andy Desmond)

GOTHIQUE
84 GEEC C 004   KRISTIANA (cassette) 10

KEVIN GOULD
70s Myrrh MYR 1028   TRUE STORIES BY (LP) 15

SANDRA GOULD
63 Philips BF 1290   Hello Melvin (This Is Mama)/My Son The Surfer 5

DALE GOULDER & LIZ DYER
70 Argo ZFB 10   JANUARY MAN (LP) 30
71 Argo ZFB 30   RAVEN & CROW (LP) 30

GRAHAM GOULDMAN
66 Decca F 12334   Stop! Stop! Stop! (Or Honey I'll Be Gone...)/Better To Have Loved And Lost 30
68 RCA Victor RCA 1667   Upstairs, Downstairs/Chestnut 15
69 Spark SRL 1026   Windmills Of Your Mind/Harvey's Theme (as Graham Gouldman Orchestra) 10
72 CBS 7739   Nowhere To Go/Growing Older 6
(see also 10cc, Whirlwinds, Mockingbirds, High Society, Frabjoy & Runcible Spoon, Manchester Mob, Garden Odyssey Enterprise, Friday Browne, Doctor Father)

GOVE
69 London HLE 10295   Sunday Morning Early/Death Letter Blues 10

GOVERNMENT ISSUE
83 Dischord 10¾   BOYCOTT STABB (LP, 500 only on pink vinyl) 12
85 Fountain Of Youth No. 17   THE FUN JUST NEVER ENDS (LP) 12

JOHN GRAAS SEPTET
54 London RE-P 1003   FRENCH HORN VOL. 1 (EP) 12

GRAB GRAB THE HADDOCK
84 Cherry Red 12CHERRY 83   THREE SONGS BY GRAB GRAB THE HADDOCK (12" EP) 8
85 Cherry Red CHERRY 86   TWO MORE SONGS BY GRAB GRAB THE HADDOCK (EP) 5
85 Cherry Red 12CHERRY 86   TWO MORE SONGS BY GRAB GRAB THE HADDOCK (12" EP) 8
(see also Marine Girls, Tracey Thorne)

MICK GRABHAM
72 United Artists UP 35391   On Fire For You Baby/Sweet Blossom Woman 5
72 United Artists UAS 29341   MICK THE LAD (LP) 12
(see also Plastic Penny, Cochise, Procol Harum)

GRACE
80 MCA MCA 628   Fire Of London/Beatnik (p/s) 12
81 MCA MCA 667   Billy Boy/Ad Mad (p/s) 8

CHARLIE GRACIE
57 Parlophone R 4290   Butterfly/Ninety-Nine Ways (initially gold lettering on label, later silver) 45/30
57 Parlophone R 4290   Butterfly/Ninety-Nine Ways (78) 10
57 Parlophone R 4313   Fabulous/Just Lookin' (initially gold lettering on label, later silver) 50/25
57 Parlophone R 4313   Fabulous/Just Lookin' (78) 7
57 London HL 8467   Wandering Eyes/I Love You So Much It Hurts (tri-centre) 18
57 London HL 8467   Wandering Eyes/I Love You So Much It Hurts (78) 7
57 London HLU 8521   Cool Baby/You Got A Heart Like A Rock (tri-centre) 25
57 London HLU 8521   Cool Baby/You Got A Heart Like A Rock (78) 15
58 London HLU 8596   Crazy Girl/Dressin' Up (tri-centre) 30
58 London HLU 8596   Crazy Girl/Dressin' Up (78) 15
59 Coral Q 72362   Doodlebug/Hurry Up, Buttercup (tri-centre) 15
59 Coral Q 72362   Doodlebug/Hurry Up, Buttercup (78) 25

Charlie GRACIE

59	Coral Q 72373	Angel Of Love/I'm A Fool, That's Why	
		(tri-centre, later round centre)	15/12
59	Coral Q 72373	Angel Of Love/I'm A Fool, That's Why (78)	30
59	Coral Q 72381	Oh-Well-A/Because I Love You So	15
59	Coral Q 72381	Oh-Well-A/Because I Love You So (78)	45
60	Columbia DB 4477	The Race/I Looked For You	18
62	London HLU 9603	Pretty Baby/Night And Day, U.S.A.	18
65	Stateside SS 402	He'll Never Love You Like I Do/Keep My Love Next To Your Heart	45
57	Parlophone GEP 8630	THE FABULOUS CHARLIE GRACIE (EP)	50
78	London HA-U 8513	CAMEO PARKWAY SESSIONS (LP)	15

GRACIOUS!

68	Polydor 56333	Beautiful/What A Lovely Rain	20
70	Vertigo 6059 009	Once On A Windy Day/Fugue In D Minor	8
70	Vertigo 6360 002	GRACIOUS! (LP, gatefold sleeve, spiral label)	45
72	Philips Intl. 6382 004	THIS IS ... GRACIOUS!! (LP, gatefold sleeve)	60

GRADUATE

80	Precision PAR 100	Elvis Should Play Ska/Julie Julie (p/s)	8
80	Precision PAR 104	Ever Met A Day/Shut Up (p/s)	10
80	Precision PAR 111	Ambition/Bad Dreams (p/s)	10
81	Precision PAR 117	Shut Up/Ever Met A Day (reissue, no p/s)	6
80s	Blue Hat 5 BHR	Mad One/Somebody Put Out The Fire	12
80	Precision PART 001	ACTING MY AGE (LP)	15

(see also Tears For Fears)

GRADUATES

79	Graduate GRAD 1	If You Want It/Hey Young Girl (p/s)	6

BILLY GRAHAM & ESCALATORS

67	Atlantic 584 073	Ooh Poo Pah Doo/East 24th Avenue	5

BOBBY/BOBBIE GRAHAM

65	Fontana TF 521	Skin Deep/Zoom Widge And Wag (as Bobbie Graham)	12
66	Fontana TF 667	Teensville/Grotty Drums (as Bobby Graham)	15

(see also Outlaws, Jimmy Page)

CHICK GRAHAM & COASTERS

64	Decca F 11859	Education/I Know	8
64	Decca F 11932	A Little You/Dance Baby Dance	8

DAV(E)Y GRAHAM

68	Decca F 12841	Both Sides Now/Tristano	8
62	Golden Guinea GGL 0224	THE GUITAR PLAYER (LP)	30
64	Decca LK 4649	FOLK, BLUES AND BEYOND (LP)	60
64	Decca LK 4652	FOLK ROOTS, NEW ROUTES (LP, with Shirley Collins)	100
66	Decca LK 4780	MIDNIGHT MAN (LP)	60
68	Decca LK/SKL 4969	LARGE AS LIFE AND TWICE AS NATURAL (LP)	50
69	Decca LK/SKL 5011	HAT (LP)	50
70	Decca SKL 5056	HOLLY KALEIDOSCOPE (LP)	50
70	President PTLS 1039	GODINGTON BOUNDARY (LP, with Holly)	30
76	Eron ERON 007	ALL THAT MOODY (LP, private pressing)	125
78	Kicking Mule SNKF 138	COMPLETE GUITARIST (LP, with tablature insert)	12
79	Kicking Mule SNKF 158	DANCE FOR TWO PEOPLE (LP, with tablature insert)	12
81	Righteous GDC 001	FOLK ROOTS, NEW ROUTES (LP, with Shirley Collins, reissue)	12

DAVY GRAHAM & ALEXIS KORNER

62	Topic TOP 70	3/4 A.D. (EP, 1st pressing credits 'Alexis Korner & Davy Graham')	each 100

(see also Alexis Korner)

DAVY GRAHAM/THAMESIDERS

63	Decca DFE 8538	FROM A LONDON HOOTENANNY (EP, 2 tracks each)	30

ERNIE GRAHAM

78	Stiff OFF 2	Romeo And The Lonely Girl/Only Time Will Tell (p/s)	5
71	Liberty LBS 83485	ERNIE GRAHAM (LP)	30

(see also Clancy, Eire Apparent, Brinsley Schwarz, Help Yourself, Nick Lowe)

KENNY GRAHAM'S AFRO-CUBISTS

60	Starlite ST45 013	Bongo Chant/Beguine	6
57	Pye Nixa NJE 1053	PRESENTING KENNY GRAHAM PART 1 (EP)	15
50s	Esquire EP 34	CARIBBEAN SUITE (EP)	12
50s	Esquire EP 68	KENNY GRAHAM'S AFRO CUBISTS (EP)	10
50s	Esquire EP 83	KENNY GRAHAM'S AFRO CUBISTS (EP)	20
56	MGM MGM-C 764	MOONDOG AND SUNCAT SUITES (LP, as Kenny Graham & His Satellites)	75
57	Nixa NJL 12	PRESENTING KENNY GRAHAM (LP)	75
50s	Esquire 20-012	KENNY GRAHAM AFRO CUBISTS (LP)	20
50s	Esquire 20-023	CARIBBEAN SUITE (LP)	20

(see also Yolanda)

LEN GRAHAM

77	Topic 12TS 334	WIND AND WATER (LP)	12

LEO GRAHAM

73	Upsetter US 399	News Flash/UPSETTERS: Flashing Echo	10
73	Summit SUM 8539	Three Blind Mice/UPSETTERS: Mice Skank	6

LOU GRAHAM

58	Coral Q 72322	Wee Willie Brown/You Were Mean Baby	450
58	Coral Q 72322	Wee Willie Brown/You Were Mean Baby (78)	100

LYNDA GRAHAM

62	Philips 326 552BF	As Long As The River Flows/When I'm Sixteen	6
63	Philips BF 1249	Without Your Love/Wait And See	7
64	Philips BF 1308	You'd Better Believe It/That's The Last Thing I'd Do	7

GRAHAM CENTRAL STATION
74	Warner Bros K 46206	GRAHAM CENTRAL STATION (LP)	12

(see also Sly & Family Stone)

RON GRAINER ORCHESTRA
60	Warner Bros WB 24	The Maigret Theme/Along The Boulevards (as Ron Grainer & His Music)	5
62	Fontana 267219 TF	A Kind Of Loving/Mild And Bitter Blues	8
62	Fontana 267232 TF	Johnny's Tune/Yeoman's Parade	8
62	Pye 7N 15411	Happy Joe/Old Ned	5
63	Decca F 11597	That Was The Week That Was/Petit Louis	7
63	Decca F 11640	Station Six Sahara/Indian Blues	8
64	HMV POP 1366	Not So Much A Programme, More A Way Of Life/Ascot Gavotte	10
67	Pye 7N 17383	A Man In A Suitcase/Andorra (red label, later blue)	18
67	RCA Victor RCA 1635	The Prisoner/Happening Sunday	60
68	RCA Victor RCA 1698	Love Theme/Detective	5
69	RCA Victor RCA 1898	The Paul Temple Theme/The Jazz Age	12
72	Pye 7N 45141	Steptoe & Son/Counting The Coaster	5
78	Casino Classics CC 5/6-12	A Touch Of Velvet — A Sting Of Brass/Theme From 'Joe 90'/ALLNIGHT BAND: The Wigan Joker/Six By Six (12", p/s, crimson vinyl, 'Disco DJ Version')	8
79	RK 1018	Tales Of The Unexpected/Paul Temple (p/s)	8
87	Six Of One LYN 18284	The Age Of Elegance/Arrival: The Awakening (Six Of One fan club flexidisc)	8
60	Warner Bros WEP 6012	THEME MUSIC FROM "INSPECTOR MAIGRET" (EP)	8
79	Six Of One 6 OF 1	THE PRISONER ARRIVAL (EP, fan club issue)	18
69	RCA Intl. INTS 1020	THEMES LIKE... (LP)	12

GLENDA GRAINGER
60s	Audio Fidelity AFSP 007	Mr. Kiss Kiss Bang Bang/Who	8

BILLY GRAMMER
58	London HLU 8752	Gotta Travel On/Chasing A Dream	12
58	London HLU 8752	Gotta Travel On/Chasing A Dream (78)	12
59	Felsted AF 121	Bonaparte's Retreat/The Kissing Tree	10
59	Felsted AF 121	Bonaparte's Retreat/The Kissing Tree (78)	15
59	Felsted AF 128	Willy, Quit Your Playing/It Takes You	10
59	Felsted AF 128	Willy, Quit Your Playing/It Takes You (78)	15
61	Brunswick 05851	Rainbow Round My Shoulder/Columbus Stockade Blues	8
59	Felsted GEP 1005	BILLY GRAMMER HITS (EP)	60

GERRY GRANAHAN
58	London HL 8668	No Chemise, Please/Girl Of My Dreams	25
58	London HL 8668	No Chemise, Please/Girl Of My Dreams (78)	15
60	Top Rank JAR 262	It Hurts/RICHIE ROBIN: Strange Dream	12

ROCCO GRANATA
59	Oriole CB 1525	Marina/Manuela	6
59	Oriole CB 1525	Marina/Manuela (78)	15
61	Oriole CB 1564	Julia/Rocco Cha Cha	5

GRAND FUNK RAILROAD
70	Capitol CL 15632	Heartbreaker/Please Don't Worry	5
70	Capitol CL 15661	Closer To Home/Aimless Lady	5
71	Capitol CL 15668	Inside Looking Out/Paranoid (33rpm)	5
71	Capitol CL 15689	I Can Feel Him In The Morning/Are You Ready/Mean Mistreater (33rpm maxi-single)	5
71	Capitol CL 15705	People, Let's Stop The War/Save The Land	5
72	Capitol CL 15738	Rock And Roll Soul/Flight Of Phoenix	5
69	Capitol E-ST 307	ON TIME (LP)	30
70	Capitol E-ST 406	GRAND FUNK (LP)	25
70	Capitol E-ST 471	CLOSER THAN HOME (LP)	25
70	Capitol E-STDW 1/2	LIVE (2-LP, gatefold sleeve)	15
71	Capitol E-SW 764	SURVIVAL (LP)	12
72	Capitol E-AS 853	E PLURIBUS FUNK (LP, circular 'silver coin' sleeve)	12
72	Capitol E-STSP 10	MARK, JOHN & MEL 1969/71 (2-LP)	15
73	Capitol E-AST 11099	PHOENIX (LP, gatefold sleeve)	12
73	Capitol E-AST 11027	WE'RE AN AMERICAN BAND (LP)	12
74	Capitol SWAE 11278	SHININ' ON (2-LP)	15
75	Capitol E-ST 11356	ALL THE GIRLS IN THE WORLD BEWARE (LP)	12
75	Capitol E-STSP 15	CAUGHT IN THE ACT (2-LP, original with custom label)	15
76	Capitol E-ST 11482	BORN TO DIE (LP)	12
76	EMI EMC 1503	GOOD SINGING, GOOD PLAYING (LP)	12

GRANDISONS
63	RCA RCA 1339	All Right/True Romance	6

GRAND PRIX
80	RCA RCA 7	Thinking Of You/Feels Good (p/s)	8
83	Chrysalis PRIXP 2	Shout/Keep On Believing (picture disc)	6
80	RCA PL 25321	GRAND PRIX — THE FIRST ALBUM (LP)	12
82	RCA RCALP 6027	THERE FOR NONE TO SEE (LP, with lyric insert)	12

(see also McAuley Schenker Group, Praying Mantis, Stratus, Uriah Heep)

GERRI GRANGER
63	London HLX 9759	Just Tell Him Jane Said Hello/What's Wrong With Me	7

ROY GRANGER ORCHESTRA
60	Top Rank JAR 320	Manhattan Lullaby/Lazy Baby	5

GRANNIE
71	SRT SRT 71138	GRANNIE (LP, private pressing, homemade sleeve)	700

MINT VALUE £

GRANNY'S INTENTIONS
67	Deram DM 158	The Story Of David/Sandy's On The Phone Again	10
68	Deram DM 184	Julie Don't Love Me Anymore/One Time Lovers	10
68	Deram DM 214	Never An Everyday Thing/Hilda The Bilda	10
70	Deram DM 293	Take Me Back/Maybe	15
70	Deram SML 1060	HONEST INJUN (LP)	45

(see also Gary Moore)

AMY GRANT
| 70s | Myrrh MYR 1124 | AGE TO AGE (LP) | 15 |

EARL GRANT
58	Brunswick 05762	The End/Hunky Dunky Doo	6
58	Brunswick 05762	The End/Hunky Dunky Doo (78)	8
59	Brunswick 05779	Evening Rain/Kathy-O	5
59	Brunswick 05779	Evening Rain/Kathy-O (78)	10
59	Brunswick 05792	Last Night (I Went Out Of My Mind)/Imitation Of Life	5
59	Brunswick 05792	Last Night (I Went Out Of My Mind)/Imitation Of Life (78)	12
60	Brunswick 05824	House Of Bamboo/Two Loves Have I	12
60	Brunswick 05824	House Of Bamboo/Two Loves Have I (78)	20
60	Brunswick 05841	Not One Minute More/Building Castles	5
62	Brunswick 05865	Tender Is The Night/Honey	5
62	Brunswick 05870	Swingin' Gently/Evening Rain	5
62	Brunswick 05877	Sweet Sixteen Bars/Learnin' The Blues	5
65	Brunswick 05945	Stand By Me/After Hours	5
60	Brunswick OE 9460	EARL GRANT (EP)	8
63	Brunswick OE 9493	SWINGING GENTLY (EP)	8
59	Brunswick LAT 8297	THE END (LP)	12
60	Brunswick LAT 8332	NOTHIN' BUT THE BLUES (LP)	12
60	Brunswick LAT 8351	THE MAGIC OF EARL GRANT (LP)	12
61	Brunswick LAT 8389	EBB TIDE (LP, also stereo STA 3051)	12/15
62	Brunswick LAT 8502	EARL AFTER DARK (LP)	12

ERKEY GRANT & EARWIGS
| 63 | Pye 7N 15521 | I'm A Hog For You/I Can't Get Enough Of You | 25 |

GOGI GRANT
55	London HLB 8192	Suddenly There's A Valley/Love Is	25
56	London HLB 8257	Who Are We/We Believe In Love	20
56	London HLB 8282	Wayward Wind/No More Than Forever	20
57	London HLB 8364	You're In Love/When The Tide Is High	18
58	London HLB 8550	The Golden Ladder/All Of Me	15
58	RCA RCA 1038	It's A Wonderful Thing To Be Loved/What A Beautiful Combination	5
58	RCA RCA 1047	Bonjour Tristesse/Johnny's Dream	5
59	RCA RCA 1101	Say A Prayer For Me Tonight/TONY MARTIN: She Is Not Thinking Of Me	5
59	RCA RCA 1105	Kiss Me Honey Honey Kiss Me/Two Dreams	7
59	RCA RCA 1105	Kiss Me Honey Honey Kiss Me/Two Dreams (78)	7
60	London HLG 9185	Goin' Home/I'm Going To Live The Life	8
56	London REB 1057	GOGI GRANT (EP, export issue)	12
57	London HA-B 2032	SUDDENLY THERE'S GOGI GRANT (LP)	22
58	RCA RD 27054	BOTH ENDS OF THE CANDLE (LP, soundtrack)	15
59	RCA RD 27097	GIGI (LP, with Tony Martin)	15
60	London HA-G 2242	IF YOU WANT TO GET TO HEAVEN — SHOUT! (LP, also stereo SAH-G 6072)	18/22

(see also Tony Martin)

JANIE GRANT
| 61 | Pye International 7N 25093 | Triangle/She's Going Steady With You | 6 |
| 62 | Pye International 7N 25148 | That Greasy Kid Stuff/Trying To Forget You | 6 |

JULIE GRANT
62	Pye 7N 15430	Somebody Tell Him/Ev'ry Letter You Write	6
62	Pye 7N 15447	So Many Ways/Unimportant Things	6
62	Pye 7N 15461	When You're Smiling/Lonely Sixteen	6
62	Pye 7N 15483	Up On The Roof/When You Ask About Love	6
63	Pye 7N 15508	Count On Me/Then, Only Then	8
63	Pye 7N 15526	That's How Heartaches Are Made/Cruel World	6
63	Pye 7N 15545	Don't Ever Let Me Down/Somebody Cares	7
63	Pye 7N 15590	Hello Love/It's Alright	6
64	Pye 7N 15684	Come To Me/Can't Get You Out Of My Mind	6
64	Pye 7N 15615	Every Day I Have To Cry/Watch What You Do With My Baby	7
64	Pye 7N 15652	You Are Nobody 'Til Somebody Loves You/I Only Care About You	6
65	Pye 7N 15756	Baby Baby (I Still Love You)/My World Is Empty Without You	7
65	Pye 7N 15812	Giving Up/Cause I Believe In You	6
65	Pye 7N 15884	Lonely Without You/As Long As I Know He's Mine	7
65	Pye 7N 15937	Stop/When The Lovin' Ends	7
62	Pye NEP 24171	THIS IS JULIE GRANT (EP)	25

LEE GRANT (& CAPITOLS)
| 66 | Parlophone R 5531 | Breaking Point/Don't Cry Baby (with Capitols) | 15 |
| 70 | Decca F 13029 | A Little Love And Understanding/I Got To Get You Out Of My Mind (solo) | 5 |

LITTLE BROTHER (GRANT)
| 70 | Torpedo TOR 27 | Baby Don't Let Me Down/Brother Strong Man (as Little Brother) | 6 |
| 70 | Torpedo TOR 28 | Let's Do It Together/Hey Man, Why (as Little Brother Grant & Zapatta Schmidt) | 6 |

(see also Equals)

NEVILLE GRANT
73	Downtown DT 509	Sick And Tired/PRINCE DJANGO: Hot Tip	25

NORMAN GRANT ORCHESTRA
61	Starlite ST45 060	Jive Medley/Speak Low	6

TOP GRANT
62	Island WI 034	Searching/David & Goliath	12
62	Island WI 052	Suzie/Jenny	12
63	Island WI 072	Riverbank Coberley (as Top-Grant)/Nancy	12
63	Island WI 074	Money Money Money/Have Mercy On Me	12
63	Island WI 077	War In Africa/The Birds	12

(see also Rhythm Aces)

GRANTCHESTER MEADOW
71	Amber ABR 004	Candlelight/Winter Blues	15

GRAPE
92	Pencil Toast PENT 001	Baby In A Plastic Bag/Listen To Your Heart (p/s)	25

(see also P.J. Harvey)

GRAPEFRUIT
68	RCA Victor RCA 1656	Dear Delilah/The Dead Boot	5
68	RCA Victor RCA 1677	Elevator/Yes	6
68	RCA Victor RCA 1716	C'mon Marianne/Ain't It Good	5
68	Stateside-Dunhill SS 8005	Someday Soon/Theme For Twiggy	6
69	Stateside-Dunhill SS 8011	Round Going Round/This Little Man	6
69	RCA Victor RCA 1855	Deep Water/Come Down To The Station	6
70	RCA Victor RCA 1907	Lady Godiva/Thunder And Lightning	5
71	Deram DM 343	Universal Party/Sha Sha	5
69	Stateside-Dunhill S(S)L 5008	AROUND GRAPEFRUIT (LP)	30
69	RCA Victor SF 8030	DEEP WATER (LP)	18

(see also Tony Rivers & Castaways, Easybeats, Fynn McCool, Sleepy)

GRAPEVINE
68	Liberty LBF 15063	Things Ain't What They Used To Be Anymore/Ace In The Hole	5

GRASSROOTS
66	RCA Victor RCA 1532	Where Were You When I Needed You/These Are Bad Times	5
67	Pye International 7N 25422	Let's Live For Today/Depressed Feeling	10
67	Pye International 7N 25431	Things I Should Have Said/Tip Of My Tongue	6
68	RCA Victor RCA 1682	Melody For You/Hey Friend	5
68	RCA Victor RCA 1737	Midnight Confessions/Who Will You Be Tomorrow	7
69	Stateside-Dunhill SS 8006	Bella Linda/Hot Bright Lights	5
69	Stateside-Dunhill SS 8012	All Good Things Come To An End/Melody For You	5
69	Stateside-Dunhill SS 8018	The River Is Wide/(You Gotta) Live For Love	5
69	Stateside-Dunhill SS 8023	Who Will You Be Tomorrow/Midnight Confessions	5
69	Stateside-Dunhill SS 8029	I'd Wait A Million Years/Fly Me To Havana	6
69	Stateside-Dunhill SS 8033	Heaven Knows/Don't Remind Me	5
70	Stateside-Dunhill SS 8037	Back To Dreamin' Again/Truck Drivin' Man	5
70	Stateside-Dunhill SS 8048	Walking Through The Country/Melinda Love	5
70	Probe PRO 503	Come On And Say It/Something's Comin' Over Me	5
71	Probe PRO 515	Temptation Eyes/Keepin' Me Down	5
69	Stateside S(S)L 5005	GOLDEN GRASS (LP)	15
70	Stateside SSL 5012	LEAVING IT ALL BEHIND (LP)	15
72	Probe SPB 1058	MOVE ALONG (LP)	12

(see also P.F. Sloan)

GRATEFUL DEAD
67	Warner Bros WB 7186	Born Cross-Eyed/Dark Star	40
70	Warner Bros WB 7410	Uncle John's Band/New Speedway Boogie	8
71	Warner Bros.	Truckin'/Johnny B. Goode (unissued)	
72	Warner Bros K 16167	One More Saturday Night (as Grateful Dead with Bobby Ace)/Bertha	5
73	Atlantic K 19301	Let Me Sing Your Blues Away/Here Comes Sunshine	5
74	United Artists UP 36030	U.S. Blues/Loose Lucy	5
77	Warner Bros SAM 79	Dark Star/Born Cross-Eyed (mail-order issue with Dark Star magazine)	15
79	Arista ARIST 236	Good Lovin'/Stagger Lee	5
87	Arista RIS 35	Touch Of Grey/My Brother Esau (grey vinyl, p/s)	5
67	Warner Bros W(S) 1689	THE GRATEFUL DEAD (LP, mono/stereo)	60/30
68	Warner Bros WS 1749	ANTHEM OF THE SUN (LP)	30
69	Warner Bros WS 1790	AOXOMOXOA (LP)	25
70	Warner Bros WS 1830	LIVE/DEAD (2-LP)	25
70	Warner Bros WS 1869	WORKINGMAN'S DEAD (LP, matt sleeve)	12
71	Warner Bros WS 1893	AMERICAN BEAUTY (LP)	12
71	Warner Bros K 66009	GRATEFUL DEAD LIVE (SKULL AND ROSES) (2-LP)	18
72	Polydor 2310 171	HISTORIC DEAD (LP)	20
72	Polydor 2310 172	VINTAGE DEAD (LP)	20
72	Warner Bros K 66019	EUROPE '72 (3-LP, triple fold-out sleeve)	20
73	Warner Bros K 46246	HISTORY OF GRATEFUL DEAD (BEAR'S CHOICE) (LP)	12
73	Warner Bros K 49301	WAKE OF THE FLOOD (LP)	12
74	Warner Bros K 56024	SKELETONS FROM THE CLOSET: THE BEST OF GRATEFUL DEAD (LP)	12
74	Warner Bros K 59302	FROM THE MARS HOTEL (LP)	12
75	United Artists UAS 29895	BLUES FOR ALLAH (LP, with insert)	12
76	United Artists UAD 60131/2	STEAL YOUR FACE (2-LP, gatefold sleeve, with sampler LP "For Dead Heads Only" [FREE 2] in inner sleeve)	30

(see also Jerry Garcia, Mickey Hart, Kingfish, Robert Hunter, Bob Weir, Keith & Donna Godchaux, Silver [U.S.], Diga Rhythm Band)

NICK GRAVENITES
69	CBS 63818	MY LABORS (LP)	18

(see also Big Brother & Holding Company)

BILLY GRAVES

59	Felsted AF 119	The Shag (Is Totally Cool)/Uncertain (export issue)	12
59	Felsted AF 119	The Shag (Is Totally Cool)/Uncertain (78, export issue)	20

CARL GRAVES

75	A&M AM 7151	Baby Hang Up The Phone/Walk Softly	6
75	A&M AM 7180	The Next Best Thing/Something Teling Me	5
76	A&M AM 7235	My Whole World Ended/Baby Don't Knock	5

GRAVY TRAIN

73	Dawn DNS 1036	Strength Of A Dream/Tolpuddle Episode	6
74	Dawn DNS 1058	Starbright Starlight/Good Time Thing	6
75	Dawn DNS 1115	Climb Aboard The Gravy Train/Sanctuary	6
70	Vertigo 6360 023	GRAVY TRAIN (LP, gatefold sleeve, spiral label)	40
71	Vertigo 6360 051	BALLAD OF A PEACEFUL MAN (LP, gatefold sleeve, spiral label)	100
73	Dawn DNLS 3046	SECOND BIRTH (LP)	30
74	Dawn DNLH 1	STAIRCASE TO THE DAY (LP)	30

BARRY GRAY (ORCHESTRA)

62	Lyntone LYN 249/250	Sabotage/Supercar Song/Supercar Twist (flexi, p/s may exist)	35+/18
64	Melodisc MEL 1591	Fireball/Zero G (by Barry Gray & His Spacemakers; some in p/s)	40/10
65	Pye 7N 17016	Thunderbirds/Parker — Well Done (some in p/s)	25/12
67	Pye 7N 17391	Captain Scarlet/The Mysterons Theme (some in p/s)	20/12
68	Pye 7N 17625	Joe 90 — Title Theme/Joe 90 — Hijacked (some in p/s)	35/15
62	Golden Guinea GGL 0106	SUPERCAR — FLIGHT OF FANCY (LP, with Edwin Astley)	50
67	United Artists (S)ULP 1159	THUNDERBIRDS ARE GO! (LP, soundtrack, mono/stereo)	80/100

(see also Century 21, Mary Jane with Barry Gray, Richard Harvey)

CLAUDE GRAY

64	Mercury 10012 MCE	COUNTRY AND WESTERN ACES (EP)	20

DOBIE GRAY

65	London HL 9953	The "In" Crowd/Be A Man	10
65	Pye International 7N 25307	See You At The Go Go/Walk With Love	12
69	London HL 10268	The "In" Crowd/Be A Man (reissue)	6
75	Black Magic BM 107	Out On The Floor/Be A Man	8

DOLORES GRAY

53	Brunswick 05111	Big Mamou/Say You're Mine (78)	6
55	Brunswick 05382	Heat Wave/After You Get What You Want, You Don't Want It	7
55	Brunswick 05407	Rock Love/One	18
55	Brunswick 05407	Rock Love/One (78)	8
57	Capitol CL 14732	There'll Be Some Changes Made/Fool's Errand	7
57	Capitol CL 14770	I'm Innocent/My Mama Likes You	6
63	Philips 326 582BF	Mornin' Train/Our Day Will Come	5

DORIAN GRAY

67	Parlophone R 5612	Behind The Tear/Walking Down A Back Street	5
68	Parlophone R 5667	I've Got You On My Mind/Move On	6
68	Parlophone R 5705	Love Is All That It Should Be/Let Me Go Home	5
68	Parlophone R 5732	Jingle Down A Hill/Get Goin' Baby	5

HERBIE GRAY

68	Giant GN 38	We're Staying Here/Life Ska	10

(see also Gene Rondo, Owen & Dandy)

JERRY GRAY & HIS ORCHESTRA

54	Brunswick 05351	The Ooh And Ah Mambo/Kettle Drum Hop	5

JOHNNIE 'THE GASH' GRAY

58	Fontana H 123	Big Guitar/Tequila	12
58	Fontana H 123	Big Guitar/Tequila (78)	8
58	Fontana H 134	Apache/Zach's Tune	12
58	Fontana H 134	Apache/Zach's Tune (78)	12
60	Melodisc 45-1500	Any Old Iron Cha Cha/Cocktails For Two Cha Cha (with His Chunks Of Mettle)	5

LORRAINE GRAY

64	Fontana TF 435	Are You Getting Tired Of Your Little Toy?/The Boy That I Want Doesn't Want Me	7
64	Fontana TF 484	The Little Girl That Cries/Talk To Him	6

OWEN GRAY

60	Starlite ST45 015	Far Love/Please Let Me Go	15
60	Starlite ST45 019	Jenny Lee/The Plea	15
60	Blue Beat BB 8	Cutest Little Woman/Running Around (with Ken Richards Band)	15
61	Blue Beat BB 43	Sinners Weep/Get Drunk (with Hersan & His City Slickers)	15
61	Starlite ST45 032	Mash It (Parts 1 & 2)	15
62	Starlite ST45 078	I Feel Good/Someone To Help Me	15
62	Starlite ST45 088	Let Me Go Free/In My Dreams	15
62	Blue Beat BB 75	Rockin' In My Feet/Nobody Else (with Jets)	15
62	Blue Beat BB 91	Millie Girl (with Buster's Group)/DERRICK MORGAN: Headache.	12
62	Blue Beat BB 103	Lonely Days/No Good Woman (with Sonny Bradshaw Quartet)	12
62	Blue Beat BB 108	Keep It In Mind/Do You Want To Jump (with Les Dawson Combo)	12
62	Blue Beat BB 113	Best Twist/Grandma-Grandpa (B-side with Hersan & His City Slickers)	12
62	Blue Beat BB 127	Pretty Girl/Twist So Fine	12
62	Blue Beat BB 136	They Got To Move/I Love Her.	15
62	Blue Beat BB 139	Tree In The Meadow/Lizebella (with Buster's Group)	15
62	Island WI 002	Patricia/Twist Baby	18
62	Island WI 020	Audrey/Dolly Baby (with Ernest Rauglin [sic] Orchestra)	15
62	Island WI 030	Midnight Trail/Time Will Tell	15
62	Island WI 048	I'm Still Waiting/Last Night	15

MINT VALUE £

62	Chek TD 101	Come On Baby/My One Desire	12
62	Dice CC 3	On The Beach/Young Lover	12
63	Blue Beat BB 147	Big Mabel/Don't Come Knocking (with Edwards' Groupe)	15
63	Blue Beat BB 188	Call Me My Pet/Give Me Your Love	15
63	Blue Beat BB 201	Snow Falling/Oowee Baby (as Owen Gray & His Big Brother)	12
64	Blue Beat BB 217	Draw Me Nearer/Daddy's Girl	15
65	Blue Beat BB 290	Daddy's Gone/BUSTER'S ALLSTARS: Johnny Dark	15
65	Aladdin WI 603	Gonna Work Out Fine/Dolly Baby	12
65	Aladdin WI 607	Can I Get A Witness/Linda Lu	12
65	Island WI 252	Shook Shimmy And Shake/I'm Going Back	12
65	Island WI 258	You Don't Know Like I Do/Take Me Serious (with Sound System)	12
66	Island WI 267	Paradise/Bye Bye Love	12
66	Blue Beat BB 365	I'm Gonna Say So Long/The Days I'm Living	10
67	Island WIP 6000	Help Me/Incense	10
67	Collins Downbeat CR 003	Collins Greetings/Rock It Down (with Sir Collins & Band)	30
67	Collins Downbeat CR 004	I'm So Lonely (with Sir Collins & Band)/EL RECO, SIR COLLINS & J. SATCH: Shock Steady	30
68	Collins Downbeat CR 007	Am Satisfy (with Sir Collins & Band)/BOB STACKIE & SIR COLLINS & BAND: Sweet Music	40
68	Collins Downbeat CR 010	I'm Gonna Take You Back (with Bob Stackie)/GLEN ADAMS: King Sized	30
68	Coxsone CS 7047	Give Me A Little Sign/Ain't Nobody Home	20
68	Coxsone CS 7053	Give It To Me/Isn't It So	20
68	Blue Cat BS 123	These Foolish Things/This I Promise	10
69	Blue Cat BS 156	I Can't Stop Loving You/Tell Me Darling	10
68	Trojan TR 632	Lovey Dovey/Grooving	10
69	Fab FAB 90	Three Coins In The Fountain/Tennessee Waltz	8
69	Fab FAB 96	Ay Ay Ay/Let It Be Me (with Rudies)	8
69	Fab FAB 120	Understand My Love/Apollo 12	8
69	Fab FAB 126	Swing Low/Release Me	8
69	Trojan TR 650	I Can't Stop Loving You/Tell Me Darling	8
69	Trojan TR 670	Too Experienced/I Really Loved You Baby	8
69	Duke DU 12	Reggae Dance/I Know	8
69	Duke DU 33	Seven Lonely Days/He Don't Love You Like I Do	7
69	Downtown DT 423	Groovin'/HERBIE GRAY & RUDIES: These Memories	7
69	Downtown DT 428	Lovey Dovey (with Dandy)/HERBIE GRAY & RUDIES: Kitty Wait	7
69	Camel CA 25	Girl What You Doing To Me/Woman A Grumble	7
69	Camel CA 34	Don't Take Your Love Away/Two Lovers	7
69	Camel CA 37	Every Beat Of My Heart/Don't Cry	7
70	Camel CA 50	Don't Sign The Paper/Packing Up Loneliness	7
70	Camel CA 51	Bring Back Your Love/Got To Come Back	7
70	Upfront UPF 3	Dream Lover/Mudda-Granma-Reggae (with Maximum Breed)	6
70	Bamboo BAM 47	I Can Feel It/I Don't Want (To Lose Your Love)	8
70	Crab CRAB 52	Just A Little Loving/DERRICK MORGAN: Take A Letter Maria	6
70	Pama PM 810	Sugar Dumpling/I Don't Know Why	6
70	Pama Supreme PS 299	I Am In Love Again/RANDY WILLIAMS: Version	6
70	Pama Supreme PS 302	Candida/When Will I Find My Way	6
70	Pama Supreme PS 310	You Gonna Miss Me/I Hear You Knocking	6
70	Supreme SUP 206	Surfin'/All The Love	6
70	Ackee ACK 102	No More/Don't Leave Me (both as Owen Gray & Omen)	7
71	Ackee ACK 123	Whispering Bells/CLANCY'S ALLSTARS: Whiplash (B-side actually "Jacket" by Dave Barker)	7
71	Camel CA 60	Groove Me/No Other One	7
71	Camel CA 73	Nothing Can Separate Us/Girl I Want You To Understand	6
71	Punch PH 87	Sincerely/Hold On I'm Coming	6
71	Pama Supreme PS 325	Summer Sand/Something To Remind Me	6
71	Pama Supreme PS 332	Greatest Hits (Parts 1 & 2)	6
72	Pama Supreme PS 351	Time/GRAHAM: Harlesden High Street	5
72	Pama Supreme PS 358	Hail The Man/I'll Follow You	5
72	Pama Supreme PS 360	Amazing Grace (with Graham Hawk)/SKETTO RICH: Don't Stay Out Late	5
70s	Rock Steady Rev. REV 004	Groovy Kind Of Love (with Elki & Rim Ram Band)/RIM RAM BAND: The Whistler	5
61	Starlite STLP 5	OWEN GRAY SINGS (LP)	135
63	Melodisc MLP 12-153	CUPID (LP)	25
69	Trojan TTL 24	REGGAE WITH SOUL (LP)	12
77	Trojan TRLS 139	FIRE AND BULLETS (LP)	12
78	Trojan TRLS 150	DREAMS OF OWEN GRAY (LP)	12

(see also Laurel & Owen, Gray Brothers, Elki & Owen, Owen & Milie, Owen & Dandy, Dennis Lowe, Survivors, Denzil & Jennifer, Brother Dan, Glen Adam)

SHANE GRAY

| 68 | Page One POF 102 | Sing Out Loud/Come Back To My Heart Again | 5 |

WARDELL GRAY

| 65 | Stateside SL 10144 | WARDELL GRAY MEMORIAL ALBUM (VOL. 1) (LP) | 12 |
| 65 | Stateside SL 10145 | WARDELL GRAY MEMORIAL ALBUM (VOL. 2) (LP) | 12 |

GRAY BROTHERS

| 68 | Blue Cat BS 124 | Always/Big Man | 12 |

(see also Owen Gray)

KATHRYN GRAYSON

53	MGM SP 1002	(All Of A Sudden) My Heart Sings/Jealousy	6
53	MGM SP 1014	Smoke Gets In Your Eyes/The Touch Of Your Hand (B-side with Howard Keel)	6
54	MGM SP 1078	I Hate Men/ANN MILLER & TOMMY RALL: Always True To You In My Way	6

MINT VALUE £

KATHRYN GRAYSON & HOWARD KEEL
53	MGM SP 1003	Why Do I Love You/Make Believe.	6
54	MGM SP 1076	So In Love/ANN MILLER: Too Darn Hot.	6
54	MGM SP 1077	We Open In Venice (with Ann Miller & Tommy Rall)/Wunderbar/	
		HOWARD KEEL: Were Thine That Special Face	6
54	MGM SP 1079	So Kiss Me Kate/KEENAN WYNN & JAMES WHITMORE:	
		Brush Up Your Shakespeare/ANN MILLER, TOMMY RALL,	
		BOBBY VAN & BOB FOSSE: From This Moment On	6

(see also Howard Keel, Ann Miller)

LARRY GRAYSON
72	York SYK 529	Shut That Door/Slack Alice	5
72	York MYK 602	WHAT A GAY DAY (LP).	12

MILTON GRAYSON
60	London HLU 9068	Forget You/The Puppet.	6

RUDY GRAYZELL
54	London HL 8094	Looking At The Moon And Wishing On A Star/The Heart That Once Was Mine.	225
54	London HL 8094	Looking At The Moon And Wishing On A Star/	
		The Heart That Once Was Mine (78).	50

GRAZINA
62	HMV POP 1094	Lover Please Believe Me/So What	12
63	HMV POP 1149	Don't Be Shy/Another Like You	12
63	HMV POP 1212	Be My Baby/I Ain't Gonna Knock On Your Door	12
64	Giv-A-Disc LYN 568	Stay Awhile/Let Me Go Lover.	8

(see also Lady Murray, Mr & Mrs Murray, Le Roys)

GREASE BAND
72	Harvest HAR 5052	Laughed At The Judge/All I Want To Do/Jesse James	5
75	Goodear EAR 602	New Morning/Pontardawe Hop	5
71	Harvest SHVL 790	THE GREASE BAND (LP).	18
75	Goodear EAR 2902	AMAZING GREASE (LP).	12

(see also Joe Cocker, Wynder K. Frog, Made In Sheffield, Henry McCullough)

JOHNNY B. GREAT (& GOODMEN)
63	Decca F 11740	School Is In/She's A Much Better Lover Than You (with Goodmen)	7
64	Decca F 11804	Acapulco 1922/You'll Never Leave Him (solo).	7

(see also Quotations, Johnny Goodison)

GREAT ACES
72	Fab FAB 191	Gold And Silver/Liberty Rock	6
72	Fab FAB 200	Liberty Rock/Rock My Soul	6
72	Fab FAB 201	I Didn't Mean It/Boots And Shoes	6
72	Fab FAB 202	Baby Girl/Version	6
73	Fab FAB 203	Banana/My Sweet Lord	6

GREAT AWAKENING
69	London HLU 10284	Amazing Grace/Silver Waterfall	6

GREAT DIVIDE
82	Wimp WIMP 004	Who Broke The Love Bank/Bless My Soul (p/s)	5

GREATEST LITTLE SOUL BAND IN THE LAND
69	MCA Soul Bag BAG 4	Tenement Halls/Flat, Black And Together	5
69	MCA Soul Bag BAG 6	Something For My People/Win Lose Or Draw.	5

(see also J.J. Jackson)

GREATEST SHOW ON EARTH
70	Harvest HAR 5012	Real Cool World/Again And Again.	15
70	Harvest HAR 5026	Tell The Story/Mountain Song	6
77	Harvest HAR 5129	Magic Touch Woman/Again And Again	8
70	Harvest SHVL 769	HORIZONS (LP)	35
70	Harvest SHVL 783	THE GOING'S EASY (LP)	35
75	Harvest SHSM 2004	THE GREATEST SHOW ON EARTH (LP)	12

(see also Living Daylights, Ian Dury & Blockheads, Fuzzy Duck, Glencoe, Naturals)

GREAT LEAP FORWARD
87	Ron Johnson ZRON 20	CONTROLLING THE EDGES OF TONE (EP)	7

(see also Big Flame)

GREAT METROPOLITAN STEAM BAND
69	MCA MNP/S 403	THE GREAT METROPLITAN STEAM BAND (LP).	30

GREAT SATURDAY NIGHT SWINDLE
77	CBS 82044	GREAT SATURDAY NIGHT SWINDLE (LP, Irish-only issue)	25

(see also Rosemary Taylor)

GREAT SOCIETY
68	CBS 63476	CONSPICUOUS ONLY IN ITS ABSENCE (LP)	22

(see also Jefferson Airplane)

GREAT UNCLE FRED
67	Strike JH 324	I'm In Love With An Ex-Beauty Queen/Singalong Version	5

R.B. GREAVES
69	Atco 226 007	Take A Letter Maria/Big Bad City.	5
70	Atco 2091 013	Fire And Rain/Ballad Of Leroy	5
71	Atlantic 2091 170	Paperback Writer/Over You Now	5
75	20th Century BTC 2191	Come On And Get Yourself Some/BMF (Beautiful)	5
70	Atco 228 034	R.B. GREAVES (LP)	12

JOE GRECH
71	Electro ES 152	Marija L-Maltija/In-Nassab (export issue)	6

JULIETTE GRECO   *AL GREEN(E)*

BUDDY GRECO

56	Vogue Coral Q 72192	They Didn't Believe Me/Here I Am In Love Again	6
57	Vogue Coral Q 72268	Paris Loves Lovers/Ain't No In Between	6
57	London HLR 8452	With All My Heart/Game Of Love (with B-G Skiffle Band)	15
57	London HLR 8452	With All My Heart/Game Of Love (with B-G Skiffle Band) (78)	10
58	London HLR 8613	I've Grown Accustomed To Her Face/On The Street Where You Live (as Buddy Greco & His Quartet)	6
58	London HLR 8613	I've Grown Accustomed To Her Face/On The Street Where You Live (78, as Buddy Greco & His Quartet)	12
60	Fontana H 255	The Lady Is A Tramp/Like Young	5
62	Fontana H 374	Twistin' The Blues/I Ain't Got Nobody	5
62	Columbia DB 4924	Mr. Lonely/Sentimental Fool	5
65	Columbia DB 7790	Mr. Kiss Kiss Bang Bang/Passing Pastels	5
60	Fontana TFE 17322	BUDDY GRECO PLAYS AND SINGS THE LADY IS A TRAMP (EP)	8
56	Vogue Coral LVA 9021	AT MISTER KELLY'S (LP)	18
60	Fontana TFL 5098	MY BUDDY (LP)	15
61	Fontana TFL 5125	SONGS FOR SWINGING LOSERS (LP, also stereo STFL 552)	15/18
62	Columbia 33SX 1441	I LIKE IT SWINGING (LP, also stereo SCX 3445)	12/15
63	Columbia 33SX 1463	LET'S LOVE (LP, also stereo SCX 3457)	12/15
63	Columbia 33SX 1478	BUDDY AND SOUL (LP, also stereo SCX 3464)	12/15
63	Columbia 33SX 1519	BUDDY'S BACK IN TOWN (LP, also stereo SCX 3482)	12/15
63	Columbia 33SX 1544	SOFT AND GENTLE (LP, also stereo SCX 3491)	12/15
64	Columbia 33SX 1590	ONE MORE TIME (LP)	12
64	Columbia 33SX 1620	SINGS FOR INTIMATE MOMENTS (LP)	12
64	Columbia 33SX 1667	ON STAGE (LP)	12
65	Columbia 33SX 1701	MODERN SOUNDS OF HANK WILLIAMS (LP)	12
65	Columbia 33SX 1766	I LOVE A PIANO (LP)	12
(see also Johnny Desmond)			

JULIETTE GRECO

54	Philips BBR 8023	JULIETTE GRECO SINGS (10" LP)	15

GREEDIES

80	Vertigo GREED 1	A Merry Jingle/A Merry Jangle (p/s)	15
(see also Professionals, Thin Lizzy, Sex Pistols)			

AL GREEN(E)

68	Stateside SS 2079	Back Up Train/Don't Leave Me (as Al Greene & Soul Mates)	12
69	Action ACT 4540	Don't Hurt Me No More/Get Yourself Together (by Al Greene)	6
70	London HLU 10300	You Say It/Gotta Find A New World	5
71	London HLU 10324	I Can't Get Next To You/Ride Sally Ride	5
71	Bell BLL 1188	Back Up Train/Don't Leave Me (as Al Green & Soul Mates, reissue)	6
73	London HLU 10426	Here I Am/I'm Glad You're Mine	5
69	Action ACLP 6008	BACK UP TRAIN (LP)	30
71	London SHU 8424	AL GREEN GETS NEXT TO YOU (LP)	15
72	London SHU 8430	LET'S STAY TOGETHER (LP)	15
72	London SHU 8443	I'M STILL IN LOVE WITH YOU (LP)	15
73	London SHU 8457	CALL ME (LP)	15
74	London SHU 8464	LIVIN' FOR YOU (LP)	15
74	London SHU 8479	EXPLORES YOUR MIND (LP)	15
(see also Annie Lennox & Al Green)			

Barry GREEN

MINT VALUE £

BARRY GREEN
63   Ember JBS 713   Together/Collective Marriage.. 6

BRIAN GREEN
68   Fontana SFJL 912   BRIAN GREEN DISPLAY (LP) 30

GARLAND GREEN
69   MCA Soul Bag BAG 9   Jealous Kinda Fella/I Can't Believe You Quit Me........................ 5

GRANT GREEN
62   Blue Note (B)BLP 84071   GREEN STREET (LP) 15
63   Blue Note (B)BLP 4111   THE LATIN BIT (LP) 15
65   Blue Note (B)BLP 4139   AM I BLUE (LP) 15
66   Blue Note (B)BLP 4202   I WANT TO HOLD YOUR HAND (LP)... 15
68   Blue Note BLP 4253   STREET OF DREAMS (LP, also stereo BST 84253).......................... 12
69   Blue Note BST 84310   GOING WEST (LP) 12

GRIZ GREEN
58   Mercury AMT 1012   Be Happy/Morocco (78) 6

HUGHIE GREEN
66   Columbia DB 8085   Cuddle Up Baby/Clap Your Hands (B-side with Monica Rose).............. 5

IAN GREEN (REVELATION)
67   Polydor 56194   Last Pink Rose/Green Blues (solo) 8
69   CBS 3997   When You Love A Man/Santa Maria....................................... 5
69   CBS 4623   Revelation/Groover's Grave.. 5
70   CBS 63840   REVELATION (LP) 15
(see also Madeline Bell, Rosetta Hightower)

JIMMY GREEN
73   Duke DU 155   Suspicion/LLOYD'S ALL STARS: Suspicion — Version 6
73   Green Door GD 4062   I'll Be Standing By/LLOYD'S ALL STARS: I'll Be Standing By "Version"......... 5
(see also Jimmy London)

KATHE GREEN
69   Deram DM 279   If I Thought You'd Ever Change Your Mind/Primrose Hill 6
69   Deram SML 1039   RUN THE LENGTH OF YOUR WILDNESS (LP)................................. 22

PETER GREEN
71   Reprise RS 27012   Heavy Heart/No Way Out 10
72   Reprise K 14141   Beast Of Burden/Uganda Woman (with Nigel Watson)..................... 10
78   PVK PV 16   Apostle/Tribal Dance (supposedly withdrawn) 8
79   PVK PV 24   In The Skies/Proud Pinto (p/s) 6
80   PVK PV 36   Walking In The Road/Woman Don't....................................... 6
80   PVK PV 41   Loser Two Times/Momma Doncha Cry 6
81   PVK PV 103   Give Me Back My Freedom/Lost My Love.................................. 6
81   PVK PV 112   Promised Land/Bizzy Lizzy... 6
70   Reprise RSLP 9006   THE END OF THE GAME (LP, with Nigel Watson).......................... 18
72   Reprise K 44106   THE END OF THE GAME (LP, with Nigel Watson, reissue)................. 12
79   PVK PVLS 101   IN THE SKIES (LP, green vinyl) 15
(see also Fleetwood Mac, Peter B's, Shotgun Express, John Mayall & Bluesbreakers, Gass, Peter Bardens, Katmandu)

SALLY GREEN
62   Philips PB 1243   It Hurts Too Much To Laugh/When's He Gonna Kiss Me.................... 5

TOM GREEN
74   Action ACT 4621   Rock Springs Railroad Station/Endless Confusion 15

PHILIP GREEN & PINEWOOD STUDIO ORCHESTRA
59   Top Rank JAR 112   Sapphire (with Johnny Dankworth)/Tiger Bay 5
60   Top Rank JAR 355   "League Of Gentlemen" March/"Golden Fleece" Theme.................... 6

GREEN ANGELS
65   Parlophone R 5390   Rockin' Red Wing/Let It Happen 7
66   Parlophone R 5512   An Exile's Dream/Hanningan's Hooley 5

NORMAN GREENBAUM
70   Reprise RS 20846   Jubilee/Skyline... 5
70   Reprise RS 20885   Spirit In The Sky/Milk Cow (cream or mustard label)............each 5
70   Reprise RS 20919   Canned Ham/Junior Cadillac.. 5
71   Reprise RS 21008   California Earthquake/Rhode Island Red 5
70   Reprise RSLP 6365   SPIRIT IN THE SKY (LP)... 15
70   Page One POLS 017   WITH DR. WEST'S MEDICINE SHOW & JUNK BAND (LP)....................... 12
(see also Dr. West's Medicine Show & Junk Band)

GREEN BEAN
69   Regal Zonophone RZ 3017   The Garden's Lovely/Sittin' In The Sunshine.......................... 5

GREENBEATS
64   Pye 7N 15718   If This World Were Mine/You Must Be The One 6
65   Pye 7N 15843   So Sad/I'm On Fire.. 5
67   Spin SP 2007   Pretty Woman/Thing... 6

GREEN BULLFROG
72   MCA MKPS 2021   GREEN BULLFROG (LP) 45
(see also Deep Purple, Ritchie Blackmore, Roger Glover, Tony Ashton, Matthew Fisher)

GREEN DAY
95   WEA W 0269CDX   Welcome To Paradise/Chump (live)/Emenius Sleepus
                            (CD, numbered in green transparent case)............................. 8
95   WEA W 0287X   Longview/Welcome To Paradise (live) (p/s, sealed with sticker sheet) 5

GREEN MAN
75   private pressing   WHAT AILS THEE? (LP).. 250

MINT VALUE £

CLAUDE 'FATS' GREENE & ORCHESTRA
66   Island WI 290   Fats Shake 'Em Up (Parts 1 & 2) (actually with Al Thomas) 10

JACK GREENE
68   Decca AD 1005   What Locks The Door/My Elusive Dreams (export issue) 7

JEANIE GREENE
69   Atlantic 584 226   Sure As Sin/I've Been A Long Time Loving You 5

LAURA GREENE
79   Grapevine GRP 135   Can't Help Loving Dat Man/It's A Good Day For A Parade 5
(see also Diane Renay)

LORNE GREENE
64   RCA RCA 1428   Ringo/Bonanza 5
63   RCA RD 7566   YOUNG... AT HEART (LP) 15
65   RCA RD 7709   THE MAN (LP) 15

GREENFIELD LEISURE
81   Strange Orch. CAMP 1   L'Orange/Sally (orange cut p/s) 4
81   Illuminated ILL 912   CANDIES (12" EP) 7

LEE GREENLEE
59   Top Rank JAR 226   Cherry, I'm In Love With You/Starlight 6

GREEN RIVER BOYS
63   Capitol ST 1810   BIG BLUEGRASS SPECIAL (LP) 20

(DAVE) GREENSLADE
73   Warner Bros K 16264   Temple Song/An English Western 5
75   Warner Bros K 16584   Catalan/Animal Farm 5
76   Warner Bros K 16828   Gangsters/Rubber Face, Lonely Eyes (as Dave Greenslade's Gangsters) 5
80   EMI EMI 5034   The Pentateuch Overture/Mischief And War (p/s, as Dave Greenslade) 5
73   Warner Bros K 46207   GREENSLADE (LP) 15
73   Warner Bros K 46259   BEDSIDE MANNERS ARE EXTRA (LP) 15
73   Warner Bros K 56055   SPYGLASS GUEST (LP, gatefold sleeve) 15
75   Warner Bros K 56126   TIME AND TIDE (LP, gatefold sleeve) 15
76   Warner Bros K 56306   CACTUS CHOIR (LP, as Dave Greenslade) 12
80   EMI EMSP 332   THE PENTATEUCH OF THE COSMOGONY (2-LP,
          with 47-page book, as Dave Greenslade) 30
(see also Wes Minster Five, Alan Price Set, Geno Washington & Ram Jam Band, Chris Farlowe, Colosseum, Samurai, Web)

ARTHUR GREENSLADE (& GEE MEN)
61   Decca F 11363   Rockin' Susannah/Eclipse (with Gee Men) 6
66   Columbia DB 7865   Watermelon Man/Serenade To A Broken Jaw 5
55   Brunswick OE 9171   CASK OF THE AMONTILLADO (EP) 8

GREEN TELESCOPE
86   Imaginary MIRAGE 001   Two By Two/Make Me Stay/Thinkin' About Toady (p/s, various designs) 6
86   Wump BIF 4811   Face In The Crowd/Thoughts Of A Madman (p/s) 5
(see also Thanes)

ELLIE GREENWICH
67   United Artists UP 1180   I Want You To Be My Baby/Goodnight, Goodnight 10
68   United Artists UP 2214   Sunshine After The Rain/A Long Time Comin' 10
70   Bell BLL 1105   I Don't Wanna Be Left Outside/Ain't That Peculiar 6
73   MGM 2315 243   LET IT BE WRITTEN, LET IT BE SUNG (LP) 15
(see also Popsicles, Raindrops [U.S.])

MICHAEL GREENWOOD
64   Oriole CB 1943   Buy Your Kid A Guitar/The Bellringer's Nightmare 5

MICK GREENWOOD
71   MCA MDKS 8003   THE LIVING GAME (LP, gatefold sleeve) 12
72   MCA MKPS 2026   TO FRIENDS (LP) 12
(see also Fotheringay, Jerry Donahue)

NICHOLAS GREENWOOD
72   Kingdom KVLP 9002   COLD CUTS (LP) 350
(see also Crazy World Of Arthur Brown, Khan, Bryn Howarth)

STOCKER GREENWOOD & FRIENDS
79   Changes   BILLY + NINE (LP) 30

BIG JOHN GREER
51   HMV JO 360   Woman Is A Five Letter Word/Got You On My Mind (78, export issue) 25

GINNY GREER
57   Brunswick 05673   Five Oranges, Four Apples/Kiss Me Hello (But Never Goodbye) 5

GREG
(see under Greg Bright)

BOBBY GREGG & FRIENDS
62   Columbia DB 4825   The Jam (Parts 1 & 2) 8

BRIAN GREGORY
65   HMV POP 1412   Give Me Your Word/The Ballad Of Dick Turpin 5

GLENN GREGORY & CLAUDIA BRÜCKEN
85   ZTT ZTAS 15   When Your Heart Runs Out Of Time/(Drumless) (p/s) 5
85   ZTT P ZTAS 15   When Your Heart Runs Out Of Time/(Drumless) (book-shaped picture disc) 6
85   ZTT 12 ZTAS 15   When Your Heart Runs Out Of Time/(Voices Of)/(6.20)/(Drumless)/
          STANLEY MYLES: Forever (What The Hell) (12", p/s) 8
(see also Heaven 17, Propaganda, Act)

MINT VALUE £

IA(I)N GREGORY
60	Pye 7N 15295	Time Will Tell/The Night You Told A Lie (as Ian Gregory)	25
61	Pye 7N 15397	Can't You Hear The Beat Of A Broken Heart/Because	25
62	Pye 7N 15435	Mr. Lovebug/Pocketful Of Dreams	25
63	Columbia DB 7085	How Many Times/Yellow Teddy Boy	10

JOHNNY GREGORY & HIS ORCHESTRA
60	Fontana H 251	Honky Tonk Train Blues/"Sons And Lovers" Theme (with Cascading Strings)	5
60	Fontana H 286	Bonanza/Maverick	8
61	Fontana H 288	Wagon Train/Bronco	8
61	Fontana H 337	Sucu Sucu/Echo For Two	5
61	Fontana H 341	Route 66/M Squad	8
61	Fontana TFE 17325	MAVERICK! (EP)	12
61	Fontana TFE 17331	BONANZA (EP)	12
62	Fontana TFE 17389	THE T.V. THRILLERS (EP)	15
61	Fontana TFL 5110	T.V. WESTERN THEMES (LP, also stereo STFL 538)	12/15
62	Fontana TFL 5170/STFL 585	CHANNEL THRILL: THE T.V. THRILLER THEMES (LP, mono/stereo)	12/15
72	Philips 6308 111	SPIES AND DOLLS (LP)	20
74	United Artists UAG 29546	A MAN FOR ALL SEASONS (LP)	12
76	Philips 6308 255	THE DETECTIVES (LP)	12

(see also Chaquito)

TONY GREGORY
66	Doctor Bird DB 1007	Baby Come On Home/Marie Elena	10
66	Doctor Bird DB 1016	Give Me One More Chance/I've Lost My Love	10
67	Island WI 3029	Get Out Of My Life/SOUL BROTHERS: Sugar Cane	12
67	Coxsone CS 7013	Only A Fool (Breaks His Own Heart)/Pure Soul	10
71	Horse HOSS 3	Bouncing All Over The World/Tell Me	5
67	Coxsone CSL 8011	TONY GREGORY SINGS (LP)	40

(see also Lloyd Charmers)

GREHAN SISTERS
66	Rex EPR 5005	THE GREHAN SISTERS (EP)	8
67	Transatlantic TRA 160	ON GALTYMORE MOUNTAINS (LP)	12

STAN GREIG'S JAZZ BAND
59	Tempo EXA 90	STAN GREIG'S JAZZ BAND (EP)	25
80s	Calligraph CLGLP 004	BLUES EVERY TIME (LP)	20
80s	Redeffusion ZS 116	BOOGIE WOOGIE (LP)	15

GREMLINS
66	Mercury MF 981	The Coming Generation/That's What I Want	18
67	Mercury MF 1004	You Gotta Believe It/I Can't Say	18

JOYCE GRENFELL
67	HMV POP 1617	Nursery School (Going Home Time)/I Wouldn't Go Back To The World I Knew	5
58	HMV 7EG 8787	AT HOME (EP)	10
59	HMV 7EG 8936	OLD TYME DANCING (EP)	8
54	Philips BBL 7004	REQUESTS THE PLEASURE (LP)	18
62	HMV CLP 1155	JOYCE GRENFELL IN A MISCELLANY (LP)	15
64	HMV CLP 1810	ENCORES (LP)	12
76	One Up OU 2149	COLLECTION (LP)	12
78	EMI DUO 128	THE NEW COLLECTION (2-LP)	20

JOEL GREY
54	MGM SPC 1	Last Night In The Back Porch/Two-Faced (export issue)	10
57	Capitol CL 14779	Everytime I Ask My Heart/Moonlight Swim	6
58	Capitol CL 14832	Be My Next/Shoppin' Around	15

RONNIE GREY & JETS
55	Capitol CL 14329	Run, Manny, Run/Sweet Baby	25

GREYHOUND
71	Trojan TR 7820	Black And White/Sand In Your Shoes	5
71	Trojan TR 7834	Follow The Leader/Funky Jamaica	5
71	Trojan TR 7848	Moon River/I've Been Trying/Pressure Is Coming On	5
72	Trojan TRLS 27	BLACK AND WHITE (LP)	15

(see also Tillermen)

GRID
89	Grid GRID 001	INTERGALACTICA (12", white label, private pressing)	18
89	Grid GRID 002	ON THE GRID (12", white label private pressing)	18
90	East West YZ 475	Floatation (Subsonic Grid Mix)/Floatation (Sonic Swing Mix) (p/s)	5
90	East West YZ 475T	Floatation (Subsonic Grid Mix)/Floatation (Sonic Swing Mix) (12", p/s)	8
90	East West YZ 475CD	Floatation (7" Version)/(Subsonic Grid Mix)/(Sonic Swing Mix) (CD)	10
90	East West YZ 498	A Beat Called Love/A Beat Called Dub (p/s)	5
90	East West YZ 498T	A Beat Called Love (3.40)/A Beat Called Club/A Beat Called Dub (12", p/s)	8
90	East West YZ 498CD	A Beat Called Love (3.40)/A Beat Called Club/A Beat Called Dub (CD)	8
91	Virgin VST 1369	Boom! (Freestyle Mix)/Boom! (707 Mix) (12", p/s)	15
93	Virgin VSCDT 1427	Heartbeat (Radio Edit)/Heartbeat (Back To The Future Mix)/ Heartbeat (Purple Heart Mix)/Heartbeat (456 Mix) (CD)	8
93	Virgin VSTX 1442	CRYSTAL CLEAR (Orb Mixes) (12", 4-track, clear vinyl)	8
94	Deconstruction CORBY 3	Texas Cowboys (Hardkiss 'Beans Is Ready, Boys' Mix) (12", promo only)	15

(see also Dave Ball, Timothy Leary Meets The Grid)

ROOSEVELT GRIER
68	Action ACT 4515	People Make The World/Hard To Forget	10
69	Pama PM 774	Who's Got The Ball	10
69	Pama PM 784	C'mon Cupid/High Society Woman	10

GRIFFIN

| 69 | Bell BLL 1075 | I Am The Noise In Your Head/Don't You Know | 25 |
| 72 | MGM 2006 088 | What Happens In The Darkness/Calling You | 8 |

(see also Heavy Jelly, Skip Bifferty, Every Which Way, Bell & Arc, Happy Magazine, Ginger Baker's Airforce)

SYLVIA GRIFFIN

88	Rocket BLAST 7	Love's A State Of Mind/Forgive The Girl (p/s, features George Harrison)	10
88	Rocket BLAST 712	Love's A State Of Mind/Forgive The Girl/Lonely Heart (12", p/s, features George Harrison)	15
88	Rocket BLACD 7	Love's A State Of Mind/Forgive The Girl/Lonely Heart (CD, card sleeve, features George Harrison)	22

GRIFFIN & SILVESTER

| 82 | Polydor POSP 466 | Please Come Into My Life/If You Give Your Love To Me (p/s) | 4 |

(see also Terry Sylvester, Hollies)

JOHNNY GRIFFIN BIG SOUL BAND

| 61 | Riverside REP 3203 | THE BIG SOUL BAND (EP, with Clark Terry & Bobby Timmons) | 8 |
| 61 | Riverside RLP 12-3331 | THE BIG SOUL BAND (LP, also stereo [RLP 9331] | 12 |

(see also Eddie 'Lockjaw' Davis)

MERV GRIFFIN

| 61 | London HLL 9339 | The Charanga/Along Came Joe | 7 |

VIRGIL GRIFFIN

| 71 | Jay Boy BOY 43 | La Da Da Da Da/Climbing | 5 |

GRIFFIN BROTHERS' ORCHESTRA

| 52 | Vogue V 2139 | Weepin' And Cryin' (with Tommy Brown)/The Teaser Boogie (78) | 15 |

ANDY GRIFFITH

55	Capitol CL 14263	Ko Ko Mo (I Love You So)/Make Yourself Comfortable	12
56	Capitol CL 14619	No Time For Sergeants/Make Yourself Comfortable	8
57	Capitol CL 14766	Mama Guitar/A Face In The Crowd	10
57	Capitol CL 14766	Mama Guitar/A Face In The Crowd (78)	7
58	Capitol CL 14936	Midnight Special/She's Bad, Bad Business (with Dixie Seven)	7
59	Capitol CL 15003	Hamlet (Parts 1 & 2)	5
56	Capitol EAP1 630	ANDY GRIFFITH (EP)	12
60	Capitol ST 1105	SHOUTS THE BLUES AND OLD TIMEY SONGS (LP, mono/stereo)	12/15

MARCIA GRIFFITHS

66	Island WI 285	Funny/KING SPARROW: Beggars Have No Choice (B-side actually by Leonard Dillon & Wailers; some copies credit Marcia Griffiths on both sides)	25
67	Studio One SO 2008	Hound Dog (actually by Norma Fraser)/HUGH GODFREY: My Time	20
67	Studio One SO 2015	After Laughter/HUGH GODFREY: Go Tell Him	18
68	Coxsone CS 7035	Mojo Girl (actually Nora Dean)/HAMLINS: Tell Me That You Love Me	20
68	Coxsone CS 7055	Feel Like Jumping/HORACE TAYLOR: Thundering Vibrations	20
68	Coxsone CS 7062	Hold Me Tight/BASIES: Home Sweet Home (B-side actually by Basses)	35
68	Studio One SO 2047	Words (as Marcia Griffiths & Jeff Dixon)/SHARKS: How Could I Live	25
68	Studio One SO 2059	Truly/SIMMS & ROBINSON: Drought	18
69	Gas GAS 111	Tell Me Now/STAN HOPE: The Weight	8
69	High Note HS 029	Talk (Parts 1 & 2) (correct title is actually "Toil")	8
69	Escort ES 808	Don't Let Me Down/REGGAEITES: Romper Room (B-side actually by Peter Tosh)	8
69	Trojan TR 693	Put A Little Love In Your Heart/J BOYS: Jay Fever	7
70	Harry J. HJ 6613	Put A Little Love In Your Heart/JAY BOYS: Bah Oop Ah	6
70	Harry J. HJ 6623	Band Of Gold/JAY BOYS: Cowboy (Version II)	6
70	Bamboo BAM 59	Shimmering Star/SOUND DIMENSION: Mun-Dun-Gu (B-side actually Im & David)	10

(see also Bob & Marcia, Peter Touch/Tosh, Roy Richards, Soul Vendor, Bob Andy, Della Humphrey, Mr. Foundation, Bob Marley)

VICTOR GRIFFITHS

| 70 | Punch PH 29 | I Am Proud Of You/KING VICTOR ALL STARS: Version | 6 |

FERRE GRIGNARD

| 68 | Atlantic 584 158 | Yellow You Yellow Me/La Si Do | 5 |
| 70 | Major Minor SMLP 72 | CAPTAIN DISASTER (LP) | 12 |

CAROL GRIMES (& DELIVERY)

70	B&C CB 129	Harry Lucky/Homemade Ruin (with Delivery)	6
74	Virgin VS 109	You're The Only One/Southern Boogie	5
74	Good Ear EAR 105	Give It Everything You've Got/Let's Do It Again (with London Boogie Band)	5
75	Good Ear EAR 605	I Betcha Didn't Know That/Dynamite	5
76	Decca FR 13674	I Betcha Didn't Know That/Dynamite (reissue)	5
77	B&C BCP 2	I Don't Wanna Discuss It/I'm Walking (with Delivery)	5
82	Polydor POSP 417	Ain't That Peculiar/Fashion Passion (p/s)	5
70	Charisma CAS 1023	FOOLS MEETING (LP, with Delivery)	50
74	Caroline CA 2001	WARM BLOOD (LP)	12
76	Decca SKL-R 5258	CAROL GRIMES (LP)	12

(see also Uncle Dog, Babylon)

TINY GRIMES & HIS R&B QUINTET

| 54 | Esquire 10-349 | Annie Laurie/Hot In Harlem (78) | 12 |

GRIMMS

75	DJM DJS 393	Backbreaker/The Masked Poet	5
76	DJM DJS 679	The Womble Bashers Of Walthamstow/The Worst Is Yet To Come/Wiggle Waggle	5
73	Island HELP 11	GRIMMS (LP)	15
73	Island ILPS 9248	ROCKIN' DUCK (LP, gatefold sleeve)	15
76	DJM DJF 20470	SLEEPERS (LP, gatefold sleeve)	12

(see also Neil Innes, Liverpool Scene, Scaffold, Mike McGear, McGough & McGear, John Gorman, Zoot Money, Patto, Viv Stanshall, Andy Roberts)

MINT VALUE £

GRIM REAPER
83	Ebony EBON 16	SEE YOU IN HELL (LP)	20
85	Ebony EBON 32	FEAR NO EVIL (LP)	18
87	RCA PL 86250	ROCK YOU TO HELL (LP)	15

GRIN
71	CBS 5239	We All Sung Together/See What A Love Can Do	5
71	CBS 7405	Everybody's Missin' The Sun/18 Faced Lover	5
72	CBS 7757	White Lies/Just To Have You	5
73	Epic EPC 1463	Ain't Love Nice/Love Or Else	5
71	Epic EPC 64272	GRIN (LP)	18
72	Epic EPC 64652	1 + 1 (LP)	18
73	Epic EPC 65166	ALL OUT (LP)	18

(see also Nils Lofgren)

GRINDERSWITCH
76	Capricorn 2089 030	Picking The Blues/Best I Can Do	5

GRINGO
71	MCA MKS 5067	I'm Another Man/Soft Mud	5
71	MCA MKPS 2107	GRINGO (LP)	18

(see also Caravan)

JOE GRINNE
69	Coxsone CS 7098	Mr Editor/How I Feel (both sides actually by Melodians)	18

GRISBY DYKE
69	Deram DM 232	The Adventures Of Miss Rosemary La Page/Mary Anne She	6

DEWEY GROOM
62	Starlite ST45 085	Butane Blues/That's All I Want Out Of Life	15
63	Starlite ST45 095	You're Tearing My Heart Out Of Me/Walking Papers	12
63	Starlite ST45 105	Heartaches For Sale/Sometimes If I'm Lucky	10

GROOP
68	CBS 3204	Woman You're Breaking Me/Mad Over You	5
68	CBS 3351	Lovin' Tree/Night Life	8
69	Bell BLL 1070	A Famous Myth/Tears And Joys	5
69	Bell BLL 1080	The Jet Song (When The Weekend's Over)/Nobody At All	5

GROOP DOGDRILL
97	Mantra MNT 23	Lovely Skin/Rockabilly Workout (p/s)	5
97	Mantra MNT 28	Oily Rag/Packmule (p/s)	5
98	Mantra MNT 33	Jackie O/Sport Of Kings (p/s)	5

GROOVE
69	Parlophone R 5783	The Wind/Play The Song	10

GROOVE
80	Trendy WHIP 1	Heart Complaint/I Wanna Be Your Pygmy	15

GROOVE FARM
87	Raving Pop Blast RPBGF 1	SORE HEADS AND HAPPY HEARTS (EP, with insert & handwritten labels)	10
87	Raving Pop Blast RPBGF 2	ONLY THE MOST IGNORANT GUTLESS SHEEP-BRAINED POLTROON CAN DENY THEM NOW (EP)	8
87	Raving Pop Blast RAVE 20	BAGISM (EP, hand-painted gatefold no'd p/s with insert, home-made labels)	5
87	Subway Org. SUBWAY 15T	GOING BANANAS WITH THE GROOVE FARM (12" EP)	8
88	Subway Organisation SUBWAY 19T	The Big Plastic Explosion! (It's Alright, It's Alright) (Dance Mix)/Nancy Sinatra/Baby Blue Marine/Riot On Sunset Strip/Red Dress (p/s)	7
88	Subway Organisation SUBWAY 22N	Driving In Your New Car (Mini Mix)/Expanding Reindeer/I Can't Dance With You/Epistle To Duppy (10", p/s)	7
88	Subway Organisation SUBWAY 22N	Driving In Your New Car (Mini Mix)/Expanding Reindeer/I Can't Dance With You/Epistle To Duppy (12", white label promos only, with press release)	20
88	Kvatch 001/LYN 18632	Baby Blue Marine/SEA URCHINS: Clingfilm (flexi, 1,000 only, 500 with p/s)	15/8
90	Woosh WOOSH 6	Heaven Is Blue/ESMERELDA'S KITE: Vampire Girl (1-sided red flexidisc free with Woosh fanzine)	6/5

GROOVERS
71	Camel CA 83	Put Me Down Easy/I Want To Go Back Home	6
71	Escort ERT 863	Bend Down Low/The Burning Feeling	6

(see also Lloyd & Groovers, Alva Lewis, Junior Byles, Dennis Walks)

GROOVE TUNNEL
95	Detour DR 023	Rainy Day/How Do You Feel (p/s, some on white vinyl)	8/5

WINSTON GROOV(E)Y
69	Grape GR 3005	Leaving Me Standing/Little Girl	8
69	Grape GR 3008	Merry X-mas/I Am Lonely	8
69	Nu Beat NB 041	Island In The Sun/Work It Up	8
69	Nu Beat NB 042	Josephine/Champagne And Wine	8
70	New Beat NB 053	Standing At The Corner/You Send Me	5
70	New Beat NB 055	Yellow Bird/For Your Love	5
70	New Beat NB 058	Here Is My Heart/Birds And Flowers	5
70	New Beat NB 066	Groovin'/Sugar Mama	5
70	New Beat NB 073	Tennessee Waltz/Old Man Trouble	5
70	Attack ATT 8019	You Can't Turn Your Back On Me/PAMA DICE: The Worm	5
70	Jackpot JP 708	Funky Chicken/CIMARRONS: Part 2 (B-side actually unknown instrumental)	7
70	Jackpot JP 709	Funny/CIMARRONS: Funny Version Two	7
70	Torpedo TOR 11	Please Don't Make Me Cry/Motion On The Ocean	5
70	Crab CRAB 63	I Like The Way/Tell Me Why	5
71	Crab CRAB 64	I've Got The Find A Way To Win Mary Back/Wanna Be There	5
71	Bullet BU 471	I Wanna Be Loved/Get Back Together	5
71	Pama PM 827	Don't Break My Heart/How Long Will This Go On	5

MINT VALUE £

71	Pama Supreme PS 323	Free The People/Not Now	5
72	Pama Supreme PS 349	What You Gonna Do/Why Did You Leave	5
72	Pama Supreme PS 364	Sylvia's Mother/Here Is My Heart	5
73	Explosion EX 2086	Nose For Trouble/RHYTHM RULERS: Version	5
74	Explosion EX 2088	Please Don't Make Me Cry/So Easy	6
69	Pama PMP 2011	FREE THE PEOPLE (LP)	15

(see also King Horror, Upsetters)

WALTER GROSS
54	MGM SP 1070	Blue Moon/Tenderly	6
54	MGM SP 1071	You Won't Forget Me (with India Adams)/Follow Me	6

G.G. GROSSETT
69	Crab CRAB 10	Run Girl Run/DENNIS WALKS: The Drifter	6
69	Crab CRAB 33	Greater Sounds/Live The Life I Love	6

STEFAN GROSSMAN
70	Big T BIG 133	Pretty Little Tune/Little Sally Walker	5
71	Big T BIG 140	'Joe Hill' — Themes	5
68	Fontana (S)TL 5463	AUNT MOLLY'S MURRAY FARM (LP)	20
69	Fontana STL 5485	THE GRAMERCY PARK SHEIK (LP)	20
70	Transatlantic TRA 217	YAZOO BASIN BOOGIE (LP)	15
70	Transatlantic TRAE 223	THE RAGTIME COWBOY JEW (2-LP)	15
71	Transatlantic TRA 246	THOSE PLEASANT DAYS (LP, with lyric insert)	12
72	Transatlantic TRA 257	HOT DOGS (LP)	12
72	Kicking Mule SNTF 627	THE GRAMERCY PARK SHEIK (LP, reissue, different sleeve)	12
73	Kicking Mule SNTF 640	AUNT MOLLY'S MURRAY FARM (LP, reissue)	12
73	Transatlantic TRA 264	LIVE! (2-LP)	15
73	Transatlantic TRA 274	GUITAR INSTRUMENTALS (LP)	12
75	Transatlantic TRA 293	BOOTLENECK SERENADE (LP)	12
75	Xtra XTRS 1151	HOW TO PLAY RAGTIME GUITAR (LP, with booklet)	12
77	Kicking Mule SNKF 129	COUNTRY BLUES GUITAR (LP)	12

(see also Jon Renbourn)

LUTHER GROSVENOR
71	Island WIP 6109	Here Comes The Queen/Heavy Day	5
72	Island WIP 6124	All The People/Waiting	5
71	Island ILPS 9168	UNDER OPEN SKIES (LP)	18

(see also Hellions, Revolution, Art, Spooky Tooth, Mott The Hoople, Widowmaker)

CARL GROSZMANN
70	Decca F 13065	Thunderbird/Missouri Woman	5
75	Ring O' 2017 103	I've Had It/C'mon And Roll	15
77	Ring O' 2017 107	Face Of A Permanent Stranger/Your Own Affair (promo p/s or company sleeve)	15/10
75	Ring O' 2320 102	CARL GROSZMANN (LP, unreleased)	

GROUND ATTACK
81	Ground Attack GAR 001	THE RED LION EP (gatefold p/s, later no p/s)	80/15

GROUNDHOGS
66	Planet PLF 104	Over You Baby/I'll Never Fall In Love Again (as John Lee's Groundhogs)	45
68	Liberty LBF 15174	You Don't Love Me/Still A Fool	15
69	Liberty LBF 15263	B.D.D./TONY McPHEE: Gasoline	10
70	Liberty LBF 15346	Eccentric Man/Status People	10
73	W. Wide Artists WWS 006	Sad Go Round/Over Blue	5
74	W. Wide Artists WWS 012	Plea Sing, Plea Sing/TONY McPHEE: Dog Me Bitch	5
76	United Artists UP 36095	Live A Little Lady/Boogie Withus	5
76	United Artists UP 36177	Pastoral Future/Live Right (as Tony McPhee & Groundhogs)	5
68	Liberty LBL/LBS 83199E	SCRATCHING THE SURFACE (LP, mono/stereo)	50/45
69	Liberty LBS 83253	BLUES OBITUARY (LP)	30
70	Liberty LBS 83295	THANK CHRIST FOR THE BOMB (LP, gatefold sleeve)	15
71	Liberty LBS 83401	SPLIT (LP, gatefold sleeve)	15
72	United Artists UAG 29347	WHO WILL SAVE THE WORLD... (LP, gatefold sleeve)	15
72	United Artists UAG 29419	HOGWASH (LP, gatefold sleeve)	12
74	United Artists UDF 31	GROUNDHOGS' BEST 1969-1972 (2-LP)	15
74	W. Wide Artists WWA 004	SOLID (LP, with lyric insert)	12
76	United Artists UAG 29917	CROSSCUT SAW (LP)	12
76	United Artists UAG 29994	BLACK DIAMOND (LP)	12
84	Psycho PSYCHO 24	HOGGIN' THE STAGE (2-LP, with EP, stickered sleeve)	25

(see also John Lee's Groundhogs, Tony McPhee, Herbal Mixture, Home, Andy Fernbach, John Lee Hooker)

GROUP
72	Charisma CB 197	Bovver Boys/Piraeus Football Club/An Open Letter To George Best	6

(see also Neil Innes)

GROUP B
67	Vocalion VF 9284	I Know Your Name Girl/I Never Really Know	18

(see also Blue Cheer)

GROUP 1850
69	Philips SBL 7884	AGEMO'S TRIP TO MOTHER EARTH (LP)	80

GROUP IMAGE
69	Stable SLE 8005	A MOUTH IN THE CLOUDS (LP)	20

GROUP ONE
58	HMV POP 463	She's Neat/Made For Each Other	18
58	HMV POP 463	She's Neat/Made For Each Other (78)	12
58	HMV POP 492	Chanson D'Amour/Londonderry Air	6
58	HMV POP 492	Chanson D'Amour/Londonderry Air (78)	6

GROUP SIX
59	Oriole CB 1488	Rock-A-Boogie/Rockin' The Blues	20
59	Oriole CB 1488	Rock-A-Boogie/Rockin' The Blues (78)	20

GROUP THERAPY
69	Philips BF 1744	River Deep Mountain High/Remember What You Said	5
69	Philips BF 1792	Can't Stop Lovin' You Baby/I Must Go	5
69	Philips SBL 7883	YOU'RE IN NEED OF GROUP THERAPY (LP)	15

GROUP TWO
68	Columbia DB 8374	It's Raining Outside/Western Man, Eastern Lady	5

GROUP X
63	Fontana 267 274 TF	There Are 8 Million Cossack Melodies — And This Is One Of Them/Teneriffe (some in p/s)	15/10
63	Fontana TF 417	Roti Calliope/Cross Beat	12

GROW UP
80	Object Music OBJ 005	THE BEST THING (LP)	12
81	Rough Trade GROW 1	WITHOUT WINDS (LP)	12

GRUMBLE
73	RCA Victor RCA 2384	Da Doo Ron Ron/Pig Bin An' Gone	5

(see also 10cc)

GRUNT FUTTOCK
72	Regal Zonophone RZ 3042	Rock 'N' Roll Christian/Free Sole	25

(see also Move, Roy Wood)

GRUVY BEATS
70	Nu Beat NB 048	Share Your Popcorn/LAUREL AITKEN: Mr. Popcorn	7
70	Nu Beat NB 049	Blue Mink/LAUREL AITKEN: I've Got Your Love	7

GRY
83	CBS A 3349	We're Like Starlight/For One More Night (unissued, promo only)	5

GRYPHON
77	Harvest HAR 5125	Spring Song/Fall Of The Leaf	5
73	Transatlantic TRA 262	GRYPHON (LP, gatefold sleeve)	15
74	Transatlantic TRA 282	MIDNIGHT MUSHRUMPS (LP)	15
74	Transatlantic TRA 287	RED QUEEN TO GRYPHON THREE (LP)	15
75	Transatlantic TRA 302	RAINDANCE (LP)	12
77	Harvest SHSP 4063	TREASON (LP, with insert)	12

(see also Richard Harvey)

G.T.O.'s
67	Polydor 56721	She Rides With Me/Rudy Vadoo	10

(see also Joey & Continentals)

G.T.O.'s (Girls Together Outrageously)
70	Straight STS 1059	PERMANENT DAMAGE (LP)	80

(see also Jeff Beck, Frank Zappa)

G.T.R.
86	Arista GTR 1	When The Heart Rules The Mind/Reach Out (p/s)	5
86	Arista GTRSD 1	When The Heart Rules The Mind/Reach Out (picture disc)	8
86	Arista GTR 121	When The Heart Rules The Mind/Reach Out (Never Say No)/Sketches In The Sun/Hackett To Bits (12", p/s)	8

(see also Genesis)

GUANA BATZ
84	Big Beat SW 89	You're So Fine/Rockin' In My Coffin/Jungle Rumble/Guana Rock (p/s)	6
84	Big Beat NS 96	The Cave/Werewolf Blues (p/s)	5
85	I.D. NOSE 4	HELD DOWN ... AT LAST (LP)	12

GUARDIANS OF THE RAINBOW
68	President PT 186	What Do You Do When You've Lost Your Love/Cry Alone	5

JOSE GUARDIOLA & ROSE MARY
63	HMV POP 1147	Algo Prodigioso/Di Papa	20

GUESS WHO
65	Pye International 7N 25305	Shakin' All Over/Till We Kissed	15
66	King KG 1044	His Girl/It's My Pride	20
67	Fontana TF 831	This Time Long Ago/There's No Getting Away From You	12
67	Fontana TF 861	Miss Felicity Grey/Flying On The Ground Is Wrong	8
69	RCA RCA 1832	These Eyes/Lightfoot	5
69	RCA RCA 1870	Laughing/Undun	5
70	RCA RCA 1925	No Time/Proper Stranger	5
70	RCA RCA 1943	American Woman/No Sugar Tonight	5
70	RCA RCA 1994	Hand Me Down World/Runnin' Down The Street	5
70	RCA RCA 2026	Share The Land/Bus Rider	5
70	RCA SF 8037	WHEATFIELD SOUL (LP)	15
70	RCA SF 8107	AMERICAN WOMAN (LP)	15
71	RCA SF 8153	SHARE THE LAND (LP)	15
71	RCA SF 8216	SO LONG BANNATYNE (LP)	12
72	RCA SF 8269	ROCKIN' (LP)	12
73	RCA SF 8329	LIVE AT THE PARAMOUNT, SEATTLE (LP)	12
73	RCA SF 8349	ARTIFICIAL PARADISE (LP)	12

EARL GUEST
62	Columbia DB 4707	Honky Tonk Train Blues/Winkle Picker Stomp	8
62	Columbia DB 4926	The Girl From The Fair Isle/Twistin' John	6
64	Columbia DB 7212	Begin The Beguine/Foxy	8

REG GUEST SYNDICATE

| 65 | Mercury MF 927 | Underworld/Guys, Guns, Dolls And Danger | 75 |
| 66 | Mercury 20089MCL | UNDERWORLD (LP) | 35 |

GUGGENHEIM

| 72 | Indigo GOLP 7001 | GUGGENHEIM (LP, private pressing) | 100 |

ISAAC GUILLORY

| 74 | Atlantic K 40521 | ISAAC GUILLORY (LP) | 12 |

(see also Shames, Sam Gopal)

GUILLOTEENS

| 65 | Pye International 7N 25324 | I Don't Believe/Hey You | 30 |

BONNIE GUITAR

58	London HLD 8591	A Very Precious Love/Johnny Vagabond	15
58	London HLD 8591	A Very Precious Love/Johnny Vagabond (78)	10
59	Top Rank JAR 260	Candy Red Apple/Come To Me, I Love You	6
58	London HA-D 2122	MOONLIGHT AND SHADOWS (LP)	22

GUITAR CRUSHER with JIMMY SPURRILL

| 69 | Blue Horizon 57-3149 | Since My Baby Hit The Numbers/Hambone Blues | 22 |

(see also Wild Jimmy Spurrill)

GUITAR RED

| 63 | Pye International 7N 25219 | Just You And I/Old Fashioned Love | 15 |

GUITAR SHORTY

| 72 | Flyright LP 500 | CAROLINA SLIDE GUITAR (LP) | 15 |

GULLIVER

70	Elektra 2101 011	Every Day's A Lovely Day/Angelina	6
70	Elektra 2101 017	Angelina/Christine	5
70	Elektra 2410 006	GULLIVER (LP)	15

(see also Daryl Hall & John Oates)

GULLIVER'S PEOPLE

66	Parlophone R 5435	Splendour In The Grass/Took This Land	6
66	Parlophone R 5464	Fi Fo Fum/Over The Hills	5
68	Parlophone R 5709	On A Day Like This/My Life	5
69	Columbia DB 8588	Somehow, Somewhere/I Found Love	5

GULLIVER'S TRAVELS

| 69 | Instant INLP 003 | GULLIVER'S TRAVELS (LP, withdrawn) | 40 |

(see also Mike D'Abo, Andrew Oldham)

GUN

68	CBS 3764	Race With The Devil/Sunshine	6
68	CBS 3764	Race With The Devil/3-4 In The Middle (different B-side)	7
69	CBS 4052	Drives You Mad/Rupert's Travels	6
69	CBS 4443	Hobo/Don't Look Back	6
69	CBS 4443	Hobo/Long Hair Wild Man (different B-side)	8
70	CBS 4952	Runnin' Wild/Drown Yourself In The River	6
69	CBS 63552	GUN (LP)	20
69	CBS 63683	GUNSIGHT (LP)	30

(see also Rupert's People, Adrian Gurvitz, Three Man Army, Knack)

GUN

89	A&M AM 505	Better Days/When You Love Somebody (p/s)	5
89	A&M AMY 505	Better Days/When You Love Somebody/Coming Home (12", p/s)	8
89	A&M CDEE 505	Better Days/When You Love Somebody/Coming Home (3" CD)	8
89	A&M AM 520	Money (Everybody Loves Her)/Prime Time (p/s, with patch)	5
89	A&M AMP 520	Money (Everybody Loves Her)/Prime Time/Dance (12", picture disc)	8
89	A&M AMCD 520	Money (Everybody Loves Her)/Prime Time/Dance(CD)	8
89	A&M AMS 531	Inside Out/Back To Where We Started (poster p/s)	5
89	A&M AMB 531	Inside Out/Back To Where We Started (box set)	8
89	A&M AMP 531	Inside Out/Back To Where We Started (picture disc)	6
89	A&M AMY 531	Inside Out/Back To Where We Started/Where Do We Go? (12", picture disc)	8
89	A&M CDEE 531	Inside Out/Back To Where We Started/Where Do We Go? (3" CD)	8
89	A&M AMCD 531	Inside Out/Back To Where We Started/Where Do We Go? (CD, picture disc)	8
90	A&M AMS 541	Taking On The World/Don't Believe A Word (p/s, with badge)	5
90	A&M AMP 541	Taking On The World/Don't Believe A Word/Better Days (12", picture disc)	8
92	A&M AMCD 851	Steal Your Fire/Don't Blame Me/Burning Down The House/Reach For Love (CD, box set)	10
92	A&M AMY 869	Higher Ground/Run/One Desire (12", poster p/s)	8
92	A&M AMY 885	Welcome To The Real World/Standing In Your Shadow/Steal Your Fire (12", picture disc)	8

GUN CLUB

82	Beggars Banquet BEG 80	Ghost On The Highway/Sex Beat (p/s)	8
82	Animal/Chry. CHCAT 2635	The Fire Of Love/walking with the beast (p/s)	8
83	Animal/Chrysalis GUN 1	Death Party/House On Highland Avenue/The Lie (p/s)	10
83	Animal/Chrysalis GUN 12	Death Party/House On Highland Avenue/The Lie/Light Of The World/Come Back Jim (12", p/s)	12
88	Red Rhino RED 89	The Breaking Hands/Crabdance (p/s)	8
88	Red Rhino RED 89 12	The Breaking Hands/Crabdance/Nobody's City (12", p/s)	10
90	Fire BLAZE 47T	The Great Divide/Crabdance/St. John's Divine Part 2 (p/s)	10

(see also Jeffrey Lee Pierce, Kid Congo Powers)

JON GUNN

| 67 | Deram DM 133 | I Just Made Up My Mind/Now It's My Turn | 8 |
| 67 | Deram DM 166 | If You Wish It/I Don't Want To Get Hung Up On You Babe | 5 |

JO JO GUNNE

(see under 'J')

MINT VALUE £

JIM GUNNER

| 60 | Decca F 11276 | Hoolee Jump/Footloose (as Jim Gunner & Echoes) | 10 |
| 61 | Fontana H 313 | Desperado/Baghdad (as Jim Gunner & His Sidekicks) | 10 |

TONY GUNNER

| 62 | London HLU 9492 | Rough Road/You Gotta Get Home | 12 |

GUNS FOR HIRE

| 80 | Korova KOW 6 | My Girlfriend's Boyfriend/I'm Famous Now (p/s) | 5 |

(see also Main T. Possee)

GUNS N' ROSES

87	Geffen GEF 22	It's So Easy/Mr Brownstone (p/s)	12
87	Geffen GEF 22T	It's So Easy/Mr Brownstone/Shadow Of Your Love/ Move To The City (12", p/s)	15
87	Geffen GEF 22TP	It's So Easy/Mr Brownstone/Shadow Of Your Love/ Move To The City (12", picture disc with stickered PVC sleeve)	50
87	Geffen GEF 30	Welcome To The Jungle/Whole Lotta Rosie (live) (red p/s)	10
87	Geffen GEF 30T	Welcome To The Jungle/Whole Lotta Rosie (live)/It's So Easy (live)/ Knockin' On Heaven's Door (live) (12", red p/s)	25
87	Geffen GEF 30TW	Welcome To The Jungle/Whole Lotta Rosie (live)/It's So Easy (live)/ Knockin' On Heaven's Door (live) (12", poster p/s)	12
87	Geffen GEF 30P	Welcome To The Jungle/Whole Lotta Rosie (live)/It's So Easy (live)/ Knockin' On Heaven's Door (live) (12", picture disc)	40
88	Geffen GEF 43	Sweet Child O' Mine/Out Ta Get Me (p/s, with wraparound sticker)	5
88	Geffen GEF 43TE	Sweet Child O' Mine/Out Ta Get Me/Rocket Queen (10", revolving p/s)	20
88	Geffen GEF 43TV	Sweet Child O' Mine/Out Ta Get Me/Rocket Queen (12", metallic p/s)	12
88	Geffen GEF 47	Welcome To The Jungle/Nightrain (p/s)	5
88	Geffen GEF 47TW	Welcome To The Jungle/Nightrain/You're Crazy (Acoustic Version) (12", poster p/s)	8
88	Geffen GEF 47TV	Welcome To The Jungle/Nightrain/You're Crazy (Acoustic Version) (12", p/s, with patch)	12
88	Geffen GEF 47TP	Welcome To The Jungle/Nightrain/You're Crazy (Acoustic Version) (12", picture disc)	12
88	Geffen GEF 47CD	Welcome To The Jungle/Nightrain/You're Crazy (Acoustic Version) (3" CD with adaptor, 5" case)	15
89	Geffen GEF 50P	Paradise City/I Used To Love Her (gun-shaped clear or white picture disc)	12/15
89	Geffen GEF 50X	Paradise City/I Used To Love Her (p/s, slotted in holster p/s)	8
89	Geffen GEF 50T	Paradise City/I Used To Love Her/Anything Goes (12", p/s)	8
89	Geffen GEF 50CD	Paradise City/I Used To Love Her/Anything Goes/Sweet Child O' Mine (3" CD)	10
89	Geffen GEF 55W	Sweet Child O' Mine (Remix)/Out Ta Get Me (stickered p/s, sealed w/ tattoo)	7
89	Geffen GEF 55P	Sweet Child O' Mine/Out Ta Get Me/Rocket Queen (shaped pic disc & sticker)	15
89	Geffen GEF 55P	Sweet Child O' Mine/Out Ta Get Me/Rocket Queen (12" uncut shaped pic disc)	100
89	Geffen GEF 55T	Sweet Child O' Mine (Remix)/Move To The City/Whole Lotta Rosie (live)/ It's So Easy (live) (12", p/s)	12
89	Geffen GEF 55CD	Sweet Child O' Mine (Remix)/Move To The City/Whole Lotta Rosie (live)/ It's So Easy (live) (3" CD)	12
89	Geffen GEF 56T	Patience/Rocket Queen/W. Axl Rose Interview (12", p/s)	10
89	Geffen GEF 56CD	Patience/Rocket Queen/W. Axl Rose Interview (3" CD, gatefold card sleeve)	12
89	Geffen GEF 60X	Nightrain/Reckless Life (live) (p/s, with patch)	8
89	Geffen GEF 60P	Nightrain/Reckless Life (live) (case-shaped picture disc, stickered PVC sleeve)	15
89	Geffen GEF 60CD	Nightrain/Knockin' On Heaven's Door (live)/Reckless Life (live) (3" CD, gatefold card sleeve)	12
91	Geffen GFSTP 6	You Could Be Mine/Civil War (12", clear vinyl with insert in PVC sleeve)	10
91	Geffen GFSTD 6	You Could Be Mine/Civil War (CD, card p/s)	8
91	Geffen GFST 9	Don't Cry/Don't Cry (Alternate Lyrics)/Don't Cry (Demo) (12", hologram p/s)	8
91	Geffen GFSTD 9	Don't Cry/Don't Cry (Alternate Lyrics)/(Demo) (CD, card gatefold p/s w/ sticker)	8
91	Geffen GFSX 17	Live And Let Die (LP Version)/Live And Let Die (live) (12", yellow/orange vinyl, die-cut p/s)	8
91	Geffen GFSTD 17	Live And Let Die (LP Version)/Live And Let Die (live)/ Shadow Of Your Love (CD, stencil p/s)	10
92	Geffen GFST 18	November Rain/Sweet Child O' Mine (live)/Patience (live) (12", p/s, 1 side etched)	10
92	Geffen GFSTD 18	November Rain/Sweet Child O' Mine (live)/Patience (live) (CD)	10

ARTHUR GUNTER

| 72 | Blue Horizon 2431 012 | BLUES AFTER HOURS (LP) | 70 |
| 70s | Contempo COLP 119 | BLACK AND BLUES (LP) | 12 |

HARDROCK GUNTER

| 52 | Brunswick 04907 | Silver And Gold/The Senator From Tennessee (78) | 12 |
| 55 | Brunswick OE 9167 | MOUNTAIN MUSIC (EP) | 30 |

(see also Red Foley, Roberta Lee)

GURU GURU

| 73 | Atlantic K 50022 | DON'T CALL US WE'LL CALL YOU (LP) | 12 |
| 74 | Atlantic K 50044 | DANCE OF THE FLAMES (LP) | 12 |

GURUS

| 66 | United Artists UP 1160 | Blue Snow Night/Come Girl | 20 |

ADRIAN GURVITZ

| 79 | Jet JET 12-140 | The Way I Feel/Drifting Star (12", clear vinyl picture disc,
stickered PVC sleeve & insert) | 8 |

(see also Knack, Rupert's People, Gun, Three Man Army, Baker-Gurvitz Army, Parish & Gurvitz)

JOHNNY GUSTAFSON

| 65 | Polydor 56022 | Just To Be With You/Sweet Day | 10 |
| 65 | Polydor 56043 | Take Me For A Little While/Make Me Your Number One | 12 |

(see also Big Three, Merseybeats, Quotations, Hard Stuff, Johnny & John, Ian Gillan Band, G-Force)

CARL GUSTAV & 84's
81	Convulsive CN 001	I Want To Kill Russians/Through Birds, Through Fire, But Not Through Glass (p/s)	5

ARLO GUTHRIE
67	Reprise RS 20644	Motorcycle Song/Now And Then	8
70	Reprise RS 20877	Alice's Rock'N'Roll Restaurant/Coming In To Los Angeles	5
70	Reprise RS 20951	Valley To Pray/Gabriel's Mother's Hiway Ballad No. 16 Blues (demo-only)	7
71	Reprise RS 20994	The Ballad Of Tricky Fred/Shackles And Chains	5
67	Reprise RLP 6267	ALICE'S RESTAURANT (LP)	15
68	Reprise RSLP 6269	ARLO (LP)	15
69	Reprise RSLP 6346	RUNNING DOWN THE ROAD (LP)	12
70	Reprise RSLP 6411	WASHINGTON COUNTY (LP)	12

GWEN GUTHRIE
86	4th + Broadway BRW 1252	Seventh Heaven/It Should Have Been You/Getting Hot (12", p/s)	12

SHEILA GUTHRIE
63	Fontana TF 399	Mirror Mirror/It Doesn't Mean A Thing	5

WOODY GUTHRIE
51	Melodisc 1141	Ramblin' Blues/Talkin' Columbia Blues (78)	12
55	Melodisc EPM7 84	HARD AIN'T IT HARD (EP)	12
55	Melodisc EPM7 85	WORRIED MAN BLUES (EP)	12
55	Melodisc EPM7 91	HEY LOLLY LOLLY (EP)	12
55	Melodisc MLP 12-106	MORE SONGS BY GUTHRIE (LP)	30
58	Topic 12T 31	BOUND FOR GLORY (LP)	30
64	RCA RD 7642	DUST BOWL BALLADS (LP)	25
65	Xtra XTRA 1012	WOODY GUTHRIE (LP)	15
66	Xtra XTRA 1064	WOODY GUTHRIE (LP)	15
66	Xtra XTRA 1065	POOR BOY (LP)	15
66	Xtra XTRA 1067	SONGS TO GROW ON VOL. 1 (LP)	15
68	Ember CW 129	WOODY GUTHRIE (LP)	15
69	Ember CW 135	CISCO HOUSTON AND WOODY GUTHRIE (LP)	15
69	Ember CW 136	BLIND SONNY TERRY & WOODY GUTHRIE (LP)	15

GUTTERSNIPES
88	Razor GUTT 1	Addicted To Love/Love's Young Dream (p/s)	8
88	Razor RAZ 42	THE POOR DRESS UP (LP)	10
	(see also Cocksparrer)		

GUV'NERS
63	Piccadilly 7N 35117	Let's Make A Habit Of This/The Kissing Had To Stop	10
	(see also Jess Conrad, Dickie Pride, Nelson Keene)		

BUDDY GUY
65	Chess CRS 8004	Let Me Love You Baby/Ten Years Ago	10
68	Fontana TF 951	Mary Had A Little Lamb/Sweet Little Angel	10
72	Atlantic K 10195	Honey Dripper/Man Of Many Words	5
65	Chess CRE 6004	CRAZY MUSIC (EP)	30
68	Vanguard SVRL 19001	COMING AT YOU (LP)	22
68	Vanguard SVRL 19002	MAN AND HIS BLUES (LP)	22
68	Vanguard SVRL 19004	BLUES TODAY (LP)	18
69	Vanguard SVRL 19008	THIS IS BUDDY GUY! (LP)	18
69	Vanguard SVRL 79290	HOT AND COOL (LP)	12
69	Chess CRL(S) 4546	I LEFT MY BLUES IN SAN FRANCISCO (LP)	18
69	Python KM 2	FIRST TIME I MET THE BLUES (LP)	30
70	Harvest SHSP 4006	BUDDY AND THE JUNIORS (LP, with Junior Mance & Junior Wells)	20
70	Red Lightnin' RL 001	IN THE BEGINNING (LP)	12
72	Atlantic K 40240	PLAY THE BLUES (LP, with Junior Wells)	15
73	Vanguard VSD 79323	HOLD THAT PLANE (LP)	12
	(see also Junior Wells, Eddie Boyd/Buddy Guy)		

DERYCK GUYLER
71	Columbia DB 8764	(You Can't Kill An Old) Desert Rat/Ruby	5

GUYS
69	Tepee TPR SP 1001	You Go Your Way/Little Girl	8
	(see also Beat Six)		

GEORGE GUZMAN
69	London HA/SH 8384	INTRODUCING GEORGE GUZMAN (LP)	12

GYGAFO
89	Holyground HG 1155	LEGEND OF THE KINGFISHER (LP, 160 copies only, posthumously designed semi-gatefold sleeve with insert)	50

GYNAECOLOGISTS
81	Teesbeat TB 2	The Red Pullover/The Offence (p/s)	5

GYPP
70s	Shy Talk	GYPP (EP)	5

GYPSIES
67	CBS 201785	Jerk It/Diamonds, Rubies, Gold And Fame	18
	(see also Flirtations, Pearly Gates)		

GYPSY
71	United Artists UAG 29155	GYPSY (LP)	15
72	United Artists UAS 29420	BRENDA AND THE RATTLESNAKE (LP)	15
	(see also Legay)		

GYRES
95	Sugar SUGA 7V	Break/Break (title die-cut sleeve)	5

JOYCE HAHN
57	London HLA 8453	Gonna Find Me A Bluebird/I Saw You, I Saw You 15
57	London HLA 8453	Gonna Find Me A Bluebird/I Saw You, I Saw You (78)........................ 8

PAUL HAIG
81	Rational	DRAMA (cassette) 15
82	Operation Twilight OPT 03	Running Away/Time (p/s)... 5
84	Island ISX 198	The Only Truth (U.S. Remix)/Instrumental/Ghost Rider (12", p/s).......... 8
80s	Masterbag	Blue (square flexidisc free with *Masterbag* magazine) 6/5
84	Island ILPS 9742	RHYTHM OF LIFE (LP) 12
85	Operation Afterglow OPA 3	THE WARP OF PURE FUN (LP, inner sleeve) 12

(see also Josef K, Rhythm Of Life, Juggernauts)

NORMAN HAINES (BAND)
70	Parlophone R 5871	Daffodil/Autumn Mobile (as Norman Haynes Band) 20
71	Parlophone SPSR 338	Den Of Iniquity/Everything You See (Mr. Armageddon) (promo only) 30
72	Parlophone R 5960	Give It To You Girl/Elaine (as Norman Haines) 20
71	Parlophone PCS 7130	DEN OF INIQUITY (LP) 325

(see also Brumbeats, Locomotive, Avalanche)

HAIR
69	Pye NSPL 18314	RAVE UP (LIVE FROM THE SHAFTESBURY THEATRE) (LP) 60

(see also Alex Harvey, Hairband)

HAIR
71	Columbia SCX 6452	HAIRPIECE (LP) 100

HAIRBAND
69	Bell BLL 1076	Big Louis/Travelling Song 12
69	Bell SBLL 69	BAND ON THE WAGON (LP)...................................... 45

(see also Alex Harvey, Hair)

HAIRCUT 100
81	Lyntone LYN 11175	Nobody's Fool (demo version) (green flexidisc free with *Flexipop*, issue 17)..... 4
82	Arista CLIP 122	Love Plus One (12", p/s) 10
82	Arista CLIP 123	Fantastic Day (live)/Ski Club Of Great Britain (12", p/s)................. 10
83	Arista CLIP 5	Whistle Down The Wind (withdrawn)............................. 10+
83	Polydor HCP	Prime Time (picture disc, no p/s)................................. 10
83	Polydor HCP2	So Tired (silver vinyl, no p/s) 10
82	Arista HCC 100	PELICAN WEST (LP, with free booklet & 2 bubblegum cards) 12
82	Arista HCC 101	BLUE HAT FOR A BLUE DAY (LP, withdrawn, test pressings only) .... 40+

HAIRPOWER
70	CBS 4961	Royal International Love-in/Be There, Be Hair 5

DENNIS HALE
55	Parlophone MSP 6153	The Butterscotch Mop/S'posin' 5

(see also Jack Parnell)

BILL HALEY (& HIS COMETS)
78s
53	London L 1190	Crazy Man, Crazy/Whatcha Gonna Do (as Bill Haley with Haley's Comets) (78, gold label lettering).. 30
53	London L 1216	Pat-A-Cake/Fractured (78, as Bill Haley with Haley's Comets, gold label) 30
54	London HL 1190	Crazy Man, Crazy/Whatcha Gonna Do (as Bill Haley with Haley's Comets) (78, reissue, silver label lettering) 30
54	London HL 1216	Pat-A-Cake/Fractured (78, reissue, silver label lettering, as Bill Haley with Haley's Comets) 30
54	Brunswick 05317	(We're Gonna) Rock Around The Clock/Thirteen Women (78, gold letting) 6
54	Brunswick 05338	Shake, Rattle And Roll/A.B.C. Boogie (78, gold or silver lettering)........... 10/8
55	Brunswick 05373	Happy Baby/Dim, Dim The Lights (I Want Some Atmosphere) (78, gold or silver lettering) 8
55	Brunswick 05405	Birth Of The Boogie/Mambo Rock (78, gold or silver lettering).............. 10/8
55	London HL 8142	Green Tree Boogie/Sundown Boogie (78) 18
55	Brunswick 05453	Two Hound Dogs/Razzle Dazzle (78) 6
55	London HLF 8161	Farewell, So Long, Goodbye/I'll Be True (78)........................ 20
55	London HLF 8194	Ten Little Indians/Rocking Chair On The Moon (78) 20
56	Melodisc 1376	I'm Gonna Dry Ev'ry Tear With A Kiss/Why Do I Cry Over You (78) 60
57	Brunswick 05641	Hook, Line And Sinker/Goofin' Around (78) 8
57	London HLF 8371	Rock The Joint/Yes Indeed! (78) 18
57	Brunswick 05658	Forty Cups Of Coffee/Choo Choo Ch'Boogie (78) 12
57	Brunswick 05688	(You Hit The Wrong Note) Billy Goat/Rockin' Rollin' Rover (78) 18
57	Brunswick 05719	Miss You/The Dipsy Doodle (78) 20
58	Brunswick 05735	Mary, Mary Lou/It's A Sin (78) 20
58	Brunswick 05742	Skinny Minnie/How Many (78) 20
58	Brunswick 05752	Lean Jean/Don't Nobody Move (78)................................ 25
58	Brunswick 05766	Whoa Mabel!/Chiquita Linda (78)................................. 25
59	Brunswick 05788	I Got A Woman/Charmaine (78) 30
59	Brunswick 05805	Shaky/Caldonia (78).. 35
59	Brunswick 05810	Joey's Song/Ooh! Look-A There, Ain't She Pretty (78) 35

SINGLES
54	Brunswick 05317	(We're Gonna) Rock Around The Clock/Thirteen Women 50/18
54	Brunswick 05338	Shake, Rattle And Roll/A.B.C. Boogie............................. 35/18
55	Brunswick 05373	Happy Baby/Dim, Dim The Lights (I Want Some Atmosphere)............ 35/18
55	Brunswick 05405	Birth Of The Boogie/Mambo Rock 35/18
55	London HL 8142	Green Tree Boogie/Sundown Boogie 120/60
55	Brunswick 05453	Two Hound Dogs/Razzle Dazzle 30/15
55	London HLF 8161	Farewell, So Long, Goodbye/I'll Be True........................ 100/50
55	London HLF 8194	Ten Little Indians/Rocking Chair On The Moon 120/60

Bill HALEY (& His Comets)

55	Brunswick 05509	Rock-A-Beatin' Boogie/Burn That Candle	30/15
56	Brunswick 05530	See You Later, Alligator/The Paper Boy (On Main Street, USA)	25/15

(When two prices are given for the above 45s, the first refers to original gold-lettering labels & the second to later lettering silver-label copies.)

56	Brunswick 05565	The Saints Rock 'N' Roll/R-O-C-K	15
56	Brunswick 05582	Rockin' Through The Rye/Hot Dog Buddy Buddy	15
56	Brunswick 05615	Rip It Up/Teenager's Mother	15
56	Brunswick 05616	Rudy's Rock/Blue Comet Blues	15
57	Brunswick 05640	Don't Knock The Rock/Calling All Comets	15
57	Brunswick 05641	Hook, Line And Sinker/Goofin' Around	15
57	London HLF 8371	Rock The Joint/Yes Indeed! (gold or silver label)	120/60
57	Brunswick 05658	Forty Cups Of Coffee/Choo Choo Ch'Boogie	15
57	Brunswick 05688	(You Hit The Wrong Note) Billy Goat/Rockin' Rollin' Rover	20
57	Brunswick 05719	Miss You/The Dipsy Doodle	18
58	Brunswick 05735	Mary, Mary Lou/It's A Sin	18
58	Brunswick 05742	Skinny Minnie/How Many	18
58	Brunswick 05752	Lean Jean/Don't Nobody Move	15
58	Brunswick 05766	Whoa Mabel!/Chiquita Linda	18
59	Brunswick 05788	I Got A Woman/Charmaine	15
59	Brunswick 05805	Shaky/Caldonia	18
59	Brunswick 05810	Joey's Song/Ooh! Look-A There, Ain't She Pretty	18

(The above 45s were originally issued with triangular centres; later round centres are worth half the value for earlier 45s to two-thirds for later 45s.)

60	Brunswick 05818	Puerto Rican Peddler/Skokiaan	10
60	Warner Bros WB 6	Candy Kisses/Tamiami	8
61	London HLU 9471	Spanish Twist/My Kind Of Woman	12
63	Stateside SS 196	Tenor Man/Up Goes My Love	7
64	Warner Bros WB 133	Rock Around The Clock/Love Letters In The Sand	10
64	Brunswick 05910	Happy Baby/Birth Of The Boogie	12
64	Brunswick 05917	The Green Door/Yeah! She's Evil	12
68	MCA MU 1013	(We're Gonna) Rock Around The Clock/Shake, Rattle And Roll	5
68	Pye International 7N 25455	Crazy Man, Crazy/Dance With A Dolly (With A Hole In Her Stocking)	15
73	Sonet SON 2016	Me And Bobby McGee/I Wouldn't Have Missed It For The World	5
74	Sonet SON 2043	Crazy Man, Crazy/Lawdy Miss Clawdy	5
74	MCA MCA 128	Rock Around The Clock/Rip It Up/Shake, Rattle And Roll	5
74	MCA MCA 142	See You Later Alligator/Rudy's Rock	5
76	MCA MCA 263	Shake, Rattle And Roll/Razzle Dazzle/Rock-A-Beatin' Boogie	5
80	Rollercoaster RRC 2004	Rock The Joint/Fractured (reissue)	5
80	Sonet SON 2202	God Bless Rock And Roll/So Right Tonight	5
81	Thumbs Up TU 103	Rocket 88/Tearstains On My Pillow	5

EXPORT SINGLES

56	Decca BM 31171	Rip It Up/Teenager's Mother	35
68	Decca AD 1010	(We're Gonna) Rock Around The Clock/Shake, Rattle And Roll	15

EPs

55	Brunswick OE 9129	DIM, DIM THE LIGHTS (EP, gold lettering label, 'stage' p/s, various colours)	30
55	Brunswick OE 9129	DIM, DIM THE LIGHTS (EP, silver lettering label, 'stage' or 'cameo' p/s) ... each	25
55	London REF 1031	ROCK AND ROLL (EP)	50
56	London REF 1049	LIVE IT UP PART 1 (EP)	40
56	London REF 1050	LIVE IT UP PART 2 (EP)	40
56	Brunswick OE 9214	ROCK AND ROLL WITH BILL HALEY (EP)	25
56	Brunswick OE 9250	ROCK AROUND THE CLOCK (EP)	20
56	Brunswick OE 9250	ROCK AROUND THE CLOCK (EP, round centre, different sleeve, same design as "Bill Haley" [OE 9459])	30
56	London REF 1058	LIVE IT UP PART 3 (EP)	35
56	Brunswick OE 9278	ROCK'N'ROLL STAGE SHOW PART 1 (EP)	25
56	Brunswick OE 9279	ROCK'N'ROLL STAGE SHOW PART 2 (EP)	25
56	Brunswick OE 9280	ROCK'N'ROLL STAGE SHOW PART 3 (EP)	25
58	Brunswick OE 9349	ROCKIN' THE OLDIES PART 1 (EP)	35
58	Brunswick OE 9350	ROCKIN' THE OLDIES PART 2 (EP)	35
58	Brunswick OE 9351	ROCKIN' THE OLDIES PART 3 (EP)	35
59	Brunswick OE 9446	ROCKIN' AROUND THE WORLD (EP)	50
59	Brunswick OE 9459	BILL HALEY (EP)	45

(The above EPs were originally issued with triangular centres, later round-centre copies are worth two-thirds these values.)

60	Warners WEP 6001	BILL HALEY AND HIS COMETS (EP)	25
61	Warners WEP 6025	BILL HALEY'S JUKE BOX (EP, also stereo WSEP 2025)	25/35
64	Warners WEP 6133	BILL HALEY VOLUME 1 (EP)	30
64	Warners WEP 6136	BILL HALEY VOLUME 2 (EP)	30

LPs

55	London H-APB 1042	LIVE IT UP (10" LP, gold or silver lettering on label)	100/60
56	Brunswick LAT 8117	ROCK AROUND THE CLOCK (LP)	30
56	Brunswick LAT 8139	ROCK AND ROLL STAGE SHOW (LP)	30
57	London HA-F 2037	ROCK THE JOINT (LP)	75
57	Brunswick LAT 8219	ROCKIN' THE OLDIES (LP)	50
57	Brunswick LAT 8268	ROCKIN' THE JOINT (LP)	50
59	Brunswick LAT 8295	BILL HALEY'S CHICKS (LP, also stereo STA 3011)	50/65
60	Brunswick LAT 8326	STRICTLY INSTRUMENTAL (LP)	45
61	Ace Of Hearts AH 13	ROCK AROUND THE CLOCK (LP, 2 slightly different sleeves)	18/15
62	Columbia 33SX 1460	TWISTIN' KNIGHTS AT THE ROUNDTABLE (LIVE!) (LP)	25
62	Ace Of Hearts AH 35	ROCKIN' THE OLDIES (LP)	15
64	Ace Of Hearts AH 66	BILL HALEY'S CHICKS (LP)	15
64	Golden Guinea GGL 0282	ROCK THE JOINT (LP)	15
65	Xtra XTRA 1027	BILL HALEY & THE COMETS (LP)	25
65	Warner Bros W 1391	BILL HALEY'S JUKE BOX (LP)	35
67	Marble Arch MAL 817	ROCK THE JOINT (LP)	12
67	Ember EMB 3386	REAL LIVE ROCK'N'ROLL (LP)	15
68	MCA MUP 318	RIP IT UP! (LP)	15

MINT VALUE £

68	Ember EMB 3396	KING OF ROCK (LP, reissued 1973)	15/12
69	Ember EMB 3401	MISTER ROCK 'N' ROLL (LP)	12
70	Valiant VS 103	BILL HALEY & THE COMETS (LP)	15
71	Coral CP 55	ROCK AROUND THE CLOCK (LP)	12
71	Sonet SNTF 623	ROCK AROUND THE COUNTRY (LP)	12
73	Sonet SNTF 645	JUST ROCK AND ROLL MUSIC (LP)	12
79	Rollercoaster ROLL 2002	ROCK THE JOINT! (10" LP)	12

(see also Kingsmen, Jodimars, Nick Nantos & His Fireballs)

HALF JAPANESE
81	Armageddon AS 009	Spy/I Know How It Feels … Bad/My Knowledge Was Wrong (p/s)	5
81	Armageddon ABOX 1	1/2 GENTLEMEN NOT BEASTS (3-LP box set with poster, booklet & lyric insert)	25
81	Armageddon ARM 7	LOUD (LP)	12

(see also Jad Fair)

HALF MAN HALF BISCUIT
86	Probe Plus TRUM 1-7	The Trumpton Riots/All I Want For Christmas Is A Dukla Prague Away Kit (p/s)	5

(see also Attempted Moustache)

HAL HOPPERS
54	London HL 8107	More Love/Do Nothin' Blues	25
54	London HL 8107	More Love/Do Nothin' Blues (78)	12
55	London HL 8129	Mother Of Pearl/Baby I've Had It	25
55	London HL 8129	Mother Of Pearl/Baby I've Had It (78)	10

BOB HALL & ALEXIS KORNER
78	Logo GO 331	Pinetop's Boogie Woogie/All I Got Is You	8

(see also Brunning Hall Sunflower Blues Band, Alexis Korner)

CAROLINE HALL
70	Major Minor MM 689	Dream Boy/Julie	5
71	Decca F 13146	Hold My Hand/Put A Light In The Window	5

DARYL HALL
86	RCA HALL 1P	Dreamtime/Let It Out (poster p/s)	5
86	RCA HALL 2P	I Wasn't Born Yesterday/What's Gonna Happen To Us (p/s, with free calendar)	5

(DARYL) HALL & (JOHN) OATES
85	RCA PB 49967	Out Of Touch/Dance On Your Knees (square picture disc)	5
88	Arista 661 730	Downtown Life/Downtown Remix/Dubtown Life/ Keep On Pushin' Love (CD, withdrawn)	8
89	RCA PD 49465	Maneater/Delayed Reaction/I Can't Go For That (No Can Do)/ Unguarded Minute (3" CD, gatefold card sleeve)	8

(see also Gulliver)

DEREK HALL & MIKE COOPER
60s	Kennet KRS 766	OUT OF THE SHADES (EP)	30

DICKSON HALL (& COUNTRY ALL-STARS)
57	MGM MGM-EP 626	OUTLAWS OF THE OLD WEST (EP)	20
58	London RE-R 1158	FABULOUS COUNTRY HITS NO. 1 (EP)	18
58	London RE-R 1159	FABULOUS COUNTRY HITS NO. 2 (EP)	18
58	London RE-R 1160	FABULOUS COUNTRY HITS NO. 3 (EP)	18
60	Fontana Z 4011	ALL-TIME COUNTRY AND WESTERN HITS (LP)	12

DOLORES HALL
72	Jay Boy BOY 77	Good Lovin' Man/W-O-M-E-N	5

(see also Jackie Lee & Dolores Hall)

DORA HALL
64	King 1003	Hello Faithless/You've Got Me Cryin'	5

GERRI HALL
66	Sue WI 4026	Who Can I Run To/I Lost A Key (unissued)	

JIMMY GRAY HALL
74	Epic EPC 2312	Be That Way/Possessed By The Moon	15

JUANITA HALL
62	Storyville SEP 382	STORYVILLE BLUES ANTHOLOGY VOL. 2 (EP)	10
64	Society SOC 971	JUANITA HALL SINGS THE BLUES (LP)	12

LANI HALL
83	A&M AM 159	Never Say Never Again/Un Chanson D'Amour (p/s)	8
74	A&M AMLS 64359	SUNDOWN LADY (LP)	15

LARRY HALL
60	Parlophone R 4625	Sandy/Lovin' Tree	8
62	Salvo SLO 1811	Ladder Of Love/The One You Left Behind (99 copies only)	15

RENE HALL'S ORCHESTRA
58	London HLU 8581	Twitchy/Flippin'	45
58	London HLU 8581	Twitchy/Flippin' (78)	12

ROBIN HALL (& JIMMY MacGREGOR)
60	Collector JDS 3	Football Crazy/Rosin The Beau	5
60	Decca F 11266	Football Crazy/Rosin The Beau (reissue, p/s)	6
60	Collector JES 5	WEE MAGIC STANE (EP)	8
60	Collector JES 6	THE BONNIE LASS O'FYVIE (EP, solo)	8
60	Collector JES 7	MACPHERSON'S RANT (EP, solo)	8
61	Collector JES 9	GLASGOW STREET SONGS VOL. 3 (EP)	8
64	Collector JES 12	ROBIN HALL (EP, solo)	8
64	Collector JES 13	ROBIN HALL SINGS AGAIN (EP, solo)	8
61	Ace Of Clubs ACL 1065	SCOTTISH CHOICE (LP, with Jimmie MacGregor)	12

(see also Galliards)

RONNIE HALL
61	Piccadilly 7N 35001	The Code Of Love/Who Cares	5
62	Piccadilly 7N 35040	My Very First Love/The Day After Forever	5
65	Fontana TF 569	I'll Stand Aside/I'm Getting Nowhere	12

ROY HALL
56	Brunswick 05531	See You Later, Alligator/Don't Stop Now (gold label lettering)	650
56	Brunswick 05531	See You Later, Alligator/Don't Stop Now (78)	100
56	Brunswick 05555	Blue Suede Shoes/Luscious	450
56	Brunswick 05555	Blue Suede Shoes/Luscious (78)	85
56	Brunswick 05627	Diggin' The Boogie/Three Alley Cats	450
56	Brunswick 05627	Diggin' The Boogie/Three Alley Cats (78)	80

TERRY HALL
94	Anxious ANX 1027 CD	Sense/God Only Knows/This Guy's In Love With You (CD)	7
97	Telstar 7 BUBBLE 1	Ballad Of A Landlord/Bang Went Forever/Interview (p/s)	5

(see also Specials, Fun Boy Three, Colourfield)

TONY HALL
77	Free Reed FRR 012	FIELDVOLE MUSIC (LP, with insert)	20

CHANCE HALLADAY
62	Vogue V 9203	John Henry/Thirteen Women	12

HALLELUJAH SKIFFLE GROUP
58	Oriole CB 1429	I Saw The Light/A Closer Walk With Thee (with Clinton Ford)	15
58	Oriole CB 1429	I Saw The Light/A Closer Walk With Thee (78, with Clinton Ford)	10

(see also Clinton Ford)

HALLIARD
67	Saga SOC 1058	IT'S THE IRISH IN ME (LP)	18
68	Broadside BRO 106	THE HALLIARD AND JON RAVEN (LP)	40

(see also Jon Raven, Nic Jones)

GERI HALLIWELL
99	EMI 12 EMDJX 542	Look At Me (Terminalhead Remix)/(Terminalhead dub) (12", die cut sleeve, promo only)	12
99	EMI CDEMDJX 542	Look At Me (CD, sealed card p/s, promo only)	12
99	EMI CD IN 122	Interview (CD, tri-fold digipak, promo only)	20
99	EMI DJ 521 0092	SCHIZOPHRENIC (CD, album sampler in sealed foil wallet, numbered sticker, promo only)	20

(see also Spice Girls)

DICK HALLMAN
56	Brunswick 05608	Two Different Worlds/Love Me As Though There Were No Tomorrow	6
60	Vogue V 9162	Born To Be Loved/Just Squeeze Me But Don't Teeze Me	6

JOHNNY HALLYDAY
62	Philips BF 1238	Shake The Hand Of A Fool/Hold Back The Sun	10
63	Philips 373 012BF	Hey Little Girl/Caravan Of Lonely Men	10
65	Philips BF 1449	Pour Moi Tu Es La Seule/They Call Him A Man	12
62	Philips 432 813BE	ROCKING (EP)	135
66	Vogue VRE 5013	JOHNNY HALLYDAY (EP)	150
61	Philips BBL 7556	SINGS AMERICA'S ROCKIN' HITS (LP)	100

HALOS
61	London HLU 9424	Nag/Copycat	25

CHRIS HAMALTON
53	London L 1177	Farmer's Boy Boogie/Celebration Rag (78)	8
53	London L 1200	Dizzy Fingers/Saturday Rag (78)	8

STUART HAMBLEN
54	HMV 7MC 20	This Ole House/When My Lord Picks Up The 'Phone (export issue)	18
54	HMV JO 413	This Ole House/When My Lord Picks Up The 'Phone (78)	7
55	HMV JO 434	Ole Pappy Time/The Toy Violin (78, export issue)	12
55	HMV 7MC 30	Go On By/Just A Man (export issue)	15
56	HMV 7M 394	Hell Train/A Few Things To Remember	12

BILLY HAMBRIC
79	Grapevine GRP 139	She Said Goodbye/I Found True Love	8

CLAIRE HAMILL
72	Island WIP 6122	When I Was A Child/Alice In The Streets Of Darlington	5
72	Island WIP 6133	Baseball Blues/Smile Your Blues Away	5
74	Konk KOS 1	Geronimo's Cadillac/Luck Of The Draw	5
81	WEA K 18440	First Night In New York/Ultraviolet Light (B-side with Gary Numan) (p/s)	7
72	Island ILPS 9182	ONE HOUSE LEFT STANDING (LP)	15
73	Island ILPS 9225	OCTOBER (LP)	15
74	Konk KONK 101	STAGE DOOR JOHNNIES (LP)	12
75	Konk KONK 104	ABRACADABRA (LP, featuring Cafe Society, with insert)	12

(see also Cafe Society, Gary Numan)

BILLY HAMILTON & STRANDSMEN
67	Philips BF 1622	Try To Remember/Don't You Believe It	5

CHICO HAMILTON QUINTET
57	Vogue V 2407	The Sage/The Morning After	6
58	Vogue LAE 12045	CHICO HAMILTON QUINTET IN HIFI (LP)	15
68	Solid State USS 7010	THE GAMUT (LP)	12

EDWARD HAMILTON & ARABIANS
80	Grapevine GRP 134	Baby Don't You Weep/I'm Gonna Love You	6

GARY HAMILTON

67	Decca F 12697	Let The Music Play/Don't Ask	5
69	CBS 4674	Easy Rider/Hare Krishna	5

(see also Hamilton & [Hamilton] Movement)

GAVIN HAMILTON

67	King KG 1067	It Won't Be The Same/Turn The Key Softly	22

GEORGE HAMILTON IV

57	London HL 8361	A Rose And A Candy Bar/If You Don't Know (gold or silver label print)	135/75
57	London HL 8361	A Rose And A Candy Bar/If You Don't Know (78)	25
57	HMV POP 429	Why Don't They Understand/Even Tho'	10
57	HMV POP 429	Why Don't They Understand/Even Tho' (78)	8
58	HMV POP 474	Now And For Always/One Heart	8
58	HMV POP 474	Now And For Always/One Heart (78)	8
58	HMV POP 505	I Know Where I'm Goin'/Who's Taking You To The Prom?	6
58	HMV POP 505	I Know Where I'm Goin'/Who's Taking You To The Prom? (78)	7
58	HMV POP 534	Your Cheatin' Heart/When Will I Know?	7
58	HMV POP 534	Your Cheatin' Heart/When Will I Know? (78)	8
60	HMV POP 813	Before This Day Ends/Loneliness Is All Around Us	6
63	RCA RCA 1353	Abilene/Oh So Many Years	6
72	Uni UNS 480	Evel Knievel/Boy From The Country	5
58	HMV CLP 1202	ON CAMPUS (LP)	18
59	HMV CLP 1263	SING ME A SAD SONG — A TRIBUTE TO HANK WILLIAMS (LP)	18

GUY HAMILTON

65	HMV POP 1418	A Lifetime Of Loneliness/Give The Game Away	8

(see also Neil Christian)

M. HAMILTON

67	Ska Beat JB 265	Something Gotta Ring/DENNIS LYNWARD & HIS GROUP: Jazz Session	12

MILTON HAMILTON

73	Explosion EX 2069	Long Long Road/Version	5

ROY HAMILTON

55	Philips PB 368	You'll Never Walk Alone/If I Loved You (78)	8
55	Philips PB 448	Unchained Melody/From Here To Eternity (78)	8
55	Philips PB 515	Forgive This Fool/You Wanted To Change Me (78)	8
56	Philips PB 551	Without A Song/Cuban Love Song (78)	8
56	Philips PB 583	Walk Along With Kings/There Goes My Heart (78)	8
58	Fontana H 113	Don't Let Go/The Right To Love	18
58	Fontana H 113	Don't Let Go/The Right To Love (78)	10
58	Fontana H 143	Crazy Feelin'/In A Dream	12
58	Fontana H 143	Crazy Feelin'/In A Dream (78)	12
59	Fontana H 180	Pledging My Love/My One And Only Love	12
59	Fontana H 180	Pledging My Love/My One And Only Love (78)	15
59	Fontana H 193	I Need Your Loving/Somewhere Along The Way	10
59	Fontana H 193	I Need Your Loving/Somewhere Along The Way (78)	25
61	Fontana H 298	You Can Have Her/Abide With Me	15
61	Fontana H 320	You're Gonna Need Magic/To The One I Love	10
63	MGM MGM 1210	Theme From "The VIPs"/The Sinner	10
64	MGM MGM 1251	There She Is/The Panic Is On	140
65	MGM MGM 1268	A Thousand Tears Ago/Sweet Violet	10
66	RCA RCA 1500	And I Love Her/Tore Up Over You	8
69	Deep Soul DS 9106	Dark End Of The Street/100 Years Ago	12
59	Fontana TFE 17160	WHY FIGHT THE FEELING (EP)	15
60	Fontana TFE 17163	THE MOOD MOVES (EP)	15
61	Fontana TFE 17170	COME OUT SWINGING (EP)	15
64	MGM MGM-C 960	WARM SOUL (LP)	25

RUSS HAMILTON

57	Oriole CB 1359	We Will Make Love/Rainbow	5
57	Oriole CB 1388	Wedding Ring/I Still Belong To You	5
57	Oriole CB 1406	I Don't Know Why/My Mother's Eyes	5
58	Oriole CB 1404	Little One/I Had A Dream	5
58	Oriole CB 1451	Drifting And Dreaming/Tip-toe Through The Tulips	5
58	Oriole CB 1459	I Wonder Who's Kissing Her Now/September In The Rain	5
58	Oriole CB 1459	I Wonder Who's Kissing Her Now/September In The Rain (78)	7
58	Oriole CB 1465	Things I Didn't Say/Strange Are The Ways Of Love	5
58	Oriole CB 1465	Things I Didn't Say/Strange Are The Ways Of Love (78)	8
59	Oriole CB 1492	The Reprieve Of Tom Dooley/Dreaming Of You	5
59	Oriole CB 1492	The Reprieve Of Tom Dooley/Dreaming Of You (78)	10
59	Oriole CB 1506	My Unbreakable Heart/I Found You	6
59	Oriole CB 1506	My Unbreakable Heart/I Found You (78)	15
59	Oriole CB 1508	Smile, Smile, Smile (And Sing, Sing, Sing)/Shadow	6
59	Oriole CB 1508	Smile, Smile, Smile (And Sing, Sing, Sing)/Shadow (78)	15
60	Oriole CB 1527	Things No Money Can Buy/Mama	6
60	Oriole CB 1527	Things No Money Can Buy/Mama (78)	15
60	Oriole CB 1531	It's A Sin To Tell A Lie/Folks Get Married In The Spring	6
60	Oriole CB 1531	It's A Sin To Tell A Lie/Folks Get Married In The Spring (78)	15
60	MGM MGM 1096	Gonna Find Me A Bluebird/Choir Girl	5
64	Ember EMBS 184	Valley Of Love/Loneliest Boy In Town	5
64	Ember EMBS 193	We Will Make Love/No One Can Love Like You	5
58	Oriole EP 7005	RUSS HAMILTON (EP)	20
58	Oriole MG 20031	WE WILL MAKE LOVE (LP)	50

SCOTT HAMILTON

66	Parlophone R 5492	Good Day Sunshine/For No One	5

HAMILTON & MOVEMENT
65	Polydor BM 56026	Really Saying Something/I Won't See You Tonight	25
67	CBS 202573	I'm Not The Marrying Kind/My Love Belongs To You	20

(see also Gary Hamilton, Paul Stewart Movement)

HAMLINS
67	Coxsone CS 7021	Trying To Keep A Good Man Down/BOB MARLEY: Oh My Darling	50
67	Coxsone CS 7022	Soul And Inspiration/ETHIOPIANS: Let's Get Together	20
68	Coxsone CS 7048	Sentimental Reasons/SOUL VENDORS: Last Waltz	20
68	Blue Cat BS 115	Sugar And Spice/SOUL VENDORS: Mercy Mercy Mercy	12

(see also Minstrels)

MARVIN HAMLISCH
77	United Artists UP 36301	Bond 77/Ride To Atlantis	5

JACK HAMMER
61	Oriole CB 1634	Young Only Once/Juliette	10
62	Oriole CB 1645	Kissin' Twist/Melancholy Boy	8
62	Oriole CB 1728	Crazy Twist/Twist Talk	10
62	Oriole CB 1753	Don't Let Baby Know/Number 2539.	10
66	Polydor 56091	Thanks/Love Ladder	10
69	United Artists UP 35029	What Greater Love/The Mason Dixon Line	30
66	Polydor	BRAVE NEW WORLD (LP)	25

HAMMERS
69	President PT 247	Baby And Me/Little Butterfly	5
69	President PT 276	Sugar Baby/Power Of Love	5

HAMMERS (Jamaica)
70	Gas GAS 162	Hotter Than Scorcher/Someday Could See You	5

(see also Joan Ross)

HAMMERSMITH GORILLAS
74	Penny Farthing PEN 849	You Really Got Me/Leavin' 'Ome	10
77	Raw RAW 2	You Really Got Me/Leavin' 'Ome (reissue, p/s)	6

(see also Clique)

PETER HAMMILL
75	Charisma CB 245	Birthday Special/Shingle Song	8
78	Charisma CB 339	The Polaroid (credited to Ricky Nadir)/The Old School Tie	10
78	Charisma PH 001	Crying Wolf/This Side Of The Looking Glass (promo only)	30
81	Virgin VS 424	My Experience/Glue (p/s).	5
82	Naive NAV 3	Paradox Drive/Now More Than Ever (p/s)	6
83	Naive NAV 8	Film Noir/Seven Wonders.	6
84	Charisma CB 414	Just Good Friends/Just Good Friends (Instrumental) (p/s)	5
86	Foundry FOUND 3	Painting By Numbers/You Hit Me Where I Live (p/s)	5
86	Foundry FOUND 312	Painting By Numbers (Extended)/You Hit Me Where I Live/Shell (12", p/s)	8
71	Charisma CAS 1037	FOOL'S MATE (LP, gatefold sleeve)	15
73	Charisma CAS 1067	CHAMELEON IN THE SHADOW OF THE NIGHT (LP, gatefold sleeve)	15
74	Charisma CAS 1083	THE SILENT CORNER AND THE EMPTY STAGE (LP, gatefold sl., with inner).	15
74	Charisma CAS 1089	IN CAMERA (LP, with inner sleeve)	15
75	Charisma CAS 1099	NADIR'S BIG CHANCE (LP, with inner sleeve)	15
77	Charisma CAS 1125	OVER (LP, some with inner lyric sleeve).	18/12
78	Charisma CAS 1137	THE FUTURE NOW (LP, with insert)	15
79	Charisma CAS 1146	pH 7 (LP, with inner sleeve)	15

(see also Van Der Graaf Generator, Le Orme, Rikki Nadir, Colin Scot)

ALBERT HAMMOND
73	MUM MUMS 65320	IT NEVER RAINS IN SOUTHERN CALIFORNIA (LP)	12
73	MUM MUMS 65554	FREE ELECTRIC BAND (LP)	12
74	MUM MUMS 80026	ALBERT HAMMOND (LP).	12

(see also Family Dogg)

CLAY HAMMOND
72	Jay Boy BOY 78	Dance Little Girl/Twin Brother	5

JOHN HAMMOND (Snr.)
72	Vanguard VRS 8523/4	JOHN HAMMOND'S SPIRITUALS TO SWING: LEGENDARY CARNEGIE HALL CONCERTS OF 1938/9 (2-LP).	15

JOHN HAMMOND
65	Fontana TF 560	Baby Won't You Tell Me/I Live The Life I Love	12
68	Atlantic 584 190	Brown Eyed Handsome Man/Crosscut Saw	8
64	Fontana TFL 6046	BIG CITY BLUES (LP)	30
65	Fontana TFL 6059	SO MANY ROADS (LP).	25
71	CBS 64365	SOURCE POINT (LP)	20
72	CBS 65051	I'M SATISFIED (LP).	20
72	Vanguard VSD 11/12	THE BEST OF JOHN HAMMOND — SOUTHERN FRIED (2-LP)	15

STEVE HAMMOND
67	Pye 7N 17275	I Think We're Alone Now/Just Call My Name.	5

CURLEY HAMNER & COOPER BROTHERS
59	Felsted SD 80061	Twistin' And Turnin'/King And Queen	8

SUSAN HAMPSHIRE
65	Decca F 12185	When Love Is True/When The World Was Our Own.	7

LIONEL HAMPTON (& HIS HAMP-TONES)
52	MGM MGM 468	Samson's Boogie/Helpless (78, & His Hamp-Tones, B-side with Sonny Parker).	8
57	Vogue V 2405	Flying Home/Perdido (with Just Jazz All Stars)	18
57	Vogue V 2406	Hamp's Boogie Woogie/The Blues (with Just Jazz All Stars)	20
56	MGM MGM-EP 552	LIONEL HAMPTON & HIS ORCHESTRA (EP)	12
54	Vogue EPV 1015	LIONEL HAMPTON TRIO (EP)	10
54	Brunswick OE 9007	JUST JAZZ (EP)	10
55	Brunswick OE 9108	JUST JAZZ CONCERT (EP)	10

MINT VALUE £

55	Philips BBE 12017	LIONEL HAMPTON & HIS ORCHESTRA (EP)	8
57	Vogue EPV 1161	GENE NORMAN PRESENTS JUST JAZZ — LIONEL HAMPTON AT THE PASADENA AUDITORIUM (EP)	12
57	Vogue EPV 1189	LIONEL HAMPTON JAM SESSION (EP)	8
57	Vogue EPV 1190	LIONEL HAMPTON AT THE PASADENA AUDITORIUM (EP)	8
56	Columbia Clef SEB 10025	LIONEL HAMPTON BIG BAND (EP)	8
56	Columbia Clef SEB 10028	LIONEL HAMPTON QUARTET/QUINTET (EP)	8
56	Columbia Clef SEB 10045	LIONEL HAMPTON BIG BAND (EP)	8
56	Columbia Clef SEB 10065	LIONEL HAMPTON QUARTET (EP)	8
57	Columbia Clef SEB 10086	LIONEL HAMPTON QUARTET (EP)	8
57	Columbia Clef SEB 10092	LIONEL HAMPTON BIG BAND NO. 3 (EP)	8
57	Felsted ESD 3026	LIONEL HAMPTON QUINTET (EP)	8
58	RCA RCX 1004	LIONEL HAMPTON (EP)	8
58	Columbia Clef SEB 10108	HAMPS BOOGIE WOOGIE (EP)	12
62	Oriole EP 7046	LIONEL HAMPTON ORCHESTRA (EP)	12
51	Brunswick LA 8527	HAMP'S BOOGIE WOOGIE (10" LP)	25
52	Brunswick LA 8551	MOONGLOW (10" LP)	25
53	Vogue LDE 043	LIONEL HAMPTON'S "JAZZ TIME PARIS" VOLUME 1 (10" LP)	20
54	Vogue LDE 051	NEW SOUNDS FROM EUROPE VOLUME 2 — FRANCE (10" LP)	20
54	Vogue LDE 063	LIONEL HAMPTON VOLUME 3 (10" LP)	20
54	Felsted EDL 87007	THE HAMP IN PARIS IN PARIS VOLUME 1 (10" LP)	20
54	Felsted EDL 87008	THE HAMP IN PARIS IN PARIS VOLUME 2 (10" LP)	20
55	Felsted PDL 85002	LIONEL HAMPTON AND HIS NEW FRENCH SOUND VOLUME 1 (10" LP)	20
55	HMV CLP 1023	HOT MALLETS (LP)	15
55	Columbia Clef 33C 9011	LIONEL HAMPTON QUARTET (10" LP)	15
55	Philips BBL 7015	APOLLO HALL CONCERT 1954 (LP)	15
56	Philips BBL 7119	HAMPTON AND THE OLD WORLD (LP)	12
56	Oriole MG 20012	HAMP 1956 (LP)	12
56	Brunswick LAT 8086	ALL AMERICAN AWARD CONCERT (LP)	12
57	RCA RD 27006	JAZZ FLAMENCO (LP)	12
61	Fontana Fortune Z 4053	THE ONE AND ONLY LIONEL HAMPTON (LP)	12

(see also Sonny Parker)

PAUL HAMPTON
| 58 | Philips PB 787 | Play It Cool/Classy Babe (78) | 20 |

SLIDE HAMPTON & HIS BAND
| 62 | London HA-K/SH-K 8008 | JAZZ WITH A TWIST (LP) | 12 |

HAMPTONS
(see under Fabulous Impact)

HERBIE HANCOCK
63	Blue Note 45-1887	Blind Man, Blind Man (Parts 1 & 2)	10
70	Warner Bros WB 7358	Fat Mama/Wiggle-Waggle	7
74	CBS 2329	Chameleon/Vein Melter	4
75	CBS 3059	Palm Grease/Butterfly	4
64	Blue Note (B)BLP 4109	TAKIN' OFF (LP)	18
64	Blue Note (B)BLP 4126	MY POINT OF VIEW (LP)	18
64	Blue Note (B)BLP 4147	INVENTIONS AND DIMENSIONS (LP)	18
65	Blue Note (B)BLP 4175	EMPYREAN ISLES (LP)	18
66	Blue Note BLP 4195	MAIDEN VOYAGE (LP, also stereo BST 84195)	15
60s	Blue Note BST 84279	SPEAK LIKE A CHILD (LP)	12
60s	Blue Note BST 84321	THE PRISONER (LP)	12
60s	Blue Note BST 89907	THE BEST OF HERBIE HANCOCK (LP)	12
71	Warner Bros WS 1834	FAT ALBERT ROTUNDA (LP)	20
71	Warner Bros K 46077	MWANDISHI (LP)	12
72	Warner Bros K 46164	CROSSINGS (LP)	12
74	Warner Bros K 46039	FAT ALBERT ROTUNDA (LP, reissue)	15
74	CBS 80193	THRUST (LP)	12
74	CBS 65582	SEXTANT (LP)	12
74	CBS 65928	HEADHUNTERS (LP)	12
75	CBS 69185	MAN CHILD (LP)	12

(see also Headhunters)

SHEILA HANCOCK
| 63 | Decca F 11618 | My Last Cigarette/Landlord And Tenant | 6 |
| 62 | Transatlantic TRA 106 | PUTTING OUT THE DUSTBIN (LP) | 18 |

SHEILA HANCOCK & MALCOLM TAYLOR
| 66 | Eyemark EMS 1007 | I'm Reformed/I Got You (die cut sleeve) | 6 |

TONY HANCOCK
63	Pye 7N 15575	Wing Commander Hancock — Test Pilot/The Threatening Letters (with Kenneth Williams)	6
61	Pye NEP 24146	LITTLE PIECES OF HANCOCK (EP)	8
62	Pye NEP 24161	LITTLE PIECES OF HANCOCK VOL. 2 (EP)	10
62	Pye NEP 24170	HANCOCK'S HALF HOUR (EP)	10
63	Pye NEP 24175	THE BLOOD DONOR (EP)	8
60	Pye NPL 18045	THIS IS HANCOCK (LP)	15
60	Pye NPL 18054	PIECES OF HANCOCK (LP)	15
61	Pye NPL 18068	THE BLOOD DONOR AND THE RADIO HAM (LP)	12
63	Piccadilly FTF 38500	FACE TO FACE (LP, interview disc)	70
65	Decca LK 4740	IT'S HANCOCK (LP)	18

(see also Sidney James, Kenneth Williams)

OWEN HAND
| 61 | Transatlantic TRA 127 | SOMETHING NEW (LP) | 80 |
| 66 | Transatlantic TRA | I LOVED A LASS (LP) | 40 |

JOHNNY HANDLE
| 61 | Topic TOP 78 | STOTTIN' DOON THE WAAL (EP) | 10 |

(see also Louise Killen & Johnny Handle)

MINT VALUE £

HANDSOME BEASTS
81	Heavy Metal HEAVY 1	All Riot Now/Mark Of The Beast (p/s)	10
81	Heavy Metal HEAVY 2	Breaker/One In A Crowd/Crazy (wraparound p/s)	8
82	Heavy Metal HEAVY 11	Sweeties/You're One Your Own (p/s, with card sheet)	8
82	Heavy Metal	BESTIALITY (LP)	18

WAYNE HANDY
58	London HL 8547	Say Yeah/Could It Be (B-side with King Sisters)	450
58	London HL 8547	Say Yeah/Could It Be (B-side with King Sisters) (78)	75

PAUL HANFORD
60	Parlophone R 4680	Itsy Bitsy Teenie Weenie Little Polka Dot Bikini/ Why Have You Changed Your Mind	5
60	Parlophone R 4694	If You Ain't Got Love/Ev'ry Little Girl	6
61	Parlophone R 4745	Everything/Cigarettes And Coffee Blues	5
61	Parlophone R 4813	Memphis Address/Flutter Flutter	6
62	Oriole CB 1779	Don't Be/Habit Of Loving You	6
63	Oriole CB 1830	Just When I Need You Most/Judy	5
63	Oriole CB 1866	The Minute You're Gone/High School Dance	8

HANGMAN'S BEAUTIFUL DAUGHTERS
87	Dreamworld DREAM 11	Love Is Blue/Popular Trend (p/s)	7
87	Dreamworld DREAM 11T	Love Is Blue/Popular Trend/Jonathan/Don't Ask My Name (12", p/s)	8
87	Yo Jo Jo 1	Darkside/Pushing Me Too Far (flexidisc, p/s)	8
88	Dreamworld BIG 5	TRASH MANTRA (mini-LP)	12

HANK & MELLOWMEN
60s	Lyntone LYN 153/154	Santa Anno/Mosology/(other artists) (Bangor University Rag flexidisc)	7
60s	Lyntone LYN 201	So In Love With You/Michael (Bangor University Rag flexidisc)	7
	(see also Roger Whittaker)		

MICHAEL HANLY & MICHAEL O'DONNEL
74	Polydor 2908 013	CELTIC FOLKWEAVE (LP, Ireland-only)	40

BOBBY HANNA
67	Decca F 12604	Thanks To You/Here I Stand	5
67	Decca F 12695	Blame It On Me/Goin' Where The Lovin' Is	8
68	Decca F 12738	Too Much Love/What Do I Want For Tomorrow	5
68	Decca F 12783	Written On The Wind/Everybody Needs Love	5
68	Decca F 12833	To Wait For Love (Is To Waste Your Life Away)/Is It Wrong	5
69	Decca F 22917	Winter Love (E' L'Amore)/Time	5

GEORGE HANNA & SARAH ANNE O'NEILL
78	Topic 12TS 372	ON THE SHORES OF LOUGH NEAGH (LP)	12

JOSH HANNA
65	Parlophone R 5385	When I Love You/Love Me, Love Me	5
66	Decca F 12532	Shut Your Mouth/Sweet To My Soul	12

HANNA BARBERA (cartoon soundtracks)
66	Hanna Barbera HBE 1	FLINTSTONES — HANSEL AND GRETEL (EP)	8
66	Hanna Barbera HBE 2	UNCLE REMUS — BRER RABBIT AND THE TAR BABY (EP)	8
66	Hanna Barbera HBE 3	FLINTSTONES — GOLDILOCKS, BEAROSAURUS (EP)	10
66	Hanna Barbera HBE 4	SNAGGLEPUSS TALES — WIZARD OF OZ (EP)	8
66	Hanna Barbera HBE 5	YOGI BEAR AND BOO BOO TELL JACK AND THE BEANSTALK (EP)	10
66	Hanna Barbera HBE 6	FRED FLINTSTONE & BARNEY RUBBLE — SONG FROM MARY POPPINS (EP)	8
67	Hanna Barbera HBE 7	TOP CAT — ROBIN HOOD (EP)	8
67	Hanna Barbera HBE 8	YOGI BEAR AND BOO BOO — LITTLE RED RIDING HOOD (EP)	8
67	Hanna Barbera HBE 9	FLINTSTONES — THREE LITTLE PIGS (EP)	8
67	Hanna Barbera HBE 10	AUGIE DOGGY AND DOGGY DADDY — SONGS FROM PINOCCHIO (EP)	8
67	Hanna Barbera HBE 11	PEBBLES AND BAMM BAMM — WE WISH YOU A MERRY CHRISTMAS (EP)	10
68	Hanna Barbera HBE 12	MERRY CHRISTMAS — ORGAN AND CHIMES (EP)	10
68	Hanna Barbera HBE 13	MAGILLA GORILLA AND OGEE — ALICE IN WONDERLAND (EP)	8
68	Hanna Barbera HBE 14	PEBBLES AND BAMM BAMM — SONGS FROM THE GOOD SHIP LOLLIPOP (EP)	8

HANNIBAL
74	B&C HB 1	Winds Of Change/Winter	6
70	B&C CAS 1022	HANNIBAL (LP)	35

LANCE HANNIBAL
69	Blue Cat BS 148	Read The News/RECO & RHYTHM ACES: Return Of The Bullet	8
	(see also Sugar Simone, Les Foster)		

HANOI ROCKS
83	Lick LIX 1	Malibu Beach/Rebel On The Run (p/s)	6
83	Lick LIXPD 1	Malibu Beach/Rebel On The Run (picture disc)	12
83	Lick LIXT 1	Malibu Beach/Taxi Driver/Rebel On The Run/Beer And A Cigarette (12", p/s)	8
83	Lick LIX 2	Until I Get You/Tragedy (p/s)	5
83	Lick LIXT 2	Until I Get You/Tragedy/Oriental Beat (12", p/s)	8
84	CBS A 4513	Up Around The Bend/Until I Get You (p/s, some with free transfer)	10/8
84	CBS DA 4513	Up Around The Bend/Until I Get You/Under My Wheels/I Feel Alright/ Train Kept A Rollin' (double pack)	15
84	CBS TA 4513	Up Around The Bend/Back To The Mystery City/Until I Get You/ Mental 84 Beat (12", p/s, some with free transfer)	10/8
84	CBS A 4732	Underwater World/Shakes (p/s)	5
84	CBS TA 4732	Underwater World/Shakes/Magic Carpet Ride (12", p/s)	10
84	CBS WA 4732	Underwater World/Shakes/Magic Carpet Ride (12", picture disc)	15
84	CBS A 4685	Don't You Ever Leave Me/Shakes (p/s)	5
84	CBS TA 4685	Don't You Ever Leave Me/Oil And Gasoline/Malibu Beach (Calypso) (12", p/s)	8
84	CBS WA 4685	Don't You Ever Leave Me/Oil And Gasoline/Malibu Beach (Calypso) (12", 3-D picture disc)	15

83	Lick LICLP 1	BACK TO THE MYSTERY CITY (LP, some on white vinyl)	15/12
83	Lick LICLP 2	BANGKOK SHOCKS, SAIGON SHAKES, HANOI ROCKS (LP)	12
83	Lick LICLP 3	ORIENTAL BEAT (LP)	12
83	Lick LICLP 4	SELF DESTRUCTION BLUES (LP)	12
84	CBS 26066	TWO STEPS FROM THE MOVE (LP, with cartoon booklet)	12
86	Lick LICLP PD4	SELF DESTRUCTION BLUES (LP, picture disc)	15
86	Lick BOOTLIC 7	ROCK'N'ROLL DIVORCE (LP)	12
88	Lick LICCD 8	THE BEST OF HANOI ROCKS (CD, with 16-page booklet)	18

(see also Fallen Angels, Dark, Idle Flowers, Urban Dogs, Suicide Twins)

HANSON
| 97 | Mercury 574 501-2 | Mmm Bop/The Man From Milwaukee (Garage Mix)/ Mmm Bop (Dust Brothers)/Mmm Bop (CD) | 12 |

HANSON & KARLSSON
67	Polydor 184 196	SWEDISH UNDERGROUND (LP)	15
69	Polydor 462 60	MONUMENT (LP)	15
69	Polydor 583 564	MAN AT THE MOON (LP)	18

(see also Bo Hansson)

BO HANSSON
| 72 | Charisma CAS 1059 | LORD OF THE RINGS (LP) | 12 |

HAPPENINGS
66	Fontana TF 735	See You In September/He Thinks He's A Hero	7
66	Fontana TF 766	Go Away Little Girl/Tea Time	7
67	Pye International 7N 25501	My Mammy/I Believe In Nothing	6
67	Stateside SS 587	Goodnight My Love/Lillies By Monet	6
67	Stateside SS 2013	I Got Rhythm/You're In A Bad Way	6
67	BT Puppy BTS 45532	Why Do Fools Fall In Love/When The Summer Is Through	6
68	BT Puppy BTS 45538	Music Music Music/When I Lock My Door	5
68	BT Puppy BTS 45540	Randy/Love Song Of Mummy And Dad	5
68	BT Puppy BTS 45543	Breaking Up Is Hard To Do/Anyway	5
68	BT Puppy BTS 45545	Crazy Rhythm/Love Song Of Mummy And Dad	5
69	BT Puppy BTS 45546	Where Do I Go/New Day Comin'	5
67	Fontana TL 5383	BYE BYE, SO LONG, FAREWELL ... SEE YOU IN SEPTEMBER (LP)	20
67	BT Puppy BTLP 1003	PSYCLE (LP)	15
68	BT Puppy BTLPS 1004	GOLDEN HITS (LP)	12

HAPPY CATS
| 78 | Grapevine 110 | Destroy That Boy/These Boots Are Made For Walking | 8 |

HAPPY CONFUSION
| 69 | Penny Farthing PEN 706 | Yes Sir/Hereditary Impediment | 5 |

HAPPY FAMILY
| 82 | 4AD AD 204 | Puritans/Innermost Thoughts/The Mistake (p/s) | 8 |
| 82 | 4AD CAD 214 | THE MAN ON YOUR STREET (LP) | 10 |

(see also Josef K, Momus)

HAPPY MAGAZINE
| 68 | Polydor 56233 | Satisfied Street/Do Right Woman Do Right Man | 8 |
| 69 | Polydor 56307 | Who Belongs To You (Ooby Dooby Doo)/Beautiful Land | 6 |

(see also Griffin)

HAPPY MONDAYS
| 87 | Factory FACT 170 | SQUIRREL & G-MAN TWENTY FOUR HOUR PARTY PEOPLE PLASTIC FACE CARNT SMILE (WHITE OUT) (LP, with "Desmond", 5,000 in plastic sleeve) | 12 |

HAPSHASH & COLOURED COAT
69	Liberty LBF 15188	Colinda/The Wall	15
67	Minit MLS 40001E	FEATURING THE HUMAN HOST AND THE HEAVY METAL KIDS (LP, with Art, initially red vinyl with insert; later copies on black vinyl)	60/40
69	Liberty LBL/LBS 83212R	THE WESTERN FLYER (LP, with Mike Batt)	25

(see also Tony McPhee, Warm Sounds, Marc Bolan/T. Rex, Art, Mike Batt)

HARBOUR LITES
65	HMV POP 1426	Come Back Silly Girl/Revenge	6
65	HMV POP 1465	I Would Give All/They Call The Wind Maria	8
66	Fontana TF 682	Run For Your Life/Lonely Journey	8

HARD CORPS
84	Hard Corps HC 01	Dirty/To Breathe (12", hand-written white labels, numbered)	35
84	Survival SUR 026	Dirty/Respirer (To Breathe) (white or printed labels, stickered plain black sleeve)	10
84	Survival SUR 12 026	Dirty/Respirer (To Breathe) (12", with sticker in plain black sleeve)	15
85	Immaculate 12 IMMAC 2	Je Suis Passée (Extended French Version)/(Extended Club Dub Mix) (12", p/s)	12
85	Polydor HARD 1	Je Suis Passée/Je Suis Passée (Instrumental Mix) (p/s)	5
85	Polydor HARDX 1	Je Suis Passée (Extended)/(Instrumental Mix)/(Dub Mix) (12", p/s)	8
85	Polydor HARDA 1	Je Suis Passée (Hard Mix)/(French Mix)/(Dub Mix) (12", gatefold PVC sleeve, various colours, with poster)	30
85	Polydor HARD 2	To Breathe/Metal And Flesh (unreleased)	35
85	Polydor HARDX 2	To Breathe/Metal And Flesh/To Breathe (Instrumental) (12", unreleased)	50
87	Rhythm King TYPE 3	Lucky Charm/Porte-Bonheur (p/s)	5
87	Rhythm King TYPE 3T	Lucky Charm/Porte-Bonheur/Lucky Charm (The Music) (12", p/s)	8
90	Concrete P. CPPRODLP 011	METAL AND FLESH (LP, clear vinyl)	20
90	Concrete P. CPPRODCD 011	METAL AND FLESH (CD)	30

(see also Craze, Skunks, T.U.F.F.)

MINT VALUE £

HARDFLOOR
92	Harthouse HARTUK 1	HARDTRANCE ACPERIENCE EP (12", 4-track)	12

EDDIE HARDIN
72	Decca F 13307	Why Does Everybody Put Me Down/Spend Your Money Honey	5
72	Decca TXS 106	HOME IS WHERE YOU FIND IT (LP)	12

(see also Hardin-York, Spencer Davis Group, Roger Glover)

TIM HARDIN
66	Verve VS 1504	Hang On To A Dream/A Reason To Believe	10
67	Verve VS 1511	The Lady Came From Baltimore/Black Sheep Boy	6
68	Verve VS 1516	Don't Make Promises/Smugglin' Man	6
69	CBS 4441	A Simple Song Of Freedom/Question Of Birth	5
71	Verve 2009 006	If I Were A Carpenter/Hang On To A Dream	5
73	CBS 1016	Do The Do/Sweet Lady	5
66	Verve (S)VLP 5018	TIM HARDIN 1 (LP)	25
67	Verve (S)VLP 6002	TIM HARDIN 2 (LP)	25
67	Atlantic 587/588 082	THIS IS TIM HARDIN (LP, plum label)	25
68	Verve (S)VLP 6010	LIVE IN CONCERT (LP)	20
69	Verve (S)VLP 6016	TIM HARDIN 4 (LP)	20
69	CBS (S/M) 63571	SUITE FOR SUSAN MOORE AND DAMIAN (LP, gatefold sleeve, mono/stereo)	15
70	CBS 64335	BIRD ON A WIRE (LP)	12
72	CBS 65209	PAINTED HEAD (LP)	12
74	GM GML 1004	NINE (LP)	12
74	Verve 2683 048	TIM HARDIN 1/2 (2-LP, gatefold reissue)	18

(Eddie) HARDIN & (Pete) YORK
69	Bell BLL 1064	Tomorrow Today/Candlelight (as Hardin-York)	5
69	Bell SBLL 125	TOMORROW TODAY (LP)	15
70	Bell SBLL 136	HARDIN & YORK (THE WORLD'S SMALLEST BIG BAND) (LP)	15
71	Bell SBLL 141	FOR THE WORLD (LP)	15
71	Decca SKL 5095	FOR THE WORLD (LP, reissue)	12

(see also Eddie Hardin, Pete York, Spencer Davis Group)

RICHARD HARDING
61	HMV POP 887	Jezebel/Temptation	20

(see also Cresters, Mike Sagar & Cresters)

ROSEMARY HARDMAN (& BOB AXFORD)
69	Folk Heritage	QUEEN OF HEARTS (LP)	100
72	Trailer LER 2075	FIREBIRD (LP)	20
71	Trailer LER 3018	SECOND SEASON CAME (LP, by Rosemary Hardman & Bob Axford)	20
75	Alida Star Cottage	JERSEY BURGER (LP)	100
78	Plant Life PLR 014	EAGLE OVER BLUE MOUNTAIN (LP, with insert)	12
80	Plant Life PLR 023	ROSIE HARDMAN (LP)	12
83	Plant Life PLR 053	THE WEAKNESS OF EVE (LP, with lyric insert)	12

HARD MEAT
69	Island WIP 6066	Rain/Burning Up Years	10
70	Warner Bros WB 8010	Ballad Of Marmalade Emma And Teddy Grimes/Yesterday, Today, Tomorrow	5
70	Warner Bros WS 1852	HARD MEAT (LP, with photo insert)	15
70	Warner Bros WS 1879	THROUGH A WINDOW (LP)	25

HARD ROAD
79	Goodstuff LP 1002	NO PROBLEM (LP, private pressing)	20

HARD STUFF
72	Purple PUR 103	Jay Time/The Orchestrator	7
73	Purple PUR 116	Inside Your Life/(It's) How Do You Do It!	7
72	Purple TPSA 7505	BULLETPROOF (LP, gatefold sleeve)	20
73	Purple TPSA 7507	BOLEX DEMENTIA (LP)	20

(see also Andromeda, Atomic Rooster, John Du Cann, Five Day Week Straw People, Johnny Gustafson, Bullet, Quatermass)

HARD TRAVELLIN'
71	Flams Ltd PR 1065	HARD TRAVELLIN' (LP, private pressing)	150

HARDWARE
79	Narc NARC 001	Speed Unit/Wall To Wall/Walking/Fire (folded p/s)	6
79	Narc NARC 002	Rubberface/Face The Flag/The Seven Minutes (p/s)	5

HARDWARE
85	Reset 7REST 7	Dance/Hey (p/s)	15
85	Reset 12REST 7	Dance/Hey (12", p/s)	25

HARDY
71	Ackee ACK 131	Glorious Morning/Hearing's Not Seeing	6

DAVE HARDY
76	Red Rag RRR 008	LEAVING THE DALES (LP)	10

FRANCOISE HARDY

64	Pye 7N 15612	Catch A Falling Star/Only Friends	8
64	Pye 7N 15653	Tous Les Garcons Et Les Filles/L'Amour S'en Va	5
64	Pye 7N 15696	Pourtant Tu M'Aimes/Jaloux	7
64	Pye 7N 15740	Et Meme/Le Temps De L'Amour	7
65	Pye 7N 15802	All Over The World/Another Place	5
66	Vogue VRS 7001	Just Call And I'll Be There/You Just Have To Say The Word	6
66	Vogue VRS 7004	So Many Friends/However Much	8
66	Vogue VRS 7010	This Little Heart/The Rose	5
66	Vogue VRS 7011	La Maison Ou J'ai Grandi/Je Ne Suis La Pour Personne	5
66	Vogue VRS 7014	Autumn Rendezvous/It's My Heart	5
66	Vogue VRS 7020	Si C'est Ca/Je Serai La Pour Toi	6
66	Vogue VRS 7025	Voila/Qui Peut Dire	7
67	Vogue VRS 7026	On Se Quitte Toujours/Les Petits Garcons	8
68	United Artists UP 1208	Now You Want To Be Loved/Tell Him You're Mine	7
68	United Artists UP 2253	Will You Love Me Tomorrow/Loving You	7
69	United Artists UP 35011	Comment Te Dire Adieu/La Mer, Les Etoiles Et Le Vent	8
70	United Artists UP 35070	All Because Of You/Time Passing By	8
70	United Artists UP 35105	Soon Is Slipping Away/The Bells Of Avignon	8
64	Pye NEP 24188	C'EST FAB (EP)	10
64	Pye NEP 24192	FRANCOISE SINGS IN ENGLISH (EP)	10
64	Pye NEP 24193	C'EST FRANCOISE (EP)	10
60s	Vogue VRE 5000	FRANCOISE (EP)	10
60s	Vogue VRE 5001	FRANCOISE HARDY (EP)	10
60s	Vogue VRE 5003	DIS LUI NON (EP)	10
60s	Vogue VRE 5008	LE TEMPS DES SOUVENIRS (EP)	10
60s	Vogue VRE 5012	CHANTE EN ALLEMAND (EP)	12
60s	Vogue VRE 5015	L'AMITIE (EP)	12
60s	Vogue VRE 5017	MON AMIE LA ROSE (EP)	12
60s	Vogue VRE 5018	AUTUMN RENDEZVOUS (EP)	12
64	Pye NPL 18094	FRANCOISE HARDY (LP)	15
64	Pye NPL 18099	IN VOGUE (LP)	15
65	Vogue VRL 3000	FRANCOISE HARDY (LP)	18
66	Vogue VRL 3021	FRANCOISE HARDY (LP)	20
66	Vogue VRL 3023	LE MEILLEUR DE FRANCOISE HARDY (LP)	15
66	Vogue VRL 3025	SINGS IN ENGLISH (LP)	15
67	Vogue VRL 3028	FRANCOISE (LP)	15
67	Vogue VRL 3031	VOILA! FRANCOISE HARDY (LP)	18
68	United Artists ULP 1207	EN ANGLAIS (LP)	25
70	United Artists UAS 29046	ONE-NINE-SEVEN-ZERO (LP)	22

LAVELL HARDY

68	Direction 58-3261	Don't Lose Your Groove/Women Of The World	6

COLIN HARE

70	Penny Farthing PEN 736	Grannie, Grannie/For Where Have You Been	6
71	Penny Farthing PEN 750	Underground Girl/Fighting For Peace	6
72	Warner Bros K 16203	Didn't I Tell You/Seek Not In The Wide World	6
71	Penny Farthing PELS 516	MARCH HARE (LP)	30

(see also Honeybus)

WINSTON HAREWOOD

71	Camel CA 64	I Will Never Fall In Love Again (actually by Winston Heywood)/ LA-FUD-DIL ALL-STARS: La-Fud-Dil (actually "La-Fud-Del")	8

(see also Winston Heywood)

RON HARGRAVE

58	MGM MGM 956	Latch On/Only A Daydream	3,000
58	MGM MGM 956	Latch On/Only A Daydream (78)	450

HARLAN COUNTY

70	Nashville 6076 002	Dr. Handy's Dandy Candy/Big Heat	5
70	Nashville 6336 002	HARLAN COUNTY (LP)	12

(see also Peter Skellern)

HARLEM HAMFATS

51	Vocalion V 1005	Weed Smoker's Dream (Why Don't You Do Now)/ ROSETTA HOWARD: Let Your Linen Hang Low (78)	15
60s	Ace Of Hearts AH 27	HARLEM HAMFATS (LP)	15

HARLEM JONNS RESHUFFLE

(see under 'J')

HARLESDEN MONKS

72	Pama Supreme PS 352	Time/Harlesden High Street	5

STEVE HARLEY (& COCKNEY REBEL)

73	EMI EMI 2051	Sebastian/Rock And Roll Parade	5
74	EMI EMI 2191	Psychomodo/Such A Dream (unreleased)	
74	EMI EMI 2191	Mr Soft/Such A Dream (with 'Orchestrated by Alan Powell' credit)	5

(The above singles are credited to Cockney Rebel.)

74	EMI EMI 2233	Big Big Deal/Bed In The Corner	12
76	EMI EMI 2539	(I Believe) Love's A Prima Donna/Sidetrack One	
77	EMI EMI 2673	The Best Years Of Our Lives (live)/Tumbling Down (live) (p/s)	6

(The above singles are credited to Steve Harley & Cockney Rebel; all subsequent singles are solo.)

77	EMI EMI 2922	Someone's Coming/Riding The Waves (For Virginia Woolf)	5
82	Chrysalis CHS 2594	I Can't Even Touch You/I Can Be Anyone (p/s)	5
89	Vital Vinyl VIT 3	When I'm With You/Theme From Babbacombe Lee (p/s)	5
93	Food For Thought	The Lighthouse/Star For A Week (CD, promo only, no cat. no.)	8

(see also Anderson Harley & Batt)

MINT VALUE £

LEE HARMER'S POPCORN
68   Page One POF 053   Love Is Coming/Hello Sunshine 8

HARMONIANS
70   Ackee ACK 107   Music Street/Group Of Girls 7
(see also Tony & Hippy Boys, Winston Shan)

HARMONICA FATS
63   Stateside SS 184   Tore Up/I Get So Tired 15
68   Action ACT 4507   Tore Up/I Get So Tired (reissue). 10

HARMONISERS
69   Duke DU 32   Mother Hen/WINSTON SINCLAIR: Chastise Them 8

HARMONIZING FOUR
66   Rymska RA 102   Who Knows/Heart Of Stone (actually by Charms) 6
(see also Charms)

HARMONY GRASS
68   RCA RCA 1772   Move In A Little Bit Closer Baby/Happiness Is Toy Shaped 6
69   RCA RCA 1828   First Time Loving/What A Groovy Day 5
69   RCA RCA 1885   I Remember/Summer Dreaming 5
70   RCA RCA 1932   Mrs. Richie/Teach Me How (withdrawn). 10
70   RCA RCA 1932   Cecilia/Mrs. Richie 5
70   RCA RCA 2011   Stand On Your Own Two Feet/Sing In The Sunshine. 5
70   RCA SF 8034   THIS IS US (LP) 15
(see also Tony Rivers & Castaways)

HARMONY TRIO
69   Emblem 7DR 323   LET'S FACE IT (LP) 12

JOE HARNELL
62   London HLR 9637   Harlem Nocturne/Fly Me To The Moon — Bossa Nova 5
78   MCA MCA 397   The Incredible Hulk Theme/Love Theme 6
62   London RER 1344   DANCE THE BOSSA NOVA (EP). 12

BILLY HARNER
71   Kama Sutra 2013 029   What About The Music/Please Spare Me This Time 8
71   Kama Sutra 2013 029   What About The Music/Please Spare MeThis Time/What About The Music
                        (Instrumental) (a few demos mispressed with extra track). 350
72   Blue Horizon 2431 013   TRIGGER FINGER (LP) 15

BUD HARPER
65   Vocalion VP 9252   Mr. Soul/Let Me Love You. 25

CHARLIE HARPER
80   Gem GEMS 35   Barmy London Army/Talk Is Cheap (p/s, green or yellow vinyl) . . . . each 5
81   Ramkup CAC 005   Freaked/Jo (p/s) 5
(see also U.K. Subs, Long Tall Shorty, Urban Dogs)

DON HARPER SEXTET
58   Pye Jazz 7NJ 2024   Hi-Diddle-Fiddle/It's The Bluest Kind Of Blues 5

DON HARPER ORCHESTRA
68   Columbia DB 8519   "World Of Sport" March/England 88 6
71   Columbia DB 8843   "World Of Sport" March/England 88 (reissue) 5
73   Columbia DB 9023   World Of Sport/"Dr. Who" Theme (as Don Harper's Homo Electronicus). 25
(see also Electricians)

JANICE HARPER
57   HMV POP 376   Bon Voyage/Tell Me That You Love Me Tonight 6
58   Capitol CL 14899   Devotion/In Time 6
59   Capitol CL 14977   I Was Hoping You'd Ask Me/I'm Making Love To You 6
59   Capitol CL 15026   Let Me Call You Sweetheart/Just Whistle 6
59   Capitol CL 15026   Let Me Call You Sweetheart/Just Whistle (78) 10
60   Capitol CL 15159   Only Once/Love Me Now, Love Me Never 6
59   Capitol T 1195   WITH FEELING (LP) 15

JESSIE HARPER
92   Kissing Spell KSLP 9203   GUITAR ABSOLUTION IN THE SHADE OF A MIDNIGHT SUN
                        (LP, reissue of acetate-only album) 20
(see also Human Instinct)

JOE 'HARMONICA' HARPER
58   MGM MGM 983   Lazy Train/Her Lips Were Like Velvet. 6
58   MGM MGM 983   Lazy Train/Her Lips Were Like Velvet (78) 8

MIKE HARPER
70   Concord CON 026   You've Got Too Much Going For You/This Time 12
76   RCA RCA 2719   Rip Off/I'm Crying 5

ROY HARPER
SINGLES
66   Strike JH 304   Take Me Into Your Eyes/Pretty Baby (some in wraparound p/s) 35/20
67   CBS 203001   Midspring Dithering/Zengem 18
68   CBS 3371   Life Goes By/Nobody's Got Any Money In The Summer 15
72   Harvest HAR 5059   Bank Of The Dead (Valerie's Song)/Little Lady (some in p/s) 8/5
74   Harvest HAR 5080   (Don't You Think We're) Forever/Male Chauvinist Pig Blues. 5
74   Harvest HAR 5089   Home (live)/Home (studio). 5
75   Harvest HAR 5096   When An Old Cricketer Leaves The Crease/Hallucinating Light
                        (Acoustic Version) (p/s) 5
75   Harvest HAR 5102   Grown-Ups Are Just Silly Children/Referendum (Legend). 5
75   EMI PSR 407   Referendum/Another Day (live)/Tom Tiddler's Ground (live)
                        (promo only) 6
77   Harvest HAR 5120   One Of Those Days In England/Watford Gap (p/s) 5

ROY HARPER

77	Harvest HAR 5140	Sail Away/Cherishing The Lonesome (as Roy Harper's Black Sheep) 7
78	Harvest HAR 5160	When An Old Cricketer Leaves The Crease/Home (studio) (p/s) 5
80	Harvest HAR 5203	Playing Games/First Thing In The Morning (p/s) 6
80	Harvest HAR 5207	Short And Sweet/Water Sports (live)/Unknown Soldier (live) (p/s) 6
82	Public PUBS 1001	No One Gets Out Here Alive/Casualty (live) (p/s) 5
83	Public PUBS 1002	I Still Care/Goodbye Ladybird (p/s) 6
85	B. Banquet BEG 131	Elizabeth (Short Version)/Advertisement (Short Version) (p/s). 6
85	B. Banquet BEG 131T	Elizabeth/Advertisement/I Hate The White Man (live) (12", p/s) 8
88	EMI EM 46	Laughing Inside/Laughing Inside (Acoustic Version) (p/s). 5

ORIGINAL ALBUMS

66	Strike JHL 105	SOPHISTICATED BEGGAR (LP). 250
67	CBS (S)BPG 63184	COME OUT FIGHTING GHENGIS SMITH (LP, mono/stereo). 25/20
69	Liberty LBL/LBS 83231	FOLKJOKEOPUS (LP, mono/stereo). 30/25
69	Harvest SHVL 766	FLAT, BAROQUE AND BERSERK (LP, gatefold sleeve; some with "H. Ash" label credit) 18
71	Harvest SHVL 789	STORMCOCK (LP, gatefold sleeve with lyric inner) 18
73	Harvest SHVL 808	LIFEMASK (LP, foldout 'door' sleeve, with insert) 18
74	Harvest SHSP 4027	VALENTINE (LP, initially with lyric booklet) 22/15
74	Harvest SHDW 405	FLASHES FROM THE ARCHIVES OF OBLIVION (2-LP, gatefold sleeve) 18
75	Harvest SHSP 4046	HQ (LP, with lyric inner sleeve) 15
77	Harvest SHSP 4060	BULLINAMINGVASE (LP, with inner sleeve & "Watford Gap"; some with 7", "Referendum"/"Another Day" (live)/"Tom Tiddler's Ground" [PSR 407]) 18/12
77	Harvest SHSP 4060	BULLINAMINGVASE (LP, 2nd pressing with "Breakfast With You") 15
77	Harvest SHSP 4077	COMMERCIAL BREAK (LP, unreleased; test pressing with proof sleeve). 200
78	Harvest SHSM 2025	HARPER 1970-1975 (LP) 12
78	Harvest	HARPER 1970-1975 (6-LP box set) 125
80	Harvest SHVL 820	THE UNKNOWN SOLDIER (LP, with inner sleeve). 12
82	Public PUBLP 5001	WORK OF HEART (LP, with inner sleeve) 12
82	Public TC PUBLP 5001	WORK OF HEART (cassette on 'real time' high quality tape, different sleeve, 250 only). 12
84	Hard Up PUB 5002	BORN IN CAPTIVITY (LP, 880 only) 35
86	Awareness AWL 1002	WORK OF HEART (cassette, different sleeve, 250 only on 'real time' quality tape). 12
92	Hard Up HU 2	BORN IN CAPTIVITY II (LIVE) (cassette) 15
93	Hard Up HUCD 003	FLAT, BAROQUE & BERSERK (CD, in box with 40-page booklet & poster, signed). 20

REISSUES

70	Young Blood SSYB 7	RETURN OF THE SOPHISTICATED BEGGAR (LP, with "Hup Hup Spiral" closed run-out groove, different sleeve) 20
73	Birth RAB 3	RETURN OF THE SOPHISTICATED BEGGAR (LP, 2nd reissue, with "Hup Hup Spiral" closed run-out groove, different sleeve). 15
75	Sunset SLS 50373	FOLKJOKEOPUS (LP) 12
77	Big Ben BBX 502	THE SOPHISTICATED BEGGAR (LP, different rear sleeve) 12
77	Embassy EMB 31544	THE EARLY YEARS (LP, reissue of "Come Out Fighting Ghengis Smith", different sleeve) 12
85	Awareness AWL 1001	BORN IN CAPTIVITY (LP, different rear sleeve) 12
86	Awareness AWL 1002	WORK OF HEART (LP, different sleeve with inner; 1st 1,000 with 2 x 7": "No One Gets Out Here Alive"/"Casualty (live)" [PUBS 1001] & "Still Care"/ "Goodbye Ladybird" [PUBS 1002]; later copies with just PUBS 1001) 15/12

(see also Rory Phare, Per Yarroh, Harry Rope)

MINT VALUE £

TIM HARPER
95	Peacefrog PF 047	I Feel A Groove (12", plain sleeve)	10

HARPER'S BIZARRE
67	Warner Bros WB 5890	59th Street Bridge Song (Feelin' Groovy)/Lost My Love Today	7
67	Warner Bros WB 7528	Come To The Sunshine/The Debutante's Ball	6
67	Warner Bros WB 7063	Anything Goes/Malibu U	6
67	Warner Bros WB 7090	Chattanooga Choo Choo/Hey You In The Crowd	6
68	Warner Bros WB 7172	Cotton Candy Sandman (Sandman's Coming)/Virginia City	6
68	Warner Bros WB 7223	Battle Of New Orleans/Green Apple Tree	6
69	Warner Bros WB 7238	I Love You, Alice B. Toklas!/Look To The Rainbow	6
70	Warner Bros WB 7388	Anything Goes/Virginia City	5
67	Warner Bros W 1693	FEELIN' GROOVY (LP)	18
67	Warner Bros W 1716	ANYTHING GOES (LP)	15
68	Warner Bros W(S) 1739	THE SECRET LIFE OF HARPER'S BIZARRE (LP)	15

SLIM HARPO
61	Pye International 7N 25098	Rainin' In My Heart/Don't Start Cryin' Now	12
63	Pye International 7N 25220	Don't Start Cryin' Now/Rainin' In My Heart	15
66	Stateside SS 491	Baby Scratch My Back/I'm Gonna Miss You (Like The Devil)	15
66	Stateside SS 527	Shake Your Hips/Midnight Blues	20
66	Stateside SS 557	I'm A King Bee/I Got Love If You Want It	18
67	Stateside SS 581	I'm Your Breadmaker Baby/Loving You (The Way I Do)	18
67	President PT 164	I'm Gonna Keep What I've Got/I've Got To Be With You Tonight	6
68	Liberty LBF 15176	Something Inside Me/PAPPA LIGHTFOOT: Wine Whisky And Women	15
68	President PT 187	Tip On In (Parts 1 & 2)	6
70	Blue Horizon 57-3175	Folsom Prison Blues/Mutual Friend	20
65	Stateside SL 10135	A LONG DRINK OF THE BLUES (LP, with Lightnin' Slim)	50
68	President PTL 1017	TIP ON IN (LP)	20
70	Blue Horizon 7-63854	HE KNEW THE BLUES (LP)	70
72	Blue Horizon 2431 013	TRIGGER FINGER (LP)	90
76	Flyright LP 520	BLUES HANGOVER (LP)	15
78	Sonet SNTF 769	HE KNEW THE BLUES (LP)	15
80	Flyright FLY 558	GOT LOVE IF YOU WANT IT (LP)	12

(see also Lightnin' Slim)

GEORGE HARRASSMENT & HOMOSEXUALS
80s	Black Noise 12 NO 6	MASAI SLEEP WALKING (LP)	10

(see also Homosexuals)

HARRIER
84	Black Horse HARR 1T	OUT ON THE STREET EP (12", p/s)	12

DERRICK HARRIOT(T) (& CRYSTALITES)
62	Blue Beat BB 131	I Care/Have Faith In Me (as Derrick Harriott & Vagabonds)	12
63	Blue Beat BB 178	Be True/I Won't Cry	12
64	Island WI 157	What Can I Do (The Wedding)/Leona	12
65	Island WI 170	I Am Only Human (as Derak Harriott)/ROY PANTON: Good Man	18
65	Island WI 237	My Three Loves/The Jerk	15
65	Island WI 245	Together/Mama Didn't Lie	12
65	Ska Beat JB 199	Monkey Ska/Derrick!	15
66	Doctor Bird DB 1002	Jon Tom/AUDREY WILLIAMS: Solas Market	12
67	Island WI 3063	The Loser/Bless You	25
67	Island WI 3064	Happy Times/You My Everything	20
67	Island WI 3077	Walk The Streets/BOBBY ELLIS: Step Softly (B-side with Desmond Miles Seven)	35
67	Island WI 3089	Solomon/BOBBY ELLIS: The Emperor (B-side with Desmond Miles Seven)	18
68	Island WI 3135	Do I Worry?/BOBBY ELLIS & CRYSTALITES: Shuntin'	18
68	Island WI 3147	Born To Love You/IKE & CRYSTALITES: Alfred Hitchcock	18
68	Island WI 3153	Tang Tang Festival Song/CRYSTALITES: James Ray	18
69	Big Shot BI 505	Standing In/Bumble Bee	10
69	Big Shot BI 511	Another Lonely Night/Been So Long	10
70	Songbird SB 1013	Riding For A Fall/I'm Not Begging	8
70	Songbird SB 1014	Sitting On Top/You Were Meant For Me	8
70	Songbird SB 1022	Go Bye Bye/Laugh It Off	8
70	Songbird SB 1028	Message From A Black Man/(Version II)	7
70	Songbird SB 1029	Psychedelic Train (w/ Chosen Few)/Psychedelic Train (Pt. 2) (with Crystalites)	7
70	Songbird SB 1033	No Man Is An Island/CRYSTALITES: No Man Is An Island Part 2	8
70	Songbird SB 1042	Groovy Situation/CRYSTALITES: The Crystal Groove	7
70	Songbird SB 1043	Psychedelic Train Chapter Three/CRYSTALITES: Groovy Situation Version II	12
71	Songbird SB 1052	Candy/CRYSTALITES: Candy Version	12
71	Songbird SB 1055	Lollipop Girl/CRYSTALITES: Lollipop Version	10
71	Songbird SB 1063	Medley In 5 (Parts 1 & 2)	6
72	Songbird SB 1065	Have You Seen Her/CRYSTALITES: Have You Seen Her — Version	6
72	Songbird SB 1068	Over The River/River (Version)	6
72	Songbird SB 1071	Since I Lost My Baby/Baby (Version)	6
72	Songbird SB 1078	Being In Love/Love (Version)	5
72	Songbird SB 1084	Don't Rock The Boat/Rock (Version)	6
73	Explosion EX 2071	Let Me Down Easy/Let Me Down Easy — Version	6
74	Harry J. HJ 6675	Some Guys Have All The Luck/Some Guys Have All The Luck — Version	5
65	Island ILP 928	THE BEST OF DERRICK HARRIOTT (LP)	120
67	Island ILP 955	DERRICK HARRIOTT'S ROCKSTEADY PARTY (LP, actually v/a LP)	140
68	Island ILP 983	THE BEST OF VOLUME TWO (LP, as Derrick Harriott & Crystalites)	100
69	Pama SECO 13	SINGS JAMAICA REGGAE (LP)	60
70	Trojan TTL 43	THE BEST OF DERRICK HARRIOTT (LP)	30
70	Trojan TTL 54	ROCKSTEADY PARTY (LP)	40
70	Trojan TBL 114	THE UNDERTAKER (LP, as Derrick Harriott & Crystalites)	25
70	Trojan TBL 141	PSYCHEDELIC TRAIN (LP, as Derrick Harriott & Crystalites)	25

JOE HARRIOTT

50s	Jazz Today JTE 106	WITH STRINGS (EP)	18
50s	Pye Jazz NJE 1003	NO STRINGS (EP)	50
50s	Melodisc EPM7 117	COOL JAZZ WITH JOE (EP)	20
57	Columbia SEG 7665	JOE HARRIOTT QUARTET (EP)	100
59	Columbia SEG 7939	BLUE HARRIOTT (EP)	30
61	Columbia SEG 8070	A GUY CALLED JOE (EP)	25
60	Jazzland JLP 49	FREE FORM (LP)	50
62	Columbia 33SX 1477	ABSTRACT (LP)	125
63	Columbia 33SX 1627	MOVEMENT (LP)	250
64	Columbia 33SX 1692	HIGH SPIRITS (LP)	100
66	Columbia S(C)X 6025	DOUBLE QUINTET (LP, with John Mayer)	25
67	Melodisc SLP 12150	SWINGS HIGH (LP)	90
67	Columbia S(C) 6122	INDO-JAZZ FUSIONS (LP, with John Mayer)	35
68	Columbia S(C)X 6215	INDO-JAZZ FUSIONS II (LP, with John Mayer)	60
68	Columbia S(C)X 6249	PERSONAL PORTRAIT (LP)	60
69	Columbia SCX 6354	HUM-DONO (LP)	125
73	One Up OU 2011	MEMORIAL 1973 (LP)	50

(see also Tony Kinsey Trio & Joe Harriott, John Mayer, Michael Garrick)

JOE HARRIOTT/DON RENDELL QUARTET

57	MGM MGM-EP 615	JAZZ BRITANNIA (EP, 2 tracks each)	20

(see also Don Rendell)

ANITA HARRIS

61	Parlophone R 4830	I Haven't Got You/Mr One And Only	6
64	Vocalion V 9223	Lies/Don't Think About Love	5
65	Decca F 12082	Willingly/At Last Love	7
65	Pye 7N 15868	Trains And Boats And Planes/Upside Down	7
65	Pye 7N 15894	I Don't Know Anymore/When I Look At You	5
65	Pye 7N 15971	London Life/I Run To Hide	5
66	Pye 7N 17069	Something Must Be Done/Funny Kind Of Feeling	10
66	CBS 2724	Just Loving You/Butterfly With Coloured Wings	5
67	CBS 2991	The Playground/B.A.D. For Me	15
68	CBS 3211	Anniversary Waltz/Old Queenie Cole	5
67	Pye NEP 24288	ANITA HARRIS (EP)	10
67	CBS EP 6359	NURSERY RHYMES FOR OUR TIMES (EP)	8

(see also Brello Cabal)

ARTIE HARRIS & HIS BOYS

63	Oriole CB 1816	Go Go Gaudeamus/Mexicana	7

BETTY HARRIS

63	London HL 9796	Cry To Me/I'll Be A Liar	12
65	Stateside SS 475	What A Sad Feeling/I'm Evil Tonight	15
67	Stateside SS 2045	Nearer To You/12 Red Roses	15
69	Action ACT 4535	Ride Your Pony/Trouble With My Lover	10
69	Action ACLP 6007	SOUL PERFECTION (LP)	40

(see also Betty Harris & Lee Dorsey)

BRENDA JO HARRIS

69	Roulette RO 503	I Can Remember/Play With Fire	6

DON 'SUGARCANE' HARRIS

70	BASF MPS 68027	KEEP ON DRIVING (LP)	12
70	BASF MPS 68028	FIDDLER ON THE ROCK (LP)	12
72	BASF MPS 68029	GOT THE BLUES (LP)	12
73	BASF MPS 68030	CUPFUL OF DREAMS (LP)	12

(see also Don & Dewey)

EDDIE HARRIS

69	Atlantic 584 218	Listen Here/Theme — In Search Of A Movie	5
69	Atlantic 584 232	It's Crazy/Live Right Now (unissued)	
74	Atlantic K 10513	Is It In?/Funkarama	5
75	Atlantic K 10561	I Need Some Money/Don't Want Nobody	5
76	Atlantic K 10741	Get On Up And Dance/Why Must We Part	5
62	Stateside SL 10009	BREAKFAST AT TIFFANY'S (LP)	15
63	Stateside SL 10018	MIGHTY LIKE A ROSE (LP)	15
63	Stateside SL 10049	GOES TO THE MOVIES (LP)	15
69	Atlantic 588 177	SILVER CYCLES (LP)	12
71	Atlantic 2466 013	FREE SPEECH (LP)	12
73	Atlantic K 40123	PLUG ME IN (LP)	12
73	Atlantic K 40482	SINGS THE BLUES (LP)	12
73	Atlantic K 40220	THE ELECTRIFYING EDDIE HARRIS (LP)	12
74	Atlantic K 50084	IS IT IN? (LP)	12
75	Atlantic K 50127	I NEED SOME MONEY (LP)	12

EMMYLOU HARRIS

79	Pye Special PKL 5577	THE LEGENDARY GLIDING BIRD ALBUM (LP)	10

(see also Gram Parsons)

JET HARRIS

62	Decca F 11466	Besame Mucho/Chills And Fever	6
62	Decca F 11488	Main Title Theme (from The Man With The Golden Arm)/Some People	6
64	Decca F 11841	Big Bad Bass/Rifka	8
67	Fontana TF 849	My Lady/You Don't Live Twice	12
75	SRT SRT 75355	Theme For A Fallen Idol/This Sportin' Life (initial pressing)	7

MINT VALUE £

75	SRT SRT 75355	Theme/This Sportin' Life (later pressing with shortened A-side title)	5
78	SRT SRT 77389	Guitar Man/Theme	6
62	Decca DFE 8502	JET HARRIS (EP)	25
78	Ellie Jay EJSP 8622	INSIDE JET HARRIS — THE LAST CONCERT (LP, 2,500 only)	20
70s	Q LPMM 1038	ANNIVERSARY ALBUM (LP)	20

(see also Shadows, Jet Harris & Tony Meehan, Keith Meehan, Peter Rawes)

JET HARRIS & TONY MEEHAN

63	Decca F 11563	Diamonds/Footstomp	5
63	Decca F 11644	Scarlett O'Hara/(Doing The) Hully Gully	5
63	Decca F 11710	Applejack/The Tall Texan	6
80	Decca F 13892	Diamonds/Scarlett O'Hara/Applejack/Man With The Golden Arm (p/s)	5
63	Decca DFE 7099	DIAMONDS (EP, export issue, existence unconfirmed)	75+
63	Decca DFE 8528	JET AND TONY (EP)	20
76	Decca REM 1	REMEMBERING (LP)	12

(see also Shadows, Jet Harris, Tony Meehan, Vipers Skiffle Group)

JOHNNY HARRIS

65	Mercury MF 942	Mynahg Hop/Here Comes The Boot	5
69	Warner Bros WB 8000	Footprints On The Moon/Lulu's Theme	6
70	Warner Bros WB 8016	Fragment Of Fear/Stepping Stones	10
70	Warner Bros WS 3002	MOVEMENTS (LP)	30
72	Warner Bros K 46054	MOVEMENTS (LP, reissue)	25
73	Warner Bros K 46187	ALL TO BRING YOU MORNING (LP)	10

JUNE HARRIS

| 65 | CBS 201774 | Over And Over Again/Stand Back | 10 |

MAJOR HARRIS

| 75 | Atlantic K 50117 | MY WAY (LP) | 12 |
| 76 | Atlantic K 50219 | JEALOUSY (LP) | 12 |

MAX HARRIS

| 60 | Fontana H 282 | Gurney Slade/Hat And Cane | 6 |
| 69 | Pye 7N 17730 | Baby Love Theme/Robert's Theme | 10 |

PAT HARRIS & BLACKJACKS

| 63 | Pye 7N 15567 | The Hippy Hippy Shake/You Gotta See Your Mama Ev'ry Night | 12 |

(see also Blackjacks)

PAUL HARRIS

| 70 | Intl. Broadcasters Society | HISTORY OF OFFSHORE RADIO (LP, radio-only) | 12 |

PHIL HARRIS

54	HMV 7M 199	I Know An Old Lady/Take Your Girlie To The Movies	8
54	HMV 7M 231	I Guess I'll Have To Change My Plan/The Persian Kitten	8
55	HMV 7M 289	I Wouldn't Touch You With A Ten-Foot Pole/There's A Lot More	8
70	Buena Vista DF 478	Thomas O'Malley Cat/SCATMAN CROTHERS: Everybody Wants To Be A Cat	5
59	RCA Camden CDN 124	THAT'S WHAT I LIKE ABOUT THE SOUTH (LP)	12

RICHARD HARRIS

68	RCA RCA 1699	MacArthur Park/Paper Chase	5
68	Stateside SS 8001	The Yard Went On Forever/Lucky Me	5
70	Stateside SS 8054	Ballad Of 'A Man Called Horse'/The Morning Of The Mourning Of Another Kennedy	5
68	RCA Victor RD/SF 7947	A TRAMP SHINING (LP)	18
68	Stateside (S)SL 5001	THE YARD WENT ON FOREVER (LP)	15
70	Stateside SSL 5019	A TRAMP SHINING (LP, reissue)	12

ROLF HARRIS

60	Columbia DB 4483	Tie Me Kangaroo Down, Sport/Nick Teen And Al K. Hall	5
60	Columbia DB 4556	Tame Eagle/Uncomfortable Yogi	6
62	Columbia DB 4888	Sun Arise/Someone's Pinched Me Winkles	6
64	Columbia DB 7349	Ringo For President/Head Hunter	6
65	Columbia DB 7669	War Canoe/Linda	5
66	Columbia DB 8014	Hev Yew Gotta Loight Boy/Animals Pop Party	5
68	Columbia DB 8475	Have A Beer/The Bloke Who Invented Beer	5
66	Columbia SEG 8531	ROLF HARRIS FAVOURITES (EP)	10

RONNIE HARRIS (& CORONETS)

54	Columbia SCM 5138	Hold My Hand/No One Can Change Destiny	7
54	Columbia SCM 5139	I Love Paris/I Still Believe	7
55	Columbia SCM 5159	Don't Go To Strangers/Surprisingly (as Ronnie Harris & Coronets)	7
55	Columbia SCM 5176	Stranger In Paradise/I Wonder	10
56	Columbia SCM 5242	I've Changed My Mind A Thousand Times/Come To Me (with Coronets)	7
56	Columbia DB 3836	That's Right/A House With Love In It	5
57	Columbia DB 3877	Armen's Theme (Yesterday And You)/Dancing Chandelier	5
57	Columbia DB 3934	Dear To Me/It's Not For Me To Say (B-side with Russ Conway)	5

(see also Coronets, Ruby Murray, Ray Burns, Russ Conway)

ROY HARRIS

| 72 | Topic 12TS 217 | THE BITTER AND THE SWEET (LP, blue label) | 15 |
| 75 | Topic 12TS 256 | CHAMPIONS OF FOLLY (LP) | 12 |

SHAKEY JAKE HARRIS

| 69 | Liberty LBS 83217 | FURTHER ON UP THE ROAD (LP) | 20 |
| 73 | Polydor 2391 015 | THE DEVIL'S HARMONICA (LP) | 20 |

SIMON HARRIS

| 88 | ffrr FFRX 4 | Bass (How Low Can You Go)/The Playback (12", p/s) | 10 |

SUE HARRIS

| 78 | Free Reed FRR 020 | HAMMERS AND TONGUES (LP) | 12 |

THURSTON HARRIS (& SHARPS)

57	Vogue V 9092	Little Bitty Pretty One/I Hope You Won't Hold It Against Me (with Sharps) 100
57	Vogue V 9092	Little Bitty Pretty One/I Hope You Won't Hold It Against Me (with Sharps) (78). . . 60
58	Vogue V 9098	Do What You Did/I'm Asking Forgiveness (as Thurston Harris & Sharps) 275
58	Vogue V 9098	Do What You Did/I'm Asking Forgiveness (78) 70
58	Vogue V 9108	Be Baba Leba/I'm Out To Getcha 325
58	Vogue V 9108	Be Baba Leba/I'm Out To Getcha (78) 90
58	Vogue V 9122	Smokey Joe's/Only One Love Is Blessed 100
58	Vogue V 9122	Smokey Joe's/Only One Love Is Blessed (78). 90
58	Vogue V 9127	Tears From My Heart/Over Somebody Else's Shoulder 85
58	Vogue V 9127	Tears From My Heart/Over Somebody Else's Shoulder (78). 70
59	Vogue V 9139	Purple Stew (as Thurston Harris & Masters)/I Hear A Rhapsody 90
59	Vogue V 9139	Purple Stew (as Thurston Harris & Masters)/I Hear A Rhapsody (78) 100
59	Vogue V 9144	You Don't Know How Much I Love You/In The Bottom Of My Heart. 85
59	Vogue V 9144	You Don't Know How Much I Love You/In The Bottom Of My Heart (78) 100
59	Vogue V 9146	Hey Little Girl/My Love Will Last 100
59	Vogue V 9146	Hey Little Girl/My Love Will Last (78). 120
59	Vogue V 9149	Runk Bunk/Bless Your Heart 165
59	Vogue V 9149	Runk Bunk/Bless Your Heart (78) 120
59	Vogue V 9151	Slip-Slop/Paradise Hill 140
59	Vogue V 9151	Slip-Slop/Paradise Hill (78) 140
66	Sue WI 4016	Little Bitty Pretty One/I Hope You Won't Hold It Against Me (reissue) 22

(see also Sharps)

WEE WILLIE HARRIS

57	Decca F 10970	Rockin' At The Two 'I's/Back To School Again. 30
57	Decca F 10970	Rockin' At The Two 'I's/Back To School Again (78) 30
58	Decca F 10980	Love Bug Crawl/Rosie Lee. 35
58	Decca F 10980	Love Bug Crawl/Rosie Lee (78) 30
58	Decca F 11044	Got A Match/No Chemise, Please!. 30
58	Decca F 11044	Got A Match/No Chemise, Please! (78) 30
60	Decca F 11217	Wild One/Little Bitty Girl 15
63	HMV POP 1198	You Must Be Joking/Better To Have Loved 10
66	Parlophone R 5504	Someone's In The Kitchen With Diana/Walk With Peter And Paul
		(some A-sides list 'Dina'). 10
66	Polydor 56140	Listen To The River Roll Along/Try Moving Baby (writing in black or white) 10
74	Decca F 13516	Together/Rock'n'Roll Jamboree 5
58	Decca DFE 6465	ROCKING WITH WEE WILLIE (EP) 125

WYNONIE 'MR BLUES' HARRIS

51	Vogue V 2006	All She Wants To Do Is Rock/Drinkin' Wine Spo-Dee-O-Dee (78) 35
52	Vogue V 2111	Luscious Woman/Lovin' Machine (78) 40
52	Vogue V 2127	Bloodshot Eyes/Lollipop Mama (78) 35
52	Vogue V 2128	Just Like Two Drops Of Water/Good Mornin' Judge (78) 45
52	Vogue V 2133	Night Train/Do It Again Please (78) 40
52	Vogue V 2134	Rock, Mr. Blues/Put It Back (78). 40
52	Vogue V 2144	Teardrops From My Eyes/Keep On Churnin' (Till The Butter Comes) (78) 40
52	Vogue V 2166	I Like My Baby's Pudding/Adam Come And Get Your Rib (78). 40
56	Vogue V 2127	Bloodshot Eyes/Lollipop Mama (triangular centre) 90
56	Vogue V 2127	Bloodshot Eyes/Lollipop Mama (round centre) 50
56	Vogue EPV 1103	WYNONIE 'MISTER BLUES' HARRIS (EP) 150
61	Blue Beat BBEP 301	BATTLE OF THE BLUES (EP). 80

WYNONIE HARRIS/EDDIE 'CLEANHEAD' VINSON

72	Polydor 2343 048	JUMP BLUES (LP) 15

(see also Tiny Bradshaw/Wynonie Harris, Eddie 'Cleanhead' Vinson)

HARRIS SISTERS

55	Capitol CL 14232	Kissin' Bug/We've Been Walkin' All Night 15
55	Capitol CL 14232	Kissin' Bug/We've Been Walkin' All Night (78) 10

DANNY HARRISON

62	Starlite ST45 77	No One To Love Me/All The World is Lonely 6
62	Starlite ST45 91	Broken Love Affair/Have I Wasted My Life 6
63	Starlite ST45 108	Have You Ever Been Lonely/Mary Ann I'm Lonesome 6
65	Coral Q 72479	Speak Of The Devil/I'm A Rollin' Stone 12
62	Starlite STEP 23	INTRODUCING DANNY HARRISON (EP) 18

EARL HARRISON

67	London HL 10121	Humphrey Stomp/Can You Forgive Me 35

GEORGE HARRISON

SINGLES

71	Apple R 5884	My Sweet Lord/What Is Life (colour 'head' p/s). 10
71	Apple R 5912	Bangla-Desh/Deep Blue (p/s [beware of new-looking counterfeits!]). 75
75	Apple R 6001	Dark Horse/I Don't Care Anymore (unissued)
75	Apple R 6001	Dark Horse/Hari's On Tour (Express) (some in lyric p/s) 12/5
75	Apple R 6007	You/World Of Stone (p/s) 10
76	Apple R 6012	This Guitar (Can't Keep From Crying)/Maya Love (no p/s) 15
76	Apple R 5884	My Sweet Lord/What Is Life (reissue, black & white 'gnome' p/s) 15
76	Dark Horse K 16856	This Song/Learning How To Love You (issued with U.S. p/s) 10
79	Dark Horse K 17327	Blow Away/Soft Touch (p/s) 6
79	Dark Horse K 17423	Faster/Your Love Is Forever (with charity stickered plain white die-cut sleeve) . . 15
79	Dark Horse K 17423	Faster/Your Love Is Forever (picture disc, stickered PVC sleeve with insert) 20
81	Dark Horse K 17837DJ	Teardrops (Edited Version)/Save The World (DJ promo only, no p/s) 15
81	Dark Horse K 17837	Teardrops/Save The World (p/s). 5
86	Ganga Publishing B.V.	Shanghai Surprise (with Vicki Brown) (unreleased, 1-sided promo only;
		no catalogue number, matrix: SHANGHAI 1). 250
87	Dark Horse W 8178	Got My Mind Set On You/Lay His Head (p/s, red or green label) 5/10
87	Dark Horse W 8178B	Got My Mind Set On You/Lay His Head (box set with 2 postcards) 6

George HARRISON

87	Dark Horse W 8178T	Got My Mind Set On You (Extended Version)/Got My Mind Set On You (Single Version)/Lay His Head (12", p/s with poster) 15
87	Dark Horse W 8178TP	Got My Mind Set On You (Extended Version)/Got My Mind Set On You (Single Version)/Lay His Head (12", picture disc) 20
88	Dark Horse W 8131B	When We Was Fab/Zig Zag (box set with fold-out poster & cut-out) 6
88	Dark Horse W 8131TP	When We Was Fab (Unextended Version)/Zig Zag/That's The Way It Goes (Remix)/When We Was Fab (Reverse End) (12", picture disc) 15
88	Dark Horse W 8131CD	When We Was Fab (Unextended Version)/Zig Zag/That's The Way It Goes (Remix)/When We Was Fab (Reverse End) (3" CD with 5" adaptor, 5" case) 10
88	Dark Horse W 7913CD	This Is Love/Breath Away From Heaven/All Those Years Ago/Hong Kong Blues (3" CD with adaptor, 5" case) 12
89	Dark Horse W 2696	Cheer Down/Poor Little Girl (p/s) 10
89	Dark Horse W 2696T	Cheer Down/Poor Little Girl/Crackerbox Palace (12", p/s) 15
89	Dark Horse W 2696CD	Cheer Down/Poor Little Girl/Crackerbox Palace (3" CD, gatefold card sleeve) 25
88	Genesis SGH 777	SONGS BY GEORGE HARRISON (Limited Edition) (EP, 33rpm, issued with limited edition book Songs By George Harrison) 275
88	Genesis SGHCD 777	SONGS BY GEORGE HARRISON (CD EP, issued with limited edition book). . . . 275
92	Genesis SGH 778	SONGS BY GEORGE HARRISON VOL. 2 (EP, with limited edition book Songs By George Harrison Vol. 2) 250
92	Genesis SGHCD 778	SONGS BY GEORGE HARRISON VOL. 2 (CD EP, with limited edition book). . . . 250

ALBUMS

68	Apple (S)APCOR 1	WONDERWALL MUSIC (LP, soundtrack; with insert, black inner sleeve, mono/stereo) 60/30
69	Zapple ZAPPLE 02	ELECTRONIC SOUND (LP, with inner sleeve) 70
71	Apple STCH 639	ALL THINGS MUST PASS (3-LP box set with poster & lyric inner sleeves; initial batch in U.K. box, later in U.S. box) 25/20
72	Apple STCX 3385	THE CONCERT FOR BANGLA DESH (3-LP box set, with booklet, featuring Bob Dylan) 22
92	Apple SAPCOR 1	WONDERWALL MUSIC (LP, reissue, gatefold sleeve with inner sleeve) 12

(see also Beatles, Traveling Wilburys, Billy Connolly & Chris Tummings, Sylvia Griffin)

KATHLEEN HARRISON

| 66 | Columbia DB 7871 | Mrs. Thursday/Call Round Any Old Time. . . . . 5 |

MIKE HARRISON

| 71 | Island ILPS 9170 | MIKE HARRISON (LP) . . . . 15 |
| 72 | Island ILPS 9209 | SMOKESTACK LIGHTNING (LP) . . . . 15 |

(see also Spirit)

NEIL HARRISON

| 74 | Deram SML 1115 | ALL DRESSED UP AND NOWHERE TO GO (LP) . . . . 12 |

(see also Driftwood)

NOEL HARRISON

65	Decca F 12001	Trees/To Ramona 6
66	Decca F 12314	A Young Girl Of Sixteen/Tomorrow Is My Turn 5
66	Decca F 12345	It's All Over Now Baby Blue/Much As I Love You 5
67	Reprise RS 20615	Suzanne/Life Is A Dream 6
68	Reprise RS 20758	Windmills Of Your Mind/Leitch On The Beach. 6
69	Decca F 12918	Love Minus Zero/Just Can't Wait 5
57	HMV 7EG 8383	NOEL HARRISON (EP) 15
65	Decca DFE 8616	NOEL HARRISON (EP) 8
65	Decca DFE 8639	TO RAMONA (EP). 12
60	Philips BBL 7399	AT THE BLUE ANGEL (LP). 15
69	Reprise RSLP 6321	THE GREAT ELECTRIC EXPERIMENT IS OVER (LP) 12

REGGIE HARRISON

| 63 | Cameo Parkway P 863 | A Lonely Piano/HIPPIES: Memory Lane . . . . 15 |

WILBERT HARRISON

59	Top Rank JAR 132	Kansas City/Listen My Darling 12
59	Top Rank JAR 132	Kansas City/Listen My Darling (78) 70
62	Island WI 031	I'm Broke/Off To School 12
65	Sue WI 363	Let's Stick Together/Kansas City Twist 15
70	London HL 10307	Let's Work Together/Stagger Lee 10
73	Action ACT 4613	Get It While You Can/Amen 5
70	London HA/SH 8415	LET'S WORK TOGETHER (LP) 25

WILBERT HARRISON/BABY WASHINGTON

| 71 | Joy JOYS 191 | BATTLE OF THE GIANTS (LP, 1 side each) . . . . 15 |

(see also Baby Washington)

YVONNE HARRISON

| 67 | Caltone TONE 102 | The Chase/Take My Hand . . . . 10 |

DEBBIE/DEBORAH HARRY

89	Chrysalis CHSCD 3369	I Want That Man (12 Inch Remix)/(7" Version)/(Instrumental)/Bike Boy (CD) . . . 8
89	Chrysalis CHSCD 3452	Brite Side/In Love With Love/Bugeye (CD) 8
89	Chrysalis CHSCCD 3452	Brite Side (Remix)/French Kissin' In The USA/In Love With Love/Bugeye (CD). . . . 8
93	Chrysalis TC-CHS 4900	I Can See Clearly/Standing In My Way (B-side with Joey Ramone) (cassette) 7
99	Chrysalis CDMAN 2000	I Want That Man (radio edit)/(Almighty Definitive Mix)/D-Bop Vocal Mix) (CD, card p/s, promo only) 15

(see also Wind In The Willows, Blondie, New York Blondes)

HARRY & RADCLIFFE

| 69 | Camel CA 26 | History/Just Be Alone . . . . 7 |
| 69 | Punch PH 8 | History/Just Be Alone . . . . 6 |

MINT VALUE £

HARRY J. ALL STARS

69	Harry J. TR 675	Liquidator/GLEN & DAVE: La La Always Stay (green or white label) .... each 5	
70	Harry J. HJ 6601	The Big Three/Lavender (B-side actually "Lavender Blue" by Lloyd Robinson) . . . 6	
70	Harry J. HJ 6608	Reach For The Sky/Interrogator. 6	
70	Harry J. HJ 6621	Return Of The Liquidator (actually "Tons Of Gold" by Val Bennett)/All Day. 10	
72	Harry J. HJ 6641	Down Side Up/Down Side Up — Version. 6	
73	Explosion EX 2073	Chirpy Chirpy Cheep Cheep/Chirpy Chirpy (Instrumental) 5	
73	Blue Mountain BM 1028	U.F.O./Reggae With The Birds 5	
70	Trojan TBL 104	THE LIQUIDATOR (LP) 20	

(see also Jay Boys, Bob Andy, John Holt, Lizzy)

HARSH REALITY

68	Philips PB 1710	Tobacco Ash Sunday/How Do You Feel. 8
69	Philips PB 1769	Heaven And Hell/Praying For Reprieve 10
69	Philips (S)BL 7891	HEAVEN AND HELL (LP, gatefold sleeve) 50

CAJUN HART

69	Warner Bros WB 7258	Got To Find A Way/Lover's Prayer 150

DERRY HART & HARTBEATS

59	Decca F 11138	Come On Baby/Nowhere In This World 15
59	Decca F 11138	Come On Baby/Nowhere In This World (78) 20

MICKEY HART

73	Warner Bros. K 46182	ROLLING THUNDER (LP) 20

(see also Grateful Dead, Diga Rhythm Band)

MIKE HART

70	Dandelion S 4781	Yawney Morning Song/Almost Liverpool 8 5
74	Deram DM 409	Son Son/Bad News Man 5
70	Dandelion 63756	MIKE HART BLEEDS (LP) 20
72	Dandelion 2310 211	BASHER, CHALKY, PONGO AND ME (LP, as Mike Hart & Comrades) 25

(see also Clayton Squares, Liverpool Scene)

TIM HART

79	Chrysalis CHR 2335	Overseas/Hillman Avenger (p/s) 7
79	Chrysalis CHR 1218	TIM HART (LP) 12

(see also Steeleye Span)

TIM HART & MADDY PRIOR

68	Tepee TPRM 104	FOLK SONGS OF OLDE ENGLAND VOL. 1 (LP, gatefold sleeve) 60
69	Tepee TPRM 105	FOLK SONGS OF OLDE ENGLAND VOL. 2 (LP, gatefold sleeve) 60
69	Ad-Rhythm ARPS 3	FOLK SONGS OF OLDE ENGLAND VOL. 1 (LP, reissue) 30
69	Ad-Rhythm ARPS 4	FOLK SONGS OF OLDE ENGLAND VOL. 2 (LP, reissue) 30
71	Charisma CAS 1035	SUMMER SOLSTICE (LP, gatefold sleeve) 20
76	Mooncrest CREST 12	SUMMER SOLSTICE (LP, reissue, gatefold or single sleeve). 15/10

(see also Steeleye Span, Maddy Prior, Silly Sisters)

CIARAN HARTE

81	Glass GLASS 003	Love Is Strange/Shimahero (p/s) 5

(see also Glass)

FRANK HARTE

67	Topic 12T 172	DUBLIN STREET SONGS (LP) 18
73	Topic 12T 218	THROUGH DUBLIN CITY (LP) 12

KEEF HARTLEY (BAND)

69	Deram DM 250	Leave It 'Till The Morning/Just To Cry 10
69	Deram DM 273	Waiting Around/Not Foolish, Not Wise 10
70	Deram DM 316	Roundabout (Parts 1 & 2) 8
73	Deram DM 380	Dance To The Music/You And Me. 7
69	Deram SML 1037	HALFBREED (LP, gatefold sleeve, 1st pressing has 'mono/stereo' holes on rear sleeve) 20
69	Deram SML 1054	THE BATTLE OF N.W.6 (LP, gatefold sleeve, 1st pressing has 'mono/stereo' holes on rear sleeve) 20
70	Deram SML 1071	THE TIME IS NEAR (LP, with booklet) 20
71	Deram SDL 2	OVERDOG (LP, gatefold sleeve). 20
71	Deram SDL 4	LITTLE BIG BAND (LP, gatefold sleeve) 20
72	Deram SDL 9	SEVENTY SECOND BRAVE (LP, gatefold sleeve) 20
73	Deram SDL 13	LANCASHIRE HUSTLER (LP, gatefold sleeve) 20
74	Deram DPA 3011/2	THE BEST OF (2-LP, gatefold sleeve) 15
70s	Deram SDN 30251/2	THE BATTLE OF N.W.6/THE TIME IS NEAR (2-LP, gatefold sleeve) 15

(see also Rory Storm & Hurricanes, Artwoods, John Mayall's Bluesbreakers, Miller Anderson, Dog Soldier, Henry Lowther, Wynder K. Frog)

HARVESTERS

78	SRT/CUS/135	TWELVE YEARS ON (LP) 12
80	private pressing	A COLLECTOR'S ITEM (LP). 12

HARVEY (Fuqua) & MOONGLOWS

58	London HLM 8730	Ten Commandments Of Love/Mean Old Blues 220
58	London HLM 8730	Ten Commandments Of Love/Mean Old Blues (78) 80

(see also Moonglows, Etta & Harvey)

HARVEY BOYS

57	London HLA 8397	Nothing Is Too Good For You/Marina Girl 25
57	London HLA 8397	Nothing Is Too Good For You/Marina Girl (78). 15

Alex HARVEY

(SENSATIONAL) ALEX HARVEY (BAND)

64	Polydor NH 52264	I Just Wanna Make Love To You/Let The Good Times Roll	25
64	Polydor NH 52907	Got My Mojo Working/I Ain't Worried Baby (as Alex Harvey & His Soul Band)	40
65	Polydor BM 56017	Ain't That Just Too Bad/My Kind Of Love (as Alex Harvey & His Soul Band)	30
65	Fontana TF 610	Agent 00 Soul/Go Away Baby	25
66	Fontana TF 764	Work Song/I Can Do Without Your Love	20
67	Decca F 12640	The Sunday Song/Horizon's	20
67	Decca F 12660	Maybe Some Day/Curtains For My Baby	25
69	Fontana TF 1063	Midnight Moses/Roman Wall Blues	20
72	Vertigo 6059 070	There's No Lights On The Christmas Tree Mother/They're Burning Big Louie Tonight/Harp	5
73	Vertigo 6059 075	Jungle Jenny/Buff's Bar Blues (as The Sensational Alex Harvey Band)	5
74	Vertigo 6059 098	The Faith Healer (Edit)/St. Anthony (as The Sensational Alex Harvey Band)	5
75	Vertigo ALEX 001	Delilah (live)/Soul In Chains (live) (p/s, as The Sensational Alex Harvey Band)	6
75	Vertigo ALEX 002	Gamblin' Bar Room Blues/Shake That Thing (p/s, as The Sensational Alex Harvey Band)	6
77	Mountain TOP 32	Mrs Blackhouse/Engine Room Boogie (p/s, as The Sensational Alex Harvey Band)	6
79	RCA PB 5199	Shakin' All Over/Wake Up Davis (p/s, as Alex Harvey - The New Band)	5
64	Polydor LPHM 46424	ALEX HARVEY AND HIS SOUL BAND (LP)	100
64	Polydor LPHM 46441	THE BLUES (LP)	120
69	Fontana (S)TL 5534	ROMAN WALL BLUES (LP)	125
73	Vertigo 6360 081	FRAMED (LP, as The Sensational Alex Harvey Band, gatefold sleeve, spiral label, later spaceship label)	60/15
73	Vertigo 6360 103	NEXT (LP, as The Sensational Alex Harvey Band, spaceship label)	12
74	Vertigo 6360 112	THE IMPOSSIBLE DREAM (LP, as The Sensational Alex Harvey Band, gatefold sleeve)	12
77	K-Tel NE 984	ALEX HARVEY PRESENTS THE LOCH NESS MONSTER (LP, withdrawn, gatefold stickered sleeve, with 16-page 'descriptive diary')	40
79	RCA PL 25257	THE MAFIA STOLE MY GUITAR (LP, as Alex Harvey - The New Band)	12
83	Power Supply AMP 2	THE SOLDIER ON THE WALL (LP)	12
84	Samurai SAH 117PD	S.A.H.B. LIVE (LP, reissue, picture disc)	12

(see also Tear Gas, Hairband, Rock Workshop, Nazareth, Michael Schenker Group, Tandoori Cassette)

FREDERIC HARVEY

60s	HMV 7EG 8847	SINGS WEST COUNTRY SONGS (EP)	10

JANCIS HARVEY

73	Pilgrim King KLPS 47	DISTANCE OF DOORS (LP)	60
75	Westwood WRS 054	TIME WAS NOW (LP)	75
76	Westwood WRS 107	A PORTRAIT OF JANCIS HARVEY (LP)	60
79	Westwood WRS 144	FROM THE DARKNESS CAME LIGHT (LP)	45

JANE HARVEY

60	Pye International 7N 25046	I'm Gonna Go Fishin'/Hundred Dreams From Now	5

LANCE HARVEY & KINGPINS

64	Pye 7N 15647	He's Telling You Lies/How Do You Fix A Broken Heart	6
64	Lyntone LYN 509	Since You Walked Out On Me/ESCORTS: I Can Tell (Keele Rag flexidisc)	15

PETER HARVEY

62	Columbia DB 4873	Rainin' In My Heart/Please Don't Tell Joe	6
63	Columbia DB 7030	Wishing You The Best Of Luck My Friend/Lovin' Can Be Lonesome	5
64	Columbia DB 7192	Heart Of Ice/Trace Of A Heartache	5
64	Columbia DB 7331	Big Man In A Big House/Date With A Heartache	5

P.J. HARVEY

91	Too Pure PURE 5	Dress/Water (demo)/Dry (demo) (12")	10
92	Too Pure PURECD 5	Dress/Water (demo)/Dry (demo) (CD)	15
92	Too Pure PURES 8	Sheela-Na-Gig/Joe (p/s, 400 only)	25
92	Too Pure PURE 8	Sheela-Na-Gig/Hair (demo)/Joe (demo) (12", p/s)	15
92	Too Pure PURECD 8	Sheela-Na-Gig/Hair (demo)/Joe (demo) (CD)	20
93	Island IS 538	50 Ft Queenie/Reeling/Mansize (demo) (p/s)	5
93	Island CID 569	Mansize/Wang Dang Doodle/Daddy (CD)	8
95	Island IS 607	Down By the Water/Lying In The Sun/Somebody's Down Somebody's Name (p/s)	5
95	Island 12IS 614	C'Mon Billy/Darling Be There/Maniac (12", p/s)	8
95	Island CID 610	Send His Love To Me/Long Time Coming (Evening Session)/Harder (CD, with postcards in envelope pack)	8
92	Too Pure PURED 10	DRY (LP, 1st 5,000 only with bonus LP, "Demonstrations", inner sleeve and no'd sticker)	35
92	Too Pure PUREDCD 10	DRY (CD, 1st 5,000 with additional "Demonstrations" LP tracks)	70
95	Island 524-178 2	THE B-SIDES CD (picture disc CD, 2,000 only, digipak)	40
95	Island CIDZ 8035	TO BRING YOU MY LOVE & THE B-SIDES CD (2-CD)	30
99	Island DESIRE CD1	IS THIS DESIRE? (CD, interview disc, slimline case, promo only)	20

(see also Automatic Dlamini, Family Cat, Grape, John Parish & Polly Jean Harvey)

RICHARD HARVEY

83	Anderburr HX 1010	Theme From Terrahawks (3.00)/Variations On The Theme (3.17) (p/s)	5
83	Anderburr HX 21010	Theme From Terrahawks (4.50)/Variations On The Theme (7.25) (12", p/s with poster)	8
75	Transatlantic TRA 292	DIVISIONS ON A GROUND (LP)	25
79	ICL 001	A NEW WAY OF SEEING (LP, private pressing)	15

(see also Gryphon, Barry Gray)

HARVEY'S PEOPLE

69	Galliard GAL 4001	LOVING AND LIVING (LP)	15

CHRISTINE HARWOOD

70	Birth RAB 1	NICE TO MEET MISS CHRISTINE (LP)	35

GORDON HASKELL

69	CBS 4509	Boat Trip/Time Only Knows	12
70	CBS 4795	Oo-La-Di-Doo-Da-Day/Born To Be Together	12
69	CBS 63741	SAILIN' MY BOAT (LP)	80
72	Atlantic K 40311	IT IS AND IT ISN'T (LP, with lyric insert)	15
73	RCA	SERVE AT ROOM TEMPERATURE (LP, unissued)	200

(see also Fleur-De-Lys, Cupid's Inspiration, Flowerpot Men, King Crimson)

JACK HASKELL (& HONEY-DREAMERS)

57	London HL 8426	Around The World/Away Out West	15
58	Oriole CB 1442	The Night Of The Senior Prom/Hungry For Love (with Honey-Dreamers)	5

MICHAEL HASLAM

65	Parlophone R 5267	There Goes The Forgotten Man/My Heart Won't Say Goodbye	5

HASSLES

67	United Artists UP 1199	You Got Me Hummin'/I'm Thinkin'	12

(see also Billy Joel)

HAT & TIE

66	President PT 105	Chance For Romance/California Jazz Club U.S.A.	10
67	President PT 122	Bread To Spend/Finding It Rough (demos credit A-side as "Bread")	60

(see also Patrick Campbell-Lyons, Nirvana)

TONY HATCH ORCHESTRA

59	Top Rank JAR 107	Chick/Side Saddle	5
59	Top Rank JAR 107	Chick/Side Saddle (78)	10
59	Top Rank JAR 165	Rhoom Ba-Cha/Stetson	5
59	Top Rank JAR 165	Rhoom Ba-Cha/Stetson (78)	12
61	Pye International 7N 25068	Tim Frazer's Theme/Girls Of Copenhagen	6
61	Pye 7N 15408	The Ghost Squad/What's That All About	5
62	Pye 7N 15434	Ben Casey Theme/Perry Mason Theme	5
62	Pye 7N 15460	Out Of This World Theme/Cyril's Tune (some in p/s)	10/5
65	Pye 7N 15754	Crossroads Theme/The Marie Celeste (some in p/s)	10/5
65	Pye 7N15972	Man Alive/Crosstown Commuter	5
66	Pye 7N 17169	Crossroads Theme/Round Every Corner (some in p/s)	10/5
67	Pye 7N 17263	Comedy Tonight/You're Lovely	10
69	Pye 7N 17814	Theme From Who-Dun-It/The Champions	30
69	Pye 7N 17864	The Doctors — Theme/Love Song	5
74	Pye 7N 45326	The World At War/Sportsnight	5
78	EMI EMI 2780	Sweeney 2/Regan's Key	15
65	Pye NPL/NSPL 18124	THE TONY HATCH SOUND (LP)	15

TONY HATCH & CHERRY CHILDREN

70	Pye 7N 17912	Yoko/Bahama Sound	5

GEORGE HATCHER BAND

77	United Artists UP 36233	Black Moon Rising/Find A New Lover (p/s)	7
77	United Artists EXP 100	HAVE BAND WILL TRAVEL (10" EP)	10
77	United Artists UAS 30090	TALKIN' TURKEY (LP)	12

(see also Budgie)

HATE

70	Famous SFMA 5752	HATE KILLS (LP)	35

BOBBY HATFIELD

68	Verve VS 570	Hang-Ups/Soul Cafe	5
68	Verve VS 576	Only You/The Wonder Of You	5
72	Warner Bros K 16163	Oo-Wee-Baby, I Love You/Rock'n'Roll Woman	10

(see also Righteous Brothers, Ringo Starr)

HATFIELD & THE NORTH

74	Virgin VS 116	Let's Eat/Fitter Stroke Had A Bath	8
74	Virgin V 2008	HATFIELD AND THE NORTH (LP, gatefold sleeve)	25
75	Virgin V 2030	THE ROTTER'S CLUB (LP)	20
79	Virgin VR 5	AFTERS (LP, withdrawn)	50

(see also Matching Mole, Egg, Khan, Camel, National Health, Caravan)

DONNY HATHAWAY

70	Atco 226 010	The Ghetto (Parts 1 & 2)	5
72	Atlantic K 10193	The Ghetto (Parts 1 & 2)/Little Ghetto Boy	5
73	Atlantic K 10354	Love Love Love/Someday We'll Be Free	5
71	Atco 2465 019	EVERYTHING IS EVERYTHING (LP)	15
71	Atlantic 2400 143	DONNY HATHAWAY (LP)	15
72	Atco K 40063	EVERYTHING IS EVERYTHING (LP, reissue)	12
72	Atlantic K 40241	DONNY HATHAWAY (LP, reissue)	12
72	Atlantic K 40369	LIVE (LP)	15
73	Atlantic K 40487	EXTENSION OF A MAN (LP)	15

(see also Roberta Flack)

HAVANA SEXTET

55	HMV 7MC 33	Elena La Cumbanchera/Eres Mi Lira Armoniosa (export issue)	5

HATS

70s	Deadly Boring HAT 001	No Time Is A Good Time/Living On The Roof (p/s, with lyric insert)	5

ALAN HAVEN

64	United Artists UP 1057	Theme From "A Jolly Bad Fellow"/Jee B'ees (with John Barry)	10
65	Fontana TF 542	Image/Romance On The North Sea	6
65	Fontana TF 590	The Knack/Satin Doll (with John Barry)	10
66	Fontana TF 658	Flamingo/Shangri-La	5
67	Fontana TF 835	Image/Romance Of The North Sea (reissue)	5

MINT VALUE £

RICHIE HAVENS

69	Big T BIG 119	Oxford Town/My Own Way	5
69	Verve VS 1512	Three Day Eternity/No Opportunity Necessary No Experience Needed	5
69	Verve VS 1519	Lady Madonna/Indian Rope Man	6
70	Verve VS 1521	Rocky Raccoon/Stop Pulling And Pushing Me	5
70	Verve VS 1523	There's A Hole In The Future/Minstrel From Gault	5
70	Verve VS 1524	Handsome Johnny/Sandie	5
72	Verve 2121 117	Freedom/Handsome Journey	5
68	Verve (S)VLP 6005	SOMETHIN' ELSE AGAIN (LP)	15
68	Verve (S)VLP 6008	MIXED BAG (LP)	15
69	Verve (S)VLP 6014	1983 (LP)	15
69	Verve (S)VLP 6021	STONEHENGE (LP)	15
69	Transatlantic TRA 187	ELECTRIC HAVENS (LP)	12
69	Transatlantic TRA 199	THE RICHIE HAVENS RECORD (LP)	12
71	Verve 2310 080	ALARM CLOCK (LP)	12
71	Verve 2304 050	STATE OF MIND (LP)	12
72	Polydor 2480 049	GREAT BLIND DEGREE (LP)	12

HAVENSTREET

76	Rissole (no cat. no.)	THE END OF THE LINE	
		(LP, private pressing with booklet)	120

PAT HAWES with DAVE CAREY'S RHYTHM

56	Tempo A 141	Snowy Morning Blues/Sheik Of Araby	6
56	Tempo LAP 9	PAT HAWES (10" LP)	15

GRAHAM HAWK & OWEN GRAY

72	Pama Supreme PS 360	Amazing Grace/SKETTO RICH: Don't Stay Out Late	5

HAWK & CO.

81	Epic EPC A 1735	Nite Life/Nite Life (Version)	5
82	Epic EPC A 2223	Livin' For The Good Times/Sweet Talker	5

(see also Shadows)

TOMMY HAWKE

60	Top Rank JAR 348	Good Gravy (I'm In Love Again)/Umpteen Years (And A Million Tears)	12

CHIP HAWKES

77	RCA PL 25044	NASHVILLE ALBUM (LP)	12

(see Tremeloes)

HAWKEYES

57	Capitol CL 14764	Someone Someday/Who Is He?	6

BUDDY BOY HAWKINS/WILLIAM MOORE

50s	Heritage RE 102	BUDDY BOY HAWKINS/WILLIAM MOORE (EP)	18

(see also Blind Lemon Jefferson)

COLEMAN HAWKINS

55	Brunswick 05459	Lucky Duck/Bye 'N' Bye	10
55	Brunswick OE 9166	THE HAWK TALKS (EP)	12
55	Mercury EP1 6029	COLEMAN HAWKINS GROUP (EP)	10
55	HMV 7EG 8057	COLEMAN HAWKINS AND HIS ORCHESTRA (EP)	8
55	Vogue EPV 1021	COLEMAN HAWKINS (EP)	10
56	Vogue EPV 1147	COLEMAN HAWKINS AND HIS ORCHESTRA (EP)	10
57	HMV 7EG 8230	THE BEAN STALKS AGAIN (EP)	8
58	HMV 7EG 8393	HAWKINS ALLSTARS (EP)	8
58	London Jazz EZ-C 19020	THE HAWK RETURNS PART 1 (EP)	10
58	Columbia Clef SEB 10106	AT THE OPERA HOUSE (EP)	8
50s	Esquire EP 192	BEAN AND THE BOYS (EP)	10
50s	London EZC 19020	THE HAWK RETURNS PT 1 (EP)	8
60	HMV 7EG 8625	COLEMAN HAWKINS AND HIS CONFRERES (EP)	8
61	Esquire EP 235	COLEMAN HAWKINS SEXTET (EP)	10
53	Capitol LC 6580	CLASSICS IN JAZZ (10" LP)	20
53	Capitol LC 6650	CAPITOL PRESENTS COLEMAN HAWKINS AND SONNY GREER	
		(10" LP)	20
54	HMV DLP 1055	TEN COLEMAN HAWKINS' SPECIALS (10" LP)	20
59	HMC CLP 1293	GENIUS OF COLEMAN HAWKINS (LP)	18
59	Felsted FJA 7005	THE HIGH AND MIGHTY HAWK	
		(LP, also stereo SJA 2005)	18
61	Esquire 32-095	SOUL (LP)	18
61	Esquire 32-102	HAWK EYES (LP)	18
61	Moodsville MV 7	COLEMAN HAWKINS (LP)	18
62	Swingsville SVLP 2001	COLEMAN HAWKINS WITH THE RED GARLAND TRIO (LP)	15
62	Swingsville SVLP 2005	THE COLEMAN HAWKINS ALL STARS (LP)	15
62	Swingsville SVLP 2013	STASCH (LP)	15
63	HMV CLP 1630	DESAFINADO (LP, also stereo CSD 1484)	15
64	Verve VLP 9044	ALIVE! AT THE VILLAGE GATE (LP)	15
64	HMV CLP 1689	TODAY AND NOW (LP)	15
64	CBS BPG 62157	BACK IN BEAN'S BAG	
		(LP, with Clark Terry)	15
64	Fontana FJL 102	SWING' (LP)	15
65	Fontana TL 5273	MEDITATION (LP)	15
66	Fontana SJL 131	CATTIN' (LP)	15
71	Xtra XTRA 1119	COLEMAN HAWKINS (LP)	12
72	Black Lion 2460 159	THE HAWK IN GERMANY (LP)	12

(see also Hines & Eldridge, Milt Jackson & Coleman Hawkins, Eddie 'Lockjaw' Davis, Sir Charles Thompson)

COLEMAN HAWKINS & LESTER YOUNG

65	Stateside SL 10117	CLASSIC TENORS (LP)	12

DALE HAWKINS

57	London HL 8482	Susie-Q/Don't Treat Me That Way	450
57	London HL 8482	Susie-Q/Don't Treat Me That Way (78)	100
58	London HLM 8728	La-Do-Dada/Cross Ties	40
58	London HLM 8728	La-Do-Dada/Cross Ties (78)	50
59	London HLM 8842	Yea-Yea/Lonely Nights	40
59	London HLM 8842	Yea-Yea/Lonely Nights (78)	75
59	London HLM 9016	Liza Jane/Back To School Blues	35
59	London HLM 9016	Liza Jane/Back To School Blues (78)	100
60	London HLM 9060	Hot Dog/Our Turn	35
69	Bell SBLL 127	L.A., MEMPHIS AND TYLER, TEXAS (LP)	12
73	Checker 6467 301	OH! SUSIE Q (LP)	12

ERSKINE HAWKINS QUINTET

60	Brunswick LAT 8374	THE HAWK BLOWS AT MIDNIGHT (LP, also stereo STA 3042)	12/15

HAWKSHAW HAWKINS

51	Vogue V 9003	Doghouse Boogie/Yesterday's Kisses (78)	12
51	Vogue V 9027	Slow Coach/Two Roads (78)	10
54	Parlophone CMSP 1	Betty Lorraine/CHARLIE GORE & LOUIS IMIS: Mexican Joe (export issue)	25
63	London HL 9737	Lonesome 7-7203/Everything Has Changed	8
58	Parlophone GEP 8742	COUNTRY AND WESTERN (EP)	30
58	Vogue VE 170117	HAWKSHAW HAWKINS — COUNTRY AND WESTERN (EP)	40
64	London HA 8181	THE ALL NEW HAWKSHAW HAWKINS (LP)	18

JUNE HAWKINS

55	Brunswick 05370	Beat Out Dat Rhythm On A Drum/MURIEL SMITH & CARMEN JONES CHORUS: Dat's Love	6

RONNIE HAWKINS (& HAWKS)

59	Columbia DB 4319	Forty Days (To Come Back Home)/One Of These Days	45
59	Columbia DB 4345	Mary Lou/Need Your Lovin' (Oh So Bad)	25
60	Columbia DB 4412	Southern Love (Whatcha-Gonna' Do)/Love Me Like You Can	15
60	Columbia DB 4442	Clara/Lonely Hours	30
63	Columbia DB 7036	Bo Diddley/Who Do You Love?	18
70	Roulette RO 512	Who Do You Love?/Bo Diddley	5
70	Atlantic 584 320	Down In The Alley/Matchbox	5
70	Atlantic 2091 007	Bitter Green/Forty Days	5
72	Monument MNT 8292	Cora Mae/Ain't That A Shame	5
60	Columbia SEG 7983	ROCKIN' WITH RONNIE (EP, also stereo ESG 7792)	100/150
60	Columbia SEG 7988	ROCKIN' WITH RONNIE (EP, also stereo ESG 7795)	100/150
60	Columbia 33SX 1238	MR. DYNAMO (LP, also stereo SCX 3315)	75/120
60	Columbia 33SX 1295	THE FOLK BALLADS OF RONNIE HAWKINS (LP, also stereo SCX 3358)	50/60
70	Roulette RCP 1003	ARKANSAS ROCK PILE (LP, with The Band)	15
70	Atlantic 2400 009	RONNIE HAWKINS (LP)	12
72	Monument MNT 65122	ROCK AND ROLL RESURRECTION (LP)	12
	(see also Band, Levon & Hawks)		

SCREAMIN' JAY HAWKINS

58	Fontana H 107	I Put A Spell On You/Little Demon (78)	150
65	Columbia DB 7460	The Whammy/Strange	18
65	Sue WI 379	I Hear Voices/Just Don't Care	25
66	Sue WI 4008	I Put A Spell On You/Little Demon (unissued)	
69	Direction 58-4097	I Put A Spell On You/Little Demon	15
80	Polydor POSP 183	I Put A Spell On You/Armpit #6 (with Keith Richards)	8
66	Planet PLL 1001	THE NIGHT AND DAY OF SCREAMIN' JAY HAWKINS (LP)	80
69	Direction (S) 8-63481	I PUT A SPELL ON YOU (LP, mono or stereo)	30
69	Mercury SMCL 20178	WHAT THAT IS (LP)	15
	(see also Keith Richards)		

WENDELL HAWKINS TRIO

61	Parlophone PMC 1157	MR. HAWKINS AT THE PIANO (LP)	12

HAWKLORDS

78	Charisma HL 1	PSI Power/Death Trap (no p/s, promo only)	12
78	Charisma CB 323	PSI Power/Death Trap (no p/s)	8
79	Charisma CB 332	25 Years/(Only) The Dead Dreams Of A Cold War Kid (no p/s)	6
79	Charisma CB 332 12	25 Years/(Only) The Dead Dreams Of A Cold War Kid/PXR 5 (12", grey vinyl; also mispressed on black vinyl)	10/12
82	Flicknife FLS 209	Who's Gonna Win The War?/Time Of (p/s)	6
78	Charisma CDS 4014	25 YEARS ON (LP, with inner sleeve, some sold with separate tour book)	15/12
	(see also Hawkwind)		

HAWKS

69	Stateside SS 2147	The Grissle/SHEEP: Hide And Seek	8

HAWKS

81	Five Believers FB 001	Words Of Hope/Sense Of Ending (p/s)	10
	(see also Lilac Time, Stephen 'Tin Tin' Duffy)		

ALAN HAWKSHAW

70	Tangerine DP 0005	Puppet On A String/Everybody Knows	5
79	BBC RESL 64	Grange Hill/Stoned	6
72	Philips 6414 310	ORGAN SOUNDS SUPER STEREO — ALAN HAWKSHAW PLAYS THE PHILICORDA (LP)	12
72	Studio Two TWO 391	27 TOP TV THEMES AND COMMERCIALS (LP)	20
72	KPM 1080	FLUTE FOR MODERNS (with Alan Parker) (LP)	30
74	Polydor 2460 218	NON-STOP HAMMOND HITS (LP)	12
	(see also Shadows)		

HAWKSWORTH-VERRELL JAZZ GROUP

56	Decca FJ 10726	Ring Dem Bells/Always	5

Johnny HAWKSWORTH

JOHNNY HAWKSWORTH (ORCHESTRA)

65	Pye 7N 15969	Lunar Walk/It's Murder (as Johnny Hawksworth Orchestra)	12
66	Columbia DB 8059	Goal/"Goal — World Cup 1966" Theme (as Sounds Of Johnny Hawksworth)	5
67	Columbia DB 8129	Wack Wack/On The Tiles	6

(see also Johnny's Jazz)

HAWKWIND

SINGLES

70	Liberty LBF 15382	Hurry On Sundown/Mirror Of Illusion	80
72	United Artists UP 35381	Silver Machine/Seven By Seven ('machine' art p/s)	10
73	United Artists (WD 3637)	Sonic Attack (1-sided promo in cloth sleeve)	175
73	United Artists UP 35566	Urban Guerilla/Brainbox Pollution	10
73	United Artists USEP 1	HURRY ON HAWKWIND (EP)	30
74	United Artists UP 35715	The Psychedelic Warlords (Disappear In Smoke)/It's So Easy	7
75	United Artists UP 35808	Kings Of Speed/Motorhead (some in p/s)	35/5
76	Charisma CB 289	Kerb Crawler/Honky Dorky	7
77	Charisma CB 299	Back On The Streets/The Dream Of Isis (p/s)	6
77	Charisma CB 305	Quark, Strangeness & Charm/Forge Of Vulcan	7
78	United Artists UP 35381	Silver Machine/Seven By Seven (reissue, black-on-white p/s)	5
78	United Artists 12UP 35381	Silver Machine/Seven By Seven (12", silver p/s)	10
80	Bronze BRO 98	Shot Down In The Night/Urban Guerilla (p/s)	5
80	Bronze BRO 98	Shot Down In The Night/Urban Guerilla (1-sided gold vinyl flexidisc)	30
80	Bronze BRO 109	Who's Gonna Win The War?/Nuclear Toy (p/s, cream or green labels)	12/5
81	RCA RCA 137	Angels Of Death/Trans-Dimensional Man (p/s)	5
82	RCA Active RCA 267	Silver Machine/Silver Machine (Full Version)/Psychedelic Warlords (p/s)	5
82	RCA Active RCAP 267	Silver/Machine/(Full Version)/Psychedelic Warlords (picture disc)	10
82	Flicknife FLS 005	Motorhead/Valium Ten (p/s)	5
82	Flicknife FLST 005	Motorhead/Valium Ten (extended) (12", p/s)	8
83	United Artists UP 35381	Silver Machine/Seven By Seven (reissue, white-on-black p/s)	5
83	Liberty UPP 35381	Silver Machine/Seven By Seven (picture disc)	12
83	Liberty UPP 35381	Silver Machine/Seven By Seven (mispressed picture disc, plays Beatles' "Ask Me Why")	18
83	Flicknife FLS 214	Hawkwind And Co: Your Last Chance (p/s, sampler with Robert Calvert & Michael Moorcock)	6
83	Flicknife FLS 025	Motorway City/Master Of The Universe (p/s)	5
84	Flicknife FLEP 104	THE EARTH RITUAL PREVIEW (12" EP)	8
85	Flicknife FLS 032	Needle Gun/Arioch (p/s)	5
85	Flicknife FLST 032	Needle Gun (extended)/Arioch (p/s)	8
86	Flicknife FLS 033	Zarozinia/Assault And Battery (live) (p/s)	5
86	Samurai HW 001	Silver Machine/Magnu (motorcycle-shaped picture disc)	15
86	Flicknife FLS 034-A	Motorhead/Hurry On Sundown (p/s with insert)	5
90	Receiver REPLAY 3014	THE EARLY YEARS LIVE (12", p/s, blue vinyl)	12
93	4 Real 4R 1	SPIRIT OF THE AGE (SOLSTICE REMIXES) (12" EP)	15
93	4 Real 4R 2	DECIDE YOUR FUTURE (12" EP)	10
94	Emerg. Broadcast EBS 110	QUARK, STRANGENESS & CHARM (12" EP, clear vinyl, 200 only)	15

ALBUMS

70	Liberty LBS 83348	HAWKWIND (LP, gatefold sleeve; blue or black labels)	30
71	United Artists UAG 29202	IN SEARCH OF SPACE (LP in foldout sleeve, some with 'log book')	25/12
72	United Artists UAG 29364	DOREMI-FASOL-LATIDO (LP, with inner sleeve, some with poster)	20/12
73	Utd. Artists UAD 60037/8	SPACE RITUAL ALIVE (2-LP, foldout sleeve with inners)	30
74	United Artists UAG 29672	HALL OF THE MOUNTAIN GRILL (LP, with inner sleeve)	15
75	United Artists UAG 29766	WARRIOR ON THE EDGE OF TIME (LP, foldout pop-up sleeve with inner)	20
76	United Artists UAK 29919	ROADHAWKS (LP, gatefold sleeve with poster & sticker)	18/12
79	Charisma CDS 4016	P.X.R.5 (LP, with family tree poster)	20
80	Charisma BG 2	REPEAT PERFORMANCE (LP)	15
80	Bronze BRON 530	LEVITATION (LP, blue vinyl)	20
81	RCA Active RCALP 6004	SONIC ATTACK (LP, with insert)	20
82	RCA Active RCALP 9004	CHURCH OF HAWKWIND (LP, with lyric booklet)	30
82	RCA Active RCALP 6055	CHOOSE YOUR MASQUES (LP)	20
83	Charisma CASMC 110	QUARK STRANGENESS AND CHARM/P.X.R.5 (double-play cassette)	10
84	Flicknife PSHARP 014	ZONES (LP, picture disc reissue)	15
84	Flicknife ZSHARP 019	INDEPENDENT DAYS (10" mini-LP)	8
84	Liberty SLP 1972921	HAWKWIND (LP, reissue, picture disc, die-cut)	15
84	Flicknife SHARP 022	STONHENGE: THIS IS HAWKWIND DO NOT PANIC (LP, with 12", gatefold sleeve or single sleeve with poster)	each 20
85	Flicknife SHARP 033	CHRONICLE OF THE BLACK SWORD (LP, with inner sleeve)	12
85	Flicknife SHARP 033CD	CHRONICLE OF THE BLACK SWORD (CD, with 3 extra tracks)	18
86	Hawkfan HWFB 2	HAWKFAN 12 (LP, with poster, sticker insert & carrier bag, 600 only)	75
86	RCA NL 71150	ANGELS OF DEATH (LP)	25
86	Samurai SMR 046	APPROVED HISTORY OF HAWKWIND 1967-1982 (3-LP, pic discs & booklet)	40
87	Flicknife HWBOX 01	OFFICIAL PICTURE LOG BOOK (4-LP box set, [3 picture discs & interview disc] with badge & insert)	40
92	Castle ESD 181	ELECTRIC TEPEE (2-LP, gatefold sleeve, 5,000 only)	15
94	Emerg. Broadcast EBS 111	THE BUSINESS TRIP (2-LP, clear vinyl, 1,500 only)	15
95	Emerg. B/cast EBSLP 118	ALIEN 4 (2-LP, gatefold sleeve)	18
95	Dojo DOJO CD 244	ELECTRIC TEPEE (CD, picture disc, unreleased)	20

(see also Hawklords, Robert Calvert, Michael Moorcock, Inner City Unit, Sphynx, Dave Brock, Steve Swindells, Tim Blake, Huw Lloyd Langton Group, Alan Davey, Motörhead, Sonic Assassins, Dr. Technical & Machines, Sam Gopal, Magic Muscle, Opal Butterfly, Nik Turner, Widowmaker, John Stevens Away, Adrian Shaw)

DEANE HAWLEY

61	Liberty LIB 55359	Pocketful Of Rainbows/That Dream Could Never Be	6

GOLDIE HAWN

72	Reprise K 14211	Carey/I'll Be Your Baby Tonight	5

BRYN HAWORTH
74   Island ILPS 9287   LET THE DAYS GO BY (LP, with inner sleeve). 12
(see also Fleur De Lys, Nicholas Greenwood)

HAYDOCK'S ROCKHOUSE
66   Columbia DB 8050   Cupid/She Thinks 30
67   Columbia DB 8135   Lovin' You/Mix A Fix 30
(see also Hollies)

BILL HAYES
53   MGM SP 1036   The Donkey Song/My Ever-Lovin' 22
55   London HL 8149   The Berry Tree/Blue Black Hair 25
55   London HL 8149   The Berry Tree/Blue Black Hair (78). 12
56   London HLA 8220   Ballad Of Davy Crockett/Farewell 35
56   London HLA 8239   Kwela Kwela/The White Buffalo 25
56   London HLA 8239   Kwela Kwela/The White Buffalo (78) 10
56   London HLA 8300   Das Ist Musik/I Know An Old Lady 20
56   London HLA 8300   Das Ist Musik/I Know An Old Lady (78) 10
56   London HLA 8325   The Legend Of Wyatt Earp/That Do Make It Nice 30
56   London HLA 8325   The Legend Of Wyatt Earp/That Do Make It Nice (78). 15
57   London HL 8430   Wringle Wrangle/Westward Ho The Wagons 15
57   London HL 8430   Wringle Wrangle/Westward Ho The Wagons (78) 8
59   London HLR 8833   Wimoweh/Goin' Down The Road Feelin' Bad
                           (with Buckle Busters). 12
59   London HLR 8833   Wimoweh/Goin' Down The Road Feelin' Bad
                           (78, with Buckle Busters). 12
56   London RE-A 1051   GREAT PIONEERS OF THE WEST (EP) 35

ISAAC HAYES
69   Stax STAX 133   Walk On By/By The Time I Get To Phoenix 5
70   Stax STAX 154   I Stand Accused/I Just Don't Know What To Do With Myself 5
71   Stax 2025 029   Never Can Say Goodbye/I Can't Help It. 5
72   Stax 2025 069   Theme From "Shaft"/Cafe Regio's. 5
72   Stax 2025 146   Men — Theme/Type Thang. 5
76   ABC ABC 4100   Disco Connection/St. Thomas Square. 5
76   ABC ABE 12007   Disco Connection/Chocolate Chip (12") 8
69   Stax SXATS 1028   HOT BUTTERED SOUL (LP). 15
70   Stax SXATS 1032   THE ISAAC HAYES MOVEMENT (LP) 15
70   Stax 2465 016   BLUE HAYES (LP) 15
71   Stax 2325 026   TO BE CONTINUED (LP) 15
71   Stax 2325 014   THE ISAAC HAYES MOVEMENT (LP, reissue) 12
71   Stax 2325 011   HOT BUTTERED SOUL (LP, reissue) 12
71   Stax 2659 007   SHAFT — ORIGINAL SOUNDTRACK
                           (2-LP, soundtrack, gatefold sleeve) 18
72   MGM 2315 115   SHAFT'S BIG SCORE! (LP, soundtrack) 18
72   Atlantic K 40327   IN THE BEGINNING (LP). 12
72   Stax 2628 004   BLACK MOSES (2-LP). 18
74   Stax 2659 026   LIVE AT THE SAHARA TAHOE (2-LP) 18
74   Stax 2325 111   JOY (LP) 12
74   Stax STXD 4001/2   TRUCK TURNER (2-LP, soundtrack) 18
74   Stax STXH 5001   TOUGH GUYS (LP) 12
75   Stax STX 1043   USE ME (LP). 12
75   ABC ABCL 5129   CHOCOLATE CHIP
                           (LP, gatefold sleeve). 12
75   ABC ABCL 5155   GROOVE-A-THON
                           (LP, gatefold sleeve). 12

LINDA HAYES
55   Parlophone MSP 6174   Please Have Mercy (with Platters)/Oochi Pachi (with Tony Williams) 275
55   Parlophone R 4038   Please Have Mercy (with Platters)/Oochi Pachi
                           (with Tony Williams) (78) 60

(see also Platters)

PETER LIND HAYES
60   Brunswick 05821   Life Gets Tee-jus Don't It/Sing Me A Happy Song. 7
(see also Peter & Mary)

TUBBY HAYES
55   Tempo A 109   May Reh/Orient Line (78) 8
55   Tempo A 113   Sophisticated Lady (78) 8
55   Tempo A 119   Fidelius/Tootsie Roll (78) 8
55   Tempo A 123   There's No You/Dance Of The Aerophagytes (78) 8
56   Tempo A 148   Ode To Ernie/No, I Woodyn't 15
56   Tempo A 148   Ode To Ernie/No, I Woodyn't (78). 8
62   Fontana H 397   Sally/I Believe In You (as Tubby Hayes Quintet) 50
55   Tempo EXA 14   THE LITTLE GIANT (EP). 60
55   Tempo EXA 17   TUBBY HAYES AND HIS ORCHESTRA (EP) 75
55   Tempo EXA 27   THE SWINGING GIANT NO. 1
                           EP, as Tubby Hayes Quartet) 80
56   Tempo EXA 28   THE SWINGING GIANT NO. 1
                           (EP, as Tubby Hayes Quartet). 80
56   Tempo EXA 36   MODERN JAZZ SCENE
                           (EP, as Tubby Hayes & His Orchestra). 50
57   Tempo EXA 55   AFTER LIGHTS OUT (EP, as Tubby Hayes Quintet) 50
57   Tempo EXA 75   TUBBY HAYES AND THE JAZZ COURIERS (EP). 50
58   Tempo EXA 82   THE EIGHTH WONDER (EP, solo) 80
57   Tempo TAP 6   AFTER LIGHTS OUT (LP, as Tubby Hayes Quintet) 200
57   Tempo TAP 15   JAZZ COURIERS (LP). 300
60   Tempo TAP 29   TUBBY'S GROOVE (LP, as Tubby Hayes Quartet). 700
61   Fontana TFL 5142   TUBBS (LP, also stereo STFL 562) 150

Tubby HAYES

61	Ember EMB 3337	AN EVENING WITH MR. PERCUSSION (LP, with Tony Kinsey)	25
61	Fontana TFL 5183	TUBBS IN NEW YORK (LP, also stereo STFL 595)	120
63	Fontana 680 998 TL	DOWN IN THE VILLAGE (LP, also stereo 886 163TY)	300
64	Fontana (S)TL 5195	RETURN VISIT! (LP)	175
64	Fontana TL 5200	LATE SPOT AT SCOTT'S (LP)	375
66	Fontana (S)TL 5221	TUBBY TOURS (LP, with Orchestra)	60
66	Fontana (S)TL 5410	100% PROOF (LP)	125
67	Wing WL 1162	TUBBS IN NEW YORK (LP, reissue)	40
69	Fontana SFJL 911	MEXICAN GREEN (LP)	225
71	Fontana 6309 002	THE TUBBY HAYES ORCHESTRA (LP)	100
72	Philips 6382 041	THIS IS JAZZ — 100% PROOF (LP)	15

(see also Jack Constanzo & Tubby Hayes, Jazz Couriers, London Jazz Quartet, Dave Lee, Ronnie Scott)

TUBBY HAYES & CLEO LAINE
61	Fontana TFL 5151	PALLADIUM JAZZ DATE (LP, also stereo STFL 570)	150
65	Wing WL 1088	PALLADIUM JAZZ DATE (LP, reissue)	75

(see also Cleo Laine)

TUBBY HAYES & PAUL GONSALVES ALLSTARS
67	Columbia SX 6003	JUST FRIENDS (LP)	120
60s	World Record Club T 631	CHANGE OF SETTING (LP)	120

(see also Paul Gonsalves)

LOU HAYLES
77	Myrrh MYR 1055	DON'T HIDE AWAY (LP)	15

DICK HAYMES
56	Capitol CL 14618	You'll Never Know/Love Walked In	5
56	Capitol CL 14659	Two Different Worlds/Love Is A Great Big Nothin'	5
57	Capitol CL 14674	Never Leave Me/New York's My Home	5
57	Capitol CL 14720	C'est La Vie/Now At Last	5
51	Brunswick LA 8516	IRVING BERLIN SONGS (10" LP)	15
51	Brunswick LA 8530	SOUVENIR ALBUM (10" LP)	15
56	Capitol LC 6823	RAIN OR SHINE (10" LP)	15

GOLDIA HAYNES
51	Capitol CL 13486	That Great Judgement Day/Travelling (78)	15
52	Capitol CL 13550	Truth In The Gospel/Oh Lord How Long (78)	18

ROY HAYNES, PHINEAS NEWBORN, PAUL CHAMBERS TRIO
61	Esquire 32-103	WE THREE (LP)	12

STEVE HAYNES BAND
78	Black Bear BLA 2008	Save Me Save Me/Strong Good Lovin' (p/s)	15

HAYSTACK
69	United Artists UP 35024	Letter To Josephine/Love You're Making A Fool Of Me	5
69	United Artists UP 35035	Tahiti Farewell/Pantomime People	5

JUSTIN HAYWARD
65	Pye 7N 17041	London Is Behind Me/Day Must Come	70
66	Parlophone R 5496	I Can't Face The World Without You/I'll Be Here Tomorrow	100
80	CBS 11-7731	The Eve Of The War/Horsell (12" picture disc)	8

(see also Wilde Three, Moody Blues)

RICK HAYWARD
71	Blue Horizon 2431 006	RICK HAYWARD (LP)	50

(see also Accent, Christine Perfect)

SUSAN HAYWARD
56	MGM MGM-EP 555	I'LL CRY TOMORROW — SOUNDTRACK SELECTION (EP)	8

JOE HAYWOOD
65	Island WI 218	Warm And Tender Love/I Would If I Could	10

LEON HAYWOOD
66	Vocalion VL 9280	Ain't No Use/Hey, Hey, Hey	12
67	Vocalion VL 9288	Ever Since You Were Sweet Sixteen/Skate Awhile	12
69	MCA Soul Bag BAG 5	Mellow Moonlight/Tennessee Waltz	7
70	Capitol CL 15634	I Wanna Thank You/I Was Sent To Love You	5
73	Pye International 7N 25611	La La Song/There Ain't Enough Hate Around To Make Me Turn Around	5
75	20th Century BTC 2191	Come On And Get Yourself Some/BMF (Beautiful)	5
75	20th Century BTC 2228	I Wanta Do Something Freaky To You/I Know What Love Is	6
78	Fantasy FTC 151	Baby Reconsider/Would I	8
67	Vocalion VAL 8064	SOUL CARGO (LP)	30
69	MCA MUPS 369	IT'S GOT TO BE MELLOW (LP)	15
73	Pye Intl. NSPL 28177	BACK TO STAY (LP)	12
75	20th Century BT 476	COME AND GET YOURSELF SOME (LP)	12

HAZE
84	Gabadon GABL 001	C'EST LA VIE (LP)	25
85	Gabadon GABC 2	CELLAR REPLAY (cassette)	10
85	Gabadon GABS 003	THE EMBER (12" EP)	8
86	Gabadon GABS 5	Tunnel Vision/Shadows (p/s)	5
87	Gabadon GABL 6	STOAT AND BOTTLE (LP)	10

HAZEL & JOLLY BOYS
67	Doctor Bird DB 1063	Stop Them/Deep Down	15

LEE HAZLEWOOD

60	London HLW 9223	Words Mean Nothing/The Girl On Death Row (with Duane Eddy)	15
66	MGM MGM 1310	Sand/My Autumn's Done Come	7
67	MGM MGM 1348	My Baby Cried All Night Long/These Boots Are Made For Walkin'	8
67	Reprise RS 20613	Ode To Billie Joe/Charlie Bill Nelson	5
68	Reprise RS 20667	Rainbow Woman/I Am, You Are	7
72	RCA RCA 2185	Big Red Balloon/Down From Dover	5
73	Stateside SS 2225	Poet/Come Spend The Morning	5
66	MGM MGM-CS 8014	THE VERY SPECIAL WORLD OF LEE HAZLEWOOD (LP)	25
68	Reprise RSLP 6297	LOVE AND OTHER CRIMES (LP)	22
69	London HA-N/SH-N 8398	TROUBLE IS A LONESOME TOWN (LP)	25
72	Reprise K 44161	REQUIEM FOR AN ALMOST LADY (LP)	18
74	Stateside SSL 10315	POET, FOOL OR BUM (LP)	22

(see also Nancy Sinatra & Lee Hazlewood, Duane Eddy)

TONY HAZZARD

66	Columbia DB 7927	You'll Never Put Shackles On Me/Calling You Home	6
68	CBS 3452	Sound Of The Candyman's Trumpet/Everything's Gone Wrong	5
69	CBS 63608	DEMONSTRATION (LP)	12
71	Bronze ILPS 9174	LOUDWATER HOUSE (LP)	12
73	Bronze ILPS 9222	WAS THAT ALRIGHT THEN? (LP)	12

MURRAY HEAD

65	Columbia DB 7635	Alberta/He Was A Friend Of Mine	6
65	Columbia DB 7771	The Bells Of Rhymney/Don't Sing No Sad Songs For Me	7
67	Columbia DB 8102	Someday Soon/You Bore Me	6
67	Immediate IM 053	She Was Perfection/Secondhand Monday	40
69	MCA MK 5019	Superstar/John 1941 (p/s, with Trinidad Singers)	6
71	MCA MKS 5019	Superstar/John 1941 (p/s, reissue)	6
73	CBS 65503	NIGEL LIVED (LP)	18
75	Island ILPS 9347	SAY IT AIN'T SO (LP)	12

ROY HEAD (& TRAITS)

65	Pye International 7N 25340	Just A Little Bit/Treat Me Right	12
65	Vocalion VP 9248	Treat Her Right/So Long, My Love	15
66	Vocalion VP 9254	Apple Of My Eye/I Pass The Day	8
66	Vocalion VP 9269	My Babe/Pain	8
66	Vocalion VP 9274	Wigglin' And Gigglin'/Driving Wheel	8
66	London HLZ 10097	To Make A Big Man Cry/Don't Cry No More	8
70	Stateside SS 8050	Mama Mama/I'm Not A Fool Anymore	6
75	London HLD 10487	The Most Wanted Woman In Town/Gingers Breadman	8
66	Pye Intl. NEP 44053	JUST A LITTLE BIT OF ROY HEAD (EP)	25
70	Stateside SSL 5033	SAME PEOPLE (LP)	15

(see also Traits)

HEADACHE

77	Lout 001	Can't Stand Still/No Reason For Your Call (p/s)	25

HEADBANGERS

81	Magnet MAG 206	Status Rock/Headbang Boogie (p/s)	5

(see also Biddu, Leaf Hound, Weapon)

THEE HEADCOATS

90	Sub Pop SP71	Time Will Tell/Davey Crockett (Gabba Hey) (p/s)	12
92	Sub Pop SP151	Ballad Of Hollis Brown/Grizzly Bear (p/s, blue vinyl)	15

(see also Milkshakes)

HEADHUNTERS (U.S.)

76	Arista ARTY 116	SURVIVAL OF THE FITTEST (LP)	25
77	Arista SPART 1046	STRAIGHT FROM THE GATE (LP)	15

(see also Herbie Hancock)

HEADHUNTERS (U.K.)

83	Shout XS 005	Impossible/Straitjacket (p/s)	4

HEADLESS CHICKENS

89	Hometown Atrocities 1	THE HOMETOWN ATROCITIES EP (wraparound p/s, 'kylie' or glossy')	200/150

HEADLINERS

59	Parlophone R 4593	The Bubble Car Song/Andy's Theme	5

HEADLINERS

65	Decca F 12209	That's The Way I Must Go/Four Seasons	6

HEAD MACHINE

70	Major Minor SMLP 79	ORGASM (LP)	125

(see also Uriah Heep)

HEAD OF DAVID

86	Blast First BFFP 5	DOGBREATH (12" EP, stickered plain sleeve)	8
89	Blast First WANT 001	WHITE ELEPHANT (LP, mail-order only)	12

TOPPER HEADON

85	Mercury MERD 201	Leave It To Luck/Casablanca//Du Cane Road/ Got To Get Out Of This Heat/S.O.S. (double pack)	8

(see also Clash)

HEADS, HANDS & FEET

71	Island ILPS 9149	HEADS, HANDS AND FEET (LP)	15
72	Island ILPS 9185	TRACKS (LP)	15

(see also Don Everly, Tony Colton, Poet & One Man Band)

HEALEY SISTERS

64	HMV POP 1313	Give Me Back My Heart/After The Party	7

JOE HEANEY
60	Collector JEI 5	MORRISSEY AND THE RUSSIAN SOLDIER (EP)	8
63	Topic 12T 91	IRISH TRADITIONAL SONGS IN GAELIC AND ENGLISH (LP)	12

HEART
77	Arista ARISTA 140	Heartless/Here Song (withdrawn)	8
86	Capitol CLP 406	Nothin' At All (Extended Remix)/The Wolf (heart-shaped picture disc)	6
87	Capitol CLP 457	Who Will You Run To?/Nobody Home (picture disc)	10
87	Capitol CDCL 473	There's The Girl (12" Remix)/Bad Animals/There's The Girl (7" Remix) (CD)	8
88	Capitol CDCL 477	These Dreams (7" Version)/Heart Of Darkness/If Looks Could Kill (live)/There's The Girl (Rock-A-Pella Version) (CD)	8
88	Capitol CDCL 482	Never (Extended Remix)/These Dreams (7" Version)/Heart Of Darkness/If Looks Could Kill (live) (CD)	8
88	Capitol CDCL 487	What About Love? (Extended Version)/Shell Shock/Crazy On You/Dreamboat Annie (CD)	8
88	Capitol CDCL 507	Nothin' At All (Remix)/I've Got The Music In Me/I Want You So Bad/Nothin' At All (Extended Remix) (CD)	8
77	Arista SPART 1024	MAGAZINE (LP, withdrawn)	15
90	Capitol HGIFT 1	HEART BOX SET (3-LP: "Heart", "Bad Animals" & "Brigade" + 24pp booklet)	18

HEART BEATS
80	Red Shadow REDS 2	Talk To Me/Don't Want Romance (p/s)	5
81	Nothing Shaking SHAD 1	Go/One Of The People (p/s, blue vinyl)	15

HEARTBREAKERS
77	Track 2094 135	Chinese Rocks/Born To Lose (p/s)	8
77	Track 2094 135T	Chinese Rocks/Born To Lose (12", p/s)	12
77	Track 2094 137	One Track Mind/Can't Keep My Eyes On You (live)/Do You Love Me (p/s)	10
77	Track 2094 142	It's Not Enough/Let Go (p/s, withdrawn)	60
79	Beggars Banquet BEG 21	Get Off The Phone (live)/I Wanna Be Loved (live) (p/s)	5
77	Track 2409 218	L.A.M.F. (LP)	20
81	Jungle FREUD 1	D.T.K. — LIVE AT THE SPEAKEASY (LP, white or pink vinyl)	18
84	Jungle FREUDP 4	L.A.M.F. REVISITED (LP, picture disc)	18
88	Jungle FREUDP 1	D.T.K. — LIVE AT THE SPEAKEASY (LP, reissue, picture disc)	18

(see also New York Dolls, Johnny Thunders)

HEARTS (U.S.)
64	Stateside SS 268	Dear Abby/Dear Abby (Instrumental)	10

HEARTS (U.K.)
64	Parlophone R 5147	Young Woman/Black Eyes	25

HEARTS & FLOWERS
67	Capitol CL 15492	Rock'N'Roll Gypsies/Road To Nowhere	8
68	Capitol CL 15549	She Sang Hymns Out Of Tune/Tin Angel	7

HEARTS OF SOUL
70	Columbia DB 8670	Waterman/Fat Jack	12

HEATERS
70	Upsetter US 329	Melting Pot/UPSETTERS: Kinky Mood	10

HEAT EXCHANGE
79	EMI EMI 2988	Shake Down/You're Gonna Love This (p/s)	4
79	EMI 12EMI 2988	Shake Down/You're Gonna Love This (12", p/s)	7
79	EMI EMC 3306	ONE STEP AHEAD (LP)	10

(see also Brian Bennett)

TED HEATH ORCHESTRA
54	Decca F 10200	Seven Eleven/Lullaby Of Birdland	8
54	Decca F 10222	Creep/Slim Jim — Creep	8
54	Decca F 10246	Skin Deep/Walking Shoes	20
54	Decca F 10272	Viva Verrell/Holiday For Strings	7
54	Decca F 10273	Lush Slide/Fascinating Rhythm	7
55	Decca F 10425	Dig Deep/Asia Minor	7
55	Decca F 10447	Peg O' My Heart (Mambo)/In The Mood (For Mambo)	7
55	Decca F 10477	Haitian Ritual/Late Night Final	7
55	Decca F 10540	Bell Bell Boogie/Amethyst	7
55	Decca F 10590	Barber Shop Jump/Look For The Silver Lining	6
55	Decca F 10624	Malaguena/Cloudburst	6
56	Decca F 10683	The Man With The Golden Arm/Paris By Night	6
56	Decca F 10746	The Faithful Hussar/Siboney	7
58	Decca F 11000	Swingin' Shepherd Blues/Raunchy	6
58	Decca F 11003	Tequila/Little Serenade	6
58	Decca F 11025	Tom Hark/Cha Cha Baby	5
59	Decca F 11111	Peter Gunn/Sermonette (78)	10
59	Decca F 11155	Jazzboat/Mah Jong (78)	10
59	Decca F 11179	Swinging Ghosts/Indian Love Call (78)	10
65	Decca F 12133	Sidewinder/Hit And Miss	5

EPs
55	Decca DFE 6025	TED HEATH AND HIS MUSIC (EP)	12
55	Decca DFE 6027	TED HEATH AND HIS MUSIC NO. 2 (EP)	12
55	Decca DFE 6120	LONDON PALLADIUM HIGHLIGHTS (EP)	8
55	Decca DFE 6159	FATS WALLER ALBUM NO. 2 (EP)	12
55	Decca DFE 6160	SELECTIONS FROM FATS WALLER ALBUM NO. 2 (EP)	8
55	Decca DFE 6189	HUNDREDTH LONDON PALLADIUM SUNDAY CONCERT VOL. 1 (EP)	8
55	Decca DFE 6190	HUNDREDTH LONDON PALLADIUM SUNDAY CONCERT VOL. 2 (EP)	8
55	Decca DFE 6191	HUNDREDTH LONDON PALLADIUM SUNDAY CONCERT VOL. 3 (EP)	8
56	Decca DFE 6290	GERSHWIN FOR MODERNS NO. 1 (EP)	8
56	Decca DFE 6300	AUSTRALIAN SUITE (EP)	12
56	Decca DFE 6304	KERN FOR MODERNS NO. 1 (EP)	8

56	Decca DFE 6305	KERN FOR MODERNS NO. 2 (EP)	8
56	Decca DFE 6306	KERN FOR MODERNS NO. 3 (EP)	8
56	Decca DFE 6317	LONDON PALLADIUM HIGHLIGHTS (EP)	8
56	Decca DFE 6323	FOUR CLASSICS (EP)	8
56	Decca DFE 6346	LONDON PALLADIUM HIGHLIGHTS NO. 3 (EP)	8
56	Decca DFE 6354	GERSHWIN FOR MODERNS NO. 2 (EP)	8
56	Decca DFE 6373	LONDON PALLADIUM HIGHLIGHTS NO. 4 (EP)	8
57	Decca DFE 6403	TED HEATH AND HIS MUSIC NO. 3 (EP)	8
57	Decca DFE 6432	TED HEATH AND HIS MUSIC NO. 4 (EP)	8
57	Decca DFE 6451	TED HEATH RECALLS THE FABULOUS DORSEYS NO. 1 (EP)	8
58	Decca DFE 6487	TED HEATH AND HIS MUSIC NO. 5 (EP)	8
58	Decca DFE 6500	OUR KIND OF JAZZ (EP)	8
58	Decca DFE 6509	HITS I MISSED NO. 1 (EP, also stereo STO 103)	8/10
58	Decca DFE 6510	TED HEATH PLAYS AL JOLSON CLASSICS NO. 1 (EP)	8
58	Decca DFE 6511	OLD ENGLISH NO. 1 (EP)	8
59	Decca STO 109	TED HEATH SWING SESSION (EP, stereo)	12
59	Decca STO 113	TED HEATH SWINGS IN HI STEREO (EP, stereo)	10
59	Decca DFE 6579	FOUR HITS FROM THE ALL TIME TOP TWELVE (EP, also stereo STO 122)	8/12
60	Decca DFE 6625	BEAULIEU FESTIVAL SUITE (EP, also stereo STO 135)	8/12
60	Decca DFE 6642	MY VERY GOOD FRIENDS THE BANDLEADERS (EP)	8
61	Decca STO 155	GREAT FILM HITS (EP, stereo)	10
63	Decca STO 8532	MOMENTS AT MONTREUX (EP, stereo)	10

LPs

51	Decca LF 1037	TEMPO FOR DANCERS (10" LP)	20
52	Decca LF 1060	LISTEN TO MY MUSIC (10" LP)	18
52	Decca LF 1064	SELECTION (10" LP)	18
53	Decca LK 4062	AT THE LONDON PALLADIUM (LP)	15
53	Decca LK 4064	STRIKE UP THE BAND (LP)	15
54	Decca LK 4074	TED HEATH'S FATS WALLER ALBUM (LP)	15
54	Decca LK 4075	TED HEATH'S 100TH LONDON PALLADIUM SUNDAY CONCERT (LP)	15
54	Decca LK 4098	GERSHWIN FOR MODERNS (LP)	12
56	Decca LK 4121	KERN FOR MODERNS (LP)	12
56	Decca LK 4134	AT THE LONDON PALLADIUM VOLUME 4 (LP)	12
56	Decca LK 4148	RODGERS FOR MODERNS (LP)	12
57	Decca LK 4165	AT CARNEGIE HALL (LP)	12
57	Decca LK 4167	FIRST AMERICAN TOUR (LP)	12
58	Decca LK 4275	HITS I MISSED (LP, also stereo SKL 4003)	12/20
58	Decca LK 4280	OLDE ENGLYSHE (LP)	12
58	Decca SKL 4023	SWINGS IN HI-STEREO (LP, stereo only)	25
59	Decca SKL 4030	SWING SESSION (LP, stereo only)	20
59	Decca SKL 4046	SHALL WE DANCE (LP)	15
59	Decca LK 4208	ALL TIME TOP TWELVE — THE BILLBOARD (LP, also stereo SKL 4054)	12/20
59	Decca LK 4307	PLAYS THE GREAT FILM HITS (LP, also stereo SKL 4055)	12/20
60	Decca LK 4324	PLAYS THE BLUES (LP, also stereo SKL 4074)	12/20
60	Decca LK 4328	THE BIG BAND DIXIE SOUND (LP, also stereo SKL 4076)	12/20
60	Decca LK 4331	IN CONCERT (LP, also stereo SKL 4079)	12/20
60	Decca LK 4344	MY VERY GOOD FRIENDS THE BAND LEADERS (LP, also stereo SKL 4090)	12/20
61	Decca LK 4374	THE INSTRUMENTS OF THE DANCE ORCHESTRA (LP, also stereo SKL 4117)	12/20
61	Decca LK 4389	GOES LATIN (LP, also stereo SKL 4389)	12/20

(Early copies of the above stereo LPs have a "ffss" circle logo at the top of the label & blue back sleeves.)

| 62 | Decca PFM 24004 | BIG BAND PERCUSSION (LP, also stereo PFS 34004) | 12/20 |

(see also Max Bygraves & Ted Heath, Joan Regan, Bobbie Britton, Johnston Brothers, Annette Klooger)

HEATHCLIFFE

| 68 | Tangerine DP 0001 | Holly Bush And Mistletoe/My World | 5 |

HEATHER

| 65 | King KG 1027 | I'll Come Softly/No One In The Whole Wide World | 6 |

HEATWAVE

| 77 | GTO GTLP 027 | CENTRAL HEATING (LP) | 10 |

HEAVENLY

| 89 | Sarah SARAH 30 | I Fell In Love Last Night/Over And Over (p/s) | 6 |

HEAVEN 17

81	Wool City Rocker LYN 9296	Something's Wrong (flexidisc free with fanzine)	8/5
81	Virgin VS 417	I'm Your Money/Are Everything (p/s)	5
82	Virgin VS 483	Height Of The Fighting (He-La-Hu)/Honeymoon In New York (unissued, no p/s)	15
83	Virgin VSP 570	Temptation/We Live So Fast (picture disc)	5
83	Virgin VSP 607	Come Live With Me/Let's All Make A Bomb (picture disc)	5
83	Virgin VSP 628	Crushed By The Wheels Of Industry/(Version) (picture disc)	5
88	Virgin VSCD 1113	The Ballad Of Go Go Brown (Extended Version)/I Set You Free/The Ballad Of Go Go Brown (7" Version)/Slow All Over (CD)	8
88	Virgin VSCD 1134	Train Of Love In Motion (7" Version)/Work/Train Of Love In Motion (The Mainline Mix)/Giving Up (3" CD, card sleeve)	8
88	Virgin CDT 19	Temptation/Who'll Stop The Rain?/We Live So Fast (3" CD, card sleeve)	8
88	Virgin CDT 21	(We Don't Need This) Fascist Groove Thang (3" CD, gatefold card sleeve)	8
84	Virgin/fan club	HOW MEN ARE (cassette, studio demo via fan club)	12
86	Virgin TCV 2383	ENDLESS (cassette, double-play in presentation box with booklet)	12

(see also B.E.F., Human League, Glenn Gregory & Claudia Brucken)

HEAVY COCHRAN

| 78 | Psycho P 2611 | I've Got Big Balls/Well, Fairly Big | 5 |
| 79 | Psycho P 2619 | I've Got A Little Prick/It's 12 Inches Long But I Don't Use It As A Rule | 6 |

(see also Lieutenant Pigeon)

MINT VALUE £

HEAVY DUTY BREAKS

85	Illuminated ILL 5512	Heavy Duty Breaks (Radio Version)/Bonus Beats (12", p/s)	8
85	Illuminated JAMS 49	HEAVY DUTY BREAKS (LP, remixes of other artists)	12

(see also Youth, Killing Joke)

HEAVY JELLY

69	Island WIP 6049	I Keep Singing The Same Old Song/Blue	20

(see also Skip Bifferty, Griffin, Graham Bell, Arc)

HEAVY JELLY

69	Head HDS 4001	Time Out Chewn In/The Long Wait	12
70	Island HELP	HEAVY JELLY (LP, promo only)	100
84	Psycho PSYCHO 30	TAKE ME DOWN TO THE WATER (LP, reissue of "Heavy Jelly")	12

(see also Jackie Lomax, Aynsley Dunbar Retaliation)

HEAVY METAL KIDS

74	Atlantic K 50047	HEAVY METAL KIDS (LP)	12
77	Rak SRAK 523	KITSCH (LP)	12

(see also Gary Holton, Kids)

HEAVYWEIGHTS

69	Spark SRL 1033	Utterly Funky/Shambala	5

BOBBY HEBB

66	Philips BF 1503	Sunny/Bread	5
66	Philips BF 1522	A Satisfied Mind/Love Love Love	8
67	Philips BF 1541	Love Me/Baby I'm Crazy	6
67	Philips BF 1570	I Love Everything About You/Some Kinda Magic	6
67	Philips BF 1610	Everything Is Coming Up Roses/Bound By Love	5
68	Philips BF 1702	You Want To Change Me/Dreamy	22
72	Philips 6051 023	Love Love Love/Sunny	5
72	Philips 6051 025	Some Kind Of Magic/Good Lovin'	5
66	Philips BL 7740	SUNNY (LP)	18

HEBREW CHILDREN & INNER CIRCLE

73	Ackee ACK 508	Dog And Bone/Version	5

DICK HECKSTALL-SMITH (QUINTET)

57	Pye Jazz NJE 1037	VERY SPECIAL OLD JAZZ (EP, as Dick Heckstall-Smith Quintet)	20
72	Bronze ILPS 9196	DUST IN THE AIR SUSPENDED MARKS THE PLACE ... WHERE A STORY ENDED (LP, gatefold sleeve with lyric inner sleeve)	15

(see also Graham Bond Organisation, John Mayall & Bluesbreakers, Alexis Korner, Colosseum, Rocket 88)

JESSE HECTOR

99	No Hit NO HIT EP 1961	Fast Train To Memphis/My Bucket's Got A Hole In It/All By Myself/Nightmares (p/s)	6

HEDGEHOG PIE

76	Rubber ADUB 8	Well I Know/Go With The Flow	6
76	Rubber TUB 12	THE LAMBTON WORM (EP, foldout sleeve)	8
72	Rubber RUB 002	HIS ROUND (LP, with Tony Capstick)	15
75	Rubber RUB 009	HEDGEHOG PIE (LP)	25
75	Rubber RUB 014	GREEN LADY (LP)	20
78	Rubber RUB 024	JUST ACT NORMAL (LP, with lyric insert)	20

(see also Dando Shaft)

HEDGEHOPPERS ANONYMOUS

65	Decca F 12241	It's Good News Week/Afraid Of Love	5
65	Decca F 12298	Don't Push Me/Please Don't Hurt Your Heart For Me	6
66	Decca F 12400	Baby (You're My Everything)/Remember	10
66	Decca F 12479	Daytime/That's The Time	6
66	Decca F 12530	Stop Press/Little Memories	7

(see also Alan Avon & Toy Shop, Jonathan King, Mick Tinsley)

HEFNER

97	Inertia INERT 0004	Car Chase/Remix (12", p/s)	10
98	Too Pure PURE 64	THE HEFNER SOUL (10" EP)	10

NEAL HEFTI & ORCHESTRA

66	RCA Victor RCA 1521	The Batman Theme/Batman Chase	15
89	RCA PB 49571PD	The Batman Theme (1966 Version)/Batman Chase (picture disc)	5
65	Warner Bros W 1599	HARLOW (LP, soundtrack)	25
65	United Artists (S)ULP 1098	HOW TO MURDER YOUR WIFE (LP, soundtrack)	30
66	RCA Victor RD 7795	BOEING BOEING (LP, soundtrack)	25
66	United Artists (S)ULP 1141	DUEL AT DIABLO (LP, soundtrack)	18
67	London HA-D 8337	BAREFOOT IN THE PARK (LP, soundtrack)	25
68	Dot (S)LPD 514	THE ODD COUPLE (LP, soundtrack)	30

LUCILLE HEGAMIN

73	VJM VLP 50	BLUE FLAME (LP)	12

DONALD HEIGHT

66	London HLZ 10062	Talk Of The Grapevine/There'll Be No Tomorrow	50
67	London HLZ 10116	Three Hundred & Sixty Five Days/I'm Willing To Wait	30
71	Avco Embassy 6105 005	Dancin' To The Music Of Love/Rags To Riches To Rags	10
71	Jay Boy BOY 32	Talk Of The Grapevine/There'll Be No Tomorrow (reissue)	6
72	Jay Boy BOY 51	Three Hundred & Sixty Five Days/I'm Willing To Wait (reissue)	5
72	Jay Boy BOY 60	We Gotta Make Up/I Can't Get Enough	5

RONNIE HEIGHT

59	Decca F 11126	Come Softly To Me/So Young, So Wise	15
59	Decca F 11126	Come Softly To Me/So Young, So Wise (78)	30
60	London HLN 9144	The One Finger Symphony/Mem'ries & Habits	6

HEINZ (& WILD BOYS)

63	Decca F 11652	Dreams Do Come True/Been Invited To A Party	15
63	Decca F 11693	Just Like Eddie/Don't You Knock At My Door	5
63	Decca F 11768	Country Boy/Long Tall Jack	6
64	Decca F 11831	You Were There/No Matter What They Say	10
64	Decca F 11920	Please Little Girl/For Loving Me This Way	15
64	Columbia DB 7374	Questions I Can't Answer/The Beating Of My Heart	15
65	Columbia DB 7482	Diggin' My Potatoes/She Ain't Comin' Back (with Wild Boys)	20
65	Columbia DB 7559	Don't Think Twice, It's All Right/Big Fat Spider	18
65	Columbia DB 7656	End Of The World/You Make Me Feel So Good	25
65	Columbia DB 7779	Heart Full Of Sorrow/Don't Worry Baby	25
66	Columbia DB 7942	Movin' In/I'm Not A Bad Guy	30
63	Decca DFE 8545	HEINZ (EP)	45
63	Decca DFE 8559	LIVE IT UP (EP)	40
64	Decca LK 4599	TRIBUTE TO EDDIE (LP)	60

(see also Tornados, Saints)

HELDEN

83	Zica ZICA 01	Holding On/Once Upon A Time In The ... (p/s)	8
83	Zica 12 ZICA 01	Holding On/Once Upon A Time In The ... (12", p/s)	15
83	In The City ITC 1	Holding On/HOI POLLOI: When It's History (free with *In The City* magazine)	8/6

(see also Ultravox)

HELEN LOVE

93	Dam. Goods DAMGOOD 18	Formula One Racing Girls/Riding High (pink vinyl, p/s)	6
93	Dam. Goods DAMGOOD 27	Joey Ramoney/I Was Your Greatest Fan (green vinyl, p/s)	6
94	Dam. Goods DAMGOOD 38	Punk Boy/Punk Boy 2 (blue vinyl, p/s)	6
94	Dam. Goods DAMGOOD 42	SUMMER POP PUNK POP EP (10", pink vinyl, p/s, 500 only)	12
95	Dam. Goods DAMPUD 33	Christmas Single/(Wat Tyler track) (olive vinyl, p/s)	12
95	Dam. Goods DAMGOOD 61	Bubblegum/Let's Go (pink vinyl, p/s)	6
95	Dam. Goods DAMGOOD 80	Ahead Of The Race/Diet Cola Race (white vinyl, p/s)	5
95	Dam. Goods DAMGOOD 89	Beat Him Up/Superboy/Supergirl (blue vinyl, p/s)	5
95	Wurlitzer Jukebox WJ 4	Il Fait Beau/BELMONDO: Metroliner (flexidisc)	5
96	Dam. Goods DAMGOOD 95	We Love You/The Girl About Town/We Love You/Punk Boy (orange vinyl, p/s)	5

RICHARD HELL (& VOIDOIDS)

76	Stiff BUY 7	(I Could Live With You In) Another World/(I Belong To The) Blank Generation/ You Gotta Lose (some with p/s, numbered, 5,000 only; later re-pressed for "The Stiff Box Set" & numbered '001')	10/6
77	Sire 6078 608	Blank Generation/Love Comes In Spurts (no p/s)	8
77	Sire 6078 608	Blank Generation/Liars Beware/Who Says? (12", p/s)	10
79	Radar ADA 30	The Kid With The Replaceable Head/I'm Your Man (p/s)	7
94	Overground OVER 36	Another World/Blank Generation/Love Comes In Spurts (p/s, reissue, 2,000 only)	5
96	Codex CODE 3X	GO NOW (10", p/s, 1,000 only, etched yellow vinyl)	8
96	Codex CODE 3	GO NOW (CD, 1,000 only)	8
92	Overground OVER 24	3 NEW SONGS (EP, 134 yellow vinyl copies)	6
77	Sire 9103 327	BLANK GENERATION (LP, some with inner sleeve)	15/12
83	I.D. NOSE 2	DESTINY STREET (LP)	12

(see also Neon Boys)

HELLANBACH

84	Neat NEAT 1006	NOW HEAR THIS (LP, with inner sleeve)	12
84	Neat NEAT 1019	THE BIG ... H (LP, with insert)	12

HELLHAMMER

84	Noise N 008	APOCALYPTIC RAIDS (12" EP, 45/33rpm)	15

DAVE HELLING

65	Stateside SS 409	It Ain't Me Babe/If You're Gonna Leave Me	7
66	Planet PLF 101	Christine/The Bells (with 'Planet' company sleeve)	20/15

HELLIONS

65	Piccadilly 7N 35213	Daydreaming Of You/Shades Of Blue	15
65	Piccadilly 7N 35232	Tomorrow Never Comes/Dream Child	15
65	Piccadilly 7N 35265	A Little Lovin'/Think It Over	15

(see also Revolution, Traffic, Roaring Sixties, Jim Capaldi, Dave Mason, Luther Grosvenor, Family, Spooky Tooth)

HELLO

72	Bell BELL 1238	You Move Me/Ask Your Mama	15
72	Bell BELL 1265	C'mon/Wench	5
73	Bell BELL 1333	Another School Day/C'mon Get Together (p/s)	15

HELL PREACHERS INC.

69	Marble Arch MALS 1169	SUPREME PSYCHEDELIC UNDERGROUND (LP)	22

BOBBY HELMS

57	Brunswick 05711	Fraulein/(Got A) Heartsick Feeling	7
57	Brunswick 05711	Fraulein/(Got A) Heartsick Feeling (78)	8
57	Brunswick 05721	My Special Angel/Standing At The End of My World	12
58	Brunswick 05730	No Other Baby/The Magic Song	10
58	Brunswick 05730	No Other Baby/The Magic Song (78)	10
58	Brunswick 05741	Love My Lady/Just A Little Lonesome	8
58	Brunswick 05741	Love My Lady/Just A Little Lonesome (78)	8
58	Brunswick 05748	Jacqueline/Living In The Shadow Of The Past	10
58	Brunswick 05748	Jacqueline/Living In The Shadow Of The Past (78)	8
58	Brunswick 05754	Schoolboy Crush/Borrowed Dreams	12
58	Brunswick 05754	Schoolboy Crush/Borrowed Dreams (78)	18
58	Brunswick 05765	Jingle Bell Rock/Captain Santa Claus	15
58	Brunswick 05765	Jingle Bell Rock/Captain Santa Claus (78)	25

Bobby HELMS

59	Brunswick 05786	Miss Memory/New River Train	7
59	Brunswick 05786	Miss Memory/New River Train (78)	20
59	Brunswick 05801	Soon It Can Be Told/I Guess I'll Miss The Prom	6
59	Brunswick 05801	Soon It Can Be Told/I Guess I'll Miss The Prom (78)	20
59	Brunswick 05813	My Lucky Day/Hurry Baby	6
59	Brunswick 05813	My Lucky Day/Hurry Baby (78)	25
61	Brunswick 05852	Sad Eyed Baby/You're The One	6
60	Brunswick OE 9461	BOBBY HELMS (EP)	50
57	Brunswick LAT 8250	SINGS TO MY SPECIAL ANGEL (LP)	75

JIMMY HELMS
63	Pye 7N 45440	Ragtime Girl/Romeo & Juliet	5
69	London HL 10255	If You Let Me/I Don't Care Who Knows It	5
73	Capitol CL 15762	My Little Devil/Magnificent Sanctuary Band	5

HELP
71	MCA MWPS 4039	SECOND COMING (LP)	50

HELPLESS HUW
78	US US 001	Still Love You (In My Heart)	5
80	US US 002	Sid Vicious Was Innocent/Going Through The Motions/ Baby We're Not In Love/When You're Weary (p/s in bag)	5

HELP YOURSELF
71	Liberty LBF 15459	Running Down Deep/Paper Leaves	8
72	United Artists UP 35355	Heaven Row/Brown Lady	8
72	United Artists UP 35466	Mommy Won't Be Home For Christmas/Johnny B. Goode	6
71	Liberty LBS 83484	HELP YOURSELF (LP)	20
72	United Artists UAS 29287	STRANGE AFFAIR (LP, with inner sleeve)	20
72	United Artists UAS 29413	BEWARE OF THE SHADOW (LP)	18
73	United Artists UDG 4001 [UAS 29487/FREE 1]	THE RETURN OF KEN WHALEY/HAPPY DAYS (2-LP, box set with individual sleeves)	30
73	United Artists UAS 29487	THE RETURN OF KEN WHALEY (LP, with inner sleeve, available separately)	15

(see also Man, Deke Leonard, Shades Of Morley Brown, Tyla Gang)

HEMLOCK
73	Deram DM 379	Mr Horizontal/Beggar Man	8
73	Deram SML 1102	HEMLOCK (LP)	45

(see also Miller Anderson, Keef Hartley Band, Dog Soldier)

BERTHA HENDERSON/ROSA HENDERSON
60	Jazz Collector JEL 14	THE FEMALE BLUES VOL. 2 (EP)	15

BILL HENDERSON
60	Top Rank JAR 412	Sweet Pumpkin/Joey, Joey, Joey	12
63	Stateside SL 10019	BILL HENDERSON (LP)	18

DICKIE HENDERSON & JUNE LAVERICK
60	Oriole CB 1536	Simpatica/It's So Nice To Sleep With No-One (78)	10

(see also June Laverick)

DORRIS HENDERSON
65	Columbia DB 7567	The Hangman/Leaves That Are Green	12
67	Fontana TF 811	Message To Pretty/Watch The Stars	8
65	Columbia SX 6001	THERE YOU GO (LP, with John Renbourn)	220
67	Fontana (S)TL 5385	WATCH THE STARS (LP, with John Renbourn)	165

(see also Eclection, John Renbourn)

EDMONIA HENDERSON
50	Jazz Collector L 21	Jelly Roll Blues/Lazy Daddy Blues (78)	10
51	Tempo R 43	Mama Don't Want A Sweet Man Any More/Hateful Blues (78)	10

FINIS HENDERSON
83	Motown TMGT 1304	Skip To My Lou/I'd Rather Be Gone/Vina Del Mar (12")	10

FLETCHER HENDERSON
50s	Jazz Collector JE 111	FLETCHER HENDERSON JAZZ GROUP (EP)	8
50s	Jazz Collector JE 115	BIG BAND STORY VOL. 1 (EP)	8
55	London AL 3547	BIRTH OF BIG BAND JAZZ (10" LP)	15
55	HMV DLP 1066	AT CONNIE'S INN (10" LP)	15
50s	Audubon AAF-AAK	FLETCHER HENDERSON (6 x 10" LP set)	60

JOE HENDERSON
63	London REU 1376	JOE HENDERSON (EP)	12

JOE 'MR. PIANO' HENDERSON
58	Pye Nixa 7N 15147	Trudie/Love Is The Sweetest Thing	5

LORNA HENDERSON
60	Oriole CB 1549	Lollipops To Lipstick/Steady Eddie	8
60	Oriole CB 1549	Lollipops To Lipstick/Steady Eddie (78)	25
60	Oriole CB 1590	A Thousand Stars/Murray, What's Your Hurry?	7

RICKIE HENDERSON
59	Embassy WB 318	One Night/High Class Baby (78)	8
59	Embassy WB 334	I Need Your Love Tonight/Never Be Anyone Else But You (78)	8
59	Embassy WB 339	Kansas City/The Heart Of A Man (78)	8
59	Embassy WB 343	A Teenager In Love/Personality (78)	8
59	Embassy WB 349	Waterloo/I Know (78)	8
59	Embassy WB 351	Waterloo/Tallahassee Lassie (78)	8
59	Embassy WB 357	Peggy Sue Got Married/The Three Bells (78)	10
59	Embassy WB 361	Dynamite/Wish It Were Me (78)	10

MINT VALUE £

60	Embassy WB 377	Starry Eyed/Why (78)	10
60	Embassy WB 382	El Paso/What More Do You Want (78)	10
60	Embassy WB 383	Delaware/Lady Luck (78)	10
60	Embassy WB 388	Do You Mind/Be Mine (78)	10
60	Embassy WB 391	He'll Have To Go/Fame And Fortune (78)	10
60	Embassy WB 399	Three Steps To Heaven/The Urge (78)	15
60	Embassy WB 406	Mais Quis/If She Should Come To You (78)	10
60	Embassy WB 419	It's Now Or Never/Save That Last Dance For Me (78)	15
60	Embassy WB 423	My Love For You/Just As Much As Ever (78)	12

RUSS HENDERSON & HIS CALYPSO BAND
57	HMV POP 333	Waiting For The Coconuts To Fall/Nobody's Business (78)	8

(see also Marie Bryant)

SKITCH HENDERSON
50s	Brunswick OE 9434	LONDON AT MIDNIGHT (EP)	10

WILLIE HENDERSON (& SOUL EXPLOSIONS)
70	MCA MU 1127	Funky Chicken/Oo Wee Baby, I Love You (with Soul Explosions)	7
73	Contempo C 18	The Dance Master (Parts 1 & 2)	6
74	Contempo CS 9005	The Dance Master (Parts 1 & 2) (reissue)	5
74	Pye International 7N 25668	Gangster Boogie Bump/Let's Merengue	5

BOBBY HENDRICKS
58	London HL 8714	Itchy Twitchy Feeling/A Thousand Dreams	50
58	London HL 8714	Itchy Twitchy Feeling/A Thousand Dreams (78)	40
59	Top Rank JAR 193	Little John Green/Sincerely, Your Lover	8
61	Mercury AMT 1163	I'm Coming Home/Every Other Night	7
64	Sue WI 315	Itchy Twitchy Feeling/Thousand Dreams (reissue, as Bobby Henricks)	15

(see also Drifters)

HUGH HENDRICKS & UPSETTERS
70	Spinning Wheel SW 103	Land Of Kinks/O'NEIL HALL: This Man	8

JON HENDRICKS
56	Brunswick 05521	Four Brothers/Cloudburst (with Dave Lambert Singers)	8
68	Verve VS 572	No More/Rainbow's End	5
71	Philips 6006 088	I Got Soul/Slow Train	5
61	Vogue EPV 1268	A GOOD GIT-TOGETHER (EP)	12
60	Vogue LAE 12231	A GOOD GIT-TOGETHER (LP)	18
70	Valiant VS 140	BOSSA MAN (LP)	12
72	Philips 6438 019	LIVE (LP)	12

(see also Dave Lambert)

JIMI HENDRIX (EXPERIENCE)
SINGLES
66	Polydor 56139	Hey Joe/Stone Free	8
67	Track 604 001	Purple Haze/51st Anniversary (white or black label)	10/6
67	Track 604 004	The Wind Cries Mary/Highway Chile	7
67	Track 604 007	Burning Of The Midnight Lamp/The Stars That Play With Laughing Sam's Dice	7
67	Decca F 22652	How Would You Feel/You Don't Want Me (with Curtis Knight, unreleased)	
67	Track 604 009	How Would You Feel/You Don't Want Me (with Curtis Knight)	8
67	London HL 10160	Hush Now/Flashing (with Curtis Knight; some in export p/s)	30/8
68	Track 604 025	All Along The Watchtower/Long Hot Summer Night	6
69	Track 604 029	Crosstown Traffic/Gypsy Eyes	8
69	Track 604 033	Let Me Light Your Fire/The Burning Of The Midnight Lamp	8
70	London HLZ 10321	Ballad Of Jimi/Gloomy Monday (with Curtis Knight)	6
70	London HL 7126	Ballad Of Jimi/Gloomy Monday (with Curtis Knight, export issue)	25
70	Track 2095 001	Voodoo Chile/Hey Joe/All Along The Watchtower (p/s; later copies have white border on sleeve; also sold without p/s)	10/7/5
71	RCA RCA 2033	No Such Animal (Parts 1 & 2) (initially in p/s, with Curtis Knight uncredited)	15/5
71	Track 2094 007	Angel/Night Bird Flying	5
71	Track 2094 010	Gypsy Eyes/Remember/Purple Haze/Stone Free (initially in p/s)	15/6
72	Polydor 2001 277	Johnny B. Goode/Little Wing	6
73	Reprise K 14286	Hear My Train A-Comin/Rock Me Baby	6
73	Polydor/Sound For Industry SFI 1572	Red House/Spanish Castle Magic (1-sided flexidisc with *Rolling Stone*)	15/5
80	Polydor 2608 001	6 SINGLES PACK (6 plain sleeve singles [2141 275-280], open-out card p/s)	20
82	CBS CBS A 2749	Fire/Are You Experienced? (p/s)	5
89	Castle Comms. HENPD 01	Hey Joe/Purple Haze/Radio One Theme (12", picture disc)	8
89	Polydor PO 33	Purple Haze/51st Anniversary (p/s, reissue)	5
89	Polydor PZCD 33	Purple Haze/51st Anniversary/All Along The Watchtower/Hey Joe (CD, card p/s)	8
90	Polydor PO 71	Crosstown Traffic/Voodoo Chile (p/s)	5
90	Polydor PO 100	All Along The Watchtower/Voodoo Chile/Hey Joe (p/s)	5
92	BMG 791 168	JIMI PLAYS BERKELEY (CD EP, available with "Jimi Plays Berkeley" video)	8

TRACK LPs
67	Track 612 001/613 001	ARE YOU EXPERIENCED (LP, mono/stereo)	60/35
67	Track 612 003	AXIS: BOLD AS LOVE (LP, laminated gatefold sleeve, some with gatefold insert, mono)	80/50
67	Track 613 003	AXIS: BOLD AS LOVE (LP, laminated gatefold sleeve, some with gatefold insert, stereo)	75/40
68	Track 612 004/613 004	SMASH HITS (LP, mono/stereo)	35/20
68	Track 612 008/009	ELECTRIC LADYLAND (2-LP, plain white non-gatefold sleeve, labels marked "Test Pressing", stereo)	1,000+
68	Track 613 008/009	ELECTRIC LADYLAND (2-LP, laminated gatefold sleeve, stereo)	60
68	Track 613 010	ELECTRIC LADYLAND PART 1 (LP, stereo only)	25
68	Track 613 017	ELECTRIC LADYLAND PART 2 (LP, stereo only)	25
70	Track Super 2406 002	BAND OF GYPSYS (LP, original 'puppet' sleeve)	50

JIMI HENDRIX

70	Track Super 2406 002	BAND OF GYPSYS (LP, repressing, gatefold 'Isle Of Wight' sleeve) 20
70	Track Super 2406 002	BAND OF GYPSYS (LP, 2nd repressing, single sleeve) 15
70	Track 2407 010	BACKTRACK 10: ARE YOU EXPERIENCED? (LP, budget reissue, mono) 15
70	Track 2407 011	BACKTRACK 11: AXIS: BOLD AS LOVE (LP, budget reissue, mono). 15
71	Track 2856 002	ELECTRIC JIMI HENDRIX (LP, mail-order only Record Club release) 600
71	Track 2408 101	THE CRY OF LOVE (LP, gatefold sleeve). 15
71	Track 2408 101	THE CRY OF LOVE
		(LP, red vinyl, factory custom pressing, 2 copies only) 1,000

POLYDOR LPs

71	Polydor 2302 016	ISLE OF WIGHT (LP) 12
71	Polydor 2302 018	HENDRIX IN THE WEST (LP, gatefold sleeve) 15
72	Polydor 2302 020	WAR HEROES (LP). 15
72	Polydor 2302 023	THE CRY OF LOVE (LP, gatefold sleeve, reissue). 12
73	Polydor 2302 268	SMASH HITS (LP, stereo reissue) 12
73	Polydor 2480 005	BAND OF GYPSYS (LP, reissue, different gatefold sleeve). 12
73	Polydor 2657 012	ELECTRIC LADYLAND (2-LP, laminated gatefold sleeve, reissue). 15
73	Polydor 2310 271	ELECTRIC LADYLAND PART 1 (LP, reissue). 12
73	Polydor 2310 272	ELECTRIC LADYLAND PART 2 (LP, reissue). 12
74	Polydor 2310 301	LOOSE ENDS (LP) 12
75	Polydor 2310 398	CRASH LANDING (LP). 12
75	Polydor 2310 415	MIDNIGHT LIGHTNING (LP). 12
78	Polydor 2612 034	THE ESSENTIAL JIMI HENDRIX (2-LP, with bonus 1-sided 33rpm 7"
		"Gloria" [JIMI 1] in special bag). 18
78	St. Michael 2102/0102	JIMI HENDRIX (LP, cat. no. also listed as Polydor 2891 139) 60
78	St. Michael/Poly. 2891 139	JIMI HENDRIX (cassette) 25
80	Polydor 2625 040	JIMI HENDRIX (13-LP box set [11 x LP + 1 x 2-LP]) 75
80	Polydor POLS 1023	NINE TO THE UNIVERSE (LP) 12
84	Polydor SPDLP 3	ELECTRIC LADYLAND
		(2-LP, non-laminate gatefold sleeve, 2nd reissue) 15
87	Polydor 833 004-1	LIVE AT WINTERLAND (2-LP, with poster) 15
88	Polydor/HMV C88 LP 1-16	ARE YOU EXPERIENCED?
		(LP, box set sold via HMV stores, 1,500 only) 12
90	Polydor 847 2311	CORNERSTONES: JIMI HENDRIX 1967-1970 (LP). 12

OTHER LPs

68	London HA/SH 8349	GET THAT FEELING (LP, with Curtis Knight) 18
68	London HA/SH 8369	STRANGE THINGS (LP, with Curtis Knight) 18
71	Ember NR 5057	EXPERIENCE — THE ORIGINAL SOUNDTRACK (LP, gatefold sleeve). 12
71	Reprise K 44159	RAINBOW BRIDGE (LP, matt gatefold sleeve, 'steamboat' label, soundtrack). 12
72	Ember NR 5061	MORE EXPERIENCE (LP, soundtrack). 12
73	Reprise K 64017	SOUNDTRACK RECORDINGS FROM THE FILM JIMI HENDRIX (2-LP). 15
73	Ember NR 5068	IN THE BEGINNING (LP, textured gatefold sleeve) 12
74	Ember EMB 3428	LOOKING BACK WITH JIMI HENDRIX (LP) 12
75	DJM DJLMD 8011	FOR REAL (2-LP, gatefold sleeve). 15
89	Castle Comms. HBLP 100	LIVE AND UNRELEASED — THE RADIO SHOW (5-LP). 30

CDs

84	Track 821 993 2	BAND OF GYPSYS (CD). 18
88	Polydor/HMV C88 LP 1-11	ARE YOU EXPERIENCED? (CD, box set via HMV stores, 1,500 only). 18
89	Castle Comms. HBCD 100	LIVE AND UNRELEASED — THE RADIO SHOW (3-CD, box set) 30
89	Polydor 831 312-2	HENDRIX IN THE WEST (CD) 18
89	Polydor 837 574-2	LOOSE ENDS (CD). 18

(see also Eire Apparent, Jayne Mansfield, McGough & McGear, Noel Redding Band, Fat Mattress, Curtis Knight, Billy Cox, Buddy Miles, Riot Squad)

MARGIE HENDRIX
66	Mercury MF 976	I Call You Lover But You Ain't Nothin' But A Tramp/The Question	6
67	Mercury MF 1001	Restless/On The Right Track	10

LARRY HENLEY
64	Hickory 45-1272	My Reasons For Living/Stickin' Up For My Baby	10

(see also Newbeats, Dean & Mark)

CHRISTIE HENNESSY
73	Westwood	CHRISTIE HENNESSY (LP)	35

HENNESSYS
69	Cambrian CLP 593	THE ROADS AND THE MILES (LP)	12
60s	Music Factory MF 106	CARDIFF AFTER DARK (LP)	20

ADRIAN HENRI
60s	Charivari	ADRIAN HENRI (LP)	12
60s	Argo PLP 1194	ADRIAN HENRI AND HUGO WILLIAMS (LP)	12

(see also Liverpool Scene, McGough & McGear)

ANN HENRY
60	Top Rank JAR 292	Like Young/Sugar Blues	5

BOB HENRY
65	Philips BF 1450	I Need Someone/Built Like A Man	10

(see also Robert Henry)

CLARENCE ('FROGMAN') HENRY
57	London HLN 8389	Ain't Got No Home/Troubles Troubles (as Clarence Henry) (gold or silver lettering)	200/100
57	London HLN 8389	Ain't Got No Home/Troubles Troubles (as Clarence Henry) (78)	50
61	Pye International 7N 25078	(I Don't Know Why) But I Do/Just My Baby And Me	6
61	Pye International 7N 25089	You Always Hurt The One You Love/Little Suzy	6
61	Pye International 7N 25108	Lonely Street/Why Can't You	7
61	Pye International 7N 25115	On Bended Knees/Standing In The Need Of Love	7
62	Pye International 7N 25123	A Little Too Much/I Wish I Could Say The Same	7
62	Pye International 7N 25141	Dream Myself A Sweetheart/Lost Without You	7
62	Pye International 7N 25169	The Jealous Kind/Come On And Dance	7
64	London HLU 9936	Little Green Frog/Have You Ever Been Lonely?	7
66	London HLU 10025	Ain't Got No Home/Baby, Ain't That Love?	7
61	Pye Intl. NEP 44007	CLARENCE 'FROGMAN' HENRY HIT PARADE (EP)	50
61	Pye Intl. NPL 28017	YOU ALWAYS HURT THE ONE YOU LOVE (LP)	50

RICHARD HENRY
68	Regal Zonophone RZ 3014	Oh Girl/Lay Your Head Upon My Shoulder	5

ROBERT HENRY
66	Philips BF 1476	Walk Away Like A Winner/That's All I Want	35

(see also Bob Henry)

HENRY COW
73	Virgin V 2005	THE LEGEND (LP)	12
74	Virgin V 2011	UNREST (LP)	12
75	Virgin V 2027	IN PRAISE OF LEARNING (LP)	12
76	Caroline CAD 3002	CONCERTS (LP)	12
79	Broadcast BC 1	WESTERN CULTURE (LP)	12

(see also Slapp Happy, Art Bears, Fred Frith, Gong/Henry Cow/Global Trucking Company)

HENRY & LIZA
73	Dragon DRA 1004	Hole Under Cratches/TIVOLIS: Hole Under Cratches (Instrumental) (actually "Hole Under Crutches")	5

(see also Max Romeo)

HENRY III
67	Island WI 3078	Thank You Girl/Take Me Back	18
67	Island WI 3081	I'll Reach The End/Won't Go Away (B-side actually "Lee's Special" by Don Tony Lee)	18
67	RCA RCA 1568	So Much Love/Sitting In The Park	12
70	Dynamic DYN 402	Out Of Time/VICEROYS: Love For Everyone (both with Hubcap & Wheels)	7

(see also Uniques)

JUDY HENSKE
66	Reprise RS 20485	Road To Nowhere/Sing A Rainbow	5
65	Reprise RS 6203	DEATH DEFYING (LP)	15

JUDY HENSKE & JERRY YESTER
69	Straight STS 1052	FAREWELL ALDEBARAN (LP)	20

ROBERT HENRY HENSLEY
68	Polydor 56295	You're Gonna See Me Cry/Montage	8

NICKY HENSON
63	Parlophone R 4976	Till I See You Cry/What Does It Mean?	6

DAVID HENTSCHEL
75	Ring O' 2017 101	Oh My My/Devil Woman	8
75	Ring O' 2320 101	ST*RTLING MUSIC (LP)	12

NAT HEPBURN
60s	Jump Up JU 516	River/Political Girl	5

HEP STARS
66	Decca F 22446	Sunny Girl/No Response	30
67	Olga OLE 001	Wedding/Consolation	15
68	Olga OLE 013	Let It Be Me/Groovy Summertime (withdrawn, supposedly reissued 1969)	40
68	Olga OLE 014	Malaika/It's Nice To Be Back (some in export p/s)	50/25

(see also Abba)

HEPTONES

66	Rio R 104	Gunmen Coming To Town/TOMMY McCOOK & SUPERSONICS: Riverton City	35
67	Ska Beat JB 266	We've Got Love/I Am Lonely	60
67	Caltone TONE 105	Schoolgirls/Ain't That Bad?	15
67	Studio One SO 2005	A Change Is Gonna Come/Nobody Knows	18
67	Studio One SO 2014	Fat Girl/DELROY WILSON: Mother Word	15
67	Studio One SO 2021	If I Knew/Festival Day	50
67	Studio One SO 2026	Why Did You Leave?/GAYLADS: Don't Try To Reach Me	18
67	Studio One SO 2027	Why Must I?/SLIM SMITH: Try Again	18
67	Studio One SO 2031	Take Me (actually by The Soul Vendors)/DELROY WILSON: I'm Not A King	18
67	Studio One SO 2033	Only Sixteen/Baby	15
68	Studio One SO 2040	Tripe Girl/DELROY WILSON: Mr. D.J.	18
68	Studio One SO 2049	Cry, Baby, Cry/Mama	18
68	Studio One SO 2052	Dock Of The Bay/KING ROCKY (ELLIS): The Ruler	18
68	Studio One SO 2055	Party Time/Oil In Your Lamp	18
68	Coxsone CS 7052	Love Won't Come Easy/Gee Wee	18
68	Coxsone CS 7068	Equal Rights/Ting-A-Ling	18
68	Coxsone CS 7082	Soul Power/Love Me Always	18
69	Coxsone CS 7092	Sweet Talking/Ob-La-Di	18
69	Studio One SO 2083	I Shall Be Released/Love Me Always	18
69	Bamboo BAM 11	I Shall Be Released/Love Me Always (Power) (reissue)	10
70	Bamboo BAM 28	Young, Gifted and Black/SOUND DIMENSION: Joyland	10
70	Bamboo BAM 39	Young Generation/You Turned Away	30
70	Bamboo BAM 43	Message From A Blackman/SOUND DIMENSION: Jamaica Underground	10
70	Upsetter US 339	Hurry Up/Thanks We Get	8
70	Banana BA 311	Be A Man/U ROY: Shock Attack	10
71	Banana BA 325	Suspicious Minds/Haven't You Any Fight Left?	10
71	Banana BA 349	Freedom Line/SOUND DIMENSION: Version	8
72	Green Door GD 4020	Hypocrite/JOHNNY LOVER: Straight To The Head	12
72	Prince Buster PB 37	Our Day Will Come/PRINCE BUSTER: Protection	12
72	Ashanti ASH 411	I'm In The Mood For Love/TOMMY McCOOK & NOW GENERATION: Eight Years After	8
72	Duke DU 143	Save The Last Dance For Me/Be The One	6
72	Pama PM 843	You've Lost That Lovin' Feelin'/RUPIE EDWARDS ALLSTARS: Feeling Version	6
72	Pama Supreme PS 367	Save The Last Dance For Me/Save The Last Dance Version	6
72	Ackee ACK 407	I Miss You (Parts 1 & 2)	10
73	Ackee ACK 414	Let Me Hold Your Hand/Version	5
73	Jaguar JAG 103	Drifting Away/BONGO LES: Zion Drum	8
73	Grape GR 3053	Old Time/G.G. ALLSTARS: Dub	5
73	Smash SMA 2328	Soul Sister/IMPACT ALLSTARS: Soul Sister (Version)	7
74	Pama Supreme PS 390	Thanks We Get/Oppression (both actually by Delroy Butler)	7
75	Faith FA 012	Party Time/Version	5
67	Studio One SOL 9002	THE HEPTONES (LP)	100
68	Studio One SOL 9010	ON TOP (LP)	100
72	Trojan TBL 183	THE HEPTONES AND THEIR FRIENDS MEET THE NOW GENERATION (LP)	25
75	Island ILPS 9297	BOOK OF RULES (LP)	12

(see also Barry Llewellyn, Soul Vendors, Ronald & Lloyd, Ed Nangle, Love Generation, Alton Ellis, Basil Daley, Ken Boothe, Jackie Mittoo)

HERB & KAY

54	Parlophone MSP 6127	This Ole House/Angels In The Sky	18
54	Parlophone R 3916	This Ole House/Angels In The Sky (78)	10
54	Parlophone CMSP 23	This Ole House/Angels In The Sky (export issue)	18
55	Parlophone CMSP 31	Coffee Blues/Juke Box Jig (export issue)	18

HERBAL MIXTURE

66	Columbia DB 8021	A Love That's Died/Tailor Made	100
66	Columbia DB 8083	Machines/Please Leave My Mind	100

(see also Tony McPhee, Groundhogs)

HERBIE & ROYALISTS

68	Saga FID 2121	SOUL OF THE MATTER (LP)	20

HERBIE'S PEOPLE

65	CBS 202005	Sweet And Tender Romance/You Thrill Me To Pieces	15
66	CBS 202058	One Little Smile/You Never Know	7
67	CBS 202584	Residential Area/Humming Bird	8

HERD

65	Parlophone R 5284	Goodbye Baby, Goodbye/Here Comes The Fool	25
65	Parlophone R 5353	She Was Really Saying Something/It's Been A Long Time Baby	35
66	Parlophone R 5413	So Much In Love/This Boy's Always Been True	35
67	Fontana TF 819	I Can Fly/Diary Of A Narcissist	8
67	Fontana TF 856	From The Underworld/Sweet William	6
67	Fontana TF 887	Paradise Lost/Come On — Believe Me (some in p/s)	12/6
68	Fontana TF 925	I Don't Want Our Loving To Die/Our Fairy Tale	6
68	Fontana TF 975	Sunshine Cottage/Miss Jones	7
69	Fontana TF 1011	The Game/Beauty Queen	7
71	B&C CB 154	You've Got Me Hangin' From Your Lovin' Tree/ I Don't Wanna Go To Sleep Again	5
72	Bumble GEX 1	From The Underworld/Paradise Lost/On My Way Home (maxi-single)	5
73	Bumble GE 120	I Don't Want Our Loving To Die/The Game	5
68	Fontana (S)TL 5458	PARADISE LOST (LP)	30
72	Bumble GEMP 5001	NOSTALGIA (LP)	18

(see also Peter Frampton, Humble Pie, Judas Jump, Andy Bown, Preachers)

HERE & NOW

78	Charly CYS 1055	End Of The Beginning/Choke A Koala (p/s) 5
79	Charly CEP 122	A Dog In Hell/Floating Anarchy Radio (p/s) 5
80	Charly NOW 1	Give And Take 5
78	Deptford Fun City DLP 02	WHAT YOU SEE ... IS WHAT YOU ARE (LP, 1 side by Alternative TV).......... 12

(see also Daevid Allen)

HERESY

86	Earache	Thanks
		(flexidisc, mail-order, 2,000 only [400 each on different coloured vinyl]).......... 10
89	In Your Face FACE 4	WHOSE GENERATION? EP (gatefold p/s)................................. 7

HERESY/CONCRETE SOX

| 87 | Manic Ears MOSH 2 | HERESY/CONCRETE SOX (LP, 1 side each) .... 12 |

HERETIC

| 84 | Thunderbolt THBE 1004 | BURNT AT THE STAKE EP (12", p/s) .... 15 |

HERITAGE

| 81 | Rondelet ROUND 8 | Strange Place To Be/Misunderstood (p/s)............................. 20 |
| 82 | Rondelet ABOUT 12 | REMORSE CODE (LP, with lyric insert)............................... 20 |

HERMAN (Chin-Loy)

71	Big Shot BI 573	El Fishy/HERMAN'S ALLSTARS: Nightmare
		(B-side actually "In The Spirit" by Lloyd Charmers)...................... 7
71	Big Shot BI 577	Tar Baby (actually "Crazy Baby" by U. Roy Jr.)/TOMMY McCOOK: Archie........ 7
71	Big Shot BI 578	New Love/AUGUSTUS PABLO: The Mood............................... 18
71	Big Shot BI 579	East Of The River Nile Version/AUGUSTO PABLO: East Of The River Nile 25
71	Duke DU 107	To The Fields/HERMAN'S VERSION MEN: Fields Version.................... 10
71	Ackee ACK 133	Dunce Cap/AQUARIANS: Version Cap................................. 6
71	Ackee ACK 140	Youth Man/AQUARIANS: Version.................................... 20
71	Explosion EX 2049	Love Brother/Uganda... 6
71	Escort ERT 854	Love Brother/Love Brother Version
		(B-side actually by Tommy McCook)................................. 6
71	Punch PH 55	Hold The Ghost/AQUARIUS SOUL BAND: Duppy Dance 6
71	Punch PH 58	Listen To The Beat/AQUARIANS: Sounds Only.......................... 6

(see also Jimbilin)

PRIEST HERMAN

| 64 | Blue Beat BB 266 | We Are Praying/BUSTER'S ALLSTARS: Dallas, Texas .... 15 |

WOODY HERMAN

78s

52	London L 1156	Celestial Blues/Early Autumn (78)................................... 8
52	London L 1160	Blues In Advance/Terrista (78)..................................... 8
53	London L 1222	Men From Mars/Beau Jazz (78) 8
54	London HL 8013	Wooftie/Moten Stomp (78, as Woody Herman & New Third Herd)............. 10
54	London HL 8031	Fancy Woman/Eight Babies To Mind
		(78, as Woody Herman's Woodchoppers) 12
55	London HL 8122	Sorry 'bout The Whole Darned Thing/Love's A Dog
		(78, with New Third Herd)... 12

SINGLES

54	London HL 8013	Wooftie/Moten Stomp (as Woody Herman & New Third Herd) 15
54	London HL 8031	Fancy Woman/Eight Babies To Mind
		(as Woody Herman's Woodchoppers) 18
54	Capitol CL 14183	Muskrat Ramble/Woodchopper's Mambo
		(Woody Herman & His Orchestra) 10
55	London HL 8122	Sorry 'Bout The Whole Darned Thing/Love's A Dog (with New Third Herd)...... 12
55	Capitol CL 14231	Mexican Hat Trick/Sleepy Serenade (as Woody Herman & His Orchestra)........ 7
55	Capitol CL 14278	My Sin Is You/Have it Your Way (with Allen Sisters) 6
55	Capitol CL 14299	Kiss The Baby/Long, Long Night (as Woody Herman & New Third Herd) 6
55	Capitol CL 14333	The Girl Upstairs/You're Here, My Love
		(as Woody Herman & His Orchestra)................................. 7
55	Capitol CL 14366	Love Is A Many Splendoured Thing/House Of Bamboo
		(as Woody Herman & His Orchestra & Singers) 6
56	Capitol CL 14522	Skinned/Skinned Again (as Woody Herman & His Orchestra)................ 5
56	Capitol CL 14578	To Love Again/For All We Know (as Woody Herman & His Orchestra) 5
57	HMV POP 371	Comes Love/Makin' Whoopee 5
60	Top Rank TR 5012	Blowin' Up A Storm/It's Coolin' Time
		(as Woody Herman Orchestra)...................................... 5
60	Philips JAZ 113	The Third Herd/Keen And Peachy 5
62	Ember JBS 702	Woodchoppers' Ball/Body And Soul 8
69	Chess CRS 8095	Hush/Light My Fire.. 7

EPs

54	London RE-P 1001	HERD FROM MARS VOL. 1
		(EP, as Woody Herman & New Third Herd) 15
55	London RE-P 1002	HERD FROM MARS VOL. 2
		(EP, as Woody Herman & New Third Herd) 15
55	Columbia SEG 7532	WOODY HERMAN AND HIS ORCHESTRA (EP)............................ 8
55	Philips BBE 12026	WOODY HERMAN AND HIS ORCHESTRA (EP)............................ 8
55	Capitol EAP1 556	SPECIALS (EP)... 8
55	Capitol EAP1 560	THE WOODY HERMAN BAND (EP) 8
55	Capitol EAP2 560	THE WOODY HERMAN BAND (EP) 8
55	Capitol EAP3 560	THE WOODY HERMAN BAND (EP) 8
56	Capitol EAP2 658	THE WOODY HERMAN ORCHESTRA (EP) 8
56	Capitol EAP3 658	THE WOODY HERMAN ORCHESTRA (EP) 8
57	Capitol EAP 1009	ROAD BAND (EP)... 8
57	Capitol EAP 1015	WOODY HERMAN'S HERD (EP)....................................... 8
57	Capitol EAP 1026	MUSIC TO DANCE TO (EP).. 8

Woody HERMAN

MINT VALUE £

LPs

52	Capitol LC 6560	CLASSICS IN JAZZ (10" LP)	15
52	MGM MGM-D 108	AT CARNEGIE HALL VOLUME 1 (10" LP)	15
53	MGM MGM-D 110	AT CARNEGIE HALL VOLUME 2 (10" LP)	15
53	London H-APB 1014	STOMPING AT THE SAVOY (10" LP, as Woody Herman & New Third Herd)	15
54	London H-APB 1018	MEN FROM MARS (10" LP, as Woody Herman & New Third Herd)	15
55	Columbia 33S 1060	HERE'S HERMAN (10" LP)	12
55	Columbia 33S 1068	SEQUENCE IN JAZZ (10" LP)	12
56	Brunswick LAT 8092	WOODCHOPPER'S BALL (LP)	12
58	Fontana TFR 6015	SUMMER SEQUENCE (10" LP)	12
59	Top Rank 35/038	THE HERD RIDES AGAIN (LP)	12
60	Top Rank BUY 009	MOODY WOODY (LP, as Woody Herman Orchestra featuring Charlie Byrd)	12
61	London Jazz LTZ-K 15200	AT THE MONTEREY JAZZ FESTIVAL (LP, also stereo SAH-K 6100)	12

(see also David Rose Orchestra)

HERMAN'S HERMITS

64	Columbia DB 7338	I'm Into Something Good/Your Hand In Mine	5
64	Columbia DB 7408	Show Me Girl/I Know Why	5
65	Columbia DB 7475	Silhouettes/Can't You Hear My Heartbeat?	5
65	Columbia DB 7546	Wonderful World/Dream On	5
65	Columbia DB 7670	Just A Little Bit Better/Take Love, Give Love	5
65	Columbia DB 7791	A Must To Avoid/The Man With The Cigar	6
66	Columbia DB 7861	You Won't Be Leaving/Listen People	5
66	Columbia DB 7947	This Door Swings Both Ways/For Love	6
66	Columbia DB 8012	No Milk Today/My Reservation's Been Confirmed	6
66	Columbia DB 8076	East-West/What Is Wrong, What Is Right?	5
67	Columbia DB 8123	There's A Kind Of Hush (All Over The World)/Gaslite Street	5
67	Columbia DB 8235	Museum/Moonshine Man	5
68	Columbia DB 8327	I Can Take Or Leave Your Loving/Marcel's	5
68	Columbia DB 8404	Sleepy Joe/Just One Girl	5
68	Columbia DB 8446	Sunshine Girl/Nobody Needs To Know	6
68	Columbia DB 8504	Something's Happening/The Most Beautiful Thing In My Life	5
69	Columbia DB 8563	My Sentimental Friend/My Lady	5
68	EMI SLES 15	No Milk Today/There's A Kind Of Hush (promo only, white label)	18
68	EMI SLES 16	London Look (promo only, white label)	18
69	Columbia DB 8626	Here Comes The Star/It's Alright Now	5
70	Columbia DB 8656	Years May Come, Years May Go/Smile Please	5
71	RCA RCA 2135	She's A Lady/Gold Mandela	5
72	RCA RCA 2265	The Man/Effen Curly	5
74	Buddah BDS 700	Train/Ride On The Water (withdrawn)	30
65	Columbia SEG 8380	HERMANIA (EP)	18
65	Columbia SEG 8440	MRS BROWN YOU'VE GOT A LOVELY DAUGHTER (EP)	15
65	Columbia SEG 8442	HERMAN'S HERMITS HITS (EP)	15
66	Columbia SEG 8477	A MUST TO AVOID (EP)	15
66	Columbia SEG 8503	MUSIC FROM THE SOUNDTRACK "HOLD ON" (EP)	18
67	Columbia SEG 8520	DANDY (EP)	18
65	Columbia 33SX 1727	HERMAN'S HERMITS (LP)	22
65	Columbia S(C)X 6303	MRS BROWN YOU'VE GOT A LOVELY DAUGHTER (LP, soundtrack, m/s)	20/25
66	Columbia SX 6084	BOTH SIDES OF HERMAN'S HERMITS (LP)	22
67	Columbia S(C)X 6174	THERE'S A KIND OF HUSH ALL OVER THE WORLD (LP)	20
60s	Regal SREG 1117	HERMAN'S HERMITS (LP, export issue)	30
60s	Columbia SCXC 27	THE BEST OF HERMAN'S HERMITS (LP, export issue)	30
60s	Columbia SCXC 32	THE BEST OF HERMAN'S HERMITS VOL. 2 (LP, export issue)	30
60s	Columbia SCXC 34	THERE'S A KIND OF HUSH ALL OVER THE WORLD (LP, export issue)	30
60s	Columbia SCXC 35	BLAZE (LP, export issue)	30

(see also Peter Noone)

CORRINE HERMES

83	Polydor POSPE 597	Words Of Love/Si La Vie Est Cadeau (p/s)	6

HEROES

75	United Artists UP 36016	Grown Up/Losing You	6

(see also Motors, Bram Tchaikovsky)

TED HEROLD

60	Polydor NH 66817	I Don't Know Why/Moonlight	25

HERON

70	Dawn DNS 1015	Take Me Back Home/Minstrel And A King	7
71	Dawn DNX 2509	Bye And Bye/Through Time/Only A Hobo/I'm Ready To Leave (p/s)	8
71	Dawn DNLS 3010	HERON (LP, with insert)	30
72	Dawn DNLS 3025	TWICE AS NICE AT HALF THE PRICE (2-LP, some with postcard)	40/30

(see also Mike Cooper)

MIKE HERON('S REPUTATION)

71	Island WIP 6101	Call Me Diamond/Lady Wonder	5
75	Neighbourhood NBH 3109	Evie/Down On My Knees After Memphis (as Mike Heron's Reputation)	5
78	Zoom ZUM 5	Sold On Your Love/Portland Rose (p/s)	5
71	Island ILPS 9146	SMILING MEN WITH BAD REPUTATIONS (LP, gatefold sleeve)	12
75	Neighborhood 80637	MIKE HERON'S REPUTATION (LP)	12

(see also Incredible String Band)

KRISTIN HERSH

93	4AD KH 2	Velvet Days (Demo)/Houdini Blues (demo) (promo only, no p/s)	10
94	4AD CADD 4002CD	HIPS & MAKERS (CD, digipak with postcards)	20

(see also Throwing Muses)

PAT HERVEY & TIARAS & ART SNIDER

67	President PT 110	Can't Get You Out Of My Mind/Givin' In	6

HERZFELD
93	Duophonic DS45 07	Two Mothers/Who The Scroungers Are (p/s, mail order only)	6

HESITATIONS
69	London HLR 10180	Born Free/Push A Little Bit Harder	15
68	London HLR 10198	The Impossible Dream (The Quest)/Nobody Knows You When You're Down And Out.	6
68	London HA-R/SH-R 8360	THE NEW BORN FREE (LP).	12

CAROLYN HESTER
65	Dot DS 16750	Ain't That Rain?/Ten Thousand Candles	5
65	Dot DS 16751	Playboys And Playgirls/High Flyin' Bird	5
65	Dot DS 26750	Come On Back/Three Young Men	5
65	Dot DS 26751	What Does It Get You?/Now He's Gone	5
66	CBS 202409	A Reason To Believe/Early Morning Rain	5
65	Dot DLP 3604	THAT'S MY SONG (LP).	15
66	Dot DLP 3638	AT TOWN HALL (LP).	15
66	CBS (S)BPG 62033	CAROLYN HESTER (LP).	15
67	Realm RM 2338	THIS LIFE I'M LIVING (LP)	12
69	Pye Intl. NSPL 28121	THE CAROLYN HESTER COALITION (LP).	12

HEWETT SISTERS
59	HMV POP 567	Baby-O/Jerri-Lee (I Love Him So)	20
59	HMV POP 567	Baby-O/Jerri-Lee (I Love Him So) (78)	12

BEN HEWITT
59	Mercury AMT 1041	You Break Me Up/I Ain't Givin' Up Nothin'	50
59	Mercury AMT 1055	For Quite A While/Patricia June.	18
59	Mercury AMT 1084	I Want A New Girl Now/My Search.	40
60	Mercury ZEP 10035	BREAK IT UP WITH BEN HEWITT (EP)	175

GARTH HEWITT
70s	Myrrh MYR 1051	LOVE SONGS FOR THE EARTH (LP).	15
70s	Myrrh MYR 1078	I'M GRATEFUL (LP)	15

PETE HEWSON
83	Reset RES 2	Take My Hand/Her (p/s)	50
83	Reset REST 2	Take My Hand/Her (12", p/s).	80

ANNE HEYWOOD
59	Top Rank JAR 130	I'd Rather Have Roses (Than Riches)/Love Is.	6
59	Top Rank JAR 130	I'd Rather Have Roses (Than Riches)/Love Is (78)	10

EDDIE HEYWOOD
58	Mercury 7MT 131	Heywood's Bounce/Soft Summer Breeze	8
64	Stateside SS 264	Theme From Film "The Prize"/Li'l Darlin'	5

(see also Hugo Winterhalter)

WINSTON HEYWOOD (& HOMBRES)
71	Dynamic DYN 424	Bam-Sa-Bo/Version	8
72	Dynamic DYN 441	Stop The War/Version.	5
72	Dynamic DYN 457	Seek And You'll Find/Version.	5
73	Attack ATT 8046	Da Doo Ron Ron/Version.	5

(see also Winston Harewood, Fud Christian All Stars)

LENNIE HIBBERT & COUNT OSSIE BAND
69	Doctor Bird DB 1113	Pure Sole/PATSY: A Man Is Two Faced	12

(see also Sound Dimension)

AL HIBBLER
55	Brunswick 05420	Unchained Melody/Daybreak	20
55	Brunswick 05454	They Say You're Laughing At Me/I Can't Put My Arms Around A Memory	12
55	London HL 8184	Now I Lay Me Down To Dream/Danny Boy	20
55	London HL 8184	Now I Lay Me Down To Dream/Danny Boy (78).	12
55	Brunswick 05492	He/Breeze (Blow My Baby Back To Me).	8
56	Brunswick 05523	The Eleventh Hour Melody/Let's Try Again	8
56	Brunswick 05552	After The Lights Go Down Low/Stella By Starlight	8
56	Brunswick 05590	Never Turn Back/Away All Boats	6
56	Brunswick 05619	Nightfall/I'm Free	6
57	Brunswick 05653	The Town Crier/Trees	6
57	Brunswick 05703	Around The Corner From The Blues/I Complain	7
57	Brunswick 05703	Around The Corner From The Blues/I Complain (78)	8
57	Columbia LB 10066	Goin' To Chicago Blues/Sent For You Yesterday And Here You Come Today (78, with Count Basie Big Band)	10
58	Brunswick 05739	When Will I Forget You?/My Heart Tells Me	6
58	Brunswick 05739	When Will I Forget You?/My Heart Tells Me (78)	8
58	Brunswick 05749	Honeysuckle Rose/Ain't Nothing Wrong With That Baby	6
58	Brunswick 05749	Honeysuckle Rose/Ain't Nothing Wrong With That Baby (78)	8
58	Brunswick 05768	Love Land/Love Me Long, Hold Me Close, Kiss Me Warm And Tender	6
58	Brunswick 05768	Love Land/Love Me Long, Hold Me Close, Kiss Me Warm And Tender (78).	8
59	London HL 7086	Danny Boy/Now I Lay Me Down To Dream (export issue).	7
55	HMV 7EG 8158	DUKE ELLINGTON AND AL HIBBLER (EP).	8
57	HMV 7EG 8326	AL HIBBLER SINGS LOVE SONGS (EP)	8
57	Brunswick OE 9331	HERE'S HIBBLER PT. 1 (EP)	10
57	Brunswick OE 9332	HERE'S HIBBLER PT. 2 (EP)	10
57	Brunswick OE 9333	HERE'S HIBBLER PT. 3 (EP)	10
56	Brunswick LAT 8140	STARRING AL HIBBLER (LP).	18

EDDIE HICKEY
59	Decca F 11153	Lady May/Cap And Gown	7
59	Decca F 11153	Lady May/Cap And Gown (78)	10
60	Decca F 11204	Who Could Be Bluer?/Plain Jane	7
60	Decca F 11241	Another Sleepless Night/Barbara	8

MINT VALUE £

ERSEL HICKEY
59	Fontana H 198	You Threw A Dart/Don't Be Afraid Of Love	50
59	Fontana H 198	You Threw A Dart/Don't Be Afraid Of Love (78)	15

DWAYNE HICKMAN
60	Capitol CL 15164	I'm A Lover, Not A Fighter/I Pass Your House	8

HICKORY
69	CBS 3963	Green Light/Key	20

(see also Equals)

COLIN HICKS (& CABIN BOYS)
57	Pye 7N 15114	Wild Eyes And Tender Lips/Empty Arms Blues (with Cabin Boys)	20
57	Pye 7N 15114	Wild Eyes And Tender Lips/Empty Arms Blues (78, with Cabin Boys)	15
57	Pye 7N 15125	La Dee Dah/Wasteland	10
57	Pye 7N 15125	La Dee Dah/Wasteland (78)	18
58	Pye 7N 15163	Little Boy Blue/Jambalaya	12
58	Pye 7N 15163	Little Boy Blue/Jambalaya (78)	30

DAN HICKS & HIS HOT LICKS
72	Blue Thumb ILPS 9204	STRIKING IT RICH (LP)	10

JIMMY HICKS
72	London HLU 10396	I'm Mr. Big Stuff/Tell Her That I Love You	10

HIDDEN STRENGTH
76	United Artists UAS 29949	HIDDEN STRENGTH (LP)	10

HIDEAWAYS
69	Action ACT 4544	Hide Out/Jolly Joe	7
71	Jay Boy BOY 29	Hide Out/Jolly Joe (reissue)	5

HI-FI
82	Butt FUNEP 3	DEMONSTRATION RECORD (12" EP)	7
83	Shanghai HAI 102	MOODS FOR MALLARDS (LP, with lyric sheet)	10

(see also Ian Matthews)

HI-FI FOUR
56	Parlophone MSP 6210	Band Of Gold/Davy, You Upset My Life	140
56	Parlophone R 4130	Band Of Gold/Davy, You Upset My Life (78)	20

HI FI'S
63	Piccadilly 7N 35130	Take Me Or Leave Me/I'm Struck	6
64	Pye 7N 15635	Will Yer Won't Yer/She's The One	6
64	Pye 7N 15710	I Keep Forgettin'/Why Can't I Stop Loving You?	20
65	Pye 7N 15788	Baby's In Black/Kiss And Run	10
66	Alp 595 010	It's Gonna Be Morning/I Wanna Hear You Say Yeah	30

LIZZIE HIGGINS
75	Topic 12TS 260	UP AND AWA WI THE LAVEROCK (LP, gatefold sleeve)	12

JOE HIGGS
67	Coxsone CS 7004	Neighbour Neighbour/MELODIANS: I Should Have Made It Up	18
67	Island WI 3026	I Am The Song/Worry No More	20
68	Island WI 3131	You Hurt My Soul/LYNN TAITT: Why Am I Treated So Bad?	20
70	Clandisc CLA 208	Mademoiselle/DYNAMITES: Lion	10
71	Big BG 312	Burning Fire/RUPIE EDWARDS ALL STARS: Version	7
71	New Beat NB 087	Mother Radio/DAWN SHARON: Little Deeds	6
71	Supreme SUP 215	Burning Fire/RUPIE EDWARDS ALL STARS: Push And Pull	6
72	Sioux SI 005	The World Is Spinning Around/THE REACTION: Hallelujah	5
72	Sioux SI 014	The Wave Of War/JUMBO STERLING: Shaft	5
72	Sioux SI 021	Lay A Foundation/JACKIE ROWLAND: Lay A Foundation (Version)	5

(see also Higgs & Wilson, Bob Marley/Wailers, Soul Vendors)

(Joe) HIGGS & (Roy) WILSON
60	Blue Beat (B)B 3	Manny Oh/When You Tell Me Baby (white label/blue writing [B3] or blue label/silver writing [BB 3]) (with Ken Richards & His Comets)	each 15
61	Starlite ST45 035	Pretty Baby/I Long For The Day	15
61	Starlite ST45 036	Lover's Song/It Is A Day	15
61	Starlite ST45 042	Come On Home/The Robe	15
61	Starlite ST45 053	Sha Ba Ba/Change Of Mind	15
62	Blue Beat BB 95	How Can I Be Sure/Mighty Man	12
63	R&B JB 109	Let Me Know/Bye And Bye	10
63	Blue Beat BB 190	If You Want Pardon/BABA BROOKS BAND: Musical Communion	15
63	Island WI 081	Last Saturday Morning/Praise The Lord	15
64	Rio R 29	Love Is Not For Me/Gone Is Yesterday	10
65	Blue Beat BB 277	Pain In My Heart/BUSTER ALL STARS: Going West	15
70	Clandisc CLA 218	Don't Mind Me/GLEN AND ROY: Angel	6

(see also Clancy Eccles)

HIGH
69	CBS 4164	Long Live The High/Beggar Man Dan	8

HIGH & MIGHTY
66	HMV POP 1548	Tryin' To Stop Cryin'/Escape From Cuba	15

HIGH BROOM
70	Island WI 6088	Dancing In The Moonlight/Percy's On The Run	15
73	Columbia DB 8969	Dancing In The Moonlight/Percy's On The Run (reissue)	7

(see also Leviathan, Mike Stuart Span, Jason Crest, Holy Mackerel)

HIGH KEYS
63	London HLK 9768	Que Sera Sera/Daddy, Ooh Long Legs	15

HIGH LEVEL RANTERS
68	Topic 12TS 186	NORTHUMBERLAND FOR EVER (LP, blue label, 2 different sleeves)	15
70	Trailer LER 2020	KEEP YOUR FEET STILL GEORDIE HINNIE (LP).	12
71	Trailer LER 2030	HIGH LEVEL (LP)	12
72	Trailer LER 2037	A MILE TO RIDE (LP)	12
75	Topic 2-12TS 271/2	THE BONNY PIT LADDIE (2-LP, blue label)	18
77	Broadside BRO 128	ENGLISH SPORTING BALLADS (LP, 1-side Martin Wyndham-Read, 2,000 only).	20

HIGHLY LIKELY
74	BBC RESL 10	Whatever Happened To You?/God Bless Everyone.	6

(see also Mike Hugg, Rodney Bewes)

HIGH NUMBERS
64	Fontana TF 480	I'm The Face/Zoot Suit (stickered demo copies £425)	350
64	Fontana TF 480	Zoot Suit/I'm The Face (re-pressing with reversed sides).	300
80	Back Door DOOR 4	I'm The Face/Zoot Suit (reissue, die cut sleeve)	15

(see also Who)

HIGH SOCIETY
66	Fontana TF 771	People Passing By/Star Of Eastern Street	15

(see also Friday Browne, Graham Gouldman, Country Gentlemen, Manchester Mob)

HIGH TIDE
69	Liberty LBS 83264	SEA SHANTIES (LP, gatefold sleeve)	60
70	Liberty LBS 83294	HIGH TIDE (LP)	50
84	Psycho PSYCHO 26	SEA SHANTIES (LP, reissue)	12
84	Psycho PSYCHO 27	HIGH TIDE (LP, reissue)	12

(see also Misunderstood, Denny Gerrard, Magic Muscle, Third Ear Band)

HIGH TIDE
81	Sunday Morning	Baby Dancing/Letter From A Coward	
	(no cat. no.)	(no p/s, mail-order only).	10
82	WEA K 18930	Dancing In My Mind/Electric Blue (p/s)	5

DEAN HIGHTOWER
60	HMV CLP 1360	TWANGY — WITH A BEAT (LP)	35

DONNA HIGHTOWER
59	Capitol CL 15048	Lover, Come Back To Me/Because Of You.	6
59	Capitol CL 15049	Ain't That Love/Forgive Them	6
60	Capitol ST 1273	GEE BABY (LP)	18

ROSETTA HIGHTOWER
68	Toast TT 506	Pretty Red Balloons/How Can You Mistreat (The One You Love)?	6
68	Toast TT 509	I Can't Give Back The Love I Feel For You/Big Bird	5
69	CBS 4584	One Heart For Sale/What Do I Do?	5
70	CBS 4758	April Fools/I'll Hold Out My Hand	5
70	CBS 4988	Persuader/Come Together	5
71	CBS 7068	Go Pray For Tomorrow/Give Me Just A Little More Line.	6
73	Philips 6006 291	The Walls Fell Down/Captain's Army.	6
71	CBS 64201	HIGHTOWER (LP)	12
71	Rediffusion ZS 88	ROSETTA HIGHTOWER (LP)	12

(see also Orlons, Ian Green [Revelation])

HIGH TREASON
80	Burlington BURLS 001	Saturday Night Special (no p/s)	30

HIGHWAY
74	EMI EMC 3019	HIGHWAY (LP)	12
75	EMI EMA 770	SMOKING AT THE EDGE (LP)	12

HIGHWAYMEN
61	HMV POP 948	The Gypsy Rover/Cotton Fields	5
62	United Artists UP 1001	Birdman (with narration from Burt Lancaster)/Cindy Oh Cindy	6

HIGH WINDOWS
68	CBS 3208	Maybe Someday/Your Eyes	5

HILARY HILARY
80	Modern STP 2	How Come You're So Dumb/Rich Kid Blues (p/s)	75

(see also Roger Taylor, Queen)

RAY HILDEBRAND
70s	Myrh MST 6508	SPECIAL KIND OF MAN (LP)	15

DIANE HILDEBRANDE
69	Elektra EKSN 45055	Jan's Blues/Early Morning Blues And Greens	7

HI LITES
65	London HL 9967	Hey Baby/Groovey	7

HI-LITERS
58	Mercury AMT 1011	Dance Me To Death/Cha Cha Rock	100
58	Mercury AMT 1011	Dance Me To Death/Cha Cha Rock (78)	80

ALEX HILL
53	Vocalion V 1027	Stompin' 'Em Down/Track Head Blues (78)	15

(see also Paramount Allstars)

BENNY HILL
55	Decca F 10442	I Can't Tell A Waltz From A Tango/Teach Me Tonight	15
55	Decca F 10442	I Can't Tell A Waltz From A Tango/Teach Me Tonight (78)	10
56	Columbia SCM 5238	Memories Are Made Of This/Who Done It? (as Benny Hill & Coronets).	12
56	Columbia SCM 5238	Memories Are Made Of This/Who Done It? (78, as Benny Hill & Coronets)	10
61	Pye 7N 15327	Gather In The Mushrooms/Pepys' Diary	5
61	Pye 7N 15359	Transistor Radio/Gypsy Rock	5

Benny HILL

62	Pye 7N 15520	Harvest Of Love/Fame	5
65	Pye 7N 15974	What A World/I'll Never Know	5
66	Pye 7N 17026	My Garden Of Love/The Andalucian Gypsies	5
92	EMI ERNPD 1	Ernie/Ting A Ling A Loo (shaped picture disc)	5
61	Pye NEP 24144	BENNY HILL PARADE VOL. 1 (EP)	8
63	Pye NEP 24174	THE HARVEST OF LOVE (EP)	8
66	Pye NPL 18133	SINGS? (LP)	15

(see also Coronets)

BUNKER HILL & RAYMEN
62	Stateside SS 135	Hide & Seek (Parts 1 & 2)	10

CHIPPIE HILL/HOCIEL THOMAS
72	Collectors Edition 1001	CHIPPIE HILL AND HOCIEL THOMAS (LP)	12

DAVID HILL
57	Vogue V 9076	All Shook Up/Melody For Lovers (with Ray Ellis Orchestra)	175
57	Vogue V 9076	All Shook Up/Melody For Lovers (78, with Ray Ellis Orchestra)	55
58	RCA RCA 1041	That's Love/Keep Me In Mind (with Joe Reisman's Orchestra & Chorus)	225
58	RCA RCA 1041	That's Love/Keep Me In Mind (78, with Joe Reisman's Orchestra & Chorus)	60

JESSIE HILL
60	London HLU 9117	Ooh Poo Pah Doo (Parts 1 & 2)	15

MIKE HILL GROUP
65	Polydor BM 56016	Silver Star/Best Of Both Worlds	5

VINCE HILL
62	Piccadilly 7N 35043	The Rivers Run Dry/Not Any More	6
62	Piccadilly 7N 35068	There You Go/Just As Long As (You Belong To Me)	6
63	Piccadilly 7N 35108	Day At The Seaside/Tricks Of The Trade	6
63	Piccadilly 7N 35118	As It Was Written/Is There Anyone At Home	5
63	Piccadilly 7N 35148	Blue Velvet/Like Anything	6
64	Piccadilly 7N 35161	If You Knew/Fools & Lovers	6
64	Piccadilly 7N 35192	It's Only Make Believe/Let The Wind Blow	6
66	Columbia SEG 8509	FOUR SIDES OF VINCE HILL (EP)	10
66	Columbia S(C)X 6018	HAVE YOU MET? (LP)	12
66	Columbia S(C)X 6046	HEARTACHES (LP)	12
67	Columbia S(C)X 6096	AT THE CLUB (LP)	12
67	Columbia S(C)X 6141	EDELWEISS (LP)	12
68	Columbia S(C)X 6185	ALWAYS YOU AND ME (LP)	12
69	Columbia S(C)X 6304	YOU FORGOT TO REMEMBER (LP)	12

(see also [Jackie &] Raindrops)

Z.Z. HILL
65	R&B MRB 5005	Someone To Love Me/Have Mercy Someone	18
69	Action ACT 4532	Make Me Yours/What Am I Living For?	12
71	Mojo 2092 019	Faithful And True/I Think I'd Do It	5
75	United Artists UP 35727	I Keep On Loving You/Whoever's Thrilling You	8
77	CBS 5553	Love Is So Good When You're Stealin' It/Need You By My Side	5
66	Sue IEP 711	GIMME GIMME (EP, 2 tracks each by Z.Z. Hill & Intentions; 2 tracks mistakenly credited to Jackie Day on sleeve; some in p/s)	175/60
69	Action ACLP 6004	WHOLE LOT OF SOUL (LP)	35
72	Mojo 2916 013	THE BRAND NEW Z.Z. HILL (LP)	20
75	Contempo CLP 515	THE BRAND NEW Z.Z. HILL (LP, reissue)	12

(see also Intentions)

STEVE HILLAGE
76	Virgin VS 161	It's All Too Much/Shimmer	5
77	Virgin VS 171	Hurdy Gurdy Man/Om Nama Shivaya	5
77	Virgin VS 197	Not Fade Away/Saucer Surfing	5
77	Virgin VDJ 23	Leylines To Glassdome/GLEN PHILLIPS: Lies (p/s, gig freebie)	6
78	Virgin VS 212	Getting Better/Palm Trees (Love Guitar) (p/s)	5
79	Virgin VS 313	Don't Dither, Do It/Getting In Tune (p/s)	5
79	Virgin SIXPACK 2	SIX PACK/SIX TRACK (EP, picture disc, 5,000 only, die-cut p/s with stand)	8
78	Virgin V 2098	GREEN (LP, green vinyl, with insert)	12
79	Virgin VR 1	RAINBOW DOME MUSICK (LP, clear vinyl)	12
83	Virgin V 2244	FOR TO NEXT (LP, with bonus instrumental LP "And Not Or")	12

(see also Gong, Khan, Arzachel, Clearlight, Radio Actors, System 7)

HILLER BROTHERS
60s	Honey Hit TB 124	Little Darlin'/Changin' My Mind (some with p/s)	8/5

JANE HILLERY
66	Columbia DB 7918	You've Got That Hold On Me/Take Me Away	15

(see also Magistrates)

MABLE HILLERY
69	Xtra XTRA 1063	IT'S SO HARD TO BE A NIGGER (LP)	18

GILLIAN HILLS
65	Vogue VRS 7005	Tomorrow Is Another Day/Look At Them	10

HILLTOPPERS
78s
52	Vogue V 9045	Trying/You Made Up My Mind (78, featuring Jimmy Sacca)	15
53	London L 1204	P.S. I Love You/I'd Rather Die Young (78)	25
54	London HL 8003	Love Walked In/To Be Alone (78)	30
54	London HL 8026	From The Vine Came The Grape/Time Will Tell (78)	25
54	London HL 8070	Poor Butterfly/Wrapped Up In A Dream (78)	25
54	London HL 8081	Will You Remember?/The Old Cabaret (78)	25
54	London HL 8092	If I Didn't Care/Bettina (78)	25
55	London HL 8116	Time Waits For No One/You Try Somebody Else (78)	25
55	London HLD 8168	The Kentuckian Song/I Must Be Dreaming (78)	20

MINT VALUE £

55	London HLD 8208	Searching/All I Need Is You (78)	20
56	London HLD 8255	My Treasure/Last Word In Love (78)	20
56	London HLD 8278	Do The Bop/When You're Alone (78)	40
56	London HLD 8298	Tryin'/D-A-R-L-I-N' (78)	15
56	London HLD 8333	So Tired/Faded Rose (78)	12
57	London HLD 8441	I'm Serious/I Love My Girl (78)	15
57	London HLD 8455	A Fallen Star/Footsteps (78)	15
57	London HLD 8528	The Joker/Chicken, Chicken (78)	10
58	London HLD 8603	You Sure Look Good To Me/Starry Eyes (78)	25

SINGLES

54	London HL 8026	From The Vine Came The Grape/Time Will Tell	50
54	London HL 8070	Poor Butterfly/Wrapped Up In A Dream	50
54	London HL 8081	Will You Remember?/The Old Cabaret	40
54	London HL 8092	If I Didn't Care/Bettina	40
55	London HL 8116	Time Waits For No One/You Try Somebody Else	40
55	London HLD 8168	The Kentuckian Song/I Must Be Dreaming	40
55	London HLD 8208	Searching/All I Need Is You	50
56	London HLD 8221	Only You (And You Alone)/(It Will Have To Do) Until The Real Thing Comes Along (gold or silver label lettering)	15/12
56	London HLD 8255	My Treasure/Last Word In Love	35
56	London HLD 8278	Do The Bop/When You're Alone	75
56	London HLD 8298	Tryin'/D-A-R-L-I-N'	25
56	London HLD 8333	So Tired/Faded Rose	25
57	London HLD 8381	Marianne/You're Wasting Your Time	18
57	London HLD 8441	I'm Serious/I Love My Girl	18
57	London HLD 8455	A Fallen Star/Footsteps	18
57	London HLD 8528	The Joker/Chicken, Chicken	25
58	London HLD 8603	You Sure Look Good To Me/Starry Eyes	15
60	London HLD 9038	Alone/The Prisoner's Song	10

EPs

55	London RE-P 1012	PRESENTING THE HILLTOPPERS (EP)	35
55	London RE-D 1030	THE HILLTOPPERS VOL. 2 (EP)	35
57	London RE-D 1099	THE HILLTOPPERS VOL. 3 (EP)	30

LPs

57	London HA-D 2029	THE TOWERING HILLTOPPERS (LP)	35
57	London HA-D 2071	TOPS IN POPS (LP)	35

(see also Sacca, Billy Vaughn)

HI-LO'S

62	Reprise RS 20095	A Taste Of Honey/My Baby Just Cares For Me	5
57	London RE-U 1077	UNDER GLASS (EP)	15
58	London RE-R 1110	THE HI-LO'S (EP)	15
50s	Philips BBE 12127	HERE ARE THE HI-LO'S (EP)	12
50s	Philips BBE 12289	AND ALL THAT JAZZ (EP)	12
50s	Philips BBE 12425	HERE ARE THE HI-LO'S (EP, also stereo SBBE 9035)	10/12
57	London HA-U 2026	UNDER GLASS (LP)	18
58	Philips BBL 7154	SUDDENLY IT'S THE HI-LO'S (LP)	15
59	Philips BBL 7288	AND ALL THAT JAZZ (LP)	15
60	Philips BBL 7411	ALL OVER THE PLACE (LP, also stereo SBBL 589)	12/15
60s	Omega XSD 11	IN STEREO (LP)	15
63	Reprise R 6034	HAPPEN TO FOLK SONGS (LP)	12

RONNIE HILTON

55	HMV 7M 285	Prize Of Gold/A Blossom Fell	18
55	HMV 7M 303	Just Say You Love Her/My Loving Hands	8
56	HMV 7M 336	Bella Notte/He	8
56	HMV 7M 358	Young And Foolish/Moments To Remember	12
56	HMV 7M 382	The Last Frontier/Here Comes My Love	7
56	HMV 7M 390	No Other Love/It's All Been Done Before (B-side with Alma Cogan)	25
56	HMV 7M 413	Who Are We/Give Me My Ranch	12
56	HMV POP 248	A Woman In Love/I Just Found Out About Love	12
56	HMV POP 274	Two Different Worlds/Constant And True	12
57	HMV POP 291	The Wisdom Of A Fool/Amore	10
57	HMV POP 307	For Your Love/Once	5
57	HMV POP 318	Heart/Penny Serenade	6
57	HMV POP 338	Around The World/I'd Give You The World	5
57	HMV POP 364	The Miracle Of Love/Wonderful! Wonderful!	8
57	HMV POP 393	Marching Along To The Blues/She	5
57	HMV POP 422	That's Why I Was Born/The Moonraker's Song	5
58	HMV POP 437	I'll Buy You A Star/You Should Belong To Me	5
58	HMV POP 446	Magic Moments/One Blade Of Grass (In A Meadow)	5
58	HMV POP 468	I May Never Pass This Way Again/Love Walked In	5
58	HMV POP 479	On The Street Where You Live/I've Grown Accustomed To Her Face	5
58	HMV POP 497	Her Hair Was Yellow/Let Me Stay With You	5
58	HMV POP 556	The Day The Rains Came/Do I Love You (Because You're Beautiful)	7
58	HMV POP 556	The Day The Rains Came/Do I Love You (Because You're Beautiful) (78)	8
58	HMV POP 559	The World Outside/As I Love You	5
58	HMV POP 559	The World Outside/As I Love You (78)	8
59	HMV POP 560	Gigi (Gaston's Soliloquy)/Keep Your Kisses	5
59	HMV POP 560	Gigi (Gaston's Soliloquy)/Keep Your Kisses (78)	8
59	HMV POP 638	The Wonder Of You/A Hundred Miles From Everywhere	5
59	HMV POP 638	The Wonder Of You/A Hundred Miles From Everywhere (78)	10
59	HMV POP 684	Happy Anniversary/The Most Wonderful Thing In The World (78)	12

MINT VALUE £

67	HMV POP 1600	If I Were A Rich Man/Laughing Gnome	5
68	Columbia DB 8506	Glory Glory Leeds United/We Shall Not Be Moved (with Leeds United AFC)	5
55	HMV 7EG 8121	THE STAR OF SONG (EP)	10
56	HMV 7EG 8149	HEY THERE (EP)	10
57	HMV 7EG 8198	FOR THOSE IN LOVE (EP)	10
57	HMV 7EG 8202	FOR THOSE IN LOVE NO. 2 (EP)	10
58	HMV 7EG 8352	The HITS FROM 'MY FAIR LADY' (EP, 1 side by Alma Cogan)	10
55	HMV DLP 1109	BY THE FIRESIDE (10" LP)	25
59	HMV CLP 1295	I'M BEGINNING TO SEE THE LIGHT (LP)	18

(see also Alma Cogan)

HILTONAIRES
| 67 | Coxsone CSL 8004 | THE BEST OF THE HILTONAIRES (LP) | 85 |

HIM & OTHERS
| 66 | Parlophone R 5510 | I Mean It/She's Got Eyes That Tell Lies | 250 |

JUSTIN HINDS/HINES (& DOMINOES)
64	Ska Beat JB 176	King Samuel/River Jordan	20
65	Ska Beat JB 187	Mother Banner/DON DRUMMOND & HIS GROUP: Apanga	30
65	Island WI 171	Botheration/Satan (as Justin Hines & Dominoes)	18
65	Island WI 174	Jump Out Of The Frying Pan/Holy Dove (as Justin Hines & Dominoes)	20
65	Island WI 194	Rub Up, Push Up/The Ark	18
65	Island WI 232	Turn Them Back/TOMMY McCOOK: Rocket Ship	20
65	Island WI 236	Peace And Love/Skalarama (B-side actually by Lyn Taitt & Comets)	18
66	Doctor Bird DB 1048	The Higher The Monkey Climbs/Fight For Your Right	15
67	Island WI 3048	On A Saturday Night/Save A Bread	18
67	Treasure Isle TI 7002	Here I Stand/No Good Rudie	12
67	Treasure Isle TI 7005	Carry Go Bring Come/Fight Too Much	12
67	Treasure Isle TI 7014	On A Saturday Night/Save A Bread	12
67	Treasure Isle TI 7017	Once A Man/TOMMY McCOOK & SUPERSONICS: Persian Cat	12
68	Treasure Isle TI 7063	Botheration/VINCENT HINDS: Mouth Trombone	8
68	Treasure Isle TI 7068	Mighty Redeemer (Parts 1 & 2)	8
69	Trojan TR 652	You Should've Known Better/TOMMY McCOOK & SUPERSONICS: Third Figure	8
70	Duke Reid DR 2511	Say Me Say/I Want It	7
70	Duke DU 67	Drink Milk/Everywhere I Go (as Justin Hines & Dominoes)	8
75	Pama PM 4001	Sinners Where You Going To Hide?/If It's Love You Need	5

(see also Lyn Taitt, Skatalites, Don Drummond)

NEVILLE HINDS
70	Duke Reid DR 2503	Sunday Gravy (as Neville Hines)/JOHN HOLT: Write Her A Letter	10
70	Camel CA 44	London Bridge/SCORCHERS: Things And Time (B-side act. by Wailing Souls)	6
70	Gas GAS 126	I Who Have Nothing/You Send Me	6
71	Explosion EX 2043	Delivered/Specially For You (B-side actually by Blake Boy)	6
72	Upsetter US 384	Blackman's Time/UPSETTERS: Version	8
73	Harry J HJ 6657	Musical Splendour/JOHN CROW GENERATION: Musical Drum & Bass	5

(see also Neville Irons & Byron Lee & The Dragonaires, Lloyd Robinson, Marvels, Alton Ellis)

RUPERT HINE
72	Purple PUR 105	Hamburgers/A Varlet Lad T'was Samuel Green (Historical Moments — Part 17)	6
76	Electric WOT 8	Snakes Don't Dance Fast/Hopi Smile	5
71	Purple TPSA 7502	PICK UP A BONE (LP, with David MacIver)	30
73	Purple TPSA 7509	UNFINISHED PICTURE (LP)	15

(see also Jon Pertwee)

EARL 'FATHA' HINES
55	HMV 7EG 8114	EARL HINES AND HIS ORCHESTRA (EP, 1 track with Billy Eckstine)	8
57	MGM MGM-EP 573	MIDNIGHT IN NEW ORLEANS (EP, as Earl Hines All Stars)	8
54	Mercury MG 25018	EARL HINES AND HIS ALL STARS (10" LP)	15
55	Vogue Coral LRA 10031	FATS WALLER SONGS (10" LP)	15
55	Columbia 33S 1063	PIANO MOODS (10" LP)	15
60	MGM MGM-C 833	EARL'S PEARLS (LP, as Earl 'Fatha' Hines Quartet)	15
65	Stateside SL 10116	SPONTANEOUS EXPLORATIONS (LP)	12
67	Fontana SFJL 902	BLUES IN THIRDS (LP)	12
67	Fontana TL 5378	JAZZ MEANS HINES! (LP)	12

(see also Louis Armstrong)

FRAZER HINES
| 68 | Major Minor MM 579 | Who's Dr. Who?/Punch And Judy Man | 30 |

JUSTIN HINES
(see under Justin Hinds)

SONNY HINES
| 65 | King KG 1009 | Anytime, Any Day, Anywhere/Nothing Like Your Love | 10 |

HINES & ELDRIDGE
| 69 | Mercury SMWL 21041 | HINES AND ELDRIDGE WITH COLEMAN HAWKINS VOLUME 2 (LP) | 12 |

(see also Coleman Hawkins, Earl Hines, Roy Eldridge)

HINES, HINES & DAD
| 68 | CBS 3667 | Something Extra/Hambone | 5 |

HINGE
| 68 | RCA RCA 1721 | Village Postman/You'd Better Go Home | 15 |

JOE HINTON
64	Vocalion VP 9224	Funny How Time Slips Away/You Gotta Have Love	10
66	Vocalion VP 9258	Just A Kid Named Joe/Pledging My Love	10
66	Vocalion VA-P 8043	FUNNY HOW TIME SLIPS AWAY (LP)	50

HI-NUMBERS
| 65 | Decca F 12233 | Heart Of Stone/Dancing In The Street | 30 |

HIPPIES
| 63 | Cameo Parkway P 863 | Memory Lane/REGGIE HARRISON: A Lonely Piano | 15 |

HIPPY BOYS
69	Trojan TR 668	Love/The Whole Family	8
69	Trojan TR 669	Michael Row The Boat Ashore/Who Is Coming To Dinner	8
69	Bullet BU 412	Hog In A Me Minte/Lorna Run	6
69	Bullet BU 413	What's Your Excuse?/Tell Me Tell	8
69	Camel CA 29	Cat Nip/Cooyah (both as Hippie Boys)	8
69	High Note HS 021	Doctor No Go/Sailing (B-side actually "Faberge" by Baba Brooks & Band)	8
69	High Note HS 030	Chicken Lickin'/BABA BROOKS: Old Man Flint	8
69	High Note HS 035	Reggae Pressure/SOUL RHYTHMS: It Hurts (B-side actually Soul Rhythms)	8
69	Unity UN 528	Dreams To Remember/Peace Maker	6
70	High Note HS 038	Piccadilly Hop/Nigeria	8
70	Duke DU 92	Cloud Burst/LLOYD CHARMERS: Message From A Black Man	7
71	Big Shot 580	Voodoo/LITTLE ROY: Hard Fighter	6
69	Big Shot BSLP 5005	REGGAE WITH THE HIPPY BOYS (LP, actually on High Note label)	35

(see also The Upsetters, Family Man, Danny Williams, Tony, Hippy Boys, Cynthia Richards, Pioneers)

HIPSTER IMAGE
| 65 | Decca F 12137 | Can't Let Her Go/Make Her Mine | 80 |

AL HIRT
60	HMV POP 749	Tin Roof Blues/The Original Dixieland One Step (as Al Hirt's Jazz Band)	5
63	RCA RCA 1380	Java/I Can't Get Started	5
67	RCA RCA 1590	Theme From "The Monkees"/Tarzan March	6
68	RCA RCA 1662	Keep The Ball Rolling/Manhattan Safari	5
68	RCA RCA 1685	The Glory Of Love/Calypsoul	5
68	RCA RD 7961	UNFORGETTABLE (LP)	12

(see also Ann-Margret)

HIS NAME IS ALIVE
| 90 | 4AD HNIA 1 | How Ghosts Affect Relationships/If July (promo only, no p/s) | 10 |
| 93 | 4AD HNIA 2 | Extracts From "Mouth To Mouth": In Every Ford/Lip/Drink, Dress And Ink/ Can't Go Wrong Without You/The Dirt Eaters (CD, promo only) | 12 |

HI-SPOTS
58	Melodisc 1457	Lend Me Your Comb/I Don't Hurt Anymore	18
58	Melodisc 1457	Lend Me Your Comb/I Don't Hurt Anymore (78)	15
58	Melodisc 1473	Secretly/I Got	10
58	Melodisc 1473	Secretly/I Got (78)	12

ALFRED HITCHCOCK
| 58 | London HA-P 2130 | MUSIC TO BE MURDERED BY (LP, music by Jeff Alexander Orchestra, also stereo SH-P 6012) | 30/40 |

ROBYN HITCHCOCK (& THE EGYPTIANS)
81	Armageddon AS 008	The Man Who Invented Himself/Dancing On God's Thumb (p/s, some with flexidisc "It's A Mystic Trip"/"Grooving On An Inner Plane" [4 SPURT 1])	12/7
82	Albion ION 103	America/It Was The Night/How Do You Work This Thing? (p/s)	8
82	Albion FREEBIE 1	52 Stations/COSMOPOLITANS: How To Keep Your Husband Happy/ MOTOR BOYS MOTOR: Little Boy And Fat Man/dB's: Amplifier (flexidisc free with "Groovy Decay" LP [ALB 110] or at gigs)	6
82	Midnight Music DING 2	Eaten By Her Own Dinner/Listening To The Higsons/Dr. Sticky (p/s)	12
82	Midnight Music DONG 2	Eaten By Her Own Dinner/Grooving On An Inner Plane/Messages Of The Dark The Abandoned Brain/Happy The Golden Prince (12", p/s)	12
84	Midnight Music DONG 8	The Bells Of Rhymney/Falling Leaves/Winter Love/ The Bones In The Ground (12", p/s)	10
85	Midnight Music DONG 12	Heaven/Dwarfbeat/Some Body (12", p/s)	10
85	Midnight Music DONG 17	Brenda's Iron Sledge (live)/Only The Stones Remain/ The Pit Of Souls (Part I-IV) (12", p/s)	8
83	Albion 12 ION 1036	Nightride To Trinidad (Long Version)/Kingdom Of Love/ Midnight Fish (12", p/s)	15
86	Glass Fish OOZE 1	If You Were A Priest/The Crawling (p/s)	5
84	Bucketfull/Brains BOB 8	Happy The Golden Prince (flexidisc free with *Bucketfull Of Brains* mag)	8/6
84	Bucketfull/Brains BOB 8	Happy The Golden Prince (hard vinyl white label test pressing, 20 only)	30
81	Armageddon ARM 4	BLACK SNAKE DIAMOND RöLE (LP)	12
84	Midnight M. CHIME 00.05S	I OFTEN DREAM OF TRAINS (LP)	10
86	Midnight Music BM 80	EXPLODING IN SILENCE (LP, picture disc)	10

(see also Soft Boys, Knox)

HI-TENSION
77	Island IPR 2007	Hi-Tension/Girl I Bet Cha (12")	8
79	Island WIP 6493	There's A Reason/If It Moves You	5
79	Island 12 WIP 6493	There's A Reason/If It Moves You (12")	10
78	Island ILPS 9564	HI-TENSION (LP, with poster)	12

HI-TONES
62	Island WI 029	Going Steady/Darlin' Elaine	18
63	Island WI 086	Ten Virgins (actually by Angelic Brothers)/Too Young To Love (actually by Larry Marshall)	18
63	R&B JB 123	You Hold The Key/DON DRUMMOND: Rock Away	25

HIT PACK
| 65 | Tamla Motown TMG 513 | Never Say No To Your Baby/Let's Dance | 70 |

HIT PARADE
84	JSH JSH 1	Forever/Stop (die-cut p/s)	8
84	JSH JSH 2	My Favourite Girl/It Rained On Monday Morning (die-cut p/s)	7
85	JSH JSH 3	The Sun Shines In Gerrards Cross/You Hurt Me Too (die-cut p/s)	6
85	JSH JSH 4	You Don't Love Me Then/Huevo's Mexicana (die-cut p/s with card)	6
86	JSH JSH 5	See You In Havana/Wipe Away The Tears (die-cut p/s)	5
87	JSH JSH 6	I Get So Sentimental/Sue (die-cut p/s)	5

HIT SQUAD
88   Eastern Bloc EASTERN 01   Wax On The Melt/SPM MC Tunes/Shure.4 (12", white label promo,
plain stickered sleeve) 60

(see also 808 State)

HITTERS
73   United Artists UP 35530   Hypocrite/The Version 20

(see also Brinsley Schwarz)

HOAX
80   Hologram HOAX 1   ONLY THE BLIND CAN SEE IN THE DARK (EP) 10
81   Hologram HOAX 3   SO WHAT (12" EP, p/s) 15
82   Hologram HOAX 4   Quiet In The Sixpenny 5 (p/s) 10

HOBBIES OF TODAY
78   Waxworks H.O.T. WAX 01   Metal Boys/Tight Rope Walker (p/s) 5

HOBBIT
71   Deroy   FIRST AND LAST (LP, private pressing) 75

HOBBITS
68   Decca AD 1004   Daffodil Days (The Affection Song)/Sunny Day Girl (export issue) ... 12
68   MCA MU 1002   Daffodil Days (The Affection Song)/Sunny Day Girl 5
67   MCA MUP 301   DOWN TO MIDDLE EARTH (LP) 18

HOBBS
78   Big SOLD 4   Bop Around The Shop/(You've Got Me In A) Whirl Girl
(gatefold p/s & insert) 6

HOBBY HORSE
72   Bell BELL 1248   Summertime, Summertime/Sweet And Low 10

(see also Mary Hopkin)

HOBBY SHOP
68   Columbia DB 8395   Why Must It Be This Way?/Talk To Me 6

LES HOBEAUX
57   HMV POP 377   Oh, Mary Don't You Weep/Toll The Bell Easy 15
57   HMV POP 377   Oh, Mary Don't You Weep/Toll The Bell Easy (78) 15
57   HMV POP 403   Mama Don't Allow/Hey, Hey, Daddy Blues 15
57   HMV POP 403   Mama Don't Allow/Hey, Hey, Daddy Blues (78) 15
58   HMV POP 444   Dynamo/Two Ships 15
58   HMV POP 444   Dynamo/Two Ships (78) 20
57   HMV 7EG 8297   SOHO SKIFFLE (EP) 40

HOBOKEN
73   Oak   HOBOKEN (LP, 6 copies only) 500

EDMUND HOCKRIDGE
53   Parlophone MSP 6027   Luck Be A Lady/I'll Know 6
53   Parlophone MSP 6028   I've Never Been In Love Before/My Time Of Day 6
56   Pye NEP 24019   EDMUND HOCKRIDGE (EP) 8
57   Pye NEP 24026   BY THE FOUNTAINS OF ROME (EP) 8

CHRIS HODGE
72   Apple APPLE 43   We're On Our Way/Supersoul (initially in p/s) 22/6
74   RCA LPBO 5007   Beautiful Love/Sweet Lady From The Sky 5
74   DJM DJS 10337   I Love You/Old James Dean 5

MARVA HODGE
70   Polydor 56792   The Ghetto/Sometimes 5

CHARLES HODGES
69   Major Minor MM 654   Try A Little Love/Someone To Love 15

(see also Outlaws, Cliff Bennett's Rebellion)

EDDIE HODGES
61   London HLA 9369   I'm Gonna Knock On Your Door/Ain't Gonna Wash For A Week 10
62   London HLA 9505   Bandit Of My Dreams/Mugmates 12
62   London HLA 9576   (Girls, Girls, Girls) Made To Love/I Make Believe It's You 6
63   MGM MGM 1232   Just A Kid In Love/Avalanche 5
65   Stateside SS 442   New Orleans/Hard Times For Young Lovers 6
65   Stateside SS 469   Love Minus Zero — No Limit/The Water Is Over My Head 8
62   London REA 1353   EDDIE HODGES (EP) 60

(see also Hayley Mills & Eddie Hodges)

JOHNNY HODGES & HIS ORCHESTRA
61   HMV CLP 1430   BLUES-A-PLENTY (LP) 12

HOFFNER BROTHERS
72   Bullet BU 513   The King Man Is Back/SHALIMAR ALL STARS: Version 5
72   Green Door GD 4039   The King Man Is Back/SHALIMAR ALL STARS: Version (reissue) 5
73   Ackee ACK 521   Open Up The Gates/Version 5
73   Grape GR 3042   Let Me Dream (Parts 1 & 2) 5

(GERALD) HOFFNUNG
60s   Decca DFE 8682   AT THE OXFORD UNION (EP) 10

ANNIE HOGAN
85   Doublevision DVR 9   PLAYS KICKABYE (12" EP) 15

(see also Marc Almond, Nick Cave, Soft Cell)

CLAIRE HOGAN
59   Top Rank JAR 161   Sing A Smiling Song/I Wonder 5
59   Top Rank JAR 161   Sing A Smiling Song/I Wonder (78) 10

(see also Teresa Brewer)

SILAS HOGAN
71	Blue Horizon 2431 008	TROUBLE AT HOME (LP)	60
70s	Flyright FLY 595	I'M A FREE-HEARTED MAN (LP)	12

HOGARTH
68	Liberty LBF 15156	Suzie's Getting Married/I've Been Dreaming	10

SMOKEY HOGG
64	Realm RM 197	I'M SO LONELY (LP)	25
72	Ember EMB 3405	SINGS THE BLUES (LP)	18
70s	Specialty SNTF 5018	U BETTER WATCH THAT JIVE (LP)	12

(see also John Lee Hooker/Lightnin' Hopkins/Smokey Hogg)

HOGS
69	Jay Boy BOY 5	It's All Coming To Me Now/Motor Cycle Rider	5

SUZI JANE HOKUM
66	MGM MGM 1323	Need All The Help I Can Get/Home	5

HOKUS POKE
72	Vertigo 6360 064	EARTH HARMONY (LP)	40

RON HOLDEN
60	London HLU 9116	My Babe/Love You So	45

FRANK HOLDER
57	Decca F 10880	The Caterpillar Bush/Red Beans And Rice	5
57	Decca F 10908	Battle Of The Century/Chinese Cricket Match	5
57	Decca F 10908	Battle Of The Century/Chinese Cricket Match (78)	8
57	Decca F 10919	Champion Calypso/Sweetie Charlie	5
57	Decca F 10919	Champion Calypso/Sweetie Charlie (78)	8
57	Pye Nixa N 15092	Victory Test Match/Murder In The Market (78)	8
58	Parlophone R 4459	Bechuanaland/Nor The Moon By Midnight	8
58	Parlophone R 4459	Bechuanaland/Nor The Moon By Midnight (78)	10
59	Pye Nixa N 15179	Watermelon/Tomato (78)	10
56	Nixa NPT 19007	CALYPSO TIME WITH FRANK HOLDER (10" LP)	12

(see also Johnny Dankworth)

RAM JOHN HOLDER
67	Columbia DB 8157	I Need Somebody/She's Alright	6
67	Columbia DB 8262	My Friend Jones/It Won't Be Long Before I Love You	6
68	Beacon BEA 108	I Just Came To Get My Baby/Yes I Do	5
69	Upfront UPF 2	Goodwill To All Mankind/BLACK VELVET: Goodwill Sermon	5
70	United Artists UP 35117	Where Do The Dreams Go?/Miracle Happens Every Day	5
63	Melodisc MLP 12-133	RAM BLUES GOSPEL AND SOUL (LP)	40
69	Beacon BEAS 2	BLACK LONDON BLUES (LP)	40
70	Beacon BEAS 17	BOOTLEG BLUES (LP)	35

(see also Ram Jam Band, Ram Holder Brothers, Black Velvet, Geno Washington)

RAM HOLDER BROTHERS
66	Parlophone R 5471	Just Across The River/Ram Blues	15

(see also Ram Jam Band, Ram John Holder)

HOLE
91	City Slang EFA 04070-45/ SLANG 013	Teenage Whore/Drown Soda (p/s, lilac, clear or green vinyl, 500 of each)	each 12
91	City Slang EFA 04070	Teenage Whore/Drown Soda (12", p/s)	8
91	City Slang EFA 04070 CD	Teenage Whore/Drown Soda (CD)	8
93	City Slang EFA 04916-45	Beautiful Son/Old Age/20 Years In The Dakota (p/s, purple vinyl)	8
94	City Slang EFA 04936-7	Miss World/Rock Star (Alternate Mix) p/s, pink vinyl)	8
96	Mirromax 573 164-7	Gold Dust Woman/N.Y. LOOSE: Spit (gatefold p/s, 2 x 1-sided 7"s, with etched B-sides, 5,000 numbered)	8
91	City Slang SLANG 012	PRETTY ON THE INSIDE (LP, blue vinyl)	18
94	City Slang EFA 04935-1	LIVE THROUGH THIS (LP, white vinyl, 3000 only)	12

BILLIE HOLIDAY
51	Vogue V 2048	Detour Ahead/Blue, Turning Grey Over You (78)	10
56	Vogue V 2048	Detour Ahead/Blue, Turning Grey Over You	6
59	MGM MGM 1033	Don't Worry About Me/Just One More Chance	6
55	Brunswick OE 9172	LADY DAY VOL. 1 (EP)	8
55	Columbia Clef SEB 10009	BILLIE HOLIDAY (EP)	8
55	Vogue EPV 1128	BILLIE HOLIDAY (EP)	10
56	Brunswick OE 9199	LADY DAY VOL. 2 (EP)	8
56	Brunswick OE 9251	LADY DAY VOL. 3 (EP)	8
56	Columbia Clef SEB 10035	AN EVENING WITH BILLIE HOLIDAY (EP)	8
56	Columbia Clef SEB 10048	BILLIE HOLIDAY SINGS (EP)	8
59	Fontana TFE 17010	LADY DAY (EP)	8
50s	Melodisc EPM7 125	EMBRACEABLE YOU (EP)	10
60	Fontana TFE 17026	BLUE (EP)	8
60	Philips BBE 12359	JAZZ GALLERY (EP)	10
54	Columbia 33S 1034	BILLIE HOLIDAY (10" LP)	18
54	Brunswick LA 8676	LOVER MAN (10" LP)	18
55	Philips BBR 8032	FAVOURITES (10" LP)	18
56	Columbia Clef 33C 9023	AT JAZZ AT THE PHILHARMONIC (10" LP)	15
56	Columbia Clef 33CX 10019	MUSIC FOR TORCHING (LP)	15

Billie HOLIDAY

57	Columbia Clef 33CX 10064	VELVET MOOD (LP)	15
57	Columbia Clef 33CX 10076	SOLITUDE (LP)	15
57	Columbia Clef 33CX 10092	LADY SINGS THE BLUES (LP)	15
59	Columbia Clef 33CX 10145	SONGS FOR DISTINGUÉ LOVERS (LP)	15
59	MGM MGM-C 792	BILLIE HOLIDAY (LP)	15
59	Fontana TFL 5032	LADY IN SATIN (LP)	15
60	Fontana TFL 5106	A BILLIE HOLIDAY MEMORIAL (LP)	15
61	HMV CLP 1414	THE UNFORGETTABLE LADY DAY (LP)	15
62	Stateside SL 10007	BILLIE HOLIDAY (LP)	15
64	Ace Of Hearts AH 64	THE LADY SINGS VOL. 3 (LP)	10
65	Fontana TL 5262	ONCE UPON A TIME (LP, with Teddy Wilson)	12
66	Fontana TL 5287	BILLIE HOLIDAY (LP)	12
66	Island ILP 929	LAST LIVE RECORDING (LP)	20

CHICO HOLIDAY
59	RCA RCA 1117	Young Ideas/Cuckoo Girl	8
59	RCA RCA 1117	Young Ideas/Cuckoo Girl (78)	15
61	Coral Q 72443	God, Country And My Baby/Fools	8
59	RCA RCX 171	CHICO HOLIDAY (EP)	60

JIMMY HOLIDAY
63	Vocalion POP V 9206	How Can I Forget/Janet	22
64	London HLY 9868	I Lied/Alison	15
66	Liberty LIB 12040	Baby I Love You/You Won't Get Away	12
67	Liberty LIB 12048	Give Me Your Love/The Turning Point	12
67	Liberty LIB 12053	Everybody Needs Help/I'm Gonna Move To The City	8
68	Minit MLF 11008	Give Me Your Love/The Beauty Of A Girl In Love	7
69	Minit MLL/MLS 40010	SPREAD YOUR LOVE (LP)	30

JIMMY HOLIDAY & CLYDIE KING
67	Liberty LIB 12058	Ready, Willing And Able/We Got A Good Thing Goin'.	20
72	United Artists UP 35371	Ready, Willing And Able/JIMMY HOLIDAY: Give Me Your Love.	5
	(see also Clydie King)		

JOHNNY HOLIDAY
| 59 | London RE 1226 | SENTIMENTAL HOLIDAY (EP) | 8 |
| 59 | London RE 1227 | HOLIDAY FOR ROMANCE (EP) | 8 |

HOLIDAYS
| 66 | Polydor 56720 | I'll Love You Forever/Makin' Up Time | 90 |
| | (see also Edwin Starr) | | |

HOLLAND
| 84 | Ebony EBON 17 | EARLY WARNING (LP) | 10 |

BRIAN HOLLAND
| 74 | Invictus INV 2553 | I'm So Glad/I'm So Glad (Version) | 8 |

EDDIE HOLLAND
| 62 | Fontana H 387 | Jamie/Take A Chance On Me | 225 |
| 63 | Oriole CBA 1808 | If It's Love (It's All Right)/It's Not Too Late | 375 |

LYNN HOLLAND
64	Ember EMB S 198	And The Angels Sing/I Can't Read Your Writing (For My Tears) (some in p/s)	8/5
65	Polydor BM 56035	Oh Darling How I Miss You/Before.	5
67	Polydor 56166	One Man In My Life/Wand'rin Boy (unissued)	
67	Polydor 56187	Come And Love/May God Help You And Protect You (unissued)	
70	Pye 7N 17926	Concerto For One Voice (Once Again)/Give The World Another Chance	5
70	Pye 7N 17967	Dreaming/She.	5
	(see also Holly)		

TONY HOLLAND
| 63 | HMV POP 1135 | Sidewalk/Time Goes By | 35 |

(Brian) HOLLAND & (Lamont) DOZIER
72	Invictus INV 525	Why Can't We Be Lovers/Don't Leave Me	8
73	Invictus INV 528	Don't Leave Me Starvin' For Your Love (Parts 1 & 2)	5
	(see also Lamont Dozier)		

MICHAEL HOLLIDAY
78s
58	Columbia DB 4155	I'll Always Be In Love With You/I'll Be Lovin' You, Too (78)	8
58	Columbia DB 4188	She Was Only Seventeen/The Gay Vagabond (78)	8
59	Columbia DB 4255	Palace Of Love/The Girls Of County Armagh (78)	8
59	Columbia DB 4307	Moments Of Love/Dearest (78)	8
59	Columbia DB 4336	For You, For You/Life Is A Circus (78)	10
59	Columbia DB 4378	Starry-Eyed/The Steady Game (78)	12

SINGLES
56	Columbia SCM 5221	Sixteen Tons/The Rose Tattoo	15
56	Columbia SCM 5252	Nothin' To Do/Perfume, Candy And Flowers	15
56	Columbia SCM 5273	Hot Diggity (Dog Ziggity)/The Gal With The Yaller Shoes	15
56	Columbia DB 3813	The Runaway Train/Ten Thousand Miles	15
57	Columbia DB 3871	Yaller Yaller Gold/I Saw Esau	10
57	Columbia DB 3919	Love Is Strange/My House Is Your House	10
57	Columbia DB 3948	Four Walls/Wringle Wrangle	10
57	Columbia DB 3973	All Of You/It's The Good Things We Remember	10
57	Columbia DB 3992	Old Cape Cod/Love You Darlin'	8
58	Columbia DB 4058	The Story Of My Life/Keep Your Heart	6
58	Columbia DB 4087	In Love/Rooney	6

58	Columbia DB 4121	Stairway Of Love/May I?	6
58	Columbia DB 4155	I'll Always Be In Love With You/I'll Be Lovin' You, Too.	6
58	Columbia DB 4188	She Was Only Seventeen/The Gay Vagabond	5
58	Columbia DB 4216	My Heart Is An Open Book/Careless Hands	5
59	Columbia DB 4255	Palace Of Love/The Girls Of County Armagh	5
59	Columbia DB 4307	Moments Of Love/Dearest	5
59	Columbia DB 4336	For You, For You/Life Is A Circus	5
59	Columbia DB 4378	Starry-Eyed/The Steady Game.	5
60	Columbia DB 4437	Skylark/Dream Talk.	5
60	Columbia DB 4475	Little Boy Lost/The One-Finger Symphony	5
60	Columbia DB 4548	Stay In Love/Catch Me A Kiss	5
61	Columbia DB 4604	I'm The One Who Loves You/Miracle Of Monday Morning	5
61	Columbia DB 4663	I Wonder Who's Kissing Her Now/Dream Boy, Dream.	5
62	Columbia DB 4819	I Don't Want You To See Me Cry/Wishin' On A Rainbow	5
62	Columbia DB 4890	Have I Told You Lately That I Love You/It Only Takes A Minute	5
63	Columbia DB 4976	Laugh And The World Laughs With You/Iron Fence	5
63	Columbia DB 7080	Between Hello And Goodbye/Just To Be With You Again	5
63	Columbia DB 7171	Drums/Can I Forget You.	5
64	Columbia DB 7265	Dear Heart/My Year Of Love.	5
64	Columbia DB 7327	My Last Date (With You)/Always Is A Long Long Time	5

EPs

56	Columbia SEG 7638	MY GUITAR AND ME (EP)	10
57	Columbia SEG 7683	MUSIC WITH MIKE (EP)	10
58	Columbia SEG 7752	RELAX WITH MIKE (EP)	10
58	Columbia SEG 7761	ALL TIME FAVOURITES (EP)	10
58	Columbia SEG 7818	MELODY MIKE (EP)	10
59	Columbia SEG 7836	SENTIMENTAL JOURNEY (EP, with Edna Savage)	10
59	Columbia SEG 7892	MIKE AND THE OTHER FELLA (EP)	10
59	Columbia SEG 7972	MIKE NO. 1 (EP, also stereo ESG 7784)	10/12
60	Columbia SEG 7986	FOUR FEATHER FALLS (EP, also stereo ESG 7793)	20/25
60	Columbia SEG 7996	MIKE NO. 2 (EP, also stereo ESG 7803)	10/12
61	Columbia SEG 8074	MIKE NO. 3 (EP, also stereo ESG 7842)	10/12
61	Columbia SEG 8101	MIKE SINGS RAGTIME (EP, also stereo ESG 7856)	10/12
61	Columbia SEG 8115	MIKE IN A SENTIMENTAL MOOD (EP, also stereo ESG 7864)	10/12
62	Columbia SEG 8161	HAPPY HOLLIDAY (EP)	10
62	Columbia SEG 8186	MORE HAPPY HOLLIDAY (EP).	10
61	Columbia SEG 8242	MIKE SINGS COUNTRY AND WESTERN STYLE (EP)	12
64	Columbia SEG 8373	MEMORIES OF MIKE (EP)	12

LPs

58	Columbia 33S 1114	HI! (10" LP)	25
59	Columbia 33SX 1170	MIKE (LP)	18
60	Columbia 33SX 1262	HOLLIDAY MIXTURE (LP, also stereo SCX 3331)	15/18
61	Columbia 33SX 1354	HAPPY HOLLIDAY (LP)	15
62	Columbia 33SX 1426	TO BING FROM MIKE (LP, also stereo SCX 3441)	15/18
64	Columbia 33SX 1586	THE BEST OF MICHAEL HOLLIDAY (LP).	15
60s	World Record Club T 792	TO BING FROM MIKE (LP).	12

(see also Edna Savage)

SU(SAN) HOLLIDAY

64	Columbia DB 7363	Dark Despair/The Other Side (demos list A-side as "[Street Of] Dark Despair").	10
64	Columbia DB 7403	Any Day Now/Don't Come Knocking At My Door	10
65	Columbia DB 7616	Sometimes/Long Haired Boy.	10
65	Columbia DB 7709	Nevertheless (I'm In Love With You)/Moonglow	10
66	Columbia SX 6067	I WANNA SAY HELLO (LP, as Su Holliday)	100

(see also Susan Singer)

TIM HOLLIER

70	Fontana TF 1080	In This Room/Love Song	5
71	Philips 6006 130	Circle Is Small/In A Corner Of My Life/Time Stood Still	5
68	United Artists (S)ULP 1211	MESSAGE TO A HARLEQUIN (LP).	18
71	Philips 6308 044	SKY SAIL (LP)	15

HOLLIES

SINGLES

63	Parlophone R 5030	(Ain't That) Just Like Me/Hey, What's Wrong With Me	20
63	Parlophone R 5052	Searchin'/Whole World Over	12
63	Parlophone R 5077	Stay/Now's The Time	7
64	Parlophone R 5104	Just One Look/Keep Off That Friend Of Mine	6
64	Parlophone R 5137	Here I Go Again/Baby That's All	6
64	Parlophone R 5178	We're Through/Come On Back.	5
65	Parlophone R 5232	Yes I Will/Nobody	5
65	Parlophone R 5287	I'm Alive/You Know He Did	5
65	Parlophone R 5322	Look Through Any Window/So Lonely	5
65	Parlophone R 5392	If I Needed Someone/I've Got A Way Of My Own	5
66	Parlophone R 5409	I Can't Let Go/Running Through The Night.	5
66	Parlophone R 5469	Bus Stop/Don't Run And Hide.	5
66	United Artists UP 1152	After The Fox (with Peter Sellers)/BURT BACHARACH: The Fox-Trot	25
66	Parlophone R 5508	Stop! Stop! Stop!/It's You.	5
67	Parlophone R 5562	On A Carousel/All The World Is Love	5
67	Parlophone R 5602	Carrie Anne/Signs That Will Never Change.	5
67	Parlophone R 5637	King Midas In Reverse/Everything Is Sunshine	7
68	Parlophone R 5680	Jennifer Eccles/Open Up Your Eyes	5
68	Parlophone R 5733	Listen To Me/Do The Best You Can	5
69	Parlophone R 5765	Sorry Suzanne/Not That Way At All	5
69	Parlophone R 5806	He Ain't Heavy, He's My Brother/'Cos You Like To Love Me	5
70	Parlophone R 5837	I Can't Tell The Bottom From The Top/Mad Professor Blyth	6
70	Parlophone R 5862	Gasoline Alley Bred/Dandelion Wine.	6

MINT VALUE £

HOLLIES

71	Parlophone R 5905	Hey Willy/Row The Boat Together	6
72	Polydor 2058 199	The Baby/Oh Granny	6
72	Parlophone R 5939	Long Cool Woman (In A Black Dress)/Cable Car	6
72	Polydor 2058 289	Magic Woman Touch/Indian Girl	6
73	Polydor 2058 403	The Day That Curly Billy Shot Down Crazy Sam McGee/Born A Man	6
74	Polydor 2058 435	The Air That I Breathe/No More Riders	5
74	Polydor 2058 476	Son Of A Rotten Gambler/Layin' To The Music	6
74	Polydor 2058 533	I'm Down/Hello Lady Goodbye	6
75	Polydor 2058 595	Sandy (Fourth Of July, Asbury Park)/Second-Hand Hangups	6
75	EMI EMI 2353	Long Cool Woman In A Black Dress/Carrie Anne	5
76	Polydor 2058 694	Boulder To Birmingham/Crocodile Woman (She Bites)	5
76	Polydor 2058 719	Star/Love Is The Thing	5
76	Polydor 2058 779	Daddy Don't Mind/C'mon	5
76	Polydor 2058 799	Wiggle That Wotsit/Corrine	5
76	Polydor 2058 880	Hello To Romance/48 Hour Parole	5
77	Polydor 2058 906	Amnesty/Crossfire	5
78	EMI EMI 2813	Look Through Any Window/I'm Alive/Just One Look	5
79	Polydor POSP 35	Something To Live For/Song Of The Sun	5
79	Polydor POSPX 35	Something To Live For/Song Of The Sun/The Air That I Breathe (12", p/s)	12
80	Polydor 2059 246	Soldier's Song/Draggin' My Heels	10
80	Polydor POSP 175	Heartbeat/Take Your Time	8
81	EMI EMI 5229	Holliedaze (A Medley)/Holliepops (Medley)	5
81	Polydor POSP 379	Take My Love And Run/Driver	5
82	Parlophome PMS 1001	He Ain't Heavy, He's My Brother/'Cos You Like To Love Me (p/s)	5
83	WEA U 9888	Stop! In The Name Of Love/Musical Pictures (p/s)	5
84	EMI G45 11	Just One Look/Here I Go Again (p/s)	5
84	Columbia DB 9110	Too Many Hearts Get Broken/You're All Woman (p/s)	5
84	Columbia 12DB 9110	Too Many Hearts Get Broken/You're All Woman/Laughter Turns To Tears (12", p/s)	8
87	Columbia DB 9146	This Is It/You Gave Me Strength (p/s)	5
87	Columbia 12DB 9146	This Is It/You Gave Me Strength/You're All Woman (12", p/s)	8
87	Columbia DB 9151	Reunion Of The Heart/Too Many Hearts Get Broken (p/s)	5
87	Columbia 12DB 9151	Reunion Of The Heart/Too Many Hearts Get Broken/Hollidaze (12", p/s)	8
88	EMI CDEM 74	He Ain't Heavy, He's My Brother/Carrie/The Air That I Breathe/Yes I Will (CD)	8
88	EMI CDEM 80	The Air That I Breathe/We're Through/King Midas In Reverse/He Ain't Heavy, He's My Brother (CD)	8
90	SRT 90LS 2407	Purple Rain/Naomi/Two Shadows (12", p/s, available only at gigs)	8
90	SRT 90C 2407	Purple Rain/Naomi/Two Shadows (cassette, available only at gigs)	6

EPs

64	Parlophone GEP 8909	THE HOLLIES (EP)	35
64	Parlophone GEP 8911	JUST ONE LOOK (EP)	40
64	Parlophone GEP 8915	HERE I GO AGAIN (EP)	40
64	Parlophone GEP 8927	WE'RE THROUGH (EP)	40
65	Parlophone GEP 8934	IN THE HOLLIES STYLE (EP)	40
65	Parlophone GEP 8942	I'M ALIVE (EP)	40
66	Parlophone GEP 8951	I CAN'T LET GO (EP)	45

LPs

64	Parlophone PMC 1220	STAY WITH THE HOLLIES (LP, also stereo PCS 3054)	30/45
65	Parlophone PMC 1235	IN THE HOLLIES STYLE (LP)	40
65	Parlophone PMC 1261	THE HOLLIES (LP)	25
66	Parlophone PMC/PCS 7008	WOULD YOU BELIEVE? (LP, mono/stereo)	20/30
66	Parlophone PMC/PCS 7011	FOR CERTAIN BECAUSE (LP, gatefold sleeve, mono/stereo)	20/25

MINT VALUE £

67	Parlophone PMC/PCS 7022	EVOLUTION (LP, mono/stereo)	25/30
67	Parlophone PMC/PCS 7039	BUTTERFLY (LP, mono/stereo)	25/30
67	Parlophone TA-PMC 7039	BUTTERFLY (reel-to-reel tape, mono)	12
67	EMI Regal SREG 2024	THE HOLLIES (LP, export compilation)	30
67	World Records ST 979	THE VINTAGE HOLLIES (LP, stereo reissue of "In The Hollies Style")	30
68	World Records ST 1035	STAY WITH THE HOLLIES (LP, record club reissue)	30
68	Parlophone PMC/PCS 7057	THE HOLLIES' GREATEST (LP)	15
68	Parlophone TA-PMC 7057	THE HOLLIES' GREATEST (reel-to-reel tape, mono)	12
69	Parlophone PMC/PCS 7078	THE HOLLIES SING DYLAN (LP, mono/stereo)	20/18
69	Regal Starline SRS 5008	REFLECTION (LP, stereo reissue of "The Hollies")	12
69	Parlophone PCS 7092	HOLLIES SING HOLLIES (LP, gatefold sleeve)	18

(The above Parlophone LPs were originally issued with yellow/black labels; 1970s pressings with silver & black labels are worth £10 each.)

70	Parlophone PCS 7116	CONFESSIONS OF THE MIND (LP, with colour insert)	18
71	Parlophone PAS 10005	DISTANT LIGHT (LP, gatefold sleeve)	18
71	Regal Starline SRS 5013	STOP! STOP! STOP! (LP, reissue of "For Certain Because")	12
71	MFP MFP 5252	THE HOLLIES (LP, budget reissue of "Evolution")	12
72	Parlophone PCS 7148	THE HOLLIES' GREATEST HITS VOL. 2 (LP)	12
72	Polydor 2383 144	ROMANY (LP, gatefold sleeve)	18
74	Polydor 2383 262	HOLLIES (LP, with lyric insert)	15
75	Polydor 2442 128	ANOTHER NIGHT (LP, gatefold sleeve)	15
76	Polydor 2442 141	WRITE ON (LP, with lyric inner)	15
76	Polydor 2383 421	RUSSIAN ROULETTE (LP, with lyric inner)	15
78	Polydor 2383 474	A CRAZY STEAL (LP, with lyric inner)	12
78	Parlophone PMC 7174	THE BEST OF THE HOLLIES' EPs (LP)	12
78	Parlophone PMC 7176	THE OTHER SIDE OF THE HOLLIES (LP)	18
79	Polydor 2442 160	FIVE THREE ONE — DOUBLE SEVEN O FOUR (LP, with lyric insert)	12
79	St. Michael 2102/0101	UP FRONT (LP, sold through Marks & Spencer in conjunction with Polydor)	50
79	St. Michael 2102/0101	UP FRONT (cassette, via Marks & Spencer/Polydor)	25
80	Polydor POLTV 12	BUDDY HOLLY (LP, with lyric insert)	12
83	WEA 2501391	WHAT GOES AROUND (LP)	12
94	Fast Forward FFCD 822	LEGENDARY TOP TENS 1963 — 1988 (CD, sold via Avon Cosmetics)	25

(see also Allan Clarke, Graham Nash, Terry Sylvester, Haydock's Rockhouse, Griffin & Sylvester, Peter Sellers & Sophia Loren)

BRENDA HOLLOWAY

64	Stateside SS 307	Every Little Bit Hurts/Land Of A Thousand Boys	30
65	Tamla Motown TMG 508	When I'm Gone/I've Been Good To You	70
65	Tamla Motown TMG 519	Operator/I'll Be Available	50
66	Tamla Motown TMG 556	Together Till The End Of Time/Sad Song	35
66	Tamla Motown TMG 581	Hurt A Little Everyday/Where Were You (demos credit Brenda Holiday)	25
67	Tamla Motown TMG 608	Just Look What You've Done/Starting The Hurt All Over Again	18
67	Tamla Motown TMG 622	You've Made Me So Very Happy/I've Got To Find It	18
69	Tamla Motown TMG 700	Just Look What You've Done/You've Made Me So Very Happy	10
68	T. Motown (S)TML 11083	THE ARTISTRY OF BRENDA HOLLOWAY (LP)	90

LOLEATTA HOLLOWAY

71	United Artists UP 35273	Bring It On Up/Rainbow '71'	5

PATRICE HOLLOWAY

66	Capitol CL 15484	Love And Desire/Ecstasy	70

STANLEY HOLLOWAY

52	HMV JH 13	Hi-De-Hi/Penny On The Drum ('Butlins' promo)	10
59	Decca F 11140	Dark Girl Dressed In Blue/Growing Old	5
59	Decca F 11140	Dark Girl Dressed In Blue/Growing Old (78)	8
60	Columbia DB 4517	Petticoat Lane/Sing A Song Of London	5
60	Pye 7N 15302	Lily Of Laguna/A Bachelor Gay	5
59	Philips BBE 12326	MY WORD YOU DO LOOK QUEER (EP)	8
59	Pye NEP 24097	NO TREES IN THE STREET (EP)	8
60	Columbia SEG 8034	ADVENTURES WITH ALBERT (EP)	8
62	Columbia SEG 8118	BRAHN BOOTS AND OTHER FAVOURITES (EP)	8
56	Columbia 33S 1093	FAMOUS ADVENTURES WITH OLD SAM & THE RAMSBOTTOMS (10" LP)	15
58	Philips BBL 7237	'ERE'S 'OLLOWAY (LP)	12
60	Pye NPL 18056	JOIN IN THE CHORUS (LP)	12

HOLLOW GROUND

80	Guardian GR/HG C57	FLYING HIGH EP (Flying High/Warlord/Rock On/Don't Chase The Dragon) (some in p/s)	150/30

HOLLOW MEN

85	Evensong EVE 107	Late Flowering Lust/Ocean Lies/Raindrop Children (p/s)	12
87	Evensong EVE 212	Gold And Ivory/Filth City Fever/Pandemonium Carousel/ Autumn Avenue (12", p/s, some with postcard)	10/8
87	Evensong EVE 212	Gold And Ivory/Filth City Fever/Pandemonium Carousel/Autumn Avenue (12", white label test pressing in unreleased proof sleeve)	50
88	Gigantic GI 101	White Train/The Man Who Would Be King (die-cut p/s, promo only)	10
89	Blind Eye BE 007	The Drowning Man/Whisper To Me/Ivory Blues (12", p/s, some signed, others with promo booklet)	10/12/7
86	Dead Man's Curve DMC 15	TALES OF THE RIVERBANK (LP)	12
88	Dead Man's Curve DMC 25	THE MAN WHO WOULD BE KING (LP)	12
88	D.M.C. VIVID ONE	THE MAN WHO WOULD BE KING (CD)	18

HOLLY

65	Fontana TF 980	On With The Game/Paradise Lost	7

(see also Lynn Holland)

HOLLY

79	Eric's ERIC'S 003	Yankee Rose/Treasure Island/Desperate Dan (p/s)	15
79	Eric's ERIC'S 007	Hobo Joe/Stars Of The Bars (p/s)	15

(see also Holly Johnson, Frankie Goes To Hollywood, Big In Japan)

MINT VALUE £

BUDDY HOLLY

78s

56	Brunswick 05581	Blue Days — Black Nights/Love Me (78)	220
57	Vogue Coral Q 72293	Peggy Sue/Everyday (78)	150
58	Coral Q 72293	Peggy Sue/Everyday (78)	12
58	Coral Q 72288	Listen To Me/I'm Gonna Love You Too (78)	25
58	Coral Q 72325	Rave On/Take Your Time (78)	25
58	Coral Q 72333	Early In The Morning/Now We're One (78)	35
58	Coral Q 72346	Heartbeat/Well ... All Right (78)	40
59	Coral Q 72360	It Doesn't Matter Anymore/Raining In My Heart (78)	40
59	Brunswick 05800	Rock Around With Ollie Vee/Midnight Shift (78)	200
59	Coral Q 72376	Peggy Sue Got Married/Crying, Waiting, Hoping (78)	200
60	Coral Q 72392	Heartbeat/Everyday (78)	400

SINGLES

56	Brunswick 05581	Blue Days — Black Nights/Love Me	650
57	Vogue Coral Q 72293	Peggy Sue/Everyday	60
58	Coral Q 72293	Peggy Sue/Everyday (reissue)	15
58	Coral Q 72288	Listen To Me/I'm Gonna Love You Too	12
58	Coral Q 72325	Rave On/Take Your Time	12
58	Coral Q 72333	Early In The Morning/Now We're One	12
58	Coral Q 72346	Heartbeat/Well ... All Right	12
59	Coral Q 72360	It Doesn't Matter Anymore/Raining In My Heart	6
59	Brunswick 05800	Rock Around With Ollie Vee/Midnight Shift	30
59	Coral Q 72376	Peggy Sue Got Married/Crying, Waiting, Hoping	15

(The above 45s were originally issued with triangular centres; reissues with round centres are worth two-thirds these values)

60	Coral Q 72392	Heartbeat/Everyday	10
60	Coral Q 72397	True Love Ways/Moondreams	10
60	Coral Q 72411	Learning The Game/That Makes It Tough	8
61	Coral Q 72419	What To Do/That's What They Say	10
61	Coral Q 72432	Baby I Don't Care/Valley Of Tears	7
61	Coral Q 72445	Look At Me/Mailman, Bring Me No More Blues	10
62	Coral Q 72449	Listen To Me/Words Of Love	10
62	Coral Q 72455	Reminiscing/Wait Till The Sun Shines, Nellie	7
63	Coral Q 72459	Brown-Eyed Handsome Man/Slippin' And Slidin'	6
63	Coral Q 72463	Bo Diddley/It's Not My Fault	6
63	Coral Q 72466	Wishing/Because I Love You	8
63	Coral Q 72469	What To Do/Umm Oh Yeah	12
64	Coral Q 72472	You've Got Love/An Empty Cup (as Buddy Holly & Crickets)	12
64	Coral Q 72475	Love's Made A Fool Of You/You're The One	10
66	Coral Q 72483	Maybe Baby/That's My Desire	20
68	Decca AD 1009	Rave On/Peggy Sue (export reissue)	30
68	MCA MU 1012	Peggy Sue/Rave On (reissue)	5
69	MCA MU 1059	Love Is Strange/You're The One	8
69	MCA MU 1081	It Doesn't Matter Anymore/Maybe Baby (reissue)	6
70	MCA MU 1116	Rave On/Umm Oh Yeah (Dearest)	5
73	MCA MMU 1198	That'll Be The Day/Well All Right/Every Day	5
74	MCA MCA 119	It Doesn't Matter Anymore/True Love Ways/Brown Eyed Handsome Man	5
75	MCA MCA 207	Oh Boy!/Every Day (as Buddy Holly & Crickets)	5
76	MCA MCA 252	True Love Ways/It Doesn't Matter Anymore/Raining In My Heart/Moondreams (p/s)	5
76	MCA MCA 253	Peggy Sue/Rave On/Rock Around With Ollie Vee/Midnight Shift (p/s)	5
76	MCA MCA 254	Maybe Baby/Think It Over/That'll Be The Day/It's So Easy (p/s, as Buddy Holly & Crickets)	5
78	MCA MCA 344	Wishing/Love's Made A Fool Of You (p/s)	5
83	MCA HR 001	That'll Be The Day/True Love Ways (as Buddy Holly & Crickets) (with/without *The History Of Rock* issue 1; 'Made In France' or 'Made In Gt. Britain' on label)	7/5
84	MCA BHB 1	THAT'LL BE THE DAY (10 x 7" box set, comprising BH1-10 in p/s)	40
89	MCA MCAV 1368	Oh Boy!/Well ... All Right/Mailman Bring Me No More Blues/Everyday (10", p/s)	5

EPs

58	Coral FEP 2002	LISTEN TO ME (EP, brown cover, sleeve shows Holly *without* glasses; disc credits title as "Buddy Holly")	350
58	Coral FEP 2002	LISTEN TO ME (EP, re-pressing, various shades of green/brown p/s, shows Holly *with* glasses; disc credits title as "Buddy Holly")	40
58	Coral FEP 2005	RAVE ON (EP, various shades of green/brown p/s)	35
59	Coral FEP 2014	IT'S SO EASY (with the Crickets) (EP)	35
59	Coral FEP 2015	HEARTBEAT (EP)	35
59	Coral FEP 2032	BUDDY HOLLY (EP)	35
59	Brunswick OE 9456	BUDDY HOLLY NO. 1 (EP)	55
59	Brunswick OE 9457	BUDDY HOLLY NO. 2 (EP)	55

(The above EPs were originally issued with tri centres; later pressings with round-centres are worth between half and two-thirds these values.)

60	Coral FEP 2044	THE LATE GREAT BUDDY HOLLY (EP, tri centre)	50+
60	Coral FEP 2044	THE LATE GREAT BUDDY HOLLY (EP, round centre)	30
64	Coral FEP 2065	BUDDY — BY REQUEST (EP)	45
64	Coral FEP 2066	THAT TEX-MEX SOUND (EP)	60
64	Coral FEP 2067	WISHING (EP)	50
64	Coral FEP 2068	SHOWCASE VOLUME 1 (EP)	60
64	Coral FEP 2069	SHOWCASE VOLUME 2 (EP)	60
65	Coral FEP 2070	BUDDY HOLLY SINGS (EP)	60

LPs

58	Vogue Coral LVA 9085	BUDDY HOLLY (LP, Vogue-Coral labels & Coral sleeve) 75
58	Coral LVA 9085	BUDDY HOLLY (LP, re-pressing with Coral labels) 30
59	Coral LVA 9105	THE BUDDY HOLLY STORY
		(LP; 'High Fidelity Coral' logo on sleeve) 20
60s	Coral LVA 9105	THE BUDDY HOLLY STORY (LP, reissue, different 'roll-neck sweater'
		sleeve with small 'Coral' logo) 40
60	Coral LVA 9127	THE BUDDY HOLLY STORY VOL. II (LP) 20
61	Ace Of Hearts AH 3	THAT'LL BE THE DAY (LP) 15
63	Coral LVA 9212	REMINISCING (LP) 18
64	Coral LVA 9222	SHOWCASE (LP) 22
65	Coral LVA 9227	HOLLY IN THE HILLS (LP, w/ Bob Montgomery, withdrawn mispressing, sleeve
		& label list "Wishing", plays "Reminiscing"; matrix no's end w/ 1B both sides) . . 35
65	Coral LVA 9227	HOLLY IN THE HILLS (LP, corrected edition, with Bob Montgomery,
		plays "Wishing", matrix numbers end with 1B on one side & 2B on other) 55
67	Ace Of Hearts AH 148	BUDDY HOLLY'S GREATEST HITS (LP) 12
68	MCA MUP(S) 312	LISTEN TO ME (LP, mono/stereo, reissue of "Buddy Holly" [LVA 9085]) 15/12
68	MCA MUP(S) 313	RAVE ON
		(LP, mono/stereo, reissue of "The Buddy Holly Story") 15/12
68	MCA MUP(S) 314	BROWN-EYED HANDSOME MAN (LP, mono/stereo,
		reissue of "Reminiscing") 15/12
68	MCA MUP(S) 315	HE'S THE ONE (LP, mono/stereo, reissue of "Showcase") 18/15
68	MCA MUP(S) 319	TRUE LOVE WAYS (LP, mono/stereo,
		reissue of "The Buddy Holly Story, Volume II") 18/15
68	MCA MUP 320	WISHING (LP, mono only, reissue of "Holly In The Hills") 20
69	MCA MUPS 371	GIANT (LP) 18

(The above MCA albums were originally issued with yellow labels; later variations exist with various twin-toned designs.)

70	Coral CP/CPS 47	BUDDY HOLLY'S GREATEST HITS VOL. 2
		(LP, reissue, mono/stereo) 12/8
75	World Records SM 301/5	THE BUDDY HOLLY STORY (5-LP box set) 30
79	MCA Coral CDMSP 807	THE COMPLETE BUDDY HOLLY (6-LP box set with sepia-tinted book) 35
80	Marks & Spencer IMP 114	HEARTBEAT (LP) 65
83	MCA MCM 1002	FOR THE FIRST TIME ANYWHERE (LP) 12
86	Rollercoaster ROLL 2013	SOMETHING SPECIAL FROM BUDDY HOLLY (LP) 20

(see also Crickets, Fireballs)

STEVIE HOLLY

66	Planet PLF 107	A Strange World/Little Man
		(initially with "Planet" company sleeve) 20/15

HOLLY GOLIGHTLY

94	Vinyl Japan PAD 13	JIGGY JIGGY (EP) 5
95	Vinyl Japan PAD 26	MARY ANN (EP) 5
96	Damaged Goods	Come The Day/In You
	Damgood 110	(picture disc) 6

HOLLY & JOEY

82	Virgin VS 478	I Got You Babe/HOLLY & ITALIANS: One More Dance (p/s) 8

(see also Ramones, Deborah Harry)

KENNY HOLLYWOOD

62	Decca F 11546	Magic Star/The Wonderful Story Of Love 30

HOLLYWOOD ARGYLES

60	London HLU 9146	Alley Oop/Sho' Knew A Lot About Love 15
60	London HLU 9146	Alley Oop/Sho' Knew A Lot About Love (78) 150
60	Top Rank JAR 530	Gun Totin' Critter Called Jack/GARY PAXTON: Bug-Eye 12

(see also Kim Fowley, Skip & Flip, Gary Paxton)

HOLLYWOOD FLAMES

57	London HL 7030	Buzz Buzz Buzz/Crazy
		(export issue) 30
58	London HL 8545	Buzz Buzz Buzz/Crazy 50
58	London HL 8545	Buzz Buzz Buzz/Crazy (78) 30
59	London HLW 8955	Much Too Much/In The Dark 50
59	London HLW 8955	Much Too Much/In The Dark (78) 60
60	London HLE 9071	If I Thought You Needed Me/Every Day Every Way 25

HOLLYWOOD FREEWAY

72	Threshold TH 10	I've Been Moved/Cool Calamares (unissued)
72	Deram DM 359	I've Been Moved/Cool Calamares 5

HOLLYWOOD HURRICANES

64	Prima PR 1009	Beavershot/Have Love Will Travel 5

HOLLYWOOD VINES

61	Capitol CL 15191	When Johnny Comes Slidin' Home/Cruisin' 8

MIKE HOLM

70	Major Minor MM 659	Mendocino/Cutey Girl 5

BILL HOLMAN OCTET

54	Capitol KC 65000	Cousin Jack/Plain Folks 6

EDDIE HOLMAN

65	Cameo Parkway P 960	This Can't Be True/A Free Country 35
69	Action ACT 4547	I Love You/I Surrender 35
70	Stateside SS 2160	(Hey There) Lonely Girl/It's All In The Game 8
70	Stateside SS 2170	Since I Don't Have You/Don't Stop Now 8
72	GSF GSZ 1	My Mind Keeps Telling Me/Stranded In A Dream 5
77	Salsoul SZ 2026	This Will Be A Night To Remember/Time Will Tell 6

MINT VALUE £

DAVID HOLMES

97	Go Beat GOB 6	Don't Die Just Yet (Mogwai Mix)/Holiday Girl (Arab Strap Mix) (p/s, 500 only)	12

(see also Mogwai)

CHRISTINE HOLMES

64	Mercury MF 813	This Is My Prayer/My Dream	6
64	Mercury MF 819	Play Me A Sad Song (Mr DJ)/Doesn't He Know	6
64	Mercury MF 831	Goodbye Boys Goodbye/Is It Love	6
65	Mercury MF 851	Many Things From Your Window/You'd Better Believe It	6
65	Mercury MF 887	Goin' Where The Lovin' Is/Where There's Smoke	6

(see also Family Dogg)

IVAN HOLMES

67	Columbia DB 8119	The Light, The Love And The Life/Cocaine	5

JAKE HOLMES

69	Polydor 56547	How Are You (Parts 1 & 2)	5
70	Ember EMB S 269	Saturday Night/Diner Song	5
70	Polydor 2066 040	So Close/Django And Friend	5
70	Polydor 583 579	JAKE HOLMES (LP)	20
70	Polydor 2425 036	SO CLOSE SO VERY FAR TO GO (LP)	15
72	CBS 64905	HOW MUCH TIME (LP)	15

JOE HOLMES & LEN GRAHAM

79	Topic 12TS 401	AFTER DAWNING (LP)	12

LEROY HOLMES & ORCHESTRA

68	United Artists UP 2222	The Good, The Bad And The Ugly/Live For Life	5

SALTY HOLMES

50	London L 663	I Found My Mama/Don't Shed Your Tears After I'm Gone (78)	8

RICHARD 'GROOVES' HOLMES

60s	Transatlantic PR 7435	SOUL MESSAGE (LP)	12
68	Transatlantic PR 7493	RICHARD 'GROOVES' HOLMES (LP)	12

HOLOCAUST

80	Phoenix PSP 1	Heavy Metal Mania/Only As Young As You Feel (p/s)	20
80	Phoenix 12 PSP 1	Heavy Metal Mania/Love's Power/Only As Young As You Feel (12", p/s)	25
80	Phoenix 12 PSP 2	Smokin' Valves/Friend Or Foe (p/s)	10
80	Phoenix 12 PSP 2	Smokin' Valves/Friend Or Foe/Out My Book (12", p/s)	15
81	Phoenix PSP 3P	HOLOCAUST LIVE (EP)	15
82	Phoenix 12 PSP 4	Comin' Through/Don't Wanna Be A Loser/Good Thing Going (12", p/s)	12
81	Phoenix PSLP 1	THE NIGHTCOMERS (LP)	20
83	Phoenix PSPLP 4	LIVE (HOT CURRY AND WINE) (LP)	25
84	Phoenix PSPLP 5	NO MAN'S LAND (LP)	15

JOHN HOLT

63	Island WI 041	I Cried A Tear/I'll Stay	18
68	Trojan TR 643	Tonight/Oh How It Hurts (B-side actually by Paragons)	15
69	Trojan TR 661	Ali Baba/I'm Your Man	10
69	Trojan TR 674	What You Gonna Do Now/Have You Ever Been To Heaven	8
69	Trojan TR 694	Have Sympathy/HARRY J ALLSTARS: Spyrone	8
69	Trojan TR 7702	Wooden Heart/All My Life	8
70	Duke Reid DR 2506	Come Out Of My Bed/WINSTON WRIGHT: Hide And Seek	10
70	Duke DU 73	Stealing, Stealing/WINSTON WRIGHT: Stealing, Stealing (Volume 2)	8
70	Duke DU 77	The Working Kind/Open Jaw	8
70	Jackpot JP 735	A Little Tear/JEFF BARNS: Get In The Groove	7
70	Bamboo BAM 44	A Love I Can Feel/JOHNNY LAST: Long Liver Man (B-side act. by Hugh Black)	10
70	Bamboo BAM 55	A Stranger In Love/WAILERS: Jailhouse (Good Rudy)	60
70	Bamboo BAM 62	Holly Holy/Do You Love Me?	8
70	Banana BA 314	Why Can't I Touch You/SOUND DIMENSION: Touching Version	8
70	Smash SMA 2303	My Heart Is Gone/PHIL PRATT ALL STARS: Version	6
70	Smash SMA 2305	I Had A Talk With My Woman/MAXINE: Life Is Not The Same Anymore	6
70	Supreme SUP 212	Share My Rest/AL BROWN: Allways	10
70	Unity UN 548	Sometimes/BUNNY LEE ALL STARS: Lash-La-Rue	6
70	Unity UN 549	Sea Cruise/LEE'S ALL STARS: Niney's Hop	8
70	Unity UN 552	Walking Along/LEE'S ALL STARS: Warefare	8
70	Unity UN 556	Give Her All The Love/BUSTY BROWN: Nobody But You	6
71	Banana BA 340	O.K. Fred/Fancy Make-Up	8
71	Banana BA 345	Build Our Dreams/LEROY SIBBLES: Love In Our Nation	8
71	Treasure Isle TI 7061	Let's Build Our Dreams/TOMMY McCOOK & SUPERSONICS: Testify Version	12
71	Treasure Isle TI 7065	Sister Big Stuff/TOMMY McCOOK & SUPERSONICS: Black River	15
71	Treasure Isle TI 7066	Paragons Medley/TOMMY McCOOK & SUPERSONICS: Medley Version	12
71	Ashanti ASH 401	Again/MUDIES ALL STARS: Ten Steps To Soul Version	6
71	Camel CA 78	Linger A While/Version	6
71	Escort ERT 847	Knock On Your Door/URIEL ALDRIDGE: Set Me Free	6
71	Jackpot JP 772	Stick By Me/It's A Pleasure	6
71	Jackpot JP 774	It's A Jam In The Streets/A Man Needs A Woman	6
71	Jackpot JP 784	Anymore/Lost Love	6
71	Moodisc MU 3513	It May Sound Silly/MUDIE ALL STARS: Instrumental	6
71	Moodisc MU 105	It May Sound Silly/MUDIE ALL STARS: Instrumental (reissue)	6
71	Punch PH 60	Strange Things/WINSTON WRIGHT: Want Money (B-side act. G.G. All Stars)	10
71	Smash SMA 2324	Mother And Father Love/AGGROVATORS: Mother Love Version	6
72	Blue Beat BB 424	O.K. Fred/BIG YOUTH: Chi Chi Run	7

72	Prince Buster PB 40	Close To Me/Version	7
72	Prince Buster PB 41	Get Ready/Version	7
72	Prince Buster PB 42	Rain From The Skies/Version	7
72	Prince Buster PB 43	The First Time/Version	7
72	Prince Buster PB 49	For Your Love/Version	7
72	G.G. GG 4529	Keep It Up/A Love Like Yours	6
72	Fab FAB 188	A Little Happiness/DELROY WILSON: Diamond Rings	10
72	Jackpot JP 790	Don't You Know/Riding For A Fall	6
72	Jackpot JP 807	Looking Back/I'll Be There	6
72	Pama PM 845	I'll Always Love You/SLIM SMITH: 3 x 7 Rock And Roll	6
72	Pama PM 852	Pledging My Love/I Will Know What To Do	6
73	Fab FAB 224	Let's Go Dancing/Version	7
73	Fab FAB 244	Let's Go Dancing/Version (reissue)	7
73	Attack ATT 8045	Time And The River/Version	5
73	Smash SMA 2329	Don't Break Your Promise/I've Been Admiring You	8
73	Ackee ACK 513	Ecstacy/Version	6
70	Bamboo BDLP 210	A LOVE I CAN FEEL (LP)	45
70s	Melodisc MLP 12170	GREATEST HITS (LP)	30
70s	Melodisc MLP 12180	OK FRED (LP)	35
70s	Melodisc MLP 12191	JOHN HOLT & FRIENDS (LP)	40
71	Trojan TRL(S) 37	STILL IN CHAINS (LP)	18
72	Trojan TRL(S) 43	HOLT (LP)	15
72	Trojan TBL 184	PLEDGING MY LOVE (LP)	15
73	Trojan TRLS 55	THE FURTHER YOU LOOK (LP)	12
74	Attack ATLP 1010	A LOVE I CAN FEEL (LP)	12
74	Trojan TRLS 75	A THOUSAND VOLTS OF HOLT (LP)	12
74	Trojan TRLS 85	DUSTY ROADS (LP)	12
75	Cactus CTLP 109	TIME IS THE MASTER (LP)	12

(see also Jay & Joya, Little John, Neville Hinds, Jeff Barnes, Danny Simpson, Hugh Roy, U Roy Junior, Don Drummond, Interns)

GARY HOLTON

84	Magnet GARY 2	Catch A Falling Star/Angel (star-shaped picture disc)	5

(see also Heavy Metal Kids, Kids, Slade)

ROOSEVELT HOLTS

68	Blue Horizon 7-63201	PRESENTING THE COUNTRY BLUES (LP)	60

HOLY MACKEREL

72	CBS 8447	Rock-A-Bye/New Black Shoes	5
72	CBS 65297	HOLY MACKEREL (LP)	20
93	Tenth Planet TP 005	CLOSER TO HEAVEN (LP, numbered, 500 only)	12

(see also Jason Crest, High Broom)

HOLY MODAL ROUNDERS

68	Elektra EKL 4026	MORAY EELS EAT THE HOLY MODALS (LP)	20
70	Transatlantic TRA 7451	HOLY MODAL ROUNDERS (LP)	25
70	Transatlantic TRA	HOLY MODAL ROUNDERS 2 (LP)	25

HOMBRES

67	Verve VS 1510	Let It Out (Let It All Hang Out)/Go Girl Go	12

HOME

69	Bell SBLL 119	JOLLIVER ARKANSAW (LP)	60

HOME

72	CBS 7809	Fancy Lady, Hollywood Child/Shady Lady	5
71	CBS 64365	PAUSE FOR A HOARSE HORSE (LP)	35
72	CBS 64752	HOME (LP)	20
73	CBS 65550	THE ALCHEMIST (LP)	18
70s	CBS	(LP, unreleased, test pressings only)	150

(see also Groundhogs, AC/DC, Wishbone Ash, Blue Rondos)

HOMER & JETHRO

53	HMV B 10258	Cold Cold Heart No. 2/Alabama Jubilee (78)	10
54	HMV B 10581	How Much Is That Hound Dog/Rudolph The Flat-Nosed Reindeer (78)	15
54	HMV 7M 211	Swappin' Partners/Crazy Mix-Up Song	10
54	HMV B 10687	Swappin' Partners/Crazy Mix-Up Song (78)	10
54	Parlophone CMSP 2	Don't Let Your Sweet Love Die/When It's Long Handle Time In Tennessee (export issue)	12
59	RCA RCA 1148	Waterloo/The Battle Of Kookamonga	5
59	RCA RCA 1148	Waterloo/The Battle Of Kookamonga (78)	30
59	Parlophone GEP 8791	WANTED FOR MURDER OF THE STANDARDS (EP)	15

HOMESICK JAMES

64	Sue WI 319	Crossroads/My Baby's Sweet	22
65	Sue WI 330	Set A Date/Can't Afford To Do It	25

HOMESICK JAMES/SNOOKY PRYOR

74	Caroline C 1502	HOMESICK JAMES AND SNOOKY PRYOR (LP)	18

HOMOSEXUALS

79	Black Noise F12 No. 2	Divorce Proceedings/Mecho Madness (12", plain sleeve with sticker)	10
79	L'Orelei PF 151	Hearts In Exile/South South Africans (p/s, with insert)	8
81	Black Noise BN 1	BIGGER THAN THE NUMBER YET MISSING THE DOT (EP, clear vinyl, fold-around hand-painted sleeve)	8
80s	Recommended RR # 18	THE HOMOSEXUALS RECORD (LP, with inserts)	12

(see also George Harrassment & Homosexuals, Ice La Bas, Amos & Sara, Nancy Sesay & Melodaires, L-Voag, Sir Alick & Phraser)

HOMUNCULUS

80s	Detrimental History DHSS 4	MORGUE DREAMS (cassette)	12

(see also Karl Blake)

MINAKO HONDA
87 Columbia DB 9153   Golden Days (English Version)/Crazy Nights (English Version)
(p/s, features Brian May) 30

HONDELLS
64 Mercury MF 834   Little Honda/Hot Rod High 15
65 Mercury MF 925   Younger Girl/All American Girl 10
66 Mercury MF 967   Cheryl's Goin' Home/Show Me Girl 12

HONEST MEN
69 Tamla Motown TMG 706   Cherie/Baby 15

HONEYBOY
71 Trojan TR 7835   Jamaica/ITALS: Sea Wave 5
72 Banana BA 375   Homeward Bound/Peace In The Land 6

HONEYBUS
67 Deram DM 131   Delighted To See You/The Breaking Up Scene 8
67 Deram DM 152   Do I Figure In Your Life/Throw My Love Away 8
68 Deram DM 182   I Can't Let Maggie Go/Tender Are The Ashes 5
68 Deram DM 207   Girl Of Independent Means/How Long 6
69 Deram DM 254   She Sold Blackpool Rock/Would You Believe 8
70 Deram DM 289   Story/The Right To Choose 6
72 Bell BLL 1205   She Is The Female To My Soul/For Where Have You Been 5
73 Warner Bros K 16250   For You/Little Lovely One 8
76 Decca F 13631   I Can't Let Maggie Go/Julie In My Heart 5
70 Deram DML/SML 1056   STORY (LP) 50
73 Warner Bros K 46248   RECITAL (LP, withdrawn) 150
(see also Pete Dello, Colin Hare, Lace, Magic Valley, Red Herring)

HONEYCOMBS
64 Pye 7N 15664   Have I The Right/Please Don't Pretend Again 5
64 Pye 7N 15705   Is It Because/I'll Cry Tomorrow 5
64 Pye 7N 15736   Eyes/If You've Got To Pick A Baby 8
65 Pye 7N 15781   Don't Love You No More/I'll See You Tomorrow (withdrawn, promo only) 100
65 Pye 7N 15827   Something Better Beginning/I'll See You Tomorrow 8
65 Pye 7N 15890   That's The Way/Can't Get Through To You 5
65 Pye 7N 15979   This Year, Next Year/Not Sleeping Too Well Lately 7
66 Pye 7N 17089   Who Is Sylvia?/How Will I Know 10
66 Pye 7N 17138   It's So Hard/I Fell In Love 10
66 Pye 7N 17173   That Loving Feeling/Should A Man Cry 12
69 Pye 7N 17741   Have I The Right/Please Don't Pretend Again (stereo reissue) 5
65 Pye NEP 24230   THAT'S THE WAY (EP) 40
64 Pye NPL 18097   THE HONEYCOMBS (LP) 45
65 Pye NPL 18132   ALL SYSTEMS GO! (LP) 75
66 Golden Guinea GGL 0350   THE HONEYCOMBS (LP, reissue in different sleeve) 18
(see also Lemmings, Dennis D'Ell, Martin Murray)

HONEYCONE
70 Hot Wax HWX 103   While You're Out Looking For Sugar/The Feeling's Gone 5
71 Hot Wax HWX 105   Girls It Ain't Easy/Take Me With You 5
71 Hot Wax HWX 107   Want Ads/We Belong Together 5
72 Hot Wax HWX 111   One Monkey Don't Stop No Show/Stick Up 5
72 Hot Wax HWX 112   The Day I Found Myself/When Will It End 5
72 Hot Wax HWX 116   Sittin' On A Time Bomb/It's Better To Have Loved And Lost 5
71 Hot Wax SHW 5002   HONEYCONE (LP) 12
71 Hot Wax SHW 5004   SWEET REPLIES (LP) 12
72 Hot Wax SHW 5005   SOULFUL TAPESTRY (LP) 12
73 Hot Wax SHW 5010   LOVE, PEACE AND SOUL (LP) 15

HONEYCRACK
95 Epic PPP 1   King Of Misery/5 Minutes (printed brown p/s, numbered, 4,000 only) ... 15
95 Epic PPP 1   King Of Misery/5 Minutes (CD) 15
(see also Wildhearts)

HONEYDEW
70 Argo AFW 101   Part Of This Game/To Make You Mine 5

HONEYDRIPPERS
84 Es Paranza 790 220-1   THE HONEYDRIPPERS VOL. ONE (10" LP) 12
(see also Robert Plant, Jeff Beck, Jimmy Page)

HONEYEND
72 Spark SRL 1072   Heartbreaker/Beautiful Downtown 5

HONEYS
63 Capitol CL 15299   Surfin' Down The Swanee River/Shoot The Curl 40
(see also American Spring, Beach Boys)

HONEYTONES
58 London HLX 8671   Don't Look Now, But.../I Know, I Know 50
58 London HLX 8671   Don't Look Now, But.../I Know, I Know (78) 35

HONEYTREE
70s Myrrh MYR 1039   EVERGREEN (LP) 15

HONG GANG
72 Sioux SI 004   Reggae Mento/MONTEGO MELON: Swan Lake 5
73 Sioux SI 025   Smoking Wild/ROOSEVELT SINGERS: Heavy Reggae 5
(see also Bob Andy)

ROBBIN HOOD
56 MGM SP 1178   The Rock-A-Bye Blues/Beautiful, Beautiful Love 10

HOOK

68	Uni UN 507	In The Beginning/Show You The Way	8

EARL HOOKER

69	Blue Horizon 57-3166	Boogie Don't Blot/Funky Blues	20
70	Blue Horizon 7-63850	SWEET BLACK ANGEL (LP)	90
70	Stateside SSL 10298	DON'T HAVE TO WORRY (LP)	35

(see also John Lee Hooker)

JOHN LEE HOOKER

78s

52	Vogue V 2102	Hoogie Boogie/Whistlin' And Moanin' Blues (78)	60
54	London HL 8037	Need Somebody/Too Much Boogie (78)	70

SINGLES

63	Stateside SS 203	Boom Boom/Frisco Blues	12
64	Stateside SS 297	Dimples/I'm Leaving	8
64	Stateside SS 341	I Love You Honey/Send Me Your Pillow	10
64	Pye International 7N 25255	High Priced Woman/Sugar Mama	10
64	Polydor NH 52930	Shake It Baby/Let's Make It Baby	12
65	Sue WI 361	I'm In The Mood/Boogie Chillun	25
66	Chess CRS 8039	Let's Go Out Tonight/In The Mood	12
66	Planet PLF 114	Mai Lee/Don't Be Messing With My Bread (with Groundhogs)	30
70	President PT 295	Dimples/Boom Boom	5
89	Silvertone ORECD 10	The Healer (Single Version)/Rockin' Chair/No Substitute/The Healer (Album Version) (3" CD, with Carlos Santana, card sleeve)	8

EPs

60	Riverside REP 3202	WEDNESDAY EVENING (EP)	20
60	Riverside REP 3207	DEMOCRAT MAN (EP)	20
64	Stateside SE 1019	THE BLUES OF JOHN HOOKER (EP)	20
64	Stateside SE 1023	I'M JOHN LEE HOOKER (EP)	20
64	Ember EP 4561	THINKING BLUES (EP)	30
65	Pye Intl. NEP 44034	LOVE BLUES (EP)	25
65	Chess CRE 6000	DOWN AT THE LANDING (EP)	25
65	Atlantic AET 6010	JOHN LEE HOOKER (EP)	25
66	Chess CRE 6007	WALKING THE BOOGIE (EP)	25
66	Chess CRE 6014	THE JOURNEY (EP)	25
66	Chess CRE 6021	REAL FOLK BLUES VOL. 3 (EP)	25
73	Impulse 9103	SERVES YOU RIGHT TO SUFFER (EP)	15

LPs

62	Riverside RLP 12-838	THE FOLK BLUES OF JOHN LEE HOOKER (LP)	35
62	Stateside SL 10014	THE FOLK LORE OF JOHN LEE HOOKER (LP)	30
63	London HA-K 8097	DON'T TURN ME FROM YOUR DOOR (LP)	50
64	Stateside SL 10053	THE BIG SOUL OF JOHN LEE HOOKER (LP)	30
64	Stateside SL 10074	I WANT TO SHOUT THE BLUES (LP)	25
64	Pye Intl. NPL 28042	HOUSE OF THE BLUES (LP)	35
64	Fontana 688 700 ZL	THE FOLK-BLUES OF HOOKER (LP)	30
65	Fontana FJL 119	BLUE! (LP)	30
65	Ember EMB 3356	SINGS THE BLUES (LP)	25
65	Riverside RLP 008	BURNING HELL (LP)	25
65	Chess CRL 4500	JOHN LEE HOOKER PLAYS AND SINGS THE BLUES (LP)	25
66	HMV CLP 5032/CSD 3542	IT SERVES YOU RIGHT TO SUFFER (LP, mono/stereo)	35/40
66	Ember (ST)EMB 3371	DRIFTIN' THROUGH THE BLUES (LP)	25
67	Chess CRL 4527	THE REAL FOLK BLUES (LP)	25
67	Marble Arch MAL 663	HOUSE OF THE BLUES (LP, reissue)	12
67	HMV CLP/CSD 3612	LIVE AT THE CAFE A GO GO (LP)	25
67	Atlantic Special 590 003	DRIFTIN' BLUES (LP)	15
68	Joy JOY(S) 101	I'M JOHN LEE HOOKER (LP)	15
68	Joy JOY(S) 124	BURNIN' (LP)	15
68	Stateside (S)SL 10246	URBAN BLUES (LP)	15
69	Joy JOYS 129	TRAVELIN' (LP)	12
69	Joy JOYS 133	THE FOLKLORE OF JOHN LEE HOOKER (LP)	15
69	Stateside (S)SL 10280	SIMPLY THE TRUTH (LP)	22
69	Joy JOYS 142	CONCERT AT NEWPORT (LP)	15
69	Joy JOYS 147	THE BIG SOUL OF JOHN LEE HOOKER (LP)	15
69	Storyville 673 005	YOU'RE LEAVIN' ME BABY (LP)	15
69	Joy JOYS 152	IN PERSON (LP)	15
60s	Advent LP 2801	JOHN LEE HOOKER AND HIS GUITAR (LP)	35
70	Storyville 673 020	TUPELO BLUES (LP)	15
70	Joy JOYS 156	THE BEST OF JOHN LEE HOOKER (LP)	15
70	Stax SXATS 1025	THAT'S WHERE IT'S AT (LP)	15
71	Probe SPB 1016	IF YOU MISS 'IM . . . I GOT 'IM (LP, with Earl Hooker)	15
71	Probe SPB 1034	ENDLESS BOOGIE (LP)	12
71	Stax 2362 017	THAT'S WHERE IT'S AT! (LP)	15
71	Xtra XTRA 1114	JOHN LEE HOOKER (LP)	15
71	United Artists UAS 29235	COAST TO COAST BLUES BAND (LP)	20
72	Speciality SNTF 5005	ALONE (LP)	15
72	Probe SPB 1057	NEVER GET OUT OF THESE BLUES ALIVE (LP)	12
73	Green Bottle GN 4002	JOHNNY LEE (LP)	15
73	Checker 6467 305	MAD MAN BLUES (LP)	12
73	Polydor 2310 256	SLIM'S STOMP (LP)	12
75	ABC ABCL 5059	FREE BEER AND CHICKEN (LP)	12
75	New World NW 6003	JOHN LEE HOOKER (LP, reissue of above with 1 extra track)	12
75	Atlantic K 40405	DETROIT SPECIAL (LP)	12
77	DJM DJD 28026	DIMPLES (2-LP)	15

(see also Canned Heat, Carlos Santana & Buddy Miles)

MINT VALUE £

JOHN LEE HOOKER/LIGHTNIN' HOPKINS/SMOKEY HOGG
73	Sonet SNTF 5013	HOOKER HOPKINS HOGG (LP)	15

(see also Lightnin' Hopkins, Smokey Hogg)

STEVE HOOKER & HEAT
77	Takeaway TAKE 1/	If You Don't Do The Business/Rock & Roll Doctor/I'm Hooked/	
	EJR 577	Marionette (stamped white sleeve with insert)	8

HOOKFOOT
69	Page One POF 144	Way Of The Musician/Hookfoot	5
71	DJM DJLPS 413	HOOKFOOT (LP)	15
72	DJM DJLPS 422	GOOD TIMES A' COMIN' (LP)	12
73	DJM DJLPS 428	COMMUNICATIONS (LP)	12

(see also Loot, Caleb, Soul Agents)

MARSHALL HOOKS & CO.
71	Blue Horizon 2096 002	I Want The Same Thing Tomorrow/Hookin' It	12
71	Blue Horizon 2431 003	MARSHALL HOOKS & CO. (LP)	50

HOOTEN(ANNY) SINGERS
64	United Artists UP 1082	Gabrielle/Darling (most copies list artist as Hooten Singers)	25

(see also Abba, Northern Lights)

BOB HOPE
50	Capitol CL 13348	Home Cookin'/Blind Date (78, with Margaret Whiting)	10
52	Capitol CL 13787	A 4-Legged Friend/There's A Cloud In My Valley Of Sunshine	
		(78, with Jimmy Wakely)	10
58	London HLU 8593	Paris Holiday/Nothing In Common (with Bing Crosby)	15
58	London HLU 8593	Paris Holiday/Nothing In Common (78, with Bing Crosby)	10
59	RCA RCA 1139	Ain't A-Hankerin'/Protection (with Rosemary Clooney)	6
59	RCA RCA 1139	Ain't A Hankerin'/Protection (78, with Rosemary Clooney)	12
63	United Artists UP 1023	Call Me Bwana/The Flipside	6
63	Brunswick LAT 8539	IN RUSSIA AND ONE OTHER PLACE (LP)	15

(see also Bing Crosby, Rosemary Clooney)

LYN(N) HOPE
57	Vogue V 9081	Blue Moon/Blues For Anna Bacca	35
57	Vogue V 9081	Blue Moon/Blues For Anna Bacca (78)	12
57	Vogue V 9082	Eleven Till Two/Blues For Mary	35
57	Vogue V 9082	Eleven Till Two/Blues For Mary (78)	12
58	Vogue V 9115	Temptation/The Scrunch	20
58	Vogue V 9115	Temptation/The Scrunch (78)	20
60	Blue Beat BB 21	Shockin'/Blue And Sentimental	15
57	Vogue VE 170103	LYNN HOPE AND HIS TENOR SAX (EP)	75
60	Vogue VE 170146	LYNN HOPE AND HIS TENOR SAX (EP)	75

PETER HOPE & RICHARD H. KIRK
85	Doublevision DVR 15	Leather Hands (Master Mix)/(Radio Mix)/(Crash Mix) (12", p/s)	8

(see also Cabaret Voltaire, Richard H. Kirk)

HOPETOWN (Lewis) & GLENMORE (Brown)
68	Fab FAB 43	Skinny Leg Girl/Live Like A King	18

MARY HOPKIN
68	Apple APPLE 2	Those Were The Days/Turn Turn Turn (later copies credit Mary Hopkins)	each 6
68	Apple APPLE 2	Those Were The Days/Turn Turn Turn (blank Apple label on A-side)	10
69	Apple APPLE 7	Lontana Dagli Occhi/Game (Europe-only, unreleased in U.K.)	
69	Apple APPLE 9	Prince En Avignon/The Game (France-only, unreleased in U.K.)	
69	Apple APPLE 10	Goodbye/Sparrow	8
69	Apple APPLE 16	Que Sera Sera/Fields Of St. Etienne (unreleased)	
69	Cambrian CSP 703	Aderyn Llwyd/Y Blodyn Gwyn (p/s)	18
70	Cambrian CSP 712	Pleserau Serch/Tyrd Yn Ôl (p/s)	18
70	Apple APPLE 22	Temma Harbour/Lontano Dagli Occhi (black or green lettering on p/s)	each 5
70	Apple APPLE 26	Knock, Knock Who's There?/I'm Going To Fall In Love Again (p/s)	5
70	Apple APPLE 27	Que Sera Sera/Fields Of St. Etienne (unreleased in U.K., acetates only)	
70	Apple APPLE 30	Think About Your Children/Heritage (p/s)	6
71	Apple APPLE 34	Let My Name Be Sorrow/Kew Gardens (p/s)	15
71	Apple APPLE 39	Water, Paper And Clay/Jefferson (p/s)	20
72	Regal Zonophone RZ 3070	Mary Had A Baby/Cherry Tree Carol	5
76	Good Earth GD 2	If You Love Me (I Won't Care) (some copies list "If You Love Me")/Tell Me Now	5
77	Good Earth GD 11	Wrap Me In Your Arms/Just A Dreamer (p/s)	5
68	Cambrian CEP 414	LLAIS SWYNOL MARY HOPKIN (EP)	15
69	Cambrian CEP 420	MARY AC EDWARD (EP, with Edward Morris Jones)	15
69	Apple (S)APCOR 5	POST CARD (LP, with black inner sleeve, mono/stereo)	18/12
71	Apple SAPCOR 21	EARTH SONG — OCEAN SONG (LP, gatefold sleeve, 'Apple' inner sleeve)	20
72	Apple SAPCOR 23	THOSE WERE THE DAYS (LP, with 'Apple' inner sleeve)	75
77	Decca SPA 546	THE WELSH WORLD OF MARY HOPKIN (LP)	25
91	Apple SAPCOR 5	POST CARD (LP, reissue, gatefold sleeve with bonus 12" [SAPCOR 52])	15
92	Apple SAPCOR 21	EARTH SONG/OCEAN SONG (LP, reissue, gatefold sleeve with inner)	15

(see also Hobby Horse, Sundance, Oasis, Elfland Ensemble, Bob Johnson & Pete Knight, Roy Budd)

JOEL & LIGHTNIN' HOPKINS
60	Heritage H 1000	BLUES FROM EAST TEXAS (LP)	80

(see also Lightnin' Hopkins)

LIGHTNIN' HOPKINS
61	Bluesville BVLP 1019	LIGHTNIN' HOPKINS (LP)	40
62	'77' LA 12/1	SAM LIGHTNIN' HOPKINS — THE ROOSTER CROWED IN ENGLAND (LP)	40
63	Stateside SL 10031	LIGHTNIN' STRIKES (LP)	30
63	Realm RM 128	LIGHTNIN' HOPKINS SINGS THE BLUES (LP)	25
63	Realm RM 171	DIRTY HOUSE BLUES (LP)	25
64	Stateside SL 10076	BLUES HOOT (LP, some tracks by Sonny Terry & Brownie McGhee)	35
65	Stateside SL 10110	HOOTIN' THE BLUES (LP)	30

			MINT VALUE £
65	Stateside SL 10155	DOWN HOME BLUES (LP)	30
65	Fontana TL 5264	THE BLUES (LP)	30
65	Fontana 688 301 ZL	LAST NIGHT BLUES (LP)	30
65	Fontana 688 801 ZL	BURNIN' IN L.A. (LP)	30
66	Fontana 688 803 ZL	BLUE BIRD BLUES (LP)	30
66	Fontana 688 807 ZL	BLUES PARTY (LP)	30
66	Ember EMB 3389	A TIME FOR BLUES (LP)	25
66	Ember EMB 3416	LIVE AT THE BIRD LOUNGE (LP)	25
67	Ember EMB 3423	I'VE BEEN BUKED AND SCORNED (LP)	25
66	Verve (S)VLP 5003	ROOTS OF HOPKINS (LP)	25
66	Verve (S)VLP 5014	LIGHTNIN' STRIKES (LP, reissue)	18
66	Saga ERO 8001	LIGHTNIN' HOPKINS (LP)	12
67	Xtra XTRA 5036	BLUES IN MY BOTTLE (LP)	18
68	Xtra XTRA 5044	GOT TO MOVE YOUR BABY (LP, reissue of Fontana 688 301 ZL)	15
68	Minit MLL/MLS 40006	EARTH BLUES (LP)	20
69	Liberty LBL 83254	KING OF DOWLING STREET (LP)	20
69	Joy JOY(S) 115	LIGHTNIN' STRIKES (LP, 2nd reissue)	15
69	Polydor 545 019	THAT'S MY STORY (LP)	15
70	Ace Of Hearts (Z)AHT 183	THE BLUES (LP)	15
70	Poppy PYS 11000	LIGHTNIN'! VOLUME 1 (LP)	15
70	Poppy PYS 11002	LIGHTNIN'! VOLUME 2 (LP)	15
71	Liberty LBS 83293	THE CALIFORNIA MUDSLIDE (AND EARTHQUAKE) (LP)	20
71	Mayfair AMLB 4000 1/2	LIGHTNIN' STRIKES (2-LP)	15
71	Blue Horizon 2431 005	LET'S WORK AWHILE (LP)	90
71	Xtra XTRA 1127	THE ROOTS OF LIGHTNIN' HOPKINS (LP)	20
71	Boulevard BLVD 4001	LIGHTNIN' HOPKINS (LP)	15
72	Carnival 2941 005	LONESOME LIGHTNIN' (LP)	15
73	Mainstream MSL 1001	DIRTY BLUES (LP)	15
74	Sonet SNTF 672	LEGACY OF THE BLUES VOLUME 12 (LP)	12
75	Mainstream MSL 1031	LOW DOWN DIRTY BLUES (LP)	15

(see also Sonny Terry & Brownie McGhee, Joel & Lightnin' Hopkins, Lightnin' Hopkins & John Lee Hooker, Big Joe Williams)

LIGHTNIN' HOPKINS & JOHN LEE HOOKER

69	Storyville 616 001	THERE'S GOOD ROCKIN' TONIGHT! (LP)	35
72	Storyville SLP 174	LIGHTNIN' HOPKINS AND JOHN LEE HOOKER (LP)	30

(see also John Lee Hooker/Lightnin' Hopkins/Smokey Hogg)

LINDA HOPKINS

61	Coral Q 72423	I Diddle Dum Dum/All In My Mind	20
62	Coral Q 72448	Mama's Doin' The Twist/My Mother's Eyes	15

LINDA HOPKINS & JACKIE WILSON

63	Coral Q 72464	Shake A Hand/Say I Do	8
65	Coral Q 72480	Yes Indeed/When The Saints Go Marching In	10

(see also Jackie Wilson)

NICKY HOPKINS

66	CBS 202055	Mr Big/Jenni	12
67	Polydor 56175	Mister Pleasant/Nothing As Yet	12
68	MGM MGM 1419	Top Pops No. 1 (Medley)/(Part 2)	5
68	Fontana TF 906	High On A Hill/Trumpet Serenade (actually by Nigel Hopkins)	5
73	CBS CBS 1328	Speed On/Sundown In Mexico	5
66	CBS (S)BPG 62679	THE REVOLUTIONARY PIANO OF NICKY HOPKINS (LP)	25
73	CBS 65416	THE TIN MAN WAS A DREAMER (LP, featuring Mick Taylor)	15

(see also Neil Christian & Crusaders, Quicksilver Messenger Service, Aquarian Age, Poet & One Man Band, Sweet Thursday)

WASH HOPKINS SINGERS

69	Action ACT 4546	He's Got Blessing/Rock In A Weary Land	6

HUGH HOPPER

73	CBS 65466	1984 (LP)	25
76	Compendium FIDARDO 4	CRUEL BUT FAIR (LP)	15
77	Compendium FIDARDO 7	HOPPERTUNITY BOX (LP)	15
78	Ogun OG 527	ROGUE ELEMENT (LP, as Hopper, Dean, Gowen, Sheen — 'Soft Heap')	12

(see also Caravan, Elton Dean, Gilgamesh, Isotope, Matching Mole, Ninesense, Soft Machine)

HOPSCOTCH

69	United Artists UP 2231	Look At The Lights Go Up/Same Old Fat Man	15
69	United Artists UP 35022	Long Black Veil/Easy To Find	6

(see also Scots Of St. James, Five Day Rain, Forever More, Glencoe, Average White Band)

HORACE & IMPERIALS

68	Nu Beat NB 012	Young Love/Days Like These	10

HORDEN RAIKES

72	Folk Heritage FHR 026	HORDEN RAIKES (LP)	20
73	Folk Heritage FHR 042	KING COTTON (LP)	15

HORIZON

81	SRT SRTS 81432	Stage Struck/Remember The Bad Boys	10

HORIZON

83	Orbit TRIP 4	Sunshine Reggae/Nightlife	8

(see also Mungo Jerry)

PAUL HORN

68	Liberty LBL 83084E	COSMIC CONSCIOUSNESS (LP)	18

LENA HORNE

55	HMV 7M 309	Love Me Or Leave Me/I Love To Love 8
55	HMV 7M 319	It's All Right With Me/It's Love 8
56	HMV 7M 423	If You Can Dream/What's Right For You (Is Right For Me) 7
56	MGM MGM 917	Can't Help Lovin' Dat Man/The Man I Love 6
56	MGM MGM 917	Can't Help Lovin' Dat Man/The Man I Love (78) 8
59	RCA RCA 1120	A New Fangled Tango/Honeysuckle Rose. 5
59	RCA RCA 1120	A New Fangled Tango/Honeysuckle Rose (78) 10
65	United Artists UP 1101	The Sand And The Sea/It Had Better Be Tonight. 5
71	Buddah 2011 078	Maybe I'm Amazed/Feels So Good 12
57	RCA RD 27021/SF 5007	AT THE WALDORF ASTORIA (LP, mono/stereo). 12/15
58	RCA RD 27063	STORMY WEATHER (LP) 12
59	RCA RD 27098/SF 5019	GIVE THE LADY WHAT SHE WANTS (LP, mono/stereo) 12/15
59	RCA RD 27141	A FRIEND OF YOURS (LP) 12
61	RCA RD 27255	LENA AT THE SANDS (LP, also stereo SF 5217) 12
63	RCA RD/SF 7530	LENA LOVELY AND ALIVE (LP) 12
64	Stateside S(S)L 10081	HERE'S LENA (LP). 12

(see also Harry Belafonte)

HANK HORNSBY

57	MGM MGM 955	Pots And Pans/Cotton 5
57	MGM MGM 955	Pots And Pans/Cotton (78) 8
58	MGM MGM 972	The Legend Of The Birds And Bees/Girls Girls Girls 5
58	MGM MGM 972	The Legend Of The Birds And Bees/Girls Girls Girls (78) 10

HORNSEY AT WAR

| 70s | War WAR 001 | DEAD BEAT REVIVAL (EP, numbered p/s) . . . . 8 |

HORRORCOMIC

77	Lightning/B&C BVZ 0007	I'm All Hung Up On Pierrepoint/The Exorcist/Sex In The Afternoon (p/s) 15
78	Lightning GIL 512	I Don't Mind/England 77 (p/s) 15
79	B&C BCS 18	Jesus Christ/Cut Your Throat (p/s). 18

HORSE

| 70 | RCA Victor SF 8109 | HORSE (LP) . . . . 80 |

(see also Saturnalia)

HORSLIPS

73	Oats OAT 1	High Reel/Furniture 5
79	DJM DJT 15001	Loneliness/Homesick (leaf-shaped green vinyl) 5
73	Oats MOO 3	HAPPY TO MEET … SORRY TO PART (LP, booklet octagonal sleeve) 20
74	Oats MOO 5	THE TAIN (LP). 15
76	Oats MOO 9	DRIVE THE COLD WINTER AWAY (LP) 12

(see also Creatures)

HORTENSE (Ellis) & ALTON (Ellis)

| 65 | Island WI 230 | Don't Gamble With Love/Something You Got (B-side act. Alton Ellis & Flames). . 18 |

(see also Hortense Ellis, Alton Ellis, Mr. Foundation)

HORTENSE (Ellis) & DELROY (Wilson)

| 66 | Rio R 119 | We're Gonna Make It/SOUL BROTHERS: Ska Shuffle. . . . . 15 |

(see also Hortense Ellis, Delroy Wilson)

HORTENSE (Ellis) & JACKIE (Opel)

| 64 | R&B JB 138 | Stand By Me/JACKIE OPEL: Solid Rock . . . . 15 |

(see also Hortense Ellis, Jackie Opel)

JOHNNY HORTON

59	Philips PB 932	The Battle Of New Orleans/All For The Love Of A Girl 6
59	Philips PB 932	The Battle Of New Orleans/All For The Love Of A Girl (78) 25
59	Philips PB 951	Sal's Got A Sugar Lip/Johnny Reb 8
59	Philips PB 951	Sal's Got A Sugar Lip/Johnny Reb (78). 40
59	Philips PB 976	Take Me Like I Am/I'm Ready If You're Willing. 6
59	Philips PB 976	Take Me Like I Am/I'm Ready If You're Willing (78) 40
60	Philips PB 995	Sink The Bismarck!/The Same Old Tale The Crow Told Me 8
60	Philips PB 1062	North To Alaska/The Mansion You Stole 6
61	Philips PB 1130	When It's Springtime In Alaska/Mr. Moonlight 7
61	Philips PB 1132	Sleepy Eyed John/They'll Never Take Her Love From Me. 8
61	Philips PB 1170	Miss Marcy/Ole Slew Foot 8
62	Philips PB 1226	Words/Honky Tonk Man 8
63	CBS AAG 132	All Grown Up/I'm A One Woman Man 8
60	Mercury ZEP 10074	THE FANTASTIC JOHNNY HORTON (EP) 45
64	Mercury 10008 MCE	COUNTRY AND WESTERN ACES (EP) 35
60	Philips BBL 7464	THE SPECTACULAR JOHNNY HORTON (LP) 30
61	Philips BBL 7536	HONKY TONK MAN (LP). 30
63	London HA-U 8096	DONE ROVIN' (LP) 40
65	Fontana FJL 306	VOICE OF JOHNNY HORTON (LP). 15
60s	Hallmark SHM 634	THE UNFORGETTABLE JOHNNY HORTON (LP). 12

ROBERT HORTON

| 60 | Pye 7N 15285 | (Roll Along) Wagon Train/Sail Ho! . . . . 5 |
| 60 | Pye NEP 24118 | SUNDAY NIGHT AT THE LONDON PALLADIUM (EP) . . . . 8 |

WALTER 'SHAKEY' HORTON

70	London HAK/SHK 8405	SOUTHERN COMFORT (LP, as Shakey Horton) 80
74	Xtra XTRA 1135	WALTER 'SHAKEY' HORTON WITH HOT COTTAGE (LP). 15
74	Sonet SNTF 677	BIG WALTER HORTON (LP, with Carey Bell). 12

LA/THE HOST

| 84 | Orbitone | THE HOST EP (cassette) . . . . 5 |
| 85 | Quiet QU 1 | The Big Sleep/Just Breaking Away (p/s) . . . . 8 |

HOT BUTTER
73	Pye NSPL 28169	POPCORN (LP)	12
73	Pye NSPL 28181	MORE HOT BUTTER (LP)	15

HOT CLUB
82	RAK 346	The Dirt That She Walks On Is Sacred Ground To Me/Heat (p/s)	10

(see also Rich Kids, Spectres)

HOTCHA TRIO
56	Philips PB 565	Bï-Ba-Butzeman-Boogie/Jazz Me Blues (78)	8

HOT CHOCOLATE (BAND)
69	Apple APPLE 18	Give Peace A Chance/Living Without Tomorrow (as Hot Chocolate Band)	30
70	Rak RAK 103	Love Is Life/Pretty Girls (with promo p/s)	8
72	Rak RAK 127	Mary Anne/Ruth	5
75	Rak RAK 199	Blue Night/You Sexy Thing	5

(see also Tony Wilson)

HOTLEGS
70	Fontana 6007 019	Neanderthal Man/You Didn't Like It Because You Didn't Think Of It	5
71	Philips 6006 140	Lady Sadie/The Loser	5
71	Philips 6308 047	THINKS: SCHOOL STINKS (LP)	18
71	Philips 6308 080	SONG (LP)	20

(see also 10cc, Mindbenders, Godley & Creme, Tristar Airbus)

HOT POTATO
73	PMTB 1	HOT POTATO (LP, private pressing)	40

HOT ROD
69	Joe's DU 41	The Judge/RON: Soul Of Soul Of Joel	8

HOT ROD ALLSTARS
69	Duke DU 59	Lick A Pop/Treasure	7
70	Duke DU 65	Paint Your Wagon/Organ Man	7
70	Duke DU 66	Return Of The Bad Man/Caysoe Reggae	7
70	Trojan TR 7732	Strong Man/Sentimental	7
70	Trojan TR 7733	Virgin Soldier/Brixton Reggae Festival	8
70	Torpedo TOR 1	Pussy Got Nine Life/BOSS SOUNDS: Lick It Back	8
70	Torpedo TOR 5	Skinheads Don't Fear/Ten Commandments From The Devil	20
70	Torpedo TOR 10	Moonhop In London/Skinhead Moondust	20
70	Torpedo TOR 14	Control Your Doggy/Follow The Stars	8
70	Hot Rod HR 104	Skinhead Speaks His Mind/CARL LEVEY: Carnaby Street	20
70	Hot Rod HR 107	Strictly Invitation/PATSY & PEGGY: Dog Your Woman	6
70	Hot Rod HR 108	Beautiful World/Shocks Of A Drugs Man	6

(see also Setters, Betty Sinclair)

HOTRODS
65	Columbia DB 7693	I Don't Love You No More/Ain't Coming Back No More	45

HOT SNAX
80s	Munch MR 2	Pressure Drop/Treat Me Right, Tonight (12")	8

HOT SPRINGS
66	Columbia DB 7821	It's All Right/All I Know About Love	12

HOT-TODDYS
59	Pye International 7N 25020	Shakin' And Stompin'/Rockin' Crickets	18
59	Pye International N 25020	Shakin' And Stompin'/Rockin' Crickets (78)	50

(see also Rockin' Rebels)

HOT TUNA
72	Grunt 65-0502	Keep On Truckin'/Water Song	5
76	Grunt RCG 1002	It's So Easy/I Can't Be Satisfied	5
70	RCA SF 8125	HOT TUNA (LP)	15
71	RCA LSP 4550	ELECTRIC LIVE (FIRST PULL UP, THEN PULL DOWN) (LP)	15
72	Grunt FTR 1004	BURGERS (LP, with purple inner sleeve)	12

(see also Jefferson Airplane)

HOT VULTURES
77	Red Rag RRR 015	THE EAST STREET SHAKES (LP)	15
70s	Plant Life PLR 018	UP THE LINE (LP)	12

HOT WATER
78	Duff	Different Morning/Premium Bondage (p/s)	8
79	Duff DWR 101	Get Lost!/Bird's Eye View (p/s)	7

HOUGHTON WEAVERS
60s	Folk Heritage FHR 106	SIT THI DOWN (LP)	15

HOUNDHEAD HENRY/FRANKIE JAXON
60	Jazz Collector JEL 10	THE MALE BLUES VOLUME 6 (EP)	15

HOUR GLASS
68	Liberty LBL/LBS 83219E	THE HOUR GLASS (LP)	20
74	United Artists USD 303/4	THE HOUR GLASS (2-LP)	15

(see also Allman Brothers)

SON HOUSE
(see under 'S')

HOUSEHOLD
67	United Artists UP 1190	I Guess I'll Learn How To Fly/Nothing You Can Do But Cry	6
68	United Artists UP 2210	Twenty First Summer/Winter's Coming On	6

HOUSEMARTINS

85	Go! Discs GOD 7	Flag Day/Stand At Ease (p/s)	5
85	Go! Discs GOD 7/GOD 9	Flag Day/Stand At Ease//Sheep/Drop Down Dead (shrinkwrapped double pack)	6
85	Go! Discs GODX 7	Flag Day/Stand At Ease/Coal Train To Hatfield Main (12", p/s)	8
86	Go! Discs GODP 9	Sheep/I'll Be Your Shelter/Drop Down Dead (picture disc)	5
86	Go! Discs GODP 11	Happy Hour/The Mighty Ship (shaped picture disc)	5
86	Go! Discs GODP 13	Think For A Minute/Who Needs The Limelight (shaped picture disc)	5
86	Go! Discs GODP 16	Caravan Of Love/When I First Met Jesus (rectangular picture disc)	5
86	Go! Discs GODB 16	THE HOUSEMARTINS' CHRISTMAS BOX SET (4 singles in foldout sleeve, some signed)	25/12
88	Go! Discs GODCD 22	There Is Always Something There To Remind Me/Get Up Off Our Knees/ Get Up Off Our Knees (live)/Johannesburg (CD)	8
84	private pressing	THEMES FROM THE WELL-DRESSED MAN (cassette)	20
84	private pressing	THE HOUSEMARTINS FROM OUTER SPACE (cassette)	20

(see also Beautiful South)

HOUSEMASTER BALDWIN

88	Koolkat KOOLT 21	DELTA HOUSE (12", p/s)	10
88	Koolkat KOOLT 22	DON'T LEAD ME (12", p/s)	10

HOUSE OF LORDS

69	B&C CB 112	In The Land Of Dreams/Ain't Gonna Wait Forever	15

HOUSE OF LOVE

87	Creation CRE 043T	Shine On/Love/Flow (12", p/s, 3,000 only)	12
87	Creation CRE 044T	Real Animal/Plastic/Nothing To Me (12", p/s, 3,000 only)	12
87	Creation CREFRE 5	Shine On (Fuck Version) (1-sided flexidisc, gig freebie)	5
88	Creation CRE 053	Christine/Loneliness Is A Gun (die-cut custom p/s)	5
88	Creation CRE 053T	Christine/The Hill/Loneliness Is A Gun (12", p/s)	8
88	Creation CRE 057	Destroy The Heart/Blind (die-cut custom sleeve)	5
88	Creation CRELP 034	HOUSE OF LOVE (LP, 1st 3,000 copies with bonus 7": "Christine [Demo Version]"/"Shine On [Demo Version]" [CREFRE 01], stickered cover)	10

(see also Colenso Parade)

BOBBI HOUSTON

74	Action ACT 4622	I Want To Make It With You (Parts 1 & 2)	8

CISCO HOUSTON

60	Top Rank 30/028	THE CISCO SPECIAL (LP)	60
68	Fontana FJL 412	I AIN'T GOT NO HOME (LP)	12
69	Ember CW 135	CISCO HOUSTON AND WOODY GUTHRIE (LP)	15

CISSY HOUSTON

70	Major Minor MM 700	He/I Believe/I'll Be There	5
70	Major Minor MM 716	The Long And Winding Road/Be My Baby	5
70	Pye International 7N 25537	I Just Don't Know What To Do With Myself/This Empty Place	15
71	Pye International 7N 25545	The Long And Winding Road/Be My Baby (reissue)	5
71	Janus 6146 003	Darling Take Me Back/Hang On To A Dream	5
72	Janus 6146 027	Midnight Train To Georgia/I'm So Glad I Can Love Again	5
70	Major Minor SMLP 80	PRESENTING CISSY HOUSTON (LP)	12
71	Pye Intl. NSPL 28146	THE LONG AND WINDING ROAD (LP)	12
78	Private Stock PVLP 1044	THINK IT OVER (LP)	12

(see also Sweet Inspirations)

DAVID HOUSTON

55	London HL 8147	Blue Prelude/I'm Sorry I Made You Cry	30
55	London HL 8147	Blue Prelude/I'm Sorry I Made You Cry (78)	18
63	Columbia DB 7159	Mountain Of Love/Poor Little Angeline	6
66	Columbia DB 7997	Almost Persuaded/We Got A Lover	5

DAVID HOUSTON & TAMMY WYNETTE

67	Columbia DB 8246	My Elusive Dreams/Marriage On The Rocks	6

(see also Tammy Wynette)

SAM HOUSTON

65	Island WI 172	My Mother's Eyes/Danny Boy	8

THELMA HOUSTON

69	Stateside SS 8026	Jumpin' Jack Flash/Sunshower	6
70	Stateside SS 8036	Save The Country/I Just Can't Stay Away	5
70	Stateside SS 8044	I Just Wanna Be Me/Crying In The Sunshine	5
72	Tamla Motown TMG 799	I Want To Go Back There Again/Pick Of The Week	5
72	Mowest MW 3001	No One's Gonna Be A Fool Forever/What If	5
73	Mowest MW 3004	Black California/I'm Letting Go (withdrawn)	10
69	Stateside (S)SL 5010	SUNSHOWER (LP)	15
72	Probe SPB 1053	SUNSHOWER (LP, reissue)	12
73	Mowest MWS 7003	THELMA HOUSTON (LP)	12

WHITNEY HOUSTON

85	Arista ARIST 614	Someone For Me/The Greatest Love Of All (p/s)	5
85	Arista ARIST 12614	Someone For Me/The Greatest Love Of All (12", p/s)	8
85	Arista ARIST 625	You Give Good Love/How Will I Know (p/s)	5
85	Arista ARIST 12625	You Give Good Love (Extended)/How Will I Know/You Give Good Love (Remix)/Someone For Me (12", p/s)	8
85	Arista ARIST 640	All At Once (promo only for 'Wogan' TV show, plain sleeve, printed white label)	10
87	Arista RISCD 1	I Wanna Dance With Somebody (Who Loves Me) (12" Remix)/Moment Of Truth/ I Wanna Dance With Somebody (Who Loves Me) (Dub Mix) (CD, card sleeve)	8
87	Arista RISCD 31	Didn't We Almost Have It All/I Wanna Dance With Somebody (Who Loves Me) (Acappella Mix)/WHITNEY HOUSTON & JERMAINE JACKSON: Shock Me (CD, card sleeve with stickered p/s)	8

87	Arista RISCD 43	So Emotional (Extended Remix)/Didn't We Almost Have It All (live)/ For The Love Of You (CD, card sleeve) 8
88	Arista 111 516P	Love Will Save The Day/Hold Me (picture disc).............................. 5
88	Arista 111 516W	Love Will Save The Day/Hold Me (tour packs, Wembley or Birmingham p/s) .... ea.ch 5
88	Arista 661 516	Love Will Save The Day (Extended Club Mix)/Love Will Save The Day (Single Version)/WHITNEY HOUSTON & TEDDY PENDERGRASS: Hold Me (CD, picture disc with gatefold card sleeve) 10
88	Arista 661 613	One Moment In Time/(KASHIF: Olympic Joy)/Rise To The Occasion/ One Moment In Time (Instrumental) (CD) 8
86	Arista WHIT 1	WHITNEY HOUSTON (LP, box set with 10 postcards, songbook & calendar)............... 12

(see also J.A.M.s, Aretha Franklin & Whitney Houston)

LARRY HOVIS
| 58 | Capitol CL 14843 | Do I Love You/We Could Have Lots Of Fun....................... 6 |
| 59 | Capitol CL 15083 | My Heart Belongs To Only You/I Want To Fall In Love..................... 6 |

BRIAN HOWARD & SILHOUETTES
62	Columbia DB 4914	Somebody Help Me/Young And Evil 15
63	Columbia DB 7067	The Worryin' Kind/Come To Me 15
64	Fontana TF 464	Back In The U.S.A./Hooked 12

JAN HOWARD
| 60 | London HL 7088 | The One You Slip Around With/I Wish I Could Fall In Love Again (export issue).. 18 |

JOHNNY HOWARD BAND
60	Decca F 11298	Up The Wall/Orbit 5
62	Decca F 11423	Mind Reader/Spanish Gipsy Dance............................ 5
64	Decca F 11925	Rinky Dink/Java 5
65	Decca F 12065	El Pussy Cat/A Tune Called Harry 5
67	Deram DML/SML 1001	THE VELVET TOUCH OF JOHNNY HOWARD (LP)................. 12

KID HOWARD
| 50s | Mono RBM 464 | KID HOWARD'S BAND (LP) .... 12 |

LES HOWARD
| 53 | HMV 7M 127 | Love Evermore/I Lived When I Met You .... 7 |
| 53 | HMV 7M 171 | Rags To Riches/From Here To Eternity .... 7 |

ROLAND S. HOWARD & LYDIA LUNCH
| 86 | 4AD BAD 210 | Some Velvet Morning/I Fell In Love With A Ghost (12", p/s, with postcard)...... 12 |

(see also Lydia Lunch, Birthday Party)

ROSETTA HOWARD
| 51 | Vocalion V 1005 | Let Your Linen Hang Low/HARLEM HAMFATS: Weed Smoker's Dream (78) ..... 15 |

WAYNE HOWARD
| 70 | Explosion EX 2042 | All Kinds Of Everything/Cool And Easy (B-side actually by Lloyd Charmers) .... 7 |

CATHERINE HOWE
71	Reflection HRS 11	Nothing More Than Strangers/It Comes With The Breezes................. 15
71	Reflection REFL 11	WHAT A BEAUTIFUL PLACE (LP) 250
75	RCA Victor SF 8407	HARRY (LP) 12

STEVE HOWE
| 75 | Atlantic K 50151 | BEGINNINGS (LP, gatefold sleeve, some with embossed 'Yes' logo) .... 15/12 |
| 79 | Atlantic K 50621 | THE STEVE HOWE ALBUM (LP, gatefold sleeve) .... 12 |

(see also In Crowd, Syndicats, Tomorrow, Bodast, Yes, Asia, Anderson Bruford Wakeman & Howe)

EDDIE HOWELL
| 76 | Warner Bros K 16701 | Man From Manhattan/Waiting In The Wings (features members of Queen)...... 12 |
| 77 | Warner Bros K 16866 | Sweet On You/Miss Amerika (features Gary Moore)........................ 6 |

(see also Queen, Gary Moore, Brian May, Freddie Mercury)

PETER HOWELL
(see under Friends, Ithaca, Alice Through The Looking Glass, Agincourt, Tomorrow Come Someday, BBC Radiophonic Workshop)

REUBEN HOWELL
| 74 | Mowest MW 3019 | Rings/I Believe When I Fall In Love It Will Be Forever .... 4 |

FRANKIE HOWERD
50	Columbia DB 2694	English As She Is Spoken/I'm The Man Who's Deputising For The Bull (78)...... 8
53	Philips PB 214	Nymphs And Shepherds/All's Going Well (78, with Margaret Rutherford)........ 8
54	Decca F 10420	(Don't Let The) Kiddy Geddin/Abracadabra........................ 10
54	Decca F 10420	(Don't Let The) Kiddy Geddin/Abracadabra (78) 8
58	Columbia DB 4230	It's All Right With Me/Song And Dance Man 7
58	Columbia DB 4230	It's All Right With Me/Song And Dance Man (78) 10
64	Decca F 12028	Last Word On The Election/Last Word On The Election (part 2) 5
70	Pye 7N 45061	Up Je T'Aime/All Through The Night 5
71	Columbia DB 8757	Up Pompeii/Salute!...................................... 5
63	Decca LK 4556	AT THE ESTABLISHMENT (LP) 18
60s	Pye NPL	SOMETHING FUNNY HAPPENED ON THE WAY TO THE FORUM (LP) 18
72	Carnival 2928 201	TELLS THE STORY OF PETER AND THE WOLF (LP) 12

CHRIS HOWLAND
58	Columbia DB 4114	Mama (Ma, He's Making Eyes At Me)/Fraulein 6
58	Columbia DB 4114	Mama (Ma, He's Making Eyes At Me)/Fraulein (78)................... 8
59	Columbia DB 4194	Susie Darlin'/The Rain Falls On Ev'rybody....................... 6
59	Columbia DB 4194	Susie Darlin'/The Rain Falls On Ev'rybody (78).................. 10

MINT VALUE £

HOWLIN' WOLF

61	Pye International 7N 25101	Little Baby/Down In The Bottom	15
63	Pye International 7N 25192	Just Like I Treat You/I Ain't Superstitious	15
64	Pye International 7N 25244	Smokestack Lightnin'/Going Down Slow	
		('Slow' or 'South' on B-side label)	15/10
64	Pye International 7N 25269	Little Girl/Tail Dragger	15
64	Pye International 7N 25283	Love Me Darling/My Country Sugar Mama	15
65	Chess CRS 8010	Killing Floor/Louise	10
65	Chess CRS 8016	Ooh Baby/Tell Me What I've Done	10
69	Chess CRS 8097	Evil/Tail Dragger	8
56	London REU 1072	RHYTHM AND BLUES WITH HOWLIN' WOLF (EP)	125
63	Pye Intl. NEP 44015	SMOKESTACK LIGHTNIN' (EP)	25
64	Pye Intl. NEP 44032	TELL ME (EP)	25
66	Chess CRE 6017	REAL FOLK BLUES (EP)	25
64	Chess CRL 4006	MOANIN' IN THE MOONLIGHT (LP)	30
65	Chess CRL 4508	POOR BOY (LP)	25
66	Ember EMB 3370	BIG CITY BLUES (LP)	20
67	Marble Arch MAL 665	MOANIN' IN THE MOONLIGHT (LP, reissue)	12
69	Chess CRLS 4543	THE HOWLIN' WOLF ALBUM (LP)	15
71	Syndicate Chapter SC 003	GOING BACK HOME (LP)	15
71	Chess 6310 108	MESSAGE TO THE YOUNG (LP)	15
71	Rolling Stones COC 49101	THE LONDON SESSIONS (LP)	12
71	Python PLP 13	HOWLIN' WOLF (LP)	40

(see also Hubert Sumlin)

HOWLIN' WOLF, MUDDY WATERS & BO DIDDLEY

68	Chess CRL 4537	THE SUPER SUPER BLUES BAND (LP)	40

(see also Muddy Waters, Bo Diddley)

HOWLIN' WOLF/JUNIOR PARKER/BOBBY BLAND

74	Polydor 2383 257	BLUES FOR MR. CRUMP (LP)	20

LINDA HOYLE

70	Vertigo 6059 018	Eli's Coming/United States Of Mind	
		(as Linda Hoyle & Affinity)	15
71	Vertigo 6360 060	PIECES OF ME	
		(LP, gatefold sleeve, spiral label)	100

(see also Affinity, Nucleus)

H.P. LOVECRAFT

67	Philips BF 1620	Wayfarin' Stranger/The Time Machine	7
68	Philips BF 1639	The White Ship (Parts 1 & 2) (unissued)	
68	Philips BF 1639	The White Ship/I've Been Wrong Before	7
67	Philips (S)BL 7830	H.P. LOVECRAFT (LP)	35
68	Philips SBL 7872	H.P. LOVECRAFT II	
		(LP, most with watermark at start of each side)	30/15
72	Philips 6336 210	THIS IS H.P. LOVECRAFT (LP)	12
72	Philips 6336 213	H.P. LOVECRAFT VOL. 2 (LP)	12

H$_2$O

81	Spock PARA 2	Hollywood Dream/Children	
		(with lyric insert)	6

FREDDIE HUBBARD

72	CTI CTL 5	STRAIGHT LIFE (LP)	12
73	CTI CTL 11	SKY DIVE (LP)	12
75	CTI CTI 6056	POLAR AC (LP)	12
75	Atlantic K 60053	THE ART OF FREDDIE HUBBARD: THE ATLANTIC YEARS (2-LP)	15
75	Blue Note BST 84056	GOIN' UP (LP)	12
75	Blue Note BST 84085	READY FOR FREDDIE (LP)	12
75	Blue Note BST 84115	HUB TONES (LP)	12
75	Blue Note BST 84172	BREAKING POINT (LP)	12
75	Blue Note BST 84196	BLUE SPIRITS (LP)	12
75	Blue Note BST 84207	THE NIGHT OF THE COOKERS VOL. 1 (LP)	12
75	Blue Note BST 84208	THE NIGHT OF THE COOKERS VOL. 2 (LP)	12
75	CBS 80478	HIGH ENERGY (LP)	12

HUBCAP & WHEELS

70	Dynamic DYN 403	One Pound Weight/VICEROYS: Come Dance	6

(see also Byron Lee & Dragonaires)

WENDY HUBER

65	Philips BF 1446	Come Away Melinda/I Belong To The Wind	6

RITA & TONY HUDD

85	Burlington BURL 022	THE WOODEN LEG ALBUM (LP)	12

ROY HUDD

66	Polydor 56136	Ramsey's Men/The Day We Won The Cup	4

R.B. HUDMAN

76	Atlantic K 10742	How Can I Be A Witness/If You Don't Cheat On Me	4

COLIN HUDSON

65	Pye 7N 15907	Girl You Don't Know Me/Little Boy Blue	4

JACK HUDSON

72	Folk Heritage FHR 041	SUMMER DAYS AND YOU (LP)	20

JOHNNY HUDSON & TEENBEATS

63	Decca F 11679	Charms/Makin' Up Is So Much Fun	8

KEITH HUDSON (& CHUCKLES)

69	Big Shot BI 528	Tambourine Man/Old Fashioned Way (both actually by Ken Boothe)	12
70	Smash SMA 2311	Don't Get Me Confused/D. SMITH: Ball of Confusion (B-side actually by Dennis Alcapone)	12
71	Smash SMA 2526	Light Of Day/I Thought You Knew	10
72	Spur SP 1	Darkest Night On A Wet Looking Road/Version	20
72	Duke DU 145	Satan Side (with Chuckles)/DON T. JUNIOR: Evil Spirit	30
72	Downtown DT 492	True True To My Heart/BIG YOUTH: Ace 90 Skank	8
73	Summit SUM 8541	Melody Maker/Uncover Me	12
75	Faith FA 025	Blackbelt Jones/Version	8

(see also Big Youth, Alton Ellis, Hugh Roy, Delroy Wilson)

KEITH HUDSON & I ROY

73	Randy's RAN 534	Silver Platter/Jean You Change Everything	15

(see also I Roy)

ROCK HUDSON

59	Brunswick 05816	Pillow Talk/Roly Poly	6
59	Brunswick 05816	Pillow Talk/Roly Poly (78)	15
70	Warner Bros WB 8006	Gone With The Cowboys/Meantime	5

HUDSON-FORD

74	A&M AMS 7096	Burn Baby Burn/Angels (p/s)	5
77	Arnakata ARN 5001	REPERTOIRE (LP, for publishers' use)	20

(see also Strawbs, Monks, Elmer Gantry's Velvet Opera)

HUDSON PEOPLE

78	Hithouse HIT 1	Trip To Your Mind (Parts 1 & 2) (12")	20
79	Ensign ENY 2712	Trip To Your Mind (Parts 1 & 2) (12", reissue)	7

HUES CORPORATION

74	RCA RCA 2444	Freedom Of The Stallion/Get Off My Cloud	5
74	RCA APL1 0323	FREEDOM OF THE STALLION (LP)	12
74	RCA APL1 0775	ROCKIN' SOUL (LP)	12

HUEYS

69	London HLU 10264	Coo-Coo Over You/You Ain't No Hippie	8

HUG

75	Polydor 2383 330	NEON DREAM (LP)	12

MIKE HUGG

72	Polydor 2058 265	Blue Suede Shoes Again/Fool No More	5
73	Polydor 2058 359	Stress And Strain/Tonight	5
72	Polydor/Sound For Industry SFI 122	Bonnie Charlie/SLADE: The Whole World's Going Crazee (33rpm flexidisc free with *Music Scene* magazine)	12/8
72	Polydor 2383 140	SOMEWHERE (LP, gatefold sleeve)	12
73	Polydor 2383 213	STRESS AND STRAIN (LP)	12

(see also Manfred Mann, Hug, Highly Likely, Elton Dean)

HUGGY BEAR

93	PUSS 002	February 14th/Into The Mission (1-sided gig freebie, w/l, plain black sleeve)	5

CAROL HUGHES

58	Columbia DB 4094	Lend Me Your Comb/First Date	10
58	Columbia DB 4094	Lend Me Your Comb/First Date (78)	8

DANNY HUGHES

69	Pye 7N 17750	Hi Ho Silver Lining/I Washed My Hands In Muddy Water	12

(see also Orange Machine)

DAVID HUGHES

59	Top Rank JAR 205	Teach Me (How To Love Him)/You Would Have Done The Same	5
60	Top Rank JAR 316	Looking High, High, High/Mi Amor	6

FRED HUGHES

65	Fontana TF 583	Oo Wee Baby I Love You/Love Me Baby	15
76	Brunswick BR 37	Baby Boy/JOHNNY JONES & KING CASUALS: Purple Haze	8
76	DJM DJS 10717	Oo Wee Baby I Love You/My Cries Oh	5

'FRIDAY' HUGHES

51	MGM MGM 422	Lazy Morning/The Devil Ain't Lazy (78)	8

GLENN HUGHES

77	Safari LONG 2	PLAY ME OUT (LP)	12

(see also Deep Purple, News, Finders Keepers, Trapeze, Roger Glover, Hughes-Thrall)

JIMMY HUGHES

63	London HL 9680	I'm Qualified/My Loving Time	18
64	Pye International 7N 25254	Steal Away/Lollipops, Lace And Lipstick	10
66	Sue WI 4006	Goodbye My Love/It Was Nice	22
66	Atlantic 584 017	Neighbour, Neighbour/It's A Good Thing	8
67	Atlantic 584 135	Hi-Heel Sneakers/Time Will Bring You Back	8
69	Stax STAX 117	Sweet Things You Do/Let 'Em Down Baby	5
69	Stax STAX 126	I'm Not Ashamed To Beg Or Plead/Chains Of Love	12
67	Atlantic 587 068	WHY NOT TONIGHT? (LP)	40
69	Stax SXATS 1010	SOMETHING SPECIAL (LP)	18

RHETTA HUGHES

70s	Polydor 184 223	RELIGHT MY FIRE (LP)	12

HUGHES-THRALL

82	Epic EPC 25052	HUGHES-THRALL (LP)	15

(see also Glenn Hughes)

MINT VALUE £

HUGO & LUIGI

57	Columbia DB 3978	Rockabilly Party/Shenandoah Rose	10
58	Columbia DB 4156	Twilight In Tennessee/Cha-Hua-Hua	7
58	Columbia DB 4156	Twilight In Tennessee/Cha-Hua-Hua (78)	8
59	RCA RCA 1127	La Plume De Ma Tante/Honolulu Lu	6
59	RCA RCA 1127	La Plume De Ma Tante/Honolulu Lu (78)	10
60	RCA RCA 1169	Just Come Home/Lonesome Stranger (78)	15

ALAN HULL

70	Big T BIG 129	We Can Swing Together/Obadiah's Grave	10
73	Charisma CB 208	Numbers (Travelling Band)/Drinking Song/One Off Pat (p/s)	6
73	Charisma CB 211	Justanothersadsong/Waiting	5
75	Warner Brothers K 16561	Dan The Plan/One More Bottle Of Wine	5
75	Warner Brothers K 16599	One More Bottle Of Wine/Squire	5
75	Warner Brothers K 16643	Crazy Woman/Golden Oldies	5
79	Rocket XPRES 12	I Wish You Well/Love Is The Answer (p/s)	5
79	Rocket XPRES 19	A Walk In The Sea/Corporation Rock	5
83	Black Crow CROS 2	Malvinas Melody/Ode To A Taxman (p/s)	5
73	Charisma CAS 1069	PIPEDREAM (LP, gatefold sleeve with booklet)	15
75	Warner Brothers K 56121	SQUIRE (LP)	12
79	Rocket TRAIN 6	PHANTOMS (LP, with inner sleeve)	12
83	Black Crow CRO 206	ON THE OTHER SIDE (LP)	12

(see also Lindisfarne, Chosen Few, Radiator)

HULLABALLOOS

64	Columbia DB 7392	I'm Gonna Love You Too/Why Do Fools Fall In Love	8
65	Columbia DB 7558	I'll Show You How To Love/Did You Ever	8
65	Columbia DB 7626	Don't Stop/I Won't Turn Away Now	8

(see also Bunch Of Fives)

GEORGE HULTGREEN

70	Warner Bros WB 8017	Say Hello/Before You Say Goodbye	5

(see Eclection, Sailor)

HUMAN BEANS

67	Columbia DB 8230	Morning Dew (Take Me For A Walk)/It's A Wonder	50

(see also Love Sculpture, Dave Edmunds)

HUMAN BEAST

70	Decca LK/SKL 5053	VOLUME ONE (LP)	150

(see also Bread Love & Dreams)

HUMAN BEINZ

68	Capitol CL 15529	Nobody But Me/Sueno	30
68	Capitol CL 15542	Turn On Your Lovelight/It's Fun To Be Clean	18

HUMAN CABBAGES

81	Boys & Girls BAG TWO	The Witch/Air-Raid Shelter (Pill Mix)/One More Fool (p/s)	4

HUMAN INSTINCT

65	Mercury MF 951	Can't Stop Around/I Want To Be Loved By You My Friend	30
66	Mercury MF 972	The Rich Man/Illusions	35
67	Mercury MF 990	Go-Go/I Can't Live Without You	25
68	Deram DM 167	A Day In My Mind's Mind/Death Of The Seaside	35
68	Deram DM 177	Renaissance Fair/Pink Dawn	35

(see also Jessie Harper)

HUMAN LEAGUE

78	Fast Product FAST 4	Being Boiled/Circus Of Death (p/s, original issue with b&w picture labels)	8
79	Fast Product FAST 10	THE DIGNITY OF LABOUR (12" EP, with spoken-word flexidisc [F10x/VF 1])	10
79	Virgin VS 294	Empire State Human/Introducing (p/s)	5
80	Virgin SV 105	HOLIDAY '80 (EP, double pack, purple & blue labels, 10,000 only)	8
80	Virgin VS 351	Empire State Human/Introducing//Only After Dark/Toyota City (Long Version) (double pack, p/s, shrinkwrapped)	20
80	Virgin VS 351	Only After Dark/Toyota City (Long Version) (p/s)	8
80	Virgin VS 351	Empire State Human/Introducing (p/s, reissue)	5
80	Virgin VS 351-12	Empire State Human/Introducing (12", p/s)	12
81	Virgin VS 395	Boys And Girls/Tom Baker (gatefold or non-gatefold p/s)	each 5
81	Virgin SV 105	HOLIDAY '80 (EP, reissue double pack, green/red labels, gatefold p/s)	7
81	Virgin SV 105	HOLIDAY '80 (reissue 3-track EP, green/red or blue/pink labels)	each 5
81	Virgin SV 105-12	HOLIDAY '80 (12", 5-track EP, withdrawn)	30+
82	Virgin VSY 522	Mirror Man/(You Remind Me Of) Gold (picture disc)	5
84	Virgin VSY 723	Louise/The Sign (Remix) (picture disc)	5
84	Virgin VS 723-12	Louise/The Sign (Extended Remix) (12", p/s with poster)	8
88	Virgin CDT 6	Hard Times/Love Action (I Believe In Love)/Hard Times Instrumental/Love Action Instrumental (3" CD, card sleeve)	10
88	Virgin VSCD 1025	Love Is All That Matters (Edit)/I Love You Too Much (Dub Version)/Love Is All That Matters (Extended Version) (CD, gatefold card sleeve)	12
88	Virgin CDT 24	(Keep Feeling) Fascination (Extended 12" version)/(Keep Feeling) Fascination (Improvisation 12" Dub Version)/Total Panic (3" CD, card sleeve)	10
90	Virgin VSCDT 1262	Heart Like A Wheel/Heart Like A Wheel (Extended Mix)/Rebound/Heart Like A Wheel (Remix) (CD)	8

90	Virgin VSCDX 1262	Heart Like A Wheel/Heart Like A Wheel (Extended Mix)/Rebound/ A Doorway (Dub Mix) (CD, numbered)	12
90	Virgin VSCDT 1303	Soundtrack To A Generation (Edit)/(Orbit Mix)/(Instrumental)/ (Pan Belgian Mix) (CD)	8
90	Virgin VSCDX 1303	Soundtrack To A Generation (Pan Belgian Dub)/(808 Mix Instrumental)/ (Dave Dodd's Mix)/(Acappella) (CD)	12
81	Virgin VP 2192	DARE! (LP, picture disc, die-cut sleeve with insert, white or black vinyl border)	10/12
88	Virgin CDHLP 1	GREATEST HITS (CD, picture disc)	18

(see also Heaven 17, Men, Philip Oakey & Giorgio Moroder, Jo Callis)

HUMANOID
88	Westside WSR 7	Stakker Humanoid (Part 1)/Stakker Humanoid (Part 2) (p/s)	5
88	Westside WSR 12	Stakker Humanoid/Radio Edit/Omen Mix (12", p/s)	8
89	Westside WSR 14	Slam/Bass Invaders/Slam Edit/Slam Hip House Version (12", p/s)	8
89	Westside HUMT 2	The Deep (Into The Abyss Mix)/The Deep (Extended LP Version)/ Cry Baby/The Deep (W5 Mix) (12", p/s)	8
92	Jumpin' & Pumpin' 12TOT 27	Stakker Humanoid (12" Orginal)/(Smart Systems Remix)/(Cobain Mix '94)/ (Snowman Mix)/(The Omen Mix)/(303 Tribe)/(Outer Limits) (12", brown or black vinyl, p/s)	10/8
92	Jumpin' & Pumpin' CDSTOT 27	Stakker Humanoid (Original Mix)/(Smart Systems Remix)/(Cobain Mix '94)/ (The Omen Mix)/(303 Mix)/(Outer Limits)/(12" Original) (CD)	10
88	Westside Human 1989	GLOBAL (LP)	12
88	Westside HUMANCD 1989	GLOBAL (CD)	18

HUMANOID featuring SHARON BENSON
| 89 | Westside HUMT 1 | TonIGHT (12", 3 mixes, p/s) | 8 |

(see also Future Sound Of London)

HUMBLEBUMS
69	Big T BIG 122	Saturday Roundabout Sunday/Bed Of Mossy Green	5
69	Big T BIG 127	Coconut Tree/Her Father Didn't Like Me Anyway	5
70	Big T BIG 130	Shoeshine Boy/My Apartment	5
69	Transatlantic TRA 186	THE FIRST COLLECTION OF MERRY MELODIES (LP)	12
69	Transatlantic TRA 201	THE NEW HUMBLEBUMS (LP)	12
70	Transatlantic TRA 218	OPEN UP THE DOOR (LP)	12
74	Transatlantic TRA 288	THE COMPLETE HUMBLEBUMS (3-LP, box set of above albums)	18

(see also Gerry Rafferty, Billy Connolly)

HUMBLE PIE
69	Immediate IM 082	Natural Born Bugie/Wrist Job (later in p/s)	8/5
70	A&M AMS 807	Big Black Dog/Strange Days	6
72	A&M AMS 7003	Hot'n'Nasty/You're So Good For Me	5
73	A&M AMS 7052	Black Coffee/Say No More	5
73	A&M AMS 7070	Get Down To It/Honky Tonk Woman	5
73	A&M AMS 7090	Oh La De Da/Outcrowd	5
75	A&M AMS 7185	Rock'n'Roll Music/Scored Out	5
80	Jet JET 180	Fool For A Pretty Face/You Soppy Pratt (p/s)	5
69	Immediate IMSP 025	AS SAFE AS YESTERDAY IS (LP)	22
69	Immediate IMSP 027	TOWN AND COUNTRY (LP)	22
70	A&M AMLS 986	HUMBLE PIE (LP)	15
71	A&M AMLS 2013	ROCK ON (LP)	15
72	A&M AMLH 63506	PERFORMANCE — ROCKIN' THE FILLMORE (2-LP)	15
72	A&M AMLS 64342	SMOKIN' (LP)	15
73	A&M AMLD 6004	EAT IT (2-LP)	18
74	A&M AMLH 63611	THUNDERBOX (LP)	15
75	A&M AMLS 68282	STREET RATS (LP)	15

(see also Steve Marriott, Small Faces, Peter Frampton, Herd, Natural Gas)

HUMBUG
| 70 | CBS 4811 | Groovin' With Mr Bloe/Marianna | 6 |
| 70 | CBS 5208 | I Got A Feeling (Vocal)/I Got A Feeling (Instrumental) | 5 |

HELEN HUMES
53	Brunswick 05078	They Raided The Joint/Loud Talking Woman (78)	10
53	Brunswick 05193	I Cried For You/Mean Way Of Loving (78)	15
56	Vogue V 2048	Million Dollar Secret/If I Could Be With You One Hour Of The Day	8
56	Vogue V 2048	Million Dollar Secret/If I Could Be With You One Hour Of The Day (78)	15
59	Contemporary CV 2415	When The Saints Come Marching In/Bill Bailey, Won't You Please Come Home (with Benny Carter's All-Stars)	6
59	Contemporary CV 2415	When The Saints Come Marching In/Bill Bailey, Won't You Please Come Home (78, with Benny Carter's All-Stars)	12
61	Contemporary LAC 12245	HELEN HUMES AND THE BENNY CARTER ALL STARS (LP)	12

(see also Benny Carter, Jimmy Witherspoon/Helen Humes)

ENGELBERT HUMPERDINCK
| 66 | Decca F 12427 | Stay/Come Over Here | 5 |
| 66 | Decca F 12496 | Dommage Dommage/When I Say Goodnight | 5 |

(see also Gerry Dorsey)

DELLA HUMPHREY
| 69 | Action ACT 4525 | Don't Make The Good Girls Go Bad/Your Love Is All I Need | 8 |
| 72 | Fab FAB 183 | Dreamland (actually by Marcia Griffiths)/Version | 6 |

LES HUMPHRIES SINGERS
| 76 | Antic K 11526 | Sing Sang Song/Just Sit Down At The Old Piano | 5 |

(see also Megaton)

HUMPY BONG
| 70 | Parlophone R 5859 | Don't You Be Too Long/We're Alright 'Till Then | 25 |

(see also Bee Gees, Morgan)

HUNGER
84	Psycho PSYCHO 14	STRICTLY FROM HUNGER (LP, reissue of U.S. LP)	15

HUNGRY WOLF
70	Philips 6308 009	HUNGRY WOLF (LP)	50

(see also Czar, Alan Parker, Ugly Custard)

GERALDINE HUNT
69	Roulette RO 515	Never Never Leave Me/Push Sweep	8
75	EMI EMI 2275	You/It's All For You	6

MARSHA HUNT
69	Track 604 030	Walk On Gilded Splinters/Hot Rod Poppa	6
69	Track 604 034	Desdemona/Hippy Gumbo	10
70	Track 604 037	Keep The Customer Satisfied/Lonesome Holy Roller	5
73	Vertigo 6059 080	Beast Day/Somebody To Love (as Marsha Hunt's 22)	5
71	Track 2410 101	WOMAN CHILD (LP)	25

MICHAEL HUNT & JOE LEATHERLAND
67	Decca LK 4902	WATER OF TYNE (LP)	12

PEE WEE HUNT & HIS ORCHESTRA
55	Capitol CL 14225	It's Never Too Late To Fall In Love/A Room In Bloomsbury	10
55	Capitol CL 14286	Save Your Love For Me/My Extraordinary Gal	10
56	Capitol CL 14515	Petunia's Patch/Vanessa	6
56	Capitol CL 14538	Lullaby Of Birdland/It's All Been Done Before	6
56	Capitol CL 14583	Swedish Rhapsody/The Object Of My Affection	6
56	Capitol CL 14630	I'll See You In Cuba/Canoodlin' Rag	6
58	Capitol CL 14884	Miss Otis Regrets/I Love Paris	6

TOMMY HUNT
62	Top Rank JAR 605	The Door Is Open/I'm Wondering	12
68	Direction 58-3216	I Need A Woman Of My Own/Searchin' For My Baby Looking Everywhere	7
72	Polydor 2058 236	Mind, Body & Soul/One More Mountain To Climb	5
74	Pye 7N 45325	Sleep Tight Honey/Time Alone Will Tell	5
75	Spark SRL 1132	Crackin' Up/Get Out	5
85	Kent TOWN 103	The Work Song/IVORYS: Please Stay	8

(see also Ivorys)

WILLIE AMOS HUNT
67	Camp 602 003	Would You Believe/My Baby Wants To Dance	30

HUNT & TURNER
72	Village Thing VTS 11	MAGIC LANDSCAPE (LP)	20

ALBERTA HUNTER
52	Jazz Collector L 94	Everybody Loves My Baby/Texas Moaner Blues (78)	10

CAROL HUNTER
73	Purple PUR 115	Look Out Cleveland/⁵/₄ March	7
73	Purple TPS 3503	THE NEXT VOICE YOU HEAR (LP)	12

DANE HUNTER
65	Oriole CB 1985	Evergreen Tree/Too Late	6

DANNY HUNTER (& GIANTS)
60	HMV POP 722	Make It Up/Little Girl (as Danny Hunter & Giants)	15
60	HMV POP 775	Who's Gonna Walk Ya Home?/Lonely And Blue	15
61	Fontana H 300	Lost Weekend/Age For Love	10

DAVE HUNTER
68	RCA RCA 1766	She's A Heartbreaker/Love Me A Lifetime	8
69	RCA RCA 1841	Don't Throw Your Love To The Wind/Hitchcock Railway	6

GREG HUNTER
66	Parlophone R 5483	Five O'Clock World/Away From Happiness	8

IAN HUNTER
75	CBS 3486	Who Do You Love/Boy	5
76	CBS 4268	All American Alien Boy (Version)/Rape	6
76	CBS 4479	You Nearly Did Me In/A Letter From Britannia To The Union Jack	15
77	CBS 5229	Justice Of The Peace/The Ballad Of Little Star (as Ian Hunter's Overnight Angels)	8
77	CBS 5497	England Rocks/Wild 'N' Free (as Ian Hunter's Overnight Angels)	5
79	Chrysalis CHS 2324	When The Daylight Comes/Life After Death (p/s, white vinyl with mask)	5
79	Chrysalis CHS 2346	Ships/Wild East (p/s)	5
79	Chrysalis CHS 2390	Cleveland Rocks/Bastard (p/s)	5
80	Chrysalis CHS 2434	We Gotta Get Out/Medley: Once Bitten Twice Shy/Bastard/Cleveland Rocks/Sons And Daughters/One Of The Boys (live double pack, gatefold p/s)	5
81	Chrysalis CHS 2542	Lisa Likes Rock 'n' Roll/Noises (p/s, clear vinyl)	5
83	CBS A 3541	All Of The Good Ones Are Taken/Death 'N' Glory Boys (p/s)	5
83	CBS TA 3541	All Of The Good Ones Are Taken/Death 'N' Glory Boys/Traitor (12", p/s)	8
83	CBS A 3855	Somethin's Goin' On/All Of The Good Ones Are Taken (Slow Version) (p/s)	5
83	CBS A 3855	Somethin' Goin' On (Radio Edit)/All Of The Good Ones Are Taken (Slow Version) (promo only, no p/s)	5
90	Mercury HRCD 1	American Music/Women's Intuition/Cool/Big Time (CD, with Mick Ronson, promo only)	8
77	CBS	YOU'RE NEVER ALONE WITH A SCHIZOPHRENIC (LP, unissued; later issued on Chrysalis CHR 1214)	

(see also Mott The Hoople, At Last The 1958 Rock & Roll Show, Apex Rhythm & Blues All Stars, Mick Ronson, Roger Taylor)

IVORY JOE HUNTER

50	MGM MGM 271	I Almost Lost My Mind/S.P. Blues (78, with Orchestra)................ 30
56	London HLE 8261	A Tear Fell/I Need You By My Side.................................. 325
56	London HLE 8261	A Tear Fell/I Need You By My Side (78)............................. 30
57	Columbia DB 3872	Since I Met You, Baby/You Can't Stop This Rockin' And Rollin'... 165
57	Columbia DB 3872	Since I Met You, Baby/You Can't Stop This Rockin' And Rollin' (78)...... 30
57	London HLE 8486	Love's A Hurting Game/Empty Arms................................. 140
57	London HLE 8486	Love's A Hurting Game/Empty Arms (78)............................ 30
61	Capitol CL 15220	I'm Hooked/Because I Love You 18
61	Capitol CL 15226	You Better Believe It, Baby/May The Man Win........................ 18

ROBERT HUNTER

74	Round RX 101	TALES OF THE GREAT RUM RUNNERS (LP) 12
75	Round RX 105	TIGER ROSE (LP)... 12
80	Dark Star DSLP 8001	JACK O'ROSES (LP) 15

(see also Grateful Dead)

SUSAN HUNTER

| 55 | Brunswick 05458 | Not Yet/Was That The Right Thing To Do? .... 7 |

TAB HUNTER

57	London HLD 8380	Young Love/Red Sails In The Sunset (gold or silver label) 25/15
57	London HLD 8410	Ninety-Nine Ways/I Don't Get Around Much Anymore 15
58	London HLD 8535	Don't Let It Get Around/I'm Alone Because I Love You 15
58	London HLD 8535	Don't Let It Get Around/I'm Alone Because I Love You (78)......... 12
60	Warner Bros WB 8	(What Can I Give) My Only Love/(I'll Be With You) In Apple Blossom Time 6
60	Warner Bros WB 20	Waitin' For The Fall/Our Love...................................... 6
61	London HLD 9381	The Wild Side Of Life/My Devotion 10
62	London HLD 9559	Born To Lose/I Can't Stop Lovin' You 8
58	London RE-D 1134	TAB HUNTER (EP) 35
61	Warner Bros WEP 6023	TAB HUNTER (EP, also stereo WSEP 2023) 25/30
60	Warner Bros WM 4008	TAB HUNTER (LP, also stereo WS 8008).......................... 35/45
61	London HA-D 2401	YOUNG LOVE (LP, also stereo SAH-G 6201) 45/55

HUNTER MUSKETT

73	Bradleys BRAD 303	John Blair/Silver Coin (p/s) 6
70	Decca Nova SDN 20	EVERY TIME YOU MOVE (LP) 150
73	Bradleys BRADL 1003	HUNTER MUSKETT (LP) 25

HUNTERS (U.K.)

60	Fontana H 276	Teen Scene/Santa Monica Flyer.................................... 10
61	Fontana H 303	Golden Ear-rings/Tally Ho 8
61	Fontana H 323	The Storm/How's M'Chicks? 8
64	Fontana TF 514	Teen Scene/Someone Else's Baby 10
61	Fontana TFL 5140	TEEN SCENE: THE HUNTERS PLAY THE BIG HITS (LP, stereo STFL 561) 40/50
62	Fontana TFL 5175	HITS FROM THE HUNTERS (LP, also stereo STFL 572)............. 40/50

(see also Dave Sampson & Hunters, Maisie McDaniel)

HUNTERS (Holland)

| 66 | RCA RCA 1541 | Russian Spy And I/Spring .... 15 |

(see also Jan Akkerman, Brainbox)

HUNTERS CLUB

| 87 | Trashcan THC 7002 | Give Me Your Soul/Angel (numbered plain sleeve) .... 4 |

HURDY GURDY

| 72 | CBS 64781 | HURDY GURDY (LP).. 150 |

RED VINCENT HURLEY

| 76 | Pye 7N 45583 | When/Just A Little Love (p/s) .... 7 |

HURRICANES

| 71 | Upsetter US 363 | Got To Be Mine/UPSETTERS: Version .... 10 |

(see also Dave Barker)

HURRICANE STRINGS

| 63 | Columbia DB 7027 | Venus/In The Carrick .... 8 |

MIKE HURST (& METHOD)

63	Philips BF 1295	The Banjo Song/Any Chance For Me 5
64	Philips BF 1319	Carol Anne/Anytime That You Want Me 5
64	Philips BF 1353	Half Heaven Half Heartache/Look In Your Eyes.................... 5
65	Philips BF 1389	Last Time You'll Walk Out On Me/Something Told Me.............. 5
65	Philips BF 1424	Show Me Around/I'm Running Away................................ 5

(see also Springfields, Remo Four, Ashton Gardner & Dyke, Sundance)

MISSISSIPPI JOHN HURT

60s	Vanguard SVRL 19005	THE IMMORTAL MISSISSIPPI JOHN HURT (LP) 20
66	Vanguard SVRL 19032	MISSISSIPPI JOHN HURT (LP)..................................... 15
67	Fontana TFL 6079	MISSISSIPPI JOHN HURT (LP)..................................... 18
71	Spokane SPL 1001	THE ORIGINAL 1928 RECORDINGS (LP) 50
71	Vanguard VSD 19/20	THE BEST OF MISSISSIPPI JOHN HURT (2-LP) 15
73	Vanguard VSD 79327	LAST SESSIONS (LP)... 15

HUSH

| 68 | Fontana TF 944 | Elephant Rider/Grey.. 120 |

HÜSKER DÜ

HÜSKER DÜ

84	SST SST 025	Eight Miles High/Masochism World (live) (p/s)	5
86	Warner Bros W 8746	Don't Want To Know If You're Lonely/All Work And No Play (p/s)	5
86	Warner Bros W 8746T	Don't Want To Know If You're Lonely/All Work And No Play/	
		Helter Skelter (live) (12", p/s)	8
86	Warner Bros W 8612	Sorry Somehow/All This I've Done For You (p/s)	5
86	Warner Bros W 8612	Sorry Somehow/All This I've Done For You//Celebrated Summer (Acoustic)/	
		Flexible Flyer (double pack, gatefold sleeve)	8
86	Warner Bros W 8612T	Sorry Somehow/All This I've Done For You/Celebrated Summer (Acoustic)/	
		Flexible Flyer/Fattie (12", p/s)	8
87	Warner Bros W 8456	Could You Be The One/Everytime (p/s)	5
87	Warner Bros W 8456T	Could You Be The One/Everytime/Charity, Chastity, Prudence, Hope	
		(12", p/s)	8
87	Warner Bros W 8276	Ice Cold Ice/Gotta Lotta (p/s)	5
87	Warner Bros W 8276T	Ice Cold Ice/Gotta Lotta/Medley	
		(12", p/s)	8

FERLIN HUSKY (& HIS HUSH PUPPIES)

57	Capitol CL 14702	Gone/Missing Persons	
		(as Ferlin Husky & His Hush Puppies)	12
57	Capitol CL 14702	Gone/Missing Persons	
		(as Ferlin Husky & His Hush Puppies) (78)	10
57	Capitol CL 14753	A Fallen Star/Prize Possession	18
57	Capitol CL 14753	A Fallen Star/Prize Possession (78)	12
57	Capitol CL 14785	This Moment Of Love/Make Me Live Again	7
57	Capitol CL 14785	This Moment Of Love/Make Me Live Again (78)	12
58	Capitol CL 14824	Wang Dang Doo/What'cha Doin' After School	20
58	Capitol CL 14824	Wang Dang Doo/What'cha Doin' After School (78)	15
58	Capitol CL 14883	Slow Down Brother/The Drunken Driver	
		(& His Hush Puppies)	15
58	Capitol CL 14916	I Feel That Old Heartache Again/I Saw God	8
58	Capitol CL 14922	The Kingdom Of Love/Terrific Together	7
58	Capitol CL 14954	I Will/All Of The Time	5
59	Capitol CL 14995	My Reason For Living/Wrong	5
59	Capitol CL 15027	Draggin' The River/Sea Sand	5
59	Capitol CL 15094	Black Sheep/I'll Always Return	5
60	Capitol CL 15160	The Wings Of A Dove/Next To Jimmy	5
57	Capitol EAP1 718	SONGS OF THE HOME AND HEART (EP)	12
57	Capitol EAP1 837	FERLIN HUSKY HITS (EP)	15
57	Capitol EAP1 921	COUNTRY MUSIC HOLIDAY (EP)	15
59	Parlophone GEP 8795	COUNTRY ROUND UP (EP)	30
60	Capitol EAP1 1280	FERLIN'S FAVOURITES (EP)	15
60	Capitol EAP2 1280	FERLIN'S FAVOURITES (EP)	15
60	Capitol EAP3 1280	FERLIN'S FAVOURITES (EP)	15
58	Capitol T 880	BOULEVARD OF BROKEN DREAMS (LP)	18
59	Capitol T 976	SITTIN' ON A RAINBOW (LP)	18
65	Fontana FJL 304	OLE OPRY FAVOURITES (LP)	12
	(see also Simon Crum)		

JACQUES HUSTIN

74	EMI EMI 2143	Fleur De Liberté/Freedom For The Man	15

HUSTLER

74	A&M AMLS 68276	HIGH STREET (LP)	12
75	A&M AMLH 33001	PLAY LOUD (LP)	12

HUSTLERS

63	Philips BF 1275	Gimme What I Want/Not Much	6
64	Mercury MF 807	Be True To You/You Can't Sit Down	6
64	Mercury MF 817	Sick Of Giving/Easy To Find	15

WILLIE HUTCH

73	Tamla Motown TMG 862	Brother's Gonna Work It Out/I Choose You	6
73	Tamla Motown STMA 8003	THE MACK (LP, soundtrack)	15
73	Tamla Motown STML 11247	FULLY EXPOSED (LP)	12
74	Tamla Motown STML 11269	FOXY BROWN (LP, soundtrack)	15
74	Tamla Motown STML 11280	THE MARK OF THE BEAST (LP)	12
75	Tamla Motown STML 12015	ODE TO MY LADY (LP)	20
76	Tamla Motown STML 12023	CONCERT IN BLUES (LP)	12

ASHLEY HUTCHINGS

72	Island HELP 5	MORRIS ON	
		(LP, actually by various folk artists)	12
76	Island HELP 24	RATTLEBONE AND ROUGHJACK	
		(LP)	20
76	Harvest SHSM 2012	SON OF MORRIS ON	
		(LP, actually by various folk artists)	12
77	Harvest SHSP 4073	KICKIN' UP THE SAWDUST	
		(LP)	20
	(see also Fairport Convention, Steeleye Span, Bunch)		

HUTCH HUTCHINS

77	Goodwood GM 12324	FEELS LIKE RAIN (LP)	30

SAM HUTCHINS

69	Bell BLL 1044	Dang Me/I'm Tired Of Pretending	6

LEROY HUTSON

75	Warner Bros K 16536	All Because Of You (Parts 1 & 2)	6
74	Buddah BDLP 4013	THE MAN (LP)	15
75	Warner Bros K 56139	HUTSON (LP)	40

J.B. HUTTO & HIS HAWKS
| 73 | Delmark DS 617 | HAWK SQUAT (LP) | 12 |

BETTY HUTTON
53	HMV 7M 103	Somebody Loves Me/Jealous (B-side with Pat Morgan)	12
53	Capitol CL 14002	Goin' Steady/No Matter How You Say Goodbye (78)	6
54	Capitol CL 14117	Banana Boat/My Cutey's Due At Two To Two Today (78)	6
54	Capitol CL 14131	I'm Nobody's Baby/Broke, Barefoot And Starry-Eyed (78)	6
56	Capitol CL 14568	Sleepy Head/Hit The Road To Dreamland	8
54	Capitol LC 6639	CAPITOL PRESENTS BETTY HUTTON (10" LP)	25

(see also Hutton Sisters, Perry Como, 'Tennessee' Ernie Ford)

DANNY HUTTON
| 66 | MGM MGM 1314 | Funny How Love Can Be/Dreamin' Isn't Good For You | 5 |
| 65 | Pye International 7N 25325 | Roses And Rainbows/Monster Shindig | 5 |

(see also Three Dog Night)

HUTTON SISTERS (Betty & Marion)
| 55 | Capitol CL 14250 | Ko Ko Mo (I Love You So)/Heart Throb | 20 |

(see also Betty Hutton)

CHARLIE HYATT
| 65 | Island IEP 706 | RASS! (EP, as Bam & Charlie Hyatt) | 15 |
| 66 | Island ILP 932 | KISS ME NECK (LP) | 35 |

HYDRA
| 74 | Capricorn 2089 008 | Glitter Queen/It's So Hard | 5 |
| 74 | Capricorn 2429 120 | HYDRA (LP) | 12 |

HYGRADES
| 65 | Columbia DB 7734 | She Cared/We're Through | 7 |

BRIAN HYLAND
78
| 60 | London HLR 9161 | Itsy Bitsy Teeny Weeny Little Polka Dot Bikini/Don't Dilly Dally, Sally | 150 |

SINGLES
60	London HLR 9113	Rosemary/Library Love Affair	18
60	London HLR 9161	Itsy Bitsy Teeny Weeny Little Polka Dot Bikini/Don't Dilly Dally, Sally	7
60	London HLR 9203	Four Little Heels/That's How Much	7
61	London HLR 9262	Lop Sided, Over Loaded/I Gotta Go ('Cause I Love You)	7
61	HMV POP 915	Let Me Belong To You/Let It Die	6
61	HMV POP 955	The Night I Cried/I'll Never Stop Wanting You	6
62	HMV POP 1013	Ginny Come Lately/I Should Be Gettin' Better	6
62	HMV POP 1051	Sealed With A Kiss/Summer Job	6
62	HMV POP 1079	Warmed Over Kisses/Walk A Lonely Mile	6
63	HMV POP 1113	I May Not Live To See Tomorrow/It Ain't That Way At All	6
63	HMV POP 1143	If Mary's There/Remember Me	6
63	HMV POP 1169	Somewhere In The Night/I Wish Today Was Yesterday	6
63	HMV POP 1188	I'm Afraid To Go Home/Save Your Heart For Me	6
63	HMV POP 1237	Let Us Make Our Own Mistakes/Nothing Matters But You	6
64	Philips BF 1326	Here's To Our Love/Two Kinds Of Girls	6
65	Philips BF 1429	Stay Away From Her/I Can't Keep A Secret	6
65	Philips BF 1486	Three Thousand Miles/Sometimes They Do	6
66	Philips BF 1508	The Joker Went Wild/I Can Hear The Rain	12
66	Philips BF 1528	Run, Run, Look And See/Why Did You Do It	6
67	Philips BF 1555	Hung Up In Your Eyes/Why Mine	6
67	Philips BF 1569	Holiday For Clowns/Yesterday I Had A Girl	6
67	Philips BF 1601	Get The Message/Kinda Groovy	7
69	Dot DOT 119	Tragedy/You Better Stop — And Think It Over	6
69	Dot DOT 124	A Million To One/It Could All Begin Again (In You)	6
69	Dot DOT 128	Stay And Love Me All Summer/Rainy April Morning	6
70	Uni UN 530	Gypsy Woman/You And Me (No. 2)	6
71	Uni UN 533	No Place To Run/So Long, Marianne	5
72	Uni UN 540	I Love Every Little Thing About You/With My Eyes Wide Open	5
72	Uni UN 545	Only Wanna Make You Happy/When' You're Lovin' Me	5

EP
| 62 | HMV 7EG 8780 | SEALED WITH A KISS (EP) | 40 |

LPs
61	London HA-R 2289	THE BASHFUL BLONDE (LP)	100
62	HMV CLP 1553	LET ME BELONG TO YOU (LP)	75
63	HMV CLP 1759	COUNTRY MEETS FOLK (LP)	45
66	Philips BL 7762	THE JOKER WENT WILD (LP)	30
68	Fontana SFL 13008	HERE'S TO OUR LOVE (LP)	18
72	Uni UNLS 118	BRIAN HYLAND (LP)	15

C. HYMAN
| 65 | Ska Beat JB 200 | The Ska Rhythm/The Ska Is Moving On | 15 |

DICK HYMAN TRIO
56	MGM SP 1164	Theme From "The Threepenny Opera"/Baubles, Bangles And Beads	8
58	MGM MGM-EP 646	DICK HYMAN SWINGS (EP)	8
69	Command SCMD 508	MOOG — THE ELECTRIC ECLECTICS OF DICK HYMAN (LP)	15
70	Command SCMD 946	THE AGE OF ELECTRONICUS (LP)	30

PHYLLIS HYMAN
| 79 | Arista ARIST 323 | You Know How To Love Me/Give A Little More (12", p/s) | 10 |

THEE HYPNOTICS
| 88 | Hipsville HIP 1 | Love In A Different Vein/All Night Long (p/s) | 8 |

JANIS IAN

IAN (Meeson) & BELINDA (Gillet)

(see also Brian May)

IAN & SYLVIA

IAN (EDWARD) & ZODIACS

(see also Koppykats, Wellington Wade)

ICARUS

ICE

(see also Affinity)

ICE

(see also Dickens)

ICE LA BAS

(see also Homosexuals)

ICICLE WORKS

(see also Ian McNabb, Melting Bear)

ICON A.D.

ICONS OF FILTH

IDEALS

IDES OF MARCH

(see also Survivors)

IDIOTS

(see also Tone Deaf & Idiots)

IDLE FLOWERS

(see also Hanoi Rocks)

IDLE RACE

67	Liberty LBF 15026	The Imposters Of Life's Magazine/Sitting In My Tree	22
68	Liberty LBF 15054	The Skeleton And The Roundabout/Knocking Nails Into My House	10
68	Liberty LBF 15101	The End Of The Road/The Morning Sunshine	10
68	Liberty LBF 15129	I Like My Toys/The Birthday (unissued)	
69	Liberty LBF 15218	Days Of Broken Arrows/Warm Red Carpet (B-side act. "Worn Red Carpet")	12
69	Liberty LBF 15242	Come With Me/Reminds Me Of You	10
71	Regal Zonophone RZ 3036	Dancing Flower/Bitter Green	10
76	United Artists UP 36060	The Skeleton And The Roundabout/Morning Sunshine	5
68	Liberty LBL/LBS 83132	THE BIRTHDAY PARTY (LP, mono/stereo)	40/35
69	Liberty LBS 83221	THE IDLE RACE (LP)	75
71	Regal Zono. SLRZ 1017	TIME IS (LP)	100
73	Sunset SLS 50354	ON WITH THE SHOW (LP)	12
76	Sunset SLS 50381	THE BIRTHDAY PARTY (LP, reissue)	12

(see also Mike Sheridan & Nightriders, Nightriders, Mike Sheridan's Lot, Lemon Tree, Jeff Lynne, Move, E.L.O., Trevor Burton, Steve Gibbons Band, Wizzard)

IDLEWILD

97	Human Condition HC 0017	Queen Of The Troubled Teens/Faster/Self Healer (p/s)	45
97	Fierce Panda NING 42	CHANDLER (p/s)	20
97	Deceptive BLUFF 057	Satan Polaroid/House Alone (p/s, numbered, 1,500 only)	18

BILLY IDOL

82	Chrysalis CHSP 2625	Hot In The City/Dead On Arrival (picture disc)	4
82	Chrysalis IDOL 1	Dancing With Myself/White Wedding (p/s, clear vinyl)	4
84	Chrysalis IDOL 2	Rebel Yell/Crank Call//White Wedding/Hot In The City (double pack, gatefold p/s)	4
84	Chrysalis IDOLP 2	Rebel Yell/Crank Call (square picture disc)	5
84	Chrysalis IDOLD 3/ CHS 2656	Eyes Without A Face/The Dead Next Door//Dancing With Myself/ Rebel Yell (double pack)	5
85	Chrysalis IDOL 5	White Wedding/Flesh For Fantasy (p/s, white vinyl)	4
85	Chrysalis IDOL 5	White Wedding (Shotgun Mix [Parts 1 & 2])/Mega-Idol-Mix (clear vinyl, PVC sl.)	4
85	Chrysalis IDOLP 6	Rebel Yell/Stand In The Shadows (live) (picture disc)	4
86	Chrysalis IDOL 8	To Be A Lover/All Summer Single (p/s, coloured vinyl)	4
87	Chrysalis IDOL 9	Don't Need A Gun/Fatal Charm (p/s, coloured vinyl)	4
88	Chrysalis IDOLCD 12	Hot In The City (Exterminator Mix)/Catch My Fall (Remix Fix)/ Soul Standing By/Mony Mony (live) (CD)	7
88	Chrysalis IDOLCD 13	Catch My Fall (The Remix Fix)/All Summer Single (CD)	7

(see also Gen[eration] X)

IDOL DEATH

80	I.D. DISPY 1234	New Lesson/Sticky Death (foldout p/s)	4

IDOLS

65	Mercury MF 840	Don't Walk Away/You Don't Care	10

(see also Mike Sax & Idols)

IDOLS

79	Ork NYC 2	You/Girl That I Love (p/s)	5

(see also New York Dolls)

IF

70	Island WIP 6083	Raise The Level Of Your Conscious Mind/I'm Reaching Out On All Sides	7
71	United Artists UP 35263	Far Beyond/Forgotten Roads	6
72	United Artists UP 35356	You In Your Small Corner/Waterfall	6
70	Island ILPS 9129	IF (LP, 1st pressing, pink label/'i' logo)	25
71	Island ILPS 9129	IF (LP, 2nd pressing, pink rim label/'palm tree' logo)	12
71	Island ILPS 9137	IF₂ (LP, pink label, pink rim label/'palm tree' logo)	18
71	United Artists UAG 29158	IF₃ (LP)	15
72	United Artists UAG 29315	IF IV (LP, gatefold sleeve with inner)	15
74	Gull GULP 1004	NOT JUST A BUNCH OF PRETTY FACES (LP)	12
75	Carley Records CR 300010	TEA BREAK OVER -- BACK ON YOUR 'EADS (LP)	15

(see also Ferris Wheel)

IF

92	MCA MCST 1627	Saturday's Angels (Justin Robertson Mixes) (12")	8

KRIS IFE

67	MGM MGM 1369	Hush/The Spectator	10
68	MGM MGM 1390	This Woman's Love/I Gotta Feeling	5
68	Music Factory CUB 3	Give And Take/Sands Of Time	6
68	Parlophone R 5741	Imagination/I'm Coming 'Round	10
69	Parlophone R 5770	Haven't We Had A Good Time?/Will I Ever Fall In Love Again?	5

(see also Quiet Five, Judd)

FRANK IFIELD

60	Columbia DB 4399	Lucky Devil/Nobody Else But You	6
60	Columbia DB 4464	Happy-Go-Lucky Me/Unchained Melody	6
60	Columbia DB 4496	Gotta Get A Date/No Love Tonight	5
61	Columbia DB 4568	That's The Way It Goes/Phoebe Snow	7
61	Columbia DB 4658	Life's A Holiday/Tobacco Road	5
61	Columbia DB 4741	Your Time Will Come/That's The Way It Is	5
62	Columbia DB 4786	Alone Too Long/Bigger Than You Or Me	5
63	Columbia DB 7131	Mule Train/One Man's Love	5
64	Columbia DB 7263	Angry At The Big Oak Tree/Go Tell It On The Mountain	5
65	Columbia DB 7319	I Should Care/Another Cup Of Coffee	5
65	Columbia DB 7355	Summer Is Over/True Love Ways	5
65	Columbia DB 7412	Don't Make Me Laugh (Don't Make Me Cry)/Without You (Tres Palabras)	5
65	Columbia DB 7520	I'm So Lonesome I Could Cry/Lonesome Number One	5
65	Columbia DB 7655	Paradise/Goodbye Now	5
65	Columbia DB 7772	I Guess/Then Came She	5
66	Columbia DB 7858	There'll Be Another Spring/Don't Be Afraid	5

Frank IFIELD

66	Columbia DB 7940	No One Will Ever Know/I'm Saving All My Love (For You)	5
66	Columbia DB 8078	Call Her Your Sweetheart/All My Daydreaming	5
67	Columbia DB 8164	You Came Along (From Out Of Nowhere)/And I Always Will Do	6
67	Columbia DB 8232	Roses, Moonlight And One Little Bottle Of Wine/Up-Up And Away	5
67	Columbia DB 8301	All The Time/In The Snow	5
68	Columbia DB 8344	Some Sweet Day/Singing The Blues	5
68	Columbia DB 8432	(You've Got) Morning In Your Eyes/Oh! Such A Stranger	5
68	Columbia DB 8478	The Swiss Maid/Baby Doll	5
69	Decca F 12893	Mary In The Morning/Let Me Into Your Life	5
69	Decca F 12966	It's My Time/I Love You Because	5
70	Decca F 13015	Three Good Reasons/I Wrapped Her In Ribbons	6
70	Decca F 13074	Easy Come, Easy Go/Tennessee Bird Walk	6
72	MAM MAM R.79	Roots And Rafters/Daddy Don't You Walk So Fast	5
74	Spark SRL 1109	Joanne/California Cotton Fields	5
76	Spark SRL 1134	Where Is Tomorrow?/Count Up To Ten	5
62	Columbia SEG 8210	FRANK IFIELD'S HITS (EP)	8
62	Columbia SEG 8254	MORE OF FRANK IFIELD'S HITS (EP)	8
63	Columbia SEG 8262	JUST ONE MORE CHANCE (EP, also stereo [ESG 7897])	10/15
63	Columbia SEG 8270	VIVA IFIELD! (EP)	10
63	Columbia SEG 8277	CONFESSIN' (EP)	8
63	Columbia SEG 8284	LUCKY DEVIL (EP)	10
63	Columbia SEG 8288	PLEASE (EP)	10
64	Columbia SEG 8300	DON'T BLAME ME (EP)	10
64	Columbia SEG 8322	BORN FREE (EP)	10
64	Columbia SEG 8343	BLUE SKIES (EP)	10
64	Columbia SEG 8359	I SHOULD CARE (EP)	10
64	Columbia SEG 8377	FRANK IFIELD SINGS (EP)	10
64	Columbia SEG 8385	FUNNY HOW TIME SLIPS AWAY (EP)	10
65	Columbia SEG 8448	LOVE WALKED IN (EP)	10
65	Columbia SEG 8456	HONG KONG BLUES (EP)	12
66	Columbia SEG 8495	GIVE HIM MY REGARDS (EP)	12
62	Columbia SCX 3460	I'LL REMEMBER YOU (LP, stereo)	15
65	Columbia 33SX 1723	PORTRAIT IN SONG (LP, also stereo SCX 3551)	12/15
65	Columbia 33SX 1751	UP JUMPED A SWAGMAN (LP)	15
66	Columbia S(C)X 6009	BABES IN THE WOOD (LP, cast recording, mono/stereo)	15/18
73	Spark SRLP 111	SOMEONE TO GIVE MY LOVE TO (LP)	15
78	FIR FIR 3781	BARBARY COAST (LP)	12
80	FIR FIR 3782	SWEET VIBRATIONS (LP)	12
80s	FIR FIR 3783	IF LOVE MUST GO (LP)	12
80s	FIR FIR 3784	AT THE SANDCASTLE (LP)	12

'IGGINBOTTOM
| 69 | Deram DML/SML 1051 | 'IGGINBOTTOM'S WRENCH (LP) | 90 |

(see also Soft Machine)

IGGY & STOOGES
(see under Stooges, Iggy Pop)

JULIO IGLESIAS
| 70 | Decca F 23005 | Gwendolyne/Bla, Bla, Bla | 12 |
| 72 | Decca FR 13339 | Un Canto A Galicia/Por Una Mujer | 5 |

IGNERANTS
| 79 | Rundown ACE 008 | Radio Interference/Wrong Place, Wrong Time (p/s) | 20 |

IGNORANTS
| 93 | Spaghetti CIOCD 8 | Phat Girls (Seven Stone Diet)/Fat Girls (Clubland Frenzy)/ Fat Girls (Bedtime Binge)/Rewind (CD) | 8 |

IGUANA
| 72 | Polydor 2383 108 | IGUANA (LP) | 15 |

IGUANAS
| 65 | RCA RCA 1484 | This Is What I Was Made For/Don't Come Runnin' To Me | 20 |

IJAHMAN
| 76 | Lucky LY 6016 | Jah Heavy Load/Heavy Dub | 10 |

I-JOG & TRACKSUITS
| 78 | Tyger TYG 1 | Red Box/Worrying Man (p/s) | 6 |

IKE (B) & CRYSTALITES
| 68 | Island WI 3134 | Illya Kuryakin/Anne Marie (B-side miscredited to Bobby Ellis & Crystalites) | 15 |
| 68 | Island WI 3151 | Try A Little Merriness/Patricia (as Ike B & Crystalites) | 15 |

IKETTES
62	London HLU 9508	I'm Blue/Find My Baby	15
65	Stateside SS 407	Peaches'N'Cream/The Biggest Players	12
65	Stateside SS 434	(He's Gonna Be) Fine Fine Fine/How Come	12
65	Sue WI 389	Prisoner Of Love/Those Words	25
66	Polydor 56506	I'm So Thankful/Don't Feel Sorry For Me	10
66	Polydor 56516	(Never More) Lonely For You/Sally Go Round The Roses	10
66	London HLU 10081	What'cha Gonna Do?/Down, Down	12
67	Polydor 56533	I'm So Thankful/Don't Feel Sorry For Me (reissue)	7
73	Mojo 2092 063	Peaches'N'Cream/Sally Go Round The Roses	5
65	Stateside SE 1033	FINE FINE FINE (EP)	75

(see also Ike & Tina Turner, P.P. Arnold)

ILANIT
| 77 | Pye International 7N 25739 | I'm No One (If You Leave Me)/I Can't Say I Love You (p/s) | 10 |

I LIFE
| 64 | R&B JB 140 | Kiss You Gave Me/No More | 10 |

ILLUSION

69	Dot DOT 122	Did You See Her Eyes?/Falling In Love	8
70	Dot DOT 133	Together/Don't Push It	5
70	Dot DOT 137	Let's Make Each Other Happy/Beside You (unissued)	
70	Paramount PARA 3007	Let's Make Each Other Happy/Beside You	5
69	Dot (S)LPD 531	ILLUSION (LP)	18
70	Dot SLPD 537	TOGETHER (AS A WAY OF LIFE) (LP)	15
70	Paramount SPFL 264	IF IT'S SO (LP, originally planned for Dot SLPD 539)	15

ILLUSIVE DREAM

| 69 | RCA Victor RCA 1791 | Electric Garden/Back Again | 20 |

(see also Christine Perfect)

SOLOMON ILORY

| 63 | Blue Note 45-1899 | Yabe E (Farewell) (Parts 1 & 2) | 10 |

I, LUDICROUS

88	Kaleid. Sound KS 707	Quite Extraordinary/At The End Of The Day (p/s)	4
88	Kaleid. Sound KS 107	Quite Extraordinary/At The End Of The Day/Kick Down The Stumps/ Mistakes (12", p/s)	7
87	Kaleid. Sound KSLP 4	IT'S LIKE EVERYTHING ELSE (LP)	10

I LUV WIGHT

| 70 | Philips 6006 043 | Let The World Wash In/Mediaeval Masquerade (some in p/s) | 75/25 |

(see also Kaleidoscope, Fairfield Parlour)

IM (Cedric Brooks) & DAVID

| 70 | Bamboo BAM 57 | Candid Eye/SOUND DIMENSION: Federated Backdrop | 20 |

IMAGE

65	Parlophone R 5281	Come To The Party/Never Let Me Go	35
65	Parlophone R 5352	Home Is Anywhere/I Hear Your Voice Again	35
66	Parlophone R 5442	I Can't Stop Myself/Let's Make The Scene	35

(see also Dave Edmunds)

IMAGES

| 65 | Polydor 56011 | I Only Have Myself To Blame/Head Over Heels | 22 |

NATALIE IMBRUGLIA

| 98 | RCA 74321 52799-2 | Torn/Contradictions/Diving In The Deep End (CD, withdrawn) | 20 |

HAMISH IMLACH

67	Xtra XTRA 1059	BEFORE AND AFTER (LP)	12
68	Xtra XTRA 1069	THE TWO SIDES OF HAMISH IMLACH (LP)	12
72	Xtra XTRA 1128	FINE OLD ENGLISH TORY TIMES (LP)	12

IMMORTALS

| 69 | Amalgamated AMG 851 | Bongo Jah/ANSELL COLLINS: My Last Waltz | 8 |

IMMORTALS

| 86 | MCA MCA 1057 | No Turning Back/No Turning Back (The Chocks-Away Mix) (p/s) | 30 |
| 86 | MCA MCAT 1057 | No Turning Back (Joy Stick Mix)/No Turning Back/No Turning Back (The Chocks-Away Mix) (12", p/s) | 35 |

(see also Queen)

IMPAC

| 66 | CBS 202402 | Too Far Out/Rat Tat Ta Tat | 70 |

IMPACT ALL STARS

71	Bullet BU 483	Dandy Shandy Version 4/Go Back Version 3	6
71	Randy's RAN 519	Go Back Version 4/Version 3	7
71	Supreme SUP 223	Go Back/Version	6

(see also Randy's All Stars, Alton Ellis, Gregory Issacs, Errol Dunkley, C. Danovan, Heptones, Dennis Brown, Horace Andy)

IMPALAS

59	MGM MGM 1015	Sorry (I Ran All The Way Home)/Fool, Fool, Fool	15
59	MGM MGM 1015	Sorry (I Ran All The Way Home)/Fool, Fool, Fool (78)	60
59	MGM MGM 1031	Oh, What A Fool/Sandy Went Away	15
60	MGM MGM 1068	Peggy Darling/'Bye Everybody	12
59	MGM MGM-EP 696	SORRY (I RAN ALL THE WAY HOME) (EP)	300

IMPERIAL POMPADOURS

| 80 | Pompadour POMP 001 | ERSATZ (LP, actually Inner City Unit with Robert Calvert & Barney Bubbles) | 40 |

(see also Inner City Unit, Robert Calvert)

IMPERIALS

| 68 | Nu Beat NB 012 | Young Love/Days Like These | 6 |

IMPERIALS (Jamaica)

| 69 | Bullet BU 417 | Black Is Soul/Always With You | 6 |

IMPERIALS

| 72 | Key KL 012 | TIME TO GET IT TOGETHER (LP) | 15 |
| 74 | Key KL 025 | FOLLOW THE MAN WITH THE MUSIC (LP) | 12 |

IMPERIALS (U.S.)

| 78 | Power Exchange PXL 029 | WHO'S GONNA LOVE ME? (LP) | 10 |

IMPERSONATORS

| 69 | Big Shot BI 524 | Make It Easy On Yourself/I've Tried Before | 8 |

(see also Moffat Allstars)

IMPLIED CONSENT

| 84 | In Tape IT 003 | Nobody In Particular/A View Of The World From A Brown Paper Bag (numbered p/s) | 5 |

IMPRESSIONS

67	HMV CLP/CSD 3631	THE FABULOUS IMPRESSIONS (LP)	30
68	Stateside (S)SL 10239	WE'RE A WINNER (LP)	20
68	Joy JOYS 104	FOR YOUR PRECIOUS LOVE (LP, with Jerry Butler)	12
69	Buddah 203 012	THIS IS MY COUNTRY (LP)	15
69	Stateside (S)SL 10279	BIG SIXTEEN (VOL. 2) (LP)	15
70	Buddah 2359 003	THE YOUNG MOD'S FORGOTTEN STORY (LP)	20
70	Buddah 2359 009	AMEN (LP)	15
71	Buddah 2318 017	CHECK OUT YOUR MIND (LP)	15
72	Buddah 2318 059	TIMES HAVE CHANGED (LP)	12
75	ABC ABCL 5104	BIG SIXTEEN (LP, reissue)	12

(see also Curtis Mayfield, Jerry Butler & Impressions)

IMPS
58	Parlophone R 4398	Dim Dumb Blonde/Let Me Lie	15
58	Parlophone R 4398	Dim Dumb Blonde/Let Me Lie (78)	20

I'M SO HOLLOW
81	Hologram ISH 002	Dreams To Fill The Vacuum/Distraction (clear vinyl, PVC sleeve)	7
81	Illuminated/Vital JAMS 5	EMOTION, SOUND, EMOTION (LP)	10

INADEQUATES
59	Capitol CL 15051	Pretty Face/Audie	7

IN-BE-TWEENS
(see under N' Betweens)

IN CAMERA
80	4AD AD 8	Die Laughing/Final Achievement (p/s)	6
80	4AD BAD 19	IV SONGS: The Conversation/The Attic/Fragments Of Fear/Legion (12" EP)	8
82	4AD BAD 205	FIN (12" EP)	8

INCAS
65	Lyntone LYN 765/6	KEELE RAG RECORD (EP, flexidisc, with 3 other bands)	40
66	Parlophone R 5551	One Night Stand/I'll Keep Holding On	12

INCOGNITO
81	Ensign ENYT 211	Incognito (remix)/Shine On (live) (12")	10

INCREDIBLE BONGO BAND
73	MGM 2006 161	Bongo Rock/Bongolia	8
72	MGM 2315 255	BONGO ROCK (LP)	30
76	DJM DJS 20452	BONGO ROCK (LP, reissue)	25

INCREDIBLE HOG
73	Dart ART 2026	Lame/Tadpole	12
73	Dart 65372	VOLUME 1 (LP)	115

INCREDIBLE KIDDA BAND
78	Psycho P 2608	Everybody Knows/No Nerve (a few in p/s)	50/30

INCREDIBLES
67	Stateside SS 2053	There's Nothing Else To Say/Heart And Soul	100
74	Contempo CS 9008	There's Nothing Else To Say/Another Dirty Deal	5
74	Contempo CLP 512	HEART AND SOUL (LP)	12

INCREDIBLE STRING BAND

SINGLES
68	Elektra EKSN 45028	Painting Box/No Sleep Blues	8
69	Elektra EKSN 45074	Big Ted/All Writ Down	8
70	Elektra 2101 003	This Moment/Black Jack Davy	6
72	Island WIP 6145	Black Jack David/Moon Hang Low	5
73	Island WIP 6158	At The Lighthouse Dance/Jigs	5

ORIGINAL LPs
66	Elektra EUK 254	THE INCREDIBLE STRING BAND (LP, 1st pressing, white label, green logo, black lettering)	80
67	Elektra EUK 257/EUKS 7257	THE 5000 SPIRITS OR THE LAYERS OF THE ONION (LP, mono/stereo, red label)	30/25
68	Elektra EUK 258/EUKS 7258	THE HANGMAN'S BEAUTIFUL DAUGHTER (LP, red label, with lyric insert)	25
68	Elektra EKL 4036/7	WEE TAM/THE BIG HUGE (2-LP, red label, gatefold sleeve, with insert; also stereo EKS 74036/7)	45
69	Elektra EKS 74057	CHANGING HORSES (LP, red label, gatefold sleeve)	20
70	Elektra EKS 74061	I LOOKED UP (LP, existence unconfirmed with this number)	
70	Elektra 2469 002	I LOOKED UP (LP, red label)	18
70	Elektra 2665 001	U (2-LP, red label, gatefold sleeve, some with foldover lyric insert)	30/25
70	Island ILPS 9140	BE GLAD FOR THE SONG HAS NO ENDING (LP, pink rim label/'palm tree' logo)	15
71	Elektra EKS 74065	RELICS OF THE INCREDIBLE STRING BAND (LP, 'butterfly' label)	12
71	Island ILPS 9172	LIQUID ACROBAT AS REGARDS THE AIR (LP, gatefold sleeve, with inner, pink rim label/'palm tree' logo)	15
72	Island ILPS 9211	EARTHSPAN (LP, with lyric inner sleeve, pink rim label/'palm tree' logo)	15
73	Island ILPS 9229	NO RUINOUS FEUD (LP, with inner sleeve, pink rim label/'palm tree' logo)	12
74	Island ILPS 9270	HARD ROPE AND SILKEN TWINE (LP, with inner sleeve, pink rim label/'palm tree' logo)	12
76	Island ISLD 9	SEASONS THEY CHANGE (2-LP, gatefold sleeve)	20

INCREDIBLE STRING BAND

REISSUE LPs

66	Elektra EUK 254	THE INCREDIBLE STRING BAND (LP, 2nd pressing, red label)	50
68	Elektra EKL 254	THE INCREDIBLE STRING BAND (LP, 3rd pressing, red label)	20
68	Elektra EKS 7257	THE 5000 SPIRITS OR THE LAYERS OF THE ONION (LP, red label)	20
68	Elektra EKL 4036	WEE TAM (LP, red label, also stereo EKS 74036)	15
68	Elektra EKL 4037	THE BIG HUGE (LP, red label, also stereo EKS 74037)	15
71	Elektra EKS 7257	THE 5000 SPIRITS OR THE LAYERS OF THE ONION (LP, 'butterfly' label)	12
71	Elektra EKS 7258	THE HANGMAN'S BEAUTIFUL DAUGHTER (LP)	12
71	Elektra K 42002	THE HANGMAN'S BEAUTIFUL DAUGHTER (LP, 'butterfly' label, with insert)	12
71	Elektra K 42037	CHANGING HORSES (LP, 'butterfly' label, gatefold sleeve)	12
72	Elektra K 42021	WEE TAM (LP, 'butterfly' label)	12
72	Elektra K 42022	THE BIG HUGE (LP, 'butterfly' label)	12
72	Elektra K 62002	U (2-LP, 'butterfly' label, gatefold sleeve, with foldover lyric insert)	15
76	Elektra K 42046	I LOOKED UP (LP, 'butterfly' label)	10

(see also Robin Williamson, Mike Heron, Famous Jug Band, C.O.B., Shirley Collins)

IN CROWD (U.K.)

65	Parlophone R 5276	That's How Strong My Love Is/Things She Says	75
65	Parlophone R 5328	Stop! Wait A Minute/You're On Your Own	45
65	Parlophone R 5364	Why Must They Criticize?/I Don't Mind	45

(see also Tomorrow, Keith West, Steve Howe, Four + One)

INCROWD (U.K.)

69	Deram DM 272	Where In The World/I Can Make Love To You	10

IN CROWD (Jamaica)

71	Spinning Wheel SW 105	Bush Jacket/Soul Face	6

INCUBUS

84	Guardian GRC 2165	TO THE DEVIL A DAUGHTER (LP)	15

INDECENT EXPOSURE

84	Index IS A1	Riots (Single Version)/A Matter Of Time (no p/s)	7

INDEPENDENTS

72	Wand WN 29	Just As Long As You Need Me (Parts 1 & 2)	5

INDIAN SUMMER

71	RCA Neon NE 3	INDIAN SUMMER (LP)	30

(see also Ross, Dodgers)

INDIGO GIRLS

89	Epic 654 907-2	Closer To Fine/History Of Us/Center Stage (CD, card sleeve)	7
89	Epic 655 135-2	Closer To Fine/Intro/Closer To Fine (live)/Mona Lisas And Mad Hatters (live)/American Tune (live) (CD, card sleeve)	7

LOS INDIOS TABAJARAS

63	RCA RCA 1365	Maria Elena/Jungle Dream	5
64	RCA RCA 1388	Always In My Heart/Moonlight And Shadows	5
64	RCA RCX 7135	A LA ORILLA DEL LAGO (EP)	8
64	RCA	LOS INDIOS TABAJARAS (LP)	12

INDO JAZZMEN

68	Saga FID 2145	RAGAS AND REFLECTIONS (LP)	15

INDUSTRIAL CHIPMUNKS/AGA ZARO PÖLOTOK

80s	Mauled By Iguana No. 1	INDUSTRIAL CHIPMUNKS/AGA ZARO PÖLOTOK (split EP, gatefold p/s)	4

INERTIA

80s	Inertial ERT 1	The Screen/4 Submarine (p/s)	5

INFANTES JUBILATE

68	Music Factory CUB 5	Exploding Galaxy/Take It Now	45

INFA RIOT

81	Secret SHH 117	Kids Of The 80s/Still Out Of Order (p/s)	10
82	Secret SHH 133	The Winner/School's Out (p/s)	10
82	Secret SEC 7	STILL OUT OF ORDER (LP)	15

(see also Infas)

INFAS

84	Panache PAN 101	Sound And Fury/Triffic Spiff Ya O.K. (p/s)	8
84	Panache PANLP 501	SOUND AND FURY (LP)	12

(see also Infa Riot)

INFINITY PROJECT

89	Fabulous FABU 004	HYPERACTIVE (12" EP, sponged cover)	10
90	Fabulous FABU 005	UPHOLD THE LAW (12" EP)	10
90	Fabulous FABU 016	TRIBADELIC MELTDOWN (12" EP)	8

IN FLAMES

72	Pama PM 842	Rocket Man/I'm All Broke Up	5

INFLUENCE

69	Orange OAS 201	I Want To Live/Driving Me Wild	10

(see also John Miles, Geordie, Smokestack Crumble)

INFORMATION
69	Beacon BEA 121	Orphan/Oh Strange Man	8
70	Evolution E 2461S	Face To The Sun/Lovely To See You	12

NICK INGHAM
75	Studio Two TWOX 1045	TERMINATOR (LP)	15

RED INGLE
50	Capitol CL 13356	Turn Your Head Little Darlin'/You Can't Be As Fit As A Fiddle (78)	8
51	Capitol CL 13485	Chew Tobacco Rag/Let Me In (78)	10
51	Capitol CL 13628	Pool/Moe Zart's Turkey Trot (78)	8
59	Capitol EAP 20052	CIGAREETS, WHUSKY AND WILD WILD WOMEN (EP)	20

JORGEN INGMANN
61	Fontana H 311	Cherokee/Anna	6
61	Fontana H 333	Milord/Oceans Of Love	6
61	Fontana H 353	Violetta/Pinetop's Boogie Woogie	6
62	Fontana 267 237 TF	Africa/Johnny's Tune	6
63	Columbia DB 7013	I Loved You (Dansevise)/Little Boy (as Grethe & Jorgen Ingmann)	5
64	Columbia SEG 8340	DRINA (EP)	15

BRIMSTONE INGRAM
78	Grapevine RED 1	What Happened To The Songs? (Vocal)/(Instrumental)	4
78	Grapevine REDC 1	What Happened To The Songs? (Vocal)/(Instrumental) (12")	7

LUTHER INGRAM
70	Stax STAX 142	My Honey And Me/Puttin' Game Down	6
70	Stax STAX 148	Home Don't Seem Like A Home/Ain't That Lovin' You?	6

INITIALS
64	London HLR 9860	School Days/Song Is Number One	12

IN-KEEPERS
68	Morgan MR 109P	IN-KEEPERS (LP)	20

INK SPOTS
54	Parlophone MSP 6063	Here In My Lonely Room/Flowers, Mister Florist, Please	18
54	Parlophone MSP 6074	Ebb Tide/If You Should Say Goodbye	18
54	Parlophone MSP 6126	Planting Rice/Yesterdays	18
55	Parlophone MSP 6152	Melody Of Love/Am I Too Late?	15
55	Parlophone R 3977	Melody Of Love/Am I Too Late? (78)	8
55	Brunswick OE 9158	SWING HIGH SWING LOW VOL. 1 (EP)	10
56	Brunswick OE 9426	THEY SOLD A MILLION NO. 10 (EP)	12
56	Brunswick OE 9427	THEY SOLD A MILLION NO. 11 (EP)	15
57	HMV 7EG 8410	CHARLIE FUQUA'S INK SPOTS (EP)	10
57	Parlophone GEP 8673	YESTERDAYS (EP)	10
50s	Britone LP 1003	THE INK SPOTS (10" LP)	20
53	Brunswick LA 8590	SOUVENIR ALBUM VOLUME ONE (10" LP)	20
55	Brunswick LA 8710	STREET OF DREAMS (10" LP)	20
	(see also Ella Fitzgerald)		

AUTREY INMAN
63	Decca DFE 8571	AMERICAN COUNTRY JUBILEE NO. 1 (EP)	15

INMATES
79	Soho SH 7	Dirty Water/Danger Zone (gatefold p/s)	6
79	Radar ADA 44	Dirty Water/Danger Zone (p/s, reissue)	5
79	Radar ADA 47	The Walk/Talkin' Woman (p/s)	5
80	Radar ADA 50	Love Got Me/Jealousy (p/s)	5
80	Radar ADA 59	So Much In Love/Tell Me What's Wrong (p/s)	5
80	Radar ADA 61	Stop It Baby/Sweet Rain (p/s)	5
81	Radar ADA 63	Heartbeat/Tallahassie Lassie (p/s)	5
81	WEA K 18850	Me And The Boys/Betty Lou (p/s)	5
79	Radar RAD 25	FIRST OFFENCE (LP)	12
80	Radar RAD 28	SHOT IN THE DARK (LP)	12

INNER CITY
92	Ten TENX 408	Praise (F.S.O.L. Conceptual)/(Intergalactic Dub)/(Mayday Mix) (12", p/s)	10
93	Virgin OVD 438	TESTAMENT 93 (EP, remixes, printed card envelope sleeve)	12
93	Virgin CDOVD 438	TESTAMENT 93 (CD EP)	10

INNER CITY EXPRESS
78	Ebony EYE 5	Fat On Funk/Sho' Dig Dancin' (12")	8

INNER CITY JAM BAND
77	Ember EMB S 355	Hurt/What I Did For Love	4

INNER CITY UNIT
79	Riddle RID 001/ICU 45	Solitary Ashtray/So Try As Id (Dub Version) (plain sleeve with colour insert)	8
79	Riddle RID 003	Paradise Beach/Amyl Nitrate (company die-cut sleeve)	8
81	Avatar AAA 113	Beer, Baccy, Bingo And Benidorm/In The Mood (Nude) (red vinyl, no p/s)	6
82	Avatar AAA 119	Bones Of Elvis/Sid's Song (no p/s)	5
85	Jettisoundz JZ 5	BLOOD AND BONE (12" EP, p/s)	8
79	Riddle RID 002	PASS OUT (THE 360° PSYCHO DELERIA SOUND) (LP)	15
81	Avatar AALP 5004	THE MAXIMUM EFFECT (LP, with insert)	12
	(see also Hawkwind, Sphynx, Radio Actors, Imperial Pompadours, Catherine Andrews, Big Amongst Sheep, Nik Turner)		

INNER MINDS
70	New Beat NB 067	Witchcraft Man/Night In Cairo	6
70	New Beat NB 069	Pum Pum Girl/Freedom	6
71	Bullet BU 465	Arawak Version/Cuffy Cuffy	6

MINT VALUE £

NEIL INNES

72	United Artists UP 35358	Slush/Rawlinson's End (unissued)	
73	United Artists UP 35495	How Sweet To Be An Idiot/The Age Of Desperation	6
73	United Artists UP 35639	Momma B/Immortal Invisible	6
74	United Artists UP 35676	Re-cycled Vinyl Blues/Fluff On The Needle	6
74	United Artists UP 35745	Lie Down And Be Counted/Bandwagon	6
75	United Artists UP 35772	What Noise Annoys An Oyster/Oo-Chuck-A-Mao-Mao	6
77	Arista ARISTA 106	Lady Mine/Crystal Balls	5
77	Arista ARISTA 123	Silver Jubilee (A Tribute)/Drama On A Saturday Night	5
78	Warner Bros K 17182	Protest Song/The Hard-To-Get	5
82	MMC MMC 100	Them/Rock Of Ages	5
82	MMC MMC 103	Mr. Eurovision/Ungawa	5
84	PRT 7P 298	Humanoid Boogie/Libido (p/s)	5
73	United Artists UAG 29492	HOW SWEET TO BE AN IDIOT (LP)	18
82	MMC MMC 001	OFF THE RECORD (2-LP)	18

(see also Grimms, Bonzo Dog [Doo Dah] Band, Rutles, World, Dirk & Stig, Group)

INN KEEPERS

71	Banana BA 328	Duppy Serenade/Sunshine Version (actually by Dennis Alcapone)	12

(see also WInston Matthews)

INNOCENCE

66	Kama Sutra KAS 203	There's Got To Be A Word!/I Don't Wanna Be Around You	5
66	Kama Sutra KAS 206	Lifetime Of Lovin' You/Mairzy Doats And Dozy Doats	6

INNOCENT BYSTANDERS

80	Rok ROK XVII/XVIII	Where Is Johnny?/DEBUTANTES: The Man In The Street (company sleeve)	5

INNOCENTS (U.S.)

60	Top Rank JAR 508	Honest I Do/My Baby Hully Gullys	22
61	Top Rank JAR 541	Gee Whiz/Please Mr Sun	22

(see also Kathy Young)

INNOCENTS (U.K.)

63	Columbia DB 7098	Stepping Stones/Grazina	8
63	Columbia DB 7173	A Fine, Fine Bird/Spanish Holiday	7
64	Columbia DB 7314	Stick With Me Baby/Not More Than Everything	7

(see also Mike Berry, Mike Sarne, Innocents & Leroys)

INNOCENTS & LEROYS

64	Regal Zonophone RZ 502	Don't Throw Your Love Away; My Girl Lollipop; I Love You Because; Not Fade Away (medley, across both sides)	8

(see also Innocents [U.K.], Le-Roys)

INNOCENTS (U.K.)

80	Kingdom KV 8010	One Way Love/Every Wednesday Night At Eight (p/s)	10

(see also Woodentops, Advertising, Secret Affair)

INQUISITIVE PEOPLE

67	Decca F 12699	Big White Chief/Rhapsody Of Spring	5

INSANE

82	Insane INSANE 1	Why Die?/War And Violence (p/s)	6
82	Riot City RIOT 3	Politics/Dead And Gone/Last Day (p/s)	4
82	No Future OI 10	El Salvador/Nuclear War/Chinese Rock (p/s)	5

INSECT TRUST

69	Capitol E-(S)T 109	THE INSECT TRUST (LP)	45

INSIDERS

80	Satellite SATS 1002	Rollin' & Strollin'/She Had To Go (features Ray Dorset)	10

(see also Ray Dorset)

INSPIRAL CARPETS

80s	own label	SONGS OF SHALLOW INTENSITY (p/s, demo cassette)	15
80s	own label	WAITING FOR OURS (p/s, demo cassette)	15
80s	own label	COW (p/s, demo cassette)	10
87	Debris DEB 06	Garage Full Of Flowers/METRO INFINITY: Stupid Friends (flexidisc, some with *Debris* fanzine)	8/4
88	Playtime AMUSE 2	Keep The Circle Around/Theme From Cow (p/s)	15
88	Playtime AMUSE 2T	PLANE CRASH (12" EP, later 'reissued' as white label without p/s)	15/7
88	Playtime AMUSE 4	Butterfly/You Can't Take The Truth (unreleased, white label promos only)	8
88	Playtime AMUSE 4T	TRAIN SURFING (12" EP, unreleased, white label test pressings only)	15
89	Cow MOO 1	PLANE CRASH (12" EP, unreleased reissue)	
89	Cow MOO 2	TRAIN SURFING (12" EP, some with rear sticker & scratched-out matrix)	7
89	Cow DUNG 4	Keep The Circle Around/Seeds Of Doubt/Joe/Causeway/Butterfly/26/ Garage Full Of Flowers/96 Tears (demo cassette)	8

(see also Too Much Texas)

INSPIRATIONS (U.S.)

67	Polydor 56730	Touch Me, Kiss Me, Hold Me/What Am I Gonna Do With You?	75

INSPIRATIONS (Jamaica)

69	Camel CA 11	Down In The Park/Love Oh Love	8
69	Camel CA 21	Wonder Of Love/Cinderella	7
70	Amalgamated AMG 857	Take Back Your Duck/Nothing For Nothing	12
70	Amalgamated AMG 861	La La/Reggae Fever	12
70	Amalgamated AMG 862	The Train Is Coming/Man Oh Man	8
70	Trojan TTL 27	REGGAE FEVER (LP)	25

(see also Untouchables, Niney)

INSTANT AGONY

82	H. Man H. Biscuit DUNK 1	THINK OF ENGLAND (EP)	5
82	H. Man H. Biscuit DUNK 2	FASHION PARADE (EP)	5
83	Flicknife FLS 022	No Sign Of Life/Taste Of Power (p/s)	5
83	Flicknife FLS 028	Nicely Does It/We Don't Need You (p/s)	5

INSTANT AUTOMATONS

80	Deleted DEP 001	PETER PAINTS HIS FENCE (EP, gatefold p/s with inserts, numbered)	5
	(see also Tronics)		

INSTANT SUNSHINE

68	Page One POF 085	Here We Go Again/Methylated	7
68	Page One POL 007	LIVE AT TIDDY DOLS (LP)	20

INSTITUTE OF FORMAL RESEARCH

97	Bubblehead BH 005	VOLUME ONE: FILE UNDER SUBCONSCIOUS (CD, features Zoot Horn Rollo)	20
	(see also Mick Taylor, Chris Spedding)		

INSYNC VS MYSTERON

95	Peacefrog PF 033	AUDIBLE ILLUSION EP (12", plain sleeve)	10

INTELLIGENT COMMUNICATIONS

91	Jumpin' & Pumpin' 12TOT 15	PRINCIPLES OF MOTION EP (12", p/s)	10
	(see also Future Sound Of London)		

INTENSIVE CARE

84	Punishment Block CELL 1	COWARDS EP (p/s)	8
87	Back To Back BTB 001	REBBELS, ROCKETS AND RUBBERMEN (12", p/s)	12

INTENTIONS (U.S.)/Z.Z. HILL

66	Sue IEP 711	GIMME GIMME (EP, 2 tracks each by Intentions & Z.Z. Hill; 2 tracks mistakenly credited to Jackie Day on sleeve; some in p/s)	165/70

INTENTIONS (U.K.)

72	Pye 7N 45123	There's Nobody I'd Sooner Love/Hurry On Home	5

INTERNATIONAL CHRYSIS

94	PWL PWLT 303	Rebel Rebel (The Hole Mix)/Rebel Rebel (Extended Mix) (12", promo only)	10
	(see also Dead Or Alive)		

INTERNATIONAL RESCUE

90	Groovy Tunes GTE 1	So Way Down/I'm Doin' Fine (p/s, 500 only)	5
90	Davy Lamp DL 12	Yeah/Never Touch The Ground (p/s)	4

INTERNS (U.K.)

64	Philips BF 1320	Don't You Dare/Here There Everywhere	10
64	Philips BF 1345	Cry To Me/There's Love For You	12
66	Parlophone R 5479	Is It Really What You Want?/Just Like Me	25
67	Parlophone R 5586	Ray Of Sunshine/Please Say Something Nice	7
	(see also Shadows)		

INTERNS (Jamaica)

70	Jackpot JP 729	See You At Sunrise/LITTLE WONDER: Out Of Reach (B-side actually "Just Out Of Reach" by John Holt)	7
	(see also Viceroys, Bob Marley & Wailers)		

INTERPLAY

82	Carrere CAR 211	Pretty Face/Terminal Vision (p/s)	4

INTESTINES

81	Altern. Capitalists ACS 1	Life In A Cardboard Box/New Recruit/Anyway (p/s)	6
	(see also Butcher)		

IN THE NURSERY

84	Paragon VIRTUE 5	Witness To A Scream/1984 (p/s)	20
85	New European BADVC 55	Sonority — A Strength (12" EP)	12
85	Sweatbox SOX 008	Temper/Breach Birth/Joaquin/Arm Me Audacity (12", p/s)	9
87	Sweatbox SOX 019	Trinity: Elegy/Trinity: Elegy (Reprise)/Blind Me (12", p/s with inner sleeve)	8
87	Sweatbox SOX 027	Compulsion/Libertaire (12", p/s)	7
83	Paragon VIRTUE 2	WHEN CHERISHED DREAMS COME TRUE (mini-LP, silk-screened g/fold p/s)	40

INTO A CIRCLE

86	Arcadia ARC 001	Rise/And In Flames/Gabriel (12", p/s, as In Two A Circle)	8
	(see also Getting The Fear, Southern Death Cult)		

INTRA VEIN

79	Bum FP 001	Speed Of The City/Sick (printed PVC sleeve or stamped plain sleeve)	40/30
	(see also Veins)		

INTRIGUES

69	London HL 10293	In A Moment/Scotchman Rock	8
72	Janus 6146 008	To Make A World/Mojo Hanna	5

INTRUDERS

59	Top Rank JAR 158	Frankfurters And Sauerkraut/Creepin'	5
59	Top Rank JAR 158	Frankfurters And Sauerkraut/Creepin' (78)	10

INTRUDERS

66	London HL 10069	Up And Down The Ladder/United	25
69	Action ACT 4523	Slow Drag/So Glad I'm Yours	8
69	Ember EMB S 254	Cowboys To Girls/Turn Back The Hands Of Time	6
72	Ember EMB S 325	Cowboys To Girls/GOOD VIBRATIONS: Shake A Hand	6
85	Streetwave MKL 6	WHO DO YOU LOVE? (LP)	12

IN TUA NUA

85	Island IS 211	Take My Hand/Fire In My Heart (p/s)	4
85	Island 12IS 211	Take My Hand/Carry Thru/Fire In My Heart (12", gatefold p/s)	7
86	Mother MOTHER 1	Comin' Thru/Laughing At The Moon (p/s)	5

INVADERS (Jamaica)

67	Columbia Bluebeat DB 105	Limbo Girl/Soul Of The Jungle	8
68	Columbia Bluebeat DB 109	Stop Teasing/Invaders At The Carnival	8
68	Studio One SO 2044	Soulful Music/SOUL VENDORS: Happy Organ	20
71	G.G. GG 4527	Got To Go Home/PAULETTE & GEE: How Long Will You Stay?	6

INVADERS (U.K.)

70s	Jovian ZIT 2	Launderama/Plastic Nose	5

INVICTAS

64	United Artists UP 1013	Green Bow Tie/Touch Of Orchid	6

INVITATIONS (U.S.)

65	Stateside SS 453	Hallelujah/Written On The Wall	35
65	Stateside SS 478	What's Wrong With Me Baby?/Why Did My Baby Turn Bad?	50
70	Jay Boy BOY 24	How'd We Ever Get This Way?/Picking Up	5
72	Mojo 2092 055	What's Wrong With My Baby?/Why Did My Baby Turn Bad? (reissue)	5
74	Polydor 2066 366	Let's Love And Find Together/Love Has To Grow	10

INVITATIONS (Jamaica)

71	Crab CRAB 66	Birmingham Cat/Now You're On Your Own	6

INXS

81	RCA RCA 89	Just Keep Walking/Scratch (some in p/s)	45/15
83	Mercury INXS 1	Don't Change/You Never Used To Cry (p/s)	18
83	Mercury INXS 121	Don't Change/You Never Used To Cry/Golden Playpen (12", p/s)	30
83	Mercury INXS 2	The One Thing/The Sax Thing (p/s)	12
83	Mercury INXS 212	The One Thing (6.10)/Black And White (12", p/s)	18
83	Mercury INXS 222	The One Thing/Black And White/Here Comes II (12", p/s)	15
84	Mercury INXS 3	Original Sin/Jan's Song (live)/To Look At You (live) (p/s)	12
84	Mercury INXS 312	Original Sin/Original Sin (Extended Version)/Jan's Song (live)/To Look At You (live) (12", p/s)	20
84	Philips PH 2	I Send A Message/Mechanical (p/s, some in envelope pack with postcard & biography)	25/6
84	Philips PH 212	I Send A Message (Long Distance)/Mechanical/I Send A Message (Local Call) (12", p/s)	25
86	Mercury INXS 4	This Time/Original Sin (Long Version) (p/s)	5
86	Mercury INXSD 4	This Time/Original Sin (Extended Version)//Burn For You (Extended Mix)/Dancing On The Jetty (double pack)	10
86	Mercury INXS 412	This Time (live)/Original Sin (Extended Version) (live)/Burn For You (live)/Dancing On The Jetty (live) (12", p/s)	8
86	Mercury INXSC 5	What You Need/Sweet As Sin (p/s, sealed with bonus promo sampler cassette)	12
86	Mercury INXS 512	What You Need (Remix)/Sweet As Sin/What You Need (live)/The One Thing (live) (12", stickered p/s)	8
86	Mercury INXSD 512	What You Need (Remix)/Sweet As Sin/What You Need (live)//The One Thing (live)/Don't Change/Johnsons Aeroplane (12", double pack)	18
86	Mercury INXSD 6	Listen Like Thieves/Begotten//One X One/XS Verbiage (double pack)	8
86	Mercury INXSP 6	Listen Like Thieves/Begotten (flag-shaped picture disc)	15
86	Mercury INXS 612	Listen Like Thieves (Extended Remix)/Listen Like Thieves (Instrumental Remix)/Listen Like Thieves (live)/Begotten (12", p/s with poster)	8
86	Mercury INXSD 7	Kiss The Dirt/6 Knots/The One Thing (live)//This Time/Original Sin (Long Version) (double pack)	7
86	Mercury INXS 712	Kiss The Dirt/6 Knots/The One Thing (live)/The Spy Of Love (12", p/s)	7
87	Mercury INXCD 8	Need You Tonight/Mediate/I'm Coming (Home) (CD, card sleeve)	12
87	Mercury INXSP 9	New Sensation/Do Wot You Do (poster p/s)	5
87	Mercury INXSR 9	New Sensation/Do Wot You Do (picture disc)	7
87	Mercury INXSP 912	New Sensation/Do Wot You Do/Love Is (What I Say)/Same Direction (12", poster p/s)	10
87	Mercury INXSR 912	New Sensation (Extended Mix)/Love Is (What I Say)/Do Wot You Do (12", p/s)	8
87	Mercury INXCD 9	New Sensation/Do Wot You Do/Love Is (What I Say)/Same Direction (CD, card sleeve)	10
88	Mercury INXS 1010	Devil Inside/On The Rocks/Dancing On The Jetty/Shine Like It Does (live) (10", p/s)	8
88	Mercury INXCD 10	Devil Inside (Re-mix Version)/Devil Inside (7" Version)/On The Rocks/What You Need (CD, card sleeve)	10
88	Mercury INXSP 11	Never Tear Us Apart/Guns In The Sky (Kick Ass Remix) (poster pack)	5
88	Mercury INXS 1100	Never Tear Us Apart/Guns In The Sky (Kick Ass Remix) (picture disc)	6
88	Mercury INXS 1110	Never Tear Us Apart/Need You Tonight/Listen Like Thieves (Extended Vocal Remix)/Guns In The Sky (Kick Ass Mix) (10", white vinyl, stickered PVC sleeve)	8
88	Mercury INXSG 1112	Never Tear Us Apart/Guns In The Sky/Burn For You/Old World World New World (12", gatefold p/s)	8
88	Mercury INXCD 11	Never Tear Us Apart/Guns In The Sky (Kick Ass Remix)/This Time (CD)	10
88	Mercury 080 396-2	Never Tear Us Apart/Guns In The Sky (Kick Ass Remix)/Different World (7" Mix) (CD Video)	12

88	Mercury INXSG 12	Need You Tonight/Move On ('magic pack' p/s with 2 photocards) 7
88	Mercury INXCD 12	Need You Tonight (Mendelssohn Mix)/Move On/Original Sin/ Don't Change (CD) 7
88	Mercury 080 394-2	Need You Tonight/Tiny Daggers/Mediate/I'm Coming (Home)/ Need You Tonight (CD Video) 12
89	Mercury INXS 1322	Mystify/Biting Bullets/Shine Like It Does (live)/Never Tear Us Apart (live) (12", 'Global Tour' 'Special Sticker Pack', with poster & postcard) 8
89	Mercury INXCD 13	Mystify/What You Need (Extended Version)/Listen Like Thieves/ Devil Inside (Extended Remix) (CD) 8
89	Mercury 080 876-2	Mystify/Need You Tonight (Ben Liebrand Mix)/Shine Like It Does (live)/ Never Tear Us Apart (live)/Mystify (CD Video) 15
91	Mercury INXSM 16	By My Side/The Other Side ('magic pack' p/s) 5
92	Mercury INSXP 19	Heaven Sent/It Ain't Easy/Eleventh Revolution/Heaven Sent (Gliding Version) (12", picture disc, gatefold PVC sleeve with insert) 8
92	Mercury INSXP 20	Baby Don't Cry/Questions (Instrumental)/Ptar Speaks/Baby Don't Cry (Vocal & Ochestral Mix) (12", picture disc) 8
97	Mercury INXSJ 3012	Searchin' (Linslee Campbell R'n'B Mix)/(Linslee Campbell Mellow Mix) (12", printed labels, die-cut 'INXS' logo p/s, promo only) 12
97	Mercury INXSJ 3012	Searchin' (Linslee Campbell R'n'B Mix)/(Linslee Campbell Mellow Mix) (12", stamped white labels, plain titles die-cut sleeve, promo only) 15
97	Mercury INXSJJ 3012	Searchin' (Lead Station Main Mix)/(Lead Station Funk Work Mix)/ (Lead Station Wiggly Worm Mix)/(Lead Station Hydroponic Mix) (12", black title p/s, promo only) 12
97	Mercury INXCD 30	Searchin'/(Lead Station Radio Mix)/(Alex Reece Mix) (CD, part 1, withdrawn) 18
97	Mercury INXDD 30	Searchin' (CD, part 2, withdrawn) 18
97	Mercury INXSD 30	Searchin' (CD, part 3, withdrawn) 18
86	Mercury MERH 82	LISTEN LIKE THIEVES (LP, with bonus LP "The Swing" [MERL 39], gatefold sleeve) 15
87	Mercury MERHP 114	KICK (LP, picture disc) 12

IONA
| 78 | Silver Scales | CUCKOO (LP) . . . . 35 |
| 70s | Celtic Music CM 001 | IONA (LP) . . . . 35 |

DON IPPOLITO ORCHESTRA
| 55 | Parlophone MSP 6187 | Camptown Racer Mambo/Can't Do It Mambo . . . . 6 |

IPSISSIMUS
| 69 | Parlophone R 5774 | Hold On/Lazy Woman . . . . 35 |

IQ
82	Red Stripe LYN 12028/9	Beef In A Box/RE-FLEX: Praying To The Beat/ASTRAKHAN: And She Smiled/ JENNY JAY: Jane (flexidisc, sampler for "Melody Maker Playback Vol. 1" LP) 10
84	Jim White/IQ PROMO 101	Awake And Nervous/Through The Corridors (12", no p/s, 500 only) 35
84	Sahara IQ 1002	Barbell Is In/Just Changing Hands (p/s) 10
84	Sahara IQ 12 1002	Barbell Is In (Lizard Mix)/Dans Le Parc Du Chateau Noir (12", p/s) 15
84	IQFREEB 1	Hollow Afternoon (1-sided, Marquee gig freebie) 40
85	Sahara IQ 1003	Corners (Remix)/Thousand Days (p/s) 10
85	Sahara IQ 12 1003	Corners/Thousand Days/The Wake (12", p/s) 15
86	STAL Other Boxer 1	Nomzamo (Demo) (1-sided fan club single) 20
86	Sahara IQSD 1	It All Stops Here/Intelligence Quotient (shaped picture disc) 20
87	Squawk VER 30	Passing Strangers/Nomzamo (p/s) 5
87	Squawk VERX 30	Passing Strangers/Colourflow/No Love Lost (12", p/s) 8
87	RLOG Another Boxer 1	Fascination/The Bold Grenadier Pt. 1 (fan club single) 20
87	Squawk VER 34	Promises/Human Nature (Edit) (p/s) 5
87	Squawk VERX 34	Promises (Extended Remix)/Promises (7" Version)/ Human Nature (Edit) (12", p/s) 12
88	RLOG One More Boxer 1	A Different Magic Roundabout (Honest!)/The Big Balls Of Bert Christ (fan club single) 15
89	Squawk VER 42	Sold On You/Through My Fingers (p/s) 5
89	Squawk VERX 42	Sold On You/Through My Fingers/Wurensh (12", p/s) 8
89	Squawk VERCD 42	Sold On You/Through My Fingers/Promises (As Years Go By)/ Colourflow (CD, card sleeve) 10
92	MIMP 00000001	BLUBA NEENY NOO: Last Human Gateway (Acoustic Middle Section)/ A Bit Of Love Lost (CD, fan club single, 361 copies only) 20
82	private pressing	SEVEN STORIES INTO EIGHT (cassette, different coloured sleeves, 40 numbered copies only) 12-15
83	private pressing	SEVEN STORIES INTO EIGHT (cassette reissue, with different intro to "Intelligence Quotient") 10
83	MRC MAJ 1001	TALES FROM THE LUSH ATTIC (LP, 1,000 copies in pale or dark blue numbered sleeve) 20
84	COSL MAJ 1001	TALES FROM THE LUSH ATTIC (LP, reissue in brown sleeve) 15
84	private pressing	SEVEN STORIES INTO EIGHT (cassette, 2nd reissue, with studio version of "For Christ's Sake") 10
85	Sahara SAH 136	THE WAKE (LP) 15
85	STAL BOXER 1	NINE IN A POND IS HERE (2-LP, 1,000 copies only) 30
86	Samurai SAMRCD 136	THE WAKE (CD) 15
86	Sahara SAMRCD 1001	TALES FROM THE LUSH ATTIC (CD) 15
86	Samurai SAMR 045	LIVING PROOF (LP) 15
86	Samurai SAMRCD 045	LIVING PROOF (CD) 30
87	Squawk VERH 43	NOMZAMO (LP) 10
89	Squawk 836 429-1	ARE YOU SITTING COMFORTABLY? (LP) 10

(see also Niadem's Ghost)

IRISH ROVERS

67	Brunswick STA 8679	FIRST OF THE IRISH ROVERS (LP)	12
68	MCA MUPS 310	THE UNICORN (LP)	12
69	MCA MUPS 353	LIVERPOOL LOU (LP)	12
69	MCA MUPS 389	TALES TO WARM YOUR MIND (LP)	12
70	MCA MUPS 406	LIFE OF THE ROVER (LP)	12

IRON BUTTERFLY

68	Atlantic 584 188	Possession/Unconscious Power	6
69	Atlantic 584 254	Soul Experience/In The Crowds	6
70	Atlantic 2091 024	In-A-Gadda-Da-Vida/Termination	5
68	Atco 2465 015	HEAVY (LP)	22
69	Atlantic 587/588 116	IN-A-GADDA-DA-VIDA (LP)	18
69	Atco 228 011	BALL (LP, gatefold sleeve)	15
70	Atlantic 2400 014	LIVE (LP)	15
71	Atlantic 2401 003	METAMORPHOSIS (LP)	12
	(see also Ramatam)		

IRON MAIDEN

70	Gemini GMS 006	Falling/Ned Kelly	10

IRON MAIDEN

79	Rock Hard ROK 1	THE SOUNDHOUSE TAPES (EP, p/s)	75
80	EMI EMI 5032	Running Free/Burning Ambition (p/s)	25
80	EMI EMI 5065	Sanctuary/Drifter (live)/I've Got The Fire (live) (uncensored p/s)	30
80	EMI EMI 5065	Sanctuary/Drifter (live)/I've Got The Fire (live) (censored p/s)	15
80	EMI EMI 5105	Women In Uniform/Invasion (p/s)	18
80	EMI 12EMI 5105	Women In Uniform/Phantom Of The Opera (live)/Invasion (12", p/s)	12
81	EMI EMI 5145	Twilight Zone/Wrathchild (p/s)	12
81	EMI EMI 5145	Twilight Zone/Wrathchild (p/s, red or clear vinyl)	25
81	EMI EMI 5145	Twilight Zone/Wrathchild (p/s, brown vinyl mispressing)	150
81	EMI TCEMI 5145	Twilight Zone/Wrathchild (cassette)	8
81	EMI EMI 5184	Purgatory/Genghis Khan (p/s)	30
81	EMI 12EMI 5219	MAIDEN JAPAN EP (12" EP, p/s)	12
82	EMI EMI 5263	Run To The Hills/Total Eclipse (p/s)	4
82	EMI EMIP 5263	Run To The Hills/Total Eclipse (picture disc)	12
82	EMI EMI 5287	The Number Of The Beast/Remember Tomorrow (live) (p/s)	4
82	EMI EMI 5287	The Number Of The Beast/Remember Tomorrow (live) (p/s, red vinyl)	10
83	EMI EMI 5378	Flight Of Icarus/I've Got The Fire (p/s)	4
83	EMI 12EMIP 5378	Flight Of Icarus/I've Got The Fire (12", picture disc)	15
83	EMI EMI 5397	The Trooper/Cross-Eyed Mary (p/s)	4
83	EMI EMI 5397	The Trooper/Cross-Eyed Mary (soldier-shaped picture disc)	20
84	EMI EMI 5489	2 Minutes To Midnight/Rainbow's Gold (p/s)	4
84	EMI 12EMI 5489	2 Minutes To Midnight/Rainbow's Gold/Mission From 'Arry (12", picture disc)	15
84	EMI EMI 5502	Aces High/King Of Twilight (p/s)	4
84	EMI 12EMIP 5502	Aces High/King Of Twilight/The Number Of The Beast (live) (12", picture disc)	15
85	EMI 12EMIP 5532	Running Free (live)/Sanctuary (live)/Murders In The Rue Morgue (live) (12", picture disc)	10
85	EMI EMI 5542	Run To The Hills (live)/Phantom Of The Opera (live) (with Xmas card)	8
85	EMI 12EMIP 5542	Run To The Hills (live)/Phantom Of The Opera (live)/ Losfer Words (The Big 'Orra) (live) (12", picture disc)	12
86	EMI EMIP 5583	Wasted Years/Reach Out (computer-shaped picture disc)	15
86	EMI 12EMI 5583	Wasted Years/Reach Out/Sheriff Of Huddersfield (12", p/s)	8
86	EMI EMI 5589	Stranger In A Strange Land/That Girl (p/s)	5
86	EMI EMI 5589	Stranger In A Strange Land/That Girl (foldout poster p/s)	6
86	EMI 12EMIP 5589	Stranger In A Strange Land/That Girl/Juanita (12", picture disc)	15
88	EMI EMS 49	Can I Play With Madness/Black Bart Blues (p/s, with sticker & transfer)	5
88	EMI EMP 49	Can I Play With Madness/Black Bart Blues (shaped picture disc)	10
88	EMI CDEM 49	Can I Play With Madness/Black Bart Blues/Massacre (CD)	10
88	EMI EMP 64	The Evil That Men Do/Prowler '88 (shaped picture disc)	8
88	EMI 12EMS 64	The Evil That Men Do/Prowler '88/Charlotte The Harlot '88 (12", poster p/s)	8
88	EMI CDEM 64	The Evil That Men Do/Prowler '88/Charlotte The Harlot '88 (CD, picture disc)	8
88	EMI EMS 79	The Clairvoyant (live)/The Prisoner (live) (clear vinyl, poster p/s)	4
88	EMI EMP 79	The Clairvoyant (live)/The Prisoner (live) (shaped picture disc)	8
88	EMI CDEM 79	The Clairvoyant (live)/The Prisoner (live)/Heaven Can Wait (live) (CD, picture disc)	8
89	EMI EM 117	Infinite Dreams (live)/Killers (live) (with free patch)	4
89	EMI EMPD 117	Infinite Dreams (live)/Killers (live) (shaped picture disc with insert)	7
90	EMI 12EMP 158	Holy Smoke/All In Your Mind/Kill Me Ce Soir (12" picture disc with insert)	8
90	EMI 12EMP 158	Holy Smoke/All In Your Mind/Kill Me Ce Soir (12", gold vinyl test pressing, promo only)	120
90	EMI EMPD 171	Bring Your Daughter ... To The Slaughter/I'm A Mover (picture disc 'brain' pack)	5
90	EMI 12EMPD 171	Bring Your Daughter ... To The Slaughter/I'm A Mover/ Communication Breakdown (12", picture disc, die-cut sleeve)	8
92	EMI 12EMP 229	Be Quick ...Or Be Dead/Nodding Donkey Blues/Space station No.5 (12" picture disc, with insert)	7
92	EMI EMPD 263	Fear Of The Dark (live)/Hooks In You (live) (shaped picture disc)	7
92	EMI EMPD 263	Fear Of The Dark (live)/Hooks In You (live) (shaped picture disc, mispressing, B-side plays "Tailgunner" [live])	10

MINT VALUE £

ALBUMS

80	EMI EMC 3330	IRON MAIDEN (LP, some with poster)	18/12
82	EMI EMCP 3400	THE NUMBER OF THE BEAST (LP, picture disc)	30
84	EMI POWERP 1	POWERSLAVE (LP, picture disc)	30
88	EMI EMDP 1006	SEVENTH SON OF A SEVENTH SON (LP, picture disc, with banner)	15
90	EMI EMPD 1017	NO PRAYER FOR THE DYING (LP, picture disc, die cut sleeve)	12
90	EMI (no cat. no.)	NO PRAYER FOR THE DYING (CD, with interview cassette, photos & bio, promo only)	75
90	EMI (no cat. no.)	THE FIRST TEN YEARS — UP THE IRONS (10 x 12" double packs, box set available by mail order with tokens from records)	65
90	EMI (no cat. no.)	THE FIRST TEN YEARS — UP THE IRONS (10 x CD, box set available by mail order with tokens from records)	65
96	EMI BEST 001	BEST OF THE BEAST (CD, Steve Harris interview disc, commercial CD, video, in 40cm x 30cm, flip-up 3D presentation box with 60-page book, 2 photographs, biography, promo only)	125
99	EMI EDHUNTER 666	ED HUNTER DEMO (CD-Rom, card p/s)	25

(see also Bruce Dickinson, A.S.A.P., Di'Anno, Gogmagog, Samson, Urchin, Xero, Lionheart, Pat Travers, Stratus, Nicko McBrain, Money, White Spirit)

NEVILLE IRONS

68	Blue Cat BS 104	Soul Glide/DYNAMICS: My Friends	25

(see also Neville Hinds)

IRON VIRGIN

74	Deram DM 416	Rebels Rule/Ain't No Clown	5

I ROY

(see under 'R')

WELDON IRVINE

75	Strata East SES 19749	IN HARMONY (LP)	12

LONNIE IRVING

60	Melodisc MEL 1546	Pinball Machine/I Got Blues On My Mind	18

(BIG) DEE IRWIN

64	Stateside SS 261	Donkey Walk/Someday You'll Understand Why	10
64	Colpix PX 11040	Heigh-ho/It's My Birthday	6
64	Colpix PX 11050	Personality/It's Only A Paper Moon	6
65	Stateside SS 450	You Satisfy My Needs/I Wanna Stay Right Here With You	50
68	Minit MLF 11013	I Can't Stand The Pain/My Hope To Die Girl (as Dee Irwin)	6

BIG DEE IRWIN & LITTLE EVA

63	Colpix PX 11010	Swinging On A Star/Another Night With The Boys (Little Eva uncredited)	6
64	Colpix PX 11021	I Wish You A Merry Christmas/Christmas Song	6
63	Colpix PXE 301	SWINGING ON A STAR (EP)	18
65	Golden Guinea GSGL 10497	SWINGING ON A STAR (LP)	15

(see also Little Eva, Suzi & Big Dee Irwin)

DAVID ISAACS

66	Island WI 261	I'd Rather Be Lonely/See That Man	15
68	Trojan TR 616	Place In The Sun/UPSETTER ALL STARS: Handy-Cap	18
69	Upsetter US 302	Good Father/SLIM SMITH: What A Situation	8
69	Upsetter US 305	I've Got Memories/I'm Leaving	8
69	Upsetter US 311	He'll Have To Go/Since You're Gone	8
69	Upsetter US 319	Who To Tell/BUSTY BROWN: I Can't See Myself Cry	8
69	Punch PH 6	I Can't Take It Anymore/LLOYD DOUGLAS: Anyway	7
71	Punch PH 84	You'll Be Sorry/Knock Three Times	7
71	Bullet BU 459	Just Enough/ROY PATIN: Standing (B-side actually by Roy Panton)	7
71	Tropical AL 006	Love Has Join Us/MAX ROMEO: Cross Over The Bridge (correct title for A-side is 'Love Has Joined Us')	6
73	Upsetter US 400	Stranger On The Shore/DILLINGER: John Devour	20
73	Bread BR 1118	Just Enough/We Are Neighbours	6

(see also Upsetters)

GREGORY ISAACS

70	Escort ERT 833	While There Is Life/HARRY YOUNG: Come On Over	6
70	Success RE 914	Too Late/KINGSTONIANS: You Can't Wine	6
71	Big Shot BI 584	Lonely Man/RUPIE EDWARDS ALL STARS: Lonely Man Version	6
73	Ackee ACK 522	I'm Coming Home/Version	5
73	Green Door GD 4054	Lonely Soldier/IMPACT ALL STARS: Version	6
74	Pyramid PYR 7012	Innocent People Cry/Version	5
74	Attack ATT 8081	Don't Go/Dubwise	5
75	Camel CA 2008	Lonely Days/Version	5
75	Bullet BU 555	Lonely Days/Version	5
75	Trojan TRLS 102	IN PERSON (LP)	15

(Joel Marvin, I Roy)

IKE ISAACS

74	Decca Eclipse ECS 2163	FOURTEEN GREAT T.V. THEMES (LP)	12

ISCA FAYRE

76	Candle CAN 761	THEN AROUND ME YOUNG AND OLD (LP)	15

JON ISHERWOOD

70	Decca LK/SKL 5051	A LAUGHING CRY (LP)	15

ANDY ISHMAEL

70s	Myrrh MYR 1005	READY SALTED (LP)	15

MINT VALUE £

ISLAND BOYS
58	London RE-R 1122	GO CALYPSO NO. 1 (EP)	8
58	London RE-R 1123	GO CALYPSO NO. 2 (EP)	8
58	London RE-R 1124	GO CALYPSO NO. 3 (EP)	8

ISLANDERS
59	Top Rank JAR 215	The Enchanted Sea/Pollyanna	7
60	Top Rank JAR 305	Blue Train/Tornado	7

ISLANDERS
65	Fontana TF 577	It Ain't Me Babe/Four Strong Winds	7
65	Fontana TF 605	Walkin' Away/Roberta Let Your Hair Hang Down	5

JIMMY ISLE
59	London HLS 8832	Diamond Ring/I've Been Waiting	60
59	London HLS 8832	Diamond Ring/I've Been Waiting (78)	50
60	Top Rank JAR 274	Billy Boy/Oh Judy	10

ISLEY BROTHERS
59	RCA RCA 1149	Shout (Parts 1 & 2)	18
59	RCA RCA 1149	Shout (Parts 1 & 2) (78)	200
60	RCA RCA 1172	Respectable/I'm Gonna Knock On Your Door	18
60	RCA RCA 1190	How Deep Is The Ocean/He's Got The Whole World In His Hands	15
60	RCA RCA 1213	Tell You Who/Say You Love Me Too	15
62	Stateside SS 112	Twist And Shout/Spanish Twist	12
62	Stateside SS 132	Twistin' With Linda/You Better Come Home	10
63	Stateside SS 218	Nobody But Me/I'm Laughing To Keep From Crying	12
63	United Artists UP 1034	Tango/She's Gone	10
64	United Artists UP 1050	Shake It With Me Baby/Stagger Lee	10
64	Atlantic AT 4010	The Last Girl/Looking For A Love	15
66	Tamla Motown TMG 555	This Old Heart Of Mine (Is Weak For You)/There's No Love Left (1st press has narrow print on label; re-pressed 1968 with wider print)	12/6
66	Tamla Motown TMG 566	Take Some Time Out For Love/Who Could Ever Doubt My Love	20
66	Tamla Motown TMG 572	I Guess I'll Always Love You/I Hear A Symphony (1st pressing with narrow print)	20/6
67	Tamla Motown TMG 606	Got To Have You Back/Just Ain't Enough Love	15
68	Tamla Motown TMG 652	Take Me In Your Arms (Rock Me A Little While)/Why When Love Is Gone	12
69	Tamla Motown TMG 683	I Guess I'll Always Love You/It's Out Of The Question	5
69	Tamla Motown TMG 693	Behind A Painted Smile/One Too Many Heartaches	5
69	Major Minor MM 621	It's Your Thing/Don't Give It Away	7
69	Tamla Motown TMG 708	Put Yourself In My Place/Little Miss Sweetness	7
69	Major Minor MM 631	I Turned You On/I Know Who You Been Socking It To	5
69	Tamla Motown TMG 719	Take Some Time Out For Love/Who Could Ever Doubt My Love (reissue)	6
70	Stateside SS 2162	Was It Good To You?/I Got To Get Myself Together	5
71	Stateside SS 2188	Warpath/I Got To Find Me One	7
71	Stateside SS 2193	Love The One You're With/He's Got Your Love	5
73	Tamla Motown TMG 877	Tell Me It's Just A Rumour, Baby/Save Me From This Misery	5
73	Epic EPC 1980	The Highways Of My Life/Don't Let Me Be Lonely Tonight	5
74	Epic EPC 2803	Need A Little Taste Of Love/If You Were There	5
76	DJM DJS 640	Twist And Shout/Time After Time (reissue)	5
79	RCA PC 9411	Shout/Respectable/Tell Me Who (12", p/s)	8
64	RCA RCX 7149	THE ISLEY BROTHERS (EP)	60
60	RCA RD 27165/SF 7055	SHOUT (LP, mono/stereo)	50/65
64	United Artists ULP 1064	THE FAMOUS ISLEY BROTHERS — TWISTING AND SHOUTING (LP)	40
66	Tamla Motown TML 11034	THIS OLD HEART OF MINE (IS WEAK FOR YOU) (LP, mono/stereo)	25/30
68	T. Motown (S)TML 11066	SOUL ON THE ROCKS (LP)	35
69	Major Minor SMLP 59	IT'S OUR THING (LP)	15
69	T. Motown (S)TML 11112	BEHIND A PAINTED SMILE (LP, mono/stereo)	22/18
70	Stateside SSL 10300	THE BROTHERS: ISLEY (LP)	15
70	RCA Intl. INTS 1098	SHOUT (LP)	12
73	M.F.P. MFP 50014	THE ISLEY BROTHERS (LP)	12
73	Epic EPC 65740	3 + 3 (LP, gatefold sleeve)	12
74	Epic EPC 80317	LIVE IT UP (LP)	12
75	Epic EPC 69139	THE HEAT IS ON (LP)	12
76	Epic EPC 81268	HARVEST FOR THE WORLD (LP)	12

ISOLATION
73	Riverside HASLP 2083	ISOLATION (LP, private pressing with insert)	600

ISOTOPE
74	Gull GULP 1002	ISOTOPE (LP)	12
74	Gull GULP 1006	ILLUSION (LP)	12
75	Gull GULP 1017	DEEP END (LP)	12

ISRAELITES
69	Downtown DT 413	Moma Moma/Melody For Two	6
69	Downtown DT 433	Seven Books/Chaka Beat	6
70	J-Dan JDN 4410	Can't Help From Crying/Can't Get Used To Losing You	8

(see also Music Doctors)

ITALS (U.K.)

71	Black Swan BW 1404	Dawn Patrol/Whisky Bonga	8
71	Black Swan BW 1407	Judgement Rock (actually by Charlie Ace)/Night West.	6

ITALS (Jamaica)

67	Giant GN 8	New Loving (with Soul Brothers)/I Told You Little Girl	15
67	Giant GN 12	Don't Throw It Away/Make Up Your Mind (both with Carib-Beats)	15
71	Big BG 325	Ba-Da-Doo-Ba-Dey/RUPIE EDWARDS ALL STARS: Version	15

(see also Alton Ellis, Honeyboy)

IT BITES

86	Virgin VS 839	All In Red/Heartbreaker (p/s)	5
86	Virgin VS 839-12	All In Red (Full Version)/All In Red (7")/Heartbreaker (12", p/s)	7
86	Virgin VSD 872	Calling All The Heroes/Strange But True//All In Red/Heartbreaker (double pack)	6
86	Virgin VSP 872	Calling All The Heroes/Strange But True (picture disc)	15
86	Virgin VSD 896	Whole New World/Black December//Calling All The Heroes (live)/ Screaming On The Beaches (live) (double pack)	5
86	Virgin VS 89612	Whole New World/Black December (12", p/s)	10
87	Virgin MIKE 94112	The Old Man And The Angel (12" Version)/Castles (12" Version)/The Old Man And The Angel (7")/Calling All The Heroes (Full Length) (CD, gatefold p/s)	8
88	Virgin VSP 983-12	Kiss Like Judas (Extended Mix)/Staring At The Whitewash/ Kiss Like Judas (7") (12", giant poster pack)	8
88	Virgin CDEP 21	Kiss Like Judas/Staring At The Whitewash/ Kiss Like Judas (12" Extended Mix) (CD)	8
88	Virgin VSS 1065	Midnight/You'll Never Go To Heaven (live) (square picture disc)	20
88	Virgin VSCD 1065	Midnight (7" Version)/You'll Never Go To Heaven (live)/ Midnight (Extended Version) (CD)	8
89	Virgin VSS 1184	Still Too Young To Remember/Vampire (shaped picture disc)	20
89	Virgin VST 1184	Still Too Young To Remember (7" Version)/(Full Length Version)/Vampire/ I'll Meet You In Spring (12", p/s)	10
89	Virgin VSCDX 1184	Still Too Young To Remember (7" Version)/(Full Length Version)/Vampire/ I'll Meet You In Spring (3" CD, 'pyramid'-shaped card sleeve)	8
89	Virgin VSCDT 1184	Still Too Young To Remember (7" Version)/(Full Length Version)/Vampire/ I'll Meet You In Spring (CD, card sleeve)	8
89	Virgin VSCD 1202	Sister Sarah/Heartbreaker/The Woman Is An Addict/Bullet In The Barrel (3" CD, card sleeve)	8
89	Virgin VSA 1215	Underneath Your Pillow (7")/Still Too Young To Remember (live)/Underneath Your Pillow (live) (10" picture disc, last track listed but not included)	10
89	Virgin VSCD 1215	Underneath Your Pillow (7" Version)/Still Too Young To Remember (live)/Underneath Your Pillow (live) (3" CD, card sleeve)	7
90	Virgin VSCD 1238	Still Too Young To Remember (7" Remix)/(Full Length Version)/ Having A Good Day/I'll Meet You In The Spring (3" CD, card sleeve)	7
89	Virgin CDVX 2591	Eat Me In St. Louis (CD, with bonus 3" CD ["Having A Good Day"/ "Reprise"/"Bullet In The Barrel"])	15
91	Virgin VGD 3516	THANKYOU AND GOODNIGHT (mini-LP, with bonus picture disc LP, in die-cut sleeve, sealed)	10

ITHACA

73	Merlin HF 6	A GAME FOR ALL WHO KNOW (LP, with insert)	600
93	Background	A GAME FOR ALL WHO KNOW (LP, reissue)	15

(see also Friends, Alice Through The Looking Glass, Agincourt, Tomorrow Come Someday, BBC Radiophonic Workshop)

IT'S A BEAUTIFUL DAY

69	CBS 4457	White Bird/Wasted Union Blues	8
70	CBS 4933	Soapstone Mountain/Do You Remember The Sun.	5
73	CBS 1625	Ain't That Lovin' You Baby/Time	5
69	CBS 63722	IT'S A BEAUTIFUL DAY (LP, gatefold sleeve)	15
70	CBS 64065	MARRYING MAIDEN (LP)	15
72	CBS 64314	CHOICE QUALITY STUFF — ANYTIME (LP)	15
73	CBS 64929	LIVE AT CARNEGIE HALL (LP)	12
73	CBS 65483	TODAY (LP).	12

IT'S IMMATERIAL

80	The Hit Machine HIT 001	Young Man (Seeks Interesting Job)/Doosha (A Success Story) (p/s)	4

IVAN

58	Coral Q 72341	Real Wild Child/Oh, You Beautiful Doll	275
58	Coral Q 72341	Real Wild Child/Oh, You Beautiful Doll (78)	150

(see also Jerry Allison, Crickets)

MINT VALUE £

JOHN-JOHN IVAN
67	United Artists UP 1155	Trouble Mountain/Games Men Play	4

IVAN D. JUNIORS
63	Oriole CB 1874	On My Mind/Catch You If I Can	12

IVANS MEADS
65	Parlophone R 5342	The Sins Of A Family/A Little Sympathy	30
66	Parlophone R 5503	We'll Talk About It Tomorrow/The Bottle	15

BURL IVES
52	Brunswick 04928	Foggy Foggy Dew/Old Uncle Ned (78)	7
52	Brunswick 04957	The Parting Song/Diesel Smoke, Dangerous Curves (with Grady Martin) (78)	8
53	Brunswick 05148	I Know An Old Lady/The Hen Is In The Haymow (78)	8
54	Columbia SCMC 5	I've Got No Use For Women/River Of Smoke (export issue)	10
56	Brunswick 05510	Ballad Of Davy Crockett/Goober Peas	12
56	Brunswick 05551	Dying Stockman/Click Go The Shears	10
56	Brunswick 05604	The Bus Stop Song/That's My Heartstrings	7
56	Decca BM 31183	Marianne/Pretty Girl (with Trinidadies) (export issue)	12
62	Brunswick 05863	A Little Bitty Tear/Shanghied	5
63	Brunswick 05868	Funny Way Of Laughin'/Mother Wouldn't Do That	6
63	HMV POP 1178	Ugly Bug Ball/On The Front Porch	5
53	Brunswick LA 8552	BALLADS AND FOLK SONGS VOL. 2 (10" LP)	18
53	Brunswick LA 8583	BALLADS AND FOLK SONGS VOL. 1 (10" LP)	18
54	Brunswick LA 8633	FOLK SONGS — DRAMATIC AND HUMOROUS (10" LP)	18
54	Brunswick LA 8641	WOMEN (10" LP)	18
55	Brunswick LAT 8048	CORONATION CONCERT (LP)	15
56	Brunswick LA 8739	AUSTRALIAN FOLK SONGS (10" LP)	18
56	Brunswick LAT 8142	DOWN TO THE SEA IN SHIPS (LP)	15
60	Brunswick LAT 8344	SONGS OF IRELAND (LP)	12
61	Brunswick LAT 8381	THE VERSATILE BURL IVES (LP)	12
62	Brunswick LAT 8395	SONGS OF THE WEST (LP)	12
62	Brunswick LAT 8404	FUNNY WAY OF LAUGHIN' (LP, also stereo STA 3063)	12/15
63	Brunswick LAT 8517	SUNSHINE IN MY SOUL (LP)	12
63	Brunswick LAT/STA 8554	SINGIN' EASY (LP, mono/stereo)	12/15
64	Brunswick LAT 8591	PEARLY SHELLS (LP)	12
66	Brunswick LAT 8665	SOMETHING SPECIAL (LP)	12

IVEYS
68	Apple APPLE 5	Maybe Tomorrow/And Her Daddy's A Millionaire	35
69	Apple APPLE 14	Dear Angie/No Escaping Your Love (unreleased; Europe & Japan only)	
68	Apple SAPCOR 8	MAYBE TOMORROW (LP, unissued; Europe & Japan only)	
92	Apple SAPCOR 8	MAYBE TOMORROW (LP, reissue, g/fold sleeve & bonus 12" [SAPCOR 82])	20
92	Apple SAPCOR 8	MAYBE TOMORROW (CD)	20

(see also Badfinger)

IVOR & SHEILA
81	Eron 027	CHANGING TIMES (LP, with insert)	30

IVORIES
85	Kent TOWN 103	Please Stay/TOMMY HUNT: The Work Song	8

(see also Tommy Hunt)

JACKIE IVORY
66	Atlantic AT 4075	Hi-Heel Sneakers/Do It To Death	10

IVY LEAGUE
64	Piccadilly 7N 35200	What More Do You Want?/Wait A Minute	10
65	Piccadilly 7N 35222	Funny How Love Can Be/Lonely Room	6
65	Piccadilly 7N 35228	That's Why I'm Crying/A Girl Like You	6
65	Piccadilly 7N 35251	Tossing And Turning/Graduation Day	5
65	Piccadilly 7N 35267	Our Love Is Slipping Away/I Could Make You Fall In Love	5
66	Piccadilly 7N 35294	Running Round In Circles/Rain Rain Go Away	6
66	Piccadilly 7N 35326	Willow Tree/One Day	8
66	Piccadilly 7N 35348	My World Fell Down/When You're Young	6
67	Piccadilly 7N 35365	Four And Twenty Hours/Arrivederci Baby	6
67	Piccadilly 7N 35397	Suddenly Things/Tomorrow Is Another Day	6
67	Pye 7N 17386	Thank You For Loving Me/In The Not Too Distant Future	6
65	Piccadilly NEP 34038	FUNNY HOW LOVE CAN BE (EP)	20
65	Piccadilly NEP 34042	TOSSING AND TURNING (EP)	20
65	Piccadilly NEP 34046	THE HOLLY AND THE IVY LEAGUE (EP)	25
66	Piccadilly NEP 34048	OUR LOVE IS SLIPPING AWAY (EP)	35
65	Piccadilly NPL 38015	THIS IS THE IVY LEAGUE (LP)	35
67	Marble Arch MAL 741	SOUNDS OF THE IVY LEAGUE (LP)	12
69	Marble Arch MALS 821	TOMORROW IS ANOTHER DAY (LP)	12

(see also Carter-Lewis, White Plains, Edison Lighthouse, Flowerpot Men, Kestrels, One & One, Johnny Shadow, Perry Ford, First Class, Friends, Warm Sensations)

IVY THREE
60	London HLW 9178	Yogi/Was Judy There	12

CLUE J. & HIS BLUES BLASTERS
60	Blue Beat BB 15	Easy Snappin'/Goin' Home (with vocal by Theophilus Beckford)............ 12
61	Blue Beat BB 37	Lovers' Jive/Wicked And Dreadful (actually with Neville Esson)............ 12
61	Blue Beat BB 60	Little Willie/Pine Juice.. 12

DAVID J. (& J. WALKERS)
81	4AD AD 112	Nothing/Armour (as David Jay & René Halkett)
		(p/s, some with lyric sheet)................................. 8/4
83	Situation 2 SIT 26	Joe Orton's Wedding/The Gospel According To Fear (p/s)............. 5
83	Situation 2 SIT 26T	Joe Orton's Wedding/Requiem For Joe/The Gospel According To Fear/
		Point Of Departure (12", p/s)............................... 7
83	Glass GLASS 031	The Promised Land/Saint Jackie (as David J. & J. Walkers) (p/s)........ 4
83	Glass GLASS 12031	The Promised Land/Saint Jackie/A Seducer, A Doctor,
		A Card You Cannot Trust (12", p/s, as David J. & J. Walkers)......... 7
84	Glass GLASS 039	I Can't Shake This Shadow Of Fear/War Game (p/s).................. 4
(see also Bauhaus)		

HARRY J. ALL STARS
(see under 'H')

TONY J.
| 75 | Stonehouse 001 | Telephone Line/Telephone Version........................... 5 |

BILLY JACK (& CIMARONS)
70	Grape GR 3018	Let's Work Together/CORPORATION: Jam Monkey................. 7
70	Big Shot BI 558	Once A Man/Soul Mood (as Billy Jack & Cimarons)............... 7
70	Big Shot BI 559	Bet Your Life I Do/CANDY & CIMARONS: Ace Of Hearts........... 7
(see also Candy)		

BOBBY JACK
| 59 | Top Rank JAR 190 | Tempting Me/Early Mornin'................................ 5 |

JACK (Bernard) & BEANSTALKS
| 69 | Supreme SUP 203 | Work It Up/Chatty Chatty................................. 8 |
| (see also Kingstonians) | | |

JACKAL
| 86 | Crim. Damage CRI 12-134 | Underneath The Arches/Thunder Machine (12", p/s)............. 10 |
| (see also Renegade Soundwave) | | |

JACKIE & BRIDIE
68	Major Minor MM 562	Come Me Little Son/We Only Needed Time..................... 5
64	Fontana TL 5212	HOLD BACK THE DAWN (LP)................................ 18
70	Concord CONS 1002	FOLK WORLD OF JACKIE AND BRIDIE (LP).................... 15
71	Galliard GAL 4009	THE PERFECT ROUND (LP)................................ 15
(see also Jacqueline & Bridie)		

JACKIE & DOREEN
| 65 | Ska Beat JB 209 | Adorable You/The New Vow................................ 15 |
| (see also Doreen Schaeffer, Jackie Opel) | | |

JACKIE (Edwards) & MILLIE (Small)
65	Island WI 253	This Is My Story/SOUND SYSTEM: Never Again................. 12
66	Island WI 265	My Desire/MILLIE: That's How Strong My Love Is............... 12
67	Island WIP 6012	In A Dream/Ooh Ooh.................................... 10
67	Island ILP 941	PLEDGING MY LOVE
		(LP, as Jackie Edwards & Millie Small)....................... 40
68	Island ILP 963	THE BEST OF JACKIE AND MILLIE VOLUME TWO (LP)............ 50
70	Trojan TTL 52	THE BEST OF JACKIE AND MILLIE VOLUME TWO
		(LP, reissue)... 12
70	Trojan TBL 155	JACKIE & MILLIE (LP)................................... 12
(see also Wilfred & Millicent, Jackie Edwards, Millie)		

JACKIE & RAINDROPS
(see under Jackie Lee & Raindrops)

JACKIE & ROY
58	Vogue V 9101	You Smell So Good/Let's Take A Walk Around The Block............. 100
58	Vogue V 9101	You Smell So Good/Let's Take A Walk Around The Block (78)......... 60
59	Vogue VE 1-70131	JACKIE AND ROY (EP).................................. 120
58	Vogue VA 1-60111	JACKIE AND ROY (LP).................................. 130

ALEXANDER JACKSON & TURNKEYS
| 65 | Sue WI 386 | The Whip/Tell It Like It Is (act. "Flea Pot"/"Sweetie Lester" by Lala Wilson)..... 25 |

BO WEAVIL JACKSON
| 52 | Jazz Collector L 81 | Some Scream High Yellow/Why Do You Moan? (78)............... 12 |
| 59 | Jazz Collector JDL 127 | Some Scream High Yellow/Why Do You Moan?.................. 5 |

BULL MOOSE JACKSON & HIS ORCHESTRA
| 53 | Vogue V 2129 | Nosey Joe/I Know Who Threw The Whisky In The Well (78)......... 20 |

CHRIS JACKSON
| 69 | Soul City SC 112 | I'll Never Forget You/Forever I'll Stay With You................. 20 |
| 70 | Soul City SC 120 | Since There's No Doubt/We Will Be Together (unissued) |

MINT VALUE £

CHUCK JACKSON

61	Top Rank JAR 564	I Don't Want To Cry/Just Once	30
62	Top Rank JAR 607	The Breaking Point/My Willow Tree	25
62	Stateside SS 102	Any Day Now/ED BRUCE: The Prophet	18
62	Stateside SS 127	I Keep Forgettin'/Who's Gonna Pick Up The Pieces	15
63	Stateside SS 171	Tell Him I'm Not Home/Getting Ready For The Heartbreak	15
64	Pye International 7N 25247	Beg Me/For All Time	15
64	Pye International 7N 25276	Any Day Now/The Prophet (reissue)	15
65	Pye International 7N 25287	Since I Don't Have You/Hand It Over	40
65	Pye International 7N 25301	I Need You/Chuck's Soul Brothers Twist	12
65	Pye International 7N 25321	If I Didn't Love You/Just A Little Bit Of Your Soul	12
66	Pye International 7N 25384	Chains Of Love/I Keep Forgettin'	40
67	Pye International 7N 25439	Shame On Me/Candy	12
68	Tamla Motown TMG 651	Girls, Girls, Girls/(You Can't Let The Boy Overpower) The Man In You	12
70	Tamla Motown TMG 729	Honey Come Back/What Am I Gonna Do Without You	8
73	Probe PRO 595	I Only Get The Feeling/Slowly But Surely	6
74	Probe PRO 617	I Can't Break Away/Just A Little Tear	6
75	All Platinum 6146 310	I've Got The Need/Beautiful Woman	6
75	Disco Demand DDS 116	These Chains Of Love/Any Day Now	5
85	Kent TOWN 104	Hand It Over/CANDY & KISSES: Mr Creator (withdrawn)	10
80s	Inferno SIN 1	Chains Of Love/Good Things Come To Those Who Wait/Hand It Over/ Any Day Now	5
66	Pye Intl. NPL 28082	TRIBUTE TO RHYTHM AND BLUES (LP)	30
68	T. Motown (S)TML 11071	CHUCK JACKSON ARRIVES! (LP)	40
69	T. Motown (S)TML 11117	GOIN' BACK TO CHUCK JACKSON (LP)	30
72	Probe SPB 1084	THROUGH ALL TIMES (LP)	18
74	Anchor ABCL 5040	THROUGH ALL TIMES (LP, reissue)	12

(see also Del[l]-Vikings)

CHUCK JACKSON & MAXINE BROWN

| 65 | Pye International 7N 25308 | Something You Got/Baby Take Me | 15 |
| 65 | Pye Intl. NPL 28091 | SAYING SOMETHING (LP) | 30 |

(see also Maxine Brown, Tammi Terrell)

DEON JACKSON

66	Atlantic AT 4070	Love Makes The World Go Round/You Said You Loved Me	10
66	Atlantic 584 012	Love Takes A Long Time Growing/Hush Little Baby	10
68	Atlantic 584 159	Ooh Baby/All On A Sunny Day	10
76	Contempo CS 9031	Love Makes The World Go Round/I Can't Go On	12

EARL JACKSON

| 76 | ABC ABC 4110 | Soul Self Satisfaction/Looking Thru' The Eyes Of Love | 5 |

GEORGE JACKSON

69	Capitol CL 15605	Find 'Em, Fool 'Em And Forget 'Em/My Desires Are Getting The Best Of Me	8
72	London HLU 10373	Aretha, Sing One For Me/I'm Gonna Wait	5
73	London HLU 10413	Let 'Em Know You Care/Patricia	6

GORDON JACKSON

69	Marmalade 598 010	Me And My Zoo/A Day At The Cottage	7
69	Marmalade 598 021	Song For Freedom/Sing To Me Woman	7
69	Marmalade 608 012	THINKING BACK (LP)	45

(see also Traffic)

HAROLD JACKSON & TORNADOES

| 58 | Vogue V 9105 | Move It On Down The Line (Parts 1 & 2) | 75 |
| 58 | Vogue V 9105 | Move It On Down The Line (Parts 1 & 2) (78) | 50 |

JACKIE JACKSON

| 74 | T. Motown STML 11249 | JACKIE JACKSON (LP) | 12 |

(see also Jacksons, Jackson 5)

JANET JACKSON

SINGLES

83	A&M AMS 8303	Come Give Your Love To Me/The Magic Is Working (p/s)	8
83	A&M AMSX 8303	Come Give Your Love To Me/The Magic Is Working (12", p/s)	12
83	A&M AM 112	Don't Mess Up This Good Thing/Young Love (p/s)	8
83	A&M AMX 112	Don't Mess Up This Good Thing/Young Love/Forever Yours (12", p/s)	12
86	A&M AMS 337	When I Think Of You/Come Give Your Love To Me//What Have You Done For Me Lately/Young Love (clear vinyl/picture disc double pack in PVC foldout cover)	12
86	A&M AMS 359	Control/Pretty Boy (p/s, with free cassette ["Nasty (Cool Summer Mix)"])	10
87	Breakout USAD 601	Let's Wait A While/Nasty (Cool Summer Mix Pt. 1)//Nasty (Original Mix)/ Control/Let's Wait A While (Remix)/Nasty (Cool Summer Mix Part 1 Fade) (picture disc/clear vinyl double pack in PVC foldout sleeve)	10
87	Breakout USAP 601	Let's Wait A While/Nasty (Cool Summer Mix Pt 1) (picture disc)	4
87	Breakout USAS 613	Funny How Time Flies (When You're Having Fun)/When I Think Of You (poster p/s)	5
89	Breakout USAS 663	Miss You Much/You Need Me (poster p/s)	4
89	Breakout USACD 663	Miss You Much (Mamma Mix 3.55)/Miss You Much (Mamma Mix 7.22)/ You Need Me (CD)	10
89	Breakout USAS 673	Rhythm Nation (7" Edit)/Rhythm Nation (C.H.R. Remix) (poster p/s)	4
89	Breakout USAPD 673	Rhythm Nation (12" House Nation Mix)/Rhythm Nation (12" United Mix)/ Rhythm Nation (United Dub) (12", picture disc)	7
89	Breakout USACD 673	Rhythm Nation (7" Edit)/(12" House Nation Mix)/(12" United Dub) (CD)	10
90	Breakout USAB 681	Come Back To Me (7" I'm Beggin' You Mix)/Alright (7" R&B mix) (box set with metal badge & foldout poster)	6
90	Breakout USAD 681	Come Back To Me (I'm Begging You Mix)/Alright (12" House Mix)/ Alright (Hip House Mix) (12", p/s with calendar poster)	7

90	Breakout USAF 681	Come Back To Me (Abandoned Heart Mix)/Alright (12" R&B Mix)/
		Alright (House Dub) (12", p/s) 7
90	Breakout USACD 681	Come Back To Me (7" I'm Beggin' You Mix)/Alright (7" R + B Mix)/
		Alright (7" House Mix With Rap) (CD) 10
90	Breakout USAP 684	Escapade (We've Got It Made 7")/Escapade (Housecapade 7")
		(picture disc with photo & discography) 5
90	Breakout USAS 693	Alright (House Mix)/Vuelve A Mi (Come Back To Me)
		(shaped picture disc with plinth in printed PVC sleeve) 8
90	A&M AMX 587	Black Cat (3 Snaps Up Mix)/Black Cat/1814 Megamix (Long Version)
		(12", with 4 postcards, leather boot badge & competition form) ... 7
95	AMPM 581 243-1	Runaway (J.R. Factory Mix)/(J.R. Tribal Mix)/When I Think Of You
		(Deep Dish Chocolate City Mix)/(Deep Dish Quiet Storm Dub)/
		(Dished Out Dub) (12", company sleeve) 8

PROMOS
95	AMPM AMPMDJ 25	Runaway (Factory Mix)/When I Think Of You (Heller & Farley Project Mix)/
		Runaway (Factory Dub)/When I Think Of You (Junior Trackhead Joint)/
		Runaway (Tribal Dub) (12", company sleeve) 10
96	AMPM 581 697-1	The Best Things In Life Are Free (The S-Man Salsoul Vibe)/(K-Klass 12")/
		(K-Klass 7")/(Roger's Nasty Dub)/(Roger's III Dub)/(Roger's Deep Dub)/
		(Bonus Beats) (12", with Luther Vandross, double pack, co. sleeve) ... 10
97	Virgin VSTXDJ 1666	Got 'Til It's Gone (Def Club Mix)/(Armand Van Helden Speedy Garagez Mix)
		(Def The Bass Mix)/(Def Instrumental)/(Armand Van Helden Bonus Beats)
		(12", double pack, title stickered sleeve) 15
97	Virgin VSTDJ 1670	Together Again: Tony Humphries Remixes/(Tony Humphries Club Mix)/
		(Tony Humphries 12" Edit Mix)/(Tony Humphries FBI Dub)/
		(Tony Humphries White And Black Dub) (12", title stickered sleeve) .. 8
97	Virgin VSTDJ 1683	I Get Lonely (Janet Vs Jason — The Club Remix)/(Janet Vs Jason —
		The Remix Sessions — Part 2)/(Jason's Special Sauce Dub)/
		(LP Version) (12", title stickered sleeve) 8

ALBUMS
83	A&M AMLH 64907	JANET JACKSON (LP) 10
84	A&M AMA 4962	DREAM STREET (LP) 10
89	A&M AMAP 3920	RHYTHM NATION 1814 (LP, picture disc, die-cut sleeve) 10
89	A&M AMAD 3920	RHYTHM NATION 1814 (CD, picture disc, no'd gatefold sleeve & poster) ... 15
93	Virgin CDVX 2720	JANET. (2-CD, with 40-page colour photo & lyric booklet) 20

JANET JACKSON & CLIFF RICHARD
84	A&M AM 210	Two To The Power Of Love/JANET JACKSON: Rock'n'Roll (p/s) 18
84	A&M AMX 210	Two To The Power Of Love/JANET JACKSON: Rock'n'Roll/Don't Mess Up
		This Good Thing (12", p/s) 22

(see also Cliff Richard)

JERMAINE JACKSON
84	Epic JMJDJ 1	Tell Me I'm Not Dreamin' (Too Good To Be True) (with Michael Jackson)/
		Come To Me/Oh Mother (promo only) 30
85	Arista ARIST 609	Do What You Do/Tell Me I'm Not Dreamin' (Too Good To Be True)
		(last track with Michael Jackson) (p/s) 5
85	Arista ARIST 12609	Do What You Do/Tell Me I'm Not Dreamin' (Too Good To Be True)
		(last track with Michael Jackson) (12", p/s) 8

(see also Jacksons, Jackson 5, Michael Jackson)

JERRY JACKSON
| 63 | London HLR 9689 | Gypsy Eyes/Turn Back .... 18 |
| 66 | Cameo Parkway P 100 | It's Rough Out There/I'm Gonna Paint A Picture .... 125 |

JIM JACKSON
| 66 | RCA RCX 7182 | R.C.A. VICTOR RACE SERIES VOL. 7 (EP) .... 15 |

JIMMY JACKSON('S ROCK 'N' ROLL SKIFFLE)
57	Columbia DB 3898	California Zephyr/I Shall Not Be Moved 15
57	Columbia DB 3898	California Zephyr/I Shall Not Be Moved (78) 8
57	Columbia DB 3937	Sittin' In The Balcony/Good Morning Blues 25
57	Columbia DB 3937	Sittin' In The Balcony/Good Morning Blues (78) 10
57	Columbia DB 3957	River Line/Lonely Road 12
57	Columbia DB 3957	River Line/Lonely Road (78) 8
57	Columbia DB 3988	White Silver Sands/Build Your Love (On A Strong Foundation) (solo) ... 8
57	Columbia DB 3988	White Silver Sands/Build Your Love (On A Strong Foundation) (solo) (78) ... 8
58	Columbia DB 4085	Love-A Love-A Love A/Photographs (solo). 8
58	Columbia DB 4085	Love-A Love-A Love A/Photographs (solo) (78) 12
58	Columbia DB 4153	Swing Down, Sweet Chariot/This Little Light Of Mine (solo) 8
58	Columbia DB 4153	Swing Down, Sweet Chariot/This Little Light Of Mine (78, solo) ... 12
58	Columbia SEG 7750	ROCK 'N' SKIFFLE (EP) 50
58	Columbia SEG 7768	COUNTRY AND BLUES (EP) 60

J.J. JACKSON (& Greatest Little Soul Band In The Land)
67	Polydor 56718	But It's Alright/Do The Boogaloo 10
67	Strike JH 329	Come See Me/Try Me 10
67	Warner Bros WB 2082	Sho Nuff (Got A Good Thing Going)/Here We Go Again 7
68	Warner Bros WB 2090	Down, But Not Out/Why Does It Take So Long? 5
68	Warner Bros WB 6029	Courage Ain't Strength/You Do It 'Cause You Wanna 5
69	Warner Bros WB 7276	Ain't Too Proud To Beg/But It's Alright 5
71	Mojo 2092 014	But It's Alright/Do The Boogaloo 7
67	Strike JLH 104	J.J. JACKSON WITH THE GREATEST LITTLE SOUL BAND (LP) 20
69	MCA SKA 100	GREATEST LITTLE SOUL BAND (LP) 15
70	RCA Victor SF 8093	J.J. JACKSON'S DILEMMA (LP). 15

(see also Greatest Little Soul Band)

J.J. JACKSON/LINDA JONES
| 77 | Loma/Warners K 56271 | THIS IS LOMA — VOL. 7 (LP, 1 side each) .... 12 |

LEVI JACKSON
| 71 | Columbia DB 8807 | This Beautiful Day/Don't You Be A Sinner............................... 40 |

(see also Solomon King)

LLOYD JACKSON
| 71 | Pama Supreme PS 308 | Cracklin' Rosie/Little Deeds Of Kindness (B-side with Scorpions)............. 6 |

MAHALIA JACKSON
51	Vogue V 301	Since The Fire Started Burning In My Soul/In My Home
		Over There (78)... 8
52	Vogue V 305	I Do, Don't You/Silent Night, Holy Night (78)........................ 8
55	Philips BB 2005	A Rusty Old Halo/The Treasures Of Love (78, export issue)............. 10
58	Philips PB 869	For My Good Fortune/Have You Any Rivers........................ 5
58	Philips PB 869	For My Good Fortune/Have You Any Rivers? (78).................... 15
59	Philips PB 933	Trouble Of The World/Tell The World About This.................... 5
60	Philips PB 1040	Onward Christian Soldiers/The Lord's Prayer....................... 5
60	Vogue V 2418	The Lord's Prayer/Bless This House............................. 5
60	Top Rank JKP 2038	IN THE UPPER ROOM VOLUME 1 (EP)............................. 8
60	Top Rank JKP 2048	IN THE UPPER ROOM VOLUME 2 (EP)............................. 8
52	Vogue LDE 005	MAHALIA JACKSON (10" LP).................................. 25
59	Philips BBL 7289	NEWPORT 1958 (LP, also stereo SBBL 547).................... 12/15
60	Top Rank 30/006	JUST AS I AM (LP).. 15
60	Philips BBL 7362	GREAT GETTIN' UP MORNING (LP)............................. 12
60	Philips BBL 7391	THE POWER AND THE GLORY (LP, also stereo SBBL 576)........... 12/15
60	Philips BBL 7435	COME ON CHILDREN LET'S SING (LP)........................... 15
61	Philips BBL 7456	I BELIEVE (LP, also stereo SBBL 610)....................... 12/15

MICHAEL JACKSON
SINGLES
72	Tamla Motown TMG 797	Got To Be There/Maria (You Were The Only One)................... 5
72	Tamla Motown TMG 816	Rockin' Robin/Love Is Here And Now You're Gone.................. 5
72	Tamla Motown TMG 826	Ain't No Sunshine/I Wanna Be Where You Are.................... 5
72	Tamla Motown TMG 834	Ben/You Can Cry On My Shoulder............................. 5
73	Tamla Motown TMG 863	Morning Glow/My Girl.................................... 5
74	Tamla Motown TMG 900	Music And Me/Johnny Raven................................ 5
75	Tamla Motown TMG 946	One Day In Your Life/With A Child's Heart..................... 5
75	Tamla Motown TMG 1006	Just A Little Bit Of You/Dear Michael......................... 5
79	Epic S EPC 7135	You Can't Win (Part 1)/You Can't Win (Part 2) (picture disc)......... 12
79	Epic 12EPC 7135	You Can't Win (Part 1)/You Can't Win (Part 2) (12").............. 10
79	Epic 12EPC 7763	Don't Stop 'Til You Get Enough/I Can't Help It (12")............... 8
79	Epic 12EPC 8206	Rock With You/Get On The Floor/You Can't Win (Extended)
		(12")... 8
81	Motown TMG 977	We're Almost There/We've Got A Good Thing Going (p/s)............. 4
81	Motown TMGT 977	We're Almost There (Album Version)/We've Got A Good Thing Going (12")...... 8
82	Epic EPCA 11-2729	The Girl Is Mine (with Paul McCartney)/
		Can't Get Outta The Rain (picture disc)....................... 15
83	Epic EPC 2906	GREATEST ORIGINAL HITS: Don't Stop 'Til You Get Enough/
		She's Out Of My Life/Off The Wall/Rock With You (EP)............. 15
83	Epic EPCA 40-2906	GREATEST ORIGINAL HITS: Don't Stop 'Til You Get Enough/
		She's Out Of My Life/Off The Wall/Rock With You (EP, cassette).............. 8
83	Motown TMG 986	Happy (Love Theme From 'Lady Sings The Blues')/We're Almost There
		(poster or standard p/s)................................ 8/4
83	Motown EPCA 112729	Happy (Love Theme From 'Lady Sings The Blues')/We're Almost There
		(picture disc)... 10
83	Motown TMGT 986	Happy (Love Theme From 'Lady Sings The Blues') (Album Version)/
		We're Almost There (12")................................. 7
83	Motown CTME 2035	MOTOWN FLIP HITS — MICHAEL JACKSON: One Day In Your Life/
		Got To Be There/Ben/Ain't No Sunshine (EP, cassette)............. 10
83	Motown M6077C	Got To Be There/Ben (cassette)............................. 6
83	Epic EPCA 3643	Thriller/JACKSONS: Things I Do For You (live) (poster p/s).......... 8
83	Epic TA 3643	Thriller (Album Version)/Thriller (Remix Short Version)/JACKSONS:
		Things I Do For You (live) (12", 'calendar' p/s)................. 50
83	Epic MJ 1 (1-9)	MICHAEL JACKSON'S 9 SINGLES PACK (9 x 7", p/s, each on red vinyl,
		in PVC foldout wallet)................................... 35
84	Motown TMGT 1342	Farewell My Summer Love (Extended)/Call On Me (12", die-cut sleeve)........ 8
84	Motown TMGT 1355	Girl You're So Together (Album Version)/Touch The One You Love/Ben/
		Ain't No Sunshine (12")................................... 8
84	Epic A 3910	P.Y.T. (Pretty Young Thing)/Working Day And Night (p/s, 2nd issue)....... 7
84	Epic EPC 450 127-4	THE 12" MIXES: Billie Jean/Beat It/Wanna Be Startin' Somethin'/Thriller/
		P.Y.T. (Pretty Young Thing) (cassette)....................... 8
84	Arista JMJDJ 1	Tell Me I'm Not Dreamin' (Too Good To Be True)/JERMAINE JACKSON:
		Come To Me/Oh Mother (promo only).......................... 25
87	Epic 650 202-0	I Just Can't Stop Loving You (with Siedah Garratt)/Baby Be Mine (poster p/s)... 10
87	Epic 650 202-6	I Just Can't Stop Loving You (with Siedah Garratt)/Baby Be Mine
		(12", p/s with poster)................................... 12
87	Epic 651 100-4	Bad (Dance Extended Mix)/Bad (Dub Version)/Bad (A Capella) (cassette)....... 7
87	Epic 651 155-6	Bad (Dance Extended Mix With False Fade)/Bad (7" Single Mix)/Bad
		(Dance Radio Edit)Bad (Dub)/Bad (A Cappella) (12", p/s, red vinyl)........ 15
87	Epic 651 275-7	The Way You Make Me Feel/The Way You Make Me Feel (Instrumental)
		(p/s, with competition leaflet, stickered sleeve)................ 5
87	Epic 651 275-3	The Way You Make Me Feel (7" Mix)/(A Cappella)/(Dance Radio Edit)/
		(Dub)/(Get Into The Groove —Put Either Side On The Turntable,
		Lower The Arm And See Which Your Needle Pix) (12, p/s, double-groove)...... 20
87	Epic 651 275-9	The Way You Make Me Feel (Dance Extended Mix)/The Way You Make Me
		Feel (Dub Version)/The Way You Make Me Feel (A Cappella) (CD, card p/s)...... 15
88	Epic 651 388-9	Man In The Mirror (Single Mix)/Man In The Mirror (Instrumental)
		(square-shaped picture disc)............................. 12

88	Epic 651 388-2	Man In The Mirror (4.55)/Man In The Mirror (Album Mix)/ Man In The Mirror (Instrumental) (CD, card sleeve). 15
88	Epic 651 388-2	Man In The Mirror/Man In The Mirror (Album Mix)/Man In The Mirror (Instrumental) (3" CD with adaptor, card sleeve) 18
88	Epic 651 546-7	Dirty Diana/Dirty Diana (p/s, with 13" cardboard figure). 6
88	Epic 652 864-6	Dirty Diana/Dirty Diana (Instrumental)/Bad (Extended Dance Mix With False Fade) (12", with tour poster p/s) 15
88	Epic 651 546-9	Dirty Diana (4.42)/Dirty Diana (Instrumental)/Bad (Dance Extended Mix Includes "False Fade") (CD, card p/s) 15
88	Epic 651 546-2	Dirty Diana (4.42)/Dirty Diana (Instrumental)/Dirty Diana (Album Version) (3" CD with adaptor, card p/s) 15
88	Epic MJ 5	THE MICHAEL JACKSON BAD SOUVENIR SINGLES PACK (5 x 7" square picture discs in foldout PVC wallet, with lyric book) 40
88	Epic 652 844-9	Another Part Of Me/(Instrumental) (p/s, with Bad tour backstage pass) 12
88	Epic 652 844-0	Another Part Of Me/Another Part Of Me (Instrumental) (poster p/s) 10
88	Epic 652 844-2	Another Part Of Me (Extended Dance Mix)/(Radio Edit)/(Drum Mix)/ (A Capella) (CD, card p/s). 18
88	Epic 652 844-3	Another Part Of Me (Extended Dance Mix)/(Radio Edit)/(Dub Mix)/ (Instrumental) (3" CD with adaptor, card p/s) 18
88	Epic 653 004-2	Another Part Of Me (Extended Dance Mix)/Another Part Of Me (Radio Edit) Another Part Of Me (Drum Mix)/Another Part Of Me (A Cappella) (CD, pic disc). . 30
88	Epic 653 026-0	Smooth Criminal/Smooth Criminal (Instrumental) (pack with 4 postcards). 15
88	Epic 653 026-8	Smooth Criminal (Extended Dance Mix)/Smooth Criminal ("Annie" Mix)/ Smooth Criminal (Radio Edit) (12", p/s) 7
88	Epic 653 170-6	Smooth Criminal (Extended Dance Mix)/Smooth Criminal Extended (Dance Mix Dub Mix)/Smooth Criminal (A Cappella) (12" w/'Moonwalker' advent calendar). . 20
88	Epic 653 026-2	Smooth Criminal (Extended Dance Mix)/Smooth Criminal ("Annie" Mix)/ Smooth Criminal (A Cappella) (CD, card p/s) 18
89	Epic 654 672-0	Leave Me Alone/Human Nature (pop-up p/s) 25
89	Epic 654 672-4	Leave Me Alone/Don't Stop 'Til You Get Enough/Human Nature (cassette, 'Moonwalker' fold-out card slip case). 8
89	Epic 654 672-2	Leave Me Alone (4.40)/Don't Stop 'Til You Get Enough (3.55)/Human Nature (4.05)/Wanna Be Startin' Something (Extended 6.30) (CD, card sleeve). 15
89	Epic 654 672-3	Leave Me Alone (4.40)/Don't Stop 'Til You Get Enough (6.04)/ Human Nature (4.05) (3" CD, gatefold card sleeve). 18
89	Tamla Motown MOTD7 0005	VINTAGE GOLD (3" CD EP, gatefold card sleeve, with Jackson 5). 10
89	Epic 654 947-9	Liberian Girl (Edit)/Girlfriend (star mobile foldout card pack) 15
89	Epic 654 947-4	Liberian Girl (Edit)/Girlfriend (cassette) 6
89	Epic 654 947-2	Liberian Girl (Edit 3.39)/Girlfriend/The Lady In My Life/Get On The Floor (CD, card p/s) 15
89	Epic 654 947-3	Liberian Girl (Edit 3.39)/Get On The Floor/Girlfriend (3" CD, g/fold card p/s). . . . 18
92	Epic 658 018-7	In The Closet (7" Edit)/The Mission (Radio Edit) (poster p/s). 4
92	Epic 658 179-7	Who Is It (Edit)/Rock With You (Masters At Work Remix) (with free die-cut portrait stand of Michael) 7
92	Epic MJ 4 (658 281-1/4)	TOUR SOUVENIR PACK (CD, 4-picture disc, box set with booklet) 40
92	Epic 658 360-7	Jam (7" Edit)/Beat It (Moby's Sub Mix) ('picture frame' pack with 2 prints). 7
92	Epic 658 360-2	Jam (7" Edit)/(Roger's Jeep Mix)/(Atlanta Techno Dub)/Wanna Be Startin' Somethin' (Brothers In Rhythm House Mix) (CD) 7
92	Epic 658 488-7	Heal The World (7" Edit)/She Drives Me Wild (poster p/s). 4
92	Epic 658 488-8	Heal The World (Album Version)/Wanna Be Startin' Somethin' (Brothers In Rhythm House Mix)/Don't Stop 'Til You Get Enough (Roger's Underground Solution/Rock With You (Masters At Work Remix) (12", p/s with poster) 7
92	Pepsi/Epic EPC 982789-4	Someone Put Your Hand Out/Dangerous Medley (promo only cassette). 8
93	Epic 659 069-7	Give In To Me/Dirty Diana (poster p/s) 4
93	Epic 659 222-7	Will You Be There (Edit)/Girlfriend (p/s, with poster). 4
96	Epic 662 950	They Don't Care About Us (jukebox issue, white labels, no p/s) 8
97	Epic 663 787	Stranger In Moscow (jukebox issue, white labels, no p/s) 8
97	Epic 664 796	History/Ghosts (jukebox issue, white labels, no p/s) 8
97	Epic	Smile (CD, withdrawn) 500

PROMOS

92	Epic XPR 1733	Remember The Time: (12" Main Mix)/(New Jack Mix)/(New Jack Main Mix)/ (Silky Soul 12" Mix)/(Silky Soul Dub)/(E-Smoov's Late Nite Mix) (12", company sleeve) 8
92	Epic XPR 1814	Jam: (More Than Enuff Mix)/(Roger's Club Mix)/(E-Smoov Jazzy Jam)/ (Atlanta Techno Mix)/(Roger's Underground Mix)/(Silky 12")/ (More Than Enuff Dub)/(Maurice's Jammin' Dub Mix)/(Roger's Club Dub)/ (Atlanta Techno Dub)/(Roger's Slam Jam Mix)/(Silky Dub)/(A Cappella Mix) (12", double pack, black & orange stickered white sleeve) 25
92	Epic XPR 1797	Who Is It (Patience Mix)/(Patience Beats)/(Most Patient Mix)/(HIS Mix)/ (The P-Man Dub) (12", company sleeve) 10
95	Epic XPR 2265	The Classic Remix Series: Wanna Be Startin' Something (Brothers In Rhythm Mix)/(Tommy D's Main Mix) (12", plain sleeve, sealed with title sticker) 15
95	Epic XPR 2266	DMC Megamix (15.40)/(11.18) (12", custom sleeve) 15
95	Epix XPR 2271	Earthsong (Hani Remixes): (Hani's Around The World Experience)/ (Hani's Club Experience)/(Hani's Extended Radio Experience)/ (Hani's Radio Experience) (12", yellow & blue title sleeve) 15
95	Epic XPR 2229	The Classic Remix Series: Rock With You (Frankie's Favorite Club Mix)/ (The Masters At Work Remix) (12", plain sleeve, sealed with title sticker). 12
95	Epic XPCD 7222	The Classic Remix Series: Rock With You (Frankie's Favorite Club Mix Radio Edit)/(Frankie's Favorite Club Mix) (CD). 20
95	Epic XPR 2184	Scream: (Classic Club Mix)/(DM R&B Extended Mix)/(Def Radio Mix)/ (Naughty Main Mix)/(Naughty Main Mix No Rap)/(Dave 'Jam' Hall's Extended Urban Remix)/(Pressurized Dub Part 1)/(Pressurized Dub Part 2)/ (Album Version)/(Single Edit No. 2)/(Naughty Pretty-Pella)/ (Naughty A Cappella) (12", double pack, red title sleeve). 20

MINT VALUE £

96	Epic XPR 2207	Mj Club Megamix (MJ Mega Remix)/(MJ Urban Megamix) (12", blue & purple title sleeve)	15
96	Epic XPR 3020	They Don't Care About Us (The Love To Infinity Mixes): Classic Paradise Mix/ Anthem Of Love/Classic Dub/Anthem Of love Dub/Hacienda Mix (12", p/s)	10
96	Epic XPR 3030	They Don't Care About Us (The R&B Mixes): Track Masters Remix/ Dallas Austin Main Mix/Charles' Full Dirty Mix/LP Edit/Love To Infinity's Walk In The Park/Track Masters' Instrumental (12", p/s)	10
96	Epic XPR 3033	The Classic Remix Series: Don't Stop Til You Get Enough (Roger's Underground Solution Mix)/Beat It (Moby's Sub Mix) (12", plain sleeve sealed with title sticker)	8
96	Epic XPR 3057	Stranger In Moscow (Todd Terry Remixes): (Tee's In House Dub Mix)/ (TNT Frozen Sun Mix)/(Album Version) (12", white title sleeve)	10
96	Epic XPR 3076	Stranger In Moscow (Hani's Remixes): (Hani's Num Club Mix)/ (Hani's Num Dub)/(Album Version (12", blue & yellow title sleeve)	10
96	Epic XPR 3073	Stranger In Moscow (The Basement Boys Remixes): (Basement Boys Dance Club Mix)/(Lonely Dub) (Album Version) (12", brown title sleeve).	10
96	Epic SAMPCD 3598	This Time Around (DM Radio Mix)/(Dallas Radio Remix)/(Maurice's Club Around Radio Mix)/(Maurice's Hip Hop Around Mix)/ (David Mitson Clean Edit) (CD)	60
97	Epic XPCD 2176	HIStory (Mix 1)/Ghosts/(HIStory (Mix 2) HIStory (Mix 3)/HIStory (Mix 4) (CD)	15
97	Epic XPR 3125	Blood On The Dancefloor (TM's Switchblade Mix)/(TM's O-Postive Dub) (12", blue title p/s)	8
97	Epic XPR 3136	Blood On The Dancefloor (Refugee Camp Mix)/(7" Version) (12", green title p/s)	8
97	Epic XPR 3149	HIStory (Marks! Phly Vocal)/(Marks! Future Dub) (12", yellow title sleeve)	8
97	Epic XPR 3159	HIStory (Tony Moran's HIStory Lesson)/(Tony Moran's HIStorical Dub)	
97	Epic XPR 3168	Is It Scary (Eddie's Love Mix)/(Eddie's Rub-A-Dub Mix)/(Eddie's Love Mix)/ (Radio Edit) (12", white embossed title p/s)	30
97	Epic XPR 3169	HIStory (Ummah Urban Mix)/(Ummah Radio Mix)/(Tony Moran's 7" HIStory Lesson Edit)/(Ummah DJ Mix) (12", green title sleeve)	8
97	Epic XPR 3196	Is It Scary (Deep Dish Dark & Scary Remix)/(Deep Dish Double-O-Jazz Dub)/ (Deep Dish Dark & Scary Remix)/(Radio Edit) (12", black embossed title p/s)	35

ALBUMS

72	Tamla Motown STML 11205	GOT TO BE THERE (LP)	10
73	Tamla Motown STML 11220	BEN (LP)	10
73	Tamla Motown STML 11235	MUSIC AND ME (LP)	10
75	Tamla Motown STMA 8022	FOREVER, MICHAEL (LP, gatefold sleeve)	10
79	Epic EPC 83458/83468	OFF THE WALL (LP, gatefold sleeve, with 7" picture disc "You Can't Win (Parts 1)/(Part 2)" [S EPC 7135], some with information sheet)	25
79	Epic SXPR 1207	EPIC HITS FROM THE JACKSONS & MICHAEL JACKSON (LP, promo only, stickered sleeve)	18
81	Motown PR 84	JACKSON 5: HISTORY OF MOTOWN (4-LP box set, with 1 Michael Jackson LP)	25
82	Epic EPC 11-85930	THRILLER (LP, picture disc in PVC sleeve)	25
82	Motown/Pickwick TMS 3511	AIN'T NO SUNSHINE (LP)	12
83	MCA MCA 70000	E.T. — THE EXTRA TERRESTRIAL (LP, box set with booklet & poster, narration & "Someone In The Dark", with music by John Williams)	70
83	MCA CAC 70000	E.T. — THE EXTRA TERRESTRIAL (cassette, box set with booklet & poster)	40
86	Motown WL 72424	LOOKING BACK TO YESTERDAY (NEVER BEFORE RELEASED MASTERS) (LP)	10
87	Epic 450 290-0	BAD (LP, picture disc)	12
87	Epic 450 290-8	BAD GIFT PACK (cassette pack, with note pad, highlighter pen & calender)	25
87	Epic 450 290-9	BAD (CD, picture disc, some sealed in long PVC blister pack)	35/25
88	Motown ZL 72622	THE ORIGINAL SOUL OF MICHAEL JACKSON (LP)	10
92	Epic 465 802-9	DANGEROUS (CD, gold disc, 10"x10" pop-up 'Collectors Edition First Printing')	30

(see also Jackson 5, Diana Ross & Michael Jackson, Paul McCartney, Jacksons, Jermaine Jackson)

MILLIE JACKSON

72	Mojo 2093 011	A Child Of God/You're The Joy Of My Life	6
72	Mojo 2093 015	Ask Me What You Want/I Just Can't Stand It	5
72	Mojo 2093 022	My Man, A Sweet Man/I Gotta Get Away (From My Own Self)	5
73	Polydor 2066 317	Breakaway/Strange Things	5
75	Polydor 2066 536	If Loving You Is Wrong/The Rap	6
75	Polydor 2006 612	Loving Arms/Left Over	7
76	Spring 2066 713	A House For Sale/There You Are	5
72	Mojo 2918 005	MILLIE JACKSON (LP)	20

(see also Elton John)

MILT JACKSON

57	Esquire EP 74	MILT JACKSON MODERN JAZZ QUARTET (EP)	8
50s	London EZ-C 19004	THE MILT JACKSON SEPTET (EP)	12
62	London RE-K 1315	THE BALLAD ARTISTRY OF MILT JACKSON (EP)	8
53	Vogue LDE 044	MILT JACKSON AND HIS NEW GROUP (10" LP)	15
55	Esquire 20-042	MILT JACKSON QUINTET (10" LP)	15
55	London Jazz LZ-C 14006	MILT JACKSON QUARTET (10" LP)	15
57	London Jazz LTZ-K 15064	BALLADS AND BLUES (LP)	12
57	London Jazz LTZ-K 15074	THE JAZZ SKYLINE (LP)	12
57	London Jazz LTZ-K 15091	JACKSONSVILLE (LP)	12
57	Vogue LAE 12046	WIZARD OF THE VIBES (LP)	12
59	London Jazz LTZ-K 15141	PLENTY, PLENTY SOUL (LP)	12
59	London Jazz LTZ-T 15172	BAGS' OPUS (LP, also stereo SAH-T 6049)	12
60	London Jazz LTZ-T 15177	BAGS AND FLUTES (LP)	12
60	London Jazz LTZ-K 15196	BEAN BAGS (LP, also stereo SAH-K 6095; with Coleman Hawkins)	12
61	London Jazz LTZ-K 15220	THE ARTISTRY OF MILT JACKSON (LP, also stereo SAH-K 6163)	12
61	London Jazz LTZ-K 15232	BAGS AND TRANE (LP, with John Coltrane; also stereo SAH-K 6192)	12
61	Philips BBL 7459	MILT JACKSON (LP)	12

MINT VALUE £

62	Esquire 32-134	MILT JACKSON MODERN JAZZ QUARTET/QUINTET (LP)	12
62	Riverside RLP (9)407	BAGS MEETS WES (LP, with Wes Montgomery)	12
63	Realm RM 119	THE MILT JACKSON QUARTET (LP)	12
63	HMV CLP 1589	STATEMENTS (LP, also stereo CSD 1455)	12
63	Realm RM 156	ROLL 'EM BAGS (LP)	12
64	Atlantic ATL/SAL 5012	VIBRATIONS (LP)	12
65	Mercury LML/SML 4008	IN A NEW SETTING (LP)	12
65	Mercury LML/SML 4016	AT THE MUSEUM OF MODERN ART (LP)	12
66	Mercury LML/SML 4028	BORN FREE (LP)	12
73	CTI CTL 8	CHERRY (LP, with Stanley Turrentine)	10
73	CTI CTL 15	SUNFLOWER (LP)	10
74	CTI CTH 1002	GOODBYE (LP, with Hubert Laws)	10
75	CTI CTH 1004	OLINGA (LP)	10
75	Atlantic K 60100	ART OF MILT JACKSON — THE ATLANTIC YEARS (LP)	10
75	Pablo/Polydor 2310 753	MILT JACKSON, OSCAR PETERSON, ETC (LP)	10

(see also Ray Charles, Modern Jazz Quartet, Stanley Turrentine, Miles Davis/Art Blakey, Coleman Hawkins)

PAPA CHARLIE JACKSON

50	Tempo R 30	Long Gone Lost John/I'm Looking For A Woman Who Knows How To Treat Me Right (78)	12
60	Heritage R 100	PAPA CHARLIE JACKSON (EP)	40
60	Heritage HLP 1011	PAPA CHARLIE JACKSON (LP)	50

(see also Paramount Allstars)

POOCH JACKSON

| 72 | Sioux SI 013 | You Just Gotta Get Ready/BROTHER DAN: Django's Valley | 5 |
| 72 | Sioux SI 016 | Once Bitten (with Harry J. Allstars)/KING REGGAE: Slave Driver | 5 |

(see also Circles)

PYTHON LEE JACKSON

(see under 'P')

RAY JACKSON

76	EMI EMI 2514	Take Some Time/Working On	5
80	Mercury MER 3	In The Night/Waiting For The Time (p/s)	5
80	Mercury MER 8	Little Town Flirt/Make It Last (p/s)	5
80	Mercury 9109 831	IN THE NIGHT (LP, with inner sleeve)	12

(see also Lindisfarne)

ROOT & JENNY JACKSON

| 69 | Beacon BEA 110 | Please Come Home/Lean On Me | 5 |
| 69 | Beacon BEA 136 | Let's Go Somewhere/If I Didn't Love You | 6 |

SHIRLEY JACKSON

| 63 | Decca F 11612 | You Gotta Love And Be Loved/Don't Play Me A Love Song | 5 |
| 63 | Decca F 11788 | Broken Home/No Greater Love Than Mine | 8 |

SHOVELVILLE K. JACKSON

| 60s | Melodisc MEL 1683 | Be Careful Of Stones That You Throw/Kentucky Blues | 10 |

SIMONE JACKSON

62	Piccadilly 7N 35087	Pop Pop Popeye/He Ain't Got No Time For Love	7
63	Piccadilly 7N 35124	Ain't Gonna Kiss Ya/Slow Motion	7
63	Piccadilly 7N 35149	Tell Me What To Do/Done What You Know Is Wrong	7

STONEWALL JACKSON

59	Philips PB 941	Waterloo/Smoke Along The Track	12
59	Philips PB 941	Waterloo/Smoke Along The Track (78)	40
60	Philips PB 1073	I'm Gonna Find You/A Little Guy Called Joe	6
65	CBS BPG 62587	GREATEST HITS (LP)	18

TONY JACKSON (& VIBRATIONS)

64	Pye 7N 15685	Bye Bye Baby/Watch Your Step	18
64	Pye 7N 15745	This Little Girl Of Mine/You Beat Me To The Punch	25
65	Pye 7N 15766	Love Potion No. 9/Fortune Teller	35
65	Pye 7N 15876	Stage Door/That's What I Want (as Tony Jackson Group)	25
66	CBS 202039	You're My Number One/Let Me Know (as Tony Jackson Group)	30
66	CBS 202069	Never Leave Your Baby's Side/I'm The One She Really Thinks A Lot Of (solo)	30
66	CBS 202297	Follow Me/Walk That Walk (solo)	45
66	CBS 202408	Anything Else You Want/Come On And Stop (solo)	30
91	Strange Things STZ 5005	JUST LIKE ME (LP)	15

(see also Searchers)

WALTER JACKSON

65	Columbia DB 7620	Welcome Home/Blowin' In The Wind	12
66	Columbia DB 7949	Tear For Tear/It's An Uphill Climb To The Bottom	20
66	Columbia DB 8054	A Corner In The Sun/Not You	12
67	Columbia DB 8154	Speak Her Name/They Don't Give Medals (To Yesterday's Heroes)	12
70	Atlantic 584 311	Any Way That You Want Me/Life Has Its Ups And Downs	5
73	Brunswick BR 5	Easy Evil/I Never Had It So Good	5

WANDA JACKSON

59	Capitol CL 15033	You're The One For Me/A Date With Jerry	15
59	Capitol CL 15090	Reaching/I'd Rather Have You	15
60	Capitol CL 15147	Let's Have A Party/Cool Love	15
61	Capitol CL 15176	Mean Mean Man/Honey Bop	15
61	Capitol CL 15223	Right Or Wrong/Funnel Of Love	8
62	Capitol CL 15234	In The Middle Of A Heartache/I'd Be Ashamed	10
62	Capitol CL 15249	If I Cried Every Time You Hurt Me/Let My Love Walk In	10
58	Capitol EAP1 1041	WANDA JACKSON (EP)	100
62	Capitol EAP1 20353	A LITTLE BITTY TEAR (EP)	60
58	Capitol T 1041	WANDA JACKSON (LP)	140

Wanda JACKSON

60	Capitol T 1384	ROCKIN' WITH WANDA (LP)	100
61	Capitol (S)T 1511	THERE'S A PARTY GOIN' ON (LP, mono/stereo)	75/100
61	Capitol T 1596	RIGHT OR WRONG (LP)	50
62	Capitol T 1776	WONDERFUL WANDA (LP)	35
64	Capitol (S)T 2030	TWO SIDES OF WANDA (LP, mono/stereo)	35/40
64	Capitol (S)T 2306	BLUES IN MY HEART (LP)	15
66	Capitol (S)T 2438	SINGS COUNTRY SONGS (LP, black label)	12
67	Capitol (S)T 2606	SALUTES THE COUNTRY MUSIC HALL OF FAME (LP, black label)	12
67	Capitol (S)T 2812	YOU'LL ALWAYS HAVE MY LOVE (LP)	12
69	Capitol (S)T 2976	CREAM OF THE CROP (LP, with Party Timers)	12
73	Word WST 9514	COUNTRY GOSPEL (LP)	12
70s	Myrrh MUR 1021	NOW I HAVE EVERYTHING (LP)	20

JACKSON & SMITH

65	Polydor 56051	Ain't That Loving You Baby/Every Day I Have The Blues	8
66	Polydor 56086	Party '66/And That's It	6

JACKSON BROTHERS

59	London HLX 8845	Tell Him No/Love Me	20
59	London HLX 8845	Tell Him No/Love Me (78)	15

JACKSON 5
SINGLES

70	Tamla Motown TMG 724	I Want You Back/Who's Loving You	5
70	Tamla Motown TMG 738	ABC/The Young Folks (some in promo only p/s)	50/5
70	Tamla Motown TMG 746	The Love You Save/I Found That Girl	5
70	Tamla Motown TMG 758	I'll Be There/One More Chance	5
71	Tamla Motown SFI 66	Chartbusters Volume 5: Going Back To Indiana (flexidisc)	8
71	Tamla Motown TMG 769	Mama's Pearl/Darling Dear (some in promo only p/s)	50/5
71	Tamla Motown TMG 778	Never Can Say Goodbye/She's Good	5
72	Tamla Motown TMG 809	Sugar Daddy/I'm So Happy	5
72	Tamla Motown TMG 825	Little Bitty Pretty One/Maybe Tomorrow	5
72	Tamla Motown TMG 833	Lookin' Through The Windows/Love Song (some in promo only p/s)	12/5
72	Tamla Motown TMG 837	THE CHRISTMAS EP: Santa Claus Is Coming To Town/	
		Someday At Christmas/Christmas Won't Be The Same This Year	5
73	Tamla Motown TMG 842	Doctor My Eyes/My Little Baby	5
73	Tamla Motown TMG 856	Hallelujah Day/To Know	5
73	Tamla Motown TMG 865	Skywriter/Ain't Nothin' Like The Real Thing (some in promo only p/s)	12/5
73	Tamla Motown TMG 878	Get It Together/Touch	5
74	Tamla Motown TMG 895	The Boogie Man/Don't Let Your Baby Catch You	5
74	Tamla Motown TMG 904	Dancing Machine/It's Too Late To Change The Time	5
74	Tamla Motown TMG 927	The Life Of The Party/Whatever You Got I Want	5
74	Lyntone LYN 2639	Talk And Sing Personally To Valentine Readers	
		(33rpm flexidisc free with 'Valentine' magazine)	15/10
75	Rice Krispies	Sugar Daddy/Goin' Back To Indiana/Who's Loving You/Mama's Pearl/	
	(no cat. nos.)	ABC/The Love You Save (6 different Rice Krispies cut-out card discs)	each 30
75	Tamla Motown TMG 942	I Am Love (Part 1)/I Am Love (Part 2)	5
75	Tamla Motown TMG 1001	Forever Came Today/I Can't Quit Your Love	5
77	Motown TMG 1081	JUKEBOX GEMS: Skywriter/I Want You Back/The Love You Save (EP)	8
80	Motown SPTMG 2	THE MOTOWN 20TH ANNIVERSARY SINGLES BOX (15 x 7")	30
83	Motown CTME 2034	MOTOWN FLIP HITS — JACKSON 5: I Want You Back/	
		I'll Be There/Lookin' Through The Windows/ABC (EP, cassette)	10
86	Motown 8000	You Can Cry On My Shoulder/Instrumental (CD)	10
87	Motown ZB 41655	THE CHRISTMAS EP: Santa Claus Is Coming To Town/	
		Someday At Christmas/Christmas Won't Be The Same This Year (EP, reissue)	5
87	Motown ZXT 41656	THE CHRISTMAS EP: I Saw Mommy Kissing Santa Claus/	
		Frosty The Snowman/Up On The House Top Roof (12" EP)	7
89	Tamla Motown ZD 41949	VINTAGE GOLD	
		(3" CD, gatefold card sleeve, as Michael Jackson & Jackson 5)	10

LPs

70	T. Motown (S)TML 11142	DIANA ROSS PRESENTS THE JACKSON 5 (LP, flipback sleeve, mono/st.)	22/18
70	T. Motown (S)TML 11156	ABC (LP, flipback sleeve, mono/stereo)	25/18
70	T. Motown STML 11168	THE JACKSON 5 CHRISTMAS ALBUM (LP, flipback sleeve)	18
71	T. Motown STML 11174	THIRD ALBUM (LP, original with flipback sleeve)	15
71	T. Motown STML 11188	MAYBE TOMORROW (LP)	15
72	T. Motown STML 11214	LOOKIN' THROUGH THE WINDOWS (LP)	12
73	T. Motown STML 11231	SKYWRITER (LP)	12
73	T. Motown STML 11243	GET IT TOGETHER (LP, with photo insert)	18
74	T. Motown STML 11275	DANCING MACHINE (LP)	15
75	T. Motown STML 11290	MOVING VIOLATIONS (LP)	18
76	Motown STML 12046	JOYFUL JUKEBOX MUSIC (LP)	12
77	T. Motown TMSP 6004	THE JACKSON 5 ANTHOLOGY (2-LP, original issue)	18
77	Motown STMX 6006	MOTOWN SPECIAL — THE JACKSON 5 (LP)	15
79	MFP MFP 50418	ZIP-A-DEE-DOO-DAH (LP)	15
81	Motown PR 84	JACKSON 5: HISTORY OF MOTOWN	
		(4-LP box set, with 1 Michael Jackson LP)	30
82	Motown/Pickwick TMS 3505	THE JACKSON 5 (LP)	20

(see also Michael Jackson, Jermaine Jackson, Jacksons)

JACKSON HEIGHTS

70	Charisma JH 1	Doubting Thomas/Insomnia	5
72	Vertigo 6059 068	Maureen/Long Time Dying	5
70	Charisma CAS 1018	KINGS PROGRESS (LP, pink label)	20
72	Vertigo 6360 067	5TH AVENUE BUS (LP, gatefold sleeve, spiral label)	30
72	Vertigo 6360 077	RAGAMUFFIN'S FOOL (LP, spiral label, some with poster)	50/35
73	Vertigo 6360 092	BUMP AND GRIND (LP, 'spaceship label')	15

(see also Nice)

JACKSONS

76	Epic S EPC 4708	Enjoy Yourself/Style Of Life	4
77	Epic S EPC 5063	Enjoy Yourself (Extended Version 5.48)/Style Of Life (12", p/s)	15
78	Epic S EPC 12-6683	Blame It On The Boogie (LP version)/Do What You Wanna (12")	10
78	Epic S EPC 12-6983	Destiny (Full Length Album Version)/Blame It On The Boogie (Special 7-Minute Extended Disco Remix)/That's What You Get (For Being Polite) (12", p/s)	10
79	Epic EPC 12-7181	Shake Your Body (Down To The Ground) (Special Disco Remix 8.40)/All Night Dancin' (6.09) (12", p/s)	10
79	Epic EPC 13-7876	Blame It On The Boogie (Album Version)/That's What You Get (For Being Polite)/Blame It On The Boogie (instrumental) (12")	10
79	Epic E 12-6983	Blame It On The Boogie (Album Version)/That's What You Get (For Being Polite) (7 Minute Remix)/Blame It On The Boogie (12")	10
80	Epic EPC 12-9391	Heartbreak Hotel (Album Version)/Different Kind Of Lady (12")	15
81	Epic EPC A 40-2627	GREATEST ORIGINAL HITS: Can You Feel It/Shake Your Body (Down To The Ground)/Show You The Way To Go/Blame It On The Boogie (EP, cassette)	6
81	Epic EPC A 1294	Walk Right Now/Your Ways (picture disc)	10
81	Epic EPC A 13-1294	Walk Right Now (Album Version)/Your Ways (12", p/s)	7
81	Epic EPC A 1902	Things I Do For You/Don't Stop 'Til You Get Enough (p/s)	5
82	Old Gold OG 4142	Shake Your Body/Blame It On The Boogie (p/s)	5
84	Epic EPC A 4431	State Of Shock/Your Ways (picture disc, with Mick Jagger)	12
84	Epic EPC 4675	Torture/Torture (Instrumental) (cassette)	5
84	Epic TA 4675	Torture (Full Length Album Version)/(Instrumental Version)/Show You The Way To Go/Blame It On The Boogie (12", p/s)	8
84	Epic A 4885	Body/Body (instrumental) (p/s)	4
84	Epic TA 4885	Body (extended)/Body (instrumental) (12", p/s)	8
85	Epic A 6185	Wait/She's Out Of My Life (live) (p/s)	4
85	Epic TA 6185	Wait (Album Version)/She's Out Of My Life (live) (12", p/s)	8
87	MCA MCA 1129	Time Out For The Burglar/DISTANCE: News At 11 (p/s)	4
87	MCA MCAS 1129	Time Out For The Burglar/DISTANCE: News At 11 (12", p/s)	7
89	Epic 654 808-2	Nothing (That Compares 2 U)/Nothing (That Compares 2 U) (The Mix)/Nothing (That Compares 2 U) (Extended Version) (CD, card sleeve)	7
89	Epic 654 570-3	SOLID GOLD (3" CD EP, gatefold card sleeve)	10
89	Epic 655 206-2	2300 Jackson Street (Album Version)/Keep Her/When I Look At You (CD, card p/s)	7
78	Epic EPC 83200	DESTINY (LP)	10
79	Epic S XPR 1207	EPIC HITS FROM THE JACKSONS & MICHAEL JACKSON (LP, promo only)	20
84	Epic EPC 86303	VICTORY (LP, picture disc)	35
85	Epic SAI 7561	A TASTE OF VICTORY (LP, picture disc, promo only via Kelloggs offer)	50

(see also Jackson 5, Michael Jackson, Jermaine Jackson)

CHUBBY JACKSON'S BIG BAND

60	Top Rank TR 5015	A Ballad For Jai/Hail, Hail, The Herd's All Here	4

JACKSON SISTERS

73	Mums MUM 18257	I Believe In Miracles/Day In The Blue	75
73	Mums MUM 1591	(Why Can't We Be) More Than Just Friends/Rockin' On My Porch	4
75	Mums MUM 2896	Boy You're Dynamite/Shake Her Loose	5
75	CBS 2896	Boy You're Dynamite/Shake Her Loose (reissue)	4
87	Urban URB 4	I Believe In Miracles/Boy You're Dynamite	8
87	Urban URBX 4	I Believe In Miracles/Boy You're Dynamite (12", p/s)	20

JACK THE LAD

73	Charisma CB 206	One More Dance/Draught Genius (Polka) (p/s)	6
73	Charisma CB 218	Why Can't I Be Satisfied/Make Me Happy	5
75	Charisma CB 242	Home Sweet Home/Big Ocean Liner	5
75	Charisma CB 253	Gentleman Soldier/Oakey Strike Evictions	5
75	Charisma CB 264	My Friend The Drink/Rocking Chair	5
74	Charisma CAS 1085	IT'S JACK THE LAD (LP)	12
74	Charisma CAS 1094	OLD STRAIGHT TRACK (LP, with lyric sheet)	12
75	Charisma CAS 1110	ROUGH DIAMONDS (LP)	12
76	United Artists UAS 29999	JACKPOT (LP)	12

(see also Lindisfarne)

JACKY

68	Philips BF 1647	White Horses/Too Many Chiefs (Not Enough Indians)	5
68	Philips BF 1689	We're Off And Running/Well That's Loving You	5
69	Page One POF 122	Love Is Now/Never Will I Be	5
68	Philips SBL 7851	WHITE HORSES (LP)	15

(see also Jackie & Raindrops, Raindrops, Jackie Lee, Emma Rede, Vince Hill)

DICK JACOBS (& HIS ORCHESTRA)

56	Vogue Coral Q 72147	Saxophone/Never Come Sunday	5
56	Vogue Coral Q 72154	"The Man With The Golden Arm" Theme/Butternut	8
56	Vogue Coral Q 72204	Petticoats Of Portugal/East Of Eden	5
57	Vogue Coral Q 72245	The Big Beat/The Tower Trot	10
57	Vogue Coral Q 72245	The Big Beat/The Tower Trot (78)	8
57	Vogue Coral Q 72260	Rock-a-billy Gal/The Golden Strings	10
57	Vogue Coral Q 72260	Rock-a-billy Gal/The Golden Strings (78)	10
57	Vogue Coral Q 72280	Fascination/Summertime In Venice	6
57	Vogue Coral LVA 9076	THE SKIFFLE SOUND (LP, as Dick Jacobs & His Skiffle Group)	35
59	Coral SVL 3008	BROADWAY SONG BOOK (LP)	12
59	Coral LVA 9102	THEMES FROM HORROR MOVIES (LP)	15

HANK JACOBS

64	Sue WI 313	So Far Away/Monkey, Hips And Rice	25

JIMMY JACOBS & NITESPOTS

60s	Gargoyle ADV 305011	SWINGIN' SOHO — JIMMY SINGS, THE NITESPOTS SWING (LP)	15

MINT VALUE £

JACQUELINE & BRIDIE
64	Fontana TL 5212	HOLD BACK THE DAWN (LP)	18

(see also Jackie & Bridie)

CHUCK JACQUES & LYNN TAITT & COMETS
67	Ska Beat JB 264	Dial 609/VIBRATORS & TOMMY McCOOK & COMETS: Wait For Me	15

(see also Wilbert Francis & Vibrators)

HATTIE JACQUES
71	Avenue NUE 143	THE BUNGLES OF BOJUN (EP)	8

(see also Eric Sykes)

ILLINOIS JACQUET & HIS ORCHESTRA
56	Vogue V 2387	Blow Illinois Blow/Destination Moon	6
53	Vogue LDE 026	ILLINOIS JACQUET (10" LP)	15
56	Columbia Clef 33C 9018	ILLINOIS JACQUET (10" LP)	15
57	Columbia Clef 33CX 10085	GROOVIN' WITH JACQUET (LP)	12
50s	Melodisc MLP 12-301	JAZZ AT THE PHILHARMONIC (LP)	12

JADE
70	DJM DJS 227	Alan's Song/Amongst Anemones	6
70	DJM DJLPS 407	FLY ON STRANGE WINGS (LP)	50

JADE WARRIOR
72	Vertigo 6059 069	The Demon Trucker/Snake	10
78	Island JAD 1	Way Of The Sun/Sun Ra	5
71	Vertigo 6360 033	JADE WARRIOR (LP, gatefold sleeve, spiral label)	40
71	Vertigo 6360 062	RELEASED (LP, gatefold sleeve, spiral label)	50
72	Vertigo 6360 079	LAST AUTUMN'S DREAM (LP, gatefold sleeve, spiral label)	40
74	Island ILPS 9290	FLOATING WORLD (LP)	15
75	Island ILPS 9318	WAVES (LP)	15
76	Island ILPS 9393	KITES (LP)	15
78	Island ILPS 9552	WAY OF THE SUN (LP)	15
79	Butt BUTT 001	REFLECTIONS (LP)	12

(see also July, Joe O'Donnell)

JADIS
83	private pressing	HOT BEANS (cassette)	10
84	private pressing	BABOON ENQUIRIES (cassette)	10
87	private pressing DEM 1	G13/Out Of Reach (cassette)	8
88	private pressing DEM 2	Don't Keep Me Waiting/In The Dark (cassette)	8
89	private pressing	Lost For Words/This Changing Face (cassette)	8
90	Back Beat 004-12	THE JADIS ALBUM (LP, numbered)	15

MAX JAFFA (& HIS ORCHESTRA)
55	Decca F 10426	Camille/The Song Of The Barefoot Contessa (My Gipsy Heart) (w/ His Violin)	5
56	Columbia SCM 5226	China Boogie/Slap Happy	6
59	Columbia SCD 2122	The Great Waltz Selection/The Vagabond Prince Selection (as Max Jaffa & Palm Court Orchestra)	5
59	Columbia SCD 2127	Black Eyes/Czardas (as Max Jaffa Trio & Orchestra)	5
59	Columbia DB 4280	Gypsy Cha Cha/Cha Cha Boogie	5
60	Columbia DB 4474	Love Is Like A Violin/Romantica (with Norrie Paramor Orchestra)	5
57	Conquest CL 1005	I'LL SEE YOU IN MY DREAMS (LP)	12

CHRIS JAGGER
73	GM GMS 3	Something New/Joy Of The Ride	6
73	GM GML 1003	CHRIS JAGGER — YOU KNOW THE NAME BUT NOT THE FACE (LP)	12

MICK JAGGER
70	Decca F 13067	Memo From Turner/Natural Magic (some in export p/s)	40/10
84	CBS TA 4431	State Of Shock/Your Ways (picture disc)	6
87	CBS 651028-0	Let's Work/Catch As Catch Can (poster p/s)	8
87	CBS THROW P1	Throwaway/Peace For The Wicked (picture disc)	10
87	CBS THROW C1	Throwaway (Remix)/(Vocal Dub)/Peace For The Wicked (CD, card sleeve)	15
70	United Artists UAS 29108	NED KELLY (LP, soundtrack)	25
70	Warner Bros WS 2554	PERFORMANCE (LP, soundtrack)	25
85	CBS 86310	SHE'S THE BOSS (CD)	15
87	CBS 460 123-2	PRIMITIVE COOL (CD)	15

(see also Rolling Stones, Jacksons, Jack Nitzsche)

JAGO
72	Duke DU 134	Rebel Train/Babylon Version	8

JAGS
61	Decca F 11397	The Hunch/Cry Wolf	7

JAGS
79	Island WIP 6501	Back Of My Hand/Double Vision (p/s)	5
80	Island WIP 6531	Woman's World/Dumb Blonde (p/s)	5
80	Island WIP 6587	Party Games/She's So Considerate (p/s)	5
80	Island WIP 6666	I Never Was A Beachboy/Tune Into Heaven (p/s)	5
80	Island WIP 6683	The Sound Of G-O-O-D-B-Y-E/The Hurt (no p/s)	5
79	Island ILPS 9603	EVENING STANDARDS (LP)	12
81	Island ILPS 9655	NO TIE LIKE THE PRESENT (LP)	12

JAGUAR
81	Heavy Metal HEAVY 10	Back Street Woman/Chasing The Dragon (p/s)	15
82	Neat NEAT 16	Axe Crazy/War Machine (p/s)	12
83	Neat NEAT 1007	POWER GAMES (LP, some on purple vinyl)	30/18
84	Roadrunner RR 9851	THIS TIME (LP)	15

JAGUARS

| 63 | Impression IMP 101 | Opus To Spring/The Beat (1,000 only) | 20 |
| 65 | Contest RGJ 152 | We'll Live On Happily/Now You Wonder Why | 200 |

JAH FISH

| 72 | Grape GR 3034 | Vampire Rock/MOD STARS: El-Sisco Rock | 5 |

JAH LLOYD

| 73 | Jaguar JAG 102 | Channel One (with Douglas Boothe)/SOUL SYNDICATES:Channel Two | 5 |
| 73 | Jaguar JAG 104 | Psalm Two/SOUL SYNDICATES: Channel Two | 5 |

JAH SCOUSE

| 85 | Better Things BETS 1 | Merge/Vegan Mix (foldout p/s) | 4 |

JAH WOBBLE

78	Virgin VS 239	STEEL LEG MEETS THE ELECTRIC DREAD (EP p/s)	7
78	Virgin VS 239-12	STEEL LEG MEETS THE ELECTRIC DREAD (12 EP, p/s)	10
78	Virgin VOLE 9	Dreadlock Don't Deal In Wedlock/Pthilius Pubis (p/s)	5
78	Virgin 12VOLE 9	Dreadlock Don't Deal In Wedlock/Pthilius Pubis (12", p/s)	8
80	Virgin VS 337	Betrayal/MR. X: Battle Of Britain (p/s)	5
80	Virgin VS 337-12	Betrayal/MR. X: Battle Of Britain (12", p/s)	8
80	Virgin VS 361-12	V.I.E.P. (12" EP)	8
81	Island WIP 6701	HOW MUCH ARE THEY? (12" EP)	8
82	Jah Wobble JAH 1	Fading/Nocturnal (p/s, as Jah Wobble With Animal)	5
82	Jah Wobble JAH 2	Long Long Way/Nocturnal (12", p/s)	8
84	Lago LAGO 5	Voodoo/East (12", p/s, with Ollie Martland & Polly Eltes)	7
85	Lago LAGO 6	Blow Out/Blow Out (Instrumental) (12", p/s)	7
80	Virgin V 2158	THE LEGEND LIVES ON (mini-LP)	10
82	Human Condition	HUMAN CONDITION (cassette only)	10
82	Human Condition	LIVE IN EUROPE (LP)	10
95	Island ILPSD 8044	HEAVEN AND EARTH (2-LP)	15
95	Island CID 8044	HEAVEN AND EARTH (CD)	18

JAH WOBBLE, THE EDGE & HOLGAR CZUKAY

| 83 | Island WOB 1 | Snake Charmer/Hold On To Your Dreams (p/s) | 5 |

(see also Don Letts & Jah Wobble, Dan MacArthur, Joolz, Public Image Ltd, Edge, Orb, Can)

JAH WOOSH

| 75 | Lucky DL 5094 | Rocking Blues/Version | 5 |
| 75 | Lucky DL 5096 | Don't Do That/That Dub | 5 |

JAKE & FAMILY JEWELS

| 70 | Polydor 2425 027 | JAKE AND THE FAMILY JEWELS (LP) | 12 |

JAKLIN

| 69 | Stable SLE 8003 | JAKLIN (LP) | 175 |

JAM

SINGLES

77	Polydor 2058 866	In The City/Takin' My Love (p/s, reissues exist with red label)	7
77	Polydor 2058 903	All Around The World/Carnaby Street (p/s)	6
77	Polydor 2058 945	The Modern World/Sweet Soul Music (live)/Back In My Arms Again (live)/ Bricks And Mortar (Part) [live] (p/s)	6
78	Polydor 2058 995	News Of The World/Aunties And Uncles (Impulsive Youths)/Innocent Man (p/s)	5
78	Polydor 2059 054	David Watts/'A' Bomb In Wardour Street (plastic moulded label, p/s)	4
78	Polydor 2059 054	David Watts/'A' Bomb In Wardour Street (white paper label, no p/s)	5
78	Polydor POSP 8	Down In The Tube Station At Midnight/So Sad About Us/The Night (p/s)	4
79	Polydor POSP 34	Strange Town/The Butterfly Collector (p/s)	4
79	Polydor POSP 69	When You're Young/Smithers-Jones (p/s)	4
79	Polydor POSP 83	The Eton Rifles/See-Saw (laminated p/s)	4

(The above singles were reissued twice in their picture sleeves; early originals have curved edges on sleeve openings whereas the reissues are straight. Lettering on the reissue labels tends to be fatter; reissues are worth £3-£4.)

80	Polydor POSP 113	Going Underground/The Dreams Of Children (laminated p/s)	4
80	Polydor POSPJ 113/ 2816 024	Going Underground/The Dreams Of Children//The Modern World (live)/ Away From The Numbers (live)/Down In The Tube Station At Midnight (live) (p/s, double pack)	8
80	Polydor 2059 266	Start!/Liza Radley (p/s)	4
81	Polydor POSP 257	Funeral Pyre/Disguises (p/s)	4
81	Polydor POSP 350	Absolute Beginners/Tales From The Riverbank (p/s, with lyric sheet)	4
82	Polydor POSP 400	Town Called Malice/Precious (p/s, red moulded label [silver label £3])	4
82	Polydor POSPX 400	Town Called Malice (live)/Precious (Extended) (12", striped die-cut sleeve)	7
82	Polydor POSPJ 540/JAM 1	Beat Surrender/Shopping//Move On Up/Stoned Out Of My Mind/ War (double pack, gatefold p/s)	6
83	Polydor 2059 482	That's Entertainment/Down In The Tube Station At Midnight (live) (U.K. reissue of European import, embossed p/s)	5
80	Lyntone LYN 9048/ Flexipop 002	Pop Art Poem/Boy About Town (version) (blue, yellow or green 1-sided flexi with Flexipop mag issue 2; add £2 with magazine & £5 with mailer p/s)	7/5/10
80	Lyntone LYN 9048	Pop Art Poem/Boy About Town (version) (same tracks both sides, hard vinyl white label, 300 only, with mail-order mailer p/s)	35/30
81	Lyntone	When You're Young (live) (1-sided fan club flexidisc, 33rpm)	20
82	Fan Club (no cat. no.)	Tales From The Riverbank (version) (33rpm 1-sided fan club flexidisc)	18
82	Polydor PAOLO 100	Move On Up (live) (flexidisc free with Melody Maker paper)	7/5
91	Polydor PO 155	That's Entertainment/Down In The Tube Station At Midnight (live) (p/s, reissue)	4
91	Polydor PZ 155	That's Entertainment/Down In The Tube Station At Midnight (live)/ Town Called Malice (Live) (12" p/s, reissue)	7
91	Polydor PZCD 155	That's Entertainment/Down In The Tube Station At Midnight (live)/ Town Called Malice (Live) (CD)	7
92	Polydor POCS 199	The Dreams Of Children/Away From The Numbers (live) (withdrawn cassette)	6
97	Polydor 2058 266	In The City (1-sided "20th anniversary party invite" promo, die-cut co. sleeve)	40
97	Polydor JAM 1	DIRECTION, REACTION, CREATION (CD, sampler, gatefold card p/s)	12

MINT VALUE £

JAM

MISPRESSINGS

78	Polydor 2058 995	News Of The World/Aunties And Uncles/Innocent Man (p/s, plays B-side on both sides)	25
78	Polydor POSP 6	Sandy/Can't Let You Go (by John Travolta, B-side mispressed with "So Sad About Us")	12
78	Polydor 2059 054	David Watts/'A' Bomb In Wardour Street (plastic moulded label; songwriting credit for "David Watts" mis-credited to "Ray Davis", p/s)	5
78	Polydor POSP 8	Down In The Tube Station At Midnight/So Sad About Us/The Night (p/s; with erroneous B-side reference to "All Mod Cons" LP)	6
78	Polydor POSP 8	Down In The Tube Station At Midnight/So Sad About Us/The Night (A-side plays John Travolta's "Sandy")	12
79	Polydor POSP 69	When You're Young/Smithers-Jones (p/s, with B-side on both sides)	25
80	Polydor 2059 266	Start!/Liza Radley (p/s, 1 side plays Village People's "Can't Stop The Music")	6
82	Polydor POSP 400	Town Called Malice/Precious (p/s, silver moulded label, both sides play "Precious")	5

ALBUMS

77	Polydor 2383 477	IN THE CITY (LP, with inner sleeve)	12
79	Polydor POLD 5028	SETTING SONS (LP, embossed sleeve with track listing sticker on back & inner sleeve)	10
80	Polydor 2683 074	IN THE CITY/THIS IS THE MODERN WORLD (2-LP, reissue, gatefold sleeve)	15
82	Polydor POLD 5055	THE GIFT (LP, with inner sleeve in pink & white candy striped bag)	10
83	Polydor SNAP 1	SNAP! (2-LP, with bonus 4-track EP 'Live At Wembley' [SNAPL 45])	15
83	Polydor SNAPC 1	SNAP! (cassette with 4 bonus 'Live At Wembley' tracks)	15
84	Polydor 821 712-2	COMPACT SNAP! (CD)	15
91	Receiver	LIVE AT THE ROXY (LP, unissued, 25 test pressings only)	150+
92	Polydor POL 900	EXTRAS (2-LP, single sleeve, with inner sleeves)	15

(see also Style Council, Paul Weller, Bruce Foxton, Time U.K., Sharp)

JAMAICA FATS

66	Blue Beat BB 368	Jacqueline/Please Come Home (actually by Al T. Joe & Celestials)	12

(see also Al T. Joe)

JAMAICAN ACTIONS

68	Coxsone CS 7070	Catch The Quinella/JACKIE MITTOO: Songbird	20

JAMAICAN EAGLES

73	Harry J HJ 6661	Country Living/Country Living (Version)	5

(see also Eagles)

JAMAICAN FOUNDATIONS

68	Coxsone CS 7036	Take It Cool/VICEROYS: Try Hard To Leave	20

JAMAICANS

66	Doctor Bird DB 1109	Cool Night/Ma And Pa	25
67	Trojan TR 007	Dedicated To You/The Things I Said To You	15
67	Treasure Isle TI 7007	Things You Say You Love/I've Got A Pain	15
67	Treasure Isle TI 7012	Baba Boom (Festival Song 1967) (actually by Baba Boom)/ TOMMY McCOOK & SUPERSONICS: Real Cool	15
67	Treasure Isle TI 7037	Peace And Love/Woman Gone Home	15
69	Escort ES 806	Early In The Morning/Mr. Lonely	7
70	Harry J. HJ 6604	Fire Parts 1 & 2	7
71	Dynamc DYN 410	Love Uprising/My Love For You	7

71	Dynamic DYN 417	Mary/CONSCIOUS MINDS: Soldier Boy	6
71	New Beat NB 084	Mary/CONSCIOUS MINDS: Soldier Boy	6
72	Dynamic DYN 430	I Believe In Music/Music (Version)	6
72	Dynamic DYN 442	Are You Sure/Are You Sure (Version)	6
72	Dynamic DYN 456	Sunshine Love/Sunshine Version	6
74	Dragon DRA 1029	My Heart Just Keeps On Breaking/	
		My Heart Just Keeps On Breaking (Instrumental)	5

(see also Norris Weir & Jamaicans, Tommy Cowan)

JAMAICAN SHADOWS

| 67 | Coxsone CS 7005 | Have Mercy/Blending Love | 20 |
| 69 | Upsetter US 320 | Dirty Dozen (actually by Upsetters)/Crying Too Long | 12 |

JAMAICA'S OWN VAGABONDS

| 64 | Decca DFE 8588 | BEHOLD (EP) | 30 |
| 64 | Decca LK 4617 | SKA TIME (LP) | 35 |

(see also Vagabonds, Jimmy James & Vagabonds)

AHMED JAMAL

59	London Jazz LTZ-M 15162	BUT NOT FOR ME (LP)	15
59	London Jazz LTZ-M 15170	AHMED JAMAL (LP)	15
62	Pye Jazz NJL 38	ALHAMBRA (LP)	12
63	Pye Jazz NJL 50	MACANUDO (LP)	12
64	Chess CRL 4001	NAKED CITY THEME (LP)	15
67	Chess CRL 4509	ROAR OF THE GREASE PAINT (LP)	15
68	Chess CRL 4530	STANDARD-EYES (LP)	12
68	Chess CRL 4532	CRY YOUNG (LP)	12
70	Impulse SIPL 521	AT THE TOP (LP)	10

JAMES

84	Factory FAC 78	JIMONE EP: What's The World/Fire So Close/Folklore (p/s)	10
85	Factory FAC 119	JAMES II: Hymn From A Village/If Things Were Perfect (p/s)	10
86	Sire JIM 3	Chain Mail/Hup Springs (p/s)	8
86	Sire JIM 3T	SIT DOWN EP: Chain Mail/Uprising/Hup Springs (12", p/s)	15
86	Sire JIM 4	So Many Ways/Withdrawn (p/s)	8
86	Sire JIM 4T	So Many Ways/Just Hipper/Withdrawn (12", p/s)	15
88	Blanco Y Negro NEG 26	Yaho/Mosquito (p/s)	6
88	Blanco Y Negro NEG 26T	Yaho/Mosquito/Left Out Of Her Will/New Nature (12", p/s)	12
88	Blanco Y Negro NEG 31	What For/Island Swing (p/s)	6
88	Blanco Y Negro NEG 31T	What For (Climax Mix)/Island Swing/Not There (12", p/s)	12
88	Blanco Y Negro NEG 31C	What For (Climax Mix)/Island Swing/Not There (cassette, in video-style box)	8
89	Rough Trade RT 225	Sit Down/Sky Is Falling (p/s)	7
89	Rough Trade RTT 225	Sit Down/Goin' Away/Sky Is Falling (12", p/s, 1st 500 with postcard)	10/7
89	Rough Trade RTT 225 CD	Sit Down/Goin' Away/Sky Is Falling (3" CD, card sleeve)	15
89	Rough Trade RT 245	Come Home/Promised Land (p/s)	6
89	Rough Trade RTT 245	Come Home (Long Version)/Come Home (7" Version)/Promised Land/	
		Slow Right Down (Demo Version) (12", p/s)	7
89	Rough Trade RTT 245 CD	Come Home (Long Version)/Come Home (7" Version)/Promised Land/	
		Slow Right Down (Demo Version) (5" CD, card sleeve)	10
90	Fontana JIMM 512	How Was It For You?/How Was It For You? (Different Mix)/Lazy/	
		Undertaker (12", p/s, with stencil)	10
90s	Lyntone	Weather Change (Demo Version) (flexidisc, with tour programme)	10/5
89	Rough Trade ONEMAN 1LP	ONE MAN CLAPPING (LP, with inner sleeve)	12
89	Rough Trade ONEMAN 1CD	ONE MAN CLAPPING (CD, with bonus track "Yaho")	15

B.B. JAMES

| 70 | Upsetter US 328 | Consider Me/Consider Me Version | 8 |

BOB JAMES

| 75 | CTI CTI 6043 | BOB JAMES ONE (LP) | 10 |
| 75 | CTI CTI 6057 | BOB JAMES TWO (LP) | 10 |

BOBBY JAMES & DAVE (Barker)

| 71 | Smash SMA 2314 | You Said It/AGGRO BAND: Hot Sauce | 7 |

BRIAN JAMES

| 68 | Olga OLE 005 | Come Back Silly Girl/It Just Happened That Way | 7 |

CALVIN JAMES

| 65 | Columbia DB 7516 | Some Things You Never Get Used To/Remember | 12 |

(pseudonym for George Underwood; see also Davie Jones & King Bees)

COL JAMES

| 62 | Oriole CB 1736 | Doesn't Anybody Make Short Movies/Oooh Looka There Ain't She Pretty | 8 |

DANNY JAMES

| 72 | Southern Sound BT 100 | Your Gravy Train/Devil Made Me Say That | 5 |

DICK JAMES

53	Parlophone MSP 6039	Mother Nature And Father Time/Don't You Care	10
53	Parlophone MSP 6047	The Joker/Guessing	7
55	Parlophone MSP 6170	Unchained Melody/Come Back (Come Back To Me)	12
55	Parlophone MSP 6190	He/So Must I Love You	10
56	Parlophone MSP 6199	Robin Hood/The Ballad Of Davy Crockett	25
56	Parlophone MSP 6230	"Summer Sing-Song" Medley	6
56	Parlophone R 4220	I Only Know I Love You/Mirabelle	6
56	Parlophone R 4241	"Sing Song Time (No. 3)" Medley	5
57	Parlophone R 4255	The Garden Of Eden/I Accuse	12
57	Parlophone R 4314	Westward Ho The Wagons!/The Gay Cavalier	7
57	Parlophone R 4375	"Skiffling Sing Song" Medley	7
58	Parlophone R 4498	Daddy's Little Girl/When You're Young	5
58	Parlophone R 4498	Daddy's Little Girl/When You're Young (78)	8
59	Parlophone R 4606	There But For Your Love Go I/Minus One Heart	5
64	Parlophone R 5212	"Sing A Song Of Beatles With Dick James" Medley (Parts 1 & 2)	6

MINT VALUE £

ELMORE JAMES

64	Sue WI 335	Dust My Blues/Happy Home	
		(as Elmore James & Broom Dusters)	25
65	Sue WI 383	It Hurts Me Too/Bleeding Heart	20
65	Sue WI 392	Knocking At Your Door/Calling The Blues (B-side actually by	
		Junior Wells & Earl Hooker)	75
66	Sue WI 4007	I Need You/Mean Mistreating Mama	20
65	Sue ILP 918	THE BEST OF ELMORE JAMES (LP)	35
65	Sue ILP 927	THE ELMORE JAMES MEMORIAL ALBUM (LP)	35
68	Bell MBLL/SBLL 104	SOMETHING INSIDE OF ME (LP)	30
68	Ember EMB 3397	THE LATE FANTASTICALLY GREAT ELMORE JAMES (LP)	20
70	United Artists UAS 29109	THE LEGEND OF ELMORE JAMES (LP)	18
70	Blue Horizon 7-66230	TO KNOW A MAN (2-LP)	70
70	Blue Horizon 7-63204	TOUGH (LP, with 4 tracks by John Brim)	50
73	Polydor 2383 200	COTTON PATCH HOTFOOTS	
		(LP, shared with Walter Horton)	15
75	DJM DJLMD 8008	ALL THEM BLUES (2-LP)	18
83	Ace CH 68	KING OF THE SLIDE GUITAR	
		(LP, yellow vinyl)	12

ETTA JAMES

60	London HLM 9139	All I Could Do Was Cry/Tough Mary	25
60	London HLM 9234	My Dearest Darling/Girl Of My Dreams	22
61	Pye International 7N 25079	At Last/I Just Want To Make Love To You	12
61	Pye International 7N 25080	Trust In Me/Anything To Say You're Mine	12
61	Pye International 7N 25113	Dream/Fool That I Am	12
62	Pye International 7N 25131	Something's Got A Hold On Me/Waiting For Charlie To Come Home	12
62	Pye International 7N 25162	Stop The Wedding/Street Of Tears	12
63	Pye International 7N 25205	Pushover/I Can't Hold It In Any More	12
65	Sue WI 359	Roll With Me Henry/Good Rockin' Daddy	25
67	Chess CRS 8052	I Prefer You/I'm So Glad (I Found Love In You)	12
67	Chess CRS 8063	Tell Mama/I'd Rather Go Blind	12
67	Chess CRS 8069	Security/I'm Gonna Take What He's Got	10
68	Chess CRS 8076	I Got You Babe/I Worship The Ground You Walk On	8
68	Chess CRS 8082	You Got It/Fire	8
72	Chess 6145 016	Tell Mama/I'd Rather Go Blind/I Found A Love	5
74	Santa Ponsa PNS 14	Just Ask Me/99 Ways	5
74	Chess 6145 033	Out On The Streets Again/Come A Little Closer	6
78	Warner Brothers K 17173	Piece Of My Heart/Lovesick Blues	5
65	Chess CRL 4502	ETTA JAMES ROCKS THE HOUSE (LP)	35
67	Chess CRL 4524	AT LAST (LP)	30
68	Ember EMB 3390	THE SOUL OF ETTA JAMES (LP)	22
68	Chess CRL 4536	TELL MAMA (LP)	30
72	Chess 6310 126	GOLDEN DECADE (LP)	12
73	Chess 6671 003	PEACHES (2-LP)	18
78	Warner Brothers K 56492	DEEP IN THE NIGHT (LP)	12
81	Ace 10CH 33	GOOD ROCKIN' MAMA (10" LP)	12
	(see also Etta & Harvey)		

ETTA JAMES & SUGAR PIE DeSANTO

| 65 | Chess CRS 8025 | Do I Make Myself Clear/Somewhere Down The Line | 12 |
| | (see also Sugar Pie DeSanto) | | |

HARRY JAMES & HIS ORCHESTRA

65	Dot DS 16729	Love Theme From In Harm's Way/Green Onions	5
54	Philips BBR 8010	SOFT LIGHTS, SWEET TRUMPET (10" LP)	12
54	Columbia 33S 1014	ALLTIME FAVOURITES (10" LP)	12
54	Columbia 33S 1031	RHYTHM SESSION WITH HARRY JAMES (10" LP)	12
55	Columbia 33S 1052	TRUMPET TIME (10" LP)	12
56	Capitol LC 6800	IN HI-FI (10" LP)	12
	(see also Rosemary Clooney)		

JASON JAMES

| 67 | CBS 2705 | Miss Pilkington's Maid/Count Me Out | 15 |

JERRY JAMES & BANDITS

| 64 | Solar SRP 101 | Sweet Little Sixteen/Three Steps To Heaven | 10 |

JESSE JAMES

| 54 | Vocalion V 1037 | Southern Casey Jones/Lonesome Day Blues (78) | 20 |

JIMMY JAMES (& VAGABONDS)

62	Dice CC 4	Bewildered And Blue/I Don't Want To Cry (solo)	15
63	R&B JB 112	Jump Children/Tell Me (solo)	15
64	Black Swan WI 437	Thinking Of You/Shirley (solo)	20
65	Columbia DB 7653	Shoo Be Doo You're Mine/We'll Never Stop Loving You	12
66	Ska Beat JB 242	Your Love/Someday (solo)	12
66	Piccadilly 7N 35298	I Feel Alright/I Wanna Be Your Everything	8
66	Piccadilly 7N 35320	Hi Diddley Dee Dum Dum (It's A Good Good Feelin')/Come To Me Softly	8
66	Piccadilly 7N 35331	This Heart Of Mine/I Don't Wanna Cry	10
66	Piccadilly 7N 35349	Ain't Love Good, Ain't Love Proud/Don't Know What I'm Gonna Do	10
67	Piccadilly 7N 35360	I Can't Get Back Home To My Baby/Hungry For Love (solo)	8
67	Piccadilly 7N 35374	No Good To Cry/You Showed Me The Way	8
68	Pye 7N 17579	Red Red Wine/Who Could Be Loving You	5
69	Pye 7N 17719	Close The Door/Why (solo)	5
71	Trojan TR 7806	Help Yourself/Why	12
72	Bamboo BAM 67	Riverboat Jenny/If I Wasn't Black	6
72	Stateside SS 2209	A Man Like Me/Survival	6

MINT VALUE £

74	People PEO 117	Help Yourself/Why (reissue)	5
75	Pye 7N 45524	Whatever Happened To The Love We Knew/Let's Have Fun	5
75	Pye 7N 45472	Hey Girl/I Am Somebody	10
66	Piccadilly NEP 34053	JIMMY JAMES AND THE VAGABONDS (EP)	40
66	Piccadilly NPL 38027	THE NEW RELIGION (LP)	35
68	Pye N(S)PL 18231	OPEN UP YOUR SOUL (LP)	25
68	Marble Arch MAL 823	THIS IS JIMMY JAMES (LP)	12
70	Marble Arch MAL 1244	THE NEW RELIGION (LP, reissue)	12
75	Pye NSPL 18457	YOU DON'T STAND A CHANCE IF YOU CAN'T DANCE (LP)	18

JIMMY JAMES & VAGABONDS/ALAN BOWN SET
| 67 | Pye N(S)PL 18156 | LONDON SWINGS — LIVE AT THE MARQUEE CLUB (LP, 1 side each) | 35 |

(see also Vagabonds, Jamaica's Own Vagabonds, Alan Bown Set)

JOHN JAMES
70	Transatlantic TRA 219	MORNING BRINGS THE LIGHT (LP)	15
71	Transatlantic TRA 242	JOHN JAMES (LP)	15
72	Transatlantic TRA 250	SKY IN MY PIE (LP)	15
75	Transatlantic TRA 305	HEAD IN THE CLOUDS (LP)	15
76	Kicking Mule SNKF 128	DESCRIPTIVE GUITAR INSTRUMENTALS (LP)	12
78	Kicking Mule SNKF 136	LIVE IN CONCERT (LP)	12
84	Stoptime STOP 101	ACOUSTICA ECLECTICA (LP)	12

JONI JAMES
53	MGM SP 1013	Why Don't You Believe Me?/Wishing Ring	18
53	MGM SP 1025	Have You Heard/Purple Shades	12
53	MGM SP 1026	Your Cheatin' Heart/I'll Be Waiting For You	15
53	MGM SP 1041	Almost Always/Is It Any Wonder?	15
53	MGM SP 1064	I'll Never Stand In Your Way/Why Can't I	15
54	MGM SP 1081	I Need You Now/You're Nearer	10
54	MGM SP 1089	I'll Be Seeing You/Am I In Love	12
54	MGM SP 1094	You're My Everything/Maybe Next Time	10
54	MGM SP 1100	In A Garden Of Roses/Every Day	10
54	MGM SP 1105	Pa Pa Pa/Mama, Don't Cry At My Wedding	10
55	MGM SP 1125	This Is My Confession/How Important Can It Be?	10
55	MGM SP 1135	When You Wish Upon A Star/Is This The End Of The Line?	10
56	MGM SP 1149	You Are My Love/My Believing Heart	10
57	MGM MGM 918	Give Us This Day/How Lucky You Are	8
57	MGM MGM 954	Only Trust Your Heart/I Need You So	7
58	MGM MGM 973	My Funny Valentine/My Darling, My Darling	6
58	MGM MGM 978	Never 'Till Now/Love Works Miracles	6
58	MGM MGM 991	There Goes My Heart/Funny	10
58	MGM MGM 991	There Goes My Heart/Funny (78)	12
59	MGM MGM 1002	There Must Be A Way/I'm Sorry For You, My Friend	8
59	MGM MGM 1002	There Must Be A Way/I'm Sorry For You, My Friend (78)	15
59	MGM MGM 1022	Perhaps/I Still Get A Thrill (Thinking Of You)	5
59	MGM MGM 1034	I Still Get Jealous/Prayer Of Love	5
59	MGM MGM 1041	Are You Sorry?/What I Don't Know Won't Hurt Me	5
59	MGM MGM 1050	Little Things Mean A Lot/I Laughed At Love	6
60	MGM MGM 1064	You Belong To Me/I Need You Now	5
60	MGM MGM 1089	We Know/They Really Don't Know You	5
60	MGM MGM 1105	Be My Love/Tall As A Tree	5
54	MGM MGM-EP 504	JONI JAMES (EP)	12
55	MGM MGM-EP 518	SINGS TO YOU (EP)	12
56	MGM MGM-EP 530	LITTLE GIRL BLUE (EP)	12
50s	MGM MGM-EP 558	LOVE LETTERS (EP)	10
60	MGM MGM-EP 728	THE SONGS OF HANK WILLIAMS (EP, also stereo MGM-ES 3501)	12/15
54	MGM MGM-D 127	LET THERE BE LOVE (10" LP)	30
59	MGM MGM-C 777	ONE HUNDRED SONGS AND JONI (LP)	22
59	MGM MGM-C 785	JONI SINGS SONGS OF HANK WILLIAMS (LP)	15
60	MGM MGM-C 809	TI VOGLIO BENE (I LOVE YOU SO) (LP)	22
60	MGM MGM-C 823/CS 6005	SINGS IRISH FAVOURITES (LP, mono/stereo)	18/22
60	MGM MGM-C 825	SWINGS SWEET (LP)	18
61	MGM MGM-C 839/CS 6015	100 STRINGS AND JONI IN HOLLYWOOD (LP, mono/stereo)	18/22
63	MGM MGM-C 933	AFTER HOURS (LP)	18

MARK JAMES
| 67 | Liberty LIB 55953 | Bimbo Knows/I Can't Let You Go | 6 |

NICKY JAMES (MOVEMENT)
65	Columbia DB 7747	Stagger Lee/I'm Hurtin' Inside (as Nicky James Movement)	20
67	Philips BF 1566	I Need To Be Needed/So Glad We Made It	5
68	Philips BF 1635	Would You Believe/Silver Butterfly	10
68	Philips BF 1694	Lookin' Through Windows/Nobody But Me	5
69	Philips BF 1755	Time/Little Bit Of Paper	6
69	Philips BF 1804	Reaching For The Sun/No Life At All	5
72	Threshold TH 12	Why/Foreign Shore	5
73	Threshold TH 16	Black Dream/She Came To Me	5
73	Threshold TH 17	I Guess I've Always Loved You/My Style	8
71	Philips 6308 069	NICKY JAMES (LP)	12
73	Threshold THS 10	EVERY HOME SHOULD HAVE ONE (LP)	15
76	Threshold THS 19	THUNDERTHROAT (LP)	12

(see also Move)

PHILIP JAMES & BLUES BUSTERS
| 65 | Island WI 219 | Wide Awake In A Dream/MAYTALS: Tell Me The Reason | 35 |

(see also Blues Busters)

MINT VALUE £

RICKY JAMES

57	HMV POP 306	Knee Deep in The Blues/Bluer Than Blue	25
57	HMV POP 306	Knee Deep in The Blues/Bluer Than Blue (78)	10
57	HMV POP 334	Party Doll/Ninety-Nine Ways	30
57	HMV POP 334	Party Doll/Ninety-Nine Ways (78)	10

ROGER JAMES FOUR

65	Columbia DB 7556	Letter From Kathy/Leave Me Alone	6
66	Columbia DB 7813	Better Than Here/You're Gonna Come Home Cryin' (withdrawn)	12
66	Columbia DB 7829	Better Than Here/You're Gonna Come Home Cryin'	10

RUBY JAMES

| 69 | Fontana TF 1051 | Gettin' Mighty Crowded/Don't Play That Song | 8 |

SIDNEY JAMES (& DEAN ROGERS/LIZ FRASER)

61	Decca F 11328	The Ooter Song/Double Bunk (with Liz Fraser)	10
61	HMV POP 886	Kids/One Last Kiss (with Dean Rogers)	7
73	Pye 7N 4528	Our House/She's Gone (solo) (p/s)	12

(see also Tony Hancock)

SKIP JAMES

65	Vanguard VSD 79219	SKIP JAMES TODAY (LP)	18
68	Vanguard VSD 79273	DEVIL GOT MY WOMAN (LP)	18
70	Spokane SPL 1003	THE ORIGINAL 1930/31 RECORDINGS (LP)	40
78	Vanguard VDP 20001	I'M SO GLAD (LP)	15
70s	Storyville 670 185	THE GREATEST OF THE DELTA BLUES SINGERS (LP)	15
83	Matchbox MSE 207	1931 COMPLETE RECORDINGS (LP)	10

SONNY JAMES

56	Capitol CL 14635	The Cat Came Back/Hello Old Broken Heart	18
56	Capitol CL 14664	Twenty Feet Of Muddy Water/For Rent (One Empty Heart)	15
57	Capitol CL 14683	Young Love/You're The Reason I'm In Love	15
57	Capitol CL 14708	First Date, First Kiss, First Love/Speak To Me	12
57	Capitol CL 14708	First Date, First Kiss, First Love/Speak To Me (78)	8
57	Capitol CL 14742	Dear Love/Lovesick Blues	8
57	Capitol CL 14788	Love Conquered (Love Came, Love Saw)/A Mighty Lovable Man	15
57	Capitol CL 14788	Love Conquered (Love Came, Love Saw)/A Mighty Lovable Man (78)	8
57	Capitol CL 14814	Uh-Huh-Mm/Why Can't They Remember?	15
57	Capitol CL 14814	Uh-Huh-Mm/Why Can't They Remember? (78)	10
58	Capitol CL 14848	Kathaleen/Walk To The Dance	8
58	Capitol CL 14848	Kathaleen/Walk To The Dance (78)	8
58	Capitol CL 14879	Are You Mine/Let's Play Love	6
58	Capitol CL 14915	You Got That Touch/I Can See It In Your Eyes	6
58	Capitol CL 14952	I Can't Stay Away From You/Let Me Be The One To Love You	5
59	Capitol CL 14991	Yo-Yo/Dream Big	10
59	Capitol CL 14991	Yo-Yo/Dream Big (78)	20
59	Capitol CL 15022	Talk Of The School/The Table	5
59	Capitol CL 15046	Pure Love/This Love Of Mine	5
59	Capitol CL 15079	Red Mud/Who's Next In Line	5
60	London HL 9132	Jenny Lou/Passin' Through	8
65	Capitol CL 15377	You're The Only World I Know/Tying The Pieces Together	5
67	Capitol CL 15494	Take Good Care Of Her/On The Fingers Of One Hand	4
69	Capitol CL 15580	Only The Lonely (Know The Way I Feel)/The Journey	4
57	Capitol EAP1 827	YOUNG LOVE (EP)	30
64	Capitol EAP1 20654	YOU'RE THE ONLY WORLD I KNOW (EP)	20
57	Capitol T 779	SOUTHERN GENTLEMAN (LP)	30
57	Capitol T 867	SONNY (LP)	30
58	Capitol T 988	HONEY (LP)	25
63	London HA-D 8049	YOUNG LOVE (LP)	70

STU(ART) JAMES (& MOJOS)

65	Decca F 12231	Wait A Minute/Wonder If She Knows (as Stu James & Mojos)	18
74	Bradleys BRAD 7406	I Only Wish I Had The Time/Back To Basingstoke (Part 1)	5
76	Bradleys BRAD 7614	I'm In The Mood/Firefly (as Stuart James)	5

(see also Mojos)

SULLIVAN JAMES BAND

| 66 | Parlophone R 5465 | Goodbye Mr. Heartache/We're Gonna Make It | 6 |

TOMMY JAMES & SHONDELLS

66	Roulette RK 7000	Hanky Panky/SHONDELLS: Thunderbolt	10
66	Pye International 7N 25398	It's Only Love/Ya! Ya!	6
67	Major Minor MM 511	I Think We're Alone Now/Gone Gone Gone	6
67	Major Minor MM 548	Out Of The Blue/Love's Closing In On Me	5
68	Major Minor MM 558	Wish It Were You/Get Out Now	7
68	Major Minor MM 567	Mony Mony/One, Two, Three And I Fell	6
68	Roulette RO 500	Do Something To Me/Somebody Cares	5
69	Roulette RO 502	Crimson And Clover/Some Kind Of Love	6
69	Roulette RO 506	Sweet Cherry Wine/Breakaway	5
69	Roulette RO 507	Crystal Blue Persuasion/I'm Alive	5
69	Roulette RO 511	Ball Of Fire/Makin' Good Time	5
70	Roulette RO 513	She/Loved One	5
70	Roulette RO 516	Come To Me/Talkin' And Signifyin'	5
70	Roulette RO 518	Ball And Chain/Candy Makers (solo)	5
68	Major Minor MMLP/SMLP 27	SOMETHING SPECIAL (LP)	25
68	Roulette RRLP/SRLP 1	MONY MONY (LP)	20
68	Roulette RRLP/SRLP 2	CRIMSON AND CLOVER (LP)	20
69	Roulette RRLP/SRLP 3	CELLOPHANE SYMPHONY (LP)	20
72	Roulette 2432 002	THE BEST OF TOMMY JAMES & THE SHONDELLS (LP)	15
72	Roulette 2432 005	MY HEAD, MY BED AND MY RED GUITAR (LP, solo)	10

TONY JAMES
68   Jolly JY 002   Treat Me Right/Me Donkey's Dead 4

WINSTON JAMES
70   Hot Rod HR 106   Prison Sentence/JANET FERRON: Darling I Need You 6

JAMES BOYS
68   Direction 58-3721   The Mule (Instrumental)/The Horse (Vocal) 5

JAMES BROTHERS
68   Page One POF 077   I Forgot To Give You Love/The Truth About It 6
68   Page One POF 088   Does It Have To Be Me/You Don't Really Love Me 6
(see also Wheels)

JAMES GANG
70   Stateside SS 2158   Funk No. 48/Collage 7
70   Stateside SS 2173   Stop/Take A Look Around (withdrawn) 12
70   Probe PRO 502   Funk 49/Thanks 6
71   Probe PRO 533   Walk Away/Yadig? 5
70   Stateside SSL 10295   YER' ALBUM (LP) 22
70   Probe SPB 6253   RIDES AGAIN (LP) 18
71   Probe SPB 1038   THIRDS (LP) 18
71   Probe SPB 1045   LIVE IN CONCERT (LP) 15
72   Probe SPB 1056   STRAIGHT SHOOTER (LP) 15
73   Probe SPB 1065   PASSIN' THRU (LP) 15
(see also Joe Walsh, Tommy Bolin)

BOBBY JAMESON
64   London HL 9921   I Wanna Love You/I'm So Lonely 20

BOBBY JAMESON
64   Decca F 12032   All I Want Is My Baby/Each And Every Day 20
65   Brit WI 1001   Rum-Pum/Please Mr. Mailman 12

STEPHEN JAMESON
70   Pye 7N 45189   Margie Make It March/Happiness Road 5
73   Dawn DNS 1035   Don't Say/Back Together Once Again 5
73   Dawn DNLS 3044   STEPHEN JAMESON (LP) 15

JAMESON RAID
80   Blackbird BRAID 001   The Hypnotist/The Raid/Gettin' Hotter/Straight From The Butchers (p/s) 60
81   GBH GBH 1   Seven Days Of Splendour/It's A Crime/Catcher In The Rye
(p/s, with lyric sheet, white sleeve, later black sleeve) 30/20

JAMIES
58   Fontana H 153   Summertime Summertime/Searching For You 30
58   Fontana H 153   Summertime Summertime/Searching For You (78) 20
62   Columbia DB 4885   Summertime Summertime/Searching For You (reissue) 15

JAMIE'S AGENT ORANGE
90   Emma EC 002   Losing My Way/Tumbling Down (no p/s) 50
91   Emma JWD 001   The Hamster Song ('Lovely Gary' Mix)/Don't Cry Chief (At Least
You're Not Stuart) (foldout p/s with free compass) 25
91   Emma JWD 001-12   The Hamster Song ('Lovely Gary' Mix)/('Two Quid' Mix)/
Don't Cry Chief (At Least You're Not Stuart) (12", p/s) 35
91   Emma JWD 002   Ooh, Lovely Gary (The Mick & Dave Rave)/Star Trek Song (p/s) 10
93   Emma JWD 003   Jamie's Porking Out (Fat Bastard Mix)/Tytherley Green Hills Of Home (p/s) 12
95   Emma JWD 005   Emma's In The Club (Rumpy Pumpy Mix)/Company Car (p/s) 6

JAMME
70   Stateside-Dunhill SS 8047   Poor Widow/She Sits There 4
70   Stateside-Dunhill SSL 5024   JAMME (LP) 10

JOE JAMMER
73   Regal Zono. SRZA 8514   BAD NEWS (LP) 20
(see also Mitchell/Coe Mysteries)

JAM ON THE MUTHA
90   Wau!/Polydor MAGXR 3   Hotel California (Orb In Cali Mix 1)/(Like Joe Never Left Mix)/
(Orbitally Ambient Mix) (12", p/s) 8

J.A.M.s
(see under Justified Ancients Of Mu Mu)

JAN & ARNIE
58   London HL 8653   Jennie Lee/Gotta Getta Date 40
58   London HL 8653   Jennie Lee/Gotta Getta Date (78) 30
(see also Jan & Dean)

JAN & DEAN
59   London HLN 8936   Baby Talk/Jeanette, Get Your Hair Done 20
59   London HLN 8936   Baby Talk/Jeanette, Get Your Hair Done (78) 90
59   London HLU 8990   There's A Girl/My Heart Sings 20
59   London HLU 8990   There's A Girl/My Heart Sings (78) 110
60   London HLU 9063   Clementine/You're On My Mind 15
61   London HLH 9395   Heart And Soul/Midsummer Night's Dream 15
62   Liberty LIB 55397   A Sunday Kind Of Love/Poor Little Puppet 8
63   Liberty LIB 55531   Linda/When I Learn How To Cry 7
63   Liberty LIB 55580   Surf City/She's My Summer Girl 6
63   Liberty LIB 55613   Honolulu Lulu/Someday You'll Go Walkin' By 8
64   Liberty LIB 55641   Drag City/Schlock Rod Pt 1 7

MINT VALUE £

64	Liberty LIB 55672	Dead Man's Curve/The New Girl In School	8
64	Liberty LIB 55704	The Little Old Lady From Pasadena/My Mighty GTO	8
64	Liberty LIB 55724	Ride The Wild Surf/The Anaheim, Azusa And Cucamonga Sewing Circle, Book Review And Timing Association	8
65	Liberty LIB 55727	Sidewalk Surfin'/When It's Over	8
65	Liberty LIB 55766	(Here They Come) From All Over The World/Freeway Flyer	8
65	Liberty LIB 55792	You Really Know How To Hurt A Guy/It's As Easy As 1, 2, 3	8
65	Liberty LIB 55833	I Found A Girl/It's A Shame To Say Goodbye	8
66	Liberty LIB 10225	Norwegian Wood/A Beginning From An End	15
66	Liberty LIB 55860	Batman/Bucket 'T'	12
66	Liberty LIB 10244	Popsicle/The Joker Is Wild	10
66	Liberty LIB 55923	The New Girl In School/School Day (Ring Ring Goes The Bell)	8
66	Liberty LIB 10252	Tennessee/Horace The Swinging School Bus Driver	12
67	CBS 202630	Yellow Balloon/A Taste Of Rain	10
65	Liberty LEP 2213	SURF 'N' DRAG HITS (EP)	30
66	Liberty LEP 2258	THE TITANIC TWOSOME (EP)	30
76	United Artists REM 402	REMEMBER JAN & DEAN (EP)	15
63	Liberty LBY 1163	SURF CITY AND OTHER SWINGING CITIES (LP)	30
64	Liberty LBY 1220	DEAD MAN'S CURVE/NEW GIRL IN SCHOOL (LP)	30
64	Liberty LBY 1229	RIDE THE WILD SURF (LP)	30
65	Liberty LBY 1279	GOLDEN HITS (LP)	20
65	Liberty LBY 1304	FOLK 'N' ROLL (LP)	20
66	Liberty LBY 1309	JAN AND DEAN MEET BATMAN (LP)	25
66	Liberty LBY 1339	FILET OF SOUL (A LIVE ONE) (LP)	18
67	Liberty LBL/LBS 83016	GOLDEN HITS (LP, reissue)	12
87	Bam Caruso KIRI 068	JAN AND DEAN MEET BATMAN (LP, reissue)	12

(see also Legendary Masked Surfers, Fantastic Baggys, Jan & Arnie)

JAN & KELLY

62	Philips 326 567 BF	Ooh! 'E Didn't/Prepare To Meet Your Fate Mate	6
62	Philips BF 1253	I Could Have Died/Make Me A Doormat	5
63	Philips BF 1265	Ooh! I Can't/Write Me A Letter	5
64	Philips BF 1323	And Then He Kicked Me/My Country And Western Lover	7
64	Philips BF 1377	There Was A Girl/There Was A Boy/And Then There Was Nothing	5
63	Philips BE 12536	TIME FOR A LAUGH (EP)	10

JAN & KJELD

59	Pye International 7N 25013	Buona Sera/Tiger Rag	6
59	Pye International N 25013	Buona Sera/Tiger Rag (78)	10
60	Ember EMB S 101	Banjo Boy/Don't Raise A Storm (some in p/s)	15/6
60	Qualiton PSP 7127	Sweet Sue/Oh! Mein Papa (as Jan & Keld)	5
60	Ember EMB S 109	Down By The Riverside/I Shall Not Be Moved	5
60	Ember EMB 3312	THE KIDS FROM COPENHAGEN (LP, label states "The Boys From ...")	22

BRUCE JANAWAY

| 78 | Deep Range SRT/CUS/216 | PURITANICAL ODES (LP, with insert) | 40 |

JAN DUKES DE GREY

| 70 | Decca Nova (S)DN 8 | SORCERERS (LP) | 35 |
| 71 | Transatlantic TRA 234 | MICE AND RATS IN THE LOFT (LP) | 60 |

JANE FROM OCCUPIED EUROPE

| 80s | Seven Per Cent JANE 001 | Ocean Run Dry/Annabel Lee/Kingdom By The Sea (p/s) | 5 |

JANE'S ADDICTION

88	WEA W 7520	Mountain Song/Jane Says (p/s)	8
88	WEA W 7520T	Mountain Song/Jane Says/Had A Dad (live) (12", p/s)	10
91	WEA W 0031TP	Classic Girl/No One's Leaving (live)/Ain't No Right (live) (12", picture disc, die-cut sleeve)	10

PETER JANES

| 67 | CBS 203004 | Emperors And Armies/Go Home Ulla (some in p/s) | 8/5 |
| 68 | CBS 3299 | Do You Believe/For The Sake Of Time | 8 |

JANGLETTIES

| 81 | Eskimo Vinyl ESK 4 | Happy All The Time/Backseat (folded, stapled p/s) | 4 |

JANIE

| 61 | Capitol CL 15180 | You Better Not Do That/Only Girls Can Tell | 8 |

(see also Jeanne Black)

JANINE

| 81 | Stiletto JAN 001 | Crazy On You (p/s) | 100 |

JOHNNY JANIS

58	London HLU 8650	The Better To Love You/Can This Be Love	12
58	London HLU 8650	The Better To Love You/Can This Be Love (78)	10
60	Philips PB 1090	Gina/If The Good Lord's Willin'	5
58	HMV 7EG 8365	JOHNNY JANIS (EP)	10
66	London HA-U 8270	ONCE IN A BLUE MOON (LP)	22

HORST JANKOWSKI

65	Mercury MF 861	Walk In The Black Forest/Nola	5
65	Mercury MF 884	Heidi/Simpel Gimpel	5
65	Mercury MF 892	Play A Simple Melody/Cruising Down The Reine	5
66	Mercury MF 966	The Spy With The Cold Nose/Black Forest Holiday	5
68	Mercury MF 1019	The Glory Of Love/Lazy	5
68	Mercury MF 1029	Un Homme Et Une Femme/Moon River	5
68	Mercury MF 1041	Zabadak/Touch Of Heidelberg	5

MINT VALUE £

BERT JANSCH

67	Big T BIG 102	Life Depends On Love/A Little Sweet Sunshine	10
73	Reprise K 14234	Oh My Father/The First Time Ever I Saw Your Face	7
74	Charisma CB 240	In The Bleak Midwinter/One For Jo	6
75	Charisma CB 267	Dance Lady Dance/Build Another Band	5
79	Kicking Mule SCK 44	Time And Time/Una Linea Di Dolcezza (as Bert Jansch Conundrum)	5
82	Logo GO 409	Heartbreak Hotel/Up To The Stars (p/s)	5
66	Transatlantic EP 145	NEEDLE OF DEATH (EP)	25
65	Transatlantic TRA 125	BERT JANSCH (LP)	15
65	Transatlantic TRA 132	IT DON'T BOTHER ME (LP)	15
66	Transatlantic TRA 143	JACK ORION (LP)	25
67	Transatlantic TRA 157	NICOLA (LP)	15
69	Transatlantic TRA 179	BIRTHDAY BLUES (LP)	20
69	Vanguard VSD 79292	STEPPING STONES (LP)	15
69	Transatlantic TRASAM 10	THE BERT JANSCH SAMPLER (LP)	15
71	Transatlantic TRA 235	ROSEMARY LANE (LP)	18
72	Transatlantic TRASAM 27	BOX OF LOVE — THE BERT JANSCH SAMPLER VOL. 2 (LP)	15
73	Reprise K 44225	MOONSHINE (LP, with lyric insert)	15
74	Charisma CAS 1090	L.A. TURNAROUND (LP, with lyric insert)	12
75	Charisma CAS 1107	SANTA BARBARA HONEYMOON (LP)	12
77	Charisma CAS 1127	A RARE CONUNDRUM (LP)	12
80	Kicking Mule SNKF 162	THIRTEEN DOWN (LP, as Bert Jansch Conundrum)	12
85	Konexion KOMA 788006	FROM THE OUTSIDE (LP, 500 only)	15
90	Run River RRA 0012	THE ORNAMENT TREE (LP)	10

BERT JANSCH & JOHN RENBOURN

66	Transatlantic TRA 144	BERT AND JOHN (LP)	15

(see also Conundrum, Pentangle, John Renbourn)

JAPAN

78	Ariola Hansa AHA 510	Don't Rain On My Parade/Stateline (solid or press-out centre, no p/s)	15
78	Ariola Hansa AHA 525	The Unconventional/Adolescent Sex (some with p/s)	20/6
78	Ariola Hansa AHA 529	Sometimes I Feel So Low/Love Is Infectious (p/s, initially on blue vinyl)	12/8
79	Ariola Hansa AHA 540	Life In Tokyo (Short Version)/Life In Tokyo Pt 2 (p/s, red vinyl)	8
79	Ariola Hansa AHAD 540	Life In Tokyo (Long Version)/(Short Version) (12", p/s, red vinyl)	15
80	Ariola Hansa AHA 559	I Second That Emotion/Quiet Life (dull red vinyl, card or paper p/s)	8/6
80	Virgin VS 379	Gentlemen Take Polaroids/The Experience of Swimming (fully autographed by band, p/s)	75
80	Virgin VS 379	Gentlemen Take Polaroids/The Experience of Swimming//The Width Of A Room/Burning Bridges (double pack, gatefold p/s)	6
82	Virgin VSY 472	Ghosts/The Art Of Parties (Version) (picture disc, stickered PVC cover)	5
82	Virgin VS 502	Cantonese Boy/Burning Bridges//Gentlemen Take Polaroids/ The Experience Of Swimming (double pack, gatefold p/s)	4
88	Virgin CDT 11	Ghosts/The Art Of Parties (Version)/Visions Of China (3" CD, card sleeve)	10
88	Virgin CDT 32	Gentlemen Take Polaroids/Cantonese Boy (12" Version)/Methods Of Dance (12" Version) (3" CD, gatefold card sleeve)	10
80	Virgin V 2180	GENTLEMEN TAKE POLAROIDS (LP, with misprinted sleeve with sticker, "Some Kind Of Fool" listed instead of "Burning Bridges")	10
81	Ariola Hansa ZCHAN 001	ASSEMBLAGE (cassette with unreleased live & remixed material)	10

(see also David Sylvian, Mick Karn, Dali's Car)

JOHNNY JAPES & HIS JESTICLES

87	Viz VIZ 1	Bags Of Fun With Buster/Scrotal Scratch Mix (p/s)	5

(see also XTC, John Otway, Mr. Partridge)

JIMMY JAQUES

58	Fontana H 100	Come Walking/Baby, Don't You Cry (78)	10
58	Fontana H 131	In My Life/Never Let You Go	10
58	Fontana H 131	In My Life/Never Let You Go (78)	10
58	Fontana H 161	Barb'ry Ann/For A Lifetime	8
58	Fontana H 161	Barb'ry Ann/For A Lifetime (78)	10
60	Parlophone R 4710	Do Me A Favour/Not To Worry	5

PEPE JARAMILLO

60	Parlophone R 4666	Fruit Salad/Ring Ding	5

JARMELS

61	Top Rank JAR 560	She Loves To Dance/Little Lonely One	18
61	Top Rank JAR 580	A Little Bit Of Soap/The Way You Look Tonight	35

COOK E. JARR

69	RCA RCA 1820	Pledging My Love/If I Were A Carpenter	5

JEAN-MICHEL JARRE

SINGLES

77	Polydor 2001 721	Oxygene 4/Oygene 6 (p/s)	4
78	Polydor POSP 20	Equinoxe 5/Equinoxe 1 (p/s, with etched autograph on run-off)	10
79	Polydor 2001 896	Equinoxe 4 (Remix)/Equinoxe 3 (p/s)	8
80	Polydor 2001 968	Jarre At The Concorde: Equinoxe 7 (live)/Equinoxe 8 (live) (p/s)	12
81	Polydor POSP 292	Magnetic Fields 2 (Remix)/Magnetic Fields 1 (Excerpt) (p/s)	7
81	Polydor POSP 363	Magnetic Fields 4 (Remix)/Magnetic Fields 1 (Excerpt) (p/s)	12
82	Polydor POSP 430	Orient Express/Fishing Junks At Sunset (p/s)	10
84	Polydor POSP 718	Zoolook/Wooloomooloo (p/s)	5
84	Polydor POSPX 718	Zoolook (Remix)/Wooloomooloo/Zoolook (Extended)/ Zoolook (Effects) (12", p/s)	20
85	Polydor POSP 740	Zoolookologie (Remix)/Ethnicolor 2 (p/s)	10
85	Polydor POSPG 740	Zoolookologie (Remix)/Ethnicolor 2//Oxygene 4/Oxygene 6 (double pack)	18
85	Polydor POSPX 740	Zoolookologie (Extended Remix)/(Remix)/Ethnicolor 2 (12", p/s)	20
86	Polydor POSPX 788	Rendezvous 4 (Special Remix)/Rendezvous 4/Moon Machine (12", 'face' or 'city skyline' p/s)	each 25

Jean-MICHEL JARRE

88	Polydor PZ 25	Revolutions (Extended Mix)/Revolutions (LP Mix)/ Industrial Revolution 2 (12", p/s)	10
88	Polydor PZCD 25	Revolutions (Extended Mix)/Revolutions/Revolutions (Single Remix) (CD, jewel case)	25
88	Polydor PZCD 32	London Kid (Full Version) (featuring Hank Marvin)/ Industrial Revolution 3/Revolutions (Remix) (CD, card sleeve)	25
89	Polydor PZCD 55	Oxygene IV (Single Version)/Industrial Revolution Overture/ Oxygene IV (live)/September (CD, card sleeve)	20
90	Polydor PZ 84	Calypso (Extended)/Calypso/Calypso Pt 2 (12", p/s)	12
90	Polydor PZCD 84	Calypso (Extended)/Calypso/Calypso Pt 2 (CD)	12

PROMOS

93	Polydor CHRONO 1	Chronologie (Black Girl Rock)/(Sunscreem 2)/(Sunscreem) (12", white 'clock' p/s)	18
93	Polydor CHRONO 2	Chronologie (Praga Kahn Dream Time Mix)/(Praga Kahn Atomium Mix) (12", black 'clock' p/s)	18
94	Polydor PZ 307DJ	Chronologie 6 (Slam Mix 1)/(Slam Mix 2) (12", pink marbled vinyl, stickered PVC sleeve)	30
94	Polydor PZ 307DJ2	Chronologie 6: Gatdecor Mixes (Main Mix)/(7" Edit Mix)/(Alternate Mix)/ (Original Mix) (12", blue marbled vinyl, stickered PVC sleeve)	30
97	Sony XPR 3117	Oxygene 8 (Sunday Club Remix)/(Sunday Club Edit) (12", stickered title p/s)	10
97	Sony SAMPMS 3984	Oxygene 8 (Hani Oxygene 101)/(Dado's Club Remix)/(Dado's Ethnic Remix)/ (Dado's FM Remix)/(Hani's Oxygene 303)/(Hani's 303 Reprise) (12", double pack, die-cut gatefold stickered sleeve)	10
97	Sony SAMPMS 3949	Oxygene 8 (Takkyu Ishino Extended Mix)/(Takkyu Ishino Edit) (12", stickered title p/s)	7
97	Sony	Oxygene 8 (3" CD)	50
97	Sony XPR 3141	Oxygene 10 (Sash Remix — Maxi Version)/Oxygene 10 (Resistance D Treatment #1)/Oxygene 10 (A 440- Remix Dub Master) (12", stickered title p/s)	7
97	Sony XPR 3145	Oxygene 10 (010 Club Mix 1)/Oxygene 10 (Resistance D Treatment # 2)/ Oxygene 10 (010 Club Mix 2)/OXY A0 A440 Xtra Dub (12", stickered title, p/s)	7
97	Sony XPCD 2166	Oxygene 10 (Sash Edit 2)/Oxygene 10 (Original Edit) (CD)	10
98	Sony XPR 3235	Rendezvous 98 (@ 440 Remix) (12", 1-sided, p/s)	15
98	Sony XPR 3228	ODYSSEY O_2: Oxygene 10 (Trancengenics 1)/Oxygene 7 (DJ Cam Remix)/Oxygene 8 (Trans Mix)/Oxygene 12 (Claude Monnet Remix) (12", title sleeve)	12

ALBUMS

81	Polydor Super POLS 1033	MAGNETIC FIELDS (LP, original pressing with inner sleeve)	10
83	Polydor PROLP 3	THE ESSENTIAL (LP, original pressing, black & white labels)	10
80	Polydor 2683 077	OXYGENE/EQUINOX (2-LP, 'double back' series)	20
80	Polydor 3574 044	OXYGENE/EQUINOX (cassette, 'double back' series)	15
87	Polydor 833 737-2	THE JEAN-MICHEL JARRE 10TH ANNIVERSARY CD BOX SET (7-CD, 5,000 only)	75
88	Polydor C88 1-3	OXYGENE (LP, HMV-only box set with booklet, 3,300 only)	25
88	Polydor C88-1-3	OXYGENE (CD, HMV-only box set with booklet, 3,500 only)	30
97	Epic EPC 489 156-2	COMPLETE OXYGENE (2-CD, with bonus track "Oxygene In Moscow", 24-page booklet, stickered shrinkwrap)	20

MAURICE JARRE

67	RCA Victor RD/SF 7876	THE PROFESSIONALS (LP, soundtrack)	50
68	Dot (S)LPD 515	VILLA RIDES (LP, soundtrack)	15

MARIAN JARVIS

75	Chelsea 2005 038	A Penny For Your Thoughts/A Good Man To Wake Up To	6

JASMINE MINKS

84	Creation CRE 004	Think!/Work For Nothing (foldaround p/s in poly bag)	10
84	Creation CRE 008	Where The Traffic Goes/Mr Magic (foldaround p/s in poly bag)	7
85	Creation CRE 018	What's Happening/Black And Blue (foldaround p/s in poly bag)	5
87	Esurient Comms. PACE 1	PURE (live EP)	4
84	Creation CRELP 003	1, 2, 3, 4, 5, 6, 7, ALL GOOD PREACHERS GO TO HEAVEN (mini-LP, red/black or yellow/black sleeve)	10

JASON & THE SCORCHERS

85	EMI EA 200	Shop It Around/Change The Tune (p/s)	5
85	EMI 12EA 200	Shop It Around/Absolutely Sweet/Change The Tune (12", p/s)	8

JASON CREST

68	Philips BF 1633	Turquoise Tandem Cycle/Good Life (some in export p/s)	60/30
68	Philips BF 1650	Juliano The Bull/Two By The Sea	25
68	Philips BF 1687	(Here We Go Round) The Lemon Tree/Patricia's Dream	35
69	Philips BF 1752	Waterloo Road/Education	15
69	Philips BF 1809	A Place In The Sun/Black Mass	100

(see also Holy Mackerel, High Broom)

JASON'S GENERATIONS

66	Polydor BM 56042	It's Up To You/Insurance Co.'s Are Very Unfair	50

JASPER

69	Spark SRLP 103	LIBERATION (LP)	200

JAWBONE

70	Carnaby CNS 4007	How's Ya Pa?/Mister Custer	10
70	Carnaby CNS 4020	Way Way Down/Bulldog Goes West	10
72	B&C CB 190	Gotta Go/Automobile Blues	6
70	Carnaby CNLS 6004	JAWBONE (LP)	80

(see also Mirage, Portobello Explosion)

BOB JAXON (& HI-TONES)

55	London HL 8156	Ali Baba/Why Does A Woman Cry (as Bob Jaxon & Hi-Tones)	30
55	London HL 8156	Ali Baba/Why Does A Woman Cry (as Bob Jaxon & Hi-Tones) (78)	20
57	RCA RCA 1019	Beach Party/(Gotta Have Something In The) Bank Frank	70
57	RCA RCA 1019	Beach Party/(Gotta Have Something In The) Bank Frank (78)	30

FRANKIE JAXON/HOUNDHEAD HENRY

| 60 | Jazz Collector JEL 10 | THE MALE BLUES VOLUME 6 (EP) | 15 |

JAY (Black)

| 64 | Coral Q 72471 | I Rise, I Fall/How Sweet It Is | 18 |
| 67 | United Artists UP 1174 | What Will My Mary Say/Return To Me (as Jay Black) | 7 |

(see also Jay & Americans)

ABNER JAY

| 63 | London HLN 9791 | Cleo/Thresher | 8 |

DAVID JAY

(see under David J.)

ERIC JAY

| 59 | London HL 9004 | The Little Drummer Boy/Blue Champagne Cha Cha | 7 |
| 59 | London HL 9004 | The Little Drummer Boy/Blue Champagne Cha Cha (78) | 15 |

LAURIE JAY COMBO

62	Ember JBS 710	Shades Of Red/Nevada Sunsets	7
63	HMV POP 1234	Teenage Idol/Think Of Me	8
64	HMV POP 1300	Love In My Heart/'Til You're Mine	6
64	HMV POP 1335	Maybe/Be Good To Me	6
65	Decca F 12083	A Song Called Soul/Just A Little Bit	20

(see also Nero & Gladiators)

LONNIE JAY & JAYNES

| 63 | Stateside SS 197 | Around And Around We Go/Somewhere | 7 |

PETER JAY (& BLUE MEN)

| 60 | Triumph RGM 1000 | Just Too Late/Friendship (as Peter Jay & Blue Men) | 30 |
| 60 | Pye 7N 15290 | Paradise Garden/Who's The Girl? | 35 |

(see also Blue Men)

PETER JAY & JAYWALKERS

62	Decca F 11531	Can Can '62/Redskins	6
63	Decca F 11593	Totem Pole/Jaywalker	6
63	Decca F 11659	Poet And Peasant/Oo La La	7
63	Decca F 11757	Kansas City/The Parade Of Tin Soldiers	8
64	Decca F 11840	You Girl/If You Love Me	8
64	Piccadilly 7N 35199	Where Did Our Love Go/Caroline	10
64	Piccadilly 7N 35212	Tonight You're Gonna Fall In Love/Red Cabbage	8
65	Piccadilly 7N 35220	Parchman Farm/What's Easy For Two Is So Hard For One	15
65	Piccadilly 7N 35259	Before The Beginning/Solitaire	12

(see also Terry Reid, Miller, Big Boy Pete)

JAY & AMERICANS

62	HMV POP 1009	She Cried/Dawning	15
63	United Artists UP 1002	This Is It/It's My Turn To Cry	7
63	United Artists UP 1018	What's The Use/Strangers Tomorrow	7
64	United Artists UP 1039	Come Dance With Me/Look Into My Eyes Maria	7
64	United Artists UP 1069	Come A Little Bit Closer/Goodbye Boys Goodbye	7
65	United Artists UP 1075	Let's Lock The Door (And Throw Away The Key)/I'll Remember You	8
65	United Artists UP 1088	Think Of The Good Times/If You Were Mine Girl	6
65	United Artists UP 1094	Cara Mia/When It's All Over	8
65	United Artists UP 1108	Some Enchanted Evening/Girl	7
66	United Artists UP 1119	Sunday And Me/Through This Doorway	7
66	United Artists UP 1129	Why Can't You Bring Me Home/Baby Stop Your Crying	6
66	United Artists UP 1132	Crying/I Don't Need A Friend	7
66	United Artists UP 1142	Livin' Above Your Head/She's The Girl (That's Messing Up My Mind)	22
66	United Artists UP 1162	(He's) Raining In My Sunshine/Reason For Living	6
67	United Artists UP 1178	You Ain't As Hip As All That Baby/Nature Boy	6
67	United Artists UP 1191	(We'll Meet In The) Yellow Forest/Got Hung Up Along The Way	30
68	United Artists UP 2211	French Provincial/Shanghai Noodle Factory	6
69	United Artists UP 2268	This Magic Moment/Since I Don't Have You	6
69	United Artists UP 35008	When You Dance/So Much In Love	6
69	United Artists UP 35026	Hushabye/No I Don't Know Her	6
70	United Artists UP 35074	Walkin' In The Rain/For The Love Of A Lady	6
65	United Artists UEP 1003	COME A LITTLE BIT CLOSER (EP)	40
66	United Artists UEP 1017	LIVING WITH JAY AND THE AMERICANS (EP)	40
66	United Artists (S)ULP 1117	JAY AND THE AMERICANS (LP)	30
66	United Artists (S)ULP 1128	SUNDAY AND ME (LP)	30
67	United Artists (S)ULP 1150	LIVIN' ABOVE YOUR HEAD (LP)	30
67	United Artists (S)ULP 1164	TRY SOME OF THIS (LP)	30

(see also Jay, Chapter Four)

JAY (John Holt) & JOYA (Landis)

| 68 | Trojan TR 633 | I'll Be Lonely/SUPERSONICS: Second Fiddle | 8 |

(see also John Holt, Joya Landis)

JAY & TECHNIQUES

67	Philips PB 1597	Apples, Peaches, Pumpkin Pie/Stronger Than Dirt	8
67	Philips PB 1618	Keep The Ball Rollin'/Here We Go Again	6
68	Philips PB 1644	Strawberry Shortcake/Still (In Love With You)	6
68	Mercury MF 1034	Baby Make Your Own Sweet Music/Help Yourself To All My Lovin'	8

MINT VALUE £

73	Mercury 6052 302	Apples, Peaches, Pumpkin Pie/Contact	5
75	Polydor 2066 473	I Feel Love Comin' On/This World Of Mine	6
71	Mercury MCF 127360	Baby Make Your Own Sweet Music/Help Yourself To All My Lovin' (reissue)	5
67	Philips (S)BL 7834	APPLES, PEACHES, PUMPKIN PIE (LP)	18

JAYBIRDS
64	Embassy WB 621	Not Fade Away/Over You	5
64	Embassy WB 624	Tell Me When/You Can't Do That	5
64	Embassy WB 625	Can't Buy Me Love/DEL MARTIN: I Love You Because.	5
64	Embassy WB 626	Good Golly Miss Molly/	5
64	Embassy WB 628	Mockin' Bird Hill/Hubble Bubble (Toil And Trouble)	5
64	Embassy WB 632	Baby Let Me Take You Home/BUD ASHTON & HIS GROUP:	
		Rise And Fall Of Fingel Blunt	5
64	Embassy WB 635	Juliet/Here I Go Again	4
64	Embassy WB 651	She's Not There/PAUL RICH: I Wouldn't Trade You For The World	5
64	Embassy WB 663	All Day And All Of The Night/Google Eye	8
64	Embassy WB 672	What Have They Done To The Rain/BUD ASHTON & HIS GROUP:	
		Genie With The Light Brown Lamp	5
65	Embassy WB 673	Go Now/TERRY BRANDON: Ferry 'Cross The Mersey	5

(see also Ray Pilgrim & Beatmen)

JAYBIRDS
| 66 | Sue WI 4013 | Somebody Help Me/The Right Kind. | 22 |

JAY BOYS
69	Trojan TR 665	Splendour Splash/TREVOR SHIELD: Please.	8
70	Harry J. HJ 6602	The Dog (Parts 1 & 2).	7
70	Harry J. HJ 6607	Jack The Ripper/Don't Let Me Down	5
70	Harry J. HJ 6609	Jay Moon Walk/Elcong.	5
70	Harry J. HJ 6610	Je T'Aime/It Ain't Me Babe.	5
70	Harry J. HJ 6617	Del Gago/Killer Version	5
70	Harry J. HJ 6618	Can't Get Next To You/(Part 2) (both actually by Charmers)	5
71	Harry J. HJ 6628	The Arcade Walk/The Arcade Walk Vers. II	5
72	Harry J. HJ 6644	African People/HARRY J. ALL STARS: African (Version)	5
72	Ashanti AHS 407	Rough Road/TREVOR SHIELD: Rough Road	6

(see also Roy Panton, Bob & Marcia, Cables)

JERRY JAYE
| 67 | London HLU 10128 | My Girl Josephine/Five Miles From Home. | 30 |

JAYE SISTERS
| 59 | London HLT 9011 | Sure Fire Love/G-3. | 45 |
| 59 | London HLT 9011 | Sure Fire Love/G-3 (78) | 50 |

JAYHAWKS
| 56 | Parlophone R 4228 | Stranded In The Jungle/My Only Darling. | 500 |
| 56 | Parlophone R 4228 | Stranded In The Jungle/My Only Darling (78) | 100 |

JAYLADS
| 71 | Punch PH 95 | Royal Chord (actually by Melodians)/Version | |
| | | (actually "In The Spirit" by Lloyd Charmers) | 6 |

(see also Melodians)

JAYNETTS
| 63 | Stateside SS 227 | Sally Go Round The Roses/Sally Go Round The Roses (Instrumental) | 8 |

JAYS
| 63 | Parlophone R 4764 | Shock A Boom/Across The Sea. | 8 |

JAYWALKERS
| 76 | Cream CRM 5003 | Can't Live Without You/Heartbroken Memories. | 6 |

JAZZATEERS
83	Rough Trade RT 138	Sixteen Reasons/Show Me The Door (p/s)	5
85	Stampede STAMP 1	Pressing On/Spiral (12", p/s)	7
84	Rough Trade ROUGH 46	JAZZATEERS (LP, with insert)	12

JAZZ BUTCHER
83	Glass GLASS 027	Southern Mark Smith/Jazz Butcher Meets Count Dracula (p/s)	5
85	Glass GLASS 12041	Real Men/The Jazz Butcher V The Prime Minister/	
		Southern Mark Smith (Original) (12", p/s)	7
86	Glass HMMM 001	Christmas With The Pygmies (p/s, promo freebie, given away at gigs)	10

JAZZ COMPOSERS ORCHESTRA
| 74 | JCOA/Virgin JDA 311 | JAZZ COMPOSERS ORCHESTRA (2-LP, gatefold sleeve) | 15 |

(see also Carla Bley, Mike Mantler, Don Cherry, Larry Coryell)

JAZZ COURIERS
57	Tempo EXA 75	JAZZ COURIERS (EP)	10
59	Tempo EXA 87	JAZZ COURIERS (EP)	10
58	Tempo TAP 22	IN CONCERT (LP).	200
59	Tempo TAP 26	THE LAST WORD (LP)	350
60	London Jazz LTZ-L 15188	THE COURIERS OF JAZZ! (LP)	225
67	M. For Pleasure MFP 1072	IN CONCERT (LP).	100

(see also Tubby Hayes, Ronnie Scott)

JAZZ CRUSADERS
| 66 | Fontana 688 149 ZL | THE THING (LP) | 15 |

(see also Crusaders)

JAZZ FIVE
| 61 | Tempo TAP 32 | THE FIVE OF US (LP). | 12 |

(see also Vic Ash Quartet, Harry Klein Quartet)

JAZZ HIP TRIO
67   Major Minor MMLP 8   JAZZ IN RELIEF (LP) 60

JAZZ MAKERS
60s   Ember FA 2023   SWINGIN' SOUNDS (LP) 12

JAZZ MODES
60   London Jazz LTZ-K 15191   THE MOST HAPPY FELLA (LP) 10
61   London Jazz LTZ-K 15203   THE JAZZ MODES (LP, also stereo SAH-K 6117) 10

JAZZ ROCK EXPERIENCE
70   Deram Nova SDN 19   JAZZ ROCK EXPERIENCE (LP) 25

J & B
66   Polydor 56095   Wow Wow Wow/There She Goes 8
(see also State Of Micky & Tommy, Foreigner)

J.B.'s
71   Mojo 2001 155   These Are The J.B.'s (Parts 1 & 2) 6
71   Mojo 2027 001   The Grunt (Parts 1 & 2) 7
72   Mojo 2093 007   Gimme Some More/The Rabbit Got The Gun 6
72   Mojo 2093 016   Hot Pants Road/Pass The Peas 6
72   Mojo 2093 021   Givin' Up Food For Funk (Parts 1 & 2) 6
72   Mojo 2918 004   PASS THE PEAS (LP) 30
72   Polydor 2391 034   FOOD FOR THOUGHT (LP) 30
74   Polydor 2391 087   DOING IT TO DEATH (LP) 30
75   Polydor 2391 194   HUSTLE WITH SPEED (LP) 30
76   Polydor 2391 204   GIVIN' UP FOOD FOR FUNK — THE BEST OF THE JB's (LP) 30
(see also Fred Wesley & JB's, James Brown, Bobby Bird)

J.D. (THE ROC)
72   Sioux SI 008   Superbad/MONTEGO MELON: Lucky Dip 6
(see also Jeff Dixon)

BOBBI JEAN
65   Mercury MF 921   Dry Your Tears/Pity The Man 7

CATHY JEAN & ROOMATES
61   Parlophone R 4764   Please Love Me Forever/Canadian Sunset 40

LANA JEAN
63   Pye International 7N 25214   It Hurts To Be Sixteen/Bad Boy 10

JEAN & GAYTONES
71   Trojan TR 7817   I Shall Sing (actually by Judy Mowatt & Gaytones)/GAYTONES: Target 6

JEAN & STATESIDES
64   Columbia DB 7287   Putty In Your Hands/One Fine Day 15
64   Columbia DB 7439   You Won't Forget Me/Cold, Cold Winter 12
65   Columbia DB 7651   Mama Didn't Lie/Just Let Me Cry 12

JEAN-ETTES
59   Pye 7N 15185   May You Always/I Saw A Light 7
59   Pye N 15185   May You Always/I Saw A Light (78) 12

JEAN-JACQUES
69   Pye International 7N 25489   Maman/Les Beaux Dimanches 5

JEANNE & JANIE
60   Capitol CL 15146   Journey Of Love/JEANNE BLACK: Lisa 6
60   Capitol CL 15165   Sleep Walkin'/JEANNE BLACK: You'll Find Out 6
(see also Jeanne Black)

JEANNIE (& BIG GUYS)
63   Piccadilly 7N 35147   Don't Lie To Me/Boys (as Jeannie & Big Guys) 10
64   Piccadilly 7N 35164   I Want You/Sticks And Stones (as Jeannie & Big Guys) 10
65   Parlophone R 5343   I Love Him/With Any Other Girl 8
(see also Cindy Cole)

JEANNIE & REDHEADS
64   Decca F 11829   Animal Duds/ANDREW OLDHAM GROUP: Funky And Fleopatra 25
(see also Andrew Oldham Orchestra)

AUDREY JEANS
56   Decca F 10768   Ticky Ticky Tick (I'm Gonna Tell On You)/Will You, Willyum 10
56   Decca F 10788   It's Better In The Dark/The Bus Stop Song (A Paper Of Pins) 6
58   Decca F 11035   Send A Letter To Jeanette — Yet!/Bad Pianna Rag 6
58   Decca F 11035   Send A Letter To Jeanette — Yet!/Bad Pianna Rag (78) 8
61   HMV POP 876   How Lovely To Be A Woman/What Did I See In Him 5

JEDDAH
83   Death RIP 2001   Eleanor Rigby (with poster, no p/s) 20

JEDI KNIGHTS
95   Clear CLR 406   MAY THE FUNK BE WITH YOU (12" EP, p/s) 15
95   Clear CLR 406X   MAY THE FUNK BE WITH YOU (12" EP, clear vinyl, embossed sleeve) 25
(see also Global Communications)

JEEPS
66   Strike JH 308   He Saw Eesaw/The Music Goes Round 5
66   Strike JH 315   Ain't It A Great Big Laugh/I Put On My Shoes 5

JEFFERSON
68   Pye 7N 17634   Montage/Did You Hear A Heartbreak Last Night 6
69   Pye 7N 17706   The Colour Of My Love/Look No Further 6
69   Pye 7N 17810   Baby Take Me In Your Arms/I Fell Flat On My Face 6
69   Pye 7N 17855   Love And All The World/I've Got To Tell Her 6
69   Pye NSPL 18316   THE COLOUR OF MY LOVE (LP) 18
(see also Rockin' Berries, Sight & Sound)

MINT VALUE £

BLIND LEMON JEFFERSON

50	Tempo R 38	Weary Dog Blues/Change My Luck Blues (78)	20
50	Tempo R 39	Lock Step Blues/Hangman's Blues (78)	20
51	Tempo R 46	Shuckin' Sugar Blues/Rabbit Foot Blues (78)	20
52	Tempo R 54	Gone Dead On You Blues/One Dime Blues (78)	20
53	Jazz Collector L 91	Shuckin' Sugar Blues/Rabbit Foot Blues (78)	15
53	Jazz Collector L 103	Jack O'Diamonds Blues/Clock House Blues (78)	15
54	Jazz Collector L 126	Gone Dead On You Blues/One Dime Blues (78)	15
50s	Poydras 99	BLIND LEMON JEFFERSON (10" EP)	30
53	London Jazz AL 3508	FOLK BLUES OF BLIND LEMON JEFFERSON (10" LP)	40
55	London Jazz AL 3546	PENITENTIARY BLUES (10" LP)	40
57	London Jazz AL 3564	SINGS THE BLUES (10" LP)	40
69	CBS 63738	THE IMMORTAL (LP)	12
70s	Roots Matchbox RL 301	BLIND LEMON JEFFERSON VOLUME 1 (LP)	12
70s	Roots Matchbox RL 306	BLIND LEMON JEFFERSON VOLUME 2 (LP)	12
70s	Roots Matchbox RL 331	BLIND LEMON JEFFERSON VOLUME 3 (LP)	12
75	Milestone M 47022	BLIND LEMON JEFFERSON (2-LP)	15

(see also Paramount Allstars)

BLIND LEMON JEFFERSON/ED BELL

| 60 | Jazz Collector JEL 13 | THE MALE BLUES VOLUME 7 (EP) | 15 |

BLIND LEMON JEFFERSON/BUDDY BOY HAWKINS

| 59 | Jazz Collector JEL 8 | THE MALE BLUES VOLUME 5 (EP) | 15 |

BLIND LEMON JEFFERSON/LEADBELLY

| 61 | Jazz Collector JEL 24 | THE MALE BLUES VOLUME 8 (EP) | 15 |

BLIND LEMON JEFFERSON & RAMBLING THOMAS

| 50s | Heritage HLP 1007 | BLIND LEMON JEFFERSON AND RAMBLING THOMAS (LP) | 60 |

EDDIE JEFFERSON

| 67 | Stateside SS 591 | Some Other Time/When You Look In The Mirror | 8 |

GEORGE PAUL JEFFERSON

| 68 | Fontana TF 923 | Looking For My Mind/Out Of Place | 12 |

MARSHALL JEFFERSON

| 88 | ffrr FFRX 18 | Open Your Eyes (Celestial Mix)/(Spiritual Mix)/ (Marhsall's Elevated Dub) (12", p/s) | 15 |

JEFFERSON AIRPLANE

67	RCA Victor RCA 1594	Somebody To Love/She Has Funny Cars	6
67	RCA Victor RCA 1631	White Rabbit/Plastic Fantastic Lover	8
67	RCA Victor RCA 1647	Ballad Of You And Me and Pooneil/Two Heads	7
68	RCA Victor RCA 1711	Greasy Heart/Share A Little Joke (With The World)	8
68	RCA Victor RCA 1736	If You Feel Like China Breaking/Triad	7
70	RCA RCA 1933	Volunteers/We Can Be Together	5
70	RCA RCA 1964	Somebody To Love/White Rabbit	5
70	RCA RCA 1989	Mexico/Have You Seen The Saucers?	5
72	Grunt 65-0500	Pretty As You Feel/Wild Turkey	6
72	Grunt 65-0506	Long John Silver/Milk Train	5
89	RCA PD 49463	White Rabbit/Plastic Fantastic Lover/Somebody To Love/ She Has Funny Cars (3" CD, gatefold card p/s)	7
67	RCA Victor RD/SF 7889	SURREALISTIC PILLOW (LP, black label, mono/stereo)	30/25
68	RCA Victor RD/SF 7926	AFTER BATHING AT BAXTERS (LP, black label, mono/stereo)	30/25
68	RCA Victor RD/SF 7976	CROWN OF CREATION (LP, black label, mono/stereo)	20/18
69	RCA RD/SF 8019	BLESS ITS POINTED LITTLE HEAD (LP)	15
69	RCA Victor SF 7889	SURREALISTIC PILLOW (LP, repressing, orange label)	12
69	RCA Victor SF 7926	AFTER BATHING AT BAXTERS (LP, repressing, orange label)	12
69	RCA Victor SF 7976	CROWN OF CREATION (LP, repressing, orange label)	12
70	RCA SF 8076	VOLUNTEERS (LP, gatefold sleeve)	15
71	RCA SF 8164	THE WORST OF JEFFERSON AIRPLANE (LP, matt sleeve)	12
71	Grunt FTR 1001	BARK (LP, bag cover with lyric sheet & brown inner sleeve)	15
71	RCA SF 8195	JEFFERSON AIRPLANE TAKES OFF (LP)	12
72	Grunt FTR 1007	LONG JOHN SILVER (LP, open-out box cover with inner lyric sleeve)	15
73	Grunt FTR 0147	30 SECONDS OVER WINTERLAND (LP, with inner sleeve)	12

(see also Jefferson Starship, Great Society, Paul Kantner, Grace Slick, Papa John Creach, Hot Tuna)

JEFFERSON STARSHIP

| 75 | Grunt FB 10367 | Miracles/Al Garimasu | 4 |
| 78 | Grunt FL 13247 | GOLD (LP, gatefold sleeve; with 7" "Light The Sky On Fire"/ "Hyperdrive" [FB 1426]) | 10 |

FRAN JEFFRIES

| 67 | Monument MON 1006 | My Lonely Corner/Life Goes On | 5 |

JEGA

| 96 | Skam SKA 6 | Phlax/Nortom Midgate/Bluette/Ionic/Evil Lee Kirtcele/Steel Drum/In With The In (12", custom sleeve) | 35 |
| 97 | Skam SKA 9 | Card Hore/Oak Hanger/Nausicaa/Stainless Steel Drum/Star Houdini (12", p/s) | 15 |

JELLYBEAN

84	EMI America EA 210	Sidewalk Talk (featuring Madonna)/Was Dog A Doughnut (p/s)	4
84	EMI America 12EA 210	Sidewalk Talk (featuring Madonna)/Was Dog A Doughnut (12", p/s)	7
84	EMI America 12EAX 210	Sidewalk Talk (featuring Madonna)/Was Dog A Doughnut/Sidewalk Talk (featuring Madonna)/Was Dog A Doughnut (12" remix, p/s)	8

(see also Madonna)

JELLY BEANS

64	Pye International 7N 25252	I Wanna Love Him So Bad/So Long	15
64	Red Bird RB 10011	The Kind Of Boy You Can't Forget/Baby Be Mine	15
75	Right On R 102	You Don't Mean Me No Good/I'm Hip To You	5

JELLYBREAD
69	Blue Horizon 57-3162	Chairman Mao's Boogaloo/No One Else	10
70	Blue Horizon 57-3169	Comment/Funky Wasp	10
70	Blue Horizon 57-3174	Rockin' Pneumonia And The Boogie-Woogie Flu/Readin' The Meters	10
70	Blue Horizon 57-3180	Old Man Hank/Faded Grace	10
71	Blue Horizon 2096 001	Creepin' And Crawlin'/The Loser/The Clergyman's Daughter	8
72	Blue Horizon 2096 006	Down Along The Cove/Sister Lucy	10
60s	Liphook 1	JELLYBREAD (mini-LP)	60
69	Blue Horizon 7-63853	FIRST SLICE (LP)	40
71	Blue Horizon 2431 002	65 PARKWAY (LP)	40
72	Blue Horizon 2931 004	BACK TO THE BEGINNING AGAIN (LP)	70

DIANNE JENKINS
76	Crystal CR 7025	Tow-A-Way-Zone/Anniversary	8

GORDON JENKINS ORCHESTRA
60	London HLR 9089	The Clock Song/Romantica	7

(see also Ella Fitzgerald)

JOHNNY JENKINS
69	Atco 226 009	The Voodoo In You/Backside Blues	5
71	Atco 2400 033	TON-TON MACOUTE (LP)	15
72	Atlantic K 40105	TON-TON MACOUTE (LP, reissue)	12

JENNIFER
69	London HLU 10278	Let The Sun Shine In/Easy To Be Hard	5
70	London HLU 10312	Cajun Train/Old Folks (Les Vieux)	6

JENNIFERS
92	Nude NUD 2T	Just Got Back/Rocks And Boulders/Danny's Song/Tomorrow's Rain (12")	15
92	Nude NUD 2CD	Just Got Back/Rocks And Boulders/Danny's Song/Tomorrow's Rain (CD)	15

(see also Supergrass)

BILL JENNINGS
55	Parlophone MSP 6146	Stuffy/Solitude (as Bill Jennings-Leo Parker Quintet)	6
55	Parlophone MSP 6156	Soft Winds/What's New? (as Bill Jennings Quartet)	6

WAYLON JENNINGS
69	RCA RCA 1866	The Days Of Sand And Shovels/Delia's Gone	6
73	RCA RCA 2322	Never Been To Spain/Sure Didn't Take Him Long	5
74	RCA RCA 2443	You Can Have Her/Gone To Denver	5
80	RCA PB 9561	The Dukes Of Hazzard Theme/Storms Never Last (p/s)	5
68	RCA SF 8003	ONLY THE GREATEST (LP)	15
70	A&M Mayfair AMLB 1006	THE COUNTRY SIDE OF WAYLON JENNINGS (LP)	12
70	RCA Victor LSA 3000	BEST OF WAYLON JENNINGS (LP)	12
72	RCA Victor LSA 3053	CEDARTOWN, GEORGIA (LP)	12
74	RCA AFL1-0240	HONKY TONK HEROES (LP)	12
74	RCA AFL1-0539	THIS TIME (LP)	12

JENNORS
67	Coxsone CS 7024	Pressure And Slide (actually by Tennors)/SOUL BROTHERS: One Stop	18

(see also Tennors)

KRIS JENSEN
62	Fontana 267 241 TF	Torture/Let's Sit Down	12
63	Fontana 267 267 TF	Don't Take Her From Me/Claudette	12
64	Hickory 45-1224	Donna Donna/Big As I Can Dream	12
64	Hickory 45-1243	Lookin' For Love/In Time	8
64	Hickory 45-1256	Come Back To Me/You've Only Got Me To Lose	8
65	Hickory 45-1285	The Little Wind-Up Doll/Somebody's Smiling While I'm Crying	8
65	Hickory 45-1311	What Should I Do/That's A Whole Lotta Love	8

KRIS JENSEN/SUE THOMPSON
65	Hickory LPE 1507	INTRODUCING KRIS JENSEN AND SUE THOMPSON (EP, 2 tracks each)	20

(see also Sue Thompson)

PAUL JENSEN & CAR THIEVES
78	Albatross TIT 3	Holiday In Spain/Always Arrive On Time (p/s)	6

JENSENS
68	Philips BF 1686	Deep Thinking/Marguerite	10

(see also Tempus Fugit)

BILL JENTIES
70	Smash SMA 2307	Stop Them (actually by Bill Gentles)/MAXINE: I Don't Care	6

(see also Bill Gentles/Bill Jentles)

BILL JENTLES
70	Pama PM 809	True True Train/JEFF BARNES: Give And Take	6

(see also Bill Jenties)

JERICHO (JONES)
71	A&M AMS 833	This Is Now/Freedom	10
72	A&M AMS 883	Don't Let Me Down/Mona Mona	10
72	A&M AMS 7017	Hey Man/Champs	10
72	A&M AMS 7037	Mama's Gonna Take You Home/So Come On	10
71	A&M AMLH 68050	JUNKIES, MONKEYS & DONKEYS (LP, as Jericho Jones)	90
72	A&M AMLS 68079	JERICHO (LP, beware of counterfeits with slightly thicker sleeves)	75

JERKS
78	Underground URA 1	Get Your Woofing Dog Off Me/Hold My Hand (p/s)	20
78	Lightning GIL 549	Cool/Jerkin' (p/s)	18
80	Laser LAS 25	Come Back Bogart (I Wish You Would)/Are You Strong Enough?/The Strangest Man Of All (p/s)	10

JERMZ
78 One Way EFP 1   Power Cut/Me And My Baby (p/s) 40

JERRY JEROME
55 MGM SP 1118   Honey/In A Little Spanish Town 5

JERRY & FREEDOM SINGERS
70 Banana BA 308   It's All In The Game (pseudonym for Winston Francis)/
IM: The Way To My Heart (pseudonym for Cedric Brooks) 10

(see also Winston Francis)

JERRY O
67 London HLZ 10162   Karate Boo-ga-loo/The Pearl 6
71 Jay Boy BOY 33   Karate Boo-ga-loo/The Pearl (reissue) 4
72 Jay Boy BOY 62   Dance What 'Cha Wanna/Afro-Twist Time 4

JERUSALEM
72 Deram DM 358   Kamakazi Moth/Frustration 10
72 Deram SDL 6   JERUSALEM (LP, gatefold sleeve) 70
(see also Pussy, Ian Gillan)

JERUSALEM
79 Praise PLP 4   JERUSALEM (LP, with insert) 40
80 Myrrh MYR 1097   VOLUME 2 (LP, with insert) 30
82 Myrrh MYR 1113   WARRIOR (LP) 40

JESS & JAMES
68 MGM MGM 1389   Move/What Was I Born For 5
68 MGM MGM 1420   Something For Nothing/I Let The Day Go By (with J.J. Band) 7
68 MGM MGM 1454   Thank You Show Biz/Motherless Child 4

JESSE GARON & DESPERADOES
86 Wild Rumpus SHEP 001   Hank Williams Is Dead/FIZZBOMBS: You Worry Me (flexidisc, p/s) 5
86 Narodnik NRK 001   Splashing Along/Presence Dear (p/s) 7
87 Narodnik NRK 002   The Rain Fell Down/I'm Up Here (p/s) 5
87 Narodnik NRK 005   BILLY THE WHIZZ (12" EP) 8
88 Velocity SPEED 002   You'll Never Be That Young Again/And If The Sky Should Fall (p/s) 4

JESTERS
62 R&L RL 15/16   Little Girl/Casa Pedro (2 different label designs) 10

JESUS & MARY CHAIN
84 Creation CRE 012   Upside Down/Vegetable Man (black, red & white wraparound p/s in
poly bag with address on rear) 12
84 Creation CRE 012   Upside Down/Vegetable Man (pink, blue or yellow wraparound p/s
in poly bag; some with small T-shirt offer insert) 8
86 Creation CRE 012   Upside Down/Vegetable Man (reissue, different printed p/s) 5
86 Creation CRE 012T   Upside Down/Vegetable Man/Upside Down (demo)
(12" white label, no sleeve) 35
85 Fierce FRIGHT 004   RIOT (EP, with 'LSD bar' & badge; 2 different sleeves) 25
85 Blanco Y Negro NEG 008   Never Understand/Suck (p/s) 5
85 Blanco Y Negro NEGT 008   Never Understand/Suck/Ambition (12", p/s) 8
85 Blanco Y Negro NEG 13   You Trip Me Up/Just Out Of Reach (p/s) 4
85 Blanco Y Negro NEGT 13   You Trip Me Up/Just Out Of Reach/Boyfriend's Dead (12", p/s) 7
85 Blanco Y Negro NEG 17F   Just Like Honey/Head//Inside Me/Just Like Honey (Demo Oct 84)
(double pack, gatefold p/s) 8
85 The Hit HOT 001   Just Like Cindy/STYLE COUNCIL: Walls Come Tumbling Down (live)/
SIMPLY RED: Every Bit Of Me/REDSKINS: Kick Over The Statues
(The Ramsey McKinnock Mix)
(p/s, free EP with *The Hit* magazine, issue 1) 4
86 Blanco Y Negro NEG 19F   Some Candy Talking/Psycho Candy/Hit/Cut Dead/You Trip Me Up/
Some Candy Talking/Psycho Candy (double pack, gatefold p/s,
2nd 7" all acoustic) 6
86 Blanco Y Negro NEGT 19   Some Candy Talking/Taste Of Cindy/Hit/Psycho Candy
(12", p/s, with poster) 7
87 Blanco Y Negro NEG 24F   April Skies/Kill Surf City//Mushroom (Live In Nuremburg 1986)/
Bo Diddley Is Jesus (double pack, stickered gatefold p/s) 5
87 Blanco Y Negro NEGB 25   Happy When It Rains/Everything Is Alright When You're Down
(box set with postcards) 7
87 Blanco Y Negro NEGTE 25   Happy When It Rains (Extended)/Shake/Everything Is Alright When You're
Down/Happy When It Rains (Demo) (10", p/s) 6
87 Blanco Y Negro NEG 29CD   Darklands/Rider/Here It Comes Again/On The Wall (Portastudio Demo) (CD) 7
88 Blanco Y Negro NEG 32CD   Sidewalking/Sidewalking (Extended Version)/Taste Of Cindy (Live In Detroit)/
Sidewalking (Chilled To The Bone) (3" CD, with 5" adaptor in 5" case) 7
89 Blanco Y Negro NEG 41TE   Blues From A Gun/Shimmer/Penetration/Break Me Down (10", gatefold p/s) 12
89 Blanco Y Negro NEG 41CD   Blues From A Gun/Shimmer/Penetration/My Girl (3" CD, gatefold card sleeve) . . . 7
89 Blanco Y Negro NEG 42/XB/Y/Z   Head On/Terminal Beach//Head On/Deviant Slice//Head On/
I'm Glad I Never//Head On/In The Black (4 x 7" box set;
each single sold separately) 15
89 Blanco Y Negro NEG 42CD   Head On/In The Black/Drop (Acoustic Re-Mix)/Break Me Down
(3" CD, gatefold card sleeve) 7
(see also Acid Angels, Primal Scream, Meat Whiplash)

JESUS HEIST
94 Religion GOD 666   Resurrection Shuffle/Forgive Them Officer, For They Know Not Wot They Do
('absolute' white vinyl, p/s) 15
95 Religion GOD 667   The Great God-Squad Swindle/Church Of The Poison Kind
(Jesus Hates You Damnation Mix) (p/s, with free rosary) 8

JESUS IS
70s Myrrh MYR 1049   JESUS IS (LP) 15

JESUS LIZARD

92	own label	Gladiator	
		(Marquee gig freebie)	8
93	Touch & Go TG 83	Puss/NIRVANA: Oh, The Guilt	
		(p/s, blue vinyl, some with poster)	25/12
93	Touch & Go TG 83	Puss/NIRVANA: Oh, The Guilt	
		(p/s, black vinyl)	18
93	Touch & Go TG 83CD	Puss/NIRVANA: Oh, The Guilt (CD)	20

(see also Nirvana)

JESUS LOVES YOU

89	More Protein PRTOX 12	After The Love (Fon Force Remix)/After The Love (Dub) (12", p/s)	10
89	More Protein PROCD 2	After The Love (10 Glorious Years Edit)/After The Love (10 Glorious Years Mix)/ After The Love (Orbital House Mix)	
		(3" CD, card sleeve)	10
90	More Protein PROCD 5	Generations Of Love (Land Of Oz 7" Mix)/Generations Of Love (Land Of Oz 12" Mix)/Generations Of Love (The 80's Mix) (CD)	8
91	More Protein PROT 1312DJ	After The Love (Prophets Of Doom Mix)/(Naughty Norman Normal's Nightie Mix)/Generations Of Love (Absolutely Queer Remix) (12", p/s, promo only)	18
91	More Protein PROCD 13	After The Love (Naughty Norman Normal's Nightie Edit)/After The Love (Prophets Of Doom 7" Edit)/After The Love (Ten Glorious Years Edit)/ Generations Of Love (Absolutely Queer Remix) (CD)	7
90	More Protein PROCD 7	One On One (Fon Force 7" Edit)/(Massive Attack Mix)/ After The Love (Danny Rampling Mix)/Generations Of Love (Oakenfold Edit) (CD, slimline jewel case)	7
91	More Protein PROCD 13	After The Love (Naught Norman Normal's Nightie Edit)/ (Prophets Of Doom 7" Edit)/(Ten Glorious Years Edit)/Generations Of Love (Absolutely Queer Remix) (CD, slimline jewel case)	7
92	Virgin VSCDX 1449	Sweet Toxic Love (Deliverance Mix)/(Hootenanny Mix)/ Am I Losing Control (Disco Mix)/Am I Losing Control (Dizzy Tequila Mix) (CD, plastic clip-shut pack with booklet)	15

(see also Boy George, Culture Club, JLY Posse)

JET

75	CBS 80699	JET (LP)	10

(see also Andy Ellison, Nice, Radio Stars, Sparks)

JETHRO TULL

SINGLES

68	MGM MGM 1384	Sunshine Day/Aeroplane (miscredited to 'Jethro Toe'; counterfeits credit 'Jethro Tull')	150
68	Island WIP 6043	A Song For Jeffrey/One For John Gee	25
68	Island WIP 6048	Love Story/A Christmas Song (2 different pink label designs)	each 7
68	Island WIP 6048	Love Story/A Christmas Song (mispressing, B-side or both sides credited to Ian Henderson)	each 10
69	Island WIP 6056	Living In The Past/Driving Song (2 different pink labels)	each 7
69	Chrysalis WIP 6070	Sweet Dream/17 (push-out or large centre hole)	7
70	Chrysalis WIP 6077	The Witch's Promise/Teacher (some in p/s)	12/5
70	Chrysalis WIP 6081	Inside/Alive And Well And Living In	10
71	Chrysalis WIP 6098	Lick Your Fingers Clean/Up To Me (unissued)	
71	Chrysalis WIP 6106	Life Is A Long Song/Up The 'Pool/Dr. Bogenbroom/From Later/Nursie (EP, p/s)	8
74	Chrysalis CHS 2054	Bungle In The Jungle/Back Door Angels	6
75	Chrysalis CHS 2075	Minstrel In The Gallery/Summerday Sands	5
76	Chrysalis CHS 2086	Too Old To Rock'n'Roll: Too Young To Die/Rainbow Blues	5
76	Chrysalis CXP 2275	Ring Out Solstice Bells/March The Mad Scientist/A Christmas Song/ Pan Dance (EP)	8
77	Chrysalis CHS 2135	The Whistler/Strip Cartoon (p/s)	7
78	Chrysalis CHS 2214	Moths/Life Is A Long Song (p/s)	10
78	Chrysalis CHS 2260	A Stitch In Time (3.30 Version)/Sweet Dream (p/s, white or black vinyl)	5/8
78	Chrysalis CHS 2260	A Stitch In Time (4.20 Version)/Sweet Dream (p/s, white or black vinyl)	5/8
79	Chrysalis CHS 2378	North Sea Oil/Elegy (p/s)	10
79	Chrysalis CHS 2394	Home/King Henry's Madrigal (Theme From Mainstream)/Warm Sporran (p/s)	12
79	Chrysalis CHS 2443	Ring Out Solstice Bells/March The Mad Scientist/A Christmas Song/ Pan Dance (EP, reissue)	7
79	Chrysalis CHS 2468	Working John, Working Joe/Flyingdale Flyer (p/s)	8
80	Chrysalis CHS 2619	Broadsword/Fallen On Hard Times (p/s)	6
80	Chrysalis CHSP 2619	Broadsword/Fallen On Hard Times (picture disc)	12
84	Chrysalis TULLD 1	Lap Of Luxury/Astronomy//Automotive Engineering/Tundra (double pack, gatefold p/s)	6
86	Chrysalis TULL 2	Coronach (with David Palmer)/Jack Frost And The Hooded Crow (p/s)	7
86	Chrysalis TULLX 2	Coronach (with David Palmer)/Jack Frost And The Hooded Crow/ Living In The Past/Elegy (12", p/s)	40
87	Chrysalis TULLP 3	Steel Monkey/Down At The End Of Your Road (picture disc)	8
87	Chrysalis ZTULL 3	Steel Monkey/Down At The End Of Your Road/Too Many Too/I'm Your Gun (cassette, numbered edition of 3,000 with competition pack)	5
87	Chrysalis TULLX 3	Steel Monkey/Down At The End Of Your Road/ Too Many Too/I'm Your Gun (12", p/s)	7
88	Chrysalis TULLP 4	Said She Was A Dancer/Dogs In The Midwinter (shaped picture disc)	10
88	Chrysalis TULLCD 4	Said She Was A Dancer/Dogs In The Midwinter/ Down At The End Of The Road/Too Many Too (CD, picture disc)	10
88	Chrysalis TULPCD 1	Part Of The Machine (Edit)/Stormy Monday Blues (live)/Lick Your Fingers Clean/ Minstrel In The Gallery (live)/Farm On The Freeway (live) (CD, picture disc)	15
89	Chrysalis TULLCD 5	Another Christmas Song/Intro —A Christmas Song (live)/Cheap Day Return — Mother Goose (live)/Outro — Locomotive Breath (live) (CD)	10

92	Chrysalis TULLCD 7	Rocks On The Road/Jack-A-Lynn (Home Demo)/Tall Thin Girl (live)/Fat Man (live)/Rocks On The Road/Bouree (live)/Mother Goose-Jack-A-Lynn (live)/ Aqualung — Locomotive Breath (live) (2-CD, boxed) 8
92	Chrysalis TULLX 7	Rocks On The Road/Jack-A-Lynn (home demo)/ Aqualung-Locomotive Breath (live) (12", picture disc) 10
93	Chrysalis 12CHS 3970	Living In The Past (Club Mix)/(7" Mix)/(Dub Ravey Master)/(Dub N.Y. Mix) (12") ... 7
93	Chrysalis 23970/1	Living In The (Slightly More Recent) Past (live)/Silver River Turning/Rosa On The Factory Floor/I Don't Want To Be Me/Living In The Past/Truck Stop Runner/Piece Of Cake/Man Of Principle (2-CD set) 8
99	Papillon BTFLYS 0001	Bends Like A Willow (edit)/Dot Com (edit)/It All Trickles Down (CD) 8

ORIGINAL LPs

68	Island ILP 985	THIS WAS (LP, 1st pressing, pink label/black & orange 'circle' logo, mono) 60
68	Island ILPS 9085	THIS WAS (LP, 1st pressing, pink label/black & orange 'circle' logo, stereo, flipback sleeve, some sleeves as mono issues with stereo stickers) 35
69	Chrysalis ILPS 9103	STAND UP (LP, 1st pressing, pop-up sleeve, pink label/black & orange 'circle' logo) 25
70	Chrysalis ILPS 9123	BENEFIT (LP, green Chrysalis or Island pink rim label/'palm tree' logo) 18
71	Island ILPS 9145	AQUALUNG (LP, with gatefold sleeve & inner bag) 18
72	Chrysalis CHR 1003	THICK AS A BRICK (LP, fold-out newspaper sleeve) 18
72	Chrysalis CJT 1	LIVING IN THE PAST (2-LP, with hard sleeve & booklet)..................... 22
73	Chrysalis CHR 1040	A PASSION PLAY (LP, with theatre booklet) 15
74	Chrysalis CHR 1067	WARCHILD (LP, with lyric inner sleeve) 12
75	Chrysalis CHR 1082	MINSTREL IN THE GALLERY (LP, with lyric inner sleeve) 12
84	Chrysalis CDLP 1461	UNDER WRAPS (LP, picture disc) 15

REPRESSINGS

68	Island ILP 985	THIS WAS (LP, pink label/'i' logo, mono) 45
69	Island ILPS 9085	THIS WAS (LP, pink label/black 'block' logo, 1st mix) 20
70	Island ILPS 9085	THIS WAS (LP, pink label/'i' logo)..................................... 20
71	Island ILPS 9085	THIS WAS (LP, pink rim label/'palm tree' logo, 2nd mix).................. 12
70	Chrysalis ILPS 9103	STAND UP (LP, pop-up sleeve, pink label/black 'block' logo or pink label/'i' logo) 15/12
70	Chrysalis ILPS 9103	STAND UP (LP, pop-up sleeve, pink rim label/'palm tree' logo) 12

(see also Ian Anderson, Mick Abrahams, Blodwyn Pig, Wild Turkey, The John Even Band)

JETLINERS

| 66 | Blue Beat BB 367 | Meditation (actually by Sugar & Dandy)/GIRL SATCHMO: Nature Of Love (actually with Jetliners) .... 12 |

JETS

| 78 | Soho SH 3 | Rockabilly Baby/James Dean .... 5 |

JET SET

| 62 | Delta DW 5001 | VC 10/Cruising 600 (some in p/s)...................................... 10/5 |

JET SET

| 64 | Parlophone R 5199 | You Got Me Hooked/True To You .... 10 |

(see also Liza & Jet Set, Soulmates)

JETSET

80s	Shadows And Reflections	What Can I Say (Demo)/Christmas Greeting (flexidisc free with fanzine) 6/5
84	Dance Network NET 1	BEST OF THE JETSET (EP)... 5
85	Dance Network NET 3	APRIL, MAY, JUNE AND THE JETSET (12" EP)............................. 7
85	Dance Network WORK 1	THERE GOES THE NEIGHBOURHOOD (LP, pink sleeve) 10

JETSTREAMS

| 59 | Decca F 11149 | Bongo Rock/Tiger .... 20 |
| 59 | Decca F 11149 | Bongo Rock/Tiger (78).. 50 |

JOAN JETT (& BLACKHEARTS)

80	Ariola ARO 227	Make Believe/Call Me Lightning (poster p/s)............................... 4
88	London LONCD 195	I Hate Myself For Loving You/I Can't Control Myself/I Hate Myself For Loving You/Love Is Pain (live) (CD, card sleeve)............................ 7
82	Epic EPC 11-85686	I LOVE ROCK'N'ROLL (LP, picture disc, as Joan Jett & Blackhearts) 10

(see also Runaways, Bangles)

JEWELS

| 64 | Colpix PX 11034 | Opportunity/Gotta Find A Way.. 12 |
| 65 | Colpix PX 11048 | But I Do/Smokey Joe .... 12 |

JIGILO JUG BAND

| 80 | Performance PERF 1 | LIVE AT THE LIMPING WHIPPET (12" EP, p/s)............................. 8 |

(see also Paul King, King Earl Boogie Band, Mungo Jerry)

JIGSAW

68	Polydor 56241	I Need Your Love/I've Gotta Get Me Some Money (as Jig-Saw Band) 5
68	Music Factory CUB 4	Mister Job/Great Idea.. 7
68	Music Factory CUB 6	Let Me Go Home/Tumblin'.. 50
68	MGM MGM 1410	One Way Street/Then I Found You.. 6
70	Philips 6006 112	One Way Street/Coffucious Confusion 12
70	Fontana 6007 017	Lollipop And Goody Man/Seven Fishes 12
71	Philips 6006 131	Jesu Joy Of Man's Desiring/No Questions Asked 6
71	Philips 6006 182	Keeping My Head Above Water/It's Nice But It's Wrong 6
73	U.K. UK 45	That's What It's All About/And I Like You 5
74	BASF BA 1002	I've Seen The Film, I've Read The Book/Mention My Name 5
74	BASF BA 1010	You're Not The Only Girl/Face The Music 5
71	Philips 6308 033	LETHERSLADE FARM (LP) 50
72	Philips 6308 072	AURORA BOREALIS (LP).. 40
73	BASF 29106-5	BROKEN HEARTED (LP, gatefold sleeve) 20
74	BASF BAP 5051	I'VE SEEN THE FILM, I'VE READ THE BOOK (LP)........................... 18

JIH
88	Jungle JUNG 32T/BOV 3	Take Me To The Girl/Come Summer Come Winter/Wake Up (12", unissue, Mayking test pressings only, white proof p/s)	20
88	Jungle JUNG 32T/BOV 3	Take Me To The Girl/Come Summer Come Winter/Wake Up (12", 'small photos' p/s, later blue art p/s)	10/7

(see also Associates)

JILL & BOULEVARDS
62	Columbia DB 4823	And Now I Cry/Eugene	15

JILL & Y'VERNS
60s	Oak RGJ 503	My Soulful Dress/Anything He Wants Me To Do	50

JILTED JOHN
78	Rabid TOSH 105	Jilted John/Going Steady (p/s)	8
78	EMI International INT 567	Jilten John/Going Steady (p/s, reissue)	5
78	EMI International INT 577	True Love/I Was A Pre-Pubescent (p/s)	7
78	EMI International INT 587	The Birthday Kiss/Baz's Party (p/s)	7
78	EMI Intl. INS 3024	TRUE LOVE STORIES (LP, with insert)	12

(see also Going Red?)

JIMBILIN
71	Bamboo BAM 68	Human Race/Let Love In (both actually by Herman Chin-Loy & Aquarians)	8

JIMBO featuring BULL
94	Trojan CDTRO 9106	Coz I Luv You (Radio Edit)/Coz I Luv You (Bull Mix)/ Coz I Luv You (Cowboy Mix) (CD)	8

(see also Slade)

JIM & JOE
64	London HL 9831	Fireball Mail/Daisy Mae	12

(see also James Burton)

JIM & MONICA
64	Stateside SS 266	Slippin' And Slidin'/Sing Along Without Jim & Monica	15

(see also Jimmy Gilmer & Fireballs)

JIMMIE & NIGHT HOPPERS
59	London HLP 8830	Cruisin'/Night Hop	20
59	London HLP 8830	Cruisin'/Night Hop (78)	40

JIVA
75	Dark Horse AMLH 22003	JIVA (LP, with inner sleeve)	12

JIV-A-TONES
58	Felsted AF 101	Flirty Gertie/Fire Engine Baby	225
58	Felsted AF 101	Flirty Gertie/Fire Engine Baby (78)	160

JIVE FIVE
61	Parlophone R 4822	My True Story/When I Was Single	140
62	Stateside SS 133	What Time Is It?/Begging You Please	50
65	United Artists UP 1106	I'm A Happy Man/Kiss Kiss Kiss	18

JIVERS (U.S.)
56	Vogue V 9060	Little Mama/Cherie	550
56	Vogue V 9060	Little Mama/Cherie (78)	80
57	Vogue V 9068	Ray Pearl/Dear Little One	550
57	Vogue V 9068	Ray Pearl/Dear Little One (78)	80

JIVERS (Jamaica)
68	Trojan TR 604	Wear My Crown/Down On The Beach	7

(see also Brother Dan Allstars)

JIVING JUNIORS
60	Blue Beat BB 4	Lollipop Girl/Dearest Darling	25
60	Blue Beat BB 5	My Heart's Desire/I Love You	25
60	Starlite ST45 028	Lovers Line/Tu-Woo-Up-Tu-Woo	45
61	Starlite ST45 049	Slop & Mash/My Sweet Angel	35
61	Blue Beat BB 36	Over The River/Hip Rub (with Hersan & His City Slickers)	25
62	Island WI 003	Sugar Dandy/Valerie	25
62	Island WI 027	Andrea/Don't Leave Me	25
63	Island WI 129	Sugar Dandy/Valerie (reissue)	20
73	United Artists UP 35494	Stay/Call Me	6

(see also Duke Reid)

J.J. ALLSTARS
68	Duke DU 3	One Dollar Of Music/CARL DAWKINS: I'll Make It Up	5
69	Trojan TR 691	Memphis Underground (Parts 1 & 2)	6
70	Duke DU 94	Collecting Coins/Cabbage Leaf	7
70	Duke DU 95	This Land (actually by Carl Dawkins)/Land Version	8
70	Escort ES 821	Mango Tree/The Removers (both actually by Winston Wright & J.J. All Stars)	8
71	Big Shot BI 570	Perseverence Version/CARL DAWKINS: Perseverance	5
71	Explosion EX 2051	I Feel Good (Version 2)/CARL DAWKINS: I Feel Good	5

(see also Lloyd Young, Bleechers, Ethiopians)

JLY POSSE
90	More Protein/Spunk JLY-1	One On One/One On One (Massive) (12", 'penis' p/s, promo only)	25

(see also Jesus Loves You, Culture Club, Boy George)

DAMITA JO
(see under 'D')

MARCY JO & EDDIE RAMBEAU
63	Stateside SS 235	Lover's Medley/When You Wore A Tulip	7

(see also Eddie Rambeau)

MINT VALUE £

ANTONIO CARLOS JOBIM
72   CTI CTL 3   STONE FLOWER (LP).. 12

JOBRIATH
73   Elektra EKS 75070   JOBRIATH (LP)... 12
74   Elektra K 42163   CREATURES OF THE STREET (LP)..................................... 12

JO'BURG HAWK
72   Charisma CB 194   Orang Utang/Dark Side Of The Moon 5
73   Charisma CAS 1064   JO'BURG HAWK (LP, gatefold sleeve)............................... 12

JOCK TAMSON'S BAIRNS
80   Temple TP 002   JOCK TAMSON'S BAIRNS (LP, with lyric insert).................... 12

JODIMARS
56   Capitol CL 14518   Well Now, Dig This/Let's All Rock Together...................... 60
56   Capitol CL 14518   Well Now, Dig This/Let's All Rock Together (78) 18
56   Capitol CL 14627   Rattle My Bones/Lotsa Love 45
56   Capitol CL 14627   Rattle My Bones/Lotsa Love (78)............................... 20
56   Capitol CL 14641   Rattle Shakin' Daddy/Eat Your Heart Out Annie 45
56   Capitol CL 14641   Rattle Shakin' Daddy/Eat Your Heart Out Annie (78)........... 20
56   Capitol CL 14642   Dance The Bop/Boom, Boom My Bayou Baby 45
56   Capitol CL 14642   Dance The Bop/Boom, Boom My Bayou Baby (78) 20
56   Capitol CL 14663   Midnight/Clarabella 45
56   Capitol CL 14663   Midnight/Clarabella (78)...................................... 20
57   Capitol CL 14700   Cloud 99/Later 40
57   Capitol CL 14700   Cloud 99/Later (78)... 20
70s Bulldog BD 16   Well Now, Dig This/Dance The Bop 5
72   Speciality SPE 6608   WELL NOW DIG THIS (LP).. 20
(see also Bill Haley & Comets)

JODY GRIND
69   Transatlantic TRA 210   ONE STEP ON (LP) 40
70   Transatlantic TRA 221   FAR CANAL (LP) 40

AL T. JOE (& CELESTIALS)
62   Dice CC 9   Rise Jamaica/I'm On My Own 12
62   Blue Beat BB 126   You Cheated On Me/This Heart Of Mine (as Al T. Joe & Celestials)... 15
63   Blue Beat BB 166   Goodbye Dreamboat/Please Forgive Me........................... 12
63   Blue Beat BB 169   Fatso/Slow Boat... 12
70   Duke DU 70   It's A Shame/Desertion 6
72   Duke DU 148   Vision/Young And Unlearned.................................... 6
72   Dynamic DYN 429   Oh What A Price/The Prisoners Song 6
(see also Jamaica Fats)

JOE & ANN
65   Black Swan WI 468   Gee Baby/Wherever You May Be 15

CALYPSO JOE
69   Escort ES 801   Adults Only/Calalue... 6

JOE & EDDIE
59   Capitol CL 15038   Green Grass/And I Believed 6
64   Vocalion V 9215   There's A Meetin' Here Tonight/Lonesome Traveller.............. 8
65   Vocalion V 9238   Gabrielle/He's Got The Whole World In His Hands 8
65   Vocalion V 9242   Depend On Yourself/With You In Mind........................... 8
65   Vocalion V-N 9246   Farewell/Hey Nelly Nelly...................................... 8
65   Vocalion V-P 9250   Walkin' Down The Line/It Ain't Me Babe 12

BILLY JOEL
72   Philips 6078 001   She's Got A Way/Everybody Loves You Now 7
74   Philips 6078 018   The Ballad Of Billy The Kid/If I Only Had The Words (To Tell You)
                                  (some in p/s)... 35/25
79   CBS 7150   Honesty/Root Beer Rag (withdrawn)............................ 20
86   CBS DA 7247   Modern Woman/Sleep With The Television On//Up Town/All For Love
                                  (double pack)... 5
72   Philips 6369 150   COLD SPRING HARBOR (LP) 15
73   Philips 6369 160   PIANO MAN (LP, withdrawn).................................... 25
73   Philips 6078 018   BALLAD OF BILLY THE KID (LP) 12
78   CBS H 82311   THE STRANGER (LP, half-speed master version)................. 15
79   CBS 66352   BILLY JOEL (3-LP box set) 18
(see also Hassles)

JOE 9T & THUNDERBIRDS
80s Gemme JOE 9T/LYN 6526   Joe 9T Theme/THEY MUST BE RUSSIANS: Psycho Analysis (p/s, white label).... 5
(see also They Must Be Russians)

JOE PUBLIC
85   Capital CLA 55   Anti CND... 20
(see also Long Tall Shorty)

JOE'S ALLSTARS
69   Joe/Duke DU 24   Hey Jude/Musical Feet... 8
69   Joe/Duke DU 28   Battle Cry Of Biafra/Funky Reggae Part 1...................... 8
69   Joe/Duke DU 50   Brixton Cat/Solitude.. 7
70   Joe JRS 9   Tony B's Theme/JOE THE BOSS: Skinhead Revolt................. 12
72   Sioux SI 012   Tony B's Theme/RAY MARTELL: She Caught The Train 6
70   Trojan TBL 106   BRIXTON CAT (LP)... 18
(see also Joe The Boss, Dice The Boss, King Horror, Pattie La Donne)

JOE SOAP
73   Polydor 2383 233   KEEP IT CLEAN (LP)... 15

JOE (Mansano) THE BOSS
70	Joe JRS 6	Son Of Al Capone/All My Enemies	10
70	Joe JRS 10	If Life Was A Thing/LLOYD KINGPIN: Daisy Bothering	7

(see also Joe's Allstars, Joe Mansano, Dice The Boss, Pama Dice)

JOEY & CONTINENTALS
70	Polydor 56520	She Rides With Me/Rudy Vadoo	10

(see also G.T.O.'s)

JOEY & GENTLEMEN
64	Fontana TF 444	Like I Love You/I'll Never Let You Go	8
64	Fontana TF 485	Dummy Dum Song/Goodbye Little Girl	5

HENRIK JOHANSEN'S JAZZ BAND
55	Tempo EXA 23	THE TRADITIONAL DANES (EP)	8
57	Tempo EXA 64	HENRIK JOHANSEN'S JAZZ BAND (EP)	8

(see also City Ramblers Skiffle Group, Al Fairweather)

ALEXSANDER JOHN
70s	Myrrh MYR 1010	DAYS GO BY (LP)	15

ANDREW JOHN
71	CBS 7017	Streets Of London/Rick Rack	5
72	CBS 64835	THE MACHINE STOPS (LP)	12

BASIL JOHN
70s	Planetone RC 12	Drink And Drive/MIKE ELLIOTT: J.K. Shuffle	10

CLIVE JOHN
75	United Artists UAS 29733	YOU ALWAYS KNOW WHERE YOU STAND WITH A BUZZARD (LP)	12

(see also Man)

DAVID JOHN & MOOD
64	Vocalion V 9220	To Catch That Man/Pretty Thing	200
65	Parlophone R 5255	Bring It To Jerome/I Love To See You Strut	165
65	Parlophone R 5301	Diggin' For Gold/She's Fine	165

(these singles do NOT feature David Bowie; see also Gagalactyca, Astral Navigations, Little Free Rock)

ELTON JOHN
PHILIPS SINGLES
68	Philips BF 1643	I've Been Loving You/Here's To The Next Time	250
69	Philips BF 1739	Lady Samantha/All Across The Havens	50

DJM SINGLES
69	DJM DJS 205	It's Me That You Need/Just Like Strange Rain (some in p/s)	80/35
70	DJM DJS 217	Border Song/Bad Side Of The Moon	20
70	DJM DJS 222	Rock And Roll Madonna/Grey Seal	20
71	DJM DJS 233	Your Song/Into The Old Man's Shoes	5
71	DJM DJS 244	Friends/Honey Roll	8
72	DJM DJX 501	Rocket Man/Holiday Inn/Goodbye (gatefold p/s)	18
72	DJM DJX 501	Rocket Man/Holiday Inn/Goodbye (plain p/s)	5
72	DJM DJS 269	Honky Cat/Lady Samantha/It's Me That You Need	6
72	DJM DJS 271	Crocodile Rock/Elderberry Wine	5
73	DJM DJS 275	Daniel/Skyline Pigeon	5
73	DJM DJX 502	Saturday Night's Alright For Fighting/Jack Rabbit/Whenever You're Ready (We'll Go Steady Again) (p/s)	5
73	DJM DJS 285	Goodbye Yellow Brick Road/Screw You	5
73	DJM DJS 290	Step Into Christmas/Ho! Ho! Ho! (Who'd Be A Turkey At Christmas)	6
74	DJM DJS 297	Candle In The Wind/Bennie And The Jets	5
74	DJM DJS 302	Don't Let The Sun Go Down On Me/Sick City	5
74	DJM DJS 322	The Bitch Is Back/Cold Highway	5
74	DJM DJS 340	Lucy In The Sky With Diamonds (featuring Dr. Winston O'Boogie [John Lennon] & His Reggae Guitars)/One Day At A Time	5
75	DJM DJS 354	Philadelphia Freedom/I Saw Her Standing There (as Elton John Band; B-side featuring John Lennon with Muscle Shoals Horns) (p/s)	8
75	DJM DJS 385	Someone Saved My Life Tonight/House Of Cards	5
75	DJM DJS 610	Island Girl/Sugar On The Floor (p/s)	6
76	DJM DJS 629	Grow Some Funk Of Your Own/I Feel Like A Bullet (In The Gun Of Robert Ford)	5
76	DJM DJS 652	Pinball Wizard/Harmony	5
77	DJM DJR 18001	FOUR FROM FOUR EYES (EP)	8
78	DJM DJS 10911	Philadelphia Freedom/Lucy In The Sky With Diamonds (reissue)	5
78	DJM EJ 12	THE ELTON JOHN SINGLES COLLECTION (12 x 7" box set [DJS 10901-12])	45
78	DJM DJT 15000	FUNERAL FOR A FRIEND (12" EP)	10
80	DJM DJS 10961	Harmony/Mona Lisas And Mad Hatters (glossy p/s)	5
81	DJM DJS 10965	I Saw Her Standing There/Whatever Gets You Thru The Night/Lucy In The Sky With Diamonds (EP, p/s, featuring John Lennon & Muscle Shoals Horns)	7

ROCKET SINGLES
76	Rocket ROKN 512	Don't Go Breaking My Heart/Snow Queen (w/ Kiki Dee, p/s)	5
76	Rocket ROKN 517	Sorry Seems To Be The Hardest Word/Shoulder Holster (p/s)	5
77	Rocket ROKN 521	Crazy Water/Chameleon	5
77	Rocket GOALD 1	The Goaldigger Song/Jimmy, Brian, Elton, Eric (mail-order, signed, 500 only)	300
77	Rocket ROKN 526	Bite Your Lip (Get Up And Dance) (Remix)/KIKI DEE: Chicago	5
77	Rocket RU 1	Bite Your Lip (Get Up And Dance) (Remix)/KIKI DEE: Chicago (12", printed sleeve)	7
78	Rocket ROKN 538	Ego/Flintstone Boy (p/s)	5
78	Rocket XPRES 1	Part Time Love/I Cry At Night (p/s)	5
79	Rocket XPRES 13	Are You Ready For Love Pts 1&2	5
79	Rocket XPRES 1312	Are You Ready For Love/Three Way Love Affair/Mama Can't Buy You Love (12", p/s)	7

ELTON JOHN

79	Rocket XPRES 20	Mama Can't Buy You Love/Strangers (p/s; withdrawn, misspelt "Mamma")	250
79	Rocket XPRES 21	The Victim Of Love/Strangers (p/s)	5
79	Rocket XPRES 24	Johnny B. Goode/Thunder In The Night (p/s)	5
79	Rocket XPRES 2412	Johnny B. Goode/Thunder In The Night (12", p/s)	8
80	Rocket XPRES 45	Dear God/Tactics (company sleeve)	25
80	Rocket ELTON 1	Dear God/Tactics//Steal Away Child/Love So Cold (double pack, p/s)	10
81	Rocket XPRES 54	Nobody Wins/Fools In Fashions (p/s)	5
81	Rocket XPRES 59	Just Like Belgium/Can't Get Over Getting Over Losing You (company sleeve)	5
82	Rocket XPRES 77	Empty Garden/Take Me Down To The Ocean (p/s)	5
82	Rocket XPPIC 77	Empty Garden/Take Me Down To The Ocean (picture disc)	8
82	Rocket XPRES 85	Princess/The Retreat (p/s)	5
82	Rocket XPRES 88	All Quiet On The Western Front/Where Have All The Good Times Gone (p/s)	7
82	Rocket XPRPO 88	All Quiet On The Western Front/Where Have All The Good Times Gone (poster p/s)	15
83	Rocket XPRES 91	That's Why They Call It The Blues/Lord Choc Ice Goes Mental ('raised musical note' sleeve with shorter A-side title)	12
83	Rocket XPRES 91	I Guess That's Why They Call It The Blues/Lord Choc Ice Goes Mental ('raised musical note' sleeve)	5
83	Rocket EJPIC 1	I'm Still Standing/Earn While You Learn (piano-shaped picture disc)	15
83	Rocket EJS 112	I'm Still Standing (Extended Mix)/Earn While You Learn (12", p/s)	8
83	Rocket EJS 2/FREEJ 2	Kiss The Bride/Dreamboat//Ego/Song For Guy (double pack, p/s)	6
83	Rocket EJS 212	Kiss The Bride (Full Version)/Dreamboat (12", p/s)	8
83	Rocket EJS 3/2	Cold As Christmas/Crystal//Don't Go Breaking My Heart/Snow Queen (double pack, gatefold p/s, 2nd 45 with Kiki Dee)	6
83	Rocket EJS 312	Cold As Christmas/Crystal/J'Veux De La Tendresse (12", p/s)	8
84	Rocket PHPIC 7	Sad Songs (Say So Much) /Simple Man (hat-shaped picture disc)	7
84	Rocket PH 712	Sad Songs (Say So Much)(Extended Version)/Simple Man (12", p/s)	7
84	Rocket EJS 512	Passengers (Extended Remix)/Lonely Boy/Blue Eyes (12", p/s)	7
84	Rocket EJS 612	Who Wears These Shoes (Extended Version)/Tortured/ I Heard It Through The Grapevine (live at Wembley) (12", p/s)	7
85	Rocket EJS 7	Breaking Hearts (Ain't what It Used To Be)/Neon (p/s)	5
85	Rocket EJS 8	Act Of War (Part 1)/(Part 2) (with Millie Jackson, 'concertina pack' of video stills)	7
85	Rocket EJSR 8	Act Of War (Part 5) (1-sided promo, p/s lists 2 tracks & 12" cat. no.)	15
85	Rocket EJSR 812	Act Of War (Part 5)/Act Of War (Part 6) (Instrumental) (12", p/s)	15
85	Rocket EJSD 9	Nikita/The Man Who Never Died//Sorry Seems To Be The Hardest Word (live)/ I'm Still Standing (live) (double pack, gatefold p/s, some pop-up)	15/8
85	Rocket EJS 10/EJS 9	Wrap Her Up/Restless (live)//Nikita/The Man Who Never Died (double pack, stickered gatefold PVC wallet with 2 separate p/s's)	7
85	Rocket EJSC 10	Wrap Her Up/Restless (live) (with George Michael, open-out 'cube' p/s)	8
85	Rocket EJSC 10	Wrap Her Up/Restless (live) (with George Michael, open-out 'cube' p/s)	8
85	Rocket EJPIC 10	Wrap Her Up/Restless (live) (with George Michael, oblong-shaped picture disc)	12
85	Rocket EJSP 10	Wrap Her Up/Restless (live) (with George Michael, oblong-shaped picture disc, with pictures on wrong sides)	25
85	Rocket EJS 1012/ELTON 1	Wrap Her Up (Extended Remix) (with George Michael)/Restless (live)/ Nikita/Cold As Christmas (12", double pack in stickered PVC sleeve)	12
86	Rocket EJSD 11	Cry To Heaven/Candy By The Pound//Rock'n'Roll Medley/Your Song (double pack, gatefold p/s)	6
86	Rocket EJSD 12	Heartache All Over The World/Highlander//Passengers/I'm Still Standing (double pack, gatefold p/s)	5
86	Rocket EJSP 13	Slow Rivers (with Cliff Richard)/Billy & The Kids (picture disc)	12
86	Rocket EJSM13	Slow Rivers (with Cliff Richard)/Billy & The Kids/Nikita/Blue Eyes I Guess That's Why They Call It The Blues (cassette)	6

86	Rocket EJS 13-12	Slow Rivers (with Cliff Richard)/Billy & The Kids/Lord Of The Flies (12", p/s) 10
87	Rocket EJS 14	Your Song (live)/Don't Let The Sun Go Down On Me (live) (p/s) 5
87	Rocket EJSM 14	Your Song/Need You To Turn To/Greatest Discovery/Don't Let The Sun Go Down On Me (all tracks live in Australia) (cassette) 5
87	Rocket EJS 1412	Your Song/Need You To Turn To/Greatest Discovery/Don't Let The Sun Go Down On Me (all tracks live in Australia) (12", p/s) 8
88	Rocket EJSP 15	Candle In The Wind (live)/Sorry Seems To Be The Hardest Word (live) (picture disc) 10
88	Rocket EJSM 15	Candle In The Wind (live)/Sorry Seems To Be The Hardest Word (live)/ Your Song (live)/Don't Let The Sun Go Down On Me (live) (cassette) 5
88	Rocket EJS 1512	Candle In The Wind (live)/Sorry Seems To Be The Hardest Word (live)/ Your Song (live)/Don't Let The Sun Go Down On Me (live) (12", p/s) 8
88	Rocket EJSCD 15	Candle In The Wind (live)/Sorry Seems To Be The Hardest Word (live)/ Your Song (live)/Don't Let The Sun Go Down On Me (live) (CD, card sleeve) 12
88	Rocket EJSIP 16	I Don't Wanna Go On With You Like That/Rope Around A Fool/ (Radio 1 interview) (33rpm, poster sleeve) 5
88	Rocket EJS 1612	I Don't Wanna Go On With You Like That (Remix)/(7" Version)/ Rope Around A Fool (12", blue vinyl factory custom pressing, no p/s) 80
88	Rocket EJSCD 16	I Don't Wanna Go On With You Like That/Rope Around A Fool/ I Don't Wanna Go On With You Like That (Extended Mix) (CD, card p/s) 10
88	Rocket EJSLB 17	Town Of Plenty (with Pete Townshend)/Whipping Boy ('look back' pack in box with 4 photos). 7
88	Rocket EJSCD 17	Town Of Plenty (with Pete Townshend)/Whipping Boy/My Baby's A Saint/ I Guess That's Why They Call It The Blues (CD, card p/s) 8
88	Rocket EJSCD 18	A Word In Spanish/Heavy Traffic/Live Medley (Song For You/Blue Eyes/ I Guess That's Why They Call It The Blues)/Daniel (live) (CD, card p/s) 8
88	Rocket 080 524 2	I Don't Wanna Go On With You Like That (CD Video) 12
88	Rocket 080 272 2	Nikita (CD Video) 12
89	Rocket EJSCD 19	Healing Hands/Sad Songs (Say So Much) (live)/Dancing In The End Zone (CD) 8
89	Rocket EJSCD 20	Sacrifice/Love Is A Cannibal/Durban Deep (CD). 8
90	Rocket EJS 21	Club At The End Of The Street/Give Peace A Chance (p/s, withdrawn) 500
90	Rocket EJSCD 21	Club At The End Of The Street/Give Peace A Chance/ I Don't Wanna Go On With You Like That (Live in Verona) (CD, withdrawn, with "Made In England" credit) 20
90	Rocket EJS 2312	Club At The End Of The Street/Whispers/I Don't Wanna Go On With You Like That (Live in Verona) (12", p/s). 8
90	Rocket EJSG 24	You Gotta Love Someone/Sacrifice (gatefold p/s with discography, dbl A-side). 5
90	Rocket EJSX 25	Step Into Xmas/Cold As Christmas/Easier To Walk Away/ I Swear I Heard The Night Talking ('Xmas EP', 33rpm, gatefold p/s). 5
92	Rocket EJSCD 28	The One/Suit Of Wolves/Fat Boys And Ugly Girls (CD, digipak) 7
92	Rocket EJSCD 30	The Last Song/The Man Who Never Died (Re-Mix)/Song For Guy (Re-Mix) (CD, digipak). 7
94	Rocket EJSJB 35	Circle Of Life (Elton's Version)/(Soundtrack Version) (jukebox issue, no p/s) 5
94	Rocket EJSMX 35	Circle Of Life (Elton's Version)/(Soundtrack Version) (cassette in heavy card box with hinged lid, with 4 mini-postcards) 6
95	Rocket EJSJB 36	Believe/The One (live) (jukebox 7", no p/s) 5
95	Rocket EJSCD 38	Blessed/Made In England (Junior's Sound Factory Mix)/ Made In England (Junior's Joyous Mix) (CD, Part 1 of a 2-CD set, withdrawn) 20
95	Rocket EJSDD 38	Blessed/Honky Cat (live)/Take Me To The Pilot (live)/ The Bitch Is Back (live) (CD, withdrawn) 25
96	Rocket LLHJB 1	Live Like Horses (Studio Version)/(Live Finale Version) (jukebox issue, no p/s). 5
97	Rocket EJSCD 41	Something About The Way You Look Tonight (Edited Version)/ I Know Why I'm In Love/No Valentines/ Something About The Way You Look Tonight (Album Version) (CD, card sleeve, unreleased) 30
97	Rocket EJSCX 41	Something About The Way You Look Tonight (Edited Version)/ I Know Why I'm In Love/You Can Make History (Young Again)/ Something About The Way You Look Tonight (Album Version) (CD, digipak, unreleased). 30

OTHER SINGLES

| 91 | Epic 657 646-5 | Don't Let The Sun Go Down On Me/I Believe (When I Fall In Love It Will Be Forever [with George Michael]) (live)/WHAM!: "Last Christmas" (12", foldout poster p/s) . . . . 7 |
| 91 | Epic 657 646-2 | Don't Let The Sun Go Down On Me/I Believe (When I Fall In Love It Will Be Forever [with George Michael]) (live)/If You Were My Woman/Fantasy (CD) . . . . . . 8 |

DJM LPs

69	DJM DJLP 403	EMPTY SKY (LP, gatefold sleeve, mono). 90
69	DJM DJLPS 403	EMPTY SKY (LP, gatefold sleeve, stereo, with 'stereo' sticker on sleeve) 12
70	DJM DJLPS 406	ELTON JOHN (LP, textured gatefold sleeve, later smooth) 15/12
70	DJM DJLPS 410	TUMBLEWEED CONNECTION (LP, gatefold sleeve with stapled booklet). 12
71	DJM DJLPS 414	17.11.70 (LP). 12
71	DJM DJLPH 420	MADMAN ACROSS THE WATER (LP, gatefold sleeve) 12
72	DJM DJLPH 423	HONKY CHATEAU (LP, gatefold sleeve, with foldover flap & pasted photo on cover) 12
76	DJM DJE 29001	GOODBYE YELLOW BRICK ROAD (2-LP, yellow vinyl, triplefold sleeve). 20
77	DJM DJLPH 20473	GREATEST HITS VOLUME TWO (LP, with inner sleeve & lyric booklet). 12
78	DJM DJV 2300	CAPTAIN FANTASTIC AND THE BROWN DIRT COWBOY (LP, picture disc). 20
78	DJM LSP 14512	ELTON JOHN (5-LP, box set) 35
80	DJM DJS 22085	LADY SAMANTHA (LP) 12

Elton JOHN

OTHER LPs

70	Warlock Music WMM 101/2	WARLOCK MUSIC SAMPLER (LP, untitled publishing sampler, 7 tracks by Elton, 4 by Linda Peters)	1,000
71	Paramount SPFL 269	FRIENDS (LP, soundtrack)	12
78	St. Michael 2094 0102	CANDLE IN THE WIND (LP, Marks & Spencer issue)	35
84	Cambra CR 130	SEASONS: THE EARLY LOVE SONGS (2-cassette set, withdrawn, includes unique track, "The Tide Will Turn For Rebecca")	15
87	Rocket EJBXL 1	LIVE IN AUSTRALIA WITH THE MELBOURNE SYMPHONY ORCHESTRA (2-LP box set, numbered banded sleeve, 3,000 only)	20

CDs

87	Rocket EJBXD 1	LIVE IN AUSTRALIA WITH THE MELBOURNE SYMPHONY ORCHESTRA (2-CD box set, 3,000 only)	25
88	Rocket 080 516 1	LIVE IN AUSTRALIA (CD Video)	15
83	DJM CD 4/8100 622	THE SUPERIOR SOUND OF ELTON JOHN 1970-1975 (CD)	15
91	Rocket 848 236-2	TO BE CONTINUED … THE VERY BEST OF ELTON JOHN (4-CD, 12" x 8" box set with large colour booklet)	90
93	Happenstance HAPP 001	PLAYS THE SIRAN (CD, private pressing, 50 only)	500+
93	Happenstance HAPP 002	THE FISHING TRIP (4-CD set, private pressing, 100 only, existence unconfirmed)	700+
97	Rocket ELTON 50	CELEBRATING ELTON JOHN'S 50TH BIRTHDAY (CD, promo only)	50
99	Mercury ADV 1999/1	AIDA (with Sir Tim Rice) (CD, box set with wallet, plinth stand, interview CD, booklet and calender cards, promo only)	75
99	Mercury ADV 1999/1	AIDA PRESS KIT (CD, card box set with wallet, plinth stand, interview CD, booklet, calender cards, scented candle and broadcast CDR, promo only)	50
99	Rocket STAR 3	ELTON JOHN'S AIDA (export CD, card p/s, promo only)	30

SESSION RECORDINGS

69	Avenue AVE 80	untitled EP (includes Elton on "Don't Forget To Remember")	8
70	Avenue AVE 93	untitled EP (includes Elton on "I Can't Tell The Bottom From The Top" & "Travellin' Band")	8
70	Avenue AVE 94	untitled EP (includes Elton on "Cottonfields")	8
70	Avenue AVE 97	untitled EP (includes Elton on "Signed Sealed Delivered" & "Natural Sinner")	8
69	Hallmark GM 635	TOP OF THE POPS (LP, includes Elton on "Snake In The Grass")	12
70	Avenue AVE 031	12 TOP HITS (LP, includes Elton on "Don't Forget To Remember")	12
70	Avenue AVE 042	ENGLAND'S 12 TOP HITS (LP, includes Elton on "I Can't Tell The Bottom From The Top" & "Young, Gifted & Black")	12
70	Avenue AVE 055	12 TOP HITS (LP, includes Elton on "Signed Sealed Delivered" & "Natural Sinner")	12
70	Marble Arch MALS 1273	CHARTBUSTERS BOOMIN' (LP, includes Elton on "She Sold Me Magic")	12
70	Marble Arch MALS 1326	CHARTBUSTERS RISIN' (LP, includes Elton on "Young, Gifted & Black")	12
70	Marble Arch MALS 1347	CHARTBUSTERS AGAIN (LP, includes Elton on "Cottonfields" & "Down The Dustpipe")	12
70	Marble Arch MALS 1357	CHARTBUSTERS TODAY (LP, includes Elton on "Signed Sealed Delivered", "Natural Sinner", "Up Around The Bend", "Rainbow" & "Neanderthal Man")	12
70	Marble Arch MALS 1397	SOUL SPECTACULAR VOL. 3 (LP, includes Elton on "Signed Sealed Delivered")	12
70	Deacon DEA 1015	PICK OF THE POPS (LP, includes Elton on "Spirit In The Sky", "I Can't Tell The Bottom From The Top", "Good Morning Freedom", "Travellin' Band")	12
70	Deacon DEA 1015	PICK OF THE POPS VOL. 4 (LP, includes Elton on "In The Summertime", "Yellow River" & "Natural Sinner")	12
70	Gallery GDEA 1015	PICK OF THE POPS VOL. 4 (LP, reissue of DEA 1015)	12
70	Gallery GDEA 1040	TOP HITS 1970 (LP, includes Elton on "In The Summertime", "Yellow River" & "Spirit In The Sky")	12
70	MFP MFP 1383	HITS 70 (LP, includes Elton on "United We Stand" & "My Baby Loves Lovin'")	12
70	Boulevard BLVD 4060	1970 TOP 12 (LP, includes Elton on "In The Summertime", "Love Of The Common People", "Lady D'Arbanville", "Yellow River")	12
70	Stereo Gold Award MER 324	CHART TOPPERS (LP, includes Elton on "Natural Sinner" & "Signed Sealed Delivered")	12
70	Windmill WMD 188	CHARTBUSTING MOTORTOWN (LP, incl. Elton on "Signed Sealed Delivered")	12

(see also [Stu Brown &] Bluesology, Bread & Beer Band, Neil Sedaka, Kiki Dee, Aretha Franklin, Jennifer Rush, Dionne Warwick)

LITTLE WILLIE JOHN

56	Parlophone R 4209	Fever/Letter From My Darling	90
56	Parlophone R 4209	Fever/Letter From My Darling (78)	45
58	Parlophone R 4396	Uh, Uh, Baby/Dinner Date (With His Girl Friend)	35
58	Parlophone R 4396	Uh, Uh, Baby/Dinner Date (With His Girl Friend) (78)	35
58	Parlophone R 4432	Talk To Me, Talk To Me/Spasms	35
58	Parlophone R 4432	Talk To Me, Talk To Me/Spasms (78)	35
58	Parlophone R 4472	Let's Rock While The Rockin's Good/You're A Sweetheart	50
58	Parlophone R 4472	Let's Rock While The Rockin's Good/You're A Sweetheart (78)	60
59	Parlophone R 4571	Leave My Kitten Alone/Let Nobody Love You	35
60	Parlophone R 4674	Heartbreak (It's Hurtin' Me)/Do You Love Me	20
60	Parlophone R 4699	Sleep/There's A Difference	25
61	Parlophone R 4728	Walk Slow/HANK BALLARD: The Hoochie Coochie Coo	20
59	Parlophone PMC 1163	SURE THINGS (LP)	120
64	London HA 8126	COME ON AND JOIN LITTLE WILLIE JOHN (LP)	60

MABLE JOHN

66	Atlantic 584 022	It's Catching/Your Good Thing (Is About To End)	10
67	Stax 601 010	Same Time Same Place/Bigger And Better (dark blue or light blue label)	12/8
68	Stax 601 034	Able Mable/Don't Get Caught	8

ROBERT JOHN

68	CBS 3436	If You Don't Want My Love/Don't	6
68	CBS 3730	Don't Leave Me/Children	5
68	A&M AMS 835	Raindrops Love And Sunshine/When The Party Is Over	8

SAMMIE JOHN
67   Stateside SS 585   Little John/Boss Bag 6

JOHN & JOHNNY
63   Decca F 11719   I Want You To Be My Girl/It's You 6

JOHN & PAUL
65   London HLU 9997   People Say/I'm Walkin' 12

JOHN LEE'S GROUNDHOGS
66   Planet PLF 104   Over You Baby/I'll Never Fall In Love Again (with Planet company sleeve) ... 50/45
(see also Groundhogs, Tony McPhee)

JOHNNY & JACK
54   HMV 7MC 21   Honey, I Need You/Goodnight, Well It's Time To Go (export issue) 18
55   HMV JO 440   Beware Of "It"/Kiss Crazy Baby (78, export) 12
56   HMV JO 456   Weary Moments/S.O.S. (78, export) 12
59   RCA RCA 1145   Sailor Man/Wild And Wicked World 6
59   RCA RCA 1145   Sailor Man/Wild And Wicked World (78) 20
50s RCA RCX 176   COUNTRY GUITAR VOL. 10 (EP) 12

JOHNNIE & JOE
58   London HLM 8682   Over The Mountain, Across The Sea/My Baby's Gone, On, On 275
58   London HLM 8682   Over The Mountain, Across The Sea/My Baby's Gone, On, On (78) 50

JOHNNY (Osborne) & ATTRACTIONS
67   Doctor Bird DB 1118   Young Wings Can Fly/DUDLEY WILLIAMSON: I'm Moving On 18

JOHNNY & CHAZ & GUNNERS
61   Decca F 11365   Bobby/Out Of Luck 20

JOHNNY & COPYCATS
64   Norco AB 102   I'm A Hog For You Baby/I Can Never See You 50
(see also My Dear Watson)

JOHNNY & HURRICANES
59   London HL 8899   Crossfire/Lazy (initially triangular-centre, later round centre) 25/20
59   London HL 8899   Crossfire/Lazy (78) 75
59   London HL 8948   Red River Rock/Buckeye (initially triangular-centre, later round centre) 10/5
59   London HL 8948   Red River Rock/Buckeye (78) 80
59   London HL 9017   Reveille Rock/Time Bomb (initially triangular-centre, later round centre). 12/5
59   London HL 9017   Reveille Rock/Time Bomb (78). 90
60   London HLI 9072   Beatnick Fly/Sand Storm 6
60   London HLI 9072   Beatnick Fly/Sand Storm (78) 100
60   London HLX 9134   Down Yonder/Sheba 6
60   London HLX 9134   Down Yonder/Sheba (78) 150
60   London HLX 9190   Rocking Goose/Revival 6
60   London HLX 9190   Rocking Goose/Revival (78) 225
60   London HL 7099   The Hep Canary/Catnip (export issue) 40
61   London HLX 9289   Ja-Da/Mr. Lonely. 6
61   London HLX 9378   High Voltage/Old Smokie 6
62   London HLX 9491   Farewell, Farewell/Traffic Jam 6
62   London HLX 7116   You Are My Sunshine/Farewell, Farewell (export issue) 25
62   London HLX 9536   Salvation/Misirlou 8
62   London HLX 9617   Minnesota Fats/Come On Train 7
63   London HLX 9660   Whatever Happened To Baby Jane/Greens And Beans 7
68   London HLX 10199   Rocking Goose/Beatnik Fly (reissue) 5
64   Stateside SS 347   Money Honey/That's All 8
76   United Artists UPS 401   Red River Rock/Sheba/Reveille Rock/Beatnik Fly (p/s) 5
61   London REX 1284   ROCKING GOOSE (EP) 30
62   London REX 1347   JOHNNY AND THE HURRICANES (EP) 30
64   London REX 1414   JOHNNY AND THE HURRICANES VOL. 2 (EP) 30
60   London HA 2227   RED RIVER ROCK (LP, plum label; reissues on black label £18) 40
60   London HA-I 2269   STORMSVILLE (LP) 35
61   London HA-X 2322   THE BIG SOUND OF JOHNNY AND THE HURRICANES (LP) 40

JOHNNY & JAMMERS
79   Big Beat NS 55   School Day Blues/You Know I Love You (p/s) 5
(see also Johnny Winter)

JOHNNY & JOHN
66   Polydor 56087   Bumper To Bumper/Scrape My Boot 12
(see also Johnny Gustafson, Big Three)

JOHNNY & JUDY
59   Vogue Pop V 9128   Bother Me Baby/Who's To Say 400
59   Vogue Pop V 9128   Bother Me Baby/Who's To Say (78) 90
(see also John Walker)

JOHNNY & SELF ABUSERS
77   Chiswick NS 22   Saints And Sinners/Dead Vandals (p/s) 15
(see also Simple Minds)

JOHNNY & VIBRATONES
63   Warner Bros WB 107   Bird Stompin'/Movin' The Bird 8

JOHNNY MOPED
76   Chiswick PROMO 3   BASICALLY, THE ORIGINAL JOHNNY MOPED TAPE (33rpm, no p/s) 12
77   Chiswick S 15   No-One/Incendiary Device (p/s) 6
78   Chiswick NS 27   Darling, Let's Have Another Baby/Something Else/It Really Digs (p/s) 5
78   Chiswick NS 41   Little Queenie/Hard Lovin' Man (p/s) 5
78   Chiswick WIK 8   CYCLEDELIC (LP, some with free single [PROMO 3]) 25/12
(see also Slime, Maxim's Trash)

MINT VALUE £

JOHNNY'S BOYS
59	Decca F 11156	Sleep Walk/Ciao Ciao Bambina	8
59	Decca F 11156	Sleep Walk/Ciao Ciao Bambina (78)	12

JOHNNY'S JAZZ
56	Decca FJ 10663	R.J. Boogie/Get Happy (featuring Johnny Hawksworth).	6

(see also Johnny Hawksworth)

BARRY JOHNS
58	HMV POP 472	Locked In The Arms Of Love/Are You Sincere	6

GLYN JOHNS
62	Decca F 11478	January Blues/Sioux Indian.	6
63	Decca F 11753	Old Deceiver Time/Dancing With You	6
65	Immediate IM 013	Mary Anne/Like Grains Of Yellow Sand.	15
65	Pye 7N 15818	I'll Follow The Sun/I'll Take You Dancing	6
60s	Westcot LYN 827/828	Today You're Gone/Such Stuff Of Dreams (freebie with jeans offer)	6

GLYNIS JOHNS
54	Columbia SCM 5149	I Can't Resist Men/Always You	7

LYNDON JOHNS (& ISRAELITES)
69	Downtown DT 444	Don't Gamble With Love/Song Bird.	6
69	Downtown DT 451	Oh Mama Oh Papa/Bring Back The Night (with The Israelites).	6

JOHN'S CHILDREN
66	Columbia DB 8030	The Love I Thought I'd Found/Strange Affair (very few in p/s)	250/90
67	Columbia DB 8124	Just What You Want — Just What You'll Get/But She's Mine	70
67	Track 604 003	Desdemona/Remember Thomas A'Beckett (some in p/s)	90/25
67	Track 604 005	Midsummer Night's Scene/Sara Crazy Child (withdrawn)	2,000
67	Track 604 005	Come And Play With Me In The Garden/Sara Crazy Child	
		(some in p/s)	100/30
67	Track 604 010	Go Go Girl/Jagged Time Lapse	35
87	Bam Caruso KIRI 095	MIDSUMMER NIGHT'S SCENE (LP).	20

(see also Marc Bolan, Andy Ellison, Radio Stars, Jook, Tyrannosaurus Rex)

AL JOHNSON & JEAN CARN
80	CBS 8545	I'm Back For More/You Are My Personal Angel	6

(see also Jean Carn)

ALEC JOHNSON
79	RFP RFP 001	Busman's Holiday (no p/s).	25

(see also Nightwing)

BARRY JOHNSON
58	HMV POP 472	Locked In The Arms Of Love/Are You Sincere (78).	10

BETTY JOHNSON
56	London HLU 8307	I'll Wait/Please Tell Me Why	40
56	London HLU 8307	I'll Wait/Please Tell Me Why (78).	18
56	London HLU 8326	Honky Tonk Rock/Say It Isn't So, Joe	150
56	London HLU 8326	Honky Tonk Rock/Say It Isn't So, Joe (78).	35
57	London HLU 8365	I Dreamed/If It's Wrong To Love You	35
57	London HLU 8365	I Dreamed/If It's Wrong To Love You (78)	20
57	London HLU 8432	1492/Little White Lies.	30
57	London HLU 8432	1492/Little White Lies (78)	20
58	London HLE 8557	Little Blue Man/Song You Heard When You Fell In Love	30
58	London HLE 8557	Little Blue Man/Song You Heard When You Fell In Love (78)	18
58	London HLE 8678	Dream/How Much.	18
58	London HLE 8678	Dream/How Much (78)	25
58	London HLE 8701	There's Never Been A Night/Mr. Brown Is Out Of Town	35
58	London HLE 8701	There's Never Been A Night/Mr. Brown Is Out Of Town (78)	30
58	London HLE 8725	Hoopa Hoola/One More Time.	30
58	London HLE 8725	Hoopa Hoola/One More Time (78)	30
59	London HLE 8839	Does Your Heart Beat For Me?/You And Only You	25
59	London HLE 8839	Does Your Heart Beat For Me?/You And Only You (78)	35
59	London RE-E 1221	DREAM (EP)	75
59	London HA-E 2163	THE SONG YOU HEARD WHEN YOU FELL IN LOVE (LP)	50

BLIND WILLIE JOHNSON
58	Fontana TFE 17052	TREASURES OF NORTH AMERICAN NEGRO MUSIC NO. 2 (EP).	15
70	Xtra XTRA 1098	BLIND WILLIE JOHNSON (LP).	15

BOB JOHNSON & PETE KNIGHT
77	Chrysalis CHR 1137	THE KING OF ELFLAND'S DAUGHTER (LP).	12

(see also Steeleye Span, Mary Hopkin)

BOBBY JOHNSON & ATOMS
67	Ember EMB S 245	Do It Again A Little Bit Slower/Tramp (some in p/s).	12/7

BROWNIE JOHNSON
62	Longhorn BLH 0004	Best Dressed Beggar/Just Pretending	8

BRYAN JOHNSON
60	Decca F 11213	Looking High, High, High/Each Tomorrow.	5
60	Decca F 11213	Looking High, High, High/Each Tomorrow (78)	12
61	Decca DFE 6664	LOOKING HIGH (EP)	18

BUBBER JOHNSON
55	Parlophone R 4105	Let's Make Every Day A Christmas Day/It's Christmas Time (78).	8
56	Parlophone R 4161	Keep A Light In The Window For Me/A Wonderful Thing Happens (78)	10
57	Parlophone R 4259	Confidential/Have A Little Faith In Me	25
57	Parlophone R 4259	Confidential/Have A Little Faith In Me (78)	12

BUDDY JOHNSON

55	Mercury MB 3231	Upside Your Head/ELLA JOHNSON: Crazy About A Saxophone (78)	10
59	Mercury ZEP 10009	BUDDY JOHNSON WAILS (EP, with Ella Johnson)	60
57	Mercury MPT 7515	ROCK AND ROLL (10" LP, with Ella Johnson)	120

BUNK JOHNSON (& HIS NEW ORLEANS BAND)

51	Jazz Man 8	Down By The River/Panama (78)	8
51	Jazz Man 9	Weary Blues/Moose March (78)	8
51	Esquire 10-151	Tiger Rag/Make Me A Pallet On The Floor (78)	8
52	Vogue V 2084	Lord, Let Me In The Lifeboat/Up In Sidney's Flat (78, with Sidney Bechet)	8
55	HMV 7M 141	When The Saints Go Marching In/Darktown Strutters' Ball	5
50s	Melodisc EPM7 52	ONE YOU LOVE (EP)	10
54	Goodtime Jazz LDG 110	BUNK JOHNSON AND THE YERBA BUENA JAZZ BAND (10" LP)	15
54	Columbia 33SX 1015	BUNK JOHNSON AND HIS NEW ORLEANS BAND (LP)	12
59	Melodisc MLP 12-112	BUNK JOHNSON AND HIS NEW ORLEANS JAZZ BAND (LP, w/ George Lewis)	15
50s	Goodtime Jazz	SPIRITUALS AND JAZZ (10" LP)	12
62	Storyville SLP 152	BUNK JOHNSON'S BAND 1944 (LP)	12
63	Goodtime Jazz LAG 545	BUNK JOHNSON AND HIS SUPERIOR JAZZ BAND (LP)	10
70s	Nola LP 3	BUNK JOHNSON AND HIS BAND (LP)	40

CAREY JOHNSON

| 72 | Banana BA 369 | Correction Train/SOUL DEFENDERS: Version | 10 |

DANIEL JOHNSON

| 65 | Island WI 250 | Come On My People/Brother Nathan | 18 |

DOMINO JOHNSON

| 72 | Green Door GD 4045 | Summertime/SWANS: Grazing | 5 |

DOMINO JOHNSON & CHAMPIONS

| 70 | Duke DU 89 | You Broke My Heart/TONY & CHAMPIONS: Tell Me The Reason | 6 |

DON JOHNSON

| 86 | Epic EPCA 650 064-8 | Heartbeat/Can't Take Your Memory (face-shaped picture disc) | 8 |
| 86 | Epic EPCA 650 203-0 | Heartache Away/Love Roulette (picture disc) | 6 |

GENERAL JOHNSON

73	Invictus INV 531	Only Time Will Tell/Only Time Will Tell (Instrumental Version)	5
76	Arista ARIST 45	All In The Family/Ready, Willing And Able	5
73	Invictus SVT 1008	GENERALLY SPEAKING (LP)	15

(see also Norman Johnson, Showmen, Chairmen Of The Board)

HOLLY JOHNSON

89	MCA DMCA 1306	Love Train (12" Mix)/Love Train (7" Mix)/Murder In Paradise (CD, card sleeve, featuring Brian May)	10
89	MCA DMCAT 1306	Love Train (Ride The 'A' Train Mix)/Love Train (Stoke It Up Mix)/Love Train (7" Mix)/Murder In Paradise (3" CD, featuring Brian May)	10
99	Pleasuredome PLDCD 005 SR	The Power Of Love (radio mix)/(Millennium Mix)/In The House Of The Rising Sun (12" mix)/(Doogs House Mix)/(DNA Mix) (CD, slimline case, promo only)	10

(see also Holly, Frankie Goes To Hollywood, Big In Japan)

HOWARD JOHNSON

| 71 | Jay Boy BOY 47 | The Slide/That Magic Touch Can Send You Flying | 4 |

JAMES P. JOHNSON

51	Melodisc MEL 1144	Everybody Loves My Baby/Found A New Baby (78)	8
54	Columbia SCM 5127	Feeling Blues/Riffs	8
56	HMV 7EG 8164	JAMES P. JOHNSON (EP)	10
57	HMV 7EG 8215	LOUISIANA SUGAR BABIES (EP, with Fats Waller)	12
57	Tempo EXA 65	JAMES P. JOHNSON (EP)	10
52	Brunswick LA 8548	DADDY OF THE PIANO (10" LP)	15
53	Brunswick LA 8622	FATS WALLER FAVOURITES (10" LP)	15
54	London AL 3511	EARLY HARLEM PIANO (10" LP)	20
55	London AL 3540	EARLY HARLEM PIANO VOLUME 2 (10" LP)	20

JAMES P. JOHNSON/LUCKEY ROBERTS

| 56 | London HB-U 1057 | HARLEM PARTY PIANO (10" LP, 1 side each) | 20 |

JIMMY JOHNSON

| 65 | Sue WI 387 | Don't Answer The Door (Parts 1 & 2) | 18 |

J.J. JOHNSON

50	Melodisc MEL 1121	Teapot/Spider's Web (78)	8
51	Jazz Parade B 14	Foxhunt/Ulysses (78, as Jay Jay Johnson's Boppers)	8
55	Vogue LDE 124	J.J. JOHNSON SEXTET (10" LP)	15
55	Vogue LDE 162	J.J. JOHNSON QUINTET (10" LP)	15
60	Fontana TFL 5041	J.J. IN PERSON (LP)	12
61	Fontana TFL 5137	BLUE TROMBONE (LP, also stereo STFL 559)	12/15
63	Verve VLP 9056	J.J.'s BROADWAY (LP)	12
65	RCA RD/SF 7721	J.J.! (LP)	12
73	United Artists UAS 29451	ACROSS 110TH STREET (LP, soundtrack, with Bobby Womack)	15

(see also Sonny Stitt)

(JOHNNY JOHNSON &) BANDWAGON

68	Direction 58-3520	Baby Make Your Own Sweet Music/On The Day We Fall In Love (as Bandwagon)	6
68	Direction 58-3670	Breaking Down The Walls Of Heartache/Dancin' Master (as Bandwagon)	6
69	Direction 58-3923	You/You Blew Your Cool And Lost Your Fool	6
69	Direction 58-4180	Let's Hang On/I Ain't Lying (withdrawn)	12
69	Direction 58-4180	Let's Hang On/Don't Let It In	6
72	Stateside SS 2207	Honey Bee/I Don't Know Why	10
69	Direction 8-63500	JOHNNY JOHNSON AND THE BANDWAGON (LP)	20
70	Bell SBLL 138	SOUL SURVIVOR (LP)	15

MINT VALUE £

JOHNSON FAMILY
91	Camden Town GNAR 001	Motorcycle/Big Bang (p/s)	5
94	Camden Town GNAR 005	Be My Rose/Kennington Vigilante (p/s)	5

JUDI JOHNSON (& PERFECTIONS)
64	HMV POP 1371	My Baby's Face/Make The Most Of It (solo)	12
65	HMV POP 1399	How Many Times/A Way Out (as Judi Johnson & Perfections)	12

LARRY JOHNSON
70	Blue Horizon 7-63851	PRESENTING THE COUNTRY BLUES (LP)	60

LAURIE JOHNSON ORCHESTRA
56	HMV 7MC 47	Buttercup/Lullaby Of The Leaves (export issue)	10
57	HMV POP 404	The Moonraker/Call Of The Casbah	6
57	HMV POP 404	The Moonraker/Call Of The Casbah (78)	10
60	Pye 7N 15251	No Hiding Place/The Deputy	6
64	Pye 7N 15599	Dr Strangelove Theme/Nevada	6
64	Pye 7N 15715	The Beautiful Jungle/Call Me Irresponsible	6
65	Pye 7N 15933	Latin Quarter/M1 (some in p/s)	7/5
65	Pye 7N 17015	The Avengers/Minor Bossa Nova (some in p/s)	35/12
69	MGM MGM 1457	There Is Another Song/Caesar Smith	12
71	Columbia DB 8826	The Jason King Theme/There Comes A Time	25
76	EMI EMI 2562	The New Avengers Theme/A Flavour Of The Avengers (some in p/s)	10/5
80	Unicorn Kachana MCPS 5	The Professionals Main Title/On Target/The New Avengers Main Title (p/s, by Laurie Johnson & London Studio Orchestra)	6
65	Pye NPL 18103	THE BIG NEW SOUND STRIKES AGAIN (LP)	15
67	Marble Arch MAL 695	THE AVENGERS AND OTHER FAVOURITES (LP)	30
68	Columbia SX 6206	SOMETHING'S COMING (LP)	12
69	MGM C(S) 8104	THEMES AND ... (LP)	18
70	Columbia SCX 6412	LAURIE JOHNSON/LONDON JAZZ ORCHESTRA — SYNTHESIS (LP, with Joe Harriott, Tubby Hayes, Stan Tracey & Tony Coe)	50
71	Columbia SCX 6464	CONQUISTADORS (LP)	12
73	Ronco RR 2006	THE BELSTONE FOX (LP, soundtrack, gatefold sleeve)	18
80	Unicorn Kachana KPM 7009	MUSIC FROM THE AVENGERS, THE NEW AVENGERS AND THE PROFESSIONALS (LP, gatefold sleeve, with London Studio Orchestra)	20

(see also Polka Dots)

LINTON KWESI JOHNSON
79	Island WIP 6494	Want Fi Goh Rave/Reality Poem (p/s)	5

LONNIE JOHNSON
51	Vogue V 2015	Drunk Again/Jelly Roll Baker (78)	25
51	Vogue V 2079	Happy New Year/Little Rockin' Chair (78)	25
51	Melodisc MEL 1138	Rocks In My Bed/Solid Blues (78)	30
51	Melodisc MEL 1186	Blues For Everybody/In Love Again (78)	30
52	Melodisc MEL 1221	Blues In My Soul/Keep What You Got (78)	30
57	Parlophone GEP 8635	LONESOME ROAD (EP)	40
57	Parlophone GEP 8663	LONNIE'S BLUES (EP)	40
58	Parlophone GEP 8693	LONNIE'S BLUES NO. 2 (EP)	40
64	Storyville SLP 162	PORTRAITS IN BLUES VOL. 6 (LP)	15
64	Storyville 616 010	SEE SEE RIDER (LP, with Otis Spann)	18
60s	Xtra XTRA 1037	LONNIE JOHNSON (LP)	22

(see also Eddie Lang & Lonnie Johnson)

LOU JOHNSON
63	London HLX 9805	Reach Out For Me/Magic Potion	20
64	London HLX 9917	(There's) Always Something There To Remind Me/Wouldn't That Be Something	20
64	London HLX 9929	A Message To Martha (Kentucky Bluebird)/The Last One To Be Loved	12
65	London HLX 9965	Please Stop The Wedding/Park Avenue	10
65	London HLX 9994	A Time To Love, A Time To Cry/Unsatisfied	45
69	London HLX 10269	(There's) Always Something There To Remind Me/Message To Martha	6
64	London REX 1438	THE MAGIC POTION OF LOU JOHNSON (EP)	70

LUTHER 'GEORGIA BOY SNAKE' JOHNSON
69	Transatlantic TRA 188	THE MUDDY WATERS BLUES BAND (LP, credits Muddy Waters on label)	15

MARGARET JOHNSON
52	Parlophone R 3506	Cushion Foot Stomp/Take Your Black Bottom Outside (78)	40
50s	Jazz Collector L 105	Death String Blues/Mistreating Man Blues (78)	8

MARV JOHNSON
59	London HLT 8856	Come To Me/Whisper	75
59	London HLT 8856	Come To Me/Whisper (78)	75
59	London HLT 9013	You Got What It Takes/Don't Leave Me	8
59	London HLT 9013	You Got What It Takes/Don't Leave Me (78)	100
60	London HLT 9109	I Love The Way You Love/Let Me Love You	18
60	London HL 7095	I Love The Way You Love/Let Me Love You (export issue)	25
60	London HLT 9165	Ain't Gonna Be That Way/All The Love I've Got	18
60	London HLT 9187	(You've Got To) Move Two Mountains/I Need You	18
61	London HLT 9265	Happy Days/Baby, Baby	18
61	London HLT 9311	Merry-Go-Round/Tell Me That You Love Me	30
65	Tamla Motown TMG 525	Why Do You Want To Let Me Go/I'm Not A Plaything	65
69	United Artists UP 35010	I Love The Way You Love/You Got What It Takes	5
68	Tamla Motown TMG 680	I'll Pick A Rose For My Rose/You Got The Love I Love	5
69	Tamla Motown TMG 713	I Miss You Baby (How I Miss You)/Bad Girl	6
70	Tamla Motown TMG 737	So Glad You Chose Me/I'm Not A Plaything	6
60	London HA-T 2271	MARVELLOUS MARV JOHNSON (LP)	100
69	T. Motown (S)TML 11111	I'LL PICK A ROSE FOR MY ROSE (LP)	25

MATT JOHNSON
81	4AD CAD 113	BURNING BLUE SOUL (LP, original 'psychedelic eye' cover)	30
81	4AD CAD 113	BURNING BLUE SOUL (LP, reissue with 'Matt' picture & inner sleeve)	10

(see also Gadgets, The The)

MIRRIAM JOHNSON
61	London HLW 9337	Lonesome Road/Young And Innocent	12

NORMAN JOHNSON (& SHOWMEN)
69	Action ACT 4529	You're Everything/Our Love Will Grow	20
69	Action ACT 4545	Take It Baby/In Paradise	30
71	Action ACT 4601	You're Everything/Our Love Will Grow (reissue)	8

(see also General Johnson, Chairmen Of The Board, Showmen)

PAUL JOHNSON
88	CBS 450640 1	PAUL JOHNSON (LP)	12

PETE JOHNSON
51	Vogue V 2007	J.J. Boogie/Yancey Special (78, red or orange label)	12/15
51	Vogue V 2008	Swanee River Boogie/St. Louis Boogie (78, red or orange label)	12/15
51	Vogue V 2019	Hollywood Boogie/Central Avenue Drag (78, orange label)	15
56	Vogue V 2007	J.J. Boogie/Yancey Special	30
56	Vogue V 2008	Swanee River Boogie/St. Louis Boogie	30
55	Vogue EPV 1039	PETE JOHNSON (EP)	30
59	Top Rank JKR 8009	ROLL 'EM BOY (EP)	20
55	London AL 3549	JUMPIN' WITH PETE JOHNSON (10" LP)	40
55	Vogue Coral LRA 10016	BOOGIE WOOGIE MOOD (LP)	25

(see also Joe Turner & Pete Johnson, Albert Ammons & Meade Lux Lewis)

PLAS JOHNSON (ORCHESTRA)
57	Capitol CL 14772	The Big Twist/Come Rain Or Come Shine	12
57	Capitol CL 14772	The Big Twist/Come Rain Or Come Shine (78)	8
57	Capitol CL 14816	Swanee River Rock/You Send Me	15
57	Capitol CL 14816	Swanee River Rock/You Send Me (78)	10
58	Capitol CL 14836	Popcorn/Hoppin' Mad	12
58	Capitol CL 14836	Popcorn/Hoppin' Mad (78)	8
58	Capitol CL 14903	Little Rockin' Deacon/Dinah	15
59	Capitol CL 14973	Robbins Nest Cha Cha/Plaz Jazz	7
57	London HB-U 1078	BOP ME DADDY (10" LP)	40

PROFESSOR JOHNSON & HIS GOSPEL SINGERS
51	Vocalion V 1013	Give Me That Old Time Religion/Where Shall I Be (78)	15
58	Brunswick OE 9352	PROFESSOR JOHNSON AND HIS GOSPEL SINGERS (EP)	15

RAY JOHNSON
57	Vogue V 9073	If You Don't Want Me Baby/Calypso Joe	40
57	Vogue V 9073	If You Don't Want Me Baby/Calypso Joe (78)	18
58	Vogue V 9093	Calypso Blues/Are You There	35
58	Vogue V 9093	Calypso Blues/Are You There (78)	18

ROBERT JOHNSON
62	Philips BBL 7539	ROBERT JOHNSON 1936-1937 (LP)	70
65	CBS BPG 62456	KING OF THE DELTA BLUES SINGERS (LP)	40
67	Kokomo K 1000	ROBERT JOHNSON (LP)	60
60s	Smokestack SS/LP 1	BLUES LEGEND 1936-1937 (LP)	45
70	CBS 64102	KING OF THE DELTA BLUES SINGERS VOL. 2 (LP)	30

ROY LEE JOHNSON
69	Action ACT 4518	So Anna Just Love Me/Boogaloo No. 3	10

RUBY JOHNSON
67	Stax 601 020	If I Ever Needed Love (I Sure Do Need It Now)/Keep On Keeping On	10

SPIDER JOHNSON & POPEYE BAND
63	Riverside RIF 106904	Doin' The Popeye/The Gospel Truth	5

TEDDY JOHNSON & PEARL CARR
57	Pye 7N 15110	Tomorrow Tomorrow/Mandolin Serenade	6
58	Pye 7N 15123	Sweet Elizabeth/Never Let Me Go	6
59	Columbia DB 4260	Petite Fleur/Missouri Waltz	5
59	Columbia DB 4260	Petite Fleur/Missouri Waltz (78)	8
59	Columbia DB 4275	Sing Little Birdie/If Only I Could Live My Life Again	5
59	Columbia DB 4275	Sing Little Birdie/If Only I Could Live My Life Again (78)	10
59	Columbia DB 4318	Tell Me, Tell Me/Viva Viva Amor	5
59	Columbia DB 4318	Tell Me, Tell Me/Viva Viva Amor (78)	10
60	Columbia DB 4397	Pazzo Pazzo (Crazy Crazy)/The Five Pennies	5
59	HMV POP 697	Pickin' Petals/When The Tide Turns	5
59	Pye NEP 24112	MEET TEDDY AND PEARL (EP)	12

THEO JOHNSON
65	Aladdin WI 604	Masters Of War/The Water Is Wide	10

TOMMY JOHNSON
60s	Saydisc SDM 224	THE LEGACY OF TOMMY JOHNSON (LP)	20

TONY JOHNSON
55	Melodisc 1331	Man Smart Woman Smarter/Give Her Banana (78)	15

WILKO JOHNSON & SOLID SENDERS
78	Virgin VS 214	Walking On The Edge/Dr. Dupree (p/s)	5
78	Virgin V 2105	SOLID SENDERS (LP, with free LP "Live" [VDJ 26])	12

(see also Dr. Feelgood, Solid Senders, Ian Dury & Blockheads)

JOHNSON ENGINEERING CO.
85 Gigantic G 103   Block Mania (die-cut company sleeve) 4

ADRIENNE JOHNSTON
75 RCA SF 8416   ADRIENNE JOHNSTON OF THE JOHNSTONS (LP) 12
(see also Johnstons)

BRUCE JOHNSTON COMBO
63 London HL 9780   Original Surfer Stomp/Pajama Party 30
(see also Beach Boys, California Music, Fantastic Baggys, Sagittarius)

JOHNSTON BROTHERS
54	Decca F 10234	The Creep/Crystal Ball	12
54	Decca F 10286	Oh Baby Mine I Get So Lonely/My Love, My Life, My Own	10
54	Decca F 10302	The Bandit/KEYNOTES: A Dime And A Dollar	20
54	Decca F 10364	Sh-Boom (Life Could Be A Dream)/Crazy 'Bout Ya Baby	15
54	Decca F 10364	Sh-Boom (Life Could Be A Dream)/Crazy 'Bout Ya Baby (78)	10
54	Decca F 10401	Mambo In The Moonlight/Papa Loves Mambo (with Ted Heath Music)	7
54	Decca F 10414	"Join In And Sing" Medley (both sides)	7
55	Decca F 10451	Majorca/Heartbroken	7
55	Decca F 10490	The Right To Be Wrong/Hot Potato Mambo	7
55	Decca F 10513	Chee Chee-Oo Chee (Sang The Little Bird)Hubble Bubble	7
55	Decca F 10526	Dreamboat/Jim, Johnny And Jonas	7
55	Decca F 10608	Hernando's Hideaway/Hey There	15
55	Decca F 10608	Hernando's Hideaway/Hey There (78)	10
55	Decca F 10636	"Join In And Sing Again" Medley (both sides)	10
56	Decca F 10721	No Other Love/Flowers Mean Forgiveness	10
56	Decca F 10747	How Little We Know/The Street Musician	7
56	Decca F 10781	In The Middle Of The House (with Keynotes)/Stranded In The Jungle	12
56	Decca F 10814	"Join In And Sing, No. 3" Medley (both sides)	10
56	Decca F 10828	Give Her My Love (When You Meet Her)/A Rose And A Candy Bar	10
57	Decca F 10860	Whatever Lola Wants (Lola Gets)/Heart	8
57	Decca F 10915	All Star Hit Parade No. 2 (with other artists)	5
57	Decca F 10939	I Like Music — You Like Music/Seven Bar Blues	7
57	Decca F 10962	"Join In And Sing, No. 4" Medley (both sides)	6
58	Decca F 10996	A Very Precious Love/Yours, Yours, Yours	5
58	Decca F 11021	Scratch, Scratch/Little Serenade	5
58	Decca F 11083	Love Is All We Need/Clementine Cha-Cha	5
58	Decca F 11083	Love Is All We Need/Clementine Cha-Cha (78)	7
56	Decca DFE 6249	JOIN THE JOHNSTON BROTHERS (EP)	10
56	Decca DFE 6311	JOIN IN AND SING WITH THE JOHNSTON BROTHERS (EP)	10
57	Decca DFE 6458	JOIN AND SING AGAIN (EP)	10
58	Decca DFE 6503	EASY NO. 1 (EP)	10
58	Decca LK 4266	EASY (LP)	15

(see also Dennis Lotis, Vera Lynn, Edmundo Ros, Joan Regan, Lita Roza, Suzi Miller, Ted Heath, Keynotes)

JOHNSTONS
66	Pye 7N 17144	Going Home/Travelling People	5
66	Pye 7N 17205	The Alamo/Life Of A Rover	5
67	Pye 7N 17205	The Curragh Of Kildare/Leaving London	5
67	Pye 7N 17430	I Never Will Marry/Banks Of Claudy	5
67	Transatlantic TRASP 17	They'll Never Get Their Man/Dublin Jack Of All Trades	5
68	Big T BIG 113	Both Sides Now/Urge For Going	5
68	Big T BIG 116	Give A Damn/Walking Out On Foggy Mornings	5
69	Big T BIG 121	My House/The Wherefore And The Why	5
70	Big T BIG 132	Streets Of London/The Spanish Lady	5
68	Transatlantic TRA 169	THE JOHNSTONS (LP)	20
68	Transatlantic TRA 184	GIVE A DAMN (LP)	18
68	Transatlantic TRA 185	THE BARLEYCORN (LP)	18
69	Marble Arch MAL 808	THE TRAVELLING PEOPLE (LP)	12
70	Transatlantic TRA 211	BITTER GREEN (LP)	15
70	Transatlantic TRASAM 16	THE JOHNSTONS SAMPLER (LP)	12
71	Transatlantic TRA 231	COLOURS OF THE DAWN (LP)	15
72	Transatlantic TRA 251	IF I SANG MY SONG (LP, gatefold sleeve)	15

(see also Adrienne Johnston)

JOHN THE POSTMAN
78 Bent BIG BENT 2   PUERILE (12" EP, stamped brown paper bag p/s, with inserts) 12
78 Bent BIG BENT 4   PSYCHEDELIC ROCK'N'ROLL FIVE SKINNERS (12" EP, white label, foldover p/s in bag) 12

JOINER, ARKANSAS, JUNIOR HIGH SCHOOL BAND
60 London HLG 9147   Big Ben/National City 7

JO JO GUNNE (U.K.)
68 Decca F 12807   Every Story Has An End/Should Live Like That 6
69 Decca F 12906   Beggin' You Baby/Bad Penny 6

JO JO GUNNE (U.S.)
72	Asylum AYM 501	Run Run Run/Shake That Fat (withdrawn)	10
72	Asylum AYM 501	Run Run Run/Take It Easy	5
72	Asylum AYM 507	Shake That Fat/I Make Love	5
73	Asylum AYM 518	Ready Freddy/Wait A Lifetime	5
74	Asylum AYM 528	I Wanna Love You/Neon City	5
74	Asylum AYM 534	Where Is The Show/Single Man	5

(see also Spirit)

JOKER
84 Lost Moment LM 018   Back On The Road/Pusher (p/s) 15

JOKERS
62 Salvo SLO 1806 — Blue Moonbeam/Dog Fight 25

JOKER'S WILD
66 Regent Sound RSR 0031 — Don't Ask Me/Why Do Fools Fall In Love (handwritten labels, 50 only) . . . . 500+
66 Regent Sound RSLP 007 — JOKER'S WILD: Don't Ask Me/Why Do Fools Fall In Love/You Don't Know What I Know/That's How Strong My Love Is (12", 1-sided, 50 copies only) . . . . 1,000+

(see also Dave Gilmour, Pink Floyd)

JOLLIVER ARKANSAS
69 Bell SBLL 119 — HOME (LP) 25

(see also Leslie West, Mountain)

JOLLY BOYS
70 Moodisc MU 3504 — On The Water/MUDIES ALL STARS: Cash Register. 10

AL JOLSON
69 MCA MU 1092 — Rockabye Your Baby With A Dixie Melody/Anniversary Song 5
54 Brunswick OE 9011 — SONGS HE MADE FAMOUS VOL. 1 (EP) 8
55 Brunswick OE 9159 — AL JOLSON MEMORIAL (EP) 8
57 Brunswick OE 9336 — SONGS HE MADE FAMOUS PT. 1 (EP) 8
57 Brunswick OE 9337 — SONGS HE MADE FAMOUS PT. 2 (EP) 8
59 Brunswick OE 9418 — THEY SOLD A MILLION NO. 2 (EP) 8
59 Brunswick OE 9419 — THEY SOLD A MILLION NO. 3 (EP) 8
58 Fontana TFE 17024 — AL JOLSON (EP) 8
50 Brunswick LA 8502 — JOLSON SINGS AGAIN (10" LP) 15
50 Brunswick LA 8509 — AL JOLSON SOUVENIR (10" LP) 15
51 Brunswick LA 8512 — JOLSON MEMORIES (10" LP) 15
53 Brunswick LA 8554 — STEPHEN FOSTER SONGS (10" LP) 15
53 Brunswick LA 8575 — AL JOLSON SOUVENIR ALBUM VOLUME 3 (10" LP) 15
53 Brunswick LA 8570 — AL JOLSON SOUVENIR ALBUM VOLUME 4 (10" LP) 15
54 Brunswick LA 8655 — AL JOLSON SOUVENIR ALBUM VOLUME 6 (10" LP) 15
57 Brunswick LAT 8220 — THE JOLSON STORY — AMONG MY SOUVENIRS (LP) 12
58 Brunswick LAT 8267 — THE IMMORTAL AL JOLSON (LP) 12
59 Brunswick LAT 8294 — AL JOLSON OVERSEAS (LP) 12
60 Brunswick LAT 8322 — THE WORLD'S GREATEST ENTERTAINER (LP) 12
61 Brunswick LAT 8387 — OSCAR LEVANT (LP) 12
61 Brunswick LAT 8403 — YOU MADE ME LOVE YOU (LP, 2 tracks with Bing Crosby) 12

JOLT
77 Polydor 2058 936 — You're Cold/All I Can Do (p/s) 5
78 Polydor 2059 008 — What'cha Gonna Do About It/Again And Again (die-cut p/s) 5
78 Polydor 2059 039 — I Can't Wait/Route 66 (p/s) 6
79 Polydor 2229 215 — Maybe Tonight/I'm In Tears/See Saw/Stop Look (p/s) 6
79 Polydor 2229 215DJ — Maybe Tonight/See Saw (promo only, no p/s) 8
78 Polydor 2383 504 — THE JOLT (LP) 12

JON
67 Parlophone R 5604 — So Much For Mary/Polly Sunday (some in p/s) 25/10
67 Columbia DB 8249 — Is It Love/Sing Out 40

(see also Titus Groan, Still Life)

JON & ALUN
63 Decca LK/SKL 4547 — RELAX YOUR MIND (LP, mono/stereo) 22/30

JON & DAVE
97 Earworm SS 1 — Land Beyond The Sun/Instrumental For Silence (p/s, pale green vinyl, 500 copies only) 8

JON & JEANNIE
68 Beacon 3-105 — Lover's Holiday/Something You Got 5
69 Beacon BEA 113 — Don't Sign The Papers/We Got Lovin' 4

JON & ROBIN & IN-CROWD
67 Stateside SS 2027 — Do It Again A Little Bit Slower/If I Need Someone It's You 7

JON & VANGELIS
81 Polydor POSP 258 — The Friends Of Mr. Cairo/Beside (p/s) 5
81 Polydor POSP 323 — State Of Independence/Beside (p/s) 5
81 Polydor POSPX 323 — State Of Independence/Beside (12", in blue plastic film cannister, promo only) 30
83 Polydor JV 3 — And When The Night Comes/Song Is (p/s) 5
83 Polydor JV 4 — He Is Sailing/Polonaise (p/s) 5
84 Polydor JV 5/POSP 246 — State Of Independence/The Friends Of Mr. Cairo/Chariots Of Fire/Eric's Theme (p/s doublepack, stickered shrinkwrapped p/s) 6
91 Arista 114 063 — Wisdom Chain/Page Of Life (with Irene Papas, p/s) 5
91 Arista 664 063 — Wisdom Chain (Edit)/Wisdom Chain (Album Version)/Page Of Life/Sing With Your Eyes (CD, with Irene Papas) 10
81 Polydor POLD 5039 — THE FRIENDS OF MR. CAIRO (LP, promo issue with b&w sleeve, raised figures & logo in left corner) 25

(see also Jon Anderson, Vangelis)

JONATHAN & CHARLES
69 Herald LLR 566 — ANOTHER WEEK TO GO (LP) 30

JONCUNO(O)
(see Juncuno)

AL JONES
58 HMV POP 451 — Mad, Mad, World/Lonely Traveller. 225
58 HMV POP 451 — Mad, Mad, World/Lonely Traveller (78) 60

AL JONES
69	Parlophone PMC/PCS 7081	ALUN ASHWORTH JONES (LP)	40
72	Village Thing VTS 19	JONESVILLE (LP)	20

(see also Anderson, Jones, Jackson)

ALLAN JONES
53	HMV 7M 111	Why Do I Love You/Make Believe	7
53	HMV 7M 135	I Believe/I Talk To The Trees	7
53	HMV 7M 161	Poppa Piccolino/Why?	7

BARBARA JONES
72	Bullet BU 507	Sad Movies/SIR HARRY: Deejay Version	6
74	Count Shelley CS 045	Baby I'm Yours/Don't Turn Your Back On Me	5
75	Dip DL 5085	Where Do I Turn/G.G. ALL STARS: Version	5

BETTY HALL JONES
50	Capitol CL 13266	This Joint's Too Hip For Me/You've Got To Have What It Takes (78)	20

BEVERLEY JONES (& PRESTONS)
63	HMV POP 1109	The Boy I Saw With You/When It Comes To Love	8
63	HMV POP 1140	Why Do Lovers Break Each Other's Heart/I'm Just An In-Between	10
63	HMV POP 1201	Wait 'Til My Bobby Gets Home/A Boy Like You	8
64	Parlophone R 5189	Heatwave/Hear You Talking (with Prestons)	12

B-LOU JONES & HIS JUPITERS
61	London HLU 9373	Anchors Aweigh (Parts 1 & 2)	7

BRENDA LEE JONES
75	UK USA 8	You're The Love Of My Life/Thread Your Needle	5

(see also Dean & Jean)

BRIAN JONES
(see under Pipes Of Pan, Rolling Stones)

CAROL JONES
60	Triumph RGM 1012	The Boy With The Eyes Of Blue/I Gave Him Back His Ring	100

CASEY JONES & ENGINEERS
63	Columbia DB 7083	One Way Ticket/I'm Gonna Love	25

CURTIS JONES
66	RCA RCX 7184	R.C.A. VICTOR RACE SERIES VOL. 9 (EP)	15
64	Decca LK 4587	CURTIS JONES IN LONDON (LP)	50
68	Blue Horizon 7-63207	NOW RESIDENT IN EUROPE (LP)	60

DAVEY JONES
65	Philips BF 1410	For Your Love/Love Bug	4

DAVIE JONES & KING BEES
64	Vocalion Pop V 9221	Liza Jane/Louie, Louie Go Home (beware of counterfeits without centres)	550
78	Decca F 13807	Liza Jane/Louie, Louie Go Home (reissue)	8

(see also David Bowie, Davy Jones, Manish Boys, Calvin James)

DAVY JONES (U.S.)
60	Pye 7N 15254	Amapola/Mighty Man	8
61	Pye 7N 15318	Shenandoah/Scenery	7
61	Pye International 7N 25072	Model Girl/Scarlet Woman	10
61	Pye International 7N 25095	Bonnie Banks/Baby Baby	8
62	Piccadilly 7N 35038	Jezebel/Don't Come Crying To Me	7

(see also Thelonious Monk)

DAVY JONES (U.K.)
65	Parlophone R 5315	You've Got A Habit Of Leaving/Baby Loves That Way	325

(see also David Bowie)

DAVY JONES (U.K.)
65	Colpix PX 784	What Are We Going To Do/This Bouquet	8
67	Pye 7N 17302	It Ain't Me Babe/Baby It's Me (some in p/s)	12/7
67	Pye 7N 17380	Theme For A New Love/Dream Girl (some in p/s)	12/7
67	Pye International 7N 25432	Theme For A New Love/Dream Girl (reissue, withdrawn)	20+
71	Bell BLL 1163	Rainy Jane/Welcome To My Love	8
77	MCA MCA 348	Life Line/It's A Jungle Out There/Gotta Get Up (from 'The Point') (p/s, last track with Micky Dolenz)	8
78	Warner Bros K 17161	(Hey Ra Ra) Happy Birthday Mickey Mouse/You Don't Have To Be A Country Boy To Sing A Country Song (p/s)	8
83	J.J. 2001	I'll Love You Forever/When I Look Back On Christmas	12
67	Pye NPL 18178	DAVY JONES (LP)	18

(see also Davy Jones & Micky Dolenz, Monkees)

DAVY JONES (U.K.) & MICKY DOLENZ
71	Bell BLL 986	Do It In The Name Of Love/Lady Jane	15

(see also Monkees, Davey Jones)

DAVY JONES (U.K.) & LOWER THIRD/MANISH BOYS
79	EMI EMI 2925	You've Got A Habit Of Leaving/Baby Loves That Way/MANISH BOYS: I Pity The Fool/Take My Tip (p/s)	5
82	Charly CYM 1	You've Got A Habit Of Leaving/Baby Loves That Way/MANISH BOYS: I Pity The Fool/Take My Tip (10", p/s)	6

(see also David Bowie, Davie Jones & King Bees, Manish Boys, Calvin James)

DILL JONES TRIO
58	Pye Jazz 7NJ 2021	Little Rock Getaway/Carolina Shout	5
56	Jazz Today JTE 104	PIANO MOODS VOL. 2 (EP)	15
50s	Pye Jazz NJE 1024	PIANO MOODS VOL. 5 (EP)	20
50s	Columbia SEG 7764	TOP OF THE POLL (EP)	10
59	Columbia SEG 7893	DILL JONES PLUS FOUR (EP)	8
60	Columbia 33SX 1336	JONES THE JAZZ (LP)	80

DOROTHY JONES

61	Philips 322 794 BF	Takin' That Long Walk Home/It's Unbearable 10

(see also Cookies)

FLOYD JONES/EDDIE TAYLOR

60s	XX MIN 712	FLOYD JONES AND EDDIE TAYLOR (EP, 2 tracks each) 15

GAYNOR JONES

69	Morgan MR 16	Mum P T Dum P T/Memories Of Summertime 4
69	Decca F 12970	Peaches And Pears/Please Take My Hand 4
72	York SYK 536	Da Doo Ron Ron/Chasing Many Roads 4

GEORGE JONES

59	Mercury AMT 1021	The Treasure Of Love/If I Don't Love You (Grits Ain't Groceries) 18
59	Mercury AMT 1021	The Treasure Of Love/If I Don't Love You (Grits Ain't Groceries) (78) 25
59	Mercury AMT 1036	White Lightning/Long Time To Forget 45
59	Mercury AMT 1058	Who Shot Sam/Into My Arms Again 18
59	Mercury AMT 1078	Big Harlan Taylor/Money To Burn 12
60	Mercury AMT 1100	Sparkling Brown Eyes/Accidentally On Purpose 12
61	Mercury AMT 1124	Candy Hearts/The Window Up Above 12
62	United Artists POP 1037	She Thinks I Still Care/Geronimo. 12
63	United Artists UP 1015	I Saw Me/Not What I Had In Mind (as George Jones with Jones Boys) 10
64	United Artists UP 1044	Your Heart Turned Left (And I Was On The Right)/My Tears Are Overdue 10
65	United Artists UP 1080	The Race Is On/She's So Lonesome Again. 12
69	Stateside SS 2145	If My Heart Had Windows/Taggin' Along 7
71	Pye International 7N 25547	It's Been A Good Year For The Roses/Let A Little Come In 6
80	Epic EPC 8560	Stranger In The House (with Elvis Costello)/A Drunk Can't Be A Man (p/s) 5
59	Mercury ZEP 10036	GEORGE JONES (EP) 90
60s	Melodisc EPM7 109	COUNTRY SONG HITS (EP) 40
64	Mercury 10009 MCE	C & W ACES (EP) 20
64	Ember EMB 4548	THE BEST OF AMERICAN COUNTRY MUSIC VOL. 4 (EP) 15
62	United Artists ULP 1007	THE NEW FAVOURITES OF GEORGE JONES (LP) 18
63	United Artists ULP 1014	MY FAVOURITES OF HANK WILLIAMS (LP) 18
63	Ember CW 101	THE CROWN PRINCE OF COUNTRY MUSIC (LP) 15
63	United Artists ULP 1037	HITS OF HIS COUNTRY COUSINS (LP) 18
64	United Artists ULP 1050	I WISH TONIGHT WOULD NEVER END (LP). 18
64	London HA-B 8125	GEORGE JONES SINGS HIS GREATEST HITS (LP) 20
64	United Artists ULP 1070	WHAT'S IN OUR HEARTS (LP, with Melba Montgomery) 15
64	Ember CW 109	THE FABULOUS COUNTRY MUSIC SOUND OF JONES (LP) 15
64	Wing WL 1175	COUNTRY & WESTERN NO. 1 MALE SINGER (LP). 12
64	United Artists ULP 1074	MORE NEW FAVOURITES (LP) 18
65	United Artists ULP 1077	BLUE GRASS HOOTENANNY (LP, with Melba Montgomery) 15
65	United Artists ULP 1091	I GET LONELY IN A HURRY (LP) 18
65	United Artists ULP 1082	JONES SINGS LIKE THE DICKENS (LP) 18
65	United Artists ULP 1101	TROUBLE IN MIND (LP) 18
65	Stateside SL 10147	GEORGE JONES AND GENE PITNEY (LP, with Gene Pitney) 22
65	Stateside SL 10157	MR. COUNTRY AND WESTERN MUSIC (LP) 15
66	London HA-B 8259	GEORGE JONES (LP, with Tommy Hill's Band) 25
66	United Artists (S)ULP 1136	THE GREAT GEORGE JONES (LP) 15
66	United Artists (S)ULP 1137	BLUE MOON OF KENTUCKY (LP, with Melba Montgomery) 15
66	Stateside SL 10173	IT'S COUNTRY TIME AGAIN (LP, with Gene Pitney) 22
66	Stateside S(S)L 10184	LOVE BUG (LP) 15
67	Stateside S(S)L 10195	WE FOUND HEAVEN RIGHT HERE ON EARTH AT '4033' (LP) 15
67	Mercury SMCL 20107	GREATEST HITS (LP). 15
67	London HA-B 8340	THE GEORGE JONES SONG BOOK (LP) 22
67	Stateside S(S)L 10215	VARIETY IS THE SPICE OF ... (LP) 15
68	Stateside S(S)L 10236	SINGS THE SONGS OF DALLAS FRAZIER (LP) 15
68	Hallmark HM 562	GEORGE JONES SINGS (LP). 12
68	Mercury SMWL 21003	THE GREAT GEORGE JONES (LP) 18
69	Stateside S(S)L 10256	IF MY HEART HAD WINDOWS (LP) 12
69	Stateside S(S)L 10283	MY COUNTRY (LP) 12
69	Fontana SFL 13202	THE GREAT GEORGE JONES (LP, reissue) 12
70	Stateside SSL 10308	I'LL SHARE MY WORLD WITH YOU (LP) 12
71	Pye Intl. NSPL 28150	THE BEST OF GEORGE JONES (LP) 12
72	Pye PKL 4412	THE BLUE SIDE OF LONESOME & OTHER COUNTRY FAVOURITES (LP). 12
72	Pye Intl. NSPL 28160	COUNTRY MUSIC '72 (LP) 12
72	CBS EQ 30802	WE GO TOGETHER
		(LP, with Tammy Wynette, quadrophonic) 12
73	Pye Intl. NSPL 28176	WRAPPED AROUND HER FINGERS (LP) 12

(see also Gene Pitney, Elvis Costello, Tammy Wynette)

GEORGE JONES/JIMMIE SKINNER

59	Mercury ZEP 10012	COUNTRY AND WESTERN (EP, 2 tracks each) 40

GLORIA JONES

66	Capitol CL 15429	Heartbeat (Parts 1 & 2). 18
66	Stateside SS 555	Finders Keepers/Run One Flight Of Stairs 30
74	Tamla Motown TMG 910	Tin Can People/So Tired 5
76	EMI EMI 2437	Get It On/Get It On (Version) 5
76	EMI EMI 2522	I Ain't Going Nowhere/Simplicity Blues 5
77	EMI EMI 2570	Go Now/Drive Me Crazy 5
77	EMI EMI 2720	Bring On The Love/Cry Baby 5
74	Tamla Motown STML 11254	SHARE MY LOVE (LP) 15
76	EMI EMC 3159	VIXEN (LP) 12

(see also Marc Bolan & Gloria Jones)

GRACE JONES

86	Island 12IS 240	Pull Up To The Bumper/La Vie En Rose (12") 8

GRANDPA JONES

MINT VALUE £

57	Brunswick 05676	Eight More Miles To Louisville/Dark As A Dungeon	25
59	Brunswick OE 9455	MOUNTAIN MUSIC VOL. 3 (EP)	30
57	Parlophone GEP 8666	MEET GRANDPA JONES (EP)	30
58	Parlophone GEP 8766	COUNTRY AND WESTERN (EP)	35
59	Parlophone GEP 8781	COUNTRY ROUND UP (EP)	30
64	London RE-U 1417	GRANDPA SINGS JIMMIE RODGERS (EP)	30
62	London HA-U/SH-U 8010	MAKES THE RAFTERS RING (LP)	35
64	London HA-U/SH-U 8119	YODELLING HITS (LP)	35

HOWARD JONES

83	WEA HOW 2/SAM 183	What Is Love?/It Just Doesn't Matter//What Can I Say (live)/Bounce Right Back (12"/7", double pack with sticker, some sealed)	15/12
84	WEA HOW 3PT	Hide And Seek/Tao Te Ching (square picture disc)	6
84	WEA HOW 3L	Hide And Seek/Tao Te Ching/China Dance (10", p/s)	6
84	WEA HOW 4P	Pearl In The Shell/Law Of The Jungle (shaped picture disc)	5
85	WEA HOW 6P	Things Can Only Get Better/Why Look For The Key (green or orange shaped picture discs)	12/5
85	WEA HOW 6P	Things Can Only Get Better/Why Look For The Key (white shaped picture disc, existence unconfirmed)	
85	WEA HOW 7TE	Look Mama (Megamamamix)/Learning How To Love/Dream Into Action (live) (12", p/s)	12
86	WEA HOW 9TF	No One Is To Blame (Extended Mix)/The Chase/No One Is To Blame (The Long Mix)//What Is Love? (Extended Version)/It Just Doesn't Matter/Hunt The Self (12", double pack, stickered p/s)	8
86	WEA HOW 10F	All I Want/Roll Right Up (gatefold booklet p/s)	4
86	WEA HOW 10D (HOW 10/SAM 316)	All I Want/Roll Right Up//(Howard Jones Interviewed by Paul Gambaccini) (double pack, non-gatefold p/s)	5
86	WEA HOW 10G (HOW 10/SAM 316)	All I Want/Roll Right Up//(Howard Jones Interviewed by Paul Gambaccini) (double pack, gatefold p/s)	8
86	WEA HOW 11C (HOW 11/SAM 329)	You Know I Love You ... Don't You?/Dig This Well Deep (p/s, shrinkwrapped with free cassette "Hide And Seek (Orchestral)"/"Look Mama (U.S. Mix)")	6
86	WEA HOW 11TF	You Know I Love You ... Don't You?/Dig This Well Deep//Hide And Seek (Orchestral) (12", p/s, double pack)	7
89	WEA HOW 13CD	Everlasting Love/The Brutality Of Fact/Power Of The Media (3" CD, g/fold p/s)	8
89	WEA HOW 13CDX	Everlasting Love (The Institute Mix)/Hide And Seek (Orchestral)/Conditioning (Live In Philadelphia) (3" CD, 'envelope' foldout card sleeve)	10
89	WEA HOW 14CD	The Prisoner/Rubber Morals/What Is Love? (The Prisoner (The Portmeiron Mix) (3" CD, gatefold sleeve)	8
92	WEA HOW 17CD	Tears To Tell/Taking The Time/Other People Are Us/You Say (CD, withdrawn)	25
90s	D-Tox D-TOX CD 1	WORKING IN THE BACKROOM (CD, private pressing, available at concerts, most autographed)	30

(see also Warrior)

JACK JONES

65	London HLR 9939	Dear Heart/Where Love Has Gone	5
65	London HLR 9956	The Race Is On/I Can't Believe I'm Losing You	6
66	London HLR 10088	Impossible Dream/A Day In The Life Of A Fool	5
67	London HLR 10108	Lady/Afraid Of Love	5
64	London HA-R 8167	WIVES AND LOVERS (LP)	15
64	London HA-R/SH-R 8191	SHE LOVES ME (LP)	15
65	London HA-R 8202	BEWITCHED (LP)	15
65	London HA-R/SH-R 8209	WHERE LOVE HAS GONE (LP)	15
65	London HA-R/SH-R 8222	SONGS OF LOVE (LP)	15
65	London HA-R/SH-R 8236	MY KIND OF TOWN (LP)	15
65	London HA-R/SH-R 8246	THE JACK JONES CHRISTMAS ALBUM (LP)	15
66	London HA-R/SH-R 8254	AND THERE'S LOVE (LP)	15

JANET JONES

74	Midas MR 005	SING TO ME LADY (LP)	75

JANIE JONES (& LASH)

65	HMV POP 1495	Witches Brew/Take-A My Tip	15
66	HMV POP 1514	Gunning For You/Go Go Away From Me	12
67	Columbia DB 8173	Tickle Me Tootsie Wootsies/High And Dry	7
68	Pye 7N 17550	Charlie Smith/Nobody's Perfect	6
68	Major Minor MM 577	The Girl's Song/I've Never Met A Boy Like You	7
70	President PT 309	Back On My Feet Again/Psycho	7
83	Big Beat NS 91	House Of The Ju-Ju Queen/Sex Machine (as Janie Jones & Lash, p/s)	7

(see also Clash)

JERRY JONES

70	Banana BA 316	Still Waters (Love)/SOUND DIMENSION: Wig Wam	15
71	Bamboo BAM 65	Still Waters (Love)/SOUND DIMENSION: Wig Wam (reissue)	15
71	Bamboo BALPS 213	LIVE AT THE KINGSTON HOTEL, JAMAICA (LP)	30

JIMMY JONES

60	MGM MGM 1051	Handy Man/The Search Is Over	5
60	MGM MGM 1051	Handy Man/The Search Is Over (78)	150
60	MGM MGM 1078	Good Timin'/Too Long Will Be Too Late	5
60	MGM MGM 1078	Good Timin'/Too Long Will Be Too Late (78)	180
60	MGM MGM 1091	I Just Go For You/That's When I Cried	7
60	MGM MGM 1103	Ready For Love/For You	6
61	MGM MGM 1123	I Told You So/You Got It	6
61	MGM MGM 1133	Dear One/I Say Love	6

61	MGM MGM 1146	Mr Music Man/Holler Hey	6
62	MGM MGM 1168	You're Much Too Young/Nights Of Mexico	6
65	Columbia DB 7592	Walkin'/Pardon Me	25
65	Cameo Parkway P 988	Don't You Just Know It	5
67	Stateside SS 2041	39-21-46/Personal Property	8
68	MGM MGM 1405	Good Timin'/Handy Man	5
60	MGM MGM-EP 745	JIMMY HANDYMAN JONES (EP)	50
61	MGM MGM-EP 787	ORIGINAL HITS (EP)	40
60	MGM MGM-C 832	GOOD TIMIN' (LP)	60

JO JONES TRIO
| 59 | Top Rank 25/039 | JO JONES (LP) | 12 |

JOE JONES
| 60 | Columbia DB 4533 | You Talk Too Much/I Love You Still | 15 |

JOHN PAUL JONES
| 64 | Pye 7N 15637 | Baja/A Foggy Day In Vietnam |
| | | (B-side actually by Andrew Oldham Orchestra) | 50 |

(see also Led Zeppelin, Tony Meehan, Andrew Oldham Orchestra)

JOHNNY JONES & KING CASUALS
68	MCA MU 1031	Soul Poppin'/Blues For The Brothers	5
76	Cream CRM 5004	Purple Haze/Horsing Around	5
76	Brunswick BR 37	Purple Haze/FRED HUGHES: Baby Boy	5
80	Sonet SNTF 821	RARE RECORDINGS (LP)	10

JONAH JONES (QUARTET)
59	Mercury AMT 15085	I Dig Chicks/Cherry	5
62	Ember JBS 704	Down By The Riverside/Stars Fell On Alabama	7
65	Brunswick LAT 8633	ON THE SUNNY SIDE OF THE STREET
		(LP, as Jonah Jones Quartet)	10

JUGGY JONES
| 76 | Contempo CS 2080 | Inside America (Parts 1 & 2) | 5 |

JUSTIN JONES
| 61 | London HLU 9463 | Dance By Yourself/Love | 50 |

KEN JONES (& HIS ROCK'N'ROLLERS)
61	Parlophone R 4763	Bluesville/On The Rebound	6
61	Parlophone R 4788	Joxville/Just Rollin'	5
58	Embassy WEP 1004	ROCK'N'ROLL TIME
		(EP, as Ken Jones & His Rock'n'Rollers)	12

KENNEY JONES
| 74 | GM GMS 027 | Ready Or Not/Woman Trouble | 5 |

(see also Small Faces, Faces, Who)

LINDA JONES
67	Warner Bros WB 2070	Hypnotised/I Can't Stop Lovin' My Baby	30
72	London HLU 10368	For Your Precious Love/Don't Go	10
75	Warner Bros WB 16621	I Just Can't Live My Life/My Heart Will Understand	8

LINDA JONES/J.J. JACKSON
| 77 | Loma/Warners K 56271 | THIS IS LOMA — VOL. 7 (LP, 1 side each) | 12 |

LITTLE JOHNNY JONES
| 73 | Pressure Beat PB 5515 | More Dub/More Dub — Chapter Two | 8 |

(see also Johnny Lover)

LLOYD JONES
| 70 | Bullet BU 429 | Rome/RHYTHM RULERS: Version | 10 |

LOUIS JONES ROCK & ROLL BAND
| 50s | Vogue VE1 70111 | ROCK AND ROLL (EP) | 80 |

MAE JONES ENSEMBLE with MARGARET BOND
| 55 | Decca F 10486 | I Walked Into The Garden/Tenderly He Watches | 6 |

MAGGIE JONES
| 70 | VJM VLP 23 | COLUMBIA RECORDINGS IN CHRONOLOGICAL ORDER VOL. 1 (LP) | 15 |
| 70 | VJM VLP 25 | COLUMBIA RECORDINGS IN CHRONOLOGICAL ORDER VOL. 2 (LP) | 15 |

MICK JONES
89	Atlantic A 8954	Everything That Comes Around/Wrong Side Of The Law
		(probably unissued)	5
89	Atlantic A 8954T	Everything That Comes Around/(extended)/Wrong Side Of The Law
		(12", probably unissued)	8

(see also Foreigner)

NIC JONES
70	Trailer LER 2014	BALLADS AND SONGS (LP, red label, later with 'highway' label)	20/12
71	Trailer LER 2027	NIC JONES (LP, red label)	15
78	Transatlantic LTRA 507	FROM THE DEVIL TO A STRANGER (LP)	12

(see also Jon Raven, Halliard)

NIGEL MAZLYN JONES
76	Isle Of Light IOL 666/1	SHIP TO SHORE (LP)	35
78	Avada AVA 105	SENTINEL (LP)	15
82	Isle Of Light IOL 0230	BREAKING COVER (LP)	15

PALMER JONES
| 68 | Direction 58-3603 | The Great Magic Of Love/Dancing Master | 6 |

MINT VALUE £

PAUL JONES

66	HMV POP 1554	High Time/I Can't Hold On Much Longer	7
67	HMV POP 1576	I've Been A Bad Bad Boy/Sonny Boy Williamson	7
67	HMV POP 1602	Thinkin' Ain't For Me/Softly (La Vita)	6
67	HMV PSR 5307	Privilege (1-sided demo)	10
67	Columbia DB 8303	Sons And Lovers/Three Sisters	6
68	Columbia DB 8379	And The Sun Will Shine/The Dog Presides	15
68	Columbia DB 8417	When I Was Six Years Old/You Have No Idea	7
68	Columbia DB 8514	Aquarius/Pisces	6
69	Columbia DB 8567	It's Getting Better/Not Before Time	6
71	Vertigo 6059 053	Life After Death/The Mighty Ship	6
78	RSO RSO 003	Sheena Is A Punk Rocker/Pretty Vacant (p/s)	5
66	HMV 7EG 8974	PRIVILEGE (EP)	18
66	HMV CLP/CSD 3586	MY WAY (LP, mono/stereo)	22/25
67	HMV CLP/CSD 3602	LOVE ME, LOVE MY FRIENDS (LP, mono/stereo)	25/30
67	HMV CLP/CSD 3623	PRIVILEGE (LP, soundtrack, with George Bean Group & Mike Leander)	25
69	Columbia SX/SCX 6347	COME INTO MY MUSIC BOX (LP, mono/stereo)	25
71	Vertigo 6360 059	CRUCIFIX IN A HORSESHOE (LP, gatefold sleeve, spiral label)	35
70s	President PTLS 1068	DRAKE'S DREAM (LP, soundtrack)	12

(see also Manfred Mann, Blues Band)

QUINCY JONES

59	Mercury AMT 1037	Tuxedo Junction/The Syncopated Clock	5
60	Mercury AMT 1111	Love Is Here To Stay/Moonglow	5
62	Mercury AMT 1195	Soul Bossa Nova/On The Street Where You Live	12
65	Mercury MF 844	Seaweed/Golden Boy Theme	5
69	RCA RCA 1850	MacKenna's Gold/Soul Full Of Gold	5
70	A&M AMS 781	Killer Joe/Oh Happy Day	5
72	A&M AMS 888	Ironside/Cast Your Fate To The Wind	5
72	Reprise K 14150	Money Runned	5
72	Atlantic K 10172	Listen To The Melody/Hot Rock Theme	5
97	EMI 7 BIGDJ 001	They Call Me Mr.Tibbs/LYN COLLINS: Mama Feelgood (promo only, some free with 'The Big Score' LP)	5
60	Mercury ZEP 10047	BIG BAND BASH (EP)	12
61	Mercury ZEP 10109	THE BIRTH OF A BAND (EP, also stereo SEZ 19017)	10/12
61	Columbia SEG 8088	DOUBLE SIX MEET QUINCY JONES (EP)	10
61	Mercury ZEP 10119	THE BIRTH OF A BAND PT. 2 (EP, also stereo SEZ 19021)	10/12
60	Mercury MMC 14038	THE BIRTH OF A BAND (LP, also stereo CMS 18026)	18/22
60	Mercury MMC 14046	THE GREAT WORLD OF QUINCY JONES (LP, also stereo CMS 18031)	18/22
61	Mercury MMC 14080	I DIG DANCERS (LP, also stereo CMS 18055)	15/18
62	HMV CLP 1581	THE QUINTESSENCE (LP, also stereo CSD 1452)	15/18
62	Mercury MMC 14098	AROUND THE WORLD (LP, also stereo CMS 18064)	15/18
63	Mercury MMC 14125	BIG BAND BOSSA NOVA (LP, also stereo CMS 18080)	15/18
63	Mercury MMC 14128	PLAYS HIP HITS (LP)	15
64	Mercury MCL 20016	EXPLORES THE MUSIC OF HENRY MANCINI (LP, also stereo SMCL 20016)	15/18
65	Columbia 33SX 1637	QUINCY'S HOME AGAIN (LP)	15
65	Mercury 20047 MCL	GOLDEN BOY (LP)	15
66	Mercury 20072 (S)MCL	"MIRAGE" (LP)	15
66	Mercury 20073 (S)MCL	PLAYS FOR PUSSYCATS (LP)	15
66	Mercury 20078 (S)MCL	QUINCY'S GOT A BRAND NEW BAG (LP)	18
66	Fontana FJL 127	FAB! (LP)	15
67	Mercury SMWL 30003	TRAVELLIN' ON THE QUINCY JONES BANDWAGON (LP)	12
68	RCA Victor RD/SF 7931	IN COLD BLOOD (LP, soundtrack)	35
68	United Artists (S)ULP 1181	IN THE HEAT OF THE NIGHT (LP, soundtrack, with Ray Charles)	40
69	Uni UNLS 103	LOST MAN (LP, soundtrack)	20
69	Paramount SPFL 256	THE ITALIAN JOB (LP, soundtrack)	80
69	RCA Victor SF 8017	MACKENNA'S GOLD (LP, soundtrack)	20
70	United Artists UAS 29128	THEY CALL ME MISTER TIBBS (LP, soundtrack)	40
70	A&M AMLS 961	WALKING IN SPACE (LP; reissued as AMLH 68050)	12
71	A&M AMLS 992	GULA MATIRA (LP)	12
71	A&M AMLS 63037	SMACKWATER JACK (LP)	15
72	WEA K 44168	THE HEIST (LP, soundtrack)	15
72	Atlantic K 40371	HOW TO STEAL A DIAMOND (LP, soundtrack)	15
73	A&M AMLS 63041	YOU'VE GOT IT BAD GIRL (LP)	12
75	A&M AMLH 64526	MELLOW MADNESS (LP)	12
75	A&M AMLP 8005	IRONSIDE (LP)	12

(see also Annie Ross, Diana Ross & Quincy Jones)

RICK JONES

73	Argo ZDA 156	HIYA MAYA (LP)	12

RONNIE JONES

64	Decca F 12012	Let's Pin A Rose On You/I Need Your Loving (B-side with Night Timers)	12
65	Decca F 12066	My Love/It's All Over	12
65	Decca F 12146	Anyone Who Knows What Love Is/Nobody But You	12
65	Parlophone R 5326	You're Lookin' Good/I'm So Clean (with Blue Jays)	25
67	CBS 2699	Little Bitty Pretty One/Put Your Tears Away	12
67	Polydor 56222	In My Love Mind/Mama Come On Home	8
68	CBS 3304	Without Love (There Is Nothing)/Little Bitty Pretty One	8

(see also Night-Timers)

SALENA JONES

66	Columbia DB 7818	A Walk In The Black Forest (Our Walk Of Love)/As Long As I Live	5
66	Columbia DB 7991	I Am Yours/I Only Know I Love You	5
67	Columbia DB 8212	When I Tell You (That I Love You)/Respect	5
73	Indigo GOPOP	Live And Let Die/Some Other World (some in p/s)	10/5
69	CBS 63613	THE MOMENT OF TRUTH (LP)	25
70	CBS 63650	EVERYBODY'S TALKIN' ABOUT SALENA JONES (LP)	15
73	RCA Victor SF 8335	ALONE & TOGETHER (LP)	20
74	RCA LPL 1 5025	THIS'N'THAT (LP)	20

SALINA JONES
65	Polydor 56012	Longing/Too Late	5

SAMANTHA JONES
65	United Artists UP 1072	It's All Because Of You/I Woke Up Crying	7
65	United Artists UP 1087	Don't Come Any Closer/Just Call And I'll Be There	8
65	United Artists UP 1105	Chained To A Memory/Just For Him	7
66	United Artists UP 1139	That Special Way/Somebody Else's Baby	7
67	United Artists UP 1185	Surrounded By A Ray Of Sunshine/How Do You Say Goodbye	25
67	United Artists UP 1200	Why Can't I Remember/Live For Life.	6
68	United Artists UP 2248	Lonely Lonely Man/Doll On A Music Box	6
68	United Artists UP 2258	And Suddenly/Go Ahead And Love Me.	15
68	Ford	Ford Leads The Way/Go Ahead And Love Me (p/s, Ford cars promo disc)	15
69	Penny Farthing PEN 703	Today (Without You)/The Feelin' That I Get	5
69	Penny Farthing PEN 708	Do I Still Figure In Your Life?/I'm Sorry, But I Think I Love You	5
70	Penny Farthing PEN 734	My Way/Darling Be Home Soon.	5
70	Penny Farthing PEN 746	Best Of Both Worlds/Guilty Of Loving You	5
68	United Artists	CALL IT SAMANTHA (LP)	12
70	Contour 2870 003	MY WAY (LP).	12

(see also Vernons Girls, Krimson Kake)

SAMMY JONES
70	Gas GAS 123	You're My Girl/HONEYBOY MARTIN: Unchained Melody	5
72	Sioux SI 002	Mendicino/RUM RUNNERS: Sugar Brown.	5
72	Sioux SI 003	Little Caeser/TWINKLE BROTHERS: Happy Song	5
72	Sioux SI 011	You're My Girl/HONEY BOY MARTIN: Unchained Melody.	5

SANDIE JONES
72	Polydor 2058 223	Music Of Love/Ceol An Ghra	15

SOLOMON JONES
70	Bullet BU 452	Be Strong/Version	5
70	Pama PM 812	Here Comes The Night/RECO RODRIGUEZ: Jaded Ramble	6

SPIKE JONES
53	HMV B 10482	I Went To Your Wedding/Lulu Had A Baby (78)	8
53	HMV 7M 121	Hot Lips/Hotter Than A Pistol (as Spike Jones & His Country Cousins)	12
53	HMV 7M 160	I Saw Mommy Kissing Santa Claus/Winter (as Spike Jones & His City Slickers)	12
54	HMV 7MC 3	Deep Purple/Dragnet (as Spike Jones & His City Slickers, export issue)	10
54	HMV 7MC 17	I Wanna Go Back To West Virginia/Little Bo-Beep Has Lost Her Sheep (as Spike Jones & His City Slickers, export issue)	10
55	HMV 7M 324	Secret Love/I'm In The Mood For Love (as Spike Jones & His City Slickers)	10
61	Warner Bros WB 34	Monster Movie Babe/Teenage Brain Surgeon.	5
57	HMV 7EG 8286	FUN IN HI FI (EP)	10
59	RCA RCX 1030	SPIKE JONES NO. 1 (EP).	10
59	RCA RCX 1037	SPIKE JONES NO. 2 (EP).	10
61	Warners W(S) EP 6044	SPIKE JONES IN HI FI (EP, mono/stereo).	10/12
60	Warner Bros WM 4004	THE BAND THAT PLAYS FOR FUN (LP, also stereo WS 8004).	12/15
60	London HA-G 2270	OMNIBUST — T.V. SCHEDULE (LP, also stereo SAH-G 6090)	12/15
61	London HA-G 2298	SIXTY YEARS OF MUSIC AMERICA HATES BEST (LP, stereo SAH-G 6106).	12/15

STAN JONES
58	Pye Disneyland DPL 39000	CREAKIN' LEATHER (LP).	20

STEVE JONES
87	MCA MCA 1184	Mercy/Through The Night (p/s)	7
89	MCA MCAT 1371	Freedom Fighter/Gimme Love/Suffragette City (12", p/s).	8
89	MCA DMCAT 1371	Freedom Fighter/Gimme Love/Suffragette City (CD, card sleeve)	8
87	MCA MCF 3384	MERCY (LP)	15
90	MCA CD45 18179	STEVE JONES LIVE (CD, promo only from unissued LP, clear PVC sleeve)	15

(see also Sex Pistols, Professionals)

TAMIKO JONES
75	Arista ARIST 6	Touch Me Baby/Creepin' On My Dreams.	6
76	Contempo CS 2079	I'm Spellbound/T.J.'s Magic	6
76	Contempo CX 15	Let It Flow/DORIS DUKE: Woman Of The Ghetto	12

THAD JONES
58	Nixa Jazz NJL 13	LEONARD FEATHER PRESENTS MAD THAD (LP, with others)	12
66	United Artists (S)ULP 1169	PRESENTING THAD JONES/MEL LEWIS AND THE JAZZ ORCHESTRA (LP, with Mel Lewis)	10

THELMA JONES
68	Sue WI 4047	Stronger/Never Leave Me.	20
69	Soul City SC 110	The House That Jack Built/Give It To Me Straight	18
76	CBS 4711	Salty Tears/You're The Song	5

THUNDERCLAP JONES
56	Oriole CB 1320	Hurricane Boogie/The Laughing Rag (78).	8
56	Oriole CB 1328	Sound Barrier Boogie/Ask For Joe (78)	8

TOM JONES
64	Decca F 11966	Chills And Fever/Breathless	35
65	Decca F 12062	It's Not Unusual/To Wait For Love (Is To Waste Your Life Away).	5
65	Decca F 12121	Once Upon A Time/I Tell The Sea.	6
65	Columbia DB 7566	Little Lonely One/That's What We'll All Do	20
65	Decca F 12191	With These Hands/Untrue	5
65	Decca F 12203	What's New Pussycat?/Rose.	5
65	Columbia DB 7733	Lonely Joe/I Was A Fool	20
65	Decca F 12292	Thunderball/Key To My Heart.	6
66	Decca F 12315	To Make A Big Man Cry/I'll Never Let You Go (export issue)	15
66	Decca F 12349	Stop Breaking My Heart/Never Give Away Love.	6
66	Decca F 12461	This And That/City Girl.	6

Tom JONES

66	Decca F 12516	Green, Green Grass Of Home/If I Had You (export issue)	15
67	Decca F 22563	Detroit City/Ten Guitars (export issue)	15
71	Decca FR 13237	Till/One Day Soon (export issue)	15
73	Decca F 13434	Today I Started Loving You Again/I Still Love You Enough	5
73	Decca F 13471	Golden Days/Goodbye, God Bless You Baby	5
74	Decca F 13490	La La La (Just Having You Here)/Love Love Love	5
74	Decca F 13564	Pledging My Love/I'm Too Far Gone (To Turn Away)	5
75	Decca F 13575	Ain't No Love/When The Band Goes Home	5
75	Decca F 13590	I Got Your Number/The Pain Of Love	5
75	Decca F 13598	Memories Don't Leave Like People Do/My Helping Hand	5
70s	Decca F 12747/12062	Delilah/It's Not Unusual (double-A-side with different number each side)	5
82	Decca JONES 1	I'll Be Here Where The Heart Is/My Last Goodbye (p/s)	5
87	Epic OLE Q1	A Boy From Nowhere/I'll Dress You In Mourning (poster p/s)	5
65	Decca DFE 8617	ON STAGE (EP)	15
65	Columbia SEG 8464	TOM JONES (EP)	40
65	Decca DFE 8668	WHAT A PARTY (EP)	15
65	Decca LK 4693	ALONG CAME JONES (LP)	12
65	Decca LK/SKL 4743	A-TOM-IC JONES (LP, mono/stereo)	12/15
66	Decca LK 4814	FROM THE HEART (LP)	12
67	Decca SKL 4855	GREEN, GREEN GRASS OF HOME (LP, stereo)	12
67	Decca SKL 4874	LIVE! AT THE TALK OF THE TOWN (LP, stereo)	12
67	Decca SKL 4909	13 SMASH HITS (LP, stereo)	12

(Mono copies of the above three albums are worth £8 each.)

68	Decca LK 4946	DELILAH (LP, mono)	12
68	Decca LK 4982	HELP YOURSELF (LP, mono)	12
69	Decca LK 5007	THIS IS TOM JONES (LP, mono)	12
69	Decca LK 5032	LIVE IN LAS VEGAS — AT THE FLAMINGO (LP, mono)	12

(All the above LPs were issued with unboxed Decca logos on the labels; later boxed label logo copies are worth £8 each.)

70	Decca LK 5045	TOM (LP, mono)	12
70	Decca LK 5072	I, WHO HAVE NOTHING (LP, mono)	12

(Stereo copies of the above two albums are worth £10 each.)

U.K. JONES

69	Deram DM 231	Let Me Tell Ya/And The Rains Came Down	6
70	Ember EMB S 298	Take Me For What I Am/Love Is Here To Stay	5

WINSTON JONES

73	Gayfeet GS 208	You Make Me Cry/Version	5

WIZZ JONES

69	United Artists (S)ULP 1029	WIZZ JONES (LP)	100
70	Village Thing VTS 4	LEGENDARY ME (LP)	20
72	CBS 64809	RIGHT NOW (LP)	50
74	Village Thing VTS 24	WHEN I LEAVE BERLIN (LP)	20
77	Plant Life PLR 009	MAGICAL FLIGHT (LP, with insert)	15

(see also Pete Stanley & Wizz Jones, Accolade)

JONES BOYS

57	Columbia DB 4046	Cool Baby/Rock-A-Hula Baby (Ukulele Lady)	10
57	Columbia DB 4046	Cool Baby/Rock-A-Hula Baby (Ukulele Lady) (78)	8
58	Columbia DB 4170	A Certain Smile/Kathy-O	7
58	Columbia DB 4170	A Certain Smile/Kathy-O (78)	8
58	Columbia DB 4217	The Day The Rains Came/Hideaway	7
58	Columbia DB 4217	The Day The Rains Came/Hideaway (78)	8
59	Columbia DB 4278	Dream Girl/Straight As An Arrow	6

(see also Four Jones Boys)

JONES GIRLS

70	Ember EMB S 294	Learn How To Love/My Own Special Way	5
71	Ember EMB S 310	Learn How To Love/My Own Special Way (reissue)	4

JONES GIRLS

82	Philadelphia Intl. PIR 2031	Nights Over Egypt/Love Don't Ever Say Goodbye	6
82	Phil. Intl. PIR 12-2031	Nights Over Egypt/Love Don't Ever Say Goodbye (12")	10
79	Phil. Intl. PIR 83831	THE JONES GIRLS (LP)	12

JONESY

73	Dawn DNS 1030	Ricochet/Every Day's The Same	5
72	Dawn DNLS 3042	NO ALTERNATIVE (LP, gatefold sleeve)	20
73	Dawn DNLS 3048	KEEPING UP (LP)	20
73	Dawn DNLS 3055	GROWING (LP, gatefold sleeve)	20

(see also Alan Bown)

JON-MARK

65	Brunswick 05929	Baby I Got A Long Way To Go/Night Comes Down	5
66	Brunswick 05952	Paris Bells/Little Town Girl	5

HARLEM JONNS RESHUFFLE

68	Fontana TF 970	You Are The One I Love/Good Lovin'	8
69	Fontana TF 1004	Everything Under The Sun/Let Love Come Between Us	6
69	Fontana (S)TL 5509	HARLEM JONNS RESHUFFLE (LP)	12

JONSTON McPHILBRY

66	Fontana TF 663	She's Gone/Woke Up At Eight	50

JOOK

72	RCA RCA 2279	Alright With Me/Do What You Can	6
73	RCA RCA 2344	Shame/City And Suburban Blues	5
73	RCA RCA 2368	Oo-Oo-Rudi/Jook's On You	5
73	RCA RCA 2431	King Capp/Rumble	5
74	RCA RCA 5024	Bish Bash Bosh/Crazy Kids	5
78	Chiswick SW 30	Watch Your Step/La La Girl/Aggravation Place/Everything I Do (EP)	6

(see also John's Children)

JOOLZ

83	Abstract 12 ABS 018	Denise/The Latest Craze/War Of Attrition/Protection (12", p/s, with Jah Wobble).. 8
84	Abstract 12 ABS 025	The Kiss/The Kiss (Club Mix)/Paved With Gold (12", p/s, with Jah Wobble).. 7
85	EMI JLZ 1	Love Is (Sweet Romance)/Musket Fife & Drum (p/s) 5
85	EMI 12 JLZ 1	Love Is (Sweet Romance)/Musket Fife & Drum/Fury (12", p/s).. 8
86	EMI EMI 5582	Mad Bad And Dangerous To Know/Legend (p/s) 5
86	EMI 12 EMI 5582	Mad Bad And Dangerous To Know/Legend/Babies (12", p/s).. 7
85	Abstract ABS 011	NEVER NEVER LAND (mini-LP)... 8
87	Columbia SCX 6711	HEX (LP) 12

(see also New Model Army, Jah Wobble)

JANIS JOPLIN

69	CBS 3683	Turtle Blues/Piece Of My Heart (withdrawn) .... 25+
71	CBS 7019	Me And Bobby McGee/Half Moon 5
71	CBS 7217	Cry Baby/Mercedes Benz.. 5
71	CBS 9136	Move Over/Cry Baby/Try/Piece Of My Heart (maxi-single) 7
72	CBS 8241	Down On Me/Bye Bye Baby... 5
76	CBS 3960	Piece Of My Heart/Kozmic Blues (p/s)................................... 6
69	CBS 63546	I GOT DEM OL' KOZMIC BLUES AGAIN, MAMA! (LP) 12
74	CBS CQ 30322/Q 64188	PEARL (LP, quadrophonic) 20

(see also Big Brother & Holding Company)

DANNY JORDAN

| 61 | Mercury AMT 1159 | Jeannie/Boom Ditty Boom... 7 |

DICK JORDAN

60	Embassy WB 358	Mack The Knife/Put Your Head On My Shoulder (78) 5
59	Embassy WB 360	Travellin' Light/Mr. Blue (78) 8
60	Embassy WB 384	Let It Be Me/Running Bear (78) 12
60	Embassy WB 394	Cathy's Clown/Don't Throw All Those Teardrops (78) 12
60	Oriole CB 1534	Hallelujah, I Love Her So/Sandy 12
60	Oriole CB 1534	Hallelujah, I Love Her So/Sandy (78) 30
60	Oriole CB 1548	Little Christine/I'll Love You Forever 12
60	Oriole CB 1548	Little Christine/I'll Love You Forever (78)......................... 30
60	Oriole CB 1566	Garden Of Eden/Alive, Alive Oh!...................................... 7
60	Oriole CB 1591	Angel On My Shoulder/The Next Train Home 10
61	Piccadilly 7N 35035	Some Of These Days/I Want Her Back 7
62	Piccadilly 7N 35057	Fortune Teller/My Angel.. 7
63	Columbia DB 7016	Stop The Music/Dream Chaser 5

(see also Don Duke)

FRED JORDAN

| 66 | Topic 12T 150 | SONGS OF A SHROPSHIRE FARM WORKER (LP, blue label) .... 12 |

JOHNNY JORDAN

| 57 | HMV POP 349 | It's Grand To Be In Love/Home At Last .... 5 |

LOUIS JORDAN (& HIS TYMPANY FIVE)

50	Brunswick 04402	Saturday Night Fish Fry (Parts 1 & 2) (78) 12
50	Brunswick 04519	Push Ka Pee Shee Pie/Hungry Man (78) 10
51	Brunswick 04770	Three-Handed Woman/Is My Pop In There? (78) 12
54	Melodisc 1031	Dad Gum Ya Hide Boy/Whiskey Do Your Stuff (78) 18
56	Melodisc 1349	Messy Bessy/I Seen What'cha Done (78) 25
60	Downbeat CHA 3	Ooo-Wee/I'll Die Happy 18
50s	Melodisc EPM7 66	LOUIS JORDAN (EP, as Louis Jordan Tympany Five, 3 different covers) .... each 80
57	Mercury MPT 7521	SOMEBODY UP THERE DIGS ME (10" LP, with Tympany Five) 50
58	Mercury MPL 6541	MAN, WE'RE WAILIN' (LP, with Tympany Five) 40
64	HMV CLP 1809	HALLELUJAH, LOUIS JORDAN IS BACK (LP).............................. 35
65	Ace Of Hearts AH 85	LET THE GOOD TIMES ROLL (LP).......................................15
68	Coral CP 59	LET THE GOOD TIMES ROLL (LP, reissue) 12

(see also Louis Armstrong)

LOUIS JORDAN & CHRIS BARBER'S BAND

| 63 | Melodisc 45-1616 | Is She Is Or Is She Ain't Your Baby/Fifty Cents...................... 12 |

(see also Chris Barber)

JORDANAIRES

57	Capitol CL 14687	Sugaree/Baby, Won't You Please Come Home? 60
57	Capitol CL 14687	Sugaree/Baby, Won't You Please Come Home? (78) 25
57	Capitol CL 14773	Summer Vacation/Each Day.. 15
57	Capitol CL 14773	Summer Vacation/Each Day (78) 20
58	Capitol CL 14921	Little Miss Ruby/All I Need Is You 18
63	Capitol CL 15281	Don't Be Cruel/Don't Worry 15
71	Ember EMB S 313	Kentucky/Teach The World To Sing 5
62	Capitol T 1742	SPOTLIGHT ON THE JORDANAIRES (LP)................................. 45

(see also Elvis Presley, Patsy Cline, Don Gibson, Marty Robbins)

JORDAN BROTHERS

59	London HLW 8908	Never, Never/Please Tell Me Now...................................... 25
59	London HLW 8908	Never, Never/Please Tell Me Now (78) 40
60	London HLW 9235	Things I Didn't Say/Polly Plays Her Kettle Drum...................... 12
61	London HLW 9308	No Wings On My Angel/Living For The Day 8

MINT VALUE £

JOSEF K

79	Absolute ABS 1	Chance Meeting/Romance (p/s, 1,000 only)	25
80	Postcard 80-3	Radio Drill Time/Crazy To Exist (live) (hand-col'd foldaround p/s, blue labels)	15
80	Postcard 80-3	Radio Drill Time/Crazy To Exist (live) (brown or cream/yellow sleeve & labels)	7/8
80	Postcard 80-5	It's Kinda Funny/Final Request (p/s in poly bag, some with picture insert)	10/6
81	Postcard 81-5	Chance Meeting/Pictures (die-cut sleeve, some with postcard)	8/6
81	Postcard 81-4/TWI 023	Sorry For Laughing/Revelation (p/s)	8
87	Supreme Intl. Edit. 87-7	Heaven Sent/Radio Drill Time/Heads Watch/Fun'n'Frenzy (12", p/s)	8
90	Supreme Intl. Edit.	Young And Stupid (CD)	12
81	Postcard 81-1	SORRY FOR LAUGHING (LP, unreleased, a few with proof sleeve)	225/80
81	Postcard 81-7	THE ONLY FUN IN TOWN (LP, with inner sleeve)	15
87	Supreme Intl. Edit. 87-6	YOUNG AND STUPID (LP)	12

(see also Orange Juice, Paul Haig, Happy Family, Rhythm Of Life)

IRVING JOSEPH

60	London HLT 9027	I Left My Love/Lorena	6

MARGIE JOSEPH (& BLUE MAGIC)

72	Stax 2025 052	Medicine Bend/Same Thing	6
74	Atlantic K 10460	Sweet Surrender/My Love	5
75	Atlantic K 10649	What's Come Over Me/You And Me (as Margie Joseph & Blue Magic)	5
72	Stax 2362 008	MAKES A NEW IMPRESSION (LP)	12
73	Atlantic K 40462	MARGIE JOSEPH (LP)	12

(see also Blue Magic)

JOSEPH & HELEN

72	Rediffusion RS 001	L'Imhabba/Gonna Be A Fun Day (p/s, export issue)	6

JOSH

69	Duke DU 41	Judge/RON: Soul Of Joemel	5

(see also Girlie)

JOSH & HERBIE

60s	Kalypso AB 107	I'm Nobody's Child/How Can I Believe In You	4

JOSHUA

73	Key KL 014	JOSHUA (LP)	120

MARVA JOSIE

66	Polydor 56711	Crazy Stockings/I'll Get By	6

JOURNEY

78	CBS CBS 6238	Wheel In The Sky/Can Do	4
78	CBS CBS 6390	Lights/Open The Door	4
80	CBS CBS 8558	Any Way You Want It/Do You Recall (p/s)	5
81	CBS CBS 9578	The Party's Over (live)/Wheel In The Sky (p/s)	5
81	CBS CBS A 1467	Who's Crying Now?/Escape (p/s)	5
82	CBS CBS A 1728	Don't Stop Believin'/Natural Thing (p/s)	5
82	CBS CBS 11A 1728	Don't Stop Believin'/Natural Thing (12", picture disc)	10
82	CBS CBS A 13-2725	Who's Crying Now?/Don't Stop Believing (12", p/s, half-speed master)	8
85	CBS DA 7095	Be Good To Yourself/Only The Young//After The Fall/Rubicon (double pack)	4
89	CBS 654 541-2	Who's Crying Now/Open Arms/Suzanne/ Don't Stop Believin' (CD, gatefold card sleeve)	7
92	Columbia 4728102	TIME3 (3-CD)	35

JOURNEYMEN

67	Ember EMB 3382	INTRODUCING THE JOURNEYMEN (LP)	12

RODDY JOY

65	Red Bird RB 10021	Come Back Baby/Love Hit Me With A Wallop	30

JOY & DAVID/DAVE

58	Parlophone R 4477	Whoopee!/My Oh My! (as Joy & David)	35
58	Parlophone R 4477	Whoopee!/My Oh My! (78, as Joy & David)	40
59	Decca F 11123	Rocking Away The Blues/If You Pass Me By (as Joy & David)	35
59	Decca F 11123	Rocking Away The Blues/If You Pass Me By (78, as Joy & David)	50
60	Triumph RGM 1002	Let's Go See Gran'ma/Believe Me (as Joy & Dave)	35
60	Decca F 11291	My Very Good Friend The Milkman/Doopey Darling (as Joy & Dave)	30
61	Parlophone R 4855	Joe's Been A-Gittin' There/They Tell Us Not To Love (as Joy & Dave)	30
61	Parlophone R 4855	Joe's Been A-Gittin' There/They Tell Us Not To Love (demo copies with alternate take of B-side)	40

JOHNNY JOYCE

76	Freedom FLP 99003	JOYCE'S CHOICE MIXTURE (LP)	20

(see also Velvet Opera, Levee Breakers)

JOYCE'S ANGELS

67	Major Minor MM 526	Flowers For My Friends/Rodney Reginald Smithfield Harvey Jo.	5

JOY DE VIVRE

81	Crass CR & SS ENVY 1	Our Wedding (flexidisc, white vinyl, no p/s, some with mailer)	22/18

(see also Crass)

JOY DIVISION

JOY DIVISION

78	Enigma PSS 139	AN IDEAL FOR LIVING (Warsaw/No Love Lost/Leaders Of Men/Failures) (EP, 1,000 only, foldout p/s; beware of counterfeits)	100
78	Anonymous ANON 1	AN IDEAL FOR LIVING (Warsaw/No Love Lost/Leaders Of Men/Failures) (12" EP reissue, 1,200 only)	60
79	Factory FAC 13	Transmission/Novelty (p/s)	5
80	Factory FAC 28	Komakino/Incubation/(As You Said) (flexidisc, 10,000 only)	5
88	Factory FACD 213	Atmosphere/Love Will Tear Us Apart/Transmission (live) (CD)	8
79	Factory FACT 10	UNKNOWN PLEASURES (LP with inner sleeve, textured sleeve)	18
81	Factory FACT 40	STILL (2-LP, hessian sleeve, card inners & white ribbon)	30

(see also New Order, Warsaw)

COL JOYE & JOYBOYS

59	Brunswick 05806	(Rockin' Rollin') Clementine/Bye Bye Baby Goodbye	8
59	Brunswick 05806	(Rockin' Rollin') Clementine/Bye Bye Baby Goodbye (78)	35
60	Top Rank JAR 529	Be My Girl/Yes Sir, That's My Baby	8

JOYFUL SINGERS & LYNN TAIT ON ORGAN

67	Master Time MT 001	Jesus Christ Is Risen/BELIEVERS: Money In The Rock	5
67	Master Time MT 002	Happy Days/He Watches Over Me	5

(see also Lyn[n] Tait)

JOY OF COOKING

72	Capitol E-ST 11050	CASTLES (LP)	12

JOY OF LIFE

85	New European BADVC 62	ENJOY (12" EP)	8

JOYRIDE

69	RCA SF 8027	FRIEND SOUND (LP)	20

JOY STRINGS

64	Regal Zonophone RZ 501	It's An Open Secret/We're Going To Set The World A'Singing	5
64	Regal Zonophone ERZ 8255	THE JOY STRINGS (EP)	8
66	Regal Zono. (S)LRZ 4016	WELL SEASONED (LP)	12
67	Regal Zonophone	CAROLS AROUND THE WORLD (LP)	12

JOY UNLIMITED

69	Page One POF 147	Daytime Night Time/Mister Pseudonym	5
69	Page One POF 160	Oh Darlin'/Feeling	5
70	Page One POLS 028	TURBULENCE (LP)	35

J.S.D. BAND

73	Cube BUG 29	Sarah Jane/Paddy Stacks (p/s)	5
71	Regal Zono. SRLZ 1018	COUNTRY OF THE BLIND (LP)	30
72	Cube HIFLY 11	J.S.D. BAND (LP)	12
73	Cube HIFLY 14	TRAVELLING DAYS (LP)	12

JUAN & JUNIOR

67	CBS 2949	The Chase/Nothing	5
68	CBS 3223	To Girls/Andurina	8

JUBILEE STOMPERS

70	Trojan TR 7725	Luciana/I Really Like It	6

MINT VALUE £

JUDAS JUMP
70	Parlophone R 5828	Run For Your Life/Beer Drinking Woman	5
70	Parlophone R 5838	This Feelin' We Feel/Hangman's Playing	6
70	Parlophone R 5873	Beer Drinking Woman/I Have The Right	5
70	Parlophone PAS 10001	SCORCH (LP)	18

(see also Herd, Amen Corner, Andy Bown)

JUDAS PRIEST
74	Gull GULS 6	Rocka-Rolla/Never Satisfied	12
76	Gull GULS 31	The Ripper/Island Of Domination	12
77	CBS S CBS 5222	Diamonds And Rust/Dissident Aggressor	7
78	CBS S CBS 6077	Better By You, Better Than Me/Invader	5
78	CBS S CBS 6719	Evening Star/Starbreaker	5
78	CBS S CBS 6794	Before The Dawn/Rock Forever	5
79	CBS S CBS 6915	Take On The World/Starbreaker	5
79	CBS S CBS 12-6915	Take On The World/Starbreaker/White Heat Red Hot (12", p/s)	8
79	CBS S CBS 7312	Evening Star/Beyond The Realms Of Death	5
79	CBS 12-7312	Evening Star/The Green Manalashi/Beyond The Realms Of Death (12", clear vinyl with picture insert)	8
79	Gull GULS 71	The Ripper/Victims Of Change	8
79	Gull GULS 7112	The Ripper/Never Satisfied/Victim Of Changes (12", p/s)	12
81	CBS A12 1153	Hot Rockin'/Steeler/You Don't Have To Be Old To Be Wise (12", no p/s)	8
82	CBS A 112611	You've Got Another Thing Comin'/Exciter (live) (picture disc)	5
82	CBS A 2822	(Take These) Chains/Judas Priest Audio File (p/s)	5
83	Gull GULS 7612	Tyrant/Rocka Rolla/Genocide (12", p/s, white vinyl)	12
86	CBS QTA 7144	Locked In (Extended)/Reckless/Desert Plains (live)/Freewheel Burning (live) (12", poster p/s)	8
88	Atlantic A 9114CD	Johnny B. Goode/Rock You All Around The World (live)/Turbo Lover (live)/Living After Midnight (live) (3" CD, with 5" adaptor in 5" case)	8
91	Columbia 656589 0	A Touch Of Evil/Between The Hammer And The Anvil (shaped disc)	7
74	Gull GULP 1005	ROCKA ROLLA (LP, original issue, 'bottle top' sleeve)	15
76	Gull PGULP 1015	SAD WINGS OF DESTINY (LP, picture disc)	15
78	Gull PGULP 1026	THE BEST OF JUDAS PRIEST (LP, picture disc)	12
78	CBS 83135	KILLING MACHINE (LP, red vinyl)	15
79	CBS 83852	UNLEASHED IN THE EAST (LP, with free single "Rock Forever"/"Hell Bent For Leather"/"Beyond The Realms Of Death" [SJP 1])	12
79	CBS 66357	BOX SET (3-LP, reissue of "Sin After Sin"/"Stained Class"/"Killing Machine")	20
86	Shanghai PGLP 1026	JUDAS PRIEST (LP, picture disc)	12

(see also Trapeze, Fancy)

JUDD
70	Penny Farthing PEN 709	Snarlin' Mumma Lion/Stronger Than A Man	5
70	Penny Farthing PEL 504	JUDD (LP)	30

(see also Kris Ife)

TERRY JUDGE & BARRISTERS
63	Oriole CB 1896	Hey Look At Her/Kind Of Girl You Can't Forget	12
64	Oriole CB 1938	I Don't Care/Try To Forget	12
65	Fontana TF 599	Come With Me And Love Me/Waitin' For The Night To Come	10

JUDGE DREAD
72	Big Shot BI 608	Big Six/One-Armed Bandit (no p/s)	5
74	Horse HOSS 62	Hey There Lonely Girl/The Planet Of The Apes (as J.D. Alex, no p/s)	5
73	Trojan TRLS 60	DREADMANIA: IT'S ALL IN THE MIND (LP)	12
74	Trojan TRLS 100	WORKING CLASS 'ERO (LP)	12
75	Cactus CTLP 113	BEDTIME STORIES (LP)	12
76	Cactus CTLP 123	LAST OF THE SKINHEADS (LP)	12
76	Klik KLP 9008	THE BEST OF JUDGE DREAD (LP)	12
78	Cactus CTLP 126	THE BEST WORST OF JUDGE DREAD (LP)	10
81	Creole CRX 3	RUB-A-DUB (LP)	10

JUDGE HAPPINESS
85	Mynah SCS 8501	Hey Judge/Pig In Pink (very few with p/s)	30/15

(see also Mock Turtles)

JUGGERNAUTS
84	Supreme Int. Editions 84-2	Come Throw Yourself/My First Million (p/s)	8

(see also Paul Haig)

JUICE ON THE LOOSE
81	Juice JJOS 1	JUICE ON THE LOOSE (LP)	12

JUICY LUCY
70	Fontana TF 1068	Who Do You Love/Walking Down The Highway (unissued)	
70	Vertigo V1/6059 001	Who Do You Love/Walking Down The Highway	6
70	Vertigo 6059 015	Pretty Woman/I'm A Thief	6
72	Polydor 2001 279	It Ain't Easy/Promised Land	5
69	Vertigo VO 2	JUICY LUCY (LP, spiral label, gatefold sleeve)	30
70	Vertigo 6360 014	LIE BACK AND ENJOY IT (LP, spiral label, gatefold poster sleeve)	30
71	Bronze ILPS 9157	GET A WHIFF OF THIS (LP)	15
72	Polydor 2310 160	PIECES (LP)	12

(see also Misunderstood, Van Der Graaf Generator, Ray Owen, Paul Williams' Big Roll Band)

JULIAN (Judy Mowatt) & CHOSEN FEW
71	High Note HS 054	Joy To The World/Joyful Version	7

JULIAN (Judy Mowatt) & GAYTONES
72	High Note HS 059	She Kept On Talking/Version	15

JULIAN (Scott)
59	Pye 7N 15236	Sue Saturday/Can't Wait	25
59	Pye N 15236	Sue Saturday/Can't Wait (78)	35

(see also Brian Bennett)

JULIAN KIRSCH
69	Columbia DB 8541	The Adventures Of A Young Cuckoo/Clever Little Man	12

JULIAN'S TREATMENT
70	Young Blood YB 1009	Phantom City/Alda, Dark Lady Of The Outer Worlds	10
70	Young Blood SYB 2	A TIME BEFORE THIS (2-LP)	80

(see also Julian Jay Savarin)

JULY
68	Major Minor MM 568	My Clown/Dandelion Seeds	70
68	Major Minor MM 580	Hello, Who's There?/The Way	70
68	M. Minor MMLP 29	JULY (LP)	275
87	Bam Caruso KIRI 097	DANDELION SEEDS (LP, reissue of above LP with extra tracks & different sleeve)	15
95	Essex 1011LP	JULY (LP, reissue with bonus 7": "Hello Who's There?"/ "The Way" [p/s, 10117])	15

(see also Jade Warrior, Tom Newman, Tomcats)

JUMBLE LANE
71	Holyground HG 115	JUMBLE LANE (LP, 99 copies only)	450

JUMP
80	Caveman CLUB 1	Shake Up/All In Vain (p/s)	5
81	Rewind REWIND 4	Tomorrow's Mine/Love In The Park	4

JUMPIN' JACKS
58	HMV POP 440	My Girl, My Girl/Tried And Tested	18
58	HMV POP 440	My Girl, My Girl/Tried And Tested (78)	15

JUMPLEADS
82	Ock OC 001	THE STAG MUST DIE (LP, with insert)	30

JUMP SQUAD
81	101 UR 2	Lord Of The Dance/Debt (p/s)	8

(see also Embryo)

JUNCO PARTNERS
65	Columbia DB 7665	As Long As I Have You/Take This Hammer	45
79	Rigid JUNK 1028	Swinging Sixties Boys/Peepin' And Hidin'	6
81	Energy NRG 4	Tall Windows/Noizez In My Head (p/s)	4
81	Energy NRGX 4	Tall Windows (Extended)/Noizez In My Head (Extended) (12", stickered white label, plain sleeve, promo only)	10
71	Philips 6308 032	JUNCO PARTNERS (LP)	40

JUNCTION 32
75	Holyground HGS 119	JUNCTION 32 (LP, 100 copies only)	500

JUNCUNO
71	Banana BA 361	The End (as Joncuno)/HORACE ANDY: See A Man's Face	15
72	Bamboo BA 69	Love Is A Stranger/When We Were Children	6

(see also Juncuno Singers)

JUNCUNO SINGERS
71	Bamboo BAM 69	Love Is Strange/When We Were Children	6
72	Banana BA 366	I'd Like To Teach The World To Sing/Rope Of Sand	6

ROSANNE JUNE
56	London HLU 8352	The Charge Of The Light Brigade/Broken Windows	22
56	London HLU 8352	The Charge Of The Light Brigade/Broken Windows (78)	12
58	Oriole CB 1430	When A Woman Cries/The Great Chicago Fire	7
58	Oriole CB 1430	When A Woman Cries/The Great Chicago Fire (78)	8

ROSEMARY JUNE
58	Fontana H 141	I'll Always Be In Love With You/Person To Person	8
58	Fontana H 141	I'll Always Be In Love With You/Person To Person (78)	8
59	Pye International 7N 25005	I'll Be With You In Apple Blossom Time/Always A Bridesmaid	6
59	Pye International N 25005	I'll Be With You In Apple Blossom Time/Always A Bridesmaid (78)	8
59	Pye International 7N 25015	With You Beside Me/I Used To Love You, But It's All Over Now	5
59	Pye International N 25015	With You Beside Me/I Used To Love You, But It's All Over Now (78)	10
59	London HLT 9014	The Village Of St. Bernadette/But Not For Me	8
59	London HLT 9014	The Village Of St. Bernadette/But Not For Me (78)	15

JUNE BRIDES
84	Pink PINKY 1	In The Rain/Sunday To Saturday (p/s)	15
84	Pink PINKY 2	Every Conversation/Disneyland (die-cut sleeve, some with insert)	8/7
85	In Tape IT 024	No Place Called Home/We Belong (p/s)	4
85	In Tape ITTI 024	No Place Called Home/On The Rocks/Josef's Gone/We Belong (12", p/s)	7
86	In Tape IT 030	This Town/Cold/Just The Same (p/s)	4
86	In Tape ITTI 030	This Town/Cold/Just The Same (12", p/s)	7
86	Pink PINKY 9	In The Rain/Sunday To Saturday/ Every Conversation/Disneyland (12", p/s)	7

(see also Phil Wilson)

JUNGLE JUICE
| 74 | Bradley's BRAD 7407 | The Zoo Gang/Monkey Business. | 5 |

HUGH ROY JUNIOR
71	Big BG 329	Papcito/RUPIE EDWARDS: I'm Gonna Live Some Life	6
71	Supreme SUP 211	Double Attack/MURPHY'S ALL STARS: Puzzle.	7
72	Ashanti ASH 405	King Of The Road/ROOSEVELT ALL STARS: Version.	7
72	Jackpot JP 806	Two Ton Guletto/Version	12

(see also U Roy Junior)

U ROY JUNIOR
72	Attack ATT 8030	This Is A Pepper/JOHN HOLT: Justice.	12
72	Sioux SI 024	The Wedding/LLOYD'S ALL STARS: Buttercup.	6
73	Randy's RAN 532	Froggie/RHYTHM RULERS: Version	6
73	Techniques TE 928	Aunt Kereba/DON RECO: Waterloo Rock	
		(B-side actually by Reco Rodriquez).	6

(see also Hugh Roy Junior)

JUNIOR (Simpson)
| 68 | Giant GN 18 | I'm Gonna Leave You Girl/I Love You I Love You. | 7 |
| 68 | Giant GN 25 | Come Cure Me/I Want Your Loving | 6 |

JUNIOR CHORALE
| 59 | Top Rank JAR 212 | Little Donkey/The Christmas Star | 5 |

JUNIORS
| 64 | Columbia DB 7339 | There's A Pretty Girl/Pocket Size. | 35 |

JUNIOR'S EYES
69	Regal Zonophone RZ 3009	Mr. Golden Trumpet Player/Black Snake	15
69	Regal Zonophone RZ 3018	Woman Love/White Light Part 2	
		(withdrawn B-side).	20
69	Regal Zonophone RZ 3018	Woman Love/Circus Days	15
69	Regal Zonophone RZ 3023	Star Child/Sink Or Swim	15
69	Regal Zono. SLRZ 1008	BATTERSEA POWER STATION	
		(LP)	45

(see also David Bowie, Tickle, Bunch Of Fives, Outsiders)

JUNIPER GREEN
| 71 | Columbia DB 8809 | Dreams In The Sky/Cascade Of Ice | 25 |

LENA JUNOFF
| 68 | Olga OLE 8 | Yesterday Has Gone/Good Kind Of Hurt | 12 |

ERIC JUPP & HIS ORCHESTRA
53	Columbia SCM 5070	Jog Trot/Doina Voda.	6
54	Columbia SCM 5081	Ooop De Ooh (Lazy Mambo)/Footsteps In The Fog	7
54	Columbia SCM 5140	They Were Doin' The Mambo/Skokiian	
		(with Coronets).	7
56	Columbia DB 3817	Theme From 'East Of Eden'/When The Lilac Blooms Again.	6
57	Columbia DB 4030	Bleep! Bleep!/Three-Two-One-Zero! (78).	8
55	Columbia SEG 7589	ERIC JUPP AND HIS ORCHESTRA (EP)	12
56	Columbia SEG 7603	RHYTHM AND BLUES (EP)	12
56	Columbia SEG 7621	THE PERFECT COMBINATION (EP).	8
56	Columbia 33S 1097	LET'S DANCE (10" LP).	15
58	Columbia 33SX 1072	MUSIC FOR SWEETHEARTS (LP)	12

(see also Coronets, Rockin' Strings)

CURT JURGENS
| 59 | Top Rank JAR 151 | Ferry To Hong Kong/Live For Love | 7 |
| 59 | Top Rank JAR 151 | Ferry To Hong Kong/Live For Love (78). | 15 |

SAMANTHA JUSTE
| 66 | Go AJ 11402 | No One Needs My Love Today/If Trees Could Talk | 12 |

JUST FOUR MEN
64	Parlophone R 5186	That's My Baby/Things Will Never Be The Same	
		(withdrawn, as Four Just Men)	70
64	Parlophone R 5208	That's My Baby/Things Will Never Be The Same.	55
65	Parlophone R 5241	There's Not One Thing/Don't Come Any Closer	55

(see also Wimple Winch, Four Just Men, Pacific Drift)

JUST FRANK
| 80 | Rok ROK III/IV | You/SPLIT SCREENS: Just Don't Try | |
| | | (die-cut company sleeve). | 6 |

JIMMY JUSTICE
60	Pye 7N 15301	I Understand Just How You Feel/Bloodshot Eyes	
		(as Jimmy Justice & Jury).	15
61	Pye 7N 15351	When Love Has Left You/The Teacher	12
61	Pye 7N 15376	A Little Bit Of Soap/Little Lonely One	10
62	Pye 7N 15421	When My Little Girl Is Smiling/If I Lost Your Love.	5
62	Pye 7N 15443	Ain't That Funny/One (some with p/s)	10/5
62	Pye 7N 15457	Spanish Harlem/Write Me A Letter	5
62	Pye 7N 15469	Parade Of Broken Hearts/Dawning	6
63	Pye 7N 15502	The World Of Lonely People/I Wake Up Crying.	6
63	Pye 7N 15509	Little Cracked Bell/Lighted Windows.	6
63	Pye 7N 15528	The Guitar Player/Don't Let The Stars Get In Your Eyes.	5
63	Pye 7N 15558	You're Gonna Need My Lovin'/Since You've Been Gone	
		(with Exchequers)	5

MINT VALUE £

63	Pye 7N 15601	Don't Say That Again/Green Leaves Of Summer	5
69	Decca F 12899	Running Out Of Time/There Goes My World	5
65	Pye 7N 15963	Only Heartbreak For Me/Everything In The Garden	5
68	RCA Victor RCA 1681	I'm Past Forgetting You/Walking Away With My Heart	20
63	Pye NEP 24159	HIT PARADE (EP)	30
62	Pye NPL 18080	TWO SIDES OF JIMMY JUSTICE (LP)	35
62	Pye NPL 18085	SMASH HITS (LP)	35

JUSTIFIED ANCIENTS OF MU MU (J.A.M.s)

87	KLF Comm. JAMS 23	All You Need Is Love (Original) (12", white label, 1-sided, 500 only)	40
87	KLF Comm. JAMS 23(s)	All You Need Is Love (Me Ru Con Mix)/(Ibo Version) (1,000 only, plain sleeve)	10
87	KLF Comm. JAMS 23T	All You Need Is Love/Ivum Naya/Rap, Rhyme And Scratch Yourself (12", 'James Anderton' p/s, 5,000 only)	15
87	KLF Comm. JAMS 24T	Whitney Joins The JAMs (120 bpm) (12", 1-sided, 'Scottish' issue, 500 only)	25
87	KLF Comm. JAMS 25T	1987 — The 45 Edits (12", p/s)	15
87	KLF Comm. JAMS 26T	BURN THE BEAT (12" EP, 5,000 for export only)	10
87	KLF Comm. JAMS 27	Down Town/118 BPM 27 (p/s)	8
87	KLF Comm. JAMS 27	Down Town (A-side Mix) (12", 1-sided, white label, 500 only)	15
87	KLF Comm. JAMS 27	Down Town (B-side Mix) (12", 1-sided, white label, 500 only)	15
87	KLF Comm. JAMS 27	Down Town (A-side Mix)/(B-side Mix) (12", white label)	12
87	KLF Comm. JAMS 27T	Down Town (118 bpm)/Down Town (12", JAMs or mispressed 'album' label, generic sleeve)	10/12
88	KLF Comm. JAMS 28T	It's Grim Up North (Original Vocal Mix) (12", grey vinyl, 1-sided, 500 only)	40
87	KLF Comm. JAMS DS 1	Deep Shit (flexidisc, unreleased)	250
91	KLF Comm. JAMS 028R	It's Grim Up North (Original Vocal Mix) (12", black vinyl, 1-sided promo)	10
88	Fierce FRIGHT 34(T)	20 GREATEST HITS (12" EP; not actually by J.A.M.s!)	25
87	KLF Comm. JAMS LP 1	1987 (WHAT THE FUCK IS GOING ON?) (LP, withdrawn)	80
87	KLF Comm. JAMS LP 1	1987 (WHAT THE FUCK IS GOING ON?) (cassette, withdrawn)	20
88	KLF Comm. JAMS LP 2	WHO KILLED THE JAMS? (LP, stickered sleeve with insert)	25
89	KLF Comm. JAMS DLP 3	SHAG TIMES (2-LP)	30
89	KLF Comm. JAMS CD 3	SHAG TIMES (CD)	40

(see also KLF, Timelords, Disco 2000, Brilliant, Space, Orb, Bill Drummond)

JAY JUSTIN

60	HMV POP 801	Nobody's Darlin' But Mine/Sweet Sensation	6
63	HMV POP 1183	Proud Of You/Love, Love Me, Baby Darling	5
68	Columbia DB 8439	I Sell Summertime/Time (withdrawn)	7

JUSTINS

| 71 | Punch PH 65 | Cholera/LLOYD ALL STARS: Black Bird | 6 |

JUSTIN CASE

| 80 | Rok ROK XIX | TV/STRAIGHT UP: One Out All Out (die-cut company sleeve) | 6 |

JUSTINE

69	Dot DOT 121	Leave Me Be/Clown	4
69	Buffalo BFS 1001	Right Now/Place Where Sorrow Hides	4
70	Uni UNS 528	She Brings Back The Morning With Her/Back To Boulder	4
70	Uni UNLS 111	JUSTINE (LP)	15

BILL JUSTIS & HIS ORCHESTRA

57	London HLS 8517	Raunchy/The Midnight Man	18
57	London HLS 8517	Raunchy/The Midnight Man (78)	10
58	London HLS 8614	College Man/The Stranger (B-side with Spinners)	18
58	London HLS 8614	College Man/The Stranger (B-side with Spinners) (78)	20
63	Mercury AMT 1201	I'm Gonna Learn To Dance/Tamoure	7

JUST PLAIN JONES

| 71 | CBS CBS 7480 | Crazy, Crazy/Should Have Stayed With Mary | 5 |

(see also Just Plain Smith, Micky Manchester, Dave Ballantyne, Mike Read, Esprit De Corps, Trainspotters)

JUST PLAIN SMITH

| 69 | Sunshine SUN 7702 | February's Child/Don't Open Your Mind (p/s) | 125 |

(see also Just Plain Jones, Micky Manchester, Esprit De Corps, Trainspotters)

JUST US

| 66 | CBS 202068 | I Can't Grow Peaches On A Cherry Tree/I Can Save You | 5 |

JUVENILES

| 66 | Pye International 7N 25349 | Bo Diddley/Yes I Believe | 75 |

JYNX

| 64 | Columbia DB 7304 | How/Do What They Don't Say | 40 |

CAROLINE K
87	Earthly Delights EARTH 1	NOW WAIT FOR LAST YEAR (LP, 1,500 only)	15

KRISSIE K
74	People PEO 110	Stick Up/Who Do You Think You Are	5

JOHNNY K & SINGIN' SWINGIN' 8
63	Fontana H 408	Lemonade/Come Closer Melinda	10

MOSES K & PROPHETS
65	Decca F 12244	I Went Out With My Baby Tonight/So Long	12
	(see also Them)		

KADDO STRINGS
80	Grapevine GRP 146	Nothing But Love/Crying Over You	8
	(see also Duke Browner, Tartans)		

KADETTES
82	Blank GET 1	Fireball XL5/Mission Impossible	6

BERT KAEMPFERT
60	Polydor NH 66639	Wonderland By Night/Dreaming The Blues	5
64	Polydor NH 59009	Red Roses For A Blue Lady/Lonely Nightingale	5
65	Polydor BM 56504	Bye Bye Blues/Remember When	5
66	Brunswick LAT/STA 8651	A MAN COULD GET KILLED (LP, soundtrack)	20

KAINE & ABEL
66	Philips BF 1472	Then You Must Know My Love/Crying In The Rain	6

KALA
73	Bradleys BRAD 302	Travelling Home/Still Got Time	5
73	Bradleys BRADL 1002	KALA (LP)	15
	(see also Quintessence)		

ALAN KALANI
59	Vogue V 9147	A Touch Of Pink/SURFERS: Mambo Jambo	12
59	Vogue V 9147	A Touch Of Pink/SURFERS: Mambo Jambo (78)	25

KALASANDRO!
60	Warner Bros WB 13	Chi Chi/Forbidden City	10

KALEIDOSCOPE (U.K.)
67	Fontana TF 863	Flight From Ashiya/Holidaymaker (some in p/s)	80/35
68	Fontana TF 895	A Dream For Julie/Please Excuse My Face	40
68	Fontana TF 964	Jenny Artichoke/Just How Much Are You	30
69	Fontana TF 1002	Do It Again For Jeffrey/Poem	30
69	Fontana TF 1048	Balloon/If You So Wish	75
67	Fontana (S)TL 5448	TANGERINE DREAM (LP)	165
69	Fontana STL 5491	FAINTLY BLOWING (LP, gatefold sleeve; most copies with watermark on beginning of each side)	175/100
87	5 Hours Back TOCK 005	TANGERINE DREAM (LP, stereo reissue)	25
87	5 Hours Back TOCK 006	FAINTLY BLOWING (LP, reissue, single sleeve)	25
	(see also Fairfield Parlour, I Luv Wight)		

KALEIDOSCOPE (U.S.)
70	CBS 64005	BERNICE (LP, as American Kaleidoscope)	15
76	Island ILPS 9462	WHEN SCOPES COLLIDE (LP)	12

KALIN TWINS
58	Brunswick 05751	When/Three O'Clock Thrill	5
58	Brunswick 05759	Forget Me Not/Dream Of Me (some B-side labels list "Dream Of You")	6
58	Brunswick 05759	Forget Me Not/Dream Of Me (78, some B-side labels list "Dream Of You")	10
59	Brunswick 05775	Oh! My Goodness/It's Only The Beginning	8
59	Brunswick 05775	Oh! My Goodness/It's Only The Beginning (78)	12
59	Brunswick 05797	Cool/When I Look In The Mirror	7
59	Brunswick 05797	Cool/When I Look In The Mirror (78)	15
59	Brunswick 05803	Moody/Sweet Sugar Lips	6
59	Brunswick 05803	Moody/Sweet Sugar Lips (78)	15
59	Brunswick 05814	The Meaning Of The Blues/Why Don't You Believe Me?	7
59	Brunswick 05814	The Meaning Of The Blues/Why Don't You Believe Me? (78)	25
60	Brunswick 05826	Chicken Thief/Loneliness	10
60	Brunswick 05844	Zing! Went The Strings Of My Heart/No Money Can Buy	7
61	Brunswick 05848	Momma Poppa/You Mean The World To Me	6
61	Brunswick 05862	One More Time/I'm Forever Blowing Bubbles	6
58	Brunswick OE 9383	WHEN (EP)	50
59	Brunswick OE 9449	THE KALIN TWINS (EP)	50

KITTY KALLEN
54	Brunswick 05261	Are You Looking For A Sweetheart/In The Chapel In The Moonlight	15
54	Brunswick 05287	Little Things Mean A Lot/I Don't Think You Love Me Anymore	50
54	Brunswick 05357	Heartless Heart/The Spirit Of Christmas	15
54	Brunswick 05359	I Want You All To Myself/(Don't Let The) Kiddy Geddin'	10
55	Brunswick 05394	A Little Lie/Take Everything But You	8
55	Brunswick 05402	Polly Pigtails/I'm A Lonely Little Petunia (In A Potato Patch)	8
55	Brunswick 05431	Kitty Who?/By Bayou Bay	8

MINT VALUE £

55	Brunswick 05447	Forgive Me/Lonely	8
55	Brunswick 05475	Let's Make The Most Of Tonight/Just Between Friends	8
55	Brunswick 05494	How Lonely Can I Get?/Sweet Kentucky Rose	8
56	Brunswick 05536	Go On With The Wedding (with Georgie Shaw)/Only Forever	10
56	Brunswick 05612	True Love/Will I Always Be Your Sweetheart?	7
57	Brunswick 05705	Long Lonely Nights/Lasting Love	7
58	Brunswick 05734	Crying Roses/I Never Was The One	6
59	Philips PB 971	If I Give My Heart To You/The Door That Won't Open	8
59	Philips PB 971	If I Give My Heart To You/The Door That Won't Open (78)	10
60	Philips PB 1028	Make Love To Me/Heaven Help Me	5
62	RCA RCA 1324	Call Me A Fool/My Colouring Book	5

(see also Georgie Shaw)

DICK KALLMAN
56	Brunswick 05608	Two Different Worlds/Love Me As Though There Were No Tomorrow	5
60	Vogue V 9162	Born To Be Loved/Just Squeeze Me But Don't Teeze Me	8
63	HMV POP 1118	Say It Isn't So/From This Day On	
		(A-side with John Barry & His Orchestra)	5
63	HMV CLP 1642	SPEAK SOFTLY (LP)	20

BOBBY KALPHAT
| 68 | Nu Beat NB 007 | Rhythm And Soul/BUNNY & RUDDY: True Romance | 8 |
| 70s | Faith FA 008 | Zion Hill/Dub Hill | 5 |

KAMARAS
| 69 | CBS 4199 | Let This Moment Pass Away/I Just Can't Break Away From This Lovin' | 6 |

AMORY KANE
68	MCA MU 1036	Reflections Of Your Face/Four Ravens	5
70	UNI UNS 518	You Were On My Mind/All The Best Songs And Marches	5
70	CBS 5111	Him Or Me/Forever Waiting	5
68	MCA MUP(S) 348	MEMORIES OF TIME UNWOUND (LP)	35
70	CBS 63849	JUST TO BE THERE (LP)	30

(see also Ron Geesin)

EDEN KANE
60	Pye 7N 15284	Hot Chocolate Crazy/You Make Love So Well	20
61	Decca F 11353	Well I Ask You/Before I Lose My Mind	5
61	Decca F 11381	Get Lost/I'm Telling You	6
62	Decca F 11418	Forget Me Not/A New Kind Of Lovin'	5
62	Decca F 11460	I Don't Know Why/Music For Strings	6
62	Decca F 11504	House To Let/I Told You	7
63	Decca F 11568	Sounds Funny To Me/Someone Wants To Know	7
63	Fontana TF 398	Tomorrow Night/I Won't Believe You (some in p/s)	10/6
63	Fontana TF 413	Like I Love You/Come Back (with Earl Preston's TTs)	8
64	Fontana TF 438	Boys Cry/Don't Come Cryin' To Me	5
64	Fontana TF 462	Rain Rain Go Away/Guess Who It Is	6
64	Fontana TF 508	Hangin' Around/Gonna Do Something About You	7
65	Fontana TF 582	If You Want This Love/Have I Done Something Wrong	7
66	Decca F 12342	Magic Town/The Whole World Was Crying	15
69	Fontana TF 1023	Boys Cry/Don't Come Cryin' To Me (p/s, reissue)	5
70	Bell BLL 1102	Reason To Believe/I Played It Like A Fool	5
62	Decca DFE 6696	WELL I ASK YOU! (EP)	25
62	Decca DFE 8503	HITS (EP)	25
64	Decca DFE 8567	SIX GREAT NEW SWINGERS (EP)	30
64	Fontana TFE 17424	IT'S EDEN (EP)	20
62	Ace Of Clubs ACL 1133	EDEN KANE (LP)	35
64	Fontana TL 5211	IT'S EDEN (LP)	35
64	Wing WL 1218	SMOKE GETS IN YOUR EYES (LP)	20

(see also Brothers Kane, Sarstedt Brothers)

GARY KANE
| 67 | Pye 7N 17334 | Too Good To Miss/Guilty Of Dreaming | 4 |

JACK KANE
| 75 | Rex Mundi S1 | God Loves Me, And So Do I/Abducted By Alien Jews | 25 |
| 73 | Rex Mundi REX 23 | BOW BEFORE ME, SON OF GOD (LP, with 'guide for the perplexed') | 200 |

LEE KANE
| 55 | Capitol CL 14297 | Ev'ry Day/How Would You Have Me? | 7 |
| 55 | Capitol CL 14328 | Around And Around/Merci Beaucoup | 7 |

MARIA KANE
| 65 | Decca F 12184 | Love Is Slipping Away/Love Is Strange | 6 |

KANSAS
| 80 | Kirshner KIR 84500 | AUDIO VISIONS (LP) | 10 |
| 82 | Kirshner KIR 85714 | VINYL CONFESSIONS (LP) | 10 |

PAUL KANTNER
71	RCA Victor SF 8163	BLOWS AGAINST THE EMPIRE (LP, gatefold sleeve with booklet, as Paul Kantner & Jefferson Starship)	12
71	Grunt FTR 1002	SUNFIGHTER (LP, gatefold sleeve with booklet & inner sleeve; as Paul Kantner, Grace Slick & Jefferson Starship)	12
73	Grunt BFL 1 0148	BARON VON TOLBOOTH (LP, with Grace Slick & David Freiberg)	12

(see also Jefferson Airplane/Starship)

KAPLAN
| 68 | Philips BF 1636 | Do You Believe In Magic/I Like | 4 |
| 68 | Philips BF 1699 | I Love It/Trousers Down | |

KAPT. KOPTER & FABULOUS TWIRLY BIRDS
73	Epic EPC 65381	KAPT. KOPTER & THE FABULOUS TWIRLY BIRDS (LP)	12

(see also Randy California)

ANTON KARAS
50	London L 760	Where Do I Go From You/I'm In The Middle Of A Riddle (78)	8
60	Decca F 9235	The "Harry Lime" Theme/The Cafe Mozart Waltz	8
50s	Decca DFE 6035	ANTON KARAS ZITHER SOLOS (EP)	10
51	Decca LF 1053	ANTON KARAS (10" LP)	15

KARINA
68	Hispavox HXS 305	Romeo Y Julieta/Fortuna Y Le Poder	5
71	United Artists UP 35205	Tomorrow I'm Coming Your Way/Something	10

MIRIAM KARLIN
67	Columbia DB 8220	Celebration/Nose For Trouble	5

KARLINS
66	Parlophone R 5457	You Mean Nothing To Me/Walkin' Away	6
66	Parlophone R 5550	The Spinning Wheel/It's Good To Be Around	6
67	Parlophone R 5607	The Hawkmoth And The Flame/Water Or The Wine	6
68	Columbia DB 8394	Everybody Wants To Go To Heaven/Stay On The Island	5

BILLY KARLOFF (& EXTREMES)
78	Wanted CULT-45-001	Back Street Billy/Crazy Paving (p/s)	8
81	Warner Bros K 17753	Headbangers/Don't Keep Me Down (p/s)	5

(see also Tom Robinson Band, Stiff Little Fingers)

BORIS KARLOFF
60	Caedmon CAL 102/1	HANS CHRISTIAN ANDERSEN (LP)	15
67	Brunswick LAT 8678	AN EVENING WITH BORIS KARLOFF AND FRIENDS (LP, soundtrack)	35

STEVE KARMEN BIG BAND
75	United Artists UP 35770	Breakaway/Breakaway (Vocal Version) (featuring Jimmy Radcliffe)	5

(see also Jimmy Radcliffe)

MICK KARN
81	RPM RPM 5118	It Doesn't Matter Anymore/Wide Boy (p/s)	4

(see also Japan, Dali's Car)

KAROO
65	Oak RGJ 193	Mamma's Out Of Town/Lonely Weekend	165

KARYN KARSH
68	RCA Victor RCA 1740	I Wasn't Born To Follow/Musty Dusty	4

KARYOBIN
(see under Spontaneous Music Ensemble)

KASENETZ-KATZ SINGING ORCHESTRAL CIRCUS
68	Pye International 7N 25472	Down In Tennessee/Mrs. Green	6
68	Pye International 7N 25476	Quick Joey Small (Run Joey Run)/Rumble '69 (unreleased)	
69	Pye International 7N 25480	We Can Work It Out/Latin Shake	5
69	Buddah 201 022	Quick Joey Small (Run Joey Run)/Rumble '69	6
69	Buddah 201 041	Embrassee/I'm In Love With You (as Kasenetz-Katz Super Circus)	5
68	Pye Int. NSPL 28119	KASENETZ-KATZ SINGING ORCHESTRAL CIRCUS (LP)	15
69	Buddah 203 018	QUICK JOEY SMALL — I'M IN LOVE WITH YOU (LP, as Kasenetz-Katz Super Circus)	12

AL KASHA
60	Coral Q 72410	Teardrops Are Falling/No Matter Where You Are	4
61	Coral Q 72420	Sing/One Of Them	4
61	Coral Q 72429	Where There's A Will There's A Way/My Arms, My Lips, My Heart	4

KATCH-22
66	Fontana TF 768	Major Catastrophe/Hold Me	25
67	Fontana TF 874	Makin' Up My Mind/While We're Friends	8
68	Fontana TF 930	The World's Gettin' Smaller/Don't Bother	8
68	Fontana TF 984	Pumpkin Mini/100,000 Years	8
69	Fontana TF 1005	Out Of My Life/Baby Love	8
69	CBS 4644	It's The Sunshine/Mrs. Jones	6
68	Saga EROS 8047	IT'S SOFT ROCK & ALLSORTS (LP, with insert)	15

KATE
68	CBS 3631	Strange Girl/I Don't Make A Sound	20
68	CBS 3815	Hold Me Now/Empty World	20
69	CBS 4123	Shout It/Sweet Little Thing	20

(see also Viv Prince, Pretty Things)

KATHY
69	Morgan MR 14	Bonjour Monsieur/Long Night	4

KATMANDU
86	Nightflite NTFL 2001	A CASE FOR THE BLUES (LP)	10

(see also Peter Green, Ray Dorset, Crane/Farlowe)

KATZ
60s	Tetlow TET 118	LIVE AT THE RUM RUNNER (EP)	75

DICK KATZ
60	Top Rank JAR 379	The Surrey With The Fringe On Top/Dreamride	6

MICKEY KATZ & HIS ORCHESTRA
56	Capitol CL 14579	David Crockett (The Ballad Of Davy Crockett)/Keneh Hora	7
58	Capitol CL 14926	The Poiple Kishke Eater/Knish Doctor	7

ARTHUR KAY'S ORIGINALS

80	Red Admiral NYMPH 1	Ska-Wars/Warska (p/s)	8
80	Red Admiral NYMPH 2	Sooty Is A Rudie/Play My Record (p/s)	10
88	Skank MLP 105	RARE 'N' TASTY (mini-LP)	10

BARBARA KAY

65	Columbia DB 8009	The Power And The Glory/I Wanna Walk In Your Sun	6
65	Pye 7N 15774	That's What Angels Are For/What's The Good Of Loving	7
65	Pye 7N 15914	Yes I'm Ready/Someone Has To Cry	8
66	Pye 7N 15997	Chips With Everything/A Lot About Love	6

JOHN KAY

72	Probe PRO 558	I'm Movin' On/Walk Beside Me	5
73	Probe PRO 593	Moonshine/Nobody Lives Here Anymore	5
73	Probe PRO 601	Easy Evil/Dance To My Song	5
72	Probe SPB 1054	FORGOTTEN SONGS AND UNSUNG HEROES (LP)	15
73	Probe SPBA 6274	MY SPORTIN' LIFE (LP)	15

(see also Steppenwolf)

KATHIE KAY(E)

55	HMV 7M 335	Suddenly There's A Valley/Teddy Bear	12
56	HMV 7M 363	Jimmy Unknown/Dreams Can Tell A Lie	12
56	HMV POP 265	A House With Love In It/To Be Sure	8
57	HMV POP 315	From The First Hello — To The Last/Every Day Is Mother's Day	6
57	HMV POP 352	We Will Make Love/Wind In The Willow	8
57	HMV POP 385	Tammy/Away From You	6
57	HMV POP 410	Be Content/My Last Love	7
58	HMV POP 485	The Secret Of Happiness/Summer Is A'Coming In (78)	8
58	HMV POP 498	Hillside In Scotland/Tomorrow Is My Birthday (78)	8
59	HMV POP 625	Goodbye Jimmy, Goodbye/Come Home To Loch Lomond And Me	5
59	HMV POP 625	Goodbye Jimmy, Goodbye/Come Home To Loch Lomond And Me (78)	15
61	HMV POP 878	In The Wee Small Hours Of The Morning/Come Home, My Darling	5

KATHIE KAY & BILLY COTTON

| 62 | Columbia DB 4896 | Til Tomorrow/Someone Nice Like You | 5 |

CAB KAYE

50	Esquire 5-061	Everything I Have Is Yours/Don't Never Stop Looking (78, with Gary Moore Trio)	8
50	Esquire 5-079	Pennies From Heaven/More Than You Know (78, with Norman Burns)	8
61	Melodisc MEL 1584	Everything Is Go/Don't You Go Away	5

DANNY KAYE

51	Brunswick 04794	Blackstrap Molasses/How D'Ye Do And Shake Hands (78, with Jane Wyman, Jimmy Durante, Groucho Marx)	8
52	Brunswick 05023	Wonderful Copenhagen/Anywhere I Wander (78)	8
52	Decca A 73013	Wonderful Copenhagen/Anywhere I Wonder (export issue)	25
54	Brunswick 05296	Knock On Wood/All About You	8
54	Brunswick 05344	The Best Things Happen While You're Dancing/Choreography (with Skylarks)	8
55	Brunswick 05414	Night Of My Nights/Not Since Ninevah (with Sonny Burke Orchestra)	7
55	Brunswick 05424	In My Neck O' The Woods/Manhattan Mambo	7
55	Brunswick 05499	I Love You Fair Dinkum (Dinky Di I Do)/Happy Ending	7
56	Brunswick 05524	Life Could Not Be Better/I'll Take You Dreaming	7
56	Brunswick 05525	Outfox The Fox/Pass The Bucket	7
56	Brunswick 05532	Little Child/Laugh It Off Upsy Daisy (as Danny & Dena Kaye)	7
56	Brunswick 05559	Delilah Jones/Molly-O	7
57	Capitol CL 14672	Love Me Do/Ciu Ciu Bella	6
58	Capitol CL 14907	The Square On The Hypotenuse/Everything Is Ticketty-Boo	6
59	Capitol CL 15061	Mommy, Gimme A Drinka Water!/Crazy Barbara	6
59	Brunswick 05023	Wonderful Copenhagen/Anywhere I Wander (reissue, tri or round centre)	10/6
59	Brunswick 05031	The Ugly Duckling/The King's New Clothes	5
60	London HL 7091	The Five Pennies/Lullaby In Ragtime (B-side with Eileen Wilson, export issue)	10
51	Brunswick LA 8507	DANNY KAYE (10" LP)	18
53	Brunswick LA 8572	HANS CHRISTIAN ANDERSEN (10" LP)	18
54	Brunswick LA 8660	DANNY KAYE AT THE PALACE (10" LP)	18
54	Brunswick LA 8668	KNOCK ON WOOD (10" LP, soundtrack)	18
56	Brunswick LAT 8097	THE COURT JESTER (LP)	15
58	Fontana TFR 6008	PURE DELIGHT (10" LP)	18
58	Capitol T 937	MOMMY, GIMME A DRINKA WATER! (LP)	12
60	Brunswick LAT 8350	FOR CHILDREN (LP)	12

(see also Bing Crosby, Groucho Marx)

DANNY KAYE & LOUIS ARMSTRONG

| 60 | London HLU 9346 | The Five Pennies Saints/Bill Bailey Won't You Please Come Home | 6 |
| 60 | London HL 7092 | The Five Pennies Saints/Bill Bailey Won't You Please Come Home (export issue) | 10 |

(see also Louis Armstrong)

DAVE KAYE (& DYKONS)

64	Decca F 11866	A Fool Such As I/It's Nice Isn't It (as Davy Kaye)	25
65	Decca F 12073	In My Way/All The Stars In Heaven (as Dave Kaye)	25
69	Major Minor MM 641	Yesterday When I Was Young/Say You Love Me (as Dave Kaye & Dykons)	10

LINDA KAYE

| 66 | Columbia DB 7915 | I Can't Stop Thinking About You/When We Meet Again | 15 |

PETER KAYE

| 60s | Aral PS 116 | Do Me A Favour/You Doll (some in p/s) | 8/4 |

SHIRLEY KAYE

| 68 | Trojan TR 015 | Make Me Yours/We Have Happiness | 12 |

MINT VALUE £

STUBBY KAYE

53	Brunswick 05098	Sit Down, You're Rocking The Boat/	
		The Oldest Established Permanent Floating Crap-Game In New York (78)	7
61	Polydor NH 66527	My Wife's A Striptease Dancer/Lydia The Tattooed Lady	6
63	Parlophone R 4996	More Humane Mikado/Cool Mikado.	5

THOMAS JEFFERSON KAYE

74	Anchor ABC 4004	American Lovers/L.A.	4
73	Probe SPB 1074	THOMAS JEFFERSON KAYE (LP)	12
74	ABC ABCL 5048	FIRST GRADE (LP).	10

TONY KAYE & HEARTBEATS

| 67 | Pye International 7N 25412 | Hey, Hey Little Orphan Annie/Dream World. | 6 |

KAYES

| 67 | Major Minor MM 515 | It's No Secret/Remember Me | 4 |
| | *(see also Kaye Sisters)* | | |

KAYE SISTERS

58	Philips PB 806	Are You Ready, Freddy?/The Pansy.	12
58	Philips PB 806	Are You Ready, Freddy?/The Pansy (78)	10
58	Philips PB 832	Stroll Me/Torero	8
58	Philips PB 877	Calla, Calla (The Bride, The Bride)/Oho-Aha	6
58	Philips PB 877	Calla, Calla (The Bride, The Bride)/Oho-Aha (78)	8
59	Philips PB 892	Jerri-Lee (I Love Him So)/Deeply Devoted	7
59	Philips PB 892	Jerri-Lee (I Love Him So)/Deeply Devoted (78)	10
59	Philips PB 925	Goodbye Jimmy, Goodbye/Dancing With My Shadow	6
59	Philips PB 925	Goodbye Jimmy, Goodbye/Dancing With My Shadow (78)	15
59	Philips PB 970	True Love, True Love/Too Young To Marry.	6
60	Philips PB 1024	Paper Roses/If Only You'd Be Mine (some in p/s)	8/5
60	Philips PB 1088	Come To Me/A Whole Lot Of Lovin' (some in p/s)	8/5
61	Philips PB 1156	Palma De Majorca/I Just Wanna Be With You	5
61	Philips PB 1189	Little Soldier/Mistletoe Kisses	6
61	Philips PB 1208	If Only Tomorrow/Mistakes	5
63	Philips PB 1273	Nine Girls Out Of Ten Girls/I Forgot More Than You'll Never Know	5
64	Philips PB 1340	Keep On Loving Me/That Little Touch Of Magic	6
66	Philips PB 1468	Life Goes On/I Should Never Know.	5
62	Philips 326 541 BF	We Won't Say Goodbye/Seven Roses	5
63	Philips 326 569 BF	Big Wide World/I'm Forever Blowing Bubbles.	5
57	Philips BBE 12166	PRESENTING THE KAYE SISTERS (EP)	15
59	Philips BBE 12256	THE KAYES AT THE COLONY (EP)	18
60	Philips BBE 12392	KAYE SISTERS FAVOURITES (EP).	18
	(see also Three Kayes/Three Kaye Sisters, Kayes, Frankie Vaughan)		

KAY GEES

| 76 | Polydor 2310 467 | HUSTLE WIT' EVERY MUSCLE (LP). | 12 |

KITZA KAZACOS

| 56 | MGM SP 1156 | You Should Know/There's Always A First Time | 5 |

ERNIE K-DOE

61	London HLU 9330	Mother-In-Law/Wanted, $10,000.00 Reward	12
61	London HLU 9390	Te-Ta-Te-Ta-Ta/Real Man	10
62	London HLU 9487	I Cried My Last Tear/A Certain Girl	12
65	Vocalion VP 9233	My Mother In Law (Is In My Hair Again)/Looking Into The Future	10
68	Action ACT 4502	Dancing Man/Later For Tomorrow	10
68	Action ACT 4512	Gotta Pack My Bags/How Sweet You Are	8

PHIL KEAGGY BAND

| 70s | Myrrh MYR 1046 | WHAT A DAY (LP). | 15 |
| 70s | Myrrh MYR 1066 | EMERGING (LP) | 15 |

SHAKE KEANE

55	HMV 7MC 38	Akinla/Fire, Fire (export issue)	6
62	Columbia SEG 8140	IN MY CONDITION (EP)	50
65	Decca SKL 4720	SHAKE KEANE WITH THE KEATING SOUND (LP)	20
66	Ace Of Clubs ACL 1219	THAT'S THE NOISE (LP).	30
69	Phase 4 Stereo PFS 4154	DIG IT (LP, with Ivor Raymonde Orchestra).	40
	(see also Marie Bryant)		

JOHNNY KEATING ORCHESTRA

62	Piccadilly 7N 35032	Theme From Z-Cars (Johnny Todd)/The Lost Patrol.	6
62	Piccadilly 7N 35071	We Three Kings/Three Beats To The Casbah.	5
63	Piccadilly 7N 35113	The Preacher/Whoop Up (as Johnny Keating & Z Men)	5
63	Piccadilly 7N 35125	Getaway/A Little Waltzing	5
71	Fly BUG 17	Theme From The Onedin Line/Taransay Lullaby.	5
62	Piccadilly NEP 34011	Z-CARS (EP, with Z-Men)	10
50s	London LTZ-15122	SWINGIN' SCOTS (LP)	25
60s	Oriole MG 20011	BRITISH JAZZ (LP).	50
64	Decca PFS 4038	SWING REVISITED (LP)	18
64	Decca PFS 4078	STRAIGHT AHEAD (LP)	30
64	Phase 4 Stereo PFS 4060	THE KEATING SOUND (LP, as Johnny Keating & 27 Men)	12
72	Studio Two TWO 393	SPACE EXPERIENCE (LP)	15
72	Studio Two Q4 TWO 393	SPACE EXPERIENCE (LP, quadrophonic)	18
74	Studio Two TWOX 1018	HITS IN HI-FI 1 (LP)	12
75	Studio Two TWOX 1044	SPACE EXPERIENCE 2 (LP).	15

KEEFERS KIDS

| 67 | King KG 1068 | Millions Of Hearts/KEEFERS: Lonely Hill | 4 |

HOWARD KEEL
57	Columbia DB 3969	Love, Wonderful Love/Parisienne	6

(see also Kathryn Grayson & Howard Keel, Vic Damone, Doris Day)

SUSAN KEELEY
69	Parlophone R 5761	Mulberry Down/I'd Fall In Love With The World	5

JOHN KEEN
72	Track 2094 103	Old Fashioned Girl/That's The Way It Is	5
73	Track 2094 108	Let Us In/Keep On The Grass	5

(see also Speedy Keen, Thunderclap Newman)

SPEEDY KEEN
71	Track 2406 105	PREVIOUS CONVICTIONS (LP)	12

(see also John Keen, Thunderclap Newman)

MARION KEENE
56	HMV 7M 395	Fortune Teller/A Dangerous Age	6
57	HMV POP 375	In The Middle Of An Island/It's Not For Me To Say	6

NELSON KEENE
60	HMV POP 771	Image Of A Girl/Ocean Of Love	7
60	HMV POP 814	Keep Loving Me/Teenage Troubles	6
61	HMV POP 916	Miracles Are Happening To Me/Poor Little Rich Boy	6

(see also Guv'ners)

REX KEENE
56	Columbia DB 3831	Rebel In Town/Happy Texas Ranger	10

ACE KEFFORD STAND
69	Atlantic 584 260	For Your Love/Gravy Booby Jamm	
		(small or large centre hole)	30/25

(see also Move, Cozy Powell, Young Blood, Big Bertha, Bedlam, Carl Wayne)

KEITH
66	Mercury MF 940	Ain't Gonna Lie/It Started All Over Again	6
67	Mercury MF 955	98.6/The Teeny Bopper Song	7
67	Mercury MF 968	Tell Me To My Face/I Can't Go Wrong	6
67	Mercury MF 989	Daylight Savin' Time/Happy Walking Around	7
67	Mercury MF 1002	Sugar Man/Easy As Pie (some in p/s)	10/5
67	Mercury MCL 20103	98.6/AIN'T GONNA LIE (LP)	25

KEITH (Poppin) & IMPACT ALL STARS
71	Randy's RAN 515	Down By The Riverside/IMPACT ALL STARS: Version Two	6

BRIAN KEITH
68	Page One POF 072	The Shelter Of Your Arms/C'est La Vie	5
68	Page One POF 103	When The First Tear Shows/When My Baby Smiles At Me	7
69	Page One POF 152	Till We Meet Again/Lady Butterfly	5

(see also Plastic Penny)

BRYAN KEITH
63	London HLU 9707	Sad Sad Song/Mean Woman	12

RON KEITH
76	A&M AMS 7217	Party Music/Gotta Go By What You Tell Me	60

KEITH & BILLIE
(see under Keith Powell & Billie Davis; see also Keith Powell, Billie Davis)

KEITH (Stewart) & ENID (Cumberland)
60	Blue Beat BB 6	Worried Over You/Everything Will Be Alright	12
60	Blue Beat BB 11	Send Me/TRENTON SPENCE GROUP: People Will Say We're In Love	12
61	Starlite ST45 047	Never Leave My Throne/Only A Pity	
		(as Keith & Enid with Caribs)	12
61	Starlite ST45 067	You're Gonna Break My Heart/What Have I Done	12
62	Blue Beat BB 125	When It's Spring/True Love	
		(with Sonny Bradshaw Orchestra)	15
63	Dice CC 14	Sacred Vow/My Dreams	12
63	Dice CC 20	Just A Closer Walk/Don't Yield To Temptation	12
64	Black Swan WI 429	Lost My Love/I Cried	15
63	Island ILP 901	KEITH & ENID SING (LP)	40
70	Trojan TTL 37	KEITH & ENID SING (LP, reissue)	18
70	Trojan TBL 154	KEITH & ENID SING (LP, 2nd reissue)	12

KEITH (Lyn) & KEN (Lazarus)
65	London HA-R/SH-R 8229	YOU'LL LOVE JAMAICA (LP)	30

KEITH (Rowe) & TEX (Dixon)
67	Island WI 3085	Tonight/LYN TAIT & JETS: You Have Caught Me	35
68	Island WI 3091	Stop That Train/BOBBY ELLIS: Feeling Peckish	
		(with Desmond Miles Seven)	30
68	Island WI 3137	Hypnotizing Eyes/Lonely Man	15
70	Explosion EX 2008	Tighten Up Your Gird/Look To The Sky	8

JERRY KELLER
59	London HLR 8890	Here Comes Summer/Time Has A Way	
		(triangular or round centre)	8/6
59	London HLR 8890	Here Comes Summer/Time Has A Way (78)	60
59	London HLR 8980	If I Had A Girl/Lovable	7
59	London HLR 8980	If I Had A Girl/Lovable (78)	60
60	London HLR 9106	Now, Now, Now/Lonesome Lullaby	7
60	London HA-R 2261	HERE COMES JERRY KELLER (LP, also stereo SAH-R 6083)	45/50

PAT KELL(E)Y

68	Giant GN 37	Little Boy Blue/You Are Not Mine (as Pat Kelley & Uniques)	15
68	Island WI 3121	Somebodies Baby (as Pat Kelly)/BEVERLY SIMMONS: Please Don't Leave Me	15
69	Gas GAS 110	The Workman Song/Never Give Up (as Pat Kelly)	6
69	Gas GAS 115	How Long/Try To Remember (as Pat Kelly)	6
69	Gas GAS 124	Festival Time (Parts 1 & 2) (as Pat Kelley)	6
69	Gas GAS 125	If It Don't Work Out/I Am Coming Home (as Pat Kelley)	6
70	Gas GAS 144	Tammy/I Am Not Your Guy (as Pat Kelley)	6
70	Gas GAS 145	Striving For The Right/When A Boy Fall In Love (as Pat Kelley)	6
70	Gas GAS 157	I Just Don't Know What To Do With Myself/What's He Got That I Ain't Got (B-side actually titled 'Lorna') (as Pat Kelley)	10
70	Jackpot JP 734	I Just Don't Know What To Do With Myself/Lorna (as Pat Kelley)	10
71	Camel CA 65	Talk About Love (as Pat Kelley)/PHIL PRATT ALL STARS: Version	10
71	Gas GAS 171	Love/With All Your Heart (as Pat Kelley)	6
71	Punch PH 88	Soulful Love (as Pat Kelly)/HUGH ROY & PARAGONS: One For All	10
72	Pama Supreme PS 353	I'm Gonna Give Her All The Love I've Got (as Pat Kelley)/MAYTONES: As Long As You Love Me	6
73	Pama Supreme PS 379	Twelfth Of Never (as Pat Kelley)/JERRY LEWIS: 5000 Watts	5
73	Pama Supreme PS 384	I Wish It Could Rain (as Pat Kelley)/PAT KELLY SINGERS: Hallelujah	5
69	Pama PMLP 12	PAT KELLEY SINGS (LP)	35
71	Pama PMP 2013	COOL BREEZING (LP)	45

(see also Wonder Boy)

MURRAY KELLUM

64	London HLU 9830	Long Tall Texan/GLEN SUTTON: I Gotta Leave This Town	15

KELLY

66	RCA RCA 1507	Be My Man/Here Comes My Baby	6

CHARLIE KELLY

68	Island WI 3155	So Nice Like Rice/STRANGER & GLADDY: Over Again	18

DAVE KELLY

69	Mercury 20151 SMCL	KEEPS IT IN THE FAMILY (LP)	90
71	Mercury 6310 001	DAVE KELLY (LP, with Jo-Ann Kelly & Brunning-Hall Sunflower Band)	140

(see also John Dummer Blues Band)

FRANK KELLY & HUNTERS

62	Fontana 267 242 TF	Send Me The Pillow That You Dream On/'Cept Me	8
63	Fontana 267 261 TF	I Saw Linda Yesterday/Good And True	8
63	Fontana 267 277 TF	What Do You Wanna Do/She Loves Me So	8
64	Fontana TF 454	Some Other Time/Why Baby Why	8

(this is not the same group as [Dave Sampson &] Hunters, also on Fontana)

GENE KELLY

51	MGM MGM 154	Ida!Sweet As Apple Cider/The Daughter Of Rosie O'Grady	8
51	MGM MGM 347	Dig Dig Dig/Heavenly Music (78)	8
51	MGM MGM 423	'S Wonderful/I'll Bring A Stairway To Paradise (78, with Georges Guetary)	8
51	MGM MGM 424	I Got Rhythm/Love Is Here To Stay (78)	8
52	MGM MGM 490	Singin' In The Rain/All I Do Is Dream Of You (78)	8
52	MGM MGM 493	Good Morning (with Debbie Reynolds, etc.)/DEBBIE REYNOLDS: All I Do Is Dream Of You (78)	8
53	MGM SP 1012	Singin' In The Rain/All I Do Is Dream Of You	12
53	MGM SP 1015	'S Wonderful (with Georges Guetary)/I Got Rhythm (with Children's Choir)	6
55	MGM MGM 829	Almost Like Being In Love/I'll Go Home With Bonnie Jean (78)	8
57	MGM MGM 965	The Happy Road (Ca Ca C'est La Vie)/My Baby Just Cares For Me	5
57	MGM MGM 965	The Happy Road (Ca Ca C'est La Vie)/My Baby Just Cares For Me (78)	10
58	RCA RCA 1068	A Very Precious Love/Uncle Samson	5
58	RCA RCA 1068	A Very Precious Love/Uncle Samson (78)	10
57	MGM MGM-EP 580	AN AMERICAN IN PARIS (EP, with George Guetary)	7
57	MGM MGM-EP 671	SINGING IN THE RAIN EXCERPTS (EP, with Donald O'Connor/Debbie Reynolds)	7
53	MGM MGM-D 117	SONG AND DANCE MAN (10" LP)	15
55	MGM MGM-D 133	S'WONDERFUL (10" LP)	15

JO-ANN KELLY

64	GW EP 1	BLUES AND GOSPEL (EP, live at the Bridge House Club)	100
66	Harlequin HAL 1/HW 349	NEW SOUNDS IN FOLK (LP, with other artists)	45
69	CBS 63841	JO-ANN KELLY (LP)	120
76	Red Rag RRR 006	DO IT (LP, with Peter Emery)	30

(see also Chilli Willi & Red Hot Peppers, Dave Kelly, Tramp)

JO-ANN KELLY & TONY McPHEE

72	Sunset SLS 50209	THE SAME THING ON THEIR MINDS (LP)	30

(see also Tony McPhee, Dave Kelly)

JONATHAN KELLY

69	Parlophone R 5805	Denver/Son John	5
70	Parlophone R 5830	Make A Stranger Your Friend/Daddy Don't Take Me Down Fishing No More	5
70	Parlophone R 5851	Don't You Believe It?/Billy	6
70	Parlophone PCS 7114	JONATHAN KELLY (LP)	30
72	RCA SF 8262	TWICE AROUND THE HOUSES (LP)	12
73	RCA SF 8353	WAIT TILL THEY CHANGE THE BACKDROP (LP)	12

(see also John Ledingham)

KEITH KELLY

60	Parlophone R 4640	(Must You Always) Tease Me/Ooh-La-La	12
60	Parlophone R 4676	Listen Little Girl/Uh-Huh	10
60	Parlophone R 4713	With You/You'll Break My Heart	7
61	Parlophone R 4797	Cold White And Beautiful/When You First Fall In Love	7
65	CBS 201794	Laurie/Save Your Love For Me	7

MARY ANN KELLY
53	London L 1195	Wilful Lies/If I Ever Fall In Love (78)	12

MONTE KELLY ORCHESTRA
53	London L 1205	Tropicana/Life In New York (78)	10
59	London HLL 8777	Willingly (Melodie Perdue)/The Blue Cha Cha	6
59	London HLL 8777	Willingly (Melodie Perdue)/The Blue Cha Cha (78)	10
60	London HLL 9085	Summer Set/Amalia	6

PAT KELLY
(see under Pat Kelley)

PAUL KELLY
65	Atlantic AT 4053	Chills And Fever/Only Your Love	20
67	Philips BF 1591	Sweet Sweet Lovin'/Cryin' For My Baby	12
72	Atlantic K 10272	Chills And Fever/Only Your Love (reissue)	6

PETE KELLY'S SOULUTION
68	Decca F 12755	Midnight Confessions/If Your Love Don't Swing	18
68	Decca F 22829	Midnight Confessions/BERNIE & BUZZ BAND: The House That Jack Built (export issue)	12

(see also Bernie & Buzz Band, Rhythm & Blues Inc.)

PETER KELLY
71	Polydor 2310 119	DEALIN' BLUES (LP)	30

SALLY KELLY
59	Decca F 11175	Little Cutie/Come Back To Me	8
59	Decca F 11175	Little Cutie/Come Back To Me (78)	10
60	Decca F 11238	He'll Have To Stay/Honey That's Alright	7
60s	Hit HIT 15	Believe In The Rain/So Much	6

SEYMOUR KELLY
68	Columbia DB 8445	Indian Scene/Worlds Apart	4

STAN KELLY
60s	Transatlantic TRASP 21	The Ballad Of Armagh Jail/Kelly The Boy From Killang	6
60	Topic TOP 27	LIVERPOOL PACKET (EP)	10
60	Topic TOP 60	SONGS FOR SWINGING LANDLORDS TO (EP)	10

WYNTON KELLY TRIO
65	Verve VLP 9103	UNDILUTED (LP)	12

KELLY BROTHERS
67	Sue WI 4034	Falling In Love Again/Crying Days Are Over	40
68	President PT 143	You Put Your Touch On Me/Hanging In There	10
70	Blue Horizon 57-3177	That's What You Mean To Me/Comin' On In	20
68	President PTL 1019	SWEET SOUL (LP)	18

REV. (Samuel) KELSEY (& CONGREGATION)
52	Vocalion V 1014	The Wedding Ceremony Of Sister Rosetta Tharpe And Russell Morrison (Parts 1 & 2) (78)	14
52	Vocalion V 1020	Little Boy/Low Down The Chariot (78)	14
53	Vocalion V 1028	I'm A Royal Child/Where Is The Lion In The Tribes Of Judea (78)	15
56	Brunswick OE 9256	REV. KELSEY (EP)	18

(see also Sister Rosetta Tharpe)

WAYNE KEMP
66	Atlantic 584 006	Watch That First Step/Little Home Wrecker	6

KEMPION
77	Broadside BRO 123	KEMPION (LP)	12
77	Sweet Folk & C. SFA 044	CAM YE O'ER FRAE FRANCE (LP)	12

KEN & NEW ESTABLISHMENT
73	Fab FAB 264	Soul Mood/Golden Locks	6

BARRY KENDALL
59	Embassy WB 364	Seven Little Girls (Sitting In The Back Seat)/JOHNNY WORTH: What Do You Want To Make Those Eyes At Me For (78)	8

(see also Johnny Worth)

JOHNNY KENDALL & HERALDS
64	RCA RCA 1416	St. James Infirmary/Little Girl	18

KENDALL SISTERS
58	London HLM 8622	Won't You Be My Baby/Yea, Yea	50
58	London HLM 8622	Won't You Be My Baby/Yea, Yea (78)	40

GRAHAM KENDRICK
73	Key KL 011	FOOTSTEPS ON THE SEA (LP)	20
73	Key KL 016	BRIGHT SIDE UP (LP)	15

LINDA KENDRICK
66	Polydor 56076	It's The Little Things/When Your Love Is Warm	18
66	Polydor 56146	I Fall Apart/Friend Of Mine	7
68	Philips BF 1660	Grey Sunny Day/In Need Of A Friend	5
69	Philips BF 1750	I Will See You There/Inside My Heart	5
69	Philips BF 1818	Hold On/Fah La La	5
70	Philips SBL 7921	LINDA KENDRICK (LP)	18

NAT KENDRICK & SWANS
60	Top Rank JAR 351	(Do The) Mashed Potatoes (Parts 1 & 2)	12
60	Top Rank JAR 387	Dish Rag (Parts 1 & 2)	12

(see also James Brown)

Eddie KENDRICKS

EDDIE KENDRICKS
73	Tamla Motown TMG 845	If You Let Me/Just Memories	5
74	Tamla Motown TMG 916	Girl You Need A Change Of Mind (Parts 1 & 2)	5
75	Tamla Motown TMG 947	Shoe Shine Boy/Hooked On Your Love	5
71	Tamla Motown STML 11186	ALL BY MYSELF (LP)	12
73	Tamla Motown STML 11213	PEOPLE ... HOLD ON (LP)	12
73	Tamla Motown STML 12245	EDDIE KENDRICKS (LP)	12

(see also Temptations)

KENICKIE
95	Slampt U.O. SLAMPT 1	CATSUIT CITY EP	30
96	Fierce Panda NING 16	Come Out 2nite/How I Was Made (p/s)	7
96	Fierce Panda NING 16CD	THE SKILLEX EP (CD)	10
96	Premier EMI DISC 001	Punka/Cowboy Song (p/s)	4
96	Premier EMI 002	Millionaire Sweeper/Girl's Best Friend (p/s)	4
97	Premier EMI 007	Punka/Brighter Shade Of Blue (picture disc in p/s)	4
98	EMI 12EMDJ 513	I Would Fix You (Kenickie Vs Mint Gun Club)/(Kenickie Vs Mint Gun Club Version)/(Kenickie Vs DJ Downfall) (12", stickered die-cut sleeve, promo only)	8

CHERYL KENNEDY
67	Columbia DB 8271	Thoroughly Modern Millie/Cradle Song	5
68	Columbia DB 8347	Love Is Blue/I Could Be Happy With You	5

DOUG KENNEDY
65	Columbia DB 7707	Julie/Jailbreak Man	4

GENE KENNEDY
65	Hickory 45-1314	You Better Take Home/Stand In Line	6

JOHN F. KENNEDY
64	Stateside SL 10064	THE PRESIDENTIAL YEARS 1960-1963 (LP)	12

LOU KENNEDY
55	Columbia SCM 5198	Stars Shine In Your Eyes/The Kentuckian Song	7
56	Columbia SCM 5216	Whisper/Sincerely Yours	7

MIKE KENNEDY
69	Major Minor MM 614	I'll Never Forget/I'll Never Get You	4
69	Major Minor MM 629	Johnny Rebel/Golden Memories	4

(see also Los Bravos)

CHRIS KENNER
61	London HLU 9410	I Like It Like That (Parts 1 & 2)	15
65	Sue WI 351	Land Of 1,000 Dances/That's My Girl	22
66	Atlantic 587 008	LAND OF 1000 DANCES (LP)	22

JAMES KENNEY
58	Pye 7N 15150	The Shrine On The Second Floor/Expresso Party	6
58	Pye 7N 15150	The Shrine On The Second Floor/Expresso Party (78)	8

TONY KENNY & SANDS SHOWBAND
67	Major Minor MM 555	Help Me Rhonda/Some Enchanted Evening	4
68	Major Minor MM 573	Yummy Yummy Yummy/Peanuts	4
71	Hit HIT 1	Knock Three Times/See You In September	4

(see also Sands)

KENNY (Everett) & (Dave) CASH
65	Decca F 12283	Knees/The B Side	12

(see also Kenny Everett)

KENNY & CORKY
59	London HLX 9002	Nuttin' For Christmas/Suzy Snowflake	8
59	London HLX 9002	Nuttin' For Christmas/Suzy Snowflake (78)	20

KENNY & DENY
65	Decca F 12138	Try To Forget Me/Little Surfer Girl	35

KENNY & WRANGLERS
64	Parlophone R 5224	Somebody Help Me/Who Do You Think I Am?	12
65	Parlophone R 5275	Doobie Doo/Moonshine	12

(see also Kenny Bernard & Wranglers)

JERRI BO KENO
75	Phil Spector Intl. 2010 001	Here It Comes (And Here I Go)/I Don't Know Why	6

AL KENT
67	Track 604 016	You Got To Pay The Price/Where Do I Go From Here	30
71	Mojo 2092 015	You Got To Pay The Price/Where Do I Go From Here (unissued)	

ENOCH KENT
59	Top Rank JAR 238	The Ballad Of Johnny Ramensky/The Bonny Lass Of Fyvie	6
60	Top Rank JAR 386	The Smashing Of The Van/Sean South Of Garryowen	5
62	Topic TOP 81	SINGS THE BUTCHER BOY AND OTHER BALLADS (EP)	8

KLARK KENT
78	Kryptone KK 1	Don't Care/Thrills/Office Girls (p/s, green or rarer black vinyl)	each 4
78	Kryptone KMS 7390	Too Kool To Kalypso/Theme For Kinetic Ritual (p/s, green vinyl)	4

(pseudonym for Stewart Copeland; see also Police, Curved Air)

PAUL KENT
71	B&C CB 165	Do You/Helpless Harry	5
70	RCA SF 8083	P.C. KENT (LP)	25
71	B&C CAS 1044	PAUL KENT (LP)	20

RICHARD KENT STYLE
66	Columbia DB 7964	No Matter What You Do/Go, Go Children	75
66	Columbia DB 8051	You Can't Put Me Down/All Good Things	45
67	Columbia DB 8182	Marching Off To War/I'm Out	40
68	MCA MU 1032	Love Will Shake The World Awake/Crocodile Tears	30
69	Mercury MF 1090	A Little Bit O' Soul/Don't Tell Lies	25

SONIA KENT
66	Parlophone R 5401	This Is My Wonderful Day/Somebody Must Care	6

(see also Diamond Twins)

SHIRLEY KENT
80	Tadpole TAD 001	My Dad/Marianne	6
66	Keele University 103	THE MASTER SINGERS AND SHIRLEY KENT SING FOR CHAREC 67 (EP)	25
89	Magic Spell 0001	FOREVER A WILLOW (LP)	12

(see also Ghost, Virginia Tree)

KENT (Brown) & DIMPLE (Hinds)
63	Island WI 046	Day Is Done/Linger A While	18

KENT (Brown) & JEANNIE with City Slickers
62	Blue Beat BB 98	Daddy/Hello Love	18

(see also Kent Brown & Rainbows)

RIK KENTON
74	Island WIP 6214	Bungalow Love/Lay It On You (no p/s)	5

(see also Roxy Music)

STAN KENTON & HIS ORCHESTRA
51	Esquire 10-113	Turmoil/Jumping For Jane (78, with His Poll Cats)	8
54	Capitol CL 14191	The Lady In Red/Skoot	7
55	Capitol CL 14247	Alone Too Long/Don't Take Your Love From Me	7
55	Capitol CL 14259	A-Ting-A-Ling/Malaguena (with Ann Richards)	10
55	Capitol CL 14269	23 Degrees North, 82 Degrees West/Falling (B-side with Ann Richards)	7
55	Capitol CL 14287	Lover Man/I've Got You Under My Skin	7
55	Capitol CL 14301	Casanova/Dark Eyes (with Ann Richards)	7
55	Capitol CL 14319	Freddy/The Handwriting's On The Wall	7
56	Capitol CL 14537	Winter In Madrid (with Ann Richards)/Baa-Too-Kee	5
56	Capitol CL 14539	Sunset Tower/Opus In Chartreuse	5
56	Capitol CL 14540	My Lady/Frank Speaking	5
56	Capitol CL 14541	Portrait Of A Count/Invention For Guitar And Trumpet	5
56	Capitol CL 14542	Cherokee/Limelight	6
57	Capitol CL 14707	His Feet Too Big For De Bed (with June Christy)/Stardust — Boogie	6
57	Capitol CL 14707	His Feet Too Big For De Bed (with June Christy)/Stardust — Boogie (78)	8
57	Capitol CL 14806	Lemon Twist/Baby You're Tough	5
57	Capitol CL 14806	Lemon Twist/Baby You're Tough (78)	8
58	Capitol CL 14847	Tequila/Cuban Mumble	5
58	Capitol CL 14847	Tequila/Cuban Mumble (78)	10
58	Capitol CL 14866	Reverie/More Love Than Your Love	5
59	Capitol CL 15029	Whistle Walk/Tamer-Lane	5
51	Capitol LC 6517	STAN KENTON'S MILESTONES (10" LP)	15
51	Capitol LC 6523	ENCORES (10" LP)	15
52	Capitol LC 6545	ARTISTRY IN RHYTHM (10" LP)	15
52	Capitol LC 6546	A CONCERT IN PROGRESSIVE JAZZ (10" LP)	15
52	Capitol LC 6548	PRESENTS (10" LP)	15
52	Capitol LCT 6006	INNOVATIONS IN MODERN MUSIC (LP)	12
53	Capitol LC 6577	CITY OF GLASS (10" LP)	15
53	Capitol LC 6595	NEW CONCEPTS OF ARTISTRY IN RHYTHM (10" LP)	15
53	Capitol LC 6602	SKETCHES ON STANDARDS (10" LP)	15
54	Capitol LC 6667	THIS MODERN WORLD (10" LP)	15
54	Capitol LC 6676	CLASSICS (10" LP)	15
54	Capitol LCT 6009	KENTON SHOWCASE (LP)	12
55	Capitol LC 6697	PORTRAITS ON STANDARDS (10" LP)	15
56	Capitol LCT 6109	IN HI-FI (LP)	12
56	Capitol LCT 6118	CUBAN FIRE (LP)	12
56	Brunswick LAT 8122	THE FORMATIVE YEARS (LP)	12
57	Capitol LCT 6138	KENTON WITH VOICES (LP)	12
58	Capitol LCT 6157	THE KENTON ERA VOLUME ONE — PROLOGUE (LP)	12
58	Capitol LCT 6158	THE KENTON ERA VOLUME TWO — GROWING PAINS (LP)	12
58	Capitol LCT 6159	THE KENTON ERA VOLUME THREE — PROGRESSIVE JAZZ (LP)	12
58	Capitol LCT 6160	THE KENTON ERA VOLUME FOUR — CONTEMPORARY (LP)	12
58	Capitol (S)T 932	RENDEZVOUS WITH KENTON (LP)	12
58	Capitol T 995	BACK TO BALBOA (LP)	12
59	Capitol (S)T 1068	BALLAD STYLE OF STAN KENTON (LP)	12
59	Capitol T 1130	LUSH INTERLUDE (LP)	12
59	Capitol (S)T 1166	THE STAGE DOOR SWINGS (LP)	12

(see also June Christy)

KEN-TONES
56	Parlophone MSP 6229	Get With It/In Port Afrique	8
57	Parlophone R 4257	I Saw Esau/Yaller, Yaller Gold	6

(see also Benny Lee)

KENTUCKY BOYS
55	HMV 7M 312	Don't Fetch It/A Little Fella Like Me	8

KENTUCKY COLONELS
74	United Artists UAS 29514	THE KENTUCKY COLONELS (LP)	12

(see also Byrds)

MINT VALUE £

BILL KENWRIGHT (& RUNAWAYS)
67	Columbia DB 8239	I Want To Go Back There Again/Walk Through Dreams (with Runaways)	7
68	MGM MGM 1430	Giving Up/Love's Black And White (solo)	6
69	MGM MGM 1463	Tiggy/House That Fell On Its Face	5
69	MGM MGM 1478	Baby I Could Be So Good At Loving You/A Boy And A Girl	5
69	Fontana TF 1065	Sugar Man/Epitaph (When Times Were Good)	5

KERBDOG
93	Vertigo VER 80	End Of Green (p/s)	8
94	Vertigo VER 83	Dry Riser/Xena Phobia/Self Inflicted (p/s)	6
94	Vertigo VERR 83	Dry Riser/Xena Phobia/Self Inflicted (p/s, clear vinyl)	8
94	Vertigo VER 86	Dummy Crusher/Too Much Too Young (p/s)	6
94	Vertigo VERX 86	Dummy Crusher/Mr. Clean/Don't Stand In Line (12", picture disc)	10
96	Fontana KER 1	J.J.'s Song/Don't Even Try (clear vinyl)	7

WOODY KERN
69	Pye 7N 17672	Biography/Tell You I'm Gone (demo)	100
69	Pye NSPL 18273	THE AWFUL DISCLOSURES OF MARIA MONK (LP)	30

MOIRA KERR
69	Beltona MBE 102	FOLK WARM AND GENTLE (LP, also stereo [SBE 102])	20
71	Beltona SBE 118	SHADOWS OF MY CHILDHOOD (LP)	20

PATRICK KERR
65	Decca F 12069	Magic Potion/It's No Trouble To Love You	8

RICHARD KERR
66	Decca F 12468	Concrete Jungle/You Got Nothing To Lose	5
66	Decca F 12538	Hard Lovin'/Auntie's Insurance Policy	5
67	Deram DM 138	Happy Birthday Blues/Mother's Blue Eyed Angel	5
73	Warner Bros K 46206	FROM NOW UNTIL THEN (LP)	18

KERRIES
67	Major Minor MM 541	Coulters Candy/Gallon Of Whisky And A Barrel Of Beer	5
67	Major Minor MMLP/SMLP 9	THE KERRIES (LP)	15

CHRIS KERRY
65	Mercury MF 957	Seven Deadly Sins/The Place	12
66	Mercury MF 985	Watermelon Man/I've Got My Pride	15

DOUG KERSHAW
69	Warner Bros WB 7304	Feed It To The Fish/You Fight Your Fight (I'll Fight Mine)	5
70	Warner Bros WB 7413	Orange Blossom Special/Swamp Rat	5
71	Warner Bros WS 1906	DOUG KERSHAW (LP)	12
73	Warner Bros K 46196	DEVIL'S ELBOW (LP)	12

(see also Rusty & Doug)

NIK KERSHAW
84	MCA NIKX 5	Human Racing/Faces (12", picture disc)	7
84	MCA NIKP 6	The Riddle/Progress (picture disc)	4
86	MCA DMCG 6016	RADIO MUSICOLA (CD)	25

(see also Fusion)

KEN KESEY
83	Psycho PSYCHO 4	THE ACID TEST (LP, 300 only)	30

BARNEY KESSEL
69	Polydor 56765	Frank Mills/Quail Bait	5
54	Vogue LDE 085	BARNEY KESSEL (10" LP)	18
55	Contemporary LDC 153	BARNEY KESSEL VOLUME 2 (10" LP)	18
59	Contemorary LAC 12214	BARNEY KESSEL PLAYS CARMEN (LP)	12
77	Phil Spector Intl. 2307 011	SLOW BURN (LP)	15

(see also Rick Nelson)

LARRY KESSLER
96	Lissey's LISS 5S	Radar Eyes/Godz Mix (p/s)	12

KESTREL
75	Cube HIFLY 19	KESTREL (LP)	100

KATE KESTREL & THE TERRAHAWKS
83	Anderburr HX 1020	S.O.S./It's So Easy (p/s)	5

KESTRELS
59	Pye 7N 15234	There Comes A Time/In The Chapel In The Moonlight	8
59	Pye 7N 15234	There Comes A Time/In The Chapel In The Moonlight (78)	15
60	Pye 7N 15248	I Can't Say Goodbye/We Were Wrong	8
61	Decca F 11391	All These Things/That's It	6
62	Piccadilly 7N 35056	Wolverton Mountain/Little Sacka Sugar	6
62	Piccadilly 7N 35079	Don't Want To Cry/Love Me With All Your Heart	6
63	Piccadilly 7N 35104	Walk Right In/Moving Up The King's Highway	6
63	Piccadilly 7N 35126	There's A Place/Little Star	6
63	Piccadilly 7N 35144	Love Me With All Your Heart/Lazy River	6
60s	Donegal MAU 500	THE KESTRELS (EP)	40
63	Piccadilly NPL 38009	SMASH HITS (LP)	30

(see also Ivy League, Flowerpot Men, White Plains)

KEYBOARD RINGS
56	Oriole CB 1331	Rhapsody In Boogie/Rainbow Rag (78)	8

KEY CHAINS
66	London HLU 10055	Morgan's Song/Scruggs	4

BERT KEYES
54	London HL 8034	Don't Break My Heart Again/Lonely (78)	10

EBONY KEYES

66	Piccadilly 7N 35358	Sitting In The Ring/If You Knew	18
67	Piccadilly 7N 35375	Cupid's House/If Our Love Should End	6
67	Piccadilly 7N 35390	Country Girl/How Many Times	6
67	Picadilly 7N 35407	Don't/Sweet Mary (Sweeter Than A Rose)	7

KAROL KEYES

64	Fontana TF 517	You Beat Me To The Punch/No-One Can Take Your Place (some in p/s)	20/10
67	Fontana TF 846	Can't You Hear The Music/The Sweetest Touch	8
66	Columbia DB 7899	A Fool In Love/The Good Love, The Bad Love	8
66	Columbia DB 8001	One In A Million/Don't Jump	22

(see also Volunteers)

TROY KEYES

68	Stateside SS 2087	Love Explosions/I'm Crying (Inside)	12
69	Stateside SS 2149	Love Explosions/I'm Crying (Inside) (reissue)	7

KEY LARGO

71	Blue Horizon 57-3178	Voodoo Rhythm/As The Years Go Passing By	15
70	Blue Horizon 7-63859	KEY LARGO (LP)	30

KEYMEN

59	HMV POP 584	Gazackstahagen/Miss You	10
59	HMV POP 584	Gazackstahagen/Miss You (78)	15
62	Columbia DB 4902	Five Weeks In A Balloon/Secretly	6
57	Vogue Coral LVA 9048	THE VOCAL SOUNDS OF THE KEYMEN (LP)	15

KEYNOTES

54	Decca F 10302	A Dime And A Dollar/JOHNSTON BROTHERS: Bandit	6
55	Decca F 10643	Relax-Ay-Voo/Steam Heat	10
56	Decca F 10693	Scotland The Brave/Lewis Bridal Song	5
56	Decca F 10745	Let's Go Steady/Chincherinchee	6

(see also Bobbie Britton, Johnston Brothers, Dave King, Suzi Miller)

KEYS

64	Oriole CB 1968	Sleep Sleep My Baby/Colour Slide	8
65	CBS 201804	Go Get Her/My Everything	6

K.G.B.

76	MCA MCF 2749	K.G.B. (LP)	12

(see also Barry Goldberg, Mike Bloomfield)

KHAN

72	Deram SDL 11	SPACE SHANTY (LP, later copies in stickered sleeve)	20

(see also Steve Hillage, Egg, Nick Greenwood, Arzachel, Hatfield & The North)

ASHISH KHAN

68	Liberty LBL 83083E	ASHISH KHAN (LP)	15
73	Elektra K 42129	JUGAL BANDI (LP, with John Barham)	12

CHAKA KHAN

80	Warner Bros K 17617	Clouds/What You Did (12", p/s)	8

(see also Rufus)

USTAD ALI AKBAR KHAN

69	HMV ASD 2367	MUSIC FROM INDIA NO. 5 (LP)	15
69	Transatlantic TRA 183	DHUN PALAS KAFI (LP)	15
71	Mushroom 100 MR 14	THE PEACEFUL MUSIC OF USTAD ALI AKBAR KHAN (LP)	50

(see also Ravi Shankar)

USTAD VILAYET KHAN

69	RCA SF 8025	THE GURU (LP, soundtrack)	15
70	Transatlantic TRA 239	RAGA TILAKKAMOD (LP)	15

KHANDARS

65	Blue Beat BB 332	Don't Dig A Hole For Me/BUSTER'S ALL STARS: Skara	20

KHANS

62	London HLU 9555	New Orleans, 2 AM/Blue Mist	10

KHARTOMB

83	Whaam! WHAAM 14	Swahili Lullaby/Teekon Warriors	7

KICK

84	Footwear FWR 01	Let's Get Back Together/A Shot In The Dark/Don't Ever Change (p/s)	5
86	Sponge SPONGE 01	Scapegoat/Flingle Bunt (live)/Leavin' Here (live) (p/s)	4

KID GUNGO

69	Escort ES 801	Hold The Pussy/KING CANNON: Wha Pen (B-side actually by Carl Bryan)	6

JOHNNY KIDD (& PIRATES)

59	HMV POP 615	Please Don't Touch/Growl	12
59	HMV POP 674	Feelin'/If You Were The Only Girl In The World (solo)	12
60	HMV POP 698	You Got What It Takes/Longin' Lips	12
60	HMV POP 753	Shakin' All Over/Yes Sir, That's My Baby	12
60	HMV POP 790	Restless/Magic Of Love	10
61	HMV POP 853	Linda Lu/Let's Talk About Us	12
61	HMV POP 919	Please Don't Bring Me Down/So What	15
62	HMV POP 978	Hurry On Back To Love/I Want That (with The Mike Sammes Singers)	10
62	HMV POP 1088	A Shot Of Rhythm And Blues/I Can Tell	8
63	HMV POP 1173	I'll Never Get Over You/Then I Got Everything	5
63	HMV POP 1228	Hungry For Love/Ecstasy	6
64	HMV POP 1269	Always And Ever/Dr. Feelgood	7

Johnny KIDD

64	HMV POP 1309	Jealous Girl/Shop Around	7
64	HMV POP 1353	Whole Lotta Woman/Your Cheatin' Heart	8
65	HMV POP 1397	The Birds And The Bees/Don't Make The Same Mistake As I Did	8
65	HMV POP 1424	Shakin' All Over '65/Gotta Travel On	12
65	HMV POP 1520	It's Got To Be You/I Hate To Get Up In The Morning (solo)	15
66	HMV POP 1559	Send For That Girl/The Fool	15
60s	HMV JO 674	Feelin'/If You Were The Only Girl In The World (export issue, black label)	25
97	Cruisin' 50 CASB 005	Shakin' All Over/Please Don't Touch (78, 300 only)	30
60	HMV 7EG 8628	SHAKIN' ALL OVER (EP)	40
64	HMV 7EG 8834	JOHNNY KIDD AND THE PIRATES (EP)	40
71	Regal Starline SRS 5100	SHAKIN' ALL OVER (LP)	15
78	EMI Nut NUTM 12	THE BEST OF JOHNNY KIDD AND THE PIRATES (LP)	12

(see also Pirates)

KIDS
| 75 | Atlantic K 50143 | ANVIL CHORUS (LP, with inner, stickered sleeve) | 12 |

(see also Heavy Metal Kids, Gary Holton)

KIDS NEXT DOOR
| 65 | London HLR 9993 | Inky Dinky Spider/Goodbye Don't Cry | 8 |

KIDZ NEXT DOOR
| 79 | Warner Bros K 17492 | What's It All About?/The Kidz Next Door (p/s) | 20 |

REGINALD KILBEY & STRINGS STARLIGHT
| 66 | HMV 7P 396 | Exotica/Edelma | 5 |

KILBURN & HIGH ROADS
74	Dawn DNS 1090	Rough Kids/Billy Bentley	10
75	Dawn DNS 1102	Crippled With Nerves/Huffety Puff	10
78	Warner Bros K 17225	Bentley/Pam's Moods	8
75	Dawn DNLS 3065	HANDSOME (LP)	20

(see also Ian Dury & Blockheads, 999, Nine Days Wonder)

ROY KILDARE
| 64 | Blue Beat BB 226 | I Won't Leave/What About It | 12 |

JUDY KILEEN
| 56 | London HLU 8328 | Just Walking In The Rain/A Heart Without A Sweetheart | 30 |
| 56 | London HLU 8328 | Just Walking In The Rain/A Heart Without A Sweetheart (78) | 15 |

KILFENORA CEILI BAND
| 74 | Transatlantic TRS 108 | KILFENORA CEILI BAND (LP) | 15 |

MERLE KILGORE
54	London HL 8103	Seeing Double, Feeling Single/It Can't Rain All The Time	165
54	London HL 8103	Seeing Double, Feeling Single/It Can't Rain All The Time (78)	35
57	London HLP 8392	Ernie/Trying To Find (Someone Like You)	275
57	London HLP 8392	Ernie/Trying To Find (Someone Like You) (78)	50
60	Melodisc MEL 1545	Dear Mama/Jimmie Bring Sunshine	15
62	Mercury AMT 1193	42 In Chicago/A Girl Named Liz	12
65	London HA-B 8244	THERE'S GOLD IN THEM THAR HILLS (LP)	20

THEOLA KILGORE
| 67 | Sue WI 4035 | I'll Keep Trying/He's Coming Back To Me | 20 |

LOUIS KILLEN
| 62 | Topic TOP 75 | NORTHUMBRIAN GARLAND (EP) | 10 |
| 66 | Topic 12T 126 | BALLADS AND BROADSIDES (LP, blue label) | 20 |

LOUIS KILLEN & JOHNNY HANDLE
62	Topic TOP 74	THE COLLIER'S RANT (EP)	10
65	Topic 12T 122	TOMMY ARMSTRONG OF TYNESIDE (LP, with Colin Ross & Tom Gilfellon, blue label with booklet)	15
68	Topic 12T 189	ALONG THE COALY TYNE (LP, with Colin Ross, blue label with booklet)	15

(see also Johnny Handle)

KILLERMETERS
| 79 | Psycho P 2620 | Why Should It Happen To Me/Cardiac Arrest (some in p/s) | 70/25 |
| 80 | Gem GEMS 22 | Twisted Wheel/SX 225 (p/s) | 18 |

KILLERS
| 78 | Satril SAT 129 | Kiler (On The Dancefloor) (no p/s) | 5 |
| 77 | Ariola ARL 5003 | KILLER (LP) | 15 |

JOHN KILLIGREW
| 71 | Penny Farthing PELS 513 | JOHN KILLIGREW (LP, with Pete Dello) | 12 |

(see also Pete Dello)

KILLING FLOOR
70	Penny Farthing PEN 745	Call For The Politicians/Acid Bean	18
69	Spark (S)RLP 102	KILLING FLOOR (LP)	120
70	Penny Farthing PELS 511	OUT OF URANUS (LP, gatefold sleeve)	110
73	Spark Replay SRLM 2004	ORIGINAL KILLING FLOOR (LP, reissue)	30

(see also Rory Gallagher)

KILLING JOKE

79	Malicious Damage MD 410	Nervous System/Turn To Red/Are You Receiving (10" EP in bag, some with picture & 4 cards)	15/10
80	Island WIP 6550	Turn To Red/Nervous System (p/s)	5
80	Island 12 WIP 6550	Almost Red/Nervous System/Are You Receiving/Turn To Red (12", p/s)	10
80	Malicious Damage MD 540	Wardance/Psyche (p/s, some with 'call up paper' insert)	10/7
80	E.G. EGMD 1.00	Requiem/Change (p/s)	4
80	E.G. EGMX 1.00	Requiem/Change/Change/Requiem (12", stamped sleeve, later in p/s)	12/10
81	E.G. EGMDS 1.01	Follow The Leaders/Tension (p/s)	4
81	E.G. EGMDX 1.01	Follow The Leaders/Follow The Leaders — Dub/Tension (10", p/s)	7
82	E.G. EGO 4	Empire Song/Brilliant (p/s)	4
82	E.G. EGO 7	Chop Chop/Good Samaritan (p/s)	4
82	E.G. EGO 10	Birds Of A Feather/Flock The B-Side (p/s)	4
82	E.G. EGOX 10	Birds Of A Feather/Flock The B-Side (12", p/s)	8
83	E.G. EGO 11	Let's All Go (To The Fire Dances)/Dominator (p/s)	4
83	E.G. EGOX 11	Let's All Go (To The Fire Dances)/The Fall Of Because (live)/ Dominator (Version) (12", p/s)	7
83	E.G. EGOD 14/KILL 1/2	Me Or You/Wilful Days//Feast Of Blaze (double pack, gatefold p/s)	5
83	E.G. EGOXD 14	Me Or You/Feast Of Blaze/Wilful Days//Let's All Go (To The Fire Dances)/ The Fall Of Because (live)/Dominator (Version) (12", sealed double pack)	15
84	E.G. EGO 16	Eighties/Eighties (Coming Mix) (p/s)	4
84	E.G. EGOX 16	Eighties (Serious Dance Mix)/Eighties/Eighties (Coming Mix) (12", p/s)	8
84	E.G. EGOX 17	A New Day (Dub Mix)/A New Day (12", p/s)	7
85	E.G. EGOY 20	Love Like Blood (Gestalt Mix)/Love Like Blood/Blue Feather (12", p/s)	10
85	E.G. EGOY 21	Kings And Queens (Knave Mix) (12", p/s)	10
85	E.G. EGOX 21	Kings And Queens (The Right Royal Mix)/The Madding Crowd/ Kings And Queens (12", p/s with poster)	7
85	E.G. EGOX 21	Kings And Queens (The Right Royal Mix)/The Madding Crowd/ Kings And Queens (12", different withdrawn p/s)	10
86	E.G. EGOD 27	Adorations/Exile//Ecstasy/Adorations (Instrumental Mix) (double pack)	4
86	E.G. EGO 30	Sanity/Goodbye To The Village (stickered p/s & "Wardance [Remix]" cassette)	12
88	E.G. EGOCD 40	America/Jihad (Beyrouth Edit)/America (Extended Mix)/Change (Original 1980 Mix) (CD)	7
88	E.G. EGOT 43	My Love Of This Land/Follow The Leaders (Dub)/Sun Goes Down (10", p/s, B-side matrix no. EGOT 43BE)	6
88	E.G. EGOT 43	My Love Of This Land/Follow The Leaders (Dub)/Sun Goes Down (10", p/s, B-side matrix no. EGOT 43B; last track plays "The Gathering")	6

(see also Youth, Brilliant, Peyr, Heavy Duty Breaks)

KILLJOYS

77	Raw RAW 3	Johnny Won't Get To Heaven/Naive (p/s, 4 different label designs)	10
91	Dam. Goods FNARR LP10	NAIVE (LP, green vinyl)	10

(see also Dexy's Midnight Runners, Girlschool)

KILOWATTS

68	Doctor Bird DB 1140	Bring It On Home/What A Wonderful World	15

(see also West Indians)

KILTIES

56	Beltona BL 2666	Teach You To Rock/Giddy-Up-A Ding Dong	15
56	Beltona BL 2666	Teach You To Rock/Giddy-Up-A Ding Dong (78)	12

KIM & KINETICS

60s	Mortonsound 3032/3033	Without A Song/Stormy Monday	40
60s	Mortonsound 3036/3033	Wee Wee Hours/Stormy Monday	40

(see also Kim Davis)

WILLIAM KIMBER

56	EFDSS LP 1001	WILLIAM KIMBER (LP, with booklet)	15
74	Topic 12T 249	THE ART OF WILLIAM KIMBER (LP, with booklet)	10

WILLIAM E. KIMBER

68	Parlophone R 5735	Kilburn Towers/Goodbye (withdrawn)	6

(see also Couriers)

STEVIE KIMBLE

66	Decca F 12378	Some Things Take A Little Time/All The Time In The World	15

KINESPHERE

76	Kinesphere KIN 5001	ALL AROUND YOU (LP)	100

KING

85	CBS CDCBS 86320	BITTERSWEET (CD)	35

(see also Reluctant Stereotypes)

AL KING

68	Sue WI 4045	Think Twice Before You Speak/The Winner	25

ALAN KING

73	Duke DU 151	Africa Wants Us All/JOE GIBBS: Liberation (B-side actually by Joe Gibbs' All Stars)	4

ALBERT KING

67	Atlantic 584 099	Crosscut Saw/Down Don't Bother Me	10
67	Stax 601 015	Born Under A Bad Sign/Personal Manager	6
68	Stax 601 029	Cold Feet/You Sure Drive A Hard Bargain	6
68	Stax 601 042	(I Love) Lucy/You're Gonna Need Me	6
73	Stax 2025 162	Breaking Up Somebody's Home/Little Brother (Make A Way)	5
67	Polydor 2343 026	TRAVELLIN' TO CALIFORNIA (LP)	25
68	Stax (S)XATS 1002	LIVE WIRE — BLUES POWER (LP)	22
69	Atlantic 588 173	KING OF THE BLUES GUITAR (LP)	22
69	Stax SXATS 1017	KING, DOES THE KING'S THINGS (LP)	18
69	Stax SXATS 1022	YEARS GONE BY (LP)	18
71	Stax 2363 003	LIVE WIRE — BLUES POWER (LP, reissue)	12
71	Stax 2325 042	LOVEJOY (LP)	15
73	Stax 2325 089	I'LL PLAY THE BLUES FOR YOU (LP)	15
74	Stax STX 1003	I WANNA GET FUNKY (LP)	15

(se also Steve Cropper & Albert King)

ANNA KING

65	Philips BF 1402	If Somebody Told You/Baby, Baby, Baby (as Anna King & Bobby Byrd)	8
65	Philips BBE 12584	BACK TO SOUL (EP)	30
65	Philips (S)BL 7655	BACK TO SOUL (LP)	50

(see also Bobby Byrd)

ANTHONY KING

70s	Peer Intl.	ELECTRICAL BAZAAR — SYNTHESIZERS UNLIMITED (LP, library issue)	25

B.B. KING

62	HMV POP 1101	Tomorrow Night/Mother's Love	15
64	Ember EMB S 196	Rock Me Baby/I Can't Lose	15
65	Sue WI 358	The Letter/You Never Know	18
66	HMV POP 1568	Don't Answer The Door (Parts 1 & 2)	10
67	HMV POP 1580	Night Life/Waitin' On You	8
67	HMV POP 1594	I Don't Want You Cuttin' Your Hair/Think It Over	8
67	Polydor 56735	Jungle/Long Gone Baby	7
68	Stateside SS 2112	Paying The Cost To Be The Boss/Having My Say	6
68	Blue Horizon 57-3144	The Woman I Love/Blues For Me	15
68	Speciality SPE 1006	Woke Up This Morning (possibly unissued)	20+
69	Stateside SS 2141	Don't Waste My Time/Get Myself Somebody	6
69	Blue Horizon 57-3161	Everyday I Have The Blues/Five Long Years	15
70	Stateside SS 2161	The Thrill Is Gone/You're Mean	6
70	Stateside SS 2169	So Excited/Confessin' The Blues	5
70	Stateside SS 2176	Hummingbird/Ask Me No Questions	5
71	Probe PRO 516	Chains And Things/King's Special	5
71	Probe PRO 528	Ask Me No Questions/Help The Poor/Humming Bird	5
72	Probe PRO 573	Summer In The City/Found What I Need	5
65	HMV CLP 1870	LIVE AT THE REGAL (LP)	30
66	HMV CLP 3514	CONFESSIN' THE BLUES (LP)	30
67	HMV CLP 3608	BLUES IS KING (LP)	30
67	Ember EMB 3379	THE R&B AND SOUL OF B.B. KING (LP)	18
68	Stateside (S)SL 10238	BLUES ON TOP OF BLUES (LP)	25
68	Blue Horizon 7-63216	THE B.B. KING STORY CHAPTER 1 (LP)	60
69	Stateside (S)SL 10272	LUCILLE (LP)	20
69	Stateside SSL 10284	HIS BEST — THE ELECTRIC B.B. KING (LP)	20
69	Blue Horizon 7-63226	THE B.B. KING STORY CHAPTER 2 — BEALE STREET BLUES (LP)	60
70	Stateside SSL 10297	LIVE AND WELL (LP)	18
70	Stateside SSL 10299	COMPLETELY WELL (LP)	18
70	Probe SPBA 6255	INDIANOLA MISSISSIPPI SEEDS (LP)	12
71	Blue Horizon 2431 004	TAKE A SWING WITH ME (LP)	65
71	Probe SPB 1032	LIVE IN COOK COUNTY JAIL (LP)	15
71	Probe SPB 1041	IN LONDON (LP)	15
72	Probe SPB 1051	L.A. MIDNIGHT (LP)	12
72	Probe SPB 1063	GUESS WHO (LP)	12
73	Probe SPB 1069	THE BEST OF B.B. KING (LP)	12
73	Probe SPB 1083	TO KNOW YOU IS TO LOVE YOU (LP)	12

(see also U2)

B.B. KING & BOBBY BLAND

74	ABC ABCD 605	TOGETHER FOR THE FIRST TIME (2-LP)	22

(see also Bobby Bland)

BEN E. KING

61	London HLK 9258	Spanish Harlem/First Taste Of Love	12
61	London HLK 9358	Stand By Me/On The Horizon	12
61	London HLK 9416	Amor, Amor/Souvenir Of Mexico	7
61	London HLK 9457	Here Comes The Night/Young Boy Blues	10
62	London HLK 9517	Ecstasy/Yes	7
62	London HLK 9544	Don't Play That Song (You Lied)/The Hermit Of Misty Mountain (later copies have Atlantic labels instead of *London* Atlantic)	each 7
62	London HLK 9586	Too Bad/My Heart Cries For You	10
63	London HLK 9631	I'm Standing By/Walking In The Footsteps Of A Fool	12
63	London HLK 9691	How Can I Forget/Gloria, Gloria	7
63	London HLK 9778	I (Who Have Nothing)/The Beginning Of Time	7
63	London HLK 9819	I Could Have Danced All Night/Gypsy	8
64	London HLK 9840	Around The Corner/Groovin'	8
64	Atlantic AT 4007	It's All Over/Let The Water Run Down	7
65	Atlantic AT 4018	Seven Letters/River Of Tears	7
65	Atlantic AT 4025	The Record (Baby I Love You)/The Way You Shake It	12
65	Atlantic AT 4043	Cry No More/(There's) No Place To Hide	15

66	Atlantic AT 4065	Goodnight My Love, Pleasant Dreams/Tell Daddy	7
66	Atlantic AT 4065	Goodnight My Love, Pleasant Dreams/I Can't Break The News To Myself (demos with blank label on different B-side)	300
66	Atlantic 584 008	So Much Love/Don't Drive Me Away	7
66	Atlantic 584 046	I Swear By The Stars Above/Get In A Hurry	6
67	Atlantic 584 069	What Is Soul?/They Don't Give Medals To Yesterday's Heroes	6
67	Atlantic 584 090	Save The Last Dance For Me (as Ben E. King & Drifters)/Stand By Me	6
67	Atlantic 584 106	Tears, Tears, Tears/A Man Without A Dream	8
68	Atlantic 584 149	Seven Letters/Goodnight My Love	7
68	Atlantic 584 184	Don't Take Your Love From Me/Forgive This Fool	15
68	Atlantic 584 205	It's Amazing/Where's The Girl	5
69	Atlantic 584 238	'Till I Can't Take It Any More/It Ain't Fair	5
70	Crewe CRW 2	Goodbye My Old Gal/I Can't Take It Like A Man	5
71	Atlantic 2091 100	It's Amazing/Tears, Tears, Tears	5
71	CBS 7397	White Moon/All Of Your Sorrows	5
72	CBS 7785	Take Me To The Pilot/I Guess It's Goodbye	5
75	Atlantic K 10565	Supernatural Things (Parts 1 & 2)	5
75	Atlantic K 10618	Happiness Is Where You Find It/Drop My Heart Off	5
63	London REK 1361	BEN E. KING (EP)	35
63	London REK 1386	I'M STANDING BY (EP)	35
64	Atlantic AET 6004	WHAT NOW MY LOVE (EP)	30
61	London HA-K 2395	SPANISH HARLEM (LP, also stereo SAH-K 6195)	40/50
62	London HA-K 8012	DON'T PLAY THAT SONG! (LP)	40
63	London HA-K/SH-K 8026	SONGS FOR SOULFUL LOVERS (LP, cover credits "*Sings* For Soulful Lovers"; mono/stereo)	40/50
65	Atlantic ATL 5016	GREATEST HITS (LP, plum label)	35
66	Atlantic 587/588 055	SONGS FOR SOULFUL LOVERS (LP, cover credits "*Sings* For Soulful Lovers"; reissue)	15
67	Atlantic 590 001	SPANISH HARLEM (LP, reissue)	15
67	Atlantic 587 072	WHAT IS SOUL? (LP)	20
68	Atlantic 588 125	SEVEN LETTERS (LP)	15
70	Crewe CRWS 203	ROUGH EDGES (LP)	12
71	CBS 64570	THE BEGINNING OF IT ALL (LP)	12
75	Atlantic K 50118	SUPERNATURAL THING (LP)	12

(see also Drifters, Soul Clan)

BRENTON KING
73	Downtown DT 505	Why Do People Have To Cry/Version	4

BOB KING & THE COUNTRY KINGS
59	Oriole CB 1497	My Petite Marie/Hey Honey	80
59	Oriole CB 1497	My Petite Marie/Hey Honey (78)	50

BUZZY KING
60	Top Rank JAR 278	Schoolboy Blues/Your Picture	18

CANNON BALL KING
69	Camel CA 14	Danny Boy/Reggae Happiness	7
70s	Junior JR 103	Reggay Got Soul/Land Of Love (actually by Soul Cats)	6

(see also Carl Bryan, King Cannon, Cannon Ball & Johnny Melody)

CARL KING
66	CBS 202407	Out Of My Depth/Keep It Coming	10
67	CBS 202553	You And Me/Satin Doll	5

CAROLE KING
62	London HLU 9591	It Might As Well Rain Until September/Nobody's Perfect	8
66	London HLU 10036	Road To Nowhere/Some Of Your Lovin'	8
72	Ode ODS 66031	Been To Canaan/Bitter With The Sweet	5
71	A&M AMLS 996	WRITER — CAROLE KING (LP)	12
72	Ode ODE 77016	RHYMES AND REASONS (LP)	12

CLAUDE KING
61	Philips PB 1173	Big River Big Man/Sweet Loving	7
61	Philips PB 1199	The Comancheros/I Can't Get Over The Way You Got Over Me	7
62	CBS AAG 108	Wolverton Mountain/Little Bitty Heart	10
62	CBS AAG 119	Burning Of Atlanta/Don't That Moon Look Lonesome	8
65	CBS EP 6067	TIGER WOMAN (EP)	25
62	CBS BPG 62114	MEET CLAUDE KING (LP)	30

CLYDIE KING
69	Minit MLF 11014	One Part, Two Part/Love Now Pay Later	8
75	UK USA 11	Punish Me/Punish Me (Instrumental Version)	5

(see also Jimmy Holiday & Clydie King, Raelets)

DANNY KING('S MAYFAIR SET)
64	Columbia DB 7276	Tossin' And Turnin'/Young Blood	25
65	Columbia DB 7456	Pretty Things/Outside Of My Room	30
65	Columbia DB 7792	Amen (My Teenage Prayer)/It's Such A Shame (as Danny King's Mayfair Set)	18

(see also Trevor Burton, Lemon Tree, Roy Wood)

DAVE KING
56	Decca F 10684	Memories Are Made Of This (& Keynotes)/I've Changed My Mind A 1000 Times	12
56	Decca F 10720	You Can't Be True To Two/A Little Bit Independent	10
56	Decca F 10741	The Birds And The Bees/Hot Chocolatta (with Keynotes)	8
56	Decca F 10791	Christmas And You/You Make Nice	12
57	Decca F 10865	Love Is A Golden Ring/If Your Heart Wants To Dance	6
57	Decca F 10910	With All My Heart/Red Shutters	6

Dave KING

57	Decca F 10947	Shake Me I Rattle/Chances Are	7
58	Decca F 10973	The Story Of My Life/I'll Buy You A Star	10
58	Decca F 11012	I Suddenly/There's Only One Of You	5
58	Decca F 11061	The Story/Home	5
58	Decca F 11061	The Story/Home (78)	10
59	Pye International 7N 25032	High Hopes/Night And Day	7
59	Pye International N 25032	High Hopes/Night And Day (78)	15
60	Pye 7N 15283	Many A Wonderful Moment/Goody Goody	5
61	Pye International 7N 25076	Young In Love/C'est La Vie, C'est L'amour	5
56	Decca DFE 6385	A DAVE KING SELECTION (EP)	12
58	Decca DFE 6514	DAVE KING NO. 2 (EP)	15
62	Ace Of Hearts ACL 1095	MEMORIES ARE MADE OF THIS (LP)	15

DAVE KING REGGAE BAND
70	Attack ATT 8014	Hey Little Girl/Why Don't You Try Me	6

DEE KING
66	Piccadilly 7N 35316	Sally Go Round The Roses/It's So Fine	6

DENNIS KING
77	EMI EMI 2578	Regan's Theme From The Film 'Sweeney'/F.J.'s Tune	12

DON KING
85	Doublevision DVR 14	Revelry/Tanajura/The Don Goes On/Never Decide/Marco Polo (12", p/s)	8

EARL (CONNELLY) KING
50s	Parlophone DP 511	Gratefully/Don't Take It So Hard (78, export issue)	20

EDDIE KING
65	Columbia DB 7572	Always At A Distance/If You Wish	6
65	Columbia DB 7654	I Wanna Love Her So Bad/If All You Need	7

FREDDY/FREDDIE KING
61	Parlophone R 4777	Hideaway/I Love The Woman	25
65	Sue WI 349	Driving Sideways/Hideaway	25
69	Atlantic 584 235	Play It Cool/Funky	7
73	A&M AMS 7076	Woman Across The River/Help Me Through The Day	5
69	Atlantic 588 186	FREDDIE IS A BLUES MASTER (LP)	25
69	Polydor 2343 009	KING OF R&B VOL. 2 (LP)	12
69	Python PLP-KM 5	FREDDY KING VOLUME 1 (LP, 99 copies only)	35
69	Python PLP-KM 7	FREDDY KING VOLUME 2 (LP, 99 copies only)	35
69	Python PLP-KM 11	FREDDY KING VOLUME 3 (LP, 99 copies only)	35

(Pre-1970 releases are usually credited to Freddy King, post-1970 releases to Freddie King.)

71	A&M AMLS 65004	GETTING READY (LP)	18
72	Polydor 2343 047	HIS EARLY YEARS VOLUME 1 (LP)	12
72	A&M AMLS 68113	TEXAS CANNONBALL (LP)	12
72	Black Bear 904	LIVE PERFORMANCES VOLUME 1 (LP)	22
72	Black Bear 905	LIVE PERFORMANCES VOLUME 2 (LP)	22
73	A&M AMLS 68919	WOMAN ACROSS THE RIVER (LP)	12
73	Atlantic K 40496	FREDDIE IS A BLUES MASTER (LP, reissue)	12
73	Atlantic K 40497	MY FEELING FOR THE BLUES (LP)	12
75	RSO 2394 163	LARGER THAN LIFE (LP)	12
77	RSO 2394 192	FREDDIE KING (1934-1976) (LP)	12

(see also Lula Reed & Freddy King)

HAMILTON KING
64	HMV POP 1289	Not Until/I Wanna Live	8
64	HMV POP 1356	Ain't It Time/Money, Money	12
65	HMV POP 1425	Bird Without Wings/Shoppin'	12
60s	Toast TT 511	This Love Of Mine/The Cup Is Fuller	5

HANK KING
63	Starlite STEP 41	COUNTRY AND WESTERN (EP)	20
66	Starlite GRK 510	COUNTRY AND WESTERN (EP, reissue)	10

JAY W. KING
66	Stateside SS 505	I'm So Afraid/I Don't Have To Worry (Not Anymore)	18

JONATHAN KING
65	Decca F 12187	Everyone's Gone To The Moon/Summer's Coming	5
65	Decca F 12234	Green Is The Grass/Creation	5
65	Decca F 12286	Where The Sun Has Never Shone/Don't Talk To Me Of Protest	5
66	Decca F 12457	Just Like A Woman/The Land Of The Golden Tree	5
66	Decca F 12517	Icicles/In A Hundred Years From Now	5
67	Decca LK/SKL 4908	OR THEN AGAIN... (LP)	15
72	Decca SKL 5127	TRY SOMETHING DIFFERENT (LP)	12
75	UK UKAL 1010	A ROSE IN A FISTED GLOVE (LP)	12
76	UK UKAL 1024	J.K. ALL THE WAY (LP)	12

(see also Weathermen, Hedgehoppers Anonymous, Pleasure Garden)

MARK KING
84	Polydor MK 1	I Feel Free/There Is A Dog (p/s)	4
84	Polydor MKX 1	I Feel Free (Extended)/There Is A Dog (12", p/s)	7
84	Polydor MKX 2-DJ	Clocks Go Forward (Long Version)/Barcelona (12", promo only, no p/s)	30
87	Polydor 823 008-2	INFLUENCES (CD)	15

(see also Level 42, Thunderthumbs & Toetsenman)

DR. MARTIN LUTHER KING
68	Pama PM 732	I Have A Dream/Top Of The Mountain	10
68	Tamla Motown TML 11076	THE GREAT MARCH TO FREEDOM (LP)	100
60s	Hallmark CHM 631	IN THE STRUGGLE FOR FREEDOM (LP)	12

P. KING
83	Red Bus RBUS 79	Hey Rosalyn/Lyin' Again	6

(see also Paul King)

PAUL KING
72	Dawn DNS 1023	Whoa Buck/Zoe	6
72	Dawn DNLS 3035	BEEN IN THE PEN TOO LONG (LP, with lyric insert)	18

(see also Mungo Jerry, P. King, P. Rufus King, King Earl Boogie Band, D'Jurann Jurran, Jigilo Jug Band, Russian Roulette)

PEE WEE KING & HIS BAND
52	HMV B 10229	Bull Fiddle Boogie (with Golden West Cowboys)/Silver And Gold (78)	8
52	HMV B 10275	Busybody (with Redd Stewart)/I Don't Mind (with Golden West Trio) (78)	8
53	HMV B 10415	Tennessee Tango/The Crazy Waltz (78)	8
54	HMV 7MC 14	Bimbo/Changing Partners (export issue)	15

(see also Hank Snow)

PETE KING CHORALE & ORCHESTRA
61	London HLR 9437	Hey! Look Me Over/Tall Hope	6

PETER KING
68	Crab CRAB 3	Reggae Limbo/DERRICK MORGAN: River To The Bank	8

P. RUFUS KING
73	Dawn DNS 1031	Look At Me Now/Nobody Knows	6

(see also Paul King, Mungo Jerry)

RAMONA KING
64	Warner Bros WB 125	It's In His Kiss/It Couldn't Happen To A Nicer Guy	10

RAY KING SOUL BAND
67	Piccadilly 7N 35394	Behold/Soon You'll Be Gone	8

REG KING
71	United Artists UP 35204	Little Boy/10,000 Miles (as Reg King & B.B. Blunder)	6
71	United Artists UAG 29157	REG KING (LP)	30

(see also Action, Andy Leigh, B.B. Blunder, Mark Charig, Elton Dean, Mighty Baby)

SAMMY KING (& VOLTAIRS)
64	HMV POP 1285	What's The Secret/Great Balls Of Fire (as Sammy King & Voltairs)	8
64	HMV POP 1330	Rag Doll/We're Through	6
65	HMV POP 1384	Only You (And You Alone)/A Kiss, A Promise	6
66	HMV POP 1540	If You Can Find Someone To Love You/Past Caring (with Voltairs)	6

SID KING & FIVE STRINGS
56	Philips PB 589	Booger Red/Oobie-Doobie (78)	220

SOLOMON KING
67	Columbia DB 8306	She Wears My Ring/Try Try (withdrawn B-side)	10
67	Columbia DB 8325	She Wears My Ring/I Get That Feeling Over You	5
68	Columbia DB 8402	When We Were Young/Those Gentle Hands	5
68	Columbia DB 8454	Somewhere In The Crowd/Hava Nagila	5
68	Columbia DB 8508	Goodbye My Old Gal/Hundred Years Or More	5
69	Columbia DB 8554	Cry Softly/Time Alone Will Tell	5
69	Columbia DB 8586	For Each Question/If I Had Three Wishes	5
70	Columbia DB 8676	Say A Prayer/This Beautiful Day	45
70	Columbia DB 8739	November Snow/Echoes Of A Million Kisses	5
71	Columbia DB 8771	Answer Me/Don't You Be A Sinner	5
68	Columbia S(C)X 6250	SHE WEARS MY RING (LP)	12
71	Columbia SCX 6458	YOU'LL NEVER WALK ALONE (LP)	12

(see also Levi Jackson)

SONNY KING
60	Pye Intl. NPL 28001	FOR LOSERS ONLY (LP)	20

TEDDI KING
56	Vogue Coral Q 72142	My Funny Little Lover/I'll Never Be The Same	6
55	Vogue LDE 142	MISS TEDDI KING WITH RUBY BRAFF (10" LP)	18
57	Vogue VA 160109	NOW IN VOGUE (LP)	15

(see also George Shearing)

TEDDY KING & BUSTER'S ALLSTARS
67	Fab FAB 27	Mexican Divorce/SOUL TOPS: Baby I Got News	12

TONY KING (& HIPPY BOYS)
69	Trojan TR 667	Proud Mary/My Devotion (as Tony King & Hippy Boys)	5
70	Gas GAS 156	Daddy, Daddy Don't Cry/I Like It	6

(see also Maytals)

KINGBEES
66	Tempo TPO 103	I'm A Kingbee/My Little Red Book (Irish-only, some in p/s)	300/200

KING BISCUIT BOY
70	Paramount SPFL 270	OFFICIAL MUSIC (LP)	20
71	Paramount SPFA 7001	GOODUNS (LP)	20

(see also Bobby Bland)

KING BROTHERS
57	Conquest CP 104	The Cradle Rock/Crazy Little Palace (78)	15
57	Conquest CP 109	Steamboat Railroad/Heart (78)	12
57	Parlophone R 4288	Marianne/Little By Little	8
57	Parlophone R 4288	Marianne/Little By Little (78)	8
57	Parlophone R 4310	A White Sport Coat (And A Pink Carnation)/Minne-Minnehaha!	8
57	Parlophone R 4338	In The Middle Of An Island/Rockin' Shoes	7
57	Parlophone R 4367	Wake Up Little Susie/Winter Wonderland	7
57	Parlophone R 4367	Wake Up Little Susie/Winter Wonderland (78)	7
57	Parlophone R 4389	Put A Light In The Window/Miss Otis Regrets	7
58	Parlophone R 4410	Hand Me Down My Walking Cane/6-5 Jive	10

MINT VALUE £

58	Parlophone R 4410	Hand Me Down My Walking Cane/6-5 Jive (78)	10
58	Parlophone R 4438	Torero/Moonlight And Roses	6
58	Parlophone R 4438	Torero/Moonlight And Roses (78)	8
58	Parlophone R 4469	Sitting In A Tree House/Father Time	5
58	Parlophone R 4469	Sitting In A Tree House/Father Time (78)	8
59	Parlophone R 4513	Leaning On A Lamp-Post/Thank Heaven For Little Girls	5
59	Parlophone R 4513	Leaning On A Lamp-Post/Thank Heaven For Little Girls (78)	8
59	Parlophone R 4554	Hop, Skip And Jump/Civilization (Bongo, Bongo, Bongo)	10
59	Parlophone R 4554	Hop, Skip And Jump/Civilization (Bongo, Bongo, Bongo) (78)	10
59	Parlophone R 4577	Makin' Love/Caribbean	5
60	Parlophone R 4639	The Waiter And The Porter And The Upstairs Maid/Standing On The Corner	5
60	Parlophone R 4672	Mais Oui/Gotta Feeling	5
60	Parlophone R 4715	Doll House/Si Si Si	5
61	Parlophone R 4737	Seventy-Six Trombones/I Like Everybody	5
61	Parlophone R 4778	Goodbye Little Darling/Tuxedo Junction	5
61	Parlophone R 4825	The Next Train Out Of Town/Sabre Dance	5
61	Parlophone R 4861	The Language Of Love/Go Tell Her For Me	5
64	Oriole CB 1978	Real Live Girl/Everytime It Rains	5
66	CBS 202030	Everytime I See You/Remember When	6
66	Page One POF 009	Symphony For Susan/My Time	6
67	Page One POF 033	My Mammy/Some Of These Days	5
57	Parlophone GEP 8638	HARMONY KINGS (EP)	10
57	Parlophone GEP 8651	SING AL JOLSON (EP)	8
57	Parlophone GEP 8665	LULLABIES OF BROADWAY (EP)	8
58	Parlophone GEP 8726	THAT'S ENTERTAINMENT (EP)	8
58	Parlophone GEP 8760	KINGS OF SONG (EP)	10
61	Parlophone GEP 8838	KING SIZE HITS (EP)	8
61	Encore ENC 106	KINGS OF SONG (EP)	12
67	Tupperware 7ES 25	THERE'S NO BUSINESS — LIKE OUR BUSINESS (EP)	8
58	Parlophone PMC 1060	THREE KINGS AND AN ACE (LP)	18

(see also Jim Dale)

KING CANNON

69	Trojan TR 663	Soul Scorcher/GLEN & DAVE: Lucky Boy	8
69	Trojan TR 644	Soul Special/TREVOR SHIELD: Moon Is Playing Tricks On Me	8
69	Crab CRAB 6	Mellow Trumpet/VAL BENNETT: Reggae City	6
71	Hillcrest HCT 2	Reggay Got Soul/SOUL CATS: Land Of Love	7
71	Moodisc HME 109	Raw Deal (as King Cannon Allout; actually by Carl Bryan)/ MUDIE'S ALL STARS: Shirley's Hide Out	6

(see also Cannon Ball & Johnny Melody, Carl Bryan, Max Romeo, Lester Sterling, Kid Gungo, Erroll Dunkley)

KING CANNONBALL

68	Trojan TR 636	Thunderstorm/BURT WALTERS: Honey Love	10

KING CHUBBY

70	Pama Supreme PS 297	What's The World Coming To/Live As One	8
70	Supreme PS 297	What's The World Coming To/Live As One (reissue)	6

(see also Junior Byles)

KING COLE TRIO

(see under Nat 'King' Cole)

KING CRIMSON

69	Island WIP 6071	The Court Of The Crimson King (Parts 1 & 2)	12
70	Island WIP 6080	Cat Food/Groon (some in p/s)	20/6
74	Island WIP 6189	The Night Watch/The Great Deceiver	5
76	Island WIP 6274	21st Century Schizoid Man/Epitaph (some in p/s)	25/7
69	Island ILPS 9111	IN THE COURT OF THE CRIMSON KING (LP, 1st pressing, pink label/'i' logo)	45
70	Island ILPS 9111	IN THE COURT OF THE CRIMSON KING (LP, 2nd pressing, pink rim label/'palm tree' logo)	15
70	Island ILPS 9127	IN THE WAKE OF POSEIDON (LP, 1st pressing, pink label/'i' logo)	25
70	Island ILPS 9127	IN THE WAKE OF POSEIDON (LP, 2nd pressing, pink rim label/'palm tree' logo)	15
70	Island ILPS 9141	LIZARD (LP, 1st pressing, pink label/'i' logo)	22
70	Island ILPS 9141	LIZARD (LP, 2nd pressing, pink rim label/'palm tree' logo)	15
71	Island ILPS 9175	ISLANDS (LP, pink rim label/'palm tree' logo, gatefold sleeve with inner)	15
72	Island HELP 6	EARTHBOUND (LP, black/pink label)	12
73	Island ILPS 9230	LARKS' TONGUE IN ASPIC (LP, pink rim label/'palm tree' logo, with inner)	12
74	Island ILPS 9275	STARLESS AND BIBLE BLACK (LP, pink rim label/'palm tree' logo, with inner)	12
74	Island ILPS 9308	RED (LP, pink rim label/'palm tree' logo, with inner sleeve)	12
75	Island ILPS 9316	U.S.A. (LP, pink rim label/'palm tree' logo, with inner)	12
76	Island ISLP 7	A YOUNG PERSON'S GUIDE (2-LP, with booklet)	15

(see also Giles Giles & Fripp, Fripp & Eno, Andy Summers & Robert Fripp, Gordon Haskell, Shame, McDonald & Giles, Emerson Lake & Palmer, Uriah Heep, Boz, Trendsetters Ltd., Pete Sinfield)

KING CRY CRY (Prince Far I)

71	Banana BA 356	I Had A Talk/BURNING SPEAR: Zion Higher	15

KING CURTIS

62	London HLU 9547	Soul Twist/Twistin' Time (as King Curtis & Noble Knights)	15
64	Capitol CL 15346	Soul Serenade/More Soul	12
67	Atlantic 584 109	Good To Me/Hold On I'm Comin'	5
67	Atlantic 584 134	Memphis Soul Stew/Blue Nocturne	6
68	Speciality SPE 1000	Wiggle Wobble/Night Train	8
69	Atlantic 584 287	Little Green Apples/La Jeanne	5
70	Atco 2091 012	Teasin'/Soulin' (as King Curtis & Delaney Bramlett, Eric Clapton & Friends)	10
60	London RE-K 1307	HAVE TENOR SAX, WILL BLOW (EP)	35
60	London HA-K 2247	HAVE TENOR SAX, WILL BLOW (LP)	40
62	RCA RD 27252	ARTHUR MURRAY'S MUSIC FOR DANCING — THE TWIST (LP)	25

MINT VALUE £

62	Esquire 32-161	THE NEW SCENE OF KING CURTIS (LP)	25
67	Atlantic 587 067	PLAYS THE GREAT MEMPHIS HITS (LP)	18
68	Ember SPE/LP 6600	SOUL SERENADE (LP)	15
68	Atlantic 587 093	KINGSIZE SOUL (LP, as King Curtis & Kingpins)	18
68	Atlantic 587/588 115	SWEET SOUL (LP)	18
69	Atco 228 002	BEST OF KING CURTIS (LP)	15
69	Atco 228 027	INSTANT GROOVE (LP)	15
70	Wand WNS 4	ETERNALLY SOUL (LP, as King Curtis & Shirelles)	12
71	Atlantic K 40214	LIVE AT FILLMORE WEST (LP)	15
72	Atlantic K 40360	EVERYBODY'S TALKIN' (LP)	12
72	Specialty SPE 6600	SOUL SERENADE (LP, reissue)	12
72	Specialty SPE 6607	MISTER SOUL (LP, reissue)	12
73	Atlantic K 40434	BLUES AT MONTREUX (LP, with Champion Jack Dupree)	12

(see also Champion Jack Dupree, Eric Clapton)

KING CURTIS, OLIVER NELSON & JIMMY FORREST
| 63 | Esquire 32-189 | SOUL BATTLE (LP) | 25 |

KING DIAMOND
| 89 | Road Runner RR 94616 | CONSPIRACY (LP, picture disc) | 20 |

KINGDOM COME (U.K.)
71	Polydor 2001 234	Eternal Messenger/I D Side To B Side The C Side	5
72	Polydor 2001 416	Spirit Of Joy/Come Alive	5
72	Polydor 2310 130	GALACTIC ZOO DOSSIER (LP, gatefold sleeve, some with poster)	40/20
72	Polydor 2310 178	KINGDOM COME (LP)	15
73	Polydor 2310 254	JOURNEY (LP)	15

(see also Arthur Brown)

KING-EARL BOOGIE BAND
72	Dawn DNS 1024	Plastic Jesus/If The Lord Don't Get You	6
72	Dawn DNS 1028	Starlight/Goin' To Germany	6
72	Dawn DNLS 3040	TROUBLE AT MILL (LP, with poster)	15

(see also Mungo Jerry, Paul King, Skeleton Crew)

KING FIGHTER
| 60s | Jump Up JU 518 | People Will Talk/Same Thing | 8 |

KINGFISH
| 76 | United Artists UAG 29922 | KINGFISH (LP) | 12 |
| 77 | United Artists UAG 30080 | LIVE AND KICKIN' (LP) | 12 |

(see also Grateful Dead, Bob Weir)

KING GEORGE
| 67 | RCA RCA 1573 | Drive On James/I'm Gonna Be Somebody Someday | 12 |

KING HARVEST
| 73 | Pye NSPL 28174 | DANCING IN THE MOONLIGHT (LP) | 10 |

KING HORROR
69	Joe/Duke DU 34	Dracula Prince Of Darkness/JOE'S ALL STARS: Honky	8
69	Grape GR 3003	Cutting Blade/Vampire	8
69	Grape GR 3006	The Hole/WINSTON GROOVY: Lover Come Back	8
69	Grape GR 3007	Lochness Monster/VISIONS: Zion I	8
69	Jackpot JP 713	Wood In The Fire/The Naked City	8
69	Jackpot JP 714	Police/PAMA DICE: Honky Tonk Popcorn	8
70	Nu Beat NB 051	Frankenstein/WINSTON GROOVY: I Can't Stand It	8

(see also Laurel Aitken)

KING KURT
82	Thin Sliced TSR 2	Zulu Beat/Rockin' Kurt (p/s, various coloured vinyls & handmade sleeves)	4-10
82	Thin Sliced TSR 2T	Zulu Beat/Rockin' Kurt (12", p/s, green vinyl)	10
83	Stiff BUY 189	Destination Zululand/She's A Hairy (shaped picture disc)	10
83	Stiff SBUY 189	Destination Zululand/She's A Hairy/A-Side Mix (12", p/s)	7
84	Stiff PBUY 199	Mack The Knife/Wreck A Party Rock (shaped picture disc)	7
84	Stiff PBUY 199	Mack The Knife/Wreck A Party Rock (picture disc)	6
84	Stiff BUY 199	Mack The Knife/Wreck A Party Rock (p/s, with free flexidisc)	5
84	Stiff SBUY 199	Mack The Knife/Wreck A Party Rock (12", p/s)	7
84	Stiff BUY 206	Banana Banana/Bo Diddley Goes East (scratch'n'sniff p/s)	4
84	Stiff PBUY 206	Banana Banana/Bo Diddley Goes East (shaped picture disc)	8
84	Stiff BUYIT 206	Banana Banana/Bo Diddley Goes East/Banana Instrumental (12", p/s, white vinyl with tattoos)	10
85	Stiff BUY 223	Billy/Back On The Dole (picture disc)	4
85	Stiff BUYIT 230	The Road To Rack And Ruin/Poppa Wobbler/Alright Mother (12", p/s)	7
85	Stiff PBUY 235	Slammers/Ape Hour (picture disc)	5
85	Stiff BUYIT 235	Slammers/Screaming Abdabs/Ape Hour (12", p/s)	7
86	Polydor KURTP 1	America/High And Mighty (shaped picture disc)	6
87	Polydor KURTG 2	The Land Of Ring Dang Doo/Zulu Beat//Horatio/Gather Your Limb (double pack)	4
86	Stiff SEEZ 62	BIG COCK (LP, red vinyl)	10
86	Stiff PSEEZ 62	BIG COCK (LP, picture disc)	10

KINGLY BAND
| 69 | Decca F 12926 | The Bitter And The Sweet/Standing At The Crossroads | 7 |

KING MIGUEL
| 73 | Bullet BU 524 | The Word Is Black/Town Talk | 10 |

KING OF THE SLUMS
| 86 | SLR SLR 001 | Spider Psychiatry/The Lodge/Losing Ground (p/s) | 6 |

MINT VALUE £

KING OLIVER
53   London AL 3510   PLAYS THE BLUES (10" LP) 20

KINGPINS (U.S.)
58   London HLU 8658   Ungaua (Parts 1 & 2) 15
58   London HLU 8658   Ungaua (Parts 1 & 2) (78). 25

KINGPINS (U.K.)
65   Oriole CB 1986   Two Right Feet/That's The Way It Should Be. 18

KINGPINS (U.K.)
67   Columbia DB 8146   Summer's Come And Gone/Another Tear Falls. 6

KING ROCK & WILLOWS
67   Caltone TONE 111   You Are The One/ALVA LEWIS: Return Home 30

KING ROCKY
68   Studio One SO 2045   The King Is Back/THREE TOPS: Vex Till Yuh Buss 18
(see also Leroy & Rocky, Clancy Eccles, Heptones)

KINGS IV
59   London HLT 8914   Some Like It Hot/The World Goes On 12
59   London HLT 8914   Some Like It Hot/The World Goes On (78). 15

KING'S HENCHMEN
59   Coral FEP 2025   ALAN FREED PRESENTS VOL. 1 (EP). 150

KING SCRATCH
70s   Ethnic ETH 16   Spiritual Whip/Version 6
70s   Ethnic ETH 30   Mash Finger/Version 6
(see also Lee Perry/Upsetters, Skatalites)

KING SISTERS
57   Capitol CL 14711   While The Lights Are Low/In Hamburg (When The Nights Are Long) 7
57   Capitol CL 14729   Imagination/You're My Thrill 7
57   Capitol CL 14777   Easy To Love/That Old Feeling 7
58   Capitol CL 14865   Deep Purple/Unbelievable 7
58   Capitol CL 14893   What's New?/The Thrill Was New. 6
58   Capitol CL 14934   Autumn In Pleasant Grove/The Guy In The Foreign Sports Car. 6
59   Capitol CL 15012   Keep Smiling (Keep Laughin', Be Happy)/The Maids Of Cadiz 6
59   Capitol CL 15069   Lovin' Up A Storm/What Would I Do Without You 6
59   Capitol CL 15096   Over The River (And Through The Woods)/Holiday Of Love (with Their Family) . . . 6
57   Capitol EAP1 919   IMAGINATION (EP) 8
57   Capitol T 808   ALOHA (LP) 15

CHARLES KINGSLEY CREATION
65   Columbia DB 7758   Summer Without Sun/Still In Love With You 60

EVELYN KINGSLEY & TOWERS
58   Capitol CL 14944   To Know Him Is To Love Him/FRANK PERRY & TOWERS: Let Me Be The One 8
(see also Towers)

KINGSMEN
58   London HLE 8735   Better Believe It/Week-End 25
58   London HLE 8735   Better Believe It/Week-End (78) 20
59   London HLE 8812   Conga Rock/The Cat Walk 30
59   London HLE 8812   Conga Rock/The Cat Walk (78) 30
59   London REE 1211   THE KINGSMEN (EP) 75
(see also Bill Haley & Comets)

KINGSMEN
63   Pye International 7N 25231   Louie Louie/Haunted Castle 10
64   Pye International 7N 25262   Little Latin Lupe Lu/David's Mood. 7
64   Pye International 7N 25273   Death Of An Angel/Searching For Love 7
65   Pye International 7N 25292   The Jolly Green Giant/Long Green 7
65   Pye International 7N 25311   The Climb/Waiting 6
65   Pye International 7N 25322   Annie Fanny/Something's Got A Hold On Me 6
66   Pye International 7N 25366   Little Latin Lupe Lu/Louie Louie 5
66   Pye International 7N 25370   Killer Joe/Little Green Thing 8
67   Pye International 7N 25406   Daytime Shadows/Trouble 7
71   Wand WN 14   Louie Louie/If I Needed Someone 5
64   Pye Intl. NEP 44023   THE KINGSMEN (EP) 25
65   Pye Intl. NEP 44040   MOJO WORKOUT (EP) 25
66   Pye Intl. NEP 44063   FEVER (EP) 20
63   Pye Intl. NPL 28050   THE KINGSMEN IN PERSON (LP, live). 20
64   Pye Intl. NPL 28054   THE KINGSMEN VOLUME II (LP) 20
65   Pye Intl. NPL 28068   THE KINGSMEN ON CAMPUS (LP) 20
66   Pye Intl. NPL 28085   GREATEST HITS (LP) 20
68   Marble Arch MAL 829   THE KINGSMEN'S GREATEST HITS (LP) 12
71   Wand WNS 6   UP AND AWAY (LP) 12

KINGS OF CARIBBEAN STEEL BAND
57   Melodisc MEL 1429   Rock 'N' Roll Susie/Down In Soho (78) 8

KING SPARROW
58   Melodisc MEL 1447   Leading Calypsonians/BILLY MOORE: Love Is Everywhere. 7
58   Melodisc MEL 1447   Leading Calypsonians/BILLY MOORE: Love Is Everywhere (78) 10
58   Melodisc MEL 1475   Familysize Cokes/Clara Honey Bunch 7
58   Melodisc MEL 1475   Familysize Cokes/Clara Honey Bunch (78) 10
59   Melodisc MEL 1491   Goaty/I Confess 7
59   Melodisc MEL 1491   Goaty/I Confess (78) 15
66   Island WI 285   Beggars Have No Choice (actually by Laurence Dillon & Wailers)/
    MARCIA GRIFFITHS: Funny 25
69   Trojan TRLS 8   SPARROW MEETS THE DRAGON (LP) 15
70s   Trojan TRLS 77   SPARROW POWER (LP). 12
(see also Mighty Sparrow, Sparrow)

KING SPORTY

70	Banana BA 321	Inspiration/Choice Of Music	10
70	Banana BA 322	Lover's Version (as Sporty & Wilson)/DUDLEY SIBLEY: Having A Party	10
70	Punch PH 44	For Our Desire/WINSTON WRIGHT: Version	12
71	Banana BA 323	D.J. Special/RICHARD & MAD: Creation Version	10
73	Green Door GD 4063	Yearful Of Sundays/Version	5

KING STITT
(see under 'S')

KINGSTON ALLSTARS

66	Dice CC 25	Happy Hunter/LITTLE NORMA: Ten Commandments Of Woman	10

KINGSTONIANS

67	Rio R 140	Winey Winey/I Don't Care	12
68	Coxsone CS 7066	Mother Miserable/I Make A Woman	18
68	Doctor Bird DB 1120	Put Down Your Fire/Girls Like Dirt	15
68	Doctor Bird DB 1123	Mummy And Daddy/False Witness	15
68	Doctor Bird DB 1126	Fun Galore/Crime Don't Pay	15
68	Trojan TR 627	Mix It Up/I'll Be Around	10
69	Big Shot BI 508	Sufferer/Kiss A Little Finger	8
69	Big Shot BI 526	Nice Nice/I'll Be Around	8
69	Crab CRAB 19	Hold Down/BARRY YORK: Who Will She Be	8
69	Bullet BU 409	I Am Just A Minstrel/Yesterday	5
69	Songbird SB 1011	The Clip/BRUCE ANTHONY: Little Miss Muffett	7
70	Songbird SB 1019	Singer Man/CRYSTALITES: Version	7
70	Songbird SB 1041	Rumble Rumble/CRYSTALITES: Version	7
70	Songbird SB 1045	Out There/CRYSTALITES: Out There Version II	10
70	Trojan TR 7708	I'll Need You Tomorrow/I'm Gonna Make It	5
70	Duke DU 88	You Can't Wine/RUPIE EDWARDS ALLSTARS: Bee Sting	8
72	Duke DU 126	Lion's Den/Version	5
70	Trojan TBL 113	SUFFERER (LP)	20

(see also Jack (Bernard) & Beanstalks, Gregory Isaacs)

KINGSTON JOE

64	Blue Beat BB 253	Time Is On My Friend (actually by Lloyd Barnes)/Wear And Tear (B-side actually by Lascelles Perkins)	15

KINGSTON PETE & BUSTER'S ALL STARS

67	Blue Beat BB 403	Little Boy Blue/I'm A Lover Try Me (actually by Larry Marshall)	35

(see also Larry Marshall)

KINGSTON TRIO

78s

59	Capitol CL 14985	Raspberries, Strawberries/Sally (78)	10
59	Capitol CL 15040	M.T.A./All My Sorrows (78)	15
59	Capitol CL 15073	San Miguel/A Worried Man (78)	20

SINGLES

58	Capitol CL 14918	Scarlet Ribbons/Three Jolly Coachmen	6
58	Capitol CL 14951	Tom Dooley/Ruby Red	6
59	Capitol CL 14985	Raspberries, Strawberries/Sally	6
59	Capitol CL 15002	The Tijuana Jail/Oh Cindy	6
59	Capitol CL 15040	M.T.A./All My Sorrows	6
59	Capitol CL 15073	San Miguel/A Worried Man	6
60	Capitol CL 15113	Green Grasses/Coo Coo U	6
60	Capitol CL 15199	El Matador/Home From The Hill	6
60	Capitol CL 15138	Bad Man's Blunder/The Escape Of Old John Webb	6
60	Capitol CL 15161	Everglades/This Mornin', This Evenin', So Soon	6
63	Capitol CL 15298	Reverend Mr. Black/One More Round	6

EPs

59	Capitol EAP1 1119	M.T.A. (EP)	12
59	Capitol EAP1 1136	TOM DOOLEY (EP)	10
59	Capitol EAP1 1182	RASPBERRIES STRAWBERRIES (EP)	10
60	Capitol EAP1 1258	HERE WE GO AGAIN (EP, also stereo SEP1 1258)	10/15
60	Capitol EAP2 1258	HERE WE GO AGAIN (EP, also stereo SEP2 1258)	10/15
60	Capitol EAP3 1258	HERE WE GO AGAIN (EP, also stereo SEP3 1258)	10/15
60	Capitol EAP1 1322	A WORRIED MAN (EP)	10
62	Capitol EAP4 2011	TIME TO THINK (EP)	10
63	Capitol EAP1 20460	GREENBACK DOLLAR (EP)	10
64	Capitol EAP1 20655	LEMON TREE (EP)	10
65	Brunswick OE 9511	THE KINGSTON TRIO (EP)	12

LPs

58	Capitol T 996	THE KINGSTON TRIO (LP)	18
59	Capitol T 1107	FROM THE HUNGRY I (LP)	15
59	Capitol T 1199	AT LARGE (LP)	15
60	Capitol (S)T 1258	HERE WE GO AGAIN (LP)	15
60	Capitol (S)T 1352	SOLD OUT (LP)	15
60	Capitol (S)T 1407	STRING ALONG (LP)	15
60	Capitol ST 1183	STEREO CONCERT (LP)	15
60	Capitol (S)T 1446	LAST MONTH OF THE YEAR (LP)	15
61	Capitol (S)T 1474	MAKE WAY! (LP)	15
61	Capitol (S)T 1564	GOIN' PLACES (LP)	15
61	Capitol (S)T 1612	ENCORES (LP)	15
61	Capitol (S)T 1642	CLOSE UP (LP)	15
62	Capitol (S)T 1658	COLLEGE CONCERT (LP)	15
62	Capitol (S)T 1705	BEST OF THE KINGSTON TRIO (LP)	12
62	Capitol (S)T 1747	SOMETHING SPECIAL (LP)	15

MINT VALUE £

63	Capitol (S)T 1809	NEW FRONTIER (LP)	15
63	Capitol (S)T 1871	NUMBER SIXTEEN (LP)	18
63	Capitol (S)T 1935	SUNNY SIDE (LP)	15
64	Capitol (S)T 2011	TIME TO THINK (LP)	15
64	Capitol (S)T 2081	BACK IN TOWN (LP)	15
64	Capitol (S)T 2180	FOLK ERA (LP)	15
64	Brunswick LAT 8597	NICK — BOB — JOHN (LP)	15
65	Brunswick LAT 8613	STAY AWHILE (LP)	15
65	Brunswick LAT/STA 8628	SOMETHIN' ELSE (LP, mono/stereo)	15/18
65	Capitol (S)T 2280	BEST OF THE KINGSTON TRIO VOL. 2 (LP)	12
66	Capitol (S)T 2614	BEST OF THE KINGSTON TRIO VOL. 3 (LP)	12
66	Brunswick LAT 8654	CHILDREN OF THE MORNING (LP)	15

(see also John Stewart)

KING TRUMAN

| 89 | Acid Jazz JAZID 9T | Like A Gun (Safe Sax Mix)/(Dub Version)/(Radio Edit) (12", p/s) | 12 |

(see also Style Council, Paul Weller)

KING TUBBY

| 76 | Klik KLP 9002 | SHALUM DUB (LP, with Aggrovators) | 15 |

KINKS

PYE SINGLES

64	Pye 7N 15611	Long Tall Sally/I Took My Baby Home	60
64	Pye 7N 15636	You Still Want Me/You Do Something To Me	90
64	Pye 7N 15673	You Really Got Me/It's All Right	7
64	Pye 7N 15714	All Day And All Of The Night/I Gotta Move	7
65	Pye 7N 15759	Tired Of Waiting For You/Come On Now	7
65	Pye 7N 15813	Everybody's Gonna Be Happy/Who'll Be The Next In Line	7
65	Pye 7N 15854	Set Me Free/I Need You	7
65	Pye 7N 15919	See My Friend/Never Met A Girl Like You Before	7
65	Pye 7N 15981	Till The End Of The Day/Where Have All The Good Times Gone	7
66	Pye 7N 17064	Dedicated Follower Of Fashion/Sittin' On My Sofa	7
66	Pye 7N 17125	Sunny Afternoon/I'm Not Like Everybody Else	7
66	Pye 7N 17222	Dead End Street/Big Black Smoke (some labels list "Deadend") each	7
67	Pye 7N 17321	Waterloo Sunset/Act Nice And Gentle	7
67	Pye 7N 17400	Autumn Almanac/Mr. Pleasant	7
68	Pye 7N 17468	Wonderboy/Polly	8
68	Pye 7N 17573	Days/She's Got Everything	7
69	Pye 7N 17724	Plastic Man/King Kong	8
69	Pye 7N 17776	Drivin'/Mindless Child Of Motherhood	15
69	Pye 7N 17812	Shangri-La/Last Of The Steam-Powered Trains (unissued, acetates only)	
69	Pye 7N 17812	Shangri-La/This Man He Weeps Tonight	15
69	Pye 7N 17865	Victoria/Mr Churchill Says	8
70	Pye 7N 17961	Lola/Berkeley Mews	7
70	Pye 7N 45016	Apeman/Rats	7
71	Pye PMM 100	You Really Got Me/Set Me Free/Wonder Boy/Long Tall Shorty (maxi-single, p/s)	7
71	Pye 7NX 8001	PERCY (33rpm 4-track maxi-single, p/s)	12
74	Pye 7N 45313	Where Have All The Good Times Gone/Lola (p/s)	20
83	PRT KPD 1	You Really Got Me/Misty Water (picture disc)	6
84	PRT KIS 003	All Day And All Of The Night/I Gotta Move (picture disc)	7

EXPORT SINGLES

65	Pye 7N 15981	Till The End Of The Day/Where Have All The Good Times Gone (export p/s)	100
66	Pye 7N 17100	Well Respected Man/Milk Cow Blues	75
67	Pye 7N 17314	Mr. Pleasant/This Is Where I Belong	50
67	Pye 7N 17405	Autumn Almanac/David Watts	50
71	Pye 7N 8001	God's Children/Moments (some in p/s)	40/20

RCA SINGLES

72	RCA RCA 2211	Supersonic Rocket Ship/You Don't Know My Name	8
72	RCA RCA 2299	Celluloid Heroes/Hot Potatoes	8
73	RCA RCA 2387	Sitting In The Midday Sun/One Of The Survivors	7
73	RCA RCA 2418	Sweet Lady Genevieve/Sitting In My Hotel	7
74	RCA RCA 5015	Mirror Of Love/Cricket	10
74	RCA RCA 5042	Mirror Of Love/He's Evil	9
74	RCA RCA 2478	Holiday Romance/Shepherds Of The Nation	7
75	RCA RCA 2546	Ducks On The Wall/Rush Hour Blues	7
75	RCA RCA 2567	You Can't Stop The Music/Have Another Drink	7
76	RCA RCM 1	No More Looking Back/Jack The Idiot Dunce/The Hard Way (p/s)	8

ARISTA SINGLES

77	Arista ARIST 153	Father Christmas/Prince Of The Punks (p/s)	8
78	Arista ARIST 189	A Rock'n'Roll Fantasy/Artificial Light	8
78	Arista ARIST 210	Black Messiah/Misfits (p/s)	7
79	Arista ARIST 300	Moving Pictures/In A Space	7
80	Arista ARIST 404	Lola (live)/Celluloid Heroes (live) (export only)	10
81	Arista ARIST 415	Better Things/Massive Reductions (p/s)	9
81	Arista ARIST 415/KINKS 1	Better Things/Massive Reductions//Lola (live)/David Watts (live) (double pack, gatefold p/s)	7
81	Arista ARIPD 426	Predictable/Back To Front (picture disc)	5
83	Arista ARIST 524	Don't Forget To Dance/Bernadette (p/s)	
83	Arista ARIST 524	Don't Forget To Dance/Bernadette//Predictable/Back To Front (shrinkwrapped with free picture disc)	12

OTHER SINGLES

84	Music Week	How Are You (freebie with *Music Week* magazine)	7
87	London LONX 132	Lost And Found/Killing Time (p/s, shrinkwrapped with bonus 7" "The Official Ray Davies Interview"/"Extracts From The LP 'Think Visual' ")	10
88	London LON 165	The Road (7" Edit)/Art Lover (p/s)	6
89	London LONCD 239	Down All The Days (Til 1992)/You Really Got Me (live)/Entertainment (CD)	12

KINKS

90	London LONCD 250	How Do I Get Close/War Is Over (CD, card sleeve)	12
91	Columbia COL 657593-2	Did Ya/Gotta Move (live)/New World/Days (1991) (CD)	12
94	Konk Grapevine KNKD 2	Waterloo Sunset 94/You Really Got Me (live)/Elevator Man/ On The Outside (CD)	7

EPs

64	Pye NEP 24200	KINKSIZE SESSION (EP)	25
64	Pye NEP 24203	KINKSIZE HITS (EP)	25
64	Pye NEP 5039	THE KINKS (EP, unreleased in U.K., Swedish only)	
65	Pye NEP 24221	KWYET KINKS (EP)	30
66	Pye NEP 24258	DEDICATED KINKS (EP)	60
68	Pye NEP 24296	THE KINKS (EP)	200
75	Pye AMEP 1001	THE KINKS (EP, 'Yesteryear' export issue, red or blue vinyl)	20

PYE LPs

64	Pye NPL 18096	THE KINKS (LP, mono)	35
64	Pye NSPL 83021	THE KINKS (LP, stereo, export only)	135
60s	Pye NSPL 15096	THE KINKS (LP, stereo, export only, reissue)	150
65	Pye NPL 18112	KINDA KINKS (LP)	35
65	Pye NPL 18131	THE KINK KONTROVERSY (LP)	30
65	Pye NSPL 18131	THE KINK KONTROVERSY (LP, reprocessed stereo with stickered catalogue number, export only)	175
66	Pye NPL 18149	FACE TO FACE (LP, mono)	30
66	Pye NSPL 18149	FACE TO FACE (LP, stereo, stickered sleeve)	60
66	Pye ZCP 18149	FACE TO FACE (cassette, original issue)	12
67	Golden Guinea GGL 0357	THE KINKS (LP, reissue, also stereo GSGL 10357)	12/15
67	Pye N(S)PL 18191	LIVE AT KELVIN HALL (LP, mono/stereo)	40/70
67	Pye N(S)PL 18193	SOMETHING ELSE BY THE KINKS (LP, mono/stereo)	100/45

(The above Pye LPs were originally issued with laminated flipback sleeves, pink labels & light blue labels)

68	Pye N(S)PL 18233	THE KINKS ARE THE VILLAGE GREEN PRESERVATION SOCIETY (LP, unissued, 12-track version, 2 test pressings only)	600+
68	Pye N(S)PL 18233	THE KINKS ARE THE VILLAGE GREEN PRESERVATION SOCIETY (LP, 15-track version, mono/stereo)	70/35
69	Pye N(S)PL 18317	ARTHUR (LP, mono/stereo)	45/20
70	Pye NPL 18326	THE KINKS (2-LP, gatefold sleeve)	18
70	Pye NSPL 18359	THE KINKS PT 1 — LOLA VS POWERMAN & THE MONEY-GO-ROUND (LP, gatefold sleeve)	18
71	Pye NSPL 18365	SOUNDTRACK FROM THE FILM 'PERCY' (LP, soundtrack)	20
73	Pye 11PP 100	ALL THE GOOD TIMES (4-LP, box set)	50
77	Pye FILD 001	THE KINKS FILE (2-LP, flip-top sleeve)	15
83	PRT KINK 1	GREATEST HITS (LP, with bonus 10" EP of unreleased material)	30

OTHER LPs

71	RCA SF 8243	MUSWELL HILLBILLIES (LP, gatefold sleeve)	18
72	RCA DPS 2035	EVERYBODY'S IN SHOWBIZ, EVERYBODY'S A STAR (2-LP, gatefold sleeve)	18
73	RCA SF 8392	PRESERVATION ACT 1 (LP)	18
74	RCA LPL2 5040	PRESERVATION ACT 2 (2-LP, gatefold sleeve)	22
75	RCA SF 8411	SOAP OPERA (LP)	15
75	RCA RS 1028	SCHOOLBOYS IN DISGRACE (LP)	15
76	RCA RS 1059	CELLULOID HEROES (LP)	15
93	Sony 472489-1	PHOBIA (LP, omits 2 tracks from CD)	50
94	Konk Grapevine KNK LP 1	TO THE BONE (LP)	15

PROMOS

98	Essential KINKS 1	GOD SAVE THE KINKS (CD, reissue sampler, gatefold white card sleeve)	20
98	Essential KINKS 2	GOD SAVE THE KINKS (CD, reissue sampler, brown card sleeve)	15
98	Essential KINKS 3	GOD SAVE THE KINKS (CD, reissue sampler, blue card sleeve)	15

(see also Dave Davies, Ray Davies, Maple Oak, Leapy Lee, Phoenix)

MINT VALUE £

DAVID KINNAIRD
60	Top Rank JAR 385	Mairi's Wedding/Northern Lights Of Aberdeen	5
60	Top Rank JAR 414	The Whistling Boy/Buttered Bannders	5

TONY KINSEY (QUARTET)
55	Decca F 10548	She's Funny That Way/Fascinatin' Rhythm	20
55	Decca F 10606	Close Your Eyes/Pierrot	10
55	Decca F 10648	Hey! There/Ballet	25
56	Decca F 10708	Stompin' At The Savoy/China Boy (with Dill Jones)	5
56	Decca F 10709	Moonglow/One O'Clock Jump	5
56	Decca FJ 10725	Starboard Bow/Body And Soul	5
56	Decca FJ 10760	Lullaby Of The Leaves/Isolation	12
56	Decca FJ 10773	In A Ditch/A Smooth One	5
57	Decca FJ 10851	Mean To Me/Supper Party	12
57	Decca F 10952	The Midgets/Blue Eyes	5
57	Decca FJ 10952	The Midgets/Blue Eyes (78)	8
62	Ember JBS 707	Girl In Blue/Weber The Great	20
56	Decca DFE 6282	PRESENTING THE TONY KINSEY QUARTET NO. 1 (EP)	40
56	Decca DFE 6285	PRESENTING THE TONY KINSEY QUARTET NO. 2 (EP)	40
58	Decca DFE 6461	MY FAIR LADY (EP)	15
59	Parlophone SGE 2004	RED BIRD — JAZZ AND POETRY (EP, stereo)	10
59	Parlophone SGE 2008	FOURSOME (EP, stereo)	10
57	Decca LK 4186	INTRODUCING THE QUINTET (LP)	90
57	Decca LK 4207	JAZZ AT THE FLAMINGO (LP)	45
58	Decca LK 4274	TIME GENTLEMEN PLEASE (LP)	90
61	Ember EMB 3337	AN EVENING WITH ... (LP)	200
63	Decca LK 4534	HOW TO SUCCEED (LP)	35

TONY KINSEY TRIO & JOE HARRIOTT
54	Esquire 10-382	How Deep Is The Ocean/Last Resort (78)	8
54	Esquire 10-392	Get Happy/Best Behavior (78)	8
54	Esquire 10-402	Raymond/Can't We Be Friends (78)	8
54	Esquire 10-412	Nice Work If You Can Get It/Jump For Me (78)	8
54	Esquire EP 36	TONY KINSEY TRIO & JOE HARRIOTT (EP)	25
54	Esquire EP 52	TONY KINSEY TRIO & JOE HARRIOTT (EP)	25
54	Esquire EP 82	TONY KINSEY TRIO & JOE HARRIOTT (EP)	25

(see also Joe Harriott)

TOMMY KINSMAN & HIS ORCHESTRA
62	Fontana 267 250 TF	Madison Time/Madison A Saint Tropez	4

KINSMEN
68	Decca F 22724	Glasshouse Green, Splinter Red/It's Started To Rain Again	12
68	Decca F 22777	It's Good To See You/Always The Loser	8

(see also Four Kinsmen)

KIPPINGTON LODGE
67	Parlophone R 5645	Shy Boy/Lady On A Bicycle	18
68	Parlophone R 5677	Rumours/And She Cried	25
68	Parlophone R 5717	Tell Me A Story/Understand A Woman	25
68	Parlophone R 5750	Tomorrow Today/Turn Out The Light	25
69	Parlophone R 5776	In My Life/I Can See Her Face	25
78	EMI NUT 2894	KIPPINGTON LODGE (EP)	7

(see also Brinsley Schwartz, Nick Lowe)

KIRBY
76	Anchor ANC 1031	Love Letters/Flasher	12
78	Hot Wax WAX 1/ANCHO 1	Bottom Line/That's Some Dream	10
78	Hot Wax HW 2	COMPOSITION (LP)	70

(see also Curved Air, Stretch)

KATHY KIRBY
60	Pye 7N 15313	Love Can Be/Crush Me	18
61	Pye 7N 15342	Danny/Now You're Crying	15
62	Decca F 11506	Big Man/Slowly	6
63	Decca F 11682	Dance On/Playboy	5
63	Decca F 11759	Secret Love/You Have To Want To Touch Him	5
64	Decca F 11832	Let Me Go, Lover!/The Sweetest Sounds	5
64	Decca F 11892	You're The One/Love Me Baby	5
64	Decca F 11992	Don't Walk Away/No Regrets	5
65	Decca F 12087	I Belong/I'll Try Not To Cry	6
65	Decca F 12177	The Way Of Love/Oh Darling, How I Miss You	6
65	Decca F 12280	Where In The World?/That Wonderful Feeling Of Love	6
66	Decca F 12338	Spanish Flea/Till The End Of Time	6
66	Decca F 12432	The Adam Adamant Theme/Will I Never Learn?	25
67	Columbia DB 8139	No One's Gonna Hurt You Anymore/My Yiddishe Momme	7
67	Columbia DB 8192	In All The World/Time	7
67	Columbia DB 8302	Turn Around/Golden Days	7
68	Columbia DB 8400	I Almost Called Your Name/Let The Music Start	8
68	Columbia DB 8521	Come Back Here With My Heart/Antonio	8
69	Columbia DB 8559	I'll Catch The Sun/Please Help Me I'm Falling	8
69	Columbia DB 8634	Is That All There Is?/Knowing When To Leave	8
70	Columbia DB 8682	Wheel Of Fortune/Lucky	8
70	Columbia DB 8721	My Way/Little Green Apples	8
71	Columbia DB 8795	So Here I Go/Yes — I've Got (A-side titled "Here I Go Again" on demos)	8
71	Decca F 13228	Bill/Can't Help Lovin' Dat Man	8
72	Columbia DB 8910	Do You Really Have A Heart/Dream On, Dreamer	8

MINT VALUE £

73	Columbia DB 8965	Little Song For You/Here, There And Everywhere	8
73	Orange OAS 216	Singer With The Band/Hello Morning	40
76	President PT 455	My Prayer/Nobody Loves Me Like You Do	6
63	Decca DFE 8547	KATHY KIRBY (EP)	12
65	Decca DFE 8596	KATHY KIRBY VOL. 2 (EP)	12
65	Decca DFE 8611	A SONG FOR EUROPE (EP)	15
65	Decca LK 4575	16 HITS FROM STARS AND GARTERS (LP)	18
67	Decca LK 4746	MAKE SOMEONE HAPPY (LP)	18
68	Ace Of Clubs ACL 1235	THE BEST OF KATHY KIRBY (LP)	15
68	Columbia S(C)X 6259	MY THANKS TO YOU (LP)	100
70	Decca PA/SPA 84	THE WORLD OF KATHY KIRBY (LP)	12

LARRY KIRBY & ENCORES

| 59 | Top Rank JAR 143 | My Baby Don't Love Me/My Rose Of Kentucky | 6 |
| 59 | Top Rank JAR 143 | My Baby Don't Love Me/My Rose Of Kentucky (78) | 15 |

PAT KIRBY

56	Brunswick 05560	Happiness Is A Thing Called Joe/Don't Tell Me Not To	6
56	Brunswick 05575	What A Heavenly Night For Love/Greensleeves	6
57	Brunswick 05697	Tammy/Don't Keep Silent	5
58	Brunswick 05731	Sayonara/Please Be Gentle With Me	5

BASIL KIRCHIN (BAND)

57	Parlophone R 4344	White Silver Sands/Waiting For The Robert E. Lee	5
58	Parlophone R 4511	Cha Cha Bells/Oh Dear What Can The Cha Cha Be (with Rock-A-Cha Cha Band)	5
58	Parlophone R 4511	Cha Cha Bells/Oh Dear What Can The Cha Cha Be (with Rock-A-Cha Cha Band) (78)	7
59	Parlophone R 4527	Rock-A-Conga/Skin Tight (as Basil Kirchin Band)	6
59	Parlophone R 4527	Rock-A-Conga/Skin Tight (as Basil Kirchin Band) (78)	8
71	Columbia SCX 6463	A WORLD WITHIN WORLDS (LP)	200

(see also Shani Wallis)

(IVOR & BASIL) KIRCHIN BAND

54	Parlophone MSP 6144	Mambo Macoco/Tangerine (as Kirchin Band)	7
55	Decca F 10434	Minor Mambo/Mother Goose Jumps (as Kirchin Band)	12
55	Parlophone R 4010	Mambo Rock/Tweedlee-Dee (as Kirchin Band) (78)	8
56	Parlophone R 4140	Rock-A-Beatin' Boogie/Stone Age Mambo (as Ivor & Basil Kirchin Band) (78)	8
56	Parlophone R 4222	The Roller/St. Louis Blues (as Ivor & Basil Kirchin)	6
56	Parlophone R 4237	Rockin' & Rollin' Thru The Darktown Strutters' Ball/Ambush	12
56	Parlophone R 4237	Rockin' & Rollin' Thru The Darktown Strutters' Ball/Ambush (78)	8
57	Parlophone R 4266	"Rock Around The World Medley" (with Shani Wallis)	10
57	Parlophone R 4266	"Rock Around The World Medley" (with Shani Wallis) (78)	10
57	Parlophone R 4284	Calypso!!/Jungle Fire Dance (as Ivor & Basil Kirchin with Wendy Windows)	5
57	Parlophone R 4284	Calypso!!/Jungle Fire Dance (with Wendy Windows) (78)	10
57	Parlophone R 4302	The High Life/Blues And The Happy Times (with Toni Sharpe) (78)	8
57	Parlophone R 4335	Teenage World/So Rare (as Kirchin Band & Bandits)	6
57	Parlophone R 4335	Teenage World/So Rare (as Kirchin Band & Bandits) (78)	12
55	Parlophone GEP 8531	KIRCHIN BANDBOX (EP)	8
56	Parlophone GEP 8569	THE IVOR AND BASIL KIRCHIN BAND (EP)	10

(see also Basil Kirchin, London Studio Group)

DEE KIRK

| 62 | Salvo SLO 1809 | I'll Cry/My Used To Be | 18 |

KEVIN KIRK

| 62 | Columbia DB 4909 | Sweet/Don't Waste Your Tears On Him | 6 |
| 62 | Columbia DB 4863 | Teenage Heartache/Midnight | 6 |

RICHARD H. KIRK

| 81 | Industrial IRC 34 | DISPOSABLE HALF TRUTHS (cassette) | 12 |
| 86 | Rough RTM 189 | UGLY SPIRIT (mini-LP) | 8 |

(see also Cabaret Voltaire, Peter Hope & Richard H. Kirk)

(RAHSAAN) ROLAND KIRK

64	Mercury 10015 MCE	THE KIRK QUARTET MEETS THE BENNY GOLSON ORCHESTRA (EP)	8
65	Mercury 10016 MCE	ROLAND SPEAKS (EP, with Benny Golson Orchestra)	8
62	Esquire 32-164	KIRK'S WORK (LP, with Jack McDuff)	18
63	Mercury MMC 14126	WE FREE KINGS (LP)	18
64	Mercury MCL 20002	THE KIRK QUARTET MEETS THE BENNY GOLSON ORCHESTRA (LP)	18
64	Mercury MCL 20021	KIRK IN COPENHAGEN (LP)	18
65	Mercury MCL 20037	WE FREE KINGS (LP, reissue)	12
65	Mercury MCL 20045	DOMINO (LP)	18
65	Fontana FJL 114	HIP! (LP)	18
66	Mercury (S)LML 4005	I TALK WITH THE SPIRITS (LP)	15
66	Mercury (S)LML 4015	RIP, RIG AND PANIC (LP)	15
67	Mercury (S)LML 4019	SLIGHTLY LATIN (LP)	15
71	Atlantic 2400 110	RAHSAAN, RAHSAAN (LP, as Rahsaan Roland Kirk)	12
72	Atlantic K 40358	BLACKNUSS (LP)	12
73	Atlantic K 40457	MEETING OF THE TIMES (LP, with Al Hibbler)	12

KIRKBYS

| 66 | RCA RCA 1542 | It's A Crime/I've Never Been So Much In Love | 70 |

(see also 23rd Turnoff, Jimmy Campbell, Rockin' Horse, Merseybeats)

KEN KIRKHAM

| 56 | Columbia SCM 5244 | It's Almost Tomorrow/No Not Much | 6 |
| 58 | Columbia DB 4116 | Now And For Always/Cathy | 6 |

JOHN KIRKPATRICK (& SUE HARRIS)

72	Trailer LER 2033	JUMP AT THE SUN (LP, with Sue Harris)	15
76	Free Reed FRR 010	PLAIN CAPERS (LP, with booklet)	12

(see also Jon Raven)

JULIAN KIRSCH
(see under 'J')

DANNY KIRWAN

75	DJM DJS 396	Ram Jam City/Hot Summer's Day	5
76	DJM DJS 666	Misty River/Rolling Hills	5
76	DJM DJS 10709	Angel's Delight	5
77	DJM DJS 10783	Hot Summer's Day/Love Can Always Bring You Happiness	5
79	DJM DJS 10896	Only You/Caroline	5
75	DJM DJLPS 454	SECOND CHAPTER (LP)	12

(see also Fleetwood Mac, Tramp)

KISS

SINGLES

75	Casablanca CBX 503	Nothin' To Lose/Love Theme From Kiss	25
75	Casablanca CBX 510	Rock And Roll All Nite/Anything For My Baby	20
76	Casablanca CBX 516	Shout It Out Loud/Sweet Pain	12
76	Casablanca CBX 519	Beth/God Of Thunder	18
77	Casablanca CAN 102	Hard Luck Woman/Calling Dr Love/Beth (initially in p/s)	30/10
77	Casablanca CAN 110	Then She Kissed Me/Hooligan/Flaming Youth	15
77	Casablanca CANL 110	Then She Kissed Me/Hooligan/Flaming Youth (12", company sleeve, some stickered)	15/12
78	Casablanca CAN 117	Rocket Ride/Love Gun (live)	8
78	Casablanca CANL 117	Rocket Ride/Detroit Rock City (live)/Love Gun (live) (12", company sleeve)	12
78	Casablanca CAN 126	Rock And Roll All Nite/C'Mon And Love Me (initially in p/s)	25/8
79	Casablanca CAN 152	I Was Made For Lovin' You/Hard Times	8
79	Casablanca CANL 152	I Was Made For Lovin' You (extended)/Charisma (12", p/s)	18
80	Casablanca NB 1001	2000 Man/I Was Made For Lovin' You/Sure Know Something (p/s)	15
80	Casablanca NBL 1001	2000 Man/I Was Made For Lovin' You/Sure Know Something (12", co. sleeve)	12
80	Casablanca MER 19	Talk To Me/She's So European (p/s)	10
80	Casablanca KISS 1	What Makes The World Go 'Round/Naked City (p/s)	10
81	Casablanca KISS 2	A World Without Heroes/Mr Blackwell (p/s)	7
81	Casablanca KISSP 002	A World Without Heroes/Mr Blackwell (picture disc)	10
82	Casablanca KISS 3	Killer/I Love It Loud (pull-out tongue p/s)	12
82	Casablanca KISS 312	Killer/I Love It Loud/I Was Made For Lovin' You (12", p/s)	15
82	Casablanca KISS 4	Creatures Of The Night/Rock And Roll All Nite (live) (p/s, pic or silver label)	10/8
82	Casablanca KISS 412	Creatures Of The Night/War Machine/Rock And Roll All Nite (live) (12", p/s)	15
82	Casablanca KISSD 4	Creatures Of The Night/Rock And Roll All Nite (live) (12", double groove, autographs engraved on 1 side)	20
83	Vertigo KISS 5	Lick It Up/Not For The Innocent (p/s)	5
83	Vertigo KISSP 5	Lick It Up/Not For The Innocent (poster p/s)	12
83	Vertigo KPIC 5	Lick It Up/Not For The Innocent (tank-shaped picture disc)	25
83	Vertigo KISS 512	Lick It Up/Not For The Innocent/I Still Love You (12", p/s)	8
84	Vertigo VER 12	Heaven's On Fire/Lonely Is The Hunter (p/s)	5
84	Vertigo VERX 12	Heaven's On Fire/Lonely Is The Hunter/All Hell's Breakin' Loose (12", p/s with poster)	10/8
85	Vertigo KISS 6	Tears Are Falling/Heaven's On Fire (live) (p/s)	5
87	Vertigo KISSP 7	Crazy Crazy Nights/No No No (poster p/s)	7
87	Vertigo KISSP 712	Crazy Crazy Nights/No No No/Heaven's On Fire/Tears Are Falling (12", picture disc)	8
87	Vertigo KISS 8	Reason To Live/Thief In The Night (p/s, with patch)	7
87	Vertigo KISSP 812	Reason To Live/Thief In The Night/Who Wants To Be Lonely/Secretly Cruel (12", picture disc)	8
87	Vertigo KISCD 8	Reason To Live/Thief In The Night/Tears Are Falling/Crazy Crazy Nights (CD, card sleeve)	8
87	Vertigo KISSP 9	Turn On The Night/Hell Or High Water (poster p/s)	5
87	Vertigo KISSP 912	Turn On The Night/Hell Or High Water/King Of The Mountain/Any Way You Slice It (12", picture disc)	8
87	Vertigo KISCD 9	Turn On The Night/Hell Or High Water/Heaven's On Fire/I Love It Loud (CD, card sleeve)	8
88	Vertigo 080 232-2	Crazy Crazy Nights/No, No, No/When Your Walls Come Down/Thief In The Night (CD Video)	15
88	Mercury 080 100-1	EXPOSED (12" CD Video)	25
89	Mercury 080 044-2	Lick It Up/Dance All Over Your Face/Gimme More/Fits Like A Glove (CD Video)	15
89	Vertigo 080 059-2	Tears Are Falling/Anyway You Slice It/Who Want To Be Lonely/Secretly Cruel (CD Video)	15
89	Vertigo KISP 1010	Hide Your Heart/Lick It Up/Heaven's On Fire (10", picture disc)	8
89	Vertigo KISCD 10	Hide Your Heart/Betrayed/Boomerang (CD)	8
90	Vertigo KISSP 11	Forever (Remix)/The Street Giveth And The Street Taketh Away (p/s, w/patch)	4
90	Vertigo KISXG 11	Forever (Remix)/The Street Giveth And The Street Taketh Away/Deuce (Demo)/Strutter (Demo) (12", gatefold p/s)	8
90	Vertigo KISCD 11	Forever (Remix)/Creatures Of The Night/Lick It Up/Heaven's On Fire (CD)	8
92	Mercury KISS 1212	Unholy/Partners In Crime/Deuce (Demo)/Strutter (Demo) (12", picture sleeve, white vinyl)	8
92	Mercury KISCD 12	Unholy/God Gave Rock'N'Roll II You Too/Deuce (Demo)/Strutter (Demo) (CD, digipak, Part 1 of 2-part pack [Part 2 unreleased])	8
90s	East West SAM 886	God Gave Rock'n'Roll To You (LP Version)/(Edit Version) (12", no p/s, promo only)	12

ALBUMS

75	Casablanca CBC 4003	KISS (LP, blue 'Bogart' label)	20
75	Casablanca CBC 4004	DRESSED TO KILL (LP, blue 'Bogart' label, embossed sleeve)	20
76	Casablanca CBC 4008	DESTROYER (LP, blue 'Bogart' label with inner sleeve)	20
76	Casablanca CBC 4011/2	ALIVE! (2-LP, blue 'Bogart' label, gatefold sleeve with insert, sleeve also lists CBSP 401)	20
77	Casablanca CALH 2001	ROCK AND ROLL OVER (LP, 'lovegun' label, red vinyl)	40
77	Casablanca CAL 2006	KISS (LP, reissue, 'lovegun' label, red vinyl)	40
77	Casablanca CAL 2007	HOTTER THAN HELL (LP, 'lovegun' label, red vinyl)	40
77	Casablanca CAL 2008	DRESSED TO KILL (LP, reissue, 'lovegun' label, red vinyl)	40
77	Casablanca CAL 2009	DESTROYER (LP, reissue, different sleeve, 'lovegun' label, red vinyl)	40
77	Casablanca CALD 5001	ALIVE! (2-LP, reissue, 'lovegun' label, red vinyl)	50
77	Casablanca CALH 2017	LOVE GUN (LP, 'lovegun' label, with picture inner sleeve)	12
77	Casablanca CALH 2017	LOVE GUN (LP, 'lovegun' label, red vinyl with picture inner sleeve)	40
77	Casablanca CALD 5004	KISS ALIVE II (2-LP, 'lovegun' label, with colour booklet & transfer sheet)	25
77	Casablanca CALD 5004	KISS ALIVE II (2-LP, 'lovegun' label, red vinyl with colour booklet)	50
78	Casablanca CALD 5005	DOUBLE PLATINUM (2-LP, 'lovegun' label, silver foil embossed sleeve & insert; sleeve & insert pressed in U.S. with U.K. cat. no. sticker)	18
79	Casablanca CALH 2051	DYNASTY (LP, 'lovegun' label, black vinyl, colour inner sleeve & poster)	12
80	Mercury 6302 032	UNMASKED (LP, with poster)	12
81	Casablanca 6302 163	(MUSIC FROM) THE ELDER (LP, single sleeve)	12
82	Casa. CANL 4/6302 219	CREATURES OF THE NIGHT (LP, 'make-up' sleeve)	12
87	Vertigo 832 903-1	CRAZY NIGHTS (LP, picture disc in stickered PVC wallet)	12

(see also Gene Simmons, Ace Frehley, Peter Criss, Paul Stanley)

KISSING SPELL
93	Essex DELUJO 1001LP	LOS PAJAROS (LP, reissue of Chilean LP, 500 only)	12

KISSING THE PINK
81	Martyrwell Music MART 271	Don't Hide In The Shadows/Hand Held Cameras (p/s)	6
83	Magnet KTPP 4	Love Lasts Forever/Underage (picture disc)	5
83	Magnet KTP 36/KTP 0	Last Film/Shine//Water In My Eye (Instrumental)/Garden Parties (double pack)	5

KATIE KISSOON
69	Columbia DB 8525	Don't Let It Rain/Will I Never See The Sun	5

(see also Peanut, Marionettes, Rag Dolls [U.K.])

MAC KISSOON
60s	Boulevard (no cat. no.)	Wear It On Your Face/In A Dream	8
69	Youngblood YB 1005	Wear It On Your Face/In A Dream (reissue)	5

(see also Marionettes, Rag Dolls [U.K.])

KITCHENS OF DISTINCTION
87	Gold Rush GRR 3	Escape/The Last Gasp Death Shuffle (p/s)	7

KIT KATS
66	London HLW 10075	That's The Way/Won't Find Better Than Me	6

EARTHA KITT
53	HMV JO 387	C'est Si Bon (with Henri René)/African Lullaby (78, export issue)	10
53	HMV B 10584	I Want To Be Evil/Annie Doesn't Live Here Any More (78)	7
54	HMV 7M 191	Under The Bridges Of Paris/Lovin' Spree	16
54	HMV 7M 198	Somebody Bad Stole De Wedding Bell/Sandy's Tune	12
54	HMV 7M 234	Santa Baby/Let's Do It (Let's Fall In Love)	12
54	HMV B 10728	Santa Baby/Let's Do It (Let's Fall In Love) (78)	8
54	HMV 7M 246	Easy Does It/Mink Shmink	12
55	HMV B 10892	Sweet And Gentle/Freddy (78, with Perez Prado)	8
55	HMV 7M 282	Monotonous/African Lullaby	12
55	HMV 7M 288	C'est Si Bon (with Henri René)/Senor	12
56	HMV 7M 422	Honolulu Rock-A-Roll-A/Je Cherche Un Homme (I Want A Man)	20
56	MGM SP 1153	Please Do It/Lady Loves	8
56	MGM SP 1178	Diamonds Are A Girl's Best Friend/Good Little Girls	10
57	HMV POP 309	Just An Old-Fashioned Girl/If I Can't Take It With Me When I Go	12
57	HMV POP 346	There Is No Cure For L'Amour/Hey Jacque	8
58	RCA RCA 1037	Take My Love/Proceed With Caution	6
58	RCA RCA 1087	Just An Old-Fashioned Girl/If I Can't Take It With Me When I Go (reissue)	8
58	RCA RCA 1093	I Want To Be Evil/Oh John!	8
58	RCA RCA 1093	I Want To Be Evil/Oh John! (78)	8
59	London HLR 8969	Love Is A Gamble/Sholem	8
59	London HLR 8969	Love Is A Gamble/Sholem (78)	20
60	RCA RCA 1180	There's No Cure For L'Amour/Let's Do It	6
63	London HL 7119	Shango/In The Evening (When The Sun Goes Down) (export issue)	15
70	Spark SRL 1039	Hurdy Gurdy Man/Catch The Wind	5
55	HMV 7EG 8079	EARTHA KITT (EP)	10
57	HMV 7EG 8258	EARTHA KITT (EP)	10
57	RCA SRC 7009	SAINT LOUIS BLUES (EP, stereo)	15
57	RCA SRC 7015	THAT BLUE EARTHA (EP, stereo)	15
60	London RE-R 1266	REVISITED (EP)	10
63	MGM MGM-EP 772	BAD BUT BEAUTIFUL NO. 1 (EP)	10
63	MGM MGM-EP 774	BAD BUT BEAUTIFUL NO. 2 (EP)	10
63	MGM MGM-EP 777	BAD BUT BEAUTIFUL NO. 3 (EP)	10
55	HMV DLP 1067	THAT BAD EARTHA (10" LP)	18
55	HMV DLP 1087	DOWN TO EARTHA (10" LP)	18
57	HMV CLP 1104	THURSDAY'S CHILD (LP)	15
58	RCA RD 27067	THAT BAD EARTHA (LP, reissue)	12
58	RCA RD 27076	ST. LOUIS BLUES (LP)	15
58	RCA RD 27084	DOWN TO EARTHA (LP, reissue)	12
59	RCA RD 27099	THURSDAY'S CHILD (LP, reissue)	12
60	London HA-R 2207	THE FABULOUS EARTHA KITT (LP, also stereo SAH-R 6058)	15/18
60	London HA-R 2296	EARTHA KITT REVISITED (LP, also stereo SAH-R 6107)	15/18
62	MGM MGM-C 878/CS 6050	BAD BUT BEAUTIFUL (LP, mono/stereo)	15/18

MINT VALUE £

KITTENS
64	Decca F 12036	Round About Way/Don't Stop Now	6

KLAN
67	Palette PG 9052	Fifi The Fly/Already Mine	6

KLAXONS
83	PRT 7P 290	Clap Clap Sound/Rippie Dance (p/s)	5

SUSIE KLEE
66	Polydor BM 56082	Mr Zero/Punch And Judy Girl	8

KLEEER
84	Atlantic 7801451	INTIMATE CONNECTION (LP)	12

KLEENEX
79	Rough Trade/Sunrise RT 9	Ain't You/Hedi's Head (poster p/s)	5
79	Rough Trade RT 014	You/U (p/s)	5

ALAN KLEIN
62	Oriole CB 1719	Striped Purple Shirt/You Gave Me The Blues	25
62	Oriole CB 1737	Three Coins In The Sewer/Danger Ahead	25
65	Parlophone R 5292	It Ain't Worth The Lonely Road Back/I've Cried So Many Tears	6
65	Parlophone R 5370	Age Of Corruption/I'm Counting On You	6
69	Page One POF 119	Honey Pie/You Turned A Nightmare Into A Dream	6
70	Decca F 13033	Dinner's In The Ice Box/Here I Am, There You Are	6
64	Decca LK 4621	WELL, AT LEAST IT'S BRITISH (LP)	15

(see also New Vaudeville Band)

HARRY KLEIN QUARTET
55	Jazz Today JTS 1502	I'm Coming Virginia/I Can't Get Started (78)	8
56	Jazz Today JTE 105	BRASH BARITONE (EP)	25
56	Nixa NJE 1009	NEW SOUND (EP)	20
56	Nixa NJE 1022	HARRY KLEIN QUARTET (EP)	20
57	Columbia SEG 7647	BARITONE SAX (EP)	15

(see also Jazz Five)

KLF
88	KLF Comms. KLF 002	Burn The Beat (II)/The Porpoise Song (p/s)	10
88	KLF Comms. KLF 002T	Burn The Bastards (LP Edit)/Burn The Beat (II) (12", p/s)	15
89	KLF Comms. KLF 004T	What Time Is Love? (Trance Mix)/What Time Is Love? (Mix 2) (12", 'Pure Trance 1', original issue with black/green p/s)	10
89	KLF Comms. KLF 004R	What Time Is Love? ('89 Primal Remix)/What Time Is Love? (Techno Slam)/What Time Is Love? (Trance Mix 1) (12", p/s)	40
89	KLF Comms. KLF 004M	What Time Is Love? (Monster Attack Mix) (12", unissued, 1-sided acetate only, 3 pressed!)	350
90	KLF Comms. KLF 004Y	What Time Is Love? (Moody Boys Vs The KLF/What Time Is Love? (Echo And The Bunnymen Mix)/What Time Is Love? (Virtual Reality Mix) (12", p/s)	8
90	KLF Comms. KLF 004P	What Time Is Love? (Live At Trancentral)/Wandafull Mix (12", w/l, 1,500 only)	10
90	KLF Comms. KLF 004X	What Time Is Love? (Live At Trancentral)/Techno Gate Mix (12", p/s, mispressing, B-side actually plays "Wandafull Mix", matrix no.: KLF 004X-B)	50
90	KLF Comms. KLF 004CD	What Time Is Love? (Radio)/(Live At Trancentral)/(Trance Mix 1) (CD, mispressing playing part of Knebworth '90 live CD)	15
90	KLF Comms. KLF 005R	3AM Eternal 'Single Edit'/Blue Danube Orbital Mix/Moody Boys Version/3PM Electro (12", original issue with stickered p/s)	12
91	KLF Comms. KLF 005S	3AM Eternal (Live At The S.S.L.) (Radio Freedom Edit) (white label, 500 only)	15
91	KLF Comms. KLF 005X	3AM Eternal (mixes) (12", white label, promo only)	15
91	KLF Comms. KLF 005Y	3AM Eternal (Moody Boys mixes) (12", white label, promo only)	15
92	KLF Comms. KLF 5 TOTP	3AM Eternal (Xmas Top Of The Pops Version) (1-sided, w/Extreme Noise Terror, mail-order only, some with insert & mailing envelope; beware of bootlegs!)	40/15
91	KLF Comms. KLF 005CD	3AM Eternal (Live At The S.S.L.)/(Guns Of Mu Mu)/(1989 Break For Love Mix) (CD)	7
89	KLF Comms. KLF 008R	Last Train To Trancentral (Remixes 1 & 2) (12", p/s, 'Pure Trance 5', 2,000 pressed, some warped)	75/10
91	KLF Comms. KLF 008X	Last Train To Trancentral (Live From The Lost Continent) (12", white label)	8
91	KLF Comms. KLF 008CD	Last Train To Trancentral (Live From The Lost Continent)/(The Iron Horse)/(The 1989 Pure Trance Original) (CD)	8
89	KLF PROMO 2	Kylie Said To Jason (Full Length)/Kylie Said Trance (12", promo & press sheet)	20
89	KLF Comms. KLF 010(S)	Kylie Said To Jason (Edit)/Kylie Said Trance (p/s)	6
89	KLF Comms. KLF 010T	Kylie Said To Jason (Full Length)/Kylie Said Trance (12", p/s)	10
89	KLF Comms. KLF 010P	Kylie Said To Jason (Full Length)/Kylie Said Trance (12", stickered p/s & pstr)	15
89	KLF Comms. KLF 010R	Kylie Said To Jason (Trance Kylie Express)/Kylie In A Trance/Kylie Said Harder (12" remix, p/s, export issue)	25
89	KLF Comms. KLF 010RR	Kylie In A Trance/Kylie Said Mu (12", p/s, export edition, 500 only, some shrinkwrapped with KLF 010R)	150/80
89	KLF Comms. KLF 010CD	Kylie Said To Jason (Full Length)/Madrugada Eterna/Kylie Said Trance (CD)	45
90	KLF Comms. KLF 011T	Madrugada Eterna (Club Mix)/Madrugada Eterna (Edit)/Madrugada Eterna (Ambient House Mix) (12", 20 only, beware of counterfeits!)	150/15
90	KLF Comms. ETERNA 1	Madrugada Eterna (Club Mix) (12", 1-sided, white label, 6 pressed, beware of counterfeits!)	200/15
91	KLF Comms. CHOC ICE 1	Justified And Ancient (All Bound For Mu Mu Land)/Justified And Ancient (Make Mine A '99') (12", white label promo)	15
91	KLF Comms. CHOC ICE 2	Justified And Ancient (Stand By The J.A.M.s)/Justified And Ancient (Let Them Eat Ice Cream) (12", white label promo)	15
91	KLF Comms. CHOC ICE 3	Justified And Ancient (Anti-Acapella Version) (12", 1-sided, w/l, 200 only)	60
91	KLF Comms. LP PROMO 1	Make It Rain/No More Tears (12", promo only, 1,729 pressed)	18
91	KLF Comms. 92PROMO 1	America: What Time Is Love/America No More (12", white label)	8
91	KLF Comms. 92PROMO 2	America: What Time Is January? (12", 1-sided, white label promo, 250 only)	80

91	KLF Comms. 3AM 1	3AM Eternal (feat. Extreme Noise Terror) (p/s, mail order only)	20
92	KLF Comms. 92PROMO 3	What Time Is Love (Acid Mix) (12", 1-sided, w/l promo, perhaps 20 only)	200
92	KLF Comms. USA 4X/	Justified And Ancient/America: What Time Is Love? (12",	
	CHOC ICE 2	'longboat' picture disc, export edition, 4,000 only)	45
92	KLF Comms. PUB 1	Justified And Ancient/America: What Time Is Love? (jukebox ed., 5,000 only)	10
97	KLF Comms.	Fuck The Millennium (4-track CD, in white carrier bag	
		"Fuck The Millennium" kit, with T-shirt, window sticker, certificate)	50
89	KLF Comms. JAMS LP 4	THE WHAT TIME IS LOVE STORY (LP)	40
89	KLF Comms. JAMS CD 4	THE WHAT TIME IS LOVE STORY (CD)	60
89	KLF Comms. JAMS LP 5	CHILL OUT (LP)	40
89	KLF Comms. JAMS CD 5	CHILL OUT (CD)	30
89	KLF Comms. JAMS LP 6	(TUNES FROM) THE WHITE ROOM (LP, 9-track white label, unreleased,	
		promo only, beware of counterfeits!)	50+
89	KLF Comms. JAMS MC 6	(TUNES FROM) THE WHITE ROOM (cassette, 10-track promo,	
		beware of counterfeits!)	50

(see also J.A.M.s, Timelords, Disco 2000, Brilliant, Bill Drummond, Space, Orb)

TONY KLINGER & MICHAEL LYONS
| 72 | Deram SML 1095 | EXTREEMS (LP, soundtrack) | 25 |

PETER KLINT (QUINTET)
| 66 | Mercury MF 997 | Walkin' Proud/Shake | 12 |
| 68 | Atlantic 584 208 | Hey Diddle Diddle/Just Holding On (solo) | 5 |

ANNETTE KLOOGER
56	Decca F 10701	The Rock And Roll Waltz/Rock Around The Island (with Ted Heath Music)	12
56	Decca F 10733	The Magic Touch/We'll Love Again (with Four Jones Boys)	10
56	Decca F 10738	Why Do Fools Fall In Love?/Lovely One (with Four Jones Boys)	12
56	Decca F 10776	Mama, Teach Me To Dance/Mama, I Long For A Sweetheart	
		(with Edmundo Ros Orchestra)	7
57	Decca F 10844	The Wisdom Of A Fool/Tra La La	7

(see also Four Jones Boys, Edmundo Ros, Ted Heath Orchestra)

EARL KLUGH
| 77 | United Artists UP 36251 | I Heard It Through The Grapevine/Kiko | 4 |
| 81 | Blue Note BNXW 642 | Living Inside Your Love/Dance With Me | 4 |

KNACK (U.K.)
65	Decca F 12234	Who'll Be The Next In Line/She Ain't No Good	25
65	Decca F 12278	It's Love Baby (24 Hours A Day)/Time Time Time	25
66	Piccadilly 7N 35315	Did You Ever Have To Make Up Your Mind?/Red Hearts	8
66	Piccadilly 7N 35322	Stop! (Before You Get Me Going)/Younger Girl	8
66	Piccadilly 7N 35347	Save All My Love For Joey/Take Your Love	8
67	Piccadilly 7N 35367	(Man From The) Marriage Guidance And Advice Bureau/Dolly Catch Her Man	8

(see also Gun, Adrian Gurvitz, Sky)

KNACK (U.S.)
| 79 | Capitol E-ST 11948 | GET THE KNACK (LP, limited white cover) | 10 |

BERNIE KNEE QUARTETTE
| 55 | HMV 7M 306 | Chocolate Whiskey And Vanilla Gin/Scrape Off De Bark | 7 |

(see also Bernie Nee)

KNEES
| 74 | United Artists UP 35773 | Day Tripper/Slow Down | 20 |

(see also Brinsley Schwarz)

KNICKERBOCKERS
66	London HLH 10013	Lies/The Coming Generation	12
66	London HLH 10035	One Track Mind/I Must Be Doing Something Right	12
66	London HLH 10061	High On Love/Stick With Me	12
66	London HLH 10093	Rumours, Gossip, Words Untrue/Love Is A Bird	12
67	London HLH 10102	Can You Help Me/Please Don't Love Him	12
73	Elektra K 12102	Lies/ELECTRIC PRUNES: I Had Too Much To Dream (Last Night)	5
66	London HA-H 8294	THE FABULOUS KNICKERBOCKERS (LP)	40

BAKER KNIGHT
| 66 | Reprise RS 20465 | Would You Believe It/Tomorrow's Good Time Girl | 8 |

CURTIS KNIGHT (& ZEUS)
69	RCA RCA 1888	Fancy Meeting You Here/Love In	8
70	RCA RCA 1950	Down In The Village/No Point Of View	6
74	Dawn DNS 1049	Devil Made Me Do It/Oh Rainbow	5
74	Dawn DNS 1065	People Places And Things/Mysterious Lady	5
74	Dawn DNLS 3060	ZEUS, THE SECOND COMING (LP)	15

(see also Jimi Hendrix, Blue Goose)

GLADYS KNIGHT (& PIPS)
SINGLES
64	Stateside SS 318	Giving Up/Maybe Maybe Baby	18
64	Stateside SS 352	Lovers Always Forgive/Another Love	18
65	Sue WI 394	Letter Full Of Tears/You Broke Your Promise	22
66	Tamla Motown TMG 576	Just Walk In My Shoes/Stepping Closer To Your Heart	40
67	Tamla Motown TMG 604	Take Me In Your Arms And Love Me/Do You Love Me Just A Little Honey	8
67	Tamla Motown TMG 619	Everybody Needs Love/Stepping Closer To Your Heart (demo-only B-side)	60
67	Tamla Motown TMG 619	Everybody Needs Love/Since I've Lost You	10
67	Tamla Motown TMG 629	I Heard It Through The Grapevine/It's Time To Go Now	12
68	Tamla Motown TMG 645	The End Of Our Road/Don't Let Her Take Your Love From Me	8
68	Tamla Motown TMG 660	It Should Have Been Me/You Don't Love Me No More	10
68	Tamla Motown TMG 674	I Wish It Would Rain/It's Summer	8
69	Tamla Motown TMG 714	The Nitty Gritty/Got Myself A Good Man	7

Gladys KNIGHT

70	Tamla Motown TMG 728	Didn't You Know (You'd Have To Cry Sometime)/Keep An Eye	6
70	Tamla Motown TMG 756	Friendship Train/You Need Love Like I Do (Don't You)	6
71	Tamla Motown TMG 765	If I Were Your Woman/The Tracks Of My Tears	6
72	Tamla Motown TMG 805	Make Me The Woman That You Go Home To/I Don't Want To Do Wrong	5
72	Tamla Motown TMG 813	Just Walk In My Shoes/I'm Losing You	5
73	Ember EMB S 326	Every Beat Of My Heart/Room In Your Heart	5
73	Tamla Motown TMG 844	The Look Of Love/You're My Everything	5
73	Tamla Motown TMG 864	Take Me In Your Arms And Love Me/No One Could Love You More	35
73	Buddah 2011 181	Midnight Train To Georgia/Window Raising Granny	5
74	Buddah BDS 401	On And On/The Making Of You	5
74	Contempo CS 2021	Why Don't You Leave Me/Maybe Baby	6
75	Tamla Motown TMG 945	You've Lost That Loving Feeling/This Child Needs A Father	5
76	Buddah BDS 441	Silent Night/Do You Hear What I Hear	5
76	DJM DJS 681	Queen Of Tears/Every Beat Of My Heart	5
89	MCA MCASP 1339	Licence To Kill/MICHAEL KAMEN: Pain (p/s with postcards & lyric sheet)	6
89	MCA MCAT 1339	Licence To Kill (Extended Version)/MICHAEL KAMEN: Pain (12", picture sleeve)	8
89	MCA DMCA 1339	Licence To Kill/MICHAEL KAMEN: Pain/Licence To Kill (Extended Version) (3" CD, card sleeve)	10

LPs

67	Music F. Pleasure MFP 1187	GLADYS KNIGHT AND THE PIPS (LP)	12
67	T. Motown (S)TML 11058	EVERYBODY NEEDS LOVE (LP)	25
68	Bell MBLL 103	TASTIEST HITS (LP)	20
68	T. Motown (S)TML 11080	FEELIN' BLUESY (LP)	25
69	T. Motown (S)TML 11100	SILK'N'SOUL (LP)	25
69	T. Motown (S)TML 11135	THE NITTY GRITTY (LP, mono/stereo)	18/15
70	Tamla Motown STML 11148	GREATEST HITS (LP, original with flipback sleeve)	15
71	Tamla Motown STML 11187	IF YOU WERE A WOMAN (LP)	12
75	Buddah BDLP 4038	2ND ANNIVERSARY (LP)	12
77	Buddah BDLP 5014	STILL TOGETHER (LP)	12
78	Buddah 11PP 602	COLLECTION (4-LP, box set)	30
79	Buddah BDLP 4056	MISS GLADYS KNIGHT (LP, solo)	12

(see also Pips, Dionne Warwick)

JASON KNIGHT

67	Pye 7N 17399	Our Love Is Getting Stronger/Standing In My Shoes	30
73	Pye 7N 45287	Our Love Is Getting Stronger/Standing In My Shoes (reissue)	4

JEAN KNIGHT

71	Stax 2025 049	Mr Big Stuff/Why Do I Keep Living These Memories	6
72	Stax 2025 103	Carry On/Do You Think You're Hot Stuff	5
73	Stax 2025 161	Do Me/Save The Last Kiss For Me	5
72	Stax 2362 022	MR. BIG STUFF (LP)	15

MARIE KNIGHT

53	Brunswick 05071	The Old Rugged Cross/Satisfied With Jesus (78)	8
53	Brunswick 05165	Does Jesus Care?/Shaded Green Pastures (78)	8
61	Fontana H 354	Nothing/Come Tomorrow	12
65	Stateside SS 419	Cry Me A River/Comes The Knight	12
60s	Soul CITY 125	You Lie So Well/That's No Way To Treat A Girl	8
85	Kent TOWN 102	That's No Way To Treat A Girl/JACK MONTGOMERY: Dearly Beloved	6
57	Brunswick OE 9283	GOSPEL SONGS VOL. 1 (EP, with Sam Price Trio)	12
64	Mercury 10001 MCE	THE STORM IS PASSING OVER (EP)	12
64	Mercury 10034 MCE	SONG OF THE GOSPEL (EP)	12
58	Mercury MPL 6546	SONGS OF THE GOSPEL (LP)	20

(see also Sister Rosetta Tharpe & Sister Marie Knight)

PETER KNIGHT ORCHESTRA/SINGERS

55	Parlophone MSP 6183	Twenty Minutes South (Medley) (both sides, as Peter Knight Singers)	8
62	Pye 7N 15472	Camel Train/Scarlett	5
67	Mercury SML 30023	SGT. PEPPER'S LONELY HEARTS CLUB BAND (LP)	12

PETER KNIGHT & KNIGHT RIDERS

61	Pye 7N 15388	Lucky Stars/Double Trouble	5
64	Pye 7N 15687	Wonderful Day Like Today/It Isn't Enough	6

ROBERT KNIGHT

62	London HLD 9496	Free Me/The Other Half Of Man	12
68	Monument MON 1008	Everlasting Love/Somebody's Baby	6
68	Monument MON 1016	Blessed Are The Lonely/It's Been Worth It All	5
68	Monument MON 1017	The Power Of Love/Love On A Mountain Top	6
68	Bell BLL 1029	Isn't It Lonely Together/We'd Better Stop	5
68	Monument LMO/SMO 5015	EVERLASTING LOVE (LP)	18
71	Monument MNT 65956	LOVE ON A MOUNTAIN TOP (LP)	15

SONNY KNIGHT

57	London HLD 8362	Confidential/Jail Bird (gold or silver label print)	300/150
57	London HLD 8362	Confidential/Jail Bird (78)	40
57	London HL 7016	Confidential/Jail Bird (export issue)	100
59	Vogue Pop V 9134	But Officer/Dear Wonderful God	150
59	Vogue Pop V 9134	But Officer/Dear Wonderful God (78)	90

TERRY KNIGHT & PACK

66	Cameo Parkway C 102	I (Who Have Nothing)/Numbers	60

TONY KNIGHT

64	Decca F 11989	Did You Ever Hear The Sound?/I Feel So Blue (as Tony Knight & Live Wires)	25
65	Decca F 12109	How Sweet/Surfer Street (as Tony Knight's Chessmen)	20

KNIGHT BROTHERS

| 65 | Chess CRS 8015 | Sinking Low/Temptation 'Bout To Get Me | 15 |
| 66 | Chess CRS 8046 | That'll Get It/She's A1 | 10 |

KNIGHTRIDER

| 87 | Omega KS 1299 | Shout Out Loud (no p/s) | 15 |

KNIGHTSBRIDGE STRINGS/BRASS CHORALE

59	Top Rank JAR 104	Io Sono Il Vento (For You My Lover)/Italian Blu	5
59	Top Rank JAR 104	Io Sono Il Vento (For You My Lover)/Italian Blu (78)	8
59	Top Rank JAR 170	Cry/The Windows Of Paris	10
59	Top Rank JAR 170	Cry/The Windows Of Paris (78)	8
59	Top Rank JAR 216	Wheel Of Fortune/Cow-Cow Boogie	10
59	Top Rank JAR 216	Wheel Of Fortune/Cow-Cow Boogie (78)	12
59	Top Rank JAR 220	Eton Boating Song/In A Shanty In Old Shanty Town	5
59	Top Rank JAR 220	Eton Boating Song/In A Shanty In Old Shanty Town (78)	10
60	Top Rank JAR 266	Ivy Will Cling/California, Here I Come	5
60	Top Rank JAR 272	Walkin' Shoes/Ring Ding	5
60	Top Rank JAR 295	Look Look Away/You Are Beautiful	5
60	Top Rank JAR 304	Misty/Tracey's Theme	5
60	Top Rank JAR 314	Two-Way Stretch/The Glad Hand	5
60	Top Rank JAR 364	The Executioner Theme/The Sioux March	5
60	Top Rank JAR 398	Make Mine Mink/Moonlight In Vermont	5
61	Top Rank JAR 532	The Singer Not The Song/Anacleto's Theme	5

KNIGHTS OF ROUND TABLE

| 68 | Pama PM 734 | Lament To Bobby Kennedy/If You Were My Girl | 6 |

K9's

| 79 | Dog Breath WOOF 1 | The K9 Hassle/Idi Amin/Sweeney Todd (numbered p/s, with insert; later reissued with different labels & insert, 500 only) | each 20 |

KNOCKER JUNGLE

| 70 | Ember EMB S 293 | I Don't Know Why/Reality (p/s) | 6 |
| 71 | Ember NR 5052 | KNOCKER JUNGLE (LP, gatefold sleeve) | 25 |

KNOCKOUTS

| 60 | Top Rank JAR 279 | Riot In Room 3C/Darling Lorraine | 20 |

DAVID KNOPFLER

83	Peach River BBPR 7	Soul Kissing/Come To Me (p/s)	8
83	Peach River BBPR 712	Soul Kissing/Come To Me/The Great Divide (12", p/s)	8
84	Fast Alley FAR 701	Madonna's Daughter/Hey Henry (p/s)	5

(see also Dire Straits)

MARK KNOPFLER

83	Vertigo DSTR 4	Going Home (Theme Of 'Local Hero')/Smooching (p/s)	5
83	Vertigo DSFM 4	Going Home (Theme Of 'Local Hero') (Cinema Version) (promo only)	12
83	Vertigo DSTR 412	Going Home (Theme Of 'Local Hero')/Smooching (12", p/s)	7
83	Vertigo DSTR 5	Themes From Local Hero: Wild Theme/Going Home (p/s)	5
84	Vertigo DSDJ 7	Joy (from 'Comfort And Joy') (unissued, 1-sided promo only, no p/s)	20
84	Vertigo DSTR 712	Joy (from 'Comfort And Joy')/Fistful Of Ice Cream (12", p/s)	25
84	Vertigo MARK ONE	Comfort And Joy (12", 1-sided promo, no p/s)	40
84	Vertigo DSTR 8	The Long Road (Theme From 'Cal')/Irish Boy (p/s)	5
84	Vertigo DSTR 812	The Long Road (Theme From 'Cal') (7.13)/Irish Boy (12", p/s)	7
86	Vertigo DSTR 14	Going Home/Wild Theme (reissue, p/s)	5
86	Vertigo DSTR 1412	Going Home/Wild Theme/Smooching (12", p/s)	7
88	Vertigo VERCD 37	Theme From 'The Princess Bride': Storybook Love (with Willy DeVille)/The Friends' Song (with Guy Fletcher)/Once Upon A Time ... Storybook Love (CD, card sleeve)	12
90	CBS 656377	Poor Boy Blues/There'll Be Some Changes Made (with Chet Atkins) (p/s)	5
90	CBS 656373	Poor Boy Blues/There'll Be Some Changes Made/So Soft Your Goodbye (CD, with Chet Atkins)	10

(see also Dire Straits, Randy Newman, Chet Atkins)

KNOPOV'S POLITICAL PACKAGE

| 80 | white label | Misadventure/You're In The Army Now | 6 |

(see also Mission)

KNOTT SISTERS

| 58 | London HLX 8713 | Undivided Attention/SHADES with KNOTT SISTERS: Sun Glasses | 35 |
| 58 | London HLX 8713 | Undivided Attention/SHADES with KNOTT SISTERS: Sun Glasses (78) | 15 |

BUDDY KNOX

57	Columbia DB 3914	Party Doll/My Baby's Gone (gold label print)	125
57	Columbia DB 3914	Party Doll/My Baby's Gone (78)	25
57	Columbia DB 3952	Rock Your Little Baby To Sleep/Don't Make Me Cry (as Lieutenant Buddy Knox, gold label print)	60
57	Columbia DB 3952	Rock Your Little Baby To Sleep/Don't Make Me Cry (as Lieutenant Buddy Knox) (78)	35
57	Columbia DB 4014	Hula Love/Devil Woman	30
57	Columbia DB 4014	Hula Love/Devil Woman (78)	30
58	Columbia DB 4077	Swingin' Daddy/Whenever I'm Lonely	30
58	Columbia DB 4077	Swingin' Daddy/Whenever I'm Lonely (78)	35
58	Columbia DB 4180	Somebody Touched Me/C'mon Baby	20
58	Columbia DB 4180	Somebody Touched Me/C'mon Baby (78)	40

MINT VALUE £

59	Columbia DB 4302	To Be With You/I Think I'm Gonna Kill Myself	20
61	London HLG 9268	Lovey Dovey/I Got You	15
61	London HLG 9331	Ling Ting Tong/The Kisses (They're All Mine)	12
61	London HLG 9472	Three-Eyed Man/All By Myself	12
62	Liberty LIB 55411	Chi-Hua-Hua/Open Your Loving Arms	10
62	Liberty LIB 55473	She's Gone/Now There's Only Me	10
63	Liberty LIB 55592	Shadaroom/Tomorrow Is Coming	8
64	Liberty LIB 55694	All Time Loser/Good Loving	8
69	United Artists UP 35019	God Knows I Love You/Night Runners	8
70	United Artists UP 35100	Party Doll/God Knows I Love You	5
57	Columbia SEG 7732	ROCK-A-BUDDY KNOX (EP)	100
62	Liberty LBY 1114	GOLDEN HITS (LP)	35
71	Sunset SLS 50206	ROCK REFLECTIONS (LP)	12

KNUCKLEHEAD
| 93 | Saucerman ART 01 | Red Eye, Dead Eye/Spirit Matter (p/s, hand-painted label, 150 copies only) | 15 |

KODIAKS
| 69 | Decca F 12942 | All Because You Wanna See Me Cry/Tell Me Rhonda | 8 |

(SPIDER) JOHN KOERNER
67	Elektra EKSN 45005	Won't You Give Me Some Love/Don't Stop	8
69	Elektra EKSN 45063	Friends And Lovers/Magazine Lady (with Willie Murphy)	8
65	Elektra EKL 290	SPIDER BLUES (LP)	25
68	Elek. EKL 4041/EKS 74041	RUNNING JUMPING STANDING STILL (LP, with Willie Murphy)	20
71	Elektra K 42026	RUNNING JUMPING STANDING STILL (LP reissue)	12

MOE KOFFMAN (QUARTET)
58	London HLJ 8549	Swingin' Shepherd Blues/Hambourg Bound	10
58	London HLJ 8549	Swingin' Shepherd Blues/Hambourg Bound (78)	8
58	London HLJ 8633	Little Pixie/Koko-Mamey	8
58	London HLJ 8633	Little Pixie/Koko-Mamey (78)	15
59	London HLJ 8813	Shepherd's Cha-Cha/The Great Healer (solo)	8
59	London HLJ 8813	Shepherd's Cha-Cha/The Great Healer (78, solo)	20
62	Palette PG 9036	Cool Ghoul/Sapphire	6
68	CBS 3544	Mighty Peculiar/Archie Buckle Up	6
58	London RE-J 1163	LITTLE PIXIE (EP)	15

KOKOMO, HIS PIANO & ORCHESTRA
| 61 | London HLU 9305 | Asia Minor/Roy's Tune | 5 |
| 62 | London HLU 9497 | Like Teen/Journey Home | 6 |

KOLETTES
| 64 | Pye International 7N 25278 | Who's That Guy?/Just How Much | 18 |
| 73 | Chess 6145 021 | Who's That Guy?/Just How Much (reissue) | 5 |

BONNIE KOLOC
72	London HLO 10377	Jazz Man/Got To Get What You Can	5
72	London HLO 10392	Burgundy Wine/We Are Ships	5
72	London SHO 8432	AFTER ALL THIS TIME (LP)	20
72	London SHO 8440	HOLD ON TO ME (LP)	15

JIMMIE KOMACK
54	Vogue Coral Q 2031	Cold Summer Blues/The Nic-Name Song	10
55	Vogue Coral Q 72061	Wabash 4-7473/An Old Beer Bottle	8
55	Vogue Coral Q 72087	Rock-A-Bye Your Baby With A Dixie Melody/This Is The Place	7

JOHN (T.) KONGOS
66	Piccadilly 7N 35341	I Love Mary/Goodtime Party Companion (as John T. Kongos)	6
69	Dawn DNS 1002	Flim Flam Pharisee/Blood	5
71	Fly BUG 8	He's Gonna Step On You Again/Sometimes It's Not Enough (purple or black label, p/s)	6
71	Fly BUG 14	Tokoloshe Man/Can Someone Please Direct Me Back To Earth	5
72	Cube BUG 22	Great White Lady/Shamarack	5
73	Cube BUG 32	Higher Than God's Hat/Would You Follow Me	5
69	Dawn DNLS 3002	CONFUSIONS ABOUT A GOLDFISH (LP)	18
72	Fly HIFLY 7	KONGOS (LP)	12

(see also Scrugg, Floribunda Rose)

KONRADS
| 65 | CBS 201812 | Baby It's Too Late Now/I'm Over You | 6 |

KONSTRUKTIVITS
| 80s | Third Mind TM 02 | PSYKO GENETIKA (LP) | 20 |
| 86 | Sterile SR 10 | GLENACAUL (LP) | 20 |

(see also Whitehouse)

KOOBAS
65	Pye 7N 17012	Take Me For A Little While/Somewhere In The Night	25
66	Pye 7N 17087	You'd Better Make Up Your Mind/A Place I Know	30
66	Columbia DB 7988	Sweet Music/Face	25
67	Columbia DB 8103	Sally/Champagne And Caviar	18
67	Columbia DB 8187	Gypsy Fred/City Girl	35
68	Columbia DB 8419	The First Cut Is The Deepest/Walking Out	35
69	Columbia S(C)X 6271	THE KOOBAS (LP)	450
88	Bam Caruso KIRI 047	BARRICADES (LP)	20

(see also Kubas, Van Der Graaf Generator, Gary & Stu, March Hare)

KOOGA
| 88 | Kooga KO 001 | Don't Break My Heart (p/s, private pressing) | 8 |

(see also Skin)

KOOL

67	CBS 203003	Look At Me, Look At Me/Room At The Top	5
69	CBS 2865	Step Out Of Your Mind/Funny (What A Fool A Man Can Be)	7
69	MCA MU 1085	Lovin'/Baby's Out Of Reach	5

KOOL & GANG

70	London HLZ 10308	Kool And The Gang/Raw Hamburgers	6
71	Mojo 2027 005	Funky Man/Kool And The Gang/Let The Music Take Your Mind	5
71	Mojo 2027 006	Love The Life You Live/The Penguin	5
72	Mojo 2027 009	Music Is The Message (Parts 1 & 2)	5
73	Polydor 2001 474	Funky Stuff/More Funky Stuff	5
74	Polydor 2001 500	Jungle Boogie/North, South, East, West	5
74	Polydor 2001 530	Hollywood Swinging/Dujii	5
74	Polydor 2001 541	Higher Plane/Wild Is Love	5
75	Polydor 2001 558	Rhyme Tyme People/Father, Father	5
75	Polydor 2001 566	Spirit Of The Boogie/Jungle Jazz	5
76	Polydor 2058 645	Love And Understanding/Sunshine And Love	5
77	Contempo CS 1001	Super Band/Open Sesame	5
77	Contempo 12 CS 1001	Super Band/Open Sesame (12")	8
81	De-Lite GANG 11	Jones Vs Jones/Summer Madness//	
		Funky Stuff/Hollywood Swinging (double pack)	5
81	De-Lite KOOL 11-12	Jones Vs Jones/Funky Stuff/Summer Madness (live)/Hollywood Swinging (12")	8
71	Mojo 2347 001	LIVE AT P.J.'S (LP)	50
71	Mojo 2347 002	THE BEST OF KOOL AND THE GANG (LP)	40
72	Mojo 2347 003	LIVE AT THE SEX MACHINE (LP)	22
73	Mojo 2347 004	MUSIC IS THE MESSAGE (LP)	25
74	Polydor 2310 299	WILD AND PEACEFUL (LP)	15
74	Polydor 2310 357	LIGHT OF WORLDS (LP)	12
75	Polydor 2310 416	SPIRIT OF THE BOOGIE (LP)	12
76	Polydor 2343 083	LIVE AT THE SEX MACHINE (LP, reissue)	12

AL KOOPER

65	Mercury MF 885	Parchman Farm/You're The Lovin' End (as Alan Kooper)	10
69	CBS 4011	You Never Know Who Your Friends Are/Soft Landing On The Moon	6
69	CBS 4160	Hey Western Union Man/I Stand Alone	8
71	CBS 5146	Brand New Lady/The Landlord (Love Theme)	5
71	CBS 7376	John The Baptist/Back On My Feet	5
72	CBS 8084	Monkey Time/Bended Knees (Please Don't Let Me Down)	6
69	CBS 63538	I STAND ALONE (LP, orange label)	15
69	CBS 63651	YOU NEVER KNOW WHO YOUR FRIENDS ARE (LP, orange label)	12
70	CBS 63797	KOOPER SESSION — WITH SHUGGIE OTIS (LP, orange label)	15
70	CBS 66252	EASY DOES IT (2-LP, orange label)	18
71	United Artists UAS 29120	THE LANDLORD (LP, soundtrack, with Staple Singers & Lorraine Ellison)	15
71	CBS 64340	NEW YORK CITY (YOU'RE A WOMAN) (LP, gatefold sleeve, orange label)	12
72	CBS 64208	A POSSIBLE PROJECTION OF THE FUTURE/CHILDHOOD'S END	
		(LP, orange label)	12
73	CBS 65193	NAKED SONGS (LP)	12

(see also Blues Project, Blood Sweat & Tears, Shuggie Otis)

AL KOOPER, MIKE BLOOMFIELD & STEPHEN STILLS

68	CBS 3770	Season Of The Witch/Albert's Shuffle	7
68	CBS 63396	SUPER SESSION (LP)	12
73	CBS CQ 30991	SUPER SESSION (LP, quadrophonic)	15

(see also Mike Bloomfield & Al Kooper, Stephen Stills)

KOPPYKATS

| 68 | Fontana SFT 13052/3 | BEATLES' BEST (2-LP) | 30 |

(see also Ian [Edward] & Zodiacs)

TAMARA KORAN WITH PERCEPTION

| 68 | Domain D 7 | Veils Of Mourning Lace/Don't Throw Our Love Away | 15 |

TOMMY KÖRBERG

| 69 | Sonet SON 2005 | Dear Mrs. Jones/Bird You Must Fly | 8 |

PAUL KORDA

66	Columbia DB 7994	Go On Home/Just Come Closer To Me	15
69	Parlophone R 5778	Seagull (West Coast Oil Tragedy Of '68)/Night Of The Next Day	5
71	MAM MAM 20	Between The Road/English Country Garden	5
71	MAM AS 1003	PASSING STRANGER (LP)	20

(see also Tim Andrews & Paul Korda, Dada, Fresh)

ALEXIS KORNER (BLUES INCORPORATED)

58	Tempo A 166	I Ain't Gonna Worry No More/County Jail	
		(as Alexis Korner Skiffle Group)	60
58	Tempo A 166	I Ain't Gonna Worry No More/County Jail (78)	50
63	Lyntone LYN 299	Blaydon Races/Up-Town (as Blues Incorporated With Alexis Korner,	
		free with women's magazine *Trio*)	125
63	Parlophone R 5206	I Need Your Loving/Please Please Please	
		(as Alexis Korner's Blues Inc.)	18
65	Parlophone R 5247	Little Baby/Roberta (as Alexis Korner's Blues Inc.)	20
65	King KG 1017	See See Rider/Blues A La King	
		(as Alexis Korner's All Stars)	30
66	Fontana TF 706	River's Invitation/Everyday (I Have The Blues)	18
67	Fontana TF 817	Rosie/Rock Me	20
75	CBS 3520	Get Off My Cloud/Strange'n'Deranged	8
76	CBS 3877	Ain't That Peculiar/Tree Top Fever	6
62	Ace of Clubs ACL 1130	R&B FROM THE MARQUEE (LP, claret labels, with Long John Baldry)	50

Alexis KORNER (BLUES INCORPORATED)

64	Transatlantic TRA 117	RED HOT FROM ALEX (LP, with Herbie Goins)	100
64	Oriole PS 40058	AT THE CAVERN (LP, live, with Herbie Goins)	125
65	Ace of Clubs ACL 1187	ALEXIS KORNER'S BLUES INCORPORATED (LP)	70
65	Spot JW 551	SKY HIGH (LP, featuring Duffy Power)	350
67	Fontana TL 5381	I WONDER WHO (LP)	50
67	Polydor Special 236 206	BLUES INCORPORATED (LP, reissue of Spot LP with fewer tracks)	35
68	Liberty LBL/LBS 83147	A NEW GENERATION OF BLUES (LP)	30
69	Transatlantic TRASAM 7	ALEXIS KORNER'S ALL STAR BLUES INCORPORATED (LP, reissue of "Red Hot From Alex", different cover)	15
71	Rak SRAK 501	ALEXIS (LP)	20
72	Rak SRAKSP 51	BOOTLEG HIM! (2-LP, with bootleg)	30
73	Transatlantic TRA 269	ACCIDENTALLY BORN IN NEW ORLEANS (LP, as Snape)	20
75	CBS 69155	GET OFF MY CLOUD (LP)	20

(see also Cyril Davies, C.C.S., Bob Hall & Alexis Korner, Herbie Goins, Duffy Power, Long John Baldry, Rocket 88, Davy Graham, Beryl Bryden, Jimmy Cotton, Ken Colyer, Jack Bruce, Snape)

ARTIE KORNFELD'S TREE
72	Neighbourhood NBH 3	Island Song/Feel	5
70	Probe SPB 1022	A TIME TO REMEMBER (LP)	15

KOROVA MILK BAR
88	Smashing SMASH 1	RONKO PRESENTS (EP, numbered p/s with raffle ticket, 2 different sleeve designs, 500 only)	8

(see also Surf Drums)

KOSMIC KOMMANDO
94	Rephlex CAT 007EP	Cat 007 (I)/Cat 007 (II)/Cat 007 (III)/Cat 007 (IV) (12", clear vinyl)	15

(see also Aphex Twin)

DAVID KOSSOFF
61	Pye 7N 15385	Alf's Blues/Please Sell No More Drink	4
61	Oriole CB 1597	I'm Shy, Mary Ellen, I'm Shy/When Father Papered The Parlour	4

PAUL KOSSOFF
73	Island ILPS 9264	BACK STREET CRAWLER (LP)	15
77	DJM DJE 29002	KOSS (2-LP, with 4-page booklet)	15
83	Street Tunes STLP 1002	CROYDON JUNE 15TH 1975 (2-LP)	15
83	St. Tunes SDLP 0012PD	MR. BIG/BLUE SOUL (LP, picture disc)	12
86	Island PKSP 100	BLUE SOUL (2-LP with 16-page booklet)	15

(see also Free, Kossoff Kirke Tetsu & Rabbit, Back Street Crawler, Creepy John Thomas)

KOSSOFF, KIRKE, TETSU & RABBIT
71	Island ILPS 9188	KOSSOFF, KIRKE, TETSU AND RABBIT (LP)	30

(see also Paul Kossoff, Rabbit, Free)

CHIM KOTHARI
66	Deram DM 108	Sitar'N'Spice/Indian Bat	12
66	Deram DML 1002	SOUND OF THE SITAR (LP)	30

LEO KOTTKE
73	Sonet SON 2034	Jesu, Joy Of Man's Desiring	4
77	Chrysalis CHS 2139	Buckaroo/Range	4
71	Capitol E-ST 682	MUDLARK (LP)	10
72	Sonet SNTF 629	LEO KOTTKE & HIS 6 & 12-STRING GUITAR (LP)	10
73	Capitol E-ST 11000	GREENHOUSE (LP)	10
73	Capitol E-ST 11164	MY FEET ARE SMILING (LP)	10
74	Capitol E-ST 11262	ICE WATER (LP)	10
75	Capitol E-ST 11335	DREAMS AND ALL THAT STUFF (LP)	10
75	Capitol E-ST 11446	CHEWING PINE (LP)	10

(see also John Fahey)

KRACKER
73	Rolling Stones RS 19106	A Song For Polly/Medicated Goo	5
74	Rolling Stones COC 49102	KRACKER BRAND (LP, gatefold sleeve)	12

KRAFTWERK
SINGLES
75	Vertigo 6147 012	Autobahn/Kometenmelodie 1	5
75	Vertigo 6147 015	Comet Melody 2/Kristallo	12
76	Capitol CL 15853	Radio Activity/Antenna (some in p/s)	12/5
77	Capitol CL 104	Showroom Dummies/Europe Endless	6
77	Capitol CLX 104	Showroom Dummies/Europe Endless (12", 'train station' p/s)	15
77	Capitol CL 15917	Trans-Europe Express/Franz Schubert	6
78	Capitol CL 15981	The Robots/Spacelab (foldout p/s)	15
78	Capitol CL 15981	The Robots (alternative mix)/Spacelab (folfout p/s)	30
78	Capitol CL 15998	Neon Lights/Trans-Europe Express/The Model	10
78	Capitol 12CL 15998	Neon Lights/Trans-Europe Express/The Model (12", luminous vinyl, dayglo sleeve)	15
78	Capitol 12CL 16098	Showroom Dummies/Spacelab/Europe Endless (12", reissue, 'red shirts' p/s)	15
81	EMI EMI 5175	Pocket Calculator/Dentaku (p/s)	5
81	EMI TCEMI 5175	Pocket Calculator/Numbers/Dentaku (cassette, 'cigarette'-pack style box)	35
81	EMI 12EMI 5175	Pocket Calculator/Numbers/Dentaku (12", p/s)	12
81	Vertigo VER 3	Kometenmelodie 2/Vom Himmel Hoch (p/s)	12
81	EMI EMI 5207	Computer Love/The Model (p/s, original issue)	6
81	EMI 12EMI 5207	Computer Love/The Model (12", p/s, original issue)	15

MINT VALUE £

81	EMI 12EMI 5207	The Model/Computer Love (12", p/s, 2nd issue, sides reversed)	7
82	EMI EMI 5272	Showroom Dummies/Numbers (p/s, some with mispressed B-side "The Model")	5/8
82	EMI 12EMI 5272	Showroom Dummies/Numbers/Pocket Calculator (12", p/s)	12
83	EMI EMI 5413	Tour De France/Tour De France (Instrumental) (p/s, red or yellow labels)	6
83	EMI TCEMI 5413	Tour De France/Tour De France (Short Version)/ Tour De France (2" Etape) (cassette)	35
83	EMI 12EMI 5413	Tour De France (Long Version)/(7" Version)/(2" Etape) (12", p/s, red or yellow labels)	20
84	EMI EMI 5413	Tour De France (Kevorkian Remix)/Tour De France (Original 7" Version) (reissue, 'Breakdance' p/s)	7
84	EMI 12EMI 5413	Tour De France (Kevorkian Remix)/Tour De France (Different Extended Version)/Tour De France (Original 7" Version) (12", reissue, 'Breakdance' p/s)	18
86	EMI EMI 5588	Musique Non-Stop/Musique Non-Stop (Different Version)	5
86	EMI 12EMI 5588	Musique Non-Stop (6.15)/Musique Non-Stop (7" Version) (12", p/s)	15
87	EMI EMI 5602	The Telephone Call/Der Telefon Anruf (p/s)	6
87	EMI 12EMI 5602	The Telephone Call (Remix)/House Phone/Der Telefon Anruf (12", p/s)	20
91	EMI EM 192	The Robots (re-recorded version)/Robotronik (p/s, red/black or white/black song title box)	5
91	EMI 12EM 192	Robotronik/The Robots (Single Mix)/The Robots (Album Version) (12", p/s, red/black or white/black song title box)	8
91	EMI CDEM 192	Robotronik/Robotnik/The Robots (Single Edit) (CD, mispressing, plays 'Robotronik [mix]' in place of 'The Robots', red/black song title box)	18
91	EMI CDEM 192	Robotronik/Robotnik/The Robots (Single Edit) (CD, white/black song title box)	18
91	EMI EM 201	Radioactivity (Francois Kevorkian Remix)/(William Orbit Mix) (p/s)	6
91	EMI TCEM 201	Radioactivity (Francois Kevorkian Remix)/(William Orbit Mix) (cassette)	5
91	EMI 12EM 201	Radioactivity (Francois Kevorkian 12" Remix)/(Francois Kevorkian 7" Remix)/ (William Orbit 12" Remix) (12", p/s)	8
91	EMI CDEM 201	Radioactivity (Francois Kevorkian 7" Remix)/(Francois Kevorkian 12" Remix)/ (William Orbit 12" Remix) (CD)	18
97	EMI KLANG DJ 101	Trans Europe Express/Trans Europe Express (Inst.) (12", p/s, promo only)	40
97	EMI KLANG DJ 102	Numbers/Numbers (12", p/s, same track both sides, promo only)	40
97	EMI KLANG DJ 103	Musique Non Stop/Musique Non Stop (12", p/s, same track both sides, promo only)	40
97	EMI KLANG DJ 104	Homecomputer/It's More Fun To Compute (12", p/s, promo only)	40
97	EMI KLANG BOX 101	KRAFTWERK (4 x 12" box set, including "Trans Europe Express", "Numbers", "Musique Non Stop" & "Homecomputer"; without T-shirt, promo only)	350
97	EMI KLANG BOX 101	KRAFTWERK (4 x 12" box set, including "Trans Europe Express", "Numbers", "Musique Non Stop" & "Homecomputer"; with separate white or black T-shirt, promo only)	500

LPs

73	Vertigo 6641 077	KRAFTWERK (2-LP, gatefold sleeve, 'spiral' or 'spacecraft' labels)	80/40
74	Vertigo 6360 616	RALF AND FLORIAN (2-LP, gatefold sleeve, 'spiral' or 'spacecraft' label)	80/40
74	Vertigo 6360 620	AUTOBAHN (LP, embossed blue sleeve)	25
75	Vertigo 6360 629	EXCELLER EIGHT (LP, some with stickered sleeve)	20
75	Vertigo 6360 629	EXCELLER EIGHT (LP, cassette)	15
76	Capitol EST 11457	RADIOACTIVITY (LP, with insert)	15
81	Vertigo 6641 077	KRAFTWERK (2-LP, reissue in single sleeve)	15
81	Vertigo 6449 006	ELEKTROKINETIK (LP)	25
81	Vertigo 6449 006	ELEKTROKINETIK (cassette)	15
83	EMI EMC 3407	TECHNOPOP (LP, unissued, sleeves only)	
91	EMI EM 1408	THE MIX (2-LP, with inner sleeves)	20

(see also Organisation, Elektric Music)

KRAKEN

| 81 | Knave EJSP 9370 | FANTASY REALITY (EP, no p/s) | 50 |

BILLY J. KRAMER & DAKOTAS

63	Parlophone R 5023	Do You Want To Know A Secret/I'll Be On My Way	5
63	Parlophone R 5049	Bad To Me/I Call Your Name	5
63	Parlophone R 5073	I'll Keep You Satisfied/I Know	6
64	Parlophone R 5105	Little Children/They Remind Me Of You	5
64	Parlophone R 5156	From A Window/Second To None	5
65	Parlophone R 5234	It's Gotta Last Forever/Don't Do It No More	6
65	Parlophone R 5285	Trains And Boats And Planes/That's The Way I Feel	6
65	Parlophone R 5362	Neon City/I'll Be Doggone	8
66	Parlophone R 5408	We're Doing Fine/Forgive Me	12
63	Parlophone GEP 8885	THE BILLY J. KRAMER HITS (EP)	22
63	Parlophone GEP 8895	I'LL KEEP YOU SATISFIED (EP)	22
64	Parlophone GEP 8907	LITTLE CHILDREN (EP)	25
64	Parlophone GEP 8921	FROM A WINDOW (EP)	35
65	Parlophone GEP 8928	BILLY J. PLAYS THE STATES (EP)	38
63	Parlophone PMC 1209	LISTEN (LP, also stereo PCS 3047)	25/35
65	Regal REG 1057	BILLY J (LP, export only)	40

(see also Dakotas)

BILLY J. KRAMER

66	Parlophone R 5482	You Make Me Feel Like Someone/Take My Hand	7
67	Parlophone R 5552	Sorry/Going Going Gone	8
67	Reaction 591 014	Town Of Tuxley Toymakers/Chinese Girl	25
68	CBS 56-3396	1941/His Love Is Just A Lie	6
68	NEMS 56-3635	A World Without Love/Going Through It	6
69	MGM MGM 1474	The Colour Of My Love/I'm Running Away	7
73	Decca F 13426	A Fool Like You/I'll Keep You Satisfied	6

Billy J. KRAMER

73	Decca F 13442	Darlin' Come To Me/Walking	6
74	BASF BA 1006	Stayin' Power/Blue Jean Queen	6
77	EMI EMI 2661	San Diego/Warm Summer Rain	5
78	EMI EMI 2740	Ships That Pass In The Night/Is There Anymore At Home Like You	5
79	Hobo HOS 010	Blue Christmas/Little Love (p/s, blue vinyl)	7
80	JM JM 1005	Silver Dream/Lonely Lady	6
82	Runaway BJK 1	Rock It/Dum Dum	6
83	Rak RAK 359	You Can't Live On Memories/Stood Up (p/s)	6

WAYNE KRAMER
| 78 | Stiffwick DEA/SUK 1 | Ramblin' Rose/Get Some (numbered p/s) | 8 |
| 79 | Radar ADA 41 | The Harder They Come/East Side Girl (p/s) | 6 |

(see also MC5)

KRAY CHERUBS
88	Fierce FRIGHT 014	No (p/s, 1-sided)	20
89	Snakeskin SS 002	Rot In Hell Mom/SAUCERMAN: Motor Drag (numbered black p/s, 300 only; later reissued in purple p/s)	20/15
89	Forced Exposure FE 18	Teen Camel/I Hate My Job (p/s)	15

(see also Art Attacks)

BILL KRENZ & HIS RAGTIMERS
| 56 | London HLU 8258 | There'll Be No New Tunes On This Old Piano/Goofus | 25 |
| 56 | London HLU 8258 | There'll Be No New Tunes On This Old Piano/Goofus (78) | 12 |

KREW KATS
| 61 | HMV POP 840 | Trambone/Peak Hour | 12 |
| 61 | HMV POP 894 | Samovar/Jack's Good | 18 |

(see also Shadows, Brian Bennett)

KREWMEN
| 86 | Lost Moment LMLP 008 | THE ADVENTURES OF THE KREWMEN (LP) | 10 |

KRIMSON KAKE
| 69 | Penny Farthing PEN 707 | Feelin' Better/Waiter | 6 |

(see also Samantha Jones, Vernons Girls)

DAVE KRISS
| 80s private pressing | | EMIGRATING (2-LP) | 20 |

SONJA KRISTINA
68	Polydor 56299	Let The Sunshine In/Frank Mills	15
80	Chopper CHOP 101	St Tropez/Mr Skin (p/s)	10
80	Chopper CHOPE 5	SONJA KRISTINA (LP)	30

(see also Curved Air)

KRIS KRISTOFFERSON
70	Monument SMO 5042	KRISTOFFERSON (LP)	15
71	Monument MNT 64636	THE SILVER TONGUED DEVIL AND ME (LP)	12
72	Monument MNT 64963	BORDER LORD (LP)	12
73	Monument MNT 64631	ME AND BOBBY McGEE (LP, reissue of "Kristofferson")	12
73	Monument MNT 65301	JESUS WAS A CAPRICORN (LP)	12
73	Monument ZQ 31909	JESUS WAS A CAPRICORN (LP, quadrophonic)	15
74	Monument MNT 69074	SPOOKY LADY'S SIDESHOW (LP)	12
75	Monument MNT 69158	WHO'S TO BLESS AND WHO'S TO BLAME (LP)	12

KRIS KRISTOFFERSON & RITA COOLIDGE
| 73 | A&M AMLH 64403 | FULL MOON (LP) | 12 |
| 75 | Monument MNT 80547 | BREAKAWAY (LP) | 12 |

KROKODIL
| 69 | Liberty LBS 83306 | KROKODIL (LP) | 22 |
| 70 | Liberty LBS 83417 | SWAMP (LP) | 22 |

KRONSTADT UPRISING
| 80s | Spider | The Unknown Revolution (p/s) | 5 |
| 85 | Dog Rock SD 108 | Part Of The Game/The Horseman (p/s) | 5 |

HARDY KRUGER
| 59 | Top Rank TR 5005 | Blind Date (I'm A Lonely Man)/PINEWOOD ORCHESTRA: Blind Date | 6 |

GENE KRUPA (& HIS ORCHESTRA)
60	HMV POP 750	Cherokee/Indiana "Montage"	5
59	HMV 7EG 8595	DRUM BOOGIE (EP)	10
55	Columbia 33S 1051	DRUMMIN' MAN (10" LP)	12
55	Columbia 33S 1064	RHYTHM PARADE (10" LP)	12
55	Columbia Clef 33C 9000	THE GENE KRUPA TRIO COLLATES (10" LP)	12
57	Columbia Clef 33C 9032	THE ROCKIN' MR. KRUPA (10" LP)	12

GENE KRUPA & BUDDY RICH
| 64 | Verve VS 503 | Perdida/Night Train | 5 |
| 62 | Verve SVLP 9014 | BURNIN' BEAT (LP) | 12 |

KRYPTON
| 78 | A&M AMS 7421 | Can You Read My Mind (Love Theme From 'Superman')/How Can I Get To Know You | 4 |

KRYPTON TUNES
78	Black & Red FIRE 1	Behind Your Smile/Coming To See You (p/s)	7
78	Lightning GIL 546	Limited Vision/All In Jail	5
79	Secret SR 009	EXTENDED PLAY (EP)	5

KRYSIA (Kocjan)
74   RCA LPL1 5052   KRYSIA (LP) 12
(see also Natural Acoustic Band, Fairport Convention)

KRYSTAL GENERATION
72   Mercury 6052 120   Wanted Dead Or Alive/Every Man Seems To Be For Himself 7

BOB KUBAN & INMEN
66   Stateside SS 488   The Cheater/Try Me Baby. 30
66   Stateside SS 514   The Teaser/All I Want 10
68   Bell BLL 1027   The Cheater/Try Me Baby (reissue) 6

KUBAS
65   Columbia DB 7451   I Love Her/Magic Potion. 15
(see also Koobas)

KUF-LINX
58   London HLU 8583   So Tough/What'cha Gonna Do. 175
58   London HLU 8583   So Tough/What'cha Gonna Do (78) 60

LENNY KUHR
69   Philips BF 1777   The Troubadour/Oh No Monsieur 15

KUKL
84   Crass 1984/1   THE EYE (LP, foldout sleeve). 18
85   Crass No. 4   HOLIDAYS IN EUROPE (LP, with inner sleeve) 15
(see also Sugarcubes)

KULA SHAKER
95   Columbia KULA 71   Tattva (Lucky 13 Mix)/Hollow Man Part 2 (thick card p/s,
                       mail-order only, 2,000 numbered copies) 10
95   Columbia KULA CD 1 Tattva (Lucky 13 Mix)/Hollow Man Part 2 (CD) 8
96   Columbia KULA 72   Grateful When You're Dead – Jerry Was There/Another Life (p/s). 7
96   Columbia KULAMC 72 Grateful When You're Dead – Jerry Was There/Another Life
                       (cassette) 5
96   Columbia KULACD 72 Grateful When You're Dead – Jerry Was There/Another Life/
                       Under The Hammer (CD) 10
96   Columbia XPCD 781 Grateful When You're Dead (Edit)/Grateful When You're Dead –
                       Jerry Was There (CD, 'J.F.K' card p/s, promo only, 941 copies) 8
96   Columbia KULA 73   Tattva/Tattva On St. George's Day/Dance In Your Shadow
                       (stickered p/s) 5
96   Columbia KULACD 3 Tattva/Dance In Your Shadow/Moonshine/Tattva (Lucky 13 Mix) (CD) 7
96   Columbia KULACD 3K Tattva On St. George's Day/Dance In Your Shadow/Red Balloon
                       (Vishnu's Eyes) (CD, stickered card sleeve with poster) 8
96   Columbia XPCD 797 Tattva/Tattva On St. George's Day (CD, stickered 'Kevin Keegan' p/s) 10
96   Columbia KULA 74   Hey Dude/Troubled Mind (jukebox issue, white label, no p/s) 4
96   Columbia KULA 75   Govinda (Radio Mix)/Gokula/Temple Of Everlasting Light
                       (p/s, states 45rpm but plays 33rpm, 5,000 only) 25
96   Columbia KULA 75   Govinda (Radio Mix)/Gokula/Temple O
                       (fan club issue, 'clock face' label p/s) 25
96   Columbia XPR 2324 Govinda (Monkey Mafia Pigsy's Mix)/(Monkey Mafia Ten To Ten
                       (12", p/s, sealed with sticker, promo only) 12
96   Columbia SHAKER 1CDK K (CD, digipak) 15

KULT
69   CBS 4276   No Home Today/Mister Number One 100

PRAMOD KUMAR
72   Philips 6460 854   THIS IS THE MUSIC OF INDIA (LP) 10

CHARLIE KUNZ
54   Decca F 10419   Charlie Kunz Piano Medley, No. 114 15
54   Decca F 10441   Charlie Kunz Piano Medley, No. 115 5
54   Decca F 10481   Charlie Kunz Piano Medley, No. 116 5

KURASS
70   Escort ES 825   Stampede/KING STITT: You Were Meant For Me
                       (B-side actually by Lee Perry) 10

FELA RANSOME KUTI (& AFRICA '70)
72   Regal Zonophone RZ 3052 Chop And Quench/Egbe Mi O (with Africa '70 & Ginger Baker). 5
72   Regal Zono. SLRZ 1023 FELI RANSOME-KUTI & THE AFRICA '70 WITH GINGER BAKER LIVE! (LP). 18
75   Creole CRLP 501   SHAKARA (LP, with Africa '70) 15
77   Creole CRLP 511   ZOMBIE (LP, with Africa '70) 12
78   Phase 4 Stereo PFS 4412 YELLOW FEVER (LP) 12
79   Creole CRLP 502   GENTLEMEN (LP). 12
79   Creole CRLP 509   EVERYTHING SCATTER (LP). 12
81   Arista SPART 1167   BLACK PRESIDENT (LP) 12
(see also Ginger Baker)

JIM KWESKIN JUG BAND
65   Fontana TFL 6036   JIM KWESKIN JUG BAND (LP) 15
67   Fontana (S)TFL 6080   SEE REVERSE SIDE FOR TITLE (LP) 12
68   Vanguard SVRL 19046 WHATEVER HAPPENED TO THOSE GOOD OLD DAYS AT CLUB 47 (LP) 12

KYTES
66   Pye 7N 17136   Blessed/Call Me Darling. 7
66   Pye 7N 17179   Frosted Panes/I'll Give You Better Love 18
68   Island WI 6027   Running In The Water/The End Of The Day 35

KYTTOCK KYND
70   Decca SKL 4782   KYTTOCK KYND (LP). 60

MINT VALUE £

L.A.
70	CBS 5017	Speak Of Peace, Sing Of Joy/Brings My Whole World Tumbling Down	5
70	CBS 64109	NEW DAY (LP)	18

(see also Love Affair)

PATTI LA BELLE (& BLUE BELLES)
64	Sue WI 324	Down The Aisle/C'est La Vie	25
65	Cameo Parkway P 935	Danny Boy/I Believe	12
65	Atlantic AT 4055	All Or Nothing/You Forgot How To Love (as Patty La Belle & Her Belles)	15
66	Atlantic AT 4064	Over The Rainbow/Groovy Kind Of Love (as Patty La Belle & Her Belles)	7
66	Atlantic 584 007	Patti's Prayer/Family Man (as Patti La Belle & Her Belles)	6
67	Atlantic 584 072	Take Me For A Little While/I Don't Want To Go On Without You (solo)	8
66	Atlantic 587 001	OVER THE RAINBOW (LP)	30

(see also Blue-Belles)

LACE
68	Columbia DB 8499	People People/The Nun	15
69	Page One POF 135	I'm A Gambler/Go Away	6

(see also Universals, Pete Dello, Honeybus, Red Herring, Gary Walker & Rain)

DAVE LACEY & CORVETTES
65	Philips BF 1419	That's What They All Say/I've Had Enough	8

LACKEY & SWEENEY
73	Village Thing VTS 23	JUNK STORE SONGS FOR SALE (LP)	15

LADDERS
83	Statik TAK 2	Gotta See Jane/Krugerrands (p/s)	6
83	Statik TAK 2-12	Gotta See Jane/Krugerrands (12", p/s)	10

LADD'S BLACK ACES
56	London AL 3556	LADD'S BLACK ACES (10" LP)	15

LA-DE-DA BAND
69	Parlophone R 5810	Come Together/Here Is Love	7

LADIES
80s	Music Of Life MOLIS 6	Turned On To You/I Knew That Love (12")	15

TOMMY LADNIER
54	London AL 3524	BLUES AND STOMPS VOLUME ONE — TOMMY LADNIER (10" LP)	25
55	London AL 3548	PLAYS THE BLUES WITH MA RAINEY & EDMONIA HENDERSON (10" LP)	25

(see also Ma Rainey)

PATTIE LA DONNE
69	Joe/Duke DU 23	Friends And Lovers/JOE'S ALLSTARS: Hot Line	7

LA DUSSELDORF
78	Radar ADA 5	La Dusseldorf/Silver Cloud (unissued, white label promos only, no p/s)	15

LADYBIRDS
64	Columbia DB 7197	Lady Bird/I Don't Care Any More	8
64	Columbia DB 7250	The White Cliffs Of Dover/It's Not The Same Without A Boy	8
64	Columbia DB 7351	Memories/Try A Little Love	8
65	Columbia DB 7523	I Wanna Fly/O.K. Fred	8

(see also Sharades, Russ Loader, Marion Davies, De Laine Sisters)

LADY JANE & VERITY
59	Pye International 7N 25036	The Slow Look/Cry Baby	6
59	Pye International N 25036	The Slow Look/Cry Baby (78)	12

LADY JUNE
74	Caroline C 1509	LADY JUNE'S LINGUISTIC LEPROSY (LP, with perforated lyric sheet)	20

(see also Kevin Ayers, Eno)

LADY LEE
64	Decca F 11961	I'm Into Something Good/When Love Comes Along	7
65	Decca F 12147	99 Times Out Of 100/I Can Feel It	5
65	Columbia DB 7121	My Whole World (Seems To Be Tumbling Down)/Girl	8

LADY LUCK & LULLABIES
62	Philips PB 1245	Young Stranger/Dance	6

LAFAYETTES
62	RCA RCA 1299	Life's Too Short/Nobody But You	6
62	RCA RCA 1308	Caravan Of Lonely Men/I Still Do	10

LA FUNK MOB
94	Mo' Wax MW 023	Ravers Suck Our Sound (Carl Craig Mix)/Motor Bass Get Phunked Up (Electofunk Remix)/Ravers Suck Our Sound (Mystic Mix)/Ravers Suck Our Sound (Gangbang Mix)/Ravers Suck Our Sound (New Mix) (2 x 10")	15

FRANCIS LAI
67	United Artists SULP 1155	A MAN AND A WOMAN (LP, soundtrack)	15
67	United Artists (S)ULP 1185	VIVRE POUR VIVRE (LIFE FOR LIFE) (LP, soundtrack)	15
67	Brunswick LAT/STA 8689	I'LL NEVER FORGET WHAT'S 'ISNAME (LP, soundtrack)	25

LAIBACH

84	East West 12 EWS 3	Panorama/Decree (12", p/s)	10
85	Cherry Red 12CHERRY 91	Die Liebe/Die Liebe Ist Grosste Kraft, Die Alles Schafft (12", p/s)	7
88	Mute PMUTE 80T	SYMPATHY FOR THE DEVIL (12" EP, picture disc)	8

CLEO LAINE

54	Parlophone MSP 6107	I Got Rhythm/I Know You're Mine (with Johnny Dankworth Orchestra)	7
55	Parlophone MSP 6147	Ain't Misbehavin'/I Got It Bad, And That Ain't Good (with Johnny Dankworth Orchestra)	7
57	Esquire 10-476	Spread A Little Happiness/You've Done Something To My Heart (78)	10
57	Esquire 10-482	Mad About The Boy/On A See Saw (78)	10
57	Pye Jazz 7NJ 2013	I'm Beginning To See The Light/Jeepers Creepers	5
58	Pye 7N 15143	Hand Me Down Love/They Were Right	5
60	Fontana H 269	Let's Slip Away/Thieving Boy	5
61	Fontana H 326	You'll Answer To Me/I Only Have Eyes For You	5
65	Fontana TF 532	Little Boat/The Exciting Mr. Fitch	5
65	Fontana TF 622	If We Live On The Top Of A Mountain/Don't You Pass Me By	5
66	Fontana TF 759	There Is Nothing Left To Say/Life Is A Wheel	5
70	Philips 6006 016	It Will Soon Be Spring/Feeling Good	5
71	Philips 6006 077	Model City's Programme/Night Owl	8
57	Parlophone GEP 8613	I GOT RHYTHM (EP)	15
57	Pye Nixa Jazz NJE 1010	CLEO LAINE (EP)	15
57	Pye Nixa Jazz NJE 1026	THE APRIL AGE (EP, as Cleo Laine & Dave Lee Quintet)	15
57	Esquire EP 102	CLEO LAINE (EP, as Cleo Laine & Keith Christie Quintet)	8
57	Esquire EP 122	CLEO LAINE (EP, as Cleo Laine & Keith Christie Quintet)	8
59	Columbia SEG 7938	CLEO SINGS ELIZABETHAN (EP)	10
61	Fontana TFE 17381	THE FABULOUS CLEO (EP)	8
64	Fontana TFE 17404	CLEO (EP)	15
55	Esquire 15-007	CLEO LAINE (10" LP)	50
58	Pye Nixa NPT 19024	CLEO'S CHOICE (10" LP)	50
58	MGM MGM-C 765	SHE'S THE TOPS (LP)	18
62	Fontana 680 992 TL	ALL ABOUT ME (LP, also stereo 886 159 TY)	25
64	Fontana (S)TL 5209	SHAKESPEARE & ALL THAT JAZZ (LP)	30
66	Fontana (S)TL 5316	WOMAN TALK (LP)	18
68	Fontana STL 5483	SOLILOQUY (LP)	30

(see also Johnny Dankworth, Tubby Hayes & Cleo Laine)

DENNY LAINE

67	Deram DM 122	Say You Don't Mind/Ask The People	5
68	Deram DM 171	Too Much In Love/Catherine's Wheel	8
69	Deram DM 227	Say You Don't Mind/Ask The People (reissue)	5
73	Wizard WIZ 104	Find A Way Somehow/Move Me To Another Place	5
77	Palladin PAL 5014	Caroline/Blues	5

(see also Moody Blues, Paul McCartney/Wings, Balls, Trevor Burton, Magic Christians, Ginger Baker's Airforce, B.L.& G)

FRANKIE LAINE

78s

51	Oriole CB 1052	Georgia On My Mind/You're Just The Kind (78, gold or silver label)	7
52	Oriole CB 1086	I'm Gonna Live 'Till I Die/The Love Of A Gypsy (78)	8
52	Oriole CB 1090	Metro Polka/The Jalopy Song (78)	8
52	Oriole CB 1091	May The Good Lord Bless And Keep You/Dear, Dear, Dear (78)	8
52	Oriole CB 1092	Get Happy/I Would Do Anything For You (78)	8
52	Oriole CB 1093	Baby, I Need You/Yes, My Dear (78)	8
52	Oriole CB 1097	The Gang That Sang "Heart Of My Heart"/You Left Me Out In The Rain (78)	8
52	Oriole CB 1098	The Day Isn't Long Enough/Isle Of Capri (78)	8
52	Oriole CB 1115	Swamp Girl/A Kiss For Tomorrow (78)	8
52	Oriole CB 1116	Wrap Your Troubles In Dreams/Black And Blue (78)	8
52	Oriole CB 1117	All Of Me/When You're Smiling (78)	8
52	Oriole CB 1118	West End Blues/I Can't Believe That You're In Love With Me (78)	8
52	Oriole CB 1119	Carry Me Back To Old Virginney/Thanks For Your Kisses (78)	8
52	Oriole CB 1120	Mule Train/A Sunday Kind Of Love (78)	8
52	Oriole CB 1121	The Cry Of The Old Goose/Black Lace (78)	8
52	Oriole CB 1122	I Get Sentimental Over Nothing/That Lucky Old Sun (78)	8
52	Columbia DB 3017	One For My Baby/She Reminds Me Of You (78)	8
53	Oriole CB 1176	Ain't Misbehavin'/That's How Rhythm Was Born (78)	8
54	Mercury MB 2946	Georgia On My Mind/You're Just The Kind (78)	8
54	Mercury MB 2958	I May Be Wrong/On The Sunny Side Of The Street (78)	8
54	Mercury MB 2959	I'm Gonna Live 'Til I Die/TONY FONTANE: The Love Of A Gypsy (78)	8
54	Mercury MB 2963	Metro Polka/The Jalopy Song (78)	8
54	Mercury MB 2964	May The Good Lord Bless And Keep You/Dear, Dear, Dear (78)	8
54	Mercury MB 2965	Get Happy/I Would Do Anything For You (78)	8
54	Mercury MB 2966	Baby, I Need You/Yes, My Dear (78)	8
54	Mercury MB 2970	The Gang That Sang "Heart Of My Heart"/You Left Me Out In The Rain (78)	8
54	Mercury MB 2971	The Day Isn't Long Enough/Isle Of Capri (78)	8
54	Mercury MB 2986	West End Blues/I Can't Believe That You're In Love (78)	8
56	Mercury MT 109	The Cry Of The Wild Goose/Mule Train (78)	8
56	Philips PB 607	Champion The Wonder Horse/Ticky Ticky Tick (I'm Gonna Tell On You) (78)	8
57	Philips PB 691	Lonely Man/Without Him (78)	8
57	Philips PB 709	Gunfight At The OK Corral/The Thief (78)	8
57	Philips PB 727	The 3:10 To Yuma/You Know How It Is (78)	8
57	Philips PB 760	The Greater Sin/East Is East (78)	8
58	Philips PB 797	Shine/Annabel Lee (78)	8
58	Philips PB 821	The Lonesome Road/My Gal And A Prayer (78)	8
58	Philips PB 836	Lovin' Up A Storm/A Kiss Can Change The World (78)	10
58	Philips PB 848	Choombala Bay/I Have To Cry (78)	10
58	Philips PB 886	When I Speak Your Name/Cottage For Sale (78)	12

Frankie LAINE

| 59 | Philips PB 905 | That's My Desire/In My Wildest Dreams (78) | 20 |
| 59 | Philips PB 965 | Rawhide/Journey's End (78) | 45 |

SINGLES

53	Columbia SCM 5016	The Ruby And The Pearl/The Mermaid	30
53	Columbia SCM 5017	Jealousy/The Gandy Dancers' Ball	35
53	Columbia SCM 5031	I'm Just A Poor Bachelor/Tonight You Belong To Me	30
53	Columbia SCM 5064	September In The Rain/Chow Willy	25
53	Columbia SCM 5073	The Swan Song/My Ohio Home	25
54	Columbia SCM 5085	Tomorrow Mountain/I'd Give My Life	25
56	Philips JK 1000	Moonlight Gambler/Only If We Love (jukebox issue)	18
57	Philips JK 1009	Love Is A Golden Ring (with Easy Riders)/There's Not A Moment To Spare	18
57	Philips JK 1017	Lonely Man/Without Him (jukebox issue)	18
57	Philips JK 1032	The Greater Sin/East Is East (jukebox issue)	18
58	Philips PB 797	Shine/Annabel Lee	7
58	Philips PB 821	The Lonesome Road/My Gal And A Prayer	7
58	Philips PB 836	Lovin' Up A Storm/A Kiss Can Change The World	8
58	Philips PB 848	Choombala Bay/I Have To Cry	6
58	Philips PB 886	When I Speak Your Name/Cottage For Sale	6
59	Philips PB 905	That's My Desire/In My Wildest Dreams	6
59	Philips PB 965	Rawhide/Journey's End	6
60	Philips PB 997	Jelly Coal Man/Rocks And Gravel	6
60	Philips PB 1011	St. James Infirmary/Et Voila!	6
60	Philips PB 1064	And Doesn't She Roll/Seven Women	6
61	Philips PB 1135	Gunslinger/Wanted Man	6
63	CBS AAG 144	Don't Make My Baby Blue/The Moment Of Truth	6
63	CBS AAG 167	And She Doesn't Roll/I'm Gonna Be Strong	6
65	Capitol CL 15373	Go On With Your Dancing/Halfway	6
67	HMV POP 1573	Ev'ry Street's A Boulevard (In Old New York)/I'll Take Care Of Your Cares	6
67	HMV POP 1590	Making Memories/The Moment Of Truth	6
67	HMV POP 1597	You Wanted Someone To Play With/The Real True Meaning Of Love	6
67	HMV POP 1606	Laura/Sometimes	6
68	Stateside SS 2091	To Each His Own/I'm Happy To Hear You're Sorry	6
69	Stateside SS 2144	You Gave Me A Mountain/The Secret Of Happiness	6
73	CBS 1156	High Noon/Cool Water (p/s)	5
74	Warner Bros K 16414	Blazing Saddles/MADELINE KAHN: I'm Tired	5
70s	Bulldog BD 24	Jezebel/Answer Me	5

EPs

54	Columbia SEG 7505	JEZEBEL (EP, company die-cut sleeve)	15
54	Philips BBE 12005	FRANKIE LAINE (I BELIEVE) (EP)	15
56	Mercury MEP 9000	FRANKIE LAINE SINGS (EP)	15
56	Mercury MEP 9500	MORE HITS BY FRANKIE LAINE (EP)	15
56	Philips BBE 12087	FRANKIE LAINE NO. 2 (EP)	15
56	Philips BBE 12103	JUBA JUBA JUBALEE (EP, as Frankie Laine & Four Lads)	12
57	Philips BBE 12130	FRANKIE LAINE NO. 3 (EP)	15
57	Mercury MEP 9520	FRANKIE LAINE SINGS VOL. 2 (EP)	15
58	Philips BBE 12216	FRANKIE LAINE (PHILIPS TV SERIES) (EP)	15
60	Mercury ZEP 10062	FRANKIE LAINE'S ALL TIME HITS (EP)	15
61	Philips BBE 12447	WESTERN FAVOURITES (EP)	15
62	CBS AGG 20003	DEUCES WILD NO. 1 (EP)	15
62	CBS AGG 20007	DEUCES WILD NO. 2 (EP)	15
62	CBS AGG 20011	DEUCES WILD NO. 3 (EP)	15
64	CBS AGG 20036	SONG OF THE OPEN ROAD (EP)	15

LPs

52	Oriole/Mercury MG 10001	MR RHYTHM SINGS (10" LP, stickered U.S. "Mr Rhythm" sleeve)	45
52	Oriole/Mercury MG 10002	SONGS BY FRANKIE LAINE (10" LP)	45
54	Mercury MG 25097	MR. RHYTHM SINGS (10" LP, reissue)	35
54	Mercury MG 25098	SONGS BY FRANKIE LAINE (10" LP, reissue)	35
54	Columbia 33S 1047	ONE FOR MY BABY (10" LP)	35
54	Philips BBR 8014	THE VOICE OF YOUR CHOICE (10" LP)	35
55	Philips BBR 8068	MR. RHYTHM (10" LP)	30
56	Mercury MPT 7007	CRY OF THE WILD GOOSE (10" LP)	30
56	Philips BBL 7080	JAZZ SPECTACULAR (LP, with Buck Clayton & His Orchestra)	18
56	Philips BBL 7111	JUBA JUBA JUBILEE (LP, with Four Lads)	18
57	Philips BBL 7155	ROCKIN' (LP)	25
57	Mercury MPT 7513	THAT'S MY DESIRE (10" LP)	30
58	Philips BBL 7238	FOREIGN AFFAIR (LP)	22
58	Philips BBL 7260	TORCHING (LP)	22
58	Philips BBL 7263	SHOWCASE OF HITS (LP, flipback or non-flipback sleeve)	25/20
59	Philips BBL 7294	REUNION IN RHYTHM (LP, with Michel Legrand, also stereo SBBL 541)	18/22
60	Philips BBL 7357	FRANKIE LAINE BALLADEER (LP)	18
61	Philips BBL 7468	HELL BENT FOR LEATHER (LP, also stereo SBBL 616)	15/20
61	Ember EMB 3334	FRANKIE LAINE SINGS (LP)	15
62	Philips BBL 7535	DEUCES WILD (LP, also stereo SBBL 663)	15/20
62	CBS (S)BPG 62052	HELL BENT FOR LEATHER (LP, reissue)	12
62	CBS (S)BPG 62082	CALL OF THE WILD (LP, mono/stereo)	18
63	CBS (S)BPG 62126	WANDERLUST (LP)	18
60s	World Records SM 531/536	THE FRANKIE LAINE SONGBOOK (6-LP box set)	35

(see also Jo Stafford & Frankie Laine, Four Lads, Doris Day, Easy Riders)

FRANKIE LAINE & JOHNNIE RAY

57	Philips JK 1026	Up Above My Head, I Hear Music In The Air/Good Evening Friends (jukebox issue)	20
57	Philips PB 708	Up Above My Head, I Hear Music In The Air/Good Evening Friends (78)	8
57	Philips BBE 12153	FRANKIE AND JOHNNIE (EP, 1 track each, 2 together)	15

(see also Johnnie Ray)

LINDA LAINE (& SINNERS)
64	Columbia DB 7204	Doncha Know, Doncha Know, Doncha Know/Ain't That Fun	8
64	Columbia DB 7370	Low Grades And High Fever/After Today	8
65	Columbia DB 7549	Don't Do It Baby/All I Want To Do Is Run	10

(see also Sinners)

SCOTT LAINE
63	Windsor WB 114	Tearaway Johnnie/John Silver	8

DENZIL LAING
71	Songbird SB 1054	Medicine Stick/CRYSTALITES: Short Cut	8

(see also Soul Vendors, Dennis Alcapone)

ALAN LAKE
70	Ember EMB S 278	Good Times/Got To Have Tenderness (p/s)	15

BONNIE LAKE & HER BEAUX
56	Brunswick 05622	Thirteen Black Cats/The Miracle Of Love	18
56	Brunswick 05622	Thirteen Black Cats/The Miracle Of Love (78)	10

(see also Jack Pleis)

GREG LAKE
75	Manticore K 13511	I Believe In Father Christmas/Humbug (p/s)	6
77	Atlantic K 10990	C'est La Vie/EMERSON, LAKE & PALMER: Jeremy Bender (p/s)	5
78	Atlantic K 11061	Watching Over You/EMERSON, LAKE & PALMER: Hallowed Be Thy Name (p/s)	5
81	Chrysalis CHS 2553	Love You Too Much/Someone (p/s)	6
82	Chrysalis CHS 2567	It Hurts/Retribution Drive	5
81	Chrysalis CHR 1357	GREG LAKE (LP, with inner sleeve)	12
83	Chrysalis CHR 1392	MANOEUVRES (LP)	12

(see also Emerson Lake & Palmer, King Crimson, Asia, Pete Sinfield, Gary Moore)

LEE LAMAR & HIS ORCHESTRA
57	London HLB 8508	Teenage Pedal Pushers/Sophia	50
57	London HLB 8508	Teenage Pedal Pushers/Sophia (78)	35

CHRIS LAMB & UNIVERSALS
65	Decca F 12176	Mysterious Land/If You Ask Me	7

(see also Universals, Gidian)

KEVIN LAMB
70	Concord CON 23	Who Is The Hero?/The Road To Antibes	6
73	Birth RAB 1004	Who Is The Hero?/Who Stole The Ice	5
72	Birth RAB 4	WHO IS THE HERO? (LP)	12

JEANNIE LAMBE
67	CBS 202636	Miss Disc/Montano Blues (with Gordon Beck Orchestra)	12
67	CBS 2731	Day After Day After Day/City At Night	7
67	CBS 3000	This Is My Love/Where Have All The Endings Gone (as Jeanne Lam)	5

DAVE LAMBERT, JON HENDRICKS & ANNIE ROSS
60	Philips BBL 7368	DAVE LAMBERT, JON HENDRICKS & ANNIE ROSS (LP, stereo SBBL 562)	10

(see also Jon Hendricks, Annie Ross)

DAVE LAMBERT & BUDDY STEWART
51	Vogue V 2039	Bopelbaby/Bopelground (78, with Al Haig)	8

TREVOR LAMBERT
72	Duke DU 132	Bald Head Teacher (act. by Max Romeo)/HEADMASTERS: Bald Head Version	6

LAMBRETTAS
79	Rocket XPRES 23	Go Steady/Listen Listen/Cortinas (p/s; later in art sleeve)	7
80	Rocket XPRES 25	Poison Ivy/Runaround (with '2-Stroke' die-cut sleeve & label)	5
80	Rocket XPRES 333	Da-a-a-ance/(Can't You) Feel The Beat (picture disc; 2 different shades, red, white & blue or pink, white & blue)	4/6
80	Rocket XPRES 36	Page 3/Steppin' Out (Of Line) (withdrawn; copies rumoured to exist, some in p/s)	120/75
80	Rocket XPRES 36	Another Day (Another Girl)/Steppin' Out (Of Line) ('emergency' p/s)	4
82	Rocket XPRES 74	Somebody To Love/Nobody's Watching Me (mispressing, crediting "Leap Before You Look" on label & sleeve)	6

TONI LAMOND
68	Philips BF 1722	Silent Voices/They Don't Give Medals (To Yesterday's Heroes)	12

LAMPLIGHTERS
55	Parlophone DP 416	Salty Dog/Ride Jockey Ride (78, export issue)	100

(see also Thurston Harris)

LAMP SISTERS
68	Sue WI 4048	A Woman With The Blues/I Thought It Was All Over	30

LANA SISTERS
58	Fontana H 148	Ring-A My Phone/Chimes Of Arcady	25
58	Fontana H 148	Ring-A My Phone/Chimes Of Arcady (78)	20
59	Fontana H 176	Buzzin'/Cry, Cry, Baby	20
59	Fontana H 176	Buzzin'/Cry, Cry, Baby (78)	15
59	Fontana H 190	Mister Dee-Jay/Tell Him No	20
59	Fontana H 190	Mister Dee-Jay/Tell Him No (78)	20
59	Fontana H 221	(Seven Little Girls) Sitting In The Back Seat (with Al Saxon)/Sitting On The Sidewalk	15
59	Fontana H 221	(Seven Little Girls) Sitting In The Back Seat (with Al Saxon)/Sitting On The Sidewalk (78)	30
60	Fontana H 235	My Mother's Eyes/You've Got What It Takes	15
60	Fontana H 235	My Mother's Eyes/You've Got What It Takes (78)	35
60	Fontana H 252	Someone Loves You, Joe/Tinatarella Di Luna	10
60	Fontana H 283	Two-some/Down South	10

(see also Al Saxon, Dusty Springfield, Chantelles)

MINT VALUE £

CYNTHIA LANAGAN
54	Columbia SCMC 8	Body And Soul/I Can't Believe You're In Love With Me (export issue)	10
57	Parlophone R 4316	Jamie Boy/Silent Lips (as Cynthia Lanigan)	7
57	Parlophone R 4383	I'm Available/(Don't Stop, Don't Stop) Tell Me More	7

STEVE LANCASTER
| 67 | Polydor 56215 | San Francisco Street/Miguel Fernando San Sebastian Brown | 6 |

LANCASTRIANS
64	Pye 7N 15732	We'll Sing In The Sunshine/Was She Tall	8
65	Pye 7N 15791	Let's Lock The Door (And Throw Away The Key)/If You're Goin' To Leave Me	7
65	Pye 7N 15846	There'll Be No More Goodbyes/Never Gonna Come On Home	7
65	Pye 7N 15927	Lonely Man/I Can't Stand The Pain	7
66	Pye 7N 17043	The World Keeps Going Round/Not The Same Anymore	15
66	Pye 7N 17072	The Ballad Of The Green Berets/My Little Rose	6

MAJOR LANCE
63	Columbia DB 7099	The Monkey Time/Mama Didn't Know	18
63	Columbia DB 7168	Hey Little Girl/Crying In The Rain	12
64	Columbia DB 7205	Um, Um, Um, Um, Um, Um/Sweet Music	10
64	Columbia DB 7271	The Matador/Gonna Get Married	18
64	Columbia DB 7365	Rhythm/Please Don't Say No More	15
65	Columbia DB 7463	I'm So Lost/Sometimes I Wonder	12
65	Columbia DB 7527	Come See/You Belong To Me, My Love	18
65	Columbia DB 7609	Pride And Joy/I'm The One	20
65	Columbia DB 7688	Too Hot To Hold/Dark And Lonely	18
65	Columbia DB 7787	Everybody Loves A Good Time/I Just Can't Help It	18
66	Columbia DB 7967	Investigate/Little Young Lover	30
67	Columbia DB 8122	Ain't No Soul (Left In These Ole Shoes)/You'll Want Me Back	30
69	Atlantic 584 277	Follow The Leader/Since You've Been Gone	7
69	Atlantic 584 302	Sweeter As The Days Go By/Shadows Of A Memory	7
69	Soul City SC 114	The Beat/You'll Want Me Back	12
70	Buddah 2011 046	Gypsy Woman/Stay Away From Me	12
72	Stax 2025 124	I Wanna Make Up/That's The Story Of My Life	10
72	Epic EPC 8404	Um, Um, Um, Um, Um, Um/Sweet Music (reissue)	5
73	Contempo C 1	The Right Track/Um, Um, Um, Um, Um, Um	5
73	Contempo C 9	Ain't No Soul (Left In These Ole Shoes)/Investigate	5
73	Contempo C 26	Dark And Lonely/My Girl	8
73	Warner Bros K 16334	Sweeter/Wild & Free	6
74	Warner Bros K 16385	Without A Doubt/Open The Door To Your Heart	6
74	Contempo CS 2017	Gimme Little Sign/How Can You Say Goodbye	5
74	Contempo CS 9015	The Right Track/Ain't No Soul (Left In These Ole Shoes)	5
75	Contempo CS 2045	Don't You Know I Love You (Parts 1 & 2)	5
75	Pye 7N 45487	You're Everything I Need (Parts 1 & 2)	5
76	Pye International 7N 25705	Nothing Can Stop Me/Follow The Leader	5
64	Columbia SEG 8318	UM UM UM UM UM UM (EP)	70
65	Columbia 33SX 1728	THE RHYTHM OF MAJOR LANCE (LP)	100
73	Contempo COLP 1001	GREATEST HITS LIVE AT THE TORCH (LP)	12
76	Epic EPC 81519	THE BEST OF MAJOR LANCE (LP)	15
78	Tamla Motown STML 12094	NOW ARRIVING (LP)	12
84	Edsel ED 124	MONKEY TIME (LP)	12

RICK LANCELOT & SEVEN KNIGHTS
| 66 | RCA RCA 1502 | Say Girl/Live Like A Lion | 6 |

LANCERS
54	London HL 8002	Sweet Mama Tree Top Tall/Were You Ever Mine To Lose (78)	10
54	London HL 8108	Live And Let Live/I Should Have Never Let You Go (78)	10
54	London HL 8027	Stop Chasin' Me Baby/Peggy O'Neil	50
54	London HL 8027	Stop Chasin' Me Baby/Peggy O'Neil (78)	15
54	London HL 8079	So High, So Low, So Wide/It's You, It's You I Love	50
54	London HL 8079	So High, So Low, So Wide/It's You, It's You I Love (78)	15
54	Vogue Coral Q 2038	Mister Sandman/The Little White Light	20
54	Vogue Coral Q 2038	Mister Sandman/The Little White Light (78)	10
55	Vogue Coral Q 72062	Timberjack/C-r-a-z-y Music	15
55	Vogue Coral Q 72081	Get Out Of The Car (as Lancers & Georgie Auld)/Close Your Eyes	15
55	Vogue Coral Q 72081	Get Out Of The Car (as Lancers & Georgie Auld)/Close Your Eyes (78)	15
55	Vogue Coral Q 72100	Jo-Ann/The Bonnie Banks Of Loch Lomon'	12
56	Vogue Coral Q 72128	Alphabet Rock/Rock Around The Island	30
56	Vogue Coral Q 72128	Alphabet Rock/Rock Around The Island (78)	25
56	Vogue Coral Q 72157	Little Fool/A Man Is As Good As His Word	10
56	Vogue Coral Q 72157	Little Fool/A Man Is As Good As His Word (78)	10
56	Vogue Coral Q 72183	The First Travelling Saleslady/Free	8
57	Vogue Coral Q 72220	Never Leave Me/I Came Back To Say I'm Sorry	8
57	Vogue Coral Q 72220	Never Leave Me/I Came Back To Say I'm Sorry (78)	8
57	Vogue Coral Q 72254	It Happened In Monterey/Ramona/Freckled-Face Sara Jane	7
57	Vogue Coral Q 72282	Charm Bracelet/And It Don't Feel Bad	8
57	Vogue Coral Q 72282	Charm Bracelet/And It Don't Feel Bad (78)	10
58	Coral Q 72300	The Stroll/Don't Go Near The Water	10
58	Coral Q 72300	The Stroll/Don't Go Near The Water (78)	15
60	Coral Q 72398	Joey, Joey, Joey/JOHNNY DESMOND: The Most Happy Fella	5
61	Warner Bros WB 39	Young In Love/Lonesome Town	5
55	London REP 1027	PRESENTING THE LANCERS (EP)	30
54	London H-APB 1029	OH SWEET MAMA (10" LP)	35
61	London HA-P 2307	CONCERT IN CONTRASTS (LP)	15

ELSA LANCHESTER
| 58 | Vogue VA 160126 | SONGS FOR A SMOKE-FILLED ROOM (LP, with Charles Laughton) | 15 |
| 59 | Vogue VA 160139 | SONGS FOR A SHUTTERED PARLOUR (LP, with Charles Laughton) | 15 |

BILLY LAND
62 Oriole CB 1750   I Go Walking/You're Too Much 7

HAROLD LAND
58 Contemporary LAC 12178   HAROLD IN THE LAND OF JAZZ (LP) 20

BOB LANDER & SPOTNICKS
62 Oriole CB 1756   My Old Kentucky Home/Home On The Range (possibly unreleased) .... 15+
62 Oriole CB 1784   Midnight Special/My Old Kentucky Home............................ 10
(see also Spotnicks)

BILL & BRETT LANDIS
59 Parlophone R 4516   Since You've Gone/Bright Eyes 8
59 Parlophone R 4516   Since You've Gone/Bright Eyes (78) 12
59 Parlophone R 4551   By You, By You/Forgive Me 8
59 Parlophone R 4570   Baby Talk/Love Me True 10

JERRY LANDIS
62 Oriole CB 1930   Carlos Dominquez/He Was My Brother 18
(see also Paul Simon)

JOYA LANDIS
68 Trojan TR 620   Kansas City/Out The Light...................................... 8
69 Trojan TR 641   Moonlight Lover/I Love You True 10
(see also Jay & Joya, Hugh Roy)

HOAGY LANDS
67 Stateside SS 2030   The Next In Line/Please Don't Talk About Me When I'm Gone ... 140
68 Stateside SS 2085   I'm Yours/Only You 12
72 Action ACT 4605   Why Didn't You Let Me Know/Do You Know What Life Is All About 10
75 UK USA 13   Friends And Lovers Don't Go Together/True Love At Last........... 5
75 UK USA 14   The Next In Line/I'm Yours 5

LANDSCAPE
78 Event Horizon EVE 137 U2XME1X2MUCH/Don't Gimme No Rebop/Sixteen (p/s) 5
78 Event Horizon EVE 139 Workers Playtime/Nearly Normal/Too Many Questions (p/s) 5
79 RCA PB 5183   Japan/Gotham City (p/s) 4
80 RCA PB 5259   Sonja Henie/Neddy Sindrum (p/s) 4
80 RCA EDM 1   European Man/Mechanical Bride (p/s)............................ 4
80 RCA EDMT 1   European Man/Mechanical Bride (12", p/s)...................... 12
82 RCA RCAT 22   Einstein A Go-Go/Japan (12", p/s)............................. 8

DES(MOND) LANE
56 Decca F 10821   Penny-Whistle Rock/Penny-Whistle Polka 8
57 Decca F 10847   Rock Mister Piper/Plymouth Rock............................... 10
59 Top Rank JAR 203   Moonbird/The Clanger March (as Des Lane Orchestra, with John Barry) 7
59 Top Rank JAR 203   Moonbird/The Clanger March (as Des Lane Orchestra, with John Barry) (78).... 12
68 Pye 7N 17546   Sadie/No More Wild Oats (as Des Lane) 5
(see also Cyril Stapleton, John Barry)

GARY LANE & GARRISONS
61 Fontana H 338   Start Walking Boy/How Wrong Can You Be 12
62 Fontana 267221 TF   I'm A Lucky Boy/A Love Like You 10

LOIS LANE
67 RCA RCA 1570   One Little Voice/Sing To Me 6
68 Mercury MF 1042   Punky's Dilemma/Lazy Summer Day................................ 6
69 Mercury MF 1092   Brontasaurus Named Bert/Windmills Of Your Mind 6
69 Mercury MF 1115   Lovin' Time/Winds Of Heaven 6
70 Philips BF 1829   Putting My Baby To Sleep/Far From The Madding Crowd............ 5
70 DJM DJS 2280   Day By Day/Cloud Of Blue 5
68 Mercury SMCL 20125   LOIS LANE (LP) 12
(see also Caravelles)

MICKEY LEE LANE
64 Stateside SS 354   Shaggy Dog/Oo Oo 7
65 Stateside SS 456   Hey Sah-Lo-Ney/Of Yesterday 25

PENNY LANE
68 Columbia DB 8377   Loving Or Losing You/Deep Down Inside 5
68 CBS 3718   The Boy Who Never Grew Up/I'm Going Back 5
70 CBS 4749   Bouzouki/Make Up Or Break Up 5
70 CBS 4905   Heartbreak House/He's Got A Hold Of My Heart.................. 5
70 CBS 5311   Rock Me In The Cradle (Of Your Loving Arms)/I'm Free 6

RONNIE LANE & SLIM CHANCE
73 GM GMS 011   How Come/Tell Everyone/Done This One Before (p/s) 5
77 Polydor 2058 944   Street In The City/Annie (with Pete Townshend) 5
77 Polydor 2058 944   Street In The City/Annie (12", with Pete Townshend) 8
79 Gem GEMS 12   Kuschty Rye/You're So Right (p/s) 5
74 GM GMS 1024   ANYMORE FOR ANYMORE (LP) 15
75 Island ILPS 9321   RONNIE LANE AND SLIM CHANCE (LP) 15
75 Island ILPS 9366   ONE FOR THE ROAD (LP) 15
76 Atlantic K 50308   MAHONEY'S LAST STAND (LP, with Ronnie Wood, soundtrack)...... 15
77 Polydor 2442 147   ROUGH MIX (LP, with Pete Townshend) 12
80 Gem GEMLP 107   SEE ME (LP, with insert) 12
88 Thunderbolt THBL 067P MAHONEY'S LAST STAND (LP, reissue, picture disc) 12
(see also Small Faces, Faces, Pete Townshend & Ronnie Lane)

ROSEMARY LANE
60 Philips PB 1041   Down By The River/My First Love Letter........................ 5
61 Philips BF 1127   Lyin' Kisses/The Nightingale Who Sang Off Key 5
61 Philips BF 1172   Who Does He Think He Is/What Is The Age....................... 5
63 Oriole CB 1871   Like You Should/Baby Please Be Kind 7

MINT VALUE £

TONY LANE & DELTONES
64	Sabre SA-45-5	It's Great/Now She's Mine	10

LANE BROTHERS
60	London HLR 9150	Mimi/Two Dozen And A Half	15

LANE SISTERS
61	Columbia DB 4671	Peek A Boo Moon/Birmingham Rag	10

DON LANG (& HIS "FRANTIC" FIVE)
78s
55	HMV POP 115	Cloudburst/Seventeen (78)	10
56	HMV POP 150	Four Brothers/I Want You To Be My Baby (solo) (78)	10
56	HMV POP 178	Rock Around The Island/Jumpin' To Conclusions (solo) (78)	10
56	HMV POP 224	Rock And Roll Blues/Stop The World I Wanna Get Off (solo) (78)	10
56	HMV POP 260	Sweet Sue — Just You/Lazy Latin (solo) (78)	10
57	HMV POP 289	Rock Around The Cookhouse/Rock Mister Piper (78)	12
57	HMV POP 335	Rock-A-Billy/Come Go With Me (B-side with Skifflers) (78)	15
57	HMV POP 350	School Day (Ring! Ring! Goes The Bell)/Six-Five Special (78)	15
57	HMV POP 382	White Silver Sands/Again 'N' Again 'N' Again (78)	12
57	HMV POP 414	Red Planet Rock/Texas Tambourine (78)	15
58	HMV POP 434	Ramshackle Daddy/6-5 Hand Jive (78)	12
58	HMV POP 465	Tequila/Junior Hand Jive (78)	15
58	HMV POP 488	Witch Doctor/Cool Baby Cool (78)	10
58	HMV POP 510	Hey Daddy!/The Bird On My Head (78)	14
58	HMV POP 547	Queen Of The Hop/La-Do-Da-Da (solo) (78)	18
59	HMV POP 585	Wiggle Wiggle/(You Were Only) Teasin' (solo) (78)	20
59	HMV POP 623	Percy Green/Phineas McCoy (solo) (78)	25
59	HMV POP 649	A Hoot An' A Holler/See You Friday (78)	30

SINGLES
56	HMV 7M 354	Four Brothers/I Want You To Be My Baby (solo)	25
56	HMV 7M 381	Rock Around The Island/Jumpin' To Conclusions (solo)	25
56	HMV 7M 416	Rock And Roll Blues/Stop The World I Wanna Get Off (solo)	22
56	HMV POP 260	Sweet Sue — Just You/Lazy Latin (solo)	15
57	HMV POP 289	Rock Around The Cookhouse/Rock Mister Piper	25
57	HMV POP 335	Rock-A-Billy/Come Go With Me (B-side with Skifflers)	22
57	HMV POP 350	School Day (Ring! Ring! Goes The Bell)/Six-Five Special	18
57	HMV POP 382	White Silver Sands/Again 'N' Again 'N' Again	12
57	HMV POP 414	Red Planet Rock/Texas Tambourine	25
58	HMV POP 434	Ramshackle Daddy/6-5 Hand Jive	18
58	HMV POP 465	Tequila/Junior Hand Jive	15
58	HMV POP 488	Witch Doctor/Cool Baby Cool	10
58	HMV POP 510	Hey Daddy!/The Bird On My Head	8
58	HMV POP 547	Queen Of The Hop/La-Do-Da-Da (solo)	12
59	HMV POP 585	Wiggle Wiggle/(You Were Only) Teasin' (solo)	8
59	HMV POP 623	Percy Green/Phineas McCoy (solo)	10
59	HMV POP 649	A Hoot An' A Holler/See You Friday	8
59	HMV POP 682	Reveille Rock/Frankie And Johnny	8
60	HMV POP 714	Sink The Bismarck!/They Call Him Cliff (solo)	15
60	HMV POP 805	Time Machine/Don't Open That Door	10
62	Decca F 11483	Wicked Women/Play Money (as Don Lang & Boulder Rollers)	7

EP
57	HMV 7EG 8208	ROCK 'N' ROLL (EP)	100

LPs
57	HMV DLP 1151	SKIFFLE SPECIAL (10" LP, by Don Lang & His Skiffle Group)	110
58	HMV DLP 1179	INTRODUCING THE HAND JIVE (10" LP)	140
62	Ace Of Clubs ACL 1111	TWENTY TOP-TWENTY TWISTS (LP)	22

(see also Gordon Langhorn)

EDDIE LANG & LONNIE JOHNSON
67	Parlophone PMC 7019	BLUE GUITARS (LP)	40
70	Parlophone PMC 7106	BLUE GUITARS VOLUME 2 (LP)	40

(see also Blind Willie Dunn's Gin Bottle Four)

k.d. lang
87	Sire W 8465	Rose Garden/High Time For A Detour (unissued in U.K.)	
88	Sire W 7841	Sugar Moon/Honky Tonk Medley (p/s)	25
88	Sire W 7841T	Sugar Moon/Honky Tonk Medley/I'm Down To My Last Cigarette (12", p/s)	50
88	Sire W 7697	Our Day Will Come/Three Cigarettes In An Ashtray (live) (p/s)	25
88	Sire W 7697T	Our Day Will Come/Three Cigarettes In An Ashtray (live)/ Johnny Get Angry (live) (12", p/s)	50
90	Warner Brothers W 9535	Ridin' The Rails/DARLENE LOVE: Mr Fix-It (p/s)	20
92	Sire W 0100	Constant Craving (Edit)/Barefoot (Rhythmic Version) (p/s)	5
92	Sire W 0100T	Constant Craving (Edit)/Barefoot (Rhythmic Version)/ Season Of Hollow Soul (12", p/s)	10
92	Sire W 0100CD	Constant Craving (Edit)/Barefoot (Rhythmic Version)/ Season Of Hollow Soul (CD)	18
92	Sire W 0135TW	Miss Chatelaine (St Tropez Mix)/Miss Chatelaine (St Tropez Edit)/Miss Chatelaine/Miss Chatelaine (Single Edit) (12", p/s with poster)	10
92	Sire W 0135CD	Miss Chatelaine (Single Version)/Miss Chatelaine (St Tropez Edit)/ Wash Me Clean (live)/The Mind Of Love (CD)	10
93	Sire W 0157CD	Constant Craving (Edit)/Wash Me Clean (live)/The Mind Of Love (live) (CD)	7
93	Sire W 0157CDX	Constant Craving (live)/Miss Chatelaine (live)/Big Boned Gal (live)/ Outside Myself (live) (CD)	8

RAY LANG & JAMAICAN ROOM ORCHESTRA
57	Brunswick 05683	Last Train (Biddi-Biddi Bum-Bum)/Keetch (Hey! Bernice)	8
57	Brunswick 05683	Last Train (Biddi-Biddi Bum-Bum)/Keetch (Hey! Bernice) (78)	8

STEVIE LANGE
81	RCA RCA 152	Remember My Name/I Don't Want To Know (1st issue, p/s)	12
81	RCA LIM 1	Remember My Name/I Don't Want To Know (2nd issue, p/s)	8
83	Jive JIVE 23	Remember My Name/Don't Want To Cry No More (no p/s)	8

LANGFORDS
60s	Torino TSP 341	Send Me An Angel/Candy (label credits to Langford Boys, some with p/s)	10/6

GORDON LANGHORN
55	Decca F 10591	Give A Fool A Chance/Don't Stay Away Too Long	12

(see also Don Lang, Cyril Stapleton)

JERRY LANGLEY
65	Parlophone R 5325	Little Grey Man/Bitter Sweets	4
67	CBS 2935	Joanna Jones/How Long	4

(see also Langleys)

MARY LANGLEY
67	CBS 2862	Stay In My World/Summer Love	6
67	CBS 3032	It Always Rains On Sunday/All My Life Is You	5

(see also Perpetual Langley, Langleys)

PERPETUAL LANGLEY
66	Planet PLF 110	We Wanna Stay Home/So Sad (with Planet company sleeve)	12
66	Planet PLF 115	Surrender/Two By Two (with Planet company sleeve)	15

(see also Mary Langley, Langleys)

LANGLEYS
64	Fontana TF 483	Snakes And Ladders/I Wander Everywhere	6
65	Fontana TF 544	Green Island/You Know I Love You	6

(see also Jerry Langley, Mary Langley, Perpetual Langley)

(HUW) LLOYD LANGTON (GROUP)
83	Flicknife FLS 021	Wind Of Change/Outside The Law (as Lloyd Langton Group, p/s)	5
83	Flicknife SHARP 015	OUTSIDE THE LAW (LP, 1,000 only with bonus 7": "Working Time"/"I See You" [FREE 001], as Huw Lloyd Langton)	12/15
86	Gas GAS 4014	LIKE AN ARROW (THROUGH THE HEART) (LP)	12

(see also Hawkwind, Widowmaker)

PHIL LANGTON TRIO
60s	Holyground	PHIL LANGTON TRIO (LP)	20

CYNTHIA LANIGAN
57	Parlophone R 4316	Silent Lips/Jamie Boy (78)	12

LESTER LANIN & HIS ORCHESTRA
62	Columbia 33SX 1442	TWISTIN' IN HIGH SOCIETY! (LP)	12

SNOOKY LANSON
50	London L 555	The Old Master Painter/Did You Ever See A Dream Walking? (78)	15
50	London L 682	Roses/Where Are You Gonna Be When The Moon Shines (78)	15
56	London HLD 8223	It's Almost Tomorrow/Why Don't You Write	100
56	London HLD 8223	It's Almost Tomorrow/Why Don't You Write (78)	12
56	London HLD 8236	Stop (Let Me Off The Bus)/Last Minute Love	165
56	London HLD 8236	Stop (Let Me Off The Bus)/Last Minute Love (78)	25
56	London HLD 8249	Seven Days/Tippity Top	165
56	London HLD 8249	Seven Days/Tippity Top (78)	25
56	London HL 7005	Seven Days/Tippity Top (export issue)	50

(see also Eve Young & Snooky Lanson, Teresa Brewer)

MARIO LANZA
53	HMV 7R 128	The First Noel/Silent Night	10
53	HMV 7R 129	Questa O Quello (Verdi)/Recondita Armonia (Puccini)	10
53	HMV 7R 130	Be My Love/The Bayou Lullaby	10
53	HMV 7R 131	Serenade (Troselli)/Serenade (Drigo)	10
53	HMV 7R 139	Because/For You Alone	10
53	HMV 7R 144	Because You're Mine/The Song Angels Sing	12
53	HMV 7R 145	Lee-Ah-Loo/You Do Something To Me	10
53	HMV 7R 146	Mi Batte Il Cor ... O Paradiso!/Mamma, Quel Vino E Generoso	10
53	HMV 7R 147	O Come, All Ye Faithful/Oh! Little Town Of Bethlehem	10
53	HMV 7R 157	Granada/Lolita	10
53	HMV 7R 168	M'Appari Tutt' Amor (Flotow)/Libiamo, Libiamo Ne' Lieti Calici (B-side with Elaine Malbin)	10
53	HMV 7R 178	Valencia/Besame Mucho	10
57	RCA RCA 1026	A Night To Remember/Behold!	5
58	RCA RCA 1045	Seven Hills Of Rome/Come Dance With Me	5
58	RCA RCA 1059	On The Street Where You Live/Younger Than Springtime	5
58	RCA RCA 1080	Love In A Home/Do You Wonder	5
58	RCA RCA 1090	Drinking Song/Serenade (Romberg)	5
58	RCA RCA 1090	Drinking Song/Serenade (Romberg) (78)	10
58	RCA RCA 1094	I'll Walk With God/The Lord's Prayer	5
58	RCA RCA 1094	I'll Walk With God/The Lord's Prayer (78)	8
60	RCA RCA 1155	O Come All Ye Faithful/Silent Night, Holy Night (78)	12
60	RCA RCA 1166	Because You're Mine/The Donkey Serenade	5
60	RCA RCA 1166	Because You're Mine/The Donkey Serenade (78)	18
53	HMV ALP 1071	THE GREAT CARUSO (LP, soundtrack)	18
54	HMV ALP 1202	OPERATIC ARIAS (LP)	18
55	HMV BLP 1071	SONGS OF ROMANCE (10" LP)	18
56	HMV ALP 1365	SERENADE (LP, soundtrack)	18
57	HMV BLP 1091	LANZA ON BROADWAY (10" LP)	18
57	HMV BLP 1094	THE TOUCH OF YOUR HAND (10" LP)	18
57	RCA RB 16002	IN A CAVALCADE OF SHOW TUNES (LP)	12

Mario LANZA

58	RCA RA 13001	THE SEVEN HILLS OF ROME (10" LP)	18
59	RCA RB 16085	SINGS A KISS AND OTHER LOVE SONGS (LP)	12
59	RCA RB 16112	THE GREAT CARUSO (LP, reissue)	12
59	RCA RB 16113	THE STUDENT PRINCE (LP, soundtrack)	12
59	RCA RB 16158	FOR THE FIRST TIME (LP, soundtrack)	12
59	RCA RB 16167	LANZA ON BROADWAY (LP, soundtrack)	12
59	RCA RB 16171/SB 2054	LANZA SINGS CHRISTMAS CAROLS (LP, mono/stereo)	12/15
60s	Readers Digest RDS 6461-6	THE BEST OF MARIO LANZA (6-LP set)	30

LARKS
64	Pye International 7N 25284	The Jerk/Forget Me	18

SAM LARNER
61	Folkways FG 3507	NOW IS THE TIME FOR FISHING (LP)	18
74	Topic 12T 244	A GARLAND FOR SAM (LP, blue label)	15

LARO
60s	Kalypso XX 21	Jamaican Referendum Calypso/Wrong Impressions Of A Soldier	8

WINSTON LARO
70	Downtown DT 461	Goodnight My Love/BOYSIE: I Don't Want To Be Hurt	6

JULIUS LA ROSA
55	London HL 8154	Mobile/Pass It On	30
55	London HL 8154	Mobile/Pass It On (78)	12
55	London HLA 8170	Domani/Mama Rosa	25
55	London HLA 8170	Domani/Mama Rosa (78)	8
55	London HLA 8193	Suddenly There's A Valley/Everytime I Kiss Carrie	30
56	HMV 7M 384	Lipstick And Candy And Rubber-Sole Shoe/Winter In New England	10
56	HMV POP 181	Lipstick And Candy And Rubber-Sole Shoe/Winter In New England (78)	10
56	London HLA 8272	No Other Love/Rosanne	22
56	London HLA 8272	No Other Love/Rosanne (78)	10
56	London HLA 8353	Jingle Bells (Campanelle)/Jingle Dingle	15
56	London HLA 8353	Jingle Bells (Campanelle)/Jingle Dingle (78)	8
58	RCA RCA 1063	Torero/Milano	6
58	Columbia DB 4218	Let Nature Take Its Course/Until He Gets A Girl	6
58	Columbia DB 4218	Let Nature Take Its Course/Until He Gets A Girl (78)	8
59	Columbia DB 4287	Where's The Girl/Protect Me	6
60	London HLR 9092	Green Fields/Caress Me	7
64	London HLA 9901	Je/Gonna Build A Mountain	6
54	London RE-P 1005	SINGS (EP)	30
57	London HA-A 2031	JULIUS LA ROSA (LP)	50

LARRY'S ALL STARS
71	Ackee ACK 130	Pre-Fight/The Prayer	7

(see also Larry Lawrence, Delroy Wilson, Hugh Roy, Sensations)

LARRY (Marshall) & ALVIN
68	Studio One SO 2065	Nanny Goat/Smell You Crep	12
68	Studio One SO 2067	Can't You Understand/Hush Up	30
69	Studio One SO 2080	Lonely Room (No One To Give Me Love)/You Mean To Me	18
69	Coxsone CS 7081	Love Got Me/BOB ANDY: Lady With The Bright Light (both sides actually by Glen [Brown] & Dave [Barker])	18

(see also Larry Marshall, Sound Dimension, Vincent Gordon)

LARRY & JOHNNY
65	Outasite 45 501	Beatle Time (Parts 1 & 2) (99 copies only)	100

(see also Larry Williams & Johnny 'Guitar' Watson)

LARRY & TOMMY
68	Polydor 56741	You've Gotta Bend A Little/Yo-Yo	8

JACK LARSON
61	Top Rank JAR 573	I Love The Way She Laughs/The Hammer Bell Song	7

DANNY LA RUE
68	Page One POF 108	On Mother Kelly's Doorstep/The Impossible Dream	4

LA'S
87	Go! Discs GOLAS 1	Way Out/Endless (p/s)	15
87	Go! Discs GOLAS 112	Way Out/Knock Me Down/Endless (12", red & silver p/s)	20
87	Go! Discs GOLAR 112	Way Out/Knock Me Down/Endless/Liberty Ship (Demo)/Freedom Song (Demo) (12", blue & silver stickered p/s listing 4 tracks)	25
87	Go! Discs GOLAR 112	Way Out/Knock Me Down/Endless/Liberty Ship (Demo)/Freedom Song (Demo) (12", blue & silver stickered p/s listing 5 tracks)	25
88	Go! Discs GOLAS 2	There She Goes/Come In Come Out (red p/s)	10
88	Go! Discs LASEP 2	There She Goes/Way Out/Who Knows/Come In Come Out (EP, blue p/s, 5,000 only)	12
88	Go! Discs GOLAS 212	There She Goes/Come In Come Out/Who Knows/Man I'm Only Human (12", p/s)	15
88	Go! Discs LASCD 2	There She Goes/Come In Come Out/Who Knows/Man I'm Only Human (CD)	18
89	Go! Discs GOLAS 3	Timeless Melody/Clean Prophet (p/s, unissued; 10 test pressings only)	60+
89	Go! Discs LASEP 3	Timeless Melody (10", unissued)	
89	Go! Discs LASDJ 312	Timeless Melody/Clean Prophet/All By Myself/Rider Yer Camel (12", promo, 500 only)	50+
89	Go! Discs LASCD 3	Timeless Melody/Clean Prophet/All By Myself/Rider Yer Camel (CD, unissued)	
89	Go! Discs GOLAS 4	Timeless Melody/Clean Prophet (blue p/s)	6
89	Go! Discs LASMC 4	Timeless Melody/Clean Prophet (cassette, green inlay)	5
89	Go! Discs GOLAS 412	Timeless Melody/Clean Prophet/Knock Me Down/Over (12", purple p/s)	8
89	Go! Discs LASCD 4	Timeless Melody/Clean Prophet/Knock Me Down/Over (CD, orange card p/s)	10
90	Go! Discs GOLAS 5	There She Goes/Freedom Song (p/s)	5

90	Go! Discs GOLAB 5	There She Goes/Freedom Song (numbered box set with badge & 3 stickers) . . . 10
90	Go! Discs LASMC 5	There She Goes/Freedom Song (cassette) 4
90	Go! Discs GOLAS 512	There She Goes/Freedom Song/All By Myself (12", p/s) 7
90	Go! Discs LASCD 5	There She Goes/Freedom Song/All By Myself (CD) 10
91	Go! Discs GOLAS 6	Feelin'/Doledrum (p/s) 4
91	Go! Discs LASMC 6	Feelin'/Doledrum (cassette) 4
91	Go! Discs GOLAB 6	Feelin'/IOU (Alternate Version)/Feelin' (Alternate Version)/Doledrum (numbered box set with badge & 3 stickers) 10
91	Go! Discs GOLAR 612	Feelin'/IOU (Alternate Version)/Feelin' (Alternate Version)/Doledrum (12") 7
91	Go! Discs LASCD 6	Feelin'/Doledrum/IOU (Alternate Version)/Liberty Ship (CD) 10
90	Go! Discs LASCD 1	THE LA'S SOUND SAMPLER (CD, promo, 1,000 only) 15
91	Go! Discs 828 202-1	THE LA'S (LP) 30
	(see also Cast)	

COUNT LASHER

| 60s | Kalypso 100 AB | Calypso Cha Cha Cha/Perseverance . . . . 5 |
| 60s | Kalypso 105 AB | Slide Mongoose/Miss Constance . . . . 5 |

LASSIES & RAY CHARLES SINGERS

| 56 | Brunswick 05571 | Sleepy Head/This I Offer You . . . . 6 |

JAMES LAST

| 72 | Polydor 2371 235 | VOODOO PARTY (LP) . . . . 15 |

LAST BANDITS

80s	Solid ROK 722	The Angels Are Calling/The Dalkey Rake (p/s) 5
86	Hotwire HWLP 8504	THE LAST BANDITS IN THE WORLD (LP) 10
	(see also Swell Maps, Nikki Sudden)	

LAST CHANT

| 81 | Chicken Jazz JAZZ 4 | Run Of The Dove/Strength Alone/Tradition (p/s) . . . . 8 |
| | *(see also Waterboys)* | |

LAST EXIT

75	Wudwink WUD 01	Whispering Voices/Evensong (no p/s) 35
75	Wudwink WUD.C.101	FIRST FROM LAST EXIT (cassette only, pink card insert, sold at gigs, 3 copies known to exist) . . . . 250+
	(see also Newcastle Big Band, Police, Sting)	

LAST FEW DAYS

| 86 | Touch TG-45 | Too Much Is Not Enough/Solemn Warnings/
If The Bonds Are Not To Burst (12", p/s) . . . . 7 |

LAST FLIGHT

| 81 | Heavy Metal HEAVY 5 | Dance To The Music/I'm Ready (p/s) . . . . 8 |

LAST POETS

| 72 | Douglas DGL 69012 | THIS IS MADNESS (LP) . . . . 12 |

LAST RESORT

| 78 | Red Meat RMRS 01 | Having Fun?/F.U.2 (die-cut printed paper sleeve) . . . . 20 |

LAST RESORT

81	own label	Violence In Our Minds/Help Hostage/Soul Boys (cassette; 4-track issue) 50
81	own label	Violence In Our Minds/Help Hostage (cassette; 3-track issue) 40
82	Last Resort LR 1	SKINHEAD ANTHEMS (LP, red vinyl; also white, blue & black vinyl) 25-30

LAST RITES

| 83 | Flicknife FLS 219 | We Don't Care/Step Down (p/s) . . . . 4 |
| 84 | Essential 004 | FASCISM MEANS WAR (EP, gatefold p/s) . . . . 4 |

LAST ROUGH CAUSE

| 86 | L.R.C. LRC 1 | THE VIOLENT FEW (EP) . . . . 7 |

LAST WORD

| 74 | Polydor 2066 429 | Keep On Bumping Before You Give Out Of Gas/Funky And Some . . . . 5 |

LAST WORDS

79	Rough Trade RT 022	Animal World/No Music In The World Today (p/s) 8
79	Remand REMAND 2	Todays Kidz/There's Something Wrong (p/s) 6
81	Armageddon ARM 2	THE LAST WORDS (LP) 12

YUSEF LATEEF

58	Esquire 32-069	THE SOUNDS OF YUSEF (LP) 20
58	Columbia Clef 33CX 10124	BEFORE DAWN (LP) 20
72	Atlantic K 40359	GENTLE GIANT (LP) 12
73	Prestige PR 24007	YUSEF LATEEF (LP) 12
74	Atlantic K 50041	PART OF THE SEARCH (LP) 12
74	Milestone ML 47009	THE MANY FACES OF YUSEF LATEEF (LP) 12
75	Atlantic K 60102	10 YEARS HENCE (LP) 12

GENE LATTER

66	Decca F 12364	Just A Minute Or Two/Dream Lover 7
66	Decca F 12397	Mother's Little Helper/Please Come Back To Me Again 12
67	CBS 202483	Something Inside Me Died/Don't Go 6
67	CBS 202655	Always/A Woman Called Sorrow 7
67	CBS 2843	A Little Piece Of Leather/Funny Face Girl 10
67	CBS 2986	With A Child's Heart/Ways 10
68	Direction 58-3245	A Tribute To Otis/Bring Your Love Home 6
68	Spark SRL 1015	My Life Ain't Easy/Angie (as Gene Latter & Detours) 5
69	Spark SRL 1022	Sign On The Dotted Line/I Love You 8
69	Spark SRL 1031	The Old Iron Bell/Holding A Dream 5
69	Parlophone R 5800	Help Me Judy, Help Me/On The Highway 5
69	Parlophone R 5815	Tiger Bay/We Can Make Out 5
70	Parlophone R 5853	Someday You'll Need My Love/Come On Home 5

Gene LATTER

71	Parlophone R 5896	Catch My Soul/Happiness	5
71	Parlophone R 5913	Sing A Song Of Freedom/Too Busy Thinking About My Baby	5
72	Spark SRL 1063	Sign On The Dotted Line/I Love You (reissue)	6
70s	Youngblood YB 1069	All Over Now/Annie's Place	5

(see also Detours)

STANLEY LAUDAN
58	Oriole CB 1434	Two Guitars/Blue Shawl	8
58	Oriole CB 1434	Two Guitars/Blue Shawl (78)	8

SIR HARRY LAUDER
59	HMV 7P 235	Harry Lauder Medley (both sides)	6
55	HMV DLP 1089	ROAMING IN THE GLOAMING (10" LP)	12

LAUGH
85	Debris DEB 01	Take Your Time Yeah!/TWANG: What's The Rub (flexidisc with *Debris* mag)	6/5
87	Remorse LOSS 5	Paul McCartney (p/s)	4

LAUGHING APPLE
81	Autonomy AUT 001	HA HA HEE HEE (EP)	8
81	Autonomy AUT 002	Participate!/Wouldn't You? (foldover p/s)	6
82	Essential ESS 001	Precious Feeling/Celebration (p/s)	8
83	Creation Artefact LYN 12903	Wouldn't You?/PASTELS: I Wonder Why! (live) (33rpm flexidisc, initially free with Legend! 7" "'73 In '83" [CRE 001], £15)	5

(see also Biff Bang Pow!, Revolving Paint Dream)

LAUGHING CACK
87	Cagon CAC8	Laugh? I Nearly Shat/Shitter Stoke Has A Laugh (brown vinyl, p/s)	8

LAUGHING CLOWNS
82	Pink Melon PM 020	Mad Flies Mad Flies/Mr Uddich (p/s)	6

LAUGHING GAS
70	RCA RCA 2006	All Shapes And Sizes/Opus No. 1	5

CYNDI LAUPER
84	Portrait WA 4290	Time After Time/I'll Kiss You (picture disc)	6
84	Portrait WA 4620	She Bop/Witness (Cyndi-shaped picture disc)	8
86	Portrait CYNDI 1P	Change Of Heart/What A Thrill (picture disc)	5
87	Epic CYNP 1	What's Going On/What's Going On (Version) (picture disc)	5
89	Epic CYNC 5	My First Night Without You/Unabbreviated Love/Iko Iko/ When You Were Mine (CD, picture disc)	8
89	Epic 655 091-1	My First Night Without You (Edited Remix)/Unabbreviated Love (3" CD, gatefold card sleeve)	8
89	Epic CDCYN 6	Heading West/Insecurious/She Bop (live)/ Money Changes Everything (live) (CD, card sleeve)	7
89	Epic CYNC 6	Heading West/What's Going On (live)/She Bop (live)/ Money Changes Everything (live) (CD, picture disc)	8

(see also Blue Angel)

LAUREL (Aitken) & OWEN (Gray)
62	Blue Beat BB 149	She's Going To Napoli/Have Mercy Mr Percy	12

(see also Laurel Aitken, Owen Gray)

LAURELS
68	RCA Victor RCA 1741	Sunshine Thursday/Threepence A Tune	4
69	RCA Victor RCA 1836	Making It Groovy/Rainmaker	4

ROD LAUREN
59	RCA RCA 1165	If I Had A Girl/No Wonder	6
59	RCA RCA 1165	If I Had A Girl/No Wonder (78)	18

HALLAM LAURENCE
98	Tyler SARK 4	Mmm, Dr. Who, I Fancy You/Go On, Kick Me (p/s)	6

ZACK LAURENCE (ORCHESTRA)
61	Parlophone R 4802	Teenage Concerto/Saratoga	6
63	Parlophone R 5000	Tempo Seven/Sleeve Shaker	6
66	HMV 7EG 8968	BEATLE CONCERTO (EP)	8

JOHN LAURENZ
55	London HL 8138	Goodbye, Stranger, Goodbye/Red Roses	30
55	London HL 8138	Goodbye, Stranger, Goodbye/Red Roses (78)	10
65	Decca F 12147	99 Times Out Of 100/I Can Feel It	5

LAURIE
66	Decca F 12347	He Understands Me/Fools Never Learn	6
66	Decca F 12424	I Love Onions/I Want Him	7

CY LAURIE JAZZ BAND
60s	Melodisc M 1479	You Make Me Love You/Dippermouth	5
61	Storyville A 45045	Don't Go Away Nobody/There'll Come A Day	5
55	Esquire EP 29	CY LAURIE BAND (EP)	20
55	Esquire EP 39	CY LAURIE BAND (EP)	10
56	Esquire EP 89	CY LAURIE BAND (EP)	10
56	Esquire EP 120	CY LAURIE BAND (EP)	20
56	Tempo EXA 32	JAZZ IN DENMARK (EP)	10
57	Esquire EP 124	CY LAURIE BAND (EP)	15
57	Esquire EP 140	CY PLAYS LIL (EP)	10
57	Melodisc EPM 7-71	CY LAURIE'S JAZZ BAND (EP)	10
58	Esquire EP 200	YOU'RE NEXT (EP)	10
59	Esquire EP 210	CY LAURIE BAND (EP)	15

60	Esquire EP 234	CY LAURIE BAND (EP)	15
60s	Parlophone GEP 8710	JUNGLE JAZZ (EP)	10
60s	Storyville SEP 395	CY LAURIE BAND VOL. 5 (EP)	8
55	Esquire 20-037	CY LAURIE JAZZ BAND (10" LP)	25
50s	Esquire 32-008	CY LAURIE JAZZ BAND (LP)	25

LINDA LAURIE
59	London HL 8807	Ambrose/Ooh, What A Lover	12
59	London HL 8807	Ambrose/Ooh, What A Lover (78)	10
60	Top Rank JAR 277	Stay With Me/All Winter Long	7

LAURIE SISTERS
| 60 | MGM MGM 1083 | Don't Forget (To Sign Your Name With A Kiss)/I Surrender Dear | 6 |
| 61 | MGM MGM 1128 | Live It Up/Lonesome And Sorry | 6 |

MISS LAVELL
| 65 | Vocalion VP 9236 | Everybody's Got Somebody/The Best Part Of Me | 18 |

ROGER La VERN & MICRONS
| 63 | Decca F 11791 | Christmas Stocking/Reindeer Ride | 35 |
| 75 | SRT SRTS/CUS/042 | Sing-A-Long Piano Party Parts 1 & 2 (maxi-single, p/s) | 8 |

(see also Tornados)

BETTY LAVETTE
67	Stateside SS 2015	I Feel Good All Over/Only Your Love Can Save Me	25
68	Pama PM 748	Only Your Love Can Save Me/I Feel Good All Over (reissue)	12
70	Polydor 56786	He Made A Woman Out Of Me/Nearer To You	7
72	Mojo 2092 030	Let Me Down Easy/I Feel Good All Over/What I Don't Know Won't Hurt Me	6
73	Atlantic K 10299	Your Turn To Cry/Soul Tambourine	10
78	Atlantic K 11198	Doin' The Best I Can Parts 1 & 2	5

AZIE LAWRENCE
59	Mezzotone ME 7001/7002	West Indians In England/Jump Up	7
59	Mezzotone ME 7004	Love In Every Land/No Dice	7
60	Starlite ST45 022	West Indians In England/Jump Up (with Carib Serenaders)	6
61	Starlite ST45 041	No Dice/Love In Every Land	6
61	Melodisc M 1563	Jamaica Blues/Come Rumble & Tumble With Me	6
61	Melodisc M 1572	You Didn't Want To Know	5
61	Blue Beat BB 71	So Far Apart/Palms Of Victory (with Melobeats)	12
64	Blue Beat BB 222	Pempelem/Lovers Understand	12

DIANE LAWRENCE
| 67 | Doctor Bird DB 1075 | I Won't Hang Around Like A Hound Dog/Read It Over | 20 |
| 68 | Jolly JY 005 | Treat Me Nice/I'll Be Loving You | 7 |

EDDIE LAWRENCE
| 59 | Coral Q 72361 | The Salesman's Philosopher/Mother Philosopher | 5 |
| 59 | Coral Q 72361 | The Salesman's Philosopher/Mother Philosopher (78) | 8 |

ELLIOTT LAWRENCE BAND
51	Vogue V 9024	Sixty-Minute Man/Quick (78)	10
52	Vogue V 9032	Lovin' Machine/Don't Leave My Poor Heart Breakin' (78)	8
58	Vogue LAE 12057	PLAYS GERRY MULLIGAN ARRANGEMENTS (LP)	12

GENE LAWRENCE
| 67 | Jump Up JU 505 | Longest Day Meringue/Bachelor Boy | 6 |
| 67 | Jump Up JU 510 | Meringue Triniana/Devil Woman | 6 |

GERTRUDE LAWRENCE
| 53 | Brunswick 05171 | Getting To Know You/YUL BRYNNER: A Puzzlement (78) | 8 |
| 53 | Brunswick 05166 | Shall We Dance (with Yul Brynner)/The King And I Overture (78) | 8 |

(see also Yul Brynner)

LARRY LAWRENCE (U.S.)
59	Pye International 7N 25042	Goofin' Off/Bongo Boogie (as Larry Lawrence & Band Of Gold)	6
59	Pye International N 25042	Goofin' Off/Bongo Boogie (as Larry Lawrence & Band Of Gold) (78)	12
60	Ember EMB S 106	Squad Car Theme/Jug-A-Roo (with Beatniks, some in art p/s)	12/7

LARRY LAWRENCE (Jamaica)
| 63 | Island WI 091 | Garden Of Eden/DERRICK MORGAN: Sendin' This Message | 15 |

(see also Larry's Allstars, McBean Scott & Champions)

LEE LAWRENCE (& CORONETS)
53	Decca F 10177	Crying In The Chapel/To Live My Life With You (78)	10
54	Decca F 10285	The Little Mustard Seed/My Love For You	10
54	Decca F 10367	The Story Of Tina/For You My Love	10
54	Decca F 10408	The Things I Didn't Do/You Still Mean The Same To Me	8
55	Decca F 10422	My Own True Love (Tara's Theme)/Beware Now!	8
55	Decca F 10438	Lights Of Paris/A Love Like Ours	7
55	Decca F 10485	Wedding Bells And Silver Horse-Shoes/Will You Be Mine Alone?	7
55	Columbia SCM 5175	Beyond The Stars/Give Me Your Word	8
55	Columbia SCM 5181	My World Stood Still/Don't Worry	8
55	Columbia SCM 5190	More Than A Millionaire/Overnight	7
55	Columbia SCM 5201	Suddenly There's A Valley/Mi Muchacha (Little Girl)	15
56	Columbia SCM 5228	Young And Foolish/Don't Tell Me Not To Love You	8
56	Columbia SCM 5254	We Believe In Love/Welcome To My Heart	7
56	Columbia SCM 5283	Come Back, My Love/Valley Valparaiso	7
56	Columbia DB 3830	From The Candy Store On The Corner/High Upon A Mountain	12
57	Columbia DB 3855	Rock 'n' Roll Opera/Don't Nobody Move	18
57	Columbia DB 3855	Rock 'n' Roll Opera/Don't Nobody Move (78)	10
57	Columbia DB 3885	Your Love Is My Love/By You, By You, By You	8
57	Columbia DB 3922	Sold To The Man With The Broken Heart/Chapel Of The Roses	7
57	Columbia DB 3981	His Servant/Lonely Ballerina	7
59	Top Rank JAR 175	The Man I Could Be/Be My Love	5

Lee LAWRENCE

58	Columbia SEG 7780	LEE LAWRENCE (EP)	18
53	Decca LF 1132	PRESENTING LEE LAWRENCE (10" LP)	25

STEVE LAWRENCE
78s
56	Vogue Coral Q 72133	Speedo/The Chicken And The Hawk (78)	15
57	Vogue Coral Q 72243	Party Doll/Pum-Pa-Lum (The Bad Donkey) (78)	10
57	Vogue Coral Q 72264	Fabulous/Can't Wait For The Summer (with Dick Jacobs Band) (78)	8
57	Vogue Coral Q 72281	Fraulein/Blue Rememberin' You (78)	8
58	Coral Q 72335	Those Nights At The Round Table (with Guinevere)/Stranger In Mexico (78)	8
59	Coral Q 72353	These Things Are Free/I Only Have Eyes For You (78)	8
60	HMV POP 689	Pretty Blue Eyes/You're Nearer (78)	40
60	HMV POP 726	Footsteps/You Don't Know (78)	50

SINGLES
53	Parlophone MSP 6038	Say It Isn't True/This Night (Madalena) (as Steve & Bernie Lawrence)	15
54	Parlophone MSP 6080	Remember Me (You Taught Me To Love)/Too Little Time	15
54	Parlophone MSP 6106	You Can't Hold A Memory In Your Arms/King For A Day	15
55	Vogue Coral Q 72114	Open Up The Gates Of Mercy/My Impression Of Janie	10
56	Vogue Coral Q 72133	Speedo/The Chicken And The Hawk	15
57	Vogue Coral Q 72228	The Banana Boat Song/If You Would Say You're Mine	10
57	Vogue Coral Q 72243	Party Doll/Pum-Pa-Lum (The Bad Donkey)	12
57	Vogue Coral Q 72264	Fabulous/Can't Wait For The Summer (with Dick Jacobs Band)	12
57	Vogue Coral Q 72281	Fraulein/Blue Rememberin' You	10
57	Vogue Coral Q 72286	Never Mind/Long Before I Knew You	10
58	Coral Q 72304	Geisha Girl/I Don't Know	5
58	Coral Q 72335	Those Nights At The Round Table (with Guinevere)/Stranger In Mexico	5
59	Coral Q 72353	These Things Are Free/I Only Have Eyes For You	6
59	HMV POP 604	Only Love Me (Angelina)/Loving Is A Way Of Living	5
60	HMV POP 689	Pretty Blue Eyes/You're Nearer	7
60	HMV POP 726	Footsteps/You Don't Know	7
60	Top Rank JAR 416	Say It Isn't True/My Shawl	5
60	HMV POP 763	Why, Why, Why/You're Everything Wonderful	5
60	London HLT 9166	Girls, Girls, Girls/Little Boy Blue	6
60	HMV POP 795	Going Steady/Come Back, Silly Girl	5
61	HMV POP 914	In Time/Oh How You Lied	5
61	HMV POP 950	Somewhere Along The Way/While There's Still Time	5
62	CBS AAG 101	The Lady Wants To Twist/Tell Her I Said Hello	5
62	CBS AAG 127	Go Away Little Girl/If You Love Her	6
62	CBS AAG 139	Don't Be Afraid Little Darlin'/Don't Come Running Back	5
63	CBS AAG 150	Poor Little Rich Girl/More	5
63	CBS AAG 166	Walking Proud/House Without Windows	5
65	CBS 201786	Last Night I Made A Little Girl Cry/Where Can I Go	6

EPs
59	Coral FEP 2010	HERE'S STEVE LAWRENCE NO. 1 (EP)	12
59	Coral FEP 2012	HERE'S STEVE LAWRENCE NO. 2 (EP)	12

LPs
60	HMV CLP 1326	SWING SOFTLY WITH ME (LP)	15
60	Top Rank BUY 033	STEVE LAWRENCE (LP)	15
61	HMV CLP 1462	THE STEVE LAWRENCE SOUND (LP, also stereo CSD 1374)	15
62	HMV CLP 1504	PORTRAIT OF MY LOVE (LP, also stereo CSD 1404)	15
63	CBS (S)BPG 62088	COME WALTZ WITH ME (LP)	12
63	United Artists (S)ULP 1022	LAWRENCE GOES LATIN (LP)	12
63	CBS BPG 62124	WINNERS (LP)	12
64	Coral LVA 9219	SONGS EVERYBODY KNOWS (LP)	15

(see also Eydie Gorme & Steve Lawrence)

BILLY (M.) LAWRIE
69	Polydor 56363	Roll Over Beethoven/Come Back Joanna (as Billy M. Lawrie)	30
73	RCA RCA 2439	Rock And Roller/Shalee Shala	6
73	RCA SF 8395	SHIP IMAGINATION (LP)	25

ELOISE LAWS
69	CBS 4056	I'd Do It All Again/To Know Him Is To Love Him	4
70	CBS 4990	You Make Me Feel Like Someone/The Only Boy In My Life	4
77	Invictus INV 5247	Love Goes Deeper Than That/Camouflage	4

RONNIE LAWS
76	Blue Note BNXW 7004	Always There/Tidal Wave	6
79	Blue Note UP 36497	Always There/Tidal Wave (reissue)	4
79	Blue Note 12UP 36497	Always There/Tidal Wave (12")	7
75	Blue Note BNLA 452	PRESSURE SENSITIVE (LP)	12
76	Blue Note UAG 20002	PRESSURE SENSITIVE (LP, reissue)	10
76	Blue Note UAG 20007	FEVER (LP)	10
77	Blue Note UAG 30079	FRIENDS AND STRANGERS (LP)	10
78	Blue Note UAG 30204	FLAME (LP)	10

LAWSON-HAGGART ROCKIN' BAND
59	Brunswick OE 9451	BOPPING AT THE HOP (EP)	60
53	Brunswick LA 8576	JELLY ROLL'S JAZZ (10" LP)	15
53	Brunswick LA 8580	BLUES ON THE RIVER (10" LP)	15
53	Brunswick LA 8593	KING OLIVER'S JAZZ (10" LP)	15
54	Brunswick LA 8635	RAGTIME JAMBOREE (10" LP)	15
54	Brunswick LA 8639	WINDY CITY JAZZ (10" LP)	15
55	Brunswick LA 8703	SOUTH OF THE MASON-DIXON LINE (10" LP)	15
59	Brunswick STA 3010	BOPPING AT THE HOP (LP)	40

JULIET LAWSON
72	Sovereign SOV 111	Only A Week Away/Weeds In The Yard	6
72	Sovereign SVNA 7257	BOO (LP)	30

(see also Trees)

SHIRLEY LAWSON
68	Soul City SC 108	The Star/One More Chance	35

JOHN LAWTON featuring Roger Glover & Guests
75	Purple PUR 128	Little Chalk Blue/RONNIE DIO: Sitting In A Dream	6

(see also Roger Glover, Ronnie Dio, Deep Purple, Uriah Heep, Lucifer's Friend)

LOU LAWTON
67	Ember EMB S 232	Doin' The Philly Dog/I Am Searching	20
68	Speciality SPE 1005	I'm Just A Fool/Wrapped In A Dream	18

LAXTON & OLIVER
69	Blue Cat BS 168	Wickeder/Stay In My Arms	12

LAY-A-BAHTS
60	Parlophone R 4641	Fings Ain't Wot They Used T'be/Layin' Abaht/The Ceiling	4

DEKE LAYNE
66	Fontana TF 774	Ringing Reindeer/Cross & Chain	5
67	Fontana TF 797	How Do You Think I Feel/I'll Be So Glad To Get Back Home	5

OSSIE LAYNE
65	R&B MRB 5006	Come Back/Never Answer That 'Phone	12

EDDIE LAYTON
58	Mercury 7MT 221	Over The Waves/Bright Lights Over Brussels	5
59	Mercury AMT 1064	Duck Walk/Doodles	7

TEDDY LAYTON JAZZ BAND
58	Parlophone R 4411	Down By The Riverside/Wooden Joe's Weary Blues	5

KEN LAZ(A)RUS (& CREW)
65	Island WI 220	Funny (as Ken Lazrus & Byron Lee Orchestra)/	
		BYRON LEE ORCHESTRA: Walk Like A Dragon	15
70	London HLJ 10301	Monkey Man/Bongo Nyah	6
71	Explosion EX 2056	Girl/TOMORROW'S CHILDREN: Sister Big Stuff	5
72	Explosion EX 2064	Hail The Man/Where Do I Go	5
72	London HLH 10379	Hail The Man/Where I Go	5
70	London HA-J 8412	REGGAE SCORCHER (LP, unissued)	
70	London LGJ/ZGJ 102	REGGAE SCORCHER (LP)	18
70	London ZGJ 107	REGGAE — GREATEST HITS VOL. 1 (LP)	15
70	London ZGJ 108	REGGAE — GREATEST HITS VOL. 2 (LP)	15

LAZY SMOKE
80s	Heyoka	CORRIDOR OF FACES (LP, reissue of U.S. LP)	15

BARBARA LEA
56	London HB-U 1058	A WOMAN IN LOVE (10" LP)	20
56	Esquire 32/043	NOBODY ELSE BUT ME (LP)	15
57	Esquire 32/063	IN LOVE (LP)	15

JIMMY LEA
85	Trojan KANE 001	Citizen Kane/Poland (p/s)	15

(see also Slade)

LEADBELLY (HUDDIE LEDBETTER)

78s
50	Capitol CL 13282	Eagle Rock Rag/Backwater Blues (78)	15
51	Melodisc 1140	How Long/Good Morning Blues (78)	20
51	Melodisc 1151	Goodnight Irene/Ain't You Glad (78)	20
51	Melodisc 1187	On A Monday/John Henry (78)	20
54	Jazz Collector L 108	New Black Snake Moan/Fore Day Worry Blues (78)	20
55	Jazz Collector L 124	Pig Meat Papa/Becky Beem (78)	20
55	HMV MH 190	Alabama Bound/Pick A Bale Of Cotton (78)	30

EPs
56	Melodisc EPM7 63	HOW LONG BLUES (EP)	20
58	Melodisc EPM7 77	LEADBELLY (EP)	20
58	Melodisc EPM7 82	SEE SEE RIDER (EP)	20
59	Melodisc EPM7 87	PARTY PLAYS AND SONGS (EP)	18
59	RCA RCX 146	ROCK ISLAND LINE (EP)	15
61	Capitol EAP1 1821	HUDDIE LEDBETTER'S BEST NO. 1 (EP)	15
61	Capitol EAP4 1821	HUDDIE LEDBETTER'S BEST NO. 2 (EP)	15
61	Capitol EAP1 20111	LEADBELLY (EP)	15
61	Storyville SEP 337	LEADBELLY (EP)	15
62	Storyville SEP 387	STORYVILLE BLUES ANTHOLOGY VOL. 7 (EP)	15

LPs
53	Capitol LC 6597	LEADBELLY SINGS CLASSICS IN JAZZ (10" LP)	25
57	Melodisc MLP 511	LEADBELLY VOL. 1 (10" LP, green & silver labels)	20
57	Melodisc MLP 512	LEADBELLY VOL. 2 (10" LP, green & silver labels)	20
58	Melodisc MLP 515	LEADBELLY VOL. 3 (10" LP, green & silver labels)	20
58	Melodisc MLP 517	PLAYS PARTY SONGS (10" LP, green & silver labels)	20
58	Melodisc MLP 12-107	THE SAGA OF LEADBELLY (LP, green & silver or blue & black labels)	20
59	Melodisc MLP 12-113	LEADBELLY'S LAST SESSIONS VOLUME 2 PART 1 (LP)	20
59	Melodisc MLP 12-114	LEADBELLY'S LAST SESSIONS VOLUME 2 PART 2 (LP)	20
62	Storyville SLP 124	A DEMON OF A MAN — BLUES ANTHOLOGY (LP)	15
63	Storyville SLP 139	LEADBELLY 2 — T.B. BLUES (LP)	15
63	Capitol T 1821	HIS GUITAR, HIS VOICE, HIS PIANO: HUDDIE LEDBETTER'S BEST (LP)	12
63	RCA Victor RD 7567	GOOD MORNING BLUES (LP)	15
65	Verve (S)VLP 5002	TAKE THIS HAMMER (LP)	15
65	Society SOC 994	LEADBELLY PLAYS AND SINGS (LP)	12
66	Elektra EKL 301/2	THE LIBRARY OF CONGRESS RECORDINGS (3-LP)	20
67	Verve (S)VLP 5011	KEEP YOUR HANDS OFF HER (LP)	15

MINT VALUE £

69	Xtra XTRA 1046	LEADBELLY SINGS FOLK SONGS (LP)	20
69	Xtra XTRA 1126	SHOUT ON (LP)	20
69	Storyville 616 003	IN THE EVENING WHEN THE SUN GOES DOWN (LP)	12
69	Storyville 616 004	GOODNIGHT IRENE (LP)	12
70	CBS 64103	LEADBELLY (LP)	12
72	Ember CW 132	LEADBELLY (LP)	12
70s	Xtra XTRAD 1017	THE LEADBELLY BOX SET (2-LP)	15

LEADBELLY/BLIND LEMON JEFFERSON
| 61 | Jazz Collector JEL 124 | THE MALE BLUES VOLUME 8 (EP) | 15 |

(see also Blind Lemon Jefferson)

HARRY LEADER BAND
| 65 | Parlophone R 5386 | Dragon Fly/Rush Hour | 5 |

LEADERBEATS
| 60 | Top Rank JAR 405 | Dance, Dance, Dance/Washington Square | 8 |

LEADERS (U.K.)
| 65 | Fontana TF 602 | Night People/Love Will Find A Way | 8 |

LEADERS (Jamaica)
| 68 | Amalgamated AMG 804 | Tit For Tat (actually by Lynn Taitt & Jets)/MARVETTS: You Take Too Long | 20 |

(see also Pioneers, Stranger Cole, Versatiles)

LEADING FIGURES
| 67 | Deram DML/SML 1006 | OSCILLATION 67! (LP) | 15 |
| 67 | Ace Of Clubs SCL 1225 | SOUND AND MOVEMENT (LP) | 35 |

(see also Jon Lord, Deep Purple)

LEAF HOUND
| 71 | Decca SKL-R 5094 | GROWERS OF MUSHROOM (LP) | 600 |

(see also Brunning Sunflower Blues Band, Black Cat Bones, Atomic Rooster, Cactus, Headbangers)

LEAGUE OF GENTLEMEN
| 65 | Columbia DB 7666 | Each Little Falling Tear/And I Do Now | 50 |
| 66 | Planet PLF 109 | How Can You Tell/How Do They Know (with Planet company sleeve) | 50 |

(see also Giles Giles & Fripp, Brain)

LEAH
| 73 | GM GMS 10 | Arise Sir Henry/Uptight Basil | 5 |

(see also Pete Dello, Red Herring)

JOE LEAHY (ORCHESTRA)
55	Parlophone MSP 6149	Desiree/Milano	6
55	Parlophone MSP 6168	Green Fire/Secretly Mine	6
57	London HBZ 1072	LOVELY LADY (10" LP)	12

MIKE LEANDER ORCHESTRA
64	Decca F 11849	The Heroes/Rang A Tang	5
69	MCA MU 1095	Ride The Wild Wild Country/Here There And Everywhere	6
69	MCA MUPS 383	MIGRATION (LP)	12

VICKY LEANDROS
72	Philips 6000 025	I Am/Love Tell Me Where Is Your Home	8
72	Philips 6000 049	Come What May (Apres Toi)/Take A Little Time	5
72	Philips 6000 066	Country Freedom/Mouth Organ Boy	12
72	Philips 6000 081	The Love In Your Eyes/You Answered My Prayer	5
73	Philips 6000 111	When Bouzoukis Played/Jacques	5
74	Philips 6000 129	Dreams Are Good Friends/Lovin' And Tenderness	12
74	Philips 6000 408	Danny, Teach Me To Dance/Love Me Tender	5
75	Philips 6000 169	More Than That/Papa's Knee	8
72	Philips 6303 019	I AM (LP)	12
72	Philips 6303 062	VICKY LEANDROS (LP)	12

(see also Vicky)

BOB LEAPER
| 65 | Pye 7N 15700 | High Wire (Theme From 'Danger Man')/The Lost World | 30 |
| 64 | Decca LK 4639 | BIG BAND, BEATLE SONGS (LP) | 12 |

LEAPERS CREEPERS SLEEPERS
| 66 | Island WI 275 | Precious Words/Ba Boo | 12 |

KEVIN 'KING' LEAR
67	Polydor 56203	Count Me Out/Pretty Woman	15
68	Page One POF 087	Power Of Love/Mr. Pearly	7
68	Page One POF 109	Cry Me A River/Shoe Shine Sam	12
69	Page One POF 132	The Snake/Man In The Funnies	10

TIMOTHY LEARY MEETS THE GRID
| 90 | Evolution EVO 1 | Origins Of Dance (Electronic Future Mix)/(Hi-Tec Pagan Mix) (12") | 10 |

(see also Grid)

LEATHERCOATED MINDS
| 67 | Fontana (S)TL 5412 | A TRIP DOWN THE SUNSET STRIP (LP) | 50 |

(see also J.J. Cale)

LEATHERHEAD
| 74 | Philips 6006 371 | Gimme Your Money Please/Epitath | 5 |

LEATHER NUN
79	Industrial IR 0006	SLOW DEATH (EP)	12
84	Subterranean SUB 40	Prime Mover/F.F.A. (p/s)	4
87	Wire WRMS 014	I Can Smell Your Thoughts (Remix)/Falling Apart/Bonus Track: 506 (Re-visited) (12", p/s, shrinkwrapped with banned poster)	7
79	Industrial IRC 27	THE LEATHER NUN AT THE SCALA CINEMA (cassette)	10

LED ZEPPELIN

BILL LEATHERWOOD
60	Top Rank JAR 506	The Long Walk/My Foolish Heart	6

LEA VALLEY SKIFFLE GROUP
57	Esquire 10-508	Streamline Train/Railroad Bill (78)	20
58	Esquire 10-518	I'm Gonna Walk And Talk With Jesus/Oh Mary, Don't You Weep (78)	20
58	Esquire EP 163	LEA VALLEY SKIFFLE GROUP (EP)	50

LEAVES
66	Fontana TF 713	Hey Joe/Funny Little World	25

OTIS LEAVILL(E)
70	Atlantic 2091 015	I Love You/I Need You	6
70	Atlantic 2091 035	Love Uprising/Glad I Met You	5
71	Atlantic 2091 160	There's Nothing Better/I'm So Jealous	8

SIMON LE BON
88	Sin DT 0001	Grey Lady Of The Sea (CD, 1-track promo, mail-order only)	70

(see also Duran Duran)

LE CHEILE
78	Inchecronin INC 7423	AIRIS (LP)	12
78	Inchecronin INC 7424	LORD MAYO (LP)	12

JOHN LEDINGHAM
68	Pye 7N 17488	Love Is A Toy/Thank You Mrs. Gilbert	6

(see also Jonathan Kelly)

LED ZEPPELIN

SINGLES
69	Atlantic 584 268	Good Times, Bad Times (unissued, 1-sided acetates only)	400
69	Atlantic 584 269	Communication Breakdown/Good Times, Bad Times (unissued, promo only)	500
69	Atlantic 584 309	Whole Lotta Love (Edit)/Livin' Lovin' Maid (She's A Woman) (withdrawn)	450
70	Atlantic 2091 043	Immigrant Song/Hey, Hey What Can I Do? (unreleased)	
73	Atlantic K 10296	D'Yer Mak'er/Over The Hills And Far Away (unreleased, promo only)	100
75	Swan Song DC 1	Trampled Underfoot/Black Country Woman (freebie, die-cut title sleeve)	20
75	Swan Song SSK 19403	Trampled Underfoot/Black Country Woman (mispressed cat. no.)	75
79	Swan Song SSK 19421	Wearing And Tearing/Darlene (cancelled Knebworth 45, existence unconfirmed)	1,000+
90	Atlantic LZ 2	Stairway To Heaven/Immigrant Song/Whole Lotta Love/ Good Times Bad Times (10", p/s, promo only)	25
90	Atlantic CD LZ 1	Stairway To Heaven/Immigrant Song/Whole Lotta Love/ Good Times Bad Times (CD, promo only, in Zeppelin-design long box)	30
90	Atlantic LZ 3	Stairway To Heaven/Whole Lotta Love (with memo, 150 copies only, promo)	100
90	Atlantic LZ 3 LC	Stairway To Heaven/Whole Lotta Love (jukebox single, push-out centre)	25
97	Atlantic PRCD 923	BBC SESSIONS SAMPLER: The Girl I Love/Whole Lotta Love/ Communicatin Breakdown (CD, promo only)	20

ALBUMS
69	Atlantic 588 171	LED ZEPPELIN (LP, 1st pressing, red/maroon label, turquoise sleeve lettering, "Superhype" publishing publising credit)	60
69	Atlantic 588 171	LED ZEPPELIN (LP, 2nd pressing, red/maroon label, orange sleeve lettering, "Warner Bros" or "Superhype" publishing publising credit)	20/15
69	Atlantic 588 198	LED ZEPPELIN II (LP, 1st pressing, red/maroon label, with "The Lemon Song" credit, light brown gatefold sleeve)	20
70	Atlantic 588 198	LED ZEPPELIN II (LP, light brown sleeve, 2nd pressing, credits "Killing Floor" instead of "The Lemon Song" on label)	20

LED ZEPPELIN

70	Atlantic Deluxe 2401 002	LED ZEPPELIN III (LP, red/maroon label, gatefold rotating-wheel sleeve, "Do What Thou Wilt" in run-off)	20
71	Atlantic Deluxe 2401 012	LED ZEPPELIN IV (FOUR SYMBOLS) (LP, red/maroon label)	20
73	Atlantic K 50014	HOUSES OF THE HOLY (LP)	12
76	Swan Song SSK 59402	PRESENCE (LP, shrinkwrapped gatefold sleeve)	12
78	Atlantic K 50008	LED ZEPPELIN IV (FOUR SYMBOLS) (LP, lilac vinyl reissue)	35
79	Swan Song SSK 59410	IN THROUGH THE OUT DOOR (LP, 6 different covers with inner sleeves; set labelled 'A' to 'F', each in individual paper outer; available separately with paper outer £10 each)	100
88	Atlantic K 50008/C 88 1-4	FOUR SYMBOLS (LP, HMV 'Classic Collection' box set, with booklet, no'd)	25
88	Atlantic 250008/C 88 1-4	FOUR SYMBOLS (CD, HMV 'Classic Collection' box set, with booklet, no'd)	25
90	Atlantic ZEP 1	REMASTERS (3-LP, triple gatefold sleeve)	18
90	Atlantic 7567 82144-1	LED ZEPPELIN (5-LP, box set)	40

(see also Jimmy Page, Robert Plant, John Paul Jones, Listen, Family Dogg, Ian Whitcomb, P.J. Proby, Lord Sutch)

ALVIN LEE

74	Chrysalis CHS 2020	The World Is Changing/Riffin' (with Mylon Le Fevre)	5
73	Chrysalis CHR 1054	ON THE ROAD TO FREEDOM (LP, with Mylon Le Fevre)	12
75	Chrysalis CHR 1094	PUMP IRON! (LP)	12
78	Chrysalis CHR 1190	LET IT ROCK (LP)	12

(see also Ten Years After)

ARTHUR LEE

72	A&M AMLS 64356	VINDICATOR (LP)	15
81	Beggars Banquet BEGA 26	ARTHUR LEE (LP)	12

(see also Love)

BENNY LEE (& KEN-TONES)

56	Parlophone MSP 6214	Love Plays The Strings Of My Banjo (with Ken-Tones)/Born To Sing The Blues	7
56	Parlophone MSP 6252	Sweet Heartaches/How Long Has This Been Going On?	7
56	Parlophone R 4245	Rock 'N' Rollin' Santa Claus/Life Was Made For Livin' (with Ken-Tones)	20

(see also Ken-Tones)

BRENDA LEE

78s

56	Brunswick 05628	I'm Gonna Lasso Santa Claus/Christy Christmas (78, as Little Brenda Lee)	80
57	Brunswick 05685	Dynamite/Love You Til I Die (78)	60
57	Brunswick 05720	Ain't That Love/One Teenager To Another (78)	50
58	Brunswick 05755	Ring-A-My-Phone/Little Jonah (Rock On Your Little Steel Guitar) (78)	70
59	Brunswick 05780	Bill Bailey, Won't You Please Come Home/Hummin' The Blues Over You (78)	70
60	Brunswick 05819	Sweet Nuthin's/Weep No More My Baby (78)	150

SINGLES

56	Brunswick 05628	I'm Gonna Lasso Santa Claus/Christy Christmas (triangular centre)	175
57	Brunswick 05685	Dynamite/Love You Til I Die (with Anita Kerr Singers, triangular centre)	125
57	Brunswick 05720	Ain't That Love/One Teenager To Another (w/ Anita Kerr Singers, tri centre)	100
58	Brunswick 05755	Ring-A-My-Phone/Little Jonah (Rock On Your Little Steel Guitar) (tri-centre)	125
58	Decca BM 31186	Fairyland/One Step At A Time (export issue, triangular centre)	60
59	Brunswick 05780	Bill Bailey, Won't You Please Come Home/Hummin' The Blues Over You (triangular or round centre)	15/12
60	Brunswick 05819	Sweet Nuthin's/Weep No More My Baby (triangular or round centre)	20/8
60	Brunswick 05823	Let's Jump The Broomstick/Rock-A-Bye Baby Blues	7
60	Brunswick 05833	I'm Sorry/That's All You Gotta Do	8
60	Brunswick 05839	I Want To Be Wanted/Just A Little	6
61	Brunswick 05847	Emotions/I'm Learning About Love	5
61	Brunswick 05849	You Can Depend On Me/It's Never Too Late	5
61	Brunswick 05854	Dum Dum/Eventually	6
61	Brunswick 05860	Fool No. 1/Anybody But Me	5
62	Brunswick 05864	Break It To Me Gently/So Deep	5
62	Brunswick 05867	Speak To Me Pretty/Lover, Come Back To Me	5
62	Brunswick 05871	Here Comes That Feeling/Everybody Loves Me But You	5
62	Brunswick 05876	It Started All Over Again/Heart In Hand	5
62	Brunswick 05880	Rockin' Around The Christmas Tree/Papa Noel	6
63	Brunswick 05882	All Alone Am I/Save All Your Lovin' For Me	5
63	Brunswick 05886	Losing You/He's So Heavenly	5
63	Brunswick 05891	I Wonder/My Whole World Is Falling Down	5
63	Brunswick 05896	Sweet Impossible You/The Grass Is Greener	5
64	Brunswick 05899	As Usual/Lonely Lonely Lonely Me	5
64	Brunswick 05903	Think/The Waiting Game	5
64	Brunswick 05911	Alone With You/My Dreams	5
64	Brunswick 05915	Is It True/What'd I Say	10
64	Brunswick 05921	Christmas Will Be Just Another Lonely Day/Winter Wonderland	6
65	Brunswick 05927	Thanks A Lot/Just Behind The Rainbow	5
65	Brunswick 05933	Truly, Truly True/I Still Miss Someone	5
65	Brunswick 05936	Too Many Rivers/No One	5
65	Brunswick 05943	Rusty Bells/If You Don't	5
66	Brunswick 05957	Too Little Time/Time And Time Again	5
66	Brunswick 05963	Ain't Gonna Cry No More/It Takes One To Know One	6
66	Brunswick 05967	Coming On Strong/You Keep Coming Back To Me	7
67	Brunswick 05970	Ride, Ride, Ride/Lonely People Do Foolish Things	5
67	Brunswick 05976	Where's The Melody/Born To Be By Your Side	7
68	Decca AD 1003	That's All Right/Baby, Won't You Please Come Home (export issue)	12
68	MCA MU 1001	That's All Right/Baby, Won't You Please Come Home	5
68	MCA MU 1021	Let's Jump The Broomstick/All Alone Am I	5
69	MCA MU 1063	Johnny One Time/I Must Have Been Out Of My Mind	5
70	MCA MU 1115	Johnny One Time/Bring Me Sunshine	5
72	MCA MU 1155	Everybody's Reaching Out For Someone/If This Is Our Last Time	5
73	MCA MUS 1189	Nobody Wins/We Had A Good Thing Going	5
73	MCA MUS 1219	Sunday Sunrise/Must I Believe	5

EPs

59	Brunswick OE 9462	ROCK THE BOP (EP, green p/s & tri centre or blue p/s & round centre) 75/45
62	Brunswick OE 9482	PRETEND (EP) 35
62	Brunswick OE 9488	SPEAK TO ME PRETTY (EP) 30
63	Brunswick OE 9492	ALL ALONE AM I (EP) 30
64	Brunswick OE 9499	BRENDA LEE'S TRIBUTE TO AL JOLSON (EP) 30
65	Brunswick OE 9510	FOUR FROM '64 (EP) 30

LPs

59	Brunswick LAT 8319	GRANDMA WHAT GREAT SONGS YOU SANG (LP) 45
60	Brunswick LAT 8347	MISS DYNAMITE (LP) 35
61	Brunswick LAT 8360	THIS IS BRENDA (LP) 30
61	Brunswick LAT 8376	EMOTIONS (LP, also stereo STA 3044) 20/25
61	Brunswick LAT 8383	ALL THE WAY (LP, also stereo STA 3048) 20/25
61	Brunswick LAT 8396	SINCERELY (LP, also stereo STA 3056) 20/25
62	Brunswick LAT/STA 8516	BRENDA, THAT'S ALL (LP, mono/stereo) 20/25
62	Brunswick LAT/STA 8530	ALL ALONE AM I (LP, mono/stereo) 18/20
63	Ace of Hearts AH 59	LOVE YOU (LP) 25
63	Brunswick LAT/STA 8548	LET ME SING (LP, mono/stereo) 20/25
64	Brunswick LAT/STA 8576	BY REQUEST (LP, mono/stereo) 20/25
64	Brunswick LAT/STA 8590	MERRY CHRISTMAS FROM BRENDA (LP, mono/stereo) 20/25
65	Brunswick LAT/STA 8603	TOP TEEN HITS (LP, mono/stereo) 20/25
65	Brunswick LAT 8614	THE VERSATILE BRENDA LEE (LP) 20
65	Brunswick LAT/STA 8622	TOO MANY RIVERS (LP, mono/stereo) 20/25
66	Brunswick LAT/STA 8649	BYE BYE BLUES (LP, mono/stereo) 20/25
67	Brunswick LAT/STA 8672	COMING ON STRONG (LP, mono/stereo) 20/25
68	MCA MUP(S) 306	REFLECTIONS IN BLUE (LP) 15
68	MCA MUP(S) 321	CALL ME (LP) 15
68	MCA MUP(S) 322	THE GOOD LIFE (LP) 12
68	MCA MUP(S) 330	MERRY CHRISTMAS FROM BRENDA LEE (LP) 12
68	MCA MUP(S) 332	BRENDA AND PETE — FOR THE FIRST TIME (LP, with Pete Fountain) 12
70	MCA MUP(S) 396	JOHNNY ONE TIME (LP) 12
71	MCA MUPS 423	MEMPHIS PORTRAIT (LP) 12
72	MCA MUPS 460	A WHOLE LOTTA BRENDA LEE (LP) 12
73	MCA MUPS 485	BRENDA (LP) 12

BUNNY LEE ALLSTARS

70	Pama PM 803	Annie Pama/Mr Magoo 6
71	Smash SMA 2304	Stanley (Parts 1 & 2) (as Bunnie Lee Allstars) 7

(see also Lloyd Charmers, Sonny Binns & Rudies, Copy Cats, John Holt, Lloyd & Doreen, Delroy Wilson)

BYRON LEE & DRAGONAIR(E)S

60	Blue Beat B 2	Dumplin's/Kissin' Gal (vocal: Buddy Davidson) (white label, blue print) 18
60	Blue Beat BB 2	Dumplin's/Kissin' Gal (vocal: Buddy Davidson) (2nd pressing, blue label, silver print) 15
61	Blue Beat BB 28	Mash! Mr. Lee/Help Me Forget (vocal: Keith Lyn) 12
61	Starlite ST45 045	Joy Ride/Over The Rainbow 10
64	Parlophone R 5124	River Bank/Musical Communion 10
64	Parlophone R 5125	Sour Apples/Hanging Up My Heart 10
64	Parlophone R 5140	Sammy Dead/Say Bye Bye (both actually by Eric Morris with Byron Lee) 10
64	Parlophone R 5177	Beautiful Garden/Too Late 10
64	Parlophone R 5182	Come Back/Jamaica Ska 10
64	MGM MGM 1256	Night Train From Jamaica/Ska Dee Wah (with Danny Davis) 15
66	Doctor Bird DB 1003	Sloopy/Gold Finger 10
67	Pyramid PYR 6015	Sloopy/Gold Finger (reissue) 7
68	Trojan TR 624	Soul Limbo/The Whistling Song 7
68	Trojan TR 631	Mr Walker/Sunset Jump Up 7
69	Major Minor MM 615	Every Day Will Be Like A Holiday/Oh What A Feeling 5
70	Trojan TR 7731	Squeeze Up (Parts 1 & 2) 6
70	Trojan TR 7736	Birth Control/Love At First Sight 6
70	Trojan TR 7747	Bond In Bliss/Musical Scorcher 6
70	Trojan TR 7761	Julianne/We Five 5
70	Duke DU 39	Elizabethan Reggae/Soul Serenade 6
70	Duke DU 91	Cashbox/WINSTON WRIGHT: Strolling Thru' The Park 6
71	Dynamic DYN 405	Hitching A Ride/Hitching A Ride Version 6
71	Dynamic DYN 409	My Sweet Lord/Shock Attack 7
71	Dynamic DYN 414	Way Back Home/Version 6
72	Dynamic DYN 435	Make It Reggae/DENNIS ALCAPONE: Go Johnny Go 6
73	Dragon DRA 1008	In The Mood/Black On 5
65	Atlantic AET 6014	SKA TIME (EP, as Byron Lee Ska Kings) 50
64	Island ILP 905	CARIBBEAN JOY RIDE (LP) 45
69	Trojan TTL 5	ROCKSTEADY EXPLOSION (LP) 25
69	Major Minor Sm 53	BYRON LEE & THE DRAGONAIRES (LP) 15
70	Trojan TRLS 18	REGGAE WITH BYRON LEE (LP) 15
70	Trojan TBL 110	REGGAE BLAST OFF (LP) 15
71	Trojan TRL 26	REGGAY SPLASHDOWN (LP) 12
72	Trojan TRL 40	REGGAY HOT COOL AND EASY (LP) 12
73	Dragon DRLS 5001	REGGAE ROUND THE WORLD (LP) 10

(see also Mighty Avengers, Ken Lazarus, Hopeton Lewis, Danny Davis Orchestra, Good Guys, Neville Hinds, Hubcaps & Wheels, Mighty Sparrow, Blues Busters)

CHRISTOPHER LEE

74	Studio Two TWOA 5001	HAMMER PRESENTS DRACULA (LP, gatefold sleeve) 12
74	Studio Two TWOA Q4 5001	HAMMER PRESENTS DRACULA (LP, gatefold sleeve, quadrophonic) 15

CURTIS LEE

60	Top Rank JAR 317	With All My Heart (I Love You)/Pure Love 40
61	London HLX 9313	Pledge Of Love/Then I'll Know 18
61	London HLX 9397	Pretty Little Angel Eyes/Gee How I Wish You Were Here 18

Curtis LEE

61	London HLX 9445	Under The Moon Of Love/Beverly Jean	18
62	London HLX 9533	A Night At Daddy Gee's/Just Another Fool	15
67	CBS 2717	Get My Bag/Everybody's Going Wild (as Curtis Lee & K.C.P.s)	20
72	Stateside SS 2208	Under The Moon Of Love/Beverly Jean (reissue)	5

DAVE LEE (& STAGGERLEES)

63	Decca F 11600	Take Four/Five To Four On	6
63	Oriole CB 1864	Dance Dance Dance/Love Me (as Dave Lee & Staggerlees)	6
63	Oriole CB 1907	Sweet & Lovely/Forever And Always (as Dave Lee & Staggerlees)	6
66	Fontana TF 723	Adam Adamant/Georgie's Theme (as Dave Lee & His Orchestra)	8

DAVE LEE

60s	Colpix PXL 550	OUR MAN CRICHTON (LP, with Tubby Hayes)	15

(see also Tubby Hayes)

DAVID H. LEE

65	Pye 7N 15809	Heaven With No Angel	6
69	Morgan MR 1	Johnny's Eyes/You're The Only One	6

DEREK LEE

66	Parlophone R 5468	Girl/You've Done Something To My Heart	8

DICK LEE

53	Columbia SCM 5066	All I Want Is A Chance/The Show Is Ended	6
53	Columbia SCM 5078	I Thought You Might Be Lonely/Happy Bells	6
54	Columbia SCM 5094	Book/Stay In My Arms Cinderella	6

DICKIE/DICKEY LEE

59	MGM MGM 1013	A Penny A Kiss — A Penny A Hug/Bermuda (as Dick Lee)	25
62	Mercury AMT 1190	Patches/More Or Less	10
62	Mercury AMT 1196	I Saw Linda Yesterday/The Girl I Can't Forget	10
62	Mercury AMT 1200	Don't Wanna Think About Paula/Just A Friend	7
65	Stateside SS 433	Laurie (Strange Things Happen)/Party Doll (as Dickey Lee)	6
65	Stateside SS 464	The Girl From Peyton Place/A Girl I Used To Know (as Dickey Lee)	6

DINAH LEE

65	Brit WI 1005	I Can't Believe What You Say/Pushin' A Good Thing Too Far (unissued)	
65	Aladdin WI 606	I'll Forgive You Then Forget You/Nitty Gritty	12
65	Aladdin WI 608	I Can't Believe What You Say/Pushin' A Good Thing Too Far	15

DON (TONY) LEE

68	Big Shot BI 504	It's Reggae Time (as Don Tony Lee)/ERROL DUNKLEY: The Clamp Is On	12
68	Doctor Bird DB 1106	Lee's Special (as Don Tony Lee)/LLOYD & GROOVERS: My Heart And Soul	15
68	Island WI 3160	It's Reggae Time (as D. Tony Lee)/ERROL DUNKLEY: The Clamp Is On	18
69	Unity UN 519	Peyton Place/Red Gal In The Ring (as Don Tony Lee)	8

EDNA LEE

68	President PT 175	I Really Think I'm Crying 'Cause I Love You/Don't Let My Friends See What You Do	4

(Freddie) 'FINGERS' LEE (& UPPER HAND)

65	Fontana TF 619	The Friendly Undertaker/Little Bit More (as 'Fingers' Lee)	18
66	Fontana TF 655	I'm Gonna Buy Me A Dog/I Can't Drive (as 'Fingers' Lee)	15
66	Columbia DB 8002	Bossy Boss/Don't Run Away (as Fingers Lee & Upper Hand)	10

(see also At Last The 1958 Rock & Roll Show)

GEORGE LEE (& MUSIC DOCTORS)

69	Downtown DT 443	Talking Boss/Jungle Fever (solo)	7
70	J-Dan JDN 4407	Johnny Dollar/Tough Of Poison (with Music Doctors)	7

(see also Desmond Riley)

HUBERT LEE

73	Ackee ACK 504	I Love Verona/Version	4
73	Downtown DT 498	Something On Your Mind/IMPACT ALL STARS: Mind Version	8
73	Green Door GD 4050	High School Dance/PRINCE TONY'S ALL STARS: Version	4
74	Ackee ACK 524	Tonight Will You Still Love Me/IMPACT ALL STARS: Version	4

JACKIE LEE (U.K.)

55	Decca F 10550	I Was Wrong/For As Long As I Live	6

JACKIE LEE (U.K.)

65	Decca F 12068	I Cry Alone/Cause I Love Him	7
65	Columbia DB 7685	Lonely Clown/Love Is Gone	7
66	Columbia DB 7860	I Know, Know, Know I'll Never Love/So Love Me	6
66	Columbia DB 8052	The Town I Live In/You Too	8
67	Decca F 12663	Born To Lose/Saying Goodbye	6
69	Pye 7N 17829	Love Is A Gamble/Something Borrowed, Something Blue	5

(see also Jacky, Jackie Lee & Raindrops, Emma Rede)

JACKIE LEE & RAINDROPS (U.K.)

62	Oriole CB 1702	I Was The Last One To Know/There's No One In The Whole World	8
62	Oriole CB 1727	There Goes The Lucky One/I Built My Whole World Around You	10
62	Oriole CB 1757	Party Lights/Midnight	8
63	Oriole CB 1800	The End Of The World/Goodbye Is Such A Lonely Word	8
63	Philips BF 1283	Down Our Street/My Heart Is Your Heart (as Jackie & Raindrops)	10
64	Philips BF 1328	Here I Go Again/Come On Dream Come On (as Jackie & Raindrops)	8

(see also Jacky, Jackie Lee [U.K.], Raindrops [U.K], Emma Rede)

JACKIE LEE (U.S.)

60	Top Rank JAR 286	Rancho/Like Sunset	7

JACKIE LEE (U.S.)

65	Fontana TF 646	The Duck/Let Your Conscience Be Your Guide	15
68	London HLM 10233	The Duck/Dancing In The Street	6
70	Jay Boy BOY 26	Do The Temptation Walk/The Shotgun And The Duck	5
71	Jay Boy BOY 28	Would You Believe/You're Everything	5

72	Jay Boy BOY 66	Oh! My Darlin'/Don't Be Ashamed	6
72	Jay Boy BOY 76	African Boo-Ga-Loo/Bring It Home	5
73	Contempo CR 5	The Duck (Parts 1 & 2)	5
85	Kent TOWN 107	Darkest Days/EDDIE BISHOP: Call Me	5
67	London HA-M 8336	THE DUCK (LP)	18
71	Joy JOYS 192	THE DUCK (LP, reissue)	12

(see also Bob & Earl, Earl Nelson, Jackie Lee & Delores Hall)

JACKIE LEE & DELORES HALL
| 69 | B&C CB 105 | Whether It's Right Or Wrong/Baby I'm Satisfied | 8 |
| 72 | Jay Boy BOY 52 | Whether It's Right Or Wrong/Baby I'm Satisfied (reissue) | 5 |

(see also Jackie Lee [U.S.], Delores Hall)

JAMIE LEE & ATLANTICS
| 63 | Decca F 11571 | In The Night/Little Girl In Blue | 35 |

JIMMY LEE
| 61 | Starlite ST45 059 | All My Life/Chicago Jump | 18 |

JOHN LEE'S GROUNDHOGS
(see under 'J')

JOHN LEE
| 72 | Explosion EX 2060 | Stagger Lee/Musical Version (both sides actually by John Holt) | 5 |

JOHNNIE LEE
59	Pye 7N 15201	Echo/It's-A Me, It's-A Me, It's-A Me My Love	7
59	Pye N 15201	Echo/It's-A Me, It's-A Me, It's-A Me My Love (78)	15
59	Pye 7N 15233	I'm Finally Free/I Fell (with The King's Men)	7
59	Pye N 15233	I'm Finally Free/I Fell (78, with the King's Men)	20
60	Fontana H 257	They're Wrong/Cindy Lou	6
60	Fontana H 280	Poetry In Motion/Let It Come True	6
61	Fontana H 306	Lonely Joe/Nobody	6
67	CBS 202591	Kiss Tomorrow Goodbye/Love No Longer Sounds	7
67	CBS 2802	I Forgot What It Was Like/Lonely Is The Willow	5
67	CBS 3112	Because You're Mine/I'll Not Forget	5

JULIA LEE (& HER BOYFRIENDS)
50	Capitol CL 13321	Nobody Knows You When You're Down And Out/Decent Woman Blues (78)	10
50	Capitol CL 13323	Cold Hearted Daddy/Snatch And Grab It (78)	10
51	Capitol LC 6535	PARTY TIME (10" LP, 2 different sleeves)	60

LAURA LEE (U.K.)
60	Triumph RGM 1030	Tell Tommy I Miss Him/I'm Sending Back Your Roses	30
62	Decca F 11513	Too Young To Be In Love/Brand New Heartbeat	10
68	Columbia DB 8495	Love In Every Room/Master Jack	8
71	Columbia DB 8770	Someone To Love Me/Look Left-Look Right	6

LAURA LEE (U.S.)
67	Chess CRS 8062	Dirty Man/It's Mighty Hard	7
68	Chess CRS 8070	As Long As I Got You/A Man With Some Backbone	7
72	Tamla Motown TMG 831	To Win Your Heart/So Will I	5
72	Hot Wax HWX 115	Rip Off/Two Lovely Pillows	5
73	Hot Wax HWX 118	Wedlock Is A Padlock/Since I Fell For You	5
73	Hot Wax HWX 119	You've Got The Love To Save Me/Crumbs Off The Table	5
74	Invictus INV 2654	I Need It Just As Bad As You/If I'm Good Enough To Love	5
71	Hot Wax SHW 5006	WOMEN'S LOVE RIGHTS (LP)	15
73	Hot Wax SHW 5009	TWO SIDES OF LAURA LEE (LP)	18

LEAPY LEE
65	Pye 7N 17001	It's All Happening/In The Meantime	6
66	Decca F 12369	King Of The Whole Wide World/Shake Hands (featuring Kinks)	35
67	CBS 202550	The Man On The Flying Trapeze/My Mixed-Up Mind	5
68	MCA MU 1028	Little Arrows/Time Will Tell	5
68	Pye 7N 17619	It's All Happening/It's Great	5

LITTLE MR. LEE & CHEROKEES
| 66 | Vocalion VP 9268 | Young Lover/I Don't Want To Go | 25 |

MANDY LEE
| 50s | Poydras 76 | I'm A Harmony Baby/If Your Man Is Like My Man (78) | 10 |

MANDY LEE
| 69 | Dandelion S 4494 | Bottle Up And Go (Parts 1 & 2) | 5 |

MARILYN LEE
| 64 | Embassy WB 636 | My Guy/DAVE CHARLES: Hello, Dolly | 5 |

MARILYN LEE & LES CARLE
| 62 | Embassy WB 540 | Keep Your Hands Off My Baby/Up On The Roof | 4 |

MICHELLE LEE
| 68 | CBS 3350 | L. David Sloan/Everybody Loves My Baby | 4 |

MICKEY LEE
| 73 | Smash SMA 2332 | Hello My Little Queen/AUGUSTUS PABLO: African Queen | 10 |

NICKIE LEE
| 69 | Deep Soul DS 9103 | And Black Is Beautiful/Faith Within | 8 |

NORMA LEE
| 67 | CBM CBM 002 | Hurt/Rollin' On | 5 |

PEGGY LEE
78s
| 54 | Brunswick 05286 | Johnny Guitar/I Didn't Know What Time It Was (78) | 8 |
| 57 | Capitol CL 14741 | Baby, Baby Wait For Me/Every Night (78) | 8 |

Peggy LEE

MINT VALUE £

57	Capitol CL 14795	Uninvited Dreams/Listen To The Rockin' Bird (78)	8
58	Capitol CL 14902	Fever/You Don't Know (78)	20
58	Capitol CL 14955	Light Of Love/Sweetheart (78)	15
59	Brunswick 05798	It Ain't Necessarily So/Swing Low, Sweet Chariot (78)	10

SINGLES

54	Brunswick 05286	Johnny Guitar/I Didn't Know What Time It Was	12
54	Brunswick 05345	Love, You Didn't Do Right By Me/Sisters	10
55	Brunswick 05360	Let Me Go, Lover/Bouquet Of Blues	12
55	Brunswick 05368	Straight Ahead/It Must Be So (with Mills Brothers)	10
55	Brunswick 05421	Baubles, Bangles And Beads/Summer Vacation	10
55	Brunswick 05435	I Belong To You/How Bitter, My Sweet	10
55	Brunswick 05461	Ooh That Kiss/Oh! No! (Please Don't Go)	10
55	Brunswick 05471	Sugar/What Can I Say After I Say I'm Sorry	10
55	Brunswick 05472	He Needs Me/Sing A Rainbow	10
55	Brunswick 05482	He's A Tramp (with Pound Hounds)/The Siamese Cat Song (with Oliver Wallace)	12
55	Brunswick 05483	Bella Notte/La La Lu.	10

(The above 45s were originally issued with gold label lettering; silver reissues are worth two-thirds these values.)

56	Brunswick 05549	Three Cheers For Mister Magoo/Mister Magoo Does The Cha Cha Cha (with Jim Backus)	7
56	Brunswick 05554	The Come Back/You've Got To See Mama Every Night	6
56	Brunswick 05593	That's All Right Honey/Love You So	6
56	Brunswick 05625	We Laughed At Love/They Can't Take That Away From Me	6
57	Brunswick 05671	Mr. Wonderful/The Gypsy With Fire In His Shoes	8
57	Brunswick 05714	I Don't Know Enough About You/Where Flamingo's Fly	6
57	Capitol CL 14741	Baby, Baby Wait For Me/Every Night	6
57	Capitol CL 14795	Uninvited Dreams/Listen To The Rockin' Bird	6
58	Capitol CL 14902	Fever/You Don't Know	7
58	Capitol CL 14955	Light Of Love/Sweetheart	6
59	Capitol CL 14984	Alright, Okay, You Win/My Man	6
59	Brunswick 05798	It Ain't Necessarily So/Swing Low, Sweet Chariot	6
59	Capitol CL 15025	Hallelujah, I Love Him So/I'm Lookin' Out The Window	6
59	Capitol CL 15058	You Came A Long Way From St. Louis/I Lost My Sugar In Salt Lake City (with George Shearing Quintet)	6
59	Capitol CL 15103	You Deserve/Things Are Swingin'	8
61	Capitol CL 15184	Till There Was You/Bucket Of Tears	6
61	Capitol CL 15214	Mañana/The Folks Who Live On The Hill	6
63	Capitol CL 15313	Doodlin' Song/Got That Magic	5
65	Capitol CL 15376	Pass Me By/That's What It Takes	5
65	Capitol CL 15413	I Go To Sleep/Stop Living In The Past	7
69	Capitol CL 15614	I'm A Woman/Me And My Shadow	5
69	Capitol CL 15614	Is That All There Is?/I'm A Woman (2nd pressing with different A-side)	7
74	Warner Bros K 10527	Let's Love/Always	6

EPs

55	Brunswick OE 9153	PETE KELLY'S BLUES NO. 1 (EP)	10
55	Brunswick OE 9154	PETE KELLY'S BLUES NO. 2 (EP)	10
56	Brunswick OE 9282	PRESENTING PEGGY LEE (EP)	10
58	Brunswick OE 9400	SEA SHELLS PT. 1 (EP)	10
58	Brunswick OE 9401	SEA SHELLS PT. 2 (EP)	10
58	Philips BBE 12172	PEGGY WITH BENNY (EP, with Benny Goodman)	8
59	Capitol EAP1 1052	FEVER (EP)	10
59	Capitol EAP1 1213	ALRIGHT OKAY YOU WIN (EP)	8
61	Capitol EAP1 1857	I'M A WOMAN (EP)	8

LPs

53	Capitol LC 6584	CAPITOL PRESENTS PEGGY LEE (10" LP)	20
53	Brunswick LA 8629	BLACK COFFEE (10" LP)	20
55	Brunswick LA 8717	SONGS IN AN INTIMATE STYLE (10" LP)	20
55	Brunswick LAT 8078	PETE KELLY'S BLUES (LP, with Ella Fitzgerald)	18
56	Brunswick LA 8731	SONGS FROM 'LADY AND THE TRAMP' (10" LP)	20
56	Capitol LC 6817	MY BEST TO YOU (10" LP)	20
56	Capitol T 864	THE MAN I LOVE (LP)	15
57	Brunswick LAT 8171	DREAM STREET (LP)	18
58	Capitol (S)T 979	JUMP FOR JOY (LP)	15
58	Brunswick LAT 8266	SEA SHELLS (LP)	15
59	Capitol T 1049	THINGS ARE SWINGIN' (LP)	15
59	Capitol (S)T 1131	I LIKE MEN! (LP)	15
59	Brunswick LAT 8287	MISS WONDERFUL! (LP)	15
60	Capitol (S)T 1219	BEAUTY AND THE BEAT! (LP, with George Shearing Quintet, mono/stereo)	12/15
60	Capitol (S)T 1290	LATIN A LA LEE (LP, mono/stereo)	12/15
60	Capitol (S)T 1401	PRETTY EYES (LP, mono/stereo)	12/15
61	Brunswick LAT 8355	THE BEST OF PEGGY LEE VOL. 1 (LP)	12
61	Brunswick LAT 8356	THE BEST OF PEGGY LEE VOL. 2 (LP)	12
61	Capitol T 1366	ALL AGLOW AGAIN! (LP)	15
61	Capitol (S)T 1423	CHRISTMAS CAROUSEL (LP)	15
61	Ace Of Hearts AH 5	BLACK COFFEE (LP, reissue)	12
62	Capitol (S)T 1520	BASIN STREET EAST PRESENTS PEGGY LEE (LP, mono/stereo)	12/15
62	Capitol (S)T 1630	IF YOU GO (LP, mono/stereo)	12/15
62	Ace Of Hearts AH 26	PEGGY LEE (LP)	12
62	Capitol (S)T1 1671	BLUES CROSS COUNTRY (LP, mono/stereo)	12/15
63	Capitol T 1743	BEWITCHING-LEE! (LP)	12
63	Ace Of Hearts AH 44	DREAM STREET (LP, reissue)	12
63	Capitol (S)T 1857	I'M A WOMAN (LP, mono/stereo)	12/15
64	Capitol (S)T 1850	MINK JAZZ (LP, mono/stereo)	12/15
64	Capitol (S)T 1969	IN LOVE AGAIN (LP, mono/stereo)	12/15
64	Ace Of Hearts AH 75	SEA SHELLS (LP, reissue)	12
64	Capitol (S)T 2096	IN THE NAME OF LOVE (LP, mono/stereo)	12/15

MINT VALUE £

65	Capitol (S)T 2320	PASS ME BY (LP)	12
66	Capitol (S)T 1475	OLE A LA LEE! (LP)	14
66	Ace Of Hearts AH 107	THE FABULOUS PEGGY LEE (LP)	12
66	Capitol (S)T 2388	THEN WAS THEN, NOW IS NOW! (LP)	12
66	Brunswick LAT 8629	BLACK COFFEE (LP, 2nd reissue)	12
67	Capitol (S)T 2469	GUITARS A LA LEE (LP)	12
67	Capitol (S)T 2475	BIG SPENDER (LP)	12
69	Capitol (S)T 21141	IS THAT ALL THERE IS? (LP)	12

(see also Bing Crosby, George Shearing)

ROBERTA LEE

52	Brunswick 04876	The Little White Cloud That Cried/Tell Me Why (78, with Grady Martin)	10
53	Brunswick 05076	Sixty Minute Man (with Hardrock Gunter)/RED FOLEY: Hot Toddy (78)	12
53	Brunswick 05116	Say It Isn't So/Dear Joe (78)	8
53	Brunswick 05123	Don't Call My Name/Hey Mister Cottonpicker (78, with Tex Williams)	8
53	Brunswick 05134	Ill Wind (You're Blowing Me No Good)/Fare-Thee-Well (78)	8
53	Brunswick 05205	Caribbean/Let's Go Home (78)	8
54	HMV 7M 261	True Love And Tender Care/When The Organ Played At Twilight	7
55	Brunswick 05388	Ridin' To Tennessee/I'll Be There If Ever You Want Me	10

(see also Red Foley, Hardrock Gunter)

ROBIN LEE

62	Reprise R 20068	Gamblin' Man/An Angel With A Broken Wing	12

ROY LEE

61	Decca F 11406	Two Initials/Honey Lies	6

TONY LEE

68	Doctor Bird DB 1106	Lee's Special/LLOYD & GROOVERS: My Heart My Soul	15

VINNY LEE & RIDERS

61	HMV POP 856	Mule Train/Gambler's Guitar	10

WARREN LEE

69	Pama PM 762	Underdog Backstreet/Come Put My Life In Order	7

WILMA LEE & STONEY COOPER

64	Hickory 45-1257	Big John's Wife/Pirate King	6

LEE & CLARENDONIANS

72	Green Door GD 4038	Night Owl/Night Owl Version	6

LEE (Perry) & JIMMY (Riley)

75	Dip DL 5075	Rasta Train/Yagga Yagga	10

LEE (Perry) & JUNIOR (Byles)

75	Dip DL 5060	Dreader Locks/Militant Rock	6

LEE & PAUL

59	Philips PB 912	The Chick/Valentina, My Valentina	6

BRAD LEEDS

60	Pye International 7N 25050	A Teenage Love Is Born/I'm Walking Behind You	6

PHIL LEEDS

66	London HLR 10044	Would You Believe It?/FRANK GALLOP: The Ballad Of Irving	5

MARK LEEMAN FIVE

65	Columbia DB 7452	Portland Town/Gotta Get Myself Together	18
65	Columbia DB 7648	Blow My Blues Away/On The Horizon	20
66	Columbia DB 7812	Forbidden Fruit/Goin' To Bluesville	20
66	Columbia DB 7955	Follow Me/Gather Up The Pieces	18

(see also Cheynes)

THOMAS LEER

78	Oblique ER 101	Private Plane/International (folded photocopied p/s, hand-stamped labels)	10
78	Company/Oblique OBCO 1	Private Plane/International (reissue, printed p/s)	6
82	Cherry Red CHERRY 52	All About You/Saving Grace (p/s)	4
82	Cherry Red 12CHERRY 52	All About You/Saving Grace (12", p/s)	7
84	Arista LERPD 121	International/Easy Way (12", picture disc)	7
82	Cherry Red ERED 26	CONTRADICTIONS EP (12", double pack)	8
79	Industrial IR 0007	THE BRIDGE (LP, with Robert Rental)	15

(see also Act, Robert Rental)

JOHN LEES

74	Polydor 2058 513	Best Of My Love/You Can't Get It	15
77	Harvest HAR 5132	Child Of The Universe/Kes (A Major Fancy)	5
73	Harvest SHVL 811	A MAJOR FANCY (LP)	12

(see also Barclay James Harvest)

RAYMOND LEFEVRE & HIS ORCHESTRA

68	Major Minor MM 559	Soul Coaxing (Ame Caline)/When A Man Loves A Woman	10

JACK LE FORGE

65	Stateside SS 444	Our Crazy Affair/Bossa Bossa Nova (withdrawn)	10

LEFT BANKE

66	Philips BF 1517	Walk Away Renee/I Haven't Got The Nerve	8
67	Philips BF 1540	Pretty Ballerina/Lazy Day	8
67	Philips BF 1575	Ivy Ivy/And Suddenly	10
67	Philips BF 1614	Desiree/I've Got Something On My Mind	7
87	Bam Caruso OPRA 023	Walk Away Renee/Ivy Ivy (DJ/jukebox issue)	6
67	Philips (S)BL 7773	WALK AWAY RENEE/PRETTY BALLERINA (LP)	35

LEFTFIELD

90	Outer Rhythm FOOT 9R	More Than I Know (10K Remix)/(More Mix)/(Even More Mix) (12")	10
91	Outer Rhythm FOOT 009	More Than I Know (12" Mix)/Not Forgotten (Hard Hands Mix) (12")	20

MINT VALUE £

92	Hard Hands HAND 001T	Release The Pressure/Release The Pressure (Instrumental)/ Release The Pressure (with Earl Sixteen) (12")	8
92	Hard Hands HAND 001R	Release The Dubs (Dub 1)/(Dub 2)/(Dub 3)/(Dub 4) (12")	12
92	Hard Hands HAND 002T	Song Of Life/Song Of Life (Dub Of Life)/Song Of Life (Fanfare Of Life) (12")	10
92	Hard Hands HAND 002R	Song Of Life (Underworld Remix)/Release The Pressure (Release The Horns Mix)/Release The Pressure (Lemon Interrupt Mix) (12")	12
94	Hard Hands LEFT EP1	LEFTISM (12", 4-track sampler, promo only)	10
95	Hard Hands LEFT EP2	Original/Original (Jam)/Filter Fish/Original (Drift) (12", double pack, as Leftfield & Halliday, promo only)	10
95	Hard Hands HAND 29P	RELEASE THE PRESSURE (12", double pack, promo only)	10
95	Hard Hands AFRO EP	AFRO-LEFT EP (12", with Djum Djum, double pack, promo only)	15

(see also Curve)

LEFT-HANDED MARRIAGE

| 67 | private pressing | ON THE RIGHT SIDE OF THE LEFT-HANDED MARRIAGE (LP) | 450 |
| 96 | Tenth Planet TP 022 | ON THE RIGHT SIDE OF THE LEFT-HANDED MARRIAGE (LP, reissue, gatefold sleeve) | 12 |

LEFT HAND DRIVE

| 79 | Bancrupt BAN 012 | Who Said Rock & Roll Is Dead/I Know Where I Am (p/s) | 5 |

LEFT SIDE

| 69 | Columbia DB 8575 | Welcome To My House/This Little Village | 4 |

LANCE LE GAULT

| 68 | United Artists UP 2255 | Billie/Louisiana Swamp Fox | 4 |

LEGAY

| 69 | Fontana TF 904 | No-One/The Fantastic Story Of The Steam Driven Banana | 80 |

(see also Gypsy)

LEGEND

69	Bell BLL 1048	National Gas/Wouldn't You	10
69	Bell BLL 1082	Georgia George Part 1/July	8
70	Vertigo 6059 021	Life/Late Last Night	8
71	Vertigo 6059 036	Don't You Know/Someday	8
69	Bell MBLL/SBLL 115	LEGEND (LP)	50
71	Vertigo 6360 019	LEGEND ('RED BOOT') (LP, gatefold sleeve, spiral label)	45
72	Vertigo 6360 063	MOONSHINE (LP, gatefold sleeve, spiral label)	50

(see also Procol Harum, Fingers)

LEGEND

| 81 | Legend LEG 1 | Hideaway/Heaven Sent (p/s) | 75 |

LEGEND

82	Workshop WR 3478	FRONTLINE EP (Frontline/Sabre & Chatila/ Stormers Of Heaven/Open The Skies) (12")	30
81	Workshop WR 2007	LEGEND (LP)	50
82	Workshop WR 3477	DEATH IN THE NURSERY (LP, with insert)	25

LEGEND!

| 83 | Creation CRE 001/ Lyntone LYN 12903 | '73 In '83/You (Chunka Chunka) Were Glamorous (foldaround p/s in poly bag, some with 33rpm flexidisc "I Wonder Why! (live)" by Pastels/"Wouldn't You?" by Laughing Apple) | 8/5 |
| 84 | Creation CRE 010 | The Legend Destroys The Blues/Arrogant Bastards (foldaround p/s in poly bag) | 6 |

TOBI LEGEND

| 78 | RK RK 1004 | Time Will Pass You By/DEAN PARRISH: I'm On My Way/ JIMMY RADCLIFFE: Long After Tonight Is All Over (p/s) | 6 |

LEGENDARY GOLDEN VAMPIRES

85	Exile EX 7001	Creeping Poison/Rebel Woman (p/s)	5
85	Exile EX 7003	Gone For Good/Train Kept A-Rollin' (p/s)	4
86	Exile EX 10EP 01	TROUBLE BOUND (10" EP)	6

LEGENDARY LONNIE

| 81 | Nervous NER 002 | Constipation Shake/Devil's Guitar (p/s) | 6 |

LEGENDARY MASKED SURFERS

| 73 | United Artists UP 35542 | Gonna Hustle You/Summertime, Summertime | 8 |

(see also Beach Boys, Jan & Dean)

LEGENDARY PINK DOTS

82	In Phaze IPNER 1	THE TOWER (LP)	18
82	In Phaze	BRIGHTER NOW (cassette)	15
83	Third Mind TMT 08	THE BASILISK (cassette)	15
83	In Phaze PHA 2	CURSE (LP)	15
84	In Phaze PHA 3	LEGENDARY PINK DOTS (LP)	15

LEGENDS

65	Pye 7N 15904	I've Found Her/Something's Gonna Happen	10
67	Parlophone R 5581	Tomorrow's Gonna Be Another Day/Nobody Laughs Anymore	25
67	Parlophone R 5613	Under The Sky/Twenty-Four Hours A Day	15

(see also First Impressions)

B. LEGGS

| 71 | Green Door GD 4004 | Drums Of Passion/Love And Emotion (Version) | 5 |

(see also Morgan's All Stars)

LEGO FEET

| 91 | Skam SKAM 1 | Untitled1/Untitled 2 (12", die cut sleeve) | 60 |

MICHEL LEGRAND

| 54 | Philips PB 261 | Me Que/Viens (78) | 8 |
| 73 | Tamla Motown TMG 848 | Love Theme From "Lady Sings The Blues"/Any Happy Home (with Gil Askey) | 5 |

MINT VALUE £

73	Tamla Motown TMG 848	Love Theme From "Lady Sings The Blues"/Any Happy Home (demo in p/s)	12
58	Philips SBBL 510	LEGRAND JAZZ (LP)	12
60s	Philips BL 7605	PLAYS RICHARD ROGERS (LP)	12
66	Philips (S)BL 7792	THE YOUNG GIRLS OF ROCHEFORT (LP, soundtrack)	20
68	United Artists SULP 1218	THE THOMAS CROWN AFFAIR (LP, soundtrack)	30
68	Sunset SLS 50519	THE THOMAS CROWN AFFAIR (LP, reissue).	12
70	United Artists UAS 29084	THE HAPPY ENDING (LP, soundtrack)	18

LE GRIFFE
83	Bullet BOL 1	Fast Bikes/Where Are You? (p/s)	8
83	Bullet BOLT 1	Fast Bikes/Where Are You?/The Actor (12", p/s)	15
84	Bullet BOL 7	You're Killing Me (p/s)	8
83	Bullet BOLT 7	You're Killing Me/E.T.A. (12", p/s)	20
84	Bullet BULP 2	BREAKING STRAIN (mini-LP)	20

LEGS AKIMBO! (& TITANICS)
80	Vindaloo UGH 1	Lederhosen/Greasy Joe's Café/Got To Get My Legs Out Of Bed/	
		Dream In A Hammock (p/s)	4
81	Vindaloo UGH 5	LAND OF THE BEARDED CRICKETERS	
		(EP, as Legs Akimbo! & Titanics; no'd p/s)	5

TOM LEHRER
60	Decca F 11243	Poisoning Pigeons In The Park/The Masochism Tango (some in p/s).	8/5
66	Reprise RS 23049	Pollution/Folk Song Army	5
58	Decca LF 1311	SONGS BY TOM LEHRER (10" LP)	15
59	Decca LF 1323	MORE OF TOM LEHRER (10" LP)	15
59	Decca LK 4332/SKL 4097	AN EVENING WASTED WITH... (LP)	12
60	Decca LK 4375	TOM LEHRER REVISITED (LP)	12
65	Reprise R 6179	THAT WAS THE YEAR THAT WAS (LP).	12

LEIBER-STOLLER ORCHESTRA
| 62 | HMV POP 1050 | Cafe Expresso/Blue Baion . . . . | 12 |

LEIBSTANDARTE SS MB
| 81 | Come Organisation | TRIUMPH OF THE WILL (LP, 500 only). . . . . . . | 80 |
| 80s | Come Organisation | WELTANSCHAUUNG (LP) . . . . | 50 |

ADELE LEIGH
| 59 | Philips PB 887 | O My Beloved Father/Voi Che Sapete (78). . . . . . . | 10 |

ANDREW LEIGH
| 70 | Polydor 2343 034 | MAGICIAN (LP). . . . . | 15 |
| | (see also Reg King) | | |

BERNIE LEIGHTON
| 63 | Pye International 7N 25177 | Lawrence Of Arabia Theme/The Wonderful World We Live In (some in p/s) . . . . . | 7/5 |

LEISURE PROCESS
82	Epic EPCA 2478	A Way You'll Never Be/Rachel Dreams (p/s)	5
82	Epic EPCA 13-2478	A Way You'll Never Be/Rachel Dreams (12", p/s).	8
	(see also Level 42)		

LEITMOTIV
| 83 | Pax PAX 17 | Silent Run/(Living In A) Tin (p/s) . . . . | 5 |
| 85 | Cryptic SPIRO 98 | Say Remain/Out Of The Way (p/s) . . . . | 4 |

GARY LeMEL
| 67 | London HLM 7124 | Beautiful People/Take Me With You (export issue) . . . . . . | 12 |

LEMMINGS
65	Pye 7N 15837	Out Of My Mind/My Little Girl	12
65	Pye 7N 15899	You Can't Blame Me For Trying/Bring Your Heart With You.	12
	(see also Honeycombs, Martin Murray)		

JACK LEMMON
| 60 | Fontana H 262 | Theme From "The Apartment"/Lemmon-Flavoured Blues . . . . . . | 6 |

LEMMY & UPSETTERS with MICK GREEN
| 90 | Sunnyside STYLE 777 | Blue Suede Shoes/Paradise (p/s) . . . . | 6 |
| | (see also Motörhead, Rockin' Vickers, Sam Gopal) | | |

LEMON DIPS
| 69 | De Wolfe DW/LP 3114 | WHO'S GONNA BUY? (LP, library issue). . . . . . . | 50 |

LEMON INTERRUPT
93	Jnr. Boys Own JBO 12002	Eclipse/Bigmouth (12")	25
93	Junior Boys Own JBO 712	Dirty/Minneapolis/Minneapolis (Airwaves) (12").	20
	(see also Underworld)		

LEMON KITTENS
79	Step Forward SF 10	SPOONFED AND WRITHING (EP)	18
81	United Dairies UD 07	CAKE BEAST (12" EP, with inner sleeve & insert)	30
80	United Dairies UD 02	WE BUY A HAMMER FOR DADDY (LP, with inner sheet)	60
83	Illuminated JAMS 131	THE BIG DENTIST (LP)	50
	(see also Danielle Dax, Shock Headed Peters, Underneath, Gland Shrouds, Karl Blake, Fur Fur)		

LEMON LINE
| 67 | Decca F 12688 | For Your Precious Love/You Made Me See The Light . . . . . . | 4 |

LEMON MEN
| 69 | Polydor 56365 | I've Seen You Cut Lemons/Lemon Strip/Lemon Walk . . . . . . | 5 |

LEMON PIPERS
68	Pye International 7N 25444	Green Tambourine/No Help From Me	6
68	Pye International 7N 25454	Rice Is Nice/Blueberry Blue.	6
68	Pye International 7N 25464	Jelly Jungle (Of Orange Marmalade)/Shoeshine Boy	8

LEMON PIPERS

68	Pye Intl. NPL 28112	GREEN TAMBOURINE (LP)	22
68	Pye Intl. NSPL 28118	JUNGLE MARMALADE (LP)	12
69	Marble Arch MAL 1120	THE LEMON PIPERS (LP)	12
	(see also Ram Jam)		

LEMON PIPERS/1910 FRUITGUM CO.
68	Pye Intl. NEP 44091	PRESENTING ... (EP, 1 side each)	15
	(see also 1910 Fruitgum Co.)		

LEMON TREE
68	Parlophone R 5671	I Can Touch A Rainbow/William Chalker's Time Machine	25
68	Parlophone R 5739	It's So Nice To Come Home/Come On Girl	10
	(see also Idle Race, Uglys, Danny King's Mayfair Set, Balls)		

LEN & HONEYSUCKERS
66	Rio R 75	One More River/Emergency Ward	8

FREDDIE LENNON
66	Piccadilly 7N 35290	That's My Life (My Love And My Home)/The Next Time You Feel Important	40
	(see also Loving Kind)		

JIMMY LENNON & ATLANTICS
64	Decca F 11825	Louisiana Mama/I Learned To Yodel	30

JOHN LENNON/PLASTIC ONO BAND
SINGLES
69	Apple APPLE 13/R 5795	Give Peace A Chance/Remember Love (p/s, as Plastic Ono Band; with Parlophone catalogue number, dark green label)	12
69	Apple APPLES 1001	Cold Turkey/Don't Worry Kyoko (Mummy's Only Looking For A Hand In The Snow) (p/s, as Plastic Ono Band)	15
69	Apple APPLES 1002	You Know My Name (Look Up The Number)/What's The New Mary Jane (as Plastic Ono Band, unreleased; vinyl test pressings only with typed Apple 'Custom Recording' labels & handwritten catalogue number)	2,000
70	Apple APPLES 1003	Instant Karma!/Who Has Seen The Wind? (p/s, as Lennon/Ono with Plastic Ono Band)	12
71	Apple R 5892	Power To The People/YOKO ONO & PLASTIC ONO BAND: Open Your Box (p/s, full apple label both sides or full/half apple label)	15
72	Apple R 5970	Happy Xmas (War Is Over) (as John & Yoko/Plastic Ono Band with Harlem Community Choir)/YOKO ONO & PLASTIC ONO BAND: Listen, The Snow Is Falling (p/s, green vinyl)	10
72	Apple R 5953	Woman Is The Nigger Of The World/Sisters O Sisters (unreleased, test pressings only)	1,000+
73	Apple R 5994	Mind Games/Meat City (p/s)	6
74	EMI PSR 369	Interview With John Lennon By Bob Mercer And Message To The Salesmen/Whatever Gets You Thru' The Night (promo only)	350
75	Apple R 6003	# 9 Dream (Edited Version)/What You Got (demo only)	50
75	Apple R 6009	Imagine/Working Class Hero (p/s)	12
84	Polydor PODJ 701	Borrowed Time (Edited Version)/YOKO ONO: Your Hands (promo only)	6
84	Polydor POSP 712	Every Man Has A Woman Who Loves Him/SEAN ONO LENNON: It's Alright (p/s, some with poster)	10/5
88	Parlophone RP 6199	Imagine/Jealous Guy (picture disc)	10
97	Parlophone IMAGINE 001	Imagine (CD, 1-track, card p/s, promo only)	10
97	Parlophone IMAGINE 002	Happy Xmas (War Is Over) (CD, 1-track, card p/s, promo only)	10
98	Parlophone LENNON 002	Happy Xmas (War Is Over) (rough mix)/Be Bop A Lula (CD, card p/s, promo only)	15

LPs
68	Apple APCOR 2	UNFINISHED MUSIC NO. 1: TWO VIRGINS (LP, with Yoko Ono, mono; black inner, no track listing, with "Merrie In England..." blurb on front sleeve)	1,000
68	Apple SAPCOR 2/ Track 613 012	UNFINISHED MUSIC NO. 1: TWO VIRGINS (LP, with Yoko Ono, stereo; black inner, with track listing & "Merrie In England..." blurb on back sleeve & Track Records logo on label)	150
69	Zapple ZAPPLE 01	UNFINISHED MUSIC NO. 2: LIFE WITH THE LIONS (LP, with Yoko Ono, with inner sleeve)	100
69	Apple SAPCOR 11	WEDDING ALBUM (LP, with Yoko Ono; gatefold sleeve in box set, includes wedding certificate glued to inside box lid, press booklet, poster, white 'Bagism' bag, passport photographs, postcard & picture of wedding cake)	175
69	Apple CORE 2001	LIVE PEACE IN TORONTO 1969 (LP, as Plastic Ono Band, with stapled calendar, some sealed)	65/45
72	Apple Q4PAS 10004	IMAGINE (LP, quadrophonic, with inner sleeve, poster & postcard)	50
81	Parlophone JLB 8	THE JOHN LENNON BOX (9-LP set)	60
84	Polydor POLH P5	MILK AND HONEY (LP, picture disc, original pressing, thin vinyl, 2,000 only)	35
84	Polydor POLH P5	MILK AND HONEY (LP, picture disc, 2nd pressing, thicker vinyl, 1,000 only)	20
98	Parlophone 8306142	ANTHOLOGY (4-CDR, jewel cases with Abbey Road studio inlays, incorrect track listing and missing "Grow Old With Me" from CD4, promo only)	500
	(see also Beatles, Yoko Ono, Bill Elliott/Elastic Oz Band, Elephant's Memory, Musketeer Gripweed, Elton John)		

JOHN LENNON & BLEECHERS (Jamaica)
70	Punch PH 23	Ram You Hard/UPSETTERS: Soul Stew	10

JULIAN LENNON
84	Charisma JLY 1	Too Late For Goodbyes/Well I Don't Know (picture disc)	10
84	Charisma JLD 2	Valotte/Too Late For Goodbyes	12
84	Charisma JLS 2	Valotte/Let Me Be (arch-shaped picture disc with stand)	12
84	Charisma JL 212	Valotte/Let Me Be/Bebop (12", poster p/s)	8
84	Charisma JLD 3	Say You're Wrong/Valotte (p/s)	12
89	Virgin VSCD 1154	Now You're In Heaven/Too Late For Goodbyes/Now You're In Heaven (Orbit Mix) (3" CD, card sleeve)	8
89	Virgin VSCD 1182	You're The One/Sunday Morning/Stand By Me (live) (3" CD, card sleeve)	8
98	Music From Another Room reg. cat. no.	PHOTOGRAPH SMILE (CD, picture frame pack, with inserts & booklet, sealed, promo only)	20

SEAN LENNON
98	Grand Royal SEAN 001	SEAN LENNON (CD, card sleeve with 16 stickers, promo only)	15

LENNON SISTERS
56	Vogue Coral Q 72176	Graduation Day/Toy Tiger	10
57	Vogue Coral Q 72259	Young And In Love/Teenage Waltz	10
57	Vogue Coral Q 72285	Shake Me I Rattle/Pocohontas	12
61	London HLD 9417	Sad Movies/I Don't Know Why	10
64	London HA-D/SH-D 8154	GREAT FOLK SONGS (LP, as Lennon Sisters & Cousins)	22

ANNIE LENNOX & AL GREEN
88	A&M CDEE 484	Put A Little Love In Your Heart (7" Version With Edits)/(Vocal Mix)/ Put A Little Love In Your Heart/SPHERES OF CELESTIAL INFLUENCE: A Great Big Piece Of Love (3" CD, in 5" card sleeve)	8

(see also Eurythmics, Al Green)

LENNY THE LION (with Terry Hall)
59	Parlophone R 4609	I Wish That I Could Be Father Christmas/I Want A Hippopotamus For Christmas	8

J.B. LENOIR (& AFRICAN HUNCH RHYTHM)
65	Sue WI 339	I Sing Um The Way I Feel/I Feel So Good (with His African Hunch Rhythm)	25
65	Bootleg 503	Man Watch Your Woman/Mama Talk To Your Daughter (99 copies only)	50
66	Blue Horizon 45-1004	Mojo Boogie/I Don't Care What Nobody Say (99 copies only)	75
68	Python PLP 25	J.B. LENOIR (LP, 99 copies only)	50
70	Polydor 2482 014	CRUSADE (LP)	20
75	Rarity LP 2	J.B. LENOIR (LP)	20
70s	CBS 62593	ALABAMA BLUES (LP)	30

ROBIN LENT
71	Nepentha 6347 002	SCARECROW'S JOURNEY (LP, gatefold sleeve, with Focus)	40

(see also Focus, Jan Akkerman)

VAL LENTON
65	Immediate IM 008	Gotta Get Away/You Don't Care	22

CHRIS LEON
72	Dynamic DYN 450	(Last Night) I Didn't Get To Sleep At All/DYNAMITES: Instrumental Version	6

LEON (Silvera) & OWEN (Gray)
62	Blue Beat BB 117	Murder (with Drumbago All Stars)/ROY PANTON: Forty Four	12

(see also Owen & Leon, Owen & Millie)

CHARLES LEONARD
71	Jay Boy BOY 39	Funky Driver On A Funky Bus (Parts 1 & 2)	4

DEKE LEONARD
73	United Artists UP 35494	Diamond Road/Turning In Circles	5
73	United Artists UP 35556	Nothing Is Happening/Sixty Minute Man (unissued)	
73	United Artists UP 35556	Nothing Is Happening/She's A Cow (unissued, demo only)	12
73	United Artists UP 35556	A Hard Way To Live/The Aching Is So Sweet	5
74	United Artists UP 35668	Louisiana Hoedown/She's A Cow	5
79	United Artists UP 36488	Map Of India/Hey There! (Lady In The Black Tuxedo) (gatefold p/s)	5
73	United Artists UAS 29464	ICEBERG (LP)	12
74	United Artists UAG 29544	KAMIKAZE (LP)	12

(see also Man, Marty Wilde, Help Yourself, Pete Brown's Piblokto, Gary Pickford-Hopkins & Friends)

ANN LEONARDO
57	Capitol CL 14723	Straws In The Wind/Travelling Stranger	5
57	Capitol CL 14755	Lottery/One And Only	5
57	Capitol CL 14797	Three Time Loser/I'll Wait Till Monday	5

TOMMY LEONETTI
54	Capitol CL 14199	That's What You Made Me/I Love My Mama	6
55	Capitol CL 14272	Ever Since You Went Away/Untied	6
56	Capitol CL 14556	Heartless/Sometime	5
56	Capitol CL 14598	It's Wild/Free	5
56	Capitol CL 14654	Too Proud/Wrong	6
58	RCA RCA 1107	Dream Lover/Moonlight Serenade	6
58	RCA RCA 1107	Dream Lover/Moonlight Serenade (78)	10

LEONIE & JOE NOLAN BAND
68	Jolly JY 015	Move And Groove/Don't Let Me Do It	4

LE ORME
(see under 'O')

LEO'S SUNSHIPP
79	Grapevine RED 3	Give Me The Sunshine/I'm Back For More	6
79	Grapevine REDC 3	Give Me The Sunshine/I'm Back For More (12")	10

LEPRECHAUN
81	Excalibur EXC 508	Loc It Up/Party Freaks (12")	8

LE RITZ
77	Breaker BS 2001	Punker/What A Sucker (p/s)	35

LEROY & ROCKY (Ellis)
68	Studio One SO 2042	Love Me Girl/WRIGGLERS: Reel Up	18

(see also King Rocky)

LE ROYS
64	Give A Disc LYN 504/505	Money/Swinging On A Star (flexidisc)	8
64	HMV POP 1274	Gotta Lotta Love (Ciribiribin)/Don't Cry Baby	8
64	HMV POP 1312	Chills/Lost Out On Love	10
64	HMV POP 1368	I Come Smiling On Through/California GL 903	7

(see also Mike Sarne, Simon Scott, John Leyton, Mike Berry, Grazina, Billie Davis, Billy Boyle, Don Spencer)

LEROYS & INNOCENTS
64   Regal Zonophone RZ 502   HOT SIX (maxi-single, plain sleeve) 10
(see also Innocents)

BILL LE SAGE
60s   World Records   PRESENTING THE BILL LESAGE/RONNIE ROSS QUARTET (LP) 10
(see also Ronnie Ross)

BONGO LES (Chen) & BUNNY (Herman)
72   Attack ATT 8041   Feel Nice (Version)/WINSTON SCOTLAND: Quick And Slick 6
(see also Bongo Herman)

LES & SILKIE
70   Torpedo TOR 13   I Don't Want To Tell You/DENZIL DENNIS: Come On In 6

LORNE LESLEY
59   Parlophone R 4518   Some Of These Days/When Love Has Let You Down 6
59   Parlophone R 4518   Some Of These Days/When Love Has Let You Down (78) 10
59   Parlophone R 4567   Warm/You Ought To Be Mine 6
59   Parlophone R 4581   So High, So Low/I Don't Know 7
60   Polydor NH 66928   Take All My Love/Ritroviamoci (Till We Meet Again) 7
60   Polydor NH 66956   Bloodshot Eyes/We're Gonna Dance 8
65   Philips BF 1403   Someone Like You/Where My Heart Never Wandered 5
65   Philips BF 1434   Rainy Days Were Made For Lonely People/Fire Down Below 5
66   Philips BF 1487   Somebody's Gonna Be Sorry/(I'm Afraid) The Masquerade Is Over 7
66   Parlophone R 5538   Little Snowflakes/Would You 5

MICHAEL LESLEY
65   Pye 7N 15835   Momma Didn't Know/I Don't Wanna Know 6
65   Pye 7N 15908   Penny Arcade/Bye Bye Baby 6
65   Pye 7N 15959   Make Up Or Break Up/She Can't See Me 10
66   Decca F 12531   Right Or Wrong/Office Girl (credited to Michael Leslie) 5

JOHN & CHRIS LESLIE
76   Cottage COT 901   THE SHIP OF TIME (LP) 15

LES RITA MITSOUKO
(see under 'R')

LES SAUTERELLES
(see under 'S')

HEDDY LESTER
77   Sonet SON 2013   The World Keeps Turning/Never Saw Him Laughing (p/s) 6

KETTY LESTER
62   London HLN 9527   Love Letters/I'm A Fool To Want You 6
62   London HLN 9574   But Not For Me/Moscow Nights 6
62   London HLN 9608   You Can't Lie To A Liar/River Of Salt 6
62   London HLN 9635   This Land Is Your Land/Love Belongs To Everyone 6
63   London HLN 9698   A Warm Summer Day/I'll Never Stop Loving You 6
64   RCA Victor RCA 1394   Some Things Are Better Left Unsaid/The House Is Haunted 60
64   RCA Victor RCA 1403   Roses Grow With Thorns/Please Don't Cry Anymore 25
64   RCA Victor RCA 1421   I Trust You Baby/Theme From "The Luck Of Ginger Coffey" 6
65   RCA Victor RCA 1460   Looking For A Better World/Pretty Eyes 6
65   Capitol CL 15427   West Coast/I'll Be Looking Back 15
66   Capitol CL 15447   When A Man Loves A Woman/We'll Be Together Again 6
62   London RE-N 1348   KETTY LESTER (EP) 30
63   London HA-N 2455   LOVE LETTERS (LP) 30
64   RCA Victor RD 7669   THE SOUL OF ME (LP) 18
65   RCA Victor RD 7712   WHERE IS LOVE (LP) 18
67   Stateside S(S)L 10196   WHEN A MAN LOVES A WOMAN (LP) 15

LAZY LESTER
64   Stateside SS 277   I'm A Lover Not A Fighter/Sugar Coated Love 18
71   Blue Horizon 2431 007   MADE UP MY MIND (LP) 90
77   Flyright FLYLP 526   THEY CALL ME LAZY (LP) 12
79   Flyright FLYLP 544   POOR BOY BLUES (LP) 12

ROBIE LESTER
62   Polydor NH 66963   Ballad Of Cheating John/Miracle Of Love 4

LES YPER SOUND
67   Fontana TF 880   Too Fortiche/Psyche Rock 60

LET'S ACTIVE
84   Bucketfull/Brains BOB 10   I Feel Funny/Wild Wild Women (flexidisc with *Bucketfull Of Brains*, issue 16) . . . 6/4

LETTERMEN
61   Capitol CL 15222   The Way You Look Tonight/That's My Desire 6
65   Capitol CL 15405   Theme From A Summer Place/Sealed With A Kiss 5
68   Capitol CL 15526   Goin' Out Of My Head/Can't Take My Eyes Off You — I Believe 5
69   Capitol CL 15609   Hurt So Bad/Traces 5
61   Capitol EAP 41669   THE LETTERMEN (EP) 10
62   Capitol (S)T 1669   A SONG FOR YOUNG LOVE (LP) 15
62   Capitol (S)T 1711   ONCE UPON A TIME (LP) 15
62   Capitol (S)T 1761   THE LETTERMEN (LP) 15
63   Capitol (S)T 1829   COLLEGE STANDARDS (LP) 15
63   Capitol (S)T 1936   IN CONCERT (LP) 15
64   Capitol (S)T 2083   LOOK AT LOVE (LP) 15
64   Capitol (S)T 2142   SHE CRIED (LP) 15
65   Capitol T 2270   PORTRAIT OF MY LOVE (LP) 15

LETTERMEN
74   Stag SG 10075   FIRST CLASS (LP, private pressing) 100

LETTERS
79	Heartbeat PULSE 9	Nobody Loves Me/Don't Want You Back (p/s)	20

DON LETTS & JAH WOBBLE
79	Virgin VS 239	Steel Leg: Stratetime & The Wide Man/Electric Dread: Haile Unlikely (p/s)	12
79	Virgin VS 239-12	Steel Leg: Stratetime & The Wide Man/Electric Dread: Haile Unlikely (12", p/s)	15

(see also Jah Wobble, PiL)

LEVEE BREAKERS
65	Parlophone R 5291	Babe I'm Leaving You/Wild About My Loving	20

(see also Beverley, Johnny Joyce)

LEVEE CAMP MOAN
69	County	LEVEE CAMP MOAN (LP, private pressing)	600
69	County	PEACOCK FARM (LP, private pressing)	600

LEVEL 42
79	Elite DAZZ 4	Sandstorm/ATMOSFEAR: Journey To The Powerline (Remix) (12", white label test pressing, no p/s)	75
80	Elite DAZZ 5	Love Meeting Love/Instrumental Love (7", unreleased)	
80	Elite DAZZ 5	Love Meeting Love/Instrumental Love (12", company die-cut stickered sleeve)	30
81	Polydor POSPX 200	(Flying On The) Wings Of Love (Remix '81)/Love Meeting (12", plain white stickered sleeve)	12
82	Polydor POSPX 500	You Can't Blame Louis (Extended Remix)/Love Games (live)/Dune Tune (live) (12", unreleased, white label test pressings only, no p/s)	25
83	Polydor POSPX 538	The Chinese Way (Extended Version)/88 (live) (12", yellow vinyl, black sl.)	15
83	Polydor POSPX 538/ Polydor POSPX 500	The Chinese Way (Extended Version)/88 (live)//Weave Your Spell (Extended Mix)/Dune Tune (live)/Love Games (live) (12", double pack, shrinkwrapped with sticker)	12
83	Polydor POSPX 538/ Polydor POSPX 396	The Chinese Way (Extended Mix)/88 (live)//Are You Hearing (What I Hear)? (Full Length)/The Return Of The Handsome Rugged Man (12", double pack, shrinkwrapped with sticker)	12
83	Polydor POPPX 570	Out Of Sight, Out Of Mind (Extended Mix)/You Can't Blame Louis (Extended Remix) (12", picture disc in PVC sleeve)	12
83	Polydor POSPX 622/ POSPX 234	The Sun Goes Down (Living It Up)/Can't Walk You Home//Love Games (Extended Mix)/Forty Two (12", shrinkwrapped double pack)	10
83	Polydor POSPX 622	The Sun Goes Down (Living It Up)/Can't Walk You Home (12", shrinkwrapped with free cassette)	10
83	Polydor POSPX 643	Micro Kid (Extended Version)/Turn It On (Extended Live Version)/ The Chinese Way (New York Remix) (12", stickered p/s)	30
83	Polydor POSPX 643/ LEVEL 643	Micro Kid (Extended Version)/Turn It On (Extended Live Version)// The Chinese Way (New York Remix)/Chinese Way (Dub Mix) (12", stickered shrinkwrapped double pack)	20
83	Lyntone LYN 12914	Love Games (live extended version) (white flexidisc free with *Melody Maker*)	6/4
84	Polydor POSPA 697	Hot Water (Master Mix)/Standing In The Light (Extended Version)/Micro-Kid (U.S. Remix) (12", stickered p/s, mispress w/ extra track, matrix: POSPA 697)	25
87	Polydor 080 156-2	It's Over (Extended Remix)/Running In The Family (Dave 'O' Remix)/ A Physical Presence (live)/It's Over (Video) (CD Video)	12
88	Polydor 080 000-2	Running In The Family (Extended Version)/Dream Crazy/Hot Water (live)/ Running In The Family (Video) (CD Video)	12
88	Polydor 080 002-2	Something About You (Sisa Mix)/Coup D'Etat (Version)/Something About You (U.S. Remix)/Something About You (Video) (CD Video)	12
88	Polydor 080 004-2	Lessons In Love (Extended Version)/Micro Kid (Remix)/ Love Games (U.S. Remix)/Lessons In Love (Video) (CD Video)	12
88	Polydor 080 218-2	Leaving Me Now (Extended Version)/I Sleep On My Heart (Remix)/ World Machine (U.S. Remix)/Leaving Me Now (Video) (CD Video)	12
89	Polydor 080 502-2	Gresham Blues (Extended Version)/Heaven In My Hands (Extended Version)/ Heaven In My Hands (7" Mix)/Heaven In My Hands (CD Video)	12
89	Polydor 080 576-2	Man (LP Version)/Take A Look (Extended Mix)/Take A Look (7" Mix)/ Take A Look (Video) (CD Video)	12
89	Polydor 080 612-2	Take Care Of Yourself (7" Mix)/Silence (live)/Man (live)/ Take A Look (Video) (CD Video)	12
91	RCA ROYAL 1	Overtime (Lorimer Instrumental) (1-sided promo, etched B-side, 500 only)	12
94	RCA LEVEL	All Over You (Pharmacy Dub)/(Full-On Instrumental)/(K-Klass Instrumental Mix)/ (K-Klass Vocal Mix)/(Mother Dub)/Forever Now (Porky Rides Again Remix)/ All Over You (Mother Slap 'N' Tickle Mix)/(K-Klass Instrumental) (12", double pack, title p/s, promo only)	12
81	Elite LEVLP 1	STRATEGY (LP, unreleased, 6 white label test pressings only)	400
84	Polydor POLHX 10	TRUE COLOURS (cassette, with bonus remix cassette [POLHX 10])	20
85	Polydor POLHX 25	WORLD MACHINE (cassette, with bonus side of remixes)	15
87	Polydor POLHB 42	RUNNING IN THE FAMILY (THE PLATINUM EDITION) (LP, with bonus 12": Lessons In Love [U.S. Remix]/Running In The Family [Dave 'O' Remix]/ It's Over [Extended Remix]/To Be With You Again [Dub Mix]/Something About You [U.S. Remix]/World Machine [U.S. Remix], with paper sash)	18
87	Polydor 833 689-2	RUNNING IN THE FAMILY (THE PLATINUM EDITION) (CD, with extra remixes)	15
89	Polydor 839-877-2	STANDING IN THE LIGHT/TRUE COLOURS/RUNNING IN THE FAMILY/ STARING AT THE SUN (4-CD box set with 16-page booklet)	30
91	Polydor 511 635-2	THE COMPLETE LEVEL 42 (9-CD box set)	75

(see also Thunderthumbs & Toetsenman, Mark King, Leisure Process)

LEVELLERS
89	Hag HAG 005	Carry Me/What's In The Way/The Last Days Of Winter/England My Home (12" EP; first 1,000 copies with Brighton contact address on p/s)	each 15
89	Hag HAG 006	Outside Inside/I Have No Answers (500 promo copies only, no p/s)	8
89	Hag HAG 126	Outside Inside/Hard Fight/I Have No Answers/Barrel Of The Gun (12", p/s with insert; initial copies with Twickenham contact address on sleeve)	each 7
91	On The Fiddle OTF EP 1	Police On My Back/Where The Hell Are We Going To Love?/Travelogue (4am Mix) (12", fan club issue, p/s)	15
92	On The Fiddle OTF LP 2	LIVE 1992 (LP, fan club issue, 2,000 only)	20

MINT VALUE £

GERRY LEVENE (& AVENGERS)
64   Decca F 11815   It's Driving Me Wild (solo)/Dr. Feelgood 35
(see also Moody Blues)

ANNABEL LEVENTON
69   Morgan MR 20   Easy To Be Hard/My Dear Friend.. 4

LEVIATHAN
68   Elektra EKSN 45052/45057   Remember The Times/Second Production/The War Machine/Time
     (double pack, A4 folder sleeve, promo only)............................ 90
68   Elektra EKSN 45052   Remember The Times/Second Production 35
68   Elektra EKSN 45057   The War Machine/Time.. 35
69   Elektra EKSN 45075   Flames/Just Forget Tomorrow 35
69   Elektra EKS 74046   LEVIATHAN (LP, unissued, acetates only)........................ 300+
(see also Mike Stuart Span, High Broom)

HANK LEVINE ORCHESTRA
61   HMV POP 947   Image (Parts 1 & 2).. 10
65   HMV POP 1390   Image (Parts 1 & 2) (reissue)...................................... 6

LEVON & HAWKS
65   Atlantic AT 4054   The Stones I Throw/He Don't Love You 30
(see also Band)

BEN LEVY
66   Ska Beat JB 245   Doren/Never Knew Love 15
66   Ska Beat JB 255   I'll Make You Glad/Keep Smiling 15

CARL LEV(E)Y & CIMARRONS
70   Hot Rod HR 100   Walk The Hot Street/PEGGY & CIMARRONS: You Say You Don't Love Me........ 8
70   Hot Rod HR 101   Remember Easter Monday/PEGGY & JIMMY: Pum Pum Lover 8
(see also Hot Rod Allstars, Rita Alston, Peggy)

JONA LEWIE
74   Sonet SON 2048   Piggy Back Sue/Papa Don't Go...................................... 5
75   Sonet SON 2056   The Swan/Custer's Last Stand 5
76   Sonet SON 2081   Hallelujah Europe (Parts 1 & 2) 5
77   Sonet SON 2117   Rocking Yobs/After We Swum 5
78   Stiff BUY 5   Big Shot — Momentarily/I'll Get By In Pittsburgh (6", p/s)............. 6
78   Stiff SEEZ 8   ON THE OTHER HAND THERE'S A FIST (LP, black or yellow vinyl) 15/12
78   Stiff SEEZ P8   ON THE OTHER HAND THERE'S A FIST (LP, picture disc)................ 15
(see also Brett Marvin & Thunderbolts)

CARL LEWIN
71   Bullet BU 456   Knock Three Times/SIDNEY ALL STARS: The Whealing Mouse................ 4
71   Punch PH 98   Nobody Told Me/WING: Don't Play That Song Again (version)............. 4

ALVA (REGGIE) LEWIS
67   Caltone TONE 111   Return Home/KING ROCK & WILLOWS: You Are The One 30
67   Island WI 3080   I'm Indebted/GROOVERS: You've Got To Cry 20
72   Upsetter US 391   Natty Natty (as Alva Reggie Lewis)/UPSETTERS: Version 7
(see also Reggae Boys, Webber Sisters, Lester Sterling, Cool Cats)

BARBARA LEWIS
63   London HLK 9724   Hello Stranger/Think A Little Sugar................................ 18
63   London HLK 9779   Straighten Up Your Heart/If You Love Her 18
64   London HLK 9832   Snap Your Fingers/Puppy Love 15
64   Atlantic AT 4013   Pushin' A Good Thing Too Far/Come Home 15
65   Atlantic AT 4031   Baby I'm Yours/Hello Stranger..................................... 10
65   Atlantic AT 4041   Make Me Your Baby/Love To Be Loved 10
66   Atlantic AT 4068   Don't Forget About Me/It's Magic.................................. 10
66   Atlantic 584 037   Make Me Belong To You/Girls Need Loving Care 8
67   Atlantic 584 061   Baby What Do You Want Me To Do/I Remember The Feeling 20
68   Atlantic 584 153   Hello Stranger/Baby I'm Yours (reissue)............................ 6
68   Atlantic 584 174   Sho Nuff (It's Got To Be Your Love)/Thankful For What I Got 8
71   Atlantic 2091 143   Someday We're Gonna Love Again/Baby I'm Yours 8
72   Atlantic K 10128   Someday We're Gonne Love Again/Baby I'm Yours (reissue)............. 5
65   Atlantic AET 6015   SNAP YOUR FINGERS (EP) 50
66   Atlantic ATL 5042   BABY I'M YOURS (LP) 35
66   Atlantic 587 002   IT'S MAGIC (LP) 30
70   Stax SXATS 1035   THE MANY GROOVES OF BARBARA LEWIS (LP) 20

BOB LEWIS
57   Parlophone R 4309   Far Away/The Mayflower Song 5

BOBBY LEWIS
61   Parlophone R 4794   Tossin' And Turnin'/Oh Yes, I Love You 18
61   Parlophone R 4831   One Track Mind/Are You Ready 15
62   Stateside SS 126   I'm Tossin' And Turnin' Again/Nothin' But The Blues 15

CAPPY LEWIS
61   Vogue V 9184   Bullfight/OLYMPICS: Little Pedro.................................. 15
(see also Olympics)

DAVE LEWIS
66   Pye Intl. NEP 44057   GIVIN' GAS (EP) 30

DAVID LEWIS
70   AX 1   SONGS OF DAVID LEWIS (LP, private pressing, paste-on sleeve)........... 325
(see also Andwella['s Dream], David Baxter)

FURRY LEWIS
69   Blue Horizon 7-63228   PRESENTING THE COUNTRY BLUES (LP) 70
70   Matchbox SDR 190   IN MEMPHIS (LP) 25

MINT VALUE £

| 71 | Xtra XTRA 1116 | FURRY LEWIS (LP). | 20 |
| 71 | Spokane SPL 1004 | THE EARLY YEARS 1927-1929 (LP) | 50 |

(see also John Estes)

GARY LEWIS & PLAYBOYS

65	Liberty LIB 10187	This Diamond Ring/Tijuana Wedding	10
65	Liberty LIB 55778	Count Me In/Little Miss Go-Go	12
65	Liberty LIB 55809	Save Your Heart For Me/Without A Word Of Warning	6
65	Liberty LIB 55818	Everybody Loves A Clown/Time Stands Still	6
66	Liberty LIB 55846	She's Just My Style/I Won't Make That Mistake Again	6
66	Liberty LIB 55865	Sure Gonna Miss Her/I Don't Wanna Say Goodnight	7
66	Liberty LIB 55880	Green Grass/I Can Read Between The Lines	7
66	Liberty LIB 55898	My Heart's Symphony/Tina	10
66	Liberty LIB 55914	(You Don't Have To) Paint Me A Picture/Looking For The Stars	10
67	Liberty LIB 55933	Where Will The Words Come From/The Best Man	6
67	Liberty LIB 55949	Loser (With A Broken Heart)/Ice Melts In The Sun	6
67	Liberty LIB 55971	Girls In Love/Let's Be More Than Friends	6
67	Liberty LBF 15025	Jill/Needles And Pins	10
68	Liberty LBF 15131	Sealed With A Kiss/Pretty Thing	6
70	Liberty LBF 15335	Orangutan/Something Is Wrong	5
75	United Artists UP 35780	My Heart's Symphony/Tina (reissue)	6
65	Liberty LBY 1259	THIS DIAMOND RING (LP)	35
66	Liberty LBY 1322	JUST OUR STYLE (LP)	25

GEORGE LEWIS & HIS NEW ORLEANS STOMPERS/BAND

SINGLES

56	Vogue V 2051	Climax Rag/Deep Bayou Blues	6
56	Vogue V 2052	Millenberg Joys/Two Jim Blues	6
56	Vogue V 2053	Just A Closer Walk With Thee/Just A Little While To Stay Here	6
56	Vogue V 2054	Fidgety Feet/Dauphine Street Blues	6
56	Vogue V 2055	Don't Go 'Way Nobody/Careless Love Blues	6
60	HMV POP 707	South Rampart Street Parade/Chinatown My Chinatown (with Band)	8

EPs

55	Vogue EPV 1066	GEORGE LEWIS AND HIS NEW ORLEANS STOMPERS (EP)	15
55	Vogue EPV 1081	GEORGE LEWIS AND HIS NEW ORLEANS STOMPERS (EP)	10
55	Tempo EXA 15	GEORGE LEWIS AND HIS NEW ORLEANS STOMPERS (EP)	12
57	Tempo EXA 62	GEORGE LEWIS (EP, as George Lewis' Ragtime Band)	8
57	Tempo EXA 66	GEORGE LEWIS (EP, as George Lewis' Ragtime Band)	8
57	Tempo EXA 70	GEORGE LEWIS' RAGTIME BAND (EP)	10
59	Tempo EXA 97	GEORGE LEWIS (EP, as George Lewis & His New Orleans Rhythm Boys)	8
59	Tempo EXA 101	GEORGE LEWIS (EP)	8
59	Vogue EPV 1220	GEORGE LEWIS IN HI-FI (EP)	10
59	Vogue EPV 1252	GEORGE LEWIS IN HI-FI (EP)	10
50s	Good Time Jazz EPG 1182	NEW ORLEANS MUSIC (EP)	8
50s	Esquire EP 125	NEW ORLEANS RAGTIME BAND VOL. 1 (EP)	12
50s	Esquire EP 135	NEW ORLEANS RAGTIME BAND VOL. 2 (EP)	12
50s	Esquire EP 155	NEW ORLEANS RAGTIME BAND VOL. 3 (EP)	12
50s	Esquire EP 175	NEW ORLEANS RAGTIME BAND VOL. 4 (EP)	12
50s	Esquire EP 209	NEW ORLEANS RAGTIME BAND VOL. 5 (EP)	10
60s	Esquire EP 211	NEW ORLEANS RAGTIME BAND VOL. 6 (EP)	10
60s	Esquire EP 215	NEW ORLEANS RAGTIME BAND VOL. 7 (EP)	10
60s	Esquire EP 219	NEW ORLEANS RAGTIME BAND VOL. 8 (EP)	10
60	Esquire EP 225	NEW ORLEANS RAGTIME BAND VOL. 9 (EP)	12
60	HMV 7EG 8540	SOUNDS OF NEW ORLEANS (EP)	8
50s	Storyville SEP 315	ICE CREAM (EP)	8
50s	Storyville SEP 321	PANAMA (EP)	8
50s	Storyville SEP 322	LOUISIANA (EP)	8
50s	Storyville SEP 325	WILLIE THE WEEPER (EP)	8
60	Storyville SEP 349	JAZZ FROM NEW ORLEANS (EP)	8
61	Storyville SEP 361	TILL WE MEET AGAIN (EP)	8
61	Storyville SEP 365	ISLE OF CAPRI (EP)	8
61	Storyville SEP 369	MUSKRAT RUMBLE (EP)	8
60s	Storyville SEP 503	HIGH SOCIETY (EP)	8
60s	Storyville SEP 504	DALLAS BLUES (EP)	8

LPs

52	Vogue LDE 012	GEORGE LEWIS AND HIS NEW ORLEANS ALLSTARS (10" LP)	20
54	Vogue LDE 082	GEORGE LEWIS JAM SESSION (10" LP)	20
55	Vogue LAE 12005	GEORGE LEWIS AND HIS NEW ORLEANS STOMPERS (LP)	50
55	London H-APB 1041	VOL. 1 JAZZ BAND (10" LP, with New Orleans Jazz Band & Quartet)	25
56	London HB-U 1045	VOL. 2 ALL STARS (10" LP, with New Orleans All Stars & Quartet)	25
57	Tempo TAP 13	GEORGE LEWIS RAGTIME BAND (LP)	80
57	Melodisc MLP 12-101	NEW ORLEANS PARADE (LP)	15
50s	Esquire 20-067	GEORGE LEWIS RAGTIME BAND (10" LP)	15
50s	Esquire 20-073	GEORGE LEWIS RAGTIME BAND (10" LP)	15
50s	'77' LA 12/28	SMILE, DARN YA, SMILE (LP, as George Lewis with Barry Martyn's Band)	20
59	Columbia Clef 33C 9042	RAGGIN' AND STOMPIN' (10" LP)	15
60	HMV CLP 1371/CSD 1309	BLUES FROM THE BAYOU (LP, mono/stereo)	25/30
61	HMV CLP 1413/CSD 1337	DOCTOR JAZZ (LP, mono/stereo)	25/30
64	London HA-K/SH-K 8165	JAZZ AT PRESERVATION HALL VOL. 4 (LP, with Band Of New Orleans)	20

GEORGE LEWIS/FREDDIE KOHLMAN

| 53 | Brunswick LA 8627 | NEW ORLEANS JAZZ CONCERT (10" LP) | 25 |

HOPETON LEWIS

67	Island WI 3054	Rock Steady/Cool Collie	18
67	Island WI 3055	Finder's Keepers/ROLAND ALPHONSO: Shanty Town Curfew	18
67	Island WI 3056	Let Me Come On Home/Hardships Of Life (with Merritone All Stars)	18
67	Island WI 3057	Run Down/Pick Yourself Up	18

67	Island WI 3059	Let The Little Girl Dance/This Music Got Soul	18
67	Island WI 3068	Rock A Shacka/I Don't Want Trouble	50
68	Island WI 3076	Everybody Rocking/Stars Shining So Bright	18
68	Fab FAB 43	Skinny Leg Girl/Live Like A King (as Hopetown Lewis & Glenmore Brown)	15
70	Duke Reid DR 2505	Boom Shaka Lacka/TOMMY McCOOK QUINTET: Dynamite	10
70	Duke Reid DR 2516	Testify/TOMMY McCOOK: Super Soul	12
71	Duke DU 112	Grooving Out Of Life (with Byron Lee & Dragonaires) (actually titled "Grooving Out On Life")/BYRON LEE & DRAGONAIRES: Fire Fire	6
71	Treasure Isle TI 7060	To The Other Man/TOMMY McCOOK: Stampede	8
72	Treasure Isle TI 7071	Judgement Day (actually by Hopeton Lewis & Dennis Alcapone)/EARL LINDO: Version Day	8
72	Attack ATT 8035	Starting All Over Again/DYNAMITES: Instrumental Version	5
72	Dynamic DYN 436	Come Together/Going Back To My Hometown	5
72	Dynamic DYN 447	Good Together/Version	5
73	Dragon DRA 1001	City Of New Orleans/The Wind Cries Mary	5
73	Dragon DRA 1011	Groovin' Out On Life/God Bless Whoever Sent You	5
67	Island ILP 957	TAKE IT EASY: ROCKSTEADY WITH HOPETON LEWIS (LP)	165
71	Trojan TRL 36	GROOVING OUT ON LIFE (LP)	20

(see also Glenmore Brown & Hopeton Lewis)

HUGH X. LEWIS

66	London HLR 10032	Looking In The Future/Too Late	5
66	London HA-R 8293	THE HUGH X. LEWIS ALBUM (LP)	15
67	London HA-R 8303	JUST BEFORE DAWN (LP)	15

JENNIFER LEWIS & ANGELA STRANGE

| 65 | Columbia DB 7662 | Bring It To Me/You Know | 8 |
| 66 | Columbia DB 7814 | I've Heard It All Before/Bad Storm Coming | 10 |

JERRY LEWIS

56	Capitol CL 14559	I Keep Her Picture Hanging Upside Down/I Love A Murder Mystery	6
56	Capitol CL 14626	Buckskin Beauty/Pardners (with Dean Martin)	6
57	Brunswick 05636	Rock-a-Bye Your Baby With A Dixie Melody/Come Rain Or Come Shine	10
57	Brunswick 05672	Let Me Sing And I'm Happy/It All Depends On You	7
57	Brunswick 05693	With These Hands/My Mammy	6
57	Brunswick 05710	By Myself/No One	6
58	Brunswick 05727	Sad Sack/Shine On Your Shoes	6
58	Brunswick 05756	Dormi, Dormi, Dormi/Love Is A Lonely Thing	6
58	Brunswick 05756	Dormi, Dormi, Dormi/Love Is A Lonely Thing (78)	8
59	Brunswick 05777	Song From "The Geisha Boy"/The More I See You	6
59	Brunswick 05777	Song From "The Geisha Boy"/The More I See You (78)	8
53	Capitol LC 6591	CAPITOL PRESENTS JERRY LEWIS (10" LP)	20

(see also Dean Martin)

JERRY LEWIS (Jamaica)

| 72 | Pama PM 862 | The Godfather/ALTON ELLIS: Some Day | 5 |
| 73 | Explosion EX 2077 | Rhythm Pleasure/AGGROVATORS: Doctor Seaton | 5 |

(see also I Roy)

JERRY LEE LEWIS

78s

57	London HLS 8457	Whole Lotta Shakin' Goin' On/It'll Be Me (78)	15
57	London HLS 8529	Great Balls Of Fire/Mean Woman Blues (78)	15
58	London HLS 8559	You Win Again/I'm Feelin' Sorry (78)	30
58	London HLS 8592	Breathless/Down The Line (78)	35
58	London HLS 8700	Break-Up/I'll Make It All Up To You (78)	40
59	London HLS 8780	High School Confidential/Fools Like Me (78)	45
59	London HLS 8840	Lovin' Up A Storm/Big Blon' Baby (78)	60
59	London HLS 8941	Let's Talk About Us/The Ballad Of Billy Joe (78)	90
59	London HLS 8993	Little Queenie/I Could Never Be Ashamed Of You (78)	150
96	Cruisin' The 50s CASS 002	Wild One/Old Black Joe (78, numbered, 300 only)	30

SINGLES

57	London HLS 8457	Whole Lotta Shakin' Goin' On/It'll Be Me	25
57	London HLS 8529	Great Balls Of Fire/Mean Woman Blues	15
58	London HLS 8559	You Win Again/I'm Feelin' Sorry	25
58	London HLS 8592	Breathless/Down The Line	12
58	London HLS 8700	Break-Up/I'll Make It All Up To You	12
59	London HLS 8780	High School Confidential/Fools Like Me	18
59	London HLS 8840	Lovin' Up A Storm/Big Blon' Baby	15
59	London HLS 8941	Let's Talk About Us/The Ballad Of Billy Joe	12
59	London HLS 8993	Little Queenie/I Could Never Be Ashamed Of You	15

(The above 45s were originally issued with triangular centres; round-centre pressings are worth two-thirds of these values.)

60	London HLS 9083	I'll Sail My Ship Alone/It Hurt Me So	8
60	London HLS 9131	Baby, Baby, Bye Bye/Old Black Joe	12
60	London HLS 9202	John Henry/Hang Up My Rock And Roll Shoes	10
61	London HLS 9335	What'd I Say?/Livin' Lovin' Wreck	6
61	London HLS 9414	It Won't Happen With Me/Cold Cold Heart	8
61	London HLS 9446	As Long As I Live/When I Get Paid	8
62	London HLS 9526	I've Been Twistin'/Ramblin' Rose	7
62	London HLS 9584	Sweet Little Sixteen/How's My Ex Treating You	7
63	London HLS 9688	Good Golly Miss Molly/I Can't Trust Me In Your Arms Anymore	7
63	London HLS 9722	Teenage Letter/Seasons Of My Heart (B-side with Linda Gail Lewis)	8
63	Mercury AMT 1216	Hit The Road Jack/Pen And Paper	6
64	Philips BF 1324	I'm On Fire/Bread And Butter Man	8
64	London HLS 9867	Lewis Boogie/Bonnie B	10
65	Philips BF 1371	Hi-Heel Sneakers/You Went Back On Your Word	6
65	Philips BF 1407	Baby Hold Me Close/I Believe In You	7
65	Philips BF 1425	Rockin' Pneumonia And The Boogie Woogie Flu/This Must Be The Place	7
65	London HLS 9980	Carry Me Back To Old Virginia/I Know What It Means	8

66	Philips BF 1521	Memphis Beat/If I Had It All To Do Over	7
67	Philips BF 1594	It's A Hang-Up Baby/Holdin' On	7
67	Philips BF 1615	Turn On Your Love Light/Shotgun Man	7
68	Mercury MF 1020	Another Place, Another Time/Walking The Floor Over You	6
68	Mercury MF 1024	Great Balls Of Fire/Whole Lotta Shakin' Goin' On	5
68	London HLS 10193	What'd I Say?/I've Been Twistin'	5
68	Mercury MF 1045	What's Made Milwaukee Famous (Has Made A Loser Out Of Me)/	
		All The Good Is Gone	5
69	Mercury MF 1088	To Make Love Sweeter For You/Let's Talk About Us	5
69	Mercury MF 1105	Long Tall Sally/Jenny, Jenny (some in p/s)	10/6
69	Mercury MF 1110	Great Balls Of Fire/Whole Lotta Shakin' Goin' On (some in p/s)	10/6
72	Mercury 6052 117	Would You Take Another Chance On Me/Me And Bobby McGee	5
72	Mercury 6052 141	Chantilly Lace/Think About It Darlin'	5
72	Mercury 6052 162	I'm Walkin'/Turn On Your Love Light	5
73	Mercury 6052 260	Drinking Wine Spo-Dee O-Dee/Rock And Roll Medley	5
73	Mercury 6052 378	(Taking My) Music To The Man/Jack Daniels (Old No. 7) (some in p/s)	8/6
79	Elektra K 12374	Rocking My Life Away/Rita May (p/s)	8
80	Elektra K 12399	Everyday I Have To Cry/Who Will The Next Fool Be	5
80	Elektra K 12432	Rockin' Jerry Lee/Good Time Charles Got The Blues	5

EXPORT SINGLES

58	London HL 7050	High School Confidential/Fools Like Me	20
62	London HL 7117	Save The Last Dance For Me/Hello Josephine	35
63	London HL 7120	Good Golly Miss Molly/I Can't Trust Me (In Your Arms Anymore)	20
63	London HL 7123	In The Mood/I'm Feelin' Sorry	35
70s	Bulldog BD 17	Bonnie B./Down The Line/Baby Baby/I'm Feeling Sorry	5

EPs

58	London RE-S 1140	JERRY LEE LEWIS — NO. 1 (EP, initially with triangular centre)	50/30
59	London RE-S 1186	JERRY LEE LEWIS — NO. 2 (EP, initially with triangular centre)	50/30
59	London RE-S 1187	JERRY LEE LEWIS — NO. 3 (EP, initially with triangular centre)	50/30
61	London RE-S 1296	JERRY LEE LEWIS — NO. 4 (EP)	35
62	London RE-S 1336	JERRY LEE LEWIS — NO. 5 (EP)	30
63	London RE-S 1351	JERRY LEE LEWIS — NO. 6 (EP)	30
63	London RE-S 1378	FOUR MORE FROM JERRY LEE LEWIS (EP)	35
66	Philips BE 12599	COUNTRY STYLE (EP)	30
84	Sun JLL EP 001	THE FABULOUS JERRY LEE LEWIS VOL. 1 (EP, Fan Club issue)	15
84	Sun JLL EP 002	THE FABULOUS JERRY LEE LEWIS VOL. 2 (EP, Fan Club issue)	15

LPs

59	London HA-S 2138	JERRY LEE LEWIS (LP)	50
62	London HA-S 2440	JERRY LEE'S GREATEST (LP)	35
64	Philips (S)BL 7622	GOLDEN HITS (LP)	15
65	Philips (S)BL 7646	LIVE AT THE STAR CLUB, HAMBURG (LP, with Nashville Teens)	20
65	Philips BL 7650	THE GREATEST LIVE SHOW ON EARTH (LP)	15
65	Philips BL 7668	THE RETURN OF ROCK (LP)	16
65	London HA-S 8251	WHOLE LOTTA SHAKIN' GOIN' ON (LP)	40
66	Philips BL 7688	COUNTRY SONGS FOR CITY FOLKS (LP)	15
66	Philips (S)BL 7706	MEMPHIS BEAT (LP)	15
66	Ember NR 5038	SUNSTROKE (LP, shared with Carl Perkins)	12
67	Philips (S)BL 7746	BY REQUEST — MORE GREATEST LIVE SHOW ON EARTH (LP, m/s)	15/18
67	London HA-S 8323	BREATHLESS (LP)	50
	(The above London LPs were originally issued with plum labels; later black label reissues are worth £15-£20.)		
68	Mercury 20117 (S)MCL	SOUL MY WAY (LP)	16
68	Fontana SFJL 964	GOT YOU ON MY MIND (LP)	15
69	Mercury 21011 SMWL	ANOTHER PLACE, ANOTHER TIME (LP)	12
69	Mercury 21047 SMCL	SHE STILL COMES AROUND (TO WHAT'S LEFT OF ME) (LP, stereo only)	12
69	Mercury 20156 SMCL	I'M ON FIRE (LP)	12
69	Mercury 20157 SMCL	SINGS THE COUNTRY MUSIC HALL OF FAME HITS VOL. 1 (LP)	12
69	Mercury 20158 SMCL	SINGS THE COUNTRY MUSIC HALL OF FAME HITS VOL. 2 (LP)	12
70	Mercury 20172 SMCL	TOGETHER (LP, with Linda Gail Lewis)	15
70	Mercury 6338 010	SHE EVEN WOKE ME UP TO SAY GOODBYE (LP)	12
71	Mercury 6338 045	THERE MUST BE MORE TO LOVE THAN THIS (LP)	12
72	Mercury 6338 071	WOULD YOU TAKE ANOTHER CHANCE ON ME? (LP)	12
72	Mercury 6336 300	ROCKIN' WITH JERRY LEE LEWIS (LP)	12
72	Mercury 6338 088	THE KILLER ROCKS ON (LP)	12
73	Mercury 6672 008	THE SESSION (2-LP)	18
73	Mercury 6338 148	LIVE AT THE INTERNATIONAL HOTEL, LAS VEGAS (LP)	12
74	Mercury 6338 452	SOUTHERN ROOTS (LP)	12
74	Mercury 6338 496	FAN CLUB CHOICE (LP)	12
84	Sun SUN 102	THE SUN YEARS (12-LP, box set with booklet)	60
	(see also Nashville Teens)		

JIMMY LEWIS

68	Minit MLF 11002	The Girls From Texas/Let Me Know	20

JOE 'CANNONBALL' LEWIS

51	MGM MGM 430	Train Whistle Nightmare/Trust Me Again (78)	12

JOHN LEWIS

60	London Jazz LTZ-K 15186	IMPROVISED MEDITATIONS AND EXCURSIONS (LP)	12
61	London Jazz LTZ-K 15218	THE GOLDEN STRIKER (LP, also stereo SAH-K 6152)	12
	(see also Modern Jazz Quartet)		

LEW LEWIS (REFORMER)

76	Stiff BUY 5	Caravan Man/Boogie On The Street (p/s, with Dr. Feelgood)	4
77	United Artists UP 36217	Out For A Lark/Watch Yourself	4
78	Lew Lewis LEW 1	Lucky Seven/Night Talk (500 only, plain white sleeve)	8
79	Stiff LEW 1	Lucky Seven/Night Talk (p/s, reissue)	4
79	Stiff BUY 48	Win Or Lose/Photo Finish (p/s, as Lew Lewis Reformer)	4
	(see also Oil City Sheiks, Dr. Feelgood, Eddie & Hot Rods)		

MINT VALUE £

LINDA LEWIS
67	Polydor 56173	You Turned My Bitter Into Sweet/Do You Believe In Love	50
71	Reprise K 14096	We Can Win/Hampstead Way	5
72	Reprise K 14209	Old Smokey/It's The Frame	5
75	Arista ARIST 17	It's In His Kiss/Walk About (p/s)	5
73	Raft RA 18502	Rock A Doodle Doo/Reach For The Truth	5
72	Reprise K 44208	LARK (LP)	15
73	Raft RA 48501	FATHOMS DEEP (LP)	12
76	Reprise K 84008	LARK/FATHOMS DEEP (2-LP, reissue)	15
79	Ariola ARL 5033	HACIENDA VIEW (LP)	12

(see also Ferris Wheel)

MARGARET LEWIS
62	Starlite ST45 081	Sometin's Wrong Baby/John De Lee	15

MEADE 'LUX' LEWIS
50	Melodisc 1130	Boogie Tidal/Yancey's Pride (78)	12
50	Melodisc 1136	Glendale Glide/Denapas Parade (78)	12
51	Melodisc 1153	Randini's Boogie/Lux's Boogie (78)	12
52	Vogue V 2123	Blues Whistle/Chicago Flyer (78)	12
54	Vogue V 2229	Six Wheel Chaser Boogie/Bass On Top Boogie (78)	12
55	Vogue EPV 1065	MEADE 'LUX' LEWIS (EP)	35
56	Melodisc EPM7 107	BOOGIE WOOGIE AND BLUES (EP)	35
56	Columbia Clef SEB 10030	BOOGIE WOOGIE PIANO AND DRUMS NO. 1 (EP)	20
56	Columbia Clef SEB 10052	BOOGIE WOOGIE PIANO AND DRUMS NO. 2 (EP)	20
57	Columbia Clef 33CX 10094	YANCEY'S LAST RIDE (LP)	20
57	HMV DLP 1176	OUT OF THE ROARING TWENTIES (10" LP)	20
60s	Philips 652 014 BL	HOUSE PARTY (LP)	20

(see also Albert Ammons, [Big] Joe Turner)

MEADE 'LUX' LEWIS & SLIM GAILLARD
56	Columbia Clef 33C 9021	JAZZ AT THE PHILHARMONIC (10" LP)	20

(see also Slim Gaillard)

MIA LEWIS
65	Decca F 12117	Wish I Didn't Love Him/This Is The End	8
65	Decca F 12240	It's Goodbye Now/The Luckiest Girl	8
66	Parlophone R 5526	Nothing Lasts Forever/(Baby) I'm Feeling Good	12
67	Parlophone R 5585	No Time For Lovin'/Onion	7
67	Parlophone R 5617	Woman's Love/You Won't Get Away	7

MICHAEL LEWIS
73	United Artists UP 35569	Theatre Of Blood Theme/Edwina's Theme	20

MONICA LEWIS
56	Parlophone R 4224	I Wish You Love/Stay After School	6

NIGEL LEWIS
86	Media Burn MB10	WHAT I FEEL NOW (LP)	20

PATTI LEWIS
56	Columbia DB 3825	Earthbound/Happiness Street (Corner Sunshine Square)	8
57	Columbia DB 3923	Your Wild Heart/A Poor Man's Roses (Or A Rich Man's Gold)	7
57	Columbia DB 3967	Pull Down De Shade/Speak For Yourself John	7

PHILLIPPA LEWIS
65	Decca F 12152	Just Like In The Movies/Get Along Without You	10

RAMSEY LEWIS (TRIO)
65	Chess CRS 8020	The 'In' Crowd/Since I Fell For You (as Ramsey Lewis Trio)	7
65	Chess CRS 8024	Hang On Sloopy/Movin' Easy (as Ramsey Lewis Trio)	7
66	Chess CRS 8029	A Hard Day's Night/'Tout A Doubt (as Ramsey Lewis Trio)	7
66	Chess CRS 8031	Hi-Heel Sneakers (Parts 1 & 2) (as Ramsey Lewis Trio)	7
66	Chess CRS 8041	Wade In The Water/Ain't That Peculiar (as Ramsey Lewis Trio)	12
66	Chess CRS 8044	Uptight (Everything's Alright)/Money In The Pocket	7
67	Chess CRS 8051	Day Tripper/Hurt So Bad	12
67	Chess CRS 8055	1-2-3/Down By The Riverside	7
67	Chess CRS 8058	Function At The Junction/Hey Mrs. Jones	7
67	Chess CRS 8060	Saturday Night After The Movies/China Gate	7
67	Chess CRS 8061	Girl Talk/Dancing In The Street	7
67	Chess CRS 8064	Soul Man/Struttin' Lightly	7
69	Chess CRS 8096	Cry Baby Cry/Wade In The Water	7
70	Chess CRS 8104	Julia/Do What You Wanna	7
72	Chess 6145 004	Wade In The Water/Ain't That Peculiar	5
72	Chess 6145 013	The 'In' Crowd/Soul Man	5
72	CBS 8280	Slipping Into Darkness/Collage	5
66	Chess CRE 6019	A HARD DAY'S NIGHT (EP, as Ramsey Lewis Trio)	20
60	Fontana SFJL 962	DOWN TO EARTH (LP)	20
65	Pye Jazz NJL 55	AT THE BOHEMIAN CAVERNS (LP)	18
65	Chess CRL 4511	THE 'IN' CROWD (LP)	18
65	Chess CRL 4518	CHOICE! THE BEST OF RAMSEY LEWIS (LP)	18
66	Chess CRL 4520	HANG ON RAMSEY! (LP)	18
66	Chess CRL 4522	WADE IN THE WATER (LP)	18
67	Chess CRL 4528	GOIN' LATIN (LP)	15
67	Chess CRL 4531	THE MOVIE ALBUM (LP)	15
68	Chess CRL(S) 4533	DANCIN' IN THE STREET (LP)	15
68	Chess CRLS 4535	UP POPS RAMSEY LEWIS (LP)	15
68	Chess CRLS 4539	MAIDEN VOYAGE (LP)	15
69	Chess CRLS 4545	MOTHER NATURE'S SON (LP)	15
72	Chess 6310 106	BACK TO THE ROOTS (LP)	12
72	Chess 6310 114	THE BEST OF RAMSEY LEWIS (LP)	12
72	Chess 6310 124	TOBACCO ROAD (LP)	12

72	CBS 64718	UPENDO NI PAMOJA (LP)	12
73	CBS 65307	FUNKY SERENITY (LP)	18
73	CBS CQ 31096	UPENDO NI PAMOJA (LP, quadrophonic)	12

(see also Young-Holt Unlimited)

RICHARD LEWIS & HIS BAND
60	Downbeat CHA 1	Hey, Little Girl/Hey, Little Boy	25

SMILEY LEWIS
53	London L 1189	Big Mamou/Play Girl (78, some copies miscredited to Smiley Davis)	100
56	London HLU 8312	One Night/Ain't Gonna Do It	750
56	London HLU 8312	One Night/Ain't Gonna Do It (78)	90
56	London HLU 8337	Down Yonder We Go Ballin'/Don't Be That Way (Please Listen To Me)	750
56	London HLU 8337	Down Yonder We Go Ballin'/Don't Be That Way (Please Listen To Me) (78)	90
57	London HLP 8367	Shame, Shame, Shame/No, No (gold or silver label lettering)	650/250
57	London HLP 8367	Shame, Shame, Shame/No, No (78)	85
70	Liberty LBF 15337	I Hear You Knocking/Play Girl	7
70	Liberty LBS 83308	SHAME, SHAME, SHAME (LP)	20

STEVIE LEWIS
65	Mercury MF 871	Take Me For A Little While/My Whole World Seems To Be Tumbling Down	8
65	Mercury MF 919	Sometimes When You're Lonely/Under The Smile Of Love	5
65	Polydor 56003	Heard It All Before/Wild	6
69	RCA RCA 1840	Take A Little Warning/I Can Try	5

TAMALA LEWIS
79	Destiny DS 1010	You Won't Say Nothing/If You Can Stand Me	5

TINY LEWIS
60	Parlophone R 4617	Too Much Rockin'/I Get Weak	100

VIC LEWIS
55	Philips PB 503	Scramble/Walk, Don't Run (78)	8
55	Philips PB 411	Barwick Green ("The Archers" Theme Tune)/Don't Say Goodbye (78)	8
60s	Columbia SEG 8202	SWINGS NELSON RIDDLE (EP)	15
55	Decca LF 1216	PROGRESSIVE JAZZ (10" LP)	20
60s	Ember CJS 807	AT THE BEAULIEU FESTIVAL (LP)	40
60s	Ember SE 8018	BIG BAND EXPLOSION (LP)	75
60s	HMV CLP 1641	PLAY BOSSA NOVA HOME AND AWAY (LP)	50
70s	DJM SPECB 103	MY LIFE MY WAY (LP)	40

LEWIS & CLARKE EXHIBITION
67	RCA Victor RCA 1633	I Feel Good/Blue Revelations	4

LEWIS SISTERS
65	Tamla Motown TMG 536	You Need Me/Moonlight On The Beach	60

DAVE LEWRY
72	Westwood WRS 019	ALL I WANT TO DO IS PLAY GUITAR (LP)	30

MONIQUE LEYRAC
68	SNB 55-3309	Time Time/Love Is Blue	5

JOHN LEYTON
60	Top Rank JAR 426	Tell Laura I Love Her/Goodbye To Teenage Love	50
60	HMV POP 798	The Girl On The Floor Above/Terry Brown's In Love With Mary Dee	90
61	Top Rank JAR 577	Johnny Remember Me/There Must Be	6
61	Top Rank JAR 585	Wild Wind/You Took My Love For Granted	7
61	HMV POP 956	Son This Is She/Six White Horses	7
62	HMV POP 992	Lone Rider/Heart Of Stone	15
62	HMV POP 1014	Lonely City/It Would Be Easy	7
62	HMV POP 1054	Down The River Nile/I Think I'm Falling In Love	8
62	HMV POP 1076	Lonely Johnny/Keep On Loving You	10
63	HMV POP 1122	Cupboard Love/Land Of Love	5
63	HMV POP 1175	I'll Cut Your Tail Off/The Great Escape	8
63	HMV POP 1204	On Lover's Hill/Lovers Lane	8
63	HMV POP 1230	I Guess You Are Always On My Mind/Beautiful Dreamer	8
64	HMV POP 1264	Make Love To Me/Missing You (as John Leyton & Le Roys)	12
64	HMV POP 1338	Don't Let Her Go Away/I Want A Love I Can See	10
64	HMV POP 1374	All I Want Is You/Every Day Is A Holiday (with Grazina Frame & Mike Sarne)	8
73	York SYK 551	Dancing In The Graveyard/Riversong	8
74	York YR 210	Rock 'N' Roll/Highway Song	8
62	Top Rank JKP 3016	JOHN LEYTON (EP)	40
62	HMV 7EG 8747	HIT PARADE (EP)	35
64	HMV 7EG 8843	BEAUTIFUL DREAMER (EP)	40
64	HMV 7EG 8854	TELL LAURA I LOVE HER (EP)	45
61	HMV CLP 1497	THE TWO SIDES OF JOHN LEYTON (LP)	45
62	HMV CLP 1664	ALWAYS YOURS (LP, with Charles Blackwell's Orchestra)	70
73	York FYK 416	JOHN LEYTON (LP)	40

(see also Le Roys)

LEYTON BUZZARDS
78	Small Wonder SMALL 7	19 And Mad/Villain/Youthanasia (p/s)	5
79	Chrysalis CHS 2288	Saturday Night Beneath The Plastic Palm Trees/Trough With You (p/s)	5
79	Chrysalis CHS 2328	I'm Hanging Around/I Don't Want To Go/No Dry Ice (p/s, green vinyl)	5
79	Chrysalis CHS 2360	We Make A Noise/Disco Romeo (p/s, as The Buzzards)	5
80	WEA K 18284	Can't Get Used To Losing You/Weird Frenz	5
79	Chrysalis CHR 1213	JELLIED EELS TO RECORD DEALS (LP, as The Buzzards)	12

(see also Modern Romance)

L.F.O.
90	Warp WAP 5	L.F.O. (The Leeds Warehouse Mix)/L.F.O. (Track 4)/ Probe (The Cuba Edit) (12")	12

MINT VALUE £

LIAISON
82	Catweazle CR 001	Play It With A Passion/Caught In A ... (some in grey or yellow p/s)	50/15
83	Liaison LIC 101	LOOKING AFTER NUMBER ONE (EP)	5
84	Liaison LSN 0020	Only Heaven Knows/Ease The Pain Away (p/s)	4

LIAR
79	Bearsville K 55524	SET THE WORLD ON FIRE (LP, picture disc)	12

LIBERACE
55	Philips PB 430	Unchained Melody/The Bridges At Toko-Ri (78)	8
56	Columbia DB 3834	I Don't Care (As Long As You Care For Me)/As Time Goes By	6
56	Columbia DB 3834	I Don't Care (As Long As You Care For Me)/As Time Goes By (78)	8
59	Coral LVA 9114	THE PIANO SONGBOOK OF MOVIE THEMES (LP)	12
60	Coral LVA 9124	THE MAGIC PIANOS OF LIBERACE & GORDON ROBINSON (LP, with Gordon Robinson)	12
60	Coral LVA 9134	MY INSPIRATION (LP)	12
61	Coral LVA 9143	LIBERACE AT THE PALLADIUM (LP)	12
61	Coral LVA 9149	MY PARADE OF GOLDEN FAVOURITES (LP)	12
62	Coral LVA 9155	AS TIME GOES BY (LP)	12
62	Coral LVA 9207	RHAPSODY BY CANDLELIGHT (LP)	12
65	Coral LVA 9225	LIBERACE PLAYS GOLDEN HITS OF HOLLYWOOD (LP)	12

LIBERATION SUITE
70s	Myrrh MYR 1027	LIBERATION SUITE (LP)	12

LIBERATORS
65	Stateside SS 424	It Hurts So Much/You Look So Fine	6

(see also Pinkerton's Assorted Colours)

EVE LIBERTINE & CRASS
84	Crass 1984/4	ACTS OF LOVE (LP, with book)	12

(see also Crass)

LIBERTY BELLES
71	Jay Boy BOY 40	Shing-A-Ling Time/Just Try Me	4

LICKS
79	Stortbeat BEAT 8	1970s EP (p/s)	12

(see also Epileptics, Flux Of Pink Indians)

LIEUTENANT BUDDY KNOX
(see under 'K')

LIEUTENANT PIGEON
73	Decca F 13403	And The Fun Goes On/Opus 302	5
73	Decca F 13440	Creativity/Oxford Bags	5
74	Decca F 13486	I'll Take You Home Again Kathleen/Big Butch Baby	5
74	Decca F 13543	You Are My Heart's Delight/Love Inflation	5
75	Decca F 13602	Rockabilly Hot Pot/Gosford Street Rag	5
76	Decca FR 13638	Good-bye (From The White Horse Inn)/I'll Sail My Ship Alone	5
77	Comet U 6313	Spangles/Opus 304	6
78	SMA SMA 1501	Disco Bells/Steam Train Stag	6
81	Shack SHA 002	Bobbing Up And Down Like This/Gordon's Rainbow Wranglers	5
73	Decca SKL 5154	MOULDY OLD MUSIC (LP)	12
74	Decca SKL 5174	PIGEON PIE (LP)	15
75	Decca SKL 5196	PIGEON PARTY (LP)	15
76	Decca SPA 414	THE WORLD OF LIEUTENANT PIGEON (LP, unreleased, test pressings only)	20

(see also Shel Naylor, Stavely Makepeace, Heavy Cochran)

LIFE
69	Polydor 56778	Hands Of The Clock/Ain't I Told You Before	6
74	Polydor 2058 500	Woman/Bless My Soul	5
74	Polydor 2383 295	LIFE AFTER DEATH (LP)	35

LIFE
73	Philips 6006 280	Cats Eyes/Death In The Family (paper or moulded label)	7/5

LIFE AFTER LIFE
85	Timetrack SRTSKL 453	LIFE AFTER LIFE (LP, private pressing)	150

LIFE 'N' SOUL
67	Decca F 12659	Ode To Billy Joe/Peacefully Asleep	15
68	Decca F 12851	Here Comes Yesterday Again/Dear Paul	7

LIFE SUPPORT
79	Slug SLUG 1	Leader Deceiver/Confusion (p/s, white labels)	6

LIFETIME
70	Polydor 2066 050	One Word/Two Worlds	6

(see also Tony Williams [Lifetime], Jack Bruce, John McLaughlin)

JOE LIGES
63	Blue Beat BB 172	Spit In The Sky/Tell Me What (both actually by Delroy Wilson)	15

(see also Delroy Wilson)

JOE LIGGINS & HONEYDRIPPERS
50	Parlophone R 3309	I've Got The Right To Cry/Blue Moods (78)	25
76	Speciality SDN 5006	Pink Champagne/Honey Dripper	6

LIGHT
78	Mint MINT 11	LIGHT (LP, Irish-only)	30

(see also Them)

LIGHT
95	Wurlitzer Jukebox WJ 12	Turning (500 on clear vinyl, 1,000 black, p/s)	5/4

BEN LIGHT

56	HMV 7M 350	Bring Me A Bluebird/You	7

ENOCH LIGHT

59	Top Rank JAR 134	With My Eyes Wide Open/I Cried For You (as Enoch Light & Light Brigade)	5
59	Top Rank JAR 134	With My Eyes Wide Open/I Cried For You (78, as Enoch Light & Light Brigade)	12
59	Top Rank JAR 234	Scarlet Ribbons/Greensleeves (as Enoch Light & His Vibrant Strings)	5
69	Studio Two TWO 312	SPACED OUT (LP)	25
70	Project 3	PERMISSIVE POLYPHONICS (LP)	15

LIGHT FANTASTIC

73	RCA RCA 2331	Jeanie/You Don't Care	20

GORDON LIGHTFOOT

62	Decca F 11527	(Remember Me) I'm The One/Daisy-Doo (as Gord Lightfoot)	7
63	Fontana 267 275TF	Negotiations/It's Too Late, He Wins (as Gordie Lightfoot)	7
63	Fontana TF 405	The Day Before Yesterday/Take Care Of Yourself (as Gordie Lightfoot)	7
65	United Artists UP 1109	Just Like Tom Thumb's Blues/Ribbon Of Darkness	7
66	Warner Bros WB 5621	I'm Not Sayin'/For Lovin' Me	5
68	President PT 138	Adios Adios/Is My Baby Blue Tonight	6
68	United Artists UP 2216	Black Day In July/Pussy Willow's Cat Tails	5
69	United Artists UP 2272	The Circle Is Small/Does Your Mother Know	5
69	United Artists UP 35020	Bitter Green/May I	5
69	United Artists UP 35036	Early Morning Rain/The Gypsy	5
72	Reprise K 14210	If You Could Read My Mind/Me And Bobby McGee/Summer Side/ Talking In Your Sleep (p/s)	5
68	United Artists SULP 1199	DID SHE MENTION MY NAME (LP)	12
69	United Artists SULP 1239	BACK HERE ON EARTH (LP)	12
69	Utd. Artists UAL/UAS 29012	EARLY LIGHTFOOT (LP)	12
71	Reprise RSLP 6392	IF YOU COULD READ MY MIND (LP)	12

PADDY LIGHTFOOT

50s	Melodisc EPM7 100	PADDY LIGHTFOOT (EP)	8

PAPA (GEORGE) LIGHTFOOT

69	Liberty LBF 15176	Wine Whiskey And Woman/SLIM HARPO: Something Inside Me	12
60s	Jan & Dil JR 451	MORE DOWN HOME BLUES (EP)	25
71	Liberty LBS 83353	NATCHEZ TRACE (LP, as Papa George Lightfoot)	18

TERRY LIGHTFOOT'S (NEW ORLEANS) JAZZMEN

57	Columbia DB 4032	I Saw Mommy Kissing Santa Claus/Winter Wonderland	6
58	Pye Jazz 7NJ 2018	My Bucket's Got A Hole In It/Good Time Swing	5
60	Columbia DB 4519	The Preacher/The Onions	5
61	Columbia DB 4696	True Love/Black Bottom Stomp	7
61	Columbia SCD 2165	King Kong/Riverside Blues	5
65	Columbia DB 7534	Alley Cat/Petite Fleur	5
56	Nixa NJE 1027	TERRY LIGHTFOOT'S JAZZMEN (EP)	12
60s	Columbia SEG 7851	PLAYS TRAD (EP)	20
60s	Columbia SEG 7917	MORE TRAD (EP)	10
60s	Columbia SEG 7976	TRAD AGAIN (EP)	10
56	Nixa Jazz NJT 503	JAZZ GUMBO VOLUME ONE (10" LP)	22
58	Columbia 33SX 1073	TRADITION IN COLOUR (LP)	15
61	Columbia 33SX 1290	TRAD PARADE (LP, with New Orleans Jazzmen, also stereo SCX 3354)	15/18
61	Columbia 33SX 1353	WORLD OF TRAD (LP)	30
62	Columbia 33SX 1449	LIGHTFOOT AT LANSDOWNE (LP)	20
65	Columbia 33SX 1721	ALLEYCAT (LP, as Terry Lightfoot's Jazzmen)	20
60s	Columbia 33SX 1551	TERRY (LP)	18

LIGHTHOUSE

69	RCA RCA 1884	Eight Miles High/If There Ever Was A Time	6
71	Vertigo 6073 150	Hats Off (To The Strangers)/Sing Sing Sing	5
72	Philips 6073 152	One Fine Morning/Little Kind Words	5
72	Philips 6073 153	Take It Slow/Sweet Lullaby	5
70	RCA SF 8103	SUITE FEELING (LP)	15
70	RCA SF 8121	PEACING IT ALL TOGETHER (LP)	12
71	Vertigo 6342 010	ONE FINE MORNING (LP, gatefold sleeve, spiral label)	25
71	Vertigo 6342 011	THOUGHTS OF MOVIN' ON (LP, gatefold sleeve, spiral label)	25

LIGHTNIN' SLIM

72	Blue Horizon 2096 013	Just A Little Bit/You're Old Enough To Understand/Mind Your Own Business	20
65	Stateside SL 10135	A LONG DRINK OF BLUES (LP, with Slim Harpo)	40
69	Python PLP 8	THE DOWNHOME BLUES PART 1 (LP, 99 copies only)	40
70	Blue Horizon 7-63863	ROOSTER BLUES (LP)	70
72	Blue Horizon 2931 005	LONDON GUMBO (LP)	75
78	Flyright FLYLP 533	TRIP TO CHICAGO (LP)	12
79	Flyright FLYLP 583	THE FEATURE SIDES 1954 (LP)	12
80	Flyright FLYLP 612	WE GOTTA ROCK TONIGHT (LP)	12

(see also Slim Harpo)

LIGHTNING LEON

60s	Jan & Dil JR 450	DOWN HOME BLUES — SIXTIES STYLE (EP)	25

LIGHTNING RAIDERS

80	Arista ARIST 341	Psychedelik Musik ('adult' version)/Views (p/s)	20
80	Arista ARIST 341DJ	Psychedelik Musik ('censored' version)/Views (promo only)	25
81	Revenge REVS 200	Criminal World/Citizens (p/s)	18
81	Revenge RSS 39	Sweet Revenge/Rowdies/Addiction/Soul Rescue (12", promo only)	12
80s	Revenge	LIGHTNING RAIDERS (12", promo sampler, die-cut company sleeve)	30

(see also Pink Fairies, Professionals)

MINT VALUE £

LIGHTNING SEEDS

89	Ghetto CDGTG 4	Pure/Fools/God Help Them/All I Want (CD, card sleeve)	10
89	Ghetto CDGTG 6	Joy/Frenzy/Control The Flame (CD, card sleeve)	8
92	Virgin VSCDG 1402	The Life Of Riley/Something In The Air/Marooned (CD, digipak)	8
92	Virgin VST 1414	Sense/Flaming Sword/Hang On To A Dream/The Life Of Riley (Remix) (12", heat sensitive p/s)	8
92	Virgin VSCDT 1414	Sense/Flaming Sword/Hang On To A Dream/The Life Of Riley (Riley) (CD, digipak)	8

(see also Big In Japan, Care, Original Mirrors)

LIGHT OF THE WORLD

80	Ensign ENY 43	London Town/Pete's Crusade	4
80	Ensign ENY 4312	London Town/Pete's Crusade (12")	8
82	EMI EMI 5319	No. 1 Girl/Don't Run	5
82	EMI 12EMI 5319	No. 1 Girl/Don't Run (12")	8
79	Ensign ENVY 7	LIGHT OF THE WORLD (LP)	12
80	Ensign ENVY 14	ROUND TRIP (LP)	12
82	EMI EMC 3410	CHECK US OUT (LP)	15

LIKE A SONG

| 73 | De Wolfe DW/LP 3273 | LIKE A SONG (LP, library issue) | 15 |

LILAC TIME

88	Swordfish LILAC 1	Return To Yesterday/Trumpets From Montparnasse (no p/s)	8
88	Swordfish 12 LILAC 1	Return To Yesterday/Railway Bazaar/Trumpets From Montparnasse/ Reunion Ball (12", p/s)	15
88	Fontana LILCD 2	Return To Yesterday/Rooftrees/Gone For A Burton/ Reunion Ball (CD, card sleeve)	10
88	Fontana LILCD 3	You've Got To Love/Railway Bazaar/Trumpets From Montparnasse (CD, card sleeve)	10
88	Fontana LILAC 4	Black Velvet/Black Dawn (p/s in Xmas card folder)	5
88	Fontana LILCD 4	Black Velvet/Tiger Tea/Street Corner/Black Dawn (CD)	8
89	Fontana LILCD 5	American Eyes/Shepherd's Plaid/The World In Her Arms/ Crossing The Line (CD)	8
89	Fontana LILCD 6	The Days Of The Week/The Queen Of Heartless/Spin A Cavalu (CD)	8
89	Fontana LILCD 7	The Girl Who Waves At Trains/If The Stars Shine Tonight (Acoustic Version)/ Ounce Of Nails/American Eyes (Acoustic Version) (CD)	8
90	Caff CAFF 12	Madresfield/Bird On The Wire (p/s, with insert)	20
88	Swordfish SWF LP 6	THE LILAC TIME (LP, original issue)	15
88	Swordfish SWF CD 6	THE LILAC TIME (CD, original issue)	30
88	Fontana 836 744-2	THE LILAC TIME (CD, reissue)	18
89	Fontana 838 641-2	PARADISE CIRCUS (CD)	20

(see also Hawks, Stephen Duffy, Tin Tin)

LIL & RENEE

| 63 | Reprise R 20206 | Tennessee Waltz/Keep A Lite | 6 |

LILYS

| 96 | Ché CHE 51 | Returns Every Morning/Touch The Water (white vinyl, p/s, 500 only) | 6 |
| 96 | Ché CHE 65 | A Nanny In Manhattan/More Than Is Deserved (coffee-coloured vinyl, p/s, 500 only) | 6 |

LIMELIGHT

| 75 | United Artists UP 35779 | I Should Have Known Better/Tell Me Why | 12 |

(see also Brinsley Schwarz)

LIMELIGHT

80	Future Earth FER 006	Metal Man/Hold Me Touch Me (p/s)	12
82	Future Earth FER 010	Ashes To Ashes/Knife In Your Back (p/s, some with insert)	12/10
80	Future Earth FER 008	LIMELIGHT (LP)	30
81	Avatar AALP 5005	LIMITED LIMELIGHT (LP, some with bonus single)	35/20

LIMELITERS

63	RCA RCX 7126	FUN FOLK (EP)	8
64	RCA RCX 7151	FOUR FOLK SONGS (EP)	8
60	Elektra EKL 180	FOLK SONGS FOR MODERNS (LP)	12
61	RCA RD 27254	SLIGHTLY FABULOUS LIMELITERS (LP)	15
63	RCA Victor RD/SF 7581	FOURTEEN 14K FOLK SONGS (LP)	12

ALISON LIMERICK

| 90 | Arista 113509 | Where Love Lives/Where Love Lives (Classic Mix) (p/s) | 4 |
| 90 | Arista 613509 | Where Love Lives/Where Love Lives (Classic Mix)/ Where Love Lives (Zone)/Where Love Lives (Cut To The Bone) (12", p/s) | 10 |

LIMEYS

65	Pye 7N 15820	I Can't Find My Way Through/Don't Cry (My Love)	6
65	Pye 7N 15909	Some Tears Fall Dry/Half Glass Of Wine	6
66	Decca F 12382	Cara-Lin/Feel So Blue	25
66	Decca F 12466	The Mountain's High/Lovin' Yourself	6

PETER LINCOLN

| 67 | Major Minor MM 520 | In The Day Of My Youth/My Monkey Is A Junkie | 8 |

(see also Peter Sarstedt, Sarstedt Brothers, Brothers Kane)

PHILAMORE LINCOLN

| 68 | NEMS 56-3711 | Running By The River/Rainy Day | 8 |

LINCOLNS

| 66 | Parlophone R 5418 | Mister Loneliness/Only Love Will Break Your Heart | 4 |

LINCOLN X

| 63 | Oriole CB 1823 | Heartaches And Happiness/Stand In For Her Past | 8 |

LINDISFARNE

BOB LIND

66	Fontana TF 670	Elusive Butterfly/Cheryl's Goin' Home	6
66	Fontana TF 702	Remember The Rain/Truly Julie's Blues (I'll Be There)	6
66	Fontana TF 750	San Francisco Woman/Oh Babe Take Me Home	6
67	Verve VS 1501	Hey Nellie Nellie/Wandering	6
66	Fontana (S)TL 5340	DON'T BE CONCERNED (LP)	25
66	Verve F'ways (S)VLP 5015	THE ELUSIVE BOB LIND (LP)	20
67	Fontana (S)TL 5395	PHOTOGRAPHS OF FEELINGS (LP)	18

ROSA LINDA

53	London L 1215	Flight 88/Taboo (78)	10

DADDY LINDBERG

67	Columbia DB 8138	Shirl/Wade In The Shade	10

(see also Crocheted Doughnut Ring, Fingers)

ANITA LINDBLOM

62	Fontana 267223 TF	Uptown/Mr Big Wheel	6

DENNIS LINDE

73	Elektra K 42149	DENNIS LINDE (LP)	12
74	Elektra K 52013	TRAPPED IN THE SUBURBS (LP)	12

KATHY LINDEN

58	Felsted AF 102	Billy/If I Could Hold You In My Arms	8
58	Felsted AF 102	Billy/If I Could Hold You In My Arms (78)	15
58	Felsted AF 105	You'd Be Surprised/Why Oh Why	8
58	Felsted AF 105	You'd Be Surprised/Why Oh Why (78)	15
58	Felsted AF 108	Oh! Johnny, Oh! Johnny Oh!/Georgie	6
58	Felsted AF 108	Oh! Johnny, Oh! Johnny Oh!/Georgie (78)	15
58	Felsted AF 111	Kissin' Conversation/Just A Sandy Haired Boy Called Sandy	8
58	Felsted AF 111	Kissin' Conversation/Just A Sandy Haired Boy Called Sandy (78)	20
59	Felsted AF 122	Goodbye Jimmy, Goodbye/Heartaches At Sweet Sixteen	6
59	Felsted AF 122	Goodbye Jimmy, Goodbye/Heartaches At Sweet Sixteen (78)	12
59	Felsted AF 124	So Close To My Heart/You Don't Know Girls	8
59	Felsted AF 124	So Close To My Heart/You Don't Know Girls (78)	20
60	Felsted AF 130	Think Love/Mary Lou Wilson And Johnny Brown	8
59	Felsted GEP 1001	KATHY (EP)	25
59	Felsted GEP 1002	KATHY'S IN LOVE VOLUME ONE (EP)	22
59	Felsted GEP 1004	KATHY'S IN LOVE VOLUME TWO (EP)	22

LINDISFARNE

SINGLES

70	Charisma CB 137	Clear White Light Part II/Knackers Yard Blues	12
71	Charisma CB 153	Lady Eleanor/Nothing But The Marvellous Is Beautiful (some with p/s)	8/5
72	Charisma CB 173	Meet Me On The Corner/Scotch Mist/No Time To Lose (p/s)	6
72	Charisma CB 191	All Fall Down/We Can Swing Together (live) (p/s)	6
72	Charisma CB 199	Court In The Act/Don't Ask Me	5
74	Charisma CB 228	Taking Care Of Business/North Country Boy	6
74	Charisma CB 232	Fog On The Tyne/Mandolin King	6
75	Warner Brothers K 16489	Tonight/No Need To Tell Me	6
75	Charisma CB 266	Lady Eleanor/Fog On The Tyne	5
78	Mercury 6007 177	Run For Home/Stick Together (p/s)	5
78	Mercury 6007 195	Brand New Day/Winter Song	5
79	Mercury 6007 205	Warm Feeling/Clear White Light (live) (p/s)	5

LINDISFARNE

79	Mercury NEWS 1	Easy And Free/When Friday Comes Along (p/s)	5
79	Mercury 6007 241	Call Of The Wild/Dedicated Hound	5
81	Hangover HANG 9	I Must Stop Going To Parties/See How They Run (p/s)	5
82	LMP LM 1	Sunderland Boys/Cruising To Disaster	5
82	LMP FOG 1	Nights/Dog Ruff (p/s)	5
83	LMP FOG 2	Do What I Want/Same Way Down (p/s)	5
85	LMP FOG 3	I Remember The Lights (Acappella Version)/Day Of The Jackal (p/s)	6
85	LMP FOG 4	CHRISTMAS (EP, sold at Christmas concerts)	6
86	River City LIND 1	Shine On/Heroes/Dance Your Live Away (Gogo Mix) (p/s)	5
87	River City LIND 2	Love On The Run/One Hundred Miles To Liverpool (p/s)	5
88	River City LIND 2A	Save Our Ales/Save Our Ales (Sub Mix) (p/s)	6
88	Charisma LADYCD 1	Lady Eleanor '88/Meet Me On The Corner/Lost In Space/Reason To Be (3" CD, gatefold card sleeve)	7
90	Best ZA 44207	Fog On The Tyne (Revisited)/Fog On The Tyne (Revisited) (Instrumental) (picture disc, by Gazza [Paul Gascoigne] & Lindisfarne)	5
93	Essential LFSCD 101	Soho Square/Think/Spoken Like A Man (CD, promo only)	7

LPs

70	Charisma CAS 1025	NICELY OUT OF TUNE (LP, pink or 'mad hatter' label)	15/12
71	Charisma CAS 1050	FOG ON THE TYNE (LP, gatefold sleeve)	12
72	Charisma CAS 1057	DINGLY DELL (LP, with inner sleeve & poster)	12
73	Charisma CLASS 2	LINDISFARNE LIVE (LP)	12
73	Charisma CAS 1076	ROLL ON RUBY (LP, gatefold sleeve & poster)	12
74	Warner Brothers K 56070	HAPPY DAZE (LP, with lyric sheet)	12
78	Mercury 9109 609	BACK AND FOURTH (LP, gatefold sleeve)	12
79	Mercury 9109 626	THE NEWS (LP, with lyric inner sleeve)	12
81	Charisma BG 5	REPEAT PERFORMANCE: THE LINDISFARNE SINGLES ALBUM (LP)	12

(see also Alan Hull, Jack The Lad, Chosen Few, Radiator, Ray Jackson)

MARK LINDSAY

69	CBS 4699	Arizona/Man From Houston	5
70	CBS 5055	Silver Bird/So Hard To Leave You	5
70	CBS 5219	And The Grass Won't Pay No Mind/Funny How Little Men Care	5
71	CBS 5408	Problem Child/Bookends	5
71	CBS 7330	Been Too Long On The Road/All I Really See Is You	5
71	CBS 7551	Are You Old Enough/Don't You Know	5
71	CBS 7690	Something Big/Pretty Pretty	5

(see also Paul Revere & Raiders)

TERRY LINDSEY

69	President PT 232	It's Over/One Day Up, Next Day Down	5

DAVID LINDUP ORCHESTRA

66	Columbia DB 7979	Informer Theme/Blue Mountain	5
66	Polydor 56106	Survival Theme/New Forest	20

LINDYS

60	Decca F 11253	The Train Of Love/You Know How Things Get Around	12
60	Decca F 11272	Boy With The Eyes Of Blue/Someone Else's Roses	15

LINES

78	Linear SJP 782	White Night/Barbican (p/s)	6
79	Illegal ILS 0011	White Night/Barbican (p/s, reissue)	4
80	RL 007	Nerve Pylon/Over The Brow (screen-printed p/s)	4

BUZZY LINHART

69	Philips SBL 7885	BUZZY (LP)	12

LINK

92	Evolution EVO 05	THE FIRST LINK EP (12", plain sleeve)	30
93	Symbiotic SYM 001	THE LINK EP (12", plain sleeve, no credits on label)	40
95	Warp WAP 59	ANTACID EP (12", p/s)	10
95	Warp WAP 59R	ANTACID REMIXES EP (12", p/s)	10

(see also Reload, Global Communications, Mystic Institute)

LINKERS

71	Big Shot BI 567	Bongo Man/FUD CHRISTIAN ALLSTARS: Creation Version	6

(see also Links)

ANSEL LINKERS & FUD CHRISTIAN ALL STARS

73	Summit SUM 8540	Memories By The Score/FUD CHRISTIAN ALL STARS: Scorer	5

(see also Links)

LINKS

72	Tropical AL 0010	Sing A Song Of Freedom/TROPICAL ALL STARS: Love Rhythm (A-side actually by Linkers)	5

ELMO LINN

63	Starlite ST45 101	Another Man's Arms/Sam Houston	10

LINN COUNTY

68	Mercury SMCL 20142	PROUD FLESH SOOTHSEER (LP)	15
69	Mercury SMCL 20165	FEVER SHOT (LP)	15
70	Philips SBL 7923	TILL THE BREAK OF DAWN (LP)	15

LINOLEUM

96	Lino Vinyl LINO 001	Dissent/Twisted (lino sleeve, some sealed, 1,000 only)	12/10
96	Lino Vinyl LINO 002	Smear/Tired (lino sleeve, some sealed, 2,000 only)	8/6

JOE LINTHECOME

50s	Poydras 87	Pretty Mama Blues/Hummingbird Blues (78)	12

LINUS & LITTLE PEOPLE

70	Evolution	Lovin' La La	8

LION
51	Sagomes SG 117	Ugly Woman/The Lost Watch (78)	12
52	Parlophone MP 114	Mary Ann/Little Mary Had No Lamb (78)	12
53	Melodisc 1236	Coronation Of Elizabeth 2/Crosby Cavalcade (78, with Caribbean Rhythm)	10

LIONHEART
85	Epic A 5001	Die For Love/Dangerous Games (p/s)	7
84	Epic EPC 26214	HOT TONIGHT (LP)	12

(see also Iron Maiden)

LIONROCK
92	M.E.R.C. 002	Roots'n'Culture (Part One)/Lionrock (12", original issue)	10
92	De Construc. 74321124381	Lionrock — The Remixes: (Most Excellent Mix)/(Roots 'n' Culture)/(A Trumpet Jamboree In Edinburgh)/)A Dubtastic Jamboree In Edinburgh) (12")	10
93	De Construc. 74321144371	Packet Of Peace (Prankster Sound System Mix)/(Instrumental)/ (No More Fucking Trumpets) (12")	8
93	De Construc. 74321144372	Packet Of Peace (Dust Brothers Mix)/(Jeff Mills Mix) (12", promo only)	20
93	Distort & Cavort	Dub Plate No. 1 (12")	10
94	De Construc. DUB PLATE 1	The Guide/Don't Be Foolish (12")	8
98	Concrete HARD 3112	Rude Boy Rock/Best Foot Forward/Push Button Cocktail (p/s)	8

LIONS
69	Polydor 56757	Twisted Nerve/My Friend The Blackbird	4

LIONS OF JUDAH
69	Fontana TF 1016	Our Love's A Growin' Thing/Katja	8

JOE LIPMAN ORCHESTRA
54	MGM SP 1108	Looking Back To See/Stop	6

LIP MOVES
79	Tichonderoga HP 1	Guest/What Is (p/s with insert, stickered white labels, some signed)	10/8

LIQUID SMOKE
70	Avco Embassy 646 6003	LIQUID SMOKE (LP)	40

LISTEN
65	CBS 202456	You'd Better Run/Everybody's Gonna Say	165

(see also Robert Plant, Led Zeppelin)

LITTER
69	Probe CLPS 4504	EMERGE (LP)	35

'BIG' TINY LITTLE
57	Vogue Coral Q 72263	School Day/That's The Only Way To Live	30
57	Vogue Coral Q 72263	School Day/That's The Only Way To Live (78)	25
60	Coral FEP 2058	HONKY TONK PIANO VOL. 1 (EP)	12
60	Coral FEP 2059	HONKY TONK PIANO VOL. 2 (EP)	12

KENNY LITTLE & LITTLE PEOPLE
65	United Artists UP 1074	A Shot In The Dark/Never On A Sunday	4

MARIE LITTLE
71	Argo ZFB 19	FACTORY GIRL (LP)	100
73	Trailer LER 2084	MARIE LITTLE (LP)	50
87	private pressing	MY ELDORADO (LP)	12

LITTLE ABNER
57	Oriole CB 1380	Not Here, Not There/You Mean Everything To Me (78)	15

LITTLE ANGELS
87	Little Angels LAN 001	LITTLE ANGELS '87 (12" EP)	60
88	Polydor LTLD 1	90 Degrees In The Shade/England Rocks (live) (poster p/s)	12
88	Polydor LTLXP 1	90 Degrees In The Shade/England Rocks (live) (shaped picture disc)	20
89	Polydor LTLCD 2	THE BIG BAD EP (CD)	15
89	Polydor LTLXV 3	Do You Wanna Riot/Move In Slow/Some Kind Of Alien (live) (10", red vinyl)	25
89	Polydor LTLX 3	Do You Wanna Riot/Move In Slow/Some Kind Of Alien (live) (12", p/s)	20
89	Polydor LTLCD 3	Do You Wanna Riot/Move In Slow/Some Kind Of Alien (live) (CD)	30
89	Polydor LTL 4	Don't Pray For Me (7" Edit)/Radical Your Lover (p/s)	10
89	Polydor LTLS 4	Don't Pray For Me (7" Edit)/Radical Your Lover (p/s, sealed with patch)	15
89	Polydor LTLXP 4	Don't Pray For Me (7" Edit)/Radical Your Lover/What Do You Want/ Don't Pray For Me (Extended Bob Clearmountain Mix) (12", poster p/s)	35
89	Polydor LTLCD 4	Don't Pray For Me (7" Edit)/Radical Your Lover/What Do You Want/ Don't Pray For Me (Extended Bob Clearmountain Mix) (CD)	20
90	Polydor LTL 5	Kickin' Up Dust/Kickin' Up Dust (live) (p/s)	7
90	Polydor LTLP 5	Kickin' Up Dust/Kickin' Up Dust (live) (picture disc, die cut sleeve)	15
90	Polydor LTLXP 5	Kickin' Up Dust/Kickin' Up Dust (live)/Pleasure Pyre (live)/Kick Hard (live) (12", picture disc, numbered)	15
90	Polydor LTLCD 5	Kickin' Up Dust/Kickin' Up Dust (live)/Pleasure Pyre (live)/Kick Hard (live) (CD)	15
91	Polydor LTLX 11	I Ain't Gonna Cry/Babylon's Burning (12", picture disc, gatefold sleeve)	15
91	Polydor LTLXG 11	I Ain't Gonna Cry/Babylon's Burning (12", in tin, numbered)	10
91	Polydor LTLXG 11	I Ain't Gonna Cry/Babylon's Burning (12", gatefold p/s)	8
87	Powerstation AMP 14	TOO POSH TO MOSH (mini-LP)	35

LITTLE ANN
98	Kent TOWN 111	What Should I Do/O.C. TALBOT: I'm Shooting High (I Reach For The Sky)	8

LITTLE ANTHONY & IMPERIALS
58	London HLH 8704	Tears On My Pillow/Two People In The World	45
58	London HLH 8704	Tears On My Pillow/Two People In The World (78)	35
59	London HL 8848	So Much/Oh Yeah	30
59	London HL 8848	So Much/Oh Yeah (78)	60
59	Top Rank JAR 256	Shimmy, Shimmy, Ko-Ko Bop/I'm Still In Love With You	15
60	Top Rank JAR 366	My Empty Room/Bayou, Bayou, Baby	15

LITTLE ANTHONY & IMPERIALS

64	United Artists UP 1065	I'm On The Outside Looking In/Please Go	10
64	United Artists UP 1073	Goin' Out Of My Head/Make It Easy On Yourself	12
65	United Artists UP 1083	Hurt So Bad/Reputation	15
65	United Artists UP 1098	Take Me Back/Our Song	7
65	United Artists UP 1112	I Miss You/Get Out Of My Life	7
66	United Artists UP 1126	Hurt/Never Again	20
66	United Artists UP 1137	Better Use Your Head/The Wonder Of It All	35
66	United Artists UP 1151	Gonna Fix You Good (Every Time You're Bad)/You Better Take It Easy Baby	35
67	United Artists UP 1189	My Love Is A Rainbow/You Only Live Twice	6
68	United Artists UP 2260	Let The Sunshine In/The Gentle Rain (as Anthony & Imperials)	6
69	United Artists UP 35017	Anthem/Goodbye Goodtimes (as Anthony & Imperials)	6
72	United Artists UP 35345	Gonna Fix You Good (Every Time You're Bad)/You Better Take It Easy Baby (reissue)	6
72	Janus 6146 005	Father Father/Each One Teach One	5
72	Janus 6146 012	Where Do I Begin/There's An Island	5
74	Avco 6105 031	La La La At The End/I Don't Have Time To Worry	5
76	United Artists UP 36118	Better Use Your Head/Gonna Fix You Good (Every Time You're Bad)	5
76	United Artists REM 405	Goin' Out Of My Head/I'm On The Outside Looking In/Hurt So Bad/ Gonna Fix You Good (Every Time You're Bad)	5
65	United Artists UEP 1004	LITTLE ANTHONY AND THE IMPERIALS (EP)	75
64	United Artists ULP 1089	I'M ON THE OUTSIDE LOOKING IN (LP)	75
66	United Artists ULP 1100	GOIN' OUT OF MY HEAD (LP)	50
(see also Anthony & Imperials)			

LITTLE ARCHIE
68	Atlantic 584 209	I Need You/I Am A Carpet	4

LITTLE BEAVER
72	President PTLS 1060	JOEY (LP)	10

LITTLE BEN'S BANJOS
60	Columbia DB 4467	There Are Just Two I's In Dixie/Silly Little Tune	5
(see also Big Ben Banjo Band, Norrie Paramor)			

LITTLE BEVERLEY
68	Pama PM 731	What A Guy/You're Mine	6
(see also Beverley Simmons)			

LITTLE BILL & BLUE NOTES
59	Top Rank JAR 176	I Love An Angel/Bye, Bye Baby	12
59	Top Rank JAR 176	I Love An Angel/Bye, Bye Baby (78)	30
(see also Blue Notes)			

LITTLE BIRD
84	Magus MGB 1	Zola/Reaching Out For Gold (p/s)	4

LITTLE BO BITCH
79	Cobra COB 1	It's Only Love/I'm Confused (p/s)	5
80	Cobra COB 4	Take It Easy (Lights Out Over London)/Lorraine, Lorraine (p/s)	5
79	Cobra CBR 1002	LITTLE BO BITCH (LP)	12

LITTLE BROTHER
(see under Little Brother Grant)

LITTLE DARLING
65	Blue Beat BB 325	No One/BUSTER'S ALL STARS: Congo Revolution	15

LITTLE DARLINGS
65	Fontana TF 539	Little Bit O' Soul/Easy To Cry	60

LITTLE DES
70	J-Dan JDN 4400	Somebody's Baby/Spy Man	6

LITTLE DIPPERS
60	Pye International 7N 25051	Forever/Two By Four	8
61	London HLG 9269	Lonely/I Wonder, I Wonder, I Wonder	15

LITTLE ESTHER
(see under Little Esther Phillips)

LITTLE EVA
62	London HL 9581	The Locomotion/He Is The Boy	5
62	London HLU 9633	Keep Your Hands Off My Baby/Where Do I Go	7
63	London HLU 9687	Let's Turkey Trot/Old Smokey Locomotion	7
63	Colpix PX 11013	The Trouble With Boys/What I Gotta Do (To Make You Jealous)	10
63	Colpix PX 11019	Please Hurt Me/Let's Start The Party Again	8
64	Colpix PX 11035	Run To Her/Making With The Magilla	8
65	Stateside SS 477	Stand By Me/That's My Man	15
63	London HA-U 8036	L-L-L-L-LOCO-MOTION (LP, original with plum label & laminated sleeve)	40
72	London SH-U 8437	L-L-L-L-LOCO-MOTION (LP, stereo reissue, plum label, boxed label logo)	12
(see also Big Dee Irwin & Little Eva)			

LITTLE FOLK
71	Studio Republic CR 1001	LEAVE THEM A FLOWER (LP)	18

LITTLE FRANKIE (& COUNTRY GENTLEMEN)
65	Columbia DB 7490	The Kind Of Boy You Can't Forget/I'm Not Gonna Do It	10
65	Columbia DB 7578	Make-A-Love/Love Is Just A Game (with Country Gentlemen)	15
65	Columbia DB 7681	It Doesn't Matter Anymore/Happy, That's Me	12
(see also Chimes featuring Denise)			

LITTLE FREDDY (McGregor)
70	Unity UN 551	Why Did My Little Girl Cry/PETER AUSTIN: Change Partners	7
(see also Freddie McGregor, Ernest Wilson)			

LITTLE FREE ROCK
69 Transatlantic TRA 608 LITTLE FREE ROCK (LP) 60
(see also David John & Mood)

LITTLE GEORGE
64 Rio R 45 Mary Anne/EDWARDS ALLSTARS: Blue Night 12

LITTLE GRANTS & EDDIE (Grant)
67 President PT 159 Rudy's Dead/Everything's Alright 5
67 President PT 172 Rock Steady '67/Bingo...5
(see also Equals, Pyramids)

LITTLE HANK
66 London HLU 10090 Mr. Bang Bang Man/Don't You Know (withdrawn)......................50
70 Monument MON 1045 Mr. Bang Bang Man/Don't You Know (reissue) 10

LITTLE JOE (& THRILLERS)
57 Philips PB 759 Peanuts/Lilly Lou (78) 60
60 Fontana H 281 Stay (as Little Joe & Thrillers)/Cherry 18
63 Reprise R 20142 Peanuts/No No I Can't Stop 12

LITTLE JOE (Jamaica)
70 Torpedo TOR 15 Bad Blood/Maxi-Mini War..6
(see also Sexy Girls)

LITTLE JOEY & FLIPS
62 Pye International 7N 25152 Bongo Stomp/Lost Love 8

LITTLE JOHN
67 Pama PM 702 Let's Get Married/Around The World 6
70 Unity UN 561 No Love/A Little Tear (both sides actually by John Holt) 6
(see also John Holt)

LITTLE JOHNNY & THREE TEENAGERS
58 Decca F 10990 Baby Lover/Rickety Rackety Rendezvous..............................12
58 Decca F 10990 Baby Lover/Rickety Rackety Rendezvous (78) 8

LITTLE LEMMY & BIG JOE
58 Decca F 11054 Little Lemmy Kwela/Kwela No. 5 5
58 Decca F 11054 Little Lemmy Kwela/Kwela No. 5 (78) 8

LITTLE LUMAN
64 Rio R 44 Hurry Harry/R. ALPHONSE: Hucklebuck (B-side actually by Roland Alphonso). . 12

LITTLE LUTHER
64 Pye International 7N 25266 Eenie Meenie Minie Moe/Twirl 40

LITTLE MACK & BOSS SOUNDS
66 Atlantic 584 031 In The Midnight Hour/You Can't Love Me (In The Midnight Hour) 7

LITTLE MILTON
65 Pye International 7N 25289 Blind Man/Blues In The Night 12
65 Chess CRS 8013 We're Gonna Make It/Can't Hold Back The Tears 12
65 Chess CRS 8018 Who's Cheating Who?/Ain't No Big Deal On You 15
66 Sue WI 4021 Early In The Morning/Bless Your Heart (actually by Roy Milton) 25
69 Chess CRS 8087 Grits Ain't Groceries/I Can't Quit You Baby.......................12
69 Chess CRS 8100 Let's Get Together/I'll Always Love You............................10
72 Stax 2025 095 That's What Love Will Make You Do/I'm Living Off The Love You Give........6
74 Stax STXS 2003 Behind Closed Doors/Bet You I Win 6
75 Stax STA 100 If That Ain't A Reason/Mr. Mailman 5
69 Chess CRLS 4552 GRITS AIN'T GROCERIES (LP) 25
72 Chess 6310 120 GOLDEN DECADE (LP) 15
74 Stax STX 1013 BLUES 'N' SOUL (LP)..15

LITTLE NORA
54 Melodisc MEL 1261 Tomato/Nora's Blues (78)..8

LITTLE RED SCHOOLHOUSE
80s Waterfall WFL 3 Aged Bee/HURT: Take My Breath (free with *Jump Away* fanzine)............5/4

LITTLE RED WALTERS
60s XX MIN 706 DARK MUDDY BOTTOM (EP)...12

LITTLE RICHARD
78s
56 London HLO 8336 Rip It Up/Ready Teddy (78).......................................15
57 London HLO 8366 Long Tall Sally/Tutti Frutti (78) 15
57 London HLO 8382 The Girl Can't Help It/She's Got It (78) 12
57 London HLO 8446 Lucille/Send Me Some Lovin' (as Little Richard & His Band) (78) ..15
57 London HLO 8470 Jenny, Jenny/Miss Ann (as Little Richard & His Band) (78) 15
57 London HLO 8509 Keep A Knockin'/Can't Believe You Wanna Leave (78) 18
58 London HLO 8560 Good Golly Miss Molly/Hey-Hey-Hey-Hey (78) 30
58 London HLO 8647 Ooh! My Soul/True, Fine Mama (78)...............................30
58 London HLO 8770 Baby Face/I'll Never Let You Go (78) 35
59 London HLU 8831 By The Light Of The Silvery Moon/Early One Morning (78) 45
59 London HLU 8868 Kansas City/She Knows How To Rock (78) 15
60 London HLU 9065 Baby/I Got It (78) 150

SINGLES
56 London HLO 8336 Rip It Up/Ready Teddy (gold label print, later silver) 80/25
50s London HLO 8336 Rip It Up/Ready Teddy (repressing, silver-top label, round centre) 15
57 London HLO 8366 Long Tall Sally/Tutti Frutti (gold label print, later silver) ..80/25
50s London HLO 8366 Long Tall Sally/Tutti Frutti (repressing, silver-top label, round centre) 15
57 London HLO 8382 The Girl Can't Help It/She's Got It (gold label print, later silver) 100/25
50s London HLO 8382 The Girl Can't Help It/She's Got It
(repressing, silver-top label, round centre)...........................15

LITTLE RICHARD

57	London HLO 8446	Lucille/Send Me Some Lovin' (as Little Richard & His Band)	20
57	London HLO 8470	Jenny, Jenny/Miss Ann (as Little Richard & His Band)	20
57	London HLO 8509	Keep A Knockin'/Can't Believe You Wanna Leave	20
58	London HLU 8560	Good Golly Miss Molly/Hey-Hey-Hey-Hey	20
58	London HLO 8647	Ooh! My Soul/True, Fine Mama	12
58	London HLU 8770	Baby Face/I'll Never Let You Go	6
59	London HLU 8831	By The Light Of The Silvery Moon/Early One Morning	7
59	London HLU 8868	Kansas City/She Knows How To Rock	10

(The above 45s were originally issued with triangular centres; later round-centres are worth around half to two-thirds these values.)

60	London HLU 9065	Baby/I Got It	15
61	Mercury AMT 1165	Joy Joy Joy (Down In My Heart)/He's Not Just A Soldier	6
62	Mercury AMT 1189	He Got What He Wanted (But He Lost What He Had)/Why Don't You Change Your Ways?	10
63	London HLK 9708	Crying In The Chapel/Hole In The Wall	10
63	London HLK 9756	Travelin' Shoes/It Is No Secret	10
64	London HL 9896	Bama Lama Bama Loo/Annie's Back	10
64	Fontana TF 519	Blueberry Hill/Cherry Red	10
64	Stateside SS 340	Whole Lotta Shakin' Goin' On/Goodnight Irene	10
64	Mercury MF 841	Joy, Joy, Joy (Down In My Heart)/Peace In The Valley	6
66	Fontana TF 652	I Don't Know What You've Got But It's Got Me (Parts 1 & 2)	15
66	Stateside SS 508	Holy Mackeral/Baby, Don'tcha Want A Man Like Me?	10
66	Sue WI 4001	Without Love/Dance What You Wanna	25
66	Sue WI 4015	It Ain't Watcha Do (It's The Way How You Do It)/Crossover	25
66	Columbia DB 7974	Poor Dog/Well	15
66	Columbia DB 8058	I Need Love/The Commandments Of Love	12
67	Columbia DB 8116	Get Down With It/Rose Mary	15
67	Columbia DB 8240	A Little Bit Of Something/Money	25
67	Columbia DB 8263	I Don't Want To Discuss It/Hurry Sundown	25
68	MCA MU 1006	She's Together/Try Some Of Mine	8
68	London HLU 10194	Good Golly Miss Molly/Lucille	5
68	President PT 201	Whole Lotta Shakin' Goin' On/Lawdy Miss Clawdy	5
69	Action ACT 4528	Baby What Do You Want Me To Do (Parts 1 & 2)	8
70	Reprise RS 20907	Dew Drop In/Freedom Blues	5
71	President PT 329	Without Love/Talkin' 'Bout Soul	5
71	Reprise K 14124	Green Power/Dancing In The Street	5
72	Reprise K 14150	Money Is/Money Runner	5

EXPORT SINGLES

57	London HL 7022	Jenny, Jenny/Miss Ann (as Little Richard & His Band)	25
58	London HL 7049	Ooh! My Soul/True, Fine Mama	18
58	London HL 7056	Baby Face/I'll Never Let You Go	18
59	London HL 7074	She Knows How To Rock/Early One Morning	25
59	London HL 7079	By The Light Of The Silvery Moon/Kansas City	20
59	London HL 7085	Whole Lotta Shakin' Goin' On/All Around The World	60
68	Decca AD 1006	She's Together/Try Some Of Mine	30

EPs

57	London RE-O 1071	LITTLE RICHARD AND HIS BAND VOL. 1 (EP, gold tri centre, later silver)	35/20
57	London RE-O 1074	LITTLE RICHARD AND HIS BAND VOL. 2 (EP, gold tri centre, later silver)	40/20
57	London RE-O 1103	LITTLE RICHARD AND HIS BAND VOL. 3 (EP)	30
57	London RE-O 1106	LITTLE RICHARD AND HIS BAND VOL. 4 (EP)	30
59	London RE-U 1208	LITTLE RICHARD AND HIS BAND VOL. 5 (EP)	30
60	London RE-U 1234	LITTLE RICHARD AND HIS BAND VOL. 6 (EP)	30
60	London RE-U 1235	LITTLE RICHARD AND HIS BAND VOL. 7 (EP)	35

(The above EPs were originally issued with triangular centres; later round-centre pressings are worth two-thirds of silver values.)

62	Summit LSE 2049	FOUR DYNAMIC NUMBERS (EP, 2 each by Little Richard & Brock Peters)	15
63	London REK 1400	HE'S BACK (EP)	30
64	Vocalion VEP 170155	MEMPHIS SLIM AND LITTLE RICHARD (EP)	60
66	Stateside SE 1042	DO YOU FEEL IT (EP)	25

LPs

57	London HA-O 2055	HERE'S LITTLE RICHARD (LP, flipback, rear sleeve initially in gloss red)	60/35
57	London HA-O 2055	HERE'S LITTLE RICHARD (LP, small flipback or non-flipback sleeve)	35/25
58	London HA-U 2126	LITTLE RICHARD VOL. 2 (LP, flipback or non-flipback sleeve)	35/30
59	RCA Camden CDN 125	LITTLE RICHARD (LP, 8 tracks only; others by Buck Ram Orchestra)	20
59	London HA-U 2193	THE FABULOUS LITTLE RICHARD (LP, flipback or non-flipback sleeve)	40/30
60	Top Rank 25/025	PRAY ALONG WITH LITTLE RICHARD VOL. 1: A CLOSER WALK WITH THEE (LP, plain white sleeve, mail-order only)	50
60	Top Rank 25/026	PRAY ALONG WITH LITTLE RICHARD VOL. 2: I'M QUITTING SHOW BUSINESS (LP, plain white sleeve, mail-order only)	100
62	Egmont EGM 9207	SINGS FREEDOM SONGS (LP, reissue of Top Rank 25/025)	15
63	Egmont EGM 9270	PRAY ALONG WITH LITTLE RICHARD (LP, reissue of Top Rank 25/026)	15
64	Stateside SL 10054	SINGS GOSPEL (LP)	20
64	Coral LVA 9220	COMING HOME (LP)	20
65	Fidelio ATL 4124	SINGS GOSPEL (LP, 4 tracks by Brock Peters but credited to Little Richard)	12
65	Summit ATL 4124	SINGS GOSPEL (LP, 4 tracks by Brock Peters, overprinted front cover)	12
65	Dial DLP 4124	SINGS GOSPEL (LP, 4 tracks by Brock Peters, correctly credited)	12
65	Mercury MCL 20036	IT'S REAL (LP)	15
65	Fontana TL 5235	IS BACK! (LP)	25
65	Ember NR 5022	REALLY MOVIN' GOSPEL (LP, 3 tracks by Sister Rosetta Tharpe)	12
66	Fontana TL 5314	GREAT HITS (LP)	15
67	Columbia SX/SCX 6136	THE EXPLOSIVE LITTLE RICHARD (LP)	12
67	Polydor 236 202	THE INCREDIBLE LITTLE RICHARD (LP, live)	12
68	Fontana SFL 13010	KING OF THE GOSPEL SINGERS (LP)	15
70	Reprise RSLP 6406	THE RILL THING (LP)	12
70	Specialty SNTF 5001	ROCK HARD, ROCK HEAVY (LP)	12
70	Union Pacific UP 003	YOU CAN'T KEEP A GOOD MAN DOWN (LP)	20

MINT VALUE £

71	Epic EPC 66285	CAST A LONG SHADOW (LP)	12
71	Reprise K 44156	THE KING OF ROCK AND ROLL (LP)	15
73	Reprise K 44204	SECOND COMING (LP)	15
75	Rhapsody RHAS 9013	KEEP A KNOCKIN' (LP)	15

(see also Canned Heat, Sister Rosetta Tharpe, Buck Ram's Ramrocks)

LITTLE ROOSTERS

79	Pye 7P 152	She Cat Sister Floozie/Roostering With Intent	6
80	Ami AIS 101	That's How Strong My Love Is/Suspicious	6
80	Ami AIS 107	I Need A Witness/The Age Of Reason	6

(see also Cocksparrer, Alison Moyet)

LITTLE ROYS

69	Camel CA 36	Bongonyah/CREATIONS: Dad Name (B-side actually "Bad Name")	7
70	Camel CA 42	Gold Digger (actually by Wailing Soul)/MATADORS: The Mine	7
70	Camel CA 57	Selassie Want Us Back/ROY AND JOY: Make It With You	8

(see also Little Roy, Hippy Boys)

LITTLE SAL with DANDY & SUPERBOYS

| 68 | Giant GN 19 | I'm In The Mood/I'm A Lover | 7 |

(see also Dandy & Superboys, Superboys)

LITTLE SISTERS

| 63 | MGM MGM 1192 | Goin' To Boston/Where Does It Lead | 4 |

LITTLE SONNY

| 71 | Stax 2363 005 | NEW KING OF THE BLUES HARMONICA (LP) | 12 |

LITTLE SUZIE

| 61 | Warner Bros WB 35 | Young Love/The Boy I Left Behind | 7 |

LITTLE TONY & HIS BROTHERS

59	Durium DC 16639	Who's That Knockin'/The Beat	15
59	Durium DC 16639	Who's That Knockin'/The Beat (78)	120
59	Durium DC 16657	Four An' Twenty Thousand Kisses/Bella Marie	10
59	Decca F 11164	I Can't Help It/Arrivederci Baby	8
59	Decca F 11164	I Can't Help It/Arrivederci Baby (78)	100
59	Decca F 11169	The Hippy Hippy Shake/Hey Little Girl	10
59	Decca F 11169	The Hippy Hippy Shake/Hey Little Girl (78)	125
59	Decca F 11190	Too Good/Foxy Little Mama	8
59	Decca F 11190	Too Good/Foxy Little Mama (78)	100
60	Decca F 21218	I Love You/The Magic Of Love	7
60	Decca F 21223	Princess/I Love You	7
60	Decca F 21247	Teddy Girl/Kiss Me, Kiss Me	10
66	Durium DRS 54008	Let Her Go/What Did I Do	8
67	Durium DRS 54012	Long Is The Lonely Night/People Talk To Me About You (as Little Tony)	8
58	Durium U 20058	PRESENTING LITTLE TONY AND HIS BROTHERS (EP)	50
65	Durium DRL 50006	I SUCCESSI DI LITTLE TONY (LP)	30
66	Durium DRL 50020	LET HER GO (LP)	25

LITTLE WALTER

60	London HLM 9175	My Babe/Blue Midnight	25
64	Pye International 7N 25263	My Babe/You Better Watch Yourself	12
56	London RE-U 1061	LITTLE WALTER AND HIS JUKES (EP)	150
64	Pye Intl. NPL 28043	LITTLE WALTER (LP)	30
67	Chess CRL 4529	SUPER BLUES (LP, with Bo Diddley & Muddy Waters)	30
68	Marble Arch MAL 815	LITTLE WALTER (LP, reissue)	12
69	Python PLP-KM 20	LITTLE WALTER AND HIS DUKES (LP, 99 copies only)	35
71	Syndicate Chapter SC 004	THUNDERBIRD (LP)	15

LITTLE WILBUR (& PLEASERS)

57	Vogue V 9091	Plaything/I Don't Care	450
57	Vogue V 9091	Plaything/I Don't Care (78)	90
58	Vogue V 9097	Heart To Heart/Alone In The Night (solo)	650
58	Vogue V 9097	Heart To Heart/Alone In The Night (solo) (78)	100

(see also Wilbur Whitfield)

LITTLE WILLIE (Francis)

| 63 | Blue Beat BB 151 | Settle Down/I'm Ashamed | 15 |

(see also Wilbert Francis & Vibrators)

LIVELY ONES

| 63 | London HA 8082 | SURF DRUMS (LP) | 40 |
| 63 | London HA/SH 8107 | SURF RIDER (LP, mono/stereo) | 35/45 |

LIVELY SET

| 65 | Pye 7N 15880 | Don't Call My Name/What Kind Of Love | 4 |
| 66 | Capitol CL 15472 | Let The Trumpets Sound/The Green Years | 4 |

LIVERPOOL FISHERMEN

| 71 | Mushroom 150 MR 9 | SWALLOW THE ANCHOR (LP) | 100 |

LIVERPOOL SCENE

68	RCA RCA 1762	Son Son/Baby	5
69	RCA RCA 1816	The Woo-Woo/Love Is	5
67	CBS 63045	THE INCREDIBLE NEW LIVERPOOL SCENE (LP)	20
68	RCA SF 7995	THE AMAZING ADVENTURES OF THE LIVERPOOL SCENE (LP)	15
69	RCA SF 8057	BREAD ON THE NIGHT (LP)	15
70	RCA SF 8100	ST. ADRIAN AND CO. BROADWAY & 3RD (LP)	15
70	RCA SF 8134	HEIRLOON (LP)	15
72	Charisma CS 3	RECOLLECTIONS (LP)	12

(see also Clayton Squares, Adrian Henri, Brian Patten, Mike Hart, Andy Roberts, Grimms)

LIVERPOOL SPINNERS
61   Topic TOP 69   SONGS SPUN IN LIVERPOOL (EP) 10
(see also Spinners [U.K.])

LIVERPOOL SUBGENII
98   Regal Stang 023   He Sets NheeGhee On Us/Living La Vida Boba (5-D foldout p/s). 25

RICKY LIVID & TONE DEAFS
64   Parlophone R 5136   Tomorrow/Nuts And Bolts 10
(see also Bill Oddie)

LIVING DAYLIGHTS
67   Philips BF 1561   Let's Live For Today/I'm Real (B-side actually titled "It's Real"). 18
67   Philips BF 1613   Always With Him/Baila Maria 25
(see also Greatest Show On Earth, Naturals)

LIVING DAYLIGHTS
79   E.S.R. S/79/CUS 523   HEARTSTOP EP (Personality Changes/Outdoor Girl/Don't Fit/Let Me Know
                                     (33¹/₃, die-cut p/s, also listed as ESR 3) 70

LIVING IN TEXAS
82   Rhythmic RMNS 2   And David Cried/And Dem Bahnhoff (fold-out photocopied p/s). 5
(see also Stephan Munson & Friends)

LIZA & JET SET
65   Parlophone R 5248   How Can I Know?/Dancing Yet 10
(see also Liza Strike, Jet Set)

LIZZIE & DELROY WILSON
71   Jackpot JP 771   Double Attack/AGGRAVATORS: The Sniper 6

LIZZY
70   Harry J HJ 6625   More Heartaches/HARRY J ALL STARS: Version 6
70   Pressure Beat PB 5508   Ten Feet Tall (actually "Wear You From The Ball"/JOE GIBBS & DESTROYERS:
                                     Chapter (actually "Harmony Hall" by Mr Nigel) 6
73   Duke DU 161   Love Is A Treasure/FREDDIE McKAY: Love Is A Treasure. 7

LIZZY & DENNIS (Alcapone)
70   Ackee ACK 114   Happy Go Lucky Girl/BOBBY & DAVE: Sammy 8

LIZZY & PARAGONS
71   Ackee ACK 118   On The Beach/DAVE BARKER: Maria 12

LLAN
66   CBS 202405   Realise/Anytime 25
(see also Vogues)

BARRY LLEWELLYN
73   Downtown DT 515   Meaning Of Life/MORWELL ESQ: Version Of Life. 8
(see also Heptones, Sound Dimension)

A.L. LLOYD
53   HMV B 10593   The Shooting Of His Dear/Lord Bateman (78). 8
53   HMV B 10594   Down In The Forest/The Bitter Withy (78) 8
60   Topic 12T 51   OUTBACK BALLADS (LP, blue label). 35
65   Topic 12T 135   BIRD IN THE BUSH
                                     (LP, with Anne Briggs & Frankie Armstrong, blue label) 50
66   Topic 12T 118   FIRST PERSON (LP, blue label) 25
67   Topic 12T 174   LEVIATHAN! (LP, blue label with booklet) 25
(see also Frankie Armstrong, Anne Briggs)

A.L. LLOYD & MARTYN WYNDHAM-READ
71   Topic 12TS 203   THE GREAT AUSTRALIAN LEGEND
                                     (LP, blue label with booklet). 60
(see also Ewan MacColl, Peggy Seeger, Martin Wyndham-Read)

CHARLES LLOYD (QUARTET)
67   Atlantic 584 125   Sombrero Sam (Parts 1 & 2) 6
67   Atlantic 587/588 077   LOVE-IN (LP) 15
68   Atlantic 587/588 101   JOURNEY WITHIN (LP). 15
68   Atlantic 588 108   IN EUROPE (LP) 12
71   Atlantic 2400 108   IN THE SOVIET UNION (LP) 10

FRED LLOYD
65   Polydor BM 56055   Girl From Chelsea/You Kissed Him 4

JERRY LLOYD
60   Top Rank JAR 411   Be Faithful, Be True/Sooner Or Later. 6

JIMMY LLOYD
58   Philips PB 827   Witch Doctor/For Your Love. 8
58   Philips PB 827   Witch Doctor/For Your Love (78) 8
58   Philips PB 871   The End/Street In The Rain 6
58   Philips PB 871   The End/Street In The Rain (78) 10
59   Philips PB 909   I Kneel At Your Throne/Sapphire 6
59   Philips PB 909   I Kneel At Your Throne/Sapphire (78) 15
60   Philips PB 1010   Teenage Sonata/Falling 7
60   Philips PB 1055   I Double Dare You/Just For A Thrill 6
61   Philips PB 1120   Pony Time/Three Handed Woman 6
61   Philips PB 1157   Yellow Bird/Without The Sun 6
61   Philips PB 1201   I'm Coming Home/You Are My Sunshine 6
62   Philips 326 527 BF   True Love/Mother Nature And Father Time 5
63   Philips 326 568 BF   Call On Me/Humma Humma Humma Humming Bird 6
59   Philips BBE 12186   FOCUS ON JIMMY LLOYD (EP) 12
62   Philips BBE 12509   YOU ARE MY SUNSHINE (EP). 12
(see also Jimmy Logsdon)

KATHY LLOYD

54	Decca F 10386	It Worries Me/Tomorrow Night	7
54	Decca F 10418	Teach Me Tonight/It's A Woman's World	7
55	Decca F 10464	Our Future Has Only Begun/Unsuspecting Heart	7
55	Decca F 10567	Experience Unnecessary/This Must Be Wrong (with Ted Heath Music)	6

PEGGY LLOYD

55	London RE-P 1017	DIXIELAND HONKY-TONK (EP, with Bill Stegmeyer & His Orchestra)	18

RUE LLOYD

72	Green Door GD 4033	Loving You/Version	6
72	Green Door GD 4036	Cheer Up/Version	6
	(see also Joe White)		

TREVOR LLOYD

70	Explosion EX 2018	Chinee Brush/DICE & CUMMIE: Real Colley	7
70	Explosion EX 2019	Give Me Back Your Love/Hold Me	7

LLOYD & BARBARA

73	Grape GR 3045	Dear Lonely Hearts/LLOYD BANTAM: I Tried To Love You	4

LLOYD & CAREY WITH G.G. ALL STARS

72	Attack ATT 8029	Scorpion/MAYTONES: Hands And Feet	7
	(see also Carey & Lloyd, Pat Satchmo)		

LLOYD & CLAUDETTE

70	Big Shot BI 546	Queen Of The World/PROPHETS: Top Of The World	10

LLOYD (Robinson) & DEVON (Russell)

67	Punch PH 14	Love Is The Key/VIRTUES: High Tide	6
69	Blue Cat BS 151	Out Of The Fire/Can't Understand (B-side actually by Austin Faithful)	12
	(see also Cobbs, Derrick Morgan)		

LLOYD & DOREEN

71	Jackpot JP 762	Midnight/BUNNY LEE'S ALL STARS: Midnight — Version	6
	(see also Lloyd Clarke/Doreen Shaeffer)		

LLOYD (Robinson) & GLEN (Brown)

67	Coxsone CS 7011	That Girl/You Got Me Wrong	18
67	Doctor Bird DB 1058	Jezebel/TOMMY McCOOK & SUPERSONICS: Jam Session	18
67	Doctor Bird DB 1071	Keep On Pushing/BOBBY AITKEN & CARIBBEATS: You Won't Regret (B-side actually by Lloyd & Glen)	18

LLOYD (Jackson) & GROOVERS

67	Caltone TONE 108	Do It To Me Baby/DIPLOMATS: Meet Me At The Corner	12
68	Caltone TONE 109	My Heart My Soul/DIPLOMATS with TOMMY McCOOK & SUPERSONICS: Going Along	12
68	Caltone TONE 112	Listen To The Music/DIPLOMATS: Strong Man	12
	(see also Groovers, Don Lett, Tony Lee)		

LLOYD & JOHNNY

68	Island WI 3158	My Argument (actually by Lloyd Terrell)/JOHNNY MELODY: Foey Man (actually by George Dekker)	20
	(see also Lloyd Terrell)		

LLOYD & JOY

71	Explosion EX 2047	Back To Africa (actually by Alton Ellis)/Born To Lose	10

LLOYD & KEN

72	Punch PH 110	Have I Sinned/Version	5
	(see also Lloyd Charmers/Ken Boothe)		

LLOYD & LARRY

70s	New Beat NB 080	Monkey Spanner/LLOYD & LARRY'S ALL STARS: Version	4

LLOYD & THE PROPHETS

70	Big Shot BI 553	Bush Beat/PATRICK & PROPHETS: Please Come Come	8
70	Big Shot BI 556	Jaco/Soul Reggae	8
	(see also Prophets [Jamaica], Patrick & Lloyd)		

LLOYD, DICE & HIS MUM

70	Joe JRS 5	Trial Of Pama Dice/NYAH SHUFFLE: Jughead Returns Version 1	8

LLOYD, DICE & THE BARRISTER

70	Joe JRS 14	Appeal Of Pama Dice/BOSS ALL STARS: Young And Strong Version 2	8

LLOYD'S ALLSTARS

69	Doctor Bird DB 1178	Love Kiss Blue/UNIQUES: Secretly	30
	(see also Justins, U Roy Junior, Jimmy Green, Victors)		

LLOYDIE & LOWBITES

73	Harry J HJ 6660	Pussy Cat/Skanky Pussy	5
71	Lowbite LOW 001	CENSORED! (LP)	18
	(see also Lloyd Tyrell/Charmers)		

LLOYD (Campbell) THE MATADOR

72	Sioux SI 010	The Train/Julia Sees Me (Exodus)	8

LLYGOD FFYRNIG

78	Pwdwr PWDWR 1	N.C.B./Sais/Cariad Y Bus Stop (p/s)	60

LOADED FORTY-FOURS

81	X-S TL 44/1	Thunderbirds (Are Go!)/T.V. Child (p/s)	4

DICKIE LOADER

61	Palette PG 9015	Heatwave/Happiness	15

RUSS LOADER

65	Columbia DB 7522	When Your Heart Is Broken/That Girl Of Mine (with Breakaways Orchestra)	7
65	Columbia DB 7643	Just Lies/Mona Lisa	6
65	Columbia DB 7696	Count The Stars/Triyng Too Hard (with Ladybirds)	8
66	Columbia DB 7839	Too Soon/Just A Little Step To Heaven	6
69	Conquest CXT 2	Just Lies/Take Me Tonight	5

(see also Mark Wirtz)

LOBO

71	Philips 6073 802	She Didn't Do Magic/I'm The Only One	4
71	Philips 6073 804	California Kid And Remo/A Little Different	4
77	Power Exchange PX 243	It's Everywhere/Someone To Love	5
77	Power Exchange PX 258	At First Sight/One More Time	6
79	MCA MCA 523	Where Were You When I Was Falling In Love/ I Don't Wanna Make Love Anymore	5
83	Young Blood Int. LOBO 1	I Don't Want To Want You/Come Looking For Me	6
71	Philips 6369 800	INTRODUCING LOBO (LP)	10
75	Philips 6369 806	A COWBOY AFRAID OF HORSES (LP)	12
77	Power Exchange PXL 014	COME WITH ME (LP)	12

JOSEF LOCKE

53	Columbia SCM 5008	My Heart And I/Goodbye	10
53	Columbia SCM 5009	Hear My Song, Violetta/The Soldier's Dream	10
92	EMI 78EM 231	Hear My Song, Violetta/Charmaine, Count Your Blessings/Goodbye (12" 78)	8

LOCKETS

63	Pye International 7N 25232	Don't Cha Know/Little Boy	10

LOCKJAW

77	Raw RAW 8	Radio Call Sign/The Young Ones (p/s)	10
78	Raw RAW 19	Journalist Jive/I'm A Virgin/A Doonga Doonga (p/s)	15

(see also Cure)

HANK LOCKLIN

60	RCA RCA 1188	Please Help Me, I'm Falling/My Old Home Town	6
60	RCA RCA 1188	Please Help Me, I'm Falling/My Old Home Town (78)	50
61	RCA RCA 1252	You're The Reason/Happy Birthday To Me	6
62	RCA RCA 1273	From Here To There To You/This Song Is Just for You	6
62	RCA RCA 1305	We're Gonna Go Fishin'/Welcome Home, Mr. Blues	6
63	RCA RCA 1336	Flyin' South/Behind The Footlights	5
63	RCA RCA 1370	Wooden Soldier/Kiss On The Door	5
64	RCA RCA 1391	You Never Want To Love Me/Followed Closely By My Teardrops	5
65	RCA RCA 1458	Faith And Truth/Forty Nine, Fifty One	5
66	RCA RCA 1510	I Feel A Cry Coming On/Insurance	5
66	RCA RCA 1548	The Last Thing On My Mind/The Best Part Of Loving You	5
67	RCA RCA 1575	It Is Love/The Upper Room	5
67	RCA RCA 1610	Wishing On A Star/Hasta Luego	5
67	RCA RCA 1641	The Country Hall Of Fame/Evergreen	5
68	RCA RCA 1678	Love Song For You/Little Geisha Girl	5
68	RCA RCA 1729	Everlasting Love/I'm Slowly Going Out Of Your Mind	5
58	RCA RCX 115	COUNTRY GUITAR VOL. 3 (EP)	15
62	RCA RCX 217	SEVEN DAYS (EP)	15
63	Parlophone GEP 8875	ENCORES (EP)	20
63	RCA RCX 7116	WALTZ OF THE WIND (EP)	15
64	RCA RCX 7150	IRISH SONGS COUNTRY STYLE (EP)	15
61	RCA RD 27201	PLEASE HELP ME, I'M FALLING (LP)	22
64	RCA RD 7623	IRISH SONGS COUNTRY STYLE (LP)	15
65	Fontana FJL 305	BORN TO RAMBLE (LP)	12

GERRY LOCKRAN

69	Decca F 12873	Hey Jude/This Train	5
69	Decca F 12919	Standing On Your Own/You're Not There	5
67	Planet PLL 1002	HOLD ON, I'M COMING (LP)	70
68	Waverley ZLP 2091	BLUES VENDETTA (LP)	30
69	Saga FID 2165	BLUES AT SUNRISE (LP)	15
69	Spark SRLP 104	THE ESSENTIAL GERRY LOCKRAN (LP)	18
72	Polydor 2383 122	WUN (LP)	10
76	Decca SKL-R 5257	RAGS TO GLADRAGS (LP)	10

GERRY LOCKRAN, REDD SULLIVAN, DAVE TRAVIS

69	Fidelity FID 2165	BLUES AT SUNRISE (LP)	15

ANNA LOCKWOOD

70	Tangent TGS 104	GLASS WORLD OF (LP)	20

MALCOLM LOCKYER ORCHESTRA

54	Decca F 10304	I'm Gonna Rock, Rock, Rock/Changing Partners (78, as Malcolm Lockyer & His Strict Tempo Music For Dancing)	5
61	HMV POP 929	"The Pursuers" T.V. Theme/Stranger Than Fiction	6
65	Columbia DB 7552	The Intelligence Men/Brighton Run	5
65	Columbia DB 7663	The Eccentric Dr. Who/Daleks And Thals	35
75	Contour 2870 439	TOP TV THEMES (LP)	10

LOCOMOTIVE

67	Direction 58-3814	Rudy A Message To You/Broken Heart	8
68	Parlophone R 5718	Rudi's In Love/Never Set Me Free	7
69	Parlophone R 5758	Mr. Armageddon/There's Got To Be A Way (some in promos p/s)	25/8
69	Parlophone R 5801	I'm Never Gonna Let You Go/You Must Be Joking	10
70	Parlophone R 5835	Movin' Down The Line/Roll Over Mary	8
71	Parlophone R 5915	Rudi's In Love/You Must Be Joking	5
69	Parlophone PCS 7093	WE ARE EVERYTHING YOU SEE (LP)	140

(see also Norman Haines Band, Dog That Bit People, Steam-Shovel)

LARRY LOEBER
84	Numa NU 2	Shivers Up My Spine/Vibrations Of The Night (p/s)	4

NILS LOFGREN
76	CBS 4339	Soft Fun/Slippery Fingers (actually by Grin)	5
79	A&M AMS 7455	Shine Silently/Kool Skool (p/s, coloured or black vinyl)	5

(see also Grin, Crazy Horse, Bruce Springsteen)

LOFT
84	Creation CRE 009	Why Does The Rain/Like (foldaround p/s in poly bag)	10
85	Creation CRE 015	Up The Hill And Down The Slope/Lonely Street (foldaround p/s in poly bag)	7

(see also Weather Prophets, Caretaker Race, Wishing Stones)

CRIPPLE CLARENCE LOFTON
59	Vogue EPV 1209	CRIPPLE CLARENCE LOFTON (EP)	50
54	London AL 3531	A LOST RECORDING DATE (10" LP)	30
55	Vogue LDE 122	JAZZ IMMORTALS NO. 1 (10" LP)	30

JIMMY LOGSDON
54	Brunswick 05226	Pa-Paya Mama/In The Mission Of St. Augustine (78)	15

CHRISTOPHER LOGUE & TONY KINSEY
58	Parlophone GEP 8765	RED BIRD JAZZ AND POETRY (EP)	25

L.O.K.
79	Fetish FET 001	Fun House/Starlet Love/Tell Me (p/s)	7

LOLITA
60	Polydor NH 66818	Sailor (Your Home Is The Sea)/La Luna (Quanda La Luna)	6

LOLLIPOPS
71	Atlantic 2091 114	Nothing's Gonna Stop Our Love/I Believe In Love	6

LAURIE LOMAN
54	London HL 8101	Whither Thou Goest/I Was The Last One To Know	35
54	London HL 8101	Whither Thou Goest/I Was The Last One To Know (78)	12

ALAN LOMAX (& RAMBLERS)
56	Decca F 10787	Dirty Old Town/Hard Case (as Alan Lomax & Ramblers)	8
56	Decca DFE 6367	OH LULA (EP)	10
58	Pye Jazz NJE 1055	SINGS (EP, with Dave Lee's Bandits)	15
58	Pye Jazz NJE 1062	MURDERER'S HOME PT. 1 (EP)	15
58	Pye Jazz NJE 1063	MURDERER'S HOME PT. 2 (EP)	15
58	Pye Jazz NJE 1064	MURDERER'S HOME PT. 3 (EP)	15
58	Pye Jazz NJE 1065	MURDERER'S HOME PT. 4 (EP)	15
59	Melodisc EPM7 88	SONGS FROM TEXAS (EP)	12
57	Nixa Jazz NJL 8	PRESENTS BLUES IN THE MISSISSIPPI NIGHT (LP, with others)	15
57	Nixa Jazz NJL 11	MURDERER'S HOME (LP)	15
58	Pye Nixa NPL 18013	PRESENTS AMERICAN SONG TRAIN VOLUME ONE (LP)	15
58	HMV CLP 1192	GREAT AMERICAN BALLADS (LP, with Guy Carawan)	12

JACKIE LOMAX
68	CBS 2554	Genuine Imitation Life/One Minute Woman	7
68	Apple APPLE 3	Sour Milk Sea/The Eagle Laughs At You	10
69	Apple APPLE 11	New Day/I Fall Inside Your Eyes	15
70	Apple APPLE 23	How The Web Was Woven/Thumbin' A Ride (some in p/s)	15/6
69	Apple (S)APCOR 6	IS THIS WHAT YOU WANT (LP, with inner sleeve, mono/stereo)	50/30
91	Apple SAPCOR 6	IS THIS WHAT YOU WANT (LP, reissue, gatefold sleeve with bonus 12" [SAPCOR 62])	15

(see also Lomax Alliance, Undertakers, Takers, Heavy Jelly, Badger)

LOMAX ALLIANCE
67	CBS 2729	Try As You May/See The People	10

(see also Jackie Lomax)

GUY LOMBARDO (& ROYAL CANADIANS)
55	Brunswick 05372	No More/Pupalina	6
55	Brunswick 05412	Softly Softly/(I'm Always Hearing) Wedding Bells	6
55	Brunswick 05413	Hey, Mr. Banjo/Blue Mirage	6
55	Brunswick 05443	Cherry Pink And Apple Blossom White/Marty	7
56	Capitol CL 14585	Charleston Parisien/Rinka Tinka Man	7
57	Capitol CL 14774	Kling-A-Ling/Rainbow Of Love (78)	6
66	Ace Of Hearts AH 86	SWEETEST MUSIC THIS SIDE OF HEAVEN (LP)	12

AL LOMBARDY & HIS ORCHESTRA
54	London HL 8076	The Blues/The Boogie	35
54	London HL 8076	The Blues/The Boogie (78)	12
55	London HL 8127	In A Little Spanish Town/Flying Home	35
55	London HL 8127	In A Little Spanish Town/Flying Home (78)	12

LONDON
77	MCA MCA 305	Everyone's A Winner/Handcuffed (no p/s)	5
77	MCA MCA 319	SUMMER OF LOVE (EP, p/s)	6
77	MCA 12 MCA 319	SUMMER OF LOVE (12" EP, p/s)	10
77	MCA MCA 336	Animal Games/Us Kids Cold (no p/s)	5
78	MCA MCF 2823	ANIMAL GAMES (LP)	15

EDDIE LONDON & CHIMES
57	Decca F 10859	Song Of The Moonlight/I'll Thank You	6

FRANCO LONDON ORCHESTRA
66	Philips BF 1470	Theme From Robinson Crusoe/Adrift	15

JIMMY LONDON

71	Randy's RAN 514	Shake A Hand/CARL MURPHY: Lick I Pipe	6
71	Randy's RAN 517	Bridge Over Troubled Waters/RANDY'S ALLSTARS: War	6
71	Randy's RAN 518	Hip Hip Hooray/IMPACT ALLSTARS: Version	6
71	Randy's RAN 520	A Little Love/IMPACT ALLSTARS: Version	6
72	Randy's RAN 521	It's Now Or Never/IMPACT ALLSTARS: Version	6
72	Randy's RAN 527	Jamaica Festival '72 (with Rocking Horse)/IMPACT ALLSTARS: Version	5
73	Explosion EX 2080	I'll Never Find Another You/IMPACT ALLSTARS: Version	6
73	Dragon DRA 1010	Jennie/I Wonder If I Care As Much (as Jimmi London)	5
74	Dragon DRA 1019	No Letter Today/The Road Is Rough	5
74	Ackee ACK 531	Till I Kiss You/Version	5
72	Trojan TRL 39	BRIDGE OVER TROUBLED WATERS (LP)	12

(see also Jimmy Green, The Inspirations)

JOE LONDON

59	London HLW 9008	Lonesome Whistle/It Might Have Been	10
59	London HLW 9008	Lonesome Whistle/It Might Have Been (78)	20

JULIE LONDON

78s

56	London HLU 8240	Cry Me A River/S'Wonderful (78)	15
56	London HLU 8279	Baby, Baby All The Time/Shadow Woman (78)	15
57	London HLU 8394	The Meaning Of The Blues/Now! Baby, Now! (78)	15
57	London HLU 8414	The Boy On A Dolphin/Tall Boy (78)	15
58	London HLU 8602	Saddle The Wind/It Had To Be You (78)	15
58	London HLU 8657	My Strange Affair/It's Easy (78)	15
58	London HLU 8769	Man Of The West/Blue Moon (78)	20
59	London HLU 8891	Come On-A My House/Must Be Catchin' (78)	40

SINGLES

56	London HLU 8240	Cry Me A River/S'Wonderful (gold label print, later silver)	40/20
56	London HLU 8279	Baby, Baby All The Time/Shadow Woman (gold label print)	30
57	London HLU 8394	The Meaning Of The Blues/Now! Baby, Now! (gold label print, later silver)	25/15
57	London HLU 8414	The Boy On A Dolphin/Tall Boy	15
58	London HLU 8602	Saddle The Wind/It Had To Be You	12
58	London HLU 8657	My Strange Affair/It's Easy	12
58	London HLU 8769	Man Of The West/Blue Moon	12
59	London HLU 8891	Come On-A My House/Must Be Catchin'	15
61	London HLG 9360	Sanctuary/Every Chance I Get	7
63	Liberty LIB 10078	There'll Be Some Changes Made/Love On The Rocks	6
63	Liberty LIB 55605	I'm Coming Back To You/When Snowflakes Fall In The Summer	8
64	Liberty LIB 55666	I Want To Find Out For Myself/Guilty Heart	6
65	Liberty LIB 10189	Send For Me/Bye Bye Blackbird	6
65	Liberty LIB 10205	Charade/Wives And Lovers	6
67	Liberty LIB 10274	Girl Talk/The Mickey Mouse March	6
83	Edsel PE 5004	Cry Me A River/February Brings The Rain (picture disc)	5

EPs

57	London RE-U 1076	JULIE SINGS FILM SONGS (EP, gold label print)	18
57	London RE-N 1092	LONDON'S GIRL FRIENDS VOL. 1 (EP)	18
58	London RE-U 1151	MAKE LOVE TO ME — PART ONE (EP)	18
58	London RE-U 1152	MAKE LOVE TO ME — PART TWO (EP)	18
58	London RE-U 1153	MAKE LOVE TO ME — PART THREE (EP)	18
59	London RE-U 1180	JULIE — PART ONE (EP)	15
59	London RE-U 1181	JULIE — PART TWO (EP)	15
59	London RE-U 1182	JULIE — PART THREE (EP)	15
63	Liberty LEP 2103	DESAFINADO (EP)	15
66	Liberty LEP 2260	ALL THROUGH THE NIGHT (EP)	15

LPs

56	London HA-U 2005	JULIE IS HER NAME (LP)	35
57	London HA-U 2038	CALENDAR GIRL (LP)	30
58	London HA-U 2083	MAKE LOVE TO ME (LP)	30
58	London HA-U 2091	ABOUT THE BLUES (LP)	30
58	London HA-U 2112	JULIE (LP)	30
59	London HA-U 2171	LONDON BY NIGHT (LP)	25
59	London HA-U 2186	JULIE IS HER NAME VOL. 2 (LP, also stereo SAH-U 6042)	25/35
60	London HA-W 2225	SWING ME AN OLD SONG (LP)	25
60	London HA-W 2229	YOUR NUMBER PLEASE (LP)	25
60	London HA-G 2280	JULIE AT HOME (LP, also stereo SAH-G 6097)	25/35
61	London HA-G 2299	AROUND MIDNIGHT (LP)	25
61	London HA-G 2353	SEND FOR ME (LP, also stereo SAH-G 6154)	25/35
62	London HA-G 2405	WHATEVER JULIE WANTS (LP, also stereo SAH-G 6205)	25/35
62	Liberty LBY 1023	THE BEST OF JULIE LONDON (LP)	15
62	Liberty (S)LBY 1083	LOVE LETTERS (LP)	18
63	Liberty (S)LBY 1113	LOVE ON THE ROCKS (LP)	18
63	Liberty (S)LBY 1136	SINGS LATIN IN A SATIN MOOD (LP)	18
64	Liberty (S)LBY 1185	THE WONDERFUL WORLD OF JULIE LONDON (LP)	18
65	Liberty LBY 1222	IN PERSON AT THE AMERICANA (LP)	18
65	Liberty (S)LBY 1251	OUR FAIR LADY (LP)	18
66	Liberty (S)LBY 1281	FEELING GOOD (LP, with Gerald Wilson Big Band)	18
66	Liberty (S)LBY 1300	ALL THROUGH THE NIGHT (LP)	18
67	Liberty (S)LBY 1334	FOR THE NIGHT PEOPLE (LP)	18
67	Liberty (S)LBY 1364	NICE GIRLS DON'T STAY FOR BREAKFAST (LP)	18
68	Liberty LBL/LBS 83049	GREAT PERFORMANCES (LP)	15
69	Liberty LBL/LBS 83183E	YUMMY, YUMMY, YUMMY (LP)	15

LAURIE LONDON

57	Parlophone R 4359	He's Got The Whole World In His Hands/The Cradle Rock	6
57	Parlophone R 4388	Handed Down/She Sells Sea Shells	6

MINT VALUE £

58	Parlophone R 4408	The Gospel Train/Boomerang	7
58	Parlophone R 4408	The Gospel Train/Boomerang (78)	8
58	Parlophone R 4426	I Gotta Robe/Casey Jones	6
58	Parlophone R 4426	I Gotta Robe/Casey Jones (78)	8
58	Parlophone R 4450	Basin Street Blues/Joshua (Fit The Battle Of Jericho)	6
58	Parlophone R 4450	Basin Street Blues/Joshua (Fit The Battle Of Jericho) (78)	8
58	Parlophone R 4474	My Mother/Darktown Strutters' Ball	6
58	Parlophone R 4474	My Mother/Darktown Strutters' Ball (78)	8
58	Parlophone R 4499	Up Above My Head/Three O'Clock	6
58	Parlophone R 4499	Up Above My Head/Three O'Clock (78)	12
59	Parlophone R 4557	Pretty-Eyed Baby (with Gitte)/Boom-Ladda-Boom-Boom	8
59	Parlophone R 4557	Pretty-Eyed Baby (with Gitte)/Boom-Ladda-Boom-Boom (78)	18
59	Parlophone R 4601	Old Time Religion/God's Little Acre	5
60	Parlophone R 4635	I'm Afraid/Roll On Spring	5
60	Parlophone R 4662	Hear Them Bells/Banjo Boy	5
61	Parlophone R 4747	Today's Teardrops/Darling Sue	5
61	Parlophone R 4801	Down By The Riverside/I'll Make Her Forget Him	5
67	CBS 202461	The Bells Of St. Mary's/Sad Songs	5
57	Parlophone GEP 8664	LAURIE LONDON (EP)	30
58	Parlophone GEP 8689	LITTLE LAURIE LONDON No. 2 (EP)	30

MARK LONDON
65	Pye 7N 15825	Stranger In The World/Moanin'.	10

MICHAEL LONDON
62	HMV POP 1026	Miracles Sometimes Happen/Stranger On The Shore (with Acker Bilk)	6
62	HMV POP 1085	Mutiny On The Bounty Love Song/For The Very Young	6

PETER LONDON
65	Pye 7N 15957	Bless You/Baby I Like The Look Of You	35

(see also Peter Cook)

LONDON & BRIDGES
66	CBS 202056	It Just Ain't Right/Leave Her Alone	25

LONDON BALALAIKA ENSEMBLE
68	Deram DML/SML 712	LONDON BALALAIKA ENSEMBLE (LP)	15

LONDON COWBOYS
83	Flicknife FLS 217	Street Full Of Soul/Let's Go Crazy (p/s)	4

LONDON JAZZ CHAMBER GROUP
72	Ember CJS 823	ADAM'S RIB SUITE (LP).	20

(see also Ken Moule's London Jazz Chamber Group, Ken Moule Seven)

LONDON JAZZ FOUR
67	Polydor 56214	It Strikes A Chord/Song For Hilary	20
67	Polydor 582 005	TAKE A NEW LOOK AT THE BEATLES (LP)	60

(see also London Jazz Quartet)

LONDON JAZZ QUARTET
66	Polydor 56092	Norwegian Wood/I Feel Fine	5
60	Tempo TAP 28	LONDON JAZZ QUARTET (LP, with Tubby Hayes & Tony Crombie)	500
60s	Ember EMB 3306	LONDON JAZZ QUARTET (LP)	200

(see also London Jazz Four, Tubby Hayes, Tony Crombie)

LONDON POPS ORCHESTRA
68	Pye 7N 17630	Eleanor Rigby/If I Only Had Time	4

LONDON PX
82	New Puritan NP 1	Orders/Eviction (p/s)	20
82	Terrapin SYD 1	Arnold Layne/Indian Summer (1-sided flexidisc)	15

LONDON STUDIO GROUP
66	De Wolfe DW/LP 2974	THE WILD ONE (10" LP, tricolour label)	25

(see also Ivor & Basil Kirchen Band)

LONDON SYMPHONY ORCHESTRA
77	20th Century BTC 2345	Star Wars (Main Title)/Cantina Band	4
72	Ode SP 88001	TOMMY (2-LP box set)	15

LONDON UNDERGROUND
81	Situation 2 SIT 9	Train Of Thought/All Too Many (p/s)	6
82	On-U Sound ON-U 3	Between The Lines/Rise And Fall (p/s)	4
82	On-U Sound ON-U 4	WATCHING WEST INDIANS IN THE COLD (10" EP)	6
83	On-U Sound ON-U 5	STRANGE (10" EP)	6

LONDON WAITS
66	Immediate IM 030	Softly Softly/Serenadio	15

LONDON ZOO
80	Gramaphone STB 80	Who's Driving This Car?/You And Your Great Ideas (stamped white labels, no p/s)	6
80	Zoom ZUM 12	Receiving End/London Zoo (p/s)	4

JOHNNY LONESOME
61	HMV POP 837	Marie Marie/Doctor Heartache	6

LONESOME PINE FIDDLERS
64	London HA-B 8143	MORE BLUEGRASS (LP)	15

LONESOME STONE
73	Reflection RL 306	LONESOME STONE (LP, stage production recording)	20

(see also Sheep)

MINT VALUE £

LONESOME SUNDOWN
71	Blue Horizon 7-63864	LONESOME LONELY BLUES (LP)	60
70s	Flyright LP 529	BOUGHT ME A TICKET (LP)	12
70s	Flyright LP 587	LONESOME WHISTLER (LP)	12

LONESOME TRAVELLERS
70s	Nebula NEB 100	THE LOST CHILDREN (LP)	15

LONE WOLF
80s	Neat NEAT 44	NOBODY'S MOVE (12" EP, p/s)	12

FITZROY D. LONG & BUSTER ALL STARS
68	Fab FAB 32	Get A New Girl/BUSTER'S ALL STARS: Come And Do It With Me	10

(see also Larry Marshall)

JOHNNY LONG ORCHESTRA
55	Parlophone MSP 6176	Silver Dollar/We'll Build A Bungalow	7

SHORTY LONG
65	Tamla Motown TMG 512	Out To Get You/It's A Crying Shame	60
66	Tamla Motown TMG 573	Function At The Junction/Call On Me (narrow print, later with wider print)	18
67	Tamla Motown TMG 600	Chantilly Lace/Your Love Is Amazing (narrow print, later with wider print)	10
68	Tamla Motown TMG 644	Night Fo' Last (Vocal)/Night Fo' Last (Instrumental)	7
68	Tamla Motown TMG 663	Here Comes The Judge/Sing What You Wanna	8
68	T. Motown (S)TML 11086	HERE COMES THE JUDGE (LP)	30
70	T. Motown STML 11144	THE PRIME OF SHORTY LONG (LP)	25

(see also Art Mooney)

LONG & SHORT
64	Decca F 11964	The Letter/Love Is A Funny Thing	18
64	Decca F 12043	Choc Ice/Here Comes The Fool	18

LONGBOATMEN
66	Polydor 56115	Take Her Any Time/Only In Her Home Town	250

LONG COLD STARE
90	Rise Above RISE 3	TIRED EYES (LP)	10

LONGDANCER
73	Rocket PIG 1	If It Was So Simple/Silent Emotions	5
74	Rocket PIG 11	Puppet Man/Cold Love	4
73	Rocket PIGL 1	IF IT WAS SO SIMPLE (LP, gatefold sleeve)	10
74	Rocket PIGL 6	TRAILER FOR A GOOD LIFE (LP, die-cut gatefold sleeve)	10

(see also Tourists, Eurythmics, Dave Stewart & Harrison)

CLAUDINE LONGET
67	A&M AMS 708	Good Day Sunshine/The Look Of Love	4

LONG HELLO
73	private pressing	THE LONG HELLO (LP, mail-order only, numbered white sleeve)	15

(see also Van Der Graaf Generator)

LONG TALL SHORTY
79	Warner Bros K 17491	By Your Love/1970's Boy (p/s, withdrawn)	25
81	Dr Creation LYN 9904	If I Was You/That's What I Want (flexidisc)	8
81	Ramkup CAC 007	Win Or Lose/Ain't Done Wrong (p/s)	35
85	Diamond DIA 002	On The Streets Again/I Fought The Law/Promises (p/s, some with poster)	12/6
86	Diamond DIA 005	What's Going On/Steppin' Stone/Win Or Lose/England (p/s)	8
88	no label or cat. no.	ROCKIN' AT THE SAVOY (LP, official bootleg, some with poster)	12/10

(see also Joe Public, Rage, Case, Charlie Harper)

LOOP
87	Head HEAD 5	16 Dreams/Head On/Burning World (12", p/s)	7
87	Head HEAD 7L	Spinning (Parts 1 & 2) (large centre, plain black die-cut sleeve)	4
87	Head HEAD 7	Spinning/Deep Hit/I'll Take You There (12", p/s)	7
88	Chapter 22 CHAPLLP 34	FADE OUT (LP, 2 x 45rpm 12", gold stickered gatefold sleeve, some signed)	15/10
90	Situation 2 SITU 27	A GILDED ETERNITY (LP, as 2 x 45rpm 12" with free 7" [Shot With A Diamond/The Nail Will Burn (Burn Out), no p/s] & foldaround sticker)	10

LOOSE ENDS
66	Decca F 12437	Send The People Away/I Ain't Gonna Eat My Heart Out Anymore	15
66	Decca F 12476	Taxman/That's It	15

LOOT
66	Page One POF 013	Baby Come Closer/Baby	8
67	Page One POF 026	I've Just Gotta Love You/You Need Someone To Love	15
67	CBS 2938	Whenever You're Ready/I Got What You Want	12
68	Page One POF 095	She's A Winner/Radio City (withdrawn B-side)	25
68	Page One POF 095	She's A Winner/Save Me	18
68	CBS 3231	Don't Turn Around/You Are My Sunshine Girl	8
69	Page One POF 115	Try To Keep It A Secret/Radio City	25

(see also Soul Agents, Hookfoot)

LINDA LOPEZ MAMBO ORCHESTRA
55	Parlophone MSP 6179	Limehouse Blues Mambo/Nursery Mambo	6

TRINI LOPEZ
63	London HL 9808	Jeanie Marie/Love Me Tonight	8
63	Reprise R 20198	If I Had A Hammer/Unchain My Heart	5
63	Reprise R 20236	Kansas City/Lonesome Traveller	5
63	Reprise R 20260	Jailer Bring Me Water/You Can't Say Goodbye	5
63	Reprise R 20276	Ya Ya/What Have I Got Of My Own	5
65	Reprise R 20238	Sad Tomorrows/I've Lost My Love For You	5
66	Reprise R 20455	I'm Coming Home Cindy/The 32nd Of May	5
66	Reprise R 20480	La Bamba/Trini's Tune	5
72	Reprise K 14205	America/If I Had A Hammer (p/s)	5

63	Reprise R(9) 6093	LOPEZ AT P.J.'s (LP, mono/stereo)	12
64	London HA 8132	TEENAGE LOVE SONGS (LP)	30
64	London HA 8160	MORE OF TRINI LOPEZ (LP)	25

DENISE LOR
54	Parlophone MSP 6120	If I Give My Heart To You/Hallo Darling	10
55	Parlophone MSP 6148	Every Day Of My Life/And One To Grow On	8

KENNY LORAN
59	Capitol CL 15081	Mama's Little Baby/Magic Star	35

L'ORANGE MECHANIK
86	Art Pop POP 44	Symphony/Intermezzo (Sprechstimme)/Scherzo (p/s)	12

(see also Times)

BOBBY LORD
64	Hickory 45-1232	Life Can Have Meaning/Pickin' White Gold	6
64	Hickory 45-1259	Take The Bucket To The Well/A Man Needs A Woman	6
65	Hickory 45-1310	That Room In The Corner Of The House/I'm Going Home Next Summer	6

BOBBY LORD/BOB LUMAN
64	Hickory LPE 1501	HICKORY SHOWCASE VOL. 2 (EP, 1 side each)	20
64	Hickory LPE 1504	HICKORY SHOWCASE VOL. 3 (EP, 1 side each)	20
64	Hickory LPM 121	CAN'T TAKE THE COUNTRY FROM THE BOYS (LP, 1 side each)	15

(see also Bob Luman)

JON LORD
76	Purple PUR 131	Bourée/Aria	7
82	Harvest HAR 5220	Bach Onto This/Going Home (p/s)	6
71	Purple TPSA 7501	GEMINI SUITE (LP)	15
74	Purple TPSA 7513	WINDOWS (LP)	15
76	Purple TPSA 7516	SARABANDE (LP, die-cut sleeve)	15
82	Harvest SHSP 4123	BEFORE I FORGET (LP)	12

(see also Artwoods, Deep Purple, [Paice] Ashton & Lord, Bernie Marsden, Wizard's Convention, Episode Six, Leading Figures, Whitesnake, Cozy Powell)

TONY LORD
66	Planet PLF 102	World's Champion/It Makes Me Sad (with Planet company sleeve)	20/15

JERRY LORDAN
59	Parlophone R 4588	I'll Stay Single/Can We Kiss	8
60	Parlophone R 4627	Who Could Be Bluer?/Do I Worry?	8
60	Parlophone R 4653	Sing Like An Angel/Ev'ry Time	8
60	Parlophone R 4695	Ring, Write Or Call/I've Still Got You	10
61	Parlophone R 4748	You Came A Long Way From St. Louis/Let's Try Again	10
62	Parlophone R 4903	One Good Solid 24 Carat Reason/Second Hand Dress	10
70	CBS 5057	The Old Man And The Sea/Harlequin Melodies	12
61	Parlophone PMC 1133	ALL MY OWN WORK (LP, also stereo PCS 3014)	75/100

(see also Lee & Jay Elvin)

LORD BEGINNER
50	Melodisc 1131	Joe Louis Calypso/Trinidad Blues (78)	10
50	Melodisc 1133	Victory Test Match — Calypso/Sergeant Brown (78)	10
50	Melodisc 1134	Straight Hair Girl/Calinda (78)	10
51	Melodisc 1164	Gold Coast Victory/Family Scandal (78)	10
51	Melodisc 1167	Family Scandal/Gold Coast Champion (78)	12
51	Melodisc 1183	Jamaica Hurricane/Pretty Woman (78)	10
51	Melodisc 1193	John Goddard Calypso/Some Girl (78)	10
51	Parlophone MP 112	Federation/Rum, More Rum (78, export)	12
51	Melodisc 1211	Australia V. West Indies/One Morning (78)	10
51	Esquire 5-034	Randolph Turpin's Victory/West Indians And The Steel Band (78, with Kenny Graham's Afro-Cubists)	15
51	Esquire 5-041	Fifty Women To One Man/1951 Festival Of Britain (78, with Kenny Graham's Afro-Cubists)	15
53	Esquire 5-091	England Regains The Ashes/Nobody Wants To Grow Old (78)	15
54	Melodisc 1333	Sir Winston Churchill Calypso/Rhythm Dance (78)	15
54	Melodisc 1334	She Walks Like You/Tambourine (78)	12
60s	Melodisc CAL 1	Victory Test Match — Calypso/Sergeant Brown (reissue)	6

LORD BRISCO(E)
64	Black Swan WI 447	Spiritual Mambo/BABA BROOKS: Fly Right	20
64	Black Swan WI 450	My Love Has Come/BABA BROOKS: Sweet Eileen	20
64	Black Swan WI 454	Trojan/I Am The Least	20
64	Island WI 131	Praise For I/Tell You The Story	20
65	Island WI 187	Jonah (The Master)/Mr. Cleveland	20

LORD BRYNNER & SHEIKS
66	Island WI 266	Congo War/Teach Me To Ska	12

(see also Roland Alphonso)

LORD BUCKLEY
60	Fontana TL 5396	BLOWING HIS MIND (AND YOURS, TOO) (LP)	15
62	Fontana 688 010ZL	IN CONCERT (LP)	15
70	Elektra 2410 002	THE BEST OF LORD BUCKLEY (LP)	12

LORD BURGESS & HIS SUN ISLANDERS
67	Pye Intl. NPL 28109	CALYPSO GO-GO (LP)	15

LORD CHARLES & HIS BAND
70s	Sound Of Jamaica JA 1	Jamaican Bits And Pieces/JA Island Soul	15

LORD COMIC
70	Bamboo BAM 66	Rhythm Rebellion/ROY RICHARDS: Reggae Children	12
70	Pressure Beat PR 5507	Jack Of My Trade/CYNTHIA RICHARDS: United We Stand	12

(see also Sir Lord Comic)

LORD CREATOR

LORD CREATOR

62	Island WI 001	Independant Jamaica Calypso/Remember (B-side is actually "Remember Your Mother And Father")	18
63	Kalypso XX 24	Peeping Tom/Second Hand Piano	8
64	Port-O-Jam PJ 4005	Rhythm Of the Blues/Simple Things	12
64	Port-O-Jam PJ 4119	Jamaica's Anniversary/Mother's Love	10
64	National Calypso NC 2001	Drive With Care/Sweet Jamaica	7
65	Blue Beat BB 292	Evening News/Good For Creator	14
65	Black Swan WI 463	Wicked Lady/MAYTALS: My Little Ruby	18
66	Doctor Bird DB 1029	Obeah Wedding/BERTRAM ENNIS COMBO: Part Two	10
67	Jump Up JU 503	Jamaica Jump Up/Laziest Man	10
67	Jump Up JU 524	Big Bamboo/Marjorie And Harry	10
76	Island WIP 6344	Big Pussy Sally/UPSETTERS: Big Pussy Dub	6

(see also Kentrick Patrick, Fabulous Flames)

LORD CRISTO

67	Jump Up JU 515	Dumb Boy And The Parrot/General Hospital	8
67	Jump Up JU 517	Election War Zone/Bad Luck Man	8

LORD DANIEL

60s	Kalypso XX 26	Small Island Gal	6

LORD FLEA & HIS CALYPSONIANS

57	Capitol CL 14704	The Naughty Little Flea/Shake Shake Senora	6
57	Capitol CL 14704	The Naughty Little Flea/Shake Shake Senora (78)	12

LORD GANDA

57	Melodisc MEL 1417	Everybody Is Rockin' & Rollin'/Landlady Don't Steal My Clothes (78)	12

LORD INVADER & HIS CALYPSO RHYTHM BOYS

59	Pye N 15162	Teddy Boy Calypso/Reincarnation (The Bed Bug) (78)	6

LORD KITCHENER

50	Parlophone MP 102	Nora/LORD BEGINNER: $ & £ (78)	12
52	Melodisc MEL 1160	Kitch/Food From The West Indies (78)	10
52	Melodisc MEL 1222	Two Timing Josephine/The Tongue Mopsie (78)	10
53	Lyragon J 717	Alec Bedser Calypso/Mistress Jacob (78)	10
55	Melodisc MEL 1325	My Wife's Nightie/Sweet Home (78)	10
56	Melodisc MEL 1400	Rock 'n' Roll Calypso/Life Begins At Forty (78)	10
56	Melodisc MEL 1401	Romeo/Kitch's Calypso Medley (78)	10
59	Melodisc MEL 1498	Black Puddin'/Piccadilly Folk	7
59	Melodisc MEL 1538	If You're Brown/Come Back In The Morning	7
60	Melodisc MEL 1577	Jamaica Turkey/Edna What You Want	7
63	Melodisc CAL 2	Kitch/Rebound Wife	6
63	Melodisc CAL 3	Muriel And The Bug/Nora And The Yankee	6
63	Melodisc CAL 4	Kitch Take It Easy/Redhead	6
63	Melodisc CAL 5	Drink A Rum/Your Wife	6
63	Melodisc CAL 6	Too Late Kitch/Saxophone Number Two	6
63	Melodisc CAL 7	Wife And Mother/Mango Tree	6
64	Melodisc CAL 10	Kitch Mambo Calypso/Ghana	6
64	Melodisc CAL 11	Life Begins At Forty/Short Skirts	6
64	Melodisc CAL 12	Romeo/Kitch Calypso Medley	6
64	Melodisc CAL 14	Federation/Alfonso In Town	6
64	Melodisc CAL 19	Black Puddin'/Piccadilly Folk	6
64	Melodisc CAL 21	Come Back In The Morning/If You're Brown	6
64	Melodisc CAL 22	Jamaica Turkey/Edna What You Want	6
64	Melodisc CAL 23	Carnival/More Rice	6
60s	Jump Up JU 504	Love In The Cemetery/Jamaica Woman	6
60s	Jump Up JU 506	Road/Neighbour	6
64	Jump Up JU 511	Dr. Kitch/Come Back Home Meh Boy	5
65	Jump Up JU 530	Kitch You So Sweet/Ain't That Fun	6
65	Aladdin WI 612	Dr. Kitch/Come Back Home Meh Boy (reissue)	8
71	Duke DU 115	Dr. Kitch/Love In The Cemetary	5
55	Melodisc MLP 500	KITCH — KING OF CALYPSO (10" LP)	20
57	Melodisc MLP 510	KING OF CALYPSO VOL. 2 (10" LP)	20
60s	Melodisc 12-129	CALYPSOS TOO HOT TO HANDLE (LP)	20
60s	Melodisc 12-130	CALYPSOS TOO HOT TO HANDLE VOL. 2 (LP)	20
60s	Melodisc 12-199	CALYPSOS TOO HOT TO HANDLE (LP, reissue with extra tracks)	20
60s	Melodisc 12-200	CALYPSOS TOO HOT TO HANDLE VOL. 2 (LP, reissue with extra tracks)	20

LORD LEBBY

58	Kalypso XX 05	Sweet Jamaica/Mama Want No Rice No Peas	12
58	Kalypso XX 05	Sweet Jamaica/Mama Want No Rice No Peas (78)	12
60	Starlite ST45 018	Caldonia/One Kiss For My Baby	50

LORD MELODY

58	Melodisc MEL 1440	The Devil/No, No	6
58	Melodisc MEL 1440	The Devil/No, No (78)	10
58	Melodisc MEL 1449	Robbery/Men Company	8
58	Melodisc MEL 1449	Robbery/Men Company (78)	10
58	Melodisc MEL 1474	Do Able/Happy Holiday	6
58	Melodisc MEL 1474	Do Able/Happy Holiday (78)	12
59	Melodisc MEL 1491	I Confess/MIGHTY SPARROW: Goaty	8
59	Melodisc MEL 1491	I Confess/MIGHTY SPARROW: Goaty (78)	12
59	Melodisc MEL 1503	Tom Dooley/Jealous Woman	6
59	Melodisc MEL 1504	Romeo/Knock On Any Door	6
60	Kalypso XX 14	Rock 'N' Roll Calypso/Bo Bo Man	5
60s	Melodisc CAL 16	Happy Holiday/Do Able	5

LORD NELSON
63	Stateside SS 189	I Got An Itch/Problems On My Mind	10
64	Stateside SS 281	It's Delinquency/Proud West Indian	10
68	Direction 58-3909	Michael/No Hot Summer	6
64	Stateside SE 1024	PROUD WEST INDIAN (EP)	25

LORD POWER
57	Kalypso XX 02	Chambolina/Penny Reel (78)	12
58	Maracas M 20001	Special Amber Calypso/Mambo La-La (78)	12
69	Coxsone CS 7079	Temptation/AL & VIBRATORS: Change Everything	18

LORD RIGBY
60s	Kalypso XX 29	The Milkman/Old Veterans	6

LORD ROCKINGHAM'S XI
58	Decca F 11024	The Squelch/Fried Onions	10
58	Decca F 11024	The Squelch/Fried Onions (78)	12
58	Decca F 11059	Hoots Mon/Blue Train	6
58	Decca F 11059	Hoots Mon/Blue Train (78)	8
59	Decca F 11104	Wee Tom/Lady Rockingham, I Presume?	10
59	Decca F 11104	Wee Tom/Lady Rockingham, I Presume? (78)	10
59	Decca F 11139	Ra-Ra Rockingham/Farewell To Rockingham	8
59	Decca F 11139	Ra-Ra Rockingham/Farewell To Rockingham (78)	15
62	Decca F 11426	Newcastle Twist/Rockingham Twist	7
58	Decca DFE 6555	OH BOY! (EP)	35
68	Columbia SCX 6291	THE RETURN OF LORD ROCKINGHAM'S XI (LP)	30

(see also Robinson Crew, Harry Robinson)

LORD ROSE
60s	Kalypso XX 25	Independent Jamaica/Twistin' Uncle	4

LORDS
67	Columbia DB 8121	Don't Mince Matters/No One Knows	60
68	Columbia DB 8367	Gloryland/Gypsy Boy	10

LORD SITAR
68	Columbia SX/SCX 6256	LORD SITAR (LP)	40

LORD SPOON
70	Escort ERT 839	Woman A Love In The Night Time/World On A Wheel	6

LORD TANAMO
60	Kalypso XX 20	Blues Have Got Me Down/Sweet Dreaming	10
64	Rio R 21	I Had A Dream/OSBOURNE GRAHAM: Be There	12
64	Ska Beat JB 177	Night Food Ska/My Business	15
65	Ska Beat JB 217	Mattie Rag/BABA BROOKS BAND: Mattie Rag	15
65	Ska Beat JB 224	I'm In The Mood For Ska/You Never Know	30
66	Ska Beat JB 243	Mother's Love/Downtown Gal	12
60s	Caribou CRC 3	I Love You Truly/If You Were Only Mine	15
71	Banana BA 319	Keep On Moving/JACKIE MITTOO: Totaly [sic] Together	12

LORD'S TAVERNERS
56	Decca F 10752	ALL STAR HIT PARADE (45, p/s, various artists)	10
57	Decca F 10915	ALL STAR HIT PARADE NO. 2 (45, p/s, various artists)	8
58	Decca F 11043	STAR BAND HIT PARADE (45, p/s, various artists)	6

SOPHIA LOREN
58	Philips PB 857	Love Song From "Houseboat"/Bing! Bang! Bong!	7

(see also Peter Sellers & Sophia Loren)

LORENZO
71	New Beat NB 094	I Will Never Let You Down/This Magic Moment	5

(see also Laurel Aitken)

LORI & CHAMELEONS
78	Zoo CAGE 006	Touch/Love On The Ganges (p/s)	6
79	Sire SIR 4025	Touch/Love On The Ganges (p/s, reissue)	4
80	Korova KOW 5	The Lonely Spy/Peru (p/s)	4
81	Korova KOW 20	Touch/The Lonely Spy (p/s)	4
81	Korova KOW 20T	Touch/The Lonely Spy/Love On The Ganges (12", p/s)	7

(see also Teardrop Explodes, Bill Drummond)

NASH LORRAINE
59	Pye N 15235	I'm New In The Ways Of Love/Belle From Barcelona (78)	8

MYRNA LORRIE
55	London HLU 8187	Underway/I'm Your Man, I'm Your Gal (B-side with Buddy DeVal)	35
55	London HLU 8187	Underway/I'm Your Man, I'm Your Gal (B-side with Buddy DeVal) (78)	12
56	London HLU 8294	Life's Changing Scene/Listen To My Heartstrings	45
56	London HLU 8294	Life's Changing Scene/Listen To My Heartstrings (78)	12

LORRIES
79	Redball RR 016	The Night/Steal You Anyway/Pushover/Idiot Dances (p/s)	4

DICK LORY
56	London HLD 8348	Cool It Baby/Ball Room Baby	550
56	London HLD 8348	Cool It Baby/Ball Room Baby (78)	85
61	London HLG 9284	My Last Date/Broken Hearted	20
62	Liberty LIB 55415	Handsome Guy/The Pain Is Here	7
63	Liberty LIB 55529	Welcome Home Again/I Got Over You	7

LOS BRAVOS
(see under 'B')

JOE LOSS (& HIS ORCHESTRA)

55	HMV 7M 329	Have You Ever Been Lonely/Remember	5
55	HMV 7M 330	Button Up Your Overcoat/Wake The Town And Tell The People	5
56	HMV 7M 341	Love Is A Many Splendoured Thing/I'll Come When You Call	5
56	HMV 7M 342	Malaguena/Autumn Leaves	5
56	HMV 7M 355	Babette/Moments To Remember	5
56	HMV 7M 377	You're The Cream In My Coffee/Young And Foolish	5
56	HMV 7M 378	The Tender Trap/April In Paris	5
56	HMV 7M 386	Zambesi/The Rose Tattoo	5
56	HMV 7M 387	Memories Are Made Of This/Who's Sorry Now	5
56	HMV 7M 398	Fortune Teller/If You Knew Susie	5
56	HMV 7M 399	The Great Pretender/Dear Love My Love	5
56	HMV 7M 409	Tear Fell/It's D'Lovely	5
56	HMV 7M 425	Laura/Monglow & Theme From "Picnic"	5
58	HMV POP 430	I'll Buy You A Star/At Last	5
58	HMV POP 431	Parlez Moi D'Amour/My Darling My Darling	5
60	HMV POP 708	Falling In Love Again/I Get A Kick Out Of Loving You (78)	8
60	HMV POP 709	Alice Blue Gown/Alexanders Ragtime Band (78)	8
61	HMV POP 959	Twistin' The Mood/Everybody Twist	5
61	HMV POP 995	The Maigret Theme/Along The Bouvelard	5
63	HMV POP 1192	Steptoe And Son/Phase Four	6
64	HMV POP 1351	March Of The Mods/Tango '65	6
65	HMV POP 1389	A Shot In The Dark/Drum Diddley	5
65	HMV POP 1470	Let's Kick/Just For Kicks	5
66	HMV POP 1500	"Thunderbirds" Theme/"The Avengers" Theme	18
66	HMV POP 1517	The World Cup March/Auld Lang Syne (March)	5
62	HMV CLP 1636/CSD 1490	MUST BE MADISON – MUST BE TWIST (LP)	12

LOST CHEREES

83	Riot RIOT 3	No Fighting No War (EP)	5
84	Mortarhate MORT 3	A MAN'S DUTY ... A WOMAN'S PLACE (EP)	5
85	Mortarhate MORT 12	UNWANTED CHILDREN (12" EP, with inner)	8
84	Fight Back FIGHT 6	ALL PART OF GROWING UP (LP, with lyric inner)	10

LOST JOCKEY

82	Operation Twilight OPT 11	Professor Slack/Rise And Fall/Animal/Behaviour And Crude Din (p/s)	8

LOTHAR & THE HAND PEOPLE

69	Capitol CL 15610	Sdrawkcab (Backwards)/Today Is Only Yesterday's Tomorrow	10
69	Capitol E-ST 247	SPACE HYMN (LP)	40

DENNIS LOTIS

54	Decca F 10287	Such A Night/Cuddle Me (with Ted Heath Music & Johnston Brothers)	15
54	Decca F 10392	Honey Love/Manhattan Mambo (with Ted Heath Music)	12
54	Decca F 10469	Face Of An Angel, Heart Of A Devil/The Golden Ring	10
55	Decca F 10471	Chain Reaction/Go, Go, Go (with Ted Heath Music)	10
56	Pye 7N 15053	Green Grows The Grass/No Other Love Can Take Your Place	7
57	Columbia DB 3993	Tammy/I Complain	6
57	Columbia DB 4056	Valentina/Good Mornin' Life	6
58	Columbia DB 4090	I May Never Pass This Way Again/Gretna Green	5
58	Columbia DB 4158	The Only Man On The Island/Guessing What The Neighbours'll Say	5
58	Columbia DB 4182	Safe In The Arms Of My Darling/Belonging To Someone	5
59	Columbia DB 4277	Moonlight Serenade/Danger Within	5
59	Columbia DB 4277	Moonlight Serenade/Danger Within (78)	10
59	Columbia DB 4339	Who Is? You Are!/Too Much	5
60	Columbia DB 4432	I Wish It Were You/Love Me A Little	5
60	Columbia DB 4507	Strangers When We Meet/Two Wrongs Don't Make A Right	5
61	Columbia DB 4626	Where Are You/Love's A Secret Game	5
69	Polydor 56346	One Woman Man/The Finger Points At You	5
56	Pye NEP 24017	PRESENTING DENNIS LOTIS (EP)	10
57	Pye NEP 24043	LET'S BE HAPPY (EP)	10
57	Pye NEP 24046	HOW ABOUT YOU (EP)	12
57	Pye NEP 24053	HOW ABOUT YOU PT. 2 (EP)	12
57	Pye NEP 24055	HOW ABOUT YOU PT. 3 (EP)	12
59	Columbia SEG 7955	HALLELUJAH IT'S DENNIS LOTIS (EP)	10
57	Nixa NPL 18002	HOW ABOUT YOU (LP)	30
58	Columbia 33SX 1089	BIDIN' MY TIME (LP)	20

(see also Johnstone Brothers)

PETER LOTIS

60	Ember EMB S 110	Doo-Dah/You're Singing Our Love Song To Somebody Else (some with p/s)	8/5

LOT 39 (STRANGERS)

60s	Eyemark EMS 1004	I'll Get Over You/I Still Love You	5

LOTUS EATERS

83	Sylvan SYL 1	The First Picture Of You/The Lotus Eater (picture disc)	4
84	Sylvan SYL 2	You Don't Need Someone New/Two Virgins Tender (picture disc)	4
84	Sylvan SYL 4	Out Of Your Own/Endless (picture disc)	4
85	Arista FS 5	It Hurts/Evidence//The Soul In Sparks/Church At Llanbadrig (double pack)	4
84	Sylvan 206 263	NO SENSE OF SIN (LP)	12

(see also Wild Swans, Care)

BONNIE LOU

53	Parlophone MSP 6021	Seven Lonely Days/Dancin' With Someone	35
53	Parlophone MSP 6036	Hand-Me-Down Heart/Scrap Of Paper	35
53	Parlophone MSP 6048	Tennessee Wig Walk/Just Out Of Reach	50
53	Parlophone MSP 6051	Pa-Paya Mama/Since You Said Goodbye	30
54	Parlophone MSP 6072	The Texas Polka/No Heart At All	25
54	Parlophone MSP 6095	Don't Stop Kissing Me Goodnight/The Welcome Mat	25

54	Parlophone MSP 6108	No One/Huckleberry Pie.	25
54	Parlophone MSP 6117	Blue Tennessee Rain/Wait For Me, Darling	25
54	Parlophone R 3895	Blue Tennessee Rain/Wait For Me, Darling (78)	8
54	Parlophone MSP 6132	Two Step — Side Step/Please Don't Laugh When I Cry	20
54	Parlophone R 3931	Two Step — Side Step/Please Don't Laugh When I Cry (78)	8
55	Parlophone MSP 6151	Tennessee Mambo/Train Whistle Blues	25
55	Parlophone R 3975	Tennessee Mambo/Train Whistle Blues (78)	10
55	Parlophone MSP 6157	Tweedle Dee/The Finger Of Suspicion Points At You	30
55	Parlophone R 3989	Tweedle Dee/The Finger Of Suspicion Points At You (78)	12
55	Parlophone R 4012	A Rusty Old Halo/Danger! Heartbreak Ahead (78)	12
55	Parlophone MSP 6173	Drop Me A Line/Old Faithful And True Love	18
55	Parlophone R 4037	Drop Me A Line/Old Faithful And True Love (78).	8
55	Parlophone MSP 6178	The Barnyard Hop/Tell The World	15
55	Parlophone R 4054	The Barnyard Hop/Tell The World (78).	8
55	Parlophone MSP 6188	Dancin' In My Socks/Daddy-O	30
55	Parlophone R 4096	Dancin' In My Socks/Daddy-O (78)	15
56	Parlophone MSP 6223	Darlin' Why/Miss The Love (That I've Been Dreaming Of).	15
56	Parlophone R 4146	Darlin' Why/Miss The Love (That I've Been Dreaming Of) (78)	8
56	Parlophone MSP 6234	Bo Weevil (A Country Song)/Chaperon	25
56	Parlophone R 4168	Bo Weevil (A Country Song)/Chaperon (78)	15
56	Parlophone MSP 6253	Lonesome Lover/Little Miss Bobby Sox	20
56	Parlophone R 4194	Lonesome Lover/Little Miss Bobby Sox (78).	15
56	Parlophone R 4215	No Rock 'N' Roll Tonight/One Track Love	18
56	Parlophone R 4215	No Rock 'N' Roll Tonight/One Track Love	15
57	Parlophone R 4350	Teenage Wedding/Runnin' Away	18
57	Parlophone R 4350	Teenage Wedding/Runnin' Away (78).	18
58	Parlophone DP 545	I'm Available/Waiting In Vain (export issue)	25

BONNIE LOU & RUSTY YORK

58	Parlophone R 4409	Let The School Bell Ring Ding-A-Ling/La Dee Dah.	60
58	Parlophone R 4409	Let The School Bell Ring Ding-A-Ling/La Dee Dah (78)	25

(see also Rusty York)

JOHN D. LOUDERMILK

61	RCA RCA 1269	The Language Of Love/Darling Jane.	5
62	RCA RCA 1287	Thou Shalt Not Steal/Mister Jones	6
62	RCA RCA 1323	Angela Jones/Road Hog	8
68	RCA RCA 1761	Sidewalks/The Odd Folks Of Okracoke.	7
62	RCA RD 27248/SF 5123	THE LANGUAGE OF LOVE (LP).	25
62	RCA Victor RD/SF 7515	TWELVE SIDES OF JOHN D. LOUDERMILK (LP)	25
67	RCA Victor RD/SF 7890	SINGS A BIZARRE COLLECTION OF SONGS (LP)	15
70	RCA LSA 3159	THE BEST OF JOHN D. LOUDERMILK (LP).	12
75	RCA LSA 3220	ENCORES (LP).	12

(see also Johnny Dee)

LOUDEST WHISPER

74	Polydor	CHILDREN OF LIR (LP, Ireland-only)	600
81	Polydor 2908 043	LOUDEST WHISPER (LP, Ireland-only)	200
83	Fiona 011	HARD TIMES (LP, with insert, Ireland-only)	200

LOUDNESS

84	Music For Nations MFN 22	DISILLUSION (LP)	12

JOE HILL LOUIS

65	Bootleg 502	Heartache Baby/I Feel Like A Million (99 copies only)	35
60s	Advent LP 2803	MEMPHIS BLUES AND BREAKDOWNS (LP).	40

JOE HILL LOUIS

74	Polydor 2383 214	BLUE IN THE MORNING (LP).	25

(see also Willie Nix)

LOUISE

96	EMI EMLH 397	Light Of My Life/Real Love (jukebox only, no p/s)	6
96	EMI CDEM 454	Light Of My Life/Real Love (Tin Tin Out Remix)/Real Love (Stonebridge Remix)/Interview with Louise (CD, with 3 prints)	8
97	EMI LOUPREM 101	SOFT & GENTLE: One Kiss From Louise Pop Megamix/Naked (Tony De Vit Mix)/Real Love (CD, promo/freebie)	12
97	EMI EMLH 490	Arms Around The World (Radio Mix)/Naked (Radio Mix) (jukebox only, no p/s)	6
97	EMI 12EMDJ 490	Arms Around The World (Rated PG Club Mix)/Arms Around The World (Rated PG Dub Mix) (12", p/s, promo only).	10
97	EMI 12DJD 490	Arms Around The World (Farley & Heller's Fire Island Vocal Mix)/Arms Around The World (Farley & Heller's Roach Motel Dub)/ArmsAround The World (T-Empo Club Mix)/Arms Around The World (T-Empo Dub Mix) (12", doublepack, p/s, promo only).	12
97	EMI EMLH 500	Let's Go Round Again/Arms Around The World (jukebox only, no p/s)	6
97	EMI 12EMDJ 500	Let's Go Round Again (Colour Systems Inc. Gold Mix)/Let's Go Round Again (Rated PG Club Mix)/(Rated PG Mr. G Dub) (12", p/s, promo only)	10
97	EMI 12EMDJD 500	Let's Go Round Again (Colour Systems Inc. Amber Vox Mix)/(187 Lockdown Dub Mix)/(Paul Gotel's Peaceful Warrior Mix)/(187 Lockdown Vocal Mix)/(Colour Systems Inc. Amber Dub)/(Paul Gotel's Warrior Dub) (12", double pack, p/s, promo only)	15
98	EMI 12EMDJD 506	All That Matters (DJ Tonka Mix)/All That Matters (Cas Roc Vocal Mix)/All That Matters (Hex Hector Dub Revisited Mix)/All That Matters (Cas Roc Vocal Mix) (12" double pack, p/s, promo only)	15

(see also Eternal)

LOUISIANA RED

64	Columbia DB 7270	Keep Your Hands Off My Woman/Don't Cry.	18
64	Sue WI 337	I Done Woke Up!/I Had A Feeling	25
64	Columbia 33SX 1612	LOWDOWN BACK PORCH BLUES (LP).	40
72	Atlantic K 40436	SINGS THE BLUES (LP).	18
72	Carnival 2941 002	THE SEVENTH SON (LP)	20

LOUISIANA SUGAR BABIES
57	HMV 7EG 8215	LOUISIANA SUGAR BABIES (EP, with Fats Waller & James P. Johnson) 15

JACQUES LOUSSIER
66	Decca F 22383	Air On A G String/Prelude No. 16 (Bach) 7
69	Decca F 22876	Air On A G String/Prelude No. 16 (Bach) (reissue) 5

LOUVIN BROTHERS
59	Capitol CL 14989	Knoxville Girl/I Wish It Had Been A Dream 7
59	Capitol CL 15078	You're Learning/My Curly Headed Baby 6
56	Capitol EAP1 769	TRAGIC SONGS OF LIFE (EP) 20
58	Capitol EAP1 910	IRA AND CHARLIE (EP) 20
59	Capitol EAP1 1106	COUNTRY LOVE BALLADS (EP) 15

LOVABLES
68	Stateside SS 2108	You're The Cause Of It/Beautiful Idea 12

LOVE
SINGLES
66	London HLZ 10053	My Little Red Book/Hey Joe. 18
66	London HLZ 10073	7 And 7 Is/No. Fourteen 18
67	Elektra EKSN 45010	She Comes In Colours/Orange Skies 15
67	Elektra EKSN 45016	Softly To Me/The Castle 12
68	Elektra EKSN 45024	Alone Again Or/Bummer In The Summer 8
68	Elektra EKSN 45026	Andmoreagain/The Daily Planet 12
68	Elektra EKSN 45038	Laughing Stock/Your Mind And We Belong Together 15
70	Elektra EKSN 45086	I'm With You/Robert Montgomery 7
70	Harvest HAR 5014	Stand Out/Doggone 7
70	Harvest HAR 5030	The Everlasting First/Keep On Shining 10
70	Elektra 2101 019	Alone Again Or/Bummer In The Summer (reissue). 5
73	Elektra K 12113	Alone Again Or/Andmoreagain 5
75	RSO 2090 151	Time Is Like A River/You Said You Would 5

ORIGINAL LPs
66	Elek. EKL 4001/EKS 74001	LOVE (LP, gold label, U.K disc in U.S. sleeve). 40
67	Elek. EKL 4005/EKS 74005	DA CAPO (LP, orange label, with U.K. or U.S. sleeve) 40
67	Elek. EKL 4013/EKS 74013	FOREVER CHANGES (LP, orange label) 45
69	Elektra EKL 4049	FOUR SAIL (LP, orange label, mono, existence unconfirmed) . . . . 40+
69	Elektra EKS 74049	FOUR SAIL (LP, orange label, stereo) 30
70	Harvest SHDW 3/4	OUT HERE (2-LP, gatefold sleeve). 25
71	Harvest SHVL 787	FALSE START (LP, gatefold sleeve) 18
71	Elektra 2469 009	LOVE REVISITED (LP, gatefold sleeve) 18
73	Elektra K 32002	LOVE MASTERS (LP) 15
74	RSO 2394 145	REEL TO REAL (LP). 12

RE-PRESSINGS
67	Elek. EKL 4001/EKS 74001	LOVE (LP, orange label, with U.K. or U.S. sleeve) 35
72	Elektra K 42068	LOVE (LP, 'butterfly' label) 12
71	Elektra EKS 74005	DA CAPO (LP, 'butterfly' label) 15
72	Elektra K 42011	DA CAPO (LP, 'butterfly' label). 12
72	Elektra K 42015	FOREVER CHANGES (LP, 'butterfly' label) 12
72	Elektra K 42030	FOUR SAIL (LP, 'butterfly' label) 12

(see also Arthur Lee)

LOVE
90	Fierce FRIGHT 036	Welsh Girl (1-sided, p/s in bag, hand-finished labels, mail-order only) 20

CHRISTOPHER LOVE
69	London HLU 10263	The Curse Goes On/You May Be The Next 8

DARLENE LOVE
63	London HLU 9725	(Today I Met) The Boy I'm Gonna Marry/Playing For Keeps 20
63	London HLU 9765	Wait 'Til My Bobby Gets Home/Take It From Me. 20
63	London HLU 9815	A Fine Fine Boy/Marshmallow World. 20
69	London HLU 10244	Wait 'Til My Bobby Gets Home/(Today I Met) The Boy I'm Gonna Marry 12
74	Warner Bros/Spector K 19011	Christmas (Baby Please Come Home)/Wait Till My Bobby Comes Home (blue vinyl) 5
77	Phil Spector Intl. 2010 019	Lord If You're A Woman/Johnny Baby 5
77	Phil Spector Intl. 2010 019	Lord If You're A Woman/Johnny Baby (12", some copies 1-sided). 15
64	London RE-U 1411	WAIT TILL MY BOBBY GETS HOME (EP) 150

(see also Bob B. Soxx & Blue Jeans, Crystals, Phil Spector, Blossoms, Allisons [U.S.], Date With Soul, Cinders)

GARFIELD LOVE & JIMMY SPRUILL
69	Blue Horizon 57-3150	Next Time You See Me/Part Time Love. 20

GEOFF LOVE ORCHESTRA
56	MGM SP 1175	Theme From Mutiny On The Bounty/Love Song From Mutiny On The Bounty 7
58	Columbia DB 4169	Brazil/Patricia 5
61	Columbia DB 4627	Coronation Street Theme/Sophia. 10
62	Columbia DB 4881	Steptoe And Son/Over The Backyard Fence 5
70	Columbia DB 8707	Coronation Street Theme/ALIRIO DIAZ: Aranjuez Mon Amour (Rodgigo) 5
74	EMI EMI 2105	Match Of The Day/Bless This House 5
75	Music For Pleasure MFP 50227	BIG BOND MOVIE THEMES (LP, 2 different sleeves; 1st design with front-facing Roger Moore illustration) . . . . each 15

(see also Mandingo, Manuel & Music Of The Mountains)

JILL BABY LOVE
76	Black Magic BM 116	My Way Or Hit The Highway (Parts 1 & 2) 4

MARY LOVE
65	King KG 1024	You Turned My Bitter Into Sweet/I'm In Your Hands 70
67	Stateside SS 2009	Lay This Burden Down/Think It Over Baby 30
68	Stateside SS 2135	The Hurt Is Just Beginning/If You Change Your Mind 18
82	Kent TOWN 501	You Turned My Bitter Into Sweet/SWEETHEARTS: This Couldn't Be Me 5

RONNIE LOVE

| 61 | London HLD 9272 | Chills And Fever/Pledging My Love | 20 |
| 78 | Grapevine GRP 108 | Let's Make Love/Nothing To It | 5 |

WILLIE LOVE/WILLIE NIX

| 66 | Highway 51 H 700 | THE TWO WILLIES FROM MEMPHIS (LP, 99 copies only) | 70 |

(see also Willie Nix)

LOVE AFFAIR

67	Decca F 12558	She Smiled Sweetly/Satisfaction Guaranteed	50
67	CBS 3125	Everlasting Love/Gone Are The Songs Of Yesterday	6
68	CBS 3366	Rainbow Valley/Someone Like Us (some in p/s)	12/6
68	CBS 3674	A Day Without Love/I'm Happy	6
69	CBS 3994	One Road/Let Me Know	6
69	CBS 4300	Bringing On Back The Good Times/Another Day	6
69	CBS 4631	Baby I Know/Accept Me For What I Am	7
70	CBS 4780	Lincoln County/Sea Of Tranquility	6
70	Pye 7N 45218	Let Me Dance/Love's Looking Out At You	8
71	Parlophone R 5887	Wake Me I Am Dreaming/That's My Home	10
71	Parlophone R 5918	Help (Get Me Some Help)/Long Way Home	10
73	CBS 1144	Everlasting Love/Bringing On Back The Good Times (p/s, 'Hall Of Fame Hits' series)	5
77	Creole CR 146	Private Lives/Let A Little Love Come In	5
68	CBS 63416	THE EVERLASTING LOVE AFFAIR (LP, mono/stereo)	15

(see also L.A., Ellis, Steve Ellis, Elastic Band, Widowmaker, Morgan, Phillip Goodhand-Tait, English Rose, Rainbow Flolly)

LOVE CHILDREN

| 69 | Deram DM 268 | Easy Squeezy/Every Little Step | 4 |
| 70 | Deram DM 303 | Paper Chase/My Turkey Snuffed It | 4 |

LOVE COMMITTEE

| 76 | Ariola AA 105 | Can't Win For Losing/Love Wins Every Time | 4 |

LOVECUT D.B.

| 91 | Suburbs Of Hell SOH 009EP | Heartspin/Heartspin (Dripping Clock Mix)/(Marisco Disco Mix)/ (Porn Cable Mix) (12", p/s) | 10 |

(see also Sarah Cracknell, St. Etienne)

LOVE DE-LUXE

| 79 | Atlantic K 11359 | Here Comes That Sound Again/Let Me Make It Up To You | 4 |
| 79 | Atlantic 12LV 17 | Here Comes That Sound Again/Here Comes That Sound Again (Version) (12") | 7 |

LOVE GENERATION (U.S.)

| 67 | Liberty LBF 15018 | She Touched Me/The Love In Me | 6 |
| 68 | Liberty LBL/LBS 83121E | LOVE GENERATION (LP) | 12 |

LOVE GENERATION (Jamaica)

| 73 | Grape GR 3046 | Money Raper/HEPTONES: The Magnificent Heptones 3 In One | 4 |
| 73 | Grape GR 3041 | Warrika Hill/Battlefield (Third And Fourth Generation) | 4 |

JOY LOVEJOY

| 72 | Chess 6145 010 | In Orbit/Uh! Hum | 5 |

LOVELITES

| 78 | Grapevine GRP 107 | Get It Off My Conscience/Oh, What A Day | 6 |

TONY LOVELLO

| 59 | Top Rank JAR 200 | Amore Mio/Dreamy Serenade | 6 |
| 59 | Top Rank JAR 200 | Amore Mio/Dreamy Serenade (78) | 10 |

LOVE OF LIFE ORCHESTRA

| 80 | Infidelity JMB 227 | EXTENDED NICETIES (12" EP) | 7 |

(see also David Byrne)

JOHNNY LOVER

| 70 | Amalgamated AMG 871 | Pumpkin Eater/Version | 15 |
| 70 | Amalgamated AMG 873 | Two Edged Sword/Version | 12 |

(see also Little Johnny Jones, Heptones)

LOVERS

| 58 | Vogue Pop V 9111 | Let's Elope/I Wanna Be Loved | 450 |
| 58 | Vogue Pop V 9111 | Let's Elope/I Wanna Be Loved (78) | 100 |

LOVE SCULPTURE

68	Parlophone R 5664	River To Another Day/Brand New Woman	20
68	Parlophone R 5731	Wang-Dang-Doodle/The Stumble	15
68	Parlophone R 5744	Sabre Dance/Think Of Love	4
69	Parlophone R 5807	Seagull/Farandole	10
70	Parlophone R 5831	In The Land Of The Few/People People	10
68	Parlophone PMC/PCS 7059	BLUES HELPING (LP, 1st pressing, yellow/black label, mono/stereo)	35/30
69	Parlophone PCS 7090	FORMS AND FEELINGS (LP, 1st pressing, yellow/black label)	30
70	Parlophone PCS 7059	BLUES HELPING (LP, 2nd pressing, silver/black label)	12
70	Parlophone PCS 7090	FORMS AND FEELINGS (LP, 2nd pressing, silver/black label)	12

(see also Human Beans, Dave Edmunds)

EDDIE LOVETTE

69	Big Shot BI 519	You're My Girl/Let Them Say	5
70	London HLU 10298	Boomerang/Together	5
70	London HLJ 10311	Too Experienced/Little Blue Bird	5
70	London HA-J 8413	TOO EXPERIENCED (LP, unissued)	
70	London LGJ/ZGJ 103	TOO EXPERIENCED (LP)	12

LOVE UNLIMITED

72	Uni UNLS 124	FROM A GIRL'S POINT OF VIEW — LOVE UNLIMITED (LP)	12
73	Pye NSPL 28179	UNDER THE INFLUENCE OF... (LP)	12
74	20th Century BT 443	IN HEAT (LP)	12

LOVEY AUSTIN BLUE SERENADERS/STATE STREET RAMBLERS
60s Collector JE 123   SMALL JAZZ BANDS VOL. 1 (EP) 8

LENE LOVICH
76	Polydor 2058 812	I Saw Mommy Kissing Santa Claus/The Christmas Song	
		(Merry Christmas To You)/Happy Christmas	10
78	Stiff BUY 32	I Think We're Alone Now/Lucky Number (p/s, 5,000 only).	4
78	Stiff BUYJ 32	I Think We're Alone Now (Japanese)/Lucky Number	
		(mail-order promo only).	8
80	Stiff BUY 69	What Will I Do Without You?/Joan//Monkey Talk/The Night/Too Tender/	
		You Can't Kill Me (p/s, with bonus live EP)	5
82	Stiff BUYP 164	It's You, Only You/Blue (picture disc).	4
78	Stiff SEEZ 7	STATELESS (LP, original pressing on black [2,000 only] or red vinyl) . . . . . each	10
78	Stiff SEEZ 7	STATELESS (LP, picture disc, 5,000 only)	12
78	Stiff LENE 1	LENE LOVICH INTERVIEW (LP, promo only)	12

(see also Diversions, Commandos)

LOVIN'
67	Page One POF 035	Keep On Believing/I'm In Command	25
67	Page One POF 041	All I've Got/Do It Again.	40

(see also Nerve)

LOVING AWARENESS
76   More Love ML 001   LOVING AWARENESS (LP, gatefold sleeve with 2 posters) 12

(see also Glencoe, Skip Bifferty, Ian Dury)

LOVING KIND
66	Piccadilly 7N 35299	Accidental Love/Nothing Can Change This Love	10
66	Piccadilly 7N 35318	I Love The Things You Do/Treat Me Nice	12
66	Piccadilly 7N 35342	Ain't That Peculiar/With Rhyme And Reason	15

(see also Noel Redding Band, Freddie Lennon)

LOVIN' SPOONFUL
65	Pye International 7N 25327	Do You Believe In Magic?/On The Road Again	8
66	Pye International 7N 25344	You Didn't Have To Be So Nice/My Gal	8
66	Pye International 7N 25361	Daydream/Night Owl Blues	5
66	Kama Sutra KAS 200	Summer In The City/Bald Headed Lena.	5
66	Kama Sutra KAS 201	Rain On The Roof/Warm Baby	5
67	Kama Sutra KAS 204	Nashville Cats/Full Measure	6
67	Kama Sutra KAS 207	Darling Be Home Soon/Darlin' Companion	5
67	Kama Sutra KAS 208	Six O'Clock/The Finale.	6
67	Kama Sutra KAS 210	She Is Still A Mystery/Only Pretty, What A Pity.	6
67	Kama Sutra KAS 211	Money/Close Your Eyes	6
68	Kama Sutra KAS 213	Never Going Back/Forever.	7
66	Kama Sutra KEP 300	DID YOU EVER HAVE TO MAKE UP YOUR MIND (EP)	18
66	Kama Sutra KEP 301	JUG BAND MUSIC (EP)	20
66	Kama Sutra KEP 302	SUMMER IN THE CITY (EP)	20
67	Kama Sutra KEP 303	DAY BLUES (EP)	20
67	Kama Sutra KEP 304	NASHVILLE CATS (EP)	20
67	Kama Sutra KEP 305	LOVIN' YOU (EP)	20
67	Kama Sutra KEP 306	SOMETHING IN THE NIGHT (EP)	20
65	Pye Intl. NPL 28069	DO YOU BELIEVE IN MAGIC? (LP).	20
66	Pye Intl. NPL 28078	DAYDREAM (LP).	20
67	Kama Sutra KLP 401	HUMS OF THE LOVIN' SPOONFUL (LP)	20
67	Kama Sutra KLP 402	YOU'RE A BIG BOY NOW (LP, soundtrack)	20
67	Kama Sutra KLP 403	THE BEST OF THE LOVIN' SPOONFUL (LP)	15
68	Kama Sutra KLP 404	EVERYTHING PLAYING (LP)	18
68	Kama Sutra K(S)LP 405	THE BEST OF THE LOVIN' SPOONFUL VOL. 2 (LP)	15
69	Kama Sutra 602 009	REVELATION: REVOLUTION '69 (LP)	15

(see also John Sebastian, Mugwumps, Zalman Yanovsky, Even Dozen Jug Band)

BRUCE LOW
56   HMV JO 464   Just Walking In The Rain/Cindy Oh Cindy (export issue) 18

LOWBITES
70   Black Swan BW 1403   I Got It/I Got It (Version). 8

ARTHUR LOWE
72	Columbia DB 8956	My Little Girl, My Little Boy/How I Won The War	4
69	World Record Club ST 1008	BLESS 'EM ALL! (LP).	10

DENNIS LOWE
70	Downtown DT 465	What's Your Name/MUSIC DOCTORS: Mr Locabe.	7
70	Downtown DT 468	Stand Up For The Sound/OWEN & DENNIS: Old Man Trouble	7

JIM LOWE
55	London HLD 8171	Close The Door/Nueva Laredo (gold label print).	45
55	London HLD 8171	Close The Door/Nueva Laredo (78)	12
56	London HLD 8276	Blue Suede Shoes/Maybellene (silver label print).	85
56	London HLD 8276	Blue Suede Shoes/Maybellene (78)	30
56	London HLD 8288	Love Is The $64,000 Dollar Question/Rene La Rue (gold label print)	50
56	London HLD 8288	Love Is The $64,000 Dollar Question/Rene La Rue (78)	15
56	London HLD 8317	The Green Door/The Little Man In Chinatown (as Jim Lowe & High Fives,	
		gold label print, later silver)	40/25
56	London HLD 8317	The Green Door/The Little Man In Chinatown (78)	10
57	London HLD 8368	I Feel The Beat/By You, By You, By You (gold label print, later silver)	30/20
57	London HLD 8368	I Feel The Beat/By You, By You, By You (78)	12
57	London HLD 8431	Four Walls/Talkin' To The Blues	25
57	London HLD 8431	Four Walls/Talkin' To The Blues (78)	15
58	London HLD 8538	Roc-A-Chicka/The Bright Light (with Billy Vaughan's Orchestra).	100
58	London HLD 8538	Roc-A-Chicka/The Bright Light (with Billy Vaughan's Orchestra) (78)	30

60	London HLD 9043	He'll Have To Go/(This Life Is Just A) Dress Rehearsal	12
65	United Artists UP 1096	Mr Moses/Make Your Back Strong	5
58	London HA-D 2108	SONGS THEY SING BEHIND THE GREEN DOOR (LP)	35
59	London HA-D 2146	WICKED WOMEN (LP)	30

(see also John Barry Seven)

PETER LOWE
57	Parlophone R 4270	The Banana Boat Song/The Wisdom Of A Fool	6

SAMMY LOWE
61	RCA RCA 1239	Hey Lawdy Lawdy Mary	12

LOWLIFE
85	Nightshift	RAIN (mini-LP)	10
88	LOLIF DEMO 1	THE DEMOS (LP, w/l test pressings only, hand-written white sleeve)	25

LOW NOISE
81	Happy Birthday UR 5	Jungle Line/Urban Tribal/Jungle Line (Instrumental) (p/s)	7
81	Happy Birthday UR 5	Jungle Line/Urban Tribal/Jungle Line (Instrumental) (12", p/s)	10

(see also Thomas Dolby)

LOW NUMBERS
79	Warner Brothers K 17493	Keep In Touch/Nine All Out (p/s)	10

LOWRELL
79	AVI AVIS 108	Mellow Mellow Right On/You're Playing Dirty	4
79	AVI AVISL 108	Mellow Mellow Right On/You're Playing Dirty (12")	8

PHILIP LOWRIE
63	Ember EMB S 179	I Might Have Known (Before)/I Might Have Known (After)	4

ART LOWRY
54	Columbia SCMC 1	The Curse Of An Aching Heart/Heart Of My Heart (export issue)	6

HENRY LOWTHER BAND
70	Deram SML 1070	CHILD SONG (LP)	50

(see also Manfred Mann, John Mayall & Bluesbreakers, Keef Hartley Band, Ricotti & Albuquerque)

MARK LOYD
65	Parlophone R 5277	I Keep Thinking About You/Will It Be The Same	5
65	Parlophone R 5332	Everybody Tries/She Said No	8
66	Parlophone R 5423	When Evening Falls/When I'm Gonna Find Her	150

JEREMY LUBBOCK
58	Parlophone R 4399	Catch A Falling Star/The Man Who Invented Love	5
58	Parlophone R 4399	Catch A Falling Star/The Man Who Invented Love (78)	8
58	Parlophone R 4421	Lemon Twist/Tonight	5
58	Parlophone R 4421	Lemon Twist/Tonight (78)	8
58	Parlophone R 4473	Odd Man Out/Too Bad You're Not Around	5
58	Parlophone R 4473	Odd Man Out/Too Bad You're Not Around (78)	8
58	Parlophone GEP 8745	JUST FOR THE FUN OF IT (EP)	15

LUCAS (& MIKE COTTON SOUND)
66	Polydor 56114	I Saw Pity In The Face Of A Friend/Dance Children Dance (solo)	8
67	Pye 7N 17313	Step Out Of Line/Ain't Love Good, Ain't Love Proud	20
68	MGM MGM 1398	Soul Serenade/We Got A Thing Going Baby	20
68	MGM MGM 1427	Jack And The Beanstalk/Mother-In-Law	8

(see also Mike Cotton Sound, Artwoods)

BUDDY LUCAS BAND
53	London L 1181	Organ Grinder's Swing/Laura (78, as Buddy Lucas & His Orchestra)	40
60	Pye International 7N 25045	I Want To Know/Deacon John	12
60	Pye International N 25045	I Want To Know/Deacon John (78)	20

FRED LUCAS
57	Columbia DB 3861	Friendly Persuasion (Thee I Love)/A Thing Of Beauty	4

TREVOR LUCAS
66	Reality RE 505	Waltzing Matilda/It's On	25
66	Reality RY 1002	OVERLANDER (LP)	275

(see also Eclection, Fotheringay, Fairport Convention, Bronco, Bunch, Sandy Denny)

LUCID DREAM
91	Euphoric E 9999T	DRIPPY EP (12", p/s)	7

LUCIFER
71	Lucifer L 001	Don't Care/Hypnosis	8
72	Lucifer L 003/004	Fuck You/Bad	8
72	Lucifer L 005/006	Prick/Want It	8
72	Lucifer L 005/006/L 003/004	Prick/Want It/Fuck You/Bad (double pack, black box set)	40
72	Lucifer LLP 1	BIG GUN (LP, private pressing, with poster/inserts, sold via *Oz* mag)	60
72	Lucifer LLP 2	EXIT (LP, private pressing, with poster, sold via *Oz* magazine)	80

LUCIFER'S FRIEND
71	Philips 6003 092	Ride The Sky/Horla	15
71	Philips 6305 068	LUCIFER'S FRIEND (LP)	15

(see also John Lawton, Uriah Heep)

JOHNNY LUCK
58	Fontana H 110	Play Rough/Buzz, Buzz, Buzz (78)	12

LUCKY MILLINDER & HIS ORCHESTRA
51	Vogue V 9007	I'm Waiting Just For You/Bongo Boogie (78)	12
51	Vogue V 9021	No One Else Could Be/The Grape Vine (78)	12
52	Vogue V 2138	Ram-Bunk-Shush/Let It Roll Again (78)	12

(see also Wynonie "Mr Blues" Harris)

LULU

LYDIA LUNCH

LUCY
77	Lightning GIL 516	Never Never/Feel So Good (p/s)	20
78	B&C BCS 8	Really Got Me Goin'/Oy (p/s)	10

(see also Def Leppard)

TOM LUCY
82	Bridgehouse BHS 15	Paris, France/Man Found Dead In Graveyard (no p/s)	6

(see also Wasted Youth)

LUCY SHOW
83	Shout XS 007	Leonardo Da Vinci/Kill The Beast (p/s)	4

LUDDITES
80s	Louder LOUD 00003	DAVIS GOES TO THE SHOPS (cassette)	8

LUDLOWS
65	Pye 7N 15946	The Last Thing On My Mind/Kisses Sweeter Than Wine	5
66	Pye 7N 17050	The Sea Around Us/The Butcher Boys	5
66	Pye 7N 17123	The Winds Thro' The Rafters/That's My Song	5
66	Pye 7N 17221	Johnny Lad/Pack Up Your Sorrows	5
67	Pye 7N 17319	Enniskillen Dragoons/Foggy Dew	5
67	Pye 7N 17384	Plaisir D'Amour/Yesterday's Dream	5
66	Pye NPL 18150	THE WIND AND THE SEA (LP)	15

(see also Jim McCann)

LUDUS
80	New Hormones ORG 4	The Visit/Lullaby Cheat/Unveil (12", p/s with insert)	8
81	New Hormones ORG 8	My Cherry Is In Sherry/Anatomy Is Not Destiny (p/s)	5
81	New Hormones CAT 1	PICKPOCKET (C-30 cassette pack with A4 book & button in PVC bag)	12
81	New Hormones ORG 12	Mother's Hour/Patient (p/s, with poster)	5
81	New Hormones ORG 16	THE SEDUCTION (2 x 12" EP, each in p/s; whole package in poly bag)	12
80s	New Hormones	LINDER SINGS BARDOT (cassette)	10
82	New Hormones ORG 20	DANGER CAME SMILING (LP)	10

LUKE & BLAKE
66	CBS 202467	Just You/Wandering Man	6

ROBIN LUKE
58	London HLD 8676	Susie Darlin'/Living's Loving You	12
58	London HLD 8676	Susie Darlin'/Living's Loving You (78)	25
58	London HLD 8771	Chicka Chicka Honey/My Girl	20
58	London HLD 8771	Chicka Chicka Honey/My Girl (78)	45
59	London RED 1222	ROBIN LUKE (EP)	100

LULU (& LUVVERS)
64	Decca F 11884	Shout/Forget Me Baby (as Lulu & Luvers)	7
64	Decca F 11965	Can't Hear You No More/I Am In Love	8
64	Decca F 12017	Here Comes The Night/That's Really Some Good	6
65	Decca F 12128	Satisfied/Surprise Surprise (as Lulu & Luvers)	7
65	Decca F 12169	Leave A Little Love/He Don't Want Your Love Anymore	5
65	Decca F 12214	Try To Understand/Not In This Whole World	5
65	Decca F 12254	Tell Me Like It Is/Stop Fooling Around	6
66	Decca F 12326	Call Me/After You	6
66	Decca F 12491	What A Wonderful Feeling/Tossin' And Turnin'	6
67	Columbia DB 8169	The Boat That I Row/Dreary Days And Nights	6
67	Columbia DB 8221	Let's Pretend/To Sir With Love	10
67	Columbia DB 8295	Love Love's To Love Love/You And I	6
68	Columbia DB 8358	Me, The Peaceful Heart/Lookout	6
68	Columbia DB 8425	Boy/Sad Memories	6
68	Columbia DB 8500	I'm A Tiger/Without Him	5

69	Columbia DB 8550	Boom Bang-A-Bang/March!. 5
69	Atco 226 008	Oh Me, Oh My (I'm A Fool For You Baby)/Sweep Around Your Own Backyard 5
70	Atco 2091 014	Hum A Song (From Your Heart)/Mr. Bojangles (with Dixie Flyers) 5
71	Atco 2091 049	Got To Believe In Love/Move To My Rhythm 6
71	Atlantic 2091 083	Everybody Clap/After The Feeling Is Gone 6
72	Atlantic K 10185	Even If I Could Change/You Ain't Wrong You Just Ain't Right 5
74	Polydor 2001 490	The Man Who Sold The World/Watch That Man 5
74	Chelsea 2005 015	The Man With The Golden Gun/A Boy Like You 10
75	Chelsea 2005 022	Take Your Mama For A Ride (Parts 1 & 2) 5
75	Chelsea 2005 031	Boy Meets Girl/Mama's Little Corner Of The World. 5
75	Chelsea 2001 048	Heaven And Earth And The Stars/A Boy Like You 5
79	Alfa ALF 1700	I Could Never Miss You (More Than I Do)/
		Dance To The Feeling In Your Heart (p/s). 5
86	Jive LULU 2	My Boy Lollipop/It's Only Love (p/s) 5
65	Decca DFE 8597	LULU (EP). 30
65	Decca LK 4719	SOMETHING TO SHOUT ABOUT (LP) 35
67	Ace Of Clubs ACL 1232	LULU! (LP) 15
67	Fontana (S)TL 5446	TO SIR, WITH LOVE (LP, soundtrack, with Ron Grainer & Mindbenders). 45
67	Columbia S(C)X 6201	LOVE LOVES TO LOVE LULU (LP). 20
69	Columbia S(C)X 6365	LULU'S ALBUM (LP) 15
69	Atco 228 031	NEW ROUTES (LP). 15
70	Atco 2400 017	MELODY FAIR (LP). 12
	(see also Luvvers)	

LULU BELLE & SCOTTY
50	London L 833	Have I Told You Lately That I Love You/Schrudle Du (78) 10

BOB LUMAN
60	Warner Bros WB 12	Dreamy Doll/Buttercup. 10
60	Warner Bros WB 18	Let's Think About Livin'/You've Got Everything 6
60	Warner Bros WB 28	Why, Why, Bye, Bye/Oh, Lonesome Me 7
61	Warner Bros WB 37	The Great Snow Man/The Pig Latin Song 7
61	Warner Bros WB 49	Private Eye/You Turned Down The Lights 7
62	Warner Bros WB 60	Louisiana Man/Rocks Of Reno (unissued)
62	Warner Bros WB 75	Hey Joe/The Fool 7
64	Hickory 45-1238	The File/Bigger Men Than I 7
64	Hickory 45-1266	(Empty Walls) A Lonely Room/Run On Home Baby Brother 6
64	Hickory 45-1277	Old George Dickel/Fire Engine Red. 7
65	Hickory 45-1289	Bad Bad Day/Tears From Out Of Nowhere 8
65	Hickory 45-1410	Come On And Sing/It's A Sin. 6
68	CBS 3602	Ain't Got Time To Be Unhappy/I Can't Remember To Forget 12
61	Warner Bros WEP 6046	LET'S THINK ABOUT LIVIN' (EP, also stereo WSEP 2046) 35/50
62	Warner Bros WEP 6055	LET'S THINK ABOUT LIVIN' NO. 2 (EP, also stereo WSEP 2055) 35/50
62	Warner Bros WEP 6102	LET'S THINK ABOUT LIVIN' NO. 3 (EP, also stereo WSEP 2102) 35/50
60	Warner Bros WM 4025	LET'S THINK ABOUT LIVIN' (LP, also stereo WS 8025) 50/60
64	Hickory LPM 124	LIVIN' LOVIN' SOUNDS (LP) 25
71	London ZGE 115	LIVIN' LOVIN' SOUNDS (LP, reissue) 12
	(see also Sue Thompson & Bob Luman)	

BOB LUMAN/BOBBY LORD
64	Hickory LPE 1501	HICKORY SHOWCASE VOL. 2 (EP, 1 side each) 20
64	Hickory LPE 1504	HICKORY SHOWCASE VOL. 3 (EP, 1 side each) 20
64	Hickory LPM 121	CAN'T TAKE THE COUNTRY FROM THE BOYS (LP, 1 side each). 15
	(see also Bobby Lord)	

RUFUS LUMLEY
66	Stateside SS 516	I'm Standing/Let's Hide Away (Me And You) 75
78	EMI International INT 556	I'm Standing/Let's Hide Away (Me And You) (reissue) 5

LUNAR TWO
60s	Spot JWS 551	Get It Take It/Don't Ever Leave Me. 7

LYDIA LUNCH
91	UFO UFOPF 1	Spooky (mono)/Spooky (stereo) (no p/s, promo only) 8
93	Clawfist X-PIG 19	Unearthly Delights/Busted (p/s). 18
82	Situation 2 SITU 6	13.13 (LP, with inner sleeve) 20
84	Doublevision DVR 5	IN LIMBO (LP, red vinyl with inner sleeve) 20
86	Widowspeak SWP 01/07	THE INTIMATE DIARIES OF THE SEXUALLY INSANE
		(cassette, box set with book, signed) 25
	(see also Eight-Eyed Spy, Roland S. Howard, No Trend)	

ART LUND
53	MGM SP 1042	If I Were A Bell/JOHNNY DESMOND: A Bushel And A Peck. 8
65	United Artists UP 1100	Branded/Gonna Have A Little Talk. 5
57	Vogue Coral LVA 9056	THIS IS ART (LP) 18

LARRY LUREX
73	EMI EMI 2030	I Can Hear Music/Goin' Back (demo). 250
73	EMI EMI 2030	I Can Hear Music/Goin' Back (press-out centre;
		beware of solid-centered counterfeits) 175
	(see also Queen)	

LURKERS
77	Beggars Banquet BEG 1	Free Admission Single: Shadow/Love Story (p/s, black vinyl;
		reissued on red, blue or white vinyl) 5/8
77	Beggars Banquet BEG 2	Freak Show/Mass Media Believer (p/s) 5
78	Beggars Banquet BEG 6	Ain't Got A Clue/Ooh Ooh I Love You (p/s, 15,000 with gold flexidisc,
		'Chaos Brothers Fulham Fallout Firty Free' [BEG 61/2]) 6/4
78	Beggars Banquet BEG 6	Ain't Got A Clue/Ooh Ooh I Love You (reissue, different p/s,
		with clear vinyl picture flexidisc). 5
79	Beggars Banquet BACK 1	Shadow/Love Story//Freak Show/Mass Media Believer (reissue double pack) 5

79	Beggars Banquet BACK 3	I Don't Need To Tell Her/Pills//Just Thirteen/Countdown (double pack)	5
82	Clay CLAY 17P	Drag You Out/Heroin (It's All Over) (picture disc)	4
78	Beggars Banquet BEGA 2	FULHAM FALLOUT (LP, gatefold sleeve, some with picture disc flexi 'Chaos Brothers Fulham Fallout Forty Free' [BEG 6½] & stickered sleeve)	15/10

(see also Pete Stride & John Plain, Fulham Furies, Rowdies)

LUSH

89	4AD JAD 911	SCAR (12", initially with inner sleeve)	7
89	4AD JAD 911	SCAR (CD, initially with inner sleeve)	8
90	4AD CAD 0017	GALA (LP, deluxe printed inner bag & sleeve)	10
92	4AD CADD 2002	SPOOKY (10", 2-LP, gatefold sleeve)	10
94	4AD CAD 4011	SPLIT (LP, with inner sleeve & postcards)	10
96	4AD CAD 6004	LOVELIFE (LP, clear vinyl, sealed with foldover sleeve in poly bag, 7,500 only)	10

DON LUSHER BAND

| 55 | Decca F 10560 | Rock 'n' Roll/On With The Don | 10 |
| 56 | Decca F 10740 | Fast And Furious/Let's Do It | 6 |

LUSTMØRD

| 82 | Sterile SR 3 | LUSTMØRD (LP, with odorous label) | 50 |

NELLIE LUTCHER (& HER RHYTHM)

50	Capitol CL 13223	Kiss Me Sweet/The Pig-Latin Song (78)	8
50	Capitol CL 13234	Fine And Mellow/Lake Charles Boogie (78)	8
50	Capitol CL 13254	There's Another Mule In Your Stall/Glad Rag Doll (78)	8
50	Capitol CL 13274	That's A Plenty/Princess Poo-Poo-Ly Has Plenty Papaya (78)	8
50	Capitol CL 13275	Can I Come In For A Second/For You My Love (78, with Nat 'King' Cole)	8
50	Capitol CL 13366	Lovable/A Maid's Prayer (78)	8
50	Capitol CL 13399	Only You/Ditto From Me To You (78)	8
50	Capitol CL 13421	Let Me Love You Tonight/Lutcher's Leap (78)	8
51	Capitol CL 13493	Chi-Chi-Chi-Chicago/Do You Or Don't You Love Me? (78)	8
51	Capitol CL 13502	Reaching For The Moon/That'll Just 'Bout Knock Me Out (78)	8
51	Capitol CL 13509	Pa's Not Home, Ma's Upstairs/I Really Couldn't Love You (78)	8
51	Capitol CL 13606	The Birth Of The Blues/I Want To Be Near You (78)	8
52	Capitol CL 13738	What A Difference A Day Made/Mean To Me (78)	8
52	Capitol CL 13770	That's How It Goes/The Heart Of A Clown (78)	8
54	Brunswick 05352	Blues In The Night/Breezin' Along With The Breeze	12
54	Brunswick 05352	Blues In The Night/Breezin' Along With The Breeze (78)	8
55	Brunswick 05437	It's Been Said/Please Come Back	15
55	Brunswick 05437	It's Been Said/Please Come Back (78)	8
55	Brunswick 05497	Whose Honey Are You?/If I Didn't Love You Like I Do	8
55	Brunswick 05497	Whose Honey Are You?/If I Didn't Love You Like I Do (78)	8
60	Capitol CL 15106	My Mother's Eyes/The Heart Of A Clown	6
60	Capitol EAP 20066	REAL GONE (EP)	45
56	Philips BBE 12045	NELLIE LUTCHER (EP)	30
51	Capitol LC 6500	REAL GONE! (10" LP)	50
57	London HA-U 2036	OUR NEW NELLIE (LP)	35
66	M. For Pleasure MFP 1038	REAL GONE (LP)	12

CLAUDE LUTER ORCHESTRA

| 59 | Vogue V 9132 | The Day That The Rains Came/La Grande Coco | 7 |
| 59 | Vogue V 9132 | The Day That The Rains Came/La Grande Coco (78) | 12 |

LUTHER

| 76 | Cotillion K 10781 | It's Good For The Soul (Parts 1 & 2) | 15 |

FRANK LUTHER

53	Brunswick 05124	I'll Ring You Up/Jig A Jig Jig (78)	8
60	Decca F 9050	The Little Red Hen (Song Story) (both sides)	5
60	Decca F 9051	The Three Billy Goats Gruff (Song Story) (both sides)	5

LUTHER & LITTLE EVA

| 57 | Parlophone R 4292 | Love Is Strange/Ain't Got No Home | 450 |
| 57 | Parlophone R 4292 | Love Is Strange/Ain't Got No Home (78) | 90 |

(do not see also Little Eva)

LUV BUG

| 86 | Roxy!-Ritz TEASE 2 | You Can Count On Me/You Can't Have It (p/s) | 7 |

LUV MACHINE

| 71 | Polydor 2058 080 | Witches Wand/In The Early Hours | 10 |
| 71 | Polydor 2460 102 | LUV MACHINE (LP) | 100 |

LUVVERS

| 66 | Parlophone R 5459 | The House On The Hill/Most Unlovely | 25 |

(see also Lulu, Peter Ross Oliver)

MICK LUVZIT

| 66 | Decca F 12421 | Long Time Between Lovers/Though I Still Love You | 7 |

GARY LUX

| 85 | Global LUX 2 | Children Of The World/Movies (p/s) | 5 |

L-VOAG

| 79 | Sesame Songs MOVE 1 | MOVE (EP, p/s with handmade labels & insert) | 12 |
| 81 | Axis No. 9 | THE WAY OUT (LP, with booklet & poster) | 15 |

(see also Homosexuals)

LYLE McGUINNESS BAND

| 83 | Cool King CKLP 03 | ACTING ON IMPULSE (LP) | 12 |

(see also McGuinness Flint, Gallagher & Lyle)

ARTHUR LYMAN GROUP

| 59 | Vogue V 9153 | Taboo/Dahil Sayo | 5 |
| 59 | Vogue V 9153 | Taboo/Dahil Sayo (78) | 20 |

61	Vogue Pop V 9183	Yellow Bird/Havali Nagilali 6
62	Vogue Pop V 9195	I Talk To The Trees/Never On Sunday 6
62	Vogue Pop V 9199	Exodus/Aloha No Honolulu 6
63	Vogue Pop V 9208	Love For Sale/It's So Right To Love 6
66	Vogue Pop V 9265	Lemon Tree/The (Jungle) Cat 5
59	Vogue VEH 70166	GREATEST HITS VOL. 1 (EP) 12
59	Vogue VEH 70167	GREATEST HITS VOL. 2 (EP) 12
59	Vogue VEH 70168	GREATEST HITS VOL. 3 (EP) 12
59	Vogue VA 160142	TABOO VOL. 1 (LP, also stereo SAV 8002) 15/18
59	Vogue VA 160149	MORE EXOTIC SOUNDS — BWANA A (LP) 15
60	Vogue VA 160166	BAHIA (LP) 15
61	Vogue VA 160171	HAWAIIAN SUNSET (LP) 15
61	Vogue VA 160174	TABOO VOL. 2 (LP, also stereo SAV 8003) 15
63	Vogue SAVH 8030	LOVE FOR SALE (LP) 15

FRANKIE LYMON (& TEENAGERS)

56	Columbia SCM 5265	Why Do Fools Fall In Love?/Please Be Mine
		(as Teenagers featuring Frankie Lymon) 45
56	Columbia DB 3772	Why Do Fools Fall In Love?/Please Be Mine (78) 10
56	Columbia SCM 5285	I Want You To Be My Girl/I'm Not A Know It All 45
56	Columbia DB 3797	I Want You To Be My Girl/I'm Not A Know It All (78) 15
56	Columbia DB 3819	Who Can Explain?/I Promise To Remember 40
56	Columbia DB 3819	Who Can Explain?/I Promise To Remember (78) 15
56	Columbia DB 3858	Share/The A.B.C.'s Of Love 40
56	Columbia DB 3858	Share/The A.B.C.'s Of Love (78) 15
57	Columbia DB 3878	I'm Not A Juvenile Delinquent/Baby, Baby 25
57	Columbia DB 3878	I'm Not A Juvenile Delinquent/Baby, Baby (78) 10
57	Columbia DB 3910	Teenage Love/Paper Castles 35
57	Columbia DB 3910	Teenage Love/Paper Castles (78) 15
57	Columbia DB 3942	Miracle In The Rain/Out In The Cold Again 35
57	Columbia DB 3942	Miracle In The Rain/Out In The Cold Again (78) 15
57	Columbia DB 3983	Goody Goody/Creation Of Love 15
57	Columbia DB 3983	Goody Goody/Creation Of Love (78) 15
57	Columbia DB 4028	My Girl/So Goes My Love 25
57	Columbia DB 4028	My Girl/So Goes My Love (78) 20
58	Columbia DB 4073	Thumb Thumb/Footsteps (solo) 20
58	Columbia DB 4073	Thumb Thumb/Footsteps (78) 20
58	Columbia DB 4134	Mama Don't Allow It/Portable On My Shoulder (solo) 18
58	Columbia DB 4134	Mama Don't Allow It/Portable On My Shoulder (78) 25
59	Columbia DB 4245	Melinda/The Only Way To Love (solo) 18
59	Columbia DB 4245	Melinda/The Only Way To Love (78) 40
59	Columbia DB 4295	Up Jumped A Rabbit/No Matter What You've Done (solo) 20
60	Columbia DB 4499	Little Bitty Pretty One/Creation Of Love (solo) 25
66	King KG 1042	Why Do Fools Fall In Love?/I'm Not A Juvenile Delinquent 8
57	Columbia SEG 7662	TEENAGE ROCK (EP) 50
57	Columbia SEG 7694	THE TEENAGERS FEATURING FRANKIE LYMON (EP) 50
57	Columbia SEG 7734	FRANKIE LYMON AND THE TEENAGERS (EP) 75
58	Columbia 33S 1127	FRANKIE LYMON IN LONDON (10" LP, solo) 140
58	Columbia 33S 1134	ROCKIN' WITH FRANKIE LYMON (10" LP, solo) 400
78	Pye NSPL 28251	WHY DO FOOLS FALL IN LOVE? (LP) 10

LEWIS LYMON & TEENCHORDS

| 58 | Oriole 45-CB 1419 | Too Young/Your Last Chance . . . . 400 |
| 58 | Oriole CB 1419 | Too Young/Your Last Chance (78) . . . . 70 |

DERMOTT LYNCH

68	Blue Cat BS 101	Hot Shot/I've Got Your Number 12
68	Blue Cat BS 122	I Got Everything/Echo 12
68	Doctor Bird DB 1115	Adults Only/Cool It 12

(see also Trevor, Carl Dawkins, Joe White)

JOE LYNCH

| 69 | Spectrum SP 107 | King Child/Johnny Appleseed . . . . 5 |

KENNY LYNCH

60	HMV POP 751	Mountain Of Love/Why Do You Treat Me This Way? 12
60	HMV POP 786	Slowcoach/You Make Love So Well 7
61	HMV POP 841	So/Love Me 7
61	HMV POP 900	The Story Behind My Tears/Steady Kind 7
61	HMV POP 985	There's Never Been A Girl/Doll Face 7
62	HMV POP 1005	It Would Take A Miracle/Strolling Blues 8
62	HMV POP 1057	Puff/Happy That's Me 8
62	HMV POP 1090	Up On The Roof/Jump On Your Broomstick 6
63	HMV POP 1136	Misery/Shut The Door 8
63	HMV POP 1165	You Can Never Stop Me Loving You/Crazy Crazes 6
63	HMV POP 1229	For You (There's Not A Thing I Wouldn't Do)/With Somebody 6
63	HMV POP 1260	Shake And Scream/Harlem Library 6
64	HMV POP 1280	Stand By Me/Baby It's True 7
64	HMV POP 1321	That's What Little Girls Are Made For/What Am I To You? 7
64	HMV POP 1367	My Own Two Feet/So Much To Love You For 12
65	HMV POP 1430	I'll Stay By You/For Loving You Baby 7
65	HMV POP 1476	Nothing But The Real Thing/Don't Ask Me To Stop Loving You 7
65	HMV POP 1496	Get Out Of My Way/One Look At You 7
66	HMV POP 1534	The World I Used To Know/Come On Come On 7
67	HMV POP 1577	I Just Wanna Love You/It's Too Late 8
67	HMV POP 1604	Movin' Away/Could I Count On You 25
68	Columbia DB 8329	Mister Moonlight/The Other Side Of Dreamland 10
68	Columbia DB 8498	Along Comes Love/Sweet Situation 10
69	Columbia DB 8599	The Drifter/Did I Stay Too Long? 12

Kenny LYNCH

70	Columbia DB 8703	In Old Kentucky/Loving You Is Sweeter Than Ever	10
63	HMV 7EG 8820	HEY GIRL (EP)	30
64	HMV 7EG 8855	KENNY LYNCH (EP)	30
65	HMV 7EG 8881	WHAT AM I TO YOU (EP)	30
63	HMV CLP 1635	UP ON THE ROOF (LP, also stereo CSD 1489)	40/50
66	Music F. Pleasure MFP 1022	WE LIKE KENNY (LP)	12

LEE LYNCH (& BLUE ANGELS)

66	Decca F 12375	You Won't See Me/You Know There's Me (as Lee Lynch & Blue Angels)	7
69	Ember EMB S 262	Stay Awhile/Bad Time To Stop Loving Me (p/s)	8
70	Ember EMB S 271	Sweet Woman/Can't Take My Eyes Off You (p/s)	8
70	Ember EMB S 282	Joe Poor Loves Daphne Elizabeth Rich/It's Love (p/s)	8

LINDA LYNDELL

| 68 | Stax 601 041 | Bring Your Love Back To Me/Here I Am | 20 |

BARBARA LYNN

64	London HLW 9918	Oh! Baby (We Got A Good Thing Goin')/Unfair	18
65	Immediate IM 011	You Can't Buy My Love/That's What A Friend Will Do	15
66	London HLU 10094	You Left The Water Running/Until I'm Free	18
67	Sue WI 4028	Letter To Mommy And Daddy/Second Fiddle Girl	25
67	Sue WI 4038	You'll Lose A Good Thing/Lonely Heartaches	25
71	Atlantic 2091 133	Take Your Love And Run/(Until Then) I'll Suffer	10
75	Oval OVAL 1006	Letter To Mommy And Daddy/You'll Lose A Good Thing	5
67	Sue ILP 949	THE BARBARA LYNN STORY (LP)	100

BOBBI LYNN

| 68 | Stateside SS 2088 | Earthquake/Opportunity Street | 30 |
| 71 | Bell BLL 1168 | Earthquake/Opportunity Street (reissue) | 6 |

CHERYL LYNN

| 84 | Streetwave KHAN 23 | Encore/Got To Be Real | 4 |
| 84 | Streetwave MKHAN 23 | Encore/Got To Be Real (12") | 8 |

KARI LYNN

| 61 | Oriole CB 1632 | Yo Yo/Summer Day | 10 |
| 61 | Oriole CB 1644 | You've Got To See Mamma Every Night/Lonesome And Sorry | 10 |

LORETTA LYNN

68	MCA MUP 338	LORETTA LYNN (LP)	12
69	MCA MUP(S) 385	GREATEST HITS (LP)	12
70	MCA MUP(S) 407	HERE'S LORETTA LYNN SINGING WINGS UPON YOUR HORNS (LP)	12
70	MCA MUPS 411	YOUR SQUAW IS ON THE WARPATH (LP)	12
71	MCA MUPS 417	WRITES 'EM AND SINGS 'EM (LP)	12
71	MCA MUPS 427	COAL MINER'S DAUGHTER (LP)	12
72	MCA MUPS 447	YOU'RE LOOKING AT COUNTRY (LP)	12

(see also Conway Twitty)

PATTI LYNN

62	Fontana H 370	I See It All Now/Someone Else's Valentine	10
62	Fontana H 391	Johnny Angel/Tonight You Belong To Me	10
62	Fontana 267 247 TF	Tell Me Telstar/Big Big Love	12
62	Fontana TFE 17392	PATTI (EP)	40

TAM(M)I LYNN

66	Atlantic AT 4071	I'm Gonna Run Away From You/The Boy Next Door	30
71	Mojo 2092 001	I'm Gonna Run Away From You/The Boy Next Door (reissue)	6
71	Mojo 2092 012	That's Understanding/Never No More	5
75	Contempo CS 9026	I'm Gonna Run Away From You/The Boy Next Door (2nd reissue)	5
71	Mojo 2916 007	LOVE IS HERE AND NOW YOU'RE GONE (LP)	20

VERA LYNN

54	Decca F 10253	Two Easter Sunday Sweethearts/Du Bist Mein Liebeshoen	7
54	Decca F 10290	The Homecoming Waltz/Humble People	7
54	Decca F 10372	My Son, My Son/Our Heaven On Earth (with Frank Weir & His Saxophone)	30
55	MGM SP 1142	From Tomorrow/Each Moment I Live	5
56	Decca F 10715	Who Are We?/I'll Be True To You	8
56	Decca F 10799	A House With Love In It/Little Lost Dog	8
57	Decca F 10846	The Faithful Hussar (Don't Cry My Love)/The One Beside You	7
57	Decca F 10903	Travellin' Home/Dear To Me	7
59	Decca F 9927	Auf Wiederseh'n, Sweetheart/From The Time You Say Goodbye	7
59	Decca F 11112	Glory Of Love/Walk With Faith In Your Heart (78)	8
59	Decca F 11129	Have I Told You Lately That I Love You/I'm A Fool To Forgive You (78)	8
59	Decca F 11157	Morgen/Time Marches On (78)	8
52	Decca LF 1022	SINCERELY YOURS, VERA LYNN (10" LP)	12
53	Decca LF 1102	SINCERELY YOURS, VERA LYNN VOL. 2 (10" LP)	12
53	Decca LF 1183	SINCERELY YOURS, VERA LYNN VOL. 3 (10" LP)	12

(see also Johnstone Brothers, Frank Weir & His Orchestra)

GLORIA LYNNE

64	London HLY 9846	I Wish You Love/Through A Long And Sleeping Night	7
64	London HLY 9888	I Should Care/Indian Love Call	7
59	Top Rank JKP 2024	MEET GLORIA LYNNE (EP, with Wild Bill Davis)	8
60	Top Rank BUY 031	LONELY AND SENTIMENTAL (LP)	18
64	London HA-Y 8112	AT THE LAS VEGAS THUNDERBIRD (LP, with Herman Foster Trio)	18
72	Mojo 2916 016	HAPPY AND IN LOVE (LP)	18

JEFF LYNNE

| 77 | Jet UP 36281 | Doin' That Crazy Thing/Goin' Down To Rio (p/s) | 5 |

(see also Nightriders, Idle Race, Move, E.L.O., Traveling Wilburys)

SUE LYNNE
68	RCA Victor RCA 1724	Reach For The Moon/All Alone	8
69	RCA Victor RCA 1822	You/Don't Pity Me	80
69	RCA Victor RCA 1874	Baby Baby Baby/You Lose Again	6

PHIL LYNOTT
80	Vertigo LYN 1	King's Call/Yellow Pearl (p/s)	5
80	Vertigo LYNT 1	King's Call/Yellow Pearl (12", p/s)	10
80	Vertigo SOLO 1	Dear Miss Lonely Hearts/Solo In Soho (p/s)	5
80	Vertigo SOLO 112	Dear Miss Lonely Hearts/Solo In Soho (12", p/s)	8
80	Vertigo SOLO 2	King's Call/Ode To A Black Man (p/s)	5
81	Vertigo SOLO 3	Yellow Pearl/Girls (p/s, yellow vinyl)	5
85	Vertigo SOLO 5	Old Town/Beat Of The Drum (p/s)	6
85	Polydor POSPD 777	19/19 (Dub Version)//THIN LIZZY: Whiskey In The Jar (live) (double pack, 2nd disc 1-sided)	10
80	Vertigo PHIL 1	SOLO IN SOHO (LP, with inner sleeve)	12
80	Vertigo PHIL 1	SOLO IN SOHO (LP, picture disc, die-cut sleeve)	15

(see also Thin Lizzy, Gary Moore & Phil Lynott, John Sykes, Rockers)

JACKIE LYNTON
61	Piccadilly 7N 35012	Over The Rainbow/High In The Sky	6
62	Piccadilly 7N 35055	Don't Take Away Your Love/Wishful Thinking	6
62	Piccadilly 7N 35064	All Of Me/I'd Steal	10
63	Piccadilly 7N 35107	I Believe/The Girl In The Wood	6
63	Piccadilly 7N 35140	Jeannie With The Light Brown Hair/Teddy Bear's Picnic	6
63	Piccadilly 7N 35156	I'm Talkin' About You/Lawdy Miss Clawdy	6
64	Piccadilly 7N 35177	Little Child/Never A Mention	6
64	Piccadilly 7N 35190	Laura/Ebb Tide	6
65	Decca F 12052	Three Blind Mice/Corrina Corrine	5
67	Columbia DB 8097	He'll Have To Go/Only You	10
67	Columbia DB 8180	Decision/Sporting Life	10
67	Columbia DB 8224	Answer Me/I Never Loved A Girl Like You	10
74	WWA WWA 012	THE JACKIE LYNTON ALBUM (LP)	15

(see also Savoy Brown Blues Band)

LYNYRD SKYNYRD
74	MCA MCA 136	Don't Ask Me No Questions/Take Your Time	6
74	MCA MCA 160	Sweet Home Alabama/Take Your Time	5
75	MCA MCA 199	Saturday Night Special/Made In The Shade	5
76	MCA MCA 229	Double Trouble/Roll Gypsy Roll	5
76	MCA MCA 251	Free Bird/Sweet Home Alabama/Double Trouble (p/s)	8
76	MCA MCA 275	Free Bird (Edit)/Gimme Three Steps (p/s)	8
78	MCA MCEP 101	DOWN SOUTH JUKIN' (EP, p/s)	7
78	MCA MCA 342	What's Your Name/I Know A Little	5
82	MCA MCA 799	I've Been Your Fool/Gotta Go (p/s)	5
82	MCA MCAT 251	Free Bird/Sweet Home Alabama/Double Trouble (12", p/s)	8
82	MCA MCATP 251	Free Bird/Sweet Home Alabama/Double Trouble (12", picture disc)	12
89	MCA DMCA 251	Free Bird/Sweet Home Alabama/Double Trouble (3" CD, card sleeve)	8
74	MCA MCG 3502	PRONOUNCED LEH-NERD SKIN-NERD (LP, gatefold sleeve)	15
77	MCA MCG 3525	STREET SURVIVORS (LP, gatefold sleeve with tour dates on inner sleeve)	12

(see also Blackfoot)

BARBARA LYON
55	Columbia SCM 5186	I Love To Dance With You/Yes You Are	10
55	Columbia SCM 5207	Whisper/Where You Are	10
56	Columbia SCM 5232	Band Of Gold/Such A Day	10
56	Columbia SCM 5276	Puppy Love/The Birds And The Bees	10
56	Columbia DB 3786	Puppy Love/The Birds And The Bees (78)	8
56	Columbia DB 3826	It's Better In The Dark/A Heart Without A Sweetheart	8
56	Columbia DB 3865	Falling In Love/Letter To A Soldier	12
56	Columbia DB 3865	Falling In Love/Letter To A Soldier (78)	8
57	Columbia DB 3931	C'est La Vie/Fire Down Below	5
57	Columbia DB 4026	Thanks For The Loan Of A Dream/Third Finger — Left Hand	5
58	Columbia DB 4137	Red Was The Moon/Ring On A Ribbon	5
60	Triumph RGM 1027	My Charlie/Tell Me	35
56	Columbia SEG 7640	MY FOUR FRIENDS (EP)	18

PATTI LYON
62	Fontana H 370	I See It All Now/Someone Else's Valentine	10

RICHARD LYON
59	Fontana H 206	All My Own/Private Eye	6
59	Fontana H 206	All My Own/Private Eye (78)	12

LYONS & MALONE
69	Jay Boy BOY 9	Doctor Gentle/She's Alright	4

LYON ST.
(see under Associates)

LYRICS
67	Coxsone CS 7003	A Get It/KEN PARKER: How Strong	20
68	Coxsone CS 7067	Music Like Dirt/TONETTES: I Give It To You	20
70	Randy's RAN 504	Give Thanks And Praises/TOMMY McCOOK: Get Ready	8
71	Randy's RAN 511	Give Thanks/RANDY'S ALL STARS: Give — Version	8

(see also Randy's All Stars, Viceroys, Jackie Mittoo)

JIMMY LYTELL
59	London HL 8873	Hot Cargo/A Blues Serenade	10

JOHNNY LYTLE
68	Minit MLF 11006	Gonna Get That Boat (Parts 1 & 2)	8

HUMPHREY LYTTELTON (& HIS BAND)

78s

56	Esquire 10-491	The Thin Red Line/Melancholy Blues (78)	8
56	Esquire 10-494	First Of Many/Blues For Two (78)	8
57	Esquire 10-501	Elizabeth/Blue For Waterloo (78)	8
57	Esquire 10-511	Cake Walkin' Babies/If You See Me Comin' (78)	8
57	Parlophone R 4277	Baby Doll/Red Beans And Rice (78)	8
58	Parlophone R 4428	Hand Me Down Love/Here And Gone (Blues In 1890) (78)	8
58	Decca F 11058	La Paloma/Bodega (78)	8
59	Parlophone R 4519	Saturday Jump/The Bear Steps Out (78)	10

SINGLES

53	Parlophone MSP 6001	Out Of The Gallion/The Old Grey Mare	7
53	Parlophone MSP 6023	Muskrat Ramble/Mamzelle Josephine (as Lyttelton Paseo Band, B-side with George Brown)	7
53	Parlophone MSP 6033	Maryland, My Maryland/Blue For Waterloo	7
53	Parlophone MSP 6034	Shake It And Break It/Jail Break	7
53	Parlophone MSP 6045	Red For Piccadilly/Kater Street Rag	7
54	Parlophone MSP 6061	Martiniquen Song (Last Year)/Ain't Cha Got Music	7
54	Parlophone MSP 6076	East Coast Trot/Breeze	7
54	Parlophone MSP 6093	Just Once For All Time/Joshua, Fit The Battle Of Jericho	7
54	Parlophone MSP 6097	Mainly Traditional/Oh! Dad (with 'Melody Maker' All Stars)	7
54	Parlophone MSP 6128	Mezzy's Tune/Jelly Bean Blues	7
56	Tempo A 10	When The Saints Go Marching In/Careless Love	6
56	Parlophone R 4212	Love, Love, Love/Echoing The Blues	6
57	Parlophone R 4262	It's Mardi Gras/Sweet And Sour	7
57	Parlophone R 4277	Baby Doll/Red Beans And Rice	7
57	Parlophone R 4333	Early Call (Bermondsey Bounce)/Creole Serenade	5
57	Parlophone R 4368	Dixie Theme/Blues At Dawn	5
58	Parlophone CMSP 41	Bad Penny Blues/Baby Doll (export issue)	25
58	Parlophone R 4392	Buona Sera/Blues In The Afternoon	5
58	Parlophone R 4428	Hand Me Down Love/Here And Gone (Blues In 1890)	5
58	Decca F 11058	La Paloma/Bodega	8
59	Parlophone R 4519	Saturday Jump/The Bear Steps Out	5
59	Parlophone R 4578	Summertime/Manhunt	5
50s	Storyville A 45041	The Thin Red Line/Ole Miss	5
50s	Summer County LYN 254	Swingin' On The Gate/Jeanie With The Light Brown Hair (flexidisc, some in p/s)	10/5

EPs

55	Parlophone GEP 8503	HUMPHREY LYTTELTON & HIS BAND (EP)	10
55	Parlophone GEP 8514	HUMPHREY LYTTELTON & HIS BAND (EP)	10
55	Parlophone GEP 8546	JAZZ WITH LYTTELTON – 1 (EP)	8
56	Parlophone GEP 8572	JAZZ WITH LYTTELTON – 2 (EP)	12
56	Parlophone GEP 8580	LIGHTLY & POLITELY (EP)	10
56	Parlophone GEP 8584	HUMPH'S BLUES (EP)	12
55	Tempo EXA 1	HUMPHREY LITTELTON & HIS BAND (EP)	60
56	Esquire EP 111	HUMPHREY LITTELTON & HIS BAND (EP)	18
57	Esquire EP 141	HUMPHREY LITTELTON & HIS BAND (EP)	18
57	Esquire EP 153	VINTAGE '49 (EP)	18
57	Parlophone GEP 8599	JAZZ WITH LYTTELTON – 4 (EP)	10
57	Parlophone GEP 8645	HUMPH'S BLUES NO. 2 (EP)	12
57	Parlophone GEP 8668	IT'S MARDI GRAS (EP)	8
58	Parlophone GEP 8700	COLOURFUL HUMPH (EP)	10
58	Parlophone GEP 8724	BLUE HUMPH (EP)	8
58	Parlophone GEP 8734	HUMPH'S JAZZ (EP)	15
58	Esquire EP 171	THAT REVIVAL SOUND (EP)	18
62	Columbia SEG 8163	DO THE BEAULIEU (EP)	15

LPs

53	Parlophone PMD 1006	JAZZ CONCERT (10" LP)	20
54	Parlophone PMC 1012	HUMPH AT THE CONWAY (LP)	25
55	Parlophone PMD 1032	JAZZ AT THE ROYAL FESTIVAL HALL (10" LP)	50
56	Parlophone PMD 1035	JAZZ SESSION WITH HUMPH (10" LP)	20
56	Parlophone PMD 1044	HUMPH SWINGS OUT (10" LP)	40
57	Parlophone PMD 1049	HERE'S HUMPH (10" LP)	20
58	Parlophone PMD 1052	KATH MEETS HUMPH (10" LP, with Kathy Stobart)	30
58	Parlophone PMC 1070	HUMPH IN PERSPECTIVE (LP)	40
58	Decca LK 4276	I PLAY AS I PLEASE (LP)	25
59	Parlophone PMC 1110	TRIPLE EXPOSURE (LP)	80
50s	Esquire 32-007	HUMPHREY LYTTELTON AND HIS BAND (LP)	25
60	Columbia 33SX 1239	BLUES IN THE NIGHT (LP)	30
60	Columbia 33SX 1305	HUMPH PLAYS STANDARDS (LP)	40
60	Columbia 33SX 1364	HUMPH MEETS CAB (LP)	70
61	Columbia 33SX 3382	HUMPH RETURNS TO THE CONWAY (LP)	30
61	Columbia SEG 8130	BIG H (EP)	10
62	Columbia 33SX 1484	LATE NIGHT FINAL (LP)	25
65	Society SOC 1003	HUMPHREY LYTTELTON AND HIS BAND (LP)	20
69	Polydor 2460 140	DUKE ELLINGTON CLASSICS (LP)	60
69	Polydor 2661 001	21 YEARS ON (LP)	25
73	Polydor 2460 233	SOUTH BANK SWING SESSION (LP)	25
74	Black Lion BLP 12149	ONCE IN A WHILE (LP)	20
78	Black Lion BLP 12173	SPREADIN' JOY (LP)	20
79	Black Lion BLP 12188	SIR HUMPH'S DELIGHT (LP)	20
79	Magnus 1	HUMPHREY'S ABOUT (LP)	20
80	Black Lion BLP 12199	ONE DAY I MET AN AFRICAN (LP)	20
82	Black Lion BLM 51011	ECHOES OF HARLEM (LP)	20

(see also Shirley Abicair, Sidney Bechet, George Brown)

M

78	Do It 640 147	Moderne Man/Satisfy Your Lust (p/s)	6
79	MCA MCAT 413	Pop Musik/M Factor (12", p/s, double groove)	7
89	Freestyle FRSCDS 1	Pop Musik 1989 (Remix)/Pop Muzik (Cabinet Remix)/	
		Pop Musik (Original 1979 Release) (CD)	7

(see also Comic Romance, Robin Scott)

MABEL

78	Sonet SON 2147	Boom Boom/FBI On The Nail (p/s)	6

MABEL JOY

75	Real RR 2004	MABEL JOY (LP)	30

MOMS MABLEY

69	Mercury MF 1127	Abraham, Martin And John/Sunny	6
71	Mercury 6052 109	That's Pops/I Surrender Dear	5

WILLIE MABON

64	Sue WI 320	Got To Have Some/Why Did It Happen To Me	20
65	Sue WI 331	Just Got Some/That's No Big Thing	20
65	Sue WI 382	I'm The Fixer/Some More	20

DAN MacARTHUR

79	Virgin VS 275	DAN MacARTHUR (EP)	5
79	Virgin VS 275-12	DAN MacARTHUR (12" EP)	8

(see also Jah Wobble, PiL)

NEIL MacARTHUR

69	Deram DM 225	She's Not There/World Of Glass	8
69	Deram DM 262	Don't Try To Explain/Without Her	8
69	Deram DM 275	It's Not Easy/12.29	8

(see also Colin Blunstone, Zombies)

MACABRE

89	Vinyl Solution SOL 18	GRIM REALITY (12" EP, with lyric insert)	8

GLO MACARI

65	Piccadilly 7N 35218	He Knows I Love Him Too Much/I've Lost You	10

MACARTHUR PARK

70	Columbia DB 8683	Taffeta Rose/Sammy	10
71	Philips 6006 086	Lottie Lottie/Love Is Coming	5

(see also Shadows)

DAVID MACBETH

59	Pye Nixa 7N 15231	Mr. Blue/Here's A Heart	6
59	Pye Nixa 7N 15231	Mr. Blue/Here's A Heart (78)	15
60	Pye 7N 15250	Tell Her From Me/Livin' Dangerously	6
60	Pye 7N 15274	Unhappy/Once Upon A Star	6
60	Pye 7N 15291	Blue Blue Blue/Pigtails In Paris	6
61	Pye 7N 15325	The Puppet Song/Angel On My Shoulder	6
61	Pye 7N 15364	Keep A-Walking/You're Free	6
61	Decca F 11402	Just A Twinkle/While I'm Away	5
62	Piccadilly 7N 35062	Roses Are Red (My Love)/Little Heart	6
62	Piccadilly 7N 35072	Have I Told You Lately That I Love You/A Brother Like You	5
63	Piccadilly 7N 35092	A Very Good Year For Girls/Broken Hearts	5
63	Piccadilly 7N 35114	My Golden Chance/Like A Falling Star	5
69	Pye 7N 17744	Does Anybody Miss Me/The Small Exception Of Me	5

MACC LADS

89	Renegade RS 1	Jingle Bells/Even Uglier Women (p/s)	5
90	FM Revolver VHF 42	Barrels Round/Jingle Bells (p/s)	4
82	Hectic House	ONE GALLON DEMO (cassette)	10
82	Hectic House	MINGE PIES AND MISTLETOE (cassette)	8
83	Hectic House	EH UP! MACC LADS (cassette)	7
85	Hectic House HH 1A	BEER AND SEX AND CHIPS'N'GRAVY (promo cassette)	8
86	Hectic House HHS 1	EH UP! MACC LADS (EP)	5
86	Hectic House HH 2	ONE GALLON DEMO (EP)	4
86	Hectic House HH 3	MINGE PIES AND MISTLETOE (EP)	4
86	Hectic House HH 5	MACC LADDS FIVE (EP, cassette)	4
87	Hectic House HH 6	FILTHY, FAT AND FLATULENT (EP, cassette)	4
88	Hectic House HH 10A	LIVE AT LEEDS — THE MACC LADS (THE WHO?) (promo cassette)	8
88	Hectic House HH 12A	FROM BEER TO ETERNITY (promo cassette)	8
85	FM Revolver FMLP 56	BEER AND SEX AND CHIPS'N'GRAVY (LP, white vinyl)	12
88	FM Revolver WKFMLP 115	LIVE AT LEEDS (LP, blue vinyl)	12

EWAN MacCOLL

58	Topic 10T 26	BARRACK ROOM BALLADS (10" LP)	30
58	Topic 10T 36	BOLD SPORTSMEN ALL (10" LP, with A.L. Lloyd)	30
58	Topic 10T 50	STILL I LOVE HIM (10" LP with booklet, with Isla Cameron)	35
60	Topic 12T 41	STREETS OF SONG (LP, with Dominic Behan, with booklet,	
		originally with blue label)	20/12
61	PRE 13004	THE BEST OF EWAN MacCOLL (LP)	12

Ewan MacCOLL

62	Topic 12T 79	JACOBITE SONGS (LP, originally with blue label)	18/12
64	Topic 12T 103	ENGLISH AND SCOTTISH FOLK BALLADS (LP, with A.L. Lloyd, originally with blue label)	18/12
67	Topic 12T 130	BUNDOOK BALLADS (LP, originally with blue label)	18/12
67	Argo RG 502	SINGING THE FISHING (LP, with Charles Parker)	20
67	Argo DA 142	SINGING THE FISHING (LP, reissue, with Charles Parker)	18
67	Argo ZFB 12	SOLO FLIGHT (LP; reissued 1972)	30
67	Xtra 1052	BLOW BOYS BLOW – SONGS OF THE SEA (LP, with A.L. Lloyd)	12
68	Argo (Z)DA 85	THE WANTON MUSE (LP, with booklet)	30
72	Argo (Z)DA 85	THE WANTON MUSE (LP, reissue)	15

(see also A.L. Loyd)

EWAN MacCOLL & PEGGY SEEGER (& CHARLES PARKER)

60s	AUEW AUEW 1	We Are The Engineers/I'm Gonna Be An Engineer (p/s)	6
57	Topic 10T 13	SHUTTLE AND CAGE (10" LP)	35
61	Topic 12T 16	CHORUS FROM THE GALLOWS (LP, originally with blue label)	18/12
64	Topic 12T 104	STEAM WHISTLE BALLADS (LP, blue label, later reissued with booklet)	18/12
65	Argo RG 474	THE BALLAD OF JOHN AXON (LP, by Ewan MacColl & Charles Parker)	25
67	Topic 12T 147	THE MANCHESTER ANGEL (LP, originally with blue label)	18/12
67	Argo DA 140	THE BIG HEWER — A RADIO BALLAD BY EWAN MacCOLL, PEGGY SEEGER, CHARLES PARKER (LP, documentary with music)	25
67	Argo (Z)DA 66	LONG HARVEST 1 (LP)	15
67	Argo (Z)DA 67	LONG HARVEST 2 (LP)	15
67	Argo (Z)DA 68	LONG HARVEST 3 (LP)	15
67	Argo (Z)DA 69	LONG HARVEST 4 (LP)	15
68	Argo (Z)DA 70	LONG HARVEST 5 (LP)	15
68	Argo (Z)DA 71	LONG HARVEST 6 (LP)	15
68	Argo (Z)DA 72	LONG HARVEST 7 (LP)	15
68	Argo (Z)DA 73	LONG HARVEST 8 (LP)	15
68	Argo (Z)DA 74	LONG HARVEST 9 (LP)	15
68	Argo (Z)DA 75	LONG HARVEST 10 (LP)	15
68	Argo (Z)DA 84	THE AMOROUS MUSE (LP)	15
68	Argo (Z)DA	THE ANGRY MUSE (LP)	15
69	Argo (Z)DA 98	THE PAPER STAGE 1 (LP, with booklet)	15
69	Argo (Z)DA 99	THE PAPER STAGE 2 (LP)	15
70	Argo DA 133	THE TRAVELLING PEOPLE (LP, with Charles Parker)	15
71	Argo DA 136	ON THE EDGE (LP)	15
72	Argo ZFB 65	THE ANGRY MUSE (LP, reissue)	12
72	Argo ZFB 66	THE AMOROUS MUSE (LP, reissue)	12

(see also Peggy Seeger, A.L. Lloyd, Isla Cameron)

KIRSTY MacCOLL
| 79 | Stiff BUY 57 | You Caught Me Out/Boys (with Boomtown Rats, unreleased, demos only) | 6 |

(see also Drug Addix)

FINN MacCUILL
| 79 | Radio Edinburgh Rel 460 | SINK YE — SWIM YE (LP) | 100 |

AIMI MACDONALD
| 67 | Polydor 56191 | Thoroughly Modern Millie/Jimmy | 4 |

BIG MACEO
| 62 | RCA RCX 203 | KINGS OF THE BLUES (EP) | 15 |

MACEO & ALL THE KING'S MEN
72	Pye International 7N 25571	Got To Get 'Cha/Thank You For Letting Me Be Myself Again (Part 1)	6
72	Mojo 2916 017	FUNKY MUSIC MACHINE (LP)	45
75	Contempo CRM 114	FUNKY MUSIC MACHINE (LP, reissue)	20

MACEO & THE MACKS
87	Urban URB 1	Cross The Tracks (We Better Go Back)/Soul Power (printed die-cut sleeve)	5
87	Urban URBX 1	Cross The Tracks (We Better Go Back) (Extended Version)/Party Part 1/ Soul Power (12", printed die-cut sleeve)	12
74	Polydor 2391 122	US (LP)	30
88	Urban URBLP 8	US (LP, reissue)	15

(see also Maceo & All The King's Men, James Brown)

MACHINE
| 67 | Granta GR 7STD | Stupidity/Please Stay (private pressing) | 20 |

MACHINE
| 69 | Polydor 56760 | Spooky's Day Off/Nobody Wants You | 6 |

(see also Swinging Soul Machine)

MACHINES
| 78 | Wax EAR 1 | True Life/Everything's Technical/You Better Hear/Evening Radio (stamped p/s, white labels) | 50 |

MACHITO
| 54 | Seeco SV 2173 | Dragnet—Mambo/Mambo Sentimental (78) | 8 |
| 50s | Columbia | AFRO CUBAN JAZZ (10" LP) | 20 |

ALURA MACK
| 50s | Poydras 84 | Everybody's Man Is Mine/Monkey Blues (78) | 8 |

JOHNNY MACK
| 70 | Columbia Blue Beat DB 116 | Reggae All Night Long/A Million Marvellous Feelings | 8 |

LONNIE MACK
63	Stateside SS 207	Memphis/Down In The Dumps	12
63	Stateside SS 226	Wham!/Susie-Q	12
64	Stateside SS 312	Lonnie On The Move/Say Something Nice To Me	10
65	Stateside SS 393	Sa-Ba-Hoola/Chickin' Pickin'	15

MINT VALUE £

67	President PT 127	Where There's A Will/Baby What's Wrong?	6
67	President PT 142	Save Your Money/Snow On The Mountain	6
68	President PT 198	Soul Express/I Found A Love	6
69	Elektra EKSN 45044	Memphis/Why (Edited Version)	7
69	Elektra EKSN 45060	Save Your Money/In The Band	6
71	Elektra EK 45715	Lay It Down/She Even Woke Me Up To Say Goodbye	5
79	Old Gold OG 9011	Memphis/CHRIS MONTEZ: Let's Dance (picture disc)	5
67	President PTL 1004	THE WHAM OF THAT MEMPHIS MAN (LP)	20
69	Elektra EKL 4040	GLAD I'M IN THE BAND (LP, orange label, also stereo EKS 74040)	20
69	Elektra EKS 74050	WHATEVER'S RIGHT (LP, orange label)	20
70	Elektra 2410 007	FOR COLLECTORS ONLY (LP, reissue of "The Wham Of That Memphis Man")	15
72	Elektra K 42097	THE HILLS OF INDIANA (LP)	15

WARNER MACK
58	Brunswick 05728	Roc-A-Chicka/Since I Lost You (with Anita Kerr Quartet)	140
58	Brunswick 05728	Roc-A-Chicka/Since I Lost You (with Anita Kerr Quartet) (78)	65
58	Decca	Roc-A-Chicka/Since I Lost You (export issue, with Anita Kerr Quartet)	70
62	London HA-R/SH-R 8002	GOLDEN COUNTRY HITS (LP)	25
63	London HA-R/SH-R 8025	GOLDEN COUNTRY HITS VOL. 2 (LP)	25
66	Brunswick LAT 8658	COUNTRY TOUCH (LP)	18
67	Brunswick LAT 8684	DRIFTING APART (LP)	18

ANDY MACKAY
74	Island WIP 6197	Ride Of The Valkyries/Time Regained	5
75	Island WIP 6243	Wild Weekend/Walking The Whippet (some in promo p/s)	10/5
78	Bronze BRO 64	A Song Of Friendship/Skill And Sweat	5
74	Island ILPS 9278	IN SEARCH OF EDDIE RIFF (LP, 2 different versions)	12

(see also Roxy Music, Rock Follies)

MAHNA MACKAY
| 69 | Parlophone R 5808 | Mah Na Mah Na/Daydream | 6 |

RABBIT MacKAY
| 68 | MCA MU 1041 | Hard Time Woman/Candy | 5 |
| 68 | MCA MUPS 351 | BUG CLOTH (LP) | 12 |

BILLY MacKENZIE (SINGS ORBIDÖIG)
82	WEA MAK 1	Ice Cream Factory/Cream Of Ice Cream Factory (p/s, as MacKenzie Sings Orbidöig)	4
82	WEA MAK 1T	Ice Cream Factory/Cream Of Ice Cream Factory (12", p/s, as MacKenzie Sings Orbidöig)	7
92	Circa YRCD 86	Baby/Sacrifice And Be Sacrificed (CH 8032 Mix)/Grooveature (D 1000 Mix)/ Colours Will Come (US 60659 Mix) (CD, solo)	7

(see also Associates, Orbidöig, Yello, B.E.F., Barry Adamson, Sweden Through The Ages)

GISELE MacKENZIE
| 53 | Capitol CL 13920 | Seven Lonely Days/Till I Waltz With You Again | 7 |
| 55 | HMV 7M 318 | Hard To Get/Boston Fancy | 6 |

JUDY MacKENZIE
| 70 | Key KL 005 | JUDY (LP) | 25 |
| 71 | Key KL 009 | PEACE AND LOVE AND FREEDOM (LP, with poster) | 25 |

MACKENZIE JET COMBO
| 70 | Torpedo TOR 18 | Milkman's Theme/Capadulah Recipe | 7 |

MACKERAL
| 66 | Columbia DB 8013 | Funny Fish/This Is Mine | 4 |
| 68 | Columbia DB 8388 | Trying Again/White Man's Burden | 4 |

KEN MACKINTOSH (& HIS ORCHESTRA)
56	HMV 7M 343	Creeping Tom/Lovers In The Dark	7
56	HMV 7M 359	Start Walking/Curtain Call	7
56	HMV 7M 379	Blues In The Night/Come Next Spring (B-side with Kenny Bardell)	7
56	HMV 7M 403	Sleepwalker/The Berkeley Hunt	7
56	HMV 7M 417	Dizzy Fingers/The Policeman's Holiday	7
56	HMV POP 270	Soft Summer Breeze/Highway Patrol	7
57	HMV POP 287	The Buccaneers/Regimental Rock	10
57	HMV POP 300	Apple-Jack/Slow Walk	15
57	HMV POP 327	Almost Paradise/Rock Man Rock	15
57	HMV POP 358	Poni Tail/Keep It Movin'	7
57	HMV POP 396	Marching Along To The Blues/Six-Five Blues	7
57	HMV POP 426	Raunchy/Mojo	7
57	HMV POP 426	Raunchy/Mojo (78)	10
58	HMV POP 441	The Stroll/The Swingin' Shepherd Blues	7
58	HMV POP 441	The Stroll/The Swingin' Shepherd Blues (78)	10
58	HMV POP 464	Big Guitar/Squatty	7
58	HMV POP 464	Big Guitar/Squatty (78)	10
58	HMV POP 506	The Swivel/Muchacha	6
58	HMV POP 506	The Swivel/Muchacha (78)	10
59	HMV POP 592	Rock-A-Conga/Hampden Park	6
59	HMV POP 592	Rock-A-Conga/Hampden Park (78)	12
59	HMV POP 656	Sleep Walk/Morgen (One More Sunrise)	6
60	HMV POP 713	No Hiding Place/Tally Ho!	6
56	HMV 7EG 8170	TEENAGER'S SPECIAL (EP)	20
58	HMV 7EG 8468	DANCING TO THE ROARING TWENTIES (EP)	10
55	HMV DLP 1093	KEN MACKINTOSH (10" LP)	15
58	HMV DLP 1178	ONE NIGHT STAND (10" LP)	25

MACK SISTERS
| 56 | London HLU 8331 | Long Range Love/Stop What You're Doing | 35 |

MINT VALUE £

PETE MacLAINE & CLAN
63   Decca F 11699 — Yes I Do/U.S. Mail 10

SHIRLEY MacLAINE
69   MCA MU 1062 — My Personal Property/Where Am I Going 4

DOUGIE MacLEAN
80   Plant Life PLR 022 — SNAIGOW (LP, with lyric insert)................................. 12

DOLINA MACLENNAN & ROBIN GRAY
61   Topic TOP 68 — BY MORMOND BRAES (EP) 8

JOHN MacLEOD'S FIRST XI
66   Fontana TF 696 — Don't Shoot The Ref/Tomato Crisps 6

JOHN MacLEOD SOUND
60s Transatlantic TRASP 12 — Russian Roulette/West Wind 4

ANGUS MacLISE
87   Fierce FRIGHT 010 — Trance (1-sided, with 'Dopechoc' & badge)....................... 10

PATRICK MacNEE & HONOR BLACKMAN
64   Decca F 11843 — Kinky Boots/Let's Keep It Friendly 30
(see also Honor Blackman)

FLORA MacNEIL
77   Tangent TGS 124 — CROABH NAN UBHAL (LP, with insert)............................. 12

UNCLE DAVE MACON
63   RCA RCX 7112 — UNCLE DAVE MACON NO. 1 (EP) 20
63   RCA RCX 7113 — UNCLE DAVE MACON NO. 2 (EP) 20
66   Ace Of Hearts AH 135 — UNCLE DAVE MACON (LP) 12

MACON JUG
70   Saga FID 8157 — IN THE SUMMERTIME (LP, with tracks by Good Earth) 12
72   Boulevard BLVD 4078 — RAY DORSET'S BEST (LP, 4 tracks by Good Earth, 6 tracks by Macon Jug) 12
(see also Ray Dorset, Mungo Jerry)

GORDON MacRAE
54   Capitol CL 14168 — How Do You Speak To An Angel?/C'est Magnifique 10
54   Capitol CL 14193 — Count Your Blessings Instead Of Sheep/Never In A Million Years 10
55   Capitol CL 14222 — Here's What I'm Here For/Love Can Change The Stars. 6
55   Capitol CL 14276 — Stranger In Paradise/High On A Windy Hill. 10
55   Capitol CL 14293 — You Forget (To Tell Me That You Love Me)/Tik-A-Tee, Tik-A-Tay 6
55   Capitol CL 14334 — Jim Bowie/Why Break The Heart That Loves You 10
55   Capitol CL 14361 — Bella Notte/Blame It On My Youth 10
56   Capitol CL 14526 — Follow Your Heart/Fate. 6
56   Capitol CL 14548 — Never Before And Never Again/Don't Blame Me. 6
56   Capitol CL 14576 — Who Are We/There's A Lull In My Life 6
56   Capitol CL 14606 — One Misty Morning/I Asked The Lord 5
56   Capitol CL 14613 — People Will Say We're In Love/The Surrey With The Fringe On Top
                         (with Ray Anthony) 6
56   Capitol CL 14622 — Woman In Love/I Don't Want To Walk Without You 6
58   Capitol CL 14818 — Lonely/Sayonora 6
58   Capitol CL 14864 — I've Grown Accustomed To Her Face/Never Till Now 6
58   Capitol CL 14920 — The Secret/A Man Once Said. 6
58   Capitol CL 14920 — The Secret/A Man Once Said (78) 10
59   Capitol CL 14983 — Fly Little Bluebird/Little Do You Know. 6
59   Capitol CL 14983 — Fly Little Bluebird/Little Do You Know (78) 10
59   Capitol CL 15021 — Palace Of Love/The Stranger. 6
62   Capitol CL 15256 — Sail Away/Face To Face 6
63   Capitol CL 15315 — Lovely/Warmer Than A Whisper. 6
52   Capitol LC 6564 — THE MERRY WIDOW (10" LP, with Lucille Norman) 15
53   Capitol LC 6592 — CAPITOL PRESENTS GORDON MACRAE (10" LP). 15
53   Capitol LC 6599 — BY THE LIGHT OF THE SILVERY MOON (10" LP, with June Hutton) 15
53   Capitol LC 6606 — THE DESERT SONG (10" LP, with Lucille Norman). 15
53   Capitol LC 6613 — THE STUDENT PRINCE (10" LP, with Dorothy Warenskjold) 15
54   Capitol LC 6663 — NAUGHTY MARIETTA (10" LP, with Lucille Norman) 15
54   Capitol LC 6666 — ROBERTA (10" LP, with Lucille Norman). 15
56   Capitol LC 6805 — ROMANTIC BALLADS (10" LP) 15
60   Capitol (S)T 1251 — SONGS FOR AN EVENING AT HOME (LP) 12
60   Top Rank 25/006 — GORDON MACRAE (LP). 12
(see also Jo Stafford, Ray Anthony, Jonathan & Darlene Edwards)

JOSH MACRAE
60   Top Rank JAR 290 — Talkin' Army Blues/Talkin' Guitar Blues. 10
60   Pye 7N 15306 — Original Talkin' Blues (Talkin' Southern Blues)/Talkin' Thro' The Mill 6
60   Pye 7N 15307 — Let Ramensky Go/Sky High Joe 6
60   Pye 7N 15308 — Wild Side Of Life/Dear John 8
61   Pye 7N 15319 — Messing About On The River/High Class Feeling. 8
61   Pye 7N 15360 — Arkansas Rambler/Never Never Man. 6
61   Pye 7N 15384 — Do It Yourself/Special Place Of Yorn 6
60   Pye NEP 24131 — WALKIN', TALKIN', SINGIN' (EP) 15
60   Top Rank JKP 2061 — JOSH MACRAE (EP). 15
66   Transatlantic TRA 150 — JOSH MACRAE (LP). 18
66   Golden Guinea GGL 0335 — MESSING ABOUT ON THE RIVER (LP) 15

M.A.D.
84   Crim. Damage CRI 12121 — Sunfeast/Craving (12", p/s) 7

JOHNNY MADARA
57   HMV POP 389 — Be My Girl/Lovesick... 7

MADCAPS
50	London L 786	Nightingale/Sleighride (78)	8
51	Brunswick 04787	Josephine/Casa Loma Stomp	6
53	Brunswick LA 8631	HARMONICATERS (10" LP)	15

MADCAPS/HARMONICATS
54	London H-APB 1016	HARMONICA RHYTHMS (10" LP, 1 side each)	15

MAD DOG
74	Chappell LPC 1053	POP SOUNDS (LP, library edition)	30

JOHNNY MADDOX (& HIS ORCHESTRA)
53	Vogue V 9047	Johnny Maddox Boogie/Little Grass Shack (78)	10
55	London MSD 1503/1504	Nickelodeon Tango/Solitude (unissued, demos only)	100
55	London HL 8056	I Don't Love Nobody/There's A Star-Spangled Banner (78)	10
55	London HL 8134	The Crazy Otto — Medley/Humoresque	20
55	London HL 8134	The Crazy Otto — Medley/Humoresque (78)	10
55	London HLD 8203	Do, Do, Do/When You Wore A Tulip (And I Wore A Big Red Rose)	20
56	London HLD 8277	Hop Scotch Boogie/Hands Off	30
56	London HLD 8277	Hop Scotch Boogie/Hands Off (78)	15
56	London HLD 8347	Heart And Soul/Dixieland Band	15
56	London HLD 8347	Heart And Soul/Dixieland Band (78)	7
58	London HLD 8540	Yellow Dog Blues/Sugar Train	15
58	London HLD 8540	Yellow Dog Blues/Sugar Train (78)	12
59	London HLD 8826	The Hurdy Gurdy Song/Old Fashioned Love	10
59	London HLD 8826	The Hurdy Gurdy Song/Old Fashioned Love (78)	15
55	London RE-P 1020	PRESENTING JOHNNY MADDOX AND THE RHYTHMASTERS (EP)	15
55	London RE-P 1040	PRESENTING JOHNNY MADDOX AND THE RHYTHMASTERS NO. 2 (EP)	15
58	London RE-D 1150	HONKY TONK JAZZ (EP)	10
61	London RE-D 1270	OLD FASHIONED LOVE (EP)	10
56	London HB-D 1060	JOHNNY MADDOX PLAYS (10" LP, with His Rhythmasters)	18
58	London HA-D 2101	MY OLD FLAMES (LP)	12

ROSE MADDOX
59	Capitol CL 15023	Gambler's Love/What Makes Me Hang Around	6

MADE IN ENGLAND
86	Red Bus RBUS 2208	Prospects/Stay Sharp (A-side with Ray Dorset, p/s)	6

(see also Ray Dorset)

MADE IN SHEFFIELD
67	Fontana TF 871	Amelia Jane/Right Satisfied	15

(see also Joe Cocker, Grease Band, Chris Stainton)

MADE IN SWEDEN
69	Sonet SLP 71	MADE IN SWEDEN (LP)	15
69	Sonet SLP 2504	SNAKES IN A HOLE (LP)	15
70	Sonet SLP 2506	LIVE AT THE GOLDEN CIRCLE (LP)	15
70	Sonet SLP 2512	MADE IN ENGLAND (LP)	15
71	Sonet SNTF 621	MAD RIVER (LP)	15

BETTY MADIGAN
54	MGM SP 1109	Always You/That Was My Heart You Heard!	6
55	MGM SP 1119	And So I Walked Home/Be A Little Darlin'.	6
55	MGM SP 1131	Salute/The Wheels Of Love	6
55	MGM SP 1137	I Had A Heart/Wonderful Words	6
55	MGM SP 1138	Teddy Bear/Strangers	6
58	Coral Q 72337	My Symphony Of Love/Dance Everyone Dance (78)	8
58	Coral Q 72348	A Lovely Night/True Love Gone (Come On Home) (78)	8
69	MGM MGM 1482	I'm Gonna Make You Love Me/Goodnight	6
58	Coral FEP 2009	JEROME KERN SONGBOOK VOL. 1 (EP)	10
59	Coral FEP 2011	JEROME KERN SONGBOOK VOL. 2 (EP)	10

MAD JOCKS & ENGLISHMEN
80	Wild Dog DOGLP 18	TONGUE IN CHEEK (LP)	12

MAD LADS (U.S.)
65	Atlantic AT 4051	Don't Have To Shop Around/Tear Maker	8
66	Atlantic AT 4083	I Want Someone/Nothing Can Break Through	10
66	Atlantic 584 038	Sugar Sugar/Get Out Of My Life Woman	8

MAD LADS (Jamaica)
69	Coxsone CS 7099	Losing You/WINSTON JARRETT: Peck Up A Pagan	18

MADNESS
SINGLES
79	2-Tone TT 3	The Prince/Madness (paper label, later plastic, company sleeve)	8/5
79	Stiff BUY IT 56	One Step Beyond/Mistakes/Nutty Theme (12", p/s)	10
79	Stiff MAD 1	Don't Quote Me On That/Swan Lake (12", promo only)	20
81	Stiff BUY IT 108	The Return Of The Los Palmas 7/My Girl (Demo)/That's The Way To Do It/Swan Lake (live) (12", p/s, with comic)	12
81	Stiff BUY IT 112	Grey Day/Baggy Trousers/Take It Or Leave It/Un Paso Adelante (12", p/s)	25
82	Stiff BUY IT 134	It Must Be Love/Mrs. Hutchinson/Shadow On The House (12", p/s credits "Limited Edition Special 12" Dance Mix", record plays standard mix)	10
82	Stiff PBUY 146	House Of Fun/Don't Look Back (picture disc)	5
82	Stiff BUY 153	Driving In My Car/Animal Farm (poster p/s)	5
82	Stiff PBUY 153	Driving In My Car/Animal Farm (picture disc)	5
82	Stiff PBUYJB 163	Our House (Special Stretch Mix)/Walking With Mr Wheeze (no'd company sl.)	6
82	Stiff PBUY 163	Our House/Walking With Mr Wheeze (picture disc)	5
82	Stiff GRAB 1	THE MADNESS PACK (6 x 7" in clear plastic folder)	20
83	Stiff PBUY 169	Tomorrow's (Just Another Day)/Madness (Is All In The Mind) (picture disc)	5
83	Stiff BUY IT 169	Tomorrow's (Just Another Day) (Warped Mix)/Blue Skinned Beast (warped mix)/Tomorrow's (Just Another Day) (Elvis Costello vocal) (12", p/s)	8

MADNESS

83	Stiff BUY IT 181	Wings Of A Dove/Behind The 8 Ball/One Second Thoughtlessness (12", p/s).....8
83	Stiff BUY IT 192	The Sun And The Rain (extended mix)/Fireball XL5/My Girl (live) (12", p/s)......8
84	Stiff BUY IT 196	Michael Caine (extended version)/Michael Caine/If You Think There's Something (12", p/s) 8
85	Zarjazz JAZZ D5	Yesterday's Men/All I Knew (square picture disc)//Yesterday's Men (Harmonica Mix)/It Must Be Love (live) (double pack, gold PVC wallet) 6
85	Zarjazz JAZZ F7	Uncle Sam/Please Don't Go ('flag bag' cloth p/s) 5
85	Zarjazz JAZZY 7	Uncle Sam/Please Don't Go/Insanity Over Christmas (picture disc) 5
86	Zarjazz JAZZ B9-12	(Waiting For) The Ghost-Train/Maybe In Another Life/Seven Year Scratch (12", p/s with 8-page booklet) 8
86	Strange Fruit SFPS 007	THE PEEL SESSIONS 14.10.79 (12" EP, p/s).............................8
88	Virgin VSX 1054	I Pronounce You/4BF/Patience/11th Hour (box with badge, 2 cards & sticker) 5
88	Virgin VSCD 1054	I Pronounce You/4BF/Patience/11th Hour (CD) 8
89	Virgin VSJ 1197	It Must Be Love/The Return Of The Los Palmas 7 (in *Tall Guy* p/s) 5

FLEXIDISCS

80	Stiff/Lyntone LYN 8680	Patches Brings You A Few Minutes Of Madness (flexi with *Patches* mag) 10/7
81	Lyntone LYN 10208	Take It or Leave It (flexidisc free with *Take It Or Leave It* magazine) 12/8
81	Lyn. LYN 10353/EVENT 2	Event — The Madness (flexidisc free with *Event* magazine) 10/7
82	Lyntone LYN 11546	My Girl (Ballad) (green or white vinyl flexidisc with *Flexipop* mag issue 19; with/without magazine) 8/6
82	Lyntone LYN 11546	My Girl (Ballad) (hard vinyl test pressing of above) 25
82	Lyntone LYN 10719	Carols On 45 (fan club flexidisc)..8
84	Lyntone LYN 15280/1	Insanity Over Christmas/Visit To Castle Dracstein (fan club flexidisc) 7
85	Lyntone LYN 16676	From Us ... To You (Mad Not Mad tour flexidisc, some with tour programme) .. 10/6
85	Lyntone LYN 16981	Live From The Mad Not Mad Tour (flexidisc)................................6
86	Lyntone LYN 18251	Ghost Train (The Demo)/The Final Goodbye (fan club flexidisc) 6

ALBUMS

84	Stiff PSEEZ 53	KEEP MOVING (LP, picture disc, U.S. running order) 15
82	Madness Info Service (no cat. no.)	THE M.I.S. RADIO PLAYERS PRESENT 30 MINUTES OF CULTURE (fan club cassette)..12
86	Madness Info Service	MADNESS LIVE (fan club cassette)..12

(see also Suggs, Fink Brothers, Argonauts, Voice Of The Beehive)

MADONNA
SIRE SINGLES

82	Sire W 9899	Everybody/Everybody (Dub Version) (no p/s)............................125
82	Sire W 9899T	Everybody/Everybody (Dub Version) (12", no p/s) 100
83	Sire W 9522	Lucky Star (Edit)/I Know It ('sunglasses' p/s, Irish only) 250
83	Sire W 9522T	Lucky Star (Full Length Version)/I Know It (12", 'sunglasses' p/s; some rumoured to come with stickered p/s & poster different to reissue).... 90/65
83	Sire W 9522TV	Lucky Star (U.S Remix)/I Know It (12", stickered plain white die-cut sleeve) 60
83	Sire W 9405	Holiday (Edit)/Think Of Me ('train' p/s).................................12
83	Sire W 9405T	Holiday (Full Length Version 6.08)/Think Of Me (12", 'train' p/s, some with 'Copyright Control' wording on label) 10
84	Sire W 9522	Lucky Star (Edit)/I Know It (reissue, 'bangles & stars' p/s)..................5
84	Sire W 9522T	Lucky Star (Full Length Version)/I Know It (12" reissue, stickered 'TV screen' p/s, some with poster) 35/15
84	Sire W 9260	Borderline (Edit)/Physical Attraction (p/s, large 'A' on paper A-side label) 5
84	Sire W 9260F	Borderline (Edit)/Physical Attraction//Holiday (Edit)/Think Of Me ('map' p/s, double pack with European p/s, copies of "Holiday", shrinkwrapped & stickered; beware of counterfeits with less-than-Mint picture sleeves!) 100
84	Sire W 9260T	Borderline (U.S. Remix)/Borderline (Dub Remix)/Physical Attraction (12", p/s, with '9-' LP catalogue numbers on rear of sleeve)................10
84	Sire W 9210T	Like A Virgin (U.S. Dance Remix)/Stay (12", p/s, some with poster & sticker)........................35/8
85	Sire W 9083	Material Girl/Pretender (p/s)..5
85	Sire W 9083T	Material Girl (Jellybean Dance Mix)/Pretender (12", p/s, some with poster) 35/8
85	Sire W 8934P	Into The Groove/Shoo-Be-Doo (heart-shaped picture disc with 2 stickers)......35
85	Sire W 8934T	Into The Groove/Everybody/Shoo-Be-Doo (12", p/s, initially with poster)......30/8
85	Sire W 9405	Holiday (Edit)/Think Of Me (reissue, 'train' p/s)..........................12
85	Sire W 9405T	Holiday (Full Length Version 6.08)/Think Of Me (12", 'cross earring' p/s reissue) 15
85	Sire W 9405P	Holiday (Full Length Version 6.08)/Think Of Me (12", picture disc) 30
85	Sire W 8881P	Angel (Edit)/Burning Up (shaped pic disc, some with cardboard plinth) 45/35
85	Sire W 8881T	Angel (Extended Dance Mix)/Burning Up (12", p/s) 8
85	Sire W 8848T	Dress You Up (12" Formal Mix)/(Casual Instrumental)/I Know It (12", p/s)......8
85	Sire W 8848TF	Dress You Up (12" Formal Mix)/(Casual Instrumental)/I Know It (12", poster p/s, '4 Track Studio' or 'Live Like A Virgin Tour' rear video advert) .... each 30
85	Sire W 8848P	Dress You Up/I Know It ('Xmas tree star'-shaped picture disc) 30
86	Sire W 9260P	Borderline/Physical Attraction (Madonna-shaped picture disc)...............50
86	Sire W 9260T	Borderline (U.S. Remix)/Borderline (Dub Remix)/Physical Attraction (12", p/s, reissue, with 'WX' LP catalogue numbers on rear of sleeve) 10
86	Sire W 8717T(W)	Live To Tell (LP Version)/(Edit)/(Instrumental) (12", p/s, some with poster).....15/8
86	Sire W 8636T(W)	Papa Don't Preach (Extended Version)/Papa Don't Preach (LP Version)/ Ain't No Big Deal (12", p/s, initially with free poster).....................15/8
86	Sire W 8636TP	Papa Don't Preach (Extended Remix)/Ain't No Big Deal (12", p/s)/Papa Don't Preach (LP version) (12", picture disc; some [maybe all] copies play last 2 tracks in wrong order) 30
86	Sire W 8550	True Blue (Extended Dance Version)/Holiday (Extended Dance Mix) (12", p/s)....8
86	Sire W 8550P	True Blue (Extended Dance Version)/Holiday (Extended Dance Mix) (12", picture disc)...25
86	Sire W 8480	Open Your Heart (Extended Version)/Open Your Heart (Dub Mix)/ Lucky Star (Full Length Version) (12", p/s)..............................8
86	Sire W 8480P	Open Your Heart (Extended Version)/Open Your Heart (Dub Mix)/ Lucky Star (Full Length Version) (12", picture disc).......................22
87	Sire W 8378	La Isla Bonita (Extended Remix)/(Extended Instrumental) (12", p/s)...........8

87	Sire W 8378P	La Isla Bonita (Extended Remix)/(Extended Instrumental) (12", picture disc).	25
87	Sire W 8341T	Who's That Girl (Extended Remix)/White Heat (12" Remix) (12", p/s)	8
87	Sire W 8341TX	Who's That Girl (Extended Version)/Who's That Girl (Dub Mix)/ White Heat (12" Remix) (12", p/s)	20
87	Sire W 8341TP	Who's That Girl (Extended Version)/White Heat (12", picture disc; beware of original decaying PVC sleeves)	50
87	Sire W 8224	Causing A Commotion (Silver Screen Single Mix)/Jimmy Jimmy (p/s, with badge shrinkwrapped to p/s)	45
87	Sire W 8224TP	Causing A Commotion (Silver Screen Mix)/Causing A Commotion (Movie House Mix)/Jimmy Jimmy (Fade) (12", picture disc).	20
87	Sire W 8115T	The Look Of Love/Love Don't Live Here Anymore/ I Know It (12", p/s & poster).	15
87	Sire W 8115TP	The Look Of Love/Love Don't Live Here Anymore/ I Know It (12", picture disc).	25
89	Sire W 7539	Like A Prayer/Act Of Contrition (p/s, with free Virgin Megastore poster)	6
89	Sire W 7539C	Like A Prayer (12" Extended Remix)/(12" Club Version)/Act Of Contrition (cassette).	4
89	Sire W 7539TX	Like A Prayer (12" Dance Mix)/(Churchapella Mix)/(7"Remix Edit) (12", p/s).	12
89	Sire W 7539TP	Like A Prayer (12" Extended Remix)/(12" Club Version)/Act Of Contrition (12", picture disc).	25
89	Sire W 7539CD	Like A Prayer/(12" Extended Remix)/(12" Club Version) (3" CD)	12
89	Sire W 2948X	Express Yourself (7" Remix)/The Look Of Love (LP) (poster p/s).	12
89	Sire W 2948W	Express Yourself (7" Remix)/The Look Of Love (LP) ('jeans zipper' p/s)	35
89	Sire W 2948C	Express Yourself (7" Remix)/The Look Of Love (LP) (cassette)	4
89	Sire W 2948CX	Express Yourself (Non-Stop Express Mix)/(Stop + Go Dubs) (cassette)	65
89	Sire W 2948TP	Express Yourself/(Non-Stop Express Mix)/(Stop + Go Dubs) (12", 'nude' picture disc)	25
89	Sire W 2948 CD	Express Yourself/(Non-Stop Express Mix)/(Stop + Go Dubs) (3" CD).	15
89	Sire W 2883TP	Cherish (Extended Version)/(7" Version)/Supernatural (12", picture disc).	25
89	Sire W 2883TP	Cherish (Extended Version)/(7" Version)/Supernatural (12", mispressed picture disc, plays "Cherish" but pictures feature Fish's "State Of Mind")	40
89	Sire W 2883 CD	Cherish (extended)/Cherish/Supernatural (3" CD)	15
89	Sire W 2668P	Dear Jessie/Till Death Do Us Part (picture disc).	10
89	Sire W 2668TW	Dear Jessie/Till Death Do Us Part/Holiday (12" Version) (12", poster p/s).	15
89	Sire W 2268CD	Dear Jessie/Till Death Do Us Part/Holiday (12" Version) (CD)	7
89	Sire W 2268CDX	Dear Jessie/Till Death Do Us Part/Holiday (12" Version) (CD, picture disc).	60
89	Sire 925 681-2	Papa Don't Preach (7" Version)/(12" Version)/Pretender (LP Version)/ Papa Don't Preach (CD Video)	65
90	Sire W 9851	Vogue/Keep It Together (Single Remix) (p/s, mispress with B-side twice).	15
90	Sire W 9851P	Vogue/Keep It Together (Single Remix) (picture disc)	10
90	Sire W 9851TW	Vogue (12" Version)/Keep It Together (12" Remix) (12", p/s, with 'Face of the 80s' poster).	12
90	Sire W 9851TX	Vogue (12" Version)/Vogue (Strike-A-Pose Dub) (12", p/s, with 'X-rated' 30" x 20" poster).	15
90	Sire W 9851TP	Vogue (12" Version)/Keep It Together (12" Remix) (12", picture disc)	25
90	Sire W 9789TP	Hanky Panky (Bare Bottom 12" Mix)/(Bare Bones Single Mix)/More (LP Version) (12", picture disc with gatefold insert & foldout poster).	15
90	Sire W 9000TP	Justify My Love (William Orbit Remix)/Justify My Love/Express Yourself (Shep's 'Spressin' Himself Remix) (12", picture disc with insert)	15
91	Sire W 0008P	Crazy For You (Remix)/Keep It Together (Single Remix) (shaped picture disc with plinth & insert).	15
91	Sire W 0008CD	Crazy For You (Remix)/Keep It Together (Shep Pettibone Remix)/ Into The Groove (Shep Pettibone Remix) (CD, picture disc).	10
91	Sire W 0037TP	Holiday/True Blue (12", clear vinyl picture disc with insert in PVC sleeve).	12
91	Sire W 0037CT	THE HOLIDAY COLLECTION (Holiday/True Blue/Who's That Girl/ Causing A Commotion) (cassette)	4
91	Sire W 0037CD	THE HOLIDAY COLLECTION (Holiday/True Blue/Who's That Girl/ Causing A Commotion) (CD).	8

MAVERICK SINGLES

92	Maverick W 0138TP	Erotica (Album Version 5.12)/Erotica (Instrumental 5.12)/Erotica (Radio Edit 4.31) (12", picture disc with gold insert, withdrawn, 138 only)	700
92	Maverick W 0146TP	Deeper And Deeper (Shep's Classic 12")/(Shep's Deep Makeover Mix)/ (Shep's Deep Beats)/(David's Klub Mix)/(David's Deep Mix)/ (Shep's Deeper Dub) (12", picture disc)	15
93	Maverick W 0168P	Fever (Edit)/Fever (Radio Edit Remix) (picture disc with numbered insert).	12
94	Maverick W 0268P	Secret (Edit)/Let Down Your Guard (Rough Mix Edit) (picture disc w/insert).	12
95	Maverick W 0278P	Take A Bow (Edit)/Take A Bow (picture disc with insert)	7
95	Maverick W 0285CDX	Bedtime Story (Junior's Single Mix)/Secret (Allstar Mix)/Secret (Some Bizarre Mix)/Secret (Some Bizarre Single Mix) (CD, booklet sleeve)	10

OTHER SINGLES

85	Geffen A 6323	Crazy For You/SAMMY HAGAR: I'll Fall In Love Again (p/s).	5
85	Geffen WA 6323	Crazy For You/SAMMY HAGAR: I'll Fall In Love Again (Madonna-shaped picture disc).	65
85	Geffen A 6585	Gambler/BLACK 'N BLUE: Nature Of The Beast (p/s).	5
85	Geffen QA 6585	Gambler/BLACK 'N BLUE: Nature Of The Beast (poster p/s).	25
85	Geffen TA 6585	Gambler (Extended Dance Mix)/Gambler (Instrumental Remix)/ BLACK 'N BLUE: Nature Of The Beast (12", p/s).	20
92	Receiver RRSP 1007	Shine A Light/On The Ground (picture disc, withdrawn)	12
92	Receiver RRSPT 1007	Shine A Light/On The Ground/Little Boy (12", p/s, withdrawn).	8

PROMOS

89	Sire SAM 641	Keep It Together (12" Remix)/(Dub)/(Extended Remix)/(12" Mix)/ (Bonus Beats)/(Instrumental) (12", no p/s)	25
96	Sire SAM 1880	Love Don't Live Here Anymore (Mark!s It's A Girl Dub)/(Mark!s It's A Boy Dub)/(Mark!s Full On Vocal) (12")	35
98	Sire SAM 3173	Frozen (Extended Club Mix)/(Stereo MC's Mix)/(Meltdown Mix — Long Version) (12")	20

MINT VALUE £

98	Sire SAM 3173	Frozen (Extended Club Mix)/(Stereo MC's Mix)/(Meltdown Mix — Long Version) (12", mispress, sleeve & labels credit "Dive Boogie" but play tracks from "Frozen" 12" promo)................................15
00	Maverick PRO 261270	American Pie (Pie Mix)/(Orbit Sugar Free Mix) (CD, tin case, promo only)......35

ALBUMS

83	Sire 923 867-1	MADONNA (LP, with inner sleeve)..15
84	Sire 925 157-1	LIKE A VIRGIN (LP, without "Into The Groove", with inner sleeve).........15
85	Sire WX 20P	LIKE A VIRGIN (LP, picture disc in die-cut sleeve)......................50
86	Sire WX 54	TRUE BLUE (LP, with tour poster)......................................10
87	Sire WX 76	YOU CAN DANCE (LP, with poster & gold 'obi')..........................10
90	Sire 7599 264932	ROYAL BOX (box set with "Immaculate Collection" CD in satin digipak, video, poster & postcards)..85

(see also Jellybean)

MADRIGAL

73	Madrigal MAD 100	BENEATH THE GREENWOOD TREE (LP, private pressing)................100

MAD RIVER

69	Capitol (S)T 2985	MAD RIVER (LP)...25

JOHNNY MAESTRO

61	HMV POP 875	What A Surprise/The Warning Voice....................................30
61	HMV POP 909	Mr. Happiness/Test Of Love..30
64	United Artists UP 1004	Before I Love Her/Fifty Million Heartbeats.............................18
71	Buddah 2011 061	Rain Came/Never Knew This Kind Of Hurt Before........................5

(see also Crests, Brooklyn Bridge)

MAGAZINE

78	Virgin VS 200	Shot By Both Sides/My Mind Ain't So Open (card or paper p/s).........5/4
78	Virgin VS 207	Touch And Go/Goldfinger (p/s)...4
78	Virgin VS 237	Give Me Everything/I Love You, You Big Dummy (p/s)....................4
79	Virgin VS 251	Rhythm Of Cruelty/T.V. Baby (p/s).....................................4
80	Virgin VS 368	Sweetheart Contract/Feed The Enemy//Twenty Years Ago/ Shot By Both Sides (stickered, shrinkwrapped double pack)...............7

(see also Buzzcocks, Barry Adamson)

MAGENTA

78	Cottage COT 821	CANTERBURY MOON (LP, with insert)..................................60
80	Little Stan LSP 811	RECOLLECTIONS (2-LP, gatefold sleeve with insert)....................80
81	Little Stan LSP 831	WOT'S NEXT THEN (LP, with insert)....................................60

MAGGIE

68	Columbia DB 8389	L. David Sloane/Too Young To Get Married..............................4

MAGIC CARPET

72	Mushroom 200 MR 20	MAGIC CARPET (LP)...100

(see also Clem Alford)

MAGIC CHRISTIANS

69	Major Minor MM 673	If You Want It/Nuts...6
69	Major Minor MM 673	Come And Get It/Nuts (2nd pressing with correct title).................8
70	Major Minor SMLP 71	THE MAGIC CHRISTIANS (LP)..30

(see also Trevor Burton, Gary Wright, Denny Laine, Steve Gibbons)

MAGICIANS

66	Decca F 12361	Wet Your Whistle/Take The A Train.....................................5
66	Decca F 12374	The Liars/Poggy Goes Pop...6
67	Decca F 12602	The Tarzan March/What A Day For A Metamorphosis.....................6
68	MCA MU 1046	Painting On Wood/Slow Motion...5

MAGIC LANTERNS

66	CBS 202094	Excuse Me Baby/Greedy Girl...5
66	CBS 202250	Rumplestiltskin/I Stumbled..25
67	CBS 202459	Knight In Rusty Armour/Simple Things..................................5
67	CBS 202637	Auntie Grizelda/Time Will Tell (If I'm A Loser).........................6
67	CBS 2750	We'll Meet Again/What Else Can It Be But Love?.........................5
68	Camp 602 007	Shame Shame/Baby I Gotta Go Now.....................................5
69	Camp 602 009	Melt All Your Troubles Away/Bossa Nova 1940 — Hello You Lovers.......5
67	CBS (S) 62935	LIT UP WITH THE MAGIC LANTERNS (LP)................................18
71	Polydor 2460 113	ONE NIGHT STAND (LP)..10

MAGIC MICHAEL

80	Atomic MAGIC 1	Millionaire/My Friend And I (p/s).......................................5

(see also Damned, Captain Sensible)

MAGIC MIXTURE

68	Saga FID 2125	THIS IS MAGIC MIXTURE (LP)..50

MAGIC MUSCLE

88	Five Hours Back TOCK 009	THE PIPE, THE ROAR, THE GRID (LP, with booklet)......................15
90	Pilgrim (no cat. no.)	LIVING WEEDS FROM ANCIENT SEEDS (cassette, box set, autographed with booklet, posters & postcard)...........................15
91	Woronzow WOO 17	GULP! (LP)..25

(see also Keith Christmas, Hawkwind, High Tide, Twink)

MAGIC MUSHROOM BAND

85	Magick Eye MUSH 001	THE MAGIC MUSHROOM BAND (cassette EP)............................10
85	Magick Eye MUSH 002	FEED YOUR HEAD (cassette)...10
86	Magick Eye MUSH 003	THE POLITICS OF ECSTASY (cassette)..................................10
86	Pagan PM 003	THE POLITICS OF ECSTASY (LP, with A3 insert, 500 only, 100 with A1 poster)......................18/12
87	Aftermath AFT 3	BOMSHAMKAR (LP)..12
89	Magick Eye MUSH 004	LIVE '89 (live cassette)...10

MINT VALUE £

| 90 | Fungus FUN 003 | PROCESS OF ILLUMINATION (LP, signed with insert & foldaround sleeve & comic in printed PVC sleeve) | 12 |
| 91 | Fungus FUN 005 | SPACED OUT (LP, foldout sleeve with A4 booklet) | 12 |

MAGIC NIGHT
| 75 | Pye 7N 25698 | If You And I Had Never Met/(version) | 8 |

MAGIC NOTES
| 60 | Blue Beat BB 9 | Album Of Memory/Why Did You Leave Me | 15 |
| 61 | Blue Beat BB 51 | Rosabel/I'm Not Worthy | 15 |

MAGIC ROUNDABOUT
72	Music F. Pleasure FP 10006	Dougal & The Blue Cat (Parts 1 & 2)	5
71	BBC Roundabout 8	MAGIC ROUNDABOUT (LP, TV soundtrack)	12
70s	Music For Pleasure	MAGIC ROUNDABOUT (LP)	12
70s	Music For Pleasure	DOUGAL AND THE BLUE CAT (LP, soundtrack)	12

MAGIC SAM
69	Python PEN 701	Twenty One Days In Jail/Easy Baby (99 copies only)	35
69	Rooster 707	MEAN MISTREATER (EP)	12
70	Blue Horizon 7-63223	MAGIC SAM: 1937-1969 (LP)	45
70	Delmark DS 615	WEST SIDE SOUL (LP, blue label)	18
71	Delmark DS 620	BLACK MAGIC (LP, blue label)	18

MAGIC SHOP
| 87 | Sha La La Ba Ba 8 | It's Time/VISITORS: Goldmining (flexidisc with various fanzines) | 7/5 |

MAGIC SLIM & TEARDROPS
| 81 | Rooster R 707 | THREE THUNDERIN' TRACKS (EP) | 7 |

MAGIC VALLEY
| 69 | Penny Farthing PEN 701 | Taking The Heart Out Of Love/Uptight Basil | 8 |

(see also Pete Dello, Honeybus)

MAGISTRATES
| 68 | MGM MGM 1425 | Here Comes The Judge/Girl | 6 |
| 68 | MGM MGM 1437 | After The Fox/Tear Down The Walls (with Jane Hillery) | 6 |

(see also Jane Hillery)

MAGITS
| 79 | Outer H. SRTS/79/CUS/401 | Fragmented/Disconnected/Disjointed/Detached (p/s) | 7 |

(see also Rudimentary Peni)

MAGMA
74	A&M AMS 7119	Mekanik Machine/Mekanik Machine (Version)	8
70	Philips 6359 051/2	MAGMA (2-LP)	15
71	Philips 6397 031	1001 CENTIGRADE (LP)	12
74	A&M AMLH 64397	MEKANIK DESTRUCTIW KOMMANDOH (LP)	12
74	A&M AMLH 68260	KOHN TARKOSZ (LP)	12

MAGNA CARTA
69	Fontana TF 1060	Romeo Jack/7 O'Clock Hymn	10
69	Mercury MF 1096	Mid-Winter/Spinning Wheels Of Time	10
70	Vertigo 6059 013	Airport Song/Elizabethan	7
71	Vertigo 6059 043	Time For The Leaving/Wayfarin'	5
72	Vertigo 6059 073	All My Life/Falkland Green	10
73	Vertigo 6059 092	Give Me Luv/Song Of Evening	8
70s	London Borough of Camden	When You're Young (charity issue for RoSPA)	5
69	Mercury SMCL 20166	MAGNA CARTA (LP)	35
70	Vertigo 6360 003	SEASONS (LP, gatefold sleeve, spiral label)	20
71	Vertigo 6360 040	SONGS FROM WASTIES ORCHARD (LP, gatefold sleeve, spiral label)	25
72	Vertigo 6360 068	IN CONCERT (LP, gatefold sleeve, spiral label)	25
73	Vertigo 6360 093	LORD OF THE AGES (LP, gatefold sleeve, spaceship label)	20
76	GTO GTLP 012	PUTTING IT BACK TOGETHER (LP)	18
77	GTO GTLP 112	TOOK A LONG TIME (LP)	15

MAGNA JAZZ BAND
| 57 | Parlophone R 4387 | Buddy's Habits/Flat Foot | 6 |

(see also Brian White & Magna Jazz Band)

ANNA MAGNANI
| 58 | HMV POP 460 | Scapricciatiello/Aggio Perouto Osuonno (78) | 8 |

MAGNETOPHONE
| 98 | Earworm WORM 26 | You Should Write Music/Monitor Rocket Science (p/s, red vinyl) | 5 |

MAGNIFICENT MEN
66	Capitol CL 15462	Peace Of Mind/All Your Lovin's Gone To My Head	20
68	Capitol CL 15530	Sweet Soul Medley (both sides)	5
68	Capitol CL 15570	Save The Country/So Much Love Waiting	6

MAGNUM
75	CBS S CBS 2959	Sweets For My Sweet/Movin' On (no p/s)	40
78	Jet SJET 116	Kingdom Of Madness/In The Beginning	5
78	Jet SJET 128	Invasion/Universe	5
79	Jet JET 155	Changes/Lonesome Star (silver p/s, some with sew-on patch)	10/8
79	Jet JET 163	Foolish Heart/Baby Rock Me (p/s)	6
80	Jet JET 175	Magnum Live [All Of My Life (live)/Great Adventure (live)/Invasion (live)/ Kingdom Of Madness (live)] (double pack, stickered p/s)	6
80	Jet JET 188	Changes (live Remix)/Everybody Needs/Changes (live) (black p/s)	7
81	Jet JET 7007	Black Nights (possibly promo only)	10+
82	Jet JET 7020	The Lights Burned Out/Long Days Black Nights (p/s)	6
82	Jet JET 7027	Back To Earth (live)/Hold Back Your Love (live)//Soldier Of The Line (live)/ Sacred Hour (live) (double pack)	8

MINT VALUE £

86	Polydor POSP 798	Lonely Night/Les Morts Dansant (live) (p/s)	5
86	Polydor POSPG 798	Lonely Night/Les Morts Dansant (live)//All England's Eyes (live)/ Hit And Run (live) (double pack)	7
86	Polydor POSPP 833	Midnight (Remix)/Back Street Kid/Kingdom Of Madness (live) (12", picture disc)	10
87	Polydor POSP 850	When The World Comes Down (Edit)/Vigilante (live) (p/s)	5
88	Polydor POSPG 910	Days Of No Trust/Maybe Tonight ('oct-o-pack', gatefold p/s)	8
88	Polydor POSPP 910	Days Of No Trust/Maybe Tonight (p/s, with sew-on patch)	7
88	Polydor POCD 910	Days Of No Trust/Maybe Tonight/Days Of No Trust (Extended Version)/ How Far Jerusalem (live) (CD, card p/s)	8
88	Polydor POSPG 920	Start Talking Love/C'est La Vie (gatefold pop-up p/s)	5
88	Polydor POSPP 920	Start Talking Love/Days Of No Trust (10", shaped picture disc)	7
88	Polydor POCD 920	Start Talking Love (7" Version)/C'est La Vie/Start Talking Love (Extended Remix)/Sacred Hour (CD, p/s)	8
88	Polydor POSPG 930	It Must Have Been Love/Crying Time ('prismatic' pack)	5
88	Polydor POCD 930	It Must Have Been Love (Edit)/Crying Time/Lonely Night (live)/ Lights Burned Out (live) (CD, card sleeve)	8
88	Polydor 080 406-2	Start Talking Love (Extended Remix)/C'est La Vie/Back To Earth (live)/ On A Storyteller's Night (live) (CD Video)	12
78	Jet JETLP 210	KINGDOM OF MADNESS (LP, original 'king' sleeve)	18
83	FM WKFMPD 111	THE ELEVENTH HOUR (LP, picture disc)	15
85	FM WKFM LP 34	ON A STORYTELLER'S NIGHT (LP, with bonus single)	15
85	FM WKFM G/C LP 34	ON A STORYTELLER'S NIGHT (LP, gold or clear vinyl)	15
86	Polydor POLD 5198	VIGILANTE (LP)	12
88	Polydor POLDP 5221	WINGS OF HEAVEN (LP, picture disc with extra track, die-cut sleeve)	12
89	FM WKFM PD 34	ON A STORYTELLER'S NIGHT (LP, picture disc reissue, with poster)	15

TEDDY MAGNUS
| 71 | Green Door GD 4008 | Flying Machine/VERSION BOYS: Machine Version | 5 |

MAGOO
95	Noisebox NBX 013	MUDSHARK EP: Tom, Lou And Me/Elsie's Skinny Arms/Hop Your Mouth (orange vinyl, numbered p/s, 500 only)	8
95	Noisebox NBX 016	ROBOT CARNIVAL EP: Robot Carnival/Sampa Calmida (Land Of Joy)/ Candle Buddah/Rocket To Spector City (blue vinyl, p/s)	6
96	Noisebox NBX 020	EYESPY EP: Eye Spy/Motel Mining/Soaterama/Polka Party No.2/ Silver Screen/Word Is Out/Diving Bell (lemon yellow vinyl, p/s, 500 only)	4

MAGPIES
| 68 | Doctor Bird DB 1129 | Lulu/Must I Be Lonely | 12 |
| 68 | Doctor Bird DB 1132 | Blue Boy/I Guess I'm Crazy | 12 |

JOHN MAGUIRE
| 73 | Leader LEE 4062 | COME DAY, GO DAY, GOD SEND SUNDAY (LP, gatefold sleeve with booklet) | 10 |

LEO MAGUIRE
| 62 | Parlophone R 4917 | Crying For The Moon/Small World | 6 |

MAGUS
| 80 | Northern Sound NSR 200 | BREEZIN' AWAY (LP, private pressing) | 70 |

(see also Blue Epitaph)

TAJ MAHAL
68	Direction 58-3547	Everybody's Got To Change Sometime/Statesboro Blues	5
69	Direction 58-4044	Ee Zee Rider/You Don't Miss Your Water	5
70	Direction 58-4586	Give Your Woman What She Wants/Further On Down The Road	5
71	CBS 7413	Diving Duck Blues/Fishin' Blues	5
67	Direction 8-63279	TAJ MAHAL (LP)	15
69	Direction 8-63397	THE NATCH'L BLUES (LP)	15
69	Direction 8-66226	GIANT STEP/DE OLE FOLKS AT HOME (2-LP)	15
71	CBS 66288	THE REAL THING (2-LP)	15
72	CBS 64447	HAPPY JUST TO BE LIKE I AM (LP)	12
73	CBS 65090	RECYCLING THE BLUES AND OTHER RELATED STUFF (LP)	12
73	CBS 65814	OOOH SO GOOD 'N BLUES (LP)	12
73	CBS 70123	SOUNDER (LP, soundtrack)	12

MAHAVISHNU ORCHESTRA
75	CBS 3007	Can't Stand Your Funk/Eternity's Breath Part 1	5
72	CBS 64717	THE INNER MOUNTING FLAME (LP, with insert)	12
74	CBS CQ 31996	BIRDS OF FIRE (LP, quadrophonic)	20
75	CBS 69108	VISIONS OF THE EMERALD BEYOND (LP, with insert)	12

(see also John McLaughlin)

MITCH MAHON & EDITIONS
| 69 | Pye 7N 17844 | You've Got What I Need/I've Thrown Our Love Away | 4 |

SKIP MAHONEY & CASUALS
| 76 | Contempo CLP 539 | LAND OF LOVE (LP) | 15 |

MAIL
| 71 | Parlophone R 5916 | Omnibus/Life Goes On | 5 |

MAINFRAME
84	YYY	INTO TROUBLE WITH THE NOISE OF ART (12", 7-track EP)	12
86	Polydor MAINA 1	5 Minutes On.../Eric's Revenge (p/s)	4
86	Polydor MAINX 1	5 Minutes On...(7.01)/He Said It/Eric's Revenge (12", p/s)	8
86	Polydor MAINF 1	5 Minutes On.../He Said It (131 bpm)/Eric's Revenge (131 bpm) (12", p/s)	7

MAINHORSE
| 71 | Polydor 2383 049 | MAINHORSE (LP) | 18 |

MAIN INGREDIENT
| 74 | RCA PB 0305 | Happiness Is Just Around The Bend/Why Can't We All Unite | 4 |
| 71 | RCA LSA 3020 | TASTEFUL SOUL (LP) | 10 |

MAINLAND
| 79 | Christy ACML 0200 | EXPOSURE (LP) | 15 |

JULIE MAIRS & CHRIS STOWELL
| 77 | Cottage COT 211 | SOFT SEA BLUE (LP) | 20 |

MAISON ROUGE
| 85 | Red Barn RBR 0001 | Questions (p/s) | 5 |

DEXTER MAITLAND
| 69 | United Artists UP 35006 | Take Ten Terrific Girls (But Only Nine Costumes)/ RUDY VALLEE: Night They Raided Minsky's | 4 |

MAJAMOOD
| 66 | Doc. Bird/W.I.R.L. DB 1052 | Two Hundred Million Red Ants/Faces Amassed | 25 |

MAJOR ACCIDENT
82	M. Melodies MAME 1001	Warboots/Terrorist Gang (unissued, test pressings only)	40
83	Step Forward SF 23	Mr. Nobody/That's You (p/s)	6
83	Flicknife FLS 216	Fight To Win/Free Man (p/s)	6
83	Flicknife FLS 023	Leaders Of Tomorrow/Dayo/Breakaway (p/s)	5
84	Flicknife FLS 026	Respectable/Man On The Wall (p/s)	5
83	Step Forward SFLP 9	MASSACRED MELODIES (LP)	12
84	Syndicate SYNLP 9	TORTURED TUNES LIVE (LP)	12

(see also Accident)

MAJORETTES
| 63 | Lyntone LYN 982 | White Levi's (flexidisc) | 10 |

MAJORITY
65	Decca F 12186	Pretty Little Girl/I Don't Wanna Be Hurt No More	5
65	Decca F 12271	A Little Bit Of Sunlight/Shut 'Em Down In London Town	8
66	Decca F 12313	We Kiss In A Shadow/Ring The Bells	5
66	Decca F 12453	Simplified/One Third	25
66	Decca F 12504	To Make Me A Man/Tears Won't Help	5
67	Decca F 12573	I Hear A Rhapsody/Wait By The Fire	5
67	Decca F 12638	Running Away With My Baby/Let The Joybells Ring	15
68	Decca F 12727	All Our Christmases/People	5

MAJORS
62	London HLP 9602	A Wonderful Dream/Time Will Tell	15
62	London HLP 9627	She's A Troublemaker/A Little Bit Now	18
63	London HLP 9693	What In The World/Tra La La	15
64	Liberty LBF 66009	Ooh Wee Baby/I'll Be There	20
63	London RE-P 1358	MEET THE MAJORS (EP)	125
63	London HA-P 8068	MEET THE MAJORS (LP)	150

MAKADOPOULOS & HIS GREEK SERENADERS
| 60 | Palette PG 9002 | In The Streets Of Athens/Festival A La Greca | 5 |
| 61 | Palette PG 9005 | Never On Sunday/Yasou (some in p/s) | 8/5 |

PETER MAKANA & HIS RHYTHM BOYS
58	Oriole CB 1445	Baboon Shepherd (with Black Duke)/Black John	5
58	Oriole CB 1445	Baboon Shepherd (with Black Duke)/Black John (78)	8
58	Oriole CB 1446	Cool Mood/Sweet Baby	5
58	Oriole CB 1446	Cool Mood/Sweet Baby (78)	8

MIRIAM MAKEBA
| 63 | London HL 9747 | Click Song/Mbube | 6 |
| 61 | London HA 2332 | MIRIAM MAKEBA (LP) | 15 |

TOMMY MAKEM
| 70 | CBS 64001 | THE BARD OF ARMAGH (LP) | 12 |

MAKIN' TIME
85	Countdown VAIN 1	Here Is My Number/Nothing Else (p/s)	5
86	Countdown TVAIN 1	Here Is My Number/Nothing Else (picture disc)	6
86	Countdown VAIN 5	Pump It Up/Walk A Thin Line (p/s)	5
85	Countdown DOWN 1	RHYTHM 'N' SOUL (LP)	15
86	Ready To Eat READY 1	NO LUMPS OF FAT OR GRISTLE GUARANTEED (LP)	15
87	Re-Elect/President ELECT 1	TIME, TROUBLE AND MONEY (LP)	15

(see also Charlatans)

MALAGON SISTERS & CHA CHA RHYTHM BOYS
| 59 | Pye International 7N 25008 | In A Little Spanish Town/Lessons In Cha-Cha-Cha | 6 |
| 59 | Pye International 7N 25008 | In A Little Spanish Town/Lessons In Cha-Cha-Cha (78) | 8 |

MAL & PRIMITIVES
| 65 | Pye 7N 15915 | Every Minute Of Every Day/Pretty Little Face | 75 |

(see also Primitives, Mal Ryder & Spirits)

MALARIA!
| 82 | Jungle JUNG 3 | NEW YORK PASSAGE (12" EP) | 7 |

CARLOS MALCOLM & AFRO CARIBS
| 65 | Island WI 173 | Bonanza Ska/Papa Luiga | 15 |

GEORGE MALCOLM
| 53 | Parlophone MSP 6058 | Bach Goes To Town/Bach Before The Mast | 8 |

HUGH MALCOLM
| 68 | Amalgamated AMG 827 | Good Time Rock/LYNN TAITT & JETS: Sleepy Ludy | 10 |
| 68 | Amalgamated AMG 829 | Mortgage/CANNONBALL BRYAN TRIO: Man About Town | 10 |

MALCOLM & ALWYN
| 70s | Key KL 022 | WILDWALL (LP) | 12 |
| 73 | Pye NSPL 18404 | FOOL'S WISDOM (LP, with poster) | 12 |

MINT VALUE £

MALLARD
77	Virgin VS 168	Harvest/Green Coyote	6
76	Virgin V 2045	MALLARD (LP)	12
77	Virgin V 2077	IN A DIFFERENT CLIMATE (LP)	10

(see also Captain Beefheart & His Magic Band)

STEPHEN MALLINDER
81	Fetish FE 12	Temperature Drop/Cool Down (12", p/s)	8
82	Fetish FM 2010	POW-WOW (LP)	10

(see also Cabaret Voltaire)

SIW MALMKVIST
59	Oriole CB 1486	Sermonette/The Preacher	5
59	Oriole CB 1486	Sermonette/The Preacher (78)	8
61	Parlophone R 4765	Wedding Cake/Red Roses And Little White Lies	5
64	Columbia DB 7411	Sole Sole Sole/Sabato Sera (as Siw Malmkvist & Umberto Marcato)	5
68	Atlantic 584 229	The Man Who Took The Valise Off The Floor/Sadie The Cleaning Lady	5

CINDY MALONE
61	RCA RCA 1254	Weird Beard/Young Marriage	6

WIL MALONE
70	Fontana STL 5541	WIL MALONE (LP)	60

(see also Motherlight, Wilson Malone Voiceband)

WILSON MALONE VOICEBAND
68	Morgan MR 112P	FUNNY SAD MUSIC (LP)	20

(see also Motherlight, Wil Malone)

RICHARD MALTBY
56	HMV 7M 393	"Man With The Golden Arm" Theme/Heart Of Paris	8
56	HMV POP 201	"Man With The Golden Arm" Theme/Heart Of Paris (78)	8
59	Philips PB 955	Theme From The FBI Story/Morgen (78)	10
61	Columbia DB 4606	The Rat Race/Walkie Talkie	8

MAMA LION
72	Philips 6078 002	Ain't Too Proud To Beg/Mr. Invitation	4
72	Philips 6369 153	MAMA LION PRESERVE WILDLIFE (LP)	10
70s	Philips	GIVE IT EVERYTHING I'VE GOT (LP)	10

MAMAS & PAPAS
66	RCA Victor RCA 1503	California Dreamin'/Somebody Groovy	6
66	RCA Victor RCA 1516	Monday, Monday/Got A Feelin'	5
66	RCA Victor RCA 1533	I Saw Her Again/Even If I Could	6
66	RCA Victor RCA 1551	Look Through My Window/Once There Was I Time I Thought	6
67	RCA Victor RCA 1564	Words Of Love/I Can't Wait	6
67	RCA Victor RCA 1576	Dedicated To The One I Love/Free Advice	6
67	RCA Victor RCA 1613	Creeque Alley/No Salt On Her Tail	6
67	RCA Victor RCA 1630	12.30/Straight Shooter	6
67	RCA Victor RCA 1649	Glad To Be Unhappy/Hey Girl	6
68	RCA Victor RCA 1710	Safe In My Garden/Too Late	5
68	RCA Victor RCA 1726	Dream A Little Dream Of Me/Midnight Voyage	6
68	RCA Victor RCA 1744	For The Love Of Ivy/Strange Young Girls	6
69	Stateside SS 8009	You Baby/My Girl	5
70	Stateside SS 8058	Go Where You Wanna Go/No Salt On Her Tail	5
72	Probe PRO 552	Shooting Star/No Dough	5
66	RCA Victor RD 7803	IF YOU CAN BELIEVE YOUR EYES AND EARS (LP)	18
66	RCA Victor RD/SF 7834	CASS, JOHN, MICHELLE, DENNY (LP)	18
67	RCA Victor RD/SF 7880	DELIVER (LP)	18
68	RCA Victor RD/SF 7960	THE PAPAS AND THE MAMAS (LP)	18
68	Stateside (S)SL 5002	THE MAMAS AND THE PAPAS GOLDEN ERA VOL. 2 (LP)	15
68	Stateside TA-SL 5002	THE MAMAS AND THE PAPAS GOLDEN ERA VOL. 2 (reel-to-reel tape, mono)	12
68	Stateside TA-SL 5007	HITS OF GOLD (reel-to-reel tape, mono)	12
70	Probe SPB 1013/14	A GATHERING OF FLOWERS (2-LP)	20
71	Probe SPB 1048	PEOPLE LIKE US (LP)	15
78	St. Michael MO 101225	CALIFORNIA DREAMIN' (LP, exclusive to Marks & Spencer)	25

(see also Mama Cass [Elliot], John Phillips, Michelle Phillips, Scott McKenzie, Barry McGuire, Mugwumps, Big Three [U.S], Spanky & Our Gang)

MAMA'S BOYS
81	Pussy	Silence Is Out Of Fashion (p/s)	10
82	Scoff DT 015	Belfast City Blues/Reach For The Top (p/s; Ireland only)	18
82	Ultra-Noise ION 1038	In The Heat Of The Night/Reach For The Top (p/s)	4
82	Ultra-Noise 12ION 1041	Needle In The Groove/Hard Headed Ways (12", p/s)	7
82	Lyntone LYN 19497	Growing Up The Hard Way (flexidisc, p/s)	4
83	Spartan 12SP 6	Too Little Of You To Love/Freedom Fighters (12", p/s, with free "Official Bootleg" LP)	18
84	Spartan SP 11	Midnight Promises/Lonely Soul (p/s)	4
84	Jive G 71	Mama We're All Crazee Now/Crazy Daisy's House Of Dreams// Runaway Rogues/Gentlemen Rogues (double pack)	4
84	Jive JIVE 71	Mama We're All Crazee Now/Crazy Daisy's House Of Dreams/ Runaway Rogues (12", p/s)	7
85	Jive JIVEP 96	Needle In The Groove/Don't Tell Mama (shaped picture disc)	5
87	Jive JIVEX 152	Waiting For A Miracle/Lightning Strikes (red vinyl, p/s)	4
87	Jive MBOYD 1	Higher Ground/Last Thing At Night/Needle In The Groove (double pack, gatefold p/s)	5
87	Jive MBOYCD 1	Higher Ground (Captain Love Mix)/Last Thing At Night/ Needle In The Groove (Album Version) (CD)	7
82	Pussy PU 010	PLUG IT IN (LP)	25
82	Albion ULTRA 1	PLUG IT IN (LP, reissue)	10
85	Jive HIP 24	POWER AND PASSION (LP, with bonus 12" picture disc)	10

MAMMATH
84	Neat NEAT 42	Rock Me/Rough 'N' Ready (p/s)	5

MAMMOTH
89	Jive MOTHX 4	All The Days/Fatman/Bet You Wish (12", picture disc, PVC sleeve, withdrawn)	20

(see also John McCoy, Gillan, Samson, Tiger, Nicky Moore Band, Hackensack)

MAN
69	Pye 7N 17684	Sudden Life/Love	12
71	Liberty LBF 15448	Daughter Of The Fireplace/Country Girl	12
74	United Artists UP 35643	Don't Go Away (possibly unissued)	15+
74	United Artists UP 35703	Taking The Easy Way Out Again/California Silks And Satins	6
74	United Artists UP 35739	Day And Night/A Hard Way To Live	5
76	MCA MCA 236	Out Of Your Head/I'm A Love Taker	5
76	United Artists REM 408	BANANAS (EP)	8
69	Pye N(S)PL 18275	REVELATION (LP, mono/stereo)	20/15
69	Dawn DNLS 3003	2 OZ'S OF PLASTIC WITH A HOLE IN THE MIDDLE (LP, orange label)	22
69	Dawn DNLS 3003	2 OZ'S OF PLASTIC WITH A HOLE IN THE MIDDLE (LP, later pressings with red & blue or purple labels)	15
70	Liberty LBG 83464	MAN (LP)	18
72	United Artists UAS 29236	DO YOU LIKE IT HERE NOW, ARE YOU SETTLING IN? (LP)	18
72	United Artists USP 100	LIVE AT THE PADGET ROOMS, PENARTH (LP)	22
72	United Artists UAG 29417	BE GOOD TO YOURSELF AT LEAST ONCE A DAY (LP, 'map' sleeve with 'family tree' inner)	15
73	United Artists UDX 205/6	CHRISTMAS AT THE PATTI (LP, 2 x 10", with other artists)	22
73	Utd Artists UAD 60053/4	BACK INTO THE FUTURE (2-LP)	18
74	United Artists UAG 29631	RHINOS, WINOS & LUNATICS (LP, gatefold sleeve)	12
74	United Artists UAG 29675	SLOW MOTION (LP, with inner sleeve)	12
75	United Artists UAG 29872	MAXIMUM DARKNESS (LP, gatefold sleeve, with poster)	12
76	MCA MCF 2753	THE WELSH CONNECTION (LP)	12
77	MCA MCF 2815	ALL'S WELL THAT ENDS WELL (LP, initially with History Of Man booklet)	18/12

(see also Bystanders, Eyes Of Blue, Ancient Grease, Big Sleep, Clive John, Alkatraz, Help Yourself, Martin Ace, Deke Leonard, Neutrons, Gary Pickford–Hopkins & Friends, Wild Turkey)

T. MAN & T. BONES
72	Sioux SI 007	True Born African (actually by Winston Jarrett & Righteous Flames)/Tropical Chief	5

(STEPHEN STILLS') MANASSAS
72	Atlantic K 60021	MANASSAS (2-LP, with 2 inner sleeves & lyric poster)	15
73	Atlantic K 40440	DOWN THE ROAD (LP)	12

(see also Stephen Stills, Crosby Stills & Nash, Flying Burrito Brothers)

MANASSEH
77	Genesis 12	MANASSEH (LP, with insert)	20

JUNIOR MANCE
60	HMV CLP 1342	JUNIOR (LP)	15
71	Atlantic 2400 028	WITH A LOTTA HELP FROM MY FRIENDS (LP)	12

STEVE MANCHA/J.J. BARNES
69	Stax SXATS 1012	RARE STAMPS (LP)	20

(see also J.J. Barnes)

MICKY MANCHESTER
75	Rainbow RBW 2001	Have You Seen Your Daughter Mrs. Jones/Chamberlain Said	4

(see also Just Plain Smith, Just Plain Jones, Trainspotters)

MANCHESTER MEKON
79	Newmarket NEW 102	No Forgetting/Have A Go-Go/Jonathan Livingstone Seafood (hand-painted p/s with insert, 1,000 only)	12

MANCHESTER MOB
67	Parlophone R 5552	Bony Maronie At The Hop/Afro Asian	25

(see also Graham Gouldman, High Society, 10cc, Friday Browne)

MANCHESTERS
66	Ember	TRIBUTE TO THE BEATLES (LP)	20

MANCHESTER'S PLAYBOYS
66	Fontana TF 745	I Feel So Good/I Close My Eyes	45

HENRY MANCINI & HIS ORCHESTRA
59	RCA RCA 1134	Peter Gunn Theme/The Brothers Go To Mother's	6
59	RCA RCA 1134	Peter Gunn Theme/The Brothers Go To Mother's (78)	10
62	RCA RCA 1285	Experiment In Terror/Tooty Twist	12
62	RCA RCA 1312	Man Of The World Theme/Fluter's Ball	8
64	RCA RCA 1414	How Soon/The Tiber Twist	5
64	RCA RCA 1431	Dear Heart/A Shot In The Dark	6
65	RCA RCA 1498	Soldier In The Rain/Moment To Moment	5
68	RCA RCA 1689	Waiting Until Dark/Norma De Alajara	10
70	RCA RCA 1934	Z-Theme/Midnight Cowboy	5
61	RCA RCX 205	BREAKFAST AT TIFFANY'S (EP)	20
62	RCA RCX 7107	HATARI! (EP)	10
64	RCA RCX 7136	THE PINK PANTHER (EP)	15
64	RCA RD 7667	THE BEST OF MANCINI (LP)	12
65	RCA RD 7759	THE GREAT RACE (LP, soundtrack)	40
66	RCA SF 7818	WHAT DID YOU DO IN THE WAR, DADDY? (LP, soundtrack)	18
66	RCA RD 7817	ARABESQUE (LP, soundtrack)	18
67	RCA RD/SF 7891	TWO FOR THE ROAD (LP, soundtrack)	18

Henry MANCINI & His Orchestra

67	RCA RD/SF 7899	GUNN (LP, soundtrack)	18
69	United Artists UAS 29049	CHICAGO, CHICAGO (LP, soundtrack)	15
70	CBS 70061	ME, NATALIE (LP, soundtrack, with Rod McKuen)	15
70	Avco Embassy 6466 002	SUNFLOWER (LP, soundtrack)	15
70	United Artists UAS 29122	MASTER OF THE ISLANDS (LP, soundtrack)	15
72	RCA Victor SF 8127	FILM THEMES A TO Z (LP)	12
73	RCA Victor SF 8366	OKLAHOMA CRUDE (LP, soundtrack)	15
73	RCA Victor SF 8379	VISIONS OF EIGHT (LP, soundtrack)	15
74	RCA Victor APL 1 0270	COUNTRY GENTLEMEN (LP, soundtrack)	15
75	RCA Red Seal RS 1010	THE RETURN OF THE PINK PANTHER (LP, soundtrack)	15
75	MCA MCF 2707	THE GREAT WALDO PEPPER (LP, soundtrack)	15
76	United Artists UAS 30012	THE PINK PANTHER STRIKES AGAIN (LP, soundtrack)	15

MANDALA BAND

75	Chrysalis CHR 1095	MANDALA BAND (LP)	12
78	Chrysalis CHR 1181	THE EYE OF WENDOR: PROPHECIES (LP, with booklet)	12

HARVEY MANDEL

74	Janus 6146 024	Uno Ino/Shangrenade	5
68	Philips SBL 7873	CRISTO REDENTOR (LP)	18
69	Philips SBL 7904	RIGHTEOUS (LP)	15
70	Philips SBL 7915	GAMES GUITARS PLAY (LP)	15
71	Dawn DNLS 3015	BABY BATTER (LP)	15
71	Philips 6336 009	CRISTO REDENTOR (LP, reissue)	12
72	London SH-O 8426	GET OFF IN CHICAGO (LP)	12
72	Janus 6310 210	THE SNAKE (LP)	12
73	Janus 6499 831	SHANGRENADE (LP)	12

(see also Canned Heat, Dewey Terry)

NELSON MANDELA

64	Ember CEL 905	WHY I'M READY TO DIE (LP, spoken word, narrated by Peter Finch)	25

MANDINGO

73	EMI EMI 2014	Medicine Man/Black Rite	10
73	EMI EMC 3010	MANDINGO 1: SACRIFICE (LP)	15
73	Studio Two TWO 400	MANDINGO 2: PRIMEVAL RHYTHM OF LIFE (LP)	30
73	Studio Two Q4TWO 400	MANDINGO 2: PRIMEVAL RHYTHM OF LIFE (LP, quadrophonic)	35
75	EMI EMC 3038	MANDINGO 3: STORY OF SURVIVAL (LP)	15
77	EMI EMC 3217	MANDINGO 4: SAVAGE RITE (LP)	15

(see also Geoff Love, Manuel & Music Of The Mountains)

MANDRAGORA

86	SAB 01	OVER THE MOON (LP)	30
91	Resonance 33-9133	HEAD FIRST (LP)	12

MANDRAKE

60	Philips PB 1093	Mandrake/The Witch's Twist	12
61	Philips BF 1153	Thank Goodness It's Friday/Queen Of Sheba	5

MANDRAKE MEMORIAL

69	RCA SF 8028	MEDIUM (LP)	30
70	RCA/Poppy PYS 11003	PUZZLE (LP)	35

MANDRAKE PADDLE STEAMERS

69	Parlophone R 5780	Strange Walking Man/Steam	60
88	Bam Caruso NRIC 033	Strange Walking Man/Steam (reissue, gatefold p/s)	5

MANDRILL

73	Polydor 2066 320	Mandrill/Hang Loose	5
73	Polydor 2066 357	Fencewalk/Polk Street Carnival	5
70	Polydor 2489 028	MANDRILL (LP)	12
72	Polydor 2391 030	MANDRILL IS (LP)	12
73	Polydor 2391 061	COMPOSITE TRUTH (LP)	12
73	Polydor 2391 092	JUST OUTSIDE OF TOWN (LP)	12

MANEATERS

82	Editions EG EGO 8	Nine To Five/SUZI PINNS: Jerusalem (withdrawn 'Adam & Toyah' p/s)	100
82	Editions EG EGO 8	Nine To Five/SUZI PINNS: Jerusalem (title p/s)	5

(see also Adam & Ants, Toyah)

MAN FRIDAY & JIVE JUNIOR

83	Malaco MAL 011	Picking Up Sounds/Picking Up Sounds (Radio Mix) (p/s, features John Deacon)	20
83	Malaco MAL 1211	Picking Up Sounds (Extended)/Picking Up Sounds (Radio Mix) (12", p/s, features John Deacon)	60

(see also Queen)

MAN FROM DELMONTE

87	Ugly Man UGLY 3	Drive Drive Drive/Twenty Two And Still In Love With You/Sun Serious (p/s)	6
87	Ugly Man UGLY 5	Water In My Eyes/Bred By You (p/s)	5
87	Ugly Man UGLY 5T	Water In My Eyes/Bred By You (12", p/s)	7
88	Ugly Man UGLY 7T	Will Nobody Save Louise/Good Things In Life/Like A Millionaire (12", p/s)	7

MANHATTANS

65	Sue WI 384	I Wanna Be (Your Everything)/Searchin' For My Baby	25
66	Carnival CAR 100	Baby I Need You/Teach Me (The Philly Dog)	10
66	Carnival CAR 101	That New Girl/Can I	10
74	CBS 2117	Soul Train/I'm Not A Run Around	5
73	London SHB 8449	A MILLION TO ONE (LP)	15
76	CBS 81513	THE MANHATTANS (LP)	12
78	CBS 81828	IT FEELS GOOD (LP)	12
79	CBS 35693	LOVE TALK (LP)	12

MANIC STREET PREACHERS

MANIACS
77	United Artists UP 36327	Chelsea 1977/Ain't No Legend (p/s) 7

(see also Rings, Physicals)

MANIAX
66	White Label WLR 101/102	Out Of Reach/The Devil's Home 10

MANIC JABS
81	Waldo's MS 009	Autophagus/The Injuns Are Comin'/Thing Wild (p/s) 4

MANIC STREET PREACHERS
SINGLES

88	SBS SBS 002	Suicide Alley/Tennessee (I Get Low) (hand-made p/s with press-cuttings glued to plain card cover) 600
88	SBS SBS 002	Suicide Alley/Tennessee (I Get Low) (blue p/s, 200 only) 500
88	SBS SBS 002	Suicide Alley/Tennessee (I Get Low) (no p/s, 100 only) 300
90	Hopelessly Devoted 1	UK Channel Boredom/LAURENS: I Don't Know What The Trouble Is (p/s flexidisc, some free with *Hopelessly Devoted* fanzine; later 're-pressed') 60/45
90	Damaged Goods YUBB 4	NEW ART RIOT EP: New Art Riot/Strip It Down/Last Exit On Yesterday/ Teenage 20/20 (12", white label, 100 copies, plain sleeves rubber-stamped with "Made In Wales") 35
90	Damaged Goods YUBB 4	NEW ART RIOT EP: New Art Riot/Strip It Down/Last Exit On Yesterday/ Teenage 20/20 (12" EP, p/s, 1st 1,000 black & white label, 2nd 1,000 black-on-yellow; later red, orange & silver & green) 18/15/12
91	Damaged Goods YUBB 004P	NEW ART RIOT EP: New Art Riot/Strip It Down/Last Exit On Yesterday/ Teenage 20/20 (12" EP, p/s, reissue on pink vinyl) 25
91	Heavenly HVN 812	Motown Junk/Sorrow 16/We Her Majesty's Prisoners (12", p/s) 40
91	Heavenly HVN 8CD	Motown Junk/Sorrow 16/We Her Majesty's Prisoners (CD) 80
91	Heavenly HVN 10	You Love Us/Spectators Of Suicide (p/s) 20
91	Heavenly HVN 1012	You Love Us/Spectators Of Suicide/Starlover/Strip It Down (live) (12", p/s) 30
91	Heavenly HVN 10CD	You Love Us/Spectators Of Suicide/Starlover/Strip It Down (live) (CD) 40
91	Columbia 657337 7	Stay Beautiful/R.P. McMurphy (p/s) 8
91	Columbia 657337 6	Stay Beautiful/R.P. McMurphy/Soul Contamination (12", p/s) 15
91	Columbia 657337 8	Stay Beautiful/R.P. McMurphy/Soul Contamination (12", stickered poster p/s) ... 18
91	Columbia 657337 2	Stay Beautiful/Soul Contamination (CD, original issue) 12
91	Columbia 657582 7	Love's Sweet Exile/Repeat (p/s) 10
91	Columbia 657582 6	Repeat (U.K.)/Love's Sweet Exile/Democracy Coma (12") 12
91	Columbia 657582 8	Repeat/Democracy Coma/Love's Sweet Exile/Stay Beautiful (live) (12", gatefold, stickered p/s) 12
91	Columbia 657582 2	Love's Sweet Exile/Repeat/Democracy Coma/Stay Beautiful (live) (CD, original issue) 12
91	Caff CAFF 15	FEMININE IS BEAUTIFUL: Repeat After Me/New Art Riot (p/s, 500 only) 125
92	Columbia 657724 7	You Love Us/A Vision Of Dead Desire (p/s) 10
92	Columbia 657724 6	You Love Us/A Vision Of Dead Desire/It's So Easy (live) (12" gatefold p/s) 20
92	Columbia 657724 2	You Love Us/A Vision Of Dead Desire/We Her Majesty's Prisoners/ It's So Easy (live) (CD, original issue) 15
92	Columbia 657873 7	Slash'N'Burn/Motown Junk (p/s) 6
92	Columbia 657873 4	Slash'N'Burn/Motown Junk (cassette) 6
92	Columbia 657873 6	Slash'N'Burn/Motown Junk/Ain't Goin' Down (12", with print, stickered p/s) 12
92	Columbia 657873 2	Slash'N'Burn/Motown Junk/Ain't Goin' Down (gold CD, digipak). 15
92	Columbia 657724 2	You Love Us/A Vision Of Dead Desire/We Her Majesty's Prisoners/ It's So Easy (live) (CD, reissue) 8
92	Columbia 658083 7	Motorcycle Emptiness/Bored Out Of My Mind (p/s) 6

MANIC STREET PREACHERS

92	Columbia 658083 4	Motorcycle Emptiness/Bored Out Of My Mind (cassette)	6
92	Columbia 658083 8	Motorcycle Emptiness/Bored Out Of My Mind/Under My Wheels (12", picture disc, stickered PVC sleeve)	25
92	Columbia 658083 2	Motorcycle Emptiness/Bored Out Of My Mind/Under My Wheels (CD, digipak)	15
92	Damaged Goods YUBB 4CD	New Art Riot/Strip It Down/Last Exit On Yesterday/Teenage 20/20 (CD, picture disc, reissue, 3,000 only)	15
92	Columbia 658382 7	Theme From M*A*S*H EP (Suicide Is Painless)/FATIMA MANSIONS: "Everything I Do (I Do It For You)" (p/s)	6
92	Columbia 658382 4	Theme From M*A*S*H EP (Suicide Is Painless)/FATIMA MANSIONS: "Everything I Do (I Do It For You)" (cassette)	5
92	Columbia 658382 6	Theme From M*A*S*H EP (Suicide Is Painless)/FATIMA MANSIONS: "Everything I Do (I Do It For You)"/Sleeping With The NME (12", p/s)	10
92	Columbia 658382 2	Theme From M*A*S*H EP (Suicide Is Painless)/FATIMA MANSIONS: "Everything I Do (I Do It For You)"/Sleeping With The NME (CD)	20
92	Columbia 658796 7	Little Baby Nothing (7" Version)/Never Want Again/Suicide Alley (p/s)	5
92	Columbia 658796	Little Baby Nothing (7" Version)/Never Want Again/Suicide Alley (cassette)	5
92	Columbia 658796 7	Little Baby Nothing (7" Version)/Never Want Again/Dead Yankee Drawl/ Suicide Alley (CD, original issue)	8
92	Columbia 658796 5	Little Baby Nothing (7" Version)/R.P. McMurphy/Tennessee (live)/ You Love Us (live) (CD)	15
93	Columbia 659727 6	From Despair To Where/Hibernation/Spectators Of Suicide (Heavenly Version) (12", p/s)	8
93	Columbia 659727 7	From Despair To Where/Hibernation/Spectators Of Suicide (Heavenly Version)/Starlover (Heavenly Version) (CD)	18
93	Columbia 659477 2	La Tristessa Durera/Patrick Bateman/What's My Name (live)/ Slash'N'Burn (CD, digipak)	15
93	Columbia 659727 7	Roses In The Hospital/Us Against You/Donkeys (red vinyl)	6
93	Columbia 659727 6	Roses In The Hospital (OG Psychovocal Mix)/(OC Psychmental Mix)/ (51 Funk Salute Mix)/(Fillet-O-Gang Mix)/(ECG Mix)/(Album Version) (12", p/s)	8
93	Columbia 659727 2	Roses In The Hospital/Us Against You/Donkeys/Wrote For Luck (CD)	15
94	Columbia 660070 2	Life Becoming A Landslide/Comfort Comes/Are Mothers Saints/ Charles Windsor (CD)	15
94	Columbia 660447 0	PCP/Faster/Sculpture Of Man (10", p/s)	15
94	Columbia 660447 2	Faster/PCP/Sculpture Of Man/New Art Riot (In E Minor) (CD)	15
94	Columbia 660686 0	Revol/Too Cold Here/You Love Us/Life Becoming A Landslide (Live in Bangkok) (10", p/s)	7
94	Columbia 660686 2	Revol/Too Cold Here/You Love Us/Life's Sweet Exile (CD)	10
94	Columbia 660686 5	Revol/Drug Drug Druggy (Live Glastonbury)/Roses In The Hospital (Live Glastonbury)/You Love Us (Live Glastonbury) (CD)	15
94	Columbia 660895 0	She Is Suffering/The Drowners (live)/Stay With Me (live) (10", p/s)	10
96	Columbia 663070	A Design For Life/Bright Eyes (jukebox issue, no p/s)	8
96	Columbia 663468	Everything Must Go/Raindrops Keep Falling On My Head (Live Acoustic Version) (jukebox issue, no p/s)	8
96	Columbia 664044	Australia/A Design For Life (jukebox issue, no p/s)	8
97	Columbia MANIC 1-6CD	SIX SINGLES FROM GENERATION TERRORISTS (6-CD box set)	90

PROMOS

91	Heavenly HVN 10P	You Love Us (Radio Edit) (promo-only, some with stickered p/s, 1-sided white label, 500 only)	30
92	Columbia XPCD 171	GERNERATION TERRORISTS (CD, 5-track sampler, digipak)	15
92	Columbia XPCD 185	Motorcycle Emptiness/Motorcycle Emptiness (Radio Edit) (CD)	18
93	Columbia XPCD 285	GOLD AGAINST THE SOUL (CD, 4-track sampler, digipak)	20
93	Columbia/Damont XPS 272	Symphony Of Tourette (1-sided, white label, no p/s)	70
96	Columbia XPR 3043	A Design For Life (Stealth Sonic Orchestra Remix)/(Instrumental) (12")	20
96	Columbia XPR 3049	Kevin Carter (Stealth Sonic Orchestra Remix) (12", white label, 1-sided, stickered card sleeve, 30 only)	30
94	Columbia	DONE AND DUSTED (12", Chemical Brothers remixes)	20
96	Columbia XPR 3094	Australia (Lionrock Remix) (12", white label, 1-sided, stickered card sleeve, 20 only)	60
99	Epic XPR 3320	Tsunami (Cornelius Remix)/(Electron Ray Tube Mix) (12", p/s, sealed with sticker, promo only)	10

ALBUMS

92	Columbia 471060 1	GENERATION TERRORISTS (2-LP, stickered gatefold sleeve with inner)	15
92	Columbia 471060 9	GENERATION TERRORISTS (2-LP, picture discs, inner sleeves, 5,000 only)	30
92	Columbia 471060 0	GENERATION TERRORISTS (CD, picture disc, 5,000 only)	40
93	Columbia 4740649 1	GOLD AGAINST THE SOUL (LP, picture disc, inner sleeve, some in custom carrier-bag)	15/10
93	Columbia 4740649 2	GOLD AGAINST THE SOUL (gold CD)	20
94	Epic 477421 1	THE HOLY BIBLE (LP)	10
94	Epic 477421 9	THE HOLY BIBLE (LP, picture disc)	20
94	Epic 4774212	THE HOLY BIBLE (CD, picture disc)	20

MANICURED NOISE

80	Pre PRE 003	Metronome/Moscow (die-cut p/s with postcard)	4
80	Pre PRE 006	Faith/Free Time (p/s)	4
	(see also Weatherman & Friends)		

MANIFESTO

80s	Fire BLAZE 66055	Pattern 26 (1-sided white/label in bag with biography)	5

BARRY MANILOW

75	Arista ARIST 9	It's A Miracle/One Of These Days	4
75	Arista ARIST 20	Could It Be Magic/I Am Your Child	4
76	Arista ARIST 40	I Write The Songs/As Sure As I'm Standing Here (some with p/s)	15/5
76	Arista ARIST 77	Weekend In New England/Riders To The Stars (p/s)	5
77	Arista ARIST 120	Looks Like We Made It/Weekend In New England/I Write The Songs (p/s)	4
78	Arista ARIST 12196	Somewhere In The Night/Copacabana (At The Copa) (Disco Version) (12", p/s, promo only)	8

MINT VALUE £

80	Arista ARIST 337	It's A Miracle/I Don't Want To Walk Without You (double pack, p/s)	4
81	Arista ARIST 406	Bermuda Triangle/One Voice (poster p/s)	4
82	Arista ARIPD 464	Stay (live)/Nickels And Dimes (picture disc)	5
82	Arista ARIST 503	I'm Gonna Sit Right Down And Write Myself A Letter/	
		Heart Of Steel (poster p/s)	4
83	Arista ARILE 542	You're Lookin' Hot Tonight (live)/Let's Get On With It (p/s)	6
83	Arista ARIST 551	Read 'Em And Weep/One Voice (live) (p/s, with Christmas card)	4
83	Arista ARISD 551	Read 'Em And Weep/One Voice (live) (shaped picture disc)	4
84	Arista ARIST 10599	When October Goes/Paradise Cafe/Interview (10", p/s)	6
89	Arista 162051	Mandy/Something's Coming Up/I Write The Songs/A Nice Boy Like Me	
		(3" CD, gatefold card sleeve)	7
73	Arista 064 96958	BARRY MANILOW (LP)	12
74	Arista ARTY 100	BARRY MANILOW II (LP)	12
76	Arista ARTY 123	TRYIN' TO GET THE FEELING (LP, with inner sleeve)	10
76	Arista ARTY 137	THIS ONE'S FOR YOU (LP)	10
78	Arista A2L8601	BARRY MANILOW'S GREATEST HITS (2-LP, shaped picture discs)	15

MANISH BOYS
| 65 | Parlophone R 5250 | I Pity The Fool/Take My Tip . . . . | 325 |
(see also David Bowie)

MANISH BOYS/DAVY JONES & LOWER THIRD
79	EMI EMI 2925	I Pity The Fool/Take My Tip/DAVY JONES & LOWER THIRD:	
		You've Got A Habit Of Leaving/Baby Loves That Way (p/s)	6
82	Charly CYM 1	I Pity The Fool/Take My Tip/DAVY JONES & LOWER THIRD:	
		You've Got A Habit Of Leaving/Baby Loves That Way (10", p/s, reissue)	6

(see also David Bowie, Davy Jones, Davie Jones & King Bees)

MAN MACHINE
90	Outer Rhythm MMAN 2T	ZEN EP (12")	8
91	Outer Rhythm MMAN 3T	Animal (Primeaval Interface)/Shout (The Communicator)/	
		Shout (Primary Contact) (12")	8

BARRY MANN
61	HMV POP 911	Who Put The Bomp/Love True Love	20
61	HMV POP 949	Little Miss U.S.A./Find Another Fool	12
62	HMV POP 1084	Hey Baby I'm Dancin'/Like I Don't Love You	12
63	HMV POP 1108	Bless You/Teenage Has Been	12
64	Colpix PX 776	Talk To Me Baby/Amy	10
66	Capitol CL 15463	Angelica/Looking At Tomorrow	7
68	Capitol CL 15538	The Young Electric Psychedelic Hippy Flippy Folk And Funky Philosophic	
		Turned On Groovy 12 String Band/Take Your Love	7
63	HMV CLP 1559	WHO PUT THE BOMP IN THE BOMP BOMP BOMP? (LP)	175

CARL MANN
59	London HLS 8935	Mona Lisa/Foolish One	22
59	London HLS 8935	Mona Lisa/Foolish One (78)	90
59	London HLS 9006	Pretend/Rockin' Love	22
59	London HLS 9006	Pretend/Rockin' Love (78)	150
60	London HLS 9170	South Of The Border/I'm Comin' Home	18
60	London HA-S 2277	LIKE MANN — CARL MANN SINGS (LP)	225

CHARLES MANN
| 73 | Probe PRO 585 | Say You Love Me Too/I Can Feel It . . . . | 5 |

GEOFF MANN
84	private pressing GM 001	CHANTS WOULD BE A FINE THING (cassette)	8
84	Food For Thought GRUB 4	I MAY SING GRACE (LP)	10
85	Wobbly WOB 1	PSALM ENCHANTED EVENING (LP)	12

GLORIA MANN
56	Brunswick 05569	Why Do Fools Fall In Love/Partners For Life	15
56	Brunswick 05569	Why Do Fools Fall In Love/Partners For Life (78)	10
56	Brunswick 05610	It Happened Again/My Secret Sin	10

HERBIE MANN
66	Atlantic 584 052	Philly Dog/DAVE PIKE: Sunny	10
66	Atlantic 584 058	Love Theme From Paris Burning/Happy Brass	5
67	Atlantic 584 112	And The Beat Goes On/Free For All	5
68	A&M AMS 719	Unchain My Heart/Glory Of Love	6
69	Atlantic 584 297	Memphis Underground/New Orleans	5
72	Atlantic K 10179	Philly Dog/Memphis Underground/It's A Funky Thing	5
75	Atlantic K 10580	Hijack/Orient Express	5
56	London EZN 19006	EAST COAST JAZZ NO. 4 PT. 1 (EP)	8
58	Fontana TFE 17113	HERBIE MANN (EP)	10
59	Columbia Clef SEB 10102	MAGIC FLUTE OF HERBIE MANN (EP)	10
58	Fontana TFL 5013	SALUTE TO THE FLUTE (LP)	15
60	Top Rank 25/015	FLUTE FOR ETERNITY (10" LP, with Buddy Collette)	15
63	London HA-K/SH-K 8043	RIGHT NOW (LP)	15
64	Atlantic ATL 5008	HERBIE MANN AT NEWPORT (LP)	15
65	Atlantic ATL/SAL 5035	THE ROAR OF THE GREASE PAINT (LP)	15
66	CBS (S)BPG 62585	LATIN MANN (LP)	12
66	Atlantic ATL/SAL 5038	STANDING OVATION AT NEWPORT (LP)	15
66	Atlantic 587/588 003	MONDAY NIGHT AT THE VILLAGE GATE (LP)	15
66	Atlantic 587/588 028	NIRVANA (LP, with Bill Evans)	15
67	Atlantic 1471	NEW MANN AT NEWPORT (LP)	12
67	Atlantic 587/588 054	HERBIE MANN AT THE VILLAGE GATE (LP)	12
67	Atlantic Special 590 013	FREE FOR ALL (LP)	12
68	Atlantic 1475	IMPRESSIONS OF THE MIDDLE EAST (LP)	15
68	Atlantic 1490	THE HERBIE MANN STRING ALBUM (LP)	12
69	Solid State USS 7007	ST. THOMAS (LP)	15

Herbie MANN

69	Atlantic 588 156	INSPIRATION I FEEL (LP)	12
69	A&M AMLS 944	GLORY OF LOVE (LP)	12
69	Atlantic 588 200	MEMPHIS UNDERGROUND (LP)	12
69	SRCP 3002	AFRO-JAZZIAC (LP)	12
70	Polydor 2465 005	CONCERTO GROSSO IN D BLUES (LP)	12
70	Polydor 2465 008	STONE FLUTE (LP)	12
71	Atco 2400 022	MUSCLE SHOALS NITTY GRITTY (LP)	12
71	Atco 2400 121	MEMPHIS TWO-STEP (LP)	12
72	Atco 2400 191	PUSH, PUSH, (LP, with Duane Allman)	15
72	Atlantic K 40385	MISSISSIPPI GAMBLER (LP)	12
73	Atlantic K 40467	HOLD ON, I'M COMIN' (LP)	12
74	Atlantic K 50020	TURTLE BAY (LP)	12
74	Atlantic K 50032	LONDON UNDERGROUND (LP)	12
75	Atlantic K 50053	REGGAE (LP)	12
75	Atlantic K 50128	DISCOTHEQUE (LP)	12
75	Atlantic K 50174	WATER BED (LP)	12

(see also Buddy Collette & Herbie Mann Group)

LORIE MANN

59	Top Rank JAR 116	A Penny A Kiss, A Penny A Hug/Dream Lover	6
59	Top Rank JAR 116	A Penny A Kiss, A Penny A Hug/Dream Lover (78)	12
59	Top Rank JAR 148	Just Keep It Up/You Made Me Care	7
59	Top Rank JAR 148	Just Keep It Up/You Made Me Care (78)	12
59	Top Rank JAR 237	So Many Ways/I Wonder	6

MANFRED MANN

63	HMV POP 1189	Why Should We Not/Brother Jack	18
63	HMV POP 1225	Cock-A-Hoop/Now You're Needing Me	15
64	HMV POP 1252	5-4-3-2-1/Without You	7
64	HMV POP 1282	Hubble Bubble (Toil And Trouble)/I'm Your Kingpin	7
64	HMV POP 1320	Do Wah Diddy Diddy/What You Gonna Do?	6
64	HMV POP 1346	Sha La La/John Hardy	6
65	HMV POP 1381	Come Tomorrow/What Did I Do Wrong?	6
65	HMV POP 1413	Oh No Not My Baby/What Am I Doing Wrong	6
65	HMV POP 1466	If You Gotta Go, Go Now/Stay Around	6
66	HMV POP 1523	Pretty Flamingo/You're Standing By	6
66	HMV POP 1541	You Gave Me Somebody To Love/Poison Ivy	10
65	HMV 7TEA 2124	There's No Living Without Your Loving/Tired Of Trying, Bored With Lying, Scared Of Dying (demo-only EP sampler)	25
66	Fontana TF 730	Just Like A Woman/I Wanna Be Rich	6
66	Fontana TF 757	Semi-Detached, Suburban Mr. James/Morning After The Party	6
67	Fontana TF 812	Ha! Ha! Said The Clown/Feeling So Good (some in p/s)	12/6
67	Fontana TF 828	Sweet Pea/One Way	7
67	Fontana TF 862	So Long, Dad/Funniest Gig	7
68	Fontana TF 897	Mighty Quinn/By Request — Edwin Garvey	6
68	Fontana TF 908	Up The Junction/Sleepy Hollow (some in p/s)	12/6
68	Fontana TF 943	My Name Is Jack/There Is A Man	6
68	Fontana TF 985	Fox On The Run/Too Many People	6
69	Fontana TF 1013	Ragamuffin Man/A 'B' Side	6
64	HMV 7EG 8848	MANFRED MANN'S COCK-A-HOOP WITH 54321 (EP)	20
65	HMV 7EG 8876	GROOVIN' WITH MANFRED MANN (EP)	15
65	HMV 7EG 8908	THE ONE IN THE MIDDLE (EP)	15
65	HMV 7EG 8922	NO LIVING WITHOUT LOVING (EP)	15
66	HMV 7EG 8942	MACHINES (EP)	18
66	HMV 7EG 8949	INSTRUMENTAL ASYLUM (EP, with Jack Bruce)	25
66	HMV 7EG 8962	AS WAS (EP)	20
66	Fontana TE 17483	INSTRUMENTAL ASSASSINATION (EP)	15
68	Philips MCF 5002	THE HITS OF MANFRED MANN (cassette EP)	12
68	Philips MCF 5005	THE HITS OF MANFRED MANN AND DDDBM&T (cassette EP)	12
64	HMV CLP 1731	THE FIVE FACES OF MANFRED MANN (LP)	30
65	HMV CLP 1911/CSD 1628	MANN MADE (LP, mono/stereo)	25/30
66	HMV CLP 3559	MANN MADE HITS (LP)	25
66	HMV TA-CLP 3559	MANN MADE HITS (reel-to-reel tape, mono)	12
66	Fontana (S)TL 5377	AS IS (LP, 'alcove' cover, mono/stereo)	18/25
66	Fontana (S)TL 5377	AS IS (LP, 'locomotive' cover, mono/stereo)	30/35
67	HMV CLP/CSD 3594	SOUL OF MANN (LP, mono/stereo)	30/35
67	HMV TA-CLP 3594	SOUL OF MANN (reel-to-reel tape, mono)	12
68	Fontana (S)TL 5460	UP THE JUNCTION — ORIGINAL SOUNDTRACK RECORDING (LP)	30
68	Fontana SFL 13003	WHAT A MANN (LP)	25
68	Fontana (S)TL 5470	MIGHTY GARVEY! (LP, mono/stereo)	20/15
70	Fontana 6852 005	UP THE JUNCTION — ORIGINAL SOUNDTRACK RECORDING (LP, reissue)	12

(see also Paul Jones, Blues Band, Mike Hugg, Henry Lowther, Mike D'Abo, McGuinness Flint, Jack Bruce, Coulson & Dean, Lyn Dobson, Paddy Klaus & Gibson)

MANFRED MANN & MIKE HUG(G)

71	Ski SKI 1	Ski 'Full-Of-Fitness' Theme/Baby Jane (some in p/s)	15/7
71	Michelin MIC+01	The Michelin Theme (Go Radial, Go Michelin) (1-sided, gatefold p/s)	15

MANFRED MANN'S CHAPTER III

70	Vertigo 6059 012	Happy Being Me/Devil Woman	6
69	Vertigo VO 3	MANFRED MANN CHAPTER III (LP, gatefold sleeve, spiral label)	20
70	Vertigo 6360 012	MANFRED MANN CHAPTER III VOL. 2 (LP, gatefold sleeve, spiral label)	30

MANFRED MANN'S EARTH BAND

70	Lyntone LYN 1981	The Maxwell House Shake (1-sided flexidisc)	7
71	Philips 6006 122	Living Without You/Tribute (as Manfred Mann)	5
71	Philips 6006 159	Mrs Henry/Prayer (as Manfred Mann)	5
72	Philips 6006 251	Meat/Glorified Magnified (as Earth Band)	5
73	Vertigo 6059 078	Get Your Rocks Off/Sadjoy (as Earth Band)	5

MINT VALUE £

79	Bronze BPO 77	Don't Kill It Carol/Blinded By The Light (picture disc)	6
71	Philips 6308 062	STEPPING SIDEWAYS (LP, unissued)	
72	Philips 6308 086	MANFRED MANN'S EARTH BAND (LP)	15
72	Philips 6308 125	GLORIFIED MAGNIFIED (LP)	15
73	Vertigo 6360 087	MESSIN' (LP, spiral label)	20

(see also Skeleton Crew)

SHADOW MANN
| 69 | Roulette RO 504 | Come Live With Me/One By One | 12 |

SHELLY MANNE
68	Atlantic 584 180	Daktari/Out On A Limb	8
54	Vogue LDE 072	SHELLY MANNE AND HIS MEN VOL. 1 (10" LP)	15
55	Contemporary LDC 143	SHELLY MANNE VOL. 2 (10" LP)	15
56	Contemporary LDC 190	SHELLY MANNE, SHORTY ROGERS AND JIMMY GIUFFRE — THE THREE (10" LP)	15
56	Contemporary LDC 192	SHELLY MANNE AND RUSS FREEMAN (10" LP)	15
56	Contemporary LAC 12075	SHELLY MANNE AND HIS FRIENDS (LP, with Andre Previn & Leroy Vinegar)	15
57	Contemporary LAC 12147	SHELLY MANNE AND HIS MEN VOL. 5 (LP)	12
57	Contemporary LAC 12232	SHELLY MANNE AND HIS MEN VOL. 6 (LP)	12
61	Contemporary LAC 12250	AT THE BLACK HAWK VOL. 1 (LP, also stereo SCA 5015)	12
61	Contemporary LAC 12255	AT THE BLACK HAWK VOL. 2 (LP, also stereo SCA 5016)	12
61	Contemporary LAC 12260	AT THE BLACK HAWK VOL. 3 (LP, also stereo SCA 5017)	12
61	Contemporary LAC 12265	AT THE BLACK HAWK VOL. 4 (LP, also stereo SCA 5018)	12
61	Contemporary LAC 12293	THE PROPER TIME (LP, soundtrack)	15
61	Contemporary LAC 12305/6	AT THE MANNE HOLE (2-LP)	15
65	Stateside SL 10125	SHELLY MANNE AND CO. (LP)	10

(see also Gerry Mulligan & Shelly Manne, Jimmy Giuffre, Shorty Rogers & His Orchestra)

BOB MANNING
54	Capitol CL 14190	I'm A Fool For You/It's All Right With Me	7
55	Capitol CL 14220	The Very Thought Of You/Just For Laughs	7
55	Capitol CL 14256	Majorca (Isle Of Love)/It's My Life	7
55	Capitol CL 14234	My Love Song To You/After My Laughter Came Tears	7
55	Capitol CL 14288	The Mission San Michel/You Are There	7
55	Capitol CL 14318	What A Wonderful Way To Die/Why Didn't You Tell Me?	7

LINDA MANNING
| 66 | King KG 1039 | Buy Me Something Pretty, Joey/Downtown Lonely Girl Blues | 6 |

MARTY MANNING & CHEETAHS
| 67 | CBS 2721 | Tarzan March/Sunny | 10 |

EDDIE MANNION
| 60 | HMV POP 804 | Just Driftin'/Quiet Girl | 7 |

WINGY MANONE ORCHESTRA
| 57 | Brunswick 05655 | Party Doll/Real Gone | 15 |
| 57 | Brunswick 05655 | Party Doll/Real Gone (78) | 15 |

MAN ON THE MOON
| 69 | Philips 88457 DE | MAN ON THE MOON (EP, spoken word, 2-part tri-foldout p/s with insert, 'historic souvenir' available via *News Of The World* newspaper) | 8 |

MANOWAR
83	M. F. Nations 12 KUT 102	Defender (featuring Orson Welles)/Gloves Of Metal (12", p/s)	15
84	10 TEN 3012	All Men Play On 10/Mountains (12", p/s, some gatefold)	18/12
87	Atlantic B 9463	Blow Your Speakers/Violence And Bloodshed (p/s)	7
87	Atlantic BT 9463	Blow Your Speakers/Violence And Bloodshed (12", embossed p/s, some with poster)	12/8

(see also Orson Welles)

JOE MANSANO
69	Blue Cat BS 150	Life On Reggae Planet/RECO & RHYTHM ACES: Z.Z. Beat	12
72	Sioux SI 022	The Trial Of Pama Dice/JACKIE ROWLAND: Lonely Man	5
70	Trojan TBL 106	BRIXTON CAT (LP)	30

(see also Joe The Boss, Joe's Allstars, Dice The Boss)

TONY MANSELL
54	Parlophone MSP 6130	The High And The Mighty/Hold My Hand (with Johnny Dankworth Orchestra)	6
56	Parlophone MSP 6222	Zambesi (Sweet African)/11th Hour Melody (with Johnny Dankworth Orchestra)	6
58	Parlophone R 4471	Impossible/Who Are They To Say	5

(see also Johnny Dankworth)

KEITH MANSFIELD ORCHESTRA
68	CBS 3895	Beautiful//Soul Thing	5
68	CBS 63426	ALL YOU NEED IS KEITH MANSFIELD (LP)	20
69	CBS 64666	RACE ON THE WIND (LP)	12
70	CBS 70073	LOOT (LP, soundtrack, with Steve Ellis)	25

JAYNE MANSFIELD
| 67 | London HL 10147 | As The Clouds Drift By/Suey (with Jimi Hendrix, demos more common, £18) | 30 |

(see also Jimi Hendrix)

CHARLES MANSON
86	Fierce FRIGHT 006	Rise/Sick City (p/s, 1 side etched, handwritten labels)	25
88	Fierce FRIGHT 012	It's Comin' Down Fast (Helter Skelter) (p/s, 1 side etched, hand-made labels)	25
86	Fierce FRIGHT 001	LOVE AND TERROR CULT (LP)	50

EDDY MANSON
| 55 | HMV 7M 325 | Oh! No!/The Lovers | 7 |

JEANE MANSON
| 79 | CBS S CBS 7222 | I've Already Seen It In Your Eyes/J'ai Deja Vu Ca Dans Tes Yeux | 15 |

MARILYN MANSON

97	Interscope INVP 95541	The Horrible People/The Not So Beautiful People (10" picture disc)	10
97	Interscope INDX 95541	The Beautiful People/The Not So Beautiful People/Snake Eyes And Sissies/ Deformography (CD)	8
97	Interscope INVP 95552	Tourniquet/(remix) (10" picture disc)	10
97	Interscope INDX 95552	Tourniquet/Lunchbox/Next MF (CD)	8
99	Interscope SAM 175 CD	I Don't Like Drugs (But The Drugs Like Me) (radio edit)/(album version) (CD, card sleeve, promo only)	20
96	Interscope IND 90086	ANTICHRIST SUPERSTAR (CD, in slipcase)	18
98	Interscope IND 90273	MECHANICAL ANIMALS (CD, in slipcase)	18
99	Interscope ADV 490 394-2	MECHANICAL ANIMALS (CD, promo, no'd, card sl., w/comic, PVC Slipcase)	40

MANSUN

95	Sci Fi Hi Fi MANSON 1	Take It Easy Chicken/Take It Easy Chicken (as Manson, same track both sides, die-cut sleeve, 1,000 only)	35
95	Regal REG 3	Skin Up Pin Up/Flourella (white vinyl)	12
95	Regal REG 3CD	Skin Up Pin Up/Flourella (CD, PVC sleeve with barcode sticker)	15
96	Parlophone R 6430	ONE EP (p/s)	8
96	Parlophone CDRS 6430	ONE EP (CD)	15
96	Parlophone R 6437	TWO EP (p/s)	8
96	Parlophone CDR 6437	TWO EP (CD)	10
96	Parlophone R 6447	Stripper Vicar/No One Knows Us (clear vinyl, p/s)	8
96	Parlophone CDRS 6447	Stripper Vicar/The Edge/Duchess (CD, card p/s with poster)	10
96	Parlophone CDR 6447	Stripper Vicar/An Open Letter/No One Knows Us/Things Keep Falling Off (CD)	12
96	Parlophone R 6453	Wide Open Space/Rebel Without A Quilt (white vinyl, foldout p/s in PVC sleeve)	7
96	Parlophone CDR 6453	Wide Open Space/Rebel Without A Quilt/Vision Impaired/ Skin Up, Pin Up (CD, digipak)	20
96	Parlophone CDRS 6453	Wide Open Space/The Gods Of Not Very Much/Moronica (Acoustic Version)/ Lemonade Secret Drinker (Acoustic Version) (CD, fold-out card p/s)	20
97	Parlophone CDRS 6482	SEVEN EP (CD, digipak with poster)	8
98	Parlophone R 6487	EIGHT EP (p/s, red vinyl)	5
99	fan club	Taxloss/Everyone Must Win (live) (fanclub only release)	20
97	Parlophone CPCS 7387	ATTACK OF THE GREY LANTERN (2-LP, gatefold sleeve)	15

JOHN MANTELL

65	CBS 201783	Remember Child/I'll See You Around	20

MIKE MANTLER

75	Watt WATT 3	13¾ (LP, with Carla Bley; with insert)	10

(see also Carla Bley, Jazz Composers Orchestra)

BOB MANTON

81	Mainstreet MS 101	No Trees In Brixton Prison/Brixton Walkabout (p/s)	8

(see also Purple Hearts)

MANTOVANI (ORCHESTRA)

53	Decca F 10168	Swedish Rhapsody/Jamaican Rumba (gold or silver label lettering)	12/7
54	Decca F 10233	Luxembourg Polka/Music Box Tango	5
54	Decca F 10250	Shadow Waltz/Moonlight Serenade	5
54	Decca F 10292	Bewitched/Dream, Dream, Dream	5
54	Decca F 10395	Lonely Ballerina/Lazy Gondolier	6
60	Decca F 9696	Charmaine/Diane	5
67	Decca F 12630	You Only Live Twice/Puppet On A String (as Mantovani Orchestra)	5

MANUEL & MUSIC OF THE MOUNTAINS

78	EMI EMI 2743	Princess Leia's Theme From Star Wars/Mountain Fire	5

(see also Geoff Love, Mandingo)

MANUFACTURED ROMANCE

81	Fresh FRESH 16	The Time Of My Life/Room To Breathe (various colours of p/s)	4

PHIL MANZANERA (& 801)

77	Polydor 2001 733	Flight 19/Car Rhumba	5
78	Polydor 2001 800	Island/Diamond Head	4
78	Polydor 2001 835	Remote Control/K Scope (1st issue)	5
78	Polydor PB 10	Remote Control/K Scope (2nd issue)	5

(see also Roxy Music, Quiet Sun, 801)

RAY MANZAREK

83	A&M AM 156	Wounds Of Fate/Roasted Swan (p/s)	4
84	A&M AM 173	Wheel Of Fortune/A Young Girl (p/s)	4
74	Mercury SRM 1703	THE WHOLE THING STARTED WITH ROCK'N'ROLL (LP)	12
83	A&M AMLX 64945	CARMINA BURANA (LP, with Philip Glass)	10

(see also Doors, Philip Glass)

MAORI QUARTET

55	Philips BB 2006	Moon Of Manakoora/Hawaiian Drinking Song (78)	8

MAPLE LEAF FOUR

56	Oriole CB 1337	The Green Door/You Must Come In At The Door (78)	8

MAPLEOAK

70	Decca F 13008	Son Of A Gun/Hurt Me So Much	15
71	Decca SKL 5085	MAPLEOAK (LP)	175

LUCILLE MAPP

57	Columbia DB 3916	Mangos/On Treasure Island	7
57	Columbia DB 3949	Jamie Boy/Moonlight In Vermont	6
57	Columbia DB 4040	I'm Available/Lovin' Ya, Lovin' Ya, Lovin' Ya	7
58	Columbia DB 4071	Love Is/The Early Birdie	5
58	Columbia DB 4168	Remember When/I'm A Dreamer, Aren't We All?	5
58	Columbia DB 4168	Remember When/I'm A Dreamer, Aren't We All? (78)	8

MINT VALUE £

59	Columbia DB 4261	Chinchilla/Follow Me (78)	8
57	Columbia SEG 7726	STREET OF DREAMS (EP)	12
57	Columbia SEG 7773	LUCILLE MAPP (EP)	12

TOMMY MARA
55	MGM SP 1128	Pledging My Love/Honey Bunch	8
55	MGM MGM 821	Pledging My Love/Honey Bunch (78)	8
58	Felsted AF 109	Where The Blues Of The Night/What Makes You So Lonely	8
58	Felsted AF 109	Where The Blues Of The Night/What Makes You So Lonely (78)	8
59	Felsted AF 116	You Don't Know/Marie	6
59	Felsted AF 116	You Don't Know/Marie (78)	10
59	Felsted AF 123	Until I Hear From You/Now Is The Hour	6
59	Felsted AF 123	Until I Hear From You/Now Is The Hour	12
58	Felsted GEP 1003	PRESENTING TOMMY MARA (EP)	18

(JOSEPH) MARAIS & MIRANDA
53	Columbia SCM 5025	Old Johnnie Goggabie/The Zulu Warrior	5
59	Fontana H 225	I-Ha-She/The Queen Bee (as Marais & Miranda)	5
59	Fontana H 225	I-Ha-She/The Queen Bee (as Marais & Miranda) (78)	8

MARATHONS
| 61 | Pye International 7N 25088 | Peanut Butter/Down In New Orleans | 12 |
| 61 | Vogue V 9185 | Peanut Butter/Talkin' Trash | 18 |

MARAUDERS
63	Decca F 11695	That's What I Want/Hey What'd You Say	10
63	Decca F 11748	Always On My Mind/Heart Full Of Tears	8
64	Decca F 11836	Lucille/Little Egypt	10
65	Fontana TF 609	Baby I Wanna Be Loved/Somebody Told My Girl	8

(see also Danny Davis)

MARBLES
68	Polydor 56272	Only One Woman/By The Light Of A Burning Candle	7
69	Polydor 56310	The Walls Fell Down/Love You	6
70	Polydor 56378	Breaking Up Is Hard To Do/I Can't See Nobody	6

(see also Graham Bonnet, Trevor Gordon, Fut)

MARBLE STAIRCASE
| 83 | Whaam! WHAAM 11 | Still Dreaming/Dark Ages (p/s) | 5 |

MARC & MAMBAS
82	Some Bizzare BZS 512	Fun City/Sleaze (Take It, Shake It)/Taking It And Shaking It (12", p/s, fan club issue, mail-order only)	20
82	Lyntone LYN 12505	Discipline (*Flexipop* flexidisc, clear or black vinyl, as Marc & Friends)	10/6
82	Some Bizzare BZS 15	Big Louise/Empty Eyes (unreleased, artwork only)	
82	Some Bizzare BZS 1512	Big Louise/Empty Eyes/The Dirt Behind The Neon (Sleaze Revisited) (12", unreleased, artwork only)	
83	Some Bizzare BZS 19	Black Heart/Your Aura (p/s, with postcard insert)	5
83	Some Bizzare BZS 1912	Black Heart/Your Aura/Mamba (12", p/s)	8
83	Some Bizzare BZSDJ 21	Torment/You'll Never See On Sunday (no p/s, promo only)	15
83	Some Bizzare BZS 2112	Torment/First Time/You'll Never See Me On A Sunday/Megamillionmania — Multimaniamix (12", p/s)	10
82	Some Bizzare BZS 13	UNTITLED (2-LP, 33rpm/45rpm)	12
83	Some Bizzare BZSL 4	TORMENT AND TOREROS (2-LP, black inner sleeves)	12
84	Gutterhearts GH 1	BITE BLACK AND BLUES — RAOUL & THE RUINED LIVE (LP, fan club issue)	30
89	Some Bizzare SOD 13	UNTITLED (2-LP, 33rpm/45rpm, reissue)	10

(see also Soft Cell, Marc Almond)

LYDIA MARCELLE
| 66 | Sue WI 4025 | Another Kind Of Fellow/I've Never Been Hurt Like This Before | 30 |

MUZZY MARCELLINO
| 56 | London HLU 8355 | Mary Lou/MR. FORD & MR. GOON-BONES: Ain't She Sweet | 25 |
| 56 | London HLU 8355 | Mary Lou/MR. FORD & MR. GOON-BONES: Ain't She Sweet (78) | 10 |

MARCELS
61	Pye International 7N 25073	Blue Moon/Goodbye To Love	8
61	Pye International 7N 25083	Summertime/Teeter Totter Love	8
61	Pye International 7N 25105	You Are My Sunshine/Find Another Fool	10
61	Pye International 7N 25114	Heartaches/My Love For You	12
62	Pye International 7N 25124	My Melancholy Baby/Really Need Your Love	10
63	Pye International 7N 25201	I Wanna Be The Leader/Give Me Back Your Love	12
61	Pye Intl. NPL 28016	BLUE MOON (LP)	125

GLORIA MARCH
| 58 | London HLB 8568 | Baby Of Mine/Nippon Wishing Well | 18 |
| 58 | London HLB 8568 | Baby Of Mine/Nippon Wishing Well (78) | 15 |

HAL MARCH
| 58 | London HLD 8534 | Hear Me Good/One Dozen Roses | 18 |
| 58 | London HLD 8534 | Hear Me Good/One Dozen Roses (78) | 15 |

JO MARCH
58	London HLR 8696	Dormi, Dormi, Dormi (Sleep, Sleep, Sleep)/Fare Thee Well, Oh Honey	8
58	London HLR 8696	Dormi, Dormi, Dormi (Sleep, Sleep, Sleep)/Fare Thee Well, Oh Honey (78)	12
58	London HLR 8763	The Virgin Mary Had One Son/I, Said The Donkey	8
58	London HLR 8763	The Virgin Mary Had One Son/I, Said The Donkey (78)	12

(LITTLE) PEGGY MARCH
63	RCA RCA 1338	I Will Follow Him/Wind Up Doll (as Little Peggy March)	7
63	RCA RCA 1350	My Teenage Castle/I Wish I Were A Princess (as Little Peggy March)	7
63	RCA RCA 1362	Hello Heartache, Goodbye Love/Boy Crazy (as Little Peggy March)	7

MINT VALUE £

64	RCA RCA 1426	Watch What You Do With My Baby/Can't Stop (as Little Peggy March)	8
65	RCA RCA 1472	Let Her Go/Your Girl	7
68	RCA RCA 1687	If You Loved Me/Thinking Through My Tears	20
68	RCA RCA 1752	I've Been Here Before/Time And Time Again	6
69	RCA RCA 1809	What Am I Going To Do Without You/Lilac Skies	6
65	RCA	IN OUR FASHION (LP, existence unconfirmed)	25

BOBBY MARCHAN
| 68 | Atlantic 584 155 | Get Down With It/Half A Mind | 6 |
| 69 | Action ACT 4533 | Ain't No Reason For Girls To Be Lonely (Parts 1 & 2) | 10 |

(see also Huey 'Piano' Smith & Clowns)

VICTOR MARCHESE
| 53 | MGM SP 1018 | Fandango/Flamingo | 6 |

MARCH HARE
| 68 | Chapter One CH 101 | Cry My Heart/With My Eyes Closed | 7 |
| 69 | Deram DM 258 | I Could Make It There With You/Have We Got News For You | 5 |

(see also Gary & Stu, Koobas)

MARCHING GIRLS
| 81 | Pop:Aural POP 011 | True Love/First In Line (p/s) | 4 |

MARCH VIOLETS
82	Merciful Release MR 013	Religious As Hell/Fodder/Children On Stun/Bon Bon Babies (p/s)	20
83	Merciful Release MR 017	Grooving In Green/Stream (p/s)	15
84	Rebirth RB 18	Crow Baby/One Two I Love You (p/s)	5
85	Rebirth RB 18-12	Crow Baby/One Two I Love You/Long Pig/Crow Bait (12", p/s)	7
84	Rebirth RB 21	Snake Dance/Slow Drip Lizard (snakeskin-embossed stickered p/s with insert)	5
84	Rebirth RB 21-12	Snake Dance/It's Hot/Slow Drip Lizard/Snake Dance (Extended) (12", p/s)	7
84	Rebirth VRB 25	NATURAL HISTORY (LP)	10

MARCIA & JEFF
| 68 | Studio One SO 2047 | Words/SHARKS: How Could I Live | 22 |

MARCUS
| 76 | United Artists UAS 30000 | MARCUS (LP) | 20 |

GUY MARDEL
| 65 | Vogue VRS 7000 | V'Avoue Jamais (actually "N'Avoue Jamais")/Si Tu N'y Crois Pas | 5 |

JANIE MARDEN
55	Decca F 10600	Soldier Boy/Hard To Get	8
55	Decca F 10605	I'll Come When You Call/Thank You For The Waltz (with Frank Weir & His Saxophone)	7
55	Decca F 10673	You Are My Love/A Teen Age Prayer	8
56	Decca F 10765	Allegheny Moon/Magic Melody	7
63	Piccadilly 7N 35128	Make The Night A Little Longer/Walk Alone	8
65	Decca F 12101	They Long To Be Close To You/This Empty Place	8
65	Decca F 12155	You Really Didn't Mean It/Only The One You Love	6

ARIF MARDIN
| 69 | Atlantic 584 295 | Glass Onion/How Can I Be Sure | 4 |

ERNIE MARESCA
62	London HLU 9531	Shout Shout/Crying Like A Baby Over You	15
62	London HLU 9579	Mary Jane/Down On The Beach	15
63	London HLU 9720	Love Express/Lorelei	12
64	London HLU 9834	Rovin' Kind/Please Be Fair	10
65	London HLU 10008	It's Their World/I Can't Dance	6
66	Stateside SS 560	Rockin' Boulevard Street/Am I Better Off Than Them	12

MARGO, Franck Oliver, Diane Solomon, Malcolm Roberts, etc.
| 85 | Sonet SON 2281 | Children, Kinder, Enfants (English)/(International)/(French) | 5 |

MARGO & MARVETTES
64	Parlophone R 5154	Say You Will/Cherry Pie	12
64	Parlophone R 5227	Copper Kettle/So Fine	10
67	Piccadilly 7N 35387	Seven Letters/That's How Love Goes	8
67	Pye 7N 17423	When Love Slips Away/I'll Be Home (When You Call)	40

(see also Liza Dulittle)

MARGUERITA
| 64 | Black Swan WI 431 | Woman Come/ERIC MORRIS: Number One | 18 |

CHARLES MARGULIS
| 59 | London HLL 8774 | Gigi/Malaguena | 8 |
| 59 | London HLL 8774 | Gigi/Malaguena (78) | 12 |

MARIANNE
| 68 | Columbia DB 8420 | As For Marionettes/You Know My Name | 8 |
| 68 | Columbia DB 8456 | You Had Better Change Your Evil Ways/Like A See Saw | 6 |

MARIANNE & MIKE
| 64 | Vocalion V 9218 | As He Once Was Mine/MARIANNE: Go On | 8 |
| 64 | Vocalion V 9225 | You're The Only One/One Good Turn Deserves Another | 8 |

(see also Friday Brown. These records do not feature Mick Jagger or Marianne Faithfull)

MARIAS & MIRANDA
| 59 | Fontana TF 225 | I He She/The Queen Bee | 6 |

MARIBELLE
| 84 | Ariola 106 235 | In Love With You/Ik Hou Van Jou | 5 |

ANNE MARIE
| 65 | Fontana TF 523 | Runaround/There Must Be A Reason | 7 |

MARIE CELESTE
| 71 | private pressing | AND THEN PERHAPS (LP) | 325 |

MARILLION
82	EMI EMI 5351	Market Square Heroes/Three Boats Down From The Candy (p/s)	5
82	EMI 12 EMI 5351	Market Square Heroes/Three Boats Down From The Candy/Grendel (12", p/s)	8
82	EMI 12 EMIP 5351	Market Square Heroes/Three Boats Down From The Candy/Grendel (12", picture disc, 3,000 only)	40
83	EMI EMI 5362	He Knows, You Know/Charting The Single (p/s, originally with blue plastic label & paper sleeve)	5
83	EMI 12 EMI 5362	He Knows, You Know/Charting The Single/He Knows, You Know (Full Length Version) (12", p/s)	8
83	EMI 12 EMIP 5362	He Knows, You Know/Charting The Single/He Knows, You Know (Full Length Version) (12", picture disc, unreleased)	
83	EMI EMI 5393	Garden Party/Margaret (live) (p/s)	5
83	EMI EMIP 5393	Garden Party/Margaret (live) ('jester'-shaped picture disc)	18
83	EMI 12 EMIS 5393	Garden Party (Extended Version)/Charting The Single (live)/Margaret (Extended Live Version) (12", p/s with poster)	15
83	EMI 12 EMI 5393	Garden Party (Extended Version)/Charting The Single (live)/Margaret (Extended Live Version) (12", p/s)	8
84	EMI MARIL 1	Punch And Judy/Market Square Heroes (New Version) (p/s)	5
84	EMI 12 MARIL 1	Punch And Judy/Market Square Heroes (New Version)/Three Boats Down From The Candy (New Version) (12", p/s)	8
84	EMI 12 MARILP 1	Punch And Judy/Market Square Heroes (New Version)/Three Boats Down From The Candy (New Version) (12", picture disc)	15
84	EMI MARIL 2	Assassing/Cinderella Search (p/s)	5
84	EMI 12 MARIL 2	Assassing (Full Length Version)/Cinderella Search (Full Length Version) (12", p/s)	15
84	EMI 12 MARILP 2	Assassing (Full Length Version)/Cinderella Search (Full Length Version) (12", picture disc)	15
85	EMI MARILP 3	Kayleigh/Lady Nina (picture disc)	10
85	EMI 12 MARILP 3	Kayleigh (Alternative Mix)/Kayleigh (Extended Version)/Lady Nina (Extended Version) (12", picture disc)	12
85	EMI 12 MARILP 4	Lavender (Remix)/Freaks/Lavender (12", picture disc)	12
85	EMI 12 MARILP 5	Heart Of Lothian (Full Length Version)/Chelsea Monday (live)/Heart Of Lothian (7" Version) (12", picture disc)	12
87	EMI 12MARILP 6	Incommunicado (LP Version)/(Alternative Mix)/Going Under (12", picture disc)	8
87	EMI CD MARIL 6	Incommunicado (LP Version)/(Alternative Mix)/Going Under (CD, gatefold p/s)	8
87	EMI MARILP 7	Sugar Mice (Radio Edit)/Tux On (picture disc with poster)	8
87	EMI 12MARILP 7	Sugar Mice (Extended Version)/(Album Version)/Tux On (12", picture disc)	12
87	EMI CD MARIL 7	Sugar Mice (Radio Edit)/Tux On/Sugar Mice (Radio Edit)/ (CD, card p/s, 3,000 only, withdrawn)	18
87	EMI 12MARILP 8	Warm Wet Circles (Full Version)/White Russian (live at Loreley)/Incommunicado (live at Loreley) (12", picture disc)	10
87	EMI CD MARIL 8	Warm Wet Circles (7" Version)/White Russian (live at Loreley)/Incommunicado (live at Loreley)/Up On Top Of A Rainbow (CD)	8
88	EMI MARIL 9	Freaks (live)/Kayleigh (live) (p/s)	5
88	EMI MARILP 9	Freaks (live)/Kayleigh (live) ('jester'-shaped picture disc)	8
88	EMI CDMARIL 9	Freaks (live)/Kayleigh (live)/Childhoods End? (live)/White Feather (live) (CD)	8
89	EMI 12MARIL 10P	Hooks In You (Meaty Mix)/Hooks In You/After Me (12", p/s with poster)	8
89	EMI CDMARIL 10	Hooks In You (Meaty Mix)/Hooks In You (Seven Mix)/After Me (CD)	8
89	EMI MARIL PD 11	Uninvited Guests/The Bell In The Sea (shaped picture disc)	6
89	EMI CDMARIL 11	Uninvited Guests (7" Version)/Uninvited Guests (12" Version)/The Bell In The Sea (CD)	8
90	EMI MARILP 12	Easter/The Release (picture disc)	8
91	EMI MARILS 14	No One Can/A Collection (box set with 4 colour pictures & badge)	5
84	EMI EMCP 3429	SCRIPT FOR A JESTER'S TEAR (LP, picture disc)	35
84	EMI MRLP 1	FUGAZI (LP, picture disc)	25
85	EMI JESTP 1	REAL TO REEL (LP, picture disc)	15
85	EMI MRLP 2	MISPLACED CHILDHOOD (LP, picture disc)	20
87	EMI EMDP 1002	CLUTCHING AT STRAWS (LP, picture disc, die-cut sleeve)	12
89	EMI EMDPD 1011	SEASON'S END (LP, picture disc, with insert)	12
99	Raw Power RAWP 2144	MARILLION.COM (CD, 3–track sampler, card p/s, promo only)	12

(see also Fish, Chemical Alice)

MARILYN SISTERS
55	Decca F 10518	Bubbles/No Chance	7
55	Decca F 10552	Genuine Love/Everything Is Big Way Down In Texas	7
55	Decca F 10604	D-a-r-l-i-n'/The Kinkajou	7

(see also Suzi Miller)

MARINE GIRLS
82	In Phaze COD 2	On My Mind/The Lure Of The Rockpools (p/s, with insert)	15
82	Cherry Red CHERRY 40	On My Mind/The Lure Of The Rockpools (reissue, different p/s)	8
83	Cherry Red CHERRY 54	Don't Come Back/You Must Be Mad (p/s)	6
80	private release	A DAY BY THE SEA (cassette, 50 copies only)	30
81	In Phaze Tapes 002	BEACH PARTY (cassette, with photocopied drawings, game & handmade sl.)	20
81	Whaam!/In Phaze COD 1	BEACH PARTY (LP, black & white sleeve & labels, with 2 inserts)	20
83	Cherry Red BRED 44	LAZY WAYS (LP, textured sleeve)	10

(see also Tracey Thorn, Everything But The Girl, Jane, Grab Grab The Haddock)

MARINERS
55	London HLA 8201	I Love You Fair Dinkum/(At The) Steamboat River Ball	25
55	London HLA 8201	I Love You Fair Dinkum/(At The) Steamboat River Ball (78)	10
55	Philips PB 467	Chee-Chee-Oo-Chee/I Didn't Come To Say Hello (78)	8
58	Fontana H 127	I Heard Ya The First Time/I Live For You	6
58	Fontana H 127	I Heard Ya The First Time/I Live For You (78)	8
56	London HA-A 2007	SPIRITUALS (LP)	15

MARINO MARINI & HIS QUARTET

57	Durium DC 16629	With All My Heart/The Pansy	6
58	Durium DC 16631	Guitar Boogie/Armen's Theme	7
58	Durium DC 16631	Guitar Boogie/Armen's Theme (78)	8
58	Durium DC 16632	Volare (Nel Blu Dipinto Di Blu)/Come Prima	6
58	Durium DC 16632	Volare (Nel Blu Dipinto Di Blu)/Come Prima (78)	8
58	Durium DC 16634	Saunabad/I Could Have Danced All Night	6
58	Durium DC 16635	Stella Stella (Star Of Love)/Lazzarella	6
58	Durium DC 16626	Gualione/La Piu' Bella Del Mondo (78)	8
59	Durium DC 16636	Ciao Ciao Bambina/Avevamo La Stessa Eta'	6
59	Durium DC 16636	Ciao Ciao Bambina/Avevamo La Stessa Eta' (78)	8
59	Durium DC 16637	Li Per Li/Io Sono Il Vento	6
59	Durium DC 16642	Guarda Che Luna/Sapra' Chi Sa'	6
59	Durium DC 16642	Guarda Che Luna/Sapra' Chi Sa' (78)	8
50s	Durium U 20007	VOLUME 1 (EP)	8
50s	Durium U 20020	VOLUME 2 (EP)	8
50s	Durium U 20028	VOLUME 3 (EP)	8
58	Durium U 20030	THAT CRAZY QUARTET (EP)	8
58	Durium U 20031	THE MARINO MARINI QUARTET VOLUME 2 (EP)	8
58	Durium U 20047	MARINO AT SAN REMO (EP)	8
55	Durium DLU 96012	HAPPY MUSIC FROM ITALY (10" LP)	12
59	Durium DLU 96034	COME PRIMA (10" LP)	12
59	Durium DLU 96039	IN SOHO (10" LP)	15
60	Durium TLU 97028	MARINO MARINI QUARTET (LP)	12

MARION (U.K.)

67	Page One POF 042	I Go To Sleep/Abyssinian Secret	6

MARION (Finland)

73	Columbia DB 8987	Tom Tom Tom/My Son John	15

MARION (U.K.)

94	Rough Trade RT 3197	Violent Men/Toys For Boys (p/s)	10
94	Rough Trade RT 3192	Violent Men/Toys For Boys/Today And Tonight (CD)	10
95	London LON 360	Sleep/Father's Day (numbered p/s)	4
95	London LONCD 360	Sleep/Father's Day/Moving Fast (CD, digipak)	7
95	London LON10 366	Toys For Boys/Down The Middle With You (10", p/s, export only)	18
96	London 828 695-1	THIS WORLD AND BODY (LP, sealed, with 1-sided single "Violent Men")	12

MARIONETTES

65	Decca F 12056	Whirlpool Of Love/Nobody But You	6
65	Parlophone R 5300	Was It Me?/Under The Boardwalk	6
65	Parlophone R 5356	Raining It's Pouring/Pick Up Your Feet (withdrawn)	12
65	Parlophone R 5374	At The End Of The Day/Pick Up Your Feet	6
66	Parlophone R 5416	Like A Man/Tonight It's Going To Storm	8

(see also Rag Dolls [U.K.], Katie Kissoon, Mac Kissoon)

JON MARK

69	Philips BF 1772	All Neat In Black Stockings/Run To Me	5

(see also Johnny Almond Music Machine, John Mayall, Mark-Almond)

MARK-ALMOND

71	Harvest SHSP 4011	MARK-ALMOND (LP)	20
73	Harvest SHVL 809	RISING (LP)	20

(see also Johnny Almond Music Machine, Jon Mark)

MARK & JOHN

64	Decca F 12044	Walk Right Back/Karen	5

MARKETTS

62	Liberty LIB 55401	Surfer's Stomp/Start (as Mar-kets)	8
62	Liberty LIB 55443	Balboa Blue/Stompede	7
64	Warner Bros WB 120	Out Of Limits/Bella Delana	10
64	Warner Bros WB 130	Vanishing Point/Borealis	6
66	Warner Bros WB 5696	The Batman Theme/Richie's Theme (some with p/s)	30/10
67	Warner Bros WB 5847	Tarzan's March/Stirrin' Up Some Soul	30
63	Warner Bros WM 8140	THE MARKETTS TAKE TO WHEELS (LP)	25
66	Warner Bros W 1642	BATMAN (LP)	40

MAR-KEYS

61	London HLK 9399	Last Night/Night Before	10
61	London HLK 9449	Morning After/Diana	8
62	London HLK 9510	Foxy/One Degree North	8
66	Atlantic AT 4079	Philly Dog/Honey Pot	10
67	Atlantic 584 074	Last Night/Night Before	6
69	Stax STAX 132	Black/Jive Man	5
62	London HA-K 8011	DO THE POP-EYE (LP)	50
66	Atlantic 587/588 024	THE GREAT MEMPHIS SOUND (LP)	20
68	Atlantic 587/588 135	MELLOW JELLY (LP)	20
69	Stax SXATS 1021	DAMNIFIKNOW! (LP)	15
69	Stax 2363 008	DAMNIFIKNOW! (LP, reissue)	12

(see also Booker T. & M.G.'s)

MARK II

60	Columbia DB 4549	Night Theme/Confusion	8

MARK IV

59	Mercury AMT 1025	Aah-Oo-Gah/I Got A Wife	10
59	Mercury AMT 1025	Aah-Oo-Gah/I Got A Wife (78)	25
59	Mercury AMT 1045	Move Over Rover/Dante's Inferno	8
59	Mercury AMT 1060	Ring, Ring, Ring Those Bells/Mairzy Doats	6

MARK FOUR

64	Mercury MF 815	Rock Around The Clock/Slow Down	30
64	Mercury MF 825	Crazy Country Hop/Try It Baby	30
65	Decca F 12204	Hurt Me If You Will/I'm Leaving	50
66	Fontana TF 664	Work All Day (Sleep All Night)/Going Down Fast	70
85	Bam-Caruso OPRA 037	LIVE AT THE BEAT SCENE CLUB (EP, 500 promos only)	12

(see also Creation)

MARK FIVE

64	Fontana TF 513	Baby What's Wrong/Tango	40

(see also Nazareth)

PIGMEAT MARKHAM

68	Chess CRS 8077	Here Comes The Judge/The Trial	7
68	Chess CRS 8085	Sock It To 'Em Judge/The Hip Judge	6

ALFRED MARKS

68	RCA RCA 1777	My Young Visitors And Me/When I Wed Miss Ethel Montiche	5

GUY MARKS

68	Stateside SS 2107	Loving You Has Made Me Bananas/Forgive Me My Love	6

MARKSMEN

63	Parlophone R 5075	Smersh/Orbit Three	12

(see also Mark Rogers & Marksmen, Houston Wells & Marksmen)

BOB MARLEY/WAILERS

SINGLES

63	Island WI 088	Judge Not/Do You Still Love Me (as Robert Marley)	225
63	Island WI 128	ERNEST RANGLIN: Exodus/ROBERT MARLEY: One Cup Of Coffee	200
65	Island WI 188	It Hurts To Be Alone/Mr. Talkative	70
65	Island WI 206	Play Boy/Your Love	70
65	Island WI 211	Hoot Nanny Hoot (actually by Peter Tosh & Wailers)/BOB MARLEY: Do You Remember (actually with Wailers)	70
65	Island WI 212	Hooligan/Maga Dog (B-side actually by Peter Tosh & Wailers)	70
65	Island WI 215	Shame And Scandal (as Peter Touch [Tosh] & Wailers)/The Jerk	60
65	Island WI 216	Donna/Don't Ever Leave Me	60
65	Island WI 254	What's New Pussycat/Where Will I Find	60
65	Ska Beat JB 186	Simmer Down/I Don't Need Your Love	60
65	Ska Beat JB 211	Lonesome Feelings/There She Goes	50
65	Ska Beat JB 226	I Made A Mistake/SOUL BROTHERS: Train To Skaville	45
66	Ska Beat JB 228	Love And Affection/Teenager In Love	60
66	Ska Beat JB 230	And I Love Her/Do It Right	60
66	Ska Beat JB 249	Lonesome Tracks/Zimmerman	60
66	Island WI 260	Jumbie Jamboree/SKATALITES: Independent Anniversary Ska (I Should Have Known Better)	60
66	Island WI 268	Put It On/Love Won't Be Mine	45
66	Island WI 3001	He Who Feels It Knows It/Sunday Morning	60
66	Island WI 3009	Let Him Go (Rude Boy Get Bail)/Sinner Man (B-side matrix: WI-3009B+)	60
66	Island WI 3009	Let Him Go (Rude Boy Get Bail)/The Masher (actually by Beverley's All Stars, or Soul Brothers) (B-side matrix: WI-3009 B+2)	60
66	Rio R 116	Dancing Shoes/Don't Look Back	40
66	Doctor Bird DB 1013	Rude Boy/ROLANDO AL & SOUL BROTHERS: Ringo's Theme (This Boy)	50
66	Doctor Bird DB 1021	Good Good Rudie (Jailhouse)/CITY SLICKERS: Oceans II	50
66	Doctor Bird DB 1039	Rasta Put It On/ROLANDO AL & SOUL BROTHERS: Ska With Ringo	50
67	Island WI 3035	Baby I Need You (credited to Ken Boothe)/KEN BOOTHE: I Don't Want To See You Cry	50
67	Island WI 3042	I Am The Toughest (by Peter Touch [Tosh] & Wailers)/MARCIA GRIFFITHS: No Faith	50
67	Island WI 3043	Bend Down Low/Freedom Time	60
67	Coxsone CS 7021	Oh My Darling/HAMLINS: Trying To Keep A Good Man Down	40
67	Doctor Bird DB 1091	Nice Time/Hypocrite	50
67	Studio One SO 2010	Have Faith In The Lord (with Heavenly Sisters; actually by Peter Austin)/JOE HIGGS: Dinah	30
67	Studio One SO 2024	I Stand Predominate/NORMA FRAZER: Come By Here	60
68	Fab FAB 34	Pound Get A Blow/Funeral (white label only)	80
68	Fab FAB 36	Thank You Lord?/Mellow Mood (white label only)	80
68	Fab FAB 37	Nice Time/Hypocrites (white label only)	80
68	Fab FAB 41	Burial/Bus Them Shut (existence unconfirmed)	
68	Trojan TR 617	Stir It Up/This Train	50
70	Bamboo BAM 55	Jailhouse (Good Rudy)/JOHN HOLT: A Stranger In Love	45

(All the above singles are credited to Wailers unless stated.)

70	Trojan TR 7759	Soul Shake Down Party/BEVERLEY'S ALLSTARS: Version	15
70	Escort ERT 842	Run For Cover/To The Rescue	60
70	Unity UN 562	Duppy Conqueror/UPSETTERS: Duppy Conqueror (Version)	30
70	Jackpot JP 730	Mr Chatterbox (as Wailing Wailers)/DOREEN SHAEFFER: Walk Thru' This World	25
70	Upsetter US 340	My Cup (solo)/LEE PERRY & WAILERS: Son Of Thunder	25
70	Upsetter US 342	Version Of Cup (solo)/UPSETTERS: Dreamland	30
70	Upsetter US 348	Doppy Conqueror (song actually titled "Duppy Conqueror" but plays "Runaway Child" by Dave Barker)/UPSETTERS: Justice	15
70	Upsetter US 349	UPSETTERS: Upsetting Station (actually plays "Dig Your Grave" by Bob Marley & Wailers/UPSETTERS: Justice (Instrumental)	25
71	Upsetter US 354	Mr. Brown/UPSETTERS: Dracula	25
71	Upsetter US 356	Kaya/UPSETTERS: Version	25
71	Upsetter US 357	Small Axe/All In One	25
71	Upsetter US 368	Picture On The Wall (as Rass Dawkins & Wailers)/UPSETTERS: Version	18
71	Upsetter US 369	More Axe (as Bob Marley)/UPSETTERS: Axe Man	25

Bob MARLEY

71	Upsetter US 371	Dreamland (as Wailers)/UPSETTERS: Version.	20
71	Upsetter US 372	More Axe (as Bob Marley, different version)/UPSETTERS: Axe Man	25
71	Bullet BU 464	Soultown/Let The Sun Shine On Me	40
71	Bullet BU 493	Lick Samba/Samba.	20
71	Punch PH 69	Small Axe/DAVE BARKER: What A Confusion	25
71	Punch PH 77	Down Presser (as Wailers)/JUNIOR BYLES: Got The Tip	35
71	Summit SUM 8526	Stop The Train/Caution (as Wailers).	30
71	Green Door GD 4005	Trench Town Rock/Grooving Kingston 12.	20
71	Green Door GD 4022	Lively Yourself Up/TOMMY McCOOK: Lively.	20
72	Green Door GD 4025	Guava Jelly/Redder Than Red	20
72	Upsetter US 392	Keep On Moving/African Herbsman	30
72	CBS 8114	Reggae On Broadway/Oh Lord, I Got To Get There (as Wailers).	15
73	Blue Mountain BM 1021	Baby Baby We've Got A Date/Stop That Train	15
73	Punch PH 101	Screw Face/Face Man	20
73	Punch PH 102	Lively Up Yourself/TOMMY McCOOK: Version.	20
73	Supreme SUP 216	I Like It Like This (as Bob Marley)/(other artist)	40
73	Island WIP 6164	Concrete Jungle/Reincarnated Soul	5
73	Island WIP 6167	Get Up, Stand Up/Slave Driver (as Wailers).	5
73	Island IDJ 2	I Shot The Sheriff/Pass It On/Duppy Conqueror (promo only)	10
74	Island 12WIP 6244	No Woman No Cry/Jamming (12", p/s)	8
74	Trojan TR 7911	Soul Shake Down Party/Caution	5
74	Trojan TR 7926	Mr Brown/Version.	5
75	Island WIP 6212	Natty Dread/So Jah Seh.	5
76	Island WIP 6478	Stir It Up/Rat Race (withdrawn, demos only)	15
77	Island IPR 2026	War/No More Trouble/Exodus (12", p/s).	8
83	Island ISP 180	Waiting In Vain/Blackman Redemption (picture disc).	6
84	Daddy Kool DK 12101	Rainbow Country (Vocal)/Rainbow Country (Dub)/	
		PABLO & UPSETTERS: Lama Lava (12", p/s)	10
84	Daddy Kool DK 12102	Natural Mystic/Natural Mystic Rhythm (12", p/s)	10
84	Island 12ISPX 169	One Love/One Love (Dub Version) (p/s)	7
84	Island 12ISP 169	One Love/One Love (Dub Version) (12", white label, p/s)	10
84	Island 12ISPP 169	One Love/One Love (Dub Version) (12", picture disc)	15
80s	Island 12 BMRM 1	Get Up Stand Up/Get Up Stand Up (live) ('Rasta' p/s, promo only)	10
99	Columbia XPR 2533	Turn Your Lights Down Low (with Lauryn Hill)/(original version)	
		(die-cut p/s, promo only)	15

(Island singles with the words "DJ Copy" stamped in the middle are worth the same as regular issues.
All the above singles are credited to Bob Marley & Wailers unless stated.)

LPs

71	Upsetter TBL 126	SOUL REBEL (LP)	45
71	Trojan TBL 126	SOUL REBEL (LP, reissue)	20
72	Island ILPS 9241	CATCH A FIRE (LP, original label, initially 'zippo lighter' sleeve).	25/12
73	Island ILPS 9256	BURNIN' (LP, original label, gatefold sleeve with photos on innner)	15
73	Trojan TRLS 62	AFRICAN HERBSMAN (LP, original issue with "12 Neasden Lane" address	
		and rough orange/white paper labels).	20
74	Trojan TRLS 89	RASTA REVOLUTION (LP, reissue of TBL 126 with 2 extra tracks)	12
75	Island ISS 3	BOB MARLEY & THE WAILERS RADIO SAMPLER	
		(LP, some with photos & press release, promo only)	30/10
78	Island ISLD 11	BABYLON BY BUS (2-LP, with inner sleeves and poster)	15
83	Island PILPS 97690	CONFRONTATION (LP, picture disc)	15
84	Island PBMW 1	LEGEND — THE BEST OF BOB MARLEY (LP, picture disc).	12

(see also Peter Tosh, Rita Marley, Ernest Ranglin, Interns, Skatalites, Rass Dawkins & Wailers, Family Man,
Norma Frazer)

RITA MARLEY

67	Rio R 108	Pied Piper/It's Alright	40
67	Island WI 3052	Come To Me/SOUL BOYS: Blood Pressure	18

(see also Soulettes, Soul Brothers)

MARLIN SISTERS/DON MILES

51	London L 851	The Girl I Left Behind/Mockin' Bird Hill (78)	8

MICKI MARLO

54	Capitol CL 14086	I'm Gonna Rock-Rock-Rock/Loves Like That (78).	10
55	Capitol CL 14198	Show Me/Every Road Must Have A Turning (78).	8
55	Capitol CL 14271	Prize Of Gold/Foolish Notion	10
55	Capitol CL 14271	Prize Of Gold/Foolish Notion (78)	8
57	London HL 8481	That's Right/What You've Done To Me (B-side with Paul Anka)	20
57	London HL 8481	That's Right/What You've Done To Me (B-side with Paul Anka) (78).	8

(see also Paul Anka)

MARLON

74	Purple PUR 120	Let's Go To The Disco/Broken Man	7

(see also Roger Glover, Ray Fenwick)

ROBERT MARLOW

83	Reset 7REST 1	Pictures Of Dorian Grey/The Tale Of Dorian Grey (p/s).	10
83	Reset 12REST 1	Pictures Of Dorian Grey/The Tale Of Dorian Grey (12", p/s).	15
83	Reset 7REST 3	I Just Want To Dance/No Heart (p/s)	10
83	Reset 7RESTP 3	I Just Want To Dance/No Heart (picture disc)	10
83	Reset 12REST 3	I Just Want To Dance/No Heart (12", p/s).	15
84	Reset 7REST 4	Claudette/This Happy World (p/s)	10
84	Reset 12REST 4	Claudette/This Happy World (12", p/s).	15
85	Reset 7REST 6	Calling All Destroyers/In Retrospect (p/s)	18
85	Reset 12REST 6	Calling All Destroyers/In Retrospect (12", p/s, existence unconfirmed).	30+

MARION MARLOWE

54	Philips PB 352	Wither Thou Goest/Kiss Me Once (78)	8
56	London HLA 8306	The Hands Of Time/Ring, Phone, Ring (withdrawn)	60
56	London HLA 8306	The Hands Of Time/Ring, Phone, Ring (78, withdrawn)	60

RITA MARLOWE
52	Oriole HB 304	Walking Down Lover's Lane/Weil Ich Bin A Yid (78)	8

MARMALADE
66	CBS 202340	It's All Leading Up To Saturday Night/Wait A Minute Baby	7
67	CBS 202643	Can't Stop Now/There Ain't No Use In Hangin' On	7
67	CBS 2948	I See The Rain/Laughing Man	12
67	CBS 3088	Man In A Shop/Cry	6
68	CBS 3412	Lovin' Things/Hey Joe	5
68	CBS 3708	Wait For Me Marianne/Mess Around	6
68	CBS 3892	Ob-La-Di, Ob-La-Da/Chains	5
69	CBS 4287	Baby Make It Soon/Time Is On My Side	6
69	CBS 4615	Butterfly/I Shall Be Released	6
69	Decca F 12982	Reflections Of My Life/Rollin' My Thing	5
70	Decca F 13035	Rainbow/The Ballad Of Cherry Flavar	5
72	CBS 7200	Man In A Shop/Cry (reissue)	5
73	CBS 8205	Ob-La-Di, Ob-La-Da/Lovin' Things (p/s, 'Hall Of Fame Hits' series)	5
84	Just Songs JST 1	Heartbreaker/I Listen To My Heart (p/s)	5
68	CBS 63414	THERE'S A LOT OF IT ABOUT (LP)	18
70	CBS SPR 36	THE BEST OF THE MARMALADE (LP)	15
70	Decca SKL 5047	REFLECTIONS OF THE MARMALADE (LP)	15
71	Decca SKL 5111	SONGS (LP)	15

(see also Dean Ford [& Gaylords], Gaylords, Junior Campbell, Chris McClure Section)

MARQUIS DE SADE
82	Out Of Town HOOT 8	Crystal Grieff/Vampire Affair (p/s)	5

MARQUIS OF KENSINGTON
67	Immediate IM 052	Changing Of The Guard/Reverse Thrust	15

HANK MARR
60	Blue Beat BB 26	Tonk Game/Hob-Nobbin	15

A MARRIAGE OF CONVENIENCE
85	Stranglers Info Service SIS2	My Young Dreams/Two Sides To Every Story (no p/s, fan club issue)	4

(see also Stranglers)

STEVE MARRIOTT
63	Decca F 11619	Give Her My Regards/Imaginary Love	85
65	Decca	Tell Me/Maybe (unissued)	
76	A&M AMS 7230	Star In My Life/Midnight Rollin'	5
85	Aura AUS 145	Wha'cha Gonna Do About It/All Shook Up	5
76	A&M AMLH 64572	MARRIOTT (LP)	15
85	Aura AUL 792	PACKET OF THREE (LP)	12

(see also Small Faces, Humble Pie, Spectrum, Pollcats)

M/A/R/R/S
87	4AD BAD 707R	Pump Up The Volume (Remix)/Anitina (The First Time I See She Dance) (Remix) (12", p/s)	8
87	4AD CAD 707R	Pump Up The Volume (Remix)/Anitina/Pump Up The Volume (12" Version)/Anitina (The First Time I See She Dance) (Remix) (CD, gatefold p/s)	15

(see also A.R. Kane, Colourbox)

BETTY MARS
72	Columbia DB 8879	Come-Comedie/Mon Café Russe	7

JOHNNY MARS
81	Ace NS 73	Born Under A Bad Sign/Horses And Places/Mighty Mars (p/s, withdrawn)	5
72	Polydor 2460 168	BLUES FROM MARS (LP)	15

BERNIE MARSDEN
81	Parlophone R 6047	Sad Clown/You And Me (p/s)	6
81	Parlophone R 6050	Look At Me Now/Always Love You So (p/s)	6
81	Parlophone R 6052	Shakey Ground/After All This Madness (p/s)	6
82	Parlophone R 6053	Thunder And Lightning/Bylbo's Shack (p/s)	6
79	Parlophone PCS 7215	AND ABOUT TIME TOO (LP, with inner sleeve)	12
81	Parlophone PCS 7217	LOOK AT ME NOW (LP, with inner sleeve)	12

(see also Jon Lord, Whitesnake, Cozy Powell, Jack Bruce, Babe Ruth, Bogdon)

BERYL MARSDEN
63	Decca F 11707	I Know/I Only Care About You	12
64	Decca F 11819	When The Lovelight Starts Shining Through His Eyes/Love Is Going To Happen To Me	12
65	Columbia DB 7718	Who You Gonna Hurt?/Gonna Make Him My Baby	12
65	Columbia DB 7797	Music Talk/Break-A-Way	12
66	Columbia DB 7888	What's She Got/Let's Go Somewhere	12

(see also Shotgun Express, She Trinity)

GERRY MARSDEN
67	CBS 2784	Please Let Them Be/I'm Not Blue	8
67	CBS 2946	Gilbert Green/What Makes Me Love You	8
68	CBS 3575	Liverpool/Charlie Girl (as Gerry Marsden & Derek Nimmo)	8
68	NEMS 56-3831	In The Year Of April/Every Day	6
69	NEMS 56-4229	Every Little Minute/In Days Of Old	6
71	Decca F 13172	I've Got My Ukelele/What A Day	5
72	Phoenix NIX 129	Amo Credo/Come Break Bread	

(see also Gerry & Pacemakers)

MARSEILLE
77	Varèse International VI 1001	Do It The French Way/Not Tonight Josephine/She Gives Me Hell (12", stickered plain sleeve, 1,000 only)	8
78	Mountain BON 1	The French Way/Cold Steel (p/s)	10
79	Mountain BON 2	Over And Over/You're A Woman/Can Can (p/s)	6

MARSEILLE

79	Mountain TOP 39	Kiss Like Rock'n'Roll/Can Can	5
79	Mountain TOP 49	Bring On The Dancing Girls/Rock Me Tonight.	5
80	Mountain TOP 51	Kites/Some Like It Hot	5
84	Ultra Noise WALK 1	Walking On A Highwire/Too Late (p/s).	5
84	Ultra Noise WALK 1	Walking On A Highwire/Too Late (silver vinyl, no p/s)	6
76	Mountain TOPC 5012	RED WHITE AND SLIGHTLY BLUE (LP).	12
79	Mountain TOPS 125	MARSEILLE (LP)	12
84	Ultra Noise ULTRA 3	TOUCH THE NIGHT (LP, with inner sleeve)	12

(see also Paul Dale)

STEVIE MARSH
59	Decca F 11181	If You Were The Only Boy In The World/Leave Me Alone.	7
59	Decca F 11181	If You Were The Only Boy In The World/Leave Me Alone (78)	18
60	Decca F 11209	You Don't Have To Tell Me (I Know)/Wish	7
60	Decca F 11244	A Girl In Love/Over And Done With.	7
62	Ember EMB S 139	I Shouldn't Be Kissing You/Time And Time Again	7

GARY MARSHALL
61	Parlophone R 4758	One Twitchy Baby/Ev'ry Chance I Get	12

JACK MARSHALL ORCHESTRA & CHORUS
58	Capitol CL 14888	Thunder Road Chase/Finger Poppin'	12

JOY MARSHALL
64	Decca F 11863	Rain On Snow/When You Hold Me Tight	5
65	Decca F 12222	My Love Come Home/When A Girl Really Loves You	6
66	Decca F 12422	The More I See You/Taste Of Honey	6

LARRY MARSHALL
67	Blue Beat BB 374	Move Your Feet/Find A New Baby	15
67	Blue Beat BB 380	Suspicion/Broken Heart.	15
67	Doctor Bird DB 1008	Snake In The Grass/ROLAND ALPHONSO: V.C. 10	25
68	Caltone TONE 126	No One To Give Me Love/PHIL PRATT: Safe Travel	25
70	Bamboo BAM 22	Girl Of My Dreams/SOUND DIMENSION: Give It Away	8
70	Bamboo BAM 52	Man From Galilee/Give It Away (as Larry Marshall & Enid Cumberland).	8
70	Banana BA 300	Stay A Little Longer/MAYTALS: He'll Provide	10
71	Banana BA 364	Maga Dog/OSSIE ROBINSON: Economical Heatwave	8
73	Pama PM 873	True Believer/FLAMES: Water Your Garden	6

(see also Larry & Alvin, Irving Brown, Fitzroy D. Long, Kingston Pete & Buster's Allstars, Max Romeo, Jackie Mittoo)

LOIS MARSHALL
59	HMV ALP 1671	BRITISH FOLK SONGS (LP).	12

WILLIE MARSHALL
70	Torpedo TOR 20	Loosen Up Strong Man/Strong Man	6

MARSHMALLOW WAY
69	United Artists UP 35031	C'mon Kitty Kitty/Michigan Mints	4

MARSHMELLOW HIGHWAY
68	London HLR 10204	I Don't Wanna Live This Way/Loving You Makes Everything Alright	4

MARSUPILAMI
70	Transatlantic TRA 213	MARSUPILAMI (LP)	35
71	Transatlantic TRA 230	ARENA (LP)	35

LENA MARTELL
61	HMV POP 958	Love Can Be/The Night The Sky Fell Down.	4
62	HMV POP 1049	The Reasons Why/To This Man	4
63	HMV POP 1152	Let The Music Play/One Boy	4
63	HMV POP 1214	I Wish You Well/Arriverderci Not Addio	4
64	Decca F 11978	I'm A Fool To Want You/All Cried Out	4

PIERA MARTELL
74	CBS S CBS 2293	My Ship Of Love/Mein Ruf Nach Dir	12

RAY MARTELL
70	Joe JRS 3	She Caught The Train/PAMA DICE: Tea House From Emperor Rosko	8
70	Attack ATT 8015	Loving Lover/Cora	6
70	Doctor Bird DB 1503	This Little Light/Lover	10
70	Trojan TR 7787	This Little Light/Lover	6
72	Sioux SI 012	She Caught The Train/JOE'S ALLSTARS: Tony B.'s Theme..........	6

MARTELLS
66	Decca F 12463	Time To Say Goodnight/The Cherry Song.	7

RALPH MARTERIE & HIS ORCHESTRA
53	Oriole CB 1199	Crazy Man, Crazy/Go Away (78).	8
54	Mercury MB 3176	Dig That Crazy Santa Claus/Rock, Rock (78).	8
54	Mercury MB 3186	Kiss Crazy Baby/Bongo Guitar (78).	8
55	Mercury MB 3220	Chicken Boogie/Silver Moon (78).	8
57	Mercury 7MT 138	Guaglione/Carla	6
57	Mercury MT 138	Guaglione/Carla (78)	8
57	Mercury 7MT 158	Tricky/Shish-Kebab	6
58	Mercury MT 204	Tequila/Pop Corn	5
58	Mercury 7MT 204	Tequila/Pop Corn (78).	10
58	Mercury 7MT 213	Night Stroll/Trombone Blues	6
58	Mercury 7MT 232	Cha-Hua-Hua/Torero.	6
58	Mercury AMT 1009	Pretend Cha Cha/Flighty	5
58	Mercury AMT 1009	Pretend Cha Cha/Flighty (78).	15
59	Mercury AMT 1042	Compulsion/Words Of Love.	5
59	Mercury AMT 1056	Wampum/Cleopatra's Dream	5
59	Mercury AMT 1074	In The Mood/Bwana	5

MINT VALUE £

57	Mercury MEP 9517	PRESENTING RALPH MARTERIE (EP)	18
60	Mercury ZEP 10040	SWINGING SOUND OF MARTERIE (EP)	10
60	Mercury ZEP 10068	MUSIC FOR A PRIVATE EYE (EP)	10

MARTHA (REEVES) & VANDELLAS

63	Oriole CBA 1814	I'll Have To Let Him Go/My Baby Won't Come Back	275
63	Oriole CBA 1819	Come And Get These Memories/Jealous Lover	100
63	Stateside SS 228	Heatwave/A Love Like Yours (Don't Come Knockin' Every Day)	45
64	Stateside SS 250	Quicksand/Darling, I Hum Our Song	35
64	Stateside SS 272	Live Wire/Old Love (Let's Try It Again)	30
64	Stateside SS 305	In My Lonely Room/A Tear For The Girl	35
64	Stateside SS 345	Dancing In The Street/There He Is (At My Door)	15
65	Stateside SS 383	Wild One/Dancing Slow	25
65	Tamla Motown TMG 502	Nowhere To Run/Motoring	15
65	Tamla Motown TMG 530	You've Been In Love Too Long/Love (Makes Me Do Foolish Things)	18
66	Tamla Motown TMG 549	My Baby Loves Me/Never Leave Your Baby's Side	18
66	Tamla Motown TMG 567	What Am I Going To Do Without Your Love/Go Ahead And Laugh	15
66	Tamla Motown TMG 582	I'm Ready For Love/He Doesn't Love Her Anymore	8
67	Tamla Motown TMG 599	Jimmy Mack/Third Finger, Left Hand (original pressing, narrow print)	7
72	Tamla Motown TMG 599	Jimmy Mack/Third Finger, Left Hand (reissue, fat print)	5
67	Tamla Motown TMG 621	Love Bug Leave My Heart Alone/One Way Out	10
68	Tamla Motown TMG 636	Honey Chile/Show Me The Way	10
68	Tamla Motown TMG 657	I Promise To Wait, My Love/Forget Me Not	10
68	Tamla Motown TMG 669	I Can't Dance To That Music You're Playing/I Tried	8
69	Tamla Motown TMG 684	Dancing In The Street/Quicksand	5
69	Tamla Motown TMG 694	Nowhere To Run/Live Wire	6
71	Tamla Motown TMG 762	Forget Me Not/I Gotta Let You Go	5
71	Tamla Motown TMG 794	Bless You/Hope I Don't Get My Heart Broke	5
65	Tamla Motown TME 2009	MARTHA AND THE VANDELLAS (EP)	100
66	Tamla Motown TME 2017	HITTIN' (EP)	90
63	Oriole PS 40052	COME AND GET THESE MEMORIES (LP)	225
65	Tamla Motown TML 11005	HEATWAVE (LP)	50
65	Tamla Motown TML 11013	DANCE PARTY (LP)	65
67	T. Motown (S)TML 11040	GREATEST HITS (LP, original with flipback sleeve, mono/stereo)	20/25
67	T. Motown (S)TML 11040	GREATEST HITS (LP, re-pressing non-flipback sleeve)	12
67	T. Motown (S)TML 11051	WATCH OUT! (LP, mono/stereo)	25/30
68	T. Motown (S)TML 11078	RIDIN' HIGH (LP)	20
69	T. Motown (S)TML 11099	DANCING IN THE STREET (LP)	18
70	T. Motown (S)TML 11134	SUGAR N' SPICE (LP)	15
70	Tamla Motown STML 11166	NATURAL RESOURCES (LP)	15
72	Tamla Motown STML 11204	BLACK MAGIC (LP)	12

MARTIN

68	Coxsone CS 7056	I Second That Emotion (actually by Martin Riley)/ROY TOMLINSON: I Stand For I	25

ALAN MARTIN

63	Rio R 3	The Party/Indeed	10
63	Rio R 6	You Came Late/Dreaming	10
63	Rio R 9	Secretly/Fame And Fortune	10
63	Rio R 10	Mother Brother/Tell Me	10
65	Rio R 66	Must Know I Love You/VIC BROWN'S COMBO: Rio Special	10
65	Rio R 67	Sweet Rosemarie/HONEY DUCKERS: Banjo Man	10
65	Rio R 68	Why Must I Cry/Shirley I Love You	10
65	Rio R 74	Since I Married Dorothy/You Promised Me	10
66	Rio R 94	Days Are Lonely/My Baby	10
66	Rio R 96	Rome Wasn't Built In A Day/I'm Hurt	10

BARRY MARTIN

61	RCA RCA 1234	Little Lonely One/Are You Sure	6

BENNY MARTIN

63	CBS RM 174	COUNTRY MUSIC'S SENSATIONAL ENTERTAINER (LP)	12

BILL MARTIN

68	Page One POF 067	Private Scotty Grant/Singing Vietnam Blues	4

BILLY RAY MARTIN

95	East West SAM 1614	Your Loving Arms (Brothers In Rhythm Mixes) (12", 2-track, promo only)	15

BOBBI MARTIN

64	Coral Q 72477	Don't Forget I Still Love You/On The Outside (Lookin' In)	7
65	Coral Q 72478	I Can't Stop Thinking About You/Million Thanks To You	6

CHRIS MARTIN

59	HMV POP 664	Lonely Street/Swing A Little Lover	6
60	HMV POP 692	Point Of No Return/I Don't Regret A Thing	6

DAVE MARTIN

64	Port-O-Jam PJ 4112	Let Them Fight/OSSIE IRVING SIX: Why I Love You	10
64	Port-O-Jam PJ 4115	All My Dreams/Take Your Belongings	10

DEAN MARTIN

78s

50	Capitol CL 13290	Choo'n Gum/Muskrat (78)	8
50	Capitol CL 13314	Just For Fun/My Own, My Only, My All (78)	8
50	Capitol CL 13331	I Don't Care If The Sun Don't Shine/Have A Little Sympathy (78)	8
50	Capitol CL 13401	Happy Feet/Don't Rock The Boat, Dear (with Margaret Whiting) (78)	8
51	Capitol CL 13433	I'm Gonna Paper All My Walls With Your Love Letters/I'll Always Love You (78)	8
51	Capitol CL 13451	If/Baby, Obey Me! (78)	8
51	Capitol CL 13494	You And Your Beautiful Eyes/Tonda Wanda Hoy (78)	8
51	Capitol CL 13503	The Money Song (with Jerry Lewis)/Bye Bye Blackbird (78)	8

Dean MARTIN

51	Capitol CL 13575	In The Cool, Cool, Cool Of The Evening/Bonne Nuite (78) 8
51	Capitol CL 13582	How D'Ya Like Your Eggs In The Morning/We Never Talk Much
		(with Helen O'Connell) 8
51	Capitol CL 13618	Hanging Around With You/I Love The Way You Say Goodnight (78) 8
51	Capitol CL 13646	Meanderin'/I'm In Love With You (with Margaret Whiting) (78) 8
52	Vogue V 9040	Santa Lucia/Hold Me (78) 12
52	Capitol CL 13672	Solitaire/I Ran All The Way Home (78) 8
52	Capitol CL 13723	Never Before/Sailor's Polka (78) 8
52	Capitol CL 13815	You Belong To Me/Hominy Grits (78) 8
52	Capitol CL 13831	Second Chance/I Know A Dream When I See One (78) 8
53	Capitol CL 13893	Kiss/There's My Lover (78) 8
53	Capitol CL 14008	That's Amore/You're The Right One (78) 10
54	Capitol CL 14021	The Christmas Blues/If I Should Love Again (78) 8
54	Capitol CL 14150	How Do You Speak To An Angel?/Ev'ry Street's A Boulevard
		In Old New York (with Jerry Lewis) (78) 8
55	Capitol CL 14215	Open Up The Doghouse (Two Cats Are Trying To Get In)
		(with Nat 'King' Cole)/Long, Long Ago (78) 8
55	Capitol CL 14255	What Could Be More Beautiful/Under The Bridges Of Paris (78) 7
58	Capitol CL 14910	Volare (Nel Blu Dipinto Di Blu)/Outta My Mind (78). 8
58	Capitol CL 14943	Once Upon A Time (It Happened)/The Magician (78) 8
59	Capitol CL 14990	It Takes So Long (To Say Goodbye)/You Were Made For Love (78) 12
59	Capitol CL 15039	On An Evening In Roma/You Can't Love 'Em All (78). 15
59	Capitol CL 15064	Ain't Gonna Lead This Life/Maybe (78) 20

SINGLES

54	Capitol CL 14123	Hey Brother, Pour The Wine/I'd Cry Like A Baby (green or purple labels). 30/18
54	Capitol CL 14138	Sway/Pretty As A Picture. 25
54	Capitol CL 14150	How Do You Speak To An Angel?/Ev'ry Street's A Boulevard
		In Old New York (with Jerry Lewis) 18
54	Capitol CL 14170	The Peddlar Man (Ten I Loved)/Try Again 18
54	Capitol CL 14180	One More Time/If I Could Sing Like Bing 15
55	Capitol CL 14215	Open Up The Doghouse (Two Cats Are Trying To Get In)
		(with Nat 'King' Cole)/Long, Long Ago 18
55	Capitol CL 14226	Let Me Go, Lover/The Naughty Lady Of Shady Lane 25
55	Capitol CL 14227	Mambo Italiano/That's All I Want From You 25
55	Capitol CL 14253	Belle From Barcelona/Confused 18
55	Capitol CL 14255	What Could Be More Beautiful/Under The Bridges Of Paris. 20
55	Capitol CL 14311	Chee Chee-Oo Chee (Sang The Little Bird)/Ridin' Into Love. 18
55	Capitol CL 14356	Relax-Ay-Voo/Two Sleepy People (with Line Renaud) 18
55	Capitol CL 14367	Simpatico/Love Is All That Matters 18
55	Capitol CL 14370	In Napoli/I Like Them All 18
		(The above 45s were originally issued with triangular centres; round-centre reissues are worth around half these values.)
56	Capitol CL 14505	When You Pretend/The Lucky Song 12
56	Capitol CL 14507	Innamorata/You Look So Familiar 15
56	Capitol CL 14519	Young And Foolish/Just One More Chance 15
56	Capitol CL 14523	Memories Are Made Of This/Change Of Heart 15
56	Capitol CL 14586	Watching The World Go By/The Lady With The Big Umbrella. 10
56	Capitol CL 14624	The Test Of Time/I'm Gonna Steal You Away. 8
56	Capitol CL 14625	Me 'N' You 'N' The Moon/The Wind, The Wind 8
56	Capitol CL 14626	Pardners (with Jerry Lewis)/Buckskin Beauty 10
56	Capitol CL 14656	Give Me A Sign/Mississippi Dreamboat 8
57	Capitol CL 14690	The Man Who Plays The Mandolino/I Know I Can't Forget 10
57	Capitol CL 14714	Bamboozled/Only Trust Your Heart 8
57	Capitol CL 14737	I Can't Give You Anything But Love/I Never Had A Chance 6
57	Capitol CL 14758	Beau James/Write To Me From Naples 10
57	Capitol CL 14782	The Triche Trache/Promise Her Anything 8
57	Capitol CL 14801	The Look/Just Kiss Me 7
57	Capitol CL 14813	Good Mornin' Life/Makin' Love Ukelele Style 8
58	Capitol CL 14844	Return To Me/Forgetting You 5
58	Capitol CL 14890	Angel Baby/I'll Gladly Make The Same Mistake Again 8
58	Capitol CL 14910	Volare (Nel Blu Dipinto Di Blu)/Outta My Mind 5
58	Capitol CL 14943	Once Upon A Time (It Happened)/The Magician 8
59	Capitol CL 14990	It Takes So Long (To Say Goodbye)/You Were Made For Love. 8
59	Capitol CL 15015	Rio Bravo/My Rifle, My Pony And Me 18
59	Capitol CL 15039	On An Evening In Roma/You Can't Love 'Em All 6
59	Capitol CL 15064	Ain't Gonna Lead This Life/Maybe. 8
59	Capitol CL 15102	(Love Is A) Career/For You. 8
60	Capitol CL 15127	Who Was That Lady?/Love Me, My Love 10
60	Capitol CL 15145	Napoli/Buttercup A Golden Hair 6
60	Capitol CL 15155	Just In Time/Humdinger. 6
60	Capitol CL 15172	Sogni D'Oro (Golden Dreams)/How Sweet It Is. 8
61	Capitol CL 15188	Sparklin' Eyes/Tu Sei Bella, Signorina. 8
61	Capitol CL 15198	All In A Night's Work/Bella Bella Bambina 10
61	Capitol CL 15209	Giuggiola/The Story Of Life 10
62	Reprise R 20058	Tik A Tee, Tik A Tay/Just Close Your Eyes 10
62	Reprise R 20076	C'est Si Bon!/The Poor People Of Paris 6
62	Reprise R 20082	Dame Su Amor/Baby O 10
63	Reprise R 20116	From The Bottom Of My Heart (Dammi, Dammi, Dammi)/
		Who's Got The Action? 10
63	Reprise R 20128	Sam's Song (with Sammy Davis Jnr)/SAMMY DAVIS JNR. & FRANK SINATRA:
		Me And My Shadow. 8
63	Capitol CL 15294	Cha Cha Cha D'Amour/I Wish You Love 5
63	Reprise R 20150	Face In A Crowd/Ain't Gonna Try Anymore. 5
63	Reprise R 20215	Via Veneto/Mama Roma 12
64	Reprise R 20217	Fugue For Tin Horns/The Oldest Established (Permanent Crap Game In
		New York) (B-side with Frank Sinatra & Bing Crosby) 6
64	Reprise R 20281	Everybody Loves Somebody Sometime/Little Voice. 6

MINT VALUE £

64	Reprise R 20307	The Door Is Still Open/Every Minute, Every Hour	5
64	Capitol CL 15363	Somebody Loves You/Hundred Years From Today	5
67	Pye DMA 1	I'm Not The Marrying Kind (Dean Martin Assoc. issue, 1-sided, promo only)	20
67	Reprise R 20538	Let The Good Times In/I'm Not The Marrying Kind	6
67	Reprise R 20601	In The Chapel In The Moonlight/Welcome To My World	6
67	Reprise R 20608	Little Ole Wine Drinker Me/I Can't Help Remembering You	6
67	Reprise R 20640	In The Misty Moonlight/Wallpaper Roses	5
68	Reprise RS 23259	Bumming Around/Home	8
68	Reprise R 20780	Not Enough Indians/Rainbows Are Back in Fashion	6
69	Reprise RS 23343	Gentle On My Mind/That Old Time Feelin'	8
69	Reprise RS 23387	By The Time I Get To Phoenix/Things	5
69	Reprise R 20841	I Take A Lot Of Pride/Drowning In My Tears	5
70	Reprise R 20893	Come On Down/Down Home	12
70	Reprise R 20973	Georgie Sunshine/For The Good Times	6
75	Capitol CL 15821	Memories Are Made Of This/That's Amore (That's Love)	5
81	Reprise K 14512	Gentle On My Mind/King Of The Road (p/s)	5

EPs

55	Capitol EAP 1-9123	DEAN MARTIN (EP)	22
55	Capitol EAP 1-481	SUNNY ITALY (EP)	20
56	Capitol EAP 1007	SWINGIN' DOWN YONDER NO. 1 (EP)	12
56	Capitol EAP 1022	SWINGIN' DOWN YONDER NO. 2 (EP)	12
56	Capitol EAP 1033	DEAN MARTIN AND JERRY LEWIS: "PARDNERS" (EP, with Jerry Lewis)	15
56	Capitol EAP 1037	SWINGIN' DOWN YONDER NO. 3 (EP)	12
57	Capitol EAP 1-806	HOLLYWOOD OR BUST — FILM SELECTION (EP)	15
57	Capitol EAP 1-840	TEN THOUSAND BEDROOMS — FILM SELECTION (EP)	20
57	Capitol EAP 1-939	RETURN TO ME (EP)	10
58	Capitol EAP 1-1027	VOLARE (EP)	8
60	Capitol EAP 1-1285	A WINTER ROMANCE PART 1 (EP)	12
60	Capitol EAP 2-1285	A WINTER ROMANCE PART 2 (EP)	12
60	Capitol EAP 3-1285	A WINTER ROMANCE PART 3 (EP)	12
61	Capitol EAP 1-20072	RELAXIN' WITH DEAN MARTIN (EP)	12
61	Capitol EAP 1-20124	DEAN MARTIN IN MOVIELAND (EP)	15
61	Capitol EAP 1-20152	I'M YOURS (EP)	12
63	Reprise R 30005	FRENCH STYLE (EP)	15
64	Reprise R 20031	DINO LATINO (EP)	15
64	Capitol EAP 6-1702	SOMEBODY LOVES YOU (EP)	10
65	Capitol EAP 7-1702	CHA CHA DE AMOUR (EP)	10
64	Reprise R 30034	EVERYBODY LOVES SOMEBODY (EP)	8
65	Reprise R 30036	WE'LL SING IN THE SUNSHINE (EP)	10
65	Reprise R 30039	ROBIN AND THE SEVEN HOODS (EP)	15
65	Reprise R 30044	I'LL BE SEEING YOU (EP)	12
65	Reprise R 30051	SEND ME SOME LOVING (EP)	10
66	Reprise R 30059	THE BIRDS AND THE BEES (EP)	10
66	Reprise R 30066	RED ROSES FOR A BLUE LADY (EP)	10
66	Reprise R 30074	LOVE LOVE LOVE (EP)	10
67	Reprise R 30078	SINGS SONGS FROM 'THE SILENCERS': THE GLORY OF LOVE (EP)	15
67	Reprise R 30084	MR. HAPPINESS (EP)	10
67	Reprise R 30090	WINTER WONDERLAND (EP)	10

ALBUMS

53	Capitol LC 6590	CAPITOL PRESENTS DEAN MARTIN (10" LP)	50
56	Britone LP 1002	DEAN MARTIN SINGS, NICOLINI LUCCHESI PLAYS (10" LP)	65
57	Capitol T 849	PRETTY BABY (LP)	20
58	Capitol T 1047	THIS IS DEAN MARTIN! (LP)	20
59	Capitol (S)T 1150	SLEEP WARM (LP, orchestra conducted by Frank Sinatra, mono/stereo)	15/18
61	Capitol (S)T 1442	THIS TIME I'M SWINGIN'! (LP, mono/stereo)	20/25
62	Encore! ENC 103	DEAN GOES DIXIE (LP)	18
62	Reprise R/R9 6021	FRENCH STYLE (LP, mono/stereo)	15/18
62	Capitol (S)T 1659	DINO (LP, mono/stereo)	20/25
63	Reprise R 6054	DINO LATINO (LP)	15
63	Capitol (S)T 1702	CHA CHA DE AMOR (LP, mono/stereo)	18/20
63	Reprise R 6061	DEAN (TEX) MARTIN COUNTRY STYLE (LP)	16
63	Reprise R 6085	DEAN (TEX) MARTIN RIDES AGAIN (LP)	16
64	Regal REG 1010	DEAN MARTIN (LP, export issue)	15
64	Reprise R 6123	DREAM WITH DEAN (LP)	15
64	Reprise R 6130	EVERYBODY LOVES SOMEBODY (LP)	12
65	Reprise R 6140	THE DOOR IS STILL OPEN TO MY HEART (LP)	12
65	Reprise R 6146	MARTIN HITS AGAIN (LP)	12
65	Reprise R/R9 6168	HOUSTON (LP, mono/stereo)	10/12
65	Reprise R/R9 6170	(REMEMBER ME) I'M THE ONE WHO LOVES YOU (LP, mono/stereo)	10/12
65	Capitol ST 490	PRETTY BABY (LP, reissue)	10
66	Reprise R 6201	SOMEWHERE THERE'S SOMEONE (LP)	12
66	Reprise R 6211	DEAN MARTIN SINGS SONGS FROM "THE SILENCERS" (LP)	15
66	Reprise RLP/RSLP 6213	THE HIT SOUND OF DEAN MARTIN (LP)	10
66	Reprise RLP 6222	THE DEAN MARTIN CHRISTMAS ALBUM (LP)	12
67	Reprise RLP/RSLP 6233	AT EASE WITH DEAN (LP)	12
67	Stateside SL/SSL 10201	LOVE IS A CAREER (LP)	15
67	Reprise RLP/RSLP 6242	HAPPINESS IS (LP)	10
67	Reprise RLP/RSLP 6250	WELCOME TO MY WORLD (LP)	10
68	Reprise RLP/RSLP 6301	DEAN MARTIN'S GREATEST HITS VOL. 1 (LP)	10
68	Reprise RLP/RSLP 6320	DEAN MARTIN'S GREATEST HITS VOL. 2 (LP)	10
69	Reprise RLP/RSLP 6330	GENTLE ON MY MIND (LP)	10
70	World Record Club ST 1001	ONE MORE TIME (LP)	10
71	Reprise RSLP 6428	FOR THE GOOD TIME (LP)	10
79	Capitol CAPS 1029	THE CLASSIC DINO (LP)	12
91	Capitol CDP 7943062	SWINGIN' DOWN YONDER (CD)	15

(see also Jerry Lewis, Line Renaud & Dean Martin, Frank Sinatra)

MINT VALUE £

DEREK MARTIN
64	Sue WI 308	Daddy Rolling Stone/Don't Put Me Down Like This (credited as Derak Martin)	25
65	Columbia DB 7694	You Better Go/You Know	25
68	Stax 601 039	Soul Power/Sly Girl	18

DON MARTIN & DANDY (& SUPERBOYS)
67	Giant GN 6	Got A Feelin'/CONNECTIONS: At The Junction	6
68	Giant GN 24	Keep On Fighting/Rock Steady Boogie (with Superboys)	12

(see also Dandy & Superboys)

GEORGE MARTIN & HIS ORCHESTRA
64	Parlophone R 5135	I Saw Her Standing There/All My Loving	7
64	Parlophone R 5166	And I Love Her/Ringo's Theme (This Boy)	7
65	Parlophone R 5222	All Quiet On The Mersey Front/Out Of The Picture	7
65	Parlophone R 5256	I Feel Fine/The Niagara Theme	6
65	Parlophone R 5375	Yesterday/Another Girl	10
66	United Artists UP 1154	By George! — It's The David Frost Theme/Double Scotch	10
66	United Artists UP 1165	Love In The Open Air/Theme From "The Family Way"	18
67	United Artists UP 1194	Theme One/Elephants And Castles	12
72	United Artists UP 35423	Pulp — Theme/Pulp — Love Theme	5
65	Parlophone GEP 8930	MUSIC FROM "A HARD DAY'S NIGHT" (EP)	25
64	Parlophone PMC 1227	OFF THE BEATLE TRACK (LP, also stereo PCS 3057)	25/30
65	Parlophone TA-PMC 1227	OFF THE BEATLE TRACK (reel-to-reel, mono only)	10
65	Columbia SX 1775	PLAYS HELP! (LP, mono)	18
65	Studio Two TWO 102	PLAYS HELP! (LP, stereo)	18
66	United Artists (S)ULP 1157	INSTRUMENTALLY SALUTES THE BEATLES GIRLS (LP)	25
66	Studio Two TWO 141	AND I LOVE HER (LP)	20
67	Decca (S)KL 4847	THE FAMILY WAY (LP)	75
68	United Artists (S)ULP 1196	BRITISH MAID (LP)	18
70	Sunset SLS 50182	BY GEORGE! (LP)	15
73	United Artists UAS 29475	LIVE AND LET DIE (LP, soundtrack, gatefold sleeve)	18
74	Polydor Super 2383 304	BEATLES TO BOND AND BACH (LP)	12
78	St. Michael IMP 105	BEATLES TO BOND AND BACH (LP, exclusive to Marks & Spencer)	25
93	EMI RNB 1	THE BEATLES — GEORGE MARTIN INTERVIEW (CD, card sl., promo only)	20

(see also Beatles, Ray Cathode)

GRADY MARTIN & SLEWFOOT FIVE
56	Brunswick 05535	Nashville/Don't Take Your Love From Me	15
56	Brunswick 05535	Nashville/Don't Take Your Love From Me (78)	8

HONEYBOY MARTIN
67	Caltone TONE 103	Dreader Than Dread (and the Voices)/DANDY: In The Mood	15
70	Gas GAS 123	Unchained Melody/SAMMY JONES: You're My Girl	5
72	Sioux SI 011	Unchained Melody/SAMMY JONES: You're My Girl (reissue)	5
72	Harry J HJ 6643	Have You Ever Seen The Rain/Spanish Harlem	5

(see also Lynn Tait & Jets)

IDO MARTIN
57	Melodisc MEL 1432	Fire Down Below/Cha Cha Cha Tres (78)	8

IRVING MARTIN
(see under Martin's Magic Sounds)

JANIS MARTIN
60	Palette PG 9000	Here Today And Gone Tomorrow Love/Hard Times Ahead	30

JEAN MARTIN
63	Decca F 11751	Ain't Gonna Kiss Ya/Three Times Three Is Love	8
64	Decca F 11897	Save The Last Dance For Me/Will You Still Love Me Tomorrow	8

JERRY MARTIN
63	London HLU 9692	Shake-A Take-A/Exchange Student	10

KERRY MARTIN
58	Parlophone R 4449	Stroll Me/Cold Hands, Warm Heart	10
58	Parlophone R 4449	Stroll Me/Cold Hands, Warm Heart (78)	10

LUCIA MARTIN
62	Parlophone R 4915	Big Jim/Star From Heaven	10

MARILYN MARTIN
86	Atlantic A 9465P	Night Moves/Wildest Dreams (shaped picture disc with plinth)	6

MARK MARTIN
67	Page One POF 020	Extraordinary Girl/Love Could Be Like Hell	6

MARY MARTIN
64	London HLR 9938	A Spoonful Of Sugar/Feed The Birds	6

MILES MARTIN FOLK GROUP
71	Amber	MILES MARTIN FOLK GROUP (LP, private pressing)	100

MILLICENT MARTIN
58	Columbia DB 4171	Our Language Of Love/Seriously	5
58	Columbia DB 4171	Our Language Of Love/Seriously (78)	8
60	Columbia DB 4466	Tintarella Di Luna/I Can Dream, Can't I?	5
63	Parlophone R 5033	Gravy Waltz/Get Lost My Love	5
64	Parlophone R 5096	In The Summer Of His Years/If I Can Help Somebody	6
64	Parlophone R 5120	Suspicion/Nothing But The Best	5

(see also Ronnie Carroll)

MOON MARTIN
79	Capitol 12CL 16076	Victim Of Romance (live)/Hot Night In Dallas (12")	7

(see also Southwind)

PAUL MARTIN
67	Sue WI 4041	Snake In The Grass/I've Got A New Love	25

RAY MARTIN (& HIS) CONCERT ORCHESTRA
53	Columbia SCM 5001	Blue Tango/Belle Of The Ball	7
53	Columbia SCM 5002	The Marching Strings/The Waltzing Cat	7
53	Columbia SCM 5020	Lady Of Spain/Ecstasy	7
53	Columbia SCM 5063	Swedish Rhapsody/Hi-Lili, Hi-Lo	5
56	Columbia SCM 5264	The Carousel Waltz/Port Au Prince	5
59	Columbia SCD 2123	The Carousel Waltz/Port Au Prince (reissue)	5
56	Columbia SEG 7639	IT'S GREAT TO BE YOUNG — FILM MUSIC (EP)	8
56	Pye Nixa NEP 24005	PRESENTING RAY MARTIN (EP)	8
53	Columbia 33S 1011	MUSIC IN THE RAY MARTIN MANNER VOL. 1 (10" LP)	15
54	Columbia 33S 1021	MUSIC IN THE RAY MARTIN MANNER VOL. 2 (10" LP)	15
64	Phase 4 Stereo PFS 4043	THE SOUND OF SIGHT (LP)	15

(see also Ray Burns)

RICKY MARTIN & TYME MACHINE
68	Olga OLE 4	Something Else/Blue Suede Shoes	10

RODGE MARTIN
67	Polydor 56725	When She Touches Me/Lovin' Machine	8

RON MARTIN & JUBILEE STOMPERS
68	Doctor Bird DB 1151	Give Your Love To Me/I Cry My Heart	8

RUPIE MARTIN
70	Punch PH 43	Death In The Arena (actually by Rupie Martin All Stars)/MAN COMETH: Julia Caesar (actually by Charlie Ace)	6

RUPIE MARTIN'S ALLSTARS
70	Torpedo TOR 24	Last Flight/Super Lotus	6
70	Torpedo TOR 26	Musical Container (Parts 1 & 2)	6

SETH MARTIN
68	Page One POF 073	Another Day Goes By/Look At Me	6
69	Page One POF 134	What A Lovely Way To Spend Forever/Mystery Lady	5

SHANE MARTIN
68	CBS 2894	You're So Young/I Need You	125

SKIP MARTIN VIDEO ALL-STARS
60	Golden Guinea GGL 0060	TV JAZZ THEMES (LP, also stereo GGLS 10060)	12/15

STEVE MARTIN
56	Columbia DB 3703	Only You/Lola	7
56	Columbia SCM 5212	Only You/Lola (78)	8
58	Philips PB 790	Crying Roses/My Darling, My Darling (78)	8
58	Philips PB 820	Stairway Of Love/Chanson D'Amour	6
58	Philips PB 820	Stairway Of Love/Chanson D'Amour (78)	8
58	Philips PB 853	The Man Inside/Blue-Eyed Sue	6
58	Philips PB 853	The Man Inside/Blue-Eyed Sue (78)	10

TONY MARTIN
53	HMV 7M 105	Tenement Symphony (both sides)	8
53	HMV 7M 136	The Golden Years/April In Portugal	12
54	HMV 7M 203	Here/I Could Write A Book	7
54	HMV 7M 258	I Love Paris/Boulevard Of Nightingales	7
55	HMV 7M 302	Stranger In Paradise/Vera Cruz	15
55	HMV 7M 320	Domani/What's The Time In Nicaragua	7
56	HMV 7M 414	Walk Hand In Hand/Flamenco Love	12
56	HMV 7MC 41	Walk Hand In Hand/Flamenco Love (export issue)	12
57	HMV POP 282	All Of You/Moderation	7
57	RCA RCA 1002	The Man From Idaho/One Is A Lonely Number	5
59	RCA RCA 1101	She Is Not Thinking Of Me/GOGI GRANT: Say A Prayer For Me Tonight	6
59	RCA RCA 1101	She Is Not Thinking Of Me/GOGI GRANT: Say A Prayer For Me Tonight (78)	8
63	HMV 7P 314	Tenement Symphony (both sides, reissue)	6
65	Stateside SS 394	Talkin' To Your Picture/Our Rhapsody	70
65	Tamla Motown TMG 537	The Bigger Your Heart Is (The Harder You'll Fall)/The Two Of Us	60
67	RCA RCA 1582	This Year/Sand Pebbles	5
54	HMV 7EG 8006	TONY MARTIN (EP)	10
55	HMV 7EG 8124	TENEMENT SYMPHONY (EP)	10
57	HMV 7EG 8205	THE DESERT SONG — SOUNDTRACK EXCERPTS (EP)	8
58	RCA RCX 130	SONGS FROM CINDERELLA (EP)	8
55	Brunswick LA 8713	TONY MARTIN SINGS VOL. 1 (10" LP)	20
56	Mercury MPT 7005	TONY MARTIN FAVOURITES (10" LP)	20
57	Mercury MPT 7516	DREAM MUSIC (10" LP)	18
57	HMV DLP 1137	SPEAK TO ME OF LOVE (10" LP)	18
57	RCA RD 27003	A NIGHT AT THE COPACABANA (LP)	15
61	London HA-D 2341	TONY MARTIN'S GREATEST HITS (LP)	15
65	Stateside SL 10113	AT CARNEGIE HALL (LP)	15

(see also Gogi Grant)

TRADE MARTIN
63	London HL 9662	Hula Hula Dancin' Doll/Something In The Wind	10

VINCE MARTIN (& TARRIERS)
56	London HLN 8340	Cindy, Oh Cindy/Only If You Praise The Lord (gold or silver label lettering)	22/12
59	HMV POP 594	Old Grey Goose (Aunt Rhodie)/Goodnight, Irene (solo)	8
59	HMV POP 594	Old Grey Goose (Aunt Rhodie)/Goodnight, Irene (solo) (78)	15

(see also Tarriers)

MARTIN & BROWNSHIRTS
78	Lightning GIL 507	Taxi Driver/Boring	20

MINT VALUE £

MARTIN & DERRICK

| 61 | Blue Beat BB 48 | Times Are Going/I Love You Baby (with Cavaliers Combo) | 15 |
| 62 | Island WI 024 | Come On/MONTY & CYCLONES: Organisation | 18 |

(see also Derrick Morgan)

MARTIN & FINLEY

| 73 | Tamla Motown TMG 867 | It's Another Sunday/Best Friends (withdrawn, demo only) | 60 |

WINK MARTINDALE

59	London HLD 8962	Deck Of Cards/Now You Know How It Feels	5
59	London HLD 8962	Deck Of Cards/Now You Know How It Feels (78)	40
60	London HLD 9042	Life Gits Tee-Jus Don't It?/I Never See Maggie Alone	6
61	London HLD 9419	Black Land Farmer/Make Him Happy	6
67	Dot DS 26753	The Shifting Whispering Sands/Trees	5
63	London RED 1370	DECK OF CARDS (EP)	20
65	Dot DEP 20000	DECK OF CARDS (EP)	12
60	London HA-D 2240	WINK MARTINDALE (LP)	25
60s	Golden Guinea GGL 0288	DECK OF CARDS (LP)	15

RAY MARTINE

| 63 | Piccadilly NPL 38007 | EAST END — WEST END (LP) | 12 |

TONY MARTINEZ QUINTET

| 54 | HMV 7M 264 | Cucusa Tune Mambo/Bernie's Tune Mambo | 6 |

MIA MARTINI

| 77 | CBS S CBS 5178 | Freedom Is Today/Libera | 5 |

AL MARTINO

78s

| 57 | Capitol CL 14680 | I'm Sorry/A Love To Call My Own (78) | 10 |
| 59 | Top Rank JAR 108 | I Can't Get You Out Of My Heart/Two Hearts Are Better Than One (78) | 15 |

SINGLES

54	Capitol CL 14128	Wanted/There'll Be No Teardrops Tonight	30/25
54	Capitol CL 14148	On And On (In Love With You)/Give Me Something To Go With The Wine	30/25
54	Capitol CL 14163	The Story Of Tina/Destiny (No One Can Change)	30/25

(The first prices for the above 45s are for green labels with triangular centres, the second for later pressings with purple labels with triangular centres.)

54	Capitol CL 14192	I Still Believe/When?	18
54	Capitol CL 14202	Not As A Stranger/No One But You	18
55	Capitol CL 14224	Don't Go To Strangers/Say It Again	18
55	Capitol CL 14284	The Snowy, Snowy Mountains/Love Is Eternal	15
55	Capitol CL 14343	The Man From Laramie/To Please My Lady	25
55	Capitol CL 14379	Come Close To Me/Small Talk	12

(All the above 45s were originally issued with triangular centres; round-centre reissues are worth around half these values.)

56	Capitol CL 14550	Journey's End/Sound Advice	8
56	Capitol CL 14614	The Girl I Left In Rome/Some Cloud Above	8
57	Capitol CL 14680	I'm Sorry/A Love To Call My Own	8
59	Top Rank JAR 108	I Can't Get You Out Of My Heart/Two Hearts Are Better Than One	10
59	Top Rank JAR 187	Darling I Love You/The Memory Of You	10
60	Top Rank JAR 312	Summertime/I Sold My Heart	7
60	Top Rank JAR 337	Mama/Dearest (Cara)	7
60	Top Rank JAR 418	Why Do I Love You/Sunday	6
60	Ember EMB S 119	Our Concerto/It's All Over But The Crying	6
61	Ember EMB S 122	My Side Of The Story/Little Boy Little Girl	5
62	Ember EMB S 147	Darling I Love You/There's No Tomorrow	6
62	Capitol CL 15260	Because You're Mine/Make Me Believe	6
63	Capitol CL 15300	I Love You Because/Merry-Go-Round	6
63	Capitol CL 15314	Painted, Tainted Rose/That's The Way It's Got To Be	6
63	Capitol CL 15324	Living A Lie/I Love You Truly	5
64	Capitol CL 15337	I Love You More And More Each Day/I'm Living My Heaven With You	5
64	Capitol CL 15349	Tears And Roses/A Year Ago Tonight	5
64	Capitol CL 15362	Always Together/Thank You For Loving Me	5
64	Capitol CL 15368	We Could/Sunrise To Sunrise	5
65	Capitol CL 15383	My Heart Would Know/Hush, Hush Sweet Charlotte	5
65	Capitol CL 15390	Somebody Else Is Taking My Place/With All My Heart	5
65	Capitol CL 15406	My Cherie/Ramona	5
65	Capitol CL 15421	Forgive Me/What Now, My Love	5
66	Capitol CL 15430	Spanish Eyes/Melody Of Love (original label)	5
66	Capitol CL 15442	Think I'll Go Somewhere And Cry Myself To Sleep/My Love, Forgive Me (Amore, Scusami)	5
66	Capitol CL 15449	Wiederseh'n/The Minute You're Gone	5
66	Capitol CL 15464	Just Yesterday/By The River Of The Roses	5
66	Capitol CL 15479	The Wheel Of Hurt/Somewhere In This World	5
67	Capitol CL 15490	Daddy's Little Girl/Devolution	5
67	Capitol CL 15504	Mary In The Morning/I Love You And You Love Me	5
67	Capitol CL 15516	More Than The Eye Can See/Red Is Red	5
68	Capitol CL 15528	Glory Of Love/The Voice In The Choir	5

EPs

55	Capitol EAP1 405	AL MARTINO SINGS (EP)	18
61	Capitol EAP1 20153	TO PLEASE MY LADY (EP)	10
63	Ember EMB 4528	DARLING I LOVE YOU (EP)	10
63	Capitol EAP4 2107	MARTINO SINGS OF LOVE (EP)	8
64	Capitol EAP1 20590	LOSING YOU (EP)	8

LPs

60	Top Rank BUY 030	AL MARTINO (LP)	18
60	Top Rank 25/025	SWING ALONG WITH AL MARTINO (LP)	18
63	Capitol (S)T 1774	THE EXCITING VOICE OF AL MARTINO (LP, mono/stereo)	15/18
63	Capitol (S)T 1914	I LOVE YOU BECAUSE (LP, mono/stereo)	15/18

MINT VALUE £

64	Capitol (S)T 1975	PAINTED, TAINTED ROSE (LP, mono/stereo)	15/18
64	Capitol (S)T 2040	LIVING A LIE (LP, mono/stereo)	15/18
64	Capitol (S)T 2107	AL MARTINO (LP, mono/stereo)	15/18
65	Capitol (S)T 2200	WE COULD (LP, mono/stereo)	15/18
65	Capitol (S)T 2312	SOMEBODY ELSE IS TAKING MY PLACE (LP, mono/stereo)	15/18
66	Capitol (S)T 2362	MY CHERIE (LP, mono/stereo)	15/18
66	Capitol (S)T 2435	SPANISH EYES (LP, mono/stereo)	15/18

MARTIN'S MAGIC SOUNDS
67	Deram DM 141	Mon Amour, Mon Amour/Midem Melody	5
67	Deram DML/SML 1014	MARTIN'S MAGIC SOUNDS (LP)	15

JOHN MARTYN
71	Island WIP 6116	May You Never/Just Now	6
77	Island WIP 6385	Over The Hill/Head And Heart	5
78	Island WIP 6414	Dancing/Dealer (Version)	5
80	Island WIP 6547	Johnny Too Bad/Johnny Too Bad (Version)	5
81	Island IPR 2046	Johnny Too Bad (Extended Dub Version)/Big Muff (Extended Mix) (12", promo)	10
82	WEA K 259987-7	Gun Money (US Remix)/Hiss On the Tape (live)	5
86	Island CID 265	Classic John Martyn: Angeline/Tight Connection To My Heart (Has Anybody Seen My Love)/May You Never/Solid Air/ Glistening Glyndebourne (CD, foldout sleeve)	20
67	Island ILP 952	LONDON CONVERSATION (LP, 1st pressing, with black 'circle' logo)	35
69	Island ILP 952	LONDON CONVERSATION (LP, 2nd pressing, 'pink rim' label, 'palm tree' logo)	18
68	Island ILP 991/ILPS 9091	THE TUMBLER (LP, 1st pressing, with black 'circle' logo, mono/stereo)	25/20
70	Island ILPS 9091	THE TUMBLER (LP, 2nd pressing, 'pink rim' label, 'palm tree' logo)	15
71	Island ILPS 9167	BLESS THE WEATHER (LP, 'pink rim' label, 'palm tree' logo)	15
73	Island ILPS 9226	SOLID AIR (LP, gatefold sleeve with lyric sheet 'pink rim' label, 'palm tree' logo)	12
73	Island ILPS 9253	INSIDE OUT (LP, gatefold sleeve with inner, 'pink rim' label, 'palm tree' logo)	12
75	Island ILPS 9296	SUNDAY'S CHILD (LP, with lyric inner sleeve, 'palm tree' label)	12
75	Island ILPS 9343	LIVE AT LEEDS (LP, mail-order, 10,000 only, numbered & signed)	25

JOHN & BEVERLEY MARTYN
70	Island WIP 6076	John The Baptist/The Ocean	6
70	Island ILPS 9113	STORMBRINGER (LP, 1st pressing, pink label with 'i' logo)	18
70	Island ILPS 9113	STORMBRINGER (LP, 2nd pressing, 'pink rim' label, 'palm tree' logo)	12
70	Island ILPS 9133	THE ROAD TO RUIN (LP, 'pink rim' label, 'palm tree' logo)	12

(see also Beverley)

KID MARTYN
62	77 77LA 12/20	IN NEW ORLEANS WITH KID SHEIK'S BAND (LP)	12

MARVELETTES
61	Fontana H 355	Please Mr Postman/So Long Baby	35
62	Fontana H 386	Twistin' Postman/I Want A Guy	60
62	Oriole CBA 1764	Beechwood 4-5789/Someday Someway	80
63	Oriole CBA 1817	Locking Up My Heart/Forever	275
64	Stateside SS 251	As Long As I Know He's Mine/Little Girl Blue	45
64	Stateside SS 273	He's A Good Guy (Yes He Is)/Goddess Of Love	40
64	Stateside SS 334	You're My Remedy/A Little Bit Of Sympathy, A Little Bit Of Love	35
65	Stateside SS 369	Too Many Fish In The Sea/Need For Love	25
65	Tamla Motown TMG 518	I'll Keep Holding On/No Time For Tears	40
65	Tamla Motown TMG 535	Danger Heartbreak Dead Ahead/Your Cheating Ways	25
66	Tamla Motown TMG 546	Don't Mess With Bill/Anything You Wanna Do	30
66	Tamla Motown TMG 562	You're The One/Paper Boy	25
67	Tamla Motown TMG 594	The Hunter Gets Captured By The Game/I Think I Can Change You	12
67	Tamla Motown TMG 609	When You're Young And In Love/The Day You Take One, You Have To Take The Other	7
68	Tamla Motown TMG 639	My Baby Must Be A Magician/I Need Someone	8
68	Tamla Motown TMG 659	Here I Am Baby/Keep Off, No Trespassing	12
69	Tamla Motown TMG 701	Reachin' For Something I Can't Have/Destination Anywhere	10
73	Tamla Motown TMG 860	Reachin' For Something I Can't Have/Here I Am Baby	5
75	Tamla Motown TMG 1000	Finders Keepers, Losers Weepers/KIM WESTON: Do Like I Do	25
65	Tamla Motown TMG 2003	THE MARVELETTES (EP)	90
65	Tamla Motown TML 11008	THE MARVELLOUS MARVELETTES (LP)	165
67	T. Motown (S)TML 11052	THE MARVELETTES (LP, mono/stereo)	35/40
69	T. Motown (S)TML 11090	SOPHISTICATED SOUL (LP)	30
70	T. Motown STML 11145	IN FULL BLOOM (LP)	18
71	T. Motown STML 11177	THE RETURN OF THE MARVELETTES (LP, unissued)	

MARVELOWS
65	HMV POP 1433	I Do/My Heart	15

MARVELS (Jamaica)
62	Dice CC 8	Come To The Wedding/Angelo	10
63	Blue Beat BB 191	Sonia/The More We Are Together	12
64	Blue Beat BB 221	Millie/Saturday	12
70	Pama PM 813	Love One Another/Falling Rain	7
70	Pama PM 817	Don't Let Him Take Your Love From Me/A Little Smile	8
70	Gas GAS 138	Sail Away/Fight A Broke	5
70	Gas GAS 139	Someday We'll Be Together/MORGAN'S ALL STARS: Instrumental	5
71	Pama PM 819	Oh Lord Why Lord/NEVILLE HINDS: Love Letter	5
71	Pama Supreme PS 338	Rocksteady/ Be My Baby	5
71	New Beat NB 081	Co Co/Hey Girl Don't Bother Me	5
72	Pama PM 832	Do You Know You Have To Cry/Love Power	5
72	Pama Supreme PS 348	What A Hurricane/If You Love Her	5

MARVELS (U.K.)
68	Columbia DB 8341	Keep On Searching/Heartache	10

MARVELS FIVE

MINT VALUE £

65	HMV POP 1423	Bye Bye Baby Bunting/In Front Of Her House	6
65	HMV POP 1452	Don't Play That Song/Forgive	6

MARVETTES

68	Amalgamated AMG 804	Tit For Tat (actually by Lyn Taitt & Jets)/You Take So Long To Know	35
68	Sacred Sound SS 001	We Are Not Divided/He Is So Real To Me	5
68	Sacred Sound SS 002	We Shall Have A Grand Time/Let The Power Fall On Me	5
68	Sacred Sound SS 003	I Was Once Lost In Sin/What A Wonderful Thing	5
68	Tabernacle TS 1001	I Want A Revival/Tell It	6
68	Tabernacle TS 1003	Sweet Jesus/When I Look Back	6
60s	Coxsone TLP 1002	IT'S REVIVAL TIME (LP)	90

BRETT MARVIN & THUNDERBOLTS

70	Sonet SON 2011	Standing On The Platform/Too Many Hot Dogs	5
71	Sonet SON 2015	Thoughts Of You/Coming Back	5
71	Sonet SON 2017	Southbound Lane/Little Red Caboose	5
70	Sonet SNTF 616	BRETT MARVIN AND THE THUNDERBOLTS (LP)	15
71	Sonet SNTF 619	12 INCHES OF BRETT MARVIN & THE THUNDERBOLTS (LP)	12
71	Sonet SNTF 620	BEST OF FRIENDS (LP)	12
72	Sonet SNTF 630	ALIAS TERRY DACTYL AND THE DINOSAURS (LP)	12
73	Sonet SNTF 651	TEN LEGGED FRIEND (LP)	12

(see also Terry Dactyl & Dinosaurs, Jona Lewie)

HANK (B.) MARVIN

68	Columbia DB 8326	London's Not Too Far/SHADOWS: Running Out Of World	10
69	Columbia DB 8552	Goodnight Dick/Wahine	10
69	Columbia DB 8601	Sacha/Sunday For Seven Days	10
69	Columbia DB 8628	Midnight Cowboy/SHADOWS: Slaughter On Tenth Avenue	15
70	Columbia DB 8693	Break Another Dawn/Would You Believe It? (demo-only, unissued B-side)	125
70	Columbia DB 8693	Break Another Dawn/Morning Star	12
78	EMI EMI 2744	Flamingo/Syndicated (as Hank Marvin Guitar Syndicate)	5
82	Polydor POSP 420	Don't Talk/Life Line (p/s)	5
83	Polydor POSP 618	Invisible Man/All Alone With Friends (p/s)	5
70	Columbia S(C)X 6352	HANK MARVIN (LP, blue/black label, mono/stereo)	25/20
70	Columbia SCX 6352	HANK MARVIN (LP, silver/black label re-pressing)	12

(see also Shadows, Marvin & Farrar, Marvin Welch & Farrar, Bruce Welch, Cliff Richard, Spaghetti Junction, Jean-Michel Jarre)

JOEL MARVIN

70	Explosion EX 2028	Too Late/Each Day (both actually by Gregory Isaacs)	8

(see also Gregory Isaacs)

MARVIN & FARRAR

73	EMI EMI 2044	Music Makes My Day/Skin Deep (with Olivia Newton-John)	8
75	EMI EMI 2335	Small And Lonely Light/Galadriel (Spirit Of Starlight)	7
73	EMI EMA 755	HANK MARVIN AND JOHN FARRAR (LP, with Olivia Newton-John)	18

(see also Shadows, Hank Marvin, Marvin Welch & Farrar)

MARVIN & JOHNNY

57	Vogue V 9074	Yak Yak/Pretty Eyes	400
57	Vogue V 9074	Yak Yak/Pretty Eyes (78)	90
58	Vogue V 9099	Smack, Smack/You're In My Heart	350
58	Vogue V 9099	Smack, Smack/You're In My Heart (78)	85
65	Black Swan WI 467	Cherry Pie/Ain't That Right	20

MARVIN, WELCH & FARRAR

71	Regal Zonophone RZ 3030	Faithful/Mr. Sun	7
71	Regal Zonophone RZ 3035	Lady Of The Morning/Tiny Robin	7
72	Regal Zonophone RZ 3048	Marmaduke/Strike A Light	12
71	Regal Zono. SRZA 8502	MARVIN, WELCH AND FARRAR (LP)	20
71	Regal Zono. SRZA 8504	SECOND OPINION (LP)	20
72	Regal Zono. Q4SRZA 8504	SECOND OPINION (LP, quadrophonic)	30

(see also Shadows, Marvin & Farrar, Bruce Welch [& Hank Marvin])

GROUCHO MARX

51	Brunswick 04794	Blackstrap Molasses/How D'ye Do And Shake Hands (78, with Jimmy Durante & Danny Kaye)	8
73	A&M AMS 7057	Show Me A Rose/Lydia The Tattooed Lady	6
72	A&M AMLS 6003	AN EVENING WITH GROUCHO MARX (2-LP)	15

(see also Danny Kaye, Jimmy Durante)

GROUCHO & CHICO MARX

69	MCA MCA 758	Ev'ryone Says I Love You/HARPO MARX: Ev'ryone Says I Love You (p/s)	7

(see also Marx Brothers)

MARX BROTHERS

70	MCA MCF 2533	ORIGINAL VOICE TRACKS FROM THEIR GREATEST MOVIES (LP)	15

(see also Groucho Marx)

MARY JANE with BARRY GRAY & SPACEMAKERS

63	Philips 326 587 BF	Robot Man/Just The Same As I Do (some in p/s)	35/15

(see also Barry Gray)

MARZIPAN

70	Trend 6099 007	My Kind Of Music/Sweet Water Mary	4

MASAI

74	Contempo CS 2007	Across The Track (We Better Go Back) (Parts 1 & 2)	40

MASAI

82	Turbo TURB 01	Stranger To Myself/Lightning (p/s)	12

MASCOTS

63	Pye International 7N 25189	Hey Little Angel/Once Upon A Love	12

BARRY MASON

DAVE MASON

HUGH MASEKELA
68	Uni UN 504	Grazing In The Grass/Bajabula Bonke.	7
69	Uni UN 510	I Haven't Slept/Where Has All The Grass Gone?	5
68	Uni UNL(S) 101	ALIVE AND WELL AT THE WHISKEY (LP)	15
69	Fontana SFL 13056	HUGH MASEKELA (LP)	15
71	Rare Earth SRE 3002	HUGH MASEKELA AND THE UNION OF SOUTH AFRICA (LP)	12
72	Blue Thumb ICD 3	HOME IS WHERE THE MUSIC IS (LP)	25

SPOKES MASHIYANE
58	Oriole CB 1441	Jika Spokes (with Ben Nkosi)/Boys Of Jo'burg (with France Pilane)	6
58	Oriole CB 1441	Jika Spokes (with Ben Nkosi)/Boys Of Jo'burg (with France Pilane) (78)	8

MASKED PHANTOM
66	Parlophone R 5437	These Clogs Are Made For Waltzing/Fried Scampi	4

MASKMAN & AGENTS
69	Direction 58-4059	One Eye Open/Y'awll	4

MASON
73	Dawn DNLS 3050	MASON (LP, export issue)	18

BARBARA MASON
65	London HL 9977	Yes, I'm Ready/Keep Him	18
68	Direction 58-3382	Oh How It Hurts/Ain't Got Nobody	12
69	Action ACT 4542	Slipping Away/Half A Love	10
72	Buddah 2011 133	Bed And Board/Yes It's You	5
73	Buddah 2011 154	Give Me Your Love/You Can Be With The One You Don't Love	6
75	Buddah BDS 425	From His Woman To You/When You Wake Up In Georgia	5
69	Action ACLP 6002	OH HOW IT HURTS (LP)	40
75	Buddah BDLP 4027	TRANSITION (LP)	15
75	Buddah BDLP 4032	LOVE'S THE THING (LP)	15

BARRY MASON
66	Decca F 12401	Misty Morning Eyes/Take Your Time	6
66	Deram DM 104	Over The Hills And Far Away/A Collection Of Recollections	40
69	Decca F 12895	I'm In Love With You, Pom Pom/Mister D.J. Play Me A Sad Song	5

(see also Sounds Of Les & Barry)

CURTISS MASON
71	Columbia DB 8800	Monkberry Moon Delight/Lot Of Lovin'	4

DAVE MASON
68	Island WIP 6032	Just For You/Little Woman	12
70	Harvest HAR 5017	World In Changes/Can't Stop Worrying, Can't Stop Lovin'	6
70	Harvest HAR 5024	Only You Know And I Know/Sad And Deep As You	6
70	Harvest SHTC 251	ALONE TOGETHER (LP)	18
72	Blue Thumb ILPS 9203	HEAD KEEPER (LP)	18
72	Island ICD 5	SCRAPBOOK (2-LP)	18
73	CBS 65258	IT'S LIKE YOU NEVER LEFT (LP, gatefold sleeve)	12

(see also Hellions, Revolution, Traffic, Fox)

DAVE MASON & CASS ELLIOT
71	Probe PRO 513	Something To Make You Happy/Next To You (as Mason & Cass, special sleeve)	5
71	Probe SPBA 6259	DAVE MASON AND CASS ELLIOT (LP)	15

(see also Dave Mason, Mama Cass [Elliot])

GLEN MASON
56	Parlophone MSP 6240	Hot Diggity (Dog Ziggity Boom)/Baby Girl Of Mine	10
56	Parlophone R 4203	Love, Love, Love/Glendora	15
56	Parlophone R 4244	The Green Door/Why Must You Go, Go, Go	15
57	Parlophone R 4271	Don't Forbid Me/Amore	7

MINT VALUE £

57	Parlophone R 4291	Round And Round/Walking And Whistling	6
57	Parlophone R 4334	Crying My Heart Out For You/Why Don't They Understand	6
57	Parlophone R 4357	By My Side/By The Fireside	5
58	Parlophone R 4390	What A Beautiful Combination/I'm Alone Because I Love You	5
58	Parlophone R 4415	I May Never Pass This Way Again/A Moment Ago	7
58	Parlophone R 4451	I Know Where I'm Going/Autumn Souvenir	6
58	Parlophone R 4451	I Know Where I'm Going/Autumn Souvenir (78)	8
58	Parlophone R 4485	The End/Fall In Love	6
58	Parlophone R 4485	The End/Fall In Love (78)	8
59	Parlophone R 4562	The Battle Of New Orleans/I Don't Know	7
59	Parlophone R 4562	The Battle Of New Orleans/I Don't Know (78)	12
60	Parlophone R 4626	You Got What It Takes/If There's Someone	6
60	Parlophone R 4723	That's What I Want!/I Like It When It Rains	6
61	Parlophone R 4834	Don't Move/Shadrack	6
62	Parlophone R 4900	St. Louis Blues/That's Life	6

MARLIN MASON
56	Vogue Coral Q 72168	Don't Throw My Love Away/The Mystery Of Love	7

NICK MASON (& RICK FENN)
85	Harvest HAR 5238	Lie For A Lie/And The Address (with Rick Fenn, p/s)	5
85	Harvest 12 HAR 5238	Lie For A Lie (Extended 12" Version)/And The Address/ Mumbo Jumbo (with Rick Fenn) (12", p/s)	8
85	EMI MAF 1	PROFILES (LP, with Rick Fenn)	10
81	Harvest SHSP 4116	FICTITIOUS SPORTS (LP, solo, with inner sleeve)	12
	(see also Pink Floyd, 10cc)		

SANDY MASON
80s	Boot BOS 7234	ONLY LOVE (LP)	10

SPENCER MASON
67	Parlophone R 5555	Flugel In Carnaby Street/Albuferia	6

MASQUERADERS
68	Bell BLL 1023	I Ain't Got To Love Nobody Else/I Got It	5
70	Now! NOW 1001	Love Peace And Understanding/Tell Me You Love Me	5
	(see also Lester Tipton)		

MASS
80	4AD AD 14	You And I/Cabbage (some with poster insert in die-cut sleeve)	15/8
81	4AD CAD 107	LABOUR OF LOVE (LP, some with inner sleeve)	15/10
	(see also Models, Rema-Rema, Wolfgang Press)		

MASSIVE ATTACK
91	Wild Bunch WBRR 2	Unfinished Sympathy (Nellee Hooper 12" Mix)/ (Nellee Hooper Instrumental Mix)/(Original) (12", p/s)	20

MASSED ALBERTS
64	Parlophone R 5159	Blaze Away/Goodbye Dolly (Gray)	6

MASTERBOY
91	Spaghetti CIAO 2	Shake It Up And Dance (Mini Live Version)/(Instrumental) (p/s)	4
91	Spaghetti CIAOC 2	Shake It Up And Dance (Mini Live Version)/(Instrumental) (cassette)	5
91	Spaghetti CIAOX	Shake It Up And Dance (Mini Live Version)/(Instrumental) (12", p/s)	8
91	Spaghetti CIAOCD 2	Shake It Up And Dance (Mini Live Version)/(Remix '91)/ (Maxi Live Version) (CD)	12

MASTERFLEET
73	Sussex LPSX 5	HIGH ON THE SEA (LP)	20

MASTERMINDS
65	Immediate IM 005	She Belongs To Me/Taken My Love	18
	(see also Badfinger)		

MASTERPLAN
78	Satril SAT 136	Love Crazy (Theme From 'Carry On Emmanuel')/ Since I've Been Away From My Love (p/s)	10

CARL MASTERS
72	Big Shot BI 604	Va Va Voom/GOD SONS: Rebel	10
	(see also Max Romeo, Dennis Alcapone)		

SAMMY MASTERS
60	Warner Bros WB 10	Rockin' Red Wing/Lonely Weekend	25
60	Warner Bros WB 10	Rockin' Red Wing/Lonely Weekend (78)	225
65	London HLR 9949	I Fought The Law (And The Law Won)/Big Man Cried	10

VALERIE MASTERS
58	Fontana H 132	Sharing/The Secret Of Happiness	8
58	Fontana H 132	Sharing/The Secret Of Happiness (78)	8
58	Fontana H 145	(Well-a, Well-a) Ding-Dong/Merci Beaucoup	8
58	Fontana H 145	(Well-a, Well-a) Ding-Dong/Merci Beaucoup (78)	8
59	Fontana H 175	Dreams End At Dawn/Wonder	7
59	Fontana H 175	Dreams End At Dawn/Wonder (78)	10
59	Fontana H 195	Jack O' Diamonds/Say When	8
59	Fontana H 195	Jack O' Diamonds/Say When (78)	15
59	Fontana H 224	If There Are Stars In My Eyes/Just Squeeze Me	7
59	Fontana H 224	If There Are Stars In My Eyes/Just Squeeze Me (78)	15
60	Fontana H 238	Oh, Gee/No One Understands	8
60	Fontana H 253	Banjo Boy/Cow Cow Boogie	8
60	Fontana H 268	Sweeter As The Day Goes By/Fools Fall In Love	7
61	Fontana H 293	Too Late For Tears/I Got Rhythm	7
61	Fontana H 322	Birmingham Rag/All The Days Of My Life	6
62	Fontana H 367	African Waltz/All Night Long	6

64	Columbia DB 7426	Christmas Calling/He Didn't Fool Me	60
65	Polydor 56056	It's Up To You/Next Train Out	5
66	Polydor 56135	Don't Ever Go/Say Hello	6
69	Columbia DB 8629	I Don't Wanna Play House/Just Wait A Little While	6

MASTER'S APPRENTICES
71	Regal Zonophone RZ 3031	I'm Your Satisfier/Because I Love Her	18
70	Regal Zono. SLRZ 1016	MASTER'S APPRENTICES (LP)	135
71	Regal Zono. SLRZ 1022	A TOAST TO PANAMA RED (LP)	100

MASTER SINGERS
60s	Parlophone R 5428	The Highway Code/Rumbletum	6
60s	Parlophone GEP 8962	THE HIGHWAY CODE (EP)	12

MASTERS OF REALITY
88	Def American DEFA 1	The Candy Song/The Blue Garden	10
88	Def American 838 474-1	THE MASTERS OF REALITY (LP)	20
88	Def American 838 474-2	THE MASTERS OF REALITY (CD)	20

MATADOR
71	Big Shot BI 594	Nyah Festival (actually "What Am I Living For" by Derrick Morgan)/ Brixton Serenade	5

MATADORS
69	Crab CRAB 27	Death A Come (actually by Lloyd Robinson)/The Sword (actually "Zylon" by Lloyd Tyrell [Charmers])	5
70	Camel CA 45	Dark Of The Sun (actually by Jackie Mittoo)/Dreader Than Dread	10
71	Green Door GD 4017	I'm Sorry(actually by Tony Brevett)/JOE WHITE: I'm Sorry Version	8

(see also Emotions, Little Roys, Ethiopians)

MATATA (AIR-FIESTA)
72	President PT 380	I Wanna Do My Thing/Wild River	10
73	President PT 406	I Feel Funky/I Want You	12
74	President PT 417	Return To You/Something On My Mind	10
75	President PT 438	Good Good Understanding/Gimme Some Lovin'	10
72	President PTLS 1052	MATATA: AIR FIESTA (LP)	40
75	President PTLS 1057	INDEPENDENCE (LP)	100

MATCHING MOLE
72	CBS 8101	O Caroline/Signed Curtain	12
72	CBS 64850	MATCHING MOLE (LP)	20
72	CBS 65260	MATCHING MOLE'S LITTLE RED RECORD (LP, with inner sleeve)	18

(see also Robert Wyatt, Soft Machine, Caravan, Hatfield & The North)

MATCHMAKERS
71	Chapter One	BUBBLEGUM A GO GO (LP)	15

(see also Mark Wirtz, Philwit & Pegasus, Fickle Finger)

MATHETAI
77	Cavs CAV 017	KNOWING (LP)	50

MIREILLE MATHIEU
67	Columbia DB 8323	La Derniere Valse/Seuls Au Monde	5
68	Columbia DB 8375	Je Ne Suis Rien Sans Toi (I'm Coming Home)/J'ai Garde L'Accent	5
68	Columbia DB 8429	When You Return/Tonight's The Night (Ce Soir Ils Vont S'Aime)	5
68	Columbia DB 8457	Sweet Souvenirs Of Stefan/An Revoir Daniel	5
68	Columbia DB 8513	Les Bicyclettes De Belsize/Sometimes	5
69	Columbia DB 8621	Hold Me/Vivre Pour Toi	5
71	Columbia DB 8775	Can A Butterfly Cry/Nobody	5
67	Fontana TE 17492	MIREILLE MATHIEU (EP)	8
66	Fontana TL 5363	MIREILLE MATHIEU (LP)	15
67	Columbia SX/SCX 6210	MIREILLE MATHIEU (LP)	12
68	Columbia SX/SCX 6328	LES BICYCLETTES DE BELSIZE (LP)	12
68	Columbia SCX 6246	LIVE AT THE PARIS OLYMPIA (LP)	12
69	Columbia SCX 6391	OLYMPIA (LP, gatefold sleeve)	12
68	Columbia SCX 6369	MIREILLE MATHIEU'S CHRISTMAS (LP)	15

COUNTRY JOHNNY MATHIS
60	Top Rank JKP 2064	COUNTRY AND WESTERN EXPRESS NO. 5 (EP)	20

JODI MATHIS
75	Capitol CL 15827	Mama/Don't You Care Anymore	5

JOHNNY MATHIS
78s
57	Philips PB 692	Warm And Tender/It's Not For Me To Say (78)	8
57	Philips PB 713	Wonderful! Wonderful!/When Sunny Gets Blue (78)	8
57	Philips PB 749	The Twelfth Of Never/Chances Are (78)	8
57	Fontana H 103	Wild Is The Wind/No Love (But Your Love) (78)	8
58	Fontana H 117	Come To Me/When I Am With You (78)	8
58	Fontana H 130	Teacher, Teacher/Easy To Love (78)	8
58	Fontana H 163	Call Me/Stairway To The Sea (78)	8
58	Fontana H 165	Winter Wonderland/Sleigh Ride (78)	10
59	Fontana H 186	Let's Love/You'd Be So Nice To Come Home To (78)	10
59	Fontana H 199	Someone/They Say It's Wonderful (78)	12
59	Fontana H 218	The Best Of Everything/Cherie (78)	15
59	Fontana H 219	Misty/The Story Of Our Love (78)	15
59	Fontana H 220	It's Not For Me to Say/Warm And Tender (78)	15

SINGLES
57	Philips JK 1029	The Twelfth Of Never/Chances Are (jukebox issue)	15
57	Fontana H 103	Wild Is The Wind/No Love (But Your Love)	7
58	Fontana H 117	Come To Me/When I Am With You	5
58	Fontana H 130	Teacher, Teacher/Easy To Love	6

Johnny MATHIS

58	Fontana H 142	A Certain Smile/Let It Rain	6
58	Fontana H 163	Call Me/Stairway To The Sea	5
58	Fontana H 165	Winter Wonderland/Sleigh Ride	5
59	Fontana H 186	Let's Love/You'd Be So Nice To Come Home To	5
59	Fontana H 199	Someone/They Say It's Wonderful	5
59	Fontana H 218	The Best Of Everything/Cherie	6
59	Fontana H 219	Misty/The Story Of Our Love	6
59	Fontana H 220	It's Not For Me to Say/Warm And Tender	5
60	Fontana H 234	You Are Beautiful/Very Much In Love	5
60	Fontana H 248	The Twelfth Of Never/Get Me To The Church On Time	5
60	Fontana H 254	Starbright/All Is Well	5
60	Fontana H 267	My Love For You/Oh That Feeling (some in p/s)	7/5
61	Fontana H 272	Maria/Hey Love	5
61	Fontana H 316	You Set My Heart To Music/Jenny	5
61	Fontana H 328	Laurie, My Love/Should I Wait (Or Should I Run To Her)	5
61	Fontana H 335	Love Look Away/When My Sugar Walks Down The Street	5
62	Fontana H 372	Sweet Thursday/One Look	5
62	CBS AAG 117	Gina/I Love Her, That's Why (with picture insert)	7
63	HMV POP 1217	Your Teenage Dreams/Come Back (some in export p/s)	12/5
63	HMV POP 1267	Bye Bye Barbara/A Great Night For Crying	5
64	HMV POP 1294	The Fall Of Love/No More	5
64	HMV POP 1318	Taste Of Tears/White Roses From A Blue Valentine	5
64	HMV POP 1365	Listen Lonely Girl/All I Wanted	5
65	HMV POP 1467	Sweetheart Tree/Mirage	5
65	HMV POP 1491	Danny Boy/This Is Love	5
66	HMV POP 1503	On A Clear Day You Can See Forever/Come Back To Me	5
66	HMV POP 1527	Moment To Moment/The Glass Mountain	5
66	HMV POP 1550	The Impossible Dream/Hurry It's Lovely Up Here	5
88	CBS 653 191-2	Daydreamin' (Remix)/Simple (Extended Version)/ Gone, Gone, Gone (CD, card sleeve)	7
88	CBS 654 773-2	Daydreamin' (7" Remix)/Once In A While/Daydreamin' (12" Extended Remix)/ Love Never Felt So Good (CD, card sleeve)	7

EPs

57	Philips BBE 12156	JOHNNY MATHIS (EP)	10
58	Fontana TFE 17011	JOHNNY MATHIS (EP)	8
58	Fontana TFE 17025	LET ME LOVE YOU (EP)	8
58	Fontana TFE 17039	COME TO ME (EP)	8
58	Fontana TFE 17047	WHILE WE'RE YOUNG (EP)	8
58	Fontana TFE 17056	THE TWELFTH OF NEVER (EP)	8
58	Fontana TFE 17064	AVE MARIA (EP)	8
58	Fontana TFE 17088	THERE GOES MY HEART (EP)	8
58	Fontana TFE 17089	SWING LOW (EP)	8
58	Fontana TFE 17091	A HANDFUL OF STARS (EP)	8
58	Fontana TFE 17162	CHRISTMAS WITH JOHNNY MATHIS (EP)	8
59	Fontana TFE 17177	MEET MISTER MATHIS (EP)	8
59	Fontana TFE 17194	IT'S DE LOVELY (EP, also stereo STFE 8001)	8/12
60	Fontana TFE 17215	SO NICE (EP, also stereo STFE 8000)	8/12
60	Fontana TFE 17275	FOUR HITS (EP)	8
60	Fontana TFE 17281	TENDERLY (EP)	8
60	Fontana TFE 17282	ELI ELI (EP)	8
60	Fontana TFE 17283	I'LL BE SEEING YOU (EP)	8
60	Fontana TFE 17285	LIKE SOMEONE IN LOVE (EP, also stereo STFE 8018)	8/12
61	Fontana TFE 17316	MOONLIGHT AND MATHIS (EP)	8
61	Fontana TFE 17317	FOUR SHOW HITS (EP)	8
61	Fontana TFE 17318	CALL ME (EP)	8
61	Fontana TFE 17319	IT'S LOVE (EP)	8
61	Fontana TFE 17334	MY LOVE FOR YOU (EP)	8
61	Fontana TFE 17354	I AM IN LOVE (EP)	8
61	Fontana TFE 17355	LET'S DO IT (EP)	8
61	Fontana TFE 17356	SECRET LOVE (EP)	8
62	Fontana TFE 17393	RING THE BELL (EP)	8
62	Fontana TFE 17394	THE PARTY'S OVER (EP)	8
62	CBS AGG 20001	LIVE IT UP VOL. 1 (EP)	8
62	CBS AGG 20006	LIVE IT UP VOL. 2 (EP)	8
62	CBS AGG 20012	LIVE IT UP VOL. 3 (EP)	8
63	CBS AGG 20028	RAPTURE (EP)	8
64	CBS AGG 20032	MATHIS ON BROADWAY (EP)	8

LPs

57	Fontana TFL 5003	WONDERFUL, WONDERFUL (LP)	20
58	Fontana TFL 5011	JOHNNY MATHIS (LP)	20
58	Fontana TFL 5015	WARM (LP, also stereo STFL 510)	15/18
58	Fontana TFL 5023	HEAVENLY (LP)	15
58	Fontana TFL 5031	MERRY CHRISTMAS (LP, also stereo STFL 506)	15/18
59	Fontana TFL 5039	SWING SOFTLY (LP, also stereo STFL 500)	15/18
59	Fontana TFL 5050	OPEN FIRE, TWO GUITARS (LP, also stereo STFL 515)	15/18
59	Fontana TFL 5058	JOHNNY'S GREATEST HITS (LP)	15
60	Fontana TFL 5061	RIDE ON A RAINBOW (LP, also stereo STFL 516)	15/18
60	Fontana TFL 5083	MORE OF JOHNNY'S GREATEST HITS (LP, also stereo STFL 517)	15/18
60	Fontana TFL 5084	FAITHFULLY (LP, also stereo STFL 522)	15/18
60	Fontana SET(S) 101	THE RHYTHMS AND BALLADS OF BROADWAY (2-LP, mono/stereo)	18/22
61	Fontana TFL 5117	JOHNNY'S MOOD (LP, also stereo STFL 545)	15/18
61	Fontana TFL 5134	I'LL BUY YOU A STAR (LP, also stereo STFL 557)	15/18
61	Fontana TFL 5153	PORTRAIT OF JOHNNY (LP, also stereo STFL 571)	15/18
62	Fontana TFL 5177	LIVE IT UP (LP, also stereo STFL 589)	12/15
62	CBS (S)BPG 62077	PORTRAIT OF JOHNNY (LP, reissue, mono/stereo)	12/15
62	CBS (S)BPG 62072	JOHNNY'S MOOD (LP, reissue, mono/stereo)	12/15

63	CBS (S)BPG 62106	RAPTURE (LP)	12
63	CBS (S)BPG 62147	JOHNNY'S NEWEST HITS (LP)	12
63	CBS (S)BPG 62172	JOHNNY (LP)	12
63	HMV CLP 1696/CSD 1521	SOUNDS OF CHRISTMAS (LP, mono/stereo)	12/15
64	CBS (S)BPG 62202	ROMANTICALLY (LP)	12
64	HMV CLP 1721	TENDER IS THE NIGHT (LP, also stereo CSD 1535)	12/15
64	CBS (S)BPG 62270	I'LL SEARCH MY SECRET HEART & OTHER GREAT HITS (LP)	12
65	HMV CSD 1553	THE WONDERFUL WORLD OF MAKE BELIEVE (LP, stereo only)	25
65	HMV CLP 1818/CSD 1578	OLÉ (LP)	50
65	HMV CLP 1859/CSD 1600	THIS IS LOVE (LP, mono/stereo)	30/18
66	HMV CLP 1926/CSD 1638	AWAY FROM HOME (LP)	40
66	CBS (S)BPG 62062	SWING SOFTLY (LP, reissue, mono/stereo)	12/15
66	CBS (S)BPG 62569	JOHNNY'S GREATEST HITS (LP, reissue)	12
66	CBS (S)BPG 62063	OPEN FIRE, TWO GUITARS (LP, reissue, mono/stereo)	12/15
66	CBS (S)BPG 62064	RIDE ON A RAINBOW (LP, reissue, mono/stereo)	12/15
66	CBS (S)BPG 62067	FAITHFULLY (LP, reissue, mono/stereo)	12/15
66	CBS (S)BPG 62105	LIVE IT UP (LP, reissue)	12
66	HMV CLP/CSD 3522	LOVE IS EVERYTHING (LP)	15
66	HMV CLP/CSD 3556	THE SHADOW OF YOUR SMILE (LP)	15
73	CBS CQ 30740	YOU'VE GOT A FRIEND — TODAY'S GREAT HITS (LP, quadrophonic)	12
73	CBS GQ 30979	JOHNNY MATHIS IN PERSON (LP, quadrophonic)	12
73	CBS CQ 31342	THE FIRST TIME EVER (I SAW YOUR FACE) (LP, quadrophonic)	12
73	CBS CQ 31626	SONG SUNG BLUE (LP, quadrophonic)	12
73	CBS CQ 32114	ME AND MRS JONES (LP, quadrophonic)	12
74	CBS CQ 32435	I'M COMING HOME (LP, quadrophonic)	12
75	CBS 66415	THE BEST OF JOHNNY MATHIS (3-LP box set, mail-order only)	20
79	CBS 66355	JOHNNY MATHIS (3-LP box set)	18
81	Readers Digest 034	THE BEST OF JOHNNY MATHIS (4-LP box set, mail-order only)	20
83	OPEN 1	THE ULTIMATE JOHNNY MATHIS (2-LP, mail-order only)	15

TONY MATOS
| 62 | Salvo SLO 5520-LP | CHA CHA! WITH TONY MATOS (LP, issued with or without sleeve) | 18/12 |

WALTER MATTHAU
| 73 | MCA MU 1185 | Love's The Only Game In Town/Pete 'N' Tillie — Love Theme | 4 |

BRIAN MATTHEW
| 61 | Pye 7N 15403 | Trad Mad/Sing With Me, Mates | 5 |

BRIAN MATTHEW & PETE MURRAY
| 60 | Decca F 11305 | What's It All About Eh?/Gee Ma, I Wanna Go Home | 5 |

IAN MATTHEWS
71	Vertigo 6059 041	Hearts/Little Known	6
71	Vertigo 6059 048	Reno, Nevada/Desert Inn	6
72	Philips 6006 197	Da Doo Ron Ron/Never Again	5
73	Vertigo 6059 081	Devil In Disguise/Thro' My Eyes	5
73	Elektra K 12111	These Days/Same Old Man	5
71	Vertigo 6360 034	IF YOU SAW THRO' MY EYES (LP, gatefold sleeve, spiral label)	18
72	Vertigo 6360 056	TIGERS WILL SURVIVE (LP, gatefold sleeve, spiral label)	18
73	Elektra K 42144	VALLEY HI (LP, gatefold sleeve)	15
74	Elektra K 42160	SOME DAYS YOU EAT THE BEAR, SOME DAYS THE BEAR EATS YOU (LP)	12
76	CBS 81316	GO FOR BROKE (LP)	12
77	CBS 81936	HIT AND RUN (LP)	12

(see also Pyramid, Fairport Convention, Matthews Southern Comfort, Plainsong, Hi-Fi)

JOE MATTHEWS
| 68 | Sue WI 4046 | Sorry Ain't Good Enough/You Better Mend Your Ways | 40 |

RANDY MATTHEWS
| 70s | Myrrh MXX 1035 | NOW DO YOU UNDERSTAND (LP, gatefold sleeve) | 20 |

TOBIN MATTHEWS
| 63 | Warner Brothers WB 117 | Can't Stop Talking About You/When You Came Along | 5 |

WINSTON MATTHEWS
| 71 | Banana BA 329 | Sun Is Shining/INN KEEPERS: My Friend (B-side actually "The Pressure Is On" by Purpleites) | 10 |

MATTHEWS SOUTHERN COMFORT
70	Uni UNS 513	Colorado Springs Eternal/The Struggle	5
70	Uni UNS 521	Ballad Of Obray Ramsey/Parting	5
70	Uni UNS 526	Woodstock/Scion	5
70	Uni UNLS 108	MATTHEWS SOUTHERN COMFORT (LP)	18
70	Uni UNLS 112	SECOND SPRING (LP, with lyric insert)	15
70	Uni MKPS 2015	LATER THAT SAME YEAR... (LP)	12

(see also Ian Matthews, Marc Ellington, Southern Comfort)

MATUMBI
| 73 | G.G. GG 4540 | Brother Louie (Parts 1 & 2) | 10 |

HARVEY MATUSOW'S JEWS HARP BAND
| 69 | Head HDS 4004 | Afghan Red/Wet Socks | 7 |
| 69 | Head HDLS 6001 | WAR BETWEEN THE FATS & THE THINS (LP) | 20 |

MAUDS
| 67 | Mercury MF 1000 | Hold On/C'mon And Move | 8 |
| 68 | Mercury MF 1062 | Soul Drippin'/Forever Gone | 6 |

SUSAN MAUGHAN
61	Philips BF 1216	Mama Do The Twist/Blue Night In Yokohama	10
62	Philips BF 1236	Baby Doll Twist/Some Of These Days	10
62	Philips 326 533BF	I've Got To Learn To Forget/I Didn't Mean To Say What I Said	7

Susan MAUGHAN

62	Philips 326 544BF	Bobby's Girl/Come A Little Closer	6
63	Philips 326 562BF	Hand A Handkerchief To Helen/I'm A Lonely One Too	6
63	Philips 326 586BF	She's New To You/Don't Get Carried Away	6
63	Philips BF 1266	The Verdict Is Guilty/Bachelor Girl	6
64	Philips BF 1301	Hey Lover/Stop Your Foolin'	6
64	Philips BF 1336	Kiss Me Sailor/Call On Me	6
64	Philips BF 1363	Little Things Mean A Lot/That Other Place	10
64	Philips BF 1382	Make Him Mine/South American Joe	7
65	Philips BF 1399	You Can Never Get Away From You/Don't Be Afraid	6
65	Philips BF 1417	When She Walks Away/Come Along Down And See	6
65	Philips BF 1445	Poor Boy/Your Girl	6
66	Philips BF 1495	Come And Get Me/Don't Love Him Too Much	6
66	Philips BF 1518	Where The Bullets Fly/I'll Never Stop Loving You	6
67	Philips BF 1564	Don't Go Home (My Little Darlin')/Somebody To Love	6
68	Philips BF 1713	Cable Car For Two/Off My Mind	6
69	Philips BF 1824	We Really Go Together/I'll Never Forget You	5
71	Spark SRL 1049	I Can't Make You Love Me/I'm Gonna Get That Guy	8
71	Spark SRL 1054	I Saw A Rainbow/Love Of The Lonely	6
62	Philips BBE 12525	HI, I'M SUSAN MAUGHAN AND I SING (EP)	20
63	Philips BBE 12549	FOUR BEAUX AND A BELLE (EP)	20
62	Philips 433 621 BE	EFFERVESCENT MISS MAUGHAN (EP)	20
63	Philips 433 641 BE	MORE OF MAUGHAN (EP)	20
63	Philips 632 300 BL	I WANNA BE BOBBY'S GIRL BUT ... (LP)	40
64	Philips BL 7577	SWINGIN' SUSAN (LP)	25
65	Philips BL 7637	SENTIMENTAL SUSAN (LP)	25
67	Wing WL 1105	BOBBY'S GIRL (LP)	15

MAU-MAUS

82	Pax PAX 6	SOCIETY'S REJECTS (EP)	7
82	Pax PAX 8	No Concern/Clampdown/Why Do We Suffer (p/s)	6
83	Pax/Paragon PAX 12	FACTS OF WAR (EP)	6
85	Rebellion REBEL 01	TEAR DOWN THE WALLS (EP)	6
85	Rebellion REBEL 1202	SCARRED FOR LIFE (12" EP)	8
83	Pax PAX 16	LIVE AT THE MARPLES (LP)	12
84	Pax PAX 20	RUNNING WITH THE PACK (LP)	12

MAUREENY WISHFULL

68	Moonshine WO 2388	THE MAUREENY WISHFULL ALBUM (LP, 300 copies, beware of counterfeits)	75

(see also Jimmy Page, Big Jim Sullivan, John Williams)

PAUL MAURIAT

67	Philips BF 1637	Love Is Blue (L'Amour Est Bleu)/Une Petite Cantate	4

MAURICE & MAC

68	Chess CRS 8074	You Left The Water Running/You're The One	10
68	Chess CRS 8081	Why Don't You Try Me/Lean On Me	12

(see also Radiants)

MAX & ELAINE

73	Ackee ACK 516	I'm Leaving/Version	5

(see also Max Romeo)

MAX & GREGORY

73	Ackee ACK 525	My Jamaican Collie/Push It Down, Rub It Up	5

(see also Max Romeo)

SMILEY MAXEDON & HIS OKAW VALLEY BOYS

54	Columbia SCMC 3	Crazy To Care/In The Window Of My Heart (export issue)	18

JOE S. MAXEY

73	Action ACT 4607	Sign Of The Crab/May The Best Man Win (actually plays Packers' "Hole In The Wall"/"Go Ahead On")	8

MAX HEADROOM & CARPARKS

80	Parlophone R 6034	Don't Panic/Rhythm And Bluebeat (p/s)	6

MAX GROUP

69	Fab FAB 110	Abraham Vision/My Heart Was Breaking	5

MAXI

73	Decca F 13394	Do I Dream/Here Today And Gone Tomorrow	8

MAXI, DICK & TWINK

70	Columbia DB 8663	Things You Hear About Me/Catch The Bride's Bouquet	4

(This single does not feature Twink from Pink Fairies.)

MAXIE (Romeo) & GLEN

71	G.G. GG 4520	Jordan River (actually by Max Romeo & Glen Adams)/GLEN ADAMS:Version Two	5

(see also Max Romeo, Ethiopians)

ERNST MAXIM

57	Parlophone R 4319	Four Walls/The Star You Wished Upon Last Night (78)	8

MAXIMILIAN

61	London HLX 9356	The Snake/The Wanderer	35

(see also Del Shannon)

MAXIM'S TRASH

79	Gimp GIMP 1	Disco Girls/Blu Shoes (plastic p/s & inner, hand-stamped white labels)	40

(see also Sunset Boys, Captain Sensible, Johnny Moped)

MAXIMUM BAND

68	Fab FAB 51	Cupid/Hold Me Tight	4

MAXIMUM BOB
92	Total 12THN 1DJ	Sucker (12", promo)	25

MAXIMUM BREED
69	Revolution REV 1	Sitting In The Park/You've Got It	4

ERNEST MAXIN ORCHESTRA
57	Parlophone R 4319	Four Walls/The Star You Wished Upon Last Night	6
60	Top Rank JAR 267	On The Beach/Take A Giant Step	6
60	Top Rank JAR 335	Conspiracy Of Hearts/No Orchids For My Lady	6

MAXINE
70	Smash SMA 2301	My Boy Lollipop/Everybody Needs Love	4

BRIAN MAXINE
72	EMI Starline SRS 5140	BRIAN MAXINE SINGS (LP)	10

(see also Fairport Convention)

MAX Q
89	Mercury MXQ 1	Way Of The World/Zero-2-O (p/s)	4
89	Mercury MXQ 112	Way Of The World (12" Mix)/Zero-2-O (Todd Terry Mix)/ Ghost Of The Year (Todd Terry Mix) (12" p/s)	7
89	Mercury MXQCD 1	Way Of The World (12" Mix)/(7" Mix)/Zero-2-O (Todd Terry Mix)/ Ghost Of The Year (Todd Terry Mix) (CD, card sleeve)	7
90	Mercury MXQP 2	Sometimes (7" Remix)/Love Man (shaped picture disc)	6
90	Mercury MXQ 212	Sometimes (Land Of Oz Mix)/Sometimes (Rock House Edit)/ Sometimes (Instrumental) (12", p/s)	7
90	Mercury MXQCD 2	Sometimes (7" Remix)/Sometimes (Land Of Oz Mix)/Love Man/ Sometimes (Rock House Edit) (CD)	7

(see also INXS)

MAX WEBSTER (BAND)
79	Capitol CLP 16079	Paradise Skies/The Party (picture disc)	5
79	Capitol 12YCL 16079	Paradise Skies/The Party/Let Your Man Fly (12")	10
81	Mercury MER 59	Battlescar/April In Toledo (p/s)	10
78	Capitol EST 11776	MEETING UP MY SLEEVE (LP)	12
79	Capitol EST 11937	A MILLION VACATIONS (LP)	12
80	Mercury 6337 144	UNIVERSAL JUVENILES (LP)	12

(see also Rush)

HOLLY MAXWELL
69	Buddah 201 056	Suffer/No-One Else	6

BILLY MAY & HIS ORCHESTRA
55	Capitol CL 14210	Loop-De-Loop Mambo/Rudolph The Red-Nosed Reindeer Mambo	5
55	Capitol CL 14266	How Important Can It Be?/Let It Happen	5
55	Capitol CL 14353	Hernando's Hideaway/Just Between Friends	5
56	Capitol CL 14551	Main Title From "The Man With The Golden Arm"/Suzette	12
56	Capitol CL 14609	Nightmare/The Beat	10
57	Capitol CL 14713	Whatever Lola Wants/Mad About The Boy	5
56	Capitol EAP 1013	IT'S BILLY MAY TIME (EP)	8
56	Capitol EAP3 677	SWINGING DRUMS (EP)	8
55	Tempo EXA 4	BILLY MAY'S DIXIELAND BAND (EP)	8
53	Capitol LC 6571	CAPITOL PRESENTS BILLY MAY AND HIS ORCHESTRA (10" LP)	12
53	Capitol LC 6623	BIG BAND BASH (10" LP)	12
54	Capitol LC 6644	BACCHANALIA (10" LP)	12
54	Capitol LC 6659	NAUGHTY OPERETTA (10" LP)	12

BRIAN MAY
83	EMI EMI 5436	Starfleet (Single Version)/Son Of Starfleet (p/s)	15
91	Parlophone R 6304	Driven By You (Single Version)/Just One Life (p/s)	5
91	Parlophone RDJ 6304	Driven By You (Edited Version)/(Pollarded Version)/(Special Version)/ (Proper Version) (promo only, no stars on p/s)	75
91	Parlophone 12R 6304	Driven By You (Single Version)/Driven By You (Ford Advert Version)/ Just One Life (Album Version)/Just One Life (Guitar Version) (12", p/s)	8
91	Parlophone CDR 6304	Driven By You (Single Version)/Driven By You (Ford Advert Version)/ Just One Life (Album Version)/Just One Life (Guitar Version) (CD)	10
91	Parlophone CDRDJ 6304	Driven By You (Edited Version)/(Pollarded Version)/(Special Version)/ (Proper Version) (CD, promo only, no stars on p/s)	100
92	Parlophone R 6320	Too Much Love Will Kill You/I'm Scared (Single Version) (p/s)	6
92	Parlophone CDRS 6320	Too Much Love Will Kill You (Album Version)/I'm Scared (Single Version)/ Too Much Love Will Kill You (Guitar Version)/Driven By You (New Version) (CD, red circular gatefold card p/s)	8
92	Parlophone MAYDJ 1	Too Much Love Will Kill You/Resurrection/Last Horizon/Driven By You (CD, promo only "Back To The Light" sampler, blue circular g/fold card p/s)	18
92	Parlophone RDJ 6329	Back To The Light (Radio Version)/Nothin' But Blue (Guitar Version) (promo only, p/s)	55
92	Parlophone CDRX 6329	Back To The Light/Starfleet/Let Me Out (CD)	8
92	Parlophone CDR 6329	Back To The Light/Nothin' But Blue (Guitar Version)/Blues Breaker (CD)	8
92	Parlophone CDRDJ 6329	Back To The Light (Radio Version)/Back To The Light (Album Version)/ Nothin' But Blue (Guitar Version) (CD)	10
93	Parlophone 12RPF 6351	Resurrection/Love Token/Too Much Love Will Kill You (Live Version) (12", with Cozy Powell, picture disc with insert in PVC sleeve)	8
93	Parlophone CDRS 6351	Resurrection/Love Token/Too Much Love Will Kill You (Live Version) (CD)	8
93	Parlophone CDR 6351	Resurrection/Driven By You/Back To The Light (live)/ Tie Your Mother Down (live, with Slash) (CD)	8
93	Parlophone R 6371	Last Horizon/39 (live)/Let Your Heart Rule Your Head (p/s)	5
93	Parlophone CDRS 6371	Last Horizon (Radio Version)/Last Horizon/We Will Rock You (live slow version)/We Will Rock You (live fast version) (CD, pop-up p/s)	8
93	Parlophone HORIZON 1	Last Horizon (CD, 1-track, promo only)	50
83	EMI SFLT 1078061	STARFLEET PROJECT (mini-LP)	15

| 93 | Parlophone 0 7777 80400 19 | BACK TO THE LIGHT (LP, textured sleeve) | 20 |
| 93 | Parlophone CDPCSD X123 | BACK TO THE LIGHT (Commemorative Issue) (gold CD, 10,000 only, stickered jewel case) | 18 |

(see also Queen, MC Spy-D & 'Friends', Eddie Howell, Holly Johnson, Jeffrey Osborne, Bad News, D-Rok, Ian & Belinda, Rock Aid Armenia, Cozy Powell, Black Sabbath)

JOHN MAYALL (& BLUESBREAKERS)
SINGLES

64	Decca F 11900	Crawling Up A Hill/Mr. James (as John Mayall & Blues Breakers)	35
65	Decca F 12120	Crocodile Walk/Blues City Shakedown	30
65	Immediate IM 012	I'm Your Witchdoctor/Telephone Blues	30
66	Purdah 45-3502	Lonely Years/Bernard Jenkins (as John Mayall & Eric Clapton, 500 copies only)	250
66	Decca F 12490	Parchman Farm (solo)/Key To Love (B-side with Bluesbreakers)	20
66	Decca F 12506	Looking Back/So Many Roads (as John Mayall's Bluesbreakers & Peter Green)	12
67	Decca F 12545	Sitting In The Rain/Out Of Reach (as John Mayall's Bluesbreakers)	10
67	Decca F 12588	Curly/Rubber Duck (as Bluesbreakers)	8
67	Decca F 12621	Double Trouble/It Hurts Me Too (as John Mayall's Bluesbreakers)	10
67	Immediate IM 051	I'm Your Witchdoctor/Telephone Blues (reissue, as John Mayall with Eric Clapton)	30
67	Decca F 12684	Suspicions (Parts 1 & 2) (as John Mayall's Bluesbreakers)	8
68	Decca F 12732	Picture On The Wall/Jenny (as John Mayall)	7
68	Decca F 12792	No Reply/She's Too Young (as John Mayall's Bluesbreakers)	7
68	Decca F 12846	The Bear/2401	6
69	Polydor 56544	Don't Waste My Time/Don't Pick A Flower	8
70	Polydor 2066 021	Thinking Of My Woman/Plan Your Revolution	8
79	DJM DJS 10918	Bottom Line/Dreamboat (p/s)	5

EP

| 67 | Decca DFE-R 8673 | THE BLUESBREAKERS WITH PAUL BUTTERFIELD (EP) | 35 |

LPs

65	Decca LK 4680	PLAYS JOHN MAYALL — LIVE AT KLOOKS KLEEK! (LP)	45
66	Decca LK 4804	BLUES BREAKERS WITH ERIC CLAPTON (LP, original label, mono)	40
67	Decca LK/SKL 4853	A HARD ROAD (LP, as John Mayall & Bluesbreakers)	25
67	Decca LK/SKL 4890	CRUSADE (LP, as John Mayall & Bluesbreakers)	25
67	Ace of Clubs ACL/SCL 1243	THE BLUES ALONE (LP)	18
68	Decca LK/SKL 4918	THE DIARY OF A BAND VOL. 1 (LP)	18
68	Decca LK/SKL 4919	THE DIARY OF A BAND VOL. 2 (LP)	18
68	Decca LK/SKL 4945	BARE WIRES (LP, gatefold sleeve, as John Mayall & Blues Breakers)	18
68	Decca LK/SKL 4972	BLUES FROM LAUREL CANYON (LP, gatefold sleeve)	18

(The above LPs were originally issued with unboxed Decca label logos. 1970s boxed-logo repressings are worth two-thirds these values.)

69	Polydor 583 571	THE TURNING POINT (LP)	18
69	Decca LK/SKL 5010	LOOKING BACK (LP)	18
69	Decca SKL 4804	BLUES BREAKERS WITH ERIC CLAPTON (LP, reissue, original label, stereo)	35
70s	Decca LK/SKL 4804	BLUES BREAKERS WITH ERIC CLAPTON (LP, reissue, boxed logo, mono/stereo)	18/15
70	Decca (S)PA 47	THE WORLD OF JOHN MAYALL (LP)	12
70	Polydor 583 580	EMPTY ROOMS (LP)	15
70	Polydor 2425 020	U.S.A. UNION (LP)	12
71	Decca SPA 138	THE WORLD OF JOHN MAYALL VOL. 2 (LP)	12
71	Polydor 2657 005	BACK TO THE ROOTS (2-LP)	18
71	Polydor 2483 016	BEYOND THE TURNING POINT (LP)	15
71	Decca SKL 5086	THRU THE YEARS (LP)	12
71	Polydor 2425 085	MEMORIES (LP)	12
72	Polydor 2425 103	JAZZ-BLUES FUSION (LP)	12
73	Polydor 2391 047	MOVING ON (LP)	12
75	ABC ABCL 5115	NEW YEAR, NEW BAND, NEW COMPANY (LP, gatefold sleeve)	12
76	Polydor 2482 272	JOHN MAYALL (LP)	12

(see also Paul Butterfield, Eric Clapton, Jack Bruce, Peter Green, McGuinness Flint, Johnny Almond Music Machine, Alan Skidmore, Mick Taylor, Dick Heckstall-Smith, Keef Hartley, Paul Williams, Ray Warleigh, Colosseum, Henry Lowther, Jon Mark, Aynsley Dunbar, Fleetwood Mac)

MAY BLITZ

| 70 | Vertigo 6360 007 | MAY BLITZ (LP, gatefold sleeve, spiral label) | 30 |
| 71 | Vertigo 6360 037 | THE 2ND OF MAY (LP, gatefold sleeve, spiral label) | 60 |

(see also Bakerloo)

MAYDAY

| 80 | Reddingtons R.R. DAN 2 | Day After Day/Love In The Spaceage (p/s) | 10 |

JOHN MAYER (GROUP)

66	Columbia DB 8037	Acka Raga (as John Mayer's I-J-7)/Gana (as John Mayer & Joe Harriott)	7
60s	National Petrol W 1	"Music For People Who Go Your Own Way" Themes 1 & 2 (p/s, with Frank Cordell)	10
67	Columbia SX 6122	INDO-JAZZ FUSIONS (LP)	35
69	Sonet SNTF 603	ETUDES (LP, as John Mayer Indo-Jazz Fusions)	20

(see also Joe Harriott & John Mayer, Radha Krishna)

NATHANIEL MAYER & FABULOUS TWILIGHTS

| 62 | HMV POP 1041 | Village Of Love/I Want A Woman | 30 |

CURTIS MAYFIELD

70	Buddah 2011 055	(Don't Worry) If There's A Hell Below We're All Going To Go (Edit)/The Makings Of You	5
71	Buddah 2011 080	Move On Up/Give It Up/Beautiful Brother Of Mine (maxi-single)	5
71	Buddah 2011 101	We Got To Have Peace/People Get Ready	5
72	Buddah 2011 119	Keep On Keepin' On/Stone Junkie	5
72	Buddah 2011 141	Freddie's Dead (Theme From "Superfly")/Underground	5

MINT VALUE £

72	Buddah 2011 156	Superfly/Give Me Your Love (Love Song)	5
73	Buddah 2011 187	Back To The World (edit)/The Other Side Of Town	5
74	Buddah BDS 402	Kung Fu/Right On For The Darkness	5
74	Buddah BDS 410	Move On Up/Give It Up	5
75	Buddah BDS 426	Mother's Son/Love Me Right In The Pocket	5
71	Buddah 2318 015	CURTIS (LP, gatefold sleeve)	18
71	Buddah 2659 004	CURTIS/LIVE (2-LP)	18
72	Buddah 2318 045	ROOTS (LP, gatefold sleeve)	15
72	Buddah 2318 065	SUPERFLY (LP, soundtrack, gatefold sleeve)	12
74	Buddah BDLP 4018	SUPERFLY (LP, soundtrack, reissue)	10
73	Buddah 2318 085	BACK TO THE WORLD (LP, gatefold sleeve)	12
73	Buddah 2318 091	CURTIS IN CHICAGO (LP, TV soundtrack, gatefold sleeve, with Impressions, Jerry Butler, Gene Chandler & Leroy Hutson)	12
74	Buddah 2318 099	SWEET EXORCIST (LP)	15
74	Buddah BDLP 2001	CURTIS/LIVE (2-LP, reissue)	15
74	Buddah BDLP 4010	CLAUDINE (LP, soundtrack, with Gladys Knight)	12
74	Buddah BDLH 5001	SWEET EXORCIST (LP, reissue)	12
74	Buddah BDLH 5005	CURTIS (LP, reissue)	12
74	Buddah BDLH 5006	ROOTS (LP, reissue)	12
74	Buddah BDLP 4015	MOVE ON UP (THE BEST OF CURTIS MAYFIELD) (LP)	12
74	Buddah BDLP 4029	GOT TO FIND A WAY (LP)	12
75	Buddah BDLP 4033	THERE'S NO PLACE LIKE AMERICA TODAY (LP)	12
76	Buddah BDLP 4042	GIVE GET TAKE AND HAVE (LP)	12

(see also Impressions, Blow Monkeys)

PERCY MAYFIELD
63	HMV POP 1185	The River's Invitation/Baby Please	7
76	Speciality SPE 5007	Please Send Me Someone To Love/The River's Invitation	5
67	HMV CLP/CSD 3572	MY JUG AND I (LP)	20

MAYFIELD'S MULE
69	Parlophone R 5817	Double Dealing Woman/(Drinking My) Moonshine (some in p/s)	25/12
70	Parlophone R 5843	I See A River/"Queen" Of Rock'n'Roll	18
70	Parlophone R 5858	We Go Rollin'/My Way Of Living	12

(see also Elastic Band, Sweet, Amen Corner, Andy Scott)

MAYHEM
82	Riot City RIOT 13	GENTLE MURDER (EP)	4
83	Riot City RIOT 24	PULLING PUPPET STRINGS (EP)	4

MAYHEM
85	Vigilante VIG 1	Bloodrush/Addictive Risk (p/s)	6
85	Vigilante VIG 1T	Bloodrush/Addictive Risk (12", p/s)	10

BILL MAYNARD
57	Decca F 10868	Hey Liley, Liley Lo/Who Needs You	7
57	Decca F 10868	Hey Liley, Liley Lo/Who Needs You (78)	15

WILSON MAYNELL
67	CBM	Mean Ole World (p/s)	10

(TOOTS &) MAYTALS
63	Blue Beat BB 176	Hallelujah/Helping Ages Past	15
64	Blue Beat BB 215	He Is Real/Domino	15
64	Blue Beat BB 220	Pain In My Belly/BUSTER'S ALL STARS: City Riot	15
64	Blue Beat BB 231	Dog War/RECO & CREATORS: I'll Be Home	20
64	Blue Beat BB 245	Little Slea (song actually "Little Flea")/Don't Talk (song actually "Pain In My Belly") (both sides miscredited as V. Maytals)	15
64	Blue Beat BB 254	Sweet Love/PRINCE BUSTER: Wings Of A Dove	15
64	Blue Beat BB 255	Judgement Day/Goodbye Jane	15
64	Blue Beat BB 270	You've Got Me Spinning/Lovely Walking	15
64	R&B JB 130	Hurry Up/Love Divide	12
64	R&B JB 141	Another Chance/FRANKIE ANDERSON: Always On A Sunday	12
64	R&B JB 153	Give Me Your Love/He Will Provide	12
64	R&B JB 164	Hello Honey/ROLAND ALPHONSO: Crime Wave	25
64	R&B JB 174	Christmas Feelings/Let's Kiss	12
65	Blue Beat BB 281	Looking Down The Street/PRINCE BUSTER: Blues Market	15
65	Blue Beat BB 299	Light Of The World/Lovely Walking	20
65	Blue Beat BB 306	Ska War (song actually "Treating Me Bad")/SKATALITES: Perhaps	20
65	Ska Beat JB 202	Let's Jump/Joy And Jean	15
65	Island WI 200	Never You Change/What's On Your Mind	18
65	Island WI 213	My New Name/It's No Use	18
65	Black Swan WI 464	John James/THEO BECKFORD: Sailing On	18
66	Doctor Bird DB 1019	If You Act This Way/SIR LORD COMIC & HIS COWBOYS: Ska-ing West	30
66	Doctor Bird DB 1038	Bam Bam/So Mad In Love	15
68	Pyramid PYR 6030	54-46, That's My Number/ROLAND ALPHONSO: Dreamland	20
68	Pyramid PYR 6043	Struggle/ROLAND ALPHONSO: Stream Of Life	12
68	Pyramid PYR 6048	Just Tell Me/Reborn	10
68	Pyramid PYR 6050	Bim Today, Bam Tomorrow/Hold On	10
68	Pyramid PYR 6052	We Shall Overcome/DESMOND DEKKER & ACES: Fu Manchu	15
68	Pyramid PYR 6055	Schooldays/Big Man	10
68	Pyramid PYR 6057	Do The Reggay/BEVERLEY'S ALLSTARS: Motoring	15
68	Pyramid PYR 6064	Scare Him/In My Heart	10
69	Pyramid PYR 6066	Don't Trouble Trouble/BEVERLEY'S ALLSTARS: Double Action	10
69	Pyramid PYR 6070	Aldina/Hold On	12
69	Pyramid PYR 6073	Pressure Drop/BEVERLEY'S ALLSTARS: Express	8
69	Pyramid PYR 6074	Sweet And Dandy/Oh Yeah	8
69	Trojan TR 7709	Pressure Drop/BEVERLEY'S ALLSTARS: Smoke Screen	7
69	Nu Beat NB 031	My Testimony/JOHNSON BOYS: One Dollar Of Soul (actually by Ethiopians)	6
70	Trojan TR 7711	Monkey Man/Night And Day	15

MINT VALUE £

70	Trojan TR 7726	Sweet And Dandy/54-46, That's My Number	7
70	Trojan TR 7741	Bla Bla Bla/Reborn	6
70	Trojan TR 7757	Water Melon/She's My Scorcher	6
70	Trojan TR 7786	Doctor Lester/Sun, Moon And Star	6
70	Summit SUM 8510	Peeping Tom/BEVERLEY'S ALLSTARS: Version	6
71	Trojan TR 7808	54-46 Was My Number/BEVERLEY'S ALLSTARS: 54-46 Instrumental	6
71	Trojan TR 7849	Johnny Cool Man/BEVERLEY's ALLSTARS: Version	5
71	Summit SUM 8513	Monkey Girl/BEVERLEY'S ALLSTARS: Version	6
71	Summit SUM 8520	One Eye Enos/BEVERLEY'S ALLSTARS: Enos Version	6
71	Summit SUM 8527	It's You/BEVERLEY'S ALLSTARS: Version	6
71	Summit SUM 8529	Walk With Love/BEVERLEY'S ALLSTARS: Version	6
71	Summit SUM 8533	Never You Change/BEVERLEY'S ALLSTARS: Version	6
72	Attack ATT 8042	It Was Written Down/Sweet And Dandy	5
72	Summit SUM 8536	Thy Kingdom Come/BEVERLEY'S ALLSTARS: Version	6
72	Summit SUM 8537	It Must Be True Love/BEVERLEY'S ALLSTARS: Version	6
72	Blue Mountain BM 1020	Christmas Song/I Can't Believe	6
72	Dynamic DYN 438	Redemption Song	6
72	Trojan TR 7865	Louie Louie/Pressure Drop '72	4
73	Dragon DRA 1007	Sit Right Down/Screwface Underground/Pomps & Pride (as Toots & Maytals)	5
73	Dragon DRA 1013	Funky Kingston/Country Road (as Toots & Maytals)	5
73	Dragon DRA 1016	In The Dark/Sailing On (as Toots & Maytals)	5
74	Dragon DRA 1021	Fever/It Was Written Down	5
74	Dragon DRA 1024	Time Tough/Time Tough Version	5
74	Dragon DRA 1026	Sailing On/If You Act This Way (as Toots & Maytals)	5
64	Ska Beat JBL 1113	PRESENTING THE MAYTALS (NEVER GROW OLD) (LP)	100
66	Doctor Bird DLM 5003	THE SENSATIONAL MAYTALS (LP)	100
70	Trojan TBL 107	MONKEY MAN (LP)	20
73	Trojan TRLS 65	FROM THE ROOTS (LP)	15
73	Dragon DRLS 5002	FUNKY KINGSTON (LP)	12
74	Dragon DRLS 5004	IN THE DARK (LP)	12
74	Prince Buster PB 11	ORIGINAL GOLDEN OLDIES VOLUME 3 (LP)	18

(see also Vikings, Flames, Philip James & Blues Busters, Don Drummond, Stranger, Lord Creator, Larry Marshall, Derrick Morgan, Brentwood Road Allstars, Roland Alphonso, Charmers)

MAYTONES

68	Blue Cat BS 149	Billy Goat/Call You Up	10
69	Blue Cat BS 152	Loving Reggae/Musical Beat	10
69	Blue Cat BS 166	Copper Girl/Love	10
69	Blue Cat BS 173	We Nah Tek You Lick/Dig Away De Money	10
69	Camel CA 27	Sentimental Reason/Lover Girl	6
69	Songbird SB 1009	I've Been Loving You/Memphis Reggae	8
69	Songbird SB 1010	Gin Gan Goolie/I'm Thirsty	6
70	Punch PH 35	Serious Love/CHARLIE ACE: Musical Combination	6
70	Explosion EX 2012	Funny Man/G.G. ALLSTARS: Champion	7
70	Explosion EX 2013	Sentimental Reason/Lover Girl	5
70	Explosion EX 2014	Barrabus/G.G. ALLSTARS: Barrabus Part 2 (B-side actually "This Kind Of Life")	8
70	Explosion EX 2027	Cecelia (actually by Keeling Beckford)/Chariot Without Horse (B-side actually "Willie My Darling")	5
70	Explosion EX 2033	Another Festival/Happy Time	5
70	Bullet BU 446	I Don't Like To Interfere/Preaching Love	5
70	Camel CA 47	Black And White/GLORIA'S ALLSTARS: Jumbo Jet	7
70	Camel CA 49	Since You Left/GLORIA'S ALL STARS: Bird Wing	6
71	Duke DU 116	Babylon A Fall/TONY KING: Version Buggy	7
71	Camel CA 61	Judas (actually by Gladstone Anderson & Followers)/Mi Nah Tek	6
71	G.G. GG 4508	Cleanliness/G.G. ALL STARS: Cleanliness Version 2	7
71	G.G. GG 4511	Let The Version Play/Lonely Nights	7
71	G.G. GG 4522	Black And White/TREVOR BROWN: Mr. Brown	6
71	G.G. GG 4525	Bongo Man Rise/ROY & BIM: Remember	6
72	G.G. GG 4530	Donkey Face/G.G. ALL STARS: Donkey Face – Version	6
72	G.G. GG 4531	As Long As You Love Me (Side One)/As Long As You Love Me (Side Two)	10
72	Attack ATT 8029	Hands And Feet/LLOYD & CAREY: Scorpion	6
72	Grape GR 3028	If Loving You Was Wrong/FLOWERS & ALVIN: In De Pum Pum	6
72	Pama PM 846	I'm Feeling Lonely/G.G. ALLSTARS: Version	6
72	Explosion EX 2076	Brown Girl/SHORTY PERRY: Half-Way-Tree Rock	6
73	Pama PM 871	All Over The World People Are Changing/Changing World (Dubwise)	6
73	Bread BR 1114	All Over The World People Are Changing/Changing World (Dubwise)	5
73	Bullet BU 528	People Get Funny/G.G. ALL STARS: Version	6

(see also Vern & Alvin, Vern & Son, Roland Alphonso, G.G. Rhythm Section, Cynthia Richards, Max Romeo, Charlie Ace, Dennis Alcapone)

MAZE (U.K.)

66	Reaction 591 009	Hello Stranger/Telephone	75
67	MGM MGM 1368	Catari Catari/Easy Street	30

(see also M.I. Five, Deep Purple)

MAZE (U.S.)

82	Capitol 12CL 211	Joy And Pain/Happy (12")	7
82	Capitol 12CL 244	Before I Let Go/Golden Time Of Day (12")	7
77	Capitol E-ST 11607	MAZE FEATURING FRANKIE BEVERLY (LP)	10

MAZZY STAR

93	R. T. Singles Club 45 rev 19	Five String Serenade/Under My Car (p/s)	10
90	Rough Trade ROUGH 158	SHE HANGS BRIGHTLY (LP)	12

JACKIE McAULEY

71	Dawn DNS 1011	Turning Green/It's Alright	6
72	Dawn DNS 1020	Rocking Shoes/One Fine Day	6
71	Dawn DNLS 3023	JACKIE McAULEY (LP)	40

(see also Them, Belfast Gypsies, Trader Horne, Freaks Of Nature)

McAULEY SCHENKER GROUP

90	EMI EMPD 127	Anytime/What We Need/Anytime (Edit) (12", picture disc)	7
90	EMI Electrola CDEM 127	Anytime (LP Version)/What We Need/Anytime (Single Edit) (CD)	8
89	EMI CDP 518941	SAVE YOURSELF SPECIMEN DISC (CD, promo, interviews/album excerpts)	18

(see also Michael Schenker, Michael Schenker Group)

GERRY McAVOY

79	Bridgehouse BHS 004	Street Talk/Many Rivers To Cross (p/s)	10

JIMMY McBEATH

67	Topic 12T 173	WILD ROVER NO MORE (LP, blue label with booklet)	12

NICKO McBRAIN

91	EMI NICKO 1	Rhythm Of The Beast/Beehive Boogie (p/s)	5
91	EMI NICKOPD 1	Rhythm Of The Beast/McBrain Damage Interview (shaped picture disc with insert & plinth)	8

(see also Iron Maiden, Pat Travers)

FRANKIE McBRIDE

67	Emerald MD 1081	Five Little Fingers/Do You Mind If You Leave Me Sleeping	5

DAN McCAFFERTY

75	Mountain TOP 1	Out Of Time/Cinnamon Girl	5
75	Mountain TOP 5	Watcha Gonna Do About It/Nightingale	5
75	Mountain DAN 1	Stay With Me Baby/Out Of Time/Watcha Gonna Do About It (p/s)	7
76	Mountain TOP 18	The Honky Tonk Downstairs/Trouble	4
79	Mountain TOP 47	Watcha Gonna Do About It/Boots Of Spanish Leather	4
75	Mountain TOPS 102	DAN McCAFFERTY (LP, with inner sleeve)	12

(see also Nazareth, Sensational Alex Harvey Band, Mitchell/Coe Mysteries, Roger Glover)

JERRY McCAIN

69	Python 02	Homogenised Love/728 Texas (99 copies only)	35

CASH McCALL

63	Ember EMB S 173	Anytime/From The Very First Rose	10
65	Ember EMB S 204	Many Are The Words (I've Left Unspoken)/Buenos Noches	10

CASH McCALL

67	Chess CRS 8056	It's Wonderful (To Be In Love)/Let's Try It Over	10

DARRELL McCALL

61	Capitol CL 15196	My Kind Of Lovin'/Beyond Imagination	6
63	Philips 304 002 BF	Dear One/I've Been Known	5
63	Philips BF 1259	Hud/No Place To Hide	5

TOUSSAINT McCALL

67	Pye International 7N 25420	Nothing Takes The Place Of You/Shimmy	12
72	Mojo 2092 035	Nothing Takes The Place Of You/Shimmy (reissue)	5

NOEL McCALLA

80	Direction 58-8731	Beggin'/Ain't That Peculiar/One More Heartache/Shake Me, Wake Me	4

DAVID McCALLUM

66	Capitol CL 15439	Communication/My Carousel	5
66	Capitol CL 15474	In The Garden/The House On Breckenridge Lane	5
66	Capitol (S)T 2432	MUSIC ... A PART OF ME (LP)	15
66	Capitol (S)T 2498	MUSIC ... A BIT MORE OF ME (LP)	15

McCALMANS

68	One Up OU 2161	McCALMANS' FOLK (LP)	12

JIM McCANN

72	Polydor 2489 053	McCANNED! (LP)	25

(see also Ludlows)

LES McCANN (LTD)

60	Vogue V 2417	Fish This Week/Vakushna (as Les McCann Ltd)	5
67	Mercury MF 973	All/Bucket O'Grease	8
69	Atlantic 584 284	With These Hands/Burnin' Coal	5
60	Vogue LAE 12238	THE TRUTH (LP)	12
69	Atlantic 588 176	MUCH LES (LP)	12
60s	Fontana 688 150ZL	THE WAILERS! (with Gerald Wilson Orchestra)	12

McCARTHY

86	Wall Of Salmon MAC 001	In Purgatory/The Comrade Era/Something Wrong Somewhere (foldover p/s in poly bag, white labels)	20
86	Pink PINKY 12	Red Sleeping Beauty/From The Damned (p/s)	5
86	Pink PINKY 12T	Red Sleeping Beauty/The Comrade Era/From The Damned/ For The Fat Lady (12", p/s with foldover insert)	8
87	Pink PINKY 17	Frans Hals/The Fall (p/s)	5
87	Pink PINKY 17T	Frans Hals/The Fall (Remix)/Kill Kill Kill Kill/Frans Hals (Version) (12", p/s)	8
87	September SEPT 1	The Well Of Loneliness/Antiamericancretin/Unfortunately (p/s)	4
87	September SEPT 1T	The Well Of Loneliness/Bad Dreams/Someone Worse Off/ Antiamericancretin/Unfortunately (12", p/s)	7

(see also Stereolab)

KEITH McCARTHY

67	Coxsone CS 7014	Everybody Rude Now/BASES: Beware	18

LYN & GRAHAM McCARTHY

65	Columbia DB 7584	Seven Doves/Out After Ale	6
66	Columbia DB 7921	I Can't Help But Wonder/There's Got To Be Love	6
66	Columbia DB 8087	The Turkey's Trial/Bitter Withy	6
68	Columbia DB 8422	I Think It's Going To Rain/Once I Was	7
68	RCA RCA 1759	Scarborough Fair — Canticle/Wild Berries	5

Mary McCARTHY

MINT VALUE £

MARY McCARTHY
| 67 | CBS 2832 | The Folk I Love/You Know He Did | 6 |
| 67 | CBS 2987 | Happy Days And Lonely Night/Easy Kind Of Love | 5 |

CECIL McCARTNEY
68	Columbia DB 8474	Hey Aleuthia I Want You/Liquid Blue	8
69	Columbia DB 8595	Orange And Green/Cloudy	6
68	Columbia S(C)X 6283	OM (LP)	20

LINDA McCARTNEY
(see under Suzy & The Red Stripes)

PAUL McCARTNEY/WINGS
SINGLES
71	Apple R 5889	Another Day/Oh Woman, Oh Why	5
71	Apple R 5914	The Back Seat Of My Car/Heart Of The Country (as Paul & Linda McCartney)	5
72	Apple R 5932	Love Is Strange/I Am Your Singer (unreleased)	
72	Apple R 5936	Give Ireland Back To The Irish/(Version) (as Wings, yellow 'Wings' die-cut sl.)	5
73	Apple R 5985	My Love/The Mess (as McCartney's Wings, later as Paul McCartney/Wings)	20/5
78	Parlophone R 6020	I've Had Enough/Deliver Your Children (p/s, as Wings)	6
80	Parlophone 12R 6039	Temporary Secretary/Secret Friend (12", p/s)	30
82	Parlophone R 6054	Ebony And Ivory/Rainclouds (unreleased sepia-toned 'studio photo' p/s; beware of clever counterfeits)	50
82	Parlophone 12R 6054	Ebony And Ivory/Rainclouds (12", unreleased sepia-toned 'studio photo' 12" p/s; beware of clever counterfeits)	125
82	Epic A 11-2729	The Girl Is Mine (with Michael Jackson)/MICHAEL JACKSON: Can't Get Outta The Rain (picture disc)	20
84	Parlophone 12RP 6080	No More Lonely Nights (Extended Version)/Silly Love Songs/No More Lonely Nights (Ballad) (12", picture disc)	8
84	Parlophone RP 6086	We All Stand Together/We All Stand Together (Humming Version) (with Frog Chorus, shaped picture disc, some in printed PVC sleeve)	10/8
85	Parlophone RP 6118	Spies Like Us/My Carnival (shaped picture disc)	12
85	Parlophone 12RP 6118	Spies Like Us (Party Mix)/Spies Like Us (Alternative Mix)/Spies Like Us (DJ Version)/My Carnival (Party Mix) (12", picture disc)	8
86	Parlophone 10R 6133	Press/It's Not True/Press (Video Edit) (10", circular foldout p/s)	10
87	Parlophone TCR 6145	Pretty Little Head/Write Away (cassette)	5
86	Parlophone R 6148/R 6018	Only Love Remains/Tough On A Tightrope//Mull Of Kintyre/Girls' School (p/s, stickered double pack in PVC sleeve, no p/s on R 6018)	7
87	Parlophone CDR 6170	Once Upon A Long Ago/Back On My Feet/Don't Get Around Much Anymore/Kansas City (CD, card sleeve with anti-static inner)	15
87	A&M FREE 21	Long Tall Sally (live)/I Saw Her Standing There (live) (p/s, free with "The Prince's Trust 10th Anniversary Birthday Party" LP [AMA 3906])	6
89	Parlophone RX 6223	This One/The Long And Winding Road (p/s, envelope pack with 6 postcards)	5

PROMO SINGLES
74	EMI R 5997	Band On The Run (Edited Version)/(Full Version) (demo)	50
74	Apple R 5999	Junior's Farm (Edited Version)/Junior's Farm (Full Version) (demo)	40
75	Apple R 5999	Sally G/Junior's Farm (reversed sides, demo)	90
76	Parlophone R 6014	Silly Love Songs (Edited Version)/Silly Love Songs (Full Version) (demo)	30
76	Parlophone R 6015	Let 'Em In (Edited Version)/Let 'Em In (Full Version) (demo)	30
77	Capitol R 6018	Mull Of Kintyre (Edited Version)/Girls' School (Edited Version) (demo)	30
77	MPL Publishing MPL 1	We've Moved! (music publishing sampler with excerpts by Wings, Peggy Lee, Gene Vincent, Frank Sinatra, etc.; some with press pack & insert)	250/200
78	Parlophone R 6019	With A Little Luck (Edited Version)/Backwards Traveller-Cuff Link (demo)	30
80	Parlophone R 6037DJ	Waterfalls (3.22) (edit)/Check My Machine (demo)	30
80	Parlophone R 6039	Temporary Secretary (1-sided demo, no p/s)	50
84	Parlophone 12RDJ 6080T	No More Lonely Nights (Mole Mix) (12", 1-sided, plain white numbered sleeve with plain white inner sleeve & insert, 250 only; beware of counterfeits with scratched [not stamped] matrix)	200
85	Parlophone RDJ 6118	Spies Like Us (DJ Version 3.46)/My Carnival (demo, white printed die-cut sleeve)	25
89	Parl. 12R LOVE 6223	This One (Lovejoy's Remix) (12", 1-sided, plain label, black die-cut sleeve)	35
89	Parlophone GOOD 1	Good Sign (6.51)/Good Sign (Groove Mix) (7.22) (12", black die-cut sleeve)	45
89	Parlophone RDJ 6235	Figure Of Eight (Edited Version 3.59)/Ou Est Le Soleil? (Edited Version 3.57) (demo, standard p/s)	25
89	Parlophone RDJ 6238	Party (Remix By Bruce Forest)/Party (different remix) (12", some copies listed as 'Party Party', some with insert)	45/35
90	Parlophone 12 SOL 1	Où Est Le Soleil? (Tub Dub Mix)/Où Est Le Soleil? (Instrumental Mix) (12", black die-cut stickered sleeve, some with insert)	35/20
93	Parlophone 12 DELIVDJ 1	Deliverance/Deliverance (Dub Mix) (12", green label, plain black die-cut sleeve)	20
93	Parlophone CDRDJ 6338	C'mon People (Radio Edit)/C'mon People (CD)	20
93	Parlophone R 6347	Biker Like An Icon/Things We Said Today (unissued)	
93	Parlophone TCR 6347	Biker Like An Icon/Things We Said Today (cassette, unissued)	
93	Parlophone CDRS 6347	Biker Like An Icon/Things We Said Today/Mean Woman Blues/Midnight Special (CD, unissued)	
93	Parlophone CDRDJ 6347	Biker Like An Icon/Things We Said Today/Mean Woman Blues/Midnight Special (CD, no inlay, jewel case with large sticker; beware of counterfeits with thicker, blurred label print & small sticker on case)	40
93	Parlophone PM LIVE 1	PAUL IS LIVE! (CD, 5-track sampler)	25
99	Parlophone PROMO WC	WORKING CLASSICAL (CD, 4-track sampler, gatefold card sleeve, promo only)	25
99	EMI RDR 004	RUN DEVIL RUN (CD, 2-track sampler, card sleeve, promo only)	15

ALBUM
| 70 | Apple TA/TD-PCS 7102 | McCARTNEY (reel-to-reel tape, jewel case, mono/stereo) | 100/50 |

856   Rare Record Price Guide 2002

PROMO ALBUMS

79	Parlophone PCTCP 257	BACK TO THE EGG (LP, as Wings, MPL in-house picture disc; die-cut sleeve, matrix numbers YEX 987-2 & YEX 988-4 or -1; beware counterfeits)	750
79	Parlophone PCTC 257	BACK TO THE EGG (LP, box set with badge, booklet, sticker, postcard & 5 cigarette cards; with or without T-shirt; beware of counterfeits with blurred printing)	250/200
79	Capitol (no cat. no.)	MPL PRESENTS (6-LP, box set, hand-numbered, 25 only)	650
88	Parlophone PMBOX 11-19	ALL THE BEST! ('Special Edition') (9 x 7" box set, in black die-cut sleeves, with signed 7" print; some with genuine signatures)	200/75
93	Parlophone CDPMCOLDJ 1	PAUL McCARTNEY COLLECTION (CD, 18-track sampler)	25

(see also Beatles, Country Hams, Percy 'Thrills' Thrillington, Fireman, Mike McGear, Suzy & The Red Stripes, George Martin, Spirit Of Play, Ferry Aid, Michael Jackson)

TOMMY McCLENNAN

75	Flyright LP 112	TRAVELIN' HIGHWAY MAN (LP)	15

DELBERT McCLINTON

62	Decca F 11541	Hully Gully/Baby Heartbreak	8

BOBBY McCLURE

(see under Bobby McLure)

CHRIS McCLURE (SECTION)

66	Decca F 12346	The Dying Swan/The Land Of The Golden Tree	7
68	Polydor 56227	Hazy People/I'm Just A Country Boy	10
68	Polydor 56259	Answer To Everything/Meditation	5
69	RCA RCA 1849	Our Song Of Love/Weather Vane	5
69	CBS 7646	You're Only Passing Time/Sing Our Song (as Chris McClure Section)	5

(see also Marmalade)

McCLUSKY BROTHERS

88	DDT DISP 15T	She Said To The Driver/Upstreet Downfall/Silent Journey (12", p/s)	7

(see also Bluebells)

BRIAN McCOLLOM FOLK GROUP

66	Pye 7N 17198	This Dusty Road/Henry Joy McCraken	5

TOMMY McCOOK (& SUPERSONICS)

63	Island WI 102	Adam's Apple/MAYTALS: Every Time (B-side actually by Tonettes)	20
63	Island WI 118	Below Zero/LEE PERRY: Never Get Weary	25
63	Island WI 124	Junior Jive/HORACE SEATON: Power	18
64	R&B JB 139	Sampson/ROY & ANNETTE: My Arms Are Waiting	25
64	R&B JB 163	Bridge View/NAOMI & CO: What Can I Do (B-side actually by Naomi & Clive)	25
64	Port-O-Jam PJ 4001	Exodus (& His Group)/LEE PERRY: Help The Weak	25
64	Port-O-Jam PJ 4003	Jam Rock/LEE PERRY: Band Minded People	25
64	Port-O-Jam PJ 4010	Road Bloack/LEE PERRY: Chatty Chatty Woman	25
64	Black Swan WI 422	Two For One/LASCELLES PERKINS: I Don't Know	20
65	Island WI 232	Rocket Ship/JUSTIN HINDS & DOMINOES: Turn Them Back	20
66	Rio R 100	Jerk Time (with Supersonics)/UNIQUES: The Journey	12
66	Rio R 101	Out Of Space (with Supersonics)/UNIQUES: Do Me Good	12
66	Rio R 103	Ska Jam/Smooth Sailing (with Supersonics)	12
66	Rio R 104	Riverton City/HEPTONES: Gunmen Coming To Town	35
66	Doctor Bird DB 1028	More Love/SILVERTONES: True Confession	18
66	Doctor Bird DB 1032	Naked City (with Supersonics)/NORMA FRASER: Heartaches	15
66	Doctor Bird DB 1047	Spanish Eyes (with Lynn Taitt)/STRANGER & HORTENSE: Loving Wine	15
66	Doctor Bird DB 1051	A Little Bit Of Heaven (& His Band)/LLOYD WILLIAMS: Sad World	15
66	Doctor Bird DB 1053	Indian Love Call (with Supersonics)/OWEN & LEON: How Would You Feel	15
66	Doctor Bird DB 1056	Danger Man (with Supersonics)/ERIC MORRIS: If I Didn't Love You	15
66	Doctor Bird DB 1061	What Now/Don't Stay Away	15
67	Doctor Bird DB 1058	Jam Session (with Supersonics)/LLOYD & GLEN: Jezebel	15
67	Island WI 3047	One Two Three Kick/TREASURE ISLE BOYS: What A Fool (B-side actually by Silvertones)	50
67	Island WI 3049	Saboo (with Supersonics)/MOVING BROTHERS: Darling I Love You	18
67	Treasure Isle TI 7017	Persian Cat/JUSTIN HINDS: Once A Man	12
67	Treasure Isle TI 7018	Saboo (with Supersonics)/MOVING BROTHERS: Darling I Love You (reissue)	15
67	Treasure Isle TI 7020	Shadow Of Your Smile/SILVERTONES: Cool Down	15
68	Treasure Isle TI 7027	Soul For Sale/SILVERTONES: In The Midnight Hour	12
68	Treasure Isle TI 7032	Venus/Music Is My Occupation (with Supersonics)	12
68	Treasure Isle TI 7039	Our Man Flint (with Supersonics)/SILVERTONES: Old Man River	12
68	Treasure Isle TI 7042	Moving (with Supersonics)/SILVERTONES: Slow And Easy	12
68	Doctor Bird DB 1135	Mad Mad World/Wonderful World (with Lloyd Williams)	15
68	Unity UN 501	Last Flight To Reggie (Reggae) City (with Stranger Cole)/Watch Dem Go	6
69	Trojan TR 642	Breaking Up/Party Time (with Supersonics) (both actually by Alton Ellis)	7
69	Trojan TR 652	Third Figure/You Should've Known Better	8
69	Trojan TR 657	When The Saints Go Marching In/SOUL OFROUS: Ease Me Up Officer (B-side actually by Righteous Flames)	8
69	Trojan TR 671	Moonshot/PHYLLIS DILLON: The Right Shot	10
69	Trojan TR 686	Tribute To Rameses/PHYLLIS DILLON: Lipstick On Your Collar	8
69	Trojan TR 7706	Black Coffee (with Supersonics)/VIC TAYLOR: Heartaches	8
69	Unity UN 506	The Avengers/LAUREL AITKEN: Donkey Man	8
69	Unity UN 534	Dream Boat/Tommy's Dream	8
69	Unity UN 535	Peanut Vendor/100,000 Tons Of Rock	8
70	Duke DU 76	The Rooster (with Supersonics) (actually by Jeff Barnes)/PHYLLIS DILLON: Walk Through This World	8
70	Duke DU 77	Open Jaw (with Supersonics)/JOHN HOLT: The Working Kind	8
70	Duke DU 78	Key To The City (with Supersonics)/DOROTHY REID: Give It To Me	8
71	Treasure Isle TI 7058	My Best Dress/PHYLISS DILLON: One Life To Live	10
71	Treasure Isle TI 7061	Testify Version/JOHN HOLT: Let's Build Our Dreams	12
71	Treasure Isle TI 7065	Black River/JOHN HOLT: Sister Big Stuff	12

Tommy McCOOK

71	Treasure Isle TI 7066	Paragon's Medley Version/JOHN HOLT: Paragon's Medley.	12
71	Treasure Isle TI 7070	Midnight Confession Version/PHYLLIS DILLON: Midnight Confession	10
71	Big Shot BI 585	Psalm Nine To Keep In Mind (with Observers)/Psalm Nine (Version).	8
71	Spinning Wheel SW 109	Crying Everynight (with Supersonics) (actually by Stranger Cole)/	
		HERMAN MARQUIS: Tom's Version	20
71	Spinning Wheel SW 110	Stupid Doctor (with Supersonics)/ROB WALKER: Grooving In Style	
		(B-side actually by Ken Parker)	18
73	Technique TE 927	Rub It Down/Rub It Down (Version) (as Tommy McCook Stars)	6
73	G.G. GG 4539	Bad Cow Skank (with Bobby Ellis)/	
		GLADSTONE ANDERSON: Drummer Roach.	5
70	Trojan TBL 111	GREATER JAMAICA (MOONWALK REGGAE) (LP, actually by various artists)	20

(see also Paragons, Alton Ellis, Herman, Karl Walker & Allstars, Denis Alcapone, Millions, Dave Barker, Dennis Brown, Heptones, Chuck & Joe White, Shenley Duffas, Dennis & Lizzy, Ethiopians, Eagles, Dynamics, Alton Ellis, Emotions, Dobby Dobson, Melodians, Mellodities, Jamaicans, Hopeton Lewis, Lloyd & Glen, Lloyd & Groovers, Bob Marley, Maytals, Millions, Hugh Roy)

JASON McCORD
65	Pye 7N 15925	It Was A Very Good Year/Song Of The Pine Tree	15

JOHN McCORMACK & EDWARD SCHNEIDER
60	HMV 7P 276	Believe Me If All Those Endearing/O Mary Dear	5

GEORGE McCORMICK
55	MGM SPC 6	Don't Fix Up The Doghouse/Gold Wedding Band (export issue)	12

McCORMICK BROTHERS
63	Polydor NH 66986	Red Hen Boogie/Blue Grass Express	45
66	Hickory LPE 1509	AUTHENTIC BLUEGRASS HITS (EP).	20

BUDD McCOY
58	RCA RCA 1106	Hiawatha/The Midnight Ride Of Paul Revere	7
58	RCA RCA 1106	Hiawatha/The Midnight Ride Of Paul Revere (78)	25

CLYDE McCOY
57	Mercury MEP 9513	DANCING TO THE BLUES (EP)	15

JOE McCOY
59	Collector JDL 81	One In A Hundred/One More Greasing	25

(JOHN) McCOY
83	Legacy LGY 9	Oh Well! (Edit)/Because You Lied (p/s)	5
83	Legacy LLM 109	MINI ALBUM (mini-LP)	10
84	Mausoleum SKULL 8373	THINK HARD (LP, with inner sleeve)	12

(see also Gillan, Samson, Mammoth, Zzebra, Split Knee Loons)

VIOLA McCOY
50s	Ristic LP 27	VIOLA McCOY 1923-1927 (10" LP).	50

McCOYS
65	Immediate IM 001	Hang On Sloopy/I Can't Explain It.	6
65	Immediate IM 021	Fever/Sorrow	6
66	Immediate IM 028	Don't Worry Mother, Your Son's Heart Is Pure/Ko-Ko	7
66	Immediate IM 029	Up And Down/If You Tell A Lie	7
66	Immediate IM 034	Runaway/Come On Let's Go	7
66	Immediate IM 037	(You Make Me Feel) So Good/Every Day I Have To Cry	6
67	Immediate IM 046	I Got To Go Back/Dynamite	10
67	London HLZ 10154	Say Those Magic Words/I Wonder If She Remembers Me.	18
68	Mercury MF 1067	Jesse Brady/Resurrection	6
69	Immediate IM 076	Hang On Sloopy/This Is Where We Came In	5
66	Immediate IMEP 002	HITS VOL. 1 (EP).	35
66	Immediate IMEP 003	HITS VOL. 2 (EP).	35
65	Immediate IMLP 001	HANG ON SLOOPY (LP)	40
68	Mercury (S)MCL 20128	THE INFINITE McCOYS (LP).	18
71	Joy JOYS 196	HANG ON SLOOPY (LP, reissue)	12

JIMMY McCRACKLIN
58	London HLM 8598	The Walk/I'm To Blame (as Jimmy McCracklin & His Band)	35
58	London HLM 8598	The Walk/I'm To Blame (as Jimmy McCracklin & His Band) (78)	25
58	London HL 7035	The Walk/I'm To Blame (export issue, as Jimmy McCracklin & His Band)	25
62	Top Rank JAR 617	Just Got To Know/The Drag.	15
65	R&B MRB 5001	I Got Eyes For You/I'm Gonna Tell Your Mother.	20
66	Outasite 45 120	Christmas Time (Parts 1 & 2) (99 copies only)	40
65	Liberty LIB 66094	Every Night, Every Day/Can't Raise Me	8
66	Liberty LIB 66129	Think/Steppin' Up In Class	8
68	Minit MLF 11003	How Do You Like Your Love/Get Together	8
68	Minit MLF 11009	Pretty Little Sweet Thing/A And I.	8
65	Vocalion VEP 170160	JIMMY McCRACKLIN (EP).	100
68	Minit MLL/MLS 40003	A PIECE OF JIMMY McCRACKLIN (LP).	20

GWEN McCRAE
74	President PT 416	It's Worth The Hurt/90% Of Me Is You	6
82	Atlantic FLAM 1	Keep The Fire Burning/Funky Sensation.	5
82	Atlantic FLAM 1T	Keep The Fire Burning/Funky Sensation (12")	8
75	President	GWEN McCRAE (LP)	12

GWEN & GEORGE McCRAE
75	President PTLS 1070	TOGETHER (LP).	10

DANNY McCULLOCH
69	Capitol CL 15607	Blackbird/Time Of Man.	5
70	Pye Intl./Festival 7N 25514	Colour Of The Sunset/Smokeless Zone	5
69	Capitol E-(S)T 174	WINGS OF A MAN (LP)	12

(see also Animals)

IAN McCULLOCH
64	Decca F11855	Come On Home/Down By The River	10

IAN McCULLOCH
84	Korowa KOW 40	September Song/Cockles & Mussels (p/s)	5
84	Korowa KOW 40L	September Song/Cockles & Mussels (10", A-side plays at 78rpm)	8
89	WEA YZ 417B	Proud To Fall/Pots Of Gold (box set, with lyric sheet & photos)	4
89	WEA YZ 417CD	Proud To Fall/Pots Of Gold/The Dead End/Proud To Fall (Long Night's Journey Mix) (3" CD, gatefold card sleeve)	7
89	WEA YZ 436CD	Faith And Healing (Remix)/Toad/Fear Of The Known/Rocket Ship (3" CD, gatefold card sleeve)	7

(see also Echo & Bunnymen)

HENRY McCULLOUGH
75	Dark Horse AMLH 22005	MIND YOUR OWN BUSINESS! (LP, some with inner sleeve)	15/12

(see also Grease Band, Eire Apparent, Paul McCartney & Wings)

GEORGE McCURN
63	London HLH 9705	I'm Just A Country Boy/In My Little Corner Of The World	10

LUKE McDANIEL
55	Parlophone CMSP 29	The Automobile Song/I Can't Steal Another's Bride (export issue)	30
55	Parlophone DP 407	The Automobile Song/I Can't Steal Another's Bride (78)	10

MAISIE McDANIEL
61	Beltona BE 2744	Christmastime In Ireland/The Old Pigsty	5
63	Fontana TF 400	Something Special/This Song Is Just For You	5
63	Fontana TE 17397	MEET MAISIE McDANIEL! (EP, with The Hunters)	12
63	Fontana TE 17398	COUNTRY STYLE (EP, with The Hunters)	10

(see also Hunters)

EUGENE McDANIELS
71	Atlantic 2465 022	OUTLAW (LP)	20

GENE McDANIELS
61	London HLG 9319	A Hundred Pounds Of Clay/Take A Chance On Love	10
61	London HLG 9396	A Tear/She's Come Back	10
61	London HLG 9448	Tower Of Strength/Secret	10
62	Liberty LIB 55405	Chip Chip/Another Tear Falls	7
62	Liberty LIB 55480	Point Of No Return/Warmer Than A Whisper	10
63	Liberty LIB 55510	Spanish Lace/Somebody's Waiting	6
63	Liberty LIB 55541	The Puzzle/Cry Baby Cry	6
63	Liberty LIB 55597	It's A Lonely Town/False Friends	15
63	Liberty LIB 10130	Anyone Else/New Love In Old Mexico	6
64	Liberty LIB 55723	In Times Like These/Make Me A Present Of You	10
65	Liberty LIB 55752	(There Goes The) Forgotten Man	12
65	Liberty LIB 55805	Walk With A Winner/A Miracle	60
61	London REG 1298	GENE McDANIELS (EP)	50
62	Liberty LEP 2054	A CHANGE OF MOOD (EP)	40
61	London HA-G 2384	A HUNDRED POUNDS OF CLAY (LP, also stereo SAH-G 6184)	50/65
62	Liberty LBY 1003	... SOMETIMES I'M HAPPY (LP)	35
62	Liberty LBY 1021	TOWER OF STRENGTH (LP)	35
63	Liberty (S)LBY 1128	SPANISH LACE (LP)	35
68	Sunset SLS 50017E	FACTS OF LIFE (LP)	15

BILL McDAVID
61	Starlite ST45 63	Kiss Me For Christmas/Little Shepherd Boy	7

CHAS McDEVITT (SKIFFLE GROUP)
57	Oriole CB 1352	Freight Train (with Nancy Whiskey)/The Cotton Song	15
57	Oriole CB 1352	Freight Train (with Nancy Whiskey)/The Cotton Song (78)	8
57	Oriole CB 1357	It Takes A Worried Man/The House Of The Rising Sun	15
57	Oriole CB 1357	It Takes A Worried Man/The House Of The Rising Sun (78)	10
57	Oriole CB 1371	Green Back Dollar (with Nancy Whiskey)/I'm Satisfied	15
57	Oriole CB 1371	Green Back Dollar (with Nancy Whiskey)/I'm Satisfied (78)	8
57	Oriole CB 1386	Face In The Rain (with Nancy Whiskey)/Sporting Life (with Tony Kohn)	12
57	Oriole CB 1386	Face In The Rain (with Nancy Whiskey)/Sporting Life (with Tony Kohn) (78)	10
57	Oriole CB 1395	Sing, Sing, Sing/My Old Man	12
57	Oriole CB 1395	Sing, Sing, Sing/My Old Man (78)	15
58	Oriole CB 1403	Johnny-O (with Nancy Whiskey)/Bad Man Stack-O-Lee	12
58	Oriole CB 1403	Johnny-O (with Nancy Whiskey)/Bad Man Stack-O-Lee (78)	12
58	Oriole CB 1405	Across The Bridge (with Shirley Douglas)/Deep Down	12
58	Oriole CB 1405	Across The Bridge (with Shirley Douglas)/Deep Down (78)	15
58	Oriole CB 1457	Real Love (with Shirley Douglas)/Juke-Box Jumble	12
58	Oriole CB 1457	Real Love (with Shirley Douglas)/Juke-Box Jumble (78)	20
59	Oriole CB 1511	Teenage Letter (with Shirley Douglas)/SHIRLEY DOUGLAS: Sad Little Girl	10
59	Oriole CB 1511	Teenage Letter/SHIRLEY DOUGLAS: Sad Little Girl (78)	25
60	Top Rank JAR 338	Dream Talk/Forever (with Shirley Douglas)	7
61	HMV POP 845	One Love/Can It Be Love (with Shirley Douglas)	6
61	HMV POP 928	Mommy Out De Light/I've Got A Thing About You (with Shirley Douglas)	5
62	HMV POP 999	Happy Family/Throwing Pebbles In A Pool (with Shirley Douglas)	5
65	Columbia DB 7595	The Most Of What Is Least/Don't Blame Me (with Shirley Douglas)	5
68	Fontana TF 957	City Smoke/One Man Band	5
57	Oriole EP 7002	CHAS AND NANCY (EP, with Nancy Whiskey)	25
57	Oriole MG 10018	THE INTOXICATING MISS WHISKEY (10" LP, with Nancy Whiskey)	50

(see also Nancy Whiskey, Cranes Skiffle Group, Coffee Bar Skifflers)

ALISTAIR McDONALD
69	Major Minor MMLP 51	BATTLE BALLADS (LP)	12

GAVIN McDONALD
72	Regal Zono. SLRZ 1027	LINES (LP)	15

(COUNTRY) JOE McDONALD

71	Vanguard 6076 252	Hold On It's Coming (Parts 1 & 2)	5
70	Vanguard (S)VRL 19057	THINKING OF WOODY GUTHRIE (LP)	15
71	Vanguard 6359 004	TONIGHT I'M SINGING JUST FOR YOU (LP)	12
71	Sonet SNTF 622	QUIET DAYS IN CLICHY (LP, soundtrack)	15
71	Vanguard VSD 79314	HOLD ON — IT'S COMING (LP)	12
71	Vanguard VSD 79315	WAR WAR WAR (LP)	12
72	Vanguard VSD 79316	INCREDIBLE! LIVE! (LP)	12
73	Vanguard VSD 79328	PARIS SESSIONS (LP)	12

(see also Country Joe & Fish)

LARRY McDONALD & DENZIL LAING

71	Clandisc CLA 228	Name Of The Game/FABULOUS FLAMES: Holly Version	6

RITCHIE McDONALD & GLEN BROWN

72	Duke DU 141	Boat To Progress/Boat To Progress — Version	8

SHELAGH McDONALD

70	B&C CAS 1019	THE SHELAGH McDONALD ALBUM (LP)	20
71	B&C CAS 1043	STAR GAZER (LP, with inner sleeve)	20

SKEETS McDONALD

56	Capitol CL 14566	Fallen Angel/It'll Take Me A Long, Long Time	25
56	Capitol CL 14566	Fallen Angel/It'll Take Me A Long, Long Time (78)	20
59	Capitol EAP1 1040	GOING STEADY WITH THE BLUES (EP)	50

TESFA McDONALD

72	Dynamic DYN 455	Life Is The Highest/Recarnate (Re-Incarnate) (actually by Bobby Ellis and Tommy McCook)	15

McDONALD & GILES

70	Island ILPS 9126	McDONALD AND GILES (LP, 1st pressing, pink label, with 'i' logo)	25
70	Island ILPS 9126	McDONALD AND GILES (LP, 2nd pressing, 'pink rim' label, 'palm tree' logo)	12
70	Polydor 2302 070	McDONALD AND GILES (LP)	15

(see also King Crimson; Giles, Giles & Fripp)

ROSE McDOWALL

88	Rio Digital 7RDS 3	Don't Fear The Reaper/Crystal Days (p/s)	5
88	Rio Digital 12RDS 3	Don't Fear The Reaper/Crystal Days (12", p/s)	8

(see also Strawberry Switchblade, Ornamental, Psychic TV, Current 93, Death In June)

(MISSISSIPPI) FRED McDOWELL

66	Bounty BY 6022	MY HOME IS IN THE DELTA (LP)	18
66	Fontana 688 806 ZL	MISSISSIPPI DELTA BLUES (LP)	18
69	CBS 63735	LONG WAY FROM HOME (LP)	18
69	Polydor 236 278	GOING DOWN SOUTH (LP)	18
70	Capitol E-ST 409	I DO NOT PLAY NO ROCK & ROLL (LP)	18
70	Transatlantic TRA 194	LONDON 1 (LP)	15
71	Transatlantic TRA 203	LONDON 2 (LP)	15
71	Revival RVS 1001	EIGHT YEARS RAMBLIN' (LP, with Johnny Woods)	15
73	Black Lion 2460 193	MISSISSIPPI DELTA BLUES (LP)	12
74	Xtra XTRA 1136	MISSISSIPPI FRED McDOWELL 1904-1972 (LP)	15

PAUL McDOWELL

62	Fontana 267228 TF	Frankie/Be A Man	6

(BROTHER) JACK McDUFF

64	Stateside SS 275	Sanctified Samba/Whistle While You Work	8
64	Stateside SS 302	Rock Candy/Real Good 'Un	8
64	Stateside SS 328	Carpetbaggers (Main Theme)/The Pink Panther (Theme)	8
66	Atlantic 584 036	Down In The Valley/A Change Is Gonna Come	6
64	Stateside SL 10060	BROTHER JACK McDUFF LIVE! (LP)	18
64	Stateside SL 10101	THE DYNAMIC JACK McDUFF (LP, as Brother Jack McDuff Quartet)	18
65	Stateside SL 10121	BROTHER JACK McDUFF QUARTET LIVE! AT THE JAZZ WORKSHOP (LP)	18
65	Stateside SL 10142	PRELUDE (LP)	18
66	Stateside SL 10165	THE CONCERT McDUFF (LP)	15
66	Atlantic 587 030	A CHANGE IS GONNA COME (LP)	18
67	Transatlantic PR 7404	SILK AND SOUL (LP)	18
67	Transatlantic PR 7476	WALK ON BY (LP)	18
68	Transatlantic	DYNAMIC JACK McDUFF (LP)	18
69	Blue Note BST 84322	DOWN HOME STYLE (LP)	15
70s	Blue Note BST 84334	MOON RAPPIN' (LP)	12
70s	Blue Note BST 84348	TO SEEK A NEW HOME (LP)	12
70s	Blue Note BST 84353	WHO KNOWS WHAT TOMORROW'S (LP)	12
72	York FYK 407	IF THE CAP FITS ... WEAR IT (LP, as Jack McDuff Band)	12
72	Prestige PR 24013	ROCK CANDY (LP)	12

(see also Roland Kirk, Kenny Burrell, Jimmy Witherspoon)

McENROE & CASH With The FULL METAL RACKETS

91	M. For Nations KUT 141	Rock'N'Roll (7" Version)/(Instrumental) (p/s)	5
91	M. For Nations 12KUT 141	Rock'N'Roll (Dance Mix)/(7" Version)/(Instrumental) (12", p/s)	10

(see also Iron Maiden, Roger Daltrey)

JOHNNY McEVOY

73	Hawk HALPX 112	JOHNNY McEVOY (LP)	15
74	Hawk HALPX 117	SOUNDS LIKE JOHNNY McEVOY (LP)	20

(see also Rambler)

BOB McFADDEN & DOR

59	Coral Q 72378	The Mummy/The Beat Generation	15
59	Coral Q 72378	The Mummy/The Beat Generation (78)	15

(see also Rod McKuen)

MC5

69	Elektra EKSN 45056	Kick Out The Jams/Motor City Is Burning.................................	20
69	Elektra EKSN 45067	Ramblin' Rose/Borderline.......................................	15
69	Elek. EKL 4042/EKS 74042	KICK OUT THE JAMS	
		(LP, red label, gatefold sleeve, mono/stereo)........................	50/40
70	Atlantic 2400 016	BACK IN THE U.S.A. (LP)......................................	20
71	Atlantic 2400 135	HIGH TIME (LP)...	18
71	Atlantic K 40223	HIGH TIME (LP, reissue)......................................	12

(see also Wayne Kramer, Destroy All Monsters, Rob Tyner & Hot Rods)

MIKE McGEAR

72	Island WIP 6131	Woman/Kill...	6
74	Warner Bros K 16446	Leave It/Sweet Baby (p/s)......................................	8
75	Warner Bros K 16520	Sea Breezes/Givin' Grease A Ride................................	5
75	Warner Bros K 16573	Dance The Do/Norton..	6
75	Warner Bros K 16658	Simply Love You/What Do We Really Know (p/s).....................	10
76	EMI EMI 2485	Doing Nothing All Day/A To Z...................................	5
80	Carrere CAR 144	All The Whales In The Ocean/I Juz What You Got — Money!	
		(some in p/s)..	25/12
81	Conn SRTS/81/CUS 1112	No Lardidar/God Save The Gracious Queen........................	30
72	Island ILPS 9191	WOMAN (LP)..	15
74	Warner Bros K 56051	*McGEAR (LP, gatefold sleeve with insert).........................	15
74	Warner Bros KMG 1	McGEAR'S LIMITED EDITION	
		(7-track white label sampler & press kit)...........................	35
80s	Centre Labs	*McGEAR (LP, 6-track reissue, 500 only, numbered & signed).........	30

(see also Grimms, Scaffold, McGough & McGear, Paul McCartney)

FRANCINE McGEE

| 78 | RCA PC 9126 | Delirium/Feelin' Good (12")..................................... | 10 |

PAT McGEEGAN

| 68 | Emerald MD 1096 | Chance Of A Lifetime/Don't Laugh At Me (If I Cry).................. | 7 |

BROWNIE McGHEE

51	Melodisc 1127	Secret Mojo Blues/Me And My Dog (78)............................	25
63	Columbia SEG 8226	BLUES ON PARADE NO. 1 (EP).................................	25
60s	Xtra 1021	BROWNIE McGHEE (LP).......................................	20
78	Magpie PY 1805	LET'S HAVE A BALL (LP)......................................	10

BROWNIE McGHEE & DAVE LEE

| 57 | Pye Jazz NJE 1060 | THE BLUEST (EP).. | 15 |

(see also Sonny Terry & Brownie McGhee)

(Roger) McGOUGH & (Mike) McGEAR

68	Parlophone PMC/PCS 7047	McGOUGH AND McGEAR (LP, with phasing on "So Much";	
		beware of counterfeits)..	225
89	Parlophone PCS 7332	McGOUGH AND McGEAR (LP, stereo reissue with inner sleeve,	
		without phasing on "So Much").................................	15
89	Parlophone CDP 7 91877-2	McGOUGH AND McGEAR (CD, without phasing on "So Much").......	25

(see also Scaffold, Adrian Henri, Mike McGear, Jimi Hendrix, Grimms)

ROGER McGOUGH & BRIAN PATTEN

| 75 | Argo ZPL 1190 | READ THEIR OWN VERSE — BRITISH POETS OF OUR TIME (LP)........... | 15 |

CHRIS McGREGOR('S BROTHERHOOD OF BREATH)

68	Polydor 184 137	VERY URGENT (LP, as Chris McGregor Group).....................	45
68	Polydor 583 072	UP TO EARTH (LP, unreleased, test pressings only).................	150+
70	RCA Neon NE 2	CHRIS McGREGOR'S BROTHERHOOD OF BREATH	
		(LP, gatefold sleeve)..	40
72	RCA SF 8260	BROTHERHOOD (LP, gatefold sleeve,	
		as Chris McGregor's Brotherhood Of Breath).....................	35
74	Ogun OG 100	LIVE, WILLISAU (LP)...	12
77	Ogun OG 521	IN HIS OWN TIME (LP).......................................	18
78	Ogun OG 524	PROCESSION (LP)...	12

(see also Brotherhood Of Breath, Tunji)

FREDDIE McGREGOR

| 73 | Fab FAB 261 | Wise Words/NEW ESTABLISHMENT: Version....................... | 12 |

(see also Soul Brothers, Young Freddie)

EDNA McGRIFF

| 60s | Gala 45XP 1014 | EDNA McGRIFF'S THE NAME (EP)................................ | 20 |

JIMMY McGRIFF

64	Sue WI 303	All About My Girl/M.G. Blues...................................	25
64	Sue WI 310	Last Minute (Parts 1 & 2)......................................	20
64	Sue WI 317	I've Got A Woman (Parts 1 & 2).................................	20
64	Sue WI 333	'Round Midnight/Lonely Avenue.................................	20
66	United Artists UP 1170	See See Rider/Hallelujah......................................	7
70	United Artists UP 35025	The Worm/What's That...	8
64	Sue ILP 907	I'VE GOT A WOMAN (LP)......................................	60
64	Sue ILP 908	GOSPEL TIME (LP)...	60
65	London HA-C 8247	BLUES FOR MISTER JIMMY (LP)...............................	40
66	London HA-C 8242	AT THE APOLLO (LP)...	40
66	United Artists (S)ULP 1158	A BAG FULL OF SOUL (LP)....................................	20
68	United Artists (S)ULP 1170	THE BIG BAND (LP)...	20
69	Solid State USS 7012	I'VE GOT A NEW WOMAN (LP).................................	12
72	Groove Merchant GM 503	GROOVE GREASE (LP).......................................	15
73	Groove Merchant GM 2205	GOOD THINGS DON'T HAPPEN EVERY DAY (LP, with Junior Parker)....	12
74	People PLEO 14	FLY DUDE (LP)..	15
74	People PLEO 19	LET'S STAY TOGETHER (LP)....................................	15

Bill McGUFFIE

BILL McGUFFIE (TRIO)

53	Parlophone MSP 6040	Concerto For Boogie/Begin The Beguine (as Bill McGuffie Trio) 7
59	Philips PB 922	Elmer's Tune/Simple Simon (78) 8
67	Philips BF 1550	Fugue For Thought (from the film 'Dalek Invasion Of Earth 2150AD')/
		Fair's Fair 35
55	Philips BBR 8054	JAZZ WITH McGUFFIE (LP) 15
56	Philips BBR 8087	McGUFFIE MAGIC (LP) 35
56	Philips BBL 7072	MORE JAZZ WITH McGUFFIE (LP) 40
58	Philips BBL 7261	CONTINENTAL TOUR (LP) 40
61	Philips BBL 7450	PLAYING FOR PLEASURE (LP) 15
68	Philips LPS 16001	LATIN OVERTONES (LP) 30
71	Rediffusion ZS 48	AN ALTO AND SOME BRASS (LP). 25
72	Rediffusion ZS 130	BILL McGUFFIE BIG BAND (LP) 25

ROGER McGUINN

74	CBS 2649	Peace On You/Without You. 6
77	CBS 5231	American Girl/Russian Hill 6
73	CBS 65214	ROGER McGUINN (LP). 12
74	CBS 81071	PEACE ON YOU (LP) 12
75	CBS 80877	ROGER McGUINN AND BAND (LP) 12
76	CBS 81369	CARDIFF ROSE (LP) 12

(see also Byrds)

McGUINNESS FLINT

70	Capitol CL 15662	When I'm Dead And Gone/Lazy Afternoon 5
71	Capitol CL 15682	Malt And Barley Blues/Rock On 5
70	Capitol EA-ST 22625	McGUINNESS FLINT (LP, gatefold sleeve) 15
71	Capitol ST 22794	HAPPY BIRTHDAY, RUTHY BABY (LP) 15
73	Bronze ILPS 9244	RAINBOW (LP, gatefold sleeve with inner) 12
74	Bronze ILPS 9302	C'EST LA VIE (LP, with inner sleeve). 12

(see also Manfred Mann, Blues Band, John Mayall, Coulson Dean McGuinness Flint, Gallagher & Lyle, Paladin, Lyle McGuinness Band)

BARRY McGUIRE

65	Ember EMB S 208	So Long Stay Well/Far Side Of The Hill 7
65	Ember EMB S 224	Greenback Dollar/One By One. 7
65	RCA Victor RCA 1469	Eve Of Destruction/What Exactly Is The Matter With Me 6
65	RCA Victor RCA 1493	Child Of Our Times/Upon A Painted Ocean 6
66	RCA Victor RCA 1497	This Precious Time/Don't You Wonder Where It's At 6
66	RCA Victor RCA 1508	Walking My Cat Named Dog/I'd Have To Be Outta My Mind 6
66	RCA Victor RCA 1525	Cloudy Summer Afternoon/You've Got To Hide Your Love Away
		(B-side with Mamas & Papas) 15
67	RCA Victor RCA 1638	Masters Of War/Why Not Stop And Dig It While You Can 7
65	Envoy VOY 9153	HERE AND NOW (LP, with New Christy Minstrels) 15
65	RCA Victor RD 7751	SINGS EVE OF DESTRUCTION (LP) 25
66	Ember EMB 3362	THE EVE OF DESTRUCTION MAN (LP, with New Christy Minstrels) 18
71	A&M AMLS 2008	BARRY McGUIRE AND THE DOCTOR (LP, with Eric Hord). 15
70s	Sparrow BIRD 105	C'MON ALONG (LP) 20
70s	Sparrow BIRD 111	HAVE YOU HEARD? (LP) 20

(see also Mamas & Papas, New Christy Minstrels)

McGUIRE SISTERS

54	Vogue Coral Q 2028	Lonesome Polecat/Muskrat Ramble 12
55	Vogue Coral Q 72050	Sincerely/No More 20
55	Vogue Coral Q 72052	Melody Of Love/Open Up Your Heart 10
55	Vogue Coral Q 72082	Something's Gotta Give/It May Sound Silly 10
55	Vogue Coral Q 72108	Christmas Alphabet/He 15
56	Vogue Coral Q 72117	Young And Foolish/Doesn't Anybody Love Me?. 10
56	Vogue Coral Q 72145	Missing/Be Good To Me (Baby, Baby) 10
56	Vogue Coral Q 72161	Delilah Jones/Picnic. 15
56	Vogue Coral Q 72188	Weary Blues/In The Alps 10
56	Vogue Coral Q 72201	My Baby's Got Such Lovin' Ways/Endless 10
56	Vogue Coral Q 72209	Tip Toe Through The Tulips With Me/Do You Remember When?. 10
56	Vogue Coral Q 72216	Goodnight My Love, Pleasant Dreams/Mommy 10
57	Vogue Coral Q 72238	Heart/Sometimes I'm Happy 10
57	Vogue Coral Q 72249	Kid Stuff/Without Him 10
57	Vogue Coral Q 72265	Rock Bottom/Beginning To Miss You. 10
57	Vogue Coral Q 72265	Rock Bottom/Beginning To Miss You (78) 10
57	Vogue Coral Q 72272	He's Got Time/Interlude 8
57	Vogue Coral Q 72296	Forgive Me/Kiss Them For Me 8
58	Coral Q 72305	Sugartime/Banana Split. 6
58	Coral Q 72305	Sugartime/Banana Split (78) 8
58	Coral Q 72327	Ding Dong/Since You Went Away To School 6
58	Coral Q 72327	Ding Dong/Since You Went Away To School (78) 8
58	Coral Q 72334	Volare/Do You Love Me Like You Kiss Me? 5
58	Coral Q 72334	Volare/Do You Love Me Like You Kiss Me? (78) 8
59	Coral Q 72356	May You Always/Achoo-Cha-Cha. 5
59	Coral Q 72356	May You Always/Achoo-Cha-Cha (78) 8
59	Coral Q 72370	Summer Dreams/Peace (withdrawn) 10
59	Coral Q 72370	Summer Dreams/Peace (78, withdrawn) 12
59	Coral Q 72379	Red River Valley/Compromise 5
59	Coral Q 72379	Red River Valley/Compromise (78) 8
60	Coral Q 72387	Lovers' Lullaby/Livin' Dangerously 5
60	Coral Q 72399	"The Unforgiven" Theme (The Need For Love)/I Give Thanks 6
60	Coral Q 72406	Nine O'Clock/The Last Dance 5
60	Coral Q 72415	I Don't Know Why/To Be Loved 5
61	Coral Q 72427	Really Neat/Just For Old Time's Sake 6
61	Coral Q 72435	Will There Be Space In The Spaceship/Tears On My Pillow 5

MINT VALUE £

61	Coral Q 72441	Just Because/I Do, I Do, I Do	5
62	Coral Q 72446	I Can Dream, Can't I/Old Devil Moon	5
62	Coral Q 72452	Sugartime Twist/More Hearts Are Broken That Way	5
64	Reprise R 20338	I'll Walk Alone/Ticket To Anywhere	5
58	Coral FEP 2001	THE McGUIRE SISTERS (EP)	15
58	Coral FEP 2006	VOLARE (EP)	15
59	Coral FEP 2033	MAY YOU ALWAYS (EP)	15
56	Vogue Coral LVA 9024	DO YOU REMEMBER WHEN? (LP)	18
57	Vogue Coral LVA 9072	CHILDREN'S HOLIDAY (LP)	18
58	Coral LVA 9073	TEENAGE PARTY (LP)	18
58	Coral LVA 9082	WHILE THE LIGHTS ARE LOW (LP)	18
59	Coral LVA 9115	MAY YOU ALWAYS (LP)	20
60	Coral LVA 9133	GOLDEN FAVORITES (LP)	18
61	Coral LVA 9140	HIS AND HERS (LP)	20

JIM McHARG'S SCOTSVILLE JAZZ BAND

| 62 | Pye Jazz 7NJ 2053 | Forgotten Dreams/St Thomas | 6 |
| 62 | Pye Jazz 7NJ 2055 | Look For A Sky Of Blue/Once In A Blue Moon | 6 |

JOHN McHUGH

| 65 | Columbia SCD 2245 | When The Stars/Strange Harmony | 4 |
| 65 | Columbia SCD 2252 | Goldsmith Of Toledo Serenade/O Vision Entrancing | 4 |

FREDDIE McKAY

71	Banana BA 348	Picture On The Wall/SOUND DIMENSION: Version	10
71	Banana BA 358	Sweet You, Sour You/High School Dance	8
71	Moodisc HM 110	Old Joe/Too Much Fire	6
72	Banana BA 370	Drunken Sailor/SOUND DIMENSION: Version	8
73	Bullet BU 525	Go On This Way/SANTIC ALL STARS: Santic Dub	5
73	Dragon DRA 1012	Our Rendezvous/Black Beauty	18
73	Grape GR 3060	Our Rendezvous/SOUL DYMAMITES: Version	8
74	Dragon DRA 1022	Dream My Life Over/YOUTH STARS: Version	5
71	Banana BALPS 01	PICTURE ON THE WALL (LP)	40
73	Attack ATLP 1013	PICTURE ON THE WALL (LP, reissue)	20
74	Dragon DRLS 5005	LONELY MAN (LP)	12

(see also Lizzy)

SCOTT McKAY

| 67 | Columbia DB 8147 | I Can't Make Your Way/Take A Giant Step | 25 |

SCOTTY McKAY

| 64 | London HLU 9885 | Cold Cold Heart/What You Wanna | 7 |

TONY McKAY

| 66 | Polydor BM 56513 | Nobody's Perfect/Detroit | 6 |

LONETTE McKEE

| 75 | Sussex SXX 4 | Save It/Do It To Me | 4 |

KENNETH McKELLAR

| 66 | Decca F 12341 | A Man Without Love/As Long As The Sun Shines | 6 |
| 66 | Decca DFE 8645 | SONGS FOR EUROPE (EP) | 8 |

McKENDREE SPRING

69	MCA MUPS 277	McKENDREE SPRING (LP)	12
71	MCA MUPS 433	SECOND THOUGHTS (LP)	12
72	MCA MUPS 454	THREE (LP)	12
73	MCA MUPS 476	TRACKS (LP)	12
75	Dawn DNLS 3067	GET ME TO THE COUNTRY (LP)	12

MAE McKENNA

| 75 | Transatlantic TRA 297 | MAE McKENNA (LP) | 12 |

(see also Contraband)

VAL McKENNA

65	Piccadilly 7N 35237	Baby Do It/I Believe In Love	8
65	Piccadilly 7N 35256	Mixed Up Shook Up Girl/Now That You've Made Up Your Mind	10
66	Piccadilly 7N 35286	I Can't Believe What You Say/Don't Hesitate	8
69	Spark SRL 1005	House For Sale/I'll Be Satisfied	7
69	Spark SRL 1023	It's All In My Imagination/Sweet Sweet Lovin'	6
70	Spark SRL 1038	Love Feeling/It's All In My Imagination	5

McKENNA MENDELSON MAINLINE

69	Liberty LBF 15235	You Better Watch Out/She's Alright	6
69	Liberty LBF 15276	Don't Give Me No Goose For Christmas/Beltmaker	5
69	Liberty LBS 83251	STINK (LP)	35

MARLENE McKENZIE

| 68 | Double D DD 106 | Left Me For Another/BOBBY AITKEN & CARIBBEATS: Cell Block Eleven | 8 |

SCOTT McKENZIE

67	CBS 2816	San Francisco (Be Sure To Wear Some Flowers In Your Hair)/	
		What's The Difference	6
67	Capitol CL 15509	Look In Your Eyes/All I Want Is You	6
67	CBS 3009	Like An Old-Time Movie/What's The Difference Chapter II	6
68	CBS 3393	Holy Man/What's The Difference (Chapter 3)	6
73	CBS 1168	San Francisco (Be Sure To Wear Some Flowers In Your Hair)/	
		Reason To Believe ("Hall Of Fame Hits" series, p/s)	5
67	CBS (S)BPG 63157	THE VOICE OF SCOTT McKENZIE (LP)	18

(see also Mamas & Papas)

TOMMY McKENZIE

| 68 | Pama PM 720 | Fiddlesticks/Please Stay | 10 |
| 71 | Pama Supreme PS 327 | Eastern Promise/Fiddlesticks (as Tommy McKenzie Orchestra) | 6 |

McKENZIE, DOUG & BOB
82 Mercury HOSER 1   Take Off/Elron McKenzie (p/s) 20
(see also Rush)

McKINLEYS
64 Columbia DB 7230   Someone Cares For Me/Million Miles Away 15
64 Columbia DB 7310   When He Comes Along/Then I'll Know It's Love. 10
64 Parlophone R 5211   Sweet And Tender Romance/That Lonely Feeling 12
65 Columbia DB 7583   Give Him My Love/Once More 15

ROD McKUEN
57 London HLU 8390   Happy Is A Boy Named Me/Jaydee 35
60 Brunswick 05828   Two Brothers/Time After Time 12
64 Capitol CL 15348   The World I Used To Know/Someplace Green. 5
66 Ember EMB 223   Soldiers Who Want To Be Heroes/Wayfarin' Stranger 5
68 RCA Victor RCA 1734 Cat Named Sloopy/Where Are We Now 5
71 Buena Vista DF 482 Pastures Green/Theme From Scandalous John/Train To Quivira (p/s) 5
67 RCA Victor RD 7897 THROUGH EUROPEAN WINDOWS (LP) 12
69 Warner Bros   LONESOME CITIES (LP) 15
69 Stateside (S)SL 10264 JOANNA (LP, soundtrack, with Mike Sarne) 15
69 Stateside (S)SL 10278 THE PRIME OF MISS JEAN BRODIE (LP, soundtrack, with Mike Redway) . . . 15
69 Warner Bros WS 1705 THE EARTH (LP) 12
70 Warner Bros WS 1720 THE SKY (LP) 12
70 Warner Bros WS 1764 HOME TO THE SEA (LP). 12
70 Warner Bros WS 1837 NEW BALLADS (LP). 12
71 Warner Bros WS 3015 THE ROD McKUEN SHOW (LP) 12
71 CBS 70078   THE BOY NAMED CHARLIE BROWN (LP, soundtrack). 15
(see also Bob McFadden & Dor, Mike Redway, Mike Sarne, Henri Mancini)

HAL McKUSICK SEXTET/QUINTET
57 Vogue Coral Q 72258 Kelly And Me (as Sextet)/When I Fall In Love (as Quintet) 6

SARAH McLACHLAN
94 Arista SARAH 1   FUMBLING TOWARDS ECSTASY (CD, sampler, promo only) 20

ALTON McLAIN & DESTINY
78 Polydor 2391 370   IT MUST BE LOVE (LP) 10

TOMMY McLAIN
66 London HL 10065   Sweet Dreams/I Need You So. 10
66 London HL 10091   Think It Over/I Can't Take No More 8

DAVE McCLAREN
71 Big BG 323   Love Is What I Bring (actually by Dave Barker & Uniques)/
                         RUPIE EDWARDS ALL STARS: Love Version (with U Roy Junior). 15

(MAHAVISHNU) JOHN McLAUGHLIN
69 Marmalade 608 007 EXTRAPOLATION (LP). 20
70 Marmalade 2343 012 EXTRAPOLATION (LP, reissue) 12
71 Douglas DGL 65075 DEVOTION (LP, gatefold sleeve) 15
71 Douglas DGL 69014 MY GOAL'S BEYOND (LP, as Mahavishnu John McLaughlin, gatefold sleeve) . . . 15
73 CBS 69037   LOVE, DEVOTION, SURRENDER (LP, by Mahavishnu John McLaughlin
                         & Carlos Santana) 12
74 CBS Q 69037   LOVE, DEVOTION, SURRENDER (LP, quadrophonic issue) 18
(see also Lifetime, Tony Williams [Lifetime], Mahavishnu Orchestra, John Surman, Santana)

DON McLEAN
72 United Artists UP 35359 Vincent/Castles In The Air (p/s) 4

NANA McLEAN
71 Banana BA 355   A Little Love/SOUND DIMENSION: Heavy Beat. 20

PHIL McLEAN
61 Top Rank JAR 597   Small Sad Sam/Chicken. 10
62 Top Rank JAR 613   Big Mouth Bill/Come With Us 10

GERALD McLEASH
71 G.G. GG 4516   False Reaper/G.G. ALL STARS: Reaping Version 7

LARIS McLENNON
67 CBM 04   Confusion/Turn Me Loose 6

ENOS McLEOD
68 Blue Cat BS 135   You Can Never Get Away/ENOS & SHEILA: La La La Bamba. 15
(see also Enos & Sheila)

VINCENT McLEOD
69 Jackpot JP 711   Too Late/SIR COLLINS: Late Night 6

OSCAR McLOLLIE & HIS HONEYJUMPERS
55 London HL 8130   Take Your Shoes Off, Pop/Love Me Tonight. 225
55 London HL 8130   Take Your Shoes Off, Pop/Love Me Tonight (78) 60

EDDIE McLOYD
75 Brunswick BR 27   Once You Fall In Love/Baby Get Down 4

BOBBY McLURE
66 Chess CRS 8048   Peak Of Love/You Got Me Baby 25
75 Island USA 006   You Bring Out The Love In Me/SURVIVAL KIT: Daybreak 10
(see also Fontella Bass)

McLYNNS
70 CBS 63836   OLD MARKET ST. (LP) 20

ROSS McMANUS
64 HMV POP 1279   Patsy Girl/I'm The Greatest 6
66 HMV POP 1543   Stop Your Playing Around/Girlie Girlie 6

MINT VALUE £

| 67 | Decca F 12618 | Can't Take My Eyes Off Of You/If I Were A Rich Man | 6 |
| 60s | Golden Guinea | SINGS ELVIS PRESLEY'S GOLDEN HITS (LP) | 12 |

(see also Day Costello)

MARGARET McMILLAN
| 65 | Decca F 12272 | You Can't Be True Dear/The Love Of My Man | 6 |

BARBARA McNAIR
| 66 | Tamla Motown TMG 544 | You're Gonna Love My Baby/The Touch Of Time | 165 |
| 64 | Warner Bros WEP 6129 | I ENJOY BEING A GIRL (EP) | 35 |

(see also Billy Williams & Barbara McNair)

CHARLIE McNAIR'S JAZZ BAND
| 60 | Waverly SLP 504 | Big House Blues/Fish Man | 4 |

HAROLD McNAIR
68	RCA Victor RCA 1742	The Hipster/Indecision	60
65	Island ILP 926	AFFECTIONATE FUNK (LP, with Ornette Coleman's Sidemen)	350
68	RCA SF 7969	HAROLD McNAIR (LP)	80
70	RCA Intl. INTS 1096	FLUTE AND NUT (LP)	50
70	B&C CAS 1016	THE FENCE (LP)	35
72	B&C CAS 1045	HAROLD McNAIR (LP)	40

(see also Ginger Baker's Airforce)

JOSEPH McNALLY
| 56 | Oriole CB 1325 | The March Hare/I'm A Sentimental One | 6 |

JOHN McNALLY
| 69 | CBS 4517 | Mary In The Morning/My Love Forgive Me | 4 |

(this is NOT John McNally of the Searchers)

TREVOR McNAUGHTON
| 72 | Hillcrest HCT 5 | No Sins At All/No Sins At All Version | 5 |

(see also The Melodians)

BIG JAY McNEELY
59	Top Rank JAR 169	There Is Something On Your Mind/...Back...Shac...Track ('vocal: Little Sonny')	30
59	Top Rank JAR 169	There Is Something On Your Mind/...Back...Shac...Track (78)	20
65	Sue WI 373	There Is Something On Your Mind/...Back...Shac...Track ('vocal: Little Sonny') (reissue)	30
64	Warner Bros WM 8143	BIG JAY'S PARTY (LP)	25

AARON McNEIL
| 73 | Action ACT 4619 | Soul Of A Black Man/Reap What You Sow | 6 |

DAVID McNEIL
| 68 | President PT 212 | Don't Let Your Chance Go By/Space Plane | 12 |

PAUL McNEILL
| 66 | Decca LK 4803 | TRADITIONALLY AT THE TROUBADOUR (LP) | 45 |

PAUL McNEILL & LINDA PETERS
| 68 | MGM MGM 1408 | You Ain't Goin' Nowhere/I'll Show You How To Sing | 6 |

(see also Linda Peters, Richard & Linda Thompson)

McPEAKE FAMILY/FOLK GROUP
64	Fontana TL 5214	IRISH FOLK! (LP, as McPeak Family)	20
65	Fontana TL 5358	AT HOME WITH THE McPEAKES (LP)	20
67	Fontana TL 5433	PLEASANT AND DELIGHTFUL (LP, as McPeak Family)	20
69	Evolution Z 1002	WELCOME HOME (LP, as McPeak Folk Group)	35
72	Windmill WMD 151	IRISH TO BE SURE (LP, as McPeak Family)	15

CLYDE McPHATTER

78s
56	London HLE 8250	Seven Days/I'm Not Worthy Of You (78)	40
56	London HLE 8293	Treasure Of Love/When You're Sincere (78)	12
57	London HLE 8462	Just To Hold My Hand/No Matter What (78)	25
57	London HLE 8476	Long Lonely Nights/Heartaches (78)	35
57	London HLE 8525	Rock And Cry/You'll Be There (78)	40
58	London HLE 8707	Come What May/Let Me Know (78)	40
58	London HLE 8755	A Lover's Question/I Can't Stand Up Alone (78)	50
59	London HLE 8878	Lovey Dovey/My Island Of Dreams (78)	50
59	London HLE 8906	Since You've Been Gone/Try Try Baby (78)	55
59	London HLE 9000	You Went Back On Your Word/There You Go (78)	80

SINGLES
56	London HLE 8250	Seven Days/I'm Not Worthy Of You	350
56	London HL 7006	Seven Days/I'm Not Worthy Of You (export issue)	100
56	London HLE 8293	Treasure Of Love/When You're Sincere (gold or silver label lettering)	200/75
57	London HLE 8462	Just To Hold My Hand/No Matter What	150
57	London HLE 8476	Long Lonely Nights/Heartaches	100
57	London HLE 8525	Rock And Cry/You'll Be There (triangular centre)	80
58	London HLE 8707	Come What May/Let Me Know	60
58	London HLE 8755	A Lover's Question/I Can't Stand Up Alone	30
59	MGM MGM 1014	I Told Myself A Lie/(I'm Afraid) The Masquerade Is Over	15
59	London HLE 8878	Lovey Dovey/My Island Of Dreams	35
59	London HLE 8906	Since You've Been Gone/Try Try Baby	35
59	MGM MGM 1040	Twice As Nice/Where Did I Make My Mistake	12
59	London HLE 9000	You Went Back On Your Word/There You Go	45
59	MGM MGM 1048	Bless You/Let's Try Again	12
60	London HLE 9079	Just Give Me A Ring/Don't Dog Me	45
60	MGM MGM 1061	Think Me A Kiss/When The Right Time Comes Along	12
60	Mercury AMT 1108	I Ain't Givin' Up Nothin' (If I Can't Get Something)/Ta Ta	10

Clyde McPHATTER

60	Mercury AMT 1120	You're For Me/I Just Want To Love You	10
61	Mercury AMT 1136	Tomorrow Is A-Comin'/I'll Love You Till The Cows Come Home	10
62	Mercury AMT 1174	Lover Please/Let's Forget About The Past	15
62	Mercury AMT 1181	Little Bitty Pretty One/Next To Me	12
66	Stateside SS 487	Everybody's Somebody's Fool/I Belong To You	7
66	Stateside SS 567	A Shot Of Rhythm And Blues/I'm Not Going To Work Today	10
67	Stateside SS 592	Lavender Lace/Sweet And Innocent	6
68	Deram DM 202	Only A Fool/Thank You Love	5
69	Deram DM 223	Baby I Could Be So Good At Loving You/Baby You've Got It	6
69	Pama PM 775	A Shot Of Rhythm And Blues/I'm Not Going To Work Today (reissue)	6
69	B&C CB 106	Denver/Tell Me	5

EPs

59	London RE-E 1202	CLYDE McPHATTER (EP)	300
60	London RE-E 1240	CLYDE McPHATTER NO. 2 (EP, unissued)	
59	MGM MGM-EP 705	TWICE AS NICE (EP)	150
60	MGM MGM-EP 739	THIS IS NOT GOODBYE (EP)	150

LPs

63	Mercury MMC 14120	LOVER PLEASE (LP)	90
64	Atlantic ATL 5001	THE BEST OF CLYDE McPHATTER (LP)	70
71	MCA MUPS 418	WELCOME HOME (LP)	15
73	Atlantic K 30033	A TRIBUTE TO CLYDE McPHATTER (LP)	15

CLYDE McPHATTER & JACKIE WILSON

| 62 | Ember JBS 705 | Tenderly/CLYDE McPHATTER: Harbour Lights | 225 |
| 62 | Ember NR 5001 | MEET BILLY WARD & HIS DOMINOES (LP, 1 side each) | 120 |

(see also Drifters, Jackie Wilson, Dominoes, Billy Ward & Dominoes)

TONY (T.S.) McPHEE

66	Purdah 45-3501	Someone To Love Me/Ain't Gonna Cry No Mo' (as T.S. McPhee)	200
80s	TS 001	Time Of Action/Born To Be With You (sold at gigs)	10
68	Liberty LBL/LBS 83190	ME AND THE DEVIL (LP)	50
71	Sunset SLS 50209	THE SAME THING ON THEIR MINDS (LP, with Jo-Ann Kelly)	25
73	World Wide Artists WWA 1	THE TWO SIDES OF TONY (T.S.) McPHEE (LP, with insert)	20

(see also Groundhogs, Champion Jack Dupree, Jo-Ann Kelly, John Dummer Blues Band, Hapshash & Coloured Coat, Herbal Mixture)

CHARLES McPHERSON

| 65 | Stateside SL 10151 | BEBOP REVISITED (LP) | 15 |
| 73 | Mainstream MSL 1004 | SIKU YA BIBI (LP) | 12 |

GILLIAN McPHERSON

| 71 | RCA Victor RCA 2089 | It's My Own Way/Is Somebody In Tune With My Song | 5 |
| 71 | RCA Victor SF 8220 | POETS AND PAINTERS AND PERFORMERS OF THE BLUES (LP) | 20 |

KEVIN McQUINN

| 62 | Top Rank JAR 598 | Every Step Of The Way/Keep Me On Your Mind | 6 |

CARMEN McRAE

55	Brunswick 05502	Love Is Here To Stay/This Will Make You Laugh	7
56	Brunswick 05588	You Don't Know Me/Never Loved Him Anyhow	6
56	Brunswick 05632	Star Eyes/I'm A Dreamer (Aren't We All)	6
57	Brunswick 05652	Whatever Lola Wants (Lola Gets)/Ooh (What 'Cha Doin' To Me) (with Dave Lambert Quartet)	8
57	Brunswick 05723	It's Like Getting A Donkey To Gallop/The Party's Over	6
58	Brunswick 05738	As I Love You/Passing Fancy	5
58	Brunswick 05761	Namely You/I'll Love You (Till I Die)	5
59	Brunswick 05789	Come On, Come In/I Love The Ground You Walk On	5
59	Brunswick 05789	Come On, Come In/I Love The Ground You Walk On (78)	8
59	London HLR 8837	Play For Keeps/Which Way Is Love	12
59	London HLR 8837	Play For Keeps/Which Way Is Love (78)	25
60	Mercury AMT 1122	The Very Thought Of You/Oh! Look At Me Now	5
75	Blue Note BNXW 7002	Who Gave You Permission/The Trouble With Hello Is Goodbye	5
57	London RE-N 1094	LONDON'S GIRL FRIENDS (EP)	15
56	Brunswick LAT 8104	BY SPECIAL REQUEST (LP)	18
56	Brunswick LAT 8133	TORCHY (LP)	18
56	Brunswick LAT 8147	BLUE MOON (LP)	18
58	Brunswick LAT 8257	AFTER GLOW (LP)	18
59	London HA-R 2185	BOOK OF BALLADS (LP)	18
66	Ember CJS 819	IN LONDON (LP)	15

(see also Sammy Davis Jnr.)

CARMEN McRAE & DAVE BRUBECK FIVE

| 62 | Fontana H 379 | Take Five/It's A Raggy Waltz | 8 |

(see also Dave Brubeck)

IAN McSHANE

| 62 | Columbia DB 4932 | The Tinker/Harry Brown | 6 |

JAY McSHANN

| 55 | Brunswick LA 8735 | KANSAS CITY MEMORIES (10" LP) | 20 |
| 73 | Black Lion 2460 201 | THE BAND THAT JUMPS THE BLUES (LP) | 10 |

MC SPY-D & 'FRIENDS'

| 95 | Parlophone 12RPD 6404 | The Amazing Spider-Man (Mastermix)/(Sad Bit)/ (The White Trouser Mix) (12", picture disc, with insert) | 7 |
| 95 | Parlophone 12RDJ 6404 | The Amazing Spider-Man (Solution Mix)/(Solution Chilled Mix)/ (B&J White Trouser Mix) (12", no p/s, promo only) | 30 |

(see also Brian May)

BLIND WILLIE McTELL

| 66 | Transatlantic PR 1040 | LAST SESSION (LP) | 15 |
| 67 | Storyville 670 816 | BLIND WILLIE McTELL 1940 (LP) | 15 |

MINT VALUE £

| 60s | Roots RL 324 | BLIND WILLIE McTELL 1929-1935 (LP) | 15 |
| 73 | Atlantic K 40400 | ATLANTA TWELVE STRING GUITAR (LP) | 15 |

RALPH McTELL

69	Big T BIG 125	Summer Comes Along	5
70	Big T BIG 131	Kew Gardens/Father Forgive Them	5
70	Big T BIG 134	Spiral Staircase/Terminus	5
71	Famous FAM 105	First And Last Man/In Some Way I Loved You	5
72	Famous FAM 111	Teacher, Teacher/Truckin' Little Baby	5
72	Reprise K 14225	Zimmerman Blues	5
74	Reprise K 14380	Streets Of London/Summer Lightning (p/s)	5
68	Transatlantic TRA 165	8 FRAMES A SECOND (LP)	15
69	Transatlantic TRA 177	SPIRAL STAIRCASE (LP, with insert)	12
69	Transatlantic TRA 209	MY SIDE OF YOUR WINDOW (LP)	12
71	Famous SFMA 5753	YOU, WELL MEANING, BROUGHT ME HERE (LP, gatefold sleeve)	12
77	Warner Bros K2 56296	RIGHT SIDE UP (LP, quadrophonic)	12

McTELLS

| 87 | Frank TRUFFAUT 303 | Jesse Man Rae/If Only/Rotten/M.T.B. (p/s in bag) | 5 |

RAY McVAY SOUND

65	Pye 7N 15777	Raunchy/Revenge	25
65	Pye 7N 15816	Kinda Kinky/Kinkdom Come	20
66	Parlophone R 5460	Genesis/House Of Clowns (as Ray MacVay Band)	6
69	Mercury MF 1121	Destination Moon/Mexican Scavenger	5
71	Philips 6006 083	They Call Me Mr. Tibbs (as Ray McVay & Orchestra)	12

CHRISTINE McVIE

| 84 | Warner Bros W 9372T | Got A Hold On Me/Who's Dreaming This Dream (12", p/s) | 7 |
| 84 | Warner Bros W 9372PT | Got A Hold On Me/Who's Dreaming This Dream (12", picture disc) | 10 |

(see also Christine Perfect, Fleetwood Mac, Chicken Shack)

CARL McVOY

| 58 | London HLU 8617 | Tootsie/You Are My Sunshine | 225 |
| 58 | London HLU 8617 | Tootsie/You Are My Sunshine (78) | 60 |

DAVID McWILLIAMS

66	CBS 202348	God And My Country/Blue Eyes	7
67	Major Minor MM 533	The Days Of Pearly Spencer/Harlem Lady	10
68	Major Minor MM 561	This Side Of Heaven/Mister Satisfied	6
69	Major Minor MM 592	The Stranger/Follow Me	7
69	Major Minor MM 616	Oh Mama Are You My Friend?/I Love Susie In The Summer	6
71	Parlophone R 5886	The Days Of Pearly Spencer/Harlem Lady (reissue)	5
72	CBS 7782	Maggie's Coming Home/Margie	5
73	Mother MOT 101	Gold/Go On Back To Momma	5
73	Dawn DNS 1044	Love Like A Lady/Down By The Dockyard	5
74	Dawn DNS 1064	You've Only Been A Stranger/Ships In The Night	5
67	Major Minor MMLP 2	SINGING SONGS BY DAVID McWILLIAMS (LP, also stereo SMLP 2)	18
67	Major Minor MMLP 10	DAVID McWILLIAMS VOL. 2 (LP, also stereo SMLP 10)	18
68	Major Minor MMLP 11	VOLUME III (LP, also stereo SMLP 11)	18
69	Major Minor MCP 5026	THE DAYS OF DAVID McWILLIAMS (LP)	18
72	Dawn DNLS 3039	LORD OFFALY (LP)	15
73	Dawn DNLS 3047	THE BEGGAR AND THE PRIEST (LP)	12
74	Dawn DNLS 3059	LIVING'S JUST A STATE OF MIND (LP)	12

M.D.C.

| 83 | Crass 121984/5 | MULTI DEATH CORPORATION (EP) | 7 |

VAUGHN MEADER

| 63 | MGM MGM 1239 | No Hiding Place/The Elephant Song | 4 |

ME & THEM

64	Pye 7N 15596	Feels So Good/I Think I'm Gonna Kill Myself	12
64	Pye 7N 15631	Everything I Do Is Wrong/Show You Mean It Too	10
64	Pye 7N 15683	Get Away/Tell Me Why	10

MEANIES

| 79 | Vendetta VD 002 | Waiting For You/It's True (p/s) | 65 |

MEAN STREET DEALERS

80	Graduate GRAD 5	Japanese Motorbikes/Tight (p/s)	6
79	Mean St. Dealers MSD 001	BENT NEEDLES (LP)	30
79	Graduate GRADLP 1	BENT NEEDLES (LP, reissue)	18

MEASLES

65	Columbia DB 7531	Casting My Spell/Bye Birdie Fly	30
65	Columbia DB 7673	Night People/Dog Rough Dan	18
66	Columbia DB 7875	Kicks/No Baby At All	25
66	Columbia DB 8029	Walkin' In/Looking For Love	18

MEAT BEAT MANIFESTO

87	Sweatbox SOX 023	Suck Hard (I Got The Fear)/Kick That Man/Kneel And Buzz (12", p/s)	12
88	Sweatbox SOX 023R	I Got The Fear (Titanium Mix)/I Got The Fear (Without Fuck) (12", p/s)	10
88	Sweatbox OX 032	Strap Down/Wall To Wall (p/s)	4
88	Sweatbox OX 032R	Strap Down (The Sound Defence Policy Remix)/Wall To Wall (p/s)	5

(see also Perennial Divide, Space Children)

MEAT LOAF

75	Ode ODS 66304	Clap Your Hands, Stamp Your Feet/Stand By Me (withdrawn)	50
78	Epic S EPC 5980	You Took The Words Right Out Of My Mouth/For Crying Out Loud (no p/s)	5
78	Epic S EPC 6281	Two Out Of Three Ain't Bad/For Crying Out Loud (no p/s)	5
78	Epic S EPC 6797	All Revved Up With No Place To Go/Paradise By A Dashboard Light (no p/s)	5
79	Epic S EPC 12-7018	Bat Out Of Hell/Heaven Can Wait (12", p/s, red vinyl)	15

81	Epic EPCA 1580	I'm Gonna Love Her For The Both Of Us/Everything Is Permitted (p/s) 5
81	Epic EPCA 11-1697	Dead Ringer For Love/More Than You Deserve (picture disc) 8
82	Epic EPCA 12-2012	Read 'Em And Weep/Meat Loaf In Conversation/Everything Is Permitted
		(12", p/s) 10
82	Epic EPCA 12-2251	MEAT LOAF IN EUROPE '82 (12" EP) 15
82	Epic EPCA 12-2251	MEAT LOAF IN EUROPE '82 (12" EP, clear vinyl, p/s, Irish issue) 50
83	Epic EPCA 2621	GREATEST ORIGINAL HITS (EP, p/s) 8
83	Epic EPCA 3357	If You Really Want To/Keep Driving (p/s) 5
83	Epic EPCA TA 3357	If You Really Want To (Alternate Version)/Lost Love/Keep Driving (12", p/s) 8
83	Epic EPCA WA 3357	If You Really Want To (Alternate Version)/Lost Love/
		Keep Driving (12", picture disc) 10
83	Epic EPCA 3511	Razor's Edge/You Can Never Be Too Sure About The Girl (p/s) 5
83	Epic EPCA WA 3511	Razor's Edge/You Can Never Be Too Sure About The Girl (picture disc) 8
83	Epic EPCA TA 3511	Razor's Edge/You Can Never Be Too Sure About The Girl/
		Don't You Look At Me Like That (12", p/s) 8
83	Epic EPCA 3748	Midnight At The Lost And Found (Remix)/Fallen Angel/Bat Out Of Hell (live)/
		Dead Ringer For Love (gatefold p/s) 6
83	Epic EPCA WA 3748	Midnight At The Lost And Found (Remix)/Fallen Angel/Bat Out Of Hell (live)/
		Dead Ringer For Love (Long Version) (picture disc) 8
83	Epic EPCA DA 3748	Midnight At The Lost And Found (Remix)/Fallen Angel//Bat Out Of Hell (live)/
		Dead Ringer For Love (Long Version) (double pack, some copies signed) 12/8
83	Epic EPCA TA 3748	Midnight At The Lost And Found (Remix)/Fallen Angel//Bat Out Of Hell (live)/
		Dead Ringer For Love (12", p/s) 7
83	Epic EPCA A 4080	Razor's Edge (Remix)/Paradise By The Dashboard Light (p/s,
		with competition insert) 6
83	Epic EPCA A 4080	Razor's Edge (Remix)/Paradise By The Dashboard Light (gatefold p/s) 6
83	Epic EPCA A 4080	Razor's Edge (Remix)/Paradise By The Dashboard Light/Read 'Em And Weep
		(12", p/s, some shrinkwrapped with tour patch and stickered sleeve) 12/8
84	Arista ARIST 585	Modern Girl/Take A Number (poster p/s) 6
84	Arista ARISDP 585	Modern Girl/Take A Number (bike-shaped picture disc,
		some with poster & plinth) 12/10
84	Arista ARIST 12585	Modern Girl (Freeway Mix)/Take A Number (Extended)
		(12", gatefold p/s with poster) 8
84	Arista ARIPD 12585	Modern Girl (Freeway Mix)/Take A Number (Extended) (12", picture disc) 10
84	Arista ARIST 12585D/	Modern Girl (Freeway Mix)/Take A Number (Extended)//Modern Girl (Freeway
	ARIPD 12585	Mix)/Take A Number (Extended) (12", double pack, 2nd 12" as picture disc) 15
85	Arista ARIPU 600	Nowhere Fast/Clap Your Hands (gatefold pop-up p/s) 6
85	Arista ARISG 600	Nowhere Fast/Clap Your Hands (gatefold p/s with booklet, some signed) 8/6
85	Arista ARISD 600	Nowhere Fast/Clap Your Hands (bike-shaped picture disc) 10
85	Arista ARIST 12600	Nowhere Fast (Re-edited Version)/Clap Your Hands/Stand By Me
		(12", p/s; with competition sticker, some with booklet) 10/8
85	Arista ARIST 603	Piece Of The Action/Sailor To A Siren (p/s, with shrinkwrapped with patch) 6
85	Arista ARIST 603/FS 603	Piece Of The Action/Sailor To A Siren//Bat Out Of Hell (live)/
		Modern Girl (U.S. Remix) (double pack) 6
85	Arista ARISD 603	Piece Of The Action/Sailor To A Siren (jaw-shaped picture disc) 10
85	Arista ARIST 12-603	Piece Of The Action (Extended Version)/Bad Attitude/Sailor To A Siren
		(12", stickered p/s, with 2-sided poster) 8
85	Arista ARIST 12-603/	Piece Of The Action (Extended Version)/Bad Attitude/Sailor To A Siren//
	FS 12-603	Bat Out Of Hell (live)/Modern Girl (U.S. Remix) (12", double pack) 10
86	Arista ARIST 666P	Rock'N'Roll Mercenaries/RPM (w/ John Parr, black guitar-shaped picture disc) . . . 8
86	Arista ARIST 666XP	Rock'N'Roll Mercenaries/RPM (w/ John Parr, white guitar-shaped picture disc) . . . 8
86	Arista ARIST 12666	Rock'N'Roll Mercenaries/RPM (with John Parr, 12", with poster) 8
86	Arista ARIST 683P	Getting Away With Murder/Rock'n'Roll Hero (camera-slide shaped picture disc) . . 8
86	Arista ARIST 10683	Getting Away With Murder/Rock'n'Roll Hero (10", circular p/s) 8
87	Arista RISCD 14	Special Girl/Dead Ringer For Love (live)/One More Kiss (Night Of The Soft
		Parade)/Paradise By The Dashboard Light (CD, card sl. with anti-static inner) . . . 10
93	Arista 660006 6	Bat Out Of Hell (Single Version)/Read 'Em And Weep/JIM STEINMAN:
		Out Of The Frying Pan/Rock'n'Roll Dreams Come Through (12", picture disc) 8
94	Virgin VSP 1479	Rock'n'Roll Dreams Come Through/Wasted Youth (picture disc) 5
98	Virgin (no cat. no.)	No Matter What (single edit)/A Kiss Is A Terrible Thing To Waste (single edit)
		(CD-R, unreleased versions, custom printed disc and folded card inlay) 25
98	Virgin VSCDJX 1718	A Kiss Is A Terrible Thing To Waste (radio edit)/(soft radio edit)
		(CD, promo only, unreleased versions, card sleeve) 15
82	Epic EPC 11 82419	BAT OUT OF HELL (LP, picture disc) 25
82	Epic EPC 82419	BAT OUT OF HELL (LP, half-speed mastered audiophile pressing with inserts) . . 20
85	Epic EPC 11 83645	DEADRINGER (LP, picture disc) 15
99	Simply Vinyl SVLP 0086	BAT OUT OF HELL (LP, 180g virgin vinyl reissue, with lyric sheet) 15
99	Virgin CDVDJ 2868	THE VERY BEST OF (2-CD, velvet digipak, embossed title, promo only) 30

(see also Stoney & Meat Loaf, Jim Steinman, Rocky Horror Show)

MEAT WHIPLASH
85	Creation CRE 020	Don't Slip Up/Here It Comes (foldaround p/s in poly bag; 1st pressing has
		photo of band by fence, 2nd pressing has band in field) 10/6

(see also Jesus & Mary Chain)

MECHANICAL HORSETROUGH
70s	Kap KAPS 96	Dogshit On Your Shoes/Jeremy Germoline/Horsetrough Hoedown (p/s) 5
75	Sonet SON 2068	When Santa Lost His Trousers/The Ballad Of Big Bruce 5

MECKENBURG ZINC
70	Orange OAS 205	Hard Working Woman/I'd Like To Help You 4

MEDALLION STRINGS
60	London HLR 9218	Green Leaves Of Summer/Spellbound 6
60	London HLR 9242	Gloria's Theme (From "Butterfield 8")/Suzie Wong 6
61	London HA-R 2331	THE SOUND OF HOLLYWOOD (LP, also stereo SAH-R 6130) 12/15

MEDDY EVILS
65	Pye 7N 15941	Find Somebody To Love/A Place Called Love 75
66	Pye 7M 17091	It's All For You/Ma's Place 75

MEDICINE HEAD

MEDIA
79	Takeaway TA 001	TV Kids/Don't Sit Back/Just For You/Rose And Crown (p/s)	6

MEDIA
80	Brain Booster Music 4	Back On The Beach Again/South Coast City Rockers (p/s)	8

MEDIATORS
70	Supreme SUP 210	When You Go To A Party (actually by Meditators)/ RUPIE EDWARDS ALLSTARS: Stop The Party	5

(see also Meditators)

MEDICINE HEAD
69	Dandelion S 4661	His Guiding Hand/This Love Of Old	15
70	Dandelion S 5075	Coast To Coast/All For Tomorrow	10
71	Dandelion DAN 7003	(And The) Pictures In The Sky/Natural Sight (also listed as K 19002) (some in p/s)	8/6
72	Dandelion 2001 276	Kum On/On The Land	6
72	Dandelion 2001 325	Only To Do What Is True/Sittin' In The Sun	6
72	Dandelion 2001 383	How Does It Feel/Morning Light	6
69	Dandelion 63757	NEW BOTTLES, OLD MEDICINE (LP)	30
71	Dandelion DAN 8005	HEAVY ON THE DRUM (LP, gatefold sleeve, also listed as K 49005; some with lyric insert)	30/25
71	Dandelion 2310 166	DARK SIDE OF THE MOON (LP, with insert)	25
73	Polydor 2310 248	ONE & ONE IS ONE (LP, gatefold sleeve)	15
74	Polydor 2383 272	THRU' A FIVE (LP)	15

(see also Ashton Gardner & Dyke, British Lions)

MEDITATIONS
68	Liberty LBF 15045	Transcendental Meditation/Beautiful Experience	6

MEDITATORS
69	Bullet BU 403	Duba Duba/CECIL NICKY THOMAS: Running Alone	5
70	Big BG 302	When You Go To A Party/Good Morning Mother Cuba	7
71	Big BG 305	Music Alone Shall Live/RUPIE EDWARDS AND ALL STARS: Music Alone — Version	6
73	Pyramid PYR 7010	Great Messiah/Nana Nana	5
73	Smash SMA 2331	Things Not Easy/BONGO HERMAN & BINGY BUNNY: Ration	6

(see also Busty Brown, Pat Satchmo)

MEDIUM
68	CBS 3404	Edward Never Lies/Colours Of The Rainbow	20

MEDIUM MEDIUM
80	APT SAP-01	Them Or Me/Freeze (p/s)	4
81	Cherry Red BRED 19	THE GLITTERHOUSE (LP)	10

BILL MEDLEY
67	Verve VS 564	That Lucky Old Sun/My Darling Clementine	6
68	MGM MGM 1418	I Can't Make It Alone/One Day Girl	6
68	MGM MGM 1432	Brown Eyed Woman/Let The Good Times Roll	6
68	MGM MGM 1456	Peace Brother Peace/Winter Won't Come This Year	8
69	MGM MGM 1475	This Is A Love Song/Something's So Wrong	5
69	MGM MGM 1491	Someone Is Standing Outside/Reaching Back	5
71	A&M AMS 898	You've Lost That Lovin' Feelin'/We've Only Just Begun	5
69	MGM MGM-C(S) 8091	BILL MEDLEY 100% (LP)	15

(see also Righteous Brothers, Garnet Mimms)

MINT VALUE £

JOE MEDLIN
59	Mercury AMT 1032	I Kneel At Your Throne/Out Of Sight, Out Of Mind	7
59	Mercury AMT 1032	I Kneel At Your Throne/Out Of Sight, Out Of Mind (78)	12

MICHAEL MEDWIN
58	HMV POP 490	The Army Game/What Do We Do In The Army? (with Bernard Bresslaw, Alfie Bass & Leslie Fyson).......................	7
58	HMV POP 490	The Army Game/What Do We Do In The Army? (78, with Bernard Bresslaw, Alfie Bass & Leslie Fyson)...................	8
59	HMV POP 645	Blankety-Blankety-Blank/Do It Yourself (with Norman Rossington)...........	5

KEITH MEEHAN
69	Marmalade 598 016	Darkness Of My Life/TONY MEEHAN: Hooker Street	15

TONY MEEHAN
64	Decca F 11801	Song Of Mexico/Kings Go Fifth....................................	10

(see also Shadows, Jet Harris & Tony Meehan, Keith Meehan, John Paul Jones)

JOE MEEK ORCHESTRA
63	Decca F 11796	The Kennedy March/The Theme Of Freedom	40

(see also Blue Men)

MEGADETH
87	Capitol CL 476	Wake Up Dead/Black Friday (live) (p/s).............................	7
87	Capitol CLP 476	Wake Up Dead/Black Friday (live) (skull-shaped picture disc with insert).......	15
87	Capitol TCDETH 1	Wake Up Dead/Black Friday (live)/Devil's Island (live) (cassette).............	5
87	Capitol 12CL 476	Wake Up Dead/Black Friday (live)/Devil's Island (live)/Wake Up Dead/ Black Friday (live) (12", p/s, some allegedly shrink-wrapped with 7" picture disc)	20/10
87	Capitol 12CL 476	Wake Up Dead/Black Friday (Tommy Vance Show)/Devil's Island (Tommy Vance Show) (12", stickered p/s, with 'Deth' certificate).............	12
88	Capitol CL 480	Anarchy In The U.K./Liar (p/s)	5
88	Capitol CLP 480	Anarchy In The U.K./Liar (U.K.-shaped picture disc)...................	12
88	Capitol TCDETH 2	Anarchy In The U.K./Liar/502 (cassette)............................	5
88	Capitol 12CL 480	Anarchy In The U.K./Liar/502 (12", p/s)	8
88	Capitol CL 489	Mary Jane/Hook In Mouth (p/s)	5
88	Capitol CLP 489	Mary Jane/Hook In Mouth (picture disc)	8
88	Capitol TCDETH 3	Mary Jane/Hook In Mouth/My Last Words (cassette)	4
88	Capitol 12CL 489	Mary Jane/Hook In Mouth/My Last Words (12", p/s)	8
90	SBK SBK 4	No More Mr. Nice Guy/DEAD ON: "Different Breed" (p/s)................	5
90	SBK SBKPD 4	No More Mr. Nice Guy/DEAD ON: "Different Breed" (chair-shaped pic disc)	8
90	SBK TCSBK 4	No More Mr. Nice Guy/DEAD ON: "Different Breed" (cassette)	4
90	SBK 12 SBKP 4	No More Mr. Nice Guy/DEAD ON: "Different Breed"/DANGEROUS TOYS: "Demon Bell [The Ballad Of Horace Pinker]" (12", poster p/s).	8
90	SBK CDSBK 4	No More Mr. Nice Guy/(DEAD ON: "Different Breed")/(DANGEROUS TOYS: "Demon Bell [The Ballad Of Horace Pinker]") (CD)...................	10
90	Capitol CLP 588	Holy Wars ... The Punishment Due/Lucretia (poster p/s)	5
90	Capitol TCCL 588	Holy Wars ... The Punishment Due/Lucretia (cassette)...................	5
90	Capitol 12CLG 588	Holy Wars ... The Punishment Due/Lucretia/(interview — Edited 6.15) (12", gatefold p/s).	8
90	Capitol 12CLPD 588	Holy Wars ... The Punishment Due/(13-minute interview) (12", picture disc)....	8
90	Capitol CDCL 588	Holy Wars ... The Punishment Due/Lucretia/(interview — Edited 6.15) (CD)	8
91	Capitol CLS 604	Hangar 18 (MJ 12 Edit)/The Conjuring (live) (p/s, shrinkwrapped with patch)...	6
91	Capitol CLPD 604	Hangar 18 (MJ 12 Edit)/The Conjuring (live) (Vic-shaped picture disc).........	8
91	Capitol 12CLG 604	Hangar 18/Hangar 18 (live)/The Conjuring (live)/Hook In Mouth (live) (12", gatefold p/s with Vic Rattlehead mask)........................	8
91	Capitol CDCL 604	Hangar 18/Hangar 18 (live)/The Conjuring (live)/Hook In Mouth (live) (CD).....	8
92	Capitol CLS 662	Symphony Of Destruction/Peace Sells (live) (yellow vinyl, stickered sleeve)	5
92	Capitol CLPD 662	Symphony Of Destruction/In My Darkest Hour (live) (picture disc)..............	5
92	Capitol 12CLS 662	Symphony Of Destruction/Breakpoint/Go To Hell (12", p/s, clear vinyl with giant autographed poster)	8
92	Capitol CDCL 662	Symphony Of Destruction/Breakpoint/Go To Hell (CD, cut-out card p/s).........	8
92	Capitol CLP 669	Skin O' My Teeth (LP Version)/Holy Wars ... The Punishment Due (The General Schwarzkopf Mix) (with giant poster & Mega game board)	5
92	Capitol CLP 669	Skin O' My Teeth (LP Version)/Holy Wars ... The Punishment Due (The General Schwarzkopf Mix)/High Speed Dirt (live)/The Passes (Mustaine Remarks On Game) (10" bronze Megadeth box with passes & game rules)	10
93	Capitol 12CL 682	Sweating Bullets (Anxiety Edit)/Countdown To Extinction (Live '92/ Ashes In Your Mouth (Live '92)/Symphony Of Destruction (Gristle Mix) (12", blue vinyl, 'paranoid pressing' plays from the middle outwards)	8
93	Capitol CDCLX 682	Sweating Bullets (Anxiety Edit)/Symphony Of Destruction (Live '92)/ Countdown To Extinction (Live '92)/Symphony Of Destruction (Gristle Edit Mix) (CD, in collector's box with room for 1st CD)	8
88	Capitol ESTP 2053	SO FAR, SO GOOD ... SO WHAT (LP, picture disc with insert)................	15
88	M. For Nations MFN 46P	KILLING IS MY BUSINESS ... AND BUSINESS IS GOOD (LP, picture disc with insert)	15
88	M. For Nations MFN 46 DM	KILLING IS MY BUSINESS ... AND BUSINESS IS GOOD (2-LP, 'Direct Metal Master' edition with poster)	15
88	Capitol ESTP 2022	PEACE SELLS ... BUT WHO'S BUYING? (LP, picture disc with insert)	15
90	Capitol ESTPD 2132	RUST IN PEACE (LP, picture disc, die cut sleeve)	15
94	Capitol EST 2244	YOUTHANASIA (LP, blue vinyl, gatefold sleeve)	12
94	Capitol ESTPD 2244	YOUTHANASIA (LP, picture disc)	15
95	Capitol CDESTS 2244	YOUTHANASIA/HIDDEN TREASURES (2-CD, card sleeve, 2,000 only).........	30
97	Capitol EST 2297	CRYPTIC WRITINGS (LP)	12

(see also Marty Friedman, Cacophony)

MEGATON
71	Deram DM-R 331	Out Of Your Own Little World/Niagara	30
71	Deram SML-R 1086	MEGATON (LP)..	275

(see also Hackensack, Les Humphries Singers)

MEGATON
81	Hot Metal HMM 69	Aluminium Lady/Diehard (p/s) 40

MEGATONS (U.S.)
65	Sue WI 325	Shimmy Shimmy Walk (Parts 1 & 2) 25
	(see also Billy Lee Riley)	

MEGATONS (Jamaica)
70	Downtown DT 464	Take It Easy/Funk The Beat 5
70	Downtown DT 469	Militant Man/MUSIC DOCTORS: Reggae Jeggae Version 5
	(see also Revelation)	

MEGATRONS
59	Top Rank JAR 146	Velvet Waters/The Merry Piper 7
59	Top Rank JAR 146	Velvet Waters/The Merry Piper (78) 10
59	Top Rank JAR 236	Tootie Flootie/Whispering Winds. 7

GEORGE MEGGIE
72	Bullet BU 504	Hard To Believe/MAX ROMEO: Softie 6
72	Punch PH 112	People Like People/MAX ROMEO: Softie 6

JOHN MEHEGAN TRIO
56	London EZC 19005	THE FIRST MEHEGAN VOLUME ONE (EP) 8
56	London EZC 19015	THE FIRST MEHEGAN VOLUME TWO (EP) 8

MEKONS
78	Fast Products FAST 1	Never Been In A Riot/32 Weeks/Heart And Soul (p/s). 10
78	Fast Products FAST 7	Where Were You?/I'll Have To Dance Then (On My Own) (p/s) 5
80	Virgin SV 101	Teeth/Guardian//Kill/Stay Cool (double pack, gatefold p/s) 5
82	CNT CNT 1	This Sporting Life (6.12)/Frustration (6.21)/(mystery live track) (12", p/s) 8
82	CNT CNT 008	This Sporting Life/Fight The Cuts (p/s) 5
82	CNT CNT 014	THE ENGLISH DANCING MASTER (12" EP) 8
80s	Catalogue CAT 075/3	Amnesia (square flexidisc with *The Catalogue* magazine). 5
	(see also Batfish Boys, Sally Timms & Drifting Cowgirls, Ut)	

(George) MELACHRINO ORCHESTRA
56	HMV B 10958	Autumn Concerto/A Woman In Love 4

MEL & DAVE
70	Upsetter US 330	Spinning Wheel/Version 8

MEL & KIM
87	Supreme SUPETP III	Respectable (The Tabloid Mix)/Respectable (7" Version)/Respectable
		(Extra Beats Version) (12", picture disc in PVC sleeve) 7

MEL & TIM
70	Concord CON 004	Backfield In Motion/Do Right Baby (pink label, later brown) 6/5
73	Stax 2025 125	Starting All Over Again/It Hurts To Want You So Bad 5
73	Stax 2025 171	What's Your Name/Free For All 5
73	Stax 2325 090	STARTING ALL OVER AGAIN (LP). 12

MELANIE
68	Buddah 201 027	Mr. Tambourine Man/Christopher Robin 5
69	Buddah 201 028	Bobo's Party/I'm Back In Town 5
69	Buddah 201 063	Tuning My Guitar/Beautiful People (withdrawn, demos may exist) . . . . 10+
69	Buddah 201 066	Beautiful People/Uptown And Down 5
70	Buddah 2011 013	Lay Down (Candles In The Rain)/Animal Crackers 5
70	Buddah 2011 039	Peace Will Come (According To Plan)/Close To It All 5
71	Buddah 2011 064	Stop! I Don't Wanna Hear It Any More/Beautiful People. 5
71	Buddah 2011 071	The Good Book/Nickel Song 5
72	Buddah 2011 093	Alexander Beetle/Christopher Robin/Animal Crackers. 5
72	Buddah 2011 115	Ring The Living Bell/Railroad 5
72	Buddah 2011 136	Some Day I'll Be A Farmer/Lay Lady Lay 5
72	Neighbourhood NBH 1	Together Alone/Summer Weaving 5
73	Neighbourhood NBH 5	Do You Believe/Stoneground Words 5
73	Neighbourhood NBH 6	Bitter Bad/Do You Believe 5
73	Neighbourhood NBH 8	Seeds/Some Say (I Got Devil) 5
73	Neighbourhood NBH 9	Will You Love Me Tomorrow/Here I Am 5
73	Lyntone LYN 2673/4	A Gift From Honey October 1973 (flexidisc, p/s). 7
75	N'hood SNBH 3789	Almost Like Being In Love/Beautiful People. 5
83	Neighbourhood NBP 1	Every Breath Of The Way/Lover's Lullaby (picture disc). 5
69	Buddah 203 019	BORN TO BE (LP, gatefold sleeve). 18
69	Buddah 203 028	AFFECTIONATELY MELANIE (LP, with inner lyric sheet) 15
70	Buddah 2318 009	CANDLES IN THE RAIN (LP, gatefold sleeve) 15
70	Buddah 2318 011	LEFTOVER WINE (LP, gatefold sleeve) 15
71	Buddah 2318 034	ALL THE RIGHT NOISES (LP, soundtrack) 15
71	Buddah 2322 001	THE GOOD BOOK (LP, gatefold sleeve, with booklet) 15
71	Buddah 2322 002	GATHER ME (LP, gatefold sleeve) 15
72	Buddah 2318 054	GARDEN IN THE CITY (LP, scratch'n'sniff sleeve) 15
72	Buddah 2659 013	THE FOUR SIDES OF MELANIE (2-LP) 18
73	Neighbourhood NHTC 251	STONEGROUND WORDS (LP, gatefold sleeve, with lyric inner & poster) 12

GIL MELLE (QUINTET)
55	Vogue LDE 141	GIL MELLE QUINTET (10" LP). 15

SUSAN MELLEN
75	MAM MAMAS 1014	THE MELLEN BIRD (LP, with insert) 30

JOHN COUGAR MELLENCAMP
86	Riva JCMDP 5	Small Town/(Version)//Hurts So Good/The Kind Of Fella I Am (p/s, double pack). . 5
86	Riva JCMXD 5	Small Town/Jack And Diane//Pink Houses/Small Town (Acoustic)
		(12" p/s, double pack) 7
87	Mercury JCMCD 9	Cherry Bomb/Shama Lama Ding Dong/Under The Boardwalk/
		Pretty Ballerina (live) (CD, card sleeve). 7

John Cougar MELLENCAMP

88	Mercury JCMCD 10	Check It Out/We Are The People/Pink Houses (Acoustic Version)/ Check It Out (live) (CD, card sleeve)	7
88	Mercury JCMCD 11	Rooty Toot Toot/Check It Out (live)/Never Too Old /Cold Sweat (CD, card sleeve)	7
89	Mercury JCMCD 12	Pop Singer/J.M.'s Question/Like A Rolling Stone (live)/Check It Out (live) (CD)	7
89	Mercury 080 212-2	Paper In Fire/Never Too Old/Under The Boardwalk/Cold Sweat/ Paper In Fire (CD Video)	15
89	Mercury 080 200-2	Pop Singer/J.M.'s Question/Check It Out (live)/Pop Singer (live)/ Pop Singer (CD Video)	15

(see also John Cougar)

MELLODITIES
64	R&B JB 179	Vacation/TOMMY McCOOK: Music Is My Occupation	15

MELLOTONES
57	Beltona BE 2673	Norah/If I Knocked The L Out Of Kelly (78)	8

MELL(O)TONES
68	Amalgamated AMG 812	Fat Girl In Red/VERSATILES: Trust The Book	12
68	Amalgamated AMG 817	Feel Good (maybe actually by Bleechers)/Soulful Mood (actually by Tommy McCook & Supersonics)	20
68	Doctor Bird DB 1136	None Such/VAL BENNETT: Popeye On The Shore	15
68	Trojan TR 612	Uncle Charlie/What A Botheration	10
68	Pyramid PYR 6060	Let's Join Together/BEVERLEY'S ALLSTARS: I Don't Know	10
69	Camel CA 18	Facts Of Life/TERMITES: I'll Be Waiting	7
70	Escort ERT 844	Work It/SOUL MAN: Good Lover	6

(see also Sexy Girls)

MELLO & MELLOTONES
72	Summit SUM 8538	Haile Selasie/Old Man River	5

(see also Mellotones)

MELLOW CANDLE
68	SNB 55-3645	Feeling High/Tea With The Sun	35
72	Deram DM 357	Dan The Wing/Silversong	35
72	Deram SDL 7	SWADDLING SONGS (LP)	400

MELLOW CATS with Count Ossie & Warrickas
61	Blue Beat BB 68	Rock A Man Soul/MONTO & CYCLONES: Lazy Lou (B-side actually by Monty [Alexander] & Cyclones)	15

(see also Melo Cats)

MELLOW FRUITFULNESS
67	Columbia SX 6242	MEDITATION (LP)	20

MELLOW LARKS
60	Blue Beat BB 16	Time To Pray (Alleluia)/Love You Baby	15
61	Blue Beat BB 38	No More Wedding/Lite Of My Life	15

(see also Basil Gabbidon)

GEORGE MELLY (& MICK MULLIGAN BAND)
51	Tempo A 96	Rock Island Line/Send Me To The 'Lectric Chair (78)	20
52	Tempo A 104	Kitchen Man/Jazzbo Brown From Memphis Town (78)	10
55	Decca F 10457	Frankie And Johnny/I'm Down In The Dumps	10
55	Decca F 10457	Frankie And Johnny/I'm Down In The Dumps (78)	10
56	Tempo A 144	Jenny's Ball/Muddy Water	10
56	Tempo A 144	Jenny's Ball/Muddy Water (78)	10
56	Tempo A 147	Death Letter/Cemetery Blues	10
56	Tempo A 147	Death Letter/Cemetery Blues (78)	10
56	Decca F 10763	Kingdom Coming/I'm A Ding Dong Daddy	10
56	Decca F 10763	Kingdom Coming/I'm A Ding Dong Daddy (78)	10
56	Decca FJ 10779	Waiting For A Train/Railroadin' Man	8
56	Decca FJ 10779	Waiting For A Train/Railroadin' Man (78)	8
56	Decca FJ 10806	My Canary Has Circles Under His Eyes/Heebie Jeebies	8
56	Decca FJ 10806	My Canary Has Circles Under His Eyes/Heebie Jeebies (78)	8
57	Decca FJ 10840	Black Bottom/Magnolia	8
57	Decca FJ 10840	Black Bottom/Magnolia (78)	8
59	Decca F 11115	Abdul Abulbul Amir/Get Away, Old Man, Get Away	5
59	Decca F 11115	Abdul Abulbul Amir/Get Away, Old Man, Get Away (78)	8
60	Pye 7N 15253	Ise A Muggin'/Run Come See Jerusalem	5
75	Warner Bros WB 16532	Ain't Misbehavin'/My Canary Has Circles Under His Eyes (p/s)	5
56	Tempo EXA 41	GEORGE MELLY WITH MICK MULLIGAN'S JAZZ BAND (EP)	12
56	Tempo EXA 47	GEORGE MELLY SINGS DOOM (EP, with Mick Mulligan's Jazz Band)	18
58	Decca DFE 6552	MICHIGAN WATER BLUES (EP)	10
58	Decca DFE 6557	ABDUL ABULBUL AMIR (EP)	10
61	Columbia SEG 8093	THE PSYCHOLOGICAL SIGNIFICANCE OF ANIMAL SYMBOLISM IN AMERICAN NEGRO FOLK MUSIC AND ALL THAT JAZZ (EP)	8

(see also Mick Mulligan Band)

MELO CATS
61	Blue Beat BB 54	Another Moses/ROLAND ALPHONSO & ALLEY CATS: Hully Gully Rock	18

(see also Mellow Cats)

MELODIANS
66	Island WI 3014	Lay It On/Meet Me	18
67	Coxsone CS 7004	I Should Have Made It Up/JOE HIGGS: Neighbour Neighbour	18
67	Treasure Isle TI 7006	You Don't Need Me/I Will Get Along	15
67	Treasure Isle TI 7022	You Have Caught Me/I Know Just How She Feels	15
67	Treasure Isle TI 7023	Last Train To Expo. '67/TOMMY McCOOK & SUPERSONICS: Expo	15
68	Treasure Isle TI 7028	Come On, Little Girl/TOMMY McCOOK & SUPERSONICS: Got Your Soul	15
68	Doctor Bird DB 1125	Little Nut Tree/You Are My Only Love	15
68	Doctor Bird DB 1139	Swing And Dine/I Could Be King	15

MINT VALUE £

68	Fab FAB 61	Sweet Rose/It Comes And Goes	25
69	Gas GAS 108	Ring Of Gold/You've Got It	7
69	Gas GAS 116	Personally Speaking/LLOYD ROBINSON: Trouble Trouble	7
69	Crab CRAB 15	When There Is You/UNIQUES: My Woman's Love	7
69	Trojan TR 660	Everybody Bawlin'/TOMMY McCOOK: Kilowatt	8
69	Trojan TR 695	Sweet Sensation/It's My Delight	5
70	Trojan TR 7720	A Day Seems So Long/BEVERLEY'S ALLSTARS: Project	6
70	Trojan TR 7764	Say Darling Say/Come Rock It To Me	8
70	High Note HS 044	Love Is A Good Thing/No Nola	6
70	Summit SUM 8505	Walking In The Rain/Rivers Of Babylon	7
70	Summit SUM 8508	Rivers Of Babylon/BEVERLEY'S ALL STARS: Babylon Version	6
71	Duke DU 128	The Sensational Melodians (Parts 1 & 2)	6
71	Summit SUM 8512	It Took A Miracle/BEVERLEY'S ALLSTARS: Miraculous Version	5
71	Summit SUM 8522	Come Ethiopians, Come/BEVERLEY'S ALL STARS: Version Two	7
71	Summit SUM 8532	My Love, My Life/My Love, My Life – Version	6
72	Summit SUM 8534	The Time Has Come/BEVERLEY'S ALL STARS: McIntosh (B-side actually "No Sins At All" by Melodians)	6
72	Bullet BU 496	Tropical Land/HUGH ROY & SLIM SMITH: Love I Bring	6
72	Duke DU 130	The Mighty Melodians (Adapted) (Parts 1 & 2)	6
72	Attack ATT 8025	This Beautiful Land/MELODIOUS RHYTHMS: Version	6
72	Attack ATT 8031	Without You (What Would I Do)/DYNAMITES: Instrumental	6
72	Punch PH 111	Round And Round/UPSETTERS: Round Version	6
73	Randy's RAN 530	Passion Love/Love Makes The World Go Round	6

(see also Gentiles, Tony Brevett, Brent Dowe, Jaylads, Trevor McNaughton, Gaylads, Joe Grinne)

JOHNNY MELODY
| 67 | Pyramid PYR 6023 | Govern Your Mouth (actually by George Dekker)/ROLAND ALPHONSO: Peace And Love | 10 |

(see also Lloyd & Johnny Melody under 'L', Lloyd Terrell)

MELODY ENCHANTERS
| 63 | Island WI 049 | Enchanter's Ball/I'll Be True | 12 |
| 63 | R&B JB 117 | Gone Gone/Blueberry Hill | 12 |

MELODY FAIR
| 68 | Decca F 12801 | Something Happened To Me/Sittin', Watchin', Waitin' | 4 |

'MELODY MAKER' ALLSTARS
(see under Humphrey Lyttleton)

MELO'S MARITIME
| 67 | Philips BF 1602 | Blow The Man Up/Maneater | 4 |

KANSAS CITY MELROSE/CASINO SIMPSON
| 72 | Chicago Piano 12-001 | KANSAS CITY MELROSE/CASINO SIMPSON (LP) | 15 |

MONIQUE MELSEN
| 71 | Decca F 23170 | The Love Beat/Pomme Pomme Pomme | 12 |

JOE MELSON
61	Polydor NH 66959	Oh Yeah!/What's The Use I Still Love You	45
61	Polydor NH 66961	Hey Mister Cupid/No One Really Cares	45
64	Hickory 45-1229	Stay Away From Her/His Girl	6

MELTING BEAR
| 85 | Beggars Banquet BEG 144 | It Makes No Difference/Nature's Way/Sea Song (unreleased, white label test pressings only) | 6 |

(see also Icicle Works)

MELTON CONSTABLE
| 70s | SIS private pressing | MELTON CONSTABLE (LP) | 250 |

HAROLD MELVIN & BLUE NOTES
72	CBS 8291	I Miss You (Parts 1 & 2)	5
72	CBS 8496	If You Don't Know Me By Now/Let Me Into Your World	5
75	Route RT 06	Get Out/You May Not Love Me	6
77	ABC 4161	Reaching For The World/Stay Together	5
73	CBS 65350	HAROLD MELVIN & THE BLUES NOTES (LP)	12
73	CBS Q 65859	BLACK AND BLUE (LP, quadrophonic)	12

MELVINS
| 90 | Tupelo TUPEP 10 | Sweet Young Thing Ain't Sweet No More/STEEL POLE BATH TUB: I Dreamed I Dream (12", p/s, green vinyl, 600 only) | 12 |

MEMBERS
78	Stiff/One Off OFF 3	Solitary Confinement/Rat Up A Drainpipe (p/s)	8
79	Virgin VS 242	The Sound Of The Suburbs/Handling The Big Jets (clear vinyl, window p/s)	5
80	Virgin VS 352	Flying Again/Disco Oui Oui/Live In A Lift/Rat Up A Drainpipe (double pack, gatefold p/s)	4

MEMBRANES
| 80 | Vinyl Drip VD 005 | Flexible Membrane: Fashionable Junkies/Almost China (flexidisc, p/s) | 6 |
| 82 | Vinyl Drip VD 007 | Muscles/Entertaining Friends/All Roads Lead To Norway (p/s) | 5 |

MEMOS
| 59 | Parlophone R 4616 | The Biddy Leg/My Type Of Girl | 75 |

MEMPHIS BEND
| 76 | United Artists UP 36132 | Ubangi Stomp/Tennessee | 8 |
| 77 | United Artists UAS 30036 | GOOD ROCKIN' TONITE (LP) | 12 |

MEMPHIS HORNS
71	Atlantic 2091 080	Woolly Bully/I Can't Turn You Loose	5
77	RCA PB 0836	Get Up And Dance/Don't Abuse It	5
71	Mojo 2466 010	THE MEMPHIS HORNS (LP)	20

MEMPHIS JUG BAND

55	HMV 7EG 8073	MEMPHIS JUG BAND (EP, withdrawn)	100
70s	Saydisc Matchbox RL 33	MEMPHIS JUG BAND (LP)	18
71	Saydisc Matchbox RL 337	MEMPHIS JUG BAND VOLUME 2 (LP)	18

MEMPHIS MINNIE

64	Heritage H 103	MEMPHIS MINNIE (EP)	50
69	Limited Edition (no cat. no.)	MEMPHIS MINNIE 1934-1936 (LP)	30
69	Limited Edition (no cat. no.)	MEMPHIS MINNIE 1934-1941 (LP)	30
69	Sunflower ET 1400	MEMPHIS MINNIE 1941-1949 (LP, 99 copies only)	35
74	Flyright LP 108	MEMPHIS MINNIE 1934-1941 (LP, reissue)	12
74	Flyright LP 109	MEMPHIS MINNIE 1941-1949 (LP, reissue)	12

MEMPHIS SLIM

53	Esquire 10-319	Harlem Bound/ST. LOUIS JIMMY R&B BAND: Holiday For Boogie (78)	30
60	Collector JDN 102	Pinetop's Blues/How Long	8
62	Storyville A 45055	Big City Girl/El Capitan	12
61	Collector JEN 5	GOING TO KANSAS CITY (EP)	20
62	Storyville SEP 385	STORYVILLE BLUES ANTHOLOGY VOL. 5 — BOOGIE WOOGIE AND THE BLUES (EP)	20
63	Vocalion VEP 170155	MEMPHIS SLIM AND LITTLE RICHARD (EP)	50
63	Summit LSE 2041	WORLD'S FOREMOST BLUES SINGERS (EP)	12
61	Collector JGN 1004	MEMPHIS SLIM IN THE U.S.A. (LP)	18
61	Collector JGN 1005	MEMPHIS SLIM (VOL. 2) (LP)	18
62	Bluesville BV 1018	JUST BLUES (LP)	20
62	Storyville SLP 118	MEMPHIS SLIM (LP)	12
62	Storyville SLP 138	THIS IS A GOOD TIME TO WRITE A SONG (LP)	12
62	Fontana 688 302 ZL	NO STRAIN (LP)	18
63	United Artists ULP 1042	BROKEN SOUL BLUES (LP)	18
64	Storyville SLP 118	TRAVELLIN' WITH THE BLUES (LP, reissue of "Memphis Slim")	15
64	Xtra XTRA 1008	MEMPHIS SLIM (LP)	15
64	Fidelio ATL 4115	THE WORLD'S FOREMOST BLUES SINGER (LP)	12
64	Fontana 688 701	ALONE WITH MY FRIENDS (LP)	20
65	Fontana TL 5254	CLAP YOUR HANDS (LP)	15
65	Melodisc MLPS 12-149	FATTENIN' FROGS FOR SNAKES (LP)	25
66	Fontana 688 315 ZL	FRISCO BAY BLUES (LP)	20
67	Polydor 623 211	PINETOP'S BLUES (LP)	15
68	Polydor 623 263	BLUESINGLY YOURS (LP, with Mickey Baker)	15
68	Xtra XTRA 5060	ALL KINDS OF BLUES (LP)	15
69	Xtra XTRA 1085	CHICAGO BLUES (LP)	15
69	Joy JOYS 143	AT THE GATE OF HORN (LP)	12
69	Beacon BEAS 6	LEGEND OF THE BLUES VOL. 2 (LP)	12
72	Barclay 920 211	BLUE MEMPHIS (LP, with Peter Green)	40
72	Barclay 920 332-3	OLD TIMES, NEW TIMES (2-LP)	15
72	Polydor 2460 155	ROCK ME BABY (LP)	12
73	Sonet SNTF 647	LEGACY OF THE BLUES: 7 (LP)	12
73	Ember EMB 3422	SOUL BLUES (LP)	12
74	Barclay 920 407	CLASSIC ALL AMERICAN MUSIC (LP)	12
70s	Xtra XTRA 5063	ALL KINDS OF BLUES (LP)	15
75	Barclay 90 034	GOING BACK TO TENNESSEE (LP)	12
76	Black Lion BLP 30196	CHICAGO BOOGIE (LP)	12

(see also Washboard Sam, Ivory Joe Hunter, Otis Spann)

MEMPHIS THREE

68	Page One POF 070	Wild Thing/She's A Yum Yum	5

MEN

79	Virgin VS 269	I Don't Depend On You/Cruel (p/s)	10
79	Virgin VS 269-12	I Don't Depend On You/Cruel (12", p/s)	15

(see also Human League, Philip Oakey & Giorgio Moroder)

MENACE

77	Illegal IL 004	Screwed Up/Insane Society (p/s)	7
77	Illegal IL 004	Screwed Up/Insane Society (12")	10
77	Small Wonder SMALL 5	G.L.C./I'm Civilized (p/s)	7
78	Illegal IL 008	I Need Nothing/Electrocutioner (p/s)	7
78	Fresh FRESH 14	The Young Ones/Tomorrow's World/Live For Today (p/s)	7
79	Small Wonder SMALL 16	Final Vinyl: Last Year's Youth/Carry No Banners (p/s)	7

(see also Aces, Vermilion & Aces)

CARLOS MENDES

72	Pye International 7N 25581	Shadows/Glow-Worm	8

SERGIO MENDES & BRASIL '66

68	A&M AMS 739	Scarborough Fair — Canticle/Canto Triste (p/s)	4
66	Pye NPL 28089	HERB ALPERT PRESENTS SERGIO MENDES AND BRASIL '66 (LP)	12
67	A&M AML(S) 902	EQUINOX (LP)	10
68	A&M AML 911	LOOK AROUND (LP)	10
69	A&M AMLS 922	FOOL ON THE HILL (LP)	10
69	A&M AMLS 948	CRYSTAL ILLUSIONS (LP)	10
70	A&M AMLS 989	LIVE AT EXPO 70 (LP)	30
70	A&M AMLS 2000	STILLNESS (LP)	20
72	A&M AMLS 64353	PRIMAL ROOTS (LP)	10
74	Bell BELLS 240	VINTAGE '74 (LP, as Sergio Mendes & Brazil '74)	12

MENDES PREY

83	MP AM 076	On To The Borderline/Runnin' For You (p/s)	50
86	Wag WAG 2	Wonderland/Can You Believe It (p/s)	25
86	Wag 12 WAG 2	Wonderland/Can You Believe It (12", p/s)	25

ENOCH & CHRISTY MENSAH
60s	Melodisc M 1569	Rebecca/Dakuku Dum	4

MENSWEAR
95	Laurel LAU 4	I'll Manage Somehow/Secondhand (p/s, 2,500 only)	8
95	Laurel LAUCD 4	I'll Manage Somehow/Secondhand (CD, 2,500 only)	15
95	Laurel LAUXDJ 5	Daydreamer (Radio Mix)/(Student Union Mix) (10", no'd white sl., 5,000 only)	10

MENTATZ
81	Naff N 001	Never Trust A Russian/Dead To The World (p/s)	4

MEN WITHOUT HATS
82	Statik STAT 13	Antarctic/Modern Dancing (p/s)	6
82	Statik STAT 14	I Got The Message/Utter Space (p/s)	5
85	Statik CDST	Folk Of The 80's Part 3 (CD)	7
87	Mercury MERCD 257	Pop Goes The World/The End (Of The World)/Pop Goes The World (Dance Mix) (CD)	7
85	Statik CDST 10	RHYTHM OF YOUTH (CD)	100

IAN MENZIES
58	Pye Jazz 7NJ 2027	Polly Wolly Doodle/In A Persian Market (with His New Stompers)	6
58	Pye Jazz NJ 2027	Polly Wolly Doodle/In A Persian Market (with His New Stompers) (78)	8
58	Pye Jazz 7NJ 2028	Bill Bailey Won't You Please Come Home/Hot Time In The Old Town Tonight (as Ian Menzies & Clyde Valley Stompers)	6
58	Pye Jazz NJ 2028	Bill Bailey Won't You Please Come Home/Hot Time In The Old Town Tonight (as Ian Menzies & Clyde Valley Stompers) (78)	8
59	Pye Jazz 7NJ 2031	The Fish Man/Salty Dog (as Ian Menzies & Clyde Valley Stompers)	5
61	Pye Jazz 7NJ 2046	Auf Wiedersehn/Taboo	10
58	Pye Jazz NJE 1049	MELODY MAKER ALL STARS (EP)	12
60	Pye Nixa NJE 1071	SWINGIN' SEAMUS (EP)	15
60	Pye Jazz NJL 26	IAN MENZIES AND THE CLYDE VALLEY STOMPERS (LP)	15

(see also Clyde Valley Stompers)

JOHNNY MERCER
53	Capitol LC 6633	CAPITOL PRESENTS JOHNNY MERCER (10" LP)	10
54	Capitol LC 6640	CAPITOL PRESENTS JOHNNY MERCER VOL. 2 (10" LP)	10
54	Capitol LC 6648	CAPITOL PRESENTS JOHNNY MERCER VOL. 3 (10" LP)	10
54	Capitol LC 6655	CAPITOL PRESENTS JOHNNY MERCER VOL. 4 (10" LP)	10

MARY MAE MERCER
65	Decca DFE 8599	MARY MAE MERCER (EP)	50

FREDDIE MERCURY
84	CBS A 4735	Love Kills/GEORGIO MORODER: Rotwang's Party (p/s)	8
84	CBS WA 4735	Love Kills/GEORGIO MORODER: Rotwang's Party (picture disc)	50
84	CBS TA 4375	Love Kills (Extended)/GEORGIO MORODER: Rotwang's Party (12", p/s)	12
85	CBS A 6019	I Was Born To Love You/Stop All The Fighting (p/s)	8
85	CBS DA 6019	I Was Born To Love You/Stop All The Fighting//Love Kills (Extended)/Stop All The Fighting (Extended) (double pack)	30
85	CBS TA 6019	I Was Born To Love You (7.03)/Stop All The Fighting (12", p/s)	20
85	CBS A 6413	Made In Heaven (Remix 3.59)/She Blows Hot And Cold (p/s)	10
85	CBS WA 6413	Made In Heaven (Remix)/She Blows Hot And Cold (shaped picture disc)	50
85	CBS WA 6413	Made In Heaven (Remix)/She Blows Hot And Cold (uncut shaped picture disc)	800
85	CBS TA 6413	Made In Heaven (Extended Remix 4.43)/Made In Heaven (Remix 3.59)/She Blows Hot And Cold (Extended Version) (12", p/s)	20
85	CBS A 6555	Living On My Own/My Love Is Dangerous (p/s)	8
85	CBS TA 6555	Living On My Own (Extended 6.38)/My Love Is Dangerous (Extended 6.25) (12", p/s)	18
85	CBS GTA 6555	Living On My Own (Extended 6.38)/My Love Is Dangerous (Extended 6.25) (12", gatefold p/s)	25
85	CBS A 6725	Love Me Like There's No Tomorrow/Let's Turn It On (p/s)	25
85	CBS TA 6725	Love Me Like There's No Tomorrow (Extended Version)/Let's Turn It On (Extended Version) (12", p/s)	45
85	CBS DTA 6725	Love Me Like There's No Tomorrow (Extended Version)/Let's Turn It On (Extended Version)//Living On My Own (Extended 6.38)/My Love Is Dangerous (Extended 6.25) (12", double pack, shrinkwrapped with stickers)	150
85	CBS TA 6725	Love Me Like There's No Tomorrow (Extended Version)/Let's Turn It On (Extended Version) (12", promo, white card sleeve, with sticker)	75
86	EMI EMI 5559	Time (From The Musical)/Time (Instrumental) (p/s, some with inner sleeve)	18/8
86	EMI 12EMI 5559	Time (From The Musical) (Extended)/Time/Time (Instrumental) (12", p/s)	15
87	Parlophone R 6151	The Great Pretender/Exercises In Free Love (Mercury Vocal) (p/s)	5
87	Parlophone RP 6151	The Great Pretender/Exercises In Free Love (Mercury Vocal) (shaped picture disc)	50
87	Parlophone RP 6151	The Great Pretender/Exercises In Free Love (Mercury Vocal) (shaped picture disc, with unfolded or folded plinth)	90/70
87	Parlophone RP 6151	The Great Pretender/Exercises In Free Love (Mercury Vocal) (uncut shaped picture disc)	500
87	Parlophone 10R 6151	The Great Pretender (Extended Version)/(7" Version)/Exercises In Free Love (7" Version) (10", 1-sided, printed white label, plain black die-cut sleeve, promo only)	40
87	Parlophone 12R 6151	The Great Pretender (Extended)/(The Great Pretender 7")/Exercises In Free Love (12", p/s)	12
87	Polydor POSP 887	Barcelona/Exercises In Free Love (Caballé Vocal) (with Montserrat Caballé, some with gatefold p/s)	8/5
87	Polydor POSPX 887	Barcelona (Single Version)/Exercises In Free Love (Caballé Vocal) (12" Version)/Barcelona (Extended) (12", some with gatefold p/s)	18/12
87	Polydor POSPP 887	Barcelona (7" Version)/Exercises In Free Love (Caballé Vocal) (7" Version)/Barcelona (Extended Version) (12", picture disc)	50

MINT VALUE £

87	Polydor POCD 887	Barcelona (7" Version)/Exercises In Free Love (Caballé Vocal) (7" Version)/ Barcelona (Extended Version) (CD, card p/s) 20
87	Polydor POCD 887	Barcelona/Exercises In Free Love (Version 2) (Caballé Vocal)/ Barcelona (Extended) (CD, autographed card p/s, promo only) .... 300+
87	Polydor PO 23 DJ	The Golden Boy (with Montserrat Caballé) (radio edit) (1-sided DJ sampler, p/s, with sticker) 150
88	Polydor POSP 23	The Golden Boy (with Montserrat Caballé)/The Fallen Priest (p/s) 10
88	Polydor POSPX 23	The Golden Boy/The Fallen Priest (Instrumental) (12", p/s) 20
88	Polydor POCD 23	The Golden Boy/The Fallen Priest/The Golden Boy (Instrumental) (CD) 30
88	Polydor POSP 29	How Can I Go On/Overture Piccante (with Montserrat Caballe) (p/s) 12
88	Polydor POSX 29	How Can I Go On/Overture Piccante (with Montserrat Caballe) (picture disc) 45
89	Polydor PZ 29	How Can I Go On/Guide Me Home/Overture Piccante (12", p/s) 25
89	Polydor PZCD 29	How Can I Go On/Guide Me Home/Overture Piccante (CD, picture disc) 30
88	Polydor CD 3 125 211	The Golden Boy/La Japanese/Barcelona (CD promo, unreleased p/s, jewel case) 75
89	Polydor 0805 548-2	Ensueno/Barcelona (Edit 4.24)/Exercises In Free Love/Barcelona (Extended Version 7.02)/Barcelona (Video) (CD Video) 60
89	Polydor 0805 580-2	The Fallen Priest/The Golden Boy (Album Version)/The Golden Boy (Instrumental Version)/The Golden Boy (Video) (CD Video) 60
92	Polydor PZCD 221	Barcelona (Single Version)/Exercises In Free Love (Caballé Vocal)/ Barcelona (Edit)/Barcelona/The Fallen Priest (TV Version) (CD) 8
92	Polydor PO 234	How Can I Go On/The Golden Boy (yellow p/s) 8
92	Polydor PZCD 234	How Can I Go On/The Golden Boy/The Fallen Priest (CD, yellow p/s) 10
92	Parlophone R 6331	In My Defence/Love Kills (Wolf Euro Mix) (p/s) 6
92	Parlophone CDR 6331	In My Defence (Original Version)/Love Kills (Wolf Euro Mix)/Mr. Bad Guy (Original Version)/Living On My Own (Underground Solutions Mix) (CD) 8
92	Parlophone CDRS 6331	In My Defence (Album Version)/In My Defence (Original Version)/Love Kills (Wolf Euro Mix)/She Blows Hot And Cold (CD) 8
93	Parlophone R 6336	The Great Pretender/Stop All The Fighting (p/s) 5
93	Parlophone CDRS 6336	The Great Pretender (Single Version)/The Great Pretender (Album Version)/ Stop All The Fighting/Exercises In Free Love (Mercury Vocal) (CD, digipak) 8
94	Parlophone R 6355	Living On My Own (Radio Version)/Living On My Own (Album Version) (p/s) 5
94	Parlophone 12R 6355	Living On My Own (Extended Version)/Living On My Own (Club Version)/ Living On My Own (Dub Version)/Living On My Own (L.A. Version) (12", p/s) 8
85	CBS 86312	MR. BAD GUY (LP, with inner sleeve) 12
85	CBS 40-86312	MR. BAD GUY (cassette, with extra remix) 12
85	CBS CD 86312	MR. BAD GUY (CD, with 3 extended mixes; beware of counterfeits) 100
94	Parlophone 7234 8 2814 10	FREDDIE MERCURY REMIXES (LP, unreleased) 40

(see also Queen, Larry Lurex, Eddie Howell, Billy Squier)

MERCY
| 69 | London HLZ 10273 | Love (Can Make You Happy)/Fireball .... 5 |

BURGESS MEREDITH
| 63 | Colpix PX 690 | Home In The Meadow/No Goodbye .... 7 |

LOTTIE MERLE
| 72 | Flyright 001 | Howling In The Moonlight/Catfish .... 5 |

ETHEL MERMAN
54	Brunswick 05346	A Husband — A Wife (with Jimmy Durante)/The Lake Song (with Ray Bolger).... 8
55	Brunswick 05381	(There's No Business Like) Show Business/Play A Simple Melody (B-side with Dan Dailey) 8
58	RCA RCA 1039	A New-Fangled Tango/Mutual Admiration Society (with Virginia Gibson) 6
58	RCA RCA 1039	A New-Fangled Tango/Mutual Admiration Society (with Virginia Gibson) (78) 8
52	Brunswick LAT 8016	SONGS FROM "CALL ME MADAM" (LP) 15
52	Brunswick 8539	CALL ME MADAM (LP, with Dick Haymes) 15
54	Brunswick LA 8636	SONGS SHE HAS MADE FAMOUS (10" LP) 18
54	Brunswick LA 8638	DUET FROM FORD 50TH ANNIVERSARY TV SHOW (LP, with Mary Martin) 15

(see also Jimmy Durante)

RAY MERRELL
60	Ember EMB S 113	Why Did You Leave Me?/Teenage Love............................. 5
60s	Aral PS 115	Battle Of Waterloo/Not Any More (some in p/s) 10/6
64	Pye 7N 15709	Where In The World/Share A Dream With Me 5
65	Pye 7N 15793	Almost There/Only In A Dream 5
67	Columbia DB 8204	Chiquita Mia/Lazy Miss Hazy................................... 5
69	Columbia DB 8643	Memories/Red Summer Roses 5
70	Jay Boy BOY 22	Tears Of Joy/Searchin' (withdrawn).............................. 150

TONY MERRICK
| 66 | Columbia DB 7913 | Lady Jane/Michelle .... 6 |
| 66 | Columbia DB 7995 | Wake Up/It's For You .... 5 |

BOB MERRILL
| 58 | Columbia DB 4086 | Nairobi/Jump When I Say Frog .... 6 |
| 58 | Columbia DB 4086 | Nairobi/Jump When I Say Frog (78)............................... 10 |

BUDDY MERRILL
| 66 | Vocalion VN 9261 | Sweet September/Sherk....................................... 12 |

ROBERT MERRILL
| 59 | RCA RCA 1109 | À Toujours/Gigi.. 5 |
| 59 | RCA RCA 1109 | À Toujours/Gigi (78)... 8 |

MERRITTS
| 70 | Hot Rod HR 113 | I Don't Want To Pt 1/HOT ROD ALL STARS: Version...................... 6 |

MERRYMEN
66	Doctor Bird DB 1004	Big Bamboo/Island Woman 10
69	Trojan TR 7707	Little Drummer Boy/Mary's Boy Child............................. 6
71	Duke DU 113	Big Bamboo/King Ja-Ja (both sides actually with Emille Straker).............. 6

MINT VALUE £

| 68 | Island ILP 984 | CARIBBEAN TREASURE CHEST (LP) | 25 |
| 60s | Merrydisc WIRL 1020 | THE MORE THE MERRIER (LP) | 15 |

(see also Soul Brothers)

JASON MERRYWEATHER
| 69 | Crystal CR 001 | My Summer Love/Abigail | 5 |

(see also Ricky Valance)

MERSEYBEATS
63	Fontana TF 412	It's Love That Really Counts/The Fortune Teller	8
64	Fontana TF 431	I Think Of You/Mister Moonlight	5
64	Fontana TF 459	Don't Turn Around/Really Mystified	6
64	Fontana TF 482	Wishin' And Hopin'/Milkman	6
64	Fontana TF 504	Last Night/See Me Back	7
65	Fontana TF 568	Don't Let It Happen To Us/It Would Take A Long Long Time	8
65	Fontana TF 607	I Love You, Yes I Do/Good Good Lovin'	6
65	Fontana TF 645	I Stand Accused/All My Life	7
69	Fontana TF 1025	I Think Of You/Wishin' And Hopin' (p/s)	5
81	Tudor CR 23	This Is Merseybeat (both sides) (p/s)	6
64	Fontana TE 17422	ON STAGE (EP)	30
64	Fontana TE 17423	I THINK OF YOU (EP)	30
64	Fontana TE 17432	THE MERSEYBEATS (EP)	25
64	Fontana TL 5210	THE MERSEYBEATS (LP)	85
65	Wing WL 1163	THE MERSEYBEATS (LP, reissue)	25
77	Look LKLP 6160	GREATEST HITS (LP)	12

(see also Merseys, Rockin' Horse, Tony Crane, Kirkbys, Quotations, Johnny Gustavson)

MERSEYBOYS
| 64 | Ace Of Clubs ACL 1169 | 15 GREAT SONGS BY JOHN, PAUL AND GEORGE (LP) | 15 |

MERSEYS
66	Fontana TF 694	Sorrow/Some Other Day	6
66	Fontana TF 732	So Sad About Us/Love Will Continue	7
66	Fontana TF 776	Rhythm Of Love/Is It Love?	7
67	Fontana TF 845	The Cat/Change Of Heart	10
68	Fontana TF 916	Penny In My Pocket/I Hope You're Happy	8
68	Fontana TF 955	Lovely Loretta/Dreaming	8
73	Philips 6006 258	Sorrow/MERSEYBEATS: I Think Of You	5

(see also Merseybeats, Crackers)

MERSEYSIPPI JAZZ BAND
57	Esquire 10-486	Ostrich Walk/Saturday Night Function (78)	8
55	Decca DFE 6251	AT THE ROYAL FESTIVAL HALL (EP)	10
55	Esquire EP 30	THE MERSEYSIPPI JAZZ BAND (EP)	15
55	Esquire EP 60	THE MERSEYSIPPI JAZZ BAND (EP)	15
56	Esquire EP 90	THE MERSEYSIPPI JAZZ BAND (EP)	15
56	Esquire EP 118	THE MERSEYSIPPI JAZZ BAND (EP)	15
57	Esquire EP 130	THE MERSEYSIPPI JAZZ BAND (EP)	15
54	Esquire 20-063	WEST COAST SHOUT (LP)	20
55	Esquire 20-083	ALL THE GIRLS (LP)	30
55	Esquire 20-088	MERSEY TUNNEL JAZZ (LP)	20
56	Esquire 20-093	ANY OLD RAGS (LP)	20

TEDDY MERTENS
| 63 | Oriole CB 1904 | Autumn Love/Try To Love Me Again | 5 |
| 63 | Oriole CB 1925 | This Is My Prayer/My River Of Memories (as Teddy Mertens' Trumpet) | 5 |

MERTON PARKAS
79	Beggars Banquet BEG 22	You Need Wheels/I Don't Want To Know You (coloured p/s with patch)	8/6
79	Beggars Banquet BEG 25	Plastic Smile/The Man With The Disguise (p/s)	5
79	Beggars Banquet BEG 30	Give It To Me Now/Gi's It (p/s)	5
80	Beggars Banquet BEG 43	Put Me In The Picture/In The Midnight Hour (p/s)	5
83	Well Suspect BLAM 002	Flat 19/Band Of Gold (p/s)	8
80s	Beggars Banquet BEG 22	You Need Wheels/I Don't Want To Know You (reissue, black & white p/s)	7
79	Beggars Banquet BEGA 11	FACE IN THE CROWD (LP)	12

(see also Style Council)

JUNIOR MERVIN
| 69 | Big Shot BI 527 | Hustler/Magic Touch | 8 |

MESS
| 80s | Reasonable MEP 1 | Tried And Trusted/I'm Falling (p/s) | 5 |

MESSAGE
| 70 | Songbird SB 1503 | Rum-Bum-A-Loo/Drummer Boy | 6 |

(see also Boris Gardner)

MESSENGERS
| 64 | Columbia DB 7344 | I'm Stealin' Back/This Little Light Of Mine | 7 |
| 65 | Columbia DB 7495 | When Did You Leave Heaven/More Pretty Girls Than One | 6 |

MESSENGERS (Jamaica)
| 73 | Attack ATT 8057 | Crowded City/Thula Thula | 5 |
| 73 | Bread BR 1116 | Cherry Baby/B.B. SEATON: Summertime | 5 |

METABOLISTS
79	Drömm DRO 1	Drömm/Slaves/Eulam's Beat (p/s, rough screen-printed & folded p/s)	12
79	Drömm DRO 1	Drömm/Slaves/Eulam's Beat (p/s, smooth printed & stapled p/s)	10
79	Drömm DRO 3	Identity/Tiz Hoz Nam (p/s)	8
70s	Metabolists	GOATMANAUT (cassette)	12
70s	Drömm D 1	GOATMANAUT (LP)	15
70s	Drömm DRO 2	HANSTEN KLORD (LP)	12

METAL BOYS
79	Rough Trade RT 016	Sweet Marilyn/Fugue For A Darkening Island (p/s)	4

(see also Metal Urbain)

METAL GURUS
90	Phonogram GURU 112	Merry Xmas Everybody/Metal Guru/Mama Weer All Crazee Now/ Gudbuy T'Jane (12", p/s)	7
90	Phonogram GURCD 1	Merry Xmas Everybody/Metal Guru/Mama Weer All Crazee Now/ Gudbuy T'Jane (CD)	7

(see also Mission, Slade)

METALLICA
SINGLES
84	Music For Nations 12 KUT 105	Jump In The Fire/Seek And Destroy (live)/Phantom Lord (live) (12", p/s, initially with beige labels [later red/yellow])	18/15
84	Music For Nations CV12 KUT 105	Jump In The Fire/Seek And Destroy (live)/Phantom Lord (live) (12", red vinyl, p/s)	30
84	Music For Nations 12 KUT 105XP	Jump In The Fire/Seek And Destroy (live)/Phantom Lord (live) (12", stickered sleeve with sew-on patch)	25
84	Music For Nations T 12 KUT 105	Jump In The Fire/Seek And Destroy (live)/Phantom Lord (live) (cassette)	10
84	M. F. N. T 12 KUT 112	Creeping Death/Am I Evil?/Blitzkrieg (cassette)	10
84	Music For Nations 12 KUT 112	Creeping Death/Am I Evil?/Blitzkrieg (12", p/s, initially with beige label, later red/yellow)	15/12
84	M. F. N. CV12 KUT 112	Creeping Death/Am I Evil?/Blitzkrieg (12", p/s, blue vinyl, red/yellow or 'Special Anniversary Edition' labels)	35
84	Music For Nations GV12 KUT 112	Creeping Death/Am I Evil?/Blitzkrieg (12", no p/s, 'Anniversary Gold Edition', gold vinyl, 3000 only; some mispressed with 1 side gold, 1 side black vinyl)	50/60
84	Music For Nations P12 KUT 112	Creeping Death/Am I Evil?/Blitzkrieg (12", picture disc, initially without barcode)	30
84	Music For Nations CD12 KUT 112	Creeping Death/Am I Evil?/Blitzkrieg Jump In The Fire/ Seek And Destroy (live)/Phantom Lord (live) (CD)	50
86	Music For Nations PKUT 105	Jump In The Fire/Phantom Lord (live) (shaped picture disc, initially without barcode)	25/20
87	Vertigo METAL 112	$5.98 EP — GARAGE DAYS RE-REVISITED: Helpless/Crash Course In Brain Surgery/The Small Hours/Last Caress - Green Hell (medley) (12", p/s, later copies allegedly add "The Wait")	20
88	Vertigo METAL 212	Harvester Of Sorrow/Breadfan/The Prince (12", p/s, some with 'skull' label)	18
88	Vertigo METAL CD 2	Harvester Of Sorrow/Breadfan/The Prince (CD, card sleeve)	20
89	Vertigo METAL 312	Jump In The Fire/Seek And Destroy (live)/Phantom Lord (live) (12", p/s, reissue)	8
89	Vertigo METAL 412	Creeping Death/Am I Evil?/Blitzkrieg (12", p/s, reissue)	10
89	Vertigo 842-219-2	Creeping Death/Am I Evil?/Blitzkrieg/Jump In The Fire/ Seek And Destroy (live)/Phantom Lord (live) (CD)	50
89	Vertigo METAL 5	One/Seek And Destroy (live) (silver/black labels, paper p/s)	8
89	Vertigo METAP 5	One/Seek And Destroy (live) (card p/s, some stickered, with rolled poster)	15
89	Vertigo METDJ 5	One/One (Edit) (unique blue cover, plus insert)	60
89	Vertigo METPD 510	One/Seek And Destroy (live) (10", picture disc with card)	25
89	Vertigo METAL 512	One (Demo Version)/For Whom The Bell Tolls (live)/Welcome Home (Sanitarium) (live) (12", p/s initially with white labels, later yellow)	15/10
89	Vertigo METAL 512	One (Demo Version)/For Whom The Bell Tolls (live)/Welcome Home (Sanitarium) (live) (12", p/s mis-labelled as "Seek and Destroy" [live])	12
89	Vertigo METG 512	One (Demo Version)/For Whom The Bell Tolls (live)/Welcome Home (Sanitarium) (live) (12", gatefold p/s, with booklet, some mispressed with B-side label both sides)	20
89	Vertigo METCD 5	One/For Whom The Bell Tolls (live)/Welcome Home (Sanitarium) (live) (CD)	20
90	Vertigo 875 487 1	THE GOOD, THE BAD AND THE LIVE — THE 6½ YEARS ANNIVERSARY COLLECTION (6 x 12", with live 4-track EP [METAL 612])	60
91	Vertigo METAL 7	Enter Sandman/Stone Cold Crazy (p/s)	5
91	Vertigo METAL 7	Enter Sandman/Stone Cold Crazy (picture disc in p/s, stickered)	15
91	Vertigo METAL 712	Enter Sandman/Stone Cold Crazy/Holier Than Thou (Demo)/ Enter Sandman (Demo) (12", p/s some with stickered sleeve)	8
91	Vertigo METBX 712	Enter Sandman/Stone Cold Crazy/Enter Sandman (Demo) (12", box with 4 photo prints)	20
91	Vertigo METCD 7	Enter Sandman/Stone Cold Crazy/Enter Sandman (Demo) (CD, picture disc in box with room for 3 more CDs)	35
91	Vertigo METAL 8	The Unforgiven/Killing Time (p/s)	4
91	Vertigo METAP 812	The Unforgiven/Killing Time /The Unforgiven (Demo) (picture disc, card insert)	10
91	Vertigo METAL 812	The Unforgiven/Killing Time/So What/The Unforgiven (Demo) (12", p/s, some stickered)	10
91	Vertigo METCD 8	The Unforgiven/Killing Time/The Unforgiven (Demo) (CD)	10
92	Vertigo METAL 9	Wherever I May Roam/Fade To Black (Live) (p/s)	4
92	Vertigo METAL 912	Wherever I May Roam/Last Caress – Am I Evil? – Battery (Live Medley)/ Wherever I May Roam (demo) (12", gatefold sleeve)	8
92	Vertigo METCD 9	Wherever I May Roam/Fade To Black (Live)/Wherever I May Roam (demo) (picture CD)	8
92	Vertigo METCB 9	Wherever I May Roam/Last Caress–Am I Evil?–Battery (Live Medley) (digipak CD)	10
92	Vertigo METAL 10	Nothing Else Matters/Enter Sandman (live) (p/s, black & white or black & silver label)	6/4
92	Vertigo METAL 1012	Nothing Else Matters/Enter Sandman (live)/Harvester Of Sorrow (live)/ Nothing Else Matters (Demo) (12", p/s)	8
92	Vertigo METCD 10	Nothing Else Matters/Enter Sandman (live)/Harvester Of Sorrow (live)/ Nothing Else Matters (Demo) (picture CD)	8
92	Vertigo METCL 10	Nothing Else Matters — Live At Wembley 20/4/92: Enter Sandman/ Sad But True/Nothing Else Matters (CD)	25

93	Vertigo METAL 11	Sad But True/Nothing Else Matters (p/s, stickered, no labels) 5
93	Vertigo METAL 1112	Sad But True/Nothing Else Matters (Elevator Version)/Creeping Death (live)/
		Sad But True (Demo) (12", p/s) 8
93	Vertigo METAL 1112	Sad But True/Nothing Else Matters (Elevator Version)/Creeping Death (live)/
		Sad But True (Demo) (12" picture disc with insert) 20
93	Vertigo METCD 11	Sad But True/Nothing Else Matters (Elevator Version)/Creeping Death (live)/
		Sad But True (Demo) (CD) 8
93	Vertigo METCH 11	Sad But True/Nothing Else Matters (live)/Sad But True (Demo) (CD, picture disc) . 8
96	Vertigo METJB 12	Until It Sleeps/Until It Sleeps (jukebox issue, no p/s) 8
96	Vertigo METAL 12	Until It Sleeps/2x4 (live)/Until It Sleeps (Moby Remix) (10" red vinyl, stickered) . . . 6
96	Vertigo METCX 12	Until It Sleeps/Kill-Ride (Medley)/Until It Sleeps (Moby Remix) (digipak CD) 10
97	Vertigo METJB 13	Hero Of The Day/Hero Of The Day (jukebox issue, no p/s) 8
96	Vertigo METCX 13	Hero Of The Day/Stone Dead Forever/Too Late Too Late/Mouldy (Demo) (CD) 7
96	Vertigo METCY 13	Hero Of The Day/Overkill/Damage Case/Stone Dead Forever/Too Late
		Too Late (CD, with poster in card cover) 10
96	Vertigo METAL 14	Mama Said/Ain't My Bitch (live) (picture disc with insert) 5

ALBUMS

83	M. For Nations MFN 7	KILL 'EM ALL (LP, 1st issue with beige labels [later red/yellow]) 25/18
84	M. For Nations MFN 27	RIDE THE LIGHTNING (LP, with inner sleeve, initially with beige labels &
		without barcode) 20
86	M. For Nations MFN 27P	RIDE THE LIGHTNING (LP, picture disc, initially lacking barcode) 25/22
86	M. For Nations MFN 7P	KILL 'EM ALL (LP, picture disc, some lacking picture on 1 side,
		initially lacking barcode) 25/22
86	M. For Nations MFN 60	MASTER OF PUPPETS (LP, with inner sleeve & insert) 18
86	M. For Nations MFN 60	MASTER OF PUPPETS (LP, mispressing, Side 1 label on both sides) 20
86	M. For Nations MFN 60P	MASTER OF PUPPETS (LP, picture disc, initially lacking barcode) 25/20
87	M. For Nations MFN 7DM	KILL 'EM ALL (2-LP, 'direct metal mastered' reissue, gatefold sleeve) 40
87	M. For Nations MFN 60DM	MASTER OF PUPPETS (2-LP, 'direct metal mastered' reissue,
		gatefold sleeve with poster) 25
87	M. For Nations MFN 27DM	RIDE THE LIGHTNING (2-LP, 'direct metal mastered' reissue,
		gatefold sleeve with insert) 25
89	Vertigo 838-140-1	RIDE THE LIGHTNING (LP, reissue, mispressing, Side 1 lists
		"Master Of Puppets" tracks) 15
90	Vertigo 888 788-1	GARAGE DAYS RE-REVISITED (mini-LP) 20
84	M. For Nations MFNCD 7	KILL 'EM ALL (CD) 30
84	M. For Nations MFN 27P	RIDE THE LIGHTNING (CD) 30
86	M. For Nations MFNCD 60	MASTER OF PUPPETS (CD) 25
91	Vertigo MECAN 1/510-022-0	THE METALLICAN (CD, gold disc in metal 'paint can' with video & T-shirt; 35,000 only) 75
93	Vertigo 518-725-0	LIVE SHIT, BINGE & PURGE (3-CD box set with 3 videos & 72-page book) 80

PROMOS

88	Vertigo MET CD 100	THE WHIPLASH SAMPLER (CD) 50
88	Vertigo METDJ 2	Harvester Of Sorrow/Harvester Of Sorrow (unique p/s) 70
89	Vertigo METDJ 512	One (Demo Version)/For Whom The Bell Tolls (live)/Welcome Home
		(Sanitarium) (live) (12", unissued, promo-only p/s) 60
91	Vertigo METDJ 7	Enter Sandman (Radio Edit)/Stone Cold Crazy (B-side actually silent) 12
96	Vertigo MET INT 1	LOAD — THE INTERVIEW (CD, with cue booklet) 50
96	Mercury MM CJ-1	MANDATORY METALLICA (CD, 7-track sampler) 40
97	Vertigo MMCJ-2	MANDATORY METALLICA 2 (2-CD, 17-track sampler) 50

METAL MIRROR

80	M&M MM 001	Rock 'N Roll Ain't Never Gonna Leave Us/English Booze (p/s) 80

METAL URBAIN

78	Radar ADA 20	Hysterie Connective/Pas Poubelle. 7
79	Rough Trade RT 001	Paris Maquis/Cle De Contact (p/s). 6
	(see also Metal Boys)	

METEORS

64	Polydor NH 52263	Get A Load Of This/Ruby Ann 4

METEORS

79	EMI EMI 5000	My Balls Ache/Action (p/s) 4

METEORS

81	Ace SW 65	METEOR MADNESS (EP, some on blue vinyl) 15/10
81	Ace SWT 65	METEOR MADNESS (10" EP, white label test pressings only, custom p/s) 80
81	Chiswick CHIS 147	Radioactive Kid/Graveyard Stomp (p/s) 10
81	Lost Soul LOST 101	The Crazed/Attack Of The Zorch Men (p/s) 10
81	Ace NS 74	Radioactive Kid/Graveyard Stomp (p/s, reissue, some clear or blue vinyl;
		most on black vinyl) 10/5
82	WXYZ ABCD 5	Mutant Rock/The Hills Have Eyes (p/s) 8
82	I.D. EYE 1	Johnny Remember Me/Fear Of The Dark/Wreckin' Crew (p/s) 5
82	I.D. EYE 1P	Johnny Remember Me/Fear Of The Dark/Wreckin' Crew (picture disc) 7
82	Lyntone LYN 12647	METEORS: Mutant Rock (Instrumental)/ANTI NOWHERE LEAGUE: World War
		Three/DEFECTS: Dance (red flexidisc with *Flexipop* magazine, issue 26) 7/5
84	Mad Pig PORK 1	I'm Just A Dog/Electro Rock (p/s) 6
85	Mad Pig PORK 1T	I'm Just A Dog (Wild Hog Mix Down)/Hoover Rock/Electro (12", p/s) 7
85	Mad Pig PORK 2	Fire, Fire/Little Red Riding Hood (p/s). 5
85	Mad Pig PORK 2T	Fire, Fire/Little Red Riding Hood/Stampede (King Ray Bat Scalator
		In The Dark Mix) (12", p/s) 8
85	Mad Pig PORK 3	Bad Moon Rising/Rhythm Of The Bell (p/s). 5
85	Mad Pig PORK 3T	Hogs And Cuties /Bad Moon Rising/Rhythm Of The Bell
		(What? Another Cover Mix) (12", p/s) 7
86	I.D. EYE 10	MUTANT ROCK (EP, green vinyl). 8
86	I.D. EYET 10	MUTANT ROCK (12" EP, green or blue vinyl) 12
86	Anagram ANA 31	Surf City/The Edge (p/s). 4
86	Anagram 12ANA 31	Surf City (Has Beens From Outer Space Mix)/The Edge/
		Johnny's Here (12", p/s). 10

MINT VALUE £

87	Anagram ANA 35	Go Buddy Go/Wildkat Ways (p/s)	5
87	Anagram 12ANA 35	Go Buddy Go (The Wonkey Donkey Mix)/Wildkat Ways/You Crack Me Up (p/s)	7
81	Ace MAD 1	THE METEORS MEET SCREAMIN' LORD SUTCH (mini-LP, 1 side each, 1,000 only, stickered cartoon print on plain card sleeve)	125
81	Lost Soul LOSTLP 3001	IN HEAVEN (LP)	20
86	Big Beat WIKA 47	TEENAGERS FROM OUTER SPACE (LP)	20
86	Big Beat WIKA 47CD	TEENAGERS FROM OUTER SPACE (CD)	18
87	Dojo LP56P	NIGHT OF THE WEREWOLF (LP, picture disc)	10

(see also Tall Boys, Clapham South Escalators, [Screamin'] Lord Sutch, Deadbeats)

METERS

69	Stateside SS 2140	Sophisticated Cissy/Sehorn's Farms	8
70	Direction 58-4751	Look-Ka-Py-Py/This Is My Last Affair	7
74	Reprise K 14367	People Say/Africa	6
75	Reprise K 14405	Fire On The Bayou/They All Asked For You	6
72	Reprise K 44242	CABBAGE ALLEY (LP)	20
74	Reprise K 54027	REJUVENATION (LP)	25
74	Island ILPS 9250	CISSY STRUT (LP)	25
75	Reprise K 54044	FIRE ON THE BAYOU (LP)	20
76	Reprise K 54076	BEST OF THE METERS (LP)	15
76	Reprise K 54078	TRICK BAG (LP)	18
77	Reprise K 56378	NEW DIRECTIONS (LP)	12
79	Pye PKL 5578	GOOD OLD FUNKY MUSIC (LP)	12

FRANK METIS ORCHESTRA

56	London REN 1048	SONGS FROM IRVING BERLIN'S 'SHOW BUSINESS' (EP)	10

METRONOME ALL STARS

51	Capitol CL 13545	Local 802 Blues/Early Spring (78, with Stan Getz & Miles Davis)	10

METROPAK

80	Metropak PAK 001	You're A Rebel/OK Let's Go/Run Run Run (numbered p/s)	6
80	Metropak PAK 002	Here's Looking At You/Walking (foldout card p/s)	5

METROPHASE

79	Neo London MS 01	In Black/Neo Beauty/Cold Rebellion (photocopied p/s with lyric insert)	8
79	Neo London MS 02	New Age/Frames Of Life (foldout p/s, stamped white labels)	8
81	Fresh FRESH 6	In Black/Neo Beauty/Cold Rebellion (reissue, better quality p/s with insert)	6

(see also Swell Maps)

METROPOLITAN POLICE BAND

66	Columbia DB 8095	Thunderbirds March/P.C. ALEXANDER MORGAN: Sussex By The Sea	10

METROTONE

97	Wurlitzer Jukebox WJ 40	Kiss Me Awake/Byddant Fel Y Ser/Four Continuous Tones (p/s, 1,000 only)	5
98	Earworm WORM 21	THE LESS YOU HAVE THE MORE YOU ARE (LP, 4 copies only on black vinyl)	40

M.E.V.

69	Polydor 583 769	MUSICA ELETTRONICA VIVA (LP)	15

ANTHONY MEYNELL

82	Hi-Lo LO 01	HITS FROM 3000 YEARS AGO (LP, purple sleeve)	10

(see also Squire)

LEE MEZA

67	Stateside SS 589	If It Happens/One Good Thing Leads To Another	20

MEZZ MEZZROW

62	Storyville SEP 394	KING JAZZ STORY (EP)	10
55	Vogue LAE 12007	PLAYEL CONCERT (LP)	12

(see also Mezzrow–Bechet Quartet)

MEZZROW–BECHET QUINTET

50	King Jazz KJ 4	De Luxe Stomp/Perdido Stomp (78)	8
50	King Jazz KJ 6	Breathless Blues/Groovin' The Minor (78)	8
51	King Jazz KJ 10	Jelly Roll/Gone Away Blues (78)	8
56	Vogue LAE 12017	THE MEZZROW-BECHET QUINTET (LP)	12

(see also Sidney Bechet)

M.F.Q.

(see under Modern Folk Quartet)

M.F.S.B.

81	Phil. Intl. PIR 12-9501	Mysteries Of The World/Manhattan Skyline (12", no p/s)	8
81	Phil. Intl. PIR 84251	Mysteries Of The World (LP)	12

M-G-M STUDIO ORCHESTRA

54	MGM SP 1099	Peddler Song/Antonia/Fisherman's Song	5
55	MGM SP 1144	Rock Around The Clock/"Blackboard Jungle" Love Theme	10
55	MGM MGM 861	Rock Around The Clock/"Blackboard Jungle" Love Theme (78)	8

MIAMI SOUND MACHINE

84	Epic A 4800	Prisoner Of Love/Toda Tuya (Toda Dia Eva Dia De Indio) (p/s)	4
84	Epic TX 4800	Prisoner Of Love/Toda Tuya (Toda Dia Eva Dia De Indio)/ Prisoner Of Love (Instrumental) (12", p/s)	7
85	Epic A 6537	Bad Boy (Shep Pettibone Remix)/Movies (p/s)	4
85	Epic DA 6537	Bad Boy (Shep Pettibone Remix)/Movies//Dr. Beat/When Someone Comes (double pack, p/s)	10
85	Epic QTA 6537	Bad Boy (Club Mix)/Bad Boy (Rubber-Club-Dub Mix)/Movies (12", p/s)	7
85	Epic TA 6361	Conga! (Dance Mix)/Conga! (Instrumental) (12", p/s)	7
86	Epic A 6956	Falling In Love (Uh-Oh)/Surrender Paradise (p/s)	4
86	Epic DTA 6956	Falling In Love (Uh-Oh)/Conga (The Stronga-Conga Remix)/ Surrender Paradise//Bad Boy (Shep Pettibone Remix)/Bad Boy (Dub Version) (12", shrinkwrapped double pack)	20

MINT VALUE £

86	Epic 650 251 7	Falling In Love (Uh-Oh) (Remix)/Surrender Paradise (p/s)	4
86	Epic TA 6956	Falling In Love (Uh-Oh)/Conga (The Stronga-Conga Remix)/ Surrender Paradise (12", p/s)	7
84	Epic EPC 26167	EYES OF INNOCENCE (LP)	10
84	Epic CDEPC 26167	EYES OF INNOCENCE (CD)	20
85	Epic EPC 26491	PRIMITIVE LOVE (LP)	10
85	Epic CDEPC 26491	PRIMITIVE LOVE (CD)	20

(see also Gloria Estefan [& Miami Sound Machine])

MICHA
| 65 | Pye 7N 15982 | Protest Singer/Serpent | 6 |

GEORGE MICHAEL
84	Epic A 4603	Careless Whisper/Careless Whisper (Instrumental) (poster p/s)	30
84	Epic QTA 4603	Careless Whisper (Extended Mix)/Careless Whisper (Special Version - Wexler)/Careless Whisper (Instrumental) (12", title p/s)	30
84	Epic WA 4603	Careless Whisper (Extended Mix)/Careless Whisper (Instrumental) (12", picture disc, clear or black rim)	each 30
87	Epic LUST QT 1	I Want Your Sex (Monogamy Mix: Rhythm 1 Lust, Rhythm 2 Brass In Love, Rhythm 3 A Last Request)/Hard Day (12", gatefold envelope p/s)	8
87	Epic CDLUST 1	I Want Your Sex (Monogamy Mix: Rhythm 1 Lust, Rhythm 2 Brass In Love, Rhythm 3 A Last Request) (CD, gatefold gard p/s)	8
87	Epic EMU C3	Faith/Faith (Instrumental)/Hand To Mouth (cassette)	6
87	Epic EMUP 3	Faith/Faith (Instrumental)/Hand To Mouth (12", picture disc)	20
87	Epic EMU 4	Father Figure/Love's In Need Of Love Today (with calendar & stickered p/s)	8
87	Epic EMUT 4	Father Figure/Love's In Need Of Love Today/Father Figure (Instrumental) (12", stickered p/s with poster)	8
88	Epic EMUP 4	Father Figure/Love's In Need Of Love Today (square picture disc in wallet)	15
88	Epic CD EMU 4	Father Figure/Love's In Need Of Love Today/Father Figure (Instrumental) (CD)	12
88	Epic CD EMU 3	Faith/Hand To Mouth/Hard Day (Remix) (CD)	12
88	Epic EMU B5	One More Try/Look At Your Hands (p/s, shrinkwrapped with badge)	12
88	Epic EMU T5	One More Try/Look At Your Hands (12", p/s with poster)	8
88	Epic EPC 651 5322	One More Try/Look At Your Hands (3" CD, 5" case with adaptor)	8
88	Epic CD EMU 5	One More Try/Look At Your Hands (CD, picture disc)	15
88	Epic EMU G6	Monkey/Monkey (A Capella) (gatefold p/s, with photo insert)	7
88	Epic CD EMU 6	Monkey (Extended Version)/(A'Capella)/(Extra Bits)/(7" Edit) (CD)	12
88	Epic CD EMU 7	Kissing A Fool/(Instr.)/A Last Request (I Want Your Sex Part 3) (CD, card p/s)	8
89	Epic Solid Gold 654 601-3	I Want Your Sex (Parts 1 & 2)/A Different Corner/Careless Whisper (3" CD)	8
90	Epic GEOC 1	Praying For Time/If You Were My Woman/Waiting (Reprise) (CD, no'd p/s)	10
90	Epic GEO C2	Waiting For That Day/Fantasy/Father Figure/Kissing A Fool (CD, picture disc)	8
90	Epic GEOC 3	Freedom '90/Mother's Pride/Freedom (Back To Reality Mix) (CD)	10
91	Epic 656 647 5	Heal The Pain/Soul Free/Hand To Mouth (CD, gatefold card p/s)	8
91	Epic XPC 4060	WEMBLEY: I Believe/Freedom (Back To Reality Mix)/If You Were My Woman/ Fantasy (cassette, concert freebie)	25
91	Epic 657 646-5	Don't Let The Sun Go Down On Me/I Believe (When I Fall In Love It Will Be Forever [with Elton John]) (live)/WHAM!: Last Christmas (12", foldout poster p/s)	7
91	Epic 657 646-2	Don't Let The Sun Go Down On Me/I Believe (When I Fall In Love It Will Be Forever [with Elton John]) (live)/If You Were My Woman/Fantasy (CD)	8
92	Epic 658 058-2	Toofunky/Crazy Man Dance/Toofunky (Extended) (CD, picture disc)	10
96	Virgin VSLH 1571	Jesus To A Child/One More Try (Live Gospel Version) (jukebox issue, no p/s)	8
96	Virgin VSLH 1579	Fastlove/I'm Your Man (jukebox issue, no p/s)	5
96	Virgin VSLH 1595	Spinning The Wheel (Radio Edit)/You Know That I Want To (jukebox issue, no p/s)	6
97	Virgin VSLH 1626	Older (Radio Edit)/I Can't Make You Love Me (jukebox issue, no p/s)	5
97	Virgin VSLH 1641	Star People '97/Everything She Wants (jukebox issue, no p/s)	7
97	Virgin VSLH 1663	You Have Been Loved/The Strangest Thing '97 (Radio Edit) (jukebox issue, no p/s)	5
99	Virgin GM 99	Roxanne (CD, 1 track, card p/s, promo only)	12
99	Virgin GMX 99	Miss Sarajevo (CD, 1 track, card p/s, promo only)	12
99	Epic XPR 3291	Outside (Hex Hector Mix)/(Dub Mix) (12", white sleeve and sticker, promo only)	20
87	Epic 460000 9	FAITH (CD, extra tracks, picture disc, PVC box, some sealed)	50/40
90	Epic 467295 2	LISTEN WITHOUT PREJUDICE VOLUME 1 (CD, picture disc, stickered case)	40
99	Epic GMCD 1	LADIES AND GENTLEMAN - THE BEST OF (CD, sampler, card case, promo only)	30
99	Epic CDVDJ 2920	SONGS FROM THE LAST MACHINE (CD, promo, card sleeve)	20

(see also Wham!, Deon Estus, Boogie Box High, Elton John, Queen)

CODY MICHAELS
| 79 | Grapevine GRP 121 | 7 Days — 52 Weeks/VIRTUE ORCHESTRA: Don't Look Back (Instrumental) | 6 |

LEE MICHAELS
68	A&M AMS 763	Heighty Hi/Want My Baby	5
71	A&M AMS 863	Do You Know What I Mean/Keep The Circle Turning	5
72	A&M AMS 882	Can I Get A Witness/You Are What You Do	5
69	A&M AML(S) 928	RECITAL (LP)	12
69	A&M AML(S) 956	LEE MICHAELS (LP)	12

MARILYN MICHAELS
| 60 | RCA RCA 1208 | Tell Tommy I Miss Him/Everyone Was There But You | 8 |

MICHAEL SCHENKER GROUP
80	Chrysalis CHS 2455	Armed And Ready/Bijou Pleasurette (p/s, clear vinyl)	6
80	Chrysalis CHS 2471	Cry For The Nations/Into The Arena (live) (p/s, clear vinyl)	5
81	Chrysalis CHS 2541	Ready To Rock/Attack Of The Mad Axeman (p/s, clear vinyl)	5
81	Sounds FREEBIE No. 1	Let Sleeping Dogs Lie/PAT BENATAR: Promises In The Dark (Edit) (flexidisc in red printed sleeve, free with *Sounds*)	6/5
82	Chrysalis CHS 2636	Dancer/Girl From Uptown (picture disc)	5

MICHAEL SCHENKER GROUP

82	Chrysalis CHS 2636	Dancer/Girl From Uptown (p/s, clear vinyl)	5
82	Chysalis PCHR 1393	ASSAULT ATTACK (LP, picture disc)	12
83	Chysalis CHRP 1441	BUILT TO DESTROY (LP, picture disc, U.S. remixes)	12

(see also McAuley Schenker Group, Michael Schenker, Scorpions, UFO, Cozy Powell, Graham Bonnet, Alex Harvey Band)

MICHELLE
66	Polydor BM 56070	Sally Fool/I Don't Know Your Name	6

MICHIGAN RAG
72	Blue Horizon 2096 009	Don't Run Away/She's Looking Good	15

MICHIGANS
63	Vogue V 9207	Intermission Riff/Tea For Two	10

MICK & MALCOLM
66	Piccadilly 7N 35344	Little Venice/In A Game Of Chess	4
67	Piccadilly 7N 35372	Big Black Smoke/Two Or Three Minutes Of My Time	4

MICKEY (Baker) & KITTY (Noble)
60	London HLE 9054	Buttercup/My Reverie	25

MICKEY (Baker) & SYLVIA
57	HMV POP 331	Love Is Strange/I'm Going Home	275
57	HMV POP 331	Love Is Strange/I'm Going Home (78)	60
58	RCA RCA 1064	Rock And Stroll Room/Bewildered	35
58	RCA RCA 1064	Rock And Stroll Room/Bewildered (78)	45
60	RCA RCA 1206	Sweeter As The Day Goes By/Mommy Out De Light	15
65	RCA Victor RCA 1487	Love Is Strange/Dearest	25
65	RCA Camden CDN 5133	LOVE IS STRANGE (LP)	120

(see also Sylvia [Robbins])

MICKEY FINN (& BLUE MEN)
64	Blue Beat BB 203	Tom Hark/Please Love Me (as 'Mickey Finn & the Blue Men')	25
64	Oriole CB 1927	Pills/Hush Your Mouth (as 'Mickey Finn & the Blue Men')	40
64	Oriole CB 1940	Reelin' & A'Rockin'/I Still Want You (as 'Mickey Finn & the Blue Men')	40
65	Columbia DB 7510	The Sporting Life/Night Comes Down (as 'The Mickey Finn')	50
66	Polydor 56719	I Do Love You/If I Had You Baby (as 'The Mickey Finn')	35
67	Direction 58-3086	Garden Of My Mind/Time To Start Loving You (as 'The Mickey Finn')	50
95	Noiseburger 3	Ain't Necessarily So/God Bless The Child (foldaround p/s in poly bag, 1,000 only, 1st 500 signed)	10/5

BOBBY "BOBCATS" MICKLEBURGH
53	Esquire 10-327	Tin Roof Blues/Jazz Me Blues (78)	10
54	Esquire 10-337	Mahogany Hall Stomp/Basin Street Blues (78)	10
55	Esquire EP 40	MICKLEBURGH'S BOBCATS (EP)	15
56	Esquire EP 73	MICKLEBURGH'S BOBCATS (EP)	15

MICROBE
69	CBS 4158	Groovy Baby/MICROBOP ENSEMBLE: Your Turn Now	4

MICRODISNEY
82	Kabuki KAMD 2	Hello Rascals/The Helicopter Of The Holy Ghost (p/s)	6
83	Kabuki KAMD 4	Pink Skinned Man/Fiction Land (p/s)	5
80s	Virgin V2505	39 MINUTES (LP)	18
80s	Rough Trade ROUGH 75	EVERYBODY IS FANTASTIC (LP)	15
80s	Rough Trade ROUGH 85	THE CLOCK COMES DOWN THE STAIRS (LP)	12
88	Rough Trade RTM 155	WE HATE YOU WHITE SOUTH AFRICAN BASTARDS (LP)	20

(see also Cathal Coughlan)

TONY MIDDLETON
65	London HLR 9983	My Little Red Book (as Burt Bacharach Orchestra with Tony Middleton)/BURT BACHARACH ORCHESTRA: What's New Pussycat	20
66	Polydor BM 56704	To The Ends Of The Earth/Don't Ever Leave Me	325
78	Grapevine GRP 115	Paris Blues/Out Of This World	8

(see also Willows, Burt Bacharach)

MIDGET
97	Radar/Pet Sounds TINY 1	Kylie And Jason/Pathetically Devoted To You (p/s, 1,000 only, some with badge)	5/4

MIDNIGHT CRUISER
77	It IT 2	Rich Bitch/Striker (p/s)	10

MIDNIGHTERS
55	Parlophone DP 399	Work With Me Annie/Sexy Ways (78, export issue)	60
55	Parlophone DP 422	Annie Had A Baby/THUNDERBIRDS: Pledging My Love (78, export issue)	60

(see also Hank Ballard)

MIDNIGHT MOVERS
72	Mojo 2092 038	Why Can't We Do It In The Road (Parts 1 & 2)	5
73	Contempo C 7	Follow The Wind (Parts 1 & 2)	6

MIDNIGHT RAGS
80	Ace ACE 005	Public Enemy/Alcatraz/Mamma Said (p/s)	8
80	Velvet Moon VM 1	The Cars That Ate New York/Oscar Automobile (p/s, withdrawn)	8

(see also Paul Roland, Weird Strings)

MIDNIGHTS
66	Ember EMB S 220	(Won'tcha) Show Me Around/Only Two Can Play	8
63	MEP 101/MN 1/EAG-EP-134	MIDNIGHTS (EP, private pressing)	125

MIDNIGHT SHIFT
66	Decca F 12487	Saturday Jump/Living Fast	15

MIDNIGHT SUN
72	MCA MKPS 2019	MIDNIGHT SUN (LP)	20
72	MCA MKPS 2024	WALKING CIRCLES (LP)	20

| 73 | MCA MCF 2687 | MIDNIGHT SUN (LP, reissue) | 15 |
| 73 | MCA MCF 2691 | WALKING CIRCLES (LP, reissue) | 15 |

M.I. FIVE
| 66 | Parlophone R 5486 | You'll Never Stop Me Loving You/Only Time Will Tell | 60 |

(see also Maze, Deep Purple)

MIGHT OF COINCIDENCE
| 72 | Entropia BM 0001 | WHY COULDN'T PEOPLE WAIT (LP) | 100 |

MIGHTY AVENGERS (U.K.)
64	Decca F 11891	Hide Your Pride/Hey Senorita	12
64	Decca F 11962	So Much In Love/Sometime They Say	12
65	Decca F 12085	Blue Turns To Grey/I'm Lost Without You	18
65	Decca F 12198	(Walkin' Thru The) Sleepy City/Sir Edward And Lady Jane	20

(see also Andrew Oldham)

MIGHTY AVENGERS (Jamaica)
| 66 | Rymska RA 101 | Scatter Shot (actually by Byron Lee & Dragonaires)/BYRON LEE: Like You Do (B-side actually "No One" by Techniques) | 15 |

MIGHTY BABY
71	Blue Horizon 2096 003	Devil's Whisper/Virgin Spring	20
69	Head HDLS 6002	MIGHTY BABY (LP, gatefold sleeve)	70
71	Blue Horizon 2931 001	A JUG OF LOVE (LP, with lyric insert)	100
84	Psycho PSYCHO 31	EGYPTIAN TOMB (LP, reissue of "Mighty Baby" in different sleeve)	15

(see also Action, Robin Scott, Habibiyya, Keith Christmas, Gary Farr, Stone's Masonry)

THEE MIGHTY CAESARS
86	Empire LWC 604	Ten Bears Of The Comanches/Baby What's Wrong (p/s)	6
86	Media Burn MB 5	Little By Little/The Swag/What You've Got/Cyclonic (12", p/s)	7
88	Swag SWG 001	She's Just Fifteen Years Old/The Swag (flexi with *Pandora's Box* fanzine)	10/7

(see also Milkshakes, Prisoners, Billy Childish, Thee Headcoats)

MIGHTY DOUGLAS
60s	Jump Up JU 501	Laziest Man/Dance Me Lover	7
60s	Jump Up JU 508	Teacher Teacher/Split Me In Two	7
60s	Jump Up JU 509	Ugliness/My Wicked Boy Child	7

MIGHTY FLEA & MICKEY BAKER
| 72 | Polydor 2058 328 | Bloodshot Eyes/Charley Stone | 5 |
| 73 | Polydor 2460 185 | LET THE GOOD TIMES ROLL (LP) | 20 |

MIGHTY FLYERS
| 74 | Myrrh MYR 1016 | LOW FLYING ANGELS (LP, with insert) | 20 |

(see also Mick Abrahams)

MIGHTY LEMON DROPS
85	Dreamworld DREAM 5	Like An Angel/Something Happens/Sympathise With Us (12", p/s)	7
86	Dreamworld DREAM 006	Like An Angel/Now She's Gone (p/s)	4
87	Tardis 004/ Lyntone LYN 18687	The Happy Head Demos: Uptight/Behind Your Back (flexidisc, stickered plain sleeve, free with *The Beast* fanzine)	7/4
89	fan club	Fall Down (Like The Rain) (Original Demo)/Breaking Down (Original Arrangement) (250 copies only)	8
90	Lyntone	Sometimes Good Guys Don't Wear White (live at the Dominion) (p/s, gig freebie flexidisc, blue or black p/s)	each 4
85	private cassette	SOME OF MY BEST FRIENDS ARE SONGS (8-song cassette, 150 only)	15

(see also Active Restraint, Another Dream, Wild Flowers)

MIGHTY MEN
| 62 | Salvo SLO 1804 | No Way Out/You Too Much (99 copies only) | 30 |

MIGHTY MIGHTY
| 86 | Girlie GAYE 001 | Everybody Knows The Monkey/You're On My Mind (foldover p/s in poly bag) | 5 |
| 86 | Sha La La 001 | Throwaway/CLOUDS: Jenny Nowhere (p/s flexi free with various fanzines) | 6 |

MIGHTY MO
| 72 | Columbia DB 8851 | Ape Call/Heavy Bear | 6 |

MIGHTY POWER
| 67 | Jump Up JU 513 | You're Wasting Your Time/Smart Barbarian | 7 |

MIGHTY SAM
66	Stateside SS 534	Sweet Dreams/Good Humor Man	10
66	Stateside SS 544	Fannie Mae/Badmouthin'	10
68	Stateside SS 2076	When She Touches Me/Just Like Old Times	10
70	Soul City SC 115	Papa True Love/I Need A Lot Of Lovin'	12
70	Soul City SCM 004	MIGHTY SOUL (LP)	35

MIGHTY SPARROW
59	Melodisc 1491	Goaty/LORD MELODY: I Confess (78)	12
60	Kalypso XX 22	Mr. Herbert/Simpson	6
68	NEMS 56-3558	Mr. Walker/Carnival In '68	6
60s	Jump Up JU 523	Village Ram/Pull Pistle Gang	6
69	Fab FAB 116	Mr. Walker/Jane	6
70	Fab FAB 147	I Don't Wanna Lose You/The Truth	6
71	Duke DU 114	Maria/Only A Fool	5
71	Jump Up JU 541	Mr Walker/Mae Mae	5
60	Kalypso XXEP 1	THIS IS SPARROW (EP)	10
60	Kalypso XXEP 2	MAN, DIG THIS SPARROW (EP)	10
60	Kalypso XXEP 3	A PARTY WITH SPARROW (EP)	10
61	Kalypso XXEP 4	THIS IS THE SPARROW AGAIN (EP)	10
61	Kalypso XXEP 5	GREETINGS FROM SPARROW (EP)	10
62	Kalypso XXEP 6	SPARROW THE CONQUEROR (EP)	10

MINT VALUE £

63	Island ILP 902	THE SLAVE (LP)	25
66	RCA RD 7516	SPARROW COME BACK (LP)	15
72	Trojan TRL 49	HOTTER THAN EVER (LP)	12

(see also Sparrow, King Sparrow, Lord Melody)

MIGHTY SPARROW/BYRON LEE & DRAGONAIRES
| 69 | Trojan TRL 8 | THE SPARROW MEETS THE DRAGON (LP, gatefold sleeve) | 8 |

(see also Byron Lee & Dragonaires)

MIGHTY TERROR & HIS CALYPSONIANS
50	Melodisc 1033	The Queen Is In/Chinese Children (78)	10
59	Pye N 15177	Women Police In England/Patricia Gone With Millicent (78)	12
59	Pye N 15178	Brown Skin Gal/Kitch Cavalcade (78)	12

MIGHTY VIKINGS
| 67 | Island WI 3060 | Do Re Mi/The Sound Of Music | 12 |
| 67 | Island WI 3074 | Rockitty Fockitty/Give Me Back My Gal (both actually with Sammy Ismay) | 12 |

MIGIL FIVE
64	Pye 7N 15597	Mockingbird Hill/Long Ago And Far Away	6
64	Pye 7N 15645	Near You/Don't Wanna Go On Shaking	6
64	Pye 7N 15677	Boys And Girls/I Saw Your Picture	6
65	Pye 7N 15757	Just Behind The Rainbow/Seven Lonely Days	6
65	Pye 7N 15874	One Hundred Years/I'm In Love Again	6
66	Pye 7N 17023	Pencil And Paper/Nevertheless (I'm In Love With You)	6
67	Columbia DB 8196	Together/Superstition	18
68	Jay Boy BOY 4	If I Had My Way/Somebody's Stolen The Moon	6
64	Pye NEP 24191	MEET THE MIGIL FIVE (EP)	20
64	Pye NPL 18093	MOCKING BIRD HILL (LP)	35

(see also Migil Four)

MIGIL FOUR
| 63 | Pye 7N 15572 | Maybe/Can't I? | 7 |

(see also Migil Five)

MIKE & MECHANICS
85	WEA U 8908	Silent Running/I Get The Feeling (art sleeve)	4
85	WEA U 8908T	Silent Running/I Get The Feeling (12", art sleeve)	7
85	WEA U 8908P	Silent Running/I Get The Feeling (engine-shaped picture disc)	8
85	WEA U 8765TP	All I Need Is A Miracle/You Are The One/A Call To Arms (12", picture disc)	10
88	WEA U 7789CD	Nobody's Perfect/Nobody's Perfect (Extended)/Nobody Knows (3" CD)	8
89	WEA U 7717CD	The Living Years/Too Many Friends/I Get The Feeling (live) (3" CD)	8
89	WEA U 7602CD	Nobody Knows (Remix)/Why Me/Nobody Knows (Album Version) (3" CD, 5" jewel case or 3" card sleeve)	8
91	Virgin VSCD 1345	Word Of Mouth/Let's Pretend It Didn't Happen (CD)	7
91	Virgin VSCDX 1345	Word Of Mouth/Taken In (live)/Let's Pretend It Didn't Happen (CD, numbered picture disc)	7
91	Virgin VSCDX 1351	A Time And Place/Yesterday Tomorrow/Word Of Mouth (East West Mix) (CD, in photo wallet with 5 prints)	7
91	Virgin VS 1359	Get Up/I Think I Got The Message (p/s, withdrawn)	6
91	Virgin VSCDG 1359	Get Up/I Think I Got The Message/Before The Next Heartache Falls (CD, withdrawn)	10
92	Virgin VSCDX 1396	Everybody Gets A Second Chance/The Way You Look At Me/At The End Of The Day (CD, with sheet music & lyrics)	7

(see also Mike Rutherford, Genesis, Paul Carrack)

MIKE & MODIFIERS
| 62 | Oriole CB 1775 | I Found Myself A Brand New Baby/It's Too Bad | 450 |

MIKE STUART SPAN
66	Columbia DB 8066	Come On Over To Our Place/Still Nights	20
67	Columbia DB 8206	Dear/Invitation	30
68	Jewel JL 01	Children Of Tomorrow/Concerto Of Thoughts	165
68	Fontana TF 959	You Can Understand Me/Baubles And Bangles	12
95	Tenth Planet TP 014	TIMESPAN (LP, gatefold sleeve, numbered, 1,000 copies only)	20

(see also Leviathan, High Defenders, Tony's Defenders, High Broom)

MIKI & GRIFF
59	Pye-Nixa 7N 15213	Hold Back Tomorrow/Deedle Dum Doo Die Day	5
59	Pye-Nixa N 15213	Hold Back Tomorrow/Deedle Dum Doo Die Day (78)	8
60	Pye 7N 15266	Long Time To Forget/Someday You'll Call My Name	5
64	Pye 7N 15614	Here Today Gone Tomorrow/Changing Partners (p/s)	5
60	Pye NEP 24116	THIS IS MIKI THIS IS GRIFF (EP)	8
60	Pye NEP 24129	HIT PARADE (EP)	8
61	Pye NEP 24145	TWO'S COMPANY (EP)	8
62	Pye NEP 24153	HIT PARADE (EP)	8
65	Pye NEP 24207	OLD ROCKING CHAIR (EP)	8
66	Pye NEP 24268	IT'S MY WAY (EP)	8
61	Pye NPL 18058	MIKI AND GRIFF (LP)	15
62	Pye NPL 18074	COUNTRY STYLE (LP)	15

BOBBY MILANO
| 55 | Capitol CL 14252 | A King Or A Slave/If You Cared | 7 |
| 55 | Capitol CL 14309 | If Tears Could Bring You Back/Make Me A Present Of You | 7 |

AMOS MILBURN
57	Vogue V 9064	Every Day Of The Week/Girl Of My Dreams (triangular or round centre)	140/60
57	Vogue V 9064	Every Day Of The Week/Girl Of My Dreams (78)	35
57	Vogue V 9069	Rum And Coca Cola/Soft Pillow (triangular centre)	165
57	Vogue V 9069	Rum And Coca Cola/Soft Pillow (78)	40
57	Vogue V 9080	Thinking Of You Baby/If I Could Be With You (One Hour Tonight) (triangular centre)	165

MINT VALUE £

57	Vogue V 9080	Thinking Of You Baby/If I Could Be With You (One Hour Tonight) (78)	50
60	Vogue V 9163	One Scotch, One Bourbon, One Beer/Bad, Bad Whiskey	100
57	Vogue VE 1-70102	ROCK AND ROLL (EP)	250
78	United Artists UAS 30203	CHICKEN SHACK BOOGIE (LP)	12

AMOS MILBURN JNR
63	London HLU 9795	Gloria/Look At Me Fool	15

PERCY MILEM
66	Stateside SS 566	Crying Baby, Baby, Baby/Call On Me	18

BARRY MILES
60	Egmont AJS 14	MILES OF GENIUS (LP)	15

BERNARD MILES
60s	Decca DFE 6415	BERNARD MILES (EP)	10
60s	Decca DFE 6559	THE RACE FOR THE RHINEGOLD STAKES (EP)	12
60s	HMV 7EG 8629	OLD ENGLISH FAIRY TALES (EP)	10
60s	HMV 7EG 8716	OVER THE GATE (EP)	12

BUDDY MILES (EXPRESS)
68	Mercury MF 1065	Train (Parts 1 & 2)	5
69	Mercury MF 1098	Miss Lady/'69 Freedom Special	5
71	Mercury 6052 036	Them Changes/Your Feeling Is Mine (solo)	5
71	Mercury 6052 077	Wholesale Love/That's The Way Life Is	5
72	Mercury 6052 127	Give Away None Of My Love/Take It Off Him And Put It On Me (solo)	5
69	Mercury 20137 SMCL	EXPRESSWAY TO YOUR SKULL (LP)	15
69	Mercury 20163 SMCL	ELECTRIC CHURCH (LP)	15
70	Mercury 6338 016	THEM CHANGES (LP)	12
71	Mercury 6338 028	WE GOT TO LIVE TOGETHER (LP)	12
71	Mercury 6338 048	A MESSAGE TO THE PEOPLE (LP)	12
72	Mercury 6641 033	LIVE (2-LP)	15
73	CBS 65406	CHAPTER VII (LP)	12
74	CBS 80349	ALL THE FACES (LP)	12

(see also Electric Flag, Jimi Hendrix, Carlos Santana & Buddy Miles)

GARRY MILES
60	London HLG 9155	Look For A Star/Afraid Of Love	12
60	London REG 1264	LOOK FOR A STAR (EP)	60

JOHN MILES
70	Orange OAS 508	Why Don't You Love Me?/If I Could See Through	5
71	Decca F 13196	Jose/You Make It So Hard	5
72	Orange OAS 207	Come Away Melinda/Walking With My Head Held High	5
72	Orange OAS 208	Yesterday (Was Just The Beginning)/Road To Freedom	5
73	Orange OAS 209	Hard Road/You're Telling Me Lies	5
73	Orange OAS 211	Jacqueline/Keep On Tryin'	5
73	Orange OAS 213	One Minute Every Hour/Hollywood Queen	6
74	Orange OAS 220	Fright Of My Life/Good Time Woman	5
74	Orange OAS 223	What's On Your Mind/Rock'n'Roll Band	5
74	Orange OAS 224	What's On Your Mind/To Be Grateful	6
83	EMI EMI 5386	The Right To Sing/Back To The Magic (picture disc)	5

(see also Influence)

JOSIE MILES
60s	Poydras 103	JOSIE MILES (EP)	8

LENNY MILES
61	Top Rank JAR 546	Don't Believe Him Donna/Invisible	12

LIZZIE MILES
56	HMV 7EG 8178	THE BLUES THEY SANG (EP, 1 side by Billy Young, both with Jelly Roll Morton)	25
59	Columbia Clef SEB 10088	SCINTILLATING LIZZIE (EP, with Bob Scobey's Band)	10
50s	Melodisc EPM7 55	NEW ORLEANS BOYS (EP, with New Orleans Boys)	18
57	Capitol T 792	A NIGHT IN NEW ORLEANS (LP)	18

SARAH MILES
65	Fontana TF 552	Where Am I/Here Of All Places	5

MILESTONES & BUTCH BAKER
75	Black Magic BM 111	The Joker (Parts 1 & 2)	5

MILKSHAKES
82	Bilko BILK-O	Please Don't Tell My Baby/It's You (p/s)	8
83	Upright UP 6	Soldiers Of Love/Shimmy Shimmy (p/s)	6
84	Big Beat NS 94	Brand New Cadillac/Commanche/Jezebel/Jaguar And Thunderbird (p/s)	5
84	Big Beat SW 105	The Ambassadors Of Love/No More/Gringles And Groyles Again/Remarkable (p/s)	5
86	Empire UXF 228	Let Me Love You/She Tells Me She Loves Me (p/s)	5
83	Big Beat NED 4	14 RHYTHM AND BEAT GREATS (LP)	18
83	Upright UPLP 1	AFTER SCHOOL SESSIONS (LP)	18
84	Milkshake HARP-O	NOTHING CAN STOP THESE MEN (LP)	18
85	Big Beat WIK 30	THEY CAME, THEY SAW, THEY CONQUERED (LP)	15
86	Milkshake MILK-O	TALKING 'BOUT MILKSHAKES (LP)	15

(see also Thee Mighty Caesars, Prisoners/Milkshakes, Pop Rivits, Len Bright Combo, Billy Childish, Thee Headcoats)

MILLER
65	Oak RGJ 190	Baby I've Got News For You/The Girl With The Castle	250
65	Columbia DB 7735	Baby I Got News For You/The Girl With The Castle	175

(see also Big Boy Pete, Peter Jay & Jaywalkers, Pete Miller, News)

ANN MILLER
54	MGM SP 1076	Too Darn Hot/KATHRYN GRAYSON & HOWARD KEEL: So In Love	6

MINT VALUE £

ANN MILLER & KATHRYN GRAYSON

| 54 | MGM SP 1078 | Always True To You In My Fashion/I Hate Men | 6 |

(see also Kathryn Grayson & Howard Keel)

BETTY MILLER

59	Top Rank JAR 115	Pearly Gates/Old Time Religion	7
59	Top Rank JAR 115	Pearly Gates/Old Time Religion (78)	8
59	Top Rank JAR 127	Jack O' Diamonds/(It Took) One Kiss	7
59	Top Rank JAR 127	Jack O' Diamonds/(It Took) One Kiss (78)	10

BOB MILLER & MILLERMEN

57	Columbia DB 4017	The Scamp/The Sack Line	5
58	Columbia DB 4140	Square Bash/Muchacha	5
59	Fontana TF 181	Dig This!/The Poacher	5
59	Fontana TF 181	Dig This!/The Poacher (78)	8
59	Fontana TF 192	Little Dipper/The Keel Row	5
59	Fontana TF 192	Little Dipper/The Keel Row (78)	10
59	Fontana TF 228	In The Mood/Joey's Song	5
59	Fontana TF 228	In The Mood/Joey's Song (78)	10
60	Fontana TF 236	The Busker's Tune/My Guy's Come Back	5
60	Fontana TF 245	77 Sunset Strip/Manhunt	5
60	Fontana TF 284	Night Theme/Last Date	5
61	Parlophone R 4779	Trouble Shooter/Hootin'	5
61	Parlophone R 4854	The "Oliver" Twist/That's It	5
65	Mercury MF 947	Uptown And Downtown/Carnaby Street Parade	6
65	Polydor 56005	6-5 Special/Dick Van Dyke Theme	8
66	Columbia DB 7877	Get Smart/Bony's Blues (as Bob Miller & His Millermen)	5

BOBBIE MILLER

65	Decca F 12064	What A Guy/You Went Away	30
65	Decca F 12252	Every Beat Of My Heart/Tomorrow	8
66	Decca F 12354	Everywhere I Go/IAN STEWART & RAILROADERS: Stu-Ball	75

(see also Mongrels, Rolling Stones)

CHUCK MILLER

56	Capitol CL 14543	Rogue River Valley/No Baby Like You	12
56	Capitol CL 14543	Rogue River Valley/No Baby Like You (78)	8
57	Mercury 7MT 153	The Auctioneer/Me Head's In De Barrel	20
57	Mercury MT 153	The Auctioneer/Me Head's In De Barrel (78)	10
57	Mercury MT 157	Bye, Bye Love/Rang Tang Ding Dong (78)	12
57	Mercury MT 181	Plaything/After Yesterday (78)	12
58	Mercury 7MT 215	Down The Road A-Piece/Mad About Her Blues	60
58	Mercury MT 215	Down The Road A-Piece/Mad About Her Blues (78)	12
59	Mercury AMT 1026	The Auctioneer/Baby Doll	12
59	Mercury AMT 1026	The Auctioneer/Baby Doll (78)	25
60	Mercury ZEP 10058	GOING GOING GONE (EP)	50

COUNT PRINCE (MILLER)

70	Downtown DT 460	I'm Gonna Keep On Trying/Girl I Need You (as Count Prince)	5
70	MCA MK 5042	Mule Train/Lucille (p/s)	5
72	Penny Farthing PEN 799	Rupert The Bear/When We Were Children	5

FRANKIE MILLER (U.S.)

59	Melodisc MEL 1519	True Blue/Black Land Farmer	15
59	Melodisc MEL 1519	True Blue/Black Land Farmer (78)	50
59	Melodisc MEL 1529	Poppin' Johnnie/Family Man	10
59	Melodisc MEL 1529	Poppin' Johnnie/Family Man (78)	50
60	Melodisc MEL 1552	Rain, Rain/Baby Rocked Her Dolly	10
62	Top Rank JKP 3013	COUNTRY MUSIC (EP)	30
64	Ember CW 107	THE TRUE COUNTRY STYLE OF FRANKIE MILLER (LP)	25

GARY MILLER

53	Philips PB 102	Congratulations/I Shall Return (78)	8
58	Pye 7N 15120	The Story Of My Life/Put A Light In The Window	6
58	Pye 7N 15136	Lollipop/Dancing With My Shadow	7
58	Pye 7N 15140	On The Street Where You Live/That's For Me (with Kenny Ball & His Jazz Band)	5
58	Pye 7N 15151	A Couple Of Crazy Kids (with Marion Ryan)/Ivanhoe Of England	7
58	Pye 7N 15164	The First Christmas Day/Nearest And Dearest	6
58	Pye 7N 15164	The First Christmas Day/Nearest And Dearest (78)	10
59	Pye 7N 15188	Jezebel/The Railroad Song	5
59	Pye 7N 15188	Jezebel/The Railroad Song (78)	10
59	Pye 7N 15207	Sing Along/Someone To Come Home To	5
59	Pye 7N 15207	Sing Along/Someone To Come Home To (78)	10
59	Pye 7N 15239	Marina/Hold Me, Thrill Me, Kiss Me	5
59	Pye 7N 15239	Marina/Hold Me, Thrill Me, Kiss Me (78)	8
64	Pye 7N 15698	Aqua Marina/Stingray	15
56	Pye NEP 24013	YELLOW ROSE OF TEXAS (EP, 2 different sleeves)	each 30
57	Pye NEP 24047	HIT PARADE VOL. 1 (EP)	18
57	Pye NEP 24057	MEET MISTER MILLER PT. 1 — ON STAGE (EP)	18
57	Pye NEP 24058	MEET MISTER MILLER PT. 2 — FOR THE YOUNG IN LOVE (EP)	18
57	Pye NEP 24059	MEET MISTER MILLER PT. 3 — FOR THE YOUNG IN LOVE (EP)	18
58	Pye NEP 24072	HIT PARADE VOL. 2 (EP)	20
60	Pye NEP 24123	FLOWER DRUM SONG (EP)	10
57	Nixa NPL 18008	MEET MISTER MILLER (LP)	35
61	Pye NPL 18059	GARY ON THE BALL (LP)	20

(see also Kenny Ball)

GLEN MILLER

| 67 | Doctor Bird DB 1089 | Where Is The Love/Funky Broadway | 60 |
| 68 | Doctor Bird DB 1128 | Rocksteady Party/Book Of Memories | 12 |

GLENN MILLER & HIS ORCHESTRA

54	Columbia SCM 5086	I Got Rhythm/Sleepy Time Gal	10
54	Columbia DB 3416	I Got Rhythm/Sleepy Time Gal (78)	8
54	HMV 7M 195	Little Brown Jug/Don't Sit Under The Apple Tree	12
54	HMV B 10662	Little Brown Jug/Don't Sit Under The Apple Tree (78)	8
58	RCA RCA 1034	Falling Leaves/So Sweet (as Glenn Miller New Orchestra)	5
58	RCA RCA 1034	Falling Leaves/So Sweet (as Glenn Miller New Orchestra) (78)	8
58	RCA RCA 1096	American Patrol/Little Brown Jug	6
58	RCA RCA 1096	American Patrol/Little Brown Jug (78)	10
59	Top Rank JAR 114	Boom Shot/You Say The Sweetest Things, Baby	6
59	Top Rank JAR 114	Boom Shot/You Say The Sweetest Things, Baby (78)	12
59	Top Rank TR 5003	Chattanooga Choo Choo/Serenade In Blue	6
65	Columbia DB 7550	Pennsylvania 6-5000/The Girl From Ipanema	5
54	HMV 7EG 8031	GLENN MILLER AND HIS ORCHESTRA (EP)	8
54	HMV 7EG 8043	GLENN MILLER AND HIS ORCHESTRA (EP)	8
54	HMV 7EG 8055	GLENN MILLER AND HIS ORCHESTRA (EP)	8
55	HMV 7EG 8067	GLENN MILLER AND HIS ORCHESTRA (EP)	8
55	HMV 7EG 8077	GLENN MILLER AND HIS ORCHESTRA (EP)	8
55	HMV 7EG 8097	THAT MILLER MUSIC (EP)	8
55	Brunswick OE 9169	COLLECTOR'S ITEMS (EP)	8
57	HMV 7EG 8204	GLENN MILLER SPECIAL (EP)	8
59	Top Rank JKR 8019	GOLDEN MILLER (EP)	8
53	HMV DLP 1012	GLENN MILLER CONCERT VOL. 1 (10" LP)	15
53	HMV DLP 1013	GLENN MILLER CONCERT VOL. 2 (10" LP)	15
53	HMV DLP 1021	GLENN MILLER CONCERT VOL. 3 (10" LP)	15
54	HMV DLP 1024	THE GLENN MILLER STORY (10" LP)	15
54	HMV DLP 1049	TIME FOR MELODY (10" LP)	15
54	HMV DLP 1059	ORCHESTRA WIVES (10" LP)	15
54	HMV RLS 599	GLENN MILLER LIMITED EDITION (5-LP, presentation set, 'snakeskin' cover)	50
55	HMV DLP 1062	SUNRISE SERENADE (10" LP)	15
55	HMV DLP 1081	GLENN MILLER CONCERT VOL. 4 (10" LP)	15
55	HMV DLP 1104	SUN VALLEY SERENADE (10" LP)	15
55	Philips BBR 8072	GLENN MILLER (10" LP)	15
56	HMV CLPC 6-10/RLS 598	GLENN MILLER LIMITED EDITION VOL. 2 (5-LP, in presentation album)	50
56	HMV RLS 637	GLENN MILLER & THE ARMY AIRFORCE BAND (5-LP, presentation box, [CLP 1077-CLP 1081])	30
56	HMV DLP 1122	MILLER MAGIC (10" LP)	15
56	Philips BBR 8092	GLENN MILLER (10" LP)	15
57	HMV DLP 1145	POLKA DOTS AND MOONBEAMS (10" LP)	15
58	RCA RD 27057	THE GLENN MILLER CARNEGIE HALL CONCERT (LP)	12
58	RCA RD 27068	THE GLENN MILLER STORY (LP)	12
58	RCA RD 27090	THE MARVELLOUS MILLER MEDLEYS (LP)	12
58	RCA RD 27096	MARVELLOUS MILLER MOODS (LP)	12
58	RCA RD 27135	GLENN MILLER ARMY AIRFORCE BAND VOL. 1 (LP)	12
59	Top Rank RX 3004	GLENN MILLER AND HIS ORCHESTRA VOL. 1 (LP)	12
59	Top Rank 35/023	GLENN MILLER AND HIS ORCHESTRA VOL. 2 (LP)	12
60	RCA RD 27146/RD 27147	FOR THE VERY FIRST TIME (2-LP)	15

JAMES MILLER

70	Trojan TR 7804	You Got To Me/2001	4

JIMMY MILLER & (NEW) BARBECUES

57	Columbia DB 4006	Sizzlin' Hot/Free Wheelin' Baby (as Jimmy Miller & Barbecues)	70
57	Columbia DB 4006	Sizzlin' Hot/Free Wheelin' Baby (as Jimmy Miller & Barbecues) (78)	20
58	Columbia DB 4081	Jelly Baby/Cry, Baby, Cry (as Jimmy Miller & New Barbecues)	50
58	Columbia DB 4081	Jelly Baby/Cry, Baby, Cry (as Jimmy Miller & New Barbecues) (78)	40

(see also Station Skiffle Group)

JODY MILLER

64	Capitol CL 15335	He Walks Like A Man/Looking At The World Through A Tear	6
64	Capitol CL 15356	The Fever/In My Room	5
65	Capitol CL 15393	Queen Of The House/The Greatest Actor	6
65	Capitol CL 15404	Silver Threads And Golden Needles/Melody For Robin	5
65	Capitol CL 15415	Home Of The Brave/This Is The Life	6
66	Capitol CL 15482	If You Were A Carpenter/Let Me Walk With You	5
66	Capitol (S)T 2446	JODY MILLER SINGS THE GREAT HITS OF BUCK OWENS (LP)	15/18

KENNY MILLER

65	Stateside SS 405	Restless/Take My Tip	30

MANDY MILLER

56	Parlophone R 4219	Nellie The Elephant/It's Time To Dream	12
56	Parlophone R 4219	Nellie The Elephant/It's Time To Dream (78)	8
58	Parlophone GEP 8776	CHILDREN'S CHOICE (EP)	8

MAX MILLER

54	Philips PB 236	Mary From The Dairy/Voulez Vous Promenade (78)	8
55	Philips PB 427	London Belongs To Me/Something Money Can't Buy (78)	8
55	Philips PB 518	Ain't It Ni–Ice/The Budgie Song (78)	10
56	Pye N 15050	The Girls I Like/The Mother Brown Story (78)	8
58	Pye 7N 15141	With A Little Bit Of Luck/Be Sincere	5
58	Pye N 15141	With A Little Bit Of Luck/Be Sincere (78)	10
59	HMV 7EG 8558	THE CHEEKY CHAPPIE (EP)	8
61	Pye NEP 25154	MAX AT THE MET (EP)	8
62	Pye NEP 25162	MAX AT THE MET VOL. 2 (EP)	8
58	Pye NPT 19026	MAX AT THE MET (10" LP)	15

(see also Lonnie Donegan)

Mitch MILLER Orchestra

MINT VALUE £

MITCH MILLER ORCHESTRA

53	Columbia SCM 5058	Just Dreaming/Without My Lover	6
59	Philips PB 937	Holiday For Lovers/This Here Goat (78)	8
59	Philips PB 948	Hey Betty Martin/Jine The Cavalry (78)	8
62	CBS AAG 118	The Longest Day/The Longest Day (Version) (p/s)	5
56	Philips BBE 12043	LISBON ANTIGUA (EP)	8

(see also Guy Mitchell)

MRS MILLER

66	Capitol CL 15444	Downtown/A Lover's Concerto	5
66	Capitol T 2494	MRS. MILLER'S GREATEST HITS (LP)	15
66	Capitol T 2579	WILL SUCCESS SPOIL MRS. MILLER (LP)	15

MRS MILLER

69	Jackpot JP 707	Feel It/LYN BECKFORD: Kiss Me Quick (actually by Keeling Beckford)	6

(see also Lloyd Terrell)

NED MILLER

63	Capitol CL 15301	Go On Back You Fool/Dark Moon	7
63	London HL 9658	From A Jack To A King/Parade Of Broken Hearts	5
63	London HL 9728	Just Before Dawn/Mona Lisa	6
63	London HL 9766	Another Fool Like Me/Magic Moon	6
64	London HL 9838	Big Love/Sunday Morning Tears	6
64	London HL 9873	Invisible Tears/Old Restless Ocean	6
64	London HL 9937	Do What You Do Do Well/Dusty Guitar	7
63	Capitol EAP1 20492	NED MILLER (EP)	25
63	London RE 1382	NED MILLER (EP)	30
63	London HA 8072	FROM A JACK TO A KING (LP)	30
66	Capitol T 2414	THE BEST OF NED MILLER (LP)	30
69	Capitol ST 2914	IIN THE NAME OF LOVE (LP)	25

PETE MILLER

97	Tenth Planet TP 030	SUMMERLAND (LP, numbered, 1000 only)	12

(see also Miller, Big Boy Pete)

ROGER MILLER

64	Philips BF 1354	Dang Me/Got 2 Again	5
64	Philips BF 1365	Chug-A-Lug/Reincarnation	5
65	Philips BF 1390	Do-Wacka-Do/Love Is Not For Me	5
65	Philips BF 1397	King Of The Road/Atta Boy Girl	5
65	Philips BF 1416	Engine Engine No. 9/The Last Word In Lonesome Is Me	5
65	Philips BF 1437	Kansas City Star/One Dyin' And Buryin'	5
65	Philips BF 1456	England Swings/The Good Old Days	5
66	Philips BF 1475	Husbands And Wives/I've Been A Long Time Leavin'	5
66	Philips BF 1498	You Can't Roller Skate In A Buffalo Herd/Train Of Life	5
66	Philips BF 1516	My Uncle Used To Love Me But She Died/You're My Kingdom	5
67	Philips BF 1560	Walkin' In The Sunshine/Home	5
69	Mercury MF 1108	England Swings/King Of The Road (p/s)	5
65	Philips BE 12578	ROGER MILLER (EP)	10
65	Camden CDN 5121	SONGS I HAVE WRITTEN (LP)	15
65	Philips BL 7667	ROGER AND OUT! (LP)	15
66	Philips BL 7669	THE RETURN OF ROGER MILLER (LP)	15
66	Philips BL 7676	THE 3RD TIME AROUND (LP)	15
66	Philips BL 7748	WORDS AND MUSIC (LP)	15
67	Philips (S)BL 7822	WALKING IN THE SUNSHINE (LP)	12
67	Philips (S)BL 7833	SINGS THE MUSIC & TELLS THE TALE OF WATERHOLE 3 (LP)	12

RUSS MILLER

57	HMV POP 391	I Sit In My Window/Wait For Me, My Love	45
57	HMV POP 391	I Sit In My Window/Wait For Me, My Love (78)	12

STEPHEN MILLER & LOL COXHILL

73	Caroline C 1503	COXHILL MILLER (LP)	12
74	Caroline C 1507	THE STORY SO FAR ... OH REALLY? (LP)	12

(see also Lol Coxhill)

STEVE MILLER BAND

68	Capitol CL 15539	Sittin' In Circles/Roll With It	12
68	Capitol CL 15564	Living In The U.S.A./Quicksilver Girl	12
69	Capitol CL 15604	My Dark Hour/Song For Our Ancestors	12
69	Capitol CL 15618	Little Girl/Don't Let Nobody Turn You Around	6
70	Capitol CL 15656	Going To The Country/Never Kill Another Man	5
72	Capitol CL 15712	My Dark Hour/The Gangster Is Back/Song For Our Ancestors (33rpm)	5
73	Capitol CL 15765	The Joker/Something To Believe In	5
74	Capitol CL 15786	Living In The U.S.A./Kow Kow Calqulator	5
68	Capitol (S)T 2920	CHILDREN OF THE FUTURE (LP, 'rainbow rim' label)	20
69	Capitol (S)T 2984	SAILOR (LP)	20
70	Capitol E-(S)T 184	BRAVE NEW WORLD (LP)	15
70	Capitol E-ST 331	YOUR SAVING GRACE (LP)	12
70	Capitol EA-ST 436	NUMBER 5 (LP)	10
82	Mercury HS 9919 916	GREATEST HITS 1974-1978 (LP, half-speed audiophile pressing)	12

(see also Boz Scaggs)

SUZI MILLER

54	Decca F 10264	The Tennessee Wig Walk/Bimbo (B-side with Johnston Brothers) (78)	7
54	Decca F 10389	Happy Days And Lonely Nights/Tell Me, Tell Me (with Johnston Brothers)	20
54	Decca F 10423	Two Step, Side Step (with Johnston Brothers)/ Hang My Heart On A Christmas Tree (with Keynotes)	12
55	Decca F 10475	Tweedlee-Dee (with Johnston Brothers)/That's All I Want From You	15
55	Decca F 10512	Dance With Me Henry (Wallflower) (with Johnston Brothers)/ Butterfingers (with Marilyn Sisters)	12

MINT VALUE £

55	Decca F 10593	The Banjo's Back In Town/Go On By	7
56	Decca F 10677	Ay-Ay-Senores/Reckless	7
56	Decca F 10722	Get Up! Get Up! (You Sleepy Head)/The Key To My Heart	7
57	Decca F 10848	I Love My Baby/The Money Tree	7

(see also Marilyn Sisters, Johnston Brothers)

MILLIE (SMALL)

63	Fontana TF 425	Don't You Know/Until You're Mine	8
64	Fontana TF 449	My Boy Lollipop/Something's Gotta Be Done	5
64	Fontana TF 479	Sweet William/Oh Henry	6
64	Fontana TF 502	I Love The Way You Love/Bring It On Home To Me	6
64	Cadbury's BNVT 01F	The Bournvita Song/Three Nights A Week (p/s)	15
65	Fontana TF 515	I've Fallen In Love With A Snowman/What Am I Living For	6
65	Fontana TF 529	See You Later Alligator/Chilly Kisses	6
65	Fontana TF 591	My Street/It's Too Late	6
65	Fontana TF 617	Bloodshot Eyes/Tongue Tied	8
65	Brit WI 1002	My Street/A Mixed Up, Fickle, Moody, Self-Centred, Spoiled Kind Of Boy	10
66	Fontana TF 740	Killer Joe/Carry Go Bring Come (as Millie Small)	7
67	Fontana TF 796	Chicken Feed/Wings Of A Dove (as Millie Small)	7
67	Island WIP 6021	You Better Forget/I Am In Love	6
68	Fontana TF 948	When I Dance With You/Hey Mr. Love	6
69	Decca F 12948	Readin' Writin' Arithmetic/I Want You Never To Stop	10
70	Pyramid PYR 6080	My Love And I/Tell Me About Yourself	6
70	Trojan TR 7744	Enoch Power/Mayfair	6
70	President PT 306	We're All In A Zoo/Piccaninny Man	5
70	Trojan TR 7801	Honey Hush/Sunday Morning	5
73	Blue Mountain BM 1026	My Boy Lollipop/I'm In Love	4
61	Blue Beat BBEP 302	MILLIE (EP, with Little Roy & Owen Gray; most without sleeve)	150/30
64	Fontana TE 17425	MY BOY LOLLIPOP (EP)	40
66	Island IEP 705	MILLIE AND HER BOYFRIENDS (EP)	75
64	Fontana (S)TL 5220	MORE MILLIE (LP, mono/stereo)	25/30
65	Fontana TL 5276	MILLIE SINGS FATS DOMINO (LP)	45
67	Island ILP 953	THE BEST OF MILLIE SMALL (LP)	35
69	Trojan TTL 17	MILLIE AND HER BOYFRIENDS (LP)	12
69	Trojan TTL 49	THE BEST OF MILLIE SMALL (LP, reissue)	12
70	Trojan TBL 108	TIME WILL TELL (LP)	12

(see also Jackie & Millie, Roy & Millie, Owen & Millie)

SPIKE MILLIGAN

58	Parlophone R 4406	Wish I Knew/Will I Find My Love Today?	8
58	Parlophone R 4406	Wish I Knew/Will I Find My Love Today? (78)	20
61	Parlophone R 4839	I'm Walking Out With A Mountain/The Sewers Of The Strand	8
62	Parlophone R 4891	Wormwood Scrubs Tango/Postman's Knock	8
64	Pye 7N 15720	The Olympic Team/Epilogue (with John Bluthal)	7
66	Parlophone R 5513	Purple Aeroplane/Nothing At All	7
66	Parlophone R 5543	Tower Bridge/Silent Night	7
69	Parlophone R 5771	The Q.5 Piano Tune/Ning, Nang, Nong	7
73	Warner Bros. K 16240	Girl On A Pony/Old Man's Protest Song	6
61	Parlophone PMC 1148	MILLIGAN PRESERVED (LP)	18
65	Decca LK 4701	MUSES WITH MILLIGAN (LP)	15
68	Pye NPL 18271	THE WORLD OF THE BEACHCOMBER (LP)	15
75	Polydor 2460 235	BADJELLY THE WITCH AND OTHER GOODIES (LP)	15

(see also Goons, Famous Eccles, Peter Sellers)

LUCKY MILLINDER & ORCHESTRA
(see under 'L')

MILLIONAIRES (Ireland)

| 66 | Decca F 12468 | Wishing Well/Chatterbox | 45 |

MILLIONAIRES (U.S.)

| 73 | Mercury 6052 301 | Never For Me/If I Had You Babe (paper or plastic label) | 7/5 |

MILLIONS

| 73 | Duke DU 154 | Murmuring/TOMMY McCOOK & BOBBY ELLIS: Murmuring — Version | 4 |
| 73 | Downtown DT 516 | Love Of Jah Jah Children/Jah Jah Version | 4 |

MILLIONS OF DEAD CHILDREN

| 85 | Radical MDC 3 | CHICKENSQUAWK EP (poster p/s) | 6 |

BARBARA MILLS

65	Hickory 45-1323	Queen Of Fools/Make It Last, Take Your Time	100
65	Hickory 45-1392	Try/Let's Make A Memory	12
75	London HLE 10491	Queen Of Fools/Make It Last, Take Your Time (reissue)	6

FREDDIE MILLS

| 57 | Parlophone R 4374 | "One For The Road" Medley (both sides) | 15 |

GARRY MILLS

59	Top Rank JAR 119	Hey Baby (You're Pretty)/You Alone	10
59	Top Rank JAR 119	Hey Baby (You're Pretty)/You Alone (78)	20
59	Top Rank JAR 219	Seven Little Girls Sitting In The Back Seat/The Night You Became 17	7
59	Top Rank JAR 219	Seven Little Girls Sitting In The Back Seat/The Night You Became 17 (78)	20
59	Oriole CB 1529	Living Lord/Big Story Breaking	5
59	Oriole CB 1529	Living Lord/Big Story Breaking (78)	8
59	Oriole CB 1530	I Am The Great I Am/Rhythm In Religion	5
59	Oriole CB 1530	I Am The Great I Am/Rhythm In Religion (78)	8
60	Top Rank JAR 301	Running Bear/Teen Angel	8
60	Top Rank JAR 336	Look For A Star/Footsteps	7
60	Top Rank JAR 393	Comin' Down With Love/I'm Gonna Find Out	8
60	Top Rank JAR 500	Top Teen Baby/Don't Cheat Me Again (some in p/s)	10/6
61	Top Rank JAR 542	Who's Gonna Take You Home Tonight?/Christina	8

MINT VALUE £

61	Decca F 11358	I'll Step Down/Your Way Is My Way	8
61	Decca F 11383	Bless You/Footprints In The Sand	7
61	Decca F 11415	Treasure Island/Sad Little Girl	7
62	Decca F 11471	Never Believed In Love/Save A Dream For Me	7
61	Top Rank JKP 3001	LOOK FOR A STAR (EP)	50

(see also Gary & Ariels)

GORDON MILLS
65	Ace Of Clubs ACL 1191	DO IT YOURSELF (LP)	12

(see also Viscounts)

HAYLEY MILLS
61	Decca F 21396	Let's Get Together/Cobbler Cobbler	5
62	Decca F 21442	Jeepers Creepers/Johnny Jingo	5
62	Decca LK 4426	LET'S GET TOGETHER (LP)	12

HAYLEY MILLS & EDDIE HODGES
63	HMV POP 1179	Flitterin'/Beautiful Beulah	4

(see also Eddie Hodges)

JEFF MILLS
60s	Ember EMB S 133	Daddy's Home/TIMMY REYNOLDS: Lullaby Of Love	10

MAUDE MILLS
60s	Vintage Jazz VEP 34	MAUDE MILLS (EP)	12

RUDY MILLS
67	Island WI 3092	A Long Story/BOBBY ELLIS: Now We Know (act. with Desmond Miles Seven)	18
68	Island WI 3136	I'm Trapped/BOBBY ELLIS & CRYSTALLITES: Dollar A Head	18
69	Big Shot BI 509	John Jones/A Place Called Happiness	10
69	Explosion EX 2007	Lemi Li/Goody Goody	8
69	Crab CRAB 20	Tears On My Pillow/I'm Trapped	5
69	Crab CRAB 24	A Heavy Load/Wholesale Love	8
69	Pama SECO 12	REGGAE HITS (LP)	40

STEPHANIE MILLS
74	Paramount PARA 3050	I Knew It Was Love/The Passion And The Pain	5
76	Tamla Motown TMG 1020	This Empty Place/I See You For The First Time (unissued, demo only)	25
76	T. Motown STML 12017	FOR THE FIRST TIME (LP)	12

MILLS BROTHERS
54	Brunswick 05325	How Blue?/Why Do I Keep Lovin' You?	10
55	Brunswick 05390	Paper Valentine/The Urge	8
55	Brunswick 05439	Smack Dab In The Middle/Opus One	12
55	Brunswick 05452	You're Nobody Till Somebody Loves You/Yes You Are	8
55	Brunswick 05487	Mi Muchacha (Little Girl)/Gum Drop	18
55	Brunswick 05488	Suddenly There's A Valley/That's All I Ask Of You	8
56	Brunswick 05522	I've Changed My Mind A Thousand Times/All The Way 'Round The World	8
56	Brunswick 05550	Dream Of You/In A Mellow Tone	7
56	Brunswick 05600	Ninety-Eight Cents/King Porter Stomp	6
56	Brunswick 05606	That's Right/Don't Get Caught (Short On Love)	8
56	Brunswick 05631	That's All I Need/Tell Me More	5
57	Brunswick 05664	In De Banana Tree/The Knocked Out Nightingale	5
57	Brunswick 05680	My Troubled Mind/Queen Of The Senior Prom	8
57	Brunswick 05680	My Troubled Mind/Queen Of The Senior Prom (78)	8
58	London HLD 8553	Get A Job/I Found A Million Dollar Baby	25
58	London HLD 8553	Get A Job/I Found A Million Dollar Baby (78)	20
60	London HLD 9169	I Got You/Highways Are Happy Ways	5
54	Brunswick OE 9014	PRESENTING THE MILLS BROTHERS (EP)	12
55	Brunswick OE 9060	THE MILLS BROTHERS NO. 2 (EP)	8
56	Brunswick OE 9239	SINGING AND SWINGING PT. 1 (EP)	8
59	London RED 1215	THE MILLS BROTHERS (EP)	15
54	Brunswick LA 8664	MEET THE MILLS BROTHERS (10" LP)	20
55	Brunswick LA 8702	FOUR BOYS AND A GUITAR (10" LP)	18
59	London HA-D 2192	THE MILLS BROTHERS' GREATEST HITS (LP, also stereo SAH-D 6046)	15
60	London HA-D 2250	THE MILLS BROTHERS SING (LP, also stereo SAH-D 6074)	15
61	London HA-D 2319	THE MILLS BROTHERS' GREATEST HITS VOLUME 2 (LP)	15
61	London HA-D 2383	SAN ANTONIO ROSE (LP, also stereo SAH-D 6183)	15
63	London HA-D/SH-D 8058	BEER BARREL POLKA (LP)	15
63	London HA-D/SH-D 8092	THE END OF THE WORLD (LP)	15

(see also Louis Armstrong)

RONNIE MILSAP
66	Pye International 7N 25392	Ain't No Soul (Left In These Old Shoes)/Another Branch From The Same Old Tree	20
69	Pye International 7N 25490	Denver/Nothing Is As Good As It Used To Be	5
72	Wand WN 26	Ain't No Soul (Left In These Old Shoes)/Another Branch From The Same Old Tree (reissue)	5

RONNIE MILSAP/ROSCOE ROBINSON
66	Pye Intl. NEP 44078	SOUL SENSATIONS (EP)	18

JOHNNY MILTON & CONDORS
61	Oriole CB 1588	Charleston Cocktail (medley) (as Johnny Milton Band)	5
64	Decca F 11862	A Girl Named Sue/Somethin' Else (as Johnny Milton & Condors)	8
64	Fontana TF 488	Cry Baby/Hurt	6

(see also Symbols)

MILVA
63	Oriole CB 1899	I Can't Believe You're Leaving Me/Loneliness Of Autumn	7
64	Oriole CB 1952	I'll Set My Love To Music/Come Sempre	7
67	Major Minor MM 510	Love Is A Feeling/Seasons Of Love	5

MILWAUKEE COASTERS

68	Pama PM 733	Treat Me Nice/Sick And Tired (Oh Babe)	5
68	Pama PMLP 2	WEST COAST ROCK'N'ROLL 1968 (LP)	15
69	Pama PSP 10	BEST PARTY ALBUM (LP, reissue of PMLP 2)	12

GARNET MIMMS (& ENCHANTERS)

63	United Artists UP 1033	Cry Baby/Don't Change Your Heart (with Enchanters)	12
63	United Artists UP 1038	Baby Don't You Weep/For Your Precious Love (with Enchanters)	12
64	United Artists UP 1048	Tell Me Baby/Anytime You Want Me (with Enchanters)	12
65	United Artists UP 1090	It Was Easier To Hurt Her/So Close	18
66	United Artists UP 1130	I'll Take Good Care Of You/Looking For You	50
66	United Artists UP 1147	It's Been Such A Long Way Home/Thinkin'	12
66	United Artists UP 1153	My Baby/It Won't Hurt Half As Much	10
66	United Artists UP 1172	All About Love/The Truth Hurts	10
67	United Artists UP 1181	Roll With The Punches/Only Your Love	10
67	United Artists UP 1186	As Long As I Have You/Yesterday	10
68	Verve VS 569	I Can Hear My Baby Crying/Stop And Think It Over	10
68	Verve VS 569	I Can Hear My Baby Crying/BILL MEDLEY: That Lucky Old Sun (mispress)	10
68	Verve VS 574	We Can Find That Love/Can You Top This	10
76	United Artists REM 403	REMEMBER GARNET MIMMS (EP)	8
63	United Artists ULP 1067	CRY BABY AND 11 OTHER HITS (LP, with Enchanters)	80
66	United Artists (S)ULP 1145	WARM AND SOULFUL (LP)	70
67	United Artists (S)ULP 1174	LIVE (LP, as Garnet Mimms & Senate)	50

MINDBENDERS

66	Fontana TF 644	A Groovy Kind Of Love/Love Is Good	6
66	Fontana TF 697	Can't Live With You, Can't Live Without You/One Fine Day	6
66	Fontana TF 731	Ashes To Ashes/You Don't Know About Love	6
66	Fontana TF 780	I Want Her, She Wants Me/The Morning After	7
67	Fontana TF 806	We'll Talk About It Tomorrow/Far Across Town	7
67	Fontana TF 869	The Letter/My New Day And Age	7
67	Fontana TF 877	Schoolgirl/Coming Back	15
68	Fontana TF 910	Blessed Are The Lonely/Yellow Brick Road	7
68	Fontana TF 961	Uncle Joe, The Ice Cream Man/The Man Who Loved Trees	8
69	Fontana H 1026	A Groovy Kind Of Love/Ashes To Ashes (p/s)	5
66	Fontana (S)TL 5324	THE MINDBENDERS (LP, mono/stereo)	30/35
67	Fontana (S)TL 5403	WITH WOMAN IN MIND (LP)	45
68	Fontana SFL 13045	THE MINDBENDERS (LP, reissue)	15

(see also Wayne Fontana & Mindbenders, Hotlegs, Lulu)

SAL MINEO

57	Philips JK 1024	Start Movin' (In My Direction)/Love Affair (jukebox issue)	30
57	Philips PB 733	Lasting Love/You Shouldn't Do That (78)	10
57	Philips PB 764	Party Time/The Words That I Whisper (78)	10
58	Fontana H 118	Little Pigeon/Cuttin' In	45
58	Fontana H 118	Little Pigeon/Cuttin' In (78)	25
58	Fontana H 135	Seven Steps To Love/A Couple Of Crazy Kids	25
58	Fontana H 135	Seven Steps To Love/A Couple Of Crazy Kids (78)	25
58	Fontana TFL 5004	SAL (LP)	60

CORINA MINETTE

| 60 | HMV POP 752 | He'll Have To Stay/TOMMY THOMAS ORCHESTRA: Young At Cha Cha | 6 |

SEXTON MING (& HIS DIAMOND GUSSETS)

| 96 | D. Goods DAMGOOD 71 | I'm In Love With Danny Edwards/Break His Spirit/Son Of Tractor Nits (p/s) | 6 |

CHARLES/CHARLIE MINGUS

60	Philips BBE 12399	CHARLES MINGUS (EP)	8
61	Philips BBE 12451	MINGUS DYNASTY (EP, as Charles Mingus Jazz Groups, also stereo SBBE 9050)	8/10
61	Philips BBE 12453	THINGS AIN'T WHAT THEY USED TO BE (EP, as Charles Mingus Jazz Groups, also stereo SBBE 9052)	8/10
63	Parlophone GEP 8786	SCENES IN THE CITY (EP)	10
65	Mercury 10021 MCE	JAZZ MAKERS (EP, as Charlie Mingus Orchestra)	8
56	Vogue LDE 178	CHARLIE MINGUS PRESENTS JAZZ WORKSHOP VOL. 2 (10" LP)	18
59	Parlophone PMC 1092	EAST COASTING (LP)	15
60	London Jazz LTZ-K 15194	BLUES AND ROOTS (LP, also stereo SAH-K 6087)	15
62	Atlantic SD 8005	CHARLES MINGUS PRESENTS CHARLES MINGUS (LP, U.K. issue of U.S. LP)	15
62	United Artists ULP 1004	JAZZ PORTRAITS (LP)	15
62	London HA-K/SH-K 8007	OH YEAH (LP, by Charlie Mingus & Jazz Group)	15
63	RCA RD/SF 7514	TIJUANA MOODS (LP)	15
63	Vocalion LAE 543	CHAZZ (LP)	15
64	HMV CLP 1694	THE BLACK SAINT AND THE SINNER LADY (LP)	15
65	United Artists ULP 1068	TOWN HALL CONCERT (LP)	15
65	Vocalion LAEF/SEAF 591	CHARLIE MINGUS QUINTET WITH MAX ROACH (LP)	15
65	HMV CLP 1742	MINGUS, MINGUS, MINGUS (LP, also stereo CSD 1545)	15
65	HMV CLP 1796	MINGUS PLAYS PIANO (LP)	15
65	Atlantic ATL/SAL 5019	CHARLIE MINGUS (LP)	15
66	Realm RM 211	JAZZ COMPOSERS WORKSHOP (NO. 1) (LP)	12
66	CBS (S)BPG 62261	MINGUS DYNASTY (LP)	12
68	Polydor 623 215	CHARLIE MINGUS (LP)	12
68	Atlantic 587 131	PITHECANTHROPUS ERECTUS (LP, as Charlie Mingus Jazz Workshop)	15
69	CBS 52543	MINGUS AH-UM! (LP)	12
69	Atlantic 587 166	REINCARNATION OF A LOVEBIRD (LP, as Charlie Mingus Jazz Workshop)	15
69	Mercury SMWL 21056	MINGUS REVISITED (LP)	12
70	Atlantic 545 111	DUKE'S CHOICE (LP, as Charlie Mingus Jazz Workshop)	12
70	Liberty LBS 83346	MY FAVOURITE QUINTET (LP)	12
72	Ember CJS 832	INTRUSIONS (LP)	12
72	CBS 24010	CHARLES MINGUS (2-LP)	15

KYLIE MINOGUE

72	CBS 64715	LET MY CHILDREN HEAR MUSIC (LP) 12
72	RCA LSA 3117	TIJUANA MOODS (LP, reissue) 12
72	Prestige PR 24010	CHARLES MINGUS (LP).. 12
73	Atlantic K 60039	THE ART OF CHARLIE MINGUS: THE ATLANTIC YEARS (2-LP) 15

MINIM
67	Polydor 582 011	WRAPPED IN A UNION JACK (LP) 20

MINISTRY
92	Sire W 0096	Jesus Built My Hotrod/T.V. Song (p/s) 10

MINISTRY OF SOUND
66	Decca F 12449	White Collar Worker/Back Seat Driver 10

LIZA MINNELLI
66	Capitol CL 15483	The Middle Of The Street/I (Who Have Nothing) 7

KYLIE MINOGUE
89	Epic ZEE C1	Losing My Mind (Remix)/(Extended Remix)/Tonight Is Forever (CD, card p/s) 8
89	Epic ZEE 2	Don't Drop Bombs (Extended Remix)/(Dub Mix)/(Acappella) (12", p/s) 10
89	Epic ZEE C2	Don't Drop Bombs (7" Version)/(Extended Remix)/(Acappella) (CD, card p/s)..... 8
89	Epic ZEE G3	So Sorry, I Said/I Can't Say Goodnight (gatefold p/s)..................... 7
89	Epic ZEE C3	So Sorry, I Said/I Can't Say Goodnight/Losing My Mind (Ultimix)/ Losing My Mind (Ultimix Dub) (CD, card sleeve) 8
89	Epic CP ZEE 3	So Sorry, I Said/I Can't Say Goodnight/Losing My Mind (Ultimix)/Losing My Mind (Ultimix Dub) (CD, 'Xmas' pack in pouch with gatefold card & envelope)... 12
90	Epic ZEE 4	Love Pains/Love Pains (Steve "Silk" Hurley's Radio Edit) (p/s) 4
90	Epic ZEEQT 4	Love Pains (Deep House Pains)/Love Pains (Steve "Silk" Hurley's Radio Edit)/ PET SHOP BOYS: Rent (12", gatefold sleeve).......................... 7
90	Epic CD ZEE 4	Love Pains/Love Pains (Steve "Silk" Hurley's Remix)/PET SHOP BOYS: Rent (CD, card sleeve) 8

(see also Pet Shop Boys)

DANNII MINOGUE
91	MCA MCSR 1529	Love And Kisses (7" Mix)/(Instrumental) (poster p/s, some signed)........ 25/4
97	Warner Bros SAM 3009	All I Wanna Do (Trouser Enthusiasts' Toys Of Desperation Mix)/ (Trouser Enthusiasts' Ultra Sensitive Dub)/(Quatara Mix)/ (Dizzy's Mix) (12", double pack, blue title sleeve, promo only)............... 15
97	Warner Bros SAM 3022	All I Wanna Do (12" Extended Mix)/(7" Mix)/(Xenomania Dream House Mix)/ (Tiny Tim & The Mekon Dream Dub)/(D-Bop's Innocent Girl Mix)/ (Trouser Enthusiasts' Toys Of Desperation Mix) (12", double pack, gold title sleeve, promo only) 20
97	Warner Bros SAM 3106	Everything I Wanted (Jupiter 6 — Soul Surround Mix)/Heaven Can Wait (D'Bop's Melt & Sparkle Mix) (10", promo only) 15
97	Warner Bros SAM 3108	Everything I Wanted (Xenomania 12" Mix)/(Radio Edit)/(Trouser Enthusiasts' Golden Delicious Mix)/(Metro's 7" Edit) (12", metallic green title sleeve, promo only) 12
97	Warner Bros SAM 3105	Everything I Wanted (Xenomania 12" Mix)/(Radio Edit)/(Trouser Enthusiasts' Golden Delicious Mix)/(Hell Fire Club Dub)/(Cloud Nine Mix)/(Liquid Silk Dub) (12" double pack, metallic pink title sleeve, promo only).................... 15

KYLIE MINOGUE

87	PWL PWLT 8R	I Should Be So Lucky (Bicentennial Mix)/(Instrumental) (12", stickered p/s)	12
88	PWL PWLT 12R	Got To Be Certain (Extra Beat Boys Mix)/Got To Be Certain (7" Mix)/Got To Be Certain (Out For A Duck Bill Platter Plus Dub Mix) (12", stickered p/s)	15
88	PWL PWCD 12	Got To Be Certain (Extended Mix)/Got To Be Certain (Instrumental)/ I Should Be So Lucky (Extended Mix 6.03) (CD)	20
88	PWL PWLT14	The Loco-Motion (Kohaku Mix)/I'll Still Be Loving You (12", p/s)	7
88	PWL PWLT 14R	The Loco-Motion (Sankie Mix)/I'll Still Be Loving You (12", stickered p/s)	18
88	PWL PWLP 21	Je Ne Sais Pas Pourquoi/Made In Heaven (poster p/s)	35
88	PWL PWLT 21R	Je Ne Sais Pas Pourquoi (Revolutionary Mix)/Made In Heaven (Maid In England Mix) (12", stickered p/s)	15
88	PWL PWCD 21	Je Ne Sais Pas Pourquoi (Moi Non Plus Mix)/Made In Heaven (Maid In England Mix)/The Loco-Motion (Sankie Mix) (CD)	20
88	PWL PWCD 24	Especially For You (7" Mix)/Especially For You (Extended)/All I Wanna Do Is Make You Mine (Extended) (CD)	18
89	PWL PWMC 35	Hand On Your Heart (7" Mix)/Hand On Your Heart (Great Aorta Mix)/ Just Wanna Love You (cassette)	6
89	PWL PWLT 35R	Hand On Your Heart (Heartache Mix)/Hand On Your Heart (Dub mix) Just Wanna Love You (12", with stickered p/s)	35
89	PWL PWCD 35	Hand On Your Heart (Great Aorta Mix)/Just Wanna Love You/ It's No Secret (Extended Mix) (CD)	15
89	PWL PWMC 42	Wouldn't Change A Thing/It's No Secret (Album Version) (cassette)	6
89	PWL PWLT 42R	Wouldn't Change A Thing (Espagna Mix)/Wouldn't Change A Thing (7" Mix)/ It's No Secret (Extended) (12", stickered p/s)	20
89	PWL PWCD 42	Wouldn't Change A Thing (7" Mix)/Wouldn't Change A Thing (Your Thang Mix)/ Je Ne Sais Pas Pourquoi (Revolutionary Mix) (CD)	15
89	PWL PWCD 45	Never Too Late (7" Mix)/(Extended)/ (Kylie Smiley Extended Mix) (6.17) (CD)	12
90	PWL PWMC47	Tears On My Pillow (7" Mix)/ We Know The Meaning Of Love (7" mix) (cassette)	6
90	PWL PWCD47	Tears On My Pillow (7" Mix)/Tears On My Pillow (Extended Mix)/We Know The Meaning Of Love (Extended Mix) (CD)	15
90	PWL PWMC 56	Better The Devil You Know (7" Mix)/I'm Over Dreaming Over You (7" Remix)/ (cassette, orange casing)	5
90	PWL PWCD 56	Better The Devil You Know (Mad March Hare Mix)/I'm Over Dreaming Over You (7" Remix) (CD)	15
90	PWL PWMC 64	Step Back In Time (7" Mix)/Step Back In Time (Instrumental) (cassette, green casing)	5
90	PWL PWCD 64	Step Back In Time (7" Mix)/Step Back In Time (Walkin' Rhythm Mix)/ Step Back In Time (Extended instrumental) (CD)	15
91	PWL PWLP 72	What Do I Have To Do (New Mix)/What Do I Have To Do (Instrumental) (stickered p/s, with postcards)	10
91	PWL PWMC 72	What Do I Have To Do (New Mix)/What Do I Have To Do (Instrumental) (cassette)	4
91	PWL PWLT 72R	What Do I Have To Do (Between The Sheets Mix) (12", withdrawn, no p/s)	80
91	PWL PWCD 72	What Do I Have To Do (New Mix)/What Do I Have To Do (Pumpin Polly Mix)/ What Do I Have To Do (Extended Instrumental) (CD)	15
91	PWL PWL P81	Shocked (DNA 7" Mix)/Shocked (Harding Curnow 7" Mix) (picture disc)	15
91	PWL PWCD 81	Shocked (DNA 7" Mix)/Shocked (DNA Extended Mix)/Shocked (Harding Curnow Extended Mix) (CD)	15
91	PWL PWLT 204R	Word Is Out (Summer Breeze Mix) (12", p/s, 1-sided, B-side etched autograph)	15
91	PWL PWCD 204	Word Is Out (Extended Mix)/Word Is Out (Instrumental)/Say The Word — I'll Be There (CD)	15
92	PWL PWLT 257	Celebration (Have A Party Mix)/Let's Get To It (Album Version) (12", Christmas "leaving PWL" promo p/s)	30
94	Polygram PSPMC 344	Hand On Your Heart/Give Me Just A Little More Time (Woolworths giveaway cassette)	20
94	De Construction 278482-0	Confide In Me (Master Mix)/Nothing Can Stop Us/ If You Don't Love Me (CD)	12
94	De Construction 21227477 JB	Confide In Me (Radio Mix)/(Truth Mix) (jukebox issue, no p/s)	10
88	PWL HFD 4	KYLIE (DAT)	50
89	PWL HFC 9	ENJOY YOURSELF (cassette, yellow casing)	10
90	PWL HF 18	RHYTHM OF LOVE (LP, with free poster)	12
90	PWL HFL 18	RHYTHM OF LOVE (LP, gold leaf sleeve, 100 only)	200
91	PWL HFCL 18	RHYTHM OF LOVE (cassette, with 3 bonus tracks, gold case)	15
91	PWL HFCDL 18	RHYTHM OF LOVE (CD, with 3 bonus tracks, gold case)	20
97	RCA 74321 57272	IMPOSSIBLE PRINCESS (CD, promo, withdrawn)	70

(see also Visionmasters)

MINORBOPS

58	Vogue V 9110	Need You Tonight/Want You For My Own	550
58	Vogue V 9110	Need You Tonight/Want You For My Own (78)	135

MINOR THREAT

85	Discord DISCORD 15	Salad Days/Stumped/Good Guys (p/s)	6

MINSTRELS

67	Studio One SO 2036	People Get Ready/HAMLINS: Everyone's Got To Be There	18
68	Studio One SO 2050	Miss Highty Tighty/WESTMORELITES: Let Me Be Yours Until Tomorrow	18

MINTS
57	London HLP 8423	Night Air/KEN COPELAND: Pledge Of Love	300
57	London HLP 8423	Night Air/KEN COPELAND: Pledge Of Love (78)	60

MINUTE MEN
61	Capitol CL 15206	Yankee Diddle/Blue Pearl	6

MINUTEMEN
83	SST SST 002	PARANOID TIME (8-track EP)	18
84	SST SST 016	BUZZ OR HOWL UNDER THE INFLUENCE OF THE HEAT (12" EP)	20
85	Homestead REFLEX-L	TOUR SPIEL (EP, live 4-track)	10

(SMOKEY ROBINSON &) MIRACLES
61	London HL 9276	Shop Around/Who's Lovin' You	45
61	London HL 9366	Ain't It Baby/The Only One I Love	70
62	Fontana H 384	What's So Good About Goodbye/I've Been So Good To You	125
63	Oriole CBA 1795	You've Really Got A Hold On Me/Happy Landing	80
63	Oriole CBA 1863	Mickey's Monkey/Whatever Makes You Happy	60
64	Stateside SS 263	I Gotta Dance To Keep From Crying/Such Is Love, Such Is Life.	30
64	Stateside SS 282	The Man In You/Heartbreak Road	25
64	Stateside SS 324	I Like It Like That/You're So Fine And Sweet.	20
64	Stateside SS 353	That's What Love Is Made Of/Would I Love You	18
65	Stateside SS 377	Come On Do The Jerk/Baby Don't You Go	25
65	Tamla Motown TMG 503	Ooo Baby Baby/All That's Good	18
65	Tamla Motown TMG 522	The Tracks Of My Tears/A Fork In The Road	25
65	Tamla Motown TMG 540	My Girl Has Gone/Since You Won My Heart	18
66	Tamla Motown TMG 547	Going To A Go-Go/Choosey Beggar	12
66	Tamla Motown TMG 569	Whole Lotta Shakin' In My Heart/Oh Be My Love	18
66	Tamla Motown TMG 584	(Come 'Round Here) I'm The One You Need/Save Me	10

(The above singles are credited to Miracles.)

67	Tamla Motown TMG 598	The Love I Saw In You Was Just A Mirage/Swept For You Baby	10
67	Tamla Motown TMG 614	More Love/Come Spy With Me (withdrawn B-side)	80
67	Tamla Motown TMG 614	More Love/Swept For You Baby	18
67	Tamla Motown TMG 631	I Second That Emotion/You Must Be Love	6
68	Tamla Motown TMG 648	If You Can Want/When The Words From Your Heart Get Caught Up In Your Throat	10
68	Tamla Motown TMG 661	Yester-Love/Much Better Off	7
68	Tamla Motown TMG 673	Special Occasion/Give Her Up	7
69	Tamla Motown TMG 687	Baby, Baby Don't Cry/Your Mother's Only Daughter.	7
69	Tamla Motown TMG 696	The Tracks Of My Tears/Come On Do The Jerk	6
70	Tamla Motown TMG 745	The Tears Of A Clown/You Must Be Love (with withdrawn B-side)	35
70	Tamla Motown TMG 745	The Tears Of A Clown/Who's Gonna Take The Blame	5
71	Tamla Motown TMG 761	(Come Round Here) I'm The One You Need/We Can Make It, We Can	5
71	Tamla Motown TMG 774	I Don't Blame You At All/That Girl	5
72	Tamla Motown TMG 811	My Girl Has Gone/Crazy 'Bout The La-La-La	5
73	Tamla Motown TMG 853	Going To A Go-Go/Whole Lotta Shakin' In My Heart/Yester-Love	5

(The above singles are credited to Smokey Robinson & Miracles.)

76	Tamla Motown TMG 1023	Nightlife/The Miracle Workers: Overture (as Miracles)	5
61	London RE 1295	SHOP AROUND (EP, as Miracles)	125
83	Tamla Motown CTME 2028	TEARS OF A CLOWN (cassette EP, as Smokey Robinson & Miracles)	7
63	Oriole PS 40044	HI! WE'RE THE MIRACLES (LP)	175
64	Stateside SL 10099	THE FABULOUS MIRACLES (LP)	140
65	Tamla Motown TML 11003	I LIKE IT THAT (LP)	60
66	Tamla Motown TML 11024	GOIN' TO A GO-GO (LP, as Smokey Robinson & Miracles, mono/stereo)	40/50
66	T. Motown (S)TML 11031	THE MIRACLES FROM THE BEGINNING (LP, mono/stereo)	40/50
67	T. Motown (S)TML 11044	AWAY WE A-GO-GO (LP, mono/stereo)	35/40

(The above albums are credited to Miracles unless otherwise stated.)

68	T. Motown (S)TML 11067	MAKE IT HAPPEN (LP)	30
68	T. Motown (S)TML 11072	GREATEST HITS (LP)	15
69	T. Motown (S)TML 11089	SPECIAL OCCASION (LP)	20
69	T. Motown (S)TML 11107	SMOKEY ROBINSON & THE MIRACLES LIVE! (LP)	18
70	T. Motown (S)TML 11129	TIME OUT FOR SMOKEY ROBINSON & MIRACLES (LP)	15
70	T. Motown STML 11151	FOUR IN BLUE (LP)	15
70	T. Motown STML 11163	WHAT LOVE HAS JOINED TOGETHER (LP, unissued)	
71	T. Motown STML 11172	POCKETFUL OF MIRACLES (LP)	15
73	T. Motown STMA 8008	1957-1972 (LP, gatefold sleeve)	12

MIRAGE
65	CBS 201772	It's In Her Kiss/What Ye Gonna Do 'Bout It	15
65	CBS 202007	Go Away/Just A Face	15
66	Philips BF 1534	Tomorrow Never Knows/You Can't Be Serious	25
67	Philips BF 1554	Hold On/Can You Hear Me	10
67	Philips BF 1571	The Wedding Of Ramona Blair/Lazy Man	50
68	Page One POF 078	Mystery Lady/Chicago Cottage	8
68	Page One POF 111	Carolyn/World Goes On Around You	8

(see also Yellow Payges, Caleb, Jawbone, Spencer Davis Group, Portobello Explosion)

MIRETTES
68	Uni UN 501	In The Midnight Hour/To Love Somebody	6
68	Uni UN 505	The Real Thing/Take Me For A Little While	6
69	MCA Soul Bag BAG 8	Whirlpool/Ain't You Trying To Cross Over	5
72	Jay Boy BOY 65	Now That I've Found You Baby/He's Alright With Me	5
69	MCA MUP(S) 344	IN THE MIDNIGHT HOUR (LP)	15

(see also Ikettes)

MIRK
79	Mother Earth MUM 1205	MODDANS BOWER (LP)	60
82	Spring Thyme SPR 1009	TAK A DRAM (LP)	25

MIRKWOOD
71	Flams Ltd PR 1067	MIRKWOOD (LP)	400
93	Tenth Planet TP 003	MIRKWOOD (LP, reissue, numbered with insert, 500 only)	20

MIRO
90	Secret Heart SH 30008	GREETINGS FROM THE GOLBORNE RD (EP, handmade col'd p/s, 1,000 only)	5
90	Secret Heart SH 4008	The World In Maps/Great Dominions (handmade p/s & mini-booklet, 1,000 only)	4

STEVE MIRO & EYES
78	Object Music OM 03	Up And About/Smiling In Reverse (p/s)	6
79	Object Music OM 10	Dreams Of Desire/Queens Of The Sea (p/s)	5
80	Object Music OBF 008	RUDE INTRUSIONS (LP)	12
81	Object Music OBJ 015	SECOND SENTENCE (LP)	10

(see also Eyes, Noyes Bros)

MIRROR
68	Philips BF 1666	Gingerbread Man/Faster Than Light	50

MIRRORS
78	Lightning GIL 503	Cure For Cancer/Nice Vice (p/s)	15
79	Lightning GIL 540	Dark Glasses/999 (p/s)	15

MISFITS (U.K.)
66	A.S.C.C. PRI 101	You Won't See Me/Hanging Around (Aberdeen Students Charities Campaign)	10

(see also Complex)

MISFITS (U.S.)
81	Plan 9/Cherry Red PLP 9	BEWARE (12" EP)	100

MISSING PRESUMED DEAD
79	Sequel PART 2	Say It With Flowers/Double Life/Driving Home/Family Tree (p/s)	5
80s	Sequel PART 4	MISSING PRESUMED DEAD (LP)	12
80s	Sequel PART 5	REVENGE (LP)	10

MISSING SCIENTISTS
80	Rough Trade RT 057	Big City, Bright Lights/Discotheque X (p/s)	10

(see also Television Personalities, Slaughter)

MISSION
86	Chapter 22 CHAP 6/7	Serpent's Kiss/Wake (p/s)	4
86	Chapter 22 CHAP 7	Garden Of Delight/Like A Hurricane (p/s)	4
86	Chapter 22 L12 CHAP 7	Like A Hurricane/Garden Of Delight/Dancing Barefoot/The Crystal Ocean (12", autographed p/s)	10
86	Mercury MYSG 1	Stay With Me/Blood Brother (autographed, gatefold p/s)	7
87	Mercury MYTHB 2	Wasteland/Shelter From The Storm (edited live version)/Serpent's Kiss (live)/1969 (live) (box set, with 5 photos)	8
87	Mercury MYTHX 22	Wasteland (Anniversary Mix)/Shelter From The Storm (live)/1969 (live)/Wake (live) (12", p/s)	8
87	Mercury MYTHP 3	Severina/Tomorrow Never Knows (p/s, with poster & numbered wraparound paper strip)	5
89	Mercury MYCDB 8	Butterfly On A Wheel/The Grip Of Disease/Kingdom Come (Forever & Again) (CD, picture disc in 12" box set, shrinkwrapped, with room for 3 other CDs)	8
90	Mercury MYCDB 9	Deliverance/Mr. Pleasant/Heaven Sends You/Deliverance (CD, picture disc)	7
88	Mercury 080 120-2	And The Dance Goes On/Garden Of Delight (Hereafter)/Tomorrow Never Knows (Amphetamix)/Wasteland/Love You To Death (Instrumental)/Wasteland (Video) (CD Video)	10
88	Mercury 080 526-2	Tower Of Strength/For Ever More/Tadeusz (1912-1988)/Dream On/Tower Of Strength (Video) (CD Video)	10
86	Mercury MERH 102	OWN MEDICINE (LP, gatefold sleeve)	10

(see also Sisters Of Mercy, Dead Or Alive, Pauline Murray, Artery, Red Lorry Yellow Lorry, Metal Gurus, Expalaires, Knopov's Political Package, TV Product)

MISSION BELLES
65	Decca F 12154	Sincerely/When A Girl Really Loves You	6

MISSISSIPPI
70	Fox FOX 1	Mr. Union Railway Man/Main Street	10

MISS JANE
68	Pama PM 704	Bad Mind People/My Heart Is Aching (B-side act. "Witch Doctor" by Coolers)	8

MISS X (Joyce Blair)
63	Ember EMB S 175	Christine/S-E-X	12

MISTER MOST
69	Downtown DT 409	Reggae Train/Pushwood	6

MISTER VERSATILE
69	Jackpot JP 701	Apple Blossom/LITTLE BOY BLUE: Dark End Of The Street (act. by Pat Kelly)	7
69	Jackpot JP 702	Devil's Disciples/ERROL DUNKLEY: Having A Party	7

(see also Lester Sterling)

MISTY
77	Cottage COT 511	MISTY (LP)	20

MISUNDERSTOOD
66	Fontana TF 777	I Can Take You To The Sun/Who Do You Love	45
69	Fontana TF 998	Children Of The Sun/I Unseen (small or large centre hole)	45/35
69	Fontana TF 1028	You're Tuff Enough/Little Red Rooster (as Misunderstood featuring Glenn "Fernando" Campbell, some in p/s)	40/25
69	Fontana TF 1041	Never Had A Girl (Like You Before)/Golden Glass (as Misunderstood featuring Glenn "Fernando" Campbell)	35
81	Cherry Red CHERRY 22	Children Of The Sun/Who Do You Love/I'll Take You To The Sun (p/s)	5
80s	Bucketfull Of Brains BOB 2	You're My Girl (flexidisc with *Bucketfull Of Brains* magazine)	8/5

(see also Juicy Lucy, High Tide, Van Der Graaf Generator, Answers)

BLUE MITCHELL
| 69 | Blue Note BST 84300 | COLLISION IN BLACK (LP) | 15 |
| 73 | Mainstream MSL 1002 | BLUE'S BLUES (LP) | 12 |

CHAD MITCHELL
| 62 | London HLR 9509 | Lizzie Borden/Super Skier | 6 |

DENNY MITCHELL SOUNDSATIONS
| 64 | Decca F 11848 | I've Been Crying/For Your Love | 6 |

(see also Preachers, Moon's Train)

GROVER MITCHELL
| 68 | London HLU 10221 | Turned On/Blue Over You | 6 |
| 76 | Vanguard VS 5003 | What Hurts/Super Hero | 25 |

GUY MITCHELL
78s
51	Columbia DB 2800	My Heart Cries For You/Me And My Imagination (78)	8
51	Columbia DB 2816	The Roving Kind/You're Not In My Arms Tonight (78)	8
51	Columbia DB 2831	Sparrow In The Treetop/Christopher Columbus (78)	8
51	Columbia DB 2871	A Begger In Love/Unless (78)	10
51	Columbia DB 2885	My Truly Truly Fair/Who Knows Love (78)	8
51	Columbia DB 2908	Belle, Belle, My Liberty Belle/Sweetheart Of Yesterday (78)	8
51	Columbia DB 2869	There's Always Room At Our House/Giddy-Ap (78)	8
52	Columbia DB 3001	Wimmin/I Can't Help It (78)	8
52	Columbia DB 3018	We Won't Live In A Castle/You're Just In Love (with Rosemary Clooney) (78)	8
52	Columbia DB 3056	Pittsburgh Pennsylvania/The Girl With The Sawdust Heart (78)	8
52	Columbia DB 3074	Gently Johnny/A Little Kiss Goodnight (78)	10
52	Columbia DB 3087	Don't Rob Another Man's Castle/Where In The World (78)	8
52	Vogue V 9033	Cabaret (with Satisfiers)/I've Got A Frame Without A Picture (78)	20
52	Columbia DB 3104	The Day Of Jubilo/You'll Never Be Mine (78)	8
52	Columbia DB 3151	Feet Up/Angels Cry (78)	8
52	Columbia DB 3180	Jenny Kissed Me/To Me You're A Song (78)	8
52	Columbia DB 3203	That's A-Why/Train Of Love (78)	8
53	Columbia DB 3238	She Wears Red Feathers/Why Should I Go Home? (78)	8
53	Columbia DB 3255	Pretty Little Black-Eyed Susie/Horn Belt Boogie (78)	8
53	Columbia DB 3311	The House Of Singing Bamboo/The Place Where I Worship (with Rosemary Clooney) (78)	8
53	Philips PB 124	Walkin' And Wonderin'/I Want You For A Sunbeam (78)	8
53	Philips PB 136	So Am I/Tell Us Where The Good Times Are (with Mindy Carson) (78)	8
53	Philips PB 162	Look At That Girl/Wise Man Or A Fool (78)	8
53	Philips PB 178	Chicka Boom/Hannah Lee (78)	8
53	Philips PB 210	Cloud Lucky Seven/Sippin' Soda (78)	8
54	Philips PB 225	The Cuff Of My Shirt/Strollin' Blues (78)	8
54	Philips PB 248	A Dime And A Doller/Tear Down The Mountains (78)	8
54	Philips PB 249	Meet A Happy Guy/Brave Man (with Rosemary Clooney) (78)	8
54	Philips PB 255	Man And A Woman (with Rosemary Clooney)/Good Intentions (78)	8
54	Philips PB 293	Bob's Yer Uncle/Got A Hole In My Sweater (78)	8
54	Philips PB 330	What Am I Doing In Kansas City/My Heaven And Earth (78)	8
54	Philips PB 387	I Met The Cutest Little Eyeful/Gee But Yer Gotta Come Home (78)	8
55	Philips PB 450	Green Grows the Grass/Solo (78)	8
55	Philips PB 452	Man Overboard/Zoo Baby (78)	8
55	Philips PB 487	Too Late/Let Us Be Sweethearts Over Again (78)	8
55	Philips PB 506	When Blinky Blows/Belonging (78)	8
56	Philips PB 556	Perfume Candy And Flowers/Ninety Nine Years (78)	8
56	Philips PB 610	Give Me A Carriage And Eight White Horses/I Used To Hate Ya (78)	8
56	Philips PB 635	I'd Like To Say A Few Words About Texas/Finders Keepers (78)	8
57	Philips PB 685	Rock-A-Billy/Got A Feeling (78)	8
57	Philips PB 712	Sweet Stuff/In The Middle Of A Dark, Dark Night (78)	8
57	Philips PB 743	Call Rosie On The Phone/Cure For The Blues (78)	8
58	Philips PB 766	C'mon Let's Go/The Unbeliever (78)	10
58	Philips PB 798	Wonderin' And Worryin'/If Ya Don't Like It, Don't Knock It (78)	12
58	Philips PB 830	Hangin' Around/Honey Brown Eyes (78)	12
58	Philips PB 858	Let It Shine, Let It Shine/Butterfly Doll (78)	15
58	Philips PB 885	My Heart Cries For You (2nd Version)/Till We're Engaged (78)	18
59	Philips PB 915	Alias Jesse James/Pride O' Dixie (78)	22
59	Philips PB 964	Heartaches By The Number/Two (78)	40

SINGLES
53	Columbia SCM 5018	Feet Up (Pat Him On The Po-Po)/Jenny Kissed Me	35
53	Columbia SCM 5022	'Cause I Love Ya, That's A-Why/Train Of Love (both with Mindy Carson)	30
53	Columbia SCM 5032	She Wears Red Feathers/Why Should I Go Home?	35
53	Columbia SCM 5037	Pretty Little Black-Eyed Susie/MITCH MILLER HORNS: Horn Belt Boogie	30
56	Philips JK 1001	Singing The Blues/Crazy With Love (jukebox issue)	50
57	Philips JK 1005	Knee Deep In The Blues/Take Me Back Baby (jukebox issue)	30
57	Philips JK 1015	Rock-A-Billy/Got A Feeling (jukebox issue)	25
57	Philips JK 1023	Sweet Stuff/In The Middle Of A Dark, Dark Night (jukebox issue)	25
57	Philips JK 1027	Call Rosie On The Phone/Cure For The Blues (jukebox issue)	25
58	Philips PB 766	C'mon Let's Go/The Unbeliever	10
58	Philips PB 798	Wonderin' And Worryin'/If Ya Don't Like It, Don't Knock It	8
58	Philips PB 830	Hangin' Around/Honey Brown Eyes	8
58	Philips PB 858	Let It Shine, Let It Shine/Butterfly Doll	8
58	Philips PB 885	My Heart Cries For You/Till We're Engaged	6
59	Philips PB 915	Alias Jesse James/Pride O' Dixie	6
59	Philips PB 964	Heartaches By The Number/Two (some with triangular centre)	10/5
60	Philips PB 998	The Same Old Me/Build My Gallows High (2nd version)	6
60	Philips PB 1026	Cry Hurtin' Heart/Symphony Of Spring	6
60	Philips PB 1050	Silver Moon Upon The Golden Sands/My Shoes Keep Walking Back To You	6
60	Philips PB 1084	Sunshine Guitar/One Way Street	6

MINT VALUE £

61	Philips PB 1131	Your Goodnight Kiss/Follow Me	6
61	Philips PB 1183	Divorce/I'll Just Pretend	6
62	Philips PB 1202	Soft Rain/Big Big Change	6
63	Pye International 7N 25179	Go, Tiger, Go/If You Ever Go Away (unreleased)	
63	Pye International 7N 25185	Have I Told You Lately That I Love You/Blue Violet	6
66	CBS 202238	Singing The Blues/Rock-A-Billy	12
67	London HLB 10173	Traveling Shoes/Every Night Is A Lifetime	6
68	London HLB 10190	Alabam/Goodbye Road, Hello Home	6
68	London HLB 10218	Before You Take Your Love From Me/Singing The Blues	6
68	London HLB 10234	Just Wish You'd Maybe Change Your Mind/If You Could Cry Me My Tears	6
86	Top Hat TPH 1	Heaven Knows/Broke But Not Busted (p/s)	5
87	Top Hat TPH 2	Always On My Mind/The Wind Beneath My Wings (p/s)	5
88	Top Hat TPH 3	Have A Nice Day/There Ain't No Worry (p/s)	5

EPs

54	Columbia SEG 7513	PRETTY LITTLE BLACK EYED SUSIE (EP, plain sleeve)	15
55	Columbia SEG 7581	MY TRULY TRULY FAIR (EP, plain sleeve)	15
55	Columbia SEG 7598	JENNY KISSED ME (EP, plain sleeve)	15
55	Philips BBE 12008	GUY MITCHELL (EP)	15
56	Philips BBE 12093	GUY MITCHELL NO. 2 (EP)	18
57	Philips BBE 12112	SINGING THE BLUES WITH GUY MITCHELL (EP)	15
58	Philips BBE 12215	GUY MITCHELL PHILIPS TV SERIES (EP)	18

LPs

54	Columbia 33S 1028	GUY MITCHELL SINGS (10" LP)	50
55	Philips BBR 8031	THE VOICE OF YOUR CHOICE (10" LP)	35
58	Philips BBL 7246	A GUY IN LOVE (LP)	30
58	Philips BBL 7265	SHOWCASE OF HITS (LP)	30
61	Philips BBL 7465	SUNSHINE GUITAR (LP)	30
66	CBS Realm RM 52336	THE BEST OF GUY MITCHELL (LP)	15
68	London HA-B 8364	TRAVELING SHOES (LP, also stereo SH-B 8364)	18/22
68	Hallmark HM 580	THE BEST OF GUY MITCHELL (LP, also stereo SHM 580)	15/20
69	Hallmark CHM 642	A GUY IN LOVE (LP, stereo reissue)	12

(see also Mindy Carson)

JONI MITCHELL

68	Reprise RS 20694	Night In The City/I Had A King	5
69	Reprise RS 23402	Chelsea Morning/Both Sides Now	6
70	Reprise RS 20906	Big Yellow Taxi/Woodstock	5
72	Asylum AYM 511	You Turn Me On, I'm A Radio/Urge For Going	5
83	Geffen DA 3122	Chinese Cafe/Ladies Man (double pack, with bonus interview 7")	5
88	Geffen GEF 37CD	My Secret Place (with Peter Gabriel)/Number One/Chinese Eyes-Unchained Melody/Good Friends (3" CD, 5" case)	7
68	Reprise RSLP 6293	JONI MITCHELL (LP, gatefold sleeve, 'steamboat' label)	18
69	Reprise RSLP 6341	CLOUDS (LP, textured single sleeve, 'steamboat' label)	18
69	Reprise RSLP 6341	CLOUDS (LP, 2nd pressing, stickered U.S. g/fold sleeve, 'steamboat' label)	18
70	Reprise RSLP 6376	LADIES OF THE CANYON (LP, gatefold sleeve, 'steamboat' label)	18
71	Reprise K 44128	BLUE (LP, gatefold sleeve, some with blue inner sleeve)	15/12
73	Asylum SYLA 8753	FOR THE ROSES (LP, gatefold sleeve)	12
74	Asylum SYLA 8756	COURT AND SPARK (LP, gatefold sleeve)	12
75	Asylum SYSP 902	MILES OF AISLES (2-LP, gatefold sleeve with inner flap)	15
79	Asylum K 53091	MINGUS (LP, gatefold sleeve)	12
80	Asylum K 62030	SHADOWS AND LIGHT (2-LP, gatefold sleeve with inners)	15
82	Asylum/Nimbus K 53018	THE HISSING OF SUMMER LAWNS (LP, audiophile pressing, mail order issue)	15

MALCOLM MITCHELL

| 54 | Parlophone MSP 6084 | The Jones Boy/Granada | 6 |

McKINLEY 'SOUL' MITCHELL

| 68 | President PT 125 | The Town I Live In/No Love Like Your Love | 6 |
| 68 | President PTL 1005 | McKINLEY 'SOUL' MITCHELL (LP) | 12 |

PHILIP MITCHELL

| 71 | Jay Boy BOY 37 | I'm Gonna Build California From All Over The World/The World Needs More People Like You | 7 |
| 72 | Jay Boy BOY 57 | Free For All/Flower Child | 7 |

RONNIE MITCHELL

| 60 | London HLU 9220 | How Many Times/The Only Love | 7 |

SINX MITCHELL

| 64 | Hickory 45-1248 | Weird Sensation/Love Is All I'm Asking For | 15 |

(see also Crickets, Earl Sinks)

VALERIE MITCHELL

65	Oak RGJ 160	There Goes My Heart Again/If I Didn't Love You (p/s)	50
65	HMV POP 1422	Bitter Tears/Forbidden	5
65	HMV POP 1462	There Goes My Heart Again/If I Didn't Love You	6
65	HMV POP 1490	Go My Way/Green Eyes	6
66	HMV POP 1509	Play With Me/Never Let It Be Said	6
66	HMV POP 1529	You Can Go/The Windmill Girls	5
67	Columbia DB 8186	Love Can Be The Sweetest Thing/I'm Sorry	5
67	Columbia DB 8265	Sunshine/You Belong To Me	5

WILLIE MITCHELL

64	London HLU 9926	20-75/Secret Home	7
65	London HLU 10004	Everything Is Gonna Be Alright/That Driving Beat	15
66	London HLU 10039	Bad Eye/Sugar T.	7
66	London HLU 10085	Mercy/Sticks And Stones	7
68	London HLU 10186	Soul Serenade/Buster Browne	6
68	London HLU 10215	Prayer Meetin'/Rum Daddy	6
68	London HLU 10224	Up Hard/Beale Street Mood	5

MINT VALUE £

69	London HLU 10246	Everything Is Gonna Be Alright/Mercy	5
69	London HLU 10282	Young People/Kitten Korner	5
70	London HLU 10313	Robbin's Nest/Six To Go	5
73	London HLU 10407	Last Tango In Paris/Six To Go	5
74	London HLU 10545	The Champion (2 parts)	5
67	London HA-U 8319	THE HIT SOUND OF WILLIE MITCHELL (LP)	20
68	London HA-U/SH-U 8365	SOUL SERENADE (LP)	18
68	London HA-U/SH-U 8368	LIVE (LP)	15
69	London HA-U/SH-U 8372	SOLID SOUL (LP)	18
70	London HA-U/SH-U 8388	ON TOP (LP)	15
70	London HA-U/SH-U 8408	SOUL BAG (LP)	15

MITCHELL/COE MYSTERIES

| 80 | RCA PL 25297 | EXILED (LP, with inner sleeve, initially with gatefold sleeve) | 15/12 |

(see also Colin Blunstone, Lesley Duncan, Dan McCafferty, Francis Rossi & Berni Frost, Ray Russell, Joe Jammer, Complex, Monsoon)

ROBERT MITCHUM

57	Capitol CL 14701	What Is This Generation Coming To?/Mama Looka Boo Boo	15
57	Capitol CL 14701	What Is This Generation Coming To?/Mama Looka Boo Boo (78)	10
62	Capitol CL 15251	The Ballad Of Thunder Road/My Honey's Lovin' Arms	12
67	Monument MON 1007	Little Ole Wine Drinker Me/Walker's Woods	7
55	Brunswick OE 9197	RACHEL AND THE STRANGER (EP)	18
67	Monument LMO 5011	THAT MAN (LP)	25

MITHRANDIR

| 82 | New Leaf SVC 01 | MAGICK EP (p/s) | 75 |
| 82 | New Leaf SVC 570 | Dreamers Of Fortune (p/s) | 50 |

JACKIE MITTO(O)

66	Island WI 293	Killer Diller (as Jackie Mitto & Soul Brothers)/ PATRICK HYTTON: Oh Lady	18
67	Rio R 114	Home Made/ETHIOPIANS: I'm Gonna Take Over Now	20
67	Rio R 123	Got My Buglaoo/ETHIOPIANS: What To Do	30
67	Coxsone CS 7002	Somebody Help Me/GAYLADS & SOUL VENDORS: The Sound Of Silence	18
67	Coxsone CS 7009	Ba Ba Boom/SLIM SMITH & FREEDOM SINGERS: Mercy Mercy	18
67	Coxsone CS 7019	Ram Jam/SUMMERTAIRES: You're Gonna Leave	15
67	Coxsone CS 7026	Something Stupid/LYRICS: Money Lover	18
68	Coxsone CS 7040	Norwegian Wood/GAYLADS: Most Peculiar Man	18
68	Coxsone CS 7042	Sure Shot/OCTAVES: The Bottle	18
68	Coxsone CS 7046	Man Pon Shot/BOP & BELTONES: Not For A Moment	18
68	Coxsone CS 7050	Napoleon Solo/CANNON BALL BRYAN: You're My Everything	18
68	Coxsone CS 7075	Mission Impossible/HEPTONES: Giddy Up (B-side actually by Actions)	18
68	Studio One SO 2043	Put It One/SOUL VENDORS: Chinese Chicken	18
68	Studio One SO 2056	Race Track/BASES: I Don't Mind	18
69	Studio One SO 2082	Hi-Jack/TREVOR CLARKE: Sufferer	18
69	Doctor Bird DB 1177	Dark Of The Sun/MATADOR ALL STARS: Bridge View	18
69	Bamboo BAM 6	Our Thing (with Sound Dimension)/C. MARSHALL: Tra La La Sweet '69	12
69	Bamboo BAM 15	Clean Up/Spring Time (as Jackie Mittoo & Sound Dimension)	12
70	Bamboo BAM 17	Dark Of The Moon/Moon Walk (as Jackie Mittoo & Sound Dimension)	12
70	Bamboo BAM 20	Gold Dust/SUPERTONES: Real Gone Loser	12
70	Bamboo BAM 31	Can I Change My Mind/BRENTFORD ALLSTARS: Early Duckling	12
70	Bamboo BAM 38	Baby Why/ETHIOPIANS: You'll Want To Come Back	8
70	Bamboo BAM 51	Dancing Groove/BLACK & GEORGE: Peanut Butter	20
70	Banana BA 315	Holly Holy/LARRY MARSHALL: I've Got To Make It	12
71	Banana BA 320	Peenie Wallie/ROY RICHARDS: Can't Go On	8
72	London HLU 10357	Wishbone/Soul Bird (as Jackie Mittoo — The Reggae Beat)	6
67	Coxsone CSL 8009	IN LONDON (LP)	75
68	Coxsone CSL 8014	EVENING TIME (LP, with Soul Vendors)	75
69	Coxsone CSL 8020	KEEP ON DANCING (LP)	90
70	Bamboo BDLP 209	NOW (LP)	50
72	London SHU 8436	WISHBONE (LP)	18

(see also Lord Tanamo, Jamaican Actions, Matadors, Jackie Opel, Soul Vendors, Winston Francis, Donna & Freedom Singers, Skatalites)

MIX BLOOD

| 80 | Creole CR 201 | Last Train To Skaville/Move And Move (p/s) | 10 |

MIXED BAG

| 69 | Decca F 12880 | Potiphar (with Ramases III Orchestra)/Million Dollar Bash | 4 |
| 69 | Decca F 12907 | Round And Round/Have You Ever Been In Love | 4 |

MIXMAN

| 90 | Citizen Kane 12KANE 2 | Bright Child (Manmix)/Bright Child (Dancemix) (12", p/s) | 10 |

MIXTURE

| 65 | Fontana TF 640 | One By One/Monkey Jazz | 6 |
| 69 | Parlophone R 5755 | Sad Old Song/Never Trust In Tomorrow | 5 |

BILLY MIZE ORCHESTRA

| 60 | Top Rank JAR 391 | Little Coco Palm/The Windward Castle | 6 |

JOHN MIZAROLLI

| 82 | Carrere CAL 142 | MESSAGE FROM THE 5TH STONE (LP) | 18 |

VIC MIZZY, HIS ORCHESTRA & CHORUS

| 65 | RCA RCA 1440 | Addams Family Main Theme/Kentucky James Main Theme | 20 |

M.J.6

| 60 | Decca F 11212 | Tracy's Theme/Private Eye | 4 |

M.J.Q.

(see under Modern Jazz Quartet)

MO & STEVE
| 66 | Pye 7N 17175 | Oh What A Day It's Going To Be/Reach Out For Your Lovin' Touch .... 4 |

MOB
68	Mercury MF 1026	Disappear/I Wish You Would Leave Me Alone 6
71	Polydor 2001 127	I Dig Everything About You/Love's Got A Hold On Me 6
71	Polydor 2001 169	Give It To Me/I'd Like To See More Of You 5
71	Polydor 2001 200	Money/Once A Man Twice A Child 5
73	MGM 2006 278	Tear The House Down/One Way Ticket To Nowhere 5
74	UK USA 4	Give It To Me/I'd LIke To See More Of You 8
71	Polydor 2344 001	MOB (LP) 12

MOB
| 80 | Kalida AKB 1/2 | Send Me To Coventry/Mobbed (p/s) .... 15 |

MOB
80	All The Madmen MAD 1	Youth/Crying Again (p/s) 7
80	All The Madmen MAD 002	Witch Hunt/Shuffling Souls/What's Going On (EP, handwritten white labels with sticker & foldout, stapled, gatefold p/s) 6
82	Crass 321984/7	No Doves Fly Here/I Hear You Laughing (foldout p/s) 5
83	All The Madmen MAD 6	The Mirror Breaks/Stay (screen-printed p/s, with lyric insert) 5
80s	All/Madmen MADPACK 1	MAD PACK 1 (3 x 7" in 12" pack) 12

HANK MOBLEY
| 61 | Blue Note BLP 4031 | HANK MOBLEY'S SOUL STATION (LP) .... 12 |
| | *(see also Wynton Kelly, Art Blakey)* | |

JOHN MOBLEY
| 62 | Stateside SS 136 | Tunnel Of Love/Work Out .... 8 |

MOBSTER
| 80 | Ensign ENY 41 | The Mobster Shuffle/Simmer Down (p/s) .... 6 |
| 81 | Ensign ENY 209 | Perfect Man/Trinidad (p/s) .... 5 |

MOBY DICK
| 82 | Ebony EBON 5 | Nothing To Fear (no p/s) .... 12 |

MOBY GRAPE
67	CBS 2953	Omaha/Hey Grandma 15
68	CBS 3555	Can't Be So Bad/Murder In My Heart For The Judge 7
69	CBS 3945	Trucking Man/Ooh Mama Ooh 8
67	CBS (S)BPG 63090	MOBY GRAPE (LP) 25
68	CBS 63271	WOW (LP, mono & stereo) 18
69	CBS 63430	'69 (LP, mono & stereo) 18
69	CBS 63698	TRULY FINE CITIZEN (LP, mono & stereo) 18
72	Reprise K 44152	20 GRANITE CREEK (LP) 12
74	CBS 64743	GREAT GRAPE (LP) 12

MOCEDADES
| 73 | Bell BELL 1303 | Touch The Wind/Eres Tu .... 6 |

MOCKINGBIRDS
65	Columbia DB 7480	That's How It's Gonna Stay/I Never Should Have Kissed You 40
65	Columbia DB 7565	I Can Feel We're Parting/The Flight Of The Mockingbird 40
65	Immediate IM 015	You Stole My Love/Skit Skat 90
66	Decca F 12434	One By One/Lovingly Yours 35
66	Decca F 12510	How To Find A Lover/My Story 35
	(see also 10cc, Graham Gouldman, Whirlwinds, Doctor Father, Hotlegs, Godley & Creme)	

MOCK TURTLES
87	Imaginary MIRAGE 003	POMONA (12" EP) 15
89	Imaginary MIRAGE 009	Wicker Man/The Willow Song/Another Jesus Walks On Water/Fionnuala (12", p/s) 10
89	Imaginary MIRAGE 015	And Then She Smiles/Calm Before The Storm/Shangri-La (12", p/s), 1st issue with pink small type; 2nd with b&w type & girl's face in pink) 8/7
90	Imaginary MIRAGE 017	Lay Me Down/Can You Dig It? (fully autographed, sold at gigs) 5
90	Imaginary MIRAGE 019	Are You Experienced?/ (Extended Mix) (12", no p/s, 500 autographed) 7
91	Imaginary FREE 001	Pale Blue Eyes/ECHO & BUNNYMEN: Foggy Notion (promo only, no p/s) 8
89	Bucketfull Of Brains BOB 26	Croppies Lie Down/SAINTS: I Dreamed Of Marie Antoinette (free with *Bucketfull Of Brains* magazine, issue 32) 6/4
	(see also Judge Happiness)	

M.O.D.
| 79 | Vertigo 6059 233 | M.O.D./M.O.D. (2) (written by D. Cook, p/s, some allegedly mispressed on 2-Tone label) .... 30/7 |
| | *(see also David Essex)* | |

MODE
| 66 | private pressing | THE MODE (EP, white labels, no p/s) .... 200 |

MODELS
| 77 | Step Forward SF 3 | Freeze/Man Of The Year (p/s) .... 8 |
| | *(see also Adam & The Ants, Mass, Rema Rema, Wolfgang Press)* | |

MODERATES
| 80 | Open Eye OEEP 1001 | FETISHES (12" EP) .... 7 |

MODERNAIRES (U.S.)
50	Columbia DB 2730	Down The Lane/DOROTHY SHAY: Home Cookin' (78) 8
54	Vogue Coral Q 2024	Teach Me Tonight/Mood Indigo (with Georgie Auld) 10
54	Vogue Coral Q 2035	New Juke Box Saturday Night/Bugle Call Rag 10
54	Vogue Coral Q 2035	New Juke Box Saturday Night/Bugle Call Rag (78) 8
55	Vogue Coral Q 72069	Birds And Puppies And Tropical Fish/Mine! Mine! Mine! 10
55	Vogue Coral Q 72084	Wine, Women And Gold/Sluefoot (with Bob Crosby Bob Cats) 10

MINT VALUE £

55	Vogue Coral Q 72112	At My Front Door/Alright, Okay, You Win	10
56	Vogue Coral Q 72135	"Let's Dance" Medley (Benny Goodman Story)	6
56	Vogue Coral Q 72158	Go On With The Wedding/Ain't She Sweet	6
56	Vogue Coral Q 72169	April In Paris/Hi-Diddlee-I-Dee	5
60	Coral FEP 2056	THE FORMER GLENN MILLER SINGERS — REUNION IN HI-FI (EP, with Tex Beneke, Marion Hutton & Ray Eberle)	8
55	Vogue Coral LVC 10012	STOP, LOOK AND LISTEN (10" LP)	20
58	Coral LVA 9080	HERE COME THE MODERNAIRES (LP)	15

(see also Four Guys, Georgie Auld, Bing Crosby)

MODERNAIRES (U.K.)

80	Illuminated ILL 2	Life In Our Times/Barbed Up (p/s)	4
81	Illuminated ILL 4	We Did It Again/And Again (p/s, red vinyl)	4

MODERN ART

84	Color Disc COLORS 1	Dreams To Live/Beautiful Truth (p/s)	25
86	Color Disc COLORS 5	Penny Valentine/One Way Ticket (1-sided, clear vinyl flexidisc, 1,000 only)	12
87	Color Disc COLOR 3	STEREOLAND (LP, hand-stencilled with insert, 300 only)	60
94	Acme 8007 LP	ALL ABOARD THE MIND TRAIN (LP, 500 only, numbered)	10

(see also Sun Dial)

MODERN ENGLISH

79	Limp LMP 2	Drowning Man/Silent World (p/s)	15
80	4AD AD 6	Swans On Glass/Incident (p/s)	7
80	4AD AD 15	Gathering Dust/Tranquility Of A Summer Moment (p/s)	6
81	4AD AD 110	Smiles And Laughter/Mesh And Lace (p/s)	5
82	4AD BAD 208	Life In The Gladhouse/The Choicest View (12", p/s)	8
82	4AD AD 212	I Melt With You/The Prize (p/s)	5
83	4AD AD 309	Someone's Calling/Life In The Gladhouse (p/s)	5
84	4AD AD 401	Chapter 12/Ringing In The Change (p/s)	4

(see also This Mortal Coil)

MODERN EON

80	Modern Eon EON 001	PIECES (EP)	20
80	Inevitable INEV 3	Euthenics/Waiting For The Cavalry (p/s)	8
81	Dinsales 2	Euthenics/Choreography/Waiting For The Cavalry/The Real Hymn (12", white label LP sampler)	30
81	DinDisc DIN 30	Euthenics (New Version)/Cardinal Signs (tri-gatefold folder p/s)	5
81	DinDisc DID 11	FICTION TALES (LP)	10

MODERN FOLK QUARTET (M.F.Q.)

64	Warner Bros WB 147	The Love Of A Clown/If You All Think	5
66	RCA RCA 1514	Night Time Girl/Lifetime (as M.F.Q.)	12
63	Warner Bros WM/WS 8135	THE MODERN FOLK QUARTET (LP)	12

MODERN JAZZ QUARTET (M.J.Q.)

57	Esquire 10-496	Delaunay's Dilemma/The Queen's Fancy (78)	8
57	Esquire 10-505	Autumn In New York/But Not For Me (78)	8
50s	Esquire EP 106	MODERN JAZZ QUARTET (EP)	8
50s	Esquire EP 109	MODERN JAZZ QUARTET (EP)	8
50s	Esquire EP 116	GERSHWIN BALLAD MEDLEY (EP)	8
50s	Esquire EP 166	FIVE WAYS OF PLAYING LA RONDE (EP)	8
50s	Fontana 469 204TE	ALL OF YOU (EP)	8
57	London Jazz EZ-C 19019	THE QUARTET (EP, as The Quartet)	8
59	London Jazz EZ-K 19046	ONE NEVER KNOWS (EP)	8
59	London Jazz EZ-K 19047	THE MODERN JAZZ QUARTET (EP)	8
61	London Jazz RE-K 1314	MODERN JAZZ QUARTET (EP)	8
61	London Jazz RE-K 1320	MODERN JAZZ QUARTET AT MUSIC INN (EP)	10
62	London Jazz RE-K 1319	MODERN JAZZ QUARTET — EUROPEAN CONCERT (EP)	10
55	Esquire 20-069	MODERN JAZZ QUARTET (10" LP)	18
55	Esquire 20-038	MODERN JAZZ QUARTET VOL. 2 (10" LP)	18
57	London Jazz LTZK 15022	FONTESSA (LP)	15
58	London Jazz LTZK 15085	AT THE MUSIC INN (LP)	12
58	London Jazz LTZ 15136	MODERN JAZZ QUARTET (LP)	12
59	London Jazz LTZ-K 15140	PLAYS ONE NEVER KNOWS (LP, also stereo SAH-K 6029)	15/18
59	London Jazz LTZK 15181	ODDS AGAINST TOMORROW (LP)	15
59	Columbia Clef 33CX 11028	MODERN JAZZ QUARTET & OSCAR PETERSON AT THE OPERA HOUSE (LP)	12
60	London Jazz LTZ-K 15193	PYRAMID (LP, also stereo SAH-K 6086)	15
61	London Jazz LTZ-K 15207	THIRD STREAM MUSIC (LP, with Beaux Arts String Quartet & Jimmy Giuffre Three)	15
61	London Jazz LTZK 15222	EUROPEAN CONCERT (LP)	12
61	Esquire 32-124	LOOKING BACK AT THE MODERN JAZZ QUARTET (LP)	12
63	London HA-K/SH-K 8016	LONELY WOMAN (LP)	15
63	London HA-K/SH-K 8046	THE COMEDY SUITE (LP)	15
64	London HA-K/SH-K 8161	THE SHERIFF (LP)	15
65	Stateside SL 10141	THE BEST OF THE MODERN JAZZ QUARTET (LP)	12
66	Atlantic 587 044	A QUARTET IS A QUARTET (LP)	12
68	Atlantic 590 012	STOCKHOLM CONCERT (LP)	12
68	Apple (S)APCOR 4	UNDER THE JASMINE TREE (LP, mono/stereo)	50/35
69	Apple SAPCOR 10	SPACE (LP, gatefold sleeve, dark green label, black inner)	40
70s	Apple SAPCOR 10	SPACE (LP, later pressing, light green label, single sl., white 'Apple' inner)	75
93	Apple SAPCOR 4	UNDER THE JASMINE TREE (LP, reissue, gatefold sleeve with inner)	20
93	Apple SAPCOR 4	UNDER THE JASMINE TREE (CD)	20

(see also John Lewis, Milt Jackson, Sonny Rollins)

MODERN JAZZ SEXTET

56	Columbia Clef 33CX 10048	MODERN JAZZ SEXTET (LP)	12

MODERN JAZZ SOCIETY

56	Columbia Clef 33CX 10038	A CONCERT OF CONTEMPORARY MUSIC (LP)	12

MO-DETTES

79	Mode/Rough Trade MODE 1	White Mice/Masochistic Opposite (pink [card or paper] or white p/s)	4/6
80	S.F.I. SFI 550/MODE 1½	Twist And Shout (gig freebie flexidisc, different label design to later issue)	4
80	Deram DET-R-1/MODE 1½	Paint It Black/Bitta Truth (with free flexidisc "Twist And Shout" & insert, black & white or blue & white p/s)	each 6
81	Deram DET 3	Tonight/Waltz In Blue Minor (p/s)	4
81	Human HUM 10	White Mice/Kray Twins (live) (p/s)	4
80	Deram SML 1120	THE STORY SO FAR (LP, with insert & free colour sticker)	15

MODIFIES

70	Punch PH 45	Bye Bye Happyness/Sufferation We Must Bear	6

MODS

64	RCA RCA 1399	Something On My Mind/You're Making Me Blue	8

MODS

80	Bootlegged Records 007	LOST TOUCH (LP; sold only in Portobello Market, London)	25

MOD '79

79	Casino Classics CC 13	Green Onions/High On Your Love	4

DOMENICO MODUGNO

58	Oriole ICB 5000	Volare (Nel Blu Dipinto Di Blu)/Nisciuno Po' Sape'	6
58	Oriole ICB 5000	Volare (Nel Blu Dipinto Di Blu)/Nisciuno Po' Sape' (78)	8
58	Oriole ICB 5001	Strada 'Nfosa/Lazzarella	6
58	Oriole ICB 5001	Strada 'Nfosa/Lazzarella (78)	7
58	Oriole CB 1460	Volare (Nel Blu Dipinto Di Blu)/Nisciuno Po' Sape'	6
58	Oriole CB 1460	Volare (Nel Blu Dipinto Di Blu)/Nisciuno Po' Sape' (78)	8
59	Oriole CB 1475	Come Prima (More Than Ever)/Mariti In Citta	5
59	Oriole CB 1475	Come Prima (More Than Ever)/Mariti In Citta (78)	8
59	Oriole CB 1479	Resta Cu'mme/Io Mammeta Et Tu	5
59	Oriole CB 1479	Resta Cu'mme/Io Mammeta Et Tu (78)	8
59	Oriole CB 1482	Strada 'Nfosa/Lazzarella	5
59	Oriole CB 1482	Strada 'Nfosa/Lazzarella (78)	8
59	Oriole CB 1489	Ciao, Ciao Bambina (Piove)/Resta Cu 'Mme	6
59	Oriole CB 1489	Ciao, Ciao Bambina (Piove)/Resta Cu 'Mme (78)	8
59	Oriole CB 1513	Notte, Lunga Notte/Sole, Sole, Sole	5
59	Oriole CB 1513	Notte, Lunga Notte/Sole, Sole, Sole (78)	10
60	Oriole CB 1543	Libero/Nuda	4
60	Oriole CB 1543	Libero/Nuda (78)	20
60	Oriole CB 1547	Hello Amore/Olimpia	4
60	Oriole CB 1547	Hello Amore/Olimpia (78)	20
57	Felsted ESD 3047	FROM THE PALERMO TO PARIS (EP)	8
59	Oriole MG 10023	DOMENICO MODUGNO (10" LP)	15

MODULATIONS

74	Buddah BDS 406	I Can't Fight Your Love/Your Love Has Locked Me Up	5
70s	Buddah	THE MODULATIONS (LP)	20

PETER MOESSER'S MUSIC

70	Stateside SS 2182	Hello/Bye Bye (withdrawn)	4

MOFFAT ALL STARS

70	Jackpot JP 719	Riot/IMPERSONATORS: Girls And Boys	6

MOGUL THRASH

70	RCA RCA 2030	Sleeping In The Kitchen/St. Peter	12
71	RCA SF 8156	MOGUL THRASH (LP)	30

(see also Colosseum, Eclection, Family, King Crimson, Average White Band)

MOGWAI

96	Rock Action RAR 01	Tuner/Lower (p/s, 500 only)	35
96	Ché CHE 059	4 TRACK 3 BAND TOUR EP (with Urusei Yatsura & Backwater, p/s, 50 only)	25
96	Ché CHE 61	Angels Vs The Aliens/DWEEB: Buzzsong (p/s, 1st 500 on green vinyl)	8/4
96	Love Train PUBE 014	Summer/Ithica 27*9 (p/s, 1,500 only)	20
97	Wurlitzer Jukebox WJ 22	New Paths To Helicon (Parts 1 & 2) (foldover p/s in polythene bag, 3,000 only)	10
97	Flotsam/Jetsam SHAG13.04	Stereo Dee/PH FAMILY: Club Beatroot Part 4 (p/s, 500 only)	20
98	Eye Q EYEUKLP 019	KICKING A DEAD PIG (2-LP)	15

ESSRA MOHAWK

75	Mooncrest CREST 24	ESSRA MOHAWK (LP, with insert)	15
77	Private Stock PVLP 1016	ESSRA (LP)	15

MOHAWKS

68	Pama PM 719	The Champ/Sound Of The Witchdoctors	12
68	Pama PM 739	Baby Hold On (Parts 1 & 2)	8
68	Pama PM 751	Sweet Soul Music/Hip Jigger	10
68	Pama PM 757	Mony Mony/Pepsi	8
69	Pama PM 758	Ride Your Pony/Western Promise	8
69	Pama PM 798	Skinhead Shuffle/RICO: Red Cow	10
70	Supreme SUP 204	Let It Be/Looking Back	6
68	Pama PMLP 5	THE CHAMP (LP)	50

MOIST

86	Debris DEB 9/LYN 19589	The Cut Up #1/KING OF THE SLUMS: Haemophiliacs On Tacks (33rpm flexidisc free with *Debris* magazine)	8/6

MOJO HANNAH

73	Kingdom KV 8008	Six Days On The Road/Moon Dog's Gonna Howl Tonight	5
73	Kingdom KVL 9001	SIX DAYS ON THE ROAD (LP)	15

MOJO MEN

65	Pye International 7N 25336	Dance With Me/The Loneliest Boy In Town	12
66	Reprise RS 20486	Hanky Panky/She's My Baby	30

MINT VALUE £

| 67 | Reprise RS 20539 | Sit Down I Think I Love You/Don't Leave Me Crying Like Before | 10 |
| 67 | Reprise RS 20580 | Me About You/When You're In Love | 12 |

MOJOS

63	Decca F 11732	They Say/Forever	10
64	Decca F 11853	Everything's Alright/Give Your Lovin' To Me	10
64	Decca F 11918	Why Not Tonight/Don/t Do It Any More	6
64	Decca F 11959	Seven Daffodils/Nothin' At All	7
65	Decca F 12127	Comin' On To Cry/That's The Way It Goes	10
67	Decca F 12557	Goodbye Dolly Gray/I Just Can't Let Her Go	12
68	Liberty LBF 15097	Until My Baby Comes Home/Seven Park Avenue	40
64	Decca DFE 8591	THE MOJOS (EP)	60

(see also Stu James & Mojos, Faron's Flamingos)

MOLES

| 68 | Parlophone R 5743 | We Are The Moles (Parts 1 & 2) | 30 |

(see also Simon Dupree & Big Sound)

MOLESTERS

| 79 | Small Wonder SMALL 14 | Disco Love/Commuter Man (p/s) | 5 |
| 79 | Small Wonder SMALL 18 | End Of Civilisation/Girl Behind The Curtain (p/s) | 5 |

MOMENT

85	Diamond DIA 004	In This Town/Just Once	6
85	Diamond DIA 008	One, Two, They Fly/Karl's New Haircut	5
80s	Tenth Floor	Poor Mr. Diamond (Parts 1 & 2)	10
89	Big Stuff	Ready To Fall (promo only)	8
86	Rave RAVE UP 1	THE WORK GETS DONE (LP, coloured vinyl)	10

MOMENTS

63	London HLN 9656	Walk Right In/Walk Right In (Instrumental)	10
72	London HLU 10378	Love On A Two Way Street/I Won't Do Anything	5
74	London HL 10449	Sexy Mama/Where Can I Find Her	5
75	All Platinum 6146 309	Look At Me/French Version	5
75	All Platinum 9109 302	SHARP (LP)	12

(see also Fabulous Impact)

MOMUS

| 91 | Creation CRECD 097 | Hippopotamomus (CD, with "Michelin Man" track & Michelin Man style inlay, withdrawn) | 28 |

(see also Happy Family)

MONARCHS

| 64 | London HLU 9862 | Look Homeward Angel/What's Made You Change Your Mind | 30 |

JULIE MONDAY

| 66 | London HLU 10080 | Come Share The Good Times With Me/Time Is Running Out For Me | 5 |

MONEY

| 69 | Major Minor MM 620 | Come Laughing Home/Power Of The Rainbow | 4 |
| 69 | Major Minor MM 669 | Welcome Me Love/Breaking Of Her Heart | 4 |

MONEY

79	Gull GULL 64	Aren't We All Searching/Where Have All The Dancers Gone	8
80	Hobo HOS 011	FAST WORLD (EP, p/s)	40
79	Gull GULP 1031	FIRST INVESTMENT (LP)	12

(see also Iron Maiden)

ZOOT MONEY('S BIG ROLL BAND)

64	Decca F 11954	The Uncle Willie/Zoot's Suit (solo)	25
65	Columbia DB 7518	Good/Bring It Home To Me	18
65	Columbia DB 7600	Please Stay/You Know You'll Cry	18
65	Columbia DB 7697	Something Is Worrying Me/Stubborn Kind Of Fellow	18
65	Columbia DB 7768	The Many Faces Of Love/Jump Back (as Paul Williams & Zoot Money Band)	20
66	Columbia DB 7876	Let's Run For Cover/Self-Discipline	18
66	Columbia DB 7975	Big Time Operator/Zoot's Sermon	12
66	Columbia DB 8090	The Star Of The Show (The La La Song)/The Mound Moves	15
67	Columbia DB 8172	Nick Knack/I Really Learnt How To Cry	15
70	Polydor 2058 020	No One But You/Prisoner	6
80	Magic Moon/MPL MACH 3	Your Feets Too Big/Ain't Nothin' Shakin' But The Bacon (solo)	10
80	Magic Moon/MPL MACH 6	The Two Of Us/Ain't Nothin' Shakin' But The Bacon (solo)	15
66	Columbia SEG 8519	BIG TIME OPERATOR (EP)	150
66	Columbia S(C)X 6075	ZOOT! — LIVE AT KLOOK'S KLEEK (LP, mono/stereo)	40/45
65	Columbia 33SX 1734	IT SHOULD'VE BEEN ME (LP)	70
68	Direction 8-63231	TRANSITION (LP)	30
70	Polydor 2482 019	ZOOT MONEY (LP)	18
80	Magic Moon/MPL LUNE 1	MR. MONEY (LP, solo)	15

(see also Paul Williams & Big Roll Band, Dantalian's Chariot, Eric Burdon & Animals, Grimms, Centipede, Ellis, Johnny Almond Music Machine)

MONGREL

73	Polydor 2058 318	Lonely Street/Sing A Little Song	5
73	Polydor 2058 347	Last Night/Twist Her Hand	5
73	Polydor 2383 182	GET YOUR TEETH INTO THIS (LP)	20

MONGRELS

| 64 | Decca F 12003 | I Long To Hear/Everywhere | 25 |
| 65 | Decca F 12086 | My Love For You/Stewball | 25 |

(see also Bobbie Miller)

MONITORS

| 69 | T. Motown (S)TML 11108 | GREETINGS WE'RE THE MONITORS (LP) | 50 |

THELONIOUS MONK

63	CBS AAG 172	Hackensack/Bye Ya	5
56	Vogue EPV 1115	THELONIOUS MONK (EP)	10
50s	Esquire EP 75	THELONIOUS MONK TRIO (EP)	8
50s	Esquire EP 148	SONNY ROLLINS AND THELONIOUS MONK (EP)	8
61	Esquire EP 236	NUTTY MONK (EP)	8
62	Esquire EP 246	BLUE MONK (EP)	8
60s	Riverside REP 3214	NUTTY (EP, as Thelonious Monk & John Coltrane)	8
60s	Riverside REP 3217	RUBY MY DEAR (EP, as Thelonious Monk & John Coltrane)	8
55	Esquire 20-039	THELONIOUS MONK QUINTET (10" LP)	18
55	Esquire 20-049	THELONIOUS MONK (10" LP)	18
56	Esquire 20-075	THELONIOUS MONK PLAYS (10" LP)	18
60	Esquire 32-109	THELONIOUS MONK QUINTETS (LP)	15
61	Esquire 32-115	WORK! (LP, with Art Blakey & Sonny Rollins)	15
61	Esquire 32-119	MONK'S MOODS (LP)	15
61	Riverside RLP 12-201	MONK PLAYS ELLINGTON (LP)	15
61	Philips BBL 1510	THELONIOUS MONK VOL. 1 (LP)	15
61	Riverside RLP 12-226	BRILLIANT CORNERS (LP)	15
61	Riverside RLP 12-262	MONK IN ACTION (LP)	15
62	Riverside RLP 12-300	AT THE TOWN HALL (LP, also stereo RLP 1138)	15/20
62	Riverside RLP 12-323	AT THE BLACK HAWK (LP, also stereo RLP 1171)	15
62	Philips BBL 1511	THELONIOUS MONK VOL. 2 (LP)	15
62	Riverside RLP 12-242	MONK'S MUSIC (LP)	15
63	Riverside RLP 201	MONK PLAYS ELLINGTON (LP, reissue)	10
63	CBS (S)BPG 62135	MONK'S DREAM (LP)	15
63	Riverside RLP 12-235	THELONIOUS HIMSELF (LP)	15
63	Riverside JLP (9)46	THELONIOUS MONK AND JOHN COLTRANE (LP)	15
64	Riverside RLP 002	IN EUROPE (VOL. 1)	15
64	CBS (S)BPG 62173	CRISS-CROSS (LP)	15
64	Blue Note (B)BLP 1510	THE GENIUS OF MODERN MUSIC (VOL. 1) (LP)	15
64	Blue Note (B)BLP 1511	THE GENIUS OF MODERN MUSIC (VOL. 2) (LP)	15
64	Riverside RLP 279	MISTERIOSO (LP)	15
64	CBS (S)BPG 62248	THELONIOUS MONK (LP)	15
65	CBS (S)BPG 62391	IT'S MONK'S TIME (LP)	15
65	Riverside RLP 305	FIVE BY MONK BY FIVE (LP)	15
65	Riverside RLP 003	IN EUROPE (VOL. 2) (LP)	15
65	CBS (S)BPG 62497	MONK (LP)	15
65	Riverside RLP 312	ALONE IN SAN FRANCISCO (LP)	15
65	Fontana FJL 113	WAY OUT! (LP)	15
65	Realm RM 52223	NICA'S TEMPO (LP, with Gigi Gryce)	12
65	CBS (S)BPG 62549	SOLO (LP)	15
65	Stateside SL 10152	THE GOLDEN MONK (LP)	15
66	Riverside RLP 004	IN EUROPE (VOL. 3)	12
66	CBS (S)BPG 62620	MISTERIOSO (LP, reissue)	10
67	CBS (S)BPG 63009	STRAIGHT, NO CHASER (LP)	12
67	Transatlantic PR 7169	WORK (LP)	12
69	CBS 63609	MONK'S BLUES (LP)	12
69	Storyville 673 014	THELONIOUS MONK PLAYS DUKE (LP)	12
69	Storyville 673 022	IN CONCERT (LP)	12
70	Storyville 673 024	THE THELONIOUS MONK (LP)	12
72	Polydor 2460 152	SOMETHING IN BLUE (LP)	12
72	Prestige PR 24006	THELONIOUS MONK (2-LP)	15
73	Black Lion 2460 197	THE MAN I LOVE (LP)	12
75	DJM DJSLM 2017	PURE MONK (LP)	12
75	CBS 88034	WHO'S AFRAID OF BIG BAD MONK (LP)	12

(see also John Coltrane, Sonny Rollins, Art Blakey, Miles Davis)

MONKEES

SINGLES

66	RCA Victor RCA 1547	Last Train To Clarksville/Take A Giant Step	8
66	RCA Victor RCA 1560	I'm A Believer/(I'm Not Your) Stepping Stone	6
67	RCA Victor RCA 1580	A Little Bit Me, A Little Bit You/The Girl I Knew Somewhere	7
67	RCA Victor RCA 1604	Alternate Title/Forget That Girl	7
67	RCA Victor RCA 1620	Pleasant Valley Sunday/Words	7
67	RCA Victor RCA 1645	Daydream Believer/Goin' Down	7
68	RCA Victor RCA 1673	Valleri/Tapioca Tundra	8
68	RCA Victor RCA 1706	D.W. Washburn/It's Nice To Be With You	8
69	RCA RCA 1802	Teardrop City/Man Without A Dream	8
69	RCA RCA 1824	Someday Man/Listen To The Band	8
69	RCA RCA 1862	Daddy's Song/The Porpoise Song	10
69	RCA RCA 1887	Mommy And Daddy/Good Clean Fun	10
70	RCA RCA 1958	Oh My My/Love You Better	12
74	Bell BLL 1354	Monkees Theme/I'm A Believer	10
80	Arista ARIST 326	THE MONKEES (EP, p/s)	9
81	Arista ARIST 402	THE MONKEES VOL. 2 (EP, p/s)	8
82	Arista ARIST 487	I'M A BELIEVER (EP, p/s)	12
84	Scoop 7SR 5035	6 TRACK HITS (EP, p/s)	15
84	Scoop 7SC 5035	6 TRACK HITS (EP, cassette)	12
86	Arista ARIST 673	That Was Then, This Is Now/(Theme From) The Monkees (p/s)	6
86	Arista ARIST 1673	That Was Then, This Is Now/(Theme From) The Monkees ('Dolenz' picture disc)	9
86	Arista ARIST 2673	That Was Then, This Is Now/(Theme From) The Monkees ('Tork' picture disc)	9
86	Arista ARIST 3673	That Was Then, This Is Now/(Theme From) The Monkees ('Jones' picture disc)	9
86	Arista ARIST 4673	That Was Then, This Is Now/(Theme From) The Monkees ('group' picture disc)	12
86	Arista ARIST 12673	That Was Then, This Is Now/Pleasant Valley Sunday/(Theme From) The Monkees/Last Train To Clarksville (12", p/s)	15
89	Arista 112 157	THE MONKEES (EP, p/s)	8
89	Arista 112 157	THE MONKEES (EP, box set, with booklet & sew-on patch)	15

MONKEES

89	Arista 112 157	THE MONKEES (10" EP, promo only, no p/s)	22
89	Arista 662 157	THE MONKEES (CD EP)	12
89	Arista 112 158	THE MONKEES VOL. 2 (EP, p/s)	8
89	Arista 112 158	THE MONKEES VOL. 2 (10" EP, promo only, no p/s)	22
89	Arista 662 158	THE MONKEES VOL. 2 (CD EP, card sleeve with anti-static inner)	15
89	Arista 162 053	Last Train To Clarksville/Take A Giant Step/I'm A Believer/(I'm Not Your) Stepping Stone (3" CD, gatefold card sleeve in blister pack)	12
97	Telstar MON 2894	Daydream Believer (promo CD single)	15

LPs

67	RCA Victor RD/SF 7844	THE MONKEES (LP, mono/stereo)	15/18
67	RCA Victor RD/SF 7868	MORE OF THE MONKEES (LP, mono/stereo)	15/18
67	RCA Victor RD/SF 7886	HEADQUARTERS (LP, mono/stereo)	15/18
67	RCA Victor RD/SF 7886	HEADQUARTERS (LP, with different 'beard' photo on back, mono/stereo)	22/28
67	RCA Victor RD/SF 7912	PISCES, AQUARIUS, CAPRICORN AND JONES LTD. (LP)	20
68	RCA Victor RD/SF 7948	THE BIRDS, THE BEES & THE MONKEES (LP)	20
		(The above albums were originally issued with black labels; later orange label copies are worth the same value.)	
69	RCA RD/SF 8016	INSTANT REPLAY (LP, mono/stereo)	28/25
69	RCA RD/SF 8051	HEAD (LP, soundtrack, mono/stereo)	75/50
73	M.F. Pleasure SPR 90032	THE MONKEES (LP, 'Sounds Superb' series, black 'circus' sleeve)	14
79	Arista MONK-1 1/2	MONKEEMANIA (LP)	25
81	Arista DARTY 12	THE MONKEES (2-LP)	18
83	Arista RS 10063	HERE COME THE MONKEES (LP, part of *Reader's Digest* v/a box set)	15
89	Circus BOY 1	IDOLISED, PLASTICISED, PSYCHOANYLYSED, STERILISED (LP, spoken-word convention issue, white vinyl)	18
89	Circus BOY 1	IDOLISED, PLASTICISED, PSYCHOANYLYSED, STERILISED (LP, spoken-word convention issue, picture disc)	20

CASSETTES

73	M.F. Pleasure SPR 80032	THE MONKEES (cassette, 'Sounds Superb' series, in blister pack)	17
74	Bell TCBEL 148	25 HITS (cassette)	15
74	Bell Y8BEL 148	25 HITS (8-track cartridge)	15
79	Arista TC-MONK-1 1/2	MONKEEMANIA (cassette)	20
83	Arista RS 10063	HERE COME THE MONKEES (cassette, part of *Reader's Digest* v/a box set)	15
86	Arista 407 708	MAGIC MOMENTS WITH THE MONKEES (cassette)	12
86	Arista 407 874	THEN AND NOW, THE BEST OF THE MONKEES (cassette)	15
93	Arista EMC 018	THE BEST OF THE MONKEES (cassette, available via Avon Cosmetics)	18

CDs

88	Platinum PLATCD 05	HEY-HEY IT'S THE MONKEES — 20 SMASH HITS (CD)	20
92	Arista 262 507	THE COLLECTION (CD)	16
93	Lightning LIGCD 5001	HEAD (CD, soundtrack)	18
93	Arista EMD 018	THE BEST OF THE MONKEES (CD, exclusive via Avon Cosmetics)	25
		(see also Micky Dolenz, Davy Jones, Michael Nesmith, Tommy Boyce & Bobby Hart)	

BOB MONKHOUSE

69	CBS 3958	I Remember Natalie/In My Dream World	6
69	CBS 4607	Another Time, Another Place, Another World/When I Found You	6
		(see also Derek Roy)	

MONKS

| 79 | EMI EMI 2999 | Johnny B. Rotten/Drugs In My Pocket (p/s) | 5 |
| | | *(see also Hudson-Ford)* | |

MONOCHROME SET

79	Rough Trade RT 005	Alphaville/He's Frank (p/s)	7
79	Rough Trade RT 019	Eine Symphonie Des Grauens/Lester Leaps In (1st 1,000 with labels on wrong sides with explanatory insert, p/s)	7/5
79	Rough Trade RT 028	The Monochrome Set/Mr Bizarro (p/s)	5
79	Disquo Bleu BL 1	He's Frank (Slight Return)/Silicon Carne/Fallout (all cuts live) (no p/s)	5
80	DinDisc DID 8	LOVE ZOMBIES (LP, with lithograph)	10
		(see also Art Attacks)	

MONOGRAMS

59	Parlophone R 4515	Juke Box Cha Cha/The Greatest Mistake Of My Life	6
59	Parlophone R 4515	Juke Box Cha Cha/The Greatest Mistake Of My Life (78)	12
59	Parlophone R 4545	Crystal/Teach Me	5

MONOPOLY

67	Polydor 56164	House Of Lords/Magic Carpet	5
67	Polydor 56188	We're All Going To The Seaside/It Isn't Easy	5
70	Pye 7N 17940	We Belong Together/Gone Tomorrow	5
		(see also Raymond Froggatt)	

MONOTONES (U.S.)

| 58 | London HLM 8625 | Book Of Love/You Never Loved Me | 50 |
| 58 | London HLM 8625 | Book Of Love/You Never Loved Me (78) | 30 |

MONOTONES (U.K.)

64	Pye 7N 15608	What Would I Do/Is It Right	7
64	Pye 7N 15640	It's Great/Anymore	7
65	Pye 7N 15761	No Waiting/Like A Lover Should	7
65	Pye 7N 15814	Something's Hurting Me/A Girl Like That	7

MATT MONRO

56	Decca F 10816	Ev'rybody Falls In Love With Someone/Out Of Sight, Out Of Mind	15
57	Decca F 10839	Gone With The Wind/My Old Flame (unreleased)	
57	Decca F 10845	The Garden Of Eden/Love Me Do	15
57	Decca F 10845	The Garden Of Eden/Love Me Do (78)	8
57	Decca F 10870	My House Is Your House/The Bean Song	15
58	Fontana H 115	I'll Never Have A Sweetheart/The Golden Age (78)	8
58	Fontana H 122	The Story Of Ireland/Another Time Another Place	12
58	Fontana H 122	The Story Of Ireland/Another Time Another Place (78)	8

58	Fontana H 167	Prisoner Of Love/Have Guitar, Will Travel	12
58	Fontana H 167	Prisoner Of Love/Have Guitar, Will Travel (78)	12
60	Parlophone R 4638	Love Walked In/I'll Know Her (as Matt Munro)	5
60	Parlophone R 4714	Portrait Of My Love/You're The Top Of My Hit Parade	5
61	Ember EMB S 120	The Ghost Of Your Past/Quite Suddenly	10
62	Parlophone R 4868	Softly As I Leave You/Is There Anything I Can Do	5
63	Parlophone R 5068	From Russia With Love/Here And Now	5
64	Parlophone R 5171	Walk Away/Around The World	5
65	Parlophone R 5348	Yesterday/Just Yesterday (Mine You Your Love Was Mine)	5
66	Capitol CL 15436	Born Free/Other People	5
66	Capitol CL 15477	Wednesday's Child/When U Become A Man	5
69	Capitol CL 15603	On Days Like These/On A Clear Day I Can See Forever	5
72	Columbia DB 8936	Curiouser/The Me I Never Knew	7
73	Columbia DB 9060	If I Never Sing Another Song/We're Gonna Change The World	7
63	Parlophone GEP 8889	SINGS THE THEME FROM THE FILM 'FROM RUSSIA FROM LOVE' (EP)	15
64	Parlophone GEP 8898	A SONG FOR EUROPE (EP)	8
57	Decca LF 1276	BLUE AND SENTIMENTAL (10" LP)	50
61	Ace Of Clubs ACL 1069	PORTRAIT (LP)	12
61	Parlophone PMC 1151	LOVE IS THE SAME ANYWHERE (LP, gold/black label, also stereo)	12/15
62	Parl. PMC 1185/PCS 3034	MATT MONRO SINGS HOAGY CARMICHAEL (LP, gold/black label)	12
65	Parlophone PMC 1250	I HAVE DREAMED (LP, yellow/black label, also stereo PCS 3067)	12/15
66	Parlophone PMC 1265	HITS OF YESTERDAY (LP, yellow/black label)	12
66	Capitol (S)T 2540	THIS IS THE LIFE! (LP)	12
67	Capitol (S)T 2608	HERE'S TO MY LADY (LP)	12
67	Capitol (S)T 2683	INVITATION TO BROADWAY (LP)	12
67	Capitol (S)T 2730	INVITATION TO THE MOVIES (LP)	12
68	Capitol (S)T 2801	THESE YEARS (LP)	12
68	Capitol (S)T 2919	THE LATE, LATE SHOW (LP)	12
69	Fontana SFL 13161	TONY BLACKBURN MEETS MATT MONRO (LP)	12
69	RCA Victor SF 8024	THE SOUTHERN STAR (LP, soundtrack, with Georges Garvarentz)	12
70	Capitol ST 22546	WE'RE GONNA CHANGE THE WORLD (LP)	12
71	World ST 1024	SOFTLY AS I LEAVE YOU (LP)	12
73	Columbia SCX 6525	FOR THE PRESENT (LP)	15
75	Columbia SCX 6578	THE OTHER SIDE OF THE STARS (LP)	15

BARRY MONROE

| 66 | Polydor 56088 | World Of Broken Hearts/Never Again | 6 |

BILL MONROE (& HIS BLUE GRASS BOYS)

56	Brunswick 05567	New John Henry Blues/Put My Little Shoes Away	12
56	Brunswick 05567	New John Henry Blues/Put My Little Shoes Away (78)	15
57	Brunswick 05681	Four Walls/A Fallen Star	10
57	Brunswick 05681	Four Walls/A Fallen Star (78)	15
59	Brunswick 05776	Gotta Travel On/No One But My Darlin'	8
59	Brunswick 05776	Gotta Travel On/No One But My Darlin' (78)	30
66	Brunswick 05960	Blue Ridge Mountain Blues/John Hardy (solo)	5
55	Brunswick OE 9160	COUNTRY DATE (EP)	18
55	Brunswick OE 9195	COUNTRY WALTZ (EP)	18
63	RCA RCX 7105	COUNTRY GUITAR VOL. 16 (EP, 2 tracks by Monroe Brothers)	12
61	Brunswick LAT 8338	I SAW THE LIGHT (LP)	15
63	Brunswick LAT/STA 8511	BLUEGRASS RAMBLE (LP, mono/stereo)	15/18
65	Brunswick LAT/STA 8579	BLUEGRASS SPECIAL (LP)	12

(see also Monroe Brothers)

GERRY MONROE

| 70 | Chapter One CHS 806 | SALLY — PRIDE OF OUR ALLEY (LP) | 12 |
| 71 | Chapter One CHS 809 | GERRY MONROE (LP) | 12 |

MARILYN MONROE

53	MGM MGM 663	Diamonds Are A Girl's Best Friend/Bye Bye Baby (78)	30
54	HMV 7M 232	The River Of No Return/I'm Gonna File My Claim	35
54	HMV B 10723	The River Of No Return/I'm Gonna File My Claim (78)	35
55	HMV B 10847	After You Get What You Want/Heat Wave (78)	35
59	London HLT 8862	I Wanna Be Loved By You/I'm Thru' With Love	25
59	London HLT 8862	I Wanna Be Loved By You/I'm Thru' With Love (78)	75
78	United Artists UP 36484	I Wanna Be Loved By You/Running Wild/I'm Thru With Love (gatefold p/s)	6
87	Zuma ZOOMP 6	When I Fall In Love/Heat Wave (picture disc)	5
55	HMV 7EG 8090	THERE'S NO BUSINESS LIKE SHOW BUSINESS — SOUNDTRACK EXCERPTS (EP, company sleeve)	40
59	London RET 1231	SOME LIKE IT HOT (EP, soundtrack; triangular centre, later round)	75/40
60	Philips BBE 12414	LET'S MAKE LOVE — FILM SOUNDTRACK (EP, with Yves Montand & Frankie Vaughan; also stereo SBBE 9031)	25/30
53	MGM MGM-D 116	GENTLEMEN PREFER BLONDES (10" LP, soundtrack with other artists)	75
59	London HA-T 2176	SOME LIKE IT HOT (LP, s/track with other artists, stereo SAH-T 6040)	65/75
60	Philips BBL 7414/SBBL 592	LET'S MAKE LOVE (LP, soundtrack, with Yves Montand & Frankie Vaughan; mono/stereo)	40/50
63	Stateside S(S)L 10048	MARILYN (LP, soundtrack, mono/stereo)	30/35
83	Liberty UASP 30226	SOME LIKE IT HOT (LP, picture disc)	12

(see also Frankie Vaughan)

VAUGHN MONROE (& HIS ORCHESTRA)

53	HMV 7M 144	Less Than Tomorrow (But More Than Yesterday)/Ruby	6
54	HMV 7M 247	They Were Doin' The Mambo/Mister Sandman	7
56	HMV 7M 332	Black Denim Trousers And Motorcycle Boots/All By Myself	18
56	HMV POP 122	Black Denim Trousers And Motorcycle Boots/All By Myself (78)	8
57	HMV POP 354	Wringle Wrangle/Westward Ho The Wagons!	8
57	HMV POP 354	Wringle Wrangle/Westward Ho The Wagons! (78)	8
59	RCA RCA 1124	The Battle Of New Orleans/Hercules	5
59	RCA RCA 1124	The Battle Of New Orleans/Hercules (78)	25

Vaughn MONROE

60	London HLT 9123	Ballerina/Love Me Forever	6
59	RCA RCX 1043	VAUGHAN MONROE'S GREATEST HITS (EP)	12
57	RCA RD 27049	FAMILY SING-SONG (LP)	12

MONROE BROTHERS

63	RCA RCX 7103	COUNTRY GUITAR VOL. 14 (EP)	15
63	RCA RCX 7104	COUNTRY GUITAR VOL. 15 (EP)	15
63	RCA RCX 7105	COUNTRY GUITAR VOL. 16 (EP, 2 tracks by Bill Monroe & Bluegrass Boys)	12

(see also Bill Monroe)

MONSOON

71	Trojan TR 7831	Hot Honolulu Night/Come Back Jane	4

MONSOON

81	Indipop IND 1	Ever So Lonely/Sunset Over The Ganges/The Mirror Of Your Mind/Shout! (Till You're Heard) (in plastic sleeve with insert)	8
83	Mobile Suit Dist. MOBIL 1	THIRD EYE (LP)	10

(see also Complex)

MONSTER MAGNET

98	A&M 582822-7	Powertrip (1-sided picture disc)	5
98	A&M 563 274-7	Space Lord/The Game (picture disc)	5

MONTANAS

65	Piccadilly 7N 35262	All That Is Mine Can Be Yours/How Can I Tell	8
66	Pye 7N 17183	That's When Happiness Began/Goodbye Little Girl	35
67	Pye 7N 17282	Ciao Baby/Anyone There	5
67	Pye 7N 17338	Take My Hand/Top Hat	8
67	Pye 7N 17394	You've Got To Be Loved/Difference Of Opinion	8
68	Pye 7N 17499	A Step In The Right Direction/Someday (You'll Be Breaking My Heart Again)	8
68	Pye 7N 17597	You're Making A Big Mistake/Run To Me	8
69	Pye 7N 17697	Roundabout/Mystery	8
69	Pye 7N 17729	Ciao Baby/Someday (You'll Be Breaking My Heart Again)	5
70	MCA MK 5036	Let's Get A Little Sentimental/Hey-Diddle-Diddle	5

(see also Trapeze)

MONTANA SEXTET

83	Virgin VS 600	Who Needs Enemies/Friendly Vibes (12")	12
87	10 TENT 204	Heavy Vibes (pts. 1 & 2) (12")	8

MONTANA SLIM

55	HMV MH 189	Broken Down Cowboy/The Old Barn Dance (78, export issue)	10
56	HMV MH 191	Where Is My Wandering Boy Tonight?/What A Friend We have In Mother (78, export issue)	10

MONTCLAIRS

74	Contempo CS 2008	Make Up For Lost Time/How Can One Man Live	5
75	Contempo CS 2036	Hung Up On Your Love/I Need You More Than Ever	6
74	Contempo CLP 503	DREAMING OF A SEASON (LP)	12

LOU MONTE

54	HMV 7M 176	A Baby Cried/One Moment More	8
54	HMV 7M 190	Darktown Strutters' Ball/I Know How You Feel	10
54	HMV 7M 249	Chain Reaction/Vera's Veranda	6
58	RCA RCA 1048	Lazy Mary (Luna Mezzo Mare)/Angelique-o	5
58	RCA RCA 1048	Lazy Mary (Luna Mezzo Mare)/Angelique-o (78)	8
59	RCA RCA 1161	Santa Nicola/All Because It's Christmas	5
59	RCA RCA 1161	Santa Nicola/All Because It's Christmas (78)	15
60	Columbia DB 4500	Oh! Oh! Rosie/(The New) Darktown Strutters' Ball	5

VINNIE MONTE

59	London HL 8947	Summer Spree/I'll Walk You Home	10
59	London HL 8947	Summer Spree/I'll Walk You Home (78)	25
63	Stateside SS 156	Joanie Don't Be Angry/Take Good Care Of Her	7

MONTEGO JOE

72	London HLP 10374	Stand Up And Be Counted/Glooey (with Seeds Of Life)	5
66	Stateside SL 10159	JARRIBA! CON MONTEGO JOE (LP)	12

MONTEGO MELON

72	Sioux SI 004	Swan Lake/HONG GANG: Reggae Mento	5

HUGO MONTENEGRO ORCHESTRA

62	Oriole CB 1765	Palm Canyon Drive/Dark Eyes	7
63	Oriole CB 1792	Get Off The Moon/Sherry	18
65	RCA Victor RD 7758	THE MAN FROM U.N.C.L.E. (LP, soundtrack)	40
66	RCA Victor RD 7832	MORE MUSIC FROM THE MAN FROM U.N.C.L.E. (LP, soundtrack)	40
67	RCA Victor RD/SF 7877	HURRY SUNDOWN (LP, soundtrack)	25
68	RCA Victor RD 7994	A FISTFUL OF DOLLARS/FOR A FEW DOLLARS MORE/THE GOOD, THE BAD AND THE UGLY (LP, soundtrack)	12
69	RCA SF 8053	MOOG POWER (LP)	35
69	Stateside S(S)L 10267	LADY IN CEMENT (LP, soundtrack)	30
70	Pye Intl. NSPL 28136	DAWN OF DYLAN (LP)	12
74	RCA APL1 0413	HUGO IN WONDERLAND (LP)	12

BOBBY MONTEZ

60	Vogue V 9165	Holiday In Havana/Jungle Stars	7

CHRIS MONTEZ

62	London HLU 9596	Let's Dance/You're The One	5
63	London HLU 9650	Some Kinda Fun/Tell Me	6
63	London HLU 9764	My Baby Loves To Dance/In An English Towne	7
66	Pye International 7N 25348	Call Me/Go 'Head On	6

Chris MONTEZ

MINT VALUE £

66	Pye International 7N 25369	The More I See You/You, I Love You	6
66	Pye International 7N 25381	There Will Never Be Another You/You Can Hurt The One You Love	6
66	Pye International 7N 23599	Time After Time/Keep Talkin'	6
67	Pye International 7N 25415	Because Of You/Elena	5
68	London HLU 10205	Let's Dance/Some Kinda Fun	5
73	CBS S CBS 1291	Come On, Let's Go/Somebody Loves You	6
73	CBS S CBS 8343	Dolores, Dolores (I Told You I'd Be Back)/When Your Heart Is Full Of Love (Your Eyes Begin To Overflow)	6
79	Old Gold OG 9011	Let's Dance/LONNIE MACK: Memphis (picture disc)	6
63	London REU 1392	LET'S DANCE (EP)	40
66	Pye Intl. NEP 44071	THE MORE I SEE YOU (EP)	20
66	Pye Intl. NEP 44080	CHRIS MONTEZ (EP)	20
63	London HA-U 8079	LET'S DANCE AND HAVE SOME KINDA FUN!!! (LP)	45
66	Pye Intl. NPL 28080	THE MORE I SEE YOU (LP)	18
67	Pye Intl. N(S)PL 28087	TIME AFTER TIME (LP)	15
68	A&M AML 906	FOOLIN' AROUND (LP)	12
68	A&M AML(S) 925	WATCH WHAT HAPPENS (LP)	12
72	CBS 65408	LET'S DANCE (LP)	15

JACK MONTGOMERY
| 85 | Kent TOWN 102 | Dearly Beloved/MARIE KNIGHT: That's No Way To Treat A Girl | 10 |
| 80s | Soul City 124 | My Dear Beloved/Do You Believe It | 8 |

LITTLE BROTHER MONTGOMERY
50	Jazz Collector L 44	No Special Rider Blues/Vicksburg Blues (78)	15
61	Columbia DB 4595	Pinetop's Boogie Woogie/Cow Cow Blues	12
61	Columbia 33SX 1289	LITTLE BROTHER MONTGOMERY (LP, with Alexis Korner)	35
62	'77' 77LA 12/21	LITTLE BROTHER MONTGOMERY/SUNNYLAND SLIM (LP)	15
65	Decca LK 4664	LITTLE BROTHER MONTGOMERY (LP)	18
66	Xtra XTRA 1018	LITTLE BROTHER MONTGOMERY (LP)	12
71	Xtra XTRA 1115	FARRO ST. JIVE (LP)	12
71	Saydisc SDR 213	LITTLE BROTHER MONTGOMERY 1930-1969 (LP)	18
72	Saydisc SDM 223	HOME AGAIN (LP)	20

MARIAN MONTGOMERY
65	Capitol CL 15375	When Sunny Gets Blue/Teach Me Tonight	5
67	Reaction 591 018	Love Makes Two People Sing/Monday Thru Saturday	10
68	Pye 7N 17533	Why Say Goodbye/Love Today — Cry Tomorrow	5

ROY MONTGOMERY
| 97 | Enraptured RAPT 4510 | Two Trajectories/Trajectory Two (p/s, 100 in handmade p/s, 280 clear vinyl, 620 black vinyl) | 6/5/4 |

STUART MONTGOMERY
| 69 | private pressing | CERTAIN SEA WORDS (LP, with insert) | 15 |

MONTROSE
74	Warner Brothers K 16382	Bad Motor Scooter/One Thing On My Mind	5
74	Warner Brothers K 16428	Rock The Nation/One Thing On My Mind	5
74	Warner Brothers/Sound For Industry SFI 175	Rock The Nation/Space Station No. 5/Good Rockin' Tonight (flexidisc)	7

(see also Sammy Hagar)

MONTY, DERRICK & PATSY
| 65 | Blue Beat BB 280 | Stir The Pot/Mercy | 15 |

(see also Monty Morris, Derrick Morgan)

MONTY (Morris) & ROY
| 61 | Blue Beat BB 61 | In And Out The Window/Tra La La Boogie (with Lumbago & His Orchestra) | 10 |
| 61 | Blue Beat BB 63 | Sweetie Pie/ROLAND ALPHONSO'S GROUP: Green Door | 15 |

(see also Monty Morris)

MONTY PYTHON('S FLYING CIRCUS)
70	BBC	Flying Sheep/Man With Three Buttocks (unissued)	
72	Charisma CB 192	Spam Song/The Concert (as Monty Python's Flying Circus, p/s)	6
72	Charisma CB 200	Eric The Half A Bee/The Yangtse Song (Extended) (as Monty Python with Niel [sic] Innes)	5
72	Python Productions	Teach Yourself Heath (flexidisc free with *Zig Zag* magazine)	12/5
74	Charisma CB 268	Lumberjack Song/Spam Song (p/s)	5
74	NME/Charisma SFI 1259	Monty Python's Tiny Black Round Thing (D.P. Gumby Presents "Election '74"/ The Lumberjack Song) (live flexidisc free with *NME*)	10/5
75	Charisma MP PROMO 1	In Store Commercial (promo only, jukebox single)	5
79	Warner Bros K 17495	Always look On The Bright Side Of Life/Brian	12
80	Charisma CB 374	I Like Chinese/I Bet You They Won't Play This Song On The Radio/Finland (p/s)	5
83	CBS WA 3495	Galaxy Song/Every Sperm Is Sacred (goldfish bowl-shaped picture disc)	5
76	Charisma MP 001	PYTHON ON SONG (EP, double pack [CBS 268/PY 2])	10
70	BBC REB 73M	MONTY PYTHON'S FLYING CIRCUS (LP, mono, pink label)	12
71	Charisma CAS 1049	ANOTHER MONTY PYTHON RECORD (LP, with 'be a great actor kit': printed inner sleeve, cut-outs sheet, cue sheet & script)	12
73	Charisma CAS 1063	MONTY PYTHON'S PREVIOUS RECORD (LP, with free flexidisc in p/s, "Teach Yourself Heath" & inner sleeve)	12
77	Charisma CAS 1134	THE MONTY PYTHON INSTANT RECORD COLLECTION (LP, foldout sleeve)	12
79	Warner Bros K 56751	LIFE OF BRIAN (LP, soundtrack, with inner sleeve)	15
80	Charisma CAS 1152	CONTRACTUAL OBLIGATION ALBUM (LP, with inner sleeve & withdrawn track "Farewell To John Denver")	15

(see also John Cleese, Rutles, Barry Booth)

MONUMENT
| 71 | Beacon BEAS 15 | THE FIRST MONUMENT (LP) | 75 |

(see also Zior)

MINT VALUE £

MOODY BLUES

MOOCHE
69	Pye 7N 17735	Hot Smoke And Sasafrass/Seen Through A Light	20

AMEIL MOODIE
69	Blue Cat BS 143	Mello Reggae/Lifeline	10
69	Blue Cat BS 164	Ratchet Knife/Bend The Tree	10

MOOD MOSAIC
66	Columbia DB 7801	A Touch Of Velvet, A Sting Of Brass/Bond Street P.M.	15
67	Columbia DB 8149	Chinese Chequers/The Real Mr. Smith	12
68	Parlophone R 5716	The Yellow Spotted Capricorn/ELMER HOCKETT'S HURDY GURDY: Fantastic Fair	8
69	Columbia DB 8618	A Touch Of Velvet, A Sting Of Brass/Bond Street P.M. (reissue)	8
67	Columbia SX 6153	MOOD MOSAIC (LP, mono)	20
67	Studio Two TWO 160	MOOD MOSAIC (LP, stereo)	20

(see also Mark Wirtz Orchestra & Chorus, Keith West)

MOOD OF HAMILTON
67	Columbia DB 8304	Why Can't There Be More Love?/King's Message	10

MOOD REACTION
70	Pama PSP 1007	LIVE AT THE CUMBERLAND (LP)	18

MOODS
63	Starlite ST45 098	Duckwalk/Easy Going	20

MOOD SIX
82	EMI EMI 5300	Hanging Around/Mood Music (p/s)	5
82	EMI EMI 5336	She's Too Far/Venus (unreleased; white label copies exist with p/s)	30
85	Psycho PSYCHO 2001	Plastic Flowers/It's Your Life (p/s)	5
85	Psycho PSYCHO 4001	PLASTIC FLOWERS (12" EP)	10
85	Psycho PSYCHO 33	THE DIFFERENCE IS... (LP)	12

(see also V.I.P.s)

CLYDE MOODY & BROWN'S FERRY FOUR
54	Parlophone CMSP 11	I Need The Prayers/Through The Pearly Gates (export issue)	12

RON MOODY
61	Decca F 11371	You've Gotta Pick A Pocket Or Two/Reviewing The Situation	7
64	Parlophone R 5205	Rinkety Tink/Bringing Home My Darling	5

MOODY BLUES
SINGLES
64	Decca F 11971	Steal Your Heart Away/Lose Your Money (But Don't Lose Your Mind) (as Moodyblues)	25
64	Decca F 12022	Go Now!/It's Easy Child	5
65	Decca F 12095	I Don't Want To Go On Without You/Time Is On My Side	6
65	Decca F 12166	From The Bottom Of My Heart (I Love You)/And My Baby's Gone	6
65	Decca F 12266	Everyday/You Don't (All The Time)	7
66	Decca F 12498	Boulevard De La Madelaine/This Is My House (But Nobody Calls)	8
67	Decca F 12543	Life's Not Life/He Can't Win (withdrawn)	40
67	Decca F 12607	Fly Me High/Really Haven't Got The Time	12
67	Decca F 12670	Love And Beauty/Leave This Man Alone	12
67	Deram DM 161	Nights In White Satin/Cities (1st issue, darker labels than later copies)	5
68	Deram DM 196	Voices In The Sky/Doctor Livingstone, I Presume	5
68	Deram DM 213	Ride My See-Saw/A Simple Game	6
69	Deram DM 247	Never Comes The Day/So Deep Within You	5

MINT VALUE £

69	Threshold TH 1	Watching And Waiting/Out And In	7
70	Threshold TH 4	Question/Candle Of Life	5
71	Threshold TH 7	Story In Your Eyes/Melancholy Man (unissued)	
72	Threshold TH 9	Isn't Life Strange/After You Came (p/s)	6
81	Threshold THPD 29	Talking Out Of Turn/Veteran Cosmic Rocker (picture disc)	7
83	Threshold TH 30	Blue World/Going Nowhere (p/s, with free T-shirt)	6
88	Threshold POCD 91	I Know You're Out There Somewhere/Miracle/Rock'n'Roll Over You (live)/	
		I Know You're Out There Somewhere (Remix) (CD, card sleeve)	7
88	Polydor 080 409-2	Miracle/Vintage Wine/Deep/I Know You're Out There Somewhere/	
		I Know You're Out There Somewhere (Video) (CD Video)	12
88	Polydor 080 022-2	Your Wildest Dreams/Talkin' Talkin'/It May Be Fire/Rock'n'Roll Over You/	
		Your Wildest Dreams (Video) (CD Video)	12

EP

65	Decca DFE 8622	THE MOODY BLUES (EP, original label or reissue with boxed Decca logo)	18/10

LPs

65	Decca LK 4711	THE MAGNIFICENT MOODIES (LP, unboxed or boxed Decca label logo)	25/12
67	Deram DML/SML 707	DAYS OF FUTURE PASSED (LP, originally with white band on sleeve & 'DSS' labels, mono/stereo)	15/12
68	Deram DML/SML 711	IN SEARCH OF THE LOST CHORD (LP, gatefold sleeve, mono/stereo)	18/12
69	Deram DML/SML 1035	ON THE THRESHOLD OF A DREAM (LP, gatefold sleeve with stapled booklet, mono/stereo)	18/12
69	Threshold THM/THS 1	TO OUR CHILDREN'S CHILDREN'S CHILDREN (LP, with insert, mono/stereo)	18/10
70	Threshold THS 3	A QUESTION OF BALANCE ('flap' gatefold sleeve with lyric sheet)	12
78	Decca TXS 129	OCTAVE (LP, blue vinyl)	12

(see also Justin Hayward, Denny Laine, Gerry Levene & Avengers, Ray Thomas)

MOOG MACHINE
69	CBS 63807	SWITCHED ON ROCK (LP)	10

MOON
68	Liberty LBF 15076	Someday Girl/Mothers And Fathers	8
70	Liberty LBF 15333	Pirate/Not To Know	8
68	Liberty LBL/LBS 83146	WITHOUT EARTH (LP)	20

(see also Beach Boys)

KEITH MOON
75	Polydor 2058 584	Don't Worry Baby/Together	10
75	Polydor 2442 134	TWO SIDES OF THE MOON (LP)	25

(see also Who)

LARRY MOON
63	Ember EMB 171	Tia Juana Ball/Bouquet Of Roses	18

PERRY MOON
63	Sway SW 002	Nine Five Baby/PLANTES: Water Front	12

TERRY MOON
63	Planetone RC 11	Moon Man/MIKE ELLIOT: This Love Of Mine	12

MOON BOYS
69	Amalgamated AMG 846	Apollo 11/PIONEERS: Love Love Everyday	10

(see also Hippy Boys)

MOONCHILD
75	Look LKSP 5010	War Orphan/Hour Glass	5

MOONDANCE
70	A&M AMS 792	Lazy River/Anna St Claire	4

MOONDOG
54	London REP 1010	ON THE STREETS OF NEW YORK (EP)	35
69	CBS 63906	MOONDOG (LP, gatefold sleeve)	20

MOONDOGS
78	Lyntone LT 002	Heads I Win/Two's A Crowd (p/s)	5

MOONDOGS
79	Good Vibrations GOT 10	She's Nineteen/Ya Don't Do Ya (foldout p/s)	5
80	Real ARE 13	Who's Gonna Tell Mary/Overcaring Parents (p/s)	4
81	Real ARE 14	Talking In The Canteen/Make Her Love Me (p/s, some with neckerchief)	6/4
81	Real ARE 16	Imposter/Baby Snatcher (p/s)	4

ART MOONEY (& HIS ORCHESTRA)
53	MGM SP 1037	I Played The Fool/I Just Couldn't Take It, Baby (with Cathy Ryan)	6
53	MGM SP 1045	Baby Don't Do It/Believe In Me (with Cathy Ryan)	6
54	MGM SP 1088	Oh Boy What Joy We Had/Silhouette D'Amour	5
55	MGM SP 1134	No Regrets/Honey Babe	5
56	MGM SP 1166	Memories Of You/I'm Looking Over	6
56	MGM MGM 899	Tutti Frutti/OCIE SMITH & CLOVERLEAFS: Our Melody (78)	20
57	MGM MGM 923	"Rebel Without A Cause" Theme/"East Of Eden" Theme	12
57	MGM MGM 923	"Rebel Without A Cause" Theme/"East Of Eden" Theme (78)	8
57	MGM MGM 943	Giant/There's Never Been Anyone Else But You	12
57	MGM MGM 943	Giant/There's Never Been Anyone Else But You (78)	8
57	MGM MGM 951	Rock And Roll Tumbleweed/Is There A Teenager In The House (with Ocie Smith)	18
57	MGM MGM 951	Rock And Roll Tumbleweed/Is There A Teenager In The House (78, with Ocie Smith)	20

(see also Ocie Smith, Shorty Long, Cloverleafs, Cathy Ryan)

HAL MOONEY ORCHESTRA
62	Oriole CB 1782	Small World/Let Us Entertain You	6

MOONGLOWS
57	London HLN 8374	I Knew From The Start/Over And Over Again	550
57	London HLN 8374	I Knew From The Start/Over And Over Again (78)	60

(see also Harvey & Moonglows, Etta & Harvey)

MOONKYTE
71	Mother SMOT 1	COUNT ME OUT (LP, with insert, spiral sleeve)	100

MOONLIGHTERS
63	Island WI 043	Going Out/Hold My Hands	18

MOONLIGHTERS
65	Columbia DB 7602	Come On Home/It's Too Late	6
66	Columbia DB 7910	We'll See It Through/Too Late To Come Home	6

MICKY MOONSHINE
74	Decca F 13555	Baby Blue/Name It You Got It.	7
75	Decca F 13555	Baby Blue/Name It You Got It (reissue, with inverted matrix number)	5

MOONSHINERS
65	Stateside SL 10137	THE MOONSHINERS BREAKOUT! (LP)	12
67	Page One POLS 004	HOLD UP (LP)	15

MOONSTONES
65	Parlophone R 5331	Heaven Fell Last Night/Little Roses	5
66	Parlophone R 5497	Violets Of Dawn/Power Of Decision	5
67	Mercury MF 1011	How Many Times/Louisville	5

MOON'S TRAIN
67	MGM MGM 1333	Deed I Do/It's In My Mind	15

(see also Peter Frampton, Denny Mitchell, Preachers)

MOONTREKKERS
61	Parlophone R 4814	Night Of The Vampire/Melodie D'Amour	20
62	Parlophone R 4888	There's Something At The Bottom Of The Well/Hatashiai	30
63	Decca F 11714	Moondust/The Bogey Man	18

MICHAEL MOORCOCK (DEEP FIX)
80	Flicknife FLS 200	Dodgem Dude/Star Cruiser (p/s)	8
82	Flicknife EJS P9831	Brothel In Rosenstrasse/Time Centre (numbered, 500 only, with autographed lyric sheet)	30
92	Cyborg (no cat. no.)	The Brothel In Rosenstrasse (cassette only)	20
75	United Artists UAG 29732	NEW WORLD'S FAIR (LP, with inner sleeve)	30

(see also Hawkwind)

ADA MOORE & JIMMY RUSHING
57	Philips BBE 12150	CAT MEETS CHICK (EP)	20

(see also Jimmy Rushing)

ALEXANDER MOORE
60	77 77LA 12-7	WHISTLING ALEX MOORE (LP)	12

ALICE MOORE
50s	Poydras MC 66	Prison Blues/My Man Blues (78)	10

ANTHONY MOORE
76	Virgin VS 144	Catch A Falling Star/Back To The Top	4
71	Polydor 2310 062	PIECES FROM THE CLOUDLAND BALLROOM (LP)	35
72	Polydor 2310 079	SECRETS OF THE BLUE BAG (LP)	35
79	Quango HMS 98	FLYING DOESN'T HELP (LP)	12
81	Do It RIDE 7	WORLD SERVICE (LP, with inner)	10

(see also Slapp Happy, A. More)

BOB MOORE & ORCHESTRA
61	London HLU 9409	Mexico/Hot Spot	6
62	London HLU 9538	Ooh La La/Aufwiedersehn Marlene	6
63	London HLU 9736	Kentucky/Flowers Of Florence	6
62	London HAU 2439	MEXICO (LP, also stereo [SAHU 6230])	12/15

BOBBY MOORE (& RHYTHM ACES)
66	Chess CRS 8033	Searching For My Love/Hey Mr D.J.	10
75	Pye International 7N 25691	Call Me Your Anything Man/Call Me Your Anything Man (Disco Version) (solo)	5
66	Chess CRL 4521	SEARCHIN' FOR MY LOVE (LP)	30

BUTCH MOORE
65	Pye 7N 15832	Walking The Streets In The Rain/I Stand Still	7

CHRISTY MOORE
69	Mercury 20170 SMCL	PADDY ON THE ROAD (LP)	175
75	Polydor 2383 344	WHATEVER TICKLES YOUR FANCY (LP)	12
76	Polydor 2383 426	CHRISTY MOORE (LP)	12

DUDLEY MOORE (TRIO)
61	Parlophone R 4772	Strictly For The Birds (solo)/Duddly Dell (B-side as Dudley Moore Trio)	6
68	Decca F 12850	30 Is A Dangerous Age, Cynthia/The Real Stuff (solo)	5
69	Decca F 12882	Keep It Up/Gently (as Dudley Moore Trio)	5
65	Decca LK 4732	THE OTHER SIDE OF DUDLEY MOORE (LP)	35
66	Decca LK 4788	GENUINE DUD (LP, as Dudley Moore Trio)	50
68	Decca LK/SKL 4923	BEDAZZLED (LP, soundtrack)	70
69	Decca LK/SKL 4976	THE DUDLEY MOORE TRIO (LP)	40
69	Decca SKL 4980	THE MUSIC OF DUDLEY MOORE (LP)	30
70	Decca SPA 106	THE WORLD OF DUDLEY MOORE (LP)	40
70	Atlantic 2465 017	FROM BEYOND THE FRINGE (LP)	35
72	Atlantic K 40397	TODAY (LP)	25

MINT VALUE £

| 73 | Decca SPA 286 | THE WORLD OF DUDLEY MOORE (LP) | 18 |
| 74 | Black Lion BLP 12151 | AT THE WAVENDON FESTIVAL (LP) | 35 |

(see also Peter Cook & Dudley Moore)

GARY MOORE

78	MCA MCA 386	Back On The Streets/Track Nine (some in p/s)	30/5
79	MCA MCA 419	Parisienne Walkways/Fanatical Fascists (p/s)	10
79	MCA MCA 534	Spanish Guitar/Spanish Guitar (instrumental) (p/s)	12
81	Jet JET 12016	Nuclear Attack/Don't Let Me Be Misunderstood/Run To Your Mama (12", company sleeve, as Gary Moore & Friends)	8
82	Kerrang!	Wishing Well/GILLAN: Purple Sky/TELEPHONE: Squeeze (flexidisc with *Kerrang!* magazine)	8/6
82	Virgin VSY 528	Always Gonna Love You/Cold Hearted (picture disc)	7
83	Virgin VSY 564	Falling In Love With You/Falling In Love With You (Instrumental) (picture disc)	7
83	Virgin VS 564	Falling In Love With You/(Instrumental) (p/s, with comic)	8
84	10 TEN 13	Hold On To Love/Devil In Her Heart (poster p/s)	5
84	10 TENS 13	Hold On To Love/Devil In Her Heart (shaped picture disc)	10
84	10 TEN 19	Shapes Of Things/Blinder (p/s, with patch)	8
84	10 TENS 19	Shapes Of Things/Blinder (explosion-shaped picture disc)	12
84	10 TEN 25	Empty Rooms/Nuclear Attack (live) (poster p/s)	5
84	10 TEN 25-12	Empty Rooms (Ext. Mix)/Empty Rooms//Nuclear Attack (live)/Empty Rooms (live)/Rockin' Every Night (live) (12", double pack, gatefold p/s with poster)	10
85	10 TEND 58	Empty Rooms ('85 Version)/Out Of My System//Parisienne Walkways (live)/Murder In The Skies (live) (double pack, gatefold p/s)	5
86	10 TENS 134	Over The Hills And Far Away/Crying In The Shadows (guitar-shaped pic disc)	12
86	10 TEND 134	Over The Hills And Far Away/Crying In The Shadows//Out In The Fields (live with Phil Lynott)/All Messed Up (live) (double pack, gatefold p/s)	5
86	10 TENG 134	Over The Hills And Far Away (Extended Mix)/Over The Hills And Far Away (7" Version)/Crying In The Shadows/All Messed Up (live) (12", gatefold p/s)	8
87	10 TEND 159	Wild Frontier/Run For Cover (live)//Wild Frontier (live)/Murder In The Skies (live) (double pack, gatefold p/s)	5
87	10 KERRY 159	Wild Frontier/Run For Cover (live)/Over The Hills And Far Away/Empty Rooms/Shapes Of Things (CD, gatefold card sleeve)	8
87	10 TENP 164	Friday On My Mind/Reach For The Sky (live) (picture disc)	5
87	10 KERRY 164	Friday On My Mind (12" Version)/Reach For The Sky (live)/Parisienne Walkways (live)/Friday On My Mind (Kool Rap Version) (CD, g/fold card sleeve)	8
87	10 TENC 178	The Loner (Extended Version)/(Edit)/Johnny Boy (PVC sleeve with patch)	5
87	10 TEND 190	Take A Little Time/Out In The Fields/All Messed Up (live)/Thunder Rising (live) (double pack, gatefold p/s)	5
88	Virgin CDT 16	Over The Hills And Far Away (Extended Version)/Crying In The Shadows/All Messed Up (3" CD, card sleeve)	8
88	Castle CD3 4	Don't Let Me Be Misunderstood/Parisienne Walkways (live)/White Knuckles/Rockin' & Rollin' (3" CD, with 5" adaptor, 5,000 only)	8
88	Virgin CDT 35	Empty Rooms (Long Version)/Parisienne Walkways (live)/Empty Rooms (Summer 1985 Version) (3" CD, gatefold card sleeve)	8
89	Virgin GMSY 1	After The War/This Thing Called Love (picture disc, stickered PVC sleeve)	6
89	Virgin GMST 1	After The War/Over The Hills And Far Away (live)/This Thing Called Love (12", p/s with patch)	8
89	Virgin GMSCD 1	After The War/This Thing Called Love/Emerald/Thunder Rising (live) (3" CD, in tin with sew-on patch)	10
89	Virgin GMSTG 2	Ready For Love (12" Version)/The Loner (live)/Wild Frontier (live) (12", gatefold p/s)	8
89	Virgin GMSCDX 2	Ready For Love (Edit)/Wild Frontier (live)/Military Man (live) (3" CD, card sleeve in 4" x 4" box with badge)	8
90	Virgin VST 1233	Oh Pretty Woman/King Of The Blues/The Stumble (12", poster p/s)	8
97	Virgin VSTDJ 1674	Rhythm Of Our Lives(Stretch Mix)/(Gary's Mix)/Always There For You (New Version) (12", white label, promo only)	10
81	Jet JETLP 245	LIVE AT THE MARQUEE (LP, withdrawn test pressing, white sleeve with Jet Info sticker)	100
82	Virgin V 2245	CORRIDORS OF POWER (LP, with free live EP [VDJ 34])	12
86	10 DIXP 16	RUN FOR COVER (LP, picture disc, die-cut sleeve)	15
87	10 DIXG 56	WILD FRONTIER (2-LP, gatefold sleeve)	15

(see also Granny's Intentions, Dr. Strangely Strange, Skid Row, Thin Lizzy, Gary Moore & Phil Lynott, Greg Lake, Eddie Howell, G-Force, Cozy Powell)

GARY MOORE & PHIL LYNOTT

85	10 TENS 49	Out In The Fields/Military Man (2 1-sided interlocking shaped picture-disc set, stickered gatefold PVC sleeve)	25
85	10 TEND 49	Out In The Fields/Military Man//Still In Love With You/Stop Messin' Around (live) (double pack)	7
85	10 TEN 49-12	Out In The Fields/Military Man/Still In Love With You (12", gatefold p/s, with poster)	10
85	10 TENC 49-12	Military Man (12", 1-sided, B-side etched with signatures, promo only)	12

(see also Gary Moore, Phil Lynott, Thin Lizzy)

GERRY MOORE

| 53 | Esquire 10-326 | Now And Then/Just You, Just Bop (78) | 8 |

JACKIE MOORE

71	Jay Boy BOY 35	Dear John/Here Am I	4
71	Atlantic 2091 054	Precious Precious/Will Power	4
71	Atlantic 2091 095	Sometimes It's Got To Rain (In Your Love Life)/Wonderful, Marvellous (with Dixie Flyers)	4
74	Atlantic K 10481	Both Ends Against The Middle/Willpower	4

JOHNNY MOORE

| 67 | Caltone TONE 101 | Sound And Soul/ROY SHIRLEY: Get On The Ball | 18 |
| 69 | Doctor Bird DB 1180 | Big Big Boss/CARL CANNONBALL BRYON: Reggae This Reggae | 12 |

(see also Cannonball & Johnny Melody, Alton Ellis)

MINT VALUE £

MATTHEW MOORE
66	Capitol CL 15467	A Face In The Crowd/St. James Infirmary	5

MERRILL E. MOORE
54	Capitol CL 14057	Bell Bottom Boogie/The House Of Blue Lights (78)	20
54	Capitol CL 14130	Nola/Fly Right Boogie (78)	20
55	Capitol CL 14369	Five Foot Two, Eyes Of Blue/Hard Top Race (as Merrill Moore)	160
55	Capitol CL 14369	Five Foot Two, Eyes Of Blue/Hard Top Race (as Merrill Moore) (78)	20
56	Capitol F 3397	King Porter Stomp/Rock Island Line (export only)	140
68	Ember EMB S 253	Down The Road A-Piece/Buttermilk Baby	12
69	B&C CB 100	Sweet Mama Tree Top Tall/Little Green Apples	6
70	Bulldog BD 20	House Of Blue Lights/Red Light	5
67	Ember EMB 3392	BELLYFUL OF BLUE-THUNDER (LP)	18
68	Ember EMB 3394	ROUGH-HOUSE 88 (LP; repressed 1973)	18
69	B&C CAS 1001	TREE TOP TALL (LP)	15

MONETTE MOORE
50s	Vocalion S 200	Rhythm For Sale/Two Old Maids In A Folding Bed (78)	20

NICKY MOORE BAND
81	Street Tunes STS 006	Year Of The Lie	10

(see also Tiger, Samson, Hackensack)

PETE MOORE'S SOLID ROCKIN' BRASS
74	Gold Star 1500 009	PETE MOORE'S SOLID ROCKIN' BRASS (LP)	15

OSCAR MOORE TRIO
55	London H-APB 1035	KENYA (10" LP)	15

ROGER MOORE
65	CBS 202014	Where Does Love Go/Tomorrow After Tomorrow (some in p/s)	8/5

SCOTTY MOORE
64	Columbia 33SX 1680	THE GUITAR THAT CHANGED THE WORLD! (LP)	40

(see also Elvis Presley)

SHELLEY MOORE (& MOORE SESSIONEERS)
55	Columbia SCM 5197	In The Wee Small Hours Of The Morning/When You Lose The One You Love	5
58	Starlite ST45 002	You've Tied Me Up/Gone On The Guy	5
58	Starlite ST45 003	Where Is The Bluebird?/Everything Is Gonna Be All Right	5
57	Starlite ST EP 1	PORTRAIT OF SHELLEY (EP)	8
58	Starlite ST EP 7	KOOOL KANARY (EP)	8

THURSTON MOORE & DON FLEMING
97	Via Satellite V.SAT 6	Telstar/E.A.R.: Sputnik	20

THURSTON MOORE, KIM GORDON & EPIC SOUNDTRACKS
92	Imaginary FREE 003	Sitting On A Barbed Wire Fence/BLUEBIRDS: Tom Thumb's Blues (12", promo)	15

(see also Sonic Youth, Epic Soundtracks)

WHISTLING ALEXANDER MOORE
63	'77' LA 12-6	WHISTLING ALEXANDER MOORE (LP)	25

ALAN MOORHOUSE ORCHESTRA
66	Pye 7N 17073	(The Ballad Of) The Green Berets/London Bridge	5
68	Page One POF 104	Stop Press/Chloe	6

MOOSE
70	Escort ERT 840	Engine No. 9/KURASS: Do It	6

BIG MOOSE (Walker)
68	Python PKM 1	Puppy Howl Blues/Rambling Woman	20

MOPEDS
68	Col. Blue Beat DB 108	Whiskey And Soda/Do It	7

(see also Cindy Starr & Mopeds)

MOQUETTES
64	Columbia DB 7315	Right String, But The Wrong Yo-Yo/You Came Along	45

SANTOS MORADOS
68	Island WIP 6034	Tonopah/Anytime	4

MORE
80	Atlantic K 11561	We Are The Band/Atomic Rock (some with p/s)	8/5
80	Atlantic K 11561T	We Are The Band/Atomic Rock (12", p/s, some with patch)	10/8
82	Atlantic K 11744	Trickster/Hey Joe (p/s)	18
81	Atlantic K 50775	WARHEAD (LP)	15

A. MORE
80	Quango HMGS 10	Judy/Lucia (p/s)	5

(see also Anthony Moore)

MORECAMBE & WISE
61	HMV POP 957	We're The Guys/Me And My Shadow	7
63	HMV POP 1240	Boom Oo Yatta Ta Ta/Why Did I Let You Go	7
64	HMV POP 1373	A-Wassailing/The Happiest Christmas Of All	6
66	HMV POP 1518	Now That You're Here/That Riviera Touch	6
67	Pye 7N 17436	Twelve Days Of Christmas/Bingle Jells	6
69	Columbia DB 8646	Bring Me Sunshine/Just Around The Corner	7
70	Philips 6006 069	Following You Around/Eric & Ernie's Theme	5
71	Columbia DB 8753	Bring Me Sunshine/Just Around The Corner (reissue)	5
74	Lyntone LYN	Happy Birthday Record (flexidisc, promotion for Maltesers/Treets, etc, p/s)	12
76	EMI EMI 2475	(We Get Along So Easily) Don't You Agree/Positive Thinking	5
64	HMV CLP 1682	MR. MORECAMBE MEETS MR. WISE (LP, also stereo CSD 1522)	18
66	Philips BL 7750	AN EVENING WITH MORECAMBE & WISE (LP)	15
71	BBC RED 128	IT'S MORECAMBE AND WISE (LP)	12

JOE MORELLO
62	RCA LSP 2486	IT'S ABOUT TIME (LP, also stereo [SF 7502])	12

MORGAN
73	RCA SF 8321	NOVA SOLIS (LP, with insert)	30

MORGAN
73	RCA SF 8321	NOVA SOLIS (LP, with insert)	30
78	Cherry Red ARED 1	THE SLEEPER WAKES (LP)	12

(see also Mott The Hoople, Love Affair, Humpy Bong)

MORGAN & MARK SEVEN
66	Polydor BM 56083	I'm Gonna Turn My Life Around/Undercover Man	7

AL MORGAN
51	London L 906	Little Red Caboose/So Long Sally (78)	10
51	London L 1129	You Can't Tell A Lie To Your Heart/Lonesome And Sorry (78)	8
52	Brunswick 04913	Mistakes/My Castle In Spain Is A Shack In The Lane (with Frankie Froba & His Boys) (78)	8
57	Philips PB 740	Easy Goin' Heart/Don't Rob Another Man's Castle (78)	8
58	London HLU 8741	Jealous Heart/Foolish Tears	10
58	London HLU 8741	Jealous Heart/Foolish Tears (78)	10
50s	London BEP 6043	AL MORGAN (EP, export issue)	10
51	London H-APB 1001	JEALOUS HEART (10" LP)	20
51	London H-APB 1003	LITTLE RED BOOK (10" LP)	20

P.C. ALEXANDER MORGAN
66	Columbia DB 8095	Sussex By The Sea/METROPOLITAN POLICE BAND: Thunderbirds March	10

DAVID/DAVY MORGAN
65	Columbia DB 7624	Tomorrow I'll Be Gone/Ain't Got Much More To See (as Davy Morgan)	35
68	Parlophone R 5692	True To Life/Dawning (as David Morgan)	10

(see also Wishful Thinking)

DERRICK MORGAN
60	Blue Beat BB 7	Fat Man/I'm Gonna Leave You	18
60	Blue Beat BB 12	Don't Cry/I Pray For You (as Derrick Morgan & Ebonies)	18
60	Blue Beat BB 18	Lover Boy/Oh My!	18
61	Blue Beat BB 31	Now We Know/Nights Are Lonely (with Trenton Spence Orchestra)	15
61	Blue Beat BB 35	Leave Earth/Wigger Wee Shuffle (with Clue J. & His Blues Busters)	15
61	Blue Beat BB 62	Shake A Leg/Golden Rule (as Derrick & Drumbago All Stars)	15
62	Blue Beat BB 76	Sunday, Monday/Be Still	12
62	Blue Beat BB 82	Don't You Know Little Girl (actually by Derrick & Basil)/ B. GABBIDON: Hully Gully Miss Molly	12
62	Blue Beat BB 85	Come On Over/Come Back My Darling (with Buster's Group)	12
62	Blue Beat BB 91	Headache/OWEN GRAY: Millie Girl	15
62	Blue Beat BB 94	Meekly Wait/Day In And Day Out (both sides with Yvonne [Sterling])	12
62	Blue Beat BB 100	In My Heart/BELL'S GROUP: Kingston 13	15
62	Blue Beat BB 110	Are You Going To Marry Me?/Troubles (as Derrick Morgan & Patsy)	12
62	Blue Beat BB 130	Should Be Ashamed/Marjorie (with Buster's Group)	12
62	Blue Beat BB 141	Joybells (with Duke Reid Group)/Going Down To Canaan (with Denzil Dennis)	15
62	Island WI 004	Travel On/Teach Me Baby	15
62	Island WI 006	The Hop/Tell It To Me	15
62	Island WI 011	Forward March/Please Don't Talk About Me (B-side actually with Eric Morris)	15
62	Island WI 013	Cherry Home/See And Blind	15
63	Blue Beat BB 148	Jezebell/Burnette	15
63	Blue Beat BB 177	Patricia My Dear/The Girl I Left Behind	15
63	Blue Beat BB 187	Tears On My Pillow/You Should Have Known	12
63	Blue Beat BB 196	Telephone/Life Is Tough (B-side actually "Tough Man Tough")	18
63	Island WI 037	Dorothy/Leave Her Alone	15
63	Island WI 051	Blazing Fire/DERRICK & PATSY: I'm In A Jam	15
63	Island WI 053	No Raise, No Praise/Loving Baby	15
63	Island WI 080	Angel With Blue Eyes/Corner Stone	15
63	Rio R 1	Blazing Fire/Edmarine	12
64	Black Swan WI 402	Street Girl/Edmarine	15
64	Black Swan WI 425	Cherry Pie (actually by Frederick Hibbert)/BOB WALLS: Beware	18
64	Blue Beat BB 233	Let Them Talk/Sleeping	12
64	Blue Beat BB 239	Miss Lulu/DERRICK & PALOY: She's So Young (B-side act. by Derrick & Patsy)	12
64	Blue Beat BB 261	The Soldier Man/BUSTER'S ALL STARS: Jet 707	20
64	Blue Beat BB 268	Katy Katy/Call On Me	12
65	Blue Beat BB 276	Weep No More/I Want A Girl	12
65	Blue Beat BB 283	Johnny Grave/BUSTER'S ALL STARS: Yeah Yeah	15
65	Blue Beat BB 311	Throw Them Away/Baby Face	12
65	Blue Beat BB 329	Sweeter Than Honey/You Never Know (with Prince Buster)	15
65	Ska Beat JB 218	Don't Call Me Daddy/BABA BROOK'S BAND: Girl's Town Ska	20
65	Island WI 193	Two Of A Kind/I Want A Lover (both actually with Naomi)	18
65	Island WI 225	Starvation/I Am A Blackhead Again	15
66	Island WI 277	It's Alright/I Need Someone (both sides actually with Blenders)	18
66	Island WI 289	Ameletia (actually by Frank Cosmo)/Don't You Worry (B-side with Patsy Todd)	12
66	Island WI 3010	Gather Together Now (Jamaican Independence Song)/Soft Hand (actually "So Hard") (both sides actually with Blenders)	18
66	Rio R 122	Cool Off Rudies/Take It Easy	15
67	Island WI 3079	Someone (actually Derrick & Pauline Morgan)/Do You Love Me (with Pauline)	12
67	Pyramid PYR 6010	Tougher Than Tough/ROLAND ALPHONSO: Song For My Father	15
67	Pyramid PYR 6013	Greedy Gal/SOUL BROTHERS: Marcus Junior	15
67	Pyramid PYR 6014	Court Dismiss/FREDERICK McCLEAN: Fine Fine Fine.	15
67	Pyramid PYR 6019	Judge Dread In Court/Last Chance	10
67	Pyramid PYR 6021	Kill Me Dead/Don't Be A Fool	10
67	Pyramid PYR 6024	No Dice/I Mean It	10
67	Pyramid PYR 6025	Do The Bang Bang/Revenge	10

Derrick MORGAN

68	Island WI 3094	Conquering Ruler/LLOYD & DEVON: Red Rum Ball	15
68	Island WI 3101	Gimme Back/VICEROYS: Send Requests	20
68	Island WI 3159	Hold You Jack/One Morning In May	12
68	Pyramid PYR 6029	I Am The Ruler/I Mean It	10
68	Pyramid PYR 6039	Woman A Grumble/Don't Be A Fool	10
68	Pyramid PYR 6040	Want More/ROLAND ALPHONSO: Goodnight My Love	10
68	Pyramid PYR 6045	Try Me/I'm Leaving (B-side with Pauline)	10
68	Pyramid PYR 6046	King For Tonight (with Pauline)/Last Chance	10
68	Pyramid PYR 6053	Me Naw Give Up/BEVERLEY'S ALLSTARS: Dreadnaught	10
68	Pyramid PYR 6056	Ben Johnson Day/MAYTALS: Ain't Got No Tip	12
68	Pyramid PYR 6061	What's Your Grouse/BEVERLEY'S ALLSTARS: I Don't Know	10
68	Pyramid PYR 6063	Johnny Pram Pram/Don't Say (B-side with Pauline Morgan)	10
68	Amalgamated AMG 824	I Want To Go Home/JACKIE ROBINSON: Let The Little Girl Dance	8
68	Crab CRAB 3	River To The Bank/PETER KING: Reggae Limbo	8
68	Trojan TR 626	Fat Man/VAL BENNETT: South Parkway Rock	8
68	Nu Beat NB 016	I Love You/JUNIOR SMITH: Searching	8
68	Big Shot BI 506	Shower Of Rain/VAL BENNETT: It Might As Well Be Spring	8
69	Crab CRAB 8	Seven Letters/TARTANS: Lonely Heartaches (B-side act. by Clarendonians)	8
69	Crab CRAB 11	My First Taste Of Love/TARTANS: Dance All Night	8
69	Crab CRAB 18	Don't Play That Song/How Can I Forget You?	7
69	Crab CRAB 23	Send Me Some Loving/Come What May	5
69	Crab CRAB 22	Mek It Tan Deah/Gimme Back	6
69	Crab CRAB 28	Hard Time/ROY RICHARDS: Death Rides A Horse	8
69	Crab CRAB 30	Man Pon Spot/What A Thing	8
69	Crab CRAB 32	Moon Hop/Harris Wheel	7
69	Jackpot JP 700	Seven Letters/Too Bad	5
69	Unity UN 507	Belly Woman/PAULETT & LOVERS: Please Stay	5
69	Unity UN 540	Derrick – Top The Pop/GLEN ADAMS: Capone's Revenge	8
70	Unity UN 546	Return Of Jack Slade/Fat Man	8
70	Unity UN 569	The Conquering Ruler/Bedweight	8
70	Crab CRAB 44	A Night Of Sin/Telephone	7
70	Crab CRAB 51	I Wish I Was An Apple/The Story	5
70	Crab CRAB 52	Take A Letter Maria/OWEN GRAY: Just A Little Loving	5
70	Crab CRAB 57	My Dickie/Brixton Hop	5
70	Crab CRAB 58	I Can't Stand It No Longer/Beyond The Wall	5
70	Crab CRAB 59	Endlessly/Who's Making Love	5
70	Crab CRAB 62	Hurt/Julia	5
70	Pama PM 822	Love Bug/My Dickie	5
71	Bullet BU 467	Nobody's Business/Standing By	5
71	Camel CA 84	I Am Just A Sufferer/We Want To Know	5
71	Crab CRAB 67	Searching So Long/MORGAN'S ALL STARS: Drums Of Passion	5
72	Grape GR 3032	Send A Little Rain/DERRICK MORGAN ALL STARS: A Little Rain (Version)	6
72	Jackpot JP 793	Let Them Talk/Bringing In the Guns	6
72	Jackpot JP 794	Won't Be This Way/Ain't No Love	6
72	Jackpot JP 797	Me Naw Run/All Night Long	6
72	Jackpot JP 802	Festival 10/Festival 10 – Version	6
72	Punch PH 107	Forward March/Plenty Of One	6
72	Buster PB 60	Tears On My Pillow/KEITH REID: Worried Over You (actually by Keith & Enid)	7
73	Attack ATT 8048	Derrick's Big Eleven/My Ding A Ling	5
73	Big Shot BI 617	Housewives Choice/Don't You Worry (both sides with Hortense Ellis)	5
73	Bread BR 1119	I Who Have Nothing/I'm Not Home	5
73	Downtown DT 520	Hey Little Girl/Don't Blame The Man	5
73	Pama Supreme PS 387	I'll Never Give Up/I Who Have Nothing	5
75	Klik KL 603	Wet Dreams Part 1/Wet Dreams Part 2	8
63	Island ILP 903	FORWARD MARCH (LP)	140
69	Doctor Bird DLMB 5014	BEST OF DERRICK MORGAN (LP)	75
69	Island ILP 990	DERRICK MORGAN AND HIS FRIENDS (LP)	70
69	Pama ECO 10	DERRICK MORGAN IN LONDON (LP)	40
69	Pama PSP 1006	MOON HOP (LP)	40
69	Trojan TTL 5	SEVEN LETTERS (LP)	20
70	Trojan TTL 38	FORWARD MARCH (LP, reissue)	18
70s	Magnet MGT 004	IN THE MOOD (LP)	18

*(see also Derrick & Lloyd; Derrick, Morris & Patsy; Derrick & Patsy; Derrick & Naomi; Derrick & Paulette;
Derrick & Pauline, Morgan's All Stars, Martin & Derrick, Larry Lawrence, Frank Cosmo, Copy Cats, Matador,
Jackie Robinson)*

FREDDY MORGAN

59	London HL 7077	Side Saddle/64 Rue Blondell (export issue)	15

GEORGE MORGAN

68	London HLB 10197	Barbara/Sad Bird	5
57	Philips BBE 12149	COUNTRY AND WESTERN SPECTACULAR (EP)	20
68	London HAB 8353	COUNTRY HITS BY CANDLELIGHT (LP)	15

JANE MORGAN (& TROUBADORS)

55	London HL 8148	Why — Oh Why/The Heart You Break (May Be Your Own)	30
55	London HL 8148	Why — Oh Why/The Heart You Break (May Be Your Own) (78)	10
57	London HLR 8395	From The First Hello To The Last Goodbye/ Come Home, Come Home, Come Home	25
57	London HLR 8436	Around The World/It's Not For Me To Say	18
57	London HLR 8436	Around The World/It's Not For Me To Say (78)	8
57	London HLR 8468	Fascination (with Troubadors)/Why Don't They Leave Us Alone	15
57	London HLR 8468	Fascination (with Troubadors)/Why Don't They Leave Us Alone (78)	8
58	London HLR 8539	I'm New At The Game Of Romance/It's Been A Long Long Time (with Troubadors)	12
58	London HLR 8539	I'm New At The Game Of Romance/It's Been A Long Long Time (78)	8
58	London HLR 8611	I've Got Bells On My Heart/Only One Love	12
58	London HLR 8611	I've Got Bells On My Heart/Only One Love (78)	8

MINT VALUE £

58	London HLR 8649	Enchanted Island/Once More, My Love, Once More	10
58	London HLR 8649	Enchanted Island/Once More, My Love, Once More (78)	8
58	London HLR 8751	The Day The Rains Came/Le Jour Ou La Pluie Viendra	6
58	London HLR 8751	The Day The Rains Came/Le Jour Ou La Pluie Viendra (78)	8
58	London HL 7064	The Day The Rains Came/I May Never Pass This Way Again (export issue)	12
59	London HLR 8810	If I Could Only Live My Life Again/To Love And Be Loved	6
59	London HLR 8810	If I Could Only Live My Life Again/To Love And Be Loved (78)	12
59	London HLR 8925	With Open Arms/I Can't Begin To Tell You	6
59	London HLR 8925	With Open Arms/I Can't Begin To Tell You (78)	25
59	London HLR 8999	Happy Anniversary/C'est La Vie, C'est L'Amour	6
59	London HLR 8999	Happy Anniversary/C'est La Vie, C'est L'Amour (78)	35
60	London HLR 9087	My Love Doesn't Love Me At All/The Bells Of St. Mary's	6
60	London HLR 9120	Romantica/I Am A Heart	7
60	London HLR 9210	Lord And Master/Where's The Boy (I Never Met)	7
60	London HLR 9249	Somebody/The Angry Sea	7
61	London HLR 9421	It Takes Love/Homesick For Old England	6
62	London HLR 9528	What Now My Love/Forever My Love	6
63	London HLR 9683	Theme From Carnival (Love Makes The World Go 'Round)/The Second Time Around	6
63	Colpix PX 700	Red Sails In The Sunset/My Special Dream	5
64	Colpix PX 713	Bless 'Em All/Does Goodnight Mean Goodbye	5
67	Columbia DB 7645	Maybe/Walking The Streets In The Rain	7
67	Columbia DB 8177	The Three Bells (Jimmy Brown Song)/I Want To Be With You	6
67	HMV POP 1608	This Is My World Without You/Somebody, Someplace	7
68	Stateside SS 2082	Masquerade/Smile	5
58	London RE-R 1161	ALL THE WAY PART 1 (EP, with Troubadours)	15
58	London RE-R 1162	ALL THE WAY PART 2 (EP, with Troubadours)	15
59	London RE-R 1204	THE DAY THAT THE RAINS CAME (EP, triangular or round centre)	15/12
61	London RE-R 1331	JANE MORGAN (EP)	18
57	London HA-R 2086	FASCINATION (LP)	25
58	London HA-R 2110	ALL THE WAY (LP, with Troubadors)	20
58	London HA-R 2133	SOMETHING OLD, SOMETHING NEW, SOMETHING BORROWED, SOMETHING BLUE (LP)	20
59	London HA-R 2136	GREAT SONGS FROM THE GREAT SHOWS OF THE CENTURY VOL. 1 (LP)	20
59	London HA-R 2137	GREAT SONGS FROM THE GREAT SHOWS OF THE CENTURY VOL. 2 (LP)	20
59	London HA-R 2158	THE DAY THE RAINS CAME (LP)	20
60	London HA-R 2244	JANE IN SPAIN (LP)	20
60	London HA-R 2316	THE BALLADS OF LADY JANE (LP)	20
61	London HA-R 2371	JANE MORGAN TIME (LP)	20
61	London HA-R 2377	THE SECOND TIME AROUND (LP, also stereo SAH-R 6177)	18/22
62	London HA-R 2430	AT THE COCONUT GROVE (LP, also stereo SAH-R 6226)	20/25
62	London HA-R/SH-R 8042	WHAT NOW MY LOVE (LP, mono/stereo)	20/25
63	London HA-R/SH-R 8069	LOVE MAKES THE WORLD GO ROUND (LP, mono/stereo)	20/25
63	Colpix PXL 460	JANE MORGAN SERENADES THE VICTORS (LP)	15
65	Columbia SX 6010	IN MY STYLE... (LP)	15

(see also Troubadors, Roger Williams)

JAYE P. MORGAN

54	London HL 8009	Life Is Just A Bowl Of Cherries/Operator 299 (78)	10
55	HMV B 10799	That's All I Want From You/Dawn (78)	8
55	HMV B 10868	Please Do It Again/Danger! Heartbreak Ahead (78)	8
55	HMV 7M 327	The Longest Walk/Swanee	10
56	HMV 7M 348	If You Don't Want My Love/Pepper Hot Baby	18
56	HMV POP 144	If You Don't Want My Love/Pepper Hot Baby (78)	8
56	HMV POP 192	Get Up Get Up (You Sleepy Head)/Sweet Lips (78)	8
56	HMV 7M 365	Not One Goodbye/My Bewildered Heart	8
56	Brunswick 05519	Have You Ever Been Lonely?/Baby Don't Do It	8
56	Brunswick 05519	Have You Ever Been Lonely?/Baby Don't Do It (78)	8
57	RCA RCA 1014	You, You Romeo/Graduation Ring	7
57	RCA RCA 1014	You, You Romeo/Graduation Ring (78)	12
59	MGM MGM 1005	Are You Lonesome Tonight?/Miss You	7
59	MGM MGM 1005	Are You Lonesome Tonight?/Miss You (78)	25
59	MGM MGM 1021	(It Took) One Kiss/My Reputation	5
59	MGM MGM 1039	Somebody Loses, Somebody Wins/Somebody Else Is Taking My Place	5
60	MGM MGM 1093	I Walk The Line/Wondering Where You Are	5
62	MGM MGM 1182	Heartache Named Johnny/He Thinks I Still Ache	5
62	MGM MGM 1190	Brotherhood Of Man/Nobody's Sweetheart	5
54	London RE-P 1013	JAYE P. SINGS (EP)	18
59	MGM MGM-C 793	SLOW AND EASY (LP)	18
50s	RCA	JUST YOU, JUST ME (LP)	18

JOHN MORGAN

| 72 | Carnaby 6302 010 | KALEIDOSCOPE (LP) | 50 |
| 70s | SWP 1007 | LIVE AT DURRANT HOUSE (LP, private pressing) | 100 |

(see also Spirit Of John Morgan)

LEE MORGAN

61	Columbia 33SX 1399	THE BIRDLAND STORY VOL. 1 (LP)	15
62	Stateside SL 10016	EXPOOBIDENT (LP)	15
65	Blue Note (B)BLP 4157	THE SIDEWINDER (LP)	15
65	Blue Note (B)BLP 4034	LEEWAY (LP)	15
66	Blue Note BLP 4199	THE RUMPROLLER (LP, also stereo BST 84199)	15
66	Blue Note BLP 4169	SEARCH FOR THE NEW LAND (LP, also stereo BST 84169)	15
69	Blue Note BST 84289	CARAMBA (LP)	12
69	Blue Note BST 84312	CHARISMA (LP)	12

MACE MORGAN THUNDERBIRDS

| 63 | Starlite STEP 36 | SHAKE AND SWING (EP) | 20 |

MARY MORGAN
56	Parlophone MSP 6204	Jimmy Unknown/You Are My Love	10
56	Parlophone R 4227	From The Candy Store On The Corner/No-One Was There But You	8
57	Parlophone R 4348	A Call To Arms/One For Sorrow, Two For Joy	6

RUSS MORGAN ORCHESTRA
55	Brunswick 05464	Alabamy Bound/SCRANTON 7: The Popcorn Song	5
55	Brunswick 05493	Dog Face Soldier/Don't Cry Sweetheart	5
55	Brunswick 05537	The Poor People Of Paris (Poor John)/Silver Moon	5
56	Brunswick 05602	Lay Down Your Arms/My Best You You	5
55	Brunswick OE 9068	MOONLIGHT MUSIC (EP)	8

SAMMY MORGAN
| 70 | Bullet BU 455 | Get Out Of This Land/SYDNEY ALL STARS: Landmark | 4 |
| 70 | Punch PH 57 | Get Out Of This Land/SYDNEY ALL STARS: Landmark | 4 |

MORGAN BROTHERS
59	MGM MGM 1007	Nola/Guiding Star	8
59	MGM MGM 1007	Nola/Guiding Star (78)	12
59	MGM MGM 1026	Kissin' On The Red Light/Milk From The Coconut	6

MORGAN TWINS
| 58 | RCA RCA 1083 | T.V. Hop/Let's Get Going | 100 |
| 58 | RCA RCA 1083 | T.V. Hop/Let's Get Going (78) | 50 |

MORGAN'S ALL STARS
| 71 | Camel CA 76 | I Love You The Most (actually by Lloyd Clarke)/I Love You The Most – Version | 6 |

(see also B. Leggs, Derrick Morgan, Marvels)

(Ron Paul) MORIN & (Luke P.) WILSON
| 72 | Sovereign SVNA 7252 | PEACEFUL COMPANY (LP) | 20 |

JOHNNY MORISETTE
| 62 | Stateside SS 107 | Meet Me At The Twistin' Place/Any Time Any Day Any Where | 8 |

ALANIS MORISSETTE
| 96 | Maverick W 0330CDDJ | All I Really Want (1-track CD, 1st issue, promo, slimline jewel case, withdrawn) | 25 |
| 96 | Maverick (no cat. no.) | All I Really Want (LP Version)/Your House (Live In Tokyo)/Wake Up (Modern Rock Live)/All I Really Want (Live From SNL) (cassette, 1st issue, promo with typed inlay, withdrawn) | 15 |

MORMON TABERNACLE CHOIR
| 59 | Philips PB 962 | Battle Hymn Of The Republic/The Lord's Prayer (78) | 8 |

MORNING
| 70 | Liberty LBS 83463 | MORNING (LP) | 15 |
| 72 | United Artists UAS 29337 | STRUCK LIKE SILVER (LP) | 12 |

MORNING AFTER
| 71 | Sky SKYLP 71014 | BLUE BLOOD (LP) | 70 |

MORNING GLORY
| 71 | Chapter One CH 140 | Green Green Grass Is Dying/Monday Song | 5 |
| 71 | Chapter One CH 148 | Green On The Other Side Of The Mountain/Marjory Daw | 5 |

MORNING GLORY
| 73 | Island ILPS 9237 | MORNING GLORY (LP) | 15 |

(see also John Surman)

GIORGIO MORODER
| 66 | Page One POF 003 | Full Stop/Believe Me | 4 |
| 67 | Page One POF 028 | How Much Longer Must I Wait/Bla Bla Diddley | 4 |

(see also Phil Oakey & Giorgio Moroder, Freddie Mercury, Giorgio)

ENNIO MORRICONE ORCHESTRA
67	RCA Victor RCA 1596	A Fistful Of Dollars/The Man With No Name	6
67	RCA Victor RCA 1634	For A Few Dollars More/La Resi Dei Conti	6
67	RCA Victor RD/SF 7875	A FISTFUL OF DOLLARS (LP, soundtrack)	20
68	United Artists (S)ULP 1197	THE GOOD, THE BAD AND THE UGLY (LP, soundtrack)	15
70	Stateside SSL 10307	THE SICILIAN CLAN (LP, soundtrack)	18
70	RCA Camden CDS 1052	A FISTFUL OF DOLLARS/FOR A FEW DOLLARS MORE (LP, soundtrack)	15
70	CBS 70067	LOVE CIRCLE (LP)	30

ERIC MORRIS
61	Starlite ST45 052	Search The World/Buster's Shack	20
61	Blue Beat BB 53	Humpty Dumpty/Corn Bread And Butter (as Eric 'Humpty Dumpty' Morris & Drumbago All Stars; [B-side actually by Drumbago All Stars])	15
62	Blue Beat BB 74	My Forty-Five/I've Tried Everybody (as Eric 'Humpty Dumpty' Morris & Drumbago All Stars)	15
62	Blue Beat BB 81	Sinners Repent And Pray/Now And Forever More (B-side act. by Alton Ellis)	18
62	Blue Beat BB 83	Money Can't Buy Life (with Buster's Group)/A. ELLIS: True Love	15
62	Blue Beat BB 105	Pack Up Your Troubles/Oh What A Smile Can Do (with D. Cosmo & Drumbago's All Stars)	12
62	Blue Beat BB 115	G.I. Lady/Going To The River	12
62	Blue Beat BB 128	Over The Hills/Lazy Woman (with Buster's Group)	12
62	Blue Beat BB 137	Miss Peggy's Grandmother/BUSTER'S GROUP: Megaton	15
62	Blue Beat BB 140	Seven Long Years/For Your Love	12
63	Blue Beat BB 153	Lonely Blue Boy/PRINCE BUSTER: Oh We	15
63	Blue Beat BB 184	Sweet Love/BUSTER, DEREK, ERIC: Country Girl	15
64	Blue Beat BB 218	Love Can Break A Man/Worried People	12
64	Blue Beat BB 273	Stitch In Time/For Ever.	12
64	Black Swan WI 412	Sampson/BABA BROOKS: Jelly Beans.	18
64	Black Swan WI 414	Solomon Grundie/BABA BROOKS: Key To The City	18
64	Black Swan WI 433	Supper In The Gutter/Words Of My Mouth	18

MINT VALUE £

64	Black Swan WI 439	River Come Down/Seek And You'll Find	18
64	Black Swan WI 445	Home Sweet Home/LESTER STERLING: '64 Special	18
64	Island WI 142	Penny-Reel/DUKE REID'S GROUP: Darling When (B-side act. Dotty & Bonnie)	18
64	Island WI 147	Mama No Fret/FRANKIE ANDERSON: Santa Lucia (B-side w/Roland Alphonso)	18
64	Island WI 150	Drop Your Sword/Catch A Fire (B-side actually by Roland Alphonso)	18
64	Island WI 151	What A Man Doeth/DUKE REID'S GROUP: Rude Boy (B-side actually by Baba Brooks)	18
64	Port-O-Jam PJ 4006	Oh My Dear/Lena Belle	12
64	Rio R 39	Little District/True And Just	12
64	Rio R 48	Live As A Man/Man Will Rule	12
65	Rio R 72	By The Sea/I Wasn't Around	12
65	Island WI 183	Love Can Make A Mansion (actually "Love Can Break A Man")/Ungodly People	20
65	Island WI 185	Suddenly/Many Long Years	20
65	Island WI 199	Fast Mouth/The Harder They Come	18
65	Island WI 234	Children Of Today/BABA BROOKS: Greenfield Ska	18
65	Blue Beat BB 298	Those Teardrops/DON DRUMMOND: Ska Town	20
66	Blue Beat BB 349	I'm The Greatest/BUSTER'S ALL STARS: Picket Line	20
60s	Fab BB 30	Humpty Dumpty (as Eric 'Humpty Dumpty' Morris & Buster All Stars)/FOLKS BROTHERS: Carolina	6

(see also Monty Morris, Byron Lee & Dragonaires, Cool Sticky, Tommy McCook, Zoot Simms, Marguerita, Cool Cats)

HAINSLEY MORRIS
| 68 | Pama PM 720 | Stay Loose | 6 |

HELMSLEY MORRIS
| 67 | Caltone TONE 104 | Love Is Strange/DON D. JUNIOR: Sir Pratt Special | 18 |

JOE MORRIS & ORCHESTRA
| 54 | London HL 8088 | I Had A Notion/Just Your Way Baby (78) | 60 |
| 54 | London HL 8098 | Travelin' Man/No, It Can't Be Done (78) | 35 |

LIBBY MORRIS
56	Parlophone R 4225	When Liberace Winked At Me/None Of That Now	8
65	RCA RCA 1499	One Of Those Songs/The Phoenix Love Theme (Senza Fine)	6
67	Polydor 56206	Ballad Of Yesterday's Idol/Bye, Yum, Pum, Pum	5

MILTON MORRIS
| 69 | Upsetter US 318 | No Bread And Butter/UPSETTERS: Soulful I | 8 |

MONTY MORRIS
67	Doctor Bird DB 1067	Play It Cool/BABA BROOKS' BAND: Open The Door	15
67	Doctor Bird DB 1081	Put On Your Red Dress/BABA BROOKS' BAND: Faberge	15
68	Doctor Bird DB 1162	Last Laugh/You Really Got A Hold On Me	25
68	Pama PM 721	Say What You're Saying/Tears In Your Eyes	12
68	Nu Beat NB 007	True Romance/BUNNY & RUDDY: Rhythm And Soul	10
68	Nu Beat NB 011	Simple Simon/BUNNY & RUDDY: On The Town	10
69	Doctor Bird DB 1176	Same Face/A Little Bit Of This	12
69	Big Shot BI 513	Deportation/Say I'm Back	8
69	Camel CA 12	Can't Get No Peace/UPSETTERS: For A Few Dollars More	8
69	Camel CA 28	No More Teardrops/Love Me Or Leave Me (as Monty Morris & Maples)	6
70	Unity UN 557	Do It My Way/Where In The World (Are You Going)	5
70	Explosion EX 2016	Higher Than The Highest Mountain/G.G. ALL STARS: Musical Shot	10
73	Ackee ACK 527	I'm Ready To Go/TOMMY McCOOK: Flower Pot	5

(see also Eric Morris, Monty, Derrick & Patsy, Monty & Roy, Alton Ellis)

ROGER MORRIS
| 72 | Regal Zono. SRZA 8509 | FIRST ALBUM (LP) | 20 |

RUSSELL MORRIS
| 69 | Decca F 22964 | The Real Thing (Parts I & II)/It's Only A Matter Of Time | 40 |
| 70 | Decca F 23066 | Rachel/Slow Joey | 5 |

VICTOR MORRIS
| 68 | Amalgamated AMG 813 | Now I'm Alone/Rise And Fall | 7 |

MORRIS & MINORS
| 80 | Round MOR 1 | STATE THE OBVIOUS (EP, p/s in poly bag) | 10 |

MORRIS & MITCH
57	Decca F 10900	Cumberland Gap/I'm Not A Juvenile Delinquent	8
57	Decca F 10900	Cumberland Gap/I'm Not A Juvenile Delinquent (78)	12
57	Decca F 10929	What Is A Skiffler?/The Tommy Rot Story	8
57	Decca F 10929	What Is A Skiffler?/The Tommy Rot Story (78)	10
58	Decca F 11086	Highway Patrol/Bird Dog	8
58	Decca F 11086	Highway Patrol/Bird Dog (78)	12
68	Trend TRE 1010	The Magical Musherishi Tourists/Mister D.J. Man	5
58	Decca DFE 6486	SIX FIVE NOTHING SPECIAL (EP)	20

MORRIS FAMILY & GOSPEL JUBILEERS
| 60 | Top Rank JAR 322 | Wake Up Jonah/He Never Complained | 6 |

CURLEY JIM MORRISON
| 61 | Starlite ST45 065 | Air Force Blues/Didn't I Tell You | 165 |

DOROTHY MORRISON
| 69 | Elektra EKSN 45070 | All God's Children Got Soul/Put A Little Love In Your Heart | 4 |

HAROLD MORRISON
| 65 | Brunswick LAT 8639 | HOSS HE'S THE BOSS (LP) | 12 |

JAMES MORRISON & TOM ENNIS
| 80 | Topic 12T 390 | JAMES MORRISON & TOM ENNIS (LP) | 12 |

MINT VALUE £

PROFESSOR MORRISON'S LOLLIPOP
68	London HLU 10228	You Got The Love/Gypsy Lady	4
69	London HLU 10254	Oo-Poo-Pah Susie/You Take It	4

TOM MORRISON
60	MGM MGM-EP 709	THE ADVENTURES OF MIGHTY MOUSE AND HIS PALS (EP)	8

VAN MORRISON
67	London HLZ 10150	Brown-Eyed Girl/Goodbye Baby (Baby Goodbye)	30
70	Warner Brothers WB 7383	Come Running/Crazy Love	5
70	Warner Brothers WB 7434	Domino/Sweet Jannie	5
70	President PT 328	Brown-Eyed Girl/Goodbye Baby (Baby Goodbye) (reissue)	12
72	Warner Brothers K 16210	Jackie Wilson Said/You've Got The Power	7
74	London HLM 10453	Brown-Eyed Girl/Goodbye Baby (Baby Goodbye) (2nd reissue)	10
74	Warner Brothers K 16392	Caldonia/What's Up, Crazy Pup	10
77	Warner Brothers K 16939	The Eternal Kansas City/Joyous Sound	5
77	Warner Brothers K 16986	Joyous Sound/Mechanical Bliss	6
79	Mercury 6001 121	Bright Side Of The Road/Rolling Hills (p/s)	5
89	Polydor VANX 2	Whenever God Shines His Light (Album Version) (with Cliff Richard)/ Cry For Home/I'd Love To Write Another Song (12", p/s)	7
89	Polydor VANCD 2	Whenever God Shines His Light (7" Version) (with Cliff Richard)/ I'd Love To Write Another Song/Cry For Home/Whenever God Shines His Light (Album Version) (CD)	7
68	London HA-Z 8346	BLOWIN' YOUR MIND (LP)	35
69	Warner Brothers WS 1768	ASTRAL WEEKS (LP, orange or green label)	18/15
70	Warner Brothers WS 1835	MOONDANCE (LP, orange or green label)	18/15
71	Warner Brothers WS 1884	HIS BAND AND STREET CHOIR (LP, green label)	15
71	President PTLS 1045	THE BEST OF VAN MORRISON (LP)	15
71	Warner Brothers K 46114	TUPELO HONEY (LP, gatefold sleeve, green label)	12
72	Warner Brothers K 46172	SAINT DOMINIC'S PREVIEW (LP, with insert, 'Burbank' label)	12
73	Warner Brothers K 46024	ASTRAL WEEKS (LP, reissue, 'Burbank' label)	12
73	Warner Brothers K 46040	MOONDANCE (LP, reissue, 'Burbank' label)	12
73	Warner Brothers K 46066	HIS BAND AND STREET CHOIR (LP, reissue, 'Burbank' label)	12
73	Warner Brothers K 46242	HARD NOSE THE HIGHWAY (LP, gatefold sleeve, 'Burbank' label)	12
74	London HSM 5008	T.B. SHEETS (LP)	12
74	Warner Brothers K 86007	IT'S TOO LATE TO STOP NOW (2-LP, gatefold sleeve, 'Burbank' label)	18
74	Warner Brothers K 56068	VEEDON FLEECE (LP, 'Burbank' label)	12
77	Bang 6467 625	THIS IS WHERE I CAME IN (LP)	12
77	Warner Brothers K 56322	A PERIOD OF TRANSITION (LP)	12
84	Mercury MERH 54	A SENSE OF WONDER (LP, white label test pressings w/"Crazy Jane On God")	25
84	Mercury MERH 54	A SENSE OF WONDER (LP, credits but doesn't play "Crazy Jane On God")	12
99	Virgin VPBCDJ 50	BACK ON TOP (CD in A4 folder, with 1-sided 7", photo and biography, promo only)	50

(see also Them)

MORRISSEY
SINGLES
88	HMV POP 1618	Suedehead/I Know Very Well How I Got My Name (p/s)	5
88	HMV TCPOP 1618	Suedehead/I Know Very Well How I Got My Name/ Hairdresser On Fire/Oh Well, I'll Never Learn (cassette)	20
88	HMV TCPOP 1618	Suedehead/I Know Very Well How I Got My Name/Oh Well, I'll Never Learn (mispressed cassette, plays "Ordinary Boys" instead of "I Know Very Well...", withdrawn)	12
88	HMV 12 POP 1618	Suedehead/I Know Very Well How I Got My Name/Hairdresser On Fire (12", p/s)	10
88	HMV CDPOP 1618	Suedehead/I Know Very Well How I Got My Name/Hairdresser On Fire/ Oh Well, I'll Never Learn (CD)	12
88	HMV POP 1619	Everyday Is Like Sunday/Disappointed (p/s)	5
88	HMV TCPOP 1619	Everyday Is Like Sunday/Sister I'm A Poet/Disappointed (cassette)	8
88	HMV 12 POP 1619	Everyday Is Like Sunday/Sister I'm A Poet/Disappointed/ Will Never Marry (12", p/s)	10
88	HMV CDPOP 1619	Everyday Is Like Sunday/Sister I'm A Poet/Disappointed/ Will Never Marry (CD)	12
89	HMV POP 1620	The Last Of The Famous International Playboys/Lucky Lisp (p/s)	5
89	HMV TCPOP 1620	The Last Of The Famous International Playboys/Lucky Lisp/ Michaels Bones (cassette)	6
89	HMV 12 POP 1620	The Last Of The Famous International Playboys/Lucky Lisp/ Michaels Bones (12", p/s)	10
89	HMV CDPOP 1620	The Last Of The Famous International Playboys/Lucky Lisp/ Michaels Bones (CD)	12
89	HMV POP 1621	Interesting Drug/Such A Little Thing Makes Such A Big Difference (p/s)	4
89	HMV TCPOP 1621	Interesting Drug/Such A Little Thing Makes Such A Big Difference (cassette)	4
89	HMV 12 POP 1621	Interesting Drug/Such A Little Thing Makes Such A Big Difference/ Sweet And Tender Hooligan (live) (12", p/s)	7
89	HMV 12 POPS 1621	Interesting Drug/Such A Little Thing Makes Such A Big Difference (12", p/s, 1 side etched)	10
89	HMV CDPOP 1621	Interesting Drug/Such A Little Thing Makes Such A Big Difference/ Sweet And Tender Hooligan (live) (CD)	12
90	HMV POP 1622	Ouija Board, Ouija Board/Yes, I Am Blind (p/s)	4
90	HMV CDPOP 1622	Ouija Board, Ouija Board/Yes, I Am Blind/East West (CD)	10
90	HMV POP 1623	November Spawned A Monster/He Knows I'd Love To See Him (p/s)	4
90	HMV TCPOP 1623	November Spawned A Monster/He Knows I'd Love To See Him (cassette, card slip case)	4
90	HMV 12 POP 1623	November Spawned A Monster/Girl Least Likely To/ He Knows I'd Love To See Him (12", p/s)	7

90	HMV CDPOP 1623	November Spawned A Monster/He Knows I'd Love To See Him/ Girl Least Likely To (CD)	10
90	HMV POP 1624	Piccadilly Palare/Get Off The Stage (p/s)	4
90	HMV TCPOP 1624	Piccadilly Palare/Get Off The Stage (cassette)	4
90	HMV 12 POP 1624	Piccadilly Palare/At Amber/Get Off The Stage (12, p/s)	7
90	HMV CDPOP 1624	Piccadilly Palare/At Amber/Get Off The Stage (CD)	12
91	HMV POP 1625	Our Frank/Journalists Who Lie (p/s)	4
91	HMV TCPOP 1625	Our Frank/Journalists Who Lie (cassette)	5
91	HMV 12 POP 1625	Our Frank/Journalists Who Lie/Tony The Pony (12", p/s)	7
91	HMV CDPOP 1625	Our Frank/Journalists Who Lie/Tony The Pony (CD)	12
91	HMV POP 1626	Sing Your Life/That's Entertainment (p/s)	4
91	HMV CDPOP 1626	Sing Your Life/That's Entertainment/The Loop (CD)	10
91	HMV POP 1627	Pregnant For The Last Time/Skin Storm (p/s)	4
91	HMV TCPOP 1627	Pregnant For The Last Time/Skin Storm (cassette)	4
91	HMV 12 POP 1627	Pregnant For The Last Time/Skin Storm/Cosmic Dancer (live)/ Disappointed (live) (12", p/s)	7
91	HMV CDPOP 1627	Pregnant For The Last Time/Skin Storm/Cosmic Dancer (live)/ Disappointed (live) (CD)	12
91	HMV CDPOP 1628	My Love Life/I've Changed My Plea To Guilty/There's A Place In Hell For Me And My Friends (live) (CD)	10
92	HMV CDPOP 1629	Certain People I Know/You've Had Her/Jack The Ripper (CD)	10
95	RCA Victor LC 0316	Dagenham Dave/Nobody Loves Us (p/s)	5
97	Island IS 667	Alma Matters/Heir Apparent (p/s)	5
97	Island IS 671	Roy's Keen/Lost (p/s)	5
97	Island IS 686	Satan Rejected My Soul/Now I Am A Was (p/s)	5

PROMOS

92	HMV POP DJ 1629	We Hate It When Our Friends Become Sucessful/We Hate It When Our Friends Become Sucessful (10", A-side plays at 45rpm, B-side at 78rpm, die-cut sleeve)	30
92	HMV POP DJ 1630	You're The One For Me, Fatty/You're The One For Me, Fatty (10", A-side plays at 45rpm, B-side at 78rpm, die-cut sleeve)	30
93	HMV POPDJ 1631	Certain People I Know/Jack The Ripper (die-cut 'Moz' p/s)	12
93	HMV POPDJ 1632	Jack The Ripper/Sister I'm A Poet (p/s)	10
95	Parlophone CDRDJ 6243	Sunny/Black-Eyed Susan/A Swallow On My Neck (CD)	12
94	Parlophone RDJ 6372	The More You Ignore, Me The Closer I Get/ Used To Be A Sweet Boy (yellow p/s)	12
94	Parlophone CDRDJ 6372	The More You Ignore, Me The Closer I Get/Used To Be A Sweet Boy/ I'd Love To (CD, yellow card p/s)	12
94	Parlophone CDRDJ 6372	The More You Ignore, Me The Closer I Get (CD, with "45rpm" logo on disc, withdrawn)	20
94	Parlophone CDRDJ 6383	Hold On To Your Friends/Moonriver (CD, card p/s)	10
95	Parlophone RDJ 6400	Have-A-Go Merchant/Whatever Happens, I Love You (p/s)	25
95	Parlophone CDRDJ 6400	Have-A-Go Merchant/Whatever Happens, I Love You (CD, 'skinhead' card p/s)	20
95	Parlophone CDRDJX 6400	Boxers/Have-A-Go Merchant/Whatever Happens I Love You (CD)	10

(see also Smiths, Durutti Column)

DICK MORRISSEY

61	'77' LEU 12/8	HAVE YOU HEARD? (LP)	250
61	Fontana TFL 5149	IT'S MORRISEY MAN! (LP)	275
67	Mercury 20093	HERE AND NOW AND SOUNDING GOOD (LP)	250
67	Mercury 20077MCL	STORM WARNING (LP)	250

(see also If, Morrissey-Mullen)

MORRISSEY-MULLEN

79	Harvest SHSP 4098	CAPE WRATH (LP)	20

(see also Dick Morrissey)

BUDDY MORROW & HIS ORCHESTRA

53	HMV 7M 145	Heap Big Beat/I Can't Get Started	6
53	HMV 7M 151	I Can't Get Started/Heap Big Beat (reissue)	6
53	HMV 7M 162	Dragnet/Your Mouth's Got A Hole In It	8
54	HMV 7M 216	Knock On Wood (with Shaye Cogan)/All Night Long	10
54	Mercury MB 3170	Rock-A-Beatin' Boogie/Mr. Sandman (78)	10
56	Mercury MT 119	Theme From "The Proud Ones" (with Whistling Elmo Tanner)/ Paradise Lost (78)	8
60	RCA RCA 1167	Staccato's Theme/Scraunchy	6
60	RCA RCA 1167	Staccato's Theme/Scraunchy (78)	20
56	Mercury MPT 7003	SHALL WE DANCE (10" LP)	15

ELLA MAE MORSE

52	Capitol CL 13666	Tennessee Saturday Night/A Little Further Down The Road (78)	18
52	Capitol CL 13727	Blacksmith Blues/Love Me Or Leave Me (78)	10
52	Capitol CL 13754	Oakie Boogie/Love Ya' Like Mad (78)	18
52	Capitol CL 13798	Male Call/Sleepin' At The Foot Of The Bed (78)	10
53	Capitol CL 13853	Jump Back Honey/Greyhound (78)	12
53	Capitol CL 13930	Big Mamou/Is It Any Wonder (78)	12
53	Capitol CL 13960	Forty Cups Of Coffee/Oh! You Crazy Moon (78)	15
54	Capitol CL 14037	T'Ain't What You Do, It's The Way That You Do It/ It Ain't Necessarily So (78)	10
54	Capitol CL 14044	The Guy Who Invented Kissin'/Good (78)	10
54	Capitol CL 14116	Goodnight, Well It's Time To Go/Sensational (78)	10
54	Capitol CL 14176	(We've Reached) The Point Of No Return/Give A Little Time (78)	12
55	Capitol CL 14223	Bring Back My Baby To Me/Lovey Dovey	50
55	Capitol CL 14223	Bring Back My Baby To Me/Lovey Dovey (78)	10
55	Capitol CL 14303	Smack Dab In The Middle/Yes, Yes I Do	45
55	Capitol CL 14303	Smack Dab In The Middle/Yes, Yes I Do (78)	12
55	Capitol CL 14332	Livin', Livin', Livin'/Heart Full Of Hope	35

MINT VALUE £

55	Capitol CL 14332	Livin', Livin', Livin'/Heart Full Of Hope (78)	10
55	Capitol CL 14341	Razzle-Dazzle/Ain't That A Shame (with Big Dave & His Music)	100
55	Capitol CL 14341	Razzle-Dazzle/Ain't That A Shame (with Big Dave & His Music) (78)	25
55	Capitol CL 14362	Seventeen/Piddily Patter Song (with Big Dave & His Music)	80
55	Capitol CL 14362	Seventeen/Piddily Patter Song (with Big Dave & His Music) (78)	18
55	Capitol CL 14376	Birmin'ham/An Occasional Man	35
55	Capitol CL 14376	Birmin'ham/An Occasional Man (78)	12

(The above 45s were originally issued with triangular centres; later round-centres are worth around two-thirds these values.)

56	Capitol CL 14508	When Boy Kiss Girl (It's Love)/Sing-Ing-Ing-Ing	20
56	Capitol CL 14508	When Boy Kiss Girl (It's Love)/Sing-Ing-Ing-Ing (78)	12
56	Capitol CL 14572	Rock And Roll Wedding/Down In Mexico	30
56	Capitol CL 14572	Rock And Roll Wedding/Down In Mexico (78)	15
57	Capitol CL 14726	What Good'll It Do Me/Mister Money Maker	18
57	Capitol CL 14726	What Good'll It Do Me/Mister Money Maker (78)	15
57	Capitol CL 14760	I'm Gone/Sway Me	18
57	Capitol CL 14760	I'm Gone/Sway Me (78)	18
55	Capitol EAP1 513	BARRELHOUSE BOOGIE AND THE BLUES (EP)	50
54	Capitol LC 6687	BARRELHOUSE BOOGIE AND THE BLUES (10" LP)	75

(see also 'Tennessee' Ernie Ford)

ELLA MAE MORSE & FREDDIE SLACK
67	Ember SPE 6605	ROCKIN' BREW (LP)	20

AZIE MORTIMER
60	London HLX 9237	Lips/Wrapped Up In A Dream	16

JELLY ROLL MORTON('S RED HOT PEPPERS)
50	Tempo R 19	Fishtail Blues/High Society (78)	8
50	Tempo R 32	Tom Cat Blues/Bucktown Blues (78)	8
50	HMV B 9979	Cannon Ball Blues/Steamboat Stomp (78)	8
51	HMV B 10048	Black Bottom Stomp/Grandpa's Spells (78)	8
51	HMV B 10151	Kansas City Stomp/Shoe Shiner's Drag (78)	8
51	HMV B 10173	Wolverine Blues/Boogaboo (78)	8
51	Tempo R 47	King Porter Stomp/Wolverine Blues (78)	8
52	Jazz Man 11	Winin' Boy Blues/Honky Tonk Music (78)	8
52	Jazz Man 12	Finger Buster/Creepy Feeling (78)	8
52	Tempo R 48	Shreveport Stomps/Stratford Hunch (78)	8
52	Tempo R 49	Tia Juana/Mamamita	8
52	Tempo R 50	Grandpa's Spells/Kansas City Stomp (78)	8
53	HMV 7M 132	The Chant/Tank Town Bump	10
53	HMV B 10456	The Chant/Tank Town Bump (78)	8
54	HMV 7M 178	Fat Frances/Pep (solo)	10
54	HMV B 10619	Fat Frances/Pep (solo) (78)	8
54	HMV 7M 187	Wild Man Blues/Smoke-House Blues	10
54	HMV B 10645	Wild Man Blues/Smoke-House Blues (78)	8
54	HMV 7M 207	Harmony Blues/Jungle Blues	10
54	HMV B 10683	Harmony Blues/Jungle Blues (78)	8
54	HMV 7M 256	Fussy Mabel/Burnin' The Iceberg	10
54	HMV B 10762	Fussy Mabel/Burnin' The Iceberg (78)	8
50s	Vogue EPV 1126	JELLY ROLL MORTON (EP)	15
50s	Collector JE 120	JAZZ ORIGINATORS VOL. 3 (EP)	12
55	HMV 7EG 8178	THE BLUES THEY SANG (EP)	15
59	RCA RCX 168	JELLY ROLL MORTON (EP)	10
60	RCA RCX 207	JELLY ROLL MORTON NO. 2 (EP)	10
60	Fontana TFE 17263	TREASURES OF NORTH AMERICAN NEGRO MUSIC VOL. 4 (EP)	10
61	Storyville SEP 379	JELLY ROLL MORTON (EP)	10
53	HMV DLP 1016	JELLY ROLL MORTON AND HIS RED HOT PEPPERS (10" LP)	18
54	HMV DLP 1044	MORTON'S RED HOT PEPPERS VOLUME 2 (10" LP)	18
54	Vogue LDE 080	NEW ORLEANS MEMORIES (10" LP)	15
54	London AL 3519	JELLY ROLL MORTON SOLOS (10" LP)	15
54	London AL 3520	JELLY ROLL MORTON'S KINGS OF JAZZ (10" LP)	15
54	London AL 3534	CLASSIC JAZZ PIANO VOL. 1 (10" LP)	15
55	HMV DLP 1071	MORTON'S RED HOT PEPPERS NO. 3 (10" LP)	18
56	London AL 3559	CLASSIC JAZZ PIANO VOL. 2 (10" LP)	15
59	RCA RD 27113	THE KING OF NEW ORLEANS JAZZ (LP)	12
61	RCA RD 27184	THE KING OF NEW ORLEANS JAZZ VOL. 2 (LP)	12
61	Riverside RLP 12-132	MR. JELLY LORD (LP)	12
62	Riverside RLP 12-111	CLASSIC PIANO SOLOS (LP)	12
65	Fontana TL 5261	JELLY ROLL MORTON (LP)	12
67	Fontana TL 5415	MORTON SIXES AND SEVENS (LP)	12
69	RCA RD 8048	I THOUGHT I HEARD BUDDY BOLDEN SAY (LP)	12

LIONEL MORTON
67	Philips BF 1578	What To Do With Laurie/I'll Just	6
67	Philips BF 1607	First Love Never Dies/Try Not To Cry	6
69	RCA RCA 1875	Waterloo Road/Floral Street	6

(see also Four Pennies)

MANDY MORTON (BAND)
79	Banshee BANS 791	Song For Me (Music Prince)/Little Inbetween (no p/s, with Spriguns)	15
80	Polydor 2382 101	Ghost Of Christmas Past/Black Nights (p/s)	6
78	Banshee BAN 1011	MAGIC LADY (LP, with lyric insert, 1,000 only)	175
78	Banshee BAN 1011	MAGIC LADY (LP, with lyric insert, blue vinyl, 20 only)	300
80	Polydor 2382 101	SEA OF STORMS (LP, solo, with insert)	20
83	Banshee	VALLEY OF LIGHT (LP, private pressing)	60

(see also Spriguns [Of Tolgus])

MIKE MORTON
69	Plexium PXM 5	I Can't Take You To The Dance/It's Been So Long (as Mike Morton 8)	5
69	Plexium PXM 7	Jennifer Jennifer/See You Around (as Mike Morton Sound)	5

MINT VALUE £

69	Plexium PXM 11	The Hokey Cokey/Time For Living (as Mike Morton Sound)	5
70	Plexium PXM 15	Butlin Shrug/Butlin Rock (as Mike Morton Sound)	5
70	Plexium PXM 19	Burning Bridges/You Gotta Be Mine (as Mike Morton Congregation)	6
71	Plexium PXM 22	See Those Hot Pants/See You Around (as Mike Morton Congregation)	5

MOSAICS
66	Columbia DB 7990	Let's Go Drag Racing/Now That You're Here	12

MOSES & JOSHUA
(see under Moses & Joshua Dillard)

MOSKOW
78	Moskow SRS 2103	Man From U.N.C.L.E./White Black (p/s)	8
81	T.W. HIT 103	Man From U.N.C.L.E./White Black (reissue in different p/s)	5

BILL MOSS
69	Pama PM 765	Sock It To 'Em Soul Brother (Parts 1 & 2)	6
70	Pama PM 796	Number One	6

BUDDY MOSS
60s	Kokomo K 1003	GEORGIA BLUES VOLUME 2 (LP)	50

JENNY MOSS
63	Columbia DB 7061	Hobbies/Big Boys	50

STIRLING MOSS
61	Redemption RLP 5004	THE STIRLING MOSS STORY (LP)	12

TEDDY MOSS/JOSH WHITE
62	Jazz Collector JEL 5	THE MALE BLUES (EP)	15

(see also Josh White)

MOST
79	SRT SRTS/CUS/570	Carefree/In And Out (no p/s, stamped lyric insert)	8

MOST
94	Detour DR 012	Days, Days, Days/Take You There/Six Fifteen/Our Time (p/s, 100 on white vinyl)	8/5

ABE MOST OCTET
55	London RE-P 1028	PRESENTING THE ABE MOST OCTET (EP)	12

MICKIE MOST (& GEAR)
63	Decca F 11664	Mr. Porter/Yes Indeed I Do	15
63	Columbia DB 7117	The Feminine Look/Shame On You Boy	12
63	Columbia DB 7180	Sea Cruise/It's A Little Bit Hot	15
64	Columbia DB 7245	Money Honey/That's Alright (as Mickey Most & Gear)	15

(see also Most Brothers)

MR MOST
69	Downtown DT 408	Push Wood/Reggae Train	7

MOST BROTHERS
57	Decca F 10968	Whistle Bait/I'm Comin' Home	15
57	Decca F 10968	Whistle Bait/I'm Comin' Home (78)	12
58	Decca F 10998	Whole Lotta Woman/Teen Angel	15
58	Decca F 10998	Whole Lotta Woman/Teen Angel (78)	12
58	Decca F 11040	Don't Go Home/Dottie	12
58	Decca F 11040	Don't Go Home/Dottie (78)	15

(see also Mickie Most, Alex Murray)

BENNY MOTEN('S KANSAS CITY ORCHESTRA)
54	HMV DLP 1057	BENNIE MOTEN PLAYS KAY-CEE JAZZ (10" LP)	15
64	RCA Victor RD 7660	K.C. JAZZ (LP)	12

MOTHER EARTH
69	Mercury MF 1081	Goodnight Melda Grebe The Telephone Company Has Cut Us Off/I Did My Part	8
71	Reprise K 14089	Temptation Took Control Of Me/I'll Be Long Gone	5
68	Mercury SMCL 20143	LIVING WITH THE ANIMALS (LP)	18
69	Mercury SMCL 20173	MAKE A JOYFUL NOISE (LP)	18
69	Mercury SMCL 20179	TRACY NELSON COUNTRY (LP)	18
71	Mercury 6338 023	SATISFIED (LP)	18
71	Reprise K 44133	BRING ME HOME (LP)	15

MOTHER GONG
81	Butt BUTT 003	ROBOT WOMEN (LP)	12
82	Shanghai HAI 100	ROBOT WOMEN 2 (LP)	12
83	Shanghai HAI 109	ROBOT WOMEN 3 (LP)	12

(see also Gong)

MOTHERLIGHT
69	Morgan Bluetown BT 5003	BOBAK, JONS, MALONE (LP)	120

(see also Will Malone [Voice Band], Orange Bicycle)

MOTHERLODE
69	Buddah 201 064	When I Die/Hard Life	5
69	Buddah 2318 043	WHEN I DIE (LP)	12

MOTHERS OF INVENTION
(see under Frank Zappa/Mothers Of Invention)

MOTHER'S RUIN
81	Spectra SPC 1	Streetfighters/Leaving You (p/s)	18
82	Spectra SPC 6	Street Lights/Turn A Corner (p/s)	20
82	Spectra SPC 7	Say It's Not True/It's Illogical (p/s)	35

MINT VALUE £

MOTHER'S SONS
70   J-Dan JDN 4415   I Want To Tell The World/Underground Man 6

MOTHER YOD
97   Prescription DRUG 1   MOTHER YOD (LP, 99 copies only) 25

MOTHMEN
79	Absurd ABSURD 6	Does It Matter Irene?/Please Let Go (p/s)	5
81	Do It DUN 12	Show Me Your House And Car/People People (p/s, deleted after 1 day)	8
81	Do It DUNIT 12	Show Me Your House And Car/People People (12", p/s, deleted after 1 day)	10
81	Do It DUN 14	Temptation/People People (p/s)	5
82	Do It DUN 19	Wadada/As They Are (p/s)	5
82	Do It RIDE 9	ONE BLACK DOT (LP)	12
80s	On-U-Sound LP 2	PAY ATTENTION (LP)	12

(see also Alberto Y Lost Trios Paranoias)

MOTHS
69   Deroy   MOTHS (LP, private pressing in plain white sleeve) 450

MOTIFFE
72   Deroy 777   MOTIFFE (LP, private pressing in hand-illustrated white sleeve) 325

MOTIONS
66   Pye International 7N 25390   Stop Your Crying/Every Step I Take 8

MOTIVATION
68   Direction 58-3248   Come On Down/Little Man 25

FRANK MOTLEY & BRIDGE CROSSINGS
98   Jazzman JM 002   Ya Ya/Ooga Boogaloo (no p/s, large centre hole) 5

MÖTLEY CRÜE
84	Elektra E 9756	Looks That Kill/Piece Of The Action (p/s)	10
84	Elektra E 9756T	Looks That Kill/Piece Of The Action/Live Wire (12", p/s with free tattoo)	12
84	Elektra E 9756TP	Looks That Kill/Piece Of The Action/Live Wire (12", picture disc)	20
84	Elektra E 9732	Too Young To Fall In Love/Take Me To The Top (p/s)	7
84	Elektra E 9732T	Too Young To Fall In Love/Take Me To The Top (12", p/s, some with poster)	12/7
86	Elektra EKR 16TP	Smokin' In The Boys' Room/Use It Or Lose It (mask-shaped pic disc & sticker)	18
86	Elektra EKR 33P	Smokin' In The Boys' Room/Home Sweet Home (2 different interlocking mask-shaped picture disc set)	30
86	Elektra EKR 33T	Smokin' In The Boys' Room/Home Sweet Home/Shout At The Devil (12", p/s with poster)	10
87	Elektra EKR 59P	Girls, Girls, Girls/Sumthin' For Nuthin' (poster p/s)	6
87	Elektra EKR 59	Girls, Girls, Girls/Sumthin' For Nuthin' ('X-rated' stickered p/s, 3,000 only)	8
87	Elektra EKR 59T	Girls, Girls, Girls/Sumthin' For Nuthin'/Smokin' In The Boys' Room (12", p/s with patch)	8
87	Elektra EKR 59B	Girls, Girls, Girls/Sumthin' For Nuthin'/Smokin' In The Boys' Room (12", box set with patch)	12
87	Elektra EKR 59TP	Girls, Girls, Girls/Sumthin' For Nuthin'/Smokin' In The Boys' Room (12", picture disc)	12
88	Elektra EKR 65TP	You're All I Need/Wild Side/Home Sweet Home/Looks That Kill (12", picture disc)	10
88	Elektra EKR 65TB	You're All I Need/Wild Side/Home Sweet Home/Looks That Kill (12", box set with poster, tour pass & patch)	10
89	Elektra EKR 97P	Dr Feelgood/Sticky Sweet (shaped picture disc)	8
89	Elektra EKR 97CD	Dr Feelgood/Sticky Sweet/All In The Name Of . . . (3" CD, gatefold card sleeve) . . .	8
83	Elektra 9602 89-1	SHOUT AT THE DEVIL (LP, with bonus 12" picture disc & poster)	20
83	Elektra 9602 89-1	SHOUT AT THE DEVIL (LP, gatefold 'pentagram' black sleeve & inner)	10

MOTÖRHEAD
SINGLES
77	Stiff BUY 9	White Line Fever/Leaving Here (p/s, "Stiff Boxed Set" 45, later mail-order)	15
77	Chiswick S 13	Motörhead/City Kids (p/s)	8
77	Chiswick NS 13	Motörhead/City Kids (12", p/s)	10
78	Bronze BRO 60	Louie Louie/Tear Ya Down (p/s)	6
79	Bronze BRO 67	Overkill/Too Late, Too Late (p/s, initially with 'Overkill' badge)	7/5
79	Bronze 12 BRO 67	Overkill/Too Late, Too Late (12", p/s)	8
79	Bronze BRO 78	No Class/Like A Nightmare (3 different sleeves) . . . . each 6
79	Bronze BRO 85	Bomber/Over The Top (p/s, some on blue vinyl)	8/5
79	Big Beat NS 13	Motörhead/City Kids (p/s, black, pink, blue, orange or white vinyl)	6-8
80	Big Beat NSP 13	Motörhead/City Kids (p/s, black & white or blue & white picture disc)	8/10
80	Bronze BRO 92	THE GOLDEN YEARS (EP)	5
80	Bronze 12 BRO 92	THE GOLDEN YEARS (12" EP)	8
80	Big Beat SWT 61	BEER DRINKERS EP (12", p/s, black, blue or scarcer pink or orange vinyl) . . .	7-10
80	Big Beat SWT 61	BEER DRINKERS EP (12", p/s, brown vinyl)	15
80	Bronze BRO 106	Ace Of Spades/Dirty Love (p/s)	5
80	Bronze BROX 106	Ace Of Spades/Dirty Love (12", 'Xmas' sleeve)	10
81	Bronze BRO 116	ST. VALENTINES DAY MASSACRE (10" EP, with Girlschool)	5
81	Lyntone LYN 9661	The Train Kept-A Rollin' (live) (blue flexi free with *Flexipop* mag, issue 7)	10/6
81	Bronze BROP 124	Motörhead (live)/Over The Top (live) (picture disc)	6
82	Bronze BRO 146	Iron Fist/Remember Me I'm Gone (p/s, blue vinyl)	12
82	Bronze BRO 151	Stand By Your Man/No Class/Masterplan (p/s, as Lemmy & Wendy O'Williams) . . .	7
83	Bronze BRO 165	I Got Mine/Turn You Round Again (p/s)	5
83	Bronze BROX 165	I Got Mine/Turn You Round Again (12", p/s)	8
83	Bronze BRO 167	Shine/Hoochie Coochie Man (live) (p/s)	5
83	Bronze BROX 167	Shine/Hoochie Coochie Man (live)/Don't Need Religion (live) (12", p/s)	8
83	Bronze BROX 167/ BROX 92	Shine/Hoochie Coochie Man (live)/Don't Need Religion (live)// THE GOLDEN YEARS (12", p/s, stickered, shrinkwrapped double pack)	18
83	Lyntone LYN 4383	In Their Own Words/BRONZ: Taken By Storm (flexi free with *Kerrang!* mag) . . .	10/5

MINT VALUE £

84	Bronze BRO 185	Killed By Death/Under The Knife (p/s) 5
84	Bronze BROP 185	Killed By Death/Under The Knife (logo skull-shaped picture disc) 15
84	Bronze BROX 185	Killed By Death (Full Length Version)/Under The Knife/Under The Knife (12", stickered p/s, some with poster) 12/8
86	GWR GWR 2	Deaf Forever/On The Road (live) (p/s, some with competition form). 6/5
87	GWR GWR 6	Eat The Rich/Cradle To The Grave (p/s) 5
88	Castle CD3-10	MOTÖRHEAD: (Ace Of Spades/Bomber/Motörhead/Overkill) (CD EP, 5,000 only). . 7
88	Sounds WAVES 1	Killed By Death (live) (p/s, with others, free with *Sounds* magazine) 8/5
88	GWR GWR 15	Ace Of Spades/Dogs/Traitor (sold at concerts & through fan club, no p/s). 12
90	Epic 656578 0	The One To Sing The Blues/Dead Man's Hand (shaped picture disc) 8

ALBUMS

77	Chiswick WIK 2	MOTÖRHEAD (LP, black & silver sleeve with inner, 600 only) 60
77	Chiswick WIK 2	MOTÖRHEAD (LP, black & white laminated sleeve with inner) 12
77	Chiswick CWK 3008	MOTÖRHEAD (LP, white vinyl). 15
79	Bronze BRON 515	OVERKILL (LP, green vinyl) 20
79	Bronze BRON 523	BOMBER (LP, 3 different shades of blue vinyl) . . . . each 15
80	Bronze BRONG 531	ACE OF SPADES (LP, gold vinyl, stickered sleeve). 15
80	Big Beat WIK 2	MOTÖRHEAD (LP, reissue, red or clear vinyl with inner sleeve) 15
81	Bronze BRONG 535	NO SLEEP 'TIL HAMMERSMITH (LP, gold vinyl, stickered sleeve). 15
84	Bronze/Pro MOTOR 1	NO REMORSE (2-LP, leather sleeve with inners) 18
84	Bronze/Pro MOTOC 1	NO REMORSE (cassette, in leather case) 12
86	Castle CLACD 121	NO REMORSE (CD, leather sleeve) 15
86	GWR GWRLP 1	ORGASMATRON (LP, picture disc) 12
91	Epic 467481-0	1916 (LP, picture disc, stickered PVC sleeve) 15
91	Epic 467481 9	1916 (CD, 'tour' picture disc shrinkwrapped with booklet, stickered case) 18

(see also Lemmy & Upsetters, Sam Gopal, Hawkwind, Girlschool, Wild Horses, Filthy Phil & Fast Eddie, Young & Moody, Rocking Vickers, Blue Goose)

MOTORS

77	Virgin VS 194	Be What You Gotta Be/You Beat The Hell Outa Me (p/s) 5
78	Virgin VS 206	Sensation/The Day I Found A Fiver (p/s, some with £5 note offer). 7/5
78	Virgin VS 219	Airport/Cold Love (live) (p/s) 6
78	Virgin VS 219-12	Airport/Cold Love (live) (12", blue vinyl, company sleeve). 8
78	Virgin VS 222-12	Forget About You/Picturama/The Middle Bit/Soul Surrender (12", red vinyl, stickered company die-cut sleeve) 8
79	Virgin VS 263	Love And Loneliness/Time For Make Up (10", red, green, blue or yellow vinyl, die-cut p/s) . . . . each 8
78	Virgin V 2089	APPROVED BY THE MOTORS (LP, withdrawn group photo & inner sleeve) 12
78	Virgin V 2089	APPROVED BY THE MOTORS (LP, red vinyl reissue, different sleeve) 10

(see also Ducks Deluxe, Snakes, Heroes, Nick Garvey, Bram Tchaikovsky, Martin Ace)

MOTORWAY

| 80 | Neat NEAT 01 | All I Wanna Be Is Your Romeo/It Ain't Easy When You're All Alone (p/s) . . . . 10 |

MOTOWN SPINNERS

(see under Detroit Spinners)

MOTT

75	CBS 3528	Monte Carlo/Shout It All Out 6
75	CBS 3741	I Can Show You How It Is/By Tonight. 5
75	CBS 4005	It Takes One To Know One/I'll Tell You Something 5

(see also Mott The Hoople)

TONY MOTTOLA

| 61 | London HAZ 2442 | STRING BAND STRUM-ALONG (LP, also stereo SAHZ 6231) . . . . 10/12 |

MOTT THE HOOPLE

69	Island WIP 6072	Rock And Roll Queen/Road To Birmingham 15
71	Island WIP 6105	Midnight Lady/The Debt (some in p/s) 10/6
71	Island WIP 6112	Downtown/Home (Is Where I Want To Be) 8
74	CBS 2439	Foxy Foxy/Trudi's Song (cherry vinyl). 6
76	CBS 3963	All The Young Dudes/Roll Away The Stone (p/s) 5
89	CBS 654853 3	All The Young Dudes/Roll Away The Stone/All The Way From Memphis/ The Golden Age Of Rock'n'Roll (3" CD, gatefold card sleeve). 7
69	Island ILPS 9108	MOTT THE HOOPLE (LP, pink label; mispress with 5 alternate mixes & "Road To Birmingham" in place of "Backsliding Fearlessly" or 1 alternate mix with "Road To Birmingham", and "Rock And Roll Queen" correctly credited) . . . 40
69	Island ILPS 9108	MOTT THE HOOPLE (LP, pink label; with "Backsliding Fearlessly" in correct order) 25
70	Island ILPS 9119	MAD SHADOWS (LP, pink label, gatefold sleeve) 18
71	Island ILPS 9144	WILD LIFE (LP, pink rim palm tree label). 18
71	Island ILPS 9178	BRAIN CAPERS (LP, pink rim palm tree label & inner sleeve, some with mask) 35/18
72	CBS 65184	ALL THE YOUNG DUDES (LP, with inner sleeve). 12
72	Island ILPS 9215	ROCK AND ROLL QUEEN (LP, 'pink rim palm tree' label). 12
73	CBS 69038	MOTT (LP, die-cut gatefold sleeve with inner). 12
80	Island IRSP 8	TWO MILES FROM HEAVEN (LP, early copies list "Moving On" on rear sl.) . . 25/15

(see also Mott, Ian Hunter, At Last The 1958 Rock & Roll Show, Morgan, Mick Ronson, British Lions, Bad Company, Luther Grosvenor, Charlie Woolfe)

KEN MOULE'S LONDON JAZZ CHAMBER GROUP

| 70 | Ember EMB S 275 | Mae West/Zsa Zsa Gabor (some in p/s) . . . . 20/10 |
| 69 | Ember CJS 823 | ADAM'S RIB SUITE (LP). . . . . 40 |

(see also London Jazz Chamber Group, Ken Moule Seven)

KEN MOULE SEVEN

55	Esquire 10-417	Hallelujah/Bensonality (78) 8
57	Decca LK 4192	KEN MOULE ARRANGES FOR (LP) 25
58	Decca LK 4261	JAZZ AT TOAD HALL (LP) 30

(see also London Jazz Chamber Group)

MATTIE MOULTRIE
67	CBS 202547	That's How Strong My Love Is/The Saddest Story Ever Told	8

MOUND CITY BLUE BLOWERS
55	HMV 7EG 8096	MOUND CITY BLUE BLOWERS (EP)	8
60	Collector JEL 1	BLUES BLOWING JAZZ VOL. 1 (EP)	10

MOUNTAIN
69	Bell BLL 1078	Dreams Of Milk And Honey/Wheels On Fire	8
70	Bell BLL 1112	Mississippi Queen/The Laird	5
70	Bell BLL 1125	Sittin' On A Rainbow/To My Friend	5
71	Island WIP 6119	Roll Over Beethoven/Crossroader	5
70	Bell SBLL 133	MOUNTAIN CLIMBING! (LP)	20
71	Island ILPS 9148	NANTUCKET SLEIGHRIDE (LP, 'pink rim palm tree' label)	15
71	Island ILPS 9179	FLOWERS OF EVIL (LP, 'pink rim palm tree' label)	15
72	Island ILPS 9199	LIVE — THE ROAD GOES ON FOREVER (LP, 'pink rim' label, 'palm tree' logo)	12

(see also West Bruce & Laing, Leslie West, Jolliver Arkansas)

VALERIE MOUNTAIN
61	Columbia DB 4660	Go It Alone/Gentle Christ	6
62	Pye 7N 15450	Some People/Yes You Did	5
62	Pye NEP 24158	SOME PEOPLE — SOUNDTRACK (EP, some tracks by Eagles)	20

(see also Eagles)

MOUNTAIN ASH
75	Witches Bane LKLP 6036	THE HERMIT (LP, private pressing with insert)	175

MOUNTAIN LINE
74	Xtra XTRA 1140	MOUNTAIN LINE (LP)	12
75	Xtra XTRA 1147	HORSEPOWER (LP)	12

MOUNT RUSHMORE
68	Dot DOT 115	Stone Free/She's No Good To Me	5

MOURNING AFTER
94	Detour DR 017	Doin' Me In/Out For The Count (p/s, 100 on blue vinyl)	8/5

MOURNING PHASE
71	Eden	MOURNING PHASE (LP, private pressing)	700
91	Eden EDEN 1	EDEN (LP, reissue of "Mourning Phase")	20

MOUSE
73	Sovereign SOV 122	We Can Make It/It's Happening To Me And You	12
74	Sovereign SOV 127	All The Fallen Teen Angels/Just Came Back	12
74	Sovereign SVNA 7262	LADY KILLER (LP)	75

(see also Ray Russell Quartet, Running Man)

MOUSE & TRAPS
68	President PT 174	L.O.V.E. Love/Beg Borrow And Steal	15
68	President PT 210	Sometimes You Just Can't Win/Crying Inside	12

MOUSEFOLK
88	Tea Time Surf's Up 01	Don't Let It Slip Away/Spinning Round (flexidisc, initially with p/s)	7/5
88	Tea Time Surf's Up 02	HAZY TAMBOURINE DAYS EP (p/s)	6
89	Flowerpot 001	Motorcycle Boy/RISK: This Year's Model (p/s flexi, foldaround p/s)	4

MOUSE ON MARS
97	Too Pure PURE 65S	Cache Coeur Naif/Schnick-Schnack (with Stereolab) (red vinyl, p/s)	6
94	Too Pure PURE 36	VULVALAND (LP, with bonus 4-track 12")	10

NANA MOUSKOURI
63	Fontana 261 365TF	The One That Got Away/No Moon At All	10
63	Fontana 261 366TF	My Heart Won't Listen To Me/Don't Go To Strangers	5

ALPHONSE MOUZON
76	United Artists UAG 20005	THE MAN INCOGNITO (LP)	12

ALPHONSE MOUZON & LARRY CORYELL
77	Atlantic K 50382	BACK TOGETHER AGAIN (LP)	12

(see also Larry Coryell)

MOVE
66	Deram DM 109	Night Of Fear/Disturbance	6
67	Deram DM 117	I Can Hear The Grass Grow/Wave The Flag And Stop The Train	6
67	Regal Zonophone RZ 3001	Flowers In The Rain/(Here We Go Round) The Lemon Tree	6
67	Regal Zonophone	Cherry Blossom Clinic/Vote For Me (unissued)	
68	Regal Zonophone RZ 3005	Fire Brigade/Walk Upon The Water	6
68	Regal Zonophone RZ 3012	Wild Tiger Woman/Omnibus	10
69	Regal Zonophone RZ 3015	Blackberry Way/Something	7
69	Regal Zonophone RZ 3021	Curly/This Time Tomorrow	7
70	Regal Zonophone RZ 3026	Brontosaurus/Lightnin' Never Strikes Twice	6
70	Fly BUG 2	When Alice Comes Back To The Farm/What?	5
71	Harvest HAR 5036	Ella James/No Time (unissued)	
71	Harvest HAR 5038	Tonight/Don't Mess Me Up	5
71	Harvest HAR 5043	Chinatown/Down On The Bay	5
72	MagniFly ECHO 104	Fire Brigade/I Can Hear The Grass Grow/Night Of Fear (p/s)	7
72	Harvest HAR 5050	California Man/Do Ya/Ella James	5
74	Harvest HAR 5086	Do Ya/No Time	5
68	Regal Zono. TRZ 2001	SOMETHING ELSE FROM THE MOVE (EP, 33rpm)	45
68	Regal Zono. (S)LRZ 1002	THE MOVE (LP, mono/stereo)	50/35
68	Regal Zono. TA-LRZ 1002	THE MOVE (reel-to-reel, mono only)	12
70	Regal Zono. SLRZ 1012	SHAZAM (LP)	30
70	Fly HIFLY 1	LOOKING ON (LP)	15
71	Harvest SHSP 4013	MESSAGE FROM THE COUNTRY (LP)	15

72	Fly TOOFA 5/6	THE MOVE/SHAZAM (2-LP reissue)	15
74	Harvest SHSP 4035	CALIFORNIA MAN (LP)	12

(see also Roy Wood, Jeff Lynne, ELO, Idle Race, Trevor Burton, Nicky James Movement, Ace Kefford Stand, Grunt Futtock, Rick Price, Uglys, Charlie Wayne)

MOVEMENT
68	Pye 7N 17443	Something You've Got/Tell Her	75
68	Target 7N 17443	Something You've Got/Tell Her (Irish issue)	75
68	Big T BIG 112	Head For The Sun/Mister Mann	75

MOVERS
65	Ska Beat JB 191	Jo-Anne/DON DRUMMOND: Don De Lion	20

MOVIES
75	A&M AMLH 33002	THE MOVIES (LP)	12

(see also Ora, Public Foot The Roman)

MOVIETONE
94	Planet PUNK 003	She Smiled Mandarine Like/Orange Zero (p/s)	6
94	Planet PUNK 009	Mono Valley/Under The 3000 Foot Red Ceiling (p/s, 1,000 only)	4

MOVING BROTHERS
67	Island WI 3049	Darling I Love You/TOMMY McCOOK & SUPERSONICS: Saboo	18
67	Treasure Isle TI 7018	Darling I Love You/TOMMY McCOOK & SUPERSONICS: Saboo (reissue)	12

MOVING FINGER
68	Mercury MF 1051	Jeremy The Lamp/Pain Of My Misfortune	20
69	Mercury MF 1077	Higher And Higher/Shake And Fingerpop	7
73	Decca F 13406	So Many People/We're Just As Happy As We Are	7

(see also Anglians)

JUDY MOWATT
73	Gayfeet GS 207	Emergency Call/Emergency Call – Version	10

(see also Jean & Gaytones)

MOWREY JNR. & WATSON
76	Riverdale RRL 1000	BUSKER (LP, with insert)	30

MOXY
77	Power Exchange PXL 011	MOXY II (LP)	10
77	Power Exchange PXL 022	RIDING HIGH (LP)	10
78	Polydor 2480 400	UNDER THE LIGHTS (LP)	10

MOZABITES
80	Rock Steady MICK 010	Soul To Save/Ananta Snake Dance	5

MICKEY MOZART QUINTET
59	Columbia DB 4308	Little Dipper/Mexican Hop	6

M-PEOPLE
94	Deconstruction OPEN 4	Open Up Your Heart (Brothers In Rhythm Mix) (12", promo only)	12

MP's
80	Moving Plastic WSP 006	Housewives' Choice/Life On The Dole (no p/s)	5

MR. BEAN & SMEAR CAMPAIGN
92	London LON 319	(I Want To Be) Elected/(Instrumental Version) (p/s, with Bruce Dickinson)	5
92	London LONCD 319	(I Want To Be) Elected/(Instrumental Version) (CD, with Bruce Dickinson)	8

(see also Bruce Dickinson)

MR. BLOE
70	DJM DJS 216	Groovin' With Mr. Bloe/Sinful	5
70	DJM DJLPS 409	GROOVIN' WITH MR. BLOE (LP)	12

MR. CALYPSON
71	Jump Up JU 40	Mohammed Ali/SAMSON DE LARK: Undemocratic Rhodesia	6

MR. DYNAMITE
67	Sue WI 4027	Sh'mon/DYNAMITE ORCHESTRA: Sh'mon (Part Two)	30

MR. FLOOD'S PARTY
71	Ember EMB S 312	Compared To What/Unbreakable Toy	10
75	Bulldog BD 6	Compared To What/Unbreakable Toy (reissue)	5

(see also Mike Corbett & Jay Hirsch)

MR. FORD & MR. GOON-BONES
56	London HLU 8355	Ain't She Sweet/MUZZY MARCELLINO: Mary Lou	25

(see also Mr. Goon-Bones & Cavaliers)

MR. FOUNDATION
67	Studio One SO 2001	Have A Good Time/KEN PARKER: See Them A Come	18
67	Studio One SO 2003	All Rudies In Jail (actually by Zoot Simms)/ HORTENSE & ALTON: Easy Squeeze	18
68	Studio One SO 2061	Time-Oh/DUDLEY SIBLEY & PETER AUSTIN: Hole In Your Soul	18
68	Studio One SO 2069	Reggae Rumble/MARCIA GRIFFITHS: You Keep Me On The Move	18
69	Supreme SUP 201	Time To Pray (actually by Lloyd Robinson)/Young Budd (by Leonard Dillon)	10

(see also Sound Dimension)

MR. FOX
70	Big T BIG 135	Little Woman/Join Us In Our Game	5
70	Transatlantic TRA 226	MR FOX (LP)	30
71	Transatlantic TRA 236	THE GIPSY (LP, gatefold sleeve)	40
75	Transatlantic TRA 303	THE COMPLETE MR FOX (2-LP, reissue of "Mr Fox" & "The Gypsy")	20

(see also Bob Pegg, Bob & Carol Pegg)

MR. GOON-BONES & CAVALIERS
50	London L 557	Pepper Pickin' Polka/Goon-Bones Polka (78)	8

(see also Mr. Ford & Mr. Goon-Bones)

MINT VALUE £

MR. MO'S MESSENGERS
67	Columbia DB 8133	Feelin' Good/The Handyman	8

MR. REJECT
71	private pressing	MR. REJECT (LP)	50

MR. RUBBISH
84	Rubbish R 2	Modern Art By Mr. Rubbish/Dog-Loo Art Group (oiled 'skin' p/s)	350
85	L.E.N. 001	FROM THE WOLF'S LAIR (cassette in deluxe 'bouffant' packaging)	250
92	M.P. MP 001	THE SEMIOTICS OF THE CRIMINAL MIND (LP, 100 only, 50 with insert)	225/180
93	M.P. MP 002	CHARLES MANSON MEETS CAPTAIN BEEFHEART!!! (LP, unissued)	750
96	M.P. MP 003	L. RON MEETS L.E.N. (CD, with 'career advice' insert, 150 only)	25

(see also Breadwinner)

MR. TWISTER & TORNADOS
63	Starlite ST45 099	Big Twist (Parts 1 & 2)	6

MRS. B., ESSEX
87	Shopping Tipps SAVE 99p	The Best Fuck I Ever Had/You'll Never Guess What (perforated coupon p/s)	250

MU
74	United Artists UAG 29709	LEMURIAN MUSIC (LP)	35

(see also Captain Beefheart, Fapardokly)

MUD
67	CBS 203002	Flower Power/You're My Mother (some in p/s)	30/20
68	CBS 3355	Up The Airy Mountain/Latter Days	12
69	Philips BF 1775	Shangri-La/House On The Hill	12
70	Philips 6006 022	Jumping Jehosaphat/Won't Let It Go	8
74	Rak RAK 187	Lonely This Christmas/I Can't Stand It (p/s)	7
75	Rak RAK 194	The Secrets That You Keep/Still Watching The Clock (p/s)	7
76	Rak RR 6	Tiger Feet/Oh Boy/Dynamite (p/s)	5
76	Private Stock PVT 65	Shake It Down/Laugh, Live, Love (p/s)	5
79	Carrere CAR 117	Drop Everything And Run/Taking The Easy Way Out (picture disc)	5

(see also Dum)

MARY MUDD
58	Columbia DB 4144	Stroll Me/Learning To Love (unreleased)	

(see also Mudlarks)

MUDHONEY
89	Blast First BFFP 46	Halloween/SONIC YOUTH: Touch Me I'm Sick (12", p/s)	8
95	Reprise 9362 458401	MY BROTHER THE COW (LP, with 6-track EP, [PRO S 7492])	18

(see also Sonic Youth)

MUD HUTTERS
79	Defensive NATO ONE	INFORMATION (EP, foldout p/s, also listed as SRTS/79/CUS 263)	5
79	Defensive NATO TWO	THE DECLARATION (EP, also listed SRTS/79/CUS 496)	5
81	Defensive NATO 3	FACTORY FARMING (LP)	10

MUDIE'S ALL STARS
70	Moodisc HM 3503	Wha Who Wha – Version/G.G. RUSSELL: Wha Who Wha	8

(see also I Roy, Eternals, King Cannon, John Holt, Niney, Jolly Boys, Jo Jo Bennett)

MUDLARKS
58	Columbia DB 4064	Mutual Admiration Society/A New Love	8
58	Columbia DB 4064	Mutual Admiration Society/A New Love (78)	10
58	Columbia DB 4099	Lollipop/Young Dove's Calling	10
58	Columbia DB 4099	Lollipop/Young Dove's Calling (78)	8
58	Columbia DB 4133	Book Of Love/Yea, Yea	10
58	Columbia DB 4133	Book Of Love/Yea, Yea (78)	8
58	Columbia DB 4190	There's Never Been A Night/Lightnin' Never Strikes Twice	7
58	Columbia DB 4190	There's Never Been A Night/Lightnin' Never Strikes Twice (78)	10
58	Columbia DB 4210	Which Witch Doctor/My Grandfather's Clock	6
58	Columbia DB 4210	Which Witch Doctor/My Grandfather's Clock (78)	12
59	Columbia DB 4250	Abdul The Bulbul Amer Cha Cha/The Love Game	7
59	Columbia DB 4250	Abdul The Bulbul Amer Cha Cha/The Love Game (78)	12
59	Columbia DB 4291	Time Flies/Tell Him No	6
59	Columbia DB 4331	Waterloo/Mary	6
59	Columbia DB 4331	Waterloo/Mary (78)	18
59	Columbia DB 4374	Tennessee/True Love, True Love	6
60	Columbia DB 4417	Never Marry A Fishmonger/Candy	6
60	Columbia DB 4513	(You've Got To) Move Two Mountains/You're Free To Go	6
61	Columbia DB 4636	When Mexico Gave Up The Rumba/Toy Balloon	6
61	Columbia DB 4708	The Mountain's High/Don't Gamble With Love	6
62	Columbia DB 4788	Them Twistin' Bones/Coney Island Washboard	6
62	Columbia DB 4861	Mañana Pasado Mañana/March Of The Broken Hearts	6
62	Decca F 11537	I've Been Everywhere/Just The Snap Of Your Fingers	6
63	Decca F 11601	The Little Cracked Bell San Raquel/La De Da	6
64	Fontana TF 495	Walk Around/Here's Another Day	5
58	Columbia SEG 7854	THE MUDLARKS! (EP)	40

(see also Mary Mudd)

MUGWUMPS
64	Warner Bros WB 144	I'll Remember Tonight/I Don't Wanna Know	8
67	Warner Bros W 1697	THE MUGWUMPS — AN HISTORICAL RECORDING (LP)	20
70	Valiant VS 134	THE MUGWUMPS — AN HISTORICAL RECORDING (LP, reissue)	12

(see also Mamas & Papas, Mama Cass Elliot, Lovin' Spoonful, Zalman Yanovsky)

BOBBY MUIR & BLUEBEATS
60	Blue Beat BB 20	Baby What You Done Me Wrong/Go Pretty Baby Go (as Blue Beats)	10
61	Blue Beat BB 44	Honey Please/That's My Girl (as Bobby Kingdom & Blue Beats)	10
62	Blue Beat BB 77	Brand New Automobile/Spanish Town Twist (as Bobby Kingdom & Blue Beats)	10

LINDSAY MUIR'S UNTAMED
66	Planet PLF 113	Daddy Long Legs/Trust Yourself A Little Bit (initially with company sleeve)	45/40

(see also Untamed)

MULCAYS
54	Polygon P 1118	My Happiness/Near You (78)	8
55	London HLF 8188	Harbour Lights/Dipsy Doodle	25
55	London HLF 8188	Harbour Lights/Dipsy Doodle (78)	12
54	London REP 1016	MERRY CHRISTMAS (EP)	15
56	London REF 1046	HARMONICS BY THE MULCAYS (EP)	15

MULDOONS
65	Decca F 12164	I'm Lost Without You/Come Back Now Baby	25

MULESKINNERS
65	Fontana TF 527	Back Door Man/Need Your Lovin'	100
65	Keepoint KEE-EP-7104	MULESKINNERS (EP, private pressing, no p/s)	750

(see also Small Faces, Faces)

ARTHUR MULLARD
67	Masquerade MSA 5001	I Love You, You Love Me/Was It Something I Said?	4

MOON MULLICAN
51	Vogue V 9013	Cherokee Boogie/Love Is The Light That Leads Me Home (78)	50
56	Parlophone MSP 6254	Seven Nights To Rock/Honolulu Rock-A Roll-A (with Boyd Bennett & His Rockets)	475
56	Parlophone R 4195	Seven Nights To Rock/Honolulu Rock-A Roll-A (with Boyd Bennett & His Rockets) (78)	75
59	Parlophone GEP 8794	COUNTRY ROUND UP (EP)	60
50s	Parlophone CGEP 15	PIANO BREAKDOWN (EP, export issue, company sleeve)	45

(see also Boyd Bennett & His Rockets)

GERRY MULLIGAN
56	Vogue V 2157	Frenesi/Nights At The Turntable	5
56	Vogue V 2158	Bernie's Tune/Freeway	5
56	Vogue V 2159	Carioca/My Funny Valentine	5
56	Vogue V 2225	Lullaby Of The Leaves/Walkin' Shoes	5
56	Vogue V 2257	Darn That Dream/I'm Beginning To See The Light	5
56	Vogue V 2258	Swing House/I May Be Wrong	5
56	Vogue V 2259	Jeru/Love Or Leave Me	5
56	Vogue V 2260	Bark For Barksdale/Moonlight In Vermont	5
56	Vogue V 2304	Carson City Stage/Cherry	5
56	Vogue V 2305	I Can't Believe That You're In Love With Me/Lady Be Good (with Lee Konitz)	5
56	Vogue V 2306	Motel/Makin' Whopee	5
56	Vogue V 2324	Soft Shoe/Aren't You Glad You're You?	5
56	Vogue V 2337	Line For Lyons/Limelight	5
59	London HLT 8901	I Want To Live — Theme/Black Nightgown (as Gerry Mulligan Combo)	6
59	London HLT 8901	I Want To Live — Theme/Black Nightgown (as Gerry Mulligan Combo) (78)	30
60	HMV POP 734	Line For Lyons/Standstill (with Paul Desmond Quartet)	5
60	HMV POP 769	I'm Gonna Go Fishin' (both sides)	5
60	Philips JAZ 102	News From Blueport/Utter Chaos (p/s)	5
55	Capitol EAP1 439	PRESENTING GERRY MULLIGAN AND HIS TENTETTE (EP)	8
55	Capitol EAP2 439	PRESENTING GERRY MULLIGAN AND HIS TENTETTE (EP)	8
58	Emarcy ERE 1553	PRESENTING THE GERRY MULLIGAN SEXTET (EP)	8
58	Emarcy ERE 1556	PRESENTING THE GERRY MULLIGAN SEXTET VOL. 2 (EP)	8
58	Emarcy ERE 1560	PRESENTING THE GERRY MULLIGAN SEXTET VOL. 3 (EP)	8
58	Emarcy ERE 1574	MAINSTREAM VOL. 1 (EP)	8
58	Emarcy ERE 1575	MAINSTREAM VOL. 2 (EP)	8
60	Mercury ZEP 10071	MULLIGAN MANIA (EP)	8
53	Capitol LC 6621	THE GERRY MULLIGAN TENTETTE — ROCKER (10" LP)	20
53	Vogue LDE 029	THE GERRY MULLIGAN QUARTET VOL. 1 (10" LP)	20
53	Vogue LDE 030	THE GERRY MULLIGAN QUARTET VOL. 2 (10" LP)	20
53	Vogue LDE 031	THE GERRY MULLIGAN QUARTET VOL. 3 (10" LP)	20
54	Vogue LDE 075	THE GERRY MULLIGAN QUARTET (10" LP)	20
54	Vogue LDE 083	THE GERRY MULLIGAN QUARTET VOL. 4 (10" LP)	20
54	Esquire 20-032	GERRY MULLIGAN ALLSTARS — MULLIGAN'S TOO (10" LP)	20
55	Vogue LDE 156	GERRY MULLIGAN QUARTET WITH LEE KONITZ (10" LP)	20
56	Esquire 32-014	GERY MULLIGAN ALLSTARS (LP)	15
56	Vogue LAE 12006	THE GERRY MULLIGAN QUARTET (LP)	18
56	Vogue LAE 12015	THE GERRY MULLIGAN QUARTET (LP)	18
56	Emarcy EJL 101	PRESENTING THE GERRY MULLIGAN SEXTET (LP)	18
57	Emarcy EJL 1259	MAINSTREAM OF JAZZ (LP, by Gerry Mulligan Sextet)	18
58	Columbia Clef 33CX 10113	GERRY MULLIGAN AND PAUL DESMOND QUARTET (LP)	15
58	HMV CLP 1204	PHIL SUNKEL'S "JAZZ CONCERTO GROSSO" (LP, with Bob Brookmeyer)	15
59	Philips SBBL 552	WHAT IS THERE TO SAY? (LP, stereo)	15
59	Vogue SEA 5006	GERRY MULLIGAN SONGBOOK (LP, stereo)	15
59	Vogue SEA 5007	REUNION WITH CHET BAKER (LP, stereo, as Gerry Mulligan Quartet)	15
59	London Jazz LTZT 15161	I WANT TO LIVE (LP, with Shelly Manne)	12
60	HMV CLP 1373	GERRY MULLIGAN MEETS BEN WEBSTER (LP)	12
61	HMV CLP 1432	THE CONCERT JAZZ BAND (LP, also stereo CSD 1351)	12/15
61	Vocalion LAE 12268	THE GENIUS OF GERRY MULLIGAN (LP)	12
62	HMV CLP 1465	GERRY MULLIGAN MEETS JOHNNY HODGES (LP, also stereo CSD 1372)	12/15
62	HMV CLP 1488	AT THE VILLAGE VANGUARD (LP, also stereo CSD 1396)	12/15
62	Riverside RLP 12-247	MULLIGAN MEETS MONK (LP, with Thelonious Monk)	15
62	HMV CLP 1549	A CONCERT IN JAZZ (LP, also stereo CSD 1432)	12/15
62	HMV CLP 1585	ON TOUR (LP, with Zoot Sims)	12
60s	Fontana FJL 133	SAXY (LP)	12

(see also Paul Desmond & Gerry Mulligan, Chet Baker, Shelly Manne, Annie Ross)

MICK MULLIGAN'S JAZZ BAND

56	Tempo A 139	In A Shanty In Old Shanty Town/Snag It	6
56	Tempo A 143	Oriental Strut/Big House Blues	6
56	Tempo A 152	Beale Street Blues/Raver's Edge	6
57	Tempo A 155	St. James' Infirmary/After A While	6
57	Tempo A 164	Old Stack-O-Lee Blues/Double Dee	6
50s	Saga STP 7020	YOUNG AND HEALTHY (EP)	18
55	Tempo EXA 25	MICK MULLIGAN'S JAZZ BAND (EP)	10
56	Tempo EXA 37	MICK MULLIGAN'S JAZZ BAND (EP)	18
56	Tempo EXA 41	GEORGE MELLY WITH MICK MULLIGAN'S JAZZ BAND (EP)	20
56	Tempo EXA 47	DOOM (EP, with George Melly)	18
57	Tempo EXA 54	MICK MULLIGAN'S JAZZ BAND (EP)	15
58	Parlophone GEP 8750	MICK BLOWS (EP)	18
57	Tempo TAP 14	JAZZ AT THE RAILWAY ARMS (LP, with George Melly)	60
59	Pye Jazz NJL 21	MEET MICK MULLIGAN (LP)	40
59	Parlophone PMC 1103	THE SAINTS MEET THE SINNERS (LP, with George Melly & Saints Jazz Band)	22

(see also George Melly)

GENE MUMFORD

58	Philips PB 862	More Than You Know/Please Give Me One More Chance	7
58	Philips PB 862	More Than You Know/Please Give Me One More Chance (78)	8

MUNGO JERRY

70	Dawn DNX 2502	In The Summertime/Mighty Man/Dust Pneumonia Blues (p/s)	8
70	Pye 7N 2502	In The Summertime/Mighty Man/Dust Pneumonia Blues (jukebox issue)	15
71	Dawn DNX 2505	Baby Jump/The Man Behind The Piano/Live From Hollywood: Maggie/Midnight Special/Mighty Man (p/s)	7
71	Dawn DNX 2510	Lady Rose/Have A Whiff On Me/Milk Cow Blues/Little Louis (p/s, withdrawn)	8
71	Dawn DNX 2510	Lady Rose/She Rowed/Milk Cow Blues/Little Louis (re-pressing with different track, p/s)	8
71	Dawn 7N 2513	You Don't Have To Be In The Army To Fight In The War/We Shall Be Free (jukebox issue)	6
71	Dawn DNX 2513	You Don't Have To Be In The Army To Fight In The War/The Sun Is Shining/O'Reilly/We Shall Be Free (p/s)	8
72	Dawn DNX 2514	Open Up/Going Back Home/I Don't Wanna Go Back To School/No Girl Reaction (p/s)	7
72	Dawn 7N 2514	Open Up/Going Back Home (jukebox issue)	10
72	Dawn DNX 2515	My Girl And Me/Summer's Gone/46 And On/It's A Goodie Boogie Woogie (p/s)	8
73	Dawn DNS 1037	Alright, Alright, Alright/Little Miss Hipshake	5
73	Dawn DNS 1051	Wild Love/Glad I'm A Rocker	5
73	Dawn DNS 1061	Long Legged Woman Dressed In Black/Gonna Bop 'Til I Drop	4
74	Dawn DNS 1092	All Dressed Up And No Place To Go/Shake 'Til I Break/Too Fast To Live And Too Young To Die/Burnin' Up (p/s)	8
75	Dawn DNS 1113	In The Summertime/She Rowed	6
75	Polydor 2058 603	Can't Get Over Loving You/Let's Go	6
75	Polydor 2058 654	Hello Nadine/Bottle Of Beer	6
76	Polydor 2058 759	Don't Let Go/Give Me Bop	6
77	Polydor 2058 868	Heavy Foot Stomp/That's My Baby	6
77	Polydor 2058 947	We're O.K./Let's Make It	6
77	Pye Big Deal BD 114	In The Summertime/Mighty Man/Baby Jump/Lady Rose (12" EP)	10
79	Pye Flashbacks FBS 7	In The Summertime/Baby Jump (yellow vinyl, p/s)	8
80	Satellite SATS 1001	What's Her Name, What's Her Number?/Why D'You Lie To Me	8
80	Satellite/Scratch HS 406	MUNGO'S SUMMER FUN PACKAGE (maxi-single, p/s)	10
83	Mach 1 MAGIC 008	There Goes My Heart Again/Thinking Of You (featuring Ray Dorset & Tarts)	8
85	Orbit TRIP 4	Sunshine Reggae/Nightlife (reissue of Horizon 45; as Mungo Jerry & Horizon)	10
87	Illegal MUNG 1	In The Summertime '87/Got A Job (as Mungo Jerry & Brothers Grimm, p/s)	5
96	Fan Club 12/1	Sugar In The Bowl/In The Summertime (fan club only, white label, autographed)	5
70	Dawn DNLS 3008	MUNGO JERRY (LP, gatefold sleeve, with 3-D glasses)	18
71	Dawn DNLS 3020	ELECTRONICALLY TESTED (LP, gatefold sleeve)	15
71	Dawn DNLS 3028	YOU DON'T HAVE TO BE IN THE ARMY (LP, gatefold sleeve, with lyric insert)	15
72	Dawn DNLS 3041	BOOT POWER (LP, with 'Dennis The Menace' or 'gun' gatefold sleeve)	15/12
73	Dawn DNLS 3045	MUNGO JERRY'S GREATEST HITS (LP)	12
74	Dawn DNLS 3501	LONG LEGGED WOMAN (LP)	12
76	Polydor 2383 364	IMPALA SAGA (LP)	12
77	Polydor 2383 435	LOVIN' IN THE ALLEYS, FIGHTIN' IN THE STREETS (LP)	12
77	Pye FILD 003	THE FILE SERIES (2-LP)	15
80	Satellite SATLP 1001	SIX-A-SIDE (LP)	12
90	Prestige CDPT 002	ALL THE HITS PLUS MORE (CD)	15

(see also Ray Dorset, Good Earth, King Earl Boogie Band, Horizon, Made In England, Jigilo Jug Band, P. King, Paul King, P. Rufus King, Russian Roulette, First Impression, Good Earth)

GARY MUNN ORCHESTRA

73	Penny Farthing PEN 820	The Original 'Big Match' Theme/Newscoop (The Original 'Grandstand' Theme)	6

RAY MUNNINGS

79	Tammi TAM 102	It Could Happen To You/Let's Boogie	12
79	Tammi TAM 103	Funky Nassau/Jump In The Water	10

CAROLINE MUNRO

67	Columbia DB 8189	Tar And Cement/The Sporting Life	8

CAROLINE MUNRO

85	Numa NU 5	Pump Me Up/The Picture (p/s)	6
85	Numa NUM 5	Pump Me Up (Ext. 6.09)/The Picture/Pump Me Up (4.00 7" Version) (12", p/s)	10

(see also Gary Numan)

HAL MUNRO

58	Embassy WB 284	Breathless/Wear My Ring Around Your Neck	6
59	Embassy WB 336	C'mon Everybody/It's Late	6
59	Embassy WB 336	C'mon Everybody/It's Late (78)	8
59	Embassy WB 340	Dream Lover/Where Were You	5
59	Embassy WB 340	Dream Lover/Where Were You (78)	8
59	Embassy WB 386	You Got What It Takes/California Here I Come	5
59	Embassy WB 386	You Got What It Takes/California Here I Come (78)	10
60	Embassy WB 401	Good Timin'/I Wanna Go Home	5
60	Embassy WB 401	Good Timin'/I Wanna Go Home (78)	12

(see also Neville Taylor)

JANET MUNRO & SEAN CONNERY

59	Top Rank JAR 163	Pretty Irish Girl/Ballamaquilty's Band	7
59	Top Rank JAR 163	Pretty Irish Girl/Ballamaquilty's Band (78)	15

LEE MUNRO

86	Numa NU 20	Stereo Headphones/Give Me Your Love (p/s)	6
86	Numa NUM 20	Stereo Headphones (Extended Version)/Give Me Your Love/ Stereo Headphones (7" Version) (12", p/s)	10

PATRICE MUNSEL

53	HMV 7M 152	Is This The Beginning Of Love/The Melba Waltz	6

ADRIAN MUNSEY

79	Virgin VS 266	C'Est Sheep (Part 1)/C'Est Sheep (Part 2) (p/s)	6
79	Virgin VS 266-12	C'Est Sheep (Part 1)/C'Est Sheep (Part 2) (12", p/s)	8

(see also Sparks)

STEPHAN MUNSON & FRIENDS

82	Rhythmic RMNS 2	And David Cried/And Dem Bahnhoff (fold-out photocopied p/s)	8

(see also Living In Texas)

JERRY MURAD'S HARMONICATS

59	Mercury ZEP 10001	IT'S CHA CHA TIME (EP)	8
67	CBS 63133	GREATEST HITS (LP)	10

MURDER INC.

80	MIL MIL 1	SOUNDS SO FALSE (EP)	8

(see also Business)

MURDER THE DISTURBED

79	Small Wonder SMALL 17	GENETIC DISRUPTION (EP)	4

BILLY MURE (ORCHESTRA)

59	Felsted AF 120	Tea & Trumpets/A String Of Trumpets	6
59	Felsted AF 120	Tea & Trumpets/A String Of Trumpets (78)	12
60	Top Rank JAR 344	Jambalaya/Kaw Liga (as Billy Mure Orchestra)	6
59	RCA RCX 158	SUPERSONICS IN FLIGHT (EP, also stereo SRC 7032)	12/20
59	Felsted GEP 1006	THE VERSATILE BILLY MURE (EP)	8
60	MGM MGM-C 800	SUPERSONIC GUITARS (LP)	12
60	MGM MGM-C 835/CS 5011	SUPERSONIC GUITARS VOL. 2 (LP, mono/stereo)	12/15

(see also Supersonics)

MURGATROYD BAND

71	Decca F 13256	Magpie (Theme From The TV Series)/Twice A Week	6

(see also Spencer Davis Group, Ray Fenwick)

MURMAIDS

63	Stateside SS 247	Popsicles And Icicles/Comedy And Tragedy	10

MICHAEL MURPHEY

72	Regal Zonophone RZ 3062	Boy From The Country/Geronimo's Cadillac	5
72	Regal Zono. SRZA 8512	GERONIMO'S CADILLAC (LP)	12
73	EMI EMA 754	COSMIC COWBOY SOUVENIR (LP)	12

ARTHUR MURPHY

59	Parlophone R 4523	Sixteen Candles/Molly Malone	6
59	Parlophone R 4523	Sixteen Candles/Molly Malone (78)	10

DELIA MURPHY

60s	HMV 7EG 8295	DELIGHTFUL DELIA (EP)	8

ELLIOT MURPHY

74	Polydor 2391 100	AQUASHOW (LP)	10

LYLE MURPHY

58	Contemporary LAC 12135	GONE WITH THE WOODWINDS (LP)	12

MARK MURPHY

57	Brunswick 05701	Goodbye Baby Blues/The Right Kind Of Woman	6
58	Capitol CL 14962	Belong To Me/Don't Cry My Love	5
58	Capitol CL 14962	Belong To Me/Don't Cry My Love (78)	8
60	Capitol CL 15117	Send For Me/Come To Me	5
63	Riverside RIF 106905	Like Love/Fly Away My Sadness	5
63	Riverside RIF 106908	Fly Me To The Moon/Why Don't You Do Right	5
65	Fontana TF 572	High On Windy Hill/Broken Heart	5
67	Fontana TF 803	(Ain't That) Just Like A Woman/Do You Wonder If I Love You	5
69	Pye 7N 17661	Come Back To Me/Dear Heart	5
57	Brunswick LAT 8172	MEET MARK MURPHY (LP)	15
60	Capitol (S)T 5011	HIT PARADE (LP)	12
64	Fontana (S)TL 5217	MARK TIME! (LP)	12
66	Immediate IMLP/IMSP 004	WHO CAN I TURN TO (LP)	35

MINT VALUE £

NOEL MURPHY
67	Fontana TL 5450	NYA-A-A-H! (LP)	12
73	Village Thing VTS 25	MURF (LP)	12

PETER MURPHY
88	B. Banquet BEGB 210	Indigo Eyes/God Sends (box set)	4

(see also Bauhaus)

ROSE MURPHY
50	Brunswick 04493	A Precious Little Thing Called Love/Me And My Shadow (78)	8
50	HMV B 9901	Busy Line/Girls Were Made To Take Care Of Boys (78)	10
53	London L 1176	Little Red Monkey/Time On My Hands (78)	12
52	Oriole/Mercury MG 10004	SONGS BY ROSE MURPHY (10" LP)	18

TURK MURPHY
50s	Philips BBL 7051	THE MUSIC OF JELLY ROLL MORTON (LP)	12

ALEX MURRAY
60	Decca F 11203	Teen Angel/Paper Doll	7
60	Decca F 11225	All On My Own/String Along	5
61	Decca F 11345	When You Walked Out/Send For Me	5

(see also Most Brothers)

LADY MURRAY
66	Clan 597 002	Mister Abercrombie Taught Me/In My Imagination	6

(see also Grazina, Mr & Mrs Murray)

MARTIN MURRAY
66	Pye 7N 17070	I Know What I Want/Goodbye Baby	7

(see also Honeycombs, Lemmings)

MICKEY MURRAY
67	Polydor 56738	Shout Bama Lama/Lonely Room	6

MISTER MURRAY
65	Fontana TF 623	Down Came The Rain/Whatever Happened To Music?	7
66	Fontana TF 674	I Drink To Your Memory/I Was A Good Song	5

(see also Mitch Murray Clan, Mr & Mrs Murray)

MITCH MURRAY CLAN
66	Clan 597 001	Skyliner/Cherokee	10

(see also Mister Murray, Mr & Mrs Murray)

MR & MRS MURRAY
68	CBS 3633	You're Outa Your Mind/A Little Bit Of You	6

(see also Mitch Murray Clan, Lady Murray, Grazina, Mister Murray)

PETE MURRAY
(see under Pascal Murray, Brian Matthew & Pete Murray)

RUBY MURRAY
55	Columbia SCM 5162	Softly, Softly/What Could Be More Beautiful	18
55	Columbia DB 3577	Let Me Go Lover/Happy Days And Lonely Nights (78)	6
55	Columbia SCM 5165	Spring, Spring, Spring/Goin' Co'tin (with Ray Burns, Diana Decker & Ronnie Harris)	10
55	Columbia SCM 5169	If Anyone Finds This, I Love You (with Anne Warren)/Before We Know It	15
55	Columbia SCM 5180	Evermore/Bambino	15
56	Columbia SCM 5222	Two Rivers/Boy Meets Girl (with Norman Wisdom)	12
56	Columbia SCM 5225	For Now, For Ever/Oh, Please Make Him Jealous	12
56	Columbia DB 3810	Teddy O'Neil/It Only Hurts For A Little While	12
57	Columbia DB 3849	Knock On Any Door/True Love	12
57	Columbia DB 3852	In Love/O'Malley's Tango	10
57	Columbia DB 3911	From The First Hello — To The Last Goodbye/Heart	10
57	Columbia DB 3933	Mr. Wonderful/Pretty, Pretty	10
57	Columbia DB 3955	Scarlet Ribbons/Macushla Mine	10
57	Columbia DB 3994	Little White Lies/Passing Strangers	7
57	Columbia DB 4042	Ain't That A Grand And Glorious Feeling/I'll Remember Today	7
58	Columbia DB 4075	Forgive Me My Darling/Keep Smiling At Trouble	7
58	Columbia DB 4108	In My Life/Nora Malone (Call Me By 'Phone)	7
58	Columbia DB 4192	Real Love/Little One	7
59	Columbia DB 4266	Nevertheless (I'm In Love With You)/Who Knows	6
59	Columbia DB 4305	Goodbye Jimmy, Goodbye/The Humour Is On Me Now	7
59	Columbia DB 4326	A Pretty Irish Girl/Connemara (with Brendan O'Dowde)	5
59	Columbia DB 4379	A Message From Jimmy/A Voice In The Choir	5
60	Columbia DB 4426	Forever/Congratulations	5
60	Columbia DB 4497	My Little Corner Of The World/Sweetheart Of All My Dreams	5
61	Columbia DB 4575	Goodbye Is The Loneliest Word/Living For The Day	5
61	Columbia DB 4701	Tammy, Tell Me True/The Faith Of A Child	5
62	Columbia DB 4771	Pianissimo/The Diamond	5
62	Columbia DB 4944	How Did He Look?/As Simple As That	5
63	Columbia DB 7028	I'm In Love With The Boy Next Door/I'll Walk The Rest Of The Way	5
63	Columbia DB 7152	Hurry Home/Something Old — Something New	5
65	Decca F 12291	The Little Pine Tree/Silent Night	5
67	Fontana TF 838	I Can't Get You Out Of My Head/Paper Mansions	5
55	Columbia SEG 7588	RUBY IS A GEM (EP)	15
56	Columbia SEG 7620	EVERYBODY'S SWEETHEART NO. 1 (EP)	12
56	Columbia SEG 7631	EVERYBODY'S SWEETHEART NO. 2 (EP)	12
56	Columbia SEG 7636	EVERYBODY'S SWEETHEART NO. 3 (EP)	12
57	Columbia SEG 7748	MUCUSHLA MINE (EP)	12
59	Columbia SEG 7952	ENDEARING YOUNG CHARMS (EP)	12
60	Columbia SEG 8052	LOVE'S OLD SWEET SONG (EP, also stereo ESG 7830)	12/15

55	Columbia 33S 1079	WHEN IRISH EYES ARE SMILING (10" LP)	18
58	Columbia 33S 1135	ENDEARING YOUNG CHARMS (10" LP)	25
60	Columbia 33SX 1201	RUBY (LP, also stereo SCX 3289)	16/20

(see also Norman Wisdom & Ruby Murray, Ray Burns, Ronnie Harris, Diana Decker)

MAC MURROUGH

72	Polydor	SHADES OF MAC MURROUGH (LP, Ireland-only)	250
74	Polydor 2908 014	MAC MURROUGH (LP, with insert, Ireland-only)	300
77	Polydor 2908 030	MERRY AND FINE (LP, Ireland-only)	150

JOHN MURTAUGH

| 70 | Polydor 2482 015 | BLUES CURRENT (LP) | 20 |

JUNIOR MURVIN

(see under Junior Soul)

MUSE

| 98 | Dangerous DREX CDEP 103 | MUSE EP (CD, 999 copies) | 30 |
| 99 | Dangerous DREX CDEP 104 | MUSCLE MUSEUM EP (CD, 999 copies) | 25 |

MUSHROOM

73	Hawk HASP 320	Devil Among The Tailors/Sun Ni Dhuibir/King Of Ireland's Daughter	25
74	Hawk HASP 340	Kings And Queens/Met A Friend	25
73	Hawk HALPX 116	EARLY ONE MORNING (LP, some with poster inner)	350/300

(see also Joe O'Donnell)

MUSICAL THEATRE

| 70 | Pye Intl. NSPL 28128 | A REVOLUTIONARY REVELATION (LP) | 12 |

MUSIC BOX

| 72 | Westwood MRS 013 | SONGS OF SUNSHINE (LP) | 30 |

MUSIC DOCTORS

69	Downtown DT 447	Music Doctor (Parts 1 & 2)	7
70	J-Dan JDN 4402	Electric Shock/KING DENNIS: Black Robin	6
70	J-Dan JDN 4403	Bush Doctor/Lick Your Stick	6
70	J-Dan JDN 4411	The Wild Bunch/ISRAELITES: Born To Be Strong	6
70	J-Dan JDN 4414	In The Summertime/Foundation	6
70	J-Dan JDN 4417	Discretion Version/Doctor Dan, Boy Friday And Friend	6
71	Downtown DT 479	The Pliers (Parts 1 & 2)	6
70	Trojan TBL 117	REGGAE IN THE SUMMERTIME (LP)	18

(see also Dennis Lowe, Audrey, Desmond Riley, Megatons, Prince Of Darkness, Gene Rondo)

MUSIC EMPORIUM

| 83 | Psycho PSYCHO 11 | MUSIC EMPORIUM (LP) | 15 |

MUSIC EXPLOSION

67	Stateside SS 2028	A Little Bit O' Soul/I See The Light	12
67	Stateside SS 2054	Sunshine Games/Can't Stop Now	5
67	Philips BF 1547	Little Black Egg/Stay By My Side	6
69	London HLP 10272	A Little Bit O' Soul/Everybody	5
67	London HA-P/SH-P 8352	A LITTLE BIT O' SOUL (LP)	20

MUSICIANS

| 66 | King KG 1055 | Jaunty Joe/The Chelsea Set | 5 |

MUSIC MACHINE

| 67 | Pye International 7N 25407 | Talk Talk/Come On In | 40 |
| 67 | Pye International 7N 25414 | The People In Me/Masculine Intuition | 30 |

MUSIC SPECIALISTS

| 70 | London HLJ 10309 | Dynamic Pressure/Flip | 6 |

MUSIC TAPES

| 98 | Earworm WORM 32 | The Television Tells Us/Freeing Song By Reindeer (p/s, pop-up sleeve with 2 inserts, 1,500 copies only) | 5 |

MUSIC THROUGH SIX

| 68 | Domain D3 | Riff Raff/ROY DOCKER: Mellow Moonlight | 6 |

(see also Jason Sims & Music Through Six)

MUSIQUE

| 78 | CBS CBS 6791 | In The Bush (2 versions) (12") | 8 |

MUSKETEER GRIPWEED & THIRD TROOP

| 66 | United Artists UP 1196 | How I Won The War/Aftermath (most copies as demos) | 90 |

(see also John Lennon)

MUSKETEERS

| 69 | Philips BF 1773 | The Fight/Magnifico | 5 |

CHARLIE MUSSELWHITE BLUES BAND

| 69 | Vanguard SVRL 19012 | STONE BLUES (LP) | 20 |

VIDO MUSSO & HIS ORCHESTRA

| 54 | London HL 8077 | Vido's Boogie/Blue Night (78) | 12 |

BOOTS MUSSULLI QUARTET

54	Capitol KC 65002	Diga Diga Doo/Lullaby In Rhythm	6
54	Capitol KC 65002	Diga Diga Doo/Lullaby In Rhythm (78)	8
55	Capitol KPL 106	THE BOOTS MUSSULLI QUARTET (10" LP)	12

(see also Stan Kenton)

MUSTANG

| 67 | Parlophone R 5579 | Why/Here, There And Everywhere | 20 |

MUS-TWANGS

| 61 | Mercury AMT 1140 | Roch Lomond/Marie | 8 |

MY BLOODY VALENTINE

MUTANTS
77	Rox ROX 002	Boss Man/Back Yard Boys (p/s)... 6
78	Rox ROX 005	School Teacher/Hard Time/Lady (p/s, red vinyl) 6

MUTE DRIVERS
80s	Mute Drivers MD 001	MUTE DRIVERS (LP, with insert in handmade painted sleeve, 300 only)....... 15
	(see also Anonymes)	

MUTT 'N' JEFF
66	Decca F 12335	Don't Nag Me Ma/Strolling The Blues 10

MU-ZIQ
93	Rephlex CAT 018	Bluff Limbo (remixes) (2 x 12", 800 only) 20

MY BLOODY VALENTINE
86	Fever FEV 5X	No Place To Go/Moonlight (p/s)... 15
86	Fever FEV 5	GEEK! (12" EP)... 20
86	Kaleid. Sound KS 101	THE NEW RECORD BY MY BLOODY VALENTINE (12" EP) 40
87	Lazy LAZY 04	Sunny Sundae Smile/Paint A Rainbow (p/s)............................... 20
87	Lazy LAZY 04T	Sunny Sundae Smile/Paint A Rainbow/Kiss The Eclipse/ Sylvie's Head (12", p/s) 40
87	Lazy LAZY 07	Strawberry Wine/Never Say Goodbye/Can I Touch You (12", p/s).............. 30
88	Creation CRE 055	You Made Me Realise/Slow (die-cut company sleeve) 6
88	Creation CRE 055T	You Made Me Realise/Slow/Thorn/Cigarette/Drive It All Over Me (12", p/s)...... 10
88	Creation CRE 061	Feed Me With Your Kiss/Emptiness Inside (plays "I Believe") (die-cut company sleeve)... 6
88	Creation CRE 061T	Feed Me With Your Kiss/I Believe/Emptiness Inside/I Need No Trust (12", p/s) 10
89	Creation CRE 085	Tremolo/To Hear Knows When (p/s) 5
89	Lyntone CAT 067	Sugar/PACIFIC: December, With The Day (square flexdisc free with *The Catalogue* magazine, issue 67) 10/7
87	Lazy LAZY 08	ECSTACY (mini-LP, 3,000 only) 30
88	Creation CRELP 040	ISN'T ANYTHING (LP, initial 3,000 copies with bonus 7", "Instrumental"/ "Instrumental" [CRE FRE 4, no p/s] & stickered sleeve) 18
89	Lazy LAZY 12	ECSTACY & WINE (LP, compilation of LAZY 07 & LAZY 08).................. 20
89	Lazy LAZY 12CD	ECSTACY & WINE (CD) 40

MY CAPTAINS
81	4AD AD 103	Fall/Converse/History/Nothing (EP)....................................... 8

MY DEAR WATSON
68	Parlophone R 5687	Elusive Face/The Shame Just Drained 20
68	Parlophone R 5737	Make This Day Last/Stop, Stop, I'll Be There............................ 20
70	DJM DJS 224	Have You Seen Your Saviour/White Line Road 8
	(see also Johnny & Copycats)	

BILLY MYLES
57	HMV POP 423	The Joker (That's What They Call Me)/Honey Bee........................ 20
57	HMV POP 423	The Joker (That's What They Call Me)/Honey Bee (78) 15

MEG MYLES
56   Capitol CL 14555   Sing On, Baby/Will You Shed A Tear For Me? 6

MY LIFE STORY
86   Think Tank CHAPTER 1   HOME SWEET ZOO EP (gatefold p/s, 500 only) 70
93   M. Tongue MOTHER 2MC   Girl A, Girl B, Boy C/You Don't Sparkle (In My Eyes)/Star Colliding/
                                You Don't Sparkle (Big Screen Soundtrack) (cassette) 6
93   M. Tongue MOTHER 2T   Girl A, Girl B, Boy C/You Don't Sparkle (In My Eyes)/Star Colliding/
                                You Don't Sparkle (Big Screen Soundtrack) (12", p/s) 15
93   M. Tongue MOTHER 2CD   Girl A, Girl B, Boy C/You Don't Sparkle (In My Eyes)/Star Colliding/
                                You Don't Sparkle (Big Screen Soundtrack) (CD) 18
94   M. Tongue MOTHER 3S   Funny Ha Ha/The Lady Is A Tramp (p/s) 6
94   M. Tongue MOTHER 3T   Funny Ha Ha/The Lady Is A Tramp/These Words Are Haunting/
                                Funny Peculiar (12", p/s) 15
94   M. Tongue MOTHER 3CD   Funny Ha Ha/The Lady Is A Tramp/These Words Are Haunting/
                                Funny Peculiar (CD) 15
94   M. Tongue MOTHER 4T   You Don't Sparkle (In My Eyes)/First Person Singular/Stood Among Friends/
                                You Don't Sparkle (Quintet) (12", p/s) 8
94   M. Tongue MOTHER 004CD   You Don't Sparkle (In My Eyes) (Radio Edit)/First Person Singular/
                                Stood Amongst Friends/You Don't Sparkle (In My Eyes) (Quintet) (CD) 15
94   M. Tongue MOTHER 005CD   MORNINGTON CRESCENT COMPANION: Checkmate/Outdoor Miner/
                                Under The Ice/Forever (CD, 2,000 only) 25
97   Parlophone 12RDJ 6474   Duchess (John '00' Fleming Remix)/(Xenomania Remix)
                                (12", title stickered sleeve, promo only) 15
95   M. Tongue MOTHERLP 1   MORNINGTON CRESCENT (LP) 12
95   M. Tongue MOTHERCD 1   MORNINGTON CRESCENT (CD) 15

MY LORDE SHERIFFE'S COMPLAINTE
79   Frog FROG 1   MY LORDE SHERIFFE'S COMPLAINTE (LP, private pressing) 20

MYND MUZIC
94   Poor Person Prod.   IMAGINE THIS (LP, handmade sleeve, 500 only) 20

ROWLAND MYRES
74   Deroy DER 1063   JUST FOR THE RECORD (LP, private pressing,
                                also listed as Music Sound Enterprise MSE 1) 150

MYRTELLES
63   Oriole CB 1805   Don't Wanna Cry Again/Just Let Me Cry 18
     (see also Sue & Sunshine, Sue & Sunny, Stockingtops)

MY RUIN
99   Snapper SMAS 106   Tainted Love/Blasphemous Girl (p/s, red vinyl, 1,000 only) 6

MYSTERE FIVE'S
80   Flicknife FLS 001   No Message/Shake Some Action (p/s) 4
81   Flicknife FLS 202   Never Say Thank You/Heart Rules The Head (p/s) 4
     (see also Wayne County & Electric Chairs)

LES MYSTERES DES VOIX BULGARES
86   4AD AD 603   Prïtourïtze Planinata/Polegnala E Todora (no p/s, promo only) 8

MYSTERIES
64   Decca F 11919   Give Me Rhythm And Blues/Teardrops 18

WILLIAM MYSTERIOUS
82   Mezzanine MEZ 1   Security Of Noise/Alright (p/s, with Fay Fife & Revettes) 6
     (see also Rezillos, Revillos)

MYSTERY GIRLS
80   Strange HAM 001   SOUNDS LIKE (EP) 5
81   Strange HAM 002   I'm A Believer/Modern Mystery Pop/Walking Backwards (p/s) 6

MYSTERY GIRLS
88   Mystery Girls MGS 2   I Promise To Rock You Forever/Nuthin' To Do (stickered w/l, promo only) 6

MYSTERY GUESTS
80   Boys Own/Heater   Wurlitzer Junction/The Merry Shark You Are
     Volume BO 1   (handmade stickered white labels) 5
81   Boys Own BO 3   The Sparrow That Ate New York/The Nude (p/s) 4

MYSTERY MAKER
77   Caves UHC 3   MYSTERY MAKER (LP, private pressing with booklet) 125

MYSTIC INSTITUTE
92   Evolution EVO 06   CYBERDON EP (12") 30
     (see also Global Communications, Reload, Link)

MYSTIC MOODS
73   Warner Bros K 16265   Cosmic Sea/Awakening 6
74   Warner Bros K 46250   AWAKENING (LP) 12

MYSTIC NUMBER NATIONAL BANK
69   Probe SPB 1001   THE MYSTIC NUMBER NATIONAL BANK (LP) 12

MYSTICS
59   HMV POP 646   Hushabye/Adam And Eve 70
59   Top Rank JAR 243   Don't Take The Stars/So Tenderly 30

MYTHRA
79   Guardian GRMA 16   DEATH & DESTINY (EP, no p/s) 8
80   Streetbeat LAMP 2   Death Or Destiny/Killer/U.F.O. (some with p/s) 100/10
80   Streetbeat 12 LAMP 2   Death Or Destiny/Killer/Overlord/U.F.O. (12", some with p/s) 120/20

NAAFI SANDWICH
80   Absurd ABSURD 8   Slice One/Slice Two (p/s) 10

NABAY
80   Grapevine GRP 143   Believe It Or Not/Believe It Or Not (Instrumental) 6

RICKY NADIR
79   Charisma CB 339   The Polaroid/PETER HAMMILL: The Old School Tie 10
(see also Peter Hammill)

NA FILI
74   Dolphin DOL 1008   CHANTER'S TUNE (LP) 10

NA H-ORGANAICH
73   Beltona SBE 145   THE GREAT GAELIC SOUND OF (LP) 15
74   Beltona SBE 160   GAEL FORCE 3 (LP) 15

JIMMY NAIL
85   Virgin VSS 764   Love Don't Live Here Anymore/Night For Day (shaped picture disc) 4

NAKED LUNCH
81   Ramkup CAC 003   Rabies/Slipping Again (p/s) 4

NAKED TRUTH
70   Deram DM 287   Two Little Rooms/Rag Doll Boy 5

NAME
80   Din Disc DIN 14   Forget Art, Let's Dance/Misfits (p/s) 5

NAMES
80   Factory FAC 29   Nightshift/I Wish I Could Speak Your Language (p/s) 4

NANETTE
70   Columbia DB 8659   Flying Machine/You're Wasting Your Time 6
70   Columbia DB 8673   Every Night When I Cry Myself To Sleep/Jamie 5
70   Columbia DB 8733   Let Me Be The One/To Be Loved 5
71   Columbia DB 8751   Everybody's Singing Right Now/Could I Forget 5
70   Columbia SCX 6398   NANETTE (LP) 15

ED NANGLE
68   Blue Cat BS 120   Good Girl/ENFORCERS: Musical Fever 15
68   Coxsone CS 7038   Whipping The Prince (actually by Ed Nangle & Alton Ellis & Soul Vendors)/
                          HEPTONES: If You Knew 25

NINO NANNI
58   London SAHD 6043   CHIC TO CHIC (LP) 12

NICK NANTOS & HIS FIREBALLERS
63   Summit LSE 2042   GUITARS ON FIRE (EP) 12
64   Summit ATL 4114   GUITARS ON FIRE (LP) 12
(see also Bill Haley & Comets)

NAOMI
70   Gayfeet GS 207   You're Not My Kind/GAYTONES: You're Not My Kind (Version II) 6
70   High Note HS 047   Natural Woman/GAYTONES: Natural Woman – Version 5
(see also Derrick Morgan, Tommy McCook)

NAPOLEON XIV
66   Warner Bros WB 5831   They're Coming To Take Me Away Ha-Haa!/
                          !Aah-Ah Yawa Em Ekat Ot Gnimoc Er'Yeht 6
66   Warner Bros WB 5853   I'm In Love With My Little Red Tricycle/Doin' The Napoleon 10
66   Warner Bros W 1661   THEY'RE COMING TO TAKE ME AWAY HA-HA-A! (LP) 50
(see also Jerry Samuels, Kim Fowley)

MARTY NAPOLEON
56   London EZ-N 19001   MARTY NAPOLEON SWINGS AND SINGS (EP) 8

PETER NARDINI
80s   Kettle KS 701   I Think You're Great/Ma Maw's A Mod (some in p/s) 15/8

NARNIA
74   Myrrh MYR 1007   NARNIA — ASLAN IS NOT A TAME LION (LP) 100
(see also After The Fire, Pauline Filby)

BILLY NASH
61   Philips PB 1181   Sunset/Nobody Loves Me Like You (as Billy Nash Combo) 4
63   Philips 370 406 BF   The Madison Step/Madison Rhythm (as Billy Nash Rock Band) 4

GENE NASH
59   Capitol CL 15042   I'm An Eskimo Too/Ja, Ja, Ja (Deutsche Rock 'N Roll) 18

GRAHAM NASH
71   Atlantic 2091 096   Chicago/Simple Man 4
71   Atlantic 2091 135   Military Madness/I Used To Be A King 4
71   Atlantic 2401 011   SONGS FOR BEGINNERS (LP) 10
(see also Hollies, Crosby Stills Nash & Young)

JOHNNY NASH

57	HMV POP 402	Ladder Of Love/I'll Walk Alone	7
57	HMV POP 402	Ladder Of Love/I'll Walk Alone (78)	12
58	HMV POP 435	Won't You Let Me Share My Love With You?/A Very Special Love	6
58	HMV POP 435	Won't You Let Me Share My Love With You?/A Very Special Love (78)	15
58	HMV POP 475	It's Easy To Say/My Pledge To You	6
58	HMV POP 475	It's Easy To Say/My Pledge To You (78)	18
58	HMV POP 553	Almost In Your Arms/Midnight Moonlight	5
58	HMV POP 553	Almost In Your Arms/Midnight Moonlight (78)	18
59	HMV POP 597	Walk With Faith In Your Heart/Roots Of Heaven	5
59	HMV POP 597	Walk With Faith In Your Heart/Roots Of Heaven (78)	25
59	HMV POP 620	As Time Goes By/Voice Of Love	5
59	HMV POP 651	And The Angels Sing/Baby, Baby, Baby	5
59	HMV POP 673	Take A Giant Step/Imagination	5
60	HMV POP 746	A Place In The Sun/Goodbye	5
60	HMV POP 822	Somebody/Kisses	5
62	Warner Bros WB 65	Don't Take Away Your Love/Moment Of Weakness	5
62	Warner Bros WB 76	Ol' Man River/My Dear Little Sweetheart	5
63	Warner Bros WB 93	Cigareets, Whiskey And Wild, Wild Women/I'm Moving On	15
64	Pye International 7N 25250	Love Ain't Nothin'/Talk To Me	15
65	Chess CRS 8005	Strange Feelin'/Rainin' In My Heart	12
66	Pye International 7N 25353	Let's Move And Groove (Together)/Understanding	5
66	Pye International 7N 25363	One More Time/Tryin' To Find Her	5
68	Regal Zono. RZ 3010	Hold Me Tight/Let's Move And Groove Together	5
68	Major Minor MM 586	You Got Soul/Don't Cry	5
69	Major Minor MM 603	Cupid/People In Love	5
69	MGM MGM 1480	(I'm So) Glad You're My Baby/Stormy	12
64	RCA Victor RCX 7163	PRESENTING JOHNNY NASH (EP)	80
59	HMV CLP 1251	JOHNNY NASH (LP)	30
59	HMV CLP 1299	QUIET HOUR WITH JOHNNY NASH (LP)	20
60	HMV CLP 1325/CSD 1288	I GOT RHYTHM (LP, mono/stereo)	25/30
62	Encore ENC 2005	LET'S GET LOST (LP)	12
69	Major Minor MMLP/SMLP 47	YOU GOT SOUL (LP)	15
69	Major Minor MMLP/SMLP 56	SOUL FOLK (LP)	15
69	Major Minor MMLP/SMLP 63	PRINCE OF PEACE (LP)	15
73	CBS Q 56449	MY MERRY GO ROUND (LP, quadrophonic)	12

JOHNNY NASH & KIM WESTON

69	Major Minor SMLP 54	JOHNNY NASH AND KIM WESTON (LP)	120

(see also Kim Weston)

TONY NASH

70	Hot Rod HR 110	Keep On Trying/WINSTON JAMES: Just Can't Do Without Your Love	6

NASH THE SLASH

81	Smash Hits (no cat. no.)	Swing-Shift (Flexi-Version)/ORCHESTRAL MANOEUVRES IN THE DARK: Pretending To See The Future (live) (blue flexidisc with *Smash Hits* mag)	6/4

NASHVILLE FIVE

62	Decca F 11427	Stand Up And Say That/Like Nashville	6
62	Decca F 11484	Some Other Love/Brainwave	6
62	Decca DFE 6706	LIKE NASHVILLE (EP)	35

NASHVILLE TEENS

64	Decca F 11930	Tobacco Road/I Like It Like That	6
64	Decca F 12000	Google Eye (some misspelled "Goggle Eye" on label)/T.N.T.	7
65	Decca F 12089	Find My Way Back Home/Devil-In-Law	7
65	Decca F 12143	The Little Bird/Whatcha Gonna Do?	6
65	Decca F 12255	I Know How It Feels To Be Loved/Soon Forgotten	6
66	Decca F 12316	The Hard Way/Upside Down	10
66	Decca F 12458	Forbidden Fruit/Revived 45 Time	12
66	Decca F 12542	That's My Woman/Words	12
67	Decca F 12580	I'm Coming Home/Searching	7
67	Decca F 12657	The Biggest Night Of Her Life/Last Minute	7
68	Decca F 12754	All Along The Watchtower/Sun-Dog	7
69	Major Minor MM 599	The Lament Of The Cherokee Reservation Indian/Looking For You	10
69	Decca F 12929	Tobacco Road/All Along The Watchtower	6
71	Parlophone R 5925	Ella James/Tennessee Woman	10
72	Parlophone R 5961	You Shouldn't Have Been So Nice/Tell The People (unissued)	
72	Enterprise ENT 001	Lawdy Miss Clawdy/Let It Rock: Break Up	6
77	Sky 1007	Tobacco Road/Chips And Peas	5
81	Go GO 2	Midnight/Live For The Summer (p/s)	5
82	Shanghai HAI 200	LIVE AT THE RED HOUSE (12" EP)	8
84	Butt FUNEP 4	Tobacco Road/Find My Way Back Home/Born To Be Wild (p/s)	5
65	Decca DFE 8600	THE NASHVILLE TEENS (EP)	45
75	New World NW 6002	THE NASHVILLE TEENS (LP)	30

(see also Arizona Swamp Company, Jerry Lee Lewis, Carl Perkins)

NASTY FACTS

81	5th Column FC 2	Drive My Car/Gotta Get To You/Crazy 'Bout You (p/s)	5

NASTY MEDIA

78	Lightning GIL 542	Spiked Copy/Winter (p/s)	10

NATCHBAND

78	Far In FARS 01	Cadillac (Made In USA)/Being From The Sky (p/s)	6

NATIONAL-ELLS

67	Parlophone R 5609	Mr. Moon/Dance, Dance	5

MINT VALUE £

NATIONAL HEAD BAND
71	Warner Bros K 46094	ALBERT 1 (LP)	25

(see also Caravan, Gary Moore, Toe-Fat, Uriah Heep)

NATIONAL HEALTH
78	Affinity AFF 6	NATIONAL HEALTH (LP)	12
78	Charly CRL 5010	OF QUEUES AND CURES (LP)	12

(see also Hatfield & The North)

NATIONAL LAMPOON
78	Island HELP 8	RADIO DINNER (LP)	10

NATIONAL PINION POLE
66	Planet PLF 111	Make Your Mark Little Man/I Was The One You Came In With	15

NATURAL ACOUSTIC BAND
73	RCA RCA 2324	Echoes/Is It True Blue	5
72	RCA SF 8272	LEARNING TO LIVE (LP, gatefold sleeve)	15
72	RCA SF 8314	BRANCHING IN (LP)	15

(see also Krysia)

NATURAL BRIDGE BUNCH
69	Atlantic 584 231	Pig Snoots (Parts 1 & 2)	5

NATURAL FOUR
75	Atlantic K 56142	HEAVEN RIGHT HERE ON EARTH (LP)	25

NATURAL GAS
76	Private Stock PVT 71	The Right Time/Miracle Mile	5
76	Private Stock PSS 1	NATURAL GAS (EP, promo only)	8
76	Private Stock PVLP 1007	NATURAL GAS (LP, with inner sleeve)	12

(see also Badfinger, Blue Goose, Humble Pie, Uriah Heep, Quiver)

NATURAL MAGIC
75	Oyster OYR 102	Strawberry Fields Forever/Isolated Lady	10

(see also Roger Glover, Eddie Hardin)

NATURALS (U.S.)
55	MGM SP 1123	The Finger Of Suspicion Points At You/You Forgot To Remember	8
57	MGM MGM 939	The Buccaneers/The Ballad Of Sir Lancelot	6
57	MGM MGM 939	The Buccaneers/The Ballad Of Sir Lancelot (78)	8

(see also Debbie Reynolds)

NATURALS (U.K.)
64	Parlophone R 5116	Daisy Chain/That Girl	6
64	Parlophone R 5165	I Should Have Known Better/Didn't I?	6
64	Parlophone R 5202	It Was You/Look At Me Now	10
65	Parlophone R 5257	Blue Roses/Shame On You	10

(see also Living Daylights, Greatest Show On Earth)

NATURE ZONE
76	London HLU 10537	Porcupine/Rhythm Will Keep Us Together	5

NAVIGATOR
96	Noisebox NBX 022	Kill Taker/Swing/We Will All Burn Together (spearmint coloured vinyl, p/s, 500 only)	7
96	Noisebox NBX 026	A Little Astronomy/At The End Of The Bay (blue vinyl, p/s, 500 only)	4
97	Noisebox NBX 027	When The Wires Fall/Impossible Without (cherry-coloured vinyl, 750 only)	4

JERRY NAYLOR
61	Top Rank JAR 591	Stop Your Crying/You're Thirteen	15
67	Stateside SS 2029	Sweet Violets/Temptation Leads Me	6
70	CBS 4882	But For Love/Angeline	5
70	CBS 5265	Marie/If I Promise	5
71	CBS 7093	Come On Love/Las Virgenese Road	5

SHEL NAYLOR
63	Decca F 11776	How Deep Is The Ocean/La Bamba	12
64	Decca F 11856	One Fine Day/It's Gonna Happen Soon	70

(see also Lieutenant Pigeon, Stavely Makepeace)

NAZARETH
72	Pegasus PGS 2	Dear John/Friends	20
72	Pegasus PGS 2	Dear John/Friends (2nd issue, PEG label, B-side lists 'Occasional Failure')	30
72	Pegasus BCP 3	Dear John/Witchdoctor Woman/Morning Dew (unreleased, promo only, stamped white labels and insert)	50
72	Pegasus PGS 4	Morning Dew/Spinning Top (PEG label)	20
72	Pegasus BCP 8	Fool About You/Woke Up This Morning/Morning Dew (unreleased, promo only, handwritten white labels)	50
72	Pegasus PGS 5	If You See My Baby/Hard Living (PEG label)	20
73	Mooncrest MOON 1	Broken Down Angel/Witchdoctor Woman (solid or push-out centre)	each 5
73	Mooncrest MOON 9	Bad Bad Boy/Hard Living/Spinning Top (initially in p/s)	10/4
73	Mooncrest MOON 14	This Flight Tonight/Called Her Name	5
74	Mooncrest MOON 22	Shanghai'd In Shanghai/Love, Now You're Gone	5
74	Mooncrest MOON 37	Love Hurts/Down	5
75	Mooncrest MOON 44	Hair Of The Dog/Too Bad, Too Sad	5
75	Mooncrest MOON 47	My White Bicycle/Miss Misery	5
75	Mountain TOP 3	Holy Roller/Railroad Boy	5
76	Mountain TOP 8	Carry Out Feelings/Lift The Lid	5
76	Mountain TOP 14	You're The Violin/Loretta	5
76	Mountain TOP 21	I Don't Want To Go On Without You/Good Love	5
77	Mountain TOP 22	Somebody To Roll/Vancouver Shakedown	5
77	Mountain NAZ 1	HOT TRACKS (EP, p/s)	5

78	Mountain NAZ 2	Gone Dead Train/Greens/Desolation Road (p/s)	5
78	Mountain TOP 37	Place In Your Heart/Kentucky Fried Blues (company sleeve)	5
78	Mountain TOP 37	Place In Your Heart/Kentucky Fried Blues (mispressing, B-side plays Bee Gees track, company sleeve)	20
79	Mountain NAZ 3	May The Sunshine/Expect No Mercy (p/s)	5
79	Mountain NAZ 4	Whatever You Want Babe/Telegram Parts 1, 2 & 3 (p/s, some purple vinyl)	10/5
79	Mountain TOP 45	Star/Born To Love (p/s)	5
80	Mountain TOP 50	Holiday/Ship Of Dreams	5
81	NEMS BSD 1	LIVE (double pack, gatefold p/s)	6
81	NEMS NES 301	Dressed To Kill/Pop The Silo (p/s)	5
81	NEMS NES 302	Morning Dew (re-recording)/Juicy Lucy (no p/s)	5
82	NEMS Int. NIS 101	Love Leads To Madness/Take The Rap (no p/s)	4
83	NEMS Int. NIS 102	Games/You Love Another (p/s)	5
83	NEMS Int. NIS 103	Dream On/Juicy Lucy (no p/s)	4
83	Mountain NEP 2	HOT TRACKS (EP, reissue, picture disc)	5
84	Vertigo VER 13	Ruby Tuesday/Sweetheart Tree (p/s)	5
84	Vertigo VERX 13	Ruby Tuesday/Sweetheart Tree/This Month's Messiah/Do You Think About It (12", p/s)	12
71	Pegasus PEG 10	NAZARETH (LP, 1st issue, Pegasus picture label/matt sleeve)	25
72	Pegasus PEG 10	NAZARETH (LP, 2nd issue, PEG label/glossy sleeve)	20
72	Pegasus PEG 14	EXERCISES (LP, gatefold sleeve)	18
74	Mooncrest CREST 10	NAZARETH (LP, reissue)	12
74	Mooncrest CREST 14	EXERCISES (LP, reissue, gatefold sleeve)	12
74	Mooncrest CREST 15	RAMPANT (LP, embossed sleeve with inner & dollar sticker insert)	12
85	Sahara SAH 130	SOUND ELIXIR (LP, Marimba label, withdrawn)	15

(see also Dan McCafferty, Mark Five, Sensational Alex Harvey Band, Tandoori Cassette, Billy Rankin)

NAZIS AGAINST FASCISM
| 79 | Truth TRUTH 1 | Sid Did It (Intelligible)/Sid Did It (Radio Version) (p/s, 2 different issues) | each 6 |

(see also Vibrators)

NAZZ
68	Atlantic 584 224	Open My Eyes/Hello It's Me (unissued)	
68	Screen Gems SGC 219001	Open My Eyes/Hello It's Me	10
69	Screen Gems SGC 219002	Hello It's Me/Crowded	10
69	Screen Gems SGC 219003	Not Wrong Long/Under The Ice	10
69	Screen Gems SGC 221001	NAZZ (LP)	35

(see also Todd Rundgren)

'N BETWEENS
| 66 | Columbia DB 8080 | You Better Run/Evil Witchman (demos credit In-Be-Tweens) | 225 |

(see also Slade, Vendors)

YOUSSOU N'DOUR & PETER GABRIEL
| 89 | Virgin VSCD 1207 | The Lion (Gaiende)/Macoy/The Lion (Gaiende) (African Mix) (3" CD, card p/s) | 7 |

(see also Peter Gabriel)

CHRIS NEAL
| 71 | Fly BUG 15 | Blame It All On Eve/All The Time In The World (p/s) | 6 |

JOHNNY NEAL & STARLINERS
| 65 | Pye 7N 15388 | And I Will Love You/Walk Baby Walk | 60 |
| 70 | Parlophone R 5870 | Put Your Hand In The Hand/Now | 5 |

(see also Storyteller)

TOMMY NEAL
| 68 | Vocalion VL 9290 | Goin' To A Happening/Tee Ta | 18 |

NEANDERTHAL
| 79 | Cave MAN 1 | Cromagnon Sucks/Hey Zal!/No Mean City | 12 |

NEARLY NORMAL
| 82 | Insurrection Now! IN 1 | Bedtime/Die Baby Die (p/s) | 5 |

NEAT CHANGE
| 68 | Decca F 12809 | I Lied To Auntie May/Sandman (some copies in foldout p/s) | 30/15 |

(see also Peter Banks, English Rose)

NECROMANDUS
| 90 | Reflection MM 09 | QUICKSAND DREAM (LP, 500 only) | 15 |

BERNIE NEE
| 58 | Philips PB 794 | Lend Me Your Comb/Medal Of Honour | 18 |
| 58 | Philips PB 794 | Lend Me Your Comb/Medal Of Honour (78) | 20 |

(see also Bernie Knee)

LOUIS NEEFS
| 69 | Columbia DB 8561 | Jennifer Jennings/I Love You | 20 |

ELGIN NEELY
| 65 | Vogue V 9240 | Four Walls/I Could Be | 6 |

NEGATIVES
| 80 | Aardvark STEAL 1 | Electric Waltz/Money Talk (p/s) | 5 |
| 81 | Aardvark STEAL 3 | Scene Of The Crime (p/s) | 8 |

FRED NEIL
| 69 | Elektra EKSN 45036 | Candy Man/The Water Is Wide | 6 |
| 69 | Capitol CL 15616 | Everybody's Talkin'/Badi-Da | 6 |

DON NEILSON
| 60 | Philips BF 1058 | The House Is Haunted/For All We Know | 6 |
| 63 | Piccadilly 7N 35103 | I Will Live My Life For You/How Do You Keep From Crying | 5 |

NEKTAR

73	United Artists NEK 1	What Ya Gonna Do?/Day In The Life Of A Preacher Pt. One (Edit) (p/s)	15
74	United Artists UP 35706	Fidgety Queen/Little Boy	10
75	United Artists UP 35853	Astral Man/Nelly The Elephant	10
73	United Artists UAD 60041/2	SOUNDS LIKE THIS (2-LP)	30
74	United Artists UAS 29499	A TAB IN THE OCEAN (LP, gatefold sleeve)	25
74	United Artists UAS 29545	REMEMBER THE FUTURE (LP)	25
74	United Artists UAG 29680	DOWN TO EARTH (LP)	25
76	Decca SKL-R 5250	RECYCLED (LP)	20

BILL NELSON('S RED NOISE)

79	Harvest HAR 5176	Furniture Music/Wondertoys That Last Forever/Acquitted By Mirrors (p/s, red vinyl)	4
79	Harvest HAR 5183	Revolt Into Style/Out Of Touch (p/s, blue vinyl)	4
85	Les Disques Du Crépuscule TWI 013	Rooms With Brittle Views/Dada Guitare (p/s, at least 2 different designs)	4
85	Cocteau JEAN 1	PERMANENT FLAME SINGLES BOX (box set of 5 singles)	12
71	Smile LAF 2182/ HG 116	NORTHERN DREAM (LP, 250 only, numbered, in foldover gatefold sleeve with booklet)	55
70s	Smile LAF 2182/HG 116	NORTHERN DREAM (LP, repressing, gatefold sleeve & lyric sheet)	10
85	Cocteau JEAN 2	TRIAL BY INTIMACY (THE BOOK OF SPLENDOURS) (4-LP, box set, with book & postcards, initial copies misspelt as "The Book Splendours")	25
86	KPM/Themes TIM	CHAMELEON — THE MUSIC OF BILL NELSON (LP, library issue)	12

(see also Astral Navigations, A To Austr, Gagalactyca, Be-Bop Deluxe, Scala)

CLARE NELSON

| 59 | MGM MGM 1025 | The Valley Of Love/You Are My Sunshine | 6 |

DAVID NELSON

| 64 | Philips BF 1321 | Somebody Loves Me/Well I Have | 8 |

EARL NELSON

| 59 | London HLW 8950 | No Time To Cry/Come On | 15 |
| 59 | London HLW 8950 | No Time To Cry/Come On (78) | 35 |

OZZIE & HARRIET NELSON

| 59 | London HA-P 2145 | OZZIE AND HARRIET NELSON (LP) | 35 |

RICK(Y) NELSON

78s

57	HMV POP 355	I'm Walkin'/A Teenager's Romance (78)	60
57	HMV POP 390	You're My One And Only Love/BARNEY KESSEL: Honey Rock (78)	70
57	London HLP 8499	Be-Bop Baby/Have I Told You Lately That I Love You (78)	30
58	London HLP 8542	Stood Up/Waitin' In School (78)	30
58	London HLP 8594	Believe What You Say/My Bucket's Got A Hole In It (78)	30
58	London HLP 8670	Poor Little Fool/Don't Leave Me This Way (78)	20
58	London HLP 8732	Someday/I Got A Feeling (78)	30
58	London HLP 8738	Lonesome Town/My Babe (78)	35
59	London HLP 8817	It's Late/Never Be Anyone Else But You (78)	35
59	London HLP 8927	Just A Little Too Much/Sweeter Than You (78)	45
60	London HLP 9021	I Wanna Be Loved/Mighty Good (78)	75
60	London HLP 9121	Young Emotions/Right By My Side (78)	90
60	London HLP 9188	Yes, Sir, That's My Baby/I'm Not Afraid (78)	120

(All the above 78s were credited to Ricky Nelson.)

SINGLES

57	HMV POP 355	I'm Walkin'/A Teenager's Romance (gold or silver label lettering)	125/75
57	HMV POP 390	You're My One And Only Love/BARNEY KESSEL: Honey Rock	100
57	London HLP 8499	Be-Bop Baby/Have I Told You Lately That I Love You	30
58	London HLP 8542	Stood Up/Waitin' In School	18
58	London HLP 8594	Believe What You Say/My Bucket's Got A Hole In It	15
58	London HLP 8670	Poor Little Fool/Don't Leave Me This Way	7
58	London HLP 8732	Someday/I Got A Feeling	7
58	London HLP 8738	Lonesome Town/My Babe	12
59	London HLP 8817	It's Late/Never Be Anyone Else But You (all black or silver-top label)	8/7
59	London HLP 8894	Just A Little Too Much/Sweeter Than You (unreleased)	
59	London HLP 8927	Just A Little Too Much/Sweeter Than You (triangular centre)	10

(The above 45s were originally issued with triangular centres; later round-centre copies are worth half to two-thirds the value.)

59	London HL 7081	Just A Little Too Much/Sweeter Than You (export issue)	10
60	London HLP 9021	I Wanna Be Loved/Mighty Good	7
60	London HLP 9121	Young Emotions/Right By My Side	6
60	London HLP 9188	Yes, Sir, That's My Baby/I'm Not Afraid	6
61	London HLP 9260	You Are The Only One/Milk Cow Blues	10
61	London HLP 9260	You Are The One And Only/Milk Cow Blues (with different label credit)	10
61	London HLP 9347	Hello Mary Lou Goodbye Heart/Travelin' Man (later copies as "Hello Marylou Goodbye Heart")	6
61	London HLP 9440	Everlovin'/A Wonder Like You	6

(The above singles were credited to Ricky Nelson; all subsequent singles were credited to Rick Nelson unless stated.)

62	London HLP 9524	Young World/Summertime	10
62	London HLP 9583	Teen Age Idol/I've Got My Eyes On You (And I Like What I See)	7
63	London HLP 9648	It's Up To You/I Need You	7
63	Brunswick 05885	I Got A Woman/You Don't Love Me Anymore	6
63	Brunswick 05889	String Along/Gypsy Woman	8
63	Brunswick 05895	Fools Rush In/Down Home	6
64	Brunswick 05900	For You/That's All She Wrote	6
64	Liberty LIB 66004	Today's Teardrops/Thank You Darling	8
64	Brunswick 05908	The Very Thought Of You/I Wonder	6
64	Brunswick 05918	Lonely Corner/There's Nothing I Can Say	6

MINT VALUE £

64	Brunswick 05924	A Happy Guy/Don't Breathe A Word	6
65	Brunswick 05939	Come Out Dancin'/Yesterday's Love	10
66	Brunswick 05964	Louisiana Man/You Just Can't Quit (as Ricky Nelson)	12
66	Liberty LIB 12033	I Need You/Wonder Like You	7
69	MCA MU 1106	She Belongs To Me/Promises	5
70	MCA MU 1124	Red Balloon/I Shall Be Released	6
71	MCA MU 1135	Life/California (with Stone Canyon Band)	6
72	MCA MU 1147	Love Minus Zero: No Limit/Gypsy Pilot (with Stone Canyon Band)	5
72	MCA MU 1165	Garden Party/So Long Mama	6
73	MCA MUS 1181	Palace Guard/A Flower Opens Gently By Itself	5
73	MCA MUS 1225	Lifestream/Evil Woman Child	5
74	MCA MCA 126	Windfall/Legacy (with Stone Canyon Band)	5
74	MCA MCA 144	One Night Stand/Lifestream (with Stone Canyon Band)	5
75	MCA MCA 198	Try (Try To Fall In Love)/Louisiana Belle (with Stone Canyon Band)	5
77	Epic S EPC 5821	You Can't Dance/It's Another Day	5

EPs

58	London RE-P 1141	RICKY PART 1 (EP)	40
58	London RE-P 1142	RICKY PART 2 (EP)	40
58	London RE-P 1143	RICKY PART 3 (EP)	40
58	London RE-P 1144	RICKY PART 4 (EP)	40
59	London RE-P 1168	RICKY NELSON PART 1 (EP)	35
59	London RE-P 1169	RICKY NELSON PART 2 (EP)	35
59	London RE-P 1170	RICKY NELSON PART 3 (EP)	35
59	London RE-P 1200	RICKY SINGS AGAIN PART 1 (EP)	35
59	London RE-P 1201	RICKY SINGS AGAIN PART 2 (EP)	35
60	London RE-P 1238	I GOT A FEELING (EP)	35
60	London RE-P 1249	RICKY SINGS SPIRITUALS (EP)	35
61	London RE-P 1300	RICKY NELSON PART 4 (EP)	40

(The above EPs were credited to Ricky Nelson; all subsequent EPs were credited to Rick Nelson.)

62	London RE-P 1339	IT'S A YOUNG WORLD (EP)	35
63	London RE-P 1362	IT'S UP TO YOU (EP)	35
63	Brunswick OE 9502	ONE BOY TOO LATE (EP)	35
64	Liberty LEP 4001	SINGS FOR YOU (EP)	35
64	Liberty LEP 4019	THAT'S ALL (EP)	40
65	Liberty LEP 4028	I'M IN LOVE AGAIN (EP)	45
65	Brunswick OE 9512	HAPPY GUY (EP)	35

LPs

57	London HA-P 2080	RICKY (LP)	50
58	London HA-P 2119	RICKY NELSON (LP)	50
59	London HA-P 2159	RICKY SINGS AGAIN (LP)	50
59	London HA-P 2206	SONGS BY RICKY (LP)	50
60	London HA-P 2290	MORE SONGS BY RICKY (LP, gatefold sleeve, also stereo SAH-P 6102)	40/50
61	London HA-P 2379	RICK IS 21 (LP, also stereo SAH-P 6179)	40/50

(The above LPs were credited to Ricky Nelson; all subsequent LPs were credited to Rick Nelson.)

62	London HA-P 2445	ALBUM SEVEN (LP, also stereo SAH-P 6236)	40/50
63	London HA-P 8066	IT'S UP TO YOU (LP)	40
63	Brunswick LAT 8545	FOR YOUR SWEET LOVE (LP, also stereo STA 8545)	35/40
64	Brunswick LAT/STA 8562	RICKY SINGS "FOR YOU" (LP, mono/stereo)	35/40
64	Liberty LBY 3027	MILLION SELLERS (LP)	30
64	Brunswick LAT/STA 8581	THE VERY THOUGHT OF YOU (LP)	35
64	Brunswick LAT/STA 8596	SPOTLIGHT ON RICK (LP)	35
65	Brunswick LAT/STA 8615	BEST ALWAYS (LP)	35
65	Brunswick LAT/STA 8630	LOVE AND KISSES (LP)	35
66	Brunswick LAT/STA 8657	BRIGHT LIGHTS, COUNTRY MUSIC (LP)	35
67	Brunswick LAT/STA 8680	COUNTRY FEVER (LP)	35
68	Liberty LBL 83020	MILLION SELLERS (LP, reissue)	12
68	MCA MUP(S) 302	ANOTHER SIDE OF RICK (LP)	18
70	MCA MUPS 409	IN CONCERT (LP, with Stone Canyon Band)	15
71	MCA MUPS 422	RICK SINGS NELSON (LP, with Stone Canyon Band)	15
72	MCA MUPS 440	RUDY THE FIFTH (LP, with Stone Canyon Band)	15
73	MCA MDKS 8009	GARDEN PARTY (LP, gatefold sleeve, with Stone Canyon Band)	15
74	MCA MCG 3516	WINDFALL (LP)	15
77	Epic EPC 81102	INTAKES (LP)	12

SANDY NELSON

59	Top Rank JAR 197	Teen Beat/Big Jump	7
59	London HLP 9015	Drum Party/The Big Noise From Winnetka	10
59	London HLP 9015	Drum Party/The Big Noise From Winnetka (78)	50
60	London HLP 9214	I'm Walkin'/Bouncy (as Sandy Nelson & His Combo)	8
61	London HLP 9377	Get With It/Big Noise From The Jungle	8
61	London HLP 9466	Let There Be Drums/Quite A Beat (as Sandy Nelson On The Drums)	5
62	London HLP 9521	Drums Are My Beat/My Girl Josephine	6
62	London HLP 9558	Drummin' Up A Storm/Drum Stomp	8
62	London HLP 9612	...And Then There Were Drums/Live It Up	7
63	London HLP 9717	Ooh Poo Pah Doo/Feel So Good	7
64	Liberty LIB 66060	Teen Beat '65/Kitty's Theme	6
66	Liberty LIB 12062	Hey Joe/Come On Let's Go	6
70	President PT 294	Teen Beat/PRESTON EPPS: Bongo Rock	6
60	Top Rank JKP 2060	RUSHING FOR PERCUSSION (EP, 2 tracks by Preston Epps)	30
62	London REP 1337	LET THERE BE DRUMS (EP)	18
63	London REP 1371	IN THE MOOD (EP)	18
65	Liberty LEP 4033	SANDY NELSON PLAYS (EP)	15
60	London HA-P 2260	TEEN BEAT (LP, also stereo SAH-P 6082)	20/25
61	London HA-P 2425	LET THERE BE DRUMS (LP, also stereo SAH-P 6221)	20/25
62	London HA-P 2446	DRUMS ARE MY BEAT! (LP, also stereo SAH-P 6237)	20/25
62	London HA-P/SH-P 8009	DRUMMIN' UP A STORM (LP)	20/25

Sandy NELSON

63	London HA-P/SH-P 8029	COMPELLING PERCUSSION (LP)	20
63	London HA-P/SH-P 8051	TEENAGE HOUSE PARTY (LP)	20
65	Liberty LBY 3007	SANDY NELSON PLAYS (LP)	15
65	Liberty LBY 3035	LIVE IN LAS VEGAS (LP)	15
66	Liberty LBY 3061	DRUMS A GO-GO (LP)	15
66	Liberty (S)LBY 3080	SUPERDRUMS (LP)	15
67	Liberty LBL/LBS 83043E	THE BEAT GOES ON (LP)	12
68	Liberty LBL/LBS 83094E	SOUL DRUMS (LP)	12
68	Liberty LBL/LBS 83110E	BOOGALOO BEAT (LP)	12
68	Liberty LBL/LBS 83131E	SUPERDRUMS (LP, reissue, different sleeve)	12
69	Liberty LBL/LBS 83165E	ROCK'N'ROLL REVIVAL (LP)	12
70	Liberty LBS 83302E	GROOVY (LP)	12

TERRY NELSON (& FIREBALLS)

65	Dice CC 23	Run Run Baby/Bonita (as Terry Nelson & Fireballs)	10
65	Dice CC 25	Bulldog Push/Pretty Little Girl (as Terry Nelson & Fireballs)	10
65	Dice CC 27	Tomorrow Will Soon Be Here/My Blue Eyed Baby	10
65	Blue Beat BB 326	Help/PRINCE BUSTER: Johnny Dollar	15
67	Halagala HG 19	That True Love Must Be Me/Bulldog Walk	7

WILLIE NELSON

63	Liberty LIB 55532	Half A Man/The Last Letter	7
64	Liberty LIB 55697	River Boy/Opportunity To Cry	7
69	RCA RCA 1867	My Own Peculiar Way/Natural To Be Gone	5
66	RCA Victor RD 7749	COUNTRY WILLIE (LP)	18
66	Liberty (S)LBY 1240	AND THEN I WROTE (LP)	18
69	RCA RD 7997	TEXAS IN MY SOUL (LP)	15

NELSON TRIO (U.K.)

| 57 | Oriole CB 1360 | Tear It Up/Roll The Carpet Up | 6 |
| 57 | Oriole CB 1360 | Tear It Up/Roll The Carpet Up (78) | 10 |

NELSON TRIO (U.S.)

| 60 | London HLL 9019 | All In Good Time/The Town Crier | 10 |
| 60 | London HLL 9019 | All In Good Time/The Town Crier (78) | 40 |

CHIITRA NEOGY

| 68 | Gemini GMX 5030 | THE PERFUMED GARDEN (LP) | 15 |

NEO MAYA

| 67 | Pye 7N 17371 | I Won't Hurt You/U.F.O. | 45 |

(see also Episode Six)

NEON BOYS

90	Overground OVER 11	TIME (EP, purple vinyl, 2,000 only)	6
90	Overground OVER 11	TIME (12" EP, 20 test pressings only)	20
91	Overground OVER 19	That's All I Know (Right Now)/Love Comes In Spurts/High Heeled Wheels/Don't Die/Time (last 2 tracks credited to Richard Hell & Voidoids [Part III]) (12", p/s, 2,000 only, clear vinyl)	8
91	Overground OVER 19	That's All I Know (Right Now)/Love Comes In Spurts/High Heeled Wheels/Don't Die/Time (Last 2 tracks credited to Richard Hell & Voidoids [Part III]) (CD, 2,000 only)	7

(see also Richard Hell, Television)

NEON HEARTS

77	Neon Hearts NEON 1	Venus Eccentric/Regulations (8" p/s)	20
78	Satril SAT 133	Answers/Armchair Thriller (p/s)	5
79	Satril SAT 139	Popular Music/Pretty As A Picture (p/s)	5
79	Satril SATL 4012	POPULAR MUSIC (LP)	12

NEPTUNE'S EMPIRE

| 71 | Polymax PXX 01 | NEPTUNE'S EMPIRE (LP) | 100 |

NERO & GLADIATORS

61	Decca F 11329	Entry Of The Gladiators/Boots	12
61	Decca F 11367	In The Hall Of The Mountain King/The Trek To Rome	12
61	Decca F 11413	Czardas/That's A Long Time Ago	15

(see also Laurie Jay, Gladiators, Screaming Lord Sutch & Savages, State Of Mickey & Tommy)

NERVE

67	Page One POF 019	No. 10 Downing Street/Georgie's March	8
68	Page One POF 055	Magic Spectacles/Come The Day	12
68	Page One POF 081	It Is/Mystery Lady	12
68	Page One POF 097	Piece By Piece/Satisfying Kind	10

(see also Lovin')

NERVES

| 78 | Lightning GIL 520 | TV Adverts/Sex Education (p/s) | 18 |

NERVES

| 81 | Good Vibrations BIG 3 | NOTRE DEMO (LP, official bootleg, foldover sleeve with booklet [matrix A1]) | 12 |

NERVOUS CHOIR

| 89 | Cathexis CRN 5407 | O'David/Tonight We Start On Witches/Alsatians/Introducing (p/s, with inserts) | 4 |

NERVOUS NORVUS

56	London HLD 8338	Ape Call/Wild Dog Of Kentucky (gold label print, later silver)	60/35
56	London HLD 8338	Ape Call/Wild Dog Of Kentucky (78)	12
57	London HLD 8383	Dig/Bullfrog Hop (gold label print, later silver)	80/40
57	London HLD 8383	Dig/Bullfrog Hop (78)	12
62	Salvo SLO 1812	Does A Chinese Chicken Have A Pigtail/ROD BARTON: Dear Old San Francisco	25

JIM NESBIT
65	Vocalion V 9241	Tiger In My Tank/I Can't Stand This Living Alone 20

MICHAEL NESMITH (& FIRST/SECOND NATIONAL BAND)
70	RCA RCA 2001	Joanne/The Crippled Lion (with First National Band)................... 8
71	RCA RCA 2053	Silver Moon/Lady Of The Valley (with First National Band)............ 8
71	RCA RCA 2086	Nevada Fighter/Here I Am (with First National Band)................... 8
76	RCA RCA 2692	Silver Moon/Lady Of The Valley (reissue) 5
76	Island IEP 4	I Fall To Pieces/Silver Moon/Some Of Shelley's Blues/Joanne (solo, p/s) 8
76	Island WIP 6373	Rio/Life, The Unsuspecting Captive (solo) 6
78	Island WIP 6398	Navajo Trail/Love's First Kiss (solo) 7
89	Awareness AWP 014	Rio/I'll Remember You (solo) (p/s) 6
70	RCA SF 8136	MAGNETIC SOUTH (LP, with First National Band) 18
71	RCA SF 8209	NEVADA FIGHTER (LP, with First National Band)................... 18
72	RCA SF 8276	TANTAMOUNT TO TREASON VOLUME ONE
		(LP, with Second National Band).............................. 18
73	RCA APL1 0164	PRETTY MUCH YOUR STANDARD RANCH STASH (LP, solo)............ 15
75	Island ILPS 9428	THE PRISON (LP, boxed with book, unreleased in U.K.)
76	RCA RS 1064	THE BEST OF MICHAEL NESMITH (LP) 15
77	Island ILPS 9439	AND THE HITS JUST KEEP ON COMIN' (LP, gatefold sleeve, solo) 12
77	Island ILPS 9486	FROM A RADIO ENGINE TO A PHOTON WING (LP, solo)................ 12

(see also Monkees, Wichita Train Whistle)

NEU
73	United Artists UP 35485	Super/Neuschnee... 8
75	United Artists UP 35874	Isi/After Eight 7
72	United Artists UAS 29396	NEU (LP)... 60
73	United Artists UAS 29500	NEU II (LP, gatefold sleeve) 60
75	United Artists UAS 29782	NEU '75 (LP, gatefold sleeve)................................ 30
82	Cherry Red BRED 27	BLACK FOREST GATEAU (LP) 25

NEUTRONS
74	United Artists UP 35704	Dance Of The Psychedelic Lounge Lizard/Suzy And The Wonder Boy 5
74	United Artists UAG 29652	BLACK HOLE STAR (LP, with inner sleeve) 15
75	United Artists UAG 29726	TALES FROM THE BLUE COCOONS (LP)......................... 15

(see also Man)

NEVILLE (Willoughby)
72	Explosion EX 2057	I Love Jamaica/Marry Me Marie................................ 5

(see also Whistling Willie)

AARON NEVILLE
67	Stateside SS 584	Tell It Like It Is/Why Worry 15
69	B&C CB 107	Tell It Like It Is/Why Worry (reissue) 6
67	Liberty LBY 3089	HERE 'TIS (LP).. 25

DEREK NEW QUINTET
63	Ember JBS 711	Scandinavian Nocturne/Nearly Ready To Begin 5

NEW AGE STEPPERS
80	On-U Sound ONU 1	Fade Away/LONDON UNDERGROUND: Learn A Language (p/s)........... 7
80	On-U Sound ONULP 1	NEW AGE STEPPERS (LP) 12

NEW-ASIA
82	Situation 2 SIT 2	Central Position/Here + There, Now + Then (p/s) 4

NEWBEATS
64	Hickory 45-1269	Bread And Butter/Tough Little Buggy (pink or black/blue label)........... each 6
64	Hickory 45-1282	Everything's Alright/Pink Dally Rue 6
65	Hickory 45-1290	Break Away/Hey O Daddy O 6
65	Hickory 45-1305	The Birds Are For The Bees/Better Watch Your Step 6
65	Hickory 45-1320	I Can't Hear You No More/Little Child 6
65	Hickory 45-1332	Run Baby Run/Mean Woolly Willie.............................. 8
66	Hickory 45-1366	Shake Hands (And Come Out Crying)/Too Sweet To Be Forgotten 8
66	Hickory 45-1387	Crying My Heart Out/Short Of Love 10
66	Hickory 45-1422	My Yesterday Love/Patent On Love 7
69	London HLE 10270	Bread And Butter/Pink Dally Rue 5
70	London HLE 10299	Groovin' (Out On Life)/Everything's Alright 5
71	London HLE 10341	Run Baby Run/Am I Not My Brother's Keeper 5
72	London HLE 10356	Thou Shalt Not Steal/Bad Dreams.............................. 5
65	Hickory LPE 1503	NEWBEATS (EP)... 20
65	Hickory LPE 1506	AIN'T THAT LOVIN' YOU BABY (EP)............................. 20
66	Hickory LPE 1510	OH! GIRLS GIRLS (EP)...................................... 25
65	Hickory LPM 120	BREAD AND BUTTER (LP).................................... 30
72	London SHE 8428	RUN, BABY, RUN (LP)....................................... 15

(see also Dean & Mark, Larry Henley)

PHINEAS NEWBORN
61	Columbia 33SX 1311	I LOVE A PIANO (LP, also stereo SCX 3370) 12/15

(see also Roy Haines)

NEW BREED
65	Decca F 12295	Friends And Lovers Forever/Unto Us 25

MICKEY NEWBURY
72	Elektra K 12047	An American Trilogy/San Francisco Mabel Joy 5

NEWBY & JOHNSON
70	Mercury 6052 027	Sweet Happiness/I Want To Give You Everything 5

NEWCASTLE BIG BAND
72	Impulse ISS NBB 106	NEWCASTLE BIG BAND (LP, white labels, 2,000 only)................ 175

(see also Last Exit, Police, Sting, Radio Actors)

NEW CHRISTY MINSTRELS

MINT VALUE £

63	CBS AAG 160	Green, Green/The Banjo	6
63	AAG 175	Saturday Night/The Wheeler Dealers	6
64	CBS AAG 234	Down The Road I Go/Gotta Get A' Goin'	5
64	CBS 201328	Three Wheels On My Wagon/Mighty Mississippi	6
65	CBS 201758	The River/Se Piangi Se Ridi	5
65	CBS EP 6057	THREE WHEELS ON MY WAGON (EP)	10
66	CBS EP 6072	EVERYBODY LOVES SATURDAY NIGHT (EP)	10
63	CBS BPG 62268	TELL TALL TALES (LP)	15
63	CBS BPG 62269	RAMBLIN' (LP)	15
65	CBS BPG 62492	SING AND PLAY COWBOYS AND INDIANS (LP)	15
66	CBS 63338	ON TOUR THROUGH MOTORTOWN (LP)	12

(see also Barry McGuire)

NEW COLONY SIX

66	London HLZ 10033	I Confess/Dawn Is Breaking	40
66	Stateside SS 522	I Lie Awake/At The River's Edge	60
68	Mercury MF 1030	I Will Always Think About You/Hold Me With Your Eyes	6
69	Mercury MF 1086	Things I'd Like To Say/Come And Give Your Love To Me	6

NEWCOMERS

72	Stax 2025 063	Pin The Tail On The Donkey/Mannish Boy	5
75	Stax STXS 2023	Keep An Eye On Your Close Friends/(Instrumental Version)	5

NEW DAWN

69	private pressing	MAINLINE (LP)	150

NEW DEAL STRING BAND

69	Argo ZDA 104	DOWN IN THE WILLOW (LP, with insert)	25

NEW DEPARTURES QUARTET

60s	Transatlantic TRA 134	THE NEW DEPARTURES QUARTET (LP, with Stan Tracey)	40

(see also Stan Tracey)

NEW ENGLAND

79	Infinity INF 110	P.U.N.K./Shoot (green vinyl, 'lightning' PVC sleeve)	4

DENNIS NEWEY

61	Philips PB 1134	Checkpoint/Title Unknown	6
61	Philips PB 1198	Border Patrol/Yes Yes	5
62	Philips 326 588 BF	The Nightriders/The Pied Piper	5

NEW FACES

65	Pye 7N 15842	So Small/Blue Mist	6
65	Pye 7N 15931	Never Gonna Love Again/You'll Be Too Late	6
66	Pye 7N 17029	Like A Man/Shake Up The Party (Myra)	8
67	Pye 7N 17335	Lace Covered Window/The Life That I Lead	6

NEW FAST AUTOMATIC DAFFODILS

90	Playtime AMUSE 7	Big (1-sided, die-cut sleeve)	4

NEW FORESTERS

65	Lyntone LYN 932/933	Travel/LIZARDS: My Love Goes On (Sheffield Students Rag record)	30

NEW FORMULA

67	Piccadilly 7N 35381	Do It Again A Little Bit Slower/I'm On The Outside Looking In	7
67	Piccadilly 7N 35401	I Want To Go Back There Again/Can't You See That She Loves Me	7
68	Pye 7N 17552	My Baby's Coming Home/Burning In The Background	6
69	Pye 7N 17818	Stay Indoors/Hare Krishna	20

NEW GENERATION

69	Spark SRL 1000	Sadie And Her Magic Mister Garland/Digger	6
69	Spark SRL 1007	Smokey Blues Away/She's A Soldier Boy	8
70	Spark SRL 1019	Police Is Here/Mister C.	5

BOB NEWHART

60	Warner Bros WM 4010	THE BUTTON-DOWN MIND OF BOB NEWHART (LP, also stereo WS 8010)	12
61	Warner Bros WM 4032	THE BUTTON-DOWN MIND STRIKES BACK (LP)	12
62	Warner Bros WM 4055	BEHIND THE BUTTON-DOWN MIND OF BOB NEWHART (LP)	12
63	Warner Bros WM/WS 8110	THE BUTTON-DOWN MIND ON TV (LP)	12
64	Warner Bros WM 8148	NEWHART FACES BOB NEWHART (LP)	12
65	Warner Bros W(W) 1588	THE WINDMILLS ARE WEAKENING (LP)	12

NEW HEARTS

77	CBS 5800	Just Another Teenage Anthem/Blood On The Knife (p/s)	7
78	CBS 6381	Plain Jane/My Young Teacher (p/s)	7

(see also Secret Affair)

NEW HERITAGE

73	Westwood WRS 028	ALL MANNER OF THINGS (LP)	40

NEW HOPE

69	London HL 10296	Won't Find Better Than Me/They Call It Love	4

NEW JAZZ GROUP

56	Tempo EXA 39	MODERN JAZZ SCENE (EP)	8

NEW JAZZ ORCHESTRA

65	Decca LK 4690	WESTERN REUNION (LONDON 1965) (LP)	45

(see also Neil Ardley, Ian Carr)

NEW JERSEY CONNECTION

82	Nitelife LIFE 1	Love Don't Come Easy/Love Don't Come Easy (Instrumental) (12")	8

NEW JUMP BAND

68	Domain D 1	The Only Kind Of Girl/Seven Kinds Of Sweet Lovin'	7

ANTHONY NEWLEY

78s

59	Decca F 11127	I've Waited So Long/Sat'day Night Rock-A-Boogie (78)	10
59	Decca F 11137	Idle On Parade/Idle Rock-A-Boogie (78)	15
59	Decca F 11142	Personality/My Blue Angel (78)	10
59	Decca F 11163	Someone To Love/It's All Over (78)	15
60	Decca F 11194	Why/Anything You Wanna Do (78)	20
60	Decca F 11220	Do You Mind/Girls Were Made To Love And Kiss (78)	25
60	Decca F 11254	If She Should Come To You/Lifetime Of Happiness (78)	25

SINGLES

59	Decca F 11127	I've Waited So Long/Sat'day Night Rock-A-Boogie	6
59	Decca F 11137	Idle On Parade/Idle Rock-A-Boogie	8
59	Decca F 11142	Personality/My Blue Angel	6
59	Decca F 11163	Someone To Love/It's All Over	5
60	Decca F 11194	Why/Anything You Wanna Do	5
60	Decca F 11220	Do You Mind/Girls Were Made To Love And Kiss	5
60	Decca F 11254	If She Should Come To You/Lifetime Of Happiness	5
60	Decca F 11295	Strawberry Fair/A Boy Without A Girl	5
61	Decca F 11331	And The Heavens Cried/Lonely Boy And Pretty Girl	5
61	Decca F 11362	Pop Goes The Weasel/Bee Bom	5
61	Decca F 11376	What Kind Of Fool Am I/Once In A Lifetime	5
62	Decca F 11419	D-Darling/I'll Walk Beside You	5
62	Decca F 11486	That Noise/The Little Golden Clown	5
63	Decca F 11636	There's No Such Thing As Love/She's Just Another Girl	5
63	Decca F 11767	The Father Of Girls/I Love Everything About You	5
64	Decca F 11818	Tribute/Lament To A Hero	10
66	RCA RCA 1518	Why Can't You Try To Didgeridoo/Is There A Way Back To Your Arms	6

EPs

59	Decca DFE 6566	SINGS FOUR SONGS FROM IDLE ON PARADE (EP)	12
60	Decca DFE 6629	TONY'S HITS (EP)	10
60	Decca DFE 6655	MORE HITS FROM TONY (EP)	10
61	Decca DFE 6687	THIS TIME THE DREAM'S ON ME (EP)	10

LPs

60	Decca LK 4343	LOVE IS A NOW AND THEN THING (LP)	18
61	Decca LK 4406	TONY (LP)	18
64	Decca LK 4600	IN MY SOLITUDE (LP)	18
64	Decca LK 4654	NEWLEY DELIVERED (LP)	18
65	RCA Victor RD/SF 7737	WHO CAN I TURN TO (LP, mono/stereo)	15/18
66	RCA Victor RD/SF 7837	NEWLEY RECORDED (LP)	18

ANDY NEWMAN

| 72 | Track 2406 103 | RAINBOW (LP) | 15 |

(see also Thunderclap Newman)

BRAD NEWMAN

62	Fontana H 357	Somebody To Love/This Time It's Love	8
62	Fontana H 369	Get A Move On/Here And Now And Evermore	7
62	Fontana 267 220TF	Stay By Me/Candy Lips	7
62	Fontana 267 243TF	Point Of No Return/Now I've Lost You	7
63	Fontana 267 273TF	I'll Find You Another Baby/No Man Should Ever Be Alone	7
64	Piccadilly 7N 35174	Please Don't Cry/Every Hour Of Living	6

COLIN NEWMAN

80	Beggars Banquet BEG 48	B/Classic Remains/Alone On Piano (p/s)	5
81	Beggars Banquet BEG 52	Inventory/This Picture (p/s)	5
82	4AD AD 209	We Means We Starts/Not To (Remix) (p/s)	7
88	4AD CN 1	Not To (We Means We Starts/Not To/You And Your Dog/H.C.T.F.R./No Doubt/The Grace You Know (free with "Provisionally Entitled The Singing Fish" CD)	7

(see also Wire)

DEL NEWMAN SOUND

| 67 | Columbia SCX 6181 | FLOWER GARDEN (LP) | 25 |

JIMMY (C.) NEWMAN

57	London HLD 8460	A Fallen Star/I Can't Go On This Way	20
57	London HLD 8460	A Fallen Star/I Can't Go On This Way (78)	15
59	MGM MGM 1009	What'cha Gonna Do/So Soon	10
59	MGM MGM 1009	What'cha Gonna Do/So Soon (78)	30
59	MGM MGM 1037	Grin And Bear It/The Ballad Of Baby Doe	8
60	MGM MGM 1085	A Lovely Work Of Art/What About Me	6
61	MGM MGM 1112	Now That You're Gone/Wanting You With Me Tonight	5
59	MGM MGM-EP 706	GRIN AND BEAR IT — COUNTRY AND WESTERN STYLE (EP)	40

JOE NEWMAN SEXTET

| 57 | Vogue Coral Q 72244 | Cocktails For Two/Later For The Happenings | 6 |
| 57 | Vogue Coral LVA 9052 | HAPPY CATS (LP) | 10 |

LIONEL NEWMAN ORCHESTRA

| 58 | Columbia DB 4150 | Hey! Eula/Two Butterflies | 6 |
| 58 | Columbia DB 4150 | Hey! Eula/Two Butterflies (78) | 5 |

PAUL NEWMAN

| 66 | Mercury MF 969 | Ain't You Got A Heart/Tears On My Pillow | 15 |

RANDY NEWMAN

68	Reprise RS 20692	Love Story/I Think It's Going To Rain Today	6
70	Reprise RS 20945	Gone Dead Train/JACK NITZSCHE: Harry Flowers	6
72	Reprise K 14155	Lonely At The Top/My Old Kentucky Home	5
72	Reprise K 14190	Sail Away/Political Science	5

Randy NEWMAN

88	Warner Bros W 7709CD	It's Money That Matters (with Mark Knopfler)/Roll With The Punches/ Short People (3" CD with adaptor, 5" case)	7
88	Warner Bros W 7578CD	Falling In Love (with Jeff Lynne & Tom Petty)/Bad News From Home (with Mark Knopfler)/Miami (3" CD with adaptor, 5" case)	7
89	Warner Bros 925 680-2	I Love L.A. (LP Version)/I'm Different (LP Version)/Miami (LP Version)/ I Love L.A. (Video) (CD Video)	10
68	Reprise R(S)LP 6286	RANDY NEWMAN CREATES SOMETHING NEW UNDER THE SUN (LP)	15
70	Reprise RSLP 6373	12 SONGS (LP)	12

(see also Harry Nilsson, Tom Petty & Heartbreakers)

TOM NEWMAN
74	Virgin VS 120	Sad Sing/Ali's Got A Broken Nose	5
75	Virgin VS 130	Don't Treat Your Woman Bad/Why Does Love Hurt So Bad	5
76	Virgin VS 133	Sleep/Darling Corey	5
76	Virgin VS 141	Ebony Eyes/Draught Guinness	5
77	Decca F 13735	Dance Of The Theena Shee (Daoine Sidhe)/The Unseelie Court (as Faerie Symphony [Tom Newman])	4
75	Virgin V 2022	FINE OLD TOM (LP, features Mike Oldfield)	15
75	Virgin V 2042	LIVE AT THE ARGONAUT (LP, unreleased, test pressings only)	80
77	Decca TXS 123	FAERIE SYMPHONY (LP, gatefold sleeve)	18
88	Oceandisc	OZYMANDIAS (LP, unissued, 20 test pressings only in proof sleeve)	25

(see also July, Mike Oldfield)

TONY NEWMAN
| 68 | Decca F 12795 | Soul Thing/Let The Good Times Roll | 8 |
| 70 | Decca F 13041 | Soul Thing/Let The Good Times Roll (reissue) | 5 |

(see also Sounds Incorporated, Flying Machine, Pinkerton['s Assorted Colours], May Blitz, Three Man Army)

NEW MODEL
| 83 | Mr. Clean MERC 001 | Chilean Warning/The World Thru Our Eyes/Totalitarian Terror (p/s, some in 7" x 10" folder) | 10/6 |

NEW MODEL ARMY
83	Shout QS 002/QF 001	Bittersweet/Betcha/Tension (p/s, some with flexi "Fashion"/"The Cause")	10/4
83	Abstract ABS 0020	Great Expectations/Waiting (p/s)	8
84	Abstract ABS 0028	The Price/1984 (p/s)	5
85	EMI 12 NMAD 1/PSLP 387	No Rest/Heroin//Vengeance (live)/The Price (live)/No Greater Love (live) (12", p/s, double pack)	8
85	EMI NMAD 2/NMA 22	The Acoustic EP: Better Than Them/No Sense//Adrenalin/Trust (double pack, gatefold p/s)	5
85	EMI 12 NMA 2	The Acoustic EP: Better Than Them/No Sense/Adrenalin/Trust (12", p/s)	8
85	EMI 12 NMAD 3/PSLP 395	Brave New World (Extended)/R.I.P. (Alternative Mix)/Brave New World 2// Young, Gifted & Skint (live)/Sex (The Black Angel) (live) (12", p/s, double pack)	8
86	EMI 12 NMAD 4/PSLP 348	51st State/Ten Commandments//Liberal Education (live)/No Rest (live)/ No Man's Land (live) (12", p/s, double pack)	8
87	EMI NMA 5	Poison Street/Courage (p/s, red vinyl)	12
	PSLP 1002	My Country (live) (12", double pack)	8
89	House Of Dolls HOD 007	125 M.P.H./EVERY NEW DEAD GHOST: She's Waiting/SANDMEN: Ship No Shore/CHALK GARDEN: Drunk Among The Trees (free with House Of Dolls magazine, issue 21)	6/4
81	own label	Aries Enterprises (cassette, with other artists)	25+

(see also Joolz)

NEW MONITORS
| 72 | Buddah 2011 118 | Fence Around Your Heart/Have You Seen Her | 8 |

NEW ORDER
81	Factory FAC 33	Ceremony/In A Lonely Place (p/s)	4
81	Factory FAC 3312	Ceremony (Re-recording)/In A Lonely Place (Extended) (12", cream & blue p/s)	7
81	Factory FAC 53	Procession/Everything's Gone Green (p/s, white writing; also other colours)	5/4
82	Factory FAC 51B	Rocking Carol/Ode To Joy (flexidisc, given away at Hacienda, 4,000 only)	10
83	Factory FAC 93	Confusion (Edit)/(same) (p/s, DJ promo only)	12
84	Factory FAC 103	Thieves Like Us (Edit)/Lonesome Tonight (Edit) (p/s, DJ promo only)	10
87	Factory FACD 187	Touched By The Hand Of God (Twelve Inch Mix)/Confusion Dub 1987/ Temptation (Original Mix) (CD, gatefold card sleeve)	10
88	Factory FAC 73RD	Blue Monday 1988/Blue Monday (DJ-only mix) (12", p/s, DJ promo only)	10
88	Factory FACD 73R	Blue Monday 1988 (12 Inch)/Beach Buggy (12 Inch)/Blue Monday 1988 (7 Inch) (CD)	7
88	Factory FACDV 73R	Blue Monday 1988 (12 Inch)/Blue Monday 1988 (7 Inch)/Beach Buggy/ Blue Monday 1988 (Video) (CD Video)	50
88	Factory FACDV 183	True Faith (Remix 12 Inch)/Evil Dust/True Faith (7 Inch) (CD Video)/ True Faith (CD Video)	15
89	Factory FAC 263DJ	Round & Round (Ben Grosse Mix)/(12" Mix)/(Detroit Mix) (12", p/s, DJ only)	10
89	Factory FACD 263R	Round & Round (Seven Inch)/Vanishing Point (Instrumental Making Out Mix)/ Round & Round (Twelve Inch)/Best & Marsh (Seven Inch) (3" CD, g/f card p/s)	8
89	Factory FAC 273/7	Run 2 (Edit)/MTO (Edit) (DJ promo only, 500 pressed)	15
89	Factory FAC 273	Run 2/Run 2 (Extended Version)/MTO/MTO (Minus Mix) (12", p/s, with inner sleeve, 20,000 only)	12
85	Factory FACTUS 12C	POWER, CORRUPTION & LIES (cassette with 2 extra tracks)	10
86	Factory FACT 150SP	BROTHERHOOD (LP, limited metallic sleeve)	10
87	Factory FACT 200	THE GATEFOLD SUBSTANCE (LP, numbered gatefold sleeve, 1,000 only)	30
87	Factory FACT 200C	SUBSTANCE (cassette, 200 only in box set with insert)	30
87	Factory FACD 150SP	BROTHERHOOD (CD, with "State Of The Nation" & metallic booklet)	20

(see also Joy Division, Electronic, Revenge)

NEW ORDER
| 80s | Come Organisation | BRADFORD RED LIGHT DISTRICT (LP) | 20+ |

(see also Come)

NEW ORLEANS ALL STAR BAND
56	Vogue V 2380	Struttin' With Some Barbecue/Basin Street Blues	10
56	Vogue V 2368	Christopher Columbus/Bugle Call Rag	6
56	Vogue V 2368	Christopher Columbus/Bugle Call Rag (78)	8

NEW ORLEANS BOOTBLACKS
54	Columbia SCM 5090	Flat Foot/Mad Dog	10

NEW ORLEANS WILD CATS
62	Storyville A 45048	Roll Along Prairie Moon/Well Well Well	5

NEWPORT JAZZ FESTIVAL ALL STARS
61	London Jazz LTZ-K 15202	NEWPORT JAZZ FESTIVAL ALL STARS (LP, also stereo SAH-K 6116)	10/12

NEW RELIGION
72	Bamboo BAM 70	In The Black Caribbean/Black Is Black	12
73	Ackee ACK 526	Walk Away Renee/What's It All About	5

NEWS
66	Decca F 12356	The Entertainer/I Count The Tears	6
66	Decca F 12477	This Is The Moment (from the TV series "Adam Adamant")/Ya Ya Da Da	15

(see also Patto, Glenn Hughes, Finders Keepers, Miller, Big Boy Pete)

NEWS FROM BABEL
86	Recommended RE 6116	NEWS FROM BABEL (LP, hand-screened sleeve)	10

BOBBY NEWSOME
72	Mojo 2093 018	Jody Come And Get Your Shoes/Post Office	5

WAYNE NEWTON
63	Capitol CL 15319	Danke Schoen/Better Now Than Later	5
65	Capitol CL 15380	Comin' On Too Strong/Red Roses For A Blue Lady	8
65	Capitol CL 15422	Keep The Lovin'/Remember When	5
68	MGM MGM 1426	Dreams Of The Everyday Housewife/The Tips Of My Fingers	5

OLIVIA NEWTON-JOHN
66	Decca F 12396	Till You Say You'll Be Mine/For Ever	175
71	Pye International 7N 25543	If Not For You/The Biggest Clown	8
76	EMI EMI 2519	Don't Stop Believin'/Greensleeves (p/s)	5
77	EMI EMI 2616	Sam/Changes (p/s)	5
77	EMI (no cat. no.)	Please Mr. Please/PILOT: Love Is (flexidisc free with *Record Mirror*)	6/5
80	Jet JET 185	Xanadu/Fool Country (gatefold p/s, with ELO)	6
80	Jet JET 10-185	Xanadu/Fool Country (10" pink vinyl, die-cut p/s, with ELO)	15
80	Jet JETP 196	Magic/Whenever You're Away From Me (picture disc)	15
88	Mercury MERCD 272	The Rumour/Winter Angel/The Rumour (12" Extended Mix) (CD, picture disc, card sleeve)	15
89	Mercury MERCD 313	When You Wish Upon A Star/Rocking/Rock A Bye Baby/ Twinkle Twinkle Little Star (CD)	15
71	Pye Intl. NSPL 28155	OLIVIA NEWTON-JOHN (LP)	15
72	Pye Intl. NSPL 28168	OLIVIA (LP)	12
74	Pye Intl. NSPL 28185	MUSIC MAKES MY DAY (LP, blue/black or white/black label)	12
74	EMI EMC 3055	FIRST IMPRESSION (LP)	12
76	EMI EMC 3124	COME ON OVER (LP, with inner sleeve)	12
77	EMI EMC 3193	MAKING A GOOD THING BETTER (LP)	12
78	EMI EMAP 789	TOTALLY HOT (LP, picture disc)	15
85	Mercury 826 169-2	SOUL KISS (CD)	25

(see also Toomorrow, Marvin & Farrar)

OLIVIA NEWTON-JOHN & CLIFF RICHARD
80	Jet JET 7002	Suddenly/You Made Me Love You (p/s)	7

(see also Cliff Richard)

NEWTOWN NEUROTICS
79	No Wonder A 45	Hypocrite/You Said No (no p/s)	25
80	No Wonder NOW 4	When The Oil Runs Out/Oh No (no p/s, some with sticker & insert)	12/7
82	CNT 4/No Wonder NOW 56	Kick Out The Tories!/Mindless Violence! (p/s)	7
82	CNT CNT 010	Licensing Hours/No Sanctuary (p/s)	7
83	Razor RZS 107	Blitzkrieg Bop/Hypocrite (New Version)/I Remember You (p/s)	5
83	Razor RAZ 6	BEGGARS CAN BE CHOOSERS (LP)	12

NEW TRENDS
67	Columbia SX 6245	THE NEW TRENDS (LP)	12

NEW VAUDEVILLE BAND
67	Fontana TF 784	Peek-A-Boo/Amy	5
67	Fontana TF 824	Finchley Central/Rosie (some in p/s)	8/5
67	Fontana TF 853	Green Street Green/Fourteen Lovely Women	5
68	Fontana TF 909	The Bonnie And Clyde/Uncle Gabriel (some in p/s)	8/5
67	Fontana TFE 17497	THOROUGHLY MODERN MILLIE (EP)	8
67	Fontana (S)TL 5386	WINCHESTER CATHEDRAL (LP)	15
67	Fontana (S)TL 5430	FINCHLEY CENTRAL (LP)	15

(see also Bonzo Dog Doo Dah Band, Alberts, Alan Klein)

NEW VENTURES
76	United Artists UP 36101	Moonlight Serenade (Parts 1 & 2)	5

NEW WANDERERS
79	Grapevine GRP 144	This Man In Love/Adam And Eve	6

NEW YORK BLONDES featuring MADAME X
79	London/Bomp HLZ 10574	Little GTO/RODNEY & BRUNETTES: Holocaust On Sunset Boulevard (no p/s)	8

(see also Blondie, Debbie Harry)

MINT VALUE £

NEW YORK DOLLS
73	Mercury 6052 402	Jet Boy/Vietnamese Baby	10
74	Mercury 6052 615	Stranded In The Jungle/Who Are The Mystery Girls	8
77	Mercury 6160 008	Jet Boy/Babylon/Who Are The Mystery Girls	5
85	Antler DOLLS 1	Personality Crisis/Subway Train (picture disc)	8
85	Antler DOLLS 2	Looking For A Kiss/Bad Girl (picture disc)	8
73	Mercury 6338 270	NEW YORK DOLLS (LP)	18
74	Mercury 6338 498	TOO MUCH TOO SOON (LP)	18

(see also Johnny Thunders, Heartbreakers, Sylvain Sylvain, Idols)

NEW YORK GONG
80	Charly CYX 203	Jungle Windo(w)/Much Too Old/Materialism (10", p/s)	6

(see also Daevid Allen, Planet Gong)

NEW YORK PORT AUTHORITY
77	Invictus INV 5312	I Got It/I Got It (Version)	5

NEW YORK PUBLIC LIBRARY
66	Columbia DB 7948	I Ain't Gonna Eat Out My Heart Anymore/Rejected	20
68	MCA MU 1025	Gotta Get Away/Time Wastin'	8
68	MCA MU 1045	Love Me Two Times/Which Way To Go	8

NEW YORK ROCK & ROLL ENSEMBLE
71	CBS 5292	Running Down The Highway/Law And Order	4
69	Atco 228 932	FAITHFUL FRIENDS (LP)	12
71	CBS 64126	ROLL OVER (LP)	10
72	CBS 64324	FREEDOMBURGER (LP)	10

NIADEM'S GHOST
87	Hibination HIDE 002	THIRST (EP, cassette)	15
86	Hibination HIDE 001	IN SHELTERED WINDS (LP)	25

(see also IQ)

NICE
67	Immediate IM 059	The Thoughts Of Emerlist Davjack/Angel Of Death	6
68	Immediate IM 068	America/The Diamond Hard Blue Apples Of The Moon (pink label, some in p/s)	12/6
68	Immediate IM 072	Brandenburger/Happy Freuds	6
70	Charisma CB 132	Country Pie/One Of Those People	5
70s	Immediate IM 068	America/The Diamond Hard Blue Apples Of The Moon (white label, reissue in p/s)	5
67	Immediate IMLP/IMSP 016	THE THOUGHTS OF EMERLIST DAVJACK (LP)	25
67	Immediate AS 2	ALBUM SAMPLER — THE THOUGHTS OF EMERLIST DAVJACK (1-sided LP, promo only)	25
68	Immediate IMSP 020	ARS LONGA VITA BREVIS (LP)	18
69	Immediate IMSP 026	THE NICE (LP)	18
70	Charisma CAS 1014	FIVE BRIDGES (LP, pink label, gatefold sleeve)	15
71	Charisma CAS 1030	ELEGY (LP, pink label)	15
72	Charisma CS 1	AUTUMN '67 AND SPRING '68 (LP)	12

(see also Keith Emerson, Emerson Lake & Palmer, Jackson Heights, Habits, Brian Davison, Refugee, Attack, Jet, P.P. Arnold)

NICK NICELY
80	Voxette VOX 1001	D.C.T. Dreams/Treeline (p/s)	8
81	EMI EMI 5256	Hillyfields (1892)/49 Cigars (p/s)	8

ALBERT NICHOLAS & AL FAIRWEATHER
56	Tempo A 129	How Long Blues/Rose Room	6

PAUL NICHOLAS
68	Polydor 56285	Where Do I Go/Here Comes The Clown	5
69	Polydor 56322	Who Can I Turn To/Sing A Sad Song For Sammy	5
70	Polydor 56374	Freedom City/Run Shaker Life	5

(see also Oscar, Paul Dean, Ivor Bird)

BILLY NICHOLLS
68	Immediate IM 063	Would You Believe/Daytime Girl (features Small Faces)	30
73	Track 2094 109	Forever's No Time At All/This Song Is Green (with Pete Townshend)	12
68	Immediate IMCP 009	WOULD YOU BELIEVE (LP, withdrawn)	1,000
74	GM GML 1011	LOVE SONGS (LP)	12

JANICE NICHOLLS
63	Decca F 11586	I'll Give It Five/The Wednesbury Madison	12

JOY NICHOLS
53	Parlophone R 3684	Little Red Monkey/Me An' Johnny (78, with Dick Bentley And Jimmy Edwards)	10

MIKE NICHOLS & ELAINE MAY
62	Mercury AMT 1192	A Little More Gauze/Merry Christmas Doctor	6
65	Mercury 20031 MCL	THE BEST OF MIKE NICHOLS & ELAINE MAY (LP)	18

RED NICHOLS & HIS PENNY SYMPHONY
55	Capitol CL 14365	The Viennese Lantern (Lights Of Vienna)/While You're Away	10
56	Capitol CL 14544	Glory, Glory/Bugler's Lament	5
56	Capitol CL 14560	Corky/The Wail Of The Winds	5
56	Capitol CL 14596	The Beautiful Girls Of Vienna/Speak Easy	5
56	Capitol CL 14596	The Beautiful Girls Of Vienna/Speak Easy (78)	8
56	Capitol CL 14617	Cool Tango/Indiana	5
56	Capitol CL 14617	Cool Tango/Indiana (78)	8
51	Capitol LC 6534	JAZZ TIME (10" LP)	12

(see also Kay Starr)

SAM NICHOLS (& MELODY RANGERS)
50	MGM MGM 225	Keep Your Motor Hot/Who Puts The Cat Out When Papa's Out Of Town? (78)	12

LEA NICHOLSON
72	Trailer LER 3010	HORSEMUSIC (LP)	15
80	Kicking Mule SNKF 165	THE CONCERTINA RECORD (LP, features Mike Oldfield)	12

ROGER NICHOLSON
74	Argo ZDA 204	THE GENTLE SOUND OF THE DULCIMER (LP)	12
76	Trailer LER 2094	TIMES & TRADITIONS FOR DULCIMER (LP, with Jake Walton & Andrew Cronshaw)	12

STEVIE NICKS
81	WEA K 79231	Stop Draggin' My Heart Around/Kind Of Woman (p/s, with Tom Petty & Heartbreakers)	6
81	WEA K 79265	Leather And Lace (edit)/Outside The Rain (p/s)	7
82	WEA K 79264	Edge Of Seventeen/Outside The Rain (p/s)	6
83	WEA U 9870	Stand Back/Garbo (p/s)	5
83	WEA U 9870T	Stand Back/Garbo/Wild Heart (12", p/s)	12
83	WEA X 9590	If Anyone Falls/Gate & Garden (p/s)	6
84	WEA U 9690	Nightbird/Nothing Ever Changes (p/s)	18
86	Parlophone R 6110	I Can't Wait/Rock A Little (long) (p/s)	4
86	Parlophone 12R 6110	I Can't Wait (Extended Mix)/Rock A Little (long)/I Can't Wait (7" Mix) (12", p/s)	10
86	Parlophone R 6124	Talk To Me/One More Big Time Rock'n'Roll Star (p/s)	4
86	Parlophone 12R 6124	Talk To Me/One More Big Time Rock'n'Roll Star/Imperial Hotel (12", p/s)	10
86	EMI EMI 5574	Has Anyone Ever Written Anything For You?/I Can't Wait (Dub Mix) (p/s)	5
86	EMI 12EMI 5574	Has Anyone Ever Written Anything For You?/No Spoken Word/ I Can't Wait (Dub Mix) (12", p/s)	12
89	EMI EM 90	Rooms On Fire/Alice (p/s)	4
89	EMI 12EM 90	Rooms On Fire (extended)/Alice/Has Anyone Ever Written Anything For You? (live) (12", p/s)	7
89	EMI 12EMP 90	Rooms On Fire (extended)/Alice/Has Anyone Ever Written Anything For You? (live) (12", poster p/s)	10
89	EMI TCEM 90	Rooms On Fire (extended)/Alice/Has Anyone Ever Written Anything For You? (live) (cassette)	5
89	EMI CDEM 90	Rooms On Fire (extended)/Alice/Has Anyone Ever Written Anything For You? (live) (CD)	8
89	EMI EM 97	Long Way To Go/Real Tears (p/s)	4
89	EMI 12EM 97	Long Way To Go (Remix)/Long Way To Go (7" Version)/Real Tears (12", p/s)	7
89	EMI 12EMG 97	Long Way To Go (7" Version)/(Remix)/Real Tears (12", gatefold p/s)	10
89	EMI CDEM 97	Long Way To Go (7" Version)/Real Tears/No Spoken Word (live)/ Long Way To Go (Remix) (CD)	7
89	EMI EM 114	Whole Lotta Trouble (remix)/Edge Of Seventeen (p/s)	4
89	EMI 12EMP 114	Whole Lotta Trouble (remix)/Edge Of Seventeen/Beauty And The Beast (live) (12", p/s with poster)	10
89	EMI CDEM 114	Whole Lotta Trouble (LP version)/Beauty And The Beast (live)/ Rooms On Fire (CD)	7
91	EMI EMP 203	Sometimes It's A Bitch/Desert Angel (portrait pack)	4
91	EMI CDEM 203	Sometimes It's A Bitch/Desert Angel/Battle Of The Dragons (CD)	7
91	EMI 12EMS 214	I Can't Wait (Time Space Mix)/I Can't Wait (Dub Mix)/Sleeping Angel (12", p/s with 2 colour photos)	7
91	EMI CDEM 214	I Can't Wait (Time Space Mix)/Edge Of Seventeen (live)/ I Can't Wait (12" Version)/Sleeping Angel (CD)	7
81	WEA 499169	BELLA DONNA (LP)	10
83	WEA 2500 7100	THE WILD HEART (LP)	10
89	EMI EMD 1008	THE OTHER SIDE OF THE MIRROR (LP, early copies with hologram)	15
89	EMI CDEMC 1008	THE OTHER SIDE OF THE MIRROR (CD, early copies with hologram)	20

(see also Fleetwood Mac, Buckingham-Nicks, Tom Petty & Heartbreakers)

NICO
65	Immediate IM 003	I'm Not Sayin'/The Last Mile	30
81	Flicknife FLS 206	Vegas/Saeta (p/s)	8
82	Immediate IMS 003	I'm Not Saying/The Last Mile (p/s, reissue)	5
82	Half 1/2 1	Procession/All Tomorrow's Parties (p/s)	5
68	Elektra EKL 4029	THE MARBLE INDEX (LP, orange label, also stereo EKS 74029)	35/30
71	Reprise RSLP 6424	DESERTSHORE (LP, with John Cale)	20
71	MGM Select 2353 025	CHELSEA GIRL (LP)	20
74	Island ILPS 9311	THE END (LP)	18
81	Aura AUL 715	DRAMA OF EXILE (LP, colour cover)	12

(see also John Cale, Velvet Underground, Ayers Cale Nico & Eno)

JIMMY NICOL (& SHUBDUBS)
64	Pye 7N 15623	Humpty Dumpty/Night Train	15
64	Pye 7N 15666	Husky/Don't Come Back (solo)	12
64	Pye 7N 15699	Baby Please Don't Go/Shub Dubbery (possibly unissued)	20+

(see also Sound Of Jimmy Nicol, Georgie Fame)

NICOLE
82	CBS A 2365	A Little Peace/Thank You, Merci (art sleeve without artist photo)	4

NICRA
77	Ogun OG 010	LISTEN/HEAR (LP)	18

(see also Keith Tippett)

NIGHTBIRDS
59	Oriole CB 1490	Cat On A Hot Tin Roof/The Square	10
59	Oriole CB 1490	Cat On A Hot Tin Roof/The Square (78)	10

NIGHTBLOOMS
90	Fierce FRIGHT 041	Crystal Eyes/Never Dream At All (p/s)	10

NIGHTCRAWLERS
67	London HLR 10109	The Little Black Egg/You're Running Wild	30

MINT VALUE £

ROBERT NIGHTHAWK
60s	XX MIN 718	ROBERT NIGHTHAWK (EP) 15

NIGHT-HAWKS
58	Fontana H 120	Cool For Cats/Time Will Tell (78) 10

NIGHTIME FLYER
69	Pye 7N 17739	Talk To Me/Spinning Wheel 5
69	Pye 7N 17798	Don't Push Me Baby/Thru' Loving You 6
71	Pye 7N 45046	Love On Borrowed Time/It's A Hurtin' Thing 5

NIGHTIME FLYER
81	Red Eye EYE 2	Out With A Vengeance/Heavy Metal Rules (p/s) 20

NIGHTINGALES
81	Rough Trade RT 075	Idiot Strength/Seconds (p/s) 4
82	Cherry Red CHERRY 34	USE YOUR LOAF (EP) 4
85	Vindaloo VILP2X	THIS PACKAGE (12" with flexi, booklet, card & lyric sheet, envelope p/s)....... 12

NIGHTMARES IN WAX
79	Inevitable INEV 0002	BIRTH OF A NATION (EP, with wraparound p/s) 20
84	KY KY 9	Black Leather/Shangri-La (12", p/s)..................................... 18
85	KY KY 9 ½	Black Leather/Shangri-La/Girls Song (12", different p/s, 3,000 only) 20
	(see also Dead Or Alive)	

NIGHTRIDERS
66	Polydor BM 56066	Love Me Right Now/Your Friend (withdrawn, issue or promo) 100/75
66	Polydor BM 56116	It's Only The Dog/Your Friend 50
	(see also Mike Sheridan & Nightriders, Mike Sheridan's Lot, Idle Race, Jeff Lynne)	

NIGHTRIDERS
79	Stardust STR 1001	I Saw Her With Another Guy/London Town (picture insert) 15

NIGHTSHIFT
65	Piccadilly 7N 35243	Corrine Corrina/Lavender Tree.. 12
65	Piccadilly 7N 35264	Stormy Monday Blues/That's My Story 15

NIGHT-TIMERS
65	Parlophone R 5355	The Music Played On/Yield Not To Temptation (featuring Herbie Goins) ... 30
	(see also Herbie Goins & Night-Timers, Ronnie Jones)	

NIGHTWING
80	Ovation OVS 1209	Barrel Of Pain/Nightwing (p/s)... 18
84	Gull GULS 75	Treading Water/Call Your Name (p/s) 7
84	Gull GULS 7512	Treading Water/Call Your Name/Barrel Of Pain (12", red vinyl, p/s) 10
84	Gull GULS 77	Night Of Mystery/Dressed To Kill (p/s) 8
84	Gull GULS 7712	Night Of Mystery/Dressed To Kill (12", p/s)............................. 12
85	Gull GULS 80	Strangers Are Welcome/Games To Play//The Devil Walks Behind You/ Cell 151 (double pack, gatefold p/s) 7
79	Ovation OV 1757	SOMETHING IN THE AIR (LP) 15
82	Gull GULP 1036	BLACK SUMMER (LP) 12
83	Gull GULP 1038	STAND UP AND BE COUNTED (LP) 12
83	Gull PGULP 1038	STAND UP AND BE COUNTED (LP, picture disc) 15
85	Gull GULP 1043	NIGHT OF MYSTERY (LP) 12
	(see also Alec Johnson Band, Nutz)	

NIHILIST SPASM BAND
85	United Dairies UD 016	1X - X = X (LP) 20

BILL NILE (& HIS GOODTIME BAND)
67	Decca F 12661	Pashionella Grundy/Bric A Brac Man 5
70	Deram DM 290	I Try Not To Laugh/Nobody Knows The Trouble I've Seen.................. 5

WILLY NILLY
84	Ad Hoc AH 1	On The Spur Of The Moment/Half A Job (p/s, with 'time-table' insert) 45

(HARRY) NILSSON
67	RCA Victor RCA 1632	You Can't Do That/Ten Little Indians 5
68	RCA Victor RCA 1675	One/Sister Marie.. 5
68	RCA RCA 1707	Everybody's Talkin'/Don't Leave Me 5
68	RCA RCA 1764	Mourning Glory/Rainmaker 5
69	RCA RCA 1864	Maybe/The Puppy Song... 5
69	RCA RCA 1876	Everybody's Talkin'/One... 5
70	RCA RCA 1913	I Guess The Lord Must Be In New York City/Good Old Desk 5
70	RCA RCA 1935	I'll Be Home/Waiting.. 5
70	RCA RCA 1987	Down To The Valley/Buy My Album 5
71	RCA RCA 2080	Are You Sleeping? 5
72	RCA RCA 2300	Me And My Arrow/Remember (Christmas)/The Lottery Song 5
74	RCA RCA 2459	Many Rivers To Cross/Don't Forget Me 5
75	RCA RCA 2504	Save The Last Dance For Me/All My Life................................ 5
79	RCA Record Year LB 2	Without You/Noel Edmonds Introduces Record Year (Lever Bros premium)... 5
84	Polydor POSP 703	Loneliness/Silver Horse (p/s)... 5
68	RCA Victor RD/SF 7928	PANDEMONIUM SHADOW SHOW (LP, mono/stereo) 15/12
68	RCA RD/SF 7973	AERIAL BALLET (LP, mono/stereo) 15/12
69	RCA SF 8010	SKIDOO (LP, soundtrack)... 18
69	RCA SF 8046	HARRY (LP) 12
70	RCA SF 8091	NILSSON SINGS NEWMAN (LP, with Randy Newman) 12
71	RCA SF 8166	THE POINT (LP, single sleeve or reissue with gatefold sleeve & book) .... each 15
73	RCA SF 8326	AERIAL PANDEMONIUM BALLET (LP)................................... 12
74	Rapple/RCA APL1-0220	SON OF DRACULA (LP, soundtrack, with Ringo Starr, fold-out sleeve)......... 15
	(see also Randy Newman, Ringo Starr, Cher)	

NILSSON TWINS
57	Capitol CL 14698	Rain On My Window/I Dance When I Walk................................. 5

LEONARD NIMOY

68	Dot (S)LPD 511	MR. SPOCK PRESENTS MUSIC FROM OUTER SPACE (LP)	20
72	Rediffusion ZS 156	MUSIC FROM OUTER SPACE (LP)	15

NINA

69	CBS 4681	Do You Know How Christmas Trees Are Grown?/The More Things Change	12

NINA & FREDERIK

59	Pye Intl. 7N 25021	Jamaica Farewell/Come Back Liza	6
59	Pye Intl. N 25021	Jamaica Farewell/Come Back Liza (78)	12
59	Pye Intl. 7N 25043	The Formula For Love (with Louis Armstrong)/LOUIS ARMSTRONG with VALMA MIDDLETON: Struttin' With Some Barbecue	5
59	Pye Intl. 7N 25043	The Formula For Love (with Louis Armstrong)/LOUIS ARMSTRONG with VALMA MIDDLETON: Struttin' With Some Barbecue	10
59	Columbia DB 4332	Listen To The Ocean/I Would Amor Her	5
59	Columbia DB 4332	Listen To The Ocean/I Would Amor Her (78)	8
59	Columbia DB 4375	Mary's Boy Child/Oh Sinner Man! (78)	10
59	Pye Intl. NEP 44002	VOLUME ONE (EP)	8
59	Pye Intl. NEP 44003	VOLUME TWO (EP)	8
59	Pye Nixa NPT 19023	NINA & FREDERICK (10" LP)	15

NINE DAYS WONDER

71	Harvest SHSP 4014	NINE DAYS WONDER (LP)	30

(see also Kilburn & High Roads)

NINE INCH NAILS

91	Island ISDJ 508	Sin (Radio Edit)/(same) (promo only, stickered p/s)	12
91	Island 9IS 508	Sin (Long)/Sin (Dub)/Get Down Make Love (9", p/s)	15
92	Island IS 552DJ	Wish (Radio Edit) (1-sided, stickered plain sleeve, promo only)	12

999

77	Labritain LAB 999	I'm Alive/Quite Disappointing (p/s)	12
77	United Artists UP 36299	Nasty Nasty/No Pity (p/s, green or black vinyl)	10/5
77	United Artists FREE 7	Nasty Nasty/No Pity (78rpm promo, 50 copies only)	60
78	Labritain 12 FREE 10	Waiting/Action (12", mail-order freebie)	8
78	United Artists UP 36399	Emergency/My Street Stinks (p/s)	5
78	United Artists UP 36376	Me And My Desire/Crazy (p/s)	4
78	United Artists UP 36435	Feelin' Alright With The Crew/Titanic (My Over) Reaction (p/s)	4
78	United Artists UP 36467	Homicide/Soldier (p/s, some on green vinyl)	5/4
79	United Artists UP 36519	I'm Alive/Quite Disappointing (p/s, reissue)	5
79	Radar ADA 46	Found Out Too Late/Lie Lie Lie (p/s)	4
80	Polydor POSP 99	Trouble/Love Made A Fool Of You (p/s)	4
81	Albion ION 1011	Obsessed/Change/Lie, Lie, Lie (live) (p/s, some with laminated sleeve and shrinkwrapped with patch)	7/4
81	Albion ION 1017	Li'l Red Riding Hood/Waiting For Your Number To Be Called/I Ain't Gonna Tell Ya (live) (p/s, with stencil; some shrinkwrapped)	7/4
81	Albion ION 1023	Indian Reservation/So Greedy (Remixed)/Taboo (Remix) (p/s, clear vinyl, with sticker)	4
82	Albion ION 1033	Wild Sun/Scandal City/Bongos On The Nile (p/s, yellow vinyl)	4
78	United Artists UAG 30199	999 (LP, with inner sleeve)	18
78	United Artists UAG 30209	SEPARATES (LP, with inner sleeve)	18

(see also Kilburn & High Roads)

NINESENSE

76	Ogun OG 900	OH! FOR THE EDGE (LP)	12
77	Ogun OG 910	HAPPY DAZE (LP)	12

(see also Elton Dean, Julie Tippetts, Keith Tippett, Mark Charig, Harold Beckett, Alan Skidmore)

NINETTE

66	Pye 7N 17039	Push A Little Button/I Just Wonder Why	5

1910 FRUITGUM CO.

68	Pye International 7N 25447	Simon Says/Reflections From The Looking Glass	6
68	Pye International 7N 25458	May I Take A Giant Step (Into Your Heart)/(Poor Old) Mr. Jensen	5
68	Pye International 7N 25468	1, 2, 3, Red Light/Sticky, Sticky	5
68	Pye International 7N 25478	Pop Goes The Weasel/The Year 2001	5
69	Buddah 201 037	Indian Giver/Liza	5
69	Buddah 201 049	Special Delivery/No-Good Annie	5
68	Pye Intl. N(S)PL 28115	SIMON SAYS (LP)	20
69	Buddah 203 014	GOODY GOODY GUMDROPS (LP)	15
70	Buddah 2359 006	HARD RIDE (LP)	15

1910 FRUITGUM CO./LEMON PIPERS

68	Pye Intl. NEP 44091	PRESENTING... (EP, 1 side each)	15

1984

69	Big T BIG 117	This Little Boy/Rosalyn	5
69	Big T BIG 120	Got To Have Your Love/Here We Are	5

9.30 FLY

72	Ember NR 5062	9.30 FLY (LP)	100

NINEY (& DESTROYERS/OBSERVERS)

70	Amalgamated AMG 856	Niney Special/Danger Zone	12
70	Pressure Beat PR 5501	Honey No Money/INSPIRATIONS: This Message To You	8
71	Big BG 317	You Must Believe/You Must Believe Version	10
71	Big Shot BI 568	Blood And Fire/Mud And Water	6
71	Big Shot BI 586	Message To The Ungodly/Message To The Ungodly — Version	6
71	Gas GAS 167	Blood And Fire/ROLAND ALPHONSO: 33 66	6
71	Moodisc HME 111	People Let Love Shine/MUDIES ALL STARS: Too Much	6
72	Big Shot BI 607	Hiding By The Riverside/The Red Sea	5
72	Big Shot BI 609	Beg In The Gutter/Beg In The Gutter Version	5

NIRVANA (U.S.)

72	Big Shot BI 610	Everyday Music (by The Observers)/Observing The Av	6
72	Bullet BU 503	Aily And Ailaloo (& Max)/Version	6
72	Downtown DT 494	Get Out My Life/Get Out My Life — Version	5
72	Downtown DT 495	Hi Diddle/Hi Diddle — Version	5

(see also Niney's All Stars, Observers)

NINEY'S ALL STARS
70	Unity UN 563	Skankee/Skankee — Version	6

(see also Niney, Observers)

NING
71	Decca F 23114	Machine/More Ning	6

NINO & EBBTIDES
61	Top Rank JAR 572	Those Oldies But Goodies/Don't Run Away	40

NIPPLE ERECTORS
78	Soho SH 1/2	King Of The Bop/Nervous Wreck (50 only with glossy p/s, later matt p/s)	20/12

(see also Nips, Pogues)

NIPS
78	Soho SH 4	All The Time In The World/Private Eyes (foldover p/s)	20
80	Soho SH 9	Gabrielle/Vengeance (no p/s)	10
80	Soho SH 9	Gabrielle/Vengeance (tour copy with 'licensed to cool' stamp)	30
80	Chiswick CHIS 119	Gabrielle/Vengeance (reissue, p/s)	10
81	Test Pressing TP 5	Happy Song/Nobody To Love (p/s)	15
80	Soho HOHO 1	ONLY AT THE END OF THE BEGINNING (LP, with insert, white labels)	25

(see also Nipple Erectors, Pogues)

NIRVANA (U.K.)
67	Island WIP 6016	Tiny Goddess/I Believe In Magic	15
67	Island WIP 6020	Pentecost Hotel/Feelin' Shattered	10
68	Island WIP 6029	Rainbow Chaser/Flashbulb	12
68	Island WIP 6038	Girl In The Park/C Side In Ocho Rios	12
68	Island WIP 6045	All Of Us (The Touchables)/Trapeze	10
69	Island WIP 6052	Wings Of Love/Requiem To John Coltrane	20
69	Island WIP 6057	Oh! What A Performance/Darling Darlene	15
70	Pye International 7N 25525	The World Is Cold Without You/Christopher Lucifer	15
71	Vertigo 6059 035	The Saddest Day Of My Life/(I Wanna Go) Home	12
71	Philips 6006 127	Pentecost Hotel/Lazy Day Drift	7
72	Philips 6006 166	Stadium/Please Believe Me	7
76	Bradleys BRAD 7602	Two Of A Kind/Before Midnight	5
76	Island WIP 6180	Rainbow Chaser/Tiny Goddess (p/s)	5
78	Pepper UP 36461	Love Is/Pascale	5
79	Pepper UP 36538	Restless Wind/Thank You And Goodnight	5
81	Zilch ZILCH 8	The Picture Of Dorian Gray/No It Isn't	5
82	Zilch ZILCH 15	Black And White Or Colour/Tall Trees	5
88	Bam Caruso OPRA 45	Black Flower/WIMPLE WINCH: Save My Soul (jukebox issue, die-cut sleeve)	5
68	Island ILP 959/ILPS 9059	THE STORY OF SIMON SIMOPATH (LP, pink label, mono/stereo)	70
68	Island ILPS 9087	ALL OF US (LP, pink label)	70
70	Pye Intl. NSPL 28132	DEDICATED TO MARKOS III (LP)	100
71	Vertigo 6360 031	LOCAL ANAESTHETIC (LP, gatefold sleeve, spiral label)	40

MINT VALUE £

| 72 | Philips 6308 089 | SONGS OF LOVE AND PRAISE (LP) | 50 |
| 87 | Bam-Caruso KIRI 061 | BLACK FLOWER (LP) | 12 |

(see also Patrick Campbell-Lyons, Ray Singer, Pica, Hat & Tie)

NIRVANA (U.S.)

89	Tupelo TUP EP8	Blew/Love Buzz/Been A Son/Stain (12", p/s)	40
89	Tupelo TUP CD8	Blew/Love Buzz/Been A Son/Stain (CD)	50
91	Tupelo TUP 25	Sliver/Dive (gatefold p/s, green vinyl only, 2,000 pressed)	25
91	Tupelo TUP EP25	Sliver/Dive/About A Girl (live) (12", p/s)	12
91	Tupelo TUP EP25	Sliver/Dive/About A Girl (live) (12", repressing, blue vinyl, p/s)	30
91	Tupelo TUP CDEP25	Sliver/Dive/About A Girl (live)/Spank Thru (live) (CD)	15
91	Geffen DGCT 5	Smells Like Teen Spirit (Edit)/Even In His Youth/Aneurysm (12", p/s)	10
91	Geffen DGCTP 5	Smells Like Teen Spirit (Edit)/Drain You (LP Version)/Aneurysm (12", picture disc, die-cut p/s)	20
91	Geffen DGCCD 5	Smells Like Teen Spirit (Edit)/Drain You/Even In His Youth/Aneurysm (CD, digipack with tour dates)	15
92	Geffen DGCTP 7	Come As You Are/Endless, Nameless/School (live) (12", picture disc, die-cut p/s)	18
92	Geffen DGCTP 9	Lithium/Been A Son (live)/Curmudgeon (12", picture disc, die-cut p/s)	15
92	Geffen DGCTP 34	In Bloom/Sliver (live)/Polly (live) (12", picture disc, die-cut p/s)	15
93	Touch & Go TG 83	Oh, The Guilt/JESUS LIZARD: Puss (p/s, blue vinyl, some with poster)	18/10
93	Touch & Go TG 83	Oh, The Guilt/JESUS LIZARD: Puss (p/s, black vinyl)	10
93	Touch & Go TGCD 83	Oh, The Guilt/JESUS LIZARD: Puss (CD)	15
93	Geffen GFST 66	All Apologies/Rape Me (12", p/s with 2 art prints)	8
94	Geffen (no cat. no.)	Penny Royal Tea (Scott Litt Mix)/Where Did You Sleep Last Night (live) (unreleased, 10 test pressings only)	800
94	Geffen NIRPRO (no cat. no.)	Penny Royal Tea (Scott Litt Mix) (CD, 1-track, no inlay, promo only)	800
89	Tupelo TUP LP 6	BLEACH (LP, 300 on white vinyl, 2,000 on green vinyl)	250/100
89	Tupelo TUP LP 6	BLEACH (LP, black vinyl)	15
89	Tupelo TUP CD 6	BLEACH (CD, original issue with extra tracks "Love Buzz" & "Downer")	20
91	Geffen DGC 24425	NEVERMIND (LP, with inner sleeve)	15
91	Geffen DGCCD 24425	NEVERMIND (CD, without uncredited bonus track "Endless, Nameless")	20
94	Geffen GED 24727	UNPLUGGED IN NEW YORK (LP, white vinyl with inner sleeve)	15

(see also Foo Fighters)

NITE-LITERS

| 72 | RCA 2214 | K-Jee/Tanga Boo Gonk | 5 |
| 72 | RCA SF 8282 | INSTRUMENTAL DIRECTIONS (LP) | 15 |

NITE PEOPLE

66	Fontana TF 747	Sweet Tasting Wine/Nobody But You	12
67	Fontana TF 808	Trying To Find Another Man/Stay As Sweet As You Are	10
67	Fontana TF 885	Summertime Blues/In The Springtime	30
68	Fontana TF 919	Morning Sun/Where You There	12
69	Page One POF 149	Love, Love, Love/Hot Smoke And Sassafras (some with insert)	12/8
69	Page One POF 159	Is This A Dream/Cream Tea	8
70	Page One POF 174	Season Of The Rain/P.M.	8
69	Page One POLS 025	P.M. (LP)	160

(see also Banana Bunch)

NITE ROCKERS

| 58 | RCA RCA 1079 | Nite Rock (Lonely Train)/Oh! Baby | 80 |
| 58 | RCA RCA 1079 | Nite Rock (Lonely Train)/Oh! Baby (78) | 75 |

NITESHADES

| 65 | CBS 201763 | Be My Guest/I Must Reveal | 7 |
| 65 | CBS 201817 | Fell So Fast/I'm Not Gonna Worry | 7 |

NITRO FUNCTION

(see under Billy Cox)

NITTY GRITTY DIRT BAND

67	Liberty LIB 55948	Buy Me For The Rain/Candy Man	6
68	Liberty LBF 15099	Collegiana/End Of Your Line	6
70	Liberty LBF 15358	Rave On/The Cure	5
71	United Artists UP 35253	House At Pool Corner/Travelin' Mood	5
71	United Artists UP 35282	Some Of Shelley's Blues/The Cure	5
72	United Artists UP 35357	Jambalaya/Hoping To Say	5
68	Liberty LBL/LBS 83122	PURE DIRT (LP)	20
69	Liberty LBL/LBS 83286	DEAD AND ALIVE (LP)	20
71	Liberty LBG 83345	UNCLE CHARLIE AND HIS DOG TEDDY (LP)	15
72	United Artists UAS 29284	ALL THE GOOD TIMES (LP)	15
74	United Artists USD 307/8	STARS AND STRIPES FOREVER (2-LP)	15

NITZER EBB

85	Power Of Voice NEP 1	Isn't It Funny How Your Body Works/The Way You Live/Crane/Cold War (12", p/s with insert)	7
85	own label	BASIC PAIN PROCEDURE (EP, cassette, given away at gig)	40
86	Power Of Voice NEB 3	Let Your Body Learn/Let Your Body Learn (Instrumental) (12", p/s)	10

JACK NITZSCHE

63	Reprise R 20202	The Lonely Surfer/Song For A Summer Night	10
63	Reprise R 20237	Night Walker/Green Grass Of Texas	7
78	MCA MCA 366	Hard Workin' Man (featuring Captain Beefheart)/Coke Machine	6
74	Warner Bros K 41211	ST GILES CRIPPLEGATE (LP)	15

(see also Date With Soul, Mick Jagger, Captain Beefheart, Randy Newman, Crazy Horse)

NIVENS

| 88 | Woosh WOOSH 1 | Let Loose Of My Knee/HOLIDAYMAKERS: Everyday (flexidisc with *Woosh* fanzine, foldaround p/s in poly bag) | 8 |
| 89 | Woosh WOOSH 5 | Yesterday/I Hope You'll Always Be My Friend (p/s) | 5 |

MINT VALUE £

REVEREND A.W. NIX
51 Decca F 9720 The Black Diamond Express To Hell (Parts 1 & 2) (78) 25

WILLIE NIX
(see under Willie Love, Joe Hill Louis)

NIX-NOMADS
64 HMV POP 1354 You're Nobody (Till Somebody Loves You)/She'll Be Sweeter Than You
(demos miscredited to Nix-Nom*ands*) 70

MEL NIXON
75 Alaska ALA 26 Every Beat Of Your Heart/ASTRA NOVA ORCHESTRA: Soul Sleeper 5

N-JOI
90 Deconstruction PT 44042 Anthem/Manic/Techno Gangsters (12", original issue) 15

RAB NOAKES
78 Ring O' 2017 115 Waiting Here For You/Restless (some in p/s) 15/8
78 Ring O' 2017 117 I Won't Let You Down/Long After Dark (unreleased)
70 Decca SKL 5061 DO YOU SEE THE LIGHTS (LP) 20
72 A&M AMLS 68119 RAB NOAKES (LP, with Stealers Wheel) 10
78 Ring O' 2339 201 RESTLESS (LP) 15

NO ARTIST
78 Deptford Fun City DFC 06 Deep Cuts/Deeper Cuts (p/s) 4

NOBELMEN
59 Top Rank JAR 155 Thunder Wagon/Dragon Walk 12
59 Top Rank JAR 155 Thunder Wagon/Dragon Walk (78) 18

LISA NOBLE
58 Decca F 11006 Maggie! — Yes Ma!/Who's Sorry Now 5
58 Decca F 11006 Maggie! — Yes Ma!/Who's Sorry Now (78) 8
58 Decca F 11051 It's A Boy/The Saints 5
58 Decca F 11051 It's A Boy/The Saints (78) 8

NICK NOBLE
57 Mercury MT 165 Fallen Star/Let Me Hold You In My Arms (78, with Dick Noel Singers) 12
60 Coral Q 72403 The Tip Of My Fingers/Sweet Love 6
60 Coral Q 72413 Island Farewell/Excuse Me (I Think I've Got A Heartache) 5
(see also Dick Noel)

PATSY ANN NOBLE
61 HMV POP 980 Good Looking Boy/The Guy Who Can Mend A Broken Heart 12
63 Columbia DB 4956 Don't You Ever Change Your Mind/Sour Grapes 8
63 Columbia DB 7008 Heartbreak Avenue/I'm Nobody's Baby 8
63 Columbia DB 7060 I Was Only Foolin' Myself/Ordinary Love 8
63 Columbia DB 7088 Accidents Will Happen/He Tells Me With His Eyes 10
63 Columbia DB 7148 It's Better To Cry Today/Don't Tell Him I Told You 8
64 Columbia DB 7258 I Did Nothing Wrong/Better Late Than Never 8
64 Columbia DB 7318 Private Property/Crack In The Door 8
64 Columbia DB 7386 Tied Up With Mary/Green Eyed People 8
65 Columbia DB 7472 Then You Can Tell Me Goodbye/If You Wanna Be More Than Friends 8
65 Polydor BM 56054 He Who Rides A Tiger/City Of Night 12
(see also Trisha Noble)

TRISHA NOBLE
67 MGM MGM 1371 Live For Life/The New Is Rarely Patchka 8
(see also Patsy Ann Noble)

CLIFF NOBLES (& CO.)
68 Direction 58-3518 The Horse/Love Is Alright 5
68 Direction 58-3738 Judge Baby, I'm Back/Horse Fever (solo) 5
69 Direction 58-4205 Switch It On/Burning Desire 5
68 Direction 8-63477 THE HORSE (LP) 15

NO CHOICE
83 Riot City RIOT 20 SADIST DREAM (EP) 5

NO COVER
82 Guardian GRC 136 200 Voices/Seen Too Much (p/s) 4

NOCTURNAL EMISSIONS
84 Sterile SR 6 NO SACRIFICE (12", p/s, 2,000 only) 15
84 CFC LP 2 CHAOS — LIVE AT THE RITZY (LP) 50
84 Illuminated JAMS LP 33 VIRAL SHEDDING (LP) 20
84 Sterile EMISS 001 TISSUE OF LIES (LP, 1st batch numbered, later in blue sleeve) 80/40
84 Sterile ION 2 FRUITING BODY (LP) 50
84 Sterile SR 4 DROWNING IN A SEA OF BLISS (LP) 70
84 Sterile SR 5 BEFEHLSNOTSTAND (LP) 50
85 Sterile SRC 003 DEATHDAY (cassette) 10
85 Sterile SR 7 SONGS OF LOVE AND REVOLUTION (LP) 20
86 Sterile SR 9 SHAKE THOSE CHAINS, RATTLE THOSE CAGES (LP) 15
87 Earhtly Delights EARTH 02 THE WORLD IS MY WOMB (LP) 20
88 Earhtly Delights EARTH 04 SPIRITFLESH (LP) 25
89 Earhtly Delights EARTH 05 BEYOND LOGIC (LP) 15
90 Earhtly Delights EARTH 06 MOUTH OF THE BABES (LP) 15

NOCTURNES
55 MGM SP 1120 Whodat? (Buck Dance)/Hey Punchinello 7
55 MGM SP 1148 Birmin'ham/Toodle-oo Igaloo 7

NOCTURNES
64 Solar SRP 102 Troika/Rawhide 15

NOCTURNES
67	Columbia DB 8158	Wish You Would Show Me Your Mind/I Do, I Do	6
67	Columbia DB 8219	Why (Am I Treated So Bad?)/Save The Last Dance For Me	6
68	Columbia DB 8332	A New Man/Suddenly Free	6
68	Columbia DB 8453	Carpet Man/Look At Me	5
68	Columbia DB 8493	Montage/Fairground Man	5
68	Columbia S(C)X 6223	THE NOCTURNES (LP)	18
68	Columbia S(C)X 6315	WANTED ALIVE (LP)	20

(see also Lyn Paul)

NOCTURNS
64	Decca F 12002	Carryin' On/Three Cool Cats	7

NODDY STORIES
53	HMV BD 1297	Noddy & Big Ears Go Shopping/Noddy Builds His House (78, picture label)	8
53	HMV BD 1298	Noddy At The Police Court/Noddy Lets The Animals Out Of The Ark (78, picture label)	8
53	HMV BD 1299	Noddy's Adventures With His Car/Noddy Is Naughty (78, picture label)	8

NO DOUBT
97	Interscope INSJB 95515	Don't Speak/Greener Pastures (jukebox issue, no p/s)	8
97	Interscope INSJB 95539	Just A Girl/Open The Gate (jukebox issue, no p/s)	8

PROFESSOR ERNEST NODE & HIS MUG & JUG BAND
67	Columbia DB 8100	The Egg Plant That Ate Chicago/I'm In The Doghouse	7

NOEL
79	Virgin VS 258	Dancing Is Dangerous/Dancing Is Dangerous (Long Version) (p/s)	5
79	Virgin VS 258-12	Dancing Is Dangerous/Dancing Is Dangerous (Long Version) (12", die-cut p/s)	8
79	Virgin VS 286	The Night They Invented Love/Au Revoir (p/s)	6
79	Virgin VP 2126	IS THERE MORE TO LIFE THAN DANCING (LP, picture disc)	10

(see also Sparks)

DICK NOEL
56	London HLH 8295	(The Same Thing Happens With) The Birds And The Bees/Birth Of The Blues	20
56	London HLH 8295	(The Same Thing Happens With) The Birds And The Bees/Birth Of The Blues (78)	15

(see also Nick Nobel)

NO ENTRY BAND
78	Kube Arts KA 1	COLD AND LONELY LIVES EP (p/s)	4

NO EXIT
83	Slug CUS 1786	Casablancan Night/Anything You Say (p/s)	5

NO FAITH
81	No Faith NF 001	Double Trouble (p/s, private pressing)	100

NOIR
71	Dawn DNLS 3029	WE HAD TO LET YOU HAVE IT (LP, with insert)	20

NO KIDDING
74	Wave	NO KIDDING (LP)	15

COLEEN NOLAN
78	Target TGT 142	Andy/Thanks For Calling	6

(see also Nolan Sisters, Young & Moody)

DENISE NOLAN
79	Pye 7P 126	Sorry Seems To Be The Hardest Word/Holding You (no p/s)	4
82	Mercury MER 103	Girls Do It, Boys Do It/Just Can't Stop The Feeling (p/s)	4
82	Mercury MER 125	In Love With Love/My Mind's Made Up On You (p/s)	5

(see also Nolan Sisters)

JOE NOLAN & HIS BAND
69	Jolly JY 013	Cool It With Reggae/Reggae With Me	7
69	Jolly JY 016	Confidential/Poison Reggae	7

(see also Bonnie Frankson)

TERRY NOLAND
58	Coral Q 72311	Oh Baby! Look At Me/Puppy Love	165
58	Coral Q 72311	Oh Baby! Look At Me/Puppy Love (78)	60

NOLAN SISTERS/NOLANS
72	Nevis NEVS 007	Blackpool/Apple Pie	10
72	Nevis NEVEP 005	SILENT NIGHT (EP)	6
74	EMI EMI 2209	But I Do/Now I'm Stuck On You	8
75	Target TGT 103	Make A Little Sunshine Shine/Have Love Will Travel	5
76	Target TGT 108	Rain/Oh My Darling	6
76	Target TGT 116	Thanks For Calling/Oh My Darling	5
76	Target TGT 121	When You Are A King/Hey What A Day	5
77	Target TGT 132	Love Transformation/Oh My Darling	4
77	Target TGT 137	Love Bandit/Don't Take Your Love Away	4
78	Target TGT 140	Don't It Make My Brown Eyes Blue/Something Tells Me (p/s)	4
78	Target SAM 84	Medley (sampler for "20 Giant Hits")	6
82	Epic EPCA 2625	GREATEST ORIGINAL HITS (EP)	4
82	Lyntone LYN 11763	Konica Pop Flexi (p/s, 1-sided flexidisc, featuring edits of Nolan Sisters' "Attention To Me" + tracks by Abba & Stars On 45)	4
84	Scoop 33 75R5032	THE NOLANS (EP)	4
72	Nevis NEVR 009	THE SINGING NOLANS (LP)	18
77	Hanover Grand HG 19751	THE NOLAN SISTERS (LP, sold only at London Room Club, Drury Lane)	25

(see also Coleen Nolan, Denise Nolan)

PIERRE NOLES
63	Oriole CB 1791	Jacqueline/Marilyn	6

MINT VALUE £

NAZ NOMAD & NIGHTMARES
84	Big Beat NS 93	I Had Too Much To Dream (Last Night)/Cold Turkey (p/s)	4
84	Big Beat WIK 21	GIVE DADDY THE KNIFE CINDY (LP, purple vinyl)	10
	(see also Damned)		

NOMADS
70	Pye 7N 17906	The Singer Sang His Song/Lovin' Him	5

NON
78	MR-00	Mode Of Infection/Knife Ladder/Soundtracks (1-sided, with two centre holes, in folded p/s in plastic bag)	80
80	Mute MUTE 7	I Can't Look Straight/SMEGMA: Flash Cards (p/s, with 2 centre holes)	6
	(see also Boyd Rice)		

NO NAMES
65	Polydor NH 59080	All Because Of You/She Is Mine	30

PETER NOONE
71	Rak RAK 114	Oh You Pretty Thing/Together Forever	5
71	Rak RAK 121	Right On Mother/Walnut Whirl	7
72	Rak RAK 129	Shoo Be Doo Wah/Because You Were There	5
72	Rak RAK 136	Should I/Each And Every Minute	5
	(see also Herman's Hermits)		

NO OTHER NAME
79	Daylight LD 500	DEATH INTO LIFE (LP, with insert)	25

NO QUARTER
83	Reel REEL 1	Survivors/Time And Space/Racing For Home (12", foldout p/s)	40

NORA/BUNNY
72	Tropical AL 0015	Butterfly/TROPICAL ALL STARS: Fly Version	5

KEN NORDINE
57	London RE-D 1091	KEN NORDINE READS (EP, with Billy Vaughn Orchestra)	20
59	London Jazz EZ-D 19040	WORD JAZZ (EP)	15
	(see also Billy Vaughn & His Orchestra)		

NORFOLK & JOY
79	Dara MPA 031	SCOTSOUNDS (LP)	30

NO RIGHT TURN
83	Chelful CHL 001	NO (LP)	25

NORKS
92	Big Jug NIP 1	A NICE PAIR (2-LP, 'nude' pop-up sleeve with free size 36-D brassiere)	100

NORMAL
78	Mute MUTE 001	T.V.O.D./Warm Leatherette (p/s)	6
	(see also Robert Rental)		

GENE NORMAN (JUST JAZZ)
51	Vogue V 2022	Hot House (Parts 1 & 2) (78, solo)	8
51	Vogue V 2047	Blue Lou (Parts 1 & 2) (78)	8
54	Vogue V 2271	One O'Clock Jump/Two O'Clock Jump (78)	8
54	Vogue V 2272	Four O'Clock Jump/Three O'Clock Jump (78)	8
56	Vogue V 2047	Blue Lou (Parts 1 & 2)	6
50s	Vogue V 2022	Hot House (Parts 1 & 2) (solo)	6
50s	Vogue V 2272	Four O'Clock Jump/Three O'Clock Jump	6

LARRY NORMAN
69	Key KL 010/Dove DOVE 64	UPON THIS ROCK (LP)	12
73	MGM 2315 135	I'M ONLY VISITING THIS PLANET (LP, with lyric sheet)	12
76	Solid Rock ROCKY 1	IN ANOTHER LAND (LP, gatefold sleeve)	15

MONTY NORMAN
55	HMV 7M 349	The Shifting, Whispering Sands/Bonnie Blue Gal	7
57	HMV POP 281	The Garden Of Eden/Priscilla	10
63	United Artists UEP 1010	DOCTOR NO (EP)	20
63	United Artists (S)ULP 1097	DOCTOR NO (LP, soundtrack, mono/stereo)	20/25

OLIVER NORMAN
67	Polydor 56176	Down In The Basement/Drowning In My Own Despair	10
68	Polydor 56247	People People/You'll Find It Will Come	5

NORMAN & HOOLIGANS
77	President PT 461	I'm A Punk/Re-Entry (no p/s)	12

NORMAN & INVADERS
64	United Artists UP 1031	Stacey/Our Wedding Day	8
64	United Artists UP 1058	Our Wedding Day/Stacey (reissue)	5
65	United Artists UP 1077	Night Train To Surbiton/Likely Lads	12

NORMAN CONQUEST
67	MGM MGM 1376	Two People/Upside Down	40
	(see also Factory, Peter & Wolves, John Pantry)		

FREDDIE NORTH
72	Mojo 2092 043	Sweeter Than Sweetness/I Did The Woman Wrong	5
72	Mojo 2916 012	FRIEND (LP)	15

ROY NORTH
63	Oak RGJ 107	Blues In Three/Blues In Five	40

NORTHERN LIGHTS
66	United Artists UP 1123	No Time/Time To Move Along	30
66	United Artists UP 1161	Through Darkness, Light/Baby Those Are The Rules	30
	(see also Hootenanny Singers, Abba)		

NORTHERN UPROAR
95	Heavenly HVN 47	Rollercoaster/Smooth Geezer (p/s) 4
95	Heavenly HVN 4710	Rollercoaster/Smooth Geezer/Rough Boy/Waiting On (Acoustic Version) (10", promo only, 500 pressed) 7

NORTH STARS
65	Fontana TF 581	For My True Love/Nothing But The Best 6
66	Fontana TF 726	She's So Far Out She's In/Eeenie Meenie Minee Mo 15

NORTHWIND
71	Regal Zono. SLRZ 1020	SISTER, BROTHER, LOVER (LP) 165

(see also Elastic Band)

NOSEBLEEDS
77	Rabid TOSH 12	Ain't Bin To No Music School/Fascist Pigs (p/s) 6

(see also Durutti Column, Ed Banger, Blue Orchids)

NOSMO
74	Pye 7N 45382	Teenage Love/Goodbye 8

NO SWEAT
79	Rip Off RIP 4	Start All Over Again/You Should Be So Lucky (p/s) 5

NOTATIONS (U.K.)
72	Chapter One SCH 174	Need Your Love/Just Nothing Left To Give 25

NOTATIONS (U.S.)
76	Curtom K 16696	Think Before You Stop/I'm Losing 6
76	Curtom K 56212	NOTATIONS (LP) 25

FREDDIE NOTES & RUDIES
69	Downtown DT 427	I Don't Wanna Lose That Girl/Train From Vietnam 8
69	Grape GR 3010	Guns Of Navarone/Yester-Me, Yester-You 7
69	Grape GR 3011	Babylon Girl/Girl I've Got A Date 7
69	Trojan TR 7713	Shanghai/Rome Wasn't Built In A Day 8
70	Bullet BU 421	The Feeling Is Fine/Girl You're Killing Me 6
70	Trojan TR 7724	Rocco/Don't Tell Your Mama 7
70	Trojan TR 7734	Down On The Farm/Easy Street 7
70	Trojan TR 7791	Montego Bay/RUDIES: Blue Mountain 5
70	Trojan TR 7810	Walk A Mile In My Shoes/JOHNNY ARTHEY ORCHESTRA: Reggae Rouser 6
70	Duke DU 63	The Bull/River Ben Come Up 7
70	Duke DU 68	Chicken Inn/Chicken Scratch 7
70	B&C CB 125	It Came Out The Sky/Well Oh Well (p/s) 5
70	Trojan TBL 109	UNITY (LP) 20
70	Trojan TBL 152	MONTEGO BAY (LP) 20

NOTHINGS
65	CBS 201779	At Times Like This/Love So Sweet 6

NO TREND/LYDIA LUNCH
85	Widowspeak WSP 3	HEART OF DARKNESS (12" EP) 7

(see also Lydia Lunch)

NOTSENSIBLES
79	Redball RR 02	(I'm In Love With) Margaret Thatcher/Little Boxes/Gary Bushell's Band Of The Week (p/s) 8
80	Bent SMALL BENT 5	Death To Disco/Coronation Street Hustle/Lying On The Sofa (p/s) 7
80	Snotty Snail NELCOL 1	(I'm In Love With) Margaret Thatcher/Little Boxes/Gary Bushell's Band Of The Week (p/s, reissue) 5
80	Snotty Snail NELCOL 3	I Thought You Were Dead/I Make A Balls Of Everything I Do/Teenage Revolution (p/s) 5
81	Snotty Snail NELCOL 6	I Am The Bishop/The Telephone Rings Again (p/s) 5
80	Bent	INSTANT CLASSICS (LP) 20
80	Snotty Snail SSLP 1	INSTANT CLASSICS (LP, reissue) 15

NOVAK
97	Enraptured WORM 2	Silver Seas/Schmaltz (p/s in outer hand-sewn cloth sleeve with embroidered "Hand-knitted by Novak" label, 200 only, each different) 25
97	Enraptured WORM 2	Silver Seas/Schmaltz (p/s, 800 only) 7
97	Kitty Kitty CHOOSY 007	Rapunzel/Almost Chinook (hand crayoned p/s, 1,000 only) 5

NOVA LOCAL
69	MCA MUPS 377	NOVA 1 (LP) 30

NOVAS
63	RCA RCA 1360	Push A Little Harder/Oh, Gee Baby! 8

NOVAS
65	London HLU 9940	The Crusher/Take 7 30

NOW
69	NEMS 56-4125	Marcia/Hands On My Clock Stand Still 15

NOW
77	Ultimate ULT 401	Development Corporations/Why (p/s, some on blue vinyl) 35/20
79	Raw RAW 31	Into The 1980s/Nine O'Clock (p/s, 800 only) 25

NOW
94	Detour DR 016	Fatal Attraction/Prying Eyes/New Direction (p/s, 100 on green vinyl) 8/5

NO WAY
78	Our Own IS/NW/1035	Breaking Point/TV Pox/30 Seconds (p/s) 4

NOW GENERATION
73	Green Door GD 4055	Alone Again, Naturally/MIND-BODY-SOUL: My Part (Version) 5
73	Pyramid PYR 7007	Baby Don't Do It/You'll Never Know 5

(see also I Roy, B.B. Seaton, Audley Rollins)

MINT VALUE £

NOYES BROTHERS
80 Object Music OBJ 009/010 SHEEP FROM GOATS (2-LP) 20
(see also Steve Miro & Eyes, Spherical Objects)

NOYS OF US
60s KPS KPS 502   He's Alright Jill/What Can I Do 30

N.R.B.Q. (New Rhythm & Blues Quintet)
69 CBS 4290   Stomp/I Didn't Know Myself 5
69 CBS 4501   C'mon Everybody/Rocket Number 9 5
73 Kama Sutra 2013 056 Ain't It All Right/Only You 5
69 CBS 63653   N.R.B.Q. (LP) 15
72 Buddah 2319 018   SCRAPS (LP) 12
(see also Carl Perkins)

N.S.U.
69 Stable SLE 8002   TURN ON OR TURN ME DOWN (LP) 120

GUITAR NUBBIT
64 Bootleg 501   Georgia Chain Gang/Hard Road (99 copies only) 35
60s XX MIN 705   GUITAR NUBBIT (EP) 15

NUCHA
90 CBS 655885 7   Together/Ha Sempre Alguem 4

NUCLEAR SOCKETTS
81 Subversive SUB 001   HONOR BEFORE GLORY (EP, folded p/s, 33rpm) 10
81 Subversive SUB 002   Play Loud/Shadow On The Map 10

NUCLEUS
70 Vertigo 6360 008   ELASTIC ROCK (LP, gatefold sleeve, spiral label, later 'spaceship' label) 35/15
71 Vertigo 6360 027   WE'LL TALK ABOUT IT LATER (LP, g/fold sl., spiral or 'spaceship' label) 45/15
72 Vertigo 6360 039   SOLAR PLEXUS (LP, 'spaceship' label) 30
73 Vertigo 6360 091   LABYRINTH (LP, 'spaceship' label) 20
73 Vertigo 6360 100   ROOTS (LP, 'spaceship' label) 20
74 Vertigo 6360 110   UNDER THE SUN (LP, 'spaceship' label) 12
75 Vertigo 6360 119   SNAKE HIPS ETCETERA (LP, 'spaceship' label) 20
75 Vertigo 6360 124   ALLEY CAT (LP, 'spaceship' label) 12
76 Vertigo 9286 019   DIRECT HITS (LP, 'spaceship' label) 12
80 Mood 24000   AWAKENING (LP) 30
(see also Ian Carr, Don Rendell, Linda Hoyle)

TED NUGENT (& AMBOY DUKES)
74 Discreet K 19200   Sweet Revenge/Ain't It The Truth (as Ted Nugent & Amboy Dukes)... 8
75 Epic S EPC 3900   Stormtroopin'/Hey Baby (some in p/s, orange label) 5
76 Epic S EPC 4796   Dog Eat Dog/Love You So I Told You A Lie 5
77 Epic S EPC 5482   Cat Scratch Fever/A Thousand Nights 5
78 Epic S EPC 9545   Homebound/Death By Misadventure (p/s) 5
75 Discreet K 59203   CALL OF THE WILD (LP) 12
(see also [American] Amboy Dukes)

NUGGETS
55 Capitol CL 14216   Quirl Up In My Arms/So Help Me, I Love You 20
55 Capitol CL 14267   Shtiggy Boom/Anxious Heart 18

GARY NUMAN
SINGLES
79 Beggars Banquet BEG 23 Cars/Asylum (p/s, orange plastic labels) 6
79 Beggars Banquet BEG 23 Cars/Asylum (p/s, 'mispressed' on dark red vinyl) 10
79 Beggars Banquet BEG 29 Complex/Bombers (live) (p/s, 'mispressed' on dark red vinyl) 12
80 Beggars Banquet SPC 7   Cars/We Are Glass (cassette, cigarette-pack style box) 8
80 Beggars Banquet BEG 35 We Are Glass/Trois Gymnopedies (1st Movement)
                                (p/s, 'mispressed' on dark red vinyl) 12
80 Beggars Banquet BEG 46 I Die, You Die/Down In The Park (Piano Version) (p/s, dark red vinyl 'mispress')... 8
80 Beggars Banquet BEG 46 I Die, You Die/Down In The Park (Piano Version) (p/s, mispressing, plays
                                "Remember I Was Vapour" & "On Broadway" [SAM 126]). 12
81 Beggars Banquet BEG 62 She's Got Claws/I Sing Rain (p/s, mispressing, plays Dollar's
                                "Hand Held In Black And White") 18
81 Beggars Banquet BEG 68 Love Needs No Disguise/Take Me Home (textured p/s, with Dramatis) 5
81 Beggars Banquet BEG 68T Love Needs No Disguise/Take Me Home/Face To Face (12", with Dramatis) 8
83 Beggars Banquet BEG 95P Warriors/My Car Slides (aeroplane-shaped picture disc) 25
84 Beggars Banquet TUB 1   This Is My Life (unissued promo for "The Plan", 300 white label
                                test pressings only) 70
84 Numa NUP 4   Berserker/Empty Bed, Empty Heart (head shaped picture disc) 5
85 Strange Fruit ST 503   JOHN PEEL SESSION ONE (poster p/s) 6
85 Strange Fruit ST 503   JOHN PEEL SESSION TWO (poster p/s) 6
85 Numa NU 7   THE LIVE EP (p/s, blue, white or black vinyl) 5
85 Numa NUM 7   THE LIVE EP (12", p/s, blue, white vinyl or black vinyl) 8
85 Numa NUM 7   THE LIVE EP (12", p/s, mispressing on multicoloured vinyl) 80
85 Numa NUP 9   Your Fascination (We Need It (picture disc) 6
85 Numa NUMP 9   Your Fascination (Extended)/We Need It/Anthem (12", picture disc) ... 10
85 Numa NUM 13   Miracles/Fear (12", 'mispressed' p/s - no red ink) 15
85 Numa NUM 13   Miracles/Fear (12", p/s, red or white vinyl) 8
86 Numa NUMX 16   This Is Love/Survival//Call Out The Dogs (Extended)/No Shelter/This Ship
                                Comes Apart (12", p/s, stickered double pack, shrinkwrapped). 12
86 Numa NUP 17   I Can't Stop/Faces (plane-shaped picture disc) 8
87 B. Banquet BEG 199P   Cars ('E' Reg Model)/Are 'Friends' Electric? (picture disc). 6
87 B. Banquet BEG 199C   Cars ('E' Reg Model)/Are 'Friends' Electric?/We Are Glass/
                                I Die, You Die (USA Mix) (cassette) 5

87	Beggars Banquet BEG 199TR	Cars ('E' Reg Extended Model)/Are 'Friends' Electric?/Cars ('E' Reg Model 7" Mix)/Cars (Motorway Mix) (12", p/s)	8
88	I.R.S. ILSP 1003	New Anger/I Don't Believe (poster p/s)	5
88	I.R.S. ILSCD 1003	New Anger/I Don't Believe/Creatures (live)/I Can't Stop (live) (CD)	15
88	I.R.S. ILSPD 1004	America/Respect (live) (picture disc)	5
88	I.R.S. ILSPD 1004	America/Respect (live) (mispressed picture disc, 'Gary' picture both sides)	30
88	I.R.S. ILSCD 1004	America (Remix)/Respect (live)/New Anger (live)/Call Out The Dogs (live) (CD)	15
89	B. Banquet BBP 5CD	SELECTION (CD EP, picture disc)	8
91	I.R.S. NUMAN 1	Heart/Icehouse (p/s, black vinyl)	5
91	I.R.S. NUMANCD 1	Heart/Icehouse/Tread Careful (CD)	8
91	Numa NUCD 22	Emotion/In A Glass House/Hanoi/Emotion (CD mix) (CD, 'mispressed' disc)	12
92	Numa NU 24DJ	Machine & Soul/Machine & Soul (fan club issue, mail-order only)	8
93	Beggars Banquet BEG 264T	Cars (Multivalve)/Cars (Endurance Model)/Cars (Top Gear Model) (12", black vinyl, promo only)	12
93	Beggars Banquet BEG 264	Cars ('93 Sprint)/Cars (Top Gear) (poster p/s)	5
93	Beggars Banquet BEG 264L	Cars ('93 Sprint)/Cars (Endurance) (McLaren F1-shaped picture disc)	8
93	Beggars Banquet BEG 264CD	Cars ('93 Sprint)/(Multivalve)/(Classic)/(Endurance)/(Top Gear)/(Motorway Mix)/ ('E' Reg Version) (CD, withdrawn, last track mispressed with 12" mix)	15
94	Salvation SACD 1	THE RADIAL PAIR (CD EP, fan club issue, mail order only)	12
94	Numa NU 26	A Question Of Faith/Whisper Of Truth (fan club issue, white label, mail-order only)	18
95	Numa NUMP 27	Absolution/Magic (Trick Mix)/Magic (extended mix) (12", picture disc)	8
95	Numa NUCDP 27	Absolution/Magic (Trick Mix)/Magic (extended mix) (CD, picture disc)	8
96	Polygram TV PRM 1	Cars (Premier Mix)/Are 'Friends' Electric? (live version) (picture disc, numbered, 5,000 only)	5
96	Polygram TV GNRAD 1	Cars (Premier Mix)/Are 'Friends' Electric? (live version)/We Are Glass (CD, promo only)	12
96	The Record Label SPIND 6	Radio (with N.R.G.)/Radio (extended mix) (CD, withdrawn)	60

ALBUMS

80	Beggars Banquet BEGA 19	TELEKON (LP, dark red vinyl 'mispressing', with stickered sl.; some with bonus single SAM 126 "Remember I Was Vapour [live]"/"On Broadway [live]")	20/15
81	Beggars Banquet BEGA 28	DANCE (LP, gatefold sleeve with poster)	12
82	Beggars Banquet BEGA 40	I, ASSASSIN (LP, initial copies at Woolworths with colour poster and merchendise sheet)	20
84	B. Banquet BEGA 55P	THE PLAN (LP, picture disc)	12
85	Numa NUMAP 1003	THE FURY (LP, with mispress pink inner sleeve)	12
86	Numa NUMAP 1003	THE FURY (LP, mispress picture disc, "Your Fascination" 12" photo on A-side)	35
86	Numa GNFCDA 1	IMAGES 1 & 2 (2-LP, fan club issue with photo inserts, mail-order only)	25
87	Numa GNFCDA 2	IMAGES 3 & 4 (2-LP, fan club issue with photo inserts, mail-order only)	25
87	Numa GNFCDA 3	IMAGES 5 & 6 (2-LP, fan club issue with photo inserts, mail-order only)	20
87	Numa GNFCDA 4	IMAGES 7 & 8 (2-LP, fan club issue with photo inserts, mail-order only)	20
87	Numa NUMAD 1007	GHOST (2-LP, fan club issue, mail-order only)	18
88	I.R.S. ILPPD 035	METAL RHYTHM (LP, picture disc)	12
89	Numa GNFCDA 5	IMAGES 9 & 10 (2-LP, fan club issue with photo inserts, mail-order only)	20
94	Numa NUMA 1010	DREAM CORROSION (3-LP, autographed gatefold sleeve; copies bought at HMV with signed 10" x 8" photo)	20
94	Numa NUMA 1011	SACRIFICE (LP, with lyric sheet, stickered sleeve & bonus single: "The Seed Of A Lie [5.26]"/"The Seed Of A Lie [7.07]")	15
86	Numa CDNUMA 1003	THE FURY (CD, with original mixes and artwork)	30
86	Numa CDNUMA 1005	STRANGE CHARM (CD)	30
88	IRS ILPCD 035	METAL RHYTHM (CD)	30
89	IRS EIRSACD 1021	METAL RHYTHM (CD, reissue)	30
89	IRS EIRSACD 1019	THE SKIN MECHANIC — LIVE (CD)	20
91	Numa NUMACD 1001	BERSERKER (CD, fan club issue, mail order only, blue text on CD & inlay)	30
91	Numa GNFCCD 11	IMAGES 11 (CD, fan club issue, mail order only)	20
92	Receiver RRLP 170	THE OTHER SIDE OF GARY NUMAN (LP, withdrawn)	12
93	Numa NUMACDX 1009	MACHINE & SOUL (CD, mispressed with 9 tracks instead of 13)	20

(see also Tubeway Army, Sharpe & Numan, Paul Gardiner, Dramatis, Claire Hamill, Radio Heart, Nicky Robson, Paper Toys, Caroline Munro, Generator, Bauhaus, Bill Sharpe)

NUMBER NINE BREAD STREET

67	Holy Ground HG 112/1109	NUMBER NINE BREAD STREET (LP, 250 copies only)	450

NUMBERS

79	Blasto SRTS 79/CUS/358	ROCK STARS (EP, with insert)	6

NUMBERS

80s	Homegrown HG 701	Here Today/Put 'Em All To Shame/Another Day/Tear You Down (photocopied or green & white sleeve; some with poster)	5/4

NU NOTES

63	HMV POP 1232	Hall Of Mirrors/Fury	18
64	HMV POP 1311	Kathy/Sunset	12

(see also Russ Sainty & Nu Notes)

NUNS

81	Butt FUN 2	Wild/Suicide Child (p/s)	5

NURSE WITH WOUND

87	Crystal/Wisewound WW 01	Crank/TERMITE QUEEN: Wisecrack (numbered plain black sleeve with printed band, 500 only)	20
88	Yangki 002	Faith's Favourites (with Current 93)/Ballad Of The Pale Girl (12", laminated p/s)	30
88	Idle Hole MIRROR 003	Cooloorta Moon/Great Empty Space (12", p/s)	20
90	Harbinger 001	Burial Of The Stoned Sardine/CURRENT 93: No Hiding From The Blackbird	15
90	United Dairies UD 031	Soresucker/Journey Through Cheese (12", p/s, 2,000 only)	20

NURSE WITH WOUND

MINT VALUE £

90	United Dairies UD 031CD	SORESUCKER (CD EP) 7
90	Shock SX 004	Sinister Senile: Human Human Human/Psychedelic Underground
		(45/33rpm, 1,000 only) 25
92	Clawfist 12	Steel Dream March Of The Metal Men/The Dadda's Intoxication
		('singles club' release, 33rpm, foldover p/s in poly bag, 1,400 only) 15
93	Clawfist 20	CRUMB DUCK (10" EP, shared with Stereolab, 1,450 only;
		50 with handmade p/s) 75/40
93	World Serpent WS 7004	Alien (1-sided, company sleeve 1,000 only) 25
95	WN 001	ALICE THE GOON (1-sided 12", p/s) 65
79	United Dairies UD 01	CHANCE MEETING ON A DISSECTING TABLE OF A SEWING MACHINE
		AND UMBRELLA (LP, 500 only) 125
80	United Dairies UD 03	TO THE QUIET MEN FROM A TINY GIRL (LP, 500 only) 75
80	United Dairies UD 04	MERZBILD SCHWET (LP, numbered, 500 only, beware of un-no'd bootlegs). 75
81	United Dairies UD 08	INSECT AND INDIVIDUAL SILENCED (LP, 1,000 only) 60
83	Mi Mort MI MORT iii	GYLLENSKOLD, GEIJERSTAM & FRIENDS, LIVE AT BAR MALDOROR
		(LP, with insert) 40
84	Third Mind TMR 03	OSTRANENIE 1913 (LP, 3,000 only). 45
85	United Dairies UD 012	HOMOTOPY TO MARIE (LP, 5,000 only). 35
86	United Dairies UD 019	AUTOMATING VOL. 1 (LP, 3,000 only) 25
86	United Dairies UD 020	A MISSING SENSE (LP, 1 side only; other side by Organum; 2,000 only) 30
87	United Dairies UD 025	DRUNK WITH THE OLD MAN OF THE MOUNTAINS
		(LP, handmade custom sleeve, around 100 only) 125
88	United Dairies UD 027	ALAS THE MADONNA DOES NOT FUNCTION (mini-LP, 45/33rpm, 3,000 only) . . . 25
88	Idle Hole MIRROR ONE	SOLILOQUY FOR LILITH (3-LP box set, 1,000 only) 60
88	Idle Hole MIRROR 1C	SOLILOQUY FOR LILITH PTS 5/6 (LP, with insert) 25
89	Idle Hole MIRROR TWO	PRESENTS THE SISTERS OF PATAPHYSICS (LP, 1,000 only) 25
89	United Dairies UD 030	AUTOMATING VOL. II (LP) 25
89	United Dairies UD 032	A SUCKED ORANGE (LP, some with full colour insert). 25/20
90	United Dairies UD 134	PSILOTRIPITAKA (3-LP [UD 01, 03 & 04], with bonus LP "Registered Nurse"
		[UD 00], 1,000 only, 30 in 'leather bondage bag') 250/60
90	United Dairies UD 134CD	PSILOTRIPITAKA (3-CD [UD 01, 03 & 04], with bonus CD "Registered Nurse"
		[UD 00CD], 1,000 only, 30 in 'leather bondage bag'). 250/60
91	United Dairies UD 038	CREAKINESS (LP, with Spasm) 20
91	United Dairies UD 09	THE 150 MURDEROUS PASSIONS (LP). 20
91	United Dairies UD 09CD	THE 150 MURDEROUS PASSIONS (CD, sealed in black plastic, 500 only) 30
93	United Dairies UD 059	CRUMB DUCK (LP, reissue of Clawfist 20, 50 pink vinyl, 500 yellow) 50/25
98	United Dairies UD 043	2nd PIRATE SESSIONS (LP, red vinyl, 500 only). 20
99	United Dairies UD 056	AN AWKWARD PAUSE (2-LP, translucent grey vinyl, 500 only,
		1 side not available on CD) 30

(see also Current 93, Whitehouse, Organum/New Blockaders, Sol Invictus)

NUTHIN' FANCY
| 80s | Dynamic Cat DC 1001 | Looking For A Good Time/Too Much Rock'n'Roll (p/s) . . . . 150 |

(see also Terraplane, Thunder)

NU TORNADOS
| 58 | London HLU 8756 | Philadelphia U .S.A./Magic Record . . . . 15 |
| 58 | London HLU 8756 | Philadelphia U.S.A./Magic Record (78) . . . . 15 |

NUTRONS
| 60s | Melodisc M 1593 | The Very Best Things/Stop For The Music. . . . . 15 |

NUTSHELL
| 70s | Myrrh MYR 1056 | FLYAWAY (LP). . . . . 15 |

MAY'F NUTTER
| 66 | Vocalion VL 1282 | Head Shrinker/Don't Know What To Do . . . . 10 |
| 73 | London HLL 10414 | I Don't Care/Hitch Hike Nightmare. . . . . 5 |

NUTTY SQUIRRELS
| 59 | Pye International 7N 25044 | Uh! Oh! (Parts 1 & 2) . . . . 6 |
| 59 | Pye International N 25044 | Uh! Oh! (Parts 1 & 2) (78). . . . . 15 |

NUTZ
74	A&M AMS 7115	As Far As The Eye Can See/Just For The Crack. 5
74	A&M AMLS 68256	NUTZ (LP). 12
75	A&M AMLS 68306	NUTZ TOO (LP). 12
77	A&M AMLH 64623	HARD NUTZ (LP) 12
77	A&M AMLH 68453	LIVE CUTZ (LP) 12

(see also Rage, Nightwing)

NYAH EARTH
| 70 | Attack ATT 8016 | Nyah Bingy/Message . . . . 5 |
| 70 | Attack ATT 8017 | Dual Heat/Night Of The Long Knives. . . . . 5 |

NYAH SHUFFLE
| 70 | Grape GR 3021 | Sting Ray/Paradise. . . . . 8 |

JUDY NYLON
| 82 | On-U-Sound LP 16 | PAL JUDY (LP) . . . . 10 |

(see also John Cale, Snatch)

LAURA NYRO
67	Verve Forecast VS 1502	Wedding Bell Blues/Stoney End 5
68	CBS 3604	Eli's Coming/Sweet Blindness. 5
68	CBS 4031	Once It Was Alright Now (Farmer Joe)/Woman's Blues 5
69	CBS 4719	Time And Love/The Man Who Sends Me Home 5
68	CBS 63346	ELI AND THE THIRTEENTH CONFESSION (LP, gatefold sleeve, orange label) . . . 15
69	CBS 63510	NEW YORK TENDABERRY (LP, orange label) 15
69	Verve Forecast SVLP 6022	THE FIRST SONGS (LP). 15
70	CBS 64157	CHRISTMAS AND THE BEADS OF SWEAT (LP, orange label) 12
71	CBS 64770	GONNA TAKE A MIRACLE (LP, orange label) 12
73	CBS 64991	THE FIRST SONGS (LP, orange label) 12

OAK
| 71 | Topic 12TS 212 | WELCOME TO OUR FAIR (LP) | 35 |

(see also Peta Webb)

OAKENSHIELD
| 82 | Acorn OAK 001 | ACROSS THE NARROW SEAS (LP) | 12 |
| 85 | Acorn OAK 002 | AGAINST THE GRAIN (LP, with insert) | 12 |

PHILIP OAKEY & GIORGIO MORODER
84	Virgin VS 713	Together In Electric Dreams/(Instrumental) (p/s)	4
84	Virgin VSY 713	Together In Electric Dreams/(Instrumental) (picture disc)	6
84	Virgin VSY 713	Together In Electric Dreams/(Instrumental) (12", p/s)	7

(see also Human League, Men)

OASIS
SINGLES
94	Creation CRE 176	Supersonic/Take Me Away (p/s)	15
94	Creation CRE 182	Shakermaker/D'Yer Wanna Be A Spaceman? (p/s)	12
94	Creation CRE 185	Live Forever/Up In The Sky (Acoustic) (numbered foldover p/s in stickered poly bag)	15
94	Creation CRE 190	Cigarettes & Alcohol/I Am The Walrus (live at Glasgow Cathouse June '94) (numbered foldover p/s in poly bag)	7
94	Creation CRECS 190	Cigarettes & Alcohol/I Am The Walrus (live at Glasgow Cathouse June '94) (cassette, flip-top 'cigarette' pack)	5
94	Creation CRE 195	Whatever/(It's Good) To Be Free (no'd foldover p/s in stickered poly bag)	5

PROMO SINGLES
93	Creation CTP 8	Columbia (Demo) (12", 1-sided, white label, 510 pressed)	150
94	Creation CRE 176TP	Supersonic/Take Me Away/I Will Believe (Live) (12", company sleeve)	60
94	Creation CRESCD 176P	Supersonic/Take Me Away/I Will Believe (Live)/ Columbia (White Label Demo) (CD)	35
94	Creation CRE 182TP	Shakermaker/D'Yer Wanna Be A Spaceman?/Alive (8 Track Demo) (12")	75
94	Creation CRESCD 182P	Shakermaker/D'Yer Wanna Be A Spaceman?/Alive (8 Track Demo)/ Bring It On Down (Live) (CD)	30
94	Creation CRE 185TP	Live Forever/Up In The Sky (Acoustic)/Cloudburst (12")	50
94	Creation CRESCD 185P	Live Forever/Up In The Sky (Acoustic)/Cloudburst/ Supersonic (Live April '94) (CD)	20
94	Creation CTP 190TP	I Am The Walrus (Live at Glasgow Cathouse June '94) (12", 250 only, co. sl.)	275
94	Creation CTP 190CL	Cigarettes & Alcohol (12", 1-sided)	75
94	Creation CTP 190CL	Cigarettes & Alcohol/I Am The Walrus (live Glasgow Cathouse June '94)/ Fade Away (12", 300 only)	60
94	Creation CRESCD 190P	Cigarettes & Alcohol/I Am The Walrus (live Glasgow Cathouse June '94)/ Listen Up/Fade Away (CD)	18
94	Creation CRE 195TP	Whatever (12", 1-sided, 560 only)	60
94	Creation CRESCD 195P	Whatever/(It's Good) To Be Free/Half The World Away/Slide Away (CD)	10
94	Creation CTP 195	(It's Good) To Be Free (12", 1-sided, 360 only)	60
95	Creation CCD 169	Slide Away (CD, 1-track Brits Awards issue, 1,000 only; beware of counterfeits)	45
95	Creation CCD 204	Some Might Say (CD, 1-track, 350 only)	75
95	Creation CCD 204P	Some Might Say/Talk Tonight/Aquiesce/Headshrinker (CD)	10
95	Creation CTP 204	Acquiesce (12", 1-sided, 570 only)	70
95	Creation CCD 204P	Acquiesce (CD, 1-track, 300 only)	80
95	Creation CTP 212	Roll With It (12", 1-sided)	40
95	Creation CRESCD 212P	Roll With It/Better People/Rockin' Chair/ Live Forever (Live at Glastonbury '95) (CD, 3,078 only)	10
95	Creation CRESCD 215P	Wonderwall/Round Are Way/The Swamp Song/The Masterplan (CD, 2,320 only)	10
95	Creation CTP 215	Round Are Way (12", 1-sided, 843 only)	50
96	Creation CTP 221X	Cum On Feel The Noize/Champagne Supernova (Lynchmob Beats Mix) (12", 1,203 pressed, plain die-cut sleeve; beware of counterfeits)	50
96	Creation CCD 221	Cum On Feel The Noize (CD, pic. disc, 1-track, with football motif, no inlay)	70
96	Creation CRESCD 221P	Don't Look Back In Anger/Step Out/Underneath The Sky/ Cum On Feel The Noize (CD)	10
96	Creation P 96/1	OASIS (Fade Away/Half The World Away/Acquiesce/The Masterplan) (CD sampler for singles box set)	30

(N.B.: the 4-track 12" "In-Store Sampler" [OASIS 1-12] is a bootleg.)

97	Creation CRESCD 256P	D'You Know What I Mean/Stay Young/Angel Child/Heroes (CD, digipak)	10
97	Creation CCD 256	D'You Know What I Mean (CD, 1-track, black card p/s)	20
97	Creation CCD 256X	D'You Know What I Mean?/Heroes (CD, 2-track, white card p/s)	20
97	Creation CTP 256	D'You Know What I Mean?/Heroes (12")	35
97	Creation CCD 219PL	Be Here Now (live)/Be Here Now (live with DJ intro) (CD)	30
97	Creation CTP 278	Stand By Me/I Got The Fever (12")	35
97	Creation CCD 278	Stand By Me (CD, 1-track, black card p/s)	18
97	Creation CCD 278X	Stand By Me (CD, 2-track, white card p/s)	20
97	Creation CRESCD 278P	Stand By Me/(I Got) The Fever/My Sister Lover/Going Nowhere (CD)	10
97	Creation CTP 282	All Around The World/Street Fighting Man (12", black die-cut sleeve)	35
97	Creation CCD 282	All Around The World (Edit) (CD, 1-track, black card sleeve)	15
97	Creation CCD 282X	All Around The World/Street Fighting Man (CD, blue card sleeve)	20

MINT VALUE £

97	Creation CRESCD 282	All Around The World/The Fame/Flashbax/Street Fighting Man (CD)	15
97	Creation (no cat. no.)	VOX BOX (9-CD, wooden guitar-amp-shaped box set in outer box, with booklets from "Silver" & "Gold" CD box sets; contains commerical issues of "Supersonic" through to "Don't Look Back In Anger"; in-house giveaway only)	450
98	Sony SAMPCM 6031	Acquiesce/Talk Tonight/Rockin' Chair/The Masterplan (CD sampler)	25
98	Sony SAMPMS 6032	Acquiesce/Underneath The Sky/I Am The Walrus/The Masterplan (CD sampler)	40
00	Creation CTP 327	Go Let It Out (12", 1-sided, p/s)	50
00	Creation CCD 327	Go Let It Out (CD, card sleeve)	20
00	Big Brother FITB 001	Fuckin' In The Bushes (12", 1-sided, white label)	65+

PROMO ALBUMS

94	Creation CRECD 169P	DEFINITELY MAYBE (CD)	50
95	Creation C-CRE 189PX	(WHAT'S THE STORY) MORNING GLORY? (cassette, 4-track sampler with "Hello"/"[What's The Story] Morning Glory"/ "Wonderwall"/"Don't Look Back In Anger")	18
95	Creation CRECD 189P	(WHAT'S THE STORY) MORNING GLORY? (CD, with "Step Out", black card p/s, withdrawn, beware of counterfeits)	60
95	Creation CRECD 189P	(WHAT'S THE STORY) MORNING GLORY? (CD, without "Step Out", black card p/s)	20
95	Creation C-CRE 189P	(WHAT'S THE STORY) MORNING GLORY? (cassette, with "Step Out", card p/s, withdrawn)	25
95	Creation C-CRE 189P	(WHAT'S THE STORY) MORNING GLORY? (cassette, without "Step Out", card p/s)	15
97	Creation (no cat. no.)	BE HERE NOW (LP, mail-order 12" box set, with "The Making Of Be Here Now" booklet, 1,000 only)	50
97	Creation (no cat. no.)	BE HERE NOW (CD, mail-order 12" box set, with "The Making Of Be Here Now" booklet, 1,000 only)	40
97	Creation C-CRE 219P	BE HERE NOW (cassette)	12
97	Creation C-CRE 219PX	BE HERE NOW (cassette, 4-track sampler with "D'You Know What I Mean?"/ "All Around The World"/"Stand By Me"/"It's Gettin' Better [Man!!]")	18
97	Creation CCD 219	BE HERE NOW (CD, black card sleeve)	30
98	Sony SAMPCD 5859	THE MASTERPLAN (CD, slimline case, p/s)	25
98	Sony SAMPCD 6034	THE MASTERPLAN INTERVIEW (CD, slimline case, no p/s)	25
00	Big Brother RKIDCD 001P	STANDING ON THE SHOULDER OF GIANTS (cassette, flip-top card box)	25
00	Big Brother RKIDCD 002P	STANDING ON THE SHOULDER OF GIANTS (CD, g/fold card sl. with insert)	35
00	Big Brother DO 1	STANDING ON THE SHOULDER OF GIANTS (promo First Aid Kit, with CD & press release)	200

*(see also Oas*s)*

OAS*S

95	Fierce Panda NING 12	WIBBLING RIVALRY (interview disc, stickered p/s, without barcode, 1000 only)	5
95	Fierce Panda CDNING 12	WIBBLING RIVALRY (CD)	7

(see also Oasis)

OBERON

71	Acorn (no cat. no.)	A MIDSUMMER NIGHT'S DREAM (LP, private pressing)	500+

HUGH O'BRIAN

58	HMV POP 539	Legend Of Wyatt Earp/Down In The Meadow	6
58	HMV POP 539	Legend Of Wyatt Earp/Down In The Meadow (78)	8
58	Oriole CB 1480	I'm Looking For A Girl/Ain't Got A Nickel	5
58	Oriole CB 1480	I'm Looking For A Girl/Ain't Got A Nickel (78)	8
58	HMV DLP 1189	TV'S WYATT EARP SINGS (10" LP)	15

ERIN O'BRIEN

58	Coral Q 72321	Honey Boy/Padre (78)	8

OBSERVERS

71	Big Shot BI 575	Brimstone And Fire/Lightning And Thunder	5
71	Big Shot BI 588	Keep Pushing/Hot Tip	20
72	Big Shot BI 610	Everyday Music/NINEY: Observing The Av	5
72	Songbird SB 1083	International Pum/Reggaematic	6

(see also Niney)

OBTAINERS

79	Dance Fools Dance (no cat. no.)	Yeh Yeh Yeh/Pussy Wussy/MAG-SPYS: Lifeblood/Bombs (stickered plain sleeve, 100 only)	65

(see also Cure)

DIERDRE O'CALLAGHAN

59	Top Rank JAR 164	The Bridal Path/I'll Walk With My Love	5
59	Top Rank JAR 164	The Bridal Path/I'll Walk With My Love (78)	12

OCCASIONALLY DAVID

79	Oven Ready OD 77901	TWIST AND SHOUT (EP)	8
80	Oven Ready OD 1/98002	I Can't Get Used To Losing You (So I'm Coming Back)/ Will You Miss Me Tonight? (foldout p/s)	6
80	Oven Read (no cat. no)	FOREVER CHANGES (cassette)	10

OCCASIONAL WORD ENSEMBLE

69	Dandelion 63753	THE YEAR OF THE GREAT LEAP SIDEWAYS (LP)	15

OCCULT CHEMISTRY

80	Bikini Girl (no. cat. no.)	Water Earth Fire Air (Rough Version) (5" clear flexidisc in stamped envelope with *Bikini Girl* magazine)	15/12
81	Dining Out TUX 4	Water Earth Fire Air/Fire Air Water Earth (handmade p/s)	8

(see also Twilight Zonerz)

OCEAN COLOUR SCENE

90	!Phffft FIT 001	Sway/Talk On (p/s)	8
90	!Phffft FITX 001	Sway (Extended)/Lullaby/Sway (7" Version)/One Of These Days (12", p/s)	12

90	!Phffft FITX 001	Sway (Extended)/Lullaby/Sway (7" Version)/One Of These Days (CD)	35
90	!Phffft	One Of These Days/Talk On (p/s, promo only)	60
90	!Phffft WAVE 1	One Of These Days/Talk On (12", p/s, promo only)	60
91	!Phffft FIT 002	Yesterday Today/Another Girl's Name/Fly Me (p/s)	6
91	!Phffft FITX 002	Yesterday Today/Another Girl's Name/Fly Me/No One Says (12", p/s)	10
91	!Phffft FITCD 002	Yesterday Today/Another Girl's Name/Fly Me/No One Says (CD)	20
92	Fontana OCSS 1	Sway/My Brother Sarah (p/s)	6
92	Fontana OCS 112	Sway/My Brother Sarah/Mona Lisa Eyes/Bellechoux (12", p/s)	8
92	Fontana OCSCD 1	Sway/My Brother Sarah/Mona Lisa Eyes/Bellechoux (CD)	12
92	Fontana OCSS 2	Giving It All Away/Third Shade Of Green (p/s)	6
92	Fontana OCS 212	Giving It All Away/Flowers/Third Shade Of Green/Don't Play (12", p/s)	8
92	Fontana OCSCD 2	Giving It All Away/Flowers/Third Shade Of Green/Don't Play (CD)	12
92	Fontana OCSS 3	Do Yourself A Favour/The Seventh Floor (p/s)	7
92	Fontana OCS 312	Do Yourself A Favour/The Seventh Floor/Patsy In Green/Suspended Motion (12", p/s)	10
92	Fontana OCSCD 3	Do Yourself A Favour/The Seventh Floor/Patsy In Green/Suspended Motion (CD)	15
95	MCA OCS 1	You've Got It Bad/You've Got It Bad (p/s, promo only)	10
96	MCA OCS 2	You've Got It Bad (Full Length Demo Version)/Mona Lisa Eyes (featuring Jimmy Miller) (p/s, mail-order only)	15
92	Fontana 512 269-1	OCEAN COLOUR SCENE (LP, with inner sleeve)	10
92	Fontana 512 269-2	OCEAN COLOUR SCENE (CD)	15

(see also Boys, Fanatics, Echo Base)

PHIL OCHS

66	Elektra EKSN 45002	I Ain't Marching Any More/That Was The President	10
68	A&M AMS 716	Outside Of A Small Circle Of Friends/Miranda	6
65	Elektra EKL 269	ALL THE NEWS THAT'S FIT TO SING (LP)	35
65	Elektra EKL 287	I AIN'T MARCHIN' ANYMORE (LP)	35
66	Elektra EKL 310	PHIL OCHS IN CONCERT (LP, gold label)	30
67	A&M AML(S) 913	PLEASURES OF THE HARBOR (LP)	20
68	A&M AMLS 919	TAPE FROM CALIFORNIA (LP)	20
69	A&M AMLS 934	REHEARSALS FOR RETIREMENT (LP)	20
70	A&M AMLS 973	GREATEST HITS (LP)	20
77	A&M AMLM 64599	CHORDS OF FAME (2-LP)	15

DES O'CONNOR

57	Columbia DB 4011	Moonlight Swim/Sailing Down The Chesapeake Bay	6
57	Columbia DB 4011	Moonlight Swim/Sailing Down The Chesapeake Bay (78)	8
62	Piccadilly 7N 35023	Thin Chow Min/Twist Drive	5

JOHNNY O'CONNOR

53	London L 1171	Fickle Fingers/GUY NELSON: When The World Was Young (78)	10

SINÉAD O'CONNOR

87	Ensign ENYCD 611	Mandinka/Drink Before The War/Mandinka (Instrumental Dub)/Still Listening (CD)	7
88	Ensign ENYCD 613	I Want Your (Hands On Me)/I Want Your (Hands On Me) (Street Mix)/I Want Your (Hands On Me)/Just Call Me Joe (live) (CD)	7
88	Ensign ENYCD 618	Jump In The River (Duet with Karen Finley)/Jump In The River (7" Version)/Never Get Old (live) (CD)	7

(see also World Party, Edge & Sinéad O'Connor)

GENE OCTOBER

83	Illegal ILS 034	Suffering In The Land/Suffering Dub (p/s)	4
84	Slipped Discs SPLAT 001	Don't Quit/Burning Sounds (p/s)	4

(see also Chelsea)

JOHNNY OCTOBER

59	Capitol CL 15070	Growin' Prettier/Young And In Love	6
60	Capitol CL 15121	So Mean/There'll Always Be A Feeling	6

OCTOPUS

69	Penny Farthing PEN 705	Laugh At The Poor Man/Girl Friend	15
70	Penny Farthing PEN 716	The River/Thief	15
73	Mooncrest MOON 7	Hey Na Na/Future Feelings	6
70	Penny Farthing PELS 508	RESTLESS NIGHT (LP, gatefold sleeve)	150
96	Essex ESSEX 1013LP	RESTLESS NIGHT (LP, reissue, gatefold sleeve)	12

(see also Cortinas)

MARTIN O'CUTHBERT

78	Esoteric EE 1	BEMS (Bug Eyed Monsters)/Fragments Of A Possessed Ego (p/s)	4
79	Esoteric EE 2	Serene Machines/Space Shall Weave Our Destiny (foldover p/s)	4

(see also Futurythm)

RAY O'DANIEL

62	Longhorn BLH 0001	What Goes Up Always Comes Down/You're The Only Love For Me	8

ANITA O'DAY

51	London L 867	Tennessee Waltz/Yea Boo (78)	8
51	London L 958	Lovesick Blues/Once There Lived A Fool (78)	8
51	London L 964	I Apologise/You Took Advantage Of Me (78)	8
51	London L 975	Black Moonlight/Something I Dreamed Last Night (78)	8
56	HMV POP 245	You're The Top/Honeysuckle Rose	5
60	HMV POP 821	Tea For Two/Sweet Georgia Brown	5
56	HMV CLP 1085	ANITA (LP)	12
56	Columbia Clef 33C 9020	ANITA O'DAY COLLATES (10" LP)	15
57	Columbia Clef 33CX 10068	AN EVENING WITH ANITA O'DAY (LP)	12
58	Columbia Clef 33CX 10125	ANITA SINGS THE MOST (LP)	12
58	HMV DLP 1169	PICK YOURSELF UP (10" LP)	15
59	HMV DLP 1203	ANITA AT MISTER KELLY'S (10" LP)	15
60	HMV CLP 1332	ANITA O'DAY SWINGS COLE PORTER WITH BILLY MAY (LP)	12

MINT VALUE £

PAT O'DAY
55	MGM SP 1129	Earth Angel (Will You Be Mine?)/A Rusty Old Halo	12
55	MGM MGM 823	Earth Angel (Will You Be Mine?)/A Rusty Old Halo (78)	8
55	MGM SP 1142	Soldier Boy/Annie Oakley	10
60	Pye International 7N 25048	I'll Build A Stairway To Your Paradise/No One Understands	5

BILL ODDIE
64	Parlophone R 5153	Nothing Better To Do/Traffic Island	6
65	Parlophone R 5346	Knitting Song/Ain't Got Rhythm	5
66	Parlophone R 5433	I Can't Get Through/Because She Is My Love	5
69	Decca F 12903	We Love Jimmy Young/Irish Get Out (as Bill Oddie & Average Mothers)	5
70	Dandelion S 4786	On Ilkla Moor Baht'at/Harry Krishna	5

(see also Ricky Livid)

ODDS
80	Double R RED 001	Saturday Night/Not Another Love Song (p/s)	6
81	JSO EAT 1	Yesterday Man/So You Think (p/s)	4
81	JSO EAT 7	Dread In My Bed/Spare Rib (with press release)	10

ODDSOCKS
| 75 | Sweet Folk & C. SFA 030 | MEN OF THE MOMENT (LP) | 15 |

(see also Bevis Frond)

ANN ODELL
| 73 | DJM DJS 10280 | Swing Song/Everything's Fine Sunshine | 6 |
| 73 | DJM DJLPS 434 | A LITTLE TASTE (LP) | 30 |

(see also Chopyn, Blue Mink)

DOYE O'DELL
| 57 | London HAP-B 1073 | DOYE (10" LP) | 12 |

MAC ODELL
| 54 | Parlophone CMSP 25 | The Stone Has Rolled Away/Heaven-Bound Gospel Train (export issue) | 20 |
| 54 | Parlophone DP 397 | The Stone Has Rolled Away/Heaven-Bound Gospel Train (78) | 10 |

RONNIE O'DELL & HIS ORCHESTRA
| 57 | London HLD 8439 | Melody Of Napoli/Struttin' Down Jane Street | 15 |
| 57 | London HLD 8439 | Melody Of Napoli/Struttin' Down Jane Street (78) | 10 |

ODIN'S PEOPLE
| 67 | Major Minor MM 501 | From A Distance/I Need You | 5 |
| 67 | Major Minor MM 506 | Tommy Jones/I Need Your Hand In Mine | 5 |

AL O'DONNELL
| 72 | Trailer LER 2073 | AL O'DONNELL (LP, red label) | 20 |
| 78 | Transatlantic LTRA 501 | AL O'DONNELL 2 (LP) | 12 |

JOE O'DONNELL
77	EMI International INT 540	Golden Earrings/Omega	5
77	Polydor 2058 930	Poets And Story Tellers/The Great Banqueting Hall	5
77	Polydor 2383 465	GAODHAL'S VISION (LP)	25

(see also Mushroom, Rory Gallagher, Jade Warrior)

ROCK O'DOODLE
| 73 | Decca F 13450 | Queen Of Rock & Roll/Woman | 4 |

(see also Patrick Campbell-Lyons)

ODYSSEY (U.K.)
| 66 | Strike JH 312 | How Long Is Time/Beware | 8 |

(see also Sons Of Fred)

ODYSSEY (U.S.)
| 73 | Mowest MWS 7002 | ODYSSEY (LP) | 25 |

OEDIPUS COMPLEX
| 68 | Philips BF 1716 | Holding My Hands Out/Brought Me Such Confusion | 6 |
| 69 | Philips BF 1771 | Up Down Round And Round/Empty Highway | 6 |

ESTHER OFARIM
| 69 | Philips BF 1807 | Saturday Night At The World/Go 'Way From My Window | 5 |
| 72 | Columbia SCXA 9253 | ESTHER OFARIM (LP) | 12 |

ESTHER & ABI OFARIM
67	Philips BF 1604	Morning Of My Life (In The Morning)/Garden	5
63	Philips BL 7617	ESTHER OFARIM & ABRAHAM (LP)	12
63	Philips 6850 012	SING-SONG (LP)	12
65	Philips BL 7690	IS IT REALLY ME (LP)	12
65	Philips BL 7698	THAT'S OUR SONG (LP)	12
67	Philips SBL 7825	2 IN 3 (LP)	12
68	Philips SBL 7868	UP TO DATE (LP)	12
68	Columbia SX 6279	SING ISRAELI BALLADS (LP)	12
69	Philips XL 4	OFARIM CONCERT LIVE 1969 (LP)	12

JAMES O'GWYNN
| 59 | Mercury AMT 1052 | How Can I Think Of Tomorrow/Were You Ever A Stranger | 10 |

O'HARA'S PLAYBOYS
66	Fontana TF 763	Start All Over/I've Been Wondering	5
68	Fontana TF 924	In The Shelter Of My Heart/Goodnight Mr. Nightfall	5
68	Fontana TF 974	I Started A Joke/Show Me	6
68	Fontana (S)TL 5461	GET READY (LP)	25

JOHN O'HARA
| 77 | President PT 465 | Starsky And Hutch/Sister Rae | 4 |

MARY O'HARA
| 77 | Chrysalis CHR 1159 | AT THE ROYAL FESTIVAL HALL (LP) | 10 |

OHIO EXPRESS
68	Pye International 7N 25459	Yummy Yummy Yummy/Zig Zag	5
69	Pye Intl. NSPL 28117	OHIO EXPRESS (LP)	15
69	Buddah 203 015	CHEWY CHEWY (LP)	15

(see also Joey Vine)

OHIO PLAYERS
69	Capitol CL 15587	Here Today And Gone Tomorrow/Bad Bargain	6
72	Janus 6146 009	Pain (Parts 1 & 2)	5
72	Janus 6146 017	Got Pleasure/I Wanna Hear From You	5
73	Westbound 6146 100	Funky Worm/Paint Me	5
74	Mercury 6167 012	Skin Tight/Heaven Must Be Like This	5
75	Mercury 6167 058	Fire/Together	5
74	Mercury 6338 497	SKIN TIGHT (LP)	12

OHR MUSIK
97	Prescription DRUG 2	OHR MUSIK (LP, 99 copies only)	25

(see also Spiral Sky)

OIL CITY SHEIKS
79	United Artists UP 36514	Don't Take But A Few Minutes/Blues Jam (p/s)	7

(see also Dr. Feelgood, Lew Lewis)

OINKLETTS
86	In Tape IT 032	The Oink Song/UNCLE PIGG: Oink Rapp (flexidisc, free with *Oink* magazine)	4

OI POLLOI
80s	Wonderful World WOW 17	OMNICIDE (EP)	5
87	Oi! OIR 011	UNITE AND WIN (LP, with lyric sheet)	10

O'JAYS
65	Liberty LIB 66102	Lipstick Traces/Think It Over Baby	35
66	Liberty LIB 66197	Stand In For Love/Friday Night	18
67	Stateside SS 2073	I'll Be Sweeter Tomorrow/I Dig Your Act	50
68	Bell BLL 1020	Look Over Your Shoulder/I'm So Glad I Found You	12
68	Bell BLL 1033	The Choice/Going Going Gone	6
70	Now! NOW 1002	Don't You Know A True Love/That's Alright	7
72	United Artists UP 35337	Working On Your Case/Hold On	7
73	Mojo 2092 052	I Dig Your Act/I'll Be Sweeter Tomorrow (reissue)	5
73	CBS 1546	Time To Get Down/Shifty Shadey Jealous Kind Of People	5
74	Power Exchange PX 101	Peace/Little Brother	5
74	Philadelphia PIR 2186	For The Love Of Money/People Keep Telling Me	6
75	Philadelphia PIR 3297	Give The People What They Want/What Am I Waiting For	6
77	Philadelphia PIR 4834	Darlin' Darlin Baby/Prayer	6
69	Sunset SLS 50038	FULL OF SOUL (LP)	12
72	CBS 65257	BACKSTABBERS (LP)	15
73	Epic EPC 65469	IN PHILADELPHIA (LP)	12

O'KAYSIONS
68	Stateside SS 2126	Girl Watcher/Deal Me In	20

JOHNNY O'KEEFE (& DEE JAYS)
58	Coral Q 72330	Shake Baby Shake/Real Wild Child (as Johnny O'Keefe & Dee Jays)	150
58	Coral Q 72330	Shake Baby Shake/Real Wild Child (as Johnny O'Keefe & Dee Jays) (78)	75
60s	Zodiac ZR 0016	Sing/Tell The Blues So Long	20

(ROGER) EARL OKIN
67	Parlophone R 5644	Yellow Petals/I Can't Face The Animals (as Roger Earl Okin)	5
69	CBS 4495	Stop And You'll Become Aware/You're Not There At All (as Earl Okin)	8

OLA (& JANGLERS)
67	Decca F 12646	I Can Wait/Eeny Meeny Miney Moe	8
68	Big T BIG 108	What A Way To Die/That's Why I Cry (solo)	6
69	Sonet SON 2004	Let's Dance/Bird, Bird	5

BABATUNDE OLATUNJI
73	Paramount PARA 3038	Soul Makossa (Parts 1 & 2)	4
73	Paramount SPFL 289	SOUL MAKOSSA (LP)	12

OLD AND IN THE WAY
75	Round RX 103	OLD AND IN THE WAY (LP)	10

(see also Jerry Garcia, Seatrain, Rowan Brothers)

MIKE OLDFIELD
SINGLES
74	Virgin VS 101	Mike Oldfield's Single ("Tubular Bells" Theme)/Froggy Went A-Courtin' (some in p/s)	20/5
75	Virgin VS 117	Don Alfonso (with David Bedford)/In Dulci Jubilo (For Maureen) (p/s rumoured to exist)	100+/12
75	Virgin VS 131	In Dulci Jubilo/On Horseback	5
76	Virgin VS 163	Portsmouth/Speak (Tho' You Only Say Farewell) (no p/s, Roger Dean or blue/red label; reissued in brown wraparound p/s)	5/10
77	Virgin VS 167	The William Tell Overture/Argiers	5
77	Virgin VS 198	The Cuckoo Song/Pipe Tune	6
78	Virgin VS 238	TAKE 4 (EP, p/s)	8
78	Virgin VS 238-12	TAKE 4 (12", white vinyl, stickered p/s)	12
79	Virgin VS 245	Guilty/Excerpt From Incantations (p/s, red/green or white/blue label)	5
79	Virgin VS 245-12	Guilty (Extended Mix)/Guilty/Excerpt From Incantations (12", blue vinyl, p/s)	10
79	Virgin VS 317	Blue Peter/Woodhenge (p/s)	6
80	Virgin VS 374	Arrival/Polka (live) (p/s)	5
80	Virgin VS 389	Wonderful Land/Sheba (p/s)	7

Mike OLDFIELD

80	Tyne Tees TT 362	"Alright Now" Theme Tune (flexidisc freebie)	50
82	Virgin VSY 464	Five Miles Out/Live Punkadiddle (picture disc)	7
82	Virgin VSY 489	Family Man/Mount Teidi (picture disc)	6
82	Virgin VS 541	Mistake/Waldberg (The Peak) (p/s)	4
82	Virgin VSY 541	Mistake/Waldberg (The Peak) (picture disc)	6
83	Virgin VSY 586	Moonlight Shadow/Rite Of Man (picture disc)	7
84	Virgin VS 648-12	Crime Of Passion (Extended)/Jungle Gardenia (12", p/s)	8
84	Virgin VS 701-12	Tricks Of The Light/Tricks Of The Light (Instrumental)/Afghan (12", p/s)	8
84	Virgin VS 731-12	Etude (Full Length Version)/Evacuation (Full Length Version) (12", p/s)	7
85	Virgin VSD 836	Pictures In The Dark/Legend//Moonlight Shadow/Rite Of Man (double pack in PVC gatefold p/s)	10
85	Virgin VS 838-12	Pictures In The Dark (Extended)/Legend/The Trap (12", p/s)	7
86	Virgin VSS 863	Shine (with Jon Anderson)/The Path (shaped picture disc)	12
86	Virgin VS 863-12	Shine (Extended) (with Jon Anderson)/The Path (12", p/s)	7
87	Virgin VS 955	In High Places (with Jon Anderson)/Poison Arrows (p/s)	6
87	Virgin VS 955-12	In High Places (with Jon Anderson)/Poison Arrows/Jungle Gardenia (12", p/s)	8
87	Virgin VSC 99012	Islands (with Bonnie Tyler)/When The Night's On Fire/The Wind Chimes Part 1 (cassette)	6
88	Virgin CDT 7	Moonlight Shadow (Extended Version)/Rite Of Man/To France/Jungle Gardenia (3" CD, card p/s)	10
89	Virgin VSCD 1189	Earth Moving (7" Version)/(Disco Mix)/Bridge To Paradise (3" CD, card p/s)	15
89	Virgin VSCD 1214	Innocent (7" Version)/(12" Mix)/(Club Version) (3" CD, card p/s)	12
90	Virgin VS 1328	Etude (The Theme Music For The "Nurofen" TV Commercial)/ONO GAGAKU KAï SOCIETY ORCHESTRA: Gakkain (p/s)	6
90	Virgin VSC 1328	Etude (The Theme Music For The "Nurofen" TV Commercial)/ONO GAGAKU KAï SOCIETY ORCHESTRA: Gakkain (cassette)	6
90	Virgin AMACD 1	AMAROK X-TRAX (3" CD EP, 'discount voucher CD' free with W.H. Smith's Insight magazine)	30/25
92	WEA YZ 708	Tattoo (Edit)/Silent Night (p/s)	6
93	WEA YZ 737	The Bell (MOC: Stanshall)/Sentinel Restructure (Trance Mix) (p/s)	4

ALBUMS

74	Virgin QV 2001	TUBULAR BELLS (LP, quadrophonic, with model plane noise at the end of side 2, stickered sleeve)	20
75	Virgin QVQS 2043	OMMADAWN (LP, quadrophonic, stickered sleeve)	20
76	Virgin QV 2043	OMMADAWN (LP, different quadrophonic mix, stickered sleeve)	20
76	Virgin VBOX 1	BOXED (4-LP box set, with booklet)	25
78	Virgin VP 2001	TUBULAR BELLS (LP, picture disc, die-cut sleeve, stereo remix of 1976 "Boxed" quadrophonic mix; with or without model plane noise)	each 15
79	Virgin V 2141	PLATINUM (LP, with inner sleeve & "Sally"; matrix reads "V 2141 B1" or "B2", withdrawn)	60
79	Tellydisc TELLY 4	IMPRESSIONS (LP, mail-order only)	25
79	Tellydisc TELLYC 4	IMPRESSIONS (cassette, mail-order only)	30

PROMOS

74	Virgin VS 112	Hergest Ridge (1-sided white label promo only, no p/s)	60
75	Virgin VDJ 9	An Extract From Ommadawn Part 1/An Extract From Ommadawn Part 2 (On Horseback) (12", no p/s, promo only)	30
84	Virgin SWALLOW 1	Etude/Moonlight Shadow/Portsmouth/In Dulci Jubilo (p/s, promo only for "The Complete Mike Oldfield")	30
97	WEA SAM 3096	Women Of Ireland (System 7 Mix)/(Lurker Mix)/(Transient Mix) (12", promo only)	12

(see also Sallyangie, David Bedford, Kevin Ayers & Whole World, Pekka, Lea Nicholson, Tom Newman)

ANDREW OLDHAM (ORCHESTRA)

64	Decca F 11878	365 Rolling Stones/Oh I Do Like To See Me On The 'B' Side	20
64	Decca F 11987	We Don't All Wear D'Same Size Boots/Right Of Way	20
64	Ace Of Clubs ACL 1180	16 HIP HITS (LP)	40
64	Decca LK 4636	LIONEL BART'S MAGGIE MAY (LP)	25
66	Decca LK/SKL 4796	THE ROLLING STONES SONGBOOK (LP)	60
82	Decca 820 186-1	THE ROLLING STONES SONGBOOK (LP, reissue)	12

(see also Aranbee Pop Symphony, Rolling Stones, Cleo, Bo & Peep, Jeannie & Her Redheads, Gulliver's Travels, Mighty Avengers, John Paul Jones)

OLDHAM TINKERS

75	Topic 12TS 276	FOR OLD TIMES SAKE (LP)	12

OLD TIMERS SKIFFLE GROUP

58	Fontana H 105	The Woman Who Loved A Swine/The Lynching Of Jeff Buckner (78)	18

JOHNNY OLENN & HIS BAND

57	London HLU 8388	I Ain't Gonna Cry No More/My Idea Of Love	325
57	London HLU 8388	I Ain't Gonna Cry No More/My Idea Of Love (78)	75
59	Mercury AMT 1050	Born Reckless/You Lovable You (as Johnny Olenn & Blockbusters)	60

O-LEVEL

78	Psycho PSYCHO 2	East Sheen/Pseudo Punk ('map' or 'schoolboy' p/s)	20/30
78	Kings Road KR 002	THE MALCOLM EP (photocopied wraparound or printed p/s)	20/10

(see also Teenage Filmstars, Times, Television Personalities)

OLIVER

69	CBS 4435	Good Morning Starshine/Can't You See	5
70	Crewe CRW 1	Jean/Good Morning Starshine (Arrangement) (p/s)	5

OLIVER

74	Oliv OL 1	STANDING STONE (LP, private pressing, withdrawn blue sleeve, later in green sleeve)	250/175
92	Tenth Planet TP 001	STANDING STONE (LP, reissue, numbered, 500 only)	20

JOHNNY OLIVER

56	MGM SP 1165	Chain Gang/These Hands	15
60	Mercury AMT 1095	What A Kiss Won't Do/That's All I'm Living For	8

SY OLIVER & HIS ORCHESTRA
58	London HL 7067	The Mardi Gras March/One More Time (export issue)	8
59	London HLJ 8776	In A Little Spanish Town Cha-Cha/The Mardi Gras March	8
59	London HLJ 8776	In A Little Spanish Town Cha-Cha/The Mardi Gras March (78)	8
53	Brunswick LA 8586	FOR DANCERS ONLY (10" LP)	12

OLIVER & TWISTERS
64	Pye Intl. NPL 28018	LOOK WHO'S TWISTIN' (LP)	30

OLIVERS
57	Columbia DB 3995	Ma Curly Headed Baby/Beautiful Dreamer	6

(see also Russ Conway)

OLLIE & NIGHTINGALES
69	Stax STAX 109	You're Leaving Me/Showered With Love	12

OLYMPICS
58	HMV POP 528	Western Movies/Well!	10
58	HMV POP 528	Western Movies/Well! (78)	20
58	HMV POP 564	(I Wanna) Dance With The Teacher/Everybody Needs Love	15
58	HMV POP 564	(I Wanna) Dance With The Teacher/Everybody Needs Love (78)	30
59	Columbia DB 4346	Private Eye/(Baby) Hully Gully	18
60	Vogue Pop V 9174	I Wish I Could Shimmy Like My Sister Kate/Workin' Hard	12
61	Vogue Pop V 9181	Dance With A Dolly/Dodge City	12
61	Vogue Pop V 9184	Little Pedro/CAPPY LEWIS: Bullfight	18
62	Vogue Pop V 9196	The Twist/Everybody Likes To Cha Cha Cha	12
62	Vogue Pop V 9198	The Stomp/Mash Them 'Taters	12
62	Vogue Pop V 9204	Baby It's Hot/The Scotch	12
63	HMV POP 1155	Sidewalk Serenade/Nothing	8
64	Sue WI 348	The Bounce/Fireworks	18
65	Warner Bros WB 157	Good Lovin'/Olympic Shuffle	10
66	Fontana TF 678	We Go Together (Pretty Baby)/Secret Agents	12
66	Fontana TF 778	Baby, Do The Philly Dog/Western Movies	10
69	Action ACT 4539	Baby, Do The Philly Dog/Mine Exclusively	10
70	Action ACT 4556	I'll Do A Little Bit More/Same Old Thing	10
71	Jay Boy BOY 27	Hully Gully/Big Boy Pete	5
72	Jay Boy BOY 56	Baby, Do The Philly Dog/Secret Agents	5
72	Jay Boy BOY 74	I'll Do A Little Bit More/Same Old Thing (reissue)	5
61	Vocalion VAH 8059	DANCE BY THE LIGHT OF THE MOON (LP)	50
67	London HA-M 8327	SOMETHING OLD, SOMETHING NEW (LP, unissued)	
67	Fontana TL 5407	SOMETHING OLD, SOMETHING NEW (LP)	40
72	Jay Boy JSX 2008	THE OLYMPICS (LP)	12

(see also Cappy Lewis)

PATRICK O'MAGICK
74	Chrysalis CHS 2041	You're A Winner/The Proposal	5

(see also Patrick Campbell-Lyons)

MICHAEL O'MARTIAN
76	Myrrh MYRA 1048	WHITE HORSE (LP, gatefold sleeve, with Larry Carlton)	12
77	Myrrh MYR 1073	SEASONS OF THE SOUL (LP, with Stormie)	15
78	Sparrow BIRD 141	MAINSTREAM (LP)	15

O.M.D.
(see under Orchestral Manoeuvres In The Dark)

OMEGA
76	Decca SKL-R 5219	HALL OF FLOATERS IN THE SKY (LP)	25
76	Decca SKL-R 5243	TIME ROBBER (LP)	25

OMEGA
85	Rock Machine MACH 1	THE PROPHET (LP)	20

OMEGA RED STAR
69	Decca LK/SKL 4974	OMEGA RED STAR (LP)	40

OMEGA TRIBE
83	Crass 221984/10	ANGRY SONGS (EP)	4

(see also Pete Fender)

OMEN SEARCHER
82	OCS 001	Too Much (p/s)	40
82	OCS 002	Teacher Of Sin (p/s)	35

ONDIOLINE BAND
66	London HL 10022	Last Bicycle To Brussels/Lovers Of Cologne	4

ONE
69	Fontana STL 5539	ONE (LP)	50

ONE & ONE
64	Decca F 11948	I'll Give You Lovin'/It's Me	7

(see also Ivy League, Flowerpot Men)

ONE EYED JACKS
78	Pennine PSS 154	TAKE AWAY (LP)	25

ONE HAND CLAPPING
80s	Curve Of Earth COTE 1	The Rich Get Rich/Running Down Greek (poster p/s)	4

101'ERS
76	Chiswick (N)S 3	Keys To Your Heart/5 Star Rock & Rock Petrol (p/s)	15
79	Big Beat NS 3	Keys To Your Heart/5 Star Rock & Rock Petrol (reissue, p/s)	5
80	Big Beat NS 63	Sweet Revenge/Rabies (From The Dogs Of Love) (p/s)	5
81	Andalucia AND 101	ELGIN AVENUE BREAKDOWN (LP)	25

(see also Clash, Alvaro

MINT VALUE £

100% PROOF
80	Smile SR 929	NEW WAY OF LIVIN' (EP)	25
81	Myrrh MYR 1107	100% PROOF (LP)	20

100% PROOF AGED IN SOUL
71	Hot Wax HWX 102	Somebody's Been Sleeping/I've Come To Save You	5
71	Hot Wax HWX 108	Somebody's Been Sleeping/I've Come To Save You (reissue)	5
72	Hot Wax HWX 113	Everything Good Is Bad/I'd Rather Fight Than Switch	5
72	Hot Wax HWX 120	Never My Love/Since You've Been Gone	5
71	Hot Wax SHW 5003	SOMEBODY'S BEEN SLEEPING IN MY BED (LP)	15

100% PURE POISON
77	EMI Intl. INS 3001	COMING RIGHT AT YOU (LP)	30

MATTY O'NEIL
51	London L 1037	Don't Sell Daddy Any More Whiskey/Little Rusty (78)	8
51	London L 1095	Whiskey Took My Daddy Away/What's This World Coming To? (78)	10
54	London L 1037	Don't Sell Daddy Any More Whiskey/Little Rusty (gold label, tri-centre)	30
54	London L 1037	Don't Sell Daddy Any More Whiskey/Little Rusty (silver label, tri-centre)	20
54	London L 1037	Don't Sell Daddy Any More Whiskey/Little Rusty (silver top, round centre)	10

JOHNNY O'NEILL
59	RCA RCA 1114	Wagon Train/Somebody, Just Like You	6
59	RCA RCA 1114	Wagon Train/Somebody, Just Like You (78)	8

ONE IN A MILLION
67	CBS 202513	Use Your Imagination/Hold On	75
67	MGM MGM 1370	Fredereek Hernando/Double Sight	250

(see also Thunderclap Newman)

ONE MILLION FUZZTONE GUITARS
82	Monsters In Orbit TVEYE 3	Heaven/Annuese (foldover p/s, at least 2 different designs)	6
83	Monsters In Orbit TVEYE 10	26 (LP)	10

ONENESS OF JUJU
79	Buddah BDS 497	Everyway But Loose/Make A Change	4
79	Buddah BDS 497	Everyway But Loose/Make A Change (12")	8

1,000 MEXICANS
83	Whaam! WHAAM 12	The Art Of Love/News For You (p/s, 1,500 only)	6

1,000 VIOLINS
85	Dreamworld DREAM 2	Halcyon Days/I Remember When Everybody Used To Ride Bikes ... Now We All Drive Cars (12", p/s, 1,000 only)	8
86	Dreamworld DREAM 8	Please Don't Sandblast My House/Time I Broke Down (p/s, 2,000 only)	4
86	Dreamworld DREAM 8T	Please Don't Sandblast My House/You Ungrateful Bastard/Though It Poured The Next Day, I Never Noticed The Rain (12", p/s)	7
86	Lyntone	You Ungrateful Bastard (fanzine flexidisc)	6

(see also Page Boys)

ONE TWO & THREE
65	Decca F 12093	Black Pearl/Bahama Lullaby	10
65	Decca LK 4682	BLACK PEARLS AND GREEN DIAMONDS (LP)	75

ONE WAY SYSTEM
82	Lightbeat WAY 1	Stab The Judge/Riot Torn City/Me And You (p/s)	8
82	Anagram ANA 1	Give Us A Future/Just Another Hero (p/s)	5
83	Anagram ANA 5	Jerusalem/Jackie Was A Jackie (p/s)	10
83	Anagram ANA 9	Cum On Feel The Noise/Breakin' In (p/s)	6
83	Anagram ANA 14	This Is The Age/Into Fires (p/s)	5
84	Anagram ANA 19	Visions Of Angels/Shine Again (p/s)	5
80s	Anagram	ALL SYSTEMS GO (LP, with lyric inner)	15
83	Anagram GRAM 008	WRITING ON THE WALL (LP, with lyric inner)	12

ONE WAY TICKET
78	President PTLS 1069	TIME IS RIGHT (LP, featuring tracks from "Five Day Rain" LP)	90

(see also Five Day Rain)

ONLOOKERS
82	Demon D 1012	You And I/Understand/Julia (p/s)	15

ONLY ONES
77	Vengeance VEN 001	Lovers Of Today/Peter And The Pets (p/s)	15
77	Vengeance VEN 001	Lovers Of Today/Peter And The Pets (12", no p/s, with 7" x 7" sticker)	12
78	CBS S CBS 6228	Another Girl, Another Planet/Special View (p/s)	8
78	CBS S CBS 6576	Another Girl, Another Planet/As My Wife Says (no p/s)	10
78	CBS S CBS 12-6576	Another Girl, Another Planet/As My Wife Says (12", p/s)	10
79	CBS S CBS 7086	You've Got To Pay/This Ain't All (It's Made Out To Be) (p/s)	8
79	CBS S CBS 7285	Out There In The Night/Lovers Of Today (no p/s)	5
79	CBS S CBS 12-7285	Out There In The Night/Lovers Of Today/Peter And The Pets (12", p/s, blue vinyl, 2 slight sleeve variations)	12
79	CBS S CBS 7963	Trouble In The World/Your Chosen Life (withdrawn 'group' black & red p/s)	350
79	CBS S CBS 7963	Trouble In The World/Your Chosen Life (standard p/s)	5
80	CBS S CBS 8535	Fools/Castle Built On Sand (p/s, with Pauline Murray)	5
83	Vengeance VEN 002	Baby's Got A Gun/PETER PERRETT: Silent Night (no p/s)	5
78	CBS 82830	THE ONLY ONES (LP, orange label)	12
79	CBS 83451	EVEN SERPENTS SHINE (LP, orange label)	15
80	CBS 84089	BABY'S GOT A GUN (LP, orange label)	12

(see also England's Glory)

YOKO ONO
71	Apple APPLE 38	Mrs. Lennon/Midsummer New York	12
72	Apple APPLE 41	Mind Train/Listen, The Snow Is Falling (p/s)	15

73	Apple APPLE 47	Death Of Samantha/Yang Yang	15
73	Apple APPLE 48	Run Run Run/Men Men Men	20
70	Apple SAPCOR 17	YOKO ONO/PLASTIC ONO BAND (LP, with inner sleeve)	40
71	Apple SAPTU 101/2	FLY (2-LP, with inner sleeves, poster & postcard)	45
73	Apple SAPDO 1001	APPROXIMATELY INFINITE UNIVERSE (2-LP, with inner sleeves)	25
73	Apple SAPCOR 26	FEELING THE SPACE (LP)	35

(see also John Lennon, Bill Elliott & Elastic Oz Band)

ONSLAUGHT
| 83 | Complete Control TROL 1 | First Strike/State Control/No More (p/s) | 8 |

ONYX
68	Pye 7N 17477	You've Gotta Be With Me/It's All Put On	15
68	Pye 7N 17622	My Son John/Step By Step	15
69	Pye 7N 17768	Tamaris Khan/So Sad Inside	50
69	CBS 4635	Time Off/Movin' In	18
71	Parlophone R 5888	Air/Our House	10
71	Parlophone R 5906	The Next Stop Is Mine/What's That You Say	10

(see also Salamander)

OOBERMAN
| 98 | Transcopic TRAN 002 | Sugarbum/Tears From A Willow (p/s, 1,000 copies only) | 10 |
| 98 | Tugboat TUGS 003 | SHORLEY WALL EP (12", clear vinyl, 500 copies only) | 12 |

OPAL BUTTERFLY
68	CBS 3576	Beautiful Beige/Speak Up	25
69	CBS 3921	Mary Anne With The Shakey Hand/My Gration Or?	50
70	Polydor 2058 041	You're A Groupie Girl/Gigging Song	50

(see also Hawkwind, Motorhead, Mott The Hoople)

JACKIE OPEL
63	Jump Up JU 512	TV In Jamaica/Worrell's Captaincy	12
64	Black Swan WI 421	You're No Good/King Liges	18
64	R&B JB 138	Stand By Me (as Jackie Opel & Hortense Ellis)/Solid Rock	15
64	R&B JB 160	Pity The Fool/The Day Will Come	15
65	King KG 1011	Cry Me A River/Eternal Love	12
65	Island WI 203	Wipe Those Tears/Don't Take Your Love	18
65	Island WI 209	Go Whey/Shelter The Storm	18
65	Island WI 227	Old Rockin' Chair/SKATALITES: Song Of Love (B-side is actually "Ska In Vienna Woods")	175
65	Ska Beat JB 190	More Wood In The Fire/Done With A Friend	20
65	Ska Beat JB 227	A Little More/The Lord Is With Thee	20
66	Island WI 264	A Love To Share/ROLAND ALPHONSO: Devoted To You	18
66	Rio R 117	I Am What I Am/JACKIE MITTOO & SKATALITES: Devil's Bug	40

(see also Jackie & Doreen, Doreen & Jackie, Hortense & Jackie)

OPEN MIND
69	Philips BF 1790	Horses And Chariots/Before My Time	50
69	Philips BF 1805	Magic Potion/Cast A Spell	200
69	Philips SBL 7893	OPEN MIND (LP)	375
86	Antar ANTAR 2	OPEN MIND (LP, reissue)	15

(see also Drag Set)

OPEN ROAD
| 72 | Greenwich GSS 102 | Swamp Fever/Lost And Found | 6 |
| 71 | Greenwich GSLP 1001 | WINDY HAZE (LP) | 30 |

(see also Warm Sounds, Denny Gerrard, Donovan)

OPERATING THEATRE
| 86 | Mother MUM 4 | Queen Of No Heart/Spring Is Coming With A Strawberry In The Mouth (p/s) | 4 |
| 86 | Mother 12MUM 4 | Queen Of No Heart/Spring Is Coming With A Strawberry In The Mouth/Part Of My Make-Up/Atlantean Satanosa (12", p/s) | 7 |

OPPRESSED
83	Firm NICK 1	NEVER SAY DIE (EP)	12
83	Oppressed OPPO 1	Work Together/Victims (p/s)	12
84	Oppressed OPLP 1	OI! OI! MUSIC (LP)	15
85	Skinhead CREW 1	FATAL BLOW (LP)	15

OPTICA
| 93 | Kinetix KINT 10 | VISIONS OF ZXYLON (12" EP) | 8 |
| 95 | Kinetix KINXLP 2 | ALL THE COLOURS OF THE RAINBOW (LP, with bonus 12") | 12 |

OPTIC EYE
| 92 | Mystic Stones RUNE LP 3 | TRANCE (LP) | 10 |
| 94 | Jump/Pumping LPTOT 17 | LIGHT SIDE OF THE SUN (LP, coloured vinyl) | 10 |

OPTIMISTS
| 81 | Armageddon AS 018 | Mull Of Kintyre/The Plumbers Song (p/s) | 6 |

OPUS
| 70 | Columbia DB 8675 | Baby, Come On/Angela Grey | 15 |

GENE O'QUIN
| 51 | Capitol CL 13600 | Boogie Woogie Fever/RAMBLIN' JIMMY DOLAN: Wine, Women, And Pink Elephants (78) | 10 |

ORA
| 69 | Tangerine OPLOP 0025 | ORA (LP) | 200 |

(see also Byzantium, Movies)

ORAL
| 85 | Conquest QUEST 6 | SEX (LP) | 10 |

MINT VALUE £

ORANGE ALABASTER MUSHROOM
| 98 | Earworm WORM 36 | The Slug/Ethel Tripped A Mean Gloss (p/s, with sticker) | 8 |

ORANGE BICYCLE
67	Columbia DB 8259	Hyacinth Threads/Amy Peate	15
67	Columbia DB 8311	Laura's Garden/Lavender Girl	15
68	Columbia DB 8352	Early Pearly Morning/Go With Goldie	15
68	Columbia DB 8413	Jenskadajka/Nicely	15
68	Columbia DB 8483	Sing This All Together/Trip On An Orange Bicycle	15
69	Parlophone R 5789	Tonight I'll Be Staying Here With You/Last Cloud Home	8
69	Parlophone R 5811	Carry That Weight/You Never Give Me Your Money/Want To B Side	8
70	Parlophone R 5827	Take Me To The Pilot/It's Not My World	8
70	Parlophone R 5854	Jelly On The Bread/Make It Rain	8
71	Regal Zonophone RZ 3029	Goodbye Stranger/Country Comforts	10
70	Parlophone PCS 7108	ORANGE BICYCLE (LP)	60
88	M'n Blue Town MBT 5003	LET'S TAKE A TRIP ON ON AN ORANGE BICYCLE (LP)	15

(see also Motherlight)

ORANGE DISASTER
| 80s | Neuter OD 1 | Something's Got To Give/Out Of The Room/Hiding From Frank | 6 |

(see also Varicose Veins, Architects Of Disaster)

ORANGE JUICE
80	Postcard 80-1	Falling And Laughing/Moscow Olympics/Moscow (foldover p/s in poly bag, some with postcard; with or without flexidisc "Felicity (live)" [I Wish I Was A Postcard 1], 963 only)	55
80	I Wish I Was A Postcard 1	Felicity (live) (freebie flexidisc, also given away with fanzines)	15
80	Postcard 80-2	Blue Boy/Lovesick (hand-coloured p/s in poly bag, blue labels)	18
80	Postcard 80-2	Blue Boy/Lovesick (brown labels & co. sleeve or yellow labels/cream co. sl.)	6/8
80	Postcard 80-6	Simply Thrilled Honey/Breakfast Time (p/s, with picture insert in poly bag)	15
80	Postcard 80-6	Simply Thrilled Honey/Breakfast Time (brown die-cut company sleeve)	6
81	Postcard 81-2	Poor Old Soul/Poor Old Soul Pt. 2 (die-cut co. sleeve, some with postcard)	10/7
81	Postcard 81-6	Wan Light/You Old Eccentric (unreleased)	
81	Polydor POSP 357	L.O.V.E. Love/Intuition Told Me Pt. 2 (p/s)	4
82	Polydor POSP 386	Felicity/In A Nutshell (p/s)	4
83	Polydor POSP 547	Rip It Up/Snake Charmer (p/s, with free live 21/4/79 cassette)	10
83	Polydor POSPD 547/OJ 2	Rip It Up/Snake Charmer//Lovesick/Sad Lament (double pack, poster p/s)	7
83	Polydor OJ 3/SFI 719	The Day I Went Down To Texas (flexidisc freebie)	5
83	Polydor OJP 4	Flesh Of My Flesh/Lord John White And The Bottleneck Train (picture disc)	5
84	Polydor OJ 5/JUICE 1	Bridge/Out For The Count (stickered p/s, with free flexidisc "Poor Old Soul [live]")	7
84	Polydor OJ 6/OJC 6	What Presence?!/A Place In My Heart (Dub) (p/s, with free cassette "The Felicity Flexi Session: The Formative Years")	8
84	Polydor OJ 7/JUICE 3	Lean Period/Bury My Head In My Hands (brown paper bag sleeve, with flexidisc, "Rip It Up"/"What Presence?!")	7
93	Postcard DUBH 934	Blue Boy/Lovesick (p/s, reissue, 1,000 only)	5
86	Polydor SPEMC 102	THE ORANGE JUICE (cassette, with extra 12" remix tracks)	10
92	Postcard DUBH 922	OSTRICH CHURCHYARD (LP, 1,000 with bonus 10" "Irritation Disc" [922TEN])	12

(see also Edwyn Collins, Paul Quinn & Edwyn Collins, Fun Four, Josef K)

ORANGE MACHINE
| 68 | Pye 7N 17559 | Three Jolly Little Dwarfs/Real Life Permanent Dream | 50 |
| 69 | Pye 7N 17680 | You Can All Join In/Dr. Crippen's Waiting Room | 50 |

(see also Danny Hughes)

ORANGE PEEL
| 71 | Reflection HRS 5 | I Got No Time/Searching For A Place To Hide | 12 |

ORANGE SEAWEED
| 68 | Pye 7N 17515 | Stay Awhile/Pictures In The Sky | 30 |

(see also Fadin' Colours)

ORB
SINGLES
89	Wau! Mr Modo MWS 010T	KISS (12" EP, 949 only, die-cut company sleeve)	40
90	Wau! Mr Modo MWS 017T	A Huge Ever Growing Pulsating Brain That Rules From The Centre Of The Ultraworld: Loving You (Orbital Mix)/(Bucket And Spade Mix)/Why Is 6 Scared Of 7? (12" p/s, B-side matrix states 'MWS 016T')	25
90	Big Life BLR 270T	A Huge Ever-Growing Pulsating Brain That Rules From The Centre Of The Ultraworld : Loving You (edited)/(Bucket And Spade Mix)/Why Is 6 Scared Of 7? (12", p/s, 8,000 only, B-side matrix: 'MWS 016T')	20
90	Big Life BLR 270CD	A Huge Ever-Growing Pulsating Brain That Rules From The Centre Of The Ultraworld : Loving You (Original Ambient House Mix) (CD)	20
90	Big Life BLR 27T	A Huge Ever-Growing Pulsating Remix (Orbital Dance Mix)/(9am Radio Mix)/(Aubrey Mix I) (12", p/s, 8,000 only)	20
90	Big Life BLR 27CD	A Huge Ever-Growing Pulsating Remix (Orbital Dance Mix)/(9am Radio Mix)/(Aubrey Mix I) (CD)	20
90	Big Life BLR 33	Little Fluffy Clouds/Ambient Mix Mk 1 (stickered die-cut p/s)	6
90	Big Life BLR 33T	Little Fluffy Clouds (Dance Mk 2)/Into The Fourth Dimension (Essenes Beyond Control)/Little Fluffy Clouds (Ambient Mk 1) (12", p/s)	10
90	Big Life BLR 33CD	Little Fluffy Clouds (Dance Mk 2)/Into The Fourth Dimension (Essenes Beyond Control)/Little Fluffy Clouds (Ambient Mk 1) (CD)	10
90	Big Life BLR 33R	Little Fluffy Clouds (Drum & Vox Version)/(Seven Inch Mk 1)/Into The Fourth Dimension (12" remix, p/s)	10
91	Big Life BLR 46	Perpetual Dawn: Solar Youth/Star 6 & 789 (Phase II) (p/s)	6

ORB

91	Big Life BLRT 46	Perpetual Dawn: Solar Flare Extended Mix/Star 6 & 789 (Phase II)/ Perpetual Dawn: Ultrabass (12", p/s)	8
91	Big Life BLR 46CD	Perpetual Dawn: Solar Youth/Star 6 & 789 (Phase II)/Perpetual Dawn: Solar Flare (CD)	8
91	Big Life BLR R46	Orb In Dub: Towers Of Dub (Ambient Mix)/Perpetual Dawn (Ultrabass II) (12" remix, stickered p/s, with Jah Wobble)	15
92	Big Life BLRDA 75	BLUE ROOM (CD, card pack with postcard & gatefold sleeve)	12
93		ASSASSIN (CD, gatefold sleeve, card pack with postcard & car sticker)	12

PROMOS

90	Wau! Mr Modo MWS 017T	A Huge Ever-Growing Pulsating Remix/From One Ear To Another/ Why Is 6 Scared Of 7? (12", white label, 100 only)	50
90	Wau! Mr Modo MWS 017R	A Huge Ever-Growing Pulsating Brain That Rules From The Centre Of The Ultraworld (Orbital Dance Mix)/(Orbital Radio Mix)/(Aubrey Mix Mk II) (12", stamped white label, 1,000 only)	30
90	Big Life ORB PROMO 1	A Huge Ever-Growing Pulsating Remix (Orbital Dance Mix)/ (9am Radio Mix)/(Aubrey Mix Mk 1) (12")	15
90	Big Life ORB PROMO 2	Little Fluffy Clouds (Dance Mk 1)/Into The Fourth Dimension/ Little Fluffy Clouds (Ambient Mk 1) (12")	12
91	Big Life ORB PROMO 3	Perpetual Dawn: Ultrabass/Perpetual Dawn: Solar Flare (12")	10
91	Big Life ORB PICTURE 3	Perpetual Dawn: Ultrabass II (12", 1-sided picture disc, 400 only, stickered PVC sleeve; later 'reissued' without sticker, 4,000 only)	20/15
91	Big Life ORB PICTURE 3	Perpetual Dawn: Ultrabass II (12", 1-sided picture disc, mispressing, plays "Towers Of Dub (Ambient)", 400 pressed but 300 allegedly destroyed)	25
91	Big Life	THE ORB SAMPLER (CD, 4-track)	10
92	Big Life ORB PROMO 4	Blue Room (Part One)/(Part Two) (12")	10
92	Big Life BLR 81D	Blue Room (Radio 7)/Assassin (Radio 7) (jukebox 7", 1,000 only)	7
92	Big Life ORB PROMO 5	Assassin (The Oasis Of Rhythms Mix)/(Another Live Version) (12", turquoise vinyl)	10
92	Big Life ORB PROMO CD 5	Assassin (Radio 7 Edit)/(Another Live Version)/ (Chocolate Hills Of Bohol Mix) (CD)	10
95	Island 12ISD 609DJ	OXBOW LAKES (12" double pack, yellow vinyl)	12

ALBUMS

91	Big Life BLRDLP 5	THE ORB'S ADVENTURES BEYOND THE UNDERWORLD (2-LP, with inner sleeve, 'classical pressing' sticker on sleeve)	20
91	Big Life BLRLP 14	THE ORB AUBREY MIXES: THE ULTRAWORLD EXCURSIONS (LP, with inner sleeve, deleted on day of release)	15
91	Big Life BLRC 14	THE ORB AUBREY MIXES: THE ULTRAWORLD EXCURSIONS (cassette)	10
91	Big Life BLRCD 14	THE ORB AUBREY MIXES: THE ULTRAWORLD EXCURSIONS (CD)	15
92	Big Life BLRLA 18	U.F.ORB (3-LP, with inner sleeves & 2 art prints in sealed blue pack)	18
92	Big Life BLV 2	ADVENTURES BEYOND THE ULTRAWORLD: PATTERNS AND TEXTURES VERSION (video with 7-track live CD from Brixton Academy)	22

(see also System 7, KLF, J.A.M.s, Jah Wobble, Apollo XI, Space)

MINT VALUE £

ORBIDÖIG

81	Situation 2 SIT 15	Nocturnal Operation/Down Periscope (p/s)	8
84	Beggars Banquet BEG 125	Nocturnal Operation/Down Periscope (reissue, p/s, newly credited to Sensational Cree.	8
84	Beggars Banquet BEG 125T	Nocturnal Operation/Down Periscope/Voyage Of The Titanic (12", p/s, newly credited to Sensational Creed)	10

(see also Billy MacKenzie)

ROY ORBISON
SINGLES

60	London HLU 9149	Only The Lonely (Know How I Feel)/Here Comes That Song Again	7
60	London HLU 9149	Only The Lonely (Know How I Feel)/Here Comes That Song Again (78)	500
60	London HLU 9207	Blue Angel/Today's Teardrops	7
61	London HLU 9307	I'm Hurtin'/I Can't Stop Loving You	7
61	London HLU 7108	I'm Hurtin'/I Can't Stop Loving You (export issue)	20
61	London HLU 9342	Runnin' Scared/Love Hurts	6
61	London HLU 9405	Cryin'/Candy Man	7
62	London HLU 9511	Dream Baby/The Actress	6
62	London HLU 9561	The Crowd/Mama	7
62	London HLU 9607	Workin' For The Man/Leah	7
63	London HLU 9676	In Dreams/Shahdaroba	6
63	London HLU 9727	Falling/Distant Drums	6
63	London HLU 9777	Blue Bayou/Mean Woman Blues	6
64	London HLU 9845	Borne On The Wind/What'd I Say	6
64	London HLU 9882	It's Over/Indian Wedding	5
64	Ember EMB S 197	Rock House/You're My Baby	10
64	Ember EMB S 200	This Kind Of Love/I Never Knew (some in p/s)	18/8
64	London HLU 9919	Oh, Pretty Woman/Yo Te Amo Maria	5
64	London HLU 9930	Pretty Paper/Summersong	5
65	London HLU 9951	Goodnight/Only With You	6
65	Ember EMB S 209	Sweet And Easy To Love/You're Gonna Cry (some in p/s)	15/7
65	London HLU 9978	(Say) You're My Girl/Sleepy Hollow	6
65	London HLU 9986	Ride Away/Wondering	7
65	London HLU 10000	Crawling Back/If You Can't Say Something Nice	5
66	London HLU 10015	Breakin' Up Is Breakin' My Heart/Wait	7
66	London HLU 10034	Twinkle Toes/Where Is Tomorrow	7
66	London HLU 10051	Lana/House Without Windows	6

(London 45s from HLU 9676 to HLU 9978, and HLU 10051, were originally issued on the London Monument label, as were later pressings of HLU 9149, 9405, 9511, and 9607)

66	London HLU 10067	Too Soon To Know/You'll Never Be Sixteen Again	5
66	London HLU 10096	There Won't Be Many Coming Home/Going Back To Gloria	6
67	London HLU 10113	So Good/Memories	7
67	London HLU 10143	Cry Softly Lonely One/Pistolero	8
67	London HLU 10159	She/Here Comes The Rain Baby	8
68	London HLU 10176	Born To Be Loved By You/Shy Away	8
68	London HLU 10206	Walk On/Flowers	7
68	London HLU 10222	Heartache/Sugar Man	7
69	London HLU 10261	My Friend/Southbound Jerico Parkway	8
69	London HLU 10285	Penny Arcade/Tennessee Owns My Soul	18
69	London HLU 10294	Break My Mind (by Roy Orbison & Art Movement)/How Do You Start Over	8
70	London HLU 10310	So Young/If I Had A Woman Like You	8
71	London HLU 10339	(Love Me Like You Did It) Last Night/Close Again	8
72	Sun 6094 001	Ooby Dooby/Devil Doll	5
72	London HLU 10358	God Love You/Changes	10
72	London HLU 10388	Memphis Tennessee/I Can Read Between The Lines	12
72	London HLU 10388	Memphis Tennessee/I Can Read Between The Lines (export issue with alternate take of A-side: matrix no. MSC-8474-T2-IL)	18
74	Mercury 6167 014	Sweet Mama Blue/Heartache	6
75	Mercury 6167 067	Hung Up On You/Spanish Nights	6
76	Monument S MNT3965	Only The Lonely/It's Over (p/s)	6
76	Monument S MNT 4247	Belinda/No Chain At All	5
76	Monument S MNT 4797	(I'm A) Southern Man/Born To Love Me	5
77	Monument S MNT 5151	Drifting Away/Under Suspicion	5
79	Asylum K 13153	Easy Way Out/Tears (p/s)	5
79	Asylum K 12391	Lay It Down/Warm Hot Spot (p/s)	5
80	WEA K 17649	That Lovin' You Feelin' Again (with Emmylou Harris)/CRAIG HUNDLEY: Lola (p/s)	5
81	WEA K 18432	Until The Night Is Over/Long Way Back To Love (p/s)	5
85	ZTT ZTAS 9	Wild Hearts (...Time)/Wild Hearts (Voiceless) (p/s)	5
85	ZTT DZTAS 9	Wild Hearts (...Time)/Wild Hearts (Voiceless)//Ooby Dooby/Crying (double pack, p/s)	25
85	ZTT 12 ZTAS 9	Wild Hearts (And Time Again)/Wild Hearts (Voiceless)/Wild Hearts (...Time)/Ooby Dooby (12", p/s)	7
89	Virgin VSG 1166	You Got It/The Only One (gatefold p/s)	5
89	Virgin VST 1166	You Got It/The Only One/Crying (with k.d. lang) (12", p/s)	15
89	Virgin VSCD 1166	You Got It/The Only One/Crying (with k.d. lang) (CD)	20
89	Virgin VS 1173	She's A Mystery To Me/Crying (with k.d. lang) (p/s)	7
89	Virgin VS T1173	She's A Mystery To Me/Crying (with k.d. lang)/Dream Baby (12", p/s)	10
89	Virgin VS CD 1173	She's A Mystery To Me/Crying (with k.d. lang)/Dream Baby (CD)	15
89	Virgin VS 1193	California Blue/Blue Bayou (live, with k.d. lang) (p/s)	7
89	Virgin VSC 1193	California Blue/Blue Bayou (live, with k.d. lang) (cassette)	6
89	Virgin VST 1193	California Blue/Blue Bayou (live, with k.d. lang) (12", p/s)	10
89	Virgin VS 1193	California Blue/Blue Bayou (live, with k.d. lang)/Leah/In Dreams (live) (CD)	15
89	Virgin VST 1224	Oh, Pretty Woman/Oh, Pretty Woman (edit)/Claudette (12", p/s, as Roy Orbison & Friends [including Jackson Browne, Elvis Costello, k.d. lang, Bonnie Raitt, Bruce Springsteen & Tom Waits])	7

89	Virgin VSCD 1224	Oh Pretty Woman (Edit) (live)/Claudette/Oh Pretty Woman (LP Version) (3" CD, card sleeve, as Roy Orbison & Friends [including Jackson Browne, Elvis Costello, k.d. lang, Bonnie Raitt, Bruce Springsteen & Tom Waits])	7
92	Virgin America VUS 63	Crying (with k.d. lang)/Falling (p/s)	5
92	Virgin America VUSC 63	Crying (with k.d. lang)/Falling (Cassette)	5
92	Virgin America VUSCD 63	Crying (with k.d. lang)/Falling/Oh, Pretty Woman (Edit)/ She's A Mystery To Me (CD)	7
92	Virgin America VUSCX 63	Crying (with k.d. Lang)/Falling/Only The Lonely/It's Over (CD)	10
92	Virgin America VUS 68	Heartbreak Radio/Crying (with k.d. lang) (p/s)	5
92	Virgin America VUSC 68	Heartbreak Radio/Crying (with k.d. lang) (cassette)	5

EPs

57	London RE-S 1089	HILLBILLY ROCK (EP, orange p/s, mauve/silver label, triangular centre)	125
57	London RE-S 1089	HILLBILLY ROCK (EP, orange p/s, mauve/silver label, round centre)	100
60	London RE-U 1274	ONLY THE LONELY (EP)	20
63	London RE-S 1089	HILLBILLY ROCK (EP, re-pressing, yellow p/s, silver-top, round centre)	75
63	London RE-U 1354	ROY ORBISON (EP)	20

(The London EPs listed below were issued on London Monument, as were the later pressings of RE-U 1274 and RE-U 1354)

63	London RE-U 1373	IN DREAMS (EP)	20
64	Ember EP 4546	SWEET AND EASY TO LOVE (EP)	60
64	Ember EP 4563	TRYIN' TO GET TO YOU (EP)	60
64	London RE-U 1435	IT'S OVER (EP)	20
64	London RE-U 1437	OH PRETTY WOMAN (EP)	20
65	London RE-U 1439	ROY ORBISON'S STAGE SHOW HITS (EP)	25
65	Ember EP 4570	DEVIL DOLL (EP)	50
65	London RE-U 1440	LOVE HURTS (EP)	25

LONDON LPs

61	London HA-U 2342	LONELY AND BLUE (LP)	35
62	London HA-U 2437	CRYIN' (LP, also stereo SAH-U 6229)	30/35
63	London HA-U/SH-U 8108	IN DREAMS (LP, mono/stereo)	25/30
64	London HA-U 8207	OH, PRETTY WOMAN (LP)	20
65	London HA-U/SH-U 8252	THERE IS ONLY ONE ROY ORBISON (LP, mono/stereo)	25/30
66	London HA-U/SH-U 8279	THE ORBISON WAY (LP, mono/stereo)	25/30
66	London HA-U/SH-U 8297	THE CLASSIC ROY ORBISON (LP, black label mono/blue label stereo)	25/30
67	London HA-U/SH-U 8318	SINGS DON GIBSON (LP, black label mono/blue label stereo)	25/30

(Unless stated, the above London LPs were originally issued with plum labels [mono] or blue labels [stereo]. Later copies were re-pressed with black labels [mono] or plum labels [stereo] with a boxed London logo. These are worth around two-thirds these values.)

68	London HA-U/SH-U 8357	CRY SOFTLY, LONELY ONE (LP)	25
68	London HA-U/SH-U 8358	SONGS FROM "THE FASTEST GUITAR ALIVE" FILM SOUNDTRACK (LP)	35
70	London HA-U/SH-U 8406	THE BIG "O" (LP, mono/stereo)	30/25
72	London SH-U 8435	ROY ORBISON SINGS (LP)	25
73	London SH-U 8445	MEMPHIS (LP)	30

OTHER LPs

64	Ember NR 5013	THE EXCITING SOUNDS OF ROY ORBISON (LP, original copies list 'Great Newport Street' address on cover; reissued 1972)	25/18
65	Allegro ALL 778	ROY ORBISON SINGS (LP, some tracks by Jerry Lee Lewis, Tommy Roe; black or blue label)	12
65	Ember FA 2005	ROY ORBISON AND OTHERS (LP, with 4 tracks by Orbison)	15

(Copies of the above LP are rumoured to exist with all tracks solely by Orbison)

67	Monument LMO/SMO 5007	ROY ORBISON'S GREATEST HITS (LP)	18
67	Monument LMO/SMO 5004	ORBISONGS (LP)	20
68	Monument LMO/SMO 5013	EARLY ORBISON (LP)	20
68	Monument LMO/SMO 5014	MORE OF ROY ORBISON'S GREATEST HITS (LP)	18
69	RCA Camden CDN 5118	SPECIAL DELIVERY (LP, with other tracks by Bobby Bare & Joey Powers)	12
70	RCA Camden CDS 1077	LITTLE RICHARD AND ROY ORBISON (LP)	12
77	Monument SMNT 81808	REGENERATION (LP)	15
79	Asylum K 53092	LAMINAR FLOW (LP)	15
70s	Fan Club	ROY ORBISON RETURNS (10" LP)	12
70s	Lone Star	THE CONNOISSEURS' ROY ORBISON VOL. 1 (LP, fan club issue)	12
70s	Lone Star	THE CONNOISSEURS' ROY ORBISON VOL. 2 (LP, fan club issue)	12
70s	Fan Club	BIG 'O' LIVE AT THE SNCO (LP, fan club issue)	12

(see also Traveling Wilburys)

WILLIAM ORBIT

93	Virgin VSCDT 1465	WATER FROM A VINE LEAF (CD)	15

ORBITAL

SINGLES

89	Oh Zone ZONE 1	Chime/Deeper (12", p/s)	25
90	ffrr FRRF 135	Chime (Edit)/Deeper (Edit) (p/s)	7
90	ffrr FRRFX 135	Chime/Deeper (12", reissue, p/s)	15
90	ffrr FRRXR 135	Chime (JZJ Remix)/Deeper (Bacardi Mix) (12", p/s)	15
90	ffrr FRRCD 135	Chime/Chime (Edit)/Deeper (Edit) (CD)	20
90	ffrr FRR 145	Omen/2 Deep (p/s)	7
90	ffrr FRRX 145	Omen/2 Deep/Open Mind (12", p/s)	15
90	ffrr FRRXR 145	The Chariot/Wheel Of Fortune/The Fool (12", p/s)	15
90	ffrr FRRCD 145	Omen (7" Version)/Omen (12" Version)/Open Mind (CD)	15
91	ffrr FRR 147	Satan/Belfast (p/s)	7
91	ffrr FRRX 149	Satan/LC1/Belfast (12", p/s)	15
91	ffrr FRRXR 149	Satan (The Rhyme & Reason Vocal Mix)/LC2 (Outer Limits Mix)/ Chime (12", p/s)	15
91	ffrr FRRCD 149	Satan/LC1/Belfast (CD)	15
92	ffrr FRRX 181	MUTATATIONS: Oolaa (Beltram Mix)/Chime (Ray Keith Mix)/ Speed Freak (Moby Mix)/Oolaa (MBM Mix) (12", p/s)	7
92	ffrr FRRXR 181	MUTATATIONS: Chime (Beltram Mix)/Steel Cube Idolatry (Angel & Dorrell Mix)/Farenheit 3D3/Chime Crime (12", p/s)	7

ORBITAL

92	ffrr FRRCD 181	MUTATIONS: Chime Crime/Oolaa (Betram Mix)/Farenheit 3D3/ Speed Freak (Moby Mix) (CD)	10
92	Internal LIARX 1	Halcyon/The Naked And The Dub (12", p/s)	8
92	Internal LIAXR 1	The Naked And The Dead/Sunday (12", p/s)	8
92	Internal LIECD 1	Halcyon/The Naked And The Dead/Sunday (CD)	10
93	Internal LIECD 7	Lush 3 — 1/Lush 3 — 2/Lush 3 — 3/Lush 3 — 4/Lush 3 — 5 (CD)	7
94	Internal LIARX 12	PEEL SESSIONS: Lush (Euro Tunnel Disaster '94)/Walk About/ Semi Detached/Attached (12", p/s)	8
94	Internal LIECD 12	PEEL SESSIONS: Lush (Euro Tunnel Disaster '94)/Walk About/ Semi Detached/Attached (CD)	10
95	Internal LIE 23	Times Fly (Slow)/Sad But New/Times Fly (Fast)/The Tranquiliser (double pack, p/s)	6
95	Internal LIARX 23	Times Fly (Slow)/Sad But New/Times Fly (Fast)/The Tranquiliser (12", double pack, p/s)	7
95	Internal LICDP 23	Times Fly (Slow)/Sad But New/Times Fly (Fast)/The Tranquiliser (CD, digipak)	7
95	Internal LIECD 25	Satan/Belfast/LC 1 (CD, re issue)	7
96	Internal LIECD 26	Midnight/Choice/Analogue Test Feb '90 (CD)	7
96	Internal LICDP 30	The Box (Part 1)/(Part 2)/(Part 3)/(Part 4) (CD, digipak)	7
96	Internal LIARX 37	Satan (Chelmsford)/Chime (Chelmsford)/Lush 3 (Boston)/The Girl With The Sun In Her Hair (Boston)/Out There Somewhere (New York)/ Chime (New York) (12", double pack, last track uncredited)	7

PROMOS

90	ffrr FRRXDJ 145	Omen (7")/Omen (12")/2 Deep/Open Mind (12")	15
91	ffrr FRRXDJ 149	Satan (2 mixes)/LC1/Belfast (12")	15
91	ffrr FRRDJ 163	Midnight (Radio Edit)/Choice (Radio Edit)	10
91	ffrr FRRXDJ 163	Midnight/Midnight (Sasha Mix)/Choice/Choice Remix (12")	15
91	ffrr FRRX 163	Midnight/Choice (12", p/s)	15
91	ffrr FRRXR 163	Midnight (Sasha Mix)/Choice (Remix) (12", p/s)	15
91	ffrr FRRCD 163	Midnight (Sasha Mix)/Choice/Analogue Test Feb '90 (CD)	18
92	ffrr FRRXDJ 181	MUTATATIONS: Chime (Beltram Mix)/Fahrenheit 3D3/Speed Freak (Moby Mix)/Chime (Ray Keith Mix) (12", plain sleeve)	8
92	Internal LIAR 1	Halcyon (Edit) (1-sided)	7
92	Internal LIXDJ 1	Halcyon/The Naked And The Dead/Sunday (12")	8
92	Internal LIXXDJ 1	The Naked And The Dub (12", 1-sided)	10
93	Internal LIARXDJ5	Lush 3 — 1/Lush 3 — 2/Walk Now (12", sampler for untitled 2nd LP)	8
93	Internal LIA DJ7	Lush 3 — 1(Edit) (1-sided)	7
93	Internal LIARX DJ7	Lush 3 — 3 (Underworld)/Lush 3 — 5 (C.J. Bolland) (12")	8
93	Internal LIAX DJ7	Lush 3 — 4 (PWOG)/Semi - Detached (12")	8
94	Internal LIARX DJ15	Are We Here — Who Are They/Do They Here/They Did it (12")	8
94	Internal LIARXDJ 19	Are We Here (Oral Mix)/(Edit)/(Laconic Dub) (12")	8
96	Internal LIE 30	The Box (Part 1)/(Part 2) (jukebox issue, no p/s)	7
96	Internal LIE 37	Satan (live)/Satan (live) (jukebox issue, no p/s)	7
97	ffrr FRR GUARD 1	Belfast/Impact USA/Sad But New/The Girl With The Sun In Her Head (CD, free with The Guardian inside 'M25 orbital')	12
97	ffrr FRR F 296	The Saint/The Sinner (Industry Standard) (jukebox issue, no p/s)	7
97	ffrr FRR FXDJ 296	The Saint/The Sinner	7
97	ffrr FRR FXXDJ 296	The Sinner (1-sided, withdrawn)	8
97	ffrr FRR FCD 296	The Saint/The Sinner (CD, custom p/s)	8
96	Internal ORB CD3	EVIL SANTA (3-CD set, including LIECD 37, LICDP 37 & LICDD 37, silver box)	20
96	Internal PromoBox TRUCD 10/LIECD 30	IN SIDES (2-CD, 245mm x 175mm burgundy box with "The Box" video)	30
97	ffrr FRR PromoBox TRCDR10/FCD 296	IN SIDES (2-CD, in 245mm x 175mm burgundy box with gold Orbital logo & "The Saint" second promo video by Activate, custom sleeve)	25

ALBUMS

91	ffrr FRR 828248 - 1	ORBITAL (2-LP, green sleeve)	15
91	ffrr FRR 828248 - 2	ORBITAL (CD, green sleeve, with bonus track)	18
93	Internal TRULP 2	ORBITAL (2-LP, brown sleeve)	15
93	Internal TRUCD 2	ORBITAL (CD, brown sleeve)	15
96	Internal TRUCD 10	IN SIDES (CD, in 145mm x 130mm black & blue box)	15

ORBIT FIVE

68	Decca F 12799	I Wanna Go To Heaven/Walking (some in p/s)	30/10

ORBITONES

73	Explosion EX 207	Memories Of Love/SONNY EARLE: In Peace	4

ORCHESTRAL MANOEUVRES IN THE DARK (O.M.D.)

79	Factory FAC 6	Electricity/Almost (black 'braille' p/s)	20
79	Din Disc DIN 2	Electricity (Re-Recorded Version)/Almost (p/s, reissue)	6
79	Din Disc DIN 2	Electricity (LP Version)/Almost (2nd reissue, diff. production details on rear sl.)	6
80	Din Disc DIN 6	Red Flame-White Light/I Betray My Friends (p/s)	5
80	Din Disc DIN 6/12	Red Flame-White Light/I Betray My Friends (12", p/s)	10
80	Din Disc DIN 15-10	Messages (Extended)/Waiting For The Man/Taking Sides Again (10", p/s)	8
80	Din Disc DIN 22-12	Enola Gay (Extended)/Annex (12", p/s)	15
80	Din Disc DIN 24-10	Souvenir (Extended)/Motion And Heart (Amazon Version)/ Sacred Heart (10", p/s)	8
81	Flexi/Smash Hits (no cat. no.)	Pretending To See The Future (Live Version)/NASH THE SLASH: Swing-Shift (Flexi-Version) (blue 33rpm 1-sided flexidisc free with *Smash Hits* mag)	20/10
82	Din Disc DIN 40-12	Maid Of Orleans (The Waltz Joan Of Arc)/Navigation/Of All Things We've Made (12", 'coin' cover; incorrectly lists "Experiments In Vertical Take-Off")	18
82	Din Disc DIN 40-12	Maid Of Orleans (The Waltz Joan Of Arc)/Navigation/Of All Things We've Made (12", 'stained glass' cover, some metallic; incorrectly lists "Experiments In Vertical Take-Off" or "Of All Things We've Done")	12/8
82	Virgin VSY 527	Genetic Engineering/4-Neu (picture disc)	6
83	Virgin VSY 580	Telegraph/66 And Fading (picture disc)	6
83	Virgin VS 580-12	Telegraph (Extended)/66 And Fading (12", p/s)	15

MINT VALUE £

84	Virgin VSX 660	Locomotion/Her Body In My Soul ('competition' p/s)	18
84	Virgin VSS 660	Locomotion/Her Body In My Soul (train-shaped picture disc)	15
84	Virgin VSY 685	Talking Loud And Clear/Julia's Song (picture disc)	6
84	Virgin TVS 70512	Tesla Girls (Remix)/Garden City/Telegraph (live)/Tesla Girls (cassette)	10
84	Virgin VSY 727	Never Turn Away/Wrappup (picture disc)	5
85	Virgin VS 766	So In Love/Concrete Hands//Maria Gallante/White Trash (live) (double pack, stickered gatefold p/s)	6
85	Virgin VS 766-13	So In Love (Extended)/Concrete Hands (Extended)/Maria Gallante (12", stickered p/s, record listed as VS 766-12)	7
85	Virgin VSY 766-14	So In Love (Extended Remix)/Concrete Hands (Extended)/ Maria Gallante (12", picture disc)	8
85	Virgin VS 796	Secret/Drift (poster p/s)	4
85	Virgin VS 796-12	Secret (Extended)/Drift//Red Frame-White Light/I Betray My Friends (12", double pack)	12
85	Virgin VSS 811	La Femme Accident/Firegun (shaped picture disc)	10
85	Virgin VSD 811-12	La Femme Accident/Firegun/La Femme Accident (12" Mix)/ Locomotion (live)/Enola Gay (12", double pack)	10
86	Virgin VSY 888	(Forever) Live And Die/This Town (picture disc)	4
86	Virgin VSD 911	We Love You/(Dub)//If You Leave/88 Seconds In Greensboro' (double pack)	6
86	Virgin VSC 911	We Love You/We Love You (Dub) (shrinkwrapped with cassette: "Souvenir"/ "Electricity"/"Enola Gay"/"Joan Of Arc"/"We Love You"/ "We Love You [Dub]")	10
87	Virgin MIKE 938-12	Shame (Extended Re-recorded Version)/Goddess Of Love/(Forever) Live And Die (12" Mix)/Messages (10" Mix) (CD, gatefold card p/s)	12
88	Virgin VSG 987	Dreaming/Satellite (foldout p/s)	4
88	Virgin VS 987-10	Dreaming (The William Orbit Remix)/Dreaming/Messages/Secret (10", numbered p/s)	8
88	Virgin VSY 987-12	Dreaming (Extended Mix)/Satellite/Gravity Never Failed (12", picture disc with poster, gatefold PVC sleeve)	8
88	Virgin VSCD 987	Dreaming (Extended Mix)/Satellite/Gravity Never Failed/Dreaming (CD)	15
88	Virgin VSCDX 987	Dreaming (Extended Mix)/Satellite/Gravity Never Failed/Dreaming (CD, trifold card digipak)	18
88	Virgin TRICD 4	Dreaming/Satellite/Gravity Never Failed (3" CD, with adaptor, no inlay)	10
88	Virgin CDT 12	Locomotion/Her Body In My Soul/The Avenue (3" CD, card sleeve)	12
88	Virgin CDT 27	Maid Of Orleans (The Waltz Joan Of Arc) (12" Version)/Joan Of Arc (12" Version)/Navigation/Of All The Things We've Made (3" CD, card sleeve)	12
91	Virgin VSCDX 1310	Sailing On The Seven Seas (Extended)/Burning/Dancing On The Seven Seas/Big Town (CD, in foldout box)	20
91	Virgin VSCDX 1331	Pandora's Box/Pandora's Box (Lost Girl Mix)/Pandora's Box (Abstract Mix)/ Pandora's Box (American Venus 7" Mix) (CD, in wooden box)	15
91	Virgin VSCDG 1368	Then You Turn Away/Sailing On The Seven Seas/Then You Turn Away (Infinite Repeat Mix)/Vox Humana (CD, in felt box with scented postcard)	15
80	Din Disc DID 2	ORCHESTRAL MANOEUVRES IN THE DARK (LP, 12" x 12" grid sleeve, black, blue or grey outer sleeves with orange, pink or red inner)	each 10
80	Din Disc DID 6	ORGANISATION (LP, stickered sleeve, with insert & 7": "Introducing Radios"/ "Distance Fades Between Us"/"Progress"/ "Once When I Was Six" [DEP 2])	15
84	Virgin V 2310	JUNK CULTURE (LP, stickered sleeve, with free 7": "[Angels Keep Turning] The Wheels Of The Universe" [JUNK 1])	15
91	Virgin V 2648	SUGAR TAX (LP, mispressing with extra track "All She Wants Is Everything" instead of "Neon Lights")	15

ORCHIDS

63	Decca F 11743	Gonna Make Him Mine/Stay At Home	15
63	Decca F 11785	Love Hit Me/Don't Make Me Mad	15
64	Decca F 11861	I've Got That Feeling/Larry	15

(see also Exceptions)

ORCHIDS

88	Sarah SARAH 002	I've Got A Habit/Give Me Some Peppermint Freedom/Apologies (foldover p/s with poster, 1,000 only)	15
88	Sarah SARAH 011	UNDERNEATH THE WINDOW, UNDERNEATH THE SINK EP (p/s)	6
89	Sarah SARAH 023	WHAT WILL WE DO NEXT EP (p/s)	4
88	Sha La La BaBaBaBaBa 5	From This Day/SEA URCHINS: Summertime (flexi, 2,500 only, 1,000 in p/s)	10/8
90	Caff CAFF 11	An Ill Wind That Blows/All Those Things (p/s, with insert)	15

ORE

82	Bandit BR 003	Your Time Will Come/Yellow River (p/s)	20

CHARLES ORGANAIRE

64	Blue Beat BB 241	How Did Moses Cross The Red Sea/You May Not Believe (as Big Charlie)	12
64	R&B JB 149	Little Village/It Happens On A Holiday	18
64	Rio R 28	Little Village/It Happens On A Holiday (reissue)	15

ORGANISATION

70	RCA SF 8111	TONE FLOAT (LP)	165

(see also Kraftwerk)

ORGANISERS

66	Pye 7N 17022	Lonesome Road/The Organiser	75

ORGANUM/NEW BLOCKADERS

80s	Aeroplane AR 7	Pulp (Parts 1 & 2) (gatefold p/s)	30

(see also Nurse With Wound)

SEAN O'RIADA & CEOLTOIRI CUALANN

61	Gael-Linn CEF 010	THE PLAYBOY OF THE WESTERN WORLD (LP)	10

ORIGINAL BARNSTORMERS SPASM BAND

ORIGINAL BARNSTORMERS SPASM BAND
59	Tempo A 168	That's All There Is/Stormin' The Barn	7
59	Tempo A 168	That's All There Is/Stormin' The Barn (78)	20
59	Tempo EXA 95	ORIGINAL BARNSTORMERS SPASM BAND (EP)	18

(see also Barnstormers Spasm Band)

ORIGINAL BLIND BOYS OF ALABAMA
65	Fontana 688 520 ZL	OLD TIME RELIGION (LP)	18

ORIGINAL CHECKMATES
62	Pye 7N 15428	Hot Toddy/Tuxedo Junction	12
62	Pye 7N 15442	Checkmate Stomp/Begin The Beguine	15
63	Decca F 11688	Union Pacific/The Spy	30

(see also Checkmates)

ORIGINAL DIXIELAND JAZZ BAND
56	HMV DLP 1065	HISTORIC RECORDS OF THE FIRST RECORDED JAZZ (10" LP)	20
56	Columbia 33S 1087	ORIGINAL DIXIELAND JAZZ BAND IN ENGLAND (1919) (10" LP)	20
56	Columbia 33S 1133	ORIGINAL DIXIELAND JAZZ BAND IN ENGLAND NO. 2 (1919-20) (10" LP)	20

ORIGINAL DOWNTOWN SYNCOPATORS
62	VJM VEP 14	ORIGINAL DOWNTOWN SYNCOPATORS (EP)	10
64	Columbia SEG 8293	IT'S JASS (EP)	10
63	J.R.T. Davies DAVLP 301/2	THE ORIGINAL DOWNTOWN SYNCOPATORS (10" LP, white labels only)	35

(see also Ron Geesin)

ORIGINAL DYAKS
67	Columbia DB 8184	Got To Get A Good Thing Going/Would You Love Me Too	8

ORIGINAL MIRRORS
79	Mercury 6007 245	Could This Be Heaven/Night Of The Angels (p/s)	4
79	Mercury 6007 251	Boys Cry/Chains Of Love (p/s)	4
81	Mercury DREAM 1	20,000 Dreamers/The Time Has Come (p/s)	4

(see Big In Japan, Care, Lightning Seeds)

ORIGINAL NEW ORLEANS RHYTHM KINGS
54	Columbia SCM 5113	Golden Leaf Strut/She's Crying For Me	8

ORIGINALS
59	London HL 8783	Sleepless Nights/Anna (unissued)	
62	Top Rank JAR 600	Gimme A Little Kiss, Will Ya, Huh/At Times Like This	25

ORIGINALS
67	Tamla Motown TMG 592	Goodnight Irene/Need Your Lovin', Want You Back	50
69	Tamla Motown TMG 702	Green Grow The Lilacs/You're The One	12
70	Tamla Motown TMG 733	Baby I'm For Real/The Moment Of Truth	10
72	Tamla Motown TMG 822	God Bless Whoever Sent You/I Like Your Style/Baby I'm For Real	6
76	T. Motown TMGT 1038	Down To Love Town/Just To Be Closer To You (12")	8
76	Tamla Motown TMG 1066	Six Million Dollar Man/Mother Nature's Best (unreleased)	
69	T. Motown (S)TML 11116	GREEN GROW THE LILACS (LP)	30

ORIGINAL SIN
80s	S1N	SHADOW (12", p/s, private pressing)	25

ORIGINAL TORNADOS
75	SRT SRTS 75350	Telstar/Red Rocket	8

(see also Tornados)

ORIGINELLS 4
64	Columbia DB 7259	My Girl/Kathy (as Origenells)	15
64	Columbia DB 7388	Nights/I Can Make You Mine	12

ORIOLES
53	London L 1180	Hold Me, Thrill Me, Kiss Me/Teardrops On My Pillow (78)	80
53	London L 1201	Crying In The Chapel/Don't You Think I Ought To Know (78)	80
54	London HL 8001	In The Mission Of St. Augustine/Write And Tell Me Why (78)	80

ORION
84	Lost Moment LM 02	Insane In Another World/Storm (p/s)	15

ORION THE HUNTER
84	Portrait PRT 25906	ORION THE HUNTER (LP)	10

(see also Boston)

ORLANDO
69	NEMS 56-4159	Am I The Same Guy/Poor Little Me	6

TONY ORLANDO
61	Fontana H 308	Halfway To Paradise/Lonely Tomorrows	12
61	Fontana H 330	Bless You/Am I The Guy	6
61	Fontana H 350	Happy Times (Are Here To Stay)/Lonely Am I	8
62	Fontana H 366	Talkin' About You/My Baby's A Stranger	6
62	Columbia DB 4871	Chills/At The Edge Of Tears	6
63	Columbia DB 4954	Beautiful Dreamer/The Loneliest	7
63	Columbia DB 4991	Shirley/Joanie	6
64	Columbia DB 7288	Tell Me What Can I Do/She Doesn't Know It	6
63	Columbia SEG 8238	BLESS YOU (EP)	75
63	Fontana TFL 5167	BLESS YOU (LP, also stereo STFL 582)	50/60

ORLONS
62	Columbia DB 4865	The Wah Watusi/Holiday Hill	12
62	Cameo Parkway C 231	Don't Hang Up/The Conservative	8
63	Cameo Parkway C 243	South Street/Them Terrible Boots	10
63	Cameo Parkway C 257	Not Me/My Best Friend	7

63	Cameo Parkway C 273	Crossfire/It's No Big Thing	8
63	Cameo Parkway C 287	Bon Doo Wah/Don't Throw Your Love Away	10
63	Cameo Parkway C 295	Shimmy Shimmy/Everything Nice	7
64	Cameo Parkway C 319	Rules Of Love/Heartbreak Hotel	10
64	Cameo Parkway C 332	Knock Knock (Who's There)/Goin' Places	10
66	Planet PLF 117	Spinnin' Top/Anyone Who Had A Heart	60
72	Mojo 2092 029	Spinnin' Top/Anyone Who Had A Heart (reissue)	6
62	Cameo Parkway C 1033	ALL THE HITS (LP)	40
63	Cameo Parkway C 1061	BIGGEST HITS (LP)	35
78	London HA-U 8504	CAMEO PARKWAY SESSIONS (LP)	15

(see also Rosetta Hightower)

LE ORME

73	Charisma CAS 1072	FELONA AND SORONA (LP)	20

(see also Peter Hammill)

ORNAMENTAL

88	One Little Indian 18TP 7	Crystal Nights/Yonilingaphonics (p/s)	4

(see also Sugarcubes, Rose McDowall)

CYRIL ORNADEL (ORCHESTRA)

55	MGM SP 1141	King Of Kings (Theme From)/El Cid (Theme From)	7

OR NOT

87	Pointless LESS 2	What A Waste Of Time/Tedium (p/s)	12

OROONIES

91	Demi Monde DMLP 1027	OF HOOF AND HORN (LP)	12

ORPHAN

86	Swoop RTLS 013	Nervous/Little England (p/s)	15

ORPHEUS

66	Red Bird RB 10-041	My Life/Music Minus Orpheus	18

ORPHEUS

68	MGM MGM 1413	I've Never Seen Love Like This/Lesley's World	5
68	MGM MGM-C(S) 8072	ORPHEUS (LP)	15

ORSON FAMILY

83	Orson Enterprises OE 1	Heartbeat/(Be My) Ball And Chain/You Shake My Soul (gatefold p/s)	6

KID ORY & HIS CREOLE JAZZ/DIXIELAND BAND

51	Jazz Man 21	South/Creole Song (78)	8
51	Jazz Man 22	Get Out Of Here/Blues For Jimmy (78)	8
52	Tempo A 106	Dippermouth Blues/Savoy Blues (78)	8
52	Tempo A 107	High Society/Ballin' The Jack (78)	8
52	Vocalion V 1012	Muskrat Ramble/High Society (78)	8
53	Columbia SCM 5047	Mahogany Hall Stomp/At A Georgia Camp Meeting	5
53	Columbia SCM 5069	Tiger Rag/The World's Jazz Crazy, Lawdy So Am I	5
53	Columbia DB 3351	Tiger Rag/The World's Jazz Crazy, Lawdy So Am I (78)	8
53	Columbia DB 3371	Bill Bailey, Won't You Please Come Home/Farewell To Storyville (78)	8
56	Tempo A 106	Dippermouth Blues/Savoy Blues	5
56	Tempo A 107	High Society/Ballin' The Jack	5
56	Vogue V 2011	Tiger Rag/Eh, La-Bas	5
56	Vogue V 2012	12th Street Rag/Savoy Blues	5
56	Good Time Jazz GV 2322	When The Saints Go Marching In/Muskrat Rumble	5
56	Good Time Jazz GV 2339	St. James Infirmary/Bill Bailey, Won't You Please Come Home	5
50s	Storyville SEP 317	KID ORY (EP)	8
55	Tempo EXA 5	KID ORY'S CREOLE JAZZ BAND (EP)	8
55	Vogue EPV 1035	KID ORY'S CREOLE JAZZ BAND (EP)	8
50s	Good Time Jazz EPG 1006	KID ORY'S CREOLE JAZZ BAND (EP)	8
59	Philips BBE 12275	KID ORY (EP)	8
60	Collector JE 117	IN THE BEGINNING (EP)	8
54	Goodtime Jazz LDG 055	KID ORY'S CREOLE JAZZ BAND 1944-1945 (10" LP)	15
54	Goodtime Jazz LDG 093	KID ORY'S CREOLE JAZZ BAND 1944-1945 VOL. 2 (10" LP)	20
56	Goodtime Jazz LDG 184	KID ORY'S CREOLE JAZZ BAND 1944-1945 VOL. 3 (10" LP)	15
56	Capitol T 389	SONG OF THE WANDERER (LP)	12
58	Columbia Clef 33CX 10116	KID ORY IN EUROPE (LP)	15
59	Columbia Clef 33CX 10134	SONG OF THE WANDERER (LP)	15
59	HMV CLP 1303	A KID FROM NEW ORLEANS — ORY, THAT IS (LP)	25
60	HMV CLP 1329	IN THE MOOD (LP)	15
60	HMV CLP 1364	KID ORY PLAYS W.C. HANDY (LP)	18
60	HMV CLP 1395/CSD 1325	DANCE WITH KID ORY — OR JUST LISTEN (LP)	25
61	HMV CLP 1422	WE'VE GOT RHYTHM (LP, with Red Allen)	20

(see also Roberta Dudley)

MIKE OSBORNE

71	Turtle TUR 300	OUTBACK (LP)	75
73	Cadillac SGC 1002	ORIGINAL (LP, as Mike Osborne & Stan Tracey)	20
77	Ogun OG 210	TANDEM — LIVE AT BRACKNELL FESTIVAL (LP, with Stan Tracey)	18
70s	Ogun OG 300	BORDER CROSSING (LP)	15
70s	Ogun OG 700	ALL NIGHT LONG (LP)	30
70s	Ogun OG 810	MARCEL'S MUSE (LP)	15

(see also Stan Tracey)

TONY OSBORNE SOUND

73	Philips 6382 069	GREAT TV THEMES (LP)	10

OSBORNE BROTHERS

62	MGM MGM 1184	The Banjo Boys/Poor Old Cora	8
59	MGM MGM-EP 691	COUNTRY PICKING AND HILLSIDE SINGING (EP)	25
62	MGM MGM-C 914	BLUE GRASS MUSIC (LP)	20

OSBORNE BROTHERS

| 63 | Brunswick LAT 8620 | VOICES IN BLUE GRASS (LP) | 15 |
| 66 | Brunswick LAT 8662 | UP THIS HILL AND DOWN (LP) | 15 |

JOHNNY OSBOURNE (& SENSATIONS)

70	Big Shot BI 549	See And Blind (solo)/THE TECHNIQUES: Scar Face	8
72	Techniques TE 916	See And Blind/TECHNIQUES ALL STARS: Rema Skank	5
70	Trojan TTL 29	COME BACK DARLING (LP, with Sensations)	20

OZZY OSBOURNE

80	Jet JET 197	Crazy Train/You Looking At Me Looking At You (p/s)	7
80	Jet JET 7003	Mr. Crowley (live)/You Said It All (live) (p/s)	8
80	Jet JET 12003	Mr. Crowley (live)/You Said It All (live)/Suicide Solution (live) (12", p/s)	10
80	Jet JETP 12003	Mr. Crowley (live)/You Said It All (live)/Suicide Solution (live) (12", picture disc)	15
81	Jet JET 7017	Over The Mountain/I Don't Know (p/s)	5
81	Jet JET 12017	Over The Mountain/I Don't Know (12", p/s)	8
82	Jet JET 7030	Symptom Of The Universe/N.I.B. (p/s)	5
82	Jet JETP 7030	Symptom Of The Universe/N.I.B. (picture disc)	10
82	Jet JET 12030	Symptom Of The Universe/N.I.B./Children Of The Grave (12", p/s)	8
83	Epic TA 3915	Bark At The Moon/One Up The B-Side (12", p/s, silver vinyl)	15
83	Epic WA 3915	Bark At The Moon/One Up The B-Side (12", picture disc, unreleased)	
84	Epic DA 4452	So Tired/Bark At The Moon (live)//Waiting For Darkness/Paranoid (live) (double pack)	8
84	Epic TA 4452	So Tired/Bark At The Moon (live)/Waiting For Darkness/Suicide Solution/Paranoid (live) (12", p/s with free patch)	8
84	Epic WA 4452	So Tired/Bark At The Moon (live)/Waiting For Darkness/Suicide Solution/Paranoid (live) (12", p/s, gold vinyl)	12
86	Epic A 6859	Shot In The Dark/Rock'n'Roll Rebel (p/s, with signature card)	6
86	Epic QA 6859	Shot In The Dark/Rock'n'Roll Rebel (poster p/s)	8
86	Epic A 7311	The Ultimate Sin/Lightning Strikes (p/s, with free patch)	5
88	Epic 652 875-2	Back To Ozz (The Ultimate Sin/Bark At The Moon/Mr. Crowley/Diary Of A Madman (CD, gatefold card sleeve with family tree)	8
88	Epic 653 063-9	Miracle Man/Crazy Babies (head-shaped picture disc)	8
88	Epic 653 063-2	Miracle Man/The Liar/Crazy Babies (CD)	8
88	Spiral Scratch 2/Ozzy 1	An Interview With… (no p/s, free with *Spiral Scratch*, issue 2, 5,000 only)	5
90	Adventure ADV TS 102	The Urpney Song/Whirlypad Launch (p/s, some with poster, with Frank Bruno/Billy Connolly)	6/5
91	Epic 657 4406	No More Tears (extended version)/S.I.N./Party With The Animals (12" picture disc)	8
93	Epic 659 3406	Changes/Changes (extended version)/No More Tears (extended version)/Desire (12" picture disc)	8
96	Epic 662 6391	Perry Mason/Living With The Enemy (picture disc)	6
86	Epic EPC 11-26404	THE ULTIMATE SIN (LP, picture disc)	12
89	Epic 463 0862	DIARY OF A MADMAN (CD, promo only with diary)	20
91	Epic 467 8592	NO MORE TEARS (CD in embossed wallet)	18
95	Epic XP CD 2007	THE BALLADS OF OZ (CD, promo only compilation)	40

(see also Black Sabbath, Lita Ford & Ozzy Osbourne)

BOB OSBURN

| 64 | London HLD 9869 | Bound To Happen/Think Of Me | 15 |

OSCAR

66	Reaction 591 003	Club Of Lights/Waking Up	15
66	Reaction 591 006	Join My Gang/Days Gone By	20
67	Reaction 591 012	Over The Wall We Go/Every Day Of My Life	20
67	Reaction 591 016	Holiday/Give Her All She Wants	15
68	Polydor 56257	Open Up The Skies/Wild Ones	15

(see also Paul Dean, Ivor Bird, Paul Nicholas)

OSCAR

| 74 | Buk BULP 2001 | OSCAR (LP) | 12 |

OSCAR BICYCLE

| 68 | CBS 3237 | On A Quiet Night/The Room Revolves Around Me | 30 |

WAVIS O'SHAVE

| 80s | Company CR 3 | DENNIS SMOKES TABS (EP) | 4 |
| 80 | Anti-Pop AP 2 | ANNA FORD'S BUM (mini LP) | 10 |

OSIBISA

71	Smoke SS 1001	Black Ant/Kotoko	5
72	MCA MKS 5079	Music For Gong Gong/Woyaya	5
72	MCA MKS 5093	Wango, Wango/Ana-Bo	5
73	Buddah 2011 179	Superfly Man/Prophets	5
71	MCA MDKS 8001	OSIBISA (LP)	15
72	MCA MDKS 8005	WOYOYA (LP)	12
72	MCA MDKS 8007	HEADS (LP)	12
73	Buddah 2318 087	SUPER FLY T.N.T. (LP, soundtrack)	12

DONNY OSMOND

72	MGM 2006 071	Go Away Little Girl/Time To Ride	4
72	MGM 2006 087	Hey Girl/I Knew You When	4
72	MGM 2006 119	Why/Lonely Boy	4
73	MGM 2006 300	Young Love/A Million To One (p/s)	4
88	Virgin VSCD 1140	If It's Love That You Want (7" Version)/Come Down/If It's Love That You Want (Extended Remix)/Soldier Of Love (7" Remix) (3" CD, pic disc, 5" g/f card p/s)	7
72	MGM 2315 055	THE DONNY OSMOND ALBUM (LP)	10

(see also Osmond Brothers, Osmonds)

OSMOND BROTHERS
63	MGM MGM 1208	Be My Little Baby Bumble Bee/I Wouldn't Know	20
63	MGM MGM 1245	Travels Of Jamie McPheeters/Aura Lee	15
63	MGM MGM-C 1011	NEW SOUND OF THE BROTHERS (LP)	35

(see also Osmonds)

OSMONDS
71	MGM 2006 021	One Bad Apple/He Ain't Heavy — He's My Brother	6
71	MGM 2006 043	Sweet And Innocent/Motown Special (Medley)	5
72	MGM 2006 115	Hold Her Tight/Love Is	5
72	Lyntone	Osmonds World (1-sided flexi)	8
73	MGM 2006 288	Goin' Home/Are You Up There	5

(see also Osmond Brothers, Donny Osmond)

OSSIAN
77	Spring Thyme SPR 1004	OSSIAN (LP)	10
79	Iona IR 001	ST. KILDA WEDDING (LP, with lyric insert)	10
81	Iona IR 002	SEAL SONG (LP, with lyric insert)	10

OSSIE & SWEET BOYS
| 67 | Polydor 56167 | Nothing Takes The Place Of You/Brixton Boo-Ga-Loo | 6 |

OSSIE & UPSETTERS
| 66 | Doctor Bird DB 1018 | Turn Me On/True Love | 15 |

(see also Upsetters, Desmond Dekkar)

BASHFUL BROTHER OSWALD
| 64 | London HA-B/SH-B 8104 | BASHFUL BROTHER OSWALD (LP, mono/stereo) | 12/15 |

GILBERT O'SULLIVAN
| 71 | Columbia DB 8779 | I Wish I Could Cry/Mr Moody's Garden | 8 |
| 73 | Columbia DB 8967 | I Wish I Could Cry/Mr Moody's Garden (reissue) | 5 |

(see also Gilbert)

OTHER BROTHERS
| 69 | Pama PM 785 | Let's Get Together/Little Girl | 6 |

OTHERS
| 64 | Fontana TF 501 | Oh Yeah/I'm Taking Her Home | 60 |

(see also Sands, Sundragon; this single does not feature Brian May)

OTHER TWO
64	Decca F 11911	I Wanna Be With You/Grumbling Guitar	10
65	RCA RCA 1465	Don't You Wanna Love Me Baby/Hold Back The Light Of Dawn	8
66	RCA RCA 1531	I'll Never Let You Go/Hot At Night	10

(see also Storyteller, J.J. Jackson)

CLYDE OTIS ORCHESTRA
| 61 | Mercury AMT 1143 | Jungle Drums/Peanut Vendor | 5 |

JOHNNY OTIS SHOW
50	Parlophone R 3291	Harlem Nocturne (solo)/SLIM GAILLARD: Jam Man (78)	40
57	Capitol CL 14794	Ma (He's Makin' Eyes At Me)/Romance In The Dark	10
58	Capitol CL 14817	Bye Bye Baby (as Johnny Otis Show with Marie Adams)/Good Golly	15
58	Capitol CL 14817	Bye Bye Baby (as Johnny Otis Show with Marie Adams)/Good Golly (78)	12
58	Capitol CL 14837	The Light Still Shines In My Window/All I Want Is Your Love (with Marie Adams)	12
58	Capitol CL 14837	The Light Still Shines In My Window/All I Want Is Your Love (78, with Marie Adams)	12
58	Capitol CL 14854	Well, Well, Well, Well!/You Just Kissed Me Goodbye (with Mel Williams)	12
58	Capitol CL 14854	Well, Well, Well, Well!/You Just Kissed Me Goodbye (78, with Mel Williams)	18
58	Capitol CL 14875	Ring-A-Ling/The Johnny Otis Hand Jive	18
58	Capitol CL 14875	Ring-A-Ling/The Johnny Otis Hand Jive (78)	30
58	Capitol CL 14941	Crazy Country Hop/Willie Did The Cha Cha	18
59	Capitol CL 15008	You/My Dear (as Johnny Otis Show with Mel Williams)	12
59	Capitol CL 15018	Castin' My Spell/Telephone Baby (as Johnny Otis Show with Marci Lee)	15
59	Capitol CL 15057	Three Girls Named Molly Doin' The Hully Gully/I'll Do The Same Thing For You	10
60	Capitol CL 15112	Mumblin' Mosie/Hey Baby, Don't You Know?	10
64	Ember EMB S 192	Hand Jive One More Time/Baby I Got News For You	10
69	Sonet SON 608	Country Girl/Signifyin' Monkey	5
72	Epic EPC 7896	The Watts Breakaway/You Can Depend On Me	6
72	Epic EPC 8071	The Watts Breakaway/Willie And The Hand Jive	6
75	Ember EMB S 345	Jaws/Good To The Last Drop	5
70s	Bulldog BD 2	Willie And The Hand Jive/Harlem Nocturne	5
59	Capitol EAP1 1134	THE JOHNNY OTIS SHOW (EP)	75
65	Vocalion VEP 170162	JOHNNY OTIS (EP)	100
58	Capitol T 940	THE JOHNNY OTIS SHOW (LP)	60
69	Sonet SNTF 613	COLD SHOT (LP)	12
71	Epic EPC 66295	LIVE AT MONTEREY (2-LP)	12
72	Ember SPE 6604	FORMIDABLE (LP)	18
73	Starline SRS 5129	PIONEERS OF ROCK VOLUME 3 (LP)	12

(see also Marie Adams)

SHUGGIE OTIS
| 70 | CBS 63996 | HERE COMES SHUGGIE OTIS (LP) | 15 |

(see also Al Kooper & Shuggie Otis)

NOIT OTNI & PITS
| 79 | Automotive AERS 107 | A Heart Can Only Be Broken Once/Moving Target (p/s) | 5 |

MINT VALUE £

KNUCKLES O'TOOLE
59	Top Rank JAR 125	If You Knew Susie/Yes, We Have No Bananas	4

NATALINO OTTO
59	Oriole CB 1515	Carina/Questo Nostro Amore	4
59	Oriole CB 1515	Carina/Questo Nostro Amore (78)	10

JOHN OTWAY
72	County COUN 215	Gypsy/Misty Mountain (private pressing, with duplicated lyric sheet)	25
76	Viking YRS CF 01	Louisa On A Horse/Beware Of The Flowers (private pressing)	30
78	Polydor 2059 001	Geneve/It's A Long Time Since I Heard Homestead On The Farm (p/s)	5
78	Polydor 2059 060	Baby's In The Club/Julie Julie Julie (p/s)	5
79	Polydor 2059 105	Frightened And Scared/Are You On My Side? (p/s)	4
79	Polydor 2059 105	Frightened And Scared (instrumental)/Are You On My Side? (p/s, only 3 copies pressed!)	100+
80	Stiff BUY 101	Green Green Grass Of Home/Wednesday Club (p/s)	4
81	Stiff BUY 115	Turning Point/Too Much Air, Not Enough Oxygen (die-cut p/s)	4
82	Empire HAM 3	In Dreams/You Ain't Seen Nothing Yet (as John Otway Sweat, p/s)	4
83	Empire HAM 6	Mass Communication/Baby It's The Real thing (p/s, green vinyl)	4
83	Strike Back SBR 1	Middle Of Winter/It Makes Me See Red (p/s)	4
86	'Warner Bros' OTWEAY 1	The New Jerusalem/The Tyger (no p/s, private pressing)	20
86	WEA YZ 95	The New Jerusalem/The Tyger (reissue, p/s)	4
88	WEA YZ 111	Whoops Apocalypse/Losing (p/s)	4
82	Empire HAMLP 1	JOHN OTWAY (ALL BALLS AND NO WILLY) (LP, with Europeans)	10

JOHN OTWAY & WILD WILLY BARRETT
73	Track 2094 111	Murder Man/If I Did	8
76	Track 2094 133	Louisa On A Horse/Misty Mountain	5
77	Polydor 2058 916	Racing Cars (Jet Spotter Of The Track)/Running From The Law (p/s)	5
77	Polydor 2058 951	Really Free/Beware Of The Flowers (Cos I'm Sure They're Going To Get You Yeh) (p/s or die-cut 'review' sleeve)	6/5
80	Polydor POSP 143	Birthday Boy/Wow, What A Woman	4
80	Polydor 2059 250	DK 50-80/JOHN OTWAY: It's A Long Time Since I Heard Homestead On The Farm/WILD WILLY BARRETT: Homestead On The Farm (p/s)	4
82	Stiff Indie STIN 1	Headbutts/Live Version Headbutts (p/s)	4
82	Empire HAM 5T	12 STITCH EP (12" EP in polythene bag with jay-card)	15
87	VM VMS 6	The Last Of The Mohicans/Fashion (brown paper bag sleeve)	5
77	Extracted EXLP 1	JOHN OTWAY AND WILD WILLY BARRETT (LP, handmade stickered sleeve)	15
77	white label OBL 1	OTWAY AND BARRETT LIVE AT THE ROUNDHOUSE (private pressing LP, freebie, handwritten labels, plain sleeve, 250 numbered copies only)	50
78	Polydor Super 2383 501	DEEP AND MEANINGLESS (LP, stickered sleeve, with free 7" "Racing Cars [Jet Spotter Of The Track]"/"Down The Road [live]" [OT 1])	10
81	Polydor POLS 1039	GONE WITH THE BIN (THE BEST OF OTWAY-BARRETT) (LP)	10
87	VM VM 7	THE WIMP AND THE WILD (LP, 1,000 only)	12

(see also Wild Willy Barrett, Johnny Japes & His Jesticles)

OUR PLASTIC DREAM
67	Go AJ 11411	A Little Bit Of Shangrila/Encapsulated Marigold	75

OUT
79	Rabid TOSH 113	Who Is Innocent/Linda's Just A Statue (p/s)	7
82	Virgin VS 308	Who Is Innocent/Linda's Just A Statue (p/s)	4

OUTCASTS
78	It IT 4	Frustration/Don't Want To Be No Adult/You're A Disease (p/s)	12
78	Good Vibrations GOT 3	Just Another Teenage Rebel/Love Is For Sops (poster p/s, various colours; 'band' p/s or 'type' p/s)	10/8
79	Good Vibrations GOT 17	Self Conscious Over You/Love You For Never (p/s)	7
81	GBH GBH 001	Magnum Force/Gangland Warfare (p/s)	6
81	Outcasts Only 0001	Programme Love/Beating And Screaming (Parts 1 & 2)/Mania (p/s)	4
79	Good Vibrations BIG 1	SELF CONSCIOUS OVER YOU (LP)	15

OUTER LIMITS
67	Elephant LUR 100	When The Work Is Thru'/5 MAN CARGO: What A Wonderful Feeling (Leeds Students Charity Rag record)	45
67	Deram DM 125	Just One More Chance/Help Me Please	15
68	Immediate IM 067	Great Train Robbery/Sweet Freedom (demo only)	60
68	Instant IN 001	Great Train Robbery/Sweet Freedom	20
71	Decca F 13176	The Dark Side Of The Moon/Black Boots	8

(see also Christie, Acid Gallery)

OUTER LIMITS
60s	Teldisc TD 154	Paradise For Two/Don't Ever Change	20

OUTER LIMITS
70s	Snow/Deroy 1049	(I'm Not) Your Stepping Stone/Great Balls Of Fire	40

OUTLAW BLUES BAND
69	Stateside SSL 10290	BREAKING IN (LP)	15

OUTLAWS
61	HMV POP 844	Swingin' Low/Spring Is Near	15
61	HMV POP 877	Ambush/Indian Brave	15
61	HMV POP 927	Valley Of The Sioux/Crazy Drums	15
62	HMV POP 990	Ku-pow!/Last Stage West	15
62	HMV POP 1074	Sioux Serenade/Fort Knox	15
63	HMV POP 1124	The Return Of The Outlaws/Texan Spiritual	10
63	HMV POP 1195	That Set The Wild West Free/Hobo	12
63	HMV POP 1241	Law And Order/Do-Da-Day	12

64	HMV POP 1277	Keep-A-Knockin'/Shake With Me	30
61	HMV CLP 1489	DREAM OF THE WEST (LP, mauve label, later black)	100/75

(see also Mike Berry, Ritchie Blackmore, Bobbie Graham, Chaps, Rally Rounders, Houston Wells [& Marksmen])

OUT OF DARKNESS
70	Key KL 006	OUT OF DARKNESS (LP)	140

OUTPATIENTS
81	Albion ION 1014	New Japanese Hairstyles/Children (p/s)	10

OUTRAGE
70	Kama Sutra 618 027	The Letter/The Way I See It	4

OUTSIDERS (U.K.)
65	Decca F 12213	Keep On Doing It/Songs We Sang Last Summer	12

(see also Bunch Of Fives, Junior's Eyes, Tickle)

OUTSIDERS (U.S.)
66	Capitol CL 15435	Time Won't Let Me/Was It Really Real?	30
66	Capitol CL 15450	Girl In Love/What Makes You So Bad, You Weren't Brought Up That Way	15
66	Capitol CL 15468	Respectable/Lost In My World	15
66	Capitol CL 15480	Help Me Girl/You Gotta Look	10
67	Capitol CL 15495	I'll Give You Time/I'm Not Tryin' To Hurt You	12

OUTSIDERS (U.K.)
77	Raw Edge RER 002	ONE TO INFINITY (EP)	20
78	Xciting Plastic	Vital Hours/Take Up (unissued)	
77	Raw Edge RER 001	CALLING ON YOUTH (LP)	25
78	Raw Edge RER 003	CLOSE UP (LP, with insert)	25

(see also Second Layer, Sound)

OUTSKIRTS OF INFINITY
87	Woronzow WOO 7	LORD OF THE DARK SKIES (LP)	15
89	Infinity INF 001	SCENES FROM THE DREAMS OF ANGELS (LP)	12
89	Infinity INF 002	STONED CRAZY (LP)	12
94	Dark Skies DSKLP 2	INCIDENT AT PILATUS (2-LP)	18

OVALTINEES
83	(no label credit) BAA 021	BRITISH JUSTICE EP (p/s)	30

OVARY LODGE
73	RCA SF 8372	OVARY LODGE (LP)	40
76	Ogun OG 600	OVARY LODGE (LP)	30

(see also Keith Tippett)

OVERDRIVE
81	Boring Grantham BGR 1	ON THE RUN (EP)	80
90	Boring Grantham BGR 11	DISHONEST WORDS (LP)	12

OVERLANDERS
63	Pye 7N 15544	Summer Skies And Golden Sands/Call Of The Wild	10
63	Pye 7N 15568	Movin'/Rainbow	5
64	Pye 7N 15619	Yesterday's Gone/Gone In The Rainbow	5
64	Pye 7N 15678	Don't It Make You Feel Good/Sing A Song Of Sadness	4
64	Pye 7N 15712	If I Gave You/I Wonder Why	5
64	Pye 7N 15719	The Leaves Are Falling/Delia's Gone	5
65	Pye 7N 15804	Along Came Jones/Walking The Soles Off My Shoes	5
65	Pye 7N 15883	Freight Train/Take The Bucket To The Well	5
65	Pye 7N 15967	Room Enough For You And Me/January	5
66	Pye 7N 17034	Michelle/Cradle Of Love	4
66	Pye 7N 17068	My Life/The Girl From Indiana	5
66	Pye 7N 17159	Go Where You Wanna Go/Don't Let It Happen Again	5
66	Pye NEP 24245	MICHELLE (EP)	30
66	Pye NPL 18138	MICHELLE (LP)	30

(see also Paul Arnold, Cuppa T)

OVERLOAD
80	MCA MCA 618	Into Overload/Follow The Lines (p/s)	7
81	MCA MCA 656	Who Are You/Drift Away	7

OVERLORD
78	Airebeat ABT 3	Lucy (p/s)	25

RUNE OVERMAN
63	Decca F 11605	Big Bass Boogie/Madison Piano	8

OVERTAKERS
68	Amalgamated AMG 803	That's The Way You Like It/The Big Take-Over	10
68	Amalgamated AMG 809	Girl You Ruff/KEITH BLAKE: Woo Oh Oh	12

OWEN (Gray) & DANDY (Livingstone)
69	Downtown DT 428	Lovey Dovey/HERBIE GRAY & RUDIES: Kitty Wait	7

OWEN (Gray) & LEON
64	Island WI 146	Nextdoor Neighbour/ROLAND ALPHONSO: Feeling Fine	18
64	Island WI 163	My Love For You/How Many Times	18
64	Island WI 164	The Fits Is On Me/SKATALITES: Good News	18
64	Island WI 165	Running Around/SKATALITES: Around The World	18
65	Ska Beat JB 189	Woman/BABA BROOKS with DON DRUMMOND: Doctor Decker	18

(see also Leon & Owen, Tommy McCook)

OWEN (Gray) & MILLIE
62	Blue Beat BB 96	Sit And Cry/Do You Know (with City Slickers Orchestra)	12
62	Island WI 014	Sugar Plum/OWEN GRAY: Jezebel	10

(see also Owen Gray, Millie, Owen & Leon, Leon & Owen)

MINT VALUE £

RAY OWEN('S MOON)
69	Fontana TF 1045	Tonight I'll Be Staying Here With You/Down, Don't Bother Me (solo)	5
71	Polydor 2058 095	Hey Sweety/Free Man (as Ray Owen's Moon)	5
71	Polydor 2325 061	RAY OWEN'S MOON (LP)	20

(see also Juicy Lucy)

REG OWEN & HIS ORCHESTRA
56	Parlophone R 4217	Comin' Thru' The Rye Bread/Harlem Swing	5
57	Parlophone R 4303	Easy Now/Sweeping The Floor	5
59	Pye International 7N 25009	Manhattan Spiritual/Ritual Blues	6
59	Pye International N 25009	Manhattan Spiritual/Ritual Blues (78)	8
59	Pye International 7N 25040	Ginchy/Kazoo	5
59	Pye International N 25040	Ginchy/Kazoo (78)	10
60	Palette PG 9004	Obsession/Sunday Morn	6
61	Palette PG 9013	Payroll/Swing A Ling-Ling	6
61	Palette PG 9022	Teen Dreams/Bye Bye Blackbird (as Reg Owen Strings)	6
62	Palette PG 9030	Hula Twist/Gonna High Life	6
56	Parlophone PMD 1045	SWING ME HIGH (10" LP)	18
59	Pye Intl. NPL 28000	MANHATTAN SPIRITUAL (LP, also stereo NSPL 93000)	18/25

BUCK OWENS (& BUCKAROOS)
59	Capitol CL 15009	Everlasting Love/Second Fiddle	7
60	Capitol CL 15123	Above And Beyond/Til These Dreams Come True	6
60	Capitol CL 15162	Excuse Me (I Think I've Got A Heartache)/I've Got A Right To Know	6
61	Capitol CL 15187	Foolin' Around/High As The Mountain	6
63	Capitol CL 15321	Love's Gonna Live Here/Getting Used To Losing You	6
64	Capitol CL 15364	Together Again/Ain't It Amazin' Gracie (as Buck Owens & Buckaroos)	6
65	Capitol CL 15379	I've Got A Tiger By The Tail/Cryin' Time	7
65	Capitol CL 15402	Before You Go/(I Want) No One But You	6
66	Capitol CL 15437	Waitin' In Your Welfare Line/In The Palm Of Your Hand	6
66	Capitol CL 15452	Think Of Me/Heart Of Glass (as Buck Owens & Buckaroos)	6
67	Capitol CL 15501	Sam's Place/Don't Ever Tell Me Goodbye (as Buck Owens & Buckaroos)	6
69	Capitol CL 15593	Johnny B. Goode/Maybe If I Close My Eyes (It'll Go Away)	5
63	Capitol EAP1 1550	FOOLIN' AROUND (EP)	20
65	Capitol EAP1 20602	ACT NATURALLY (EP)	20
64	Capitol (S)T 2105	THE BEST OF BUCK OWENS (LP)	15
65	Capitol T 2135	TOGETHER AGAIN/MY HEART SKIPS A BEAT (LP)	15
66	Capitol (S)T 2353	BEFORE YOU GO/NO ONE BUT YOU (LP)	15
66	Capitol (S)T 2443	ROLL OUT THE RED CARPET (LP)	15
66	Fontana FJL 307	BUCK OWENS WITH FERLIN HUSKY & FARON YOUNG (LP)	15
66	Capitol (S)T 2283	I'VE GOT A TIGER BY THE TAIL (LP)	15
66	Capitol (S)T 20861	YOURS, COUNTRY STYLE (LP)	18
67	Capitol (S)T 2556	CARNEGIE HALL CONCERT (LP)	15
68	Capitol (S)T 2760	YOUR TENDER LOVING CARE (LP, with His Buckaroos)	15
68	Capitol (S)T 2841	IT TAKES PEOPLE LIKE YOU TO MAKE PEOPLE LIKE ME (LP)	15
68	Capitol (S)T 2897	THE BEST OF BUCK OWENS VOL. 2 (LP)	12
69	Capitol (S)T 2994	THE GUITAR PLAYER (LP)	12
69	Capitol E-(S)T 131	I'VE GOT YOU ON MY MIND AGAIN (LP)	12
69	Capitol E-(S)T 232	BUCK OWENS IN LONDON (LP)	12
70	Capitol E-ST 212	TALL DARK STRANGER (LP)	12
71	Capitol E-ST 628	I WOULDN'T LIVE IN NEW YORK CITY (LP)	12
71	Capitol E-ST 685	BRIDGE OVER TROUBLED WATER (LP)	12
72	Capitol E-ST 795	BUCK OWENS' RUBY (LP)	12
72	Capitol E-ST 11039	BUCK OWENS LIVE AT THE NUGGET (LP)	12
73	Capitol E-ST 11136	IN THE PALM OF YOUR HAND (LP)	12
73	Capitol E-ST 11180	AIN'T IT AMAZING, GRACIE (LP)	12

DONNIE OWENS
58	London HLU 8747	Need You/If I'm Wrong	20
58	London HLU 8747	Need You/If I'm Wrong (78)	30
59	London HLW 8897	Ask Me Anything/Between Midnight And Dawn (unissued)	

OWL
68	United Artists UP 2240	Run To The Sun/Shades Of Blue And Green Water Flies	20

TONY OXLEY (QUARTET)
69	CBS 52664	THE BAPTISED TRAVELLER (LP)	80
70	CBS 64071	4 COMPOSITIONS FOR SEXTET (LP, with Derek Bailey)	80
71	RCA SF 8215	ICHNOS (LP)	45
70s	Incus 8	TONY OXLEY (LP)	50
70s	Incus 18	FEBRUARY PAPERS (LP)	18
80s	Bead 25	THE GLIDER & THE GRINDER (LP)	25

(see also Derek Bailey)

OXY & MORONS
81	Music For The Deaf MFD 1	Dirty Harry In The Falls Road/Nice To Be Back (printed brown paper bag p/s)	6
82	Music For The Deaf MFD 2	Work/The Good Life (no p/s)	4

OXYM
80	Cargo CRS 003	Music Power/Mind Key (p/s)	30

OZRIC TENTACLES
94	Dovetail DOVEBOX 1	VITAMIN ENHANCED (6-CD box set)	30
98	Snapper SMALP 410	CURIOUS CORN (LP)	12

(see also Eat Static)

AUGUSTUS PABLO
71	Big Shot BI 578	The Mood/HERMAN CHIN-LOY: New Love	25
71	Big Shot BI 579	East Of The River Nile/HERMAN CHIN-LOY: East Of River Nile Version (B-side actually by Aquarians)	20
71	Creole CR 1004	405 (actually "The Mood" by Tommy McCook)/Duck It Up (actually "Confidential Version" by Charmers)	8
71	Ackee ACK 134	Still Yet/AQUARIANS: Version	12
71	Ackee ACK 138	Snowball And Pudding/AQUARIANS: Version	12
71	Duke DU 122	Reggae In The Fields/TOMMY McCOOK: Love Brother	10
73	Randy's RAN 536	Bedroom Mazurka (as Augustus Pablo & Fay)/Melodica Version	12
75	Island WIP 6226	King Tubby Meets The Rockers Uptown/Baby I Love You So	5
75	Island 12 WIP 6226	King Tubby Meets The Rockers Uptown/Baby I Love You So (12")	8
78	Rough Trade RT 002	Pablo Meets Mr. Bassie/Mr. Bassie Special (with Rockers All Stars) (no p/s with colour sticker)	5
75	Trojan TRLS 115	ITAL DUB (LP, original issue with "12 Wealdon Lane" address on sleeve and rough orange/white paper labels)	15

(see also Mickey Lee, I Roy)

PACESETTERS
70	Big Chief BC 101	Cool Coffee/Israelites	7
70	Escort ERT 829	Bits And Pieces/Nimrod Leap	6

PACIFIC DRIFT
70	Deram DM 304	Water Woman/Yes You Do	7
70	Deram Nova (S)DN 13	FEELIN' FREE (LP)	30

(see also Wimple Winch, Just Four Men)

PACIFIC GAS & ELECTRIC (P.G. & E.)
70	CBS 5039	Are You Ready?/Staggolee	6
70	CBS 5204	Father Come On Home/Elvira	5
69	B&C CAS 1003	GET IT ON (LP)	20
69	CBS 63822	PACIFIC GAS & ELECTRIC (LP, orange label)	18
70	CBS 64026	ARE YOU READY (LP, orange label)	18
71	CBS 64295	HARD BURN (LP, orange label)	18

PACK
65	Columbia DB 7702	Do You Believe In Magic?/Things Bring Me Down	25

PACK
79	SS PAK 1	Brave New Soldiers/Heathen (p/s, 2,500 only)	12
79	Rough Trade RT 025	King Of Kings/Number 12 (p/s)	10
80	SS SS 1N2/SS 2N1	KIRK BRANDON AND THE PACK OF LIES (EP, with printed inner sleeve)	15
82	Cyclops CYCLOPS 1	LONG LIVE THE PAST (EP)	7
82	Donut DONUT 2	THE PACK LIVE, 1979 (cassette)	12

(see also Theatre Of Hate, Spear Of Destiny, Senate)

PACKABEATS
61	Parlophone R 4729	Gypsy Beat/Big Man	15
62	Pye 7N 15480	Evening In Paris/The Traitors	20
63	Pye 7N 15549	Dream Lover/Packabeat	20

PACKERS
66	Pye International 7N 25343	Hole In The Wall/Go 'Head On	12
69	Soul City SC 111	Hole In The Wall/Go 'Head On (reissue)	10
70	Soul City SCM 003	HOLE IN THE WALL (LP)	30

PAC-KEYS
67	Speciality SPE 1003	Stone Fox/Diggin'	10

PADDY GOES TO HOLLYHEAD
87	Jackeen PAD 1	Green Green Grass Of Home/(Telling Me) All Those Lies (p/s)	5
87	Rage PADDY 1	Green Green Grass Of Home/(Telling Me) All Those Lies (reissue, p/s)	4

PADDY, KLAUS & GIBSON
65	Pye 7N 15906	I Wanna Know/I Tried	18
66	Pye 7N 17060	No Good Without You Baby/Rejected	30
66	Pye 7N 17112	Teresa/Quick Before They Catch Us	18

(see also Manfred Mann, Big Three, Rory Storm & Hurricanes, Kingsize Taylor)

BILLY PAGE
65	London HLU 10006	It's Pop/American Girl	6

CHRIS PAGE
66	Cameo Parkway CP 751	Wait And See/Mine Mine Mine	7

GENE PAGE
75	Atlantic K 10574	Satin Soul/Cream Corner	4

HOT LIPS PAGE & HIS ORCHESTRA
55	Parlophone MSP 6172	Ain't Nothing Wrong With That Boy/The Cadillac Song	25
55	Parlophone R 4030	Ain't Nothing Wrong With That Boy/The Cadillac Song (78)	10

JIMMY PAGE
65	Fontana TF 533	She Just Satisfies/Keep Moving	375

Jimmy PAGE

88	Geffen GEF 41	Wasting My Time/Writes Of Winter (p/s, withdrawn)	8
91	Fontana TFCD 533	She Just Satisfies/Keep Moving (CD, in 'Led Zeppelin Celebration' pack)	10

(see also Led Zeppelin, Page & Plant, Firm, Yardbirds, Paul, Carter-Lewis & Southerners, Neil Christian & Crusaders, Bobby Graham, Robert Plant, Honeydrippers, Brian Auger, Cartoone, Maureeny Wishfull)

LARRY PAGE (ORCHESTRA)

57	Columbia DB 3965	Cool Shake/Start Movin' (In My Direction)	18
57	Columbia DB 3965	Cool Shake/Start Movin' (In My Direction) (78)	15
58	Columbia DB 4012	That'll Be The Day/Please Don't Blame Me	18
58	Columbia DB 4012	That'll Be The Day/Please Don't Blame Me (78)	15
58	Columbia DB 4080	Under Control/This Is My Life	15
58	Columbia DB 4080	Under Control/This Is My Life (78)	15
59	Saga SAG 45-2902	Big Blon' Baby/I Vibrate	20
60	Saga SAG 45-2903	How'm I Doing, Hey Hey/Throw All Your Lovin' My Way	10
60	Saga SAG 45-2904	Little Old Fashioned You/Marylin	8
66	Decca F 12320	Waltzing To Jazz/Jo Jo (as Larry Page Orchestra)	5
66	Decca F 12368	Peyton Place Theme/Leanda's Theme (as Larry Page Orchestra)	5
68	Page One POF 068	Take Five/Michelle	5
68	Page One POF 096	Hey Jude/Those Were The Days (as Larry Page Orchestra)	5
60	Saga STP 1024	SINGS HIS PERSONAL CHOICE (EP)	10
65	Decca LK 4692	KINKY MUSIC (LP, as Larry Page Orchestra)	70
68	Page One POL(S) 002	EXECUTIVE SUITE (LP, as Larry Page Orchestra)	12
68	Page One POLS 004	FROM LARRY, WITH LOVE (LP)	12
69	Page One POLS 601	LARRY PAGE ORCHESTRA (LP)	12

MALLY PAGE

66	Pye 7N 17105	The Life And Soul Of The Party/You Can Be Wrong About Boys	6

PATTI PAGE

78s

51	Oriole CB 1046	The Tennessee Waltz/Long, Long Ago (78)	8
51	Oriole CB 1047	Mockin' Bird/I Love You Because (78)	8
51	Oriole CB 1059	Ever True Ever More/Down The Trail Of Achin' Hearts (78)	8
51	Oriole CB 1060	Detour/Who's Gonna Shoe My Pretty Little Feet (78)	8
51	Oriole CB 1061	And So To Sleep Again/One Sweet Letter (78)	8
52	Oriole CB 1065	All My Love/Roses Remind Me Of You (78)	8
52	Oriole CB 1099	Come What May/Retreat (78)	8
52	Oriole CB 1114	Love, Where Are You Now/Whispering Minds (78)	8
52	Oriole CB 1129	I Went To Your Wedding/You Belong To Me (78)	8
53	Oriole CB 1145	Why Don't You Believe Me/Conquest (78)	8
53	Oriole CB 1146	Once In A While/I'm Glad That You're Happy With Somebody Else (78)	8
53	Oriole CB 1156	How Much Is That Doggie In The Window/My Jealous Eyes (78)	10
53	Oriole CB 1190	Oo What You Do To Me/Now That I'm In Love (78)	8
53	Oriole CB 1213	This Is My Song/Butterflies (78)	8
53	Oriole CB 1230	Father — Father/The Lord's Prayer (78)	8
53	Oriole CB 1231	My World Is You/Milwaukee Polka (78)	8
54	Oriole CB 1251	Where Did My Snowman Go?/I'll Keep The Love-Light Burning (78)	8
54	Oriole CB 1254	Changing Partners/Streets Of Laredo (78)	8
54	Oriole CB 1269	Cross Over The Bridge/My Restless Lover (78)	8
54	Oriole CB 1278	Arfie, The Doggie In The Window (Parts 1 & 2) (78)	10
54	Mercury MB 3125	Don't Get Around Much Anymore/Lonely Days (78)	8
54	Mercury MB 3149	What A Dream/I Cried (78)	8
54	Mercury MB 3161	I Can't Tell A Waltz From A Tango/The Mama Doll Song (78)	8
55	Mercury MB 3182	Let Me Go Lover/Hocus-Pocus (78)	8
55	Mercury MB 3201	Everlovin'/You Too Can Be A Dreamer (78)	8
55	Mercury MB 3232	Keep Me In Mind/Little Crazy Quilt (78)	8
56	Mercury MT 104	Go On With The Wedding/Too Young To Go Steady (78)	8
56	Mercury MT 112	Allegheny Moon/My First Formal Gown (78)	8
56	Mercury MT 116	Born To Be With You/Come Rain Or Come Shine (78)	12
57	Mercury MT 134	Mama From The Train/Married I Can Always Get (78)	8
57	Mercury MT 142	The Wall/A Poor Man's Roses (78)	8
57	Mercury MT 160	Old Cape Cod/Wondering (78)	8
58	Mercury MT 184	I'll Remember Today/My, How The Time Goes (78)	8
58	Mercury MT 200	Bring Us Together/Belonging To Someone (78)	8
58	Mercury MT 206	These Worldly Wonders/Another Time, Another Place (78)	8
58	Mercury MT 223	Left Right Out Of Your Heart/Longing To Hold You Again (78)	10
58	Mercury AMT 1000	Fibbin'/You Will Find Your Love (In Paris) (78)	12
59	Mercury AMT 1022	Trust In Me/Under The Sun Valley Moon (78)	15
59	Mercury AMT 1054	My Mother's Eyes/With My Eyes Wide Open I'm Dreaming (78)	30

SINGLES

58	Mercury 7MT 184	I'll Remember Today/My, How The Time Goes	8
58	Mercury 7MT 200	Bring Us Together/Belonging To Someone	8
58	Mercury 7MT 206	These Worldly Wonders/Another Time, Another Place	8
58	Mercury 7MT 223	Left Right Out Of Your Heart/Longing To Hold You Again	10
58	Mercury AMT 1000	Fibbin'/You Will Find Your Love (In Paris)	6
59	Mercury AMT 1022	Trust In Me/Under The Sun Valley Moon	6
59	Mercury AMT 1038	The Walls Have Ears/My Promise	6
59	Mercury AMT 1054	My Mother's Eyes/With My Eyes Wide Open I'm Dreaming	6
60	Mercury AMT 1089	Promise Me Thomas/Two Thousand, Two Hundred And Twenty-Three Miles	6
60	Mercury AMT 1102	One Of Us (Will Weep Tonight)/What Will My Future Be	6
60	Mercury AMT 1112	I Wish I'd Never Been Born/I Need You	6
63	CBS AAG 136	Just A Simple Melody/Pretty Lonely Boy	6

EPs

56	Mercury MEP 9502	PATTI PAGE (EP)	15
59	Mercury ZEP 10006	PATTI PAGE ONE (EP)	15
59	Mercury ZEP 10017	PATTI PAGE TWO (EP)	15

MINT VALUE £

59	Mercury ZEP 10032	PATTI PAGE THREE (EP)	15
59	Mercury ZEP 10045	PATTI PAGE FOUR (EP)	15
60	Mercury ZEP 10073	PATTI PAGE FIVE (EP)	15
61	Mercury ZEP 10092	THE LADY IS NO TRAMP (EP, also stereo [SEZ 19008])	10/15
61	Mercury ZEP 10114	MY KINDA LOVE (EP, also stereo [SEZ 19020])	12/15

LPs

54	Mercury MG 25101	FOLK SONG FAVOURITES (10" LP)	25
55	Mercury MG 25197	PATTI'S SONGS (10" LP)	25
56	Mercury MPT 7510	CHRISTMAS WITH PATTI PAGE (10" LP)	25
57	Mercury MPT 7531	I'M GETTING SENTIMENTAL OVER YOU (10" LP)	25
57	Mercury MPT 7535	PATTI'S SONGS (10" LP, reissue)	15
57	Emarcy EJL 1252	PATTI PAGE IN THE LAND OF HI-FI (LP)	15
57	Mercury MPL 6506	MANHATTAN TOWER (LP)	15
58	Mercury MPL 6521	YOU GO TO MY HEAD (LP)	15
58	Mercury MPL 6524	PAGE 1 — A COLLECTION OF HER MOST FAMOUS SONGS (LP)	15
59	Mercury MMC 14000	LET'S GET AWAY FROM IT ALL (LP)	15
59	Mercury MMC 14007	I'VE HEARD THAT SONG BEFORE (LP)	15
59	Mercury MMC 14013	I'LL REMEMBER APRIL (LP)	15
59	Mercury MMC 14017	INDISCRETION (LP)	15
59	Mercury CMS 18004	PATTI PAGE IN THE LAND OF HI-FI (LP, stereo reissue)	15
60	Mercury MMC 14036	THREE LITTLE WORDS (LP)	15
61	Mercury MMC 14064	ROMANCE IN RHYTHM (LP)	12

(see also Pete Rugolo)

PAGE & PLANT
| 94 | Fontana PRCDJ 1 | Gallows Pole (CD, in special brown or red sleeve, promo only) | 18/15 |
| 94 | Fontana PPDD 2 | Gallows Pole/Four Sticks/What Is And What Should Never Be (CD, picture disc, digipak) | 10 |

(see also Jimmy Page, Robert Plant)

PAGEBOYS (U.S.)
| 65 | London HLU 9948 | When I Meet A Girl Like You/I Have Love | 6 |

PAGE BOYS (U.K.)
| 83 | Whaam! WHAAM 10 | You're My Kind Of Girl/In Love With You (p/s, 1,000 only) | 10 |

(see also 1,000 Violins)

PAGE FIVE
| 66 | Parlophone R 5426 | Let Sleeping Dogs Lie/I Know All About Her | 20 |

PAGE TEN
| 65 | Decca F 12248 | Boutique/Colour Talk | 8 |

CARLOS PAIAO
| 81 | EMI EMI 5174 | Playback (English)/Playback (Portuguese) | 7 |

PAICE, ASHTON & LORD
| 77 | Polydor/Oyster 2391 269 | MALICE IN WONDERLAND (LP, with inner sleeve) | 12 |

(see also Deep Purple, Jon Lord, Ashton & Lord, Ashton Gardner & Dyke, Elf, Bernie Marsden)

ELAINE PAIGE
| 86 | RCA CHESS 7D | Nobody's Side (Remix)/Embassy Lament/I Know Him So Well/Chess (Theme) (double pack) | 5 |
| 89 | Siren SRNCD 110 | Radio Ga Ga (Radio Edit)/Love Of My Life/Play The Game/Radio Ga Ga (Full-Length Version) (3" CD, gatefold card sleeve) | 7 |

(see also Colours Of Love)

HAL PAIGE & WHALERS
| 60 | Melodisc MEL 1553 | Going Back To My Home Town/After Hours Blues | 35 |

JOEY PAIGE
| 65 | Fontana TF 554 | Cause I'm In Love With You/Yeah Yeah Yeah | 15 |

ROSALIND PAIGE
55	London HL 8120	When The Saints Go Marching In/Nobody's Sweetheart Now	20
55	London HL 8120	When The Saints Go Marching In/Nobody's Sweetheart Now (78)	10
57	MGM MGM 937	Love, Oh Careless Love/That Funny Melody	8
57	MGM MGM 937	Love, Oh Careless Love/That Funny Melody (78)	8

PAINTBOX
| 70 | Young Blood YB 1013 | Get Ready For Love/Can I Get To Know You | 6 |
| 71 | Young Blood YB 1029 | Get Ready For Love/Can I Get To Know You (reissue) | 5 |

(see also Easybeats, Haffy's Whiskey Sour)

PAINTED SHIP
| 67 | Mercury MF 988 | Frustration/I Told Those Little White Lies | 50 |

PAISLEYS
| 83 | Psycho PSYCHO 7 | COSMIC MIND AT PLAY (LP, reissue) | 15 |

PALACE COURT BRIGADE
| 69 | CBS 4643 | Whistlin' In The Sunshine/Girls Grow Up | 4 |

PALADIN
71	Bronze WIP 6108	Anyway/Giving All My Love	5
73	Bronze BRO 3	Sweet Sweet Music/Get One Together	5
71	Bronze ILPS 9150	PALADIN (LP)	20
72	Bronze ILPS 9190	CHARGE (LP, gatefold sleeve)	25

(see also Glass Menagerie, McGuinness Flint)

PALE FOUNTAINS
| 82 | Operation Twilight OPT 09 | Just A Girl/(There's Always) Something On My Mind (p/s) | 12 |
| 85 | Virgin VS 750 | From Across The Kitchen Table/Bicycle Thieves//Thank You/Just A Girl (double pack) | 6 |

(see also Shack)

MINT VALUE £

PALE SAINTS
88	Panic PANIC FIRST	Children Break/SAVLONS: ...And What's More/KERRY FIDDLES: Shiver Me Timbers (33rpm flexidisc, stickered card sleeve, some with postcard)	7
89	4AD BAD 910	BARGING INTO THE PRESENCE OF GOD: Sight Of You/She Rides The Waves/ Mother Might (12" EP)	7
91	4AD PS ONE	Porpoise (12", no p/s)	8
92	4AD PS 2CD	EXTRACTS FROM IN RIBBONS: Throwing Back The Apple/Featherframe/ Babymaker/A Thousand Stars Burst Open (CD, card sleeve)	10
90	4AD CAD 0002	COMFORTS OF MADNESS (LP, with postcards)	10
92	4AD CAD 2004	IN RIBBONS (LP, with free 7" "A Thousand Stars Burst Open"/ "A Revelation" [RIB 1])	10

TOM PALEY
69	Argo ZFB 3	SUE COW (LP)	12

PALEY BROTHERS
78	Sire SRE 4005	Come On Let's Go/Magic Power (p/s)	10

(see also Ramones)

PALI GAP
82	Sinister SYN 001	Under The Sun/The Knives Are Out (p/s, with insert)	35

MORTY PALITZ & ACES
59	London HLJ 8778	The Grocer's Cha Cha Cha/Eso Es El Amor (This Is Love)	7
59	London HLJ 8778	The Grocer's Cha Cha Cha/Eso Es El Amor (This Is Love) (78)	12

PALLAS
78	Sue-i-cide PAL/101	THE PALLAS EP (stamped plain die-cut sleeve)	60
82	Granite Wax GWS 1	Arrive Alive/Stranger (On The Edge Of Time) (two different p/s)	35
83	Cool King CK 010	Paris Is Burning/The Hammer Falls (p/s)	6
83	Cool King 12 CK 010	Paris Is Burning/The Hammer Falls/ Stranger At The Edge Of Time (12", p/s)	10
84	EMI Harvest PLS 1	Eyes In The Night (Arrive Alive)/East West (p/s)	5
84	EMI Harvest PLSP 1	Eyes In The Night (Arrive Alive)/East West (picture disc)	8
84	EMI Harvest 12 PLS 1	Eyes In The Night (Arrive Alive)/East West/Crown Of Thorns (12", p/s)	10
84	EMI Harvest 12 PLSP 1	Eyes In The Night (Arrive Alive)/East West/Crown Of Thorns (12", picture disc, unreleased)	
84	EMI Harvest PLS 2	Shock Treatment/March On Atlantis (poster p/s)	8
84	EMI Harvest 12 PLS 2	Shock Treatment/March On Atlantis/Heart Attack (12", p/s)	8
85	Harvest PLS 3	Strangers/Nightmare/Sanctuary (p/s)	6
85	Harvest 12 PLS 3	THE KNIGHTMOVES EP (Strangers/Nightmare/Sanctuary) (12", p/s)	8
85	Harvest 12 PLSP 3	THE KNIGHTMOVES EP (12", picture disc)	12
85	Harvest 12 PLSD 3	THE KNIGHTMOVES EP (12", with free 7" "Mad Machine"/"Stitch In Time" in sealed plastic sleeve)	20
86	Harvest PLS 4	Throwing Stones At The Wind/Cut And Run (live) (p/s)	5
86	Harvest 12 PLS 4	Throwing Stones At The Wind/Cut And Run (live)/Crown Of Thorns (live) (12", p/s)	8
83	Cool King CKLP 002	ARRIVE ALIVE (LP)	18
84	Harvest SHSP 2400 121	THE SENTINEL (LP, some with poster and sticker)	15/12
86	Harvest SHVL 850	THE WEDGE (LP)	12

EARL PALMER & HIS TEN PIECE ROCKIN' BAND
58	Capitol CL 14859	Drum Village (Parts 1 & 2)	8
61	Liberty LBY 1008	DRUMSVILLE (LP)	18

EDDIE PALMER
57	Decca F 10873	The Sky/The Twilight Theme	6

JACK PALMER
50	London L 605	Sweet Jennie Lee/All My Baby's Got To Wear Is Minks (78)	8

RICK PALMER
59	London HLL 8900	You Threw A Heart/My Greatest Wish (unreleased)	

ROBERT PALMER
75	Island WIP 6250	Which Of Us Is The Fool/Get Outside	5
76	Island WIP 6272	Gimme An Inch Girl/Pressure Drop	5
76	Island WIP 6345	Man Smart, Woman Smarter/From a Whisper To A Scream	5
78	Island WIP 6425	Every Kinda People/Keep In Touch	5
78	Island WIP 6445	Best Of Both Worlds/Where Can It Go	5
79	Island WIP 6481	Bad Case Of Loving You (Doctor Doctor)/Love Can Run Faster (p/s)	5
81	Island WIP 6678	Not A Second Time/Woke Up Laughing (p/s)	5
82	Island PWIP 6754	Some Guys Have All The Luck/Too Good To Be True (picture disc)	5
82	Island 12PWIP 6754	Some Guys Have All The Luck/Style Kills/Si Chatouillieux/ What Do You Care (12", picture disc)	7
82	Island PWIP 6833	Pride/Pride (Instrumental) (picture disc)	5
83	Island ISP 121	You Can Have It (Take My Heart)/The Silver Gun (picture disc)	5
85	Island ISD 256	Riptide/Johnny And Mary//Trick Bag/No Not Much/ Back In My Arms (double pack)	5
86	Island ISP 270	Addicted To Love/More (shaped picture disc)	5
86	Island CID 283	I Didn't Mean To Turn You On/Addicted To Love/Get It Through Your Heart/ You Are in My System (Remix)/Johnny And Mary (CD, g/f card p/s, withdrawn)	20
88	Island CIDX 352	Sweet Lies/Want You More/Riptide (3" CD, with adaptor in 5" case)	7

(see also Alan Bown [Set], Dada, Vinegar Joe, Power Station)

ROY PALMER & STATE STREET RAMBLERS
54	London AL 3518	A CHICAGO SKIFFLE SESSION (10" LP)	30

PALMETTO KINGS
60	Starlite ST45 021	Ten Rum Bottles/Home Cookin' Mama	6

Rare Record Price Guide 2002

PAMA DICE
69	Jackpot JP 715	Bongo Man/Bear De Pussy	8
69	Jackpot JP 716	Sin, Sun And Sex/Reggae Pop-Corn	8
70	Reggae REG 3001	Brixton Fight/OPENING: Tea House	10

(see also Winston Groovy, King Horror, Ray Martell)

PAN
89	Ton Son Ton SON 14	Bana Bana (After Midnight Mix)/Bana Nana (Before Midnight Mix) (p/s)	6
89	Ton Son Ton SONL 14	Bana Bana (After Midnight 12" Club Mix)/Bana Nana (Before Midnight 12" Club Mix)/Bana Nana (Original Version) (12", p/s)	8

PANACHE
83	Mach 1 MAGIC 004	I Wanna Dance/Crazy For Your Love (with Ray Dorset)	7

(see also Ray Dorset)

PANAMA FRANCIS BLUES BAND
64	Stateside SL 10070	TOUGH TALK!! (LP)	15

PANAMA LIMITED (JUG BAND)
69	Harvest HAR 5010	Lady Of Shallot/Future Blues	25
70	Harvest HAR 5022	Round And Round/Rotting Wooden In A White Collar's Grave	25
69	Harvest SHVL 753	PANAMA LIMITED JUG BAND (LP)	85
70	Harvest SHVL 779	INDIAN SUMMER (LP, as Panama Limited)	75

GENE PANCHO
68	Giant GN 21	I Like Sweet Music/Seven Days (with Sandy & Superboys)	7

(see also Gene Rondo)

PANDEMONIUM
67	CBS 202462	Season Of The Witch/Today I'm Happy	35
67	CBS 2664	No Presents For Me/The Sun Shines From His Eyes	70
68	CBS 3451	Chocolate Buster Dam/Fly With Me Forever	35

PANDIT PRANNATH
69	Transatlantic TRA 193	EARTH GROOVE (LP)	20

PANHANDLE
72	Decca SKL 5105	PANHANDLE (LP)	20

(see also Chris Spedding)

JOHNNY PANIC & THE BIBLE OF DREAMS
91	Fontana PAN CD 1	Johnny Panic And The Bible Of Dreams (Mix 1) (Mix 2) (CD)	12

(see also Tears For Fears)

PANIK
77	Rainy City SHOT 1	IT WON'T SELL (EP)	15

BILL PANNELL
50	London L 623	A Heart Of Stone/I Miss My Miss From Mississippi (78)	10

PAN'S PEOPLE
74	Epic EPC 2606	You Can Really Rock'n'Roll Me/The Singer Not The Song	4
75	Epic EPC 3339	He's Got Magic/Sooner Or Later	4
79	GM GMS 9052	Club Lido/Club Lido (Instrumental Mix)	4

GARY PANTER & JAY COTTON
90	Blast First FU 7	ONE HELL SOUNDWICH (LP, picture disc)	20

JAN PANTER
65	Oriole CB 1938	My Two Arms Minus You Equals Tears/Does My Heart Show	15
65	CBS 201810	Let It Be Now/Stand By And Cry	12
66	Pye 7N 17097	Scratch My Back/Put Yourself In My Place	18
69	President PT 241	Si Si Senor/Stella In Lights	6

PANTHER BURNS
81	Rough Trade RT 077	Train Kept A Rollin'/Red Headed Woman (p/s)	15

(see also Tav Falco's Panther Burns, Alex Chilton)

ROY PANTON
63	Blue Beat BB 182	Mighty Ruler/Run Old Man	12
64	Blue Beat BB 219	Good From The Bad/Hell Gate	15
64	Rio R 19	Cherita/Seek And You Shall Find	12
64	Rio R 33	You Don't Know Me/KING EDWARD'S ALLSTARS: Doctor No	15
64	Island WI 137	Goodbye Peggy Darling (actually "Goodbye Peggy" by Stranger Cole)/BABA BROOKS: Portrait Of My Love	12
70	Harry J HJ 6624	The Same Old Life/JAYBOYS: Life Version	6

(see also Roy & Annette, Roy & Millie, Roy & Paulette, Roy & Yvonne, Roy & Duke Allstars, Roy & Patsy, Derrick Harriot, Leon & Owen, Charmers)

JOHN PANTRY
72	Philips 6006 250	Net Of Concern/Words	5
72	Philips 6308 129	JOHN PANTRY (LP)	15
73	Philips 6308 138	LONG WHITE TRAIL (LP)	15

(see also Factory, Peter & Wolves, Norman Conquest, Sounds Around, Bunch)

PAOLA
69	Decca F 22916	Bonjour Bonjour/Valse D'Amour	7

NIKKI PAPAS
59	Parlophone R 4590	49 State Rock/Try Again	15
60	Parlophone R 4652	By The River/Don't Leave Me Alone	12

PAPER BLITZ TISSUE
67	RCA Victor RCA 1652	Boy Meets Girl/Grey Man	100

(see also Cupid's Inspiration

MINT VALUE £

PAPER BUBBLE
70	Deram DML/SML 1059	SCENERY (LP)	25

PAPER DOLLS
68	Pye 7N 17456	Something Here In My Heart/All The Time In The World	6
68	Pye 7N 17547	My Life Is In Your Hands/There's Nobody I'd Sooner Love	6
68	Pye 7N 17655	Someday/Any Old Time You're Lonely And Sad	5
70	RCA RCA 1919	My Boyfriend's Back/Mister Good Time Friday	5
70	RCA RCA 2007	Remember December/Same Old Story	5
68	Pye N(S)PL 18226	PAPER DOLLS HOUSE (LP)	20

PAPER DRAGON
69	Bell BLL 1054	April Fool/Get Something Going	4

PAPERHOUSE
91	Mystic Stones RUNE LP 11	SPONGY COMESTIBLES (LP)	10

PAPER TOYS
90	Armada ARMAP 003	Cold Surrender (Winston Club Mix)/Cold Surrender (D-Day 7" Radio Mix)/Cold Surrender (Outland Mix) (numbered p/s, 500 only)	10

(see also Gary Numan)

PARADE
67	A&M AMS 701	Sunshine Girl/This Old Melody	8
67	A&M AMS 720	Radio Song/I Can See Love	5

VANESSA PARADIS
87	Polydor POSPG 902	Joe Le Taxi/Varvara Pavlovna (poster p/s)	25
87	Polydor POSPX 902	Joe Le Taxi (Version Longue)/Joe Le Taxi/Varvara Pavlovna (12", p/s)	7
88	Polydor 080 466-2	Joe Le Taxi/Manolo Manolete/Joe Le Taxi (Version Espagnole)/Joe Le Taxi (Version Longue)/Joe Le Taxi (Video) (CD Video)	35
88	Polydor PO 16	Marilyn And John (English Version)/(French Version) (p/s)	7
88	Polydor PZ 16	Marilyn And John (English Version)/(French Version)/Soldat (12", p/s)	12
88	Polydor 080 468-2	Marilyn And John (Version Français) (4.40)/Soldat/Marilyn And John (Version Anglais)/Marilyn And John (Version Français) (5.44)/Marilyn And John (Version Français) (Video) (CD Video)	30
88	Polydor 081 312-2	Coup Coup (Remix)/Maxou/Marilyn And John/Coup Coup (Remix) (Video) (CD Video)	40
88	Polydor PO 38	Maxou (Remix)/Le Bon Dieu Est Un Marin (p/s)	6
88	Polydor PZ 38	Maxou (Remix)/Soldat/Le Bon Dieu Est Un Marin (12", p/s)	12
89	Polydor 871 225-2	Maxou (Remix)/Soldat/Le Bon Dieu Est Un Marin (CD)	15
92	Polydor PZCDD 235	Be My Baby/The Future Song/Joe Le Taxi (CD, with video picture insert)	6
88	Polydor POLD 5232	M + J (LP)	12
92	Polydor 513 954-1	VANESSA PARADIS (LP)	12

JOE PARADISE
59	Top Rank JAR 195	From The French/CLAUDE DAUPHON: From The French	5

PARADONS
60	Top Rank JAR 514	Diamonds And Pearls/I Want Love	120

PARADOX
68	Polydor 56275	The Wednesday Theme/Ring The Changes	70

(see also David Walker)

PARAFFIN JACK FLASH LTD
68	Pye NSPL 18252	MOVERS AND GROOVERS (LP)	15

PARAGONS
66	Doctor Bird DB 1060	Happy-Go-Lucky Girl/Love Brings Pain	20
67	Island WI 3045	On The Beach/CAROL & TOMMY McCOOK: Sweet And Gentle (B-side actually by Tommy McCook & Supersonics)	20
67	Island WI 3067	Talking Love/If I Were You	20
67	Treasure Isle TI 7009	Only A Smile/The Tide Is High	15
67	Treasure Isle TI 7011	Mercy, Mercy, Mercy/Riding On A High And Windy Day	15
67	Treasure Isle TI 7013	The Same Song/TOMMY McCOOK & SUPERSONICS: Soul Serenade	15
67	Treasure Isle TI 7025	Wear You To The Ball/You Mean The World To Me	15
68	Treasure Isle TI 7034	Silver Bird/My Best Girl	15
68	Island WI 3138	Memories By The Score/The Number One For Me	15
69	Studio One SO 2081	Have You Ever Been In Love/Change Your Style	15
69	Duke DU 7	Left With A Broken Heart/I've Got To Get Away	12
67	Doctor Bird DLM 5010	ON THE BEACH (LP)	100

(see also Rosalyn Sweat & Paragons, John Holt, Lester Sterling)

PARALEX
80	Reddingtons R.R. DAN 4	Travelling Man, Black Widow, White Lightning (12", green vinyl)	40

PARAMETER
70	Deroy	GALACTIC RAMBLE (LP)	300

NORRIE PARAMOR & HIS ORCHESTRA
53	Columbia SCM 5023	Cotton Reel/Pink Plank Plonk	6
53	Columbia SCM 5034	Fandango/Penny Whistle	6
53	Columbia SCM 5051	April In Portugal/The Song From Moulin Rouge (Where Is Your Heart)	6
53	Columbia SCM 5068	Man Between/Callaghan's Monkey	6
54	Columbia SCM 5126	Johnny Guitar/Paramambo	6
54	Columbia SCM 5136	High And Mighty/Rip Van Twinkle	6
56	Columbia SCM 5251	Theme From The Threepenny Opera/Poor John	6
60	Columbia DB 4419	Summer Place (Theme)/Half Pint	6
62	Columbia DB 4789	Z Cars (Theme)/Ballad Of A Soldier (Theme)	5
65	Columbia DB 7446	Dance Of The Warriors/Dragon Dance	6

PARAMOUNTS

70	Polydor 56375	Randall And Hopkirk (Deceased)/A Summer Palace........................ 50
55	Columbia 33S 1076	JUST WE TWO (10" LP) 15
66	Columbia SX 6012	SHADS IN LATIN (LP, also stereo Studio Two TWO 107) 12/15
67	Studio Two TWO 172	PLAYS THE HITS OF CLIFF RICHARD (LP).............................. 100

(see also Big Ben Banjo Band, Harry Gold)

PARAMOUNT ALL-STARS
50	Tempo R 20	Hometown Skiffle (Parts 1 & 2) (78)................................. 25

(see also Blind Blake, Will Ezell, Georgia Tom, Alex Hill, Papa Charlie Jackson, Blind Lemon Jefferson, Charlie Spand)

PARAMOUNTS
63	Parlophone R 5093	Poison Ivy/I Feel Good All Over...................................... 10
64	Parlophone R 5107	Little Bitty Pretty One/A Certain Girl 15
64	Parlophone R 5155	I'm The One Who Loves You/It Won't Be Long 18
64	Parlophone R 5187	Bad Blood/Do I.. 12
65	Parlophone R 5272	Blue Ribbons/Cuttin' In 15
65	Parlophone R 5351	You Never Had It So Good/Don't Ya Like My Love 15
64	Parlophone GEP 8908	THE PARAMOUNTS (EP) 200

(see also Procol Harum)

PARANOIA
84	Rot ASS 8	Dead Man's Dreams/Man In Black (p/s)................................. 4

PARANOIDS
79	Hurricane FIRE 8	Stupid Guy/Road To Ruin (p/s) 5
80	Hurricane FIRE 14	The Love Job/Theme From Gravity's Rainbow (p/s)...................... 4

PARCEL OF ROGUES
(see under Villagers)

PARCHMENT
72	Pye 7N 45178	Light Up The Fire/Let There Be Light (p/s) 6
72	Pye 7N 45214	Where Can I Find You/Working Man 5
73	Pye 7N 45233	You Were On My Mind/Rock'n'Roll Part Time 5
73	Pye 7N 45261	You Are My Morning/Getting Out Of This Town......................... 5
72	Pye NSPL 18388	LIGHT UP THE FIRE (LP, with poster insert) 15
73	Pye NSPL 18409	HOLLYWOOD SUNSET (LP)... 12
75	Myrrh MYR 1028	SHAMBLEJAM (LP) 20
77	Pilgrim GRAPEVINE 106	REHEARSAL FOR A REUNION (LP)................................... 15

TONY PARENTI
50	Esquire 10-048	The Entertainer's Rag/Cataract Rag (78)............................... 8
52	Vogue V 2115	Hysteric's Rag/Sunflower Slow Drag (78, With Ralph Sutton) 8
57	London EZ V 19022	RAGTIME (EP) 10
57	London LTZU 15072	RAGTIME (LP) 22

PAULA PARFITT
69	Beacon BEA 135	I'm Gonna Give You Back Your Ring/Love Is Wonderful 40
70	Upfront UPF 4	Peace Of Mind/Baby You Give Me A Song To Sing 5

TINY PARHAM
50s	Audubon AAC	TINY PARHAM (10" LP) 25

MINT VALUE £

PARIS
72	Avalanche AV 67312	I've Lost The Way/Long Time	5
84	Bluebird BR 9	I Choose You/Punkin' Funkin' (p/s)	5
84	Bluebird BRT 9	I Choose You/Punkin' Funkin' (12", p/s)	8

BOBBY PARIS
68	Polydor 56747	Per So Nal Ly/Tragedy	50
69	Polydor 56762	Let The Sun Shine In/You	7
77	London HLU 10553	Night Owl/YVONNE BAKER: You Didn't Say A Word	5
79	Capitol CL 16067	I Walked Away/H.B. BARNUM: Heartbreaker	5

PRISCILLA PARIS
74	Rak RAK 184	I Love How You Love Me/Over You	7

(see also Paris Sisters, Priscilla Paris)

PARIS SISTERS
61	Top Rank JAR 588	I Love How You Love Me/I'll Be Crying Tomorrow	80
64	MGM MGM 1240	Dream Lover/Lonely Girl	30

(see also Date With Soul, Priscilla Paris)

JOHN PARISH & POLLY JEAN HARVEY
96	Island IS 648	That Was My Veil/Losing Ground (p/s)	6
96	Island CIDX 8051	DANCE HALL AT LOUSE POINT (CD, 5,000 in digipak with insert)	20

(see also P.J. Harvey)

PARISH HALL
70	Liberty LBS 83374	PARISH HALL (LP)	15

ALAN PARKER
70	Aristocrat AR 1022	GUITAR FANTASY (LP)	15
73	MCA MUPS 471	BAND OF ANGELS (LP)	12

(see also Hungry Wolf, Ugly Custard)

BENNY PARKER & DYNAMICS
64	Decca F 11944	Boys And Girls/You'll Be On Your Way	35

BILLY PARKER
63	Decca F 11668	Thanks A Lot/Out Of Your Heart	6

BOBBY PARKER
61	London HLU 9393	Watch Your Step/Steal Your Heart Away	30
64	Sue WI 340	Watch Your Step/Steal Your Heart Away (reissue)	25
69	Blue Horizon 57-3151	It's Hard But It's Fair/I Couldn't Quit My Baby	30

CHARLIE PARKER
SINGLES
50	Savoy 928	Buzzy/Donna Lee (78)	12
50	Esquire 10-079	Relaxing At Camarillo/Crazeology—3 Ways Of Playing A Chorus (78)	8
51	Esquire 10-108	Quasimodo/Dewey Square (78, with Miles Davis)	10
51	Esquire 10-139	Klactoveedsedstene/Charlie's Wig (78, with Miles Davis)	10
52	Vogue V 2132	How Deep Is The Ocean/Schmourphology (78)	8
55	Columbia LB 10006	K.C. Blues/She Rote (78)	8
56	Columbia LB 10034	Laura/Dancing In The Dark (78)	8
57	Columbia LB 10051	Laird Baird/I Hear Music (78)	8
57	Columbia LB 10074	Just One Of Those Things/My Heart Belongs To Daddy (78)	10
60	HMV POP 747	Kim/Cosmic Eyes (as Charlie Parker Quartet)	5

EPs
55	Vogue EPV 1011	CHARLIE PARKER PLAYS (EP)	25
55	Columbia Clef SEB 10002	THE MAGNIFICENT CHARLIE PARKER NO. 1 (EP)	8
56	Columbia Clef SEB 10026	NOW'S THE TIME (EP)	12
56	Columbia Clef SEB 10032	PLAYS SOUTH OF THE BORDER (EP)	8
56	Columbia Clef SEB 10038	THE MAGNIFICENT CHARLIE PARKER NO. 2 (EP, as Charlie Parker Group)	10
57	Columbia Clef SEB 10053	THE MAGNIFICENT CHARLIE PARKER NO. 3 (EP)	8
50s	Esquire EP 57	CHARLIE PARKER QUINTET (EP)	20
60	Vogue EPV 1264	ALL STAR QUINTET/SEXTET (EP)	20
60	HMV 7EG 8626	CHARLIE PARKER BIG BAND (EP)	8
64	Realm REP 4008	PARKER'S MOOD (EP, as Charlie Parker All Stars)	8

LPs
52	Vogue LDE 004	CHARLIE PARKER VOLUME ONE (10" LP)	60
53	Vogue LDE 016	CHARLIE PARKER VOLUME TWO (10" LP)	60
50s	Vogue LAE 12002	CHARLIE PARKER MEMORIAL ALBUM (LP, gatefold sleeve w/ 2 inserts)	18
55	Melodisc MLP 12-105	BIRD AT ST. NICK'S (LP)	35
55	Columbia Clef 33CX 10004	CHARLIE PARKER BIG BAND (LP)	75
56	Columbia Clef DIZ 9026	BIRD AND DIZ (10" LP, with Dizzy Gillespie)	75
57	Columbia Clef 33CX 10081	APRIL IN PARIS (LP, as Charlie Parker With Strings)	40
57	Columbia Clef 33CX 10090	CHARLIE PARKER PLAYS COLE PORTER (LP)	35
58	Columbia Clef 33CX 10117	CHARLIE PARKER JAZZ PERENNIAL (LP)	20
58	London Jazz LTZ-C 15104	THE IMMORTAL CHARLIE PARKER VOL. 1 (LP)	20
58	London Jazz LTZ-C 15105	THE IMMORTAL CHARLIE PARKER VOL. 2 (LP)	20
58	London Jazz LTZ-C 15106	THE IMMORTAL CHARLIE PARKER VOL. 3 (LP)	20
58	London Jazz LTZ-C 15107	THE IMMORTAL CHARLIE PARKER VOL. 4 (LP)	20
58	Mercury MPL 12-105	BIRD AT NICK'S (LP)	15
60	Collector JGN 1002	CHARLIE PARKER IN SWEDEN (LP)	50
61	HMV CLP 1538	THE ESSENTIAL CHARLIE PARKER (LP)	15
62	Verve VLP 9105	"BIRD" SYMBOLS (LP, with insert for Egmont AJS 3)	15
62	Storyville SLP 27	IN SWEDEN 1950 (LP)	18
62	Esquire 32-157	'BIRD' IS FREE (LP)	22
62	Eros ERL 50054	MEMORIAL VOL. 1 (LP)	10
62	Eros ERL 50057	MEMORIAL VOL. 2 (LP)	10
62	Eros ERL 50060	MEMORIAL VOL. 3 (LP)	10
62	Eros ERL 50065	MEMORIAL VOL. 4 (LP)	10

MINT VALUE £

63	Realm RM 131	MEMORIAL VOL. 5 (LP)	10
63	Columbia 33SX 1555	PORTRAIT OF THE BIRD (LP)	15
64	MGM MGM-C 986	HISTORICAL MASTERPIECES VOL. 1 (LP)	10
64	MGM MGM-C 987	HISTORICAL MASTERPIECES VOL. 2 (LP)	10
64	MGM MGM-C 988	HISTORICAL MASTERPIECES VOL. 3 (LP)	10
65	Realm RM 214	MEMORIAL VOL. 6 (LP)	10
71	Xtra XTRA 1118	CHARLIE PARKER VOL. 2 (LP)	10

(see also Dizzy Gillespie & Charlie Parker, Sir Charles Thompson)

DAVID PARKER
| 71 | Polydor 2460 101 | DAVID PARKER (LP) | 40 |

(see also Andwella's Dream)

DEAN PARKER & REDCAPS
| 62 | Decca F 11555 | Stormy Evening/Blue Eyes And Golden Hair | 40 |

EDDIE PARKER (U.K.)
| 55 | Columbia SCM 5211 | Far Away From Everybody/Bella Notte | 6 |
| 56 | Columbia DB 3804 | Love Me As Though There Were No Tomorrow/Rich In Love | 5 |

EDDIE PARKER (U.S.)
| 79 | Grapevine GRP 119 | Love You Baby (Parts 1 & 2) (some in p/s) | 10/5 |

EULA PARKER
| 58 | Oriole CB 1411 | Silhouettes/Hedgehopper | 18 |
| 58 | Oriole CB 1411 | Silhouettes/Hedgehopper (78) | 12 |

(see also Frank Weir)

FESS PARKER
| 57 | Oriole CB 1378 | Wringle Wrangle/Ballad Of John Colter | 10 |
| 57 | Philips PB 654 | Yaller Yaller Gold/King Of The River (78) | 6 |

JIMMY PARKER
| 62 | Top Rank JAR 608 | We Gonna/No Word From Betty | 12 |

JOHNNY PARKER
55	Pye Nixa NJE 1000	JOHNNY PARKER WASHBOARD BAND (EP)	8
56	Metronome MEP 1092	BARRELHOUSE (EP)	8
57	Storyville SEP 366	JOHNNY PARKER (EP)	8

(LITTLE) JUNIOR PARKER
61	Vogue V 9179	Stand By Me/I'll Forget About You (as Little Junior Parker)	20
62	Vogue V 9193	Mary Jo/Annie Get Your Yo-Yo (as Little Junior Parker)	20
66	Vocalion VP 9256	These Kind Of Blues (Parts 1 & 2)	18
66	Vocalion VP 9275	Goodbye Little Girl/Walking The Floor Over You	15
67	Mercury SMCL 20097	LIKE IT IS (LP)	30
72	Groove Merchant GM 502	BLUE SHADOWS FALLING (LP)	12
73	Groove Merchant GM 2205	GOOD THINGS DON'T HAPPEN EVERY DAY (LP, with Jimmy McGriff)	12
73	Vogue LDM 30163	MEMORIAL (LP)	15
73	People PLEO 4	YOU DON'T HAVE TO BE BLACK TO LOVE THE BLUES (LP)	15

(see also Howlin' Wolf, Bobby Bland)

KEN PARKER
67	Island WI 3082	How Could I/SONNY BURKE: Choo Choo Train	18
67	Studio One SO 2001	See Them A-Come/MR FOUNDATION: Have A Good Time	18
68	Island WI 3096	Down Low/Sad Mood	18
68	Island WI 3105	Lonely Man/ERROL DUNKLEY: I Am Going Home	25
68	Giant GN 34	Change Is Gonna Come/VAL BENNETT: Jumping With Val	12
69	Bamboo BAM 1	My Whole World Is Falling Down/The Chokin' Kind	10
69	Amalgamated AMG 847	It's Alright/COBBS: One One	12
69	Amalgamated AMG 853	Only Yesterday/COBBS: Joe Gibbs Mood	12
70	Duke DU 79	I Can't Hide/TOMMY McCOOK: Kansas City	8
70	Unity UN 553	When You Were Mine/CLAREDONIANS: The Angels (song actually "The Angels Listened In")	6
71	Duke Reid DR 2504	Sugar Pantie (as Ken Parker & Tommy McCook; actually by Andy Capp)/TOMMY McCOOK: All Afire	8
71	Duke Reid DR 2521	Jimmy Brown/Version	5
71	Big BG 332	Ain't Misbehaving/Genuine Love	5
72	Jackpot JP 805	Guilty/AGGROVATORS: Guilty (Version)	5
72	Pama PM 844	Shake It Loose/TOMMY McCOOK: Shake It Loose — Version (actually titled "Help Me Make It Through The Night")	5
72	Treasure Isle TI 7073	Help Me Make It Through The Night/TOMMY McCOOK & ALLSTARS (Version)	5
73	Dragon DRA 1003	Will The Circle Be Unbroken/DYNAMITES: Instrumental	5
73	Dragon DRA 1015	Say Wonderful Things/It's True	5
74	Attack ATT 8063	Kiss An Angel/TOMMY McCOOK: Inez	5
74	Attack ATT 8073	Count Your Blessings/Count Your Blessings (Version)	4
74	Trojan TRLS 80	JIMMY BROWN (LP)	12

(see also Lyrics, Scotty)

RAYMOND PARKER
| 66 | Sue WI 4024 | Ring Around The Roses/She's Coming Home | 18 |

ROBERT PARKER
66	Island WI 286	Barefootin'/Let's Go Baby	10
66	Island WI 3008	Happy Feet/The Scratch	12
74	Island USA 991	Get Ta Steppin'/Get Right On Down	7
66	Island ILP 942	BAREFOOTIN' (LP)	40

(see also Huey 'Piano' Smith & Clowns)

SONNY PARKER
| 56 | Vogue V 2392 | My Soul's On Fire/Disgusted Blues | 300 |
| 56 | Vogue V 2392 | My Soul's On Fire/Disgusted Blues (78) | 50 |

(see also Lionel Hampton)

MINT VALUE £

WILLIE PARKER
67   President PT 171   You Got Your Finger In My Eye/I Love The Life I Live 5

WINFIELD PARKER
72   Mojo 2093 019   Stop Her On Sight/I'm On My Way 6

PARKING LOT
69   Parlophone R 5779   Carpet Man/World Spinning Sadly 30

JIMMY PARKINSON
56	Columbia SCM 5236	The Great Pretender/Hand In Hand	25
56	Columbia SCM 5267	Walk Hand In Hand/Cry Baby	18
56	Columbia DB 3808	Gina/A Lover's Quarrel	12
56	Columbia DB 3833	In The Middle Of The House/You To Me	18
57	Columbia DB 3876	But You/Together (You And I)	8
57	Columbia DB 3912	Round And Round/Whatever Lola Wants (Lola Gets)	10
57	Columbia DB 3912	Round And Round/Whatever Lola Wants (Lola Gets) (78)	10
57	Columbia 33S 1109	SOLO (10" LP)	40

BERNICE PARKS
55   Coral Q 72056   Lovin' Machine/Only Love Me 10

LLOYD PARKS
70	Harry J. HJ 6603	Feel A Little Better/I'll Be Your Man	12
72	Randy's RAN 524	Stars/Stars – Version	10
74	Fab FAB 273	Schooldays/Version	6

(see also L. Sparks)

SONNY PARKS
63   Warner Bros WB 100   New Boy In Town/Us Kids Have Got To Make Up Our Minds 6

VAN DYKE PARKS
| 66 | MGM MGM 1301 | Number Nine/Do What You Wanta . . . . | 8 |
| 69 | Warner Bros W(S) 1727 | SONG CYCLE (LP) . . . . | 12 |

PARLET
79   Casablanca CAL 2052   INVASION OF THE BOOTY SNATCHERS (LP) 15

(see also Parliament)

PARLIAMENT
71	Invictus INV 513	The Silent Boatman/Livin' The Life	15
72	Invictus INV 522	Come In Out Of The Rain/Little Ole Country Boy	12
75	Casablanca CBX 505	Up On The Down Stroke/Presence Of A Brain	5
76	Casablanca CBX 518	Tear The Roof Off The Sucker (Give Up The Funk)/P. Funk	6
77	Casablanca CAN 103	Tear The Roof Off The Sucker (Give Up The Funk)/Dr. Funkenstein/P. Funk	4
78	Casablanca CAN 115	Bop Gun/I've Been Watching You	4
78	Casablanca CANL 115	Bop Gun/I've Been Watching You (12")	8
78	Casablanca CAN 136	Aqua Boogie/Water Sign	4
79	Casablanca CAN 154	Deep/Flashlight	4
79	Casablanca CANL 154	Deep/Flashlight (12")	8
80	Casablanca CANL 188	Theme From Black Hole/Big Bang Theory (12")	8
81	Casablanca CAN 223	Agony Of De Feet/The Freeze	4
81	Casablanca CANL 223	Agony Of De Feet/The Freeze (12")	7
71	Invictus SVT 1004	OSMIUM (LP)	60
74	Casablanca NBLP 7002	UP ON THE DOWN STROKE (LP)	20
75	Casablanca NBLP 7014	CHOCOLATE CITY (LP)	15
76	Casablanca CBC 4009	MOTHERSHIP CONNECTION (LP)	15
74	Casablanca CAL 2003	THE CLONES OF DR. FUNKENSTEIN (LP)	12
74	Casablanca CAL 2011	UP ON THE DOWN STROKE (LP, reissue)	10
75	Casablanca CAL 2012	CHOCOLATE CITY (LP, reissue)	10
77	Casablanca CAL 2013	MOTHERSHIP CONNECTION (LP, reissue)	10
77	Casablanca CALD 5002	PARLIAMENT LIVE — P. FUNK EARTH TOUR (2-LP, with poster & transfer)	15
78	Casablanca CALH 2021	FUNKENTELECHY VS. THE PLACEBO SYNDROME (LP, with poster)	10
79	Casablanca CALN 2044	MOTOR BOOTY AFFAIR (LP)	12
79	Casablanca CALN 2044	MOTOR BOOTY AFFAIR (LP, picture disc)	12

(see also Parliaments, Funkadelic, Parlet, Brides Of Funkenstein, Bootsy's Rubber Band, P-Funk Allstars)

PARLIAMENTS
| 67 | Track 604 013 | I Wanna Testify/I Can Feel The Ice Melting . . . . | 20 |
| 69 | Track 604 032 | I Wanna Testify/I Can Feel The Ice Melting (reissue) . . . . | 12 |

(see also Parliament, Funkadelic)

PARLOPHONE POPS ORCHESTRA
56   Parlophone R 4250   Giddy Up A Ding Dong/(We're Gonna) Rock Around The Clock 10

PARLOUR BAND
72   Deram SDL 10   IS A FRIEND? (LP) 55

JACK PARNELL ORCHESTRA
50	Decca F 9374	Jukebox Jumba/Quickie (78)	8
53	Parlophone MSP 6009	Waltzing The Blues/Catherine Wheel (as Jack Parnell Band)	8
53	Parlophone MSP 6031	Night Train/Hawk Talks (as Jack Parnell & His Music Makers)	8
53	Parlophone MSP 6046	Cotton Tail/April In Paris	7
53	Parlophone MSP 6054	Dragnet/Fuller Bounce (as Jack Parnell & His Music Makers)	7
54	Parlophone MSP 6066	Route 66/The Creep	7
54	Parlophone MSP 6078	Skin Deep/Devil's Eyes (B-side with Dennis Hale)	20
54	Parlophone MSP 6094	Knock Out/Blowin' Wild (B-side with Dennis Hale)	7
54	Parlophone MSP 6102	The Bandit (with Dennis Hale)/Annie's Blues (with Annie Ross)	7
54	Parlophone MSP 6138	Sky Blue Shirt And Rainbow Tie/Trip To Mars	7
55	Parlophone R 3986	Shake Rattle And Roll/Fanfare Boogie (78)	8
58	Parlophone R 4500	Topsy/Cha Cha Rock	5

MINT VALUE £

58	Parlophone R 4500	Topsy/Cha Cha Rock (78).. 10
59	HMV POP 630	Kansas City/The Golden Stalker 7
60	Philips PB 1005	77 Sunset Strip/Teen Ride 6
74	Bradley BRAD 7420	Spy Glass/Razor's Edge 5
76	EMI EMI 2480	Gotham City Municipal Swing Band/Kiss 5
55	Parlophone GEP 8532	JACK PARNELL AND HIS ORCHESTRA (EP) 8
52	Decca LF 1065	THE JACK PARNELL QUARTET (10" LP) 20
58	Parlophone PMD 1053	TRIP TO MARS (10" LP) 60
70s	Sounds Superb SPR 90082	MUSIC OF THE GIANTS (LP) 25

(see also Dennis Hale)

CATHERINE PARR
| 65 | Decca F 12210 | You Belong To Me/He's My Guy .... 8 |

DEAN PARRISH
66	Stateside SS 531	Tell Her/Fall On Me.. 20
66	Stateside SS 550	Turn On Your Lovelight/Determination 50
67	Stateside SS 580	Skate (Parts 1 & 2) 15
75	UK USA 2	I'm On My Way/Watch Out 5

PARRISH & GURVITZ
| 71 | Regal Zono. SRZA 8506 | PARRISH & GURVITZ (LP) .... 18 |

(see also Baker Gurvitz Army, Three Man Army, Adrian Gurvitz, Frampton's Camel)

SAM PARRY
| 73 | Argo ZDA 155 | IF SADNESS COULD SING (LP)................................. 60 |

ALAN PARSONS PROJECT
76	Charisma CB 293	(The System Of) Doctor Tarr And Professor Fether/
		A Dream Within A Dream....................................... 4
76	Charisma CB 298	The One In Paradise/The Cask Of Amontillado................ 4
84	Arista ARISD 553	Don't Answer Me/You Don't Believe (shaped picture disc) 5

BILL PARSONS & HIS ORCHESTRA
| 59 | London HL 8798 | The All American Boy/Rubber Dolly .... 12 |
| 59 | London HL 8798 | The All American Boy/Rubber Dolly (78)....................... 40 |

(see also Bobby Bare)

GENE PARSONS
| 74 | Warner Bros K 46257 | KINDLING (LP) .... 12 |

(see also Byrds, Flying Burrito Brothers)

GRAM PARSONS
73	Reprise K 14245	The New Soft Shoe/She... 5
73	Reprise K 44228	GP (LP, gatefold sleeve).. 22
74	Reprise K 54018	GRIEVOUS ANGEL (LP, with Emmylou Harris) 22
76	A&M AMLH 65478	SLEEPLESS NIGHTS (LP, with Flying Burrito Brothers & Emmylou Harris) 18

(see also Byrds, Flying Burrito Brothers, Emmylou Harris)

PARTICULAR PEOPLE
| 68 | Big T BIG 105 | Boys Cry/What's The Matter With Juliet .... 5 |

PARTISANS
| 63 | E.R.S. EP 63:33 | THE PARTISANS (EP, private pressing)......................... 75 |

PARTISANS
82	No Future OI 2	Police Story/Killing Machine (p/s, with lyric insert) 12
82	No Future OI 12	17 Years Of Hell/The Power And The Greed/Bastards In Blue (p/s) 12
83	Cloak & Dagger PART 1	Blind Ambition/Come Clean (p/s) 12
83	No Future PUNK 4	PARTISANS (LP).. 18
84	Cloak & Dagger PARTLP 1	THE TIME WAS RIGHT (LP) 18

PARTISANS
| 88 | Hotwire HWS 863 | Open Your Eyes/Partisan (p/s).................................. 8 |

(see also Blades)

MR. PARTRIDGE
| 80 | Virgin V 2145 | TAKEAWAY — THE LURE OF THE SALVAGE (LP)................ 10 |

(see also XTC, Three Wise Men, Dukes Of Stratosphere, Johnny Japes & His Jesticles, Colonel)

DON PARTRIDGE
68	Columbia DB 8330	Rosie/Going Back To London 5
68	Columbia DB 8416	Blue Eyes/I've Got Something For You 5
68	Columbia DB 8484	Top Man/We Have Ways Of Making You Laugh 5
69	Columbia DB 8538	Breakfast On Pluto/Stealin' 5
69	Columbia DB 8583	Colour My World/Homeless Bones 5
69	Columbia DB 8617	Going To Germany/Ask Me Why 5
60s	CFP CFP 001/002	SINGING SOHO STYLE (EP) 15
68	Columbia S(C)X 6280	DON PARTRIDGE (LP) 15

(see also Accolades)

PARTRIDGE FAMILY
71	Bell BELL 1150	Doesn't Somebody Want To Be Wanted/You Are Always On My Mind 5
72	Bell MABEL 1	Breaking Up Is Hard To Do/I Think I Love You/I'll Meet You Halfway
		(p/s, maxi-single) 5

(see also David Cassidy)

PARTY BOYS
87	Epic 651230 7	He's Gonna Step On You Again/She's A Mystery (p/s) 4
87	Epic 651230 0	He's Gonna Step On You Again/She's A Mystery (shaped picture disc) 12
87	Epic 651230 6	He's Gonna Step On You Again (Stomp Mix)/She's A Mystery (12", p/s) 8

(see also Status Quo)

FRANCOISE PASCAL
| 68 | SNB 55-3634 | When It Comes To Love/Got It Badly........................... 4 |

MINT VALUE £

JEAN CLAUDE PASCAL
61　HMV POP 861　Nous Les Amoureux/Les Oubliettes 7

PASCAL MURRAY
69　MCPS ATV 1　T.V. THEMES (EP, Pascal Fruits promo presented by Pete Murray) 10

PASCALIS, MARIANNA, ROBERT & BESSY
77　Power Exchange PX 254　A Music Lesson/Mathema Solfege 8

PASHA
69　Liberty LBF 15199　Someone Shot The Lollipop Man/Pussy Willow Dragon 100
(see also Searchers)

PASSAGE
78　Object Music OM 02　NEW LOVE SONGS (EP) 5
79　Object Music OM 08　ABOUT TIME (EP). 4
82　Lyntone LYN 1183/84　Born Every Minute/BLANCMANGE: Living On The Ceiling/Sad Day (excerpt)
　(black 33rpm flexidisc free with *Melody Maker* magazine) 10/5
80　Object Music OBJ 11　PINDROP (LP) 10
(see also Contact)

PASSENGERS
95　Island IS 625　Miss Sarajevo/One (live) (7", with poster in 12" card in PVC p/s) 6
95　Island CID 625　Miss Sarajevo/One (live)/Bottoms (Zoo Station Remix)/
　Via Davidoff (CD, with shrinkwrapped poster, withdrawn) 30
96　Island OST 3　Your Blue Room (CD, 1-track promo, card sleeve, export issue) 45
95　Island OST 2　ORIGINAL SOUNDCHAT 1 (2-CD, music & interview disc,
　fold-out digipaks, with cue sheet, promo only) 125

(see also U2, Brian Eno)

PASSIONS (U.S.)
58　Capitol CL 14874　My Aching Heart/Jackie Brown 35

PASSIONS (U.S.)
59　Top Rank JAR 224　Just To Be With You/Oh Melancholy Me. 45
60　Top Rank JAR 313　I Only Want You/This Is My Love 50

PAST AND PRESENT
79　Rook CUS 423　FIRST TIME OUT (LP, private pressing) 25

PAST SEVEN DAYS
86　4AD AD 102　Raindance/So Many Others/Nothing (p/s) 10

PASTELS
82　Whaam! WHAAM 005　Songs For Children: Heavens Above!/Tea Time Tales (p/s) 25
83　Rough Trade RT 137　I Wonder Why/Supposed To Understand (p/s) 20
83　Creation Artefact/Lyntone　I Wonder Why! (live)/LAUGHING APPLE: Wouldn't You? (33rpm flexidisc,
　LYN 12903　initially free with Legend 7" "'73 In '83" [CRE 001]) 5
84　Creation CRE 005　Something Going On/Stay With Me Till Morning (foldaround p/s in poly bag). . . . 20
84　Creation CRE 011T　A Million Tears/Baby Honey/Surprise Me (12", p/s). 10
85　Villa 21 VILLA 3　Heavens Above!/Tea Time Tales/I Wonder Why (live)/
　Tea Time Tales (live) (p/s). 30
85　Creation CRE 023T　I'm Alright With You/Couldn't Care Less/What It's Worth (12", p/s) 8
86　Glass GLASS 048　Truck Train Tractor/Breaking Lines (p/s) 5
86　Glass GLASS 12 048　Truck Train Tractor/Truck Train Tractor (2)/Breaking Lines (12", green p/s) . . . 7
87　Glass GLASS 053　Comin' Through/Sit On It Mother (p/s, with print) 5
87　Glass PASTEL 001　Truck Train Tractor/Truck Train Tractor (2)/Breaking Lines//Crawl Babies/
　Empty House/The Day I Got Certified (12", double pack). 10
90　Overground OVER 06　Heavens Above!/Tea Time Tales/Something Going On (demo)/
　Until Morning Comes (demo) (p/s; 2,604 blue vinyl, 200 clear vinyl,
　157 green vinyl) 5/6/8
(see also Vaselines, Buba & Shop Assistants)

PASTEL SIX
63　London HLU 9651　The Cinnamon Cinder/Bandido 10

PASTORAL SYMPHONY
68　President PT 202　Love Machine/Spread A Little Love Around 7

PAT
71　Gas GAS 158　Teach Me (actually "Words Of Temptation" by Earl Lawrence)/
　RHYTHM RULERS: Sea Breeze (actually by Im & David) 6

PAT & MARIE
66　Ska Beat JB 234　I Try Not To Tell You/PAT RHODEN: Don't Blame It On Me. 10
66　Ska Beat JB 235　You're Really Leaving/PAT RHODEN: Broken Heart 10
(see also Pat Rhoden)

PAT & ROXIE
65　Caribou CRC 2　Sing To Me/Things I Used To Do 7

PATCHES
72　Warner Bros K 16201　Living In America. 8

JOHNNY PATE ORCHESTRA
58　Parlophone R 4404　Swinging Shepherd Blues/The Elder (as Johnny Pate Quartet). 5
58　Parlophone R 4437　Musketa/Pretty One (as Johnny Pate Quintet) 5
59　Parlophone PMD 1057　JAZZ GOES IVY LEAGUE (10" LP) 12
59　Parlophone PMD 1072　SWINGIN' FLUTE (10" LP) 12
60s　MGM　OUTRAGEOUS (LP) 25
73　Probe SPB 1077　SHAFT IN AFRICA (LP, soundtrack, with Four Tops) 25
74　ABC ABCL 5035　SHAFT IN AFRICA (LP, soundtrack, reissue) 20

PATHETIX
78　No Records NO 001　Aleister Crowley/Don't Touch My Machine/Snuffed It (p/s, with insert) 20
79　TJM TJM 12　THE PATHETIX EP (no p/s) 25

PATHFINDERS
64	Decca F 12038	I Love You Caroline/Something I Can Always Do	12

PATHFINDERS
65	Parlophone R 5372	Don't You Believe It/Castle Of Love	12

(see also [White] Trash, Poets)

PATHFINDERS
64	Hayton SP 138/139	What Do You Do/What'd I Say (private pressing)	20

PATHWAY TO YOUR MIND
68	Major Minor SMLP 19	PREPARING THE MIND AND BODY FOR MEDITATION (LP, spoken word)	40

PATIENCE & PRUDENCE
56	London HLU 8321	Tonight You Belong To Me/A Smile And A Ribbon	25
57	London HLU 8369	Gonna Get Along Without Ya Now/The Money Tree	20
57	London HL 7017	Gonna Get Along Without Ya Now/The Money Tree (export issue)	20
57	London HLU 8425	Dreamer's Bay/We Can't Sing Rhythm And Blues	18
57	London HLU 8425	Dreamer's Bay/We Can't Sing Rhythm And Blues (78)	15
57	London HLU 8493	You Tattletale/Very Nice Is Bali Bali	15
57	London HLU 8493	You Tattletale/Very Nice Is Bali Bali (78)	15
58	London HLU 8773	Tom Thumb's Tune/Golly Oh Gee	15
58	London HLU 8773	Tom Thumb's Tune/Golly Oh Gee (78)	25
57	London REU 1087	A SMILE AND A SONG (EP)	60

LEON PATILLO
70s	Maranatha MM 0049	DANCE CHILDREN (LP)	15
70s	Myrrh MYR 1136	LIVE EXPERIENCE (LP)	15

BOBBY PATRICK BIG SIX
64	Decca F 11898	Shake It Easy Baby/Wildwood Days	20
64	Decca F 12030	Monkey Time/Sweet Talk Me Baby	20
64	Decca DFE 8570	TEENBEAT 3 (FROM STAR CLUB, HAMBURG) (EP)	100

(see also Beat Brothers, Tony Sheridan & Beat Brothers)

DAN PATRICK
67	Stateside SS 2004	Tiger Lee/Call Of The Wild	8

KENTRICK PATRICK
63	Island WI 066	Man To Man/ROLAND ALFONSO: Blockade (B-side actually "Hit And Run")	20
63	Island WI 079	Don't Stay Out Late/Forever And Ever	20
63	Island WI 104	The End Of The World/Little Princess	18
63	Island WI 119	Golden Love/Beyond	20
64	Island WI 132	Take Me To The Party/I'm Sorry	25
64	Island WI 140	I Am Wasting Time/RANDY'S GROUP: Royal Charley	75

(see also Lord Creator)

PATRICK & LLOYD
70	Big Shot BI 550	Return Of The Pollock/PROPHETS: Concorde	8

(see also Lloyd & Prophets)

PATRIOTS
66	Fontana TF 650	Prophet/I'll Be There	8

PATRON OF THE ARTS
66	Page One POF 012	The True Patron Of The Arts/Eleanor Rigby (B-side actually by Queen City Show Band)	20

PATSY
68	Doctor Bird DB 1122	Little Flea/The Retreat Song	10

(see also Patsy Todd, Derrick & Patsy, Stranger & Patsy, Emotions)

PATSY & PEGGY
70	Hot Rod HR 107	Dog Your Woman/HOT ROD ALLSTARS: Strictly Invitation	6

BRIAN PATTEN
70	Caedmon TC 1300	BRIAN PATTEN (LP)	12
71	Tangent TGS 116	VANISHING TRICK (LP)	25
77	Argo ZSW 607	SLY CORMORANT (LP)	12

(see also Liverpool Scene, Roger McGough & Brian Patten)

PATTERN PEOPLE
68	MGM MGM 1429	Love Is A Lover/Loving To Be Loved	6

BOBBY PATTERSON (& MUSTANGS)
68	Pama PM 735	Broadway Ain't Funky No More/I Met My Match (with Mustangs)	12
68	Pama PM 743	The Good Ol' Days/Don't Be So Mean	6
68	Pama PM 754	Busy Busy Bee/Sweet Taste Of Love (with Mustangs)	6
69	Pama PM 763	T.C.B. Or T.Y.A./What A Wonderful Night For Love (with Mustangs)	8
69	Pama PM 773	My Thing Is Your Thing/Keep It In The Family	6
72	Action ACT 4604	I'm In Love With You/Married Lady	10
72	Mojo 2092 037	How Do You Spell Love/She Don't Have To See You	8

DON PATTERSON
64	Transatlantic PR 733	THE EXCITING NEW ORGAN SOUND OF (LP)	12
67	Transatlantic PR 7430	SATISFACTION! (LP)	12

MANLEY PATTERSON
72	Pama Supreme PS 337	I Stayed Away Too Long/Country Boy	5

OTTILIE PATTERSON
55	Decca F 10472	I Hate A Man Like You/Reckless Blues (with Chris Barber's Jazz Band)	8
55	Decca F 10472	I Hate A Man Like You/Reckless Blues (78, with Chris Barber's Jazz Band)	8
55	Decca F 10621	Weeping Willow Blues/Nobody Knows You When You're Down And Out	8
55	Decca F 10621	Weeping Willow Blues/Nobody Knows You When You're Down And Out (78)	8
57	Pye 7N 15109	Kay-Cee Rider/I Love You Baby	6

Ottilie PATTERSON

57	Pye 7N 15109	Kay-Cee Rider/I Love You Baby (78)	8
58	Pye Jazz 7NJ 2015	Jailhouse Blues/Beale Street Blues	8
58	Pye Jazz NJ 2015	Jailhouse Blues/Beale Street Blues (78)	8
58	Pye Jazz 7NJ 2025	Trombone Cholly/Lawdy, Lawdy Blues	5
61	Columbia DB 4760	Blueberry Hill/I'm Crazy 'Bout My Baby	25
62	Columbia DB 4834	I Hate Myself/Come On Baby	15
63	Columbia DB 7140	Jealous Heart/Won't Be Long	5
63	Columbia DB 7208	Baby Please Don't Go/I Feel So Good (with Sonny Boy Williamson)	25
65	Columbia DB 7332	Tell Me Where Is Fancy/Oh Me What Eyes	8
69	Marmalade 598 016	Spring Song/Sound Of The Door As It Closes	6
69	Marmalade 598 020	Bitterness Of Death/Spring Song	5
55	Jazz Today JTE 102	THAT PATTERSON GIRL (EP)	15
56	Decca DFE 6303	BLUES (EP)	18
56	Pye Jazz Today NJE 1012	THAT PATTERSON GIRL (EP, reissue)	30
56	Pye Jazz Today NJE 1023	THAT PATTERSON GIRL VOL. 2 (EP)	30
60s	Columbia SEG 7915	OTTILIE (EP)	15
60s	Columbia SEG 7998	SWINGS THE IRISH (EP)	20
59	Pye NPL 18028	OTTILIE'S IRISH NIGHT (LP)	18
69	Marmalade 608 011	3000 YEARS WITH OTTILIE (LP)	15
69	Polydor 2384 031	SPRING SONG (LP)	50

(see also Chris Barber)

PATTERSONS
70s	CBS 63522	AGAIN (LP)	12
70s	CBS 63335	TRAVELLING PEOPLE (LP)	12

ROBERT PATTERSON SINGERS
60s	United Artists UAS 2903	THE SOUL OF GOSPEL (LP)	15
65	Fontana 688 516 ZL	I'M SAVED (LP)	12

PATTERSON'S PEOPLE
66	Mercury MF 913	Shake Hands With The Devil/Deadly Nightshade	12

PATTI & PATETTES
75	Dart ART 2053	Bill/It's My Party	5
76	United Artists UP 36077	Summer Heartbreak/Too Much	5

HUBERT PATTISON
66	Pye 7N 17207	Bare Back Rider/The Baby 1 & 2 Problem	4
67	Fontana TF 859	My Home's In My Pocket/Saturday Morning Bride	4

LITTLE JOHN PATTISON
64	Giv-A-Disc LYN 510	Needles And Pins/All My Loving (flexidisc free with *Giv-A-Disc* booklet)	15/10

(MIKE) PATTO
66	Columbia DB 8091	Can't Stop Talking About My Baby/Love (as Mike Patto)	50
74	Goodear EAR 106	Sitting In The Park/Get Up And Dig It (as Mike Patto)	5
70	Vertigo 6360 016	PATTO (LP, gatefold sleeve, spiral label)	40
71	Vertigo 6360 032	HOLD YOUR FIRE (LP, spiral label, foldout sleeve)	100
72	Island ILPS 9210	ROLL 'EM SMOKE 'EM PUT ANOTHER LINE OUT (LP)	25

(see also Bo Street Runners, Breakaways, Boxer, News, Chicago Line, Timebox, Felder's Orioles, Steve York, Centipede, Grimms, V.I.P.s)

ALEXANDER PATTON
66	Capitol CL 15461	A Lil Lovin' Sometimes/No More Dreams	90

CHARLIE PATTON
50s	Heritage REU 4	CHARLIE PATTON (EP)	40

JOHN PATTON
64	Blue Note 45-1889	I'll Never Be Free/Along Came John	8

PATTY & EMBLEMS
64	Stateside SS 322	Mixed Up Shook Up Girl/Ordinary Guy	30

PATTY FLABBIE'S COUGHED ENGINE
69	Stateside SS 2136	Billy's Got A Goat/Tin Can Eater	4

PAUL
65	Polydor BM 56045	Will You Follow Me/Head Death	50

(see also Jimmy Page)

ANDY PAUL
84	Proto ENA 117	Anna Mari-Elena (Greek)/Anna Mari-Elena (English)/Bistepsememe (p/s, all copies mispressed with Greek version of A-side included twice)	12

BILLY PAUL
73	Epic EPC 1055	Me And Mrs. Jones/Your Song	4
73	Epic EPC 65351	360 DEGREES OF BILLY PAUL (LP)	10
73	Epic EPC 65456	EBONY WOMAN (LP)	10
74	Phil. Intl. PIR 65861	WAR OF THE GODS (LP, gatefold sleeve)	10

BUNNY PAUL
54	London HL 8008	Magic Guitar/Never Let me Go (78)	10
54	Columbia SCM 5102	New Love/You'll Never Leave My Side	10
54	Columbia SCM 5112	Such A Night/I'm Gonna Have Some Fun	12
54	Columbia DB 3469	Such A Night/I'm Gonna Have Some Fun (78)	10
54	Columbia SCM 5131	Lovey Dovey/Answer The Call	18
54	Columbia DB 3510	Lovey Dovey/Answer The Call (78)	10
54	Columbia SCM 5151	You Came A Long Way From St. Louis/You Are Always In My Heart	10
55	Capitol CL 14279	Please Have Mercy (On A Fool)/These Are The Things We'll Share	10
55	Capitol CL 14304	Leave My Heart Alone/Two Castanets	8
55	Capitol CL 14368	Song Of The Dreamer/For The Very First Time	8

CLARENCE PAUL
75	London HLU 10492	I'm In Love Again/Blue Tuesday	4

DARLENE PAUL
64	Capitol CL 15344	Act Like Nothing Happened/Little Bit Of Heaven	12

EUGENE PAUL
70	Pama Supreme PS 303	Don't Let The Tears Fall/Another Saturday Night	5
70	Pama Supreme PS 305	I Found A Man In My Bed/So Many Things	5
71	Pama Supreme PS 317	Farewell My Darling/Whole Lot Of Woman	5
71	Pama Supreme PS 329	Somebody's Changing My Sweet Baby's Mind/Hard Minded Neighbour	5
72	Pama PM 838	Beautiful Sunday/Take Care Son	5
72	Pama Supreme PS 357	I'll Take You There/Beautiful Baby	5
73	Pama Supreme PS 382	Power To All Our Friends/RANNY WILLIAMS ALLSTARS: Wicked And Dreadful	5

EUGENE PAUL & PILOTS
70	Torpedo TOR 17	Sugar Dumpling/I May Dwell	5

JASON PAUL
69	Pye 7N 17710	Shine A Little Light Into My Room/Paradise Pudding	4
	(see also Svensk)		

JOHN E. PAUL
67	Decca F 12685	Prince Of Players/I Wanna Know	25

JOYCE PAUL
54	London L 1232	Caribbean/I Forgot More Than You'll Never Know (78)	8

LES PAUL (& MARY FORD)
78s
51	Brunswick 04798	Guitar Boogie/Steel Guitar Rag (as Les Paul & His Trio) (78)	8
54	Brunswick 05311	Guitar Boogie/Steel Guitar Rag (as Les Paul & His Trio) (78, reissue)	8
55	Capitol CL 14212	Mister Sandman/That's What I Like (78)	8
56	Capitol CL 14577	Send Me Some Money/Say The Words I Love To Hear (78)	8
56	Capitol CL 14665	Runnin' Wild/Blow The Smoke Away (78)	8
57	Capitol CL 14710	Cinco Robles (Five Oaks)/Ro-Ro-Robinson (78)	8
57	Capitol CL 14809	(I'm Keeping My Heart Away From) Fire/A Pair Of Fools (78)	8
58	Capitol CL 14839	Bewitched/The Night Of The Fourth (as Les Paul solo) (78)	8
58	Philips PB 873	Put A Ring On My Finger/Fantasy (78)	12
58	Philips PB 882	Jealous Heart/Big Eyed Girl (78)	12

SINGLES
54	Capitol CL 14185	Mandolino/Whither Thou Goest	15
55	Capitol CL 14212	Mister Sandman/That's What I Like	18
55	Capitol CL 14233	Someday Sweetheart/Song In Blue	15
55	Capitol CL 14300	No Letter Today/Genuine Love	15
55	Capitol CL 14342	Goodbye My Love/Hummingbird	15
56	Capitol CL 14502	Alabamy Bound/Texas Lady	10
56	Capitol CL 14521	Magic Melody/Amukiriki (The Lord Willing)	10
56	Capitol CL 14534	Theme From "The Threepenny Opera" (Moritat)/Nuevo Laredo	10
56	Capitol CL 14577	Send Me Some Money/Say The Words I Love To Hear	8
56	Capitol CL 14593	San Antonio Rose/Cimarron (Roll On)	8
56	Capitol CL 14665	Runnin' Wild/Blow The Smoke Away	8
57	Capitol CL 14710	Cinco Robles (Five Oaks)/Ro-Ro-Robinson	7
57	Capitol CL 14738	Hummin' And Waltzin'/Tuxedos And Flowers	6
57	Capitol CL 14776	Strollin' Blues/I Don't Want You No More	8
57	Capitol CL 14809	(I'm Keeping My Heart Away From) Fire/A Pair Of Fools	8
58	Capitol CL 14839	Bewitched/The Night Of The Fourth (as Les Paul solo)	7
58	Capitol CL 14858	More And More Each Day/Small Island	6
58	Philips PB 873	Put A Ring On My Finger/Fantasy	10
58	Philips PB 882	Jealous Heart/Big Eyed Girl	7
59	Philips PB 906	At The Sav-A-Penny Super Store/All I Need Is You	7
61	Philips PB 1155	Jura/It's Been A Long Long Time	5

EPs
55	Capitol EAP1 9121	PRESENTING LES PAUL AND MARY FORD (EP)	10
55	Capitol EAP1 540	SITTING ON TOP OF THE WORLD (EP)	12
60	Capitol EAP1 20048	MR AND MRS MUSIC (EP)	12
61	Capitol EAP1 20145	NOLA (EP)	8
65	Capitol EAP1 20540	JAZZ ME BLUES (EP)	10

LPs
51	Capitol LC 6514	THE NEW SOUND (10" LP)	20
53	Capitol LC 6581	THE NEW SOUND VOL. 2 (10" LP)	20
55	Capitol LC 6701	LES AND MARY (10" LP)	20
55	Capitol LC 6704	LES AND MARY PART 2 (10" LP)	20
56	Capitol LC 6806	BYE BYE BLUES! (10" LP)	18
50s	Capitol T 416	HIT MAKERS (LP)	12
57	Capitol T 802	TIME TO DREAM (LP)	12
50s	Capitol T 1276	LOVER (LP)	12
59	Philips BBL 7306	LOVER'S LUAU (LP)	12
61	Capitol T 1476	HITS OF LES AND MARY (LP)	12
68	Decca LK 4924	LES PAUL NOW (LP, also stereo Phase 4 PFS 4138)	12

LYN PAUL
74	Polydor 2058 472	Sail The Summer Winds/Lay Me Down (with John Barry)	6
75	Polydor 2383 340	GIVE ME LOVE (LP)	10
	(see also Nocturnes)		

RIM D. PAUL
68	Philips BF 1737	Thousand Hours/Downstairs To Meet Her	4

SHELLEY PAUL
69   Jay Boy BOY 10   Clowns Are Coming In/Take Me To Your Heart 4

PAUL & LINDA
69   Page One POF 140   You're Taking My Bag/When I Hear Your Name 4
(this single is not by Paul & Linda McCartney)

PAUL & PAULA
63   Philips 304 012 BF   Hey Paula/Bobby Is The One 6
63   Philips 304 016 BF   Young Lovers/Ba-hey-be 6
63   Philips BF 1256   First Quarrel/School Is Thru. 6
63   Philips BF 1269   Something Old, Something New/Flipped Over You. 6
63   Philips BF 1281   First Day Back At School/A Perfect Pair 7
64   Philips BF 1380   No Other Baby/Too Dark To See 7
63   Philips BBE 12639   YOUNG LOVERS (EP). 25
63   Philips 652 026BL   SING FOR YOUNG LOVERS (LP) 35
63   Philips BL 7573   WE GO TOGETHER (LP). 30
63   Philips BL 7587   HOLIDAY FOR TEENS (LP). 30

PAUL & RITCHIE & CRYING SHAMES
66   Decca F 12483   September In The Rain/Come On Back 100
(see also Cryin' Shames, Gary Walker & Rain)

PAULA & JETLINERS
66   Rainbow RAI 102   The Great Pretender/The Legend Of The Man From U.N.C.L.E. 10
66   Rainbow RAI 105   I Know Someday/Something On My Mind (B-side with Carols) 6

PAULETTE (Williams)
68   Major Minor MM 565   One Love In My Heart/Must We Say Goodbye. 5
73   Summit SUM 8543   Every Day Is The Same Kind Of Thing/SHORTY PERRY:
                               The Sweat Of Your Brow 6
(see also Paulette & Gee)

PAULETTE & DELROY
63   Island WI 120   Little Lover/Lovin' Baby 18
(see also Paulette, Paulette & Gee)

PAULETTE & GEE
70   G.G. GG 4506   Hold On Tight/G.G. ALL STARS: Tight Version 6
(see also Paulette, Sister, Winston Wright)

PAULETTE SISTERS
55   Capitol CL 14294   Dream Boat/Leave My Honey Be 15
55   Capitol CL 14310   Ring-A-Dang-A-Doo/Lonely One 15
55   Capitol CL 14347   You Win Again/Mama, El Baion 15

PAUL'S DISCIPLES
65   Decca F 12081   See That My Grave Is Kept Clean/Sixteen Tons. 20

PAUL'S TROUBLES
67   Ember EMB S 233   You'll Find Out/You've Got Something 20

PAUPERS
68   Verve Forecast VS 1514   Think I Care/White Song 5
69   Verve Forecast VS 1520   Southdown Road/Numbers 5
68   Verve Forecast (S)VLP 6017 ELLIS ISLAND (LP, mono/stereo). 18

PAVEMENT
69   Crystal CR 7005   Double Decker Of A Man/Saffron. 4

PAVEMENT
92   Ablaze 8   My First Mine/FLUFF: "Us" (flexi, free with *Ablaze* magazine). 10/7
92   Big Cat ABB 38   WATERY, DOMESTIC (Texas Never Whispers/Frontwards/Feed Them To The
                               Lions [Linden]/Shoot The Singer [1 Sick Verse]) (12" EP) 8
92   Big Cat ABB 38P   WATERY, DOMESTIC (12" EP, picture disc). 10
94   Big Cat ABB 56L   CROOKED RAIN CROOKED RAIN (LP, with inner sleeve & free 7":
                               "Haunt You Down"/"Jam Kids"). 12

RITA PAVONE
64   RCA RCA 1415   Remember Me/Just Once More 5
66   RCA RCA 1553   Heart/The Man Who Made Music 5
66   RCA RCA 1561   You Only You/Before You Go 5
73   Decca F 13462   He (Didn't Remember My Name)/(Vado Via) Last Summer 5

PAX EXTERNAL
71   Decca F 13167   A Second Chance Mr. Jones/You See Him As Your Brother. 6

GARY PAXTON
62   Liberty LIB 55485   Stop Twistin' Baby/Alley Oop Was A Two Dab Man. 10
(see also Skip & Flip)

TOM PAXTON
66   Elektra EKSN 45001   The Last Thing On My Mind/Goin' To The Zoo. 6
66   Elektra EKSN 45003   One Time And One Time Only/Bottle Of Wine. 7
67   Elektra EKSN 45006   Leaving London/All The Way Home. 6
69   Elektra EKSN 45021   Jennifer's Rabbit/The Marvellous Toy 7
69   Elektra EKSN 45049   Victoria Dines Alone/Clarissa Jones 5
69   Elektra EKSN 45064   Crazy John/Things I Notice Now 5
67   Elektra EPK 802   TOM PAXTON (EP) 15
66   Elektra EKL 277/EKS 7277 RAMBLIN' BOY (LP, U.K. pressing in U.S. sleeve). 20
66   Elektra EKL 298/EKS 7298 AIN'T THAT NEWS (LP, U.K. pressing in U.S. sleeve) 20
66   Elektra EKL 317/EKS 7317 OUTWARD BOUND (LP). 15
68   Elek. EKL 4019/EKS 74019 MORNING AGAIN (LP, red label) 15
69   Elektra EKS 74043   THINGS I NOTICE NOW (LP, red label) 12
70   Elektra EKS 74066   TOM PAXTON 6 (LP; also listed as 2469 003) 12
71   Reprise K 44129   HOW COME THE SUN (LP). 12

DAVEY PAYNE & MEDIUM WAVE
69	Ember EMB S 265	Walk In The Sunshine/Looking Towards The Sky (p/s)	5

FREDA PAYNE
62	HMV POP 1091	He Who Laughs Last/Slightly Out Of Tune	12
70	Invictus INV 502	Band Of Gold/The Easiest Way To Fall	6
70	Invictus INV 505	Deeper And Deeper/Unhooked Generation	5
71	Invictus INV 509	Cherish What Is Dear To You (While It's Near To You)/The World Don't Owe You A Thing	5
71	Invictus INV 512	Rock Me In The Cradle (Of Your Lovin' Arms)/Now Is The Time To Say Goodbye	5
71	Invictus INV 515	Bring Home The Boys/Odds And Ends	5
71	Invictus INV 518	You've Got To Love Somebody/Mama's Gone	5
72	Invictus INV 520	You Brought Me Joy/Suddenly It's Yesterday	5
72	Invictus INV 526	Unhooked Generation/Come Back	5
73	Invictus INV 529	I Shall Not Be Moved/Thru' The Memory Of My Mind	5
73	Invictus INV 533	Band Of Gold/The Easiest Way To Fall (reissue, withdrawn)	10
75	ABC ABC 4087	You/Lost In Love	5
78	Capitol 12CL 15959	Love Magnet/Bring Back The Joy (12", promo only)	7
80s	Inferno FIRE 14	Band Of Gold (Original Version)/(Extended Version Alternate Take) (gold vinyl)	5
70	Invictus SVT 1001	BAND OF GOLD (LP)	25
71	Invictus SVT 1005	CONTACT (LP)	20
72	Invictus SVT 1007	THE BEST OF FREDA PAYNE (LP)	15
78	Capitol E-ST 11864	SUPERNATURAL HIGH (LP)	12
70s	MGM 2351 004	FREDA PAYNE (LP)	12

LEON PAYNE
51	Capitol CL 13474	I Love You Because/KEN MARVIN: Why Don't You Haul Off And Love Me? (78)	7
64	London HA-B 8136	AMERICANA (LP)	12

PAZ
79	Magnus 2	PAZ AT CHICHESTER (LP)	25
83	Spotlight SPJ 507	KANDEEN LOVE SONG (LP)	12
83	Spotlight SPJ 518	PAZ ARE BACH (LP)	10
83	Paladin PALP 001	LOOK INSIDE (LP)	10

EDDIE PEABODY
55	London RE-D 1034	THE MAN WITH THE BANJO (EP)	10

DAVE PEACE QUARTET
69	Saga FID 2155	GOOD MORNING MR. BLUES (LP)	20

(see also Birmingham)

PEACEFUL COMPANY
(see under Morin & Wilson)

PEACHES & HERB
67	CBS 202509	Let's Fall In Love/We're In This Thing Together	10
67	CBS 2711	Close Your Eyes/I Will Watch Over You	6
67	CBS 2866	For Your Love/I Need Your Love So Desperately	12
67	Direction 58-3096	Love Is Strange/Two Little Kids	6
68	Direction 58-3415	Let It Be Me/I Need Your Love So Despeartely	6
68	Direction 58-3548	United/Thank You	5
68	Direction 58-3829	Let's Make A Promise/Me And You	5
69	Direction 58-4085	When He Touches Me/Thank You	5
70	Direction 58-4909	Satisfy My Hunger/It's Just A Game, Love	5
70	Direction 58-5249	Soothe Me With Your Love/We're So Much In Love	6
71	CBS 5249	Soothe Me With Your Love/We're So Much In Love (reissue)	4
77	Epic EPC 4903	Soothe Me With Your Love/Satisy My Hunger (coloured vinyl)	5
67	CBS 62966	LET'S FALL IN LOVE (LP)	20
67	CBS 63119	FOR YOUR LOVE (LP)	20
68	Direction 8-63263	GOLDEN DUETS (LP)	18

ANNETTE PEACOCK
72	RCA SF 8255	I'M THE ONE (LP)	12
78	Aura AUL 702	X DREAMS (LP)	12
78	Aura AUL 707	THE PERFECT RELEASE (LP)	15
70s	Aura	LIVE IN PARIS (LP)	25
83	Aura AUL 722	THE COLLECTION (LP)	12

ANNETTE PEACOCK & PAUL BLEY
72	Freedom 2383 105	DUAL UNITY (LP)	20

(see also Paul Bley, Bley-Peacock Synthesiser Show, Annette Peacock)

BERNIE PEACOCK
53	Vogue V 2168	Dog Days/My Blue Heaven (78)	8

TREVOR PEACOCK
61	Decca F 11414	I Didn't Figure On Him To Come Back/Can I Walk You Home	10

PEANUT
65	Pye 7N 15901	Thank Goodness For The Rain/I'm Not Sad	6
65	Pye 7N 15963	Home Of The Brave/I Wanna Hear It Again	10
66	Columbia DB 8032	I'm Waiting For The Day/Someone's Gonna Be Sorry	12
67	Columbia DB 8104	I Didn't Love Him Anyway/Come Tomorrow	12

(see also Katie Kissoon, Ragdolls U.K.)

PEANUT BUTTER CONSPIRACY
67	CBS 2981	It's A Happening Thing/Twice Is Life	6
68	CBS 3543	Turn On A Friend/Captain Sandwich	6
69	London HLH 10290	Back In L.A./Have A Little Faith	7
68	CBS 63277	THE GREAT CONSPIRACY (LP)	25

MINT VALUE £

BOB PEARCE BLUES BAND
| 74 | Westwood WRS 040 | LET'S GET DRUNK AGAIN (LP)................................15 |
| 79 | Forest Tracks FT 3015 | COLOUR BLIND (LP)....................................12 |

(see also Brother Bung)

PEARL JAM
92	Epic 657 572-7	Alive/Once (white vinyl p/s)................................10
92	Epic 657 572-6	Alive/Once/Wash (12", poster p/s)...........................15
92	Epic 657 857-8	Even Flow/Dirty Frank/Oceans (12", white vinyl, p/s).............15
92	Epic 658 258-7	Jeremy/Alive (live) (white vinyl, p/s).........................8
92	Epic 658 258-4	Jeremy/Alive (live) (cassette, jewel case with outer card sleeve).....5
92	Epic 658 258-6	Jeremy/Alive (live)/Footsteps (12", picture disc)................8
92	Epic 658 258-2	Jeremy/Yellow Ledbetter/Alive (live) (CD, picture disc)...........15
92	Epic 468 884-0	TEN (LP, picture disc)....................................18
92	Epic 468 884-5	TEN (CD, with 3 bonus tracks, in metallic yellow digipak)..........20

(see also Temple Of The Dog)

PEARLS
| 62 | Embassy EMB 564 | He's So Fine/BUD ASHTON: Scarlett O'Hara.....................4 |

(see also Bud Ashton)

PEARLS BEFORE SWINE
68	Fontana STL 5503	BALAKLAVA (LP)......................................22
68	Fontana STL 5505	ONE NATION UNDERGROUND (LP)..........................20
69	Reprise RSLP 6364	THESE THINGS TOO (LP)................................18
70	Reprise RSLP 6405	THE USE OF ASHES (LP)................................18
71	Reprise RSLP 6442	CITY OF GOLD (LP)....................................18
71	Reprise RSLP 6467	BEAUTIFUL LIES YOU COULD LIVE (LP).....................12

BUSTER PEARSON BAND
| 73 | Action ACT 4612 | Big Funky/Pretty Woman..................................8 |

DUKE PEARSON
| 60s | Polydor | ANGEL EYES (LP)......................................60 |

JOHNNY PEARSON
66	Columbia DB 7851	Rat Catcher's Theme/Weaver's Green Theme...................15
75	Pye 7N 45537	Red Alert/Midland Parade..................................5
78	Rampage RAM 2	All Creatures Great And Small/Love Dream....................6

(see also John Barry Seven)

KEITH PEARSON'S RIGHT HAND BAND
| 76 | Eron ER 014 | KEITH PEARSON'S RIGHT HAND BAND (LP)....................12 |

RONNIE PEARSON
| 58 | HMV POP 489 | Flippin' Over You/Teen-Age Fancy..........................650 |
| 58 | HMV POP 489 | Flippin' Over You/Teen-Age Fancy (78)......................175 |

PEASANTS
| 65 | Columbia DB 7642 | Got Some Lovin' For You Baby/Let's Get Together...............100 |

PEBBLES
68	Major Minor MM 574	40 Miles Inside Your Heart/Get Around.......................5
69	Decca F 22944	Incredible George/Playing Chess.............................7
70	Deram DM 305	Stand Up And Be Counted/May In The Morning..................5
71	Parlophone R 5900	Goodnight Ma/Sadness Of A Summer's Afternoon................5
71	Parlophone R 5921	First Time Loving/Party....................................5

PEBBLES & BAMM BAMM
| 66 | Pye International 7N 25382 | Daddy/The World Is Full Of Joys...........................5 |

PEDDLERS
64	Philips BF 1375	Let The Sunshine In/True Girl..............................6
65	Philips BF 1404	Whatever Happened To The Good Times/Song For The Blues.........6
65	Philips BF 1455	Over The Rainbow/You Must Be Having Me On..................6
66	Philips BF 1506	Adam's Apple/Anybody's Fool...............................6
66	Philips BF 1530	I've Got To Hold On/Gassin'................................6
67	Philips BF 1557	What'll I Do/Delicious Lady.................................6
67	CBS 2947	Irresistible You/Murry's Mood...............................5
67	CBS 3055	You're The Reason I'm Living/Nine Miles High...................5
68	CBS 3333	Handel With Care/Horse's Collar.............................5
68	CBS 3734	Comin' Home Baby/Empty Club Blues.........................5
69	CBS 4045	That's Life/Wasting My Time................................5
69	CBS 4449	Birth/Steel Mill..5
70	CBS 4720	Girlie/P.S. I Love You....................................5
66	Philips BE 12954	SWINGING SCENE (EP)..................................10
67	Philips (S)BL 7768	LIVE AT THE PICKWICK (LP)..............................15
67	CBS (S)BPG 63183	FREE WHEELERS (LP)...................................12
68	CBS 63411	THREE IN A CELL (LP)..................................12
68	Fontana SFL 13016	THE FANTASTIC PEDDLERS (LP)...........................12
70	CBS 63682	BIRTHDAY (LP).......................................12
70	Philips 6308 028	THREE FOR ALL (LP)...................................12
71	Philips 6386 066	GEORGIA ON MY MIND (LP)..............................12
72	Philips 6308 102	SUITE LONDON (LP, with London Symphony Orchestra)..........12

MIKE PEDICIN QUINTET
| 62 | HMV POP 1001 | When Cats Come Twistin' In/Gotta Twist......................7 |

BOBBY PEDRICK
| 58 | London HLX 8740 | White Bucks And Saddle Shoes/Stranded......................30 |
| 58 | London HLX 8740 | White Bucks And Saddle Shoes/Stranded (78).................30 |

ANN PEEBLES
70	London HLU 10322	Part Time Love/I Still Love You	5
71	London HLU 10328	I Pity The Fool/Heartaches, Heartaches	5
71	London HLU 10346	Slipped, Tripped And Fell In Love/99 lbs	5
72	London HLU 10361	Breaking Up Somebody's Home/Troubles, Heartaches And Sadness	5
72	London HLU 10385	Somebody's On Your Case/I've Been There Before	5
73	London HLU 10405	I'm Gonna Tear Your Playhouse Down/One Way Street	5
74	London HLU 10428	I Can't Stand The Rain/I've Been There Before	5
74	London HLU 10468	(You Keep Me)/Hangin' On/Run Run Run	5
75	London HLU 10484	Beware/You Got To Feed The Fire	5
75	London HLU 10508	Come On Mama/I'm Leaving You	5
72	London SHU 8434	STRAIGHT FROM THE HEART (LP)	12
74	London SHU 8468	I CAN'T STAND THE RAIN (LP)	12
76	London SHU 8490	TELLIN' IT (LP)	12

PAUL PEEK
61	Pye International 7N 25102	Brother In Law/Through The Teenage Years	12
66	CBS 202073	Pin The Tail On The Donkey/Rockin' Pneumonia	10

(see also Gene Vincent & Blue Caps)

DAVID PEEL (& LOWER EAST SIDE)
68	Elektra EKL 4032	HAVE A MARIJUANA (LP, red label, also stereo EKS 74032)	18/20
70	Elektra 2401 001	AMERICAN REVOLUTION (LP)	15

PEELERS
72	Polydor Folk Mill 2460 165	BANISHED MISFORTUNE (LP)	125

PEELS
66	Stateside SS 513	Juanita Banana/Fun	7
66	Audio Fidelity AFSP 527	Scrooey Mooey/Time Marches On	12

PEENUTS
67	Ember EMB S 242	The Theme For "The Monkees"/The World's Been Good To Me Tonight (some in p/s)	15/7

PEEPS
65	Philips BF 1421	Now Is The Time/Got Plenty Of Love	10
65	Philips BF 1443	What Can I Say?/Don't Talk About Love	12
66	Philips BF 1478	Gotta Get A Move On/I Told You Before	8
66	Philips BF 1509	Tra La La/Loser Wins	8

(see also Martin Cure & Peeps, Sabres, Rainbows)

PEEP SHOW
67	Polydor 56196	Your Servant, Stephen/Mazy	60
68	Polydor 52226	Esprit De Corps/Mino In A Mix Up	15

DONALD PEERS
53	HMV B 10411	Barrels 'N' Barrels Of Roses/Lulu Had A Baby (78, B-side with Tanner Sisters)	8
58	Oriole CB 1431	Oh! Oh! I'm Falling In Love Again/I Need Somebody	8

BEV PEGG (& HIS GOIN' NOWHERE BAND)
70s	Beaujangle DB 0007	NOSTALGIA IS A THING OF THE PAST (LP, private pressing, with booklet, 100 only; as Bev Pegg & His Goin' Nowhere Band)	12
70s	Beaujangle DB 0008	THE FOUNDRY DITTY AND THE INDUSTRIAL AIR (LP, private pressing, 500 only)	10

(see also David Cartwright, Away From The Sand, Brindley Brae)

BOB PEGG
74	Transatlantic TRA 280	THE SHIPBUILDER (LP, with Nick Strutt)	15
75	Transatlantic TRA 299	ANCIENT MAPS (LP, with insert)	15

BOB & CAROL PEGG
71	Trailer LER 3016	HE CAME FROM THE MOUNTAIN (LP, red label)	20
72	Galliard GAL 4017	AND NOW IT IS SO EARLY — THE SONGS OF SYDNEY CARTER (LP)	30

(see also Carol Pegg, Mr. Fox)

BOB PEGG & NICK STRUTT
73	Transatlantic TRA 265	BOB PEGG & NICK STRUTT (LP)	15

CAROL PEGG
73	Transatlantic TRA 266	CAROL PEGG (LP, gatefold sleeve)	40

(see also Bob & Carol Pegg)

PEGGY
70	Trojan TR 7752	All Kinds Of Everything Part 1/CARL LEVEY: Instrumental Version	6
70	Hot Rod HR 103	I Shall Follow The Star/CARL LEVEY: Gifted At The Top	6

PEGGY & JIMMY
70	Hot Rod HR 101	Pum Pum Lover/CARL LEVY: Remember Easter Monday	8

PEGGY'S LEG
73	Bunch	William Tell Overture (Irish only)	30
73	Bunch BAN 2001	GRINILLA (LP, Irish only, with insert)	400

(see also Skid Row, Jimi Slevin)

PEG LEG SAM
74	Flyright LP 507/8	THE LAST MEDICINE SHOW (2-LP)	15

BERNARD PEIFFER
54	Felsted ED 82010	Strip Tease/Who Is Me? (78)	10

PEKKA
77	Virgin V 2084	THE MATHEMATICIANS AIR DISPLAY (LP, features Mike Oldfield)	18

DAVE PELL OCTET
54	London RE-P 1008	IRVING BERLIN GALLERY VOL. 1 (EP)	12
55	London RE-P 1018	RODGERS AND HART (EP)	12

MINT VALUE £

TRACY PENDARVIS
| 60 | London HLS 9059 | A Thousand Guitars/Is It Too Late | 20 |
| 60 | London HLS 9213 | Is It Me/South Bound Line | 20 |

MIKE PENDER
| 86 | Sierra FED 23 | It's Over/Brothers And Sisters (p/s) | 6 |
| 86 | Sierra FED 23T | It's Over/Brothers And Sisters (12", p/s) | 8 |

PENDLEFOLK
| 70 | Folk Heritage FHR 007 | PENDLEFOLK (LP) | 20 |

PENDRAGON
82	private pressing	VICTIMS OF LIFE (demo cassette)	8
83	private pressing	ALASKA (demo cassette)	8
87	Awareness AWS 101	Red Shoes/Searching/Contact (p/s)	4
87	Awareness AWSX 101	Red Shoes/Searching/Contact (12", p/s)	7
89	Toff PENDS 7S	Saved By You/Lady Luck (p/s)	8
89	Toff PENDS 12S	Saved By You/Lady Luck/Elephants Never Grow Old (12", p/s)	8
84	Elusive ARRMP 001	FLY HIGH FALL FAR (12" mini-LP)	8
85	Elusive ARRLP 100	FIRE IN HARMONY (LP)	10
85	Elusive ARRLP 101	THE JEWEL (LP)	10

PENDULUMS
| 64 | Pye 7N 15701 | The Weaver/The Slow Weaver | 4 |

PENETRATION
77	Virgin VS 192	Don't Dictate/Money Talks (p/s)	8
78	Virgin VS 213	Firing Squad/Never (p/s)	5
78	Virgin VS 226	Life's A Gamble/V.I.P. (p/s)	4
79	Virgin VS 257	Danger Signs/Stone Heroes (live) (p/s)	4
79	Virgin VS 268	Come Into The Open/Lifeline (p/s)	4
78	Virgin V 2109	MOVING TARGETS (LP, 15,000 on luminous vinyl)	12
79	Virgin V 2131	COMING UP FOR AIR (LP)	10
79	Virgin/Clifdayn PEN 1	RACE AGAINST TIME (LP, official bootleg)	15

PENGUINS
55	London HL 8114	Earth Angel/Hey Senorita (gold label print, triangular centre)	1,350
55	London HL 8114	Earth Angel/Hey Senorita (silver label print, tri-centre, existence unconfirmed)	800
55	London HL 8114	Earth Angel/Hey Senorita (large centre hole, export issue)	800
55	London HL 8114	Earth Angel/Hey Senorita (78)	120

DAWN PENN
66	Rio R 113	Long Days Short Night/Are You There	35
67	Studio One SO 2030	You Don't Love Me/SOUL VENDORS: Portobello Road	30
68	Island WI 3097	I'll Never Let You Go/MARK BROWN: Brown Low Special	18
	(see also Max Romeo, Viceroys)		

TONY PENN
| 62 | Starlite ST45 083 | That's What I Like/I Won't Cry Anymore | 30 |

PENNSYLVANIA SIXPENCE
| 67 | Pye 7N 17326 | Love Of The Common People/Midweek Excursion | 6 |

PENNY
| 61 | Piccadilly 7N 35009 | Who Does He Think He Is/Sparks | 6 |
| 62 | Piccadilly 7N 35045 | Shall I Take My Heart And Go/What'd I Do? | 6 |

GEORGE A. PENNY
| 68 | Trojan TR 625 | Win Your Love/VAL BENNETT: All In The Game | 10 |

HANK PENNY
| 56 | Parlophone MSP 6202 | Bloodshot Eyes/Wham! Bam! Thank You Ma'am | 50 |
| 56 | Parlophone R 4120 | Bloodshot Eyes/Wham! Bam! Thank You Ma'am (78) | 20 |

PENNY PEEPS
| 68 | Liberty LBF 15053 | Little Man With A Stick/Model Village | 40 |
| 68 | Liberty LBF 15114 | I See The Morning/Curly, The Knight Of The Road | 10 |

PENNY SERENADERS
| 58 | Columbia DB 4164 | Whistle Kwela/Fluitjie Vastrap (78) | 8 |

GAYLA PEEVEY
| 53 | Philips PB 211 | I Want A Hippopotamus For Christmas/Are My Ears On Straight? (78) | 7 |

LYDIA PENSE & COLD BLOOD
| 70s | ABC ABC 4109 | I Get Off On You/We Came Down Here/Cold Blood Smoking | 6 |

PENTAD
65	Parlophone R 5288	Silver Dagger/Nothing But Love	15
65	Parlophone R 5368	Don't Throw It All Away/Too Many Ways	8
66	Parlophone R 5424	Something Other People Call Love/It Better Be Me	8

PENTAGONS
| 61 | London HLU 9333 | To Be Loved Forever/Down At The Beach | 60 |

PENTANGLE
68	Big T BIG 109	Travellin' Song/Mirage (some in title die-cut sleeve)	8/5
69	Big T BIG 124	Once I Had A Sweetheart/I Saw An Angel	5
70	Big T BIG 128	Light Flight/Cold Mountain	5
73	Big T BIG 567	Light Flight/Market Song/The Time Has Come	5
68	Transatlantic TRA 162	THE PENTANGLE (LP)	20
68	Transatlantic TRA 178	SWEET CHILD (2-LP)	20
69	Transatlantic TRA 205	BASKET OF LIGHT (LP, gatefold sleeve)	20
70	Transatlantic TRA 228	CRUEL SISTER (LP, gatefold sleeve)	20
71	Transatlantic TRA 240	REFLECTION (LP, gatefold sleeve with inner sleeve)	18
72	Reprise K 44197	SOLOMON'S SEAL (LP, with lyric insert)	30

MINT VALUE £

| 72 | Transatlantic TRASAM 23 | HISTORY BOOK (LP) | 15 |
| 73 | Transatlantic TRASAM 29 | PENTANGLING (LP) | 15 |

(see also Bert Jansch, John Renbourn, Duffy's Nucleus)

PEOPLE
69	Capitol CL 15553	I Love You/Somebody Tell Me My Name	8
69	Capitol CL 15599	Ulla/Turnin' Me In	6
70	RCA RCA 2028	I Am (The Preacher)/September's Son	5
71	Deram DM 346	In Ancient Times/Glastonbury	6
70	Paramount SPFL 261	THERE ARE PEOPLE AND THERE ARE PEOPLE (LP)	15

PEOPLE BAND
| 70 | Transatlantic TRA 214 | THE PEOPLE BAND (LP, with Charlie Watts) | 40 |

(see also Charlie Watts, Battered Ornaments)

PEOPLE'S CHOICE
| 71 | Mojo 2092 024 | I Like To Do It/Big Ladies Man | 6 |
| 73 | London HLU 10404 | Let Me Do My Thing/On A Cloudy Day | 5 |

PEPPER
| 68 | Pye 7N 17569 | We'll Make It Together/I'm On The Way Down | 8 |

ART PEPPER
54	Vogue LDE 067	ART PEPPER QUARTET (10" LP)	15
50s	London HLZ V 14038	ART PEPPER QUARTET (10" LP)	60
60	Contemporary LAC 12229	MODERN JAZZ CLASSICS (LP, as Art Pepper Eleven)	12

(see also Chet Baker)

JIM PEPPER
| 71 | Atlantic 2400 149 | PEPPER'S POW WOW (LP) | 20 |

KEN PEPPER
| 61 | Top Rank JAR 535 | Just A Little At A Time/I Get The Blues When It Rains | 6 |

DANNY PEPPERMINT (& JUMPING JACKS)
61	London HLL 9478	The Peppermint Twist/Somebody Else Is Taking My Place (with Jumping Jacks)	8
62	London HLL 9516	One More Time/La Dee Dah	8
62	London HLL 9614	Maybe Tomorrow But Not Today/Passing Parade	8
62	London HA-L 2438	TWIST WITH DANNY PEPPERMINT (LP)	40

PEPPERMINT CIRCUS
67	Olga OLE 007	All The King's Horses/It Didn't Take Long	10
68	Polydor 56288	I Won't Be There/Keeping My Head Above Water	6
69	Polydor 56312	Please Be Patient/Take My Love	6
69	A&M AMS 765	One Thing Can Lead To Another/It's So Easy	5
70	A&M AMS 778	Let Me Go/School Days	5

PEPPERMINT RAINBOW
68	MCA MU 1034	Walking In Different Circles/Pink Lemonade	5
69	MCA MU 1076	Will You Be Staying After Sunday/And I'll Be There	5
69	MCA MU 1091	Don't Wake Up In The Morning, Michael/Rosemary	5

PEPPERMINT TROLLEY COMPANY
| 68 | Dot DOT 110 | Baby You Come Rolling 'Cross My Mind/Nine O'Clock Business Man | 6 |

PEPPI
62	Decca F 11520	Stories/When I Think Of You	6
63	Decca F 11638	Can You Waddle/I Never Danced Before	7
64	Decca F 11991	Pistol Packin' Mama/Roll On Baby	8
64	Fontana TF 446	So Used To Loving You/Don't Trust My Friend	7
65	Decca F 12055	The Skip/Do The Skip	6

PERCELLS
| 63 | HMV POP 1154 | Cheek To Cheek/What Are Boys Made Of? | 8 |

LANCE PERCIVAL
63	Parlophone R 5032	Rivera Cafe/You're Joking Of Course	5
63	Parlophone R 5071	Dancing In The Streets Tonight/The Beetroot Song	5
66	Parlophone R 5517	End Of The Season/Our Jim	5
67	Parlophone R 5587	The Maharajah Of Brum/Taking The Maharajah Apart	6

NORMAN PERCIVAL
| 67 | United Artists UP 1197 | Theme From "Billion Dollar Brain"/Shades Of Green | 7 |

PERCY PAVILION
| 83 | Pavil. In Splendour PIS 1 | CRICKET (EP) | 7 |
| 84 | Dead Good Dolly P. DMS 2 | Gower Power/You're An Extra Baby (p/s) | 4 |

(see also Captain Sensible)

PEREGRINE
| 72 | Westwood WRS 016 | SONGS OF MINE (LP) | 90 |

RAY PEREIRA
| 70 | Baf BAF 5 | Don't Mess With Cupid/CATS: Falling In Love | 6 |
| 70 | Baf BAF 6 | On Broadway/Hey Chick | 6 |

PERENNIAL DIVIDE
86	Sweatbox SOX 018	BURN DOWN EP (12", p/s)	8
88	Sweatbox SOX 020	Bee Head (1-sided, promo only)	6
88	Sweatbox SOX 020	Bee Head/World Spread/Gentle As A Fawn Is Warm/Clamp (12", p/s)	7

(see also Meatbeat Manifesto)

PERERIN
| 80 | Gwerin SYWM 215 | HAUL AR YR EIRA (LP, with insert) | 180 |

PERET
| 74 | Pye International 7N 25645 | Canta Y Se Feliz/Tocale Las Palmas | 5 |

MINT VALUE £

PERE UBU

79	Chrysalis CHS 2372	The Fabulous Sequel (Have Shoes Will Walk)/Humour Me (live)/	
		The Book Is On The Table (p/s)	8
80	Rough Trade RT 049	Final Solution/My Dark Ages (p/s)	8
81	Rough Trade RT 066	Not Happy/Lonesome Cowboy Dave (p/s)	8
78	Radar RDR 1	DATAPANIK IN THE YEAR ZERO (12" EP)	10
78	Blank BLANK 001	THE MODERN DANCE (LP)	15
80	Rough Trade ROUGH 14	THE ART OF WALKING (LP, original with "Miles" & "Arabia")	12

(see also David Thomas)

CHRISTINE PERFECT

69	Blue Horizon 57-3165	When You Say/No Road Is The Right Road	12
70	Blue Horizon 57-3172	I'm Too Far Gone (To Turn Around)/Close To Me	15
70	Blue Horizon 7-63860	CHRISTINE PERFECT (LP)	50
82	CBS 32198	CHRISTINE PERFECT (LP, reissue)	12

(see also Christine McVie, Fleetwood Mac, Illusive Dream, Chicken Shack, Rick Hayward)

PERFECT PEOPLE

69	MCA MU 1079	House In The Country/Polyanna	10

PERFORMANCE

73	Polydor 2058 324	Funny Little Things/Rejoice	6

PERFORMERS

69	Action ACT 4552	I Can't Stop You/L.A. Stomp	8

EMILIO PERICOLI

58	Parlophone DP 536	Chella Lla!/La Più Bella Del Mondo (78, export issue)	8

PERISHERS

68	Fontana TF 965	How Does It Feel/Bye Bye Baby	20

(see also Seftones)

NICK PERITO ORCHESTRA

60	London HLT 9221	Green Leaves Of Summer/Jennifer	7
62	HMV POP 1032	Jessica/Gina	5

CARL PERKINS

78s

56	London HLU 8271	Blue Suede Shoes/Honey Don't (78)	50
57	London HLS 8408	Matchbox/Your True Love (78)	35
57	London HLS 8527	Glad All Over/Forever Yours (78)	60
58	London HLS 8608	Lend Me Your Comb/That's Right (78)	80
59	Philips PB 983	I Don't See Me In Your Eyes Anymore/One Ticket To Loneliness (78)	120

SINGLES

56	London HLU 8271	Blue Suede Shoes/Honey Don't	200
57	London HLS 8408	Matchbox/Your True Love	130
57	London HLS 8527	Glad All Over/Forever Yours	90
58	London HLS 8608	Lend Me Your Comb/That's Right	90
59	Philips PB 983	I Don't See Me In Your Eyes Anymore/One Ticket To Loneliness	15
61	Philips PB 1179	Anyway The Wind Blows/The Unhappy Girls	15
64	Brunswick 05905	Help Me Find My Baby/I Wouldn't Have You	10
64	Brunswick 05909	Big Bad Blues/Lonely Heart (with Nashville Teens)	10
64	Brunswick 05923	The Monkey Shine/Let My Baby Be	12
67	Stateside SS 599	A Country Boy's Dream/If I Could Come Back	10
68	London HLP 7125	A Country Boy's Dream/Shine Shine Shine (export issue)	20
68	Spark SRL 1009	Lake County, Cotton Country/It's You	8
68	London HLS 10192	Blue Suede Shoes/Dixie Fried (unissued)	
68	London HLS 10192	Blue Suede Shoes/Matchbox	7
69	CBS 3932	Restless/11.43	7
70	CBS 4991	All Mama's Children/Step Aside (with N.R.B.Q.)	6
77	Mercury ELV 15	The E.P. Express/Big Bad Blues (p/s)	6
78	Jet UP 36365	Blue Suede Shoes/That's All Right/Rock On Around The World (p/s)	5
78	Jet SJET 117	Mustang Wine/The Whole World Misses You (p/s)	5
80	Jet JET 182	Love Sick Blues/Turn Around/Miss Misunderstood/Blue Suede Shoes (p/s)	5

LPs

59	London HA-S 2202	THE DANCE ALBUM OF CARL PERKINS	
		(LP, flipback/non-flipback sleeve)	100/75
66	Ember NR 5038	SUNSTROKE (LP, shared with Jerry Lee Lewis)	15
66	CBS Realm 52305	WHOLE LOTTA CARL PERKINS (LP, boxed square logo on originals)	40/18
68	CBS 63309	KING OF ROCK (LP)	18
68	London HA-P/SH-P 8366	COUNTRY BOY'S DREAM (LP)	25
69	CBS 63676	CARL PERKINS' GREATEST HITS (LP)	15
70	CBS 63826	BOPPIN' THE BLUES (LP, with N.R.B.Q.)	15
74	Mercury 6338 475	MY KIND OF COUNTRY (LP)	12
78	Jet JETLP 208/UATV 30146	OL' BLUE SUEDE'S BACK (LP, record & spine list UATV cat. no.)	12
82	Sun BOX 101	THE SUN YEARS (3-LP, box set with booklet)	25

(see also N.R.B.Q.)

JOE PERKINS

63	London HLU 9794	Little Eeefin Annie/Encle Eeef	7
72	Mojo 2092 047	Wrapped Up In Your Love/Looking For A Woman	5

LASCELLES PERKINS

61	Blue Beat BB 41	Creation/Lonely Robin	12
63	Island WI 038	Tango Lips (with Yvonne)/DENNIS SINDREY: Rub Up	
		(B-side actually plays "Jamaica's Song")	12
64	R&B JB 175	I Am So Grateful/When I Survey	12
70	Escort ES 814	Please Stay/MATADORS: Voyage From The Moon	7
71	Banana BA 317	Tell It All Brothers/SOUND DIMENSION: Polkadots	10

(see also Tommy McCook)

POLLY PERKINS

63	Decca F 11583	I Reckon You (as Polly Perkins & Bill)/The Girls Are At It Again	5
63	Oriole CB 1869	Sweet As Honey/I've Gotta Tell You	6
63	Oriole CB 1929	Young Lover/You Too Can Be A Beatle	6
63	Oriole CB 1979	Faling In Love Again/I Went By Your House Today	6
73	Chapter One CMS 1018	LIBERATED WOMAN (LP)	12

(see also Academy)

TONY PERKINS

57	RCA RCA 1018	Moonlight Swim/First Romance	8
57	RCA RCA 1018	Moonlight Swim/First Romance (78)	20

PERMANENTS

63	London HLU 9803	Oh Dear, What Can The Matter Be/Let Me Be Baby	8

JEAN-JACQUES PERREY

72	Vanguard VAN 1005	Gossipo Perpetuo/Moog Indigo	8
73	Vanguard VAN 1008	Minuet Of The Robots/Porcupine Rock	8
71	Vanguard VSD 6525	KALEIDOSCOPIC VIBRATIONS — SPOTLIGHT ON THE MOOG (LP, 'kaleidoscope' sleeve, with Gershon Kingsley)	30
72	Vanguard VSD 6549	MOOG INDIGO (LP, title sleeve)	35
73	Vanguard VSD 79222	THE IN SOUND FROM WAY OUT! (LP, green/black 'starburst' sleeve, with Gershon Kingsley)	30
73	Vanguard VSD 79286	THE AMAZING NEW ELECTRONIC POP SOUND OF... (LP)	25
74	Vanguard DPS 2051	THE BEST OF THE MOOG (2-LP)	35
96	Beat Goes Public BGPZ 1103	MOOG INDIGO (LP, mono vinyl reissue, 3,000 only)	15

PAT PERRIN

68	Island WI 3115	Over You/LLOYD TERRELL: Lost Without You	18

PERRI'S

59	Oriole CB 1481	Jerri-Lee/Ballad Of A Happy Heart	10
63	Oriole CB 1481	Jerri-Lee/Ballad Of A Happy Heart (78)	15

BARBARA PERRY

70	Pama PM 795	Say You Need Me/Unloved	5

JEFF PERRY

76	Arista ARIST 51	Love Don't Come No Stronger/I've Got To See You Right Away	5

KING PERRY

(see under Lee Perry)

LEE 'SCRATCH' PERRY (& UPSETTERS)

63	R&B JB 102	Prince In The Black/Don't Copy	25
63	R&B JB 104	Old For New/Prince And Duke	25
63	R&B JB 106	Mad Head/Man And Wife	30
63	R&B JB 135	Royalty/Can't Be Wrong	25
63	Island WI 118	Never Get Weary/TOMMY McCOOK: Below Zero	25
64	Port-O-Jam PJ 4001	Help The Weak/TOMMY McCOOK: Exodus	25
64	Port-O-Jam PJ 4003	Bad Minded People/TOMMY McCOOK & HIS GROUP: Jam Rock	30
64	Port-O-Jam PJ 4010	Chatty Chatty Woman/TOMMY McCOOK & HIS GROUP: Road Block	30
65	Island WI 210	Please Don't Go/Bye, St. Peter (both sides with Soulettes)	25
65	Island WI 223	Country Girl/Strange Country (as Upsetters; both act. by Ossie & Upsetters)	15
65	Ska Beat JB 201	Roast Duck/Hand To Hand, Man To Man	25
65	Ska Beat JB 203	Trail And Crosses/Jon Tom	25
65	Ska Beat JB 212	Wishes Of The Wicked/Hold Down	25
65	Ska Beat JB 215	Open Up/ROLAND ALPHONSO: Twin Double	25
66	Ska Beat JB 251	The Woodman/Give Me Justice	25
66	Island WI 259	Just Keep It Up/ROLAND ALPHONSO: James Bond	25
66	Island WI 292	Doctor Dick (as King Perry)/SOUL BROTHERS: Magic Star	25
66	Island WI 298	Rub And Squeeze (as King Perry & Soulettes)/SOUL BROTHERS: Here Comes The Minx	25
67	Doctor Bird DB 1073	Run For Cover/Something You've Got (as Lee 'King' Perry & Sensations)	30
67	Doctor Bird DB 1098	Whop Whop Man/Wind-Up Doll (with Dynamites)	25
68	Amalgamated AMG 808	The Upsetter/Thank You Baby	35
68	Doctor Bird DB 1146	People Funny Boy/BURT WALTERS: Blowing In The Wind	12
68	Trojan TR 644	Uncle Desmond/Bronco (with Upsetters)	10
69	Upsetter US 303	People Funny Fi True/UPSETTERS: Ten To Twelve	10
69	Upsetter US 324	Yakety Yak/Tackio (with Upsetters)	10
70	Upsetter US 325	Kill Them All/Soul Walk (with Upsetters)	10
71	Bullet BU 461	All Combine Pts 1& 2 (as Lee Perry & Upsetters)	12
72	Upsetter US 385	French Connection (with Upsetters)/UPSETTERS: Version	10
72	Upsetter US 389	Back Biter (with Dennis Alcapone)/UPSETTERS: Version	12
73	Upsetter US 397	Jungle Lion/Freakout Skank	10
73	Upsetter US 398	Cow Thief Skank (actually by Lee Perry & Charlie Ace)/Seven And Three Quarters Skank	10
73	Bread BR 1111	Station Underground/CARLTON & SHOES: Better Days	20
73	Downtown DT 513	Bucky Skank/Mid East Rock	12
73	Jackpot JP 812	Justice To The People/UPSETTERS: Version	10
74	Dip DL 5037	Dub A Pum Pum (with Silvertones)/Version	7
74	Dip DL 5060	Dreader Locks (& Junior Byles)/Militant Rock	6
79	Trojan TRL 166	AFRICAN BLOOD (LP)	25
79	Cactus CTLP 112	REVOLUTION DUB (LP)	20

(see also Upsetters, Defenders, Roland Alphonso, Bob Marley/Wailers, King Scratch, Punchers, Roy Shirley, Pioneers, Desmond Dekker)

MINT VALUE £

MAL PERRY
58	Fontana H 125	Lollipop/Love Me Again (78)	12
58	Fontana H 133	That's When Your Heartaches Begin/Make Me A Miracle	10
58	Fontana H 133	That's When Your Heartaches Begin/Make Me A Miracle (78)	12
58	Fontana H 149	Too Young To Love/Who Are They To Say	10
58	Fontana H 149	Too Young To Love/Who Are They To Say (78)	12
58	Fontana H 157	Things I Didn't Say/The Girl Next Door	10
58	Fontana H 157	Things I Didn't Say/The Girl Next Door (78)	12
59	Fontana H 172	Richer Than I/Willingly	10
59	Fontana H 172	Richer Than I/Willingly (78)	15

MARK PERRY
80	Deptford Fun City DFC 09	You Cry Your Tears/Music Death? (with Dennis Burns, unissued)	
80	NB NB 7	You Cry Your Tears/Music Death? (with Dennis Burns, p/s in poly bag)	4
80	Deptford Fun City DFC 12	Whole World's Down On Me/I Live — He Dies (p/s)	4
80	Deptford Fun City DLP 06	SNAPPY TURNS (LP)	12

SHORT(L)Y PERRY
72	Attack ATT 8043	Musical Goat/WINSTON GRENNON & J. JACKSON: Stinging Dub	6
72	Explosion EX 2067	Sprinkle Some Water/FLOWERS & ALVIN: Howdy And Tenky	5
72	Bullet BU 512	Sprinkle Some Water/FLOWERS & ALVIN: Howdy And Tenky	5
73	Bullet BU 529	Yama Skank/U ROY JUNIOR: Doctor Run Come Quick	7
73	Downtown DT 517	Dedicated To Illiteracy/G.G. ALL STARS: Illiteracy Dub	6
73	Grape GR 3052	Abusing And Assaulting (by Flowers & Alvin)/Food Control	6
73	Green Door GD 4043	President Mash Up The Resident/President Mash Up The Resident Part Two	6

(see also Shorty, Cornell Campbell, Maytones, Paulette Williams)

STEVE PERRY
60	HMV POP 745	Step By Step/Because They're Young	8
62	Decca F 11462	Ginny Come Lately/Two Of A Kind	8
62	Decca F 11526	Young And In Love/Let It Come True	7
63	Decca F 11656	Find Me A Girl/My Dad	6
64	Decca F 11895	Crooked Little Man/Day Dreams	6

PERRY SISTERS
59	Brunswick 05802	Fabian/Willie Boy	20
59	Brunswick 05802	Fabian/Willie Boy (78)	20

PERSIAN RISK
81	SRT SRTS/81/CUS/1146	Calling For You/Chasing The Dragon (p/s)	175
83	Neat NEAT 24	Ridin' High/Hurt You (p/s)	10
86	Metal Masters METALLP 2	RISE UP (LP)	12

PERSIANS
69	Pama PM 772	I Only Have Eyes For You	6
72	Capitol CL 15726	Baby Come Back Home/I Want To Go Home	5

PERSIMMON'S PECULIAR SHADES
68	Major Minor MM 554	Watchmaker/Coplington	15

PERSONALITIES
65	Dice CC 30	I Remember/Suffering	10
66	Blue Beat BB 354	Push It Down/BUSTER'S ALL STARS: Blues Market	15

PERSONALITY CRISIS
90	Overground OVER 09	Twilight's Last Gleaming/The Jam (live) (p/s, 1,000 only)	5

PERSUADERS (U.S.)
72	Atlantic K 40370	THE THIN LINE BETWEEN LOVE AND HATE (LP)	15
73	Atlantic K 40476	THE PERSUADERS (LP)	12

PERSUADERS (U.K.)
93	Detour DR 001	Finished Forever/In The Night (p/s, 300 only)	20
94	Detour DR 011	Waiting For The Nowhere Express/Girl/The Paperchase (p/s, 100 on red vinyl)	8/5

PERSUASIONS (U.K.)
65	Columbia DB 7560	I'll Go Crazy/Try Me	18
65	Columbia DB 7700	Big Brother/Deep Down Love	20
66	Columbia DB 7859	La, La, La, La, La/Opportunity	20

PERSUASIONS (U.S.)
69	Minit MLF 11017	Party In The Woods/It's Better To Have Loved And Lost	6
70	Straight STS 1062	A CAPPELLA (LP)	30
72	Island ILPS 9201	STREET CORNER SYMPHONY (LP)	12

MORRIS PERT
75	Chantry ABM 21	LUMINOS/CHROMOSPHERE/4 JAPANESE VERSES (LP)	40
80	Chantry CHT 001	LUMINOS/CHROMOSPHERE/4 JAPANESE VERSES (LP, reissue)	30
82	Chantry CHT 007	BOOK OF LOVE/FRAGMENTI I/ULTIMATE DECAY (LP)	30

JON PERTWEE
72	Purple PUR 111	Who Is The Doctor/Pure Mystery	15
85	Safari DOCTOR 1	Who Is The Doctor/Doctor Blood Donor (p/s)	5
70s	Phillips BBL 7558	SONGS FOR VULGAR BOATMEN (LP)	15

(see also Rupert Hine, Derek Roy, BBC Radiophonic Workshop, Blood Donor)

PESKY GEE!
69	Pye 7N 17708	Where Is My Mind/A Place Of Heart Break	12
69	Pye N(S)PL 18293	EXCLAMATION MARK (LP)	40

(see also Black Widow, Agony Bag)

PETALS
63	Decca F 11650	Let's Do The Tamoure/Look At Me	6

PETER & GORDON

64	Columbia DB 7225	A World Without Love/If I Were You	5
64	Columbia DB 7292	Nobody I Know/You Don't Have To Tell Me	5
64	Columbia DB 7356	I Don't Want To See You Again/I Would Buy	6
64	Columbia DB 7407	I Go To Pieces/Love Me Baby	6
65	Columbia DB 7524	True Love Ways/If You Wish	5
65	Columbia DB 7617	To Know You Is To Love You/I Told You So	5
65	Columbia DB 7729	Baby I'm Yours/When The Black Of Your Eyes Turns To Grey	5
66	Columbia DB 7834	Woman/Wrong From The Start	6
66	Columbia DB 7951	Don't Pity Me/To Show I Love You	6
66	Columbia DB 8003	Lady Godiva/Morning's Calling	6
66	Columbia DB 8075	Knight In Rusty Armour/The Flower Lady	6
67	Columbia DB 8159	Sunday For Tea/Start Trying Someone Else	6
67	Columbia DB 8198	The Jokers/Red, Cream And Velvet	6
68	Columbia DB 8398	I Feel Like Going Out/The Quest For The Holy Grail	6
68	Columbia DB 8451	You've Had Better Times/Sipping My Wine	6
69	Columbia DB 8585	I Can Remember (Not Too Long Ago)/Hard Time, Rainy Day	6
64	Columbia SEG 8337	JUST FOR YOU (EP, 2 tracks by Freddie & Dreamers)	18
64	Columbia SEG 8348	NOBODY I KNOW (EP)	25
64	Columbia 33SX 1630	PETER AND GORDON (LP, also stereo SCX 3518)	18/25
64	Columbia 33SX 1660	IN TOUCH WITH PETER AND GORDON (LP, also stereo SCX 3532)	18/25
65	Columbia 33SX 1761	HURTIN 'N' LOVIN' (LP, also stereo SCX 3565)	18/25
66	Columbia S(C)X 6045	PETER AND GORDON (LP, mono/stereo)	30/35
66	Columbia S(C)X 6097	SOMEWHERE... (LP, mono/stereo)	18/25
65	Columbia SCXC 25	I GO TO PIECES (LP, export issue)	50
66	Columbia SCXC 29	WOMAN (LP, export issue)	50
66	Columbia SCXC 33	LADY GODIVA (LP, export issue)	60

(see also Gordon Waller)

PETER & HEADLINES

64	Decca F 11980	Don't Cry Little Girl/It Was Love	12
64	Decca F 12035	Tears And Kisses/I've Got My Reasons	12

(see also Count Downe & Zeros)

PETER & PAUL

66	Blue Beat BB 364	Hosana/Schoolgirl	12

PETER & PAVEL

68	Page One POF 112	Laska/Wenceslas Square	4

PETER & PERSUADERS

65	Oak RGJ 197	The Wanderer/Wine Glass Rock/Oh My Soul/Cross My Heart (EP)	25

(see Legendary Lonnie)

PETER & TEST TUBE BABIES

81	No Future OI 4	Banned From The Pubs/Moped Lads/Peacehaven Wild Lads (p/s)	10
82	No Future OI 15	Run Like Hell/Up Yer Bum (p/s)	10
83	Trapper EARS 1	Zombie Creeping Flesh/No Invitation/Smash And Grab (p/s)	8
83	Trapper 12 EARS 1	Zombie Creeping Flesh/No Invitation/Smash And Grab (12", p/s)	8
83	Trapper EARS 2	The Jinx/Trapper Ain't Got A Bird (p/s)	8
83	Trapper 12 EARS 2	The Jinx/Trapper Ain't Got A Bird (12", p/s)	8
84	Trapper EARFIT 1	Pressed For Cash/Blown Out Again (Blender Version)/FITS: Peace And Quiet But Never Dreamed It Was Going To Be Like This (12", p/s)	8
85	Jungle JUNG 21T	ROTTING IN THE FART-SACK (12" EP, white vinyl)	10
85	Trapper EARS 3	Whimpeez/Never Made It (p/s)	5
86	Hairy Pie TTB 1	Keys To The City/Keith Moon (p/s)	5
86	Hairy Pie TTB 121	Keys To The City/Keith Moon/Work Hard (12", p/s)	7
82	No Future Punk 3	PISSED AND PROUD (LP)	15
83	Trapper THIN 1	MATING SOUNDS OF SOUTH AMERICAN FROGS (LP, with lyric inner)	15

PETER & WOLVES

67	MGM MGM 1352	Little Girl Lost And Found/Is Me	10
68	MGM MGM 1374	Lanternlight/Break Up-Break Down	10
68	MGM MGM 1397	Julie/Birthday	8
70	UPC UPC 104	Something In The Way She Moves/The Lady And Me	6

(see also Factory, Norman Conquest, John Pantry, Sounds Around, Bunch)

PETER B's

66	Columbia DB 7862	If You Wanna Be Happy/Jodrell Blues	50

(see also Tony Colton, Peter Bardens, Peter Green, Cheynes, Shotgun Express)

PETER, JAN & JOHN

65	HMV POP 1442	Mountain Boy/I'm Lookin' Out	4

PETER, PAUL & MARY

63	Warner Bros WB 95	Puff (The Magic Dragon)/Pretty Mary	5
63	Warner Bros WSE 6119	MOVING (EP, stereo)	8
63	Warner Bros WSE 6122	PETER, PAUL AND MARY (EP, stereo)	8
63	Warner Bros WM 4064	PETER, PAUL AND MARY (LP, also stereo WS 9064)	12
63	Warner Bros WM/WS 8124	MOVING (LP)	12
64	Warner Bros WM/WS 8142	IN THE WIND (LP)	12
65	Warner Bros WM/WS 8158	IN CONCERT VOL. 1 (LP)	12
65	Warner Bros WM/WS 8159	IN CONCERT VOL. 2 (LP)	12
65	Warner Bros (W)S 1589	A SONG WILL RISE (LP)	12
66	Warner Bros (W)S 1615	SEE WHAT TOMORROW BRINGS (LP)	12
66	Warner Bros W(S) 1648	PETER, PAUL & MARY ALBUM (LP)	12
67	Warner Bros W(S) 1700	ALBUM 1700 (LP)	12
68	Warner Bros W(S) 1751	LATE AGAIN (LP)	12

PETER ROSS OLIVER

68	Pro PRO 101	THREE'S COMPANY (LP, private pressing)	10

(see also Luvvers)

MINT VALUE £

PETER'S FACES
64	Piccadilly 7N 35178	Why Did You Bring Him To The Dance/She's In Love	8
64	Piccadilly 7N 35196	Try A Little Love My Friend/I Don't Care	8
64	Piccadilly 7N 35205	Wait/Just Like Romeo And Juliet	12
65	Piccadilly 7N 35225	De-Boom-Lay-Boom/Suzie Q	7

(see also Flowerpot Men, White Plains)

JANICE PETERS & PLAYBOYS
58	Columbia DB 4222	This Little Girl's Gone Rockin'/Kiss Cha Cha	30
58	Columbia DB 4222	This Little Girl's Gone Rockin'/Kiss Cha Cha (78)	30
59	Columbia DB 4276	A Girl Likes/You're The One	25
59	Columbia DB 4276	A Girl Likes/You're The One (78)	40

LENNIE PETERS
63	Oriole CB 1887	And My Heart Cried/For A Lifetime	7
64	Oriole CB 1956	Let The Tears Begin/Love Me, Love Me	7

LINDA PETERS
70	Warlock Music WMM 101/2	WARLOCK MUSIC SAMPLER (LP, sampler, 7 tracks by Elton John)	1,000

(see also Paul McNeill & Linda Peters, Richard & Linda Thompson)

MARK PETERS & SILHOUETTES
63	Oriole CB 1836	Fragile (Handle With Care)/Janie	18
64	Oriole CB 1909	Cindy's Gonna Cry/Show Her	18
64	Piccadilly 7N 35207	Don't Cry For Me/I Told You So	10

(see also Rats)

WENDY PETERS
68	Saga OPP 1	Morning Dew/I Don't Understand	12

PAUL PETERSEN
62	Pye International 7N 25153	Keep Your Love Locked/Be Everything To Anyone You Love	6
62	Pye International 7N 25163	Lollipops And Roses/Please Mr Sun	6
63	Pye International 7N 25173	My Dad/Little Boy Sad	6
63	Pye International 7N 25196	Amy/Goody Goody	6
68	Tamla Motown TMG 670	A Little Bit For Sandy/Your Love's Got Me Burnin' Alive	20

PAUL PETERSEN & SHELLEY FABARES
62	Pye International 7N 25133	She Can't Find Her Keys/Very Unlikely	8

(see also Shelley Fabares)

BOBBY PETERSON (QUINTET)
59	Top Rank JAR 232	The Hunch/Love You Pretty Baby (as Bobby Peterson Quintet)	18
64	Sue WI 342	Rockin' Charlie (Parts 1 & 2) (solo)	18
65	Sue WI 346	Piano Rock/One Day (solo)	18

OSCAR PETERSON
57	HMV POP 366	Soft Sands/Echoes	5
60	HMV POP 706	Jive At Five/Blues For Basie	5
61	HMV POP 850	Woody 'N' You/Liza	5
55	Columbia Clef SEB 10005	OSCAR PETERSON (EP)	8
56	Columbia Clef SEB 10022	OSCAR PETERSON NO. 2 (EP)	8
55	Columbia 33C 1037	PLAYS PRETTY (10" LP)	40
55	Columbia 33C 9012	PLAYS PRETTY (10" LP, reissue)	12
55	Columbia 33C 1038	THE OSCAR PETERSON QUARTET (10" LP)	15
55	Columbia Clef 33C 9013	THE OSCAR PETERSON QUARTET (10" LP, reissue)	15
55	Columbia 33C 1039	OSCAR PETERSON SINGS (10" LP)	15
55	Columbia Clef 33C 9014	OSCAR PETERSON SINGS (10" LP, reissue)	12
55	Columbia Clef 33CX 10012	PLAYS DUKE ELLINGTON (LP)	18
55	Columbia Clef 33CX 10016	PLAYS COLE PORTER (LP)	12
55	Columbia Clef 33CX 10028	PLAYS RICHARDS RODGERS (LP)	35
55	Columbia Clef 33CX 10039	PLAYS COUNT BASIE (LP)	12
56	Columbia Clef 33C 9025	O LADY BE GOOD (10" LP)	25
56	HMV CLP 1086	IN ROMANTIC MOOD (LP)	12
57	Columbia Clef 33CX 10062	KEYBOARD (LP)	12
57	Columbia Clef 33CX 10073	PLAYS HAROLD ARLEN (LP)	12
58	Columbia Clef 33CX 10096	STRATFORD (CANADA SHAKESPEAREAN FESTIVAL) (LP)	12
59	Columbia Clef 33CX 10135	A NIGHT ON THE TOWN (LP)	12
59	HMV CLP 1278	THE OSCAR PETERSON TRIO SWINGS "MY FAIR LADY" (LP)	12
59	HMV CLP 1317	OSCAR PETERSON AT THE CONCERTGEBOUW (LP)	12
60	HMV CLP 1355	JAZZ PORTRAIT OF SINATRA (LP)	12
60	HMV CLP 1403/CSD 1326	SWINGING BRASS (LP)	12
61	HMV CLP 1429	THE JAZZ SOUL OF OSCAR PETERSON (LP)	12
62	HMV CLP 1563	WEST SIDE STORY (LP)	12
63	Verve VLP 9052	NIGHT TRAIN (LP)	12

(see also Louis Armstrong, Lester Young, Ella Fitzgerald, Sonny Stitt)

RAY PETERSON
59	RCA RCA 1131	The Wonder Of You/I'm Gone	10
59	RCA RCA 1131	The Wonder Of You/I'm Gone (78)	40
59	RCA RCA 1154	Shirley Purley/Come And Get It	15
59	RCA RCA 1154	Shirley Purley/Come And Get It (78)	60
60	RCA RCA 1175	Answer Me/Goodnight My Love, Pleasant Dreams	10
60	RCA RCA 1195	Tell Laura I Love Her/Wedding Day	8
60	London HLX 9246	Corrine, Corrina/Be My Girl	10
61	London HLX 9332	Sweet Little Kathy/You Didn't Care	8
61	London HLX 9379	Missing You/You Thrill Me	7
62	London HLX 9489	I Could Have Loved You So Well/Why Don't You Write Me	10
62	London HLX 9569	You Didn't Care/You Know Me Much Too Well	7
63	London HLX 9746	Without Love/Give Us Your Blessing	8
64	MGM MGM 1249	Oh No/If You Were Here	5

64	MGM MGM 1258	Across The Street/When I Stop Dreaming	5
65	MGM MGM 1273	House Without Windows/Wish I Could Say No To You	5
65	MGM MGM 1288	I'm Only Human/One Lonesome Rose	5
66	MGM MGM 1303	Everybody/Love Hurts	5
61	London REX 1293	CORRINE CORRINA (EP)	75

PETER, SUE & MARC & PFURI, GORPS & KNIRL

| 79 | EMI EMI 2940 | Second Hand Company/Troedler & Co | 6 |

PETEY, PATTY, PEGGY & BRUCE

| 59 | Top Rank JAR 250 | The Happy Penguins/IRVING KRASE ORCHESTRA: The Happy Penguin Waltz | 5 |

PET HATE

| 84 | Heavy Metal HMRLP 23W | BAD PUBLICITY (LP, white vinyl) | 12 |

(see also Silverwing)

PETITES

| 60 | Philips PB 1035 | Get Your Daddy's Car Tonight/Sun Showers | 7 |

MARY PETTI

| 61 | RCA RCA 1239 | Hey! Lawdy Lawdy/Gee, But It Hurts | 35 |

PETS

58	London HL 8652	Cha-Hua-Hua/Cha-Kow-Ski	20
58	London HL 8652	Cha-Hua-Hua/Cha-Kow-Ski (78)	20
59	Pye International 7N 25004	(You Wandered) Beyond The Sea/Wow-ee!!!	7
59	Pye International N 25004	(You Wandered) Beyond The Sea/Wow-ee!!! (78)	10

(see also Seph Acre & Pets)

PET SHOP BOYS

SINGLES

84	Epic A 4292	West End Girls/Pet Shop Boys (p/s)	35
84	Epic TA 4292	West End Girls (Extended)/Pet Shop Boys (12", p/s)	50
85	Parlophone R 6097 (matrix: A-3-1-2)	Opportunities (Let's Make Lots of Money)/In The Night (1st mix, white p/s)	25
85	Parlophone 12R 6097	Opportunities (Let's Make Lots of Money) (Dance Mix)/In The Night (Extended) (12", white p/s)	40
85	Parlophone 12RA 6097	Opportunities (Let's Make Lots of Money) (Version Latina)/(Dub For Money Remix)/In The Night (Extended Mix) (12", large picture labels, die-cut p/s)	80
85	Parlophone 12R 6097	Opportunities (Let's Make Lots of Money) (Dance Mix)/In The Night (Extended) (12", p/s, mispressing, B-side plays "Opportunities [Dub For Money Remix]")	50
85	Parlophone 12R 6097	Opportunities (Let's Make Lots of Money) (Dance Mix)/In The Night (Extended) (12", p/s, 2nd mispressing, A-side plays "Opportunities [Version Latina]")	50
85	Parlophone R 6115	West End Girls/A Man Could Get Arrested (4.36 Mix) (glossy p/s)	6
85	Parlophone 10R 6115	West End Girls (Untitled Mix)/A Man Could Get Arrested (4.09 Mix)/West End Girls (7" Mix) (10", foldout round p/s some sealed; some stickered)	75/65/60
85	Parlophone 12R 6115	West End Girls (Dance Mix)/A Man Could Get Arrested (4.36 Mix)/West End Girls (7" Mix) (12", standard p/s, standard labels)	10
85	Parlophone 12R 6115	West End Girls (Dance Mix)/A Man Could Get Arrested (4.09 Mix)/West End Girls (7" Mix) (12", 4" die-cut hole in front or front & back of p/s, 4" picture labels)	10
85	Parlophone 12R 6115	West End Girls (Dance Mix)/A Man Could Get Arrested (4.09 Mix)/West End Girls (7" Mix) (12", with 6" die-cut holes in p/s, 6" picture labels)	12
86	Parlophone 12RA 6115	West End Girls (Shep Pettibone Mastermix)/West End Dub/A Man Could Get Arrested (4.09 Mix) (12", black/blue/red p/s, standard labels)	18
86	Parlophone 12RA 6115	West End Girls (Shep Pettibone Mastermix)/West End Dub/A Man Could Get Arrested (4.09 Mix) (12", same as above with 6" yellow circle on sleeve)	18
86	Parlophone 12RA 6115	West End Girls (Shep Pettibone Mastermix)/West End Dub/A Man Could Get Arrested (4.09 Mix) (12", stickered black/blue/red p/s with 6" die-cut hole & 6" yellow picture labels)	18
86	Parlophone R 6116	Love Comes Quickly/That's My Impression (glossy p/s)	5
86	Parlophone 10R 6116	Love Comes Quickly (Dance Mix)/That's My Impression (Disco Mix) (10", PVC sleeve with poster)	80
86	Parlophone 12R 6116	Love Comes Quickly (Dance Mix)/That's My Impression (Disco Mix) (12", standard p/s)	12
86	Parlophone 12R 6116	Love Comes Quickly (Dance Mix)/That's My Impression (Disco Mix) (12", large picture labels, die-cut white sleeve)	20
86	Parlophone R 6129	Opportunities (Let's Make Lots of Money)/Was That What It Was (p/s)	4
86	Parlophone 12R 6129	Opportunities (Let's Make Lots of Money) (7.18 Shep Pettibone Mastermix)/Opportunities (4.27 Reprise)/Opportunities (6.44 Original Dance Mix)/Was That What It Was (12", stickered silver title sleeve)	15
86	Parlophone R 6140	Suburbia/Paninaro (p/s)	4
86	Parlophone RD 6140	Suburbia/Paninaro//Love Comes Quickly (Shep Pettibone Remix)/Jack The Lad/Suburbia Part Two (double pack, gatefold p/s)	18
86	Parlophone TR 6140	Suburbia/Paninaro/Jack The Lad/Love Comes Quickly (Shep Pettibone Remix) (cassette)	12
86	Parlophone TR 6140	Suburbia/Paninaro/Jack The Lad/Love Comes Quickly (Shep Pettibone Remix) (cassette, mispressed with TCR 6140 tracks)	15
86	Parlophone TCR 6140	Suburbia (The Full Horror)/Paninaro/Jack The Lad/Love Comes Quickly (Shep Pettibone Remix) (cassette)	12
86	Parlophone 12R 6140	Suburbia (The Full Horror)/Paninaro/Jack The Lad (12", p/s, some with inner sleeve)	10/8
87	Parlophone RS 6158	It's A Sin/You Know Where You Went Wrong (p/s, with inner sleeve)	8
87	Parlophone TCR 6158	It's A Sin (7" version)/You Know Where You Went Wrong/It's A Sin (Disco Mix) (cassette)	8
87	Parlophone 12R 6158	It's A Sin (Disco Mix)/You Know Where You Went Wrong (7" Version) (12", p/s with inner sleeve)	15
87	Parlophone 12RX 6158	It's A Sin (Ian Levine Remix)/You Know Where You Went Wrong (Rough Mix) (12", 'video still' p/s)	15

PET SHOP BOYS

87	Parlophone CDR 6158	It's A Sin (7" Version)/You Know Where You Went Wrong/ It's A Sin (Disco Mix) (CD, card sleeve)........................... 18
87	Parlophone TCR 6163	What Have I Done To Deserve This? (Extended Mix) (with Dusty Springfield)/ A New Life/What Have I Done To Deserve This? (Disco Mix) (cassette)........ 8
87	Parlophone CDR 6163	What Have I Done To Deserve This? (Extended Mix) (with Dusty Springfield)/ A New Life/What Have I Done To Deserve This? (Disco Mix) (CD, card sleeve)... 18
87	Parlophone TCR 6168	Rent (Extended Mix)/Rent (Dub)/I Want A Dog (cassette)................. 8
87	Parlophone 12R 6168	Rent (Extended Mix)/Rent (Dub)/I Want A Dog (12", p/s)................ 10
87	Parlophone CDR 6168	Rent (Extended Mix)/Rent (Dub)/I Want A Dog (CD, card sleeve)............ 18
87	Parlophone RS 6171	Always On My Mind/Do I Have To? (p/s, with inner sleeve)................ 7
87	Parlophone TCR 6171	Always On My Mind (Extended Dance Mix)/Do I Have To?/ Always On My Mind (Edit) (cassette)........................... 8
87	Parlophone 12RS 6171	Always On My Mind (Extended Dance Mix)/Do I Have To?/ Always On My Mind (Edit) (12", p/s with inner sleeve).................. 15
87	Parlophone 12RX 6171	Always On My Mind (Phil Harding Remix)/Do I Have To?/ Always On My Mind (Dub) (12", title sleeve)...................... 15
87	Parlophone CDR 6171	Always On My Mind (Extended Dance Version)/Do I Have To?/ Always On My Mind (Edit) (CD)........................... 20
88	Parlophone R 6177	Heart/I Get Excited (You Get Excited Too) ('Neil' or 'Chris' p/s)........... each 4
88	Parlophone TCR 6177	Heart (Disco Mix)/I Get Excited (You Get Excited Too)/Heart (Dance Mix) (cassette).................................. 8
88	Parlophone 12R 6177	Heart (Disco Mix)/I Get Excited (You Get Excited Too)/Heart (Dance Mix) (12", 'Neil' or 'Chris' p/s)........................... each 8
88	Parlophone 12RX 6177	Heart (Julian Mendelssohn Remix)/Heart (Dub Mix)/I Get Excited (You Get Excited Too) (12", p/s).......................... 12
88	Parlophone CDR 6177	Heart (Disco Mix)/I Get Excited (You Get Excited Too)/Heart (Dance Mix) (CD, card sleeve)............................. 18
88	Parlophone TCR 6190	Domino Dancing (Disco Mix)/Don Juan (Disco Mix)/Domino Dancing (Alternative Mix) (cassette)........................... 8
88	Parlophone 12RS 6190	Domino Dancing (Disco Mix)/Don Juan (Disco Mix)/Domino Dancing (Alternative Mix) (12", 'van' p/s with inner sleeve)............... 8
88	Parlophone 12RX 6190	Domino Dancing (Remix)/Don Juan (Demo)/Domino Dancing (Demo) (12", 'hotel' p/s)............................. 20
88	Parlophone CDR 6190	Domino Dancing (Disco Mix)/Don Juan (Disco Mix)/Domino Dancing (Alternative Mix) (CD, card sleeve with inner)................. 20
88	Parlophone TCR 6198	Left To My Own Devices/Left To My Own Devices (The Disco Mix)/ The Sound Of The Atom Splitting (cassette, with outer slip case)......... 8
88	Parlophone 12RS 6198	Left To My Own Devices (The Disco Mix)/Left To My Own Devices/ The Sound Of The Atom Splitting (12", p/s with inner sleeve)........... 10
88	Parlophone CDR 6198	Left To My Own Devices/Left To My Own Devices (The Disco Mix)/ The Sound Of The Atom Splitting (CD, yellow card p/s, some with inner) 20/15
89	Parlophone RS 6220	It's Alright/One Of The Crowd/Your Funny Uncle (p/s, with wraparound strip) 4
89	Parlophone TCR 6220	It's Alright/One Of The Crowd/Your Funny Uncle (cassette)................. 5
89	Parlophone 10R 6220	It's Alright (Alternative Mix)/It's Alright (Extended Dance Mix) (10", black title sleeve with poster)..................... 15
89	Parlophone 12RS 6220	It's Alright (Extended)/One Of The Crowd/Your Funny Uncle (12", p/s, with Obi)........................... 8
89	Parlophone 12RX 6220	It's Alright (The Tyree Mix)/It's Alright (The Sterling Void Mix) (12", p/s)........ 12
89	Parlophone CDR 6220	It's Alright (Seven Inch Vocal)/One Of The Crowd/Your Funny Uncle/ It's Alright (Extended Version) (CD, card sleeve)................. 12
90	Parlophone 12RX 6269	So Hard (7" Mix)/So Hard/It Must Be Obvious (UFO Mix) (CD, card sleeve)............................. 8
90	Parlophone CDR 6275	Being Boring/We All Feel Better In The Dark/Being Boring (Extended Mix) (CD)................................ 15
91	Parlophone CDR 6283	Jealousy (7" Version)/Lose My Mind (Disco Mix)/Jealousy (Extended Mix) (CD) .. 12
91	Parlophone CDRS 6283	Jealousy (Extended Version)/This Must Be The Place I Waited Years To Leave (Extended Mix)/So Hard (Eclipse Mix) (CD, gatefold digipak)............. 22
91	Parlophone TCRX 6301	DJ Culturemix (Grid Remix)/Music For Boys Part 3/ Overture To Performance (cassette)....................... 5
91	Parlophone 12RX 6301	DJ Culturemix (Grid Remix)/Music For Boys Part 3/ Overture To Performance (12", p/s)....................... 7
91	Parlophone CDRX 6301	DJ Culturemix (Grid Remix)/Music For Boys Part 3/ Overture To Performance (CD)......................... 20
93	Parlophone R 6348	Can You Forgive Her? (7" Version)/Hey Headmaster (red vinyl, factory custom pressing, p/s)....................... 500
93	Parlophone 12R 6348	Can You Forgive Her? (MK Remix)/Can You Forgive Her? (MK Dub) (12", p/s) ... 10
93	Parlophone CDRS 6348	Can You Forgive Her? (MK Remix)/I Want To Wake Up (1993 Remix)/ What Keeps Mankind Alive/Can You Forgive Her? (MK Dub) (CD, with wallet) ... 15
93	Parlophone CDRS 6370	I Wouldn't Normally Do This Kind Of Thing (LP Version)/Too Many People/ Violence (Hacienda Version)/West End Girls (Sasha Remix) (CD, PVC pack) 12
93	Parlophone CDRS 6386	Yesterday When I Was Mad (Coconut 1 Remix)/If Love Were All)/ Can You Forgive Her? (Swing Version)/Yesterday When I Was Mad (Jam & Spoon Mix) (CD, card sleeve)................... 12
93	Parlophone CDR 6386	Yesterday When I Was Mad (Coconut 1 Remix)/Junior Vasquez Factory Dub)/ (R.A.F. Zone Dub)/Some Speculation (CD, card sleeve)............. 15
95	Parlophone 12RX 6614	Paninaro '95 — The Remixes Part 1 (Tracy's 12" Mix)/(Sharon's Sexy Boyz Dub)/ (Tin Tin Out Mix)/(Pet Shop Boys Extended Mix) (12", 'Neil' p/s)......... 15
95	Parlophone 12R 6614	Paninaro '95 — The Remixes Part 2 (Angel Morales Dub Dance Mix)/ (Angel Morales Girls Boys In Dub)/(Angel Morales The Hot 'N' Spycy Dub) (12", 'Chris' p/s)........................... 15
96	Parlophone 12RX 6431	Before (Underground Mix)/(Bonus Dub)/(Underground Instrumental)/ (Bonus Beats)/(Classic Paradise Mix)/(Afrodisiac Mix)/(Hedboys Mix)/ (Hedboys Dub)/(Joey Negro Extended Mix) (3 x 12", each in p/s, box set) 25
96	Parlophone 12RD 6443	Se A Vida É (That's The Way Life Is) (Mark's Deep And Dark Vocal)/ (Mark's Deep And Dark Instrumental)/(Mark's Shelter Dub)/ (Deep Dish Liquid Remix)/(Pink Noise Mix)/(Deep Dish Dub)/(7" Version) (12", double pack, yellow & green vinyl, p/s, 2 inner sleeves)............. 15

PET SHOP BOYS

ALBUMS

87	Parlophone PCSDX 104	ACTUALLY (LP, with U.S. import "Always On My Mind" 12", stickered sleeve) . . . 12
87	Parlophone PCSDX 104	ACTUALLY (cassette, with U.S. import "Always On My Mind" cassette) 10
87	Parlophone CDPCSDX 104	ACTUALLY (CD, with U.S. import "Always On My Mind" CD single). 35
88	Parlophone PCSX 7325	INTROSPECTIVE (LP, 3 x clear vinyl 12" factory custom pressing, with wraparound paper strip, 10 copies only). 450
93	Parlophone CDPSDX 143	VERY (CD, with 6-track bonus CD "Relentless" in foldout 'bubble' wallet) 45

PROMOS

85	Parlophone R 12R 6097	Opportunities (Let's Make Lots of Money)/In The Night (12", "photocopy" sl.) . . . 50
85	Parlophone R 6097 (matrix: A-1U-1-1-1)	Opportunities (Let's Make Lots of Money) (New Mix)/In The Night (2nd mix, stickered plain sleeve). 100
86	Parlophone R 6116	Love Comes Quickly (1-sided, p/s) 75
86	Parlophone 12R 6129	Opportunities (Let's Make Lots of Money) (7.18 Shep Pettibone Mastermix)/ Opportunities (4.27 Reprise)/Opportunities (6.44 Original Dance Mix)/ Was That What It Was (12", autographed black die-cut sleeve, some with press release) 45/40
86	Parlophone 12R 6140	Suburbia (The Full Horror)/Paninaro/Jack The Lad (12", blank red labels) 20
88	Parlophone 12RDJ 6198	Left To My Own Devices (The Disco Mix)/Left To My Own Devices/ The Sound Of The Atom Splitting (12", unique title sleeve) 25
90	Parlophone 12RXDJ 6275	Being Boring (Remix)/We All Feel Better In The Dark (After Hours Climax)/ We All Feel Better In The Dark (Ambient) (12", black die-cut sleeve). 15
91	Parlophone 12R 6283A	Lose My Mind (Disco Version) (12", 1-sided, no p/s) 15
91	Parlophone 12RDJ 6301A	D.J. Culture (12", 1-sided, no p/s) 15
91	Parlophone MFB 1	Music For Boys (12", 3 untitled mixes, hand-stamped white label, no p/s) 45
91	Parlophone 12MFBX 1	Music For Boys (12", 2 untitled mixes, white label, no p/s) 25
92	Parlophone CDRX 6332	Go West (7" Version)/West End Girls (Sacha Mix)/Forever/Go West (Extended Dance Mix) (cassette, title sleeve) 250
93	Parlophone 12RXDJ 6348	Can You Forgive Her? (MK Remix)/(MK Bicycle Dub)/I Want To Wake Up (Johnny Marr 1993 Remix)/(Johnny Marr Groove Mix) (12", no p/s). 40
93	Parlophone 12RDJ 6348	Can You Forgive Her (Rollo Remix)/(Rollo Dub) (12", no p/s) 12
93	Abbey Road	COMPILED EP (CD-R, Abbey Road title sleeve; autographed by The Boys, 20 only) 1000
94	Parlophone 12RDJ 6386	Yesterday When I Was Mad (Jam & Spoon Mix)/(Junior Vasquez Factory Dub)/ (Junior Vasquez Fabulous Dub)/(Junior Vasquez Body Dub)/(Coconut 12" Mix)/ (RAF Zone Mix)/(RAF Zone Dub)/Euroboy/Some Speculation (12", double pack, unique p/s) 30
95	Parlophone RLH 6414	Paninaro '95/In The Night (jukebox issue, no p/s). 10
95	Parlophone 12RDJX 6614	Paninaro '95 — The Remixes Part 1 (Tracy's 12" Mix)/(Sharon's Sexy Boyz Dub)/ (Tin Tin Out Mix)/(Pet Shop Boys Extended Mix) (12", 'close-ups' p/s) 12
95	Parlophone 12RDJ 6614	Paninaro '95 — The Remixes Part 2 (Angel Morales Dub Dance Mix)/ (Angel Morales Girls Boys In Dub)/(Angel Morales The Hot 'N' Spycy Dub) (12", different 'close-ups' p/s) 12
96	Parlophone RLH 6431	Before/The Truck Driver And His Mate (jukebox issue, no p/s) 10
96	Parlophone 12RDJD 6431	Before (Classic Paradise Mix)/(Afrodisiac Mix)/(Hedboys Mix)/ (Dub)/(Extended Mix) (2 x 12", blue 'penis' p/s) 45
96	Parlophone 12RJD 6431	Before (Underground Mix)/(Bonus Dub)/(Underground Instrumental)/ (Bonus Beats) (12", red 'penis' p/s) 35
96	Parlophone CDRDJ 6431	Before/The Truck Driver & His Mate/Hit & Miss/In The Night 1995 (CD, slimline jewel case) 10
96	Parlophone 12RDJS 6443	Se A Vida É (That's The Way Life Is) (Mark Picchiotti's Deep And Dark Vocal)/ (Mark Picchiotti's Shelter Deep And Dark Instrumental)/ (Mark Picchiotti's Shelter Dub) (12", purple p/s). 12

PET SHOP BOYS

Year	Label/Cat. No.	Title	Value
96	Parlophone 12RDJ 6443	Se A Vida É (That's The Way Life Is) (Deep Dish Liquid Remix)/(Pink Noise Mix)/(Deep Dish Dub)/(Radio Mix) (12", yellow vinyl, p/s)	15
97	Parlophone 12 BARDJ 2	The Truck Driver & His Mate/Before (Love To Infinity Classic Paradise Mix) (12", nasty 'two knobs' p/s, 150 copies)	125
97	Parlophone 12RDJ 6460	A Red Letter Day (Trouser Enthusiasts Autoerotic Decapitation Mix)/(Trouser Enthusiasts Congo Dongo Dubstramental) (12", no p/s)	10
97	Parlophone 12RDJX 6460	A Red Letter Day (Basement Jaxx Vocal Mix)/(Motiv8 Cyber Dub Mix)/The Boy Who Couldn't Keep His Clothes On (On Stage At Twilo) (12", no p/s)	10
97	Parlophone 12RDJZ 6460	A Red Letter Day (Motiv8 Twelve-Inch Master Mix)/(Basement Jaxx Nite Dub)/(PSB Extended Edit)/The Boy Who Couldn't Keep His Clothes On (The Far & Away Dub) (12", no p/s)	10
97	Parlophone 12BOYDJ 101	The Boy Who Couldn't Keep His Clothes On (Main Vocal)/(INT... Club Mix)/(Banji Girlfriend Beats)/(On Stage At Twilo)/(Radio Edit) (12", die-cut sleeve)	65
97	Parlophone CDRDJ 6460	A Red Letter Day/The Boy Who Couldn't Keep His Clothes On (CD, card p/s)	10
97	Parlophone 12RDJX 6452	Discoteca (Baby Doc Mix)/Single-Bilingual (Baby Doc Mix)/Single-Bilingual (Baby Doc Mix) (Original Baby Doc Mix) (12", yellow title p/s)	15
97	Parlophone 12RDJ 6452	Discoteca (Pet Shop Boys Extended Mix)/Discoteca (Trouser Enthusiasts Adventures Beyond The Stellar Empire Mix) (12", green title p/s)	12
97	Parlophone 12RDJD 6470	Somewhere (Forthright Club Mix)/(Trouser Enthusiasts Mix)/To Step Aside (Brutal Bill Mix)/Somewhere (Forthright Dub)/To Step Aside (Ralphi's Old School Dub)/To Step Aside (Davidson Ospina Dub) (12" double pack, title p/s)	25
99	Parlophone 12 RDJX 6523	I Don't Know What You Want (6 mixes) (2 x 12", gatefold p/s)	25
99	Parlophone 12 CDRDJX 6523	I Don't Know What You Want (7 mixes) (CD, double card sleeve)	75
99	Parlophone 12 RDJD 6533	You Only Tell Me You Love Me When You're Drunk (Brother Brown's Mix)/(Attaboy Mix)/(T-Total Mix)/(Brother Brown's Dub) (12", p/s)	25
99	Parlophone 12 CDRDJ 6533	You Only Tell Me You Love Me When You're Drunk (1-track CD, card sleeve)	10
99	Parlophone 12 CDRDJ Y6533	You Only Tell Me You Love Me When You're Drunk (Brother Brown's Newt Mix) (1-track CD, card sleeve)	55
99	Parlophone 12 CDRDJX 6533	You Only Tell Me You Love Me When You're Drunk (5 Mixes) (CD, card sleeve)	50
99	Parlophone 12 RDJ 6525	New York City Boy (Superchumbo's Uptown Mix)/(Superchumbo's Downtown Dub) (12", p/s)	18
99	Parlophone 12 RDJX 6525	New York City Boy (Almighty Definitive Mix)/(Man On A Mission Mix) (12", p/s)	18
99	Parlophone 12 RDJY 6525	New York City Boy (Morales Mix)/(Thunderpuss 2000 Mix) (12", p/s)	18
99	Parlophone 12 RDYZ 6525	New York City Boy (Lange Mix) (1-sided 12", p/s)	20
99	Parlophone 12 RDJS 6525	NEW YORK CITY BOY (all the mixes) (4 x 12", in slip case)	70
99	Parlophone 12 CDRDJ 6525	New York City Boy (CD, card slipcase)	10
99	Parl. 12 CDRDJX 6525	NEW YORK CITY BOY (6 mixes) (CD, double card sleeve)	45
99	Parlophone (no cat. no.)	New York City Boy (Almighty Definitive Mix 8:54) (CD-R, title sleeve)	175
99	Parlophone (no cat. no.)	NIGHTLIFE (10" x 10" box in PVC slip case, contains interview CD, music CD, book, EPK & 3 photographs)	175
88	Parlophone (no cat. no.)	INTROSPECTIVE (cassette, video-style case, with lyric booklet)	75
89	Parlophone CDPCSD 113	BEHAVIOUR (CD, commercial issue, different inlay, in white monogrammed pouch, with full-album cassette & chronology)	90
91	Parlophone CDPSBDJ 1	DISCOGRAPHY (CD, with Mark Goodyear spoken-word introductions)	30
93	Parlophone DF 118	RELENTLESS (3 x 12", on pink/yellow/blue vinyl)	80
96	Parlophone BILING 1	BILINGUAL (A4 yellow box set, including "A Taste Of Bilingual" CD: [Discoteca/Electricity/A Red Letter Day/It Always Comes As A Surprise/Se A Vida É], with 2 photos & insert)	125
96	Parlophone PSBCDDJ 1	BILINGUAL (A4 pale blue launch party promo box set including "A Taste Of Bilingual" CD [Before/Se A Vida É], & album cassette, unique inlay)	250
99	Parlophone CDIN 126	INTERVIEW (CD, slipcase)	85

(see also Eighth Wonder, Dusty Springfield, Absolutely Fabulous, Cicero, Electronic, Liza Minnelli, Ian Wright)

FRANK PETTY TRIO

Year	Label/Cat. No.	Title	Value
53	MGM SP 1010	St. Louis Blues (Boogie Woogie)/Somebody Stole My Girl	15
53	MGM SP 1033	Side By Side/Who's Sorry Now	7
53	MGM SP 1038	Sugar/Sioux City Sue	7
53	MGM SP 1053	Sweet Jenny Lee/Yes Sir That's My Baby	6
54	MGM SP 1092	Loch Lomond/Pino Pantaloni	6
54	MGM SP 1112	Mr Pogo/Sunday	6

NORMAN PETTY TRIO

Year	Label/Cat. No.	Title	Value
54	HMV 7M 274	Mood Indigo/Petty's Little Polka	15
54	HMV B 10792	Mood Indigo/Petty's Little Polka (78)	10

TOM PETTY (& HEARTBREAKERS)

Year	Label/Cat. No.	Title	Value
77	Shelter WIP 6377	American Girl/Wild One Forever	5
77	Shleter WIP 6396	Anything That's Rock'n'Roll/Fooled Again (I Don't Like It)	4
77	Shleter WIP 12-6396	Anything That's Rock'n'Roll/Fooled Again (I Don't Like It) (live) (12", no p/s)	10
77	Shelter WIP 12-6403	American Girl/Luna (live) (12", no p/s)	10
80	MCA Backstreet MCA 596/ MSAM 4	Don't Do Me Like That/Century City//Something Else (live)/Stories We Could Tell (live) (double pack)	6
82	MCA MCAP 778	Refugee/Insider (picture disc)	4
85	MCA MCAT 1047	Refugee (live)/Don't Do Me Like That (live)/Here Comes My Girl/The Waiting (12", p/s)	10

(The above releases are by Tom Petty & the Heartbreakers. Those listed below are solo releases.)

Year	Label/Cat. No.	Title	Value
89	MCA MCA 1334	I Won't Back Down/The Apartment Song (no'd pack with 4 postcards)	5
89	MCA DMCAX 1334	I Won't Back Down/The Apartment Song/Don't Threat Me Like A Stranger (CD, in 6" black embossed plastic pouch)	8
89	MCA MCA 1359	Runnin' Down A Dream/Alright For Now (no'd pack with 4 postcards)	6
89	MCA DMCAX 1359	Runnin' Down A Dream/Alright For Now/Down The Line (CD, numbered envelope-shaped card pack with square polystyrene insert)	8
89	MCA MCA 1381	Free Fallin'/Love Is A Long Road (numbered gatefold p/s)	6
89	MCA DMCAX 1381	Free Fallin'/Love Is A Long Road/Free Fallin' (live) (CD, 6" gatefold hardback book sleeve with 8-page biography)	8
76	Shelter 1DJ 24A	OFFICIAL LIVE BOOTLEG (LP, with Heartbreakers, 1-sided 5-track, promo only)	35

(see also Stevie Nicks, Randy Newman, Traveling Wilburys, k.d. lang & Roy Orbison)

PEYR
(see under Theyr)

P.F.M.
73	Manticore K 43502	PHOTOS OF GHOSTS (LP, gatefold sleeve)	20
74	Manticore K 53502	THE WORLD BECAME THE WORLD (LP)	20
75	Manticore K 53506	COOK (LP)	20
76	Manticore K 53508	CHOCOLATE KINGS (LP, gatefold sleeve with lyric sheet)	18
77	Manticore K 53511	JET LAG (LP)	15

PHANTOM
| 78 | Cool Ghoul COOL 1 | Lazy Fascist/Power Dub (no p/s) | 6 |

(see also Tom Robinson, Blazing Sons)

PHANTOM CHORDS
| 92 | Camden Town GNAR 003 | Town Without Pity/She's A Bad Motorcycle (p/s, 2,000 only) | 5 |

(see also Damned)

PHANTOMS
| 61 | Palette PG 9014 | Phantom Guitar/Cachina | 15 |
| 60s | Arc ARC | GREAT GUITAR HITS (LP) | 30 |

PHARAOHS
| 58 | Decca DFE 6522 | THE PHARAOHS (EP) | 800 |
| 86 | Ace SW 116 | THE PHARAOHS (EP, reissue) | 10 |

RORY PHARE
| 88 | Parlophone RP 1 | Laughing Inside/Laughing Inside (actually by Roy Harper; p/s, promo only) | 7 |

(see also Roy Harper)

PHASE 4
66	Decca F 12327	What Do You Say About That/Think I'll Sit Down And Cry (1st issue)	12
66	Fab FAB 1	What Do You Say About That/I'm Gonna Sit Down And Cry (2nd issue)	12
67	Fab FAB 6	Man Am I Worried?/Listen To The Blues	35

(see also Mike Batt)

PHASE 5
| 70 | Polydor 2058 063 | Star Trek/Enterprise | 20 |

JAMES PHELPS
| 72 | Paramount PARA 3019 | Check Yourself/My Lover's Prayer | 8 |

PHENOMENA
85	Bronze BRO 193	Dance With The Devil/Hell On Wings (p/s)	7
85	Bronze BROX 193	Dance With The Devil (Midnight Mix)/Hell On Wings (12", p/s with poster)	10
87	Arista RIS 42	Did It All For Love/Double 6, 55, 44... (box set with insert)	5

(see also Trapeze, Whitesnake, Cozy Powell, Black Sabbath, Thin Lizzy, Budgie, A-Ha)

PHILADELPHIA SOCIETY
| 75 | Gull GULS 21 | 100 South Of Broadway (Parts 1 & 2) | 4 |

PHIL & FLINTSTONES
| 64 | Bedrock PR 5371 | Love Potion No. 9/Honey Don't (private pressing) | 45 |

PHILIP & HIS FOETUS VIBRATIONS
| 82 | Self Immol. WOMB KX 07 | Tell Me, What Is The Bane Of Your Life/Mother I've Killed The Cat (p/s) | 25 |

(see also You've Got Foetus On Your Breath, Foetus Art Terrorism, Foetus Über Frisco, Foetus Under Glass, Scraping Foetus Off The Wheel, Foetus Summertime Seaside Special)

ANTHONY PHILLIPS
78	Arista ARIST 192	We're All As We Lie/Squirrel/Sitars And Nebulous (no p/s)	10
79	Arista ARIST 252	Um & Aargh/Souvenir (p/s)	10
81	RCA RCA 102	Prelude '84/Anthem '84	8
84	Street Tunes JJ 102-12	Sally/Exocet/Women Were Watching (12", p/s)	8
88	PRT PYS 18	The Anthem From Tarka/The Rising Spring (p/s)	10
88	PRT PYD 18	The Anthem From Tarka (Single Mix)/The Rising Spring/Excerpt From Tarka (Movement 1)/(Movement 3)/The Anthem From Tarka (Ext. Single Mix) (CD)	15
79	Arista SPART 1085/AFLP 1	SIDES (LP, 1st 500 copies sealed with free LP "Private Parts & Pieces")	20
85	Cherry Red BRED 66	HARVEST OF THE HEART (LP)	10
89	Occasional (no cat. no.)	FINGER PAINTING — MISSING LINKS VOL. 1 (cass., 1,000 copies, m/order only)	10

(see also Genesis)

CONFREY PHILLIPS (TRIO)
55	Columbia DB 3664	Seventeen/Song Of The Dreamer (78)	8
56	Columbia SCM 5223	Love And Marriage/The Others I Like	5
57	Decca F 10835	Am I Going Out Of My Mind?/Afterglow	5
57	Decca F 10866	Shotgun Rock 'n' Roll/Hokey-Kokey Rock 'n' Roll (as Confrey Phillips Trio)	12
57	Decca F 10866	Shotgun Rock 'n' Roll/Hokey-Kokey Rock 'n' Roll (as Confrey Phillips Trio) (78)	12
58	Decca DFE 6518	SWINGING DOWN BROADWAY (EP)	8

EDDY/EDWIN PHILLIPS
| 76 | Charisma CB 283 | Limbo Jimbo/Change My Ways (as Eddy Phillips) | 5 |
| 85 | T-Mac UEZT 003 | Life On Earth/(Radio Mix)/(Instrumental) (12", as Edwin Phillips) | 7 |

(see also Creation, Mark Four, Spectrum)

(LITTLE) ESTHER (PHILLIPS)
62	Stateside SS 140	Release Me/Don't Feel Rained On	8
63	Ember EMB S 174	Am I That Easy To Forget/I Really Don't Want To Know (as Little Esther Phillips)	7
65	Sue WI 395	The Chains/Feel Like I Wanna Cry (as Esther Philips)	18
65	Atlantic AT 4028	And I Love Him/Shangri-La	10
65	Atlantic AT 4048	Let Me Know When It's Over/I Saw Me	10
66	Atlantic AT 4077	I Could Have Told You/Just Say Goodbye	40
66	Ember EMBS 221	Release Me/Be Honest With Me (as Little Esther Phillips)	7
66	Atlantic 584 013	When A Woman Loves A Man/Ups And Downs	6
67	Atlantic 584 062	Someone Else Is Taking My Place/When Love Comes To The Human Race	6

(Little) Esther (PHILLIPS)

67	Atlantic 584 103	And I Love Him/Shangri-La (reissue)	5
67	Atlantic 584 126	I'm Sorry/Cheater Man	5
69	Roulette RO 505	Too Late To Worry, Too Blue To Cry/I'm In The Mood For Love (Moody's Mood For Love)	5
69	Roulette RO 508	Tonight I'll Be Staying Here With You/Sweet Dreams	5
72	Atlantic K 10168	Catch Me I'm Falling/Release Me	6
72	Kudu KUS 4000	Home Is Where The Hatred Is/Til My Back Ain't Got No Bone	8
73	Kudu KUS 4002	I've Never Found A Man/Cherry Red	5
63	Ember CW 103	REFLECTIONS OF GREAT COUNTRY AND WESTERN STANDARDS (LP)	25
65	Atlantic ATL 5030	AND I LOVE HIM (LP)	40
67	Atlantic 587/588 010	ESTHER PHILLIPS SINGS (LP)	25
72	Kudu KUL 2	FROM A WHISPER TO A SCREAM (LP)	20
73	Kudu KUL 6	ALONE AGAIN, NATURALLY (LP)	12
75	Kudu KU 18	PERFORMANCE (LP)	12
76	Atlantic K 50521	CONFESSIN' THE BLUES (LP, gatefold sleeve)	12

GLENN PHILLIPS

75	Caroline C 1519	LOST AT SEA (LP)	12

GREGORY PHILLIPS

63	Pye 7N 15546	Angie/Please Believe Me	8
64	Pye 7N 15593	Everybody Knows/Closer To Me (with Remo Four)	7
64	Pye 7N 15633	Don't Bother Me/Make Sure That You're Mine	7
65	Immediate IM 004	Down In The Boondocks/That's The One	15

(see also Remo Four)

JOHN PHILLIPS

70	Stateside SS 8046	Mississippi/April Anne	6
70	Stateside-Dunhill SSL 5027	JOHN PHILLIPS: THE WOLFKING OF L.A. (LP)	18

(see also Mamas & Papas)

LESLIE PHILLIPS

59	Parlophone R 4610	The Navy Lark/The Disc	7
69	Columbia DB 8562	The Man Most Likely To/Marigold	6

MICHELLE PHILLIPS

76	A&M AMS 7250	No Love Today/Aloha Louie	5
77	A&M AMS 7340	Victim Of Romance/Lady Of Fantasy	6
77	A&M AMLS 64651	VICTIM OF ROMANCE (LP)	12

(see also Mamas & Papas)

PHIL PHILLIPS & TWILIGHTS

59	Mercury AMT 1059	Sea Of Love/Juella	25
60	Mercury AMT 1072	Take This Heart/Verdi Mae	10
60	Mercury AMT 1093	Your True Love Once More/What Will I Tell My Heart	12
61	Mercury AMT 1139	I Love To Love You/No One Else But You	15

SHAWN PHILLIPS

65	Columbia DB 7611	Hey Nelly Nelly/Solitude	8
65	Columbia DB 7699	Doesn't Anybody Know My Name?/Nobody Listens	8
65	Columbia DB 7789	Little Tin Soldier/London Town	6
66	Columbia DB 7956	Summer Came/Storms	6
67	Parlophone R 5606	Stargazer/Woman Mine	35
70	A&M AMS 819	Christmas Song/Lovely Lady	4
65	Columbia 33SX 1748	I'M A LONER (LP)	100
66	Columbia S(C)X 6006	SHAWN (LP)	60
70	A&M AMLS 978	CONTRIBUTION (LP)	12
71	A&M AMLS 2006	SECOND CONTRIBUTION (LP, with insert)	12
72	A&M AMLS 64324	COLLABORATION (LP)	12
73	A&M AMLS 64363	FACES (LP)	12
74	A&M AMLH 68278	FURTHERMORE (LP)	12
74	A&M AMLH 64402	BRIGHT WHITE (LP)	12
75	A&M AMLH 64539	DO YOU WONDER (LP)	12
76	A&M AMLH 64582	RUMPLESTILTSKIN'S RESOLVE (LP)	12
77	A&M AMLH 64650	SPACED (LP, with inner sleeve)	15

SID PHILLIPS BAND

56	HMV 7M 372	Bugle Call Rag/Memories Of You	6
56	HMV 7M 396	Rockin' Thru' The Rye/Everybody Step	6
56	HMV 7M 406	Juke Box Baby/My Honey's Lovin' Arms	6
56	HMV 7M 418	Mamma Don't Allow/Glad Rag Doll	6
56	HMV POP 269	Farewell Blues (Rock 'N' Roll Style)/It Goes Like This	5
57	HMV POP 416	The Midgets/Tropical Twilight	5
58	HMV POP 456	Varsity Drag/The Lolly Rag (78)	8
58	HMV POP 525	Happy Days Are Here Again/Nobody's Sweetheart (78)	8
59	HMV POP 549	Weekend/Enchiladas-Cha-Cha	5
59	HMV POP 549	Weekend/Enchiladas-Cha-Cha (78)	10
57	HMV 7EG 8253	DIXIELAND RAMBLINGS (EP)	18
59	HMV 7EG 8425	DIXIE SPECIAL (EP)	12
59	HMV 7EG 8461	DIXIE BEAT (EP)	12
61	HMV 7EG 8645	DIXIELAND EXPRESS (EP)	12
50s	HMV DLP 1102	HORS D'OEUVRES (10" LP)	18
50s	HMV DLP 1164	DOWN DIXIELAND HIGHWAY (10" LP)	15
50s	HMV DLP 1194	CRUISING DOWN TO DIXIE (10" LP)	12
50s	HMV DLP 1212	FLYING DOWN TO DIXIE (10" LP)	12
70	Fontana 6438 026	RHYTHM IS OUR BUSINESS (LP)	12

STU PHILLIPS

58	London HL 8673	The Champlain And St. Lawrence Line/The Priest Who Slept 100 Years	10
58	London HL 8673	The Champlain And St. Lawrence Line/The Priest Who Slept 100 Years (78)	15

MINT VALUE £

60	Pye International 7N 25062	Strangers When We Meet/BOB MERSEY ORCHESTRA: Song Of India 6
67	RCA RCA 1601	Angel Of Love/The Great El Tigre 5
59	Pye Intl. NEP 44001	STU PHILLIPS (EP). 10

TEDDY PHILLIPS & HIS ORCHESTRA
50	London L 524	Charley My Boy/Are You Kissin' Someone Else (78). 8
50	London L 686	Circus Rag/Oo-La-La Some More (78). 8
50	London L 773	Big Brown Eyes/Nevertheless (78) 8
54	London HL 8032	Ridin' To Tennessee/Alone Tonight 45
54	London HL 8032	Ridin' To Tennessee/Alone Tonight (78). 15
54	Parlophone CMSP 4	Down Boy/Meet "Miss Pippin" (export issue) 15
54	Parlophone CMSP 12	The Old Red Barn/JIMMY BLUE CREW: The Old Shoe Cobbler (export issue) . . . 15
54	Parlophone CMSP 28	Life Is Like A Slice Of Cake/One-Sided Love Affair (export issue). 15

WARREN PHILLIPS & THE ROCKETS
| 69 | Decca (S)PA 43 | WORLD OF ROCK 'N' ROLL (LP). . . . . 20 |

(see also Savoy Brown, Foghat)

WOOLF PHILLIPS & HIS ORCHESTRA
54	Melodisc M 1284	Rock, Rock, Rock/Merci Beaucoup (78). 10
54	Decca F 10416	Count Your Blessings Instead Of Sheep/Your Heart, My Heart
		(B-side with Dennis Morley — Vocal) 6

VINCE PHILPOTT & DRAGS
| 64 | Decca F 11997 | The Cramp/Eenie Meenie Miny Mo . . . . 15 |

PHILWIT & PEGASUS
70	Chapter One CHR 130	And She Came — Final Thought/Pauper's Son. 7
70	Chapter One CHR 131	And I Try/Pauper's Son. 7
70	Chapter One CHR 137	The Elephant Song/Pseudo Phoney Mixed Up Croney. 7
70	Chapter One CHSR 805	PHILWIT AND PEGASUS (LP) 30

(see also Mark Wirtz)

PHOENIX
| 69 | President PT 246 | Tour De France/Time To Go . . . . 4 |

PHOENIX
| 76 | CBS 81621 | PHOENIX (LP). . . . . 12 |
| 80 | Charisma CAS 1150 | IN FULL VIEW (LP) . . . . 12 |

(see also Argent, Kinks, Michael Des Barres)

PAT PHOENIX
| 62 | HMV POP 1030 | The Rovers Chorus/Coronation Street Monologue. . . . . 12 |

PHONES SPORTSMAN BAND
| 81 | Rather GEAR 9 | I REALLY LIKE YOU (EP) . . . . 8 |

(see also Swell Maps)

PHOTOGRAPHED BY LIGHTNING
| 86 | Fierce FRIGHT 008 | Sleep's Terminator/Winter Trees (foldaround p/s, hand-coloured labels). . . . . 30 |

PHUTURE PHANTASY
| 88 | Low Fat Vinyl LFV 1 | SLAM (12", no p/s). . . . . 15 |

PHYSICALS
| 78 | Physical PR 001 | ALL SEXED UP (EP). . . . . 6 |

(see also Maniacs)

EDITH PIAF
53	Columbia DCF 152	Soeur Anne/Misericorde (78) 20
60	Columbia DC 754	Milord/Je Sais Comment (export issue) 5
61	Columbia DB 4596	Non, Je Ne Regrette Rien/Les Amants D'Un Jour. 5
61	Columbia DB 4642	Exodus/No Regrets 5
63	Columbia DB 7149	Polichinelle/Le Billiard Electrique 5
63	Columbia SEG 8220	GREAT PIAF (EP) 8
64	Columbia SEG 8308	NON, JE NE REGRETTE RIEN (EP) 8
65	Columbia SEG 8387	QU'IL ETAIT TRISTE (EP). 8
57	Columbia SCX 5	MEA CULPA (LP) 15
60	Columbia 33SX 1276	SINCERELY ... EDITH PIAF (LP) 12
61	Columbia 33SX 1330	PIAF AT THE PARIS OLYMPIA (LP) 12

PIANO RED
52	HMV B 10244	Rockin' With Red/Red's Boogie (78) 20
52	HMV B 10246	Just Right Bounce/Hey, Good Lookin' (78) 20
52	HMV B 10316	Count The Days I'm Gone/Bouncin' With Red (78) 20
52	HMV JO 244	Rockin' With Red/Red's Boogie (78, export issue) 20
52	HMV JO 276	Layin' The Boogie/Baby What's Wrong (78, export issue). 20
52	HMV JO 296	My Gal Jo/Let's Have A Good Time (78, export issue) 20
53	HMV JO 334	Voo Doopee Doo/Everybody's Boogie (78, export issue) 20
53	HMV 7M 108	Rockin' With Red/Red's Boogie 200
64	RCA RCX 7138	RHYTHM AND BLUES VOL. 2 (EP) 40

(see also Dr. Feelgood [U.S.])

PIBLOKTO
(see under Pete Brown & Piblokto)

PICA
| 70 | Polydor 2058 056 | Take The Barriers Down/Insurance Man . . . . 6 |
| 71 | Philips 6006 129 | Rainbow Chaser/Ad Lib. . . . . 6 |

(see also Nirvana [UK])

PIC & BILL
67	Page One POF 024	All I Want Is You/It's Not You 8
67	Page One POF 037	This Is It/Nobody But My Baby 6
68	Page One POF 052	Sad World Without You/Just A Tear 8

PICADILLY LINE

67	CBS 2785	At The Third Stroke/How Could You Say You're Leaving Me	8
67	CBS 2958	Emily Small (The Huge World Thereof)/Gone Gone Gone	8
68	CBS 3595	Yellow Rainbow/Evenings With Corrina	6
68	CBS 3595	Yellow Rainbow/I Know, She Believes (reissue with different B-side)	10
68	CBS 3743	Evenings With Corrina/My Best Friend	6
67	CBS (S)BPG 63129	THE HUGE WORLD OF EMILY SMALL (LP, some with promo insert)	45

(see also Edwards Hand)

PICCADILLY STRINGS

| 61 | Piccadilly 7N 35013 | Sir Francis Drake Theme/Our House | 5 |

BUSTER PICKENS

| 60s | Heritage HLP 1008 | TEXAS PIANO (LP) | 40 |

BOBBY (BORIS) PICKETT & CRYPT-KICKERS

| 62 | London HLU 9597 | Monster Mash/Monsters' Mash Party | 12 |
| 73 | London ZGU 133 | MONSTER MASH (LP) | 18 |

DAN PICKETT

| 60s | XX MIN 710 | DAN PICKETT (EP) | 15 |

NICK PICKETT

| 72 | Warner Bros K 14156 | America/Lady Luck | 5 |
| 72 | Warner Bros K 44172 | SILVERSLEEVES (LP) | 15 |

(see also John Dummer Blues Band)

KENNY PICKETT

| 80 | F-Beat PRO 2 | Got A Gun (1-sided, promo only) | 10 |

(see also Creation)

WILSON PICKETT

63	Liberty LIB 10115	It's Too Late/I'm Gonna Love You	18
65	Atlantic AT 4036	In The Midnight Hour/I'm Not Tired	15
65	MGM MGM 1286	Let Me Be Your Boy/My Heart Belongs To You (DJ copies £80)	45
65	Atlantic AT 4052	Don't Fight It/It's All Over	10
66	Atlantic AT 4072	634-5789/That's A Man's Way	10
66	Atlantic 584 023	99 And A Half (Won't Do)/Danger Zone	7
66	Atlantic 584 039	Land Of 1000 Dances/You're So Fine	5
66	Atlantic 584 066	Mustang Sally/Three Time Loser	5
67	Atlantic 584 101	Everybody Needs Somebody To Love/Nothing You Can Do	5
67	Atlantic 584 107	New Orleans/Soul Dance III	5
67	London HLU 10146	Billy The Kid/I Don't Want No Part-Time Love (with Falcons)	7
67	Atlantic 584 130	Funky Broadway/I'm Sorry About That	5
67	Atlantic 584 142	Stag-O-Lee/I'm In Love	5
68	Atlantic 584 150	In The Midnight Hour/Danger Zone	5
68	Atlantic 584 173	That Kind Of Love/I've Come A Long Way	5
68	Atlantic 584 183	She's Looking Good/We've Got To Have Love	5
68	Atlantic 584 203	I'm A Midnight Mover/Deborah	5
68	Atlantic 584 221	I Found A True Love/For Better Or Worse	5
69	Atlantic 584 236	Hey Jude/Night Owl	5
69	Atlantic 584 261	Mini-Skirt Minnie/Back In Your Arms	5
69	Atlantic 584 281	Hey Joe/Born To Be Wild	5
70	Atlantic 584 313	You Keep Me Hangin' On/Now You See Me, Now You Don't	5
70	Atlantic 2091 005	Sugar, Sugar/Cole, Cooke And Redding	5
70	Atlantic 2091 032	(Get Me Back On Time) Engine No. 9/International Playboy	6
71	Atlantic 2091 086	Fire And Water/Don't Let The Green Grass Fool You	5
71	Atlantic 2091 124	Don't Know My Love (Parts 1 & 2)	5
72	Atlantic K 10166	Don't Let The Green Grass Fool You/Covering The Same Old Ground	5
72	Atlantic K 10181	Funk Factory/One Step Away	5
72	President PT 319	If You Need Me/I'm Gonna Love You	5
73	President PT 322	I Can't Stop/Down To My Last Heartbreak	7
65	Atlantic ATL 5037	IN THE MIDNIGHT HOUR (LP)	40
66	Atlantic 587/588 029	THE EXCITING WILSON PICKETT (LP)	25
66	Atlantic 587 032	IN THE MIDNIGHT HOUR (LP, reissue)	15
67	Atlantic 587/588 057	THE WICKED PICKETT (LP)	18
67	Atlantic 587/588 080	THE SOUND OF WILSON PICKETT (LP)	18
68	Atlantic 587/588 092	THE BEST OF WILSON PICKETT (LP)	15
68	Atlantic 587/588 107	I'M IN LOVE (LP)	18
68	Atlantic 587/588 111	MIDNIGHT MOVER (LP)	18
69	Atlantic 588 170	HEY JUDE (LP)	15
70	Atlantic 2465 002	RIGHT ON (LP)	15
70	Joy JOYS 181	IF YOU NEED ME (LP)	12
71	Atlantic 2400 026	ENGINE NO. 9 — IN PHILADELPHIA (LP)	18
72	Atlantic K 40319	DON'T KNOCK MY LOVE (LP)	12
75	RCA APL 2 0669	LIVE IN JAPAN (LP)	12

(see also Falcons)

PICKETTYWITCH

| 70 | Pye NSPL 18357 | PICKETTYWITCH (LP) | 12 |

(see also Polly Brown)

GARY PICKFORD-HOPKINS & FRIENDS

| 83 | Spartan SP 143 | Why? (The Song)/Why? (The Story) (p/s) | 8 |
| 83 | Spartan SP 143T | Why? (The Song)/Why? (The Story) (12", p/s) | 10 |

(see also Deke Leonard, Man, Andy Fairweather-Low, Alan Ross, Big Sleep, Eyes Of Blue)

PICKWICKS

64	Decca F 11901	Apple Blossom Time/I Don't Wanna Tell You Again	10
64	Decca F 11957	You're Old Enough/Hello Lady	10
65	Warner Bros WB 151	Little By Little/I Took My Baby Home	50

PICTURES FROM THE GREAT EXHIBITION
80s Recommended RE/ARC   The Housewife's Nightmare (silkscreened, 1-sided, gatefold p/s) 6

PIED PIPERS
54   Parlophone CMSP 21   Kissin' Drive Rock/Please Understand (export issue) 15

PIED PIPERS
66   Columbia DB 7883   Ragamuffin/Fat Marie... 6

BILLY & DEDE PIERCE/JIM ROBINSON
64   London HA-K/SH-K 8163   JAZZ AT PRESERVATION HALL VOL. 2 (LP)............................ 12

JEFFREY LEE PIERCE
85   Statik TAK 36   Love And Desperation/Spoken word tracks 5
85   Statik STAT LP 25   WILDWEED (LP, with free 7": "Open The Door Osiris"/"The Fertility Goddess"/
    "Portrait Of the Artist In Hell"/"Chris And Maggie Meet Blind Willie McTell At
    The James Brown Concert" [no p/s]) 12

(see also Gun Club)

WEBB PIERCE
50s	Decca BM 311368	We'll Find A Way/Any Old Time (export issue)	20
56	Brunswick 05630	Teenage Boogie/Any Old Time............................	150
56	Brunswick 05630	Teenage Boogie/Any Old Time (78)	35
57	Brunswick 05682	Bye, Bye Love/Honky Tonk Song..........................	30
57	Brunswick 05682	Bye, Bye Love/Honky Tonk Song (78).....................	25
59	Brunswick 05809	I Ain't Never/Shanghaied	12
59	Brunswick 05809	I Ain't Never/Shanghaied (78)	20
60	Brunswick 05820	No Love Have I/Whirlpool Of Love	8
60	Brunswick 05842	Drifting Texas Sand/All I Need Is You	8
56	Brunswick OE 9253	WEBB PIERCE PT. 1 (EP).................................	20
56	Brunswick OE 9254	WEBB PIERCE PT. 2 (EP).................................	20
56	Brunswick OE 9255	WEBB PIERCE PT. 3 (EP).................................	20
62	Ember EMB 4520	COUNTRY AND WESTERN FAVOURITES VOL. 1 (EP)...........	15
59	Parlophone GEP 8792	COUNTRY ROUND UP (EP)...............................	30
55	Brunswick LA 8716	THE WONDERING BOY (10" LP)	35
60	Brunswick LAT 8324	WEBB! (LP)	20
65	Brunswick LAT 8540	HIDEAWAY HEART (LP)	20
65	Brunswick LAT 8551	CROSS COUNTRY (LP)	15
69	MCA MUPS 364	IN THE JAILHOUSE NOW (LP).............................	12

(see also Red Sovine & Webb Pierce)

PIGEON FLYERS
68   Columbia DB 8449   The Heaven We Shared Together/Keep On Sayin'................... 4

BILLY PIGG
71   Leader LEA 4006   THE BORDER MINSTREL (LP, gatefold sleeve with booklet) 12

PIGGLESWICK FOLK
77   Acorn CF 256   PIG IN THE MIDDLE (LP) 12

PIGS
77   Bristol Recorder NBR 01   Youthenasia/They Say/Psychopath/National Front (p/s)................. 7

PIGSTY HILL LIGHT ORCHESTRA
70   Village Thing VTS 1   PHLOP! (LP).. 15
72   Village Thing VTS 8   PIGGERY JOKERY (LP) 15

DAVE PIKE
63   Starlite ST45 094   Melvalita/Ginha... 5
66   Atlantic 584 052   Sunny/HERBIE MANN: Philly Dog 10
66   Atlantic 588 005   JAZZ FOR THE JET SET (LP)....................................... 15

PiL
(see under Public Image Ltd)

RAY PILGRIM (& BEATMEN)
60   Oriole CB 1557   Baby Doll/Gambler's Guitar (solo).................................. 10
61   Oriole CB 1616   Little Miss Makebelieve/Granada (solo).............................. 10
64   Embassy WB 645   Kissin' Cousins (with Beatmen)/
    JAYBIRDS: Some Day We're Gonna Love Again....................... 8

(see also Bud Ashton, Jaybirds, Typhoons)

PILTDOWN MEN
60   Capitol CL 15149   McDonald's Cave/Brontosaurus Stomp 7
61   Capitol CL 15175   Piltdown Rides Again/Bubbles In The Tar 7
61   Capitol CL 15186   Goodnight Mrs Flintstone/The Great Imposter........................ 6
61   Capitol CL 15211   Gargantua/Fossil Rock 10
62   Capitol CL 15245   A Pretty Girl Is Like A Melody/Big Lizard 10
61   Capitol EAP1 20155   GOODNIGHT MRS. FLINTSTONE (EP)................................ 40

SIR HUBERT PIMM
55   London HL 8155   Goodnight And Cheerio/Honky Tonk Train Blues 25
55   London RE-U 1032   PIMM'S PARTY (EP, with Ellen Sutton) 20
(see also Duke & Duchess)

PINEAPPLE CHUNKS
65   Mercury MF 922   Drive My Car/Dream About 8

PINEWOOD STUDIO ORCHESTRA with PHILIP GREEN
59   Top Rank TR 5005   Blind Date/HARDY KRUGER: Blind Date............................. 6
59   Top Rank JAR 112   Sapphire/Tiger Bay 5
59   Top Rank JAR 112   Sapphire/Tiger Bay (78)... 8
60   Top Rank JAR 355   'League Of Gentlemen' March/'Golden Fleece' Theme 5
60   Top Rank JAR 361   French Horn Blues (Augie's Theme)/Elevator Ride.................... 5
(see also Johnny Dankworth Orchestra)

PINEWOOD TOM

PINEWOOD TOM/TOM TALL
59	Jazz Collector JEL 5	THE MALE BLUES VOLUME 4 (EP)	15

'PING PING' & AL VERLANE
60	Oriole CB 1589	Sucu Sucu/Maria Della Montagna	5

PINKERTON'S ('ASSORTED' COLOURS)
65	Decca F 12307	Mirror Mirror/She Don't Care (as Pinkerton's 'Assorted' Colours)	7
66	Decca F 12377	Don't Stop Loving Me Baby/Will Ya? (as Pinkerton's 'Assorted' Colours)	7
66	Decca F 12493	Magic Rocking Horse/It Ain't Right (as Pinkerton's Colours)	18
67	Pye 7N 17327	Mum And Dad/On A Street Car (as Pinkerton's Colours)	8
67	Pye 7N 17414	There's Nobody I'd Sooner Love/Look At Me (as Pinkerton's)	8
68	Pye 7N 17574	Kentucky Woman/Behind The Mirror (as Pinkerton's)	8

(see also Flying Machine, Liberators, Tony Newman)

PINK FAIRIES
71	Polydor 2058 089	The Snake/Do It	15
72	Polydor 2059 302	Well Well Well/Hold On	12
76	Stiff BUY 2	Between The Lines/Spoiling For A Fight (p/s)	5
71	Polydor 2383 045	NEVERNEVERLAND (LP, printed PVC outer & gatefold card inner, in yellow bag with photos & notes)	35
71	Polydor 2383 045	NEVERNEVERLAND (LP, printed PVC outer & gatefold card inner, pink vinyl & "pink plastic" in text on rear sleeve, around 100 pressed)	350
71	Polydor 2383 045	NEVERNEVERLAND (LP, black vinyl, standard sleeve)	12
72	Polydor 2383 132	WHAT A BUNCH OF SWEETIES (LP)	25
73	Polydor 2383 212	KINGS OF OBLIVION (LP, with poster)	15
84	Big Beat WIK 14	LIVE AT THE ROUNDHOUSE '75 (LP, pink vinyl, with inner sleeve)	12

(see also Twink, Larry Wallis, Deviants, Lightning Raiders, Shagrat)

PINK FLOYD
SINGLES
67	Columbia DB 8156	Arnold Layne/Candy And A Currant Bun	30
67	Columbia DB 8214	See Emily Play/Scarecrow	30
67	Columbia DB 8310	Apples And Oranges/Paintbox	45
68	Columbia DB 8401	It Would Be So Nice/Julia Dream	45
68	Columbia DB 8511	Point Me At The Sky/Careful With That Axe, Eugene	50
79	Harvest HAR 5194	Another Brick In The Wall (Part Two)/One Of My Turns (initial pressing, plain B-side label without 'window' picture, no p/s)	6
81	Harvest HAR 5217	Money (Edit)/Let There Be More Light (unreleased)	
81	Harvest 12HAR 5217	Money (Full Length)/Let There Be More Light (12", unreleased)	
82	Harvest HAR 5222	When The Tigers Broke Free/Bring The Boys Back Home (gatefold p/s)	7
82	Harvest HAR 5222	When The Tigers Broke Free/Bring The Boys Back Home (standard p/s)	8
87	EMI EMDJ 26	Learning To Fly (Edited Version)/One Slip (Edited Version)/Terminal Frost (no p/s, mispressing without "One Slip", 1,000 only on pink vinyl, 50 on black)	12/20
87	EMI EM 26	Learning To Fly (Edited Version)/One Slip (Edited Version)/Terminal Frost (p/s)	4
87	EMI 12EM 26	Learning To Fly (Edited Version)/One Slip (Edited Version)/Terminal Frost (DYOL Version) (12", p/s)	7
87	EMI CDEM 26	Learning To Fly (Edited Version)/One Slip (Edited Version)/Terminal Frost (Album Version)/Terminal Frost (DYOL Version) (CD, card sleeve & inner)	15
87	EMI EM 34	On The Turning Away (Album)/Run Like Hell (Live Version) (p/s)	5
87	EMI EMP 34	On The Turning Away (Album)/Run Like Hell (Live Version) (p/s, pink vinyl, 1000 only)	8
87	EMI 12EMP 34	On The Turning Away (Album)/Run Like Hell (Live Version)/On The Turning Away (Live Version) (12", poster p/s)	12
87	EMI CDEM 34	On The Turning Away/Run Like Hell (Live Version)/On The Turning Away (Live Version) (CD)	15
88	EMI EM 52	One Slip/Terminal Frost (p/s)	5
88	EMI EMG 52	One Slip/Terminal Frost (pink vinyl, gatefold p/s with ticket application)	8
88	EMI 12EMP 52	One Slip/Terminal Frost/The Dogs Of War (live) (12", poster p/s)	8
88	EMI CDEM 52	One Slip/Terminal Frost/The Dogs Of War (live) (CD)	8
94	EMI EM 309	Take It Back (Edit)/Astronomy Domine (live) (jukebox issue, black vinyl, no p/s)	8
94	EMI EM 309	Take It Back (Edit)/Astronomy Domine (live) (red vinyl, p/s)	7
94	EMI CDEMS 309	Take It Back (Album Version)/Astronomy Domine (live)/Take It Back (Edit) (CD, picture disc, with poster)	8
94	EMI EM 342	High Hopes (Radio Edit)/Keep Talking (Radio Edit) (clear vinyl, poster p/s)	4
94	EMI 12EM 342	High Hopes (Album Version)/Keep Talking (Album Version)/One Of These Days (live) (12", 1-sided, laser-etched blue vinyl, p/s in outer gatefold p/s with 7 postcards)	8
94	EMI CDEM 342	High Hopes (Radio Edit)/Keep Talking (Radio Edit)/One Of These Days (live) (CD, with 7 postcards)	8

ALBUMS
67	Columbia S(C)X 6157	THE PIPER AT THE GATES OF DAWN (LP, blue/black label, mono/stereo)	165/80
68	Columbia S(C)X 6258	A SAUCERFUL OF SECRETS (LP, blue/black label, mono/stereo)	165/70
70	Columbia SCX 6157	THE PIPER AT THE GATES OF DAWN (LP, re-pressing, silver & black label)	20
70	Columbia SCX 6258	A SAUCERFUL OF SECRETS (LP, re-pressing, silver & black label)	20
69	Columbia SCX 6346	SOUNDTRACK FROM THE FILM 'MORE' (LP, laminated flipback sleeve, 'couple facing west' photo on green-tinted rear sleeve)	25
70s	Columbia SCX 6346	SOUNDTRACK FROM THE FILM 'MORE' (LP, laminated non-flipback sleeve, 'couple facing west' photo on black-tinted rear sleeve)	18
70s	Columbia SCX 6346	SOUNDTRACK FROM THE FILM 'MORE' (LP, laminated non-flipback sleeve, 'couple facing east' photo on black-tinted rear sleeve)	30
69	Harvest SHDW 1/2	UMMAGUMMA (2-LP, laminated gatefold sleeve)	20
70	MGM 2315 002	ZABRISKIE POINT (LP, soundtrack, with Jerry Garcia/Kaleidoscope, et al.)	18
70	Harvest SHVL 781	ATOM HEART MOTHER (LP, gatefold sleeve)	15
71	Harvest SHVL 795	MEDDLE (LP, gatefold sleeve)	12
71	Starline SRS 5071	RELICS (LP, white textured sleeve)	12
72	Harvest SHSP 4020	OBSCURED BY CLOUDS (LP, rounded sleeve)	18

73	Harvest SHVL 804	THE DARK SIDE OF THE MOON (LP, blue & black label, gatefold sleeve with black inner, 2 posters & 2 stickers, some with stickered sleeve) 15/12
70s	Harvest SHVL 804	THE DARK SIDE OF THE MOON (LP, repressing, blue & white label, gatefold sleeve with black inner, 2 posters & 2 stickers) 12
73	Harvest Q4 SHVL 781	ATOM HEART MOTHER (LP, quadrophonic, gatefold sleeve, initially with 'quadrophonic' logo on front sleeve, later inside)............ 30/25
73	Harvest Q4 SHVL 804	THE DARK SIDE OF THE MOON (LP, quadrophonic, gatefold sleeve, without inserts) 30
73	Harvest SHDW 403	A NICE PAIR (2-LP, gatefold sleeve, with 2 inner sleeves; early copies with 'Mr Phang' dentist cover)........................... 20/15
75	Harvest SHVL 814	WISH YOU WERE HERE (LP, with inner sleeve, postcard & black cellophane wraparound with sticker).......................... 15
76	Harvest Q4 SHVL 814	WISH YOU WERE HERE (LP, quadrophonic, with inner sleeve) 35
77	Harvest SHVL 815	ANIMALS (LP, picture labels, non-barcode gatefold sleeve with inner)...... 12
78	Harvest SHDW 411	THE WALL (2-LP, plastic stickered gatefold sleeve, with inners)......... 15
79	Harvest PF 11	THE FIRST XI (11-LP set, original sleeves, plus exclusive "Dark Side Of The Moon" & "Wish You Were Here" picture discs, 1,000 only) 200
83	Harvest SHPF 1983	THE FINAL CUT (LP, gatefold sleeve with title sticker)............... 10
87	EMI EMD 1003	A MOMENTARY LAPSE OF REASON (LP, gatefold sleeve with inner) 10
93	EMI CDDSOM 20	THE DARK SIDE OF THE MOON (CD, 20th anniversary box set with booklet & 5 art cards) 18
94	EMI EMD 1055	THE DIVISION BELL (LP, gatefold sleeve, with inner).............. 10
95	EMI EMD 578	PULSE (4-LP box set in slipcase with hardback book)............. 35
97	EMI 859 857-1	THE PIPER AT THE GATES OF DAWN (LP, reissue, gatefold sleeve with inner sleeve, mono) 10
97	EMI CDEMD 1110	THE PIPER AT THE GATES OF DAWN (CD, mono, 30th anniversary box set with prints).................................... 18
97	EMI SIGMA 630	'97 VINYL COLLECTION (7-LP set, die-cut box, includes "The Piper At The Gates Of Dawn" [EMD 1110], "The Wall" [EMD 1111], "Atom Heart Mother" [EMD 1112]", "Relics" [EMD 1113], "The Dark Side Of The Moon" [EMD 1114], "Wish You Were Here" [EMD 1115], each in stickered gatefold sleeves & inners [no inner on EMD 1111], withdrawn) 80
97	EMI CDEMD 1118	THE FIRST THREE SINGLES (CD, mono, mini album in card gatefold sleeve) .. 20

PROMOS
67	Columbia DB 8156	Arnold Layne/Candy And A Currant Bun (demo copy in promo-only p/s)...... 650
67	Columbia DB 8214	See Emily Play/Scarecrow (demo copy in promo-only p/s) 650
67	Columbia DB 8310	Apples And Oranges/Paintbox (demo copy in promo-only p/s)........... 650
81	Harvest HAR 5217	Money (Edited Version) (1-sided, pink vinyl, 200 only) 30
81	Harvest HAR 5217	Money (Edited Version) (1-sided, pink vinyl, mispressing with "Let There Be More Light" label on B-side)................ 50
87	EMI EMDJ 34	On The Turning Away (edit)/On The Turning Away (album) (stickerd p/s)....... 8
88	EMI 12PF 1	Delicate Sound Of Thunder Sampler: Another Brick In The Wall Part 2/ One Of These Days/Run Like Hell (12", black & pink sleeve) 20
88	EMI PSLP 1026	Pink Floyd In Europe '88: Money/Shine On/Another Brick In The Wall Part 2/ One Slip/On The Turning Away/Learning To Fly (12", with "Another Brick ... Part 1" miscredit on back p/s)....................... 20
88	EMI CDPINK 1	Wish You Were Here/Learning To Fly/Run Like Hell (CD) 20
92	EMI SHINE 1	SELECTED TRACKS FROM "SHINE ON" (CD, card sleeve) 18

(see also Syd Barrett, Roger Waters, Dave Gilmour, Rick Wright, Nick Mason, Joker's Wild, Ron Geesin)

PINK INDUSTRY
82	Zulu ZULU 1	Is This The End?/47/Don't Let Go/Final Cry (12", p/s)............. 8
83	Zulu ZULU 2	LOW TECHNOLOGY (LP)........................... 10
83	Zulu ZULU 4	WHO TOLD YOU — YOU WERE NAKED (LP)................. 10

(see also Pink Military, Big In Japan)

PINK KROSS
| 94 | Bouvier BV 909 | PUNK OR DIE (EP, 400 only, silkscreened 'swirl' die-cut sleeve) .... 6 |

PINK MILITARY
79	Last Trumpet LT 001	BUDDHA WALKING DISNEY SLEEPING (EP, foldout sleeve)................ 8
79	Eric's ERIC'S 002	BLOOD AND LIPSTICK (12" EP, die-cut p/s)................... 8
80	Eric's ERIC'S 005	Did You See Her/Everyday (p/s)........................ 4
80	Virgin/Eric's ERIC'S 004	DO ANIMALS BELIEVE IN GOD? (LP).................... 10

(see also Pink Industry, Big In Japan, Ambrose Reynolds)

PINK PEOPLE
| 64 | Philips BF 1355 | Psychologically Unsound/Cow Catcher .... 20 |
| 64 | Philips BF 1356 | Indian Hate Call/I Dreamt I Dwelt In..................... 15 |

(see also Four Squares)

PINKY (& FELLAS)
65	Polydor BM 56009	All Cried Out/Back Where I Belong 6
68	Decca F 12748	Manchester And Liverpool/Come Back Again (as Pinky & Fellas)........... 5
69	Polydor BM 56338	Let The Music Start/Oh, A Beautiful Day (as Pinky & Fellas) 5

PINKY & PERKY
58	Decca F 11095	Tom Dooley/The Velvet Glove (Pinky & Perky Theme) (some in p/s)......... 8/5
58	Decca F 11095	Tom Dooley/The Velvet Glove (Pinky & Perky Theme) (78, some in 10" p/s)... 20/12
59	Decca F 11116	The Little Mountaineer/Does Your Chewing Gum Lose Its Flavour (some in p/s) 25/15
59	Decca F 11116	The Little Mountaineer/Does Your Chewing Gum Lose Its Flavour (78, some in 10" p/s) 20/8
59	Decca F 11174	Pinky And Perky's Sing Song Medley (both sides).............. 5
59	Decca F 11174	Pinky And Perky's Sing Song Medley (both sides) (78) 25
60	Columbia DB 4538	Eeny Meeney Miney Mo/The Ugly Duckling 5
61	Columbia DB 4710	What's New At The Zoo?/Dream Your Tears Away............. 5

PINKY & PERKY

65	Columbia DB 7548	Hole In My Bucket/Glow Worm	5
60	Columbia SEG 8058	CHILDREN'S CHOICE (EP)	8
61	Columbia SEG 8122	CHRISTMAS WITH PINKY & PERKY (EP)	8
62	Columbia SEG 8152	PINKY & PERKY OUT WEST (EP)	8
63	Columbia SEG 8261	DOWN ON THE FARM (EP)	8
63	Columbia SEG 8344	NURSERY ROMP (EP)	8
68	MFP MFP 1282	HIT PARADE (LP)	12

PINNACLE
74	Stag HP 125	ASSASSIN (LP)	80

PIONEERS
66	Rio R 102	Good Nannie/Doreen Girl	12
66	Rio R 106	Too Late/Give Up	12
68	Blue Cat BS 100	Shake It Up/Rudies Are The Greatest	12
68	Blue Cat BS 103	Give It To Me/LEADERS: Someday Someway	12
68	Blue Cat BS 105	Whip Them/Having A Bawl	12
68	Blue Cat BS 139	Reggae Beat/Miss Eva	12
68	Caltone TONE 119	I Love No Other Girl/MILTON BOOTHE: I Used To Be A Fool	12
68	Amalgamated AMG 811	Give Me A Little Loving/This Is Soul (B-side actually by Lyn Tait & Jets)	12
68	Amalgamated AMG 814	Long Shot/Dip And Fall Back	12
68	Amalgamated AMG 821	Jackpot/CREATORS: Kimble (B-side actually by Lee Perry)	25
68	Amalgamated AMG 823	No Dope Me Pony/LORD SALMONS: Great — Great In '68	12
68	Amalgamated AMG 826	Tickle Me For Days/VERSATILES: The Time Has Come	10
68	Amalgamated AMG 828	Catch The Beat/SIR GIBB'S ALLSTARS: Jana (B-side actually Immortals' "Jane Anne")	12
68	Amalgamated AMG 830	Sweet Dreams/DON DRUMMOND JUNIOR: Caterpillar Rock	12
68	Pyramid PYR 6062	Easy Come, Easy Go/BEVERLEY'S ALLSTARS: Only A Smile (B-side actually by Lyn Tait & Jets)	12
69	Pyramid PYR 6065	Pee Pee Cluck Cluck/BEVERLEY'S ALLSTARS: Exclusively	10
69	Amalgamated AMG 833	Don't You Know/Me Naw Go A Believe	10
69	Amalgamated AMG 835	Mama Look Deh/BLENDERS: Decimal Currency	10
69	Amalgamated AMG 840	Who The Cap Fits/I'm Moving On	10
69	Amalgamated AMG 850	Alli Button/HIPPY BOYS: Death Rides	10
69	Trojan TR 672	Long Shot Kick The Bucket/RICO: Jumping The Gun	6
69	Trojan TR 685	Black Bud/Too Late	6
69	Trojan TR 698	Poor Rameses/BEVERLEY'S ALLSTARS: In Orbit	6
70	Trojan TR 7781	Money Day/BEVERLEY ALL STARS: Ska Ba Do	7
71	Summit SUM 8511	Starvation/BEVERLEY'S ALLSTARS: Version	6
72	Summit SUM 8535	Story Book Children/SIDNEY, GEORGE AND JACKIE: Gorgeous, Marvellous	6
68	Amalgam. AMGLP 2003	GREETINGS FROM THE PIONEERS (LP)	60
70	Trojan TBL 103	LONGSHOT (LP)	18
70	Trojan TBL 139	BATTLE OF THE GIANTS (LP)	15
71	Trojan TRL 24	YEAH! (LP)	15

(see also Sir Gibbs, Rebels [Jamaica], Jackey Robinson, Moonboys, Sidney George & Jackie)

PIPES OF PAN
67	Page One POF 038	Monday Morning Rain/Monday Morning Rain (Instrumental Mix)	5

PIPES OF PAN
71	Rolling Stones COC 49100	BRIAN JONES PLAYS WITH THE PIPES OF PAN AT JOUJOUKA (LP, gatefold sleeve with foldout insert; front cover with misprinted title)	80
71	Rolling Stones COC 49100	BRIAN JONES PRESENTS THE PIPES OF PAN AT JOUJOUKA (LP, gatefold sleeve with foldout insert; "Presents" sticker on misprinted cover)	65
71	Rolling Stones COC 49100	BRIAN JONES PRESENTS THE PIPES OF PAN AT JOUJOUKA (LP, gatefold sleeve with foldout insert; corrected title on front cover)	60

(see also Rolling Stones)

PIPKINS
(see under Sweet)

PIPS
61	Top Rank JAR 574	Every Beat Of My Heart/Room In Your Heart	30

(see also Gladys Knight & Pips)

PIRATES
64	HMV POP 1250	My Babe/Casting My Spell	25
66	Polydor BM 56712	Shades Of Blue/Can't Understand	20
77	Warner Bros K 17002	Sweet Love On My Mind/You Don't Own Me (p/s)	10
78	Warner Bros K 17113	All In It Together/Dr. Feelgood (p/s)	8
78	Warner Bros K 17231	Shakin' All Over/Saturday Night Shoot Out	5
79	Sound For Industry SFI 431	All By Myself/Cat Clothes (1-sided fan club flexidisc, gold vinyl)	5
79	Cube Hi Fly 33	HAPPY BIRTHDAY ROCK N' ROLL (LP, with flexidisc [PIR 2])	10

(see also Johnny Kidd & Pirates, [Billy J. Kramer &] Dakotas)

PISCES
71	Trailer LER 2025	PISCES (LP)	25

HARRY PITCH
68	MOR MR 101P	HARMONICA JEWEL BOX (LP)	20

PITCH PIKES
57	Mercury MT 171	Come Back To Me/How Will I Know (78)	8

GENE PITNEY
SINGLES
61	London HL 9270	(I Wanna) Love My Life Away/I Laughed So Hard I Cried	15
61	HMV POP 933	Every Breath I Take/Mr Moon, Mr Cupid & I	15
61	United Artists POP 952	Town Without Pity/Air Mail Special	12
62	United Artists POP 1018	The Man Who Shot Liberty Valance/Take It Like A Man	12

MINT VALUE £

62	United Artists UP 1005	If I Didn't Have A Dime/Only Love Can Break A Heart	7
63	United Artists UP 1012	Half Heaven, Half Heartache/Tower Tall	7
63	United Artists UP 1021	Mecca/Teardrop By Teardrop	7
63	United Artists UP 1030	True Love Never Runs Smooth/Donna Means Heartbreak	6
63	United Artists UP 1035	24 Hours From Tulsa/Lonely Night Dreams (blue or black label)	5
64	United Artists UP 1045	That Girl Belongs To Yesterday/Who Needs It?	6
64	United Artists UP 1055	I'm Gonna Find Myself A Girl/Lips Are Redder On You	10
64	United Artists UP 1063	It Hurts To Be In Love/Hawaii	7
64	Stateside SS 358	I'm Gonna Be Strong/Aladdin's Lamp	6
64	Stateside SS 365	It Hurts To Be In Love/Hawaii (reissue)	6
65	Stateside SS 390	I Must Be Seeing Things/Save Your Love	6
65	Stateside SS 420	Lookin' Thru The Eyes Of Love/Last Chance To Turn Around	6
65	Stateside SS 471	Princess In Rags/Amore Mio	6
66	Stateside SS 490	Backstage/In Love Again	6
66	Stateside SS 518	Nobody Needs Your Love/Dream World	6
66	Stateside SS 558	Just One Smile/The Boss's Daughter	6
67	Stateside SS 597	(In The) Cold Light Of Day/Flower Girl	6
68	Stateside SS 2118	Love Grows/Conquistador	6
68	Stateside SS 2131	Yours Until Tomorrow/She's A Heartbreaker	8
70	Stateside SS 2177	Shady Lady/Billy, You're My Friend	6
71	Pye International 7N 25564	Run Run Road Runner/Rain Maker	5
72	Pye International 7N 25579	I Just Can't Help Myself/Beautiful Sounds	5

EPs

63	HMV 7EG 8832	TOWN WITHOUT PITY (EP)	60
64	United Artists UEP 1001	TWENTY FOUR HOURS FROM TULSA (EP)	12
64	United Artists UEP 1002	THAT GIRL BELONGS TO YESTERDAY (EP)	12
65	Stateside SE 1027	TWENTY FOUR HOURS FROM TULSA (EP, reissue)	15
65	Stateside SE 1028	THAT GIRL BELONGS TO YESTERDAY (EP, reissue)	12
65	Stateside SE 1030	I MUST BE SEEING THINGS (EP)	15
65	Stateside SE 1032	GENE ITALIANO (EP)	18
66	Stateside SE 1036	GENE PITNEY SINGS JUST FOR YOU (EP)	12
66	Stateside SE 1040	BACKSTAGE (EP)	15
66	Stateside SE 1041	SAN REMO WINNERS AND OTHERS (EP)	15
67	Stateside SE 1045	THERE'S NO LIVING WITHOUT YOUR LOVING (EP)	12
60s	Bravo BR 375	GENE PITNEY (EP)	10

LPs

62	HMV CLP 1566	THE MANY SIDES OF GENE PITNEY (LP)	40
63	United Artists (S)ULP 1028	ONLY LOVE CAN BREAK A HEART (LP, mono/stereo)	25/30
63	United Artists ULP 1043	GENE PITNEY SINGS JUST FOR YOU (LP)	20
64	United Artists ULP 1061	BLUE GENE (LP)	20
64	United Artists ULP 1064	GENE PITNEY MEETS THE FAIR YOUNG LADIES OF FOLKLAND (LP)	20
64	United Artists ULP 1073	GENE PITNEY'S BIG SIXTEEN (LP)	20
65	Stateside SL 10118	GENE PITNEY'S BIG SIXTEEN (LP, reissue)	15
65	Stateside SL 10119	BLUE GENE (LP, reissue)	15
65	Stateside SL 10120	I'M GONNA BE STRONG (LP)	18
65	Stateside SL 10132	GENE PITNEY'S MORE BIG SIXTEEN (VOL. 2) (LP)	20
65	Stateside SL 10147	GEORGE JONES AND GENE PITNEY (LP, with George Jones)	20
65	Stateside SL 10148	LOOKING THRU THE EYES OF LOVE (LP)	18
65	Stateside SL 10156	SINGS THE GREAT SONGS OF OUR TIME (LP)	20
66	Stateside SL 10173	IT'S COUNTRY TIME AGAIN (LP, with George Jones)	20
66	Stateside S(S)L 10181	BEING TOGETHER (LP, with Melba Montgomery)	18
66	Stateside S(S)L 10183	NOBODY NEEDS YOUR LOVE (LP)	18
67	Stateside S(S)L 10194	YOUNG, WARM AND WONDERFUL (LP)	18
67	Stateside S(S)L 10199	GENE PITNEY'S BIG SIXTEEN (VOL. 3) (LP)	20
67	Stateside S(S)L 10212	JUST ONE SMILE (LP)	18
67	Stateside S(S)L 10216	GOLDEN GREATS (LP)	15
68	Stateside S(S)L 10242	PITNEY TODAY (LP)	18
69	Stateside S(S)L 10286	THE BEST OF GENE PITNEY (LP)	15
71	Pye Intl. NSPL 28148	TEN YEARS LATER (LP)	15
72	Pye Intl. NSPL 28165	THE NEW SOUNDS OF GENE PITNEY (LP)	15

(see also Marc Almond & Gene Pitney, George Jones)

PETE PITTERSON

52	Esquire 5-058	West Indian Folk Music/Bali Game (78)	10

PIXIES

88	4AD BAD 805CD	Gigantic/River Euphrates/Vamos (live)/In Heaven (Lady In The Radiator Song) (live) (CD)	10
89	4AD AD 904	Monkey's Gone To Heaven/Manta Ray (p/s)	4
89	4AD BAD 904CD	Monkey's Gone To Heaven/Manta Ray/Weird At My School/ Dancing The Manta Ray (CD)	10
90	4AD C 0009	Velouria/Make Believe (cassette)	4
89	4AD PIX ONE	DOOLITTLE SAMPLER: Debaser/Wave Of Mutilation/I Bleed/Gouge Away (12", 1-sided, title sleeve, promo only)	12
89	4AD PIX 2	Into The White/Wave Of Mutilation (U.K. Surf) (12", 1-sided, promo only, no p/s)	10
90	4AD PIX 3	EXTRACTS FROM BOSSANOVA: Allison/Rock Music/Down To The Well/ The Happening (12", 1-sided, promo only, no p/s)	8
91	4AD PIX 4	EXTRACTS FROM TROMPE LE MONDE: U-Mass/Letter To Memphis/ Subbacultcha (10", same track both sides, promo only, no p/s)	8
89	4AD CAD 905	DOOLITTLE (LP, with lyric booklet & postcard, some in carrier bag)	15/12
90	4AD CAD 0010	BOSSANOVA (LP, with booklet)	10

(see also Breeders, Frank Black)

PIXIES THREE

63	Mercury AMT 1214	Birthday Party/Our Love	10

P.J. HARVEY
(see under 'H')

MINT VALUE £

PLACEBO

95	Fierce Panda NING 13	Bruise Pristine/SOUP: M.E.L.T.D.O.W.N. (foldover p/s)	15
96	Deceptive BLUFF 024	Come Home/Drowning By Numbers (p/s)	10
96	Deceptive BLUFF 024	Come Home/Drowning By Numbers (CD)	10
96	Elevator FLOOR 1	36 Degrees/Dark Globe (p/s)	6
96	Elevator FLOOR 3	Teenage Ankst/Been Smoking Too Long/Hug Bubble (p/s, double pack)	4
96	Elevator FLOOR 4	Nancy Boy/Slackerbitch (p/s)	4

PLAGUE

68	Decca F 12730	Looking For The Sun/Here Today, Gone Tomorrow	60

PLAID

92	GPR GENP(X) 7	Scoobs In Columbia (remixes) (12", custom sleeve)	30
94	Clear CLR 409	ANDROID (12" EP, p/s, clear or black vinyl)	25/15
95	Rumble RUMBLE 01	MIND OVER RHYTHM MEET THE MEN FROM PLAID (3 x 10" in p/s)	20
92	Black Dog Productions LP 1	MBUKI MVUKI (LP)	75

(see also Black Dog)

PLAIN CHARACTERS

(see under Gadgets)

PLAINSONG

72	Elektra K 12976	Even The Guiding Light/Yoko Man/Call The Tune	5
72	Elektra K 42120	IN SEARCH OF AMELIA EARHART (LP, gatefold sleeve with lyric insert)	12
73	Elektra K 42136	PLAINSONG II (LP, white label, promo only)	100

(see also Andy Roberts, Ian Matthews)

PLANET GONG

77	Affinity AF 5101	Opium For The People/Poet For Sale (p/s)	8
78	Charly CYX 202	Opium For The People/Stoned Innocent Frankenstein (10", p/s)	6

(see also Daevid Allen, New York Gong, Gong)

PLANET P PROJECT

83	Geffen A 3204	Why Me?/Only You And Me (p/s)	6
83	Geffen GEF 25367	PLANET P PROJECT (LP, with inner sleeve)	12
85	MCA MCSP 311	PINK WORLD (2-LP, gatefold sleeve)	15

(see also Tony Carey, Rainbow)

PLANETS

60	Palette PG 9008	Like Party/Ippy Yippy Beatnik (some in p/s)	15/10

PLANETS

60	HMV POP 818	Chunky/Screwball	12
61	HMV POP 832	Jam Roll/Delaney's Theme	12
61	HMV POP 895	Jungle Street/The Grasshopper	15

ROBERT PLANT

66	CBS 202656	Our Song/Laughin', Cryin', Laughin'	165
66	CBS 202858	Long Time Coming/I've Got A Secret	165
82	Swan Song SSK 19429T	Burning Down One Side/Moonlight In Samosa (12", p/s)	10
83	WEA B 9848	Big Log/Log (p/s)	5
85	Es Paranza B 9621 F	Little By Little (Remix)/Doo Doo A Do Do//Easily Lead (live)/Rockin' At Midnight (live) (double pack)	8
88	Es Paranza A 9373 TB	Heaven Knows (Extended Remix)/Walking Towards Paradise/Heaven Knows (Astral Mix) (12", stickered sealed box set with colour poster & 2 prints)	8
88	Es Paranza A 9373 CD	Heaven Knows/Walking Towards Paradise/Big Log (3" CD & adaptor, 5" case)	8
88	Es Paranza A 9348 CD	Tall Cool One/White, Clean And Neat/Tall Cool One (Extended Version)/Little By Little (3" CD, with adaptor, 5" case)	8
88	Es Paranza A 9281 CDB	Ship Of Fools/Helen Of Troy (live)/Dimples (live) (3" CD, with adaptor & 5" case, inside 5" box set with card, foldout lyric sheet & 2-page biography)	8
90	Es Paranza A 8985P	Hurting Kind (I've Got My Eyes On You)/I Cried (shaped picture disc)	5
93	Fontana FATX 2	I Believe (CD picture disc)	10
90	Es Paranza WX 339X	MANIC NIRVANA (LP, gatefold sleeve)	12

(see also Led Zeppelin, Listen, Jimmy Page, Page & Plant, Honeydrippers)

PLANXTY

73	Polydor 2383 186	PLANXTY (LP)	12
73	Polydor 2383 232	THE WELL BELOW THE VALLEY (LP)	12
74	Polydor 2383 301	COLD BLOW AND RAINY NIGHT (LP)	12
76	Polydor 2389 387	THE PLANXTY COLLECTION (LP, gatefold sleeve)	12

PLASMATICS

80	Stiff SEEZ 24	NEW HOPE FOR THE WRETCHED (LP, yellow & red vinyl)	10

(see also Wendy & Lemmy)

PLASTIC GANGSTERS

83	Secret SHH 144	Plastic Gangsters/Sretsgnag Citsalp (7", 12", no p/s, unissued, DJ copies only)	each 250

(see also 4 Skins)

PLASTIC ONO BAND

(see under John Lennon, Yoko Ono)

PLASTIC PENNY

67	Page One POF 051	Everything I Am/No Pleasure Without Pain My Love	5
68	Page One POF 062	Nobody Knows It/Just Happy To Be With You	6
68	Page One POF 079	Your Way To Tell Me Go/Baby You're Not To Blame	10
69	Page One POF 107	Hound Dog/Currency	6
69	Page One POF 146	She Does/Genevieve	6
68	Page One POL(S) 005	TWO SIDES OF THE PENNY (LP)	40
69	Page One POLS 014	CURRENCY (LP)	40
70	Page One POLS 611	HEADS YOU WIN, TAILS I LOSE (LP)	35

(see also Universals, Circles, Brian Keith, Mick Grabham)

PLASTIKMAN
94	NovaMute L NO MU 37	MUSIK (2-LP, with bonus 1-sided etched 12") 20

PLATFORM SIX
65	Piccadilly 7N 35255	Money Will Not Mean A Thing/Girl Down Town 15

EDDIE PLATT
58	Columbia DB 4101	Tequila/Pop Corn 7
58	Columbia DB 4101	Tequila/Pop Corn (78) 8

PLATTERS
78s
55	Parlophone DP 433	Voo-Vee-Ah-Bee/STRANGERS: Just Don't Care (78, export issue) 50
56	Parlophone DP 506	Beer Barrel Boogie/Roses Of Picardy (78, export issue) 50
56	Mercury MT 107	(You've Got) The Magic Touch/Winner Takes All (78) 20
56	Mercury MT 117	The Great Pretender/Only You (And You Alone) (78)..................... 8
57	Mercury MT 143	On My Word Of Honor/One In A Million (78).......................... 8
57	Mercury MT 145	I'm Sorry/She's Mine (78).. 8
57	Mercury MT 156	My Dream/I Wanna (78).. 10
58	Mercury MT 197	Helpless/Indiff'rent (78).. 15
58	Mercury MT 205	Don't Let Go/Are You Sincere? (78)................................. 10
58	Mercury MT 214	Twilight Time/Out Of My Mind (78).................................. 8
58	Mercury MT 227	You're Making A Mistake (featuring Tony Williams)/My Old Flame (78) 12
58	Mercury AMT 1001	I Wish/It's Raining Outside (78) 20
58	Mercury AMT 1016	Smoke Gets In Your Eyes/No Matter What You Are (78) 25
59	Mercury AMT 1039	Enchanted/The Sound And The Fury (78)............................. 30
59	Mercury AMT 1053	Remember When/Love Of A Lifetime (featuring Tony Williams) (78) 35
60	Mercury AMT 1081	Harbour Lights/(By The) Sleepy Lagoon (78) 40

SINGLES
56	Mercury MT 117	The Great Pretender/Only You (And You Alone) (export issue) 30
58	Mercury 7MT 197	Helpless/Indiff'rent... 35
58	Mercury 7MT 205	Don't Let Go/Are You Sincere? 25
58	Mercury 7MT 214	Twilight Time/Out Of My Mind 12
58	Mercury 7MT 227	You're Making A Mistake (featuring Tony Williams)/My Old Flame 18
58	Mercury AMT 1001	I Wish/It's Raining Outside....................................... 15
58	Mercury AMT 1016	Smoke Gets In Your Eyes/No Matter What You Are..................... 8
59	Mercury AMT 1039	Enchanted/The Sound And The Fury 6
59	Mercury AMT 1053	Remember When/Love Of A Lifetime (featuring Tony Williams)........... 6
59	Mercury AMT 1066	My Blue Heaven/Wish It Were Me 7
60	Mercury AMT 1076	My Secret/What Does It Matter 6
60	Mercury AMT 1081	Harbour Lights/(By The) Sleepy Lagoon 6
60	Mercury AMT 1098	Ebb Tide/(I'll Be With You In) Apple Blossom Time (featuring Tony Williams) .. 6
60	Mercury AMT 1106	Red Sails In The Sunset/Sad River (featuring Tony Williams)............. 6
60	Mercury AMT 1118	To Each His Own/Down The River Of Golden Dreams 6
61	Mercury AMT 1128	If I Didn't Care/True Lover 6
61	Mercury AMT 1154	I'll Never Smile Again/You Don't Say................................ 6
62	Ember JBS 701	Only You/Tell The World 200
66	Stateside SS 511	I Love You 1000 Times/Hear No Evil, Speak No Evil, See No Evil........... 18
66	Stateside SS 568	I'll Be Home/(You've Got) The Magic Touch.......................... 8
67	Stateside SS 2007	With This Ring/If I Had A Love.................................... 12
67	Stateside SS 2042	Washed Ashore (On A Lonely Island In The Sea)/
		What Name Shall I Give You My Love 12
67	Stateside SS 2067	Sweet Sweet Lovin'/Sonata 12
69	Stateside SS 2150	With This Ring/If I Had A Love (reissue) 6
71	Pye Intl. 7N 25559	Sweet Sweet Lovin'/Going Back To Detroit........................... 5
71	Pye Intl. 7N 25569	With This Ring/I Washed Ashore (On A Lonely Island In The Sea)............ 5

EPs
56	Mercury MEP 9504	THE FABULOUS PLATTERS (EP) 15
57	Mercury MEP 9514	THE FABULOUS PLATTERS VOL. II (EP) 18
57	Mercury MEP 9524	THE FABULOUS PLATTERS VOL. III (EP) 20
58	Mercury MEP 9526	THE FLYING PLATTERS VOL. I (EP)................................. 20
58	Mercury MEP 9528	THE FLYING PLATTERS VOL. II (EP) 20
58	Mercury MEP 9537	THE PLATTERS (EP) 20
59	Mercury ZEP 10000	PICK OF THE PLATTERS NO. 1 (EP) 20
59	Mercury ZEP 10008	PICK OF THE PLATTERS NO. 2 (EP) 20
59	Mercury ZEP 10025	PICK OF THE PLATTERS NO. 3 (EP) 20
59	Mercury ZEP 10031	PICK OF THE PLATTERS NO. 4 (EP) 20
59	Mercury ZEP 10042	PICK OF THE PLATTERS NO. 5 (EP) 20
60	Mercury ZEP 10056	PICK OF THE PLATTERS NO. 6 (EP) 22
60	Mercury ZEP 10070	PICK OF THE PLATTERS NO. 7 (EP) 22
61	Mercury ZEP 10112	HARBOUR LIGHTS (EP)... 25
62	Mercury ZEP 10126	THE PLATTERS ON A PLATTER (EP) 25

LPs
57	Mercury MPL 6504	THE PLATTERS (LP) 40
57	Mercury MPL 6511	THE PLATTERS VOL. 2 (LP) 40
58	Mercury MPL 6528	THE FLYING PLATTERS (LP)....................................... 35
58	Parlophone PMD 1058	THE PLATTERS (10" LP) 350
59	Mercury MMC 14009	AROUND THE WORLD WITH THE FLYING PLATTERS (LP)............... 35
59	Mercury MMC 14010	THE PLATTERS ON PARADE (LP)................................... 35
59	Mercury MMC 14014	REMEMBER WHEN? (LP).. 30
60	Mercury MMC 14045	REFLECTIONS (LP) 25
61	Mercury MMC 14072	LIFE IS JUST A BOWL OF CHERRIES (LP)............................ 25
62	Ember EMB 3339	THE BEST OF THE PLATTERS (LP).................................. 12
62	Mercury MMC 14091	GOLDEN HITS (LP)... 15
64	Mercury MCL 20000	THE PLATTERS SING LATINO (LP) 15
64	Concert Hall CJ 1255	THE PLATTERS (LP) 12
66	Wing WL 1044	REFLECTIONS (LP, reissue) 12

PLATTERS

67	Stateside S(S)L 10208	GOING BACK TO DETROIT (LP)	15
67	Wing WL 1174	TENTH ANNIVERSARY ALBUM (LP)	12
68	Stateside S(S)L 10227	THE NEW GOLDEN HITS OF THE PLATTERS (LP)	12
68	Stateside S(S)L 10245	SWEET, SWEET LOVIN' (LP)	15
68	Polydor Special 236 223	ONLY YOU (LP)	12
68	Fontana SFL 13040	THE PLATTERS SING LATINO (LP, reissue)	12
71	Pye Intl. NSPL 28149	OUR WAY (LP)	12

(see also Buck Ram's Ramrocks, Linda Hayes)

PLAYBOY CLUB BUNNIES
| 68 | Decca F 12832 | Keep The Ball Rollin'/I Only Want To Be With You | 6 |

PLAYBOYS (U.S.)
| 58 | London HLU 8681 | Over The Weekend/Double Talk | 35 |
| 58 | London HLU 8681 | Over The Weekend/Double Talk (78) | 30 |

PLAYBOYS (U.K)
| 60s | Lyntone LYN 549/550 | THE PLAYBOYS FOR CHARITY (EP, flexidisc, no p/s) | 15 |

PLAYBOYS (U.S.)
| 69 | Capitol CL 15621 | Let's Get Back To Rock And Roll/Homemade Cookin' | 4 |

PLAYBOYS (Jamaica)
| 71 | Tropical AL 007 | Change Change/TROPICAL ALL STARS: Version 2 | 6 |

(see also Rad Bryan)

PLAY DEAD
81	Fresh FRESH 29	Poison Takes A Hold/Introduction (p/s)	7
81	Fresh FRESH 38	T.V. Eye/Final Epitaph (p/s)	7
83	Jungle JUNG 002	Propaganda/Propaganda (Mix) (p/s)	8
83	Situation 2 SIT 28	Shine/Promise (p/s)	5
83	Situation 2 SIT 28T	Shine/Promise/Gaze (12", p/s)	8
84	Clay CLAY 31	Break/Blood Stains (p/s)	8
84	Clay 12CLAY 31	Break/Blood Stains/Pleasure (12", p/s)	7
84	Clay CLAY 35	Isabel/Solace (p/s)	4
84	Clay 12CLAY 35	Isabel/Solace (12", p/s)	7
85	Tanz TANZ 1	This Side Of Heaven (unissued, white label promos only)	7

PLAYERS
| 63 | Oriole CB 1861 | Mockingbird/Bizet As It May | 12 |

PLAYGIRLS (U.S.)
| 59 | RCA RCA 1133 | Hey Sport/Young Love Swings The World | 15 |
| 59 | RCA RCA 1133 | Hey Sport/Young Love Swings The World (78) | 25 |

PLAYGIRLS (Jamaica)
| 65 | Black Swan WI 456 | Looks Are Deceiving/BABA BROOKS: Dreadnaught | 18 |

PLAYGROUND
| 67 | MGM MGM 1351 | At The Zoo/Yellow Balloon | 7 |

PLAYMATES
53	London L 1198	My Love Was Wasted On You/You Never Get Too Old To Fall In Love (78)	12
57	Columbia DB 3941	Pretty Woman/Barefoot Girl	10
57	Columbia DB 4033	Island Girl/Darling, It's Wonderful	10
58	Columbia DB 4084	Jo-Ann/You Can't Stop Me From Dreaming	8
58	Columbia DB 4127	Let's Be Lovers/Give Me Another Chance	7
58	Columbia DB 4127	Let's Be Lovers/Give Me Another Chance (78)	8
58	Columbia DB 4151	Can't You Get It Through Your Head/Don't Go Home	7
58	Columbia DB 4151	Can't You Get It Through Your Head/Don't Go Home (78)	8
58	Columbia DB 4207	While The Record Goes Around/The Day I Died	7
58	Columbia DB 4207	While The Record Goes Around/The Day I Died (78)	8
58	Columbia DB 4224	Beep Beep/Your Love	7
58	Columbia DB 4224	Beep Beep/Your Love (78)	12
59	Columbia DB 4288	Star Love/The Thing-A-Ma-Jig	6
59	Columbia DB 4338	What Is Love?/I Am	8
59	Columbia DB 4389	On The Beach/First Love	6
60	Columbia DB 4468	Parade Of Pretty Girls/Jubilation T. Cornpone	6
60	Columbia DB 4551	Wait For Me/Eyes Of An Angel	6
61	Columbia DB 4628	Little Miss Stuck Up/Real Life	6
59	Columbia SEG 7949	PARTY PLAYMATES NO. 1 (EP)	10
59	Columbia SEG 7966	PARTY PLAYMATES NO. 2 (EP)	10
60	Columbia 33SX 1215	BROADWAY SHOW STOPPERS (LP, also stereo SCX 3300)	12/15

PLAYTHINGS
| 70 | Pye 7N 45212 | Stop What You're Doing To Me/Sad Songs (re-pressed 1973) | 6 |
| 73 | Pye 7N 45399 | Surrounded By A Ray Of Sunshine/Dance The Night Away | 5 |

BOBBY PLEASE
| 57 | London HLB 8507 | Your Driver's Licence, Please (unissued, 1-sided demo only) | 275 |
| 57 | London HLB 8507 | Your Driver's Licence, Please/Heartache Street (78) | 100 |

PLEASERS
77	Solid Gold SGR 104	You Know What I'm Thinking/Hello Little Girl (no p/s)	8
77	Arista ARIST 21	Girl I Know/Don't Go Breaking My Heart (p/s)	4
77	Arista ARIST 152	You Keep Tellin' Lies/I'm In Love/Who Are You (p/s)	4
78	Arista ARIST 180	The Kids Are Alright/Stay With Me (p/s)	5

PLEASURE
| 75 | Fantasy FTC 115 | Dust Yourself Off/Midnight At The Oasis | 5 |
| 78 | Fantasy FT 543 | GET TO THE FEELIN' (LP) | 12 |

PLEASURE FAIR
| 68 | Uni UN 500 | Morning Glory Blues/Fade Out Fade In | 5 |
| 67 | Uni UNL(S) 100 | PLEASURE FAIR (LP) | 12 |

(see also Bread)

PLEASURE GARDEN

60s	Sound For Industry SFI 31H/32H	Permissive Paradise/EMPEROR ROSKO & JONATHAN KING: Young London (flexidisc, art sleeve)	30

PLEASURES

65	Sue WI 357	Music City/If I Had A Little Money	20

PLEBS

64	Decca F 12006	Bad Blood/Babe I'm Gonna Leave You	40
60s	Oak	THE PLEBS (LP, 1-sided, private pressing)	600

JACK PLEIS & HIS ORCHESTRA

50	London L 611	Ragging The Scale/Story Of The Stars (78)	8
50	London L 762	Ragamuffin/La Petite Valse (78)	8
51	London L 853	I'll Always Be In Love With You/Caravan (78)	8
51	London L 871	Autumn Leaves/Sophisticated Lady (78)	8
51	London L 898	Stardust/The Sheik Of Araby (78)	8
51	London L 985	Hurry Home To Me/Shenandoah Waltz (78)	8
56	Brunswick 05534	The Trouble With Harry (with Bonnie Lake & Her Beaux)/Pauline	6
57	Brunswick 05634	Giant (with Ralph Young)/Lonesome Without You	6
59	Brunswick 05795	Theme From "Compulsion"/Romantico	5
59	Brunswick 05795	Theme From "Compulsion"/Romantico (78)	10
61	Brunswick 05846	Pepe/Theme From "The Sundowners"	5

(see also Ralph Young, Bonnie Lake & Her Beaux)

PLEXUS

78	Look LKLP 6175	PLEXUS (LP)	60
79	Hill & Dale HD004	LIFE UP THE CREEK (LP)	50

PLONE

97	Wurlitzer Jukebox WJ 36	Press A Key/Electronic Beauty Parlour (1,500 black vinyl, 300 red, p/s)	6/4

PLUGS

79	Cathedral CATH 1	Too Late/UFO/Sally (gatefold p/s)	8

JEAN PLUM

76	London HLU 10514	Look At The Boy/Back At You	8

PLUMMERS

64	Blue Beat BB 260	Johnny/Little Stars (actually by Plamers)	15

PLUS

70	Probe SPB 1009	SEVEN DEADLY SINS (LP)	20

PLUTO

71	Dawn DNS 1017	Rag A Bone Joe/Stealing My Thunder	15
72	Dawn DNS 1026	I Really Want It/Something That You Loved	20
71	Dawn DNLS 3030	PLUTO (LP)	50

(see also Dry Ice, Foundations)

NICK PLYTAS & ANN PIGALLE

82	Illuminated ILL 1210	HOT SAGAS (10" EP)	7

PNEUMONIA

79	Plastic PLAS 001	Exhibition/Coming Attack/U.K. DECAY: U.K. Decay/Carcrash (folded p/s)	18

(see also U.K. Decay)

POCO

71	Epic EQ 30209	DELIVERIN' (LP, quadrophonic)	12

(see also Buffalo Springfield, Au Go-Go Singers)

POEMS

81	Polka DOT 1	ACHIEVING UNITY (EP, initially with booklet)	8

(see also Strawberry Switchblade)

POET & ONE MAN BAND

69	Verve Forecast SVLP 6012	THE POET AND THE ONE MAN BAND (LP)	35

(see also Tony Colton, Nicky Hopkins, Heads Hands & Feet)

POETS (U.K.)

64	Decca F 11995	Now We're Thru/There Are Some	12
65	Decca F 12074	That's The Way It's Got To Be/I'll Cry With The Moon	50
65	Decca F 12195	I Am So Blue/I Love Her Still	30
65	Immediate IM 006	Call Again/Some Things I Can't Forget	60
66	Immediate IM 024	Baby Don't You Do It/I'll Come Home	60
67	Decca F 12569	Wooden Spoon/In Your Tower	165
71	Strike Cola SC 1	Heyla Hola/Fun Buggy	40
88	Bam Caruso OPRA 088	I Love Her Still/GHOST: Time Is My Enemy (company sleeve, promo only)	7

(see also Pathfinders, [White] Trash, Blue)

POETS (Ireland)

68	Pye 7N 17668	Locked In A Room/Alone Am I	60
68	Target 7N 17668	Locked In A Room/Alone Am I (Irish issue, different label)	60

POETS (U.S.)

(see under American Poets)

POGUE MAHONE

84	Pogue Mahone PM 1	Dark Streets Of London/The Band Played Waltzing Mathilda (no p/s)	10
84	Pogue Mahone PM 1	Dark Streets Of London/The Band Played Waltzing Mathilda (white label tour copy with 'harp' sticker, 237 only)	50

(see also Pogues)

MINT VALUE £

POGUES

84	Stiff BUY 207	Dark Streets Of London/The Band Played Waltzing Mathilda (reissue of Pogue Mahone, no p/s) 10
84	Stiff BUY 212	Boys From The County Hell/Repealing Of The Licensing Laws (green-tinted p/s) 10
84	Stiff BUY 212	Boys From The County Hell/Repealing Of The Licensing Laws (A-label promos in blue-tinted p/s) 12
84	Stiff BUY 207/BUY 212	Dark Streets Of London/The Band Played Waltzing Mathilda//Boys From The County Hell/Repealing Of The Licensing Laws (shrinkwrapped double pack) ... 20
85	Stiff BUY 220	A Pair Of Brown Eyes/Whiskey You're The Devil (p/s) 6
85	Stiff DBUY 220	A Pair Of Brown Eyes/Whiskey You're The Devil (picture disc) 15
85	Stiff BUYIT 220	A Pair Of Brown Eyes/Whiskey You're The Devil/Muirshin Durkin (12", p/s) ... 15
85	Stiff BUY 212/BUY 220	Boys From The County Hell/Repealing Of The Licensing Laws//A Pair Of Brown Eyes/Whiskey You're The Devil (shrinkwrapped double pack) 15
85	Stiff BUY 224	Sally MacLennane/Wild Rover (wraparound poster p/s, some green vinyl) 10/7
85	Stiff BUY 224	Sally MacLennane/Wild Rover (standard p/s) 6
85	Stiff PBUY 224	Sally MacLennane/Wild Rover (shaped picture disc) 10
85	Stiff BUYIT 224	Sally MacLennane/Wild Rover/The Leaving Of Liverpool (12", p/s) 8
85	Stiff BUYC 224	Sally MacLennane/Wild Rover/The Leaving Of Liverpool/ Wild Cats Of Kilkenny (cassette) 12
85	Stiff PBUY 229	Dirty Old Town/A Pistol For Paddy Garcia (picture disc) 10
85	Stiff BUYIT 229	Dirty Old Town/A Pistol For Paddy Garcia/The Parting Glass (12", some with poster & stickered p/s) 20/15
85	Stiff MAIL 3	Dirty Old Town (live)/Sally MacLennane (live)/(interview) (12", mail-order) ... 12
86	Stiff PBUY 243	POGUETRY IN MOTION (EP, picture disc) 5
86	MCA MCAT 1084	Haunted/Junk Theme/Hot Dogs With Everything (12", p/s, with poster) 7
87	Stiff/Hell BLOOD 1	The Good, The Bad & The Ugly/Rake At The Gates Of Hell (unreleased)
87	Stiff/Hell BLOODY 1	The Good, The Bad & The Ugly/Rake At The Gates Of Hell (12", unreleased)
88	Pogue Mahone SGG 1-12	ST. PATRICK'S NIGHT EP (12" EP) 7
89	WEA SAM 553	Misty Morning Albert Bridge/(same track) (12" promo, green vinyl, no p/s) 8

(see also Pogue Mahone, Nips, Nipple Erectors, Radiators From Space)

POGUES featuring KIRSTY MacCOLL

87	Pogue Mahone CDNY 7	A Fairytale Of New York/The Battle March Medley/Shane Bradley (CD) 7

POINTED STICKS

79	Stiff BUY 59	Out Of Luck/What Do You Want Me To Do/Somebody's Mom (p/s) 6

POISON

87	M. F. Nations P12 KUT 125	Talk Dirty To Me/We Want Some Need Some/Interview (12", picture disc) 7
87	Music For Nations P12 KUT 127	Cry Tough/Cry Tough (U.S. Mix)/Look What The Cat Dragged In (12", picture disc) 7
88	Capitol CLP 486	Nothin' But A Good Time/Look But You Can't Touch (poster p/s) 4
88	Capitol CLP 486	Nothin' But A Good Time/Look But You Can't Touch (picture disc) 5
89	Capitol CLP 520	Every Rose Has Its Thorn/Back To The Rocking Horse (shaped picture disc) 6
89	Capitol CLS 523	Your Mama Don't Dance/Tearin' Down The Walls (p/s, green vinyl) 4

POISON GIRLS

79	Small Wonder WEENY 4	HEX (12" EP, with lyric insert) 7
80	Crass/Xntrix 421984/1	Persons Unknown/CRASS: Bloody Revolutions (folded 21" x 14" poster p/s) 5
81	Crass 421984/10	Pretty Polly/Bully Boys (live) (square red or clear flexidisc free with *In The City* fanzine, with/without magazine) 6/4
81	Crass 421984/8	All Systems Go/Promenade Immortelle/Dirty Work (p/s with lyrics) 5
83	Illuminated ILL 23	One Good Reason/Cinnamon Gardens (p/s) 4
83	Illuminated ILL 25	Are You Happy Now?/Cream Dream (p/s) 4
80	Crass 421984/2	CHAPPAQUIDICK (LP, with free flexidisc "Statement" [421984/7]) 10

(see also Crass, Fatal Microbes/Poison Girls)

POISON IDEA

91	Vinyl Solution VS 29	Plastic Bomb/We Got The Beat/Harder They Come/Lawdy Miss Clawdy (double pack, p/s) 8

POISON IVY

64	Granta GR 7EP 1011	CLINGING MEMORIES (EP) 100

POLECATS

81	Nervous NER 001	Rockabilly Guy/Chicken Shack (p/s) 12
81	Mercury POLE 4	Make A Circuit With Me/Juvenile Delinquent (p/s) 5
81	Mercury POLE 10	John I'm Only Dancing/All Night Long/Big Green Car (10", p/s, pink vinyl) 8
81	Lyntone LYN 10138/9	We Say Yeah/GRAHAM BONNET: Night Games/THIN LIZZY: Song For Jimmy/ WAY OF THE WEST: Monkey Love (orange flexi with *Flexipop*, issue 10). 8/4

ROLO POLEY

69	Jackpot JP 704	Zapatoo The Tiger/Music House (both sides actually by Lester Sterling) 6

POLICE

77	Illegal IL 001	Fall Out/Nothing Achieving (black & white p/s, red & black label, various designs). 15
78	A&M AMS 7348	Roxanne/Peanuts (2.52) ('telephone' p/s, typed matrix no., 'All Rights ...' on top half of label) 7
78	A&M AMS 7348	Roxanne/Peanuts (12", 'telephone' p/s) 15
78	A&M AMS 7381	Can't Stand Losing You/Dead End Job (glossy p/s, original issue, label credited to 'Police', mid-blue or rarer black vinyl). 10/7
78	A&M AMS 7402	So Lonely/Time This Time (p/s, miscredited flip, label credited to 'Police') 5
79	A&M AMS 7348	Roxanne/Peanuts (3.54) (reissue, 'group' p/s, handwritten matrix number, blue or black vinyl) 6/4
79	A&M AMS 7348	Roxanne/Peanuts (2.52) (reissue, 'group' p/s, typed matrix number, blue or black vinyl) 6/4
79	A&M AMSP 7348	Roxanne/Peanuts (12", reissue, 'group' p/s) 10

79	A&M AMS 7381	Can't Stand Losing You/Dead End Job (reissue, label credited to 'The Police'; dark blue or light blue vinyl) .... each 5
79	A&M AMS 7381	Can't Stand Losing You/Dead End Job (p/s, reissue, red, yellow, green or white vinyl) 10-12
79	A&M AMS 7381	Can't Stand Losing You/Dead End Job (p/s, mispressed B-side, plays "No Time This Time") .... 20+
79	A&M AMS 7474	Message In A Bottle/Landlord (p/s, green vinyl) 4
79	Illegal IL 001	Fall Out/Nothing Achieving (reissue, various label designs, green/black p/s) 8
79	Illegal IL 001	Fall Out/Nothing Achieving (reissue, various label designs, purple/blue p/s) 15
79	Illegal IL 001	Fall Out/Nothing Achieving (reissue, various label designs, black & orange p/s) 30
80	A&M AMPP 6001	POLICE PACK (6 x 7" printed foldout PVC pack [AMS 7348, 7381, 7402, 7474 & 7494] & "The Bed's Too Big Without You"/"Truth Hits Everybody" [AMPP 6001/E]; all on blue vinyl with 6 inserts) 25
80	A&M SAMP 5	SIX-TRACK RADIO SAMPLER (custom p/s, promo radio sampler) 15
81	A&M AMS 8194	Spirits (In The Material World)/Low Life (poster p/s, some with badge) 8/4
83	A&M AM 117	Every Breath You Take/Murder By Numbers (p/s, with free badge) 4
83	A&M AM 117/AM 01	Every Breath You Take/Murder By Numbers//Truth Hits Everybody/ Man In A Suitcase (double pack, gatefold p/s) 15
83	A&M AMSP 117	Every Breath You Take/Murder By Numbers (picture disc). 8
83	A&M AMP 127	Wrapped Around Your Finger/Someone To Talk To (Sting picture disc). 6
83	A&M AMP 127	Wrapped Around Your Finger/Someone To Talk To (Andy Summers or Stewart Copeland picture disc, 1,000 each)...................... each 8
88	A&M AMCD 905	COMPACT HITS (CD EP) 7
78	A&M AMLN 68502	OUTLANDOS D'AMOUR (LP, blue vinyl) 15

(see also Sting, Klark Kent, Radio Actors, Zoot Money's Big Roll Band, Last Exit, Newcastle Big Band, Eberhard Schoener, Andy Summers & Robert Fripp)

POLIPHONY
| 73 | Zella JHLPS 136 | POLIPHONY (LP, private pressing) .... 175 |

POLITICIANS
| 72 | Hot Wax HWX 114 | Love Machine/Free Your Mind .... 5 |
| 72 | Hot Wax SHW 5007 | THE POLITICIANS (LP) .... 18 |

FRANK POLK
| 65 | Capitol CL 15389 | Trying To Keep Up With The Joneses/Welcome Home, Baby .... 25 |

POLKA DOTS
58	Pye Nixa 7N 15144	Don't Make Small Talk Baby/There Will Never Be Another 6
58	Pye Nixa N 15144	Don't Make Small Talk Baby/There Will Never Be Another (78) 8
59	Pye Nixa 7N 15194	Hey Liley, Liley Lo/Go Chase A Moonbeam 6
59	Pye Nixa N 15194	Hey Liley, Liley Lo/Go Chase A Moonbeam (78) 10
59	Pye Nixa 7N 15211	Girls In Arms/You've Done Something To My Heart (with Laurie Johnson Orch.). . 6
59	Pye Nixa N 15211	Girls In Arms/You've Done Something To My Heart (78) 10
59	Columbia SEG 7894	SINGIN' AND SWINGIN' (EP) 18
61	Philips BBE 12487	THE POLKA DOTS (EP, also stereo SBBE 9074) 10/15
62	Philips BBE 12528	STRICTLY FOR KICKS (EP) 10
62	Philips BE 12534	RELAX AWHILE (EP) 10
62	Philips 433 625 BE	VOCAL SPECTACULAR (EP) 10
63	Philips BL 7576	NICE WORK AND YOU CAN BUY IT (LP) 150

(see also Teddy Johnson, Laurie Johnson)

RAY POLLARD
| 65 | United Artists UP 1111 | The Drifter/Let Him Go (And Let Me Love You) .... 150 |
| 66 | United Artists UP 1133 | It's A Sad Thing/All The Things You Are. .... 80 |

(see also Wanderers)

POLLCATS
| 90 | Community Charge AXT 1 | Poll Tax Blues/Poll Tax Blues (same track both sides, p/s). .... 10 |

(see also Steve Marriott)

MICHAEL POLNAREFF
66	Vogue VRS 7012	La Poupée Qui Fait Non/Beatnik 5
66	Vogue VRS 7013	No No No No No No/Beatnik 5
66	Vogue VRS 7019	Love Me Please Love Me/L'Amour Avec Toi 6

POLYGON WINDOW
| 92 | Warp WARP LP 7 | SURFING ON THE SINE WAVES (2-LP) .... 20 |
| 92 | Warp WARP LP 7LTD | SURFING ON THE SINE WAVES (LP, clear vinyl)................... 40 |

(see also Aphex Twin)

POLYPHEMUS
| 95 | Acme AC 8010LP | SCRAPBOOK OF MADNESS (LP, reissue with insert, 500 only) .... 15 |
| 95 | Acme AC 8016LP | STONEHOUSE (LP, gatefold sleeve, 700 only) .... 12 |

HERB POMEROY BIG BAND
| 57 | Columbia SX 1091 | LIFE IS A MANY SPLENDOURED GIG (LP). .... 12 |

POMPHEY
| 72 | Green Door GD 4029 | Jamaica Skank/JOHNNY MOORE: Bing Comes To Town .... 6 |

PONI-TAILS
58	HMV POP 516	Born Too Late/Come On Joey, Dance With Me (as Pony-Tails). 10
58	HMV POP 516	Born Too Late/Come On Joey, Dance With Me (as Pony-Tails) (78) 12
58	HMV POP 558	Close Friends/Seven Minutes In Heaven. 10
58	HMV POP 558	Close Friends/Seven Minutes In Heaven (78) 15
59	HMV POP 596	Early To Bed/Father Time 10
59	HMV POP 596	Early To Bed/Father Time (78) 20
59	HMV POP 644	Moody/Oom Pah Polka..................................... 10

MINT VALUE £

| 59 | HMV POP 663 | I'll Be Seeing You/I'll Keep Tryin' | 10 |
| 58 | HMV 7EG 8427 | THE PONI-TAILS (EP) | 125 |

JEAN-LUC PONTY
| 69 | Liberty LBL/LBS 83262 | ELECTRIC CONNECTION (LP) | 12 |
| 70 | Liberty LBL/LBS 83375 | KING KONG (LP) | 12 |

POOGY
| 74 | EMI EMI 2136 | She Looked Me In The Eye (I Gave Her My Life)/Morris And His Turtle | 15 |

POOH STICKS
88	Fierce FRIGHT 011	On Tape (p/s, 1-sided, etched B-side)	35
88	Fierce FRIGHT 021	1-2-3 Red Light (p/s, 1-sided)	20
88	Fierce FRIGHT 021-025	FIERCE BOX SET (5 x 1-sided etched discs, hand-coloured labels, with insert)	45
88	Fierce FRIGHT 026	ALAN McGEE (CD EP, with FRIGHT 021-025 tracks plus "On Tape"/ "Please Hue, Please", some in 7" box with booklet)	20/10
89	Fierce FRIGHT 034	Dying For It (p/s, sold at U.L.U. gig, 300 only, some signed)	25/15
89	Fierce FRIGHT 034	Dying For It (1-sided, different p/s to above)	15
89	Cheree CHEREE 3	Go Go Girl/Simon E (flexidisc with foldout *Cheree* fanzine/sleeve)	8
89	Woosh WOOSH 007/ WOOSH 6	Hard On Love (yellow flexi with Pooh Sticks fanzine)// GROOVE FARM: Heaven Is Blue/ESMERALDA'S KITE: Vampire Girl (red flexi) (with *Woosh* fanzine 3)	12
89	Anonymous ANON 2	ENCORES (EP, numbered box set, multi-coloured 1-sided 7" with sweet watch, badge, sticker & booklet)	8
92	Fierce/BMG FRIGHT 42	Million Seller (1-sided, no p/s)	6
89	53rd & 3rd AGAMC 5	ORGASM (LP, a few on pink vinyl with insert for export)	20/10
89	Fierce FRIGHT 025	THE POOH STICKS (mini-LP, with inner, black & white sleeve, 1-sided, side 2 etched)	12
89	Fierce FRIGHT 035	TRADE MARK OF QUALITY (LP, mail-order only, plain stickered sleeve with insert, numbered)	20

(see also Dumb Angels)

BRIAN POOLE
66	Decca F 12402	Hey Girl/Please Be Mine	6
66	CBS 202349	Everything I Touch Turns To Tears/I Need Her Tonight	8
67	CBS 202661	That Reminds Me Baby/Tomorrow Never Comes	6
67	CBS 3005	Just How Loud/The Other Side Of The Sky	10
69	President PT 239	Send Her To Me/Pretty In The City (as Brian Poole & Seychelles)	5
69	President PT 264	What Do Women Most Desire/Treat Her Like A Woman (with Seychelles)	5

(see also Brian Poole & Tremeloes)

BRIAN POOLE & TREMELOES
62	Decca F 11455	Twist Little Sister/Lost Love	10
62	Decca F 11515	That Ain't Right/Blue	8
63	Decca F 11567	A Very Good Year For Girls/Meet Me Where We Used Meet	7
63	Decca F 11616	Keep On Dancing/Run Back Home	7
63	Decca F 11694	Twist And Shout/We Know	5
63	Decca F 11739	Do You Love Me?/Why Can't You Love Me?	5
63	Decca F 11771	I Can Dance/Are You Loving Me At All	6
64	Decca F 11823	Candy Man/I Wish I Could Dance	5
64	Decca F 11893	Someone, Someone/Till The End Of Time	5
64	Decca F 11951	Twelve Steps To Love/Don't Cry	6
64	Decca F 12037	Three Bells/Tell Me How To Care	5
65	Decca F 12124	After A While/You Know	7
65	Decca F 12197	I Want Candy/Love Me Baby	10
65	Decca F 12274	Good Lovin'/Could It Be You	7
64	Decca DFE 8566	BRIAN POOLE AND THE TREMELOES (EP)	30
65	Decca DFE 8610	BRIAN POOLE AND THE TREMELOES (EP)	30
63	Ace of Clubs ACL 1146	BIG BIG HITS OF '62 (LP)	25
63	Decca LK 4550	TWIST AND SHOUT WITH BRIAN POOLE AND THE TREMELOES (LP)	35
65	Decca LK 4685	IT'S ABOUT TIME (LP)	45

(see also Brian Poole, Tremeloes)

LOU & LAURA POOLE
| 72 | Jay Boy BOY 63 | Only You And I Know/Look At Me | 7 |

POOR SOULS
| 65 | Decca F 12183 | When My Baby Cries/My Baby She's Not There | 12 |
| 66 | Alp ALP 595 004 | Love Me/Please Don't Change Your Mind | 35 |

GROOVY JOE POOVEY
| 70 | Injun 100 | Ten Long Fingers On The 88 Keys/Thrill Of Love | 8 |

IGGY POP
77	RCA PB 9093	China Girl/Baby	4
77	RCA PB 9160	Success/The Passenger	5
77	RCA PB 9160	Some Weird Sin/The Passenger	4
78	RCA PB 9213	Sixteen/I Got A Right	4
78	Radar ADA 4	Kill City (with James Williamson)/I Got Nothin'	4
79	Arista ARISP 274	Five Foot One/Pretty Flamingo (picture disc)	6
80	Arista ARIST 327	Loco Mosquito/Take Care Of Me (p/s)	4
82	Chrysalis/Melody Maker	Extracts From "Zombie Birdhouse"/STIFF LITTLE FINGERS: Excerpts From "Now Then" (flexidisc, free with *Melody Maker*)	6/4
88	A&M AMCD 909	COMPACT HITS (EP)	7
90	Virgin America VUSCD 18	Livin' On The Edge Of The Night (Edit)/The Passenger/Nightclubbing/ China Girl (3" CD, card sleeve)	7
73	CBS 65586	RAW POWER (LP, with inner, orange label, as Iggy & Stooges)	30
78	Radar RAD 2	KILL CITY (LP, as Iggy Pop & James Williamson)	10

(see also Stooges)

POPCORNS
63 Columbia DB 4968   Zero Zero/Chinese Twist 10

DAVE POPE
70s Myrrh MYR 1003   TIME TO TAKE ACCOUNT (LP). 15

TIM POPE
84 Fiction FICS 21   I Want To Be A Tree/The Double Crossing Of Two Faced Fred (p/s) 15
84 Fiction FICSX 21   I Want To Be A Tree/(Elephant) Song/The Double Crossing Of
Two Faced Fred (12", p/s) 25

(see also Cure)

POP GROUP
79 Radar ADA 29   She Is Beyond Good And Evil/3.38 (p/s) 6
79 Radar ADA 1229   She Is Beyond Good And Evil/3.38 (12", p/s) 8
79 Rough Trade RT 023   We Are All Prostitutes/Amnesty International Report On
British Army Torture Of Irish Prisoners (p/s) 5
80 Rough Trade RT 039/ Y Y1   Where There's A Will There's A Way/SLITS:
In The Beginning There Was Rhythm (p/s) 5
79 Radar RAD 20   Y (LP, with foldout colour poster) 15
80 Rough Trade ROUGH 9   FOR HOW MUCH LONGER DO WE TOLERATE MASS MURDER?
(LP, with 4 black-and-white posters) 12
80 Y/Rough Trade ROUGH 12   WE ARE TIME (LP, plain black sleeve). 12
(see also Slits)

POP GUNS
80s La Di Da LA-DI-DA 001   Where Do You Go/HOW MANY BEANS MAKE FIVE: Another Friendly Face
(flexidisc, 33rpm, p/s). 5
89 Medium Cool MC 019T   LANDSLIDE (12" EP) 8
(see also Wedding Present)

POPINJAYS
88 Big Cat BBA 02   Don't Go Back/So Close/Move To Perish (12", p/s). 7

POPPIES
66 Columbia DB 7879   Lullaby Of Love/I Wonder Why. 15

KEITH POPPIN
73 Randy's RAN 531   Kick The Bucket/I'm A Man Of My Word 5

POPPY FAMILY
70 Decca (S)KL-R 5022   WHICH WAY YOU GOING BILLY? (LP, mono/stereo). 15/12
72 Decca SKL 5114   POPPY SEEDS (LP) 12

POPPYHEADS
88 Sha La La Ba Ba Ba Ba 4   POSTCARD FOR FLOSSY (EP, 1-sided flexidisc, p/s in poly bag) 8
88 Sarah SARAH 006   Cremation Town/Pictures You Weave/Dreamboat
(foldaround p/s with large poster in poly bag) 8

POP RIVETS
79 Hypocrite HEP 001   POP RIVITS (EP, no p/s) 12
79 Hypocrite HEP 002   Pop Rivits/Sulphate 15
79 Hypocrite JIM 1   FUN IN THE U.K. (EP, no p/s, double pack) 30
79 Hypocrite HIP-O   EMPTY SOUNDS FROM ANARCHY RANCH (LP, col'd back, stamped labels). . . . 30
80 Hypocrite HIP 007   THE POP RIVETS GREATEST HITS (LP, screen-printed sleeve). 15
(see also Milkshakes)

POPSICLES
65 Vogue V 9243   I Don't Want To Be Your Baby Anymore/Baby I Miss You 15
(see also Ellie Greenwich, Raindrops)

POPULAR 5
68 Minit MLF 11011   I'm A Lovemaker/Little Bitty Pretty One 10

POP WILL EAT ITSELF
86 Desperate SRT 1   POPPIES SAY GRRR! (EP, stamped white labels in brown paper bag) 8
86 Desperate DAN 1   POPPIES SAY GRRR! (EP, reissue, orange sleeve) 5
86 Chapter 22 CHAP 9   POPPIECOCK (EP). 4
87 Chapter 22 LCHAP 13   Love Missile F1-11(Designer Grebo Mix)/(Original Poppies Mix)/Orgone
Accumulator (Original Version)/Everything That Rises (New Version) (p/s). 8
87 Chapter 22 LCHAP 16   Beaver Patrol/Bubbles (numbered p/s, clear vinyl in stickered PVC sleeve). 6
87 Chapter 22 LCHAP 16   Beaver Patrol/Bubbles (no'd p/s, signed, pink vinyl in stickered PVC sleeve). . . . 10
88 Chapter 22 LCHAP 20   There Is No Love Between Us Anymore/Picnic in The Sky (picture disc) 5
88 Chapter 22 CLUB CHAP 20   There Is No Love Between Us Anymore (Speciality Extended High Mix)/
Hit The Hi-Tech Groove (The M & K Mix) (12", die-cut sleeve) 8
89 RCA PB 42729   Can U Dig It/Poison To The Mind (p/s, shrinkwrapped to 10" card with patch) 5
89 RCA PB 43021   VERY METAL NOISE POLLUTION (EP, pink or yellow gatefold sleeve) 4/5
89 RCA PT 43022   VERY METAL NOISE POLLUTION (EP, shaped picture disc) 4
89 House Of Dolls HOD 009   Wake Up! Time To Die.../WILD POPPIES: The Last Thing/BLOW UP: Slip Into
Something (Rough Mix)/GODSPEED: Radiate (freebie with *House Of Dolls*). . . . 6/4
(see also Wild & Wandering)

POP WORKSHOP
68 Page One POF 091   Fairyland/When My Little Girl Is Happy. 5
69 Page One POF 129   Punch And Judy Man/Love Is A One Way Highway 5

PORCUPINE TREE
89 Delerium DELC 0002   TARQUIN'S SEAWEED FARM (cassette, 1st issue, around 50 only) 30
91 Delerium DELC 0002   TARQUIN'S SEAWEED FARM (cassette, 2nd issue, silver print,
with A4 booklet, red/black text, 200 only) 25
91 Delerium DELC 0002   TARQUIN'S SEAWEED FARM (cassette, silver print, with photocopied
A5 booklet, label on Side 1, 200 only). 20
91 Delerium DELC 0003   THE NOSTALGIA FACTORY (cassette, silver print, with A4 booklet,
red/black text, 200 only). 20

MINT VALUE £

91	Delerium DELC 0003	THE NOSTALGIA FACTORY (cassette, with photocopied A5 booklet, label on Side 1, 200 only)	20
92	Delerium DELEC 008	ON THE SUNDAY OF LIFE (2-LP, gatefold sleeve)	20
92	Delerium DELEC EP 007	VOYAGE 34 (Astralasia Remix) (12", p/s)	10
92	Delerium DELEC EP 010	VOYAGE 34 (12", p/s)	15
92	Delerium DELECD EP 010	VOYAGE 34 (CD)	15
94	Delerium DELEC EP 032	Stars Die/Moonloop (12", p/s)	8
92	Delerium DELEC 008	ON THE SUNDAY OF LIFE (2-LP, gatefold sleeve)	20
92	Delerium DELEC CD 008	ON THE SUNDAY OF LIFE (CD)	20
94	Magic Gnome MG 4299325	YELLOW HEADGROW DREAMSCAPE (CD, 2,500 only)	50
95	Delerium DELEC LP 028	THE SKY MOVES SIDEWAYS (LP, 2,000 on blue vinyl w/poster)	15

PORK DUKES

77	Wood WOOD 9	Bend And Flush/Throbbing Gristle (p/s)	6
77	Wood BRANCH 9	Making Bacon/Tight Pussy (12", p/s, yellow vinyl)	8
78	Wood Standard WOOD 56	Telephone Masturbator/Melody Makers (p/s)	6
78	Wood PORK 001	THE PORK DUKES (LP, pink vinyl with warning sticker & postcard)	15
80	Wood PORK 2	PIG OUT OF HELL (LP)	15
82	Butt PORK 1	PIG IN A POKE (LP)	15

DAVID PORTER

70	Stax STAX 150	One Part — Two Parts/Can't I See You When I Want To	4
70	Stax SXATS 1034	GRITTY, GROOVY AND GETTIN' IT (LP)	10
71	Stax 2362 006	INTO A REAL THING (LP)	10

NOLAN PORTER

| 72 | Probe PRO 580 | If I Could Only Be Sure/Work It Out In The Morning | 10 |
| 72 | Probe SPB 1067 | NOLAN (LP) | 12 |

PORTER CUNNINGHAM

| 72 | Folk Heritage FHR 027 | OBSERVATIONS (LP) | 80 |

PORTION CONTROL

82	In Phaze POR CON 006	Surface And Be Seen/Spinola (Blotch)/Terror Leads To Better Days/ Simple As ABC/Monstrous Bulk/He Is A Barbarian (12", p/s, with plastic outer sleeve)	15
84	Illuminated ILL 2612	Raise The Pulse/Collapse/Bite My Head (12", p/s)	10
84	Illuminated ILL 3212	Rough Justice/The Man Who Did Backwards Somersaults (12", p/s with inner)	8
85	Illuminated ILL 4312	Go-Talk/Upside Down/Drag Down (12", p/s)	8
85	Rhythmic/Havoc 7RMIC 7	The Great Divide/Totall Recall (p/s)	4
85	Rhythmic/Havoc 12RMIC 7	The Great Divide/Divided/Bolt It Down (12", p/s)	7
85	Rhythmic/Havoc 12RMICX 7	The Great Divide (Julian Mendelsohn Remix)/Divided/Bolt It Down (12", p/s)	12
86	Dead Man's Curve DMC 1	PRESENT PURGE (12" EP)	8
83	In Phaze EZ 2	HIT THE PULSE (mini-LP, 45/33rpm)	15
84	Illuminated JAMS 44	STEP FORWARD (LP)	12
86	Dead Man's Curve DMC 8	PSYCHO-BOD SAVES THE WORLD (LP, with inner sleeve)	10
85	In Phaze PHA 5	SIMULATE SENSUAL (LP, clear vinyl, PVC sleeve with insert)	20

PORTISHEAD

| 94 | Go Beat 828 522 | DUMMY (LP) | 12 |

PORTOBELLO EXPLOSION

| 69 | Carnaby CNS 4001 | We Can Fly/Hot Smoke And Sasafrass (label credits *Portebello Explosion*) | 25 |

(see also Mirage, Jawbone, Spencer Davis Group)

PORTRAIT

| 69 | CBS 4520 | Sh-Sh-Sh-Sheila/Hurt Bad By Love | 4 |
| 70 | Pye 7N 45043 | Tokaido Links/Cuddle Me Closer | 4 |

SANDY POSEY

66	MGM MGM 1321	Born A Woman/Caution To The Wind	6
66	MGM MGM 1330	Single Girl/Blue Is My Best Colour	6
67	MGM MGM 1335	What A Woman In Love Won't Do/Shattered	6
67	MGM MGM 1342	I Take It Back/The Boy I Love	6
67	MGM MGM 1364	Are You Never Coming Home/I Can Show You How To Live	6
67	MGM MGM-C(S) 8035	BORN A WOMAN (LP)	20
67	MGM MGM-C(S) 8042	SINGLE GIRL (LP)	20
68	MGM MGM-C(S) 8051	SANDY POSEY (LP)	20
68	MGM MGM-C 8060	THE BEST OF SANDY POSEY (LP, original with blue label)	15
68	MGM MGM-C(S) 8073	LOOKING AT YOU (LP)	18

POSITIVE FORCE

| 79 | Sugarhill SH 102 | We Got The Funk/Tell Me What You See (12", no p/s) | 7 |

ROBERT POSS

| 80s | Sonic Life 001/LYN 21552 | O Five O (33rpm flexidisc, mail order only) | 4 |

(see also Band Of Susans)

HOWIE POST & SWIFTIES

| 63 | Fontana TF 421 | Tom Swift/The Elephant | 8 |

MIKE POST COALITION

| 72 | MGM PPSP 11 | The Rockford Files (Parts 1 & 2) | 4 |
| 75 | Warner Bros K 16588 | Afternoon Of The Rhino/Bubble Gum Breakthrough | 4 |

ADRIENNE POSTER

63	Oriole CB 1890	Only Fifteen/There's Nothing You Can Do About That	15
63	Decca F 11797	Only Fifteen/There's Nothing You Can Do About That (reissue)	12
64	Decca F 11864	Shang A Doo Lang/When A Girl Really Loves You	15
65	Decca F 12079	He Doesn't Love Me/The Way You Do The Things You Do	12
65	Decca F 12181	The Winds That Blow/Back Street Girl	10
66	Decca F 12329	Something Beautiful/So Glad You're Mine	8
66	Decca F 12455	They Long To Be Close To You/How Can I Hurt You (as Adrienne Posta)	6

POST MORTEM
82	Regime RM 006	AGAINST ALL ODDS (EP)	5

POTATOES
66	Fontana TF 756	The Bend/Bend Ahead..	6

KEITH POTGER
69	Mercury MF 1073	The World Would Never Turn Again/Santa Marie (some in p/s)	12/6

(see also Seekers, Judith Durham)

POTLIQUOR
72	Janus 6146 011	Cheer/Chatanooga	5
70	Dawn DNLS 3016	FIRST TASTE (LP, withdrawn)	80
72	Janus 6310 202	LEVEE BLUES (LP)	12
72	Janus 6310 203	FIRST TASTE (LP, reissue)	12

PHIL POTTER
76	Genesis GEN 10	MY SONG IS LOVE UNKNOWN (LP)	20
79	Dove DOVE 61	THE RESTORER (LP)	12

POUND HOUNDS
55	Brunswick 05484	Home Sweet Home/MELLOMEN: Lady	8

(see also Peggy Lee)

ALLEN POUND'S GET RICH
66	Parlophone R 5532	Searchin' In The Wilderness/Hey You (most copies as demos).............	325

POWDER
95	Parkway PARK 001X	20th Century Gods/Dizco Girl (embossed p/s, numbered, 2,000 only)	10
95	Parkway PARK 002	Afrodiziak/Shave Me (p/s, 2,000 only)	4

BOBBY POWELL
72	Mojo 2092 034	Peace Begins Within/Question	6

BUD POWELL (TRIO)
58	Columbia LB 10086	That Old Black Magic/Someone To Watch Over Me (78)...................	8
64	Blue Note 45-1712	Buster Rides Again/Dry Soul..	7
55	Vogue EPV 1030	BUD POWELL TRIO (EP)	70
55	Vogue EPV 1033	BUD POWELL'S MODERNISTS (EP)	70
55	Vogue EPV 1036	BUD POWELL TRIO (EP)	60
55	Columbia Clef SEB 10013	BUD POWELL (EP)..	70
57	Columbia Clef SEB 10074	GENIUS OF BUD POWELL (EP)...	70
58	Columbia Clef SEB 10094	GENIUS OF BUD POWELL NO. 2 (EP)	60
52	Vogue LDE 010	THE BUD POWELL TRIO (10" LP)	30
54	Vogue LDE 053	JAZZ AT THE MASSEY HALL VOL. 2 (10" LP)	25
56	Columbia Clef 33C 9016	BUD POWELL TRIO (10" LP)	30
57	Columbia Clef 33CX 10069	JAZZ ORIGINAL (LP)	40
58	Columbia Clef 33CX 10123	BLUES FOR BUD (LP)	75
59	HMV CLP 1294	THE LONELY ONE (LP)	60
63	Blue Note (B)BLP 1503	THE AMAZING BUD POWELL VOL. 1 (LP)..................................	15
63	Vogue LAE 558	THE BUD POWELL TRIO (LP)	15
63	Columbia 33SX 1575	THE BUD POWELL TRIO FEATURING MAX ROACH (LP)	60
64	Blue Note (B)BLP 1504	THE AMAZING BUD POWELL VOL. 2 (LP)..................................	15
64	Fontana FJL 903	HOT HOUSE (LP)	100
65	Columbia 33SX 1701	THE RETURN OF POWELL (LP)...	12
65	Xtra XTRA 1011	BOUNCING WITH BUD (LP)	12
65	Verve VLP 9075	THE VINTAGE YEARS (LP)	12
68	Fontana SFJL 901	BLUES FOR BOUFFEMONT (LP)...	90
69	Fontana SFJL 924	AT THE BLUE NOTE CAFE, PARIS 1961 (LP)	12

COZY POWELL
73	Rak RAK 164	Dance With The Devil/And Then There Was Skin...........................	5
73	Rak 4C 006 94962	Dance With The Devil/And Then There Was Skin (export issue, p/s, RAK 164 in run out groove)............................	12
74	Rak RAK 173	The Man In Black/After Dark..	5
74	Rak RAK 180	Na Na Na/Mistral (as Cozy Powell's Hammer).............................	5
79	Ariola ARO 189	Theme One/Over The Top Part 1 (p/s, red vinyl)	6
79	Ariola AROD 189	Theme One/Over The Top (full version) (12", company sleeve)	10
79	Ariola ARO 205	The Loner/El Sid (p/s, blue vinyl).......................................	6
80	Ariola ARO 222	Heidi Goes To Town/Over The Top Part 2 (p/s, clear vinyl)	6
81	Polydor POSP 328	Sooner Or Later/The Blister (p/s)	5
80	Ariola ARL 5038	OVER THE TOP (LP)	12
81	Polydor POLD 5047	TILT (LP, with inner sleeve)...	12

(see also Rainbow, Young Blood, Big Bertha, Ace Kefford Stand, Bedlam, Bernie Marsden, Phenomena, Black Sabbath, Jeff Beck,Whitesnake, Michael Schenker Group, Donovan, Gary Moore, Young & Moody, Brian May, Chick Churchill, Graham Bonnet, Forcefield, Emerson Lake & Powell, Jack Bruce)

JANE POWELL
53	MGM SP 1061	Something Wonderful/I Whistle A Happy Tune	6
53	MGM SP 1062	Hello, Young Lovers/We Kiss In A Shadow	6
56	HMV POP 267	True Love/Mind If I Make Love To You	8
59	MGM MGM-EP 701	JANE POWELL SINGS (EP)	18
54	Capitol LC 6665	THREE SAILORS AND A GIRL (10" LP)	20
57	HMV CLP 1131	JANE POWELL (LP)	20

JIMMY POWELL (& DIMENSIONS)
62	Decca F 11447	Sugar Babe (Parts 1 & 2) (solo)..	8
62	Decca F 11544	Tom Hark/Dance Her By Me (solo)......................................	8
63	Decca F 11570	Remember Them/Everyone But You (solo)	6
64	Pye 7N 15663	That's Alright/I'm Looking For A Woman	35
64	Pye 7N 15735	Sugar Babe/I've Been Watching You (as Jimmy Powell & 5 Dimensions)	15

Jimmy POWELL (& DIMENSIONS)

66	Strike JH 309	I Can Go Down/Love Me Right	8
67	Decca F 12664	Unexpected Mirrors/Time Mends Broken Hearts (with Dimensions)	7
68	Decca F 12751	I Just Can't Get Over You/Real Cool (with Dimensions)	7
68	Decca F 12793	Sugar Babe (Parts 1 & 2)	7
69	Young Blood YB 1002	I Can Go Down/Captain Man	5
69	Young Blood YB 1006	House Of The Rising Sun/That's Love	5
70	Young Blood YB 1019	Witness To A War/Strangers On A Train	5

JUDITH POWELL
| 67 | RCA RCA 1569 | Greener Days/No Goodbyes | 5 |

KEITH POWELL (& VALETS)
63	Columbia DB 7116	The Answer Is No!/Come On And Join The Party (with Valets)	10
64	Columbia DB 7229	Tore Up/You Better Let Him Go (with Valets)	12
64	Columbia DB 7366	I Should Know Better (But I Don't)/Too Much Monkey Business (with Valets)	25
65	Piccadilly 7N 35235	People Get Ready/Paradise	6
65	Piccadilly 7N 35249	Come Home Baby/Beyond The Hill	6
66	Piccadilly 7N 35275	Goodbye Girl/It Was Easier To Hurt Her	6
66	Piccadilly 7N 35300	Victory/Some People Only	6
66	Piccadilly 7N 35353	It Keeps Rainin'/Song of The Moon	7

(see also Move, Carl Wayne & Vikings)

KEITH (POWELL) & BILLIE (DAVIES)
66	Piccadilly 7N 35288	When You Move, You Lose/Tastes Sour, Don't It? (as Keith & Billie)	7
66	Piccadilly 7N 35321	You Don't Know Like I Know/Two Little People	8
66	Piccadilly 7N 35340	Swingin' Tight/That's Really Some Good	6

(see also Keith Powell, Billie Davis)

MARILYN POWELL
64	Fontana TF 448	All My Loving/After The Party	8
65	Fontana TF 526	Please Go Away/Where Did I Go Wrong	7
65	Fontana TF 557	As Long As You Come Back To Me/Go Away	6
65	Fontana TF 687	Showdown/Came The Day	7
68	CBS 2331	Something To Hold On To/Kiss Me Again	8
69	CBS 4440	Have Another Dream On Me/Afraid To Love You	5
70	CBS 5290	Dear Madame/Home	5

DUFFY POWER
59	Fontana H 194	Dream Lover/That's My Little Suzie	12
59	Fontana H 194	Dream Lover/That's My Little Suzie (78)	25
59	Fontana H 214	Kissin' Time/Ain't She Sweet	12
59	Fontana H 214	Kissin' Time/Ain't She Sweet (78)	25
59	Fontana H 230	Starry-Eyed/Prettier Than You	10
59	Fontana H 230	Starry-Eyed/Prettier Than You (78)	30
60	Fontana H 279	Whole Lotta Shakin' Goin' On/If I Can Dream	20
61	Fontana H 302	I've Got Nobody/When We're Walking Close	15
61	Fontana H 344	No Other Love/What Now	12
63	Parlophone R 4992	It Ain't Necessarily So/If I Get Lucky Someday	15
63	Parlophone R 5024	I Saw Her Standing There (with Graham Bond Quartet)/Farewell Baby	30
63	Parlophone R 5059	Hey Girl/Woman Made Trouble	15
64	Parlophone R 5111	Parchman Farm/Tired, Broke And Busted (with Paramounts)	20
64	Parlophone R 5169	Where Am I?/I Don't Care	30
67	Parlophone R 5631	Davy O'Brien (Leave That Baby Alone)/July Tree	20
70	CBS 5176	Hell Hound/Hummingbird	12
71	Epic EPC 7139	Hummingbird/Hell Hound (reissue)	8
73	GSF GSZ 6	River/Little Soldiers	6
73	GSF GSZ 8	Liberation/Song About Jesus	6
71	Transatlantic TRA 229	INNOVATIONS (LP)	30
73	GSF GS 502	DUFFY POWER (LP)	18
73	Spark SRLM 2005	DUFFY POWER (LP)	20
76	Buk BULP 2010	POWERHOUSE (LP, revised reissue of GSF GS 502)	15

(see also Alexis Korner, John McLaughlin, Jack Bruce, Graham Bond, Duffy's Nucleus)

JIMMY POWER
| 76 | Topic 12TS 306 | IRISH FIDDLE PLAYER (LP) | 12 |

POWERHOUSE
| 66 | Decca F 12471 | Chain Gang/Can You Hear Me? | 12 |
| 66 | Decca F 12507 | Raindrops/La Bamba | 6 |

POWERPACK
66	CBS 202335	It Hurts Me So/What You Gonna Do	25
67	CBS 202551	I'll Be Anything For You/The Lost Summer	12
69	Polydor 56319	Hannibal Brooks/Juliet Simkins	6
70	Polydor 2001 077	Oh Calcutta/Soul Searchin'	7
69	Polydor 583 057	SOUL CURE (LP)	15

(see also Procol Harum, Emperor Rosko & Power Pack)

JETT POWERS
| 70 | Liberty LBS 83320 | CALIFORNIA LICENCE (LP) | 50 |

(see also P.J. Proby)

KID CONGO POWERS
| 89 | Night Shift NISHI 208T | In The Heat Of The Night/Cat Tabu/La Historia Des Un Amour (12", p/s) | 8 |

(see also Gun Club)

JOEY POWERS
| 63 | Stateside SS 236 | Midnight Mary/Where Do You Want The World Delivered | 8 |

POWERS OF BLUE
| 67 | CBS 62953 | FLIP OUT! (LP) | 10 |

POWER STATION
85	Parlophone 12 RP 6091	Some Like It Hot (Full Length Version)/The Heat Is On/	
		Some Like It Hot (12", picture disc)	7
85	Parlophone 12R 6114	Communication (Extended Remix)/Murderess (12", p/s)	8

(see also Duran Duran, Robert Palmer)

P.P. & PRIMES
96	Nice (no cat. no.)	Understanding/STEVIE'S BUZZ: Autumn Stone (promo only)	5

(see also Primal Scream, P.P. Arnold)

PEREZ 'PREZ' PRADO & HIS ORCHESTRA
54	HMV 7M 255	Skokiaan — Mambo/The High And The Mighty	7
55	HMV 7M 295	Cherry Pink And Apple Blossom White/Maria Elena	10
55	HMV POP 102	Marilyn Monroe Mambo/C'est Si Bon (78)	8
55	HMV 7MC 29	Mambo De La Telefonista/En Las Calles De La Habana (export issue)	10
58	RCA RCA 1067	Patricia/Why Wait	6
58	RCA RCA 1067	Patricia/Why Wait (78)	8
58	RCA RCA 1082	Guaglione/Paris	8
58	RCA RCA 1082	Guaglione/Paris (78)	12
59	RCA RCA 1129	Tic Toc Polly Woc/My Roberta	5
59	RCA RCA 1129	Tic Toc Polly Woc/My Roberta (78)	10
60	RCA RCA 1199	Rockambo Baby/Oh, Oh, Rosie	5
55	HMV 7EG 8104	KING OF MAMBO (EP)	8
58	RCA SRC 7004	PREZ (EP)	8
59	RCA RCX 140	PRADO PLAYS PATRICIA (EP)	8
59	RCA RCX 1001	PEREZ PRADO (EP)	8
60	RCA RD 27046	LATIN SATIN (LP)	12
64	Parlophone PMC 1226	A CAT IN LATIN (LP)	12

PRAG VEC
78	Spec SP 001	Wolf/Cigarettes/Existential/Bits! (p/s)	4
79	Spec SP 002	Expert/The Follower! (p/s)	4
81	Spec RESPECT 1	NO COWBOYS (LP, with insert)	12

PRAMS
81	Product/Ltd. Edition TAKE 3	Nowhere's Safe/TV PRODUCT: Jumping Off Walls (foldout p/s)	15

PRAISE
76	No Seven 001	BLESSED QUIETNESS (LP)	40

ANDY PRATT
69	Polydor 2489 003	RECORDS ARE LIKE LIFE (LP)	12

PHIL PRATT
69	Jolly JY 008	Sweet Song For My Baby/THRILLERS: I'm Restless	12

(see also Charlie Ace, Larry Marshall, Don Drummond)

PHIL PRATT ALL STARS
70	Jackpot JP 748	Cut Throat/KEN BOOTHE: You Left The Water Running	15
71	Punch PH 94	Winey Winey (actually "Kingstonians Medley" by Kingstonians)/	
		There Is A Place (actually by Barrington Spence)	6

(see also Dennis Alcapone, Horace Andy, Dennis Brown, Ken Boothe, Erroll Dunkley, John Holt, Delroy Wilson)

PRAYING MANTIS
79	Ripper/Harvest HAR 5201	THE SOUNDHOUSE TAPES PART 2: Captured City/	
		Johnny Cool (some in p/s)	70/10
79	Ripper/Harvest 12HAR 5201	THE SOUNDHOUSE TAPES PART 2 (12", no p/s)	15
80	Gem GEMS 36	Praying Mantis/High Roller (p/s, some with transfer)	8/6
80	Arista ARIST 378	Cheated/Thirty Pieces Of Silver (gatefold p/s, with bonus single)	8
81	Arista ARIST 397	All Day And All Of The Night/Beads Of Ebony (p/s)	10
82	Jet JET 7026	Tell Me The Nightmare's Wrong/A Question Of Time/Turn The Tables (p/s)	20
81	Arista SPART 1153	TIME TELLS NO LIES (LP, with inner sleeve)	20

(see also Stratus, Grand Prix, Uriah Heep)

PREACHERS
65	Columbia DB 7680	Hole In My Soul/Too Old In The Head	45

(see also Herd, Peter Frampton, Denny Mitchel & Soundsations, Moon's Train)

PRECIOUS FEW
68	Pye 7N 17510	Young Girl/Little Children Sleep	5
68	Pye 7N 17641	Pleasure Of You/Little Children Sleep	5

PRECISIONS
67	Track 604 014	If This Is Love/You'll Soon Be Gone	10
79	Grapevine GRP 129	Such Misery/A Lovers Plea	6

PREDATOR
78	Bust! SOL 2	Punk Man/Paperboy Song (with insert, no p/s)	90

PREDATOR
85	CTM C 001	Don't Stop/Shotdown (some in p/s)	65/15

PREDATUR
82	Quicksilver QUICK 5	Take A Walk/Seen You Here (p/s)	90

PREFAB SPROUT
82	Candle CANDLE 1	Lions In My Own Garden (Exit Someone)/Radio Love (no p/s)	20
83	Kitchenware SK 4	Lions In My Own Garden (Exit Someone)/Radio Love (p/s, reissue,	
		black labels)	5
88	Kitchenware SKQ 35	Cars And Girls/Real Life (Just Around The Corner)/Vendetta (10", no'd p/s)	7
88	Kitchenware CDDSK 35	Cars And Girls/Faron Young (Truckin' Mix)/Real Life	
		(Just Around The Corner)/Vendetta (CD, picture disc)	7

PREGNANT INSOMNIA
67	Direction 58-3132	Wallpaper/You Intrigue Me	30

PRELUDE
70s	Crotchet	PRELUDE (LP, private pressing)	40

PRELUDE
73	Dawn DNLS 3052	HOW LONG IS FOREVER (LP, gatefold sleeve)	12
74	Dawn DNLS 3061	DUTCH COURAGE (LP)	12
75	Dawn DNLH 3	OWL CREEK INCIDENT (LP)	12

PREMIERS (U.K.)
64	Silver Phoenix 1002	Tears, Tears/Bye Bye Johnny	25

PREMIERS (U.S.)
64	Warner Bros WB 134	Farmer John/Duffy's Blues	10
64	Warner Bros W 1565	FARMER JOHN "LIVE" (LP)	35

YVONNE PRENOSILOVA
65	Pye 7N 15775	When My Baby Cries/Come On Home	7

PRESENCE
76	NC SLCW 1031	PRESENCE (LP)	35

PRESENCE
91	Reality LOL 1	In Wonder/Soft (p/s, withdrawn)	4
91	Reality LOLX 1	In Wonder/Soft/In Wonder (Didgeribdub Mix) (12", p/s, withdrawn)	7
91	Reality LOLCD 1	In Wonder/Soft/In Wonder (Didgeribdub Mix)/In Wonder (Millies Mix) (CD)	7
(see also Cure)			

PRESIDENTS
64	Decca F 11826	Candy Man/Let The Sunshine In	30

PRESIDENTS
72	A&M AMS 856	5-10-15-20 Years Of Love/Triangle Of Love	4
72	Sussex AMLS 65001	5-10-15-20-25-30 (LP)	15

ELVIS PRESLEY

HMV 78s
56	HMV POP 182	Heartbreak Hotel/I Was The One (78)	20
56	HMV POP 213	Blue Suede Shoes/Tutti Frutti (78)	25
56	HMV POP 235	I Want You, I Need You, I Love You/My Baby Left Me (78)	25
56	HMV POP 249	Hound Dog/Don't Be Cruel (78)	20
56	HMV POP 253	Love Me Tender/Anyway You Want Me (That's How I Will Be) (78)	25
56	HMV POP 272	Blue Moon/I Don't Care If The Sun Don't Shine (78)	25
57	HMV POP 295	Mystery Train/Love Me (78)	30
57	HMV POP 305	Rip It Up/Baby, Let's Play House (78)	30
57	HMV POP 330	Too Much/Playing For Keeps (78)	25
57	HMV POP 359	All Shook Up/That's When Your Heartaches Begin (78)	12
57	HMV POP 378	Paralyzed/When My Blue Moon Turns To Gold Again (78)	25
57	HMV POP 408	Tryin' To Get To You/Lawdy, Miss Clawdy (78)	30
58	HMV POP 428	I'm Left, You're Right, She's Gone/How Do You Think I Feel? (78)	30

HMV SINGLES: PURPLE LABEL/GOLD PRINT
56	HMV 7M 385	Heartbreak Hotel/I Was The One ('removable/replaceable' or solid centre)	350/200
56	HMV 7M 405	Blue Suede Shoes/Tutti Frutti	250
56	HMV 7M 424	I Want You, I Need You, I Love You/My Baby Left Me	150
56	HMV POP 249	Hound Dog/Don't Be Cruel	80
56	HMV POP 253	Love Me Tender/Anyway You Want Me (That's How I Will Be)	80
56	HMV POP 272	Blue Moon/I Don't Care If The Sun Don't Shine ('removable/replaceable' centre or solid centre)	150/100
57	HMV POP 295	Mystery Train/Love Me ('removable/replaceable' centre or solid centre)	300/250
57	HMV 7MC 42	Mystery Train/I Forgot To Remember To Forget (U.K. issue of export single, gold label print only, smooth edge to labels)	275
57	HMV POP 305	Rip It Up/Baby, Let's Play House ('removable/replaceable' centre or solid centre)	225/175
57	HMV POP 330	Too Much/Playing For Keeps	100
57	HMV POP 359	All Shook Up/That's When Your Heartaches Begin (push-out centre or solid centre)	150/80
57	HMV POP 378	Paralyzed/When My Blue Moon Turns To Gold Again	60

HMV SINGLES: PURPLE LABEL/SILVER PRINT
56	HMV 7M 385	Heartbreak Hotel/I Was The One	200
56	HMV 7M 405	Blue Suede Shoes/Tutti Frutti	250
56	HMV 7M 424	I Want You, I Need You, I Love You/My Baby Left Me	150
56	HMV POP 249	Hound Dog/Don't Be Cruel	100
56	HMV POP 253	Love Me Tender/Anyway You Want Me (That's How I Will Be)	125
56	HMV POP 272	Blue Moon/I Don't Care If The Sun Don't Shine	125
57	HMV POP 295	Mystery Train/Love Me	250
57	HMV POP 305	Rip It Up/Baby, Let's Play House	175
57	HMV POP 330	Too Much/Playing For Keeps	125
57	HMV POP 359	All Shook Up/That's When Your Heartaches Begin ('removable/replaceable' centre or solid centre)	175/25
57	HMV POP 378	Paralyzed/When My Blue Moon Turns To Gold Again	75
57	HMV POP 408	Tryin' To Get To You/Lawdy, Miss Clawdy	50
58	HMV POP 428	I'm Left, You're Right, She's Gone/How Do You Think I Feel?	50

HMV EXPORT SINGLES
57	HMV 7MC 42	Mystery Train/I Forgot To Remember To Forget (gold label print, serrated edge to labels)	250
57	HMV 7MC 45	I Want You, I Need You, I Love You/My Baby Left Me (gold label print)	275
57	HMV 7MC 50	Hound Dog/Don't Be Cruel (gold label print)	275

ELVIS PRESLEY

57	HMV JO 465	Love Me Tender/Anyway You Want Me (That's How I'll Be) (gold label print)	300
57	HMV JO 466	Too Much/Playing For Keeps (gold label print)	250
57	HMV JO 473	All Shook Up/That's When Your Heartaches Begin (gold label print)	225

RCA 78s

57	RCA RCA 1013	(Let Me Be Your) Teddy Bear/Loving You (78)	20
57	RCA RCA 1020	Party/Got A Lot O' Livin' To Do (78)	25
57	RCA RCA 1025	Santa Bring My Baby Back (To Me)/Santa Claus Is Back In Town (78)	30
58	RCA RCA 1028	Jailhouse Rock/Treat Me Nice (78)	20
58	RCA RCA 1043	Don't/I Beg Of You (78)	30
58	RCA RCA 1058	Wear My Ring Around Your Neck/Doncha' Think It's Time (78)	40
58	RCA RCA 1070	Hard Headed Woman/Don't Ask Me Why (78)	35
58	RCA RCA 1081	King Creole/Dixieland Rock (78)	45
58	RCA RCA 1088	All Shook Up/Heartbreak Hotel (78)	120
58	RCA RCA 1095	Hound Dog/Blue Suede Shoes (78)	120
59	RCA RCA 1100	One Night/I Got Stung (78, composing credit: Bartholomew or Bartholemew)	70
59	RCA RCA 1113	(Now And Then There's) A Fool Such As I/I Need Your Love Tonight (78)	90
59	RCA RCA 1136	A Big Hunk O' Love/My Wish Came True (78)	100
60	RCA RCA 1187	Stuck On You/Fame And Fortune (78)	400
60	RCA RCA 1194	A Mess Of Blues/The Girl Of My Best Friend (78)	800

ORIGINAL RCA SINGLES: BLACK LABELS

57	RCA RCA 1013	(Let Me Be Your) Teddy Bear/Loving You	20
57	RCA RCA 1020	Party/Got A Lot O' Livin' To Do	15
57	RCA RCA 1025	Santa Bring My Baby Back (To Me)/Santa Claus Is Back In Town	20
58	RCA RCA 1028	Jailhouse Rock/Treat Me Nice	10
58	RCA RCA 1043	Don't/I Beg Of You	10
58	RCA RCA 1058	Wear My Ring Around Your Neck/Doncha' Think It's Time	10
58	RCA RCA 1070	Hard Headed Woman/Don't Ask Me Why	10
58	RCA RCA 1081	King Creole/Dixieland Rock	10
58	RCA RCA 1088	All Shook Up/Heartbreak Hotel	40
58	RCA RCA 1095	Hound Dog/Blue Suede Shoes	40
59	RCA RCA 1100	One Night/I Got Stung	8
59	RCA RCA 1113	(Now And Then There's) A Fool Such As I/I Need Your Love Tonight	10
59	RCA RCA 1136	A Big Hunk O' Love/My Wish Came True	10

(The above RCA 45s were issued with triangular centres, round-centre re-pressings are worth half to two-thirds these values.)

Elvis PRESLEY

60	RCA RCA 1187	Stuck On You/Fame And Fortune	7
60	RCA RCA 1194	A Mess Of Blues/The Girl Of My Best Friend	7
60	RCA RCA 1207	It's Now Or Never (O Sole Mio)/Make Me Know It	4
61	RCA RCA 1216	Are You Lonesome Tonight?/I Gotta Know	4
61	RCA RCA 1226	Wooden Heart/Tonight Is So Right For Love	4
61	RCA RCA 1227 *	Surrender (Torna A Surriento)/Lonely Man	5
61	RCA RCA 1244	Wild In The Country/I Feel So Bad	5
61	RCA RCA 1258	(Marie's The Name) His Latest Flame/Little Sister	5
62	RCA RCA 1270	Rock-A-Hula Baby/Can't Help Falling In Love	4

ORIGINAL RCA VICTOR SINGLES: BLACK LABELS

63	RCA Victor RCA 1337	One Broken Heart For Sale/They Remind Me Too Much Of You	6
63	RCA Victor RCA 1355	(You're The) Devil In Disguise/Please Don't Drag That String Around	5
63	RCA Victor RCA 1374	Bossa Nova Baby/Witchcraft	6
63	RCA Victor RCA 1375	Kiss Me Quick/Something Blue	6
64	RCA Victor RCA 1390	Viva Las Vegas/What'd I Say	6
64	RCA Victor RCA 1404	Kissin' Cousins/It Hurts Me	5
64	RCA Victor RCA 1411	Such A Night/Never Ending	8
64	RCA Victor RCA 1422	Ain't That Loving You Baby/Ask Me	5
64	RCA Victor RCA 1430	Blue Christmas/White Christmas	5
65	RCA Victor RCA 1443	Do The Clam/You'll Be Gone	6
65	RCA Victor RCA 1455	Crying In The Chapel/I Believe In The Man In The Sky	5
65	RCA Victor RCA 1489	Tell Me Why/Puppet On A String	8
66	RCA Victor RCA 1504	Blue River/Do Not Disturb	6
66	RCA Victor RCA 1509	Frankie And Johnny/Please Don't Stop Loving Me	10
66	RCA Victor RCA 1526	Love Letters/Come What May	6
66	RCA Victor RCA 1545	All That I Am/Spinout	6
66	RCA Victor RCA 1557	If Every Day Was Like Christmas/How Would You Like To Be?	5
67	RCA Victor RCA 1565	Indescribably Blue/Fools Fall In Love	7
67	RCA Victor RCA 1593	The Love Machine/You Gotta Stop	15
67	RCA Victor RCA 1616	Long-Legged Girl (With The Short Dress On)/That's Someone You Never Forget	15
67	RCA Victor RCA 1628	Judy/There's Always Me	50
67	RCA Victor RCA 1642	Big Boss Man/You Don't Know Me	8
68	RCA Victor RCA 1663	Guitar Man/Hi-Heel Sneakers	15
68	RCA Victor RCA 1688	U.S. Male/Stay Away	10
68	RCA Victor RCA 1714	Your Time Hasn't Come Yet Baby/Let Yourself Go	15
68	RCA Victor RCA 1747	You'll Never Walk Alone/We Call On Him	20
68	RCA Victor RCA 1768	A Little Less Conversation/Almost In Love	15

RCA VICTOR SINGLES: BLACK LABEL REISSUES

64	RCA Victor RCA 1020	Party/Got A Lot O' Livin' To Do	30
64	RCA Victor RCA 1025	Santa Bring My Baby Back (To Me)/Santa Claus Is Back In Town	30
64	RCA Victor RCA 1028	Jailhouse Rock/Treat Me Nice	25
64	RCA Victor RCA 1043	Don't/I Beg Of You	15
64	RCA Victor RCA 1058	Wear My Ring Around Your Neck/Doncha' Think It's Time	25
64	RCA Victor RCA 1070	Hard Headed Woman/Don't Ask Me Why	30
64	RCA Victor RCA 1081	King Creole/Dixieland Rock	30
64	RCA Victor RCA 1088	All Shook Up/Heartbreak Hotel	30
64	RCA Victor RCA 1095	Hound Dog/Blue Suede Shoes	30
64	RCA Victor RCA 1100	One Night/I Got Stung	15
64	RCA Victor RCA 1113	(Now And Then There's) A Fool Such As I/I Need Your Love Tonight	15
64	RCA Victor RCA 1136	A Big Hunk O' Love/My Wish Came True	15
64	RCA Victor RCA 1187	Stuck On You/Fame And Fortune	8
64	RCA Victor RCA 1194	A Mess Of Blues/The Girl Of My Best Friend	7
64	RCA Victor RCA 1207	It's Now Or Never (O Sole Mio)/Make Me Know It	5
64	RCA Victor RCA 1216	Are You Lonesome Tonight?/I Gotta Know	4
64	RCA Victor RCA 1226	Wooden Heart/Tonight Is So Right For Love	4
64	RCA Victor RCA 1227	Surrender (Torna A Surriento)/Lonely Man	5
64	RCA Victor RCA 1244	Wild In The Country/I Feel So Bad	5
64	RCA Victor RCA 1258	(Marie's The Name) His Latest Flame/Little Sister	5
64	RCA Victor RCA 1270	Rock-A-Hula Baby/Can't Help Falling In Love	4
62	RCA Victor RCA 1280	Good Luck Charm/Anything That's Part Of You	5
62	RCA Victor RCA 1303	She's Not You/Just Tell Her Jim Said Hello	4
62	RCA Victor RCA 1320	Return To Sender/Where Do You Come From	4

RCA VICTOR SINGLES: ORANGE LABEL REISSUES

69	RCA Victor RCA 1088	All Shook Up/Heartbreak Hotel	50
69	RCA Victor RCA 1095	Hound Dog/Blue Suede Shoes	50
69	RCA Victor RCA 1207	It's Now Or Never (O Sole Mio)/Make Me Know It	50
69	RCA Victor RCA 1216	Are You Lonesome Tonight?/I Gotta Know	50
69	RCA Victor RCA 1226	Wooden Heart/Tonight Is So Right For Love	50
69	RCA Victor RCA 1688	U.S. Male/Stay Away	100
71	RCA MAXI 2104	Heartbreak Hotel/Hound Dog/Don't Be Cruel ('Maximillion' sleeve)	5
71	RCA MAXI 2153	Jailhouse Rock/Are You Lonesome Tonight?/(Let Me Be Your) Teddy Bear/Steadfast, Loyal And True ('Maximillion' sleeve)	8
75	RCA MAXI 2601	Blue Moon/You're A Heartbreaker/I'm Left, You're Right, She's Gone ('Maximillion' sleeve)	8

ORIGINAL RCA VICTOR ORANGE LABEL SINGLES

69	RCA Victor RCA 1795	If I Can Dream/Memories	7
69	RCA Victor RCA 1831	In The Ghetto/Any Day Now	5
69	RCA Victor RCA 1869	Clean Up Your Own Backyard/The Fair's Moving On	5
69	RCA Victor RCA 1900	Suspicious Minds/You'll Think Of Me (p/s)	7
70	RCA Victor RCA 1916	Don't Cry Daddy/Rubberneckin' (p/s)	7
70	RCA Victor RCA 1949	Kentucky Rain/My Little Friend (p/s)	7
70	RCA Victor RCA 1974	The Wonder Of You/Mama Liked The Roses	4
70	RCA Victor RCA 1999	I've Lost You/The Next Step Is Love	5
71	RCA Victor RCA 2046	You Don't Have To Say You Love Me/Patch It Up	4

71	RCA Victor RCA 2060	There Goes My Everything/I Really Don't Want To Know (p/s) 7
71	RCA Victor RCA 2084	Rags To Riches/Where Did They Go, Lord (p/s) 7
71	RCA Victor RCA 2125	I'm Leavin'/Heart Of Rome 5
71	RCA Victor RCA 2158	I Just Can't Help Believin'/How The Web Was Woven 10
72	RCA Victor RCA 2188	Until It's Time For You To Go/We Can Make The Morning (p/s) 7
72	RCA Victor RCA 2229	American Trilogy/The First Time Ever I Saw Your Face 10
72	RCA Victor RCA 2267	Burning Love/It's A Matter Of Time 4
72	RCA Victor RCA 2304	Always On My Mind/Separate Ways 10
73	RCA Victor RCA 2359	Polk Salad Annie/See See Rider 6
73	RCA Victor RCA 2393	Fool/Steamroller Blues 6
73	RCA Victor RCA 2435	Raised On Rock/For Ol' Times Sake 6
74	RCA Victor APBO 0196	Take Good Care Of Her/I've Got A Thing About You Baby (solid centre, no p/s; most copies as U.S. imports with large centre hole in U.S. p/s) 200/15
74	RCA Victor APBO 0280	If You Talk In Your Sleep/Help Me 5
74	RCA Victor RCA 2458	My Boy/Loving Arms 5
74	RCA Victor PB 10074	Promised Land/It's Midnight (1st pressing) 4
74	RCA Victor PB 10074	Promised Land/It's Midnight And I Miss You (2nd pressing with correct B-side title) 15
75	RCA Victor RCA 2562	T-R-O-U-B-L-E/Mr. Songman 4
75	RCA Victor RCA 2635	Green Green Grass Of Home/Thinking About You 4
76	RCA Victor RCA 2674	Hurt/For The Heart 20

RETROSPECTIVE RCA BLUE LABEL SINGLES

78	RCA PB 9265	Don't Be Cruel/Hound Dog (p/s) 4
78	RCA PB 9334	Old Shep/Paralysed (p/s) 4
80	RCA RCA 4	It's Only Love/Beyond The Reef (p/s) 4
80	RCA RCA 16	Santa Claus Is Back In Town/I Believe (p/s) 4
81	RCA RCA 43	Guitar Man/Faded Love (with matt U.K. p/s [cat. no. RCA 43]) 30
81	RCA RCA 43	Guitar Man/Faded Love (with glossy U.S. p/s [cat. no. PB 12158]) 4
82	RCA RCA 196	Are You Lonesome Tonight? (Laughing Version)/ From A Jack To A King (p/s) 4

OTHER RCA SINGLES

82	RCA RCAP 232	The Sound Of Your Cry/I'll Never Know (picture disc) 5
83	RCA RCAP 1028	Jailhouse Rock/The Elvis Medley (without "Hound Dog" credit on B-side) (reissue, picture disc) 5
83	RCA RCAP 1028	Jailhouse Rock/The Elvis Medley (with "Hound Dog" credit on B-side) (reissue, picture disc) 25
83	RCA RCAP 332	Baby, I Don't Care/One-Sided Love Affair/Tutti Frutti (picture disc) 5
83	RCA RCA 369	I Can Help/The Lady Loves Me (p/s) 4
83	RCA RCAT 369	I Can Help/If Every Day Was Like Christmas/The Lady Loves Me (10", p/s) 15
83	RCA RCAP 369	I Can Help/If Every Day Was Like Christmas/The Lady Loves Me (10", picture disc) 15
84	RCA RCA 405	Green Green Grass Of Home/Release Me (And Let Me Love Again)/ Solitaire (p/s, some with poster) 20/4
84	RCA RCA 459	The Last Farewell/It's Easy for You (p/s) 4
84	RCA RCAT 459	The Last Farewell/It's Easy for You (10", p/s) 15
85	RCA RCA 476	The Elvis Medley/Blue Suede Shoes (p/s) 4
85	RCA PB 49943	Always On My Mind (Alternate Version)/Tomorrow Night (p/s) 4
87	RCA ARON 1	Bossa Nova Baby/Ain't That Loving You Baby (p/s) 4
87	RCA ARONT 1	Bossa Nova Baby/Ain't That Loving You Baby (12", p/s) 15
87	RCA ARON 2	Love Me Tender/If I Can Dream (p/s) 4
87	RCA ARONT 2	Love Me Tender/If I Can Dream (p/s) (12", p/s) 15
88	RCA PB 49177	Are You Lonesome Tonight/Reconsider Baby (p/s) 4
88	RCA PB 49177	Are You Lonesome Tonight/Reconsider Baby (12", p/s) 8
88	RCA PB 49473	Mean Woman Blues/I Beg Of Of You (p/s) 10
88	RCA PT 49474	Mean Woman Blues/I Beg Of Of You (12", p/s) 15
88	RCA PB 49545	Stuck On You/Any Way You Want Me (p/s) 4
88	RCA PT 49546	Stuck On You/Any Way You Want Me (12", p/s) 8
88	RCA PB 49943	Always On My Mind/Tomorrow Night (p/s) 8
88	RCA PT 49944	Always On My Mind/Tomorrow Night (12", p/s) 20
89	RCA PD 49467	Heartbreak Hotel/I Was The One/Don't Be Cruel (To A Heart That's True)/ Hound Dog (3" CD, gatefold card sleeve) 7

SINGLES BOX SET

| 77 | RCA (no cat. no.) | PRESLEY GOLD — 16 NUMBER ONES (16 x 7", each in p/s, black box set) . . . . . 40 |

OTHER SINGLES & FLEXIDISCS

57	Weekend Mail (no cat. no.)	THE TRUTH ABOUT ME (1-sided 6" 78 rpm, mail-order only, some in mailer) . 90/60
75	Reader's Digest/RCA RD ELV 785/65	Brian Matthew Introduces Excerpts From Elvis Presley's Greatest Hits (6" flexidisc, some with newsletter & advertising leaflet) 7/5
77	RCA Victor 2694-2709	"GOLD 16" SERIES (16 x p/s 7" in foldout cardboard carrier) 35
79	RCA LB 1	The Wonder Of You/Noel Edmonds Introduces Record Year (Lever Brothers premium) 15
81	Chiswick NS 71	Press Conference 1957/DEKE RIVERS: Elvis Presley Medley (picture disc) 6
83	Buttons BUT 3	A.F.N. RADIO INTERVIEW (p/s, fan club interview flexidisc) 4
83	Buttons BUT 4	NEW YORK PRESS CONFERENCE (orange vinyl fan club flexidisc, free with *Elvis Monthly Collector's Special*, issue 2) 4
83	Buttons BUT 5	INTERVIEW BETWEEN ELVIS, PETER NOONE AND TOM MOFFETT (fan club flexidisc free with *Elvis Monthly Collector's Special*, issue 4) 4
84	Buttons BUT 6	GERMAN RADIO INTERVIEW (fan club flexidisc free with *Elvis Monthly Collector's Special*, issue 6) 4
84	Buttons BUT 7	ELVIS' 1964 GREETING TO HIS BRITISH FANS/THE TRUTH ABOUT ME (fan club flexi with *Elvis Monthly Collector's Special*, issue 8) 4
85	Buttons BUT 8	1956 NEW ORLEANS INTERVIEW (fan club flexidisc free with *Elvis Monthly Collector's Special*, issue 10) 4
85	Buttons BUT 9	JACKSON, FLORIDA 1955 INTERVIEW/MEMPHIS 1957 INTERVIEW (fan club flexidisc free with *Elvis Monthly Collector's Special*, issue 10) 4

Elvis PRESLEY

MINT VALUE £

HMV EPs

57	HMV 7EG 8199	LOVE ME TENDER (soundtrack, round or removeable/replaceable centre)	150/175
57	HMV 7EG 8256	GOOD ROCKIN' TONIGHT (round centre only)	175

RCA EPs: TRIANGULAR CENTRES

57	RCA RCX 101	PEACE IN THE VALLEY	30
57	RCA RCX 104	ELVIS PRESLEY	20
58	RCA RCX 106	JAILHOUSE ROCK (soundtrack)	20
58	RCA RCX 117	KING CREOLE VOL. 1 (soundtrack, black label, cream or white rear p/s)	25
58	RCA RCX 118	KING CREOLE VOL. 2 (soundtrack, cream or white rear sleeve)	20
58	RCA RCX 121	ELVIS SINGS CHRISTMAS SONGS (1st issue, single sleeve)	75
58	RCA RCX 131	ELVIS SAILS (interview record, sleeve laminated front & back)	40
59	RCA RCX 135	ELVIS IN TENDER MOOD (with red print on rear sleeve)	45

*(The above RCA EPs were originally issued with **laminated front and back** sleeves; later copies with **front-only** laminate are worth three quarters of these values.)*

59	RCA RCX 1045	A TOUCH OF GOLD (laminated front sleeve only)	50
59	RCA RCX 175	STRICTLY ELVIS	40
60	RCA RCX 1048	A TOUCH OF GOLD VOL. 2	120

RCA EPs: ROUND CENTRE RE-PRESSINGS

60s	RCA RCX 101	PEACE IN THE VALLEY	20
60s	RCA RCX 104	ELVIS PRESLEY	15
60s	RCA RCX 106	JAILHOUSE ROCK (soundtrack)	15
60s	RCA RCX 117	KING CREOLE VOL. 1 (soundtrack)	18
60s	RCA RCX 118	KING CREOLE VOL. 2 (soundtrack)	15
60s	RCA RCX 121	ELVIS SINGS CHRISTMAS SONGS (gatefold p/s)	100
60s	RCA RCX 131	ELVIS SAILS (interview record)	25
60s	RCA RCX 135	ELVIS IN TENDER MOOD	20
60s	RCA RCX 1045	A TOUCH OF GOLD	25
60s	RCA RCX 175	STRICTLY ELVIS	12
60s	RCA RCX 1048	A TOUCH OF GOLD VOL. 2	50

ORIGINAL RCA EPs: ROUND CENTRES

60	RCA RCX 190	SUCH A NIGHT	25
62	RCA RCX 211	FOLLOW THAT DREAM (soundtrack)	10
62	RCA RCX 211	FOLLOW THAT DREAM (mispressing, 2nd side features Jim Reeves)	100
62	RCA RCX 7109	KID GALAHAD (soundtrack)	14
64	RCA Victor RCX 7141	LOVE IN LAS VEGAS (soundtrack)	20
64	RCA Victor RCX 7142	ELVIS FOR YOU VOL. 1	60
64	RCA Victor RCX 7143	ELVIS FOR YOU VOL. 2	60
65	RCA Victor RCX 7173	TICKLE ME (soundtrack)	40
65	RCA Victor RCX 7174	TICKLE ME VOL. 2 (soundtrack)	45
67	RCA Victor RCX 7187	EASY COME, EASY GO (soundtrack)	60

RCA VICTOR EPs: BLACK LABEL RE-PRESSINGS

64	RCA Victor RCX 101	PEACE IN THE VALLEY	20
64	RCA Victor RCX 104	ELVIS PRESLEY	15
64	RCA Victor RCX 106	JAILHOUSE ROCK (soundtrack)	25
64	RCA Victor RCX 117	KING CREOLE VOL. 1 (soundtrack)	15
64	RCA Victor RCX 118	KING CREOLE VOL. 2 (soundtrack)	15
64	RCA Victor RCX 121	ELVIS SINGS CHRISTMAS SONGS (single p/s)	45
64	RCA Victor RCX 131	ELVIS SAILS (interview record)	40
64	RCA Victor RCX 135	ELVIS IN TENDER MOOD	30
64	RCA Victor RCX 1045	A TOUCH OF GOLD	25
64	RCA Victor RCX 175	STRICTLY ELVIS	15
64	RCA Victor RCX 1048	A TOUCH OF GOLD VOL. 2	40
64	RCA Victor RCX 190	SUCH A NIGHT	10
64	RCA Victor RCX 211	FOLLOW THAT DREAM (soundtrack)	10
64	RCA Victor RCX 7109	KID GALAHAD (soundtrack)	8

RCA VICTOR EPs: ORANGE LABEL RE-PRESSINGS

69	RCA Victor RCX 101	PEACE IN THE VALLEY (push-out or solid centre)	12/25
69	RCA Victor RCX 104	ELVIS PRESLEY (push-out or solid centre)	15/10
69	RCA Victor RCX 106	JAILHOUSE ROCK (soundtrack, push-out or solid centre)	15/10
69	RCA Victor RCX 117	KING CREOLE VOL. 1 (soundtrack, push-out or solid centre)	15/10
69	RCA Victor RCX 118	KING CREOLE VOL. 2 (soundtrack, push-out or solid centre)	15/10
69	RCA Victor RCX 131	ELVIS SAILS (interview record, push-out or solid centre)	each 15
69	RCA Victor RCX 135	ELVIS IN TENDER MOOD (push-out or solid centre, with different take of "Lover Doll")	each 15
69	RCA Victor RCX 1045	A TOUCH OF GOLD (push-out or solid centre)	20/15
69	RCA Victor RCX 175	STRICTLY ELVIS (push-out or solid centre)	each 15
69	RCA Victor RCX 1048	A TOUCH OF GOLD VOL. 2 (push-out or solid centre)	20/15
69	RCA Victor RCX 190	SUCH A NIGHT (push-out or solid centre)	15/10

EP BOX SETS

82	RCA EP 1	THE EP COLLECTION (11-EP box set, reissues, with booklet)	60
83	RCA EP 2	THE EP COLLECTION VOL. 2 (11-EP box set, reissues, with booklet)	80

LPs: HMV ISSUES

56	HMV CLP 1093	ROCK 'N' ROLL	400
57	HMV CLP 1105	ROCK 'N' ROLL NO. 2	500
57	HMV DLP 1159	THE BEST OF ELVIS (10" LP)	350

LPs: ORIGINAL BLACK/SILVER SPOT RCA ISSUES

57	RCA RC 24001	LOVING YOU (10" LP, soundtrack)	100
57	RCA RD 27052	ELVIS' CHRISTMAS ALBUM (laminated front & back covers with 4 pictures on back cover)	75
58	RCA RD 27088	KING CREOLE (soundtrack)	35

59	RCA RD 27120	ELVIS	60
59	RCA RD 27128	A DATE WITH ELVIS	45
60	RCA RD 27159	ELVIS' GOLDEN RECORDS VOL. 2	30
60	RCA RD 27171/SF 5060	ELVIS IS BACK! (gatefold sleeve, mono/stereo)	30/50
60	RCA RD 27192/SF 5078	G.I. BLUES (soundtrack, mono/stereo)	15/40
61	RCA RD 27211/SF 5094	HIS HAND IN MINE (mono/stereo)	25/40
61	RCA RD 27224/SF 5106	SOMETHING FOR EVERYBODY (mono/stereo)	18/40
61	RCA RD 27238/SF 5115	BLUE HAWAII (soundtrack, mono/stereo)	18/30
62	RCA RD 27265/SF 5135	POT LUCK (mono/stereo)	15/30

LPs: SILVER SPOT/'RED SEAL' RCA ISSUES

58	RCA RB 16069	ELVIS' GOLDEN RECORDS (maroon 'silver spot' label, gatefold sleeve with stapled-in 4-page photo booklet)	100
60	RCA RB 16069	ELVIS' GOLDEN RECORDS ('Red Seal'/'silver spot' label, gatefold sleeve with stapled-in 2-page photo booklet)	35
63	RCA RB 16069	ELVIS' GOLDEN RECORDS ('Red Seal'/'black spot' label, no booklet, gatefold sleeve)	25
67	RCA RB 16069	ELVIS' GOLDEN RECORDS ('Red Seal'/'black spot' label, no booklet, single sleeve)	18

LPs: ORIGINAL BLACK/SILVER SPOT RCA VICTOR ISSUES

63	RCA Victor RD/SF 7534	GIRLS! GIRLS! GIRLS! (soundtrack, mono/stereo)	18/40
63	RCA Victor RD/SF 7565	IT HAPPENED AT THE WORLD'S FAIR (soundtrack, mono/stereo)	18/40
63	RCA Victor RD/SF 7609	FUN IN ACAPULCO (soundtrack, mono/stereo)	18/40

LPs: ORIGINAL BLACK/RED SPOT RCA VICTOR ISSUES

64	RCA Victor RD/SF 7630	ELVIS' GOLDEN RECORDS VOL. 3 (mono/stereo)	18/40
64	RCA Victor RD/SF 7645	KISSIN' COUSINS (soundtrack, mono/stereo)	18/40
64	RCA Victor RD/SF 7678	ROUSTABOUT (soundtrack, mono/stereo)	16/40
65	RCA Victor RD/SF 7714	GIRL HAPPY (soundtrack, mono/stereo)	18/40
65	RCA Victor RD 7723	FLAMING STAR AND SUMMER KISSES (soundtrack, mono only, black label)	100
65	RCA Victor RD/SF 7752	ELVIS FOR EVERYONE (mono/stereo, 'orange shirt' sleeve)	40/60
65	RCA Victor RD/SF 7767	HAREM HOLIDAY (soundtrack, mono/stereo)	20/30
66	RCA Victor RD/SF 7793	FRANKIE AND JOHNNY (soundtrack, mono/stereo)	25/40
66	RCA Victor RD/SF 7810	PARADISE, HAWAIIAN STYLE (soundtrack, mono/stereo)	25/40
66	RCA Victor RD/SF 7820	CALIFORNIA HOLIDAY (soundtrack, mono/stereo)	25/40
67	RCA Victor RD/SF 7867	HOW GREAT THOU ART (mono/stereo)	25/40
67	RCA Victor RD/SF 7892	DOUBLE TROUBLE (soundtrack, mono/stereo)	20/30
68	RCA Victor RD/SF 7917	CLAMBAKE (soundtrack, mono/stereo)	20/30
68	RCA Victor RD/SF 7924	ELVIS' GOLD RECORDS VOLUME 4 (with "Never Ending" listed on sleeve instead of "Love Letters"; mono/stereo)	40/60
68	RCA Victor RD/SF 7924	ELVIS' GOLD RECORDS VOLUME 4 (corrected sleeve, mono/stereo)	18/20
68	RCA Victor RD/SF 7957	SPEEDWAY (soundtrack, with Nancy Sinatra, mono/stereo)	25/30

LPs: ORIGINAL ORANGE RCA VICTOR ISSUES

69	RCA Victor RD 8011	ELVIS ("TV Special" Soundtrack)	15
69	RCA Victor RD/SF 8029	FROM ELVIS IN MEMPHIS (mono/stereo)	15/12
70	RCA Victor SF 8080/1	FROM MEMPHIS TO VEGAS — FROM VEGAS TO MEMPHIS (2-LP, with 2 x 10"x8" photos, glossy or matt cover)	30/25
70	RCA SF 8128	ON STAGE, FEBRUARY 1970 (with 30" x 20" colour poster; glossy or matt cover)	15/12
70	RCA LPM 6401	WORLDWIDE 50 GOLD AWARD HITS VOL. 1 — A TOUCH OF GOLD (4-LP, box set with 20-page photo book)	40
71	RCA LPM 6402	THE OTHER SIDES — WORLDWIDE 50 GOLD AWARD HITS VOL. 2 (4-LP, box set with material patch & colour portrait)	40
71	RCA Victor SF 8162	THAT'S THE WAY IT IS (glossy or matt cover)	15/12
71	RCA Victor SF 8172	I'M 10,000 YEARS OLD — ELVIS COUNTRY (with colour print, glossy or matt cover)	15/10
71	RCA Victor SF 8202	LOVE LETTERS FROM ELVIS	12
71	RCA Victor SF 8221	ELVIS SINGS THE WONDERFUL WORLD OF CHRISTMAS	25
72	RCA Victor SF 8266	ELVIS NOW	20
72	RCA Victor SF 8275	HE TOUCHED ME	20
72	RCA Victor SF 8296	ELVIS AS RECORDED AT MADISON SQUARE GARDEN	12
73	RCA Victor SF 8378	ELVIS (with "Fool" sticker)	30
73	RCA DPS 2040	ALOHA FROM HAWAII VIA SATELLITE (2-LP)	16
73	RCA APL1 0388	RAISED ON ROCK/FOR OL' TIMES SAKE (U.K. disc in U.K. sleeve)	200
74	RCA CPL1 0341	ELVIS — A LEGENDARY PERFORMER VOL. 1	15
74	RCA APL1 0475	GOOD TIMES (back cover credits "Loving Arms" or "Lovin' Arms")	15
74	RCA APL1 0606	ELVIS AS RECORDED ON STAGE IN MEMPHIS	12
74	RCA LPL1 7527	HITS OF THE 70s	12
75	RCA APL1 0873	PROMISED LAND	12
75	RCA APM1 0818	HAVING FUN WITH ELVIS ON STAGE	40
75	RCA RS 1011	TODAY	15
76	RCA CPL1 1349	ELVIS — A LEGENDARY PERFORMER VOL. 2	25
76	RCA RS 1060	FROM ELVIS PRESLEY BOULEVARD, MEMPHIS, TENNESSEE	12
77	RCA LP 3021	MOODY BLUE	10
77	RCA PL 02587	ELVIS IN CONCERT	15
77	RCA PL 12274	WELCOME TO MY WORLD	12
77	RCA PL 12772	HE WALKS BESIDE ME	12
77	RCA PL 42003	ELVIS IN DEMAND	15
80	RCA CPL8 3699	ELVIS ARON PRESLEY (8-LP, box set)	60
83	RCA RCALPP 9020	JAILHOUSE ROCK/LOVE IN LAS VEGAS (picture disc)	10
84	RCA PLP 89287	I CAN HELP (picture disc)	10
84	RCA PL 85172	A GOLDEN CELEBRATION (6-LP box set with inserts)	25

LPs: BLACK/SILVER SPOT RCA VICTOR RE-PRESSINGS

| 64 | RCA Victor RC 24001 | LOVING YOU (10" LP, mono only) | 75 |
| 64 | RCA Victor RD 27052 | ELVIS' CHRISTMAS ALBUM (laminated front & back covers, no pictures on back cover, mono only) | 60 |

Elvis PRESLEY

64	RCA Victor RD/SF 7528	ROCK 'N' ROLL NO. 2 (reissue of HMV LP, mono/stereo)	18/25
64	RCA Victor RD 27088	KING CREOLE (soundtrack, mono only)	35
64	RCA Victor RD 27120	ELVIS (mono only)	35
64	RCA Victor RD 27128	A DATE WITH ELVIS (mono only)	20
64	RCA Victor RD 27159	ELVIS' GOLDEN RECORDS VOL. 2 (mono only)	15
64	RCA Victor RD 27171	ELVIS IS BACK! (gatefold sleeve, mono)	30
64	RCA Victor SF 5060	ELVIS IS BACK! (gatefold sleeve, stereo)	40
64	RCA Victor RD 27192	G.I. BLUES (soundtrack, mono)	15
64	RCA Victor SF 5078	G.I. BLUES (soundtrack, stereo)	30
64	RCA Victor RD 27211	HIS HAND IN MINE (mono)	25
64	RCA Victor SF 5094	HIS HAND IN MINE (stereo)	30
64	RCA Victor RD 27224	SOMETHING FOR EVERYBODY (mono)	18
64	RCA Victor SF 5106	SOMETHING FOR EVERYBODY (stereo)	30
64	RCA Victor RD 27238	BLUE HAWAII (soundtrack, mono)	18
64	RCA Victor SF 5115	BLUE HAWAII (soundtrack, stereo)	25
64	RCA Victor RD 27265	POT LUCK (mono)	15
64	RCA Victor SF 5135	POT LUCK (stereo)	30

LPs: BLACK/RED SPOT RCA VICTOR RE-PRESSING

64	RCA Victor RD/SF 7528	ROCK 'N' ROLL NO. 2 (reissue of HMV LP, mono/stereo)	18/25

LPs: 'SMALL' ORANGE RCA VICTOR MONO RE-PRESSINGS

69	RCA Victor RD 27052	ELVIS' CHRISTMAS ALBUM	40
69	RCA Victor RD 27088	KING CREOLE (soundtrack)	30
69	RCA Victor RD 27120	ELVIS	30
69	RCA Victor RD 27128	A DATE WITH ELVIS	30
69	RCA Victor RD 27159	ELVIS' GOLDEN RECORDS VOL. 2	30
69	RCA Victor RD 27171	ELVIS IS BACK! (gatefold sleeve)	30
69	RCA Victor RD 27192	G.I. BLUES (soundtrack)	30
69	RCA Victor RD 27211	HIS HAND IN MINE	30
69	RCA Victor RD 27224	SOMETHING FOR EVERYBODY	30
69	RCA Victor RD 27238	BLUE HAWAII (soundtrack)	30
69	RCA Victor RD 7528	ROCK 'N' ROLL NO. 2	30
69	RCA Victor RD 7630	ELVIS' GOLDEN RECORDS VOL. 3	30
69	RCA Victor RD 7723	FLAMING STAR AND SUMMER KISSES (soundtrack)	350
69	RCA Victor RD 7810	PARADISE, HAWAIIAN STYLE (soundtrack)	30
69	RCA Victor RD 7867	HOW GREAT THOU ART	30
69	RCA Victor RD 7917	CLAMBAKE (soundtrack)	40
69	RCA Victor RD 7924	ELVIS' GOLD RECORDS VOLUME 4	30
69	RCA Victor RD 7957	SPEEDWAY (soundtrack, with Nancy Sinatra)	30

LPs: 'LARGE' ORANGE RCA VICTOR STEREO RE-PRESSINGS

72	RCA Victor SF 8232	ELVIS FOR EVERYONE ('blue shirt'/'TV Special' sleeve)	40

LPs: GREEN RCA INTERNATIONAL ISSUES

69	RCA Intl. INTS 1012	ELVIS SINGS FLAMING STAR	15
70	RCA Intl. INTS 1103	LET'S BE FRIENDS	15
72	RCA Intl. INTS 1414	BURNING LOVE AND HITS FROM HIS MOVIES (U.K. disc in U.K. sleeve)	40

OTHER LPs

78	St. Michael IMP 113	ELVIS (exclusive to Marks & Spencer)	40
78	St. Michael IMPD 204	THE WONDERFUL WORLD OF ELVIS PRESLEY (2-LP, via Marks & Spencer)	60
79	Hammer HMR 6002	THE KING SPEAKS (green sleeve)	30
84	Imperial Records DR 1124	AMERICAN TRILOGY (3-LP, box set)	25

CDs

84	RCA PD 89061/2/3	THE LEGEND (3-CD, gold box set, with booklet, numbered, 5,000 only)	300
84	RCA PD 89061/2/3	THE LEGEND (3-CD, silver box set, 5,000 only, with booklet, numbered)	350

PROMO CDs

92	BMG ELVIS 58	Love Letters (1-track, plain PVC sleeve, no inlay)	200
94	BMG 74321 24079/2	SELECTIONS FROM AMAZING GRACE (sampler)	100
96	BMG 74321 36570/2	Twelfth Of Never/Walk A Mile In My Shoes ('live' picture disc, box set sampler)	50
97	BMG ELVIS DJ 1/97	Always On My Mind (Orchestral Version)/Are You Lonesome Tonight (Laughing Version)/Moody Blue/Way Down (numbered digipak)	250
97	BMG 74321 46658/2	OFF CAMERA (compilation)	50
99	BMG/RCA 74321 68133 2	ARTIST OF THE CENTURY SAMPLER (10-track European sampler, digipak, promo only)	250

(see also Jordanaires, Scotty Moore, Bill Black's Combo)

REG PRESLEY

69	Page One POF 131	Lucinda Lee/Wichita Lineman	10
73	CBS 1478	'S Down To You Marianne/Hey Little Girl	10

(see also Troggs, Suzi Quatro)

RAY PRESSLEY

62	Longhorn BLH 0002	Living, Learning, Trying To Forget/Half A Love	8

PRESSURE CO.

82	Paradox SOLID 1	LIVE IN SHEFFIELD 19 JAN '82 (LP)	10

(see also Eric Random, Cabaret Voltaire)

PRESSURE GROUP

80s	Kirple KIRP 1	EDHEARING (cassette)	10

BILLY PRESTON

66	Sue WI 4012	Billy's Bag/Don't Let The Sun Catch You Cryin'	15
66	Capitol CL 15458	In The Midnight Hour/Advice	6
66	Capitol CL 15471	Sunny/Let The Music Play	6
69	President PT 263	Billy's Bag/Don't Let The Sun Catch You Crying (reissue)	5
69	President PT 263	Billy's Bag/Goldfinger (different B-side)	5
69	Apple APPLE 12	That's The Way God Planned It/What About You (p/s)	6
69	Apple APPLE 19	Everything's Alright/I Want To Thank You	7

MINT VALUE £

70	Apple APPLE 21	All That I've Got/As I Get Older (some in p/s) 20/5
70	Apple APPLE 29	My Sweet Lord/Long As I Got My Baby (unreleased)
70	President PT 298	If I Had A Hammer/Goldfinger (possibly unreleased) 7
70	President PT 298	If I Had A Hammer/Ferry 'Cross The Mersey 5
70	Soul City SC 107	Greazee (Parts 1 & 2) 12
73	A&M AMS 7049	Will It Go Round In Circles/Blackbird 5
75	A&M AMS 7198	Fancy Lady/Song Of Joy 5
67	Capitol (S)T 2532	THE WILDEST ORGAN IN TOWN (LP) 18
67	Sue ILP 935	THE MOST EXCITING ORGAN EVER (LP) 40
69	President PTLS 1034	APPLE OF MY EYE (LP) 12
69	Apple SAPCOR 9	THAT'S THE WAY GOD PLANNED IT (LP) 20
70	Apple SAPCOR 14	ENCOURAGING WORDS (LP) 25
70	Soul City SCM 002	GREAZEE SOUL (LP) 25
72	A&M AMLH 63507	I WROTE A SIMPLE SONG (LP) 12
91	Apple SAPCOR 9	THAT'S THE WAY GOD PLANNED IT (LP, gatefold sleeve, with bonus 12" [SAPCOR 92]) 15
93	Apple SAPCOR 14	ENCOURAGING WORDS (LP, gatefold sleeve with bonus 12" [SAPCOR 142]) ... 15

(see also Beatles)

EARL PRESTON

| 63 | Fontana TF 406 | I Know Something/Watch Your Step (as Earl Preston & T.T.'s) .... 18 |
| 64 | Fontana TF 481 | Raindrops/That's For Sure (as Earl Preston & Realms) .... 18 |

(see also Realm)

JOHNNY PRESTON

60	Mercury AMT 1079	Running Bear/My Heart Knows 7
60	Mercury AMT 1079	Running Bear/My Heart Knows (78) 100
60	Mercury AMT 1092	Cradle Of Love/City Of Tears (some in p/s) 18/7
60	Mercury AMT 1104	Feel So Fine/I'm Starting To Go Steady 10
60	Mercury AMT 1114	Charming Billy/Up In The Air 12
61	Mercury AMT 1129	Leave My Kitten Alone/Do What You Did 15
61	Mercury AMT 1145	Big Chief Heartbreak/Madre De Dios (Mother Of God) 12
61	Mercury AMT 1164	New Baby For Christmas/Rock And Roll Guitar 12
61	Mercury AMT 1167	Free Me/Kissing Tree 12
60	Mercury ZEP 10078	RUNNING BEAR (EP) 75
60	Mercury ZEP 10098	RING TAIL TOOTER (EP) 100
61	Mercury ZEP 10116	TOKEN OF LOVE (EP) 125
60	Mercury MMC 14051	JOHNNY PRESTON — RUNNING BEAR (LP) 85

MIKE PRESTON

58	Decca F 11053	A House, A Car And A Wedding Ring/My Lucky Love 10
58	Decca F 11053	A House, A Car And A Wedding Ring/My Lucky Love (78) 12
58	Decca F 11087	Why, Why, Why/Whispering Grass 8
58	Decca F 11087	Why, Why, Why/Whispering Grass (78) 12
59	Decca F 11120	Dirty Old Town/In Surabaya 8
59	Decca F 11120	Dirty Old Town/In Surabaya (78) 10
59	Decca F 11167	Mr. Blue/Just Ask Your Heart 6
59	Decca F 11167	Mr. Blue/Just Ask Your Heart (78) 12
60	Decca F 11222	A Girl Like You/Too Old 6
60	Decca F 11222	A Girl Like You/Too Old (78) 15
60	Decca F 11255	I'd Do Anything/Where Is Love? 6
60	Decca F 11255	I'd Do Anything/Where Is Love? (78) 20
60	Decca F 11287	Togetherness/Farewell My Love 6
60	Decca F 11335	Marry Me/Girl Without A Heart 5
61	Decca F 11366	It's All Happening/Just As I Am 5
62	Decca F 11440	Innocent Eyes/I've Got All The Time In The World 5
62	Decca F 11498	It's A Sin To Tell A Lie/Careless Love 5
63	Decca F 11613	Punish Her/From The Very First Rose 5
66	Emerald MD 1028	Forgive Me/Our Love Will Go On 6
60	Decca DFE 6635	FOUR SONGS BY RAY NOBLE (EP) 30
61	Decca DFE 6679	MARRY ME (EP) 30

PRETENDERS

| 81 | Lyntone LYN 9650 | Whatcha Gonna Do About It/Stop Your Sobbin' (orange flexi with Flexipop 6) .. 6/4 |
| 87 | WEA YZ 149TX | If There Was A Man/Where Has Everybody Gone/Into Vienna (12", p/s) .... 7 |

(see also Jimmy Edwards)

PRETTY BOY FLOYD & GEMS

78	Montreco EPM RC 3005	HOLD TIGHT EP (12") 15
79	Rip Off RIP OFF 1	Spread The Word Around/Hold Tight (p/s) 12
79	Rip Off RIP 10	Sharon/The Instigator (p/s) 12
81	Heavenly Sound P. HSP 4	Look At Her Dancin'/Take Me I'm Yours (no p/s) 12

PRETTY THINGS

64	Fontana TF 469	Rosalyn/Big Boss Man 15
64	Fontana TF 503	Don't Bring Me Down/We'll Be Together 10
65	Fontana TF 537	Honey I Need/I Can Never Say 10
65	Fontana TF 585	Cry To Me/Get A Buzz 10
65	Fontana TF 647	Midnight To Six Man/Can't Stand The Pain 12
66	Fontana TF 688	Come See Me/£.s.d. 10
66	Fontana TF 722	A House In The Country/Me Needing You 10
66	Fontana TF 773	Progress/Buzz The Jerk 12
67	Fontana TF 829	Children/My Time 12
67	Columbia DB 8300	Defecting Grey/Mr. Evasion 25
68	Columbia DB 8353	Talkin' About The Good Times/Walking Through My Dreams 30
68	Columbia DB 8494	Private Sorrow/Balloon Burning 25
69	Fontana TF 1024	Rosalyn/Don't Bring Me Down (p/s) 6
70	Harvest HAR 5016	The Good Mr. Square/Blue Serge Blues 7
70	Harvest HAR 5031	October 26/Cold Stone 7

MINT VALUE £

71	Harvest HAR 5037	Stone-Hearted Mama/Summertime/Circus Mind	7
72	Warner Bros K 16225	Over The Moon/Havana Bound	5
64	Fontana TE 17434	THE PRETTY THINGS (EP)	40
65	Fontana TE 17442	RAININ' IN MY HEART (EP)	40
66	Fontana TE 17472	ON FILM (EP)	125
65	Fontana TL 5239	THE PRETTY THINGS (LP)	50
65	Fontana TL 5280	GET THE PICTURE (LP)	100
67	Wing WL 1164	BEST OF THE PRETTY THINGS (LP)	30
67	Fontana (S)TL 5425	EMOTIONS (LP, mono/stereo)	40
67	Wing WL 1167	THE PRETTY THINGS (LP, stereo reissue)	18
68	Columbia S(C)X 6306	S.F. SORROW (LP, gatefold sleeve, blue/black label, mono/stereo)	60/50
70	Columbia SCX 6306	S.F. SORROW (LP, gatefold sleeve; silver/black label re-pressing, stereo)	30
70	Harvest SHVL 774	PARACHUTE (LP, gatefold sleeve)	25
72	Fontana Special SFL 13140	EMOTIONS (LP, reissue)	15
72	Warner Bros K 46190	FREEWAY MADNESS (LP, gatefold sleeve)	15
74	Swan Song SSK 59400	SILK TORPEDO (LP, gatefold sleeve with insert)	15
75	Harvest SHDW 406	S.F. SORROW/PARACHUTE (2-LP)	18
75	Swan Song SSL 59401	SAVAGE EYE (LP, gatefold sleeve with inner)	15
77	Harvest SHSM 2022	THE SINGLES A's & B's (LP)	12
82	G.I. WAX 6	PARACHUTE (LP, reissue, 1,000 only)	12

(see also Electric Banana, Twink, Viv Prince, Sunshine, Fenmen, Kate, Zac Zolar & Electric Banana)

DORY PREVIN

70	United Artists UAG 29176	ON MY WAY TO WHERE (LP)	12
71	United Artists UAG 29186	MYTHICAL KINGS & IGUNAS (LP, gatefold sleeve)	12
71	United Artists UAG 29346	REFLECTIONS IN A MUD PUDDLE (LP, stickered sleeve with poster)	12
72	United Artists UAG 29435	MARY C. BROWN & THE HOLLYWOOD SIGN (LP, gatefold sleeve)	12
72	Sunset SLS 50385	ON MY WAY TO WHERE (LP, reissue)	12
73	United Artists UAD 60045/6	LIVE AT CARNEGIE HALL (2-LP, gatefold sleeve)	18
74	Warner Bros K 56066	DORY PREVIN (LP)	12
76	Warner Bros K 56213	WE'RE CHILDREN OF COINCIDENCE AND HARPO MARX (LP, with insert)	12
77	United Artists UAS 30070	ONE A.M. PHONECALLS (LP)	12

EDDIE PREVOST BAND

78	Matchless MR 1	LIVE VOLUME 1 (LP, private pressing)	15

(see also Amm)

JOEL PREVOST

78	CBS SCBS 6300	Somewhere Sometime/Il Y Aura Toujours Des Violins	10

ALAN PRICE (SET)

65	Decca F 12217	Any Day Now (My Wild Beautiful Baby)/Never Be Sick On Sunday	5
66	Decca F 12367	I Put A Spell On You/Iechyd-Da	5
66	Decca F 12442	Hi-Lili, Hi-Lo/Take Me Home	5
66	Decca F 12518	Willow Weep For Me/Yours Until Tomorrow	5
67	Decca F 12570	Simon Smith And His Amazing Dancing Bear/Tickle Me	5
67	Decca F 12641	The House That Jack Built/Who Cares	5
67	Decca F 12691	Shame/Don't Do That Again	5
68	Decca F 12731	Don't Stop The Carnival/The Time Has Come	5
68	Decca F 12774	When I Was A Cowboy/Tappy Turquoise (export issue)	8
68	Decca F 12808	Love Story/My Old Kentucky Home	5
69	Deram DM 261	Trimdon Grange Explosion/Falling In Love Again	5
70	Decca F 13017	Sunshine And Rain (The Name Of The Game)/Is There Anybody Out There? (solo)	5
73	Warner Bros K 16266	O Lucky Man!/Pastoral	5
78	Jet UP 36358	Just For You/I'm A Gambler (p/s, heart-shaped disc, red vinyl; solo)	5
67	Decca DFE 8677	THE AMAZING ALAN PRICE (EP)	30
66	Decca LK 4839	THE PRICE TO PLAY (LP)	25
67	Decca LK/SKL 4907	A PRICE ON HIS HEAD (LP)	15
73	Warner Bros K 46227	O LUCKY MAN! (LP, soundtrack)	18

(see also Animals, Paul Williams Set, Johnny Almond Music Machine, Dave Greenslade)

BILL PRICE

72	Folk Heritage FHR 038	THE FINE OLD YORKSHIRE GENTLEMAN (LP)	20

KENNY PRICE

66	Stateside SS 554	Walking On New Grass/Wasting My Time	6

LLOYD PRICE (ORCHESTRA)

78s

57	London HL 8438	Just Because/Why (78)	30
59	HMV POP 580	Stagger Lee/You Need Love (78)	50
59	HMV POP 598	Where Were You (On Our Wedding Day)?/Is It Really Love? (78)	55
59	HMV POP 626	Personality/Have You Ever Had The Blues? (78)	60
59	HMV POP 650	I'm Gonna Get Married/Three Little Pigs (78)	60
59	HMV POP 672	Won'tcha Come Home/Come Into My Heart (78)	75
60	HMV POP 712	Lady Luck/Never Let Me Go (78)	85
60	HMV POP 772	Question/If I Look A Little Blue (as Lloyd Price Orchestra) (78)	100

SINGLES

57	London HL 8438	Just Because/Why (triangular or round centre)	100/60
59	HMV POP 580	Stagger Lee/You Need Love	10
59	HMV POP 598	Where Were You (On Our Wedding Day)?/Is It Really Love?	7
59	HMV POP 626	Personality/Have You Ever Had The Blues?	7
59	HMV POP 650	I'm Gonna Get Married/Three Little Pigs	7
59	HMV POP 672	Won'tcha Come Home/Come Into My Heart	7
60	HMV POP 712	Lady Luck/Never Let Me Go	7
60	HMV POP 741	For Love/No If's — No And's	7
60	HMV POP 772	Question/If I Look A Little Blue (as Lloyd Price Orchestra)	8
60	HMV POP 799	Just Call Me (And I'll Understand)/Who Coulda' Told You (They Lied)	8

Lloyd PRICE (ORCHESTRA)

MINT VALUE £

Year	Label	Title	Value
61	HMV POP 826	Know What You're Doin'/That's Why Tears Come And Go (as Lloyd Price Orchestra)	8
61	HMV POP 926	Boo Hoo/I Made You Cry	8
62	HMV POP 983	Be A Leader/'Nother Fairy Tale	7
62	HMV POP 1100	Under Your Spell, Again/Happy Birthday Mama	7
71	Wand WN 17	Hooked On A Feeling/If You Really Love Him	5
71	Wand WN 21	Natural Sinner/Mr & Mrs Untrue	5
73	GSF GSZ 5	Love Music/Just For Baby	7
73	GSF GSZ 11	Trying To Slip Away/They Get Down	5

EP

| 59 | HMV 7EG 8538/GES 5784 | THE EXCITING LLOYD PRICE (EP, mono/stereo) | 60/75 |

LPs

59	HMV CLP 1285	THE EXCITING LLOYD PRICE (LP)	50
59	HMV CLP 1314	MR. PERSONALITY (LP)	45
60	London HA-U 2213	LLOYD PRICE (LP)	50
60	HMV CLP 1361	MR. PERSONALITY SINGS THE BLUES (LP)	40
60	HMV CLP 1393	THE FANTASTIC LLOYD PRICE (LP, also stereo CSD 1323)	40/50
62	HMV CLP 1519	COOKIN' (LP, also stereo CSD 1413)	40/50
63	Encore ENC 2004	PRICE SINGS THE MILLION DOLLAR SELLERS (LP)	20
69	Major Minor SMLP 57	LLOYD PRICE NOW (LP)	18
70	Regal Starline SRS 5025	THE BEST OF LLOYD PRICE (LP)	12
71	Joy JOYS 202	STAGGER LEE (LP)	12

MALCOLM PRICE (TRIO)

61	Oak RGJ 106	PICKIN' ON THE COUNTRY STRINGS! (EP)	20
64	Decca LK 4627	COUNTRY SESSION (LP, as Malcolm Price Trio)	12
65	Decca LK 4665	WAY DOWN TOWN (LP)	12
69	Saga FID 2156	HIS SONGS, HIS GUITARS (LP)	12
75	Sweet Folk & C. SFA 017	THEN WE ALL GOT UP AND WALKED AWAY (LP)	12

RAY PRICE

| 57 | Philips BBE 12137 | RAY PRICE (EP) | 30 |

(ROCKIN') RED PRICE

56	Decca F 10822	Rocky Mountain Gal/Rock O' The North (as Red Price & His Rockin' Rhythm)	12
56	Decca F 10822	Rocky Mountain Gal/Rock O' The North (78)	15
57	Woodbine	Woodbine Rock (78, some in p/s, promo only)	25/15
58	Pye 7N 15169	Weekend/The Sneeze	10
58	Pye N 15169	Weekend/The Sneeze (78)	30
60	Pye 7N 15262	Wow!/My Baby's Door	10
61	Parlophone R 4789	Theme From "Danger Man"/Blackjack (as Red Price Combo)	18

(see also Cherry Wainer)

RED PRICE & BLUE BEATS

| 64 | Blue Beat BB 209 | Blue Beats Over (The White Cliffs Of Dover)/Kiss The Baby (When You Grow Too Old To Dream) | 10 |

RICK PRICE

70	Gemini GMS 012	Davey Has No Dad/Bitter Sweet	7
71	Gemini GMS 017	Top Ten Record/Beautiful Sally	6
70	Gemini GME 1002	THIS IS TO CERTIFY THAT (LP, as Rick Price & Gemini)	20
71	Gemini GME 1017	TALKING TO THE FLOWERS (LP)	18

(see also Move, Sheridan-Price, Sight & Sound)

RIKKI PRICE

58	Fontana H 162	Tom Dooley/(It Looks Like Rain In) Cherry Blossom Lane	6
58	Fontana H 162	Tom Dooley/(It Looks Like Rain In) Cherry Blossom Lane (78)	8
59	Fontana H 171	Honey, Honey/The Very Thought Of You	7
59	Fontana H 171	Honey, Honey/The Very Thought Of You (78)	8
59	Fontana H 217	Mr. Blue/Man On My Trail	6
59	Fontana H 217	Mr. Blue/Man On My Trail (78)	12
62	Fontana H 371	You're For Real/When You Pass By	6
58	Fontana TFE 17100	RIKKI PRICE (EP)	18

(see also Sheridan-Price)

SAMMY PRICE

63	Storyville A 45 068	Boogieing With Big Sid/133 Street Boogie (some with p/s)	30/20
57	Columbia SEG 7679	ORIGINAL SAMMY BLUES (EP)	20
58	Vogue EPV 1146	SAMMY PRICE (EP)	60
58	Vogue EPV 1151	SAMMY PRICE'S BLUESICIANS (EP)	60
58	Vogue LAE 12027	SWINGIN' PARIS STYLE (LP)	25
62	London Jazz LTZ-R 15240	THE BLUES AIN'T NOTHIN' (LP, also stereo SAH-R 6234)	25/30

(see also SIster Rosetta Tharpe)

VINCENT PRICE

| 77 | EMI EMI 2659 | The Monster Mash/The Bard's Own Recipe | 6 |
| 59 | Columbia 33SX 1141 | VINCENT PRICE (LP) | 35 |

CHARLEY PRIDE

| 69 | RCA RCA 1796 | The Little Folks/Kaw Liga | 5 |
| 68 | RCA RD 7966 | MAKE MINE COUNTRY (LP) | 12 |

DICKIE PRIDE

59	Columbia DB 4283	Slippin' 'N' Slidin'/Don't Make Me Love You	30
59	Columbia DB 4296	Fabulous Cure/Midnight Oil	20
59	Columbia DB 4340	Frantic/Primrose Lane	20
60	Columbia DB 4403	Betty, Betty (Go Steady With Me)/No John	12
60	Columbia DB 4451	You're Singin' Our Love Song To Somebody Else/Bye Bye Blackbird	6
59	Columbia SEG 7937	SHEIK OF SHAKE (EP)	200
61	Columbia 33SX 1307	PRIDE WITHOUT PREJUDICE (LP, also stereo SCX 3369)	100/120

(see also Guvners)

MINT VALUE £

LOUIS PRIMA (& HIS ORCHESTRA)

52	Columbia DB 3070	Ooh–Dahdily–Dah/Eleanor (78)	18
53	Columbia DC 604	Chili Sauce/One Mint Julep (78, export issue)	25
53	Columbia DC 609	Bigger The Figure/Honey Bones (78, export issue)	20
54	Brunswick 05314	The Happy Wanderer/LOUIS PRIMA & KEELY SMITH: Until Sunrise (78)	10
56	Capitol CL 14669	5 Months, 2 Weeks, 2 Days/Banana Split For My Baby	25
56	Capitol CL 14669	5 Months, 2 Weeks, 2 Days/Banana Split For My Baby (78)	15
58	Capitol CL 14821	Buona Sera/Beep! Beep!	15
58	Capitol CL 14821	Buona Sera/Beep! Beep! (78)	15
60	London HLD 9230	Ol' Man Moses (with Sam Butera's Witnesses)/Wonderland By Night	10
64	Prima PR 1000	Robin Hood/Angelina (with Gia Maione)	5
64	Prima PR 1001	Fee Fie Fo O (Parts 1 & 2)	5
64	Prima PR 1006	Spoonful Of Sugar/Stay Awake	5
64	Prima PR 1009	Robin Hood/Angelina	5
59	Capitol EAP1 1132	STRICTLY PRIMA (EP)	12
57	Capitol T 755	THE WILDEST (LP)	30
58	Capitol T 836	THE CALL OF THE WILDWEST (LP)	20
58	Capitol T 1010	LAS VEGAS PRIMA STYLE (LP)	18
62	Ember EMB 3348	LOUIS PRIMA SWINGS (LP)	15
60s	Dot GTL 0287	HIS GREATEST HITS (LP)	12

(see also Sam Butera's Witnesses)

LOUIS PRIMA & KEELY SMITH

50	Polygon P 1001	Oh Babe!/LOUIS PRIMA: Piccolina Lena (78)	15
54	Columbia SCM 5092	Take A Little Walk Around The Block/LOUIS PRIMA: Oh! Cumari	20
54	Columbia DB 3431	Take A Little Walk Around The Block/LOUIS PRIMA: Oh! Cumari (78)	10
58	Capitol CL 14862	The Lip/KEELY SMITH: Foggy Day	6
58	Capitol CL 14862	The Lip/KEELY SMITH: Foggy Day (78)	20
58	Capitol CL 14948	That Old Black Magic/KEELY SMITH: You Are My Love	6
58	Capitol CL 14948	That Old Black Magic/KEELY SMITH: You Are My Love (78)	8
59	Capitol CL 14994	I've Got You Under My Skin/KEELY SMITH: Don't Take Your Love From Me	5
59	London HLD 8923	Bei Mir Bist Du Schon/I Don't Know Why	10
59	London HLD 8923	Bei Mir Bist Du Schon/I Don't Know Why (78)	30
60	London HLD 9084	I'm Confessin' (That I Love You)/Night And Day	8
60	London HA-D 2243	LOUIS AND KEELY (LP)	20
61	London HA-D 2350	ON STAGE (LP, also stereo SAH-G 6149)	20/25
62	Capitol T 1531	THE HITS OF LOUIS & KEELY (LP)	15

(see also Keely Smith)

PRIMAL SCREAM

85	Creation CRE 017	All Fall Down/It Happens (foldaround p/s in poly bag)	25
86	Creation CRE 026	Crystal Crescent/Velocity Girl (p/s)	10
86	Creation CRE 026T	Crystal Crescent/Velocity Girl/Spirea X (12", p/s)	12
87	Elevation ACID 3	Gentle Tuesday/Black Star Carnival (p/s)	5
87	Elevation ACID 3T	Gentle Tuesday/Black Star Carnival/I'm Gonna Make You Mine (12", p/s)	10
87	Elevation ACID 5	Imperial/Star Fruit Surf Rider (p/s)	6
87	Elevation ACID 5T	Imperial/Star Fruit Surf Rider/So Sad About Us/Imperial (demo) (12", some in poster p/s with 'special price' sticker)	12/10
90	Creation CRE 070X	LOADED EP (12", black die-cut stickered sleeve, 5,000 only)	8
91	Creation CRESCD 096	Higher Than The Sun (7" Edit)/Higher Than The Sun (12")/Higher Than The Orb (CD)	8
98	Creation CRE 284	If They Move, Kill 'Em/MY BLOODY VALENTINE: Arkestra (p/s, 2,000 only)	4
98	Creation CRE 284CD	If They Move, Kill 'Em/MY BLOODY VALENTINE: Arkestra (CD, 2,000 only)	8
89	Creation CRELP 054	PRIMAL SCREAM (LP, with bonus 45 "Split Wide Open #1"/"Lone Star Girl #1" [CREFRE 6, no p/s])	15

(see also Jesus & Mary Chain, Revolving Paint Dream, P.P. & Primes)

PRIMETTES

68	Ember EMBS 3398	LOOKING BACK WITH THE PRIMETTES AND EDDIE FLOYD (LP, 1 side each)	40
70s	Windmill WMD 192	LOOKING BACK WITH THE PRIMETTES AND EDDIE FLOYD (LP, reissue)	12

(see also Supremes, Eddie Floyd)

PRIME-MATES

69	Action ACT 4530	Hot Tamales (Versions 1 & 2)	6

PRIMITIVES

64	Pye 7N 15721	Help Me/Let Them Tell	165
65	Pye 7N 15755	You Said/How Do You Feel	180

(see also Mal & Primitives)

PRIMITIVES

86	Head HEAD 010	Thru The Flowers/Across My Shoulder/Lazy/She Don't Need You (12", unreleased, white label test pressings only)	30
86	Lazy LAZY 01	Thru The Flowers/Across My Shoulder/She Don't Need You/Lazy (12", p/s)	10
86	Lazy LAZY 02	Really Stupid/We Found A Way To The Sun (p/s)	5
86	Lazy LAZY 02T	Really Stupid/We Found A Way To The Sun/Where The Wind Blows (12", p/s)	7
86	Lazy LAZY 03	Stop Killing Me/Buzz Buzz Buzz (p/s, with postcard, sleeves printed back-to-front; also a very few with badge)	5/4
87	Lazy LAZY 05	Ocean Blue/Shadow (2,000 only, given free at London Astoria gig, no p/s)	6
88	RCA PB 41761X	Crash/I'll Stick With You/Crash (Live In Studio) (10", 1,500 signed, gatefold p/s)	5
88	RCA PB 42209E	Way Behind Me/All The Way Down (no'd [3,000 each in red, blue, green & yellow], foldover p/s in poly bag, postcard & badge, with bubble bath)	4

PRIMO & HOPETON

67	Rio R 139	Your Safekeep/Loving And Kind	10
68	Pama PM 753	Peace On Earth/SCHOOL BOYS: Love Is A Message	5

PRIMROSE CIRCUS

70	President PT 314	P.S. Call Me Lulu/In My Mind	5

PRINCE (& THE REVOLUTION)
SINGLES

79	Warner Bros K 17537	I Wanna Be Your Lover/Just As Long As We're Together (no p/s)	10
79	Warner Bros K 17537T	I Wanna Be Your Lover/Just As Long As We're Together (12", co. sleeve)	18
80	Warner Bros K 17590	Sexy Dancer/Bambi (die-cut company sleeve)	30
80	Warner Bros K 17590T	Sexy Dancer (Remix)/Bambi (12", die-cut company sleeve)	45
81	Warner Bros K 17768	Do It All Night/Head (die-cut company sleeve)	30
81	Warner Bros K 17768T	Do It All Night/Head (12", die-cut company sleeve)	60
81	Warner Bros K 17819	Gotta Stop (Messin' About)/Uptown (p/s)	75
81	Warner Bros K 17819	Gotta Stop (Messin' About)/I Wanna Be Your Lover (p/s)	75
81	Warner Bros LV 47	Gotta Stop (Messin' About)/Uptown/Head (12", stickered p/s)	130
81	Warner Bros LV 47	Gotta Stop (Messin' About)/I Wanna Be Your Lover/Head (12", stickered p/s)	130
81	Warner Bros K 17866	Controversy/When You Were Mine (p/s)	40
81	Warner Bros K 17866T	Controversy/When You Were Mine (12", p/s)	60
82	Warner Bros K 17922	Let's Work/Ronnie, Talk To Russia (p/s)	40
82	Warner Bros K 17922T	Let's Work (Extended)/Ronnie, Talk To Russia (12", p/s)	130
83	Warner Bros W 9896	1999/How Come U Don't Call Me Anymore (paper labels, p/s, some with free cassette mini-album in card p/s: "1999 (Edit)"/"Uptown"/ "Controversy"/"Dirty Minds"/"Sexuality")	40/10
83	Warner Bros W 9896T	1999/How Come U Don't Call Me Anymore/D.M.S.R. (12", p/s)	25
83	Warner Bros W 9688	Little Red Corvette/Lady Cab Driver (p/s)	10
83	Warner Bros W 9688T	Little Red Corvette (Full Length Version)/Automatic/International Lover (12", stickered p/s, some with poster insert)	60/25
83	Warner Bros W 9436	Little Red Corvette/Horny Toad (poster calendar p/s)	55
83	Warner Bros W 9436	Little Red Corvette/Horny Toad (standard p/s)	40
83	Warner Bros W 9436T	Little Red Corvette (Full Length Version)/Horny Toad/D.M.S.R. (12", p/s)	30
83	Warner Bros W 9436T	Little Red Corvette (Full Length Version)/Horny Toad/D.M.S.R. (12", p/s, with spiral-bound calendar or poster)	85/75
84	Warner Bros W 9286C	When Doves Cry/17 Days/1999/D.M.S.R. (cassette, some with paper labels)	10/8
84	Warner Bros W 9286T	When Doves Cry/17 Days (12", p/s)	8
84	Warner Bros W 9286T	When Doves Cry/17 Days//1999/D.M.S.R. (12", stickered shrinkwrapped double pack)	70
84	Warner Bros W 9174P	Purple Rain/God (motorbike-shaped picture disc)	70
84	Warner Bros W 9174T	Purple Rain/God (instrumental)/God (12", p/s, initially with poster)	20/8
84	Warner Bros W 9121	I Would Die 4 U/Another Lonely Christmas (paper labels, p/s)	5
84	Warner Bros W 9121T	I Would Die 4 U/Another Lonely Christmas (12", p/s)	10
84	Warner Bros W 9121TE	I Would Die 4 U (U.S. Remix)/Another Lonely Christmas (U.S. Remix) (12", p/s)	30
85	Warner Bros W 2000	Let's Go Crazy/Take Me With U (paper labels, p/s)	5
85	Warner Bros W 2000T	Let's Go Crazy (Extended)/Take Me With U/Erotic City (12", stickered p/s)	10
85	Paisley Park W 9052	Paisley Park/She's Always In My Hair (p/s)	4
85	Paisley Park W 9052P	Paisley Park/She's Always In My Hair (shaped picture disc)	35
85	Paisley Park W 9052T	Paisley Park/She's Always In My Hair/Paisley Park (Remix) (12", p/s)	12
85	Paisley Park W 9052T	Paisley Park/She's Always In My Hair/Paisley Park (Remix) (12", p/s, mispressing with repeated 2nd track "She's Always In My Hair")	25
85	Paisley Park W 8929	Raspberry Beret/Hello (paper label, p/s)	5
85	Paisley Park W 8929T	Raspberry Beret (Extended Remix)/Hello (Extended Remix) (12", p/s)	12
85	Paisley Park W 8858	Pop Life/Girl (paper label, p/s)	5
85	Paisley Park W 8858T	Pop Life (Extended)/Girl (12", p/s)	15
86	Paisley Park W 8751P	Kiss/Love Or Money (shaped picture disc with plinth)	30
86	Paisley Park W 8751T	Kiss (Extended)/Love Or Money (12", p/s, some with poster)	15/8
86	Paisley Park W 8711	Mountains/Alexa De Paris (paper label, p/s)	4
86	Paisley Park W 8711TE	Mountains (Ext.)/Alexa De Paris (Extended) (10", white vinyl in PVC sleeve)	40
86	Paisley Park W 8711T	Mountains (Extended 9.56)/Alexa De Paris (12", p/s, some with poster)	20/10
86	Paisley Park W 8586	Girls And Boys (Edit)/Under The Cherry Moon (paper label, p/s)	4
86	Paisley Park W 8586F	Girls And Boys (Edit)/Under The Cherry Moon//She's Always In My Hair/ 17 Days (double pack, gatefold p/s)	15
86	Paisley Park W 8586P	Girls And Boys (Edit)/Under The Cherry Moon (shaped picture disc)	45
86	Paisley Park W 8586T	Girls And Boys/Under The Cherry Moon/Erotic City (12", p/s, some with poster advertising London gigs)	18/10
86	Paisley Park W 8521W	Anotherloverholenyohead/I Wanna Be Your Lover (paper or plastic labels, poster p/s)	15
86	Paisley Park W 8521T	Anotherloverholenyohead (Extended)/I Wanna Be Your Lover (12", p/s)	10
87	Paisley Park W 8399TP	Sign O' The Times (Extended)/La La La He He Hee (Extended) (12", picture disc)	30
87	Paisley Park W 8334W	If I Was Your Girlfriend/Shockadelica (poster p/s)	10
87	Paisley Park W 8334E	If I Was Your Girlfriend/Shockadelica (peach vinyl, PVC cover, with postcards & stickers)	15
87	Paisley Park W 8334TP	If I Was Your Girlfriend/Shockadelica (Extended) (12", picture disc)	25
87	Paisley Park W 8289TP	U Got The Look (Long Look)/Housequake (7 min MoQuake)/ U Got The Look (Single Cut) (12", picture disc)	25
87	Paisley Park W 8288TP	I Could Never Take The Place Of Your Man/Hot Thing (Remixed Edit)/ Hot Thing (Extended) (12", picture disc)	25
88	Paisley Park W 7900CD	Alphabet Street (Album Version)/This Is Not Music, This Is A Trip (Alphabet Street) (Extended) (3" CD, with adaptor, 5" case)	20
88	Paisley Park W 7806CD	Glam Slam (Edit)/Escape (Free Yo Mind) (Edit)/Glam Slam (Remix) (3" CD, with adaptor, 5" case)	20
88	Paisley Park W 7745	I Wish U Heaven (Edit)/Scarlet Pussy (Edit) (poster p/s)	10
88	Paisley Park W 7745TW	I Wish U Heaven (Parts 1/2/3)/CAMILLE: Scarlet Pussy (Edit) (12", p/s with poster)	15
88	Paisley Park W 7745CD	I Wish U Heaven (Parts 1/2/3)/CAMILLE: Scarlet Pussy (Edit) (3" CD, with adaptor, 5" case)	25
89	Paisley Park W 2924TP	Batdance (LP Version)/200 Balloons (12", picture disc, PVC sleeve)	12
89	Paisley Park W 2924CD	Batdance (LP Version)/200 Balloons (3" CD, card sleeve)	10
89	Paisley Park W 2924CDX	Batdance (LP Version)/200 Balloons (3" CD, oval card sleeve)	15
89	Paisley Park W 2814TP	Partyman (Video Mix)/Feel U Up (Long Stroke) (12", picture disc, PVC sleeve)	12

89	Paisley Park W 2814CD	Partyman (Video Mix)/Feel U Up (Long Stroke) (3" CD, gatefold card sleeve in outer plastic pouch). 8
89	Paisley Park W 2814CDX	Partyman (Video Mix)/Feel U Up (Long Stroke) (3" CD, octagonal foldout sleeve with film stills). 15
89	Paisley Park W 2814CDT	Partyman (The Purple Party Mix)/(Partyman Music Mix)/(The Video Mix)/ Feel U Up (Short Stroke) (3" CD, card sleeve) 8
89	Paisley Park W 2757TP	The Arms Of Orion (5.03)/I Love U In Me/The Arms Of Orion (3.52) (12", with Sheena Easton, picture disc, PVC sleeve) 10
89	Paisley Park W 2757CD	The Arms Of Orion (5.03)/I Love U In Me/The Arms Of Orion (3.52) (3" CD, with Sheena Easton, gatefold card sleeve). 8
89	Paisley Park W 2757CDX	The Arms Of Orion (5.03)/I Love U In Me/The Arms Of Orion (3.52) (CD, shrinkwrapped tri-fold stickered sleeve, some with sticker insert) 15/12
88	Paisley Park W 8751TP	Kiss/Love Or Money (shaped picture disc, 're-promoted' edition with longer, extended version of B-side & without plinth) 25
90	Paisley Park W 9751TP	Thieves In The Temple/Thieves In The Temple (Thieves In The House Mix)/ (Temple House Dub) (12", picture disc with insert) 8
90	Paisley Park W 9525TP	New Power Generation/New Power Generation (Melody Cool Extended Remix)/ Part II (12", picture disc with insert) 8
92	Paisley Park W 0091TP	Money Don't Matter 2 Night/Push/Call The Law (12", picture disc with insert) 8
92	Paisley Park W 0113TP	Thunder/Violet The Organ Grinder/Gett Off (Thrust Dub) (12", 1-sided picture disc, with numbered insert). 10
92	Paisley Park W 0123TP	Sexy M.F./Strollin' (shaped picture disc with insert). 8
94	Paisley Park W 0260P	Let It Go/Solo (picture disc with numbered insert). 5

ALBUMS

83	Warner Bros 923 809-1	1999 (LP, original issue, single disc). 30
84	Warner Bros 925 110-1	PURPLE RAIN — MUSIC FROM THE MOTION PICTURE (LP, purple vinyl with poster). 25
86	Paisley Park WX 39P	PARADE — MUSIC FROM "UNDER A CHERRY MOON" (LP, pic. disc, die-cut sl.). 50
89	Paisley Park WX 281P	BATMAN (LP, picture disc, die-cut sleeve) 15
89	Paisley Park 927 489-2	BATMAN (CD, picture disc) 20
89	Paisley Park 925 978-2	BATMAN (CD, picture disc in 'Bat' tin with booklet) 25

(The Revolution are credited on all recordings from "Purple Rain" to "Anotherloverholenyohead")
(see also Wendy & Lisa)

VIV PRINCE

66	Columbia DB 7960	Light Of The Charge Brigade/Minuet For Ringo 30

(see also Pretty Things, Bunch Of Fives, Kate, Vamp, Chicago Line)

PRINCE & PRINCESS

65	Aladdin WI 609	Ready Steady Go/Take Me Serious 15

PRINCE BUSTER (& ALL STARS)

61	Starlite ST45 052	Buster's Shack (as Buster's Group)/ERIC MORRIS: Search The World 18
62	Blue Beat BB 101	My Sound That Goes Around/They Got To Go (with Torchlighters) 15
62	Blue Beat BB 116	Independence Song (with Bluebeats)/RICO & BLUEBEATS: August 1962 15
62	Blue Beat BB 133	Time Longer Than Rope/Fake King (with Voice Of The People) 15
62	Blue Beat BB 138	One Hand Washes The Other/Cowboy Comes To Town 15
63	Blue Beat BB 150	Run Man Run/Danny, Dane And Lorraine 15
63	Blue Beat BB 158	Open Up, Bartender/Enjoy It (B-side actually "Enjoy Yourself"). 15
63	Blue Beat BB 162	Money/SCHOOL BOYS: Little Boy Blue. 15
63	Blue Beat BB 163	King, Duke, Sir/I See Them In My Sight. 15
63	Blue Beat BB 167	The Ten Commandments (with All Stars)/Buster's Welcome 15
63	Blue Beat BB 170	Madness/PRINCE BUSTER ALL STARS: Toothache. 15
63	Blue Beat BB 173	Burning Creation/PRINCE BUSTER ALL STARS: Boop 15
63	Blue Beat BB 180	Three More Rivers To Cross/RAYMOND HARPER & PRINCE BUSTER ALL STARS: African Blood 15
63	Blue Beat BB 186	Fowl Thief/Remember Me. 15
63	Blue Beat BB 189	Watch It Blackhead/Hello My Dear. 15
63	Blue Beat BB 192	Rollin' Stone (with Charmers)/RICO & HIS BLUES BAND: This Day. 15
63	Blue Beat BB 197	Window Shopping/Sodom And Gomorrah 15
63	Blue Beat BB 199	Spider And Fly/Three Blind Mice. 18
63	Blue Beat BB 200	Wash All Your Troubles Away/RICO & BLUE BEATS: Soul Of Africa 15
63	Dice CC 6	They Got To Come/These Are The Times (with Voice Of The People). 15
63	Dice CC 11	Blackhead Chinaman/You Ask (I Had A Girl) 15
63	Dice CC 18	World Peace/The Lion Roars (as Prince Buster & Hazel) 15
64	Stateside SS 335	30 Pieces Of Silver/Everybody Ska 12
64	Blue Beat BB 210	Wash All Your Troubles Away/RICO & BLUE BEATS: Soul Of Africa (reissue) . . . 15
64	Blue Beat BB 211	Bluebeat Spirit/Beggars Are No Choosers 15
64	Blue Beat BB 216	You're Mine/Tongue Will Tell 15
64	Blue Beat BB 225	Three Blind Mice/I Know 15
64	Blue Beat BB 232	Sheep On Top (song actually titled "She Pon Top")/Midnight. 15
64	Blue Beat BB 234	She Loves You/Healing. 15
64	Blue Beat BB 243	Jealous/Buster's Ska 15
64	Blue Beat BB 248	Thirty Pieces Of Silver/The National Dance 15
64	Blue Beat BB 254	Wings Of A Dove/MAYTALLS: Sweet Love 18
64	Blue Beat BB 262	Old Lady/Dayo Ska. 15
64	Blue Beat BB 271	No Knowledge In College/In The Middle Of The Night 15
64	Blue Beat BB 274	I May Never Love You Again/Hey Little Girl. 15
65	Blue Beat BB 278	Blood Pressure/Islam. 15
65	Blue Beat BB 281	Blues Market/MAYTALS: Looking Down The Street 15
65	Blue Beat BB 282	Big Fight/Red Dress. 15
65	Blue Beat BB 293	Agua Fumar/Long Winter (with Charmers) 15
65	Blue Beat BB 302	Ling Ting Tong/Walk Along 15
65	Blue Beat BB 307	Bonanza/Wonderful Life. 18
65	Blue Beat BB 309	Here Comes The Bride (with Patsy Todd, as Jamaica's Greatest)/ BUSTER'S ALLSTARS: Burkes' Law 15
65	Blue Beat BB 313	Everybody Yeah Yeah (as Jamaica's Greatest)/ BUSTER'S ALLSTARS: Gun The Man Down 15

Year	Label	Title	Value
65	Blue Beat BB 314	Float Like A Butterfly/Haunted Room	20
65	Blue Beat BB 316	Sugar Pop/Feel Up (as Prince & Jamaica's Greatest)	15
65	Blue Beat BB 317	Come Home/I Thank You (as Jamaica's Greatest)	15
65	Blue Beat BB 321	My Girl/BUSTER'S ALL STARS: The Fugitive	15
65	Blue Beat BB 324	Al Capone/One Step Beyond (as Prince Buster's Allstars) (blue label or other label colours)	8/5
65	Blue Beat BB 328	Ambition/BUSTER'S ALL STARS: Ryging	15
65	Blue Beat BB 330	Rum And Coca Cola/I Love Her	20
65	Blue Beat BB 334	The Ten Commandments/BUSTER'S ALL STARS: Sting Like A Bee (reissue)	10
65	Blue Beat BB 335	Respect/BUSTER'S ALL STARS: Virginia (B-side actually "Dance Jamaica" by Val Bennett & Prince Buster's All Stars)	15
66	Blue Beat BB 338	Big Fight (Prince Buster Versus Duke Reid)/Adios, Senorita	15
66	Blue Beat BB 339	Under Arrest (But Officer)/PRINCE BUSTER'S ALLSTARS: Say Boss Man	15
66	Blue Beat BB 343	Don't Throw Stones/Prince Of Peace	40
66	Blue Beat BB 352	Day Of Light (song actually "Dayo")/It's Too Late	15
66	Blue Beat BB 355	Sunshine With My Girl/Girl Answer Your Name	20
66	Blue Beat BB 357	I Won't Let You Cry/Hard Man Fe Dead	15
66	Blue Beat BB 359	The Prophet (actually "Feel The Spirit" with Slim Smith)/BUSTER'S ALL STARS: Lion Of Judah	35
66	Blue Beat BB 362	To Be Loved/BUSTER'S ALLSTARS: Set Me Free	20
66	Rainbow RAI 107	Your Turn (Sad Song)/If You Leave Me (with Allstars)	12
67	Blue Beat BB 370	Shanty Town (Get Scanty)/BUSTER'S ALL STARS: Duppy	20
67	Blue Beat BB 373	Knock On Wood/And I Love Her	15
67	Blue Beat BB 377	Dark End Of The Street/Love Oh Love	15
67	Blue Beat BB 378	Drunkard's Psalm (Wise Man)/7 Wonders Of The World (as Prince Buster All Stars)	35
67	Blue Beat BB 382	Sit And Wonder (with His All Stars)/ROLAND ALFONSO: Sunrise In Kingston	25
67	Blue Beat BB 383	Sharing You/You'll Be Lonely On The Blue Train (as Prince Buster's Allstars; A-side actually by Prince Buster, B-side actually by Rico's Band)	15
67	Blue Beat BB 384	Take It Easy/Why Must I Cry (2nd issue, B-side actually by Hopeton Lewis)	12
67	Blue Beat BB 387	Judge Dread (Judge Four Hundred Years)/FITZROY CAMPBELL & PRINCE BUSTER ALL STARS: Waiting For My Rude Girl	12
67	Blue Beat BB 388	Dance Cleopatra/All In My Mind	35
67	Blue Beat BB 390	Soul Serenade/Too Hot	15
67	Blue Beat BB 391	Land Of Imagination/The Appeal (B-side actually "The Barrister Appeal")	15
67	Blue Beat BB 393	Johnny Dollar/Rude Boys Rule	15
67	Blue Beat BB 395	This Gun's For Hire/Yes, Daddy	15
67	Blue Beat BB 400	All In My Mind/Judge Dread Dance (The Pardon)	15
67	Blue Beat BB 402	Vagabond/PRINCE BUSTER ALL STARS: Come Get Me	15
67	Philips BF 1552	The Ten Commandments/Don't Make Me Cry	10
67	Fab FAB 10	Shakin' Up Orange Street/Black Girl (with Allstars)	12
67	Fab FAB 11	Johnny Cool (Parts 1 & 2) (with Allstars)	15
67	Fab FAB 16	Bye Bye Baby/Human (with Allstars)	12
67	Fab FAB 25	Train To Girls Town/Give Love A Try (with Allstars)	12
67	Fab FAB 26	Going To The River (as Prince Buster & Allstars)/PRINCE BUSTER'S ALLSTARS: Julie On My Mind	15
68	Fab FAB 31	Kings Of Old (My Ancestors)/Sweet Inspiration (with Allstars)	12
68	Fab FAB 35	Try A Little Tenderness/All My Loving (with Allstars)	12
68	Fab FAB 36	The Glory Of Love/Another Sad Nite	12
68	Fab FAB 37	This Is A Hold Up/Julie On My Mind (with Allstars)	8
68	Fab FAB 38	Free Love (with Allstars)/DALTONS: All Over The World	12
68	Fab FAB 40	Rough Rider (with Allstars)/PRINCE BUSTER: 127 Orange Street (B-side actually by Prince Buster Allstars)	18
68	Fab FAB 41	Shepherd Beng Beng (with Teddy King)/TENNORS: Ride Your Donkey	15
68	Fab FAB 47	Going To Ethiopia (as Prince Buster & Allstars)/PRINCE BUSTER ALLSTARS: Shakin' Up Orange Street	10
68	Fab FAB 49	Glory Of Love/WAILERS: Mellow Mood (possibly white labels only)	50
68	Fab FAB 56	Intensified Dirt/Don't You Know I Love You (with Allstars)	10
68	Fab FAB 57	Green Green Grass Of Home (as Prince Buster's Allstars; actually by Prince Buster & Allstars)/SOUL MAKERS: Girls Like You	8
68	Fab FAB 58	We Shall Overcome/Keep The Faith (as Prince Buster's Allstars; actually by Prince Buster & Allstars)	10
68	Fab FAB 64	Cool Stroker/It's You I Love (B-side actually by Little Roy)	10
68	Fab FAB 80	Hypocrite/New Dance (B-side actually by Little Roy)	10
68	Fab FAB 81	Wine And Grind/The Scorcher (with Allstars)	10
69	Unity UN 522	30 Pieces Of Silver/Everybody Ska (reissue)	10
69	Fab FAB 82	Dr. Rodney (Black Power)/Taxation	8
69	Fab FAB 92	Pharaoh House Crash/Ob-La-Di, Ob-La-Da	8
69	Fab FAB 93	Ob-La-Di, Ob-La-Da/Wreck A Pum Pum	6
69	Fab FAB 94	Hey Jude/Django Fever	8
69	Fab FAB 102	Black Soul/CALEDONIANS: Oh Baby (B-side actually by Claredonians)	8
69	Fab FAB 108	Wine And Grind/The Scorcher (with Allstars) (reissue)	8
69	Fab FAB 118	Bull Buck/ROLAND ALPHONSO: One Heart	8
69	Fab FAB 119	Let Her Go/Tie The Donkey's Tail	8
69	Fab FAB 122	Stand Up/Happy Reggae (with Allstars)	7
70	Fab FAB 127	Young Gifted And Black/PRINCE BUSTER'S ALLSTARS: The Rebel	7
70	Fab FAB 131	That's All/The Preaching (B-side actually titled "The Preacher")	7
70	Fab FAB 132	Ganja Plant/Creation	7
70	Fab FAB 140	Hit Me Back/Give Peace A Chance	10
70	Fab FAB 150	Big Five/Musical College	5
70	Prince Buster PB 1	Big Five/Musical College (reissue)	5
70	Prince Buster PB 2	Rat Trap/Black Organ (B-side with Allstars but actually by Ansell Collins & Prince Buster's Allstars)	7
71	Fab FAB 162	Baby Version (with Jan Fender)/Holly	6
71	Fab FAB 176	Police Trim Rasta (with Allstars)/Smooth (B-side actually by Ansell Collins & Prince Buster Allstars)	7

PRINCE BUSTER

71	Prince Buster PB 4	Fishey/More Fishey	7
71	Prince Buster PB 7	I Wish Your Picture Was You/PRINCE BUSTER ALLSTARS: It Mash Up — Version (B-side actually by Dennis Alcapone)	7
71	Prince Buster PB 8	Sons Of Zion (actually by Dennis Alcapone)/ANSELL COLLINS: Short Circuit	7
71	Prince Buster PB 9	My Happiness/Human (with Allstars)	7
72	Prince Buster PB 14	Big Sister Stuff/Satta Massagana (with Allstars)	10
72	Prince Buster PB 15	Protection/Cool Operator (with Allstars)	7
72	Prince Buster PB 16	I Stand Accused/My Heart is Gone (with Allstars)	7
72	Prince Buster PB 19	Four In One Medley/Drums Drums (as Prince Buster & Allstars, B-side actually by Prince Buster Allstars)	7
72	Prince Buster PB 32	Still/Sister Big Stuff (with Allstars)	7
72	Prince Buster PB 36	South Of The Border/South Of The Border (Version) (with Allstars)	7
72	Fab FAB 36	South Of The Border/South Of The Border (Version) (with Allstars)	7
72	Prince Buster PB 47	Baldhead Pum Pum/Giver Her (with Allstars)	7
79	Blue Beat DDBB 324	Al Capone/One Step Beyond (12", p/s)	7
79	Blue Beat DDBB 334	THREE OF THE BEST (12" EP, p/s)	7
79	Blue Beat DDPB 1	Big Five/FOLK BROTHERS: Carolina/ PRINCE BUSTER: Shaking Up Orange Street (12", p/s)	7
79	Blue Beat DDPB 2	PICK OF THE PUNCH (12" EP, p/s, 2 tracks each by Tennors & Prince Buster)	7
79	Blue Beat DDPB 3	NAUGHTY BUT NICE (12" EP, p/s)	7
79	Blue Beat DDPB 4	BEHIND BARS (12" EP, p/s)	7
63	Blue Beat BBLP 802	I FEEL THE SPIRIT (LP)	80
65	Blue Beat BBLP 805	SKA-LIP-SOUL (LP, with His All Stars)	150
65	Blue Beat BBLP 806	IT'S BURKE'S LAW — JAMAICA SKA EXPLOSION! (LP, as Prince Buster All Stars; 2 different sleeves, laminated plain and unlaminated 'explosion')	140
67	Blue Beat BBLP 807	WHAT A HARD MAN FE DEAD — PRINCE BUSTER SINGS FOR THE PEOPLE (LP, with Baba Brooks)	150
67	Blue Beat BBLP 808	ON TOUR (LP)	75
67	Blue Beat BBLP 809	JUDGE DREAD (LP)	80
67	Blue Beat BBLP 820	SHE WAS A ROUGH RIDER (LP)	60
68	Fab BBLP 820	SHE WAS A ROUGH RIDER (LP, reissue on Fab label)	25
68	Fab BBLP 821	WRECK A PUM PUM (LP)	35
69	Fab BBLP 822	THE OUTLAW (LP, title listed as "Queen Of The Outlaws" on disc)	50
70	Fab MS 1	FABULOUS GREATEST HITS (LP, original issue with 'West Brothers Printers' credit on rear of sleeve)	12
70	Fab MS 2	I FEEL THE SPIRIT (LP)	35
70	Fab MS 6	TUTTI FRUTTI (LP)	30
72	Melodisc MLP 12-156	SISTER BIG STUFF (LP)	30
72	Melodisc MLP 12-157	BIG FIVE (LP)	20
73	Prince Buster PB 9	ORIGINAL GOLDEN OLDIES VOLUME 1 (LP)	15

(see also Buster's Allstars, Buster's Group, Dennis Alcapone, Jim Dakota, Hortense Ellis, Heptones, Eric Morris, Terry Nelson, Schoolboys, Protege)

PRINCE CHARLIE
69	Coxsone CS 7101	Hit And Run/Darling, There I Stand	15

PRINCE HAROLD
66	Mercury MF 952	Forget About Me/Baby You've Got Me	8

PRINCE JAZZBO
73	Grape GR 3047	Free From Chains/LLOYD & PATSY: Papa Do It Sweet	6
73	Techniques TE 921	Mr. Harry Skank/GLEN BROWN: Telavid Drums	7
74	Ackee ACK 532	Kick Boy Face/Version	6
74	Dip DL 5036	Penny Reel/Good Things	7

(see also Earl George)

PRINCE OF DARKNESS
69	Downtown DT 441	Burial Of Long Shot/MUSIC DOCTORS: Burial Of Long Shot	8
69	Downtown DT 448	Meeting Over Yonder/MUSIC DOCTORS: Ghost Rider	8
71	Downtown DT 467	Sound Of Today/MUSIC DOCTORS: Red Red Wine Version	8

PRINCE PATO EXPEDITION
70s	Beacon BEAS 18	FIREBIRD (LP)	25

PRINCESS & SWINEHERD
68	Oak RGJ 633	PRINCESS AND THE SWINEHERD (LP, plain black sleeve)	30

PRINCIPAL EDWARDS MAGIC THEATRE
69	Dandelion S 4405	Ballad Of The Big Girl Now/Lament For The Earth	6
73	Deram DM 391	Captain Lifeboy/Nothing	5
73	Deram DM 398	Weekdaze/Whizzmore Kid	5
69	Dandelion 63752	SOUNDTRACK (LP)	25
71	Dandelion DAN 8002	THE ASOMOTO RUNNING BAND (LP, gatefold sleeve)	20
74	Deram SML 1108	ROUND ONE (LP)	20

JOHN PRINE
72	Atlantic K 40357	JOHN PRINE (LP)	12
72	Atlantic K 40427	DIAMONDS IN THE ROUGH (LP)	12
74	Atlantic K 40524	SWEET REVENGE (LP)	12
75	Atlantic K 50137	COMMON SENSE (LP)	12

MADDY PRIOR
78	Chrysalis CHS 2232	Baggy Pants/Woman In The Wings	6
80	EMI EMI 5903	Wake Up England/Paradise (p/s, as Maddy Prior Band)	6
82	Plant Life PLRS 001	Face To Face/Half Listening (p/s, as Maddy Prior Band)	6
83	RCA/Spindrift RCA 379	Deep In The Darkest Night/Western Movies (p/s)	6
85	Making Waves SURF 108	Stookie/Incidental Music From Stookie (p/s)	6
85	Making Waves SURF 109	Deep In The Darkest Night/Western Movies (p/s, reissue)	6
90	Parks PRKS 3	Happy Families/Who's Sorry Now (p/s, with Rick Kemp)	5
90	Parks PRKS 7	Who's Sorry Now/Happy Families (p/s, with Rick Kemp)	5

| 92 | Park PRKCD 16 | I Saw Three Ships (Dance Doctor's Christmas Remix)/The Boar's Head/ Poor Little Jesus/I Saw Three Ships (CD) | 8 |
| 78 | Chrysalis CHR 1185 | WOMAN IN THE WINGS (LP, with insert) | 12 |

(see also Steelye Span,Tim Hart & Maddy Prior)

PRISONERS

83	Big Beat NS 90	Hurricane/Tomorrow (She Said) (p/s)	10
84	Big Beat SW 98	ELECTRIC FIT (EP)	8
82	Own Up OWN UP U2	A TASTE OF PINK (LP)	20
85	Own Up OWN UP U2	A TASTE OF PINK (LP, reissue in pink sleeve on pink vinyl)	25
85	Own Up OWN UP U3	THE LAST FOURFATHERS (LP)	15
86	Countdown DOWN 2	IN FROM THE COLD (LP)	12
89	Hangman HANG 23 UP	RARE AND UNISSUED (LP)	10

(see also James Taylor Quartet)

PRISONERS/MILKSHAKES

| 86 | Empire MIC 001 | THE LAST NIGHT AT THE MIC CLUB (LP, live, 1 side each) | 15 |
| 86 | Media Burn MB 17 | THEE MILKSHAKES VS. THE PRISONERS (LP, live, 1 side each) | 12 |

(see also Milkshakes, Thee Mighty Caesars)

PRIVATE DICKS

| 79 | Heartbeat PULSE 6 | She Said So/Private Dicks (p/s) | 6 |
| 80 | Heartbeat PULSE 9 | Follow My Lead/You Want It You Got It (p/s) | 6 |

PRIVATE SECTOR

| 78 | TJM TJM 8 | Just Just (Wanna) Stay Free/Things Get Worse (p/s) | 6 |

P.J. PROBY

62	Liberty LIB 55367	Try To Forget Her/There Stands The One	10
64	Decca F 11904	Hold Me/The Tips Of My Fingers	6
64	Decca F 11967	Together/Sweet And Tender Romance	6
64	Liberty LIB 10182	Somewhere/Just Like Him	5
65	Liberty LIB 10188	I Apologise/What's On Your Mind	6
65	Liberty LIB 10206	Let The Water Run Down/I Don't Want To Hear It Anymore	7
65	Liberty LIB 10215	That Means A Lot/My Prayer	10
65	Liberty LIB 10218	Maria/She Cried	5
66	Liberty LIB 10223	You've Come Back/It Ain't Necessarily So	6
66	Liberty LIB 10236	To Make A Big Man Cry/Wicked Woman	6
66	Fab FAB 7	You've Got Me Cryin'/I Need Love (some in die-cut p/s)	12/6
66	Liberty LIB 10250	I Can't Make It Alone/Sweet Summer Wine	6
67	Liberty LIB 55936	Nicki Hoeky/Good Things Are Coming My Way	7
67	Liberty LIB 55974	You Can't Come Home Again/Work With Me Annie	12
68	Liberty LIB 15046	It's Your Day Today/I Apologise Baby	6
68	Liberty LBF 15085	What's Wrong With My World/Why Baby Why	7
68	Liberty LBF 15152	The Day That Lorraine Came Down/Mery Hoppkins Never Had Days Like These (B-side features Led Zeppelin)	12
69	Liberty LBF 15245	Hanging From Your Loving Tree/Empty Bottles	12
70	Liberty LBF 15280	Today I Killed A Man/It's Too Good To Last	12
70	Liberty LBF 15386	It's Goodbye/Gift Of Love	12
72	Columbia DB 8874	We'll Meet Again/Clown Shoes	8
73	Ember EMB S 328	Put Your Head On My Shoulder/Momma Married A Preacher	7
74	Seven Sun SSUN 13	The Champ (Parts 1 & 2)	8
81	Rooster RONS 101	You've Got It All/Starting All Over Again (with Polly Brown)	5
87	Savoy PJS 6	M97002: Hardcore/Elvis Was Not The White Nigger — I Was (Hardcore Reprise) (12", p/s)	8
64	Liberty LEP 2192	P. J. PROBY (EP)	10
65	Liberty LEP 2229	SOMEWHERE (EP)	10
65	Liberty LEP 2239	CHRISTMAS WITH P. J. (EP)	15
66	Liberty LEP 2251	P. J.'s HITS (EP)	20
67	Liberty LEP 2267	PROBY AGAIN (EP)	22
65	Liberty LBY 1235	I AM P. J. PROBY (LP)	25
65	Liberty LBY 1264	P. J. PROBY (LP)	25
66	Liberty LBY 1291	P. J. PROBY IN TOWN (LP)	20
67	Liberty LBY 1361	ENIGMA (LP)	20
67	Liberty LBL/LBS 83018	P. J. PROBY IN TOWN (LP, blue label reissue)	12
67	Liberty LBL/LBS 83032	ENIGMA (LP, blue label reissue)	15
67	Liberty LBL/LBS 83045	PHENOMENON (LP)	20
68	Liberty LBL/LBS 83087	BELIEVE IT OR NOT (LP)	25
69	Liberty LBS 83219E	THREE WEEK HERO (LP, featuring Led Zeppelin on "Jim's Blues")	45
73	Ember NR 5069	I'M YOURS (LP)	18
78	Astoria 1	ELVIS (LP; sold at theatres)	30

(see also Jett Powers, Marc Almond)

PROCESSION

68	Mercury MF 1053	Every American Citizen/Essentially Susan (p/s)	6
68	Mercury MF 1070	One Day In Every Week/Wigwam City	5
69	Mercury SMCL 20132	PROCESSION (LP)	12

PROCOL HARUM

67	Deram DM 126	A Whiter Shade Of Pale/Lime Street Blues (1st issue with darker labels)	6
67	Regal Zonophone RZ 3003	Homburg/Good Captain Clack	5
68	Regal Zonophone RZ 3007	Quite Rightly So/In The Wee Small Hours Of Sixpence	5
69	Regal Zonophone RZ 3019	A Salty Dog/Long Gone Geek	5
72	Fly Magni Fly ECHO 101	A Whiter Shade Of Pale/A Salty Dog/Homburg (p/s)	7
79	RCA LB 6	A Whiter Shade Of Pale/Noel Edmonds Introduces Record Year (Lever Brothers premium)	5
67	Regal Zono. LRZ 1001	PROCOL HARUM (LP)	25
67	Regal Zono. TA-LRZ 1001	PROCOL HARUM (LP, reel-to-reel, mono only)	12
68	Regal Zono. (S)LRZ 1004	SHINE ON BRIGHTLY (LP, mono/stereo)	18/15
68	Regal Zono. TA-LRZ 1004	SHINE ON BRIGHTLY (reel-to-reel, mono only)	12
69	Regal Zono. SLRZ 1009	A SALTY DOG (LP)	20

MINT VALUE £

| 70 | Regal Zono. SLRZ 1014 | HOME (LP, with lyric sheet) | 18 |
| 71 | Chrysalis ILPS 9158 | BROKEN BARRICADES (LP, gatefold sleeve) | 12 |

(see also Paramounts, Legend, Matthew Fisher, Robin Trower, Matthew Ellis, Freedom, Mick Grabham, Power Pack)

JUDD PROCTOR
61	Parlophone R 4769	Rio Grande/Plainsman	8
61	Parlophone R 4809	Palamino/Nola	8
61	Parlophone R 4841	Speakeasy/Clearway	8
62	Parlophone R 4885	The Turk/Mad	8
62	Parlophone R 4920	Backfire/It's Bluesy	8
64	Parlophone R 5126	Better Late/Boots	8
60s	Morgan MR 103P	GUITARS GALORE (LP)	40
70s	Gemini GMX 5004	GUITARS GALORE (LP, reissue)	12

MIKE PROCTOR
| 67 | Columbia DB 8254 | Mr. Commuter/Sunday, Sunday, Sunday | 35 |

PRODIGY
91	XL XLT 17	WHAT EVIL LURKS EP (What Evil Lurks/We Gonna Rock/Android/Everybody In The Place) (12", company sleeve)	100
91	XL XLS 21	Charly (Original Mix) (p/s)	5
91	XL XLS 26	Everybody In The Place (Fairground Edit)/G-Force (Energy Flow) (p/s)	5
92	XL XLS 30	Fire (Edit)/Jericho (Original Version) (p/s)	5
92	XL XLS 35	Out Of Space/Ruff In The Jungle Bizness (Uplifting Vibes Remix) (p/s)	5
93	XL XLS 39	Wind It Up (Rewound)/We Are The Ruffest (p/s)	5
95	XL SC 1	SCIENIDE (12", white label, 500 hand-stamped promos only)	40
96	XL XLT 70LC	Firestarter/Molotov Bitch (jukebox issue, 500 copies only)	10
96	XL XLT 70P	Firestarter/Firestarter (Instrumental)/Firestarter (Emprion Mix)/Molotov Bitch (12", 'photocopied' molotov cocktail sleeve, promo only)	15
96	XL 76 XLC 76	Minefields (Radio Edit)/Minefields (Monkey Mafia Mix)/Minefields (Headrock Beats)/Minefields (Full Length) (cassette, promo only, 50 copies with photocopied inlay)	60
96	XL XLT 76	Minefields (Radio Edit)/(Monkey Mafia Mix)/(Headrock Beats)(Full Length Version) (12", unreleased, 10 test pressings only)	200+
96	XL XLS 76CD	Minefields (Radio Edit)/(Monkey Mafia Mix)/(Headrock Beats)(Full Length Version) (CD, unreleased, advance copy only)	80
97	XL XLS 80LC	Breathe (Edit)/The Trick (jukebox issue, no p/s)	10
98	XL XLT 98	Smack My Bitch Up (Slacker mix) (12", promo only)	30
92	XL XLLP 110	THE PRODIGY EXPERIENCE (2-LP)	15
94	XL XLLP 114	MUSIC FOR THE JILTED GENERATION (LP)	15
96	XL XLS 70CDP	FIRESTARTER (Firestarter/Charly/Everybody In The Place/Out Of Space/Wind It Up/Firestarter/One Love/No Good/Voodoo People/Poison/Firestarter) (CD, no inlay, in-store promo only, 1000 only)	15

PROFESSIONALS
80	Virgin VS 353	Just Another Dream/Action Man (p/s)	5
80	Virgin VS 376	1-2-3/White Light White Heat/Baby I Don't Care (p/s, with giant foldout poster in stickered PVC sleeve)	5
80	Virgin VS 376	1-2-3/White Light White Heat/Baby I Don't Care (p/s, signed by Cook & Jones, sold via Red Rhino)	15
81	Virgin VS 426	Join The Professionals/Has Anybody Got An Alibi (gatefold p/s)	4
81	Virgin VS 456	The Magnificent/Just Another Dream (p/s)	4
81	Sounds FREEBIE No. 2	Little Boys In Blue (extract)/GILLAN: I'll Rip Your Spine Out (extract) (33rpm 1-sided flexi, printed die-cut sleeve, free with *Sounds*)	5
81	Virgin V 2220	I DIDN'T SEE IT COMING (LP)	12

(see also Sex Pistols, Greedies, Lightning Raiders, Steve Jones)

PROFESSOR LONGHAIR
65	Sue WI 397	Baby Let Me Hold Your Hand/Looka' No Hair	25
78	Harvest HAR 5154	Mess Around/Tipitina	10
60s	XX MIN 708	PROFESSOR LONGHAIR (EP)	15
72	Speakeasy 10-78	NEW ORLEANS 88 (10" LP)	45
72	Atlantic K 40402	NEW ORLEANS PIANO (LP)	25
78	Harvest SHSP 4086	LIVE ON THE QUEEN MARY (LP)	22
83	Stateside SSL 6004	LIVE ON THE QUEEN MARY (LP, reissue)	12

PROFIL
| 80 | CBS S CBS 8574 | Hey Music Man/Jour De Chance (p/s) | 10 |

PROFILE
65	Mercury MF 875	Haven't They Got Better Things To Do/Touch Of Your Hand	8
65	Mercury MF 981	Got To Find A Way/Don't Say Goodbye	8
69	Philips BF 1757	Politician Man/Where Is Love	5

(see also Karl Stuart & Profiles, Voice)

PROLES
| 79 | Rock Against Racism RAR 1 | Stereo Love/Thought Crime/CONDEMNED: Soldier Boys/Endless Revolution (p/s) | 10 |
| 79 | Small Wonder SMALL 23 | Softground/SMK (p/s) | 6 |

PROPAGANDA
85	ZTT ZTAS 2	Dr. Mabuse/Dr. Mabuse Der Spieler ('white glove' p/s)	5
85	ZTT ZTAS 2 (matrix: 2A X1)	Dr. Mabuse (Instrumental Mix)/Dr. Mabuse Der Spieler ('dark photo' p/s)	7
85	ZTT CTIS 101	Das Testaments Des Mabuse/The Last Word/Dr. Mabuse (cassette, "Femme Fatale" is listed but doesn't appear)	12
85	ZTT 12 ZTAS 2	Das Testaments Des Mabuse/Femme Fatale (The Woman With The Orchid)/The 9th Life (Of Dr. Mabuse) (12", white p/s)	8
85	ZTT 12 ZTAS 2 (matrix: 2A 2U)	Das Testaments Des Mabuse/Femme Fatale/The 9th Life (Of Dr. Mabuse) (12", white p/s, title sticker reads "13th Life New Mix")	18
85	ZTT 12 ZTAS 2	Das Testaments Des Mabuse (The Third Side)/Femme Fatale (The Woman With The Orchid) The Fourth Side (12", 'dark photo' p/s)	12
85	ZTT P ZTAS 8	Duel/Jewel (Rough Cut) (ZTT logo-shaped picture disc)	12
85	ZTT DUAL 1	Duel/Jewel//Lied/The Lesson (double pack, gatefold ZTT sleeve)	10

85	ZTT 12 ZTAS 8/12 ZTAS 2	Duel (Bittersweet)/Jewel (Cut Rough) (12", p/s, shrinkwrapped with "Dr. Mabuse" 12" [ZTT sleeve])	20
85	ZTT PROP 1	Bejewelled (12", 1-sided, white label, stickered title sleeve, promo only)	15
85	ZTT CTIS 108	DO WELL: The First Cut/Duel (7")/(Cut Rough)/Wonder/Bejewelled (cassette)	12
85	ZTT PZTAS 12	P-Machinery/Frozen Faces (clear vinyl, printed PVC sleeve)	6
85	ZTT ZTAS 21	P-Machinery (Beta Wraparound)/Frozen Faces (purple die-cut p/s)	4
85	ZTT 12X ZTAS 12	P-Machinery (Beta)/Complete Machinery/Frozen Faces (12", 'sofa' p/s)	12
85	ZTT 12 ZTAS 21/12 ZTAS 8	P-Machinery (Polish)/P-Machinery (Passive)/Frozen Faces (12", p/s, shrinkwrapped with "Duel" 12")	20
85	ZTT 12P ZTAS 12	P-Machinery (Polish)/P Machinery (Passive)/Frozen Faces (12", p/s, clear vinyl, printed PVC sleeve)	10
85	ZTT 12X ZTAST 12	P-Machinery (Beta)//Complete Machinery/Frozen Faces//P-Machinery (Polish)/P-Machinery (Passive)/Frozen Faces (12", clear vinyl/black vinyl double pack, gatefold PVC sleeve with poster)	25
85	ZTT CTIS 12	COMPLETE MACHINERY: Introduction/P-Machinery (Connected)/ P-Machinery (Separation)/Frozen Faces (cassette)	12

(see also Act, Ralph Dorper, Claudia Brücken, Glen Gregory & Claudia Brücken)

ORVAL PROPHET
63	London HLL 9729	Run Run Run/My Lois And Me	10

REX PROPHET
55	Brunswick OE 9144	CANADIAN PLOWBOY (EP)	15

PROPHETS (U.S.)
69	Mercury MF 1097	I Got The Fever/Soul Control	20

(see also Creation [U.S.])

PROPHETS (Jamaica)
70	Big Shot BI 554	Crystal Blue Persuasion (Parts 1 & 2)	7
70	Big Shot BI 555	Tumble Time (Parts 1 & 2)	7
70	Big Shot BI 557	Revenge Of Eastwood Version One/Version Two	8
70	Jackpot JP 712	Let's Fall In Love/Purple Moon	5

(see also Lloyd & Prophets, Claudette, Lloyd & Claudette, Patrick & Lloyd)

PROS & CONS
66	CBS 202341	Bend It/No Time	6

PROTEGUE (& PRINCE BUSTER'S ALL STARS)
67	Blue Beat BB 398	Foul Dance/PRINCE BUSTER'S ALL STARS: This Is It	20

PROTEX
78	Good Vibrations GOT 6	Don't Ring Me Up/(Just Want) Your Attention/ Listening In (wraparound p/s)	8
79	Rough Trade GOT 1	Don't Ring Me Up/(Just Want) Your Attention/Listening In (reissue, p/s)	5
79	Polydor 2059 124	I Can't Cope/Popularity (p/s)	8
79	Polydor 2059 167	I Can Only Dream/Heartache (p/s)	8
80	Polydor 2059 245	A Place In Your Heart/Jeepster (p/s)	8

PROTOS
82	Airship AP 391	ONE DAY A NEW HORIZON (LP)	140

PROVIDENCE
73	Threshold TH 14	Fantasy Fugue/Island Of Light	5
72	Threshold THS 9	EVER SENCE THE DAWN (LP, gatefold sleeve with insert)	15

PROWLER
85	SRT SRT5KS/368	Alcatraz (p/s)	30

PRUDES
89	Yo Yo PRU 1	P.S. I'm Leaving/Lighthouse Keeper's Daughter (p/s, white vinyl)	5
90	Imaginary RED TWO	Never Penetrate (p/s, 1-sided)	4

PRUNES
70	Songbird SB 1023	Come A Little Closer/Come A Little Closer Version II	7

(see also Eric Donaldson, West Indians)

SNOOKY PRYOR
70	Flyright LP 100	SNOOKY PRYOR (LP)	15

ARTHUR PRYSOCK
65	CBS 201820	It's Too Late, Baby Too Late/My Special Prayer	10
66	CBS EP 6076	AGAIN (EP)	18
78	Polydor 2383 481	DOES IT AGAIN (LP)	12

RED PRYSOCK
54	Mercury MB 3158	Blow Your Horn/Happy Feet (78)	25
57	Mercury MT 154	Teen-Age Rock/Paquino Walk (78)	30
59	Mercury AMT 1028	Chop Suey/Margie	12
59	Mercury AMT 1028	Chop Suey/Margie (78)	20
58	Mercury MPL 6535	THE BEAT (LP)	45
58	Mercury MPL 6550	FRUIT BOOTS (LP)	40

PSEUDO EXISTORS
80	Dead Good DEAD 2	Pseudo Existence/Coming Up For Air/New Modern Warfare (rubber-stamped folded p/s, pink/white label; later red/black label & stamped white sleeve)	35/30

PSYCHEDELIC FURS
79	Epic EPC 8005	We Love You/Pulse (green, pink or orange p/s)	5
80	CBS 8179	Sister Europe/(untitled) (p/s)	4
80	CBS 9059	Mr. Jones/Susan's Strange (p/s)	4
81	CBS A 1166	Dumb Waiters/Dash (1st 5,000 with playable p/s)	4
81	CBS WA 1327	Pretty In Pink/Mack The Knife (picture disc)	4
81	CBS A 13 1327	Pretty In Pink/Mack The Knife/Soap Commercial (12", no p/s, shrinkwrapped with free T-shirt)	7
82	CBS A 2549	Love My Way/Aeroplane (5,000 in gatefold p/s)	4

MINT VALUE £

PSYCHIC TV

84	CBS A 4300	Heaven (Parts 1 & 2) (with poster in plastic wrap)	4
84	CBS WA 4470	The Ghost In You/Another Edge (picture disc)	4
84	CBS TA 4300	Heaven/Heartbeat (12", p/s with poster)	7
84	CBS DA 4654	Heartbeat/My Time//Heaven (U.S. Remix)/Here Come The Cowboys (U.S. Remix) (double pack)	4
86	CBS DA 7242	Pretty In Pink/Love My Way//Heaven/Heartbeat (double pack)	4
86	CBS 6501830	Heartbreak Beat/New Dream (shrinkwrapped with free cassette: "Sister Europe"/"Into You Like A Train"/"President Gas")	5
87	CBS FURS C3	Angels Don't Cry/No Release (with cassette "We Love You"/"Pretty In Pink"/ "Love My Way")	5

(see also Unwanted)

PSYCHIC TV

82	Some Bizzare PTV 1	Just Drifting/Breakthrough (p/s)	8
82	Some Bizzare PTV 1T	Just Drifting/Just Drifting (Midnight) (12", p/s)	15
84	Temple TOPY 001	Unclean/Mirrors (12", p/s)	10
86	Temple TOPY 009	Godstar/Godstar (BJ Mix) (p/s)	6
86	Temple TOPYS 009	Godstar/Godstar (BJ Mix)/Discopravity/Yes It's The B Side (double pack, gatefold p/s)	8
86	Temple TOPIC 009	Godstar/Godstar (California Mix) (12", picture disc)	15
86	Temple TOPY 023	Good Vibrations/Roman P (p/s)	8
86	Temple TOPYD 023	Good Vibrations/Interzone/Roman P/Hex-Sex/Godstar (Ugly Mix)/Je T'Aime (double pack, gatefold p/s)	6
86	Temple TOPYT 023	Roman P (Fireball Mix)/Interzone/Good Vibrations (Kundalini Mix)/Hex-Sex (Voodoo Mix) (12", p/s)	8
87	Temple TOPY 022	Papal Breakdance/Magick Defends Itself (12", p/s)	8
87	Temple TOPY 030	Temporary Temple/Temporary Temple (12", p/s)	8
88	Temple TOPY 037	Tune In (Turn On To Thee Acide House) (12", p/s, as (Psychic TV/Jack The Tab)	10
88	DC DC 23	Superman/Jack The Tab (12", p/s, no artist credit on label)	20
89	Temple TOPY 048	Love, War, Riot/Eve Of Destruction (Vocoder Mixes) (12", p/s)	10
90	Temple TOPY 050	Je T'Aime/Wicked (12", p/s)	8
90	Temple TOPYT 051	Beyond Thee Infinite Beat/Beyond Thee Infinite Beat (12", p/s)	8
90	Temple TOPY 051CD	Beyond Thee Infinite Beat/Beyond Thee Infinite Beat (CD)	8
90	Temple TOPYT 058	IC Water (versions)/Alien Be In (12", p/s)	8
93	Temple TOPY 070	Remind/Tibal (12", p/s)	8
94	Temple TOPY 077	Tribal (Four Versions) (12")	8
94	Tribal TOPY 077CD	Tribal (Four Versions) (CD)	8
82	Some Bizzare PSY 1	FORCE THE HAND OF CHANCE (LP, with bonus LP & double-sided poster, featuring Marc Almond)	35
83	CBS 25737	DREAMS LESS SWEET (LP, with inner sleeve, some with free 12" EP [XPR 1251])	20/25
84	Temple TOPY 003	PAGAN DAY (LP, picture disc, 999 copies)	50
84	Gramm GRAMM 23	THOSE WHO DO NOT (2-LP, 5000 copies)	30
85	Temple TOPY 004	THEMES 2 (LP)	15
85	Temple TOPY 008	THEMES 3 (LP)	15
85	Temple TOPY 010	MOUTH OF THE NIGHT (LP)	15
85	Temple TOPIC 010	MOUTH OF THE NIGHT (LP, picture disc)	20
88	Temple TOPY 031	PSYCHIC TV (LP, picture disc)	15
88	Temple TOPY 032	ALBUM 10 (LP, picture disc)	15
88	Temple TOPY 038	ALLEGORY AND SELF (LP, blue vinyl)	20
89	Temple TOPY 046	KONDOLE / COPYCAT (LP)	15
89	Temple TOPY 047	LIVE AT THE PYRAMID NYC (LP)	15

(see also Throbbing Gristle, Coil, Monte Cazazza, Rose McDowall)

PSYCHOPATHS

| 91 | Elicit 12 ELIC 2 | NIGHTMARES (12") | 8 |

PSYCHO'S MUM

| 89 | Woronzow W 011 | A SIBILANT SIN (LP, with insert) | 15 |

PSYKYK VOLTS

79	Ellie Jay EJPS 9262	Totally Useless/Horror Story No. 5 (also listed as MHG GHM 109) (p/s)	50

PUBLIC ENEMY

87	Def Jam 651 245-0	Rebel Without A Pause (Vocal Mix)/(Instrumental) (picture disc)	8
87	Def Jam 651 245-8	Rebel Without A Pause (Vocal Mix)/(Instrumental)/Bring The Noise (Noise Version)/Sophisticated Bitch (12", no p/s)	7
87	Def Jam 651 335-6	Bring The Noise (No Noise Version)/(No Noise Instrumental A Cappella)/ Sophisticated Bitch/(Instrumental) (12", p/s)	7
87	Def Jam 651 335-8	Bring The Noise/Bring The Noise (No Noise Version)/(No Noise Instrumental A Cappella)/Sophisticated Bitch/(Instrumental) (12", p/s, with sticker)	7
88	Def Jam 652 833-0	Don't Believe The Hype/Prophets Of Rage (p/s, with patch).	4
88	Def Jam 653 089-7	Night Of The Living Baseheads/Terminator X To The Edge Of Panic (p/s, badge pack)	4

PUBLIC FOOT THE ROMAN

73	Sovereign SVNA 7259	PUBLIC FOOT THE ROMAN (LP)	25

(see also Movies)

PUBLIC IMAGE LTD (PiL)

78	Virgin VS 228	Public Image/The Cowboy Song (foldout 'newspaper' p/s)	8
79	Virgin VS 274	Death Disco/And No Bird Do Sing (p/s)	4
79	Virgin VS 274-12	Death Disco/And No Bird Do Sing (½ Mix)/Death Disco Megamix (12", p/s, 5,000 only)	8
86	Virgin VSD 855	Home/Round//Rise/Rise (Instrumental) (double pack)	4
87	Virgin VS 988	Seattle/Selfish Rubbish (box set with 7", badge, postcard & sew-on patch)	6
88	Virgin CDT 14	This Is Not A Love Song/Blue Water/This Is Not A Love Song (Remixed Version)/ Public Image (3" CD, card sleeve)	7
89	Virgin VSCD 1181	Disappointed/Same Old Story/Disappointed (12" Version) (3" CD, picture disc, card sleeve in 3" envelope-shaped plastic pouch)	8
89	Virgin VSCD 1195	Warrior (Edit)/U.S.L.S.I. (Extended Mix) (3" CD, card sleeve)	7
79	Virgin METAL 1	METAL BOX (LP, 3 x 12" with circular paper dividers & inner sheet in round tin). 20
90	Virgin TPAK 5	METAL BOX (CD, in round tin with insert).	20

(see also Sex Pistols, Jah Wobble, Don Letts & Jah Wobble, Dan MacArthur, Vivien Goldman, Time Zone)

GARY PUCKETT (& UNION GAP)

68	CBS 3365	Young Girl/I'm Losing You (as Union Gap featuring Gary Puckett)	6
68	CBS 3551	Lady Willpower/Daylight Stranger	6
68	CBS 3713	Over You/If The Day Would Come	5
69	CBS 4505	This Girl Is A Woman Now/His Other Woman	5
69	CBS 4122	Don't Give In To Him/Could I	5
70	CBS 4885	Let's Give Adam & Eve Another Chance/Beggar	5
70	CBS 4345	I Just Don't Know What To Do With Myself/All That Matters (solo)	5
71	CBS 7021	Keep The Customer Satisfied/No-One Really Knows (solo)	5
73	CBS 8202	Young Girl/Woman, Woman (p/s, 'Hall Of Fame Hits' series)	5
68	CBS (S) 63342	YOUNG GIRL (LP).	20
68	CBS (S) 63429	INCREDIBLE (LP)	20
70	CBS 63794	THE NEW GARY PUCKETT AND THE UNION GAP ALBUM (LP)	20

PUDDING

67	Decca F 12603	The Magic Bus/It's Too Late	40

TITO PUENTE

58	RCA SF 5008	MUCHO PUENTE (LP)	12

LEROY PULLINS

66	London HLR 10056	I'm A Nut/Knee Deep	12

PULLOVER

95	Fierce Panda NING 09	This Is The Life/The Great Pretender (1,000 only in poly bag with foldover p/s)	5
95	Fierce Panda NING 14	White Horses And Shooting Stars (1,000 only in poly bag with foldover p/s). . . .	5
96	Fierce Panda NING 20	Holiday/Last Christmas (p/s)	4

PULP

79	Pulp Music PB 1	Low Flying Aircraft/Something Just Behind My Back/So Lo (blank labels, some numbered up to 2,000 & signed, some with handmade sleeve)	25/20

PULP

83	Red Rhino RED 32	My Lighthouse (Remix)/Looking For Life (p/s)	45
83	Red Rhino RED 37	Everybody's Problem/There Was (p/s).	30
85	Fire BLAZE 5	Little Girl (With Blue Eyes)/Simultaneous/Blue Glow/The Will To Power (12", p/s)	25
86	Fire BLAZE 10	Dogs Are Everywhere/The Mark Of The Devil/97 Lovers/Aborigine/ Goodnight (12", p/s).	20
87	Fire BLAZE 17	They Suffocate At Night (Edited Version)/Tunnel (Cut Up Version) (p/s)	15
87	Fire BLAZE 17T	They Suffocate At Night (Uncut Version)/Tunnel (Full Length Version) (12", p/s)	20
87	Fire BLAZE 21T	Master Of The Universe (Sanitised Version)/Manon/Silence (12", p/s)	20
90	Fire BLAZE 44T	My Legendary Girlfriend/Is This House?/This House Is Condemned (12", p/s). . .	15
91	Fire BLAZE 51T	Countdown/Death Goes To The Disco/Countdown (Radio Edit) (12", p/s)	15
92	Gift GIF 1	O.U. (Gone Gone)/Space/O.U. (Gone Gone) (Radio Edit) (12", p/s).	12
92	Gift GIF 1CD	O.U. (Gone Gone) (Radio Edit)/Space/O.U. (Gone Gone) (CD)	20
92	Caff CAFF 17	My Legendary Girlfriend/Sickly Grin/Back In L.A. (foldover p/s with insert in poly bag, 500 only).	25
92	Gift GIF 3	Babies/Styloroc (Nites Of Suburbia)/Sheffield: Sex City (12", p/s).	10
92	Gift GIF 3CD	Babies/Styloroc (Nites Of Suburbia)/Sheffield: Sex City/ Sheffield: Sex City (Instrumental) (CD)	18
93	Gift 7GIF 6	Razzmatazz/Inside Susan (Abridged Version) (p/s)	8
93	Gift GIF 6	Razzmatazz/Inside Susan: A Story In 3 Songs (Stacks/Inside Susan/ 59 Lyndhurst Grove) (12", p/s)	10
93	Gift GIF 6CD	Razzmatazz/Inside Susan: A Story In 3 Songs (Stacks/Inside Susan/ 59 Lyndhurst Grove) (CD)	15
94	Island IS 595	THE SISTERS EP (numbered gatefold p/s)	5

MINT VALUE £

94	Island 12IS 595	THE SISTERS EP (12", p/s with print)	18
96	Island ISC 574	Do You Remember The First Time/Street Lites (reissue, brown vinyl, p/s)	5
96	Island ISC 567	Lipgloss/You're A Nightmare (reissue, red vinyl, p/s)	5
96	Island ISC 595	THE SISTERS E.P.: Babies/Your Sisters Clothes/Seconds/	
		His 'N' Hers (reissue, white vinyl, gatefold p/s)	5
96	Island ISC 613	Common People/Underwear (reissue, yellow vinyl, p/s)	5
96	Island ISC 620	Sorted For E's & Wizz/Mis-shapes (reissue, blue vinyl, p/s)	5
96	Island ISC 623	Disco 2000/Ansaphone (reissue, orange vinyl, p/s)	5
96	Island ISJB 632	Something Changed/Disco 2000 (7" Mix) (jukebox issue, no p/s)	8
96	Island ISC 632	Something Changed/Mile End (reissue, pink vinyl, p/s)	5
97	Island ISJB 679	Help The Aged/Tomorrow Never Lies (jukebox issue, no p/s)	8
84	Red Rhino REDLP 29	IT (mini-LP)	20
94	Cherry Red CDMRED 112	IT (CD, with extra tracks; withdrawn, 1,000 only)	20

PULSAR
| 76 | Decca SKL-R 5228 | POLLEN (LP) | 18 |
| 77 | Decca TXS 119 | STRANDS OF THE FUTURE (LP) | 15 |

PULSE
| 70 | Major Minor SMLP 64 | PULSE (LP) | 40 |

PUMPHOUSE GANG
| 77 | Kitsch FAD 1 | Motorcity Fantasy/Cocaine (p/s) | 7 |

PUNCHERS
| 70 | Punch PH 46 | Sons Of Thunder (actually by Lee Perry & The Upsetters)/ | |
| | | Only If You Understand | 7 |

PUNCHIN' JUDY
| 73 | Transatlantic TRA 272 | PUNCHIN' JUDY (LP) | 15 |

PUNCTURE
| 77 | Small Wonder SMALL 1 | Mucky Pup/Can't Rock'n'Roll (p/s) | 6 |

PUNISHMENT OF LUXURY
78	Small Wonder SMALL 8	Puppet Life/The Demon (p/s)	5
79	United Artists UP 36507	Engine Of Excess/Jellyfish (p/s)	5
79	United Artists UP 36537	Secrets/Brainbomb (p/s)	5
79	United Artists BP 317	Laughing Academy/Baby Jump (p/s)	5
79	United Artists UAG 30258	LAUGHING ACADEMY (LP, gatefold sleeve)	12

PUNKETTES
| 77 | Response SR 511 | Going Out Wiv A Punk/Polythene (no p/s) | 8 |

PUPILS
66	Wing WL 1150	A TRIBUTE TO THE ROLLING STONES (LP)	75
69	Fontana SFL 13087	A TRIBUTE TO THE ROLLING STONES (LP, reissue)	50
	(see also Eyes)		

PUPPETS
63	Pye 7N 15556	Poison Ivy/Everybody's Talking	35
64	Pye 7N 15634	Baby Don't Cry/Shake With Me	35
64	Pye 7N 15625	Shake With Me/Three Boys Looking For Love (existence unconfirmed)	40+

FRANK PURCELL
| 73 | Paramount PAS 6064 | JAMES BOND'S GREATEST HITS (LP) | 18 |

DANNY PURCHES
55	Columbia SCM 5183	Mama/Just One More Time	10
58	Columbia DB 4129	The Shrine On The Second Floor/He	8
58	Columbia DB 4129	The Shrine On The Second Floor/He (78)	10

(BERNARD) PRETTY PURDIE
68	Direction 58-3301	Funky Donkey/Caravan	6
68	Direction 58-3628	Soul Clappin'/Blow Your Lid	6
71	Philips 6073 708	Good Livin' Good Lovin'/Day Dreaming	5
68	Direction 8-63290	SOUL DRUMS (LP)	50
71	Philips 6369 421	SOUL IS ... (LP)	20

PURE HELL
| 78 | Golden Sphinx GSX 002 | These Boots Are Made For Walking/No Rules (p/s) | 20 |

PURE LOVE & PLEASURE
| 70 | Stateside SSL 5026 | A RECORD OF PURE LOVE AND PLEASURE (LP) | 10 |

PURESSENCE
| 92 | Rough TradE 45rev9 | Siamese/Scapa Flow (p/s, 'singles club' release) | 5 |

PURGE
| 69 | Corn CP 101 | The Mayor Of Simpleton Hall/The Knave (p/s) | 125 |

JAMES & BOBBY PURIFY
66	Stateside SS 547	I'm Your Puppet/So Many Reasons	8
67	Stateside SS 595	Wish You Didn't Have To Go/You Can't Keep A Good Man Down	8
67	Stateside SS 2016	Shake A Tail Feather/Goodness Gracious	10
67	Stateside SS 2039	I Take What I Want/Sixteen Tons	8
67	Stateside SS 2049	Let Love Come Between Us/I Don't Want To Have To Wait	15
68	Stateside SS 2093	Do Unto Me/Everybody Needs Somebody	8
68	Bell BLL 1008	I Can't Remember/I Was Born To Lose Out	6
68	Bell BLL 1024	Help Yourself To All My Lovin'/Last Piece Of Love	6
69	Bell BLL 1043	Untie Me/We're Finally Gonna Make It	6
69	Bell BLL 1056	Let Love Come Between Us/Shake A Tail Feather	6
69	Bell BLL 1067	Do Unto Me/Wish You Didn't Have To Go	5
72	Mojo 2092 056	I'm Your Puppet/Wish You Didn't Have To Go	5
67	Stateside SL 10206	JAMES AND BOBBY PURIFY (LP)	30
67	Bell MBLL/SBLL 101	THE PURE SOUND OF THE PURIFYS (LP)	20

ALTON PURNELL
70　Dixie DIX 4　　　　　　　　　TRAVELLING LIGHT (LP) 30
(see also Bonnie Raitt)

PURPLE ALGAE
95　Poor Person Prod. PPPR 7　ADRIFT ON A SEA OF SOUND (LP, handmade sleeve & insert, no'd, 500 only) . . 15

PURPLE FOX
71　Gold Award MER 340　　　TRIBUTE TO JIMI HENDRIX (LP) 15

PURPLE GANG
67　Big T BIG 101　　　　　　Granny Takes A Trip/Bootleg Whisky 8
68　Big T BIG 111　　　　　　Kiss Me Goodnight Sally Green/Auntie Monica 6
68　Transatlantic　　　　　　THE PURPLE GANG STRIKES (LP) 30

PURPLE HAZE
85　S.R.S. SRS 6　　　　　　Hear It On The Radio (p/s) 30

PURPLE HEARTS
79　Fiction FICS 003　　　　Millions Like Us/Beat That! (p/s) 5
79　Fiction FICS 007　　　　Frustration/Extraordinary Sensations (p/s) 5
80　Fiction FICS 9　　　　　Jimmy/What Am I Gonna Do (p/s) 5
80　Safari SAFE 30　　　　　My Life's A Jigsaw/The Guy Who Made Her A Star/Just To Please You
　　　　　　　　　　　　　　　(initially in foldout jigsaw p/s) 8/4
82　Road Runner RR 1　　　Plane Crash/Scooby Doo/Gun Of Life (p/s) 12
80　Fiction FIX 002/2383 568　BEAT THAT! (LP) 12
(see also Bob Manton, Rage)

PUSSY
72　Deram DM 368　　　　　Feline Woman/Ska Child 18
(see also Jerusalem)

PUSSY
69　Morgan Bluetown BT 5002　PUSSY PLAYS (LP) 300
(see also Angel Pavement, Fortes Mentum)

PUSSYFOOT
66　Decca F 12474　　　　　Freeloader/Things That Still Remind Me 12
67　Decca F 12561　　　　　Mr Hyde/Hasty Words 12
68　Pye 7N 17520　　　　　Good Times/Till You Don't Want Me Anymore 12
(see also Rare Breed)

ASHA PUTHLI
73　CBS 65804　　　　　　ASHA PUTHLI (LP) 15
75　CBS 80978　　　　　　SHE LOVES TO HEAR THE MUSIC (LP) 15
76　CBS 81443　　　　　　THE DEVIL IS LOOSE (LP) 15

PUZZLE
69　Stateside SS 2146　　　Hey Medusa/Make The Children Happy 5
69　Stateside SSL 10285　　PUZZLE (LP) 15

PVC 2
77　Zoom ZUM 2　　　　　Put You In The Picture/Pain/Deranged, Demented and Free (p/s) ... 7
(see also Midge Ure, Slik, Zones)

NATASHA PYNE
66　Polydor 56713　　　　　It's All In Your Head/I'm A Dreamer 7

PYRAMID
67　Deram DM 111　　　　　Summer Of Last Year/Summer Evening 15
(see also Fairport Convention, Ian Matthews)

PYRAMIDS (U.S.)
64　London HLU 9847　　　Penetration/Here Comes Marsha 25

PYRAMIDS (U.K.)
65　Polydor BM 56028　　　Baby's Gone Away/Kiss And Dance With You 4

PYRAMIDS (Jamaica)
67　President PT 161　　　　Train Tour To Rainbow City/John Chewey 5
68　President PT 177　　　　Wedding In Peyton Place/Girls Girls Girls 5
68　President PT 195　　　　All Change On The Bakerloo Line/Playing Games 5
68　President PT 206　　　　Mexican Moonlight/Mule 5
68　President PT 225　　　　Tisko My Darling/Movement All Around 5
69　President PT 243　　　　Do-Re-Mi/I'm Outnumbered 5
69　President PT 274　　　　I'm A Man/Dragon Fly 5
69　Doctor Bird DB 1307　　Stay With Him/Chicken Mary 12
70　Duke DU 80　　　　　　Geronimo/Feel Alright 7
70　Trojan TR 7755　　　　Feel Alright/Telstar 6
70　Trojan TR 7770　　　　To Sir With Love/Reggae Shuffle 6
71　Trojan TR 7803　　　　All For You/All For You Version 5
71　Creole CR 1003　　　　Mosquito Bite/Mother's Bath 6
71　Creole CR 1006　　　　Can't Leave Now/Teardrops 5
68　President PTL 1021　　THE PYRAMIDS (LP) 20
(see also Symarip, Equals, Little Grants & Eddie, Seven Letters, Bruce Ruffin)

PYTHAGORAS THEOREM
70　Pye 7N 17924　　　　　Give A Damn/London Bridge 4
70　Pye 7N 17990　　　　　Our House/Free Like Me 4

PYTHON LEE JACKSON
70　Young Blood YB 1017　In A Broken Dream/Doing Fine 6
76　Young Blood YB 1077　The Blues/Cloud Nine 5
80　Young Blood YB 0089　In A Broken Dream/The Blues 6
80　Young Blood YEP 89　In A Broken Dream (mono)/In A Broken Dream (stereo)/The Blues/
　　　　　　　　　　　　　Cloud Nine (EP, "Kelly Girl" Employment Agency advert on p/s) 12
74　Young Blood YB 3001　IN A BROKEN DREAM (LP, featuring Rod Stewart) 15
(see also Rod Stewart)

Q-CHASTIC
92	Rephlex 002EP	Q-CHASTIC EP (double pack)	80

(see also Aphex Twin)

QUAD
97	Acme AC 8020LP	QUAD (LP, clear vinyl in printed clear PVC cover)	15
97	Prescription DRUG 3	QUAD (LP, 99 copies only, handmade sleeve, mail-order only)	25

(see also Sun Dial)

CHRISTINE QUAITE
62	Oriole CB 1739	Guilty Eyes/Oh My!	12
62	Oriole CB 1772	Your Nose Is Gonna Grow/Our Last Chance	12
63	Oriole CB 1845	Mister Heartache/Whisper Wonderful Words	12
63	Oriole CB 1876	In The Middle Of The Floor/Tell Me Mama	12
63	Oriole CB 1921	I Believe In Love/Here She Comes	12
64	Oriole CB 1945	Mister Stuck Up/Will You Be The Same Tomorrow	12
65	Stateside SS 435	If You've Got A Heart/So Near So Far	10
66	Stateside SS 482	Long After Tonight Is All Over/I'm Hoping	30

QUAKER CITY BOYS
59	London HLU 8796	Teasin'/Won't Y' Come Out, Mary Ann	12
59	London HLU 8796	Teasin'/Won't Y' Come Out, Mary Ann (78)	15

QUAKERS
65	Oriole CB 1992	I'm Ready/Down The Road A Piece	100
65	Studio 36 KSP 109/110	She's Alright/Talk To Me	325

QUARRY MEN
81	'Percy Philips, Kensington' (no cat. no.)	That'll Be The Day/In Spite Of All The Danger (78rpm, private pressing reproduction of 1958 demo disc, repro Parlophone co. sleeve, 25 only)	10,000+
81	'Percy Philips, Kensington' (no cat. no.)	That'll Be The Day/In Spite Of All The Danger (45rpm, private pressing reproduction of 1958 demo disc, repro Parlophone co. sleeve, 25 only)	10,000+

(see also Beatles, Trad Grads)

JOE QUARTERMAN & FREE SOUL
73	GSF GSZ 3	So Much Trouble In My Mind (Parts 1 & 2)	7
74	GSF GSZ 12	Thanks Dad (Parts 1 & 2)	4
73	GSF GS 504	JOE QUARTERMAN & FREE SOUL (LP)	40

QUARTER NOTES
57	Parlophone R 4365	My Fantasy/Ten Minutes To Midnight	7
57	Parlophone R 4365	My Fantasy/Ten Minutes To Midnight (78)	8

QUARTET
69	Decca F 12974	Now/Will My Lady Come	5
70	Decca F 13072	Joseph/Mama Where Did You Fail	5

QUARTZ
77	Jet UP 36290	Sugar Rain/Street Fighting Lady/Mainline Riders	15
77	Jet UP 36317	Street Fighting Lady/Mainline Riders	12
80	Reddingtons R.R. DAN 1	Nantucket Sleighride/Wildfire (p/s, white or blue vinyl; also black vinyl)	10/5
80	Jet SJET 189	Street Fighting Lady/Mainline Riders (p/s, reissue)	7
80	Logo GO 387	Satan's Serenade/Bloody Fool (p/s)	5
80	Logo GOT 387	Satan's Serenade/Bloody Fool/Roll Over Beethoven (live) (12", p/s, blue or red vinyl)	20/12
80	Sound For Industry SFI 549	Satan's Serenade (flexidisc)	7
80	MCA MCA 642	Stoking The Fires Of Hell/Circles (p/s)	7
81	MCA MCA 661	Stand Up And Fight/Charlie Snow (p/s)	10
83	Heavy Metal HEAVY 17	Tell Me Why/Streetwalker (p/s)	7
77	Jet UAG 30081	QUARTZ (LP, with inner sleeve)	25
79	Jet JETLP 233	DELETED (LP, in sealed brown paper bag)	12
80	Reddingtons R.R. REDD 001	QUARTZ LIVE — COUNT DRACULA (LP, some in b&w 'live' sleeve)	15/12
80	MCA MCF 3080	STAND UP AND FIGHT (LP, with lyric insert)	12
83	Heavy Metal HMRLP 9	AGAINST ALL ODDS (LP, with inner sleeve)	12
83	Heavy Metal HMRPD 9	AGAINST ALL ODDS (LP, picture disc)	18

(see also Black Sabbath, Copperfield, Bandy Legs)

QUATERMASS
70	Harvest SVHL 775	QUATERMASS (LP, gatefold sleeve)	50
75	Harvest SHSM 2002	QUATERMASS (LP, reissue, different sleeve)	12

(see also Ian Gillan Band, Episode Six, Strapps)

QUATRAIN
69	Polydor 583 743	QUATRAIN (LP)	12

SUZI QUATRO
72	Rak RAK 134	Rolling Stone/Brain Confusion (For All The Lonely People)	20
75	Rak RAK 200	I Bit Off More Than I Could Chew/Red Hot Rosie	5
75	Rak RAK 215	I May Be Too Young/Don't Mess Around	5
75	Rak RAK 256	Roxy Roller/I'll Grow On You	5
73	Rak PSR 355	Primitive Love/Shakin' All Over (promo only)	40
78	Rak RAK 285	Stumblin' In/Stranger With You (with Chris Norman) (p/s)	5
79	Rak RAK 285	Stumblin' In/Stranger With You (with Chris Norman) (clear vinyl, different p/s)	5

MINT VALUE £

79	Rak RAK 299	She's In Love With You/Space Cadets (p/s)	5
81	Dreamland DLSP 8	Glad All Over/Ego In The Night (no p/s)	5
81	Dreamland DLSP 10	Lipstick/Woman Cry (p/s)	5
83	Polydor PSOP 555	Main Attraction/Transparent (red or silver label)	5
84	Rak/Golden 45 G 45 35	Can The Can/Devilgate Drive (Rak label, p/s)	5
84	Rak RAK 372	I Go Wild/I'm A Rocker (p/s)	5
84	Rak 12RAK 372	I Go Wild/I'm A Rocker (12", p/s)	8
85	Rak RAK 384	Tonight I Could Fall In Love/Good Girl (Looking For A Bad Time) (p/s)	5
85	Rak 12RAK 384	Tonight I Could Fall In Love (Extended Mix)/ Good Girl (Looking For A Bad Time) (12", p/s)	8
86	First Night SCORE 3	I Got Lost In His Arms/You Can't Get A Man With A Gun (p/s)	5
86	PRT 7P 367	Wild Thing/I Don't Want You (with Reg Presley) (p/s)	5
86	PRT 12P 367	Wild Thing (Extended)/I Don't Want You (with Reg Presley) (12", p/s)	8
87	Rak/Golden 45 G 45 35	Can The Can/Devilgate Drive (reissue, black label, no p/s)	5
87	Hackenbacker HACK 101	Am I Dreaming/Who Needs Chairs/Will You Take This Woman (only available at pantomime show)	10
89	Teldec 247 008-7/ WEA YZ 406	Baby You're A Star/Baby You're A Star (Instrumental) (p/s, early pressings with German labels & sticker "U.K. Cat. No. YZ 406"; later WEA copies)	6/5
89	WEA YZ 406T	Baby You're A Star/(Extended)/(Instrumental)/(Radio Version) (12", p/s)	7
74	Rak SRAK 509	QUATRO (LP, white label test pressing with longer intro on "The Wild One")	18
80	Rak GMTV 24	GREATEST HITS (LP, white label test pressing, with different, slower version of "Tear Me Apart")	20

QUAZAR
78	Arista ARIST 224	Funk 'N' Roll/Savin' My Love For A Rainy Day	4
83	Tabitha QUAZ 1	Silver Stallion/Dated And Signed	4

IKE QUEBEC
64	Blue Note 45-1749	Buzzard Lope/Blue Friday	8
63	Blue Note (B)BLP 4098	BLUE AND SENTIMENTAL (LP)	15
64	Blue Note (B)BLP 4114	BOSSA NOVA — SOUL SAMBA (LP)	15
65	Blue Note BLP 4105	IT MIGHT AS WELL BE STRING (LP)	15

QUEEN
SINGLES
73	EMI EMI 2036	Keep Yourself Alive/Son And Daughter (no p/s)	25
74	EMI EMI 2121	Seven Seas Of Rhye/See What A Fool I've Been (no p/s)	8
74	EMI EMI 2229	Killer Queen/Flick Of The Wrist (no p/s)	6
75	EMI EMI 2256	Now I'm Here/Lily Of The Valley (no p/s)	10
75	EMI EMI 2375	Bohemian Rhapsody/I'm In Love With My Car (p/s; beware counterfeits with 'computer-scanned' logo)	30
76	EMI EMI 2494	You're My Best Friend/39 (no p/s)	6
76	EMI EMI 2565	Somebody To Love/White Man (p/s, beware of recent counterfeit sleeves)	15
77	EMI EMI 2593	Tie Your Mother Down/You And I (no p/s)	8
77	EMI EMI 2623	QUEEN'S FIRST EP: Good Old Fashioned Lover Boy/Death On Two Legs/ Tenement Funster/White Queen (As It Began) (p/s)	12
77	EMI EMI 2708	We Are The Champions/We Will Rock You (p/s)	7
78	EMI EMI 2575	Spread Your Wings/Sheer Heart Attack (p/s)	8
78	EMI EMI 2870	Bicycle Race/Fat Bottomed Girls (p/s)	8
78	EMI EMI 2870	Bicycle Race/Fat Bottomed Girls (different p/s for export to Belgium)	150
79	EMI EMI 2910	Don't Stop Me Now/In Only Seven Days (p/s)	7
79	EMI EMI 2959	Love Of My Life (live)/Now I'm Here (live) (no p/s)	20
79	EMI EMI 5001	Crazy Little Thing Called Love/We Will Rock You (live) (p/s)	5
80	EMI EMI 5022	Save Me/Let Me Entertain You (live) (p/s)	6
80	EMI EMI 5076	Play The Game/A Human Body (p/s, beige label with red 'EMI' logo or white label with large black 'Queen' logo)	each 8
80	EMI EMI 5102	Another One Bites The Dust/Dragon Attack (p/s)	7
80	EMI EMI 5126	Flash/Football Fight (p/s)	5
81	EMI EMI 5250	Under Pressure (with David Bowie)/Soul Brother (p/s)	5
82	EMI EMI 5293	Body Language/Life Is Real (Song For Lennon) (p/s)	5
82	EMI EMI 5316	Las Palabras De Amor (The Words Of Love)/Cool Cat (p/s)	6
82	EMI EMI 5325	Backchat/Staying Power (p/s)	8
82	EMI 12EMI 5325	Backchat (Extended)/Staying Power (12", p/s)	25
84	EMI QUEEN 1	Radio Ga Ga (Edit)/I Go Crazy (p/s)	5
84	EMI 12QUEEN 1	Radio Ga Ga (Ext. Version)/Radio Ga Ga (Instrumental)/I Go Crazy (12", p/s)	10
84	EMI QUEEN 2	I Want To Break Free (Remix)/Machines (Back To Humans) ('Freddie' p/s, gold or white lettering)	15/8
84	EMI QUEEN 2	I Want To Break Free (Remix)/Machines (Back To Humans) ('Brian', 'Roger' or 'John' p/s, each with gold lettering)	12/18/20
84	EMI 12QUEEN 2	I Want To Break Free (Extended Remix)/Machines (Back To Humans) (12", p/s, with red background with gold or black lettering)	20/12
84	EMI 12QUEEN 2	I Want To Break Free (Extended Remix)/Machines (Back To Humans) (12", p/s, with white background)	10
84	EMI QUEEN 3	It's A Hard Life/Is This The World We Created...? (p/s)	6
84	EMI QUEEN 3	It's A Hard Life/Is This The World We Created...? ('Roger Taylor' overprinted photo p/s)	25
84	EMI 12QUEEN 3	It's A Hard Life (Extended)/It's A Hard Life/ Is This The World We Created...? (12", no p/s)	25
84	EMI 12QUEENP 3	It's A Hard Life/Is This The World We Created...? (12", picture disc)	18
84	EMI QUEEN 4	Hammer To Fall (Edit)/Tear It Up ('live' p/s, withdrawn)	125
84	EMI QUEEN 4	Hammer To Fall (Edit)/Tear It Up (red p/s)	5
84	EMI 12 QUEEN 4	Hammer To Fall (The Headbangers Mix)/Tear It Up (12", 'live' p/s, withdrawn)	125
84	EMI 12 QUEEN 4	Hammer To Fall (The Headbangers Mix)/Tear It Up (12", red p/s)	12
84	EMI QUEEN 5	Man On The Prowl/Keep Passing The Open Windows (unreleased, white label test pressings only)	250
84	EMI QUEEN 5	Thank God It's Christmas/Man On The Prowl/ Keep Passing The Open Windows (p/s)	8

Year	Label/Cat No	Description	Value
84	EMI 12QUEEN 5	Thank God It's Christmas/Man On The Prowl (Extended Version)/ Keep Passing The Open Windows (Extended Version) (12", p/s)	18
85	EMI QUEEN 6	One Vision (7" Mix)/Blurred Vision (p/s, some with red lyric inner sleeve)	7/5
85	EMI 12QUEEN 6	One Vision (Extended Vision)/Blurred Vision (12", p/s, some with red inner)	12/10
85	EMI 12QUEEN 6	One Vision (Extended Vision)/Blurred Vision (12", printed PVC sl. & red inner)	35
86	EMI QUEEN 7	A Kind Of Magic/A Dozen Red Roses For My Darling (p/s)	5
86	EMI 12QUEEN 7	A Kind Of Magic (Ext. Version)/A Dozen Red Roses For My Darling (12", p/s)	12
86	EMI 12QUEENP7	A Kind Of Magic (Extended Version)/Don't Lose Your Head (Instrumental Version) (12", picture disc)	50
86	EMI QUEEN 8	Friends Will Be Friends/Seven Seas Of Rhye (p/s)	6
86	EMI QUEEN P8	Friends Will Be Friends/Seven Seas Of Rhye (picture disc)	40
86	EMI 12QUEEN 8	Friends Will Be Friends (Extended Version)/Friends Will Be Friends (7" Version)/Seven Seas Of Rhye (12", p/s)	10
86	EMI QUEEN 9	Who Wants To Live Forever/Killer Queen (p/s)	8
86	EMI 12QUEEN 9	Who Wants To Live Forever (7" Version)/(Album Version)/Killer Queen/ Who Wants To Live Forever (Piano Version) (12", p/s)	15
89	Parlophone QUEEN 10	I Want It All/Hang On In There (p/s)	6
89	Parlophone QUEEN C10	I Want It All/Hang On In There (cassette)	8
89	Parlophone 12QUEEN 10	I Want It All (Single Version)/Hang On In There/ I Want It All (Album Version) (12", p/s)	12
89	Parlophone CDQUEEN 10	I Want It All (Album Version)/Hang On In There/I Want It All (Single Version) (CD, picture disc)	20
89	Parlophone QUEEN 11	Breakthru' (7" Mix)/Stealin' (p/s)	5
89	Parlophone QUEEN PD 11	Breakthru' (7" Mix)/Stealin' (shaped picture disc, 12" PVC sleeve with insert)	20
89	Parlophone QUEEN C11	Breakthru' (7" Mix)/Stealin' (cassette)	5
89	Parlophone 12QUEEN 11	Breakthru' (12" Version)/Breakthru' (Single Version)/Stealin' (12", p/s)	12
89	Parlophone CD QUEEN 11	Breakthru' (12" Version)/Stealin'/Breakthru' (7" Mix) (CD)	25
89	Parlophone QUEEN 12	The Invisible Man/Hijack My Heart (black vinyl, p/s)	8
89	Parlophone QUEEN X12	The Invisible Man/Hijack My Heart (clear vinyl, p/s)	12
89	Parlophone QUEEN C12	The Invisible Man/Hijack My Heart (cassette)	8
89	Parlophone 12QUEEN 12	The Invisible Man (12" Version)/(7" Version)/Hijack My Heart (12", p/s)	12
89	Parlophone 12QUEENX12	The Invisible Man (12" Version)/The Invisible Man (7" Version)/ Hijack My Heart (12", clear vinyl, PVC sleeve with insert)	18
89	Parlophone CD QUEEN 12	The Invisible Man (12" Version)/Hijack My Heart/ The Invisible Man (Single Version) (CD)	30
89	Parlophone QUEEN 14	Scandal/My Life Has Been Saved (p/s)	8
89	Parlophone QUEEN P14	Scandal/My Life Has Been Saved (poster p/s)	15
89	Parlophone QUEEN C14	Scandal/My Life Has Been Saved (cassette, card sleeve)	8
89	Parlophone 12QUEEN 14	Scandal (12" Version)/Scandal (7" Version)/My Life Has Been Saved (12", p/s)	10
89	Parlophone 12QUEENS 14	Scandal (12" Version)/My Life Has Been Saved/Scandal (7" Version)/ (12", p/s, 1-sided, B-side etched with group's signatures)	25
89	Parlophone CD QUEEN 14	Scandal (12" Version)/My Life Has Been Saved/Scandal (7" Version) (CD)	35
89	Parlophone QUEEN 15	The Miracle/Stone Cold Crazy (live) (p/s)	8
89	Parlophone QUEEN H15	The Miracle/Stone Cold Crazy (live) (hologram p/s)	12
89	Parlophone QUEEN C15	The Miracle/Stone Cold Crazy (live) (cassette)	8
89	Parlophone 12QUEEN 15	The Miracle/Stone Cold Crazy (live)/My Melancholy Blues (live) (12", yellow p/s)	15
89	Parlophone 12QUEENP 15	The Miracle/Stone Cold Crazy (live)/My Melancholy Blues (live) (12", turquoise p/s with insert print)	18
89	Parlophone QUEENCD 15	The Miracle/Stone Cold Crazy (live)/My Melancholy Blues (live) (CD)	25
91	Parlophone QUEEN 16	Innuendo/Bijou (p/s)	5
91	Parlophone QUEEN C16	Innuendo/Bijou (cassette)	4
91	Parlophone 12QUEEN 16	Innuendo (Explosive Version)/Under Pressure/Bijou (12", p/s)	8
91	Parl. 12QUEEN PD16	Innuendo (Explosive Version)/Under Pressure/Bijou (12", picture disc, PVC sleeve with insert)	20
91	Parl. CDQUEEN PD16	Innuendo (Explosive Version)/Under Pressure/Bijou (CD)	8
91	Parlophone QUEEN 17	I'm Going Slightly Mad/The Hitman (p/s)	7
91	Parlophone QUEEN PD 17	I'm Going Slightly Mad/The Hitman (shaped picture disc with insert)	20
91	Parlophone QUEEN C17	I'm Going Slightly Mad/The Hitman (cassette)	6
91	Parlophone 12QUEENG 17	I'm Going Slightly Mad/The Hitman/Lost Opportunity (12", gatefold p/s)	15
91	Parlophone CDQUEEN 17	I'm Going Slightly Mad/The Hitman/Lost Opportunity (CD)	15
91	Parlophone 12QUEEN 18	Headlong/All God's People/Mad The Swine (12", p/s)	8
91	Parlophone 12QUEEN PD18	Headlong/All God's People/Mad The Swine (12", clear vinyl picture disc, with insert in PVC sleeve)	18
91	Parlophone CD QUEEN 18	Headlong/All God's People/Mad The Swine (CD)	15
91	Parlophone QUEEN 19	The Show Must Go On/Keep Yourself Alive (p/s)	5
91	Parlophone QUEEN C19	The Show Must Go On/Keep Yourself Alive (cassette)	25
91	Parlophone 12QUEENSG 19	The Show Must Go On/Keep Yourself Alive/Queen Talks (12", 1-sided, B-side etched with group's signatures, gatefold p/s)	18
91	Parlophone CDQUEEN 19	The Show Must Go On/Keep Yourself Alive/Queen Talks/Body Language (CD)	10
91	Parlophone CDQUEENS 19	The Show Must Go On/Now I'm Here/Fat Bottomed Girls/Las Palabras De Amor (The Words Of Love) (CD, in box with foldout poster, 10,000 only)	25
91	Parlophone QUEEN 19/20	The Show Must Go On/Bohemian Rhapsody (unissued, no p/s)	350
91	Parlophone QUEEN 20	Bohemian Rhapsody/These Are The Days Of Our Lives (p/s)	5
93	Parlophone CDR 6340	FIVE LIVE EP: Killer/Papa Was A Rolling Stone (PM Dawn Remix)/ Somebody To Love/These Are The Days Of Our Lives (as Queen featuring George Michael & Lisa Stansfield) (CD, picture disc, silver inlay)	10
95	Parlophone CDQUEENS 21	Heaven For Everyone (Single Version)/It's A Beautiful Day/Heaven For Everyone (Album Version) (CD)	8
95	Parlophone CDQUEENS 22	A Winter's Tale/Thank God It's Christmas/Rock In Rio Blues (CD, 'Merry Christmas' box)	8
96	Parlophone QUEEN 23	Too Much Love Will Kill You/We Will Rock You/We Are The Champions (p/s, pink vinyl)	5
96	Parlophone QUEENPD 24	Let Me Live/Fat Bottomed Girls/Bicycle Race (picture disc with poster)	5
97	Parlophone QUEEN 26	No-One But You (Only The Good Die Young)/Princes Of The Universe/ We Will Rock You (Rick Rubin 'Ruined' Remix)/ Gimme The Prize (Instrumental 'Eye' Remix) (unissued 7")	100

QUEEN

97	Parlophone QUEENPD 27	No-One But You (Only The Good Die Young)/We Will Rock You (Rick Rubin 'Ruined' Remix)/Tie Your Mother Down/Gimme The Prize (Instrumental 'Eye' Remix) (picture disc) 5

3" CD SINGLES

88	Parlophone QUECD 1	Seven Seas Of Rhye/See What A Fool I've Been/Funny How Love Is (3" CD) 15
88	Parlophone QUECD 2	Killer Queen/Flick Of The Wrist/Brighton Rock (3" CD) 12
88	Parlophone QUECD 3	Bohemian Rhapsody/I'm In Love With My Car/You're My Best Friend (3" CD) . . . 12
88	Parlophone QUECD 4	Somebody To Love/White Man/Tie Your Mother Down (3" CD) 12
88	Parlophone QUECD 5	QUEEN'S FIRST EP: Good Old Fashioned Lover Boy/Death On Two Legs/ Tenement Funster/White Queen (As It Began) (3" CD) 12
88	Parlophone QUECD 6	We Are The Champions/We Will Rock You /Fat Bottomed Girls (3" CD) 15
88	Parlophone QUECD 7	Crazy Little Thing Called Love/Spread Your Wings/Flash (3" CD) 12
88	Parlophone QUECD 8	Another One Bites The Dust/Dragon Attack/Las Palabras De Amor (3" CD) 12
88	Parlophone QUECD 9	Under Pressure/Soul Brother/Body Language (3" CD) 18
88	Parlophone QUECD 10	Radio Ga Ga/I Go Crazy/Hammer To Fall (3" CD) 15
88	Parlophone QUECD 11	I Want To Break Free/Machines (Back To Humans)/It's A Hard Life (3" CD) 12
88	Parlophone QUECD 12	A Kind Of Magic/A Dozen Red Roses For My Darling/One Vision (3" CD) 15

(The above 3" CDs were all issued in card sleeves with generic plastic EMI outer packages.)

QUEEN

MINT VALUE £

ALBUMS

78	EMI EMA 788	JAZZ (LP, gatefold sleeve with poster)	12
81	EMI EMTV 30	GREATEST HITS (LP, mispress, side 2 plays "Anne Murray's Greatest Hits").	15
85	EMI QB 1	THE COMPLETE WORKS (14-LP, box set including "Complete Vision" LP of non-LP tracks, 2 booklets & map, numbered; 600 autographed)	500/80
89	Band Of Joy BOJLP 001	QUEEN AT THE BEEB (LP)	12
91	Parlophone PMTV 2	GREATEST HITS 2 (2-LP, embossed gatefold sleeve)	20
91	Parlophone PCSD 115	INNUENDO (LP)	12
92	Parlophone PCSP 725	LIVE AT WEMBLEY (2-LP, gatefold sleeve)	25
92	Parlophone CDQTEL 0001	BOX OF TRIX (CD, box set, with video, book, poster, T-shirt, patch & badge)	60
92	Parlophone CQTEL 0001	BOX OF TRIX (cassette, box set, with video, book, poster, T-shirt, patch & badge)	45

PROMOS

77	EMI SP SLP 241 A1U	We Will Rock You/We Are The Champions/Spread Your Wings (12", 1-sided, no p/s)	200
78	EMI EMI 2375	Bohemian Rhapsody/I'm In Love With My Car (EMI 'Queen's Award For Export' in-house edition, blue vinyl, Queen crest label, hand-numbered, purple p/s)	2,500
78	EMI EMI 2375	Bohemian Rhapsody/I'm In Love With My Car (as above, with outer 'EMI International' carrying envelope)	3,000
78	EMI EMI 2375	Bohemian Rhapsody/I'm In Love With My Car (as above, with invites, matches, pen, ticket, menu, outer card sleeve, scarf & EMI goblets in card box)	3,500

(The blue vinyl "Bohemian Rhapsody" was limited to 200 numbered copies)

84	EMI QUEEN 1	Radio Ga Ga (Edit)/I Go Crazy ('video shoot' p/s, unreleased, proofs only)	500
84	EMI QUEENDJ 5	Man On The Prowl/Thank God It's Christmas	150
84	Flexi Ltd. (no cat. no.)	Excerpts From Their New Album 'The Works' (flexidisc sampler, p/s)	12
86	Parlophone EMCDV 2	THE HIGHLANDER SELECTION (CD Video, 50 only)	450
86	(no label or cat. no.)	A Message From Queen (cassette, 1st Fan Club Convention issue)	20
89	Flexi Ltd. (no cat. no.)	A Message From Queen (flexidisc, 4th Fan Club Convention issue)	25
89	Parlophone TEASER 1	THE TEASER TAPE (cassette, edits sampler for "The Miracle")	15
95	EMI QUEEN DJ95	Bohemian Rhapsody/I'm In Love With My Car (purple vinyl, hand numbered, p/s, 10th anniversary Fan Club Convention issue, 2,000 only)	175
95	Parlophone QUEENLHDJ 21	Heaven For Everyone (Album Version)/Heaven For Everyone (Single Version) (jukebox issue, plain white sleeve, with poster, fold-out card & jukebox strip)	20
95	Parlophone QUEENDJ 22	A Winter's Tale/Thank God It's Christmas (jukebox issue, plain white sleeve, with jukebox strip)	10
96	Parlophone QUEENDJ 23	Too Much Love Will Kill You/We Are The Champions (jukebox issue, plain white sleeve, with jukebox strip)	8
96	Parlophone VIRGIN 1	Heaven For Everyone/Heaven For Everyone (12", white label, Virgin Radio 'Queen Day' competition prize, black 'Queen crest' p/s with handwritten details; mispressing with same track both sides, unreleased)	
96	Parlophone VIRGIN 2	Heaven For Everyone (12", 1-sided, white labels, Virgin Radio 'Queen Day' competition prize, 'Queen crest' p/s w/ handwritten details, 15 copies only)	600+
96	Parlophone VIRGIN 3	A Winter's Tale (12", 1-sided, white labels, Virgin Radio 'Queen Day' competition prize, 'Queen crest' p/s with handwritten details, 15 only)	600+
96	Parlophone VIRGIN 4	Mother Love (12", 1-sided, white labels, Virgin Radio 'Queen Day' competition prize, 'Queen crest' p/s with handwritten details, 15 only)	600+
96	Parlophone VIRGIN 5	Let Me Live (12", 1-sided, white labels, Virgin Radio 'Queen Day' competition prize, 'Queen crest' p/s with handwritten details, 15 only)	600+
96	Parlophone VIRGIN 6	You Don't Fool Me (12", 1-sided, white labels, Virgin Radio 'Queen Day' competition prize, 'Queen crest' p/s with handwritten details, 15 only)	600+
96	Parlophone VIRGIN 7	It's A Beautiful Day (12", 1-sided, white labels, Virgin Radio 'Queen Day' competition prize, 'Queen crest' p/s with handwritten details, 15 only)	600+
96	Parlophone VIRGIN 8	I Was Born To Love You (12", 1-sided, white labels, Virgin Radio 'Queen Day' competition prize, 'Queen crest' p/s with handwritten details, 15 only)	600+
99	EMI QUEENWL 28	Under Pressure (Remixes) (with David Bowie) (12", white label, unreleased mix, promo only)	60
99	EMI QUEEN DJ 28	Under Pressure (Rah Mix)/(Mike Spencer Mix)/The Show Must Go On (CD, card p/s, promo only)	15
73	EMI (no cat. no.)	QUEEN (LP, white label, EMI conference custom issue, die-cut sleeve, with/without outer envelope)	400/200
77	EMI (no cat. no.)	NEWS OF THE WORLD (LP, box set, with factory sample sticker, 5 photos, bio, badge & demo copy of "We Are The Champions"/"We Will Rock You", 50 only)	300
91	Parlophone (no cat. no.)	HINTS OF INNUENDO (cassette, edits/out-takes sampler for "Innuendo")	30
91	Parlophone (no cat. no.)	EIGHT GOOD REASONS TO BUY GREATEST HITS 2 (cassette, segued excerpts)	30
91	Parlophone (no cat. no.)	A SAMPLE OF MAGIC (CD, segued excerpts from "Greatest Hits 2")	100
94	EMI CD DIG 1	DIGITAL MASTER SAMPLER (CD, picture disc)	45
97	Parlophone CDQT 1	QUEEN ROCKS (CD, Brian May interview)	75

MISPRESSINGS

75	EMI EMI 2378	Bohemian Rhapsody/I'm In Love With My Car (2nd issue, with incorrect cat. no.)	12
78	EMI EMI 2870	Bicycle Race/Fat Bottomed Girls (p/s, B-side plays Crystal Gayle's "3 O'Clock In The Morning" or Dollar track)	each 10
79	EMI EMI 2975	CLIFF RICHARD: We Don't Talk Anymore/Count Me Out (A-side plays "Bohemian Rhapsody")	12
79	EMI EMI 5001	Crazy Little Thing Called Love/We Will Rock You (live) (p/s, both sides play "We Will Rock You")	15
80	EMI EMI 5076	Play The Game/A Human Body (p/s, both sides play "A Human Body")	12
86	Parlophone RP 5452	BEATLES: Paperback Writer/Rain (picture disc, A-side plays "Friends Will Be Friends")	75

(see also Freddie Mercury, Brian May, Roger Taylor, Larry Lurex, Cross, Immortals, Hilary Hilary, Eddie Howell, Man Friday & Jive Junior)

QUEEN B
89	London LON 223	Red Top Hot Shot/Gardening (p/s)	5

QUEENSRYCHE
83	EMI America 12EA 162	Queens Of The Reich/Nightrider/Blinded/Lady Wore Black (12", p/s)	12
84	EMI America EA 183	Take Hold Of The Flame/Nightrider (p/s)	12
86	EMI America EA 22	Gonna Get Close To You/Prophecy (p/s)	12
86	EMI America EAD 22	Gonna Get Close To You/Prophecy//Queen Of The Reich (live)/ Deliverance (live) (double pack)	12
88	EMI Manhattan 10QR 1	OVERSEEING THE OPERATION (10" EP)	12
89	EMI USA MT 65	Eyes Of A Stranger/Queen Of The Reich (p/s)	5
89	EMI USA 12MT 65	Eyes Of A Stranger/Queen Of The Reich/Walk In The Shadows/ Take Hold Of The Flame (12", p/s)	8
89	EMI USA 12MTG 65	Eyes Of A Stranger/Queen Of The Reich/Walk In The Shadows/ Take Hold Of The Flame (12", gatefold p/s)	12
89	EMI USA CDMT 65	Eyes Of A Stranger/Take Hold Of The Flame/Queen Of The Reich/ Prophecy (CD)	8
90	EMI USA MTPD 90	Empire/Scarborough Fair (shaped picture disc)	8
91	EMI USA MTS 94	Silent Lucidity (LP Version)/The Mission (live) (box set, 5 portraits & 2 stencils)	5
91	EMI USA 10MT 97	Best I Can/I Dream In Infrared (1991 Acoustic Remix)/Prophecy (10", box set with poster & badge)	8
91	EMI USA MTPD 98B	Jet City Woman/Empire (live) (shaped picture disc)	5
91	EMI USA 12MTS 98	Jet City Woman/Walk In The Shadows (live)/Empire (live) (12", box set with tour laminate & poster)	8

? & MYSTERIANS
66	Cameo Parkway C 428	96 Tears/Midnight Hour	20
66	Cameo Parkway C 441	I Need Somebody/'8' Teen	18
67	Cameo Parkway C 467	Can't Get Enough Of You, Baby/Smokes	12
67	Cameo Parkway C 479	Girl (You Captivate Me)/Got To	12
67	Cameo Parkway C 496	Do Something To Me/Love Me Baby	12
76	London HLU 10534	96 Tears/'8' Teen	8

QUESTIONS
68	Decca F 22740	We Got Love/Something Wonderful	20

TOMMY QUICKLY (& REMO FOUR)
63	Piccadilly 7N 35137	Tip Of My Tongue/Heaven Only Knows (solo)	30
63	Piccadilly 7N 35151	Kiss Me Now/No Other Love	7
64	Piccadilly 7N 35167	Prove It/Haven't You Noticed	7
64	Piccadilly 7N 35183	You Might As Well Forget Him/It's As Simple As That	7
64	Pye 7N 15708	The Wild Side Of Life/Forget The Other Guy	7
64	Pye 7N 15748	Humpty Dumpty/I'll Go Crazy	15

(see also Remo Four)

QUICKSAND
70	Carnaby CNS 4015	Passing By/Cobblestones	8
73	Dawn DNS 1046	Time To Live/Empty Street, Empty Heart	6
74	Dawn DNLS 3056	HOME IS WHERE I BELONG (LP)	30

QUICKSILVER MESSENGER SERVICE
76	Capitol CL 15859	Gypsy Lights/Witches' Moon	5
68	Capitol (S)T 2904	QUICKSILVER MESSENGER SERVICE (LP, black label with rainbow rim)	30
69	Capitol E-(S)T 120	HAPPY TRAILS (LP)	25
70	Capitol E-ST 391	SHADY GROVE (LP)	18
70	Capitol EA-ST 498	JUST FOR LOVE (LP)	15
71	Capitol EA-ST 630	WHAT ABOUT ME? (LP)	15
72	Capitol E-SW 819	QUICKSILVER (LP)	12
72	Capitol EA-ST 11002	COMIN' THRU (LP)	12
75	Capitol E-ST 11462	SOLID SILVER (LP)	12
83	Psycho PSYCHO 10	MAIDEN OF THE CANCER MOON (2-LP)	50

(see also Dino Valenti, Nicky Hopkins)

QUICKSPACE (SUPERSPORT)
94	Love Train PUBE 04	Found A Way/Do It My Own Way (12", p/s, 1,500 only)	12
95	Kitty Kitty Corp. CHOOSY 1	Quickspace Happy Song (#1)/Unique Slippy (as Quickspace Supersport, hand painted/stamped p/s, 1000 only)	6
96	Kitty Kitty Corp. CHOOSY 4	Friend/Good Timez (as Quickspace, painted wallpaper sleeve, 500 only)	6
97	Kitty Kitty Corp. CHOOSY 8	QUICKSPACE (LP, die-cut spray-painted sleeve, 1000 only)	10

QUIET FIVE
65	Parlophone R 5273	When The Morning Sun Dries The Dew/Tomorrow I'll Be Gone (some in p/s)	20/5
65	Parlophone R 5302	Honeysuckle Rose/Let's Talk It Over	7
66	Parlophone R 5421	Homeward Bound/Ain't It Funny What Some Lovin' Can Do	7
66	Parlophone R 5470	I Am Waiting/What About The Time For Me	7
67	CBS 202586	Goodnight Sleep Tight/Just For Tonight	6

(see also Kris Ife, Patrick Dane, Richard Barnes)

QUIET SUN
75	Island HELP 19	MAINSTREAM (LP)	12

(see also Phil Manzanera, Roxy Music)

QUIET WORLD
69	Dawn DNS 1001	Miss Whittington/There Is A Mountain (as Quiet World Of Lea & John)	25
70	Dawn DNS 1005	Children Of The World/Love Is Walking	25
70	Pye 7N 45005	Rest Comfortably/Gemima	10

MINT VALUE £

| 71 | Pye 7N 45074 | Visitor/Sam | 8 |
| 70 | Dawn DNLS 3007 | THE ROAD (LP) | 60 |

(see also Steve Hackett, Genesis)

QUIK
67	Deram DM 121	Love Is A Beautiful Thing/Bert's Apple Crumble	30
67	Deram DM 139	King Of The World/My Girl	15
67	Deram DM 155	I Can't Sleep/Soul Full Of Sorrow	30

(see also Meddy Evils)

QUILLER
| 75 | BBC RESL 25 | Quiller/General Direction (no p/s) | 10 |

QUINCEHARMON
| 71 | Columbia DB 8798 | On The Buses/Don't You Tell Me It's Over | 4 |

QUINCICASM
| 73 | Saydisc SDL 249 | QUINCICASM (LP) | 20 |

ANTHONY QUINN
| 70 | Capitol CL 15649 | I Love You And You Love Me/Sometimes (I Just Can't Stand You) | 4 |

CARMEL QUINN
| 55 | Philips PB 474 | The Whistling Gypsy/Doonaree (78) | 8 |
| 57 | MGM MGM 967 | Who Are You Foolin' Now/You Can't Run Away From Your Heart (78) | 8 |

MIKE QUINN
66	Fontana TF 761	Someone's Slipping Into My Mind/I Know What You Know	6
69	CBS 4506	Apple Pie/There's A Time	5
69	Jay Boy BOY 7	Toothbrush Nell/Fairy Cakes	5

PAUL QUINN & EDWYN COLLINS
| 84 | Swamplands SWP 1 | Pale Blue Eyes (Edited Version)/Burro (p/s) | 5 |
| 84 | Swamplands SWX 1 | Pale Blue Eyes/Pale Blues Eyes (Western)/Burro (12", original with 'film' p/s, inner sleeve & yellow obi) | 10/7 |

(see also Edwyn Collins, Orange Juice, Vince Clarke & Paul Quinn)

QUINTESSENCE
70	Island WIP 6075	Notting Hill Gate/Move Into The Light	6
71	Neon NE 1003	Sweet Jesus/You Never Stay The Same (some in p/s)	15/6
69	Island ILPS 9110	IN BLISSFUL COMPANY (LP, pink label)	30
70	Island ILPS 9128	QUINTESSENCE (LP, pink label)	30
70	Island ILPS 9143	DIVE DEEP (LP)	15
72	RCA SF 8273	SELF (LP)	12
72	RCA SF 8317	INDWELLER (LP)	12

(see also Kala)

QUINTET OF HOT CLUB OF FRANCE
| 53 | Decca LF 1139 | SWING FROM PARIS (10" LP) | 15 |

(see also Django Reinhardt)

QUIREBOYS
88	Survival SUR 043	Mayfair/Misled (p/s)	5
88	Survival SURT 043	Mayfair/Misled/Man On The Loose (12", p/s)	8
88	Survival SUR 46	There She Goes Again/How Do Ya Feel (p/s)	5
88	Survival PDSUR 46	There She Goes Again/How Do Ya Feel (picture disc)	8
88	Survival SURT 46	There She Goes Again/How Do Ya Feel/Sex Party (12", p/s)	8
89	Parlophone CDR 6230	Seven O'Clock/Pretty Girls/How Do You Feel? (CD, picture disc, with gatefold insert)	8
89	Parlophone CDR 6241	Hey You/Sex Party/Hoochie Coochie Man (live) (CD, picture disc, with gatefold insert)	8
89	Parlophone CDR 6248	I Don't Love You Anymore/Mayfair (Original Version)/Hey You (CD, picture disc, with gatefold insert)	8

DARYL QUIST
63	Pye 7N 15538	Thanks To You/Keep Moving (some in p/s)	12/6
63	Pye 7N 15563	Goodbye To Love/All Through The Night	6
64	Pye 7N 15605	True To You/Above And Beyond	7
64	Pye 7N 15656	See The Funny Little Clown/When She Comes To You	6
65	Decca F 12058	Put Away Your Teardrops/Across The Street	6

QUIVER
72	Warner Bros K 16165	Green Tree/I Might Stumble	5
71	Warner Bros K 46089	QUIVER (LP)	15
72	Warner Bros K 46153	GONE IN THE MORNING (LP)	15

(see also Bridget St. John, Natural Gas, Village)

QUODLING'S DELIGHT
| 76 | Fanfare FR 2179 | AMONG THE LEAVES SO GREEN (LP) | 25 |

QUOTATIONS (U.S.)
| 61 | HMV POP 975 | Imagination/Ala Men Say | 45 |

QUOTATIONS (U.K.)
64	Decca F 11907	Alright Baby/Love You All Over Again	15
68	CBS 3710	Cool It/Mark Of Her Head	10
69	CBS 4378	Hello Memories/Pretend	6

(see also Fleur De Lys, Johnny B. Great, Johnny Gustafson, Merseybeats, Johnny Goodison)

QUOTING MARX
| 77 | Full Stop PUNC 28 | Opening And Closing/66 And 99 | 12 |

QUO VARDIS
(see under Vardis)

RABBI JOSEPH GORDAN
85 Bam Caruso Intl. NRICO 30 Competition/Belief In Him (large centre hole, plain beige sleeve) 15
(see also Julian Cope)

RABBIT
73 Island WIP 6161   Broken Arrows/Blues My Guitar 5
73 Island ILPS 9238   BROKEN ARROWS (LP).. 12
74 Island ILPS 9289   DARK SALOON (LP)... 12
(see also Free; Kossoff, Kirke, Tetsu & Rabbit)

RABID
82 Fallout FALL 007   BLOODY ROAD TO GLORY (EP) 5

MIKE RABIN (& DEMONS)
64 Columbia DB 7350   Head Over Heels/Leaving You (as Mike Rabin & Demons) 40
65 Polydor BM 56007   If I Were You/What Do You Do.. 18

OSCAR RABIN & HIS BAND
53 Polygon P 1086   Crazy Man Crazy/Forgive Me (B-side with Mel Gaynor) (78) 8
(see also David Ede Band)

TREVOR RABIN
79 Chrysalis CHS 2282 Painted Picture/Stay With Me (p/s) 5
79 Chrysalis CHS 2362 Don't You Ever Lose/Stay With Me/Getting To Know You Better (p/s)........... 5
81 Chrysalis CHS 2508 Take Me To A Party/Looking For A Lady (p/s, coloured vinyl) 5
78 Chrysalis CHR 1196 TREVOR RABIN (LP) 12
79 Chrysalis CHR 1221 FACE TO FACE (LP) 12
(see also Yes)

JOSEPH RACAILLE
80s Recommended RRA 16.5 6 PETITES CHANSONS (EP, clear vinyl, foldaround p/s) 6

STEVE RACE
60 KP Music KP 042   A Piano In Love/Easy Walk (78) 7
61 Parlophone R 4808   Crosstrap/Stop Look Listen.. 10
62 Parlophone R 4894   Nicola/Ring Ding 5
63 Parlophone R 4981   The Pied Piper/Here And Now 5
63 World Records TP 285 DANCE TO THE TV THEMES (LP) 40
65 World Records TP 453 TAKE ONE (LP)... 25
65 World Records TP 456 LATE RACE (LP).. 12

RACE DANS
68 Trojan TR 610   Bookie Man/UNIQUES: More Love..................................... 8

YANK RACHELL TENNESSEE JUG BUSTERS
64 '77' LA 12-23   MANDOLIN BLUES (LP)... 20

RADAR
83 House Of Wax WAX 1 Leave Her Alone (p/s)... 25

JIMMY RADCLIFFE
65 Stateside SS 374   Long After Tonight Is Over/What I Want I Can Never Have................... 35
73 Pye International 7N 25614 Long After Tonight Is Over/What I Want I Can Never Have (reissue) 6
77 DJM DJS 10772   Long After Tonight Is Over/What I Want I Can Never Have (2nd reissue) 5
(see also Steve Karmen Big Band)

RADHA KRISHNA
71 Columbia SCX 6462 RADHA KRISHNA (LP, composed & directed by John Mayer) 35
(see also John Mayer)

RADHA KRISHNA TEMPLE (LONDON)
69 Apple APPLE 15   Hare Krishna Mantra/Prayer To The Spiritual Masters
                              (p/s, as Radha Krishna Temple [London], some with insert)............. 20/10
70 Apple APPLE 25   Govinda/Govinda Jai Jai (p/s) 15
71 Apple SAPCOR 18   THE RADHA KRSNA TEMPLE (LP, gatefold sleeve) 35
93 Apple SAPCOR 18   THE RADHA KRSNA TEMPLE (LP, reissue, gatefold sleeve with inner)......... 18

RADIANTS
64 Chess CRS 8002   Voice Your Choice/If I Only Had You 15
68 Chess CRS 8073   Hold On/I'm Glad I'm The Loser....................................... 10
(see also Maurice & Mac, Caston & Majors)

RADIATOR
77 Rocket ROKN 533   Isn't It Strange/Dancing On The Judgement Day 4
77 Rocket ROLL 14   ISN'T IT STRANGE (LP) 10
(see also Alan Hull, Lindisfarne)

RADIATORS (FROM SPACE)
77 Chiswick S 10   Television Screen/Love Detective (p/s, original issue)..................... 5
77 Chiswick NS 10   Television Screen/Love Detective (p/s, repressing) 4
77 Chiswick NS 19   Enemies/Psychotic Reaction (p/s)..................................... 4
78 Chiswick NS 24   Prison Bars/(Why Can't I Be A) Teenager In Love (unreleased, promo only
                              white label in stamped white sleeve & loose printed labels) 25
78 Chiswick NS 29   Million Dollar Hero (In A Five And Ten Cents Store)/Blitzin' At The Ritz
                              (as Radiators) (p/s).. 4

RADIATORS (FROM SPACE)

79	Chiswick NS 45	Walkin' Home Alone Again/Try And Stop Me/The Hucklebuck (unreleased; white label test pressings exist with loose labels; as Radiators)	20
79	Chiswick CHIS 144	Song Of The Faithful Departed/They're Looting In The Town (Irish-only)	8
79	CBS 5572	Sunday World/(Why Can't I Be A) Teenager In Love (p/s, Irish-only)	20
77	Chiswick WIK 4	TV TUBE HEART (LP)	20

(see also Pogues)

RADICAL SHEIKS

85	Red Door AB 1	Flip, Flop And Fly/My Babe/Don't Start Me Talking/Get On The Right Track/Just What I Want/Willie And The Hand Jive (EP)	4

(see also Bo Street Runners)

MARK RADICE

72	Paramount PARA 3024	Hey My Love/Your Love Is Like Fire	6
72	Paramount PARA 3025	New Day/Take Me To The Park	6
72	Paramount SPFA 7004	MARK RADICE (LP)	15

RADIO ACTORS

79	Charly CYS 1058	Nuclear Waste/Digital Love (p/s, reissue of Fast Breeder & Radio Actors single, 2 slightly different label designs)	8
79	DB DBS 5	Nuclear Waste/Digital Love (different p/s, 2nd reissue)	8

(see also Fast Breeder & Radio Actors, Sting, Newcastle Big Band, Police, Gilli Smyth, Inner City Unit, Steve Hillage, Sphynx)

RADIO BIRDMAN

78	Sire 6078 617	What Gives/Anglo Girl Desire (no p/s)	10
78	Sire 9103 332	RADIOS APPEAR (LP, with inner sleeve)	25
78	Sire SRK 6050	RADIOS APPEAR (LP, reissue)	12

RADIOHEAD

92	Parlophone TCR 6312	DRILL EP (Prove Yourself/Stupid Car/You/Thinking About You) (cassette, 3,000 only)	25
92	Parlophone 12R 6312	DRILL EP (Prove Yourself/Stupid Car/You/Thinking About You) (12", p/s, 3,000 only)	75
92	Parlophone CDR 6312	DRILL EP (Prove Yourself/Stupid Car/You/Thinking About You) (CD, 3,000 only)	125
92	Parlophone TCR 6078	Creep/Lurgee/Inside My Head/Million $ Question (cassette, 6,000 only)	12
92	Parlophone 12R 6078	Creep/Lurgee/Inside My Head/Million $ Question (12", p/s, 6,000 only)	25
92	Parlophone CDR 6078	Creep/Lurgee/Inside My Head/Million $ Question (CD, 6,000 only)	40
93	Parlophone TCR 6333	Anyone Can Play Guitar/Faithless, The Wonder Boy/Coke Babies (cassette)	8
93	Parlophone 12R 6333	Anyone Can Play Guitar/Faithless, The Wonder Boy/Coke Babies (12", p/s)	20
93	Parlophone CDR 6333	Anyone Can Play Guitar/Faithless, The Wonder Boy/Coke Babies (CD)	30
93	Parlophone TCR 6345	Pop Is Dead/Banana Co. (Acoustic)/Creep (live)/Ripcord (live) (cassette)	5
93	Parlophone 12R 6345	Pop Is Dead/Banana Co. (Acoustic)/Creep (live)/Ripcord (live) (12", g/fold p/s)	12
93	Parlophone CDR 6345	Pop Is Dead/Banana Co. (Acoustic)/Creep (live)/Ripcord (live) (CD)	35
93	Parlophone RS 6359	Creep/Yes I Am/Blow Out (Remix)/Inside My Head (live) (p/s, clear vinyl)	12
93	Parlophone TCR 6359	Creep/Yes I Am/Blow Out (Remix)/Inside My Head (live) (cassette)	6
93	Parlophone 12RG 6359	U.S. LIVE EP (Creep [Acoustic KROQ]/You [live]/Vegetable [live]/Killer Cars [live]) (12", numbered gatefold p/s)	20
93	Parlophone CDR 6359	Creep/Yes I Am/Blow Out (Remix)/Inside My Head (live) (CD, digipak)	25
93	Parlophone 12RDJ 6369	Ripcord/Prove Yourself/Faithless, The Wonderboy/Stop Whispering (Album Version) (12", p/s, promo only)	25
93	Parlophone CDRDJ 6369	Stop Whispering (U.S. Version)/Prove Yourself/Lurgee (CD, promo only, card p/s & inner sleeve)	15
94	Parlophone TCR 6394	My Iron Lung/The Trickster/Lewis (Mistreated)/Punchdrunk Lovesick Singalong (cassette)	5
94	Parlophone 12R 6394	My Iron Lung/Punchdrunk Lovesick Singalong/The Trickster/Lewis (Mistreated) (12", numbered p/s)	12
94	Parlophone CDRS 6394	My Iron Lung/Punchdrunk Lovesick Singalong/Lozenge Of Love (CD)	15
94	Parlophone CDR 6394	My Iron Lung/The Trickster/Lewis (Mistreated)/Permanent Daylight/You Never Wash Up After Yourself (CD)	15
95	Parlophone CDRS 6411	Fake Plastic Trees/India Rubber/How Can I Be Sure? (CD)	10
95	Parlophone CDR 6411	Fake Plastic Trees/Fake Plastic Trees (Acoustic)/Bulletproof...I Wish I Was (Acoustic)/Street Spirit (Fade Out) (CD, with poster)	20
95	Parlophone CDR 6415	Just/Bones (live)/Planet Telex (live)/Anyone Can Play Guitar (live) (CD, box set with 2 prints)	20
95	Parlophone 8 83115 2	The Bends/My Iron Lung (Live At Forum)/Bones (Live At Forum) (CD, for export to Ireland, slimline jewel case)	25
95	Parlophone 8 83115 2	The Bends/My Iron Lung (Live At Forum)/Bones (Live At Forum) (CD, for export to Ireland, mispressed with "Planet Telex" instead of "The Bends", slimline jewel case)	25
96	Parlophone R 6419	Street Spirit (Fade Out)/Bishop's Robes (die-cut p/s, white vinyl)	8
96	Parlophone R 6419LH	Street Spirit (Fade Out)/Bishop's Robes (jukebox issue, black vinyl, no p/s)	10
96	Parlophone CDR 6419	Street Spirit (Fade Out)/Bishop's Robes (CD, with poster)	20
97	Parlophone NODATALH 03	Karma Police (Album Version)/Lull (jukebox issue, black vinyl, no p/s)	10
97	Parlophone NODATALH 04	No Surprises/Palo Alto (jukebox issue, black vinyl, no p/s)	10
97	Parlophone NODATA 2	OK COMPUTER (2-LP, gatefold sleeve with inner sleeves)	15

RADIO HEART

87	GFM GFMP 109	Radio Heart/Radio Heart (Instrumental) (picture disc)	5
87	GFM GFMG 109	Radio Heart/Radio Heart (Instrumental) (radio-shaped picture disc)	6
87	GFM GFMP 112	London Times/Rumour (picture disc)	5
87	GFM GFMX 112	London Times/Rumour (oblong picture disc)	6
87	NBR CDNBR 1	All Across The Nation (extended remix)/(radio mix)/(Instrumental)/River (CD, card sleeve)	10
87	NBR NBRL 1	RADIO HEART (LP, withdrawn)	12

(see also Gary Numan)

RADIOPHONIC WORKSHOP
73 BBC RESL 13   Moonbase 3/World Of Dr. Who..18
(see also BBC Radiophonic Workshop)

RADIO STARS
77 Chiswick (N)S 9   Dirty Pictures/Sail Away (p/s) 4
77 Chiswick SW 17   STOP IT! (EP) 4
77 Chiswick NS 23   Nervous Wreck/Horrible Breath (p/s)...4
77 Chiswick NST 23   Nervous Wreck/Horrible Breath (12", p/s, numbered).......................7
78 Chiswick NS 36   From A Rabbit/The Beast No. 2 (p/s, 2 different mixes of B-side:
                          matrix numbers 5288-1T & 5288-2T)..4
78 Chiswick NS 36   From A Rabbit/To A Beast (6" 'hip pocket' issue, p/s) 6
82 Snap ECG 001   My Mother Said/2 Minutes Mr Smith (p/s)..................................5
82 Moonlight MNS 001   Good Personality/Talking 'Bout You (p/s) 5
77 Chiswick WIK 5   SONGS FOR SWINGING LOVERS (LP, shrinkwrapped with free single:
                          "No Russians In Russia"/"Dirty Pictures" [PROMO 2, no p/s]) 12
78 Chiswick CWK 3001   THE HOLIDAY ALBUM (LP) 10
82 Moonlight MNA 001   TWO MINUTES MR SMITH (LP) 10
(see also John's Children, Andy Ellison, Trevor White)

JACKIE RAE
58 Fontana H 155   More Than Ever/Hello Ma Baby 5
58 Fontana H 155   More Than Ever/Hello Ma Baby (78) 8
58 Fontana H 170   Day By Day/Take A Deep Breath 5
58 Fontana H 170   Day By Day/Take A Deep Breath (78) 8
60 Fontana H 242   Summer Place/The Moon Got In My Eyes...............................5
60 Fontana H 275   Dreamy/Close...5
67 Coral Q 72495   Believe In Love/Lonely One...5
(see also Janet Scott & Jackie Rae)

RAELET(T)S
67 HMV POP 1591   One Hurt Deserves Another/One Room Paradise (as Raelets) 10
71 Tangerine 6121 002   Bad Water/That Goes To Show You 5
71 Tangerine 6121 003   Here I Go Again/Leave My Man (Woman) Alone 5
(see also Ray Charles, Clydie King, Merry Clayton)

GERRY RAFFERTY
71 Transatlantic TRA 241 CAN I HAVE MY MONEY BACK? (LP) 10
(see also Humblebums, Fifth Column)

RAG DOLLS (U.S.)
64 Cameo Parkway P 921   Society Girl/Ragen (with Caliente Combo) 10
65 Stateside SS 398   Dusty/Hey Hoagy 10

RAG DOLLS (U.K.)
67 Columbia DB 8289   Never Had So Much Loving/Any Little Bit..............................6
68 Columbia DB 8378   My Old Man's A Groovy Old Man/They Didn't Believe Me 6
(see also Marionettes, Peanut, Katie Kissoon, Mac Kissoon)

RAGE
80 Carrere CAR 159   Money/Thank That Woman (p/s)..5
80 Carrere CAR 159CT   Money/Thank That Woman (10", red vinyl, stickered clear sleeve)..........10
81 Carrere CAR 182   Out Of Control/Double Dealer (p/s)....................................5
81 Carrere CAR 182CT   Out Of Control (Extended Version)/Double Dealer (12", yellow vinyl,
                          PVC sleeve) 10
83 Carrere CAR 304   Cry From A Hill (p/s) 10
81 Carrere CAL 124   OUT OF CONTROL (LP) 12
82 Carrere CAL 138   NICE N' DIRTY (LP) 12
83 Carrere CAL 149   RUN FOR THE NIGHT (LP) 12
(see also Nutz)

RAGE
86 Diamond RAGE 1   Looking For You/Come On Now (p/s) 4
86 Diamond RAGE 112   Looking For You/Come On Now/Great Balls Of Fire/Hallelujah I Love Her So
                          (12", unissued, test pressings only) 75
(see also Long Tall Shorty, Case, Purple Hearts, Chords)

RAGGAMUFFINS
67 London HLU 10134   Four Days Of Rain/It Wasn't Happening At All 4

RAGGED HEROES
83 Celtic CM 013   ANNUAL (LP) 25

RAGING STORMS
62 London HLU 9556   The Dribble/Hound Dog..20

LOU RAGLAND
73 Warner Bros K 16312   Since You Said You'd Be Mine/I Didn't Mean To Love You..............20

RAGPICKERS
59 Saga SAG 45-2906   Fifi/Cat On A Cool Tin Roof (p/s)......................................5
(see also Bert Weedon)

RAIDERS
70 CBS 4801   Just Seventeen/Sorceress With Blue Eyes 4
70 CBS 5016   Gone Movin' On/Interlude 4
71 CBS 7126   Indian Reservation/Terry's Tune 4
71 CBS 7474   Birds Of A Feather/The Turkey...4
72 CBS 7808   Country Wine/It's So Hard Gettin' Up Today 4
72 CBS 8129   Powder Blue Mercedes Queen/Golden Girls Sometimes 4
70 CBS 63973   COLLAGE (LP)...10
71 CBS 64471   INDIAN RESERVATION (LP)..10
(see also Paul Revere & Raiders)

RAIN

85	Jive Alive JA 002	Once/Tom Paine (with insert)	7
88	Medium Cool MC 012	First Of May	4
88	Medium Cool MC 012T	First Of May (12")	7

RAINBEAUS

60	Vogue V 9161	That's All I'm Asking Of You/Maybe It's Wrong (triangular centre)	100

(RITCHIE BLACKMORE'S) RAINBOW

74	Oyster OYR 103	Man On The Silver Mountain/Snake Charmer (as Ritchie Blackmore's Rainbow)	6
77	Polydor 2066 845	Kill The King (live)/Man On The Silver Mountain (live)/Mistreated (live) (p/s)	6
78	Polydor 2066 913	Long Live Rock'n'Roll/Sensitive To Light (p/s)	6
78	Polydor 2066 968	L.A. Connection/Lady Of The Lake (p/s, initially on red vinyl)	10/5
79	Polydor POSP 70	Since You've Been Gone/Bad Girl (p/s)	4
80	Polydor POSP 104	All Night Long/Weiss Heim (p/s)	4
81	Polydor POSP 221	I Surrender/Vieleicht Das Nachster Zeit (p/s)	4
81	Polydor POSP 251	Can't Happen Here/Jealous Lover (p/s)	4
82	Polydor POSP 421	Stone Cold/Rock Fever (p/s)	4
82	Polydor POSPX 421	Stone Cold (Long Version)/Rock Fever (12", p/s)	7
83	Polydor POSP 631	Street Of Dreams/Anybody There? (p/s)	5
83	Polydor POSPP 631	Street Of Dreams/Anybody There? (picture disc, 2000 only)	20
83	Polydor POSPX 631	Street Of Dreams/Anybody There?/Power (live) (12", p/s)	10
83	Polydor POSP 654	Can't Let You Go/All Night Long (live) (p/s)	5
83	Polydor POSPP 654	Can't Let You Go/All Night Long (live) (guitar-shaped picture disc)	15
83	Polydor POSPX 654	Can't Let You Go/All Night Long (live)/Stranded (live) (12", p/s)	10
75	Oyster OYA 2001	RITCHIE BLACKMORE'S RAINBOW (LP, gatefold sleeve, as Ritchie Blackmore's Rainbow)	12
77	Polydor 2808 010 010	RAINBOW ON STAGE (LP, music & interview disc, with insert, promo only)	75
79	Polydor POLD 5023	DOWN TO EARTH (LP, clear vinyl, with inner sleeve)	15

(see also Ritchie Blackmore, Deep Purple, Elf, Dio, Graham Bonnet, Cozy Powell, Roger Glover, Wild Horses, Tony Carey)

RAINBOW FFOLLY

68	Parlophone R 5701	Go Girl/Drive My Car	30
67	Parlophone PMC/PCS 7050	SALLIES FFORTH (LP)	150

(see also Love Affair)

RAINBOW PEOPLE

68	Pye 7N 17582	Walk'll Do You Good/Dream Time	10
68	Pye 7N 17624	The Sailing Song/Rainbows	5
69	Pye 7N 17759	Living In A Dream World/Happy To See You Again	6

RAINBOWS

69	CBS 3995	Rainbows/Nobody But You	8
69	CBS 4568	New Day Dawning/Days And Nights	5

(see also Peeps, Martin Cure & Peeps)

RAINCOATS

79	Rough Trade RT 013	Fairytale In The Supermarket/In Love/Adventures Close To Home (p/s)	4
82	Rough Trade RT 093	No-One's Little Girl/Running Away (p/s)	4
79	Rough Trade ROUGH 3	THE RAINCOATS (LP, some with lyric booklet)	12/10
81	Rough Trade ROUGH 13	ODYSHAPE (LP)	10

(see also Slits)

RAINCHECKS

64	Solar SRP 104	Something About You/You're My Angel	12
65	R&B MRB 5002	How Are You Boy/Bye Bye Baby	25

RAINDROPS (U.K.)

59	Parlophone R 4559	Italian Style/Along Came Jones	8
60	Oriole CB 1544	Let's Make A Foursome/If I Had My Life To Live Over	8
60	Oriole CB 1544	Let's Make A Foursome/If I Had My Life To Live Over (78)	12
60	Oriole CB 1555	Banjo Boy/Crazy Rhythm	7
61	Oriole CB 1595	Will You Love Me Tomorrow/Raindrops	8
62	Oriole CB 1707	Paintin' The Town With Teardrops/A Letter From Anne	7
67	CBS 202669	Foolman/Got To Find A Reason (credited to Raindrops '67)	6

(see also Jackie & Raindrops, Jackie Lee, Jacky, Emma Rede, Vince Hill)

RAINDROPS (U.S.)

63	London HL 9718	What A Guy/It's So Wonderful	12
63	London HL 9769	The Kind Of Boy You Can't Forget/Even Though You Can't Dance	15
64	London HL 9825	That Boy John/Hanky Panky	10
64	Fontana TF 463	The Book Of Love/I Won't Cry	12
64	London RE 1415	WHAT A GUY (EP)	80
64	London HA 8140	THE RAINDROPS (LP)	60

(see also Ellie Greenwich, Popsicles)

CLAIRE RAINE

68	Jolly JY 010	La-La-La/I Want You	7

LORRY RAINE

51	London L 899	Spin The Bottle/Who'll Take My Place When I'm Gone (78)	12
51	London L 1081	Sometime, Somewhere/Why Cry (78)	10
53	London L 1220	I've Gotta Have Love/A Wooin' We Will Go (78)	12
54	London HL 8043	You Broke My Broken Heart/I'm In Love With A Guy	25
54	London HL 8043	You Broke My Broken Heart/I'm In Love With A Guy (78)	12
55	London HL 8132	Love Me Tonight/What Would I Do	25
55	London HL 8132	Love Me Tonight/What Would I Do (78)	12

MA RAINEY

50	Jazz Collector L 16	Don't Fish My Sea/Soon This Morning (78)	10
50	Jazz Collector L 20	Jealous Hearted Blues/See See Rider Blues (78)	10
50	Jazz Collector L 35	Blues The World Forgot (Parts 1 & 2) (78)	10

MINT VALUE £

50	Jazz Collector L 42	New Bo-Weavil Blues/Moonshine Blues (78)	10
50	Jazz Collector L 48	Barrel House Blues/Walking Blues (78)	10
50	Jazz Collector L 52	Misery Blues/Dead Drunk Blues (78)	10
50	Jazz Collector L 57	Morning Hour Blues/Weepin' Woman Blues (78)	10
50	Jazz Collector L 66	Moonshine Blues/Southern Blues (78)	10
51	Jazz Collector L 73	Stack O'Lee Blues/Yonder Come The Blues (78)	10
52	Jazz Collector L 78	Those Dogs Of Mine/Lucky Rock Blues (78)	10
52	Jazz Collector L 82	Honey Where Have You Been So Long/Ma Rainey's Mystery Record (78)	10
52	Jazz Collector L 87	Slave To The Blues/Oh My Babe Blues (78)	10
52	Jazz Collector L 98	Blues Oh Blues/Oh Papa Blues (78)	10
54	Jazz Collector L 107	Lawd Send Me A Man Blues/South Bound Blues (78)	10
55	Jazz Collector L 120	Gone Daddy Blues/Slow Driving Moan (78)	10
50s	Signature 908	Yonder Come The Blues/Stack O'Lee Blues (78)	8
53	London AL 3502	MA RAINEY VOLUME 1 (10" LP)	30
55	London AL 3538	MA RAINEY VOLUME 2 (10" LP)	30
56	London AL 3558	MA RAINEY VOLUME 3 (10" LP)	30
50s	Ristic LP 13	MA RAINEY (10" LP)	35
50s	Ristic LP 19	MA RAINEY (10" LP)	35
62	Riverside RL 12-108	MA RAINEY SINGS THE BLUES (LP)	20
64	Riverside RLP 8807	MOTHER OF THE BLUES (LP, gatefold sleeve with booklet)	18
70	CBS 52798	MA RAINEY AND THE CLASSIC BLUES SINGERS (LP)	12
75	Milestone M 47021	MA RAINEY (2-LP)	15

MA RAINEY & IDA COX
| 60 | Jazz Collector JEL 12 | THE FEMALE BLUES VOL. 1 (EP) | 15 |
| 64 | Jazz Collector JEL 22 | THE FEMALE BLUES VOL. 3 (EP, with Trixie Smith) | 15 |

(see also Ida Cox, Tommy Ladnier)

MA RAINEY & PAPA CHARLIE JACKSON
| 50s | Poydras 11 | Ma And Papa Poorhouse Blues/Big Feeling Blues (78) | 8 |

RAIN PARADE
| 83 | Enigma BOB 4/LYN 15263 | Sad Eyes Kill (3.16) (1-sided flexi with Bucketfull Of Brains mag, issue 10) | 6/4 |
| 83 | Enigma BOB 4/LYN 15263 | Sad Eyes Kill (3.16) (hard vinyl white label test pressing) | 15 |

MARVIN RAINWATER
55	MGM SP 1150	Tennessee Houn' Dog Yodel/Albino (Pink-Eyed) Stallion	50
55	MGM MGM 876	Tennessee Houn' Dog Yodel/Albino (Pink-Eyed) Stallion (78)	20
56	MGM MGM 929	What Am I Supposed To Do/Why Did You Have To Go And Leave Me	20
56	MGM MGM 929	What Am I Supposed To Do/Why Did You Have To Go And Leave Me (78)	15
57	MGM MGM 961	Gonna Find Me A Bluebird/So You Think You've Got	20
57	MGM MGM 961	Gonna Find Me A Bluebird/So You Think You've Got (78)	15
58	MGM MGM 974	Whole Lotta Woman/Baby, Don't Go	8
58	MGM MGM 974	Whole Lotta Woman/Baby, Don't Go (78)	8
58	MGM MGM 980	I Dig You Baby/Two Fools In Love (B-side with Sister Patty)	8
58	MGM MGM 980	I Dig You Baby/Two Fools In Love (B-side with Sister Patty) (78)	8
58	MGM MGM 988	Dance Me Daddy/Because I'm A Dreamer (B-side with Sister Patty)	12
58	MGM MGM 988	Dance Me Daddy/Because I'm A Dreamer (B-side with Sister Patty) (78)	15
59	MGM MGM 1030	Half-Breed/A Song Of New Love	12
59	MGM MGM 1030	Half-Breed/A Song Of New Love (78)	25
60	MGM MGM 1052	Nothin' Needs Nothin' (Like I Need You)/The Valley Of The Moon	15
61	London HLU 9447	Boo Hoo/I Can't Forget	90
58	MGM MGM-EP 647	MEET MARVIN RAINWATER (EP)	50
58	MGM MGM-EP 662	WHOLE LOTTA MARVIN (EP)	60
59	MGM MGM-EP 685	MARVIN RAINWATER (EP)	60
63	Ember EMB 4521	COUNTRY AND WESTERN FAVOURITES VOL. 2 (EP)	30
58	MGM MGM-D 152	SONGS BY MARVIN RAINWATER (10" LP)	80
72	Philips 6414 110	MARVIN RAINWATER GETS COUNTRY FEVER (LP)	12

(see also Connie Francis & Marvin Rainwater)

RAINY DAY
| 84 | EMI EMI 5472 | Painting Pictures/Welche Farbe Hat Der Sonnenschein (p/s) | 12 |

RAINY DAZE
67	CBS 3200	What Do You Think/Autumn Leaves	10
67	Polydor 56731	That Acapulco Gold/In My Mind Lives A Forest	8
68	Polydor 56737	Blood Of Oblivion/Stop Sign	12
68	CBS 56731	THAT ACAPULCO GOLD (LP, unissued in U.K.)	

RAISINS
68	Major Major MM 540	Ain't That Lovin' You Baby/Stranger Things Have Happened	7
69	Major Minor MM 602	I Thank You/Don't Leave Me Like This	5
68	Major Minor MMLP 20	THE RAISINS (LP, also stereo SMLP 20)	15

BONNIE RAITT
72	Warner Bros K 16226	Too Long At The Fair/Under The Falling Sky	5
72	Warner Bros K 46189	GIVE IT UP (LP)	12
73	Warner Bros K 46261	TAKIN' MY TIME (LP)	12
74	Warner Bros K 56075	STREETLIGHTS (LP)	12
75	Warner Bros K 56160	HOME PLATE (LP)	12

(see also Roy Orbison, Alton Purnell)

RAJAH
| 73 | Philips 6006 284 | The Godfather Theme/The Deadeye Dick | 4 |

RALFI (Pagan)
| 74 | Island USA 003 | Wonderful Thing/Gambler | 4 |

DON RALKE ORCHESTRA
| 59 | Vogue V 9152 | Maverick/Travellin' West | 6 |
| 59 | Vogue V 9152 | Maverick/Travellin' West (78) | 12 |

Don RALKE Orchestra

60	Warner Brothers WB 2	77 Sunset Strip (as Big Sound Of Don Ralke)/	
		PETE CANDOLI & HIS ORCHESTRA: 77 Sunset Strip Cha-Cha.	6
60	Warner Brothers WM 4014	DANCE CAPER IN HI-FI (LP)	12
60	Warner Brothers WS 8007	YOU'VE NEVER HEARD GERSHWIN WITH BONGOS (LP)	12

TOMMY RALL, ANN MILLER, BOBBY VAN & BOB FOSSE
54	MGM SP 1079	From This Moment On/So Kiss Me Kate (by Kathryn Grayson & Howard Keel)/	
		Brush Up Your Shakespeare (by Keenan Wynn & James Whitmore)	6

RALLY ROUNDERS
64	Lyntone LYN 573/574	Bike Beat Part 1/Bike Beat Part 2 (actually the Outlaws) (p/s, flexidisc)	50

(see also Outlaws, Ritchie Blackmore)

RALPH & PONYTAILS
80	Pony Tunes RATP 1	James Bond/James Bond (Different Version) (p/s)	5
80	Pony Tunes RATP 2	Illogical Rhythm/Hawaii Five Oh!/Splendid Stories (p/s)	4

BUCK RAM'S RAMROCKS
63	London HLU 9677	Benfica/Odd Man Theme	12

(see also Little Richard, Platters)

RAMASES
71	Philips 6113 001	Ballroom/Muddy Water.	7
71	Philips 6113 003	Jesus Come Back/Hello Mister	7
71	Vertigo 6360 046	SPACE HYMNS (LP, foldout sleeve, spiral label, later 'spaceship' label)	25/15
75	Vertigo 6360 115	GLASS TOP COFFIN (LP, gatefold sleeve, spiral label).	15

(see also 10cc, Ramases & Seleka, Ramases & Selket)

RAMASES & SELEKA
70	Major Minor MM 704	Love You/Gold Is The Ring.	18

(see also Ramases)

RAMASES & SELKET
68	CBS 3717	Crazy One/Mind's Eye	70

(see also Ramases)

RAMATAM
72	Atlantic K 40415	RAMATAM (LP)	10

(see also Iron Butterfly)

EDDIE RAMBEAU
62	Stateside SS 116	Summertime Guy/Last Night Was My Last Night	7
64	Stateside SS 301	Come Closer/She's Smilin' At Me	6
65	Stateside SS 448	My Name Is Mud/I Just Need Your Love	6
66	Stateside SS 486	The Train/Yesterday's Newspapers	7
66	Stateside SS 501	I'm The Sky/I Just Need Your Love	5
66	Stateside SS 561	The Clock/If I Were You	5

(see also Marcy Jo & Eddie Rambeau)

RAMBLER
66	Pye 7N 17164	Love Minus Zero No Limit/An Bonnan Bui	6

(see also Johnny McEvoy)

RAMBLERS
63	Decca F 11775	Dodge City/Just For Chicks.	30

RAMBLERS TWO
65	Pye 7N 15989	Today Is The Highway/The Mountains And The Sea	4

RAMBLETTES
65	Brunswick 05932	Thinking Of You/On Back Street	8

RAMBLIN' JIMMY DOLAN
51	Capitol CL 13600	Wine, Women And Pink Elephants/GENE O'QUIN: Boogie Woogie Fever (78).	10
53	Capitol CL 13982	Playin' Dominoes And Shootin' Dice/	
		The Wheel That Does The Squeekin' (78).	10

SID RAMIN
69	CBS	STILETTO (LP, soundtrack)	25

CARLOS RAMIREZ
54	MGM SP 1072	I Had To Kiss You/Little More Of Your Armour.	6

RAM JAM
76	Epic EPC 82215	RAM JAM (LP)	10
77	Epic EPC 82628	PORTRAIT OF THE ARTIST (LP)	10

(see also Lemon Pipers)

RAM JAM BAND
65	Columbia DB 7621	Shake Shake Senora/Akinla.	12

(see also Geno Washington & Ram Jam Band, Ram John Holder, Ram Holder Brothers)

RAMLEH
83	Broken Flag BF V4	THE HAND OF GLORY (EP).	15
91	Shock SX 013	Slammers/Black Moby Dick (p/s, numbered, 500 only).	8
92	Dying Earth DE 003	Loser Patrol/Tracers (p/s, numbered, 500 only, 1st 30 in red sleeve)	15/8
93	Dying Earth DE 007	Say Fuck/Slackjaw (wraparound p/s, numbered, 500 only)	8
94	Format Supremacy	Welcome/Pristine Womankind (cardboard p/s, 500 only)	8
	(no cat. no.)		
83	Broken Flag BF V2	A RETURN TO SLAVERY (LP, with Libertarian Recordings).	40
91	Shock Records SX D14	BLOWHOLE (LP)	12

(see also Skullflower)

RAMON & CRYSTALITES
71	Songbird SB 1053	Golden Chickens/Stranger Version	15

DEE DEE RAMONE

| 97 | Blackout BLK 5000-7 | I Am Seeing UFOs (featuring Joey Ramone)/Bad Horoscope (2,500 copies only) . . . . 5 |

DEE DEE RAMONE & ICLC

| 94 | Rough Trade/World Service RDT 157.1757.2 | Chinese Bitch/I Don't Want To Get Involved With You/ That's What Everybody Else Does/We're A Creepy Family (CD) . . . . 10 |

(see also Ramones)

RAMONES

76	Sire 6078 601	Blitzkrieg Bop/Havana Affair (some with p/s). 80/8
77	Sire 6078 603	I Remember You/California Sun (live)/I Don't Wanna Walk Around With You (live) (p/s) 20
77	Sire RAM 001 (6078 606)	Sheena Is A Punk Rocker/Commando/I Don't Care 8
77	Sire RAM 001 (6078 606)	Sheena Is A Punk Rocker/Commando/I Don't Care (12", with or without T-shirt offer on perforated centre of no'd p/s, 12,000 only) 20/15
77	Sire 6078 607	Swallow My Pride/Pinhead/Let's Dance (live) (p/s) 10
77	Sire 6078 611	Rockaway Beach/Teenage Lobotomy/Beat On The Brat (p/s). 10
77	Sire 6078 611	Rockaway Beach/Teenage Lobotomy/Beat On The Brat (12", p/s, some with poster) 20/10
78	Sire 6078 615	Do You Wanna Dance?/It's A Long Way Back To Germany/Cretin Hop (p/s) 8
78	Sire (no cat. no.)	Questioningly/Don't Come Close/Sedated/I Just Want To Have Something To Do (p/s, promo only, with spoken intros by Joey Ramone) 12
78	Sire SRE 1031	Don't Come Close/I Don't Want You (p/s, some on yellow vinyl) 10/8
78	Sire SRE 1031	Don't Come Close/I Don't Want You (12", p/s, yellow or red vinyl) 12/15
79	Sire SIR 4009	She's The One/I Wanna Be Sedated (p/s) 10
79	Sire SIR 4021	Rock'n'Roll High School/Rockaway Beach (live)/Sheena Is A Punk Rocker (live) (p/s). 10
80	Sire SIR 4031	Baby, I Love You/High Risk Insurance (cassette) 8
80	RSO RSO 70 (2090 512)	I Wanna Be Sedated/The Return Of Jackie And Judy (p/s). 8
80	Sire SREP 1	MELTDOWN WITH THE RAMONES: I Just Want To Have Something To Do/ Here Today Gone Tomorrow/I Wanna Be Your Boyfriend/Questioningly (EP). 15
81	Sire SIR 4051	We Want The Airwaves/You Sound Like You're Sick (p/s). 10
81	Sire SIR 4052	She's A Sensation/All Quiet On The Eastern Front (p/s) 8
83	Sire W 9606	Time Has Come Today/Psycho Therapy (p/s) 15
83	Sire W 9606T	Time Has Come Today/SHeena Is A Punk Rocker/Teenage Lobotomy/ Rock'n'Roll Radio (12", p/s). 25
85	Beggars Banquet BEG 128	Chasing The Night/Howling At The Moon (p/s) 6
85	Beggars Banquet BEG 128D	Chasing The Night/Howling At The Moon//Smash You/Street Fighting Man (double pack, gatefold sleeve). 12
85	Beggars Banquet BEGTP 128	Chasing The Night/Howling At The Moon//Smash You/Street Fighting Man (12", p/s) 15
85	Beggars Banquet BEG 140	Bonzo Goes To Bitburg/Go Home Ann (p/s) 8
85	Beggars Banquet BEG 140T	Bonzo Goes To Bitburg/Go Home Ann/Daytime Dilemma (12", p/s) 10
86	Beggars Banquet BEG 157	Somebody Put Something In My Drink/Something To Believe In (p/s). 6
86	Beggars Banquet BEG 157T	Somebody Put Something In My Drink/(You) Can't Say Anything Nice/ Something To Believe In (12", p/s, some with poster) 15/8
87	Beggars Banquet BEG 198	Real Cool Time/Life Goes On (p/s) 6
87	Beggars Banquet BEG 198T	Real Cool Time/Life Goes On/Indian Giver (12", p/s) 10
87	Beggars Banquet BEG 201	I Wanna Live/Merry Christmas (p/s) 8
92	Chrysalis 0946 3 23917 66	Poison Heart/Chinese Rock/Sheena Is A Punk Rocker (live)/ Rockaway Beach (live) (12", yellow vinyl). 12
76	Sire 9103 253	RAMONES (LP, with insert) 22
76	Sire 9103 254	RAMONES LEAVE HOME (LP, with "Carbona Not Glue" or "Babysitter", both with inner sleeve) 35/20
77	Sire 9103 255	ROCKET TO RUSSIA (LP, with inner sleeve) 18
78	Sire SRK 6063	ROAD TO RUIN (LP, yellow vinyl) 20
79	Sire SRK2 6074	IT'S ALIVE (2-LP) 15
80	Sire SRK 6077	END OF THE CENTURY (LP) 12
81	Sire SRK 3571	PLEASANT DREAMS (LP) 12
90	Beggar's Banquet (no cat. no.)	END OF THE DECADE (6 x 12" singles, box set with t-shirt, postcards & poster, 2,500 copies only) 50
93	Chrysalis CHR 6052	ACID EATERS (LP). 15

(see also Paley Brothers & Ramones, Holly & Joey, Dee Dee Ramone)

MICHEL RAMOS

| 51 | Esquire 5-036 | Boucle Blonde/Maia (78) . . . . 8 |

RAM RAM KINO

| 85 | Temple TOPY 006 | Advantage — Tantric Routines 1-4 (3.23)/(Basket Mix) (4.00)/ Into The Bush (3.26)/Special (3.56) (12", p/s) . . . . 7 |

(see also Crispy Ambulance)

RAMRODS (U.S.)

61	London HLU 9282	Riders In The Sky/Zig Zag 7
61	London HLU 9355	Loch Lomond Rock/Take Me Back To My Boots And Saddle. 12
61	London RE-U 1292	RIDERS IN THE SKY (EP). 100

RAMRODS (U.K.)

| 65 | United Artists UP 1113 | Overdrive/Stalker . . . . 8 |

BILL RAMSEY

| 62 | Polydor NH 66812 | Go Man Go/Rocking Mountain. . . . . 10 |

RANCHERS

| 65 | Cavern Sound IMSTL 2 | An American Sailor At The Cavern/Sidetracked . . . . 20 |

(see also Phil Brady & Ranchers)

RANCID

| 94 | Epitaph 86434-1 | LET'S GO (LP, 2 x 10", gatefold sleeve, white vinyl) . . . . 12 |

MINT VALUE £

ELLIOTT RANDALL
| 71 | Polydor 2489 004 | RANDALL'S ISLAND (LP) | 12 |

FREDDY RANDALL & HIS BAND
50	Tempo A 45	Dark Night Blues/Washington And Lee Swing (78)	8
51	Tempo A 49	Riverside Blues/Jazz Club Stomp (78)	8
50	Tempo A 55	Georgia Cake Walk/Sugar Foot Strut (78)	8
53	Parlophone MSP 6007	Clarinet Marmalade/Original Dixieland One-Step	5
53	Parlophone MSP 6030	At The Jazz Band Ball/Way Down Yonder In New Orleans	5
53	Parlophone MSP 6043	Twelve For Six/Copenhagen	5
54	Parlophone MSP 6087	Carolina In The Morning/Tin Roof Blues	5
54	Parlophone MSP 6098	Muskrat Ramble/Shine	5
54	Parlophone MSP 6137	Someday Sweetheart/Hotter Than That	5
58	Parlophone GEP 8715	CHICAGO JAZZ (EP)	12
58	Parlophone PMD 1046	DR JAZZ (LP)	15

TEDDY RANDAZZO (& DAZZLERS)
59	HMV POP 578	It's Magic/Richer Than I	7
59	HMV POP 578	It's Magic/Richer Than I (78)	12
60	HMV POP 806	Journey To Love/Misery	6
61	HMV POP 866	Happy Ending/But You Broke My Heart	6
61	HMV POP 925	Let The Sunshine In/Broken Bell	6
62	HMV POP 1067	Dance To The Locomotion/Cottonfields (as Teddy Randazzo & Dazzlers)	8
63	HMV POP 1119	Echoes/It Wasn't A Dream	6
63	Pye International 7N 25181	Big Wide World/Be Sure, My Love	6
62	HMV CLP 1527	JOURNEY TO LOVE (LP, also stereo CSD 1421)	50/60
63	HMV CLP 1601	TEDDY RANDAZZO TWISTS (LP, with Dazzlers)	70

(see also Three Chuckles)

LYNNE RANDELL
| 67 | CBS 2847 | Ciao Baby/Stranger In My Arms | 150 |
| 67 | CBS 2927 | That's A Hoe Down/I Need You Boy | 12 |

RAN-DELLS
| 63 | London HLU 9760 | The Martian Hop/Forgive Me Darling | 18 |

(see also Jeff Wayne)

DON RANDI
| 65 | London HLU 9963 | Mexican Pearls/I Don't Wanna Be Kissed | 6 |

BARBARA RANDOLPH
67	Tamla Motown TMG 628	I Got A Feelin'/You Got Me Hurtin' All Over	35
71	Tamla Motown TMG 788	I Got A Feelin'/You Got Me Hurtin' All Over (reissue)	7
79	Tamla Motown TMG 1133	Can I Get A Witness/You Got Me Hurtin' All Over	8

BOOTS RANDOLPH
62	London HLU 9567	Bluebird Of Happiness/Keep A Light In Your Window Tonight	6
63	London HLU 9685	Yakety Sax/I Really Don't Want To Know	10
63	London HLU 9798	Windy And Warm/Lonely Street	6
64	London HLU 9891	Hey, Mr. Sax Man/Baby Go To Sleep	7
66	London HLU 10017	Theme From A Dream/King Of The Road	5
66	London HLU 10028	These Boots Are Made For Walking/Honey In Your Heart	5
67	Monument MON 1001	The Shadow Of Your Smile/I'll Just Walk Away	5
67	Monument MON 1011	Big Daddy/Love Letters	5
69	Monument MON 1028	Games People Play/By The Time I Get To Phoenix	5
63	London RE-U 1365	THE YAKETY SAX OF BOOTS RANDOLPH (EP)	30
63	London HA-U 8106	YAKETY SAX (LP)	25
66	London HA-U 8280	MORE YAKETY SAX (LP, as Boots Randolph & His Combo)	25
67	Monument LMO/SMO 5002	HIP BOOTS (LP)	15
67	Monument LMO/SMO 5003	BOOTS WITH STRINGS (LP)	15
68	Monument LMO/SMO 5012	THE FANTASTIC BOOTS RANDOLPH (LP)	15
69	Monument LMO/SMO 5022	SAXSATIONAL (LP)	15
70	Monument LMO/SMO 5040	YAKETY REVISITED (LP)	12

CHARLES RANDOLPH GREEN SOUND
| 69 | London HLD 10283 | Quintin's Theme/Number One At The Blue Whale | 4 |
| 76 | UK USA 15 | Star Trek/The Hustle | 4 |

ERIC RANDOM
80	New Hormones ORG 6	THAT'S WHAT I LIKE ABOUT ME (12" EP)	5
81	D. du Crepescule TW 1029	23 Skidoo/Subliminal (p/s)	5
81	New Hormones ORG 11	Dow Chemical Company/Skin Deep (p/s)	4
80	New Hormones CAT 4	LIVE IN EUROPE (cassette)	10
82	New Hormones ORG 18	EARTHBOUND GHOST NEED (LP, as Eric Random Meets Bedlamites)	10
85	Doublevision DVR 11	TIME SPLICE (LP)	10

(see also Tiller Boys, Cabaret Voltaire, Free Agents, Pressure & Co.)

RANDY & RAINBOWS
| 63 | Stateside SS 214 | Denise/Come Back | 35 |

RANDY'S ALLSTARS
70	Randy's RAN 500	I'm The One, You're The One/End Us	5
70	Randy's RAN 501	Pepper Pot (act. with Count Machuki)/	
		Same Thing (B-side actually by Gaylads)	8
70	Randy's RAN 502	Dixie/Five Cents (B-side actually	
		"A Lover's Question" by Winston Samuels)	5
70	Randy's RAN 505	Emperor Waltz/War	6
70	Randy's RAN 506	Blue Danube Waltz/Together (B-side actually by Delroy Wilson)	6
70	Randy's RAN 507	Bridge Over Troubled Water (actually by Lyrics)/Waterfall	5
71	Explosion EX 2052	Hold On Girl (actually by Lyrics)/Hold On Girl (Version)	5

(see also Impact Allstars, Lyrics, Dave Barker, Ethiopians, Jimmy London)

RANEE & RAJ
68	Fontana TF 920	Feel Like A Clown/Rainbow Land	8
68	Fontana TF 941	Don't Tell Me I Must Go/Razor Edge	6

SUE RANEY
57	Capitol CL 14757	The Careless Years/What's The Good Word, Mr. Bluebird	6
57	Capitol CL 14792	Please Hurry Home/Don't Take My Happiness	6
58	Capitol CL 14923	My, My, How The Time Goes By/Periwinkle Blue	6
59	Capitol CL 14980	Ever/The Restless Sea	6
59	Capitol CL 15045	Swingin' In A Hammock/I Don't Look Right Without You	6
60	Capitol CL 15132	Biology/I Stayed Too Long At The Fair	6
58	Capitol T 964	WHEN YOUR LOVER HAS GONE (LP)	18

WAYNE RANEY (STRING BAND)
53	Parlophone DP 333	If You Never Slip Around/The Child's Side Of Life (78, export issue)	10
54	Parlophone CSMP 20	Adam/The Roosters Are Crowing (export issue)	25
54	Parlophone DP 380	Adam/The Roosters Are Crowing (78, export issue)	25
55	Parlophone DP 413	Mama/Trying To Live Without You (78, export issue)	8
58	Parlophone GEP 8746	COUNTRY AND WESTERN (EP)	40

RANGLERS
68	Trend TRE 1007	You Never Said Goodbye/Step Down	15

ERNEST RANGLIN
62	Island WI 015	Harmonica Twist/Mitty Gritty (as Ernest Ranglin Orchestra)	15
63	Island WI 128	Exodus/ROBERT MARLEY: One Cup Of Coffee	200
66	Black Swan IEP 704	ERNEST RANGLIN & THE G.B.'s (EP, some with p/s)	100/35
64	Island ILP 909	WRANGLIN' (LP)	90
64	Island ILP 915	REFLECTIONS (LP)	60

(see also Owen Gray, Graham Bond)

MASSIMO RANIERI
71	CBS 7207	Goodbye My Love/The Sun Shining Down On Me	12

BILLY RANKIN
83	A&M AM 172	Baby Come Back/Part Of The Scenery (p/s)	6

(see also Nazareth)

KENNY RANKIN
60	Brunswick 05845	As Sure As You're Born/Teasin' Heart	6

FELA RANSOME KUTI
(see under 'K')

RAOUL & RUINED
84	Gutter Hearts GH 1	BITE BACK + BLUES (LP, fan-club only issue)	50

(see also Marc Almond)

RAPED
78	Parole KNIT 1	PRETTY PAEDOPHILES (EP)	6
78	Parole PURL 1	Cheap Night Out/Foreplay Playground (p/s, with ad sheet)	6
84	Iguana PILLAGED 1	PHILES AND SMILES (LP, official bootleg, with booklet)	15

RAPEMAN
88	Fierce FRIGHT 031	Hated Chinee/Marmoset (p/s)	30

(see also Big Black)

RAPHAEL
65	Pye 7N 25362	Yo Soy Aquel/Es Verdad	5
66	Hispavox HXS 303	Please Speak To Me Of Love/Hablemos Del Amor	15
67	Hispavox HXL 106	CANTA RAPHAEL (LP)	12
67	Hispavox HXL 109	RAPHAEL (LP)	12

JOHNNY RAPHAEL
58	Vogue V 9104	We're Only Young Once/The Lonely Road To Nowhere	75
58	Vogue V 9104	We're Only Young Once/The Lonely Road To Nowhere (78)	25

RAPIERS
60s	Ilford Sound ILF 272	The Phantom Stage/Valencia	12

RAPIERS
86	Off Beat NS 112A	The Closing Theme/Still I Cry	10
83	Red Door RA 001	THE RAPIERS VOL. 1 (EP)	20
84	Twang RA 002	THE RAPIERS VOL. 2 (EP)	15
85	Twang RA 003	THE RAPIERS VOL. 3 (EP)	15
86	Twang RA 004	THE RAPIERS VOL. 4 (EP)	12
85	Off Beat WIK 40	STRAIGHT TO THE POINT (LP)	20
87	Off Beat WIK 67	1961 (LP)	20

BRIAN RAPKIN & KELVIN JONES
70s	MSR	DREAMS OF THE BEAST (LP)	20

MARIE RAPP
53	London L 1207	When A Man Loves A Woman/When I'm With You (78)	15

RARE AMBER
69	Polydor BM 56309	Malfunction Of The Engine/Blind Love	10
69	Polydor 583 046	RARE AMBER (LP)	70

RARE BIRD
70	Charisma CB 120	Sympathy/Devil's High Concern	5
70	Charisma CB 138	What You Want To Know/Hammerhead	6
72	Charisma CB 179	Sympathy/Devil's High Concern/What Do You Want To Know/Hammerhead (p/s)	7
73	Polydor 2058 402	Virgina/Lonely Street	5

RARE BIRD

74	Polydor 2058 471	Body And Soul/Redman 5
74	Polydor SH 1041/2	Diamonds/BARCLAY JAMES HARVEST:
		Negative Earth (flexi, with *Sounds*) 10/5
75	Polydor 2058 591	Don't Be Afraid/Passin' Through 5
75	Charisma CB 262	Sympathy/Beautiful Scarlet 5
69	Charisma CAS 1005	RARE BIRD (LP) 20
70	Charisma CAS 1011	AS YOUR MIND FLIES BY (LP) 20
72	Polydor 2442 101	EPIC FOREST (LP & poster, some with bonus EP "Roadside Welcome"/
		"Four Grey Walls"/"You're Lost" [2814 011], p/s) 30/20
73	Polydor 2383 211	SOMEBODY'S WATCHING (LP) 12
74	Polydor 2383 274	BORN AGAIN (LP) 12
	(see also Fields, Fruit Machine)	

RARE BREED

66	Strike JH 316	Beg, Borrow And Steal/Jeri's Theme 20
	(see also Pussyfoot)	

RARE EARTH

70	Tamla Motown TMG 742	Get Ready/Magic Key 10
71	Rare Earth RES 102	I Just Want To Celebrate/The Seed 5
72	Rare Earth RES 104	Hey Brother/Under God's Light 5
72	Rare Earth RES 105	Born To Wander/Here Comes The Night 5
73	Rare Earth RES 109	Good Time Sally/Love Shines Down 5
70	T. Motown STML 11165	GET READY (LP) 20
71	T. Motown STML 11180	ECOLOGY (LP) 18
71	Rare Earth SREA 4001	ONE WORLD (LP) 12
72	Rare Earth SRESP 301	IN CONCERT (2-LP, satchel sleeve) 15
73	Rare Earth SRE 3008	WILLIE REMEMBERS (LP, gatefold sleeve) 12
73	Rare Earth SRE 3010	MA (LP) 12

RASCALS

68	Atlantic 584 182	A Beautiful Morning/Rainy Day 6
68	Atlantic 584 210	People Got To Be Free/My World 5
69	Atlantic 584 255	Heaven/Baby I'm Blue 5
69	Atlantic 584 274	See/Away Away 5
69	Atlantic 584 292	Carry Me Back/Real Thing 5
70	Atlantic 584 307	Hold On/I Believe 5
70	Atlantic 2091 029	Glory, Glory/You Don't Know 5
71	CBS 7363	Love Me/Happy Song 5
71	CBS 7672	Lucky Day/Love Letter 5
68	Atlantic 587/588 098	ONCE UPON A DREAM (LP) 18
68	Atlantic 587/588 120	TIME PEACE — RASCALS' GREATEST HITS (LP) 15
69	Atlantic 588 183	FREEDOM SUITE (LP) 15
70	Atlantic 588 210	SEE (LP) 12
71	Atlantic 2400 113	SEARCH AND NEARNESS (LP) 15
72	CBS 64756	THE ISLAND OF REAL (LP) 12
	(see also Young Rascals)	

RENATO RASCEL

60	RCA RCA 1177	Romantica/Dimmelo Con Un Fiore 10

RASPBERRIES

72	Capitol CL 15718	I Don't Want To Say Goodbye/Rock And Roll Mama 5
72	Capitol CL 15730	Go All The Way/With You In My Life 5
73	Capitol CL 15740	I Wanna Be With You/Goin' Nowhere Tonight 5
74	Capitol CL 15801	Overnight Sensation/Hands On You 5
72	Capitol E-ST 11036	THE RASPBERRIES (LP) 15
72	Capitol E-ST 11123	FRESH RASPBERRIES (LP) 15
73	Capitol E-ST 11220	SIDE THREE (LP) 15
74	Capitol E-ST 11329	STARTING OVER (LP) 12
	(see also Choir)	

RAT & WHALE

80	Rewind REWIND 5	Wheels On Fire/Wheels On Fire (Long Version) (p/s) 5
	(see also Alternative TV, Rat Scabies)	

BASIL RATHBONE

60s	Caedmon TC 1028	EDGAR ALLAN POE (LP) 15

RATIO

70	Big Chief BC 102	Let There Be Peace In The World/Pharaoh's Walk 6

ARMAN RATIP

73	Regal Zono. SLRZ 1038	THE SPY FROM ISTANBUL (LP) 25

RATS

64	Oak RGJ 145	Spoonful (1-sided, some with foldout p/s) 250/150
65	Columbia DB 7483	Spoonful/I've Got My Eyes On You Baby 90
65	Columbia DB 7607	I Gotta See My Baby Everyday/Headin' Back (To New Orleans) 50
95	Tenth Planet TP	THE RISE AND FALL OF BERNIE GRIPPLESTONE &
		THE SPIDERS FROM HULL (LP, gatefold sleeve, 1,000 only) 15
	(see also Beat Boys, Mark Peters; the above singles do not feature Mick Ronson)	

RATS

64	Oriole CB 1967	Parchman Farm/Every Day I Have The Blues 90
65	CBS 201740	Sack Of Woe/Gimme That Wine 60

RATS

74	Goodear EARLH 5003	FIRST (LP) 15
	(see also World of Oz)	

RATT
85	Atlantic A 9546P	Lay It Down/Got Me On The Line (shaped picture disc)	6
86	Atlantic A 9502P	You're In Love/Between The Eyes (shaped picture disc)	8

RATTLES
63	Philips BF 1277	The Stomp/Zip A Dee Doo Dah	10
64	Decca F 11873	Bye Bye Johnny/Roll Over Beethoven	15
64	Decca F 11936	Tell Me What I Can Do/Sunbeam At The Sky	10
65	Fontana TF 618	Come On And Sing/Candy To Me	10
66	Fontana TF 724	Say All Right/Love Of My Life	10
70	Decca F 23058	The Witch/Geraldine	5
71	Decca F 23119	You Can't Have Sunshine Every Day/Where Is The Friend?	5
71	Decca F 13243	Devil's On The Loose/I Know You Don't Know	5
64	Decca DFE 8568	TEENBEAT FROM THE STAR CLUB HAMBURG (EP)	100
64	Philips BL 7614	TWIST AT THE STAR CLUB HAMBURG (LP)	75
67	Mercury MG 1127	GREATEST HITS (LP)	25
71	Decca SKL-R 5088	THE RATTLES (LP)	18

(see also Wonderland)

CARL RAVAZZA
51	HMV B 10202	Rock, Rock, Rock/Like A Dream (78)	12

CHRIS RAVEL & RAVERS
63	Decca F 11696	I Do/Don't You Dig This Kind Of Beat	12

(see also Chris Andrews)

RAVEN
70	CBS 5043	Children At Our Feet/Here Comes A Truck	5

RAVEN
80	Neat NEAT 06	Don't Need Your Money/Wiped Out (p/s)	8
81	Neat NEAT 11	Hard Ride/Crazy World (p/s)	7
82	Neat NEAT 15	Crash Bang Wallop (no p/s)	5
82	Neat NEAT 15	CRASH BANG WALLOP (12" EP, mauve splattered vinyl)	12
83	Neat NEAT 28	Break The Chain/Ballad Of Marshall (p/s)	5
83	Neat NEAT 29P	Born To Be Wild/Inquisitor (with Udo Dirkschneider) (picture disc)	6
83	Neat NEAT 2912	Break The Chain/Born To Be Wild/Inquisitor (with Udo Dirkschneider) (12", p/s)	8
81	Neat NEAT 1001	ROCK UNTIL YOU DROP (LP, with lyric insert)	15
81	Neat NEAT 1004	WIPED OUT (LP)	12
83	Neat NEATP 1001	ROCK UNTIL YOU DROP (LP, reissue, picture disc)	15
83	Neat NEAT 1011	ALL FOR ONE (LP)	12

JON RAVEN
70s	Broadside	HARVEST (LP, with book)	15
71	Argo ZFB 29	KATE OF COALBROOKDALE (LP, as Jon & Mike Raven with Jean Ward)	25
73	Trailer LER 2083	SONGS OF A CHANGING WORLD (LP, with Nic Jones & Tony Rose, red label with insert)	25
76	Broadside BRO 118	THE ENGLISH CANALS (LP, with John Kirkpatrick & Sue Harris)	12

(see also Halliard, Black Country Three, John Kirkpatrick)

SIMON RAVEN
66	Piccadilly 7N 35301	I Wonder If She Remembers Me/Sea Of Love	40

RAVENS (U.S.)
53	Oriole CB 1148	Rock Me All Night Long/Write Me One Sweet Letter (with Jimmy Ricks) (78)	35
53	Oriole CB 1149	Begin The Beguine/Looking For My Baby (with Jimmy Ricks) (78)	35
53	Oriole CB 1258	Who'll Be The Fool?/Rough Ridin' (with Jimmy Ricks) (78)	35

RAVENS
63	Oriole CB 1910	I Just Wanna Hear You Say/Send Me A Letter	12

RAVENS ROCK GROUP
61	Pye International 7N 25077	The Ghoul Friend/Career Girl	12

RAVE ONS
60s	Sounds Good MT 103	She's A Spoon/Keep Wrong	75

RAVERS
69	Upsetter US 312	Badam Bam/UPSETTERS: Medical Operation	8

RAW DEAL
81	White Witch WIT 701	Out Of My Head/In The Mood (no p/s)	125
81	Neat NEAT 12	Lonewolf/Take The Sky (p/s)	6

RAW DEAL
95	Mental Disorder MAD 666	THE LEGENDARY RAW DEAL (10" LP)	12

PETER RAWES
87	Official OFFA 5	Why Should I Ask Her To Stay?/Theme From Shark/Theme From Forever (with Jet Harris) (p/s)	4

(see also Jet Harris)

RAW HERBS
86	Medium Cool MC 002	Old Joe/That's How It Is (1-sided flexidisc in card sleeve with stuck-on prints, 2 different colour sleeves, 33rpm)	7
87	Medium Cool MC 003	She's A Nurse But She's Alright/So Wired! (p/s)	5
87	Medium Cool MC 006	Don't Bury Me Yet/I'm Falling (p/s)	4
87	Medium Cool MC 006T	Don't Bury Me Yet/I'm Falling/In My Bones (12", p/s)	7

RAW MATERIAL
69	Evolution E 2441	Time And Illusion/Bobo's Party	30
70	Evolution E 2445	Hi There Hallelujah/Days Of The Fighting Cock	25
71	RCA Neon NE 1002	Ride On Pony/Religion	15

RAW MATERIAL

70	Evolution Z 1006	RAW MATERIAL (LP)	175
71	RCA Neon NE 8	TIME IS (LP)	140

(see also Shoot)

LOU RAWLS

65	Capitol CL 15398	Three O'Clock In The Morning/Nothing Really Feels The Same	5
66	Capitol CL 15465	Love Is A Hurtin' Thing/Memory Lane	6
67	Capitol CL 15488	You Can Bring Me All Your Heartaches/A Woman Who's A Woman	5
67	Capitol CL 15499	Dead End Street/Yes It Hurts Doesn't It	6
67	Capitol CL 15507	Show Business/When Loves Goes Wrong	5
67	Capitol CL 15515	Hard To Get Thing Called Love/(How Do You Say) I Don't Love You Anymore	6
67	Capitol CL 15522	Little Drummer Boy/Child With A Toy	5
68	Capitol CL 15533	My Ancestors/Evil Woman	5
68	Capitol CL 15548	You're Good For Me/Soul Serenade	6
68	Capitol CL 15560	Down Here On The Ground/I'm Satisfied	5
69	Capitol CL 15583	It's You/Sweet Charity	5
69	Capitol CL 15611	Your Good Thing (Is About To End)/Season Of The Witch	5
70	Capitol CL 15630	You've Made Me So Very Happy/Let's Burn Down The Cornfield	5
74	Bell BLL 1390	She's Gone/Hourglass	5
63	Capitol EAP-1 20646	LOST AND LOOKIN' (EP)	40
65	Capitol T 1824	BLACK AND BLUE (LP)	18
66	Capitol (S)T 2459	LIVE (LP)	18
67	Capitol (S)T 2566	SOULIN' (LP)	18
67	Capitol (S)T 2632	CARRYIN' ON! (LP)	15
68	Capitol (S)T 2864	FEELIN' GOOD (LP)	15
69	Capitol ST 2927	YOU'RE GOOD FOR ME (LP)	15
71	MGM 2315 054	NATURAL MAN (LP)	12

CLYDE RAY

57	Columbia DB 3875	Follow Me/Steady As A Rock	6
57	Columbia DB 3875	Follow Me/Steady As A Rock (78)	10
58	Columbia DB 4106	Locked In The Arms Of Love/I'm Not Afraid Anymore	6
58	Columbia DB 4106	Locked In The Arms Of Love/I'm Not Afraid Anymore (78)	8

DIANE RAY

63	Mercury AMT 1209	Please Don't Talk To The Lifeguard/That's All I Want From You	7

FROGGIE RAY

71	Big BG 313	Uncle Charlie/Party Version	10
71	Big BG 314	Half Moon/RUPIE EDWARDS ALL STARS: Full Moon	6

JAMES RAY

62	Pye International 7N 25126	If You Gotta Make A Fool Of Somebody/It's Been A Drag	12
62	Pye International 7N 25147	Itty Bitty Pieces/You Remember The Face	10

JAMES RAY & PERFORMANCE

86	Merciful Release MRAY 52R	Mexico Sundown Blues (Edit)/(Instrumental) (p/s, promo only)	8
86	Merciful Release MRAY 52	Mexico Sundown Blues/Edie Sedgwick (12", p/s)	8
87	Merciful Release MRAY 38	Texas/Mountain Voices (p/s)	4
87	Merciful Release MRAY 38/T	Texas/Mountain Voices/Johnny Goodbye (12", p/s)	7
80s	Merciful Release MRAY 101	WITHOUT CONSCIENCE (12", p/s, with flexidisc "Live In Leeds")	7

(see also Sisterhood)

JOHNNIE RAY

78s

52	Columbia DB 2995	Cry (with Four Lads)/The Little White Cloud That Cried (78)	8
55	Philips PB 449	Flip, Flop And Fly/Thine Eyes Are As The Eyes Of A Dove (78)	8
57	Philips PB 683	So Long/I Miss You So (78)	8
57	Philips PB 686	Yes, Tonight, Josephine/No Wedding Today (78)	8
57	Philips PB 721	Build Your Love (On A Strong Foundation)/Street Of Memories (78)	8
57	Philips PB 762	Pink Sweater Angel/Texas Tambourine (78)	8
58	Philips PB 785	Miss Me Just A Little/Soliloquy Of A Fool (78)	8
58	Philips PB 808	Strollin' Girl/Plant A Little Seed (78)	8
58	Philips PB 829	Lonely For A Letter/Endlessly (78)	8
58	Philips PB 849	Up Until Now/No Regrets (78)	10
58	Philips PB 884	What More Can I Say/You're The One Who Knows (78)	12
59	Philips PB 901	When's Your Birthday, Baby/ One Man's Love Song Is Another Man's Blues (78)	20
59	Philips PB 918	Call Me Yours/Here And Now (78)	30
59	Philips PB 952	I'll Never Fall In Love Again/You're All That I Live For (78)	40

SINGLES

53	Columbia SCM 5015	Walkin' My Baby Back Home/The Lady Drinks Champagne (B-side with Four Lads)	35
53	Columbia SCM 5033	Mama Says, Pa Says/A Full Time Job (with Doris Day)	25
53	Columbia SCM 5041	Whiskey And Gin/Tell The Lady I Said Goodbye	45
53	Columbia SCM 5074	Please Don't Talk About Me When I'm Gone/Coffee And Cigarettes (B-side with Four Lads)	35
54	Columbia SCM 5111	Nobody's Sweetheart/I Can't Escape From You	25
54	Columbia SCM 5122	She Didn't Say Nothin' At All/I'm Just A Shadow Of Myself	25
57	Philips JK 1004	You Don't Owe Me A Thing/Look Homeward, Angel (jukebox issue)	30
57	Philips JK 1011	So Long/I Miss You So (jukebox issue)	25
57	Philips JK 1016	Yes, Tonight, Josephine/No Wedding Today (jukebox issue)	30
57	Philips JK 1025	Build Your Love (On A Strong Foundation)/Street Of Memories (jukebox issue)	20
57	Philips JK 1033	Pink Sweater Angel/Texas Tambourine (jukebox issue)	25
58	Philips PB 785	Miss Me Just A Little/Soliloquy Of A Fool	8
58	Philips PB 808	Strollin' Girl/Plant A Little Seed	5
58	Philips PB 829	Lonely For A Letter/Endlessly	7
58	Philips PB 849	Up Until Now/No Regrets	7
58	Philips PB 884	What More Can I Say/You're The One Who Knows	7

59	Philips PB 901	When's Your Birthday, Baby/One Man's Love Song Is Another Man's Blues	7
59	Philips PB 918	Call Me Yours/Here And Now	5
59	Philips PB 952	I'll Never Fall In Love Again/You're All That I Live For	7
60	Philips PB 990	Wagon Wheels/When It's Springtime In The Rockies	7
60	Philips PB 1025	Before You/I'll Make You Mine	6
60	Philips PB 1047	Tell Me/Don't Leave Me Now	6
60	London HLA 9216	In The Heart Of A Fool/Let's Forget It Now	7
61	Philips PB 1126	An Ordinary Couple/Cool Water	5
61	United Artists POP 902	How Many Nights How Many Days/I'll Bring Along My Banjo	6
62	London HLG 9484	I Believe (with Timi Yuro)/TIMI YURO: Smile	12
63	Brunswick 05884	Lookout Chatanooga/After My Laughter Came Tears	5
69	Pye 7N 17691	Wise To The Ways Of The World/Since I Lost You Baby	6
69	Pye 7N 17760	Long And Lonely Nights/Brokenhearted Me, Evilhearted You	6

EPs

54	Columbia SEG 7511	JOHNNIE RAY (EP, company sleeve)	15
55	Philips BBE 12006	JOHNNIE RAY (EP)	15
57	Philips BBE 12115	WALKING AND CRYING (EP)	15
58	Philips BBE 12192	YES TONIGHT (EP)	18
58	Philips BBE 12217	T.V. SERIES (EP)	15
61	Philips BBE 12460	ON THE TRAIL (EP)	18

LPs

54	Philips BBR 8001	AT THE LONDON PALLADIUM (10" LP, red or blue sleeve)	35/25
55	Philips BBR 8062	THE VOICE OF YOUR CHOICE (10" LP)	25
57	Philips BBL 7148	THE BIG BEAT (LP)	30
58	Philips BBL 7254	AT THE DESERT INN — LAS VEGAS (LP)	30
58	Philips BBL 7264	SHOWCASE OF HITS (LP)	25
59	Philips BBL 7285	TILL MORNING (LP, also stereo SBBL 555)	30/35
59	Philips BBL 7348	A SINNER AM I (LP)	35
60	Philips BBL 7363	ON THE TRAIL (LP)	30
62	Liberty LBY 1020	JOHNNIE RAY (LP)	25
66	CBS Realm 52317	THE BEST OF JOHNNIE RAY (LP)	12

(see also Four Lads, Frankie Laine & Johnnie Ray, Timi Yuro)

RICARDO RAY
| 68 | Roulette RO 501 | Nitty Gritty/Mony Mony | 7 |

WADE RAY
| 63 | London HL 9700 | Burning Desire/Two Red Red Lips | 12 |

RAY & COLLUNEY
| 71 | Westwood WRS 001 | TYRANTS OF ENGLAND (LP) | 40 |

CHRIS(TINE) RAYBURN
63	Parlophone R 5098	Slow Loving Woman/Same Old Places	7
64	Parlophone R 5144	I've Cried My Last Tear/You Forgot To Say When	7
66	Parlophone R 5422	I Wanna Be In Love Again/Another Night Alone	7
68	Music Factory CUB 2	One Way Ticket/Photograph Of Love	6
69	Pye 7N 17679	Skip A Rope/Starlight (as Christine Rayburn)	6

MARGIE RAYBURN
56	Capitol CL 14532	The Wedding Song/That's The Chance I've Got To Take	8
57	London HLU 8515	I'm Available/If You Were	18
57	London HLU 8515	I'm Available/If You Were (78)	12
58	London HLU 8648	I Would/Alright, But It Won't Be Easy	18
58	London HLU 8648	I Would/Alright, But It Won't Be Easy (78)	20

ANTHONY RAYE
| 80 | Grapevine GRP 147 | Give Me One More Chance/Hold On To What You've Got | 6 |

SOL RAYE
| 63 | Oriole CB 1855 | Dear Michelle/I Love You Because | 7 |
| 67 | Deram DM 154 | While I'm Here/To Be With You | 6 |

BILLY RAYMOND
58	HMV POP 503	Making Love/I Would	6
58	HMV POP 503	Making Love/I Would (78)	10
58	HMV POP 526	One In Particular/Seven Daughters	6
58	HMV POP 526	One In Particular/Seven Daughters (78)	10
59	HMV POP 614	Charlie Is Their Darling/Loch Lomond	6

DANNY RAYMOND
| 71 | Big Shot BI 587 | Sister Big Stuff/BOY FRIDAY: Free Man | 6 |

LEE RAYMOND with COSTELLO SISTERS
| 55 | Brunswick 05438 | Foolishly Yours/Baby Darling | 12 |

MARK RAYMOND & CROWD
| 64 | Columbia DB 7308 | Girls/Remember Me To Julie | 6 |

TONY RAYMOND
59	Fontana H 213	Broken-Hearted Melody/This Earth Is Mine	6
59	Fontana H 213	Broken-Hearted Melody/This Earth Is Mine (78)	10
62	Oriole CB 1777	The Infant King/Because Of You	7

IVOR RAYMONDE & HIS ORCHESTRA
| 65 | Mercury MF 866 | Feelin' Fruggy/Grotty | 6 |

RAYMONDE'S MAGIC ORGAN
| 69 | Deram SML 1032 | SIXTIES HITS (LP) | 12 |

JULIE RAYNE
| 59 | HMV POP 665 | Waltz Me Around/Love Where Can You Be? | 8 |
| 60 | HMV POP 785 | Bim Bam Bom/One More Time | 8 |

Julie RAYNE

61	HMV POP 868	Green With Envy Purple With Passion/My First Romance	8
63	Windsor WPS 123	Faithfully/Free To Love	8
64	Windsor WPS 128	You Can't Come Back/Straight To Your Arms	8

LISA RAYNE
| 65 | Fontana TF 563 | Don't Ever Change/It Had To Be You | 7 |

MARTIN RAYNOR & SECRETS
| 65 | Columbia DB 7563 | Candy To Me/You're A Wonderful One | 20 |

(see also Secrets, Simon's Secrets, Clifford T. Ward)

MIKE RAYNOR & CONDORS
67	Decca F 12605	Turn Your Head/Lazy Day	6
67	Decca F 22690	Is She A Woman Now?/My Shy Serenade	5
68	Decca F 22790	Wonderful Day/On Top Of The World	5
69	Decca F 22864	Ob-La-Di, Ob-La-Da/I'm Goin' Down (as Mike Raynor & Sky; Danish export issue)	8

RAY O VACS
| 50 | Brunswick 04511 | Sentimental Me/Once Upon A Time (78) | 15 |

RAYS
| 57 | London HLU 8505 | Silhouettes/Daddy Cool | 30 |
| 57 | London HLU 8505 | Silhouettes/Daddy Cool (78) | 25 |

RAY'S PEOPLE
| 70 | Philips 6006 044 | Run To The Park/I Spy | 4 |

RAZORCUTS
86	Subway Org. SUBWAY 5	Big Pink Cake/I'll Still Be There (foldover p/s with insert, poly bag, 2,000 only)	8
86	Subway Org. SUBWAY 8	Sorry To Embarrass You/Summer In Your Heart (p/s, with insert, 2,000 only)	5
86	Subway Organisation SUBWAY 8T	Sorry To Embarrass You/Summer In Your Heart/Snowbirds Don't Fly/Mary Day (12", p/s, 2,000 only)	7
87	Sha La La BaBaBaBaBa 02	Sad Kaleidoscope/TALULAH GOSH: I Told You So (flexidisc p/s, 2,500 only)	6
87	Legend LEG 100/ LYN 18042	Sad Kaleidoscope/WOLFHOUNDS: Rats On A Raft (flexidisc, free with *The Legend* & other fanzines, 500 only)	4
80s	Caff CAFF 10	Sometimes I Worry About You/For Always/Sorry To Embarrass You/Music From The Big Pink (foldaround p/s with insert, 500 only)	12

(see also Cinematics, Red Chair Fadeaway)

RAZOR'S EDGE
| 66 | Stateside SS 532 | Let's Call It A Day, Girl/April | 12 |

CHRIS REA
74	Magnet MAG 10	So Much Love/Born To Lose (no p/s)	30
78	Magnet MAG 111	Fool (If You Think It's Over)/Midnight Love	4
78	Magnet MAG 121	Whatever Happened To Benny Santini?/Three Angels (red vinyl)	4
82	Magnet 12 MAG 233	Let It Loose/Sierra Sierra/Urban Samurai (12", p/s, with 7": "Fool (If You Think It's Over)"/"The Closer You Get"/"Diamonds"/"Guitar Street" [CHRIS 1])	7
84	Magnet MAGT 255	I Don't Know What It Is But I Love It/Mystery Man (12", p/s)	7
84	Magnet MAGT 259	Bombolini/Excerpts From Bombolini/True Love (12", p/s)	7
79	Magnet MAGL 5028	DELTICS (LP, blue vinyl, stickered sleeve)	10

REACTA
| 79 | Battery Operated WAC 1 | Stop The World/SUS (p/s) | 40 |

(see also Television Personalities)

REACTION
| 68 | President PT 208 | That Man/Falling In Love With You | 5 |

REACTION
| 70 | Columbia Blue Beat DB 119 | Oh Me, Oh My/RECO: It's Love | 10 |
| 70 | Attack ATT 8022 | You Yes You/CIMARONS: Be There | 8 |

(see also Ezz Reco, Joe Higgs)

REACTION
| 78 | Island WIP 6437 | I Can't Resist/I Am A Case (p/s) | 8 |

(see also Talk Talk)

AL READ
56	HMV POP 278	Though We Haven't Got The Money/What Is A Home?	7
59	HMV POP 575	That's Life/Our Maggie's Going To Get Married	6
59	HMV POP 575	That's Life/Our Maggie's Going To Get Married (78)	8
59	HMV 7EG 8440	SUCH IS LIFE (EP)	12

MIKE READ
| 78 | Satril SAT 131 | Are You Ready/London Town (p/s) | 4 |

(see also Just Plain Smith, Just Plain Jones, Micky Manchester, Trainspotters, Esprit De Corps)

PAT READER
60	Triumph RGM 1024	Ricky/Dear Daddy	30
62	Piccadilly 7N 35077	Cha Cha On The Moon/May Your Heart Stay Young Forever	40
63	Oriole CB 1903	Helpless/Lover's Lane	12

BERTICE READING
55	Parlophone R 4045	My One Sin (In Life)/Frankie And Johnnie (78)	10
55	Parlophone R 4057	Songs From "Jazz Train" Parts 1 & 2 (78, with Edric Connor)	10
55	Parlophone R 4057	Songs From "Jazz Train" Parts 3 & 4 (78)	10
55	Parlophone R 4064	Bessie Smith Blues/Everybody's Somebody's Fool (78)	10
57	Decca F 10965	No Flowers By Request/September In The Rain	8
58	Parlophone R 4462	Rock Baby Rock/It's A Boy	35
58	Parlophone R 4462	Rock Baby Rock/It's A Boy (78)	18
58	Parlophone R 4487	My Big Best Shoes/No More In Life	20
58	Parlophone R 4487	My Big Best Shoes/No More In Life (78)	12

RONALD REAGAN
81   Magic ABRA 1   THE WIT & WISDOM OF RONALD REAGAN (LP, completely silent!) 10

REALITY FROM DREAM
75   (no label) CP 109   REALITY FROM DREAM (LP, private pressing). 50

REAL KIDS
78   Bronze BRO 54   All Kindsa Girls/Common At Noon (p/s) 6
78   Bronze BRON 509   REAL KIDS (LP) 12

REALM
66   CBS 202044   Hard Time Loving You/Certain Kind Of Girl 18
    (see also Earl Preston & Realms)

REAL McCOY
67   Fontana TF 794   Show Me How You Milk A Cow/I Paid For My Laughs. 6
68   Pye 7N 17618   I Get So Excited/Somebody's Taken Maria Away 5
69   Pye 7N 17669   Quick Joey Small/Happiness Is Love 5
69   Pye 7N 17704   Round The Gum Tree/I Will. 5
69   Pye 7N 17772   Gitarzan/Anytime You Need Me 5
69   Pye 7N 17850   Many The Memories/She's Different, She's Beautiful 5
70   Marble Arch MAL 1251   THIS IS THE REAL McCOY (LP). 25
    (see also Tony Colton)

REAL THING
72   Bell BLL 1232   Vicious Circles (Parts 1 & 2) 4
    (see also Chants)

REBEL
81   Bridge House BHS 2   Rocka Shocka/Drift Away (p/s) 12
86   Flying Pig REBS 1   Valentino/Lonely Traveller (p/s, with free single). 12

REBEL ROUSERS
68   Fontana TF 973   Should I?/As I Look 25
    (see also Cliff Bennett & Rebel Rousers, Soul Sounds)

REBELS (U.K.)
67   Page One POF 017   Hard To Love You/Call Me. 15

REBELS (Jamaica)
70   Bullet BU 440   Nice Grind/SIDNEY ALL STARS: Nice Grind — Version 6
70   Trojan TR 7779   It's All In The Game/Easy Come. 12
    (see also The Pioneers)

REBOUNDS
64   Fontana TF 461   Help Me/The World Is Mine 15

REBS
58   Capitol CL 14932   Bunky/Renegade 8

RECO
69   Downtown DT 417   Quando Quando/Reg 'A' Jeg (as Reco & Rudies). 10
69   Jackpot JP 710   Memory Of Don Drummond/THE TOBIES: Resting. 8
69   Treasure Isle TI 7052   The Lion Speaks/ANDY CAPP: Pop A Top. 8
69   Pama ECO 14   RECO IN REGGAE LAND (LP) 40
    (see also Reaction, Don Reco, Rico Rodriguez, Father Sketto, Joe Monsano, Slim Smith, Laurel Aitken)

DON RECO
71   Big Shot BI 597   Waterloo Rock/LLOYD'S ALL STARS: Walls Soul 6
    (see also U Roy Junior)

EZZ RECO & LAUNCHERS
64   Columbia DB 7217   King Of Kings/Blue Beat Dance. 10
64   Columbia DB 7222   Little Girl/The Bluest Beat 10
64   Columbia DB 7290   Please Come Back/At A Party 10
64   Columbia SEG 8326   JAMAICAN BLUE BEAT (EP) 35
    (see also Reaction)

RECORD PLAYERS
78   Wreckord WRECK 001   DOUBLE C SIDE (EP, label also listed as Aerco AERO 1104) 7
80   Wreckord WRECK 002   Give An Inch/Squirming In The Vermin By The Bonny Banks Of Clyde/
                                                 67/Parasite (p/s) 6

RECORDS
79   Virgin V 2122   SHADES IN BED (LP, with bonus 12" EP "High Heels") 10

RED
83   Jigsaw SAW 2   RED (LP, private pressing). 25

TAMPA RED
65   RCA Victor RCX 7160   RHYTHM AND BLUES VOL. 3 (EP). 22
60s   Memory TR 1   TAMPA RED (LP) 30

TAMPA RED & GEORGIA TOM
59   Collector JE 13   MALE BLUES NO. 2 (EP) 15

RED ALERT
80   Guardian GM-RA/B 61   BORDER GUARDS (EP) 60
82   No Future OI 5   In Britain/Screaming At The Nation/Murder Missile (p/s) 10
82   No Future OI 13   Take No Prisoners/Empire Of Crime/Sell Out (p/s) 10
83   No Future OI 20   City Invasion/Negative Reaction (p/s) 8
83   No Future OI 27   THERE'S A GUITAR BURNING (12" EP) 15
83   No Future PUNK 5   WE'VE GOT THE POWER (LP, with inner) 15

RED ALERT
82   Steel City AJS7R   Run To Ground (no p/s) 10

MINT VALUE £

OTIS REDDING

RED ALLIGATOR

OTIS REDDING
SINGLES

64	London HLK 9833	Pain In My Heart/Something Is Worrying Me	18
64	London HLK 9876	Come To Me/Don't Leave Me This Way	18
65	Atlantic AT 4024	Mr Pitiful/That's How Strong My Love Is	12
65	Sue WI 362	Shout Bamalama/Fat Girl	20
65	Atlantic AT 4029	I've Been Loving You Too Long/Winter Wonderland (unissued, demos only)	40+
65	Atlantic AT 4039	Respect/I've Been Loving You Too Long	10
65	Atlantic AT 4050	My Girl/Down In The Valley	8
66	Atlantic AT 4080	(I Can't Get No) Satisfaction/Any Ole Way	7
66	Atlantic 584 019	My Lover's Prayer/Don't Mess With Cupid	6
66	Atlantic 584 030	I Can't Turn You Loose/Just One More Day	6
66	Atlantic 584 049	Fa-Fa-Fa-Fa-Fa (Sad Song)/Good To Me	6
67	Atlantic 584 070	Try A Little Tenderness/I'm Sick Y'all	6
67	Atlantic 584 091	Respect/These Arms Of Mine	5
67	Atlantic 584 092	My Girl/Mr Pitiful	6
67	Stax 601 005	Day Tripper/Shake (dark blue labels, later copies with light blue labels)	8/5
67	Stax 601 007	Let Me Come On Home/I Love You More Than Words Can Say (dark blue labels, later copies with light blue labels)	8/5
67	Stax 601 011	Shake (live)/634-5789 (live)	7
67	Stax 601 017	The Glory Of Love/I'm Coming Home	6
67	Stax 601 027	(I Can't Get No) Satisfaction/I've Been Loving You Too Long	6
68	Stax 601 031	(Sittin' On) The Dock Of The Bay/My Sweet Lorene	6
68	Stax 601 040	The Happy Song/Open The Door	5
68	Pye International 7N 25463	She's All Right/Gama Lama	8
68	Atlantic 584 199	Hard To Handle/Amen	5
68	Atlantic 584 220	Champagne And Wine/I've Got Dreams To Remember	6
68	Atlantic 584 234	Papa's Got A Brand New Bag/Direct Me	6
69	Atlantic 584 249	A Lover's Question/You Made A Man Out Of Me	5
69	Atco 226 001	Love Man/That's How Strong My Love Is	6
69	Atco 226 002	Free Me/Higher And Higher	6
69	Evolution E 2442	She's All Right/Tuff Enuff	8
70	Atco 226 012	Look At The Girl/That's A Good Idea	5
70	Atco 2091 020	Wonderful World/Security	5
71	Atlantic 2091 062	I've Been Loving You Too Long/Try A Little Tenderness	5
71	Atlantic 2091 112	(Sittin' On) The Dock Of The Bay/Respect/Mr Pitiful (reissue)	5
72	Atlantic K 10206	White Christmas/Merry Christmas, Baby	5

EP

| 66 | Sue IEP 710 | EARLY OTIS REDDING (EP) | 80 |

LPs

65	Atlantic ATL 5029	THE GREAT OTIS REDDING SINGS SOUL BALLADS (LP)	45
66	Atlantic ATL 5041	OTIS BLUE: OTIS REDDING SINGS SOUL (LP)	40
66	Atlantic 587 011	THE SOUL ALBUM (LP)	25
66	Atlantic 587 035	THE GREAT OTIS REDDING SINGS SOUL BALLADS (LP, reissue)	18
66	Atlantic 587/588 036	OTIS BLUE: OTIS REDDING SINGS SOUL (LP, reissue, mono/stereo)	18
67	Atlantic 587/588 050	THE OTIS REDDING DICTIONARY OF SOUL (LP)	25
67	Atlantic 587 042	PAIN IN MY HEART (LP)	18
67	Stax VOLT 418	THE HISTORY OF OTIS REDDING (LP)	18
68	Stax 589 016	OTIS REDDING IN EUROPE (LP)	18
68	Stax 230 001/231 001	THE DOCK OF THE BAY (LP)	18
68	Atlantic 587/588 113	THE IMMORTAL OTIS REDDING (LP)	18
68	Atlantic 587/588 148	OTIS REDDING AT THE WHISKEY A GO GO, LOS ANGELES (LP)	18
69	Atco 228 001	THE HISTORY OF OTIS REDDING (LP, reissue)	12
69	Atco 228 022	THE DOCK OF THE BAY (LP, reissue)	12
69	Atco 228 017	OTIS REDDING LIVE IN EUROPE (LP, reissue)	12
69	Atco 228 025	LOVE MAN (LP)	15
71	Atco 2400 018	TELL THE TRUTH (LP)	15
72	Atlantic K 60015	THE BEST OF OTIS REDDING (LP)	12

OTIS REDDING & CARLA THOMAS

67	Stax 601 012	Tramp/Oooh Carla, Oooh Otis (with Carla Thomas)	6
67	Stax 601 021	Knock On Wood/Let Me Be Good To You	5
68	Stax 601 033	Lovey Dovey/OTIS REDDING: New Year's Resolution	5
67	Stax 589 007	THE KING AND QUEEN OF SOUL (LP)	25

(see also Carla Thomas)

RED DIRT

| 70 | Fontana STL 5540 | RED DIRT (LP) | 400 |

HELEN REDDY

| 78 | Capitol CL 16007 | Poor Little Fool/We'll Sing In The Sunshine | 5 |

EMMA REDE

| 67 | Columbia DB 8136 | Just Like A Man/I Gotta Be With You | 12 |

(see also Jacky, Jackie Lee, Jackie & Raindrops, Raindrops)

TEDDY REDELL

| 60 | London HLK 9140 | Judy/Can't You See | 60 |

MICHAEL REDGRAVE

| 50 | Topic TRC 12 | A New World Will Be Born/ALAN KANE: Me Without You (78) | 12 |

VANESSA REDGRAVE

| 64 | Topic STOP 111 | Hanging On A Tree/Where Have All The Flowers Gone (some in title sleeve) | 8/5 |

RED HERRING

| 73 | GMS GMS 007 | I'm A Gambler/Working Class Man | 4 |

(see Pete Dello, Lace, Leah)

MINT VALUE £

RED HOT CHILI PEPPERS
85	EMI America EA 205	Hollywood (Africa)/Never Mind (p/s)	10
85	EMI America 12EA 205	Hollywood (Africa) (Remix)/Hollywood	
		(Africa) (Dub Mix)/Never Mind (12", p/s)	12

RED HOUSE PAINTERS
93	4AD RHP 1 CD	I Am A Rock/New Jersey (CD, tracing paper p/s, promo only)	10

RED LETTERS
70s	Burning Bing CPS 025	SACRED VOICES EP (p/s)	50

RED LIGHTS
78	Free Range PF 5	Never Wanna Leave/Seventeen (p/s)	8

RED LONDON
83	Razor RZS 105	Sten Guns In Sunderland/This Is England/Soul Train/Revolution Times (p/s)	8

RED LORRY YELLOW LORRY
82	Red Rhino RED 20	Beating My Head/I'm Still Waiting (p/s)	6
83	Red Rhino RED 28	Take It All/Happy (p/s)	5
83	Red Rhino RED 39	He's Read/See The Fire (p/s)	4

(see also Mission)

ROY REDMOND
67	Warner Bros WB 2075	Good Day Sunshine/That Old Time Feeling	6

RED ONION JAZZ BABIES
60	Collector JE 19	RED ONION JAZZ BABIES (EP)...	8

(see also Louis Armstrong)

JEAN REDPATH
66	Bounty BY 6004	LOVE LILT AND LAUGHTER (LP)...	15
77	Trailer LER 2106	THERE WERE MINSTRELS (LP)...	12

RED RAGE
80	Flicknife FLS 203	Total Control/I Give You This (p/s)	40

RED RIVER BAND
70	Banana BA 35	I'm Gonna Use What I've Got/Shame Shame	7

REDSKINS
82	CNT CNT 007	Lev Bronstein/The Peasant Army (p/s)	12
83	CNT CNT 016	Lean On Me!/Unionize! (p/s)	7
83	CNT CNTX 016	Lean On Me! (Northern Mix)/Unionize! (Break Mix) (12", p/s).............	7
84	Decca F 1	Keep On Keepin' On!/Reds Strike The Blues! (p/s)......................	4
84	Decca FX 1	Keep On Keepin' On! (Die On Your Feet Mix)!/16 Tons (Coal Not Dole)/Reds	
		Strike The Blues! (12", with inner, some shrinkwrapped with free 7")	10/8
85	Decca FDP 2	Bring It Down! (This Insane Thing)/You Want It They've Got It/Turnin' Loose	
		(The Furious Flames)/Take No Heroes (live)/Go Get Organized (live)	
		(double pack, stickered gatefold p/s)	5
85	The Hit HOT 001	Kick Over The Statues (The Ramsey McKinnock Mix)/JESUS & MARY CHAIN:	
		Just Like Cindy/STYLE COUNCIL: Walls Come Tumbling Down (live)/	
		SIMPLY RED: Every Bit Of Me (p/s, freebie EP with *The Hit* mag, issue 1)......	8/4
86	Decca FXT 3	THE POWER IS YOURS ... THE BOOTLEG EXCERPTS PROPAGANDA EP	
		(10", 33rpm, stickered plain black die-cut sleeve)	5
86	Decca FXT 4	It Can Be Done/Let's Make It Work! (live)/K.O.! K.O.! (live)/A Plateful Of	
		Hateful (10" 'Russian Import', no'd stickered plain white die-cut sleeve)	7
86	Jamming!/London J 1	You Want It They've Got It (Red Soul & Fury Unleased Mix)/THEN JERICO:	
		The Big Sweep/DAINTEES: Watch The Running Water/COMMUNARDS:	
		Breadline Britain (free with *Jamming!* magazine, no p/s)	8/6

RED SQUARES
67	Columbia DB 8160	Mountain's High/Pity Me	6
67	Columbia DB 8257	True Love Story/Lollipop	6

RED TELEVISION
71	Brecht Times	RED TELEVISION (LP, private pressing with insert)	200

REDUCERS
78	Vibes XP 1/VR 001	Things Go Wrong/We Are Normal (p/s).................................	30
79	Vibes VR 003	Man With A Gun/Vengeance/Can't Stop Now (p/s)	20

MIKE REDWAY
63	Embassy WB 549	That's What Love Will Do/TYPHOONS: Please Please Me	5
63	Embassy WB 579	Just Like Eddie/Bad To Me..	5
63	Embassy WB 589	I Want To Stay Here/TYPHOONS: Surf City.............................	5
63	Embassy WB 604	It's Almost Tomorrow/TYPHOONS: This Boy.............................	5
64	Oriole CB 1948	Many People/It's So Funny I Could Cry.................................	6
65	CBS 201755	Darling Take Me Back/That's The Way Love Goes.......................	7
65	CBS 202017	Magic Rocking Chair/When You Go	5
66	CBS 202092	One Day/Let Me Be The Someone	5
67	Deram DM 124	Have No Fear, Bond Is Here (Casino Royale)/My Poem For You	8
67	Deram DM 157	Don't Speak Of Me/Sometimes I Remember	5

(see also Rod McKuen, Typhoons, Bud Ashton)

REDWOODS
62	Columbia DB 4859	Please Mr Scientist/Where You Used To Be.............................	15

DIZZY REECE QUINTET
56	Tempo A 140	Chorus/Basie Line	5
58	Tempo EXA 84	A VARIATION ON MONK (EP)..	250
59	Tempo EXA 86	NOWHERE TO GO (EP)..	150
59	Tempo EXA 89	ON THE SCENE (EP)	25
55	Tempo LAP 3	A NEW STAR... (10" LP)..	15

| 57 | Tempo TAP 9 | PROGRESS REPORT (LP) .... 550 |
| 58 | Esquire 32 185 | ASIA MINOR (LP) .... 45 |

(see also Victor Feldman, Ronnie Scott)

CHUCK REED

57	Brunswick 05646	Whispering Heart/Another Love Has Ended 10
57	Brunswick 05646	Whispering Heart/Another Love Has Ended (78) 8
58	Columbia DB 4113	No School Tomorrow/Let's Put Our Hearts Together 15
58	Columbia DB 4113	No School Tomorrow/Let's Put Our Hearts Together (78) 12
62	Stateside SS 108	Just Plain Hurt/Talking No Trash 10

DEAN REED

| 59 | Capitol CL 14986 | The Search/Annabelle .... 6 |
| 59 | Capitol CL 15030 | I Kissed A Queen/A Pair Of Scissors (And A Pot Of Glue)......... 6 |

DENNY REED

| 61 | London HLK 9274 | A Teenager Feels It Too/Hot Water .... 15 |

JERRY REED

58	Capitol CL 14851	Bessie Baby/Too Young To Be Blue 220
58	Capitol CL 14851	Bessie Baby/Too Young To Be Blue (78) 70
69	RCA RCA 1798	Oh What A Woman/Claw 5
70	RCA RCA 2025	Georgia Sunshine/Singing '69 5
71	RCA RCA 2063	Amos Moses/The Preacher And The Bear......................... 5
69	RCA SF 8006	ALABAMA WILD MAN (LP) 12

JIMMY REED

60	Top Rank JAR 333	Baby What You Want Me To Do/Caress Me Baby................. 18
60	Top Rank JAR 394	Found Love/Where Can You Be................................. 15
60	Top Rank JAR 533	Hush-Hush/Going By The River................................. 15
63	Stateside SS 205	Shame Shame Shame/Let's Get Together 12
64	Stateside SS 330	Shame Shame Shame/Let's Get Together (reissue) 6
66	Sue WI 4004	Odds And Ends/Going By The River Pt. II (B-side actually Pt. I) ... 20
67	HMV POP 1579	Two Ways To Skin A Cat/Got Nowhere To Go 10
64	Stateside SE 1016	BLUES OF JIMMY REED (EP) 25
64	Stateside SE 1026	I'M JIMMY REED (EP)... 25
62	Stateside SL 10012	JIMMY REED AT CARNEGIE HALL (LP) 35
64	Stateside SL 10055	JUST JIMMY REED (LP)....................................... 35
64	Stateside SL 10069	SINGS THE BEST OF THE BLUES (LP) 25
64	Stateside SL 10086	PLAYS 12-STRING GUITAR BLUES (LP) 25
64	Stateside SL 10091	THE BOSS MAN OF THE BLUES (LP) 25
65	Fontana 688 514 ZL	THINGS AIN'T WHAT THEY USED TO BE (LP)..................... 20
67	HMV CLP/CSD 3611	THE NEW JIMMY REED (LP) 20
68	Stateside S(S)L 10221	SOULIN' (LP) 20
69	Action ACLP 6011	DOWN IN VIRGINIA (LP)....................................... 30
69	Joy JOY(S) 111	THE LEGEND — THE MAN (LP).................................. 12
69	Joy JOY(S) 120	AT CARNEGIE HALL (LP, reissue)............................... 12
69	Joy JOYS 127	AT SOUL CITY (LP) 12
69	Joy JOYS 132	PLAYS THE 12-STRING GUITAR BLUES (LP, reissue)............... 12
69	Joy JOYS 141	ROCKIN' WITH REED (LP)...................................... 12
69	Joy JOYS 146	JUST JIMMY REED (LP, reissue) 12
69	Joy JOYS 151	JIMMY REED SINGS THE BEST OF THE BLUES (LP)............... 12
69	Joy JOYS 155	THE BEST OF JIMMY REED (LP)................................ 12
76	DJM DJD 28033	BIG BOSS MAN (MEMORIAL ALBUM NO. 1) (2-LP, gatefold sleeve) ... 15

JIMMY REED & EDDIE TAYLOR

| 60s | XX MIN 704 | JIMMY REED & EDDIE TAYLOR (EP)............................. 15 |

JOE REED

| 71 | Dawn DNS 1012 | Ain't That A Shame/Follow Me.................................. 5 |

LES REED

62	Piccadilly 7N 35080	Theme From Dr. Finlay's Casebook/The Saint (as Les Reed Strings) 6
64	Fontana TF 455	Spanish Armada/Madrid (as Les Reed Combo) 5
70	Chapter One CH 126	Man Of Action/Madrid (as Les Reed Orchestra) 5
72	Chaoter One SCH 189	Man Of Action/Lest We Forget (as Les Reed Orchestra) 5

LOU REED

72	RCA RCA 2240	I Can't Stand It (unissued)
72	RCA RCA 2240	Walk And Talk It/Wild Child 8
73	RCA RCA 2318	Vicious/Satellite Of Love 8
73	MGM 2006 283	Candy Says/I'm Waiting For The Man/Run Run Run (with Velvet Underground) ... 8
74	RCA APBO 0221	Caroline Says (Parts 1 & 2) 5
74	RCA APBO 0238	Sweet Jane/Lady Day... 5
74	RCA RCA 2467	Sally Can't Dance/Ennui 5
76	RCA RCA 2666	Charley's Girl/Nowhere At All 5
89	Sire W 7547CD	Dirty Blvd/Last Great American Whale/The Room (3" CD) 7
89	RCA PD 49453	Walk On The Wild Side/Satellite Of Love (3" CD, gatefold card sleeve) 7
72	RCA SF 8281	LOU REED (LP, orange label) 12
73	RCA RS 1002	BERLIN (LP, orange label with insert).......................... 12
75	RCA CPL 2 1101	METAL MACHINE MUSIC (2-LP, U.S. import with U.K. sticker) 30

(see also Velvet Underground)

LULU REED

| 55 | Parlophone CMSP 34 | Troubles On Your Mind/Bump On A Log (export issue) .... 30 |
| 55 | Parlophone DP 408 | Troubles On Your Mind/Bump On A Log (78, export issue) ...... 15 |

LULU REED & SYL JOHNSON

| 63 | Ember EMB EP 4535 | RHYTHM & BLUES BLUE BEAT STYLE (EP) .... 50 |

LULU REED & FREDDIE KING

| 63 | Ember EMB 4536 | LULA REED AND FREDDIE KING (EP)........................... 35 |

(see also Freddie King)

NANCY REED
53	London L 1179	You Never Tell Me You Love Me/It's Written All Over Your Face (78)	12

OLIVER REED
61	Decca F 11390	The Wild One/Lonely For A Girl	15
62	Piccadilly 7N 35037	Sometimes/Ecstasy	10

TAWNY REED
65	Pye 7N 15935	Needle In A Haystack/I've Got A Feeling	7
66	Pye 7N 17078	You Can't Take It Away/My Heart Cries	6

VIVIEN REED
68	Direction 58-3574	I Wanna Be Free/Yours Until Tomorrow	4
71	CBS 5422	Lean On Me/Missing You	4

WINSTON REED
72	Pama Supreme PS 365	Breakfast In Bed/RANNY WILLIAMS: Guitar Shuffle	5
73	Pama PM 863	Big Eight/RANNY WILLIAMS & CLASSICS: Big Eight – Version	5

REEF
95	Sony S2 XPS 273	Good Feeling (p/s, promo only)	8

VALA REEGAN & VALARONS
66	Atlantic 584 009	Fireman/Living In The Past	140

REEGS
89	Imaginary MIRAGE 006	See My Friends/Is There A Mother-In-Law In The Club/	
		The Savage Garden (12", blue or green p/s)	each 7

(see also Chameleons)

DELLA REESE
57	London HL 7024	I Cried For You (Now It's Your Turn To Cry Over Me)/And That Reminds Me	
		(export issue)	12
58	London HLJ 8687	You Gotta Love Everybody/I Wish	12
58	London HLJ 8687	You Gotta Love Everybody/I Wish (78)	15
59	London HLJ 8814	Sermonette/Dreams End At Dawn	10
59	London HLJ 8814	Sermonette/Dreams End At Dawn (78)	15
59	RCA RCA 1160	Not One Minute More/Soldier Won't You Marry Me	5
59	RCA RCA 1160	Not One Minute More/Soldier Won't You Marry Me (78)	25
60	RCA RCA 1185	Someday/Let's Get Away From It All	5
60	RCA RCA 1192	Everyday/There's No Two Ways About It	5
60	RCA RCA 1204	And Now/There's Nothing Like A Boy	5
64	RCA RCA 1407	Forbidden Games/If Ever I Would Leave You	5
66	HMV POP 1504	Home/Her Little Heart Went To Loveland	5
66	HMV POP 1553	It Was A Very Good Year/Solitary Woman	5
68	Stateside SS 2128	It Was A Very Good Year/I Had To Know My Way Around	5
72	Avco Embassy 6105 010	If It Feels Good, Do It/Good Lovin' (Makes It Right)	5
74	People PEO 106	Who Is She And What Is She To You/If Loving You Is Wrong	5
59	London LTZ-J 15163	THE HISTORY OF THE BLUES (LP)	20
60	RCA RD 27167/SF 5057	DELLA (LP)	15
61	RCA RD 27208/SF 5091	DELLA DELLA CHA-CHA-CHA (LP)	15
62	RCA RD 27234/SF 5112	SPECIAL DELIVERY (LP)	15
63	RCA Victor RD/SF 7508	ON STAGE (LP)	15
63	RCA Victor RD/SF 7584	WALTZ WITH ME, DELLA (LP)	12
64	RCA RD/SF 7628	AT BASIN STREET EAST (LP)	12
65	RCA RD 7695	MOODY (LP)	12
65	HMV CLP 1923	C'MON AND HEAR (LP, also stereo CSD 1636)	12
66	HMV CLP/CSD 3540	I LIKE IT LIKE DAT! (LP)	12
66	HMV CLP/CSD 3573	LIVE (LP, with Bill Doggett & others)	12
67	HMV CLP/CSD 3605	ONE MORE TIME! (LP)	12
68	Stateside S(S)L 10230	THE BEST OF DELLA REESE (LP)	12
68	Stateside S(S)L 10261	I GOTTA BE ME ... THIS TRIP OUT (LP)	12

TONY REESE
59	London HLJ 8987	Just About This Time Tomorrow/Lesson In Love	10
59	London HLJ 8987	Just About This Time Tomorrow/Lesson In Love (78)	20

DEL REEVES
65	United Artists UP 1092	Girl On The Billboard/Eyes Don't Come Crying To Me	6
66	United Artists UP 1122	Women Do Funny Things To Me/My Half Of Our Past	6
66	United Artists UP 1145	Gettin' Any Feed For Your Chickens/Plain As The Tears On My Face	6

EDDIE REEVES
62	London HL 9548	Cry Baby/Talk Talk	12

JIM REEVES
78s
54	London HL 8014	Bimbo/Gipsy Heart (78)	30
54	London HL 8030	Mexican Joe/I Could Cry (with Circle O Ranch Boys) (78)	30
54	London HL 8055	Butterfly Love/It's Hard To Love Just One (with String Band) (78)	30
54	London HL 8064	Echo Bonita/Then I'll Stop Loving You (with Louisiana Hayride Band) (78)	30
54	London HL 8105	Padre Of Old San Antone/Mother Went A-Walkin' (78)	20
55	London HL 8118	Penny Candy/I'll Follow You (with Louisiana Hayride Band) (78)	30
55	London HL 8159	Drinking Tequila/Red-Eyed And Rowdy (78)	40
55	London HLU 8185	Tahiti/Give Me One More Kiss (78)	30
56	London HLU 8351	The Wilder Your Heart Beats, The Sweeter You Love/	
		Where Does A Broken Heart Go (78)	30
57	RCA RCA 1005	Four Walls/I Know And You Know (78)	25
58	RCA RCA 1074	Blue Boy/Theme Of Love (78)	30
59	RCA RCA 1144	Partners/I'm Beginning To Forget You (78)	40
60	RCA RCA 1168	He'll Have To Go/In A Mansion Stands My Love (78)	60

SINGLES

54	London HL 8014	Bimbo/Gipsy Heart	180
54	London HL 8030	Mexican Joe/I Could Cry (with Circle O Ranch Boys)	180
54	London HL 8055	Butterfly Love/It's Hard To Love Just One (with String Band)	180
54	London HL 8064	Echo Bonita/Then I'll Stop Loving You (with Louisiana Hayride Band)	180
54	London HL 8105	Padre Of Old San Antone/Mother Went A-Walkin'	120
55	London HL 8118	Penny Candy/I'll Follow You (with Louisiana Hayride Band)	170
55	London HLU 8185	Tahiti/Give Me One More Kiss	170
55	London HL 8159	Drinking Tequila/Red-Eyed And Rowdy	240

(All the above 45s were issued with gold label print)

56	London HLU 8351	The Wilder Your Heart Beats, The Sweeter You Love/ Where Does A Broken Heart Go	175
57	RCA RCA 1005	Four Walls/I Know And You Know	30
58	RCA RCA 1074	Blue Boy/Theme Of Love	18
59	RCA RCA 1144	Partners/I'm Beginning To Forget You (triangular or round centre)	18/12
60	RCA RCA 1168	He'll Have To Go/In A Mansion Stands My Love	6
60	RCA RCA 1197	I'm Getting Better/I Know One	6
60	RCA RCA 1214	Am I Losing You/I Missed Me	6
61	RCA RCA 1223	Whispering Hope/I'd Like To Be	5
61	RCA RCA 1233	Danny Boy/The Blizzard	5
61	RCA RCA 1261	You're The Only Good Thing (That's Happened To Me)/ Oh, How I Miss You Tonight	5
62	RCA RCA 1293	Adios Amigo/Letter To My Heart	5
62	RCA RCA 1317	I'm Gonna Change Everything/Pride Goes Before A Fall	5
63	RCA RCA 1330	Missing Angel/Is This Me?	6
63	RCA RCA 1364	Guilty/Little Ole You	5
65	RCA RCA 1448	Don't Let Me Cross Over/The World You Left Behind	6

EPs

54	London RE-P 1015	THE BIMBO BOY (EP)	75
55	London RE-P 1033	THE BIMBO VOL. 2 (EP)	75

LPs

60	RCA RD 27176	HE'LL HAVE TO GO (LP)	18
61	RCA RD 27193	THE INTIMATE JIM REEVES (LP, also stereo SF 5079)	15/18
62	RCA Camden SDN 5100	THE COUNTRY SIDE OF JIM REEVES (LP, stereo [mono £8])	12
62	London HA-U 8015	BIMBO (LP)	20
62	RCA Victor SF 7521	A TOUCH OF VELVET (LP, stereo [mono £8])	12
63	RCA Victor SF 7541	GENTLEMAN JIM (LP, stereo [mono £8])	12
63	RCA Victor SF 7577	THE INTERNATIONAL JIM REEVES (LP, stereo [mono £8])	12
64	RCA Victor RD 7636	GOD BE WITH YOU (LP)	12
64	RCA Victor RD 7637	WE THANK THEE (LP)	12
65	RCA Victor SF 7639	MOONLIGHT AND ROSES (LP, stereo [mono £8])	12
65	RCA Victor RD 7663	TWELVE SONGS OF CHRISTMAS (LP)	12
66	RCA Victor RD 7666	THE BEST OF JIM REEVES (LP)	12
66	RCA Victor SF 7694	THE JIM REEVES WAY (LP, stereo [mono £8])	12
66	RCA Victor RD/SF 7781	KIMBERLEY JIM (LP, mono/stereo)	12/15
66	RCA Victor SF 7814	DISTANT DRUMS (LP, stereo [mono £8])	12
67	RCA Victor RD/SF 7906	YOURS SINCERELY, JIM REEVES (LP)	15

(All the above LPs were originally issued with black labels, later orange label reissues are worth around £6 each.)

69	RCA Victor RD/SF 7978	A TOUCH OF SADNESS (LP, mono/stereo)	12
69	RCA Victor RD/SF 8022	JIM REEVES AND SOME FRIENDS (LP)	12
69	RCA Victor RD/SF 8047	JIM REEVES 'ON STAGE' (LP)	12
71	RCA Victor SF 8146	MY CATHEDRAL (LP)	12
71	RCA Victor SF 8176	JIM REEVES WRITES YOU A RECORD (LP)	12
71	RCA Victor SF 8203	SOMETHING SPECIAL (LP)	12
72	RCA Victor SF 8258	MY FRIEND (LP)	12
72	RCA Victor SF 8303	MISSING YOU (LP)	15
74	RCA APL1 0537	I'D FIGHT THE WORLD (LP)	12
75	RCA SF 8444	SONGS OF LOVE (LP)	12
77	RCA PL 11224	I LOVE YOU BECAUSE (LP)	12
77	RCA PL 12309	IT'S NOTHIN' TO ME (LP)	12
78	RCA PL 12720	NASHVILLE '78 (LP)	12
79	RCA PL 13454	DON'T LET ME CROSS OVER (LP)	12

MARTHA REEVES & VANDELLAS
(see under Martha & Vandellas)

REFLECTION

68	Reflection RL 3015	THE PRESENT TENSE: SONGS OF SYDNEY CARTER (LP)	20

(see also Sounds Of Salvation)

REFLECTIONS (U.S.)

64	Stateside SS 294	(Just Like) Romeo & Juliet/Can't You Tell By The Look In My Eyes	30
65	Stateside SS 406	Poor Man's Son/Comin' At You	10
74	Tamla Motown TMG 907	(Just Like) Romeo & Juliet/Can't You Tell By The Look In My Eyes (reissue)	6
77	ABC ABC 4181	Like Adam And Eve/AUGUST & DENEEN: We Go Together	5
65	Stateside SE 1034	POOR MAN'S SON (EP)	50

REFLECTIONS (U.K.)

74	Purple PUR 124	Love And Affection/No More	7
75	Purple PUR 127	Moon Power/Little Star	7

REFLECTIONS (U.K.)

82	Cherry Red CHERRY 33	4 Countries/The Coroner And The Inquest (p/s)	4
82	Cherry Red BRED 22	SLUGS AND TOADS (LP)	10

(see also Alternative TV)

REFUGEE

74	Charisma CAS 1087	REFUGEE (LP)	15

(see also Nice, Yes, Patric Moraz)

MINT VALUE £

JOAN REGAN

54	Decca F 10362	Wait For Me, Darling (with Johnston Brothers)/Two Kinds Of Tears (gold or silver lettering)	25/20
54	Decca F 10373	If I Give My Heart To You/Faded Flowers	15
54	Decca F 10397	This Ole House/Can This Be Love?	12
55	Decca F 10432	Prize Of Gold/When You're In Love	15
55	Decca F 10474	Open Up Your Heart And Let The Love In (with Rusty Regan)/ If You Learn To Love Each Other	15
55	Decca F 10505	Danger! Heartbreak Ahead/Don't Be Afraid Of Love	10
55	Decca F 10521	Just Say You Love Her/Nobody Danced With Me	10
55	Decca F 10598	The Shepherd Boy/The Rose And The Flame	8
56	Decca F 10659	Love And Marriage/Cross Of Gold (Croce Di Oro)	12
56	Decca F 10710	Don't Take Me For Granted/The Boy With The Magic Guitar	7
56	Decca F 10742	Honestly/I'd Never Leave You Baby (B-side with Johnston Brothers)	7
56	Decca F 10757	Sweet Heartaches/Second Fiddle (with Ted Heath)	7
56	Decca F 10801	Gone/Make Me A Child Again	7
57	Decca F 10871	Nearer To Me/Cross My Ever-Loving Heart	6
57	Decca F 10911	Wonderful! Wonderful!/Speak For Yourself John	6
57	Decca F 10934	7½ Cents/Good Evening Friends (with Max Bygraves)	6
57	Decca F 10942	Soft Sands/Love Me To Pieces	6
58	Decca F 11009	I May Never Pass This Way Again/Breezing Along With The Breeze	6
58	HMV POP 555	Love Like Ours/Take Me In Your Arms	6
58	HMV POP 555	Love Like Ours/Take Me In Your Arms (78)	8
59	HMV POP 593	May You Always/Have You Ever Been Lonely?	5
59	HMV POP 593	May You Always/Have You Ever Been Lonely? (78)	10
59	Pye Nixa 7N 15238	Happy Anniversary/So Close To My Heart	5
59	Pye Nixa N 15238	Happy Anniversary/So Close To My Heart (78)	12
60	Pye 7N 15259	If Only You'd Be Mine/O Dio Mio	5
60	Pye 7N 15278	Papa Loves Mama/When You Know Someone Loves You	6
60	Pye 7N 15310	One Of The Lucky Ones/My Thanks To You	5
60	Pye 7N 15303	Must Be Santa/Will Santa Come To Shanty Town	5
61	Pye 7N 15367	We Who Are In Love/My Foolish Heart	5
61	Pye 7N 15400	Surprisin'/In The Arms Of My Love (some with p/s)	8/5
66	CBS 202100	Don't Talk To Me About Love/I'm No Toy	35
67	CBS 2657	No-One Beside Me/A Love So Fine	18
55	Decca DFE 6235	JOAN REGAN SUCCESSES (EP)	15
56	Decca DFE 6278	JOAN REGAN SUCCESSES VOL. 2 (EP)	15
54	Decca LF 1182	THE GIRL NEXT DOOR (10" LP)	25
56	Decca LK 4153	JUST JOAN (LP)	20

RUSS REGAN

59	Capitol CL 15084	Adults Only/Just The Two Of Us	4

TOMMY REGAN

64	Colpic PX 725	I'll Never Stop Loving You/This Time I'm Losing You	75

REGENTS (U.S.)

61	Columbia DB 4666	Barbara Ann/I'm So Lonely	18
61	Columbia DB 4694	Runaround/Laura My Darling	18

REGENTS (U.K.)

63	Oriole CB 1912	Bye Bye Johnny/Come Along	20

(see also Buddy Britten)

REGENTS (U.K.)

66	CBS 202247	Words/Worryin' Kind	25

REGENTS (U.K.)

79	Rialto TREB 111	7 Teen (Uncensored Version)/Hole In The Heart (p/s)	8

REGGAE BOYS

69	Amalgamated AMG 841	Me No Born Ya/The Wicked Must Survive	12
69	Amalgamated AMG 843	The Reggae Train/Dolly House On Fire	12
69	Gas GAS 135	Ba Ba/GLEN ADAMS: Power Cut	6
69	Unity UN 530	What You Gonna Do/HEDLEY BENNETT: Hot Coffee	6
70	Bullet BU 431	Pupa Live On Eye Top/Give Me Faith	6
70	Gas GAS 122	Phrases/Give Me Faith	6
70	Upsetter US 339	Hurry Up/Thanks We Get	10
70	Pressure Beat PR 5503	Walk By Day, Fly By Night/JOE GIBBS & DESTROYERS: Unknown Tongue	8

(see also Glen Adams, Alva Lewis, Upsetters)

REGGAE STRINGS

73	Trojan TRLS 54	REGGAE STRINGS (LP)	10

(see also Horace Faith)

AL REID

69	Blue Cat BS 161	Vietcong/MAX ROMEO: Me Want Man	10
69	Blue Cat BS 163	Darling/MAX ROMEO: It's Not The Way	10

LOU REICHNER BAND

80	ESR Records S/80/CUS 733	Photograph/I Sit And Stare/The End Of The World/Out On The Streets (also listed as ESR 4, 300 only, some with insert)	50/20

ALTYMAN REID

72	Green Door GD 4026	A Sugar/A Sugar Part Two (with Roy Shirley)	6

(see also Roy Shirley)

BERYL REID

65	HMV POP 1489	Love Makes The World Go Round/When The Circus Comes To Town	4

CARLTON REID

66	Ska Beat JB 254	Funny/Turn On The Lights	12
69	Blue Cat BS 162	Leave Me To Cry/Warning	8

CLARENCE REID
69	Atlantic 584 290	Nobody But You Babe/Send Me Back My Money	4
69	Atlantic 584 301	I'm Gonna Tear You A New Heart/I'm A Man Of My Word	4

DUKE REID (& HIS GROUP)
60	Blue Beat BB 24	Duke's Cookies (with His Group)/JIVING JUNIORS: I Wanna Love	15
62	Blue Beat BB 119	Twelve Minutes To Go (actually by Don Drummond)/	
		HORTENSE ELLIS: Midnight Train	15
63	Duke DK 1002	Pink Lane Shuffle (with His Group)/LAUREL AITKEN: Low Down Dirty Girl	12
67	Master's Time MT 003	Religious Service At Bond Street Gospel Hall/Religious Service At Bond	
		Street Gospel Hall (Continued)	7
67	Trojan TR 001	Judge Sympathy (actually by Freedom Singers & Duke Reid All Stars)/	
		ROLAND ALPHONSO: Never To Be Mine	20
72	Duke Reid DR 2522	Hurt (Parts 1 & 2) (actually by Eagles [Jamaica])	5

(see also Chuck & Darby, Derrick Morris, Stranger)

LEYROY REID
68	Blue Cat BS 125	The Fiddler/LOVELETTES: Shook	12
68	Blue Cat BS 127	Great Surprise/TEN(N)ORS: Khaki	12

(see also Nehemiah Reed)

MARC REID
66	CBS 202244	For No One/Lonely City Blues	6
67	CBS 202581	Magic Book/My World Turns Around	6
67	CBS 2950	We Should Live Together/Sale By Auction	6

MIKE REID
76	Pye 7N 45584	Swinging On A Star/Winkle Picker Annie	5
76	Pye 7N 45645	All The Love In The World/It's A Small World (with His Little Friends)	5

NEHEMIAH REID('S ALL STARS)
68	Island WI 3102	Family War/Give Me That Love	15
70	Hot Shot HS 03	Hot Pepper/Seawave (as Nehemiah Reid's All Stars)	8
70s	Torpedo TOR 23	Mafia/H.E.L.L. 5 (as Nehemiah Reid's All Stars)	6

(see also Leyroy Reid, Cynthia Richards)

P. REID
65	Ska Beat JB 197	Redeemed/Goodbye World	15

PATTI REID
87	Fellside FE 061	PATTI REID (LP)	12

TERRY REID (& JAYWALKERS)
67	Columbia DB 8166	The Hand Don't Fit The Glove/This Time (as Terry Reid & Jaywalkers)	12
68	Columbia DB 8409	Better By Far/Fires Alive	15
69	Columbia PSRS 323	Superlungs (promo only, as "Terry Reid Is Superlungs")	18
76	ABC 4137	Oooh Baby/Brave Awakening	5
79	Capitol CL 16071	Ain't No Shadow/Bowangi	5
69	Columbia SCX 6370	TERRY REID (LP)	25
71	M. For Pleasure MFP 5220	THE MOST OF TERRY REID (LP)	12
73	Atlantic K 40340	RIVER (LP, gatefold sleeve)	15
76	ABC ABCL 5162	SEED OF MEMORY (LP)	12
79	Capitol E-ST 11857	ROGUE WAVES (LP)	12

(see also Peter Jay & Jaywalkers)

REIGN
70	Regal Zonophone RZ 3028	Line Of Least Resistance/Natural Lovin' Man	30

(see also Yardbirds, Keith Relf, Renaissance, Armageddon, Illusion)

JOHN REILLY
78	Topic 12T 359	THE BONNY GREEN TREE (LP, with booklet)	12

TOMMY REILLY & TRADESMEN
63	Oriole CB 1833	Dakota/S.O.S.	6

DJANGO REINHARDT
53	Decca F 10219	Le Soir/Deccaphonie (78)	8
50s	Collector JEN 6	SWING GUITARS (EP)	8
50s	Collector JEN 8	IMPROVISATION (EP)	8
55	HMV 7EG 8132	DJANGO REINHARDT (EP)	8
54	Oriole/Mercury MG 10019	DJANGO (10" LP)	15
54	Vogue LDE 049	DJANGO REINHARDT VOL. 1 (10" LP)	18
54	Vogue LDE 084	DJANGO REINHARDT VOL. 2 (10" LP)	18
54	Vogue LDE 106	DJANGO REINHARDT VOL. 3 (10" LP, as Django Reinhardt Quintet)	18
54	HMV DLP 1045	DJANGO REINHARDT (10" LP)	18
54	Felsted EDL 87005	NUAGES (10" LP, as Django Reinhardt & His Rhythm)	18
59	HMV CLP 1249	DJANGO (LP)	15
60	HMV CLP 1340	THE ART OF DJANGO (LP)	15
60	HMV CLP 1389	DJANGO — THE UNFORGETTABLE (LP)	15
60s	Ember CJS 810	REQUIEM FOR A JAZZMAN (LP)	12
71	Xtra XTRA 1117	DJANGO REINHARDT VOL. 2 (LP)	12

(see also Quintet Of Hot Club Of France)

JOE REISMAN ORCHESTRA
55	HMV B 10891	Bo Diddley/Bubble Boogie (78)	10
56	HMV 7M 364	Robin Hood/His Name Was Judas	5
60	Columbia DB 4553	The World Of Suzi Wong (Theme)/Melodie D'Amour	5
61	Pye International 7N 25087	The Guns Of Navarone/Yassu	5

REIVERS
59	Top Rank JAR 244	The Wee Magic Stane/The Wreck Of The John B	5
60	Top Rank JAR 283	Down In The Mines/Govan Is A Busy Place	6

MINT VALUE £

REJOICE!
| 69 | Stateside SS 8010 | November Snow/Quick Draw Man | 5 |
| 69 | Stateside S(S)L 5009 | REJOICE! (LP) | 12 |

BOB RELF
| 75 | Black Magic BM 101 | Blowin' My Mind To Pieces/PAULA RUSSELL: Blowin' My Mind To Pieces | 4 |
| | (see also Bob & Earl) | | |

JANE RELF
| 71 | Decca F 13231 | Without A Song From You/Make My Time Pass By | 20 |
| | (see also Stairway, Renaissance) | | |

KEITH RELF
66	Columbia DB 7920	Mr. Zero/Knowing	25
66	Columbia DB 8084	Shapes In My Mind/Blue Sands	40
	(see also Yardbirds, Jim McCarty, Renaissance, Reign, Together, Armageddon)		

RELIGIOUS OVERDOSE
80	Glass GLASS 004	Control Addicts/25 Minutes (p/s, initially with green labels)	6/5
81	Glass GLASS 009	I Said Go/Alien To You (p/s)	4
82	Glass GLASS 018	In This Century/The Girl With The Disappearing Head (12", p/s)	7

RELOAD
92	Evolution EVO 01	RELOAD EP (12", plain sleeve)	30
92	Evolution EVO 02	AUTO RELOAD EP (12", with E 621)	30
92	Evolution EVO 03	RELOAD EP (12", 1-side credited to E 621)	25
93	Infonet INF 13	AURO RELOAD EP Volume 2 (12", p/s)	15
93	Infonet INF 04LP	A COLLECTION OF SHORT STORIES (2-LP, some with colour booklet)	25/20
93	Infonet INF 04CD	A COLLECTION OF SHORT STORIES (CD, some with colour booklet)	25/20
95	Warp WARPLP 29	THE THEORY OF EVOLUTION (2-LP, gatefold sleeve)	18
95	Surreal Sound TAPE 2	THE BIOSPHERE (cassette, free with initial copies of 'Surreal Sound' magazine)	15
	(see also Global Communications, Link, Mystic Institute)		

RELUCTANT STEREOTYPES
| 79 | Oval OVAL 1013 | The Lull/The Rounds/Fetch Mr. Clifford, The Political Boys Are On Us (p/s) | 4 |
| | (see also King) | | |

R.E.M.
I.R.S. SINGLES
83	I.R.S. PFP 1017	Radio Free Europe/There She Goes Again (p/s)	50
83	I.R.S. PFP 1026	Talk About The Passion/Talk About The Passion (plain sleeve, promo only)	30
83	I.R.S. PFSX 1026	Talk About The Passion/Shaking Through/Carnival Of Sorts (Box Cars)/1,000,000 (12", p/s)	25
84	I.R.S. IRS 105	S. Central Rain (I'm Sorry)/King Of The Road (p/s)	12
84	I.R.S. IRSX 105	S. Central Rain (I'm Sorry)/Voice Of Harold/Pale Blue Eyes (12", p/s)	18
84	I.R.S. IRS 107	(Don't Go Back To) Rockville/Wolves (p/s)	20
84	I.R.S. IRSX 107	(Don't Go Back To) Rockville/Wolves/9 - 9 (Live Version)/Gardening At Night (live) (12", p/s)	20
85	I.R.S. IRM 102	Can't Get There From Here/Bandwagon (p/s)	10
85	I.R.S. IRT 102	Can't Get There From Here (sleeve states 'Extended Mix', label states 'LP Version', but actually 3.39 edit)/Bandwagon/Burning Hell (12", p/s, some with printed banner crediting unissued tracks)	25/15
85	I.R.S. IRM 105	Wendell Gee/Crazy (p/s)	12
85	I.R.S. IRMD 105	Wendell Gee/Crazy//Ages Of You/Burning Down (double pack)	15
85	I.R.S. IRT 105	Wendell Gee/Crazy/Driver 8 (live) (12", p/s)	15
86	I.R.S. IRM 121	Fall On Me/Rotary Ten (p/s, blue, gold or silver label)	8
86	I.R.S. IRMT 121	Fall On Me/Rotary Ten/Toys In The Attic (12", p/s)	15
86	I.R.S. IRM 128	Superman/White Tornado (p/s, gold or silver label)	8
86	I.R.S. IRMT 128	Superman/White Tornado/Femme Fatale (12", p/s)	12
86	I.R.S. DIRM 128	Superman/White Tornado/Femme Fatale (CD, unissued)	
87	I.R.S. IRM 145	It's The End Of The World As We Know It (And I Feel Fine) (2.59 edit)/This One Goes Out (live) (p/s, gold or metallic blue label)	7
87	I.R.S. IRMT 145	It's The End Of The World As We Know It (And I Feel Fine)/This One Goes Out (live)/Maps And Legends (live) (12", p/s)	12
87	I.R.S. DIRM 145	It's The End Of The World As We Know It (And I Feel Fine) (CD, withdrawn)	25
87	I.R.S. IRM 146	The One I Love/Last Date (live) (bronze label, glossy p/s; silver label, matt p/s)	7
87	I.R.S. IRMT 146	The One I Love/Last Date/Disturbance At The Heron House (live) (12", p/s)	12
87	I.R.S. DIRM 146	The One I Love/Last Date/Disturbance At The Heron House (live) (CD)	20
88	I.R.S. IRM 161	Finest Worksong/Time After Time, Etc. (live) (stickered p/s)	6
88	I.R.S. IRMT 161	Finest Worksong (Lengthy Club Mix)/Finest Worksong (Other Mix)/Time After Time, Etc. (live) (12", stickered p/s)	12
88	I.R.S. DIRM 161	Finest Worksong (LP Version)/Time After Time, Etc. (live)/It's The End Of The World As We Know It (And I Feel Fine) (CD, numbered stencilled 7" box, 5,000 only)	22
88	I.R.S. IRM 178	The One I Love/Fall On Me (p/s, reissue)	4
88	I.R.S. IRMT 178	The One I Love/Fall On Me/S. Central Rain (12", p/s, reissue)	8
88	I.R.S. DIRM 178	The One I Love/Fall On Me/S. Central Rain (CD, reissue)	15
91	I.R.S. IRM 178	The One I Love/Crazy (2nd reissue, jukebox pressing with black label)	4
91	I.R.S. DIRMT 178	The One I Love/This One Goes Out (live)/Maps And Legends (CD, with 10-page insert)	7
91	I.R.S. DIRMX 178	The One I Love/Driver 8 (live)/Disturbance At The Heron House (live) (CD, with 4-page discography)	7
92	I.R.S. DIRM 180	It's The End Of The World As We Know It (And I Feel Fine)/Radio Free Europe (Hib-Tone Version) (gold or silver labels, p/s)	4
92	I.R.S. DIRMX 180	It's The End Of The World As We Know It (And I Feel Fine)/Radio Free Europe (Hib-Tone Version)/Last Date/White Tornado (CD, withdrawn)	12

WARNER BROS SINGLES

88	Warner Bros W 7652CD	Orange Crush/Memphis Train Blues/(Eleventh Untitled Song) (3" CD, unissued)	
89	Warner Bros W 7577	Stand/Memphis Train Blues (p/s)	5
89	Warner Bros W 7577X	Stand/Memphis Train Blues (recycled paper p/s)	5
89	Warner Bros W 7577T	Stand/Memphis Train Blues/(The Eleventh Untitled Song) (12", p/s)	8
89	Warner Bros W 7577CD	Stand/Memphis Train Blues/(The Eleventh Untitled Song) (3" CD, card sleeve)	10
89	Warner Bros W 7577CDX	Stand/Memphis Train Blues/(The Eleventh Untitled Song) (3" CD, 'maple-leaf' pack)	25
89	Warner Bros W 2960	Orange Crush/Ghost Riders (p/s)	4
89	Warner Bros W 2960X	Orange Crush/Ghost Riders (recycled paper p/s)	5
89	Warner Bros W 2960B	Orange Crush/Ghost Riders ('The Green Package' box set with poster)	12
89	Warner Bros W 2960C	Orange Crush/Ghost Riders (cassette)	5
89	Warner Bros W 2960T	Orange Crush/Ghost Riders/Dark Globe (12", p/s)	8
89	Warner Bros W 2960CD	Orange Crush/Ghost Riders/Dark Globe (3" CD, gatefold card sleeve)	15
89	Warner Bros W 2833	Stand/Pop Song '89 (Acoustic) (reissue, p/s)	7
89	Warner Bros W 2833W	Stand/Pop Song '89 (Acoustic) (stencil die-cut p/s)	12
89	Warner Bros W 2833T	Stand/Pop Song '89 (Acoustic)/Skin Tight (live) (12", p/s)	12
89	Warner Bros W 2833CD	Stand/Pop Song '89 (Acoustic)/Skin Tight (live) (3" CD, gatefold card sleeve)	15
89	Warner Bros W 2833CDX	Stand/Pop Song '89 (Acoustic)/Skin Tight (live) (3" CD, black die-cut sleeve in Velcro seal envelope)	20
91	Warner Bros W 0015	Losing My Religion/Rotary Eleven (some with large centre, p/s)	5
91	Warner Bros W 0015C	Losing My Religion/Rotary Eleven (cassette)	5
91	Warner Bros W 0015T	Losing My Religion/Rotary Eleven/After Hours (live) (12", p/s)	8
91	Warner Bros W 0015CD	Losing My Religion/Rotary Eleven/After Hours (live) (CD)	10
91	Warner Bros W 0015CDX	Losing My Religion/Stand (live)/Turn You Inside-Out (live)/World Leader Pretend (live) (CD, with fold-out poster)	25
91	Warner Bros W 0027CDX	Shiny Happy People/I Remember California (live)/Get Up (live)/Pop Song '89 (live) (CD)	12
91	Warner Bros W 0055CDX	Near Wild Heaven/Tom's Diner (live)/Low (live)/Endgame (live) (CD)	8
91	Warner Bros W 0072CDX	Radio Song/You Are The Everything (live)/Orange Crush (live)/Belong (live) (CD, with collector's slipcase)	10
95	Warner Bros W 0281X	Crush With Eyeliner (Album Version)/(Instrumental Version) (orange vinyl, with calendar, numbered p/s)	4
95	Warner Bros W 0290X	Strange Currencies (Album Version)/(Instrumental Version) (yellow vinyl, with metal 'Monster' badge, numbered p/s)	4
95	Warner Bros W 0308X	Tongue (Album Version)/(Instrumental Version) (numbered p/s, with 14-page 'tour souvenir')	4

OTHER RELEASES

85	Bucketfull Of Brains BOB 5	Tighten Up (flexidisc [LYN 15742] with *Bucketfull Of Brains* magazine)	15
85	Bucketfull Of Brains BOB 5	Tighten Up (hard vinyl test pressing, 50 only)	60
92	Lyntone BOB 32	Academy Fight Song (live)/COAL PORTERS: Watching Blue Grass Burn (p/s, free with *Bucketfull Of Brains* magazine, double issue 39/40)	15
92	Lyntone BOB 32	Academy Fight Song (live)/COAL PORTERS: Watching Blue Grass Burn (white label test pressing, no p/s)	25
92	Warner Bros 2-45122	AUTOMATIC FOR THE PEOPLE (CD, in wooden box with 16 vellum cards)	25

PROMOS

94	Warner Bros REM 1	SAMPLER FROM THE BEST OF REM (CD, Brit Awards nomination issue)	50
95	Warner Bros SAM 1558	POP SONGS 89 — 95 (CD, 18-track sampler)	25
95	Warner Bros PRO CD 7888	SONGS THAT ARE LIVE (CD, 4 unreleased live tracks)	30
99	Warner Bros SAM 00132	POP SONGS (CD, slimline case, promo only)	50

(see also Full Time Men)

REMA-REMA

| 80 | 4AD BAD 5 | WHEEL IN THE ROSES: Feeback Song/Rema-Ream/Instrumental/Fond Affections (12" EP, blue labels) | 18 |

(see also Adam & The Ants, Mass, Models)

REMAINS

| 84 | Lyntone LYN 14086/LARM 1 | Talkin' 'Bout You (U.K. flexi, originally with Swedish *Larm* mag, issue 17) | 7/4 |

REMAYNS

| 85 | Bam Caruso NRIC 029 | FIRST (EP, coloured vinyl) | 5 |

HERBIE REMINGTON

| 66 | Fontana FJL 313 | REMINGTON RIDES AGAIN (LP) | 12 |

REMO FOUR

64	Piccadilly 7N 35175	I Wish I Could Shimmy Like My Sister Kate/Peter Gunn	15
64	Piccadilly 7N 35186	Sally Go Round The Roses/I Know A Girl	15
67	Fontana TF 787	Live Like A Lady/Sing Hallelujah	50

(see also Tommy Quickly, Johnny Sandon, Gregory Phillips, Ashton Gardner & Dyke, Mike Hurst, George Harrison)

RENAISSANCE (U.S.)

| 68 | Polydor BM 56736 | Mary Jane (Get Off The Devil's Merry-Go-Round)/Daytime Lovers | 30 |

RENAISSANCE (U.K.)

70	Island WIP 6079	Island/The Sea	10
78	Sire SRE 1022	Northern Lights/Opening Out (picture disc, export issue)	15
79	Sire SIR 4019	Jekyll And Hyde/Forever Changing (withdrawn)	15
69	Island ILPS 9114	RENAISSANCE (LP, pink label)	20
71	Island HELP 27	ILLUSION (LP, withdrawn, export only)	40
72	Sovereign SVNA 7253	PROLOGUE (LP)	12
73	Sovereign SVNA 7261	ASHES ARE BURNING (LP)	12
79	Sovereign CAPACK 3	PROLOGUE/ASHES ARE BURNING (2-LP, shrinkwrapped)	15
75	BTM BTM 1000	TURN OF THE CARDS (LP)	12
75	BTM BTM 1006	SCHEHERAZADE AND OTHER STORIES (LP)	12
76	BTM BTM 2001	LIVE AT CARNEGIE HALL (2-LP)	15

(see also Jim McCarty, Keith Relf, Jane Relf, Yardbirds, Rupert's People, Reign, Stairway)

LINE RENAUD

53	Columbia SCM 5055	April In Portugal/The Song From Moulin Rouge	7
55	Capitol CL 14230	If I Love You /Pam-Pou-De (Pam-Poo-Day) (triangular centre)	15
56	Columbia SCM 5268	Flamenco Love/To You, My Love	7
56	Columbia DB 3824	Strange/You Can't Keep Running	6
58	Columbia DB 4193	Irma La Douce/Disc-Donc, Disc-Donc	5
60	Columbia DB 4485	Mon Coeur Au Portugal/Jeremy	5

LINE RENAUD & DEAN MARTIN

61	Capitol EAP1 20060	LINE AND DINO (EP)	15

(see also Dean Martin)

RENAULTS

60	Warner Bros WB 11	Meloncolie/Stella	6

DIANE RENAY

64	Stateside SS 270	Navy Blue/Unbelievable Guy	10
64	Stateside SS 290	Kiss Me Sailor/Soft Spoken Guy	10
64	MGM MGM 1262	Watch Out Sally/Billy Blue Eyes	10
65	MGM MGM 1274	Troublemaker/I Had A Dream	10

(see also Laura Greene)

JOHN RENBOURN

65	Transatlantic TRA 135	JOHN RENBOURN (LP)	18
66	Transatlantic TRA 149	ANOTHER MONDAY (LP)	20
68	Transatlantic TRA 167	SIR JOHN ALOT OF MERRIE ENGLANDE'S MUSICK THYNGE AND YE GREENE KNIGHT (LP)	18
70	Transatlantic TRA 224	THE LADY AND THE UNICORN (LP)	18
72	Transatlantic TRA 247	FARO ANNIE (LP)	18
73	Transatlantic TRA 336	THE HERMIT (LP)	18
73	Transatlantic TRASAM 20	THE JOHN RENBOURN SAMPLER (LP)	15
73	Transatlantic TRASAM 28	SO CLEAR — THE JOHN RENBOURN SAMPLER VOL. 2 (LP)	15

(see also Pentangle, Stefan Grossman, Bert Jansch & John Renbourn, Steve Tilston, Dorris Henderson)

JOHN RENBOURN & STEFAN GROSSMAN

70s	Kicking Mule SNKF 139	JOHN RENBOURN & STEFAN GROSSMAN (LP)	12
70s	Kicking Mule SNKF 161	UNDER THE VOLCANO (LP)	12

(see also John Renbourn, Stefan Grossman)

DON RENDELL

55	Tempo EXA 11	DON RENDELL QUARTET (EP)	125
55	Tempo EXA 12	DON RENDELL SEXTET (EP)	125
55	Tempo EXA 16	DON RENDELL SEXTET/DAMIAN ROBINSON TRIO (EP, 2 tracks each)	20
56	Tempo EXA 20	DON RENDELL QUINTET (EP)	50
57	Pye Jazz NJE 1044	DON RENDELL JAZZ SIX (EP)	30
58	Decca DFE 6501	PACKET OF BLUES (EP, as Don Rendell Jazz Six)	15
54	Vogue LDE 050	MUSIC IN THE MAKING (10" LP)	100
55	Vogue LDE 144	DON RENDELL IN PARIS (10" LP, with Bobby Jaspa)	30
55	Tempo LAP 1	MEET DON RENDELL (10" LP)	350
57	Nixa Jazz Today NJL 7	DON RENDELL PRESENTS THE JAZZ SIX (LP)	200
58	Decca LK 4265	PLAYTIME (LP, as Don Rendell Jazz 6)	40
62	Jazzland JLP 51	ROARIN' (LP, as Don Rendell New Jazz Quintet [with Graham Bond])	125
72	Columbia SCX 6491	SPACEWALK (LP, as Don Rendell Quintet)	70

DON RENDELL & IAN CARR QUINTET

65	Columbia 33SX 1733	SHADES OF BLUE (LP)	250
66	Columbia S(C)X 6064	DUSK FIRE (LP)	275
68	Columbia S(C)X 6214	PHASE III (LP)	150
69	Columbia S(C)X 6316	LIVE (LP)	150
69	Columbia SCX 6368	CHANGE IS 1 (LP)	150

(see also Neil Ardley, Ian Carr, Nucleus)

DON RENDELL QUARTET/JOE HARRIOT QUARTET

57	MGM MGM-EP 615	JAZZ BRITANNIA (EP, 2 tracks each)	15

(see also Joe Harriott)

GOOGIE RENE COMBO

60	London HLY 9056	Forever/Ez-zee	15
66	Atlantic AT 4076	Smokey Joe's La La/Needing You	30
66	Atlantic 584 015	Chica-Boo/Mercy Mercy (Too Much For The Soul)	8

HENRI RENE

55	HMV 7M 308	Enchantment/Crystal Chandelier (with Hugo Winterhalter Orchestra)	6
59	London HLP 8960	La Shabla (The Shovel)/Destiny (with His Orchestra & Chorus)	6
59	London HLP 8960	La Shabla (The Shovel)/Destiny (with His Orchestra & Chorus) (78)	20

RENE & HIS ALLIGATORS

66	Decca F 22324	She Broke My Heart/I Can Wait	12

RENE & RENE

65	HMV POP 1468	Chantilly Lace/I'm Not The Only One	7
67	Island WIP 6001	Loving You Could Hurt Me So Much/Little Diamonds	5

RENEGADE

80	White Witch WIT 1	LONELY ROAD (12" EP, with insert)	100

RENEGADES

66	Polydor BM 56508	Cadillac/Every Minute Of The Day	20
66	President PT 106	Thirteen Women/Walking Down The Street	60
67	Parlophone R 5592	Take A Message/Second Thoughts	15
68	Columbia DB 8383	No Man's Land/Sugar Loaf Mountain	12

RENIA
73   Transatlantic TRA 261   FIRST OFFENDERS (LP) 18

JON RENNARD
70   Tradition TSR 003   BRIMBLEDON FAIR (LP) 12
71   Tradition TSR 010   THE PARTING GLASS (LP) 12

DON RENNIE
56   Parlophone MSP 6218   To Love, To Love Is Wonderful/One Girl — One Boy.............. 7
56   Parlophone MSP 6237   Who Are We?/Can You Find It In Your Heart? 7

DON RENO & RED SMILEY
58   Parlophone GEP 8777   COUNTRY AND WESTERN (EP)................................... 30
61   Melodisc MLP 12-123   HYMNS SACRED GOSPEL SONGS (LP) 12
64   Ember CW 104   SING SWEET BALLADS OF THE WEST (LP) 12

GERRY RENO
62   Decca F 11477   Don't Ever Change/What Would You Do 7
62   Decca F 11516   Who's Fooling You/Three Deadly Sins......................... 7
63   Decca F 11774   It Only Happens In The Movies/One Lonely Guy................ 7

PAUL RENO
63   Oriole CB 1872   Lonely Little Girl/Angela 7

TEDDY RENO
59   RCA RCA 1108   Ciao Ciao Bambino/Li Per Li (78) 10

ROBERT RENTAL
78   Regular ER 102   Paralysis/A.C.C. (photocopied black & white foldover p/s) 10
78   Company/Regular RECO 2   Paralysis/A.C.C. (reissue, different colour p/s)............... 5
79   Industrial IR 0007   THE BRIDGE (LP, with Thomas Leer) 15
80   Rough Trade ROUGH 17   ROBERT RENTAL AND THE NORMAL (LP, 1-sided, plain red sleeve) .. 12
      (see also Thomas Leer, Normal)

R.E.O. SPEEDWAGON
72   Epic EPC 8044   157 Riverside Avenue/Five Men Were Killed Today.............. 5
72   Epic EPC 64813   R.E.O. SPEEDWAGON (LP) 12
75   Epic EPC 80175   LOST IN A DREAM (LP) 12

REPARATA & DELRONS
65   Stateside SS 382   Whenever A Teenager Cries/He's My Guy....................... 18
65   Stateside SS 414   Tommy/Momma Don't Allow 12
68   Bell BLL 1002   Captain Of Your Ship/Toom Toom Is A Little Boy 7
68   RCA Victor RCA 1691   I Can Hear The Rain/Always Waitin'........................... 10
68   Bell BLL 1014   Saturday Night Didn't Happen/Panic.......................... 20
68   Bell BLL 1021   Weather Forecast/You Can't Change A Young Boy's Mind......... 5
72   Bell BLL 1252   Captain Of Your Ship/Toom Toom Is A Little Boy (reissue) 4
73   Dart ART 2006   Octopus's Garden/Your Life Is Gone........................... 5
72   Avco 6467 250   ROCK AND ROLL REVOLUTION (LP) 15

REPERCUSSIONS
92   Mo'Wax MW 001   Promise/(dub)/Field Trippin' (12") 20

RESERVE
88   Sha La La   Wherever You Go/SIDDELEYS: The Sun Slid Down/Behind The Tower
      Ba Ba Ba-Ba Ba 006   (flexidisc, foldover p/s) 6

RESIDENTS
80   Pre PRE 009   THE COMMERCIAL SINGLE (p/s) 10
84   Korova KOW 36   It's A Man's Man's Man's World/I'll Go Crazy (p/s, 5,000 only) 7
83   London RALPH 1   INTERMISSION (12" EP)....................................... 8
88   Torso TORSOCD 322   KAW-LIGA (CD) 8
89   Torso TORSOCD 355   Double Shot/Loss Of Loved One (Extended Version)/
                                   Kiss Of Flesh (Instrumental) (3" CD, picture disc) 8
89   Torso TORSOCD 421   Diskomo/Whoopy Snorp/Saint Nix/Diskomo Live (CD)............ 8
79   Virgin VR 3   NIBBLES (LP, 5,000 only).................................... 12
80   Pre PRE X2   PICNIC BOY — THE COMMERCIAL ALBUM (LP, 5,000 only,
                                   with incorrect song order).................................. 15
84   Korova CODE 9   GEORGE AND JAMES (cassette with extra track) 10
84   Doublevision DV 9   THE MOLE SHOW/WHATEVER HAPPENED TO VILENESS FATS (cassette)...... 20
85   Doublevision DVR 17   THE PAL TV LP (LP, red vinyl, 5,000 only).................... 15
      (see also Snakefinger)

RESISTANCE 77
82   Riot City RIOT 18   NOWHERE TO PLAY (EP).. 7
84   Resistance RESIST 1   You Reds/Young And Wrong (p/s) 5

RESISTORS
80   Break SMASH 1   For Jeanie/Takeaway Love/End Of The Line (p/s)............... 5

JOHNNY RESTIVO
59   RCA RCA 1143   The Shape I'm In/Ya Ya (initially with triangular centre, later round) 25/12
59   RCA RCA 1143   The Shape I'm In/Ya Ya (78) 100
59   RCA RCA 1159   I Like Girls/Dear Someone 12
59   RCA RCA 1159   I Like Girls/Dear Someone (78) 100
60   Ember EMB S 135   Look Here Now/Sweet Sweet Lovin' 12

RESTLESS ONES
65   Herald HSR 2521   The Restless Ones/He's Everything To Me (p/s) 10

RESTRICTED HOURS
79   Stevenage   Getting Things Done/Still Living Out The Car Crash/SYNDICATE: One Way
                                   Or Another/I Want To Be Somebody (white label, foldover p/s) 8

      (see also Astronauts)

RETREADS

MINT VALUE £

RETREADS
81	Eddi Osmo EO 101	Would You Listen Girl/One After 909/You Said You Knew (p/s, with mini-poster insert)	40

RETURN TO FOREVER
74	Polydor 2310 283	HYMN OF GALAXY (LP)	10
74	Polydor 2310 354	WHERE HAVE I KNOWN YOU BEFORE (LP)	10
75	Polydor 2310 378	NO MYSTERY (LP)	10

(see also Chick Corea)

MARTIN REV
85	New Rose ROSE 52	CLOUDS OF GLORY (LP, red vinyl)	10

(see also Suicide)

REVELATION
70	Trojan TR 7727	Suffering/MEGATONS: Crazy Elephant	6

REVELLERS
66	Columbia DB 8093	Believe, Believe/Love Is The Greatest Thing	5
67	Spin LP 1703	REVELLERS AGAIN (LP)	30

REVELS
59	Top Rank JAR 235	Midnight Stroll/Talking To My Heart	25

REVELLS
71	CBS 7050	Mind Party/Indian Ropeman	8

DIGGER REVELL'S DENVERMEN
63	Decca F 11657	Surfside/Lisa Marie	15

REVENGE
76	Normal QS 000	Go Away/Game	12
70s	Blood CUS 614	Don't Tell Me Lies/Gimme The Good Times	10

REVENGE
78	Loony LOO 1	Our Generation	120
78	Loony LOO 2	We're Not Gonna Take It/Pornography (p/s)	60

REVENGE
89	Factory FACD 247	7 Reasons/Jesus ... I Love You (Edit)/Bleach Boy/Jesus ... I Love You (CD)	7

(see also New Order)

PAUL REVERE & RAIDERS (featuring Mark Lindsay)
61	Top Rank JAR 557	Like Long Hair/Sharon	18
65	Sue WI 344	Like Long Hair/Sharon (reissue)	18
65	CBS 202003	Steppin' Out/Blue Fox	7
66	CBS 202027	Just Like Me/B F D R F Blues	10
66	CBS 202205	Kicks/Shake It Up	8
66	CBS 202253	Hungry/There She Goes	6
66	CBS 202411	The Great Airplane Strike/In My Community	8
67	CBS 202502	Good Thing/Undecided Man	8
67	CBS 202610	Ups And Downs/Leslie	7
67	CBS 2737	Him Or Me — What's It Gonna Be?/The Legend Of Paul Revere	8
67	CBS 2919	I Had A Dream/Upon Your Leaving	5
67	CBS 3186	Mo'reen/Oh! To Be A Man	5
68	CBS 3310	Too Much Talk/Happening '68 (featuring Mark Lindsay)	5
68	CBS 3586	Don't Take It So Hard/Observation From Flight 285 (featuring Mark Lindsay)	6
68	CBS 3757	Cinderella Sunshine/Theme From It's Happening (featuring Mark Lindsay)	5
69	CBS 4025	Mr. Sun, Mr. Moon/With You (featuring Mark Lindsay)	5
69	CBS 4260	Let Me/I Don't Know (featuring Mark Lindsay)	6
69	CBS 4504	We Gotta All Get Up Together/Frankfurt Side Street (featuring Mark Lindsay)	5
66	CBS (S)BPG 62406	JUST LIKE US (LP)	20
66	CBS (S)BPG 62797	MIDNIGHT RIDE (LP)	20
67	CBS (S)BPG 62963	GOOD THING (LP)	20
68	CBS (S)BPG 63095	REVOLUTION (LP)	20
69	CBS 63265	GOIN' TO MEMPHIS (LP, mono/stereo)	18
69	CBS 63649	HARD 'N' HEAVY (LP)	18

(see also Raiders, Mark Lindsay)

REVILLOS
79	Snatzo/Dindisc DIN 1	Where's The Boy For Me/The Fiend (p/s)	6
79	Snatzo/Dindisc DIN 5	Motor Bike Beat/No Such Luck (p/s)	5
80	Snatzo/Dindisc DINZ 16	Scuba Scuba/Scuba Boy Bop (p/s)	6
80	Snatzo/Dindisc DINZ 20	Hungry For Love/Voodoo 2 (p/s, label also lists SP 703)	5
82	Superville SV 1001	She's Fallen In Love With A Monster Man/Mind Bending Cutie Doll (p/s)	6
82	Superville SV 2001	Bongo Brain/Hip City — You Were Meant For Me (p/s)	4
82	Aura AUS 135	Tell Him/Graveyard Groove (p/s)	6
83	EMI RVL 1	Bitten By A Love Bug/Cat Call	5
83	EMI 12 RVL 1	Bitten By A Love Bug (Extended Version)/Cat Call (12", p/s)	8
84	EMI RVL 2	Midnight/Z-X-7 (p/s)	5
84	EMI 12 RVL 2	Midnight (Extended Version)/Midnight (7" Version)/Z-X-7 (12", p/s)	8
80	Snatzo/Dindisc DID X 3	REV UP (LP, green or pink titles)	25
82	Superville SV 4001	ATTACK! (LP, withdrawn)	25+

(see also Rezillos)

REVOLUTION
66	Piccadilly 7N 35289	Hallelujah/Shades Of Blue	30

(see also Hellions, Luther Grosvenor, Family, Traffic, Dave Mason & Cass Elliot, Spirit)

REVOLUTIONARY ARMY OF INFANT JESUS
87	Probe Plus PROBE 12	THE GIFT OF TEARS (LP)	35

REVOLUTIONARY BLUES BAND
70 MCA MUP(S) 402   REVOLUTIONARY BLUES BAND (LP). 15

REVOLUTIONARY CORPS OF TEENAGE JESUS VS SUICIDE
96 Creeping Bent BENT 005 FRANKIE TEARDROP EP (Frankie Teardrop [126 b.p.m.]/U.S.A. '95/
                            Frankie Teardrop [114 b.p.m.]/Womb # 17) (12", p/s, 1,000 only) 10

(see also Suicide, Future Pilot A.KA.)

REVOLVER
69 Young Blood YB 1006   Frisco Annie/Imaginations. 8

REVOLVING PAINT DREAM
84 Creation CRE 002   Flowers In The Sky/In The Afternoon (foldaround p/s in poly bag) 15

(see also Laughing Apple, Primal Scream)

REVS
91 Major Label BIG 002   I've Got News For You/Ten Years On/Nothing That I've Said/A Day Like Today 5
93 Detour DR 009   Do The Right Thing/Stay In Touch/Anna (p/s, some on blue vinyl) 8/5

KIMBERLEY REW
80 Armageddon AS 004   Stomping All Over The World/Nothing's Going To Change In Your Life/
                            Fighting Someone's War (p/s) 5
81 Armageddon AS 012   My Baby Does Her Hairdo Long/Fishing (p/s, with dB's) 4

(see also Soft Boys, Waves)

ROBERTA REX
68 Fontana TF 967   Joey/I Can Feel It 4

REX (Morris) & MINORS
60 Triumph RGM 1023   Chicken Sax/Snake Eyes 35

ALVINO REY
61 London HLD 9431   Original Mama Blues/Steel Guitar Rag 10
62 London HA-D 2414   ALVINO REY'S GREATEST HITS (LP) 20

LITTLE BOBBY REY & HIS BAND
60 Top Rank JAR 525   Rockin' "J" Bells/Dance Of The New Year 7

REYNARD
76 Pilgrim/Grapevine GRA 102 FRESH FROM THE EARTH (LP) 40

AMBROSE REYNOLDS
82 New Hormones CAT 4   WORLD'S GREATEST HITS (cassette with 'Assassination Calendar'). 10
83 Zulu ZULU 3   GREATEST HITS (LP). 12

(see also Pink Military)

DEBBIE REYNOLDS
55 MGM SP 1127   Carolina In The Morning/Never Mind The Noise In The Market
                          (B-side as Debbie Reynolds' Naturals) 12
56 MGM SP 1155   (Love Is) The Tender Trap/Canoodlin' Rag. 8
56 MGM MGM 881   (Love Is) The Tender Trap/Canoodlin' Rag (78) 8
57 Vogue Coral Q 72274   Tammy/French Heels 8
58 MGM MGM 968   All Grown Up/Wall Flower 6
58 MGM MGM 968   All Grown Up/Wall Flower (78). 10
58 Coral Q 72297   A Very Special Love/I Saw A Country Boy 6
58 Coral Q 72297   A Very Special Love/I Saw A Country Boy (78) 10
58 Coral Q 72324   This Happy Feeling/Hillside In Scotland 6
58 Coral Q 72324   This Happy Feeling/Hillside In Scotland (78) 10
58 Coral Q 72345   Hungry Eyes/Faces There Are Fairer. 6
58 Coral Q 72345   Hungry Eyes/Faces There Are Fairer (78) 12
59 MGM MGM 1019   The Mating Game/Right Away 5
59 MGM MGM 1019   The Mating Game/Right Away (78) 15
59 MGM MGM 1043   It Started With A Kiss/Love Is A Gamble. 5
60 London HLD 9028   Am I That Easy To Forget?/Ask Me To Go Steady 5
60 London HLD 9128   City Lights/Just For A Touch Of Your Love 5
61 London HLD 9351   Lonely People/Just A Little Girl. 5
58 MGM MGM-EP 670   DEBBIE REYNOLDS (EP). 15
58 MGM MGM-EP 671   SINGING IN THE RAIN (EP, with Gene Kelly & Donald O'Connor) 12
59 MGM MGM-EP 694   DELIGHTFUL DEBBIE REYNOLDS (EP) 15
60 MGM MGM-EP 725   FROM DEBBIE WITH LOVE (EP) 15
59 London HA-D 2200   DEBBIE (LP, also stereo SAH-D 6051) 25/30
60 London HA-D 2294   AM I THAT EASY TO FORGET? (LP, also stereo SAH-D 6106). 25/30
61 London HA-D 2326   FINE AND DANDY (LP). 25
63 London HA-D/SH-D 8075 GREAT FOLK HITS (LP, mono/stereo) 25/30

(see also Naturals [U.S.])

DONN REYNOLDS
57 HMV POP 314   Hasta Luego/Lorelei. 6
58 MGM MGM 971   Rose Of Ol' Pawnee/All Alone (With No One By My Side) 6
58 MGM MGM 996   Blue Eyes Crying In The Rain/Bella Belinda 6
58 MGM MGM 996   Blue Eyes Crying In The Rain/Bella Belinda (78) 8
58 Pye 7N 15122   Swing Low Sweet Chariot/Ramona 6
58 Pye N 15122   Swing Low Sweet Chariot/Ramona (78) 8
59 Pye NEP 24098   THE DONN REYNOLDS SONGBAG (EP) 18

ELI REYNOLDS
70 Punch PH 37   Mr Car Man/Chiney Man. 6

JODY REYNOLDS
58 London HL 8651   Endless Sleep/Tight Capris 20
58 London HL 8651   Endless Sleep/Tight Capris (78) 25

L.J. REYNOLDS (& CHOCOLATE SYRUP)
72 Avco Embassy 6105 014 The Penguin Breakdown (with Chocolate Syrup)/YOUNGHEARTS: Ooh La Wee . . 4
82 Capitol CL 260   Special Effects/Key To The World 5

TIMMY REYNOLDS
62	Ember EMB S 133	Lullaby Of Love/JEFF MILLS: Daddy's Home	10

REZILLOS
77	Sensible FAB 1	Can't Stand My Baby/I Wanna Be Your Man (p/s, 15,000 only, 5,000 no'd)	12/7
77	Sensible FAB 2	Flying Saucer Attack/(My Baby Does) Good Sculptures (p/s, unissued)	
77	Sire 6078 612	Flying Saucer Attack/(My Baby Does) Good Sculptures (p/s)	7
78	Sire 6198 215	Cold Wars/William Mysterious Overture (unissued)	
78	Sire SIR 4001	Top Of The Pops/20,000 Rezillos Under The Sea (p/s)	7
78	Sire SIR 4008	Destination Venus/Mystery Action (p/s)	6
79	Sire SIR 4014	Cold Wars (live)/Flying Saucer Attack (live)/Twist & Shout (live) (p/s)	8
79	Sensible FAB 1 (Mark 2)	Can't Stand My Baby/I Wanna Be Your Man (reissue, new p/s, run out groove reads "Come Back John Lennon")	6
79	Sensible FAB 1 (Mark 2)	Can't Stand My Baby/I Wanna Be Your Man (reissue, p/s, mispressing, B-side plays "(My Baby Does) Good Sculptures (live)", run-off groove reads "De-sire-able product?", 4,000 only)	6
81	Sire SPC 3	Top Of The Pops/Destination Venus (cassette, flip-up box)	5
78	Sire K 56530	CAN'T STAND THE REZILLOS (LP, with inner sleeve & postcard insert)	25
78	Sire SRK 6069	MISSION ACCOMPLISHED ... BUT THE BEAT GOES ON (LP, live)	25

(see also Revillos, Shake, Jo Callis, William Mysterious)

RHABSTALLION
81	Rhab RHAB 001	Day To Day/Breadline (p/s, some with badge)	25/20

RHINOCEROS
69	Elektra EKSN 45051	You're My Girl (I Don't Want To Discuss It)/Apricot Brandy	6
69	Elektra EKSN 45058	I Will Serenade You/Belbuekul	6
70	Elektra EKSN 45080	Back Door/In A Little Room	6
70	Elektra 2101 009	Old Age/Let's Party	5
69	Elektra EKL 4030	RHINOCEROS (LP, orange label, also stereo EKS 74030)	20
69	Elektra EKL 4056	SATIN CHICKENS (LP, also stereo EKS 74056)	18
70	Elektra 2469 006	BETTER TIMES ARE COMING (LP)	15

RHODA with SPECIAL A.K.A.
82	2-Tone CHS TT 18	The Boiler/Theme From The Boiler (p/s)	5
82	2-Tone CHS TT 1218	The Boiler/Theme From The Boiler (12", p/s)	8

(see also Special A.K.A.)

JAN RHODE
60	Qualiton Offbeat PSP 7128	Come Back Baby/So Shy	8

PAT RHODEN
68	Trojan TR 606	Woman Is Greedy/Endlessy	6
70	Pama PM 811	Maybe The Next Time/Got To See You	5
70	Pama Supreme PS 298	Do What You Gotta Do/Crying Won't Help You	5
70	Mary Lyn ML 101	Time Is Tight/MILTON & DENZIL: I Like It Like That	5
73	Pama Supreme PS 378	Out Of Time/Put A Little Rain Into My Life	5

(see also Pat Riden, Pat & Marie, Denzil & Pat)

WINSTON RHODEN
66	Blue Beat BB 360	Send Your Love/Make Believe	10

EMITT RHODES
71	Probe PRO 520	Fresh As A Daisy/You Take The Dark Out Of The Night	5
71	Probe PRO 529	With My Face On The Floor/Somebody Made For Me	5
71	A&M AMS 865	You're A Very Lovely Woman/Till The Day After	5
72	Probe PRO 565	Tame The Lion/Golden Child Of God	5
71	Probe SPBA 6256	EMITT RHODES (LP, gatefold sleeve)	12
71	A&M AMLS 64254	AMERICAN DREAM (LP)	15
71	Probe SPBA 6262	MIRROR (LP)	12
72	Probe SPBA 6266	FAREWELL TO PARADISE (LP)	12

TODD RHODES ORCHESTRA
55	Parlophone R 4029	Specks/Silver Sunset (78)	12
55	Parlophone MSP 6171	Specks/Silver Sunset	25

RHUBARB RHUBARB
68	President PT 229	Rainmaker/Moneylender	25

RHYTHM ACES
61	Starlite ST45 061	A Thousand Teardrops/Wherever You May Go	18
61	Starlite ST45 066	Please Don't Go Away/Oh My Darling	15
62	Blue Beat BB 134	I'll Be There/DON DRUMMOND: Dewdrops	18
62	Island WI 032	C-H-R-I-S-T-M-A-S/TOP GRANT: A Christmas Drink	18

RHYTHM & BLUES INC.
65	Fontana TF 524	Louie Louie/Honey Don't	45

RHYTHMETTES
59	Coral Q 72358	Page From The Future/I'll Be With You In Apple Blossom Time	6
59	Coral Q 72358	Page From The Future/I'll Be With You In Apple Blossom Time (78)	12

RHYTHM FORCE
72	Tropical AL 0013	Satta Call/Satta Version	6

RHYTHM HERITAGE
76	ABC 4095	Theme From S.W.A.T./I Wouldn't Treat A Dog	5
76	ABC ABCL 5174	DISCO-FIED (LP)	12

RHYTHM INVENTION
92	Warp WAP 21	CAN'T TAKE IT (12")	7

RHYTHM KINGS
63	Vocalion POP V 9212	Blue Soul/Exotic	15

RHYTHM OF LIFE
81	Rational RATE 6	Soon/Summertime (p/s; label also lists Rhythm RHYTHM 1) 7
82	Rational RATE 7	Uncle Sam/Portrait Of The Heart (p/s; label also lists Rhythm RHYTHM 2) 6

(see also Josef K, Paul Haig)

RHYTHM MAKERS
76	Polydor 2001 651	Zone/Prime Cut 6

RHYTHM RULERS
70	Bullet BU 447	Second Pressure/Sammy Dead 6

(see also Lloyd Jones, U Roy Junior, Matadors, Winston Groovy, Pat, Winston Wright)

RIALTO
96	Jealous COUP 005	Skyscraper/DOGGER: Bitter Almonds (CD, stickered slimline green case) 8

RIBS
78	Aerco AERS 101	Man With No Brain/Long Time Coming (p/s) 10

RICARDO
52	Melodisc MEL 1210	Grenada (Land Of Spice)/Banana Song (78) 10

BOYD RICE & FRIENDS
90	New European BADVC 1969	MUSIC, MARTINIS AND MISANTHROPY (LP, with inner sleeve) 25

(see also Non, Death In June, Current 93)

MACK RICE
69	Atlantic 584 250	Love's A Mother Brother/Coal Man 4

MANDY RICE-DAVIES
64	Ember EMB 4537	MANDY (EP) 40

TIM RICE & WEBBER GROUP
69	RCA RCA 1895	Come Back Richard (Your Country Needs You)/Roll On Over The Atlantic 4

(see also Tales Of Justine, Nightshift)

BUDDY RICH
67	Fontana TF 836	Norwegian Wood/The Monitor Theme 5
56	Columbia Clef SEB 10024	BUDDY RICH (EP) 8
57	Columbia Clef SEB 10071	SWINGING BUDDY RICH (EP) 8
56	HMV CLP 1092	BUDDY RICH SINGS JOHNNY MERCER (LP) 15
56	Columbia Clef 33CX 10052	THE WAILING BUDDY RICH (LP) 15
57	Columbia Clef 33CX 10071	THIS ONE'S FOR BASIE (LP) 15
57	Columbia Clef 33CX 10080	BUDDY AND SWEETS (LP, with Harry 'Sweets' Edison) 30
58	HMV CLP 1185	BUDDY RICH JUST SINGS (LP) 12
59	Columbia Clef 33CX 10138	BUDDY RICH AT MIAMI (LP) 12
68	Liberty LBL/LBS 83090	TAKE IT AWAY! (LP) 12
80	Pye NSPL 18620	THE MAN FROM PLANET JAZZ (LP) 20

BUDDY RICH & MAX ROACH
60	Mercury MMC 14031	RICH VERSUS ROACH (LP, also stereo CMS 18021) 12

(see also Max Roach)

CHARLIE RICH
60	London HLU 9107	Lonely Weekends/Everything I Do Is Wrong 30
62	London HLS 9482	Just A Little Bit Sweet/It's Too Late 25
65	RCA RCA 1433	Too Many Teardrops/It's All Over Now 8
65	Philips BF 1432	Mohair Sam/I Washed My Hands In Muddy Water 8
67	London HLU 10104	Love Is After Me/Pass On By (silver-top label, later boxed logo label) 20/7
69	Mercury MF 1109	Mohair Sam/I Washed My Hands In Muddy Water (reissue) 4
65	RCA RD 7719	THAT'S RICH (LP) 35
66	Philips BL 7695	THE MANY NEW SIDES OF CHARLIE RICH (LP) 20
73	Epic Q 65716	BEHIND CLOSED DOORS (LP, quadrophonic) 12
75	London ZGU 136	CHARLIE RICH SINGS THE SONGS OF HANK WILLIAMS & OTHERS (LP) 12
75	Epic EPC 80532	THE SILVER FOX (LP) 12
76	Epic EPC 69206	SILVER LININGS (LP) 12

DAVE RICH
58	RCA RCA 1092	Burn On Love Fire/City Lights 15
58	RCA RCA 1092	Burn On Love Fire/City Lights (78) 15
66	Polydor BM 56113	Last Two People On Earth/I Just Wanna Dance 5

JOHNNY RICH
64	Mercury MF 836	Dream On/Together 4

LEWIS RICH
66	Parlophone R 5434	I Don't Want To Hear It Anymore/Shedding Tears 8

PAUL RICH (& BEATMEN)
59	Embassy WB 322	Smoke Gets In Your Eyes/Problems 5
59	Embassy WB 327	Does Your Chewing Gum Lose Its Flavour (On The Bedpost Overnight)/
		Stagger Lee 5
59	Embassy WB 330	Venus/Wonderful Secret Of Love 5
59	Embassy WB 345	Battle Of New Orleans/BUD ASHTON: Peter Gunn 5
59	Embassy WB 353	I'm Gonna Get Married/Mona Lisa 5
59	Embassy WB 363	Makin' Love/GORDON FRANKS SEXTET: Red River Rock 5
60	Embassy WB 374	Heartaches By The Number/BUD ASHTON: Some Kinda Earthquake 5
60	Embassy WB 374	Heartaches By The Number/BUD ASHTON: Some Kinda Earthquake (78) 8
60	Embassy WB 378	Little White Bull/Harbour Lights 5
60	Embassy WB 378	Little White Bull/Harbour Lights (78) 8
60	Embassy WB 387	My Old Man's A Dustman/Fings Ain't Wot They Used To Be 5
60	Embassy WB 387	My Old Man's A Dustman/Fings Ain't Wot They Used To Be (78) 10
60	Embassy WB 403	What A Mouth/Itsy Bitsy Teeny Weeny Yellow Polka Dot Bikini 5
60	Embassy WB 403	What A Mouth/Itsy Bitsy Teeny Weeny Yellow Polka Dot Bikini (78) 12
60	Embassy WB 411	Tell Laura I Love Her/Lorelei 5

MINT VALUE £

60	Embassy WB 411	Tell Laura I Love Her/Lorelei (78)	15
61	Embassy WB 479	Tower Of Strength/Hit The Road Jack	5
62	Embassy WB 548	Don't You Think It's Time/Little Town Flirt	5
62	Embassy WB 567	Young Lovers (as Paul Rich & Kay Barry)/JOAN BAXTER: I Will Follow Him	5
64	Embassy WB 637	No Particular Place To Go (as Paul Rich & Beatmen)/ TERRY BRANDON & BEATMEN: I Love You Baby	5
65	Embassy WB 678	Keep Searchin' (as Paul Rich & Beatmen)/BURT SHANE: The Special Years	5

(see also Bud Ashton, Jaybirds, Jean Campbell)

RICHIE RICH
89	ffrr FX 113	Salsa House (Silver On Black Mix)/(Original Mix)/(Orbital Mix) (12")	15
89	ffrr FXR 156	You Used To Salsa/You Used To Hold Me (12", remix)	25

SKETTO RICH
70	Pama PM 806	Hound Dog/Black Girl	6
71	Big Shot BI 596	Know Your Friend/Know Your Friend — Version	6

(see Ruddy & Sketto, Father Sketto, Owen Gray)

TONY RICH
66	Piccadilly 7N 35291	Save Your Love/Don't Mention Your Name	6
66	Piccadilly 7N 35323	It's All Up To You Now/See Saw	6

(see also Tony Sheveton)

RICHARD & GLEN
72	Duke DU 141	Boat To Progress (Parts 1 & 2)	8

RICHARD & YOUNG LIONS
66	Philips BF 1520	Open Up Your Door/Once Upon Your Smile	40

RICHARD BROTHERS
63	Island WI 060	I Need A Girl/Desperate Lover	15
63	Island WI 109	I Shall Wear A Crown/BABA BROOKS: Robin Hood	18

(see also Joe White)

CLIFF RICHARD (& DRIFTERS/SHADOWS)
78s
58	Columbia DB 4178	Move It!/Schoolboy Crush (78)	50
58	Columbia DB 4203	High Class Baby/My Feet Hit The Ground (78)	45
59	Columbia DB 4249	Livin' Lovin' Doll/Steady With You (78)	100
59	Columbia DB 4290	Mean Streak/Never Mind (78)	120
59	Columbia DB 4306	Living Doll/Apron Strings (78)	50

(The above 78s were credited to Cliff Richard & Drifters)

59	Columbia DB 4351	Travellin' Light/Dynamite (78)	70
60	Columbia DB 4398	A Voice In The Wilderness/Don't Be Mad At Me (78)	90
60	Columbia DB 4431	Fall In Love With You/Willie And The Hand Jive (78, existence unconfirmed)	150+

(The above 78s were credited to Cliff Richard & Shadows)

COLUMBIA SINGLES
58	Columbia DB 4178	Move It!/Schoolboy Crush (green label, later black)	15/35
58	Columbia DB 4203	High Class Baby/My Feet Hit The Ground (green label, later black)	15/35
59	Columbia DB 4249	Livin' Lovin' Doll/Steady With You (green label, later black)	20/40
59	Columbia DB 4290	Mean Streak/Never Mind (green label, later black)	12/35
59	Columbia DB 4306	Living Doll/Apron Strings (green label, later black)	6/30

(The above singles were credited to Cliff Richard & Drifters)

59	Columbia DB 4351	Travellin' Light/Dynamite	6
60	Columbia DB 4398	A Voice In The Wilderness/Don't Be Mad At Me	6
60	Columbia DB 4431	Fall In Love With You/Willie And The Hand Jive	6
60	Columbia DB 4479	Please Don't Tease/Where Is My Heart	6
60	Columbia DB 4506	Nine Times Out Of Ten/Thinking Of Our Love	7
60	Columbia DB 4547	I Love You/"D" In Love	6
61	Columbia DB 4593	Theme For A Dream/Mumblin' Mosie	6
61	Columbia DB 4667	A Girl Like You/Now's The Time To Fall In Love	6
61	Columbia DB 4716	When The Girl In Your Arms Is The Girl In Your Heart/ Got A Funny Feeling (solo)	6
62	Columbia DB 4761	The Young Ones/We Say Yeah (green label, later black)	5/7
62	Columbia DB 4828	I'm Lookin' Out The Window/Do You Want To Dance?	6
62	Columbia DB 4886	It'll Be Me/Since I Lost You	6

(The above 45s were originally green labels; later black label copies are worth at least twice the listed values unless stated.)

62	Columbia DB 4950	The Next Time/Bachelor Boy	5
63	Columbia DB 4977	Summer Holiday/Dancing Shoes	5
63	Columbia DB 7034	Lucky Lips/I Wonder	5
63	Columbia DB 7089	It's All In The Game/Your Eyes Tell On You (solo)	5
63	Columbia DB 7150	Don't Talk To Him/Say You're Mine	5
64	Columbia DB 7203	I'm The Lonely One/Watch What You Do With My Baby	5
64	Columbia DB 7272	Constantly (solo)/True True Lovin'	5
64	Columbia DB 7305	On The Beach/A Matter Of Moments	6
64	Columbia DB 7372	The Twelfth Of Never/I'm Afraid To Go Home (solo)	5
64	Columbia DB 7420	I Could Easily Fall (In Love With You)/I'm In Love With You	5

(The above singles were credited to Cliff Richard & Shadows unless stated; the singles listed below were solo unless stated.)

64	Columbia DB 7435	This Was My Special Day/I'm Feeling Oh So Lovely (withdrawn, credited to Cliff Richard, Audrey Bayley, Joan Palethorpe & Faye Fisher)	40
65	Columbia DB 7496	The Minute You're Gone/Just Another Guy	5
65	Columbia DB 7596	On My Word/Just A Little Bit Too Late	6
65	Columbia DB 7660	The Time In Between/Look Before You Love (as Cliff Richard & Shadows)	6
65	Columbia DB 7745	Wind Me Up (Let Me Go)/The Night	5
66	Columbia DB 7866	Blue Turns To Grey/Somebody Loses (as Cliff Richard & Shadows)	6
66	Columbia DB 7968	Visions/What Would I Do (For The Love Of A Girl?)	6
66	Columbia DB 8017	Time Drags By/La La La Song (as Cliff Richard & Shadows)	5
66	Columbia DB 8094	In The Country/Finders Keepers (as Cliff Richard & Shadows)	6

MINT VALUE £

67	Columbia DB 8150	It's All Over/Why Wasn't I Born Rich?	6
67	Columbia DB 8210	I'll Come Runnin'/I Get The Feelin'	10
67	Columbia DB 8245	The Day I Met Marie/Our Story Book	5
67	Columbia DB 8293	All My Love/Sweet Little Jesus Boy	5
68	Columbia DB 8376	Congratulations/High 'N' Dry	5
68	Columbia DB 8437	I'll Love You Forever Today/Girl, You'll Be A Woman Soon	10
68	Columbia DB 8476	Marianne/Mr Nice	8
68	Columbia DB 8503	Don't Forget To Catch Me/What's More (I Don't Need Her)	8
69	Columbia DB 8548	Good Times (Better Times)/Occasional Rain	7
69	Columbia DB 8581	Big Ship/She's Leaving You	10
69	Columbia DB 8615	Throw Down A Line (as Cliff & Hank)/Reflections	6
69	Columbia DB 8641	With The Eyes Of A Child/So Long	7
70	Columbia DB 8657	Joy Of Living (as Cliff & Hank)/CLIFF RICHARD: Leave My Woman Alone/HANK MARVIN: Boogatoo	7
70	Columbia DB 8685	Goodbye Sam, Hello Samantha/You Never Can Tell	5
70	Columbia DB 8708	I Ain't Got Time Anymore/Monday Comes Too Soon	6
71	Columbia DB 8747	Sunny Honey Girl/Don't Move Away (with Olivia Newton-John)/I Was Only Fooling Myself	10
71	Columbia DB 8774	Silvery Rain/Annabella Umbrella/Time Flies	10
71	Columbia DB 8797	Flying Machine/Pigeon	10
71	Columbia DB 8836	Sing A Song Of Freedom/A Thousand Conversations	5
72	Columbia DB 8864	Jesus/Mister Cloud	10
72	Columbia DB 8917	Living In Harmony/Empty Chairs	6
72	Columbia DB 8957	Brand New Song/The Old Accordion	15

EXPORT SINGLES

61	Columbia DC 756	Gee Whiz It's You/I Cannot Find A True Love	8
63	Columbia DC 758	What'd I Say/Blue Moon	300
65	Columbia DC 762	Angel/Razzle Dazzle	100

EMI SINGLES

73	EMI EMI 2012	Power To All Our Friends/Come Back Billie Joe	5
73	EMI EMI 2022	Help It Along/Tomorrow Rising/The Days Of Love/Ashes To Ashes (some in p/s)	12/6
73	EMI EMI 2088	Take Me High/Celestial Houses	5
74	EMI PSR 368	Nothing To Remind Me/The Learning (promo only)	40
74	EMI EMI 2150	(You Keep Me) Hangin' On/Love Is Here	5
75	EMI EMI 2279	It's Only Me You've Left Behind/You're The One	15
75	EMI EMI 2344	Honky Tonk Angel/(Wouldn't You Know It) Got Myself A Girl	20
76	EMI EMI 2376	Miss You Nights/Love Is Enough (later available with p/s in box set)	6/5
76	EMI EMI 2458	Devil Woman/Love On (Shine On)	5
76	EMI EMI 2499	I Can't Ask For Anything More Than You/Junior Cowboy	5
76	EMI EMI 2559	Hey Mr Dream Maker/No One Waits	5
77	EMI EMI 2584	My Kinda Life/Nothing Left For Me To Say	5
77	EMI EMI 2633	When Two Worlds Drift Apart/That's Why I Love You	5
78	EMI EMI 2730	Yes! He Lives/Good On The Sally Army	15
78	EMI EMI 2832	Please Remember Me/Please Don't Tease	8
78	EMI EMI 2885	Can't Take The Hurt Anymore/Needing A Friend (p/s)	6
79	EMI EMI 2920	Green Light/Imagine Love (some in p/s)	30/5
79	EMI EMI 2975	We Don't Talk Anymore/Count Me Out (p/s)	4
79	EMI EMI 2975	We Don't Talk Anymore/Count Me Out (p/s, mispress, A-side plays Queen's "Bohemian Rhapsody")	12
79	EMI EMI 5003	Hot Shot/Walking In The Light (p/s)	4
80	EMI EMI 5006	Carrie/Moving In (p/s)	4
82	EMI EMI 5341	Where Do We Go From Here/Discovering (p/s)	4
82	EMI EMIP 5348	Little Town/Love And A Helping Hand/You Me And Jesus (picture disc)	6
83	EMI 12EMI 5415	Never Say Die (Give A Little Bit More)/Lucille (12", p/s)	10
83	EMI EMI 5437	Please Don't Fall In Love/Too Close To Heaven (p/s)	5
84	EMI EMI 5457	Ocean Deep/Baby You're Dynamite (different version) (blue p/s, A & B-sides reversed)	15
84	EMI 12EMI 5457	Baby You're Dynamite (Extended Mix)/Ocean Deep (12", p/s)	12
84	EMI RICHP 1	Shooting From The Heart/Small World (heart-shaped picture disc)	12
85	EMI RICHP 2/RICHP 1	Heart User/I Will Follow You//Shooting From The Heart/Small World (shrinkwrapped double pack, 2nd single as shaped picture disc)	12
85	EMI 12 RICH 2	Heart User (Extended)/I Will Follow You (12", poster p/s)	10
86	WEA YZ 65P	Living Doll (with Young Ones)/YOUNG ONES: (All The Little Flowers Are) Happy (picture disc)	8
86	WEA YZ 65T	Living Doll (The Disco Funk Get Up Get Down Go To The Lavatory Mix) (with Young Ones)/YOUNG ONES: (All The Little Flowers Are) Happy (12", p/s)	7
85	EMI EMI 5531	She's So Beautiful/(Special Mix) (p/s, some with 'Time' inner sleeve)	6/4
85	EMI 12EMI 5531	She's So Beautiful (Extended Mix)/She's So Beautiful (12", p/s)	7
85	EMI EMI 5537	It's In Every One Of Us/Alone (p/s, some with 'Time' inner sleeve)	6/4
86	EMI EMI 5545	Born To Rock And Roll/Law Of The Universe (p/s, some with 'Time' inner)	6/4
86	EMI 12EMI 5545	Born To Rock And Roll (Special Extended Mix)/Born To Rock And Roll/Law Of The Universe (12", p/s)	8
87	EMI EMG 4	My Pretty One/Love Ya (gatefold p/s)	5
87	EMI 12EMP 4	My Pretty One/Love Ya/Under The Gun (12", p/s with poster)	7
87	EMI EMG 18	Some People/One Time Lover Man (gatefold p/s with booklet)	5
87	EMI EMP 18	Some People/One Time Lover Man (Cliff-shaped picture disc)	10
87	EMI EM 31	Remember Me/Another Christmas Day (gold-embossed p/s)	6
87	EMI 12EMP 31	Remember Me/Another Christmas Day/Brave New World (12", gold embossed p/s)	10
87	EMI 12EMT 31	Remember Me/Another Christmas Day/Brave New World (12", poster p/s)	7
87	EMI CDEM 31	Remember Me/Some People/Another Christmas Day/Remember Me (12" Version) (CD, card sleeve with inner)	10
87	EMI EMP 42	Two Hearts/Yesterday, Today, Forever (double heart-shaped picture disc)	10
87	EMI EMG 42	Two Hearts/Yesterday, Today, Forever (gatefold p/s)	5
87	EMI 12EMG 42	Two Hearts/Yesterday, Today, Forever/Wild Geese (12", gatefold p/s)	8

Cliff RICHARD

Year	Catalogue	Description	Value
88	EMI CDEM 42	Two Hearts/Yesterday, Today, Forever/Two Hearts (Ext.)/Wild Geese (CD)	10
88	EMI EMS 78	Mistletoe And Wine/Marmaduke/True Love Ways (p/s)	4
88	EMI EMP 78	Mistletoe And Wine/Marmaduke (poster/calendar p/s)	5
88	EMI 12EMX 78	Mistletoe And Wine/Marmaduke/Little Town (12", Advent calendar p/s)	12
88	EMI CDEM 78	Mistletoe And Wine/Marmaduke/Little Town/La Gonave (CD, with Christmas card)	10
89	EMI EM 92	The Best Of Me/Move It/Lindsay Jane (gold '100th Single' p/s)	6
89	EMI 12EM 92	The Best Of Me/Move It/Lindsay Jane/High Class Baby (12", gold '100th Single' p/s)	8
89	EMI CDEM 92	The Best Of Me/Move It/Lindsay Jane/High Class Baby (CD)	8
89	EMI CDEMS 92	The Best Of Me/Move It/Lindsay Jane/High Class Baby (CD, gold '100th Single' card sleeve)	10
89	EMI EM 101	I Just Don't Have The Heart/Wide Open Space (p/s, white label)	5
89	EMI 12EM 101	I Just Don't Have The Heart/Wide Open Space/I Just Don't Have The Heart (Instrumental) (12", p/s, white label)	7
89	EMI 12EMP 101	I Just Don't Have The Heart/Wide Open Space/I Just Don't Have The Heart (Instrumental) (12", poster p/s)	7
89	EMI 12EMX 101	I Just Don't Have The Heart (Remix)/Wide Open Space /I Just Don't Have The Heart (Instrumental) (12", plain black sleeve)	10
89	EMI CDEM 101	I Just Don't Have The Heart/Wide Open Space/ I Just Don't Have The Heart (Instrumental) (CD)	10
89	EM EMPD 105	Lean On You/Hey Mister (Cliff-shaped picture disc)	8
89	EM CDEM 105	Lean On You (Extended Mix)/Lean On You/Hey Mister (CD)	10
89	EMI EM 129	Stronger Than That/Joanna (p/s, with 3 postcards pack)	7
89	EMI 12EM 129	Stronger Than That (Extended Version)/Joanna/Stronger Than That (12" p/s, some with 'signed' print)	8/7
89	EMI CDEM 129	Stronger Than That (Extended Version)/Joanna/Stronger Than That (CD)	10
89	EMI EMS 152	Silhouettes/The Winner ('photoframe' p/s with stand)	5
89	EMI 12EM 152	Silhouettes/The Winner/All The Time You Need (12", p/s)	7
89	EMI CDEM 152	Silhouettes/The Winner/All The Time You Need (CD)	8
90	EMI EMPD 155	From A Distance/I Could Easily Fall (picture disc, PVC sleeve)	5
90	EMI 12EMP 155	From A Distance/Lindsay Jane II/Wired For Sound (12", poster p/s)	8
90	EMI CDEM 155	From A Distance/Lindsay Jane II/Wired For Sound (CD)	8
90	EMI XMAS P90	Saviour's Day/Oh! Boy Medley ('Xmas' pack, envelope p/s with 5 photos)	7
90	EMI 12XMAS 90	Saviour's Day/Oh! Boy Medley/Where You Are (12", p/s)	7
90	EMI CDXMAS 90	Saviour's Day/Oh! Boy Medley/Where You Are (CD)	10
91	EMI EM 205	More To Life/Mo's Theme (Intrumental) (p/s)	4
91	EMI CDEM 205	More To Life/Mo's Theme (Intrumental) (CD)	8
91	EMI XMAS G91/XMAS 91	We Should Be Together/Miss You Nights (live)//We Should Be Together/ Twelve Days Of Christmas/Mistletoe And Wine/The Holly And The Ivy (Acapella Version) (double pack, gatefold p/s, discs sold separately)	7
91	EMI CDXMAS 91	We Should Be Together/Miss You Nights (live)/Mistletoe And Wine (CD)	8
91	EMI EM 218	This New Year/Scarlet Ribbons (p/s, 1 side etched with autograph)	5
91	EMI 12EMP 218	This New Year/Scarlet Ribbons/We Don't Talk (12", p/s with poster)	7
91	EMI CDEM 218	This New Year/Scarlet Ribbons/We Don't Talk (CD)	8
92	EMI EM 255	I Still Believe In You/Bulange Downpour (p/s)	4
92	EMI CDEMS 255	I Still Believe In You/Bulange Downpour/There's No Power In Pity (CD)	8
92	EMI CDEM 255	I Still Believe In You/Remember (Worlds Drift Apart)/ Ocean Deep (CD)	10
93	EMI CDEMS 265	Peace In Our Time/Somebody Loves You/That's Alright Mama (CD)	7
93	EMI CDEM 265	Peace In Our Time (7" Remix)/Peace In Our Time (Gospel Mix)/Livin' Doll (live)/Peace In Our Time (Instrumental) (CD)	7
93	EMI CDEMS 267	Human Work Of Art/Move It ('92 Live Version)/Never Even Thought (CD)	7
93	EMI CDEM 267	Human Work Of Art (7" Version)/Devil Woman/Ragged/Free (Live Version) (CD)	7
93	EMI EM 281	Never Let Go/Congratulations (p/s, with poster)	4
93	EMI CDEMS 281	Never Let Go/Congratulations/The Young Ones/You've Got Me Wondering (CD, box set with three prints)	8
93	EMI CDEM 294	Healing Love/Healing (12" Remix)/Yesterday's Memories/Some People (CD, box set, with badge & signed print)	8
93	EMI CDEMS 294	Healing Love/Carrie/Daddy's Home/Some People (CD)	7
94	EMI CDEMS 359	All I Have To Do Is Dream (with Phil Everly)/Miss You Nights/When Will I Be Loved/Tribute To The Legends (Medley) (CD)	7
94	EMI CDEM 359	All I Have To Do Is Dream (with Phil Everly)/Miss You Nights/True Love Ways/ Party Megamix (CD)	7

POLYDOR SINGLES

Year	Catalogue	Description	Value
86	Polydor POSPX 802	All I Ask Of You (with Sarah Brightman)/ROYAL PHILHARMONIC ORCHESTRA: Phantom Of The Opera Overture (Act II)/Over You (12", p/s)	7
89	Polydor VANCD 2	Whenever God Shines His Light (7" Version) (with Van Morrison)/ VAN MORRISON: I'd Love To Write Another Song/Cry For Home/ Whenever God Shines His Light (Album Version)	7
89	Polydor VANX 2	Whenever God Shines His Light (Album Version) (with Van Morrison)/ VAN MORRISON: Cry For Home/I'd Love To Write Another Song (12", p/s)	7

FLEXIDISCS & OTHER RELEASES

Year	Catalogue	Description	Value
60	Serenade Magazine/ Rainbow (no cat. no.)	Serenade Presents Cliff Richard's Personal Message To You (turquoise flexidisc free with magazine)	25/20
60s	Serenade Magazine	Cliff's Rock Party (flexidisc with magazine)	30/20
60s	Boyfriend Magazine	untitled flexidisc with magazine	30/20
60s	Rainbow Magazine	Music From America (flexidisc with magazine)	35/25
60s	New Spotlight	Star Souvenir Greetings (208 Radio Luxembourg flexidisc)	20
73	Lyntone LYN SF 1218	The Cliff Richard Story (World Record Club 1-sided flexidisc)	6
73	Spree (no cat. no.)	Good News (plain black flexidisc with spoken/sung introduction from Cliff, other side by Johnny Cash)	20
70s	Lyntone LYN 14745	The Best Of Cliff Richard And The Shadows (preview flexidisc)	8
80s	Weetabix	Children's Hospital Appeal (spoken-word cassette)	5
98	Cruisin' The 50's CASB 007	Breathless/Lawdy Miss Clawdy (10" 78, p/s, with 6 inserts)	15

CLIFF RICHARD

EPs

59	Columbia SEG 7895	SERIOUS CHARGE (EP, soundtrack)	30
59	Columbia SEG 7903	CLIFF NO. 1 (EP, also stereo ESG 7754)	30/60
59	Columbia SEG 7910	CLIFF NO. 2 (EP, also stereo ESG 7769)	30/60
59	Columbia SEG 7971	EXPRESSO BONGO (EP, soundtrack, also stereo ESG 7783)	20/40
60	Columbia SEG 7979	CLIFF SINGS NO. 1 (EP, also stereo ESG 7788)	25/55
60	Columbia SEG 7987	CLIFF SINGS NO. 2 (EP, also stereo ESG 7794)	25/55
60	Columbia SEG 8005	CLIFF SINGS NO. 3 (EP, also stereo ESG 7808)	25/55
60	Columbia SEG 8021	CLIFF SINGS NO. 4 (EP, also stereo ESG 7816)	25/55
60	Columbia SEG 8050	CLIFF'S SILVER DISCS (EP)	18
60	Columbia SEG 8065	ME AND MY SHADOWS NO. 1 (EP, also stereo ESG 7837)	25/50
61	Columbia SEG 8071	ME AND MY SHADOWS NO. 2 (EP, also stereo ESG 7481)	25/50
61	Columbia SEG 8078	ME AND MY SHADOWS NO. 3 (EP, also stereo ESG 7843)	25/50
61	Columbia SEG 8105	LISTEN TO CLIFF NO. 1 (EP, also stereo ESG 7858)	25/50
61	Columbia SEG 8119	DREAM (EP, also stereo ESG 7867)	18/50
61	Columbia SEG 8126	LISTEN TO CLIFF NO. 2 (EP, also stereo ESG 7870)	25/50
62	Columbia SEG 8133	CLIFF'S HIT PARADE (EP)	18
62	Columbia SEG 8151	CLIFF RICHARD (EP)	30
62	Columbia SEG 8159	HITS FROM 'THE YOUNG ONES' (EP)	15
62	Columbia SEG 8168	CLIFF RICHARD NO. 2 (EP)	30

(The above EPs were originally issued with turquoise labels, later blue/black label copies are worth two-thirds these values.)

62	Columbia SEG 8203	CLIFF'S HITS (EP)	18
63	Columbia SEG 8228	TIME FOR CLIFF AND THE SHADOWS (EP, mono)	22
63	Columbia ESG 7887	TIME FOR CLIFF AND THE SHADOWS (EP, stereo, turquoise or blue/black)	55/45
63	Columbia SEG 8246	HOLIDAY CARNIVAL (EP, also stereo ESG 7892)	18/45
63	Columbia SEG 8250	HITS FROM 'SUMMER HOLIDAY' (EP, also stereo ESG 7896)	15/40
63	Columbia SEG 8263	MORE HITS FROM 'SUMMER HOLIDAY' (EP, also stereo ESG 7898)	25/40
63	Columbia SEG 8269	CLIFF'S LUCKY LIPS (EP)	18
63	Columbia SEG 8272	LOVE SONGS (EP, also stereo ESG 7900)	18/55
64	Columbia SEG 8290	WHEN IN FRANCE (EP)	22
64	Columbia SEG 8299	CLIFF SINGS 'DON'T TALK TO HIM' (EP)	22
64	Columbia SEG 8320	CLIFF'S PALLADIUM SUCCESSES (EP)	30
64	Columbia SEG 8338	WONDERFUL LIFE (EP, also stereo ESG 7902)	18/45
64	Columbia SEG 8347	A FOREVER KIND OF LOVE (EP)	25
64	Columbia SEG 8354	WONDERFUL LIFE NO. 2 (EP, also stereo ESG 7903)	20/45
64	Columbia SEG 8376	HITS FROM 'WONDERFUL LIFE' (EP, also stereo ESG 7906)	22/50
65	Columbia SEG 8384	WHY DON'T THEY UNDERSTAND? (EP)	25
65	Columbia SEG 8395	CLIFF'S HITS FROM 'ALADDIN AND HIS WONDERFUL LAMP' (EP)	18
65	Columbia SEG 8405	LOOK IN MY EYES, MARIA (EP)	25
65	Columbia SEG 8444	ANGEL (EP)	35
65	Columbia SEG 8450	TAKE FOUR (EP)	35
66	Columbia SEG 8474	WIND ME UP (EP)	25

Cliff RICHARD

66	Columbia SEG 8478	HITS FROM 'WHEN IN ROME' (EP)	60
66	Columbia SEG 8488	LOVE IS FOREVER (EP)	40
66	Columbia SEG 8510	THUNDERBIRDS ARE GO! (EP, 3 tracks by Cliff & Shadows, 1 solo)	60
66	Columbia SEG 8517	LA LA LA LA LA (EP, 1 track by Bruce Welch & Hank Marvin)	35
67	Columbia SEG 8527	CINDERELLA (EP)	100
67	Columbia SEG 8533	CAROL SINGERS (EP)	35
68	Columbia SEG 8540	CONGRATULATIONS (EP)	25
77	EMI PSR 410	EVERY FACE TELLS A STORY (Promo EP)	20
77	EMI PSR 414/415	40 GOLDEN GREATS (EP, double pack promo, issued to shops only)	30

COLUMBIA LPs

59	Columbia 33SX 1147	CLIFF (LP, green labels, later blue/black labels)	45/30
59	Columbia 33SX 1192	CLIFF SINGS (LP, green labels, later blue/black labels)	40/30
60	Columbia 33SX 1261	ME AND MY SHADOWS (LP, also stereo SCX 3330)	30/60
61	Columbia 33SX 1320	LISTEN TO CLIFF! (LP, also stereo SCX 3375)	25/60
61	Columbia 33SX 1368	21 TODAY (LP, also stereo SCX 3409)	25/60
61	Columbia 33SX 1384	THE YOUNG ONES (LP, soundtrack with inner, also stereo SCX 3397)	18/35
62	Columbia 33SX 1431	32 MINUTES AND 17 SECONDS WITH... (LP, also stereo SCX 3436)	25/60

(The above LPs were originally issued with green labels, later blue/black copies are worth two-thirds the value unless stated.)

63	Columbia 33SX 1472	SUMMER HOLIDAY (LP, soundtrack with inner sleeve, mono)	15
63	Columbia SCX 3462	SUMMER HOLIDAY (LP, stereo, initially green labels, later blue/black)	30/20
63	Columbia SX 1512	CLIFF'S HIT ALBUM (LP)	15
63	Columbia SX 1541	WHEN IN SPAIN (LP, also stereo SCX 3488)	20/30
64	Columbia SX 1628	WONDERFUL LIFE (LP, soundtrack, mono, with inner sleeve)	15
64	Columbia SCX 3515	WONDERFUL LIFE (LP, soundtrack, stereo, with inner sleeve)	25
64	Columbia SX 1676/ SCX 3522	ALADDIN AND HIS WONDERFUL LAMP (LP, with stage cast, gatefold sleeve, mono/stereo)	18/25
65	Columbia SX 1709	CLIFF RICHARD (LP, also stereo SCX 3546)	35/40
65	Columbia SX 1737	MORE HITS BY CLIFF (LP, also stereo SCX 3555)	14/18
65	Columbia SX 1762	WHEN IN ROME (LP)	35
65	Columbia SX 1769	LOVE IS FOREVER (LP, also stereo SCX 3569)	22
66	Columbia S(C)X 6039	KINDA LATIN (LP, mono/stereo)	30/35
66	Columbia S(C)X 6079	FINDERS KEEPERS (LP, soundtrack, with inner sleeve, mono/stereo)	15/20
67	Columbia S(C)X 6103	CINDERELLA (LP, with stage cast)	35
67	Columbia S(C)X 6133	DON'T STOP ME NOW (LP)	30
67	Columbia S(C)X 6167	GOOD NEWS (LP)	18
67	Columbia JSX 6167	GOOD NEWS (LP, export issue)	35
68	Columbia S(C)X 6244	CLIFF IN JAPAN (LP, blue/black labels, later white/black labels)	30/20
68	Columbia S(C)X 6262	TWO A PENNY (LP, blue/black labels, later white/black labels)	25/18
68	Columbia S(C)X 6282	ESTABLISHED 1958 (LP, gatefold sleeve, half tracks by Shadows, mono/stereo)	18/15

(The above Columbia LPs were originally issued with blue/black labels;
white/black copies are worth half the value unless stated)

69	Columbia S(C)X 6343	THE BEST OF CLIFF (LP)	15
69	Columbia S(C)X 6357	SINCERELY CLIFF RICHARD (LP, mono/stereo)	25/20
70	Columbia SCX 6408	ABOUT THAT MAN (LP, 4 songs plus narration)	125
70	Columbia SCX 6435	TRACKS 'N' GROOVES (LP)	25
70	Columbia SCX 6443	HIS LAND (LP, documentary soundtrack, with Cliff Barrows)	60
71	Columbia SCX 1512	CLIFF'S HIT ALBUM (LP, stereo reissue)	10
72	Columbia SCX 6519	THE BEST OF CLIFF VOLUME 2 (LP)	15

EMI ALBUMS

73	EMI EMC 3016	TAKE ME HIGH (LP, soundtrack, some with poster)	25/15
74	EMI EMA 768	HELP IT ALONG (LP, gatefold sleeve)	25
74	EMI EMC 3048	THE 31ST OF FEBRUARY STREET (LP)	30
74	EMI TC EXSP 1601	THE MUSIC AND LIFE OF CLIFF RICHARD (6-cassette box set, music & interviews, with Brian Bennett, Olivia Newton-John, Cilla Black etc.)	25
82	EMI PSLP 350	CLIFF (LP, promo-only sampler)	40
83	EMI EMC 1077 871/881	SILVER/ROCK'N'ROLL SILVER (2-LP, box set, with booklet)	20
84	EMI CLIFF 2	THE ROCK CONNECTION (LP)	12
84	EMI TC CLIFF 2	THE ROCK CONNECTION (cassette)	10
87	EMI EMDB 1004	ALWAYS GUARANTEED (LP, box set, some in embossed sleeve with free 7" "Another Christmas Day")	15/12
89	EMI CR 1	THE 30TH ANNIVERSARY PICTURE RECORD COLLECTION (2-LP, picture discs, gatefold sleeve, mail-order only)	50
90	EMI CRTVB 31	FROM A DISTANCE ... THE EVENT (LP, box set, includes 6 prints, engraved 7" "Miss You Nights (A Capella Version)" & lyric poster)	15
90	EMI CRTVBC 31	FROM A DISTANCE ... THE EVENT (cassette, box set, includes 6 prints, engraved 7" "Miss You Nights (A Capella Version)" & lyric poster)	12
91	EMI EMD 1028	TOGETHER WITH CLIFF (LP, with inner sleeve)	10
93	EMI EMD 1043	CLIFF RICHARD — THE ALBUM (LP, with innner sleeve)	10

OTHER LPs

62	World R. Club STP 1051	CLIFF RICHARD (LP)	60
63	Elstree Studios	SUMMER HOLIDAY (2-LP, full soundtrack recording, 80 copies only)	300
64	Elstree Studios	WONDERFUL LIFE (2-LP, full soundtrack recording, 150 copies only)	300
64	World Record Club (S)T 643	HOW WONDERFUL TO KNOW (LP, mono/stereo)	20/25
64	EMI Regal SREG 1120	ME AND MY SHADOWS (LP, export issue)	70
69	Regal Starline SRS 5011	IT'LL BE ME (LP, reissue of "32 Minutes And 17 Seconds With Cliff Richard")	12
70	MFP MFP 1420	ALL MY LOVE (LP)	12
70	Regal Starline SRS 5031	CLIFF 'LIVE' AT THE TALK OF THE TOWN (LP)	12
72	World R. Club SM 255-260	THE CLIFF RICHARD STORY (6-LP box set with booklet)	30
72	World R. Club CSM 255-260	THE CLIFF RICHARD STORY (6-cassette box set with booklet)	30
73	Sounds Superb SPR 90018	IT'LL BE ME (LP, 2nd reissue, different cover)	12
75	Sounds Superb SPR 90070	EVERYONE NEEDS SOMEONE TO LOVE (LP)	12
70s	Readers Digest	THE BEST OF CLIFF RICHARD AND THE SHADOWS (8-LP box set)	50
80	World R. Club ALBUM 26	THE CLIFF RICHARD SONGBOOK (6-LP box set)	35

MINT VALUE £

80	WRC CASSETTE 26	THE CLIFF RICHARD SONGBOOK (6-cassette box set)	25
85	Tellydisc TELLY 28	FROM THE HEART (2-LP, gatefold sleeve, mail-order only)	25
85	Myrrh MYR 1176	WALKING IN THE LIGHT (LP, with insert)	15
85	Myrrh MYRC 1176	WALKING IN THE LIGHT (cassette)	10
85	Myrrh MYRCD 1176	WALKING IN THE LIGHT (CD)	20
86	Word WRD R 3017	HYMNS AND INSPIRATIONAL SONGS (LP)	25
86	Word WRD C 3017	HYMNS AND INSPIRATIONAL SONGS (cassette)	10
88	Myrrh MYR R 1209	IT'S A SMALL WORLD (LP)	35
88	Myrrh MYR C 1209	IT'S A SMALL WORLD (cassette)	10
88	Word WRD R 3034	CAROLS (LP)	25
88	Word WRD C 3034	CAROLS (cassette)	10
88	Word WRD R 3036	SMALL CORNERS (LP, reissue)	25
88	Word WRD C 3036	SMALL CORNERS (cassette, reissue)	10

REEL-TO-REEL TAPES

63	Columbia TA-SX 1512	CLIFF'S HIT ALBUM (mono only)	10
65	Columbia TA-SX 1737	MORE HITS BY CLIFF (mono only)	10
66	Columbia TA-SX 6079	FINDERS KEEPERS (mono only)	10
66	Columbia TA-SX 6039	KINDA LATIN (mono only)	10
67	Columbia TA-SX 6133	DON'T STOP ME NOW ... (mono only)	10
67	Columbia TA-SX 6167	GOOD NEWS (mono only)	10
68	Columbia TA-SX 6244	CLIFF IN JAPAN (mono only)	10
68	Columbia TA-SX 6282	ESTABLISHED 1958 (mono only)	10

(see also Drifters [U.K.], Shadows, Olivia Newton-John, Sheila Walsh, Janet Jackson, Elton John, Phil Everly)

WENDY RICHARD & DIANA BERRY

| 63 | Decca F 11680 | We Had A Dream/Keep 'Em Looking Around | 15 |

(see also Mike Sarne)

BARRY RICHARDS

| 73 | MAM R 198 | Durango (parts 1 & 2) | 5 |

CYNTHIA RICHARDS

69	Clandisc CLA 203	Foolish Fool/KING STITT: On The Street	8
70	Clandisc CLA 210	Conversation/DYNAMITES: Conversation Version II	8
70	Clandisc CLA 216	Can't Wait/Promises	6
70	Clandisc CLA 220	Foolish Fool/CLANCY & STITT: Dance Beat	8
71	Clandisc CLA 229	Stand By Your Man (actually by Merlene Webber)/DYNAMITES: Version 2	5
71	Big Shot BI 581	I'm Moving On/HIPPY BOYS: I'm Moving On – Version	6
71	Escort ERT 861	Love & Unity/MAYTONES: Wah Noh Dead	6
71	G.G. GG 4528	Place In My Heart/You've Got A Friend (act. Irving [Brown] & Cynthia Richards)	7
72	Pama Supreme PS 366	Mr Postman/SKIN, FLESH AND BONES: Version	8
73	Attack ATT 8047	Aily I/REID'S ALL STARS: Aily I – Version	5
70	Trojan TBL 123	FOOLISH FOOL (LP, actually Clancy Eccles productions compilation)	20

(see also Bobby Aitken, Lord Comic, Sir Lord Comic)

JOHN RICHARDS

57	HMV POP 401	Let Me Be Loved/By The Fireside	5
65	Oriole CB 312	Folks Get Married In The Spring/Then I'll Be There	5
66	Polydor BM 56705	I Will Go Again To Ireland/Midnight Sky	5

JOHNNY RICHARDS

| 59 | Esquire 32-076 | THE RITES OF DIABLO (LP) | 15 |

KEITH RICHARDS

79	Rolling Stones RSR 102	Run Rudolph Run/The Harder They Come (p/s)	15
86	Arista ARIST 678P	Jumping Jack Flash/Integrity (with Aretha Franklin) (shaped pic disc & plinth)	12
88	Virgin VS 1125	Take It So Hard/I Could Have Stood You Up (p/s)	4
88	Virgin VST 1125	Take It So Hard/I Could Have Stood You Up/It Means A Lot (12", p/s)	7
88	Virgin VSCD 1125	Take It So Hard/I Could Have Stood You Up/It Means A Lot (3" CD, 4" x 4" gatefold card sleeve)	8
89	Virgin VS 1179	Make No Mistake (Edit)/It Means A Lot (p/s)	4
89	Virgin VST 1179	Make No Mistake (Extended Version)/(LP Version)/It Means A Lot (12", p/s)	7
89	Virgin VSCD 1179	Make No Mistake/It Means A Lot/Make No Mistake (Extended Version) (3" CD, card sleeve)	8
88	Virgin KEITH 1234	Make No Mistake/Locked Away/Struggle/Big Enough (4 x 1-sided 7", "Talk Is Cheap" sampler box set, promo only)	75
88	Virgin V 2334	TALK IS CHEAP (LP)	10
88	Virgin 2-91047 A/B/C	TALK IS CHEAP (3 x 3" CDs in tin)	40

(see also Rolling Stones, Aranbee Pop Symphony Orchestra, Dirty Strangers, Screamin' Jay Hawkins)

LISA RICHARDS

| 65 | Vocalion VP 9244 | Mean Old World/Take A Chance | 20 |

LLOYD RICHARDS

| 64 | Port-O-Jam PJ 4004 | Be Good/I Need You | 10 |

ROY RICHARDS

66	Doctor Bird DB 1012	Contact/Maureen	15
66	Island WI 297	Green Collie/MARCIA GRIFFITHS: You No Good	12
66	Island WI 283	Double Trouble/FITSY & FREDDY: Why Did You Do It	12
66	Island WI 299	Western Standard Time/(JA) EAGLES: What An Agony	12
66	Island WI 3000	South Viet Nam/You Must Be Sorry (Vocal)	12
67	Island WI 3027	Rub-A-Dub/SHARKS: Baby Come Home	12
67	Island WI 3037	Hopeful Village Ska/DELROY WILSON: Ungrateful Baby	18
67	Island WI 3050	Port-O-Jam/DELROY WILSON: Get Ready	18
67	Studio One SO 2020	Hanky Panky/ALTON ELLIS: I Am Still In Love	30

(see also Roland Alphonso, Lord Comic, Soul Vendors, Jackie Mittoo, Derrick Morgan, Righteous Flames)

RUSTY RICHARDS

| 60 | Top Rank JAR 297 | Middle Hand Road/Golden Moon (China Night) | 6 |

TRUDY RICHARDS
57	Capitol CL 14728	Wishbone/Hangin' Around	6
57	Capitol CL 14744	Weaker Than Wise/I Want A Big Butter And Egg Man	5
58	Capitol CL 14857	Somebody Just Like You/The Night When Love Was Born	5
57	Capitol EAP 1 1087	CRAZY IN LOVE (EP)	8
57	Capitol T 838	CRAZY IN LOVE (LP)	15

WINSTON RICHARDS
| 67 | Rio R 124 | Studio Blitz/Don't Up | 25 |

JOE 'GROUNDHOG' RICHARDSON
| 69 | Major Minor MM 632 | Take It Off/Blues To Take It Off | 4 |

MARK RICHARDSON
| 65 | Stateside SS 440 | Baby, I'm Sorry/Blanket Fair | 6 |
| 65 | Stateside SS 467 | See It My Way/Think | 6 |

RICHENEL
| 86 | 4AD BAD 601 | L'Esclave Endormi/L'Esclave Endormi (12", p/s) | 7 |

RICH KIDS
78	EMI EMI 2738	Rich Kids/Empty Words (red vinyl, p/s)	10
78	EMI EMI 2803	Marching Men/Here Comes The Nice (p/s)	8
78	EMI EMI 2848	Ghosts Of Princes In Towers/Only Arsenic (no p/s)	8
78	EMI EMC 3263	GHOSTS OF PRINCES IN TOWERS (LP)	18

(see also Sex Pistols, Ultravox, Slik, Spectres, Swingers, Visage)

JONATHAN RICHMAN & MODERN LOVERS
75	United Artists UP 36006	Road Runner/It Will Stand	7
77	Beserkley BZZ 1	Road Runner (Once)/Road Runner (Twice) (p/s)	5
77	Beserkley BSERK 9	ROCK 'N' ROLL WITH THE MODERN LOVERS (LP)	10
77	Beserkley BSERK 2	JONATHAN RICHMAN AND THE MODERN LOVERS (LP)	10
77	Beserkley BSERK 12	MODERN LOVERS LIVE (LP)	10
77	Beserkley BSERK 17	BACK IN YOUR LIFE (LP)	10

RICHMOND
73	Dart ART 2008	Candy Dora/Willow Farm	5
73	Dart ART 2025	Frightened/Breakfast	5
73	Dart ART 2031	Raise Your Heads To The Wind/All I Really Need	5
74	Dart ART 2044	Peaches/Work For My Baby	5
73	Dart ARTS 65371	FRIGHTENED (LP)	20

BEN RICHMOND
| 63 | Piccadilly 7N 35132 | You Gotta Have Love/I Don't Care | 5 |

JANET RICHMOND
60	Top Rank JAR 288	You Got What It Takes/Not One Minute More	7
60	Top Rank JAR 378	June Bride/My One And Only Love	6
61	Top Rank JAR 536	Senora/I Need You	6

RICH MOUNTAIN TOWER
| 72 | London HLO 10359 | Thank You, Maggie/Uncle Bob White | 4 |

RICHUS FLAMES
| 67 | Fab FAB 17 | Need To Be Loved/I Am Going Home | 8 |

(see also Righteous Flames)

RICK & KEENS
| 61 | Mercury AMT 1150 | Peanuts/I'll Be Home | 35 |

BERESFORD RICKETTS
60	Starlite ST45 025	Cherry Baby/I Want To Know	12
60	Starlite ST45 029	Baby Baby/When I Woke Up	12
61	Starlite ST45 048	Hold Me Tight/Dream Girl (as Ricketts & Rowe)	12
62	Starlite ST45 079	I'm Going To Cry/Waiting For Me	12
62	Blue Beat BB 107	You Better Be Going/I've Been Walking (as Beresford Ricketts & Blue Beats)	12
63	Dice CC 12	Oh Jean/Rivers Of Tears (as Lauren Aitken's Group)	10
66	Blue Beat BB 350	Jailer Bring Me Water/Careless Love	12

WAKEY RICKMAN
| 74 | M&A QUAP-779955 | JOURNEY TO THE CENTRE OF THE ROUND TABLE OF THE SIX WIVES OF KING ARTHUR VIII (ON ICE) (7-LP, quadrophonic, 'fold-in' tangram sleeve, some copies with free dinosaur) | 600/400 |

RICO (RODRIGUEZ)
61	Blue Beat BB 56	Luke Lane Shuffle (as Rico Rodrigues & Buster's All Stars)/ BUSTER'S GROUP: Little Honey	18
62	Island WI 022	Rico Special (as Emanuel Rodrigues Orchestra; some copies may credit Reco & His Happy Orchestra)/BUNNY & SKITTER: A Little Mashin'	18
62	Planetone RC 1	London Here I Come/Midnight In Ethiopia	18
62	Planetone RC 4	Planet Rock/You Win	10
62	Planetone RC 5	Youth Boogie/Western Serenade (as Rico's Combo)	10
67	Fab FAB 12	Jingle Bells/Silent Night (with His Boys)	5
68	Pama PM 706	Soul Man/It's Not Unusual (as Reco Rodriguez)	8
68	Pama PM 715	Tender Foot Ska/Memories (as Reco Rodriguez)	8
69	Blue Cat BS 160	The Bullet/Rhythm In (as Reco Rodriguez & His Rhythm Aces)	8
69	Doctor Bird DB 1302	Baby Face (as Reco & Rudies)/RUDIES: News	8
69	Bullet BU 407	Tribute To Don Drummond/Japanese Invasion (as Rico Rodriquez)	7
71	Duke DU 96	Surprise Package (as Rico & Satch)/PETE JOHNSON: I'm Sorry	7
80	2-Tone CHS TT 15	Sea Cruise/Carolina (p/s, paper label)	4
82	2-Tone CHS TT 19	Jungle Music/Rasta Call (paper label, 2-Tone sleeve, with Special A.K.A.)	4
82	2-Tone CHS TT 1219	Jungle Music/Rasta Call/You/Easter Island (12", p/s, with Special A.K.A.)	7

69	Trojan TTL 12	BLOW YOUR HORN (LP, as Rico & Rudies)	30
78	Island ILPS 9485	MAN FROM WARREIKA (LP)	12
70s	Ghetto Rockers PRE 1	WARREIKA DUB (LP)	12

(see also Special A.K.A., Reco, Andy Capp, Don Reco, Reco, Prince Buster, Pioneers, Stramger)

RICOTTI & ALBUQUERQUE
71	Pegasus PEG 2	FIRST WIND (LP)	12

(see also Frank Ricotti, Henry Lowther)

FRANK RICOTTI
69	CBS 52668	OUR POINT OF VIEW (LP)	15

(see also Ricotti & Albuquerque)

DON RIDDELL FOUR
63	Decca F 11651	Casablanca/The Four Corners Of The Earth	4

NELSON RIDDLE ORCHESTRA
55	Capitol CL 14241	Vera Cruz/You Won't Forget Me	10
55	Capitol CL 14305	Run For Cover (with Bob Graham)/Make Believe That You're In Love With Me (with Pat Auld)	10
56	Capitol CL 14510	Robin Hood/In Old Lisbon (Lisboa Antigua)	7
58	Capitol CL 14911	Volare (Del Blu Dipinto Di Blu)/Walkin'	5
59	Capitol CL 15016	Blue Safari/De Guello (No Quarter)	5
62	Capitol CL 15253	Route 66 Theme/Lolita Ya Ya	5
63	Capitol CL 15309	Supercar/The Dick Van Dyke Theme	12
66	Stateside SS 517	Batman Theme (from the T.V. series)/Nelson's Riddler	18
61	Capitol EAP4 1771	ROUTE 66 AND OTHER T.V. THEMES (EP)	12
58	Capitol ST 915	SEA OF DREAMS (LP)	12
60	Capitol SW 1301	CAN CAN (LP, soundtrack)	12
62	Capitol (S)T 1771	ROUTE 66 AND OTHER GREAT T.V. THEMES (LP)	15
64	Stateside SL 10090	WHAT A WAY TO GO! (Nelson Riddle)	12
66	Stateside S(S)L 10179	BATMAN (LP, TV soundtrack)	50
67	Columbia S(C)X 6155	EL DORADO (LP, soundtrack)	25
69	Paramount SPFL 257	PAINT YOUR WAGON (LP, gatefold sleeve)	12

(se also Shirley Bassey)

RIDDLERS
66	Polydor BM 56716	Batman Theme/Weegie Walk	15

PAT RIDEN & BROTHER LLOYD'S ALL STARS
69	Mercury MF 1072	I Need Help/Let The Red Wine Flow (actually by Pat Rhoden)	4

(see also Pat Rhoden)

JACKIE RIDING & IMESON SOUND
66	Fab FAB 4	Don't Wanna Leave/The Wave	7

NICOLE RIEU
75	Barclay BAR 31	Live For Love/Et Bonjour A Toi L'Artiste	12

RIFF
64	Blue Beat BB 242	Oh What A Feeling/Primitive Man	12

EDDIE RIFF
80	Fleetville FV 301	My Baby's Gone Away/Ain't That Loving You Baby	5

RIFF-RAFF
73	RCA RCA 2396	Copper Kettle/You Must Be Joking	5
73	RCA SF 8351	RIFF-RAFF (LP)	15
74	RCA LPL1 5023	ORIGINAL MAN (LP)	15

RIFF RAFF
78	Chiswick SW 34	I WANNA BE A COSMONAUT (EP)	8
70s	Geezer GZ 1	Every Girl/You Shared House	4
70s	Geezer GZ 2	Kitten/Fantocide	4
70s	Geezer GZ 3	Little Girls Know/She Don't Matter	4
70s	Geezer GZ 4	New Home Town/Richard	4
79	Albion DEL 6	Barking Park	4

(see also Billy Bragg)

RIFKIN
68	Page One POF 071	Continental Hesitation/We're Not Those People Any More	50

ELEANOR RIGBY
85	Waterloo Sunset RUSS 101	I Want To Sleep With You/Till The End Of The Day (p/s, with Durex & sticker, 1,000 only)	8
85	Waterloo Sunset RUSS 102	Take Another Shot Of My Heart/1995 (p/s, with signed story)	8

BRAM RIGG SET
67	Stateside SS 2020	Take The Time Be Yourself/I Can Only Give You Everything	70

DIANA RIGG
72	RCA RCA 2178	Sentimental Journey/Forget Yourself	10

JACKIE RIGGS
56	London HLF 8244	The Great Pretender/His Gold Will Melt	25
56	London HLF 8244	The Great Pretender/His Gold Will Melt (78)	8

RIGHTEOUS BROTHERS
63	London HL 9743	Little Latin Lupe Lu/I'm So Lonely	7
63	London HL 9814	My Babe/Fee-Fi-Fidily-I-Oh	6
65	London HL 9943	You've Lost That Lovin' Feelin'/There's A Woman	6
65	Pye International 7N 25297	Bring Your Love To Me/Try To Find Another Man	6
65	Pye International 7N 25304	Something's Got A Hold On Me/Night Owl	6
65	London HL 9962	Just Once In My Life/The Blues (withdrawn)	50
65	London HL 9975	Hung On You/Unchained Melody	7

MINT VALUE £

65	Pye International 7N 25323	Let The Good Times Roll/B Flat Blues	6
65	Pye International 7N 25334	For Your Love/My Tears Will Go Away	6
65	London HL 10011	Ebb Tide/(I Love You) For Sentimental Reasons	6
66	Pye International 7N 25358	Georgia On My Mind/My Tears Will Go Away	6
66	Verve VS 535	(You're My) Soul And Inspiration/B Side-Blues	7
66	Verve VS 537	He/He Will Break Your Heart	6
66	Sue WI 4018	You Can Have Her/Justine	18
66	London HL 10066	Just Once In My Life/The Blues (reissue)	6
66	Verve VS 542	Go Ahead And Cry/Things Didn't Go Your Way	5
66	London HL 10086	The White Cliffs Of Dover/Baby She's Mine	6
66	Verve VS 547	Island In The Sun/What Now My Love	5
67	Verve VS 554	Melancholy Music Man/Don't Give Up On Me	5
67	Verve VS 560	Stranded in The Middle Of No Place/Been So Nice	5
69	London HL 10241	You've Lost That Lovin' Feelin'/Unchained Melody	5
77	Phil Spector International 2010 022	You've Lost That Lovin' Feelin'/RIGHTEOUS BROTHERS BAND: Rat Race (Instrumental)	5
65	Pye Intl. NEP 44043	THE RIGHTEOUS BROTHERS (EP)	25
66	Verve VEP 5024	SOUL AND INSPIRATION (EP)	20
66	Verve VEP 5025	THE RIGHTEOUS BROTHERS (EP, reissue)	18
65	Pye Intl. NPL 28056	SOME BLUE-EYED SOUL (LP)	30
65	London HA-U 8226	YOU'VE LOST THAT LOVIN' FEELIN' (LP)	30
65	Pye Intl. NPL 28059	RIGHT NOW! (LP)	20
65	London HA 8245	JUST ONCE IN MY LIFE (LP)	30
66	London HA 8278	BACK TO BACK (LP)	25
66	Verve (S)VLP 9131	SOUL AND INSPIRATION (LP)	20
66	Sue ILP 937	IN ACTION! (LP)	40
66	Verve (S)VLP 9140	GO AHEAD AND CRY (LP)	15
67	Verve (S)VLP 9168	SAYIN' SOMETHIN' (LP)	15
67	Verve (S)VLP 9183	THE RIGHTEOUS BROTHERS GREATEST HITS (LP)	12
68	Verve (S)VLP 9190	SOULED OUT (LP)	20
68	Verve (S)VLP 9204	THE RIGHTEOUS BROTHERS STANDARDS (LP)	15
68	Verve (S)VLP 9228	ONE FOR THE ROAD (LP)	15
69	Verve (S)VLP 9240	GREATEST HITS VOLUME 2 (LP)	12
70	Verve (S)VLP 9249	RE-BIRTH (LP)	15

(see also Bill Medley, Bobby Hatfield)

RIGHTEOUS FLAMES

67	Fab FAB 18	Gimme Some Sign Girl/Let's Go To The Dance (B-side act. by Prince Buster)	15
67	Fab FAB 30	When A Girl Loves A Boy	12
68	Coxsone CS 7061	You Don't Know/ROY RICHARDS & SOUL VENDORS: Summertime	12
71	High Note HS 052	Run To The Rock/GAYTONES: Run To The Rock Version	8
71	Nu Beat NB 083	Love And Emotion/Version	6

(see also Richus Flames, Alton Ellis, Flames, Soul Vendors)

RIGHTEOUS HOMES (FLAMES)

68	Coxsone CS 7049	I Was Born To Be Loved/NORMA FRAZER: Heartaches	18
68	Blue Cat BS 112	Seven Letters (actually by Winston Jarrett)/SOUL VENDORS: To Sir With Love	12

RIGHTEOUS SOULS

71	Supreme SUP 217	Mount Zion/ECCLE & NEVILL: All Over	6

RIGHTEOUS TWINS

69	Blue Cat BS 174	If I Could Hear My Master/Satan Can't Prevail	10

RIGOR MORTIS

73	Track 2094 107	Made In Japan/Hound Dog	6
73	Track 2406 106	RIGOR MORTIS SETS IN (LP)	18

(see John Entwistle, Who)

RIKKI & CUFFLINKS

79	Different HAVE 17	Nervous Breakdown/Steamin' On (no p/s)	5

RIKKI & THE LAST DAYS OF EARTH

77	(own label)	Oundle 29/5/77 (1-sided)	25
77	DJM DJS 10814	City Of The Damned/Victimized (p/s)	10
77	DJM DJF 20526	FOUR MINUTE WARNING (LP)	12

RIKKI & NUMBERS

77	Rainbow RAIS 1001	The Heartbreak Kid/Headlines (no p/s)	4

BILLY LEE RILEY

65	King KG 1015	I've Been Searchin'/Everybody's Twistin'	12
69	Stax STAX 120	Going Back To Memphis/Family Portrait	10
72	CBS 8182	I Got A Thing About You Baby/You Don't Love Me	5

(see also Megatons)

BOB RILEY

58	MGM MGM 977	The Midnight Line/Wanda Jean	60
58	MGM MGM 977	The Midnight Line/Wanda Jean (78)	25

DESMOND RILEY

69	Downtown DT 432	Tear Them/GEORGE LEE & RUDIES: Chaka Ground	7
69	Downtown DT 435	Tears On My Pillow/RUDIES: Man Pon Spot	7
69	Downtown DT 436	If I Had Wings/AUDREY: You'll Lose A Good Thing	7
69	Downtown DT 438	Out Your Fire/No Return	7
69	Downtown DT 450	Skinhead, A Message To You/MUSIC DOCTORS: Going Strong	10
69	Downtown DT 454	If I Had Wings/AUDREY: You'll Lose A Good Thing (reissue)	5

HOWARD RILEY (TRIO)

68	Opportunity CP 2499	DISCUSSIONS (LP with insert, as Howard Riley Trio)	1,500
69	CBS 52669	ANGLE (LP)	35
70	CBS 64077	THE DAY WILL COME (LP)	60

71	Turtle TUR 301	FLIGHT (LP, gatefold sleeve)	275
76	Incus INCUS 13	SYNOPSIS (LP, as Howard Riley Trio with Tony Oxley & Barry Guy)	50
79	Spotlite	THE OTHER SIDE (LP)	12

(see also Colosseum, Karyobin)

JEANNIE C. RILEY
68	Polydor 56748	Harper Valley P.T.A./Yesterday All Day Long Today	6
68	Polydor 56756	The Girl Most Likely/My Scrapbook	6
69	Polydor 56782	Things Go Better With Love/Back Side Of Dallas	5
69	Polydor 583 716	HARPER VALLEY P.T.A. (LP)	12
69	Polydor 583 733	YEARBOOKS AND YESTERDAYS (LP)	12
70	Polydor 583 753	THINGS GO BETTER WITH LOVE (LP)	12

JIMI/JIMMY RILEY
71	Supreme SUP 217	Mount Zion (actually by Jimi Riley & Stranger Cole)/ ECCLE & NEVIL: All Over	7
75	Dip DL 5067	Ram Goat Liver/OMAR & MARSHA PERRY: Ram Goat Dub	7

(see also Martin Riley, Sensations, Uniques)

MARTIN RILEY
69	Gas GAS 114	Walking Proud/LLOYD CHARMERS: Why Baby	6
69	Punch PH 7	Trying To Be Free/I've Got It Bad	6
70	Camel CA 53	Catch This Sound/Suspense	6
70	Escort ES 823	It Grows (actually "It's Growing")/We Had A Good Thing Going	6
71	Camel CA 77	When Will We Be Paid/WILLIE FRANCIS: He's Got The Whole World In His Hands	6

(see also Slim Smith, Slickers)

TERRY RILEY
71	CBS 64259	CHURCH OF ANTHRAX (LP, with John Cale)	15
71	CBS 64564	A RAINBOW IN CURVED AIR (LP)	12
71	CBS 64565	IN "C" (LP)	12
72	Shandar 83501/2	PERSIAN SURGERY DERVISHES (2-LP)	15

(see also John Cale)

WINSTON RILEY
73	Techniques TE 922	Woman Don't You Go Astray/Travelling Man	5

(see also The Techniques)

RILEY'S ALLSTARS
71	Banana BA 343	Glory Of Love (actually "Mystic Blue" by Hugh Hendricks & Buccaneers)/ We'll Cry Together — Version	7

(see also Bobby Davis, Techniques)

SHANE RIMMER
59	Columbia DB 4293	(Roll Along) Wagon Train/A Touch Of Pink	6
59	Columbia DB 4343	The Three Bells (Jimmy Brown Song) (as Shane Rimmer & Spinners)/ I Want To Walk You Home	6

RINGS
77	Chiswick S 14	I Wanna Be Free/Automobile (p/s)	5

(see also Maniacs, Twink)

RINGS & THINGS
68	Fontana TF 987	Strange Things Are Happening/To Me:To Me:To Me	50

RINKY DINKS
58	London HLE 8679	Early In The Morning/Now We're One (as Rinky-Dinks featuring Bobby Darin)	40
58	London HLE 8679	Early In The Morning/Now We're One (78)	45
59	London HLE 8793	Mighty Mighty Man/You're Mine (as Bobby Darin with Rinky Dinks)	30
59	London HLE 8793	Mighty Mighty Man/You're Mine (78)	45
59	Capitol CL 14999	Catch A Little Moonbeam/Choo Choo Cha Cha	8

(see also Bobby Darin)

BOBBY RIO (U.S.)
63	Stateside SS 211	Don Diddley/I Got You	12

BOBBY RIO (& REVELLES)
65	Pye 7N 15790	Boy Meets Girl/Don't Break My Heart And Run Away	35
65	Pye 7N 15897	Everything In The Garden/When Love Was Young	35
65	Pye 7N 15958	Value For Love/I'm Not Made Of Clay	35
66	Piccadilly 7N 35303	Ask The Lonely/Be Lonely Little Girl (solo)	8
66	Piccadilly 7N 35337	Angelica/Lovin' You (solo)	8

RIO GRANDES
66	Pyramid PYR 6001	Soldiers Take Over/Moses	8

RIOT
81	Elektra K 12565	Outlaw (Remix)/Rock City (p/s)	6
81	Elektra K 12565T	Outlaw (Remix)/Rock City (12", p/s)	7
77	Ariola ARL 5007	ROCK CITY (LP)	10
78	Capitol E-ST 12081	NARITA (LP)	10

RIOT CLONE
82	Riot Clone RC 001	THERE'S NO GOVERNMENT LIKE NO GOVERNMENT (EP)	5
82	Riot Clone RC 002	DESTROY THE MYTH OF MUSICAL DESTRUCTION (EP)	5
84	Riot Clone RCR 004	BLOOD ON YOUR HANDS (EP)	5

RIOTS
65	Island WI 176	Telling Lies/Don't Leave Me (actually by Techniques)	18
65	Island WI 195	You Don't Know (actually by Techniques)/DON DRUMMOND & DRUMBAGO: Treasure Island	18
65	Island WI 197	I Am In Love/When You're Wrong (actually by Techniques)	18
65	Island WI 247	Yeah Yeah/BABA BROOKS: Virginia Ska	15

(see also Techniques)

RIOT SQUAD

65	Pye 7N 15752	Any Time/Jump	25
65	Pye 7N 15817	I Wanna Talk About My Baby/Gonna Make You Mine.	35
65	Pye 7N 15869	Nevertheless/Not A Great Talker	30
66	Pye 7N 17041	Cry Cry Cry/How Is It Done	35
66	Pye 7N 17092	I Take It We're Through/Working Man.	35
66	Pye 7N 17130	It's Never Too Late To Forgive/Try To Realise	35
67	Pye 7N 17237	Gotta Be A First Time/Bitter Sweet Love.	40

(see also Graham Bonney, Jimi Hendrix Experience, Blue Aces)

RIOT SQUAD

| 82 | The THE 001 | Total Onslaught (p/s) | 7 |

RIOT SQUAD

82	Rondelet ROUND 23	Fuck The Tories/Civil Destruction (p/s)	6
82	Rondelet ROUND 25	Riot In The City/Religion (p/s)	5
83	Rot ASS 1	DON'T BE DENIED (EP)	6
83	Rot ASS 2	I'm OK Fuck You/In The Future/Friday Night (p/s)	6
84	Rot ASS 3	THERE AIN'T NO SOLUTION (EP)	6
84	Rot ASS 13	NO POTENTIAL THREAT (LP, with free single [ASS3], stickered sleeve)	12

RIP CHORDS

63	CBS AAG 143	Here I Stand/Karen	10
63	CBS AAG 162	Gone/She Thinks I Still Care	10
64	CBS AAG 181	Hey Little Cobra/The Queen.	15
64	CBS AAG 202	Three Window Coupe/Hot Rod USA	15
64	CBS BPG 62228	HEY LITTLE COBRA (LP).	45

(see also Terry Day)

RIPCORD

| 89 | private pressing | HARVEST HARDCORE (EP, foldout sleeve) | 8 |

RIPLEY WAYFARERS

| 72 | Tradition TSR 013 | FIVE WELLS (LP) | 20 |

RIP 'N' LAW

| 71 | Crab CRAB 64 | In The Ghetto/Something Sweet | 6 |

RIPPERS

| 68 | Saga | HONESTLY (LP) | 25 |

RISING MOON

| 74 | Theatre Projects | RISING MOON (LP). | 30 |

RISING SONS (U.S.)

| 65 | Stateside SS 426 | You're My Girl/Try To Be A Man | 12 |

RISING SONS (U.K.)

| 68 | Pye 7N 17554 | Hold Me Just A Little While Longer/Fountain Of Love | 4 |

RITA

| 69 | Major Minor MM 653 | Erotica/Sexologie | 20 |

RITA (Alston)

| 69 | Jackpot JP 718 | Love Making/NAT COLE: My Love. | 6 |

(see also Rita Alston)

LES RITA MITSOUKO

89	Virgin VS 1163	Singing In The Shower (with Sparks)/Smog (p/s)	4
89	Virgin VST 1163	Singing In The Shower (with Sparks)/Smog/Hip Kit (12" p/s).	7
89	Virgin VSCD 1163	Singing In The Shower (with Sparks)/Smog/Hip Kit (3" CD).	18
90	Virgin VS 1296	Hipkit (William Orbit Remix) (with Russell Mael)/Andy Live (p/s).	4
90	Virgin VST 1296	Hipkit (William Orbit Remix) (with Russell Mael)/ Andy Live (Fat Freddy Remix) (12", p/s)	7

(see also Sparks)

RITA & TIARAS

| 79 | Destiny DS 1002 | Gone With The Wind Is My Love/Wild Times (p/s) | 5 |

JEAN RITCHIE

| 53 | Argo ARS 1009 | SONGS FROM KENTUCKY (10" LP) | 15 |

TEX RITTER

51	Capitol CL 13490	Blood On The Saddle/Bad Brahma Bull(78)	8
52	Capitol CL 13778	High Noon/Boogie Woogie Cowboy (78)	8
54	Capitol CL 14175	Is There A Santa Claus?/Old Tex Kringle.	12
55	Capitol CL 14277	A Whale Of A Tale/High On A Mountain Top	12
55	Capitol CL 14335	Marshal Of Wichita/September Song.	12
56	Capitol CL 14536	The Last Frontier/These Hands	7
56	Capitol CL 14581	The Wayward Wind/Gunsmoke	12
56	Capitol CL 14581	The Wayward Wind/Gunsmoke (78)	8
56	Capitol CL 14605	The Searchers (Ride Away)/Remember The Alamo.	10
56	Capitol CL 14660	The Last Wagon/Paul Bunyan Love	8
57	Capitol CL 14684	Green Grow The Lilacs/The Touch Of The Master's Hand.	6
57	Capitol CL 14715	Children And Fools/I Leaned On A Man	6
57	Capitol CL 14715	Children And Fools/I Leaned On A Man (78).	8
57	Capitol CL 14805	Here Was A Man/It Came Upon The Midnight Clear	6
58	Capitol CL 14900	Jealous Heart/Burning Sand	6
58	Capitol CL 14933	I Look For A Love/The History Song.	5
59	Capitol CL 15041	Rye Whisky/Conversation With A Gun	5
60	Capitol EAP1-1323	DECK OF CARDS (EP)	15
52	Capitol LC 6552	COWBOY FAVOURITES (10" LP)	18
59	Capitol T 1100	PSALMS (LP)	12
60	Capitol (S)T 1292	BLOOD ON THE SADDLE (LP).	15

BOB RITTERBUSH

59	Top Rank JAR 118	I Wish That You Were Mine/Darling Corey	6
59	Top Rank JAR 118	I Wish That You Were Mine/Darling Corey (78)	10

RIVALS

78	Sound On Sound SOS 100	Skateboarding In The UK/Top Of The Pops (no p/s)	8

RIVALS

80	Ace ACE 007	Future Rights/Flowers (p/s)	20
80	Oakwood/Ace ACE 011	Here Comes The Night/Both Sides (p/s)	12

HECTOR RIVERA

67	Polydor 65728	At The Party/Do It To Me	25

ROYD RIVERS & CLIFF AUNGIER

65	Decca LK 4696	WANDERIN' (LP)	30

(see also Cliff Aungier)

CLIFF RIVERS

63	London HLU 9739	True Lips/Marsha	25

(pseudonym for Joey Castle)

DANNY RIVERS

60	Top Rank JAR 408	Hawk/I Got	20
60	Decca F 11294	Can't You Hear My Heart/I'm Waiting For Tomorrow	18
61	Decca F 11357	Once Upon A Time/My Baby's Gone Away (with Alexander Combo)	25
64	Decca F 11865	There Will Never Be Anyone Else/	
		I Don't Think You Know How I Feel	10
62	HMV POP 1000	We're Gonna Dance/Movin' In (as Danny Rivers & River Men)	35

DEKE RIVERS

62	Oriole CB 1735	One Kiss/Outsider	12
81	Chiswick NS 71	Elvis Presley Medley/ELVIS PRESLEY:	
		Press Conference Vancouver 1957 (picture disc)	6

JOHNNY RIVERS

62	Pye International 7N 25118	Blue Skies/That Someone Should Be Me	7
64	Liberty LIB 66032	Memphis/It Wouldn't Happen With Me	6
64	Liberty LIB 66056	Maybellene/Walk Myself On Home	6
64	Liberty LIB 66075	Mountain Of Love/Moody Love	6
64	Liberty LIB 66087	Midnight Special/Cupid	7
65	Liberty LIB 66112	Seventh Son/Un-Square Dance	5
65	Liberty LIB 12021	He Don't Love You Like I Love You/Where Have All The Flowers Gone	5
66	Liberty LIB 66144	Under Your Spell Again/Long Time Man	5
66	Liberty LIB 12023	Secret Agent Man/Tom Dooley	7
66	Liberty LIB 66175	I Washed My Hands In Muddy Water/Roogalator	8
66	Liberty LIB 66205	The Poor Side Of Town/Baby She's Mine	10
67	Liberty LIB 66227	Baby I Need Your Lovin'/Getting Ready For Tomorrow	6
67	Liberty LIB 66244	The Tracks Of My Tears/Rosecrans Blvd.	7
68	Liberty LBF 15041	Summer Rain/Memory Of The Coming Good	6
68	Liberty LBF 15078	Look To Your Soul/Something Strange	5
68	Liberty LBF 15163	Right Relations/Better Life	5
69	Liberty LBF 15239	John Lee Hooker (Parts 1 & 2)	5
69	Liberty LBF 15241	Muddy River/Resurrection	5
70	Liberty LBF 15364	Into The Mystic/Jesus Is A Soul Man	5
74	Atlantic K 10469	Six Days On The Road/Artists And Poets	6
75	Atlantic K 10544	Sitting In Limbo/Geronimo's Cadillac	6
75	Epic EPC 3482	Help Me Rhonda/New Lovers And New Friends	6
66	Liberty LEP 4049	MORE JOHNNY RIVERS (EP)	18
64	Liberty LBY 3031	AT THE WHISKY A GO-GO (LP)	20
65	Liberty LBY 3036	HERE WE A GO-GO AGAIN (LP)	18
65	Liberty LBY 3056	MEANWHILE BACK AT THE WHISKY A GO-GO (LP)	18
66	Liberty LBY 3064	RIVERS ROCKS THE FOLK (LP)	18
67	Liberty (S)LBY 3087	CHANGES (LP)	15
67	Liberty LBL/LBS 83040	REWIND (LP)	15
68	Liberty LBL/LBS 83118	REALIZATION (LP)	12
69	Liberty LBS 83141	A TOUCH OF GOLD (LP)	12
70	Liberty LBS 83383	SLIM SLO RIDER (LP)	12
72	United Artists UAS 29253	HOME GROWN (LP)	12
75	Epic EPC 80987	HELP ME RHONDA (LP)	15

MAVIS RIVERS

60	Capitol CL 15120	So Rare/Longing, Longing, Longing	6
63	Reprise RS 20115	Slightly Out Of Tune/Footsteps Of A Fool	5

TONY RIVERS & CASTAWAYS

63	Columbia DB 7135	Shake Shake Shake/Row Row Row	12
64	Columbia DB 7224	I Love The Way You Walk/I Love You	8
64	Columbia DB 7336	Life's Too Short/Tell On Me	8
65	Columbia DB 7448	She/Till We Get Home	8
65	Columbia DB 7536	Come Back/What To Do	8
66	Columbia DB 7971	God Only Knows/Charade	8
66	Parlophone R 5400	Nowhere Man/The Girl From New York City	7
66	Immediate IM 027	Girl Don't Tell Me/The Girl From Salt Lake City	15
68	Polydor 56245	I Can Guarantee Your Love/Pantomime	6

(see also Grapefruit, Harmony Grass, Capability Brown, Senators)

RIVIERA

69	Pye 7N 17712	Baby Won't Leave Me Alone/The Love Story	4

RIVIERAS

60	HMV POP 773	Blessing Of Love/Moonlight Cocktails	40

RIVIERAS
64	Pye International 7N 25237	California Sun/H B Goose Step	20

RIVINGTONS
62	Liberty LIB 55427	Papa Oom Mow Mow/Deep Water	30
63	Liberty LIB 55553	The Bird's The Word/I'm Losing My Grip	30
66	CBS 202088	Rose Growing In The Ruins/Tend To Business	35

FREDDIE ROACH
67	Transatlantic PR 7490	THE SOUL BOOK (LP)	12

MAX ROACH (& CLIFFORD BROWN GROUP)
54	Vogue V 2270	Orientation/Mobleyzation (78)	8
55	Vogue V 2329	Just One Of Those Things/Drum Conversation (78)	8
50s	Vogue EPV 1074	MAX ROACH AND CLIFFORD BROWN (EP)	8
50s	Vogue EPV 1083	MAX ROACH AND CLIFFORD BROWN (EP)	8
50s	Vogue EPV 1091	MAX ROACH AND CLIFFORD BROWN (EP)	8
58	Emarcy ERE 1572	MAX ROACH AND CLIFFORD BROWN (EP, withdrawn)	15
55	Vogue LDE 117	MAX ROACH & CLIFFORD BROWN IN CONCERT VOL. 1 (10" LP)	18
55	Vogue LDE 128	MAX ROACH & CLIFFORD BROWN IN CONCERT VOL. 2 (10" LP)	18
58	Emarcy EJL 1282	JAZZ IN THREE-QUARTER TIME (LP)	15
59	Emarcy MMB 12005	MAX ROACH, NEWPORT (LP, by Max Roach)	15
59	Emarcy MMB 12009	THE MAX ROACH FOUR PLUS FOUR (LP, by Max Roach)	15
60	Mercury MMC 14041	I REMEMBER CLIFFORD (LP)	12
60	Mercury MMC 14054	QUIET AS IT'S KEPT (LP, by Max Roach)	12

(see also Clifford Brown, Buddy Rich)

ROAD
73	Rare Earth SRE 3006	ROAD (LP)	15

ROADRUNNERS
65	Cavern Sound 2BSNL 7	PANTOMANIA (EP, with tracks by Chris Edwards & Clive Wood)	30

ROADSTER
81	Mayhem SRTS81	Fantasy/45 Mph (p/s)	25

ROADSTERS
64	Stateside SS 293	Joy Ride/Drag	15

ROARING SIXTIES
66	Marmalade 598 001	We Love The Pirates/I'm Leaving Town	30

ROBAN'S SKIFFLE GROUP
61	Storyville A45 062	Careless Love/Frankie And Johnny (some with p/s)	30/15

E.G. ROBB
63	Columbia DB 7100	Stage To Cimarron/Jezebel	10

ROBBIE & RAY
66	Decca F 12452	This Little Bird/You Better Move On	4

IAN ROBBINS
66	Mercury MF 933	Ain't I Met You Somewhere Before/Like Any Other Girl	4

KATE ROBBINS
78	Anchor ANC 1054	Tomorrow/Crowds Of You (demos more common £10)	15
78	Bright BULB 6	That First Love/That First Love (Instrumental Mix)/When You Go	4

MARTY ROBBINS
78s
56	Philips PB 590	Long Tall Sally/Mr. Teardrop (78)	30
57	Philips PB 696	A White Sport Coat (And A Pink Carnation)/Grown-Up Tears (78)	25
57	Philips PB 741	Please Don't Blame Me/Teen-Age Dream (78)	25
58	Fontana H 102	The Story Of My Life/Once-A-Week Date (78)	20
58	Fontana H 128	Stairway Of Love/Just Married (78)	30
58	Fontana H 150	Sittin' In A Tree House/She Was Only Seventeen (78)	35
59	Fontana H 184	The Hanging Tree (from film)/The Blues Country Style (78)	40
59	Fontana H 212	Cap And Gown/Last Night About This Time (78)	40
59	Fontana H 229	Big Iron/Cool Water (78)	50
59	Fontana H 233	El Paso/Running Gun (78)	60

SINGLES
57	Philips JK 1019	A White Sport Coat (And A Pink Carnation)/Grown-Up Tears (jukebox issue)	40
58	Fontana H 128	Stairway Of Love/Just Married	20
58	Fontana H 150	Sittin' In A Tree House/She Was Only Seventeen	12
59	Fontana H 184	The Hanging Tree (from film)/The Blues Country Style	8
59	Fontana H 212	Cap And Gown/Last Night About This Time	7
59	Fontana H 229	Big Iron/Cool Water	7
59	Fontana H 233	El Paso/Running Gun	6
60	Fontana H 263	I Told My Heart/Is There Any Chance	6
60	Fontana H 270	Ballad Of The Alamo/Five Brothers (some in p/s)	10/6
61	Fontana H 301	Don't Worry/Like All Other Times	6
61	Fontana H 324	Ghost Train/Jimmy Martinez	6
61	Fontana H 342	It's Your World/You Told Me So	6
62	CBS AAG 114	Devil Woman/April Fool's Day	6
63	CBS AAG 128	Ruby Ann/Won't You Forgive	8
63	CBS AAG 141	Cigarette And Coffee Blues/Teenager's Dad	6
63	CBS AAG 151	No Signs Of Loneliness Here/I'm Not Ready Yet	6
63	CBS AAG 164	Not So Long Ago/I Hope You Learn A Lot	5
65	CBS 201729	Whole Lot Easier/I Eish Tay Mah Su	5
65	CBS 201789	Ribbon Of Darkness/Little Robin	5
65	CBS 202012	While You're Dancing/Lonely Too	5
67	CBS 2955	Tonight Carmen/No Tears Milady	5
68	CBS 3585	Love Is In The Air/I've Been Leaving Every Day	5
68	CBS 3828	I Walk Alone/Lily Of The Valley	5

EPs

59	Fontana TFE 17161	MARTY'S BIG HITS (EP)	30
59	Fontana TFE 17168	WEDDING BELLS (EP)	12
60	Fontana TFE 17167	SONG OF THE ISLANDS (EP)	12
61	Fontana TFE 17224	GUNFIGHTER (EP)	15
61	CBS AGG 20004	JUST A LITTLE SENTIMENTAL (EP)	12
61	CBS AGG 20013	JUST A LITTLE SENTIMENTAL VOL. 2 (EP)	12
66	CBS AGG 20049	MARTY ROBBINS (EP)	12

LPs

59	Fontana TFL 5063	GUNFIGHTER BALLADS AND TRAIL SONGS (LP)	25
60	Fontana TFL 5086	MARTY'S GREATEST HITS (LP)	16
61	Fontana TFL 5113	MORE GUNFIGHTER BALLADS AND TRAIL SONGS (LP, stereo STFL 541)	25/30
61	Fontana TFL 5145	MORE GREATEST HITS (LP, also stereo STFL 565)	16/22
61	Fontana TFL 5162	JUST A LITTLE SENTIMENTAL (LP, with Jordanaires, also stereo STFL 579)	20/25
62	CBS (S)BPG 62041	MARTY AFTER MIDNIGHT (LP)	20
63	CBS (S)BPG 62113	DEVIL WOMAN (LP, mono/stereo)	15/18
63	CBS BPG 62131	PORTRAIT OF MARTY (LP, mono/stereo)	15/18
63	CBS (S)BPG 62169	HAWAII'S CALLING ME (LP, mono/stereo)	15/18
64	CBS (S)BPG 62190	THE RETURN OF THE GUNFIGHTER (LP, mono/stereo)	15/18
64	CBS (S)BPG 62297	ISLAND WOMAN (LP, mono/stereo)	15/18
65	CBS (S)BPG 62437	R.F.D. (LP, mono/stereo)	15/18
65	CBS (S)BPG 62499	TURN THE LIGHTS DOWN LOW (LP)	15
65	CBS (S)BPG 62359	GUNFIGHTER BALLADS AND TRAIL SONGS (LP, reissue, mono/stereo)	12/15
66	CBS (S)BPG 62070	MORE GUNFIGHTER BALLADS AND TRAIL SONGS (LP, reissue, m/s)	12/15
66	CBS (S)BPG 62075	MORE GREATEST HITS (LP, reissue)	12
66	CBS (S)BPG 62689	WHAT GOD HAS DONE (LP)	15
66	CBS (S)BPG 62782	THE DRIFTER (LP)	20
67	CBS (S)BPG 62962	MY KIND OF COUNTRY (LP)	15
67	CBS (S)BPG 63116	TONIGHT CARMEN (LP)	15
68	CBS 63295	BY THE TIME I GET TO PHOENIX (LP, mono/stereo)	12
68	CBS 63354	CHRISTMAS WITH MARTY ROBBINS (LP, mono/stereo)	18
69	CBS 66211	A PORTRAIT OF MARTY (2-LP)	15
69	CBS 63431	I WALK ALONE (LP, mono/stereo)	12
70	CBS 64066	MY WOMAN, MY WOMAN, MY WIFE (LP)	15
72	CBS 64810	TODAY (LP)	12

(see also Jordanaires)

MEL ROBBINS

59	London HLM 8966	Save It/To Know You (initially triangular centre, later round centre)	450/275
59	London HLM 8966	Save It/To Know You (78)	120

SYLVIA ROBBINS

60	London HLJ 9118	Frankie And Johnny/Come Home	18

(see also Mickey & Sylvia)

ROBBS

67	Mercury MF 983	Rapid Transit/Cynthia Loves	4

ROBERT & REMOULDS

79	Black & White BW 1	X No. 1/Do Eyes Ever Meet? (p/s)	6

ANDY ROBERTS

73	Elektra K 12109	Baby Baby/All Around My Grandmothers Floor	5
70	RCA SF 8086	HOME GROWN (LP)	18
71	Charisma CAS 1034	HOME GROWN (LP, reissue, different sleeve)	12
71	Pegasus PEG 5	NINA AND THE DREAM TREE (LP)	18
73	Elektra K 42139	URBAN COWBOY (LP, with insert)	12
73	Elektra K 42151	ANDY ROBERTS AND THE GREAT STAMPEDE (LP, gatefold sleeve)	12

(see also Clayton Squares, Liverpool Scene, Everyone, Plainsong)

ALAN ROBERTS

70s	Plant Life PLR 012	CALEDONIA (LP, with Dougie Maclean)	12

BOB ROBERTS

70	Explosion EX 2021	Stick By Me/TOMMY McCOOK: The Designer	6

HUGH ROBERTS

70	Explosion EX 2041	California Dreaming/One Woman (both sides actually by Lloyd Charmers)	5

J. ROBERTS

70	Bamboo BAM 30	Someday We'll Be Together/SOUND DIMENSION: Everyday People	6

JOHN ROBERTS

68	Sue WI 4042	Sockin' 1, 2, 3, 4/Sophisticated Funk	18
68	Action ACT 4511	I'll Forget You/Be My Baby	12

KEITH ROBERTS

72	Trailer LER 3031	PIER OF THE REALM (LP)	20

KENNY ROBERTS

57	Brunswick 05638	I'm Looking For The Bully Of The Town/Broken Teenage Heart	10

KENNY ROBERTS

65	Pye 7N 15882	Say, Do You Mean It/Since My Love Has Gone	6
66	Pye 7N 17054	Run Like The Devil/Where Goes My Heart	18

(see also Kenny Damon)

KIM ROBERTS

64	Decca F 11813	I'll Prove It/For Loving Me This Way	70

PADDY ROBERTS

62	Decca F 11552	Got 'N Idea/Merry Christmas You Suckers	5
59	Decca DFE 6584	STRICTLY FOR GROWN-UPS (EP)	8

Paddy ROBERTS

60	Decca DFE 6641	STRIKES AGAIN (EP) 8
60	Decca DFE 6701	PADDY (EP) 12
59	Decca LF 1322	STRICTLY FOR GROWN-UPS (10" LP) 12
60	Decca LK 4358	PADDY ROBERTS TRIES AGAIN (LP) 12
61	Decca LK 4410	PADDY ROBERTS AT THE BLUE ANGEL (LP) 12

RENEE ROBERTS
| 62 | Oriole CB 1731 | I Want To Love You/Aching Heart .... 6 |

RICK ROBERTS
| 72 | A&M AMLH 64372 | WINDMILLS (LP) .... 12 |

(see also Flying Burrito Brothers)

DALE ROBERTSON
| 60 | RCA SF 5064 | PRESENTS HIS ALBUM OF WESTERN CLASSICS (LP) .... 12 |

DON ROBERTSON
50	London L 629	Gamblin' Fever/On The Hudson Bay Line (78, with Lou) 12
56	Capitol CL 14575	The Happy Whistler/You're Free To Go (B-side with Lou Dinning) 8
56	Capitol CL 14629	Every Day That I Live (with Lou Dinning)/You 6
59	Capitol CL 15088	Fine Day/The Merry Men 6
59	Capitol CL 15088	Fine Day/The Merry Men (78) 12

JEANNIE ROBERTSON
59	Topic 10T 52	I KEN WHERE I'M GOING (10" LP) 18
59	Topic 12T 96	JEANNIE ROBERTSON (LP, blue label, with card insert) 15
60	Collector JFS 4001	LORD DONALD (LP) 15

JIM ROBERTSON
| 55 | MGM SPC 7 | Pride Of My Heart/Walkin' And Talkin' With The Lord (export issue) .... 12 |

ROBBIE ROBERTSON
| 88 | Geffen GEF 46CD | Fallen Angel (LP Version) (with Peter Gabriel)/Hell's Half Acre (LP Version)/ Testimony (Remix)/Somewhere Down The Crazy River (Radio Remix) (3" CD, with adaptor, 5" case) .... 7 |

(see also Band)

PAUL ROBESON
52	HMV 7P 113	Ol' Man River/I Suits Me 6
57	HMV DLP 1155	THE INCOMPARABLE VOICE OF PAUL ROBESON (10" LP) 12
57	HMV DLP 1165	EMPEROR OF SONG (10" LP) 12

IVO ROBIC
| 60 | Polydor NH 23923 | Morgen/Ay, Ay, Ay Paloma .... 6 |
| 60 | Fontana H 239 | The Happy Muleteer/Rhondaly .... 5 |

DAVE ROBIN
| 65 | Eyemark EMS 1003 | You I Don't Want To Share/Life's Too Short .... 5 |

RICHIE ROBIN
| 60 | Top Rank JAR 262 | Strange Dream/GERRY GRANAHAN: It Hurts .... 12 |

TINA ROBIN
57	Vogue Coral Q 72284	Over Somebody Else's Shoulder/Lady Fair 15
57	Vogue Coral Q 72284	Over Somebody Else's Shoulder/Lady Fair (78) 15
57	Vogue Coral Q 72294	Never In A Million Years/Ça C'est L'Amour 10
57	Vogue Coral Q 72294	Never In A Million Years/Ça C'est L'Amour (78) 12
58	Coral Q 72309	Everyday/Believe Me 12
58	Coral Q 72309	Everyday/Believe Me (78) 15
58	Coral Q 72323	No School Tomorrow/Sugar Blues 12
58	Coral Q 72323	No School Tomorrow/Sugar Blues (78) 15
62	Mercury AMT 1199	Get Out Of My Life/Why Did You Go 7

ROBIN HOODS
| 65 | Mercury MF 865 | Wait For The Dawn/Love You So .... 5 |

ROBINS
| 60 | Vogue V 9168 | Cherry Lips/Out Of The Picture .... 120 |
| 60 | Vogue V 9173 | Just Like That/Whole Lot Imagination .... 100 |

(see also Coasters)

JIMMY ROBINS
| 68 | President PT 118 | I Can't Please You/I Made It Over .... 80 |

ALVIN ROBINSON
64	Pye International 7N 25248	Something You Got/Searchin'
64	Red Bird RB 10010	Down Home Girl/Fever 15
66	Strike JH 307	You Brought My Heart Right Down To My Knees/Whatever You Had 12

BROTHER CLEOPHUS ROBINSON
| 57 | Vogue EPV 1196 | BROTHER CLEOPHUS ROBINSON (EP) .... 20 |

EDDIE ROBINSON
| 71 | Ember EMB S 301 | Hey Blackman (Parts 1 & 2) .... 5 |
| 70s | Myrrh MYR 1013 | REFLECTIONS OF THE MAN INSIDE (LP) .... 15 |

ELZADIE ROBINSON
50	Tempo R 33	The Santa Claus Crave/St. Louis Cyclone Blues (78) 12
50	Tempo R 36	Arkansas Mill Blues/Gold Mansion Blues (78, with Will Ezell) 12
50	Tempo R 37	Rowdy Man Blues/Going South Blues (78) 12

(see also Will Ezell)

FLOYD ROBINSON
| 59 | RCA RCA 1146 | Makin' Love/My Girl (initially with triangular centre, later round) .... 10/6 |
| 59 | RCA RCA 1146 | Makin' Love/My Girl (78) .... 40 |

Floyd ROBINSON

60	RCA RCA 1179	I Believe In Love/Tattletale	6
60	RCA RD 27166	FLOYD ROBINSON (LP)	45

FREDDY ROBINSON
| 72 | Stax 2325 085 | AT THE DRIVE-IN (LP) | 12 |

HARRY ROBINSON
| 60 | Top Rank JAR 325 | The Skirl/Wimoweh (as Harry Robinson "String Sound") | 6 |
| 61 | Decca F 11319 | Heavy Date/Sentimental Journey (as Harry Robinson's XV) | 5 |

(see also Lord Rockingham's XI)

JACKEY ROBINSON
| 70 | Punch PH 50 | Heart Made Of Stone (actually by Jackie Bernard)/BOB TAYLOR: I May Never See My Baby Anymore | 35 |

(see also Jackie Robinson, Pioneers)

JACKIE ROBINSON
| 68 | Amalgamated AMG 819 | Over And Over/Woman Of Samaria | 10 |
| 68 | Amalgamated AMG 824 | Let The Little Girl Dance/DERRICK MORGAN: I Want To Go Home | 8 |

JIM ROBINSON NEW ORLEANS BAND
| 61 | Riverside RLP 369 | NEW ORLEANS: THE LIVING LEGENDS (LP) | 15 |
| 64 | Riverside RLP 393 | PLAYS SPIRITUAL AND BLUES (LP) | 15 |

J.P. ROBINSON
| 72 | Atlantic K 10149 | George Jackson/Wall To Wall Love | 6 |
| 72 | Atlantic K 10209 | What Can I Tell Her/Please Accept My Call | 5 |

JUNE ROBINSON
| 56 | Oriole CB 1319 | 45 Men In A Telephone Box/Oo-Shoo-Be-Doo-Be (78) | 12 |

LLOYD ROBINSON
62	Blue Beat BB 122	Give Me A Chance/When You Walk	15
63	Blue Beat BB 159	I Need Your Love/You Told Me	15
69	Duke DU 5	Cuss Cuss/Lavender Blue	20
70	Camel CA 41	The Worm/NEVILLE HYNES: Afro (actually by Neville Hinds)	6
72	Green Door GD 4028	I Can't Forget/LLOYD AND THE NOW GENERATION: I Can't Forget – Version	6

(see also Lloyd Clarke, Lloyd Charmers, Harry J. Allstars, Matadors, Melodians)

M. ROBINSON
| 64 | Port-O-Jam PJ 4114 | Who Are You/Follow You | 15 |

ROSCO ROBINSON
66	Pye International 7N 25385	That's Enough/One More Time	20
72	Wand WN 27	That's Enough/One More Time (reissue)	6
73	Contempo C 16	We're Losing It Baby/We Got A Good Thing Going	5

SUGAR CHILE ROBINSON
50	Capitol CL 13393	Christmas Boogie/Rudolph The Red Nosed Reindeer (78)	8
51	Capitol CL 13589	After School Blues/Caldonia (78)	8
51	Capitol CL 13636	Green Grass/Baby Blues (78)	8
52	Capitol CL 13796	Lazy Boy's Boogie/Whop Whop (78)	10
53	Capitol LC 6586	CAPITOL PRESENTS SUGAR CHILE ROBINSON (10" LP)	45

TOM ROBINSON (BAND)
75	Chebel SRT/CUS 015	GOOD TO BE GAY (EP, as Bradford Gay Liberation Front)	25
78	EMI EMI 2749	Don't Take No For An Answer/Glad To Be Gay (2-track jukebox issue)	5
79	EMI EMI 2946	All Right All Night/Black Angel (withdrawn, demo-only)	10
79	Deviant DEVIANT 1	Stand Together/A Dyke's Gotta Do (with Gay Pride)	7
82	Panic PROMO 2	Now Martin's Gone (live)/Atmospherics (live) (flexidisc)	6

(see also Cafe Society, Phantom, Billy Karloff [& Extremes])

VICKI SUE ROBINSON
| 76 | RCA RCA 2673 | Turn The Beat Around/Common Thief | 4 |

ROBINSON CREW
| 63 | Decca F 11706 | Taxi (Theme From TV Series)/Stormalong | 7 |

(see also Lord Rockingham's XI)

CARSON ROBISON (& HIS PLEASANT VALLEY BOYS)
53	MGM SP 1004	Lady Round The Lady/Pokeberry Promenade	8
53	MGM SP 1024	Square Dance Jitterbug/Keep On Circlin' 'Round	12
58	MGM MGM-EP 669	LIFE GETS TEEJUS (EP)	12
61	MGM MGM-EP 755	SQUARE DANCE — WITH CALLS (EP)	10
52	MGM MGM-D 101	EIGHT SQUARE DANCES (10" LP)	15

RALPH ROBLES
| 69 | London HA/SH 8385 | TAKING OVER (LP) | 12 |

ROBOTNIK
| 81 | Neutron NT 004 | SPACE RACE (EP) | 5 |

NICKY ROBSON
| 80 | Scratch SCR 006 | Stars/Eye To Eye (p/s) | 20 |
| 80 | Scratch SCRT 006 | Stars (Extended)/Eye To Eye (12", no p/s) | 50 |

(see also Gary Numan)

ROCAMARS
| 65 | King KG 1031 | All In Black Woman/Give Me Time | 12 |

TONY ROCCO
| 62 | Parlophone R 4886 | Stalemate/Keep A Walking | 12 |
| 62 | Parlophone R 4946 | Torture/Competition | 8 |

HARRY ROCHE CONSTELLATION
| 67 | CBS 202653 | Casino Royale/In The Pad Of The Mountain King | 7 |
| 67 | CBS SBPG 63013 | CASINO ROYALE (LP) | 25 |

71	Studio Two TWO 340	SPINDRIFT (LP)	20
73	Pye Intl. NSPL 41024	SPIRAL (LP)	50
73	Pye QUAD 1022	SOMETIMES (LP, quadrophonic)	25

ROCHEE & SARNOS
| 85 | Nervous NERD 018 | UNDERSTANDING SARNO (LP) | 12 |

JACKIE ROCHELLE
| 68 | Olga OLE 011 | Till The End/Grown Up Games | 5 |

ROCKABILLY PSYCHOSIS
| 84 | Big Beat WIK 18 | ROCKABILLY PSYCHOSIS AND THE GARAGE DISEASE (LP) | 15 |
| 89 | Big Beat CDWIK 18 | ROCKABILLY PSYCHOSIS AND THE GARAGE DISEASE (CD) | 18 |

DICKIE ROCK & MIAMI SHOWBAND
63	Piccadilly 7N 35154	Boys/There's Always Me	6
64	Piccadilly 7N 35202	From The Candy Store/Twenty Flight Rock	8
65	Pye 7N 15750	Round And Around/Little Baby	5
65	Pye 7N 15855	Every Step Of The Way/Rock And Roll Music	5
65	Pye 7N 17063	Come Back To Stay/Can't Make Up My Mind (p/s)	12
65	Pye NEP 24251	COME BACK TO STAY (EP)	15

ROCK AID ARMENIA
89	Life Aid Armenia ARMEN 01	Smoke On The Water/BLACK SABBATH: Paranoid (1970) (p/s)	5
89	L. A. Armenia ARMEN T01	Smoke On The Water/BLACK SABBATH: Paranoid (1970) (12", blue or white p/s)	8
89	Life Aid Armenia ARMENCD 01	Smoke On The Water (Radio Mix)/Smoke On The Water (Extended Mix)/BLACK SABBATH: Paranoid (1970) (CD)	10
90	L. A. Armenia ARMEN 002	Smoke On The Water '90 (Radio Edit)/BLACK SABBATH: Paranoid ('90) (p/s)	5

(see also Brian May, Roger Taylor, Ritchie Blackmore, Dave Gilmour, Black Sabbath, Rush, Bryan Adams, Bruce Dickinson, Ian Gillan, Free, Bad Company, Firm, Yes, Keith Emerson, Eighth Wonder)

ROCK-A-TEENS
| 59 | Columbia DB 4361 | Woo-Hoo/Untrue | 30 |

ROCK BROTHERS
| 56 | Parlophone MSP 6201 | Dungaree Doll/Livin' It Up | 70 |
| 56 | Parlophone R 4119 | Dungaree Doll/Livin' It Up (78) | 30 |

ROCKERS
| 59 | Oriole CB 1501 | Get Cracking/Counter Melody | 15 |
| 59 | Oriole CB 1501 | Get Cracking/Counter Melody (78) | 20 |

ROCKERS
| 83 | CBS A 3929 | We Are The Boys (Who Make All The Noise)/Rockin' On Stage (p/s) | 8 |
| 83 | CBS TA 3929 | We Are The Boys (Who Make All The Noise) (Extended Version)/Rockin' On Stage (12", p/s) | 12 |

(see also Phil Lynott, Roy Wood, Status Quo)

ROCKET 88
| 81 | Atlantic K 50776 | ROCKET 88 (LP) | 20 |

(see also Charlie Watts, Alexis Korner, Jack Bruce, Dick Heckstall-Smith)

ROCKET FROM THE CRYPT
93	Southern Studios PUS 007	Glazed/Pressures/Cut It Loose (white label test pressing, 5-10 copies only)	30
95	Elemental ELM 32S	Born in 69/Ciao Patsy (p/s)	5
96	Elemental ELM 33S	Young Livers/Burning Army Men (p/s)	5
96	Dinked 1	Used/Lose Your Clown (in-store giveaway)	25
98	Elemental ELM 47PIC	When In Rome/Tarzan/Tiger Feet Tonight (picture disc)	7
98	Elemental ELM 48S	Lipstick/Hot Heart (p/s)	5
98	Elemental ELM 49S	Break It Up/Turkish Revenge (p/s)	5
95	Elemental ELM 27LP	HOT CHARITY (LP)	12

ROCKETS
60	Philips PB 982	Gibraltar Rock/Walkin' Home	15
60	Philips PB 982	Gibraltar Rock/Walkin' Home (78)	40
61	Zodiac ZR 0010	Warrior/Countdown	15

ROCK FOLLIES
76	Island WIP 6293	Glenn Miller Is Missing/Talkin' Pictures (no p/s)	4
76	Island WIP 6310	Sugar Mountain/War Brides (no p/s)	6
77	Polydor 2001 714	O.K./B-Side	4

(see also Andy McKay, Julie Covington)

ROCKIN' BERRIES
63	Decca F 11698	Wah Wah Wah Woo/Rockin' Berry Stomp	25
63	Decca F 11760	Itty Bitty Pieces/The Twitch	18
64	Piccadilly 7N 35197	I Didn't Mean To Hurt You/You'd Better Come Home	6
64	Piccadilly 7N 35203	He's In Town/Flashback	5
64	Piccadilly 7N 35217	What In The World's Come Over You/You Don't Know What To Do	5
65	Piccadilly 7N 35236	Poor Man's Son/Follow Me	5
65	Piccadilly 7N 35254	You're My Girl/Brother Bill	7
65	Piccadilly 7N 35270	The Water Is Over My Head/Doesn't Time Fly	7
66	Piccadilly 7N 35304	I Could Make You Fall In Love/Land Of Love	6
66	Piccadilly 7N 35327	Midnight Mary/Money Grows On Trees	8
67	Piccadilly 7N 35373	Sometimes/Needs To Be	6
67	Piccadilly 7N 35400	Smile/Breakfast At Sam's	8
67	Pye 7N 17411	Dawn (Go Away)/She's Not Like Any Girl	8
68	Pye 7N 17519	When I Reach The Top/Pain	8
68	Pye 7N 17589	Mr. Blue/Land Of Love	6
73	Satril SAT 9	Day To Day/Big Louis' Birthday	5
74	Pye 7N 45394	Rock-A-Bye Nursery Rhyme/Long Time Ago	5
65	Piccadilly NEP 34039	I DIDN'T MEAN TO HURT YOU (EP)	30

65	Piccadilly NEP 34043	NEW FROM THE BERRIES (EP)	30
65	Piccadilly NEP 34045	HAPPY TO BE BLUE (EP)	50
64	Piccadilly NPL 38013	IN TOWN (LP)	75
65	Piccadilly NPL 38022	LIFE IS JUST A BOWL OF BERRIES (LP)	75
76	Satril SATL 4002	BLACK GOLD (LP)	12

(see also Jefferson)

ROCKIN' DUPSEE
70s	Flyright FLY 592	ROCKIN' WITH DUPSEE (LP)	12

ROCKIN' FOO
70	Stateside SS 2168	Rochester River/Stranger In The Attic	5
70	Stateside SSL 10303	ROCKIN' FOO (LP)	15

ROCKIN' HENRI & HAYSEEDS
63	Decca F 11700	Sally/Sweet Adeline	6

ROCKIN' HORSE
71	Philips 6006 156	The Biggest Gossip In Town/You Say	6
72	Philips 6006 200	Julian The Hooligan/Stayed Out Late Last Night	6
70	Philips 6308 075	YES IT IS (LP)	25

(see also Jimmy Campbell, 23rd Turnoff, Kirkbys, Merseys)

ROCKING HORSE
71	Camel CA 75	Running Back Home/SOUL SYNDICATE BAND: Running Back — Version	6
72	Randy's RAN 522	Hard Time/Change Your Ways	6
73	Randy's RAN 535	I'm So Fed Up/I'm So Fed Up — Version	5
74	Pyramid PYR 7009	New Situation/New Version	5

ROCKIN' RAMRODS
60s	Polydor BM 56512	Don't Fool With Fu Manchu/Tears Melt The Stone	15

ROCKIN' REBELS
63	Stateside SS 162	Wild Weekend/Wild Weekend Cha Cha	12
63	Stateside SS 187	Rockin' Crickets/Hully Gully Rock (both sides actually by Hot-Toddys)	12

(see also Hot-Toddys)

ROCKIN' R's
59	London HL 8872	The Beat/Crazy Baby	35
59	London HL 8872	The Beat/Crazy Baby (78)	50

ROCKIN' SAINTS
60	Brunswick 05843	Cheat On Me, Baby/Half And Half	100

ROCKIN' STRINGS
59	Columbia DB 4349	Red Sails In The Sunset/Autumn Leaves	6

(see also Eric Jupp)

ROCKIN' VICKERS
64	Decca F 11993	I Go Ape/Someone Like You (as Rocking Vickers)	20
66	CBS 202051	It's Alright/Stay By Me	40
66	CBS 202241	Dandy/I Don't Need Your Kind	30

(see also Sam Gopal, Motörhead)

ROCK MACHINE
73	T.I.M.	THEMES (LP)	50

(see also Ugly Custard)

ROCK'N'ROLL REVIVAL SHOW
68	Decca F 12752	Midnight Train/Oh Boy (both sides featuring Tommy Bishop)	7

(see also Tommy Bishop's Ricochets)

ROCK-OLGA
60	Ember EMB S 105	Red Sails In The Sunset/My Dixieland Doll (some in p/s)	10/5

ROCKSTEADYS
67	Giant GN 2	Squeeze And Freeze/JUNIOR SMITH: I'm A Good Boy	8

ROCKSTONES
70	Trojan TR 7762	A.B.C. Reggae/BEVERLEY'S ALLSTARS: Be Yours	5
70	Summit SUM 8501	Everything Is Beautiful/BEVERLEY'S ALLSTARS: Give Up	5

(see also Gaylads)

ROCK WORKSHOP
70	CBS 5046	You To Lose/Born In The City	6
71	CBS 7252	Very Last Time/Light Is Light	5
70	CBS 64075	ROCK WORKSHOP (LP, orange label)	30
71	CBS 64394	THE VERY LAST TIME (2-LP, orange label)	30

(see also Alex Harvey)

ROCKY & MUTATIONS
83	Cool Ghoul COOL 003	Thatcher Rap/Crisis! (no p/s)	5

ROCKY FELLERS
63	Stateside SS 175	Killer Joe/Lonely Treardrops	7
63	Stateside SS 212	Great Big World/Like The Big Guys	7
63	Pye International 7N 25225	Ching A Ling Baby/Hey Little Donkey	7

ROCKY HORROR SHOW
75	Ode ODS 66305	Science Fiction Double Feature/Time Warp	8
74	Ode ODE 77026	THE ROCKY HORROR SHOW (LP, original US Roxy cast)	15
75	Ode ODE 78332	THE ROCKY HORROR PICTURE SHOW ALBUM (LP, soundtrack)	15
83	Ode OSVP 78332	THE ROCKY HORROR PICTURE SHOW ALBUM (LP, soundtrack, picture disc)	20
86	Ode ODE 21653	THE ROCKY HORROR PICTURE SHOW ALBUM (LP, soundtrack, reissue)	12
87	Ode OSVP 21653	THE ROCKY HORROR PICTURE SHOW ALBUM (LP, soundtrack, reissue, picture disc)	20

TOMMY ROE

87	Ode ODE 9009	THE ROCKY HORROR SHOW (LP, reissue of original U.S. cast, with inner sleeve)	15
87	Ode RHBXLP 1	THE ROCKY HORROR BOX SET ALBUMS (4-LP, box set, with inserts)	25
90	Ode RHBXCD 1	THE ROCKY HORROR PICTURE ALBUMS (15th ANNIVERSARY) (4-CD, with booklet)	45

(see also Meat Loaf, Original Soundtracks)

GENE RODDENBERRY
| 76 | CBS 4692 | Star Trek Theme/Star Trek Philosophy | 12 |

RODD-KEN & CAVALIERS
| 60 | Triumph RGM 1001 | Magic Wheel/Happy Valley | 35 |

(see also Blue Men)

CLODA(GH) RODGERS
62	Decca F 11534	Believe Me I'm No Fool/End Of The Line	6
63	Decca F 11607	Sometime Kind Of Love/I See More Of Him	6
63	Decca F 11667	To Give My Love To You/I Only Live To Love You	6
64	Decca F 11812	Mister Heartache/Time	6
65	Columbia DB 7468	Wanting You/Johnny Come Home	6
66	Columbia DB 7926	Every Day Is Just The Same/You'll Come A Running	6
66	Columbia DB 8038	Stormy Weather/Lonely Room	7
69	RCA RCA 1891	Biljo/Spider	5
69	RCA SF 8033	CLODAGH RODGERS (LP)	15
69	RCA SF 8071	MIDNIGHT CLODAGH (LP)	15
71	RCA SF 8180	RODGERS AND HART (LP)	15
72	RCA SF 8271	IT'S DIFFERENT NOW (LP)	15
74	RCA SF 8394	YOU ARE MY MUSIC (LP)	15
77	Polydor 2383 473	SAVE ME (LP)	12

EILEEN RODGERS
58	Fontana H 136	Careful, Careful/I'm Alone Because I Love You	10
58	Fontana H 136	Careful, Careful/I'm Alone Because I Love You (78)	10
58	Fontana H 156	Treasure Of Your Love/Little Bit Bluer	10
58	Fontana H 156	Treasure Of Your Love/Little Bit Bluer (78)	12
61	London HLR 9271	Sailor/Wait Till Tomorrow	12

JEAN RODGERS
| 65 | Columbia DB 7637 | Take What I Have/Baby What You Gonna Do? | 6 |

JIMMIE RODGERS (The Blue Yodeller)
56	HMV MH 192	Blue Yodel No. 4/Waiting For A Train (78, export issue)	12
56	HMV MH 194	Blue Yodel No. 9/Jimmie The Kid (78, export issue)	12
58	HMV 7EG 8163	JIMMIE RODGERS (EP)	20
60	RCA RCX 1058	LEGENDARY JIMMIE RODGERS (EP)	15
59	RCA RD 27110	TRAIN WHISTLE BLUES (LP)	20
59	RCA RD 27138	NEVER NO MO' BLUES (JIMMIE RODGERS MEMORIAL ALBUM) (LP)	20
61	RCA RD 27203	MY ROUGH AND ROWDY WAYS (LP)	20
61	RCA RD 27241	JIMMIE THE KID (LP)	20

62	RCA RD 7505	COUNTRY MUSIC HALL OF FAME (LP)	20
63	RCA RD 7562	THE SHORT BUT BRILLIANT LIFE OF JIMMIE RODGERS (LP)	20
64	RCA RD 7644	MY TIME AIN'T LONG (LP)	20

JIMMIE RODGERS

57	Columbia DB 3986	Honeycomb/Their Hearts Were Full Of Spring (as Jimmy Rodgers)	15
57	Columbia DB 4052	Kisses Sweeter Than Wine/Better Loved You'll Never Be	7
58	Columbia DB 4078	Oh-Oh, I'm Falling In Love Again/The Long Hot Summer	7
58	Columbia DB 4130	Secretly/Make Me A Miracle	7
58	Columbia DB 4130	Secretly/Make Me A Miracle (78)	8
58	Columbia DB 4175	Are You Really Mine/The Wizard	7
58	Columbia DB 4175	Are You Really Mine/The Wizard (78)	8
58	Columbia DB 4206	Women From Liberia/Girl In The Wood	7
58	Columbia DB 4206	Women From Liberia/Girl In The Wood (78)	10
59	Columbia DB 4235	Bimbombey/You Understand Me	6
59	Columbia DB 4235	Bimbombey/You Understand Me (78)	8
59	Columbia DB 4281	Because You're Young/I'm Never Gonna Tell	6
59	Columbia DB 4327	Soldier, Won't You Marry Me?/Ring-A-Ling-A-Lario	6
59	Columbia DB 4327	Soldier, Won't You Marry Me?/Ring-A-Ling-A-Lario (78)	12
59	Columbia DB 4362	Tucumcari/The Night You Became Seventeen	6
60	Columbia DB 4401	Waltzing Matilda/T.L.C. — Tender Loving Care	6
60	Columbia DB 4447	Joshua Fit The Battle Of Jericho/Just A Closer Walk With Thee	6
61	Columbia DB 4617	Little Shepherd Of Kingdom Come/When Love Is Young	6
62	Columbia DB 4847	English Country Garden/Little Dog Cried	5
62	Columbia DB 4904	The Fox And The Goose/Soldier, Won't You Marry Me	6
62	London HLD 9582	No One Will Ever Know/Because	7
63	London HLD 9654	Rhumba Boogie/Rainbow At Midnight	6
63	London HLD 9697	Face In A Crowd/Lonely Tears	6
63	London HLD 9752	I'm Gonna Be The Winner/Poor Little Raggedy Ann	7
64	London HLD 9904	I Forgot More Than You'll Ever Know/The World I Used To Know (unissued)	
64	Pye International 7N 25253	I Forgot More Than You'll Ever Know/The World I Used To Know	6
58	Columbia SEG 7770	JIMMIE RODGERS (EP)	20
58	Columbia SEG 7811	JIMMIE RODGERS SINGS (EP)	18
59	Columbia SEG 7911	JIMMIE RODGERS NO. 2 (EP)	20
63	Columbia SEG 8253	ENGLISH COUNTRY GARDEN (EP)	8
65	Dot DEP 20007	JIMMIE RODGERS FAVOURITES (EP)	12
58	Columbia 33SX 1082	JIMMIE RODGERS (LP)	30
58	Columbia 33SX 1097	THE NUMBER ONE BALLADS (LP)	25
59	Columbia 33SX 1144	SINGS FOLK SONGS (LP)	18
59	Columbia 33SX 1176	JIMMIE RODGERS FAVOURITES (LP)	18
59	Columbia 33SX 1206	IT'S CHRISTMAS ONCE AGAIN (LP)	18
60	Columbia 33SX 1217	TWILIGHT ON THE TRAIL (LP, also stereo SCX 3302)	15/18
60	Columbia 33SX 1236	WHEN THE SPIRIT MOVES YOU (LP, also stereo SCX 3313)	15/18
61	Columbia 33SX 1292	AT HOME WITH JIMMIE RODGERS (LP, also stereo SCX 3355)	12/15
61	Columbia 33SX 1393	THE FOLK SONG WORLD OF ... (LP, also stereo SCX 3425)	12/15
63	London HA-D 8040	NO ONE WILL EVER KNOW (LP)	25
65	London HA-D/SH-D 8116	HONEYCOMB (LP)	25
66	Dot DLP 3710	COUNTRY MUSIC 1966 (LP)	15

RODNEY & BRUNETTES

| 79 | London/Bomp HLZ 10574 | Holocaust On Sunset Boulevard/NEW YORK BLONDES featuring MADAME X: Little GTO (no p/s) | 8 |

(see also Blondie, Debbie Harry)

RODS (U.K.)

| 77 | Island WIP 12-6401 | Do Anything You Wanna Do/Schoolgirl Love (12", stickered plain sleeve) | 7 |

(see also Eddie & Hot Rods)

RODS (U.S.)

| 82 | Arista ARIPD 467 | You Keep Me Hangin' On/Wings Of Fire (picture disc) | 5 |

TOMMY ROE (& ROEMANS)

62	HMV POP 1060	Sheila/Save Your Kisses	6
62	HMV POP 1092	Susie Darlin'/Piddle De Pat	6
63	HMV POP 1117	Gonna Take A Chance/Don't Cry Donna	6
63	HMV POP 1138	The Folk Singer/Count On Me	6
63	HMV POP 1174	Kiss And Run/What Makes The Blues	6
63	HMV POP 1207	Everybody/There's A Day A Coming	6
64	HMV POP 1290	Be A Good Little Girl/Carol	6
63	HMV POP 1259	Come On/There Will Be Better Years	6
64	HMV POP 1364	Little Miss Heartbreak/You Might As Well Forget Him (with Roemans)	6
65	HMV POP 1386	Diane From Manchester Square/Party Girl (as Tommy Roe & Roemans)	6
65	HMV POP 1469	Doesn't Anybody Know My Name/I'm A Rambler, I'm A Gambler	6
66	HMV POP 1539	Sweet Pea/Much More Love	6
66	HMV POP 1556	Hooray For Hazel/Need For Love	6
67	HMV POP 1574	It's Now Winter's Day/Kick Me Charlie	6
67	HMV POP 1611	Melancholy Mood/Paisley Dreams	6
69	Stateside SS 2143	Dizzy/The You I Need	5
69	Stateside SS 2152	Heather Honey/Money Is My Pay	5
69	Stateside SS 2156	Jam Up Jelly Tight/Moontalk	5
70	Stateside SS 2165	Stir It Up And Serve It/Firefly	5
70	Stateside SS 2174	Pearl/A Dollar's Worth Of Pennies	5
71	Probe PRO 527	Greatest Love/King of Fools	5
71	Probe PRO 538	Stagger Lee/Back Streets And Alleys	5
72	Probe PRO 555	We Can Make Music/Gotta Keep Rolling Along	6
72	MGM 2006 134	Mean Little Woman, Rosalie/Skyline	6
63	HMV 7EG 8806	THE FOLK SINGER (EP)	30
63	HMV CLP 1614	SHEILA (LP)	40
64	HMV CLP 1704	EVERYBODY LIKES TOMMY ROE (LP)	35

65	HMV CLP 1860	BALLADS AND BEAT (LP)	25
69	Stateside S(S)L 10282	DIZZY (LP)	15
70	Stateside SSL 10296	TOMMY ROE'S GREATEST HITS (LP)	15
70	Probe SPB 1021	WE CAN MAKE MUSIC (LP)	12
72	Probe SPB 1046	BEGINNINGS (LP)	12

ROGER ROGER & HIS ORCHESTRA
| 63 | Fontana 2567 268TF | The Desperadoes/Song Of Mexico | 4 |

ROGER ME RIGID
| 78 | Roger's TOOL 069 | Taming The Trouser Lion/Premiere Bush-Bunny (10", 78rpm, 'rude' p/s) | 35 |
| 78 | Roger's SENSELESS 001 | SLIP IT UP IN BETWEEN (LP, with diaphragm insert) | 80 |

BILL ROGERS
| 52 | Melodisc 1230 | Nice Woman, Ugly Man/B.G. BARGEE: Shanto (78) | 12 |

CE CE ROGERS
| 89 | WEA A 8852T | Forever/Someday (12", 3-track) | 25 |

DANE ROGERS & NU BEATS
| 64 | Pye 7N 15621 | Mary Jane/Jeanette | 7 |

DEAN ROGERS
60	Parlophone R 4732	End Of Time (as Dean Rogers & Hi-Fi's)/Keep The Miracle Going	7
61	Parlophone R 4835	Timber/High In A Misty Sky	7
(see also Sydney James)			

ERIC ROGERS
| 59 | Decca F 11151 | Joanna/Lingering Lovers (78) | 8 |
| 63 | Decca F 11585 | The Iron Maiden/Fly-Wheel | 6 |

IKE ROGERS
| 50 | Jazz Collector L 55 | It Hurts So Good/Screenin' The Blues (78) | 10 |

JULIE ROGERS
64	Mercury MF 809	It's Magic/Without Your Love	7
64	Mercury MF 820	The Wedding (La Novia)/The Love Of A Boy	5
65	Mercury MF 838	Like A Child/Our Day Will Come	5
65	Mercury MF 849	Hawaiian Wedding Song/Turn Around, Look At Me	6
65	Mercury MF 858	Sudden Love/Play The Music	6
65	Mercury MF 868	Day By Day/I'm Walking Behind You	6
65	Mercury MF 895	Another Year, Another Love, Another Heartache/ Don't Waste Young Years On Him	6
65	Mercury MF 901	In My Room/Three Unspoken Words	6
65	Mercury MF 917	I Love Him/Lullaby For Lovers	6
65	Mercury MF 950	While The Angel Was Ringing/Climb Every Mountain	6
66	Mercury MF 980	These Gentle Hands/When Two Worlds Collide	6
66	Mercury MF 993	Bless You/Go On Home	6
68	Mercury MF 1015	Let Me Belong To You/You Never Told Me	6
69	Ember EMB S 267	Almost Close To You (O Mio Angelo)/This Is Me (C'est Ton Nom) (p/s)	7
69	Ember EMB S 273	Which Way To Nowhere/Love Theme From The Motion Picture "Michael And Helga" (p/s)	7
70	Ember EMB S 287	Children Of My Mind/Once More With Feeling (p/s)	7
70	Ember EMB S 300	Baby Don't You Leave Me/Where Do You Go (p/s)	7
64	Mercury 10023 MCE	JULIE ROGERS (EP)	12
65	Mercury 10028 MCE	THE SOUND OF JULIE (EP)	12
65	Mercury 20048 (S)MCL	THE SOUND OF JULIE (LP, mono/stereo)	20/25
66	Mercury 20086 (S)MCL	CONTRASTS (LP, mono/stereo)	20/25
67	Mercury 20100 (S)MCL	SONGS OF INSPIRATION (LP, mono/stereo)	20/25

KENNY ROGERS (& FIRST EDITION)
69	Reprise RS 20829	Ruby Don't Take Your Love To Town/Girl Get A Hold Of Yourself	5
70	Reprise RS 20888	Something's Burning/Momma's Waiting	5
70	Reprise RS 20923	Tell It All Brother/Just Remember You Are My Sunshine	5
70	Reprise RS 20953	Heed The Call/Stranger In My Place	5
70	Reprise RS 20999	Someone Who Cares/Mission Of San Nohero	5
72	Reprise K 14009	Ruby Don't Take Your Love To Town/Girl Get A Hold Of Yourself (p/s)	5
72	Reprise K 14206	Ruby Don't Take Your Love To Town/Me And Bobby McGee/ Reuben James/Something's Burning (maxi-single)	5
69	Reprise RSLP 6352	RUBY DON'T TAKE YOUR LOVE TO TOWN (LP)	15
70	Reprise RSLP 6385	SOMETHING'S BURNING (LP)	12
70	Reprise RSLP 6412	TELL IT ALL BROTHER (LP)	12
(see also First Edition)			

LINCOLN ROGERS
| 73 | Phoenix NIX 137 | Let Love Come Between Us/She Looked At Me With Love | 8 |

LYNNE ROGERS
| 65 | RCA RCA 1479 | Sometimes/I Shouldn't Care | 6 |

MARK ROGERS & MARKSMEN
| 63 | Parlophone R 5045 | Bubble Pop/Hold It! | 12 |
| *(see also Marksmen, Mark Wirtz)* | | | |

PAUL ROGERS
| 61 | HMV POP 872 | Four An' Twenty Thousand Kisses/Free To Love | 6 |
| 63 | HMV POP 1121 | Always/Joanie Don't Be Angry | 6 |

PAULINE ROGERS
| 54 | Columbia SCM 5106 | Spinnin' The Blues/But Good | 8 |

PIERCE ROGERS & OVERLANDERS
| 61 | Parlophone R 4838 | Do You Still Love Me?/That Someone | 10 |

ROY ROGERS

50	HMV MH 109	Oh Dem Golden Slippers/Lucky Leather Breeches (78, export issue)	10
51	HMV BD 1267	Me And My Teddy Bear/Buffalo Billy (78)	10
51	HMV BD 1286	A Four Legged Friend/There's A Cloud In My Valley Of Sunshine (78)	10
55	HMV 7EG 8145	KING OF THE COWBOYS (EP)	18
55	HMV 7EG 8182	HAPPY TRAILS (EP)	18

ROY ROGERS & DALE EVANS

50s	Gala Goldentone GG 2	Me And My Teddy Bear/Buffalo Billy (6", some in p/s, orange vinyl, 78rpm)	10/8
50s	Gala Goldentone GG 3	Happy Trails To You/A Cowboy Needs A Horse (6", some in p/s, orange vinyl, 33rpm)	10/8
53	HMV MH 174	Hazy Mountains/You've Got A Rope Around My Heart (78, export issue)	10
54	HMV 7MC6	Old Rugged Cross/In The Garden (export issue)	6

SHORTY ROGERS & HIS ORCHESTRA

54	HMV 7M 267	Tale Of An African Lobster/Sweetheart Of Sigmund Freud	5
54	HMV 7EG 8044	SHORTY ROGERS AND HIS ORCHESTRA (EP)	10
52	Capitol LC 6549	MODERN SOUNDS (10" LP, as Shorty Rogers & His Giants)	12
54	HMV DLP 1030	COOL AND CRAZY (10" LP, featuring Giants)	12
54	HMV DLP 1058	EIGHT SHORTY ROGERS' NUMBERS (10" LP)	12
56	Contemporary LDC 190	SHELLY MANNE, SHORTY ROGERS AND JIMMY GIUFFRE — THE THREE (10" LP, with Shelly Manne & Jimmy Giuffre)	15

(see also Boots Brown, Bud Shank, Shelly Manne, Jimmy Giuffre)

SIDNEY ROGERS

73	Techniques TE 923	Don't Throw Stones/Toughness	5

TIMMIE ROGERS

53	Capitol CL 13991	Nothin's Wrong With Nothin'/Oh, Yeah! (78)	8
57	London HLU 8510	Back To School Again/I've Got A Dog Who Loves Me	60
57	London HLU 8510	Back To School Again/I've Got A Dog Who Loves Me (78)	30
58	London HLU 8601	Take Me To Your Leader/Fla-Ga-La-Pa	75
58	London HLU 8601	Take Me To Your Leader/Fla-Ga-La-Pa (78)	35

TRACY ROGERS

65	Polydor 56029	How Love Used To Be/When I Realise	5
65	Polydor 56037	Love Story/I Remember When I Loved You	5
66	Polydor 56077	Baby/Through Thick And Thin	6
67	Polydor 56197	Back With You Baby/In The Morning	8

VERN ROGERS & HI-FI'S

62	Oriole CB 1785	That Ain't Right/Be Everything	10
63	Oriole CB 1826	He's New To You/Can't Complain	7
63	Oriole CB 1885	I Will/One Way Love Affair	10
63	Oriole CB 1923	Anna/Pride	7

ROGUES (U.S.)

65	CBS 201731	Everyday/Rogers Reef	8

ROGUES (U.K.)

67	Decca F 12718	Memories Of Missy/And You Let Her Pass By	6

(see also Terry Day)

ROKES

67	RCA RCA 1587	Let's Live For Today/Ride On	15
67	RCA RCA 1646	Hold My Hand/Regency Sue	30
68	RCA RCA 1694	When The Wind Arises/The Works Of Bartholemew	50

ROKKA

80	Rock Trax RT 01	Come Back (no p/s)	10

CHERRY ROLAND

63	Decca F 11579	Handy Sandy/Stay As I Am	6
63	Decca F 11648	What A Guy/Just For Fun	7

(see also Cherry Rowland)

PAUL ROLAND

82	Aristocrat ARC 1389	Doctor Strange/Madelaine (p/s)	8
82	Scoff DT 020	Doctor Strange/Madelaine (p/s, Irish-only)	10
83	Aftermath AEP 12011	Blades Of Battenburg (Remix)/Captain Blood/Puppet Master/Cavalier (12", p/s)	10
85	Aftermath AEP 12012	Death Or Glory (Revamped Version)/The Great Edwardian Air Raid/Beau Brummel/The Curious Case Of Richard Fielding (12", p/s)	8
86	Aftermath AEP 12013	Gabrielle/Berlin/Sword & Sorcery (p/s)	8
86	Imaginary MIRAGE 002	Demon In A Glass Case/In The Opium Den (oversized p/s)	7
87	Bam Caruso OPRA 081	Madame Guillotine/UNITED STATES OF EXISTENCE: Gone (radio jukebox promo, company sleeve)	5
87	Bam Caruso PABL 094	Alice's House/Go Down You Murderers/Happy Families/Jumbee (demo) (p/s)	8
87	Bucketfull Of Brains BOB 14	Madhouse (Demo)/GIANT SAND: Wishing Well (flexidisc free with *Bucketfull Of Brains* magazine)	6/4
87	Bucketfull Of Brains	Madhouse (Demo)/GIANT SAND: Wishing Well (hard vinyl test pressing)	10
85	Aftermath SCOOP 2	BURNT ORCHIDS (mini LP)	12
80	Ace ACE 013	THE WEREWOLF OF LONDON (LP)	18
81	Armageddon ARM 9	THE WEREWOLF OF LONDON (Revamped Version) (LP, different sleeve)	12
87	Bam Caruso KIRI 052	DANSE MACABRE (LP)	10
87	Bam Caruso KIRI 052CD	DANSE MACABRE (CD)	15
94	Gaslight CACD 501	SARABANDE (CD)	15

(see also Weird Strings, Midnight Rags, Beau Brummel)

WALTER ROLAND/GEORGIA SLIM

59	Jazz Collector JEL 2	THE MALE BLUES VOL. 1 (EP)	15

BARRY ROLFE

73	Philips 6006 384	Beam Me Aboard, Mr. Spock/Boadicea	4

ROLLER

| 95 | Poor Person Prod. | LIFE IN THE DAY OF... (LP, handmade sleeve with insert, numbered, 500 only) .... 12 |

ROLLERS

| 61 | London HLG 9340 | Continental Walk/I Want You So .... 12 |

ROLLING STONES

DECCA SINGLES

63	Decca F 11675	Come On/I Want To Be Loved 18
63	Decca F 11742	Poison Ivy/Fortune Teller (release cancelled; U.K. solid-centre copies are possibly record-club or export issues) 400
63	Decca F 11764	I Wanna Be Your Man/Stoned 10
63	Decca F 11764	I Wanna Be Your Man/Stones (B-side mis-spelled) 12
64	Decca F 11845	Not Fade Away/Little By Little 6
64	Decca F 11934	It's All Over Now/Good Times, Bad Times 6
64	Decca F 12014	Little Red Rooster/Off The Hook 6

(The above singles were originally issued with 'Recording First Published ...' text & 'wide' label lettering.)

65	Decca F 12104	The Last Time/Play With Fire 6
65	Decca F 12220	(I Can't Get No) Satisfaction/The Spider And The Fly 6
65	Decca F 12263	Get Off Of My Cloud/The Singer Not The Song 6
66	Decca F 12331	19th Nervous Breakdown/As Tears Go By 6
66	Decca F 12395	Paint It, Black/Long Long While 7

(The above singles were originally issued with a round Decca logo; later boxed-logo pressings are worth £4 each.)

66	Decca F 12497	Have You Seen Your Mother, Baby, Standing In The Shadow?/ Who's Driving Your Plane 6
67	Decca F 12546	Let's Spend The Night Together/Ruby Tuesday 6
67	Decca F 12654	We Love You/Dandelion 6
68	Decca F 12782	Jumping Jack Flash/Child Of The Moon 6
69	Decca F 12952	Honky Tonk Women/You Can't Always Get What You Want (some in demo-only p/s) 40/5
71	Decca F 13195	Street Fighting Man/Surprise Surprise/Everybody Needs Somebody To Love (33rpm maxi-single) 5
71	Decca F 13203	Street Fighting Man/Surprise Surprise (jukebox edition) 15
73	Decca F 13404	Sad Day/You Can't Always Get What You Want 6
74	Decca F 13517	It's All Over Now/Paint It Black (release cancelled, demo-only) 120
75	Decca F 13584	I Don't Know Why I Love You (credited to either 'Jagger/Richard/Taylor' or 'Stevie Wonder')/Try A Little Harder 12/8
75	Decca F 13597	Out Of Time/Jiving Sister Fanny 5
76	Decca F 13635	Honky Tonk Women/Sympathy For The Devil 6
70s	Decca F 11934	It's All Over Now/Good Times, Bad Times (repressing, with stereo mix on A-side, [ZXDR instead of XDR matrix no.] boxed Decca logo) 5
87	Decca F 102	Jumping Jack Flash/Child Of The Moon (p/s, reissue) 6
87	Decca FX 102	Jumping Jack Flash/Child Of The Moon/Sympathy For The Devil (12", p/s, reissue) 8

EXPORT SINGLES

65	Decca F 12104	The Last Time/Play With Fire (with Dutch or Scandinavian p/s) 25
65	Decca F 22180	Heart Of Stone/What A Shame (some in p/s) 50/25
65	Decca F 12220	(I Can't Get No) Satisfaction/Under Assistant West Coast Promotional Man (some with p/s) 30/15
65	Decca F 22265	Get Off My Cloud/I'm Free (some in p/s) 30/15
66	Decca F 12331	19th Nervous Breakdown/As Tears Go By (with Dutch p/s) 25
66	Decca F 12395	Paint It, Black/Long Long While (p/s) 25
67	Decca F 12546	Let's Spend The Night Together/Ruby Tuesday (p/s) 25
67	Decca F 12654	We Love You/Dandelion (p/s) 25
67	Decca F 22706	2,000 Light Years From Home/She's A Rainbow 30
68	Decca F 22825	Street Fighting Man (remix)/No Expectations (some in p/s) 80/25
69	Decca F 12952	Honky Tonk Women/You Can't Always Get What You Want (p/s) 45
71	Decca F 13126	Little Queenie/Love In Vain (some in p/s) 30/15
71	Decca F 13195	Street Fighting Man/Surprise Surprise/Everybody Needs Somebody To Love (33rpm maxi-single, p/s) 25
71	Decca F 13204	Street Fighting Man/Everybody Needs Somebody To Love (some in p/s) 25/15
63	Decca AT 15005	I Wanna Be Your Man/Stoned 75
64	Decca AT 15006	Not Fade Away/Little By Little 75
64	Decca AT 15032	Come On/Tell Me (You're Coming Back) 100
64	Decca AT 15035	Empty Heart/Around And Around 100
65	Decca AT 15039	Time Is On My Side/Congratulations 100
65	Decca AT 15040	Little Red Rooster/Off The Hook 100
65	Decca AT 15043	(I Can't Get No) Satisfaction/Under Assistant West Coast Promotional Man (p/s) 100

SINGLES BOX SETS

| 80 | Decca STONE 1-12 | SINGLE STONES (12-single box set) .... 60 |
| 80 | Decca BROWSE 1 | SINGLE STONES (in-store, 3 x 12-single box set [STONE 1-12], with poster & badge, also available via mail-order) .... 200 |

ROLLING STONES LABEL SINGLES

71	Rolling Stones RS 19100	Brown Sugar/Bitch/Let It Rock (some in p/s) 20/5
72	Rolling Stones RS 19103	Tumbling Dice/Sweet Black Angel 4
73	Rolling Stones RS 19105	Angie/Silver Train 4
74	Rolling Stones RS 19114	It's Only Rock 'N' Roll/Through The Lonely Nights 5
76	Rolling Stones RS 19121	Fool To Cry/Crazy Mama 4
78	Rolling Stones EMI 2802	Miss You/Faraway Eyes (p/s) 4
78	R. Stones 12EMI 2802	Miss You (8.26)/Faraway Eyes (12", p/s, pink vinyl) 8
78	Rolling Stones EMI 2861	Respectable/When The Whip Comes Down (p/s) 4
80	Rolling Stones RSR 105	Emotional Rescue/Down The Hole (p/s) 4
80	Rolling Stones RSR 106	She's So Cold/Send It To Me (p/s) 4
81	Rolling Stones RSR 109	Waiting On A Friend/Little T & A (p/s) 4

81	Rolling Stones	Beast Of Burden/Everything Is Turning Gold (unreleased)	
82	Rolling Stones RSR 111	Time Is On My Side (live)/Twenty Flight Rock (live) (p/s)	5
82	Rolling Stones 12RSR 111	Time Is On My Side (live)/Twenty Flight Rock (live)/	
		Under My Thumb (live) (12", p/s)	10
83	R. Stones RSR 112 (DJ)	Let's Spend The Night Together (live)/Start Me Up (live) (no p/s, promo only)	18
83	Rolling Stones RSR 113	Undercover Of The Night/All The Way Down (p/s)	4
83	Rolling Stones 12RSR 113	Undercover Of The Night/All The Way Down/Feel On Baby (12", p/s)	8
84	Rolling Stones RSR 114	She Was Hot/I Think I'm Going Mad (p/s)	4
84	Rolling Stones RSRP 114	She Was Hot/I Think I'm Going Mad (shaped picture disc)	15
84	Rolling Stones SUGAR 1	Brown Sugar/Bitch (p/s, reissue)	6
84	Rolling Stones SUGARP 1	Brown Sugar/Bitch (shaped picture disc)	15
93	Rolling Stone RS LH 1	Brown Sugar/Start Me Up (jukebox issue, no p/s)	15
93	Rolling Stone ORDER LH 1	Gimme Shelter/TOM JONES: Gimme Shelter (jukebox issue, no p/s)	15

OTHER SINGLES

| 74 | Atlantic K 19107 | Brown Sugar/Happy/Rocks Off (possibly unissued) | 75+ |
| 72 | Sound For Industry 107 | Mick Jagger Introduces 'Exile On Main Street' (flexidisc free with *NME*) | 12/7 |

CBS SINGLES

86	CBS QA 6864	Harlem Shuffle/Had It With You (poster p/s)	8
86	CBS TA 6864	Harlem Shuffle (N.Y. Mix)/(London Mix)/Had It With You (12", p/s)	10
86	CBS QTA 6864	Harlem Shuffle (N.Y. Mix)/(London Mix)/Had It With You (12", p/s)	15
86	CBS A 7160	One Hit (To The Body)/Fight (p/s)	4
86	CBS TA 7160	One Hit (To The Body) (London Mix)/Fight (12", p/s)	7
89	CBS 655 193-2	Mixed Emotions (7" Version)/Mixed Emotions (Chris Kimsey's 12")/	
		Fancyman Blues (CD, picture disc, card sleeve)	10
89	CBS 655 193-5	Mixed Emotions (7" Version)/Fancyman Blues/Tumbling Dice/Miss You	
		(CD, picture disc, in circular tin with 'tongue' logo sticker)	30
89	CBS 655 193-6	Mixed Emotions (Chris Kimsey's 12")/Fancyman Blues (12", p/s)	10
89	CBS 655 193-6	Mixed Emotions (Chris Kimsey's 12")/Fancyman Blues/	
		Mixed Emotions (7" Version) (12", p/s)	10
89	CBS 655 214-2	Mixed Emotions (7" Version)/Fancyman Blues/Shattered/Waiting On A Friend	
		(CD, picture disc, in circular tin with 'tongue' logo sticker)	30
89	CBS 655 422-7	Rock And A Hard Place/Cook Cook Blues (p/s)	5
89	CBS 655 422-6	Rock And A Hard Place (Dance Mix)/Emotional Rescue/Some Girls/	
		Rock And A Hard Place (Hard Dub Mix)/Cook Cook Blues (12", p/s)	10
89	CBS 655 422-5	Rock And A Hard Place (Michael Brauer Mix)/Rock And A Hard Place	
		(Bonus Beats Mix)/Rock And A Hard Place (Edited 7" Version) (2nd 12", p/s)	8
89	CBS 655 422-8	Rock And A Hard Place (Dance Mix)/(Hard Dub Mix)/Cook Cook Blues	
		(3rd 12", p/s)	10
89	CBS 655 422-2	Rock And A Hard Place (7" Version)/(Dance Mix)/(Bonus Beats Mix)/	
		Cook Cook Blues (CD, picture disc, card sleeve)	15
89	CBS 655 422-3	Rock And A Hard Place (Dance Mix)/Cook Cook Blues/Rock And A Hard Place	
		(Hard Dub Mix) (2nd CD)	10
89	CBS 655 448-2	Rock And A Hard Place (7" Version)/Cook Cook Blues/It's Only Rock'n'Roll	
		(But I Like It)/Rocks Off (3rd CD, picture disc, 7" box set with poster)	20
89	CBS 655 448-5	Rock And A Hard Place (7" Version)/Cook Cook Blues/Emotional Rescue/	
		Some Girls (CD, tongue-shaped card sleeve)	25
90	CBS 656 065-6	Almost Hear You Sigh/Beast Of Burden/Angie/Fool To Cry (12", gatefold p/s)	7
90	CBS 656 065-2	Almost Hear You Sigh/Beast Of Burden/Angie/Fool To Cry (CD, gold disc)	20
90	CBS 656 065-5	Almost Hear You Sigh/Miss You/Waiting On A Friend/Wish I'd Never Met You	
		(CD, in tin with 'Urban Jungle' sticker)	30
90	CBS 656 122-6	Terrifying (12" Dance Remix)/Rock And A Hard Place (Dance Mix)/	
		Harlem Shuffle (London Mix) (12", p/s)	10
90	CBS 656 122-2	Terrifying (7" Remix Edit)/(12" Remix)/Rock And A Hard Place (7" Version)/	
		Harlem Shuffle (LP Version) (CD)	10
90	CBS 656 122-5	Terrifying (7" Remix Edit)/Start Me Up/Shattered/If You Can't Rock Me	
		(2nd CD, card p/s)	10
91	CBS 656 756-6	Highwire/2,000 Light Years From Home (live)/Sympathy For The Devil (live)/	
		I Just Wanna Make Love To You (live) (12", gatefold p/s)	10
91	CBS 656 756-2	Highwire/2,000 Light Years From Home (live)/Sympathy For The Devil (live)/	
		I Just Wanna Make Love To You (live) (CD)	10
91	CBS 656 756-5	Highwire/Play With Fire (live)/Factory Girl (live) (CD)	12
91	CBS 656 892-6	Ruby Tuesday/Play With Fire (live)/You Can't Always Get What You Want	
		(live)/Rock And A Hard Place (live) (12", p/s)	12
91	CBS 656 892-2	Ruby Tuesday/Play With Fire (live)/You Can't Always Get What You Want	
		(live)/Undercover Of The Night (live) (CD)	10
91	CBS 656 892-5	Ruby Tuesday/Harlem Shuffle (live)/Winning Ugly (CD)	10
91	CBS 657 334-2	Sex Drive (single edit)/(Dirty Hands Mix)/(Club Version) (91)	10

VIRGIN SINGLES

94	Virgin VS 1503	Love Is Strong/The Storm (numbered p/s, 7,000 only)	10
94	Virgin VSCDT 1503	Love Is Strong/The Storm/So Young/Love Is Strong (Bob Clearmountain Mix)	
		(CD)	10
94	Virgin VSCDX 1503	Love Is Strong (Teddy Riley Radio Remix)/(Teddy Riley Extended Remix)/	
		(Teddy Riley Extended Rock Remix)/(Teddy Riley Dub Remix)/	
		(Joe The Butcher Club Mix)/(Teddy Riley Instrumental) (CD, stickered cover)	7
94	Virgin VS 1518	You Got Me Rocking/Jump On Top Of Me (numbered p/s, 7,000 only)	8
94	Virgin VST 1518	You Got Me Rocking (Perfecto Mix)/(Sexy Disco Dub Mix)/(Trance Mix)	
		(12", p/s)	12
94	Virgin VSCDG 1518	You Got Me Rocking/Jump On Top Of Me/You Got Me Rocking (Perfecto Mix)/	
		You Got Me Rocking (Sexy Disco Dub Mix) (CD, gatefold digipak)	7
94	Virgin VS 1524	Out Of Tears/I'm Gonna Drive (numbered p/s, 7,000 only)	8
94	Virgin VSCDX 1524	Out Of Tears (Don Was Edit)/I'm Gonna Drive/Sparks Will Fly (Radio Clean)/	
		Out Of Tears (Bob Clearmountain Remix Edit) (CD, tear-shaped card p/s)	10
94	Virgin VSCDG 1524	Out Of Tears (Don Was Edit)/I'm Gonna Drive/So Young/The Storm/	
		Jump On Top Of Me (CD, digipak, numbered, 4,000 only, withdrawn)	350
94	Virgin VSP 1539	I Go Wild/I Go Wild (live) (picture disc)	8

MINT VALUE £

94	Virgin VSCDX 1539	I Go Wild/I Go Wild (Scott Litt Remix)/I Go Wild (live)/I Go Wild (Luis Resto Straight Vocal Mix) (CD, with 4 postcards)	7
96	Virgin VS 1578	Wild Horses/Tumbling Dice/Gimme Shelter (unreleased)	
96	Virgin VSCDT 1578	Wild Horses/Tumbling Dice/Gimme Shelter (CD, unreleased)	
97	Virgin VS 1653	Anybody Seen My Baby? (LP Edit)/(Soul Solution Remix Edit) (numbered picture disc, p/s, 7,500 only)	15
97	Virgin VST 1653	Anybody Seen My Baby? (Armand's Rolling Steelo Mix)/(Soul Solution Remix)/ (Bonus Roll) (12", p/s)	30
98	Virgin VSY 1667	Saint Of Me (Radio Edit)/Anyway You Look At It (picture disc)	10
98	Virgin VSTX 1667	Saint Of Me (remixes)/Anybody Seen My Baby? (remixes) (12", double pack, stickered p/s)	15
98	Virgin VSTTDT 1667	Saint Of Me (remixes)/Anybody Seen My Baby? (remixes) (12", double pack, stickered p/s)	15
98	Virgin VSY 1700	Out Of Control (Album Radio Edit)/(In Hand With Fluke Radio Edit)	8

PROMO ONLY SINGLES

91	CBS A 026/B 027	Highwire/Sympathy For The Devil (live) (12")	10
93	EMI ORDERLH 1	Gimme Shelter (live) (1-sided jukebox issue)	20
93	Virgin STONES 1	JUMP BACK (EP)	25
94	Virgin VSCDJ 1518	You Got Me Rocking (Original Version)/(Perfecto Mix) (CD)	15
95	Virgin VSCDJ 1539	I Go Wild (CD, 1-track)	25
95	Virgin VSCDJ 1562	Like A Rolling Stone (Edit)/(Album Version) (CD)	15
96	Virgin VSCDJ 1578	Wild Horses (Edit) (CD, 1-track)	25
97	Virgin VSCDJ 1653	Anybody Seen My Baby? (LP Edit)/(Don Was Radio Remix) (CD)	15
97	Virgin VSCDXJ 1653	Anybody Seen My Baby? (Armand's Rolling Steelo Mix)/(Soul Solution Remix)/ (Bonus Roll) (CD)	15
98	Virgin VSCDJ 1667	Saint Of Me (Radio Edit)/(Album Version) (CD)	15
98	Virgin VSCDJX 1667	Saint Of Me (Deep Dish Grunge Garage Remix Edit) (CD, 1-track)	8
98	Virgin VSTDJ 1667	Saint Of Me (Deep Dish Grunge Garage Remix) (Part 1)/(Part 2) (Grunge Garage Dub)/(Rolling Dub)/Anyone Seen My Baby? (Armand's Rolling Steelo Mix)/Anybody Seen My Baby? (Bonus Roll) (12", double pack, stickered sleeve)	15
98	Virgin VSP 1700	Out Of Control (Bi-Polar At The Controls)/(Bi-Polar Outer Version) (withdrawn brown label or silver label)	50/12
98	Virgin VSTDJ 1700	Out Of Control (In Hand With Fluke)/(In Hand Full Version)/ (Bi-Polar's Fat Controller Mix)/(Bi-Polar At The Controls) (12")	15
98	Virgin VSTDDJ 1700	Out Of Control (In Hand With Fluke Instrumental)/(In Hand Full Version)/ (Bi-Polar's Fat Controller Mix)/(Bi-Polar At The Controls) (12")	15
98	Virgin VSCDJ 1700	Out Of Control (Album Radio Edit)/(Album Version) (CD)	15
98	Virgin VSCDXJ 1700	Out Of Control (In Hand With Fluke Edit)/(In Hand With Fluke Instrumental)/ (Bi-Polar At The Controls)/(Bi-Polar's Fat Controller Mix) (CD)	18
98	Virgin VSCDF 1700	Out Of Control (Album Radio Edit)/(In Hand With Fluke)/ (In Hand With Fluke Instrumental)/(Bi-Polar At The Controls) (CD)	18
98	Virgin VSCDJ 1700	Out Of Control (Album Radio Edit)/(Saber Master With Fade)/ (In Hand With Fluke Radio Edit) (CD)	20

EPs

64	Decca DFE 8560	THE ROLLING STONES (EP, with unboxed or later boxed Decca logo)	15/8
64	Decca DFE 8590	FIVE BY FIVE (EP, with unboxed or later boxed Decca logo)	15/8
65	Decca DFE 8620	GOT LIVE IF YOU WANT IT! (EP, with unboxed or later boxed Decca logo)	15/8
83	Decca DFEX 8560	THE ROLLING STONES (12" EP, reissue)	10
83	Decca DFEX 8590	FIVE BY FIVE (12" EP, reissue)	10
83	Decca DFEX 8620	GOT LIVE IF YOU WANT IT (12" EP, reissue)	10

EXPORT EPs

64	Decca SDE 7260	ROLLING STONES (EP)	80
64	Decca SDE 7501	THE ROLLING STONES VOLUME 2 (EP)	70
65	Decca SDE 7502	GOT LIVE IF YOU WANT IT! (EP)	65
65	Decca DFE 8620	GOT LIVE IF YOU WANT IT! (EP, red label, some with yellow titles on p/s)	each 80
65	Decca SDE 7503	ROLLING STONES (EP, with "Out Of Our Heads [U.K. version]" sleeve)	80

DECCA LPs

64	Decca LK 4605	ROLLING STONES (LP, 1st pressing, plays 2.52 version of "Tell Me"; Side 2 matrix: XARL 6272-1A)	100
64	Decca LK 4605	ROLLING STONES (LP, 2nd pressing, plays 4.06 version of "Tell Me"; a few sleeves list "Mona", most list "I Need You, Baby" instead)	80/50
65	Decca LK 4661	ROLLING STONES NO. 2 (LP)	50
	(The above LPs were simultaneously pressed with both flipback and non-flipback sleeves. Values are the same.)		
65	Decca LK/SKL 4733	OUT OF OUR HEADS (LP, mono/stereo)	40/50
66	Decca TXL/TXS 101	COULD YOU WALK ON THE WATER (LP, unreleased, proof sleeves exist)	
66	Decca LK/SKL 4786	AFTERMATH (LP, mono/stereo)	40/50
66	Decca TXL/TXS 101	BIG HITS (HIGH TIDE AND GREEN GRASS) (LP, 1st pressing, gatefold sleeve, with stapled 12" x 12" picture booklet, mono/stereo)	30/35
67	Decca TXL/TXS 101	BIG HITS (HIGH TIDE AND GREEN GRASS) (LP, 1st pressing, gatefold sleeve, without booklet, mono/stereo)	20/15
67	Decca LK/SKL 4852	BETWEEN THE BUTTONS (LP, mono/stereo)	40/50
67	Decca TXL/TXS 103	THEIR SATANIC MAJESTIES REQUEST (LP, promo padded silk sleeve)	1,000+
67	Decca TXL/TXS 103	THEIR SATANIC MAJESTIES REQUEST (LP, 3-D gatefold sleeve with red inner, mono/stereo)	50/80
68	Decca LK/SKL 4955	BEGGARS BANQUET (LP, gatefold sleeve, with Stones Decca label insert, mono/stereo)	50/40
68	Decca LK/SKL 4955	BEGGARS BANQUET (LP, gatefold sleeve, no insert, mono/stereo)	40/30
69	Decca LK/SKL 5019	THROUGH THE PAST, DARKLY (BIG HITS VOL. 2) (LP, octagonal gatefold sleeve, mono/stereo)	40/25
69	Decca LK 5025	LET IT BLEED (LP, mono, red inner, w/poster, some with stickered sleeve)	60/50
		LET IT BLEED (LP, mono, red inner, without poster or sticker)	35
69	Decca SKL 5025	LET IT BLEED (LP, stereo, blue inner, w/poster, some w/ stickered sleeve)	35/30
		LET IT BLEED (LP, stereo, blue inner, without poster or sticker)	20

| 69 | Decca TXL/TXS 103 | THEIR SATANIC MAJESTIES REQUEST (LP, 2nd pressing, gatefold sleeve with red inner, mono/stereo, stereo disc in stickered mono sleeve) ...... each 50 |

(The above LPs were originally pressed with Decca labels with a large-print logo without a box surrounding it; later pressings with smaller print & boxed logo are worth between half the value for earlier LPs to two-thirds the value for later LPs and three-quarters for "Let It Bleed".)

69	Decca RSM. 1	PROMOTIONAL ALBUM (LP, U.K. disc in U.S. sleeve [lists RSD-1], 200 copies pressed [100 each for U.K. & U.S.], promo only) 800
70	Decca SKL 5065	GET YER YA-YA'S OUT! (LP) 15
71	Decca SKL 5084	STONE AGE (LP) 12
71	Decca SKL 5101	GIMME SHELTER (LP) 10
72	Decca SKL 5098	MILESTONES (LP) 12
72	Decca SKL 5149	ROCK 'N' ROLLING STONES (LP) 12
73	Decca SKL 5165	GOLDEN B-SIDES (LP, unreleased, test pressings only) 600
73	Decca SKL 5173	NO STONE UNTURNED (LP) 12

(Except where noted, the above Decca LPs were originally issued with dark blue labels & laminated sleeves; later copies are worth two-thirds the value.)

75	Decca SKL 5212	METAMORPHOSIS (LP, dark blue label, matt sleeve) 12
70s	Decca TXS 101	BIG HITS (HIGH TIDE AND GREEN GRASS) (LP, 2nd pressing, gatefold sleeve, later issue with foldout insert & later Decca logo, stereo only) 12
70s	Decca TXS 103	THEIR SATANIC MAJESTIES REQUEST (LP, 3rd pressing, gatefold sleeve, stereo only) 15
70s	Decca SKL 4733	OUT OF OUR HEADS (LP, 2nd pressing, light green sleeve, box Decca logo) ... 30
75	Decca (no cat. no.)	THE HISTORY OF THE ROLLING STONES (3-LP box set; 3x12" pink label test pressings exist, no sleeves, matrices read: ZAL 12996/7, ZAL 12998/9 & ZAL 13000/1; release cancelled in favour of "Rolled Gold" 2-LP) 800
75	Decca ROST 3/4	LIVE STONES (2-LP, compilation, pink label test pressings only, follow-up to "Rolled Gold", unreleased) 500
83	Decca ROLL 1	THE FIRST EIGHT STUDIO ALBUMS (8-LP set, with 192-page book; wraparound card box, each LP has star printed on rear sleeve) 225
80s	Decca TXS 103	THEIR SATANIC MAJESTIES REQUEST (LP, 3-D gatefold sleeve, boxed logo) ... 15

EXPORT LPs

65	Decca LK/SKL 4725	OUT OF OUR HEADS (LP, with U.S. track listing & cover design, laminated flipback sleeve & unboxed Decca label logo, mono/stereo, withdrawn) 80/100
66	Decca LK/SKL 4838	HAVE YOU SEEN YOUR MOTHER, LIVE (LP, laminated sleeve & unboxed Decca label logo, mono/stereo) 100/120
70	Decca SKL 4786	AFTERMATH (LP, white label, black print, supposedly for export) 15
70	Decca TXS 103	THEIR SATANIC MAJESTIES REQUEST (LP, gatefold sleeve, white label, black print, supposedly for export) 15
70	Decca SKL 5065	GET YER YA-YA'S OUT! (LP, white label, black print, supposedly for export) 15
70s	Decca LK/SKL 4838	HAVE YOU SEEN YOUR MOTHER, LIVE (LP, later pressing, boxed logo, laminated sleeve) 70
67	Decca LK/SKL 4888	FLOWERS (LP, laminated sleeve, unboxed Decca label logo) 125
70s	Decca LK/SKL 4888	FLOWERS (LP, later pressing, laminated sleeve, boxed Decca label logo) 70

ROLLING STONES LABEL LPs

71	Rolling Stones COC 59100	STICKY FINGERS (LP, zip sleeve with insert) 12
72	Rolling Stones COC 69100	EXILE ON MAIN STREET (2-LP, with inners, some with postcard inserts) 30/15
77	Rolling Stones COC 89101	LOVE YOU LIVE (2-LP, gatefold sleeve & inner bags) 15
78	Rolling Stones CUN 39108	SOME GIRLS (LP, with uncensored inner sleeve) 12
82	R. Stones CUNP 39115	STILL LIFE (AMERICAN CONCERT 1981) (LP, picture disc, a few mispressed with wrong tracks) 125/12

OTHER ALBUMS

83	R. Digest GROLA 119	THE GREAT YEARS (4-LP, box set) 25
89	Abkco 820900-1	ROLLING STONES SINGLES COLLECTION/LONDON YEARS (4-LP set) 40
89	CBS 466 918 2	COLLECTION 1971-1989 (15-CD box set, w/ bonus CD, 'Collector's Edition') ... 120
89	CBS SAMPC 1347	SAY AHHH! (LP, promo only compilation) 150
89	CBS (no catalogue no.)	STEEL WHEELS - THE ALBUM OF THE TOUR (box set, with LP, CD, cassette and "Terrifying" 12", European tour dates & sticker, promo only) 125
91	Sony 468 135-9/468 135-2	FLASHPOINT/INTERVIEW 1990 (2-CD pack, shrinkwrapped with tongue logo sticker, numbered) 35
94	Virgin V 2750	VOODOO LOUNGE (2-LP) 15
95	Virgin V 2801	STRIPPED (2-LP) 15
95	Virgin IVDG 2801	STRIPPED (2-CD, interview disc & album, fold-out digipak, promo only) 50
97	Virgin V 2840	BRIDGES TO BABYLON (2-LP, with inner sleeves) 15
97	Virgin CDVDJ 2840	BRIDGES TO BABYLON (CD, with spoken word intros, 200 only, promo only) ... 60
97	Virgin IVDG 2840	BRIDGES TO BABYLON INTERVIEW (2-CD, interview disc & album, fold-out digipak, promo only) 50
97	Virgin (no catalogue no.)	BRIDGES TO BABYLON (CD in promo press box, with "Anybody Seen My Baby?" promo CD, press release, bottle opener, notebook and sheet of stamps, 200 only, promo only) 150
99	Virgin CDVDJ 2880	NO SECURITY ALBUM SAMPLER (CD, card p/s, promo only) 20
99	Virgin CDIDJ 2880	NO SECURITY (3-CD [2 interview discs], foldout digipak, promo only) 60

(see also Mick Jagger, Keith Richards, Pipes Of Pan, Bill Wyman, Charlie Watts, Mick Taylor, Andrew Oldham, Bobbie Miller)

AUDLEY ROLLINS

72	Explosion EX 2062	Repatriation/HUGH ROY JUNIOR: Repatriation – Version 6
73	Attack ATT 8060	Without You In My World/It's Flowing (actually "It's Growing") 5
73	Harry J HJ 6654	What's Your Name/NOW GENERATION: What's Your Name – Version 5

BIRD ROLLINS

| 72 | Mojo 2092 049 | Love Man From Carolina/She Needs Loving All The Time .... 5 |

HENRY ROLLINS

91	Vinyl Solution VS 30	Let There Be Rock/Carry Me Down (12", p/s, as Henry Rollins & Hard-Ons) 15
91	Vinyl Solution VS 30CD	Let There Be Rock/Carry Me Down (CD, as Henry Rollins & Hard-Ons) 15
92	Imago 72787250187	Tearin' (poster p/s) 5
94	Imago 7432323057	Liar (poster p/s) 8
92	Quarter Stick QS 13CD	DEEP THROAT (4-CD box set, spoken-word) 45

SONNY ROLLINS

56	Esquire EP 94	SONNY ROLLINS AND THE MODERN JAZZ QUARTET (EP)	10
57	Esquire EP 148	SONNY ROLLINS WITH THELONIUS MONK (EP)	10
58	Esquire EP 198	WAILING MISTER ROLLINS (EP)	20
60	Esquire EP 228	VALSE HOT (EP, as Sonny Rollins Plus Four)	10
61	Esquire EP 238	ROLLINS AND BROWNIE (EP, with Clifford Brown)	8
62	Esquire EP 248	SAINT THOMAS (EP)	10
56	Esquire 20-050	SONNY ROLLINS QUARTET (10" LP)	30
57	Esquire 20-080	SONNY ROLLINS QUINTET (10" LP)	22
57	Esquire 32-025	SONNY ROLLINS PLUS FOUR (LP)	30
57	Esquire 32-035	PERSPECTIVES (LP, with Modern Jazz Quartet)	35
58	Esquire 32-038	SONNY ROLLINS QUARTET (LP)	40
58	Esquire 32-045	SAXOPHONE COLOSSUS (LP, as Sonny Rollins Four)	70
58	Contemporary LAC 12118	WAY OUT WEST (LP)	35
58	Esquire 32-058	TENOR MADNESS (LP)	40
59	Esquire 32-075	SONNY ROLLINS QUINTET (LP)	25
59	Esquire 32-085	TOUR-DE-FORCE (LP)	18
59	MGM MGM-C 776	SONNY ROLLINS AND THE BIG BRASS (LP)	15
60	Contemporary SCA 5013	SONNY ROLLINS AND THE CONTEMPORARY LEADERS (LP, stereo only)	20
61	Riverside RLP 12-241	THE SOUND OF SONNY (LP)	15
61	Blue Note BLP 1558	SONNY ROLLINS VOL. 2 (LP)	20
62	Riverside RLP 12-258	FREEDOM SUITE (LP)	15
62	Esquire 32-155	MOVIN' OUT (LP)	30
62	RCA RD/SF 7504	THE BRIDGE (LP)	15
63	Esquire 32-175	SONNY BOY (LP)	25
63	RCA RD/SF 7524	WHAT'S NEW (LP)	15
63	RCA RD/SF 7546	OUR MAN IN JAZZ (LP)	15
64	RCA RD/SF 7593	SONNY MEETS HAWK (LP, with Coleman Hawkins)	15
64	Blue Note (B)BLP 4001	NEWK'S TIME (LP)	20
64	RCA RD/SF 7626	SONNY ROLLINS & CO. (LP)	15
64	Blue Note (B)BLP 1581	A NIGHT AT THE VILLAGE VANGUARD (LP)	20
65	RCA RD 7670	NOW'S THE TIME (LP)	15
65	Blue Note (B)BLP 1542	THE SONNY ROLLINS QUARTET (LP)	20
65	Fontana FJL 124	BLOW! (LP)	25
66	HMV CLP 1915	ROLLINS ON IMPULSE (LP)	15
66	Stateside SL 10164	SAXOPHONE COLOSSUS (LP, reissue)	12
67	RCA RD/SF 7736	STANDARD SONNY ROLLINS (LP)	15
67	HMV CLP/CSD 3529	SONNY PLAYS ALFIE (LP)	20
67	HMV CLP/CSD 3610	EAST BROADWAY RUNDOWN (LP)	15
72	Prestige PR 24004	SONNY ROLLINS (2-LP)	15

(see also Modern Jazz Quartet, Thelonious Monk, Clifford Brown, Coleman Hawkins)

ROLL MOVEMENT

67	Go AJ 11410	I'm Out On My Own/Just One Thing	12

ROLL-UPS

80	Bridgehouse BHS 6	Blackmail/Hold On (p/s)	4
79	Bridgehouse BHLP 004	LOW DIVES FOR HIGHBALLS (LP)	15

DICK ROMAN

59	MGM MGM 1004	Party Girl/My Greatest Mistake	6
59	MGM MGM 1004	Party Girl/My Greatest Mistake (78)	8
65	London HLU 10007	The Truth Hurts/What Good Does It Do Me	6
66	Coral Q 72485	Green Years/Ivy	5
63	Stateside SL 10023	TOUCH OF LOVE (LP)	12

LYN ROMAN

74	Brunswick BR 11	Stop, I Don't Need No Sympathy/Where Do You Go	4

MARK ROMAN

68	Columbia DB 8360	Gonna Get Along Without Ya Now/Cuddly Toy	4

MIMI ROMAN

61	Warner Bros WB 55	Johnny Will/Let It Be Me	5

MURRAY ROMAN

69	Track 613 007	YOU CAN'T BEAT PEOPLE UP AND HAVE THEM SAY I LOVE YOU (LP)	18
69	Track 613 015	A BLIND MAN'S MOVIE (LP)	15
70	Track 2407 013	YOU CAN'T BEAT PEOPLE UP AND HAVE THEM SAY I LOVE YOU (LP, 'Backtrack' reissue)	10

SANDY ROMAN

66	Columbia DB 7931	Dale Anne/Home Is Where The Heart Is	6

TONY ROMAN

67	Stateside SS 2022	Shadows On A Foggy Day/Maggie	4

MAX ROMEO

68	Island WI 3104	Put Me In The Mood/My One Girl	12
68	Island WI 3111	Walk Into The Room/DAWN PENN: I'll Get You	15
68	Island WI 3124	Twelfth Of Never (actually by Pat Kelly)/VAL BENNETT: Caledonia	15
68	Unity UN 503	Wet Dream/She's But A Little Girl	6
69	Blue Cat BS 161	We Wान Man/AL REID: Vietcong	10
69	Blue Cat BS 163	It's Not The Way/AL REID: Darling	10
69	Nu Beat NB 022	Blowing In The Wind/LARRY MARSHALL: Money Girl	10
69	Trojan TR 656	Sweet Chariot/Far Far Away (with Hippy Boys)	8
69	Unity UN 507	Belly Woman (actually by Derrick Morgan)/PAULETT & LOVERS: Please Stay	7
69	Unity UN 511	Twelfth Of Never (actually by Pat Kelly)/TARTONS: Solid As A Rock (actually by Tartans)	7
69	Unity UN 516	Wine Her Goosie/KING CANNON: Fire Ball	7
69	Unity UN 532	Mini-Skirt Vision/Far Far Away	6

70	Unity UN 545	Clap Clap (with Hippy Boys)/Death Rides A Horse	7
70	Unity UN 547	What A Cute Man/Buy You A Rainbow	12
70	Unity UN 560	Fish In The Pot/Feel It	7
71	Bullet BU 478	Mother Oh Mother/Dreams Of Passion (actually "Judgement Rock" by Charlie Ace)	6
71	Pama Supreme PS 328	Ginal Ship/UPSETTERS: Version 2	6
71	Pama Supreme PS 306	Let The Power Fall On I/The Raid	6
71	Pama Supreme PS 318	Don't You Weep/Weeping (Version)	6
71	Punch PH 73	Chie Chie Bud/Version	6
71	Unity UN 571	Macabee (Version)/SOUL SYNDICATE: Music Book	6
71	Camel CA 82	The Coming Of Jah/Watch And Pray	6
72	Camel CA 85	Rasta Bandwagon/When Jah Speaks	6
72	Camel CA 86	Public Enemy Number One/How Long Must We Wait	6
72	Big BG 334	Are You Sure/RUPIE EDWARDS ALL STARS: Are You Sure – Version	6
72	Dynamic DYN 444	We Love America/SOUL RHYTHM: We Love Jamaica Version	5
72	G.G. GG 4535	Is It Really Over?/MAYTONES: Born To Be Loved	6
72	High Note Hs 058	Pray For Me (with Gaytones)/GAYTONES: Pray For Me — Version	5
72	Pama PM 836	Wet Dream/("Bang Bang Lulu" by Lloyd Tyrell)/("Birth Control" by Lloyd Tyrell)/ "Sex Education" by Classics) (Maxi-Single)	5
72	Pama Supreme PS 345	Pray For Me/Version	5
72	Pama Supreme PS 359	Are You Sure/CARL MASTERS: Va-Va-Voom	6
72	Prince Buster PB 11	River Jordan/Words Sound And Power	6
73	Dragon DRA 1028	No Joshua No/JOSHUA'S ALL STARS: No Joshua No (Version)	5
73	Magnet MA 032	Murder In The Place/Version	5
73	Magnet MA 032	I Woke Up In Love/Version	5
73	Pama PM 875	Pussy Watchman/You Are My Sunshine	5
73	Pama Supreme PS 383	Hide Away/SOUL SYNDICATE: Sweet And Gentle	5
73	Pama Supreme PS 385	Everyman Aught To Know/Version	5
73	Unity UN 572	Rent Crisis/Version	5
74	Ackee ACK 529	Sixpence/Eating Competition	5
69	Pama PMLP 11	A DREAM (LP)	25
71	Pama PMP 2010	LET THE POWER FALL (LP)	25

(see also Max & Elaine, Maxie & Glen, Al Read, Henry & Lisa, Dennis Alcapone, George Meggie, David Isaacs)

ROMEO & EMOTIONS
67	Caltone TONE 106	Don't Want To Let You Go/I Can't Do No More	12

CHAN ROMERO
59	Columbia DB 4341	The Hippy Hippy Shake/If I Had A Way	60
60	Columbia DB 4405	My Little Ruby/I Don't Care Now	100

RONALD & LLOYD
74	Magnet MG 042	Back In My Arms/HEPTONES: Drifting Away	8

RONALD & RUBY
58	RCA RCA 1053	Lollipop/Fickle Baby	25
58	RCA RCA 1053	Lollipop/Fickle Baby (78)	20

RONNIE RONALDE
53	Columbia SCM 5006	Song Of The Mountains/If I Were A Blackbird	12
53	Columbia SCM 5007	In A Monastery Garden/Bells Across The Meadow	12
56	Columbia SCM 5214	Ballad Of Davy Crockett/Hair Of Gold	12
56	Columbia SCM 5241	Robin Hood/Happy Trails	12
56	Columbia SCM 5262	The Yarmouth Song/Macnamara's Band	7
55	Columbia SEG 7512	RONNIE RONALDE (EP)	8
56	Columbia SEG 7651	YODELLING, WHISTLING AND SINGING (EP)	8
57	Columbia SEG 7678	BEAUTIFUL DREAMER (EP)	8
58	Columbia SEG 7784	T.V. TOP FOUR (EP)	8
58	Columbia SEG 7838	STORY OF CHRISTMAS (EP)	8
59	Columbia SEG 7945	RONNIE (EP)	8
60	Columbia SEG 7990	LITTLE BOY BLEW (EP, also stereo ESG 7797)	8/10
61	Columbia SEG 8087	YODELLING (EP, also stereo ESG 7850)	8/10
63	Golden Guinea GGL 0193	THE INIMITABLE RONNIE RONALDE (LP)	12

RONDELLS
58	London HLU 8716	Good Good/Dreamy (with Ned Jr.)	100
58	London HLU 8716	Good Good/Dreamy (with Ned Jr.) (78)	40

RONDELS
61	London HLU 9404	Back Beat No. 1/Shades Of Green	15

DON RONDO
56	Columbia DB 3854	Two Different Worlds/He Made You Mine	7
57	Columbia DB 3909	The Love I Never Had/Don't	7
57	London HLJ 8466	White Silver Sands/Stars Fell On Alabama	10
58	London HLJ 8567	What A Shame/Made For Each Other	12
58	London HLJ 8567	What A Shame/Made For Each Other (78)	12
58	London HLJ 8610	I've Got Bells On My Heart/School Dance	10
58	London HLJ 8610	I've Got Bells On My Heart/School Dance (78)	15
58	London HLJ 8641	Blonde Bombshell/Her Hair Was Yellow	15
58	London HLJ 8641	Blonde Bombshell/Her Hair Was Yellow (78)	15
58	London HLJ 8695	Dormi, Dormi, Dormi (Sleep, Sleep, Sleep)/In Chi Chi Chihuahua	7
58	London HLJ 8695	Dormi, Dormi, Dormi (Sleep, Sleep, Sleep)/In Chi Chi Chihuahua (78)	12
58	London HLJ 8749	City Lights/I Could Be A Mountain	7
58	London HLJ 8749	City Lights/I Could Be A Mountain (78)	20
59	London HLJ 8808	Song From "The Geisha Boy"/Gretna Green	7
59	London HLJ 8808	Song From "The Geisha Boy"/Gretna Green (78)	20
60	London HLL 9217	The King Of Holiday Island/Wanderlust	6
59	London RE-J 1154	RONDO PT. 1 (EP)	20
59	London RE-J 1155	RONDO PT. 2 (EP)	20

GENE RONDO

68	Giant GN 39	Ben Nevis/Grey Lies	8
68	Jolly JY 004	Mary, Mary/Baby, Baby	7
69	Downtown DT 422	A Lover's Question/HERBIE GRAY & RUDIES: Blue Moon	6
69	Downtown DT 431	Sentimental Reasons/Then You Can Tell Me Goodbye	6
70	Downtown DT 459	Spreading Peace/MUSIC DOCTORS: Guitar Riff	6
72	Downtown DT 490	Wanna Be Like Daddy/STUDIO SOUND: A Little More	5
72	Count Shelly CS 005	Happy Birthday Sweet Sixteen/Meditation	5
73	Magnet MA 001	Prisoner Of Love/How Many Times Girl	6
73	Magnet MA 006	Each Moments/If You Do Want Me	5
73	Magnet MA 028	Oh Sweet Africa/This Is Love	6
73	Magnet MA 035	Valley Of Tears/He'll Break Your Heart	5

(see also Gene Pancho)

RONETTES

63	London HLU 9793	Be My Baby/Tedesco And Pitman	6
64	London HLU 9826	Baby I Love You/Miss Joan And Mr Sam	8
64	London HLU 9905	(The Best Part Of) Breakin' Up/Big Red	12
64	London HLU 9922	Do I Love You?/When I Saw You	10
64	London HLU 9931	(Walking) In The Rain/How Does It Feel?	10
65	London HLU 9952	Born To Be Together/Blues For Baby	15
65	London HLU 9976	Is This What I Get For Loving You?/You Baby	15
66	London HLU 10087	I Can Hear Music/When I Saw You (withdrawn)	50
69	London HLU 10240	Be My Baby/Baby I Love You	5
69	A&M AMS 748	You Came, You Saw, You Conquered/I Can Hear Music	7
75	Phil Spector Intl. 2010 009	I'm A Woman In Love/When I Saw You	6
77	Phil Spector Intl. 2010 017	I Wonder/Walking In The Rain	6
64	London HA-U 8212	PRESENTING THE FABULOUS RONETTES FEATURING VERONICA (LP, originally on plum label, later on black label)	100/50
65	Colpix PXL 486	THE RONETTES (LP)	90
75	Phil Spector Intl. 2307 003	SING THEIR GREATEST HITS (LP)	12

(see also Ronnie Spector, Joey Dee & Starlighters)

RONNIE & DEL AIRES

64	Coral Q 72473	Drag/Wigglin' 'N' Wobblin'	18

RONNIE & HI-LITES

62	Pye International 7N 25140	I Wish That We Were Married/Twistin' And Kissin'	18

RONNIE & RAINBOWS

61	London HL 9345	Loose Ends/Sombrero	12

RONNIE & ROBYN

80	Grapevine GRP 137	As Long As You Love Me/Sidra's Theme (unissued)	

RONNIE & ROY

59	Capitol CL 15028	Big Fat Sally/Here I Am	100

RONNO

71	Vertigo 6059 029	Fourth Hour Of My Sleep/Powers Of Darkness	25

(see also Mick Ronson, Rats)

RONNY

64	Decca F 21908	Oh! My Darling Caroline/Lu La Lu	8

RONNY & DAYTONAS

64	Stateside SS 333	G.T.O./Hot Rod Baby	12
64	Stateside SS 367	California Bound/Hey Little Girl	10
65	Stateside SS 391	Bucket T/Little Rail Job	15
65	Stateside SS 432	Beach Boy/No Wheels	15
66	Stateside SS 484	Sandy/Sandy (Instrumental)	12

MICK RONSON

74	RCA APBO 0212	Love Me Tender/Only After Dark	5
74	RCA 11474 XSP	Love Me Tender/Slaughter On 10th Avenue (1-sided red or black interview flexidisc, included in press kits)	10
74	RCA LPBO 5022	Slaughter On 10th Avenue/Leave My Heart Alone	5
75	RCA RCA 2482	Billy Porter/Seven Days	5
74	RCA APL1 0353	SLAUGHTER ON 10TH AVE (LP)	12
75	RCA APL1 0681	PLAY, DON'T WORRY (LP)	12
94	Epic (no cat. no.)	MICK RONSON ALUM (advance cassette for "Heaven And Hull", with extra track "Indian Summer")	15
94	Epic EPC 474742 1	HEAVEN AND HULL (LP, picture disc)	18

(see also Ronno, Rats, David Bowie, Mott The Hoople, Slaughter & The Dogs, Ian Hunter)

LINDA RONSTADT

69	Capitol CL 15590	The Long Way Round/The Dolphins	5
69	Capitol CL 15612	Baby You've Been On My Mind/I'll Be Your Baby Tonight	5
79	Asylum K 13149	Alison/All That You Dream (picture disc)	5
87	MCA MCAP 1172	Somewhere Out There/(Fievel's Version)/(Instrumental) (with James Ingram) (picture disc)	5
69	Capitol E-ST 208	HOME SOWN, HOME GROWN (LP)	12
70	Capitol E-ST 407	SILK PURSE (LP)	12
72	Capitol EA-ST 635	LINDA RONSTADT (LP)	12
73	Asylum SYL 9012	DON'T CRY NOW (LP)	12
73	Capitol E-ST 11358	HEART LIKE A WHILE (LP)	12
73	Asylum SYL 8761	PRISONER IN DISGUISE (LP)	12
78	Asylum K 53085	LIVING IN THE USA (LP, red vinyl)	12

(see also Stone Poneys)

ROOFTOP SINGERS
63	Fontana 271 700 TF	Walk Right In/Cool Water 6
63	Fontana 271 702 TF	Tom Cat/Hey Boys 5
63	Fontana TF 411	Mama Don't Allow/It Don't Mean A Thing 5
63	Fontana 680 999 TL	WALK RIGHT IN (LP) 15
66	Fontana TFL 6065	RAINY RIVER (LP) 12

(see also Tarriers)

ROOGALATOR
77	Do It RIDE 1	PLAY IT BY EAR (LP) 10

(see also Disco Brothers)

ROOM
70	Deram SML 1073	PRE-FLIGHT (LP) 220

ROOM
80	Box BOX 001	Motion/Waiting Room (p/s) 6
80	Box BOX 002	Bitter Reaction (cassette) 8
81	Box BOX 003	In Sickness And Health/Bated Breath (p/s) 5

ROOM 10
65	Decca F 12249	I Love My Love/Going Back 4

ROOM 13
82	Woronzow W 002	Murder Mystery/Need Some Dub (12", p/s) 30

(see also Bevis Frond)

ROOM 101
84	Norwood NRW ERL S102	Tokyo Nights/I'm Not Your Kind (p/s) 4

MICKEY ROONEY
57	RCA RD 27038	MICKEY ROONEY SINGS GEORGE M. COHAN (LP) 18

(see also Judy Garland)

MARY ROOS
72	CBS 7959	Wake Me Early In The Morning/When You're Singing (Don't Forget) 6

ROOSEVELT SINGERS
73	Sioux SI 025	Heavy Reggae/HONG GANG: Smoking Wild 5

ROOT BOYS
70	C'mbia Blue Beat DB 115	Please Don't Stop The Wedding/Your Love, Your Love 8

HARRY ROPE
88	Regal Zonophone HR 1	Laughing Inside/Laughing Inside (p/s, promo only; actually by Roy Harper) 7

(see also Roy Harper)

RO RO
70	Parlophone R 5920	Here I Go Again/What You Gonna Do 10
72	Regal Zonophone RZ 3056	Goin' Round My Head/Down On The Road 10
73	Regal Zonophone RZ 3076	Blackbird/Feel It Coming 10
72	Regal Zono. SRZA 8510	MEET AT THE WATER (LP) 150

(see also Ross)

EDMUNDO ROS (& HIS ORCHESTRA)
53	Decca F 10214	Blowin' Wind/Istanbul (B-side as Edmundo Ros & Johnston Brothers) 7
54	Decca F 10263	Somebody Bad Stole De Wedding Bell/Chili Sauce 7
55	Decca F 10480	Cherry Pink And Apple Blossom White/Ole Mambo 7
55	Decca F 10669	Sixteen Tons/Robin Hood 7
56	Decca F 10716	Mister Cuckoo/Don't Ringa Da Bell 5
57	Decca F 10834	I Saw Esau/Jamaica Farewell (Kingston Town) 5

(see also Johnston Brothers, Annette Klooger, Annie Ross)

ROSITA ROSANO
54	Melodisc M 1308	Down In The Indies/Admiral's Daughters (78) 10
55	Melodisc M 1320	Pull Down The Shade, Marie/Cutest Little Dinghy (78) 8
57	Melodisc M 1436	Queer Things/Little Boy 8
57	Melodisc M 1436	Queer Things/Little Boy (78) 12

ANDY ROSE
58	London HLU 8761	Lov-A Lov-A Love/Just Young 20
58	London HLU 8761	Lov-A Lov-A Love/Just Young (78) 6

DAVID ROSE ORCHESTRA
53	MGM SP 1009	Harlem Nocturne (with Woody Herman)/Vanessa 5
56	MGM SP 1181	Forbidden Planet/The Portuguese Washerwomen 5
56	MGM MGM 1158	The Stripper/Ebb Tide 5
65	MGM MGM-C(S) 8002	THE VELVET BEAT (LP) 15

(see also Woody Herman, Rush Adams)

DUSTY ROSE
55	London HLU 8162	The Birds And The Bees/It Makes Me So Mad 40
55	London HLU 8162	The Birds And The Bees/It Makes Me So Mad (78) 20
57	London RE-U 1078	COUNTRY SONGS (EP) 50

JOHNNY ROSE
60	Capitol CL 15166	Linda Lee/The Last One To Know 6

MONICA ROSE
74	Windmill WMD 223	OH YOU BEAUTIFUL DOLL (LP) 10

TIM ROSE
67	CBS 202631	Morning Dew/You're Slipping Away From Me 6
68	CBS 3277	I Got A Loneliness/Long Time Man 20
68	CBS 3478	I Guess It's Over/Hello Sunshine 5
68	CBS 3598	Long-Haired Boy/Looking At A Baby 5

Tim ROSE

69	CBS 4209	Roanoke/Baby You Turn Me On	5
70	CBS 2631	Morning Dew/You're Slipping Away From Me (reissue)	5
70	Capitol CL 15664	I've Gotta Get A Message To You/Ode To An Old Ball	5
67	CBS (S)BPG 63168	TIM ROSE (LP)	20
69	CBS 63636	THROUGH ROSE COLOURED GLASSES (LP)	15
71	Capitol ST 22673	LOVE — A KIND OF HATE STORY (LP)	12
74	Dawn DNLS 3062	TIM ROSE (LP)	15
75	Atlantic K 50183	MUSICIAN (LP, with lyric insert)	12

TONY ROSE
| 70 | Trailer LER 2013 | YOUNG HUNTING (LP) | 12 |
| 72 | Trailer LER 2024 | UNDER THE GREENWOOD TREE (LP) | 12 |

ROSE GARDEN
| 68 | Atlantic 584 163 | Next Plane To London/Flower Town | 7 |

ROSEHIPS
87	Subway Organisation SUBWAY 10	Room In Your Heart/Thrilled To Bits/Dead End (foldaround p/s with insert in poly bag)	5
87	Subway Organisation SUBWAY 10T	Room In Your Heart/Middle Of Next Week/Thrilled To Bits/So Naive/ Just Another Girl/Dead End (12", p/s)	8
87	Subway Organisation SUBWAY 16	I Shouldn't Have To Say/Loophole/Wastin' My Time/All Mine/ Sad As Sunday (p/s, with insert)	4
87	Subway Organisation SUBWAY 16T	I Shouldn't Have To Say/Loophole/Wastin' My Time/All Mine/ Sad As Sunday (12", p/s with insert)	7
88	Sweet William BILLY 001	Ask Johnny Dee/FAT TULIPS: You Opened My Eyes (33rpm flexidisc, p/s)	4

JIMMY ROSELLI
| 62 | Pye International 7N 25134 | The Sheik Of Araby/A Fool In Love | 6 |
| 62 | Pye International 7N 25156 | I'm Gonna Sit Right Down And Write You A Letter/I Love You | 6 |

LEONARD ROSENMAN ORCHESTRA
| 57 | London HA-P 2040 | A TRIBUTE TO JAMES DEAN (LP) | 18 |

ROSE OF VICTORY
| 83 | No Future OI 24 | Suffragette City/Overdrive (p/s) | 7 |
| | (see also Blitz) | | |

ROSE TATTOO
78	Carrere CAL 125	Bad Boy For Love/Tramp (p/s)	6
78	Carrere CAL 125	Bad Boy For Love/Tramp (12", p/s)	8
78	Epic EPC 9411	Rock 'N' Roll Outlaw/One Of The Boys (p/s)	5
80	Repeal PRS 2724	Release Legalise/COL PATERSON: Bong On Aussie (500 only)	50
81	Mirage PR 405	Rock 'N' Roll Is King/Sidewalk Sally (12", promo only)	10
81	Carrere CAR 200P	Rock 'N' Roll Outlaw/Remedy (picture disc)	5
81	Carrere CAR 220	Assault And Battery/Astra Wally//One Of The Boys/Manzil Madness (double pack, gatefold p/s)	5
83	Carrere CARP 263	It's Gonna Work Itself Out/Fightin' Sons (picture disc)	5
82	Albert Productions AP 854	We Can't Be Beaten/Fightin' Sons (no p/s)	5
82	Albert Productions AP 898	Branded/Dead Set (no p/s)	5
82	Albert Productions AP 1007	It's Gonna Work Itself Out/Sydney Girls	8
84	Albert Productions AP 1299	I Wish/Wild One (no p/s)	6
82	Albert Productions AP 1384	Freedom's Flame/Never Too Loud (p/s)	6
84	Albert Productions AP 1444	No Secrets/Let Us Live (no p/s)	4
85	Mushroom K 9837	Born To Be Wild/Suns Gonna Shine (p/s)	7
85	Mushroom K 9837	Born To Be Wild/Suns Gonna Shine (12", promo only)	12
86	Mushroom K 66	Calling/Win At Any Cost	4
86	Mushroom K 187	Get It Right/Michael O'Reilly (p/s)	6
87	Mushroom K 248	Falling/Winnie Mandela (p/s)	5
88	CBS 651 556	You're Not Alone/You're Not Alone (Instrumental) (as Angry Anderson of Rose Tattoo, p/s)	4

ROSIE (& ORIGINALS)
| 61 | London HLU 9266 | Angel Baby/Give Me Love (as Rosie & Originals) | 30 |
| 61 | Coral Q 72426 | Lonely Blue Nights/We'll Have A Chance | 18 |

ROSIEBUNS
| 69 | Plum P2 | A Posteriori/Gluteus Maximus | 35 |
| 71 | Spank 60 W | ROLL THOSE BUNS (LP, gatefold with deep centre crease) | 60 |

ROSKO
70	Trojan TR 7758	Al Capone/Kaiser Bill	6
70	Philips 6009 070	Grab The Rabbit/Mohammed Ben Ali	5
	(see also Emperor Rosko & Power Pack)		

EMPEROR ROSKO & POWER PACK
69	Polydor 56316	Opposite Lock (Parts 1 & 2)	4
71	B&C CB 148	The Customs Man/Take It In Your Stride	4
	(see also Rosko, Power Pack, Pleasure Garden)		

FRANK ROSOLINO SEXTET
| 54 | Capitol KC 65001 | That Old Black Magic/Yo Yo | 7 |

ROSS
74	RSO 2090 125	Alright By Me/Carolina	4
74	RSO 2394 127	ROSS (LP)	12
75	RSO 2394 144	THE PIT AND THE PENDULUM (LP)	12
	(see also Alan Ross, Indian Summer, Gary Pickford-Hopkins, Ro Ro)		

ALAN ROSS
77	Ebony EBY 1000	ARE YOU FREE ON A SATURDAY (LP, with insert)	10
78	Ebony EBY 1003	RESTLESS NIGHTS (LP)	10
	(see also Ross)		

ANNIE ROSS

54	Esquire 10-334	Annie's Lament/Twisted (78, with Teacho Wiltshire, Art Blakey)	8
54	Esquire 10-344	Jackie/The Song Is You (78, with Quincy Jones)	10
55	Decca F 10514	Mama (He Treats Your Daughter Mean)/The Fish	12
55	Decca F 10637	I Want You To Be My Baby (with Tony Crombie)/TONY CROMBIE & HIS ORCHESTRA: Three Little Words	10
55	Decca F 10637	I Want You To Be My Baby (with Tony Crombie)/TONY CROMBIE & HIS ORCHESTRA: Three Little Words (78)	8
56	Decca F 10680	Cry Me A River/Only You	8
72	Columbia DB 8912	Straight On Till Morning/God Bless The Child	10
57	Pye Jazz NJE 1035	NOCTURNE FOR VOCALIST (EP)	8
50s	Esquire EP 1	WITH THE TEACHO WILTSHIRE GROUP (EP)	30
50s	Pieces Of Eight PEP 604	WITH THE TONY CROMBIE FOURTET (EP)	12
64	Transatlantic TRAEP 112	GO TO THE WALL (EP)	8
57	Nixa Jazz NJT 504	ANNIE BY CANDLELIGHT (10" LP)	225
59	Vogue LAE 12203	ANNIE ROSS (LP, with Gerry Mulligan Quintet)	30
60	Vogue LAE 12233	A GASSER (LP, with Zoot Sims)	30
63	Ember NR 5008	A HANDFULL OF SONGS (LP)	80
63	Transatlantic TRA 107	LOGUERRHTHMS (LP)	25
65	Pye GGL0316	ANNIE BY CANDLELIGHT (LP)	100
66	Xtra XTRA 1049	ANNIE ROSS WITH THE TONY KINSEY QUINTET (LP)	60

(see also Tony Crombie, Dave Lambert, Gerry Mulligan, Zoot Sims, Jack Parnell, Teacho Wiltshire, Art Blakey, Quincy Jones)

DAVID ROSS

57	Embassy WB 252	Last Train To San Fernando/Diana (78)	8
57	Embassy WB 261	Wake Up Little Susie/Be My Girl (78)	8
58	Oriole CB 1416	Pit-A-Patter Boom Boom/Everybody's Got A Girl But Tino (as Dave Ross)	10
58	Oriole CB 1416	Pit-A-Patter Boom Boom/Everybody's Got A Girl But Tino (78, as Dave Ross)	8

DIANA ROSS

70	Tamla Motown TMG 743	Reach Out And Touch (Somebody's Hand)/Dark Side Of The World	5
70	Tamla Motown TMG 751	Ain't No Mountain High Enough/Can't It Wait Until Tomorrow	5
71	Tamla Motown TMG 768	Remember Me/How About You	5
71	Tamla Motown TMG 781	I'm Still Waiting/Reach Out I'll Be There	5
71	Tamla Motown TMG 792	Surrender/I'm A Winner (mono)	5
79	Motown TMG 1136	Pops, We Love You/Pops, We Love You (Instrumental) (p/s, with Smokey Robinson, Marvin Gaye & Stevie Wonder)	5
79	Motown 12TMG 1136	Pops, We Love You/Pops, We Love You (Instrumental) (12", p/s, with Smokey Robinson, Marvin Gaye & Stevie Wonder)	7
81	Tamla Motown TMG 1248	Tenderness/Supremes Medley (picture disc)	5
82	Capitol CLP 247	Work That Body/Two Can Make It (picture disc)	5
83	Motown CTME 2021	DIANA ROSS (cassette EP)	5
84	Capitol CLP 337	Touch By Touch/Fight For It (picture disc)	5
85	Motown TMGT 1380	Love Hangover/Remember Me (12")	12
73	Tamla Motown TMSP 1131	LADY SINGS THE BLUES (2-LP, soundtrack, brown inner sleeves)	15

DIANA ROSS & MICHAEL JACKSON

78	MCA MCA 396	Ease On Down The Road/QUINCY JONES: Poppy Girls (p/s)	8
78	MCA MCAT 12-396	Ease On Down The Road (U.S. Version)/THE WIZ: Poppy Girls (12", p/s)	15
78	MCA MCA 898	Ease On Down The Road/QUINCY JONES: Poppy Girls (p/s, reissue)	6
78	MCA MCAT 12-898	Ease On Down The Road (Extended Version)/THE WIZ: Poppy Girls (12", reissue, p/s)	12

(see also [Diana Ross &] Supremes, Michael Jackson, Quincy Jones)

DOCTOR (Isaiah) ROSS

66	Blue Horizon LP 1	THE FLYING EAGLE (LP, 99 copies only)	800
66	Xtra XTRA 1038	DOCTOR ROSS (LP, reissue of "The Flying Eagle")	40
70s	Bounty BY 6020	CALL THE DOCTOR (LP)	25
72	Polydor 2460 169	LIVE AT MONTREUX (LP)	20
75	Big Bear BEAR 2	THE HARMONICA BOSS (LP)	15

ERROL ROSS

80	Carrere CAR 149	Round And Round In Circles/Reggae Music Of Today (p/s)	6

GENE ROSS

58	Parlophone R 4434	Endless Sleep/The Only One	20
58	Parlophone R 4434	Endless Sleep/The Only One (78)	15

JACK ROSS

62	London HLD 9534	Cinderella/Margarita	4
62	London HLD 9485	Happy Jose/Sweet Georgia Brown	4

JACKIE ROSS

64	Pye International 7N 25259	Selfish One/Everything But Love	35
64	Chess CRS 8003	Jerk And Twine/New Lover	18

JOAN ROSS

70	Crab CRAB 61	Band Of Gold/HAMMERS: Midnight Sunshine	6

RICKY ROSS

83	Sticky Music GUM 8	SO LONG AGO (cassette only, existence unconfirmed)	
93	Sticky Music GUM 8CD	SO LONG AGO (CD, reissue)	30

(see also Deacon Blue)

RONNIE ROSS

58	Parlophone PMC 1079	DOUBLE EVENT (LP)	30
61	Ember EMB 3323	STOMPIN' (LP)	50
60s	Ember FA 2023	THE SWINGIN' SOUNDS OF THE JAZZ MAKERS (LP, with Allan Ganley)	30
69	Fontana SFJL 915	CLEOPATRA'S NEEDLE (LP)	80

(see also Bill Le Sage)

MINT VALUE £

SONNY ROSS
71 Mojo 2093 001 — Alakazam/The Piper Must Be Paid 4

SPENCER ROSS
60 Philips PB 992 — Tracy's Theme/Thanksgiving Day Parade 5
60 London HLX 9141 — Theme Of A Lonely Evening/Bobby's Blues 6

T.T. ROSS
75 Dip DL 5079 — Single Girl/Funny What Love Can Do 4
76 Dip DL 5104 — Last Date/I Am Sorry 4
76 Lucky LY 6000 — No Charge/When I Was A Little Girl 4
76 Lucky LY 6014 — Baby Why/TOUGH GANG: Part 2 4
76 Lucky LY 6017 — Misty Blue/Version 4
76 House Of Eve 001 — Let The World Go Away/Part 2 4
76 House Of Eve 002 — Piece Of My Heart/Part 2 4
77 Lovers Rock CJ 622 — I Will/I Will Dub 4

LEON ROSSELSON
70 Acorn CF 206 — SONGS FOR SCEPTICAL CIRCLES (reissue) 15
71 Trailer LER 3015 — THE WORD IS HUGGA MUGGA CHUGGA HUMBUGGA BOOM CHIT
(LP, with Roy Bailey & Martin Carthy) 12
75 Acorn CF 249 — PALACES OF GOLD (LP) 15
75 Acorn CF 251 — THAT'S NOT THE WAY IT'S GOT TO BE (LP, with Roy Bailey) 12
(see also Three City Four, Roy Bailey)

NITA ROSSI
65 Piccadilly 7N 35258 — Every Little Day Now/Untrue Unfaithful 10
66 Piccadilly 7N 35307 — Here I Go Again/Something To Give 20
66 Piccadilly 7N 35354 — The Daddy Christmas Song/Our Love Was Meant To Be 6
67 Piccadilly 7N 35384 — Misty Blue/Come Around 7

(Francis) ROSSI & (Bernard) FROST
85 Vertigo VER 17/FROS 1 — Modern Romance (I Want To Fall In Love Again)/I Wonder Why (p/s) 6
85 Vertigo VERX 17/FROSX 1 — Modern Romance (I Want To Fall In Love Again) (Extended Remix)/
I Wonder Why (Extended Remix) (12", p/s) 12
85 Vertigo VER 24 — Jealousy/Where Are You Now? (p/s) 5
85 Vertigo VERX 24 — Jealousy/Where Are You Now?/That's Alright (12", p/s) 10
(see also Status Quo, Mitchell/Coe Mysteries)

LEONARD ROSSITER & RIGSBYETTES
80 Chip CHI 101 — Rising Damp/Damp Disco (p/s) 4

NINI ROSSO
65 Durium DRS 54000 — Il Silenzio/Il Clown 4

JOHN HENRY ROSTILL
71 Columbia DB 8794 — Funny Old World/Green Apples 60
(see also Shadows)

STEVE ROSTRON
74 Sweet Folk & Country
SFA 009 — NO STRANGER'S FACE 30

ROTARY CONNECTION
68 Chess CRS 8072 — Soul Man/Ruby Tuesday 6
69 Chess CRS 8103 — The Weight/Respect 6
70 Chess CRS 8106 — Want You To Know/Memory Band 6
68 Chess CRL 4538 — ROTARY CONNECTION (LP) 18
69 Chess CRL(S) 4547 — ALADDIN (LP) 20
69 Chess CRLS 4551 — SONGS (LP) 18

DAVID LEE ROTH
86 Warner Bros W 8656P — Yankee Rose/Shy Boy (pin-up shaped picture disc) 15
88 Warner Bros W 8119TP — Just Like Paradise/The Bottom Line/Yankee Rose (12", picture disc) 7
88 Warner Bros W 8119CD — Just Like Paradise/The Bottom Line/Yankee Rose (3" CD with adaptor) 7
88 Warner Bros W 7753W — Damn Good (Edit)/Stand Up (7" in 12" x 12" card p/s with poster) 6
88 Warner Bros W 7650 — California Girls (LP Version)/Just A Gigolo/I Ain't Got Nobody (Medley)/
Yankee Rose (Spanish Version) (CD) 7
91 Warner Bros W 0016P — Sensible Shoes/California Girls
(5" 'backstage tour pass'-shaped picture disc) 10
85 Warner Bros 925 2221 — CRAZY FROM THE HEAT (mini LP) 10
(see also Van Halen)

ROTHCHILDS
66 Decca F 12411 — You've Made Your Choice/It's Love 8
66 Decca F 12488 — Artificial City/I Let Her Go 10

LINDA ROTHWELL
73 Chapter One SCH 180 — Write Me A Letter/Tell Me 4

ROUGH JUSTICE
80s Rough Justice RJ 001 — MILLION TO ONE (EP, p/s) 100

ROULETTES
62 Pye 7N 15467 — Hully Gully Slip 'N' Slide/La Bamba 12
63 Parlophone R 5072 — Soon You'll Be Leaving Me/Tell Tale Tit 10
64 Parlophone R 5110 — Bad Time/Can You Go 8
64 Parlophone R 5148 — I'll Remember Tonight/You Don't Love Me 8
64 Parlophone R 5218 — Stubborn Kind Of Fellow/Melody 8
65 Parlophone R 5278 — I Hope He Breaks Your Heart/Find Out The Truth 10
65 Parlophone R 5382 — The Long Cigarette/Junk 10
66 Parlophone R 5419 — The Tracks Of My Tears/Jackpot 12
66 Oak RGJ 205 — I Can't Stop (1-sided, some with p/s) 120/60

66	Parlophone R 5461	I Can't Stop/Yesterday, Today And Tomorrow	10
67	Fontana TF 822	Rhyme Boy, Rhyme/Airport People	12
67	Fontana TF 876	Help Me To Help Myself/To A Taxi Driver	12
65	Parlophone PMC 1257	STAKES AND CHIPS (LP)	450

(see also Adam Faith, Unit 4 + 2, Argent)

ROUND ROBIN

64	London HLU 9908	Kick That Little Foot Sally Ann/Slauson Party	35

ROUNDTABLE

69	Jay Boy BOY 18	Saturday Gigue/Scarborough Fair	5
69	Jay Boy JSL 2	SPINNING WHEEL (LP)	22

DEMIS ROUSSOS

72	Philips 6009 230	Life In The City/I Just Don't Know What to Do	5
72	Philips 6009 249	My Reason/When I'm A Kid	5
73	Philips 6009 331	Forever And Ever/Velvet Morning	5
74	Philips 6009 463	Goodbye My Love Goodbye/When I'm A Kid	5
74	Philips 6009 534	My Friend The Wind/Forever And Ever	5
74	Philips 6009 543	With You/When Forever Has Gone	5

(see also Aphrodite's Child, Forminx)

ROUTERS

62	Warner Bros WB 77	Let's Go/Mashy	8
63	Warner Bros WB 91	Make It Snappy/Half Time	7
63	Warner Bros WB 97	Stingray/Snap Happy	10
63	Warner Bros WB 108	Big Band/A Ooga	7
64	Warner Bros WB 139	Stamp And Shake/Ah Ya	7
73	Warner Bros K 16156	Let's Go/Mashy (reissue)	5
63	Warner Bros WM/WS 8126	LET'S GO! WITH THE ROUTERS (LP, features Scott Walker)	35
64	Warner Bros WM/WS 8144	PLAY 1963'S GREAT INSTRUMENTALS (LP)	20
65	Warner Bros WM/WS 8162	CHARGE! (LP)	20

(see also Scott Walker)

JONATHAN ROUTH

57	Nixa NPT 19016	CANDID MIKE (10" LP)	10

ROVERS

55	Capitol CL 14283	Ichi-Bon Tami, Dachi/Why Oh-h (Why Do You Lie To Me?)	120
55	Capitol CL 14283	Ichi-Bon Tami, Dachi/Why Oh-h (Why Do You Lie To Me?) (78)	40

ROVING KIND

65	Decca F 12264	Ain't It True/Don't Tell Me The Time	6
66	Decca F 12381	Lies A Million/How Many Times	6

ROWAN & MARTIN

69	CBS 63490	ROWAN AND MARTIN'S LAUGH-IN (LP)	12
69	Atlantic 588 151	ROWAN AND MARTIN AT WORK (LP)	12

ROWAN BROTHERS

73	CBS 1125	All Together/Lady Of Laughter	4

(see also Earth Opera, Old & In The Way)

ROWDIES

78	Birds Nest BN 109	A.C.A.B. (All Coppers Are Bastards)/Negative Malfunction/Freeze Out	6
79	Teenage Depression TD 1/2	She's No Angel/Had Me A Real Good Time (p/s)	8

(see also Cockney & Westerns, Boys, Lurkers, Steve Sharp & Cleancuts)

NORMIE ROWE

66	Polydor 56132	It's Not Easy/Mary Mary	6
66	Polydor 56144	Ain't Nobody Home/Ooh La La	5
67	Polydor 56159	Going Home/I Don't Care (Just Take Me There) (some in p/s)	8/5

MAJOR ROWELY

65	Stateside SS 438	There's A Riot Going On/Do It The Right Way	10

JEFF ROWENA GROUP

61	Pye 7N 15328	Peanut Vendor/Bullfight	5
61	Pye 7N 15365	Ambush/John Peel	5
62	Pye 7N 15423	La Cucuracha/Ten Ton Caroline	5
63	Oriole CB 1787	Dance Baby Dance/Diddle De Dum (as Jeff Rowena Five)	6
63	Oriole CB 1797	Dance Baby Dance/Love Me Once Again	6
63	Oriole CB 1810	Diddle De Dum/Lovely Water Melon	6
67	CBS 202460	Eleanor/Short Skirts (solo)	5

(see also Big Joe Smith)

CHERRY ROWLAND

63	Fontana TF 420	Nobody But Me/Boys	7
74	Decca F 13491	Here Is Where The Love Is/I Can Give You Back Yourself	8

(see also Cherry Roland)

JACKIE ROWLAND

72	Sioux SI 015	Indian Reservation/JUNIOR SMITH: I'm In A Dancing Mood	5
72	Sioux SI 022	Lonely Man/JOE MANSANO: The Trial Of Pama Dice	5

(see also Joe Higgs)

KEVIN ROWLAND

88	Mercury DEXYB 1412	Walk Away/The Way You Look Tonight/Even When I Hold You/Walk Away (Instrumental) (12", with 6-page gatefold biography)	8
88	Mercury DEXCD 14	Walk Away/Even When I Hold You/The Way You Look Tonight/Because Of You (CD, card sleeve)	7
88	Mercury ROWCD 1	Tonight (Remix)/DEXY'S MIDNIGHT RUNNERS: Celtic Soul Brothers/ DEXY'S MIDNIGHT RUNNERS: Come On Eileen/Kevin Rowland's Band (CD, card sleeve)	7

Kevin ROWLAND

| 88 | Mercury ROWCD 2 | Young Man/A One Way Ticket To Palookaville/DEXY'S MIDNIGHT RUNNERS: Show Me/DEXY'S MIDNIGHT RUNNERS: Jackie Wilson Said (I'm In Heaven When You Smile) (CD, card sleeve) | 7 |

(see also Dexy's Midnight Runners)

STEVE ROWLAND
| 67 | Fontana TF 844 | So Sad/I See Red | 8 |

(see also Family Dogg)

JOHN ROWLES
| 68 | MCA MU 1000 | If I Only Had Time/Now Is The Hour | 5 |
| 69 | MCA MKPS 2001 | THAT LOVIN' FEELING (LP) | 15 |

ROX
82	Teenteeze ROX 100	HOT LOVE IN THE CITY (EP)	25
83	M. For Nations 12 KUT 103	KRAZY KUTZ (12" EP)	7
83	Music For Nations MFN 11	VIOLENT BREED (LP)	10

ROXETTE
89	EMI CDEM 87	The Look (Head Drum Mix)/The Look (7" Version)/Silver Blue (Demo Version)/Sleeping Single (Demo Version) (CD)	20
89	EMI EM 96	Dressed For Success/The Look (white p/s)	5
89	EMI TCEM 96	Dressed For Success/The Look (cassette)	4
89	EMI 12EM 96	Dressed For Success (The Mark McGuire Mix)/The Look (Big Red Mix)/Dressed For Success (7" Version) (12", white p/s)	12
89	EMI CDEM 96	Dressed For Success (7" Version)/The Look (7" Version)/Dressed For Success — The Remix/Dressed For Success — The Voice (CD, white inlay)	20
90	EMI CDEM 108	Listen To Your Heart (Single Mix)/Dressed For Success (New Radio Mix)/(I Could Never) Give You Up/Never Ending Love (live) (CD)	18
90	EMI CDEM 141	It Must Have Been Love/Paint/Cry (live)/Surrender (live) (CD)	18
90	EMI CDEM 149	Listen To Your Heart (Swedish Single Mix)/Listen To Your Heart (U.S. Club Edit Mix)/Listen To Your Heart (Dangerous LP Mix) (CD)	18
91	EMI CDEM 162	Dressed For Success (Single Version)/(New Radio Mix)/The Look (Big Red Mix)/The Voice (CD)	20
91	EMI CDEM 177	Joyride (7" Version)/Come Back (Before You Leave)/Joyride (Magicfriendmix) 12" Version/Joyride (U.S. Remix) (CD)	8
91	EMI CDEM 190	Fading Like A Flower (Every Time You Leave) (Gatica Remix)/The Look/Physical Fascination (Guitar Solo Version)/I Remember You (CD)	10
91	EMI CDEM 204	The Big L (Album Version)/The Big L (The Bigger The Better Mix)/One Is Such A Lonely Number (Demo)/It Must Have Been Love (CD)	10
91	EMI EM 215	Spending My Time/Listen To Your Heart (poster p/s)	6
91	EMI CDEM 215	Spending My Time (Single Version)/(Electric Dance Remix)/The Sweet Hello, The Sad Goodbye/Listen To Your Heart (7" Edit) (CD)	15
92	EMI CDEM 227	Church Of Your Heart/I Call Your Name/Come Back (Before You Leave) (Demo)/Fading Like A Flower (Every Time You Leave) (3.54) (CD)	15
92	EMI CDEMS 227	Church Of Your Heart/I Call Your Name/Soul Deep (Tom Lord-alge Remix)/The Roxette Megamix (CD, digipak)	15
92	EMI CDEM 241	How Do You Do/Fading Like A Flower(live)/Knockin' On Every Door (Bomkrash) (12" Remix)/How Do You Do (Bomkrash 12" Remix) (CD)	10
92	EMI EM 253	It Must Have Been Love/It Must Have Been Love (p/s)	15
92	EMI CDEMS 253	Queen Of Rain (Radio Edit)/Pearls Of Passion/Interview With Roxette (CD)	12
92	EMI CDEM 253	Queen Of Rain/It Must Have Been Love/Paint/Dangerous (CD)	12
93	EMI 12EMPD 268	Almost Unreal/The Heart Shaped Sea/Fingertips '93 (12", picture disc, PVC sleeve with card insert)	7
95	EMI 12EMDJ 406	The Look '95 (Rapino Club Mix)/(Rapino Dub Mix)/(Chaps Donna Bass Mix) (12", promo only)	12
98	EMI CDEMDJ 537	Wish I Could Fly (CD in box with photos and retrospective CD [ROXHITS 001], promo only)	80

ROXY
70	Elektra EKSN 45084	Rock And Roll Circus/Somebody Told You	4
70	Elektra EKSN 45087	Love, Love, Love/Yesterday's Song	4
70	Elektra EKS 74063	ROXY (LP)	10

ROXY MUSIC
72	Island WIP 6144	Virginia Plain/The Numberer (no p/s, initially pink labels, later orange)	each 5
73	Island WIP 6159	Pyjamarama/The Pride And The Pain (no p/s)	5
74	Island WIP 6173	Street Life/Hula Kula (no p/s)	5
74	Island WIP 6208	All I Want Is You/Your Application's Failed (no p/s)	5
75	Island WIP 6248	Love Is The Drug/Sultanesque (no p/s)	5
76	Island WIP 6262	Both Ends Burning/For Your Pleasure (no p/s)	5
76	Island WIP 6306	Do The Strand/Warbrides (unissued)	
77	Polydor/EG 2001 739	Virginia Plain/Pyjamarama (p/s)	4
78	Polydor/EG 2001 756	Do The Strand/Editions Of You (no p/s)	4
78	Polydor/EG 2001 756	Do The Strand/Editions Of You (12", p/s)	7
79	Polydor/EG POSP 32	Trash/Trash 2 (p/s)	4
79	Polydor/EGPOSPX 67	Angel Eyes (Extended 6.39)/My Little Girl (12", p/s)	7
82	E.G. ROXYX 3	More Than This/India (12", p/s)	8
86	E.G. EGOX 26	Love Is The Drug/Let's Stick Together (12", p/s, promo only)	15
72	Island ILPS 9200	ROXY MUSIC (LP, gatefold sleeve)	12
76	Island ILPS 9400	VIVA! ROXY MUSIC (LP)	12
79	Polydor/E.G. EGPD 001	MANIFESTO (LP, picture disc)	12
79	Polydor/E.G. EGPD 001	MANIFESTO (LP, picture disc, mispress, 1 side plays Gordon Giltrap's "Fear Of The Dark" LP)	12
79	Polydor/E.G. EG 001	MANIFESTO (LP, with normal versions of "Angel Eyes" & "Dance Away", different inner sleeve to later issue)	12
81	Polydor/E.G. EGBS 001	THE FIRST SEVEN ALBUMS (7-LP box set plus insert)	50
81	Polydor/E.G. EGBS 001	THE FIRST SEVEN ALBUMS (7-cassette box set)	35
83	E.G. 815 849-2	THE ATLANTIC YEARS 1973-1980 (CD)	15

(see also Brian Eno, Bryan Ferry, Andy Mackay, Phil Manzanera, Dumbelles, 801, Fripp & Eno)

ROXY MUSIC

DEREK ROY

57	Oriole CB 1415	Derek Roy's All-Star Party (with Bob Monkhouse, Richard Murdoch, Jon Pertwee, Ted Ray & others)	10
57	Oriole CB 1415	Derek Roy's All-Star Party (78)	8

(see also Jon Pertwee, Bob Monkhouse)

HUGH ROY (JUNIOR)

70	Supreme SUP 211	Double Attack/Puzzle	6
70	Explosion EX 2040	Whisper A Little Prayer (actually by Audley Rollins)/ Rain A Fall (actually by Melanie)	6
70	Punch PH 34	Scandal/Son Of The Wise	8
70	Duke Reid DR 2509	Wake The Town/Big Boy And Teacher	10
70	Duke Reid DR 2510	Rule The Nation/NORA DEAN: Ay Ay Ay Ay	10
70	Duke Reid DR 2513	Wear You To The Ball (with John Holt)/EARL LINDO: The Ball	10
70	Duke Reid DR 2514	You'll Never Get Away/TOMMY McCOOK QUINTET: Rock Away	10
70	Duke Reid DR 2515	Version Galore/TOMMY McCOOK: Nehru	8
71	Duke Reid DR 2516	Testify/TOMMY McCOOK: Super Soul	10
71	Duke Reid DR 2517	Tom Drunk (with Hopeton Lewis)/TOMMY McCOOK: Wailing	10
71	Duke Reid DR 2518	True True/On The Beach	8
71	Duke Reid DR 2519	Flashing My Whip/Do It Right	8
71	Treasure Isle TI 7059	Drive Her Home (Parts 1 & 2) (with Hopeton Lewis)	10
71	Treasure Isle TI 7062	Behold/Way Back Home (with Tommy McCook)	10
71	Treasure Isle TI 7064	Everybody Bawlin'/Ain't That Loving You	10
71	Upsetter US 375	Earthquake/Suspicious Minds	8
71	Duke DU 105	Love I Tender/JOYA LANDIS: When The Lights Are Low	8
71	Big BG 329	Papacito (as Hugh Roy Junior)/RUPIE EDWARDS: I'm Gonna Live Some Life	5
71	Supreme SUP 211	Double Attack (as Hugh Roy Junior)/MURPHY'S ALL STARS: Puzzle	6
72	G.G. GG 4532	Way Down South/BILLY DYCE: Be My Guest	6
72	Ashanti ASH 405	King Of The Road (as Hugh Roy Junior)/ROOSEVELT ALL STARS: Version	6
72	Jackpot JP 806	Two Ton Guletto/Version (as Hugh Roy Junior)	6

MINT VALUE £

72	Duke DU 137	Live It Up/DENNIS BROWN: Baby Don't Do It	6
72	Jackpot JP 806	Two Ton Gulleto/Version	6
72	Dynamic DYN 448	Festival Wise/Festival Wise Part 2	6
72	Banana BA 367	Keep On Running/LARRY'S ALL STARS: Version	8
72	Grape GR 3026	On Top The Peak/TYPHOON ALLSTARS: Race Attack	6
72	Pama PM 835	Way Down South/BILLY DYCE: Be My Guest	8
72	Punch PH 104	Nannyscrank (title actually "Nanny Skank")/PITTSBURG ALLSTARS: Scank Version	6
72	Green Door GD 4034	Hudson Affair/KEITH HUDSON: Hot Stick — Version	8
73	Green Door GD 4052	King Tubby's Special/Here Come The Heartaches	7
73	Gayfeet GS 210	Hard Feeling/Regular Style	6
73	Duke DU 157	Higher The Mountain/OLD BOYS INC.: Version	6
73	Harry J. HJ 6651	Treasure Isle Skank/Words Of Wisdom	5

(see also U Roy, Jeff Barnes, Melodians, Delroy Wilson)

I ROY

71	Moodisc MU 3509	Musical Pleasure/JO JO BENNETT: Hot Pop	8
71	Moodisc MU 3510	Heart Don't Leap (as I. Roy & Dennis Walks)/DENNIS WALKS & MUDIE'S ALLSTARS: Snow Bird	8
71	Moodisc MU 3512	Let Me Tell You Boy (with Ebony Sisters)/MUDIE'S ALLSTARS: Version	7
71	Moodisc HM 104	The Drifter (with Dennis Walks)/JO JO BENNETT: Snowbird	7
72	Green Door GD 4030	Hot Bomb (with Jumpers)/JUMPERS: The Bomb	6
72	Green Door GD 4044	Make Love/STAGE: Tic Toc Bill	6
73	Pyramid PYR 7001	Tip From The Prince/Fat Beef Skank	6
73	Attack ATT 8050	Space Flight/JERRY LEWIS: Burning Wire	10
73	Downtown DT 503	Blackman's Time/High Jacking	8
73	Downtown DT 519	Clapper's Tail/Live And Learn	8
73	Duke DU 156	Buck And The Preacher/PETE WESTON ALLSTARS: Preacher — Version	8
73	Smash SMA 2337	The Magnificent Seven/Leggo Beast	8
73	Smash SMA 2338	Rose Of Sheron/Slip Out	8
73	Techniques TE 926	Pauper And The King/GREGORY ISAACS: Loving Pauper	8
73	Techniques TE 930	Monkey Fashion/Medley Mood	6
73	Ackee ACK 503	Great Great Great (with Ken Parker)/RUPIE EDWARDS ALLSTARS: Version	7
73	Ackee ACK 510	Sound Education/AUGUSTUS PABLO: Cinderella In Black	10
73	Harry J HJ-6655	Musical Drum Sound/NOW GENERATION: Musical Drum — Version	5
73	Pama PM 854	Cowtown Skank/AUGUSTUS PABLO: Cowtown Skank Version	7
74	Atra ATRA 017	Yah Ma Ride/SWEET HARMONY: Mexican Rockin'	5
74	Ashanti ASH 412	Mood For Love (Parts 1 & 2)	8
75	Bullet BU 551	Step Right Up/ANDY'S ALLSTARS: Banjo Serenade	5
75	Lucky DL 5098	I Man Time/Version	6
76	Dip DL 5107	Padlock/Lock And Key (copies also exist with Lucky label)	each 6
70s	Nationwide NW 005	Tea Pot/Tea Cup	5
73	Trojan TRLS 63	PRESENTING I ROY (LP, original issue with "12 Neasden Lane" address and rough orange/white paper labels)	18
74	Trojan TRLS 71	HELL AND SORROW (LP, original issue with "12 Neasden Lane" address and rough orange/white paper labels)	15
74	Trojan TRLS 91	I ROY (LP, original issue with "12 Neasden Lane" address and rough orange/white paper labels)	15

(see also Keith Hudson & I Roy)

LEE ROY

| 54 | Philips PB 226 | The Creep/B.O. Plenty (78) | 10 |
| 65 | Island WI 251 | Oh Ee Baby/My Loving Baby Come Back | 10 |

LITTLE ROY

69	Crab CRAB 39	Without My Love (actually by Roy & Joy)/WINSTON SAMUELS: Here I Come Again	6
70	Bullet BU 445	Keep Trying/THE MATADORS: Version II	6
70	Camel CA 43	Scrooge/In The Days Of Old	6
70	Camel CA 46	You Run Come/THE LITTLE ROYS: Skank King (actually "Skank Me" by Little Roy)	6
70	Camel CA 52	Fight Them/Dreadlock	6
71	Escort ERT 850	Yester-Me Yester-You Yesterday/MATADOR ALL-STARS: Yes Sir	6
71	Punch PH 75	Hard Fighter/COUNT OSSIE: Back To Africa Version	6

(see also Roy & Joy, Little Roys)

MAD ROY

70	Banana BA 324	Nanny Version (actually by Dennis Alcapone)/BIGGER D: Freedom Version	8
71	Banana BA 326	Home Version (actually by Dennis Alcapone)/SOUND DIMENSION: One Time	8
71	Banana BA 327	Universal Love/ROLAND ALPHONSO: Shelly Belly	8
71	Banana BA 328	Duppy Serenade/Sunshine Version (both sides actually by Dennis Alcapone)	10

(pseudonym for Leroy Wallace; see also Dennis Alcapone)

U ROY (JUNIOR)

72	Duke Reid DR 2520	Rock To The Beat/Love Is Not A Gamble (both actually by Dennis Alcapone)	6
72	Attack ATT 8030	This Is A Pepper (as U Roy Junior)/JOHN HOLT: Justice	6
72	Sioux SI 024	The Wedding (as U Roy Junior)/LLOYD'S ALL STARS: Buttercup	6
73	Randy's RAN 532	Froggie (as U Roy Junior)/RHYTHM RULERS: Version	5
73	Techniques TE 928	Aunt Kereba (as U Roy Junior)/DON RECO: Waterloo Rock (B-side actually by Reco Rodriquez)	6
71	Duke Reid DR 2517	Tom Drunk/Wailing (B-side actually by Tommy McCook)	8
71	Trojan TBL 161	VERSION GALORE (LP)	15
73	Attack ATLP 1006	U ROY (LP)	10

(see also Hugh Roy, Dennis Alcapone, Sir Harry, Shorty Perry, Heptones, Herman Chin-Loy)

ROY & ANNETTE

| 63 | R&B JB 107 | My Baby/Go Your Ways | 12 |

(see also Tommy McCook, Lester Sterling)

ROY & DUKE ALL STARS
68	Blue Cat BS 113	Pretty Blue Eyes (Parts 1 & 2)	10
68	Blue Cat BS 117	The Train (Parts 1 & 2)	10

(see also Roy Panton)

ROY & ENID
68	Coxsone CS 7063	Rocking Time/RALPH BLAKE: High Blood Pressure	18
68	Coxsone CS 7069	He'll Have To Go/CARLTON & SHOES: Love Is A Treasure	18
69	Coxsone CS 7088	Reggae For Days/SOUND DIMENSION: Holy Moses	18

(Little) ROY & JOY
73	Camel CA 107	Rainy Weather/THE DEN BROTHERS: Version	5

(see also Little Roys)

ROY (Panton) & MILLIE
62	Island WI 005	We'll Meet/ROLAND ALPHONSO: Back Beat (B-side act. with City Slickers)	18
63	Island WI 050	This World/Never Say Goodbye	18
63	Island WI 090	There'll Come A Day/I Don't Want You	18
63	Blue Beat BB 154	Over And Over/I'll Go (with Prince Buster All Stars)	18
64	Black Swan WI 409	Cherry I Love You/You're The Only One	12
64	Black Swan WI 410	Oh Merna/DON DRUMMOND: Dog War Bossa Nova	12
64	Black Swan WI 427	Oh Shirley/Marie	12

(see also Roy Panton, Millie [Small])

ROY (Panton) & PATSY
62	Blue Beat BB 118	My Happy Home/In Your Arms Dear (with Hersang & His Combo)	12

(see also Roy Panton)

ROY (Richards) & PAULETTE
63	Island WI 067	Have You Seen My Baby/Since You're Gone	15

ROY (Panton) & YVONNE (Harrison)
64	Blue Beat BB 258	Little Girl/No More	12
64	Black Swan WI 436	Two Roads/Join Together	15

(see also Roy Panton)

BILLY JOE ROYAL
62	Oriole CB 1751	Never In A Hundred Years/We Haven't A Moment To Lose	12
65	CBS 201802	Down In The Boondocks/Oh! What A Night	7
65	CBS 201983	You Make Me Feel Like A Man/I've Got To Be Somebody	6
65	CBS 202009	I Knew You When/Steal Away	6
66	CBS 202052	It's A Good Time/Don't Wait Up For Me Mama	6
66	CBS 202087	Heart's Desire/Everybody's Gotta Cry	25
66	Atlantic 584 002	Never In A Hundred Years/We Haven't A Moment To Lose (reissue)	5
66	CBS 202400	High On A Hilltop/I'm Gonna Get Right Tonight	5
67	CBS 202548	Yo Yo/We Tried	6
67	CBS 2861	The Greatest Love/These Are Not My People	5
67	CBS 3044	Hush/Watching From The Bandstand	5
68	CBS 3402	Don't You Be Ashamed/Don't You Think It's Time	5
68	CBS 3644	Storybook Children/Just Between You And Me	5
68	CBS 3858	Gabriel/Movies In My Mind	5
69	CBS 4470	Cherry Hill Park/Helping Hand	5
66	CBS BPG 62590	INTRODUCING BILLY JOE ROYAL (LP)	18

BOBBY ROYAL
63	HMV POP 1253	Big Big Star/Little Word Of Love	6

JAMES ROYAL (& HAWKS)
65	Parlophone R 5290	She's About A Mover/Black Cloud (as James Royal & Hawks)	12
65	Parlophone R 5383	Work Song/I Can't Stand It	15
67	CBS 202525	Call My Name/When It Comes To My Baby	7
67	CBS 2739	It's All In The Game/Green Days	7
68	CBS 2959	Take Me Like I Am/Sitting In The Station	5
68	CBS 3232	I Can't Stand It/Little Bit Of Rain	6
68	CBS 3450	Hey Little Boy/Thru' The Love	12
68	CBS 3624	A Woman Called Sorrow/Fire	12
69	CBS 3797	Time Hangs On My Mind/Anna-Lee	6
69	CBS 3915	House Of Jack/Which Way To Nowhere	5
69	CBS 4139	I've Something Bad On My Mind/She's Independent	6
69	CBS 4463	Send Out Love/I've Lost You	10
70	CBS 5032	And Soon The Darkness/I'm Going Home	5
70	Carnaby CNS 4021	Carolina/Big Heat On The Loose	6
71	Carnaby 6151 002	Carolina/A Woman Called Sorrow	5
72	Carnaby 6151 006	Two Of Us/Who Are We (with Liz Christian)	5
69	CBS 63780	CALL MY NAME (LP)	20
70	Carnaby CNLS 6008	ONE WAY (LP)	35
72	Carnaby 6302 011	THE LIGHT AND SHADE OF JAMES ROYAL (LP)	25

ROBBIE ROYAL
65	Mercury MF 923	Only Me/I Don't Need You	7
65	Decca F 12097	Within My Lonely Heart/When I Found You	5

ROYAL AIR FORCE CENTRAL BAND
56	HMV B 10957	"Reach For The Sky" Theme/The Jolly Airman	5
57	Decca F 10932	High Flight/Out Of The Blue	5
61	HMV 7P 287	The Dambusters March/Lilliburlero	5
57	HMV 7EG 8265	R.A.F. CENTRAL BAND (EP)	8

ROYAL BLUES
69	Pye 7N 17670	Mountain Of Love/Wishful Thinking	5
69	Pye 7N 17732	Mendocino/Hi-Lili Hi-Lo	5

MINT VALUE £

| 69 | Pye 7N 17769 | Proud Mary/Sunny Girl Friend | 5 |
| 69 | Pye 7N 17847 | High As A Mountain/Wildwood Flower | 5 |

ROYALETTES
65	MGM MGM 1272	Poor Boy/Watch What Happens	12
65	MGM MGM 1279	It's Gonna Take A Miracle/Out Of Sight Out Of Mind	20
65	MGM MGM 1292	I Want To Meet Him/Never Again	18
66	MGM MGM 1302	You Bring Me Down/Only When You're Lonely	18
66	MGM MGM 1324	It's A Big Mistake/I Want To Meet Him	12
68	Big T BIG 106	River Of Tears/Something Wonderful	12
66	MGM MGM-C 8028	THE ELEGANT SOUND OF THE ROYALETTES (LP)	50

ROYAL GUARDSMEN
67	Stateside SS 574	Snoopy Vs The Red Baron/I Needed You	6
67	Stateside SS 2010	The Return Of The Red Baron/Sweetmeats Slide	6
67	Stateside SS 2035	Airplane Song/OM	6
67	Stateside SS 2051	Wednesday/So Right (To Be In Love)	7
67	London HLP 10171	Snoopy's Christmas/It Kinda Looks Like Christmas	6
68	London HLP 10211	Snoopy For President/Down Behind The Lines	6
68	London HLP 10235	Baby Let's Wait/So Right (To Be In Love)	5
68	London HLP 10182	I Say Love/I'm Not Gonna Stay	5
67	Stateside S(S)L 10202	SNOOPY VS THE RED BARON (LP)	25
68	London HA-P/SH-P 8351	THE RETURN OF THE RED BARON (LP)	25

ROYAL HOLIDAYS
| 58 | London HLU 8722 | Margaret/I'm Sorry (I Did You Wrong) | 90 |
| 58 | London HLU 8722 | Margaret/I'm Sorry (I Did You Wrong) (78) | 45 |

ROYAL ROCKERS
| 60 | Top Rank JAR 326 | Jet II/Swinging Mambo | 12 |

ROYALS
64	Blue Beat BB 259	Save Mama/Out De Fire	15
68	Amalgamated AMG 831	Never See Come See/CANNONBALL BRYAN TRIO: Jumping Jack	10
69	Trojan TR 662	Pick Out Me Eye/Think You Too Bad	8
69	Duke DU 29	Never Gonna Give You Up/Don't Mix Me Up	8
73	Dip DL 5016	Promised Land/Every Jamaican Is A Rebel	5

ROYAL SHOWBAND, WATERFORD
| 64 | HMV POP 1377 | Huckle Buck/I Ran All The Way Home | 6 |

ROYAL TEENS
58	HMV POP 454	Short Shorts/Planet Rock	30
58	HMV POP 454	Short Shorts/Planet Rock (78)	30
59	Capitol CL 15068	Little Cricket/Believe Me	18

ROYALTONES
58	London HLJ 8744	Poor Boy/Wail!	15
58	London HLJ 8744	Poor Boy/Wail! (78)	25
61	London HLU 9296	Flamingo Express/Tacos	12
64	Stateside SS 309	Our Faded Love/Holy Smokes	10

ROYALTY
| 69 | CBS 4181 | That Kind Of Girl/Will You Be Staying After Sunday | 4 |

EARL ROYCE & OLYMPICS
| 64 | Columbia DB 7433 | Que Sera Sera/I Really Do | 18 |
| 65 | Parlophone R 5261 | Guess Things Happen That Way/Sure To Fall | 18 |

ROY'S BOYS
| 64 | Columbia DB 7425 | Do Wah Diddy Diddy—I'm Into Something Good—I Want To Hold Your Hand/Oh! Pretty Woman—Have I The Right?—It's All Over Now | 6 |

LITA ROZA
51	Decca F 9731	Allentown Jail/I Wish I Knew (78)	10
51	Decca F 9785	I'm Gonna Wash That Man Right Outta My Hair/A Wonderful Guy (78)	10
52	Decca F 9955	Oakie Boogie/Raminay (78)	12
53	Decca F 10070	(How Much Is) That Doggie In The Window/Tell Me We'll Meet Again (78)	15
53	Decca F 75082	(How Much Is) That Doggie In The Window/Tell Me We'll Meet Again (export issue)	35
53	Decca F 10128	Seven Lonely Days/No-One Will Ever Know (78)	10
53	Decca F 10144	Crazy Man, Crazy/Oo! What You Do To Me (78)	7
54	Decca F 10363	Skinnie Minnie (Fishtail)/My Kid Brother	10
54	Decca F 10240	Changing Partners/Just A Dream Or Two Ago (B-side with Stargazers)	12
54	Decca F 10269	Bell Bottom Blues (with Johnston Brothers)/Make Love To Me (both with Ted Heath Orchestra)	10
54	Decca F 10277	Young At Heart/Secret Love	10
54	Decca F 10393	Call Off The Wedding/The "Mama-Doll" Song	10
55	Decca F 10427	Heartbeat/Leave Me Alone	10
55	Decca F 10431	Let Me Go, Lover!/Make Yourself Comfortable	10
55	Decca F 10479	Tomorrow/Foolishly	10
55	Decca F 10536	Two Hearts, Two Kisses (Make One Love)/Keep Me In Mind	10
55	Decca F 10541	The Man In The Raincoat/Today And Ev'ry Day	8
55	Decca F 10611	Hey There/Hernando's Hideaway	15
56	Decca F 10679	Jimmy Unknown/The Rose Tattoo	15
56	Decca F 10728	Too Young To Go Steady/You're Not Alone	8
56	Decca F 10761	No Time For Tears/But Love Me (Love But Me)	8
56	Decca F 10792	Innismore/The Last Waltz	8
56	Decca F 10830	Hey! Jealous Lover/Julie	8
57	Decca F 10861	Lucky Lips/Tears Don't Care Who Cries Them	10
57	Decca F 10884	Tonight My Heart She Is Crying/Five Oranges, Four Apples	7
57	Decca F 10921	I Need You/You've Changed	7

MINT VALUE £

58	Pye 7N 15119	Pretend You Don't See Him/Ha-Ha-Ha!	6
58	Pye 7N 15133	I Need Somebody/You're The Greatest	6
58	Pye 7N 15139	I Could Have Danced All Night/The Wonderful Season Of Love.	6
58	Pye 7N 15149	Sorry, Sorry, Sorry/Hillside In Scotland.	6
58	Pye 7N 15155	Nel Blu Dipinto Di Blu (Volare)/It's A Boy	6
58	Pye N 15155	Nel Blu Dipinto Di Blu (Volare)/It's A Boy (78).	10
59	Pye 7N 15190	This Is My Town/Oh Dear What Can The Matter Be.	6
59	Pye N 15190	This Is My Town/Oh Dear What Can The Matter Be (78).	10
59	Pye 7N 15204	Allentown Jail/Once In A While	6
59	Pye N 15204	Allentown Jail/Once In A While (78).	10
59	Pye 7N 15241	Let It Rain, Let It Rain/Maybe You'll Be There	6
59	Pye N 15241	Let It Rain, Let It Rain/Maybe You'll Be There (78).	12
63	Ember EMB S 168	Mama (He Treats Your Daughter Mean)/	
		(He's My) Dreamboat (as Lisa Rosa)	10
65	Columbia DB 7785	What Am I Supposed To Do/Where Do I Go From Here	5
65	Columbia DB 7689	Keep Watch Over Him/Stranger Things Have Happened	6
57	Decca DFE 6386	LITA ROZA SELECTION (EP)	30
57	Decca DFE 6399	LITA ROZA (EP)	25
58	Decca DFE 6443	BETWEEN THE DEVIL AND THE DEEP BLUE SEA NO. 1 (EP)	25
54	Decca LF 1187	PRESENTING LITA ROZA (10" LP)	75
56	Decca LF 1243	LISTENING IN THE AFTER HOURS (10" LP)	100
57	Decca LK 4171	LOVE IS THE ANSWER (LP)	35
57	Decca LK 4218	BETWEEN THE DEVIL AND THE DEEP BLUE SEA (LP)	35
58	Pye Nixa NPL 18020	ME ON A CAROUSEL (LP, also stereo NSPL 83003)	30/35
60	Pye NPL 18047	DRINKA LITA ROZA DAY (LP)	50
64	Ember NR 5009	LOVE SONGS FOR NIGHT PEOPLE (LP).	18

(see also Stargazers, Johnston Brothers)

RPM
| 94 | Mo' Wax MW018 | 2,000/Sorti Des Ombres/(dub) (12", 3 different covers, full colour, | |
| | | green and purple or blue) | 20/12/6 |

RUB-A-DUBS WITH DANDY
| 65 | Blue Beat BB 304 | Without Love/I Know | 18 |

(see also Dandy)

RUBBER BAND
73	Youngblood YB 1052	Moonwalker/Wichita.	5
69	Major Minor SMCP 5045	CREAM SONGBOOK (LP)	15
69	Major Minor SMCP 5048	HENDRIX SONGBOOK (LP)	15

RUBBER BOOTZ
| 67 | Deram DM 134 | Joy Ride/Chicano | 10 |

RUBELLA BALLET
82	Xntrix XN 2005	The Ballet Dance/Something To Give/	
		Unemployed/Krak Trak (p/s)	4
82	Xntrix ZN 2004	BALLET DOG (C-30 cassette with insert)	6

RUBETTES
74	Polydor 2058 529	Juke Box Jive/When You're Falling In Love (p/s)	5
76	State STAT 27	Under One Roof/Sign Of The Times (p/s)	5
77	Polydor 2058 943	Come On Over/Let Him Bleed (p/s)	5
78	Polydor 2059 042	Goodbye Dolly Gray/Great Be The Nation (p/s).	5
78	Polydor 2059 059	Movin'/San Andreas (p/s).	5
79	Polydor 2059 100	Lola/Truth Of The Matter (p/s)	5
79	Polydor 2059 173	Kid Runaway/Southbound Train (p/s)	5
82	V-Tone VTONE 004	Don't Come Crying/Breakdown	5
74	Polydor 2489 090	WEAR IT'S AT (LP, gatefold sleeve, with paper hat insert)	12

(see also Baskin & Copperfield)

RUBIN
| 75 | MCA MU 196 | You've Been Away/Baby, You're My Everything | 5 |

RUBAIYATS
| 68 | Action ACT 4516 | Omar Khayam/Tomorrow | 10 |

RUBY
| 77 | PBR Intl. PBRL 5001 | RUBY (LP) | 10 |
| 78 | PBR Intl. PBRL 5003 | ROCK'N'ROLL MADNESS (LP) | 10 |

(see also Tom Fogerty)

RUBY & GLORIA
71	Big Shot BI 583	Worried Over You/Worried Over You – Version	7
71	Black Swan BW 1409	Talk To Me Baby/LLOYD'S ALL STARS:	
		Talk To Me Baby — Version	7

RUBY & ROMANTICS
63	London HLR 9679	Our Day Will Come/Moonlight And Music	10
63	London HLR 9734	My Summer Love/Sweet Love And Sweet Forgiveness	12
63	London HLR 9771	Hey There Lonely Boy/Not A Moment Too Soon	12
63	London HLR 9801	Young Wings Can Fly/Day Dreaming	10
64	London HLR 9881	Our Everlasting Love/Much Better Off Than I've Ever Been.	8
64	London HLR 9916	Baby Come Home/Every Day's A Holiday	12
64	London HLR 9935	When You're Young And In Love/I Cry Alone.	12
65	London HLR 9972	Your Baby Doesn't Love Me Anymore/We'll Meet Again.	12
69	A&M AMS 750	Hurting Each Other/Baby I Could Be So Good At Loving You	6
63	London RE-R 1389	OUR DAY WILL COME (EP)	75
64	London RE-R 1427	HEY THERE LONELY BOY (EP)	75
63	London HA-R 8078	OUR DAY WILL COME (LP)	60
66	London HA-R 8282	GREATEST HITS (LP).	50

(see also Danny Davis Orchestra)

MINT VALUE £

RUDDY & SKETTO
71 Supreme SUP 218   Every Night/Ethiopia 5
(see also Sketto Rich)

RUDE BOYS
67 Island WI 3088   Rock Steady Massachusetts/Going Home 10

RUDI
78	Good Vibrations GOT 1	Big Time/Number 1 (folded p/s, 3,000 only). 5
79	Good Vibrations GOT 12	I Spy/Genuine Reply/Sometimes/Ripped In Two (p/s) 5
81	Jamming! CREATE 1	When I Was Dead/The Pressure's On (p/s) 5
82	Jamming! CREATE 3	Crimson/14 Steps (p/s) 5

RUDIES (FANATICS)
68	Blue Cat BS 107	The 7-11 Go To The Go Go Club (Parts 1 & 2). 10
68	Blue Cat BS 109	Cupid/RECO'S ALLSTARS: Wise Message 10
68	Nu Beat NB 001	Train To Vietnam/Skaville To Rainbow City 7
68	Nu Beat NB 005	Engine 59/My Girl. 6
68	Fab FAB 46	I Wanna Go Home/La Mer 5
68	Fab FAB 70	Give Me The Rights/I Do Love You (as Rudies Fanatics) 5
68	Fab FAB 71	Mighty Meaty/Go (as Rudies Fanatics) 5
69	Doctor Bird DB 1301	Sin Thing/What's Your Name 7
69	Doctor Bird DB 1302	Boss Sound/RECO & RUDIES: Peace 10
69	Fab FAB 104	Brixton Market/Rudie's Joy 6
70	Pama PM 789	Give Peace A Chance/Theme From She 5
70	Trojan TR 7798	Patches/Split 5
71	Spinning Wheel SW 106	My Sweet Lord/Devil's Lead Soup. 6

(see also Freddie Notes, Sonny, Binns & Rudies, Rico, Dandy, Owen & Dandy, Downtown All Stars, Desmond Riley)

RUDIMENTARY PENI
81	Outer Himalayan OH 003	RUDIMENTARY PENI (EP, A4 foldout p/s with booklet, later 14" x 7"). 12/10
82	Crass 211984/2	FARCE (EP, initially in 21" x 14" foldout black & white p/s). 10/7
83	Corpus Christi CHRISTITS 6	DEATH CHURCH (LP). 12

(see also Magits)

RUD(D)Y (Grant) & SKETTO (Rich)
62	Dice CC 5	Summer Is Just Around The Corner/Nothing Like Time (as Ruddy & Sketto & Reco's All Stars) 15
62	Dice CC 7	Little Schoolgirl/Hush Baby (as Ruddy & Sketto & Baron Twist & His Knights) 15
62	Dice CC 10	Mr Postman/Christmas Blues (as Rudy & Sketto with Laurel's Group). 10
63	Dice CC 16	Hold The Fire/Good Morning Mr Jones 15
63	Dice CC 19	Never Set You Free/Brothers And Sisters 15
63	Blue Beat BB 198	Was It Me/Minna Don't Deceive Me 15
64	Blue Beat BB 208	Show Me The Way To Go Home/Let Me Dream 10
64	Blue Beat BB 230	Ten Thousand Miles From Home/I Need Someone (as Ruddy & Sketto) 10
64	Blue Beat BB 252	I Love You/If Only Tomorrow 15
65	Blue Beat BB 297	See What You Done/Heart's Desire (as Ruddy & Sketto) 15
65	Blue Beat BB 310	Oh Dolly/You're Mine (as Ruddy & Sketto) 15

(see also Ruddy & Sketto)

RUEFREX
80	Good Vibrations GOT 8	One By One/Cross The Line/Don't Panic (foldover p/s, 2 different designs). . . . . each 6
83	Kabuki KAR 7	Capital Letters/April Fool (p/s). 5
84	One By One 1X1	Paid In Kind/The Perfect Crime (p/s) 4
86	Kasper KAS 2	The Wild Colonial Boy/Even In The Dark Hours (p/s) 4
86	Kasper KAS 3	In The Traps/Leaders Of The Last Resort (p/s) 4

RAY RUFF & CHECKMATES
64 London HLU 9889   I Took A Liking To You/A Fool Again 20

RUFFIANS
71 Banana BA 359   Room Full Of Tears (actually by Sensations)/Black Soul (actually "Black And White — Version" by Riley's Allstars) 8

(see Al Brown, Sensations)

BRUCE RUFFIN
69	Songbird SB 1002	Long About Now/Come See About Me (as Bruce Ruffin & Temptations). 12
69	Trojan TR 7704	Dry Up Your Tears/BEVERLEY'S ALLSTARS: One Way Street 5
70	Trojan TR 7737	I'm The One/Who's Gonna Be Your Man? 5
70	Trojan TR 7776	Cecelia/BEVERLEY ALL STARS: Stand Up. 5
70	Summit SUM 8509	O-o-h Child/Bitterness Of Life 5
71	Summit SUM 8516	Candida/Are You Ready 5
71	Trojan TR 7814	Rain/THE PYRAMIDS: Geronimo (B-side actually by Pyramids) 5
71	Trojan TR 7814	Rain/THE PYRAMIDS: Off Limits (B-side actually by Aquarians). 5
71	Trojan TR 7832	One Big Happy Family (Parts 1 & 2) 5
72	Trojan TRM 9000	Songs Of Peace/You Are The Best/We Can Make It 5
71	Trojan TRL 23	RAIN (LP) 12
72	Rhino SRNO 8001	BRUCE RUFFIN (LP) 12

(see also Bruce Downer)

DAVID RUFFIN
69	Tamla Motown TMG 689	My Whole World Ended (The Moment You Left Me)/I've Got To Find Myself A Brand New Baby. 7
69	Tamla Motown TMG 711	I've Lost Everything I've Ever Loved/We'll Have A Good Thing Going On 6
76	Tamla Motown TMG 1022	Heavy Love/Me And Rock And Roll Are Here To Stay 5
69	T. Motown (S)TML 11118	MY WHOLE WORLD ENDED (LP). 30
70	T. Motown (S)TML 11139	FEELIN' GOOD (LP) 25
73	Tamla Motown STML 11228	DAVID RUFFIN (LP) 12

(see also Temptations)

JIMMY RUFFIN

66	Tamla Motown TMG 577	What Becomes Of The Broken-Hearted?/Baby I've Got It (small print, later large)	10/6
67	Tamla Motown TMG 593	I've Passed This Way Before/Tomorrow's Tears	10
67	Tamla Motown TMG 603	Gonna Give Her All The Love I Got/World So Wide, Nowhere To Hide	7
67	Tamla Motown TMG 617	Don't You Miss Me A Little Bit Baby/I Want Her Love	10
68	Tamla Motown TMG 649	I'll Say Forever My Love/Everybody Needs Love	8
68	Tamla Motown TMG 664	Don't Let Him Take Your Love From Me/Lonely Lonely Man Am I	8
69	Tamla Motown TMG 703	I've Passed This Way Before/Tomorrow's Tears	5
70	Tamla Motown TMG 726	Farewell Is A Lonely Sound/If You Let Me, I Know I Can	5
70	Tamla Motown TMG 740	I'll Say Forever My Love/Everybody Needs Love	5
70	Tamla Motown TMG 753	It's Wonderful (To Be Loved By You)/Maria (You Were The Only One)	5
71	Tamla Motown TMG 767	Let's Say Goodbye Tomorrow/Living In A World I Created For Myself	5
71	Tamla Motown TMG 784	On The Way Out (On The Way In)/Honey Come Back	6
73	Mojo 2092 060	Mother's Love/Waiting For You	5
74	Polydor 2058 433	Tell Me What You Want/Going Home (p/s)	5
67	T. Motown (S)TML 11048	THE JIMMY RUFFIN WAY (LP)	35
69	T. Motown (S)TML 11106	RUFF 'N' READY (LP)	25
70	T. Motown STML 11161	JIMMY RUFFIN ... FOREVER (LP)	20
73	Polydor 2383 240	JIMMY RUFFIN (LP)	12
70s	Sounds Superb SPR 90041	I'VE PASSED THIS WAY BEFORE (LP)	12

(see also Council Collective)

JIMMY & DAVID RUFFIN

71	Tamla Motown STML 11176	I AM MY BROTHER'S KEEPER (LP)	18

(see also David Ruffin, Temptations)

RUFUS

74	ABC ABC 4022	You Got The Love/Rags To Rufus	4
75	ABC ABC 4038	Stop On By/Rufusized	4
75	ABC ABC 4055	Once You Get Started/Right Is Right (p/s)	4
84	Warner Bros RCKT 1	Ain't Got You/Stop On By/Don't Go To Strangers (12", with Chaka Khan)	8
75	ABC ABCL 5151	RUFUS WITH CHAKA KHAN (LP)	10

(see also Chaka Khan)

RUGBYS

69	Polydor 56781	You And I/Stay With Me	40
70	Polydor 56789	Wendegahl The Warlock/Light	10

PETE RUGOLO (& DIAMONDS)

61	Mercury AMT 1147	Marie/Moonglow And Theme From Picnic (as Pete Rugolo & His Perfect Presence Sound Orchestra)	5
58	Emarcy ERE 1577	MUSIC FOR HI-FI BUGS VOL. 1 (EP)	8
58	Emarcy ERE 1578	MUSIC FOR HI-FI BUGS VOL. 2 (EP)	8
59	Mercury ZEP 10020	THE DIAMONDS MEET PETE RUGOLO (EP)	25
60	Mercury ZEP 10084	RUGOLO PLAYS KENTON (EP, also in stereo SEZ 19000)	7/8
61	Mercury ZEP 10097	PETE RUGOLO LEADS THE DIAMONDS (EP, also stereo SEZ 19012)	25/30
61	Mercury ZEP 10099	THE MASTERPIECES OF KENTON (EP, also stereo SEZ 19015)	7/8
54	Philips BBR 8024	PETE RUGOLO AND HIS ORCHESTRA (10" LP)	12
57	Mercury MPL 6517	BRASS IN HI-FI (LP)	12
57	Emarcy EJL 1254	FOR HI-FI BUGS (LP)	12
58	Emarcy EJL 1274	OUT ON A LIMB (LP)	12
59	Mercury MMC 14012	ADVENTURES IN SOUND — REEDS IN HI-FI (LP)	12
60	Mercury MMC 14034	"RICHARD DIAMOND" MUSIC (LP, also stereo CMS 18025)	12/15
60	Warner Bros WM 4001	BEHIND BRIGITTE BARDOT — COOL SOUNDS FROM HER HOT SCENES (LP, also stereo WS 8001)	20

(see also Diamonds, Patti Page)

BARBARA RUICK

53	MGM SP 1044	Delishious/The Price I Paid For Loving	6

RULERS

66	Rio R 105	Don't Be A Rude Boy/Be Good	12
66	Rio R 107	Copasetic/Too Late	12
67	Rio R 132	Wrong Embryo/Why Don't You Change	12
67	Rio R 135	Well Covered/CARL DAWKINS: Help Time	10
67	Rio R 138	Be Mine/CARL DAWKINS: Hot And Sticky	12
69	Trojan TR 696	Got To Be Free/Situation	8

RUMBLERS

63	London HLD 9684	Boss/I Don't Need You No More	20
65	King KG 1021	Soulful Jerk/Hey Did A Da Da	35
63	London RE-D 1396	BOSSOUNDS (EP)	200
63	London HA-D/SH-D 8081	BOSSOUNDS (LP, mono/stereo)	80/100

RAMBLING SYD RUMPO

67	Parlophone R 5638	The Ballad Of The Wogglers Moulie/Green Grow My Nadgers Oh!	5
68	Parlophone GEP 8965	RAMBLING SYD RUMPO IN CONCERT VOL. 1 (EP)	12
68	Parlophone GEP 8966	RAMBLING SYD RUMPO IN CONCERT VOL. 2 (EP)	12
70	Starline SRS 5034	THE BEST OF RAMBLING SYD RUMPO (LP)	15

(see also Kenneth Williams)

RUMPLESTILTSKIN

70	Bell BLL 1101	Squadron Leader Johnson/Rumplestiltskin	7
71	Bell BLL 1157	Wimoweh/Through My Looking Glass	7
70	Bell SBLL 130	RUMPLESTILTSKIN (LP, gatefold sleeve)	35

(see also Blue Mink, Clem Cattini)

RUNAWAYS

76	Mercury 6167 392	Cherry Bomb/Blackmail	10
77	Mercury 6167 493	Queens Of Noise/Born To Be Bad	6

RUNAWAYS

77	Mercury 6167 587	School Days/Wasted (p/s)	8
79	Cherry Red CHERRY 8	Right Now/Black Leather (p/s)	12
76	Mercury 9100 029	THE RUNAWAYS (LP, with gatefold sleeve & lyric sheet; U.S. pressing, with cat. no. SRM 1 1090, in U.K. sleeve)	12
77	Mercury 9100 032	QUEENS OF NOISE (LP, with lyric sheet)	15
77	Mercury 9100 046	LIVE IN JAPAN (LP)	12
77	Mercury 9100 047	WAITIN' FOR THE NIGHT (LP)	12
79	Cherry Red ARED 38	AND NOW ... THE RUNAWAYS (LP, 1,000 copies each in yellow, red, blue & orange vinyl)	each 25
80	Cherry Red BRED 9	FLAMING SCHOOLGIRLS (LP)	15

(see also Joan Jett, Cherie Currie, Lita Ford & Ozzy Osbourne)

TODD RUNDGREN

72	Bearsville K 15502	I Saw The Light/Marlene	4
82	Avatar AVAB 1	TIME HEALS (EP, picture disc)	4
73	Bearsville K 45513	A WIZARD, A TRUE STAR (shaped gatefold sleeve with lyric inner)	10
74	Bearsville K 85501	TODD (2-LP, with giant poster)	15
75	Bearsville K 55504	INITIATION (LP, with lyric inner)	10
81	Island ILPS 9567	HEALING (LP, with bonus 7" "Time Heals"/ "Tiny Diamonds" [PSR 455])	10

(see also Nazz, Utopia, Runt)

RUN DMC

86	London LONX 104	Walk This Way/Walk This Way (Instrumental) (both with Aerosmith)/ My Adidas (12", p/s)	8
86	London LON 118	You Be Illin'/Hit It And Run (p/s, with 'Dictionary Of Rap' booklet)	4
87	London LONG 163	Christmas In Hollis/Peter Piper (gatefold p/s)	4
85	4th + B'dway PBRLP 504	KING OF ROCK (LP, picture disc)	10

RUNESTAFF

85	FM VHF 5	Road To Ruin/Last Chances (p/s)	7
85	FM VHF 17	Do It!/Runestaff (no p/s)	6
85	Heavy Metal HMRLP 26	RUNESTAFF (LP)	15

RUNNING MAN

72	RCA Neon NE 11	THE RUNNING MAN (LP)	100

(see also Ray Russell Quartet, Mouse)

RUNRIG

83	Ridge RRS 103	Loch Lomond/Tuireadh Iain Ruaida (p/s)	20
84	Simple SIM 4	Dance Called America/Na H Uain A's T-Earrach (p/s)	10
84	Simple 12 SIM 4	Dance Called America/Na H Uain A's T-Earrach/Ribhinn (12", p/s)	20
84	Simple SIM 8	Skye/Hey Mandu (p/s)	20
86	Ridge RRS 006	The Work Song/This Time Of Year (p/s)	20
86	Ridge RRS 007	Alba/Worker For The Wind (p/s)	15
88	Chrysalis CHS 3284	Protect And Survive/Hearts Of Olden Glory (live) (p/s)	10
88	Chrysalis CHS 12 3284	Protect And Survive/Hearts Of Olden Glory (live)/ Protect And Survive (live) (12", p/s)	15
88	Chrysalis CHSCD 3284	Protect And Survive/Hearts Of Olden Glory (live)/ Protect And Survive (live) (CD)	20
89	Chrysalis CHS 3404	News From Heaven/Chi Mi'n Tir (p/s)	5
89	Chrysalis CHS 12 3404	News From Heaven/Chi Mi'n Tir/The Times They Are A'Changing (12", p/s)	12
89	Chrysalis CHS 12T 3404	News From Heaven/Chi Mi'n Tir/The Times They Are A'Changing (12", picture disc)	15
89	Chrysalis CHSCD 3404	News From Heaven/Chi Mi'n Tir/The Times They Are A'Changing (CD)	20
89	Chrysalis CHS 3451	Every River/This Time Of Year (p/s)	5
89	Chrysalis CHS 12 3451	Every River/This Time Of Year/Our Earth Was Once Green (12", p/s)	15
89	Chrysalis CHSCD 3451	Every River/This Time Of Year/Our Earth Was Once Green (CD)	20
90	Chrysalis CHSCD 3594	CAPTURE THE HEART EP: Stepping Down The Glory Road/Satellite Flood/ Harvest Moon/The Apple Came Down (10", p/s)	10
90	Chrysalis CHSCD 3594	CAPTURE THE HEART EP: Stepping Down The Glory Road/Satellite Flood/ Harvest Moon/The Apple Came Down (CD)	10
90	Chrysalis CHSGCD 3754	HEARTHAMMER EP: Hearthammer/Pride Of The Summer (live)/ Loch Lomond (live)/Solus Na Madainn (CD, with booklet)	10
90	Chrysalis CHSCD 3805	Flower Of The West/Ravenscraig/Ch Mi'n Greamhradh/ Harvest Moon (CD, digipak)	12
78	Neptune NA 105	RUNRIG PLAY GAELIC (LP)	20
78	Neptune NA 105	RUNRIG PLAY GAELIC (cassette)	10
79	Ridge RR 001	THE HIGHLAND CONNECTION (LP)	12

RUNT

71	Bearsville K 44505	RUNT (LP)	15
71	Bearsville K 44506	RUNT — THE BALLAD OF TODD RUNDGREN (LP)	15

(see also Todd Rundgren, Utopia, Nazz)

R.U.1.2.

78	SRTS/78/CUS 131	She's Gone/Purely Physical/Teenage Girl (p/s)	8

RUN 229

80	MM JR 7040S	Soho/Dance/In This Day And Age (no p/s)	25

RUPERT BEAR

73	Philips 6006 289	My Name's Rupert Bear/Little Motor Car	4

RUPERT'S PEOPLE

67	Columbia DB 8226	Reflections Of Charles Brown/Hold On	30
67	Columbia DB 8278	A Prologue To A Magic World/Dream In My Mind	40
68	Columbia DB 8362	I Can Show You/I've Got The Love	50

(see also Renaissance, Fleur-De-Lys, Gun, Adrian Gurvitz, Sweet Feeling)

RUSH (Australia)

67	Decca F 12614	Happy/Once Again	5
67	Decca F 12635	Make Mine Music/Enjoy It	6

RUSH (Canada)

77	Mercury RUSH 7	Closer To The Heart/Bastille Day/Temples Of Syrinx (metallic blue or beige labels)	15/6
78	Mercury RUSH 12	Closer To The Heart/Anthem/Bastille Day/Temples Of Syrinx (12", p/s)	10
80	Mercury RADIO 7	Spirit Of Radio/The Trees (p/s)	6
80	Mercury RADIO 12	Spirit Of Radio/The Trees/Working Man (12", p/s)	10
81	Mercury VITAL 7	Vital Signs/In The Mood (p/s)	5
81	Mercury VITAL 12	Vital Signs/In The Mood/A Passage To Bangkok/Circumstances (12", p/s)	8
81	Mercury EXIT 7	Tom Sawyer (live)/A Passage To Bangkok (live) (p/s)	5
81	Mercury EXIT 12	Tom Sawyer (live)/A Passage To Bangkok (live)/Red Barchetta (live) (12", p/s)	8
81	Mercury RUSH 1	Closer To The Heart (live)/The Trees (live) (p/s)	5
82	Mercury RUSH 8	New World Man/Vital Signs (live) (p/s)	5
82	Mercury RUSH 812	New World Man/Vital Signs (live)/Freewill (live) (12", p/s)	8
82	Mercury RUSH 9	Subdivisions/Red Barchetta (live) (p/s)	5
82	Mercury RUSH P9	Subdivisions/Red Barchetta (live) (picture disc)	8
82	Mercury RUSH 912	Subdivisions/Red Barchetta (live)/Jacob's Ladder (live) (12", p/s)	8
82	Mercury RUSH 10	Countdown/New World Man (p/s)	5
82	Mercury RUSH 10 PD	Countdown/New World Man (shaped picture disc)	25
82	Mercury RUSH 1012	Countdown/New World Man/Spirit Of Radio (live)/Interview Excerpts (12", p/s)	10
84	Vertigo RUSH 11	The Body Electric/The Analog Kid (p/s)	6
84	Vertigo RUSH 1110	The Body Electric/The Analog Kid/Distant Early Warning (10", p/s, red vinyl)	8
84	Vertigo RUSH 1112	The Body Electric/The Analog Kid/Distant Early Warning (12", p/s)	50
85	Vertigo RUSH D12	The Big Money/Territories//Closer To The Heart/Spirit Of Radio (double pack)	8
85	Vertigo RUSH G12	The Big Money/Middletown Dreams (gatefold 'window' p/s)	10
87	Vertigo RUSH 13	Time Stand Still/Force Ten (p/s, red label)	10
87	Vertigo RUSH D13	Time Stand Still/Force Ten (cut-out p/s)	6
87	Vertigo RUSH P1312	Time Stand Still/Force Ten/The Enemy Within (live) (12", picture disc)	8
87	Vertigo RUSH CD 13	Time Stand Still/Force Ten/The Enemy Within (live)/Witch Hunt (live) (CD, card sleeve)	12
88	Vertigo RUSH R14	Prime Mover/Distant Early Warning (live) (p/s, white vinyl)	7
88	Vertigo RUSH R1412	Prime Mover/Tai Shan/Distant Early Warning (live)/New World Man (live) (12", 3-D p/s)	8
88	Vertigo RUSH 1412	Prime Mover/Tai Shan/Distant Early Warning (live)/New World Man (live) (12", p/s)	12
88	Vertigo RUSH CD 14	Prime Mover/Tai Shan/Distant Early Warning (live)/New World Man (live) (CD, numbered card sleeve)	12
88	Old Gold OG 9767	Spirit Of Radio/Closer To The Heart (no p/s)	6
89	Vertigo 080 084-2	The Big Money/Red Sector A (live)/Marathon/The Big Money (video) (CD Video)	25
92	Atlantic A 7524	Roll The Bones/Dreamline (p/s)	5
92	Atlantic A 7524 CD	Roll The Bones/Anagram/Interview (CD, hologram sleeve)	8
92	Atlantic A 7491	Ghost Of A Chance/Dreamline (p/s)	5
92	Atlantic A 7491CD	Ghost Of A Chance/Dreamline/Chain Lightning/Red Tide (CD, slimline case)	8
78	Mercury 9100 059	HEMISPHERES (LP, mispressing, both sides play Side 1)	100
85	Vertigo VERHP 31	POWER WINDOWS (LP, picture disc, with discography on sleeve)	20

(see also McKenzie Doug & Bob, Max Webster Band)

JENNIFER RUSH & ELTON JOHN

87	CBS 650 865-8	Flames Of Paradise (Extended Version)/Flames Of Paradise (Instrumental)/Call My Name (solo) (12", p/s)	7

(see also Elton John)

MERRILEE RUSH & TURNABOUTS

68	Bell BLL 1013	Angel Of The Morning/Reap What You Sow	5
68	Bell BLL 1026	That Kind Of Woman/Sunshine And Roses	5
69	Bell BLL 1041	Reach Out I'll Be There/Love Street	6
68	Bell MBLL/SBLL 109	MERRILEE RUSH (LP)	15

OTIS RUSH

66	Vocalion V-P 9260	Homework/I Have To Laugh	20
69	Blue Horizon 57-3159	All Your Love/Double Trouble	18
68	Blue Horizon 7-63222	THIS ONE'S A GOOD UN (LP)	55
69	Atlantic 588 188	MOURNING IN THE MORNING (LP)	35
70s	Atlantic K 40495	MOURNING IN THE MORNING (LP, reissue)	15
70	Python KM 3	GROANING THE BLUES (LP)	40
76	Delmark DS 63?	COLD DAY IN HELL (LP)	12
78	Sonet SNTF756	TROUBLES, TROUBLES (LP)	15

TOM RUSH

67	Elektra EKSN 45004	Who Do You Love/On The Road Again	6
67	Elektra EKSN 45015	On The Road Again/Love's Made A Fool Of You	6
68	Elektra EKSN 45025	No Regrets/Shadow Dream Song	5
68	Elektra EKSN 45032	Something In The Way She Moves/Rockport Sunday	5
66	Xtra XTRA 5024	BLUES, SONGS & BALLADS (LP)	20
66	Xtra XTRA 5053	I GOT A MIND TO RAMBLE (LP)	20
67	Elektra EKL 308	TAKE A LITTLE WALK WITH ME (LP, also stereo EKS 7308)	30
68	Elektra EKL 4018	THE CIRCLE GAME (LP, red label, also stereo EKS 74018)	20
69	Elektra EKL 4062	CLASSIC RUSH (LP, red label, also stereo EKS 74062)	20
70	CBS 63940	TOM RUSH (LP)	12
70	CBS 64268	WRONG END OF A RAINBOW (LP)	12
71	Elektra EKS 74062	CLASSIC RUSH (LP, reissue, 'butterfly' label)	12
72	CBS 64887	MERRIMACK COUNTRY (LP)	12

MINT VALUE £

PATRICE RUSHEN
77   Prestige PR 10101   SHOUT IT OUT (LP) 10

MARTIN RUSHENT
79   Albion DEL 1   Give It All You've Got/Why Bother To Fight (p/s) 4

JIMMY RUSHING (& ADA MOORE)
57	Philips BBE 12150	CAT MEETS CHICK (EP, as Jimmy Rushing, Buck Clayton & Ada Moore)	20
57	Vanguard EPP 14003	LITTLE JIMMY ALL STAR BAND (EP)	15
57	Parlophone GEP 8597	JIMMY RUSHING (EP)	15
58	Parlophone GEP 8695	THE WAY I FEEL (EP)	15
63	Ember EMB 4523	JIMMY RUSHING (EP)	15
55	Vanguard PPT 12002	SINGS THE BLUES (10" LP)	12
57	Vanguard PPT 12016	SHOWCASE (10" LP)	30
57	Philips BBL 7105	CAT MEETS CHICK (LP, with Ada Moore & Buck Clayton)	25
57	Philips BBL 7166	THE JAZZ ODYSSEY OF JAMES RUSHING ESQ (LP, with Buck Clayton)	20
58	Vanguard PPL 11008	IF THIS AIN'T THE BLUES (LP)	20
58	Philips BBL 7252	LITTLE JIMMY RUSHING AND THE BIG BRASS (LP, also stereo SBBL 524)	18
60	Philips BBL 7360	RUSHING LULLABIES (LP)	20
61	Philips BBL 7484	THE SMITH GIRLS — BESSIE, CLARA (LP, also stereo SBBL 631) ...	20/25
66	Ace Of Hearts AH 119	BLUES I LOVE TO SING (LP)	18
67	Golden Guinea GGL 0384	FIVE FEET OF SOUL (LP)	15
67	Fontana FJL 405	LISTEN TO THE BLUES (LP)	12
67	HMV CLP/CSD 3632	EVERYDAY I HAVE THE BLUES (LP)	15
71	Vanguard VRS 8513	IF THIS AIN'T THE BLUES (LP, reissue)	15
72	Vanguard VRS 8518	GOING TO CHICAGO (LP)	12

(see also Count Basie, Dave Brubeck)

JIMMY RUSHING/CHAMPION JACK DUPREE
64   Ember CJS 800   TWO SHADES OF BLUE (LP, 1 side each) 20

(see also Champion Jack Dupree)

BARBARA RUSKIN
65	Piccadilly 7N 35224	Halfway To Paradise/I Can't Believe In Miracles	7
65	Piccadilly 7N 35246	You Can't Blame A Girl For Trying/No More To Fall	8
66	Piccadilly 7N 35274	Well How Does It Feel/Wishing Your Life Away	7
66	Piccadilly 7N 35296	Song Without End/Love Came Too Late	7
66	Piccadilly 7N 35328	Light Of Love/At Times Like These Mama	7
67	Parlophone R 5571	Take It Easy/Sunshowers	6
67	Parlophone R 5593	Euston Station/Hear That Telephone	6
67	Parlophone R 5642	Come Into My Arms Again/Just A Little While Longer	8
68	Parlophone R 5685	Is This Another Way/The Night Of The Spanish Tightrope Walker ...	5
68	President PT 217	Pawnbroker Pawnbroker/Almost	5
69	President PT 238	Gentlemen Please/24th Of July	5
69	President PT 261	Hail Love/Lady Of Leisure	5
70	President PT 280	A Little Bit Of This (And A Little Bit Of That)/Where Are We	5

ROGER RUSKIN SPEAR
72   United Artists UAG 29381   ELECTRIC SHOCKS (LP) 18

(see also Bonzo Dog Doo-Dah Band, Topo D. Bill)

LONNIE RUSS
62   Fontana 267263 TF   Something Old Something New/My Wife Can't Cook 6

THANE RUSSAL (& THREE)
66	CBS 202049	Security/Your Love Is Burning Me (some with p/s)	150/50
66	CBS 202403	Drop Everything And Run/I Need You (solo)	75

ANDY RUSSELL
58	RCA RCA 1076	Seven Daughters/A Certain Smile	5
58	RCA RCA 1076	Seven Daughters/A Certain Smile (78)	8

BOBBY RUSSELL
68	Bell BLL 1019	Dusty/I Made You This Way	4
68	Bell BLL 1034	1432 Franklin Pike Circle Hero/Let's Talk About It	4
69	Bell BLL 1050	Carlie/Ain't Society Great?	4

BRENDA RUSSELL
79   A&M AMLJ 739   BRENDA RUSSELL (LP) 10

CONNIE RUSSELL
54	Capitol CL 14171	No One But You/One Arabian Night	10
54	Capitol CL 14197	Love Me/Papa's Puttin' The Pressure On	8
55	Capitol CL 14214	Foggy Night In San Francisco/This Is My Love	8
55	Capitol CL 14236	Ayuh, Ayuh/I'm Making Believe	15
55	Capitol CL 14246	Snow Dreams/Green Fire	8
55	Capitol CL 14268	Farewell, Farewell/The Magnificent Matador	8
57	Capitol CL 14676	All Of You/This Is My Love	6

DAVE RUSSELL
66   Columbia DB 7828   When I Grow Too Old To Dream/All The Tears In The World 4

(see also Dave & Diamonds)

DOROTHY RUSSELL
71   Duke Reid DR 2524   You're The One I Love/Version 5

JANE RUSSELL
51	London L 956	Dear Dear Dear/I Can't Get Started With You (78)	15
51	London L 969	Five Little Miles From San Berdoo/You'll Know (78)	15
53	Columbia SCM 5043	Please Do It Again/Two Sleepy People (B-side with Bob Lowery) ...	15

53	Columbia DB 3293	Please Do It Again/Two Sleepy People (B-side with Bob Lowery) (78)	18
53	MGM MGM 662	A Little Girl From Little Rock/When Love Goes Wrong (78)	15
53	MGM MGM 664	Bye Bye Baby/Ain't There Anyone Here For Love? (78)	15
56	Capitol CL 14590	If You Wanna See Mamie Tonight/Keep Your Eyes On The Hands	12
59	MGM MGM-EP 702	JANE RUSSELL (EP)	25

JOHNNY RUSSELL
| 60 | MGM MGM 1074 | Lonesome Boy/Baby Won't You Tell Me So | 7 |

KEITH RUSSELL
| 65 | Piccadilly 7N 35235 | People Get Ready/Paradise | 5 |

LEON RUSSELL
65	Dot DS 16771	Everybody's Talkin' 'Bout The Young/It's Alright With Me	10
70	A&M AMS 788	Roll Away The Stone/Hummingbird	5
71	A&M AMS 806	Delta Lady/Apple Pisces Lady	5
71	A&M AMS 841	Ballad Of Mad Dogs And Englishmen/CLAUDIA LINNEAR: Let It Be (p/s)	5
70	A&M AMLS 982	LEON RUSSELL (LP, with Shelter People)	12
71	A&M AMLS 65003	LEON RUSSELL AND THE SHELTER PEOPLE (LP)	12
72	A&M AMLS 68089	ASYLUM CHOIR II (LP, as Leon Russell & Asylum Choir, with Marc Benno)	12
72	A&M AMLS 68911	CARNEY (LP)	12

(see also Asylum Choir)

PAULA RUSSELL
| 75 | Black Magic BM 101 | Blowin' My Mind To Pieces/BOB RELF: Blowin' My Mind To Pieces | 4 |

PEE WEE RUSSELL & RUBY BRAFF
| 50 | Melodisc MEL 1137 | Baby Won't You Please Come Home/Dinah (78) | 8 |
| 57 | London Jazz LTZ-C 15061 | JAZZ AT STORYVILLE VOL. 2 (LP) | 12 |

RAY RUSSELL QUARTET
68	CBS Realm 52586	TURN CIRCLE (LP)	18
69	CBS Realm 52663	DRAGON HILL (LP)	18
71	RCA SF 8214	JUNE 11TH 1971 (LP)	15
71	CBS 64271	RITES AND RITUALS (LP)	30
73	Black Lion BLP 12100	SECRET ASYLUM (LP)	12

(see also Running Man, Mouse, Chopyn)

ROLAND RUSSELL
| 68 | Nu Beat NB 019 | Rhythm Hips/RHYTHM FLAMES: Deltone Special | 8 |

ROSALIND RUSSELL & EDITH ADAMS
| 55 | Brunswick 05406 | Ohio/Little Bit Of Love | 5 |

RUSSELL FAMILY
| 75 | Topic 12TS 251 | OF DOOLIN COUNTY CLARE (LP, with insert) | 12 |

RUSSIAN ROULETTE
| 84 | Red Bus RBUS 86 | Come Into My Room/Lyin' Again (p/s) | 5 |

(see also Paul King, Mungo Jerry)

CHARLIE RUSSO
| 63 | Stateside SS 165 | Preacherman/Teresa | 6 |

RUSTIKS
| 64 | Decca F 11960 | What A Memory Can Do/Hello Anne | 7 |
| 65 | Decca F 12059 | I'm Not The Loving Kind/Can't You See | 6 |

RUSTLERS
| 61 | Pye 7N 15398 | High Strung/Matter Of Who | 8 |

RUSTY & DOUG (Kershaw)
59	Oriole CB 1510	Hey Mae!/Why Don't You Love Me	175
59	Oriole CB 1510	Hey Mae!/Why Don't You Love Me (78)	100
59	London HL 8972	I Like You (Like This)/Dancing Shoes	25
59	London HL 8972	I Like You (Like This)/Dancing Shoes (78)	50
62	Polydor NH 66970	Hey Mae!/Sweet Thing	40
62	Fontana 267 238 TF	Cajun Joe (The Ballad Of The Bayou)/Sweet Sweet Girl To Me	12

(see also Doug Kershaw)

RUSTY HARNESS
| 70 | Ember EMB S 283 | Ain't Gonna Get Married/Goodbye (some in p/s) | 10/5 |
| 73 | Ember SE 8024 | DISCOTHEQUE EXPLOSION (LP) | 10 |

RUSTY NAIL
| 60s | Hi-Fi MEP 3093 | RUSTY NAIL (EP, some in p/s) | 100/40 |

RUTH
| 67 | Columbia DB 8216 | Leaf In The Wind/Society's Child | 6 |
| 68 | Columbia DB 8386 | Cherish/Until It's Time For You To Go | 6 |

MIKE RUTHERFORD
| 80 | Charisma CB 364 | Time And Time Again/At The End Of The Day (p/s, correct B-side & label) | 6 |
| 80 | Charisma CB 364 | Time And Time Again/Overnight Job (p/s, with new label on B-side, credits & plays "Overnight Job") | 5 |

(see also Genesis, Mike & Mechanics)

RUTLES
| 78 | Warner Bros K 17125 | I Must Be In Love/Cheese And Onions/With A Girl Like You (p/s) | 5 |
| 78 | Warner Bros K 17180 | Let's Be Natural/Piggy In The Middle | 6 |

(see also Dirk & Stig, Neil Innes, Monty Python, Beach Boys, Patto)

RUTS (D.C.)
79	People Unite SJP 795	In A Rut/H-Eyes (1,000 only, black-ringed label)	20
79	People Unite RUT 1	In A Rut/H-Eyes (repressing)	5
79	Virgin VS 285	Something That I Said/Give Youth A Chance (p/s)	4

MINT VALUE £

79	Virgin VS 298	Jah War/I Ain't Sofisticated (p/s)	5
80	Virgin VS 327	Staring At The Rude Boys/Love In Vain (gatefold p/s with competition sticker, or normal p/s)	6/4
80	Virgin VS 370	West One (Shine On Me)/The Crack (p/s)	4
80	RSO RSO 71	Babylon's Burning/XTC: Take This Town (p/s)	6
81	Virgin VS 396	Different View/Formula Eyes (p/s, as Ruts D.C.)	5
82	Bohemian BO 2	Whatever We Do/Push Yourself — Make It Work (p/s, as Ruts D.C.)	12
83	Bohemian BO 3	Weak Heart/Militant (white label, with paper insert; as Ruts D.C., promo only)	15
83	Bohemian BO 4	Stepping Bondage/Lobotomy/Rich Bitch (p/s)	12
83	Virgin VS 583-12	Babylon's Burning/Something That I Said/Staring At The Rude Boys/West One (Shine On Me) (12" EP, p/s)	7
87	Strange Fruit SFPSC 011	PEEL SESSION 14.5.79 (EP, cassette)	5
79	Virgin V 2132	THE CRACK (LP, stickered '£3.99 pay no more')	10
80	Virgin V 2188	GRIN AND BEAR IT (LP, with photo insert, stickered '£3.99 pay no more')	10
81	Virgin V 2193	ANIMAL NOW (LP, as Ruts D.C., stickered 'Ruts D.C. list price £3.99')	10
82	Bohemian BOLP 4	RHYTHM COLLISION (LP, as Ruts D.C.)	10

(see also Laurel Aitken, Typhoons, Pete Zear)

BARRY RYAN (& MAJORITY)

68	MGM MGM 1423	Goodbye/I'm So Sad	5
68	MGM MGM 1442	Eloise/Love I Almost Found You (as Barry Ryan & Majority)	5
68	MGM MGM 1464	Love Is Love/I'll Be On My Way Dear	6
69	Polydor 56348	The Hunt/No Living Without Her	6
70	Polydor 56370	Magical Spiel/Caroline	5
70	Polydor 2001 035	Kitsch/Give Me A Sign	5
71	Polydor 2001 154	It Is Written/Annabella	5
72	Polydor 2001 335	From My Head To My Toes/Alimony Money Blues	5
69	MGM MGM-C(S) 8106	SINGS PAUL RYAN (LP)	25
69	Polydor 583 067	BARRY RYAN (LP)	18

(see also Paul & Barry Ryan)

CATHY RYAN

53	MGM SP 1051	Show Me The Way To Go Home/If I Had You	6

(see also Art Mooney)

KRIS RYAN (& QUESTIONS)

64	Mercury MF 818	Miss Ann/She Told Me Lies (as Kris Ryan & Questions)	7
64	Mercury MF 832	Don't Play That Song/If You Don't Come Back	8
64	Mercury MF 852	Marie Marie/I've Had Enough Of You Baby	7
65	Mercury MF 877	Tell Me How/She Belongs To Me	7
65	Mercury 10024 MCE	ON THE RIGHT TRACK (EP, as Kris Ryan & Questions)	40

MARION RYAN

57	Pye N 15105	Ding Dong Rock-A-Billy Wedding/That's Happiness (78)	8
58	Pye 7N 15121	Love Me Forever/Make The Man Love Me	10
58	Pye 7N 15130	Oh Oh, I'm Falling In Love Again/Always And Forever	7
58	Pye 7N 15138	Stairway Of Love/I Need You	7
58	Pye N 15138	Stairway Of Love/I Need You (78)	8
58	Pye 7N 15157	The World Goes Around And Around/Please Don't Say Goodnight	5
58	Pye 7NSR 15157	The World Goes Around And Around/Please Don't Say Goodnight (stereo)	15
59	Pye 7N 15184	Wait For Me/Jeepers Creepers	5
59	Pye N 15184	Wait For Me/Jeepers Creepers (78)	10
59	Pye 7N 15200	Jo-Jo The Dog-Faced Boy/Doin' What Comes Naturally	7
59	Pye N 15200	Jo-Jo The Dog-Faced Boy/Doin' What Comes Naturally (78)	10
59	Pye 7N 15216	Too Much/Promise Me	5
59	Pye N 15216	Too Much/Promise Me (78)	12
60	Columbia DB 4448	Sixteen Reasons/Mangos	7
60	Columbia DB 4550	It's You That I Love/Somebody	5
62	Columbia DB 4857	No Love But Your Love/An Occasional Man (A-side with John Barry & Orch.)	6
68	Philips BF 1721	Better Use Your Head/The Seasons Change	6
57	Pye Nixa NEP 24041	THAT RYAN GIRL! (EP)	10
58	Pye NEP 24079	MARION RYAN HIT PARADE (EP)	25
59	Pye N(S)PL 18030	A LADY LOVES! (LP, mono/stereo)	20
			40/50

(see also Ray Ellington, Gary Miller)

PAT RYAN

77	Folk Heritage FHR 094	LEA BOY'S LASSIE (LP)	15

PAUL & BARRY RYAN

65	Decca F 12260	Don't Bring Me Your Heartaches/To Remind Me Of Your Love	6
66	Decca F 12319	Have Pity On The Boy/There You Go	6
66	Decca F 12391	I Love Her/Gotta Go Out To Work	6
66	Decca F 12445	I Love How You Love Me/Baby I'm Sorry	6
66	Decca F 12494	Have You Ever Loved Somebody?/I'll Tell You Later	6
66	Decca F 12520	Missy, Missy/Rainbow Weather	6
67	Decca F 12567	Keep It Out Of Sight/Who Told You?	6
67	Decca F 12633	Claire/I'll Make It Worth Your While	8
67	MGM MGM 1354	Heartbreaker/Night Time	7
68	MGM MGM 1385	Pictures Of Today/Madrigal	7
67	Decca LK 4878	THE RYANS — TWO OF A KIND (LP)	30
68	MGM MGM-C(S) 8081	PAUL AND BARRY RYAN (LP)	25

(see also Barry Ryan)

PHIL RYAN & CRESCENTS
64	Columbia DB 7406	Mary Don't You Weep/Yes I Will	6
65	Columbia DB 7574	Gypsy Woman/Be Honest With Yourself	12

BOBBY RYDELL
59	Top Rank JAR 181	Kissin' Time/You'll Never Tame Me	12
59	Top Rank JAR 181	Kissin' Time/You'll Never Tame Me (78)	75
59	Top Rank JAR 227	We Got Love/I Dig Girls	10
60	Columbia DB 4429	Wild One/Little Bitty Girl	6
60	Columbia DB 4471	Swingin' School/Ding-A-Ling	7
60	Columbia DB 4495	Volare/I'd Do It Again	8
60	Columbia DB 4545	Sway/Groovy Tonight	6
61	Columbia DB 4600	Good Time Baby/Cherie	6
61	Columbia DB 4651	Don't Be Afraid/That Old Black Magic	6
61	Columbia DB 4690	The Fish/The Third House	6
61	Columbia DB 4731	I Wanna Thank You/The Door To Paradise	6
62	Columbia DB 4785	I've Got Bonnie/Lose Her	6
62	Columbia DB 4858	I'll Never Dance Again/Gee, It's Wonderful	6
63	Cameo Parkway C 108	Forget Him/Hey Ev'rybody (some in p/s)	10/6
63	Cameo Parkway C 129	It's Time We Parted/Too Much Too Soon	6
63	Cameo Parkway C 228	Cha Cha Cha/The Best Man Cried	5
63	Cameo Parkway C 242	Butterfly Baby/Love Is Blind	6
63	Cameo Parkway C 272	Since We Fell In Love/Childhood Sweetheart	5
64	Cameo Parkway C 309	Make Me Forget/Darling Jennie	5
65	Capitol CL 15371	I Can't Say Goodbye/Two Is The Loneliest Number	6
65	Capitol CL 15424	When I See That Girl Of Mine/It Takes Two	8
66	Cameo Parkway CP 601	Until I Met You/New Love	6
60	Top Rank JKP 2059	LOVINGEST (EP)	40
63	Cameo Parkway CPE 551	SWAY WITH BOBBY RYDELL (EP)	25
63	Cameo Parkway CPE 553	BOBBY RYDELL (EP)	25
63	Summit LSE 2036	BEST OF BOBBY RYDELL (EP)	12
60	Columbia 33SX 1243	WILD ONE (LP)	45
61	Columbia 33SX 1308	SINGS AND SWINGS (LP)	20
61	Columbia 33SX 1352	SALUTES "THE GREAT ONES" (LP)	20
62	Columbia 33SX 1425	RYDELL AT THE COPA (LP)	50
62	Cameo Parkway C 1019	ALL THE HITS (LP)	25
63	Cameo Parkway C 1040	ALL THE HITS VOL. 2 (LP)	25
63	Cameo Parkway C 1043	BYE BYE BIRDIE (LP)	15
63	Cameo Parkway C 1055	WILD (WOOD) DAYS (LP)	25
65	Capitol T 2281	SOMEBODY LOVES YOU (LP)	18

(see also Chubby Checker & Bobby Rydell)

RUTH RYDELL
54	London HL 8016	On The Carousel/Someone Is Crying (78)	10

FREDDIE RYDER
65	Mercury MF 864	To Get Your Love Back/A Little Thing Called Love	5
65	Mercury MF 879	Some Kind Of Wonderful/Slow Down	10
65	Mercury MF 935	Man Of The Moment/My Block	5
68	Columbia DB 8335	Shadows (I Can't See You)/Airport	5
68	Columbia DB 8427	Worst That Could Happen/World Of My Own	5

(see also Freddie Self, Trends)

MAL RYDER (& SPIRITS)
63	Decca F 11669	Cry Baby/Take Over (as Mal Ryder & Spirits)	15
64	Vocalion V 9219	See The Funny Little Clown/Slow Down	60
64	Piccadilly 7N 35209	Your Friend/Forget It (as Mal Ryder & Spirits)	20
65	Piccadilly 7N 35234	Lonely Room/Tell Your Friend	18

(see also Mal & Primitives)

MITCH RYDER (& DETROIT WHEELS)
66	Stateside SS 481	Jenny Take A Ride/Baby Jane	7
66	Stateside SS 498	Little Latin Lupe Lu/I Hope	7
66	Stateside SS 521	Breakout/I Need Help	15
66	Stateside SS 549	Devil With A Blue Dress On (Medley)/I Had It Made	7
67	Stateside SS 596	Sock It To Me Baby/I Never Had It Better	7
67	Stateside SS 2023	Too Many Fish In The Sea — Three Little Fishes/One Grain Of Sand	10
67	Stateside SS 2037	Joy/I'd Rather Go To Jail (solo)	6
67	Stateside SS 2063	What Now My Love/Blessing In Disguise (solo)	15
68	Stateside SS 2075	You Are My Sunshine/Wild Child (solo)	5
68	Stateside SS 2096	Personality/Chantilly Lace/I Make A Fool Of Myself (solo)	6
69	Dot DOT 129	Sugar Bee/I Believe (There Must Be Someone)	5
71	Avco 6105 001	Jenny Take A Ride/I Never Had It Better	5
72	Paramount PARA 3022	It Ain't Easy/Long Neck Goose	5
75	Pye Disco Demand DDS 113	You Get Your Kicks/Breakout	5
66	Stateside SE 1039	RIDIN' (EP)	40
66	Stateside S(S)L 10178	TAKE A RIDE ... (LP)	25
67	Stateside S(S)L 10189	BREAKOUT... !! (LP)	30
67	Stateside S(S)L 10204	SOCK IT TO ME (LP)	25
68	Stateside S(S)L 10229	WHAT NOW MY LOVE (LP, solo)	15
69	Bell MBLL/SBLL 114	ALL MITCH RYDER HITS (LP)	12

(see also Detroit)

RYE & QUARTERBOYS
82	Replay REPLAY 001	Fantasy/Private Number (no p/s)	4

TONY RYMOND
62	Oriole CB 1708	Handful Of Songs/She'll Have To Go	6

MINT VALUE £

SAGRAM
72 Windmill WMD 118   POP EXPLOSION SITAR STYLE (LP) 30
(see also Clem Alford, Magic Carpet)

SAHARA
73 Dawn DNLS 3068   SUNRISE (LP) 15

MORT SAHL
59 HMV CLP 1252   THE FUTURE LIES AHEAD (LP) 12

DOUG SAHM
73 Atlantic K 10293   Is Anybody Going To San Antoine/Don't Turn Around 4
73 Atlantic K 40466   DOUG SAHM AND BAND (LP) 10
(see also Sir Douglas Quintet, Bob Dylan)

OLIVER SAIN (& SHIRLEY BROWN)
72 Mojo 2092 031   St. Louis Breakdown/I Ain't Gonna Tell (with Shirley Brown) 6
74 Contempo CS 2026   Bus Stop/Nightime (solo) 6
75 Contempo CS 2057   London Express/Blowing For Love (solo) 5
(see also Shirley Brown, Fontella Bass)

ST. CHRISTOPHER
84 Bluegrass GM 001   Crystal Clear/My Fond Farewell (p/s) 12
86 Bluegrass GM 003   Go Ahead Cry/Charmelle (p/s) 10
87 Veston VOD 001   Forevermore Stars Here/Remember Me To Her/
Sinking Ships (flexidisc, p/s) 7
88 Clarity CLARITY 1   Josephine Why?/I Wish I Hadn't Hurt Her/Tell The World
(flexidisc, foldaround p/s, 33rpm) 5
89 Sarah SARAH 015   You Deserve More Than A Maybe/The Kind Of Girl/The Summer Of Love
(foldaround p/s with poster in poly bag) 4
89 Sarah SARAH 020   All Of A Tremble/My Fortune/The Hummingbird
(foldaround p/s with poster in poly bag) 4

CHERYL ST. CLAIR
66 CBS 202041   My Heart Is Not In It/We Want Love 10
66 Columbia DB 8077   What About Me/I'll Forget You Tonight 8
(see also Alison Wonder)

SAINT ETIENNE
90 Heavenly HVN 2   Only Love Can Break Your Heart/Only Love Can Break Your Heart
(Version) (p/s) 6
90 Heavenly HVN 212   Only Love Can Break Your Heart/Only Love Can Break Your Heart
(Original Version) (12", p/s) 10
90 Heavenly HVN 212R   Only Love Can Break Your Heart (A Mix Of Two Halves)/
The Official Saint Etienne World Cup Theme (12", die-cut p/s) 12
90 The Catalogue CAT 084   Only Love Can Break Your Heart (remixed by Flowered Up)/FLOWERED UP:
It's On (The Posh Facker Mix) (square flexidisc with *The Catalogue* mag) 5/4
90 Heavenly HVN 4   Kiss And Make Up/Sky's Dead (p/s) 5
90 Heavenly HVN 412   Kiss And Make Up/Sky's Dead (12", p/s) 10
90 Heavenly HVN 412R   Kiss And Make Up (Midsummer Madness Remix)/Kiss And Make Up
(Midsummer Dubness Mix) (12", p/s) 12
90 Heavenly HVN 4CD   Kiss And Make Up (7")/Kiss And Make Up (12")/Sky's Dead (CD) 18
91 Heavenly HVN 912R   Speedwell (Flying Mix)/Speedwell (Project Mix)/Nothing Can Stop Us
(Instrumental)/3D Tiger (12", p/s) 8
91 Heavenly HVN 9CD   Nothing Can Stop Us/Speedwell/
Nothing Can Stop Us (Instrumental) (CD) 15
92 Heavenly HVN 12CD   Only Love Can Break Your Heart/Only Love Can Break Your Heart
(A Mix Of Two Halves)/Filthy (CD) 8
92 Heavenly HVN 22   Live — Paris '92 (clear flexidisc, gig freebie, 1,000 only) 10
93 Heavenly HVN 2912   Hobart Paving/Who Do You Think You Are (12", p/s, mispressed with
"Hobart Paving" & "Your Head My Voice" on both sides) 15
95 Heavenly HVN 41   XMAS '95: A Christmas Gift To You/Driving Home For Christmas/
A Message In A Bottle (CD, signed fan club edition) 75
93 Heavenly HVNCDX 6   SO TOUGH/YOU NEED A MESS
OF HELP TO STAND ALONE (2-CD) 18
95 Heavenly HVNLP 9CD   I LOVE TO PAINT (CD, fan club edition, 600 only) 200
95 Heavenly HVNCD 10   TOO YOUNG TO DIE (CD, with bonus CD "Too Young To Die
— The Remix Album" [HVN LP 10CDR]) 25
(see also 50 Year Void, Sarah Cracknell, Lovecut D.B.)

SAINT ORCHESTRA
78 Pye 7N 46127   Return Of The Saint/Funko (p/s) 12

BARRY ST. JOHN
64 Decca F 11933   A Little Bit Of Soap/Thing Of The Past 10
64 Decca F 11975   Bread And Butter/Cry To Me 10
65 Decca F 12111   Mind How You Go/Don't You Feel Proud 12
65 Decca F 12145   Hey Boy/I've Been Crying 10
65 Columbia DB 7783   Come Away Melinda/Gotta Brand New Man 8
66 Columbia DB 7868   Everything I Touch Turns To Tears/Sounds Like My Baby 45
68 Major Minor MM 587   Cry Like A Baby/Long And Lonely Night 6
69 Major Minor MM 604   By The Time I Get To Phoenix/Turn On Your Light 6
69 M. Minor MMLP/SMLP 43   ACCORDING TO ST. JOHN (LP) 30

BRIDGET ST. JOHN
69 Dandelion K 4404   To B Without A Hitch/Autumn Lullaby 7
70 Warner Bros WB 8019   If You've Got Money/Yep 8
72 Polydor 2001 280   Fly High/There's A Place I Know/Suzanne (p/s) 8
72 Polydor 2001 361   Nice/Goodbye Baby Goodbye 6
73 MCA MUS 1203   Passing Thru'/The Road Was Lonely On My Own 7
69 Dandelion 63750   ASK ME NO QUESTIONS (LP, gatefold sleeve) 35

Bridget ST. JOHN

CRISPIAN ST. PETERS

BUFFY SAINTE-MARIE

71	Dandelion DAN 8007	SONGS FOR THE GENTLE MAN
		(LP, gatefold sleeve, also listed as K 49007) 30
72	Dandelion 2310 193	THANK YOU FOR... (LP, gatefold sleeve) 30
74	Chrysalis CHR 1062	JUMBLE QUEEN (LP) 12
	(see also Ron Geesin, Quiver)	

TAMMY ST. JOHN

64	Pye 7N 15682	Boys/Hey Hey Hey Hey 7
65	Pye 7N 15762	He's The One For Me/I'm Tired Of Just Looking At You 7
65	Pye 7N 15948	Dark Shadows And Empty Hallways/I Mustn't Cry 7
66	Pye 7N 17042	Nobody Knows What's Goin' On (In My Mind But Me)/
		Stay Together Young Lovers 25
69	Tangerine DP 0007	Concerning Love/Sound Of Love 6
	(see also Trends)	

ST. LOUIS JIMMY

53	Esquire 10-319	Harlem Bound/MEMPHIS SLIM: Holiday For Boogie (78) 25

ST. LOUIS UNION

66	Decca F 12318	Girl/Respect 20
66	Decca F 12386	Behind The Door/English Tea. 30
66	Decca F 12508	East Side Story/Think About Me 40

OLIVER ST. PATRICK & DIAMONDS

67	Trojan TR 005	I Want To Be Loved By You/Tulips 10

CRISPIAN ST. PETERS

65	Decca F 12080	At This Moment/Goodbye, You'll Forget Me. 10
65	Decca F 12207	No No No/Three Goodbyes 10
65	Decca F 12287	You Were On My Mind/What I'm Gonna Be. 6
66	Decca F 12359	The Pied Piper/Sweet Dawn My True Love 6
66	Decca F 12480	Changes/My Little Brown Eyes 6
66	Decca F 12525	But She's Untrue/Your Ever Changin' Mind. 6
67	Decca F 12596	Almost Persuaded/You Have Gone 6
67	Decca F 12677	Free Spirit/I'm Always Crying 7
68	Decca F 12761	That's The Time/The Silent Times 7
68	Decca F 12861	Carolina/That's Why We Are Through 7
69	Mencap MEN 002	Monumental Queen/Soft As A Rose 7
70	Decca F 13055	So Long/My Little Brown Eyes (withdrawn) .... 12+
70	Square SQ 2	Wandering Hobo/Love, Love, Love 6
74	Santa Ponsa PNS 17	Do Daddy Do/Every Time You Sinned 6
67	Decca DFE 8678	ALMOST PERSUADED (EP). 45
66	Decca LK 4805	FOLLOW ME... (LP) 35
70	Square SQA 102	SIMPLY... CRISPIAN ST. PETERS (LP) 18

KIRBY ST. ROMAIN

63	Stateside SS 199	Summer's Comin'/Miss You So 6

SAINT STEVEN

69	Probe SPB 1005	OVER THE HILLS/THE BASTICH (LP) 50

ST. VALENTINE'S DAY MASSACRE

67	Fontana TF 883	Brother Can You Spare A Dime/Al's Party (some with p/s) 100/40
	(see also Artwoods)	

ST. VITUS DANCE

80s	Lyntone LYN 17627	Meet Mohammed/BLAH BLAH BLAH: Heavenly View (1-sided 33rpm
	Good Vibes H 002	flexidisc with *Helden* fanzine). 5/4

BUFFY SAINTE-MARIE

65	Fontana TF 574	Until It's Time For You To Go/The Flower And The Apple Tree	5
65	Fontana TF 614	The Universal Soldier/Cripple Creek	5
66	Fontana TF 695	Timeless Love/Lady Margret	5
72	Vanguard VRS 35143	I'm Gonna Be A Country Girl Again/Piney Wood Hills	5
75	Vanguard VS 5002	I'm Gonna Be A Country Girl Again/Now That The Buffalo's Gone	5
65	Fontana TFL 6040	IT'S MY WAY! (LP)	15
65	Fontana TFL 6047	MANY A MILE (LP)	15
66	Fontana (S)TFL 6071	LITTLE WHEEL SPIN AND SPIN (LP)	15
71	Vanguard VSD 79311	SHE USED TO WANNA BE A BALLERINA (LP)	12
71	Vanguard VSD 79250	FIRE & FEET & CANDLELIGHT (LP)	12
71	Vanguard VSD 79300	ILLUMINATIONS (LP)	12
72	Vanguard VSD 79280	I'M GONNA BE A COUNTRY GIRL AGAIN (LP)	12
72	Vanguard VSD 79312	MOONSHOT (LP)	12
73	Vanguard VSD 3/4	THE BEST OF BUFFY SAINTE-MARIE (2-LP)	15
73	Vanguard VSD 79330	QUIET PLACES (LP)	12
74	Vanguard VSD 79340	NATIVE NORTH AMERICAN CHILD (LP)	12
74	MCA MCG 3517	BUFFY (LP)	12
75	MCA MCF 2594	CHANGING WOMAN (LP)	12
76	ABC ABCL 5168	SWEET AMERICA (LP)	15

SAINTS (U.K.)

63	Pye 7N 15548	Wipe Out/Midgets	20
63	Pye 7N 15582	Husky Team/Pigtails	20

(see also Tornados, Heinz)

SAINTS (U.K.)

64	MJB BEV 73/4	SAINTS (10" LP, private pressing)	350
64	MJB BEVLP 127/8	SAINTS ALIVE! (LP, private pressing)	350

SAINTS (Jamaica)

66	Doctor Bird DB 1009	Brown Eyes/BABA BROOKS & HIS BAND: King Size	15
69	Big Shot BI 522	Windy Part One/Windy Part Two	8

SAINTS (Jamaica)

73	Count Shelley CS 043	How Long/Feeling Good	5

SAINTS (Australia)

76	Power Exchange PX 242	I'm Stranded/No Time (p/s)	7
77	Power Exchange PXE 101	I'm Stranded/(STANLEY FRANK: 2 tracks) (p/s)	5
77	Harvest HAR 5123	Erotic Neurotic/One Way Street (no p/s)	5
77	Harvest HAR 5130	This Perfect Day/L-I-E-S (no p/s)	5
77	Harvest 12 HAR 5130	This Perfect Day/L-I-E-S/Do The Robot (12", with 'disclaimer' stickered p/s)	8
77	Harvest HAR 5137	1, 2, 3, 4 (EP, p/s)	5
77	Harvest HAR 5137	1, 2, 3, 4 (EP, double pack, gatefold p/s)	8
78	Harvest HAR 5148	Know Your Product/Run Down (no p/s)	5
78	Harvest HAR 5166	Security/All Times Through Paradise (p/s)	5
89	Bucketfull Of Brains BOB 26	I Dreamed Of Marie Antoinette/MOCK TURTLES: Croppies Lie Down (free with *Bucketfull Of Brains* magazine, issue 32)	6/4
77	Harvest SHSP 4065	I'M STRANDED (LP)	25
78	Harvest SHSP 4078	ETERNALLY YOURS (LP, with inner sleeve)	20
78	Harvest SHSP 4094	PREHISTORIC SOUNDS (LP)	20

SAINTS JAZZ BAND

51	Parlophone R 3427	I Want A Girl Just Like The Girl That Married Dear Old Dad/CRANE RIVER JAZZ BAND: I'm Travelling (78)	8
51	Parlophone R 3427	I Want A Girl Just Like The Girl That Married Dear Old Dad/CRANE RIVER JAZZ BAND: I'm Travelling	10
53	Parlophone MSP 6042	Hey Lawdy Papa/Who Walks In When I Walk Out?	8
56	Parlophone R 4240	Mahogany Hall Stomp/Stack O' Lee Blues	7
57	Parlophone R 4260	Blue Turning Grey Over You/'Till We Meet Again	6
57	Parlophone R 4304	How Come You Do Me Like You Do/Willie The Weeper	6
58	Parlophone R 4417	Swingin' The Blues/I've Found A New Baby	7
58	Parlophone R 4417	Swingin' The Blues/I've Found A New Baby (78)	8
56	Parlophone GEP 8560	SAINTS PLAY JAZZ (EP)	20
56	Parlophone GEP 8577	SAINTS JAZZ BAND (EP)	15

RUSS SAINTY (& NU NOTES)

60	Top Rank JAR 381	Happy-Go-Lucky-Me/Standing Around	10
60	Decca F 11270	Race With The Devil/Too Shy (solo)	10
61	Decca F 11325	Don't Believe Him, Donna/Your Other Love (solo)	7
62	HMV POP 1055	Keep Your Love Locked/I've Got A Girl (as Russ Sainty & Nu Notes)	6
62	HMV POP 1069	Send Me The Pillow That You Dream On/What Do You Know About That (solo)	6
63	HMV POP 1181	Unforgettable Love/The Twinkle In Your Eye (solo)	6
64	Parlophone R 5168	That's How I'm Gonna Love You/Lonesome Town (as Russ Sainty & Nu-Notes)	6
64	Columbia DB 7394	This Is My Lovely Day/Bless You, Girl (as Russ Sainty & Nu-Notes)	6
65	Columbia DB 7521	It Ain't That Easy/And Then (solo)	6
65	Columbia DB 7708	Saving My Tears (For A Rainy Day)/She (solo)	6
60s	Society SOC 1035	THE GENIUS OF LENNON AND McCARTNEY (LP)	15

(see also Nu Notes)

SIR SIDNEY SAITHESWAITE & GARBAGE COLLECTORS

67	Parlophone R 5591	Tea Lovely Tea/I Like Knees	4
67	Parlophone R 5636	Our Mabel/Chase Me Round The Garden	4

KYU SAKAMOTO

63	HMV POP 1171	Sukiyaki/Anoko No Namae Wa Nantenkana	5
63	HMV POP 1211	China Nights/Benkyo No Cha Cha Cha	5
64	HMV POP 1342	Rose Rose I Love You/Sayonara Tokyo	5
62	HMV CLP 1674	SUKIYAKI (LP)	15

RUICHI SAKAMOTO
80	Island IPR 2048	Riot In Lagos/Iconic Storage (12", company sleeve)	8

(see also David Sylvian, Yellow Magic Orchestra)

(BOB) SAKER
68	Polydor BM 56231	Still Got You/Imagination (as Bob Saker)	5
68	Parlophone R 5740	Foggy Tuesday/Ooh Nana Na (as Bob Saker)	8
69	Parlophone R 5752	Hey Joe!/Christianity	8
71	CBS 7010	What A Beautiful World/City Of The Angels	5
71	CBS 7399	Even Though We Ain't Got Money/Wild Winds Are Blowing	5

SALAMANDER
70	CBS 5102	Crystal Ball/Billy	15

(see also Onyx)

SALAMANDER
71	Youngblood SSYB 14	THE TEN COMMANDMENTS (LP, gatefold sleeve)	100

SALEM
82	Hilton FMR 056	Cold As Steel/Reach To... (no p/s)	60

SOUPY SALES
65	HMV POP 1432	The Mouse/Pachalfaka	5

SALLY & ALLEY CATS
64	Parlophone R 5183	Is It Something I Said/You Forgot To Remember	8

SALLYANGIE
69	Big T BIG 126	Two Ships/Colours Of The World	15
72	Philips 6006 259	Child Of Allah/Lady Go Lightly	15
68	Transatlantic TRA 176	CHILDREN OF THE SUN (LP, gatefold sleeve)	45
78	Transatlantic TRA 176	CHILDREN OF THE SUN (LP, reissue, different single sleeve)	20

(see also Mike Oldfield)

DOUG SALMA & HIGHLANDERS
63	Philips BF 1279	Highland Fling/The Scavenger	6

SALMONTAILS
85	Oblivion OBL 001	SALMONTAILS (LP)	15

SALOME
69	Page One POF 137	Vivo Cantando/Amigos Amigos	6

SALT
78	Grapevine GRA 111	BEYOND A SONG (LP, with insert)	18

SALT & PEPPER
61	London HLU 9338	High Noon/Come Softly To Me	8

SAL SALVADOR
55	KPL 105	SAL SALVADOR QUARTET (10" LP)	12

SALVATION
69	United Artists UP 35048	Cinderella/The Village Shuck	5
69	United Artists UAS 29062	SALVATION (LP)	20

SALVATION
83	Merciful Release MR 025	Girlsoul/Evelyn (p/s)	10
83	Merciful Release MRX 025	Girlsoul/Evelyn/Dust Up (12", p/s)	12
86	Batfish Inc. BF 103	Jessica's Crime/The Shining (p/s)	6
86	Batfish Inc. USS 104	Jessica's Crime (Extended Mix)/The Shining/Shattered Sky (12", p/s)	8
86	Ediesta CALC 4	Seek: Strange Fruit/Lady Faith (p/s)	5
86	Ediesta CALCT 4	Seek: Strange Fruit/Lady Faith/Angel Pain/The Answer (12", p/s)	7
88	Karbon KAR 609	Sunshine Superman/Payola (plain sleeve)	5

RINO SALVIATI
55	Durium DC 16579	Canto Nella Valle/Ersa Do Mare (78)	8

SAMMY SALVO
58	RCA RCA 1032	Oh Julie/Say Yeah	20
58	RCA RCA 1032	Oh Julie/Say Yeah (78)	30
59	London HLP 8997	Afraid/Marble Heart	10
59	London HLP 8997	Afraid/Marble Heart (78)	50
62	Polydor NH 66974	Billy Blue/French Poodle	8

SAM & BILL
66	Pye International 7N 25355	Fly Me To The Moon/Treat Me Right	10
67	Brunswick 05973	I Feel Like Cryin'/I'll Try	20

SAM & DAVE
66	King KG 1041	No More Pain/You Ain't No Big Thing Baby	10
66	Atlantic AT 4066	You Don't Know Like I Know/Blame Me, Don't Blame My Heart	10
66	Atlantic 584 003	Hold On I'm A Comin'/I Got Everything I Need	7
66	Atlantic 584 047	If You Got The Loving (I Got The Time)/Said I Wasn't Gonna Tell Nobody	6
67	Atlantic 584 064	You Got Me Hummin'/Sleep Good Tonight	7
67	Atlantic 584 086	You Don't Know Like I Know/Blame Me, Don't Blame My Heart (reissue)	6
67	Stax 601 004	Soothe Me/Sweet Pains (initially dark blue label, later light blue)	8/5
67	Stax 601 006	When Something Is Wrong With My Baby/A Small Portion Of Your Love (initially with dark blue labels, later light blue)	8/5
67	Stax 601 023	Soul Man/May I Baby	6
68	Stax 601 030	I Thank You/Wrap It Up	5
68	Atlantic 584 192	You Don't Know What You Mean To Me/This Is Your World	6
68	Atlantic 584 211	Can't You Find Another Way/Still Is The Night	6
68	Atlantic 584 228	Everybody's Got To Believe In Somebody/If I Didn't Have A Girl Like You	5
69	Atlantic 584 237	Soul Sister, Brown Sugar/Come On In	5

69	Atlantic 584 247	You Don't Know Like I Know/Hold On I'm A Comin'.	5
69	Atlantic 584 303	Ooh, Ooh, Ooh/Holdin' On	5
70	Atlantic 584 324	Baby, Baby, Don't Stop Now/I'm Not An Indian Giver	5
66	King KGL 4001	SAM AND DAVE (LP)	30
66	Atlantic 587/588 045	HOLD ON, I'M A COMIN' (LP)	20
67	Stax 589 003	DOUBLE DYNAMITE (LP)	20
68	Stax 589 015	SOUL MEN (LP)	20
68	Major Minor MCP 5000	SAM AND DAVE (LP)	18
69	Atlantic 588 154	I THANK YOU (LP).	15
69	Atlantic 588 155	THE BEST OF SAM AND DAVE (LP)	12
69	Atlantic 587/588 181	DOUBLE TROUBLE (LP)	18
69	Atlantic 588 185	SOUL MEN (LP, reissue)	12

SAM & KITTY
| 80 | Grapevine GRP 132 | I've Got Something Good/Love Is The Greatest | 8 |

SAM APPLE PIE
69	Decca F 22932	Tiger Man (King Of The Jungle)/Sometime Girl.	10
73	DJM DJS 274	Call Me Boss/Old Tom	5
69	Decca LK-R/SKL-R 5005	SAM APPLE PIE (LP)	80
73	DJM DJLPS 429	EAST 17 (LP)	25

SAME
| 79 | Wessex WEX 267 | Wild About You/Movements (p/s) | 8 |
| 80 | Blue Print BLU 2008 | Movements/Wild About You (reissue with reversed sides & blue print on p/s) | 5 |

SAM, ERV & TOM
| 68 | Direction 58-3339 | Soul Teacher/Hard To Get. | 6 |

(see also Diplomats)

SAM GOPAL
(see under 'G')

MIKE SAMMES & HIS SINGERS
58	Fontana H 159	Heartaches/The Gang That Sang Heart Of My Heart (78)	8
59	Fontana G 232	Little Drummer Boy/Comin' Through The Rye (78)	8
59	Top Rank JAR 166	Upstairs And Downstairs/IVOR RAYMONDE: Mylene	6
62	Oriole CB 1738	Oh My Twisted Bach/Al Of A Twist	7

SAMMY
72	Philips 6006 227	Goo Ger Woogie/Big Lovin' Woman.	4
72	Philips 6006 249	Sioux Eyed Lady/70 Days	4
72	Philips 6308 136	SAMMY (LP)	20

SAMPLES
| 80 | Sample | VENDETTA (EP) | 10 |
| 84 | No Future OI 14 | Dead Hero/Fire Around Round/Suspicion (p/s). | 7 |

DAVE SAMPSON & HUNTERS
60	Columbia DB 4449	Sweet Dreams/It's Lonesome	15
60	Columbia DB 4502	If You Need Me/See You Around.	15
61	Columbia DB 4597	Why The Chicken?/1999.	10
61	Columbia DB 4625	Easy To Dream/That's All	12
62	Fontana H 361	Wide, Wide World/Since Sandy Moved Away (solo)	10
61	Columbia SEG 8095	DAVE (EP, also stereo ESG 7853)	100/125

(see also Hunters [U.K.])

TOMMY SAMPSON
58	Melodisc MEL 1411	Rockin'/Rock'n'Roll Those Big Brown Eyes (with His Strongmen)	18
58	Melodisc MEL 1411	Rockin'/Rock'n'Roll Those Big Brown Eyes (with His Strongmen) (78)	25
58	Parlophone R 4458	Lazy Train/Smooth Mood (as Tommy Sampson Orchestra)	6
58	Parlophone R 4458	Lazy Train/Smooth Mood (as Tommy Sampson Orchestra) (78)	15

SAMSON
| 69 | Instant INSP 004 | ARE YOU SAMSON (LP) | 30 |

(see also Strider)

SAMSON
| 70 | Parlophone R 5867 | Venus/Wool And Water. | 6 |

SAMSON
78	Lightning GIL 547	Telephone/Leavin' You (p/s)	35
79	Lightning GIL 553	Mr. Rock'n'Roll/Drivin' Music (p/s).	35
79	Laser LAS 6	Mr. Rock'n'Roll (remix)/Primrose Shuffle (no p/s)	12
80	EMI EMI 5061	Vice Versa (Edit)/Hammerhead (p/s, withdrawn, 1,000 demos only).	30
80	Gem GEMS 34	Vice Versa (Edit)/Hammerhead (reissue, p/s, some with sticker).	8/5
80	Gem GEMS 38	Hard Times (Remix)/Angel With A Machine Gun (p/s).	5
81	RCA RCA 67	Riding With The Angels (Edit)/Little Big Man	5
81	RCA RCA 67	Riding With The Angels (Edit)/Little Big Man (picture disc)	10
82	Polydor POSPP 471	Losing My Grip/Pyramid To The Stars (picture disc)	6
82	Polydor POSPX 471	Losing My Grip/Pyramid To The Stars/Mr. Rock'n'Roll (live)/Tomorrow Or Yesterday (live) (12" EP)	8
82	Polydor POSPG 519/ SAM 1	Life On The Run/Drivin' With ZZ!!/Walking Out On You (live)/Bright Lights (live) (double pack, gatefold p/s)	6
82	Polydor SAM 2	Red Skies/Young Idea (unissued, promo only)	18
83	Polydor PODJ 554	Red Skies (DJ Edit) (1-sided promo)	12
83	Polydor POSPP 554	Red Skies/Livin', Lovin', Lyin' (picture disc)	6
83	Polydor POSPX 554	Red Skies/Livin', Lovin', Lyin'/Running Out Of Time (12", p/s)	8
84	Polydor POSP 670	Are You Ready?/Front Page News (p/s)	5
84	Polydor POSPP 670	Are You Ready?/Front Page News (picture disc)	8
84	Polydor POSPX 670	Are You Ready?/Front Page News/La Grange (12", p/s)	8
84	Polydor POSP 680	The Fight Goes On/Riding With The Angels (re-recording) (p/s)	5

84	Polydor POSPX 680	The Fight Goes On (Long Version)/Riding With The Angels (re-recording)/	
		Vice Versa (live) (12", p/s)	8
84	Thunderbolt THBE 1.003	Mr Rock'n'Roll/Primrose Shuffle/Telephone/Leavin' You (12", p/s)	8
86	Capitol CL 395	Vice Versa (Remix)/Losing My Grip (Remix) (p/s)	5
86	Capitol 12CLP 395	Vice Versa (Remix)/Losing My Grip (Remix) (12", picture disc)	8
87	Metal Hammer METAL 1	One Day's Heroes (as Paul Samson's Empire)/CHARIOT: Life On The Line/	
		HEAVY PETTIN': Heaven Sent/STRANGEWAYS: Never Gonna Lose It	
		(EP, with/without *Metal Hammer* magazine)	6/4
79	Laser LAP 1	SURVIVORS (LP)	15
80	Gem GEMLP 108	HEAD ON (LP, 2 different mixes, A1/B1 or A2/B2 in matrix;	
		each with insert, some with free patch)	15/12
80	Gem GEMLP 108	HEAD ON (LP, mispress with A1/B2 matrix)	20
81	Gem GEMLP 113	SHOCK TACTICS (LP, release cancelled)	
81	RCA LP 5031	SHOCK TACTICS (LP, with insert)	15
82	Polydor POLS 1077	BEFORE THE STORM (LP, initially with poster, stickered sleeve)	12
84	Polydor POLD 5132	DON'T GET MAD, GET EVEN (2-LP, white labels, 2 different mixes	
		of same album, promo only)	35

(see also Bruce Dickinson, Iron Maiden, John McCoy, Tiger, Colin Town[e]s, Thunderstick, Nicky Moore, Mammoth, Egypt)

SAM THE SHAM & PHARAOHS

65	MGM MGM 1269	Woolly Bully/Ain't Gonna Move	8
65	MGM MGM 1278	Ju Ju Hand/Big City Lights	7
65	MGM MGM 1285	Ring Dang Doo/Don't Try It	7
66	MGM MGM 1298	Red Hot/Long Long Way	7
66	MGM MGM 1315	Li'l Red Riding Hood/Love Me Like Before	7
66	MGM MGM 1326	The Hair On My Chinny Chin Chin/The Out Crowd	6
66	MGM MGM 1331	How Do You Catch A Girl/The Love You Left Behind	6
67	MGM MGM 1337	Oh That's Bad No That's Good/Take What You Can Get	6
67	MGM MGM 1343	Black Sheep/My Day's Gonna Come	10
68	MGM MGM 1379	Yakety Yak/Let Our Lovelight Shine	6
69	MGM MGM 1473	Woolly Bully/Ring Dang Doo	5
66	MGM MGM-EP 794	RED HOT (EP)	50
65	MGM MGM-C 1007	WOOLY BULLY (LP)	35
66	MGM MGM-C(S) 8032	LI'L RED RIDING HOOD (LP)	30
71	Atco 2400 146	SAM HARD AND HEAVY (LP, as Sam Samudio)	12

LEROY SAMUEL
72	Punch PH 113	Trying To Wreck My Life/JOHN HOLT: Pride And Joy	6

(Phillip) SAMUEL THE FIRST
71	Summit SUM 8515	Sounds Of Babylon/BEVERLEY'S ALL STARS: Second Babylon Version	8

JERRY SAMUELS
56	HMV 7M 411	Puppy Love/The Chosen Few	12
56	HMV POP 219	Puppy Love/The Chosen Few (78)	12

(see also Napoleon XIV)

WINSTON SAMUELS
64	Columbia DB 7405	You Are The One/Angela	8
64	Rio R 26	Follow/I'm So Glad	12
64	Black Swan WI 419	Luck Will Come My Way/LLOYD BREVITT: One More Time	12
64	Black Swan WI 426	You Are The One/Gloria Love (B-side actually by Beltones)	12
65	Ska Beat JB 196	Be Prepared/Jericho Wall	15
65	Ska Beat JB 213	My Bride To Be/LLOYD PREVITT: Wayward Ska	15
65	Ska Beat JB 214	Never Again/My Angel	15
66	Ska Beat JB 238	What Have I Done/Broken Hearted	15
66	Ska Beat JB 241	Ups And Downs/Come What May	15
66	Ska Beat JB 244	Time Will Tell/I'm Sorry	15
67	Island WI 3051	The Greatest/FREDDIE & FITZY: Truth Hurts	15
67	Island WI 3053	I Won't Be Discouraged/FREDDIE & FITZIE: Why Did My Little Girl Cry	15

SAMURAI
69	United Artists UP 2242	Good Morning Starshine/Temple Of Gold	4

SAMURAI
71	Greenwich GSLP 1003	SAMURAI (LP)	90

(see also Greenslade, Web)

SAMURAI
84	Ebony EBON 25	Fires Of Hell/Dreams Of The World (p/s)	10
84	Ebony EBON 24	SACRED BLADE (LP)	10

ALEX SANDERS
70	A&M AMLS 984	A WITCH IS BORN (LP, foldout sleeve with warning sticker, withdrawn)	40

GARY SANDERS
66	Warner Bros WB 5676	Ain't No Beatle/Ain't I Good To You	8

GEORGE SANDERS
58	HMV 7EG 8395	THE GEORGE SANDERS TOUCH (EP)	8

PHAROAH SANDERS
71	Probe SPB 1019	DEAF, DUMB AND BLIND (LP)	15
73	Impulse AS 9199	DEAF, DUMB AND BLIND (LP, reissue)	12
73	Impulse AS 9219	BLACK UNITY (LP)	12
73	Impulse AS 9227	LIVE AT THE EAST (LP)	12
73	Impulse AS 9229-2	THE BEST OF PHAROAH SANDERS (LP, original issue)	12
76	Impulse IMPL 8023	WISDOM THROUGH MUSIC (LP)	12
77	Impulse AS 9138	TAUHID (LP)	12
77	Impulse AS 9181	KARMA (LP)	12
77	Impulse AS 9190	JEWELS OF THOUGHT (LP)	12
77	Impulse AS 9206	THEMBI (LP)	12

RAY SANDERS
60	London HLG 7106	A World So Full Of Love/A Little Bitty Tear (export issue)	15

TOMMY SANDERSON & SANDMEN
61	Ember EMB 131	Deadline/Candelglow	8
62	Ember EMB 152	Ding Dong Rag/Piano A-Go Go	8

CHRIS SANDFORD (& CORONETS)
63	Decca F 11778	Not Too Little — Not Too Much/I'm Lookin'	6
64	Decca F 11842	You're Gonna Be My Girl/Don't Leave Me Now (with Coronets)	6
65	Fontana TF 633	I Wish They Wouldn't Always Say I Sound Like The Guy From The U.S.A. Blues/Little Man, Nobody Cares	7

FLO SANDON
59	Durium DC 16641	La Strada Dell Amore/Passion Flower (78)	8

GERRY SANDON
96	Twangsville TW 001	JUST GERRY (EP)	8

JOHNNY SANDON (& REMO FOUR)
63	Pye 7N 15542	Lies/On The Horizon (as Johnny Sandon & Remo Four)	10
63	Pye 7N 15559	Magic Potion/Yes (as Johnny Sandon & Remo Four)	10
64	Pye 7N 15602	Sixteen Tons/The Blizzard	8
64	Pye 7N 15665	Donna Means Heartbreak/Some Kinda Wonderful	8
64	Pye 7N 15717	The Blizzard/(I'd Be A) Legend In My Time	7

(see also Remo Four)

SAND PEBBLES
67	Track 604 015	Love Power/Because Of Love	12
68	Toast TT 505	If You Didn't Hear Me The First Time/Flower Power	6
69	Track 604 028	Love Power/Because Of Love (reissue)	5

SANDPIPERS
66	Pye International 7N 25396	Louie Louie/Things We Said Today	6

SANDRA
86	10 TEN 78	(I'll Never Be) Maria Magdalena/Party Games/Little Girl (3-track issue, p/s)	4
86	10 TEN 78-12	(I'll Never Be) Maria Magdalena/Party Games/Little Girl (12", p/s)	7
86	10 TENY 78-12	(I'll Never Be) Maria Magdalena/Party Games/Little Girl (12", picture disc)	15
86	10 TEN 113	In The Heat Of The Night/Heatwave (Instrumental) (p/s)	4
86	10 TEN 113-12	In The Heat Of The Night/Heatwave (Instrumental) (12", p/s)	7
86	10 TEN 113-12/TENY 78-12	In The Heat Of The Night/Heatwave (Instrumental)//(I'll Never Be) Maria Magdalena/Party Games/Little Girl (12", double pack, including picture disc, gatefold PVC sleeve)	30
88	10 TEN 149	Everlasting Love/Stop For A Minute (p/s)	4
89	Siren SRN 85	Everlasting Love/Stop For A Minute (reissue, p/s)	4
89	Siren SRNCD 85	Everlasting Love/Stop For A Minute/Everlasting Love (Remix)/ (I'll Never Be) Maria Magdalena (CD)	18
89	Siren SRNT 104	Heaven Can Wait (Extended Version)/Heaven Can Wait (Dub Mix)/ Heaven Can Wait (4.05) (12", p/s)	7
89	Siren SRNCD 104	Heaven Can Wait (Single Version 4.05)/(Dub Mix)/Heaven's Theme (Instrumental)/Heaven Can Wait (Extended Version) (3" CD, card sleeve)	20

SANDROSE
73	Polydor 2480 137	SANDROSE (LP)	100

SANDS (U.K.)
67	Reaction 591 017	Mrs. Gillespie's Refrigerator/Listen To The Sky	200

(see also Others, Sundragon)

SANDS (Ireland)
70	Major Minor MM 681	Venus/Cara Mia	12

SANDS
69	Tribune TRS 122	Dance Dance Dance/The Cheater	8
69	Tribune	SAND DOIN'S (LP)	40

(see also Tony Kenny & Sands)

SANDS
72	RCA RCA 2210	Salvation Sally/She Is Me	5

CLIVE SANDS
69	CBS 3955	Lo Muchco Que Te Quiro/Picture On The Wall	5
69	S.N.B. 55-4058	Hooked On A Feeling/Marie	6
69	S.N.B. 55-4431	Whitchi Tai Yo/In A Dream	10
69	CBS 4672	A Very Lonely Man/You Made Me What I Am	5

(see also Brothers Kane, Sarstedt Brothers, Wes Sands)

DAVEY SANDS & ESSEX
65	Decca F 12170	Please Me Mine/All The Time	12
67	CBS 202620	Advertising Girl/Without You I'm Nothing	10

EVIE SANDS
65	Red Bird BC 118	Take Me For A Little While/Run Home To Mama	30
66	Cameo Parkway C 413	Picture Me Gone/It Makes Me Laugh	70
68	A&M AMS 736	Shadow Of The Evening/Until It's Time For You To Go	6
69	A&M AMS 748	I'll Hold Out My Hand/One Fine Summer Morning	6
69	A&M AMS 760	Anyway That You Want Me/I'll Never Be Alone	6
75	Capitol CL 15818	You Brought The Woman Out In Me/Early Morning Sunshine	6

JODI(E) SANDS
57	London HL 8456	With All My Heart/More Than Only Friends (as Jodi Sands)	12
57	London HL 8530	Please Don't Tell Me (Sayonara)/If You're Not Completely Satisfied	15

57	London HL 8530	Please Don't Tell Me (Sayonara)/If You're Not Completely Satisfied (78)	25
58	Starlite ST45 005	All I Ask Of You/The Way I Love You	10
58	HMV POP 533	Someone (You'll Want Me To Want You)/Always In My Heart.	6
58	HMV POP 533	Someone (You'll Want Me To Want You)/Always In My Heart (78)	10

TOMMY SANDS

78s

57	Capitol CL 14695	Teen-Age Crush/Hep Dee Hootie (Cutie Wootie) (78)	8
57	Capitol CL 14724	Ring-A-Ding-A-Ding/My Love Song (78)	8
57	Capitol CL 14745	Goin' Steady/Ring My 'Phone (78)	10
57	Capitol CL 14781	Let Me Be Loved/Fantastically Foolish (78)	8
57	Capitol CL 14811	Man, Like Wow!/A Swingin' Romance (78)	15
58	Capitol CL 14834	Sing, Boy, Sing/Crazy 'Cause I Love You (78)	15

SINGLES

57	Capitol CL 14695	Teen-Age Crush/Hep Dee Hootie (Cutie Wootie)	18
57	Capitol CL 14724	Ring-A-Ding-A-Ding/My Love Song	15
57	Capitol CL 14745	Goin' Steady/Ring My 'Phone	12
57	Capitol CL 14781	Let Me Be Loved/Fantastically Foolish	10
57	Capitol CL 14811	Man, Like Wow!/A Swingin' Romance	15
58	Capitol CL 14834	Sing, Boy, Sing/Crazy 'Cause I Love You.	12
58	Capitol CL 14872	Hawaiian Rock/Teen-Age Doll	18
58	Capitol CL 14889	After The Senior Prom/Big Date.	10
58	Capitol CL 14925	Blue Ribbon Baby/I Love You Because (as Tommy Sands & Raiders)	18
59	Capitol CL 14971	The Worryin' Kind/Bigger Than Texas	20
59	Capitol CL 15013	Is It Ever Gonna Happen/I Ain't Gittin' Rid Of You	18
59	Capitol CL 15047	Sinner Man/Bring Me Your Love	8
59	Capitol CL 15071	That's The Way I Am/I'll Be Seeing You	8
60	Capitol CL 15109	I Gotta Have You/You Hold The Future.	8
60	Capitol CL 15143	The Old Oaken Bucket/These Are The Things You Are	8
61	Capitol CL 15219	Love In A Goldfish Bowl/I Love My Baby	7
63	HMV POP 1193	Connie/Young Man's Fancy	7
63	HMV POP 1247	Only 'Cause I'm Lonely/Cinderella	7
66	Liberty LIB 55842	The Statue/Lolita	20

EPs

57	Capitol EAP1 848	STEADY DATE WITH TOMMY SANDS PT. 1 (EP)	40
57	Capitol EAP2 848	STEADY DATE WITH TOMMY SANDS PT. 2 (EP)	40
57	Capitol EAP3 848	STEADY DATE WITH TOMMY SANDS PT. 3 (EP)	40
57	Capitol EAP1 851	TEENAGE CRUSH (EP)	40
59	Capitol EAP1 1081	SANDS STORM PART 1 (EP)	40
59	Capitol EAP2 1081	SANDS STORM PART 2 (EP)	45
59	Capitol EAP3 1081	SANDS STORM PART 3 (EP)	45
59	Capitol EAP1 1123	THIS THING CALLED LOVE (EP)	30

LPs

57	Capitol T 848	STEADY DATE WITH TOMMY SANDS (LP).	45
58	Capitol T 929	SING, BOY, SING (LP, soundtrack).	45
59	Capitol T 1081	SANDS STORM! (LP)	40
59	Capitol T 1123	THIS THING CALLED LOVE (LP)	25
60	Capitol (S)T 1239	WHEN I'M THINKING OF YOU (LP, mono/stereo)	20/25
61	Capitol T 1426	A DREAM WITH TOMMY SANDS (LP)	25

TONY SANDS & DRUMBEATS

| 60s | Studio 36 NSRS EP 1/22 | Shame Shame Shame/I Got A Feeling. | 200 |

WES SANDS

| 63 | Columbia DB 4996 | There's Lots More Where This Came From/Three Cups | 35 |

(see also Brothers Kane, Sarstedt Brothers, Clive Sands)

SANDS OF TIME

| 66 | Pye 7N 17140 | Where Did We Go Wrong/When I Look Back. | 6 |
| 67 | Pye 7N 17236 | One Day/Ev'ry Time We Say Goodbye | 6 |

PAT SANDY

| 69 | Attack ATT 8000 | Gentle On My Mind/BIG L: Soulful. | 6 |

SANDY & TEACHERS

| 64 | Columbia DB 7244 | Listen With Mammy/Real Sweet. | 5 |

(see also Sandy Brown)

SANDY COAST

71	Polydor 2121 046	True Love/That's A Wonder	7
73	Polydor 2001 457	Blackboard Jungle Lady/Don't Get Me Wrong	7
69	Page One POLS 020	FROM THE STEREO WORKSHOP (LP)	100
69	Page One MORS 201	SHIPWRECK (LP)	100
73	Polydor 2310 277	STONEWALL (LP).	15

SAN FRANCISCO EARTHQUAKE

| 68 | Mercury MF 1036 | Fairy Tales Can Come True/Su Su | 8 |

CLAUDE SANG

| 70 | Sugar SU 105 | I'm In Love Again/You'll Never Fool Me Again | 6 |
| 70 | Sugar SUM 1 | THE WORLD OF REGGAE VOL. 1 (LP) | 12 |

SAN REMO STRINGS

71	Tamla Motown TMG 795	Festival Time/All Turned On.	5
72	Tamla Motown TMG 807	Reach Out, I'll Be There/Hungry For Love.	5
73	Tamla Motown STML 11216	SAN REMO STRINGS SWING (LP).	12

BOBBY SANSOM (& GIANTS)

63	Oriole CB 1837	There's A Place/Lucille (as Bobby Sansom & Giants)	12
63	Oriole CB 1888	Where Have You Been/Do You Promise (as Bobby Sansom & Giants)	10
70	Decca F 13104	Lady One And Only/Handbags And Gladrags.	5

71	Decca F 13151	I Believe In Music/The Valley Of The Shadows Of Tears	5

MONGO SANTAMARIA
63	Riverside RIF 106909	Watermelon Man/Don't Bother Me No More	10
65	CBS 201766	El Pussycat/Black Eyed Peas And Rice	5
69	Direction 58-4086	Cloud Nine/Son Of A Preacher Man	5
69	Direction 58-4430	Twenty Five Miles/El Tres	6
71	CBS 63904	WORKING ON A GROOVY THING (LP)	12
71	Atlantic 2400 140	MONGO'S WAY (LP)	12

SANTANA
69	CBS 4593	Persuasion/Savor	6
70	CBS 4940	Evil Ways/Jin-Go-Lo-Ba	6
70	CBS 5325	Black Magic Woman/Hope You're Feeling Better.	6
71	CBS 7046	Oye Como Va/Samba Pa Ti.	5
71	CBS 7546	Everybody's Everything/Guajira	5
73	CBS 1155	Oye Como Va/Black Magic Woman (p/s, 'Hall Of Fame Hits' series)	5
89	CBS 654 568-3	SOLID GOLD (3" CD EP, gatefold card sleeve)	8
99	Arista ASCD 3662	SANTANA (CD, 5-track album sampler, digipak, promo only)	12
69	CBS 63015	SANTANA (LP, laminated sleeve original, orange label)	18
70	CBS 63815	SANTANA (LP, non-laminated sleeve reissue, orange label)	12
70	CBS 64087	ABRAXAS (LP, orange label)	12
71	CBS 69015	SANTANA (III) (LP, gatefold sleeve, some stickered, orange label)	12
72	CBS CQ 30595	SANTANA (III) (LP, gatefold sleeve, quadrophonic).	18
72	CBS 65299	CARAVANSERAI (LP, gatefold sleeve, orange label)	12
73	CBS CQ 31610	CARAVANSERAI (LP, gatefold sleeve, quadrophonic)	18
73	CBS 69040	WELCOME (LP, embossed gatefold sleeve)	12
74	CBS CQ 32445	WELCOME (LP, embossed gatefold sleeve, quadrophonic)	15
75	CBS 66325	LOTUS (3-LP, triple-gatefold sleeve, with inners)	18
75	CBS CQ 30130	ABRAXAS (LP, gatefold sleeve, quadrophonic)	18
75	CBS Q 69081	GREATEST HITS (LP, quadrophonic).	18
75	CBS Q 69084	BORBOLETTA (LP, quadrophonic)	18
76	CBS Q 86005	AMIGOS (LP, quadrophonic)	18

CARLOS SANTANA & BUDDY MILES
72	CBS 8338	Evil Ways/Them Changes	5
83	CBS A 3359	They All Went To Mexico (with Willie Nelson)/BUDDY MILES: Mudbone (p/s)	5
72	CBS 65142	CARLOS SANTANA & BUDDY MILES LIVE (LP, gatefold sleeve)	12
73	CBS CQ 31308	CARLOS SANTANA & BUDDY MILES LIVE (LP, quadrophonic)	18

(see also Santana, Buddy Miles, Mahavishnu Orchestra, John McLaughlin, John Lee Hooker)

SANTELLS
66	Sue WI 4020	So Fine/These Are Love	20

SANTIAGO
75	Buk BU 3007	I Want To Be Sure/New Guitar (p/s)	5

DAVID SANTO
68	London HLK 10219	Jingle Down A Hill/Rising Of Scorpio	4

SANTO & JOHNNY
59	Pye International 7N 25037	Sleep Walk/All Night Diner	10
59	Pye International N 25037	Sleep Walk/All Night Diner (78)	50
60	Parlophone R 4619	Tear Drop/The Long Walk Home	8
60	Parlophone R 4644	Caravan/Summertime	7
61	Pye International 7N 25111	Theme From Come September/Hopscotch	7
61	Parlophone R 4844	Bullseye!/Twistin' Bells	8
62	Parlophone R 4865	Birmingham/The Mouse	7
62	Stateside SS 110	Spanish Harlem/Stage To Cimarron	7
64	Stateside SS 253	Three Cabelleros/Manhattan Spiritual	6
64	Stateside SS 292	In The Still Of The Night/Song For Rosemary	6
60	Parlophone GEP 8806	SANTO AND JOHNNY NO. 1 (EP)	25
60	Parlophone GEP 8813	SANTO AND JOHNNY NO. 2 (EP)	25
59	Parlophone	SANTO AND JOHNNY (LP, existence unconfirmed)	50
64	Stateside S(S)L 1008	HAWAII (LP)	20
67	Philips (S)BL 7759	PULCINELLA (LP)	15
67	Philips (S)BL 7760	MONA LISA (LP).	15

SAPPHIRE
82	Sapphire Rocks SRR 001	Jealousy (p/s)	150

SAPPHIRES
63	Stateside SS 223	Where Is Johnny Now/Your True Love	30
64	Stateside SS 267	Who Do You Love/Oh So Soon	30
65	HMV POP 1441	Gotta Have Your Love/Gee Baby I'm Sorry	100
65	HMV POP 1461	Evil One/How Could I Say Goodbye	125
72	Probe PRO 556	Gotta Have Your Love/Gee Baby I'm Sorry (reissue)	5
74	Probe PRO 609	Slow Fizz/Our Love Is Everywhere	5
78	ABC 4221	Gonna Be A Big Thing/EDDIE REGAN: Playin' Hide And Seek	5

SARABAND
73	Folk Heritage FHR 050	CLOSE TO IT ALL (LP)	25

SARACEN
82	Nucleus SAR 1	No More Lonely Nights/Rock Of Ages (p/s, some with patch).	8/6
83	Neat NEAT 30	We Have Arrived/Face In The Crowd (p/s).	7
82	Nucleus MPGR 492	HEROES, SAINTS AND FOOLS (LP)	12
84	Neat NEAT 1016	CHANGE OF HEART (LP, with lyric insert)	10

SARAH JANE
66	Pye 7N 17114	Listen People/The World Is Round	6

MINT VALUE £

DON SARGENT
60	Vogue Pop V 9160	St. James' Infirmary/Gypsy Boots (triangular centre)	350

SARI & SHALIMARS
68	United Artists UP 2235	It's So Lonely (Being Together)/You Walked Out On Me Before	15

DEREK SARJEANT
61	Oak RGJ 101	FOLK SONGS SUNG BY DEREK SARJEANT (EP)	15
61	Oak RGJ 103	SONGS WE LIKE TO SING (EP, with tracks by Lisa Turner & Mick Wells)	15
61	Oak RGJ 105	FOLK SONGS SUNG BY DEREK SARJEANT VOL. 2 (EP)	15
63	Oak RGJ 117	MAN OF KENT (EP)	15

MIKE SARNE
62	Parlophone R 4902	Come Outside (with Wendy Richards)/Fountain Of Love	6
62	Parlophone R 4932	Will I What (with Billie Davis)/Bird, You Know I Love Ya	6
62	Parlophone R 4974	Just For Kicks/Don't You Phone Me, I'll Phone You	6
63	Parlophone R 5010	Code Of Love/Are You Satisfied	6
63	Parlophone R 5060	Please Don't Say/Now You've Moved	6
63	Parlophone R 5090	Hello Lover Boy/Baby I'm On My Way	6
64	Parlophone R 5129	Out And About/A Place To Go	7
64	Parlophone R 5170	Love Me Please/You've Got Something (as Mike Sarne & Le Roys)	6
63	Parlophone DP 558	Just Like Eddie/Slow Twistin' Round The Totem Pole (export issue)	80
63	Parlophone GEP 8879	MIKE SARNE HIT PARADE (EP, as Mike Sarne & Innocents)	50
62	Parlophone PMC 1187	COME OUTSIDE (LP)	40

(see also Wendy Richards, Innocents, Le Roys, Billie Davis, Rod McKuen)

SAROFEEN & SMOKE
71	Pye International 7N 25556	Susan Jane/Tomorrow	5
71	Pye Intl. NSPL 28153	DO IT (LP)	15

SAROLTA
68	Island WIP 6035	Open Your Hands/L.O.V.E.	4
69	President PT 248	I Am A Woman/Change Of Heart	4

PETER SARSTEDT
69	United Artists UP 2262	Morning Mountain/Step Into The Candelight (unissued)	
69	United Artists UP 2262	Where Do You Go To (My Lovely)/Morning Mountain	5
69	United Artists UP 35021	Frozen Orange Juice/Arethusa Loser	6
69	United Artists (S)ULP 1219	PETER SARSTEDT (LP)	15
69	United Artists UAL 29037	AS THOUGH IT WERE A MOVIE (LP)	15
71	United Artists UAS 29247	EVERY WORD YOU SAY (LP)	15

(see also Sarstedt Brothers, Brothers Kane, Peter Lincoln)

SARSTEDT BROTHERS
73	Regal Zonophone RZ 3081	Chinese Restaurant/Beloved Illusions	5
73	Regal Zono. SRZA 8516	WORLDS APART TOGETHER (LP, gatefold sleeve)	15

(see also Brothers Kane, Peter Sarstedt, Eden Kane, Clive Sands, Wes Sands)

SASPARELLA
69	Decca F 12892	Spooky/Come Inside	5

SASSAFRAS
74	Polydor 2058 497	Oh My (Don't It Make You Want To Cry)/Kansas City Wine	5
73	Polydor 2383 245	EXPECTING COMPANY (LP)	15

SASSENACHS
64	Fontana TF 518	That Don't Worry Me/All Over You	20

SATAN
82	Guardian GRC 145	Kiss Of Death/Heads Will Roll (some with p/s)	120/25
85	Neat NEAT 1012	COURT IN THE ACT (LP)	20

SATANIC RITES
81	Heavy Metal HEAVY 8	Live To Ride/Hit And Run (p/s)	12
85	Chub CHUBLP 001	WHICH WAY THE WIND BLOWS (LP)	15
87	Chub CHUBLP 002	NO USE CRYING (LP)	18

SATAN'S RATS
77	DJM DJS 10819	In My Love For You (p/s)	18
77	DJM DJS 10821	Year Of The Rats/Louise (p/s)	15
78	DJM DJS 10840	You Make Me Sick/Façade (p/s)	15
89	Overground OVER 01	Year Of The Rats/Louise (p/s, 600 yellow vinyl, 400 white vinyl, 25 gold vinyl, numbered test pressings)	6/7/15
89	Overground OVER 02	In My Love For You/Facade (p/s, 600 yellow vinyl, 400 white vinyl, 25 gold vinyl, numbered test pressings)	6/7/15
91	Overground OVER 14	You Make Me Sick (p/s, clear vinyl, 567 copies only)	7

SATAN'S SAUSAGE
82	Blood RITE 002	Pain In The Pentangle/Rite Up Me Passage (first 666 with p/s & cocktail sausage "pitchfork")	200/150

YOUNG SATCH
70	Black Swan BW 1401	Bongo Bongo/BOYS: Ramba	6

GIRL SATCHMO
61	Blue Beat BB 45	Satchmo's Mash Potato/Darling	10
62	Blue Beat BB 79	Twist Around Town/My New Honey (with Karl Rowe & Bluebeats)	10
63	Blue Beat BB 156	Don't Be Sad/Brother Joe (with Les Dawson Combo)	10
64	Blue Beat BB 227	Rhythm Of The New Beat/Blue Beat Chariot	10
69	Fab FAB 111	Take You For A Ride/I'm Coming Home	6
69	Trojan TR 676	Taken For A Ride/I'm Coming Home	5

(see also Pat Satchmo, Sugar & Dandy)

PAT SATCHMO
69	Punch PH 9	Hello Dolly/ERIC DONALSON: Never Get Away	5
69	Upsetter US 316	Hello Dolly/King Of The Trombone	5
70	Punch PH 24	Wonderful World/MEDITATORS: Purple Mast	7
70	Songbird SB 1039	A Handful Of Friends/CRYSTALITES: Handful — Version	5
72	Attack ATT 8024	What's Going On/LLOYD & CAREY: Tubby's In Full Swing	8

(see also Girl Satchmo, Hortense Ellis)

SATIN BELLS
68	Pye 7N 17531	Baby You're So Right For Me/When You're Ready	5
68	Pye 7N 17608	Da-Di-Da-Da/Oh No Oh Yes	5
69	Decca F 22937	I Stand Accused (Of Loving You)/Sweet Darlin'	8
70	Decca F 23044	The Power Of Love/Baby Come Back	5
71	CBS S 7220	The Belle Telephone Song/Losing You	5

(see also Three Bells)

SATISFACTION
71	Decca F 13129	Love It Is/Cold Summer	8
71	Decca F 13207	Don't Rag The Lady/Gregory Shan't	8
71	Decca SKL 5075	SATISFACTION (LP)	45

(see also Mike Cotton Sound)

SATISFIERS
57	Vogue Coral Q 72247	Where'll I Be Tomorrow Night?/Come Away, Love	12
57	Vogue Coral Q 72247	Where'll I Be Tomorrow Night?/Come Away, Love (78)	10
57	Vogue Coral LVA 9068	THE SATISFIERS (LP)	20

LONNIE SATTIN
56	Capitol CL 14552	Trapped (In The Web Of Love)/Your Home Can Be A Castle	8
56	Capitol CL 14638	High Steel/What Time Does The Sun Go Down?	7
57	Capitol CL 14771	I'll Never Stop Loving You/Whoo-Pie Shoo-Pie	7
57	Capitol CL 14771	I'll Never Stop Loving You/Whoo-Pie Shoo-Pie (78)	8
58	Capitol CL 14831	Ring Around The Moon/My Heart's Your Home	6
60	Warner Bros WB 15	I'll Fly Away/Any More Than I	6

LON SATTON
74	CBS 2016	The Love I See In Your Eyes/Do You Need My Love	5

SATURNALIA
69	Matrix TRIX 1	MAGICAL LOVE (LP, picture disc, with booklet & ticket)	30
69	Matrix TRIX 1	MAGICAL LOVE (LP, test pressing on black vinyl)	70
73	Matrix TRIX 1	MAGICAL LOVE (LP, picture disc, reissue)	12

(see also Horse)

SAUCERMAN
88	Fierce FRIGHT 029	Scatterbrain/Beyond Repair (12", p/s with inner, 1 side etched, 1,000 only)	20
88	Fierce FRIGHT 029P	Scatterbrain (Long Gone Rancid Mix) (acetate, 2 only)	30
89	Fierce FRIGHT 035	I Will Be King/Sid James Rules (withdrawn)	25
95	UFO UFO 01	Hot Wire/Bronx (p/s)	5
96	UFO UFO 02	Mean/Shake Your Ass For Me (p/s)	5

(see also Kray Cherrubs)

JACK SAUNDERS & ROBERT FARNON ORCHESTRA
59	Top Rank 35/021	MIKE TODD'S BROADWAY (LP)	15

LARRY SAUNDERS
74	London HLU 10469	On The Real Side/Let Me Be The Special One	15

MAHALIA SAUNDERS
71	Moodisc HME 112	Down The Aisle/IAN ROBINSON: Three For One	6
71	Upsetter US 374	Pieces Of My Heart/UPSETTERS: Version	8

MERL SAUNDERS
73	Fantasy FT 514	FIRE UP (LP)	10

TUPPER SAUSSY
63	London HAU 8127	DISCOVER TUPPER SAUSSY (LP)	12

LES SAUTERELLES
68	Decca F 22824	Heavenly Club/Dream Machine	40

SAUTER-FINEGAN ORCHESTRA
54	HMV B 10690	The Honey Jump/Doodletown Races (78)	8
55	HMV B 10818	Eddie And The Witchdoctor/Midnight Sleighride (78)	8

SAVAGE
82	Ebony EBON 10	Ain't No Fit Place (no p/s)	7
84	Zebra 12RA 4	We Got The Edge/Running Scared/She Don't Need You (12", p/s)	7
84	Carrere CAR 350	Only You/Turn Around (p/s)	4
84	Carrere CART 350	Only You/Turn Around (12", p/s)	7
83	Ebony EBON 12	LOOSE 'N' LETHAL (LP)	12
85	Zebra ZEB 4	HYPERACTIVE (LP)	12

EDNA SAVAGE
55	Parlophone MSP 6175	Stars Shine In Your Eyes/A Star Is Born	12
55	Parlophone MSP 6181	Candlelight/In The Wee Small Hours Of The Morning	12
55	Parlophone MSP 6189	Arrivederci Darling/Bella Notte	12
56	Parlophone MSP 6217	Tell Me, Tell Me, Tell Me That You Love Me/Please Hurry Home	10
56	Parlophone R 4226	My Prayer/Me 'n' You 'n' The Moon	10
56	Parlophone R 4253	Never Leave Me/Don't Ever Go (I Need You)	7
57	Parlophone R 4301	Me Head's In De Barrel/Five Oranges, Four Apples	7
57	Parlophone R 4360	Let Me Love/Diano Marina	7
57	Parlophone R 4360	Let Me Love/Diano Marina (78)	8
58	Parlophone R 4420	My Shining Star/Once	5

MINT VALUE £

58	Parlophone R 4420	My Shining Star/Once (78)... 8
58	Parlophone R 4489	Why, Why, Why/Near You 5
58	Parlophone R 4489	Why, Why, Why/Near You (78) 10
59	Parlophone R 4572	Maybe This Year/Beautiful Love....................................... 5
60	Parlophone R 4648	All I Need/Everyday 5

(see also Michael Holliday)

JOAN SAVAGE

57	Columbia DB 3929	Five Oranges, Four Apples/Bamboozled.................................. 8
57	Columbia DB 3968	With All My Heart/Love Letters In The Sand 8
57	Columbia DB 4039	Shake Me, I Rattle/Lula Rock-A-Hula................................... 15
57	Columbia DB 4039	Shake Me, I Rattle/Lula Rock-A-Hula (78) 10
58	Columbia DB 4159	Hello Happiness, Goodbye Blues/Left Right Out Of My Heart 8
58	Columbia DB 4159	Hello Happiness, Goodbye Blues/Left Right Out Of My Heart (78) 8

SAVAGE PENCIL

| 88 | Blast First FU 3LP | ANGEL DUST (LP, picture disc, 1,000 only) .... 20 |

SAVAGE RESURRECTION

| 68 | Mercury MF 1027 | Thing In E/Fox Is Sick .... 15 |
| 68 | Mercury SMCL 20123 | SAVAGE RESURRECTION (LP) .... 75 |

SAVAGE ROSE

68	Polydor 184 144	SAVAGE ROSE (LP) 12
68	Polydor 184 206	IN THE PLAIN (LP) 12
69	Polydor 184 316	TRAVELLIN' (LP) 12
71	RCA SF 8169	YOUR DAILY GIFT (LP)... 12

SAVAGES

| 63 | Decca DFE 8546 | EVERYBODY SURF! WITH THE SURFIN' SAVAGES (EP)................... 225 |

(see also Soul Sounds, Screaming Lord Sutch, Circles, Tony Dangerfield & Thrills)

TERRY SAVALAS

| 72 | Jam JAM 5 | We All End Up The Same/We Both Knew It Was Over .... 5 |
| 72 | Jam JAL 102 | THIS IS TELLY SAVALAS (LP) .... 12 |

JULIAN JAY SAVARIN

70s	Lyntone LYN 3426	I Am You/Kizeesh (Corgi Books sampler)............................... 10
73	Birth RAB 2	WAITERS ON THE DANCE (LP, with insert)............................. 150
87	Five Hours Back TOCK 002	WAITERS ON THE DANCE (LP, reissue) 12

(see also Julian's Treatment)

JIMMY SAVILLE

| 62 | Decca F 11493 | Ahab The Arab/Very Unlikely.. 8 |
| 63 | Decca F 11576 | The Bossa Nova/Don't Do Anything I Like .... 6 |

(see also Vernons Girls)

RONNIE SAVOY

| 61 | MGM MGM 1122 | And The Heavens Cried/Big Chain .... 4 |
| 61 | MGM MGM 1131 | Bewitched/It's Gotta Be Love.. 4 |

SAVOY BROWN (BLUES BAND)

66	Purdah 45-3503	I Tried/Can't Quit You Baby (as Savoy Brown's Blues Band) 200
67	Decca F 12702	Taste And Try, Before You Buy/Someday People
		(as Savoy Brown Blues Band)... 15
68	Decca F 12797	Walking By Myself/Vicksburg Blues 10
69	Decca F 12843	Train To Nowhere/Tolling Bells 18
69	Decca F 12978	I'm Tired/Stay With Me Baby 15
70	Decca F 13019	A Hard Way To Go/Waiting In The Bamboo Grove....................... 12
70	Decca F 13098	Poor Girl/Master Hare 10
71	Decca F 13247	Tell Mama/Let It Rock 8
73	Decca F 13372	So Tired/The Saddest Feeling 6
73	Decca F 13431	Coming Down Your Way/I Can't Find You 6
67	Decca LK/SKL 4883	SHAKE DOWN (LP) 45
68	Decca LK/SKL 4925	GETTING TO THE POINT (LP) 40
69	Decca LK/SKL 4994	BLUE MATTER (LP, mono/stereo)................................... 30/25
69	Decca LK/SKL 5013	A STEP FURTHER (LP, mono/stereo).............................. 30/25
70	Decca LK/SKL 5043	RAW SIENNA (LP, mono/stereo, gatefold sleeve)................. 30/25
70	Decca SKL 5066	LOOKING IN (LP, gatefold sleeve)...................................... 25
71	Decca TXS 104	STREET CORNER TALKING (LP, gatefold sleeve)....................... 20
72	Decca TXS 107	HELLBOUND TRAIN (LP, gatefold sleeve) 18
73	Decca SKL 5152	LION'S SHARE (LP) 18
73	Decca TXS 112	JACK THE TOAD (LP) 15
74	Decca SKL 5186	BOOGIE BROTHERS (LP) 15

(see also Warren Philips & The Rockets, Chris Youlden, Stone's Masonry, Jackie Lynton, Foghat)

TOM SAWYER

| 69 | CBS 4243 | Cookbook/Gates .... 4 |

(see also Unit 4 + 2)

'ACE' DINNING SAX

| 59 | Top Rank JAR 184 | Mulholland Drive/My Love .... 10 |
| 59 | Top Rank JAR 184 | Mulholland Drive/My Love (78) .... 15 |

MIKE SAX & IDOLS

| 65 | Mercury MF 886 | My Little One/Come Back To Me .... 4 |

(see also Idols)

SAXON

79	Carrere SAM 109	Big Teaser/Stallions Of The Highway (12", promo only) 12
79	Carrere CAR 118	Big Teaser/Stallions Of The Highway (p/s) 10
79	Carrere CAR 118	Big Teaser/Stallions Of The Highway (p/s) 10
79	Carrere CAR 129	Backs To The Wall/Militia Guard (p/s).................................. 8

80	Carrere CAR 151	747 (Strangers In The Night)/See The Light Shining (p/s)............ 5
80	Carrere CAR 151	747 (Strangers In The Night)/See The Light Shining (12", p/s)....... 10
80	Carrere HM 5	Big Teaser/Stallions Of The Highway (p/s, reissue)............. 4
80	Carrere HM 6	Backs To The Wall/Militia Guard (p/s, reissue)................ 4
80	Carrere CAR 165	Suzie Hold On/Judgement Day (live) (p/s)................... 5
81	Carrere CAR 180P	And The Bands Played On/Hungry Years/Heavy Metal Thunder (picture disc) ... 7
81	Carrere CAR 204/ SAM 134	Never Surrender/20,000 Feet (Remix)//Bap-shoo-ap! (live)/
		Street Fighting Gang (double pack) 5
83	Carrere CARP 284P	Nightmare/Midas Touch (picture disc)..................... 10
83	Carrere SAXON 1	The Power And The Glory/See The Light Shining (live) (poster p/s)..... 7
83	Carrere SAXON P 1	The Power And The Glory/See The Light Shining (live) (pic disc, 600 signed) .. 10/6
83	Carrere SAXON T 1	The Power And The Glory/See The Light Shining (live) (12", p/s)...... 8
84	Carrere CAR 323	Do It All For You/Just Let Me Rock (p/s).................... 5
84	Carrere CART 323	Do It All For You/Just Let Me Rock (12", p/s)................ 8
85	Parlophone RP 6103	Back On The Streets/Live Fast Die Young (shaped picture disc)...... 7
85	Parlophone 12RA 6103	Back On The Streets (Extended Version)/Back On The Streets/
		Live Fast Die Young (12", p/s with poster & sticker)............ 8
85	Parlophone 12R 6103	Back On The Streets (Club Mix)/Back On The Streets/Live Fast Die Young
		(12", promo only) 15
86	Parlophone R 6112	Rock 'n' Roll Gypsy/Krakatoa (poster p/s) 5
86	Parlophone RP 6112	Rock 'n' Roll Gypsy/Krakatoa (picture disc)................. 7
86	EMI EMIP 5587	Rock The Nations/747/And The Bands Played On (shaped picture disc)... 7
86	EMI 12EMI 5587	Rock The Nations/747/And The Bands Played On (12", clear vinyl, st'krd p/s) ... 10
88	EMI EMP 43	Ride Like The Wind/Red Alert (shaped picture disc) 10
88	EMI CDEM 43	Ride Like The Wind/Red Alert/Rock The Nations (live)/
		Back On The Streets (live) (CD) 10
88	EMI EMP 54	I Can't Wait Anymore/Broken Heroes (live)
		(pouch pack, with discography & poster)................... 6
80s	Din Disc DINSY 105	We Will Remember/Altar Of The Gods (shaped picture disc)........ 6
82	Carrere CAL 137	THE EAGLE HAS LANDED (LP, picture disc)................. 12
83	Carrere CAL 147	THE POWER AND THE GLORY (LP, picture disc)............. 12
84	Carrere CALP 200	CRUSADER (LP, picture disc) 15
85	Parlophone SAXONP 2	INNOCENCE IS NO EXCUSE (LP, picture disc) 15
87	EMI EMS 1163	DENIM AND LEATHER (LP, blue vinyl reissue) 12

(see also Son Of A Bitch)

AL SAXON

57	Fontana H 111	Dreamboy/You, All You (78) 8
58	Fontana H 138	Where The Black-Eyed Susans Grow/She Screamed 6
58	Fontana H 138	Where The Black-Eyed Susans Grow/She Screamed (78) 8
58	Fontana H 164	The Day The Rains Came (Le Jour Ou La Pluie Viendra)/You're The Top-Cha 6
58	Fontana H 164	The Day The Rains Came (Le Jour Ou La Pluie Viendra)/You're The Top-Cha
		(78) 10
59	Fontana H 188	Chattanooga Choo-Choo/Chip Off The Old Block............. 4
59	Fontana H 188	Chattanooga Choo-Choo/Chip Off The Old Block (78) 8
59	Fontana H 205	Only Sixteen/I'm All Right, Jack 7
59	Fontana H 205	Only Sixteen/I'm All Right, Jack (78) 10
59	Fontana H 222	Linda Lu/Heart Of Stone 6
59	Fontana H 222	Linda Lu/Heart Of Stone (78) 12
59	Fontana H 231	Marina/Me Without You.............................. 6
59	Fontana H 231	Marina/Me Without You (78) 12
60	Fontana H 244	The Piper Of Love/Believe Me 5
60	Fontana H 261	I've Heard That Song Before/Someone Like You 5
60	Fontana H 278	Blue-Eyed Boy/Don't Push Your Luck 5
61	Piccadilly 7N 35002	Can You Keep A Secret/Promises 5
61	Piccadilly 7N 35011	There, I've Said It Again/You Came A Long Way From St. Louis 5
62	Parlophone R 4966	But I Do/I Got A Girl 5
58	Fontana TFE 17014	THOSE YOU'VE NEVER HEARD (EP)...................... 12
59	Fontana TFE 17202	BIG DEAL (EP) 12
60	Fontana TFE 17271	THE BATTLE OF THE SEXES (EP) 12

(see also Lana Sisters, Ella Stone & Moss)

SKY 'SUNLIGHT' SAXON

87	Fierce FRIGHT 009	Dog=God (p/s, with badge, piece of shirt, sugar 'skycubes' & inserts) 20
84	Psycho PSYCHO 29	STARRY EYED (LP) 20

(see also Seeds)

LINDA SAXONE

64	Pye 7N 15624	Love Is A Many Splendoured Thing/The Other Side Of The Street........ 7
65	Polydor BM 56015	I've Got To Say No/Another Day Another Night 6
65	Polydor BM 56032	Only Last Night/Lucky Girl 6

SAXONS

63	Ace Of Clubs ACL 1173	MEET THE SAXONS (LP)............................. 100

SAXONS

65	Decca F 12179	Saxon War Cry/Click-Ete-Clack 45

(see also Tornados)

JOHNNY SAYLES

66	Liberty LIB 12042	Deep Down In Your Heart/Anything For You 15

RAT SCABIES

84	Paradiddle Music HIT 1	Let There Be Rats/Wiped Out/Drums Drums Drums (mail-order only, no p/s)..... 6

(see also Damned, Rat & Whale, Pete Zear)

SCABS

79	Clubland Records SJP 799	Amory Building/Leave Me Alone/Don't Just Sit There/U.R.E.
		(blue/black or red/black fold out 'envelope' p/s, 2 inserts)................ 60/40

MINT VALUE £

SUE SCADDING
82	Speed FIRED 5	Simple Love/Poland (p/s)	5

(see also Slade)

SCAFFOLD
66	Parlophone R 5443	2 Day's Monday/3 Blind Jellyfish	8
66	Parlophone R 5548	Goodbat Nightman/A Long Strong Black Pudding	10
68	Parlophone R 5679	Do You Remember?/Carry On Krow	6
68	Parlophone R 5703	1-2-3/Today	6
69	Parlophone R 5784	Charity Bubbles/Goose	6
69	Parlophone R 5812	Gin Gan Goolie/Liver Birds	8
70	Parlophone R 5847	All The Way Up/Please — Sorry	8
70	Parlophone R 5866	Busdreams/If I Could Start All Over Again	8
71	Parlophone R 5922	Do The Albert/Commercial Break	8
74	Warner Bros K 16400	Liverpool Lou/Ten Years On After Strawberry Jam	8
68	Parlophone PMC/PCS 7051	AN EVENING WITH ... — LIVE AT QUEEN ELIZABETH HALL (LP, black/yellow label)	18
69	Parlophone PMC/PCS 7077	L THE P (LP, black/yellow label)	15
73	Island ILPS 9234	FRESH LIVER (LP)	15

(see also McGough-McGear, Roger McGough, Mike McGear, Liverpool Scene, Grimms, John Gorman)

BOZ SCAGGS
71	CBS 7219	We Were Always Sweethearts/Painted Bells	5
71	CBS 7401	Near You/Downright Woman	5
72	CBS 7803	Up To You/Runnin' Blue	5
88	CBS 651 559-2	Heart Of Mine/You'll Never Know/Soul To Soul?/What Can I Say? (CD, card sl.)	7
69	Atlantic 588 205	BOZ SCAGGS (LP, plum label)	18
71	CBS 64248	MOMENTS (LP, plain orange label)	12

(see also Steve Miller Band, Steve York's Camelo Pardalis)

SCALA
88	Cocteau COQ CD21	Theme From "Brond" (3" CD, picture disc with 5" adaptor, 5" case)	7

(see also Bill Nelson)

HARVEY SCALES & 7 SOUND
67	Atlantic 584 146	Get Down/Love It Is	6

SCAMPS
59	London HLW 8827	Petite Fleur/Naomi	10
62	Ace Of Clubs ACL 1116	TEEN DANCE AND SING ALONG PARTY (LP)	12

SCARAB
81	Inferno HEADBANGER 1	Rock Night/Wicked Women (no p/s)	30
84	Pharaoh PR-001	Poltergeist/Hell On Wheels (p/s)	50

SCARECROW
78	Spilt Milk SMFM 11278	SCARECROW LIVE (LP, numbered foldout sleeve with insert; beware of watermarked unnumbered copies)	40

SCARFO
95	Fierce Panda NING 08	Skinny/Lifeline (p/s)	8

SCARLETS
64	Philips BF 1376	Let's Go/Tambourine Shake	5

CHARLES FRANCIS SCARRATT III
59	Felsted AF 113	Two Innocent Lovers/Lovemobile	6
59	Felsted AF 113	Two Innocent Lovers/Lovemobile (78)	10

SCARS
79	Fast Product FAST 8	Horrorshow/Adult-ery (p/s)	8
81	I.D. ID-1	Your Attention Please (gold vinyl flexidisc with *ID* magazine, issue 3)	8

SCENE
80	Inferno BEAT 2	I've Had Enough/Show 'Em Now (p/s)	7

SCENE
80	Hole In The Wall HS 1	Hey Girl/Reach The Top (p/s)	10

SCENE
80	GTO GT 277	Driving It Home (Stacks Of Soul)/Da Na Na Na (p/s)	4
80	GTO	PUSHING AN' A SHOVING EP (12", p/s)	8

SCENE
83	Diamond DIA 001	Looking For A Love/Let Me Know (p/s)	6
85	Diamond DIA 003	Something That You Said/Stop-Go (p/s)	4

(see also Diplomats)

HAL SCHAEFER ORCHESTRA & CHORUS
58	London HLT 8692	March Of The Vikings/March Of The Parisian Bakers	7
58	London HLT 8692	March Of The Vikings/March Of The Parisian Bakers (78)	15

SCHEER
93	Son BUACD 293	Wish You Were Dead/Green Room Sex Kitten/Don't Know Why (p/s)	20

MICHAEL SCHENKER
94	EMI 724382861 1423	THE STORY OF MICHAEL SCHENKER (2-CD)	20
97	Michael Schenker Records MSR CD 1/2	THE MICHAEL SCHENKER STORY LIVE (2-CD)	20

(see also McAuley Schenker Group, Michael Schenker Group, Scorpions, UFO)

LALO SCHIFRIN
63	MGM MGM 1203	The Good Life/Broken Date	5
66	MGM MGM 1329	Our Venetian Affair/Venice After Dark	5
68	Dot DOT 103	Mission: Impossible/Jim On The Move	15
74	20th Century BTC 2150	Ape Shuffle (Theme From 'Planet Of The Apes')/Escape From Tomorrow	8

76	CTI CTSP 5	Jaws Theme/Quiet Village	5
68	Dot (S)LPD 503	'MISSION: IMPOSSIBLE' — MUSIC FROM THE TV SERIES (LP, TV soundtrack)	40
69	Paramount SPFL 252	MORE 'MISSION: IMPOSSIBLE' (LP, TV soundtrack)	40
70s	Verve 2304 051	ROCK REQUIEM (LP)	12

SCHMETTERLINGE
77	Pye International 7N 25743	Boom Boom Boomerang/Mr Moneymaker's Music Show	10

ZAPPATA SCHMIDT
71	President PTLS 1041	IT'S GONNA GET YOU (LP)	15

(see also Equals)

OLIVER LINDSEY SCHMITT
72	private pressing	GRAFFENSTADDEN (LP)	50

EBERHARD SCHOENER
79	Harvest HAR 5196	Video Magic/Code Word Elvis (p/s)	7
79	Harvest SHSM 2030	VIDEO FLASHBACK (LP)	12

(see also Police)

SCHOLARS
64	Stagesound SDE 29370/1	THE SCHOLARS (EP, no p/s)	15

SCHOLARS
70s	Unicorn 254	VERSATILITY OF THE SCHOLARS (LP)	10

ARTHUR SCHOLEY & DONALD SWANN
60s	Galliard GAL 4014	THE SONG OF CAEDMON (EP)	10

SCHOOL BOYS
63	Blue Beat BB 162	Little Boy Blue/PRINCE BUSTER: Money	15
63	Blue Beat BB 174	Little Dilly/The Joker (B-side actually by Prince Buster's Allstars)	15
64	Port-O-Jam PJ 4000	Dream Lover/I Want To Know	12

(see also Bill Gentles)

SCHOOLERS
69	Doctor Bird DB 1170	Ugly Man (actually by Scorchers)/Whip Cracker (actually by Vincent Gordon)	15

SCHOOLGIRL BITCH
78	Garage!/Aerco AERS 102	Abusing The Rules/Thinking For Yourself (no p/s)	40

SCHOOL GIRLS
63	Blue Beat BB 168	Love Another Love/Little Keithie	10
63	Blue Beat BB 185	Live Up To Justice/Give Up	10
64	Blue Beat BB 214	Sing And Shout/Last Time	12
64	Blue Beat BB 263	Never Let You Go/BUSTER'S ALL STARS: Supercharge	15

SCHOOL TIES
81	School Ties SCF 01	No Future	6

DON SCHROEDER
62	Philips BF 3040033	Quicksand/My Kind Of Woman	5

JOHN SCHROEDER ORCHESTRA
65	Piccadilly 7N 35240	The Fugitive Theme/Don't Break The Heart Of Kimble (some in p/s)	8/5
65	Piccadilly 7N 35253	You've Lost That Lovin' Feeling/Funny How Love Can Be	6
66	Piccadilly 7N 35280	Ave Maria No Morro/Peter Popgunn	5
66	Piccadilly 7N 35285	Hungry For Love/Soul Destroyer	8
65	Piccadilly 7N 35271	Agent 00 Soul/Night Rider	10
66	Piccadilly 7N 35319	On The Ball (Theme For The World)/The Britannia March	5
67	Piccadilly 7N 35362	Soul For Sale/Loving You Girl	12
69	Pye 7N 17862	The Virgin Soldiers' March/Sweet Soul Talk	6
66	Piccadilly N(S)PL 38025	JOHN SCHROEDER'S WORKING IN THE SOULMINE (LP)	20
67	Piccadilly N(S)PL 38036	THE DOLLY CATCHER! (LP)	15
68	Marble Arch MAL 839	WORKING IN THE SOULMINE (LP, reissue)	12
71	Pye NSPL 18362	WITCHI-TAI-TO (LP)	12
71	Polydor 2460 134	DYLAN VIBRATIONS (LP)	12
72	Polydor 2460 149	TV VIBRATIONS (LP)	18
73	Polydor 2460 188	THEMES FROM TELEVISION (LP)	18

IVY SCHULMAN & BOWTIES
57	London HLN 8372	Rock, Pretty Baby/BOWTIES: Ever Since I Can Remember	50
57	London HLN 8372	Rock, Pretty Baby/BOWTIES: Ever Since I Can Remember (78)	30

KLAUS SCHULZE
75	Caroline CA 2003	BLACK DANCE (LP)	10

(see also Tangerine Dream)

(Voices Of) WALTER SCHUMANN
54	HMV 7M 229	Haunted House/I Only Have Eyes For You	6
55	HMV 7M 323	The Man From Laramie/Let Me Hear You Whisper	6

SCHUNGE
72	Regal Zonophone RZ 3066	Misty/Joseph Demanio	6
73	Regal Zonophone RZ 3077	Ballad Of A Simple Love/Enter The Violins	6
72	Regal Zono. SLRZ 1033	BALLAD OF A SIMPLE LOVE (LP)	15

ARMANDO SCIASCIA ORCHESTRA
66	Ember EMB S 228	Theme From 'The Liars'/World Tomorrow Theme	4

SCIENCE POPTION
67	Columbia DB 8106	You've Got Me High/Back In Town	45

SCIENTIST
69	Amalgamated AMG 848	Professor In Action/SUPERSONICS: Reflections Of Don D	12

MINT VALUE £

SCIENTISTS
85	Karbon KAR 007	You Only Live Twice/If It's The Last Thing I Do (p/s)	8
85	Karbon KAR 101 L	YOU GET WHAT YOU DESERVE (LP)	15
86	Karbon KAR 103 L	WEIRD LOVE (LP)	18
87	Karbon KAR 105 L	THE HUMAN JUKEBOX (LP)	18

SCI-FI SEX STARS
86	Who Am I WM 1001 7	Rock It Miss U.S.A./Teenage Thunder (p/s)	8
86	Who Am I WM 1001	Rock It Miss U.S.A. (Death Wish IV)/Commercial Break/Teenage Thunder (Spitstyle)/Suicide (12", stickered p/s)	8

(see also Sigue Sigue Sputnik)

SCISSOR FITS
79	Dubious DUB 1/SJP 793	TAUT? TENSE? ANGULAR? AND OTHER BRITISH RAIL SANDWICHES (EP, gatefold sleeve)	6
79	Tortch TOR 005	SOON AFTER DARK (EP)	5

JOANNE SCOONI
59	Philips PB 936	Constantly/Scibidou (78)	10

SCOOP
80	Sharp POINT 1	You Can Do It/Disco/My Friend Tony/Anonymity (p/s)	5

SCORCHED EARTH
85	Carrere CAR 342	Tomorrow Never Comes/Questions (promo only, no p/s)	35
85	Carrere CART 342	Tomorrow Never Comes/Questions/So Long/Where Do We Go From Here (12", initially black sleeve, later red sleeve with insert)	50/35

SCORCHERS
69	Camel CA 17	Hold On Tight/THE ROYALS: 100 Lbs Of Clay	6
69	Duke DU 26	Hear Ya/VIBRATORS: Live Life	7

(see also Neville Hinds)

SCORE
66	Decca F 12527	Please Please Me/Beg Me	120

SCORPION & BORIS GARDINER HAPPENING
73	Dragon DRA 1002	Deadly Sting/BORIS GARDINER HAPPENING: Boing Boing	5

SCORPIONS (U.K.)
61	Parlophone R 4740	(Ghost) Riders In The Sky/Torquay	15
61	Parlophone R 4768	Rockin' At The Phil/Scorpio	15

SCORPIONS (Jamaica)
72	Green Door GD 4019	Breaking Your Heart/IN CROWD BAND: Breaking Your Heart Version	5

(see also Bill Gentles, Lloyd Jackson)

SCORPIONS (Germany)
77	RCA PB 5556	He's A Woman, She's A Man/Suspender Love	8
79	Harvest HAR 5185	Is Anybody There?/Another Piece Of Meat (p/s, green vinyl)	6
79	Harvest HAR 5185	Is Anybody There?/Another Piece Of Meat (12", p/s)	8
79	Harvest HAR 5188	Love Drive/Coast To Coast (p/s)	5
79	Harvest 12HAR 5188	Love Drive/Coast To Coast (12", p/s)	8
79	RCA PC 9402	All Night Long/Fly To The Rainbow/Speedy's Coming/In Trance (12", p/s)	8
80	Harvest HAR 5206	Make It Real/Don't Make No Promises (p/s)	4
80	Harvest HAR 5212	The Zoo/Holiday (p/s)	4
82	Harvest HAR 5219	No One Like You/Now! (p/s)	4
82	Harvest HARP 5219	No One Like You/Now! (picture disc)	6
82	Harvest HAR 5221	Can't Live Without You/Always Somewhere (p/s, clear vinyl)	4
84	Harvest HAR 5225	Rock You Like A Hurricane/Coming Home (p/s)	4
84	Harvest HAR 5231	Big City Nights/Bad Boys Running Wild (p/s)	4
84	Harvest 12HAR 5231	Big City Nights/Bad Boys Running Wild (12", p/s)	7
84	Harvest 12HARP 5231	Big City Nights/Bad Boys Running Wild (12", picture disc)	8
85	Harvest HAR 5232	Still Loving You/Holiday (p/s)	4
85	Harvest 12HAR 5232	Still Loving You/Holiday/Big City Night (12", p/s)	7
85	Harvest 12HAR 5232	Still Loving You/Holiday/Big City Night (12", picture disc)	10
88	Harvest HARX 5240	Rhythm Of Love/We Let It Rock (box set with postcards)	5
88	Harvest HARP 5240	Rhythm Of Love/We Let It Rock (picture disc)	6
89	Harvest CDHAR 5242	Passion Rules The Game (3.42)/Every Minute Every Day/Is There Anybody There?/Passion Rules The Game (5.18) (CD)	7
91	Vertigo VER 54	Wind Of Change/Restless Nights (p/s, red vinyl)	5
91	Vertigo VERXP 54	Wind Of Change/Restless Nights/Hit Between The Nights/Blackout (live) (12", picture disc)	8
79	Harvest LP SHSP 4097	LOVE DRIVE (LP)	12
82	H.M. Worldwide HMILP 2	LONESOME CROW (LP, clear vinyl)	12
82	H.M. Worldwide HMIPD 2	LONESOME CROW (LP, picture disc)	12
86	EMI CDP 7461 552	WORLD WIDE LIVE (CD)	15
88	Harvest SHSPP 4125	SAVAGE AMUSEMENT (LP, picture disc, with lyric sheet)	15
97	Mercury 314 534 788 2	WORLD WIDE LIVE (CD, reissue)	18

(see also Michael Schenker, Michael Schenker Group)

COLIN SCOT
71	United Artists UP 35216	Hey Sandy/Nite People	4
71	United Artists UAG 29154	COLIN SCOT WITH FRIENDS (LP, gatefold sleeve, with Peter Hammill & Peter Gabriel)	10
73	Warner Bros K 46236	JUST ANOTHER CLOWN (LP, gatefold sleeve)	10

(see also Peter Hammill, Peter Gabriel)

WINSTON SCOTLAND
72	Green Door GD 4027	My (Girl) Little Filly/BUNNY BROWN: My Girl	6
72	Punch PH 100	Butter Cup/RONALD WILSON: I Care	6

(see also Bunny Flip, Big Youth, Bongo Les, Lennox Brown, Dennis Alcapone)

SCOTS OF ST. JAMES
66	Go AJ 111404	Gypsy/Tic Toc	80
67	Spot JW 1	Timothy/Eiderdown Clown	70

(see also Hopscotch, Forever More, Average White Band, Five Day Rain)

ANDY SCOTT
75	RCA RCA 2629	Lady Starlight/Where D'Ya Go (p/s)	12
83	Static TAK 10	Krugerrands/Face (p/s)	8
84	Static TAK 24	Let Her Dance/Suck It And See (p/s)	10
84	Static TAK 24-12	Let Her Dance (Full Version)/(Instrumental)/Suck It And See (12", p/s)	10
84	Static TAK 31	Invisible/Never Too Young (clear vinyl, stickered PVC sleeve)	7
84	Statik TAK 31-12	Invisible (Single Version)/(Instrumental)/Invisible (Extended Version)/	
		Never Too Young (12", clear vinyl, stickered PVC sleeve)	10

(see also Sweet, Elastic Band, Mayfield's Mule, G.O.S.H.)

ARTIE SCOTT ORCHESTRA
70	Major Minor MM 670	March Of The Skinheads/Love At First Sight	8

BILLY SCOTT
58	London HLU 8565	You're The Greatest/That's Why I Was Born	18
58	London HLU 8565	You're The Greatest/That's Why I Was Born (78)	15
60	Top Rank JAR 270	Carole/Stairway To The Stairs	6

BOBBY SCOTT
56	London HL 8254	Chain Gang/Shadrack	40
56	London HL 8254	Chain Gang/Shadrack (78)	25
55	London Jazz LZ-N 14001	BOBBY SCOTT TRIO (10" LP)	15

BRUCE SCOTT
65	Mercury MF 857	I Made An Angel Cry/Don't Say Goodbye To Me	15
65	MGM MGM 1291	Once A Thief Twice A Thief/So Much To Live For	6

DEREK SCOTT ORCHESTRA
63	Pye 7N 15500	Hancock's Tune/Spying Tonight	6

FREDDIE SCOTT
63	Colpix PX 692	Hey Girl/The Slide	18
63	Colpix PX 709	I Got A Woman/Brand New World	18
67	London HLZ 10103	Are You Lonely For Me/Where Were You	8
67	London HLZ 10123	Cry To Me/No One Could Ever Love You	6
67	London HLZ 10139	Am I Grooving You?/Never You Mind	6
67	London HLZ 10172	He Ain't Give You None/Run Joe	6
69	Roulette RO 509	Sugar Sunday/Johnny's Hill	6
71	Jay Boy BOY 34	Just Like A Flower/Spanish Harlem	5
72	Jay Boy BOY 59	Are You Lonely For Me Baby/The Woman Of My Love	5
70s	Upfront UP 1	The Great If/Deep In The Night	5
71	Joy JOYS 215	ARE YOU LONELY FOR ME (LP)	20

GERRY SCOTT
62	Parlophone R 4908	Stay With Me/Summer Love	4

HAZEL SCOTT
53	Capitol LC 6607	LATE SHOW (10" LP)	20

JACK SCOTT (& CHANTONES)
78s
58	London HLU 8626	My True Love/Leroy (78)	30
58	London HLL 8765	With Your Love/Geraldine (as Jack Scott with Chantones) (78)	50
59	London HLL 8804	Goodbye Baby/Save My Soul (as Jack Scott with Chantones) (78)	55
59	London HLL 8851	I Never Felt Like This/Bella (78)	60
59	London HLL 8912	The Way I Walk/Midgie (78)	70
59	London HLL 8970	There Comes A Time/Baby Marie (78)	100

SINGLES
58	London HLU 8626	My True Love/Leroy	10
58	London HLL 8765	With Your Love/Geraldine (as Jack Scott with Chantones)	15
59	London HLL 8804	Goodbye Baby/Save My Soul (as Jack Scott with Chantones)	15
59	London HL 7069	Goodbye Baby/Save My Soul (export issue)	12
59	London HLL 8851	I Never Felt Like This/Bella	15
59	London HLL 8912	The Way I Walk/Midgie (triangular or round centre)	20/15
59	London HLL 8970	There Comes A Time/Baby Marie (triangular or round centre)	18/15
60	Top Rank JAR 280	What In The World's Come Over You/Baby, Baby	8
60	Top Rank JAR 375	Burning Bridges/Oh, Little One	10
60	Top Rank JAR 419	Cool Water/It Only Happened Yesterday	10
60	Top Rank JAR 524	Patsy/Old Time Religion	10
61	Top Rank JAR 547	Is There Something On Your Mind/Found A Woman	10
61	Capitol CL 15200	A Little Feeling/Now That I	10
61	Capitol CL 15216	Strange Desire/My Dream Come True	12
62	Capitol CL 15236	One Of These Days/Steps 1 And 2	12
62	Capitol CL 15261	Sad Story/I Can't Hold Your Letters In My Arms	15
63	Capitol CL 15302	Meo Myo/All I See Is Blue	15

EPs
59	London RE-I 1205	MY TRUE LOVE (EP, initially triangular centre, later round centre)	100/75
61	Top Rank JKP 3002	WHAT IN THE WORLD'S COME OVER YOU (EP)	60
61	Top Rank JKP 3011	I REMEMBER HANK WILLIAMS (EP)	50
64	Capitol EAP 20035	BURNING BRIDGES (EP, existence unconfirmed)	250

LPs
58	London HA-L 2156	JACK SCOTT (LP)	100
60	Top Rank BUY 034	I REMEMBER HANK WILLIAMS (LP)	30
60	Top Rank 25-024	WHAT IN THE WORLD'S COME OVER YOU (LP)	65
61	Top Rank 35-109	THE SPIRIT MOVES ME (LP)	55
64	Capitol (S)T 2035	BURNING BRIDGES (LP, mono/stereo)	50/60

JANET SCOTT & JACKIE RAE
60	Fontana TFE 17203	SWEET TALK (EP, also stereo STFE 8009)	7/8
60	Fontana TFL 5102	WE LOVE LIFE! (LP, also stereo STFL 533)	10/12

(see also Jackie Rae)

JIMMY SCOTT
69	Revolution REV 002	Ob-La-Di, Ob-La-Da/Story Part 2 — Allulo & Doh	5

JOHN SCOTT
60	Parlophone R 4697	Hi-Flutin' Boogie/Peace Pipe	5

JOHN(NY) SCOTT
60	Oriole CB 1542	Darlin'/Why Don't You Write Me? (as Johnny Scott)	6
60	Philips PB 1056	They Say/How About That (as John Scott)	5

JOHNNY SCOTT QUINTET
67	Columbia S(C)X 6149	COMMUNICATION (LP)	12
70	Fontana 6383 002	PURCELL VARIATIONS FOR FIVE (LP)	12

JUDI SCOTT
68	Page One POF 066	Billy Sunshine/Happy Song	10

JUDY SCOTT
57	Brunswick 05687	The Game Of Love (A-One And A-Two)/With All My Heart	7
57	Brunswick 05704	Parlour Piano Theme/A Tender Word	7

JULIAN SCOTT
61	Columbia DB 4571	My Steady Date/So Tired	5

KEVIN SCOTT
59	Parlophone R 4520	Wait For Me/Love Of My Life	5
59	Parlophone R 4520	Wait For Me/Love Of My Life (78)	8
59	Parlophone R 4540	Ciao Ciao Bambina (Piove)/Broken-Hearted Clown	5
60	HMV POP 731	You Are Beautiful/Love Look Away	5

LINDA SCOTT
60	Columbia DB 4638	I've Told Every Little Star/Three Guesses	6
61	Columbia DB 4692	Don't Bet Money, Honey/Starlight Starbright	6
61	Columbia DB 4748	I Don't Know Why/It's All Because	7
61	Columbia DB 4829	Count Every Star/Land Of Stars	7
62	Pye International 7N 25146	Never In A Million Years/Through The Summer	7
63	London HLR 9802	Let's Fall In Love/I Know It, You Know It	8
61	Columbia 33SX 1386	STARLIGHT, STARBRIGHT (LP)	60

LINDA SCOTT
69	CBS 4528	The Composer/You Made A Fool Out Of Me	6
69	CBS 4246	First Of All/The Answer's In My Eyes	6

McBEAN SCOTT & CHAMPIONS
70	Jackpot JP 744	Top Of The World/LARRY LAWRENCE & CHAMPIONS: Everybody Reggae	6

MIKE SCOTT
65	Mercury MF 906	I Am A Rock/I'm Gonna Be Somebody Someday	6

NEIL SCOTT
61	Pye International 7N 25096	Bobby/I Haven't Found It With Another	6

NICKY SCOTT
67	Immediate IM 044	Big City/Everything's Gonna Be Alright	20
67	Immediate IM 045	Backstreet Girl/Chain Reaction	20
69	Pye 7N 17688	Honey Pie/No More Tomorrow	6

(see also Diane Ferraz & Nicky Scott)

PEGGY SCOTT
69	Polydor 56722	Every Little Bit Hurts/You Can Never Get Something For Nothing	6
79	Pinnacle PIN 73	You've Got It All/Let Me Unite You (p/s)	5

(see also Peggy Scott & Jo Jo Benson)

PEGGY SCOTT & JO JO BENSON
68	Polydor 56745	Lover's Holiday/Here With Me	6
69	Polydor 56750	Pickin' Wild Mountain Berries/Pure Love And Pleasure	5
69	Polydor 56761	Soulshake/We Were Made For Each Other	5
69	Polydor 56773	We Got Our Own Bag/I Want To Love You Babe	5
71	Atlantic 2091 066	I Thank You/Spreadin' Love	5
69	Polydor 583 731	SOULSHAKE (LP)	12
70	Polydor 583 756	LOVER'S HEAVEN (LP)	12

(see also Peggy Scott)

RAMBLIN' TOMMY SCOTT
54	Parlophone CMSP 15	Ain't Love Grand/What Do You Know — I Love Her (export issue)	18

RAYMOND SCOTT
54	London L 1229	Naked City/Shadow Dance (78)	12

ROBIN SCOTT
69	Head HDS 4003	The Sailor/Sound Of The Rain	25
69	Head HDLS 6003	WOMAN FROM THE WARM GRASS (LP, with insert)	120

(see also Mighty Baby, M)

RONNIE SCOTT
51	Esquire 10-154	Crazy Rhythm/El Sino (78)	8
51	Esquire 10-185	Close Your Eyes/I Didn't Know What Time It Was (78, with Ronnie Ball)	8
53	Esquire 10-321	Stomping At The Savoy/Body Beautiful (78)	8
54	Esquire 10-335	Night And Day	8
56	Decca FJ 10712	Basie Talks/Flying Home (as Ronnie Scott Orchestra)	8
57	Tempo A 153	I'll Take Romance/Speak Low (as Ronnie Scott New Quintet)	30

MINT VALUE £

57	Tempo A 153	I'll Take Romance/Speak Low (as Ronnie Scott New Quintet) (78). 8
55	Esquire EP 31	RONNIE SCOTT ORCHESTRA (EP) 20
55	Esquire EP 51	RONNIE SCOTT QUARTET (EP). 20
55	Esquire EP 61	RONNIE SCOTT ORCHESTRA (EP) 20
55	Esquire EP 65	RONNIE SCOTT QUINTET (EP) 10
56	Esquire EP 81	RONNIE SCOTT ORCHESTRA (EP) 20
56	Esquire EP 85	RONNIE SCOTT ORCHESTRA (EP) 25
56	Esquire EP 95	RONNIE SCOTT ORCHESTRA (EP) 15
56	Tempo EXA 45	RONNIE SCOTT BLOWS WITH THE DIZZY REECE QUARTET (EP) 150
52	Esquire 20-006	RONNIE SCOTT QUARTET (10" LP) 50
54	Esquire 32-001	THE RONNIE SCOTT JAZZ CLUB VOLUME 1 (LP) 45
54	Esquire 32-002	THE RONNIE SCOTT JAZZ CLUB VOLUME 2 (LP) 45
54	Esquire 32-003	THE RONNIE SCOTT JAZZ CLUB VOLUME 3 (LP) 45
54	Esquire 32-006	THE RONNIE SCOTT JAZZ CLUB VOLUME 4 (LP) 45
56	Decca LF 1261	AT THE ROYAL FESTIVAL HALL (10" LP) 45
57	Philips BBL 7153	PRESENTING THE RONNIE SCOTT SEXTET (LP) 100
66	Fontana TL 5332	THE NIGHT IS SCOTT AND YOU'RE SO SWINGABLE (LP). 75
69	CBS Realm Jazz 523661	LIVE AT RONNIE SCOTT'S (LP) 40
74	RCA Victor LPL1	SCOTT AT RONNIE'S (LP) 40
77	Pye NSPL 18542	SERIOUS GOLD (LP) 30

(see also Jazz Couriers, Tubby Hayes, Dizzy Reece)

SHIRLEY SCOTT

66	Transatlantic PR 7205	HIP SOUL (LP) 20
69	Atlantic 588 175	SOUL SONG (LP) 15
71	Chess 6310 109	MYSTICAL LADY (LP) 15

SIMON SCOTT (& LE ROYS)

64	Parlophone R 5164	Move It Baby/What Kind Of Woman (with Le Roys) 7
64	Parlophone R 5207	My Baby's Got Soul/Midnight (with Le Roys) 6
65	Parlophone R 5298	Tell Him I'm Not Home (as Simon Scott & All Nite Workers)/Heart Cry 12
69	Polydor 56355	Brave New World/I'm The Universe 5

(see also Le Roys)

TERRY SCOTT (& June Whitfield)

62	Parlophone R 4967	My Brother/Don't Light The Fire 'Til After 12
66	Pye 7N 17093	Juanita Banana/I Like Birds. 6
76	DJM DJS 665	A Bed Full Of Foreigners/Nicholas The Circus Clown 5

TOMMY SCOTT

62	Decca F 11474	Angela/Did You (as Jay & Tommy Scott) 6
64	Decca F 11839	Who Will It Be?/If It's Me That You Want 6
64	Decca F 11942	Wrap Your Troubles In Dreams/Blueberry Hill 6

TONY SCOTT

69	Escort ES 805	What Am I To Do/Bring Back That Smile 8
69	Escort ES 816	Darling If You Love Me/Saturday Night 6

SCOTT BROTHERS

61	Fontana H 317	Travellin' Home/Susie Black 6
63	Decca F 11539	Yuggi Duggi/Our Time 6

GIL SCOTT-HERON (& BRIAN JACKSON)

73	Philips 6073 705	Lady Day And John Coltrane/When You Are Who You Are 5
75	Arista ARIST 23	(What's The Word) Johannesburg/Fell Together 5
78	Arista ARIST 169	The Bottle (live)/Hello Sunday, Hello Road 6
79	Inferno HEAT 23	The Bottle (Drunken Mix)/The Bottle (Sober Mix) (with Brian Jackson). . . . 5
79	Inferno HEAT 23-12	The Bottle (Drunken Mix)/The Bottle (Sober Mix) (12", with Brian Jackson) 8
81	Champagne VAT 302	The Bottle (Drunken Mix)/The Bottle (Sober Mix) (reissue) 4
81	Champagne VATS 302	The Bottle (Drunken Mix)/The Bottle (Sober Mix) (12", reissue). 7
73	Philips 6369 415	PIECES OF A MAN (LP) 25
74	RCA SF 8428	THE REVOLUTION WILL NOT BE TELEVISED (LP) 15
75	Arista ARTY 106	FIRST MINUTES OF A NEW DAY (LP) 12
76	Arista ARTY 121	FROM SOUTH AFRICA TO SOUTH CAROLINA (LP, with Brian Jackson). . . . 10
76	Arista DARTY 1	IT'S YOUR WORLD (LP, with Brian Jackson). 35
77	Arista SPARTY 1031	BRIDGES (LP, with Brian Jackson) 10
78	Arista SPARTY 1073	SECRETS (LP, with Brian Jackson). 10

MICHELLE SCOTTI

64	Philips BF 1384	Little Drummer Boy/Lonely Lonely Lonely 7

SCOTT'S WASHBOARD BAND

60	Columbia 33SX 1232	HARLEM WASHBOARD (LP) 10

SCOTTY (David Scott)

70	Songbird SB 1044	Sesame Street/CRYSTALITES: Version 15
71	Duke DU 106	Donkey Skank (with Tennors)/MURPHY'S ALLSTARS: Version 6
71	Songbird SB 1049	Riddle I This/Musical Chariot. 7
71	Songbird SB 1051	Jam Rock Style/Jam Rock Style Version (with Crystalites) 8
71	Songbird SB 1056	Penny For Your Song/CRYSTALITES: Version 6
72	Songbird SB 1080	Clean Race/CRYSTALITES: Version Train 6
72	Harry J. HJ 6642	Skank In Bed/BONGO HERMAN: African Breakfast 5
73	Count Shelley CS 036	Salvation Train/KEN PARKER: Message To Mary 8
71	Trojan TRL 33	SCHOOLDAYS (LP) 40

(see also Lloyd Charmers, Joe White)

SCRAPING FOETUS OFF THE WHEEL

81	Womb WOMB-OYBL-2	HOLE (LP, gatefold sleeve with lyrics, also listed as FDL 3) 40

(see also Foetus, You've Got Foetus On Your Breath, Philip & His Foetus Vibrations)

SCREAMING DEAD

82	Skull DEAD 1	Valley Of The Dead/Schoolgirl Junkie (p/s) 4

MINT VALUE £

SCRITTI POLITTI
78	St. Pancras SCRIT 1	Skank Bloc Bologna/Is And Ought Of The Western World/28.8.78 (photocopied stapled foldout p/s, hand-stamped white labels)	6
79	Rough Trade RT 027T	4 A SIDES (12" EP)	5
79	Rough Trade	Songs To Remember/The Cassette Interview (cassette, with 12-page booklet & 2 photos, promo only)	10
79	St. Pancras SCRIT 2/RT 034	PEEL SESSIONS (EP, with photcopied inserts)	5
99	Virgin PROMO 5 2884	ANOMIE AND BONHOMIE (CD, 5 track album sampler, card p/s with inner sleeve, promo)	12

SCROTUM POLES
79	Scrotum Poles ERECT 1	Revelation: Why Don't You Come Out Tonight?/Night Train/ Pick The Cat's Eyes Out/Helicopter Honeymoon/Radio Tay (handwritten labels, 2 p/s designs)	each 35
80s	One-Tone ERECT 1	AUCHMITHY CALLING (cassette)	15

SCRUGG
68	Pye 7N 17451	I Wish I Was Five/Everyone Can See	25
68	Pye 7N 17551	Lavender Popcorn/Sandwichboard Man	40
69	Pye 7N 17656	Will The Real Geraldine Please Stand Up/Only George	25

(see also Floribunda Rose, John T. Kongos)

EARL SCRUGGS
72	CBS 7877	Brand New Tennessee Waltz/Foggy Mountain Breakdown	5
72	CBS 64777	EARL SCRUGGS: HIS FAMILY AND FRIENDS (LP, with Byrds, Joan Baez, Bob Dylan, etc.)	15

(see also Flatt & Scruggs, Byrds)

IRENE SCRUGGS
50s	Poydras 80	You've Got What I Want/My Back To The Wall (78)	8

MR. JOHNNY SEA
60s	Fontana FJL 315	EVERYBODY'S FAVOURITE (LP)	12

SEA-DERS
67	Decca F 22576	Thanks A Lot/Undecidedly	35
67	Decca DFE-R 8674	THE SEA-DERS (EP, export issue)	200

(see also Cedars)

DAVE SEALEY
69	DJM DJS 210	Picking Up The Pieces/I Can't Go On Living Without You	6

MILT SEALEY TRIO
60s	Duc. Thompson DEP 95017	MILTON SEALEY AND KANSAS FIELDS (EP)	8

PHIL SEAMAN
68	Verve (S)VLP 9220	PHIL SEAMAN NOW ... LIVE (LP)	150
60s	Decibel BSN 103	PHIL SEAMAN STORY (LP)	40
60s	Saga OPP 102	MEETS EDDIE GOMEZ (LP)	100
74	77 Records 77 SEU 12/53	PHIL ON DRUMS (LP)	35

SEARCHERS
63	Pye 7N 15533	Sweets For My Sweet/It's All Been A Dream	6
63	Philips BF 1274	Sweet Nuthins/What'd I Say	10
63	Pye 7N 15566	Sugar And Spice/Saints And Searchers (dark maroon or lighter pink label)	10/5
64	Pye 7N 15594	Needles And Pins/Saturday Night Out	6
64	Pye 7N 15630	Don't Throw Your Love Away/I Pretend I'm With You	5
64	Pye 7N 15670	Someday We're Gonna Love Again/No One Else Could Love You	5
64	Pye 7N 15694	When You Walk In The Room/I'll Be Missing You	6
64	Pye 7N 15739	What Have They Done To The Rain/This Feeling Inside (maroon or lighter pink label)	7/5
65	Pye 7N 15794	Goodbye My Love/Till I Met You	5
65	Pye 7N 15878	He's Got No Love/So Far Away	6
65	Pye 7N 15950	When I Get Home/I'm Never Coming Back	5
65	Pye 7N 15992	Take Me For What I'm Worth/Too Many Miles (a few in export p/s)	25/6
66	Pye 7N 17094	Take It Or Leave It/Don't Hide It Away	6
66	Pye 7N 17170	Have You Ever Loved Somebody/It's Just The Way	6
67	Pye 7N 17225	Popcorn, Double Feature/Lovers	12
67	Pye 7N 17308	Western Union/I'll Cry Tomorrow	12
67	Pye 7N 17424	Secondhand Dealer/Crazy Dreams	25
68	Liberty LBF 15159	Umbrella Man/Over The Weekend	30
69	Liberty LBF 15340	Kinky Kathy Abernathy/Suzanna	40
71	Pye PMM 101	Needles And Pins/Take It Or Leave It/Sweets For My Sweet/Alright (p/s, maxi-single)	5
71	RCA RCA 2057	Desdemona/The World Is Waiting For Tomorrow	12
71	RCA RCA 2139	Love Is Everywhere/And A Button	8
72	RCA RCA 2231	Sing Singer Sing/Come On Back To Me	8
72	RCA RCA 2248	Needles And Pins/When You Walk In The Room/Come On Back To Me	8
72	RCA RCA 2288	Vahevala/Madman	12
73	RCA RCA 2330	Solitaire/Spicks And Specks	5
79	Sire SIR 4029	Hearts In Her Eyes/Don't Hang On (p/s)	8
80	Sire SIR 4036	It's Too Late/This Kind Of Love Affair (p/s)	6
81	Sire SIR 4046	Love's Melody/Changing (p/s)	10
81	Sire SIR 4049	Another Night/Back To The War (p/s)	8
80s	private pressing	Don't Make Promises	10
80s	private pressing	Four Strong Winds	10

EPs
63	Pye NEP 24177	AIN'T GONNA KISS YA (EP)	15
63	Pye NEP 24183	SWEETS FOR MY SWEET (EP, some copies with white & maroon label)	12
64	Pye NEP 24184	HUNGRY FOR LOVE (EP)	15
64	Pye NEP 24201	THE SEARCHERS PLAY THE SYSTEM (EP)	18

SEARCHERS

64	Pye NEP 24204	WHEN YOU WALK IN THE ROOM (EP)	20
65	Pye NEP 24218	BUMBLE BEE (EP)	18
65	Pye NEP 24222	SEARCHERS '65 (EP)	20
65	Pye NEP 24228	FOUR BY FOUR (EP)	20
66	Pye NEP 24263	TAKE ME FOR WHAT I'M WORTH (EP)	80

LPs

62	private pressing	THE SEARCHERS (LP)	150+
63	Pye NPL 18086	MEET THE SEARCHERS (LP)	20
63	Pye NPL 18089	SUGAR AND SPICE (LP)	18
64	Pye NPL 18092	IT'S THE SEARCHERS (LP)	18
65	Pye NPL 18111	SOUNDS LIKE SEARCHERS (LP)	18
65	Pye NPL 18120	TAKE ME FOR WHAT I'M WORTH (LP)	25
67	Marble Arch MAL 640	SMASH HITS VOL. 1 (LP)	12
67	Marble Arch MAL(S) 673	SMASH HITS VOL. 2 (LP, mono/stereo)	12
72	RCA SF 8289	SECOND TAKE (LP)	15
79	Sire SRK 6082	SEARCHERS (LP)	12
80	Sire SRK 6086	THE SEARCHERS (LP)	12
81	Sire SRK 3523	PLAY FOR TODAY (LP)	12
83	PRT DOW 11	LOVE LIES BLEEDING (10" LP)	12

(see also Tony Jackson & Vibrations, Chris Curtis, Pasha)

AL SEARS
52	Vogue V 21242	Berry Wells/Steady Eddie (78)	10

SEA STONE
78	Plankton PKN 101	MIRRORED DREAMS (LP, with insert)	80

SEATHROUGH
70s	private pressing	LALA LAPLA (LP)	40

B.B. SEATON
72	Big BG 336	I Want Justice/RUPIE EDWARD'S ALL STARS: Justice (Version)	6
72	Bullet BU 514	I Miss My Schooldays/CONSCIOUS MINDS: School Days — Version	6
72	Camel CA 100	Lean On Me/NOW GENERATION: Samba Pati	6
72	Pama PM 864	I Want Justice/RUPIE EDWARD'S ALL STARS: Justice — Version	6
72	Pama Supreme PS 374	Sweet Caroline/Eleanor Rigby	5
73	Trojan TRLS 59	THE THIN LINE BETWEEN LOVE AND HATE (LP)	20

(see also Bibby, Winston & Bibby, Gaylads, Messengers)

HORACE SEATON
63	Island WI 123	I'm So Glad/Tell Me	18
64	R&B JB 143	Hold On/LESTER STERLING: Peace And Love	12

(see also Bibby, B.B. Seaton, Tommy McCook)

SEA & CAKE
95	Lissy's LIS 1	Glad You're Right/Tiger Partner/Crimson Wing (p/s, 500 only)	8

(see also Tortoise)

SEA TRAIN
68	A&M AMS 737	Let The Duchess Know/As I Lay Losing	4
69	A&M AMLS 941	SEA TRAIN (LP)	15
71	Capitol EA-ST 659	SEA TRAIN (LP)	12
72	Capitol EA-ST 829	MARBLEHEAD MESSENGER (LP, gatefold sleeve)	12
73	Warner Bros K 46222	WATCH (LP)	10

(see also Blues Project, Old & In The Way)

SEA URCHINS

87	Sha La La Ba Ba Ba Ba Ba 5	Summershine/ORCHIDS: From This Day (flexidisc, 2,500 only, 1,000 w/p/s)	10/5
87	Sarah SARAH 001	Pristine Christine/Sullen Eyes/Everglades (foldaround p/s with 14" x 10" poster in poly bag, 1,600 only)	35
88	Sarah SARAH 008	Solace/Please Rain Fall (foldaround p/s in poly bag)	15
88	Kvatch KVATCH 001/ Lyntone LYN 18632	Clingfilm/GROOVE FARM: Baby Blue Marine (flexidisc, 1,000 only, 500 in p/s)	15/8
89	Fierce FRIGHT 032	30.10.88 (live) (1-sided, p/s)	10
91	Cheree CHEREE 15	Please Don't Cry/Time Is All I've Seen (die-cut company sleeve)	4

SEAWIND

78	CTI CTSP 13	One Sweet Night/Countin' The Days	8

JOHN SEBASTIAN

54	London HL 8029	Inca Dance/Foolish Waltz	25
54	London HL 8029	Inca Dance/Foolish Waltz (78)	12
55	London HL 8131	Stranger In Paradise/Autumn Leaves	20
55	London HL 8131	Stranger In Paradise/Autumn Leaves (78)	5

JOHN (B.) SEBASTIAN

69	Kama Sutra 618 026	She's A Lady/The Room Nobody Lives In	6
70	Reprise RS 20902	Magical Connection/Fa-Fana-Fa	5
70	Reprise RSLP 6379	JOHN B. SEBASTIAN (LP, gatefold sleeve)	18
70	Buddah 2361 003	JOHN SEBASTIAN SONGBOOK VOLUME ONE (LP, with Lovin' Spoonful)	15
71	Reprise K 44149	THE FOUR OF US (LP, gatefold sleeve)	15

(see also Lovin' Spoonful, Even Dozen Jug Band)

HARRY SECOMBE

60	Philips PB 974	Jerusalem/The Holy City (78)	8

(see also Goons)

SECOND CITY SOUND

65	Decca F 12310	Tchaikovsky One/Shadows	5
66	Decca F 12366	Greig One/In A Mist	5
66	Decca F 12406	Love's Funny/Tell Me Where I'm Going	5
69	Major Minor MM 600	The Dream Of Olwyn/A Touch Of Velvet, A Sting of Brass	6

SECOND COMING

71	Mercury 6338 030	SECOND COMING (LP)	15

SECONDHAND

69	Polydor 56308	Fairy Tales	15
68	Polydor 583 045	REALITY (LP, labels on early copies credit band as Moving Finger)	60
72	Mushroom MR 2006	DEATH MAY BE YOUR SANTA CLAUS (LP, some copies omit "Funeral")	100

(see also Andreas Thomopoulos, Fungus, Chillum, Vulcans, Seventh Wave)

SECOND LAYER

79	Tortch-r TOR 001	FLESH AS PROPERTY (EP, white p/s, black printed labels)	12
80	Tortch TOR 006	State Of Emergency/I Need Noise/The Cutting Motion (p/s)	8
81	Tortch/Fresh FRESH 5	FLESH AS PROPERTY (EP, reissue, yellow p/s & white labels)	10
81	Cherry Red CHERRY 21	FLESH AS PROPERTY (EP, 2nd reissue, unreleased)	
82	Cherry Red BRED 14	WORLD OF RUBBER (LP, with inner)	12

(see also Outsiders, Sound)

SECOND VISION

80	Chrysalis CHR 1289	FIRST STEPS (LP, with insert)	10

MIKE SECREST

57	MGM MGM 960	The Gift/Do You Promise (78)	8

SECRET

77	Arista ARIST 142	The Young Ones/Handel A Vandel	7
78	Arista ARIST 173	Do You Really Care?/I Wanna Car Like That	4

SECRET AFFAIR

79	I-Spy SEE 1	Time For Action/Soho Strut (brown p/s, black print or black p/s, white print)	5/4
79	I-Spy SEE 3	Let Your Heart Dance/Sorry Wrong Number (p/s)	4
80	I-Spy SEE 5	My World/So Cool (paper labels, some with badge)	6/4
80	I-Spy SEE 8	Sound Of Confusion/Take It Or Leave It (p/s)	4
81	I-Spy SEE 10	Do You Know?/Dance Master (keyhole company sleeve, paper labels)	4
82	I-Spy SEE 11	Lost In The Night (Mack The Knife)/The Big Beat (p/s)	5
79	I-Spy I SPY 1	GLORY BOYS (LP, with 2 inserts)	15
80	I-Spy I SPY 2	BEHIND CLOSED DOORS (LP, with inner sleeve)	15
82	I-Spy I SPY 3	BUSINESS AS USUAL (LP, stickered sleeve)	12

(see also New Hearts, Advertising, Innocents [U.K.])

SECRET GOLDFISH

81	Postcard 81-11	Hey Mister/Poorest Boy In Town (unreleased)	

SECRET OYSTER

74	CBS 80489	SEA SON (LP)	10

SECRETS

64	Philips BF 1298	The Boy Next Door/Learnin' To Forget	12
64	Philips BF 1318	Hey Big Boy/Other Side Of Town	12

SECRETS

66	CBS 202466	I Suppose/Such A Pity	20
67	CBS 202585	Infatuation/She's Dangerous	20
67	CBS 2818	I Intend To Please/I Think I Need The Cash	20

(see also Simon's Secrets, Clifford T. Ward, Martin Raynor & Secrets)

SECT

81	Shoestring SHOE 1	This is Your Life/Private Eye (p/s)	4

SECTION 25
81	Factory FACT 45	ALWAYS NOW (LP, in envelope/folder)	10

NEIL SEDAKA
59	RCA RCA 1099	The Diary/No Vacancy	15
59	RCA RCA 1099	The Diary/No Vacancy (78)	65
59	RCA RCA 1115	I Go Ape/Moon Of Gold	12
59	RCA RCA 1115	I Go Ape/Moon Of Gold (78)	65
59	RCA RCA 1130	You've Got To Learn Your Rhythm And Blues/Crying My Heart Out For You	15
59	RCA RCA 1130	You've Got To Learn Your Rhythm And Blues/ Crying My Heart Out For You (78)	85
59	London HLW 8961	Ring A Rockin'/Fly Don't Fly On Me	45
59	London HLW 8961	Ring A Rockin'/Fly Don't Fly On Me (78)	100

(The above RCA 45s were originally issued with triangular centres; later round-centres are worth two-thirds these values.)

59	RCA RCA 1152	Oh! Carol/One Way Ticket (triangular centre or round centre)	12/6
59	RCA RCA 1152	Oh! Carol/One Way Ticket (78)	175
60	RCA RCA 1178	Stairway To Heaven/Forty Winks Away	6
60	RCA RCA 1178	Stairway To Heaven/Forty Winks Away (78)	175
60	RCA RCA 1198	Run Samson Run/You Mean Everything To Me	6
60	RCA RCA 1198	Run Samson Run/You Mean Everything To Me (78)	175
61	RCA RCA 1220	Calendar Girl/The Same Old Fool	6
61	RCA RCA 1236	Little Devil/I Must Be Dreaming	6
61	RCA RCA 1250	Sweet Little You/I Found My World In You	6
61	RCA RCA 1266	Happy Birthday, Sweet Sixteen/Don't Lead Me On	6
62	RCA RCA 1282	King Of Clowns/Walk With Me	6
62	Stateside SS 105	Oh Delilah/MARVELS: Neil's Twist	12
62	RCA RCA 1298	Breaking Up Is Hard To Do/As Long As I Live	6
62	RCA RCA 1319	Next Door To An Angel/I Belong To You	6
63	RCA RCA 1331	Circulate/Alice In Wonderland	6
63	RCA RCA 1343	Let's Go Steady Again/Waiting For Never	6
63	RCA RCA 1359	The Dreamer/Look Inside Your Heart	7
63	RCA RCA 1368	Bad Girl/Wait 'Til You See My Baby	7
65	RCA RCA 1475	World Through A Tear/High On A Mountain	10
74	Polydor 2058 532	Bad Blood/Hey Mister Sunshine (with Elton John)	5
59	RCA RCX 166	NEIL SEDAKA (EP)	40
60	RCA RCX 186	NEIL SEDAKA VOL. 2 (EP)	30
62	RCA RCX 212	NEIL SEDAKA VOL. 3 (EP)	30
59	RCA RD 27140	NEIL SEDAKA (LP)	80
60	RCA RD 27207/SF 5090	CIRCULATE (LP, mono/stereo)	45/50

(see also Sam Cooke, Paul Anka, 10cc)

MIKE SEDGEWICK
68	Parlophone R 5694	The Good Guys In The White Hats Never Lose/ Woman (She's Got To Be Treated Right)	4

(see also Adam Mike & Tim)

SEDUCER
83	Sticky SSR 0017	Call Your Name (no p/s)	50
85	Thunderbolt THBL 016	CAUGHT IN THE ACT (LP)	10

TOMMY SEEBACH
79	EMI EMI 2934	Disco Tango (English)/Disco Tango (Danish)	4

RUDY SEEDORF
65	Island WI 189	One Million Stars/Mr. Blue	8

SEEDS
66	Vocalion VN 9277	Pushin' Too Hard/Try To Understand	30
67	Vocalion VN 9287	Can't Seem To Make You Mine/Daisy Mae	25
67	Vocalion VAN 8062	A WEB OF SOUND (LP)	45
67	Vocalion VAN/SAVN 8070	FUTURE (LP)	45
78	Sonet SNTF 746	THE SEEDS (LP)	12
89	Bam Caruso STRANGEP 1	THE BEST OF THE SEEDS (LP, picture disc)	12

(see also Sky Saxon, Ya Ho Wa 13)

MIKE SEEGER
65	Fontana TFL 6039	MIKE SEEGER (LP)	15

(see also Peggy & Mike Seeger)

PEGGY SEEGER
57	Topic TRC 107	Freight Train/Cumberland Gap (78)	30
65	Decca F 12282	Pretty Little Baby/My Love And I Are One	6
50s	Pye Jazz NJE 1043	ORIGINS OF SKIFFLE (EP)	20
60	Topic TOP 38	SHINE LIKE A STAR (EP)	10
61	Topic TOP 72	TROUBLED LOVE (EP)	10
61	Topic TOP 73	EARLY IN THE SPRING (EP)	8
61	PRE 13005	THE BEST OF PEGGY SEEGER (LP)	15
64	Topic 12T 113	WHO'S GOING TO SHOE... (LP, with Tom Paley)	18
69	Argo (Z)DA 63	PEGGY ALONE (LP)	18
72	Argo ZFB 63	PEGGY ALONE (LP, reissue)	12
72	Argo ZFB 64	FEMALE FROLIC (LP, with Frankie Armstrong & Sandra Kerr)	15

(see also Al Lloyd)

PEGGY SEEGER & GUY CARAWAN
58	HMV CLP 1174	AMERICA AT PLAY (LP)	18

(see also Guy Carawan)

PEGGY & MIKE SEEGER
68	Argo (Z)DA 80	PEGGY 'N' MIKE (LP)	18
72	Argo ZFB 62	PEGGY 'N' MIKE (LP, reissue)	10

(see also Ewan MacColl & Peggy Seeger, Mike Seeger)

Pete SEEGER

PETE SEEGER

60	Top Rank TR 5020	Careless Love/LEON BIBB: Times Are Getting Hard (p/s)	10
63	CBS AAG 187	Little Boxes/Mail Myself To You	5
58	Melodisc EPM7 78	TRIBUTE TO LEADBELLY (EP)	12
58	Topic TOP 33	PETE AND FIVE STRINGS (EP)	10
59	Topic TOP 37	HOOTENANNY NEW YORK CITY (EP, with Sonny Terry)	15
64	CBS AGG 20055	IN CONCERT (EP)	8
65	CBS EP 6065	HEALING RIVER (EP)	8
66	Ember EP 4560	D-DAY DODGERS (EP)	8
61	Philips BBL 7507	PETE SEEGER STORY SONGS (LP)	12
63	Folklore F-LAUT 1	PETE SEEGER IN CONCERT (LP)	12
63	Folklore F-LAUT 2	PETE SEEGER IN CONCERT VOL. 2 (LP)	12
64	CBS (S)BPG 62209	WE SHALL OVERCOME (LP)	15
65	Xtra XTRA 1005	SING WITH SEEGER (LP)	12
65	CBS (S)BPG 62462	I CAN SEE A NEW DAY (LP)	12
65	CBS (S)BPG 62528	STRANGERS AND COUSINS (LP)	12
66	Xtra XTRA 1016	BROADSIDES (LP)	12
66	Xtra XTRA 1034	FOLK SINGER'S GUITAR GUIDE (LP, with 16-page booklet)	12
66	Verve (S)VLP 5004	IN PERSON (LP)	12
68	Ember CW 130	PETE SEEGER (LP)	12
68	Xtra XTRA 1066	ABIYOYO AND OTHER SONGS (LP)	12

(see also Big Bill Broonzy, Sonny Terry [& Brownie McGhee], Weavers)

PETE SEEGER & BIG BILL BROONZY

64	Xtra XTRA 1006	IN CONCERT — PETE SEEGER & BIG BILL BROONZY (LP)	20
66	Verve Folkways VLP 5006	IN CONCERT (LP, reissue, also ST SVLP 506)	12/15

(see also Big Bill Broonzy)

SEEKERS

65	Oriole CB 1935	With A Swag On My Shoulder/Myra	12
65	Decca F 22167	Chilly Winds/Kumbaya	8
66	Columbia DB 7867	Someday, One Day/Nobody Knows The Trouble I've Seen	5
66	Columbia DB 8000	Walk With Me/We're Moving On	5
67	Columbia DB 8134	Georgy Girl/The Last Thing On My Mind	5
67	Columbia DB 8273	When Will The Good Apples Fall/Myra	5
67	Columbia DB 8313	Music Of The World A Turnin'/Emerald City	5
68	Columbia DB 8407	Days Of My Life/Study War No More (as Seekers with Judith Durham)	5
68	Columbia DB 8460	Love Is Kind, Love Is Wine/All I Can Remember	5
68	Columbia DB 8509	Island Of Dreams/Red Rubber Ball	5
69	Columbia DB 8609	Colours Of My Life/Rattler	5
81	Lyntone LYN 2359	A World Of Their Own (flexidisc sampler for World Record Club box set)	5
65	Columbia SEG 8425	THE SEEKERS (EP)	8
65	Columbia SEG 8465	THE SEEKERS (EP)	8
66	Columbia SEG 8496	HITS FROM THE SEEKERS (EP)	8
67	Columbia SEG 8522	MORNINGTOWN RIDE (EP)	8
65	Decca LK 4694	THE SEEKERS (LP)	12
65	Columbia 33SX 1722	A WORLD OF OUR OWN (LP, blue/black label)	12
66	Columbia S(C)X 6093	COME THE DAY (LP, blue/black label, mono/stereo)	12/15
67	Columbia S(C)X 6193	SEEN IN GREEN (LP, blue/black label, gatefold sleeve)	12
68	Columbia S(C)X 6278	LIVE AT THE TALK OF THE TOWN (LP, blue/black label)	12

(see also Judith Durham, Keith Potger)

JEANNIE SEELY

66	London HLU 10052	Don't Touch Me/You Tied Tin Cans To My Heart	4
68	Monument MON 1023	How Is He?/Little Unfair	4

SEFTONS

66	CBS 202491	I Can See Through You/Here Today	20

(see also Perishers)

VIVIENNE SEGAL & HAROLD LANG

54	Columbia SCM 5114	Den Of Iniquity/BARBARA ASHLEY: That Terrific Rainbow	6

BOB SEGER (SYSTEM)

68	Capitol CL 15574	Ramblin' Gamblin' Man/Tales Of Lucy Blue (as Bob Seger System)	6
70	Capitol CL 15642	Lucifer/Big River (as Bob Seger System)	8
72	Reprise K 14208	If I Were A Carpenter/Jesse James	5
73	Reprise K 14243	Rosalie/Back In '72	5
74	Reprise K 14364	Get Out Of Denver/Long Song Comin'	5
78	Capitol CL 16004	Hollywood Nights/Brave Strangers (silver vinyl, special sleeve)	5
83	Capitol CLD 284	Even Now/Little Victories//We've Got Tonight/ Brave Strangers (double pack)	5
83	Capitol TC-CL 284	Even Now/We've Got Tonight (cassette)	5
86	Capitol CLD 396	American Storm/Fortunate Son//Hollywood Nights/ Hollywood Nights (live) (double pack)	5
72	Reprise K 44214	SMOKIN' O.P.'s (LP)	15
73	Reprise K 44227	BACK IN '72 (LP)	12
77	Capitol CAPS 1010	MONGREL (LP)	12

LLOYD SEIVRIGHT

70	Creole CR 1001	Mary's Boy Child/And Glory Walked Among Men	6

SEIZE

81	Why Not? NOT 001	Grovelands Road/Why? (p/s)	15
82	Why Not? NOT 002	EVERYBODY DIES EP (p/s)	15

RICHARD SELANO

69	Jolly JY 019	All Of The Time/Broken Romance	6

SELECTED FOUR

71	Banana BA 351	Selection Train/SOUND DIMENSION: Version Train	8

SELECTER
79	2-Tone CHS TT 4	On My Radio/Too Much Pressure (paper label, company sleeve) 4
82	Flexipop 001/SFI 566	Ready Mix Radio (1-sided clear flexidisc with *Flexipop* mag, issue 1) 8/4

(see also Special A.K.A.)

FREDDIE SELF
64	Mercury MF 839	Don't Cry/Why Should I? 6

(see also Freddie Ryder, Trends)

RONNIE SELF
58	Philips PB 810	Bop-A-Lena/Ain't I A Dog (78) 300

SELF ABUSE
84	Radical Change RC 5	SOLDIER (EP). 5

SELF DESTRUCT
91	Retch RR 12004	AFFRAY (12" EP) 7

BROTHER JOHN SELLERS
56	Vanguard EPP 14002	BLUES AND SPIRITUALS (EP). 12
57	Columbia SEG 7740	BLUES AND SPIRITUALS (EP). 12
57	Decca DFE 6457	BROTHER JOHN SELLERS IN LONDON (EP) 10
56	Vanguard PPT 12008	BROTHER JOHN SELLERS SINGS BLUES AND FOLK SONGS (10" LP). . . . 20
57	Vanguard PPT 12017	JACK OF DIAMONDS AND OTHER FOLK SONGS AND BLUES (10" LP). . . . 20

PETER SELLERS (& SOPHIA LOREN)
52	Parlophone R 3785	Jakka And The Flying Saucers (An Interplanetary Fairy Tale) (both sides) (78) . . 10
54	HMV B 10724	Dipso-Calypso/Never Never Land (78). 25
57	Parlophone R 4337	Any Old Iron/Boiled Bananas And Carrots 7
57	Parlophone R 4337	Any Old Iron/Boiled Bananas And Carrots (78) 8
58	Parlophone R 4491	I'm So Ashamed/A Drop Of The Hard Stuff 6
58	Parlophone R 4491	I'm So Ashamed/A Drop Of The Hard Stuff (78) 20
59	Parlophone R 4605	Puttin' On The Smile/My Old Dutch 6
59	Parlophone R 4605	Puttin' On The Smile/My Old Dutch (78) 25
60	Parlophone R 4702	Goodness Gracious Me! (with Sophia Loren)/Grandpa's Grave 5
61	Parlophone R 4724	Bangers And Mash (with Sophia Loren)/SOPHIA LOREN: Zoo Be Zoo Be Zoo . . . 5
65	Parlophone R 5393	A Hard Day's Night/Help! 6
66	United Artists UP 1152	After The Fox (as Peter Sellers & Hollies)/
		BURT BACHARACH: The Fox-Trot. 25
79	United Artists BP 335	There Are Camels Where The Taxis Used To Be/Night And Day 5
59	Parlophone GEP 8770	BEST OF SELLERS NO. 1 (EP) 8
59	Parlophone GEP 8784	BEST OF SELLERS NO. 2 (EP) 8
59	Parlophone GEP 8809	BEST OF SELLERS NO. 3 (EP) 8
59	Parlophone GEP 8822	SONGS FOR SWINGIN' SELLERS (EP, also stereo SGE 2013) 10/12
59	Parlophone GEP 8827	SONGS FOR SWINGIN' SELLERS NO. 2 (EP, also stereo SGE 2016) 10/12
61	Parlophone GEP 8832	SONGS FOR SWINGIN' SELLERS NO. 3 (EP, also stereo SGE 2019) 10/12
61	Parlophone GEP 8835	SONGS FOR SWINGIN' SELLERS NO. 4 (EP, also stereo SGE 2020) 10/12
61	Parlophone GEP 8843	PETER AND SOPHIA NO. 1 (EP, with Sophia Loren, also stereo SGE 2021). . . 10/12
61	Parlophone GEP 8845	PETER AND SOPHIA NO. 2 (EP, with Sophia Loren, also stereo SGE 2022). . . 10/12
61	Parlophone GEP 8848	PETER AND SOPHIA NO. 3 (EP, with Sophia Loren, also stereo SGE 2023). . . 10/12
61	Parlophone GEP 8853	TWO PETERS (EP, with Peter Ustinov, 1 side each) 10
58	Parlophone PMD 1069	THE BEST OF SELLERS (10" LP) 15
59	Parlophone PMC 1111	SONGS FOR SWINGIN' SELLERS (LP, also stereo PCS 3003). 12/15
60	Parlophone PMC 1131	PETER AND SOPHIA (LP, with Sophia Loren, also stereo PCS 3012) 15/18
60s	United Artists UAG 30266	SELLERS' MARKET (LP) 15

PETER SELLERS, SPIKE MILLIGAN & HARRY SECOMBE
64	Philips AL 3464	HOW TO WIN AN ELECTION (LP). 18

(see also Goons, Spike Milligan, Sophia Loren, Hollies, Harry Secombe, Peter Ustinov)

SELOFANE
68	CBS 3413	Girl Called Fantasy/Happiness Is Love 4
68	CBS 3700	Shingle I.A.O./Chase The Face. 4

SEMA 4
79	Pollen PBM 022	4 FROM SEMA 4 (EP, 2 different coloured sleeves, 500 only, numbered) 30
79	Pollen PBM 024	UP DOWN AROUND (EP, 1,000 only) 20

ARCHIE SEMPLE
60	Columbia 33SX 1240	JAZZ FOR YOUNG LOVERS (LP) 50
62	Columbia 33SX 1450	EASY LIVING (LP) 50
63	Columbia 33SX 1580	THE TWILIGHT COMETH (LP) 18
64	77 LEU 12/6	THE CLARINET OF ARCHIE SEMPLE (LP) 30

SEMPRINI
53	HMV 7M 104	Variations On Boogie/Kitten On The Keys 6
54	HMV 7M 169	Selection From "Bangwagon" (both sides). 5
54	HMV 7M 225	Dancing To The Piano, No. 23 (medley, both sides) 5
61	HMV POP 842	Exodus — Main Title Theme/Lark In The Clear Air 6

SENATE
67	Columbia DB 8110	I Can't Stop/Ain't As Sweet As You 15
68	United Artists (S)ULP 1180	THE SENATE SOCK IT TO YOU ONE MORE TIME (LP) 20

(see also Garnet Mimms)

SENATOR BOBBY
62	Cameo Parkway P 127	Wild Thing/SENATOR EVERETT McKINLAY: Wild Thing 8

SENATORS
64	Dial DSP 7001	She's A Mod/Lot About You 45
64	Oriole CB 1957	When Day Is Done/Breakdown 25
65	CBS 201768	The Tables Are Turning/Stop Wasting Time 20

(see also Tony Rivers & Castaways)

MINT VALUE £

RAY SENDIT & HIS ROCKEY TEAM
57 Felsted SD 80052   Rocket 0869/Spike's Rock 6

LOS SENORS
63 Cameo Parkway C 290   Amapola/Acapulco 4

SENSATIONAL ALEX HARVEY BAND
(see under Alex Harvey)

SENSATIONAL CREED
84 Beggars Banquet BEG 125   Nocturnal Operation/Down Periscope (p/s, reissue of Orbidöig single) 8
84 Beggars Banquet BEG 125T Nocturnal Operation/Down Periscope/Voyage Of The Titanic (12", p/s,
                              reissue of Orbidöig single) 10

(see also Orbidöig)

SENSATIONS (featuring Yvonne) (U.S.)
61 Pye International 7N 25110 Music, Music, Music/A Part Of Me (as Sensations featuring Yvonne) 10
62 Pye International 7N 25128 Let Me In/Oh Yes I'll Be True 10
(see also Yvonne Baker)

SENSATIONS (U.K.)
66 Decca F 12392   Look At My Baby/What A Wonderful Feeling 7

SENSATIONS (Jamaica)
67 Doctor Bird DB 1074   A Thing Called Soul/BOBBY LEE & SENSATIONS: I Was Born A Loser 15
67 Doctor Bird DB 1100   Right On Time/Lonely Lover 15
67 Doctor Bird DB 1102   Born To Love You/Your Sweet Love 15
68 Duke DU 2   Those Guys/I'll Never Fall In Love 12
68 Island WI 3110   Long Time Me No See You Girl/ROY SHIRLEY: Million Dollar Baby 18
69 Camel CA 31   The Warrior (actually by Johnny Osbourne & Sensations)/
                              JOHNNY ORGAN: Don Juan 8
70 Techniques TI 902   War Boat/Mr Blue 7
71 Duke DU 120   Remember/LARRY'S ALLSTARS: Madhouse 6
71 Duke DU 121   What Are You Doing Sunday/RUFFIANS: Sweet Dream 6
(see also Roy Shirley, Baba Dise, Winston Wright)

SENSELESS THINGS
88 Yo Jo Jo 3   I'm Moving/Low Time/(All You've Got To Do Is) Stay Together
                              (flexidisc, p/s) 5
91 Way Cool WC 006CD   UP AND COMING (CD, reissue, export-only, with extra tracks
                              "Girlfriend" & "Standing In The Rain") 7
90 What Goes On GOES ON 37   Andi In A Karmann (12" EP, white label, unreleased) 20

SEPTIC DEATH
85 Pusmort 0012-01D   NOW THAT I HAVE THE ATTENTION... (LP, with inner, 18 tracks) 15

SEPULTURA
96 Roadrunner RR 23145   Ratamahatta/War/Slave New World (Live)/Amen/Inner Self (Live) (CD, digipak) ... 8
91 Roadracer RO 9328-8   ARISE (LP, picture disc) 15
94 Roadrunner RR 90000 0   CHAOS A.D. (CD, limited edition tin box; CD has embossed cover & different
                              sleeve, Brazilian flag & 2 bonus tracks, "Policia" & "Inhuman Nature") ... 20

SERENADERS
59 Top Rank JAR 111   Sudden Holiday/Tango Madeira 6
59 Top Rank JAR 111   Sudden Holiday/Tango Madeira (78) 8

SERENDIPITY
68 CBS 3733   Through With You/I'm Flying 70
69 CBS 4428   If I Could/Castles 50

SERENDIPITY SINGERS
64 Philips BF 1333   Don't Let The Rain Come Down (Crooked Little Man)/Freedom's Star 5

SERFS
69 Capitol E-ST 207   THE SERFS (LP) 12

WILL SERGEANT
82 WEA K 19238   Favourite Branches/RAVI SHANKAR & BILL LOVEDAY: Himalaya (p/s) 25
95 Ochre OCH 003   Cosmos/Venus In Flares (p/s, orange vinyl) 15
78 (no label or cat. no.)   WEIRD AS FISH (cassette, 7 copies only, each with a different cover) .... 50+
83 92 Happy Cust. HAPLP 1   THEMES FOR "GRIND" (LP) 10
(see also Echo & Bunnymen)

SERGIO & ESTIBALIZ
75 Epic S EPC 3187   Love Come Home/Tu Volveras 12

SESAME STREET
72 CBS 5366   Rubber Duckie (Ernie)/Sesame Street 4

NANCY SESAY & MELODAIRES
81 It's War Boys S 1   C'est Fab/The Ballad Of Hong Kong/National Honk (gatefold p/s) 6
(see also Homosexuals)

SESSILE WANDERER
88 Metal Gnu GNU 023   THEY CAME AND ATE US (LP, with free 'liquid glass insect' print, 50 only) 90

SETTERS
70 Duke DU 65   Paint Your Wagon/Organ Man (both sides actually by Hot Rod All Stars) 8
70 Trojan TR 7738   Virgin Soldier/Brixton Reggae Festival (both actually by Hot Rod All Stars) 7

SET THE TONE
83 Island ILPS 9736-DJ   Prove It/Start The Bus/All Tied Up (12", unreleased, DJ copies only) 7

SETTLERS
64 Decca F 11938   Settle Down/Sassafras 6
65 Decca F 12123   When's It Gonna Be My Turn?/Good News 6
65 Pye 7N 15965   A Woman Called Freedom/I Know I'm Right 5

66	Pye 7N 17065	Nowhere Man/Call Again	5
66	Pye 7N 17104	Early Morning Rain/Without You	5
66	Pye 7N 17171	'Til Winter Follows Spring/Do You Want To Know The Reason Why	5
66	Pye 7N 17213	On The Other Side/Can't Stop Following You	5
67	Pye 7N 17375	Major To Minor/I Love 'Oo Kazoo	5
68	Columbia DB 8424	As Long As There's Love/Penny To My Name	5
69	Columbia DB 8570	Keep Movin' On/Love Is More Than Words	5
70	Columbia DB 8695	Nessie The Monster/Jesus Met The Woman At The Well	5
71	York FYK 505	The Lightning Tree/Just This Side Of Nowhere	5
64	Decca LK 4645	SING OUT (LP)	12
67	Island ILP 947	EARLY SETTLERS (LP)	20
70	Columbia SCX 6381	SETTLERS ALIVE (LP)	12
72	York FYK 405	LIGHTNING TREE (LP)	12
70s	Myrrh MST 6507	SING A NEW SONG (LP)	20

SEVEN AGES OF MAN
| 72 | Rediffusion ZS 115 | SEVEN AGES OF MAN (LP) | 15 |

(see also Madeline Bell, Gordon Beck)

SEVEN LETTERS/SYMARIP
69	Doctor Bird DB 1189	People Get Ready/The Fit (as Seven Letters)	12
69	Doctor Bird DB 1194	Please Stay/Special Beat (as Seven Letters)	12
69	Doctor Bird DB 1195	Flour Dumpling/Equality (as Seven Letters [Symarip])	12
69	Doctor Bird DB 1206	Mama Me Want Girl/Sentry (as Seven Letters)	12
69	Doctor Bird DB 1207	Soul Crash/Throw Me Things (as Seven Letters)	12
69	Doctor Bird DB 1208	There Goes My Heart/Wish (as Seven Letters)	12
69	Doctor Bird DB 1209	Bam Bam Baji/Hold Him Joe (as Seven Letters [Symarip])	12
69	Doctor Bird DB 1306	Fung Sure/Tomorrow At Sundown (as Symarip)	12
69	Treasure Isle TI 7050	Skinhead Moonstomp/Must Catch A Train (as Symarip)	8
70	Treasure Isle TI 7054	Parson's Corner/Redeem (as Symarip)	10
70	Treasure Isle TI 7055	La Bella Jig/Holidays By The Sea (as Symarip)	8
70	Attack ATT 8013	I'm A Puppet/Vindication (as Symarip)	5
70	Trojan TBL 102	SKINHEAD MOONSTOMP (LP, as Symarip)	20

(see also Pyramids, Equals, Laurel Aitken)

7 SECONDS
| 82 | Alt. Tentacles VIRUS 15 | SKIN, BRAINS AND GUTS (EP, with insert) | 12 |

SEVENTEEN
| 80 | Vendetta VD 001 | Don't Let Go/Bank Holiday Weekend (p/s) | 50 |

(see also Alarm)

SEVENTH SEAL
| 97 | Acme ACLP 8018LP | THE SEVENTH SEAL (LP) | 10 |

SEVENTH SON
82	Rising Son FMR 067	Man In The Street (some in p/s)	50/15
84	Rising Son SRT4KS 282	Metal To The Moon (no p/s)	20
87	Music Factory MF 0043	Northern Boots (p/s)	18
89	Rising Son SRT9KLS	What More Do You Want (12", p/s)	10

SEVENTH WAVE
| 75 | Gull GULS 14 | Manifestations/Only The Beginning (Part 1) | 5 |

(see also Second Hand, Fungus)

SEVENTH WONDER
| 80 | Grapevine GRP 130 | Captain Of My Ship/Pharaoh | 5 |

SEVERED HEADS
| 83 | Plastic Canvas PC 002 | Heavy Metal/Killin' The Kidz (p/s) | 4 |

SEVERINE
71	CBS 7230	Chance In Time/Nothing Bad Can Be This Good	8
71	Philips 6009 135	Un Banc, Un Arbre, Une Rue/Viens	5
71	Philips 6009 151	La La Melodie/Je Ferme Les Yeux, Je Compte Dix	5

DAVID SEVILLE & HIS ORCHESTRA (& CHIPMUNKS)
57	London HLU 8359	Armen's Theme/Carousel In Rome (initially gold label print, later silver)	15/8
57	London HLU 8411	The Gift/The Donkey And The Schoolboy	10
57	London HLU 8411	The Gift/The Donkey And The Schoolboy (78)	12
57	London HLU 8485	Gotta Get To Your House/Camel Rock	10
57	London HLU 8485	Gotta Get To Your House/Camel Rock (78)	15
58	London HLU 8582	Bonjour Tristesse/Dance From "Bonjour Tristesse"	10
58	London HLU 8582	Bonjour Tristesse/Dance From "Bonjour Tristesse" (78)	8
58	London HLU 8619	Witch Doctor/Don't Whistle At Me Baby	8
58	London HLU 8619	Witch Doctor/Don't Whistle At Me Baby (78)	8
58	London HLU 8659	The Bird On My Head/Hey There Moon	8
58	London HLU 8659	The Bird On My Head/Hey There Moon (78)	8
58	London HLU 8736	Little Brass Band/Take Five	7
58	London HLU 8736	Little Brass Band/Take Five (78)	10
58	London HLG 8762	Almost Good/CHIPMUNKS: The Chipmunk Song	6
58	London HLG 8762	Almost Good/CHIPMUNKS: The Chipmunk Song (78)	8
59	London HLU 8823	Alvin's Harmonica (with Chipmunks)/Mediocre	5
59	London HLU 8823	Alvin's Harmonica (with Chipmunks)/Mediocre (78)	10
59	London HLU 8893	Judy/Maria From Madrid	7
59	London HLU 8893	Judy/Maria From Madrid (78)	15
59	London HLU 7083	Alvin's Harmonica/Ragtime Cowboy Joe	6
59	London HLG 8916	Ragtime Cowboy Joe (with Chipmunks)/Flip Side	5
59	London HLG 8916	Ragtime Cowboy Joe (with Chipmunks)/Flip Side (78)	10
60	London HLG 9061	Alvin's Orchestra (with Chipmunks)/Copyright 1960 (B-side as Music Of David Seville)	5
60	London HLG 9061	Alvin's Orchestra (with Chipmunks)/Copyright 1960 (78)	18

David SEVILLE & His Orchestra

60	London HLG 9125	Coming 'Round The Mountain/Sing A Goofy Tune (with Chipmunks)	5
60	London HLG 9193	Alvin For President (with Chipmunks)/Sack Time	5
61	London HLU 9329	Oh Judge, Your Honour, Dear Sir/Freddy, Freddy	5
57	London RE-U 1085	DAVID SEVILLE & HIS ORCHESTRA (EP)	25
59	London RE-U 1219	WITCH DOCTOR AND FRIENDS (EP)	25
63	Liberty LEP 2057	SING ALONG WITH THE CHIPMUNKS (EP)	10
63	Liberty LEP 2117	SING AGAIN WITH THE CHIPMUNKS (EP)	10
59	London HA-U 2153	THE WITCH DOCTOR PRESENTS DAVID SEVILLE AND HIS FRIENDS (LP)	30

(see also Chipmunks, Alfi & Harry)

ALEC SEWARD

56	Vogue LDE 165	CITY BLUES (10" LP)	25

SEX AIDS

83	Riot City RIOT 23	BACK ON THE PISS AGAIN (EP)	5

(see also Vice Squad)

SEX BEATLES

79	Charly CYS 1061	Well You Never/Fatal Fascination (p/s)	5

SEX PISTOLS

76	EMI EMI 2566	Anarchy In The U.K./I Wanna Be Me (black p/s, with Chris Thomas production credit on B-side)	35
76	EMI EMI 2566	Anarchy In The U.K./I Wanna Be Me (no p/s, Dave Goodman production credit on B-side)	15
77	A&M AMS 7284	God Save The Queen/No Feelings (withdrawn, no p/s, some in brown envelope with press release)	2,500/2,000
77	Virgin VS 181	God Save The Queen/Did You No Wrong (p/s)	5
77	Virgin VS 184	Pretty Vacant/No Fun (p/s, some with push-out centre)	each 5
77	Virgin VS 191	Holidays In The Sun/Satellite (withdrawn p/s)	10
77	Virgin/Lyntone LYN 3261	Lentilmas — A Seasonal Offering To You From Virgin Records (flexidisc, Xmas freebie to journalists; some with Xmas card)	125/90
78	Virgin VS 220	No-One Is Innocent (A Punk Prayer By Ronald Biggs)/SID VICIOUS: My Way (p/s)	4
78	Virgin VS 220	No-One Is Innocent (mispress, plays Motors track)/SID VICIOUS: My Way (p/s)	15
78	Virgin VS 22012	The Biggest Blow (A Punk Prayer By Ronald Biggs)/(Interview)/SID VICIOUS: My Way (12", p/s [matrix: VS 22012A3] or without [VS 22012 A1])	20/10
79	Virgin VS 240	Something Else/Friggin' In The Riggin' (p/s)	4
79	Virgin VS 240	Something Else/Friggin' In The Riggin' (p/s, mispressing, black & white labels A-side plays "Silly Thing")	15
79	Virgin VS 290	The Great Rock 'n' Roll Swindle/Rock Around The Clock (vocals by Tenpole Tudor) (withdrawn 'American Express' p/s)	5
79	Virgin VS 290	The Great Rock 'n' Roll Swindle (mispressing with 'lawyers' telephone conversation' track)/Rock Around The Clock ('American Express' p/s)	12
80	Virgin VS 339	(I'm Not Your) Stepping Stone/Pistols Propaganda (p/s)	4
80	Virgin VS 339	(I'm Not Your) Stepping Stone/Pistols Propaganda (p/s, mispressing, B-side plays "Substitute")	15
80	Virgin VS 339	(I'm Not Your) Stepping Stone/Pistols Propaganda (p/s, mispressing, plays Gillan track)	12
80	Virgin SEX 1	PISTOLS PACK (6 x 7" in p/s; all in plastic wallet)	25
81	Virgin VS 443	Who Killed Bambi?/Rock Around The Clock (by Tenpole Tudor & Pistols, p/s)	6
85	Virgin CDT 3	Anarchy In The U.K./EMI/No Fun (CD, 3" or 5")	each 7
85	Chaos DICK 1	Submission/No Feelings (p/s, 5,000 only, blue, pink or yellow vinyl)	7/6/5
85	Chaos EXPORT 1	Submission/Anarchy In The U.K. (Dave Goodman version) (12", p/s, black, pink, red, white, green, clear or yellow vinyl)	7
85	Chaos	Submission (12", 1-sided test pressing, die-cut sleeve, label has big red 'A')	45
85	Chaos	Pretty Vacant (unreleased, 20 copies only)	40
86	Archive 4 TOF 104	THE ORIGINAL SEX PISTOLS LIVE (4-track 12", p/s, 5,000 only)	8
88	Virgin CDT 3	Anarchy In The U.K./No Fun/EMI (3" CD, card sleeve)	10
88	Virgin CDT 37	God Save The Queen/Did You No Wrong/Don't Give Me No Lip Child (3" CD, gatefold card sleeve)	12
88	Counterpoint CDEP 13	CLASSIC TRACKS (CD, live EP, as Original Pistols)	7
88	Spiral Scratch SCRATCH 4	Pretty Vacant (Demo)/I Wanna Be Me (Demo) (no p/s, with *Spiral Scratch* magazine, issue 4, B-side actually plays "Seventeen")	6/4
96	Virgin VUSCDJ 113	Pretty Vacant (live) (CD, promo only, card sleeve)	20
77	Virgin V 2086/SPOTS 001	NEVER MIND THE BOLLOCKS, HERE'S THE SEX PISTOLS (LP, black rear sleeve, with poster & 1-sided single, "Submission" [VDJ 24], shrinkwrapped with sticker)	125
78	Virgin V 2086	NEVER MIND THE BOLLOCKS, HERE'S THE SEX PISTOLS (LP, pink rear sleeve with no track listing)	12
78	Virgin VP 2086	NEVER MIND THE BOLLOCKS, HERE'S THE SEX PISTOLS (LP, picture disc)	35
79	Virgin VD 2510	THE GREAT ROCK 'N' ROLL SWINDLE (2-LP, including "Watcha Gonna Do About It", with card insert)	40
79	Virgin VD 2510	THE GREAT ROCK 'N' ROLL SWINDLE (2-LP, "I Wanna Be Me" and "Who Killed Bambi" replace "Watcha Gonna Do About It", with spoken overdubs on "God Save The Queen Symphony")	18
80	Factory FACT 30	THE HEYDAY (gold interview cassette in satin pouch with Xmas card)	25
86	Virgin CDV 2086	NEVER MIND THE BOLLOCKS, HERE'S THE SEX PISTOLS (CD, mispressing, plays country music titles)	20
89	Link LINKLP 063	LIVE AND LOUD (LP, green or marbled pink vinyl)	12/10
92	Baktabak CINT 5008	INTROSPECTIVE: SEX PISTOLS (interview CD, unreleased)	

(see also Public Image Ltd, Professionals, Rich Kids, Steve Jones, Cash Pussies, Spectres (UK), Swingers)

SEXY GIRLS

69	Fab FAB 100	Pom-Pom Song/LITTLE JOE & BUSTER'S ALLSTARS: Hy There (B-side actually by Melltones)	7
69	Dice CC 100	Pom-Pom Song/LITTLE JOE & BUSTER'S ALLSTARS: Hy There (B-side actually by Melltones) (reissue)	7

DENNY SEYTON & SABRES

64	Mercury MF 800	Tricky Dicky/Baby What You Want Me To Do	15
64	Mercury MF 814	Short Fat Fanny/Give Me Back My Heart	18
64	Mercury MF 824	The Way You Look Tonight/Hands Off	30
65	Parlophone R 5363	Just A Kiss/In The Flowers By The Trees (as Denny Seyton Group)	30
65	Wing WL 1032	IT'S THE GEAR (14 HITS) (LP)	35

SHA-BOOM

89	WEA 244 970-1	DANCING IN THE FIRE — THE RE-MIX ALBUM (LP)	10

SHACK

88	Ghetto GTG B 1	Emergency/Liberation (p/s)	4
88	Ghetto GTG T 1	Emergency/Liberation/Faith (12", p/s)	7
88	Ghetto GTG CD 1	Emergency/Liberation/Faith/What's It Like (CD)	10
89	Ghetto GTG B 2	High Rise Low Life/Who Killed Clayton Square? (p/s)	4
89	Ghetto GTG T 2	High Rise Low Life/Who Killed Clayton Square?/High Rise Low Life (Bert Hardy Mix) (12", p/s)	7
89	Ghetto GTG CD 2	High Rise Low Life/Who Killed Clayton Square?/High Rise Low Life (Bert Hardy Mix) (CD)	10
90	Ghetto GTG B 11	I Know You Well/I Feel No Way (p/s)	4
90	Ghetto GTG 11T	I Know You Well (Extended Mix)/I Feel No Way/(If You Want It Mix) (12", p/s)	7
90	Ghetto GTG CD 11	I Know You Well (7" Version)/(If You Want It Mix)Feel No Way/(Ext. Mix) (CD)	10
88	Ghetto GHETT 1	ZILCH (LP, distributed by Epic, or later independent issue)	10/12
88	Ghetto GHETT D 1	ZILCH (CD)	18
	(see also Pale Fountains)		

SHADE JOEY & NIGHTOWLS

64	Parlophone R 5180	Bluebirds Over The Mountain/That's When I Need You Baby	50

SHADES (U.S.)

58	London HLX 8713	Sun Glasses (with Knott Sisters)/KNOTT SISTERS: Undivided Attention	35
58	London HLX 8713	Sun Glasses (with Knott Sisters)/KNOTT SISTERS: Undivided Attention (78)	25

SHADES

62	Starlite ST45 074	Weird Walk/Joe's Shuffle	20

SHADES (Jamaica)

69	Gas GAS 119	Never Gonna Give You Up/Let Me Remind You (both actually by Techniques)	7
	(see also Techniques)		

SHADES OF BLUE (U.K.)

65	Parlophone R 5270	Voodoo Blues/Luceanne	40
65	Pye 7N 15988	Where Did All The Good Times Go/I Ain't No Use	10
	(see also Toby Twirl)		

SHADES OF BLUE (U.S.)

66	Sue WI 4022	Oh! How Happy/Little Orphan Boy	18

SHADES OF JOY

69	Fontana STL 5498	SHADES OF JOY (LP)	12

SHADES OF MORLEY BROWN

66	Mercury MF 896	In Time/Walking Proud	6
68	Mercury MF 1054	Silly Girl/Pretty Blue Bird	5
	(see also Help Yourself)		

JOHNNY SHADOW (& DANNY GAVIN)

63	Pye 7N 15506	Golli Golli/I'm Coming Home To You (with Danny Gavin) (some in p/s)	10/6
63	Pye 7N 15529	Golli Guitar/Week (with Danny Gavin)	6
65	Parlophone R 5286	Kiss Me Now/What Colour Is The Wind	6
65	Parlophone R 5308	Atom Bomb Song Part 3/Talented Man	6
	(see also Ivy League)		

SHADOWS (U.S.)

58	HMV POP 563	Jungle Fever/Under Stars Of Love	75
58	HMV POP 563	Jungle Fever/Under Stars Of Love (78)	75

SHADOWS (U.K.)

SINGLES

59	Columbia DB 4387	Saturday Dance/Lonesome Fella	35
59	Columbia DB 4387	Saturday Dance/Lonesome Fella (78)	200
60	Columbia DB 4484	Apache/Quartermaster's Stores (green label, later black)	6/8
60	Columbia DB 4530	Man Of Mystery/The Stranger	7
61	Columbia DB 4580	F.B.I./Midnight	6
61	Columbia DB 4637	The Frightened City/Back Home	6
61	Columbia DB 4698	Kon-Tiki/36-24-36	6
61	Columbia DB 4726	The Savage/Peace Pipe	6
62	Columbia DB 4790	Wonderful Land/Stars Fell On Stockton	6
62	Columbia DB 4870	Guitar Tango/What A Lovely Tune	6
	(The above singles were originally issued with green labels; later black label copies are worth £12-£15 unless otherwise stated.)		
62	Columbia DB 4948	Dance On!/All Day	6
63	Columbia DB 4984	Foot Tapper/The Breeze And I	6
63	Columbia DB 7047	Atlantis/I Want You To Want Me	6
63	Columbia DB 7106	Shindig/It's Been A Blue Day	7
63	Columbia DB 7163	Geronimo/Shazam	6
64	Columbia DB 7231	Theme For Young Lovers/This Hammer	6
64	Columbia DB 7261	The Rise And Fall Of Flingel Bunt/It's A Man's World	6
64	Columbia DB 7261	The Rise And Fall Of Flingel Bunt/It's A Man's World (mispressing with A-side on both sides)	12
64	Columbia DB 7342	Rhythm 'n' Greens/The Miracle	7
64	Columbia DB 7416	Genie With The Light Brown Lamp/Little Princess	7

SHADOWS

65	Columbia DB 7476	Mary Anne/Chu-Chi 7
65	Columbia DB 7588	Stingray/Alice In Sunderland (some in export p/s) 20/7
65	Columbia DB 7650	Don't Make My Baby Blue/My Grandfather's Clock (some in export p/s) 20/6
65	Columbia DB 7769	The War Lord/I Wish I Could Shimmy Like My Sister Arthur 7
66	Columbia DB 7853	I Met A Girl/Late Night Set 8
66	Columbia DB 7952	A Place In The Sun/Will You Be There 8
66	Columbia DB 8034	The Dreams I Dream/Scotch On The Socks 8
67	Columbia PSR 305	Thunderbirds Are Go (1-sided advance promo) 50
67	Columbia DB 8170	Maroc 7/Bombay Duck 7
67	Columbia PSR 308	Maroc 7 (1-sided demo with spoken-word intro) 50
67	Columbia PSR 310	Chelsea Boot/Jigsaw (demo only) 60
67	Columbia DB 8264	Tomorrow's Cancelled/Somewhere 12
68	Columbia DB 8326	Running Out Of World/HANK MARVIN: London's Not Too Far 10
68	Columbia DB 8372	Dear Old Mrs. Bell/Trying To Forget The One You Love 10
69	Columbia DB 8628	Slaughter On Tenth Avenue/HANK MARVIN: Midnight Cowboy 15
72	Columbia DB 8958	Apache/Wonderful Land/F.B.I. 5
72	Lyntone LYN 10099	The Shadows (flexidisc sampler from World Record Club box set) 6
73	EMI EMI 2081	Turn Around And Touch Me/Jungle Jam 5
75	EMI EMI 2269	Let Me Be The One/Stand Up Like A Man 5
75	EMI EMI 2269	Stand Up Like A Man/Let Me Be The One (sides reversed) 7
75	EMI EMI 2310	Run Billy Run/Honourable Puff-Puff 6
76	EMI EMI 2461	It'll Be Me Babe/Like Strangers 7
77	EMI EMI 2573	Apache/Wonderful Land/F.B.I. (reissue) 5
77	EMI EMI 2660	Another Night/Cricket Bat Boogie 6
78	EMI EMI 2838	Love Deluxe/Sweet Saturday Night 6
78	EMI EMI 2890	Don't Cry For Me Argentina/Montezuma's Revenge (p/s) 5
79	EMI EMI 2939	Theme From "The Deer Hunter"/Bermuda Triangle (p/s) 5
79	EMI EMI 5004	Rodrigo's Guitar Concerto/Song For Duke (p/s) 5
80	EMI EMI 5083	Heart Of Glass/Return To The Alamo (p/s) 5
80	Polydor POSP 148	Equinoxe (Part V)/Fender Bender (p/s) 5
80	Polydor POSP 187	Mozart Forte/Midnight Creepin' (no p/s) 5
81	Polydor POSP 255	The Third Man/The Fourth Man (no p/s) 5
81	Polydor POSP 316	Telstar/Summer Love '59 (no p/s) 5
81	Polydor POSP 376	Imagine — Woman (Medley)/Hats Off To Wally (no p/s) 5
82	Polydor POSP 439	Treat Me Nice/Spot The Ball (p/s) 6
82	Polydor POSP 485	The Theme From "Missing"/The Shady Lady (p/s) 5
83	Polydor POSP 629	Diamonds/Elevensis (p/s) 6
83	Polydor POSP 657	Going Home/Cat 'N' Mouse (p/s) 5
86	Polydor POSPX 808	Dancing In The Dark (12" Remix)/Dancing In The Dark (7" Version)/
		Turning Point (12", p/s) 15
89	Polydor PZCD 47	Mountains Of The Moon/Stack-It/Turning Point (CD) 8
89	Polydor PZCD 61	SHADOWMIX (CD, megamix) 7

EPs

61	Columbia SEG 8061	THE SHADOWS (EP, also stereo ESG 7834) 12/30
61	Columbia SEG 8094	THE SHADOWS TO THE FORE (EP) 12
62	Columbia SEG 8135	SPOTLIGHT ON THE SHADOWS (EP) 15
62	Columbia SEG 8148	THE SHADOWS NO. 2 (EP, only some sleeves list "No. 2") 15
62	Columbia SEG 8166	THE SHADOWS NO. 3 (EP) 15
62	Columbia SEG 8171	WONDERFUL LAND OF THE SHADOWS (EP) 15

(The above EPs were originally issued with turquoise labels; later blue/black label copies are worth two-thirds the values listed.)

62	Columbia SEG 8193	THE BOYS (EP, mono) 12
62	Columbia ESG 7881	THE BOYS (EP, stereo, turquoise labels, later black/blue labels) 35/30
63	Columbia SEG 8218	OUT OF THE SHADOWS (EP, mono) 15
63	Columbia ESG 7883	OUT OF THE SHADOWS (EP, stereo, turquoise or black/blue labels) 35/30
63	Columbia SEG 8233	DANCE ON WITH THE SHADOWS (EP) 15
63	Columbia SEG 8249	OUT OF THE SHADOWS NO. 2 (EP, also stereo ESG 7895) 15/30
63	Columbia SEG 8268	FOOT TAPPING WITH THE SHADOWS (EP) 15
63	Columbia SEG 8278	LOS SHADOWS (EP, 2 different sleeves) 15
63	Columbia SEG 8286	SHINDIG WITH THE SHADOWS (EP) 18
64	Columbia SEG 8321	THOSE BRILLIANT SHADOWS (EP) 18
64	Columbia SEG 8342	DANCE WITH THE SHADOWS (EP) 18
64	Columbia SEG 8362	RHYTHM AND GREENS (EP, also stereo ESG 7904) 15/30
64	Columbia SEG 8375	DANCE WITH THE SHADOWS NO. 2 (EP) 18
65	Columbia SEG 8396	THEMES FROM "ALADDIN AND HIS WONDERFUL LAMP" (EP) 18
65	Columbia SEG 8408	DANCE WITH THE SHADOWS NO. 3 (EP) 20
65	Columbia SEG 8445	ALICE IN SUNDERLAND (EP) 20
65	Columbia SEG 8459	THE SOUND OF THE SHADOWS (EP) 20
66	Columbia SEG 8473	THE SOUND OF THE SHADOWS NO. 2 (EP) 20
66	Columbia SEG 8494	THE SOUND OF THE SHADOWS NO. 3 (EP) 20
66	Columbia SEG 8500	THOSE TALENTED SHADOWS (EP) 20
66	Columbia SEG 8510	THUNDERBIRDS ARE GO! (EP, with Cliff Richard) 50
67	Columbia SEG 8528	THE SHADOWS ON STAGE AND SCREEN (EP) 30

LPs

61	Columbia 33SX 1374	THE SHADOWS (LP, also stereo SCX 3414) 15/30
62	Columbia 33SX 1458	OUT OF THE SHADOWS (LP, also stereo SCX 3449) 18/25

(The above LPs were originally issued with green labels; later blue/black label copies are worth two-thirds the values listed.)

63	Columbia 33SX 1522	GREATEST HITS (LP) 12
64	Columbia 33SX 1619	DANCE WITH THE SHADOWS (LP, also stereo SCX 3511) 15/20
65	Columbia 33SX 1736	THE SOUND OF THE SHADOWS (LP, also stereo SCX 3554) 18/22
65	Columbia 33SX 1791	MORE HITS! (LP, also stereo SCX 3578) 12
66	Columbia 33SX/SCX 6041	SHADOW MUSIC (LP) 15
67	Columbia S(C)X 6148	JIGSAW (LP) 18
67	Columbia S(C)X 6199	FROM HANK, BRUCE, BRIAN AND JOHN (LP) 18
68	Columbia S(C)X 6282	ESTABLISHED 1958 (LP, half by Cliff Richard, mono/stereo) 18/15

(The above LPs were originally issued with blue/black labels; later silver/black label copies are worth half the values listed.)

MINT VALUE £

70	M. For Pleasure MFP 1388	WALKIN' WITH THE SHADOWS (LP, royal blue sleeve & red lettering)	12
70	Columbia SCX 6420	SHADES OF ROCK (LP)	12
72	World Records ALBUM 72	THE SHADOWS (6-LP box set)	30
73	EMI EMA 762	ROCKIN' WITH CURLY LEADS (LP)	15
77	EMI EMTV 3	TWENTY GOLDEN GREATS (LP, mispressing, side 2 plays Pink Floyd's "Animals")	12

CDs

86	Roll Over/Polydor 832 797-2	GUARDIAN ANGEL (CD)	15
86	Polydor 833 452-2	HITS RIGHT UP YOUR STREET (CD)	15

REEL-TO-REEL TAPES

60s	Columbia TA-SX 1374	THE SHADOWS (mono only)	10
60s	Columbia TA-SX 1458	OUT OF THE SHADOWS (mono only)	10
60s	Columbia TA-SX 1522	GREATEST HITS (mono only)	10
60s	Columbia TA-SX 1619	DANCE WITH THE SHADOWS (mono only)	10
60s	Columbia TA-SX 1736	THE SOUND OF THE SHADOWS (mono only)	10
60s	Columbia TA-SX 1791	MORE HITS! (mono only)	10
60s	Columbia TA-SX 6041	SHADOW MUSIC (mono only)	10
60s	Columbia TA-SX 6148	JIGSAW (mono only)	10
60s	Columbia TA-SX 6199	FROM HANK, BRUCE, BRIAN AND JOHN (mono only)	10

(see also Cliff Richard, Drifters, Five Chesternuts, Hank Marvin, Marvin Welch & Farrar, Bruce Welch, John Henry Rostill, Brian Bennett, Jet Harris, Tony Meehan, Vipers Skiffle Group, Marty Wilde, Krew Kats, Interns, Strangers, Wasp, MacArthur Park, Thunder Company, Alan Hawkshaw)

SHADOWS OF KNIGHT

66	Atlantic AT 4085	Gloria/Dark Side	25
66	Atlantic 584 021	Oh Yeah/Light Bulb Blues	20
66	Atlantic 584 045	Bad Little Woman/Gospel Zone	20
67	Atlantic 584 136	Someone Like Me/Three For Love	20
69	Buddah 201 024	Shake/From Way Out To Way Under	15
79	Radar ADA 11	GLORIA (LP)	20

SHADROCKS

67	Island WI 3061	Go Go Special/Count Down	10
68	Jay Boy BOY 2	There Is/Jigsaw	5

DOREEN SHAEFFER

69	Unity UN 536	No Matter What/Walk Through This World	6
69	Unity UN 538	How Much Is That Doggy In The Window/As Long As He Needs Me	6

(see also Bob Marley/Wailers, Lloyd Clarke)

JOHN SHAFT

72	Downtown DT 488	Forever Music/BLOSSOM JOHNSON: The Boy I Love	6

SHAFTESBURY

80	O.K. SRT CUS 025	Hit Man (no p/s)	5
80	O.K. OKA 001	THE LULL BEFORE THE STORM (LP, with insert)	20
81	O.K. OKA 002	WE ARE THE BOYS (LP)	12

BOBBY SHAFTO

62	Parlophone R 4870	Over And Over/I Want My Bed	8
62	Parlophone R 4958	Feel So Blue/I Haven't Got A Girl	8
64	Parlophone R 5130	She's My Girl/Wonderful You	8
64	Parlophone R 5167	Love, Love, Love (Don't Let Me Down)/I Don't Love You Anymore	8
64	Parlophone R 5184	Who Wouldn't Love A Girl Like That/I Remember	8
65	Parlophone R 5252	How Could You Do A Thing Like That To Me/Baby Then	8
66	Parlophone R 5403	Lonely Is As Lonely Does/The Same Old Room	8
66	Parlophone R 5481	A Little Like You/See Me Cry	8

SHAG NASTY

79	Shag Nasty SN 1	No Bullshit Just Rock 'n' Roll/Looking For A Love? (p/s)	12

SHAGRAT

90	Shagrat ORC 001	Amanda/Peppermint Flickstick (p/s, 500 only, some autographed)	5/7
91	Shagrat ENT 001	NOTHING EXCEEDS LIKE EXCESS (mini LP, as Steve Took's Shagrat, numbered, 400 only)	10

(see also Tyrannosaurus Rex, Pink Fairies, Larry Wallis, Tools You Can Trust)

SHAKE

79	Sire SIR 4016	Culture Shock/Dream On (no p/s)	5
79	Sire SIR 4016-10	Culture Shock/Glass House/Dream On/(But) Not Mine (10", p/s)	7
80	Sire SIR 4035	Invasion Of The Gamma Men/Night By Night (p/s)	4

(see also Rezillos, Jo Callis, TV 21)

SHAKEOUTS

65	Columbia DB 7613	Every Little Once In A While/Well Who's That	40

SHAKERS (U.K.)

63	Polydor NH 52158	Money/Memphis Tennessee	18
63	Polydor NH 52213	Hippy Hippy Shake/Dr. Feelgood	18
63	Polydor NH 66991	Hippy Hippy Shake/Dr. Feelgood	18
63	Polydor NH 52258	Money/Hippy Hippy Shake	18
63	Polydor NH 52272	Whole Lotta Lovin'/I Can Tell	18
63	Polydor 237 139	LET'S DO THE SLOP, TWIST, MADISON, HULLY GULLY WITH THE SHAKERS (LP)	60

(see also Kingsize Taylor & Dominoes)

SHAKERS (U.S.)

73	Probe PRO 582	One Wonderful Moment/Love, Love, Love	6
74	ABC ABC 4018	One Wonderful Moment/Love, Love, Love (reissue)	4

CHRIS SHAKESPEARE GLOBE SHOW

69	Page One POF 113	Ob-La-Di, Ob-La-Da/Tin Soldier	15

(see alslo Globe Show)

SHAKESPEARES
68   RCA Victor RCA 1695   Something To Believe In/Burning My Fingers 25
(see also Fynn McCool)

SHAKESPEAR'S SISTER
88   London LON 200   Break My Heart (You Really)/Heroine (p/s) 4
88   London LONX 200   Break My Heart (You Really) (Extended Version)/Heroine (Extended Version)/
Break My Heart (You Really) (Acidic Mix) (12", p/s) 7
88   London LONXR 200   Break My Heart (You Really) (The Shep Pettibone House Mix)/Heroine
(Heavenly Remix)/Break My Heart (You Really) (Dub Mix) (12", p/s) 8
88   London LONCD 200   Break My Heart (You Really) (The Shep Pettibone House Mix)/(7" Version)/
Heroine (Extended Version) (CD) 20
89   ffrr FPD 112   You're History/Dirty Mind (picture disc in p/s) 4
89   ffrr FBCD 119   Run Silent/Mr. Wrong/Run Silent (The Run Deep Mix)
(CD in pull-apart card case) 15

(see also Bananarama)

SHAKEY JAKE
69   Liberty LBL 83217E   FURTHER ON UP THE ROAD (LP) 25

SHAKEY VICK
69   Pye N(S)PL 18276   LITTLE WOMAN, YOU'RE SO SWEET (LP) 50

SHAKIN' PYRAMIDS
81   Cuba Libre DRINK 2   Reeferbilly Boogie/Wake Up Little Suzie/Harmonica Lisa (p/s) 7
81   Virgin VS 404   Take A Trip/Hellbent On Rockin'//Reeferbilly Boogie/I & Others
(double pack) 7

SAM SHAM
69   Blue Cat BS 157   Drumbago's Dead/SPARTERS: Song Of The Year 8

SHAMANIC TRIBES ON ACID
93   Ambient Space Acid 1202   SHAMANIC TRIBES ON ACID EP (12", blue vinyl) 8

ALEXANDER SHAMBER BOYS
58   HMV POP 496   Dintho (Kwela)/Holom Toe (Kwela) 5
58   HMV POP 496   Dintho (Kwela)/Holom Toe (Kwela) (78) 8

SHAME
67   MGM MGM 1349   Don't Go Away Little Girl/Dreams Don't Bother Me 50
(see also Shy Limbs, King Crimson, Gods, Emerson Lake & Palmer)

SHAME
85   Fierce FRIGHT 003   Real Tears (1-sided, possibly unissued) . . . . 30+

SHAMEN
86   One Big Guitar OBG 003T   THEY MAY BE RIGHT ... BUT THEY'RE CERTAINLY WRONG (12" EP) 7
86   Skipping Kitten   WAYWARD WEDNESDAY IN MAY AFFAIR ("Four Letter Girl"/"Stay In Bed")
(no cat. no.)   (33rpm 1-sided flexidisc, with insert, free with *Skipping Kitten* fanzine) 6/4
88   Ediesta CALC CD 069   Jesus Loves Amerika/Darkness In Zion/Do What You Will/
Sub Knature Dub (CD) 15
89   The Catalogue CAT 074   Purple Haze/SLEEPING DOGS WAKE: This Little Piggy/SUGARCUBES:
Cindy/KITCHENS OF DISTINCTION: Margaret's Injection/HAM: Voulez Vous
(square flexidisc with *The Catalogue* magazine) 5/4
89   Moksha SOMA 6CD   You, Me And Everything (Evil Edit)/Reraptyouare (Evil Edit)/
Ed's Bonus Beats (CD, no inlay) 10
89   Moksha SOMACD 3   PHORWARD (CD) 20
(see also Alone Again Or)

SHAMES
66   CBS 202344   Sugar And Spice/Ben Franklin's Almanac 20
66   CBS 202450   I Wanna Meet You/We Could Be Happy 6
67   CBS 2704   Mr Unreliable/Georgia 7
67   CBS 2929   It Could Be We're In Love/I Was Lonely When 5
68   CBS 3820   Greenburg, Glickstein, Charles, David, Smith And Jones/Warm 7
(see also Isaac Guillory)

SHAM 69
77   Step Forward SF 4   I Don't Wanna/Ulster/Red London (black & white photo p/s) 8
77   Step Forward SF 412   I Don't Wanna/Ulster/Red London (12", black & white photo p/s) 10
77   Polydor (no cat. no.)   Song Of The Streets/Fanx (1-sided concert freebie, red brick-wall label;
white label copies are counterfeits) 15
78   Polydor 2058 966   Borstal Breakout/Hey Little Rich Boy (p/s) 6
78   Polydor 2059 023   Angels With Dirty Faces/The Cockney Kids Are Innocent (p/s) 5
78   Polydor 2059 050   If The Kids Are United/Sunday Morning Nightmare (p/s) 5
78   Polydor POSP 7   Hurry Up Harry/No Entry (p/s) 5
79   Step Forward SF 4   I Don't Wanna/Red London/Ulster (reissue, yellow p/s) 5
79   Step Forward SF 412   I Don't Wanna/Red London/Ulster (12" reissue, yellow p/s) 8
79   Polydor POSP 27   Questions And Answers/I Gotta Survive/With A Little Help
From My Friends (p/s) 5
79   Polydor POSP 64   Hersham Boys/I Don't Wanna (live)/Tell Us The Truth (live) (p/s) 5
79   Polydor POSPX 64   Hersham Boys/I Don't Wanna (live)/Rip Off (live)/I'm A Man, I'm A Boy (live)/
Tell Us The Truth (live) (12", p/s) 8
79   Polydor POSP 82   You're A Better Man Than I/Give A Dog A Bone (p/s) 5
80   Polydor POSP 136   Tell The Children/Jack (p/s) 5
80   Polydor 2059 259   Unite And Win/I'm A Man (p/s) 5
87   Legacy LGY 70   Ban The Gun/Ban The Gun (no p/s, withdrawn) 8
79   Polydor POLD 5025   THE ADVENTURES OF THE HERSHAM BOYS (LP, with 12" EP [2812 045],
stickered sleeve) 12
80   Polydor 2383 596   THE FIRST, THE BEST AND THE LAST (LP, with live EP [RIOT 1/2816 028]) 12
(see also Jimmy Edwards)

SHAMROCKS
65	Polydor BM 56503	La La La La La/And I Need You	8

SHA NA NA
70	Kama Sutra 2013 010	Little Darlin'/Teenager In Love	5
71	Kama Sutra 2013 022	Only One Song/Yakety Yak/Jailhouse Rock	5
72	Kama Sutra 2013 042	Rock'n'Roll Is Here To Stay/At The Hop/Duke Of Earl/FLAMIN' GROOVIES: Gonna Rock Tonite/Keep A-Knockin'	6
72	Kama Sutra 2013 045	Sea Cruise/Vote Song	5
70	Buddah 2361 001	ROCK AND ROLL IS HERE TO STAY (LP)	12
71	Buddah 2319 007	SHA NA NA (LP)	12
72	Buddah 2319 019	THE NIGHT IS STILL YOUNG (LP)	12

SHA NA NETTES
75	Disco Demand DDS 114	Romeo And Juliet/Flint Nit Rock	5

WINSTON SHAN(D)
69	Bullet BU 399	Throw Me Corn/Darling Remember (B-side actually by Pat Edwards)	7
69	Bullet BU 411	Matilda (as Wilston Shan)/HARMONIANS: Come To Me	7
70	Moodisc MU 3505	I'll Run Away/Time Is The Master	7
72	Camel CA 88	Audrey (as Winston Shan)/So Nice (as Winston Shan)	7

DAVE SHAND & HIS ROCKIN' RHYTHM
56	Oriole CB 1321	Rockin' The Boat/LIZZIE BORDEN: You Can't Chop Your Poppa Up In Massachusetts (actually by Derek Nimmo) (78)	10

SHANE & SHANE GANG
64	Pye 7N 15662	Whistle Stop/Who Wrote That Song	12

JOHN SHANE
77	Full Moon	CROSS MY PALM WITH SILVER (LP)	12

VALERIE SHANE
58	Philips PB 833	When The Boys Talk About The Girls/Careful, Careful	7
58	Philips PB 879	Meet Me Tonight In Dreamland/One Billion Seven Million Thirty-Three	8
59	Philips PB 929	Make Love To Me/Baisez-Moi (Kiss Me)	6
59	Philips PB 929	Make Love To Me/Baisez-Moi (Kiss Me) (78)	10

SHANES
65	Columbia DB 7601	I Don't Want Your Love/New Orleans	40

SHANGAANS
65	Columbia DB 7551	Genzene (What Have I Done)/Yeh Girl	6

SHANGRI-LAS
64	Red Bird RB 10008	Remember (Walking In The Sand)/It's Easier To Cry	6
64	Red Bird RB 10014	Leader Of The Pack/What Is Love?	8
65	Red Bird RB 10018	Give Him A Great Big Kiss/Twist And Shout	10
65	Red Bird RB 10025	Out In The Streets/The Boy	10
65	Red Bird RB 10030	Give Us Your Blessings/Heaven Only Knows	12
65	Red Bird RB 10036	Right Now And Not Later/Train From Kansas City	18
66	Red Bird RB 10043	I Can Never Go Home Anymore/Bulldog	10
66	Red Bird RB 10048	Long Live Our Love/Sophisticated Boom Boom	12
66	Red Bird RB 10053	He Cried/Dressed In Black	12
66	Red Bird RB 10068	Past, Present, And Future/Paradise	15
67	Mercury MF 962	The Sweet Sound Of Summer/I'll Never Learn	8
67	Mercury MF 979	Take The Time/Footsteps On The Roof	8
73	Buddah 2011 164	Give Him A Great Big Kiss/TRADEWINDS: New York Is A Lonely Town/ AD LIBS: The Boy From New York City	5
73	Philips 6051 027	Train From Kansas City/Past Present & Future	5
65	Red Bird RB 40 002	THE SHANGRI-LAS (EP)	75
66	Red Bird RB 40 004	I CAN NEVER GO HOME ANYMORE (EP, unreleased)	
65	Red Bird RB 20 101	THE SHANGRI-LAS — LEADER OF THE PACK (LP)	60
66	Mercury MCL 20096	GOLDEN HITS OF THE SHANGRI-LAS (LP)	15

BUD SHANK
56	Vogue V 2376	Royal Garden Blues/It Had To Be You (with Bill Perkins Quintet)	6
56	Vogue V 2383	When Your Lover Has Gone/There's A Small Hotel (with Bob Brookmeyer)	6
56	Vogue V 2385	Shank's Pranks/Left Bank (with Shorty Rogers Quintet)	6
59	Vogue LAE 12248	LATIN CONTRASTS (LP)	20
	(see also Shorty Rogers)		

ANANDA SHANKAR
69	Reprise RSLP 6398	ANANDAR SHANKAR (LP)	50
70	Reprise K 44092	ANANDAR SHANKAR (LP, reissue)	40

RAVI SHANKAR
66	Fontana TF 712	Song From The Hills/Dhun	8
72	Apple APPLE 37	Joi Bangla/Oh Bhaugowan/Raga Mishri-Jhinjhoti (p/s)	15
74	Dark Horse AMS 7133	I Am Missing You/Lust (as Shankar Family & Friends)	5
59	Vogue VA 160156	INDIA'S MASTER MUSICIAN (LP)	20
62	HMV ASD 463	MUSIC OF INDIA (LP)	15
63	Melodisc MLP 12-151	THE EXCITING MUSIC OF RAVI SHANKAR (LP)	15
65	Fontana TF 5253	INDIA'S MASTER MUSICIAN (LP, reissue)	15
66	Fontana TL 5285	PORTRAIT OF GENIUS (LP)	15
66	Fontana TL 5357	SOUND OF THE SITAR (LP)	15
67	Fontana TL 5424	IN NEW YORK (LP)	15
67	HMV ASD 2304	DUETS: RAVI SHANKAR & ALI AKBAR KHAN (LP)	12
67	HMV ASD 2341	MUSIC OF INDIA NO. 4 (LP)	12
68	HMV ASD 2418	MUSIC OF INDIA NO. 8 (LP)	12
68	Liberty LBL/LBS 83076	IMPROVISATIONS (LP)	12
68	Liberty LBL/LBS 83077	IN CONCERT (LP)	12

Ravi SHANKAR

68	Liberty LBL/LBS 83078	INDIA'S MASTER MUSICIAN (LP, 2nd reissue)	12
68	Liberty LBL/LBS 83079	PORTRAIT OF GENIUS (LP, reissue)	12
68	Liberty LBL/LBS 83080	SOUND OF THE SITAR (LP, reissue)	12
68	Liberty LBL/LBS 83081	IN NEW YORK (LP, reissue)	12
68	Columbia S(C)X 6273	LIVE AT THE MONTEREY POP FESTIVAL (LP)	15
69	Transatlantic TRA 182	A SITAR RECITAL (LP)	12
69	Transatlantic TRA 183	DHUN PALAS KAFI (LP, with Ali Akbar Khan)	12
70	Columbia SCX 6382	RAVI SHANKAR IN SAN FRANCISCO (LP)	12
71	Mushroom 300 MR 8	FOUR RAGA MOODS (2-LP)	30
72	United Artists UAG 29379	AT THE WOODSTOCK FESTIVAL (LP)	12
73	Apple SAPDO 1002	IN CONCERT — 1972 (2-LP, with Ali Akbar Khan, gatefold sleeve)	150
74	Dark Horse AMLH 22002	SHANKAR FAMILY & FRIENDS (LP)	15
76	Dark Horse AMLH 22007	RAVI SHANKAR'S MUSIC FESTIVAL FROM INDIA (LP)	20
96	Apple SAPDO 1002	IN CONCERT — 1972 (2-LP, reissue)	25
96	Apple SAPDO 1002	IN CONCERT — 1972 (CD)	20

(see also Ali Akbar Khan, Will Sergeant)

JOHNNY SHANLY
| 60 | Columbia DB 4425 | This Day I Promise/Makin' Love To You | 6 |
| 60 | Columbia DB 4526 | I Wonder/It Happens That Way | 6 |

DEAN SHANNON
| 60 | HMV POP 820 | Blinded With Love/Jezebel | 15 |
| 62 | HMV POP 1103 | Ubangi Stomp/Blowing Wild | 20 |

DEL SHANNON
SINGLES
61	London HLX 9317	Runaway/Jody	6
61	London HLX 9317	Runaway/Jody (mispressed B-side, plays "The Snake" by Maximilian)	18
61	London HLX 9402	Hats Off To Larry/Don't Gild The Lily, Lily	6
61	London HLX 9462	So Long Baby/The Answer To Everything	6
62	London HLX 9515	Hey! Little Girl/You Never Talked About Me	6
62	London HLX 9587	Cry Myself To Sleep/I'm Gonna Move On	6
62	London HLX 9609	The Swiss Maid/Ginny In The Mirror	6
63	London HLX 9653	Little Town Flirt/The Wamboo	6
63	London HLX 9710	Two Kinds Of Teardrops/Kelly	6
63	London HLX 9761	Two Silhouettes/My Wild One	7
63	London HLU 9800	Sue's Gonna Be Mine/Since She's Gone	7
64	London HLU 9858	That's The Way Love Is/Time Of The Day	8
64	Stateside SS 269	Mary Jane/Stains On My Letter	7
64	Stateside SS 317	Handy Man/Give Her Lots Of Lovin'	7
64	Stateside SS 349	Do You Want To Dance/This Is All I Have To Give	7
65	Stateside SS 368	Keep Searchin' (We'll Follow The Sun)/Broken Promises	6
65	Stateside SS 395	Stranger In Town/Over You	7
65	Stateside SS 430	Break Up/Why Don't You Tell Him	7
65	Stateside SS 452	Move It On Over/She Still Remembers Tony	12
66	Stateside SS 494	I Can't Believe My Ears/I Wish I Wasn't Me Tonight	12
66	Liberty LIB 55866	The Big Hurt/I Got It Bad	10
66	Liberty LIB 55889	For A Little While/Hey Little Star	12
67	Liberty LIB 55939	She/What Makes You Run	12
67	Liberty LIB 10277	Mind Over Matter/Led Along	10
67	Liberty LBF 15020	Runaway '67/Show Me	10
68	Liberty LBF 15061	Thinkin' It Over/Runnin' On Back	12
68	Liberty LBF 15079	Gemini/Magical Musical Box	12
69	Stateside SS 8025	Comin' Back To Me/Sweet Mary Lou	10
70	Stateside SS 8040	Sister Isabelle/Colorado Rain	10
72	United Artists UP 35460	What's A Matter, Baby/Early In The Morning	8
73	United Artists UP 35535	Kelly (live)/Coppersville Yodel	8
74	United Artists UP 35740	And The Music Plays On/In My Arms Again	7
83	Demon D 1017	Cheap Love/Distant Ghost (p/s)	6
83	Demon D 1019	Sea Of Love/Help Me (p/s)	6

EPs
62	London RE-X 1332	RUNAWAY WITH DEL SHANNON (EP)	25
63	London RE-X 1346	DEL SHANNON NO. 2 (EP)	25
63	London RE-X 1383	DEL'S OWN FAVOURITES (EP)	25
63	London RE-X 1387	FROM DEL TO YOU (EP)	30
65	Stateside SE 1029	DEL SHANNON'S HITS (EP)	25
67	Liberty LEP 2272	THE NEW DEL SHANNON (EP)	40

LPs
61	London HA-X 2402	RUNAWAY WITH DEL DHANNON (LP)	40
63	London HA-X 8071	HATS OFF TO DEL SHANNON (LP)	35
63	London HA-X 8091	LITTLE TOWN FLIRT (LP)	40
65	Stateside SL 10115	HANDY MAN (LP)	40
65	Stateside SL 10130	DEL SHANNON SINGS HANK WILLIAMS (LP)	35
65	Stateside SL 10140	ONE THOUSAND SIX HUNDRED AND SIXTY-ONE SECONDS WITH DEL SHANNON (LP)	35
66	Liberty (S)LBY 1320	THIS IS MY BAG (LP, mono/stereo)	20/25
66	Liberty (S)LBY 1335	TOTAL COMMITMENT (LP, mono/stereo)	20/25
68	Liberty LBL/LBS 83114E	THE FURTHER ADVENTURES OF CHARLES WESTOVER (LP)	50
73	United Artists UAS 29474	LIVE IN ENGLAND (LP)	15

(see also Maximilian)

LINDA SHANNON
| 59 | Parlophone R 4603 | Goodbye Charlie/If You Only Knew | 5 |

MIKE SHANNON & STRANGERS
(see under Strangers)

DEL SHANNON

HELEN SHAPIRO

SHAPE OF THE RAIN
71	RCA Neon NE 1001	Woman/Wasting My Time.	7
71	RCA Neon NE 7	RILEY, RILEY, WOOD & WAGGETT (LP, gatefold sleeve).	35

SHAPES
79	Sofa SEAT 1/FRR 004	THE SHAPES EP (no p/s, with insert)	15
79	Good Vibrations GOT 13	Blast Off/Airline Disasters (p/s).	15

SHAPES & SIZES
66	Decca F 12441	A Little Lovin' Somethin'/Rain On My Face.	6

HELEN SHAPIRO
SINGLES
61	Columbia DB 4589	Don't Treat Me Like A Child/When I'm With You	6
61	Columbia DB 4670	You Don't Know/Marvellous Lie.	6
61	Columbia DB 4715	Walkin' Back To Happiness/Kiss 'N' Run.	6
62	Columbia DB 4782	Tell Me What He Said/I Apologise	6
62	Columbia DB 4824	Let's Talk About Love/Sometime Yesterday.	7
62	Columbia DB 4869	Little Miss Lonely/I Don't Care	7
62	Columbia DB 4908	Keep Away From Other Girls/Cry My Heart Out	7
63	Columbia DB 4966	Queen For Tonight/Daddy Couldn't Get Me One Of Those.	8
63	Columbia DB 7026	Woe Is Me/I Walked Right In.	8
63	Columbia DB 7072	Not Responsible/No Trespassing	8
63	Columbia DB 7130	Look Who It Is/Walking In My Dreams.	8
64	Columbia DB 7190	Fever/Ole Father Time	10
64	Columbia DB 7266	Look Over Your Shoulder/You Won't Come Home	8
64	Columbia DB 7340	Shop Around/He Knows How To Love Me.	60
64	Columbia DB 7395	I Wish I'd Never Loved You/I Was Only Kidding.	10
65	Columbia DB 7517	Tomorrow Is Another Day/It's So Funny I Could Cry	10
65	Columbia DB 7587	Here In Your Arms/Only Once	10
65	Columbia DB 7690	Something Wonderful/Just A Line.	10
66	Columbia DB 7810	Forget About The Bad Things/Wait A Little Longer	10
66	Columbia DB 8073	In My Calendar/Empty House	10
67	Columbia DB 8148	Make Me Belong To You/The Way Of The World.	10
67	Columbia DB 8256	She Needs Company/Stop And You Will Become Aware	60
68	Pye 7N 17600	You'll Get Me Loving You/Silly Boy (I Love You)	10
69	Pye 7N 17714	Today Has Been Cancelled/Face The Music	10
69	Pye 7N 17785	You've Guessed/Take Me For A While	12
70	Pye 7N 17893	Take Down A Note Miss Smith/Couldn't You See	10
70	Pye 7N 17975	Waiting On The Shores Of Nowhere/A Glass Of Wine	10
83	Oval HELEN 25	Let Yourself Go/Funny (p/s).	5
83	Oval HELEN 25/10	Let Yourself Go/Cry Me A River/Funny (10", p/s)	6
84	Oval OVAL 26	Brickyard Blues/Just Another Weekend (p/s)	6

EPs
61	Columbia SEG 8128	HELEN (EP, mono, 'smiling' or 'cross-armed' sleeve)	each 15
61	Columbia ESG 7872	HELEN (EP, stereo, 'smiling' or 'cross-armed' sleeve)	each 20
61	Columbia SEG 8136	HELEN'S HIT PARADE (EP)	15
62	Columbia SEG 8170	A TEENAGER SINGS THE BLUES (EP, also stereo ESG 7880).	20/25
62	Columbia SEG 8174	MORE HITS FROM HELEN (EP).	15
62	Columbia SEG 8209	EVEN MORE HITS FROM HELEN (EP).	15
63	Columbia SEG 8229	'TOPS' WITH ME NO. 1 (EP, also stereo ESG 7888)	20/30
63	Columbia SEG 8243	'TOPS' WITH ME NO. 2 (EP, also stereo ESG 7891)	20/30

LPs
62	Columbia 33SX 1397	'TOPS' WITH ME (LP, also stereo SCX 3428)	18/30
63	Columbia 33SX 1494	HELEN'S SIXTEEN (LP, also stereo SCX 3470)	30/40

MINT VALUE £

63	Columbia 33SX 1561	HELEN IN NASHVILLE (LP)	30
64	Columbia 33SX 1561	HELEN HITS OUT (LP, also stereo SCX 3533)	30/40
65	EMI Encore! ENC 209	12 HITS AND A MISS HELEN SHAPIRO (LP)	20
74	Columbia SCX 6565	THE VERY BEST OF HELEN SHAPIRO (LP)	12

(see also Ella Stone & Moss)

SHARADES
| 64 | Decca F 11811 | Dumb Head/Boy Trouble | 75 |

(see also Ladybirds, Breakaways)

BILLY SHA RAE
| 71 | Action ACT 4602 | Do It/Crying Clown | 12 |

(BILLY) SHARI
| 58 | Decca F 11069 | Going Home For Christmas/Count Every Star (as Shari) | 6 |
| 68 | United Artists UP 2235 | It's So Lonely Being Together/You Walked Out On Me Before | 5 |

SHARKEY & HIS KINGS OF DIXIELAND
57	Capitol CL 14767	Look Sharp, Be Sharp/Sharkey Strut	5
51	Capitol LC 6531	SHARKEY'S SOUTHERN COMFORT (10" LP)	12
53	Capitol LC 6600	MIDNIGHT ON BOURBON STREET (10" LP)	12
54	Melodisc MLP 503	SHARKEY'S KINGS OF DIXIELAND (10" LP)	12

SHARKS
| 68 | RCA RCA 1776 | Goodbye Lorene/Funkology | 7 |

(see also Marcisa & Jeff, Roy Richards)

SHARKS
| 73 | Island ILPS 9233 | FIRST WATER (LP, 'pink rim palm tree' label with inner sleeve) | 12 |
| 74 | Island ILPS 9271 | JAB IT IN YORE EYE (LP, 'palm tree' label with inner sleeve) | 12 |

(see also Chris Spedding, Andy Fraser Band)

RALPH SHARON
53	Decca LF 1107	SPRING FEVER (10" LP)	12
53	Decca LF 1138	AUTUMN LEAVES (10" LP)	30
53	Lyragon AF 1	COCKTAIL TIME (10" LP)	15

(see also Tony Bennett)

SHARONETTES
| 75 | Black Magic BM 102 | Papa Ooh Mow Mow/Papa Ooh Mow Mow (Instrumental Version) | 4 |
| 75 | Black Magic BM 104 | Going To A Go Go/Going To A Go Go (Instrumental Version) | 4 |

SHARONS
| 70 | Emblem JDR 325 | SOMEONE TO TURN TO (LP, Irish only) | 50 |

SHARP
| 86 | Unicorn-Kanchana PHZ 5 | Entertain Me/So Say Hurrah (The Emperor's New Clothes) (p/s) | 4 |

(see also Jam)

BOBBY SHARP & OTHERS
| 65 | Stateside SS 404 | Blues For Mr. Charlie (Parts 1 & 2) (with Paul Sindap, Joe Lee Wilson & Little Butler) | 7 |

DEE DEE SHARP
62	Columbia DB 4818	Mashed Potato Time/Set My Heart At Ease	10
62	Columbia DB 4874	Gravy (For My Mashed Potatoes)/Baby Cakes	10
62	Cameo Parkway C 230	Ride/Night	7
63	Cameo Parkway C 244	Do The Bird/Lover Boy	12
63	Cameo Parkway C 260	Rock Me In The Cradle Of Love/You'll Never Be Mine	10
63	Cameo Parkway C 274	Wild/Why Doncha Ask Me	7
65	Cameo Parkway C 375	I Really Love You/Standing In The Need Of Love	50
65	Cameo Parkway C 382	It's A Funny Situation/There Ain't Nothing I Wouldn't Do (demo-only)	100
66	Atlantic 584 056	My Best Friend's Man/Bye Bye Baby	10
69	Action ACT 4522	What Kind Of Lady/You're Gonna Miss Me	25
79	London HA-U 8514	CAMEO PARKWAY SESSIONS (LP)	12

(see also Chubby Checker & Dee Dee Sharp)

STEVE SHARP & CLEANCUTS
| 80 | Happy Face MM 122 | We Are The Mods/He Wants To Be A Mod (no p/s) | 75 |

(see also Rowdies)

BILL SHARPE
| 85 | Polydor 825 497-2 | FAMOUS PEOPLE (CD) | 16 |

(see also Sharpe & Numan)

RAY SHARPE
59	London HLW 8932	Linda Lu/Red Sails In The Sunset (triangular or round centre)	40/25
59	London HLW 8932	Linda Lu/Red Sails In The Sunset (78)	50
63	United Artists UP 1032	Hey Little Girl/Day You Left Me	15

ROCKY SHARPE & REPLAYS
| 82 | Chiswick DICE 9 | Heart/Mary (Won't You Marry Me) (withdrawn, approx. 100 only) | 10 |

SHARPE & NUMAN
85	Polydor POSPP 722	Change Your Mind/Remix, Remake, Remodel (picture disc)	5
85	Polydor POSPX 722	Change Your Mind (Extended Mix)/Remix, Remake, Remodel/Fools In A World Of Fire (12", picture disc)	8
86	Numa NU 19	New Thing From London Town/Time To Die (p/s, 1,000 autographed)	6
86	Numa NUP 19	New Thing From London Town/Time To Die (picture disc)	4
86	Numa NUM 19	New Thing From London Town/Time To Die (12", picture disc)	8
88	Polydor POSP B/W/T 894	No More Lies/Voices (p/s, blue, white or clear vinyl)	5
88	Polydor POCD 894	No More Lies (Extended Mix)/Voices/Change Your Mind/ No More Lies (7" Version) (CD, card sleeve, some autographed)	12/10
89	Polydor POPB 43	I'm On Automatic/No More Lies ('89 Remix) (poster p/s)	5

MINT VALUE £

89	Polydor POPD 43	I'm On Automatic/Love Like A Ghost (picture disc) 5
89	Polydor PZPD 43	I'm On Automatic (Extended Mix)/Love Like A Ghost (12", picture disc) 8
89	Polydor PZCD 43	I'm On Automatic (12" Remix)/Love Like A Ghost/Voices ('89 Remix) (CD)...... 10
89	Polydor 839 520-0	AUTOMATIC (CD, with bonus tracks "No More Lies" [12" Version] & "I'm On Automatic" [12" Version]) 20

(see also Gary Numan, Bill Sharpe)

SHARPEES
66	Stateside SS 495	Tired Of Being Lonely/Just To Please You. 50
73	President PT 389	Do The 45/Make Up Your Mind 5
73	President PT 399	Tired Of Being Lonely/Just To Please You (reissue) 5

BOB SHARPLES & HIS (DANCE) MUSIC/ORCHESTRA
55	Decca F 10450	Capitano/Time Remembered 6
56	Decca F 10707	Hurricane Boogie/Concetta 6
56	Decca F 10748	The Portuguese Washerwoman/Sadie's Shawl 5

SHARPS
57	Vogue V 9086	Lock My Heart/Love Is Here To Stay 550
57	Vogue V 9086	Lock My Heart/Love Is Here To Stay (78). 75
58	Vogue V 9096	Shufflin'/What Will I Gain 500
58	Vogue V 9096	Shufflin'/What Will I Gain (78) 75

(see also Thurston Harris)

S-HATERS
| 81 | Outer Himmilayan OHR 02 | Death Of A Vampire/Research (p/s). .... 5 |
| 81 | Outer Himmilayan OHR 05 | STORIES AS COLD AS THE IRISH SEA (EP, foldover p/s) .... 4 |

SHAVED FISH
| 87 | Antar ANTAR 4501 | Two Minutes Silence/Two Minutes Silence (Demo Version) (p/s) .... 4 |

SHAVERS, GETZ, COLE, NORVO, BELLSON, MILLER, etc
| 52 | Vogue V 2104 | Charlie Got Rhythm (Parts 1 & 2) (78). .... 8 |

ADRIAN SHAW
| 96 | Woronzow W0027 | TEA FOR THE HYDRA (LP, 299 copies only, in hand-finished sleeves) .... 15 |

(see also Hawkwind, Bevis Frond)

ARTIE SHAW
54	MGM EPC 3	ARTIE SHAW (EP, export issue). 8
54	Brunswick LA 8677	SPEAK TO ME OF LOVE (10" LP) 15
55	Columbia Clef 33C 9006	ARTIE SHAW AND HIS GRAMERCY FIVE (10" LP) 15
58	RCA RD 27065	ANY OLD TIME (LP) 12

GEORGIE SHAW
55	Brunswick 05356	Give Me The Right/Yearning (Just For You). 6
55	Brunswick 05362	Unsuspecting Heart/Let Me Go, Devil 6
55	Brunswick 05426	I'll Step Aside/The Water Tumbler Tune 6
55	Brunswick 05476	Banjo Woogie/I Can Tell 7

(see also Kitty Kallen)

MARLENA SHAW
67	Chess CRS 8054	Mercy Mercy Mercy/Go Away Little Boy 10
73	United Artists UP 35517	Last Tango In Paris/Save The Children 5
76	United Artists UP 36125	It's Better Than Walking Out/Be For Real 5
76	Blue Note UP 36163	Love Has Gone Away/No Hiding Place 5
77	CBS 5550	Go Away Little Boy/Look At Me Look At You 5

NINA SHAW
68	CBS 3239	Woven In My Soul/Love So Fine 7
68	CBS 3556	From Now Till Then/Window Of My Mind........................ 5
69	CBS 3943	Stop The Music/Celebration Of The Year 5
69	CBS 4227	One Fine Day/Somewhere In The World 5
69	CBS 4673	In One Hour/I Will Come To You. 5

RICKY SHAW
| 62 | London HLU 9606 | No Love But Your Love/Be Still, Be Still, My Own. .... 8 |

ROLAND SHAW ORCHESTRA
54	Decca F 10407	No One But You (with Kim Bennett)/The High And The Mighty 6
55	Decca F 10449	Softly, Softly (with Kim Bennett)/A Trumpeter's Lullaby 6
67	Decca F 12595	The Look Of Love/Have No Fear, Mr Bond Is Here 5
66	Decca DFE 8670	I SPY (EP). 18
65	Decca LK 4730	JAMES BOND IN ACTION (LP). 20
66	Decca LK 4765	THEMES FOR SECRET AGENTS (LP, mono). 18
66	Phase 4 Stereo PFS 4094	THEMES FOR SECRET AGENTS (LP, stereo) 18
67	Phase 4 Stereo PFS 4125	MORE JAMES BOND IN ACTION (LP) 18
71	Decca Phase 4 SPA 158	THE WORLD OF JAMES BOND ADVENTURE (LP) 10
72	Decca Phase 4 SPA 213	PHASE 4 WORLD OF SPY THRILLERS (LP) 10

SANDIE SHAW
SINGLES
64	Pye 7N 15671	As Long As You're Happy Baby/Ya-Ya-Da-Da 30
64	Pye 7N 15704	(There's) Always Something There To Remind Me/Don't You Know 5
64	Pye 7N 15743	I'd Be Far Better Off Without You/Girl Don't Come 5
65	Pye 7N 15783	I'll Stop At Nothing/You Can't Blame Him. 5
65	Pye 7N 15841	Long Live Love/I've Heard About Him. 5
65	Pye 7N 15940	Message Understood/Don't You Count On It. 5
65	Pye 7N 15987	How Can You Tell/If Ever You Need Me 6
66	Pye 7N 17036	Tomorrow/Hurting You 5
66	Pye 7N 17086	Nothing Comes Easy/Stop Before You Start 5
66	Pye 7N 17163	Run/Long Walk Home 6
66	Pye 7N 17212	Think Sometimes About Me/Hide All Emotion 6

Sandie SHAW

67	Pye 7N 17239	I Don't Need Anything/Keep In Touch 6
67	Pye 7N 17272	Puppet On A String/Tell The Boys (pink label, later blue) 5/6
67	Pye 7N 17346	Tonight In Tokyo/You've Been Seeing Her Again 5
67	Pye 7N 17378	You've Not Changed/Make Me Cry 5
68	Pye 7N 17441	Today/London (pink label, later blue) . . . . each 6
68	Pye 7N 17504	Don't Run Away/Stop 6
68	Pye 7N 17564	Show Me/One More Life 6
68	Pye 7N 17587	Together/Turn On The Sunshine 6
68	Pye 7N 17611	Those Were The Days/Make It Go 6
69	Pye 7N 17675	Monsieur Dupont/Voice In The Crowd 5
69	Pye 7N 17726	Think It All Over/Send Me A Letter 6
69	Pye 7N 17821	Heaven Knows I'm Missing Him Now/So Many Things To Do. 6
70	Pye 7N 17894	By Tomorrow/Maple Village 6
70	Pye 7N 17954	Wight Is Wight/That's The Way He's Made. 6
71	Pye 7N 45040	Rose Garden/Maybe I'm Amazed. 6
71	Pye 7N 45073	The Power And The Glory/Dear Madame. 6
72	Pye 7N 45118	Where Did They Go/Look At Me. 6
72	Pye 7N 45164	Father And Son/Pity The Ship 6
77	CBS 5371	One More Night/Still So Young 6
77	Epic EPC 5513	Just A Disillusion/Your Mama Wouldn't Like It 6
82	Virgin VS 484	Anyone Who Had A Heart/Anyone Who Had A Heart (instrumental) (p/s) 12
84	Rough Trade RT 130	Hand In Glove/I Don't Owe You Anything (p/s, with The Smiths) 4
84	Rough Trade RTT 130	Hand In Glove/I Don't Owe You Anything/Jeanne (12", p/s, with The Smiths) 10
88	Rough RTT 220CD	Please Help The Cause Against Loneliness/Jeanne/Lover Of The Century/ I Will Remain (Alternative Mix) (CD) 15
88	Rough RTT 230CD	Nothing Less Than Brilliant (Remix)/I Don't Owe You Anything/ Where Were You/I Love Peace (CD) 15

EPs

64	Pye NEP 24208	(THERE'S) ALWAYS SOMETHING THERE TO REMIND ME (EP) 15
65	Pye NEP 24220	LONG LIVE LOVE (EP). 15
65	Pye NEP 24232	TALK ABOUT LOVE (EP) 15
65	Pye NEP 24234	SANDIE (EP). 15
66	Pye NEP 24236	MESSAGE UNDERSTOOD (EP) 15
66	Pye NEP 24247	TOMORROW (EP) 20
66	Pye NEP 24254	NOTHING COMES EASY (EP) 20
66	Pye NEP 24264	RUN WITH SANDIE SHAW (EP) 20
67	Pye NEP 24271	SANDIE SHAW IN FRENCH (EP) 35
67	Pye NEP 24273	SANDIE SHAW IN ITALIAN (EP). 35
67	Pye NEP 24281	TELL THE BOYS (EP) 20

LPs

65	Pye NPL 18110	SANDIE SHAW (LP) 20
65	Pye NPL 18122	ME (LP). 20
66	Golden Guinea GGL 0360	THE GOLDEN HITS OF SANDIE SHAW (LP) 15
67	Golden Guinea GGL 0378	SANDIE SINGS (LP) 15
67	Pye N(S)PL 18182	PUPPET ON A STRING (LP) 20
67	Pye N(S)PL 18205	LOVE ME, PLEASE LOVE ME (LP). 20
68	Marble Arch MAL(S) 781	THE GOLDEN HITS OF SANDIE SHAW (LP) 12
68	Pye N(S)PL 18232	THE SANDIE SHAW SUPPLEMENT (LP) 20
69	Pye N(S)PL 18323	REVIEWING THE SITUATION (LP) 25

SANDY SHAW
| 58 | Starlite ST45 007 | Hello, Goodbye/TERRY TAYLOR: The Only Way . . . . 6 |

THOMAS SHAW
| 72 | Xtra XTRA 1132 | THOMAS SHAW (LP) . . . . 15 |

TIMMY SHAW & STERNPHONES
| 64 | Pye International 7N 25239 | Gonna Send You Back To Georgia/I'm A Lonely Guy . . . . 10 |

TREVOR SHAW
| 81 | CMS PR 26 | WHEELS IN MOTION (LP) . . . . 20 |

DOROTHY SHAY
| 53 | Capitol LC 6618 | THE PARK AVENUE HILLBILLIE (10" LP) . . . . 10 |

SHE
| 85 | Neat NEAT 5012 | Never Surrender/Breaking Away/On My Way (12", p/s). 7 |

GEORGE BEVERLY SHEA
54	HMV 7M 184	Robe Of Calvary/I Found A Friend 6
54	HMV 7M 204	I'd Rather Have Jesus/Tenderly He Watches. 6
54	HMV 7M 205	If You Know The Lord/The King Of All Kings. 6
54	HMV 7M 218	He Bought My Soul At Calvary/Each Step Of The Way. 6

LEE SHEARIN
| 50 | London L 695 | Give A Broken Heart A Chance To Cry/I Need You (78) . . . . 8 |

GEORGE SHEARING (QUINTET)
53	MGM SP 1006	I'll Remember April/Jumping With Symphony Sid 5
53	MGM SP 1017	There's A Lull In My Life/Bassic English. 5
53	MGM SP 1031	Night Flight/Love (Your Magic Spell Is Everywhere) (B-side with Teddi King). . . . 5
53	MGM SP 1035	How High The Moon/So This Is Cuba 5
53	MGM SP 1046	Body And Soul/The Lady Is A Tramp. 5
53	MGM SP 1047	Love Is Just Around The Corner/Point And Counterpoint 5
54	MGM SP 1066	Tiempo De Cencerro (both sides) 5
54	MGM SP 1080	Rap Your Troubles In Drums/Love Is Here To Stay 5
54	MGM SP 1090	Spring Is Here/Easy To Love 5
54	MGM SP 1103	Mambo Inn/I've Never Been In Love Before 5
56	MGM SP 1113	Lullaby Of Birdland/Get Off My Bach 6
56	MGM SP 1161	I'll Never Smile Again/If You Were The Only Girl In The World 5
56	MGM SP 1171	I Wished On The Moon/It's Easy To Remember (with Teddi King) 5
54	MGM EPC 4	GEORGE SHEARING (EP, export issue) 8

56	MGM EP 563	WHEN LIGHTS ARE LOW (EP)	8
50s	London BEP 6029	PIANOLOGY (EP, export issue)	8
50s	London BEP 6030	THE GEORGE SHEARING TRIO (EP, export issue)	8
50s	London BEP 6031	THE GEORGE SHEARING TRIO (EP, export issue)	8
50s	Vogue EPV 1145	THE GEORGE SHEARING QUINTET (EP)	8
51	Decca LF 1036	THE NEARNESS OF YOU (10" LP, as George Shearing Trio)	12
52	MGM MGM-D 103	YOU'RE HEARING GEORGE SHEARING (10" LP)	12
53	MGM MGM-D 118	I HEAR MUSIC (10" LP)	12
54	MGM MGM-D 129	TOUCH OF GENIUS (10" LP)	12
56	Vogue LDE 188	THE VERY FIRST SESSION (10" LP)	12
56	Capitol LC 6803	THE SHEARING SPELL (10" LP)	12
59	Capitol T/ST 1275	LATIN AFFAIR (LP)	12

(see also Peggy Lee)

SHEDS
| 85 | John Wayne's S/bags 1 | BIMBO EP (cassette, shrinkwrapped with free packet of tomato seeds) | 75 |

(see also Super 8)

SHED SEVEN
94	Polydor YORK 1	Mark/Casino Girl (p/s)	10
94	Polydor YORKX 1	Mark/Casino Girl/Mobile 10 (12", p/s)	10
94	Polydor YORKCD 1	Mark/Casino Girl/Mobile 10 (CD)	12
94	Polydor YORK 2	Dolphin/Immobilise (p/s, purple vinyl)	4
94	Polydor YORKCD 2	Dolphin/Immobilise/Dolphin (Forward) (CD)	7
94	Polydor YORK 3	Speakeasy/Around Your House (p/s, coloured vinyl)	4
94	Polydor YORK 4	Ocean Pie/Never Again (p/s, clear vinyl)	4
96	Polydor 576 214-7	Going For Gold/Making Waves (withdrawn 'nude' gatefold p/s, some without disc)	20/10

SHEEBA
| 81 | Ritz RITZ 6 | Horoscopes/You Came Through Love With Me (p/s) | 4 |

BOBBY SHEEN
| 66 | Capitol CL 15455 | Dr. Love/Sweet, Sweet Love | 60 |
| 72 | Capitol CL 15713 | Dr. Love/Sweet, Sweet Love (reissue) | 6 |

(see also Bob B. Soxx & Blue Jeans)

SHEEP (U.S.)
| 66 | Stateside SS 493 | Hide And Seek/Twelve Months Later | 15 |
| 69 | Stateside SS 2147 | Hide And Seek/HAWKS: The Grissle | 8 |

SHEEP (U.K.)
| 73 | Myrrh MYR 1000 | SHEEP (LP, with insert) | 25 |

(see also Lonesome Stone)

IREEN SHEER
70	Bell BLL 1129	Hey Pleasure Man/You Walked Away	5
71	Parlophone R 5930	Many Rivers/Is It Me	5
74	Polydor 2041 533	Bye Bye I Love You/Roseberry Avenue	6

SHEER KHAN
| 84 | SRT 4KS 140 | Last Generation (p/s) | 100 |

SHEFFIELDS
64	Pye 7N 15600	It Must Be Love/Say Girl	40
64	Pye 7N 15627	I Got My Mojo Working/Hey Hey Lover Boy	60
65	Pye 7N 15767	Bag's Groove (Skat Walking)/Plenty Of Love	60

SHEIKS (U.S.)
| 59 | London HLW 9012 | Très Chic/Little French Doll | 12 |
| 59 | London HLW 9012 | Très Chic/Little French Doll (78) | 40 |

SHEIKS (U.K.)
| 66 | Parlophone R 5500 | Missing You/Tell Me Bird | 8 |

SHEILA & JENNY
| 64 | Ember EMB S 3202 | When The Boy's Happy/Please Don't Break Her Heart (some in p/s) | 10/6 |

ERNIE SHELBY
| 73 | Mojo 2093 026 | Bend Over Backwards/Punish Me | 5 |

DOUG SHELDON
61	Decca F 11368	The Book Of Love/Play Me The Blues	7
61	Decca F 11398	Runaround Sue/Come With Me	6
61	Decca F 11416	Your Ma Said You Cried In Your Sleep/You're Only Fooling Yourself	7
62	Decca F 11433	My Kingdom For A Girl/You Never Had It So Good	6
62	Decca F 11463	A Big Big Baby/If You'd Be Mine	6
62	Decca F 11514	Lollipops And Roses/One Way To Say Goodbye	6
62	Decca F 11529	Live Now Pay Later/Me	6
63	Decca F 11564	I Saw Linda Yesterday/My Billy	7
63	Decca F 11654	Let's Make A Habit Of This/I Was Alone	7
63	Decca F 11790	Mickey's Monkey/Falling In Love With Love	8
65	Sue WI 332	Take It Like A Man/Lonely Boy	15
65	Pye 7N 17011	It's Because Of You/How Can I Tell Her?	6
63	Decca DFE 8527	HERE I STAND (EP)	60

SANDI SHELDON
| 76 | Epic EPC 4186 | You're Gonna Make Me Love You/Baby You're Mine | 6 |

SHELL
| 66 | Columbia DB 8082 | Goodbye Little Girl/Little Bit Of Lovin' | 8 |

SHELLEY
64	Pye 7N 15711	I Will Be Wishing/Why Don't You Say You Love Me	10
65	Pye 7N 15773	Stairway To A Star/I Heard A Whisper	7
65	Pye 7N 15913	Where Has Your Smile Gone/Paradise	7

MINT VALUE £

LIZ SHELLEY
65	Brunswick 05940	Make Me Your Baby/You Made Me Hurt	7
66	Brunswick 05953	No More Love/I Can't Find You	7

PETE SHELLEY
82	Lyntone 10952/53	Qu'est-Ce Que C'est, Qu'est Que Ça (Dub)/ANIMAL MAGNET: More (hard vinyl test pressing, numbered, some with info sheet/letter)	15/12
80	Groovy STP 2	SKY YEN (mini-LP)	12

(see also Buzzcocks, Free Agents, Tiller Boys)

SHELLS
61	London HLU 9288	Baby, Oh Baby/Angel Eyes	40
62	London HLU 9644	It's A Happy Holiday/Deep In My Heart	35

ALAN SHELLY & MANU DIBANGO'S BROTHERS
69	Philips BF 1709	Lady Black Wife/Give Me Time	12

ANNE SHELTON
78s
54	HMV B 10732	Juke Box Rag/Love Him So Much I Could Scream (78)	8
58	Philips PB 852	Volare/Do You Love Me Like You Kiss Me? (78)	8
58	Philips PB 878	Hurry Home/I.T.A.L.Y. (I Trust And Love You) (78)	8
59	Philips PB 969	The Village Of St. Bernadette/You're Not Living In Vain (78)	15

SINGLES
53	HMV 7M 164	Answer Me (Mutterlein)/The Bridge Of Sighs	12
54	HMV 7M 186	The Book/Why Does It Have To Be Me	12
54	HMV 7M 197	Cross Over The Bridge/(O Baby Mine) I Get So Lonely	12
54	HMV 7M 240	Goodnight, Well It's Time To Go/If I Give My Heart To You	12
54	HMV 7M 279	My Gypsy Heart/Teach Me Tonight	12
57	Philips JK 1012	Absent Friends/Seven Ages Of Man (jukebox issue)	15
58	Philips PB 779	Until They Sail/Ha! Ha! Ha!	7
58	Philips PB 815	The Girl He Left Behind/Sail Along, Silv'ry Moon	7
58	Philips PB 852	Volare/Do You Love Me Like You Kiss Me?	7
58	Philips PB 878	Hurry Home/I.T.A.L.Y. (I Trust And Love You)	7
59	Philips PB 920	Just Love Me/Could I Love You More	6
59	Philips PB 956	Now Hear This!/To Love And Be Loved	6
59	Philips PB 969	The Village Of St. Bernadette/You're Not Living In Vain	6
60	Philips PB 994	The Angels' Lullaby/Where Can I Go	6
60	Philips PB 1042	Papa Loves Mama/Come Back Again	6
61	Philips PB 1096	Sailor/A Souvenir Of Ireland (some with p/s)	8/5
61	Philips PB 1165	Don't Forget/Aidios, My Love	5
66	Philips BF 1464	The Carnival Is Closed Today/The Sounds Of Summer	5

EPs
50s	London BEP 6043	ANNE SHELTON WITH ORCHESTRAL ACCOMPIANIMENT (EP, export issue)	10
56	Decca DFE 6321	FOUR STANDARDS (EP)	12
56	Philips BBE 12090	ANNE SHELTON (EP)	18
58	Philips BBE 12169	THE SHELTON SOUND (EP)	10
58	Philips BBE 12205	ITALIAN TOUCH (EP)	10
58	Philips BBE 12218	ANNE SHELTON (EP)	10
59	Philips BBE 12292	JUST LOVE ME (EP)	10
60	Philips BBE 12344	SONGS OF FAITH (EP)	10
60	Philips BBE 12347	MY YIDDISHE MOMMA (EP, also stereo SBBE 9003)	10/15
61	Philips BBE 12430	FAVOURITES (EP)	10
62	Philips BBE 12526	SPRING FEVER (EP)	10

LPs
52	Decca LF 1023	FAVOURITES (10" LP)	30
53	Decca LF 1106	FAVOURITES VOL. 2 (10" LP)	30
57	Philips BBL 7188	THE SHELTON SOUND (LP)	20
59	Philips BBL 7291	SONGS FROM THE HEART (LP)	20
60	Philips BBL 7393	ANNE SHELTON SHOWCASE (LP)	20
62	Philips BBL 7541	A SOUVENIR OF IRELAND (LP, also stereo SBBL 664)	15/20
62	Ace Of Clubs ACL 1101	ANNE (LP)	15

JO SHELTON
59	Top Rank JAR 124	Tread Softly (You're Stepping On My Heart)/More, More, More Romancing	7
59	Top Rank JAR 124	Tread Softly (You're Stepping On My Heart)/More, More, More Romancing (78)	10
59	Top Rank JAR 245	If There Are Stars In My Eyes/I Need Your Arms Around Me	7

ROSCOE SHELTON
65	Sue WI 354	Strain On My Heart/Question (A- & B-side labels reversed)	20

CAROL SHELYNE
65	Liberty LIB 55794	The Girl With The Horn Rim Glasses/Boys Do Make Passes At Girls Who Wear Glasses	6

DEANNA SHENDEREY
65	Decca F 12090	Comin' Home Baby/I've Got That Feeling	7

SHENLEY (Duffas) & ANNETTE
61	Blue Beat BB 72	Million Dollar Baby/The First Time I Met You	12

SHENLEY (Duffas) & HYACINTH (Brown)
66	Rio R 80	The World Is On A Wheel/ROY & CORNELL: Salvation	12

(see also Baba Brooks)

SHENLEY (Duffas) & (Little) LUNAN
65	Rio R 52	Something On Your Mind/The Rain Came Tumbling Down	10

(see also Shenley Duffas)

SHEP & LIMELITES
61	Pye International 7N 25090	Daddy's Home/This I Know	75
61	Pye International 7N 25112	Ready For Your Love/You'll Be Sorry	50

JEAN SHEPARD
53	Capitol CL 13986	A Dear John Letter/I'd Rather Die Young	5
59	Capitol CL 15031	Jeopardy/Better Love Next Time	5
56	Capitol EAP 1030	SONGS OF A LOVE AFFAIR NO. 1 (EP)	8
56	Capitol EAP2 728	SONGS OF A LOVE AFFAIR NO. 2 (EP)	8
60	Capitol T 1253	THIS IS JEAN SHEPARD (LP)	12

BILLY SHEPHARD
59	Felstad AF 117	You Call Everybody Darling/Somebody Stole My Gal	5
59	Felstad AF 117	You Call Everybody Darling/Somebody Stole My Gal (78)	10

BILL SHEPHERD ORCHESTRA
58	Pye Nixa 7N 15137	Big Guitar/Tequila	7
58	Pye Nixa N 15137	Big Guitar/Tequila (78)	8
59	Pye Nixa 7N 15180	"Inn Of The 6th Happiness" Theme/DR. BARNARDO'S CHILDREN: This Old Man	5
59	Pye Nixa N 15180	"Inn Of The 6th Happiness" Theme/DR. BARNARDO'S CHILDREN: This Old Man (78)	6

PAULINE SHEPHERD
57	Columbia DB 4010	Love Me To Pieces/Just Between You And Me	10

SHEPHERD BOYS (& GIRLS)
56	Columbia SCM 5282	Little Girls And Little Boys/Teenage Love (as Shepherd Boys & Girls)	8
56	Columbia DB 3793	Little Girls And Little Boys/Teenage Love (as Shepherd Boys & Girls) (78)	8
56	Columbia DB 3816	Summer Sweetheart/Song For A Summer Night	6

SHEPHERD/SHEPPARD SISTERS
57	HMV POP 411	Alone (Why Must I Be Alone)/Congratulations To Someone	8
57	HMV POP 411	Alone (Why Must I Be Alone)/Congratulations To Someone (78)	8
58	Mercury 7MT 196	Gettin' Ready For Freddy/Best Thing There Is (Is Love) (as Sheppard Sisters)	10
58	Mercury MT 196	Gettin' Ready For Freddy/Best Thing There Is (Is Love) (78)	10
58	Mercury 7MT 218	Eating Pizza/A Boy And A Girl (as Sheppard Sisters)	6
58	Mercury MT 218	Eating Pizza/A Boy And A Girl (as Sheppard Sisters) (78)	10
58	Mercury AMT 1005	Dancing Baby/Is It A Crime?	6
58	Mercury AMT 1005	Dancing Baby/Is It A Crime? (78)	12
63	London HLK 9681	Don't Mention My Name/What Makes Little Girls Cry	15
63	London HLK 9758	Talk Is Cheap/Greatest Lover	12

TOM SHEPLEY'S BAND
78	Tradition TSR 031	HOW DO YOU DO? (LP)	10

ARCHIE SHEPP
66	HMV CLP/CSD 3524	FOUR FOR TRANE (LP)	15
66	HMV CLP/CSD 3561	ON THIS NIGHT (LP)	15
67	HMV CLP/CSD 3600	LIVE IN SAN FRANCISCO (LP)	15
67	Polydor 623 235	ARCHIE SHEPP AND THE NEW YORK CONTEMPORARY FIVE (LP)	12
67	Fontana 681 014 ZL	RUFUS (LP, with John Tchicai)	12
68	Impulse MIPL/SIPL 508	MAMA TOO TIGHT (LP)	12
68	Polydor 623 267	NEW YORK CONTEMPORARY FIVE VOL. 2 (LP)	12
69	Impulse MILP/SIPL 512	THE MAGIC OF JU-JU (LP)	12
69	Impulse MIPL/SIPL 516	THE WAY AHEAD (LP)	12
69	Atlantic 583 732	ONE FOR THE TRANE (LP)	12
69	Impulse SIPL 520	THREE FOR A QUARTER, ONE FOR A DIME (LP)	12

(see also John Coltrane)

SHEPPARDS
71	Jay Boy BOY 30	How Do You Like It/Stubborn Heart	10

SHEPPERTON FLAMES
69	Deram DM 257	Take Me For What I Am/Goodbye	8

(see also Mike Berry)

SHERIDAN
70	Gemini GMS 001	Follow Me Follow/When Love Breaks Your Heart	12

(see also Sheridan-Price, Mike Sheridan & Night Riders, Mike Sheridan's Lot)

DANI SHERIDAN
66	Planet PLF 106	Guess I'm Dumb/Songs Of Love	18

MIKE SHERIDAN & NIGHT RIDERS
63	Columbia DB 7141	Tell Me What'cha Gonna Do/No Other Guy	35
63	Columbia DB 7183	Please Mr. Postman/In Love	25
64	Columbia DB 7302	What A Sweet Thing That Was/Fabulous	25
65	Columbia DB 7462	Here I Stand/Lonely Weekends	25
84	Edsel ED 120	BIRMINGHAM BEAT (LP)	12

(see also Roy Wood, Idle Race, Mike Sheridan's Lot, Nightriders, Sheridan-Price, Sight & Sound)

MIKE SHERIDAN'S LOT
65	Columbia DB 7677	Take My Hand/Make Them Understand	25
66	Columbia DB 7798	Don't Turn Your Back On Me, Babe/Stop, Look, Listen	25

(see also Roy Wood, Idle Race, Mike Sheridan & Night Riders, Nightriders, Sheridan-Price, Sight & Sound)

TONY SHERIDAN & BEAT BROTHERS
64	Polydor NH 52315	Jambalaya/Will You Still Love Me Tomorrow (with Beat Brothers)	12
64	Polydor NH 52927	Skinny Minny/You'd Better Move On (with Beat Brothers)	12
75	Buk BU 3026	Lonely/I Should Have Stayed (solo)	5

(see also Bobby Patrick Big Six, Beat Brothers, Pete Best Four)

TONY SHERIDAN & BEATLES
(see under Beatles)

SHERIDAN-PRICE
70	Gemini GMS 009	Sometimes I Wonder (as Sheridan & Rick Price)/SHERIDAN: Lightning Never Strikes Twice	5
70	Gemini GME 1002	THIS IS TO CERTIFY THAT... (LP, gatefold sleeve)	18

(see also Rick Price, Mike Sheridan & Nightriders, Mike Sheridan's Lot, Idle Race, Sight & Sound, Sheridan)

ROGER SHERLOCK
78	Inchecronin INC 7419	MEMORIES OF SLIGO (LP)	12

ALLAN SHERMAN
64	Warner Bros WEP 6148	YOUR MOTHER'S HERE TO STAY (EP)	12

BOBBY SHERMAN
69	Pye International 7N 25498	Little Woman/One Too Many Mornings	4

GARRY SHERMAN ORCHESTRA
70	United Artists UP 35055	Alice's Restaurant Massacree/The Let Down	4

JOE SHERMAN
58	Fontana H 129	Miraculous Music Box/Make Me Laugh	6
58	Fontana H 129	Miraculous Music Box/Make Me Laugh (78)	8
58	Fontana H 147	Buttermilk/Please Don't Say Goodnight	6
58	Fontana H 147	Buttermilk/Please Don't Say Goodnight (78)	8

BILLY SHERRILL
61	Mercury AMT 1131	Like Making Love/Rules Of The Game	6

SHERRYS
62	London HLW 9625	Pop Pop Pop-Pie/Your Hand In Mine	12
63	London HL 9686	Let's Stomp Again/Slop Time	15
63	London RE 1363	DO THE POPEYE (EP)	75

SHERWOOD
86	Sherwood SRT6KL 901	RIDING THE RAINBOW (12" EP)	40

BOBBY SHERWOOD
55	Vogue Coral Q 72097	The Kentuckian Song/Far Away Places	6

HOLLY SHERWOOD
71	Bell BLL 1180	Day By Day/Great Golden Day	5

ROBERTA SHERWOOD
56	Brunswick 05572	Lazy River/This Train	7
57	Brunswick 05654	Tears Don't Care Who Cries Them/You're Nobody Till Somebody Loves You	7
57	Brunswick 05670	Mary Lou/What Does It Matter	7
57	Brunswick 05670	Mary Lou/What Does It Matter (78)	8
63	Stateside SS 154	You Always Hurt The One You Love/In San Francisco	6
63	Stateside SL 10039	ON STAGE (LP)	18

TONY SHERWOOD TRIO
60s	Zodiac ZR 010	Piano Boogie Twist/Tom Dooley	12

SHERWOODS
61	Pye International 7N 25097	Nanette/El Scorpion	10

SHERWOODS
64	Solar SRP 105	Memories/Some Other Time	10

SHERWOODS
67	Major Minor MM 516	Here's To You Sir Francis/Butcher Boy	4

SHE TRINITY
66	Columbia DB 7874	He Fought The Law/The Union Station Blues	10
66	Columbia DB 7943	Have I Sinned/Wild Flower	7
66	Columbia DB 7959	Wild Flower/The Man Who Took The Valise Off The Floor Of Grand Central Station At Noon	7
66	Columbia DB 7992	Yellow Submarine/Promise Me You'll Never Cry	12
67	CBS 2819	Across The Street/Over And Over Again	6
70	President PT 283	Hair/Climb That Tree	5

(see also Shotgun Express, Beryl Marsden, Gilded Cage)

SHEVELLES
63	Oriole CB 1915	Ooh Poo Pa Doo/Like I Love You	12

SHEVELLS
64	United Artists UP 1059	I Could Conquer The World/How Would You Like Me To Love You	18
65	United Artists UP 1076	Walking On The Edge Of The World/Not So Close	18
65	United Artists UP 1081	Watermelon Man/Taking Over Your Life	18
66	United Artists UP 1125	Come On Home/I Gotta Travel All Over	35
68	Polydor 56239	Big City Lights/Coffee Song	12

(see also Mike Stevens & Shevells)

TONY SHEVETON
62	Oriole CB 1705	Lullaby Of Love/I Have A Feeling	12
62	Oriole CB 1726	Lonely Heart/Foolish Doubts	12
62	Oriole CB 1766	Hey Little Girl/Kissing Date	20
63	Oriole CB 1788	Runaround Sue Is Getting Married/I Love The Girl Next Door	20
63	Oriole CB 1895	Million Drums/Dance With Me	8
64	Oriole CB 1975	Excuses/Is It Me, Is It You?	12

(see also Tony Rich)

SHIDE & ACORN
73	private pressing	UNDER THE TREE (LP)	400
94	Acme AC 8006LP	UNDER THE TREE (LP, reissue, 500 only, numbered)	15

(see also Jeremy Cahill)

SHIELA
71   Nu Beat NB 079   Only Heaven Knows/GRANT & RICHARDS: Freedom Psalm 6

TREVOR SHIELD
69   Trojan TR 664   The Moon Is Playing Tricks On Me/KING CANNON: Soul Special 8
69   Trojan TR 665   Please/JAY BOYS: Splendour Splash 8
72   Ashanti ASH 407   Rough Road/JAY BOYS: Rough The Road 6
(see also Beltones, Trevor)

SHIELDS
58   London HLD 8706   You Cheated/That's The Way It's Gonna Be......................... 35
58   London HLD 8706   You Cheated/That's The Way It's Gonna Be (78) 40

KEITH SHIELDS
67   Decca F 12572   Hey Gyp (Dig The Slowness)/Deep Inside Your Mind 30
67   Decca F 12609   The Wonder Of You/Run, Run, Run 10
67   Decca F 12666   So Hard Livin' Without You/Baby Do You Love Me 12
(see also Marty Wilde [& Wildcats])

SHILLELAGH SISTERS
84   CBS WA 217   Give Me My Freedom/Cheatin' Teasin' Man (picture disc) 5

SHINDIGS
65   Parlophone R 5316   One Little Letter/What You Gonna Do 30
65   Parlophone R 5377   A Little While Back/Why Say Goodbye 30

SHINDOGS
67   Fontana TF 790   Who Do You Think You Are/Yes, I'm Going Home 8
(see also Delaney & Bonnie, James Burton)

JOHNNY SHINES
69   Blue Horizon 7-63212   LAST NIGHT'S DREAM (LP, with Otis Spann, mono or stereo) 70
74   Xtra XTRA 1142   COUNTRY BLUES (LP).. 20

DON SHINN (& SOUL AGENTS)
66   Polydor BM 56075   A Minor Explosion/Pits Of Darkness (with Soul Agents) 40
69   Columbia S(C)X 6319   TEMPLES WITH PROPHETS (LP).. 25
69   Columbia SCX 6355   DEPARTURES (LP)... 20
(see also Soul Agents)

SHIP
72   Elektra K 42122   THE SHIP — A CONTEMPORARY FOLK JOURNEY (LP, gatefold sleeve) 10

SHIRALEE
67   Fontana TF 855   I'll Stay By Your Side/Penny Wren 10

SHIRELLES
SINGLES
58   Brunswick 05746   I Met Him On A Sunday/I Want You To Be My Boyfriend 60
58   Brunswick 05746   I Met Him On A Sunday/I Want You To Be My Boyfriend (78) 50
60   London HL 9233   Tonight's The Night/The Dance Is Over............................. 18
60   Top Rank JAR 540   Will You Love Me Tomorrow/Boys 10
61   Top Rank JAR 549   Dedicated To The One I Love/Look-A-Here Baby 10
61   Top Rank JAR 567   Mama Said/Blue Holiday 10
61   Top Rank JAR 578   What A Sweet Thing That Was/A Thing Of The Past 10
61   Top Rank JAR 590   Big John/Twenty One.. 10
62   Top Rank JAR 601   Baby It's You/The Things I Want To Hear 12
62   HMV POP 1019   Soldier Boy/Love Is A Swingin' Thing 10
62   Stateside SS 119   Welcome Home Baby/Mama Here Comes The Bride...................... 12
62   Stateside SS 129   Stop The Music/It's Love That Really Counts 12
63   Stateside SS 152   Everybody Loves A Lover/I Don't Think So......................... 10
63   Stateside SS 181   Foolish Little Girl/Not For All The Money In The World 10
63   Stateside SS 213   Don't Say Goodnight And Mean Goodbye/I Didn't Mean To Hurt You 10
63   Stateside SS 232   What Does A Girl Do/Don't Let It Happen To Us 10
63   Pye International 7N 25229 It's A Mad, Mad, Mad, Mad World/31 Flavours........................ 6
64   Pye International 7N 25233 Tonight You're Gonna Fall In Love With Me/20th Century Rock And Roll 7
64   Pye International 7N 25240 Sha La La/His Lips Get In The Way 8
64   Pye International 7N 25279 Maybe Tonight/Lost Love 15
65   Pye International 7N 25288 Are You Still My Baby/I Saw A Tear 7
66   Pye International 7N 25386 Shades Of Blue/When The Boys Talk About The Girls 7
67   Pye International 7N 25425 Too Much Of A Good Thing/Bright Shiny Colours 12
69   Mercury MF 1093   There's A Storm Going On In My Heart/Call Me (If You Want Me)....... 15
71   United Artists UP 31592   Take Me/Dedicated To The One I Love.............................. 6
75   Pye Disco Demand DDS 115 Last Minute Miracle/March.. 5

EP
61   Top Rank JKP 3012   THE SHIRELLES SOUND FEATURING
                               "WILL YOU LOVE ME TOMORROW" (EP)................................ 80

LP
61   Top Rank 35-115   THE SHIRELLES SING — TO TRUMPET AND STRINGS (LP) 80
62   Stateside SL 10006   BABY IT'S YOU (LP)... 60
63   Stateside SL 10041   THE SHIRELLES' HITS (LP) 50
70   Wand WNS 4   ETERNALLY SOUL (LP, with King Curtis) 15
71   Wand WCS 1001   TONIGHT'S THE NIGHT (LP) 15
72   RCA Victor SF 8237   HAPPY AND IN LOVE (LP)... 15
72   RCA Victor SF 8279   THE SHIRELLES (LP)... 15
72   Wand WCS 1009   REMEMBER WHEN VOL. 1 (LP) 12
72   Wand WCS 1010   REMEMBER WHEN VOL. 2 (LP) 12
(see also Shirley & Shirelles, Shirley Alston)

DON SHIRLEY
61   London HLA 9391   Water Boy/Freedom, I'm On My Way 6
62   London HLA 9503   I'll Drown My Own Tears/Lonesome Road............................ 6

Don SHIRLEY

56	London HA-A 2003	PIANO PERSPECTIVES (LP)	15
56	London HA-A 2004	TONAL EXPRESSIONS (LP)	15
62	London HAA 2448	DROWN IN MY OWN TEARS (LP, also stereo [SAHA 6238])	12/15
63	London HAA 8038	PIANIST EXTRAORDINARY (LP)	12

ROY SHIRLEY

66	Ska Beat JB 253	Paradise/Calling	18
66	Doctor Bird DB 1068	Hold Them/Be Good	18
67	Doctor Bird DB 1079	I'm A Winner/Sleeping Beauty	18
67	Doctor Bird DB 1088	Prophet/What To Do	18
67	Doctor Bird DB 1093	Musical Field/LEE PERRY & DYNAMITES: Trial And Crosses	20
67	Doctor Bird DB 1108	Thank You/Touch Them	15
67	Caltone CAL 101	Get On The Ball/JOHNNY MOORE: Sound And Soul	18
67	Island WI 3070	People Rock Steady/I'm Trying To Find A Home (actually by Uniques)	20
67	Island WI 3071	Musical War/Soul Voice	18
67	Island WI 3120	Girlie/GLEN ADAMS: She's So Fine	18
68	Doctor Bird DB 1165	Hush A Bye/Musical Dinner	12
68	Doctor Bird DB 1168	Dance The Reggae/The Agreement	12
68	Giant GN 32	Dance Hall Arena/The Musical Train	10
68	Giant GN 33	Warming Up The Scene/GLEN ADAMS: Lonely Girl	10
68	Island WI 3098	Thank You/Touch Them	15
68	Island WI 3108	Move All Day/Rollin' Rollin'	15
68	Island WI 3110	Million Dollar Baby/SENSATIONS: Long Time No See You Girl	18
68	Island WI 3118	Good Is Better Than Bad/Fantastic Lover	15
68	Island WI 3119	Facts Of Life/Lead Us Not Into Temptation (as Roy Shirley & Uniques; B-side actually by Roy Shirley & Slim Smith)	15
68	Island WI 3125	If I Did Know/Good Ambition	15
68	Amalgamated AMG 815	The World Needs Love/Dance The A	10
68	Fab FAB 54	Think About The Future/Golden Festival	10
69	Duke DU 18	Life/I Like Your Smile	8
71	Nu Beat NB 090	Hold Them One/Two Three Four	6
72	Punch PH 103	Don't Be A Loser/Jamaican Girl	6
72	Punch PH 108	A Sugar/ALTYMAN REID: A Sugar — Version	6
75	R&JJ 001	Heart Breaking Jepsey/Version	5

(see also Val Bennett, Glen Adams, Shirley & Charmers, Sensations, Denzil, Errol & His Group, Ronsig, Stranger & Gladys, Untouchables)

SUSAN SHIRLEY

68	Mercury MF 1038	Sun Shines Out Of Your Shoes/Tomorrow Today	5
69	Mercury MF 1087	Too Many Tears/Boy From Boston Massachusetts USA	5
70	Philips 6006 037	Really Into Somethin'/My Friend The Clown	12
71	Columbia DB 8835	Jealous Guy/Oh Yoko	6
72	Columbia DB 8937	The Other Side Of Me/Imagine	5

SHIRLEY & CHARMERS

| 72 | Bullet BU 502 | Rum Rhythm/LLOYD CHARMERS: Rhythm (Version) | 6 |

(see also Roy Shirley)

SHIRLEY & JOHNNY

64	Parlophone R 5149	It Must Me Love/I Don't Want To Know	6
65	Parlophone R 5246	Only Once/Make Me An Offer	6
65	Parlophone R 5319	Day Dreamin' Of You/Till You Say You'll Be Mine	6
66	Parlophone R 5411	I'm Sorry/Breakaway	6
67	Parlophone R 5630	And I Don't Want Your Love/There Go The Heartaches	6
69	Mercury MF 1074	Don't Make Me Over/Baby Baby Baby	5
69	Mercury MF 1114	Just Say Goodbye/The Sunshine After The Rain	5

SHIRLEY & LEE

78s

56	Vogue V 9059	Let The Good Times Roll/Do You Mean To Hurt Me So (78)	45
57	Vogue V 9063	I Feel Good/Now That It's Over (78)	45
57	Vogue V 9067	That's What I Wanna Do/When I Saw You (78)	50
57	Vogue V 9072	Rock All Nite/Don't You Know I Love You (78)	50
57	Vogue V 9084	Rockin' With The Clock/The Flirt (78)	60
57	Vogue V 9088	I Want To Dance/Marry Me (78)	50
57	Vogue V 9094	Feel So Good/You'd Be Thinking Of Me (78)	50
58	Vogue V 9103	I'll Thrill You/Love No One But You (78)	50
58	Vogue V 9118	Everybody's Rockin'/Don't Leave Me Here To Cry (78)	70
59	Vogue V 9129	All I Want To Do Is Cry/Come On And Have Your Fun (78)	50
59	Vogue V 9135	A Little Word/That's What I'll Do (78)	50
59	Vogue V 9137	I'll Do It/Lee's Dream (78)	50
59	Vogue V 9156	True Love/When Day Is Done (78)	60

SINGLES

56	Vogue V 9059	Let The Good Times Roll/Do You Mean To Hurt Me So	125
57	Vogue V 9063	I Feel Good/Now That It's Over	80
57	Vogue V 9067	That's What I Wanna Do/When I Saw You	75
57	Vogue V 9072	Rock All Nite/Don't You Know I Love You	100
57	Vogue V 9084	Rockin' With The Clock/The Flirt	110
57	Vogue V 9088	I Want To Dance/Marry Me	70
57	Vogue V 9094	Feel So Good/You'd Be Thinking Of Me	70
58	Vogue V 9103	I'll Thrill You/Love No One But You	75
58	Vogue V 9118	Everybody's Rockin'/Don't Leave Me Here To Cry	90
59	Vogue V 9129	All I Want To Do Is Cry/Come On And Have Your Fun	70
59	Vogue V 9135	A Little Word/That's What I'll Do	70
59	Vogue V 9137	I'll Do It/Lee's Dream	70

(The above 45s were originally issued with triangular centres; later round-centre issues are worth two-thirds of these values.)

| 59 | Vogue V 9156 | True Love/When Day Is Done | 60 |

(Later Vocalion pressings of the above singles are worth two-thirds the values listed.)

60	London HLI 9186	I've Been Loved Before/Like You Used To Do	22
60	London HLI 9209	Let The Good Times Roll/Keep Loving Me	18
65	Island WI 257	Let The Good Times Roll/I'm Gone	15

EPs

| 57 | Vogue VE 1-70101 | ROCK 'N' ROLL (EP, triangular centre, later round) | 275/200 |
| 60 | Vogue VE 1-70145 | SHIRLEY AND LEE (EP) | 225 |

LP

| 71 | Jay Boy JSX 2005 | LET THE GOOD TIMES ROLL (LP) | 20 |

SHIRLEY & RUDE BOYS

| 67 | Blue Beat BB 375 | Gently Set Me Free/BUSTER'S ALL STARS: Rock Steady | 15 |

SHIRLEY & SHIRELLES

69	Bell BLL 1049	Look What You've Done To My Heart/A Most Unusual Boy	8
69	Bell BLL 1065	Plaything/Looking Glass	5
72	Bell BLL 1251	Look What You've Done To My Heart/A Most Unusual Boy (reissue)	5

(see also Shirelles)

SHIVA

82	Heavy Metal HEAVY 13	Rock Lives On/Sympathy For The Devil (p/s)	12
82	Heavy Metal HEAVY 16	Angel Of Mons (p/s)	10
82	Heavy Metal HMRLP 6	FIREDANCE (LP)	20

BUNNY SHIVEL

| 67 | Capitol CL 15487 | You'll Never Find A Love Like Mine/The Slide | 8 |

SHOCK

| 80 | RCA RCA 14 | Angel Face/R.E.R.B. (p/s) | 5 |

JOYCE SHOCK

58	Philips PB 780	Pit A Patter Boom Boom/Bells In My Heart (78)	10
58	Philips PB 824	Take Your Foot From The Door!/I've Got Bells On My Heart	8
58	Philips PB 824	Take Your Foot From The Door!/I've Got Bells On My Heart (78)	10
58	Philips PB 872	Hoopa Hoola/You're Not Losing A Daughter, Mama	7
58	Philips PB 872	Hoopa Hoola/You're Not Losing A Daughter, Mama (78)	8
59	Philips PB 934	Personality/I Can't Love You Anymore	6
59	Philips PB 934	Personality/I Can't Love You Anymore (78)	15
59	Philips PB 957	Cry, Baby, Cry/Dear Diary	6
59	Philips PB 957	Cry, Baby, Cry/Dear Diary (78)	15

SHOCK HEADED PETERS

84	él EL 1	I, Blood Brother Be/Truth Has Come (p/s)	6
84	él ONET	I, Blood Brother Be/Truth Has Come/Katabolism/Hate On Sight (12", p/s)	8
85	él Benelux ELT 3	The Kissing Of Gods/Heartbreak Hotel/Always Be Waiting/Mr. Very Big (12", p/s)	7
86	Beach Culture 3BC	LIFE EXTINGUISHER (12" EP)	7
85	él Benelux FIN 1	NOT BORN BEAUTIFUL (LP, with inner sleeve)	12
87	Produkt Korps PKLP 0020	FEAR ENGINE (LP)	12

(see also Lemon Kittens, Underneath, Karl Blake, Sol Invictus)

SHOCKING BLUE

69	Olga OLE 015	Send Me A Postcard/Harley Davidson (demo only)	40
69	Penny Farthing PEN 702	Venus/Hot Sand	5
70	Penny Farthing PEN 713	Mighty Joe/Wild Wind	5
70	Penny Farthing PEN 721	Never Marry A Railroad Man/Roll Engine Roll	5
70	Penny Farthing PEN 744	Sally Was A Good Old Girl/Long And Lonesome Road	5
71	Penny Farthing PEN 758	Shocking You/Waterloo	5
72	Polydor 2001 266	Out Of Sight Out Of Mind/I Like You	5
72	Polydor 2001 298	Inkpot/Give Me Love In The Sunrise	5
70	Penny Farthing PELS 500	SHOCKING BLUE AT HOME (LP)	20
70	Penny Farthing PELS 510	SCORPIO'S DANCE (LP)	20

SHOES (Holland)

| 68 | Polydor BM 56739 | Farewell In The Rain/What In The World Is Love | 4 |

SHOES FOR INDUSTRY

| 79 | Fried Egg EGG 001 | Falling In Love Again (Can't Help It)/Laughing Song (Laughbeat) (p/s) | 5 |
| 81 | Fried Egg EGG 004 | Spend/Sheepdog Trials Inna Babylon (p/s) | 4 |

SHOGUN

| 86 | Attack ATA 913 | High In The Sky (p/s) | 20 |
| 86 | Attack ATA 006 | SHOGUN (LP) | 40 |

TROY SHONDELL

61	London HLG 9432	This Time/Girl After Girl	10
62	Liberty LIB 55398	Island In The Sky/Tears From An Angel	10
63	London HL 9668	I Got A Woman/Some People Never Learn	12
64	London HAY 8128	MANY SIDES OF TROY SHONDELL (LP)	70

SHONDELLS

| 64 | Ember EMB S 191 | My Love/Don't Cry My Soldier Boy | 12 |

SHOOT

| 73 | EMI EMI 2026 | On The Frontier/Ships And Sails | 4 |
| 72 | EMI EMA 73 | ON THE FRONTIER (LP) | 12 |

(see also Yardbirds, Raw Material)

SHOOTER

| 78 | EMI Intl. INS 3020 | SHOOTER (LP) | 12 |

SHOP ASSISTANTS

| 85 | Subway Organisation SUBWAY 1 | All Day Long/All That Ever Mattered/It's Up To You/Switzerland (red foldaround hand-coloured p/s in poly bag, later blue) | 12/6 |
| 85 | Subway Organisation GVP 007 | Home Again/CHESTERFIELDS: Nose Out Of Joint (33rpm flexidisc, with *The Underground* issue 4, *Screed* or *The Legend!* fanzine) | 8/5 |

MINT VALUE £

86	53rd & 3rd AGAAR 1	Safety Net/Somewhere In China/Almost Made It (p/s)	4
86	53rd & 3rd AGAAR 112	Safety Net/Somewhere In China/Almost Made It (12", p/s)	7
90	Avalanche AGAP 001C	Here It Comes/I'd Rather Be With You//You Trip Me Up/The Other One (with 33rpm Flexi Records flexidisc)	4
90	Avalanche AGAP 001B	Here It Comes/Look Out/I'd Rather Be With You/Adrenalin (12", box set with flexidisc, badge, postcard & lyric sheet, 1st 200 numbered)	6/4

(see also Buba & Shop Assistants)

DINAH SHORE

53	HMV 7M 119	Keep It A Secret/Bella Musica	15
53	HMV 7M 139	Sweet Thing/Three-Cornered Tune	12
54	HMV 7M 183	Changing Partners/Think	12
54	HMV 7M 221	This Must Be The Place/Come Back To My Arms	12
54	HMV 7M 236	Three Coins In The Fountain/Pakistan	15
54	HMV 7M 250	If I Give My Heart To You/Let Me Know	15
56	HMV 7M 352	Love And Marriage/Compare	10
56	HMV POP 148	Love And Marriage/Compare (78)	10
57	RCA RCA 1003	The Cattle Call/Promises, Promises (Skip Redwine)	8
57	RCA RCA 1003	The Cattle Call/Promises, Promises (Skip Redwine) (78)	8
58	RCA RCA 1054	Thirteen Men/I'll Never Say "Never Again" Again	6
58	RCA RCA 1054	Thirteen Men/I'll Never Say "Never Again" Again (78)	8
58	RCA RCA 1060	The Secret Of Happiness/I've Never Left Your Arms	6
58	RCA RCA 1060	The Secret Of Happiness/I've Never Left Your Arms (78)	8
58	RCA RD 27072	HOLDING HANDS AT MIDNIGHT (LP)	20
59	Capitol (S)T 1247	DINAH, YES INDEED! (LP)	15
60	Fontana Fortune Z 4026	BUTTONS AND BOWS (LP)	15
60	Capitol (S)T 1296	SOMEBODY LOVES ME (LP)	15
60	Capitol (S)T 1354	DINAH SINGS SOME BLUES WITH RED (LP, with Red Norvo)	15

(see also Doris Day)

BRIAN SHORT

| 71 | Transatlantic TRA 245 | ANYTHING FOR A LAUGH (LP, gatefold sleeve) | 20 |

(see also Black Cat Bones)

J.D. SHORT

| 73 | Sonet SNTF 648 | THE LEGACY OF THE BLUES VOL. 8 (LP) | 12 |

SHORT KUTS with Eddie Harrison

| 68 | United Artists UP 2233 | Your Eyes May Shine/Letting The Tears Tumbling Down | 15 |

SHORTWAVE (BAND)

75	RCA Victor SF 8400	SHORTWAVE BAND (LP, with lyric sheet)	12
77	Crescent/Avada ARS 111	GREATEST HATS (LP)	20
79	Pye 2CN 111	SHORTWAVE (LP)	12

SHORTY (THE PRESIDENT)

| 73 | Ackee ACK 509 | Aquarius Pressure/Halfway Tree Pressure (as Shorty The President) | 8 |
| 73 | Ackee ACK 517 | Jelly-Belly-Nelly/Message Of Love (as Shorty) | 5 |

(see also Shorty Perry)

SHORTY & THEM

| 64 | Fontana TF 460 | Pills Or Love's Labours Lost/Live Laugh And Love | 25 |

SHOTGUN EXPRESS

66	Columbia DB 8025	I Could Feel The Whole World Turn Round/Curtains	45
67	Columbia DB 8178	Funny 'Cos Neither Could I/Indian Thing	45
83	See For Miles CYM 2	I Could Feel The Whole World Turn Round/Curtains/Funny 'Cos Neither Could I/Indian Thing (10", p/s)	7

(see also Rod Stewart, Peter Bardens, Spencer Davis, Brian Auger, She Trinity, Beryl Marsden, Fleetwood Mac)

SHOTS

| 65 | Columbia DB 7713 | Keep A Hold Of What You've Got/She's A Liar | 30 |

(see also Smoke)

SHOUT

| 72 | Explosion 2058 | Life Is Rough/Life Is Rough – Version | 6 |

SHOUTS

| 64 | React EA 001 | She Was My Baby/That's The Way It's Gonna Be | 10 |

SHOWBIZ KIDS

| 80s | Top Secret CON 1 | She Goes To Finos/I Don't Want To Discuss That (p/s) | 35 |

(see also Toy Dolls)

SHOW BOYS

| 69 | Gas GAS 129 | People Are Wondering/Long Time | 6 |

SHOWMEN

62	London HLP 9481	It Will Stand/Country Fool	70
62	London HLP 9571	The Wrong Girl/I Love You Can't You See	100
69	Pama PM 767	Action/What Would It Take	8

(see also Norman Johnson, General Johnson, Chairmen Of The Board)

SHOW OF HANDS

| 70 | Elektra EKS 74084 | FORMERLY ANTHRAX (LP, gatefold sleeve) | 10 |

SHOWSTOPPERS

68	Beacon 3-100	Ain't Nothing But A House Party/What Can A Man Do (red swirly label)	7
68	Beacon 3-106	Shake Your Mini/Heartbreaker	5
68	MGM MGM 1436	Eeny Meeny/How Easy Your Heart Forgets Me	5
69	Beacon BEA 110	Don't Leave Me Standing In The Rain/Do You Need My Love	5
69	Beacon BEA 130	Just A Little Bit Of Lovin'/School Prom	5
70	Beacon BEA 100	Ain't Nothing But A House Party/What Can A Man Do (reissue, yellow label)	5

SHOWTIMERS
64	HMV POP 1328	You Must Be Joking/Don't Say Goodbye	6

SHOX
80	Axis AXIS 4	No Turning Back/Lying Here (p/s)	15
80	Beggars Banquet BEG 33	No Turning Back/Lying Here (p/s, reissue)	8

MARK SHREEVE
85	Jive Electro T 102	Legion (Razor Mix)/Legion (Space Mix)/Legion (Satan Mix) (12", p/s)	8
81	Uniton U 001	THOUGHTS OF WAR (LP)	15
83	Uniton U 021	ASSASSIN (LP)	15
84	Jive Electro HIP 21	ASSASSIN (LP, reissue)	10
85	Jive Electro HIP 28	LEGION (LP)	10
88	Jive Electro HIP 42	CRASH HEAD (LP)	10

SHUBERT
68	Fontana TF 942	Until The Rains Come/Let Your Love Go	12

SHREDS
95	Detour DR 026	Brutally You/The Love I Knew/Never Too Late (p/s, some on white vinyl)	8/5

MORT SHUMAN
59	Decca F 11184	Turn Me Loose/I'm A Man (initially triangular centre, later round)	45/25
59	Decca F 11184	Turn Me Loose/I'm A Man (78)	60
66	Fontana TF 685	Cry A Little/She Ain't Nothing But A Little Child	6
67	Immediate IM 048	Monday Monday/Little Children	12

SHUSHA
74	United Artists UP 35699	Barun Baruneh/Wild Flowers	5
74	United Artists UP 35759	Ev'ry Time We Say Goodbye/Siren's Call	5
71	Tangent TGS 108	PERSIAN LOVE SONGS AND MYSTIC CHANTS (LP)	20
72	Tangent TGS 114	SONGS OF LONG TIME LOVERS (LP)	15
74	United Artists UAS 29575	SHUSHA (LP)	12
74	United Artists UAS 29684	THIS IS THE DAY (LP)	12
75	United Artists UAS 29879	BEFORE THE DELUGE (LP)	12
78	Tangent TGS 138	FROM EAST TO WEST (LP)	15

SHUTDOWNS
63	Colpix PX 11016	Four In The Floor/Beach Buggy	20

SHY
83	Ebony EBON 15	ONCE BITTEN TWICE SHY (LP)	30

SHY LIMBS
69	CBS 4190	Reputation/Love	60
69	CBS 4624	Lady In Black/Trick Or Two	60

(see also Shame)

SHY ONES
63	Oriole CB 1848	Nightcap/Carry Me Back	15
64	Oriole CB 1924	La Route/Susanna	12

(see also Spotnicks)

SHYSTER
68	Polydor 56202	Tick Tock/That's A Hoe Down	100

(see also Fleur-De-Lys)

SHYWOLF
82	MRS SW 001	Lucretia (p/s)	35

LEROY SIBBLES & ROCKY ELLIS
68	Studio One SO 2042	Love Me Girl/WRIGGLERS: Reel Up	18

(see also John Holt, King Rocky)

DUDLEY SIBLEY
67	Coxsone CS 7010	Run Boy Run/Message Of Old (B-side actually by Joe Higgs & Ken Boothe)	25
67	Island WI 3034	Gun Man/Monkey Speaks His Mind (B-side actually by Dinsdell Thorpe)	18

(see also Delroy & Sporty, King Sporty, Mr. Foundation)

SICKIDZ
84	Big Beat SWT 97	I COULD GO TO HELL FOR YOU (EP)	5

SICK THINGS
83	Chaos CH 3	THE LEGENDARY SICK THINGS (EP)	10

SIDDELEYS
86	Sha La La Ba Ba Ba 006	Wherever You Go/RESERVE: The Sun Slid Down (flexidisc with fanzines, p/s)	8/6
87	Medium Cool MC 005	What Went Wrong This Time? (p/s)	5
88	Sombrero THREE	Sunshine Thuggery/Are You Still Evil When You're Sleeping/Falling Off My Feet Again (12", p/s)	7

FRANK SIDEBOTTOM
85	EMI/Regal Zonophone Z39	SINGS FRANK'S FIRM FAVOURITES (EP, with lyric sheet)	12
87	In Tape IT 048	TIMPERLEY SUNSET (EP)	5
87	Go! Discs	The Beastie Puppets (p/s, unreleased, demos only)	8

(see also Chris Sievey, Freshies)

SIDEKICKS
66	RCA RCA 1538	Suspicions/Up On The Roof	10

ANN SIDNEY
65	HMV POP 1411	The Boy In The Woolly Sweater/Lonely Doll	6

SIDNEY, GEORGE & JACKIE
71	Summit SUM 8528	Lady Of My Complexion/No Sad Song	5
72	Summit SUM 8535	Story Book Children/Gorgeous Marvellous	5

(see also Pioneers)

MINT VALUE £

PAUL SIEBEL
70	Elektra EKSN 45085	Bride 1945/Miss Cherry Lane.	4
70	Elektra EKS 74064	WOODSMOKE AND ORANGES (LP)	10
71	Elektra EKS 74081	JACK-KNIFE GYPSY (LP)	10

SIEGE
85	Siege THM 1	Goddess Of Fire (no p/s)	20

SIEGEL-SCHWALL BAND
68	Vanguard SVRL 19044	SHAKE (LP)	15
72	RCA SF 8246	THE SIEGEL-SCHWALL BAND (LP)	12

CHRIS SIEVEY
79	Rabid TOSH 109	Baiser/Last (p/s)	4
79	Razz RAZZXEP 1	BAISER (33rpm EP, 2 tracks each by Sievey & Freshies, handwritten labels).	10
80	Razz RAZZ 4	My Tape's Gone/Moon Midsummer (some with *True Life Revealing Confessions Of Romance And Love* fanzine)	6/4
81	Razz RAZZ 5	Hey/FRESHIES: We're Like You (p/s)	4
82	Razz RAZZ 8	RED INDIAN MUSIC (EP)	5
82	Razz RAZZ 9	Skip The Flight/Jim Baiser ("Baiser"/"Last" with new labels & sleeve)	5
83	Random RND 1	Camouflage/(ZX 81 Programme "Camouflage")/Flying Train/F.T. (p/s, 'computer' single, B-side at 33rpm, 2,000 only)	5
80s	CV CVS 1	If You Really Love Me, Buy Me A Shirt/I Am The Walrus (with Freshies)	4
75	Hey Boss (no. cat. no.)	GIRL IN MY BLUE JEANS (16-track cassette, 250 only)	20
76	Razz CS-1	ALL SLEEPS SECRETS (cassette, 1,000 only)	12
80	Razz (no cat. no.)	NO GO DEMOS (cassette, with "Complete Book Of Rejection Slips" booklet, 400 only)	12
82	Razz RAZZ 4	DENIGRATION NOW (cassette, with booklet, 500 only)	10
85	11.37 ETS-S	DENIGRATION NOW (cassette, reissue with 2 extra tracks, 250 only)	12
86	Cordelia ERICAT 015	CHRIS SIEVEY'S BIG RECORD (LP, with free 7" "Baiser"/"Last" [TOSH 109])	10

(see also Freshies, Frank Sidebottom, Going Red?)

LABI SIFFRE
70	Pye Intl. NSPL 28135	LABI SIFFRE (LP)	12
71	Pye Intl. NSPL 28147	THE SINGER AND THE SONG (LP, gatefold sleeve)	20
72	Pye Intl. NSPL 28163	CRYING, LAUGHING, LOVING, LYING (LP, gatefold sleeve with lyric insert)	12
75	EMI EMC 3065	REMEMBER MY SONG (LP)	40
98	EMI/Mr. Bongo MRBLP 011	REMEMBER MY SONG (LP, reissue)	12

RON SIG
71	Camel CA 58	1970's/Version	6
71	Camel CA 59	You Girl/ROY SHIRLEY & SLIM SMITH: Facts Of Life	6

SIGHT & SOUND
68	Fontana TF 927	Ebenezer/Our Love (Is In The Pocket)	12
68	Fontana TF 982	Alley Alley/Little Jack Monday	12

(see also Jefferson, Sheridan & Price, Mike Sheridan)

BUNNY SIGLER
67	Cameo Parkway P 153	Let The Good Times Roll — Feel So Good/There's No Love Left	15
73	Epic S EPC 1177	Tossin' And Turnin'/Picture Us	5
76	London HLU 10518	Let The Good Times Roll/Girl Don't Make Me Wait	5

SIGNS
66	Decca F 12522	Ain't You Got A Heart/My Baby Comes To Me	8

SIGUE SIGUE SPUTNIK
86	Parlophone 12 SSS 1	Love Missile F1-11 (Extended Version)/(Dance Mix)/Hack Attack (12", p/s, 'Russian' or 'Japanese' obi sleeve bands)	each 7
86	Parlophone 12 SSS 1	Love Missile F1-11 (Bangkok Remix)/(Dance Mix)/Hack Attack (Dub Mix) (12", p/s, 'German' or 'Spanish' obi sleeve bands)	each 8
86	Parlophone 12 SSSX 1	Love Missile F1-11 (Trailer Mix):Love Missile F1-11 (Video Mix)/Love Missile F1-11 & Actuality Sound/Hack-Attack (12", p/s, with 6 poster inserts)	10
86	Parlophone SSS 2	21st Century Boy/Buy EMI (foldout 'crucifix' p/s)	4
88	Parlophone 12 SSSW 3	Success (Extended)/(Seven Inch)Frankenstein Cha-Cha-Cha (Extended) (12", 'Pete Waterman' p/s, withdrawn)	20
88	Parlophone 12 SSSP 3	Success (Extended)/Frankenstein Cha-Cha-Cha (Extended)/Nightmare Of Neal X/Success Sputnik Style (12", picture disc, unissued)	
88	Parlophone CD SSS 3	Success (Seven Inch)/Frankenstein Cha-Cha-Cha/Last Temptation Of Sputnik (CD)	8
89	Parlophone SSS 5	Dancerama/Barbarandroid (p/s)	4
89	Parlophone CD SSS 5	Dancerama (7" Mix)/(12" Extended)/(Album Mix Extended) (CD)	10
89	Parlophone CD SSS 4	Albinoni Vs Star Wars (Part 1 — 7" Version)/(Part 1 — Extended Version)/(Part 2 — Extended Version) (Bonus Beats) (CD)	8
89	Parlophone CD SSS 6	Rio Rocks (7 Inch)/Rio Rocks (Extended)/Rio Rocks (Samba) (CD)	8
86	Parlophone PCSS 7305	FLAUNT IT (LP, box set with insert)	12
86	Parlophone TCPCSS 7305	FLAUNT IT (cassette, mounted on backing card with insert)	10

(see also Sci Fi Sex Stars, Generation X, Sisters Of Mercy)

SILENT MAJORITY
71	Hot Wax HWX 110	Frightened Girl/Colours Of My Love	4

SILENT MOVIES
79	ESR Records ESR 1	Ain't No Van Gough/What Did Ya Say? (p/s)	40

SILENT NOISE
79	Silent Noise/Easy ER 02	I've Been Hurt (Too Many Times Before)/Heart To Heart.	10

SILHOUETTES (U.S.)
58	Parlophone R 4407	Get A Job/I Am Lonely	35
58	Parlophone R 4407	Get A Job/I Am Lonely (78)	40
58	Parlophone R 4425	Headin' For The Poorhouse/Miss Thing	75
58	Parlophone R 4425	Headin' For The Poorhouse/Miss Thing (78)	50

SILHOUETTES (Jamaica)

| 69 | Sound System SSR 103 | In Times Like These (actually by Lloyd Jackson & Groovers)/ In Times Like These | 6 |

ERIC SILK (& His Southern Jazz Band)

56	Esquire EP 70	AND HIS SOUTHERN JAZZ BAND (EP)	15
56	Esquire EP 100	AND HIS SOUTHERN JAZZ BAND (EP)	10
57	Esquire EP 110	AND HIS SOUTHERN JAZZ BAND (EP)	10
57	Esquire EP 128	AND HIS SOUTHERN JAZZ BAND (EP)	15
57	Esquire EP 150	AND HIS SOUTHERN JAZZ BAND (EP)	15
57	Esquire 20-065	SOUTHERN JAZZ (LP)	30
58	Esquire 20-095	THE SILKEN TOUCH (LP)	30
60s	Polydor 582 002	OFF THE CUFF (LP)	25

SILKIE

65	Fontana TF 556	Blood Red River/Close The Door Gently	6
65	Fontana TF 603	You've Got To Hide Your Love Away/City Winds	7
66	Fontana TF 659	Keys To My Soul/Leave Me To Cry	6
66	Fontana TF 709	Born To Be With You/So Sorry Now	6
65	Fontana TL 5256	THE SILKIE SING THE SONGS OF BOB DYLAN (LP)	18

JUDEE SILL

72	Asylum AYM 502	Jesus Was A Cross Maker/The Phantom Cowboy	5
72	Asylum AYM 509	Enchanted Sky Machines/My Man On Love	5
73	Asylum AYM 513	The Kiss/Down Where The Valleys Are Low	5
72	Asylum SYLA 8751	JUDEE SILL (LP, gatefold sleeve)	15
73	Asylum SYL 9006	HEART FOOD (LP)	15

SILLY SISTERS

| 76 | Chrysalis CHR 1101 | SILLY SISTERS (LP, with lyric insert) | 12 |

(see also Steeleye Span, Maddy Prior, June Tabor)

SILVER (Jamaica)

68	Jolly JY 006	Baby Oh Yeah/Rock Steady Is Here To Stay (as Silver & Magnets)	8
68	Jolly JY 012	Things/Sweet Lovin'.	7
68	Jolly JY 017	I Need A Girl/Lost And Found	8
70	Columbia Blue Beat DB 117	Love Me Forever/Sugar, Sugar (B-side as Silver & Noreen)	8
71	Fab FAB 163	Change Has Got To Come/Magnet Stomp (as Silver & Magnets)	6

SILVER (U.S.)

| 76 | Arista ARIST 79 | Musician (It's Not An Easy Life)/Right On Time | 6 |
| 76 | Arista ARTY 144 | SILVER (LP, U.S. disc & inner [AL 4076] in U.K. sleeve) | 10 |

(see also Grateful Dead)

ANDEE SILVER

64	HMV POP 1297	Too Young To Go Steady/Sleeping Beauty	7
64	HMV POP 1344	The Boy I Used To Know/What Do You Do	7
66	Fontana TF 666	Only Your Love Can Save Me/Window Shopping	8
69	Decca F 22872	Go Now/You're Just What I Was Looking For Today	6
69	Decca F 22953	With A Little Love/Te Quiero (unreleased)	
70	Decca F 23071	Love Me/You're Breaking My Heart (export issue)	8
70	Decca SKL-R 5059	A HANDFUL OF SILVER (LP)	30

EDDIE SILVER

58	Parlophone R 4439	Seven Steps To Love/Put A Ring On Her Finger	15
58	Parlophone R 4439	Seven Steps To Love/Put A Ring On Her Finger (78)	12
58	Parlophone R 4483	Rockin' Robin/The Ways Of A Woman In Love	12
58	Parlophone R 4483	Rockin' Robin/The Ways Of A Woman In Love (78)	25

HORACE SILVER QUINTET/TRIO

61	Blue Note 45-1750	Sister Sadie/Break City	8
63	Blue Note 45-1873	Too Much Sake (Parts 1 & 2)	8
63	Blue Note 45-1902	Let's Get To The Nitty Gritty/Silver's Serenade	8
64	Blue Note 45-1903	Sweet Sweetie Dee/Dragon Lady	8
54	Vogue LDE 065	THE HORACE SILVER TRIO (10" LP)	18
69	Blue Note BST 84277	SERENADE TO A SOUL SISTER (LP)	15

LORRAINE SILVER

| 65 | Pye 7N 15922 | Lost Summer Love/I'll Know You'll Be There | 70 |
| 66 | Pye 7N 17055 | The Happy Faces/When The Love Light Starts Shining Thru His Eyes | 40 |

SILVER BIRCH

| 73 | Brayford BRO 2 | SILVER BIRCH (LP, private pressing) | 225 |

SILVER BULLITT

| 72 | Philips 6073 808 | Willpower Weak, Temptation Strong/Hittin' On You | 4 |

SILVER BYKE

| 68 | London HLZ 10200 | Who Needs Tomorrow/I've Got Time | 5 |

SILVER EAGLE

| 67 | MGM MGM 1345 | Theodore/True As A Brand New Lie | 15 |

SILVERHEAD

72	Purple PUR 104	Ace Supreme/Oh No No No	7
72	Purple PUR 110	Rolling With My Baby/In Your Eyes	7
73	Purple TPSA 7506	SILVERHEAD (LP)	12
73	Purple TPSA 7511	SIXTEEN AND SAVAGED (LP)	12

(see also Michael Des Barres, Blondie)

SILVER MOUNTAIN

| 83 | Road Runner RR 9884 | SHAKIN' BRAINS (LP) | 15 |

SILVERS

| 66 | Polydor BM 56094 | What A Way To Start A Day/Blue Blue Eyes | 6 |

MINT VALUE £

PHIL SILVERS
57   Fontana Fortune Z 4040   BUGLE CALLS FOR BIG BAND (LP) 15

SILVER SISTERS
60   Parlophone R 4669   Waiting For The Stars To Shine/When A Boy Meets A Girl 8

DOOLEY SILVERSPOON
76   Seville SEV 1022   Game Players/Believe In Me 5

SILVERSTARS
69   Trojan TR 646   Old Man Say/Promises 8

SILVER STARS STEEL BAND
63   Island ILP 904   THE SILVER STARS STEEL BAND (LP) 30
(see also Clancy Eccles)

SHEL SILVERSTEIN
73   CBS 65452   FREAKIN' AT THE FREAKER'S BALL (LP, with Dr. Hook) 12
(see also Dr. Hook)

SILVERTONES
66   Doctor Bird DB 1028   True Confession (with Duke Reid)/TOMMY McCOOK & SUPERSONICS:
      More Love. 18
66   Doctor Bird DB 1041   It's Real (with Lynn Tait & Boys)/LYNN TAIT & BOYS: Storm Warning ... 18
66   Rymska RA 105   True Confession/GRANVILLE WILLIAMS ORCHESTRA: Honky Tonk Ska 25
67   Treasure Isle TI 7020   Cool Down/TOMMY McCOOK & SUPERSONICS: Shadow Of Your Smile 15
68   Treasure Isle TI 7027   In The Midnight Hour/TOMMY McCOOK & SUPERSONICS: Soul For Sale ... 12
68   Treasure Isle TI 7039   Old Man River/TOMMY McCOOK & SUPERSONICS: Our Man Flint 12
68   Treasure Isle TI 7042   Slow And Easy/TOMMY McCOOK & SUPERSONICS: Moving 12
69   Trojan TR 7705   Intensified Change/Marie 8
71   Clandisc CLA 234   Tear Drops Will Fall/DYNAMITES: Tear Drops — Version 6
73   Techniques TE 924   That's When It Hurts/I'll Take You Home 6
71   Trojan TRLS 69   SILVER BULLETS (LP) 20
(see also Valentines, Tommy McCook, Vincent Gordon, Alton Ellis, Carl Bryon, Charmers)

SILVERWING
80   Mayhem SILVER 1   Rock'n'Roll Are Four-Letter Words/High Class Woman (no p/s). 7
82   Mayhem SILV 02   Sittin' Pretty/Teenage Love (p/s) 8
82   Mayhem SILV 212   Sittin' Pretty/Teenage Love/Flashbomb Fever/Rock'n'Roll Mayhem (12") .. 10
82   Mayhem SILV 3   That's Entertainment/Flashbomb Fever (poster p/s) 6
83   Bullet BULP 1   ALIVE AND KICKING (LP) 15
(see also Pet Hate, Big Amongst Sheep)

VICTOR SILVESTER & HIS ROCK 'N' ROLL RHYTHM
57   Columbia DB 3888   Rockin' Rhythm Roll/Society Rock 10
57   Columbia DB 3907   Alligator Roll/Off Beat Rock. 10
57   Columbia DB 3907   Alligator Roll/Off Beat Rock (78) 10

SIMBA
71   Fire FIR 100   Louie Louie/Movin'. 4

HARRY SIMEONE CHORALE
59   Top Rank JAR 101   The Little Drummer Boy/JUNIOR CHORALE: Die Lorelei 6
59   Top Rank JAR 101   The Little Drummer Boy/JUNIOR CHORALE: Die Lorelei (78) 8
59   Top Rank JAR 109   In The Valley Of Love/The Beat O' My Heart 5
59   Top Rank JAR 109   In The Valley Of Love/The Beat O' My Heart (78) 8
59   Top Rank JAR 222   The Little Drummer Boy/The Toy Drum 5
59   Top Rank JAR 222   The Little Drummer Boy/The Toy Drum (78) 10
60   Top Rank JAR 397   Onward Christian Soldiers/Won't You Marry Me? 5

BEVERLEY SIMMON(D)S
68   Pama PM 716   Mr. Pitiful/That's How Strong My Love Is. 6
73   Pama Supreme PS 380   You're Mine/What A Guy (as Beverley Simmonds) 5
69   Pama PMLP/PMSP 9   REMEMBER OTIS (LP) 15
(see also Little Beverly)

(JUMPIN') GENE SIMMONS
64   London HLU 9913   Haunted House/Hey, Hey Little Girl 15
64   London HLU 9933   The Jump/The Dodo. 15

GENE SIMMONS
79   Casablanca CAN 134   Radioactive/When You Wish Upon A Star (p/s, red vinyl with mask,
      picture label) 20
79   Casablanca CAN 134   Radioactive/When You Wish Upon A Star (p/s, black vinyl) 12
(see also Kiss)

JEFF SIMMONS
69   Straight STS 1057   LUCILLE HAS MESSED UP MY MIND (LP) 45
(see also Frank Zappa)

LITTLE MAC SIMMONS
66   Outasite OSEP 1   BLUES FROM CHICAGO (EP, 99 copies only) 175

(Zoot) SIMMS & (Lloyd) ROBINSON
62   Blue Beat BB 143   White Christmas/Searching 10

JASON SIMMS & MUSIC THROUGH SIX
68   Domain D 5   It's Got To Be Mellow/MUSIC THROUGH SIX: Floppy Ears 8
(see also Music Through Six)

ZOOT SIMMS (Jamaica)
63   Blue Beat BB 183   Press Along/PRINCE BUSTER ALLSTARS: 100 Ton Megaton
      (B-side actually "Mighty As A Rose" by Raymond Harper) 15
63   Blue Beat BB 193   Golden Pen/ERIC MORRIS: So You Shot Reds 15

64	Port-O-Jam PJ 4007	Please Don't Do It/Don't Do It (as Simms & [Lloyd] Robinson)	15
68	Blue Cat BS 118	Bye Bye Baby/AL & THRILLERS: Heart For Sale	12
69	Coxsone CS 7095	Tit For Tat/We Can Talk It Over (as Simms & Elmond)	18

SEIJA SIMOLA
78	Sonet SON 2145	Give Love A Chance/Little Smile (p/s)	12

SIMON
67	RCA Victor RCA 1609	I Like The Way/Little Tin Soldier	5
68	RCA Victor RCA 1668	Dream Seller/Sweet Reflections Of You	5
69	Plum PLS 002	Mrs Lillyco/There's No More You	25

JOE SIMON
66	London HLU 10057	Teenager's Prayer/Long Hot Summer	20
67	Monument MON 1004	My Special Prayer/Travelin' Man	7
68	Monument MON 1010	Nine Pound Steel/The Girl's Alright With Me	7
68	Monument MON 1014	No Sad Songs/Come On And Get It	6
68	Monument MON 1019	You Keep Me Hangin' On/What Makes A Man Feel Good	6
68	Monument MON 1025	Message From Maria/I Worry About You	6
69	Monument MON 1029	Looking Back/Standing In The Safety Zone	6
69	Monument MON 1032	The Chokin' Kind/Come On And Get It	5
69	Monument MON 1038	San Francisco Is A Lonely Town/It's Hard To Get Along	5
70	Monument MON 1042	Moon Walk (Parts 1 & 2)	5
70	Monument MON 1044	Further Down The Road/Wounded Man	5
70	Monument MON 1049	Yours Love/I Gotta Whole Lot Of Lovin'	7
70	Monument MON 1051	That's The Way I Want Our Love/When	10
71	Polydor 2066 066	Your Time To Cry/I Love You More (Than Anything)	7
71	Mojo 2006 098	Help Me Make It Through The Night/Most Of All	5
71	Mojo 2093 003	You Are The One/I Ain't Givin' Up	5
72	Mojo 2093 008	Drowning In A Sea Of Love/Let Me Be The One	5
72	Mojo 2093 014	You Are Everything/Pool Of Bad Luck	5
73	Mojo 2093 024	Trouble In My Home/I Found My Dad	5
74	Mojo 2093 030	Step By Step/Talk Don't Bother Me	5
75	Polydor 2006 551	Get Down Get Down/In My Baby's Arms	5
67	Monument LMO/SMO 5005	SIMON PURE SOUL (LP)	15
68	Monument LMO/SMO 5017	NO SAD SONGS (LP)	15
69	Monument LMO/SMO 5026	SIMON SINGS (LP)	15
70	Monument LMO/SMO 5030	THE CHOKIN' KIND (LP)	15
70	Monument LMO/SMO 5033	BETTER THAN EVER (LP)	15
71	Mojo 2918 001	THE SOUNDS OF SIMON (LP)	15
72	Mojo 2918 003	DROWNING IN THE SEA OF LOVE (LP)	15

PAUL SIMON
65	CBS 201797	I Am A Rock/Leaves That Are Green	20
73	CBS 1545	Kodachrome (withdrawn, any pressed?)	15+
65	CBS (S) 62579	THE PAUL SIMON SONGBOOK (LP)	30
72	CBS CQ 30750/Q 69007	PAUL SIMON (LP, quadrophonic)	18
74	CBS CQ 32280/Q 69035	THERE GOES RHYMIN' SIMON (LP, quadrophonic)	18
75	CBS Q 86001	STILL CRAZY AFTER ALL THESE YEARS (LP, quadrophonic)	18

(see also Simon & Garfunkel, Jerry Landis, Tom & Jerry)

TONY SIMON
67	Track 604 012	Gimme A Little Sign/Never Too Much To Love	15

SIMON & GARFUNKEL
SINGLES
65	CBS 201977	The Sound Of Silence/We've Got A Groovy Thing Goin'	7
66	CBS 202045	Homeward Bound/Leaves That Are Green	7
66	CBS 202303	I Am A Rock/Flowers Never Bend With The Rainfall	7
66	CBS 202285	The Dangling Conversation/The Big Bright Green Pleasure Machine	15
66	CBS 202378	A Hazy Shade Of Winter/For Emily, Whenever I May Find Her	7
67	CBS 202608	At The Zoo/The 59th Street Bridge Song (Feelin' Groovy)	10
67	CBS 2911	Fakin' It/You Don't Know Where Your Interest Lies	10
68	CBS Special Prods. WB 73	The Sound Of Silence/GEORGIE FAME: By The Time I Get To Phoenix (p/s)	5
68	CBS Special Prods. WB 728	The 59th Street Bridge Song (Feelin' Groovy)/TREMELOES: Here Comes My Baby (p/s, mail-order only with Pepsi Cola tokens)	7
69	CBS 4162	The Boxer/Baby Driver (p/s)	7
73	CBS 1159	Mrs. Robinson/Bookends Theme (p/s, 'Hall Of Fame Hits' series)	5

EPs
65	CBS EP 6053	WEDNESDAY MORNING 3AM (EP)	18
66	CBS EP 6074	I AM A ROCK (EP)	18
67	CBS EP 6360	FEELING GROOVY (EP)	18
68	CBS EP 6400	MRS ROBINSON (EP)	15

LPs
66	CBS (S)BPG 62690	THE SOUNDS OF SILENCE (LP)	18
66	CBS (S)BPG 62860	PARSLEY, SAGE, ROSEMARY AND THYME (LP)	12

(The above LPs were originally issued with flipback sleeves & textured orange labels.)

67	Allegro ALL 836	SIMON AND GARFUNKEL (LP)	20
68	CBS (S) 70042	THE GRADUATE (LP, soundtrack, blue label, mono/stereo)	18/15
68	CBS (S) 63370	WEDNESDAY MORNING 3AM (LP, flipback sleeve, textured orange label, mono/stereo)	18/15
72	CBS CQ 30995	BRIDGE OVER TROUBLED WATER (LP, quadrophonic)	18

(see also Paul Simon, Art Garfunkel, Tom & Jerry)

NINA SIMONE
SINGLES
59	Parlophone R 4583	I Loves You Porgy/Love Me Or Leave Me	10
59	Pye International 7N 25029	Solitaire/Chilly Winds Don't Blow	6
59	Pye International N 25029	Solitaire/Chilly Winds Don't Blow (78)	20

MINT VALUE £

63	Colpix PX 200	You Can Have Him/Return Home	6
64	Colpix PX 799	Exactly Like You/The Other Woman	6
65	Philips BF 1388	Don't Let Me Be Misunderstood/Monster	5
65	Philips BF 1415	I Put A Spell On You/Gimme Some	7
66	Philips BF 1465	Either Way I Lose/Break Down And Let It Out	8
67	RCA Victor RCA 1583	Do I Move You?/Day And Night	5
68	RCA Victor RCA 1697	Why? (The King Of Love Is Dead) (Parts 1 & 2)	5
68	RCA Victor RCA 1743	Ain't Go No — I Got Life/Do What You Gotta Do	5
68	RCA Victor RCA 1779	To Love Somebody/I Can't See Nobody	5
68	Pye International 7N 25466	The Other Woman/Exactly Like You	5
69	Philips BF 1736	I Put A Spell On You/Don't Let Me Be Misunderstood	5

EPs

61	Parlophone GEP 8844	MY BABY JUST CARES FOR ME (EP)	15
62	Parlophone GEP 8864	INTIMATE NINA SIMONE (EP)	12
64	Colpix PXE 303	FINE AND MELLOW (EP)	12
66	Colpix PXE 306	JUST SAY I LOVE HIM (EP)	12
66	Colpix PXE 307	I LOVE TO LOVE (EP)	12
65	Philips BE 12585	DON'T LET ME BE MISUNDERSTOOD (EP)	10
65	Philips BE 12589	STRANGE FRUIT (EP)	10

LPs

61	Pye Intl. NPL 28014	AT THE TOWN HALL (LP)	18
62	Pye Jazz NJL 36	FORBIDDEN FRUIT (LP)	18
64	Colpix PXL 419	FORBIDDEN FRUIT (LP, reissue)	15
64	Colpix PXL 421	NINA AT THE VILLAGE GATE (LP)	15
65	Colpix PXL 465	FOLKSY NINA (LP)	15
65	Fontana SFJL 954	TELL ME MORE (LP)	12
65	Philips BL 7662	BROADWAY . . . BLUES . . . BALLADS (LP)	15
65	Philips BL 7671	I PUT A SPELL ON YOU (LP)	15
65	Philips BL 7678	IN CONCERT (LP)	15
66	Philips BL 7683	PASTEL BLUES (LP)	15
66	Philips (S)BL 7722	LET IT ALL OUT (LP)	15
66	Philips (S)BL 7726	WILD IS THE WIND (LP)	15
67	Philips (S)BL 7764	HIGH PRIESTESS OF SOUL (LP)	15
67	RCA RD/SF 7883	SINGS THE BLUES (LP)	15
68	RCA RD/SF 7967	SILK AND SOUL (LP)	12
69	RCA RD/SF 7979	NUFF SAID! (LP)	12
71	RCA	BLACK GOLD (LP)	12
71	RCA SF 8192	HERE COMES THE SUN (LP)	12
72	Mojo 2383 110	GIFTED AND BLACK (LP)	12
73	RCA SF 8304	EMERGENCY WARD (LP)	12

SUGAR SIMONE

66	Rainbow RAI 103	Is It Because/I Want To Know	10
67	Rainbow RAI 115	I Love My Baby/I'll Keep You Satisfied	8
67	Sue WI 4029	Suddenly/King Without A Throne	25
67	Go AJ 11409	It's Alright/Take It Easy	12
68	CBS 3250	The Vow/Spinning Wheel	6
69	Doctor Bird DB 1192	Black Is Gold/The Invitation	15
69	Doctor Bird DB 1193	The Squeeze Is On/Tell Me	15
69	Doctor Bird DB 1201	Come And Try/Don't Listen To What They Say	15
69	Fab FAB 106	Boom Biddy Boom/RUDIES: What Can I Do	8
69	Fab FAB 107	I Need A Witness/Johnny Dollar	8
69	Upfront UPF 1	Turns On The Heatwave/Crying Blues	5
70	Beacon BEA 156	Keep On Trying/Only The Lonely	5
70	Beacon BEA 174	Why Can't I Touch You/Gotta Get It Off My Mind	5

(see also Sugar & Dandy, Les Foster, Larry Foster & Soul Explosion, Lance Hannibal)

SIMON PLUG & GRIMES

70	Deram DM 296	Is This A Dream?/I'm Going Home	8
70	President PT 310	Way In, Way Out/Long Long Summer	5
71	President PT 354	Pull Together/I'll Keep Smiling	5

SIMON'S SECRETS

| 68 | CBS 3406 | Naughty Boy/Sympathy | 20 |
| 68 | CBS 3856 | I Know What Her Name Is/Keeping My Head Above Water | 20 |

(see also Secrets, Clifford T. Ward, Martin Raynor & Secrets)

SIMON SISTERS

| 64 | London HLR 9893 | Winkin', Blinkin' And Nod/So Glad I'm Here | 12 |
| 65 | London HLR 9984 | Cuddlebug/No One To Talk My Trouble To | 10 |

NIC SIMPER'S FANDANGO

| 79 | Gull GULP 1033 | SLIPSTREAMING (LP) | 20 |

(see also Deep Purple, Warhorse)

SIMPLE IMAGE

| 70 | Carnaby CNS 4013 | Spinning Spinning Spinning/Shy Boy | 4 |

SIMPLE MINDS

79	Zoom ZUM 10	Life In A Day/Special View (p/s)	8
79	Zoom ZUM 11	Chelsea Girl/Garden Of Hate (p/s)	7
80	Arista ARIST 325	Changeling/Premonition (live) (p/s)	10
80	Arista ARIST 372	I Travel/New Warm Skin (p/s, some with blue vinyl flexidisc: "Kaleidoscope"/"Film Theme Dub")	12/4
80	Arista ARIST 12372	I Travel (Mix)/Film Theme (12", p/s)	8
81	Arista ARIST 394	Celebrate/Changeling (p/s)	7
81	Arista ARIST 12394	Celebrate (Mix)/Changeling/I Travel (12", stickered sleeve)	10
81	Virgin VS 410	The American/League Of Nations (p/s)	4
81	Virgin VS 410-12	The American/League Of Nations (12", p/s)	7

SIMPLE MINDS

86	Virgin MIKE 907-12	Ghostdancing (A Special Extended 12" Remix)/Jungleland (A Special Extended 12" Remix)/Ghostdancing (Instrumental)/Jungleland (Instrumental) (CD, gatefold card sleeve)	7
88	Virgin CDT 2	Don't You (Forget About Me)/A Brass Band In African Chimes (3" CD, card sleeve)	7
89	Virgin SMXCD 3	Ballad Of The Streets (3" CD EP, card sleeve)	7
89	Virgin SMXCD 4	This Is Your Land (Full Length Version) (with Lou Reed)/Saturday Girl/ Year Of The Dragon (CD)	7
89	Virgin SMXCD 5	Kick It In (LP Version)/Waterfront ('89 Remix)/Big Sleep (live) (CD)	7
89	Virgin SMXCD 6	THE AMSTERDAM EP (Let It All Come Down/Sign O' The Times/Jerusalem) (3" CD, card sleeve)	7
89	Virgin SMXX 6	THE AMSTERDAM EP (Let It All Come Down/Sign O' The Times/ Sign O' The Times [C.J. Mackintosh Mix]/Jerusalem) (CD)	7
79	Zoom ZULP 1	LIFE IN A SIMPLE DAY (LP, original issue)	10
80	Arista SPART 1109	REAL TO REAL (CACOPHONY) (LP, original issue)	10
80	Arista SPART 1140	EMPIRES AND DANCE (LP, original issue)	10
81	Virgin V 2207	SONS AND FASCINATION/SISTER FEELINGS CALL (2-LP, stickered & shrinkwrapped)	18
84	Virgin V 2300	SPARKLE IN THE RAIN (LP, white vinyl, stickered sleeve)	15
85	Virgin V 2364	ONCE UPON A TIME (LP, picture disc, gatefold sleeve)	14
87	Virgin SMDL 1	LIVE IN THE CITY OF LIGHT (2-LP, with booklet & gold embossed sleeve)	14
89	Virgin SMBXC 1	STREET FIGHTING YEARS (box set w/ interview cassettes & songbook, no'd)	18

(see also Johnny & Self Abusers)

SIMPLICITY PEOPLE

73	Grape GR 3062	Murderer/BIG YOUTH: The Killer	15
73	Harry J HJ 6649	Time Is Getting Harder/HARRY J ALLSTARS: Time Is Getting Harder	5

SIMPLY RED

85	Lyntone LYN 15914	Something's Burning/10,000 MANIACS: Grey Victory (33rpm 1-sided clear flexidisc free with Jamming magazine, issue 29)	12/6
85	Elektra EKR 9	Money's Too Tight (To Mention)/Open Up The Red Box (die-cut rear sleeve)	4
85	Elektra EKR 9P	Money's Too Tight (To Mention)/Open Up The Red Box (picture disc)	8
85	Elektra EKR 19	Come To My Aid/Valentine (die-cut p/s)	4
85	Elektra EKR 19T	Come To My Aid (extended)/Granma's Hands/Valentine (12", p/s)	8
85	Elektra EKR 19TX	Come To My Aid (Survival Mix)/Granma's Hands/Come To My Aid (Heavy Dub Mix)/Valentine (12", p/s)	12
85	Elektra EKR 29	Holding Back The Years/I Won't Feel Bad (p/s)	5
85	Elektra EKR 29F	Holding Back The Years/I Won't Feel Bad (gatefold p/s, with poster)	7
85	Elektra EKR 29P	Holding Back The Years/I Won't Feel Bad (shaped picture disc)	25
85	Elektra EKR 29T	Holding Back The Years (Extended)/I Won't Feel Bad/ Drowning In My Own Tears (12", p/s)	12
86	WEA YZ 63R	Jericho/Jericho The Musical (red vinyl in clear PVC sleeve)	6
86	WEA YZ 63T	Jericho (12" Extended Mix)/Jericho The Musical/Money's Too Tight (To Mention) (live)/Heaven (live) (12", p/s)	8

MINT VALUE £

86	WEA YZ 75B	Open Up The Red Box (Remix)/Look At You Now (foldout box p/s) 8
86	WEA YZ 75F	Open Up The Red Box (Remix)/Look At You Now//Holding Back The Years/ I Won't Feel Bad (shrinkwrapped double pack) 8
86	WEA YZ 75T	Open Up The Red Box (Remix) (Extended)/Look At You Now (live)/ Heaven The Movie (live) (12", p/s) 7
86	WEA YZ 75TF	Open Up The Red Box (Remix)/Look At You Now (live)/Heaven The Movie (live)//Holding Back The Years (Extended)/Drowning In My Own Tears/ Picture Book In Dub (12", double pack) 15
87	WEA YZ 103F	The Right Thing/There's A Light//Holding Back The Years/ Drowning In My Own Tears (double pack) 6
87	WEA YZ 103TP	The Right Thing (Extended Version)/There's A Light/Ev'rytime We Say Goodbye (12", clear vinyl picture disc) 8
87	WEA YZ 114TP	Infidelity (Stretch Mix)/Love Fire (Massive Red Mix)/Lady Godiva's Room (12", picture disc with insert in stickered PVC sleeve) 8
87	WEA YZ 141T	Maybe Someday.../Broken Man/Let Me Have It All (Remix) (12", p/s) 8
87	WEA YZ 161TE	Ev'ry Time We Say Goodbye/Love For Sale (live in studio)/Sad Old Red/ Broken Man (10", stitched cardboard die-cut sleeve) 12
87	WEA YZ 161TW	Ev'ry Time We Say Goodbye/Ev'ry Time We Say Goodbye (live in studio)/Love For Sale (live in studio) (12", envelope pack with sheet music & 4 postcards) . . . 20
87	WEA YZ 161CD	Ev'ry Time We Say Goodbye (live)/Love For Sale (live in the studio)/Ev'ry Time We Say Goodbye (live)/Sad Old Red (CD, red or silver discs) 12/10
88	WEA YZ 172CD	I Won't Feel Bad (Arthur Baker Remix)/The Right Thing/I Won't Feel Bad (Edit)/Lady Godiva's Room (Ellis Hucknall Mix) (3" CD, with adaptor, 5" case) . . . 10
89	WEA YZ 349TE	It's Only Love (Valentine Mix)/Turn It Up/I'm Gonna Lose You (10", numbered stitched cardboard die-cut sleeve) 8
89	WEA YZ 349 CD	It's Only Love (4.00 remix)/Turn It Up/X/The Right Thing (3" CD, with adaptor, 5" case) 8
89	WEA YZ 349 CDX	It's Only Love (4.00 remix)/Turn It Up/X/The Right Thing (3" CD, 'criss-cross' box pack) 12
89	WEA YZ 377TE	If You Don't Know Me By Now/Move On Out (live)/The Great Divide (S.H.T.G.) (10", stitched cardboard die-cut sleeve) 8
89	WEA YZ 377CD	If You Don't Know Me By Now/Move On Out (live)/Shine (live)/Sugar Daddy (3" CD, gatefold p/s in protective plastic case) 8
89	WEA YZ 377CDX	If You Don't Know Me By Now/Move On Out (live)/Shine (live)/Sugar Daddy (3" CD, 'criss-cross' box pack) 10
89	WEA YZ 404TE	A New Flame/More/I Asked Her For Water (live)/Funk On Out (instrumental) (live) (10", numbered stitched cardboard die-cut sleeve) 8
89	WEA YZ 404CD	A New Flame/More/I Asked Her For Water (live)/Resume (live) (3" CD, gatefold card sleeve) 8
89	WEA YZ 404CDX	A New Flame/More/I Asked Her For Water (live)/Resume (live) (3" CD, 'criss-cross' box pack) 8
89	WEA YZ 424TE	You've Got It/Holding Back The Years (Live Acoustic Version)/I Wish/ I Know You Got Soul (live) (10", numbered stitched cardboard sleeve) 7
89	WEA YZ 424CD	You've Got It/Holding Back The Years (Live Acoustic Version)/I Wish (live) (3" CD, gatefold card sleeve) 7
85	Elektra EKT 27P	PICTURE BOOK (LP, picture disc, die-cut sleeve) 20

(see also Frantic Elevators)

BILL SIMPSON
| 64 | Piccadilly 7N 35179 | I Love You For Sentimental Reasons/My Love Is Like A Red Red Rose (p/s) . . . . . 5 |

DANNY SIMPSON
| 69 | Trojan TR 653 | Outa Sight/JOHN HOLT: I Want You Closer . . . . 6 |

DUDLEY SIMPSON ORCHESTRA
| 78 | BBC RESL 58 | Blake's 7/The Federation March (p/s) . . . . 8 |

HOKE SIMPSON
| 58 | HMV POP 442 | I Finally Found You/Gi-Gi . . . . 7 |

JEANETTE SIMPSON
67	Giant GN 16	Rain/Whatcha Gonna Do About It 6
68	Giant GN 29	My Baby Just Cares For Me/Don't Let Me Cry No More (with Superboys) 8
68	Giant GN 35	Through Loving You/Send Me Some Lovin' (with Missions) 8

LEO SIMPSON
| 65 | Blue Beat BB 351 | I Love Her So/Good To Be Seen (as Leo Simmo) . . . . 12 |
| 73 | Pyramid PYR 7004 | Waxy Doodle/Go Away . . . . 5 |

(see also Lionel Simpson)

LIONEL SIMPSON
65	Ska Beat JB 205	Tell Me What You Want/Love Is A Game 15
65	Ska Beat JB 221	Red River Valley/Eight People 15
66	Ska Beat JB 233	Give Over/Never Before 15

(see also Leo Simpson)

MARTIN SIMPSON
| 76 | Trailer LER 2099 | GOLDEN VANITY (LP) . . . . 12 |

RED SIMPSON
| 66 | Capitol ST 2468 | ROLL TRUCK ROLL (LP) . . . . 12 |

VALERIE SIMPSON
| 72 | Tamla Motown STML 11194 | EXPOSED (LP) . . . . 15 |

CHUCK SIMS
| 58 | London HLR 8577 | Little Pigeon/Life Isn't Long Enough . . . . 325 |
| 58 | London HLR 8577 | Little Pigeon/Life Isn't Long Enough (78) . . . . 50 |

FRANKIE LEE SIMS
| 71 | Speciality SPE 5009 | Married Woman Blues/Lucy Mae Blues . . . . 5 |
| 71 | Speciality SNTF 5004 | LUCY MAE BLUES (LP) . . . . 15 |

JOAN SIMS

63	Parlophone R 5021	Oh Not Again Ken/Hurry Up Gran	6
67	CBS 202635	Sweet Lovely Whatsisname/The Lass With The Delicate Hair	6

KELLY SIMS

60	Top Rank JAR 321	Betrayed By Love/A Girl In Love	6

SYLVIA SIMS

58	Brunswick 05771	The Night They Invented Champagne/The Nature Of Things	5
58	Brunswick 05771	The Night They Invented Champagne/The Nature Of Things (78)	8

ZOOT SIMS (U.S.)

51	Esquire 10-107	Yellow Duck/Boot It Zoot (78)	8
50s	Esquire EP 183	ZOOT! (EP)	20
50s	Esquire EP 204	ZOOT'S CASE (EP)	20
52	Esquire 20-002	ZOOT SIMS QUARTET/QUINTET (10" LP)	50
53	Esquire 20-010	ZOOT SIMS ALLSTARS (10" LP)	20
53	Esquire 20-018	ZOOT SIMS QUARTET/QUINTET (10" LP)	20
54	Vogue LDE 056	ZOOT SIMS GOES TO TOWN (10" LP)	250
55	Esquire 20-040	ZOOT SIMS QUARTET/QUINTET (10" LP)	60
50s	Esquire 32-040	ZOOT SIMS SEPTET (LP)	30
58	HMV CLP 1165	GEORGE HANDY COMPOSITIONS (LP)	18
58	HMV CLP 1188	PLAYS FOUR ALTOS (LP)	20
61	Vogue LAE 12309	CHOICE (LP)	20
61	Fontana TFL 5176	ZOOT AT RONNIE SCOTT'S (LP)	350
62	Fontana (S)TFL 588	ZOOT AT RONNIE SCOTT'S (LP, reissue)	150
62	Fontana 886 151 TY	SOLO FOR ZOOT (LP)	50
65	Fontana FJL 123	COOKIN'! (LP)	150
60s	Xtra XTRA 5001	TROTTING! (LP)	15

(see also Sims-Wheeler Vintage Jazz Band)

SIMS TWINS/VALENTINOS

68	Soul City SCM 001	THE VALENTINOS/THE SIMS TWINS (LP, 1 side each)	20

SIMS-WHEELER VINTAGE JAZZ BAND

60	Polydor NH 66638	Never On A Sunday/Ma Curly Headed Baby	4

(see also Zoot Sims)

FRANK SINATRA

78s

50	Columbia DX 1666	Soliloquy (Parts 1 & 2) (12" 78)	12
51	Columbia LB 104	If She'd Only Look My Way/London By Night (78)	12
53	Columbia DB 3347	I Whistle A Happy Tune/Hello Young Lovers (78)	8
54	Capitol CL 14120	Three Coins In The Fountain/I Could Have Told You (78)	8
54	Philips PB 364	My Blue Heaven/Should I (78)	10
55	Philips PB 363	It's Only A Paper Moon/When You're Smiling (78)	10
56	Capitol CL 14503	Love And Marriage/Look To Your Heart (78)	8
57	Capitol CL 14719	So Long, My Love/Crazy Love (78)	8
57	Capitol CL 14750	Something Wonderful Happens In Summer/You're Cheatin' Yourself (78)	8
57	Capitol CL 14804	Mistletoe And Holly/Jingle Bells (78)	8
57	Philips PB 734	Once In Love With Amy/I Am Loved (78)	12
57	Philips PB 756	Full Moon And Empty Arms/Autumn In New York (78)	12
57	Philips PB 763	White Christmas/Christmas Dreaming (78)	12
58	Capitol CL 14819	Witchcraft/Tell Her You Love Her (78)	8
58	Capitol CL 14863	Nothing In Common/How Are Ya Fixed For Love (with Keely Smith) (78)	8
58	Capitol CL 14904	The Song From "Kings Go Forth" (Monique)/The Same Old Song And Dance (78)	8
58	Fontana H 109	I Could Write A Book/Nevertheless (I'm In Love With You) (78)	10
58	Fontana H 140	If I Forget You/I'm A Fool To Want You (78)	12
58	Capitol CL 14956	Mr. Success/Sleep Warm (78)	8
59	Capitol CL 14997	Time After Time/French Foreign Legion (78)	10
59	Capitol CL 15006	To Love And Be Loved/No-One Ever Tells You (78)	12
59	Capitol CL 15052	High Hopes/All My Tomorrows (78)	20
59	Capitol CL 15086	Talk To Me/They Came To Cordura (78)	25

SINGLES

53	Columbia SCM 5052	Birth Of The Blues/Why Try To Change Me Now?	30
53	Columbia SCM 5060	You Do Something To Me/Lover	30
53	Columbia SCM 5076	Santa Claus Is Comin' To Town/My Girl	35
54	Capitol CL 14064	Young-At-Heart/Take A Chance	18
54	Capitol CL 14120	Three Coins In The Fountain/I Could Have Told You	25
54	Capitol CL 14174	White Christmas/The Christmas Waltz	25
54	Capitol CL 14188	When I Stop Loving You/It Worries Me	15
55	Capitol CL 14221	Someone To Watch Over Me/The Gal That Got Away	15
55	Capitol CL 14238	Melody Of Love/I'm Gonna Live Till I Die	15
55	Columbia SCM 5167	S'posin'/How Deep Is The Ocean	20
55	Capitol CL 14240	You, My Love/Just One Of Those Things	15
55	Capitol CL 14270	Don't Change Your Mind About Me/Why Should I Cry Over You	15
55	Capitol CL 14292	Two Hearts, Two Kisses (Make One Love)/From The Bottom To The Top	15
55	Capitol CL 14296	Learnin' The Blues/If I Had Three Wishes	15
55	Capitol CL 14326	Not As A Stranger/How Could You Do A Thing Like That To Me	15
55	Capitol CL 14352	My Funny Valentine/I Get A Kick Out Of You	12
55	Capitol CL 14360	It Never Entered My Mind/In The Wee Small Hours Of The Morning	12
55	Capitol CL 14373	Fairy Tale/Same Old Saturday Night	12

(The above Capitol 45s were originally issued with triangular centres; later round-centre copies are worth half these values.)

56	Capitol CL 14503	Love And Marriage/Look To Your Heart	10
56	Capitol CL 14511	(Love Is) A Tender Trap/Weep They Will	8
56	Capitol CL 14564	You'll Get Yours/Flowers Mean Forgiveness	7
56	Capitol CL 14584	Five Hundred Guys/(How Little It Matters) How Little We Know	6
56	Capitol CL 14607	"Johnny Concho" Theme (Wait For Me)/Hey! Jealous Lover	6

MINT VALUE £

56	Capitol CL 14620	The Impatient Years/Our Town	6
56	Capitol CL 14644	Who Wants To Be A Millionaire? (with Celeste Holm)/ Mind If I Make Love To You?	7
56	Capitol CL 14646	You're Sensational/You Forgot All The Words	6
57	Capitol CL 14696	Can I Steal A Little Love?/Your Love For Me	6
57	Capitol CL 14719	So Long, My Love/Crazy Love	6
57	Capitol CL 14750	Something Wonderful Happens In Summer/You're Cheatin' Yourself	6
57	Capitol CL 14800	All The Way/Chicago	5
57	Capitol CL 14804	Mistletoe And Holly/Jingle Bells	5
58	Capitol CL 14819	Witchcraft/Tell Her You Love Her	6
58	Capitol CL 14863	Nothing In Common/How Are Ya Fixed For Love (with Keely Smith)	5
58	Capitol CL 14904	The Song From "Kings Go Forth" (Monique)/The Same Old Song And Dance	5
58	Fontana H 140	If I Forget You/I'm A Fool To Want You	10
58	Capitol CL 14956	Mr. Success/Sleep Warm	5
59	Capitol CL 14997	Time After Time/French Foreign Legion	5
59	Capitol CL 15006	To Love And Be Loved/No-One Ever Tells You	5
59	Capitol CL 15052	High Hopes/All My Tomorrows	5
59	Capitol CL 15086	Talk To Me/They Came To Cordura	5
62	Reprise RS 20063	Ev'rybody's Twistin'/Nothing But The Best	5
66	Reprise RS 20531	That's Life/I've Got You Under My Skin	5
69	Reprise RS 20817	My Way/Blue Lace	5

EPs

54	HMV 7EG 8004	TOMMY DORSEY & HIS ORCHESTRA (EP, plain sleeve, 2 tracks with Sinatra)	10
54	HMV 7EG 8070	FRANK SINATRA (EP, plain sleeve)	8
54	Capitol EAP1-488	SONGS FOR YOUNG LOVERS NO. 1 (EP)	8
55	HMV 7EG 8128	MOONLIGHT SINATRA (EP)	12
55	Columbia SEG 7565	FRANK SINATRA (EP, plain sleeve)	8
55	Columbia SEG 7582	SINATRA SERENADE (EP, plain sleeve)	10
55	Columbia SEG 7597	FRANKIE'S FAVOURITES (EP, plain sleeve)	10
55	Capitol EAP 2-488	SONGS FOR YOUNG LOVERS NO. 2 (EP)	8
55	Capitol EAP 1-571	SONGS FROM "YOUNG AT HEART" (EP)	8
56	Capitol EAP 1-590	MELODY OF LOVE (EP)	8
56	Capitol EAP 1-629	SESSION WITH SINATRA (EP)	8
56	Capitol EAP 1025	OUR TOWN (EP)	8
56	Capitol EAP 2-488	YOUNG AT HEART (EP)	8
60	Fontana TFE 17273	'BYE BABY (EP)	12
61	Capitol SEP1-221	NO ONE CARES (EP, stereo)	12
61	Capitol SEP2-1221	NO ONE CARES NO. 2 (EP, stereo)	12
61	Capitol SEP3-1221	NO ONE CARES NO. 3 (EP, stereo)	12

CAPITOL LPs

54	Capitol LC 6654	SONGS FOR YOUNG LOVERS (10" LP)	25
54	Capitol LC 6689	SWING EASY (10" LP)	25
55	Capitol LC 6702	IN THE WEE SMALL HOURS VOL. 1 (10" LP)	20
55	Capitol LC 6705	IN THE WEE SMALL HOURS VOL. 2 (10" LP)	20
56	Capitol LCT 6106	SONGS FOR SWINGIN' LOVERS (LP)	15
56	Capitol LCT 6111	FRANK SINATRA CONDUCTS TONE POEMS OF COLOUR (LP)	18
57	Capitol LCT 6123	THIS IS SINATRA (LP)	15
57	Capitol LCT 6130	CLOSE TO YOU (LP)	15
57	Capitol LCT 6135	A SWINGIN' AFFAIR (LP)	15
57	Capitol LCT 6144	A JOLLY CHRISTMAS FROM FRANK SINATRA (LP)	15
58	Capitol (S)LCT 6152	WHERE ARE YOU? (LP, mono/stereo)	15/18
58	Capitol LCT 6155	THIS IS SINATRA VOL. 2 (LP)	15
58	Capitol (S)LCT 6168	FRANK SINATRA SINGS FOR ONLY THE LONELY (LP, mono/stereo)	15/18
59	Capitol (S)LCT 6179	COME DANCE WITH ME (LP)	15
59	Capitol LCT 6181	LOOK TO YOUR HEART (LP)	15
59	Capitol (S)LCT 6185	NO ONE CARES (LP)	15
60	Capitol W 587	SWING EASY (LP)	15
61	Capitol W(S) 1417	NICE'N'EASY (LP, mono/stereo)	15/18
61	Capitol W(S) 1491	SINATRA'S SWINGIN' SESSION! (LP, mono/stereo)	15/18
62	Capitol W(S) 1594	COME SWING WITH ME! (LP, mono/stereo)	15/18
62	Capitol W(S) 1676	POINT OF NO RETURN (LP, mono/stereo)	15/18
62	Capitol T 20389	LONDON BY NIGHT (LP)	15
62	Capitol W(S) 1538	ALL THE WAY (LP, mono/stereo)	15/18
63	Capitol W(S) 1729	SINATRA SINGS ... OF LOVE AND THINGS! (LP, mono/stereo)	15/18
63	Capitol W 1/2/3-1762	THE GREAT YEARS (3-LP)	20
63	Capitol W 1825	FRANK SINATRA SINGS RODGERS AND HART (LP)	20
64	Capitol T 20577	MY FUNNY VALENTINE (LP)	15
65	Capitol W 20652	SINGING AND SWINGING (LP)	15
65	Capitol (S)T 1919	TELL HER YOU LOVE HER (LP)	15
65	Capitol T 20734	THE CONNOISSEUR'S SINATRA (LP)	15
66	Capitol T 20757	SINATRA FOR THE SOPHISTICATED (LP)	15
67	Capitol (S)T 2700	THE MOVIE SONGS (LP)	15
85	Capitol SINATRA 20	FRANK SINATRA: THE CAPITOL YEARS (20-LP, box set)	80
90	Capitol C1-94777	THE CAPITOL YEARS (5-LP, box set)	30

PHILIPS/FONTANA LPs

54	Philips BBR 8003	SING AND DANCE WITH FRANK SINATRA (10" LP)	30
55	Philips BBR 8038	FABULOUS FRANK (10" LP)	25
55	Philips BBR 8040	YOUNG AT HEART (10" LP, with Doris Day)	25
57	Philips BBR 8114	CHRISTMAS DREAMING (10" LP)	30
57	Philips BBL 7137	DORIS AND FRANK (LP, 6 tracks each by Doris Day & Frank Sinatra)	25
57	Philips BBL 7168	FRANKIE (LP)	20
57	Philips BBL 7180	THAT OLD FEELING (LP)	20
58	Fontana TFL 5000	THE VOICE (LP)	25
58	Fontana TFL 5006	ADVENTURES OF THE HEART (LP)	20
58	Fontana TFL 5030	THE FRANK SINATRA STORY (LP)	18

59	Fontana TFL 5048	PUT YOUR DREAMS AWAY (LP)	25
59	Fontana TFL 5054	THE BROADWAY KICK (LP)	20
60	Fontana TFL 5074	LOVE IS A KICK (LP)	18
60	Fontana TFL 5082	COME BACK TO SORRENTO (LP)	18
60	Fontana TFL 5107	REFLECTIONS (LP)	15
61	Fontana TFL 5138	SINATRA SOUVENIR (LP)	15
61	Fontana SET 303	SINATRA PLUS (2-LP)	15

REPRISE LPs

61	Reprise R 1001	RING-A-DING-DING! (LP)	15
61	Reprise R(9) 1002	SINATRA SWINGS (LP, mono/stereo)	12/15
62	Reprise R(9) 1003	I REMEMBER TOMMY... (LP, die-cut gatefold sleeve, mono/stereo)	12/15
62	Reprise R(9) 1004	SINATRA AND STRINGS (LP, mono/stereo)	12/15
62	Reprise R(9) 1005	SINATRA AND SWINGIN' BRASS (LP, mono/stereo)	12/15
62	Reprise R(9) 1006	SINATRA SINGS GREAT SONGS FROM GREAT BRITAIN (LP, mono/stereo)	30/45
63	Reprise R 1007	ALL ALONE (LP)	12
63	Reprise R(9) 1008	SINATRA-BASIE (LP)	12
63	Reprise R(9) 1009	THE CONCERT SINATRA (LP)	12
63	Reprise R 1010	SINATRA'S SINATRA (LP)	12
64	Reprise R(9) 1011	FRANK SINATRA SINGS "DAYS OF WINE AND ROSES" & OTHER ACADEMY AWARD WINNERS (LP)	12
64	Reprise R(9) 1012	IT MIGHT AS WELL BE SWING (LP, with Count Basie)	12
64	Reprise R 2022	TWELVE SONGS OF CHRISTMAS (LP, with Bing Crosby, Fred Waring, etc)	12
65	Reprise R(9) 1013	SOFTLY AS I LEAVE YOU (LP)	12
65	Reprise R(9) 1014	SEPTEMBER OF MY YEARS (LP)	12
65	Reprise R(9) 6167	SINATRA '65 (LP)	12
66	Reprise R(9) 1015	MY KIND OF BROADWAY (LP)	12
66	Reprise R(9) 1016	SINATRA: A MAN AND HIS MUSIC (2-LP)	15
66	Reprise R(9) 1017	STRANGERS IN THE NIGHT (LP)	12
66	Reprise R(9) 1018	MOONLIGHT SINATRA (LP)	15
66	Reprise R(S)LP 1019	IN CONCERT: SINATRA AT 'THE SANDS' (2-LP, with Count Basie)	15
67	Reprise R(S)LP 1020	THAT'S LIFE (LP)	12
67	Reprise R(S)LP 1021	FRANCIS ALBERT SINATRA — ANTONIO CARLOS JOBIM (LP)	12
67	Reprise R(S)LP 1022	FRANK SINATRA (LP)	12
68	Reprise R(S)LP 1024	FRANCIS A. EDWARD K. (LP, with Duke Ellington)	12
69	Reprise R(S)LP 1027	CYCLES (LP)	12
69	Reprise R(S)LP 1030	A MAN ALONE — THE WORDS AND MUSIC OF ROD McKUEN (LP)	12
70	Reprise R(S)LP 1031	WATERTOWN (LP)	15
71	Reprise RSLP 1033	SINATRA AND COMPANY (LP)	12
77	Reprise K 94003	SINATRA — THE REPRISE YEARS (4-LP, box set)	18

OTHER LPs

56	HMV DLP 1123	IT'S D-LOVELY (LP, with Tommy Dorsey Orchestra)	25
58	RCA RD 27069	FRANKIE AND TOMMY (LP, with Tommy Dorsey Orchestra)	20
61	Encore ENC 101	WHEN YOUR LOVER HAS GONE (LP)	12
61	World Record Club TP 81	LOOK OVER YOUR SHOULDER (LP)	12
66	World Record C. (S)T 545	CLOSE TO YOU (LP, reissue)	12
67	World Record C. (S)T 635	SEPTEMBER SONG (LP)	12
68	CBS 63172	THE ESSENTIAL FRANK SINATRA VOL. 1 (LP)	12
68	CBS 63173	THE ESSENTIAL FRANK SINATRA VOL. 2 (LP)	12
68	CBS 63174	THE ESSENTIAL FRANK SINATRA VOL. 3 (LP)	12
69	World Records SM 137-142	THE SINATRA TOUCH (6-LP, box set, mail-order only)	30
70	Valiant VS 144	FRANK SINATRA WITH COUNT BASIE (LP, reissue)	12
81	World Records ALBUM 47	THE SINATRA TOUCH (4-LP, box set, mail-order only)	20

(see also Nancy Sinatra, Count Basie, Tommy Dorsey, Dean Martin, Doris Day)

FRANK SINATRA & BONO

| 93 | Capitol DUETS 1 | I've Got You Under My Skin (CD, 1-track, promo only, card p/s) | 15 |

(see also U2)

FRANK & NANCY SINATRA

| 67 | Reprise REP 30082 | SOMETHING STUPID (EP) | 8 |
| 69 | Reprise R(S)LP 1026 | THE SINATRA FAMILY WISH YOU A HAPPY CHRISTMAS (LP) | 20 |

NANCY SINATRA

61	Reprise RS 20017	Cuff Links And Tie Clips/Not Just Your Friend	12
62	Reprise RS 20045	To Know Him Is To Love Him/Like I Do	10
63	Reprise RS 20144	I See The Moon/Put Your Head On My Shoulder	8
64	Reprise RS 20335	True Love/The Answer To Everything	7
65	Reprise RS 20407	So Long Babe/If He'd Loved Me	7
66	Reprise RS 20432	These Boots Are Made For Walkin'/The City Never Sleeps At Night	5
66	Reprise RS 20461	How Does That Grab You Darlin'/I Move Around	6
66	Reprise RS 20491	Friday's Child/Hutchinson Jail	6
66	Reprise RS 20514	In Our Time/Leave My Dog Alone	6
66	Reprise RS 20527	Sugar Town/Summer Wine	6
67	Reprise RS 20559	Love Eyes/Coastin'	6
67	Reprise RS 20595	You Only Live Twice/Jackson	6
67	Reprise RS 20620	Lightning's Girl/Until It's Time For You To Go	6
68	Reprise RS 20670	100 Years/See The Little Children	6
68	Reprise RS 20756	Happy/Nice 'N Easy	6
68	Reprise RS 20789	Good Time Girl/Old Devil Moon	6
69	Reprise RS 20813	God Knows I Love You/Just Being Plain Old Me	6
69	Reprise RS 20851	Drummer Man/Home	6
69	Reprise RS 20869	The Highway Song/Are You Growing Tired Of My Love	5
75	Private Stock PVT 27	Annabell Of Mobile/She Played Piano And He Beat The Drums	6
77	Private Stock PVT 114	It's For My Dad/A Gentle Man Like You	15
66	Reprise REP 30069	RUN FOR YOUR LIFE (EP)	15
66	Reprise REP 30072	I MOVE AROUND (EP)	15
67	Reprise REP 30080	SORRY 'BOUT THAT (EP)	15
67	Reprise REP 30086	NASHVILLE NANCY (EP)	12

MINT VALUE £

66	Reprise R 6202	BOOTS (LP)	15
66	Reprise R 6207	HOW DOES THAT GRAB YOU? (LP)	15
66	Reprise R(S)LP 6221	NANCY IN LONDON (LP)	15
67	Reprise RLP 6239	SUGAR (LP)	15
67	Reprise R(S)LP 6251	COUNTRY, MY WAY (LP)	15
68	Reprise R(S)LP 6277	MOVIN' WITH NANCY (LP)	15
69	Reprise RSLP 6333	NANCY (LP)	15
72	RCA DPS 2037	THIS IS NANCY SINATRA (LP)	15
73	RCA SF 8331	WOMAN (LP)	15

(see also Elvis Presley)

NANCY SINATRA & LEE HAZLEWOOD
67	Reprise RS 20629	Lady Bird/Sand	6
67	Reprise RS 23215	Some Velvet Morning/Tony Rome	6
71	Reprise K 14093	Did You Ever?/Back On The Road Again	5
67	Reprise REP 30083	JACKSON (EP)	15
68	Reprise R(S)LP 6273	NANCY & LEE (LP)	15
72	RCA Victor SF 8240	DID YOU EVER? (LP)	15

(see also Lee Hazlewood, Frank Sinatra)

SINATRAS
81	Dining Out TUX 6	Happy Feeling/You May Be An Angel (p/s, red vinyl)	4
82	Transmanor CBV 1	You Make Me Feel Like I'm Wearing New Clothes (All The Time)/ Finding Your Own Level (p/s)	4

BETTY SINCLAIR
70	Torpedo TOR 19	Why Why Why/HOT ROD ALL STARS: Fistful Of Dollars	8

JIMMY SINCLAIR & TRENTON SPENCE ORCHESTRA
61	Blue Beat BB 47	Verona/To Prove My Love	15

STEPHEN SINCLAIR
62	HMV POP 1066	Mister Sandman/Part Lights	6

WINSTON SINCLAIR
69	Nu Beat NB 026	Another Heartache/Come On Little Girl	5

(see also Harmonisers)

SINDELFINGEN
73	Medway	ODGIPIG (LP, private pressing, with insert)	500
90	Cenotaph CEN 111	ODGIPIG/TRIANGLE (2-LP, reissue with live album, 300 only)	20

TONY SINDEN, ALAN BAKER & INSECTS
79	Piano SING 001	Magnificent Cactus Trees/Cast Shadows	5

SINEWAVE
72	Chapter One SCH 172	Clochemerle/Star Trek	4

PETE SINFIELD
73	Manticore K 43501	STILL (LP, textured gatefold sleeve)	25

(see also Emerson Lake & Palmer, King Crimson, Greg Lake)

SINGAROUND
69	G. Guinea GSGL 10436	SINGAROUND (LP)	15

RAY SINGER
64	Ember EMB S 187	Tell Me Now/I'm Comin' Home	6
64	Ember EMB S 199	It's Gotta Be/Hey, Who?	6
65	Ember EMB S 215	I'm The Richest Man Alive/Pretty Little Rambling Rose (some in p/s)	10/6
65	Fontana TF 621	You'll Come Crying To Me/Who Can I Talk To About You	6
67	Ember EMB S 231	What's Done Has Been Done/Won't It Be Fine	8
60s	Ember NR	RAY SINGER (LP)	25

(see also Nirvana [U.K.])

SUSAN SINGER
62	Oriole CB 1703	Gee It's Great To Be Young/Hello First Love	12
62	Oriole CB 1741	Bobby's Loving Touch/Johnny Summertime	20
62	Oriole CB 1778	Love Me With All Your Heart/Autumn Leaves	12
63	Oriole CB 1802	Lock Your Heart Away/Answer To A Prayer	12
63	Oriole CB 1882	I Know/That Old Feeling	12

(see also Susan Holiday)

SINGING BELLES
60	Top Rank JAR 350	The Empty Mailbox/Someone Loves You, Joe	7

SINGING DOGS
56	Pye Nixa N 15065	Barking Dog Boogie/Rock Around The Dogs (78)	8
57	Pye NEP 24029	SINGING DOGS (EP)	15

SINGING NUN
63	Philips BL 7593	SOEUR SOURIRE (LP)	12
63	Philips BL 7607	HER JOY — HER SONGS (LP)	12

SINGING POSTMAN
70s	Starline SRS 5063	THE BEST OF (LP)	15

SINGING PRINCIPAL
73	Action ACT 4608	Thank You Baby/Women's Lib	4

SINGING REINDEER
60	Capitol CL 15124	The Happy Birthday Song/I Wanna Be An Easter Bunny	4

(see also "Dancer, Prancer & Nervous")

MARGIE SINGLETON
60	Melodisc 45-1544	Angel Hands/The Eyes Of Love	10
62	Mercury AMT 1197	Magic Star/Only Your Shadow Knows	15
68	Fontana TL 5646	SINGS COUNTRY WITH SOUL (LP)	15

VALERIE SINGLETON
69   Pye 7N 17800   Solomon Centipede/Jimmy Giraffe 4

SINISTER DUCKS
83   Situation 2 SIT 25   Suicide: March Of The Sinister Ducks/
                             Homicide: Old Gangsters Never (foldout p/s) 10

(see also Bauhaus)

EARL SINK(S)
61   Warner Bros WB 38   Look For Me, I'll Be There/Super Market (as Earl Sink) 12
61   Warner Bros WB 51   Superstitious/Little Suzie Parker 18
63   Capitol CL 15310   Looking For Love/Raining On My Side Of Town (as Earl Sinks) 15

(see also Crickets, Sinx Mitchell)

SINNER
79   Whitetower AMC 705   Need Your Love (foldout p/s) 60

SINNERMAN & SARA
68   MGM MGM-C(S) 8099   SINNERMAN AND SARA (LP) 10

SINNERS
63   Columbia DB 7158   I Can't Stand It/If You Leave Me Now 8
64   Columbia DB 7295   It's So Exciting/Leave Him 10

(see also Linda Laine & Sinners)

SIOUXSIE & BANSHEES
78   Polydor 2059 052   Hong Kong Garden/Voices (10,000 only in gatefold p/s; beige plastic,
                             silver plastic, red plastic or red paper label) 12-16
78   Polydor 2059 052   Hong Kong Garden/Voices (p/s) 7
79   Polydor POSP 9   The Staircase (Mystery)/20th Century Boy (p/s) 6
79   Polydor POSP 59   Playground Twist/Pull To Bits (p/s, some with red paper label) 7/5
79   Polydor 2059 151   Mittageisen (Metal Postcard)/Love In A Void (p/s) 8
80   Polydor POSP 117   Happy House/Drop Dead/Celebration (p/s) 5
80   Polydor 2059 249   Christine/Eve White, Eve Black (p/s, plastic moulded or red paper label) . . . each 5
80   Polydor 2059 249   Christine/Eve White, Eve Black (with Nigel Gray credit on B-side, p/s) 6
80   Polydor POSP 205   Israel/Red Over White (plain gold sleeve) 4
80   Polydor POSPX 205   Israel (Extended)/Red Over White (Extended) (12", no p/s, a few with
                             'Made In England' credit, most with 'Made In France' credit) 10/8
81   Polydor POSP 273   Spellbound/Follow The Sun (p/s) 4
81   Polydor POSPX 273   Spellbound/Follow The Sun/Slap Dash Snap (12", p/s) 7
81   Polydor POSP 309   Arabian Knights/Supernatural Thing (p/s) 4
81   Polydor POSPX 309   Arabian Knights/Supernatural Thing/Congo Conga (12", p/s) 7
82   Polydor POSPG 450   Fireworks/Coal Mind (gatefold p/s) 5
82   Polydor POSP 510   Slowdive/Cannibal Roses (p/s, red paper label) 6
83   Wonderland SHEG 4   Dear Prudence/Tattoo (foldout p/s) 8
84   Wonderland SHEX 6   Swimming Horses/Let Go/The Humming Wires (12", p/s with poster) 8
85   Wonderland SHE 8   Overground/Placebo Effect (p/s) 5
85   Wonderland SHE 9   Cities In Dust/An Execution (poster p/s) 5
85   Wonderland SHEX 9   Cities In Dust/An Execution/Quarterdrawing Of The Dog (12", p/s,
                             'banned' picture label) 8
86   Wonderland SHEDP 10   Candyman/Lullaby (with free 2nd single, gatefold p/s, 2,000 only) 12
87   Wonderland SHEG 11   This Wheel's On Fire/Shooting Sun/Sleepwalking (On The High Wire)/
                             She's Cracked (numbered double pack, gatefold p/s) 6
87   Wonderland SHEG 12   The Passenger/She's Cuckoo (poster p/s) 5
87   Wonderland SHEP 13   Song From The Edge Of The World/The Whole Price Of Blood (picture disc) 4
87   Wonderland SHEPC 13   Song From The Edge Of The World/The Whole Price Of Blood/Mechanical
                             Eyes/Song From The Edge Of The World (Columbus Mix) (cassette). 6
87   Wonderland SHESP 1/2/3 The Passenger/Hall Of Mirrors//Your Lost Little Girl/Sea Breezes//This Town
                             Ain't Big Enough For The Both Of Us/Gun (promo, 3 x 7" pack in PVC wallet). . . 20
88   Wonderland SHEG 14   Peek-A-Boo/False Face (gatefold p/s, numbered) 4
88   Wonderland SHECD 14   Peek-A-Boo/False Face/Catwalk/Peek-A-Boo (Big Spender Mix) (CD, card p/s) . . 7
88   Polydor 080 398-2   Peek-A-Boo/False Face/Catwalk/Peek-A-Boo (Big Spender Mix)/
                             Peek-A-Boo (Video) (CD Video) 15
88   Wonderland SHEG 15   The Killing Jar/Something Wicked (This Way Comes) (clear vinyl,
                             stickered gatefold p/s, numbered) 5
88   Wonderland SHEP 15   The Killing Jar/Something Wicked (This Way Comes) (picture disc) 4
88   Wonderland SHECD 15   The Killing Jar/Something Wicked (This Way Comes)/Are You Still
                             Dying Darling?/The Killing Jar (Lepidopteristic Mix) (CD) 7
88   Wonderland SHEG 16   The Last Beat Of My Heart/El Dia De Los Muertos
                             (stickered gilded p/s, no'd) 4
88   Wonderland SHECD 16   The Last Beat Of My Heart/El Dia De Los Muertos/Sunless/
                             El Dia De Los Muertos (Espiritu Mix) (CD) 7
89   Wonderland SHEX 19   Kiss Them For Me (Snapper Mix)/Staring Back/Return (p/s) (12", gatefold p/s) . . 10
92   Wonderland SHEX 21   Face To Face (Catatonic Mix)/Hot Head (picture disc) 4
83   Fan Club FILE 1   Head Cut/Running Town (freebie, p/s) 40
88   Spiral Scratch SCRATCH 2 An Interview With... (free with *Spiral Scratch* mag, 5,000 only, no p/s). 6/4
78   Polydor POLD 5009   THE SCREAM (LP, with inner sleeve; some with labels reversed) 10/12
87   Wonderland SHELP 4   THROUGH THE LOOKING GLASS (LP, mispressing, 1 side plays
                             Jimi Hendrix's "War Heroes") 25

(see also Creatures, Cure, Glove)

SIR ALEC & HIS BOYS
67   Deram DM 116   I'm A Believer/Green Green Grass Of Home 6

SIR ALICK & PHRASER
82   Recommended/Black   In Search Of The Perfect Baby/PROLIFIKURDS: Nursery Crymes
      Noise 7 NO 5   (printed p/s in PVC sleeve or standard p/s) 10

(see also Homosexuals)

SIR CHAUNCEY AND HIS EXCITING STRINGS
60   Warner Bros. WB 9   Beautiful Obsession/Tenderfoot 6

(see also Ernie Freeman)

SIR (Clancy) COLLINS BAND

MINT VALUE £

68	Collins Downbeat CR 005	Sock It Softly (with Bob Stackie)/LESTER STERLING, SIR COLLINS & BAND: Three Wise Men	30
68	Collins Downbeat CR 0011	Collins And The Boys/Bob Stackie In Soho (both with Bob Stackie)	30
68	Collins Downbeat CR 0017	Soul Feelings/SIR COLLINS: Hello Stella	30
69	Duke DU 46	Black Panther/I Want To Be Loved	8
69	Duke DU 47	Black Diamonds (with Diamonds)/DIAMONDS: I Remember	8
69	Duke DU 55	Brother Moses/Funny Familiar Feeling (both with Earthquakes)	8

(see also Bob Stackie, Earthquakes, Collins Band, Owen Gray)

SIR D's GROUP

| 61 | Blue Beat BB 66 | Hey Diddle Diddle (with K. Brown)/Pocket Money (with Mossman & Zeddze) | 15 |

(see also Kent Brown & Rainbows)

SIR DOUGLAS QUINTET

65	London HLU 9964	She's About A Mover/We'll Take Our Last Walk Tonight	8
65	London HLU 9982	The Tracker/Blue Norther	8
65	London HLU 10001	The Story Of John Hardy/In Time	7
66	London HLU 10019	The Rains Came/Bacon Fat	7
69	London HLU 10248	She's About A Mover/The Rains Came	5
69	Mercury MF 1079	Mendocino/I Wanna Be Your Mama Again	7
69	Mercury MF 1129	Dynamite Woman/Too Many Dociled Minds	7
65	London RE-U 1441	SHE'S ABOUT A MOVER (EP, unissued)	
65	London HA-U 8311	THE SIR DOUGLAS QUINTET (LP)	70
69	Mercury SMCL 20160	MENDOCINO (LP)	20
69	Mercury SMCL 20186	TOGETHER AFTER FIVE (LP)	18

(see also Doug Sahm)

SIREN

71	Dandelion DAN 7002	Strange Locomotion/I'm All Aching (label also lists K 19004)	6
69	Dandelion 63755	SIREN (LP)	20
71	Dandelion DAN 8001	STRANGE LOCOMOTION (LP, gatefold sleeve, label also lists K 49001)	20

(see also Kevin Coyne, Clague)

SIR GIBBS

| 68 | Amalgamated AMG 822 | People Grudgeful/Pan Ya Machet (both sides actually by Pioneers) | 10 |

SIR HARRY

71	Duke DU 127	Last Call/ORGAN D: Hot Organ	6
72	Duke DU 136	Apples To Apples/DRUM BEAT ALL STARS: Good Life	6
72	Bullet BU 519	Mr. Parker's Daughter/U.ROY: On Top Of The Peak	6
72	Downtown DT 493	Meet The Boss/Musical Light	8
73	Downtown DT 504	Apollo 17 (& Cables)/Uptown Rock	8

(see also Barbara Jones)

SIR HENRY (& HIS BUTLERS)

68	Columbia DB 8351	Camp/Pretty Style (as Sir Henry & His Butlers)	12
68	Columbia DB 8497	The Rolo Sensation (Camp)/Pretty Style (reissue, as Sir Henry & His Butlers)	5
70	Columbia DB 8740	Annie Got A Date/Like A Rose	5

SIR HORATIO

| 82 | Rock Steady/666 Mix 1T | Abracadubra/Sommadub (12", plain sleeve) | 15 |

(see also A Certain Ratio)

SIR LORD COMIC

| 67 | Doctor Bird DB 1070 | The Great Wuga Wuga (with Cowboys)/THREE TOPS: Feel So Lonesome | 20 |
| 70 | Pressure Beat PR 5507 | Jack Of My Trade/CYNTHIA RICHARDS: United We Stand | 20 |

(see also Lord Comic)

SIR WASHINGTON

| 69 | Star ST 1 | Apollo 12/When You Kiss Me | 6 |
| 70 | Big Chief BC 100 | Apollo 13/Space | 6 |

SIR WILLIAM

| 67 | Stateside SS 583 | Shakespeare's Shrew/Patsy | 4 |

SISTER

| 70 | Camel CA 55 | Feel It/MAYTONES: Serious | 6 |
| 73 | Camel CA 106 | Every Day Is The Same Kind Of Thing/Sweat Of Your Brow | 5 |

(see also Paulette & Gee, Ebony Sisters)

SISTERHOOD

| 86 | Merciful Release SIS 010 | Giving Ground (RSV)/Giving Ground (AV) (p/s) | 6 |

(see also Sisters Of Mercy, James Ray & Performance)

SISTER SLEDGE

73	Atlantic K 10375	Mama Never Told Me/Neither One Of Us	5
75	Atlantic K 10551	Love Don't You Go Through No Changes On Me/Don't You Miss Me	5
75	Atlantic K 10683	Love Has Found Me/Love Ain't Easy	5
77	Cotillion K 10876	Cream Of The Crop/Love Ain't Easy	5

SISTERS LOVE

70	A&M AMS 772	Forget It, I've Got It/Eye To Eye	5
70	A&M AMS 808	The Bigger Your Love/Piece Of My Heart	6
72	Tamla Motown TMG 828	Mr. Fix It Man/You've Got To Make Your Choice	5
73	Mowest MW 3009	I'm Learning To Trust My Man/Try It You'll Like It	6
75	Tamla Motown TMG 1002	I'm Learning To Trust My Man/Try It You'll Like It (reissue)	5

SISTERS OF MERCY

80	Merciful Release MR 7	The Damage Done/Watch/Home Of The Hitmen (p/s, 1,000 only; beware of counterfeits without 'MR 7' matrix number)	100
82	CNT CNT 002	Body Electric/Adrenochrome (p/s)	60
82	Merciful Release MR 015	Alice/Floorshow (white background p/s)	25
83	Merciful Release MR 019	Anaconda/Phantom (p/s)	5

MINT VALUE £

83	Merciful Release MR 021	Alice/Floorshow/1969/Phantom (12", p/s)	7
83	Merciful Release MR 023	THE REPTILE HOUSE (12" EP, with lyric sheet)	10
83	Merciful Release MR 027	Temple Of Love/Heartland (p/s)	4
83	Merciful Release MRX 027	Temple Of Love (Extended)/Heartland/Gimme Shelter (12", without bardcode on p/s)	7
84	Merciful Release MR 029	Body And Soul/Train (p/s)	8
84	Merciful Release MR 029T	Body And Soul/Body Electric/Train/Afterhours (12", p/s)	10
84	Merciful Release/WEA	ALICE/TEMPLE OF LOVE/REPTILE HOUSE/BODY AND SOUL (4 x 12" box set, promo only)	150
84	Merciful Release MR 033	Walk Away/Poison Door (p/s, some with flexidisc "Long Train" [SAM 218])	15/8
84	Merciful Release MR 033T	Walk Away/Poison Door/On The Wire (12", p/s, with flexi "Long Train")	15/8
85	Merciful Release MR 335	No Time To Cry/Blood Money (p/s)	8
85	Merciful Release MR 035T	No Time To Cry/Blood Money/Bury Me Deep (12", p/s)	10
87	Merciful Release MR 39	This Corrosion/Torch (p/s, with 3 postcards, 5,000 only)	10
87	Merciful Release MR 39C	This Corrosion/Torch/Colours (cassette)	4
87	Merciful Release MR 39CD	This Corrosion (11.15)/Torch/Colours (CD, black disc, gatefold card sleeve with gauze inner, some without 'WEA' logo on back sleeve)	12
88	Merciful Release MR 43C	Dominion/Untitled/Sandstorm/Ozymandias (cassette in presentation box)	6
88	Merciful Release MR 43TB	Dominion (Extended)/Untitled/Sandstorm/Emma (12", box set with poster)	8
88	Merciful Release MR 43CD	Dominion (Extended)/Untitled/Sandstorm/Ozymandias (3" CD, black disc with adaptor, 5" case)	8
88	Merciful Release MR 44CD	Lucretia My Reflection (Extended 9.52)/Long Train (1984) (3" CD, with adaptor, 5" case)	8
90	Merciful Release MR 47CD	More/More (Extended)/You Could Be The One (CD)	8
90	Merciful Release MR 47CDX	More/More (Extended)/You Could Be The One (CD, 12" foldout p/s)	10
90	Merciful Release MR 51TX	Doctor Jeep (Extended)/Burn (live)/Amphetamine Logic (live) (12", p/s, 6,000 only)	8
92	Merciful Release MR 53CDX	Temple Of Love (1992) (Touched By The Hand Of Ofra Haza)/I Was Wrong (American Fade)/Vision Thing (Canadian Club Remix)/When You Don't See Me (German Release) (CD, box set with 4 postcards)	7
85	Merciful Release MR 337L	FIRST AND LAST AND ALWAYS (LP, gatefold sleeve, beware of copies with faked autographs!)	15
87	Merciful Release MR 441L	FLOODLAND (LP, numbered sleeve with lyric sheet)	10

(see also Mission, Sisterhood, James Ray & Performance, Ghost Dance, Fur Bible, Dead Or Alive)

SITUATION
66	CBS 202392	Situation Now/Time	8

SIVUCA
74	Vanguard VSD 79337	SIVUCA (LP)	10

SIX OF ONE
64	Mercury MF 812	He's The One You Love/I Love My Little Girl	6

SIXPENCE
67	London HLJ 10124	You're The Love/What To Do	4

SIX TEENS
56	London HLU 8345	A Casual Look/Teen Age Promise	400
56	London HLU 8345	A Casual Look/Teen Age Promise (78)	70

60 FOOT DOLLS
94	Townhill TIDY 001	Happy Shopper/London Breeds (p/s)	12
95	Rough Trade R 3797	White Knuckle Ride/No. 1 Pure Alcohol (p/s, double-A-side, numbered, 500 clear vinyl, 500 white vinyl)	8
95	Indolent DOLLS 001	Pig Valentine/British Racing Green (p/s, pink vinyl)	4
96	Indolent DOLLS 002	Stay/The Main Dee Run (p/s, swirly green vinyl, numbered, 2,000 only)	5

64 SPOONS
78	Bushbaby	LADIES DON'T HAVE WILLIES (EP)	5

SIZE SEVEN GROUP
65	Mercury MF 845	Where Do We Go From Here/Till I Die	8
65	Mercury MF 854	In Time/Walking Proud	6
65	Mercury MF 896	It's Got To Be Love/I Met Her In The Rain	6

SKA CHAMPIONS
65	Blue Beat BB 305	My Tears/Yesterday's Dreams	15

SKA CITY ROCKERS
80	Inferno BEAT 1	Time Is Tight/Roadrunner/You Don't Know Like I Know (p/s)	6
80	Inferno BEAT 1	Time Is Tight/Roadrunner/You Don't Know Like I Know (12", p/s)	10

SKA-DOWS
80	Cheapskate CHEAP 1	Apache/The Tune That Time Forgot (p/s)	6
80	Cheapskate CHEAP 4	Telstar/Yes Yes Yes (p/s)	7
81	Cheapskate CHEAP 25	Yes Yes Yes/Twice (p/s)	7
81	Penthouse PENT 7	Ska's On 45/Rhapsody In Buh (plain stickered sleeve)	4
81	Penthouse PENT 127	Ska's On 45/The Ska-Dows Live (Let's Twist Again/Everybody Knows It's Shocking/Aye-Ho — Kinky Reggae (12", p/s)	10
81	Cheapskate CHEAP 36	Ska's On 45/Rhapsody In Buh (p/s, reissue)	6
81	Cheapskate CHEAPT 36	Ska's On 45/The Ska-Dows Live (Let's Twist Again/Everybody Knows It's Shocking/Aye-Ho — Kinky Reggae (12", p/s, reissue)	8
82	Cheapskate CHEAP 41	We Gotta Get Out Of This Place/Ska'd For Life (no p/s)	5
82	Cheapskate SKATE 3	SKA'D FOR LIFE (LP)	15

SKA KINGS
64	Atlantic AT 4003	Jamaica Ska (actually by Keith Lynn & Ken Lazarus, & Byron Lee/Dragonaires)/Oil In My Lamp (actually by Eric Morris with Byron Lee & Dragonaires)	12
65	Parlophone R 5338	Bimbo/Ska'ville	10

SKATALITES (Jamaica)
65	Island WI 161	Trip To Mars/DOTTIE & BONNIE: Bunch Of Roses	25

MINT VALUE £

65	Island WI 164	Good News/OWEN & LEON: The Fits Is On Me	18
65	Island WI 168	Guns Of Navarone (actually by Roland Alphonso & Studio One Orchestra)/ Marcus Garvey (actually "Where's Marcus Garvey" by Bongoman Byfield)	8
65	Island WI 175	Dragon Weapon/DESMOND DEKKER & FOUR ACES: It Was Only A Dream	20
65	Island WI 191	Dr. Kildare/Sucu Sucu	18
65	Island WI 207	Ball O' Fire/LINVAL SPENCER: Can't Go On	18
65	Island WI 226	Dick Tracy/RITA & SOULETTES: One More Chance	20
65	Island WI 228	Beardman Ska/BONNIE & RITA: Bless You	18
65	Island WI 244	Lucky Seven/JUSTIN HINDS & DOMINOES: Never Too Young	18
66	Island WI 260	Independent Anniversary Ska (I Should Have Known Better)/ WAILERS: Jumbie Jamboree	70
65	Ska Beat JB 177	Latin Goes Ska/LORD TANAMO: Night Food Ska	30
65	Ska Beat JB 178	Silver Dollar/My Business	18
65	Ska Beat JB 182	Street Corner/DREAMLETS: Really Now	18
65	Ska Beat JB 206	Timothy/KING SCRATCH & DYNAMITES: Gumma	35
73	Trojan Maxi TRM 9008	Guns Of Navarone/Bonanza Ska/Napolean Solo	5
67	Studio One SOL 9006	SKA AUTHENTIC (LP)	90

(see also Justin Hinds, Deltas, Four Aces, Maytals, Jackie Opel, Joe White, Jackie Mittoo)

SKATALITES (U.K.)

| 68 | Decca F 12743 | Don't Knock It/I Know | 6 |
| 69 | Spark SRL 1034 | 'Cos You're The One I Love/Please Let Me Hide | 8 |

SKAVENGERS

| 80 | Identity Discs ID 001 | Party Girls/Go To Pieces/Happy (no p/s) | 5 |

SK'BOO

| 70s | Cuecumber CUE 1001 | It's A Hard Road/Music Is Life/Talking Pictures/God's Peace In Mind | 4 |

(see also Them)

BOBBY SKEL

| 64 | London HLU 9942 | Kiss And Run/Say It Now | 10 |

SKELETAL FAMILY

83	Luggage RRP 00724	Trees/Just A Friend (foldout p/s)	12
83	Red Rhino RED 36	The Night/Waiting Here (p/s)	8
84	Red Rhino RED 41	She Cries Alone/The Wind Blows (p/s)	5
84	Red Rhino RED 43	So Sure/Batman (p/s)	4
85	Red Rhino RED 54	Promised Land/Stand By Me (p/s)	4

(see also Ghost Dance)

SKELETON CREW

| 87 | B# BS 1 | BOOGIE-WOOGIE, SKIFFLE & BLUES (12" EP, p/s) | 15 |
| 88 | B# BS 2 | House Of The Rising Sun/Hurricane Janine (white label promo only) | 15 |

(see also King Earl Boogie Band, Manfred Mann's Earth Band)

PETER SKELLERN

| 72 | Decca SKL 5151 | PETER SKELLERN (LP) | 12 |
| 74 | Decca SKL 5178 | NOT WITHOUT A FRIEND (LP) | 12 |

(see also Harlan County)

SKEPTIX

82	Zenon SKEP 001	Routine Machine/Curfew (p/s)	5
83	Zenon SKEP 002	Scarred For Life/Born To Lose/Peaceforce (p/s)	5
83	Zenon SKEP 003	RETURN TO HELL (EP)	5

SKERNE

| 81 | Guardian GRC 81 | BETTER LATE THAN NEVER (LP, private pressing) | 15 |

FATHER SKETTO

| 73 | Pama PM 877 | Big Nine/RECO'S GROUP: Old Lady | 6 |

(see also Sketto Rich, Ruddy & Sketto)

SKIDDY & DETROIT

| 72 | Grape GR 3030 | The Exile Song/BUNNY GALE: In The Burning Sun Joh-Ho | 6 |

ALAN SKIDMORE (QUINTET)

| 69 | Deram Nova SDN 11 | ONCE UPON A TIME (LP) | 100 |
| 71 | Philips 6308 041 | T.C.B. (LP) | 120 |

(see also John Mayall's Bluesbreakers, Brian Bennett, Centipede)

JIMMY SKIDMORE

| 72 | DJM DJSL 026 | SKID MARKS (LP) | 50 |

SKID ROW (Ireland)

70	CBS 4893	Sandie's Gone (Parts 1 & 2)	15
71	CBS 7181	Night Of The Warm Witch/Mr. Deluxe	10
70	CBS 63965	SKID (LP, orange label, red & blue sleeve)	50
71	CBS 64411	34 HOURS (LP, orange label)	45

(see also Gary Moore, Thin Lizzy, Peggy's Leg, UFO)

SKID ROW (U.S.)

89	Atlantic A 8935W	Youth Gone Wild/Sweet Little Sister (poster p/s)	6
89	Atlantic A 8935B	Youth Gone Wild/Sweet Little Sister (box set)	6
89	Atlantic A 8935P	Youth Gone Wild/Rattlesnake Shake (Live) (guitar-shaped picture disc)	10
89	Atlantic A 8935T	Youth Gone Wild/Sweet Little Sister/Makin' A Mess (Live) (12", p/s)	8
90	Atlantic A 8886X	I Remember You/Makin' A Mess (p/s, with tattoo pack)	5
90	Atlantic A 8886TE	I Remember You/Makin' A Mess (10", clear vinyl)	6
90	Atlantic A 8886TW	I Remember You/Makin' A Mess (12", poster p/s)	8
90	Atlantic A 8886CD	I Remember You/Makin' A Mess/Big Guns (Live) (CD)	8
90	Atlantic A 8883P	18 And Life/Midnight Tornado (shaped picture disc)	8
91	Atlantic A 7673SP	Monkey Business/Slave To The Grind (die-cut picture disc)	6
91	Atlantic A 7603TX	Slave To The Grind/C'mon And Love Me/Creepshow/Beggars Day (12", "rubberised" p/s)	10

SKIDS

78	No Bad NB 1	Charles/Reasons/Test Tube Babies (p/s)	6
78	Virgin VS 227	Sweet Suburbia/Open Sound (p/s, white vinyl)	5
78	Virgin VS 232	The Saints Are Coming/Of One Skin (p/s)	4
78	Virgin VS 232-12	WIDE OPEN (12" EP, red vinyl)	7
79	Virgin VS 241	Into The Valley/TV Stars (p/s, white vinyl)	4
79	Virgin VS 262	Masquerade/Out Of Town//Another Emotion/Aftermath Dub (double pack)	5
79	Virgin VS 306	Working For The Yankee Dollar/Vanguard's Crusade//All The Young Dudes/ Hymns From A Haunted Ballroom (double pack)	5
80	Virgin VS 373	Goodbye Civilian/Monkey McGuire Meets Specky Potter Behind The Lochore Institute (poster p/s in poly bag)	4
80	Virgin VSP 373	Goodbye Civilian/Monkey McGuire Meets Specky Potter Behind The Lochore Institute (picture disc)	4
81	Virgin VSK 101	Woman In Winter/Working For The Yankee Dollar (p/s, with comic booklet)	4
92	Virgin VSCDT 1411	THE SKIDS VS THE RUTS EP (EP, shared with Ruts)	10
79	Smash Hits HIT 002	The Olympian/XTC: Ten Feet Tall (33rpm red flexi with *Smash Hits* mag)	6/4
79	Virgin V 2116	SCARED TO DANCE (LP, blue vinyl, withdrawn)	40
79	Virgin V 2138	DAYS IN EUROPA (LP, with insert, 1st pressing with withdrawn cover featuring German 'gothic' lettering & 1936 Olympics picture)	10
80	Virgin V 2174	THE ABSOLUTE GAME (LP, with free LP "Strength Through Joy" [VDJ 33])	10

(see also Big Country)

BJORN SKIFS

78	EMI EMI 2785	When The Night Comes/Don't Stop Now	6
81	EMI EMI 5172	Haunted By A Dream/Fangad I En Drom	8

SKILLETS

70	Pantonic PAN 6303	BOTH SIDES NOW (LP)	15

SKIN ALLEY

70	CBS 5045	Tell Me/Better Be Blind	10
72	Transatlantic BIG 506	You Got Me Danglin'/Skin Valley Serenade	8
72	Transatlantic BIG 511	In The Midnight Hour/Broken Eggs	8
69	CBS 63847	SKIN ALLEY (LP)	35
70	CBS 64140	TO PAGHAM AND BEYOND (LP)	25
72	Transatlantic TRA 260	TWO QUID DEAL (LP, with inner sleeve & poster)	30
73	Transatlantic TRA 273	SKIN TIGHT (LP)	20

SKIN DEEP

85	Enemy ENEMY 1	FOOTBALL VIOLENCE (EP)	40

SKIN, FLESH & BONES

74	Pyramid PYR 7014	Butter Te Fish/Bammie And Fish	4

(see also Vincent Gordon, Cynthia Richards)

JIMMIE SKINNER

59	Mercury AMT 1030	Walkin' My Blues Away/Dark Hollow	6
59	Mercury AMT 1030	Walkin' My Blues Away/Dark Hollow (78)	30
59	Mercury AMT 1062	John Wesley Hardin/Misery Loves Company	6
60	Mercury AMT 1088	Riverboat Gambler/Married To A Friend	5
60	Mercury AMT 1117	Reasons To Live/I'm A Lot More Lonesome Now	5
64	London RE-B 1421	KENTUCKY COLONEL VOL. 1 (EP)	20
64	London RE-B 1422	KENTUCKY COLONEL VOL. 2 (EP)	20
64	London RE-B 1423	KENTUCKY COLONEL VOL. 3 (EP)	20

JIMMIE SKINNER/GEORGE JONES

59	Mercury ZEP 10012	COUNTRY AND WESTERN (EP, 2 tracks each)	40

J. SCOTT SKINNER

75	Topic 12T 280	THE STRATHSPEY KING (LP)	10

SKI PATROL

80	Clever Metal VIN 1	Everything Is Temporary/Silent Screams (p/s)	4
80	Malicious Damage MD 2	Agent Orange/Driving (p/s, with insert)	8
81	Malicious Damage MD 3	Cut/Faith In Transistion (p/s)	4

(see also Wall)

SKIP & FLIP

59	Top Rank JAR 156	It Was I/Lunch Hour	8
59	Top Rank JAR 156	It Was I/Lunch Hour (78)	25
59	Top Rank JAR 248	Fancy Nancy/It Could Be	7
60	Top Rank JAR 358	Cherry Pie/(I'll Quit) Cryin' Over You	8

(see also Gary Paxton, Skip Battin, Hollywood Argyles)

SKIP BIFFERTY

67	RCA Victor RCA 1621	On Love/Cover Girl	15
67	RCA Victor RCA 1648	Happy Land/Reason To Live	10
68	RCA Victor RCA 1720	Man In Black/Mr. Money Man	20
68	RCA Victor RD/SF 7941	SKIP BIFFERTY (LP, black label, later orange)	75/60

(see also Chosen Few, Heavy Jelly, Griffin, Graham Bell, Arc, Bell & Arc, Every Which Way, Loving Awareness)

SKITZO

87	Nervous NERD 028	SKITZO MANIA (LP)	10

SKREWDRIVER

77	Chiswick S 11	You're So Dumb/Better Off Crazy (orange or green p/s)	15
77	Chiswick NS 18	Anti-Social/19th Nervous Breakdown (p/s)	10
78	Chiswick NS 28	Streetfight/Unbeliever (unissued, white label acetates only)	100+
80	TJM TJM 4	Built Up, Knocked Down/A Case Of Pride/Breakout (p/s)	20
82	Skrewdriver SKREW 1T	BACK WITH A BANG (12", p/s)	35
83	White Noise WN 1	White Power/Smash The I.R.A./Shove The Dove (p/s)	35
83	White Noise WN 2	Voice Of Britain/Sick Society (p/s)	35
77	Chiswick CH 3	ALL SKREWED UP (mini-LP, 12-track, 45rpm, 3 different colour sleeves)	25
77	Chiswick WIK 3	ALL SKREWED UP (LP, 15-track, 33rpm, unissued in U.K.; German-only)	

MINT VALUE £

SKROTEEZ
82	Skroteez SPILL 1	OVERSPILL (EP)..	5

SKULLFLOWER
86	Broken Flag BF V9	BIRTHDEATH (12" EP)..	30
89	Shock SX 001	(I Live) In The Bottomless Pit/Bo Diddley's Shitpump (foldaround p/s in poly bag, 500 only, 75 copies in 'burns victim' sleeve)	20/12
90	Toe Jam	Rotten Sun/Spook Rise (p/s, numbered, 500 only)	8
92	Dying Artefact DE 002	Bad Alchemy/Blues For H.M. (p/s in poly bag, numbered, 500 only)	8
94	Freak Records RR 001	White Fang # 2/Glassy Essence (wraparound sleeve, stamped label)...........	7
89	Shock SX 008	XAMAN (LP)	12
89	Broken Flag BFV 10	FORM DESTROYER (LP)	20

(see also Ramleh)

SKULLS
89	Snake Skin SS 001	Graveyard Signal/Idols And Dolls (p/s, 300 only)	10

SKULLSNAPS
73	GSF GSZ 7	My Hang Up Is You/It's A New Day................................	12

SKUNKS
78	Eel Pie EPS 001	Good From The Bad/Back Street Fightin' (2,000 only, die-cut 'swirl' sleeve)	6

(see also Craze, Hard Corps)

SKY
68	United Artists UP 2234	Air-O-Plane Ride/Weather Forecast..............................	4
69	Decca F 12971	On Our Way/The Singer Is Singing His Song	4

SKY
71	RCA RCA 2070	Goodie Two Shoes/Make It On Time (as U.S. Sky)	4
71	RCA SF 8168	DON'T HOLD BACK (LP, as U.S. Sky)	10

(see also Knack)

PATRICK SKY
65	Vanguard VSD 79179	PATRICK SKY (LP)	20
70	Vanguard SVRL 19054	A HARVEST OF GENTLE CLANG (LP)	20

SKYBIRD
74	Holyground HGS 118	SUMMER OF '73 (LP, 250 copies only)	50

SKY HIGH
80	Circus CIRC 5	Ghettos Of Your Own Kind/Passing By/Moving To The Music/Red Light (p/s).....	5

SKYLARK
73	Capitol CL 15764	Wildflower/Writing On the Wall	5
72	Capitol E-ST 11048	SKYLARK (LP)	10

SKYLINERS
59	London HLB 8829	Since I Don't Have You/One Night, One Night	150
59	London HLB 8829	Since I Don't Have You/One Night, One Night (78)	100
59	London HLU 8924	This I Swear/Tomorrow	60
59	London HLU 8924	This I Swear/Tomorrow (78)...................................	100
59	London HLU 8971	It Happened Today/Lonely Way	30
59	London HLU 8971	It Happened Today/Lonely Way (78).............................	120
60	Polydor NH 66951	Pennies From Heaven/I'll Be Seeing You.........................	12
61	Pye International 7N 25091	I'll Close My Eyes/The Door Is Still Open	12

SKYSOUNDS
66	Anglo TPMA 101/102	Two Timer/No Matter Where I Wander (private pressing)	4

FREDDIE SLACK (& Orchestra)
50	Capitol 13340	Whatever Happened To Ol' Jack?/Is I Gotta Practice, Ma? (78)	8
50	Capitol 13379	Be-Bop Boogie/On The Road To Mandolin (78).....................	8
51	Capitol LC 6529	FREDDIE SLACK'S BOOGIE WOOGIE (10" LP).....................	30

(see also Ella Mae Morse & Freddie Slack)

SLACK ALICE
74	Philips 6308 214	SLACK ALICE (LP)...	12

(see also Sandra Alfred, Sandra Barry)

SLADE
SINGLES
69	Fontana TF 1056	Wild Winds Are Blowing/One Way Hotel (credited to The Slade)..............	60
70	Fontana TF 1079	Shape Of Things To Come/C'mon C'mon	60
70	Polydor 2058 054	Know Who You Are/Dapple Rose................................	60
71	Polydor 2058 112	Get Down With It/Do You Want Me/The Gospel According To Rasputin (initially with writing credit: Holder/Hill/Lea/Powell/Penniman; some copies repressed as "Get Down And Get With It", credited to Bobby Marchant)	8
74	Polydor 2058 453	Everyday/Good Time Gals (mispressed with Hollies' "The Air That I Breathe" on A-side)	6
74	Polydor 2058 522	Far Far Away/O.K. Yesterday Was Yesterday (p/s)	5
75	Polydor 2058 547	How Does It Feel?/So Far So Good (p/s)........................	6
75	Polydor 2058 585	Thanks For The Memory (Wham Bam Thank You Mam)/ Raining In My Champagne.................................	5
75	Polydor 2058 663	In For A Penny/Can You Just Imagine (p/s)......................	8
76	Polydor 2058 690	Let's Call It Quits/When The Chips Are Down	5
76	Polydor 2058 716	Nobody's Fool/L.A. Jinx	6
77	Barn 2014 105	Gypsy Roadhog/Forest Full Of Needles	5
77	Barn 2014 106	Burning In The Heat Of Love/Ready Steady Kids	15
77	Barn 2014 114	My Baby Left Me; That's Alright/O.H.M.S. (p/s)	10
78	Barn 2014 121	Give Us A Goal/Daddio	6
78	Barn 2014 127	Rock'n'Roll Bolero/It's Alright By Me	15

MINT VALUE £

79	Barn BARN 002	Ginny Ginny/Dizzy Mama (no p/s, yellow vinyl only, some with sticker)	12/10
79	Barn BARN 010	Sign Of The Times/Not Tonight Josephine (no p/s)	15
79	Barn BARN 011	Okey Cokey/My Baby's Got It (no p/s)	6
80	RSO RSO 051	Okey Cokey/My Baby's Got It (withdrawn reissue, existence unconfirmed)	50
80	S.O.T.B. SUPER 45 3	SIX OF THE BEST — NIGHT STARVATION (12" EP, die-cut sleeve)	15
80	Cheapskate CHEAP 5	ALIVE AT READING '80 (EP, die-cut sleeve)	7
80	Cheapskate CHEAP 11	Merry Xmas Everybody/Okey Cokey/Get Down And Get With It (as Slade & Reading Choir, some in die-cut p/s)	8/5
80	Polydor 2058 422	Merry Xmas Everybody/Don't Blame Me (reissue, green background, 'holly leaf' design, colour group photo p/s)	5
81	Cheapskate CHEAP 16	We'll Bring The House Down/Hold On To Your Hats (p/s)	7
81	Cheapskate CHEAP 21	Wheels Ain't Comin' Down/Not Tonight Josephine (p/s)	5
81	Cheapskate CHEAP 24	Knuckle Sandwich Nancy/I'm Mad (p/s)	7
81	RCA RCA 124	Lock Up Your Daughters/Sign Of The Times (no p/s)	5
81	Polydor POSP 399	CUM ON FEEL THE NOIZE (EP)	6
81	Polydor POSPX 399	CUM ON FEEL THE NOIZE (Cum On Feel The Noize/Coz I Luv You/ Tak Me Bak 'Ome/Gudbuy T'Jane) (12" EP, p/s)	10
82	RCA RCA 191	Ruby Red/Funk Punk And Junk (p/s)	10
82	RCA RCAD 191	Ruby Red/Funk Punk And Junk//Rock And Roll Preacher (live)/ Take Me Bak 'Ome (live) (double pack, gatefold p/s)	5
82	RCA RCA 291	(And Now The Waltz) C'est La Vie/Merry Xmas Everybody (p/s)	5
82	Speed SPEED 201	Okey Cokey/Get Down And Get With It (no p/s)	8
82	Speed SPEEDP 201	Okey Cokey/Get Down And Get With It (picture disc)	5
83	RCA RCA 373	My Oh My/Merry Xmas Everybody (live)/Keep Your Hands Off My Power Supply (3-track edition, p/s)	5
83	RCA RCA 373	My Oh My/Merry Xmas Everybody (live)/Keep Your Hands Off My Power Supply (12", p/s)	8
84	RCA RCAT 455	All Join Hands/My Oh My/Here's To... (The New Year)/ Merry Xmas (Live & Kickin') (12", stickered p/s)	8
85	RCA RCA 475	Seven Year Bitch/Leave Them Girls Alone (p/s)	5
85	RCA RCAT 475	Seven Year Bitch/Leave Them Girls Alone/ We'll Bring The House Down (live) (12", p/s)	8
85	RCA PB 40027	Myzterious Mizster Jones/Mama Nature Is A Rocker (p/s)	5
85	RCA PB 40027	Myzterious Mizster Jones/Mama Nature Is A Rocker (picture disc, PVC sleeve)	10
85	RCA PT 40028	Myzterious Mizster Jones (Extended Version)/Mama Nature Is A Rocker/ My Oh My (Piano And Vocal Version) (12", p/s)	8
85	RCA PB 40449/PB 40549	Do You Believe In Miracles/My Oh My (Swing Version)//Santa Claus Is Coming To Town/Auld Lang Syne/You'll Never Walk Alone (double pack, gatefold PVC sleeve, 2nd 45 without p/s)	12
85	RCA PT 40450D (PT 40450/PT 40550)	Do You Believe In Miracles/My Oh My (Swing Version)/Time To Rock/ Santa Claus Is Coming To Town/Auld Lang Syne/You'll Never Walk Alone (12", 'Slade Xmas' double pack, separate sleeves in gatefold PVC cover)	20
87	RCA PB 41137	Still The Same/Gotta Go Home (p/s)	5
87	RCA PB 41147D	Still The Same/Gotta Go Home//The Roaring Silence/Don't Talk To Me About Love (21st anniversary double pack, gatefold p/s)	10
87	RCA PT 41138	Still The Same/Gotta Go Home (12", p/s)	5
87	RCA PB 41271	That's What Friends Are For/Wild Wild Party (p/s)	5
87	RCA PT 41272	That's What Friends Are For/Hi Ho Silver Lining/Wild Wild Party/ Lock Up Your Daughters (live) (12", p/s)	8
87	Cheapskate BOYZ 1	You Boyz Make Big Noize/Boyz Instrumental (p/s, B-side plays U.S.A. Mix)	5
87	Cheapskate TBOYZ 1	You Boyz Make Big Noize (Noize Remix)/(Instrumental Boyz Mix)/ (The USA Mix) (12", p/s)	8
87	Cheapskate BOYZ 2	We Won't Give In/Ooh La La On LA (p/s)	5
88	Cheapskate BOYZ 3	Let's Dance (1988 Remix)/Standing On The Corner (p/s)	5
88	Cheapskate BOYZCD 3	Let's Dance (1988 Remix)/Far Far Away/How Does It Feel/ Standing On The Corner (3" CD, with adaptor, 5" case)	8
88	Counterpoint CDEP 12 C	How Does It Feel/Far Far Away//(WIZZARD: 2 tracks) (CD)	10
89	RCA PD 42637	My Oh My/Keep Your Hands Off My Power Supply/Run Runaway/ Two Track Stereo, One Track Mind (CD)	8
89	Cheapskate CD BOYZ 4	Merry Xmas Everybody/Don't Blame Me/Far Far Away (CD)	8
80s	Polydor 2058 422	Merry Xmas Everybody/Don't Blame Me (export p/s from various artist box set, green background, 4 individual photos)	25
80s	SLADE 1	An Interview With Slade (picture disc, 2,000 only, PVC sleeve)	10
91	Polydor PO 189	Universe/Red Hot/Merry Xmas Everybody (p/s)	5
91	Polydor POCS 189	Universe/Red Hot/Merry Xmas Everybody (cassette)	5
91	Polydor PZ 189	Universe/Red Hot/Gypsy Roadhog/Merry Xmas Everybody (12", stickered p/s)	8
91	Polydor PZCD 189	Universe/Red Hot/Merry Xmas Everybody (CD)	8

FLEXIDISCS

72	Polydor/Sound For Industry SFI 122	The Whole World's Going Crazee/MIKE HUGG: Bonnie Charlie (33rpm flexidisc free with *Music Scene* magazine)	18/8
73	Lyntone LYN 2645	Slade talk to *Melanie* readers (flexidisc with *Melanie* magazine)	15/8
74	Lyntone LYN 2797	Slade exclusive to all *19* readers (flexidisc with *19* magazine)	15/8
75	Lyntone LYN 3156/7	Far Far Away/Thanks For The Memory (flexidisc with Smith's Crisps offer)	8
75	Fan Club LYN 2645/2797	Slade talk to *Melanie* readers/Slade talk to *19* readers (flexidisc)	10
74	Polydor 2058 492	The Bangin' Man/She Did It To Me (export p/s)	25

PROMOS

72	Polydor 2814 008	Hear Me Calling/Get Down With It (33rpm sampler for "Slade Alive", 500 only)	100
75	Polydor 2058 585	Thanks For The Memory (with altered lyrics)/Raining In My Champagne (promo issue)	25
77	Barn 2014 105	Gypsy Roadhog/Forest Full Of Needles (mono, DJ copy)	25
80	S.O.T.B. SUPER 3	Night Starvation/When I'm Dancing I Ain't Fightin'	45
91	Polydor PO 180 DJ	Radio Wall Of Sound /Radio Wall Of Sound (no p/s)	15
91	Polydor PZ 180 DJ	Radio Wall Of Sound /Lay Your Love On The Line/Cum On Feel The Noize (12", no p/s)	15

SLADE

ALBUMS

70	Polydor 2383 026	PLAY IT LOUD (LP)	12
72	Polydor 2383 101	SLADE ALIVE (LP, gatefold sleeve)	12
73	Polydor 2442 119	SLADEST (LP)	12
73	Polydor 2383 261	OLD NEW BORROWED AND BLUE (LP, gatefold sleeve)	12
74	Polydor 2442 126	SLADE IN FLAME (LP, gatefold sleeve)	12
76	Polydor 2383 377	NOBODY'S FOOLS (LP, with lyric inner sleeve)	12
77	Barn 2314 103	WHATEVER HAPPENED TO SLADE (LP, with lyric sheet)	20
78	Barn 2314 106	SLADE ALIVE VOLUME 2 (LP)	20
79	Barn NARB 003	RETURN TO BASE (LP)	20
83	Action Replay REPLAY 1000	SLADE IN FLAME (LP, reissue)	40
85	RCA PD 70604	ROGUES GALLERY (CD)	12
87	RCA PD 71260	YOU BOYS MAKE BIG NOIZE (CD)	18

(see also Ambrose Slade, Steve Brett, 'N Betweens, Vendors, Dummies, Jimmy Lea, Gary Holton, China Dolls, Sue Scadding, Clout, Jimbo Featuring Bull, Gang Of Angels, Metal Gurus, Blessings In Disguise)

PRENTIS SLADE

61	Parlophone R 4850	I Can Tell/Looking For A Friend	7

SLAM CREEPERS

68	Olga OLE 009	Saturday/Hold It Baby	15
73	Sonet SON 2003	We Are Happy People/Yansbro Memories	5

SLAM SLAM

89	MCA DMCA 1346	Move (Dance All Night) (7" Version)/(Club Mix)/Dream On/ Move (Dance All Night) (Vocal Dub) (3" CD, card sleeve)	7
91	MCA MCA 10147	FREE YOUR FEELINGS (LP, with inner sleeve)	10
91	MCA CDMCA 10147	FREE YOUR FEELINGS (CD)	15

(see also Style Council)

SLANES

65	Blue Beat BB 300	It Takes Time/LIGES: Have Mercy Baby (B-side actually by Frank Cosmo)	15

IVOR SLANEY ORCHESTRA

61	HMV POP 943	The Sir Francis Drake Theme/Midsummer Madness	5
63	HMV POP 1210	The Carlos Theme/Chant Espana	5
64	HMV POP 1347	High Wire/Sacramento	10
66	Columbia DB 8020	Long Weekend/Eleven Up (as Slaney Strings)	5

SLAPP HAPPY

74	Virgin VS 105	Casablanca Moon/Slow Moon's Rose	6
75	Virgin VS 124	Johnny's Dead/Mr. Rainbow (p/s)	6
83	Half Cat HC 001	Everybody's Slimmin' (Even Men And Women!)/Blue-Eyed Villain (p/s)	5
72	Polydor 2310 204	SORT OF (LP, with insert)	120
74	Virgin V 2014	SLAPP HAPPY (LP)	10
74	Virgin V 2024	DESPERATE STRAIGHTS (LP, with Henry Cow)	10
86	Recommended RRS 5	SORT OF (LP, reissue)	15

(see also Henry Cow, Peter Blegvad, Anthony Moore, Art Bears)

FELIX SLATKIN ORCHESTRA

61	London HLG 9256	Sundowners (Theme)/Gaythers Gone	6

SLAUGHTER (& THE DOGS)

77	Rabid TOSH 101	Cranked Up Really High/The Bitch (p/s, blue, later cream plastic labels)	10
77	Rabid TOSH 101	Cranked Up Really High/The Bitch (p/s, repressings with b&w paper label)	10
77	Decca FR 13723	Where Have All The Boot Boys Gone/You're A Bore (paper label)	8

MINT VALUE £

77	Decca LF 13723	Where Have All The Boot Boys Gone/You're A Bore (12", p/s, 10,000 only)	12
77	Decca FR 13743	Dame To Blame/Johnny T (no p/s)	6
78	Decca FR 13758	Quick Joey Small/Come On Back (no p/s, with Mick Ronson)	6
79	TJM TJM 3	It's Alright/Edgar Allen Poe/Twist & Turn/UFO (12", p/s)	12
79	DJM DJS 10927	You're Ready Now/Runaway (p/s)	6
80	Decca FR	Where Have All The Boot Boys Gone/You're A Bore (reissue, p/s)	10
80	DJM DJS 10936	East Side Of Town/One By One (p/s, as Slaughter)	6
80	DJM DJS 10945	I'm The One/What's Wrong Boy? (live)/Hell In New York (p/s, as Slaughter)	5
82	Thrush THRUSH 1	HALF ALIVE (12" EP)	10
88	Damaged Goods FNARR 1	Where Have All The Boot Boys Gone/You're A Bore/Johnny T. (p/s, 1,000 only: 500 on green vinyl, 500 on red vinyl)	each 6
78	Decca SKL 5292	DO IT DOG STYLE (LP)	20
78	Rabid HAT 23	LIVE SLAUGHTER RABID DOGS (LP, plain white sleeve with large sticker)	12
80	DJM DJF 20566	BITE BACK (LP, as Slaughter)	10
89	Damaged Goods FNARRLP 2	DO IT DOG STYLE (LP, reissue, 1,000-only, multi-coloured vinyl, numbered, with 2 multi-coloured stickers)	10

(see also Studio Sweethearts, Ed Banger)

SLAUGHTER JOE

85	Creation CRE 019	I'll Follow You Down/Napalm Girl (foldaround p/s in poly bag)	5
87	Kaleidoscope S. KLSLP 003	ALL AROUND MY HOBBY HORSE'S HEAD (LP)	10

(see also Television Personalities, Missing Scientists)

SLAVE

84	Cotillion BT 6955	Just A Touch Of Love/Wait For Me (12")	10
77	Cotillion K 50358	SLAVE (LP)	10

MARTIN SLAVIN & HIS GANG

60	Oriole CB 1587	Rock-A-Charleston/The Charleston's Gonna Rock The Hop	7

(see also Martinas & His Music)

FRANK SLAY ORCHESTRA

62	Top Rank JAR 599	Flying Circle/Cincinnati	7

SLAYER

84	Roadrunner RR 2444 2	HAUNTING THE CHAPEL (12" EP)	10
87	London LON 133	Criminally Insane (Remix)/Aggressive Perfector ('cross' p/s, some on red vinyl with patch)	20/6
89	Roadrunner RR 2444 2	Haunting The Chapel/Chemical Warfare/Captor Of Sin (CD, reissue)	8
87	Enigma 720151	LIVE UNDEAD (LP, picture disc)	12
87	London LONPP 34	REIGN IN BLOOD (LP, picture disc)	12

JAKE SLAZENGER

95	Clear CLR 410	MAKE A RACKET (2-LP)	15

F. SLEDGE

67	Blue Beat BB 386	Red Eye Girl/Try To Love Again (actually by "Go On Girl"/"Giving You A Try Girl" by Freddie McKay & Buster's Group)	20

PERCY SLEDGE

66	Atlantic 584 001	When A Man Loves A Woman/Love Me Like You Mean It	6
66	Atlantic 584 034	Warm And Tender Love/Sugar Puddin'	6
66	Atlantic 584 055	Heart Of A Child/My Adorable One	7
67	Atlantic 584 071	It Tears Me Up/Oh, How Happy	6
67	Atlantic 584 080	Baby, Help Me/You've Lost That Something Wonderful	7
67	Atlantic 584 108	Out Of Left Field/It Can't Be Stopped	6
67	Atlantic 584 140	Pledging My Love/You Don't Miss Your Water	6
68	Atlantic 584 177	Take Time To Know Her/It's All Wrong But It's Alright	6
68	Atlantic 584 225	Come Softly To Me/You're All Around Me	5
69	Atlantic 584 264	Any Day Now/The Angels Listened In	6
69	Atlantic 584 286	Kind Woman/Woman Of The Night	5
69	Atlantic 584 300	True Love Travels On A Gravel Road/Faithful And True	5
72	Atlantic K 10144	Rainbow Road/Standing on The Mountain	5
72	Atlantic K 10165	Baby, Help Me/Warm And Tender Love/Take Time To Know Her	5
74	Capricorn 2089 009	I'll Be Your Everything/Walkin' In The Sun	5
67	Atlantic 587/588 048	WARM AND TENDER SOUL (LP)	25
67	Atlantic 587/588 081	THE PERCY SLEDGE WAY (LP)	20
68	Atlantic 587/588 105	WHEN A MAN LOVES A WOMAN (LP)	20
69	Atlantic 587/588 153	THE BEST OF PERCY SLEDGE (LP)	15

SLEDGEHAMMER

79	Slammer SRTS79CUS 395	Sledgehammer/Feel Good (no p/s)	12
80	Slammer CELL 2	Living In Dreams/Fantasia (p/s)	10
80s	Slammer MRSB 2	In The Middle Of The Night (no p/s)	10
80	Valiant STRONG 1	Sledgehammer/Feel Good (p/s, reissue)	8
80	Valiant ROUND 2	Sledgehammer/Feel Good (p/s, 2nd reissue)	6
85	Illuminated ILL 33	In The Queue/Oxford City (shaped picture disc)	12
85	Illuminated JAMS 32	BLOOD ON THEIR HANDS (LP)	30

SLEEPWALKERS

59	Parlophone R 4580	Sleep Walk/Golden Mile	12

SLEEPY

68	CBS 3592	Love's Immortal Fire/Is It Really The Same	20
68	CBS 3838	Rosie Can't Fly/Mrs. Bailey's Barbecue And Grill	20

(see also Grapefruit, Fynn McCool)

SLENDER PLENTY

67	Polydor BM 56189	Silver Tree Top School For Boys/I've Lost A Friend And Found A Lover	25

SLENDER THREAD

80	Rock MHMS 193	I See The Light (no p/s)	50

MINT VALUE £

JIMI SLEVIN
82   Claddagh CCF 7   FREEFLIGHT (LP). 25
(see also Peggy's Leg)

GRACE SLICK
74   Grunt BFL1 0347   MANHOLE (LP, with booklet) 10
(see also Jefferson Airplane, Jefferson Starship, Paul Kantner, Great Society)

RICKY SLICK
72   Dynamic DYN 449   Family Man/Family Man — Version 6

SLICKERS
68   Blue Cat BS 133   Wala Wala/LESTER STERLING: Super Special 12
68   Blue Cat BS 134   Nana (actually by George Dekker)/MARTIN RILEY:
                           I May Never See My Baby Anymore. 12
69   Blue Cat BS 154   Frying Pan/RARFIELD WILLIAMS: Code It 8
69   Amalgamated AMG 852 Man Beware/Matty Matty 10
69   Amalgamated AMG 866 Money Reaper/Man Beware 10
70   Bullet BU 449   Coolie Girl/BIGGIE: Bawling Baby. 6
70   Trojan TR 7718   Run Fattie/Hoola Bulla (song actually "Bulla Man") 8
71   G.G. GG 4524   Oh My Baby/WINSTON WRIGHT: Change Of Love Version. 5
71   Punch PH 59   Johnny Too Bad/Johnny Too Bad — Version 6
71   Dynamic DYN 406   Johnny Too Bad/ROLAND ALFONSO: Saucy Horde (act. by Roland Alphonso) . . . 8
71   Dynamic DYN 419   You Can't Win/Don't Fight The Law 5
72   Explosion EX 2061   Bounce Me Johnny/Bounce Me 'Version' (actually "Say You"). 5
(see also G.G. Allstars, Clancy Eccles, Viceroys)

SLIK
75   Bell BELL 1414   The Boogiest Band In Town/Hatche. 4
75   Bell BELL 1464   Forever And Ever/Again My Love (p/s) 5
76   Arista ARIST 83   Don't Take Your Love Away/This Side Up 4
(see also PVC 2, Zones, Rich Kids, Midge Ure)

SLIM & FREEDOM SINGERS
70   Banana BA 304   Do Dang Do (actually by Leroy Sibbles)/
                           JACKIE MITTOO & SOUND DIMENSION: Hot Milk 8

SLIME
78   Toadstool GOOD 1   Controversial/Loony (p/s) 7
(see also Johnny Moped)

SLITS
79   Island WIP 6505   Typical Girls/I Heard It Through The Grapevine (p/s) 5
79   Island 12 WIP 6505   Typical Girls (Brink Style)/I Heard It Through The Grapevine/
                           Liebe And Romanze (12", p/s) 7
80   Rough Trade RT 039/Y Y 1 In The Beginning There Was Rhythm/POP GROUP:
                           Where There's A Will There's A Way (p/s) 5
79   Island ILPS 9573   CUT (LP, with inner sleeve) 18
80   Rough Trade/Y Y 3   BOOTLEG RETROSPECTIVE (LP, plain sleeve) 22
81   CBS 85269   THE RETURN OF THE GIANT SLITS (LP, some with bonus 45
                           "American Radio Interview"/"Face Dub" [XPS 125]) 22/18

(see also Raincoats)

P.F. SLOAN
65   RCA Victor RCA 1482 Sins Of A Family/This Mornin'. 6
67   RCA Victor RCA 1623 Sunflower Sunflower/The Man Behind The Red Balloon 6
72   Epic EPC 65179   RAISED ON RECORDS (LP). 12
(see also Grass Roots)

SAMMI SLOAN
68   Columbia DB 8480   Yes I Would/Be His Girl 8

SLOWBONE
74   Rare Earth RES 119   Get What You're Given/Oh Man 6
(see also Roll Ups)

SLOWBURNER
89   Burn BURN LP 001   AN EMOTIONAL BUSINESS (LP). 10

SLY & FAMILY STONE
(see under Sly [& Family] Stone)

SMACK
78   Asprin 001   Edward Fox/Came Again (p/s, original issue) 4

JOAN SMALL
56   Parlophone MSP 6219 Change Of Heart/Come Next Spring 10
56   Parlophone R 4211   Love Is A Stranger/Autumn Concerto 7
57   Parlophone R 4269   Gonna Get Along Without You Now/You Can't Say I Love You To A
                           Rock & Roll Tune 12
57   Parlophone R 4269   Gonna Get Along Without You Now/You Can't Say I Love You To A
                           Rock & Roll Tune (78) 10
58   Parlophone R 4431   Afraid/How Many Times (Can I Fall In Love) 15
58   Parlophone R 4431   Afraid/How Many Times (Can I Fall In Love) (78) 15
60   Parlophone R 4622   The Big Hurt/Ask Me To Go Steady 15

KAREN SMALL
66   Vocalion V 9281   To Get You Back Again/That's Why I Cry 10

MARY SMALL
56   Vogue Coral Q 72196 None Of That Now/Dino 4
56   Vogue Coral Q 72196 None Of That Now/Dino (78) 8

MILLIE SMALL
(see under Millie)

SMALL FACES
SINGLES

65	Decca F 12208	Whatcha Gonna Do About It?/What's A Matter, Baby?	12
65	Decca F 12276	I've Got Mine/It's Too Late	15
66	Decca F 12317	Sha-La-La-La-Lee/Grow Your Own	10
66	Decca F 12393	Hey Girl/Almost Grown	12
66	Decca F 12470	All Or Nothing/Understanding (curved or boxed Decca logo)	10
66	Decca F 12500	My Mind's Eye (alternate demo mix, matrix no. ends T1-1C)/I Can't Dance With You (withdrawn)	25
66	Decca F 12500	My Mind's Eye (matrix no. ends T2-1C)/I Can't Dance With You	7
67	Decca F 12565	I Can't Make It/Just Passing	15
67	Decca F 12619	Patterns/E Too D.	50
67	Immediate AS 1	Small Faces (1-sided sampler for "Small Faces", promo only)	125
67	Immediate IM 050	Here Comes The Nice/Talk To You	8
67	Immediate IM 057	Itchycoo Park/I'm Only Dreaming	8
67	Immediate IM 062	Tin Soldier/I Feel Much Better (some in p/s)	40/15
68	Immediate IM 064	Lazy Sunday/Rollin' Over	8
68	Immediate IM 069	The Universal/Donkey Rides, A Penny A Glass (lilac label, later pink)	10/6
69	Immediate IM 077	Afterglow (Of Your Love)/Wham Bam, Thank You Mam (demos [& perhaps some copies] have demo version of B-side)	35/7
75	Immediate IM 064	Lazy Sunday/Rollin' Over (p/s, reissue with white label)	8
80	Virgin VS 367	Tin Soldier/Tin Soldier (live)/Rene.	6
86	Archive 4 TOF 103	Itchycoo Park/Lazy Sunday/Sha-La-La-La-Lee/Here Comes The Nice (12", p/s)	8
88	Castle Comms. Special Edition CD 3-9	THE SMALL FACES (Itchycoo Park/Lazy Sunday/All Or Nothing (live)/ Autumn Stone) (3" CD EP, with adaptor, 5" case, 5,000 only)	8

LPs

66	Decca LK 4790	SMALL FACES (LP, original red label)	70
67	Decca LK 4879	FROM THE BEGINNING (LP, original red label)	70
67	Immediate IMLP/IMSP 008	SMALL FACES (LP, mono/stereo)	100/120
68	Immediate IMLP/IMSP 012	OGDENS' NUT GONE FLAKE (LP, lilac label, circular foldout sleeve, mono/stereo)	50/40
68	Immediate IMLP/IMSP 012	OGDENS' NUT GONE FLAKE (LP, pink label, circular foldout sl., m/s)	45/35
69	Decca LK 4790	SMALL FACES (LP, boxed Decca label)	35
69	Decca LK 4879	FROM THE BEGINNING (LP, boxed Decca label)	35
69	Immediate IMLP/IMSP 022	IN MEMORIAM (LP, export issue [German copies more common, £50])	125
69	Immediate IMAL 01/02	THE AUTUMN STONE (2-LP, gatefold sleeve)	35
75	Immediate/NEMS IML 1001	OGDENS' NUT GONE FLAKE (LP, reissue, round sleeve, white label)	15
76	NEMS AML 1008	MAGIC MOMENTS (LP)	15
77	Immediate/NEMS IML 2001	OGDENS' NUT GONE FLAKE (LP, reissue, square sleeve)	12
77	Decca ROOTS 5	ROCK ROOTS — THE DECCA SINGLES (LP)	12
78	Charly CR 300005	OGDENS' NUT GONE FLAKE (LP, export release, square sleeve)	12
78	Charly CR 300025	THE SMALL FACES — LIVE U.K. 1969 (LP, export release)	12
80	Virgin/Immediate V 2166	SMALL FACES: BIG HITS (LP, gatefold sleeve)	12
80	Virgin/Immediate V 2178	FOR YOUR DELIGHT, THE DARLINGS OF WAPPING WHARF LAUNDERETTE (LP)	15
97	Castle CLA 016	OGDENS' NUT GONE FLAKE (LP, reissue, round sleeve with obi)	10
91	Castle CLACT 016	OGDENS' NUT GONE FLAKE (CD, in round tin box with beer mats & booklet)	40

(see also Faces, Steve Marriott, Humble Pie, Jimmy Winston & His Reflections, Winston's Fumbs, Billy Nicholls, Kenney Jones)

SMALL HOURS

80	Automatic K 17708	The Kid/Business In Town/Midnight To Six/End Of The Night (p/s)	30
80	Automatic K 17708X	The Kid/Business In Town/Midnight To Six/End Of The Night (10", p/s)	20

SMALL WORLD

81	Whaam! WHAAM 003	Love Is Dead/Liberty (p/s)	40
83	Valid VC 001	First Impressions/Stupidity Street/Tomorrow Never Comes (p/s)	40

SMART

82	Complex CPX 001	This Time (p/s)	35

SMART ALEC

79	B&C BCS 20	Scooter Boys/Soho (p/s)	20

S*M*A*S*H

93	Popcor POPCOR 001	Real Surreal/Drugs Again/Revisited No. 3 (wraparound p/s in poly bag, 1,000 only)	5
93	Popcor POPCOR 002	WHEELERS DEALERS & CHRISTINE KEELERS (EP,cassette, b/w 5 tracks by These Animal Men, 200 only, photocopied green paper inlay)	5
94	Popcor POPCOR 003	Lady Love Your Cunt/Shame (wraparound p/s in poly bag, 1,500 only)	4
94	Popcor POPCOR 003	Lady Love Your Cunt/Shame (pink vinyl, wraparound p/s in poly bag, 500 only)	5
94	Popcor POPCOR 003V	Lady Love Your Cunt/Shame ('St. Valentine's Day' edition, 1-sided, red vinyl, blank labels, metallic red wraparound p/s, 1,000 only)	6

SMASHING PUMPKINS

91	Hut	I Am One (1-sided blue flexidisc)	40
91	Caroline SMASH 1	Siva/Rhinoceros (no p/s, promo only)	40
91	Hut HUTT 6	Siva/Window Paine (12", p/s, 5,000)	30
92	Hut HUTT 10	LULL EP (Rhinoceros/Blue/Slunk/Bye June [Demo]) (12", p/s)	10
92	Hut CDHUT 10	LULL EP (Rhinoceros/Blue/Slunk/Bye June [Demo]) (CD)	7
92	Hut HUTC 017	PEEL SESSIONS: Siva/A Girl Named Sandoz/Smiley (cassette EP)	5
92	Hut HUTT 017	PEEL SESSIONS: Siva/A Girl Named Sandoz/Smiley (12" EP, p/s)	12
92	Hut HUTEN 018	I Am One/Terrapin (live)/Bullet Train To Osaka (10", p/s, 6,000 only)	20
92	Hut HUTT 18	I Am One/Plume/Starla (12", p/s)	12
93	Sup Pop SP 90	Tristessa/La Dolly Vita/Honeyspider (12", 5,000 only)	35
93	Hut HUT 31	Cherub Rock/Purr Snickety (p/s, clear vinyl, numbered, 5,000 only)	20

MINT VALUE £

93	Hut HUTT 31	Cherub Rock/Pissant/French Movie Theme/(Star Spangled Banner) (12", p/s, last track uncredited)	7
93	Hut HUT 37	Today/Apathy's Last Kiss (p/s, red vinyl, 5,000 only)	15
93	Hut HUTT 37	Today/Hello Kitty Kat/Obscured (12", p/s)	8
94	Hut HUT 43	Smile (Disarm/Siamese Dream) (stickered p/s, purple vinyl)	10
94	Hut HUTL 48	Rocket/Never Let Me Down (box set, salmon pink vinyl, 1,500 only)	35
93	Hut HUTTDJ 73	Zero (12", promo only)	12
94	Hut SPBOX 1	SIAMESE SINGLES (Rocket/Never Let Me Down//Cherub Rock/Purr Snickety// Today/Apathy's Last Kiss/Smile [Disarm/Siamese Dream]) (4 x 7" box set, black vinyl, 6,000 only)	40

ROY SMECK

54	Brunswick LA 8649	SONGS OF THE RANGE (10" LP)	15
65	London (S)HAR 8273	WIZARD OF THE STRINGS (LP)	10

PHILIP LLOYD SMEE & DONATO CINICOLO III

71	Deroy PLS 1	DAS LUNE/SYNTHI-A (LP, private pressing, handmade sleeve, 2 copies only)	400

K. SMILEY

72	Pressure Beat PB 5514	Tipatone/Do It To Me	6

SMILEY

72	Philips 6006 206	Penelope/I Know What I Want	5
	(see also Creation)		

SMILIN' JOE

54	London HL 8106	A.B.C.'s (Parts 1 & 2) (78)	100

SMITH

69	Stateside-Dunhill SS 8028	Baby It's You/I Don't Believe	5
70	Stateside-Dunhill SS 8042	Take A Look Around/Mojalesky Ridge	5
70	Stateside-Dunhill SS 8055	What Am I Gonna Do/Born In Boston	5
69	Stateside-Dunhill SSL 5016	A GROUP CALLED SMITH (LP)	15
70	Stateside-Dunhill SSL 5031	MINUS-PLUS (LP)	15

ADAM (Eric) SMITH

62	Island WI 057	I Wonder Why/My Prayer	18

ALEXANDER MURRAY SMITH & BLACK O'TOWN SYNCOPATORS

63	Decca F 11604	"Steptoe And Son" Theme/Ragtime Tuba	6

A.S.A.P. (Adrian Smith & Project)

89	EMI 12 EMPD 107	Silver And Gold/Blood Brothers (12", no p/s, silver & gold vinyl)	7
90	EMI EMPD 131	Down The Wire (Crossed Line Mix)/When She's Gone (shaped picture disc)	6
	(see also Iron Maiden, Urchin)		

ARTHUR 'GUITAR BOOGIE' SMITH (& HIS CRACKERJACKS)

50	MGM MGM 254	Mule Train/ROY LEAR & BETTY SMITH: Dime A Dozen (78)	8
50	MGM MGM 329	Guitar Boogie/Be Bop Rag (78)	10
51	MGM MGM 363	Mandolin Boogie/The Memphis Blues (78)	8
52	MGM MGM 484	Alabama Jubilee/Fiddle-Faddle (78, with Crackerjacks)	10
52	MGM MGM 518	Guitar And Piano Boogie/Banjo Buster (78)	8
52	MGM MGM 555	Express Train Boogie/River Rag (78)	10
53	MGM SP 1008	Guitar Boogie/Be Bop Rag	25
53	MGM SP 1021	Five String Banjo Boogie/South	18
53	MGM MGM 599	Five String Banjo Boogie/South (78)	10
53	MGM SP 1039	Express Train Boogie/River Rag	18
53	MGM MGM 630	Recitation Sonny Smith: In Memory Of Hank Williams/HANK WILLIAMS & HIS DRIFTING COWBOYS: I Saw The Light (78)	10
53	MGM MGM 660	Big Mountain Shuffle/KEN CURTIS: The Call Of The Faraway Hills (78)	8
53	MGM MGM 695	Three D Boogie/He Went That-A-Way (78)	8
54	MGM SP 1096	Oh, Baby Mine, I Get So Lonely/Outboard	18
54	MGM MGM 755	Oh, Baby Mine, I Get So Lonely/Outboard (78)	10
54	MGM SP 1110	Redheaded Stranger/Texas Hop	18
54	MGM MGM 779	Redheaded Stranger/Texas Hop (78)	12
54	MGM MGM 3011	Guitar Boogie/Boomerang (78)	12
55	MGM SP 1122	Hi Lo Boogie/Truck Stop Grill	18
55	MGM MGM 805	Hi Lo Boogie/Truck Stop Grill (78)	12
54	MGM MGM-EP 510	ARTHUR 'GUITAR BOOGIE' SMITH AND HIS CRACKERJACKS (EP)	22
54	MGM MGM EPC 5	ARTHUR 'GUITAR BOOGIE' SMITH (EP, export issue)	25
59	MGM MGM-EP 695	ARTHUR 'GUITAR BOOGIE' SMITH AND HIS CRACKERJACKS (EP)	22
63	Stateside SE 1005	MISTER GUITAR (EP)	20
53	MGM MGM-D 111	FINGERS ON FIRE (10" LP)	30
54	MGM MGM-D 131	FOOLISH QUESTIONS (10" LP)	30
71	MGM 2354 009	GUITAR BOOGIE (LP)	12

BARRY SMITH

74	People PEO 114	Hold On To It (Parts 1 & 2)	15

BEASLEY SMITH & HIS ORCHESTRA

56	London HLD 8235	Goodnight, Sweet Dreams/Parisian Rag	25
56	London HLD 8273	My Foolish Heart/Old Spinning Wheel	25

BESSIE SMITH

51	Columbia DB 2796	Empty Bed Blues (Parts 1 & 2) (78)	25
58	Philips BBE 12202	EMPRESS OF THE BLUES (EP)	15
59	Philips BBE 12231	EMPRESS OF THE BLUES NO. 2 (EP)	15
59	Philips BBE 12233	EMPRESS OF THE BLUES NO. 3 (EP)	15
60	Philips BBE 12360	BESSIE SMITH (EP)	12
55	Philips BBL 7019	THE BESSIE SMITH STORY VOLUME 1 (LP, with Louis Armstrong)	25
55	Philips BBL 7020	THE BESSIE SMITH STORY VOLUME 2 (LP)	25

55	Philips BBL 7042	THE BESSIE SMITH STORY VOLUME 3 (LP)	25
55	Philips BBL 7049	THE BESSIE SMITH STORY VOLUME 4 (LP)	25
62	Philips BBL 7513	BESSIE'S BLUES 1923-1924 (LP)	30
66	CBS BPG 62377	THE BESSIE SMITH STORY VOLUME 1 (LP)	12
66	CBS BPG 62378	THE BESSIE SMITH STORY VOLUME 2 (LP)	12
66	CBS BPG 62379	THE BESSIE SMITH STORY VOLUME 3 (LP)	12
66	CBS BPG 62380	THE BESSIE SMITH STORY VOLUME 4 (LP)	12
71	CBS 66258	THE WORLD'S GREATEST BLUES SINGER (2-LP, some with booklet)	20/15
71	CBS 66262	ANY WOMAN'S BLUES (2-LP)	15
71	CBS 66273	EMPTY BED BLUES (2-LP)	15
72	CBS 66264	THE EMPRESS (2-LP)	15
73	CBS 67232	NOBODY'S BLUES BUT MINE (2-LP)	15
70s	Empress 10006	THE COMPLETE ST. LOUIS BLUES SOUNDTRACK (10" LP)	12

BETTY SMITH SKIFFLE GROUP

| 57 | Tempo A 162 | There's A Blue Ridge Round My Heart, Virginia/Double Shuffle | 12 |
| 57 | Tempo A 162 | There's A Blue Ridge Round My Heart, Virginia/Double Shuffle (78) | 8 |

(see also Betty Smith Quintet)

BETTY SMITH QUINTET

57	Tempo A 163	Sweet Georgia Brown/Little White Lies	20
57	Tempo A 163	Sweet Georgia Brown/Little White Lies (78)	12
58	Decca F 10986	Hand Jive/Bewitched (as Betty Smith Group)	8
58	Decca F 10986	Hand Jive/Bewitched (as Betty Smith Group) (78)	10
58	Decca F 11031	Will The Angels Play Their Harps For Me/Betty's Blues	8
58	Decca F 11031	Will The Angels Play Their Harps For Me/Betty's Blues (78)	10
58	Decca F 11071	Begin The Beguine/Song Of The Boulevards	6
58	Decca F 11071	Begin The Beguine/Song Of The Boulevards (78)	10
59	Decca F 11124	Song Of India/Stormy Weather	6
59	Decca F 11124	Song Of India/Stormy Weather (78)	12
57	Tempo EXA 74	BETTY SMITH QUINTET (EP)	15
57	Decca DFE 6446	BETTY SMITH QUINTET (EP)	15

(see also Betty Smith Skiffle Group)

BIG JOE SMITH & REGGAE ROUSERS

| 70 | Major Minor MM 702 | Lovely Watermelon/Tomahawk | 4 |

(see Jeff Rowena)

BUSTER SMITH

| 61 | London Jazz LTZ-K 15206 | THE LEGENDARY BUSTER SMITH (LP) | 12 |

CAL SMITH

| 74 | MCA MCA 143 | Country Bumpkin/It's Not The Miles You Travelled | 5 |
| 75 | MCA MCA 222 | The Ghost Of Jim Bob Wilson/Mama's Face | 5 |

CARL SMITH

52	Columbia DB 3077	Let's Live A Little/Me And My Broken Heart (78)	10
53	Columbia DC 608	Our Honeymoon/Sing Her A Love Song (78, export issue)	7
56	Philips PB 572	Loose Talk/More Than Anything Else In The World (78)	12
59	Philips PB 943	Ten Thousand Drums/The Tall, Tall Gentlemen	8
59	Philips PB 943	Ten Thousand Drums/The Tall, Tall Gentlemen (78)	30
60	Philips BBL 7437	THE CARL SMITH TOUCH (LP)	15

CLARA SMITH

69	VJM VLP 15	CLARA SMITH VOLUME 1 (LP)	15
69	VJM VLP 16	CLARA SMITH VOLUME 2 (LP)	15
69	VJM VLP 17	CLARA SMITH VOLUME 3 (LP)	15

CLARA SMITH & FLETCHER HENDERSON

| 61 | Philips BBE 12491 | BLUES BY CLARA SMITH 1926-1928 (EP) | 15 |

CONNIE SMITH

66	RCA Victor RD 7785	CUTE AND COUNTRY (LP)	15
71	RCA LSA 3042	WHERE IS MY CASTLE (LP)	12
73	RCA LSA 3150	IT AIN'T LOVE (LP)	12

COUNTY SMITH

| 68 | Decca F 12818 | Low Bad Hurting/No Longer Mine | 4 |

DAVE SMITH & ASTRONAUTS

| 67 | C'mbia Blue Beat DB 104 | A Lover Like You/Cup Of Love | 8 |

DICK SMITH BAND

| 80 | Hol-O-Gram HOL 001 | Way Of The World/Giving The Game Away (p/s) | 35 |

EDDIE SMITH

| 55 | Parlophone MSP 6186 | Silver Star Stomp/Stumbling (as Eddie Smith & Chiefs) | 12 |
| 60 | Top Rank JAR 285 | Upturn/Border Beat (as Eddie Smith & Hornets) | 12 |

EDGEWOOD SMITH & FABULOUS TAILFEATHERS

| 67 | Sue WI 4037 | Ain't That Lovin'/Yeah | 40 |

EFFIE SMITH

| 66 | Sue WI 4010 | Dial That Telephone (Parts 1 & 2) | 20 |

ELSON SMITH

| 61 | Fontana H 291 | Flip Flop/Are You Ready For That | 18 |

ERNIE SMITH

71	Duke DU 119	Bend Down/Heaven Help Us All	6
71	Horse HOSS 6	Sunday Morning/One Three	5
73	London SHS 8442	ERNIE SMITH (LP)	12

ETHEL SMITH

| 55 | Brunswick 05470 | Hernando's Hideaway/Lemon Merengue | 7 |

MINT VALUE £

(LITTLE) GEORGE (HARMONICA) SMITH

65	Blue Horizon 45-1002	Blues In The Dark/Telephone Blues (as Little George Smith).	75
70	Blue Horizon 57-3170	Someone You're Gonna Learn/Before You Do Your Thing (as George Smith).	15
69	Liberty LBL/LBS 83218E	BLUES WITH FEELING — A TRIBUTE TO LITTLE WALTER (LP, with Chicago Blues Band)	30
70	Blue Horizon 7-63856	NO TIME TO JIVE (LP)	75
71	Deram SML 1082	ARKANSAS TRAP (LP)	45

(see also Bacon Fat)

GLORIA SMITH

59	London HLU 8903	Playmates/Don't Take Your Love From Me.	12
59	London HLU 8903	Playmates/Don't Take Your Love From Me (78)	30

GORDON SMITH

69	Blue Horizon 57-3156	Too Long/Funk Pedal	12
69	Blue Horizon 7-63211	LONG OVERDUE (LP)	60

(see also Kevin Coyne)

HAROLD SMITH'S MAJESTIC CHOIR

69	Chess CRS 8100	We Can All Walk A Little Bit Prouder/Why Am I Treated So Bad	6

HUEY 'PIANO' SMITH & CLOWNS

58	Columbia DB 4138	Don't You Just Know It/High Blood Pressure	50
58	Columbia DB 4138	Don't You Just Know It/High Blood Pressure (78).	50
60	Top Rank JAR 282	Don't You Just Know Kokomo/FRANKIE FORD: Cheatin' Woman	20
62	Top Rank JAR 614	Pop-Eye/Scald-Dog (as Huey Smith)	15
65	Sue WI 364	If It Ain't One Thing It's Another/Tu-Ber-Cu-Lucas And The Sinus Blues.	20
65	Sue WI 380	Rockin' Pneumonia And The Boogie Woogie Flu (Parts 1 & 2).	20
78	Chiswick NS 43	Rockin' Pneumonia And The Boogie Woogie Flu (unissued)	
65	Sue ILP 917	ROCKIN' PNEUMONIA AND THE BOOGIE WOOGIE FLU (LP, titled "Havin' A Good Time" on labels)	40
78	Chiswick CH 9	ROCKIN' PNEUMONIA AND THE BOOGIE WOOGIE FLU (LP)	10

(see also Frankie Ford, Lee Allen, Bobby Marchan, Robert Parker)

HURRICANE SMITH

71	Columbia DB 8785	Don't Let It Die/The Writer Sings His Songs	5
72	Columbia DB 8878	Oh Babe What Would You Say/Getting To Know You.	5
72	Columbia DB 8916	Who Was It/Take Suki Home	5

(see also Amos Gherkin Quartet)

IAN SMITH & INNER MIND

71	Bullet BU 490	Devil Woman/Nenn Street Rub.	6

(see also Smithy All Stars)

JENNIE SMITH

59	Philips PB 924	Huggin' My Pillow (Sweet Side)/Huggin' My Pillow (Sweet Beat Side).	5
59	Philips PB 924	Huggin' My Pillow (Sweet Side)/Huggin' My Pillow (Sweet Beat Side) (78)	30

JIMMY SMITH

SINGLES

62	HMV POP 1025	Walk On The Wild Side (Parts 1 & 2)	10
65	Verve VS 509	Hobo Flats (Parts 1 & 2).	5
65	Verve VS 521	Who's Afraid Of Virginia Woolf (Parts 1 & 2).	6
65	Verve VS 523	The Cat/Basin Street Blues	10
65	Verve VS 531	The Organ Grinder's Swing/I'll Close My Eyes	6
66	Verve VS 534	Slow Theme From "Where The Spies Are" (Parts 1 & 2).	6
66	Verve VS 536	Got My Mojo Working (Parts 1 & 2).	6
66	Verve VS 540	I'm Your Hoochie-Coochie Man (Parts 1 & 2)	7
67	Verve VS 551	Cat In A Tree (Parts 1 & 2)	6
67	Verve VS 562	Mickey Mouse (Parts 1 & 2)	6

EPs

64	Verve VEP 5008	WALK ON THE WILD SIDE (EP)	12
65	Verve VEP 5021	CREEPER (EP)	12
65	Verve VEP 5016	PLAYS THE BLUES (EP).	12
65	Verve VEP 5022	SWINGING WITH THE INCREDIBLE JIMMY SMITH (EP)	12

LPs

62	Verve CLP 1596/CSD 1462	BASHIN' THE UNPREDICTABLE (LP, Verve label with HMV number)	15
63	Verve (S)VLP 9039	HOBO FLATS (LP)	15
64	Verve VLP 9057	ANY NUMBER CAN WIN (LP).	15
64	Verve VLP 9068	WHO'S AFRAID OF VIRGINIA WOOLF (LP).	15
64	Verve (S)VLP 9079	THE CAT (LP).	15
65	Verve (S)VLP 9093	MONSTER (LP).	15
66	Verve (S)VLP 9108	ORGAN GRINDER SWING (LP)	15
66	Verve (S)VLP 9123	GOT MY MOJO WORKING (LP).	15
66	Verve (S)VLP 9142	HOOCHIE COOCHIE MAN (LP)	15
67	Verve (S)VLP 9159	PETER & THE WOLF (LP).	15
67	Verve (S)VLP 9160	THE DYNAMIC DUO (LP, with Wes Montgomery)	15
67	Verve (S)VLP 9182	RESPECT (LP)	15
68	Verve (S)VLP 9218	STAY LOOSE (LP).	15
68	Verve (S)VLP 9227	LIVIN' IT UP (LP).	15
68	Verve (S)VLP 9231	CHRISTMAS COOKIN' (LP)	15
69	Verve (S)VLP 9241	FURTHER ADVENTURES OF JIMMY AND WES (LP, with Wes Montgomery)	15
71	Verve 2304 020	I'M GON' GIT MYSELF TOGETHER (LP)	15
71	Verve 2304 021	OTHER SIDE (LP).	15
71	Verve 2304 033	THE BEST OF JIMMY SMITH (LP)	12
72	Verve 2304 044	THE BEST OF JIMMY SMITH VOL. 2 (LP)	12
73	Decca SKL 5146	AT THE LOWERY ORGAN (LP).	12
74	Verve 2304 167	PORTUGUESE SOUL (LP).	12
75	DJM DJLPS 451	BLACK SMITH (LP).	12

(see also Kenny Burrell)

JOEY SMITH & BABA BROOKS BAND
64	R&B JB 131	Maybe Once/Tell Me You're Mine	12

JOHNNY SMITH & STAN GETZ
52	Vogue V 2137	Tabou/Moonlight In Vermont (78)	8

(see also Stan Getz)

JUDI SMITH
65	Decca F 12132	Leaves Come Tumbling Down/Come My Way	10

JUNIOR SMITH
67	Giant GN 1	Cool Down Your Temper/I'm Groovin'	8
68	Giant GN 18	I'm Gonna Leave You Girl/I Love You, I Love You	8
68	Giant GN 25	Come Cure Me/I Want Your Lovin'	8
68	Gas GAS 132	Gimme Little/Trip To War Land	6
69	Crystal CR 7002	Put On The Pressure/I Don't Know	5
72	Sioux SI 019	Saturday Child/JUMBO STERLING: Hot Dog	5
72	Sioux SI 023	You Don't Know/JUMBO STERLING: My Sugar Ain't Sweet	5

(see also Stranger Cole, Derrick Morgan, Rocksteadys)

KEELY SMITH (& LOUIS PRIMA)
57	Capitol CL 14717	Hurt Me/High School Affair	7
57	Capitol CL 14739	Young And In Love/You Better Go Now	7
57	Capitol CL 14754	Good Behaviour/You'll Never Know	7
57	Capitol CL 14754	Good Behaviour/You'll Never Know (78)	5
57	Capitol CL 14803	Autumn Leaves/I Keep Forgetting	7
57	Capitol CL 14803	Autumn Leaves/I Keep Forgetting (78)	8
58	Capitol CL 14862	Foggy Day/The Lip (B-side with Louis Prima)	6
58	Capitol CL 14885	The Whippoorwill/Sometimes	5
58	Capitol CL 14948	That Old Black Magic (with Louis Prima)/You Are My Love	6
58	Capitol CL 14948	That Old Black Magic (with Louis Prima)/You Are My Love (78)	20
59	Capitol CL 14994	I've Got You Under My Skin (with Louis Prima)/Don't Take Your Love From Me	6
59	London HLD 8984	If I Knew I'd Find You (I'd Climb The Highest Mountain)/ Don't Let The Stars Get In Your Eyes	10
59	London HLD 8984	If I Knew I'd Find You (I'd Climb The Highest Mountain)/ Don't Let The Stars Get In Your Eyes (78)	30
60	London HLD 9240	Here In My Heart/Close	8
64	Reprise R 20346	You're Breaking My Heart/Crazy	5
64	Reprise R 20356	If I Fell/Do You Want To Know A Secret	5
65	Reprise R 20402	Somethin' Wonderful Happened/Have You Ever Been Lonely	5
65	Reprise R 20482	If I Fell/Do You Want To Know A Secret (reissue)	5
65	Reprise R 23048	Standing In The Ruins/That Old Black Magic	5
65	Capitol CL 15385	S'posin'/The Song Is You	5
66	Reprise R 20482	The Wonder Of You/Who's Afraid	30
61	London RE-D 1269	YOU LOVERS (EP)	10
65	Capitol EAP 1-20629	IT'S MAGIC (EP)	12
65	Reprise R 30042	JOHN LENNON, PAUL McCARTNEY SONGBOOK VOL. 1 (EP)	12
65	Reprise R 30045	THE SUCCESS OF KEELY SMITH (EP)	8
65	Reprise R 30046	JOHN LENNON, PAUL McCARTNEY SONGBOOK VOL. 2 (EP)	12
66	Reprise R 30053	SOMEBODY LOVES ME (EP)	8
66	Reprise R 30062	I'VE GOT THE WORLD ON A STRING (EP)	8
58	Capitol (S)T 914	I WISH YOU LOVE (LP, mono/stereo)	15/18
59	Capitol T 1073	POLITELY (LP)	14
59	Capitol T 1145	SWINGIN' PRETTY (LP)	14
59	Capitol T 1160	HEY BOY! HEY GIRL! (LP, soundtrack, with Louis Prima)	20
64	Reprise R 6086	LITTLE GIRL BLUE, LITTLE GIRL NEW (LP)	15
65	Reprise R 6132	THE INTIMATE SMITH (LP)	15
65	Reprise R 6142	THE JOHN LENNON-PAUL McCARTNEY SONGBOOK (LP)	15
65	Reprise R 5012	YOU'RE BREAKING MY HEART (LP)	15
66	Reprise R 6175	THAT OLD BLACK MAGIC (LP)	12

(see also Louis Prima, Frank Sinatra)

LONNIE LISTON SMITH (& COSMIC ECHOES)
75	RCA RCA 2568	Expansions (Parts 1 & 2) (& Cosmic Echoes)	6
76	RCA RCA 2668	Chance For Peace/Sunset	5
76	RCA RCA 2727	Get Down Everybody/Inner Beauty	5
79	RCA PB 9450	Expansions/A Chance For Peace	5
79	RCA PC 9450	Expansions/A Chance For Peace (12", reissue)	10
75	RCA SF 8434	EXPANSIONS (LP, with Cosmic Echoes)	12
76	RCA SF 8461	VISIONS OF A NEW WORLD (LP)	12
76	RCA RS 1053	REFLECTIONS OF A GOLDEN DREAM (LP, with Cosmic Echoes)	12
77	RCA PL 11822	RENAISSANCE (LP, with Cosmic Echoes)	12

LONNIE SMITH
67	CBS 63146	FINGER LICKIN' GOOD (LP)	15
70s	Blue Note BST 84290	THINK (LP)	20
70s	Blue Note BST 84313	TURNING POINT (LP)	12
70s	Blue Note BST 84326	MOVE YOUR HAND (LP)	25
70s	Blue Note BST 84351	DRIVES (LP)	12

LORENZO SMITH
66	Outasite 45-503	(Too Much) Firewater/Count Down (99 copies only)	50

LOU SMITH
60	Top Rank JAR 520	Cruel Love/Close To My Heart	8

MARTHA SMITH
65	Pye 7N 15778	As I Watch You Walk Away/It Always Seems Like Summer	6
65	Pye 7N 15860	Love Means Nothing To You/The Song Is Love	6

MINT VALUE £

MARVIN SMITH
66	Coral Q 72486	Time Stopped/Have More Time	30
74	Contempo CS 2034	Let The Good Times Roll/Ain't That A Shame	4

MEL SMITH
81	Mercury MEL 1	Mel Smith's Greatest Hits/Richard & Joey (p/s, with Roger Taylor)	20

MICK SMITH
76	Midas MFHR 078	SOMEBODY NOBODY KNOWS (LP)	35
77	Alida Star AS 771	WORDS AND MUSIC (LP)	30
79	Repercussion RR 1000	RAINDANCE (LP, as Mike Smith)	25

MIKE SMITH
85	Proto ENA 130	Medley (7" version)/Bits And Pieces (some in p/s)	7/5
85	Proto ENAT 130	Medley (12" version)/Glad All Over (12", p/s)	12
90	Mooncrest MOON 1010	You Gotta Play Rock'N'Roll/Operator	6

(see also Dave Clark 5, Smith & D'Abo)

MURIEL SMITH & CARMEN JONES CHORUS
55	Brunswick 05370	Dat's Love/JUNE HAWKINS: Beat Out Dat Rhythm On A Drum	7

O.C. (OCIE) SMITH
57	London HLA 8480	Lighthouse/Too Many (as Ocie Smith)	60
57	London HLA 8480	Lighthouse/Too Many (as Ocie Smith) (78)	40
68	CBS 3343	The Son Of Hickory Holler's Tramp/On A Clear Day You Can See Forever	5
70	CBS 5203	Baby I Need Your Loving/San Francisco Is A Lonely Town	6
68	CBS (S) 63147	THE DYNAMIC O.C. SMITH (LP)	20
68	CBS (S) 63362	HICKORY HOLLER REVISITED (LP)	15
69	CBS 63805	AT HOME (LP)	12

(see also Art Mooney)

OTELLO SMITH & TOBAGO BAD BOYS
67	Direction 58-3082	My Home Town/Trouble	4
68	Direction 8-63242	THE BIG ONES GO SKA (LP)	10

PATTI SMITH (GROUP)
76	Arista ARIST 47	Gloria (In Excelsis Deo) (Edit)/My Generation (p/s)	4
77	Arista ARIST 12135	Gloria (In Excelsis Deo)/My Generation (live) (12", Rough Trade copies in brown paper bag with titles in felt pen)	10/7
78	Arista ARIST 181	Because The Night/God Speed (p/s)	6
78	Sire 6078 614	Hey Joe (Version)/Piss Factory (p/s)	15
78	Arista ARIST 197	Privilege (Set Me Free)/Ask The Angels (p/s)	4
78	Arista ARIST 12197	Privilege (Set Me Free)/Ask The Angels/25th Floor (Live Version)/Babelfield (12", p/s)	10
79	Arista ARIST 264	Frederick/Fire Of Unknown Origin (p/s)	4
79	Arista ARIST 281	Dancing Barefoot/5-4-3-2-1 (live) (p/s)	4
79	Arista ARIST 291	So You Want To Be A Rock'n'Roll Star/Frederick (live) (p/s)	5
88	Fierce FRIGHT 017	Brian Jones/Stockinged Feet/Jesus Christ (1-sided, white label, no p/s)	15
75	Arista ARTY 122	HORSES (LP, blue label)	10
76	Arista SPARTY 1001	RADIO ETHIOPIA (LP, as Patti Smith Group, with lyric insert)	12
78	Arista SPARTY 1043	EASTER (LP, as Patti Smith Group, with lyric insert)	10
79	Arista SPARTY 1086	WAVE (LP, as Patti Smith Group, with lyric insert)	10

PAUL SMITH
65	Columbia DB 7636	Piccadilly Paper Boy/Yakety Yak	6

PHOEBE SMITH
70	Topic 12T 93	ONCE I HAD A TRUE LOVE (LP)	10

PINE TOP SMITH
50	Brunswick 04426	I'm Sober Now/Jump Steady Blues (78)	12

RAY SMITH
51	London L 857	When The Saints Go Marching Home/You Gotta Walk The Straight & Narrow (78)	12
51	London L 1002	It's No Secret/All Alone Neath The Blue Grass (78)	12
60	London HL 9051	Rockin' Little Angel/That's All Right	60

ROY SMITH (& STARGAZERS) (U.K.)
55	Decca F 10529	Red Roses (For My Lady Fair)/The Devil's In Your Eyes	6
55	Decca F 10644	He/Glengarry (solo)	6

(see also Stargazers)

ROY SMITH (Jamaica)
70	Grape GR 3013	See Through Craze/TERRY CARL & DERRICK: I'm The One	6
70	Jackpot JP 723	The Wedding/Air Balloon	6

SIMON SMITH
67	Columbia DB 8213	And This Is My Beloved/I Just Can't Live Without You	4

SLIM SMITH (& UNIQUES)
66	Island WI 3023	I've Got Your Number/The New Boss	25
67	Coxsone CS 7016	Hip Hug/FREEDOM SINGERS: I Want Money	20
67	Coxsone CS 7034	Rougher Yet/I'll Never Let Go	20
67	Coxsone CS 7009	Mercy Mercy/JACKIE MITTOO: Baba Boom	20
68	Trojan TR 619	Watch This Sound/Out Of Love (as Slim Smith & Uniques)	12
69	Unity UN 504	Everybody Needs Love/JUNIOR SMITH: Come Back Girl	7
69	Unity UN 508	For Once In My Life/Burning Desire	7
69	Unity UN 510	Zip A Dee Doo Dah/On Broadway	5
69	Unity UN 513	Let It Be Me/Love Makes Me Do Foolish Things (both with Paulette)	5
69	Unity UN 515	Somebody To Love/Confusion	7
69	Unity UN 520	Slip Away/Spanish Harlem	7
69	Unity UN 524	Sunny Side Of The Sea/A Place In The Sun	7
69	Unity UN 527	Blessed Are The Meek/Conversation	7

69	Unity UN 537	Keep That Light Shining On Me/Build My World Around You	7
69	Unity UN 539	Love Me Tender/This Feeling	7
69	Unity UN 542	Honey/There's A Light	7
69	Jackpot JP 703	If It Don't Work Out/Love Power	7
69	Gas GAS 132	The Vow (& Doreen Shaeffer)/JAMES NEPHEW: Why Don't You Say	5
70	Gas GAS 150	What Kind Of Life/MARTIN RILEY: It's All In The Game	7
70	Unity UN 570	Jenny/The Race	7
71	Supreme SUP 219	Stay/You're My Everything	7
71	Pama Supreme PS 334	Send Me Some Loving/I'm Lost	7
71	Camel CA 81	Spanish Harlem/Slip Away	6
71	Escort ERT 851	My Love Come True/This Feeling	6
71	Escort ERT 852	Life Keeps Turning/My Girl	6
71	Escort ERT 859	My Girl/RECO: Plus One	6
71	Jackpot JP 779	Keep Walking/Will You Still Love Me Tomorrow	6
72	Jackpot JP 786	I Need Your Loving/You've Got What It Takes	7
72	Jackpot JP 788	Take Me Back/Where Do I Turn	6
72	Jackpot JP 789	Rain From The Skies/You're No Good	15
72	Jackpot JP 798	Closer Together/Blinded By Love	6
72	Jackpot JP 799	Turning Point/Money Lover	6
72	Dynamic DYN 428	Just A Dream/Send Me Some Loving	6
72	Pama PM 850	The Time Has Come/RECO & HIS BAND: Version	6
72	Pama Supreme PS 373	A Place In The Sun/Stranger On The Shore	6
72	Camel CA 89	Take Me Back/Where Do I Turn	6
72	Explosion EX 2074	The Time Has Come/Blessed Is The Man	6
73	Explosion EX 2078	Stand Up And Fight/The Sunny Side Of The Sea	6
73	Green Door GD 4058	Let Me Love You/If It Don't Work Out	8
73	Bullet BU 523	A Place In The Sun/Burning Fire	6
69	Pama ECO 9	EVERYBODY NEEDS LOVE (LP)	35
72	Trojan TBL 186	JUST A DREAM (LP)	20
73	Trojan TBL 198	GREATEST HITS (LP)	20
70s	Lord Koos KLP 1	SLIM SMITH (LP)	20

(see also Wonder Boy, Pioneers, Uniques, Roy Shirley, Ron Sig, Dakota Jim, Dennis Alcapone, David Isaacs, John Holt, Heptones, Melodians, Count Ossie, Winston Williams)

SOMETHIN' SMITH & REDHEADS

58	Fontana H 112	I'm Gonna Wrap Up All My Heartaches/ Ev'ry Night At Nine O'Clock (78)	8
58	Fontana H 154	I Don't Want To Set The World On Fire/You Made Me Love You	8
58	Fontana H 154	I Don't Want To Set The World On Fire/You Made Me Love You (78)	8
58	Fontana TFR 6005	PUT THE BLAME ON ME (10" LP)	18

STUART SMITH

68	Polydor 56271	She's A Woman Now/Where Did Holly Go	5
69	Polydor 56336	My Head Goes Around/Where You Are	5

TAB SMITH & HIS ORCHESTRA

53	Vogue V 2141	On The Sunny Side Of The Street/Milk Train (78)	7
53	Vogue V 2172	Ace High/Deejay Special (78)	10
54	Vogue V 2203	Down Beat/Boogie Joogie (78)	10
54	Vogue V 2282	Cuban Boogie/Red Hot And Blue (78)	10
55	Vogue V 2299	All My Life/Seven Up (78)	10
56	Vogue V 2410	Jump Time/Rock City	12
56	Vogue V 2410	Jump Time/Rock City (78)	8
56	Vogue V 2416	My Mother's Eyes/These Foolish Things (78)	8
59	London HLM 8801	Smoke Gets In Your Eyes/My Happiness Cha-Cha	10
59	London HLM 8801	Smoke Gets In Your Eyes/My Happiness Cha-Cha (78)	15
60	Vogue V 2416	My Mother's Eyes/These Foolish Things	7
62	Vogue V 2299	All My Life/Seven Up	7

TERRY SMITH

69	Philips (S)BL 7871	FALL OUT (LP)	12
77	Lambert LAM 002	TERRY SMITH AND TONY LEE TRIO (LP)	22

(see also If)

TRIXIE SMITH

51	Tempo R 42	Black Bottom Stomp/He Likes It Slow (78)	25
52	Vocalion V 1006	Freight Train Blues/Trixie's Blues (78)	30
52	Vocalion V 1017	My Daddy Rocks Me (Parts 1 & 2) (78)	30
53	Jazz Collector L 102	The World's Jazz Crazy And So Am I/Railroad Blues (78)	12
50s	Poydras 101	TRIXIE SMITH (10" EP, 45 rpm)	12
50s	Ristic 12	TRIXIE SMITH (10" EP, 45 rpm)	12
50s	Audubon AAE	TRIXIE SMITH (10" LP)	25

TRIXIE SMITH/MA RAINEY

64	Jazz Collector JEL 22	FEMALE BLUES VOL. 3 (EP, 2 tracks each)	12

TRULY SMITH

66	Decca F 12373	My Smile Is Just A Frown Turned Upside Down/Love Is Me, Love Is You	20
66	Decca F 12415	I Love Him/Buttermilk Hill	5
66	Decca F 12489	You Are The Love Of My Life/The Merry Go Round Is Slowing	5
67	Decca F 12554	Windows And Doors/Take A Broken Heart	5
67	Decca F 12645	I Wanna Go Back There Again/Window Cleaner	10
67	Decca F 12700	The Boy From Chelsea/Little Man With A Stick	6
68	MGM MGM 1431	This Is The First Time/Taking Time Off	8

VERDELLE SMITH

66	Capitol CL 15234	In My Room/Like A Man	5
66	Capitol CL 15456	Tar And Cement/A Piece Of The Sky	6
66	Capitol CL 15481	I Don't Need Anything/If You Can't Say Anything Nice	10
67	Capitol CL 15516	There's So Much Love Around Me/Baby Baby	6

WARREN SMITH

MINT VALUE £

60	London HL 7101	I Don't Believe I'll Fall In Love/Cave-In (export issue)	30
61	London HLG 7110	Odds And Ends/A Whole Lot Of Nothin' (export issue)	30
64	Liberty LIB 55699	Blue Smoke/Judge And Jury	15

WHISPERING SMITH

72	Blue Horizon 2431 015	OVER EASY (LP)	60

WHISTLING JACK SMITH

67	Deram DM 112	I Was Kaiser Bill's Batman/The British Grin And Bear	5
68	Decca F 12741	Havah Nagilah/RUDI BENNETT: I'm So Proud	5
67	Deram DML 1009	AROUND THE WORLD WITH WHISTLING JACK SMITH (LP)	12

(see also Rudi Bennett)

WILLIE 'THE LION' SMITH

72	Polydor 2460 156	PORK AND BEANS (LP)	10

SMITH & D'ABO

76	CBS 81583	SMITH & D'ABO (LP)	15

(see also Manfred Mann, Dave Clark Five, Band Of Angels, Mike Smith)

SMITH & JONES

89	Alias ALE 02	Pete And Ben/Amnesty/Duel To The End (p/s, with postcard insert)	8

SMITH BROTHERS (U.K.)

51	London L 959	Castles In The Sand/Little Small Town Girl (78)	12
56	Decca F 10759	Smith (What A Name To Be Stuck With)/Bacon Barbecue	5

(see also Five Smith Brothers)

SMITHFIELD MARKET

73	Gloucester GLS 0435	LONDON IN 1665 (LP, private pressing, gatefold sleeve)	800
74	Globe/Gloucester GLS 0443	AFTER SHAKESPEARE (LP, private pressing, die-cut sleeve, with insert)	700

SMITH, PERKINS & SMITH

72	Island ILPS 9198	SMITH, PERKINS & SMITH (LP)	10

SMITHS

SINGLES

83	Rough Trade RT 131	Hand In Glove/Handsome Devil (p/s, original pressing with Manchester address on rear sleeve; later issue with London address)	15/10
83	Rough Trade RT 131	Hand In Glove/Handsome Devil (later pressing with misprinted blue/negative p/s)	600
83	Rough Trade RT 136	Reel Around The Fountain/Jeane (unissued, white label test pressings only)	950
83	Rough Trade RT 136	This Charming Man/Jeane (with 'Smiths' credit; Rough Trade 'tower' or plain logo on p/s)	7
83	Rough Trade RT 136	This Charming Man/Jeane (without 'Smiths' credit & with either Rough Trade 'tower' or later plain logo on p/s)	7
83	Rough Trade RTT 136	This Charming Man (Manchester)/This Charming Man (London)/Accept Yourself/Wonderful Woman (12", with or without "Smiths" credit on p/s)	12
83	Rough Trade RTT 136NY	This Charming Man (New York Mix)/This Charming Man (London Mix)/Accept Yourself/Wonderful Woman (12", p/s)	25
84	Rough Trade RT 146	What Difference Does It Make?/Back To The Old House ('Morrissey' or 'Terence Stamp' p/s)	10/8
84	Rough Trade RTT 146	What Difference Does It Make?/Back To The Old House/These Things Take Time (12", Morrissey or Terence Stamp p/s)	15/12
84	Rough Trade RT 166	William, It Was Really Nothing/Please Please Please Let Me Get What I Want (original issue with 'man on bed' p/s)	5
84	Rough Trade RTT 166	William, It Was Really Nothing/How Soon Is Now?/Please Please Please Let Me Get What I Want (12", original with green 'man on bed' p/s)	8
85	Rough Trade RTT 176	How Soon Is Now?/Well I Wonder/Oscillate Wildly (12", p/s)	8
85	Rough Trade RTT 181	Shakespeare's Sister/What She Said/Stretch Out And Wait (12", p/s & inner)	8
85	Rough Trade RTT 186	MEAT IS MURDER (live EP, unissued, test pressings only)	1000+
85	Rough Trade RTT 186	MEAT IS MURDER (live 12" EP, unissued, test pressings only)	1000+
85	Rough Trade RTT 186	That Joke Isn't Funny Anymore/Nowhere Fast (live)/Stretch Out And Wait (live)/Shakespeare's Sister (live)/Meat Is Murder (live) (12", p/s)	8
86	Rough Trade RT 193	Panic/Vicar In A Tutu (p/s, with 'Hang The DJ' stickers)	10
86	Rough Trade RTT 193	Panic/Vicar In A Tutu/The Draize Train (12", p/s, with 'Hang The DJ' stickers)	12
86	Rough Trade RT 194C	Ask/Cemetry Gates/Golden Lights (cassette with picture inlay)	12
87	Rough Trade RTT 195	Shoplifters Of The World Unite/Half A Person/London (12", p/s, mispressing, A-side plays "You Just Haven't Earned It Yet Baby")	75
87	Rough Trade RTT 195	Shoplifters Of The World Unite/Half A Person/London (12", p/s in carrier bag)	10
87	Rough Trade RTT 197C	Girlfriend In A Coma/Work Is A Four Letter Word/I Keep Mine Hidden (cassette with picture inlay)	12
87	Rough Trade RTT 198C	I Started Something I Couldn't Finish/Pretty Girls Make Graves/Some Girls Are Bigger Than Others/What's The World (live) (cassette)	12
87	Rough Trade RTT 166	William, It Was Really Nothing/How Soon Is Now?/Please Please Please Let Me Get What I Want (12", reissue, 'Billie Whitelaw' p/s)	15
88	Spiral Scratch SCRATCH 3	An Interview With The Smiths (with *Spiral Scratch* magazine, issue 3)	4

PROMOS

84	Rough Trade RT 61 DJ	Still Ill/You've Got Everything Now (no p/s)	25
88	Rough Trade RTT 171	Barbarism Begins At Home (Edited Version)/Barbarism Begins At Home (12", 1-sided, p/s)	35

REISSUE CDs

88	Rough Trade RTT 146CD	What Difference Does It Make?/Back To The Old House/These Things Take Time (CD)	25
88	Rough Trade RTT 156CD	Heaven Knows I'm Miserable Now/Girl Afraid/Suffer Little Children (CD)	18
88	Rough Trade RTT 166CD	William, It Was Really Nothing/How Soon Is Now?/Please, Please, Please Let Me Get What I Want (CD)	25
88	Rough Trade RTT 171CD	Barbarism Begins At Home/Shakespeare's Sister/Stretch Out And Wait (CD)	30

SMITHS

88	Rough Trade RTT 191CD	The Boy With The Thorn In His Side/Rubber Ring/Asleep (CD)	25
88	Rough Trade RTT 193CD	Panic/Vicar In A Tutu/The Draize Train (CD)	20
88	Rough Trade RTT 194CD	Ask/Cemetery Gates/Golden Lights (CD)	15
88	Rough Trade RTT 200CD	Last Night I Dreamt Somebody Loved Me/Rusholme Ruffians/ Nowhere Fast/William, It Was Really Nothing (CD)	18
88	Rough Trade RTT 215CD	The Headmaster Ritual/Nowhere Fast (live)/Stretch Out And Wait (live)/ Meat Is Murder (live) (CD)	65

ALBUMS

84	Rough Trade ROUGH 76	HATFUL OF HOLLOW (LP, original issue, gatefold sleeve & inner sleeve)	10
85	Rough Trade ROUGHCD 81	MEAT IS MURDER (CD, original issue)	20
86	Rough Trade ROUGHCD 61	THE SMITHS (CD, original issue)	20
86	Rough Trade ROUGHCD 96	THE QUEEN IS DEAD (CD, original issue)	20
87	R. Trade ROUGHCD 101	THE WORLD WON'T LISTEN (CD, original issue)	20
87	R. Trade ROUGHCD 106	STRANGEWAYS HERE WE COME (CD, original issue)	20
87	R. Trade RT 225	LOUDER THAN BOMBS (2-LP, gatefold sleeve)	20
88	R. Trade ROUGH CD 76	HATFUL OF HOLLOW (CD, original sleeve)	20
88	R. Trade ROUGH 126D	RANK (DAT)	25

(see also Morrissey, Sandie Shaw, The The, Electronic)

SMITHY ALL STARS
71	Hillcrest HCT 3	Witchfinder General/Deserted	5

(see also Ian Smith & Inner Mind)

SALLY SMITT & HER MUSICIANS
80	Groovy STP 3	SOUNDTRACK OF THE FILM HANGAHAIR (LP)	10

SMOG
95	City Slang EFAD 49517	A Hit/Wine Stained Lips (p/s, yellow vinyl)	5

SMOKE
67	Columbia DB 8115	My Friend Jack/We Can Take It	15
67	Columbia DB 8252	If The Weather's Sunny/I Would If I Could, But I Can't	15
67	Island WIP 6023	It Could Be Wonderful/Have Some More Tea	40
68	Island WIP 6031	Utterly Simple/Sydney Gill (unreleased)	
70	Revolution Pop REVP 1002	Dreams Of Dreams/My Birth	12
71	Pageant SAM 101	Ride Ride Ride/Guy Fawkes	8
72	Regal Zonophone RZ 3071	Sugar Man/That's What I Want	15
74	Decca FR 13484	Shagalagalu/Gimme Good Loving	5
74	Decca FR 13514	My Lullaby/Looking High	5
88	M. Blue Town MBT 5001	MY FRIEND JACK (LP)	15

(see also Shots)

SMOKESTACK LIGHTNIN'
69	Bell BLL 1046	Light In My Window/Long Stemmed Eyes	5
69	Bell MBLL/SBLL 116	OFF THE WALL (LP)	25

SMOKEY BABE
62	'77' LA 12-12	SMOKEY BABE AND HIS FRIENDS (LP)	25

SMOKEY CIRCLES
70	Carnaby CNS 401	Long Long Long/Love Me While You Can	5
70	Carnaby CNLS 6006	THE SMOKEY CIRCLES ALBUM (LP)	30

SMOKIE & HIS SISTER
67	CBS 202605	Creators Of Rain/In Dreams Of Silent Seas	4

SMOKIN' ROADIE
83	Zone To Zone ZON 3	Midnight/Ripp Off (p/s)	50

SMOKEY SMOTHERS
69	Polydor 623 239	THE DRIVING BLUES (LP)	30

DES SMYTH & COLLEGEMEN
65	Pye 7N 15867	The Pillow That Whispers/Lonely Streets	6
65	Pye 7N 15996	Wedding Bells/All For The Love Of A Girl	6

GILLI SMYTH & MOTHER GONG
78	Charly CRL 5007	MOTHER (LP, with insert)	15

(see also Gong)

DONALD SMYTHE
71	Punch PH 83	Where Love Goes/HURRICANES: You Can Run	30

GLORIA SMYTHE
60	Vogue V 9159	I'll Be Over After A While/Gee Baby Ain't I Good To You	10

SNAFU
74	WWA WWS 007	Dixie Queen/Monday Morning	5
74	WWA WWA 003	SNAFU (LP)	15
74	WWA WWA 013	SITUATION NORMAL (LP)	15

(see also Whitesnake, Freedom)

SNAIL'S PACE
77	Brian MR 76575	I Left My Trail In San Francisco/Shell Out Slug (foldout p/s)	25

SNAKEBITE
83	Astor ASTOR 1	Blow You Away (no p/s)	50

SNAKEFINGER
79	Virgin VS 312	Kill The Great Raven/What Wilbur (p/s)	5
79	Virgin V 2140	CHEWING HIDES THE SOUND (LP)	12

(see also Residents)

SNAKES
75	Dynamite DYR45 006	Teenage Head/Lights Out	6

(see also Motors)

SNAPE
73	Transatlantic TRA 269	ACCIDENTALLY BORN IN NEW ORLEANS (LP)	20

(see also Alexis Korner)

SNAPPERS
59	Top Rank JAR 167	Big Bill/If There Were	12
59	Top Rank JAR 167	Big Bill/If There Were (78)	50

SNAPPERS
67	CBS 2719	Upside Down Inside Out/Memories	10

SNATCH
78	Lightning LIG 502	Stanley/I.R.T. (p/s)	4
78	Lightning LIG 505	All I Want/When I'm Bored ('foil' p/s)	5
80	Fetish FET 004	Shopping For Clothes/Joey/Red Army (12", die-cut p/s)	8

(see also Johnny Thunders, Judy Nylon)

SNEAKY PETES
60	Decca F 11199	Savage (Parts 1 & 2)	10

SNEEKERS
64	Columbia DB 7385	I Just Can't Get To Sleep/Bald Headed Woman	60

LEN SNIDER
63	London HLU 9790	Everyone Knows/I'll Be Coming Home Tonight	6

SNIFF 'N' THE TEARS
79	Chiswick NS 40	Driver's Seat (cancelled, test pressings only)	10

SNIVELLING SHITS
77	Ghetto Rockers PRE 2	Terminal Stupid/I Can't Come (p/s)	15
89	Damaged Goods FNARR 4	Isgodaman?/Terminal Stupid/I Can't Come (p/s)	4
89	Dam. Goods FNARR4B	Isgodaman?/Terminal Stupid/I Can't Come (box set with badge & inserts, pink vinyl in stamped plain white sleeve)	7
90	Dam. Goods FNARR LP 3	I CAN'T COME (LP, brown vinyl)	10

(see also Doctor Dark, John Ellis)

SNOBS
64	Decca F 11867	Buckle Shoe Stomp/Stand And Deliver	20

SNOOKY & MOODY
66	Blue Horizon 45-1003	Snooky And Moody's Blues/Telephone Blues (99 copies only)	60

HANK SNOW (& RAINBOW RANCH BOYS)
52	HMV B 10203	Down The Trail Of Achin' Hearts/PEE WEE KING: Slow Coach (78)	8
52	HMV B 10284	My Two Timin' Woman/The Rhumba Boogie (78)	8
52	HMV B 10354	Lady's Man/I Went To Your Wedding (78)	8
54	HMV 7MC 7	Why Do You Punish Me (For Loving You)/When Mexican Joe Meets Jole Blon (with Rainbow Ranch Boys) (export issue)	15
54	HMV 7MC 15	Spanish Fire Ball/Between Fire And Water (with Rainbow Ranch Boys) (export issue)	15
54	HMV 7MC 24	My Arabian Baby/I Don't Hurt Anymore (with Rainbow Ranch Boys) (export issue)	15
54	HMV 7MC 25	My Religion's Not Old-Fashioned (But It's Real Genuine)/The Alphabet (with Rainbow Ranch Boys) (export issue)	15
54	HMV 7MC 31	Yellow Roses/Would You Mind (with Rainbow Ranch Boys) (export issue)	15
59	RCA RCA 1151	Old Shep/The Last Ride	5
59	RCA RCA 1151	Old Shep/The Last Ride (78)	30
61	RCA RCA 1248	Poor Little Jimmie/Beggar To A King	7
58	RCA RCX 116	COUNTRY GUITAR NO. 4 (EP)	12
59	RCA RCX 142	COUNTRY GUITAR NO. 7 (EP)	15
63	RCA RCX 7125	WHEN TRAGEDY STRUCK (EP)	12
64	RCA RCX 7154	THAT COUNTRY GENTLEMAN (EP)	15
59	RCA RD 27115	WHEN TRAGEDY STRUCK (LP)	15
62	RCA Camden CDN 164	SOUTHERN CANNONBALL (LP)	12
63	RCA Camden CDN 5102	THE ONE AND ONLY HANK SNOW (LP)	12
63	RCA RD/SF 7579	RAILROAD MAN (LP)	15
64	RCA RD/SF 7607	I'VE BEEN EVERYWHERE (LP)	15
64	RCA Victor RD 7658	SONGS OF TRAGEDY (LP)	15
65	RCA Camden CDN 5124	THE OLD AND GREAT SONGS (LP)	12
66	RCA Victor RD 7741	SINGS YOUR FAVOURITE COUNTRY HITS (LP)	15
67	RCA Victor RD 7831	GOSPEL TRAIN (LP)	12
68	RCA RD/SF 7945	HANK IN HAWAII (LP)	12

(see also Chet Atkins)

SNUFF
89	Workers Playtime PLAY 008	Not Listening/Dead And Buried/That's Enough/ For Both Sides & No-One Home (p/s)	5
95	Deceptive BLUFF 019	Theme From Whatever Happened To The Likely Lads (1-sided, 1,000 only, 'Merry Christmas' card p/s)	7

BILL SNYDER & HIS (MAGIC PIANO &) ORCHESTRA
51	London L 868	Bewitched/Drifting Sands (B-side with Ralph Sterling)	8
51	London L 869	Ridin' The Offbeat/Dream Concerto (78)	8
51	London L 870	My Silent Love/Choppin' Up Chopin (78)	10
51	London L 971	The Very Thought Of You/I Can't Believe That You're In Love (78)	8
52	London L 1075	Unless/My Dearest (78)	8
53	Parlophone MSP 6005	Bewitched/Drifting Sands (B-side with Ralph Sterling)	6
56	Brunswick 05578	The March Hare/The Eleventh Hour	5
54	London REP 1011	BEWITCHED (EP)	15
51	London H-APB 1004	BEWITCHED (10" LP)	18

MINT VALUE £

54	Brunswick LA 8667	THE STARLIT HOUR (10" LP)	15
57	Brunswick LAT 8200	CAFE RENDEZVOUS (LP)	12
58	Brunswick LAT 8254	SWEET AND LOVELY (LP)	12

RON SNYDER
63	Parlophone R 4993	Oh My Twisted Bach/Narcissus	6

ERROL SOBERS
70	Beacon BEA 159	Sugar Shaker/You're In Love	5

(see also Bobby Bridger)

SOCIALITES
64	Warner Bros WB 148	Jive Jimmy/You're Losing Your Touch	15

SOCIAL SECURITY
78	Heartbeat PULSE 1	I Don't Want My Heart To Rule My Head/ Stella's Got A Fella/Cider/Choc Ice (p/s)	8

SOCIETIE
67	Deram DM 162	Bird Has Flown/Breaking Down	25

SOCRATES
72	Deram DM 362	Eating Momma's Cookin'/Dearest Agnes	4

SODS
79	Tap TAP 1	Moby Grape/Negative Positive (p/s)	12
79	Stortbeat SB 5	No Pictures Of Us/Plaything (p/s)	6
79	Step Forward SFLP 3	MINUTES TO GO (LP)	12

SOFT BOYS
77	Raw RAW 5	GIVE IT TO THE SOFT BOYS (EP, test pressing with withdrawn track, "Vyrna Knowl Is A Headbanger" in place of "Ventilator", 2 copies only)	100
77	Raw RAW 5	GIVE IT TO THE SOFT BOYS (EP)	20
78	Radar ADA 8	(I Want To Be An) Anglepoise Lamp/Fat Man's Son (p/s)	8
79	Raw RAW 37	GIVE IT TO THE SOFT BOYS (EP, unreleased reissue)	
79	Raw RAW 41	Where Are The Prawns (unreleased)	
80	Armageddon AEP 002	NEAR THE SOFT BOYS (EP)	8
80	Armageddon AS 005	I Wanna Destroy You/I'm An Old Pervert (Disco) (p/s)	8
81	Armageddon AS 029	Only The Stones Remain/The Asking Tree (p/s)	8
82	Bucketfull Of Brains BOB 1	Love Poisoning/When I Was A Kid (p/s, with/without Bucketfull Of Brains magazine)	15/12
83	Midnight Music DING 4	He's A Reptile/Song No. 4 (p/s, 2 different designs)	8
87	Bucketfull Of Brains BOB 17	Deck Of Cards/ROBYN HITCHCOCK & PETER BUCK: Flesh No. 1 (flexidisc with Bucketfull Of Brains magazine, issue 23)	6/4
89	Overground OVER 4	The Face Of Death/The Yodelling Hoover (p/s, 600 yellow vinyl, 400 white vinyl, 15 gold test pressings)	6/15
85	Delorean SOFT 1P	WADING THROUGH A VENTILATOR (12" EP, as picture disc)	10
79	Two Crabs CLAW 1001	A CAN OF BEES (LP, original issue, black & white labels)	20
80	Aura AUL 709	A CAN OF BEES (LP, reissue)	10
80	Armageddon ARM 1	UNDERWATER MOONLIGHT (LP)	12
82	Armageddon BYE 1	TWO HALVES FOR THE PRICE OF ONE (LP)	12
83	M. Music CHIME 0002	INVISIBLE HITS (LP)	10
84	Two Crabs CLAW 1001	A CAN OF BEES (LP, 2nd reissue, black & red labels)	10

(see also Robyn Hitchcock, Kimberley Rew)

SOFT CELL
80	Big Frock ABF 1	MUTANT MOMENTS (EP, plain p/s with postcard; beware of counterfeits without postcard & in wraparound p/s!)	75
81	Some Bizzare HARD 1	A Man Can Get Lost/Memorabilia (p/s, 10,000 only)	10
81	Some Bizzare HARD 12	Memorabilia (Extended)/Persuasion (Extended) (12", p/s)	10
81	Some Bizzare BZS 212	Tainted Love/Where Did Our Love Go/Tainted Dub/Memorabilia (12", p/s, limited edition with 4 tracks)	8
81	Lyntone LYN 10410	Metro Mr. X/B-MOVIE: Remembrance Day (red or green flexidisc, with/without Flexipop magazine, issue 12)	8/6
82	Some Bizzare CELBX 1	THE 12" SINGLES (6 x 12" box set, with booklet)	50
83	Some Bizzare BZS 2020	Soul Inside/You Only Live Twice//Loving You — Hating Me/ Her Imagination (double pack)	6
84	Some Bizzare BZSR 2212	Down In The Subway (Remix)/Disease And Desire/Born To Lose (12", p/s)	18
91	Some Bizzare SOFCP 1	Say Hello, Wave Goodbye — '91/Numbers/Torch (Original Extended Version) (CD, picture disc)	8
91	Some Bizzare SOFCP 2	Tainted Love—Where Did Our Love Go/Loving You — Hating Me/ Where The Heart Is (CD, in different colours of leather pouch)	10
91	Some Bizzare (no cat. no.)	Megamix '91 (12", promo only, custom p/s)	12
83	Lyntone (no cat. no.)	Say Hello, Wave Goodbye (live) (flexidisc, blue vinyl, fan club issue, 500 only)	18
84	Lyntone (no cat. no.)	Ghostrider (live '83) (flexidisc, blue, black or green vinyl, fan club issue)	15

(see also Marc Almond, Marc & Mambas, Bronski Beat with Marc Almond, Dave Ball, Anne Hogan)

SOFTIES
77	Charly CYS 1036	Suicide Pilot/C.I. Angel (p/s)	5

(see also Captain Sensible)

MICK SOFTLEY
65	Immediate IM 014	I'm So Confused/She's My Girl	18
67	CBS 202469	Am I The Red One/That's Not My Kind Of Love	35
70	CBS 5130	Can You Hear Me Now/Time Machine	6
71	CBS 7337	Goin' Down The Road/Gypsy	6
72	CBS 8269	Lady Willow/From The Land Of The Crab	6
65	Columbia 33SX 1781	SONGS FOR SWINGIN' SURVIVORS (LP)	90
70	CBS 64098	SUNRISE (LP, gatefold sleeve)	25
71	CBS 64395	STREET SINGER (LP)	22
72	CBS 64841	ANY MOTHER DOESN'T GRUMBLE (LP)	22

SOFT MACHINE

67	Polydor 56151	Love Makes Sweet Music/Reelin' Feelin' Squeelin'	100
78	Harvest HAR 5155	Soft Space (Parts 1 & 2) (p/s)	8
69	Probe SPB 1002	THE SOFT MACHINE VOLUME TWO (LP)	25
70	CBS 66246	THIRD (2-LP)	20
71	CBS 64280	FOURTH (LP)	15
72	CBS 64806	FIFTH (LP)	15
73	CBS 68214	SIX (2-LP)	15
73	CBS 65799	SEVEN (LP, gatefold sleeve)	15
75	Harvest SHSP 404	BUNDLES (LP, with inner sleeve)	12
76	Harvest SHSP 4056	SOFTS (LP)	12
77	Harvest SHTW 800	TRIPLE ECHO (3-LP, box set, with colour booklet)	40
78	Harvest SHSP 4083	ALIVE & WELL (LP)	12

(see also Robert Wyatt, Kevin Ayers, Hugh Hopper, Elton Dean, Daevid Allen, Matching Mole, 'Igginbottom, Lyn Dobson)

SOFT PEDALLING

70	Decca F 23034	It's So Nice/Rolling On Home	4

SOFT SHOE

78	Aardvark AARD 1	FOR THOSE ALONE (LP, with insert)	100

SOHEP

81	Merciful Release MR 3	So Much Fun/You Could Be So Nice Dear (p/s)	10

SOHO SKIFFLE GROUP

57	Melodisc 1403	Give Me A Big Fat Woman/The Midnight Special (78)	18
57	Melodisc 1421	Frankie And Johnny/Streamline Train (78)	18
57	Melodisc EMP 7 72	SOHO SKIFFLE GROUP (EP)	80

MARTIAL SOLAL

63	RCA Victor RD/SF 7614	AT NEWPORT '63 (LP)	12

SOLAR PLEXUS

73	Polydor 2383 222	SOLAR PLEXUS (LP)	12

SOLDIER

82	Heavy Metal HEAVY 12	Sheralee/Force (p/s)	15

SOLID GOLD CADILLAC

73	RCA SF 8311	SOLID GOLD CADILLAC (LP)	20
73	RCA SF 8365	BRAIN DAMAGE (LP)	18

(see also Chris Spedding, Mike Westbrook)

SOLID ROCK BAND

78	Chapel Lane RWA 1	FOOTPRINTS ON THE WATER (LP, gatefold sleeve)	20

SOLID SENDERS

(see under Wilko Johnson)

SOL INVICTUS

90	Cerne 004	Abbatoirs Of Love/CURRENT 93: This Ain't The Summer Of Love (live in Japan, gig freebie, 93 only with insert & gig ticket [200 without insert])	25/20
91	Shock SX 016	See The Dove Fall/Somewhere In Europe (numbered foldover p/s in poly bag, 1,000 only)	10
91	World Serpent WS7 002	Looking For Europe (1-sided, etched B-side, foldover sleeve in poly bag)	10
89	SVL SVL 009	IN THE JAWS OF THE SERPENT (LP, with insert)	15

(see also Current 93, Death In June, Nurse With Wound, Karl Blake, Shock Headed Peters)

SOLITAIRES

58	London HLM 8745	Walking Along/Please Kiss This Letter	125
58	London HLM 8745	Walking Along/Please Kiss This Letter (78)	50

BOBBY SOLO

64	Fontana TF 456	Una Lacrima Sul Viso/Ora Che Se I Già Una Donna (some in p/s)	10/6
65	Fontana TF 573	Se Piangi Se Ridi/Saro Un Illuso	6

SANDY SOLO

53	London L 1178	It Really Doesn't Matter/I'm Through With Love (78)	12
53	London L 1182	I D'Wanna Hear Sweet Music Tonight/Close Your Dreamy Eyes (78)	12

SOLSTICE

82	private pressing	MORNING LIGHT (cassette)	10
83	Roke RO 001C	New Life/Peace For The New Age (cassette)	6
84	Equinox EQRLP 001	SILENT DANCE (LP, gatefold sleeve)	25

SOLUTION

72	Decca SKL-R 5124	SOLUTION (LP)	12

SOME CHICKEN

77	Raw RAW 7	New Religion/Blood On The Wall (p/s)	12
78	Raw RAW 13	Arabian Daze/No. 7 (p/s)	8
78	Raw RAWT 13	Arabian Daze/No. 7 (12", no p/s)	8
78	Raw RAWT 17	Arabian Daze/No. 7 (12", no p/s, reissue)	10

SOMEONE'S BAND

70	Deram DM 313	Story/Give It To You	10
70	Deram SML 1068	SOMEONE'S BAND (LP)	120

GORDON SOMERS & HIS GROUP

64	Top Ten TPSX 101	THE SOUND OF THE BEATLES (EP)	7

VIRGINIA SOMERS

54	Decca F 10301	Lovin' Spree/Cross Over The Bridge	8

SOMETHING HAPPENS!

86	Prophet PRS 002	TWO CHANCES (EP, p/s)	12
86	Cooking Vinyl WILD 001	TWO CHANCES (EP, reissue, p/s with insert)	10

ELKE SOMMER
61	Columbia DB 4688	Be Not Notty/The Faithfull Hussar	5

JOANIE SOMMERS
60	Warner Bros WB 23	Be My Love/Why Don't You Do Right?	6
61	Warner Bros WB 31	Ruby Duby Du/Bob White	6
61	Warner Bros WB 44	One Boy/I'll Never Be Free	6
62	Warner Bros WB 71	Johnny Get Angry/Summer Place	7
62	Warner Bros WB 78	Passing Strangers/When The Boys Get Together	7
63	Warner Bros WB 85	Goodbye Joey/Bobby's Hobbies	7
63	Warner Bros WB 105	Little Girl Bad/Wishing Well	8
65	Warner Bros WB 150	If You Love Him/I Think I'm Gonna Cry	8
60	Warner Bros WEP 6013	POSITIVELY THE MOST (EP, also stereo WSEP 2013)	15/20
61	Warner Bros WEP 6047	THE VOICE OF THE SIXTIES (EP, also stereo WSEP 2047)	15/20
64	Warner Bros W(S)EP 6121	JOHNNY GET ANGRY No. 1 (EP, mono/stereo)	15/20
64	Warner Bros W(S)EP 6123	JOHNNY GET ANGRY No. 2 (EP, mono/stereo)	15/20
61	Warner Bros WM 4045	THE VOICE OF THE 60s (LP, also stereo WS 8045)	20/25
62	Warner Bros WM 4062	FOR THOSE WHO THINK YOUNG (LP, also stereo WS 8062)	20/25
63	Warner Bros WM 8107	JOHNNY GET ANGRY (LP, also stereo WS 8107)	25/30
64	Warner Bros WM 8119	LET'S TALK ABOUT LOVE (LP, also stereo WS 8119)	18/20

(see also Ed Byrnes)

ROY SONE
59	Decca F 11159	Jenny/Why Do You Doubt Our Love	5
59	Decca F 11159	Jenny/Why Do You Doubt Our Love (78)	8

SONGSTERS
54	London HL 8100	Bahama Buggy Ride/It Isn't Right	25
54	London HL 8100	Bahama Buggy Ride/It Isn't Right (78)	10

SON HOUSE
60s	Saydisc Roots SL 504	THE VOCAL INTENSITY OF SON HOUSE (LP)	30
66	CBS (S)BPG 62604	THE LEGENDARY FATHER OF FOLK BLUES (LP)	30
70	Liberty LBS 83391	JOHN THE REVELATOR (LP)	40

SON HOUSE/J.D. SHORT
69	Xtra XTRA 1080	DELTA BLUES (LP)	30

SONIC ASSASSINS
81	Flicknife FLEP 101	SONIC ASSASSINS (12" EP, p/s)	7

(see also Hawkwind)

SONIC BOOM
90	Silvertone SONIC 1	Octaves/Tremeloes (10", orange vinyl PVC sleeve, mail-order only)	20
91	Silvertone SONIC 2	(I Love You) To The Moon And Back/Capo Waltz (live) (gig freebie in black die-cut sleeve, promo only, 33rpm, p/s later available separately)	12/8
90	Silvertone ORE ZLP 506	SPECTRUM (LP, gatefold rotating plastic disc sleeve with inner)	20

(see also Spacemen 3, Spectrum)

SONIC GIT
77	Cider GIT 001	Ain't Nuffink In My Pants (1-sided sewage-coloured flexidisc, some with *My School's A Cunt* fanzine)	40/20

SONIC YOUTH
82	Zensor ND 01	THE BURNING SPEAR (12" EP)	25
83	Zensor ZENSOR 10	KILL YOUR IDOLS (EP)	18
86	Blast First BFFP 3	Flower/Halloween (12", p/s, some on yellow vinyl)	20/12
86	Blast First BFFP 3	Flower/Rewolf (12", p/s, censored version)	25
86	Blast First BFFP 3(B)	(Savage Pencil etch)/Halloween II (12", p/s, A-side engraved, 1st 100 signed)	40/20
86	Blast First BFFP 3X	Flower/Halloween/Satan Supermix (12", unreleased)	
86	Blast First BFFP 7	Starpower (edit)/Bubblegum (p/s, some with badge & poster)	12/4
88	Fierce FRIGHT 015/016	Stick Me Donna Magick Momma/Making The Nature Scene (live) (p/s, 2 x 1-sided 7" with etched B-sides)	25
88	Fierce FRIGHT 015/016	Stick Me Donna Magick Momma/Making The Nature Scene (live) (p/s, single disc reissue)	15
88	Catalogue CAT 064	Teenage Riot (square flexidisc sewn into 'The Catalogue' magazine)	12/8
89	Blast First BFFP 46	Touch Me I'm Sick/MUDHONEY: Be We Halloween (12", p/s)	8
89	Blast First BFFP 48	Providence (stereo)/Providence (mono) (no p/s, promo only)	5
92	Geffen 7-19664 DJ	Personality Crisis/Dirty Boots (no p/s, DJ promo only)	8
83	Neutral NEUTRAL 9	CONFUSION IS SEX (LP)	20
85	NOT NOT 1/BUT 2	WALLS HAVE EARS (2-LP, 2,000 copies only, numbered)	50
87	Blast First CHAT 1	SISTER INTERVIEW DISC (LP)	18
88	Blast First BFFP 34	DAYDREAM NATION (2-LP, 1st 1,000 with signed poster)	25

(see also Thurston Moore, Kim Gordon & Epic Soundtracks, Ciccone Youth, Mudhoney)

SONNY
71	Ackee ACK 127	Love And Peace/LARRY & ALVIN: Throw Me Corn	8

SONNY (& SONNY'S GROUP)
65	Atlantic AT 4038	Laugh At Me/Tony (as Sonny & Sonny's Group)	4
65	Atlantic AT 4060	The Revolution Kind/Georgia And John Quetzal (as Sonny & Sonny's Group)	4
67	Atlantic 584 131	I Told My Love To Go Away/Misty Roses (solo)	4

(see also Sonny & Cher)

SONNY (Burke) & YVONNE
64	Island WI 134	Life Without Fun/SONNY BURKE GROUP: Mount Vesuvius	15

(see also Sonny Burke)

SONNY & CHER
64	Reprise R 20309	Baby Don't Go/Walkin' The Quetzal	7
65	Atlantic AT 4035	I Got You Babe/It's Gonna Rain	5
65	Atlantic AT 4047	But You're Mine/Hello	5

65	Vocalion VL 9247	The Letter/Spring Fever (B-side by 'Sonny & Cher (Instrumental)')	6
66	Atlantic AT 4069	What Now My Love/I Look For You	6
66	Atlantic 584 018	Have I Stayed Too Long/Leave Me Be	5
66	Atlantic 584 040	Little Man/Monday	5
66	Atlantic 584 057	Living For You/Turn Around	5
67	Atlantic 584 078	The Beat Goes On/Love Don't Come	6
67	Atlantic 584 110	Podunk/Beautiful Story	6
67	Atlantic 584 129	It's The Little Things/Plastic Man	6
68	Atlantic 584 162	Good Combination/You And Me	6
68	Atlantic 584 168	Circus/SONNY BONO: I Would Marry You Today	6
68	Atlantic 584 215	You Gotta Have A Thing Of Your Own/I Got You Babe	6
70	Atco 2091 021	Get It Together/Hold You Tighter	5
71	MCA MU 1139	Real People/Somebody	5
72	MCA MU 1154	A Cowboy's Work Is Never Done/Somebody	5
72	MCA MU 1164	When You Say Love/Crystal Clear/Muddy Waters	5
73	MCA MUS 1211	The Greatest Show On Earth/You Know Darn Well	5
65	Reprise R 30056	CAESAR AND CLEO (EP, 2 tracks each by Sonny & Cher, Caesar & Cleo)	18
64	Atlantic ATL/STL 5036	LOOK AT US (LP, mono/stereo)	15/20
66	Atlantic 587 006	THE WONDROUS WORLD OF SONNY AND CHER (LP)	15
67	Atlantic 587/588 052	IN CASE YOU'RE IN LOVE (LP)	15
72	MCA MUPS 435	LIVE (LP)	12
72	MCA MUPS 452	ALL I EVER NEED IS YOU (LP)	12

(see also Caesar & Cleo, Cher, Sonny, Date With Soul)

SONNY & DAFFODILS

63	Ember EMB EP 4538	SONNY & DAFFODILS (EP)	60

SONS & LOVERS

67	Camp 602 002	Matters/Peaceful Is The River	6
68	Beacon 3-101	Help Me (I'm On Top Of The World)/Feel Alright	5
68	Beacon 3-107	Happiness Is Love/Things You Do	5

SON OF A BITCH

96	Hengest SOABCDS 1	Treacherous Times/Victim You (CD, stickered jewel case)	10

(see also Saxon)

SONS OF DEMENTED CHILDREN

87	Hatter MAD 003	Spoof Dealer/Busking (p/s, with insert)	18

SONS OF FRED

65	Columbia DB 7605	Sweet Love/I'll Be There	75
65	Parlophone R 5391	I, I, I (Want Your Lovin')/She Only Wants A Friend	40
66	Parlophone R 5415	Baby What Do You Want Me To Do/You Told Me	80

(see also Odyssey)

SONS OF MAN

67	Oak RGJ 612	SONS OF MAN (EP, no p/s)	350

(see also Aubrey Small)

SONS OF MOSES

75	MCA MCA 169	Soul Symphony/Fatback	4

SONS OF PILTDOWN MEN

63	Pye International 7N 25206	Mad Goose/Be A Party	15

SONS OF PIONEERS

54	HMV 7EG 8069	SONS OF THE PIONEERS (EP)	12
57	RCA RD 27016	FAVOURITE COWBOY SONGS (LP)	15

SONS OF SOUL

66	Doctor Bird DB 1037	Yeah Yeah Baby/So Ashamed	15

SONSONG

76	Zebra ZM 5761	SONSONG (LP)	30

SOPHOMORES

60s	Seeco CELP 451	THE SOPHOMORES (LP)	25

SOPWITH CAMEL

66	Kama Sutra KAS 205	Hello Hello/Treadin'	5
74	Reprise K 44251	THE MIRACULOUS HUMP RETURNS FROM THE MOON (LP)	15

SORE THROAT

78	Hub Cap SPIN 1	Complex/I Dunno (p/s)	4

SORROWS

65	Piccadilly 7N 35219	I Don't Wanna Be Free/Come With Me	30
65	Piccadilly 7N 35230	Baby/Teenage Letter	30
65	Piccadilly 7N 35260	Take A Heart/We Should Get Along Fine	10
66	Piccadilly 7N 35277	You've Got What I Want/No, No, No (a few with export p/s)	25/12
66	Piccadilly 7N 35309	Let The Live Live/Don't Sing No Sad Songs For Me	25
66	Piccadilly 7N 35336	Let Me In/How Love Used To Be	30
67	Piccadilly 7N 35385	Pink, Purple, Yellow And Red/My Gal	60
66	Piccadilly N(S)PL 38023	TAKE A HEART (LP, mono/stereo)	135/200

(see also Don Fardon)

SORT SOL

81	4AD AD 101	Marble Station/Misguided (p/s)	10

S.O.U.L. (Sounds Of Unity & Love)

72	Pye Intl. NSPL 28162	CAN YOU FEEL IT (LP)	30
70s	Pye Intl.	WHAT IS IT (LP)	60

HORATIO SOUL

68	Island WI 3132	Ten White Horses/Angela (Sweet Sweet)	10
69	Crystal CR 7006	Nobody's Gonna Sleep Tonight/Turn Around Baby	6

JIMMY SOUL
62	Stateside SS 103	Twistin' Matilda/I Can't Hold Out Any Longer	8
63	Stateside SS 178	If You Wanna Be Happy/Don't Release Me	10
64	Stateside SS 274	I Hate You Baby/Change Partners	8
64	Stateside SE 1010	IF YOU WANNA BE HAPPY (EP)	30

JUNIOR SOUL (Murvin)
68	Doctor Bird DB 1112	Miss Cushie/LYNN TAITT & JETS: Dr. Paul	15
68	Big Shot BI 503	Chattie Chattie/The Magic Touch	8
69	Big Shot BI 527	The Hustler/The Magic Touch	8
70	Gayfeet GS 205	Jennifer/Slipping	7

SHARON SOUL
65	Stateside SS 411	How Can I Get To You/Don't Say Goodbye Love	50

SOUL AGENTS (U.K.)
64	Pye 7N 15660	I Just Wanna Make Love To You/Mean Woman Blues	35
64	Pye 7N 15707	Seventh Son/Let's Make It Pretty Baby	40
65	Pye 7N 15768	Don't Break It Up/Gospel Train	35
	(see also Loot, Don Shinn, Hookfoot)		

SOUL AGENTS (Jamaica)
67	Coxsone CS 7007	Get Ready It's Rocksteady/BOB & BELTONES: Smile Like An Angel	
		(B-side actually by Bop & Beltones)	15
67	Coxsone CS 7018	For Your Education/SUMMERTAIRES: Tell Me	18
67	Coxsone CS 7027	Lecture/SOUL BOYS: Blood Pressure	18

SOUL BOYS
67	Island WI 3052	Blood Pressure/RITA MARLEY: Come To Me	18
	(see also Soul Agents [Jamaica])		

SOUL BROTHERS (U.K.)
65	Mercury MF 916	Gotta Get A Goof Thing Going/Good Lovin' Never Hurt	6
65	Decca F 12116	I Keep Ringing My Baby/I Can't Take It	8
65	Parlophone R 5321	I Can't Believe It/You Don't Want To Know	12

SOUL BROTHERS (Jamaica)
65	Ska Beat JB 226	Train To Skaville/WAILERS: I Made A Mistake	40
66	Rio R 118	Crawfish/RITA MARLEY: You Lied	35
66	Rio R 121	Mr T.N.T/MARCIA GRIFFITHS: Mr Everything	15
66	Island WI 282	Green Moon/E Gal OK	18
66	Island WI 294	Ska-Bostello/DON DRUMMOND: Looking Through The Window	18
66	Island WI 296	Sound One/MARTINE: Grandfather's Clock	
		(B-side actually by Emille Straker & Merrymen or Martinis)	18
66	Island WI 3013	More & More/DELROY WILSON: Dancing Mood	18
66	Island WI 3016	Mr Flint/Too Young To Love (B-side actually by Freddie McGregor)	18
67	Island WI 3036	Sound Pressure/ETHIOPIANS: For You	18
67	Island WI 3039	Hi-Life/DELROY WILSON: Close To Me	18
67	Coxsone CS 7001	Take Ten/HUGH GODFREY: Deh Pon Dem	18
67	Coxsone CS 7020	Hey Windell/KEN BOOTHE: Home Home Home	18
67	Coxsone CS 7024	One Stop/TENNORS: Pressure And Slide	18
67	Studio One SO 2006	Hot And Cold/TERMITES: Mercy Mr. Percy	18
67	Studio One SO 2016	Honeypot/VICEROYS: Lose And Gain	18
70	Pressure Beat PR 5506	Pussy Catch A Fire (actually by Soul Twins)/DESTROYERS:	
		Follow This Beat (B-side actually "Secret Weapon" by Ansell Collins)	10
67	Coxsone CSL 8001	HOT SHOT SKA (LP)	100
67	Coxsone CSL 8002	CARIB SOUL (LP)	75
	(see also Earl Van Dyke & Soul Brothers, Soul Twins, Lee Perry, Tony Gregory, Ethiopians, Itals, Hortense & Delroy, Gaylads, Jennors, Derrick Morgan, Summertaires, Delroy Wilson)		

SOUL BROTHERS SIX
67	Atlantic 584 118	Some Kind Of Wonderful/I'll Be Loving You	25
69	Atlantic 584 256	Some Kind Of Wonderful/Somebody Else Is Loving My Baby	6
72	Atlantic K 10204	Some Kind Of Wonderful/Check Yourself	5
74	Atlantic K 10471	Thank You For Loving Me/Somebody Else Is Loving My Baby	5

SOUL CATS
69	Camel CA 23	Keep It Moving/Your Sweet Love	6
69	Gas GAS 109	Choo Choo Train/The Load (actually "Swinging For Joy" by Count	
		Ossie Band)	6
71	Hillcrest HCT 2	Reggay Got Soul (actually by Carl Bryan)/Land Of Love	7
70s	Junior JR 103	Reggay Got Soul (actually by Carl Bryan)/Land Of Love (reissue)	6

SOUL CHILDREN
69	Stax STAX 137	The Sweeter He Is (Parts 1 & 2)	5
71	Stax 2025 050	Give Me One Good Reason/Bring It Here	5
72	Stax 2025 102	Hearsay/Don't Take My Sunshine	5
74	Stax STXS 2006	Love Makes It Right/Love Makes It Right (mono)	5
72	Stax 2325 076	GENESIS (LP)	12
74	Stax STX 1005	FRICTION (LP)	12

SOUL CITY
62	Cameo Parkway P 103	Everybody Dance Now/Who Knows	35

SOUL CITY EXECUTIVES
69	Soul City SC 109	Happy Chatter/Falling In Love	8

SOUL CLAN
68	Atlantic 584 202	Soul Meeting/That's How It Feels (some in p/s)	10/6
	(see also Solomon Burke, Arthur Conley, Don Covay, Ben E. King, Joe Tex)		

MINT VALUE £

SOUL DEFENDERS
| 71 | Banana BA 354 | Way Back Home/SOUL REBELS: Stand For Your Rights | 8 |
| 72 | Ackee ACK 147 | Sound Almighty/COUNT OSSIE: Meditation | 8 |

(see also Eric Donaldson, Carey Johnson)

SOUL DIRECTIONS
| 70 | Attack ATT 8011 | Su Su Su/Better Herring | 7 |

GEORGE SOULE
| 75 | United Artists UP 35771 | Get Involved/Everybody's Got A Song To Sing | 8 |

SOULETTES
65	Ska Beat JB 204	Opportunity/DIZZY JOHNNY & STUDIO 1 ORCHESTRA: Sudden Destruction	15
70	Upsetter US 337	Let It Be/UPSETTERS: Big Dog	10
71	Jackpot JP 766	My Desire/Bring It Up	8
71	Jackpot JP 767	All Of Your Loving/LLOYD CLARKE: Love Me	10
73	Attack ATT 8044	This World/Same Thing	6

(see also Rita Marley, Ken Boothe, Roland Alphonso, Uniques)

SOUL EXPLOSION
| 69 | Downtown DT 455 | Let's Try It Again/Gumpton Rock | 5 |
| 70 | J-DAN JDN 4405 | My Mother's Eyes/Gum Pot | 7 |

SOUL FLAMES
| 68 | Nu Beat NB 020 | Mini Really Fit Dem/Soul Train | 8 |

SOULFUL STRINGS
67	Chess CRS 8068	Burning Spear/Within You, Without You	15
69	Chess CRS 8094	I Wish It Would Rain/Listen Here	6
69	Chess CRLS 4534	GROOVIN' WITH THE SOULFUL STRINGS (LP)	18

SOUL KINGS
| 69 | Blue Cat BS 169 | The Magnificent Seven/RUPIE EDWARDS: Long Lost Love | 12 |

SOUL LEADERS
| 67 | Rio R 134 | Pour On The Sauce/Beauty Is Only Skin Deep | 10 |

SOULMATES (U.K.)
65	Parlophone R 5334	Too Late To Say You're Sorry/Your Love	8
66	Parlophone R 5407	Bring Your Love Back Home (with Jet Set)/When Love Is Gone	8
66	Parlophone R 5506	Mood Melancholy/Sayin' Something	7
67	Parlophone R 5601	Is That You?/Time's Run Out	6

(see also Liza Strike)

SOULMATES (Jamaica)
69	Amalgamated AMG 836	Them A Laugh And A Ki Ki/The Hippys Are Here (B-side actually by Hippy Boys)	8
69	Amalgamated AMG 842	On The Move/Jump It Up (B-side actually by Viceroys)	12
69	Camel CA 33	Beware Of Bad Dogs/Short Cut (actually by Glen Adams)	7
70	Unity UN 555	Ten Cent/DOREEN SHAFFER: Stay With Me Forever	6

SOUL MERCHANTS
| 67 | President PT 166 | Whole Lot Of Lovin'/Stormy Weather | 4 |

SOUL PARTNERS
| 69 | Pama PM 766 | Walk On Judge/Lose The One You Love | 5 |

SOUL PEOPLE
| 68 | Island WIP 6040 | Hummin'/Soul Drink | 8 |

SOUL PROPRIETORS
| 65 | Concord CON STD 74 | All/Lonely Separation (private pressing) | 200 |

SOUL REBELS
| 72 | Banana BA 374 | Listen And Observe/What's Love | 40 |

(see also Soul Defenders)

SOUL RHYTHMS
69	Bullet BU 404	Work Boy Work/CECIL THOMAS: Girl Lonesome Fever	6
69	High Note HS 013	National Lottery/Round Seven	8
69	Gas GAS 113	Soul Call/Musical Gate	6

(see also Hippy Boys, Max Romeo)

SOUL RUNNERS
| 67 | Polydor 56732 | Grits 'n' Cornbread/Spreading Honey | 8 |

SOUL SEARCHERS
| 74 | Sussex SXX 2 | Blow Your Whistle (Parts 1 & 2) | 5 |
| 74 | Sussex LPSX 4 | SALT OF THE EARTH (LP) | 20 |

SOUL SISTERS (U.S.)
64	Sue WI 312	I Can't Stand It/Blueberry Hill	30
64	Sue WI 336	Loop De Loop/Long Gone	25
65	London HLC 9970	Foolish Dreamer/Good Time Tonight	25
72	United Artists UP 35388	Good Time Tonight/Some Soul Food	6
64	Sue ILP 913	THE SOUL SISTERS (LP)	100

SOUL SISTERS (Jamaica)
| 69 | Amalgamated AMG 839 | Wreck A Buddy/VERSATILES: Push It In | 8 |

(see also Dennis Brown)

SOUL SOUNDS
| 67 | Columbia S(C)X 6158 | SOUL SURVIVAL (LP) | 18 |

(see also Savages, Rebel Rousers)

SOUL STIRRERS
| 69 | Duke DU 25 | Come See About Me/LLOYD CHARMERS: 5 To 5 | 10 |

(see also Sam Cooke)

SOUL SURVIVORS
67	Stateside SS 2057	Expressway To Your Heart/Hey Gyp	15
68	Stateside SS 2094	Explosion (In Your Soul)/Dathon's Theme	10
69	Atlantic 584 275	Mama Soul/Tell Daddy	5

SOUL SYNDICATE
| 72 | Green Door GD 4021 | Riot (actually by Vincent Gordon & Soul Syndicate)/Smoke Without Fire (actually by Keith Hudson) | 8 |

(see also Rockin' Horse)

SOUL TONES
| 70 | Pama PM 790 | Dancing Time/BUNNY BARRETT: Love Locked Out | 6 |

SOUL TWINS (Jamaica)
| 70 | High Note HS 043 | Little Suzie/Cherrie | 6 |
| 72 | Clandisc CLA 238 | Don't Call Me Nigga/DYNAMITES: Joe Louis | 6 |

SOUL TWINS (U.S.)
| 77 | Grapevine GRP 101 | Quick Change Artist/Give The Man A Chance | 6 |

SOUL VENDORS
67	Coxsone CS 7028	You Troubled Me/BOP & BELTONES: Love	22
67	Coxsone CS 7029	Fat Fish/MARCIA GRIFFITHS: Call To Me	22
67	Studio One SO 2018	Rocking Sweet Pea/JOE HIGGS: Change Of Plans	22
67	Studio One SO 2022	Cool Shade/RICHARD ACE: I Need You	22
67	Studio One SO 2028	Just A Little Bit Of Soul/ALTON ELLIS: I Am Just A Guy	20
67	Studio One SO 2031	Take Me/DELROY WILSON: I'm Not A King	22
67	Studio One SO 2032	Pe Da Pa/ERNEST WILSON: Money Worries	22
67	Studio One SO 2034	Hot Rod/GAYLADS: Africa (We Want To Go)	22
67	Studio One SO 2035	Pupa Lick/ETHIOPIANS: Leave My Business Alone	22
68	Studio One SO 2038	Psychedelic Rock/Gaylads: I'm Free	22
68	Studio One SO 2043	Chinese Chicken/JACKIE MITTOO: Put It On	22
68	Studio One SO 2044	Happy Ogan (actually titled "Happy Organ")/INVADERS: Soulful Music	22
68	Studio One SO 2048	Evening Time/RIGHTEOUS FLAMES: Ease Up	22
68	Studio One SO 2058	Frozen Soul/ERNEST WILSON: If I Were A Carpenter	22
68	Studio One SO 2066	Soul Joint/Soul Limbo	22
68	Coxsone CS 7037	Grooving Steady/ROY RICHARDS: Warm And Tender Ska	22
68	Coxsone CS 7038	Whipping The Prince (actually by Ed Hangle & Alton Ellis)/HEPTONES: If You Knew	22
68	Coxsone CS 7048	Last Waltz/HAMLINS: Sentimental Reasons	22
68	Coxsone CS 7057	Real Rock/AL CAMPBELL: Don't Run Away	22
68	Coxsone CS 7071	West Of The Sun/ALTON ELLIS: A Fool	22
69	Coxsone CS 7084	Sixth Figure/DENZIL LAING: Man Payaba	22
69	Studio One SO 2070	Captain Cojoe/JACKIE MITTOO: Drum Song	22
67	Coxsone CSL 8010	ON TOUR (LP)	100

(see also Dobby Dobson)

SOUND
79	Tortch TOR 003	PHYSICAL WORLD (EP)	18
80	Korova KOW 10	Heyday/Brute Force (p/s)	6
81	Korova KOW 21	Sense Of Purpose/Point Of No Return (p/s)	6
79	Tortch TOR 008	THE SOUND (LP, possibly unissued)	20+
80	Korova KODE 2	JEOPARDY (LP)	12

(see also Outsiders, Second Layer)

SOUND BARRIER
| 68 | Beacon BEA 109 | She Always Comes Back To Me/Groovin' Slow | 10 |

SOUND CEREMONY
80s	Celestial Sound	You're Breaking My Heart (p/s)	5
79	Celestial Sound RWG 001	GUITAR STAR (LP)	15
79	Celestial Sound RWG 002	RON WARREN GANDERTON & SOUND CEREMONY (LP)	15
81	Celestial Sound RWG 003	PRECIOUS AS ENGLAND (LP)	15

(see also Ron Warren Ganderton)

SOUND DIMENSION
69	Coxsone CS 7083	Scorcia/CECIL & JACKIE: Breaking Up (B-side actually "Hold Me Baby" by Basil Daley)	20
69	Coxsone CS 7085	Soul Trombone (Suffering Stink)/LARRY & ALVIN: Your Cheating Heart	20
69	Coxsone CS 7090	Soulful Strut/Breaking Up	20
69	Coxsone CS 7093	More Scorcha/LENNIE HIBBERT: Village Soul	20
69	Coxsone CS 7097	Time Is Tight/BARRY LLEWELLYN: Sad Song	20
69	Bamboo BAM 5	Doctor Sappa Too/Soul Eruption (B-side actually by Roy Richards & Sound Dimension)	10
69	Bamboo BAM 7	Baby Face/GLADIATORS: Anywhere	10
69	Bamboo BAM 9	Jamaica Rag/C. MARSHALL: I Need Your Loving	10
69	Bamboo BAM 13	Whoopee/NORMA FRAZER: Working (B-side actually by Marcia Griffiths)	10
69	Bamboo BAM 14	Black Onion/Bitter Blood	10
70	Bamboo BAM 18	Poison Ivy/Botheration — Version	8
70	Banana BA 313	In The Summertime/In The Summertime — Version	8
70	Banana BA 338	My Sweet Lord (Instrumental)/DENNIS BROWN: Silky (B-side actually by Monty Alexander & Cyclones)	8
70	Supreme SUP 202	More Games/MR. FOUNDATION: Maga Dog (actually by Invaders)	8
72	Ackee ACK 149	Solas/GLADIATORS: Sonia	10

(see also Brentford Road Allstars, Jackie Mittoo, Bob Andy, Horace Andy, John Holt, Larry Marshall, Irving Brown, Heptones, Freedom Singers, Winston Francis, Jerry Jones, Ethiopians, Cables, Alton Ellis, Gladiators, Ken Boothe)

SOUNDGARDEN
| 89 | A&M AM 574 | Loud Love/Big Dumb Sex (Dub Version)/Get On The Snake/Fresh Deadly Roses (p/s) | 5 |
| 89 | A&M AMY 574 | Loud Love/Big Dumb Sex (Dub Version)/Get On The Snake/Fresh Deadly Roses (12", p/s, 1 side etched) | 8 |

SOUNDGARDEN

90	A&M AMX 560	Hands All Over/Come Together/Heretic/Big Dumb Sex (10", foldout pack)	8
90	A&M AMCD 560	Hands All Over/Come Together/Heretic/Big Dumb Sex (CD)	8
91	A&M AM 691	Jesus Christ Pose/Stray Cat Blues (picture disc)	4
91	A&M AM 691	Jesus Christ Pose/Stray Cat Blues (poster pack)	6
91	A&M AM 691	Jesus Christ Pose/Stray Cat Blues/Into The Void (Sealth)/Somewhere (12", 1 side etched, die-cut p/s with inner)	7
91	A&M AMCD 691	Jesus Christ Pose/Stray Cat Blues/Into The Void (Sealth)/Somewhere (CD, no'd digipak with black inner, 5,000 only)	7

SOUND OF JIMMY NICOL
65	Decca F 12107	Clementine/Bim Bam	12

(see also Jimmy Nicol)

SOUND NETWORK
65	Mercury MF 944	Watching/How About Now	20

SOUNDS AROUND
66	Piccadilly 7N 35345	What Does She Do?/Sad Subject	12
67	Piccadilly 7N 35396	Red White And You/One Of Two	12

(see also Peter & Wolves, John Pantry, Norman Conquest, Factory)

SOUNDS COMBINE
71	Escort ERT 862	African Museum/African Museum — Version	6

SOUNDS GALACTIC
70	Phase 4 Stereo PFS 4208	AN ASTRONOMICAL ODYSSEY (LP)	15

SOUNDS INCORPORATED
61	Parlophone R 4815	Mogambo/Emily	12
62	Decca F 11540	Sounds Like Locomotion/Taboo	6
63	Decca F 11590	Stop/Go	7
63	Decca F 11723	Order Of The Keys/Keep Moving	18
64	Columbia DB 7239	The Spartans/Detroit	6
64	Columbia DB 7321	Spanish Harlem/Rinky Dink	6
64	Columbia DB 7404	William Tell/Bullets	6
65	Columbia DB 7545	Time For You/Hall Of The Mountain King	6
65	Columbia DB 7676	My Little Red Book/Justice Neddi	6
65	Columbia DB 7737	On The Brink/I'm Comin' Thru	25
67	Polydor 56209	How Do You Feel/Dead As You Go	5
64	Columbia SEG 8360	TOP GEAR (EP)	20
64	Columbia 33SX 1659	SOUNDS INCORPORATED (LP, also stereo SCX 3531)	20/25
65	EMI Regal SREG 1071	RINKY DINK (LP, export issue)	18
66	Studio Two TWO 144	SOUNDS INCORPORATED (LP)	15

(see also Tony Newman)

SOUND SIXTY-SIX
66	Decca F 12323	Flight 4864/The Bouncer	7

SOUNDS NICE
69	Parlophone R 5797	Love At First Sight/Love You Too ('featuring Tim Mycroft')	5
69	Parlophone R 5821	Sleepless Night/Continental Exchange ('featuring Tim Mycroft')	5
69	Parlophone PMC/PCS 7089	LOVE AT FIRST SIGHT (LP)	20

(see also Third Ear Band, Chris Spedding, Clem Cattini Ork)

SOUNDS OF JOHNNY HAWKSWORTH
66	Columbia DB 8059	Goal/"Goal — World Cup 1966" Theme	6

(see also Johnny Hawksworth)

SOUNDS OF MODIFICATION
68	Stateside SL/SSL 10262	SOUNDS OF MODIFICATION (LP)	15

SOUNDS OF SALVATION
74	Reflection RL 310	SOUNDS OF SALVATION (LP, with booklet)	80

(see also Reflection)

SOUNDS OF ZION
60s	Tabernacle TEP 1	HOME TO GLORY (EP)	8

SOUNDS ORCHESTRAL
66	Piccadilly 7N 35284	Thunderball/Mr Kiss Kiss Bang Bang	10
65	Pye NPL 38016	THUNDERBALL — SOUNDS ORCHESTRAL MEET JAMES BOND (LP, some in gatefold sleeve)	30/20

SOUNDS PROGRESSIVE
70	Eyemark EMCL 1009S	KID JENSEN INTRODUCES SOUNDS PROGRESSIVE (LP)	25

SOUNDS SENSATIONAL
67	HMV POP 1584	Love In The Open Air/Night Cry	12

SOUND SYSTEM
65	Island WI 258	You Don't Know Like I Do/Take Me Serious	12

(see also Owen Gray)

EPIC SOUNDTRACKS
81	Rough Trade RT 084	Popular, Classical: Jelly Babies/A 3-Acre Floor/Pop In Packets (p/s)	4

(see also Swell Maps, Thurston Moore Kim Gordon & Epic Soundtracks)

SOUP DRAGONS
86	Popshop 001/ Lyntone LYN 16674	If You Were The Only Girl In The World/LEGEND: Talk Open (33rpm flexi with *Pure Popcorn* fanzine, later with *The Legend* fanzine)	8/6/5
86	Subway Organisation SUBWAY 2	THE SUN IS IN THE SKY (EP, unreleased, 1,000 only, foldaround p/s in poly bag)	15
86	Subway Organisation SUBWAY 4	Whole Wide World/I Know Everything (with insert in poly bag, orange or blue foldaround p/s)	4

86	Raw TV Products RTV 1	Hang Ten!/Slow Things Down (p/s, blue or red vinyl)	4
89	Raw TV Products	DEEP TRASH (cassette, withdrawn)	15
90	Raw TV SOUPLP 2	LOVEGOD (LP, with foiled sleeve & lyric sheet)	10

(see also BMX Bandits, Future PIlot A.K.A.)

SOUP GREENS

65	Stateside SS 457	That's Too Bad/Like A Rolling Stone	40

SOUPHERBS

65	Oak RGJ 601	SOUPHERBS (LP)	200

HARRY SOUTH ORCHESTRA

75	EMI EMI 2252	The Sweeney (TV Theme) (Parts 1 & 2)	20
67	Mercury 20081 MCL	PRESENTING HARRY SOUTH (LP)	22

JOE SOUTH

62	Oriole CB 1752	Masquerade/I'm Sorry For You	10
63	MGM MGM 1206	Same Old Song/Standing Invitation	7
65	MGM MGM 1267	Concrete Jungle/Last One To Know	7
65	HMV POP 1474	I Want To Be Somebody/Deep Inside Me	6
68	Capitol CL 15535	Birds Of A Feather/It Got Away	6
69	Capitol CL 15568	Don't Throw Your Love To The Wind/Redneck	6
69	Capitol CL 15579	Games People Play/Mirror Of Your Mind	6
69	Capitol CL 15594	Leanin' On You/Don't Be Ashamed	5
69	Capitol CL 15602	Birds Of A Feather/These Are Not My People	5
69	Capitol CL 15608	Don't It Make You Want To Go Home/Heart's Desire	6
70	Capitol CL 15625	Walk A Mile In My Shoes/Shelter	5
70	Capitol CL 15636	The Clock Up On The Wall/What Makes Lovers Hurt One Another	5
70	Capitol CL 15666	Hush/Party People	6
69	Capitol E-(S)T 108	INTROSPECT (LP)	15
70	Capitol ST 21548	WALK A MILE IN MY SHOES (LP)	12

SOUTH COAST SKA STARS

80	Safari SAFE 27	South Coast Rumble/Head On (p/s)	8

JERI SOUTHERN

51	London L 1070	I'm In Love Again/You're The Cause Of It All (78)	20
54	Brunswick 05276	That Old Devil Called Love/Autumn In My Heart (78)	8
54	Brunswick 05343	Remind Me/Little Boy Grown Tall	12
55	Brunswick 05367	The Man That Got Away/Speak Softly To Me	12
55	Brunswick 05490	An Occasional Man/It's D'Lovely	12
56	Brunswick 05529	Where Walks My True Love?/Don't Explain	10
57	Brunswick 05665	Fire Down Below/Smoke Gets In Your Eyes	7
57	Brunswick 05665	Fire Down Below/Smoke Gets In Your Eyes (78)	10
57	Brunswick 05709	Scarlet Ribbons (For Her Hair)/Would I	7
57	Brunswick 05722	Bells Are Ringing/Just In Time	7
58	Brunswick 05737	I Waited So Long/The Mystery Of Love	7
58	Brunswick 05737	I Waited So Long/The Mystery Of Love (78)	10
59	Capitol CL 14993	Senor Blues/Take Me Back Again	6
59	Capitol CL 15054	Run/Don't Look At Me That Way	7
59	Brunswick OE 9438	CARESSES (EP)	15
59	Columbia SEG 7935	RIDIN' HIGH (EP)	15
55	Brunswick LA 8699	WARM (10" LP)	30
56	Brunswick LAT 8100	THE SOUTHERN STYLE (LP)	25
57	Brunswick LAT 8209	JERI GENTLY JUMPS (LP)	25
58	Columbia 33SX 1110	SOUTHERN BREEZE (LP)	20
58	Columbia 33SX 1134	COFFEE, CIGARETTES AND MEMORIES (LP)	20
59	Columbia 33SX 1155	JERI SOUTHERN MEETS JOHNNY SMITH (LP)	18
59	Capitol (S)T 1173	JERI SOUTHERN MEETS COLE PORTER (LP, mono/stereo)	15/18
60	Capitol (S)T 1278	AT THE CRESCENDO (LP, mono/stereo)	15/18

JOHNNY SOUTHERN & HIS WESTERN RHYTHM KINGS

57	Melodisc MEL 1413	We Will Make Love/Crazy Heart	8
57	Melodisc MEL 1413	We Will Make Love/Crazy Heart (78)	8
57	Melodisc MEL 1434	She's Long, She's Tall/Lonesome Whistle	8
57	Melodisc MEL 1434	She's Long, She's Tall/Lonesome Whistle (78)	8

SOUTHERN COMFORT

71	Harvest SHSP 4012	FROG CITY (LP)	15
72	Harvest SHSP 799	SOUTHERN COMFORT (LP)	15
72	Harvest SHSP 4021	STIR DON'T SHAKE (LP)	12

(see also Matthews Southern Comfort)

SOUTHERN DEATH CULT

86	Beggars Banquet BEGA 46	THE SOUTHERN DEATH CULT (LP)	10

(see also Cult, Death Cult, Into A Circle, Getting The Fear)

SOUTHERN SOUND

66	Columbia DB 7982	Just The Same As You/I Don't Wanna Go	200

SOUTHERN TONES

58	Jazz Collector JEN 10	WAITING FOR THE LORD (EP)	10

SOUTHLANDERS

55	Parlophone R 4025	The Crazy Otto Rag/Earth Angel (Will You Be Mine?) (78)	8
55	Parlophone MSP 6182	Ain't That A Shame/Have You Ever Been Lonely	20
55	Parlophone R 4069	Ain't That A Shame/Have You Ever Been Lonely (78)	10
56	Parlophone MSP 6236	Hush-A-Bye Rock/The Wedding Of The Lucky Black Cat	18
56	Parlophone R 4171	Hush-A-Bye Rock/The Wedding Of The Lucky Black Cat (78)	10
57	Decca F 10946	Alone/Swedish Polka	6
57	Decca F 10958	Peanuts/I Never Dreamed	7
58	Decca F 10982	Put A Light In The Window/Penny Loafers And Bobby Socks	15

SOUTHLANDERS

58	Decca F 10982	Put A Light In The Window/Penny Loafers And Bobby Socks (78)	12
58	Decca F 11014	Down Deep/Wishing For Your Love	6
58	Decca F 11014	Down Deep/Wishing For Your Love (78)	8
58	Decca F 11032	I Wanna Jive Tonight/Torero	15
58	Decca F 11032	I Wanna Jive Tonight/Torero (78)	10
58	Decca F 11067	The Mole In A Hole/Choo-Choo-Choo-Choo Cha-Cha-Cha	15
58	Decca F 11067	The Mole In A Hole/Choo-Choo-Choo-Choo Cha-Cha-Cha (78)	12
60	Top Rank JAR 403	Imitation Of Love/Charlie	6
58	Decca DFE 6508	THE SOUTHLANDERS NUMBER ONE (EP)	30

SOUTHSIDE JOHNNY & ASBURY DUKES
77	Epic EPC 5230	Little Girl So Fine/I Ain't Got The Fever (withdrawn)	20

SOUTH SIDE MOVEMENT
73	Pye International 7N 25615	I Been Watchin' You/Have A Little Mercy	5

SOUTHWEST F.O.B.
68	Stax STAX 107	Smell Of Incense/Green Skies	6

SOUTHWIND
70	Harvest HAR 5019	Boogie Woogie Country Girl/Honky Tonkin'	5

(see also Moon Martin)

SOVEREIGNS
66	King KG 1050	Bring Me Home Love/That's The Way Love Is	6

SOVIET-FRANCE
82	Red Rhino RED 12	SOVIET-FRANCE (12" EP, printed hessian sleeve)	15
83	Red Rhink RED 23	NORSCHE (LP)	10
84	Red Rhink RED 40	MOHNOMISCHE (LP)	10
84	Red Rhino REDLP 45	ELSTRE (LP)	10

RED SOVINE
56	Brunswick 05513	Why Baby Why? (with Webb Pierce)/Sixteen Tons	30
56	Brunswick 05513	Why Baby Why? (with Webb Pierce)/Sixteen Tons (78)	18
62	Top Rank JKP 3015	COUNTRY MUSIC (EP)	20
66	London HA-B 8288	GIDDY-UP GO (LP)	15
67	London HA-B 8343	I DIDN'T JUMP THE FENCE (LP)	15
69	London HA-B 8379	TELL MAUDE I SLIPPED (LP)	15

(see also Webb Pierce)

BOB B. SOXX & BLUE JEANS
63	London HLU 9646	Zip-A-Dee-Doo-Dah/Flip And Nitty	10
63	London HLU 9694	Why Do Lovers Break Each Other's Heart?/Dr Kaplan's Office	12
63	London HLU 9754	Not Too Young To Get Married/Annette	15
69	London HLU 10243	Zip-A-Dee-Doo-Dah/Why Do Lovers Break Each Other's Heart?	5
63	London HA-U 8121	ZIP-A-DEE-DOO-DAH (LP)	100
75	Phil Spector Intl. 2307 004	BOB B. SOXX & THE BLUE JEANS (LP)	15

(see also Darlene Love, Bobby Sheen, Blossoms, Crystals, Phil Spector)

SPACE
79	Pye NSPH 28725	JUST BLUE (LP, picture disc)	20

(see also Madeline Bell)

SPACE
90	Space LP 1	SPACE (LP)	40
90	Space CD 1	SPACE (CD, beware of counterfeits)	50

(see also J.A.M.S., KLF, Timelords, Disco 2000)

SPACE
93	Hug HUG 1T	If It's Real/Lookin'/I'm Free (12", p/s with free 'fortune fish')	30
95	Home Rec. CAHOME 1	Money (7" Radio Edit)/Kill Me (7" Radio Edit) (cassette)	4
95	Home Recordings 12HOME 1	Money (Space Club Mix)/Kill Me (Space Club Mix)/Money (7" Radio Edit)/Kill Me (7" Radio Edit) (12", p/s)	10
95	Home Recordings 12HOMEX 1	Money Remixes By Consolidated: Money (Lost In Space Remix)/(Still Lost In Space/Safe Bass Mix)/(Space Club Mix)/(Instrumental) (12", p/s, yellow vinyl)	12
95	Home Recordings CDHOME 1	Money (7" Radio Edit)/Kill Me (7" Radio Edit)/Money (Space Club Mix)/Kill Me (Space Club Mix) (CD)	15
96	Gut CDGUT 1	Neighbourhood (Radio Edit)/Turn Me On To Spiders/Rejects/Neighbourhood (Live It Club Mix) (CD)	10

SPACE ART
77	Arista AHAL 8001	SPACE ART (LP)	15

SPACE CHILDREN
88	Sweatbox SOX 038	LET'S GO DISCO (12" EP)	10

(see also Meat Beat Manifesto)

SPACEMEN
59	Top Rank JAR 228	The Clouds/The Lonely Jet Pilot	15

SPACEMEN 3
86	Glass GLAEP 105	Walkin' With Jesus (Sound Of Confusion)/Rollercoaster/Feel So Good (12" maxi-single, p/s, some with numbered insert)	55/50
87	Glass GLAEP 108	Transparent Radiation/Ecstasy Symphony/Transparent Radiation (Flashback)/Things'll Never Be The Same/Starship (12" maxi-single, p/s)	40
88	Glass GLASS 12054	Take Me To The Other Side/Soul 1/That's Just Fine (12", p/s)	25
89	Fire THREEBIE 3	Revolution/Suicide/Repeater/Love Intro Theme (Xtacy) (12", mail-order only, numbered p/s)	25
89	Cheree CHEREE 5	Extract From A Contemporary Sitar Evening (p/s, flexi with *Cheree* fanzine)	12
89	Fire BLAZE 36T	Hypnotized/Just To See You Smile (Honey Pt 2)/The World Is Dying (12", with poster)	10
89	Fire BLAZE 36CD	Hypnotized/Just To See You Smile (Honey Pt 2)/The World Is Dying (3" CD, with adaptor, 5" case)	8

SPACE

90	Fire BLAZE 41TR	Big City (Remix)/I Love You (Remix) (12", unissued, white label promo, 50 only) 50
86	Glass GLALP 018	SOUND OF CONFUSION (LP) 20
87	Glass GLALP 026	THE PERFECT PRESCRIPTION (LP, gold/silver or bronze/silver sleeve) 20
87	Glass GLAMC 026	THE PERFECT PRESCRIPTION (cassette) 10
88	Glass GLALP 030	PERFORMANCE (LP) 15
88	Glass GLACD 030	PERFORMANCE (CD) 18
90	Fierce FRIGHT 042	DREAMWEAPON/ECSTASY IN SLOW MOTION (LP) 15
90	Fierce FRIGHT 042CD	DREAMWEAPON/ECSTASY IN SLOW MOTION (CD) 18

(see also Sonic Boom, Spiritualized, Darkside, Spectrum)

SPACEPIMP

95	Clear CLR 415	The Pimp/Spacechace/K9 Law (12", p/s, some on clear vinyl) 15/10

SPAGHETTI HEAD

75	RCA RCA 2513	Big Noise From Winnetka/Spunky Axe 5

(see also Clem Cattini Ork, Tornados)

SPAGHETTI JUNCTION

72	Columbia DB 8935	Work's Nice — If You Can Get It/Step Right Up 12

(see also Hank Marvin)

CHARLIE SPAND

50s	Jazz Collector L 18	She's Got Good Stuff/Big Fat Mama Blues (78) 5

(see also Paramount Allstars)

SPANDAU BALLET

82	Chrysalis CHSP 2602	Instinction/Gently (picture disc) 4
82	Chrysalis CHSP 2642	Lifeline/Live And Let Live (picture disc) 4
83	Chrysalis CHSP 2668	Communication (Parts 1 & 2) (picture disc) 4
83	Reformation SPANP 1	True/Lifeline (picture disc) 4
83	Reformation SPANP 2	Gold (Parts 1 & 2) (picture disc) 4
84	Reformation SPANP 3	Only When You Leave/Paint Me Down (picture disc) 4
84	Reformation SPANP 4	I'll Fly For You/To Cut A Long Story Short (live) (5 different picture discs) .. each 4
84	Reformation SPAN 5	Highly Strung (Parts 1 & 2) (p/s, silver vinyl) 4
84	Reformation SPAN 6	Round And Round/True (gatefold p/s, with booklet). 5
84	Reformation SPANX 6	Round And Round/True/Gold (12", p/s, gold vinyl). 7
84	Reformation SPANX 6	Round And Round/True/Gold (12", p/s, poster, sticker, postcard & 5 photos)..... 8
88	CBS SPANS C3	Raw/Raw (Flip)/Raw (Extended Mix) (CD, card sleeve) 7
88	CBS SPANS D3	Raw/Raw (Flip)/Raw (Amnesia Mix) (CD, picture disc) 7
89	CBS SPANS C4	Be Free With Your Love/Be Free With Your Love (Dance Mix Edit)/ Through The Barricades (CD, card sleeve) 7
89	CBS SPANS P4	Be Free With Your Love/Be Free With Your Love (Dance Mix Edit)/ Raw (Extended 12" Mix) (CD, picture disc) 7
89	CBS SPANS C5	Empty Spaces/With The Pride — Gold (live)/Chant No. 1 (live) (CD, card sleeve) .. 7
89	CBS SPANS D5	Empty Spaces/With The Pride — Gold (live)/True (live) (CD, picture disc) 7
90	CBS SPANS C6	Crashed Into Love/How Many Lies (live)/Through The Barricades (live) (CD, card sleeve) 7
90	CBS SPANS D6	Crashed Into Love/With The Pride — Gold (live)/True (live) (CD, gatefold insert) .. 7
82	Chrysalis/Lyntone	Smash Hits (flexidisc free with Smash Hits) 5/4
82	Chrysalis C BOX 1353	DIAMOND (LP, box set as 4 x 12" singles, with posters & lyric sheet) 15

(see also Tony Hadley)

SPANIELS

60	Joy JOYS 197	THE SPANIELS (LP) 18

MUGGSY SPANIER & DIXIELAND/RAGTIME BAND

56	Tempo A 36	Tin Roof Blues/Muskrat Rumble	6
55	Tempo EXA 3	MUGGSY SPANIER'S DIXIELAND BAND (EP)	10
53	Vogue LDE 015	MUGGSY SPANIER BROADCASTS "THIS IS JAZZ" (10" LP)	18
54	London AL 3528	MUGGSY SPANIER AND THE BUCKTOWN FIVE (10" LP)	15
54	HMV DLP 1031	MUGGSY SPANIER AND HIS RAGTIME BAND (10" LP)	15
55	Brunswick LA 8722	MUGGSY SPANIER AND HIS BAND (10" LP)	15
57	Mercury MPL 6516	MUGGSY SPANIER AND HIS DIXIELAND BAND (LP)	12
63	MGM MGM-C 936	THE GEM OF THE OCEAN (LP)	12

(see also Sidney Bechet)

SPANISH BOYS

65	Blue Beat BB 331	I Am Alone/BUSTER'S ALL STARS: Vera Cruz	20

SPANISHTONIANS

67	Pyramid PYR 6005	Kisses/ROLAND ALPHONSO: Women Of The World	12
67	Pyramid PYR 6009	Suffer Me Not/ROLAND ALPHONSO: Guantanamera Ska	10
67	Pyramid PYR 6018	Rudie Gets Plenty/ROLAND ALPHONSO: Sock It To Me	10

SPANISHTOWN SKABEATS

65	Blue Beat BB 315	Oh My Baby (actually by Charmers)/Stop That Train	15
65	Blue Beat BB 320	King Solomon/BUSTER'S ALLSTARS: Devil's Daffodil	15

SPANKY & OUR GANG

67	Mercury MF 982	Sunday Will Never Be The Same/Distance	8
67	Mercury MF 999	Making Every Minute Count/If You Could Only Be Me	8
67	Mercury MF 1010	Lazy Day/It Ain't Necessarily Byrd Avenue	8
68	Mercury MF 1018	Sunday Mornin'/Echoes	5
68	Mercury MF 1023	Like To Get To Know You Well/Three Ways From Tomorrow	5
69	Mercury MF 1123	And She's Mine/Leopard Skin Phone	5
67	Mercury 20114 (S)MCL	SPANKY AND OUR GANG (LP)	20
68	Mercury 20121 SCML	LIKE TO GET TO KNOW YOU (LP)	15
69	Mercury 20150 SCML	ANYTHING YOU CHOOSE B/W WITHOUT RHYME OR REASON (LP)	15

(see also Mama & Papas)

OTIS SPANN

64	Decca F 11972	Stirs Me Up/Keep Your Hand Out Of My Pocket	12
68	Blue Horizon 57-3142	Bloody Murder/Can't Do Me No Good	12
69	Blue Horizon 57-3155	Walkin'/Temperature Is Rising (with Fleetwood Mac)	18
64	Decca LK 4615	THE BLUES OF OTIS SPANN (LP)	70
64	Storyville SLP 157	GOOD MORNING MR. BLUES (LP)	30
64	Storyville SLP 168	PIANO BLUES (LP, with Memphis Slim)	30
65	Decca LK 4661	BLUES NOW (LP)	30
66	Stateside SL 10169	THE BLUES NEVER DIE (LP)	30
67	HMV CLP/CSD 3609	BLUES ARE WHERE IT'S AT (LP)	30
67	Storyville 670 157	PORTRAITS IN BLUES VOL. 3 (LP, reissue of SLP 157)	18
67	Polydor 545 030	NOBODY KNOWS MY TROUBLES (LP)	30
67	Bounty BY 6037	NOBODY KNOWS MY TROUBLES (LP)	20
68	Stateside (S)SL 10255	BOTTOM OF THE BLUES (LP)	30
69	Chess CRLS 4556	FATHERS AND SONS (LP)	20
69	Blue Horizon 7-63217	BIGGEST THING SINCE COLOSSUS (LP, with Fleetwood Mac)	75
69	Deram DML/SML 1036	CRACKED SPANNER HEAD (LP)	45
69	Python KM 4	RAISED IN MISSISSIPPI (LP, 99 copies only, with Robert Jnr. Lockwood)	50
70	Vanguard VSD 6514	CRYIN' TIME (LP)	15

(see also Fleetwood Mac, Memphis Slim, Johnny Shines, Lonnie Johnson)

SPANNER THRU MA BEATBOX

87	Earthly Delights EARTH 3	SPANNER THRU MA BEATBOX (LP)	15

SPARKERS

69	Blue Cat BS 155	Dig It Up/DELROY WILSON: This Life Makes Me Wonder	12

(see also Samuel Edwards)

LOU SPARKES

69	Gayfeet GS 203	By The Time I Get To Phoenix/Lover Boy	8
70	Gayfeet GS 208	We Will Make Love/ROLAND ALPHONSO: Sticker	8

(see also Eric Boswell)

SPARKS

72	Bearsville K 15505	Wonder Girl/(No More) Mr. Nice Guy	12
74	Bearsville K 15516	Girl From Germany/Beaver O'Lindy (brown or white label)	10/7
74	Island WIP 6211	Never Turn Your Back On Mother Earth/Alabamy Right (p/s)	8
76	Island WIP 6282	I Want To Hold Your Hand/England (withdrawn after 1 day)	20
77	Island WIP 6193	This Town Ain't Big Enough For The Both Of Us/Barbecutie (reissue, orange sunset label)	25
77	CBS 5593	A Big Surprise/Forever Young	5
79	Virgin VS 244-12	The Number One Song In Heaven/The Number One Song In Heaven (Long Version) (12, p/s, blue or red vinyl)	10
79	Virgin VS 270-12	Beat The Clock/Beat The Clock (Long Version) (12", black, blue, orange, yellow or pink vinyl picture disc, die-cut p/s)	each 10
79	Virgin VS 289-12	Tryouts For The Human Race/Tryouts For The Human Race (Long Version) (12", p/s, orange, yellow, blue or green picture disc, die-cut p/s)	each 10
79	Island WIP 6532	This Town Ain't Big Enough For The Both Of Us/Looks, Looks, Looks	7
80	Virgin VS 343-12	Young Girls (Disco Version)/Young Girls (Long Version)/Just Because You Love Me (12", p/s)	10
81	Why Fi WHYT 1	Tips For Teens/Don't Shoot Me (12", p/s)	10
83	Atlantic A 9866	Cool Places/Sports (no p/s)	5
86	Epic A 6671	Armies Of The Night/EVELYN KING: Give It Up (p/s)	5
94	Finiflex FF 1004	National Crime Awareness Week (13 Minutes In Heaven)/National Crime Awareness Week (Perkins Playtime) (12", p/s)	15

94	Finiflex FFCD 1004	National Crime Awareness Week (Psycho Cut)/National Crime Awareness Week (Highly Strung Hoedown)/National Crime Awareness Week (Complete Psycho)/National Crime Awareness Week (13 Minutes In Heaven) (CD) 25
94	Logic 74321 24302-2	Excerpts From Gratuitous Sax & Senseless Violins (CD, picture disc, gatefold card p/s, promo only). 50
97	Roadrunner RR 2262-6	The Number One Song In Heaven (Tin Tin Out Mix)/part 2/(Heavenly Dub) (with Jimmy Somerville) (12", diecut sleeve) 10
99	Winney CD IFPI LAE 1	The Cute Candidate/This Town Ain't Big Enough For The Both Of Us (1920 Archival Recording)/The Winney Empire/The Cute Candidate On TV/The Race For President (CD, fan club only issue). 10
76	Bearsville K 85505	TWO ORIGINALS OF SPARKS (2-LP, gatefold sleeve with 12-page booklet). 15
79	Virgin V 2115	NO. 1 IN HEAVEN (LP, yellow vinyl with lyric inner sleeve) 12

(see also Les Rita Mitsouko, Noel, Adrian Musey, Trevor White)

L. SPARKS
| 72 | Big Shot BI 601 | You Don't Care/TONY'S ALL STARS: Must Care (Version) . . . . 6 |
| 72 | Pama PM 833 | You Don't Care/TONY'S ALL STARS: Must Care (Version) . . . . 6 |

(see also Lloyd Parks, Termites)

RANDY SPARKS
| 59 | HMV POP 683 | Birmingham Train/A Girl Like You . . . . 6 |
| 59 | HMV 7EG 8531 | RANDY SPARKS (EP) . . . . 8 |

CANDY SPARLING
| 62 | Piccadilly 7N 35046 | When's He Gonna Kiss Me?/Lonely For You . . . . 8 |
| 63 | Piccadilly 7N 35096 | Can You Keep A Secret/Charm Bracelet . . . . 8 |

SPARROW (U.S.)
| 66 | CBS 202342 | Tomorrow's Ship/Isn't It Strange . . . . 40 |

(see also Steppenwolf)

SPARROW (Jamaica)
60	Kalypso XX 10	Carnival Boycott/Gloria (with Lord Melody) 5
60	Kalypso XX 17	The Sack/Round And Around 5
60s	Melodisc CAL 15	Leading Calypsonians/Love Is Everywhere 5
60s	Melodisc CAL 17	Clara Honey Bunch/Family Sized Cokes. 5
60s	Melodisc CAL 18	Goaty/I Confess 5

(see also Mighty Sparrow, King Sparrow)

JACK SPARROW
| 66 | Doctor Bird DB 1005 | Ice Water/ROLAND ALPHONSO: Ska-Culation . . . . 20 |
| 66 | Doctor Bird DB 1027 | More Ice Water/ROLAND ALPHONSO: Miss Ska-Culation . . . . 30 |

SPARTA
| 81 | Suspect SUS 1 | Fast Lane (some in p/s). . . . . 50/12 |
| 81 | Suspect SUS 2 | Angel Of Death (wraparound p/s) . . . . 40 |

SPARTANS
| 62 | Stateside SS 117 | Can You Waddle? (Parts 1 & 2) . . . . 7 |

ROGER RUSKIN SPEAR
71	United Artists UP 35221	REBEL TROUSER (EP). 5
74	United Artists UP 35683	On Her Doorstep Last Night 5
74	United Artists UP 35720	I Love To Bumpity Bump/When Yuba Plays The Rumba 5
72	United Artists UAG 29381	ELECTRIC SHOCKS (LP). 18
74	United Artists UAS 29508	UNUSUAL (LP) 18

(see also Bonzo Dog [Doo Dah] Band)

SPEAR OF DESTINY
83	Epic SPEAR 13-1	Flying Scotsman (Extended)/Africa/The Man Who Tunes The Drums (12", p/s, with poster, some autographed). 10
83	Epic WA 3372	The Wheel/The Hop (picture disc) 4
83	Epic DA 3372	The Wheel/The Hop//Grapes Of Wrath (live)/The Preacher (live) (double pack). . . . 4
84	Epic DA 4068	Prisoner Of Love//Rosie//Rainmaker (live)/Don't Turn Away (live) (double pack) . . . 4
85	Epic DTA 6445	Come Back (Dub Mix)/Cole Younger//Young Men (Return Of)/ Come Back (WL Remix) (12", double pack) 7
86	Dale DALE 2	BOTTOM DRAWER (EP, p/s, white label, 500 only, numbered) 6

(see also Theatre Of Hate, Pack)

SPECIAL DUTIES
81	Charnel H. SARCOPHAGI 2	Violent Society/Colchester Council (wraparound p/s) 8
82	Rondelet ROUND 15	VIOLENT SOCIETY (EP). 7
82	Rondelet ROUND 20	POLICE STATE (EP) 7
82	Rondelet ROUND 24	Bullshit Crass/You're Doing Yourself No Good (p/s) 7
83	Expulsion OUT 1	Punk Rocker/Too Much Talking (p/s) 7
82	Rondelet ABOUT 9	77 IN 82 (LP) 12

SPECIALS (SPECIAL A.K.A.)
79	2-Tone TT 1/TT 2	Gangsters (as Special A.K.A.)/SELECTER: The Selecter (paper label, some in stamped plain white sleeve; matrix numbers TT1-3 & TT2-1) 8/6
79	2-Tone TT 1/TT 2	Gangsters (as Special A.K.A.)/SELECTER: The Selecter (paper label, die-cut 2-Tone sleeve, 2nd issue with Chrysalis CHS TT 1/2 matrix no.) 5
79	2-Tone CHS TT 5	Message To You Rudy/Nite Klub (paper label, company sleeve, as Specials featuring Rico) 5
80	2-Tone CHS TT 7	THE SPECIAL A.K.A. LIVE (EP, p/s, paper label). 5
80	2-Tone CHS TT 11	Rat Race/Rude Boys Outa Jail (p/s, paper label, as Specials) 5
80	2-Tone CHS TT 13	Stereotype/International Jet Set (p/s, paper label, as Specials) 5
80	2-Tone CHS TT 16	Do Nothing/Maggie's Farm (p/s, paper label, as Specials) 5
82	2-Tone CHS TT 1023	War Crimes (The Crime Is Still The Same)/War Crimes (The Crime Is Still The Same) (Version) (10", p/s, as Special A.K.A.). 6
83	2-Tone CHS TPTT 23	Racist Friend/Bright Lights (picture disc, as Special A.K.A.) 5
84	2-Tone CHS TT 27	What I Like Most About You Is Your Girlfriend/Can't Get A Break//War Crimes (The Crime Is Still The Same)/(Version) (double pack, as Special A.K.A.) 5

MINT VALUE £

84	2-Tone CHS TPTT 27	What I Like Most About You Is Your Girlfriend/Can't Get A Break (picture disc)	6
84	2-Tone CHS TT 1227	What I Like Most About You Is Your Girlfriend/Can't Get A Break (12", poster p/s with free single)	8
87	Strange Fruit SFPSC 018	PEEL SESSION 23.5.79 (cassette EP)	5
80	2-Tone CDL TT 5001	MORE SPECIALS (LP, with poster & 7": Roddy Radiation & Specials' "Braggin' And Tryin' Not To Lie"/Judge Roughneck's "Rude Buoys Outa Jail" [TT 999])	12

(see also Terry Hall, Fun Boy Three, Colourfield, Selecter, Rhoda, Rico; Terry, Blair & Anouchka)

SPECIMEN
83	London LON 24	Returning From A Journey/Kiss Kiss Bang Bang (bat-shaped disc)	8

(see also Diskord Datkord)

SPECKLED RED
60s	Storyville SEP 384	STORYVILLE BLUES ANTHOLOGY VOL. 4 (EP)	15
63	Esquire 32-190	THE DIRTY DOZENS (LP)	35
66	Storyville DL 601	THE DIRTY DOZENS (LP, reissue)	12
71	VJM LC 11	OH RED (LP)	18

PHIL SPECTOR
63	London HA-U 8141	A CHRISTMAS GIFT FOR YOU (LP, various artists, Spector as producer; plum label, later black label)	40/18
72	Apple APCOR 24	PHIL SPECTOR'S CHRISTMAS ALBUM (LP, reissue of London HA-U 8141)	25
74	Warner Bros K 59010	PHIL SPECTOR'S CHRISTMAS ALBUM (LP, 2nd reissue, some w/ poster)	18/12
76	Phil Spector Intl. 2307 008	RARE MASTERS VOL. 1 (LP, various artists, Spector as producer)	18
76	Phil Spector Intl. 2307 009	RARE MASTERS VOL. 2 (LP, various artists, Spector as producer)	12
80	Phil Spector Intl. 2307 015	PHIL SPECTOR '74/'79 (LP, various artists, Spector as producer)	12
81	Phil Spector Intl. WOS 001	WALL OF SOUND (9-LP box set, various artists, Spector as producer)	50

(see also Ronettes, Crystals, Darlene Love, Bob B. Soxx & Blue Jeans, Teddy Bears)

RONNIE SPECTOR
71	Apple APPLE 33	Try Some, Buy Some/Tandoori Chicken (initially with p/s)	30/8
77	Epic EPC 5185	Say Goodbye To Hollywood/Baby Please Don't Go (with E Street Band)	5
81	Red Shadow MS 488	Darlin'/Settin' The Woods On Fire (p/s)	5
81	Red Shadow LP 002	SIREN (LP)	12

(see also Ronettes)

SPECTRES (Ireland)
65	Lloyd Sound UED QU 1	The Facts Of Life/Whirlpool	200

SPECTRES (U.K.)
66	Piccadilly 7N 35339	I (Who Have Nothing)/Neighbour, Neighbour	250
66	Piccadilly 7N 35352	Hurdy Gurdy Man/Laticia	225
67	Piccadilly 7N 35368	We Ain't Got Nothin' Yet/I Want It	225

(see also Traffic Jam, Status Quo)

SPECTRES (U.K.)
80	Direct Hit DH 1	This Strange Effect/Getting Away With Murder (p/s)	15
81	Demon D 1002	Stories/Things (p/s)	4

(see also Rich Kids, Swingers)

SPECTRUM
65	Columbia DB 7742	Little Girl/Asking You	5
67	RCA RCA 1589	Samantha's Mine/Saturday's Child	5
67	RCA RCA 1619	Portobello Road/Comes The Dawn	8
67	RCA RCA 1651	Headin' For A Heatwave/I Wanna Be Happy With You	5
68	RCA RCA 1700	London Bridge Is Coming Down/Tables And Chairs	6
68	RCA RCA 1753	Little Red Boat By The River/Forget Me Not	5
68	RCA RCA 1775	Ob-La-Di, Ob-La-Da/Music Soothes The Savage Beast	5
69	RCA RCA 1853	Free/The Tale Of Wally Toft	5
69	RCA RCA 1883	Glory/Nodnol	5
70	RCA RCA 1976	Portobello Road/Comes The Dawn (reissue)	6
71	Parlophone R 5908	I'll Be Gone/Launching Place — Pt II	6
69	RCA Intl. INTS 118	THE LIGHT IS DARK ENOUGH (LP)	40

SPECTRUM
85	Phoenix Modernist 7-THE-1	All Or Nothing (Contemporary Version)/All Or Nothing (Traditional Version) (p/s)	4
85	Phoenix Modernist THE 1	All Or Nothing (Contemporary Version)/All Or Nothing (Traditional Version) (12", p/s; distributed by Stiff)	7
87	Phoenix Modernist THE 1	All Or Nothing (Contemporary Version)/All Or Nothing (Traditional Version) (12", p/s with 2 inserts & free 7", distributed by Nine Mile & Cartel)	7

(see also Steve Marriott, Chris Farlowe, P.P. Arnold, Creation)

SPECTRUM
92	Beechwood TT 015e	Taste The Ozone/MOONSHAKE: Night Tripper (no p/s)	5
94	Silvertone	Tempter (demo)/STEREOLAB: Tone Burst (demo) (unreleased, with colour photocopied wraparound p/s, 25 test pressings only)	450+

(see also Spacemen 3, Sonic Boom)

CHRIS SPEDDING
70	Harvest HAR 5013	Rock'n'Roll Band/BATTERED ORNAMENTS: Goodbye We Loved You (Madly)	12
75	Island WIP 6225	My Bucket's Got A Hole In It/I Can't Boogie	5
76	RAK RAK 246	Pogo Dancing/Pose (p/s)	6
70	Harvest SHSP 4004	BACKWOOD PROGRESSION (LP)	20
72	Harvest SHSP 4017	THE ONLY LICK I KNOW (LP)	20

(see also Sharks, Nucleus, Sounds Nice, Panhandle, Solid Gold Cadillac, Matthew Ellis, Vibrators, Battered Ornaments, IOFR)

SPEED (Jamaica)
71	Bullet BU 477	There's A Train/Blue Moon	6

SPEED
78	It IT 1	Big City/All Day And All The Night (some in p/s)	40/15

(see also Cobra, Tearjerkers)

SPEEDBALL(S)
80	No Pap/Dirty Dick DD 1/2	No Survivors/Is Somebody There? (miscredited as 'Speedballs' on label, some in withdrawn printed sleeve)	25/15

SPEEDOMETERS
78	Mascot NICE 1	Disgrace/Work (p/s)	4
78	Mascot NICE 2	Liverpool Ladies (p/s)	4

SPEEDY J
93	Warp WARP LP 14	GINGER (LP, ginger vinyl)	10

DAVEY SPEIRS
69	Beltona LBA/LBS 61	A MAN OF CONSTANT SORROW (LP)	15

SPELLBINDERS
66	CBS 202453	Help Me (Get Myself Back Together)/Danny Boy	15
67	CBS 202622	Chain Reaction/For You	15
67	CBS 2776	Since I Don't Have You/I Believe	6
69	Direction 58-3970	Help Me/Chain Reaction	6

BENNY SPELLMAN
62	London HLP 9570	Lipstick Traces/Fortune Teller	45

JOHNNY SPENCE
61	Parlophone R 4736	Wheels/First Romance	6
62	Parlophone R 4872	Dr. Kildare Theme/Midnight Theme	7
68	Verve (S)VLP 9222	WHY NOT? (LP, as Johnnie Spence Big Band)	15

KENTY SPENCE
73	Ackee ACK 505	I Have A Party/Party Trouble	5

DON SPENCER
62	HMV POP 1087	Fireball/I'm All Alone Again (blue or black labels)	15/12
63	HMV POP 1186	Busy Doing Nothing/The Joker	6
63	HMV POP 1205	Worried Mind/Give Give A Little	6
64	HMV POP 1306	Pride Is Such A Little Word/For Love (with Le Roys)	6
66	Page One POF 006	Why Don't They Understand/Marriage Is For Old Folks	5

(see also Le Roys)

DON SPENCER/XL5
63	HMV 7EG 8802	FIREBALL AND OTHER TITLES (EP, 2 tracks each)	40

JEREMY SPENCER (Band)
70	Reprise RS 27002	Linda/Teenage Darling	6
79	Atlantic K 11363	Travelling/Cool Breeze (as Jeremy Spencer Band)	5
70	Reprise RSLP 9002	JEREMY SPENCER (LP)	40
71	Reprise K 44105	JEREMY SPENCER (LP, reissue)	25
73	CBS 65387	JEREMY SPENCER AND THE CHILDREN OF GOD (LP)	12

(see also Fleetwood Mac)

JO SPENCER
71	Dynamic DYN 415	Bed Of Roses/Forgive Me	6

SONNY SPENCER
59	Parlophone R 4611	Oh Boy/Gilee	20

JON SPENCER BLUES EXPLOSION
94	Matador OLE 077	Afro/Relax Her (p/s)	6
95	Matador OLE 111	Bellbottoms/Miss Elaine (p/s, white vinyl)	5
95	Matador OLE 111.1	Bellbottoms/Flavor (12", p/s)	8
96	Mute MUTE 202.2	2 Kindsa Love/Let's Smerf (pink vinyl)	5
97	Mute MUTE 204	Wail/Judah Love Theme/Radio Spot (grey vinyl)	5
97	Mute MUTE 204	Wail/Flavor (green vinyl)	5
98	Mute MUTE 222	Magical Colors/Confused (red vinyl)	5
98	Mute MUTE 226	Talk About The Blues/Wait A Minute (orange vinyl)	5
91	Hut HUTLP 3	THE JON SPENCER BLUES EXPLOSION (LP)	15

JOHN SPENCER'S LOUTS
78	Beggars Banquet BEGA 3	THE LAST LP (LP)	10

BRINDLEY D. SPENDER
68	Domain D 8	The Company I Keep/On A Day Like Today	6

SPERMICIDE
79	No Wonder NOW 3	Femme Prothèse/Belgique (p/s with lyrics)	6

SPHERES
78	Sphere	FESTIVAL AND SUNS (LP, with insert)	25

(see also Jimmy Winston)

SPHERICAL OBJECTS
78	Object Music OM 01	The Kill/The Knot (p/s)	5
78	Object Music OM 04	Seventies Romance/Sweet Tooth (p/s)	5
78	Object Music PBJ 001	PAST & PARCEL (LP)	10
79	Object Music OBJ 004	ELLIPTICAL OPTIMISM (LP)	10
80	Object Music OBJ 012	FURTHER ELLIPSES (LP)	10
81	Object Music OBJ 016	NO MAN'S LAND (LP)	10

(see also Alternomen Unlimited, Noyes Brothers)

SPHYNKTA
83	Sultanic SUL 666	In The Shade Of The Gods/Jesus Bless My Upside-Down Cross (p/s, red vinyl, with 'devil' tattoo)	60
83	Sultanic SUL 999	Death And Violence/Ritual Slaughter (Of Your Daughter) (p/s, red vinyl)	40
84	Sultanic SUL 000	Spike Up My Sphynkta/No Pain No Gain (unissued)	100+

SPHYNX
78	Charisma CDS 4011	XITINTODAY (LP, some with booklet)	25/15

(see also Inner City Unit, Gong, Radio Actors)

SPICE (Sweden)
68	Olga OLE 013	Union Jack/Delicious	40

SPICE (U.K.)
68	United Artists UP 2246	What About The Music?/In Love (demo only)	60

(see also Uriah Heep, Godz, Toe-Fat)

SPICE GIRLS
96	Virgin VSLH 1588	Wannabe/Bumper To Bumper (jukebox issue, no p/s, large centre hole)	8
96	Virgin VSTDJ 1588	Wannabe/Wannabe (Vocal Slam)/Wannabe (Dub Slam)/Wannabe (Instrumental Slam) (12" promo, stickered title p/s)	12
96	Virgin VSCXD 1588	Wannabe (Radio Edit)/Wannabe (Dave Way Alternative Mix)/Wannabe (Dub Slam)/Wannabe (Instrumental) (CD, fold-out postcard inlay, stickered case)	35
96	Virgin VSLH 1601	Say You'll Be There/Take Me Home (jukebox issue, no p/s, large centre hole)	6
96	Virgin VSTDJ 1601	Say You'll Be There (Junior's Main Pass)/Say You'll Be There (Junior's Dub Girls)/Say You'll Be There (Junior's X-Beats Mix)/Say You'll Be There (Kurt's Dub) (12" promo, stickered title sleeve)	10
96	Virgin VSCDG 1601	Say You'll Be There (Single Mix)/Say You'll Be There (Spice Of Life Mix)/Say You'll Be There (Linslee's Extended Mix)/Say You'll Be There (Junior Vasquez's Dub Girls) (CD, digipak, with foldout poster in envelope)	18
96	Virgin VSLH 1607	2 Become 1/One Of These Girls (jukebox issue, no p/s, large centre hole)	6
96	Virgin VSTDJ 1607	2 Become 1 (Dave Way Remix Edit)/Wannabe (Junior Vasquez Remix Edit)/(Junior Vasquez Gomis Dub) (12" promo, stickered title p/s)	10
97	Virgin VSLH 1623	Mama/Who Do You Think You Are (jukebox issue, no p/s, large centre hole)	6
97	Virgin VSTDJ 1623	Who Do You Think You Are (Morales Club Mix)/Who Do You Think You Are (Morales Dub Mix)/Who Do You Think You Are (Morales Bonus Mix) (12" promo, stickered title sleeve)	10
97	Virgin VSLH 1660	Spice Up Your Life (Stent Radio Mix)/(Morales Radio Mix) (jukebox issue, no p/s, large centre hole)	6
97	Virgin SGPC 97	Step To Me (7" Mix)/(Matthew's Disco Steppin' Mix)/(Matthew's Extra Spicey Dub)/(Extended Mix) (CD, mail order only via Pepsi offer, card p/s or slimline jewel case)	each 15
97	Virgin VSLH 1669	Too Much (Radio Edit) (jukebox issue, no p/s, large centre hole)	6
98	Virgin VSTDJ1679	Stop (Morales Remix)/Stop (Stretch 'N' Vern's Rock & Roll Mix)/Stop (Morales Dub)/Stop (Stretch 'N' Vern's Dub) (12", doublepack, title stickered sleeve, promo only)	15
98	Virgin CDLIC 116	Move Over-Generation Next (CD, 1-track, mail order only via Pepsi offer, card p/s)	12
96	Virgin CDVDJ 2812	SPICE (CD, promo only, with spoken-word intros by Andi Peters, card sleeve)	30
96	Virgin SGCDR 1	FIVE GO MAD IN CYBERSPACE (CD ROM, promo only, card sl., Mac format)	60

(see also Geri Halliwell)

GEORGE SPICER
74	Topic 12T 235	BLACKBERRY FOLD (LP)	12

SPIDELLS
66	Sue WI 4019	Find Out What's Happening/That'll Make My Heart Break	25

SPIDER
66	Decca F 12430	The Comedown Song/Blow Ya Mind	15

SPIDER
80	Alien ALIEN 14	Children Of The Street/Down 'N' Out (some in p/s)	30/8
80	Alien ALIEN 16	College Luv/Born To Be Wild (some in p/s)	20/6
80	Dreamland 2090 441	New Romance/Cross Fire (p/s)	4
80	Dreamland DSLP 4	Everything Is Alright/Shady Lady (p/s)	4
81	Dreamland DSLP 11	Better Be Good To Me/I Love (p/s)	4
81	City NIK 7	All The Time/Feel Like A Man (p/s)	10
82	RCA RCA 268	Rock 'N' Roll Will Forever Last/Did Ya Like It Baby?//Amazin' Grace Medley (Parts 1 & 2) (double pack, separate sleeves)	5
84	A&M AMP 180	Here We Go Rock'n'Roll/Death Row (web-shaped picture disc)	8
86	PRT 7PX 344	Gimme Gimme It All/Rock Tonite//Live Recording From Kerrang Corner (double pack)	4

SPIDER-MAN
73	Buddah 2318 075	FROM BEYOND THE GRAVE (LP)	15

SPIDERS (U.S.)
54	London HL 8086	I'm Slippin' In/I'm Searching (78)	90

SPIDERS (U.K.)
66	Philips BF 1531	Sad Sunset/Hey Boy	40

SPIDERS FROM MARS
75	Pye 7N 45549	White Man Black Man/National Poll	5
76	Pye 7N 45578	I Don't Wanna Limbo/Can't Be Fair	5
76	Pye NSPL 18479	SPIDERS FROM MARS (LP)	12

(see also David Bowie, Mick Ronson)

BERND SPIER
65	Oriole CB 1987	A Million And One Times/My Mistake	5

ARTHUR SPINK BAND
68	Beltona BL 2766	Beatles Och Aye/Harry Lauder Medley	4

SPINNERS (U.K.)
57	Columbia DB 4048	On Ilkla Moor Baht'at/Green Grow The Rushes O.	6
59	Columbia DB 4243	This Old Man/Alive And Kicking	5

59	Columbia DB 4243	This Old Man/Alive And Kicking (78)	10
59	Columbia DB 4267	The "I Had A Dream, Dear" Rock/Pedro The Fisherman	5
59	Columbia DB 4267	The "I Had A Dream, Dear" Rock/Pedro The Fisherman (78)	12
64	Fontana TF 450	Maggie May/Linstead Market	5
64	Fontana TF 494	Dirty Old Town/Fi-Li-Mi-Oo-Re-Ay	5
64	Fontana (S)TL 5201	THE SPINNERS (LP)	12

(see also Liverpool Spinners, Shane Rimmer)

SPINNERS (U.S.)

61	Columbia DB 4693	That's What Girls Are Made For/Heebie Jeebies	150
65	Tamla Motown TMG 514	Sweet Thing/How Can I? (demos with 'Spinners' or 'Detroit Spinners' credit)	100
65	Tamla Motown TMG 514	Sweet Thing/How Can I?	150

(see also Detroit Spinners)

SPINNING WHEEL

79	private pressing	JACOB'S FLEECE (LP)	25

(see also Dragonsfire)

SPIRALS

58	Capitol CL 14958	The Rockin' Cow/Everybody Knows	15

SPIRAL SKY

93	Acme AC 8002LP	SPIRAL SKY (LP, numbered & sealed with insert, 500 only)	15

(see also Sun Dial, Ohr Musik)

SPIRAL STARECASE

68	CBS 3507	Baby What I Mean/Makin' Your Mind Up	10
69	CBS 4187	More Today Than Yesterday/Broken Hearted Man	25
69	CBS 4524	No One For Me To Turn To/Sweet Little Thing	10

SPIRIT

68	CBS 3523	Uncle Jack/Mechanical World	6
69	CBS 3880	I Got A Line On You/She Smiles	6
69	CBS 4511	Dark Eyed Woman/Ice	5
69	CBS 4565	Dark Eyed Woman/New Dope In Town	5
70	CBS 4773	1984/Sweet Stella Baby	6
70	CBS 5149	Animal Zoo/Red Light Roll On	6
72	CBS 8083	Cadillac Cowboys/Darkness	5
73	Epic EPC 7082	Mr. Skin/Nature's Way	5
84	Mercury MER 1626	Fresh Garbage/Mr Skin (6", p/s)	5
78	Sound For Industry SFI 326	Midnight Train/Potatoland Theme (flexidisc free with *Dark Star* magazine)	8/5
68	CBS 63278	SPIRIT (LP, orange label)	15
68	CBS 63523	THE FAMILY THAT PLAYS TOGETHER (LP, orange label)	15
69	CBS 63729	CLEAR (LP, orange label)	20
71	Epic EPC 64191	THE TWELVE DREAMS OF DR. SARDONICUS (LP, g/fold sleeve, yellow label)	15
72	Epic EPC 64507	FEED-BACK (LP, yellow label)	12
81	Beggars Banquet BEGA 23	POTATOLAND (LP, with cartoon book)	15
88	Chord CHDAT 010	POTATOLAND (DAT)	15

(see also Kapt. Kopter & Fabulous Twirlybirds, Randy California, Jo Jo Gunne)

DARIEN SPIRIT

73	Charisma CAS 1065	ELEGY TO MARILYN (LP)	18

SPIRIT OF JOHN MORGAN

69	Carnaby CNS 4005	Ride On/Along Came John	8
71	RCA RCA 2085	Floating Opera Show/Never Let Go	6
69	Carnaby CNLS 6002	THE SPIRIT OF JOHN MORGAN (LP)	50
70	Carnaby CNLS 6007	AGE MACHINE (LP)	50
71	Carnaby 6437 503	THE SPIRIT OF JOHN MORGAN (LP, reissue)	25

(see also John Morgan)

SPIRIT OF MEMPHIS QUARTET

58	Parlophone PMD 1070	NEGRO SPIRITUALS (10" LP)	20
65	Vogue LAE 1033	NEGRO SPIRITUALS (LP, reissue)	15

SPIRIT OF PLAY

88	Release KIDS 1988	Children In Need/Children In Need (Instrumental) (with Paul McCartney) (p/s)	20

SPIRITUALIZED

90	Dedicated ZB 43783	Anyway That You Want Me/Step Into The Breeze (p/s)	8
90	Dedicated ZT 43784	Anyway That You Want Me (Extended)/Step Into The Breeze 1 & 2 (12", p/s)	18
90	Dedicated ZT 43780	Anyway That You Want Me (Remix)/Step Into The Breeze 1 & 2 (12", p/s)	20
90	Dedicated ZD 43784	Anyway That You Want Me/Step Into The Breeze 1 & 2 (CD)	25
91	Dedicated SPIRT 002	Run/I Want You (clear vinyl, p/s)	6
91	Dedicated SPIRT 002CD/ ZD 44846	Run/Luminescence (Stay With Me)/I Want You/ Effervescent (Chimes) (CD)	8
91	Dedicated SPIRT 003	Why Don't You Smile Now?/Sway (clear vinyl, p/s)	6
91	Fierce FRIGHT 053	Feel So Sad/I Want You (gig freebie, no p/s, stamped plain white sleeve with date & venue details)	25
92	Dedicated SPIRT 004	LAZER GUIDED MELODIES (LP, sampler, some with bonus 7", mail-order only)	12
92	Dedicated SPIRT 005	Medication/Smile (p/s)	4
96	Dedicated 7432 13 11782	Lay Back In The Sun/The Slide Song/Spread Your Wings/ Lay Back In The Sun (CD)	7
93	Dedicated DEDLP 008	FUCKED UP INSIDE (LP, mail-order only)	25
92	Dedicated SPIRT 004CD	LAZER GUIDED MELODIES (CD, sampler, mail-order only)	10
97	Dedicated DEDCD 034S	LADIES AND GENTLEMAN WE ARE FLOATING IN SPACE (12 x 3" CD, in blister packs in card box with insert)	80

(see also Spacemen 3)

SPIROGYRA

MINT VALUE £

SPIROGYRA
72	Pegasus PGS 3	Dangerous Dave/Captain's Log	10
71	B&C CAS 1042	ST. RADIGUND'S (LP, with lyric inner)	70
72	Pegasus PEG 13	OLD BOOT WINE (LP)	80
73	Polydor 2310 246	BELLS, BOOTS AND SHAMBLES (LP)	250

(see also Caravan)

SPITFIRE & BLACKFIRE BARMIES
82	Carrere CAR 253	So You Want To Be A Rock'n'Roll Star/Spitfire Boogie (no p/s)	25

SPITFIRE BOYS
77	RK RK 1001	British Refugee/Mein Kampf (push-out centre, no p/s)	25
77	RK RK 1001	British Refugee/Mein Kampf (reissue, solid centre, p/s)	20

(see also Frankie Goes To Hollywood)

SPITZBROOK
70s	Ace SPIT 1	Stranger/Looking At You (p/s)	40

CHARLIE SPIVAK & HIS ORCHESTRA
54	Parlophone CMSP 14	Red Lilacs/Sentimental Trumpet (export issue)	8
50s	London BEP 6036	CHARLIE SPIVAK AND HIS ORCHESTRA (EP, export issue)	10

VICTORIA SPIVEY
60	Fontana TFE 17264	TREASURES OF NORTH AMERICAN NEGRO MUSIC NO. 5 (EP)	15
56	HMV 7EG 8190	VICTORIA SPIVEY (EP)	20
65	Xtra XTRA 1022	VICTORIA SPIVEY (LP)	25

SPIZZ (OIL/ENERGI)
79	Rough Trade RTSO 1	6000 Crazy/1989/Fibre (p/s)	5
79	Rough Trade RTSO 2	Cold City/Red And Black/Solarisation (Shun)/Platform 3 (as Spizz Oil) (p/s)	5
79	Rough Trade RTSO 3	Soldier Soldier/Virginia Plain (as Spizz Energi) (p/s)	6
79	Rough Trade RTSO 4	Where's Captain Kirk?/Amnesia (as Spizz Energi) (p/s)	5

S.P.K. (SEPPUKU/SURGICAL PENIS KLINIK)
80	Industrial IR 0011	MEAT PROCESSING SECTION (Mekano/Slogun) (p/s, labels list "Slogan"/ "Factory", with insert, as Surgical Penis Klinik)	18
83	Side Effekts SER 003	Dekompositiones (12", p/s, as Seppuku)	15
84	WEA YZ 24	Junk Funk/High Tension (p/s, as S.P.K.)	4
84	WEA YZ 24T	Junk Funk/High Tension (12", p/s, as S.P.K.)	8
85	Desire WANT 1	Metal Dance/Will To Power (p/s, as S.P.K.)	4
85	Desire WANTX 1	Metal Dance/Will To Power (12", p/s, as S.P.K.)	8
86	Side Effekts SFX 01	In Fragrante Delicto/Invocation (12", p/s, as S.P.K.)	8
81	Side Effekts SER 01	INFORMATION OVERLOAD UNIT (LP, 1st 1,000 with booklet & poster)	30/20
80s	Side Effekts SER 002	LEICHENSCHREI (LP)	15
86	Sterile SRC 4	LIVE AT THE CRYPT (cassette)	12

SPLAT!
83	Ron Johnson RON 1	Yeah... The Dum Dum/Book Face/Biggles Bloodbath (foldaround p/s & stamped white label)	5

SPLINTER
74	Dark Horse AMS 7135	Costafine Town/Elly May	5
75	Dark Horse AMS 5502	China Light/Drink All Day	8
75	Dark Horse AMS 5501	Drink All Day/Haven't Got Time	5
75	Dark Horse AMS 5503	Which Way Will I Get Home/Green Bus Line	5
76	Dark Horse AMS 5506	Half Way There/What Is It (If You Never Ever Tried It Yourself)	5
77	Dark Horse K 17009	Round And Round/I'll Bend For You	5
77	Dark Horse K 17116	New York City (Who Am I)/Baby Love	5
78	Barn BARN 4	Danger Zone/Swear To God	10
76	Dark Horse DH 3	SPLINTER (LP, promo only, plain white sleeve)	75

(see also Elastic Oz Band)

SPLINTERED
91	Fourth Dimension	Mouth Clamp/CINDYTALK: In Sunshine (numbered freebie with *Grim Humour* fanzine, Vol. 2, No. 1)	7/5

SPLIT BEAVER
81	Heavy Metal HEAVY 7	Savage/Hound Of Hell (some with p/s)	18/5
82	Heavy Metal HMRLP 3	WHEN HELL WON'T HAVE YOU (LP)	15

SPLIT CROW
84	Guardian GRC 2167	ROCKSTORM (LP)	12

SPLIT ENZ
76	Chrysalis CHS 2120	Late Last Night/Walking Down The Road (p/s)	4
77	Chrysalis CHS 2131	Another Great Divide/Stranger Than Fiction (p/s)	4
77	Chrysalis CHS 2170	My Mistake/Crosswords (p/s)	5
77	Chrysalis CHS 2170-12	My Mistake/Crosswords/The Woman Who Loves You (12", p/s)	10
79	Illegal ILS 19	I See Red/Give It A Whirl/Hermit McDermitt (p/s)	7
80	A&M AMS 7546	I Got You/Double Happy (p/s)	5
80	A&M AMS 7574	Nobody Takes Me Seriously/Choral Sea (p/s)	5
81	A&M AMS 8101	Poor Boy/Missing Person (live) (p/s)	6
81	A&M AMS 8128	History Never Repeats/Shark Attack/What's The Matter With You (p/s, laser etched)	5
81	A&M AMS 8146	One Step Ahead/In The Wars (p/s, laser etched)	5
76	Chrysalis CHR 1131	MENTAL NOTES (LP)	10
77	Chrysalis CHR 1145	DIZRYTHMIA (LP)	10
80	A&M AMLH 64822	TRUE COLOURS (LP, some copies laser etched)	12/10
81	Chrysalis CHR 1329	BEGINNING OF THE ENZ (LP)	10

(see also Crowded House, Tim Finn)

SPLIT IMAGE
82	Heroes ER 01	Now That We've Parted (no p/s)	25

SPLIT KNEE LOONS
81	Avatar AAA 111	THE SPECIAL COLLECTORS EP (p/s, brown vinyl, some with badge) 10/8

(see also Gillan, Bernie Tormé, John McCoy, Colin Town[e]s)

SPLIT SCREENS
78	Rok ROK III/IV	Just Don't Try/JUST FRANK: You (no p/s) 5

SPLODGENESSABOUNDS
81	Deram BUM 3	COWPUNK MEDLUM (EP, p/s, with free flexi [BUMF 3]) 5

SPOILT BRATZ
88	Spoilt Bratz SB 1	SPOILT BRATZ: (Not So) Hot/You Talk Too Much/I Could Die/She's A Drag (cassette, private issue, 200 only) 50
88	Spoilt Bratz SB 2	GASOLINE & SUICIDE: Sex Doll, Love Cramp/Going Down Again/ Stuck In A Rut/Crawling On Broken Glass (cassette, private issue, 200 only) . . . 50
89	Spoilt Bratz BRAT 3	BE MY GUEST: Pain Reliever/Past Times/Ignorance (cassette, private issue). . . . 50

(see also Terrorvision)

SPOKESMEN
65	Brunswick 05941	The Dawn Of Correction/For You Babe 6
65	Brunswick 05948	It Ain't Fair/Have Courage Be Careful 5
66	Brunswick 05950	Michelle/Better Days Are Yet To Come. 6
66	Brunswick 05958	Today's The Day/Enchanté. 5

SPONTANEOUS COMBUSTION
71	Harvest HAR 5046	Lonely Singer/200 Lives/Leaving. 15
72	Harvest HAR 5060	Gay Time Night/Spaceship. 10
73	Harvest HAR 5066	Sabre Dance/Part 2 8
72	Harvest SHVL 801	SPONTANEOUS COMBUSTION (LP) 35
72	Harvest SHVL 805	TRIAD (LP, with insert). 30

(see also Time)

SPONTANEOUS MUSIC ENSEMBLE
66	Eyemark EMP L1002	CHALLENGE (LP). 75
68	Island ILP 979	KARYOBIN ... ARE THE IMAGINARY BIRDS SAID TO LIVE IN PARADISE (LP, pink label) 60
69	Marmalade 608 008	SPONTANEOUS MUSIC ENSEMBLE (LP) 20
71	Tangent TNGS 107	SOURCE FROM AND TOWARDS (LP) 12
72	Marmalade 2384 009	SPONTANEOUS MUSIC ENSEMBLE (LP, reissue) 12
73	Tangent TNGS 118	SO WHAT DO YOU THINK (LP) 12

(see also Howard Riley Trio)

SPOOKY TOOTH
67	Island WIP 6022	Sunshine Help Me/Weird 10
68	Island WIP 6037	Love Really Changed Me/Luger's Grove 8
68	Island WIP 6046	The Weight/Do Right People 8
69	Island WIP 6048	Nobody There At All/ART: Room With A View (unissued, white labels only) 40
69	Island WIP 6060	Son Of Your Father/I've Got Enough Heartache 7
73	Island WIP 6168	All Sewn Up/As Long As The World Keeps Turning 6
68	Island ILP 980/ILPS 9080	IT'S ALL ABOUT (LP, pink or palm tree label) 40/18
69	Island ILPS 9098	SPOOKY TWO (LP, pink label) 30
69	Island ILPS 9107	CEREMONY (LP, with Pierre Henry, pink label, gatefold sleeve) 25
70	Island ILPS 9117	THE LAST PUFF (LP, pink label) 25
73	Island ILPS 9227	YOU BROKE MY HEART SO I BUSTED YOUR JAW (LP, pink rim label). 20
73	Island ILPS 9255	WITNESS (LP, pink rim label). 18
74	Good Ear EARL 2001	THE MIRROR (LP) 12
74	Island ILPS 9292	THE MIRROR (LP, export issue). 18

(see also Gary Wright, V.I.Ps, Art, Luther Grosvenor, Hellions, Revolution, State Of Mickey & Tommy, Mike Harrison, Foreigner)

COOL SPOON
67	Coxsone CS 7031	Yakety Yak/SOUL VENDORS: Drum Song (both act. by Jeff Dixon & Alton Ellis) . 15

SPOTLIGHTERS
59	Vogue Pop V 9130	Please Be My Girlfriend/Whisper (with Bob Thompson & His Band) 450
59	Vogue Pop V 9130	Please Be My Girlfriend/Whisper (with Bob Thompson & His Band) (78) 100

SPOTLIGHTS
66	Philips BF 1485	Batman And Robin/Day Flower 8

SPOTNICKS
62	Oriole CB 1724	Orange Blossom Special/The Spotnicks Theme. 6
62	Oriole CB 1755	Galloping Guitars/The Rocket Man 6
63	Oriole CB 1790	Hava Nagila/High Flyin' Scotsman 6
63	Oriole CB 1818	Just Listen To My Heart/Pony Express 7
63	Oriole CB 1844	Valentina/Save The Last Dance For Me/No Yaga Daga Blues 6
63	Oriole CB 1886	Anna/The Sailor's Hornpipe 12
64	Oriole CB 1953	Lovesick Blues/The Space Creatures 12
64	Oriole CB 1981	Donner Wetter/Shamus O'Toole. 12
63	Oriole EP 7075	ON THE AIR (EP) 15
64	Oriole EP 7078	SPOTNICKS IN PARIS (EP) 18
64	Oriole EP 7079	SPOTNICKS AT THE OLYMPIA PARIS (EP) 20
63	Oriole PS 40036	OUT-A SPACE: THE SPOTNICKS IN LONDON (LP, also stereo SPS 40037). . . 25/40
64	Oriole PS 40054	THE SPOTNICKS IN SPAIN (LP). 25
65	Oriole PS 40064	THE SPOTNICKS IN BERLIN (LP) 35
81	Air CHM 1171	THE VERY BEST OF THE SPOTNICKS (LP) 12

(see also Bob Lander & Spotnicks, Shy Ones)

JACK SPRATT & LEROY SIBBLES & HEPTONES
69	Coxsone CS 7100	Give Me Your Love/LARRY & ALVIN: Magic Moments. 15

MINT VALUE £

SPREADEAGLE
72	Charisma CB 183	How Can We Be Lost/Nightmare	5
72	Charisma BCP 7	Nightingale Lane/Liar (p/s)	5
72	Charisma CAS 1055	THE PIECE OF PAPER (LP)	12

SPREDTHICK
78	An Actual ACT 003	SPREDTHICK (LP, with insert)	18

SPRIGUNS (OF TOLGUS)
76	Decca F 13676	Nothing Else To Do/Lord Lovell	8
77	Decca F 13739	White Witch/Time Will Pass	8
74	private pressing	ROWDY DOWDY DAY (cassette, as Spriguns Of Tolgus)	50
75	Alida Star C'tage ASC7755	JACK WITH A FEATHER (LP, as Spriguns Of Tolgus)	700
76	Decca SKL 5262	REVEL WEIRD & WILD (LP, with lyric insert)	100
77	Decca SKL 5286	TIME WILL PASS (LP, with lyric insert)	100
92	Kissing Spell KSLP 002	ROWDY DOWDY DAY (LP, reissue)	15
	(see also Mandy Morton Band)		

SPRING
71	RCA Neon NE 6	SPRING (LP, foldout sleeve)	100

SPRINGBOARD
69	Polydor 545007	SPRINGBOARD (LP)	30

DUSTY SPRINGFIELD
SINGLES
63	Philips BF 1292	I Only Want To Be With You/Once Upon A Time	5
64	Philips BF 1313	Stay Awhile/Something Special	5
64	Philips BF 1348	I Just Don't Know What To Do With Myself/My Colouring Book	5
64	Philips BF 1369	Losing You/Summer Is Over	5
64	Philips BF 1381	Oh Holy Child/SPRINGFIELDS: Jingle Bells (some with p/s)	10/5
65	Philips BF 1396	Your Hurtin' Kinda Love/Don't Say It Baby	5
65	Philips BF 1418	In The Middle Of Nowhere/Baby Don't You Know	5
65	Philips BF 1430	Some Of Your Lovin'/I'll Love You For A While	5
66	Philips BF 1466	Little By Little/If It Hadn't Been For You	5
66	Philips BF 1482	You Don't Have To Say You Love Me/Every Ounce Of Strength	5
66	Philips BF 1502	Goin' Back/I'm Gonna Leave You	5
66	Philips BF 1510	All I See Is You/Go Ahead On (some with p/s)	8/5
67	Philips BF 1553	I'll Try Anything/The Corrupt Ones	7
67	Philips BF 1577	Give Me Time/The Look Of Love	5
67	Philips BF 1608	What's It Gonna Be/Small Town Girl	10
68	Philips BF 1682	I Close My Eyes And Count To Ten/No Stranger Am I	5
68	Philips BF 1706	I Will Come To You/The Colour Of Your Eyes	6
68	Philips BF 1730	Son Of A Preacher Man/Just A Little Lovin'	5
69	Philips BF 1811	Am I The Same Girl/Earthbound Gypsy	6
69	Philips BF 1826	Brand New Me/Bad Case Of The Blues	6
70	Philips BF 1835	Morning Please Don't Come (with Tom Springfield)/TOM SPRINGFIELD: Charley	6
70	Philips 6006 045	How Can I Be Sure/Spooky	6
72	Philips 6006 214	Yesterday When I Was Young/I Start Counting	6
73	Philips 6006 295	Who Gets Your Love/Of All The Things	6
74	Philips 6006 325	Learn To Say Goodbye/Easy Evil	6
74	Philips 6006 350	What's It Gonna Be/Bring Him Back	6
75	Philips 6006 446	Yesterday When I Was Young/The Look Of Love	7
78	Mercury DUSTY 1	A Love Like Yours (Don't Come Knocking Every Day)/Hollywood Movie Girls	6
78	Mercury DUSTY 002	That's The Kind Of Love I've Got For You/Sandra	6
79	Mercury DUSTY 003	I'm Coming Home Again/Save Me Save Me	6
79	Mercury DUSTY 4	Baby Blue/Get Yourself To Love (p/s)	7
79	Mercury DUSTY 412	Baby Blue (Disco Version)/Baby Blue (7" Version) (12")	8
80	Mercury DUSTY 5	Your Love Still Brings Me To My Knees/ Let Me Love You Once Before You Go (withdrawn)	8
80	Mercury DUSTY 5	Your Love Still Brings Me To My Knees/I'm Your Child	5
84	Allegiance ALES 3	Private Number (with Spencer Davis)/SPENCER DAVIS: Don't Want You No More	6
85	Hippodrome HIPPO 103	Sometimes Like Butterflies/I Wanna Control You (p/s)	8
85	Hippodrome 12 HIPPO 103	Sometimes Like Butterflies (Extended Mix)/Sometimes Like Butterflies/ I Wanna Control You (12", p/s)	12
89	Parlophone RG 6207	Nothing Has Been Proved/Nothing Has Been Proved (Instrumental) (g/fold p/s)	5
89	Parlophone 12RG 6207	Nothing Has Been Proved (Dance Mix)/Nothing Has Been Proved/ Nothing Has Been Proved (Instrumental) (12", gatefold p/s)	8
89	Parlophone CDR 6207	Nothing Has Been Proved (Dance Mix)/Nothing Has Been Proved/ Nothing Has Been Proved (Instrumental) (CD, with Pet Shop Boys, card p/s)	15
89	Parlophone R 6234	In Private/In Private (Instrumental version) (p/s)	5
89	Parlophone 12RX 6234	In Private (Remix)/In Private (Dub)/In Private (Bonus Beats) (12", p/s)	7
89	Parlophone CDR 6234	In Private (12" Version)/(7" Version)/(Instrumental version) (CD)	10
90	Parlophone R 6253	Reputation/Rep U Dub 1 (p/s)	5
90	Parlophone 12R 6253	Reputation (Lots Of Fun 12" Mix)/Rep U Dub 1/Rep U Dub 2 (p/s)	8
90	Parlophone 12RX 6253	Reputation (The Alternative Mix)/Reputation (Lots Of Fun Single Mix)/ Getting It Right (12", p/s)	8
90	Parlophone 12R 6266	Reputation/Reputation (Lots Of Fun 12" Mix)/Rep U Dub 2 (CD)	8
90	Parlophone R 6266	Arrested By You/Arrested By You (Instrumental) (p/s)	5
90	Parlophone 12R 6266	Arrested By You (Extended Version)/Born This Way (12" Remix)/ Arrested By You (Instrumental) (12", p/s)	8
90	Parlophone CDR 6266	Arrested By You (7" Version)/Arrested By You (Extended Version)/ Born This Way (12" Version)/Getting It Right (CD)	8
93	Columbia 659856 7	Heart And Soul (with Cilla Black)/CILLA BLACK: A Dream Come True (p/s)	5
93	Columbia 659856 2	Heart And Soul (with Cilla Black) (7" Version)/A Capella Remix/Instrumental/ CILLA BLACK: A Dream Come True (CD)	7

94	Philips SPRCD 1	Goin' Back/Son Of A Preacher Man/Let Me Love You Once Before You Go/ What Are You Doing The Rest Of Your Life (CD)	7

EPs
64	Philips BE 12560	I ONLY WANT TO BE WITH YOU (EP)	15
64	Philips BE 12564	DUSTY (EP)	15
65	Philips BE 12572	DUSTY IN NEW YORK (EP)	15
65	Philips BE 12579	MADEMOISELLE DUSTY (EP)	25
68	Philips BE 12605	IF YOU GO AWAY (EP)	15
68	Philips 6850 751	STAR DUSTY (EP, Audio Club Of Great Britain release)	12
68	Philips MCP 1004	THE HITS OF THE WALKER BROTHERS AND DUSTY SPRINGFIELD (EP, cassette)	10
71	Philips MCP 100	THE HITS OF DUSTY SPRINGFIELD (EP, cassette)	10

LPs
64	Philips (S)BL 7594	A GIRL CALLED DUSTY (LP, mono/stereo)	18/20
65	Philips (S)RBL 1002	EVERYTHING'S COMING UP DUSTY (LP, gatefold sleeve with booklet, mono/stereo)	18/20
66	Philips (S)BL 7737	GOLDEN HITS (LP)	15
67	Philips (S)BL 7820	WHERE AM I GOING? (LP)	18
68	World Record Club ST 848	DUSTY SPRINGFIELD (LP)	15
68	Philips (S)BL 7864	DUSTY... DEFINITELY (LP)	18
69	Wing WL 1211	STAY AWHILE (LP)	15
69	Philips SBL 7889	DUSTY IN MEMPHIS (LP)	18
70	Philips SBL 7927	FROM DUSTY... WITH LOVE (LP)	18
71	Philips 6382 016	THIS IS DUSTY SPRINGFIELD (LP)	15
71	Audio Club/G.B. 6850 002	STAR DUSTY (LP)	15
71	Audio Club/G.B. 6856 020	SHEER MAGIC (LP)	40
72	Philips 6308 117	SEE ALL HER FACES (LP)	15
73	Philips 6382 063	THIS IS DUSTY SPRINGFIELD VOL. 2 — MAGIC GARDEN (LP)	15
73	Philips 6308 152	CAMEO (LP)	15
75	Philips 6382 105	SINGS BURT BACHARACH AND CAROLE KING (LP)	15
78	Mercury 9109 607	IT BEGINS AGAIN (LP)	15
79	Mercury 9109 617	LIVING WITHOUT YOUR LOVE (LP)	15

CDs
94	Philips 522 254-2	THE LEGEND OF DUSTY SPRINGFIELD (4-CD boxed set, 2,000 only)	75
96	DSB/Zone X001	WE WISH YOU A MERRY CHRISTMAS (with Springfields) (CD, Bulletin charity issue)	15

(see also Lana Sisters, Springfields, Tom Springfield, Pet Shop Boys)

RICK SPRINGFIELD
72	Capitol EA-ST 80001	BEGINNINGS (LP)	10

TOM SPRINGFIELD (& HIS) ORCHESTRA
63	Philips BF 1294	The Moon Behind The Hill/The Londonderry Air	5
64	Philips BF 1331	Brazilian Shake/Brazilian Blues	5
65	Philips BF 1423	The Mogul Theme/Homage To Spewdley Parsons	5
69	Philips BF 1759	Theme From From The Troubleshooters/Homage To Spewdley Parsons (some with p/s)	8/5
69	Decca LK/SKL 5003	LOVE'S PHILOSOPHY BY... (LP, featuring Dusty Springfield)	25

(see also Springfields, Dusty Springfield)

SPRINGFIELD PARK
68	CBS 3775	Never An Everyday Thing/I Can See The Sun Shine	4

SPRINGFIELD PARK
87	Matzo MATZ 001	Stamford Hill Cowboy (Belz Mix)/Swing That Shaytl For Me (no p/s)	7

SPRINGFIELDS
61	Philips PB 1145	Dear John/I Done What They Told Me To	6
61	Philips PB 1168	Breakaway/Good News	5
61	Philips PB 1178	Bambino/Star Of Hope (some with p/s)	10/5
62	Philips PB 1241	Silver Threads And Golden Needles/Aunt Rhody	5
62	Philips 326 536 BF	Swahili Papa/Gotta Travel On	8
62	Philips 326 557 BF	Island Of Dreams/The Johnson Boys	5
63	Philips 326 577 BF	Say I Won't Be There/Little Boat	5
61	Philips BBE 12476	THE SPRINGFIELDS (EP, also stereo SBBE 9068)	15/20
62	Lyntone P125E	CHRISTMAS WITH THE SPRINGFIELDS (EP, mail-order via *Woman's Own*)	10
62	Philips 433 622 BE	KINDA FOLKSY (EP)	15
63	Philips 433 623 BE	KINDA FOLKSY No. 2 (EP)	15
63	Philips 433 624 BE	KINDA FOLKSY No. 3 (EP)	15
63	Philips BBE 12538	HIT SOUNDS (EP)	10
63	Philips 433 643 BE	FOLK SONGS FROM THE HILLS (EP)	8
62	Philips BBL 7551/SBBL 674	KINDA FOLKSY (LP, mono/stereo)	15/20
63	Philips 632 304 BL	FOLK SONGS FROM THE HILLS (LP)	15
64	Philips BET 606	THE SPRINGFIELDS STORY (2-LP)	20
69	Fontana SFL 13098	THE SPRINGFIELDS SING AGAIN (LP)	15

(see also Dusty Springfield, Lana Sisters, Tom Springfield, Mike Hurst)

SPRINGFIELDS
88	Sarah SARAH 010	Sunflower/Clown/Are We Gonna Be Alright? (foldaround p/s with 14" x 10" poster in poly bag; yellow p/s, later orange p/s)	12/8

BRUCE SPRINGSTEEN
SINGLES
75	CBS A 3661	Born To Run/Meeting Across The River	8
76	CBS A 3940	Tenth Avenue Freeze-Out/She's The One	12
78	CBS A 6424	Prove It All Night/Factory	15
78	CBS A 6532	Badlands/Something In The Night	12
78	CBS A 6720	Promised Land/Streets Of Fire	40
80	CBS A 9309	Hungry Heart/Held Up Without A Gun (p/s, blue or black lettering)	15/10

Bruce SPRINGSTEEN

80	CBS A 9568	Sherry Darling/Be True (p/s)	10
81	CBS A 1179	The River/Independence Day (p/s)	10
81	CBS A 13-1179	The River/Born To Run/Rosalita (12", p/s, some sleeves credit 'East Street Band')	15/10
81	CBS A 1557	Cadillac Ranch/Wreck On The Highway (p/s)	25
82	CBS A 2794	Atlantic City/Mansion On The Hill (p/s)	25
82	CBS A 2969	Open All Night/The Big Pay Back (p/s)	25
84	CBS WA 4436	Dancing In The Dark/Pink Cadillac (Cadillac-shaped picture disc)	30
84	CBS A 4662	Cover Me/Jersey Girl (live) (poster p/s)	10
84	CBS WA 4662	Cover Me/Jersey Girl (live) (Bruce-shaped picture disc with plinth, withdrawn)	25
84	CBS DA 4662/A 4436	Cover Me/Jersey Girl (live)//Dancing In The Dark/Pink Cadillac (shrinkwrapped double pack, both 45s in p/s)	12
84	CBS DA 4662/A 7077	Cover Me/Jersey Girl (live)//Born To Run/Meeting Across The River (shrinkwrapped double pack, no p/s on 2nd 45)	12
84	CBS QTA 4662	Cover Me (Undercover Mix)/Cover Me (Dub)/Shut Out The Light/ Dancing In The Dark (Dub)/Jersey Girl (12", p/s)	7
84	CBS A 6773	My Hometown/Santa Claus Is Comin' To Town (p/s)	4
85	CBS A 7077	Born To Run/Meeting Across The River (reissue, blue p/s, withdrawn)	25
85	CBS A 6342	I'm On Fire/Born In The U.S.A. (p/s, with competition postcard)	8
85	CBS WA 6342	I'm On Fire/Born In The U.S.A. (p/s, flag-shaped picture disc)	15
85	CBS TA 6342	I'm On Fire/Rosalita/Born In The U.S.A. (Freedom Mix)/ Johnny Bye Bye (12", p/s)	10
85	CBS QTA 6375	Glory Days/Stand On It/Sherry Darling/Racing In The Street (12", poster p/s)	8
85	CBS BRUCE 1	BORN IN THE U.S.A. — THE 12" COLLECTION (4 x 12" & 7", box with poster)	25
86	CBS 650 193-0	War (live)/Merry Xmas Baby (live)/My Home Town (live)/ Santa Claus Is Coming To Town (live) (shrinkwrapped double pack, both 45s in p/s)	12
86	CBS 650 193-6	War/Merry Xmas Baby (live)/Incident On 57th Street (live) (12", poster p/s)	8
87	CBS 650 381-7	Fire (live)/For You (live) (p/s)	6
87	CBS 650 381-6	Fire (live)/For You (live)/Born To Run (live)/No Surrender (live)/ 10th Avenue (live) Freeze-Out (live) (12", p/s)	8
87	CBS BRUCE B2	Born To Run/Spirit In The Night//Johnny 99/Because The Night (double pack box set)	10
87	CBS BRUCE BP 2	Born To Run (live)/Johnny 99 (live) (p/s, badge pack)	4
87	CBS BRUCE C2	Born To Run (live)/Spirit In The Night (live)/Johnny 99 (live)/Seeds (live) (CD, card sleeve with gauze inner)	10
87	CBS 651 141-0	Brilliant Disguise/Lucky Man (gatefold p/s)	7
87	CBS 651 295-7	Tunnel Of Love/Two For The Road (p/s)	4
87	CBS 651 295-0	Tunnel Of Love/Two For The Road (postcard-shaped picture disc)	15
87	CBS 651 295-8	Tunnel Of Love/Two For The Road/Santa Claus Is Coming To Town (12", p/s with poster)	10
87	CBS 651 295-2	Tunnel Of Love/Santa Claus Is Coming To Town (live)/Two For The Road (CD, card sleeve)	45
88	CBS BRUCE 3	Tougher Than The Rest/Tougher Than The Rest (live) (p/s, with patch)	6
88	CBS BRUCE C3	Tougher Than The Rest/Roulette/Be True (Live)/Born To Run (New Live) (CD, card sleeve)	10
88	CBS BRUCE Q4	Spare Parts/Cover Me (live)/Spare Parts (live)/I'm On Fire (live) (12", different p/s)	15
88	CBS BRUCE C4	Spare Parts/Pink Cadillac/Spare Parts (live)/Chimes Of Freedom (live) (CD, card sleeve)	12
88	CBS BRUCE B4	Spare Parts/Pink Cadillac/Spare Parts (live)/Chimes Of Freedom (live) (CD, BRUCE C4 disc in silver tin)	25
92	Sony 658 138-5	57 Channels (And Nothin' On)/Stand On It/Janey, Don't You Lose Heart (CD, picture disc, digipak)	25
92	Sony 658 369-2	Leap Of Faith/Leap Of Faith (live)/30 Days Out (CD)	7

LPs

73	CBS 65480	GREETINGS FROM ASBURY PARK, N.J. (LP, cutaway gatefold sleeve, orange label)	10
74	CBS 65780	THE WILD, THE INNOCENT AND THE E STREET SHUFFLE (LP, orange label, yellow lettering on sleeve; some with "Ashbury" mis-spelled on label)	15/12
75	CBS 69170	BORN TO RUN (LP, with "John Landau" misprint on rear sleeve)	12
79	CBS 66353	BRUCE SPRINGSTEEN (3-LP, box set)	30
84	CBS 11-86304	BORN IN THE U.S.A. (LP, picture disc)	35
87	CBS 460 270-0	TUNNEL OF LOVE (LP, picture disc)	15
87	CBS CDCBS 460 270-9	TUNNEL OF LOVE (CD, picture disc)	20
92	Sony 471 423-0	HUMAN TOUCH (LP, picture disc)	10
92	Sony 471 424-0	LUCKY TOWN (LP, picture disc)	10

(see also Nils Lofgren, Roy Orbison)

SPRINGTIME

78	Sonet SON 2143	Mrs Caroline Robinson/Honey Bye Bye (p/s)	6

SPROG & WIDGIT

72	Diddley Do DIDLP 02	32 ENGLISH FOLK SONGS IN THE SILLY TRADITION (2-LP, gatefold sleeve)	15

SPRONG & NYAH SHUFFLE

69	Grape GR 3001	Moonwalk/Think	7

BILLY SPROUD & ROCK 'N' ROLL SIX

57	Columbia DB 3893	Rock Mr. Piper/If You're So Smart (How Come You Ain't Rich)	40
57	Columbia DB 3893	Rock Mr. Piper/If You're So Smart (How Come You Ain't Rich) (78)	20

SPROUTS

58	RCA RCA 1031	Teen Billy Baby/Goodbye, She's Gone	75
58	RCA RCA 1031	Teen Billy Baby/Goodbye, She's Gone (78)	35

SPROUT-U-LIKE
86	Cab-bab-babbage CH 4	Swamp Gas Saturday/Sulphurous Sunday (flexidisc with scratch'n'sniff p/s) . . .	10

SPUD
75	Philips 9108 002	A SILK PURSE (LP)	20
75	Philips 9108 003	A HAPPY HANDFUL (LP)	25
77	Sonet SNTF 742	SMOKING IN THE BOG (LP, with lyric sheet)	15

WILD JIMMY SPURRILL
60s	XX MIN 717	NOBLE 'THIN MAN' WATTS AND WILD JIMMY SPURRILL (EP)	15

(see also Noble 'Thin Man' Watts, Guitar Crusher)

SPYS
79	No Bad NB 3	The Young Ones/Heavy Scene (p/s)	5

SQUAD
79	Squad SQS 1	Red Alert/£8 A Week (die cut p/s)	20

SQUADRONAIRES
54	Decca F 10248	Coach Call Boogie/Donegal Cradle Song	10
54	Decca F 10274	Wolf On The Prowl/Mudhopper	10
57	Columbia DB 3882	Rock And Roll Boogie/Right Now, Right Now	12
57	Columbia DB 3882	Rock And Roll Boogie/Right Now, Right Now (78)	12
53	Decca LF 1141	CONTRASTS IN JAZZ (10" LP)	15

(see also Ronnie Aldrich)

SQUEEZE
77	BTM SBT 107	Take Me I'm Yours/No, Disco Kid, No (unreleased)	
77	Deptford Fun City DFC 01	PACKET OF THREE (EP, red & blue photo p/s)	6
77	Deptford Fun City DFC 01	PACKET OF THREE (12" EP, plain pink die-cut sleeve, 500 only)	10
78	A&M AMSP 7335	Take Me I'm Yours/Night Nurse (12", p/s)	7
78	A&M AMS 7360	Bang Bang/All Fed Up (p/s, green vinyl)	4
78	A&M AMS 7398	Goodbye Girl/Saints Alive (3-D p/s)	5
79	A&M AMS 7426	Cool For Cats/Model (p/s, brilliant pink vinyl, 5,000 only)	6
79	A&M AMS 7426	Cool For Cats/Model (p/s, red vinyl, 1,000 only)	8
79	A&M AMSP 7426	Cool For Cats/Model (12", p/s, pale pink vinyl)	10
79	A&M AMS 7495	Christmas Day/Going Crazy (p/s, white vinyl)	4
79	A&M AMS 7507	Another Nail In My Heart/Pretty Thing (p/s, clear vinyl)	4
80	Lyntone LYN 7010/1	Wrong Way (green vinyl flexidisc, free with *Smash Hits*)	6/4
81	A&M AMS 8147	Tempted/Yap Yap Yap (p/s, with free U.S. 5" single "Another Nail In My Heart"/"If I Didn't Love You", p/s, shrinkwrapped)	5
81	A&M AMS 8166	Labelled With Love/Squabs On Forty Five (withdrawn p/s)	15

SQUIBBY & REFLECTIONS
68	Direction 58-3453	Ragamuffin/For A Little While	5
68	Direction 58-3606	Loving You Has Made My Life Worthwhile/Better Off Without You	5
69	Direction 58-4073	You Got It/Come Back To Me	5

BILLY SQUIER
82	Capitol CL 231	Too Daze Gone/Whadda You Want From Me (p/s, coloured vinyl)	4
82	Capitol CL 261	Emotions In Motion/Catch 22 (p/s)	12
82	Capitol CL 261	Emotions In Motion/Catch 22 (picture disc)	15
84	Capitol SQD 1	Rock Me Tonite/Can't Get Next To You//She's A Runner/Listen To The Heart (double pack)	6
86	Capitol CL 433	Love Is The Hero/Learn How To Live (live) (p/s)	7
86	Capitol 12CL 433	Love Is The Hero (extended version with Freddie Mercury intro)/ Learn How To Live (live) (12", p/s)	65

(see also Freddie Mercury, Roger Taylor)

SQUIRE
79	Rok ROK I/II	Get Ready To Go/COMING SHORTLY: Doing The Flail (company sleeve)	12
79	I-Spy SEE 4	The Face Of Youth Today/I Know A Girl (keyhole company sleeve, paper or plastic labels)	4/6
80	Stage One STAGE 2	My Mind Goes Round In Circles/Does Stephanie Know? (p/s)	6
82	Hi-Lo HI 001	No Time Tomorrow/Don't Cry To Me (p/s)	4
82	Hi-Lo HI 002	Girl On A Train/Every Trick In The Book (p/s)	4
83	Hi-Lo HI 003	Every Trick In The Book/Every Trick In The Book (Instrumental) (p/s)	4
83	Hi-Lo HIT 003	Every Trick In The Book/Every Trick In The Book (Elastic Mix) (12", p/s)	7
83	Hi-Lo HI 004	Jesamine/When I Try, I Lie (p/s)	4
84	Hi-Lo HI 005/SFC 2	The Young Idea/It's Getting Better (Squire Fan Club issue)	10
85	Hi-Lo LOX 1	Does Stephanie Know? (flexidisc)	8
94	Detour DR 020	The Place I Used To Live/Make Love To You/Over You (p/s, 900 only, 50 on white vinyl: 2nd pressing of 250 copies, white labels & purple print: 3rd pressing, 588 copies on clear splattered vinyl)	10/5/5/5
83	Hi-Lo LO 01	HITS FROM 3,000 YEARS AGO (LP)	10
83	Hi-Lo LO 02	GET SMART (LP, with poster)	10
85	Hi-Lo LO 03	THE SINGLES ALBUM (LP)	10

(see also Anthony Meynell)

CHRIS SQUIRE
75	Atlantic K 50203	FISH OUT OF WATER (LP, with inner sleeve & poster)	12

(see also Yes)

DOROTHY SQUIRES
57	Columbia DB 3985	Song Of The Valley/Our Song	6
58	Columbia DB 4070	Bewitched/A Secret That's Never Been Told	6
58	Pye 7N 15154	Torremelinos/This Is My Mother's Day	5
58	Pye 7N 15199	Sticks And Stones/Don't Search For Love	5
58	Pye N 15199	Sticks And Stones/Don't Search For Love (78)	10
62	Columbia DB 4942	Are You/Moonlight And Roses	5
57	Pye NEP 24036	DOROTHY SQUIRES (EP)	15

MINT VALUE £

58	Pye Nixa NPL 18015	SINGS BILLY REID (LP)	20
67	Ace Of Clubs SCL-R 1230	THIS IS MY LIFE (LP)	12
68	Marble Arch MAL(S) 1211	REFLECTIONS (LP, mono/stereo)	12/15
68	President PTL(S) 1023	SAY IT WITH FLOWERS (LP)	12
69	President PTL(S) 1032	SEASONS OF DOROTHY SQUIRES (LP)	12
70	President PTLS 1043/4	AT THE LONDON PALLADIUM (2-LP)	15
73	Pye NSPL 18425	CHEESE'N'WINE (LP, with Dennis Lotis)	12
73	EMI EMC 3004	LONDON PALLADIUM 1972 (LP)	15
74	Pye NSPD 501	LIVE AT THEATRE ROYAL, DRURY LANE (LP)	12

ROSEMARY SQUIRES

56	Decca F 10685	Band Of Gold/Where You Are	7
58	HMV POP 462	Happy Is The Bride/Give Me The Simple Life	6
58	HMV POP 541	There Goes My Lover/Please Be Kind	5
64	HMV POP 1288	Bluesette/Nothing's Changed	6
56	MGM MGM-EP 640	MY LOVE IS A WANDERER (EP)	15
60	HMV 7EG 8588	ROSEMARY (EP)	12
65	HMV CLP 1832	SOMETHING TO REMEMBER ME BY (LP)	18

(see also Streamliners & Joanne)

S.R.C.

69	Capitol CL 15576	Black Sheep/Morning Mood	15
87	Bam Caruso OPRA 063	Black Sheep/BRAIN: Nightmares In Red (jukebox issue, die-cut co. sleeve)	5
69	Capitol (S)T 2991	S.R.C. (LP)	35
69	Capitol E-(S)T 134	MILESTONES (LP)	25
70	Capitol E-(S)T 273	TRAVELLER'S TALE (LP)	35

STACCATOS (U.K.)

| 61 | Parlophone R 4828 | Main Line/Topaz | 12 |

STACCATOS (U.S.)

| 66 | Capitol CL 15478 | Let's Run Away/Face To Face (With Love) | 8 |
| 67 | Capitol CL 15505 | Half Past Midnight/Weatherman | 8 |

STACCATOS (U.K.)

| 68 | Fontana TF 966 | Butchers And Bakers/Imitations Of Love | 15 |

CLARENCE STACEY

| 59 | Pye International 7N 25025 | Just Your Love/Lonely Guy | 8 |
| 59 | Pye International N 25025 | Just Your Love/Lonely Guy (78) | 20 |

GWEN STACEY

| 65 | RCA RCX 7166 | INTRODUCING GWEN STACEY (EP) | 60 |

BOB STACKIE

| 68 | Collins Downbeat CR 009 | Grab It Hold It Feel It (with Sir Collins Band)/DAN SIMMONDS: Way Out Sound | 30 |

(see also Sir Collins [Band], Owen Gray)

STACKRIDGE

71	MCA MKS 5065	Dora, The Female Explorer/Everyman	5
72	MCA MKS 5103	Anyone For Tennis?/Amazingly Agnes	5
71	MCA MDKS 8002	STACKRIDGE (LP, gatefold sleeve)	30
72	MCA MKPS 2025	FRIENDLINESS (LP)	12
74	MCA MCG 3501	THE MAN IN THE BOWLER HAT (LP, gatefold sleeve)	12
76	MCA MCF 2747	DO THE STANLEY (LP)	12
76	Rocket ROLL 3	MR. MICK (LP)	12

STACKWADDY

70	Dandelion S 5119	Roadrunner/Kentucky	10
72	Dandelion 2001 331	You Really Got Me/Willie The Pimp	8
71	Dandelion DAN 8003	STACKWADDY (LP, gatefold sleeve with inner sleeve; also listed as K 49003)	30
72	Dandelion 2310 231	BUGGER OFF! (LP)	60

STADIUM DOGS

| 77 | Audiogenic A 17 | Easy Beat/Android Rocker/Media Withdrawl (die cut p/s) | 10 |

JO STAFFORD

78s

51	Columbia DB 2802	Tennessee Waltz/My Heart Cries For You (B-side with Gene Autry) (78)	8
51	Columbia DB 2939	Kissing Bug Boogie/Hawaiian War Chant (78)	8
51	Columbia DB 2961	Allentown Jail/FRANKIE LAINE: Love Is Such A Cheat (78)	8
53	Capitol CL 13970	Diamonds Are A Girl's Best Friend/The Stanley Steamer (78)	8
58	Philips PB 812	Sweet Little Darlin'/Star Of Love (78)	10
58	Philips PB 818	With A Little Bit Of Luck/Wouldn't It Be Loverly (78)	8
58	Philips PB 876	Hibiscus/How Can We Say Goodbye (78)	12
59	Philips PB 935	Pine Top's Boogie Woogie/All Yours (78)	25

SINGLES

53	Columbia SCM 5011	Star Of Hope/Somebody	15
53	Columbia SCM 5012	It Is No Secret/He Bought My Soul At Calvary	15
53	Columbia SCM 5013	You Belong To Me/Jambalaya (On The Bayou)	25
53	Columbia SCM 5026	Keep It A Secret/Once To Every Heart	15
53	Columbia SCM 5046	Something To Remember You By/Blue Moon	12
53	Columbia SCM 5064	September In The Rain/JO STAFFORD & FRANKIE LAINE: Chow, Willy	25
57	Philips JK 1003	On London Bridge/Perfect Love (jukebox issue)	15
58	Philips PB 818	With A Little Bit Of Luck/Wouldn't It Be Loverly	7
58	Philips PB 876	Hibiscus/How Can We Say Goodbye	5
59	Philips PB 898	My Heart Is From Missouri/It Won't Be Easy	5
59	Philips PB 935	Pine Top's Boogie Woogie/All Yours	10
60	Philips PB 991	It Is No Secret/He Bought My Soul At Calvary (reissue)	6
60	Philips PB 1034	Candy/Indoor Sport	5
61	Capitol CL 15225	The Old Rugged Cross/In The Gloaming (with Gordon McRae)	5
62	Pye International 7N 25127	Adios My Love/Misty	5

MINT VALUE £

| 62 | Pye International 7N 25139 | Symphony/If My Heart Had A Window............................ | 5 |

EPs

54	Columbia SEG 7516	WITH NELSON EDDY (EP, plain sleeve)............................	10
54	Columbia SEG 7548	SHOW SONGS (EP, plain sleeve)................................	10
55	Philips BBE 12014	JO STAFFORD No. 1 (EP)..	15
57	Philips BBE 12138	JO STAFFORD No. 2 (EP)..	15
57	Philips BBE 12141	JO STAFFORD WITH THE ART VAN DAMME QUINTET (EP)..........	12
57	Philips BBE 12147	JO STAFFORD SINGS SACRED SONGS (EP)......................	8
58	Philips BBE 12163	SINGS SONGS OF SCOTLAND (EP).............................	8
58	Philips BBE 12198	JO STAFFORD SINGS SACRED SONGS No. 2 (EP)...............	8
58	Philips BBE 12214	T.V. SERIES (EP)..	15
60	Philips BBE 12378	JO STAFFORD SINGS SACRED SONGS No. 3 (EP)...............	8
60	Capitol EAP 20049	THE JO STAFFORD TOUCH (EP)...............................	12
61	Capitol EAP 20154	SIMPLE MELODY (EP)..	10
61	Philips BBE 12459	JO + JAZZ (EP)...	12

LPs

50	Capitol LC 6500	AMERICAN FOLK SONGS (10" LP)...............................	25
51	Capitol LC 6515	KISS ME KATE (10" LP, with Gordon MacRae)...................	18
53	Capitol LC 6575	CAPITOL PRESENTS JO STAFFORD (10" LP)....................	25
53	Capitol LC 6611	SUNDAY EVENING SONGS (10" LP, with Gordon MacRae)........	20
54	Capitol LC 6635	CAPITOL PRESENTS JO STAFFORD, VOL. 2 (10" LP)............	25
54	Columbia 33S 1024	AS YOU DESIRE ME (10" LP)..................................	30
54	Philips BBR 8011	MY HEART'S IN THE HIGHLANDS (10" LP)......................	20
56	Philips BBR 8076	THE VOICE OF YOUR CHOICE (10" LP).........................	20
56	Philips BBL 7100	HAPPY HOLIDAY (LP, soundtrack).............................	15
57	Philips BBL 7169	ONCE OVER LIGHTLY (LP).....................................	15
57	Philips BBL 7187	SKI TRAILS (LP)..	15
58	Philips BBL 7243	SWINGIN' DOWN BROADWAY (LP)...............................	15
59	Philips BBL 7290	I'LL BE SEEING YOU (LP).....................................	15
59	Philips BBL 7327	BALLAD OF THE BLUES (LP)..................................	15
60	Philips BBL 7395	JO STAFFORD SHOWCASE (LP)................................	18
61	Philips BBL 7428	JO + JAZZ (LP, also stereo SBBL 595)......................	15/18
62	Capitol (S)T 1653	AMERICAN FOLK SONGS (LP, reissue, mono/stereo)...........	12/15
62	Capitol (S)T 1696	WHISPERING HOPE (LP, with Gordon MacRae)..................	12
63	Encore ENC 144	JO STAFFORD'S SMOKE DREAMS (LP)..........................	12
64	Capitol (S)T 1921	THE HITS OF JO STAFFORD (LP).............................	12

(see also Jonathan & Darlene Edwards, Gordon MacRae, Tommy Dorsey)

JO STAFFORD & FRANKIE LAINE

| 53 | Columbia SCM 5014 | Settin' The Woods On Fire/Piece A-Puddin'.................... | 25 |
| 55 | Philips BBR 8075 | FLOATIN' DOWN TO COTTON TOWN (10" LP).................... | 35 |

(see also Frankie Laine)

TERRY STAFFORD

63	Stateside SS 225	Heartache On The Way/You Left Me Here To Cry................	10
64	London HLU 9871	Suspicion/Judy..	8
64	London HLU 9902	Playing With Fire/I'll Touch A Star.........................	10
64	London HLU 9923	Follow The Rainbow/Are You A Fool Like Me...................	10
64	London RE-U 1436	SUSPICION (EP)...	75
64	London HA-U 8200	SUSPICION (LP)...	60

STAINED GLASS

| 74 | Sweet Folk & C. SFA 019 | OPEN ROAD (LP).. | 80 |

CHRIS STAINTON & GLEN TURNER

| 76 | Decca SKL-R 5259 | TUNDRA (LP).. | 12 |

(see also Made In Sheffield, Joe Cocker, Grease Band)

STAIRS

| 92 | Imaginary MIRAGE 029 | Weed Bus (12", unissued, test pressings only, proof p/s)..... | 15 |

STAIRSTEPS

71	Buddah 2011 092	Stay Close To Me/I Made A Mistake..........................	7
71	Buddah 2359 021	STEP BY STEP BY STEP (LP).................................	12
71	Buddah 2365 015	STAY CLOSE TO ME (LP).....................................	12
72	Buddah 2365 016	THE STAIRSTEPS (LP).......................................	12

(see also Five Stairsteps)

STAIRWAY

87	New World NWC 143	AQUAMARINE (cassette)......................................	12
88	New World NWCD 168	MOONSTONE (CD)..	18
88	New World NWC 168	MOONSTONE (cassette)......................................	12
89	New World NWC 179	CHAKRA DANCE (cassette)...................................	10

(see also Jane Relf, Yardbirds, Renaissance)

STAKKER

| 88 | Westside WSRT 12 | HUMANOID (12").. | 10 |
| 88 | Westside WSRCD 12 | HUMANOID (3" CD)... | 10 |

(see also Future Sound Of London, Art Science Technology)

TERRY STAMP

| 75 | A&M AMLH 63329 | FAT STICKS (LP).. | 15 |

(see also Third World War)

STAMPEDE

82	Polydor POSP 507	Days Of Wine And Roses/Photographs (p/s)....................	10
82	Polydor POSP 507	Photographs/Days Of Wine And Roses (A-side switched, no p/s)..	25
82	Polydor POSPX 507	Days Of Wine And Roses/Photographs (12", p/s)...............	30
83	Polydor POSP 592	The Other Side/The Runner (p/s)............................	10
82	Polydor ROCK 1	OFFICIAL BOOTLEG (LP).....................................	12
83	Polydor POLS 1083	HURRICANE TOWN (LP).......................................	12

MINT VALUE £

VIVIAN STANSHALL

STAMPEDERS
72	Stateside SS 2202	Monday Morning Choo Choo/Then Came The White Man	5
72	Regal Zonophone RZ 3069	Johnny Lightning/Today's The Beginning Of The Rest Of Your Life.	5
73	Regal Zonophone RZ 3079	Oh My Lady/No Destination	5
72	Regal Zono. SLRZ 1032	THE STAMPEDERS (LP)	15
74	Regal Zono. SLRZ 1039	FROM THE FIRE (LP)	15

JOE STAMPLEY
73	Dot DOT 145	Soul Song/Not Too Long Ago	8

JEAN STANBACK
69	Deep Soul DS 9101	I Still Love You/If I Ever Needed Love	15

STANDELLS
64	Liberty LIB 55722	I'll Go Crazy/Help Yourself	20
66	Capitol CL 15446	Dirty Water/Rari	20
65	Liberty LBY 1243	THE STANDELLS IN PERSON AT P.J.'s (LP)	50

JOHNNY STANDLEY
56	Capitol EAP 1020	IT'S IN THE BOOK (EP)	10

ARNOLD STANG
59	Fontana H 226	Where Ya' Calling From, Charlie/Ivy Will Cling	7
59	Fontana H 226	Where Ya' Calling From, Charlie/Ivy Will Cling (78)	10

STANLEY
73	Action ACT 4615	I'll Go Down And Getcha (Parts 1 & 2)	4

PAUL STANLEY
79	Casablanca CAN 140	Hold Me Touch Me/Goodbye (p/s)	12
79	Casablanca CAN 140	Hold Me Touch Me/Goodbye (p/s, purple vinyl with mask & picture label, most with mispressed B-side: "Love in Chains")	20

(see also Kiss)

PETE STANLEY & WIZZ JONES
65	Columbia DB 7776	The Ballad Of Hollis Brown/Riff Minor	15
66	Columbia SX 6083	SIXTEEN TONS OF BLUEGRASS (LP)	90

(see also Wizz Jones)

PETE STANLEY & ROGER KNOWLES
70s	Xtra TRANS 1146	PICKING AND SINGING (LP)	25

STANLEY BROTHERS
61	Melodisc MLP 12-118	MOUNTAIN SONG FAVOURITES (LP)	10
61	Melodisc MLP 12-122	SACRED SONGS FROM THE HILLS (LP)	10

ROY STANNARD ORCHESTRA
87	SS SS 100	The Peanut Vendor/'Swingin' 'The Blues	5

STEVE STANNARD
60	Embassy WB 375	Reveille Rock/BOBBY BRITTON: Dance With Me	5
60	Embassy WB 375	Reveille Rock/BOBBY BRITTON: Dance With Me (78)	8
60	Embassy WB 385	Theme From A Summer's Place/RIKKI HENDERSON: What In The World	5
60	Embassy WB 385	Theme From A Summer's Place/RIKKI HENDERSON: What In The World (78)	8
60	Embassy WB 400	Down Yonder/RIKKI HENDERSON: Ain't Misbehavin'.	5
60	Embassy WB 400	Down Yonder/RIKKI HENDERSON: Ain't Misbehavin' (78)	8
60	Embassy WB 415	Walk Don't Run/Never On Sunday.	5
60	Embassy WB 415	Walk Don't Run/Never On Sunday (78)	10

(see also Bud Ashton, Matt Bryant & Linda Joyce, Bobby Britton, Ricki Henderson)

LISA STANSFIELD

81	Devil DEV 2	Your Alibis/Thought Police (p/s)	6

(see also Blue Zone)

VIV(IAN) STANSHALL

70	Liberty LBF 15309	Labio-Dental Fricative/Paper Round (with Sean Head Show Band featuring Eric Clapton)	25
71	Fly BUG 4	Suspicion (with Gargantuan Chums)/Blind Date (with biG GRunt)	12
74	Warner Bros K 16424	Lakonga/Baba Tunde	7
76	Harvest HAR 5114	Young Ones/Are You Havin' Any Fun/Question	7
80	Charisma CB 373	Terry Keeps His Clips On/King Cripple (p/s)	6
81	Charisma CB 382	Calypso To Colapso/Smoke Signals At Night (p/s)	5
74	Warner Bros K 56052	MEN OPENING UMBRELLAS AHEAD (LP)	30
78	Charisma CAS 1139	SIR HENRY AT RAWLINSON END (LP, soundtrack, with insert)	20
81	Charisma CAS 1153	TEDDY BOYS DON'T KNIT (LP)	15

(see also Bonzo Dog [Doo Dah] Band, Grimms)

STAPLE SINGERS

64	Riverside 106902 RIF	Hammer And Nails/Glory Land	10
67	Columbia DB 8292	For What It's Worth/Are You Sure?	10
69	Soul City SC 117	For What It's Worth/Are You Sure? (reissue)	8
69	Stax STAX 118	I See It/The Ghetto	5
71	Stax 2025 019	Heavy Makes You Happy/Love Is Plentiful	5
72	Stax 2025 068	Respect Yourself/You're Gonna Make Me Cry	5
72	Stax 2025 110	I'll Take You There/Just Another Soldier	5
62	Riverside REP 3220	THE SAVIOUR IS BORN (EP)	10
63	Stateside SL 10015	SWING LOW (LP)	25
63	Riverside RLP 3501	HAMMER AND NAILS (LP)	25
65	Fontana 688 515 ZL	UNCLOUDY DAY (LP)	20
66	Columbia SX 6023	FREEDOM HIGHWAY (LP)	20
69	Stax (S)XATS 1004	SOUL FOLK IN ACTION (LP)	15
69	Stax SXATS 1018	WE'LL GET OVER (LP)	15
71	Stax 2362 005	THE STAPLE SINGERS (LP)	12
71	Stax 2362 011	SOUL FOLK IN ACTION (LP, reissue)	10
72	Stax STX 1001	CITY IN THE SKY (LP)	12
72	Stax 2325 069	BEALTITUDE/RESPECT YOURSELF (LP)	12

CYRIL STAPLETON & HIS ORCHESTRA

54	Decca F 10293	Long Distance Love/There'll Be No Teardrops Tonight	7
55	Decca F 10456	Tango Mambo/Mexican Madness	7
55	Decca F 10470	Fanfare Boogie/Time After Time	8
55	Decca F 10488	Elephant Tango/Gabrielle	10
55	Decca F 10559	Blue Star (The "Medic" Theme) (with Julie Dawn)/Honey Babe (with Gordon Langhorn)	10
56	Decca F 10703	The Italian Theme/Come Next Spring	10
56	Decca F 10735	The Happy Whistler (with Desmond Lane)/Tiger Tango	8
56	Decca F 10793	Highway Patrol/Maids Of Madrid	7
57	Decca F 10883	Rock, Fiddle, Rock/Chantez, Chantez	7
57	Decca F 10912	Forgotten Dreams/It's Not For Me To Say	6
58	Decca F 10979	Monday Blues (Parts 1 & 2)	5
58	Decca F 11094	Nick Nack Paddy Whack/The Inn Of The Sixth Happiness	5
59	Decca F 11180	North West Frontier/Third Man Theme	5
59	Decca F 11180	North West Frontier/Third Man Theme (78)	8
66	Pye 7N 17040	The Theme From The Power Game/'Lil (some in p/s)	8/5
68	Pye 7N 17629	The Forsyte Saga/The Lonely Sea And The Sky (some in p/s)	8/5
69	Pye 7N 17807	Department S (Theme)/W. Somerset Maugham TV Theme (some in p/s)	30/15
54	Decca DFE 6288	PRESENTING CYRIL STAPLETON (EP)	8
54	Decca DFE 6340	PRESENTING CYRIL STAPLETON NO. 2 (EP)	8
55	Decca DFE 6454	DANCING IN THE DARK NO. 1 (EP)	8
55	Decca DFE 6455	DANCING IN THE DARK NO. 2 (EP)	8
62	Ace Of Clubs ACL 1114	COME TWISTIN' (LP)	20

(see also Gordon Langhorn, Desmond Lane)

STA-PREST

80	Avatar AAA 103	Schooldays/Tomorrow (p/s)	18

BUDDY STARCHER

64	London RE-B 1424	BUDDY STARCHER AND HIS MOUNTAIN GUITAR VOL. 1 (EP)	20
64	London RE-B 1425	BUDDY STARCHER AND HIS MOUNTAIN GUITAR VOL. 2 (EP)	20
64	London RE-B 1426	BUDDY STARCHER AND HIS MOUNTAIN GUITAR VOL. 3 (EP)	20

ALVIN STARDUST

75	Magnet MAG 21	Good Love Can Never Die/The Danger Zone (p/s)	6

(see also Shane Fenton & Fentones)

STARFIGHTERS

80	Motor City MCR 105	I'm Calling (some in p/s)	30/7
81	Jive JIV 003	Alley Cat Blues/Don't Touch Me (p/s)	7
81	Jive JIVET 6	Power Crazy/I Want You (p/s)	6
81	Jive JIVET 6	Power Crazy/I Want You/Get Out While You Can (12", p/s)	8
82	Jive HOP 200	POWER CRAZY (LP)	10

STARGAZERS

53	Decca F 10047	Broken Wings/Make It Soon (78)	20
54	Decca F 10213	I See The Moon/Eh Cumpari	25
54	Decca F 10259	The Happy Wanderer/Till We Two Are One	18
54	Decca F 10379	365 Kisses/I Need You Now	8
54	Decca F 10412	Rose Of The Wildwood/Come The Morning	8
55	Decca F 10437	Somebody/(My Baby Don't Love Me) No More (& Sonny Farrar Banjo Band)	15
55	Decca F 10523	The Crazy Otto Rag/Hey, Mr. Banjo	15

MINT VALUE £

55	Decca F 10569	At The Steamboat River Ball/I Love You A Mountain (with Sonny Farrar Banjo Band)	7
55	Decca F 10594	Close The Door/I've Got Four Big Brothers	15
55	Decca F 10626	Twenty Tiny Fingers/An Old Beer Bottle	15
55	Decca F 10668	(Love Is) The Tender Trap/When The Swallows Say Goodbye	7
56	Decca F 10696	Zambesi/When The Swallows Say Goodbye	10
56	Decca F 10731	Hot Diggity (Dog Ziggity Boom)/Rockin' And Rollin'	12
56	Decca F 10775	She Loves To Rock/John Jacob Jingleheimer Smith	12
57	Decca F 10867	You Won't Be Around/Mangos	6
57	Decca F 10898	Honky Tonk Song/Golly!	6
57	Decca F 10916	Who Is It? (It's The Milkman)/Sorry, You'll Have To Wait	6
57	Decca F 10969	The Skiffling Dogs/Out Of This World	6
57	Decca F 10969	The Skiffling Dogs/Out Of This World (78)	8
58	Decca F 11034	Big Man/Lonely For A Letter	5
58	Decca F 11034	Big Man/Lonely For A Letter (78)	8
59	Decca F 11105	My Blue Heaven/How Ja Lika	5
59	Decca F 11105	My Blue Heaven/How Ja Lika (78)	8
60	Palette PG 9003	Manhattan Spiritual/Three Beautiful Words	5
56	Decca DFE 6341	THE STARGAZERS (EP)	25
56	Decca DFE 6362	ROCKIN' AND ROLLIN' (EP)	22
54	Decca LF 1186	PRESENTING THE STARGAZERS (10" LP)	40
59	Decca LK 4309	SOUTH OF THE BORDER (LP)	30

(see also Roy Smith & Stargazers, Lita Roza, Dickie Valentine)

STARJETS

78	Epic S EPC 6902	Here She Comes Again/Watch Out	5
79	Epic S EPC 6968	It Really Doesn't Matter/Schooldays	5
79	Epic S EPC 7123	Run With The Pack/Watch Out	5
79	Epic S EPC 6968/7123	It Really Doesn't Matter/Schooldays//Run With The Pack/Watch Out (double pack, die cut sleeves, promo only)	8
79	Epic S EPC 7417	Ten Years/One More Word (p/s)	5
79	Epic S EPC 7417	Ten Years/One More Word (Manchester gig issue, stamped white labels)	8
79	Epic S EPC 7770	War Stories/Do The Push (p/s)	5
79	Epic S EPC 7986	Schooldays/What A Life (p/s)	5
80	Epic S EPC 8276	Shiraleo/Standby 19 (p/s)	5
79	Epic EPC 83534	GOD BLESS STARJETS (LP)	12

(see also Tango Brigade)

STARLIGHTERS

50	Capitol CL 13263	Rag Mop/If Not Bad (78)	8

STARLINGS

64	Embassy WB 612	Baby I Love You/MARILYN LEE: As Usual	4
64	Embassy WB 648	I Get Around/Thinking Of You Baby	4
64	Embassy WB 653	Where Did Our Love Go/TYPHOONS: I'm Into Something Good	4

STARLINGS

80s	Ruffin A-M 029	NEW BLOOD (EP)	4

STARLITES

73	Downtown DT 502	You're A Wanted Man/G.G. ALL STARS: Back To Dubwise	5
74	Big Shot BI 629	Mama Dee Part One/Mama Dee Part Two	6
75	Bullet BU 554	Healing In The Barnyard/G.G. ALL STARS: Version	5

(see also Bellfield)

CINDY STARR

68	C'mbia Blue Beat DB 107	Pain Of Love/Hippy Ska (as Cindy Starr & Rude Boys)	8

(see also Mopeds, Teardrops)

EDWIN STARR

66	Polydor BM 56702	Stop Her On Sight (S.O.S.)/I Have Faith In You	15
66	Polydor BM 56717	Headline News/Harlem	12
67	Polydor BM 56726	It's My Turn Now/Girls Are Getting Prettier	18
68	Polydor BM 56753	Stop Her On Sight (S.O.S.)/Headline News (reissue)	7
67	Tamla Motown TMG 630	I Want My Baby Back/Gonna Keep On Tryin' Till I Win	18
68	Tamla Motown TMG 646	I Am The Man For You Baby/My Weakness Is You	18
68	Tamla Motown TMG 672	Twenty Five Miles/Mighty Good Lovin'	7
69	Tamla Motown TMG 692	Way Over There/If My Heart Could Tell The Story	10
70	Tamla Motown TMG 725	Time/Running Back And Forth	8
70	Tamla Motown TMG 754	War/He Who Picks A Rose	6
71	Tamla Motown TMG 764	Stop The War Now!/Gonna Keep On Tryin' Till I Win	6
71	Tamla Motown TMG 790	Agent 00-Soul/Back Street	7
72	Tamla Motown TMG 810	Funky Music Sho' Nuff Turns Me On/Cloud Nine	5
75	Bradleys BRAD 7520	Stay With Me/I'll Never Forget You	5
75	Bradleys BRAD 7531	Pain/Party	5
76	GTO GT 65	Accident/Eavesdropper	5
69	T. Motown (S)TML 11094	SOUL MASTER (LP)	30
69	T. Motown (S)TML 11115	25 MILES (LP)	25
70	T. Motown (S)TML 11131	JUST WE TWO (LP, as Edwin Starr & Blinky)	18
72	Tamla Motown STML 11199	INVOLVED (LP)	15
72	Tamla Motown STML 11209	THE HITS OF EDWIN STARR (LP)	15
74	Tamla Motown STML 11260	HELL UP IN HARLEM (LP)	12

(see also Blinky & Edwin Starr, Holidays)

FRANK STARR

62	London HLU 9545	Little Bitty Feeling/Lost In A Dream	12

FREDDIE STARR & MIDNIGHTERS

63	Decca F 11663	Who Told You?/Peter Gunn Locomotion	25
63	Decca F 11786	It's Shaking Time/Baby Blue	30
64	Decca F 12009	Never Cry On Someone's Shoulder/Just Keep On Dreaming	35

MINT VALUE £

71	A&M AMS 838	Naomi/Free To Carry On (solo)	5
78	PVK PVK 004	FREDDIE STARR (LP)	12
	(see also Howie Casey & Seniors)		

JIMMY STARR

58	London HL 8731	It's Only Make Believe/Ooh Crazy	30
58	London HL 8731	It's Only Make Believe/Ooh Crazy (78)	30

KAY STARR

78s

50	Capitol CL 13295	If I Could Be With You/Flow Gently Sweet Afton (78, with Red Nichols)	8
50	Capitol CL 13420	Oh Babe/The Texas Song (78)	8
51	Vogue V 9009	Ain't Misbehavin'/Good For Nothin' Joe (78)	10
51	Vogue V 9010	Them There Eyes/What Is This Thing Called Love? (78)	10
52	Capitol CL 13658	On A Honky Tonk Floor/Someday Sweetheart (78)	8
52	Capitol CL 13808	Comes A-Long A-Love/Three Letters (78)	8
58	RCA RCA 1065	Stroll Me/Rockin' Chair (78)	10

SINGLES

54	Capitol CL 14151	Am I A Toy Or A Treasure?/Fortune In Dreams	18
54	Capitol CL 14167	Fool, Fool, Fool/Allez-Vous En	18
55	HMV 7M 300	If Anyone Finds This, I Love You/Turn Right	12
55	HMV 7M 307	Foolishly Yours/For Better Or Worse	12
55	HMV 7M 315	Where, What Or When?/Good And Lonesome	12
56	HMV 7M 371	Rock And Roll Waltz/I've Changed My Mind 1,000 Times	18
56	HMV 7M 420	Second Fiddle/Love Ain't Right	12
57	HMV POP 345	A Little Loneliness/Touch And Go	8
57	HMV POP 357	Jamie Boy/The Things I Never Had	8
58	RCA RCA 1065	Stroll Me/Rockin' Chair	7
60	Capitol CL 15105	Riders In The Sky/Night Train	6
60	Capitol CL 15137	Wheel Of Fortune/If You Love Me (Really Love Me)	7
60	Capitol CL 15154	Just For A Thrill/Out In The Cold Again	5
61	Capitol CL 15194	Foolin' Around/Kay's Lament	6
61	Capitol CL 15213	Nobody/I'll Never Be Free	5
63	Capitol CL 15293	Swingin' At The Hungry O/Bossa Nova Cassanova	5
63	Capitol CL 15308	No Regrets/Cherche La Rose	5
64	Capitol CL 15354	It's Happening All Over Again/Dancing On My Tears	5

EPs

55	Vogue EPV 1014	KAY STARR (EP)	15
56	HMV 7EG 8165	WHAT A STAR IS KAY (EP)	12
56	HMV 7EG 8184	KAY STARR'S AGAIN (EP)	12
60	Top Rank JKP 2042	HEAVENLY KAY STARR (EP)	15
60	Capitol EAP1 1254	MOVING (EP)	10
60	Capitol EAP2 1254	MOVING PT. 2 (EP)	10
60	Capitol EAP3 1254	MOVING PT. 3 (EP)	15
61	Capitol EAP 1-20063	WHEEL OF FORTUNE (EP)	18
62	Capitol EAP 1-20210	WELL I ASK YOU (EP)	10

LPs

53	Capitol LC 6574	CAPITOL PRESENTS KAY STARR (10" LP)	25
54	Capitol LC 6630	THE KAY STARR STYLE (10" LP)	25
56	Capitol LC 6835	THE HITS OF KAY STARR (10" LP)	20
57	Capitol T 580	IN A BLUE MOOD (LP)	18
57	London HA-U 2039	SWINGING WITH THE STARR (LP)	35
58	RCA RD 27056	BLUE STARR (LP)	18
60	Capitol (S)T 1254	MOVIN'! (LP)	15
60	Capitol (S)T 1303	LOSERS, WEEPERS (LP)	15
60	Capitol (S)T 1374	MOVIN' ON BROADWAY (LP)	15
61	Capitol T 1358	ONE MORE TIME (LP)	15
61	Capitol (S)T 1438	JAZZ SINGER (LP)	15
62	Capitol T 1468	ALL STARR HITS! (LP)	15
62	Capitol (S)T 1681	I CRY BY NIGHT (LP)	15
63	Capitol (S)T 1795	JUST PLAIN COUNTRY (LP)	15
64	Capitol (S)T 2106	THE FABULOUS FAVOURITES (LP)	15
60s	World Record Club T 100	WISH UPON A STARR (LP)	12ª

LUCILLE STARR

64	London HL 9900	The French Song/Sit Down And Write Me A Letter	7

LUCKY STARR

62	Parlophone R 4963	I've Been Everywhere/Wrong	7

MAXINE STARR

63	London HLU 9712	Wishing Star/Sailor Boy	8

RANDY STARR

57	London HL 8443	After School/Heaven High (Man So Low)	40
57	London HL 8443	After School/Heaven High (Man So Low) (78)	20
58	Felsted AF 106	Pink Lemonade/Count On Me	15
58	Felsted AF 106	Pink Lemonade/Count On Me (78)	30
60	Top Rank JAR 264	Workin' On The Santa Fe/You're Growing Up	7

RINGO STARR

71	Apple R 5898	It Don't Come Easy/Early 1970 (p/s, B-side with Ringo or George Harrison production credit)	6/5
72	Apple R 5944	Back Off Boogaloo/Blindman (p/s, blue label)	5
73	Apple R 5992	Photograph/Down And Out (p/s)	6
74	Apple R 5995	You're Sixteen/Devil Woman (p/s)	5
74	Apple R 6000	Only You/Call Me (p/s)	5
75	Apple R 6004	Snookeroo/Oo-wee	8
76	Apple R 6011	Oh My My/No No Song	12

Ringo STARR

76	Polydor 2001 694	A Dose Of Rock 'N' Roll/Cryin'	8
76	Polydor 2001 695	You Don't Know Me At All/Cryin' (unissued in U.K., Europe only)	
76	Polydor 2001 699	Hey Baby/Lady Gaye	8
77	Polydor 2001 734	Drowning In The Sea Of Love/Just A Dream	75
78·	Polydor 2001 782	Lipstick Traces/Old Time Relovin' (unissued in U.K., Europe only)	
78	Polydor 2001 795	Tonight/Heart On My Sleeve	75
72	R.O.R. ROR 2001	Steel (1-sided promo only interview disc for 'Ringo Or Robin' reception at Liberty's department store, p/s)	700
74	Parlophone PSR 374	Interview By Bob Mercer With Ringo For The Salesmen And Uxbridge Road/Only You (promo only)	275
70	Apple PCS 7101	SENTIMENTAL JOURNEY (LP)	18
70	Apple TD-PCS 7101	SENTIMENTAL JOURNEY (reel-to-reel tape, jewel case)	25
70	Apple PAS 10002	BEAUCOUPS OF BLUES (LP, gatefold sleeve)	18
78	Polydor 2480 429	SCOUSE THE MOUSE (LP, with Adam Faith, Donald Pleasance etc.; some with stickered sleeve & printed [not photocopied!] competition insert)	100/25
78	Polydor 3194 429	SCOUSE THE MOUSE (cassette)	40
90	EMI EMS 1375	RINGO STARR & HIS ALL STARR BAND (LP)	20

(see also Beatles, Harry Nilsson, Billy Connolly & Chris Tummings, Traveling Wilburys)

STELLA STARR
67	Piccadilly 7N 35366	Bring Him Back/Say It	30

TONY STARR
64	Decca F 11847	I'll Take A Rocket To The Moon/Next Train Leaving	45

STARR BOUNDS
75	Horse HOSS 95	Heavenly (parts 1 & 2)	8

STARS OF HEAVEN
85	Hotwire HWS 853	Clothes Of Pride/All About You (beige or black label, some with p/s)	12/7

STARS OF THE LID
98	Earworm WORM 11	Manouvering The Nocturnal Hum (12", silk screened sleeves, 1,000 only)	10

STARTIME KIDS
59	Fontana H 182	The Railroad Song/I Don't Want To Walk Without You, Baby	5
59	Fontana H 182	The Railroad Song/I Don't Want To Walk Without You, Baby (78)	8

STATE OF MICKEY & TOMMY
67	Mercury MF 996	With Love From One To Five/I Know What I Will Do	60
67	Mercury MF 1009	Frisco Bay/Nobody Knows Where You've Been	60

(see also Spooky Tooth, Nero & Gladiators, Foreigner)

STATESMEN
63	Studio Republic	FIVE PLUS ONE (LP, private pressing)	100

STATESMEN
63	Decca F 11687	Look Around/I'm Wondering	6
64	Fontana TF 432	I've Just Fallen In Love/It's All Happening	6

STATE STREET RAMBLERS
50	Tempo R 18	Weary Way Blues/Cootie Stomp (78)	8
60s	Collector JE 123	SMALL JAZZ BAND VOL. 1 (EP, shared with Lovey Austin Blue Serenaders)	8

STATE STREET SWINGERS/CHICAGO BLACK SWANS
73	Collectors Items 003	STATE STREET SWINGERS (LP)	12

STATIC
67	Page One POF 039	When You Went Away/Let Me Tell You	8

STATIC
81	Eeyo EEYO 1	Voice On The Line/Stealin' (no p/s, 1,000 only)	10

(see also White Lightning)

STATION SKIFFLE GROUP
57	Esquire 10-503	Don't You Rock Me Daddy-O/Hugged My Honey (78)	20
57	Esquire 10-516	Steamboat Bill/Titanic (78)	20
58	Esquire EP 161	STATION SKIFFLE GROUP (EP)	60

(see also Jimmy Miller)

STATLER BROTHERS
65	CBS 201796	Flowers On The Wall/Bill Christian	5
66	CBS BPG 62713	FLOWERS ON THE WALL (LP)	15

(see also Johnny Cash)

CANDI STATON
69	Capitol CL 15601	I'd Rather Be An Old Man's Sweetheart/For You	6
69	Capitol CL 15620	Heart On A String/I'm Just A Prisoner	5
70	Capitol CL 15646	Sweet Feeling/Evidence	5
70	Capitol CL 15658	Stand By Your Man/How Can I Put Out The Flame (When You Keep The Fire Burning)	5
75	United Artists UP 35823	Love Chain/I'm Gonna Hold On	6
70	Capitol ST 21631	I'M JUST A PRISONER (LP)	12

DAKOTA STATON
55	Capitol CL 14314	Don't Leave Me Now/A Little You	12
55	Capitol CL 14339	I Never Dreamt/Abracadabra	8
58	Capitol CL 14828	Trust In Me/The Late, Late Show	5
58	Capitol CL 14870	The Party's Over/Invitation	6
59	Capitol CL 14917	Confessin' The Blues/(I'm Left With The) Blues In My Heart (with George Shearing Quintet)	8
59	Capitol CL 14931	My Funny Valentine/A Foggy Day	6
59	Capitol EAP1 1054	THE DYNAMIC DAKOTA STATON (EP)	10

59	Capitol EAP2 1054	THE DYNAMIC DAKOTA STATON (EP).. 10
59	Capitol EAP3 1054	THE DYNAMIC DAKOTA STATON (EP).. 10
58	Capitol T 876	THE LATE, LATE SHOW (LP)... 15
59	Capitol (S)T 1054	THE DYNAMIC DAKOTA STATON (LP).. 15
59	Capitol T 1170	CRAZY HE CALLS ME (LP).. 15
60	Capitol (S)T 1325	MORE THAN THE MOOD (LP).. 15
60	Capitol (S)T 1387	BALLADS AND THE BLUES (LP).. 15
61	Capitol (S)T 1241	TIME TO SWING (LP).. 15
62	Capitol (S)T 1597	'ROUND MIDNIGHT (LP)... 12
62	Capitol (S)T 1649	DAKOTA AT STORYVILLE (LP)... 12

STATUES

60	London HLG 9192	Blue Velvet/Keep The Hall Burning 40

STATUS QUO

PYE SINGLES

68	Pye 7N 17449	Pictures Of Matchstick Men/Gentleman Joe's Sidewalk Café (some with '75c Minimum' on B-side label credit) 8
68	Pye 7N 17497	Black Veils Of Melancholy/To Be Free.. 20
68	Pye 7N 17581	Ice In The Sun/When My Mind Is Not Live...................................... 6
68	Pye 7N 17650	Technicolor Dreams/Paradise Flat (withdrawn, demos more common £300) . . . 700
69	pink 7N 17665	Make Me Stay A Bit Longer/Aunt Nellie....................................... 25
69	Pye 7N 17728	Are You Growing Tired Of My Love/So Ends Another Life 25
69	Pye 7N 17825	The Price Of Love/Little Miss Nothing.. 25
70	Pye 7N 17907	Down The Dustpipe/Face Without A Soul (blue, red, black or reissue Precision labels)... 5/4/5/5
70	Pye 7N 17998	In My Chair/Gerdundula (some with p/s) 60/8
71	Pye 7N 45077	Tune To The Music/Good Thinking... 20
73	Pye 7N 45229	Mean Girl/Everything (blue labels)... 5
73	Pye 7N 45253	Gerdundula/Lakky Lady (red label or PRT reissue)........................... 8/5
77	Pye BD 103	Down The Dustpipe/Mean Girl/In My Chair/Gerdundula (12", generic sleeve)..... 7
79	Pye Flashbacks FBS 2	Pictures Of Matchstick Men/Down The Dustpipe (reissue, yellow vinyl, p/s)..... 8
79	Pye 7P 103	In My Chair/Gerundula (p/s).. 8
79	Pye QUO 1/SFI 434	In My Chair (flexi, concert freebie, some with *Record Mirror* Quo special)..... 15/7

VERTIGO SINGLES

72	Vertigo 6059 071	Paper Plane/Softer Ride (spiral label, solid centre or large centre hole) 12/8
73	Vertigo 6059 085	Caroline/Joanne (with B-side miscredited to Lancaster) 6
74	Vertigo 6059 101	Break The Rules/Lonely Night (mispressed, B-side labels on both sides) 7
75	Vertigo QUO 13	STATUS QUO LIVE! (EP) 5
76	Vertigo 6059 153	Wild Side Of Life/All Through The Night (brown plastic labels) 4
77	Vertigo 6059 184	Rockin' All Over The World/Ring Of A Change (p/s, some with small poster).. 25/12
78	Vertigo QUO 2	Accident Prone/Let Me Fly (p/s, silver plastic label)......................... 5
79	Vertigo 6059 242	Whatever You Want/Hard Ride (p/s)... 5
79	Vertigo 6059 248	Livin' On An Island/Runaway (p/s).. 5
80	Vertigo QUO 4	Lies/Don't Drive My Car (p/s, with B-side misspellings 'MyiCar' or 'Caf')...... 10/8
81	Vertigo QUO 5	Something 'Bout You Baby I Like/Enough Is Enough (red or blue p/s) 5
81	Vertigo QUO JB 6	Rock 'n' Roll/Hold You Back (no p/s, jukebox issue, B-side at 45rpm).......... 10
82	Vertigo QUO 8	She Don't Fool Me/Never Too Late (p/s) 4
82	Vertigo QUO 9	Jealousy/Calling The Shots (unreleased in U.K.; Irish promos only) .... 150+
82	Vertigo QUOP 10	Caroline (Live At The NEC)/Dirty Water (picture disc) 8
82	Vertigo QUOP 1012	Caroline (Live At The NEC)/Dirty Water (live)/Down Down (live) (12", p/s)...... 10
83	Vertigo QUO 11	Ol' Rag Blues/Stay The Night (p/s).. 7
83	Vertigo QUOB 11	Ol' Rag Blues/Stay The Night (blue vinyl, different rear to p/s) 7
83	Vertigo QUO 1112	Ol' Rag Blues (Extended Remixed Edition)/Stay The Night/ Whatever You Want (12", p/s)....................................... 12
83	Vertigo QUO 12	A Mess Of Blues/Big Man (reversed p/s with 'table' picture on rear).......... 15
83	Vertigo QUO 1212	A Mess Of Blues (Extended)/Big Man/Young Pretender (12", p/s)............. 14
83	Vertigo QUO 14	Marguerita Time/Resurrection (p/s, white paper label)........................ 4
83	Vertigo QUOP 14	Marguerita Time/Resurrection (picture disc).................................. 18
83	Vertigo QUO 1414	Marguerita Time/Resurrection/Caroline/Joanne (double pack, gatefold p/s) ... 25
84	Vertigo QUO 15	Too Close To The Ground/I Wonder Why (release cancelled)
84	Vertigo QUO 15	Going Down Tonight/Too Close To The Ground (p/s) 4
84	Vertigo QUOP 16	The Wanderer/Can't Be Done (12" clear vinyl, picture labels) 20
85	Vertigo QUO 17	Naughty Girl (actually "Dreamin' ") (unreleased)
86	Vertigo QUO 18	Rollin' Home/Lonely (p/s, blue or bronze moulded labels) 5/4
86	Vertigo QUOPD 18	Rollin' Home/Lonely ('Q'-shaped picture disc) 15
86	Vertigo QUO 19	Red Sky/Don't Give It Up (p/s, blue moulded labels) 5
86	Vertigo QUODP 19	Red Sky/Don't Give It Up/Rockin' All Over The World/Whatever You Want (double pack, gatefold p/s) 10
86	Vertigo QUOPB 191	Red Sky/Don't Give It Up/The Milton Keynes Medley (12", 'Wembley Souvenir Pack') 20
86	Vertigo QUO 20	In The Army Now/Heartburn (stickered p/s, with sew-on patch, shrinkwrapped) . 10
86	Vertigo QUOPD 20	In The Army Now/Heartburn (picture disc) 25
86	Vertigo QUODP 20	In The Army Now/Heartburn//Marguerita Time/ What You're Proposing (double pack, gatefold p/s) 10
86	Vertigo QUO 2012	In The Army Now (Military Mix)/Heartburn/Late Last Night (12", stickered p/s, shrinkwrapped with poster) 25
86	Vertigo QUOP 21	Dreamin'/Long-Legged Girls (p/s, with foldout poster/calendar) 12
88	Vertigo QUOH 22	Ain't Complaining/That's Alright ('History Pack' with family tree in envelope) 5
88	Vertigo QUOCD 22	Ain't Complaining (Extended)/That's Alright/Lean Machine/ In The Army Now (Remix) (CD, card sleeve) 12
88	Vertigo QUOH 23	Who Gets The Love?/Hallowe'en ('History Pack' with family tree part 2, in envelope p/s)... 6
88	Vertigo QUOCD 23	Who Gets The Love? (7.09)/Hallowe'en/The Reason For Goodbye/ The Wanderer (Sharon The Nag Mix) (CD, card sleeve) 12
88	Vertigo QUACD 1	Running All Over The World (Extended)/Magic/Whatever You Want (CD, card sleeve) 12

STATUS QUO

88	Vertigo QUOCD 25	Burning Bridges (On And Off And On Again) (Extended Version)/ Whatever You Want/Marguerita Time (CD)	10
89	Vertigo 080 630-2	Burning Bridges (On And Off And On Again) (Extended Version)/ Whatever You Want (Extended Version)/Marguerita Time/ Who Gets The Love?/Burning Bridges (Video) (CD Video)	20
89	Vertigo 080 322-2	Ain't Complaining (Extended)/That's Alright/Lean Machine/ In The Army Now (Remix)/Ain't Complaining (Video) (CD Video)	20
89	Vertigo QUOCD 26	Not At All/Everytime I Think Of You/Gone Thru The Slips (CD)	10
90	Vertigo QUOP 27	Little Dreamer/Rotten To The Bone (p/s, shrinkwrapped with sew-on patch)	5
90	Vertigo QUOCD 27	Little Dreamer/Rotten To The Bone/Doing It All For You (CD)	10
90	Vertigo QUODJ 28	Anniversary Waltz (Parts 1 & 2) (p/s, promo only)	20
90	Vertigo QUOG 28	Anniversary Waltz Part One/The Power Of Rock (p/s, silver vinyl, with booklet)	8
90	Vertigo QUO 2812	Anniversary Waltz/The Power Of Rock/Perfect Remedy (12", p/s, mispressing, B-side plays "Little Lady" (live) & exclusive "Paper Plane" re-recording)	40
90	Vertigo QUO 2812	Anniversary Waltz/The Power Of Rock/Perfect Remedy (12", p/s, mispressing, A-side plays "The Power Of Rock [Full Version]")	40
91	Vertigo STATUS 30	Can't Give You More (Radio Edit)/Dead In The Water (promo only)	20
91	Vertigo QUOCDJ 30	Can't Give You More (Radio Edit)/Dead In The Water/ Mysteries From The Ball (CD, promo only)	20
91	Vertigo QUO 31	Fakin' The Blues (Edit)/Heavy Daze (p/s, spiral label, release cancelled, approximately 25 copies only)	200
91	Vertigo QUO 3112	Fakin' The Blues (Edit)/Fakin' The Blues (Album Version)/Heavy Daze/ Better Times (12", spiral label, p/s, cancelled, approx. 25 copies only)	200
91	Vertigo QUOCD 31	Fakin' The Blues (Edit)/Fakin' The Blues (Album Version)/Heavy Daze/Better Times (CD, unissued, 2,000 later sent out by fan club, no inlay)	30
92	Vertigo QUO 3212	Rock 'Til You Drop/Medley/Forty-Five Hundred Times (12", p/s, mispressing, omits "Forty-Five Hundred Times")	12

OTHER SINGLES

72	Phonogram DJ 005	Roadhouse Blues/BLACK SABBATH: Children Of The Grave (promo, 100 only)	375
75	Lyntone LYN 3154/5	Down Down/Break The Rules (Smiths Crisps flexidisc, a few with 'Smiths' p/s)	15/6
80s	Lyntone QUO 1-4	Interview picture discs (4-single pack)	20

LPs

68	Pye N(S)PL 18220	PICTURESQUE MATCHSTICKABLE MESSAGES (LP, mono/stereo)	70/60
69	Pye N(S)PL 18301	SPARE PARTS (LP, blue label, mono/stereo)	75/60
69	Marble Arch MAL(S) 1193	STATUS QUO-TATIONS (LP)	50
70	Pye NSPL 18344	MA KELLY'S GREASY SPOON (LP, very early copies with poster)	25/15
71	Pye NSPL 18371	DOG OF TWO HEAD (LP, gatefold sleeve, blue label; 5 other labels)	15/12
72	Vertigo 6360 082	PILEDRIVER (LP, spiral label, gatefold sleeve)	15
73	Vertigo 6360 098	HELLO! (LP, spaceship label, with inner sleeve & poster)	15
74	Vertigo 9102 001	QUO (LP, with poster/lyric sheet; also Record Club issue [ACB 00217])	10/25
75	Vertigo 9102 002	ON THE LEVEL (LP, gatefold sleeve, with inner sleeve)	12
76	Vertigo 9102 006	BLUE FOR YOU (LP, gatefold sleeve, with inner sleeve)	12
77	Pye FILD 005	THE FILE SERIES (2-LP, single sleeve, with inner sleeve; later re-pressed with Precision label)	20
77	PRT FILD 005	THE STATUS QUO FILE SERIES (2-LP, different sleeve)	18
79	Pye NPSL 18607	JUST FOR THE RECORD (LP, red vinyl)	15
82	Phonogram PRO LP 1	FROM THE MAKERS OF... (3-LP, with insert in cardboard box, some no'd)	20/18
82	Phonogram PRO BX 1	FROM THE MAKERS OF... (3-LP, with insert in round metal tin, some no'd)	20/18
82	Phonogram PRO BX 1	FROM THE MAKERS OF... (3-LP, 20 copies in bronze tin for in-house use)	300+
83	Vertigo VERH 10	BACK TO BACK (LP, in-store promo copies with poster insert)	12
88	PRT PYX 4007	FROM THE BEGINNING (LP, picture disc)	18

CDs

83	Vertigo 800 035-2	1+9+8+2 (CD)	30
83	Vertigo 800 053-2	NEVER TOO LATE (CD)	30
83	Vertigo 814 66-2	BACK TO BACK (CD)	15

(see also Spectres, Traffic Jam, Rossi & Frost, Rockers, Bob Young, Andy Bown, John Du Cann, Party Boys, Stretch)

STAVELY MAKEPEACE

69	Pyramid PYR 6072	(I Want To Love You Like A) Mad Dog/Greasy Haired Woman	6
70	Pyramid PYR 6082	Tarzan Harvey/Reggae Denny (unissued, test pressings exist)	10
70	Concord CON 008	Edna (Let Me Sing My Beautiful Song)/Tarzan Harvey ('fried egg' or multi-coloured label)	5
70	Concord CON 013	Smokey Mountain Rhythm Revue/Rampant On The Rage	5
71	Concord CON 018	Give Me That Pistol/The Sundance	5
72	Spark SRL 1066	Walking Through The Blue Grass/Swings And Roundabouts	5
72	Spark SRL 1081	Slippery Rock 70's/Don't Ride A Pillion Paula	5
73	Spark SRL 1085	Prima Donna/Swings And Roundabouts	5
73	Deram DM 386	Cajun Band/Memories Of Your Love	5
74	Deram DM 423	Runaround Sue/There's A Wall Between Us	5
77	Unigram U 6312	Baby Blue Eyes/Big Bad Baby Blondie	5
78	Barn 2014 118	No Regrets/You're Talking Out Of Your Head	5
79	Barn BARN 001	Coconut Shuffle/Napoleon Brandy	5
80	Hammer HS 304	Songs Of Yesterday/Storm	5

(see also Lieutenant Pigeon, Shel Naylor)

STAVERTON BRIDGE

70s	Saydisc SDL 266	STAVERTON BRIDGE (LP, with lyrics)	30

STEAM

69	Fontana TF 1058	Na Na Hey Hey Kiss Him Goodbye/It's The Magic In You Girl	6

STEAMHAMMER

69	CBS 4141	Junior's Wailing/Windmill	8
69	CBS 4496	Autumn Song/Blues For Passing People	7
71	Reflection HRS 9	Junior's Wailing/You'll Never Know	7
68	CBS (S) 63611	STEAMHAMMER (LP)	40
70	CBS (S) 63694	STEAMHAMMER MK. II (LP)	30

70	B&C CAS 1024	MOUNTAINS (LP)	30
70	Reflection REFL 1	STEAMHAMMER (LP, reissue, different sleeve)	25
71	Reflection REFL 12	STEAMHAMMER MK. II (LP, reissue)	20

(see also Armageddon)

STEAM-SHOVEL
| 68 | Trojan/Big Bear TR 635 | Rudi, The Red Nosed Reindeer/White Christmas | 7 |
| 68 | Decca F 22863 | Rudi, The Red Nosed Reindeer/White Christmas (export issue) | 10 |

(see also Locomotive)

STEEL
| 81 | Neat NEAT 14 | Rock Out/All Systems Go (p/s) | 10 |

BETTE ANNE STEELE
| 55 | Capitol CL 14315 | Barricade/Give Me A Little Kiss Will Ya, Huh? | 8 |

DORIS STEELE
| 59 | Oriole CB 1468 | Why Must I?/Never Again | 8 |
| 59 | Oriole CB 1468 | Why Must I?/Never Again (78) | 12 |

JAN STEELE & JOHN CAGE
| 76 | Obscure OBS 5 | VOICES AND INSTRUMENTS (LP) | 12 |

LAURIE STEELE COMBO & WORTH SCHOOL CHOIR
| 70 | Deram Nova SDN 23 | MAKE MUSIC TO THE LORD (LP) | 12 |

SONDRA & JON STEELE
| 55 | Parlophone MSP 6166 | I'm Crazy With Love/Fill My Heart With Happiness | 7 |

TOMMY STEELE (& STEELMEN)
78s
56	Decca F 10795	Rock With The Caveman/Rock Around The Town (with Steelmen) (78)	8
58	Decca F 11026	It's All Happening/What Do You Do (78)	8
58	Decca F 11072	Come On Let's Go/Put A Ring On Her Finger (78)	8
58	Decca F 11089	A Lovely Night/Marriage Type Love (78)	5
58	Weekend Mail (no cat. no.)	THE TRUTH ABOUT ME (6" 78 in envelope, mail-order only)	25
59	Decca F 11117	Hiawatha/The Trial (78)	8
59	Decca F 11152	Tallahassee Lassie/Give! Give! Give! (78)	20
59	Decca F 11162	You Were Mine/Young Ideas (78)	12
59	Decca F 11177	Little White Bull/Singing Time (78)	20
60	Decca F 11245	What A Mouth (What A North And South)/Kookaburra (78)	30

SINGLES
56	Decca F 10795	Rock With The Caveman/Rock Around The Town (with Steelmen)	35
56	Decca F 10808	Doomsday Rock/Elevator Rock	30
56	Decca F 10819	Singing The Blues/Rebel Rock (with Steelmen)	18
57	Decca F 10849	Knee Deep In The Blues/Teenage Party (with Steelmen)	12
57	Decca F 10877	Butterfingers/Cannibal Pot	8
57	Decca F 10896	Shiralee/Grandad's Rock	10
57	Decca F 10923	Water Water/A Handful Of Songs	7
57	Decca F 10941	Hey You!/Plant A Kiss	8
58	Decca F 10976	Happy Guitar/Princess	6
58	Decca F 10991	Nairobi/Neon Sign	6
58	Decca F 11026	It's All Happening/What Do You Do	5
58	Decca F 11041	The Only Man On The Island/I Puts The Lightie On	6
58	Decca F 11072	Come On Let's Go/Put A Ring On Her Finger	6
58	Decca F 11089	A Lovely Night/Marriage Type Love	5
59	Decca F 11117	Hiawatha/The Trial	6
59	Decca F 11152	Tallahassee Lassie/Give! Give! Give!	8
59	Decca F 11162	You Were Mine/Young Ideas	6
59	Decca F 11177	Little White Bull/Singing Time (some in p/s)	10/5

(The above 45s were originally issued with triangular centres; later round-centre copies are worth two-thirds the values listed.)

60	Decca F 11245	What A Mouth (What A North And South)/Kookaburra	5
60	Decca F 11258	Drunken Guitar/Light Up The Sky (unreleased)	
60	Decca F 11275	Happy Go Lucky Blues/(The Girl With The) Long Black Hair	5
60	Decca F 11299	Must Be Santa/Boys And Girls	5
61	Decca F 11361	My Big Best Shoes/The Dit Dit Song	5
61	Decca F 11372	Writing On The Wall/Drunken Guitar	5
62	Decca F 11479	Hit Record/What A Little Darling	5
62	Decca F 11551	He's Got Love/Green Eyes	5
63	Decca F 11532	Where Have All The Flowers Gone/Butter Wouldn't Melt in Your Mouth	5
63	Decca F 11615	Flash, Bang, Wallop!/She's So Far Above Me	5
63	Columbia DB 7070	Egg And Chips/The Dream Maker (with John Barry)	8

EPs
56	Decca DFE 6388	YOUNG LOVE (EP)	15
56	Decca DFE 6389	SINGING THE BLUES (EP)	15
57	Decca DFE 6398	THE TOMMY STEELE STORY NO. 1 (EP)	15
57	Decca DFE 6424	THE TOMMY STEELE STORY NO. 2 (EP)	15
57	Decca F 10915	ALL STAR HIT PARADE NO. 2 (EP, with other artists)	10

(The above EPs were originally issued with triangular centres; later round-centre reissues are worth two-thirds the values listed.)

58	Decca DFE 6472	THE DUKE WORE JEANS (EP)	12
58	Decca DFE 6551	C'MON LET'S GO (EP)	15
59	Decca DFE 6592	SWEET GEORGIA BROWN (EP)	12
59	Decca DFE 6607	TOMMY THE TOREADOR (EP)	10
60	Decca DFE 6660	WHAT A MOUTH (EP)	10

LPs
| 57 | Decca LF 1287 | THE TOMMY STEELE STAGE SHOW (10" LP) | 30 |
| 57 | Decca LF 1288 | THE TOMMY STEELE STORY (10" LP) | 20 |

MINT VALUE £

58	Decca LF 1308	THE DUKE WORE JEANS (10" LP, soundtrack)	18
60	Decca LK 4351	GET HAPPY WITH TOMMY (LP)	12
60s	RCA Victor RB/SB 6735	HALF A SIXPENCE (LP, soundtrack, gatefold sleeve)	15

STEELEYE SPAN

71	B&C CB 164	Rave On/Reels/Female Drummer (p/s)	7
72	Pegasus PGS 6	JIGS AND REELS (maxi-single, some with p/s)	10/6
72	Chrysalis CHS 2005	John Barleycorn/Bride's Favourite/Tansey's Fancy	5
72	Chrysalis CHS 2007	Gaudete/The Holly And The Ivy (p/s)	6
74	Chysalis CHS 2026	Thomas The Rhymer/The Mooncoin Jig	5
75	Chysalis CHS 2061	New York Girls/Two Magicians	5
76	Mooncrest MOON 50	Rave On/False Knight On The Road	5
76	Chrysalis CHS 2085	Hard Times Of Old England/Cadgwith Anthem	6
76	Chrysalis CHS 2085	Hard Times Of Old England/Sum Waves (Tunes) (alternate B-side)	5
76	Chrysalis CHS 2107	London/Sligo Maid	5
76	Chrysalis CHS 2125	Fighting For Strangers/The Mooncoin Jig	5
77	Chrysalis CHS 2129	The Boar's Head Carol/Gaudete/Some Rival (p/s)	6
78	Chrysalis CHS 2233	Rag Doll/Saucy Sailor	5
80	Chrysalis CHS 2479	Sails Of Silver/Senior Service (p/s)	5
81	Chrysalis CHS 2503	Gone To America/Let Her Go Down (p/s)	5
82	Chrysalis CHS 2658	All Around My Hat/Fighting For Strangers/Gaudete/The Boar's Head Carol (p/s)	5
82	Chrysalis CHSDJ 2658	All Around My Hat/Gaudete (promo only)	5
89	Flutterby FLUT 3	Padstow/First House In Connaught/Sailor's Bonnet (Reel) (p/s, later pressed as Dover FLUT 3)	5/4
70	RCA SF 8113	HARK! THE VILLAGE WAIT (LP, with insert)	25
71	United Artists UAG 29160	HARK! THE VILLAGE WAIT (LP, reissue)	12
71	B&C CAS 1029	PLEASE TO SEE THE KING (LP, initially in 'hessian' textured sleeve)	15/12
72	Charisma CS 5	INDIVIDUALLY AND COLLECTIVELY (LP)	15
72	Pegasus PEG 9	TEN MAN MOP, OR MR. RESERVOIR BUTLER RIDES AGAIN (LP, gatefold sleeve, initially with 8-page booklet)	18/12
72	Chrysalis CHR 1008	BELOW THE SALT (LP, gatefold sleeve)	12
73	Charisma CS 12	ALMANACK (LP)	12
73	Chrysalis CHR 1046	PARCEL OF ROGUES (LP, gatefold sleeve, with lyric insert)	12
74	Mooncrest CREST 8	PLEASE TO SEE THE KING (LP, reissue)	12
74	Chrysalis CHR 1053	NOW WE ARE SIX (LP, with lyric inner sleeve)	12
74	Mooncrest CREST 9	TEN MAN MOP, OR MR. RESERVOIR BUTLER RIDES AGAIN (LP, initially in gatefold sleeve, later single)	15/12
75	Chrysalis CHR 1071	COMMONER'S CROWN (LP)	12
77	Chrysalis CHR 1151	STORM FORCE TEN (LP, with lyric insert)	12

(see also Maddy Prior, Tim Hart & Maddy Prior, Gay & Terry Woods, Ashley Hutchings, Fairport Convention, Martin Carthy, Silly Sisters, Bob Johnson & Pete Knight)

STEEL MILL

71	Penny Farthing PEN 770	Green Eyed God/Zang Will	8
72	Penny Farthing PEN 783	Get On The Line/Summer's Child	8
75	Penny Farthing PEN 894	Green Eyed God/Zang Will (reissue)	6
71	Penny Farthing PELS 549	GREEN EYED GOD (LP)	120

STEEL PULSE

77	private pressing	Nyah Luv/Luv Nyah (12")	10
77	Anchor ANC 1046	Nyah Luv/Luv Nyah	5

STEELY DAN

72	Probe PRO 562	Dallas/Sail The Waterway	6
73	Probe PRO 577	Do It Again/Fire In The Hole	5
73	Probe PRO 587	Reelin' In The Years/Only A Fool	5
73	Probe PRO 602	Show Biz Kids/Razor Boy	5
73	Probe PRO 606	My Old School/Pearl Of The Quarter	5
74	Probe PRO 622	Rikki Don't Lose That Number/Any Major Dude Will Tell You	5
79	ABC ABC 4241	Rikki Don't Lose That Number/Any Major Dude Will Tell You (p/s, reissue, yellow vinyl)	5
73	Probe SPB 1062	CAN'T BUY A THRILL (LP, original)	12
73	Probe SPD 1079	COUNTDOWN TO ECSTASY (LP, original)	12
80s	MCA 203 16009	GAUCHO (LP, audiophile pressing)	12
82	MCA MCF 3165	GOLD (LP, with free EP [MSAMT 21])	12
80s	MCA 203 16016	GOLD (LP, audiophile pressing)	12

(see also Donald Fagen)

WOUT STEENHUIS

65	Columbia DB 7722	Desert Island/Teran Boelan	5
66	Columbia DB 8027	Nivram/Bay Of Paradise	5
65	Columbia SEG 8487	HAWAII (EP)	8
64	Columbia 33SX 1585	SURFIN' WITH STEENHUIS (LP)	15
65	Columbia 33SX 1695	HAWAIIAN SURF RIDE (LP)	15
66	Columbia SX 6024	PARADISE ISLAND (LP, mono)	12
66	Studio Two TWO 116	PARADISE ISLAND (LP, stereo)	12
74	Studio Two TWOX 1017	BEYOND THE REEF (LP)	12

STEEPLECHASE

71	Polydor 2489 001	LADY BRIGHT (LP)	12

STEERPIKE

68	(no label credit) ADM 417	STEERPIKE (LP, private pressing)	500

BILL STEGMEYER & HIS ORCHESTRA

54	London HL 8078	On The Waterfront (From The Film)/We Just Couldn't Say Good-Bye	30

LOU STEIN

57	London HLZ 8419	Almost Paradise/Soft Sands	20
58	Mercury 7MT 226	Who Slammed The Door/Got A Match?	8

JIM STEINMAN

81	Epic EPCA 1236	Rock And Roll Dreams Come Through/Love And Death And An American Guitar (p/s)	5
81	Epic EPCA 13-1236	Rock And Roll Dreams Come Through/Love And Death And An American Guitar/The Storm (12", p/s, blue vinyl)	8
81	Epic EPCA 1561	Lost Boys And Golden Girls/Left In The Dark (p/s)	5
81	Epic EPCA 1707	Dance In My Pants/Dance In My Pants (unissued, promo only)	6
84	MCA MCA 889	Tonight Is What It Means To Be Young/Hold That Snake (p/s)	5
84	MCA MCA T889	Tonight Is What It Means To Be Young/Hold That Snake (12", p/s)	12
81	Epic EPC 11-84361	BAD FOR GOOD (LP, picture disc)	15

(see also Meat Loaf)

STEINWAYS

85	Kent TOWN 106	You've Been Leading Me On/JOHNNY CASWELL: You Don't Love Me No More	8

STELLA

82	President PT 504	Si Tu Aimes Ma Musique/If You Do Like My Music (p/s)	7

STAN STENNETT

60s	Audio JDT 1	STYLE (EP)	8

MALCOLM STENT

70s	Starline SWL 2002	GO AND PLAY UP YOUR OWN END (LP)	15

STEP

80	Epic/Direction S DIR 8733	Love Letter/Land Of 1,000 Dances (p/s)	4
80	Epic/Direction S DIR 8944	Let Me Be The One/634 5789 (p/s)	4
80	Epic/Direction S DIR 9311	Tears That I Cry/Shake (p/s)	4
81	Epic EPC A 1291	Chain Gang/In The House (p/s)	4
81	Epic EPC A 1412	Model Soldiers/Hightime Havana (p/s)	4

EWAN STEPHENS

71	Decca F 13219	Queen Of The Good Times/We Can Give It A Try	4
72	Decca F 13299	Brother, Surely We Can Work It Out/Long, Long Summer	4

(see also Turquoise)

LEIGH STEPHENS

69	Philips SBL 7897	RED WEATHER (LP)	25
71	Charisma CAS 1040	AND A CAST OF THOUSANDS (LP)	20

(see also Blue Cheer)

STEPPENWOLF

68	RCA RCA 1679	Sookie Sookie/Take What You Need	10
68	RCA RCA 1735	Born To Be Wild/Everybody's Next One	10
68	Stateside-Dunhill SS 8003	Magic Carpet Ride/Sookie Sookie	8
69	Stateside-Dunhill SS 8013	Rock Me/Jupiter Child	6
69	Stateside-Dunhill SS 8017	Born To Be Wild/Everybody's Next One (reissue)	5
69	Stateside-Dunhill SS 8027	Magic Carpet Ride/Sookie Sookie (reissue)	5
70	Stateside-Dunhill SS 8035	Monster/Move Over	6
70	Stateside-Dunhill SS 8038	The Pusher/Your Wall's Too High	6
70	Stateside-Dunhill SS 8049	Hey Lawdy Mama/Twisted	6
70	Stateside-Dunhill SS 8056	Screaming Night Hog/Spiritual Fantasy	5
70	Probe PRO 510	Who Needs Ya/Earschplittenloudenboomer	5
71	Probe PRO 525	Snowblind Friend/Hippo Stomp	5
71	Probe PRO 534	Ride With Me/For Madmen Only	6
71	Probe PRO 544	For Ladies Only/Sparkle Eyes	5
68	RCA RD/SF 7974	STEPPENWOLF (LP, initially white sleeve, later silver sleeve)	25/18
68	Stateside (S)SL 5003	STEPPENWOLF THE SECOND (LP)	18
69	Stateside (S)SL 5011	AT YOUR BIRTHDAY PARTY (LP)	15
69	Stateside (S)SL 5015	EARLY STEPPENWOLF (LP)	15
69	Stateside (S)SL 10276	CANDY (LP, soundtrack, 2 tracks by Steppenwolf, 1 track by Byrds)	25
70	Stateside-Dunhill SSL 5020	STEPPENWOLF (reissue)	12
70	Stateside-Dunhill SSL 5021	MONSTER (LP, gatefold sleeve)	15
70	Stateside-Dunhill SSL 5029	STEPPENWOLF 'LIVE' (2-LP, gatefold sleeve)	15
70	Probe SPBA 6254	STEPPENWOLF 7 (LP)	15
71	Probe SPBA 6260	FOR LADIES ONLY (LP)	12
71	Probe SPBA 1033	GOLD (LP)	12
72	Probe SPBA 1059	REST IN PEACE (LP)	12

(see also Sparrow, John Kay)

STEPPES

79	South Circular SGS 108	The Beat Drill/FIFTY FANTASTICS: God's Got Religion (p/s, white label)	10

(see also Fifty Fantastics, Disco Zombies)

STEPPING TALK

79	Eustone/Rough Trade TO1	Alice In Sunderland/Health And Safety/Common Problems/John Turtles (p/s, with stamped inner)	6

STEPTOE & SON

(see under Wilfred Brambell & Harry H. Corbett)

STEREOLAB

SINGLES

91	Duophonic DS 45-01	SUPER 45: The Light That Will Cease To Fail/Au Grand Jour/Brittle/Au Grand Jour! (10" EP, with insert, mail-order only, 40 with hand-painted p/s, 500 only in poly bag)	100/80
91	Too Pure PURE 4	SUPER ELECTRIC: Super-Electric/High Expectation/The Way Will Be Opening/Contact (10" EP, with red on yellow sleeve)	10
91	Duophonic DS 45-02	STUNNING DEBUT ALBUM: Doubt/Clanger (p/s, mail-order only, gatefold p/s with insert in poly bag; multicoloured vinyl export issue for France, withdrawn due to pressing fault/warping, 200 only)	200

STEREOLAB

91	Duophonic DS 45-02	STUNNING DEBUT ALBUM: Doubt/Clanger (p/s, mail-order only, gatefold p/s with insert in poly bag; 985 copies on clear vinyl) 60
92	Duophonic DS 45-04	Harmonium/Farfisa (p/s, mail-order only, 1,306 copies on transparent amber vinyl, with insert & fluorescent sticker) 40
92	Too Pure PURE 14	Low Fi/Varoom!/Laissez-Faire/Elektro (He Held The World In His Iron Grip) (10", p/s, clear vinyl, 2,000 only) 25
93	Spacewatch FLX 2107	Ronco Symphony (demo)/SUBMARINER: Lyricist Downer/ Seeming And The Meaning (demo) (clear vinyl flexi with paper strip insert) 15
93	Elektra 7-64615	Golden Ball/Jenny Ondioline (promo only, 3,200 on clear vinyl) 12
93	Duophonic D-UHF-D 01	Jenny Ondioline (Part 1)/Golden Ball (Studio) (10", factory custom pressings; 5 copies on multicoloured vinyl; 36 on 'thin' clear vinyl, later endorsed & signed by band; no p/s) . . . . 100+/80
93	Duophonic D-UHF-CD 01	Jenny Ondioline/Fruition/Golden Ball/French Disko (CD) 15
93	Clawfist 20	CRUMB DUCK (10" EP, shared with Nurse With Wound, 1,450 only; 50 with handmade p/s) 80/60
93	Duophonic D-UHF-D 03	French Disko/Jenny Ondioline ('teaser' single, p/s, 1,500 only) 35
93	Duophonic D-UHF-D 01P	French Disko/Jenny Ondioline (CD, 1,000 only, hand-made p/s) 25
94	Duophonic D-UHF-D 04S	Ping Pong/Moogie Wonderland (p/s, 2,150 on pink vinyl, 3,322 on green) 12/8
94	Silvertone	Tone Burst (demo)/Tempter (demo)/SPECTRUM: Soul Kiss Glide Divine (unreleased, with colour photocopied wraparound p/s, 25 test pressings only) . . . . 450+
94	Duophonic D-UHF-07	Wow And Flutter/Heavy Denim (3,000 only with hand-painted p/s) 12
95	Wurlitzer Jukebox WJ 3	The Eclipse/Yes Sir! I Can Moogie/CAT'S MIAOW: Shoot The Moon (flexidisc, 1,000 only) 15
95	Duophonic Super 45s DS 45-10	Long Hair Of Death/YO LA TENGO: Evanescent Psychic Pez Drop (gig single, fluorescent yellow vinyl, plain white stickered card sleeve, 3,000 only) 20
95	Flying Nun STEREO 1	French Disko/Super Electric (CD, also listed as B 8595, promo only) 10
95	Duophonic STEREO 2	John Cage Bubblegum/Revox (CD, also listed as B 8895, promo only) 6
96	Duophonic D-UHF-D 10	Cybele's Reverie/Les Yper Yper Sound/Brigitte/Young Lungs (10", p/s, 2,000 only) 12
96	Lissy's LISS 15	You Used To Call Me Sadness/FUXA: Skyhigh (p/s, 400 on white vinyl, 1,500 on black) 15/6
96	Duophonic D-UHF-D 12	Speedy Car/TORTOISE: Yaus (gig freebie, blue vinyl, p/s, 3,000 only) 20
97	Duophonic D-UHF-D 15	Metronomic Underground (Wagon Christ Mix)/Percolations (12", plain red sleeve, 2,500 only) 12
97	Duophonic DS 4517	Splitting The Atom (Parts 1 & 2) (with Sonic Boom)/ Monkey Brain (p/s, 2,500 only) 10
97	Duophonic D-UHF-D 18	Iron Man/The Incredible He Woman (red vinyl, p/s, only available at gigs, 1,000 only) 10
97	Duophonic Super 45s DS 3311	Simple Headphone Mind/NURSE WITH WOUND: Trippin' With The Birds (12", 5,000 copies, 1,000 copies on yellow vinyl, in sealed foil sleeve) 25/15
97	Duophonic Super 45s CD 3311	Simple Headphone Mind/NURSE WITH WOUND: Trippin' With The Birds (CD, sealed foil sleeve) 20
98	Duophonic D-UHF-D 19	Refractions In The Plastic Pulse/Contronatura (12", die-cut stickered sleeve, yellow or black vinyl) 12/8

LPs

93	Duophonic D-UHF-D 02	TRANSIENT RANDOM NOISE-BURSTS WITH ANNOUNCEMENTS (2-LP, with inner sleeves, poor playing-quality gold vinyl, with stickered sleeve, 1,500 only) 35
93	United Dairies UD 059	CRUMB DUCK (LP, shared with Nurse With Wound, reissue of Clawfist EP, 50 copies on pink vinyl, 500 on fluorescent yellow vinyl) 50/25
95	Duophonic D-UHF-D 05X	MARS AUDIAC QUINTET (2-LP, gatefold sleeve, 1st 1,000 copies with bonus coloured vinyl single "Klang Tone"/"Ulan Bator" [D-UHF-06]) 35
95	Duophonic D-UHF-CD 05	MARS AUDIAC QUINTET (CD, 1st 1,000 with bonus CD "Klang Tone"/"Ulan Bator" [D-UHF-CD 06]) 30
95	Duophonic D-UHF-D 09	REFRIED ECTOPLASM (Switched On Volume 2) (2-LP, amber vinyl, 4,000 only) 15
95	Duophonic D-UHF-D 08	MUSIC FOR THE AMORPHOUS BODY STUDY CENTRE (10" LP, 3,000 only) 20
95	Duophonic D-UHF-CD 08	MUSIC FOR THE AMORPHOUS BODY STUDY CENTRE (CD, first issue with white cover & "1st edtion" printed on disc available at Charles Long art exhibition; reissue has yellow sleeve) 30/20
97	Duophonic D-UHF-D 17	DOTS AND LOOPS (2-LP, green & white vinyl) 15
99	Duophonic D-UHF-D 23	COBRA AND PHASES GROUP PLAY VOLTAGE IN THE MILKY NIGHT (2-LP) 15

(see also McCarthy, Spectrum, Mouse On Mars)

STEREOPHONICS

96	V2 SPH 1	Looks Like Chaplin/More Life In A Tramp's Vest (p/s, 500 only) 25
96	V2 SPHD 1	Looks Like Chaplin/More Life In A Tramp's Vest/Raymond's Shops (CD) 35
96	V2 SPH 2	Local Boy In The Photograph/Too Many Sandwiches (p/s, 2,000 only) 8
99	V2 no catalogue number	PERFORMANCE AND COCKTAILS (7 x 10" box set, mail order only) 50
97	Banana VVR 1000431	WORD GETS AROUND (LP, with bonus 12") 25

STEREOS

61	MGM MGM 1143	Please Come Back To Me/I Really Love You 25
61	MGM MGM 1149	The Big Knock/Sweet Water 25
66	MGM MGM 1328	Sweet Water/The Big Knock (reissue) 15

STEREOTYPES

80	Art Theft AT 001	Calling All The Shots/Lovers Of The Future (p/s) 8

DEAN STERLING & TEENBEATS

61	Pye 7N 15345	Send Me A Girl/Lost Love 8

FITZROY STERLING

68	Gas GAS 102	Got To Play It Cool/Jezebel 7
70	Bullet BU 422	That's My Life/Queen Of Hearts. 6

70	Bullet BU 438	Freedom Street/FITZROY ALL STARS: Freedom Street Version.	6
71	Escort ERT 858	Girl Tell Me What To Do/Be Careful	6
71	Pama PM 820	My Sweet Lord/Darling That's Right	6

LESTER STERLING (& HIS GROUP)

63	Island WI 121	Clean The City/Long Walk Home (B-side actually by Charmers)	18
63	R&B JB 111	Air Raid Shelter/ROY & ANNETTE: I Mean It.	12
63	R&B JB 115	Gravy Cool/WINSTON & BIBBY: Lover Lover Man	12
64	R&B JB 143	Peace And Love/HORACE SEATON: Hold On	18
64	R&B JB 150	Hot Cargo/MAYTALS: Marching On	15
64	R&B JB 155	Baskin' Hop (as Lester Sterling & His Group)/MAYTALS: Shining Light	15
64	R&B JB 172	Indian Summer (as Lester Sterling & His Group)/STRANGER & PATSY: I'll Forgive You	15
66	Doctor Bird DB 1057	Inez (with Tommy McCook & Supersonics)/GLORIA CRAWFORD: Sad Movies	15
67	Doctor Bird DB 1107	Soul Voyage/ALVA LEWIS: Revelation	25
67	Collins Downbeat CR 001	Sir Collins Special/Lester Sterling '67.	25
68	Coxsone CS 7080	Africkaan Beat/PARAGONS: My Satisfaction	20
68	Blue Cat BS 116	Zigaloo/Wiser Than Solomon.	20
68	Unity UN 502	Bangarang (with Stranger Cole)/STRANGER COLE: If We Should Ever Meet	6
69	Unity UN 505	Reggae On Broadway/CLIQUE: Love Can Be Wonderful	6
69	Unity UN 509	Spoogy/TOMMY McCOOK: Monkey Fiddle	6
69	Unity UN 512	Regina/Bright As A Rose.	6
69	Unity UN 517	1,000 Tons Of Megaton/KING CANNON: Five Card Stud.	6
69	Unity UN 518	Man About Town/Man At The Door	6
69	Unity UN 531	Lonesome Feeling/Bright As A Rose	6
69	Big Shot BI 507	Forest Gate Rock/RAVING RAVERS: Rock Rock And Cry	8
69	Gas GAS 103	Reggae In The Wind/SOUL SET: Try Me One More Time (B-side actually by Stranger & Gladdy).	6
70	Unity UN 562	Slip Up/DAVE BARKER: On Broadway	6
71	Nu Beat NB 095	Iron Side Part 1/COXSON'S ALL STARS: Iron Side Part 2	6
71	Smash SMA 2321	Sir Collins Special/Version (actually "Heart Of The Knight" by Gaytones)	6
72	Ashanti ASH 409	Iron Side Part 1/COXSON'S ALL STARS: Iron Side Part 2	6
72	Ashanti ASH 410	War Is Not The Answer/COXSON'S ALL STARS: Version	6
69	Pama SECO 15	BANGARANG (LP)	40

(see also Mister Versatile, Bobby Aitken, Eric Morris, Sir Collins Band, Slickers, Uniques)

NINA STERN

65	Pye 7N 15823	Take It From Me/Please Come Back To Me	4

STEROID KIDDIES

70s	Steroid/Grundinga SK 001	THE KIDDIES EP (p/s)	20

STEROIDS

78	Radar ADA 11	In The Colonies/Sha La La Loo Ley (p/s)	6

STEVE 'N' BONNIE

72	Young Blood SSYB 16	BRIEF ENCOUNTER (LP)	12

STEVE & EYDIE

(see under Eydie Gorme & Steve Lawrence)

STEVE & STEVIE

68	Toast TLP 2	STEVE AND STEVIE (LP)	25

(see also Tin Tin, Fut)

APRIL STEVENS

53	Parlophone MSP 6060	C'est Si Bon/Soft Warm Lips	10
54	Parlophone MSP 6088	How Could Red Riding Hood (Have Been…)/You Said You'd Do It.	10
67	MGM MGM 1366	Falling In Love Again/Wanting You	50
76	MGM 2006 586	Wanting You/Falling In Love Again (reissue).	5

(see also Nino Tempo & April Stevens)

BOBBY STEVENS

60	Embassy WB 390	Fall In Love With You/Wild One	5
60	Embassy WB 390	Fall In Love With You/Wild One (78).	10
60	Embassy WB 392	Stuck On You/Clementine	5
60	Embassy WB 392	Stuck On You/Clementine (78).	12
60	Embassy WB 397	Cradle Of Love/Heart Of A Teenage Girl	5
60	Embassy WB 397	Cradle Of Love/Heart Of A Teenage Girl (78).	10
60	Embassy WB 404	Shakin' All Over/Angela Jones	5
60	Embassy WB 404	Shakin' All Over/Angela Jones (78).	12
60	Embassy WB 412	A Mess Of Blues/Tie Me Kangaroo Down Sport	5
60	Embassy WB 412	A Mess Of Blues/Tie Me Kangaroo Down Sport (78)	12

CAT STEVENS

66	Deram DM 102	I Love My Dog/Portobello Road.	6
66	Deram DM 110	Matthew And Son/Granny	6
67	Deram DM 118	I'm Gonna Get Me A Gun/School Is Out	6
67	Deram DM 140	Bad Night/Laughing Apple	6
67	Deram DM 156	Kitty/Blackness Of The Night.	6
68	Deram DM 178	Lovely City/Image Of Hell	6
68	Deram DM 211	Here Comes My Wife/It's A Supa (Dupa) Life	6
69	Deram DM 260	Where Are You/The View From The Top	6
70	Island WIP 6086	Lady D'Arbanville/Time/Fill My Eyes (some in p/s)	8/5
67	Deram DML/SML 1004	MATTHEW AND SON (LP)	20
67	Deram DML/SML 1018	NEW MASTERS (LP)	20
67	Deram	CATS AND DOGS (LP, unreleased, test pressings only).	30
75	Island ILPS 9310	GREATEST HITS (LP, with calendar & poster)	12

MINT VALUE £

CHUCK STEVENS
57	Columbia DB 3883	Take A Walk/The Way I Do	7
57	Columbia DB 3938	My London/Couldn't Care More	7

CONNIE STEVENS
60	Warner Bros WB 3	Sixteen Reasons (with Don Ralke)/Little Sister (with Buddy Cole Trio)	7
60	Warner Bros WB 17	Too Young To Go Steady/A Little Kiss Is A Kiss, Is A Kiss	6
60	Warner Bros WB 25	Apollo/Why Do I Cry For Joey	6
61	Warner Bros WB 41	And This Is Mine/Make-Believe Lover	6
61	Warner Bros WB 47	The Greenwood Tree/If You Don't, Somebody Else Will	6
62	Warner Bros WB 63	Why'd You Wanna Make Me Cry/Just One Kiss	6
62	Warner Bros WB 73	Mr. Songwriter/I Couldn't Say No	6
64	Warner Bros WB 128	They're Jealous Of Me/A Girl Never Knows	8
60	Warner Bros WEP 6007	CONNIE STEVENS AS CRICKET (EP, also stereo WSEP 2007)	15/20
63	Warners WEP/WSE 6105	CONNIE STEVENS AS CRICKET NO. 2 (EP, mono/stereo)	15/20
63	Warners WEP/WSE 6112	CONNIE STEVENS AS CRICKET NO. 3 (EP, mono/stereo)	15/20
62	Warner Bros WM 4061	CONNIE (LP, also stereo WS 8061)	20/25
63	Warner Bros WM/WS 8111	THE HANK WILLIAMS SONG BOOK (LP)	18
	(see also Edward Byrnes)		

DODIE STEVENS
59	London HLD 8834	Pink Shoe Laces/Coming Of Age	20
59	London HLD 8834	Pink Shoe Laces/Coming Of Age (78)	35
60	London HLD 9174	No/A-Tisket A-Tasket	7
61	London HLD 9280	Yes, I'm Lonesome Tonight/Too Young	8
63	London HLP 9672	Don't Send Me Roses/Daddy Couldn't Get Me One Of Those	7
64	Liberty LIB 83	I Wore Out Our Record/You Don't Have To Prove A Thing	6

JOHNNY STEVENS & LES DAWSON SYNDICATE
50s	Melodisc M 1586	Last Chicken In The Shop/Oh Yeah	6

JOHNNY STEVENS & BLUE BEATS
64	Blue Beat BB 229	Shame/Ball And Chain	12

KIRK STEVENS
57	Decca F 10863	Once/This Silver Madonna	8

MEIC STEVENS
65	Decca F 12174	Did I Dream/I Saw A Field (as Mike Stevens)	15
70	Warner Bros WB 8007	Ballad Of Old Joe Blind/Blue Sleep	15
70	Warner Brothers WS 3005	OUTLANDER (LP, with insert)	140
79	Tic Toc	CANAEON CYNNAR (LP, private pressing)	200
97	Tenth Planet TP 028	GHOST TOWN (LP, gatefold sleeve, numbered, 1000 only)	12
	(see also Gary Farr)		

MICK STEVENS
71	Deroy (no cat. no.)	SEE THE MORNING (LP, private pressing)	150
75	Deroy (no cat. no.)	NO SAVAGE WORD (LP, private pressing)	100

MIKE STEVENS (& SHEVELLS)
65	Decca F 12174	Did I Dream/I Saw A Field (solo)	6
66	Pye 7N 17243	Cathy's Clown/Go-Go Train (as Mike Stevens & Shevells)	6
68	Polydor 56269	Guaranteed To Drive You Wild/Hog-Tied (as Mike Stevens & Shevells)	6
	(see also Shevells)		

MORT STEVENS & HIS ORCHESTRA
70	Capitol CL 15655	"Hawaii Five-O" Theme/McGarrett's Theme	5

PAUL STEVENS
68	Page One POF 080	Sometimes You Love Me/Hey Mr. Love	4

RAY STEVENS
58	Capitol CL 14881	Chickie-Chickie Wah Wah/Crying Goodbye	12
61	Mercury AMT 1158	Jeremiah Peabody's Polyunsaturated Quick Dissolving Fast Acting Pleasant Tasting Green And Purple Pills/Teen Years	7
62	Mercury AMT 1184	Ahab The Arab/It's Been So Long	7
63	Mercury AMT 1207	Harry The Hairy Ape/Little Stone Statue	7
66	London HLU 10027	Devil May Care/Make A Few Memories	6
71	Mercury 6052 072	Bubble Gum The Bubble Dancer/Jeremiah Peabody's Polyunsaturated Quick Dissolving Fast Acting Pleasant Tasting Green And Purple Pills	5

RICKY STEVENS
61	Columbia DB 4739	I Cried For You/I Am	6
62	Columbia DB 4778	Forever/Now, It's All Over	6
63	Columbia DB 4981	My Mother's Eyes/I'll Get By	6
62	Columbia SEG 8172	I CRIED FOR YOU (EP)	50

ROY STEVENS
66	London HLU 10016	Party People/ABC	4

SHAKIN' STEVENS (& SUNSETS)
SINGLES
70	Parlophone R 5860	Spirit Of Woodstock/Down On The Farm	45
72	Polydor 2058 213	Sweet Little Rock'n'Roller/White Lightning	30
74	Emerald MD 1176	Honey Honey/Holey Moley 2001	25
76	Mooncrest MOON 51	Jungle Rock/Girl In Red	18
77	Track 2094 134	Never/You Always Hurt The One You Love	15
77	Track 2094 136	Somebody Touched Me/Way Down Yonder In New Orleans (some in p/s)	18/10
78	Track 2094 141	Justine/Wait And See	25
78	Epic SEPC 6567	Treat Her Right/I Don't Want No Other Baby	15
79	Epic SEPC 6845	Endless Sleep/Fire	15
79	Epic SEPC 7235	Spooky/I Don't Want No Other Baby	15
80	Epic SEPC 8090	Hot Dog/Apron Strings (p/s)	15

MINT VALUE £

80	Epic SEPC 8573	Hey Mae/I Guess I Was A Fool (some in p/s)	12/5
80	Epic SEPC 8725	Marie Marie/Baby If We Touch (p/s)	5
80	Epic SEPC 8778	Solid As A Rock/Generation X (p/s)	6
80	Epic SEPC 9064	Shooting Gallery/Make It Right Tonight (p/s)	15
81	Epic SEPC 9555	This Ole House/Let Me Show You How (p/s)	5
81	Epic EPCA 1165	You Drive Me Crazy/Baby You're A Child (p/s)	5
81	Battle Of The Bands BOB 2	Jungle Rock/Girl In Red (p/s, reissue, as Shakin' Stevens & Sunsets)	8
81	Epic EPCA 1354	Green Door/Don't Turn Your Back (p/s)	5
81	Mint CHEW 51	No Other Baby/Manhattan Melodrama (p/s)	7
81	Epic A 1643	It's Raining/You And I Were Meant To Be (picture disc)	10
81	Solid Gold SGR 107	Shaky Sings Elvis (Parts 1 & 2) (medley) (p/s)	12
82	Epic EPCA 1742	Oh Julie/I'm Knocking (poster p/s)	6
82	Epic EPCA 40-2620	GREATEST ORIGINAL HITS (cassette EP)	7
82	Epic EPCA 2656	Give Me Your Heart Tonight/Thinkin' Of You (p/s, with poster)	6
82	Epic EPCA 2656	Give Me Your Heart Tonight/Thinkin' Of You (picture disc)	8
82	Everest/Premier RAY 1	Tiger/Give Me A Break (p/s)	7
82	Everest/Premier EV 1000	Tiger/Sweet Little Sixteen/Give Me A Break (picture disc)	8
83	Epic A 3565	It's Late/It's Good For You Baby (p/s)	5
83	Epic WA 3565	It's Late/It's Good For You Baby (feet-shaped picture disc)	12
83	Epic WA 3774	Cry Just A Little Bit/Love Me Tonight (picture disc)	8
83	Kelloggs KELL 1	Oh Julie/ABBA: I Have A Dream (free with Kelloggs' 'Rice Krispies')	8
84	Epic A 4291	A Love Waiting For You/As Long As I Have You (live) (poster p/s)	10
84	Epic QA 4677	A Letter To You/Come Back And Love Me (p/s, with free post bag game)	6
84	Epic DA 4882	Teardrops/You Shake Me Up//Shakin' Stevens Party Mix (Parts 1 & 2) (double pack)	10
85	Epic GA 6072	Breakin' Up My Heart/I'll Give You My Heart (gatefold pop-up p/s)	5
85	Epic TA 6072	Breakin' Up My Heart/I'll Give You My Heart (12", p/s)	7
85	Epic GTA 6769	Merry Christmas Everyone/With My Heart (12", advent calendar p/s)	7
86	Epic QA 6819	Turning Away/Diddle (poster p/s)	5
86	Epic SHAKY 2	Because I Love You/Tell Me One More Time (2 picture sleeves, sealed together on edge with sticker, with autograph)	8
86	Epic SHAKY G2	Because I Love You/Tell Me One More Time (gatefold p/s)	6
86	Epic GA 6769	Merry Christmas Everyone/Blue Christmas (reissue, gatefold p/s)	6
87	Epic SHAKY C3	A Little Boogie Woogie (In The Back Of My Mind)/If You're Gonna Cry (cassette)	5
87	Epic SHAKY Q4	Come See About Me/Boppity Bop (12", p/s with patch, sealed)	7
87	Epic SHAKY 5	What Do You Want To Make Those Eyes At Me For/You're Evil (p/s, with competition entry form)	5
87	Epic SHAKY P5	What Do You Want To Make Those Eyes At Me For/You're Evil (picture disc)	6
87	Epic SHAKY G5	What Do You Want To Make Those Eyes At Me For/You're Evil + 2 (g/fold p/s)	5
88	Epic SHAKY Q6	Feel The Need In Me/If I Can't Have You (poster p/s)	5
88	Epic SHAKY C6	Feel The Need In Me (12" Mix)/Feel The Need In Me (Single Version)/If I Can't Have You (CD, card p/s)	7
88	Epic SHAKY 7	How Many Tears Can You Hide/If I Really Knew (p/s, with poster)	5
88	Epic SHAKY Q7	How Many Tears Can You Hide/If I Really Knew (p/s, shrinkwrapped w/ badge)	8
88	Epic SHAKY C7	How Many Tears Can You Hide (Remix)/If I Really Knew/How Many Tears Can You Hide (Dance Mix) (CD, card sleeve)	7
88	Epic SHAKY Q8	True Love/Come On Little Girl (poster p/s)	5
88	Epic SHAKY C8	Special Christmas CD: True Love/Come On Little Girl/Merry Xmas Everyone (Extended Version)/Blue Christmas (CD, card sleeve)	7
89	Epic SHAKY Q9	Jezebel/As Long As I Have You (p/s, with competition entry form)	4
89	Epic SHAKY P9	Jezebel/As Long As I Have You (poster p/s)	4
89	Epic SHAKY C9	Jezebel (Remix)/As Long As I Have You/Jezebel (Monster Remix) (CD, card p/s)	7
89	Epic SHAKY M10	Love Attack/As Long As I Have You (live) (cassette)	4
89	Epic SHAKY C10	Love Attack/Love Attack (Extended Version)/As Long As I Have You (live) (CD, card sleeve)	7

EPs

81	Magnum Force MFEP 001	Memphis Earthquake/You Mostest Girl/Evil Hearted Ada/My Bucket's Got A Hole In It (EP, p/s)	8
82	Magnum Force MFEP 007	Frantic/Ready Teddy/Tear It Up/Monkey's Uncle (EP, p/s)	8
83	Magnum Force MFEP 010	Justine/Jungle Rock/Story Of The Rockers/My Baby Died (EP, p/s)	8
83	Epic 40-2620	GREATEST ORIGINAL HITS (EP, cassette)	10

LPs

70	Parlophone PCS 7112	A LEGEND (LP)	50
71	CBS 52901	I'M NO J.D. (LP)	40
72	Contour 2870 152	ROCKIN' AND SHAKIN' (LP)	18
73	Emerald GES 1121	SHAKIN' STEVENS AND THE SUNSETS (LP)	15
78	Track 2406 011	SHAKIN' STEVENS (LP)	15
80	Epic EPC 83978	TAKE ONE (LP)	12
80	Epic EPC 84547	MARIE MARIE (LP, withdrawn)	18
81	Epic EPC 10027	SHAKY (LP, feet-shaped picture disc)	12
83	Epic BX 86301	THE BOP WON'T STOP (LP & cassette, box set, with Shaky autograph book)	18
85	CJS CJS 1	MANHATTAN MELODRAMA (LP)	12

SHAKIN' STEVENS & BONNIE TYLER

| 83 | Epic WA 4071 | A Rockin' Good Way/Why Do You Treat Me This Way (picture disc) | 7 |

(see also Bonnie Tyler)

TERRI STEVENS

59	Felsted AF 112	My Wish Tonight/All Alone	8
59	Felsted AF 112	My Wish Tonight/All Alone (78)	15
59	Felsted AF 126	Adonis/Vieni, Vieni	7
59	Felsted AF 126	Adonis/Vieni, Vieni (78)	30

VIKKI STEVENS

| 60 | Embassy WB 410 | As Long As He Needs Me/Where Is Love? | 5 |
| 60 | Embassy WB 410 | As Long As He Needs Me/Where Is Love? (78) | 8 |

Richard STEVENSEN

RICHARD STEVENSEN
70	Pye NSPL 18358	GATES OF ME (LP)	15

MICKEY STEVENSON
72	Ember EMBS 320	Here I Am/Joe Poor Loves Daphne Elizabeth Richard	5
72	Ember NR 5063	HERE I AM (LP)	12

STEVIE'S BUZZ
96	Nice (no cat. no.)	Autumn Stone/P.P. & PRIMES: Understanding (promo only, large centre hole)	5

(see also Buzzcocks)

AL STEWART
66	Decca F 12467	The Elf/Turn To Earth	100
67	CBS 3034	Bedsitter Images/Swiss Cottage Manoeuvres	7
70	CBS 4843	Electric Los Angeles Sunset/My Enemies Have Sweet Voices	7
70	CBS 5351	The News From Spain/Elvaston Place	6
72	CBS 7763	You Don't Even Know Me/I'm Falling	6
72	CBS 7992	Amsterdam/Songs Out Of Clay	6
88	Enigma ENVCD 4	King Of Portugal/Josephine Baker/Bad Reputation/King Of Portugal (3" CD, card sleeve)	7
67	CBS (S)BPG 63087	BED SITTER IMAGES (LP)	75
69	CBS (S) 63460	LOVE CHRONICLES (LP, gatefold sleeve)	25
70	CBS 63848	ZERO SHE FLIES (LP, gatefold sleeve)	25
70	CBS 64023	FIRST ALBUM (BED SITTER IMAGES) (LP, remixed reissue, different track listing)	25
72	CBS 64739	ORANGE (LP)	15
73	CBS 65726	PAST, PRESENT AND FUTURE (LP, gatefold sleeve)	12
75	CBS 80477	MODERN TIMES (LP)	12

(see also Jimmy Page)

ANDY STEWART
60	Top Rank JAR 427	Donald, Where's Your Troosers?/Dancing In The Kyle	7
60	Top Rank JAR 512	A Scottish Soldier/The Muckin' O' Geordie's Brye	5
61	Top Rank JAR 565	The Battle's O'er/Tunes Of Glory	5
61	Top Rank JAR 594	Take Me Back/The Road And The Miles To Dundee	5
62	Top Rank JAR 616	Cowboy Jock From Skye/The Highland Twist	6
65	HMV POP 1454	Dr. Finlay/Oh! What A Ceilidh	5
61	Top Rank JKP 3009	ANDY SINGS (EP)	8

BILLY STEWART
62	Pye International 7N 25164	Reap What You Sow/Fat Boy	8
63	Pye International 7N 25222	Strange Feeling/Sugar And Spice	7
65	Chess CRS 8009	I Do Love You/Keep Loving	10
65	Chess CRS 8017	Sitting In The Park/Once Again	10
66	Chess CRS 8028	Because I Love You/Mountains Of Love	12
66	Chess CRS 8038	Love Me/Why Am I Lonely	12
66	Chess CRS 8040	Summertime/To Love To Love	7
66	Chess CRS 8045	Secret Love/Look Back And Smile	10
66	Chess CRS 8050	Ole Man River/Every Day I Have The Blues	12
67	Chess CRS 8067	Cross My Heart/Why (Do I Love You So)	6
69	Chess CRS 8092	Summertime/I Do Love You	6
72	Chess 6145 017	Sitting In The Park/Summertime	5
66	Chess CRE 6010	IN CROWD (EP)	25
67	Chess CRE 6024	I DO LOVE YOU (EP)	20
66	Chess CRL 4523	UNBELIEVABLE (LP)	30
72	Chess 6310 125	GOLDEN DECADE (LP)	15

BOB STEWART
55	MGM SP 1114	It's A Woman's World/I Went Out Of My Way	6

BOB STEWART
75	Argo ZDA 207	THE UNIQUE SOUND OF THE PSALTERY (LP)	12

DAVID A. STEWART
92	Anxious ZT 43046	LILY WAS HERE (12", with 2 Orb mixes, featuring Candy Dulfer, p/s)	8

(see also Eurythmics, Tourists, Longdancer, Stewart & Harrison)

DAVIE STEWART
78	Topic 12T 293	DAVIE STEWART (LP, with insert)	12

DELANO STEWART
68	Doctor Bird DB 1138	That's Life/Tell Me Baby	15
68	High Note HS 004	Let's Have Some Fun/Dance With Me	10
69	High Note HS 014	Rocking Sensation/GAYTONES: One Look	25
70	High Note HS 027	Got To Come Back/Don't Believe In Him	5
70	High Note HS 034	Hallelujah/I Wish It Could Last	5
70	High Hote HS 039	Wherever I Lay My Hat/Don't Believe Him (B-side actually by Gladstone Anderson & Gaytones)	8
70	High Note HS 041	Stay A Little Bit Longer/Stay A Little Bit Longer (Version II) (B-side actually by Gladstone Anderson & Gaytones)	10
70	Trojan TBL 138	STAY A LITTLE BIT LONGER (LP)	20

(see also Winston Stewart, Gaylads, Patsy Todd)

GRAHAM STEWART SEVEN
59	Tempo EXA 91	GRAHAM STEWART SEVEN (EP)	8

JAMES STEWART
65	Brunswick 05938	The Legend Of Shenandoah/CHARLES 'BUD' DANT CHORUS: We're Ridin' Out Tonight	10

JAMES STEWART & HENRY FONDA
70	Stateside SS 2179	Rolling Stone/Theme From Cheyenne Social Club	8

AL STEWART

ROD STEWART

JOHN STEWART
69	Capitol CL 15589	July, You're A Woman/Shackles And Chains	5
69	Capitol E-(S)T 203	CALIFORNIA BLOODLINES (LP)	12
70	Capitol E-ST 540	WILLARD (LP)	12

(see also Kingston Trio, Cumberland Three)

JOHNNY STEWART
| 58 | HMV POP 480 | Wishing For Your Love/Promise Me | 6 |

PAUL STEWART (MOVEMENT)
| 66 | Philips BF 1513 | Queen Boadicea/Talkin' | 6 |
| 67 | Decca F 12577 | Saturday Morning Man/Too Too Good (as Paul Stewart Movement) | 10 |

(see also Hamilton & [Hamilton] Movement)

RAPHAEL STEWART & HOT TOPS
| 71 | Punch PH 71 | Put Your Sweet Lips/JUSTINS: Stand By Me | 6 |

ROD STEWART (& FACES)
SINGLES
64	Decca F 11996	Good Morning Little Schoolgirl/I'm Gonna Move To The Outskirts Of Town	75
65	Columbia DB 7766	The Day Will Come/Why Does It Go On?	100
66	Columbia DB 7892	Shake/I Just Got Some	100
68	Immediate IM 060	Little Miss Understood/So Much To Say	75
70	Vertigo 6086 002	It's All Over Now/Jo's Lament	12
73	Mercury 6052 371	Oh No Not My Baby/Jodie (tartan sleeve)	6
73	NME SF1 139	Dishevelment Blues/Ooh La La Preview (with Faces, flexidisc free with *NME*)	8/5
74	Warner Bros K 16494	You Can Make Me Dance, Sing Or Anything/As Long As You Tell Him (as Rod Stewart & Faces, p/s)	5
76	Mercury 6160 006	Maggie May/You Wear It Well/Twistin' The Night Away (p/s)	5
77	Mercury 6160 007	Mandolin Wind/Girl From The North Country/Sweet Little Rock'N'Roller	5
76	Mercury 6167 327	It's All Over Now/Handbags And Gladrags	5
77	Riva RIVA 1	You're Insane/You're Insane (DJ copy, 500 only)	20
77	Riva RIVA 3	Tonight's The Night/The First Cut Is The Deepest (withdrawn B-side)	10
77	Riva RIVA 8	THE FACES (EP, p/s)	5
78	Riva RIVA 9	Sailing/Stone Cold Sober (p/s)	5
78	Riva RIVA 9	Sailing/Stone Cold Sober (HMS Ark Royal Commemorative issue, blue vinyl, p/s)	80
78	Riva RIVA 15	Ole Ola/I'd Walk A Million Miles — Que Sera Sera (p/s)	5
80	Riva RIVA 23	If Lovin' You Is Wrong/Last Summer (p/s)	5
80	Virgin VS 366	Little Miss Understood/So Much To Say (p/s, reissue)	5
80	Riva W 7929TP	Excerpts From "Foolish Behaviour" (flexidisc free w/ *London Evening News*)	8/5
80	Riva RIVA 26T	Passion (Extended Version)/Better Off Dead (12", p/s)	7
81	Riva RIVA 29M	Oh God I Wish I Was Home Tonight/Somebody Special (cassette)	5
82	Riva RIVA 35	How Long/Jealous (p/s, with free sticker)	5
82	Decca F 11996	Good Morning Little Schoolgirl/I'm Gonna Move To The Outskirts Of Town (reissue)	8
82	Immediate IM 060	Little Miss Understood/So Much To Say (reissue, p/s)	5
83	Warner Bros W 9440P	Sweet Surrender/Ghetto Blaster (picture disc)	5
83	Warner Bros W 96564T	Baby Jane/Ready Now/If Lovin' You Is Wrong (live) (12", p/s, with poster)	7
84	Warner Bros SAM 194	Infatuation (1-sided picture disc in wallet with interview cassette)	15
86	Warner Bros W 8668TP	Love Touch/Heart Is On The Line/Hard Lesson To Learn (12", picture disc)	7
86	Warner Bros W 8625TE	Every Beat Of My Heart (Tartan Mix)/Trouble/Some Guys Have All The Luck/I Don't Want To Talk About It (live) (12", p/s with poster)	8
87	Geffen RODS 1	Twistin' The Night Away/Let's Get Small (p/s)	4
88	Warner Bros WX 152TP	Lost In You (Extended Remix)/Lost In You (Fade)/Almost Illegal (12", pic disc)	7

Rod STEWART

88	Warner Bros W 7927CD	Lost In You (Fade)/Almost Illegal/Lost In You (Extended Remix)/Baby Jane (3" CD, with adaptor, 5" case)	7
88	Warner Bros W 7796CD	Forever Young (LP Version)/Days Of Rage/Forever Young (Remix)/ Every Beat Of My Heart (LP Version) (3" CD, with adaptor, 5" case)	7
89	Warner Bros W 7729CD	My Heart Can't Tell You No/The Wild Horse/Passion (live) (3" CD)	7
89	Warner Bros W 2686P	This Old Heart Of Mine/Ain't Love A Bitch/Tonight I'm Yours (Don't Hurt Me) (with Ronald Isley, shaped picture disc)	6
89	Warner Bros W 2686CD	This Old Heart Of Mine/Ain't Love A Bitch/Tonight I'm Yours (Don't Hurt Me) (with Ronald Isley, 3" CD, gatefold card sleeve)	7
89	Warner Bros W 2647TG	Downtown Train/Stay With Me/Cindy Incidentally/To Love Somebody (12", gatefold p/s)	7
70s	Mercury BRAUN 3	MAGGIE MAY (EP, freebie)	6

LPs

70	Vertigo VO 4	AN OLD RAINCOAT WON'T EVER LET YOU DOWN (LP, g/fold sl., spiral label)	18
70	Vertigo 6360 500	GASOLINE ALLEY (LP, gatefold sleeve, spiral label)	18
71	Mercury 6338 063	EVERY PICTURE TELLS A STORY (LP, black label)	12
72	Mercury 6499 153	NEVER A DULL MOMENT (LP, gatefold sleeve)	12
75	Riva RVLP 4	ATLANTIC CROSSING (LP, gatefold sleeve, blue vinyl)	12
78	St. Michael 21020 102	REASON TO BELIEVE (LP, only available in Marks & Spencer)	30
84	Warner Bros 9250 951	CAMOUFLAGE (LP, with bonus 1-sided picture disc "Infatuation" in wallet with interview tape [SAM 194])	20

(see also Jeff Beck, Shotgun Express, Faces, Python Lee Jackson, Long John Baldry, Ted Wood, Atlantic Crossing Drum & Pipe Band)

ROMAN STEWART

72	Songbird SB 1075	Changing Times (with Dave)/CRYSTALITES: Changing Times Version	10
73	Downtown DT 518	Try Me/BIG YOUTH: Rhythm Style	25
73	Techniques TE 932	Tonight I'm Staying Here (& Tennors)/Lady Love (& Tennors)	5
75	Camel CA 2002	Wolverton Mountain/PITTERSON ALL STARS: Version	5

SANDY STEWART

58	London HLE 8683	A Certain Smile/Kiss Me Richard	15
58	London HLE 8683	A Certain Smile/Kiss Me Richard (78)	20
63	Pye International 7N 25176	My Colouring Book/I Heard You Cried Last Night	6

SONNY STEWART & HIS SKIFFLE KINGS

57	Philips PB 719	The Northern Line/Black Jack (78)	25
57	Philips PB 773	Let Me Lie/Mama Don't Allow It (78)	25

TINGA STEWART

71	Songbird SB 1048	Hear That Train/CRYSTALITES: Hear That Train — Version	6
72	Tropical AL 0018	A Brand New Me/BROWNS ALL STARS: Nice Version	6
74	Dragon DRA 1025	The Message/Dub	10

WINSTON STEWART

64	R&B JB 147	But I Do/MAYTALS: Four Seasons	15
64	Port-O-Jam PJ 4002	All Of My Life/How Many Times	15

(see also Andy & Clyde, Gaylads, Delano Stewart, Winston & Tonettes)

WYNN STEWART

60	London HL 7087	Wishful Thinking/Uncle Tom Got Caught (export issue)	25

(Dave) STEWART & HARRISON

70	Multicord MULT SH 1	GIRL (EP)	15

(see also Longdancer, Tourists, Eurythmics, David A. Stewart)

REX STEWART'S LONDON FIVE

55	Tempo EXA 8	REX STEWART'S LONDON FIVE (EP)	8

STICKERS

71	Bullet BU 492	One Night Of Sin/Sin (Version) (both sides actually by Jackie Brown)	6

(see also Jackie Brown)

COOL STICKY

68	Amalgamated AMG 825	Train To Soulsville/ERIC MONTY MORRIS: Cinderella	12

ARBEE STIDHAM

70s	Mainstream MSL 1011	A TIME FOR BLUES (LP)	12

STIFF LITTLE FINGERS

78	Rigid Digits SRD-1	Suspect Device/Wasted Life (hand-made p/s, 500 only, red label with catalogue number on right-hand side)	15
78	Rigid Digits SRD-1	Suspect Device/Wasted Life (re-pressing, different machine-cut p/s, various colour labels/yellow labels)	6/10
78	Rough Trade RT 004	78 R.P.M./Alternative Ulster (p/s, A & B-sides reversed)	8
78	Rough Trade RT 004	Alternative Ulster/78 R.P.M. (p/s)	5
78	Rough Trade RT 006	Suspect Device/Wasted Life (reissue)	5
79	Rough Trade RT 015	Gotta Getaway/Bloody Sunday (p/s)	5
82	Chrysalis CHSDJ 2580	Listen/Two Guitars Clash (p/s, jukebox issue)	8
82	Chrysalis/Melody Maker [no cat. no.]	Excerpts From "Now Then"/IGGY POP: Excerpts From "Zombie Birdhouse" (flexidisc, free with *Melody Maker*)	6/4
87	Strange Fruit SFPSC 004	THE PEEL SESSION (EP, cassette)	6
89	Limited Ed. LTD EDT 3LP	LIVE IN SWEDEN (LP, green vinyl)	10
92	Essential! EPDLP 171	FLAGS AND EMBLEMS (LP, picture disc)	10

(see also Billy Karloff & Extremes)

STIFFS

79	Dork UR 1	Standard English/S.C. Rip/Brookside Riot Squad (die cut sleeve)	8
79	Dork UR 2	Inside Out/Kids On the Street (die cut sleeve or later Zonophone Z3 p/s)	8
80	Zonophone Z 14	Volume Control/Nothing To Lose (p/s)	7
80	Stiff BUT 86	Goodbye My Love/Magic Roundabout (p/s)	7
85	Dork UR 7(12)	The Young Guitars/Yer Under Attack (12", p/s)	8

STILETTOS
| 80 | Ariola ARO 200 | This Is The Way/Who Can It Be (p/s) | 8 |

STILL LIFE
| 68 | Columbia DB 8345 | What Did We Miss/My Kingdom Cannot Lose | 25 |
| 71 | Vertigo 6360 026 | STILL LIFE (LP, gatefold sleeve, spiral label) | 100 |

(see also Jon, Tutus Groan)

STEPHEN STILLS
71	Atlantic 2091 046	Love The One You're With/To A Flame	5
71	Atlantic 2091 069	Sit Yourself Down/We Are Not Helpless	5
71	Atlantic 2091 117	Change Partners/Relaxing Town	5
71	Atlantic 2091 141	Marianne/Nothing To Do But Today	5
70	Atlantic 2401 004	STEPHEN STILLS (LP)	15
71	Atlantic 2401 013	STEPHEN STILLS 2 (LP, gatefold sleeve)	12

(see also Buffalo Springfield, Al Kooper Mike Bloomfield & Stephen Stills, Crosby Stills Nash & Young, Manassas, Stills-Young Band)

STILLWATER TRIO
| 70s | Sharon 330 | LIFE'S RAILROAD (LP) | 15 |

STILLS-YOUNG BAND
76	Reprise K 14446	Long May You Run/12-8 Blues	5
76	Reprise K 14482	Like A Hurricane (edit)/Hold Back The Tears	5
76	Reprise K 54081	LONG MAY YOU RUN (LP)	12

(see also Stephen Stills, Manassas, Neil Young, Buffalo Springfield, Crosby Stills Nash & Young)

STING
87	A&M AMCD 410	We'll Be Together (Extended Mix 5.54)/(Previous Version 4.28)/ Conversation With A Dog/We'll Be Together (Instrumental Version) (3" CD, with adaptor in plastic tray in gatefold card sleeve)	10
87	A&M AMCD 431	Englishman In New York/Ghost In The Strand (Instrumental)/Bring On The Night-When The World Is Running Down (live) (CD)	10
88	A&M AMCD 439	Fragile/Fragile (Portuguese Version)/Fragilidad/Mariposa Libre (CD)	7
88	A&M AMCD 911	COMPACT HITS (CD EP)	7
88	A&M AMCD 458	They Dance Alone (Gueca Solo) (with Eric Clapton & Mark Knopfler)/ Ellas Damzon Solas (Gueca Solo)/St. Estamos Juntos (CD)	7
88	A&M AMCDR 580	Englishman In New York/Englishman In New York (Ben Liebrand Mix)/If You Love Somebody Set Them Free (Jellybean Dance Mix) (CD, picture disc)	7
85	A&M DREAMP 1	THE DREAM OF THE BLUE TURTLES (LP, picture disc, die-cut sl., with insert)	10
91	A&M 397 171-2	ACOUSTIC LIVE IN NEWCASTLE (CD, box set with book)	20

(see also Police, Last Exit, [Fast Breeder &] Radio Actors, Newcastle Big Band)

STINGERS
| 72 | Upsetter US 395 | Preacher Man/UPSETTERS: Version | 8 |

STINGRAY (TV series)
(see under Century 21)

STING-RAYS
82	Big Beat SW 82	Dinosaurs/Math Of Trend/Another Cup Of Coffee/You're Gonna Miss Me (white label test pressing, 100 Club gig freebie, 80 only)	20
83	Big Beat SW 82	Dinosaurs/Math Of Trend/Another Cup Of Coffee/You're Gonna Miss Me (p/s)	6
84	Big Beat NS 95	Escalator/Loose Lip Synch Ship/Escalator (Instrumental) (p/s)	5
85	Big Beat NS 109	Don't Break Down/Don't Break Down (Version) (p/s)	4
85	Big Beat NST 109	Don't Break Down/Don't Break Down (Version) (12", p/s)	7
85	Media Burn MB 2/ Lyntone LYN 16436	Bonus Track/I Want My Woman/Flash On You (33 rpm, red vinyl flexidisc with *The Sting-Rays Story* magazine)	5
86	ABC ABCS 009T	June Rhyme/Militant Tendency/Wedding Ring (12", p/s)	7
86	Kaleidoscope Sound 702	Behind The Beyond (EP)	5
86	Kaleidoscope Sound 102	BEHIND THE BEYOND (12" EP)	7
83	Big beat WIKM 16	DINOSAURS (LP)	10
84	Media Burn MB 1	LIVE RETALIATION (LP, white or black vinyl)	15/10
87	K'scope Sound KSLP 1	CRYPTIC AND COFFEE TIME (LP)	10
88	Media Burn MB 18	GOODBYE TO ALL THAT — LIVE VOL. 2 (LP, red or black vinyl)	15/10

STINKY TOYS
| 77 | Polydor 2056 630 | Boozy Creed/Driver Blues (p/s) | 6 |
| 77 | Polydor 2393 174 | STINKY TOYS (LP) | 15 |

(PETER) LEE STIRLING (& BRUISERS)
63	Columbia DB 4992	My Heart Commands Me/Welcome Stranger (as Lee Stirling & Bruisers)	7
63	Parlophone R 5063	I Could If I Wanted To/Right From The Start (as Lee Stirling & Bruisers)	7
64	Parlophone R 5112	Now That I've Found You/I Believe (as Peter Lee Stirling & Bruisers)	7
64	Parlophone R 5158	Sad, Lonely And Blue/I'm Looking For Someone To Love (as Peter Lee Stirling & Bruisers)	7
64	Parlophone R 5198	Everything Will Be Alright/You'll Be Mine (as Peter Lee Stirling & Bruisers)	7
66	Decca F 12433	The Sweet And Tender Hold Of Your Love/Everybody Needs A Someone	6
66	Decca F 12535	Oh What A Fool/I'm Sportin' A New Baby	7
67	Decca F 12628	You Don't Live Twice/8.35 On The Dot	6
67	Decca F 12674	Goodbye Thimblemill Lane/Hey Conductor	6
69	MCA MU 1093	Big Sam/Mr. Average Man	6
70	MCA MK 5027	Goodbye Summer Girl/Judas In Blue	5

(see also Bruisers, Hungry Wolf)

STITCHED-BACK FOOT AIRMAN
| 87 | Very Mouth EAT 10 | Wouldn't You Like To Know/Sinking Ship/Neverbend Manchester/ Some People (p/s) | 4 |
| 86 | Very Mouth EAT 9 | SEVEN EGG-TIMING GREATS (mini-LP, with insert) | 8 |

GARY STITES
| 59 | London HLL 8881 | Lonely For You/Shine That Ring | 25 |
| 59 | London HLL 8881 | Lonely For You/Shine That Ring (78) | 30 |

Gary STITES

59	London HLL 9003	Starry Eyed/Without Your Love	12
59	London HLL 9003	Starry Eyed/Without Your Love (78)	50
60	London HLL 9082	Lawdy, Miss Clawdy/Don't Wanna Say Goodbye	18

KING STITT

69	Clandisc CLA 200	Who Yea/DYNAMITES: Mr Midnight	8
69	Clandisc CLA 202	Vigerton Two/On The Street	8
69	Clandisc CLA 203	On The Street/CYNTHIA RICHARDS: Foolish Fool	8
69	Clandisc CLA 206	The Ugly One/CLANCY ECCLES: Dance Beat	8
70	Clandisc CLA 207	Herbsman Shuffle (with Andy [Capp])/HIGGS & WILSON: Don't Mind Me	8
70	Clandisc CLA 223	King Of Kings/DYNAMITES: Reggaedelic	7
71	Clandisc CLA 235	Merry Rhythm/CLANCY ECCLES: John Crow Skank	6
71	Banana BA 332	Back Out Version/VEGETABLES: Holly Rhythm	8
71	Banana BA 334	Rhyming Time/Reality	8
	(see also Kurass)		

SONNY STITT

53	Esquire 20-013	SONNY STITT-BUD POWELL QUARTET (10" LP)	18
58	Esquire 32-049	S.P.J. JAZZ (LP, with Bud Powell & J.J. Johnson)	15
58	Columbia Clef 33CX 10114	NEW YORK JAZZ (LP)	15
59	Esquire 32-078	STITT'S BITS (LP)	15
59	HMV CLP 1280	ONLY THE BLUES (LP)	12
60	HMV CLP 1363	PERSONAL APPEARANCE (LP)	12
60	HMV CLP 1384	SONNY STITT WITH THE OSCAR PETERSON TRIO (LP)	12
61	HMV CLP 1420/CSD 1341	BLOWS THE BLUES (LP, mono/stereo)	12/15
	(see also Oscar Peterson, J.J. Johnson)		

ALAN STIVELL

72	Philips 6009 208	Wind Of Keltia/Pop Plinn	5
72	Philips 6414 406	RENAISSANCE OF THE CELTIC HARP (LP)	12
73	Fontana 6399 005	A L'OLYMPIA (LP)	12
74	Fontana 6399 008	REFLECTIONS (LP)	12
74	Philips 6325 304	FROM CELTIC ROOTS (LP)	12

STOCKER, GREENWOOD & FRIENDS

79	Changes	BILL + NINE (LP)	25
	(see also Slack Alice)		

STOCKINGTOPS

68	Toast TT 500	You're Never Gonna Get My Lovin'/You Don't Know What Love Is All About	6
68	CBS 3407	I Don't Ever Wanna Be Kicked By You/The World We Live In Is A Lonely Place	6
	(see also Sue & Sunny, Sue & Sunshine, Myrtelles)		

STOICS

68	RCA RCA 1745	Earth, Fire, Air And Water/Search Of The Sea	4

STOKES

65	London HLU 9955	Whipped Cream/Pie Crust	10

SIMON STOKES & NIGHTHAWKS

70	Elektra EKSN 45082	Voodoo Woman/Can't Stop Now	5

RHET STOLLER (& HIS ECHOES)

60	Decca F 11271	Walk Don't Run/All Rhet	15
60	Decca F 11302	Chariot/Night Theme	10
63	Decca F 11738	Countdown/Over The Steppes (as Rhet Stoller & His Echoes)	10
64	Melodisc MEL 1595	Beat That/Treble Gold + One	18
64	Windsor PS 118	Bandit/Tonight (unissued)	
64	Windsor PS 119	Caravan/Short Cut	18
64	Windsor PS 130	Ricochet/Knockout	18
66	Columbia DB 8013	Uncrowned King/Surf Ride (unissued, demos only)	25
69	Mosaic MOSAIC 1	SUNSHINE ANYTIME (EP, as Rhet Stoller & Music)	12
67	Coronet EC 101	THE INCREDIBLE RHET STOLLER (LP)	30

JACKIE STOLLINGS (& NASHVILLE BOYS)

62	Starlite ST45 092	Footsteps Of A Fool/And Then I Knew (B-side with Nashville Boys)	6

MORRIS STOLOFF (& COLUMBIA PICTURES ORCHESTRA)

56	Brunswick 05553	Theme From "Picnic"/Moonglow	7
56	Brunswick 05597	Theme From "The Solid Gold Cadillac"/Sweet Sue Just You	6
57	Brunswick 05618	Exactly Like You/Wanna Go Back To You	5
57	Brunswick 05666	Theme From "Fire Down Below"/Theme From "Full Of Life"	6

STOMPERS

62	Fontana H 385	Quarter To Four Stomp (Surf Stompin')/Foolish One	15

ALEXANDER STONE

70	Gemini GMS 003	I Try To Make You Good/Man In A Suitcase	4

CLIFFIE STONE & HIS ORCHESTRA

55	Capitol CL 14330	Barracuda/The Popcorn Song (with Billy Strange & Speedy West)	100
55	Capitol CL 14330	Barracuda/The Popcorn Song (with Billy Strange & Speedy West) (78)	30
56	Capitol CL 14666	Jingle Bells/Rudolph The Red Nosed Reindeer	6
58	Capitol CL 14928	Near You/Nobody's Darlin' But Mine	6
59	Capitol CL 14982	Maybe/I Don't Want To Walk Without You	5
59	Capitol CL 14996	Blood On The Saddle/Cool Water	6
59	Capitol T 1080	THE PARTY'S ON ME (LP)	15
	(see also Jeanne Gayle, Billy Strange)		

ECKERSLEY STONE

75	Nad NARDS 00	Fat Girls Of Gurningsthwaite/By 'Eckaslahk, Tha Knows ('black pudding' p/s)	15
80	Fat LARD 47	WHIPPET DRIPPING BUTTIE (LP, some on pallid vinyl)	30/20

ELLA STONE & MOSS
70s Phoenix SNIX 128   The Prophet/Now Or Never 6
(see also Helen Shapiro, Al Saxon)

GEORGE STONE
65	Stateside SS 479	Hole In The Wall/My Beat	8

KIRBY STONE QUARTET/FOUR
56	Vogue Coral Q 72129	Honey Hush/Lassus Trombone	12
56	Vogue Coral Q 72129	Honey Hush/Lassus Trombone (78).	10
59	Philips PB 903	That "I Had A Dream, Dear" Rock/Sweet Nothings	5
59	Philips PB 903	That "I Had A Dream, Dear" Rock/Sweet Nothings (78)	10
63	Warner Bros WB 102	The Great Escape (March)/Fancy Dan	5
63	Warner Bros WB 118	Washington Guitar/Blue Guitar	5
59	London HA-A 2164	MAN, I FLIPPED WHEN I HEARD THE KIRBY STONE FOUR (LP). . . .	15

MARK STONE
58	London HLR 8543	Ever Since I Met Lucy/The Stroll	75
58	London HLR 8543	Ever Since I Met Lucy/The Stroll (78)	40

SLY (& FAMILY) STONE
68	Columbia DB 8369	Dance To The Music/Let Me Hear It From You	35
68	Direction 58-3568	Dance To The Music/Let Me Hear It From You (reissue)	5
68	Direction 58-3707	M'Lady/Life	6
69	Direction 58-3938	Everyday People/Sing A Simple Song	6
69	Direction 58-4279	Stand!/I Want To Take You Higher.	6
69	Direction 58-4471	Hot Fun In The Summertime/Fun.	6
70	Direction 58-4782	Thank You (Falettinme Be Mice Elf Agin)/Everybody Is A Star.	6
70	CBS 5054	I Want To Take You Higher/You Can Make It If You Try	6
71	Epic EPC 7632	Family Affair/Luv n' Haight	5
72	Epic EPC 7810	Running Away/Brave And Strong	5
73	Epic EPC 1148	Family Affair/Dance To The Music (p/s, 'Hall Of Fame Hits' series)	4
73	Epic EPC 1655	If You Want Me To Stay/Thankful & Thoughtful	5
74	Epic EPC 2530	Time For Livin'/Small Talk (as Sly Stone)	5
75	Epic EPC 2882	Loose Booty/Can't Strain My Brain (as Sly Stone)	5
68	Direction 8-63412	DANCE TO THE MUSIC (LP).	18
68	Direction 8-63461	M'LADY (LP).	18
69	Direction 8-63655	STAND! (LP, CBS sleeve with Direction label).	18
70	Epic EPC 69002	GREATEST HITS (LP, gatefold sleeve).	12
72	Epic EPC 64613	THERE'S A RIOT GOING ON (LP, gatefold sleeve, with free EP/newspaper)	15
73	CBS Q 69002	GREATEST HITS (LP, quadrophonic, gatefold sleeve)	15
73	Epic EPC 69039	FRESH (LP, gatefold sleeve)	12
74	Epic EPC 69070	SMALL TALK (LP).	12
75	Epic EPC 22004	HIGH ENERGY (2-LP, gatefold sleeve).	15
75	Epic EPC 69165	HIGH ON YOU (LP, as Sly Stone)	12
76	Epic EPC 81641	HEARD YA MISSED ME, WELL I'M BACK (LP).	12

(see also Rosie Banks)

STONE ANGEL
75	SSLP 04	STONE ANGEL (LP, private pressing)	200
94	Acme AC 8008 LP	STONE ANGEL (LP, reissue, 500 only)	15

(see also Ken Saul)

STONED AID
80s Hit STONE 1   Are You Going To Stonehenge/Magical Carpet Ride (p/s). 5
(see also Cannibals)

STONEFIELD TRAMP
74	Acorn/Tramp CF 247	DREAMING	150

(see also Terry Friend, Rob Van Spyk)

STONEGROUND
71	Warner Bros K 16126	You Must Be One Of Us/It Takes A Lot To Laugh	5
71	Warner Bros K 46087	STONEGROUND (LP).	15
71	Warner Bros K 53999	FAMILY ALBUM (LP).	15

STONEGROUND BAND
70s Nut   SUNSTRUCK!! (LP, stickered sleeve) 30

HARRY STONEHAM
70	Studio Two TWO 326	HIGH POWER HAMMOND (LP)	12
71	Contour 2870 112	HAMMOND MY WAY (LP)	12
71	Studio Two TWO 345	SOLID GOLD HAMMOND (LP)	12
72	Studio Two Q4TWO 375	HAMMOND HITS THE HIGHWAY (LP, quadrophonic)	12
75	Studio Two TWOX 1046	HAMMOND HEATWAVE (LP)	12

STONEHENGE MEN
62	HMV POP 981	Big Feet/Pinto.	40

STONEHOUSE
71	RCA SF 8197	STONEHOUSE CREEK (LP)	65

E.V. STONEMAN
63	London HA-B/SH-B 8089	E.V. STONEMAN AND THE STONEMAN FAMILY (LP)	10

STONEPILLOW
69	Phase 4 Stereo PFS 4163	ELEAZAR'S CIRCUS (LP)	10

STONE PONEYS
67	Capitol CL 15523	A Different Drum/I've Got To Know	7

(see also Linda Ronstadt)

STONE ROSES

STONE ROSES

SINGLES

85	Thin Line THIN 001	So Young/Tell Me (12", p/s, 1,200 only; beware of counterfeits!) 75
87	Black/Revolver 12 REV 36	Sally Cinnamon/Here It Comes/All Across The Sand (12", 'Printed In England' on rear p/s & no barcode, "All Across The Sands" listed on label; different mixes of 2 tracks to later reissue) 20
88	Silvertone ORE 1	Elephant Stone/The Hardest Thing In The World (catalogue number in black print on rear of p/s) 7
88	Silvertone ORE 1T	Elephant Stone (4.48)/Elephant Stone (7" Version) (3.00)/Full Fathom Five/ The Hardest Thing In The World (12", p/s, cat. no. in black print on rear of p/s) . . 12
89	Silvertone ORE 2	Made Of Stone/Going Down (p/s, cat. no. in black print on rear of p/s). 5
89	Silvertone ORE 2T	Made Of Stone/Going Down/Guernica (12", p/s, catalogue number in black print on rear of p/s) 8
89	Silvertone ORE 6	She Bangs The Drums/Standing Here (p/s). 4
89	Silvertone OREX 6	She Bangs The Drums/Standing Here (p/s, with postcard, 3,000 only) 7
89	Silvertone OREZ 6	She Bangs The Drums/Mersey Paradise/Standing Here (12", p/s with colour print, 5,000 only) 12
89	Silvertone ORE 13	What The World Is Waiting For/Fools Gold 4.15 (paper label, with postcard stickered p/s credits "What The World Is Waiting For") 6
89	Silvertone ORE 13	Fools Gold 4.15/What The World Is Waiting For (repressing, p/s credits "Fools Gold"). 4
89	Silvertone ORET 13	What The World Is Waiting For/Fools Gold 9.23 (12", stickered p/s credits "What The World Is Waiting For", with print). 10
89	Silvertone ORECD 13	Fools Gold 9.23/What The World Is Waiting For/Fools Gold 4.15 (CD, inlay credits "What The World Is Waiting For") 8
89	Black/Revolver REV 36	Sally Cinnamon/Here It Comes (p/s) 5
90	Silvertone ORE 1	Elephant Stone (7" Version)/The Hardest Thing In The World (catalogue number in *red* print on rear of p/s) 4
90	Silvertone ORE 2	Made Of Stone/Going Down (p/s, cat. no. in blue print on rear of p/s). 4
90	Fierce FRIGHT 044	SPIKE ISLAND EP (fan interviews, P.A. announcements & fireworks, with cigarette, badge, bag of grass & banana sweet) 15
91	Silvertone ORE 31	I Wanna Be Adored (3.28)/Where Angels Play (p/s) 4
91	Silvertone OREZ 31	I Wanna Be Adored (4.52)/Where Angels Play/ Sally Cinnamon (live at the Hacienda) (12", stickered p/s with print) 7
92	Silvertone ORE 35	Waterfall (7" Version 3.31)/One Love (7" Version 3.40) (p/s). 4
92	Silvertone OREZT 35	Waterfall (12" Version 5.23)/One Love (Adrian Sherwood 12" Version 7.10) (12", p/s with print). 8
92	Silvertone ORE 40	I Am The Resurrection (Pan And Scan Radio Version)/I Am The Resurrection (Highly Resurrected Dub) (p/s) 5
92	Silvertone ORET 40	I Am The Resurrection (Extended 19:9 Ratio Club Mix)/(Original LP Version)/ Fools Gold (Bottom Won Mix) (12", some with print). 15/8
93	Silvertone ORECD 37	So Young/Tell Me (CD, from "CD Singles Collection") 12
92	Silvertone SRBX 2	12" SINGLES COLLECTION (10 x 12" singles box set, 1,000 only) 60
92	Silvertone SRBX 1	CD SINGLES COLLECTION (8 x CD singles box set, 1,000 only) 60

PROMOS

90	Silvertone OREZ 13	Fools Gold (The Top Won Mix!)/(The Bottom Won Mix!) (12", promo only) 18
90	Silvertone OREZCD 13	Fools Gold (The Top Won Mix!)/(The Bottom Won Mix!) (gold CD). 12
90	Silvertone OREZ 17	One Love (Paul Schroeder Mix 7.08)/Something's Burning (12", promo only) 7
90	Silvertone STONE ONE	Fools Gold (A Guy Called Gerald Remix)/Elephant Stone (DJ Mix) (12", white label, promo only). 18
95	Silvertone OREDJ 71	Fools Gold (The Tall Paul Remix)/Fools Gold 9.23/ Fools Gold (Cricklewood Ballroom Mix) (12", promo only) 10
95	Geffen WGFSX 22060	Begging You (Album Version)/(Chic Mix)/(Stone Corporation Vox)/ (Young American Primitive Remix) (12", no p/s, promo only) 7
95	Geffen WGFST 22060	Begging You (Album Version)/(Cox's Ultimatum Mix)/(Overworld Mix)/ (Lakota Mix) (12", no p/s, promo only) 7
95	Geffen WGFTD 22060	Begging You (Radio Edit)/(Chic Mix) (CD, promo only). 7

ALBUMS

89	Silvertone ORE LP 502	THE STONE ROSES (LP, U.S. disc with "Elephant Stone" in U.K. embossed sleeve with gold lettering) 10
91	Silvertone ORE ZLP 502	THE STONE ROSES (2-LP, reissue, numbered gatefold sleeve with silver lettering) 15
95	Silvertone OREZCD 535	THE COMPLETE STONE ROSES (2-CD) 18

STONE'S MASONRY

66	Purdah 45-3504	Flapjacks/Hot Rock (99 copies only) 175

(see also Action, Mighty Baby, Savoy Brown)

STONE THE CROWS

70	Polydor 2066 060	Mad Dogs & Englishmen/Sad Mary. 5
72	Polydor 2058 301	Good Time Girl/On The Highway 5
70	Polydor 2425 017	STONE THE CROWS (LP). 25
70	Polydor 2425 042	ODE TO JOHN LAW (LP) 20
71	Polydor 2425 701	TEENAGE LICKS (LP) 15
72	Polydor 2391 043	ONTINUOUS PERFORMANCE (LP) 15

(see also White Trash, Maggie Bell)

STONEY & MEAT LOAF

71	Rare Earth RES 103	What You See Is What You Get/The Way You Do The Things You Get. 12
79	Prodigal PROD 10	What You See Is What You Get/The Way You Do The Things You Do (reissue, no p/s) 8
72	Rare Earth SRE 3005	STONEY AND MEAT LOAF (LP). 25
79	Prodigal PDL 2010	MEAT LOAF (FEATURING STONEY & MEAT LOAF) (LP, revised reissue of "Stoney And Meat Loaf" with different tracks) 15
86	Motown ZL 72217	MEAT LOAF (FEATURING STONEY & MEAT LOAF) (LP, 2nd reissue) 12

(see also Meat Loaf)

STOOGES

89	Spiral Scratch SCRATCH 5	She Creatures Of Hollywood Hills/Untitled (as Iggy & Stooges, no p/s, free with *Spiral Scratch* magazine, issue 5)	6/4
69	Elektra EKS 74051	THE STOOGES (LP, orange label)	50
70	Elektra EKS 74071	FUN HOUSE (LP, orange label)	45
70	Elektra 2410 009	FUN HOUSE (LP, reissue, red label)	20
73	CBS 65586	RAW POWER (LP, as Iggy & Stooges, plain orange label, with inner sleeve)	15
77	Elektra K 42032	THE STOOGES (LP, reissue, 'butterfly' label)	15
77	Elektra K 42051	FUN HOUSE (LP, reissue, 'butterfly' label)	15

(see also Iggy Pop)

STOP

80	Elite CAB 101	I Can Feel It/Iauwata (12")	12

STOREY SISTERS

58	London HLU 8571	Bad Motorcycle/Sweet Daddy	100
58	London HLU 8571	Bad Motorcycle/Sweet Daddy (78)	50

BILLY STORM

59	Philips PB 916	I've Come Of Age/This Is Always	7
59	Philips PB 916	I've Come Of Age/This Is Always (78)	25
60	London HLK 9236	Sure As You're Born/In The Chapel In The Moonlight	10

DANNY STORM (& STROLLERS)

62	Piccadilly 7N 35025	Honest I Do/Sad But True (some in p/s)	10/6
62	Piccadilly 7N 35053	Just You/I Told You So	8
62	Piccadilly 7N 35091	I Just Can't Fool My Heart/Thinking Of You	10
63	Piccadilly 7N 35143	Say You Do/Let The Sunshine In (as Danny Storm & Strollers)	10

GALE STORM

56	London HLD 8222	I Hear You Knocking/Never Leave Me	40
56	London HLD 8222	I Hear You Knocking/Never Leave Me (78)	12
56	London HLD 8232	Memories Are Made Of This/A Teen-Age Prayer	35
56	London HLD 8232	Memories Are Made Of This/A Teen-Age Prayer (78)	10
56	London HLD 8283	Ivory Tower/I Ain't Gonna Worry	40
56	London HLD 8283	Ivory Tower/I Ain't Gonna Worry (78)	12
56	London HLD 8286	Why Do Fools Fall In Love/I Walk Alone	35
56	London HLD 8286	Why Do Fools Fall In Love/I Walk Alone (78)	10
56	London HL 7008	Why Do Fools Fall In Love/I Walk Alone (export issue)	18
56	London HLD 8311	Don't Be That Way (Please Listen To Me)/Tell Me Why	30
56	London HLD 8311	Don't Be That Way (Please Listen To Me)/Tell Me Why (78)	12
56	London HLD 8329	A Heart Without A Sweetheart/Now Is The Hour	20
56	London HLD 8329	A Heart Without A Sweetheart/Now Is The Hour (78)	15
57	London HLD 8393	Lucky Lips/On Treasure Island	30
57	London HLD 8393	Lucky Lips/On Treasure Island (78)	18
57	London HLD 8413	Orange Blossoms/My Heart Belongs To You	20
57	London HLD 8413	Orange Blossoms/My Heart Belongs To You (78)	15
57	London HLD 8424	Dark Moon/A Little Too Late	20
58	London HLD 8570	Love Theme From "Farewell To Arms"/I Get That Feeling	10
58	London HLD 8570	Love Theme From "Farewell To Arms"/I Get That Feeling (78)	18
58	London HLD 8632	You/Angry	15
58	London HLD 8632	You/Angry (78)	20
56	London HB-D 1056	PRESENTING GALE STORM (10" LP)	60
58	London HA-D 2104	SENTIMENTAL ME (LP)	45

RORY STORM & HURRICANES

63	Oriole CB 1858	Dr. Feelgood/I Can Tell	30
64	Parlophone R 5197	America/Since You Broke My Heart	18

(see also Keef Hartley, Paddy Klaus & Gibson)

STORM BUGS

70s	Storm Bugs	STORM BUGS (EP, white label, foldout insert, plain white sleeve)	5

ROBB STORME (& WHISPERS)

60	Decca F 11282	1000, 900 And When/I Don't Need Your Love Anymore	12
61	Decca F 11313	Music/Five Minutes More (as Robb Storme & Whispers)	7
61	Decca F 11364	Near You/Lonely Town (as Robb Storme & Whispers)	7
61	Decca F 11388	Transistor Sister/Earth Angel	12
62	Decca F 11432	Pretty Hair And Angel Eyes/A Mile Of Broken Hearts	10
63	Pye 7N 15515	Sixteen Years Ago Tonight/Surprise Surprise	7
63	Piccadilly 7N 35133	Happens Ev'ryday/Surprise Surprise	6
63	Piccadilly 7N 35160	To Know Her Is To Love Her/Bu Bop A Lu Bop A Lie	6
65	Pye 7N 15819	Love Is Strange/Shy Guy	6
65	Columbia DB 7756	Where Is My Girl?/Double Oh Seven (as Robb Storme & Whispers)	8
66	Columbia DB 7993	Here Today/Don't Cry (as Robb Storme Group)	8
62	Decca DFE 6700	WHEELS (EP)	100

STORMER

78	Ring O' 2017 113	My Home Town/Shake It Baby (some in promo p/s)	20/15

STORMTROOPER

78	Solent SS 047	I'm A Mess/It's Not Me (some in stamped plain sleeve with insert)	30/15

STORMTROOPER

80	Heartbeat BEAT 1	Pride Before A Fall/Still Comin' Home (p/s)	35

STORYTELLER

71	CBS 7182	Remarkable/Laugh That Came Too Soon	5
70	Transatlantic TRA 220	STORYTELLER (LP)	25
71	Transatlantic TRA 232	MORE PAGES (LP)	30

(see also Johnny Neal & Starliners, Terry Durham, Other Two, Andy Bown)

MINT VALUE £

STORYTELLER
85 Storyteller ZELSP 438 — Mystery Girl (p/s) 35

BABE STOVALL
76 Southern Sound SD 203 — THE BABE STOVALL STORY (LP) 12

STOWAWAYS
79 Supermusic SUP 27 — I Wanna Be Me/My Friends/You'll Tie Me Down (p/s) 75

STP 23
89 Wau! Mr. Modo WMS 001R — Let Jimi Take Over/Let Jimi Take Over (Remix By Youth) (12", p/s) 10

STRAIGHT EIGHT
78 Eel Pie EPS 003 — Modern Times/Tell Me If You Wanna Bleed (p/s) 12
79 Warner Bros K 18049 — Spread It Around/It Ain't Easy/Oh No (p/s) 5
80 Logo DEAL 1 — I'm Sorry/Satisfied (p/s) 7
80 Logo DEAL 2 — Tombstone/On The Rebound (p/s) 5
82 Logo GO 416 — Tomorrow/Faded Stars/You Are What You Are (p/s) 4
79 Eel Pie EPRP 001 — NO NOISE FROM HERE (LP) 10
80 Logo LOGO 1032 — STRAIGHT TO THE HEART (LP) 10
80 Logo FLUSH 1 — SHUFFLE'N''CUT (LP) 12

STRAIGHT UP
80 Rok XX/XIX — One Out All Out/JUSTIN CASE: T.V. (no p/s) 5

STRAITJACKET FITS
90 Rough Trade G5SFI — Hail/GALAXIE 500: Blue Thunder/Victory Garden (promo only, stickered sleeve). . 8

EMILLE STRAKER & HIS MERRYMEN
(see under Merrymen)

PETER STRAKER
69 Polydor 56345 — Breakfast In Bed/The Right To Cry 5
69 Polydor 56362 — I Never Thought I'd Fall In Love/Birdie Told Me 5
70 Polydor 2058 039 — Carousel/It's A New Day 5
77 EMI EMI 2700 — Ragtime Piano Joe/Saddest Clown 10
78 EMI EMI 2758 — Jackie/I've Been To Hell And Back 12
80 Rocket XPRES 35 — Late Night Taxi Dancer/Real Natural Man (p/s) 5
77 EMI EMC 3204 — THIS ONE'S ON ME (LP) 18

STRANGE
94 Detour DR 015 — I Don't Care/Mint Sensation/Bad Scene (p/s, 100 on pink vinyl) 8/5

BILLY STRANGE (& CHALLENGERS)
61 London HLG 9321 — Where Your Arms Used To Be/Sadness Done Come 10
64 Vocalion V-N 9228 — The James Bond Theme/007 Theme 12
64 Vocalion V-N 9231 — Goldfinger/"Munsters" Theme 20
66 Vocalion V-N 9257 — Thunderball/"Ninth Man" Theme 12
66 Vocalion V-N 9259 — Get Smart/Run Spy, Run 15
67 Vocalion V-N 9289 — "A Few Dollars More" Theme/You Only Live Twice 10
63 Vocalion VA/SVN 8022 — 12-STRING GUITAR (LP) 15
64 Vocalion VAN 8026 — MR GUITAR (LP) 15
64 Vocalion VAN/SAVN 8032 — THE JAMES BOND THEME (LP) 20
65 Vocalion VAN/SAVN 8038 — GOLDFINGER (LP) 20
65 Vocalion VAN/SAVN 8042 — ENGLISH HITS OF '65 (LP) 15
65 Vocalion VAN/SAVN 8045 — STRANGE PLAYS THE HITS (LP) 15
66 Vocalion VAN/SAVN 8050 — FOLK-ROCK HITS (LP) 15
66 London HA-F/SH-F 8274 — THE FUNKY 12 STRING GUITAR (LP, as Billy Strange & Transients) ... 12
66 Vocalion VAN/SAVN 8065 — BILLY STRANGE & THE CHALLENGERS (LP) 15
70 London ZGL 104 — GREAT WESTERN THEMES (LP) 15
(see also Cliffie Stone)

GILES STRANGE
66 Stateside SS 570 — Watch The People Dance/You're Goin' Up To The Bottom 50

STEVE STRANGE
82 Palace PALACE 1 — In The Year 2525/Strange Connexions (white label, unreleased) 60
82 Palace PALACE 1 — In The Year 2525/Strange Connexions (p/s, available separately) 35
(see also Visage)

STRANGE DAYS
75 Retreat RTS 263 — Monday Morning/Joe Soap 5
75 Retreat RTL 6005 — NINE PARTS TO THE WIND (LP) 20

STRANGE FRUIT
71 Village Thing VTSX 1001 — Cut Across Shorty/Shake That Thing 12

STRANGELOVE
92 Sermon SERT 001 — Visionary/Front/Chances/Snakes (12", p/s, 1,000 only) 30
93 Sermon SERT 002 — Hysteria/Unknown/My Dark Walls/Sea (12", some in p/s) 18/7
93 Sermon SERT 002CD — Hysteria/Unknown/My Dark Walls/Sea (CD) 25
93 R. T. Singles Club 45REV 18 — Zoo'd Out/Circles (p/s) 15
94 Kennel Club VTDOG 10 — Wolf's Story:TINDERSTICKS: Girl On Death Row/GOD MACHINE:
The Devil Song/BREED: Diamonds Are Forever (10", numbered, 1,500 only,
free with *Purr* magazine, issue 2) 10/8
94 Food 12FOOD 49 — Time For The Rest Of Your Life/Motorpsycho Nitemare/It's So Easy (12", p/s) 7
94 Food CDFOOD 49 — Time For The Rest Of Your Life/Motorpsycho Nitemare/It's So Easy (CD) 8
94 M. Tongue MOTHER 1F — All Because Of You/MY LIFE STORY: "Under The Ice" (flexidisc) 8
95 Food FOODDJ 62 — World Outside (live)/Hysteria Unknown (live) (gig freebie,
some with jukebox centre) 6
96 Food FOODLP 15 — LOVE AND OTHER DEMONS (LP, with 12 page booklet) 10

STRANGELOVES
65 Stateside SS 446 — I Want Candy/It's About My Baby 15
65 Immediate IM 007 — Cara-Lin/Roll On Mississippi 12

MINT VALUE £

66	London HLZ 10020	Night Time/Rhythm Of Love	20
66	London HLZ 10063	Hand Jive/I Gotta Dance	8
69	London HLZ 10238	Honey Do/I Wanna Do It	8

(see also Beach-Nuts)

STRANGER (Cole)

63	Blue Beat BB 165	Rough And Tough (with Duke Reid Band)/DUKE REID BAND: The Mood I Am In	12
63	Blue Beat BB 195	Miss Reamer/RICO & HIS BLUES BAND: Blues From The Hills	15

(see also Stranger Cole)

STRANGER (Cole) & GLADY (Anderson)

67	Island WI 3128	Love Me Today/Over Again	18
68	Amalgamated AMG 806	Seeing Is Knowing/ROY SHIRLEY: Music Is The Key	12
71	Clandisc CLA 230	Tomorrow (as Stranger & Gladdy)/DYNAMITES: Tomorrow Version	6
71	Supreme SUP 227	My Application (as Stranger & Gladdy)/TADDY & DIAMONDS: Oh No, My Baby	6
73	Count Shelley CS 015	Don't Give Up The Fight (as Stranger & Gladdy)/TIDALS: Stand Firm	5
73	Dragon DRA 1014	Conqueror/Conqueror (Instrumental Version)	12

(see also Stranger Cole, Gladdy & Followers, Gladstone Anderson, Gladdy & Stranger)

STRANGER (Cole) & HORTENSE (Ellis)

74	Count Shelley CS 049	Mocking Bird/Corra Bella Baby	4

STRANGER (Cole) & KEN (Boothe)

63	R&B JB 120	Thick In Love/All Your Friends	12

(see also Stranger Cole, Ken Boothe)

STRANGER (Cole) & PATSY (Todd)

63	Blue Beat BB 171	When I Call Your Name/Take My Heart (with Duke Reid All Stars)	12
63	Island WI 113	Senor And Senorita/DON DRUMMOND: Snowboy	18
64	Island WI 141	Oh Oh I Need You/DON DRUMMOND: J.F.K.'s Memory	18
64	Island WI 144	Tom, Dick And Harry/We Two, Happy People	18
64	Island WI 152	Yeah Yeah Baby/BABA BROOKS: Boat Ride	18
64	Island WI 160	Miss B/Thing Come To Those Who Wait	18
65	Black Swan WI 462	Hey Little Girl/CORNELL CAMBELL: Make Hay	18
66	Rio R 81	Give Me One More Chance/Fire In Cornfield	12
66	Doctor Bird DB 1050	Give Me The Right/Tonight	18
67	Doctor Bird DB 1084	Tell It To Me/Your Photograph	18
67	Doctor Bird DB 1087	Down The Trainlines/Sing And Pray	15
69	Escort ES 807	My Love/SWEET CONFUSION: Windsor Castle	6
69	Escort ES 811	Why Did You/Do You Remember	6

(see also Stranger Cole, Patsy)

STRANGERS (with Mike Shannon)

64	Philips BF 1335	One And One Is Two/Time And The River (as Strangers with Mike Shannon)	30
64	Philips BF 1378	Do You Or Don't You/What Can I Do	7

(see also Shadows)

STRANGERS

67	Pye 7N 17240	Look Out (Here Comes Tomorrow)/Mary Mary	15
67	Pye 7N 17351	You Didn't Have To Be So Nice/Daytime Turns To Night	6
68	Pye 7N 17585	I'm On An Island/Step Inside	6

STRANGEWAYS

78	Real ARE 2	Show Her You Care/You're On Your Own (p/s)	10
79	Real ARE 7	All The Sounds Of Fear/Wasting Time (p/s)	10

(see also Ada Wilson)

STRANGLERS

SINGLES

77	United Artists UP 36211	(Get A) Grip (On Yourself)/London Lady (paper p/s, later in card p/s)	5/4
77	United Artists UP 36248	Peaches/Go Buddy Go ('group' p/s with 'blackmail' lettering, withdrawn)	275
77	United Artists UP 36248	Peaches/Go Buddy Go ('peach' p/s)	6
77	United Artists UP 36277	Something Better Change/Straighten Out (p/s)	6
77	United Artists UP 36300	No More Heroes/In The Shadows (p/s, 'wreath' label)	5
79	United Artists STR 1	DON'T BRING HARRY (EP, 33rpm)	4
80	United Artists 12-BP 344	Bear Cage (Extended)/Shah Shah A Go Go (Extended) (12", p/s)	12
81	Liberty BP 383	Thrown Away/Top Secret (p/s)	5
81	Liberty BP 393	Just Like Nothing On Earth/Maninwhite (p/s)	7
83	Epic EPCA 11-2893	European Female/Savage Breast (picture disc)	5
84	Epic A 4738	Skin Deep/Here And There ('skin-feel' p/s, with 'Skin Deep' tattoo, 10,000 only)	6
84	Epic EPC GA 4921	No Mercy/In One Door//Hot Club (Riot Mix)/Head On The Line (double pack)	8
84	Epic WA 4921	No Mercy/In One Door (ear-shaped picture disc)	7
85	Epic EPC QTA 6045	Let Me Down Easy (Extended)/Achilles Heel/Place De Victories (Instrumental)/Vladimir Goes To Havana/The Aural Sculpture Manifesto (12", p/s with poster)	7
86	Epic 650 055-0	Nice In Nice/Since You Went Away (shaped picture disc)	6
86	Epic SOLAR P1	Always The Sun/Norman Normal (shaped picture disc)	5
86	Epic SOLAR D1	Always The Sun/Norman Normal//Nice In Nice/Since You Went Away (double pack, shrinkwrapped & stickered)	6
86	Epic HUGE P1	Big In America/Dry Day (shaped picture disc)	5
86	Epic HUGE D1	Big In America/Dry Day//Always The Sun/Norman Normal (double pack, shrinkwrapped & stickered)	5
87	Epic SHEIK P1	Shakin' Like A Leaf/Hit Man (shaped picture disc)	7
87	Epic SHEIK Q1	Shakin' Like A Leaf (Jelly Mix)/Hit Man/Was It You? (live) (12", p/s with poster)	7
88	Epic VICE 1	All Day And All Of The Night/¡Viva Vlad! ('Monica Couglan' p/s, withdrawn sold via fan club)	6
88	Epic VICE P1	All Day And All Of The Night/¡Viva Vlad! (shaped picture disc)	7
88	Epic VICE QT1	All Day And All Of The Night/¡Viva Vlad!/Who Wants The World (live) (12", p/s with poster)	7
88	Epic CDVICE 1	All Day And All Of The Night (Jeff Remix)/¡Viva Vlad!/Who Wants The World (live)/Strange Little Girl (live) (CD, card sleeve, 5,000 only)	10

STRANGLERS

89	Liberty EMR 84	Grip '89 — (Get A) Grip (On Yourself)/Waltzinblack (p/s, red vinyl with poster in gatefold PVC wallet, 5,000 only) 5
89	Liberty CDEM 84	Grip '89 (Gripping Stuff 12" Mix)/Grip '89 (Single Mix)/Waltzinblack/ Tomorrow Was The Hereafter (CD) 15
90	Epic TEARS Q1	96 Tears/Instead Of This (in embossed stickered tin) 5
90	Epic TEARS P1	96 Tears/Instead Of This/Poisonality (CD, picture disc) 7

FLEXIS & FREEBIES

77	United Artists FREE 3	Choosey Susie/Peasant In The Big Shitty (S.I.S. fan club reissue, black p/s with "Ello 'Elen" in run-off groove, later pressed with Liberty label) 5/4
77	United Artists FREE 4	Peaches (radio version)/Go Buddy Go (promo only, no p/s) 75
77	United Artists FREE 8	No More Heroes (1-sided radio edit, promo only) 40
79	United Artists UA STR 1 DJ	Don't Bring Harry/HUGH CORNWELL: Wired (45rpm, promo only) 20
80	Stranglers Info Service SIS 001	Tomorrow Was The Hereafter/Bring On The Nubiles (Cocktail Version) (fan club issue, originally without p/s; 2nd pressing with push-out centre & "Nubiles" on label) 5/4
80	Stranglers Info Service SIS 001	Tomorrow Was The Hereafter/Bring On The Nubiles (Cocktail Version) (fan club issue, 3rd pressing, solid centre, 1,000 with numbered p/s) 8
83	Epic/S.I.S. XPS 167	Aural Sculpture (reissue, 1-sided fan club issue) 4
91	Stranglers Info S. SIS 004	New Day Today (flexidisc with *Strangled* fan magazine, issue 32) 5

MISPRESSINGS

78	United Artists UP 36248	Peaches/Go Buddy Go (p/s, mispressing, B-side plays Buzzcocks' "Oh Shit") . . 30
78	United Artists UP 36379	Nice 'N' Sleazy/Shut Up (p/s, mispressing, B-side plays tracks by other artist) . . 30
81	Liberty BP 393	Just Like Nothing On Earth/Maninwhite (p/s, mispressing, plays A-side both sides) 20
82	United Artists BP 407	Golden Brown/Love 30 (B-side plays "Everybody Samba") 20

ALBUMS

77	United Artists UAG 30045	RATTUS NORVEGICUS (LP, 10,000 with 7" "Choosey Susie"/"Peasant In The Big Shitty" (live) [FREE 3, red p/s, "What Do You Expect ..." in run-off groove]) 15
78	United Artists UAK 30222	BLACK AND WHITE (LP, 75,000 with white vinyl 7" "Walk On By"/"Tits"/ "Mean To Me" [FREE 9, black die-cut sleeve & card insert], a few freebies mispressed on blue or beige vinyl) 25/10
79	United Artists UAG 30224	LIVE CERT X (LP, with inner sleeve) 10
79	United Artists UAG 30262	THE RAVEN (LP, 20,000 with 3-D cover & inner sleeve) 18
79	United Artists UAG 30262	THE RAVEN (LP, mispressing, 2nd side plays country & western [B-side matrix: UAK 30263]) 15
82	Liberty LBG 30353	THE COLLECTION '77-82 (LP, withdrawn 'dark' sleeve) 25
83	Epic EPC 25237	FELINE (LP, with bonus 1-sided 7" "Aural Sculpture" [XPS 167]) 12
83	Epic 40 25237	FELINE (cassette, initial copies with "Midnight Summer Dream" remix) 10
86	Epic EPC 26648	DREAMTIME (LP, picture disc) 12

(see also Jean Jacques Burnel [& Dave Greenfield], Celia & Mutations, Marriage Of Convenience, Fools Dance)

STRAPPS

76	Harvest HAR 5108	In Your Ear/Rita B (p/s) 7
76	Harvest SHSP 4055	STRAPPS (LP) 12
77	Harvest SHSP 4064	SECRET DAMAGE (LP, with inner sleeve) 12

(see also Episode Six, Gillan, Quatermass)

STRAPS

80	Donut DONUT 1	Just Can't Take Anymore/New Age (p/s) 6
82	Donut DONUT 3	Brixton/No Liquor (p/s) 8
83	Cyclops CYC 2	THE STRAPS ALBUM (LP) 15

(see also Public Image Ltd.)

STRATEGY

| 82 | Ebony EBON 7 | Technical Overflow/Astral Planes (p/s) . . . . 12 |

STRATE JACKET

| 70s | Wessex | You're A Hit (stamped plain sleeve) . . . . 6 |

STRATUS

| 85 | Steel Trax STEEL 31001 | THROWING SHAPES (LP) . . . . 18 |

(see also Grand Prix, Uriah Heep, Iron Maiden, Praying Mantis)

SYD STRAW

| 89 | Virgin America VUSCD 6 | Future 40's (String Of Pearls) (with Michael Stipe)/ Taken/Learning The Game (3" CD, card sleeve) . . . . 7 |

STRAWBERRY ALARM CLOCK

67	Pye International 7N 25436	Incense And Peppermints/The Birdman Of Alkatrash 15
68	Pye International 7N 25446	Tomorrow/Birds In My Tree 12
68	Pye International 7N 25456	Sit With The Guru/Pretty Song From Psych-Out 12
69	MCA MU 1080	Good Morning Starshine/Me And The Township 8
68	Pye Intl. N(S)PL 28106	INCENSE AND PEPPERMINTS (LP) 35

STRAWBERRY CHILDREN

| 67 | Liberty LBF 15012 | Love Years Coming/One Stands Here . . . . 12 |

(see also Jim Webb)

STRAWBERRY JAM

| 69 | Pye 7N 17711 | Per-Son-Al-Ly/This Is To A Girl . . . . 6 |

STRAWBERRY SWITCHBLADE

83	92 Happy Customers HAP 1	Trees And Flowers/Go Away (p/s) 10
83	92 Happy Cust. HAPT 1	Trees And Flowers/Go Away/Trees And Flowers (Just Music) (12", p/s) 10
85	Korova KOW 38TP	Since Yesterday/By The Sea/Sunday Mornings (12", picture disc) 8
85	Korova KOW 39	Let Her Go/Beautiful End (shaped picture disc) 7
85	Korova KOW 42	Jolene/Being Cold (strawberry-shaped picture disc) 8
85	Korova/Flexi FLX 388-1	Strawberry Switchblade LP sampler (clear vinyl square flexidisc sewn into gatefold booklet; cat. no. only visible in run-off groove) 6
85	Korova KODE 11	STRAWBERRY SWITCHBLADE (LP, with bonus 7" "Trees And Flowers", initially mispressed with some tracks playing twice & others out of order) . . . 15/10

(see also Poems, Rose McDowall)

STRAWBS

68	A&M AMS 725	Oh How She Changed/Or Am I Dreaming	7
68	A&M AMS 738	The Man Who Called Himself Jesus/Poor Jimmy Wilson	8
70	A&M AMS 791	Forever/Another Day	8
71	A&M AMS 837	Witchwood/Keep The Devil Outside/We'll Meet Again Sometime (live) (withdrawn)	10
71	A&M AMS 874	Benedictus/Keep The Devil Outside	6
72	A&M AMS 7002	Here It Comes/Tomorrow	5
73	A&M AMS 7047	Part Of The Union/Will You Go (p/s)	5
76	Polydor 2066 751	So Close And Yet So Far Away/The Soldier's Tale	5
78	Arista ARIST 183	I Don't Want To Talk About It/Last Resort	5
80	L.O. LO 1	The King/Ringing Down The Years (with Maddy Prior, title sleeve)	10
91	Strawbs Fan Club	Might As Well Be On Mars/The King (fan club cassette)	5
69	private pressing	STRAWBERRY MUSIC SAMPLER NO. 1 (LP, publisher's sampler, 100 only)	500
69	A&M AMLS 936	STRAWBS (LP; disc inserted in middle or at edge of sleeve)	25/15
70	A&M AMLS 970	DRAGONFLY (LP, with lyric insert, mustard label)	20
70	A&M AMLS 994	JUST A COLLECTION OF ANTIQUES AND CURIOS (LP, gatefold sleeve, mustard label; 2 different rear sleeves)	20
71	A&M AMLH 64304	FROM THE WITCHWOOD (LP, gatefold sleeve)	15
72	A&M AMLH 68078	GRAVE NEW WORLD (LP, triple gatefold sleeve, with 12-page booklet)	15
73	A&M AMLH 68144	BURSTING AT THE SEAMS (LP, with inner sleeve)	12
73	Hallmark SHM 813	ALL OUR OWN WORK (LP, with Sandy Denny)	15
74	A&M AMLS 63607	HERO AND HEROINE (LP, with inner sleeve)	12
74	A&M AMLH 68259	BY CHOICE (LP, gatefold sleeve)	12
75	A&M AMLH 68277	GHOSTS (LP, with inner sleeve)	12
76	A&M AMLH 68331	NOMADNESS (LP, with lyric insert)	12
76	Oyster 2391 234	DEEP CUTS (LP, with lyric insert)	12
77	Oyster 2391 287	BURNING FOR YOU (LP, with inner sleeve)	12

(see also Dave Cousins, Sandy Denny, Fire, Foggy, Monks, Davey & Morris, Hudson-Ford)

STRAWHEAD

70s	Tradition TSR 032	FORTUNES OF WAR (LP)	10

STRAY

72	Big T BIG 141	Our Song/Mama's Coming Home	5
70	Transatlantic TRA 216	STRAY (LP, die-cut sleeve)	25
71	Transatlantic TRA 233	SUICIDE (LP)	20
72	Transatlantic TRA 248	SATURDAY MORNING PICTURES (LP, gatefold sleeve)	15
73	Transatlantic TRA 268	MUDANZAS (LP, gatefold sleeve)	15
74	Transatlantic TRA 281	MOVE IT (LP, die-cut sleeve with inner)	12
75	Transatlantic TRA 3066	TRACKS (LP)	12
75	Dawn DNLS 3066	STAND UP AND BE COUNTED (LP)	12
76	Pye NSPL 18482	HOUDINI (LP)	12
76	Pye NSPL 18512	HEARTS OF FIRE (LP)	12

STRAY CATS

81	Arista CSCAT 2	Rock This Town/Can't Hurry Love (cassette, flip-top case)	6
81	Arista SCAT 4	You Don't Believe Me/Cross That Bridge (p/s)	4
81	Arista SCAT 5	Little Miss Prissy/Sweet Love On My Mind (live)/Something Else (live) (p/s)	7
83	Arista SCAT 123	Stray Cat Strut/Built For Speed/Sweet Love On My Mind (live)/Drink That Bottle Down (live) (12", p/s, reissue)	8
83	Arista SCAPD 6	(She's Sexy) And 17/Lookin' Better Every Beer (shaped picture disc)	10
83	Arista SCAT 126	(She's Sexy) And 17/Lookin' Better Every Beer/Cruisin'/Lucky Charm (12", p/s)	8
83	Arista SCAT 7	Rebels Rule/Lookin' Through My Back Door (p/s, with stickers)	6
83	Arista SCAT 127	Rebels Rule/Lookin' Through My Back Door/Look At That Cadillac (12", p/s)	8
89	EMI USA MT 62	Bring It Back Again/Runaway Boys (live) (p/s)	4
89	EMI USA MTS 62	Bring It Back Again/Runaway Boys (live) (p/s, with 3 postcards)	5
89	EMI USA CDMT 62	Bring It Back Again/Runaway Boys (live)/I Fought The Law (CD)	7
89	EMI USA 12MTP 67	Gina/Two Of A Kind (p/s)	4
89	EMI USA 12MTP 67	Gina/Two Of A Kind/Stray Cat Strut (Live Version) (12", poster p/s)	8
89	EMI USA CDMT 67	Gina/Two Of A Kind/Stray Cat Strut (Live Version) (CD)	7
92	Pump 907 047-0	Elvis On Velvet (Radio Edit)/Lust'n'Love (p/s)	4
92	Pump 907 047-2	Elvis On Velvet (Radio Edit)/Lust'n'Love/Elvis On Velvet (Album Version) (CD)	7

STRAY DOG

74	Manticore K 43506	STRAY DOG (LP)	12
74	Manticore K 53504	WHILE YOU'RE DOWN THERE (LP)	12

(see also Emerson Lake & Palmer)

STREAK

73	Deram DM 376	Bang Bang Bullet/Black Jack Man	4

STREAMLINERS & JOANNE

61	Columbia DB 4689	Frankfurter Sandwiches/Pachalafaka	8
62	Columbia DB 4808	Everybody's Doin' The Twist/Do Something	8

(see also Rosemary Squires)

STREET

69	London HLU 10275	Apollo... Amen/Why Concern Yourself	4

DANNY STREET

65	Philips BF 1387	Don't Go To Him/As It's Meant To Be	5
60s	Domino DO 114	Melanie/Birds An' Bees An' Things	5
71	London HLU 10342	My Little Guy/You Blew It	6

GARY STREET & FAIRWAYS

68	Domain D 2	Flipperty Flop/Hold Me Closer	6

(see also Fairways)

HILLARD STREET

58	Capitol CL 14960	River Love/It Will Never Happen Again	6

JOHN STREET & INMATES OF NO. 12
| 67 | Deram DM 147 | Keep A Little Love/My Kind Of Luck | 6 |

JUDY STREET
| 78 | Grapevine GRP 106 | What/You Turn Me On | 5 |

STREETFIGHTER
| 82 | J.R. JR 7049S | CRAZY DREAM (EP) | 35 |

STREET LEGAL
| 84 | Weird Brothers SLW 1 | Rollin' On (p/s) | 60 |

STREET PEOPLE
| 70 | Stateside SS 2163 | Jennifer Tomkins/All Night Long | 4 |

STREETWALKERS
74	Reprise K 54017	STREETWALKERS (LP, with lyric sheet)	10
75	Vertigo 6360 123	DOWNTOWN FLIER (LP)	10
76	Vertigo 9102 010	RED CARD (LP, red vinyl with poster & lyric sheet, numbered)	12
77	Vertigo 9102 012	VICIOUS BUT FAIR (LP)	10

(see also Roger Chapman, Family)

BARBRA STREISAND
SINGLES
62	CBS AAG 130	My Colouring Book/Lover Come Back To Me	6
63	CBS AAG 179	Happy Days Are Here Again/Down With Love	6
64	CBS AAG 223	People/Draw Me A Circle	6
64	CBS AAG 233	Funny Girl/I Am A Woman	6
64	CBS 201543	People/I Am A Woman You Are Man (p/s)	12
65	CBS 201754	People/Funny Girl	6
65	CBS 201787	Why Did I Choose You/My Love	6
65	CBS 201998	Where Am I Going/You Wanna Bet	5
65	CBS 202001	Autumn/How Much Of The Dream Comes True	5
65	CBS 202025	Second Hand Rose/He Touched Me	5
66	CBS 202077	Sam, You Made The Pants Too Long/Where Am I Going	5
66	CBS 202387	Free Again/I've Been Here	5
66	CBS 202417	Sleep In Heavenly Peace (Silent Night)/Gounod's "Ave Maria" (p/s)	7
67	CBS 2989	Stout Hearted Men/Look	6
68	CBS 3863	Our Corner Of The Night/He Could Show Me	6
68	CBS 3705	Funny Girl/I'd Rather Be Blue Over You	6
69	CBS 3931	My Man/Don't Rain On My Parade	7
69	CBS 4497	Honey Pie/Little Tin Soldier	6
70	CBS 5321	Stoney End/I'll Be Home	6
71	CBS 7123	Time And Love/No Easy Way Down	5
71	CBS S 7396	Where You Lead/Since I Fell For You	5
71	CBS S 7584	Mother/The Summer Knows	5
72	CBS S 7687	Space Captain/One Less Bell To Answer/A House Is Not A Home	5
73	CBS 1149	People/Second Hand Rose (p/s, Hall Of Fame single)	5
73	CBS S CBS 1202	Didn't We/On A Clear Day	7
74	CBS S CBS 1915	The Way We Were/What Are You Doing	5
74	CBS S CBS 2394	All In Love Is Fair/Medley: My Buddy/How About Me	6
75	CBS S CBS 3613	My Father's Song/By The Way	5
76	CBS 3955	The Way We Were/People (p/s, Hall Of Fame single)	6
76	CBS S CBS 4027	Shake Me, Wake Me/Widescreen	5
77	CBS S CBS 5392	My Heart Belongs To Me/Answer Me	5
78	CBS S CBS 6169	Superman/Lullaby For Myself	5
78	CBS S CBS 6476	Love Breakdown/Honey Can I Put On Your Clothes	5
78	CBS S CBS 6657	Love Theme From "The Eyes Of Laura Mars" (Prisoner)/Laura & Neville (instrumental)	5
79	CBS S CBS 7073	Stoney End/I'll Be Home (reissue, Golden Decade series)	5
79	CBS S CBS 7286	Superman/A Man I Loved	5
79	CBS S CBS 7714	The Main Event/Fight/Instrumental	5
79	CBS 12 7714	The Main Event/Fight/Instrumental (12" picture label)	10
79	Casablanca CAN 174	No More Tears (with Donna Summer)/Donna Summer: "My Baby Understands"	5
79	Casablanca CAN 174	No More Tears (with Donna Summer)/Donna Summer: "Lucky"	4
79	CBS 13 8000	No More Tears (with Donna Summer)/Wet (12", p/s)	7
81	CBS S CBS 9517	What Kind Of Fool/Make It Like A Memory (with Barry Gibb)	4
81	CBS A 1203	Promises/Never Give Up	4
81	CBS A 1660	The Love Inside/Never Give Up (p/s)	4
82	CBS A 1789	Comin' In And Out Of Your Life/Lost Inside Of You (p/s)	5
83	CBS BARB 1	Memory/Evergreen (p/s reissue)	5
83	CBS A 3888	The Way He Makes Me Feel (Studio Version)/The Way He Makes Me Feel (Film Version) (p/s)	4
83	CBS A 4125	No Matter What Happens (Studio Version)/No Matter What Happens (Original Soundtrack Version) (p/s)	5
84	CBS A 4754	Left In The Dark/Here We Are At Last (p/s)	4
84	CBS TA 4754	Left In The Dark/Here We Are At Last/Woman In Love/Guilty Memory (12", p/s, withdrawn)	50
85	CBS A 4994	Make No Mistake, He's Mine (with Kim Carnes)/Clear Sailing (p/s)	4
85	CBS A 4994	Make No Mistake, He's Mine (with Kim Carnes)/Clear Sailing//Memory/Evergreen (p/s, shrinkwrapped double pack)	8
85	CBS A 6707	Somewhere/Not While I'm Around (p/s)	4
86	CBS A 6988	Send In The Clowns/Being Alive/	4
86	CBS DA 6988	Send In The Clowns/Being Alive//Somewhere/Not While I'm Around (p/s, shrinkwrapped double pack)	10
88	CBS CD BARB 2	Till I Loved You (Love Theme From Goya) (Album Version) (with Don Johnson)/Guilty (with Barry Gibb)/Left In The Dark/Two People (CD, card p/s)	8
89	CBS BARB 3	All I Ask Of You/On My Way To You (p/s)	5

89	CBS CD BARB 3	All I Ask Of You (from "The Phantom Of The Opera")/On My Way To You/ Life Story/Emotion (CD, card sleeve)	8
89	CBS CP BARB 3	All I Ask Of You (from "The Phantom Of The Opera")/Somewhere/ Memory/Send In The Clowns (CD, picture disc, 2,000 only)	20
89	CBS BARB QT 3	All I Ask Of You/On My Way To You/Make No Mistake, He's Mine (with Kim Carnes)/Since I Fell For You (12", p/s with poster, 3,000 only)	12
89	CBS BARBQT 4	We're Not Makin' Love Anymore/Wet/No More Tears (Enough Is Enough) (12", p/s)	7
89	CBS BARB 4	We're Not Makin' Love Anymore (7" Version)/Till I Loved You (with Don Johnson)/ Kiss Me In The Rain/The Places You Find Love (CD, card sleeve)	8
89	CBS BARB C4	We're Not Makin' Love Anymore/Wet/No More Tears (Enough Is Enough) (with Donna Summer) (CD, picture disc)	12
92	Columbia 657794 7	Places That Belong To You/For All We Know (p/s)	4
92	Columbia 657794 9	Places That Belong To You/Warm All Over/I Know Him So Well/ You'll Never Know (CD, picture disc)	15
93	Columbia 659342 7	With One Look/Memory (p/s)	4
94	Columbia 659738 2	The Music Of The Night/Children Will Listen/Move On (CD)	8
94	Columbia 660357 7	As If We Never Said Goodbye/Guilty (with Barry Gibb) (p/s)	4

EPs

63	CBS AGG 320042	LOVER COME BACK TO ME (EP)	15
63	CBS AGG 320054	BARBRA STREISAND (EP)	10
64	CBS EP 6048	EN FRANÇAIS (EP)	12
65	CBS EP 6068	MY MAN (EP)	12
66	CBS EP 6150	SECOND HAND ROSE (EP)	10

LPs

64	Capitol (S)W 2059	FUNNY GIRL (LP, original cast recording, mono/stereo)	12
66	CBS (S)BPG 62784	HAROLD SINGS ARLEN (WITH FRIEND) (LP, mono/stereo)	12
66	Hallmark SHM 871	PEOPLE (LP)	12
68	CBS S 70044	FUNNY GIRL (LP, soundtrack, gatefold sleeve)	12
69	EMI Stateside SSL 10292	HELLO, DOLLY! (LP, gatefold sleeve)	12
70	CBS 70075	ON A CLEAR DAY YOU CAN SEE FOREVER (LP, with Yves Montand, gatefold sleeve)	15
71	CBS 70081	THE OWL AND THE PUSSYCAT (LP, gatefold sleeve)	15
71	CBS CQ 30378	STONEY END (LP, quadrophonic)	15
71	CBS 64459	BARBRA JOAN STREISAND (LP, gatefold stickered sleeve & poster)	12
71	CBS CQ 30792	BARBRA JOAN STREISAND (LP, quadrophonic)	15
73	CBS SQ 30992	FUNNY GIRL (LP, soundtrack, quadrophonic)	15
73	CBS CQ 31760	LIVE CONCERT AT THE FORUM (LP, quadrophonic)	15
74	CBS 69079	BUTTERFLY (LP, gatefold sleeve)	12
75	Arista ARTY 101	FUNNY LADY (LP, soundtrack, gatefold sleeve)	15
77	CBS 66349	BARBRA STREISAND DELUXE BOX SET ("Greatest Hits Volume 1"/ "Stoney End"/"Streisand Superman")	25
78	CBS 70163	EYES OF LAURA MARS (LP, soundtrack)	12
79	CBS 66349	BARBRA STREISAND: 3-RECORD BOX SET ("Greatest Hits Volume 1", "Volume 2" & "Wet")	25
83	CBS Cameo 32265	I CAN GET IT FOR YOU WHOLESALE (LP, original cast recording)	12
88	CBS 651379 6	NUTS (LP, soundtrack)	15
88	CBS 462943 1	TILL I LOVED YOU (LP)	12
91	Columbia 468734 2	JUST FOR THE RECORD (4-CD box set with 92-page booklet)	50
94	Columbia 4775 992	BARBRA — THE CONCERT (2-CD)	20
94	Columbia XPCD 147	THE EVENT OF THE DECADE, A RETROSPECTIVE (2-CD, promo only)	200

'TEXAS' BILL STRENGTH

| 55 | Capitol CL 14357 | Cry, Cry, Cry/The Yellow Rose Of Texas | 15 |
| 55 | Capitol CL 14357 | Cry, Cry, Cry/The Yellow Rose Of Texas (78) | 8 |

STRETCH

75	Anchor ANC 1021	Why Did You Do It/Write Me A Note	5
75	Anchor ANC 1027	That's The Way The Wind Blows/Hold On	5
75	Anchor ANC 1034	Love's Got A Hold On Me/If The Cap Fits	5
78	Hot Wax WAX 2	Forget The Past/Fooling Me	5
75	Anchor ANCL 2014	ELASTIQUE (LP)	15
76	Anchor ANCL 2016	YOU CAN'T BEAT YOUR BRAIN FOR ENTERTAINMENT (LP)	12
77	Anchor ANCL 2023	LIFE BLOOD (LP)	18
78	Hot Wax HW 1	FORGET THE PAST (LP)	25

(see also Elmer Gantry, Kirby, Status Quo, Clifford Davis, Legs)

STRETCHHEADS

| 88 | Moksha SOMA 5 | BROS ARE PISH (EP, stamped brown sleeve with insert) | 5 |

WILLIAM R. STRICKLAND

| 69 | Deram DML/SML 1041 | WILLIAM R. STRICKLAND IS ONLY THE NAME (LP) | 15 |

PETE STRIDE & JOHN PLAIN

| 80 | Beggars Banquet BEGA 17 | NEW GUITARS IN TOWN (LP, with inner sleeve) | 10 |

(see also Lurkers)

STRIDER

73	GM GMS 002	Higher And Higher/Ain't Got No Love	5
74	GM GMS 023	Seems So Easy/Arthur Hydrogen	5
73	GM GML 1002	EXPOSED (LP)	18
74	GM GML 1012	MISUNDERSTANDING (LP)	15

(see also Samson)

STRIFE

| 77 | Outlaw OUT 1 | School/Go/Feel So Good (p/s) | 4 |

LIZA STRIKE

| 68 | Parlophone R 5725 | All's Quiet On West 23rd/Mr Daddy-Man | 6 |

(see also Liza & Jet Set, Soulmates, Vice Versa)

STRING-A-LONGS

MINT VALUE £

61	London HLU 9278	Wheels/Am I Asking Too Much	6
61	London HLU 9354	Panic Button/Brass Buttons	7
61	London HLU 9394	Should I/Take A Minute	6
61	London HLU 9452	Scottie/Ming Bird	10
62	London HLD 9535	Sunday/Twistwatch	10
62	London HLD 9588	Spinning My Wheels/My Blue Heaven	10
63	London HLD 9652	Mathilda/Replica	10
61	London RE-U 1322	THE STRING-A-LONGS (EP)	40
63	London RE-D 1350	THE STRING-A-LONGS (EP)	40
63	London RE-D 1398	STRINGALONG WITH THE STRING-A-LONGS (EP)	35
63	London HA-D/SH-D 8054	THE STRING-A-LONGS (LP, mono/stereo)	40/45
69	London HAU/SHU 8371	WIDE WORLD HITS (LP)	30

STRING CHEESE

72	RCA SF 8222	STRING CHEESE (LP)	20

STRING DRIVEN THING

70	Concord CON 7	Another Night/Say What You Like	15
72	Charisma CB 195	Eddie/Hooked On The Road	5
70	Concord CON 1001	STRING DRIVEN THING (LP)	125
72	Charisma CAS 1062	STRING DRIVEN THING (LP, pink label)	20
73	Charisma CAS 1070	THE MACHINE THAT CRIED (LP, pink label, gatefold sleeve)	15
74	Charisma CAS 1097	PLEASE MIND YOUR HEAD (LP, with lyric sheet)	12
76	Charisma CAS 1112	KEEP YOUR 'AND ON IT (LP)	12

STRIPES OF GLORY

62	Vogue V 9194	The Denial/O' Send The Fire	15

SYLVIA STRIPLIN

80s	Streetwave	Give Me Your Love/Give Me Your Love (Version) (12")	10

STROLLERS

58	Vogue V 9113	Jumping With Symphony Sid/Swinging Yellow Rose Of Texas	35
58	Vogue V 9113	Jumping With Symphony Sid/Swinging Yellow Rose Of Texas (78)	20
58	Vogue V 9124	Little Bitty Pretty One/Flute Cha-Lypso	35
58	Vogue V 9124	Little Bitty Pretty One/Flute Cha-Lypso (78)	40

STROLLERS

61	London HLL 9336	Come On Over/There's No One But You	15

STROLLERS

65	Fontana TF 598	Cuckoo/Rich And Rambling Boy	5
	(see also David & Toni Arthur)		

BARRETT STRONG

60	London HLU 9088	Money (That's What I Want)/Oh I Apologise	150
76	Capitol CL 15864	Man Up In The Sky/Gonna Make It Right	6

CHAD STUART & JEREMY CLYDE

(see under Chad & Jeremy)

GLEN STUART

60s	Honey Hit TB 126	Make Me An Angel/Walking To Heaven (some with p/s)	10/6
62	Melodisc MEL 1581	Make Me An Angel/Walking To Heaven	6

GLEN STUART & CLANSMEN

59	Pye 7N 15232	Weepy Willow/Della Darling	5
59	Pye N 15232	Weepy Willow/Della Darling (78)	8

KARL STUART & PROFILES

65	Mercury MF 870	Love Of My Eyes/Not A Girl In A Million	6
65	Mercury MF 875	Haven't They Got Better Things To Do/The Touch Of Your Hand	6
	(see also Profile, Voice)		

MIKE STUART SPAN

(see under 'M')

NAT STUCKEY

67	Pye International 7N 25403	Sweet Thang/Paralyze My Mind	6
69	RCA RCA 1833	Loving You/Joe And Mabel's 12th Street Bar And Grill	5
69	RCA RCA 1890	Cut Across Shorty/Understand, Little Man	5

STUD

70	Deram SML-R 1084	STUD (LP)	40
	(see also Taste, Family, Blossom Toes, Eric Burdon & Animals)		

STUDIO G's

70	LPSG 100	BETA GROUP (LP, library edition)	100
96	Tenth Planet TP 023	BEAT GROUP (LP, 600 only)	15

STUDIO ONE ALLSTARS

67	Island WI 3038	Sherry (actually by Bumps Oakley)/Out Of My Mind (actually by Soul Junior)	18

STUDIO SIX

66	Polydor 56131	When I See My Baby/Don't Tell Lies	6
67	Polydor 56162	Bless My Soul (I've Been And Gone And Done It)/People Say	6
67	Polydor 56189	Times Were When/I Can't Sleep	6
67	Polydor 56219	Strawberry Window/Falling Leaves	20
69	Polydor 56361	Bless My Soul/People Say	5

STUDIO SWEETHEARTS

79	DJM DJS 10915	I Believe/It Isn't Me (p/s)	10
	(see also Cult, Slaughter & Dogs)		

STUKAS

77	Sonet SON 2134	I Like Sport/I'll Send You A Postcard/Dead Lazy (p/s)	6

STUMP
86	Ron Johnson ZRON 6	MUD ON A COLON (12" EP)	8
88	Ensign CHEN 9	A FIERCE PANCAKE (LP, with inner lyric sleeve)	12

STUPIDS
85	Children Of Rev. COR 3	VIOLENT NUN (EP, some mispressed)	15

STYLE COUNCIL
83	Polydor TSCX 2	Money-Go-Round/Money-Go-Round (Dance Mix) (12", white label, promo)	8
85	Polydor TSDJ 8	Walls Come Tumbling Down! (censored)/The Whole Point II/Blood Sports (12", no p/s, promo only)	8
85	Polydor TSCG 9	Come To Milton Keynes/(When You) Call Me (alternate gatefold p/s)	4
85	Polydor TSC DP 10	The Lodgers (re-recorded)/You're The Best Thing (live)/Big Boss Groove (live)// You're The Best Thing/Long Hot Summer (stickered, shrinkwrapped dble pack)	5
86	Polydor CINE 1/CINEC 1	Have You Ever Had It Blue/Mr. Cool's Dream//Have You Ever Had It Blue/ Uncut Version/With Everything To Lose (live in London) (p/s, with free cassette & insert in printed PVC sleeve)	6
87	Polydor TSCCD 14	Wanted/Cost Of Loving (Instrumental)/Cost Of Loving (Vocal) (CD, card p/s)	10
87	Polydor TSCCD 101	CAFE BLUE (CD EP, card sleeve)	10
87	Polydor TSCEP 2	THE BIRDS & THE B's (EP, p/s)	4
87	Polydor TSCCD 102	THE BIRDS & THE B's (CD EP, card sleeve)	10
87	Polydor TSCEP 3	MICK TALBOT IS AGENT '88 (EP, p/s)	4
87	Polydor TSCCD 103	MICK TALBOT IS AGENT '88 (CD EP, card sleeve)	8
88	Polydor TSCCD 15	Life At A Top People's Health Farm (7" Version)/Spank! (Life At A Top People's Health Club)/Sweet Loving Ways/Life At A Top People's Health Farm (Um & Argh Mix) (CD, card sleeve)	10
88	Polydor TSCCD 16	1-2-3-4 EP: How She Threw It All Away/Love The First Time/ Long Hot Summer (Tom Mix)/I Do Like To Be B-Side The A-Side (CD)	8
88	Polydor 080 400-2	1-2-3-4 EP: How She Threw It All Away/Love The First Time/ Long Hot Summer (Tom Mix)/How She Threw It All Away (Video) (CD Video)	15
88	Polydor 080 336-2	Have You Ever Had It Blue (Uncut Version)/Mr. Cool's Dream/With Everything To Lose (live in London)/Have You Ever Had It Blue (Video) (CD Video)	15
88	Polydor 080 206-2	Long Hot Summer (Extended Version)/Party Chambers/The Paris Match/ Le Depart/Long Hot Summer (Video) (CD Video)	15
88	Polydor 080 560-2	Life At A Top People's Health Farm (Extended Remix)/Spank! (Life At A Top People's Health Club)/Sweet Loving Ways/Life At A Top People's Health Farm (7" Version) (Video) (CD Video)	15
89	Polydor TSCB 17	Promised Land (Juan Atkins Mix)/Can You Still Love Me (stickered box set, with numbered 7" & poster)	5
89	Polydor TSC XS 17	Promised Land (Joe Smooth's Alternate Club Mix)/Can You Still Love Me (Club Vocal)/Can You Still Love Me (12 O'clock Dub) (12", orange p/s)	7
89	Polydor TSCCD 17	The Promised Land (Longer Version Juan Atkins Mix)/(Pianopella)/ Can You Still Love Me? (Dub)/(Vocal) (CD)	8
89	Polydor TSCD 17	The Promised Land (Radio Edit)/The Promised Land (Longer Version)/ Can You Still Love Me? (Vocal)/Can You Still Love Me? (Dub) (CD)	10
89	Polydor LHSCD 1	Long Hot Summer '89 Mix/Everybody's On The Run (Version One)/ Everybody's On The Run (Version Two) (CD)	10
84	Lyntone LYN 15344/45	It Just Came To Pieces In My Hands (Coventry)/Speak Like A Child (London) (33rpm fan club flexidisc)	12
87	Polydor COST 2	Angel/Heaven's Above (12", no p/s, promo only)	10
87	Polydor TSCLP 4	THE COST OF LOVING (LP, single disc)	10
87	Polydor 831 443-2	THE COST OF LOVING (CD)	15
88	Polydor TSCIN 1	INTERVIEW WITH THE STYLE COUNCIL (LP, promo only)	15
98	Polydor TSCLP 6 (/2)	MODERNISM: A NEW DECADE (LP or 2 x 12", both in p/s, promo only)	each 60

(see also Council Collective, Paul Weller, Jam, Merton Parkas, Slam Slam, King Truman)

STYLISTICS
72	Avco/Embassy 6105 015	I'm Stone In Love With You/The Point Of No Return	5

STYLOS
64	Liberty LBS 10173	Head Over Heels/Bye Bye, Baby, Bye Bye	75

POLY STYRENE
80	United Artists BP 370	Talk In Toytown/Sub Tropical (p/s)	5
86	Awesome AOR 7	Trick Of The Witch/Paramatma (p/s)	4
86	Awesome AOR 7T	GODS AND GODDESSES (12" EP)	7
80	United Artists UAG 30320	TRANSLUCENCE (LP, with lyric inner)	10

(see also X-Ray Spex, Mari Elliott)

STYX
75	RCA RCA 2518	Lady/Children Of The Land	4
78	A&M AMS 7388	Blue Collar Man/Superstars (12", coloured vinyl)	6
79	A&M AMS 7446	Renegade/Sing For The Day (p/s, red vinyl)	4
81	A&M AMS 8102	The Best Of Times/Light (p/s, laser etched)	4
81	A&M AMS 8118	Too Much Time On My Hands/Queen Of Spades (p/s, coloured vinyl)	4
83	A&M AM 120	Don't Let It End/Rockin' The Paradise (shaped picture disc)	5
78	A&M AMLH 64724	PIECES OF EIGHT (LP, translucent vinyl)	10

SUBHUMANS
81	Spiderleg SDL 3	Religious Wars/Love Is.../Work Experience/It's Gonna Get Worse (p/s)	5

SUBMARINER
93	Spacewatch FLX 2107	Lyricist Downer/Seeming And The Meaning (demo)/STEREOLAB: Ronco Symphony (demo) (clear vinyl flexi with paper strip insert)	15

SUBMARINES
87	Head HEAD 4	Grey Skies Blue/I Saw The Children (p/s)	6

SUBS
78	Stiff OFF 1	Gimme Your Heart/Party Clothes (p/s)	5

(see also Larry Wallis)

SUBSTITUTE
79	Ignition IR 2	The One/Look Sharp (some in p/s)	15/7

(see also Vibrators)

SUBTERRANEANS
87	Mother MUM 6	Slum/Maxi Joy (p/s)	4
87	Mother 12MUM 6	Slum/Maxi Joy/Head For The Light (12", p/s)	7

SUBURBAN STUDS
77	Pogo POG 001/LYN 44845	No Faith/Questions (p/s, 'with horns' version, withdrawn)	15
77	Pogo POG 001/LYN 44845	No Faith/Questions (p/s)	6
78	Pogo POG 002	I Hate School/Young Power (p/s)	6
78	Pogo POW 001	SLAM (LP)	15

SUBWAY SECT
78	Braik BRS 01	Nobody's Scared/Don't Split It (p/s)	12
79	Rough Trade RT 007	Ambition/A Different Story (initially in yellow p/s, later orange)	7/6

(see also Vic Godard [& Subway Sect])

NIKKI SUDDEN
81	Rather GEAR 11	Back To The Start/Ringing On My Train (p/s)	5
82	Abstract ABS 009	Channel Steamer/Chelsea Embankment (p/s)	4
80s	Rather RATHER 10	BEAU GESTE (cassette, with insert)	12
85	Hotwire HWLP 8504	THE LAST BANDITS IN THE WORLD (LP)	10

(see also Swell Maps, Last Bandits, Jeremy Gluck)

(A) SUDDEN SWAY
80	Chant CHANT 1	Jane's Third Party/Don't Go (p/s, as A Sudden Sway)	15
80	own label	Jane's Third Party/Don't Go (cassette, as A Sudden Sway)	8
81	Chant CHANT 2/EJSP 9692	TO YOU, WITH REGARD (12" EP, with insert)	10
84	Chant CHANT 3	The Traffic Tax Scheme (12" with badge & inserts in folder)	12
86	WEA BYN 8B	Spacemate (2 x 12" box set with stickers, info sheets, 2 booklets & poster)	12
87	Strange Fruit SFPSC 005	PEEL SESSION 16.11.83 (EP, cassette)	5

SUE & MARY
62	Decca F 11517	Traitor In Disguise/I Love You	5

SUE & SUNNY
65	Columbia DB 7748	Every Ounce Of Strength/So Remember	7
67	Columbia DB 8099	You Can't By-Pass Love/I Like Your Style	8
68	CBS 3874	Little Black Book/The Show Must Go On	8
68	Island WIP 6043	Set Me Free/NIRVANA ORCHESTRA: City Of The South	8
69	CBS 4567	Let Us Break Bread/Stop Messing About With My Heart	6
70	CBS 4757	You Devil, Cotton-Eyed Joe/Night In The City	6
70	Deram DM 318	Ain't That Telling You People/Didn't I Blow Your Mind	5
71	Deram DM 328	Freedom/Break Up	5
71	Reflection HRS 10	Let Us Break Bread Together/Michael From Mountains	5
72	Deram DM 355	I'm Gonna Make You Love Me/High On The Thought Of You	5
70	CBS 63740	SUE AND SUNNY (LP)	15
70	Reflection REFL 4	SUE AND SUNNY (LP)	25

(see also Sue & Sunshine, Myrtelles, Stockingtops, Brotherhood Of Man)

SUE & SUNSHINE
64	Columbia DB 7409	A Little Love/If You See Me Crying	7
65	Columbia DB 7533	We're In Love/Don't Look Behind	6

(see also Sue & Sunny, Myrtelles, Stockingtops)

SUEDE
91	RML RML 001	Be My God/Art (12", unissued, 50 white label copies only, no p/s; later counterfeited with off-white labels)	125/20
92	Nude NUD 1S	The Drowners (Radio Edit)/To The Birds (p/s)	15
92	Nude NUD 1CD	The Drowners (Radio Edit)/To The Birds/My Insatiable One (CD, promo only)	15
93	Nude SUEDE 1	My Insatiable One (clear flexidisc, fan club/gig freebie)	10
94	Nude NUD 11CD 2	The Wild Ones/Eno's Introducing The Band/Asda Town (CD)	15
95	Nude NUD 12CD 2	New Generation/Animal Nitrate (live)/The Wild Ones (live)/Pantomime Horse (live) (CD, digipak)	15
96	Nude NUD 21S	Trash/Europe Is Our Playground (p/s, mail order only)	12
93	Nude NUDE 1LP	SUEDE (LP, with inner sleeve & carrier bag from Chain With No Name stores)	15
99	Nude INT 1 CD	HEAD MUSING (CD, 2-track interview, promo only)	40

(see also Elastica)

SUGAR (Simone) & DANDY (Livingstone)
63	Carnival CV 7006	One Man Went To Mow/Cryin'	6
64	Carnival CV 7009	Oh Dear What Can The Matter Be/Tra La La	6
64	Carnival CV 7015	What A Life/Time And Tide	6
64	Carnival CV 7016	I'm Not Crying Now/Blues Got A Hold On Me	6
65	Carnival CV 7023	Let's Ska/Only Heaven Knows	6
65	Carnival CV 7024	I'm Into Something Good/Crazy For You	6
65	Carnival CV 7027	Think Of The Good Times/Girl Come See	6
65	Carnival CV 7029	I Want To Be Your Lover/I Don't Know What I'm Going To Do Now	6
66	Blue Beat BB 367	Meditation (as Jetliners)/GIRL SATCHMO & JET LINERS: Nature Of Love	8
67	Page One POF 044	Let's Ska/Only Heaven Knows	5
64	Carnival CX 1000	THE SKA'S THE LIMIT (LP)	25
67	Page One FOR 006	THE SKA'S THE LIMIT (LP, reissue)	12

(see also Sugar Simone)

SUGAR & PEE WEE
58	Vogue Pop V 9112	One, Two, Let's Rock/Just A Few Little Words	550
58	Vogue Pop V 9112	One, Two, Let's Rock/Just A Few Little Words (78)	150

SUEDE

SUGAR & SPICE
69	London HLU 10259	Cruel War/Not To Return	6

SUGARBEATS
66	Polydor BM 56069	I Just Stand Here/The Ballad Of Ole Betsy	6
66	Polydor BM 56120	Alice Designs/Sunny Day Girl	6

SUGARCUBES
87	One Little Indian 7 TP 7	Birthday/Birthday (Icelandic) (p/s)..................................	6
87	One Little Indian 12 TP 7	Birthday/Birthday (Icelandic)/Cat (Icelandic) (12", p/s)...............	8
87	One Little Indian 7TP 7CD	Birthday/Motorcrash/Cat (Icelandic)/Birthday (Icelandic) (CD).........	10
87	One Little Indian L12 TP 9	Cold Sweat (Remix)/Birthday (Original Demo Version)/	
		Dragon (Icelandic)/Traitor (Icelandic) (12", p/s, 5,000 only)	8
87	One Little Indian 7TP 9CD	Cold Sweat/Dragon (Icelandic)/Traitor (Icelandic)/Revolution (CD)	8
88	One Little Indian 10 TP 10	Deus (Remix)/Luftgitar (Icelandic) (with Johnny Triumph)/	
		Organic Prankster (10", p/s)	6
88	One Little Indian 7TP 10CD	Deus/Organic Prankster/Luftgitar (12" Version)/Night Of Steel (CD)	7
88	One Little Indian 12TP 11L	BIRTHDAY CHRISTMAS MIX (12" EP, double groove, with Jesus & Mary Chain) ..	7
88	One L. Indian 12TP 11CDL	BIRTHDAY CHRISTMAS MIX (CD EP, with Jesus & Mary Chain)	7
89	House Of Dolls HOD 010	Dark Disco/HOST: Homelands/MURRUMBRIDGE WHALERS: Giving Away To	
		Trains/SHARK TABOO: Tinsel Town (live) (no p/s, with *House Of Dolls* mag)....	6/4
90	One Little Indian TP BOX 2	7.8 (8 x 7" box set)...	25
90	One Little Indian TP BOX 1	12.11 (11 x 12" box set)	40
90	One Little Indian TP BOX 3	CD.6 (6 x CD box set)...	45
88	One Little Indian DTPLP 5	LIFE'S TOO GOOD (DAT)	20
89	One Little Indian TPLP 15SP	HERE TODAY, TOMORROW NEXT WEEK! (LP, gatefold sleeve with sticker, silver vinyl & inner)	15
89	One Little Indian TPLP 15L	SYKURMOLARNIR ILLUR ARFUR! (LP, as Sykurmolarnir, gatefold sleeve)	15
	(see also Björk, Kukl, Ornamental)		

SUGAR SHOPPE
68	Capitol CL 15555	Skip-A-Long Sam/Let The Truth Come Out	6

SUGARLOAF
70	Liberty LBF 15401	Green-Eyed Lady/West Of Tomorrow.................................	4
71	Liberty LBS 83415	SUGARLOAF (LP)...	15
74	United Artists UAS 29165	SPACESHIP EARTH (LP)	12
75	Polydor 2310 394	DON'T CALL US, WE'LL CALL YOU (LP, with Jerry Corbetto)	15

SUGARLUMPS
69	Jay Boy BOY 16	Sugar Sugar/Can't We Be Friends..................................	4
70	Jay Boy BOY 20	Satan's People/Shame	4

SUGARPLUMS
70	Fab FAB 160	Red River Reggae/Too Much	7

SUGGS
95	WEA YZ 975	I'm Only Sleeping/Off On Holiday (7", unreleased).....................	10
	(see also Madness)		

SUICIDAL TENDENCIES
87	Virgin VS 967-12	Possessed To Skate/Human Guinea Pig/Two Wrongs Don't Make A Right (12", picture disc)...	7

SUICIDE
77	Sound For Industry SFI 323	Johnny/(Real Kids track) (flexidisc via *Circuit* magazine)	8
78	Red Star/Bronze BRO 57	Cheree/I Remember (p/s)...	8

SUICIDE

MINT VALUE £

78	Red Star/Bronze 12 BRO 57	Cheree/I Remember (12", 'limited edition', p/s)	10
79	Island WIP 6543	Dream Baby Dream/Radiation (p/s)	6
79	Island 12 WIP 6543	Dream Baby Dream (Long Version)/Radiation (12", p/s)	10
86	Demon D 1046	Cheree/I Remember (promo only)	5
89	Chapter 22 12CHAP 42	SUICIDE (12", unissued)	
77	Red Star/Bronze BRON 508	SUICIDE (LP)	12
78	Red Star FRANKIE 1	24 MINUTES OVER BRUSSELS (LP, official bootleg, 1,000 only, no p/s)	30
80	Ze/Island ILPS 7007	SUICIDE: ALAN VEGA/MARTIN REV (LP, with printed inner sleeve)	10
98	Blast First BFFP 133 1/2	SUICIDE (2-LP)	15

(see also Alan Vega, Martin Rev)

SUICIDE TWINS
86	Lick LICLP 9	SILVER MISSILES AND NIGHTINGALES (LP)	12

(see also Hanoi Rocks)

BIG JIM SULLIVAN
61	Decca F 11387	You Don't Know What You've Got/Hot Hiss Of Steam (as Big Jim Sullivan Combo)	8
65	Mercury MF 928	She Walks Through The Fair/Don't Know What I'm Doing (as Jim Sullivan Sound)	20
73	MAM MAM 100	Out Of The Question/Alone Again	5
67	Mercury SML 30001	SITAR A GO-GO (LP)	25

(see also Maureeny Wishfull, Brian Bennett, Tiger)

MAXINE SULLIVAN
54	Parlophone MSP 6086	Boogie Woogie Maxine/Piper In The Glen (with Vic Ash)	8
54	Parlophone MSP 6086	Boogie Woogie Maxine/Piper In The Glen (78, with Vic Ash)	8

PHIL SULLIVAN with LONZO & OSCAR'S PEAPICKERS
59	Melodisc MEL 1512	Love Never Dies/Luckiest Man In Town	4

YMA SUMAC
52	Capitol CL 13746	Suray Surita/Zana (78)	10
52	Capitol CL 13766	Wimoweh/Babalu (78)	10
54	Capitol CL 14094	Ripui (Farewell)/Llulla Mak'ta (Andean Don Juan) (78)	10
55	Capitol EAP1 564	YMA SUMAC MAMBO (EP)	30
55	Capitol EAP2 564	YMA SUMAC MAMBO (EP)	30
57	Capitol EAP1 770	LEGEND OF JIVARO PT. 1 (EP)	30
57	Capitol EAP2 770	LEGEND OF JIVARO PT. 2 (EP)	30
57	Capitol EAP3 770	LEGEND OF JIVARO PT. 3 (EP)	30
53	Capitol LC 6522	VOICE OF THE XTABY (10" LP)	50
54	Capitol LC 6609	LEGEND OF THE SUN VIRGIN (10" LP)	20
64	Regal REG 2007	VOICE OF THE XTABY (LP)	15
72	London HLU/SHU 8431	MIRACLES (LP)	40

HUBERT SUMLIN
65	Blue Horizon 45-1000	Across The Board/Sumlin Boogie (99 copies only)	100

(see also Howlin' Wolf)

DONNA SUMMER
74	People PEO 115	The Hostage/Let's Work Together Now	6
79	Casablanca SANL 151	Hot Stuff/Journey To The Centre Of Your Heart (12", red vinyl)	15
84	Casablanca FEEL 12	I Feel Love/I Feel Love (Version) (12")	12
87	WEA U 8237P	Dinner With Gershwin (Parts 1 & 2) (12", picture disc)	8
89	WEA U 7780P	This Time I Know It's For Real/Whatever Your Heart Desires (shaped picture disc)	4

(see also Donna Gaines, John Barry)

SUMMERHILL
69	Polydor 583 746	SUMMERHILL (LP)	20

ANDY SUMMERS & ROBERT FRIPP
82	A&M (no cat. no.)	Hardy Country/Stultified/Yellow Leader/I Advance Masked (clear flexidisc)	6

(see also Police, King Crimson)

BOB(BY) SUMMERS
59	Capitol CL 15063	Rattle Rhythm/Excitement (as Bob Summers)	7
60	Capitol CL 15130	Little Brown Jug/Twelfth Street Rag (as Bobby Summers)	8

SUMMER SET
66	Columbia DB 8004	Farmer's Daughter/Papa-Oom-Mow-Mow	15
66	Columbia DB 8004	Farmer's Daughter/What Are You Gonna Do (2nd issue with different B-side)	15
67	Columbia DB 8215	Overnight Changes/It's A Dream	50

(see also Candy Choir)

SUMMERTAIRES
66	Ska Beat JB 258	My Heart Cries Out/SOUL BROTHERS: James Bond Girl	15

(see also Jackie Mittoo, Soul Agents)

SUN
78	Capitol EMC 3262	LIVE ON DREAM ON (LP)	12

SUN
96	Polydor 575 113-1	THE SUN EP (yellow vinyl, p/s)	8
96	Polydor 575 113-2	THE SUN EP (CD)	8

(see also Silver Sun)

SUN ALSO RISES
70	Village Thing VTS 2	THE SUN ALSO RISES (LP)	20

SUN & MOON
88	Geffen GEF 39	The Speed Of Life/Death Of Imagination (p/s)	5
88	Geffen GEF 39T	The Speed Of Life/Death Of Imagination/The Boy Who Sees Everything/I Love You, You Bastard (12", p/s)	8

| 89 | Midnight Music DONG 44CD | ALIVE; NOT DEAD (CD EP) | 12 |
| 89 | Geffen 9241 882 | THE SUN AND THE MOON (CD) | 15 |

(see also Chameleons)

SUNBIRD
| 70 | Philips 6006 046 | Brother Bird/Love Of The Free | 4 |

SUNDAE TIMES
68	President PT 203	Baby Don't Cry/Aba-Aba	5
68	President PT 219	Jack Boy/I Don't Want Nobody	5
70	President PT 285	Live Today/Take Me Higher Baby	5
70	Joy JOYS 159	US COLOURED KIDS (LP)	20

SUNDANCE
73	Decca F 13423	Coming Down/Eagles	5
73	Decca F 13461	Stand By/Willie The Gambler	5
74	Decca F 13494	Loving You/Can You Feel It	5
73	Decca TXS 111	RAIN STEAM SPEED (LP, with insert)	15
74	Decca SKL 5183	CHUFFER (LP)	15

SUNDAY AFTERNOONS
| 70s | Longman | SUNDAY AFTERNOONS (LP) | 80 |

SUNDAYS
89	Rough Trade RTX 218	Can't Be Sure/I Kicked A Boy (export issue, brown p/s)	6
89	Rough Trade RTTX 218	Can't Be Sure/I Kicked A Boy/Don't Tell Your Mother (12", export issue, brown p/s)	8
89	Rough Trade RTT 218CD	Can't Be Sure/I Kicked A Boy/Don't Tell Your Mother (3" CD, card sleeve)	8
90	Catalogue CAT 076	I Won (square flexidisc with *The Catalogue* magazine)	4
90	Rough Trade ROUGH 148P	READING, WRITING AND ARITHMETIC (LP, picture disc, stickered sleeve)	15

SUNDAY SING TRIO
| 70s | Sharon SHLP 1221 | ONE OF THESE DAYS (LP) | 15 |

SUN DIAL
90	Bucketfull Of Brains BOB 30	Visitation/JEFF DAHL & AMERICAN RUSE: One Track Mind (flexidisc free with *Bucketfull Of Brains* magazine, issue 36)	6/4
91	Tangerine TANGERINE 111	Exploding In Your Mind (Colour Mix)/Otherside/Slow Motion (12", unreleased, 80 white label test pressings only)	30
91	UFO PF 2	Fireball/Only A Northern Song ('Pre-Flight' 7", no p/s, promo only)	30
90	Tangerine MM 07	OTHER WAY OUT (LP, with insert, some signed in silver ink)	20/30
91	UFO UFO 1LP	OTHER WAY OUT (LP, reissue in gatefold sleeve)	10
92	UFO UFO 8	REFLECTER (LP, clear vinyl)	10
94	Acme AC 8001	RETURN JOURNEY (LP, official bootleg; 200 promos with inserts, 500 numbered commercial copies)	20/12

(see also Modern Art, Spiral Sky, Quad)

SUNDOWNERS
63	Piccadilly 7N 35142	Baby Baby/House Of The Rising Sun	7
64	Piccadilly 7N 35162	Come On In/Shot Of Rhythm And Blues	7
65	Parlophone R 5243	Where Am I/Gonna Make The Future Bright	6
68	Columbia DB 8339	Dr. J. Wallace-Brown/Love Is In The Air	8
68	Spark SRL 1016	Gloria The Bosom Show/Don't Look Back	5

SUNDOWN PLAYBOYS
| 72 | Apple APPLE 44 | Saturday Nite Special/Valse De Soleil Couche (some in p/s) | 25/8 |
| 72 | Apple APPLE 44 | Saturday Nite Special/Valse De Soleil Couche (10", 78rpm, pink-patterned die-cut sleeve) | 175 |

SUNDRAGON
68	MGM MGM 1380	Green Tambourine/I Need All The Friends I Can Get	8
68	MGM MGM 1391	Blueberry Blue/Far Away Mountain	8
68	MGM MGM 1458	Five White Horses/Look At The Sun	6
68	MGM MGM-C(S) 8090	GREEN TAMBOURINE (LP)	60

(see also Sands, Others)

SUN ELECTRIC
| 90 | Wau! Mr Modo MWS 020T | O'Locco — Karma Sutra/O'Locco —Space Therapy/ O'Locco (Orbital Therapy Part 1)/(Orbital Therapy Part 2)/ (Orbital Therapy Part 3)/(Orbital Therapy Part 4) (12", p/s) | 10 |

SUNFIGHTER
| 76 | EMI EMI 2493 | Drag Race Queen/Riding On Your Star | 5 |
| 76 | EMI EMI 2553 | Such A Lovely Night/Don't Get Me Wrong | 5 |

SUNFOREST
| 70 | Deram Nova (S)DN 7 | SOUND OF SUNFOREST (LP, mono/stereo) | 75/60 |

SUNLIGHT ORCHESTRA
| 70s | Myrrh MYR 1036 | PLAYS LOVE AND OTHER GREATS (LP) | 15 |

SUNNY & HI-JUMPERS
| 65 | Carnival CV 7022 | Tarry Till You're Better/Dance Til You're Better | 6 |
| 65 | Carnival CV 7025 | Going To Damascus/Sweet Potatoes | 6 |

SUNNY & SUNGLOWS/SUNLINERS
| 63 | London HL 9792 | Talk To Me (as Sunny & Sunglows)/Every Week, Every Month, Every Year (as Sunny & Sunliners) | 20 |

SUNNYLAND SLIM
65	'77' LA 12-23	CHICAGO BLUES SESSION (LP, with Little Brother Montgomery)	25
65	Storyville SLP 169	I DONE YOU WRONG (LP)	22
68	Storyville 670 169	PORTRAITS IN BLUES (LP, reissue of SLP 169)	18
69	Liberty LBS 83237	SLIM'S GOT THIS THING GOIN' ON (LP)	25
69	Blue Horizon 7-63213	MIDNIGHT JUMP (LP)	50
74	Sonet SNTF 671	THE LEGACY OF THE BLUES VOL. II (LP)	12

MINT VALUE £

SUNNYSIDERS
55	London HL 8135	Hey! Mr. Banjo/Zoom, Zoom, Zoom	50
55	London HL 8135	Hey! Mr. Banjo/Zoom, Zoom, Zoom (78)	6
55	London HL 8160	Oh Me Oh My Oh/(Let's Gather Round) The Parlour Piano	30
55	London HL 8160	Oh Me Oh My Oh/(Let's Gather Round) The Parlour Piano (78)	6
55	London HLU 8180	Banjo Woogie/She Didn't Even Say Goodbye	30
55	London HLU 8180	Banjo Woogie/She Didn't Even Say Goodbye (78)	6
55	London HLU 8202	I Love You Fair Dinkum/Stay On The Sunny Side	25
55	London HLU 8202	I Love You Fair Dinkum/Stay On The Sunny Side (78)	6
56	London HLU 8246	Doesn't He Love Me/Humdinger	30
56	London HLU 8246	Doesn't He Love Me/Humdinger (78)	6

SUN RA ARKESTRA
82	Y RA 1	NUCLEAR WAR (12" EP)	25
70s	Delmark DL 411	SUN SONG (LP)	15
70s	Delmark DL 414	SOUND OF JOY (LP)	15
71	Black Lion 2460 106	PICTURES OF INFINITY — IN CONCERT (LP)	15
71	Byg 529 341	THE SOLAR MYTH APPROACH VOL. 2 (LP)	15
78	Affinity AFF 10	S-M APPROACH (LP, with Solar-Myth Ark)	12
79	Cobra COB 37001	FATE IN A PLEASANT MOOD (LP)	12

SUNRAYS
65	Capitol CL 15416	I Live For The Sun/Bye, Baby, Bye	7
66	Capitol CL 15433	Andrea/You Don't Phase Me	7

SUNRISE
76	Grapevine GRA 105	BEFORE MY EYES (LP)	30

SUNSCREEM
92	Sony XPR 1825	Perfect Motion (Boys Own Mix)/(Vocal Mix)/(Once Down Mix) (12", promo)	30

SUNSET BOYS
79	Gimp GIM 1234	Wreck My Bed/Tutti Frutti/Copy Cat (Blues)/Wreck My Bed (Hippy Version) (p/s)	5
	(see also Maxim's Trash)		

SUN SET
67	Polydor BM 56193	East Baby/You Can Ride My Rainbow	4

SUNSETS
61	Ember EMB S 125	Cry Of The Wild Goose/Manhunt	15

SUNSHINE
72	Warner Brothers K 46169	SUNSHINE (LP)	12
	(see also Pretty Things)		

MONTY SUNSHINE
55	Tempo A 125	Wild Cat Blues/St. Philips St. Breakdown (78)	10
62	Pye Jazz 7NJ 2011	Hushabye/Whistling Rufus (with His Jazz Band)	5
62	London HLR 9629	Gonna Build A Mountain/Hushabye (with His Band)	6
63	London HLR 9822	Carnival — From "Black Orpheus"/Charmaine (with His Orchestra)	6
57	Pye Nixa NJE 1050	THE MONTY SUNSHINE SHOWCASE (EP)	8
61	Columbia SEG 8059	MONTY (EP)	10
61	Columbia SEG 8127	SUNSHINE (EP)	15
63	London RE-R 1368	GONNA BUILD A MOUNTAIN (EP, with His Band)	12
63	London HAR 8037	MONTY SUNSHINE AND HIS BAND (LP, also stereo [SHR 8037])	18
64	London HAR 8158	BLACK MOONLIGHT & SUNSHINE (LP, also stereo [SHR 8158])	18
60s	Major Minor SMCP 5062	SHADES OF SUNSHINE (LP)	18
70s	DJM DJB 26088	A TASTE OF SUNSHINE (LP)	15
	(see also Lonnie Donegan)		

MR. SUNSHINE
56	MGM SP 1160	Along The China Coast/MRS. SUNSHINE: Two Car Garage	6

SUNSHINE COMPANY
67	Liberty LBF 15008	Happy/Blue May	5
67	Liberty LBF 15034	Back On The Street Again/A Year Of Janie's Time	5
68	Liberty LBF 15060	Look Here Comes The Sun/It's Sunday	5
68	Liberty LBF 15149	On A Beautiful Day/To Put Up With You	5
68	Liberty LBL/LBS 83120	THE SUNSHINE COMPANY (LP)	15
69	Liberty LBL/LBS 83159	SUNSHINE AND SHADOWS (LP)	15

SUNSPOTS
63	Decca F 11672	Paella/Vancouver	6

SUNSTROKE
78	Hot Stuff HS 004	SUNSTROKE (EP)	4

SUNTREADER
73	Island HELP 13	ZIN ZIN (LP)	12
	(see also Stomu Yamashta)		

SUPERBOYS
68	Giant GN 22	Ain't That A Shame/Do It Right Now	7
68	Giant GN 31	You're Hurtin' Me/Funky Soul	7
	(see also Dandy & Superboys, Little Sal)		

SUPER 8
95	García POUM 001	Billy The Kid/It Doesn't Matter/How Can I Understand The Flies? ('hairloss' p/s, 500 only, 37 sold)	4
	(see also Sheds)		

SUPERGRASS

SUPER FURRY ANIMALS

95	Ankst ANKST 057	LLANFAIRPWLLGWYNGYLLGOGERYCHWYRNDROBWLLANTYSILIO-GOGOGOCHYNYGOFOD (IN SPACE) (EP, 7", p/s)	8
95	Ankst ANKST 62	LLANFAIRPWLLGWYNGYLLGOGERYCHWYRNDROBWLLANTYSILIO-GOGOGOCHYNYGOFOD (IN SPACE) (EP, cassette)	5
95	Ankst ANKST 62	MOOG DROOG EP (EP, p/s)	8
95	Ankst ANKST 62	MOOG DROOG EP (CD)	10
96	Creation CRE 247	The Man Don't Give A Fuck (p/s, 1- sided, blue vinyl)	10
96	Creation CRE 247 T	The Man Don't Give A Fuck/(Howard Marks Mix)/(Wishmountain Mix)/(Darren Price Mix) (12", p/s)	10
96	Creation CRESCD 247	The Man Don't Give A Fuck/(Howard Marks Mix)/(Wishmountain Mix) (CD)	15
96	Debiel SS 01	(Nid) Hon Yw'r Gan Sy'n Mynd I Achub Yr Laith (1-sided gig freebie)	15
98	Creation CRECD 229 L	OUT SPACED (CD, rubber pack [black, green or blue])	15

SUPERGRASS

94	Backbeat (no cat. no.)	Caught By The Fuzz/Strange Ones (hand-stamped labels, no p/s; 1,000 only, later re-pressed)	15
94	Backbeat (no cat. no.)	Mansize Rooster/Sitting Up Straight (luminous green vinyl, printed green cardboard or plain die-cut sleeve, 500 only)	12/8
94	Backbeat (no cat. no.)	Mansize Rooster/Sitting Up Straight (marbled green vinyl, plain sleeve)	7
94	Parlophone R 6396	Caught By The Fuzz/Strange Ones (p/s, reissue)	6
94	Parlophone 12R 6396DJ	Caught By The Fuzz/Strange Ones (12", p/s, promo only)	12
94	Parlophone CDR 6396	Caught By The Fuzz/Strange Ones/Caught By The Fuzz (Acoustic) (CD)	7
95	Parlophone R 6402	Mansize Rooster/Sitting Up Straight (p/s, red vinyl)	4
95	Parlophone CDR 6402	Mansize Rooster/Sitting Up Straight/Odd (CD)	7
95	Parlophone GRASS 2	Sofa (Of My Lethargy) (Radio Edit)/(Album Vers.) (CD, promo only, card p/s)	7
97	Parlophone GRASS 9497	THE SINGLES 1994-1997 (8 x 7" black vinyl 'grass'-covered box set, with signed & numbered insert, promo only)	40
95	Parlophone PCSX 7373	I SHOULD COCO (LP, with bonus single "Stone Free"/"Odd?" [PCSS 7373])	12
97	Parlophone 12RDJ 6469	Sun Hits The Sky (Bentley Rhythm Ace Sun Hits The Sky Mix) (12", no p/s, promo only)	12
99	EMI CDIN 125	INTERVIEW (CD, tri-fold digipak, promo only)	15
	(see also Jennifers)		

SUPERMATIX

81	MC 4	BAD TIMING EP (p/s)	6

MINT VALUE £

SUPERSISTER

72	Polydor 2001 379	No Tree Will Grow/She Was Naked	5
71	Dandelion 2310 146	TO THE HIGHEST BIDDER (LP, gatefold sleeve)	25
71	Polydor 2419 030	SUPER STARSHINE 3 (LP)	15
72	Polydor 2419 061	PRESENT FROM NANCY (LP)	15
73	Polydor 2480 153	PUDDING & YESTERDAY (LP)	15
73	Polydor 2925 021	ISKANDER (LP, gatefold sleeve with lyric sheet)	12

SUPERSONICS

53	London L 1197	New Guitar Boogie Shuffle/The Sheik Of Araby (78)	15
54	London HL 8022	Cherokee/Linger Awhile (B-side with Arlene James) (78)	15

SUPERTONES

70	Banana BA 312	Freedom Blues/First Time I Met You	10

(see also Jackie Mittoo)

SUPERTRAMP

74	A&M AMS 7101	Land Ho/Summer Romance	5

(see also John Andrews & Lonely Ones, Argosy)

(DIANA ROSS &) SUPREMES

SINGLES

64	Stateside SS 257	When The Lovelight Starts Shining Thru' His Eyes/Standing At The Crossroads Of Love	40
64	Stateside SS 327	Where Did Our Love Go/He Means The World To Me	6
64	Stateside SS 350	Baby Love/Ask Any Girl	6
65	Stateside SS 376	Come See About Me/(You're Gone But) Always In My Heart	12
65	Tamla Motown TMG 501	Stop! In The Name Of Love/I'm In Love Again	7
65	Tamla Motown TMG 516	Back In My Arms Again/Whisper You Love Me Boy	12
65	Tamla Motown TMG 527	Nothing But Heartaches/He Holds His Own	15
65	Tamla Motown TMG 543	I Hear A Symphony/Who Could Ever Doubt My Love	7
66	Tamla Motown TMG 548	My World Is Empty Without You/Everything Is Good About You	10
66	Tamla Motown TMG 560	Love Is Like An Itching In My Heart/He's All I Got	25
66	Tamla Motown TMG 575	You Can't Hurry Love/Put Yourself In My Place	6
66	Tamla Motown TMG 585	You Keep Me Hangin' On/Remove This Doubt	6
67	Tamla Motown TMG 597	Love Is Here And Now You're Gone/There's No Stopping Us Now	6
67	Tamla Motown TMG 607	The Happening/All I Know About You	6

(The singles listed above are credited to Supremes.)

67	Tamla Motown TMG 616	Reflections/Going Down For The Third Time (push-out or solid centre)	7/6
67	Tamla Motown TMG 632	In And Out Of Love/I Guess I'll Always Love You	5
68	Tamla Motown TMG 650	Forever Came Today/Time Changes Things	5
68	Tamla Motown TMG 662	Some Things You Never Get Used To/You've Been So Wonderful To Me	5
68	Tamla Motown TMG 677	Love Child/Will This Be The Day?	5
69	Tamla Motown TMG 695	I'm Living In Shame/I'm So Glad I Got Somebody (Like You Around)	6
69	Tamla Motown TMG 704	No Matter What Sign You Are/The Young Folks	5
69	Tamla Motown TMG 721	Someday We'll Be Together/He's My Sunny Boy	5

(The singles listed above are credited to Diana Ross & Supremes.)

70	Tamla Motown TMG 735	Up The Ladder To The Roof/Bill, When Are You Coming Back	5
70	Tamla Motown TMG 747	Everybody's Got The Right To Love/But I Love You More	5
71	Tamla Motown TMG 760	Stoned Love/Shine On Me	5
71	Tamla Motown TMG 782	Nathan Jones/Happy (Is A Bumpy Road)	5

(The singles listed above are credited to Supremes and do not feature Diana Ross.)

EPs

65	Tamla Motown TME 2008	THE SUPREMES HITS (EP; originally with flipback sl. & push-out centre)	25/15
66	Tamla Motown TME 2011	SHAKE (EP)	60

LPs

64	Stateside SL 10109	MEET THE SUPREMES (LP)	30
65	Tamla Motown TML 11002	WITH LOVE — FROM US TO YOU (LP)	40
65	Tamla Motown TML 11012	WE REMEMBER SAM COOKE (LP)	45
65	Tamla Motown TML 11018	THE SUPREMES SING COUNTRY, WESTERN AND POP (LP)	45
65	Tamla Motown TML 11020	MORE HITS BY THE SUPREMES (LP)	18
66	T. Motown (S)TML 11026	THE SUPREMES AT THE COPA (LP, mono/stereo)	15/20
66	T. Motown (S)TML 11028	I HEAR A SYMPHONY (LP, mono/stereo)	15/18
66	T. Motown (S)TML 11039	SUPREMES A-GO GO (LP, mono/stereo)	15/18
67	T. Motown (S)TML 11047	THE SUPREMES SING MOTOWN (LP)	18
67	T. Motown (S)TML 11054	THE SUPREMES SING RODGERS AND HART (LP)	18

(The LPs listed above are credited to Supremes.)

68	T. Motown (S)TML 11063	GREATEST HITS (LP, original pressing with flipback laminated sleeve)	12
68	T. Motown (S)TML 11070	'LIVE' AT LONDON'S TALK OF THE TOWN (LP)	12
68	T. Motown (S)TML 11073	REFLECTIONS (LP)	15
69	T. Motown (S)TML 11088	SING & PERFORM FUNNY GIRL (LP, mono/stereo)	15/12
69	T. Motown (S)TML 11095	LOVE CHILD (LP, mono/stereo)	15/12
69	T. Motown (S)TML 11114	LET THE SUNSHINE IN (LP, mono/stereo)	15/12
70	T. Motown (S)TML 11137	CREAM OF THE CROP (LP, mono/stereo)	15/12
70	Tamla Motown STML 11157	RIGHT ON (LP, as Supremes)	12
71	Tamla Motown STML 11189	TOUCH (LP)	12
73	T. Motown STML 11222	THE SUPREMES PRODUCED AND ARRANGED BY JIMMY WEBB (LP)	12

(The LPs listed above are credited to Diana Ross & Supremes unless otherwise stated.
All the albums listed above were originally issued with flipback sleeves; later pressings are worth two-thirds these values.)

SUPREMES & FOUR TOPS

71	Tamla Motown TMG 777	River Deep, Mountain High/It's Gotta Be A Miracle (This Thing Called Love)	4
71	Tamla Motown TMG 793	You Gotta Have Love In Your Heart/I'm Glad About It	4
71	T. Motown STML 11179	THE SUPREMES AND THE FOUR TOPS — MAGNIFICENT 7 (LP)	10

DIANA ROSS & SUPREMES & TEMPTATIONS

69	Tamla Motown TMG 685	I'm Gonna Make You Love Me/A Place In The Sun	5
69	Tamla Motown TMG 709	I Second That Emotion/The Way You Do The Things You Do	5
70	Tamla Motown TMG 730	Why (Must We Fall In Love)/Uptight (Everything Is Alright)	5

MINT VALUE £

69	T. Motown (S)TML 11096	DIANA ROSS & THE SUPREMES JOIN THE TEMPTATIONS (LP)	12
69	T. Motown (S)TML 11110	THE ORIGINAL SOUNDTRACK FROM TCB (LP, gatefold laminated sleeve)	15
70	T. Motown STML 11122	TOGETHER (LP, flipback sleeve)	12

(see also Primettes, Diana Ross, Temptations, Four Tops, Florence Ballard)

SURFARIS
63	London HLD 9751	Wipe Out/Surfer Joe.	7
63	Brunswick 05894	Waikiki Run/Point Panic.	8
64	Brunswick 05902	Scatter Shield/Bat Man	10
66	Dot DS 26756	Wipe Out/Surfer Joe (reissue)	6
73	Paramount PARA 3034	Wipe Out/Shake	5
63	London RE-D 1405	WIPE OUT (EP)	50
63	London HA-D 8110	WIPE OUT (LP)	40
63	Brunswick LAT/STA 8561	THE SURFARIS PLAY (LP, mono/stereo)	25/35
64	Brunswick LAT/STA 8567	HIT CITY '64 (LP, mono/stereo)	25/35
64	Brunswick LAT 8582	FUN CITY (LP)	30
65	Brunswick LAT 8605	HIT CITY '65 (LP)	30
65	Brunswick LAT 8631	IT AIN'T ME BABE (LP, also stereo STA 8631)	25/35
66	Dot DLP 3535	WIPE OUT (LP, reissue)	20

SURF DRUMS
| 85 | Swordfish SWF 003 | Take It With Me/Stone And Silver/These Seven Years/Everything (12", p/s). | 8 |

(see also Korova Milk Bar)

SURFERS
| 59 | Vogue V 9147 | Mambo Jambo/ALAN KALANI: A Touch Of Pink. | 15 |

SURFING DEAD
| 95 | Mental Disorder MAD 017 | POWERTWANG (10" EP) | 10 |

LES SURFS
64	RCA RCA 1432	Just For The Boy/Stop	7
65	RCA RCA 1461	Go Your Way/Chained To A Memory	7
67	Fontana TF 832	When I Tell You (That I Love You)/I Want To Be Free	5

SURFSIDERS
| 67 | Allegro ALL 867 | THE SURFSIDERS SING THE BEACH BOYS SONGBOOK (LP) | 10 |

SURGEONS
| 79 | Surgery S-100 | Sid Never Did It/Breaking Rocks On Ricker's Island (no p/s). | 12 |

JOHN SURMAN (Trio)
69	Deram DM 224	Obeah Wedding/Can't Stop The Carnival.	40
68	Deram DML/SML 1030	JOHN SURMAN (LP)	60
69	Deram DML-R/SML-R 1045	HOW MANY CLOUDS CAN YOU SEE? (LP)	90
70	Futura GER 12	ALORS! (LP)	40
71	Dawn DNLS 3006	THE TRIO (LP)	60
71	Dawn DNLS 3018	WHERE FORTUNE SMILES (LP, with insert, with John McLaughlin, Karl Berger, Stu Martin & Dave Holland)	40
71	Dawn DNLS 3022	CONFLAGRATION (LP)	50
71	Deram SML 1094	TALES OF THE ALGONQUIN (LP, with John Warren)	90
72	Island HELP 10	WESTERING HOME (LP)	20
73	Island ILPS 9237	MORNING GLORY (LP)	20

(see also Morning Glory, Trio, Mike Westbrook, John McLaughlin, Alan Skidmore/Mike Osborne/John Surman)

SURPLUS STOCK
| 79 | Outatune OUT 7911 | Spiv/Vips (p/s) | 15 |

SURPRISES
| 79 | Dead Dog DEAD 01 | Jeremy Thorpe Is Innocent/Flying Attack/Little Sir Echo (p/s) | 10 |

SURVIVORS
| 65 | Rio R 55 | Take Charge/Ska-Ology | 8 |
| 65 | Rio R 70 | Rawhide Ska/OWEN GRAY: Girl I Want You. | 8 |

SUSSED
| 80 | Graduate GRAD 7 | I've Got Me A Parka/Myself, Myself And I Repeated (p/s, paper labels; later reissued [1986] with silver labels). | 6 |
| 81 | Shoestring LACE 002 | I Like You/Tango/The Perv (p/s) | 8 |

(SCREAMING) LORD SUTCH (& SAVAGES)
61	HMV POP 953	Till The Following Night/Good Golly Miss Molly	15
63	Decca F 11598	Jack The Ripper/Don't You Just Know It	15
63	Decca F 11747	I'm A Hog For You/Monster In Black Tights.	15
64	Oriole CB 1944	She's Fallen In Love With A Monster Man/Bye Bye Baby	35
64	Oriole CB 1962	Dracula's Daughter/Come Back Baby	40
65	CBS 201767	The Train Kept A-Rollin'/Honey Hush (as Lord Sutch)	45
66	CBS 202080	The Cheat/Black And Hairy	35
70	Atlantic 584 321	'Cause I Love You/Thumping Beat.	12
70	Atlantic 2091 006	'Cause I Love You/Thumping Beat (reissue)	8
70	Atlantic 2091 017	Election Fever/Rock The Election	10
72	Atlantic K 10221	Gotta Keep A-Rockin'/Flashing Lights/Hands Of Jack The Ripper.	10
76	SRT SRTS 76361	Monster Ball/Rang-Tang-A-Lang	6
76	SRT SRTS 76375	I Drink To Your Health Marie (Parts 1 & 2)	6
77	Decca F 13697	Jack The Ripper/I'm A Hog For You.	5
81	Ridgemount RMR 45 010	LOONABILLY (EP, p/s, with bonus "Loon Party" single).	8
81	Ace SW 70	SCREAMING LORD SUTCH AND THE SAVAGES (EP)	8
94	Bareface 1	I'm Still Raving/Radio Edit/Loony Mix (12", no p/s)	8
70	Atlantic 2400 008	LORD SUTCH AND HIS HEAVY FRIENDS (LP)	25

Lord SUTCH & Savages

72	Atlantic K 40313	HANDS OF JACK THE RIPPER (LP, as Lord Sutch & Heavy Friends)	25
81	Ace MAD 1	THE METEORS MEET SCREAMING LORD SUTCH (mini-LP, 1 side each, stickered cartoon print on plain grey card sleeve, 1,000 only)	60

(see also Savages, Meteors, Led Zeppelin, Cliff Bennett & Rebel Rousers, Circles, Nero & Gladiators, Neil Christian & Crusaders)

GLEN SUTTON
(see under Murray Kellum)

RALPH SUTTON
53	Lyragon LF 2	STRIDE PIANO (10" LP)	10

(see also Tony Parenti)

SUZANNE
77	Ring O' 2017 108	Born On Hallowe'en/Like No One Else (some in promo p/s)	25/12
78	Ring O' 2017 111	You Really Got A Hold On Me/You Could Be Right This Time (no p/s)	10
78	Ring O' 2017 115	single (unreleased)	
78	Ring O' 2320 105	SUZANNE (LP, unreleased)	

SUZI & BIG DEE IRWIN
66	Polydor BM 65715	Ain't That Lovin' You Baby/I Can't Get Over You	12

(see also Big Dee Irwin)

PAT SUZUKI
58	RCA RCA 1069	Daddy/Just One Of Those Things	7
60	RCA RCA 1171	I Enjoy Being A Girl/Sunday	8

SUZY & THE RED STRIPES
77	A&M AMS 7461	Seaside Woman/B-side To The Seaside (yellow vinyl, die-cut p/s)	12
79	A&M AMSP 7461	Seaside Woman/B-side To The Seaside (yellow vinyl, die-cut p/s, in box set with badge & 10 'saucy' mini-postcards)	40
80	A&M AMS 7548	Seaside Woman/B-side To The Seaside (reissue, cartoon p/s, as Linda McCartney alias Suzy & Red Stripes)	10
80	A&M AMSP 7548	Seaside Woman/B-side To The Seaside (12", as Linda McCartney alias Suzy & Red Stripes)	12
86	EMI EMI 5572	Seaside Woman/B-side To The Seaside (p/s)	6
86	EMI 12EMI 5572	Seaside Woman/B-side To The Seaside (12", p/s)	10

(see also Paul McCartney [& Wings])

SVANTE
68	United Artists UP 2224	Baby I Need Your Lovin'/Just One Word From You	6

SVENSK
67	Page One POF 036	Dream Magazine/Getting Old	20
67	Page One POF 050	You/All I Have To Do Is Dream	15

(see also Jason Paul)

SWALLOWS
56	Vogue EPV 1113	RHYTHM AND BLUES (EP, 2 tracks by Dominoes)	275

SWALLOWS with SONNY THOMPSON
52	Vogue V 2136	Roll, Roll Pretty Baby/It Ain't The Meat (78)	40

SWAMP DOGG
74	Island USA 002	Did I Come Back Too Soon/I Wouldn't Leave Here	5
72	Mojo 2916 014	TOTAL DESTRUCTION TO YOUR MIND (LP)	12

(see also Jerry Williams, Brooks & Jerry)

BILLY SWAN
75	Monument MNT 80615	I CAN HELP (LP)	12
75	CBS 69162	ROCK & ROLL MOON (LP)	12
76	Monument MNT 81387	BILLY SWAN (LP)	12

SWAN ARCADE
73	Trailer LER 2032	SWAN ARCADE (LP)	20

SWANEE RIVER BOYS
52	Parlophone DP 391	When I Move/I've Got A Date To Meet An Angel (78, export issue)	8
54	Parlophone CMSP 7	Do You Believe/Gloryland Boogie (export issue)	12
54	Parlophone DP 385	Was He Quiet Or Did He Cry/I Have Desire (78, export issue)	12

BETTYE SWANN
67	CBS 2942	Make Me Yours/I Will Not Cry (demos in p/s)	60
67	CBS 2942	Make Me Yours/I Will Not Cry	35
69	Capitol CL 15586	Don't Touch Me/(My Heart Is) Closed For The Season	20
72	Atlantic K 10174	Victim Of A Foolish Heart/Cold Day In Hell	10
72	Atlantic K 10273	Today I Started Loving You Again/I'd Rather Go Blind	8
73	Mojo 2092 059	Make Me Yours/I Will Not Cry (reissue)	6
75	Atlantic K 10622	Doing It For The One I Love/All The Way In Or All The Way Out	5
76	Atlantic K 10851	Heading In The Right Direction/Be Strong Enough To Hold On	10

(see also Sam Dees & Bettye Swann)

SWANS
63	Stateside SS 224	He's Mine/You Better Be A Good Girl Now	15
64	Cameo Parkway C 302	The Boy With The Beatle Hair/Please Hurry Home	18

BENRICE SWANSON
65	Chess CRS 8008	Lying Awake/Baby I'm Yours	25

DAVE SWARBRICK
67	Bounty BYI 6030	RAGS, REELS AND AIRS (LP, with Martin Carthy & Diz Disley)	80
67	Polydor Special 236 514	RAGS, REELS AND AIRS (LP, reissue, with Martin Carthy & Diz Disley)	35
76	Transatlantic TRA 337	SWARBRICK (LP)	12
77	Transatlantic TRA 341	SWARBRICK 2 (LP)	12
78	Sonet SNTF 763	LIFT THE LID AND LISTEN (LP)	12

78	Sonet SNTF 764	THE CEILIDH ALBUM (LP, as Dave Swarbrick & Friends)	12
81	Logo LOGO 1029	SMIDDYBURN (LP)	12

(see also Martin Carthy & Dave Swarbrick, Fairport Convention, Young Tradition, Vashti Bunyan, Ian Campbell)

DAVE SWARBRICK & SIMON NICOL
81	White Bear WBR 001	LIVE AT THE WHITE BEAR (LP)	20
83	Woodworm WR 006	CLOSE TO THE WIND (LP)	15

(see also Dave Swarbrick, Fairport Convention, Young Tradition)

SWARBRIGG (PLUS TWO)
75	MCA MCA 179	That's What Friends Are For/Love Is	7
75	MCA MCA 202	Shuffle Into My Heart/Sing It Again	5
75	MCA MCA 214	Funny/To Love	5
77	EMI EMI 2606	It's Nice To Be In Love Again/Here We Are Again (as Swarbrigg Plus Two)	5

ROSALYN SWEAT & PARAGONS
73	Duke DU 160	Blackbird Singing/Always	6
74	Horse HRLP 703	BLACKBIRD SINGING (LP)	15

(see also Paragons)

SWE-DANES
60	Warner Bros WB 7	Scandinavian Shuffle/Hot Toddy	7
60	Warner Bros WB 22	Swe-Dane Shuffle/At A Georgia Camp Meeting	7
61	Warner Bros WEP 6017	THE SWE-DANES (EP; also stereo SWEP 2017)	18/25

(see also Alice Babbs)

SWEDEN THROUGH THE AGES
86	Snappy SW 001	IT HELPS TO CRY EP (12", p/s)	10

(see also Billy MacKenzie)

SWEDISH MODERN JAZZ GROUP
61	Tempo TAP 31	SAX APPEAL (LP)	220

SWEENEY'S MEN
67	Pye 7N 17312	Old Maid In The Garrett/Derby Ram	10
68	Pye 7N 17459	Waxies Dargle/Old Woman In Cotton	10
69	Transatlantic TRASP 19	Sullivan's John/Rattlin' Roarin' Willy	8
68	Transatlantic TRA 170	SWEENEY'S MEN (LP)	50
69	Transatlantic TRA 200	THE TRACKS OF SWEENEY (LP)	75
76	Transatlantic TRASAM 37	SWEENEY'S MEN (LP, reissue)	15
77	Transatlantic TRASAM 40	THE TRACKS OF SWEENEY (LP, reissue)	15

(see also Gay & Terry Woods, Dr. Strangely Strange)

JIM SWEENY
58	Philips PB 811	The Midnight Hour/Till The Right One Comes Along	6
58	Philips PB 811	The Midnight Hour/Till The Right One Comes Along (78)	12

SWEET
SINGLES
68	Fontana TF 958	Slow Motion/It's Lonely Out There	400
69	Parlophone R 5803	The Lollipop Man/Time	80
70	Parlophone R 5826	All You'll Ever Get From Me/The Juicer	30
70	Parlophone R 5848	Get On The Line/Mr. McGallagher	60
71	RCA RCA 2051	Funny Funny/You're Not Wrong For Loving Me	5
71	Parlophone R 5902	All You'll Ever Get From Me/The Juicer (reissue)	15
71	RCA RCA 2121	Alexander Graham Bell/Spotlight	5
73	RCA RCA 2403	Ballroom Blitz/Rock & Roll Disgrace (mispressed at wrong speed, 49rpm; matrix: 2403-A-1E)	15
74	RCA RCA 2480	Turn It Down/Someone Else Will	4
76	RCA RCA 2641	The Lies In Your Eyes/Cockroach	4
76	RCA RCA 2748	Lost Angels/Funk It Up	5
77	RCA PB 5011	Fever Of Love/A Distinct Lack Of Ancient	6
77	RCA PB 5046	Stairway To The Stars/Why Don't You Do It To Me	8
78	Polydor POSP 5	California Nights/Show Me The Way (unreleased)	
79	Polydor POSP 36	Call Me/Why Don't You	7
79	Polydor POSP 73	Big Apple Waltz/Why Don't You	30
80	RCA PE 5226	Fox On The Run/Hellraiser/Ballroom Blitz/Blockbuster (EP, p/s)	15
80	Polydor POSP 131	Give That Lady Some Respect/Tall Girls	7
80	Polydor POSP 160	Sixties Man/Tall Girls	5
80	Polydor POSP 160	Sixties Man/Oh Yeah	15
80	Polydor POSP 160	Sixties Man/Oh Yeah (mispressing, B-side plays "Tall Girls")	20
81	RCA GOLD 524	Blockbuster/Hellraiser (pink 'Golden Groove' p/s)	8
81	RCA GOLD 551	Ballroom Blitz/Wig Wam Bam (pink 'Golden Groove' p/s)	8
84	Anagram ANA 27	The Sixteens/Action (p/s)	5
84	Anagram ANA 28	It's The Sweetest Mix/Fox On The Run (p/s)	5
84	Anagram 12 ANA 28	It's The Sweetest Mix/Fox On The Run (12" p/s; matrix no. 12 ANA 28 AI)	8
84	Anagram 12 ANA 28	It's The Sweetest Mix/Fox On The Run (12" p/s; matrix no. 12 ANA 28.A)	10
85	Anagram ANA 29	Sweet 2th — The Wig Wam-Willy Mix/The Teen Action Mix (p/s)	5
85	Anagram ANA 29	Sweet 2th — The Wig Wam-Willy Mix/The Teen Action Mix (12", p/s)	8
89	RCA PB 43337	Wig Wam Bam/Little Willy	15

LPs
71	MFP MFP 5248	GIMME DAT DING (LP, 1 side each by Sweet & Pipkins)	12
71	RCA SF 8288	FUNNY HOW SWEET CO-CO CAN BE (LP)	25
75	RCA SPC 0001	STRUNG UP (2-LP, with insert)	15
76	RCA RS 1036	GIVE US A WINK (LP)	12
77	RCA PL 25072	OFF THE RECORD (LP, with inner sleeve)	15
79	Polydor POLD 5022	CUT ABOVE THE REST (LP, with inner sleeve)	15
80	Polydor POLS 1021	WATER'S EDGE (LP)	15
82	Polydor 2311 1179	IDENTITY CRISIS (LP)	20
84	Anagram P GRAM 16	SWEET SIXTEEN (LP, picture disc)	40

(see also Brian Connolly, Mayfield's Mule, Elastic Band, Andy Scott)

SWEET CHARIOT

SWEET CHARIOT
69	MCA MK 5010	Heavenly Road/Wish I Were A Child 5
72	De Wolfe DWLP 3230	SWEET CHARIOT & FRIENDS (LP, library issue only) 40

SWEET CHARLES
88	Urban URB 15	Yes It's You/LYN COLLINS: Rock Me Again And Again And Again (die-cut sleeve) 4
88	Urban URBX 15	Yes It's You/LYN COLLINS: Rock Me Again And Again And Again/
		Think About It (12", die-cut sleeve)... 10
88	Urban URBLP 9	FOR SWEET PEOPLE FROM SWEET CHARLES (LP)...................... 15

SWEET CONFUSION
69	Escort ES 809	Elizabeth Serenade/Don At Rest... 6
69	Escort ES 812	Hotter Scorcher/Conquer Lion 6
	(see also Stranger & Patsy)	

SWEET CORPORALS
59	Top Rank JAR 217	The Same Old Army/Warm And Willing....................................... 4

SWEET CREAM
77	Ember EMB S 364	Skunk Funk/Don't Know What To Do.. 4

SWEET DREAMS
74	Bradleys BRADL 1008	WE'LL BE YOUR MUSIC (LP).. 12
	(see also Polly Brown, Jimmy Thomas)	

SWEET DREAMS
83	Ariola AROPD 333	I'm Never Giving Up/Two Way Mirror (picture disc) 5

SWEET FEELING
67	Columbia DB 8195	All So Long Ago/Charles Brown 75
	(see also Rupert's People)	

SWEETHEARTS
65	Blue Beat BB 389	Sit Down And Cry (act. with Clinton & Rufus)/PRINCE BUSTER: Ghost Dance .. 40

SWEET INSPIRATIONS
67	Atlantic 584 117	Why (Am I Treated So Bad)/I Don't Want To Go On Without You............. 6
67	Atlantic 584 132	Let It Be Me/When Something Is Wrong With My Baby 6
68	Atlantic 584 167	Sweet Inspiration/I'm Blue... 6
68	Atlantic 584 233	What The World Needs Now Is Love/You Really Didn't Mean It 6
69	Atlantic 584 241	Sweet Inspiration/I'm Blue... 5
69	Atlantic 584 279	Sweets For My Sweet/Get A Little Older..................................... 5
70	Atlantic 584 312	(Gotta Find) A Brand New Lover (Parts 1 & 2) 5
71	Atlantic 2091 073	Evidence/Change Me Not.. 5
68	Atlantic 587/588 090	THE SWEET INSPIRATIONS (LP)... 15
69	Atlantic 587/588 137	WHAT THE WORLD NEEDS NOW IS LOVE (LP) 12
69	Atlantic 587/588 194	SWEETS FOR MY SWEET (LP) 12
70	Atlantic 2465 003	SWEET SWEET SOUL (LP) 12
	(see also Cissy Houston)	

SWEET JESUS
91	Chapter 22 CHAP 63	Cat Thing/Honey Loving Honey/Peach/Baby Blue (12" EP,
		unreleased, 25 test pressing only) 10

SWEET LITTLE BUNTY
75	Ackee ACK 540	I (Who Have Nothing)/Oh Me Oh My 5

SWEET PAIN
71	United Artists UP 35268	Timber Gibbs/Chain Up The Devil 5
69	Mercury 20146 SMCL	SWEET PAIN (LP)... 50

SWEET PLUM
69	Middle Earth MDS 103	Lazy Day/Let No Man Steal Your Thyme 20
70	Middle Earth MDS 105	Set The Wheels In Motion/Catch A Cloud 20

SWEET SAVAGE
81	Park PRK 1001	Take No Prisoners/Killing Time (p/s)....................................... 90
80s	Crashed CAR 48	Straight Through The Heart/Teaser (no p/s) 150
80s	private pressing	The Raid/Prosecutors Of Greed (possibly unreleased) .... 50+

SWEETSHOP
68	Parlophone R 5707	Barefoot And Tiptoe/Lead The Way 10
	(see also Mark Wirtz)	

SWEET SLAG
71	President PTLS 1042	TRACKING WITH CLOSE-UPS (LP) 50

SWEET THUNDER
78	Fantasy FTC 158	Everybody's Singin' Love Songs/Joyful Noise 4

SWEET THURSDAY
69	Polydor 2310 051	SWEET THURSDAY (LP)... 20
	(see also Nicky Hopkins, Mark-Almond)	

SWEGAS
70	Trend 6099 001	What You Gonna Do/There Is Nothing In It 5
71	Trend 6480 002	CHILD OF LIGHT (LP, gatefold sleeve) 20

SWELL MAPS
78	Rather GEAR ONE	Read About Seymour/Ripped And Torn/Black Velvet (p/s) 15
79	Rough Trade RT 010/	Read About Seymour/Ripped And Torn/Black Velvet (p/s,
	Rather GEAR ONE MK. 2	reissue, different back sleeve)... 6

79	R. Trade RT 012/GEAR 3	Dresden Style/Mystery Track/Ammunition Train/Full Moon (Dub) (p/s) 6
79	R. Trade RT 021/GEAR 6	Real Shocks/English Verse/Monlogues (p/s, 2 different colours) 6
79	R. Trade RT 036/GEAR 7	Let's Build A Car/Big Maz In The Country/...Then Poland (p/s) 6
81	Rough Trade RT 012/ Rather GEAR 3	Dresden Style (new vocal)/Ammunition Train/Full Moon (Dub) (p/s, reissue, different back sleeve) 7
79	Rough Trade ROUGH 2/ Rather TROY 1	A TRIP TO MARINEVILLE (LP, with inner sleeve, some with bonus EP in die-cut sleeve [Rather GEAR FIVE]) 15/10
80	Rough Trade ROUGH 15	SWELL MAPS IN 'JANE FROM OCCUPIED EUROPE' (LP) 10
81	Rough Trade ROUGH 21	WHATEVER HAPPENS NEXT... (2-LP) 18
84	Rough Trade ROUGH 41	SWELL MAPS IN 'COLLISION TIME' (LP). 10

(see also Cult Figures, Nikki Sudden, Steve Treatment, Phones Sportsman Band, Epic Soundtracks, Metrophase, Last Bandits)

ANTHONY SWETE
69	RCA RCA 1905	Backfield in Motion/Soul Deep 4

JONATHAN SWIFT
70	MCA MU 1130	Afraid Of Tomorrow/I Haven't Got Anything Better To Do. 5
72	CBS 7931	Corinna/Just This Morning 5
71	CBS 64412	INTROVERT (LP, nude cover) 12
72	CBS 64751	SONGS (LP, with lyric insert) 12

TUFTY SWIFT
77	Free Reed FRR 017	HOW TO MAKE A BAKEWELL TART (LP, with booklet). 15
85	Shark SHARK 04	YOU'LL NEVER DIE FOR LOVE (LP, private pressing) 10

ALAN SWIMMER & DEE DAVIDSON
70s	Fab FAB 242	Take Me Back To Jamaica/Thousands Of Children. 5

SWINDLEFOLK
68	Deroy	A-ROVIN' (LP, private pressing) 70
69	Deroy	SWINDLED (LP, private pressing) 70

STEVE SWINDELLS
74	RCA LPL1 5057	MESSAGES (LP, with insert) 15

(see also Hawkwind)

SWINGERS
60	Vogue V 9158	Love Makes The World Go Round/Jackie 18

SWINGERS
81	Magnet MAG 202	Be My Baby/Swinging (no p/s) 5

(see also Spectres, Rich Kids)

SWINGING BLUE JEANS
63	HMV POP 1170	It's Too Late Now/Think Of Me 10
63	HMV POP 1206	Do You Know/Angie 12
63	HMV POP 1242	Hippy Hippy Shake/Now I Must Go 6
64	HMV POP 1273	Good Golly Miss Molly/Shakin' Feelin' 6
64	HMV POP 1304	You're No Good/Don't You Worry About Me 5
64	HMV POP 1327	Promise You'll Tell Her/It's So Right. 7
64	HMV POP 1375	It Isn't There/One Of These Days 7
65	HMV POP 1409	Make Me Know You're Mine/I've Got A Girl 7
65	HMV POP 1477	Crazy 'Bout My Baby/Good Lovin'. 10
66	HMV POP 1501	Don't Make Me Over/What Can I Do Today 10
66	HMV POP 1533	Sandy/I'm Gonna Have You 10
66	HMV POP 1564	Rumours, Gossip, Words Untrue/Now The Summer's Gone 10
67	HMV POP 1596	Tremblin'/Something's Coming Along. 10
67	HMV POP 1605	Don't Go Out Into The Rain/One Woman Man 10
64	HMV 7EG 8850	SHAKE WITH THE SWINGING BLUE JEANS (EP) 40
64	HMV 7EG 8868	YOU'RE NO GOOD MISS MOLLY (EP) 45
64	HMV CLP 1802	BLUE JEANS A' SWINGING (LP, also stereo CSD 1570) 50/75
64	Regal SREG 1073	TUTTI FRUTTI (LP, export issue) 50
67	MFP MFP 1163	SWINGING BLUE JEANS (LP, reissue of HMV CLP 1802). 15
74	Dart BULL 1001	BRAND NEW AND FADED (LP) 18

(see also Ray Ennis & Blue Jeans, Blue Jeans, Escorts, Terry Sylvester)

SWINGING CATS
80	Two Tone CHS TT 14	Mantovani/Away (p/s). 4

SWINGIN' MEDALLIONS
66	Philips BF 1500	Double Shot Of My Baby's Love/Here It Comes Again. 6
66	Philips BF 1515	She Drives Me Out Of My Mind/You Gotta Have Faith 6

SWINGING SOUL MACHINE
69	Polydor 56760	Spooky's Day Off/Nobody Wants You 6

(see also Machine)

SWING OUT SISTER
88	Mercury 080 122-2	Breakout/Fooled By A Smile/Communion/Surrender (12" Version)/ Breakout (Video) (CD Video) 7

(see also Teresa Del Fuego)

SYD & JOE
72	Bullet BU 498	Three Combine/I'm The Nearest To Your Heart 5

SYDNEY (Crooks) ALL STARS
70	Bullet BU 436	The Return Of Batman/In Action 6
70	Bullet BU 437	Outer Space/Full Moon 6

(see also Pioneers, Junior English, Sammy Morgan)

Eric SYKES & Hattie Jacques

ERIC SYKES & HATTIE JACQUES
62	Decca F 11512	Doctor Kildare/Bedtime Story 7

(see also Eric & Hattie, Goons)

JOHN SYKES
82	MCA MCA 792	Please Don't Leave Me/(Instrumental) (with Phil Lynott, some in p/s) 35/10

(see also Thin Lizzy, Phil Lynott, Tygers Of Pan Tang, Whitesnake)

ROOSEVELT SYKES
50	Jazz Collector L 40	Three, Six And Nine/We Can Sell That Thing (78) 12
56	Vogue V 2389	Fine And Brown/Too Hot To Hold 75
56	Vogue V 2389	Fine And Brown/Too Hot To Hold (78) 30
56	Vogue V 2393	Walkin' This Boogie/Security Blues 75
56	Vogue V 2393	Walkin' This Boogie/Security Blues (78) 30
66	Delmark DJB 2	BACK TO THE BLUES (EP). 30
59	Encore ENC 183	BIG MAN OF THE BLUES (LP) 18
61	Columbia 33SX 1343	FACE TO FACE WITH THE BLUES (LP) 30
62	Columbia 33SX 1422	THE HONEYDRIPPER (LP, with Alexis Korner) 40
67	'77' 77LEU 12-50	BLUES FROM BAR ROOMS (LP) 18
67	Riverside RLP 8819	MR SYKES' BLUES 1929-1932 (LP) 25
67	Ember EMB 3391	ROOSEVELT SYKES SINGS THE BLUES (LP). 18
60s	Bluesville BVLP 1006	THE RETURN OF ROOSEVELT SYKES (LP) 30
71	Barclay 920 294	THE HONEYDRIPPERS' DUKE'S MIXTURE (LP) 12
70s	Delmark DL 607	HARD DRIVIN' BLUES (LP, blue label) 12

(see also Robert Pete Williams)

SYKO & CARBIS
64	Blue Beat BB 213	Do The Dog/Jenny 10
64	Blue Beat BB 223	Big Boy/Sugar Baby. 10

SYLSESTRA ABSURD
80s	Spangle SPANG 3	Dog-Faced Nun Living On The Edge/Heavy Whip Scene 6

SYLTE SISTERS
63	London HLU 9753	Summer Magic/Well It's Summertime 10

SYLVAIN SYLVAIN
80	RCA PB 9500	Every Boy And Every Girl/Emily 4

(see also New York Dolls)

SYLVAN
65	Columbia DB 7674	We Don't Belong/Life's Colours Have Gone 15

FOSTER SYLVERS
73	MGM 2006 292	Misdemeanour/So Close 6

C. SYLVESTER & PLANETS
64	Blue Beat BB 206	Going South/LITTLE JOYCE: Oh Daddy 12

ROLAND SYLVESTER
64	Carnival CV 7018	Grandfather's Clock/SANDRA MURRAY: Nervous 6

TERRY SYLVESTER
74	Polydor 2383 394	I BELIEVE (LP, with insert). 10

(see also Escorts, Swinging Blue Jeans, Hollies, Griffin & Sylvester)

SYLVIA (U.K.)
67	Fontana TF 884	Make Me A Woman/Without Your Love 6
68	Fontana TF 932	Down Hill/A Few Sweet Moments Of Love 7

SYLVIA (U.S.)
68	Soul City SC 103	I Can't Help It/It's A Good Life 12

DAVID SYLVIAN
84	Virgin VSY 633	Red Guitar/Forbidden Colours (Version) (picture disc) 5
84	Virgin VS 700	The Ink In The Well (Remix)/Weathered Wall (Instrumental) (poster p/s) 4
84	Virgin VS 700-12	The Ink In The Well/Weathered Wall (Instrumental) (12", poster p/s) 7
84	Virgin VS 717	Pulling Punches (7" Mix)/Backwaters (Remix) (p/s, with 3 postcards). 4
84	Virgin VSY 717	Pulling Punches (7" Mix)/Backwaters (Remix) (picture disc) 7
84	Virgin VS 717-12	Pulling Punches (Extended Mix)/Backwaters (Remix) (12", p/s, & 3 postcards) . . . 7
85	Virgin VS 835-12	WORDS WITH THE SHAMAN (12" EP, p/s). 7
86	Virgin VSS 815	Taking The Veil/Answered Prayers (rectangular picture disc, stickered PVC sleeve) 7
86	Virgin VS 895	Silver Moon/Gone To Earth (p/s) 4
86	Virgin VSP 895	Silver Moon/Gone To Earth (gatefold p/s) 6
88	Virgin CDT 23	Words With The Shaman: Part 1 — Ancient Evening/Part 2 — Incantation/ Part 3 — Awakening (Songs From The Tree Tops) (3" CD, gatefold card p/s) 12
89	Virgin VSCD 1221	Pop Song/A Brief Conversation Ending In Divorce/ The Stigma Of Childhood (Kin) (3" CD, card sleeve) 10
89	Virgin VSCDX 1221	Pop Song/A Brief Conversation Ending In Divorce/ The Stigma Of Childhood (Kin) (CD, presentation card pack) 20
89	Virgin DSCD 1	WEATHERBOX (5-CD box set, with poster & booklet) 75
98	Virgin CDIVDJ 2876	DEAD BEES ON A CAKE - PROMOTIONAL INTERVIEW CD (CD, card p/s, promo only) 20

DAVID SYLVIAN & RYUICHI SAKAMOTO
82	Virgin VS 510	Bamboo Houses (7" Mix)/Bamboo Music (7" Mix) (some with gatefold p/s). 5/4
83	Virgin VSY 601	Forbidden Colours/RYUICHI SAKAMOTO: The Seed And The Sower
88	Virgin CDT 18	Forbidden Colours/Bamboo Houses/Bamboo Music (3" CD, card sleeve) 15
92	Virgin VUSDG 57	Heartbeat (Tainai Kaiki II)/Nuages/Forbidden Colours/Heartbeat I (CD box set, with postcards) 10

(see also Japan, Yellow Magic Orchestra)

SYLVIN & GLENROY
70	Torpedo TOR 25	What You Gonna Do 'Bout It/KEN JONES: Sad Mood.	6

SYMARIP
(see under Seven Letters/Symarip, see also Pyramids)

SYMBOLS
65	Columbia DB 7459	One Fine Girl/Don't Go	8
65	Columbia DB 7664	You're My Girl/Why Do Fools Fall In Love.	8
66	President PT 104	See You In September/To Make You Smile Again	5
66	President PT 113	Canadian Sunset/The Gentle Art Of Loving	6
67	President PT 128	You'd Better Get Used To Missing Her/Hideaway	5
67	President PT 144	Bye Bye Baby/The Things You Do To Me.	5
67	President PT 173	(The Best Part Of) Breaking Up/Again.	6
68	President PT 190	Lovely Way To Say Goodnight/Pretty City	6
68	President PT 216	Do I Love You/Schoolgirl	6
75	Crystal CR 7021	Canadian Sunset (Instrumental)/Canadian Sunset (Vocal Recording).	6
68	President PTL 1018	THE BEST PART OF THE SYMBOLS (LP)	20

(see also Johnny Milton & Condors)

SYMON & PI
68	Parlophone R 5662	Sha La La La Lee/Baby Baby.	12
68	Parlophone R 5719	Got To See The Sunrise/Love Is Happening To Me	8

SYMPHONICS
73	Polydor 2058 341	Heaven Must Have Sent You/Using Me	8

SYMPHONIC SLAM
76	A&M AMLH 69023	SYMPHONIC SLAM (LP).	40

SYMPOSIUM
96	Infectious INFECT 30S	Drink The Sunshine/Disappear (p/s, 750 only)	12
96	Infectious INFECT 30CD	Drink The Sunshine/Disappear (CD, 1,000 only)	15
97	Infectious INFECT 34SX	Farewell To Twilight/Xanthein/Song/Easily Scared (p/s, orange vinyl)	5
97	Infectious INFECT 49CD	ONE DAY AT A TIME EP (CD)	15

PAT SYMS
64	Oriole CB 1971	It's Got To Be You Or No One/Lost.	6

SYLVIA SYMS
58	Brunswick 05744	I Could Have Danced All Night/Be Good (To Me)	6
58	Brunswick 05744	I Could Have Danced All Night/Be Good (To Me) (78).	8

SYN
67	Deram DM 130	Created By Clive/Grounded	70
67	Deram DM 145	14-Hour Technicolour Dream/Flowerman	70

(see also Syndicats, Yes, Peter Banks)

SYNCHROMESH
80	Rok ROK XI/XII	October Friday/E.F. BAND: Another Day Gone (company die-cut sleeve)	25

SYNCOPATORS
61	Decca F 11359	Everything Stops For Tea/If I Had A Talking Picture Of You	6

SYNDICATE
79	Stevenage/Rock Against Racism	One Way Or Another/I Want To Be Somebody/RESTRICTED HOURS: Getting Things Done/Still Living Out The Car Crash (white label, foldover p/s)	8

(see also Astronauts)

SYNDICATE OF SOUND
66	Stateside SS 523	Little Girl/You	20
66	Stateside SS 538	Rumours/The Upper Hand	12
66	Stateside S(S)L 10185	LITTLE GIRL (LP)	40

SYNDICATS
64	Columbia DB 7238	Maybellene/True To Me.	125
65	Columbia DB 7441	Howlin' For My Baby/What To Do.	125
65	Columbia DB 7686	On The Horizon/Crawdaddy Simone	400

(see also Tomorrow, Syn, Yes, Peter Banks)

SYNANTHESIA
69	RCA SF 8058	SYNANTHESIA (LP)	80

SYREETA
(see under Syreeta Wright)

SYRUP
70	Amity OTS 501	Gentlemen Joe's Sidewalk Café/Love Is Love	4

SYSTEM
77	Tash	THE OTHER SIDE OF TIME (LP, 250 copies only)	100

SYSTEM 7
90	10 TENX 335	Sunburst (Flutter Mix)/Sunburst (Paradise Mix) (12", p/s)	10
91	10 TENDJ 381	Miracle (12", promo only, clear vinyl)	15
91	10 TENX 385	Habibi (Another World Mix)/Miracle/Habibi (7" Edit) (12", p/s)	10
91	10 TENY 385	Habibi (Tex Mix)/(Legian Beach Mix)/Mia (Ultraworld Colony Mix) (12", clear vinyl, clear sleeve)	12

(see also Orb, Steve Hillage)

SYZYGY
85	Taptag TAP 3	LADY IN GREY (mini-LP)	15

(see also Blackthorn)

GABOR SZABO
66	HMV CLP 3614	JAZZ RAGA (LP).	25

T. & UNKNOWN
80   Carrere CAR 142   My Generation/Woodstock Rock (p/s) 5

ERROL T. & ROOSEVELT ALL STARS
72   Ashanti ASH 406   Jamaica Born And Bred/Version 6

TABLE
77   Virgin VS 176   Do The Standing Still/Magical Melon Of The Tropics (p/s) 7
78   Chiswick NS 31   Sex Cells/The Road Of Lyfe (p/s) 6

TABLE TOPPERS
62   Starlite ST45 069   Rocking Mountain Dew/My Wild Irish Rose Rock 15

CHARLIE TABOR
63   Island WI 061   Blue Atlantic/Red Lion Madison 12

JUNE TABOR
76   Topic 12TS 298   AIRS AND GRACES (LP) 15
77   Topic 12TS 360   ASHES AND DIAMONDS (LP) 15
     (see also Silly Sisters)

TAD & SMALL FRY
62   London HLU 9542   Checkered Continental Pants/Pretty Blue Jean Baby 10

TADPOLES
69   High Note HS 032   Rasta/Like Dirt 7

TAGES
66   Columbia DB 8019   Crazy 'Bout My Baby/In My Dreams 8
66   HMV POP 1515   So Many Girls/I'm Mad 30
67   Parlophone R 5640   Treat Me Like A Lady/Wanting 8
68   Parlophone R 5702   There's A Blind Man Playin' Fiddle In The Street/Like A Woman 8
68   MGM MGM 1443   Halcyon Days/I Read You Like An Open Book 8
     (see also Blond)

BLIND JOE TAGGART
52   Tempo R 55   Religion Is Something Within You/Mother's Love (78) 20
55   Jazz Collector L 129   Religion Is Something Within You/Mother's Love (78, reissue) 15

TAGMEMICS
80   Index INDEX 003   Chimneys/(Do The) Big Baby/Take Your Brain Out For A Walk (p/s, with insert) . . 12
     (see also Art Attacks)

JACQUELINE TAIEB
68   Fontana TF 952   Tonight I'm Going Home/7 A.M. 40

LYN(N) TAIT(T) (& JETS)
66   Doctor Bird DB 1006   Vilma's Jump Up (as Lyn Taitt & Comets)/GLEN MILLER &
                                    HONEYBOY MARTIN: Dad Is Home 15
66   Doctor Bird DB 1047   Spanish Eyes (with Tommy McCook)/STRANGER & HORTENSE: Loving Wine . . 15
67   Island WI 3066   Something Stupid/Blue Tuesday (as Lyn Tait & Jets) 18
67   Island WI 3075   I Don't Want To Make You Cry/Nice Time (as Lyn Tait & Jets) 20
68   Island WI 3139   Napoleon Solo/Pressure And Slide (as Lyn Tait & Jets) 20
68   Amalgamated AMG 810   El Casino Royale/Dee's Special (as Lyn Tait & Jets) 12
68   Pama PM 723   Soul Food/Music Flames (as Lyn Tait & Jets) 10
68   Island ILP 969   SOUNDS ROCK STEADY (LP, as Lyn Tait & Jets) 75
68   Big Shot BBTL 4002   GLAD SOUNDS (LP, as Lynn Taitt & Jets) 50
     (see also Justin Hines, Mike Thompson Jnr, ALton Ellis, Ken Boothe, Baba Brooks)

TAJ MAHAL
     (see under 'M')

TAKE FIVE
60s D.S.C.A (no cat. no.)   MY GIRL (EP, oversized p/s; Dundee Students Charity Appeal record) 40

TAKE IT
80s Fresh Hold TRI   Man Made World/Taking Sides/How It Is (p/s) 4
80   Fresh Hold FHR 1   Twenty Lines/Armchairs/Friends And Relations (p/s) 4

'TAKERS
64   Pye 7N 15690   If You Don't Come Back/Think 15
     (see also Undertakers, Jackie Lomax)

TAKE THAT
91   Dance U.K. DUK 2   Do What U Like/Waiting Around (p/s) 20
91   Dance U.K. CADUK 2   Do What U Like/Waiting Around (cassette) 15
91   Dance U.K. 12DUK 2   Do What U Like (Club Mix)/Do What U Like (Radio Mix)/Waiting Around
                                    (12", p/s; most with wrong tracks listed on sleeve) 35
91   RCA PB 45085   Promises/Do What U Like (p/s) 5
91   RCA PB 45085P   Promises/Do What U Like (poster p/s) 12
91   RCA PK 45085   Promises/Do What U Like (cassette) 5
91   RCA PT 45086   Promises (12" Mix)/Do What U Like (12" Mix) (12", p/s) 12
92   RCA PB 45257   Once You've Tasted Love/Guess Who Tasted Love (p/s) 5
92   RCA PB 45265   Once You've Tasted Love/Guess Who Tasted Love
                                    (spined p/s with pull-out hexagonal pop-up calendar) 20

92	RCA PK 45257	Once You've Tasted Love/Guess Who Tasted Love (cassette with stencil) 8
92	RCA PB 45258	Once You've Tasted Love (Aural Mix)/Guess Who Tasted Love (Guess Who Mix)/Once You've Tasted Love (Radio Version) (12" picture disc, with insert) 20
92	RCA 74321 10100 7	It Only Takes A Minute/Satisfied (p/s, with Mark & Robbie prints) 15
92	RCA 74321 10101 7	It Only Takes A Minute/It Only Takes A Minute (Royal Rave Mix) (different p/s, with Jason & Howard prints & paper frame) 12
92	RCA 74321 10100 4	It Only Takes A Minute/Satisfied (cassette) 4
92	RCA 74321 10814 7	I Found Heaven (7" Radio Mix)/(Mr. F's Garage Mix) (poster p/s) 12
92	RCA 74321 10813 7B	I Found Heaven (7" Radio Mix)/I'm Out (picture disc) 12
92	RCA 74321 10813 4	I Found Heaven/I'm Out (cassette) 4
92	RCA 74321 11600 7	A Million Love Songs/A Million Love Songs (The Lovers Mix) (p/s, with tattoos) . 12
92	RCA 74321 11600 4	A Million Love Songs/A Million Love Songs (The Lovers Mix) (cassette) 4
92	RCA 74321 11630 7	THE LOVE SONGS (EP) 5
92	RCA 74321 112313 1	Could It Be Magic (Deep In Rapino's Club Mix)/Take That Club Megamix/ Could It Be Magic (Mr F Mix) (12", poster p/s) 12
93	RCA 74321 13311 7	Why Can't I Wake Up With You (Radio Edit)/Promises (live)/ Clap Your Hands (live) (EP) 4
95	RCA (no cat. no.)	Every Guy (CD, unreleased, 1-track promo only) 25
92	RCA 74321 10923-19	TAKE THAT AND PARTY (LP, with poster) 10
93	RCA 74321 16926-1	EVERYTHING CHANGES (LP, picture disc) 10
	(see also Robbie Williams)	

TALBOT BROTHERS

59	Melodisc MEL 1507	Bloodshot Eyes/She's Got Freckles 10
60s	Melodisc CAL 20	Bloodshot Eyes/She's Got Freckles (reissue). 6

ZIGGY TALENT

55	Brunswick 05506	Cheek To Cheek (Cha Cha)/Bozooki Blues 7

TALES OF JUSTINE

67	HMV POP 1614	Albert/Monday Morning (some in p/s) 90/30
97	Tenth Planet TP 034	PETALS FROM A SUNFLOWER (LP, gatefold sleeve, numbered, 1,000 only) 12
	(see also Tim Rice)	

TALISKER

75	Caroline CA 1513	DREAMING OF GLENISLA (LP) 12

TALISMAN

73	Argo AFW 110	Stepping Stones/Dr Jazz 5
72	Argo ZFB 33	PRIMROSE DREAMS (LP) 25
73	Argo ZDA 161	STEPPING STONES (LP) 25

TALISMEN

65	Stateside SS 408	Masters Of War/Casting My Spell 30

TALKING HEADS

77	Sire 6078 604	Love Goes To Building On Fire/New Feeling (p/s) 7
77	Sire 6078 610	Psycho Killer/I Wish You Wouldn't Say That (p/s) 5
77	Sire 6078 610	Psycho Killer/Psycho Killer (Acoustic)/I Wish You Wouldn't Say That (12", p/s) . . . 8
78	Sire 6078 620	Pulled Up/Don't Worry About The Government (p/s) 5
79	Sire SIR 4004	Take Me To The River/Found A Job (p/s). 4
79	Sire SIR 4004/SAM 87	Take Me To The River/Found A Job//Love Goes To Building On Fire/ Psycho Killer (double pack, gatefold p/s) 6
79	Sire SIR 4027	Life During Wartime/Electric Guitar (p/s) 4
79	WEA SPC 9	Take Me To The River/Psycho Killer (cassette) 4
80	Sire SIR 4033	I Zimbra/Paper (p/s) 4
80	Sire SIR 4040	Cities/Cities (live) (p/s) 4
80	Sire SIR 4040T	Cities/Cities (live)/Artists Only (live) (12", p/s) 7
80	Sire SIR 4050	Houses In Motion (Special Re-Mixed Version)/Air (p/s) 4
84	Sire W 9451T/SAM 176	This Must Be The Place (Full Version)/Moon Rocks//Slippery People (Remix)/ Making Flippy Floppy (Remix) (12", p/s, double pack) 8
85	EMI 12EMID 5520	The Lady Don't Mind/Give Me Back My Name//Slippery People (live)/ This Must Be The Place (Naive Melody) (live) (12", p/s, double pack) 7
85	EMI EMIP 5530	Road To Nowhere/Television Man (picture disc). 5
85	EMI 12 EMID 5530/ 12 EMI 5504	Road To Nowhere/Television Man (Extended)//Slippery People (Long Live Version)/Naive Melody (live) (12", stickered double pack) 8
86	EMI 12 EMIP 5543	And She Was (Extended Mix)/And She Was/Perfect World (12", picture disc) 7
87	EMI EMD 1	Radio Head/Hey Now (Movie Version)//Radio Head (Movie Version)/ Radio Head (Extended Remix) (double pack, gatefold p/s) 5
87	EMI CDEM 1	Radio Head (LP Version)/Hey Now (Movie Version)/Radio Head (Extended Remix)/Radio Head (Movie Version)/Hey Now (Milwaukee Mix) (CD) 7
88	EMI CDEM 68	Blind (Vocal Mix)/Blind/Bill (CD) 7
88	EMI 10EM 53	(Nothing But) Flowers/Facts Of Life/Ruby Dear/Mommy, Daddy, You And I (10", numbered p/s) 6
88	EMI CDEM 53	(Nothing But) Flowers/(Nothing But) Flowers (Lilywhite Mix)/ Ruby Dear (Bush Mix)/Mommy, Daddy, You And I (CD). 7
89	Sire 921 135-2	Love Goes To Building On Fire/Psycho Killer/Once In A Lifetime/ Burning Down The House (3" CD, card sleeve) 7
79	Sire K 56707	FEAR OF MUSIC (LP, with free single "Psycho Killer"/"New Feeling" [SAM 108]) 12
79	Sire SRK 6076	FEAR OF MUSIC (LP, re-pressing, with bonus single "Psycho Killer [live]") . . . 10
83	EMI 9237711	SPEAKING IN TONGUES (LP, clear vinyl in special cover) 15
	(see also David Byrne, Dinosaur)	

TALK TALK

82	EMI EMI 5265	Mirror Man/Strike Up The Band (p/s). 8
82	EMI 12EMI 5314	Today (Extended)/It's So Serious (12", p/s). 12
82	EMI EMIP 5352	Talk Talk (Remix)/Mirror Man (picture disc). 7
82	EMI EMIP 5352	Talk Talk (Extended)/Talk Talk (BBC Version) (12", p/s). 12
83	EMI 12EMI 5373	My Foolish Friend (Extended)/Call In The Nightboys/ My Foolish Friend (12", p/s). 12

MINT VALUE £

TALK TALK

TOM TALL

TALL BOYS

TALMY/STONE BAND

TALULAH GOSH

TAMANGOE'S
79	Grapevine GRP 122	I Really Love You/You've Been Gone So Long (withdrawn)	8

JAMES TAMLIN
65	Columbia DB 7438	Is There Time/Main Line Central Station	10
65	Columbia DB 7577	Yes I Have/Now There Are Two	6

TAMPA RED
50	Jazz Collector L 58	Easy Rider Blues/Come On Mama Do That Dance (78)	20
52	HMV JO 301	Pretty Baby Blues/Since Baby's Been Gone (78, export issue)	40
50s	Square M 2	Moot It Boy/She Rocks Me (With One Steady Roll) (78)	50
64	RCA RCX 7160	R & B VOL. 3 (EP)	30

TAMPA RED/GEORGIA TOM
59	Jazz Collector JEL 3	THE MALE BLUES VOLUME 2 (EP)	15

TAMS
63	Stateside SS 146	Untie Me/Disillusioned	12
63	HMV POP 1254	What Kind Of Fool Do You Think I Am/Laugh It Off	12
64	HMV POP 1298	It's All Right, You're Just In Love/You Lied To Your Daddy	10
64	HMV POP 1331	Hey Girl Don't Bother Me/Take Away	35
65	HMV POP 1464	Concrete Jungle/Till The End Of Time	10
69	Stateside SS 2123	Be Young, Be Foolish, Be Happy/That Same Old Song	10
70	Capitol CL 15650	Too Much Foolin' Around/How Long Love	10
75	ABC ABC 4020	Hey Girl Don't Bother Me/Be Young, Be Foolish, Be Happy	5
68	Stateside (S)SL 10258	A LITTLE MORE SOUL (LP)	30
70	Stateside SSL 10304	BE YOUNG, BE FOOLISH, BE HAPPY (LP)	22
74	Probe SPB 1044	THE BEST OF THE TAMS (LP)	15
74	ABC ABCL 5118	THE BEST OF THE TAMS (LP, reissue)	12

JOCK TAMSON'S BAIRNS
(see under 'J')

TANAMO
63	Island WI 108	Come Down/I Am Holding On (actually by Lord Tanamo)	18

TANDOORI CASSETTE
83	IKA IKA 001	Angel Talk/Third World Brief Case (p/s, 5,000 only)	15

(see also Nazareth, Alex Harvey, Tear Gas)

SHARON TANDY
65	Mercury MF 898	Love Makes The World Go Round/By My Side	15
65	Pye 7N 15806	Now That You've Gone/Hurtin' Me	12
65	Pye 7N 15939	I've Found Love/Perhaps Not Forever	7
67	Atlantic 584 098	Toe Hold/I Can't Get Over It	15
67	Atlantic 584 124	Stay With Me/Hold On	25
67	Atlantic 584 137	Our Day Will Come/Look And Find	20
68	Atlantic 584 166	Fool On The Hill/For No One	20
68	Atlantic 584 181	Love Is Not A Simple Affair/Hurry Hurry Choo-Choo	18
68	Atlantic 584 194	You've Gotta Believe It/Border Town	18
68	Atlantic 584 214	The Way She Looks At You/He'll Hurt Me	18
68	Atlantic 584 219	Hold On/Daughter Of The Sun	40
69	Atlantic 584 242	Gotta Get Enough Time/Somebody Speaks Your Name	18

(see also Fleur-De-Lys, Tony & Tandy)

NORMA TANEGA
66	Stateside SS 496	Walkin' My Cat Named Dog/I'm In The Sky	6
66	Stateside SS 537	Bread/Waves	5
66	Stateside S(S)L 10182	WALKIN' MY CAT NAMED DOG (LP)	20

TANGERINE DREAM
74	Virgin PR 214	Phaedra (Edit)/Mysterious Semblance At The Strand Of Nightmares (promo)	20
76	Virgin VDJ 17	Stratosfear/The Big Sleep In Search Of Hades (promo only)	20
77	MCA PSR 413	Betrayal (Sorceror Theme)/Search (promo only)	22
77	Virgin VS 199	Encore/Hobo March (no p/s)	5
81	Virgin VS 444	Chronozon/Network 23 (p/s)	8
84	Jive Electro P 74	Warsaw In The Sun/Polish Dance (map-shaped picture disc)	10
84	Jive Electro T 74	Warsaw In The Sun (Parts 1 & 2)/Polish Dance/Rare Bird (12", p/s)	8
85	Jive Electro T 101	STREETHAWK (12" EP)	6
87	Jive Electro 143	Tyger/21st Century Common Man II (p/s)	10
87	Jive Electro T 143	Tyger/Tyger (7" Version)/21st Century Common Man II (12", p/s)	10
89	Private 663 747	ORANGES DON'T DANCE (CD EP, promo only)	30
74	Polydor Super 2383 297	ATEM (LP)	15
75	Polydor Super 2383 314	ALPHA CENTAURI (LP)	15
79	Virgin V 2111	FORCE MAJEURE (LP, clear vinyl)	18
80	Virgin VBOX 2	TANGERINE DREAM '70-80 (4-LP box set)	25
80	Virgin TCVX 2	TANGERINE DREAM '70-80 (4-cassette box set)	25
81	Virgin V 2212	EXIT (LP, 1st 1,000 with poster)	12
84	MCA MCF 3233	FIRESTARTER (LP, soundtrack)	12
84	Jive Electro HIPX 22	POLAND — THE WARSAW CONCERT (2-LP, picture disc)	25
85	Heavy Metal HMI PD 29	FLASHPOINT (LP, soundtrack, picture disc)	15
85	Heavy Metal HMXD 29	FLASHPOINT (CD, soundtrack; playable CD [most copies faulty])	50
86	Jive Electro TANG 1	IN THE BEGINNING (6-LP box set, with booklet)	25
87	Jive CHIP 26	LE PARC (CD, U.K. pressing [most copies pressed in Europe])	15
90	Virgin TD AK 11	TANGERINE DREAM (3-CD, 'Collector's Edition' box set)	25

(see also Edgar Froese, Klaus Schulze)

TANGERINE PEEL
67	United Artists UP 1193	Every Christian Lion-Hearted Man Will Show You/Trapped	15
68	CBS 3402	Solid Gold Mountain/Light Across The River	5
68	CBS 3676	Talking To No One/Wishing Tree	6

MINT VALUE £

69	MGM MGM 1470	Never Say Never Again/A Thousand Miles Away	6
69	MGM MGM 1487	Play Me A Sad Song And I'll Dance/Wish You Could Be Here With Me	5
70	RCA RCA 1936	Move Into My World/In Between	5
70	RCA RCA 1990	Soft Delights/Thinking Of Me	5
70	RCA RCA 2036	What Am I To Do?/Don't Let Me Be Misunderstood	5
70	RCA LSA 3002	SOFT DELIGHTS (LP)	20

TANGO BRIGADE
81	Epic S EPC 9398	Donegal/In Vain (p/s)	5

(see also Starjets)

TANK
81	Kamaflage KAM 1	Don't Walk Away/Shellshock/Hammer On (p/s, some with cover mounted patch)	7/5
82	Kamaflage KAM 3	Turn Your Head Around/Steppin' On A Landmine (p/s)	15
82	Kamaflage KAM 7	Crazy Horses/Filth Bitch Boogie (p/s)	5
82	Kamaflage KAP 1	(He Fell In Love With A) Stormtrooper/Blood Guts And Beer (picture disc)	5
82	Kamaflage KAMLP 1	FILTH HOUNDS OF HADES (LP, with bonus p/s 7" "Don't Walk Away (live)"/ "The Snake" [KAM F1])	15
83	Music For Nations MFN 3P	THIS MEANS WAR (LP, picture disc)	15

(see also Damned)

TANNAHILL WEAVERS
76	Plant Life PLR 001	ARE YE SLEEPING MAGGIE? (LP, with lyric insert)	12
78	Plant Life PLR 010	THE OLD WOMAN'S DANCE (LP)	12

HOLLY TANNEN & PETE COOPER
79	Plant Life PLR 015	FROSTY MORNING (LP)	12

PHIL TANNER
68	EDF SSLP 1005	PHIL TANNER (LP, with lyric book)	25

TANNER SISTERS
55	Mercury MB 3214	Bambino/Penelope Jane (78)	8
55	Mercury MB 3225	Dreamboat/Blow Hot, Blow Cold (78)	8

(see also Max Bygraves)

TANTONES
57	Vogue V 9085	So Afraid/Tell Me	650
57	Vogue V 9085	So Afraid/Tell Me (78)	120

TANTOR
99	Rogue FANT 12	Quay Hai!/TEMBOLI: Cheese Me Up ('knitted' p/s)	8

TANTRUM
80	Ovation OV 1247	RATHER BE ROCKIN' (LP)	10

TANZ DER YOUTH
78	Radar ADA 19	I'm Sorry, I'm Sorry/Delay (p/s)	5

(see also Brian James, Damned)

TAO JONES INDEX
97	RCA 512541	Pallas Athena (live)/V-2 Schneider (live) (12", p/s)	7

(see also David Bowie)

TAPESTRY
67	London HLZ 10138	Carnaby Street/Taming Of The Shrew	8
68	NEMS 56-3679	Like The Sun/Florence	5

DEMETRISS TAPP
64	Coral Q 72470	Lipstick Paint A Smile On Me/If You Find Love	6

TARA
78	Polydor 2066 009	Happy/El Amor De Una Mujer	6

TARANTULA
70	A&M AMLS 959	TARANTULA (LP)	15

JIMMY TARBUCK
65	Immediate IM 018	Someday/(We're) Wastin' Time	7

TARHEEL SLIM & LITTLE ANN
65	Sue WI 390	You Make Me Feel So Good/Got To Keep On Lovin' You	22

TARRIERS
56	London HLN 8340	Cindy, Oh Cindy/Only If You Praise The Lord (as Vince Martin & Tarriers)	25
56	London HLN 8340	Cindy, Oh Cindy/Only If You Praise The Lord (as Vince Martin & Tarriers) (78)	8
57	Columbia DB 3891	The Banana Boat Song/No Hidin Place	7
57	Columbia DB 3961	Tom Dooley/Everybody Loves Saturday Night	7
57	Columbia DB 4025	Dunya/Quinto (My Little Pony)	6
58	Columbia DB 4148	I Know Where I'm Going/Acres Of Clams	6
58	Columbia DB 4148	I Know Where I'm Going/Acres Of Clams (78)	8
58	London HLU 8600	Lonesome Traveller/East Virginia	15
58	London HLU 8600	Lonesome Traveller/East Virginia (78)	20
60	London RET 1236	HARD TRAVELIN' VOLUME 1 (EP)	8
60	London RET 1237	HARD TRAVELIN' VOLUME 2 (EP)	8
57	Columbia 33S 1115	THE TARRIERS (10" LP)	18

(see also Vince Martin, Rooftop Singers)

TARTAN HORDE
75	United Artists UP 35891	Bay City Rollers, We Love You/Rollers Theme	12

(see also Nick Lowe, Rat Scabies, Roogalator, Disco Brothers)

TARTANS
67	Island WI 3058	Dance All Night/What Can I Do	15
68	Caltone TONE 115	Awake The Town (with Lynn Taitt's Band)/LYNN TAITT & JETS: The Brush	10

| 68 | Caltone TONE 117 | Coming On Strong/It's Alright (with Tommy McCook's Band) | 10 |
| 71 | Escort ERT 843 | A Day Will Come/ROBI'S All STARS: Version | 5 |

(see also Devon & Tartans, Kaddo Strings, Max Romeo, Derrick Morgan)

TASAVALLAN PRESIDENTI
| 73 | Sonet SNTF 636 | LAMBERTLAND (LP) | 12 |
| 74 | Sonet SNTF 658 | MILKY WAY MOSES (LP, with insert) | 12 |

TASSELS
59	London HL 8885	To A Soldier Boy/The Boy For Me	80
59	London HL 8885	To A Soldier Boy/The Boy For Me (78)	50
59	Top Rank JAR 229	To A Young Lover/My Guy And I	30

TASTE
68	Major Minor MM 560	Blister On The Moon/Born On The Wrong Side Of Time	10
69	Polydor 56313	Born On The Wrong Side Of Time/Same Old Story	6
70	Major Minor MM 718	Born On The Wrong Side Of Time/Blister On The Moon	6
69	Polydor 583 042	TASTE (LP)	20
70	Polydor 583 083	ON THE BOARDS (LP)	20
71	Polydor 2310 082	LIVE TASTE (LP)	15
72	Polydor 2383 120	TASTE — LIVE AT THE ISLE OF WIGHT (LP)	15

(see also Rory Gallagher, Stud)

TASTE OF HONEY
| 69 | Rim RIM 19 | 8.05/Charleston | 5 |

BUDDY TATE
| 58 | Felsted FAJ 7004 | SWINGING LIKE TATE (LP) | 30 |

HOWARD TATE
66	Verve VS 541	Ain't Nobody Home/How Come My Bulldog Won't Bark	8
67	Verve VS 549	Look At Granny Run Run/Half A Man	10
67	Verve VS 552	Get It While You Can/Glad I Knew Better	6
67	Verve VS 555	Baby I Love You/How Blue Can You Get	7
67	Verve VS 556	I Learned It All The Hard Way/Part Time Love	6
68	Verve VS 565	Stop/Shoot 'Em All Down	6
68	Verve VS 571	Night Owl/Every Day I Have The Blues	8
70	Major Minor MM 696	My Soul's Got A Hole In It/It's Too Late	5
67	Verve (S)VLP 9179	GET IT WHILE YOU CAN (LP)	18

PHIL TATE ORCHESTRA
58	Oriole CB 1438	Dream Lover/Zing, Went The Strings Of My Heart	5
58	Oriole CB 1438	Dream Lover/Zing, Went The Strings Of My Heart (78)	8
59	Oriole CB 1514	Countdown (Jive)/Green Turtle	5
59	Oriole CB 1514	Countdown (Jive)/Green Turtle (78)	12
60	Oriole CB 1539	Falling In Love Again/Dancing On The Ceiling	5
60	Oriole CB 1539	Falling In Love Again/Dancing On The Ceiling (78)	15
60	Oriole CB 1568	Moulin Rouge Waltz/I Won't Dance (78)	10
60	Oriole CB 1585	I Came I Saw I Conga'd/Cokey Cokey (78)	10
61	Oriole CB 1601	Are You Lonesome Tonight/Whispering Tango	6
61	Oriole CB 1601	Are You Lonesome Tonight/Whispering Tango (78)	25
63	Oriole CB 1832	Hi-Lili, Hi-Lo/Theme From 'Dr. Kildare'	5
63	Oriole CB 1878	Devils Horn (Twist)/Hitch Hike (Twist)	5
62	Oriole EP 7052	PARTY DANCES (EP)	8
62	Oriole EP 7060	TUNES FOR TWISTERS (EP)	10

TOMMY TATE
| 66 | Columbia DB 8046 | Big Blue Diamonds/A Lover's Reward | 25 |

TATTY OLLITY
| 70s | Tatty TR 101 | Punktuation | 4 |

ART TATUM
51	Melodisc MEL 1157	Fine And Dandy/Ja Da (78)	6
54	Vogue EPV 1008	ART TATUM (EP)	8
55	Columbia SEG 7540	ART TATUM (EP)	8
50s	Melodisc EPM7 108	ART TATUM TRIO (EP)	8
55	Columbia Clef SEB 10003	ART TATUM (EP)	12
56	Columbia Clef SEB 10027	TATUM-CARTER-BELLSON TRIO (EP, with Benny Carter & Louis Bellson)	8
57	Columbia Clef SEB 10062	TATUM-CARTER-BELLSON TRIO (EP, with Benny Carter & Louis Bellson)	8
57	Philips BBE 12136	UNFORGETTABLE ART (EP)	8
57	Vogue EPV 1212	ART TATUM (EP)	8
58	Columbia Clef SEB 10084	ART TATUM AT HOLLYWOOD BOWL (EP)	7
58	Columbia Clef SEB 10101	ART TATUM — BUDDY DE FRANCO QUARTET (EP)	7
59	Columbia Clef SEB 10116	DELICATE TOUCH OF ART TATUM (EP)	7
60	Fontana TFE 17235	ART TATUM NO. 1 (EP)	7
60	Fontana TFE 17236	ART TATUM NO. 2 (EP)	8
60	Fontana TFE 17237	ART TATUM NO. 3 (EP)	7
60	HMV 7EG 8604	THE GREATEST PIANO OF THEM ALL (EP)	7
60	HMV 7EG 8619	ART TATUM — BUDDY DE FRANCO QUARTET (EP)	7
61	HMV 7EG 8684	INCOMPARABLE MUSIC OF ART TATUM (EP)	7
62	Ember EMB 4502	MEMORIES OF ART TATUM (EP)	7
51	Capitol LC 6524	ART TATUM (10" LP)	18
53	Capitol LC 6625	OUT OF NOWHERE (10" LP)	40
54	Vogue LDE 081	ART TATUM "JUST JAZZ" (10" LP)	30
55	Vogue Coral LRA 10011	THE ART TATUM TRIO (10" LP)	15
55	Columbia Clef 33CX 10005	THE GENIUS OF ART TATUM (LP)	12
55	Capitol LC 6638	ART TATUM ENCORES (10" LP)	15
56	Columbia Clef 33CX 10053	THE GENIUS OF ART TATUM (NO. 2) (LP)	12
57	Columbia Clef 33C 9033	THE GENIUS OF ART TATUM (NO. 3) (10" LP)	15
57	Columbia Clef 33C 9039	PRESENTING THE ART TATUM TRIO (10" LP)	15

Art TATUM

MINT VALUE £

57	Vogue Coral LVA 9047	HERE'S ART TATUM (LP)	12
58	Columbia Clef 33CX 10115	ART TATUM (LP)	12
59	Columbia Clef 33CX 10137	ART TATUM-BEN WEBSTER QUARTET (LP)	40
60	Top Rank 35/067	ART TATUM DISCOVERIES (LP)	10
61	Brunswick LAT 8358	THE ART OF TATUM (LP)	10
61	Ember EMB 3314	MEMORIES OF ART TATUM (LP)	10
61	Ember EMB 3326	MEMORIES OF ART TATUM VOL. 2 (LP)	10
64	Xtra XTRA 1007	ART TATUM (LP)	10
67	Fontana FJL 904	ART (LP)	15

BERNIE TAUPIN
| 71 | DJM DJLPS 415 | TAUPIN (LP) | 12 |

TAVARES
74	Capitol CL 15795	She's Gone/To Love You	4
75	Capitol CL 15809	Remember What I Told You To Forget/My Ship	4
76	Capitol CL 15848	Free Ride/In The Eyes Of Love	4
76	Capitol CL 15867	Love I Never Had/In The City	4
77	Capitol E-ST 11628	LOVE STORM (LP)	10

JOHN TAVENER
70	Apple SAPCOR 15	THE WHALE (LP, gatefold sleeve)	50
71	Apple SAPCOR 20	CELTIC REQUIEM (LP, gatefold sleeve, with insert & 'Apple' inner sleeve)	90
77	Ring O' 2320 104	THE WHALE (LP, reissue, different single sleeve)	50
92	Apple SAPCOR 15	THE WHALE (LP, 2nd reissue, gatefold sleeve with inner sleeve)	20
93	Apple SAPCOR 20	CELTIC REQUIEM (LP, reissue, gatefold sleeve with inner sleeve)	20
93	Apple SAPCOR 20	CELTIC REQUIEM (CD)	20

TAVERNERS
69	Saga EROS 8146	SELDOM SOBER (LP)	18
73	Trailer LER 2080	BLOWING SANDS (LP)	15
74	Folk Heritage FHR 062	TIMES OF OLD ENGLAND (LP)	25
78	Folk Heritage FHR 101	SAME OLD FRIENDS (LP, with insert)	12

TAW FOLK
| 75 | Sentinel SENS 1030 | DEVONSHIRE CREAM AND CIDER (LP) | 12 |

CYRIL TAWNEY
69	Polydor 236 577	THE OUTLANDISH KNIGHT (LP)	20
70	Argo ZFB 4	SINGS CHILDREN'S SONGS FROM DEVON AND CORNWALL (LP)	20
72	Argo ZFB 28	TAWNEY IN PORT (LP)	12
73	Argo ZFB 87	I WILL GIVE MY LOVE (LP)	12
76	Trailer LER 2095	DOWN AMONG THE BARLEY STRAW (LP)	12

TAXI GIRL
| 80 | Virgin VS 467 | Cherchez Le Garçon/Jardin Chinois (p/s) | 4 |

ALLAN TAYLOR
71	Liberty LBF 15447	Sometimes/Song For Kathy	5
73	United Artists UP 35541	My Father's Room/Always You	5
71	Liberty LBS 83483	SOMETIMES (LP, gatefold sleeve)	18
72	United Artists UAS 29275	THE LADY (LP)	12
73	United Artists UAG 29468	THE AMERICAN ALBUM (LP, gatefold sleeve)	12
(see also Fairport Convention)			

AUSTIN TAYLOR
| 60 | Top Rank JAR 511 | Push Push/A Heart That's True | 15 |

BILLY TAYLOR (TRIO)
50s	Esquire EP 115	BILLY TAYLOR (EP)	15
50s	Esquire EP 169	BILLY TAYLOR TRIO (EP)	20
54	Felsted EDL 87009	JAZZ AT STORYVILLE (10" LP)	25
54	Esquire 20-053	AT THE TOWN HALL 1954 (LP)	25
54	Esquire 32-010	A TOUCH OF TAYLOR (LP)	25
60	Vogue LAE 12192	TAYLOR MADE PIANO (LP)	25

BOBBY TAYLOR
| 64 | Columbia DB 7282 | Temptation/Mod Bod | 7 |

BOBBY TAYLOR (& VANCOUVERS)
68	Tamla Motown TMG 654	Does Your Mama Know About Me/Fading Away (with Vancouvers)	35
73	Epic EPC 1720	I Can't Quit Your Love/Queen Of The Ghetto (solo)	5
69	T. Motown (S)TML 11093	BOBBY TAYLOR AND THE VANCOUVERS (LP)	40
70	T. Motown (S)TML 11125	TAYLOR MADE SOUL (LP, solo)	60

BRYAN TAYLOR
| 61 | Piccadilly 7N 35018 | The Donkey's Tale/Let It Snow On Christmas Day | 35 |

CECIL TAYLOR JAZZ UNIT
| 60s | Fontana SFJL 926 | NEFERTITI, THE BEAUTIFUL ONE HAS COME (LP) | 12 |

CECIL TAYLOR QUARTET
| 60 | Contemporary LAC 12216 | LOOKING AHEAD! (LP) | 15 |

CHIP TAYLOR
62	Warner Bros WB 82	Here I Am/I Love You But I Know	5
73	Buddah 2011 151	Angel Of The Morning/Swear To God, Your Honor	5
73	Buddah 2318 074	GASOLINE (LP)	12
74	Warner Bros K 56032	CHIP TAYLOR'S LAST CHANCE (LP)	12

DUFFY TAYLOR BLUES
| 69 | Page One POF 130 | You Wrecked My Life/I'll Be There | 6 |

EDDIE TAYLOR
| 65 | Big Bear BEAR 6 | READY FOR EDDIE (LP) | 10 |

EDDIE TAYLOR & FLOYD JONES
60s	XX MIN 712	EDDIE TAYLOR & FLOYD JONES (EP) 15

EDDIE TAYLOR & JIMMY REED
60s	XX MIN 704	EDDIE TAYLOR & JIMMY REED (EP) 15

(see also Jimmy Reed)

ELIZABETH TAYLOR
63	Colpix PXL 459	IN LONDON (LP, TV soundtrack, music by John Barry, mono/stereo) 40/50

(see also John Barry)

FELICE TAYLOR
67	President PT 120	It May Be Winter Outside/BOB KEENE ORCHESTRA: Winter Again 5
67	President PT 133	I'm Under The Influence/BOB KEENE ORCHESTRA: Love Theme 5
67	President PT 155	I Feel Love Comin' On/BOB KEENE ORCHESTRA: Comin' On Again 5
68	President PT 193	Captured By Your Love/I Can Feel Your Love (Coming Down On Me) 6
68	President PT 220	Suree-Surrender/All I Want To Do Is Love You 6

GEOFF TAYLOR
50s	Esquire EP 55	GEOFF TAYLOR SEXTET (EP) 8
50s	Esquire EP 105	GEOFF TAYLOR ALL STARS (EP) 8

GLORIA TAYLOR
70	Polydor BM 56788	You Gotta Pay The Price/Loving You And Being Loved By You 8

HOUND DOG TAYLOR
66	Outasite 45-504	Christine/Alley Music (99 copies only) 60

JAMES TAYLOR
70	Apple APPLE 32	Carolina In My Mind/Something's Wrong 10
68	Apple (S)APCOR 3	JAMES TAYLOR (LP, gatefold sleeve, black inner, orange cover lettering, mono/stereo) 60/35
70	Apple SAPCOR 3	JAMES TAYLOR (LP, 2nd issue, gatefold sleeve, 'Apple' inner sleeve, black cover lettering) 25
70	Warner Bros WS 1843	SWEET BABY JAMES (LP, orange label, later green label) . . . . each 15
71	Warner Bros WS 2561	MUD SLIDE SLIM AND THE BLUE HORIZON (LP, g/fold sleeve, green label) 15
72	Warner Bros K 46043	SWEET BABY JAMES (LP, reissue, green label) 12
72	Warner Bros K 46085	MUD SLIDE SLIM AND THE BLUE HORIZON (LP, reissue, gatefold sleeve, green label) 12
73	Warner Bros K 46185	ONE MAN DOG (LP, green label, with insert & stickered sleeve) 12
91	Apple SAPCOR 3	JAMES TAYLOR (LP, reissue, gatefold sleeve) 20
91	Apple SAPCOR 3	JAMES TAYLOR (CD) 20

JAMES TAYLOR QUARTET
87	Re-Elect President FORD 1	Blow Up/One Mint Julep (p/s) 7
88	Urban URB 24	Starsky And Hutch Theme//(Version) 4
88	Urban URBX 24	Starsky And Hutch Theme//(Version) (12") 7
92	Big Life JTQ 7 PROMO 1	Absolution (live) (gig freebie, plain black sleeve with postcard, 1 side etched) . . . 4
90s	Big Life	Hope And Pray (p/s) 4
87	Re-Elect Pres. REAGAN 2	MISSION: IMPOSSIBLE (mini-LP, 45rpm) 10
87	Re-Elect Pres. KENNEDY 1	THE MONEY SPYDER (LP) 10
95	Acid Jazz JAZIDLP 115L	IN THE HANDS OF THE INEVITABLE (LP, with bonus 2-track 12") 10

(see also Prisoners, Daggermen)

JEREMY TAYLOR
62	Decca F 11502	Ag. Pleeze Daddy/Jo'burg Talking Blues 5
68	Fontana TF 962	Red Velvet Steering Wheel/Nasty Spider 5
64	Decca DFE 8581	"WAIT A MINIM" SONGS (EP) 12
66	Decca LK 4731	ALWAYS SOMETHING NEW (LP) 40
68	Fontana (S)TL 5475	HIS SONGS (LP) 15
69	Fontana (S)TL 5523	MORE OF HIS SONGS (LP) 15
72	Galliard GAL 4018	PIECE OF GROUND (LP) 35
73	Canon CPT 3982	JOBSWORTH (LP) 12
75	Spark SRLP 115	COME TO BLACKPOOL (LP) 12

JOHN TAYLOR
71	Turtle	PAUSE AND THINK AGAIN (LP) 40

JOHNNIE TAYLOR
67	Stax 601 003	Ain't That Lovin' You/Outside Love (dark blue label, later light blue) 8/5
68	Stax STAX 106	Who's Makin' Love/I'm Trying 5
69	Stax STAX 114	Take Care Of Your Homework/Hold On This Time 6
69	Stax STAX 122	(I Wanna) Testify/I Had To Fight With Love 5
69	Stax STAX 129	I Could Never Be President/It's Amazing 5
70	Stax STAX 141	Love Bones/Separation Line 5
70	Stax STAX 150	Steal Away/Friday Night 8
70	Stax STAX 156	I Am Somebody (Parts 1 & 2) 5
71	Stax 2025 021	Jody's Got Your Girl And Gone/A Fool Like Me 5
73	Stax 2025 083	Standing In For Jody/Shackin' Up 5
73	Stax 2025 194	I Believe In Love/Love Depression 5
75	Stax STXS 2021	It's September/Just One Moment 5
75	Stax STXS 2025	Friday Night/I Ain't Particular 7
76	CBS 4886	Disco Lady/Sombody's Gettin' It (blue vinyl) 5
67	Stax 589 008	WANTED, ONE SOUL SINGER (LP) 25
69	Stax (S)XATS 1006	WHO'S MAKING LOVE (LP) 22
69	Stax 228 008	LOOKING FOR JOHNNIE TAYLOR (LP) 20
69	Stax SXATS 1024	THE J.T. PHILOSOPHY CONTINUES (LP) 20
70	Soul City SCB 2	ROOTS OF JOHNNIE TAYLOR (LP) 30
71	Stax 2363 009	WHO'S MAKING LOVE (LP, reissue) 10
71	Stax 2362 015	GREATEST HITS (LP) 12

Johnnie TAYLOR

74	Stax STXH 5003	SUPER TAYLOR (LP) 15
75	Stax STS 3014	TAYLORED IN SILK (LP)... 15
78	CBS 82776	EVER READY (LP) 12

(LITTLE) JOHNNY TAYLOR

65	Vocalion V 9234	Part Time Love/Somewhere Down The Line 12
66	Vocalion VP 9264	One More Chance/Looking At The Future................................ 12
72	Mojo 2092 033	Everybody Knows About My Good Thing (Parts 1 & 2) 5
72	Mojo 2092 044	It's My Fault Darling/There's Something On Your Mind 5
65	Vocalion VA-F 8031	LITTLE JOHNNY TAYLOR (LP)... 40
72	Mojo 2916 015	EVERYBODY KNOWS ABOUT MY GOOD THING (LP)...................... 20
73	Contempo COLP 1003	OPEN HOUSE AT MY HOUSE (LP) 12
74	Contempo CLP 502	SUPER TAYLORS (LP, with Ted Taylor) 12

JOSEPH TAYLOR

72	Leader LEA 4050	UNTO BRIGG FAIR (LP, gatefold sleeve with booklet) 20

KINGSIZE TAYLOR (& DOMINOS)

64	Polydor NH 66990	Memphis Tennessee/Money (reissue of Shakers single) 18
64	Polydor NH 66991	Hippy Hippy Shake/Dr. Feelgood (reissue of Shakers single) 18
64	Decca F 11874	Stupidity/Bad Boy 20
64	Decca F 11935	Somebody's Always Trying/Looking For My Baby (solo) 25
65	Polydor BM 56152	Thinkin'/Let Me Love You.. 20
63	Polydor EPH21 628	TWIST AND SHAKE (EP, manufactured in Germany) 100
64	Decca DFE 8569	TEENBEAT 2 — FROM THE STAR CLUB, HAMBURG (EP) 100

(see also Shakers, Paddy Klaus & Gibson)

KO KO TAYLOR

66	Chess CRS 8035	Wang Dang Doodle/Blues Heaven...................................... 12
72	Chess 6145 018	Violent Love/The Egg Or The Hen/Wang Dang Doodle..................... 5

LIVINGSTON TAYLOR

71	Warner Bros WB 8022	Carolina Day/Doctor Man.. 4
72	Warner Bros K 16138	Get Out Of Bed/Mom, Dad 4
70	Warner Bros WS 3006	LIVINGSTONE TAYLOR (LP)... 12

MICK TAYLOR

65	CBS 201770	London Town/Hoboin' 15

MICK TAYLOR

79	CBS 82600	MICK TAYLOR (LP, with inner sleeve) 12
90	Maze 084 649	STRANGER IN THIS TOWN (LP).. 12

(see also Rolling Stones, Gods, Institute Of Formal Research)

MIKE TAYLOR

65	Columbia SX 6042	PENDULUM (LP)... 100
66	Columbia SX 6137	TRIO (LP) 100

(see also Jack Bruce)

MONTANA TAYLOR

52	Vocalion V 1011	Indiana Avenue Stomp/ROMEO NELSON: Head Rag Hop (78)............. 12

NEVILLE TAYLOR (& CUTTERS)

58	Parlophone R 4447	House Of Bamboo/Mercy, Mercy, Percy (solo) 18
58	Parlophone R 4447	House Of Bamboo/Mercy, Mercy, Percy (solo) (78) 25
58	Parlophone R 4476	Tears On My Pillow/I Don't Want To Set The World On Fire (solo) 15
58	Parlophone R 4476	Tears On My Pillow/I Don't Want To Set The World On Fire (solo) (78) 20
58	Parlophone R 4493	A Baby Lay Sleeping/The Miracle Of Christmas (solo)................... 8
58	Parlophone R 4493	A Baby Lay Sleeping/The Miracle Of Christmas (solo) (78) 10
59	Parlophone R 4524	Crazy Little Daisy/The First Words Of Love (solo) 15
59	Parlophone R 4524	Crazy Little Daisy/The First Words Of Love (solo) (78) 30
60	Oriole CB 1546	Dance With Dolly/Free Passes... 8
60	Oriole CB 1546	Dance With Dolly/Free Passes (78) 50
60	Embassy WB 373	It Ain't Necessarily So/BOBBIE BRITTON: Woman Is A Sometime Love 5
60	Embassy WB 373	It Ain't Necessarily So/BOBBIE BRITTON: Woman Is A Sometime Love (78) 8
60s	Honey Hit TB 127	Joshua Fit The Battle Of Jericho/It's Me, It's Me, It's Me, My Love (some p/s) .. 10/5

(see also Hal Munro, Bobbie Britton)

PEGGY TAYLOR

60	Top Rank JAR 421	(Won't You Come Home) Bill Bailey/So Similar.......................... 5

R. DEAN TAYLOR

68	Tamla Motown TMG 656	Gotta See Jane/Don't Fool Around 6
71	Tamla Motown TMG 763	Indiana Wants Me/Love's Your Name................................... 4
71	Tamla Motown TMG 786	Ain't It A Sad Thing/Backstreet (unissued)
71	Rare Earth RES 101	Ain't It A Sad Thing/Backstreet 10
72	Rare Earth RES 106	Taos New Mexico/Shadow 4
74	Tamla Motown TMG 896	There's A Ghost In My House/Let's Go Somewhere...................... 4
74	Tamla Motown TMG 909	Don't Fool Around/Poor Girl 4
71	Tamla Motown STML 11185	INDIANA WANTS ME (LP) 20

ROGER TAYLOR

77	EMI EMI 2679	I Wanna Testify/Turn On The TV (no p/s) 60
81	EMI EMI 5157	Future Management/Laugh Or Cry (p/s) 12
81	EMI EMI 5200	My Country (Edit)/Fun In Space (p/s) 25
84	EMI EMI 5478	Man On Fire/Killing Time (p/s) 12
84	EMI 12 EMI 5478	Man On Fire (Extended)/Killing Time (12", p/s)........................ 50
84	EMI EMI 5490	Strange Frontier/I Cry For You (Remix) (p/s).......................... 15
84	EMI 12 EMI 5490	Strange Frontier (Extended)/I Cry For You (Extended Remix)/ Two Sharp Pencils (Get Bad) (12", p/s) 65
94	Parlophone R 6379	Nazis 1994/Nazis 1994 (Version) (red vinyl, numbered p/s) 4
94	Parlophone 12RC 6379	Nazis 1994 (Single Version)/(Radio Mix)/(Makita Mix — Extended)/ (Big Science Mix) (12", clear vinyl, with numbered insert in PVC sleeve) 7

94	Parlophone CDR 6379	Nazis 1994 (Single Version)/(Radio Mix)/(Kick Mix)/(Schindler's Mix — Extended)/(Makita Mix — Extended)/(Big Science Mix) (CD)	8
94	Parlophone NAZIS 1	Nazis 1994 (Radio Mix)/Nazis 1944 (Kick Mix) (12", black vinyl, p/s, promo only)	30
94	Parlophone NAZIS 3	Nazis 1994 (Radio Mix)/(Kick Mix)/(Big Science Mix)/(Makita Mix) (12", black vinyl, p/s, promo only)	30
94	Parlophone NAZIS 4	Nazis 1994 (Schindler's Mix)/(Big Science Mix)/(Makita Mix — Extended) (12", black vinyl, p/s, promo only)	30
94	Parlophone R 6389	Foreign Sand (Single Version)/You Had To Be There (as Roger Taylor & Yoshiki) (blue vinyl, numbered p/s)	6
94	Parlophone 12R 6389	Foreign Sand (Single Version)/(Album Version)/You Had To Be There/Final Destination (as Roger Taylor & Yoshiki) (12", picture disc, with no'd insert)	7
94	Parlophone R 6399	Happiness/Ride The Wild Wind (live) (green vinyl, numbered p/s)	6
94	Parlophone 12R 6399	Happiness/Dear Mr. Murdoch/Everybody Hurts Sometime (live)/Old Friends (live) (12", picture disc, with no'd insert)	7
81	EMI EMC 3369	FUN IN SPACE (LP)	15
84	EMI RTA 1	STRANGE FRONTIER (LP)	15
93	Parlophone PCSD 157	HAPPINESS? (LP, some numbered)	40

(see also Queen, Cross, Hilary Hilary, Ian Hunter, Fox, Kansas, Camy Todorow, Mel Smith, Billy Squier)

ROSEMARY TAYLOR

| 75 | JD 2009 | TAYLORMAID (LP, private pressing with insert) | 200 |

(see also Great Saturday Night Swindle)

SAM ('THE MAN') TAYLOR

| 54 | MGM SP 1106 | Please Be Kind/This Can't Be Love (as Sam 'The Man' Taylor & Cat Men) | 25 |
| 56 | MGM MGM-EP 531 | SAM TAYLOR ORCHESTRA (EP) | 30 |

(see also Claude Cloud)

TED TAYLOR FOUR

58	Oriole CB 1464	Son Of Honky Tonk/Farrago	10
58	Oriole CB 1464	Son Of Honky Tonk/Farrago (78)	10
60	Oriole CB 1573	M.1./You Are My Sunshine	10
61	Oriole CB 1574	Fried Onions/Yellow Rock Of Texas	10
61	Oriole CB 1628	Cat's Eyes/Canyon	7
61	Oriole CB 1630	Flyover/Haunted Pad	12
62	Oriole CB 1713	Jericho/Everytime We Say Goodbye	12
62	Oriole CB 1767	Surfrider/Talent Spot	18

VERNON TAYLOR

| 59 | London HLS 8905 | Today Is A Blue Day/Breeze (unreleased) | |
| 60 | London HLS 9025 | Mystery Train/Sweet And Easy To Love | 65 |

VIC TAYLOR

| 67 | Treasure Isle TI 7021 | Heartaches/When It Comes To Loving You I'm Alright (B-side actually "Loving Pauper" by Dobby Dobson) | 12 |
| 71 | Trojan TRLS 38 | DOES IT HIS WAY (LP) | 15 |

(see also Tommy McCook)

VINCE TAYLOR (& HIS PLAYBOYS)

58	Parlophone R 4505	Right Behind You Baby/I Like Love (solo)	40
58	Parlophone R 4505	Right Behind You Baby/I Like Love (solo) (78)	100
59	Parlophone R 4539	Brand New Cadillac/Pledging My Love	30
60	Palette PG 9001	I'll Be Your Hero/Jet Black Machine	20
61	Palette PG 9020	Move Over Tiger/What'cha Gonna Do	20
76	Chiswick (N)S 2	Brand New Cadillac/Pledging My Love (no p/s)	5
97	Cruisin' 50 CASB 006	Brand New Cadillac/Right Behind You Baby (78, 300 only)	25

WALTER TAYLOR

| 50s | Poydras 2 | Thirty-Eight And Plus/Diamond Ring Blues (78) | 8 |

TAYLOR MAIDS

| 55 | Capitol CL 14322 | Po-Go Stick/Theme From "I Am A Camera" (Why Do I) | 10 |

T-BONES

| 64 | Columbia DB 7401 | How Many More Times/I'm A Lover Not A Fighter | 35 |
| 65 | Columbia DB 7489 | Won't You Give Him (One More Chance)/Hamish's Express Relief | 30 |

(see also Gary Farr & T-Bones, Kevin Westlake)

BRAM TCHAIKOVSKY

79	Radar ADA 28	Girl Of My Dreams/Come Back/Robber (live)/Whiskey & Wine (live) (double pack, gatefold p/s)	5
79	Radar ADA 37	I'm the One That's Leaving/Amelia (picture disc)	5
79	Criminal DSWAG 3	Sarah Smiles/Turn On The Lights/Bloodline (12", p/s)	8

(see also Motors, Heroes)

T. CONNECTION

| 77 | T.K. XC 9109 | Do What You Wanna Do/Got To See My Baby (12") | 7 |

TEA

74	Vertigo 6147 006	Good Times/Judy	5
75	Philips 6305 238	TEA (LP)	12
75	Philips 9118 001	THE SHIP (LP)	12

TEA & SYMPHONY

69	Harvest HAR 5005	Boredom/Armchair Theatre	8
69	Harvest SHVL 761	AN ASYLUM FOR THE MUSICALLY INSANE (LP, gatefold sleeve)	50
70	Harvest SHVL 785	JO SAGO (LP)	60

TEACHO & HIS STUDENTS

| 58 | Felsted AF 104 | Rock-et/Stop | 45 |
| 58 | Felsted AF 104 | Rock-et/Stop (78) | 60 |

MINT VALUE £

TEA COMPANY
68	Mercury SMCL 20127	COME AND HAVE SOME TEA WITH THE TEA COMPANY (LP)	25

ANTHONY TEAGUE
62	Decca F 11548	Like I Don't Love You/My Guardian Angel	6

TEAM DOKUS
94	Tenth Planet TP 007	TEAM DOKUS (LP, numbered, 500 only)	15

TEARDROP EXPLODES
79	Zoo CAGE 003	Sleeping Gas/Camera Camera/Kirkby Workers' Dream Fades (red or blue p/s)	12/10
79	Zoo CAGE 005	Bouncing Babies/All I Am Is Loving You (p/s)	10
80	Zoo CAGE 008	Treason (It's Just A Story)/Read It In Books (p/s)	8
80	Mercury TEAR 1	When I Dream/Kilimanjaro (p/s)	4
81	Mercury TEAR 312	Treason (It's Just A Story) (Remix)/Traison (C'est Juste Une Histoire)/Use Me (12", p/s)	8
81	Mercury TEAR 4	Ha Ha I'm Drowning/Poppies In The Field (some in withdrawn p/s)	30/5
81	Mercury TEAR 44	Ha Ha I'm Drowning/Poppies In The Field/Bouncing Babies/Read It In Books (double pack, gatefold p/s)	8
81	Mercury TEAR 44	Ha Ha I'm Drowning/Poppies In The Field/Bouncing Babies/Read It In Books (double pack, withdrawn gatefold p/s)	40
81	Mercury TEAR 512	Passionate Friend/Christ Versus Warhol (12", no p/s)	8
81	Mercury TEAR 6	Colours Fly Away/Window Shopping For A New Crown Of Thorns (p/s & insert)	5
81	Mercury TEAR 612	Colours Fly Away/East Of The Equator/Window Shopping (12", p/s)	8
82	Mercury TEAR 7	Tiny Children/Rachael Built A Steamboat (p/s)	5
82	Mercury TEAR 7G	Tiny Children/Rachael Built A Steamboat (gatefold p/s)	5
82	Mercury TEAR 712	Tiny Children/Rachael Built A Steamboat/Sleeping Gas (live) (12", p/s)	7
83	Mercury TEAR 88	You Disappear From View/Suffocate//Ouch Monkey's/Soft Enough For You/The In-Psychlopedia (double pack, gatefold p/s)	6
90	Fontana DROCD 1	Serious Danger/Sleeping Gas/Seven Views Of Jerusalem (CD)	7
90	Fontana DROCD 2	Count To Ten And Run For Cover/Reward/Poppies/Just Like Leila Khaled Said (CD)	8
80	Mercury 6359 035	KILIMANJARO (LP, original issue, 'group photo' on cover & inner sleeve)	12

(see also Julian Cope, Rabbi Joseph Gordan, Lori & Chameleons)

TEARDROPS (Jamaica)
71	Ackee ACK 126	Let Me Be Free/CINDY STARR: Sentimental Girl	6
71	Big Shot BI 582	Two In One/LAURIE'S ALL STARS: Rock-A-Boogie	8

TEARDROPS
78	Bent BIGB 3	LEAVE ME NO CHANCE (12" EP, p/s in poly bag)	7
79	TJM TJM 9	Seeing Double/Teardrops And Heartaches (p/s)	4
80s	Illuminated JAMS 2	FINAL VINYL (LP)	10

TEAR GAS
70	Famous SFMA 5751	PIGGY GO-GETTER (LP)	40
71	Regal Zono. SLRZ 1021	TEAR GAS (LP)	100

(see also Alex Harvey, Tandoori Cassette)

TEARJERKERS
80	Back Door DOOR 1	Murder Mystery/Heart On The Line (die cut p/s with insert)	4
81	Good Vibrations GOT 9	Love Affair/Bus Stop (p/s)	5
80s	Gray GRC 1	TEARJERKERS (cassette)	10

(see also Speed)

TEARS FOR FEARS
81	Mercury IDEA 1	Suffer The Children/Wind (p/s, original issue with light labels)	5
81	Mercury IDEA 12	Suffer The Children (Remix)/Wind/Suffer The Children (Instrumental) (12", p/s)	10
82	Mercury IDEA 2	Pale Shelter (You Don't Give Me Love)/The Prisoner (p/s, original issue with light labels)	4
82	Mercury IDEA 212	Pale Shelter (You Don't Give Me Love) (Extended)/Pale Shelter/The Prisoner (12", original p/s)	8
82	Mercury IDEA 33	Mad World/Mad World (World Remix) (withdrawn 'fishing net' sleeve)	150
82	Mercury IDEA 33	Mad World/Mad World (World Remix)//Suffer The Children/Ideas As Opiates (double pack)	12
82	Mercury IDEA 4	Change/The Conflict (poster p/s)	8
83	Mercury IDEA W/G 5	Pale Shelter/We Are Broken (p/s, white or green vinyl)	6/4
83	Mercury IDEA R/B 5	Pale Shelter/We Are Broken (p/s, red or blue vinyl)	each 6
83	Mercury IDEAP 5	Pale Shelter/We Are Broken (picture disc)	6
83	Mercury IDEA 6	(The) Way You Are/The Marauders (p/s, with poster, existence unconfirmed)	
83	Mercury IDEAS 6	(The) Way You Are/The Marauders//Change (Live)/Start Of The Breakdown (live) (shrinkwrapped double pack)	10
83	Mercury IDEA 612	(The) Way You Are (Extended)/The Marauders/Start Of The Breakdown (live) (12", p/s)	8
84	Mercury IDEA 7	Mother's Talk/Empire Building (clear vinyl picture disc)	5
84	fan club	Mother's Talk/Interview	8
85	Mercury IDEC 8	Shout/The Big Chair (calendar pack with 6 cards)	8
84	Mercury IDEA 810	Shout/The Big Chair (10", p/s)	6
85	Mercury IDEA 99	Everybody Wants To Rule The World/Pharaohs//Everybody Wants To Rule The World (Urban Mix)/Interview (double pack)	5
85	Mercury IDEAP 10	Head Over Heels (Remix)/When In Love With A Blind Man (poster p/s)	5
85	Mercury IDEP 10	Head Over Heels (Remix)/When In Love With A Blind Man (clover-shaped picture disc)	10
85	Mercury IDEA 11	I Believe/Sea Song (p/s, sealed with set of postcards, withdrawn)	10
85	Mercury IDEA 1111	I Believe (A Soulful Re-Recording)/Sea Song/I Believe (Original Version)/Shout (Dub Version) (double pack, gatefold p/s)	5
89	Fontana IDCDL 12	Sowing The Seeds Of Love (Full Version)/Tears Roll Down/Shout (U.S. Remix) (3" CD, red/yellow plastic sunflower pack)	15

89	Fontana IDSUN 13	Woman In Chains/Always In The Past/My Life In The Suicide Ranks/ Woman In Chains (Instrumental) (3" CD, gold card 'sun' pack) 15
88	Mercury 080 032-2	Everybody Wants To Rule The World/The Marauders/When In Love With A Blind Man/Pharaohs/Everybody Wants To Rule The World (Video) (CD Video) 15
88	Mercury 080 064-2	Shout/Everybody Wants To Rule The World (Urban Mix)/Shout (U.S.A. Mix)/ Shout (Video) (CD Video) 15
88	Mercury 080 062-2	Head Over Heels/Sea Song/The Working Hour/Mother's Talk (U.S.A.)/ Head Over Heels (Video) (CD Video) 15
88	Mercury 080 068-2	I Believe (A Soulful Re-Recording)/Start Of The Breakdown/ Ideas As Opiates/Change/I Believe (Video) (CD Video) 15
89	Fontana 081 376-2	Sowing The Seeds Of Love (Full Version)/Tears Roll Down/ Shout (U.S. Remix)/Sowing The Seeds Of Love (Video) (CD Video) 15
95	Mercury FFFCJ 1	Raoul And The Kings Of Spain/God's Mistake/Falling Down/Secrets (CD, sampler, promo only, card sleeve, withdrawn) 20
93	Mercury	THE ELEMENTAL INTERVIEW (CD, promo only) 20

(see also Graduate)

TEARS ON THE CONSOLE

| 75 | Holyground HG 120 | TEARS ON THE CONSOLE (LP, with booklet, 120 demo copies only) .... 150 |
| 90 | Magic Mixture MM 3 | TEARS ON THE CONSOLE (LP, reissue, 425 only, with insert) .... 10 |

(Band's name is actually Chick Shannon & Last Exit)

TEASER

| 89 | LTW 9KS 2049 | Here Tonight .... 15 |

TEA SET

| 66 | King KG 1048 | Join The Tea Set/Ready Steady Go! .... 12 |

TEA SET

78	Waldo's Beat Series 003	CUPS AND SAUCERS (EP, with stapled lyric book sleeve) 5
79	Waldo's Beat PS 006	Parry Thomas/Tri-X Pan (gatefold p/s with poster 'mystery' envelope) 5
80	Demon D 1009	South Pacific/The Preacher (foldout p/s with inserts) 4
80	Mainly Modern STP 3	Keep On Running (Big Noise From The Jungle)/Flaccid Pot (p/s) 4

TECHNIQUES (U.S.)

| 58 | Columbia DB 4072 | Hey! Little Girl/In A Round About Way .... 40 |
| 58 | Columbia DB 4072 | Hey! Little Girl/In A Round About Way (78) .... 40 |

TECHNIQUES (Jamaica)

65	Island WI 231	Little Did You Know/DON DRUMMOND: Cool Smoke 18
67	Treasure Isle TI 7019	Queen Majesty/Fighting For The Right 20
67	Treasure Isle TI 7026	Love Is Not A Gamble/Bad-Minded People 18
68	Treasure Isle TI 7031	My Girl/Drink Wine (with Tommy McCook & Supersonics) 20
68	Treasure Isle TI 7038	Devoted/Bless You (with Tommy McCook & Supersonics) 18
68	Treasure Isle TI 7040	It's You I Love/Travelling Man (with Tommy McCook & Supersonics) 18
68	Duke DU 1	I Wish It Would Rain/There Comes A Time 10
69	Duke DU 6	A Man Of My Word/The Time Has Come 10
69	Duke DU 22	What Am I To Do/You're My Everything. 8
69	Duke DU 60	Where Were You/Just One Smile 8
69	Camel CA 10	Who You Gonna Run To/Hi There (B-side act. "Look Who's Back" by Carl Bryan). . 7
69	Camel CA 19	Everywhere Everyone/Find Yourself Another Fool 7
67	Treasure Isle TI 7001	You Don't Care (with Tommy McCook & Supersonics Band)/ TOMMY McCOOK & SUPERSONICS BAND: Down On Bond Street 18
70	Treasure Isle TI 7054	He Who Keepeth His Mouth/One Day (act. by Johnny Osborne & Sensations). . . 8
70	Techniques TE 904	Lonely Man/I Feel Alive 8
70	Techniques TE 906	Feel A Little Better (actually by Techniques Allstars)/You'll Get Left. 8
70	Big Shot BI 536	He Who Keepeth His Mouth/One Day (act. by Johnny Osborne & Sensations). . 6
71	Banana BA 350	Since I Lost You/RILEY'S ALLSTARS: Version 8

(see also Techniques All Stars, Riots, Tommy McCook, Mighty Avengers, Gaylads, Rad Bryan)

TECHNIQUES ALL STARS

70	Big Shot BI 543	Come Back Darling/Move Over (act. by Johnny Osborne & Sensations) 7
70	Big Shot BI 545	Elfrego Bacca (actually by Dave Barker)/TECHNIQUES: Iron Joe (B-side actually by Techniques All Stars) 6
70	Techniques TE 900	Something Tender/CANNONBALL: Bewitch 6
70	Trojan TR 7728	El Dora/TECHNIQUES: If It's Not True (B-side actually by Techniques All Stars). . . 6

(see also Dennis Alcapone, Ansell Collins)

TEDDIE & TIGERS

| 67 | Spin SP 2004 | Hold On I'm Comin'/First Love Never Dies .... 20 |

TEDDY

| 71 | Upsetter US 353 | Elusion/UPSETTERS: Big John Wayne .... 12 |

TEDDY & CONQUERORS

| 71 | High Note HS 053 | Homebound/GAYTONES: Homebound Chapter 3 .... 6 |

TEDDY & FRAT GIRLS

| 85 | Alternative Tentacles VIRUS 19 | I Wanna Be A Man/I Owe It All To The Girls/Clubnite/ Alophen Baby/The Eggman Don't Cometh (p/s) .... 4 |

TEDDY & PEARL

(see under Teddy Johnson & Pearl Carr)

TEDDY & TWILIGHTS

| 63 | Stateside SS 167 | I'm Just Your Clown/Bikini Bimbo .... 10 |

TEDDY BEARS

58	London HL 8733	To Know Him Is To Love Him/Don't You Worry, My Little Pet 10
58	London HL 8733	To Know Him Is To Love Him/Don't You Worry, My Little Pet (78). 15
59	London HLP 8836	I Don't Need You Anymore/Oh Why 20

MINT VALUE £

59	London HLP 8836	I Don't Need You Anymore/Oh Why (78)	35
59	London HLP 8889	You Said Goodbye/If You Only Knew.	30
59	London HLP 8889	You Said Goodbye/If You Only Knew (78)	60
59	London HA-P 2183	THE TEDDY BEARS SING! (LP)	175

(see also Phil Spector, Carol Connors)

WILLIE TEE
67	Atlantic 584 116	Thank You John/Walking Up A One-Way Street	18
71	Mojo 2092 025	Walking Up A One-Way Street/Thank You John/Teasin' You	6
78	Contempo CS 8002	Walking Up A One-Way Street/Thank You John (unissued)	

TEENAGE FANCLUB
90	Paperhouse PAPER 003	Everything Flows/Primary Education/Speeeder (1,500 only, die-cut p/s)	10
90	Paperhouse PAPER 005	The Ballad Of John And Yoko (p/s, 1-sided, 5,000 only, 2nd side engraved)	8
90	Paperhouse PAPER 007	God Knows It's True/So Far Gone (p/s)	4
91	Creation CRE 105L	Star Sign/Like A Virgin (p/s, with reversed colours)	4
91	Creation CRELP 096	THE KING (LP, available for 1 week only, sprayed plain sleeve)	12
91	Creation CRECD 096	THE KING (CD, available for 1 week only, sprayed plain sleeve)	15

(see also Boy Hairdressers, BMX Bandits, Clouds)

TEENAGE FILMSTARS
79	Clockwork COR 002	(There's A) Cloud Over Liverpool/Sometimes Good Guys Don't Follow Trends (1st 150 with foldout p/s)	75/15
80	Wessex WEX 275	The Odd Man Out/I Apologise (no p/s)	15
80	Blueprint BLU 2013	The Odd Man Out/I Apologise (reissue, p/s)	10
80	Fab Listening FL 1	I Helped Patrick McGoohan Escape/We're Not Sorry (p/s)	10

(see also Television Personalities, Times, O Level)

TEENAGERS
| 57 | RCA RCX 102 | THE TEENAGERS (EP) | 50 |

TEENAGERS featuring FRANKIE LYMON
(see under Frankie Lymon)

TEEN BEATS (U.S.)
| 60 | Top Rank JAR 342 | The Slop Beat/Califf Boogie (featuring Don Rivers & Califfs) | 15 |

TEENBEATS (U.K.)
| 79 | Safari SAFE 17 | I Can't Control Myself/I Never Win (p/s) | 6 |
| 79 | Safari SAFE 19 | Strength Of The Nation/I'm Gone Tomorrow (p/s) | 5 |

TEEN QUEENS
| 65 | R&B MRB 5000 | Eddie My Love/Just Goofed | 45 |

TEEN STARLETS
| 61 | Top Rank JAR 583 | The Children's Picnic Song/Theme From 'Spinster' | 4 |

TEESIDE FETTLERS
| 74 | Tradition TSR 016 | RING OF IRON (LP) | 10 |

TEETH
| 79 | Soho SH 8 | Say Hello To Suzy/Human Bondage (p/s) | 5 |

JAHN TEIGEN
| 83 | Epic EPC A 3391 | Do Re Mi (English)/Do Re Mi (Norwegian) (unissued, promo only) | 7 |

TELESCOPES
87	private cassette	THE TREE 'ATES EP (demo cassette)	10
88	Cheree CHEREE 1	Forever Close Your Eyes/LOOP: Soundhead (33rpm flexi, p/s, 1,000 only)	6
89	Cheree CHEREE 2	Kick The Wall/This Is The Last Of What's Coming Now (p/s, with insert, 1,000 only, light grey/blue p/s)	5
89	Cheree CHEREE 2	Kick The Wall/This Is The Last Of What's Coming Now (numbered re-pressing, 500 only, red p/s)	8
90	Fierce FRIGHT 039	TRADE MARK OF QUALITY (LP)	10
90	Fierce FRIGHTCD 039	TRADE MARK OF QUALITY (CD)	15

TELEVISION
77	Elektra K 12252	Marquee Moon (Parts 1 & 2) (no p/s)	4
79	Ork/WEA NYC 1T	Little Johnny Jewel Parts 1 & 2/Little Johnny Jewel (live) (12", p/s)	8
78	Elektra K 52072	ADVENTURE (LP, red vinyl with lyric insert)	15

(see also Neon Boys)

TELEVISION PERSONALITIES
78	Teen '78 SRTS/CUS/77/089	14th Floor/Oxford Street W1 (p/s, various different sleeve designs)	35-45
78	Kings Road LYN 5976/7	WHERE'S BILL GRUNDY NOW? (EP, hand-stamped label, 2,000 only)	15
78	Kings Road LYN 5976/7	WHERE'S BILL GRUNDY NOW? (EP, white labels, various sleeves)	10
79	Rough Trade RT 033	WHERE'S BILL GRUNDY NOW? (EP, reissue, different p/s, printed labels)	7
80	Rough Trade RT 051	Smashing Time/King & Country (p/s)	12
81	Rough Trade RT 063	I Know Where Syd Barrett Lives/Arthur The Gardener (p/s)	10
82	Whaam! WHAAM 4	Three Wishes/Geoffrey Ingram/And Don't The Kids Just Love It (p/s, 2 different sleeve designs, 2,000 only)	12
82	Creation Artefact 002/ Lyntone LYN 13546	Biff Bang Pow!/A Picture Of Dorian Gray (1-sided flexidisc, some with *Communication Blur* fanzine)	25/18
83	Rough Trade RT 109	A Sense Of Belonging/Paradise Estate (p/s)	14
86	Dreamworld DREAM 4	How I Learnt To Love The Bomb/Then God Snaps His Fingers/Now You're Just Being Ridiculous (12", p/s, 3,700 only)	12
86	Dreamworld DREAM 10	How I Learnt To Love The Bomb/Grocer's Daughter/Girl Called Charity (7", reissue, p/s, 1,000 only)	15
87	Dreamworld DREAM 13(T)	Privilege/Me And My Desires (unreleased)	
89	Overground OVER 03	14th Floor/Oxford Street W1 (numbered p/s, 600 yellow vinyl, 400 white vinyl; 1,000 black vinyl)	6/7/4
89	Caff CAFF 5	I Still Believe In Magic/Respectable (p/s, in poly bag, 500 only)	25
90	Overground OVER 13	I Know Where Syd Barrett Lives/Arthur The Gardener (reissue, p/s, 2000 only)	6
90	Overground OVER 15	Silly Girl (unissued, 100 test pressings only)	18

Rare Record Price Guide 2002

TELEVISION PERSONALITIES

81	Rough Trade ROUGH 24	AND DON'T THE KIDS JUST LOVE IT (LP, 1st 1,000 with insert) 30/25
81	Whaam! WHAAM 3	MUMMY YOU'RE NOT WATCHING ME (LP, 3,500 only, 1st 1,000 with insert) 30/25
82	Whaam! BIG 5	THEY COULD HAVE BEEN BIGGER THAN THE BEATLES (LP, 2,500 only, hand-painted sleeve) 25
83	Whaam! BIG 10	TURN ON ... TUNE IN (LP, unreleased)
84	Dreamworld HWDS 001	I KNOW WHERE DAN TREACY LIVES (live at Forum 20/9/84) (cassette only, fan club issue) 35
85	Illuminated JAMS 37	THE PAINTED WORD (LP) 25
86	Dreamworld BIG DREAM 2	THEY COULD HAVE BEEN BIGGER THAN THE BEATLES (LP, reissue with insert) 15
86	Dreamworld BIG DREAM 4	MUMMY YOU'RE NOT WATCHING ME (LP, reissue with insert) 15
87	Dreamworld BIG DREAM 6	PRIVILEGE (LP, unreleased)

(see also Teenage Filmstars, Times, O Level, Missing Scientists, Reacta, Dry Rib, Slaughter, Gifted Children)

TELEX

78	Sire SIR 4006	Twist A Saint-Tropez/Le Fond De L'Air (p/s) 4
79	Sire SIR 4017	Moskow Diskow/Twist A Saint-Tropez (p/s) 6
79	Sire SIR 4017T	Moskow Diskow (Disco Version)/Twist A Saint-Tropez (Disco Version) (12", no p/s) 10
79	Sire SIR 4020	Rock Around The Clock/Moskow Diskow (no p/s) 4
79	Sire SIR 4020T	Rock Around The Clock (Extended Version)/Moskow Diskow (Disco Version) (12", no p/s) 7
80	Sire SIR 4039	Eurovision (English Version)/Eurovision (French Version) (p/s) 4
80	Sire SIR 4043	Getting Old (New Mix)/Tropical (p/s) 6
80	Sire SIR 4047	Soul Waves/Soul Waves (instrumental) (p/s) 6
80	Sire SIR 4047T	Soul Waves (Extended)/Dance To The Music (Remix)/ Colonel Olrick (12", no p/s) 12
82	Interdisc IN 1	Haven't We Met Somewhere Before/Dummy (p/s) 4
82	Interdisc IN 1X12	Haven't We Met Somewhere Before/Dummy/ Exercise Is Good For You (12", p/s) 10
82	Interdisc IN 2	L'Amour Toujours/Trains Et Sifflets (p/s) 5
82	Interdisc IN 2X12	L'Amour Toujours/Trains Et Sifflets/The Man With The Answer (12", p/s) 10
85	WEA X 9175	L'Amour Toujours/I Don't Like Music (p/s) 4
79	Sire SRK 6072	LOOKING FOR ST. TROPEZ (LP, with lyric inner sleeve) 10
80	Sire SRK 6090	NEUROVISION (LP) 10
82	Interdisc INTO 1	BIRDS AND BEES (LP) 12

TELHAM TINKERS
84   Eron ERON 031   HOT IN ALICE SPRINGS (LP, with insert) 10

TELLERS
74   Pyramid PYR 7011   No Work, No Pay/Version 5
74   Dragon DRA 1031   Ta It Deh/Hit Dib 5

TELSTARS
62   Oriole CB 1754   I Went A' Walkin'/A Rose And A Thorn 10

TEMPERANCE SEVEN
61   Parlophone R 4757   You're Driving Me Crazy/Charley My Boy 5
61   Parlophone R 4781   Pasadena/Sugar 7
63   Parlophone R 5070   From Russia With Love/P.C.Q. (Please Charleston Quietly) 6
61   Argo EAF 14   THE TEMPERANCE SEVEN INCH RECORD (EP) 10
61   Argo RG 11   THE TEMPERANCE SEVEN PLUS ONE (LP) 18
61   Parlophone PMC 1152 THE TEMPERANCE SEVEN 1961 (LP, also stereo PCS 3021) 20
       (see also Ted Wood)

TEMPEST
73   Bronze ILPS 9220   TEMPEST (LP, foldover cover with lyric inner sleeve) 25
74   Bronze ILPS 9267   LIVING IN FEAR (LP, die-cut cover with inner sleeve) 20
       (see also Colosseum)

BOBBY TEMPEST
59   Decca F 11125   Love Or Leave/Don't Leave Me 10
59   Decca F 11125   Love Or Leave/Don't Leave Me (78) 20

BOB TEMPLE
57   Parlophone R 4264   Come Back, Come Back/Vim Vam Vamoose 100
57   Parlophone R 4264   Come Back, Come Back/Vim Vam Vamoose (78) 20

GERRY TEMPLE
61   HMV POP 823   No More Tomorrows/So Nice To Walk You Home 30
61   HMV POP 939   Seventeen Come Sunday/Tell You What I'll Do 25
63   HMV POP 1114   Angel Face/Since You Went Away 30
68   RCA Victor RCA 1670 Lovin' Up A Storm/Everything I Do is Wrong 12

RICHARD TEMPLE
70   Jay Boy BOY 31   That Beatin' Rhythm/Could It Be 6

SHIRLEY TEMPLE
59   Top Rank JAR 139   On The Good Ship Lollipop/Animal Crackers In My Soup 7
59   Top Rank JAR 139   On The Good Ship Lollipop/Animal Crackers In My Soup (78) 40
59   Top Rank JKR 8003   I REMEMBER (EP) 15

TEMPLEAIRES
60s Vogue V 2421   He Spoke/What Will Heaven Have In Store For Me 12

TEMPLE OF THE DOG
92   A&M AM 0091   Hunger Strike/All Night Thing (picture disc) 12
92   A&M AMY 0091   Hunger Strike/Your Saviour/All Night Thing (12", p/s, with poster) 12
92   A&M AMCD 0091   Hunger Strike/Your Saviour/All Night Thing (CD, digipak) 10
       (see also Pearl Jam)

NINO TEMPO
57   London HLU 8387   Tempo's Tempo/June's Blues (as Nino Tempo & His Band) 300
57   London HLU 8387   Tempo's Tempo/June's Blues (as Nino Tempo & His Band) (78) 60
75   A&M AMS 7190   Come See Me Round Midnight/High On Music (as Nino Tempo & 5th Avenue) . . . 5
58   London HB-U 1075   ROCK 'N' ROLL BEACH PARTY (10" LP) 225
       (see also Nino Tempo & April Stevens, April Stevens, Top Notes)

NINO TEMPO & APRIL STEVENS
62   London HLK 9580   Sweet And Lovely/TOP NOTES: Twist And Shout 10
63   London HLK 9782   Deep Purple/I've Been Carrying A Torch For You So Long
                             That I Burned A Great Big Hole In My Heart 5
64   London HLK 9829   Whispering/Tweedle Dee 5
64   London HLK 9859   Stardust/1-45 6
64   London HLK 9890   Tea For Two/I'm Confessin' (That I Love You) 6
66   London HLU 10084   All Strung Out/I Can't Go On Living Baby Without You 8
67   Atlantic 584 048   Coldest Night Of The Year/Ooh La La (as April Stevens & Nino Tempo) 7
67   London HLU 10106   The Habit Of Lovin' You Baby/You'll Be Needing Me Baby 8
67   London HLU 10130   My Old Flame/Wings Of Love 6
68   Atlantic 584 151   Deep Purple/Sweet And Lovely 5
68   London HLU 10209   Ooh Poo Pah Doo/Let It Be Me 6
69   London HLU 10245   All Strung Out/My Old Flame 6
69   Bell BLL 1087   Sea Of Love/On The Dock Of The Bay/Twilight Time 5
73   A&M AMS 7075   Put It Where You Want It/I Can't Get Over You Baby 5
64   London RE-K 1412   DEEP PURPLE (EP) 18
64   London HA-K 8168   NINO TEMPO AND APRIL STEVENS — DEEP PURPLE (LP) 35
64   Atlantic (S)AL 5006 SING THE GREAT SONGS (LP, mono/stereo) 25/30
67   London HA-U/SH-U 8314 ALL STRUNG OUT (LP) 20
       (see also Nino Tempo, April Stevens)

TEMPOS
59   Pye International 7N 25026 See You In September/Bless You My Love 50
59   Pye International N 25026 See You In September/Bless You My Love (78) 60

TEMPREES
72   Stax 2025 147   Explain To Her Mama/Dedicated To The One I Love 5
74   Stax STS 2027   At Last/I'll Live Her Life 5
72   Stax 2325 083   LOVE MEN (LP) 15
74   Stax STX 1040   THREE (LP) 18

TEMPTATIONS

60	Top Rank JAR 384	Barbara/Someday 30

TEMPTATIONS

SINGLES

64	Stateside SS 278	The Way You Do The Things You Do/Just Let Me Know 40
64	Stateside SS 319	I'll Be In Trouble/The Girl's Alright With Me. 40
64	Stateside SS 348	Why You Wanna Make Me Blue/Baby Baby I Need You 50
65	Stateside SS 378	My Girl/(Talking 'Bout) Nobody But My Baby 35
65	Tamla Motown TMG 504	It's Growing/What Love Has Joined Together 30
65	Tamla Motown TMG 526	Since I Lost My Baby/You've Got To Earn It 25
65	Tamla Motown TMG 541	My Baby/Don't Look Back 25
66	Tamla Motown TMG 557	Get Ready/Fading Away. 20
66	Tamla Motown TMG 565	Ain't Too Proud To Beg/You'll Lose A Precious Love 12
66	Tamla Motown TMG 578	Beauty Is Only Skin Deep/You're Not An Ordinary Girl 10
66	Tamla Motown TMG 587	(I Know) I'm Losing You/Little Miss Sweetness. 8
67	Tamla Motown TMG 610	All I Need/Sorry Is A Sorry Word 12
67	Tamla Motown TMG 620	You're My Everything/I've Been Good To You 8
67	Tamla Motown TMG 633	(Loneliness Made Me Realise) It's You That I Need/I Want A Love I Can See. 25
68	Tamla Motown TMG 641	I Wish It Would Rain/I Truly, Truly Believe 8
68	Tamla Motown TMG 658	I Could Never Love Another (After Loving You)/
		Gonna Give Her All The Love I've Got. 6
68	Tamla Motown TMG 671	Why Did You Leave Me Darling/How Can I Forget 7
69	Tamla Motown TMG 688	Get Ready/My Girl 5
69	Tamla Motown TMG 699	Ain't Too Proud To Beg/Fading Away 5
69	Tamla Motown TMG 707	Cloud Nine/Why Did She Have To Leave Me (Why Did She Have To Go). 6
69	Tamla Motown TMG 716	Runaway Child, Running Wild/I Need Your Lovin'. 6
70	Tamla Motown TMG 722	I Can't Get Next To You/Running Away (Ain't Gonna Help You) 5
70	Tamla Motown TMG 741	Psychedelic Shack/That's The Way Love Is. 5
70	Tamla Motown TMG 749	Ball Of Confusion (That's What The World Is Today)/It's Summer 5
71	Tamla Motown TMG 773	Just My Imagination (Running Away With Me)/You Make Your Own Heaven
		And Hell Right Here On Earth 5
71	Tamla Motown TMG 783	It's Summer/Unite The World (Ungena Za Ulimwengu) 5
72	Tamla Motown TMG 800	Superstar/Gonna Keep Tryin' Till I Win Your Love 5
72	Tamla Motown TMG 808	Take A Look Around/Smooth Sailing (From Now On) 5
72	Tamla Motown TMG 832	Smiling Faces Sometimes/Mother Nature 5
73	Tamla Motown TMG 839	Papa Was A Rolling Stone (Parts 1 & 2) 5

EPs

65	Tamla Motown TME 2004	THE TEMPTATIONS (EP) 35
66	Tamla Motown TME 2010	IT'S THE TEMPTATIONS (EP) 30

LPs

65	Tamla Motown TML 11009	MEET THE TEMPTATIONS (LP) 100
65	Tamla Motown TML 11016	SING SMOKEY (LP) 40
66	T. Motown (S)TML 11023	THE TEMPTIN' TEMPTATIONS (LP, mono/stereo) 35/40
66	T. Motown (S)TML 11035	GETTIN' READY (LP, mono/stereo) 35/40
67	T. Motown (S)TML 11042	GREATEST HITS (LP). 18
67	T. Motown (S)TML 11053	THE TEMPTATIONS LIVE! (LP). 18
67	T. Motown (S)TML 11057	WITH A LOT O'SOUL (LP) 20
68	T. Motown (S)TML 11068	IN A MELLOW MOOD (LP) 25
68	T. Motown (S)TML 11079	THE TEMPTATIONS WISH IT COULD RAIN (LP) 30
69	T. Motown (S)TML 11104	THE TEMPTATIONS LIVE AT THE COPA (LP) 18
69	T. Motown (S)TML 11109	CLOUD NINE (LP). 18
70	T. Motown (S)TML 11133	PUZZLE PEOPLE (LP) 20
70	T. Motown (S)TML 11141	'LIVE' AT LONDON'S TALK OF THE TOWN (LP). 15
70	Tamla Motown STML 11147	PSYCHEDELIC SHACK (LP). 20
70	Tamla Motown STML 11170	GREATEST HITS Vol. 2 (LP) 12
71	Tamla Motown STML 11184	THE SKY'S THE LIMIT (LP) 15
72	Tamla Motown STML 11202	SOLID ROCK (LP). 12
72	Tamla Motown STML 11218	ALL DIRECTIONS (LP) 12
73	Tamla Motown STML 11229	MASTERPIECE (LP). 12

(see also David Ruffin, Eddie Kendricks, Diana Ross)

TEMPUS FUGIT

69	Philips BF 1802	Come Alive/Emphasis On Love 20

(see also Jensens)

10cc

72	UK UK 22	Johnny Don't Do It/4% Of Something 6
74	UK UK 57	The Worst Band In The World/18 Carat Man Of Means 6
73	UK UKAL 1005	10cc (LP) 12
80s	Mercury HS 9102 500	THE ORIGINAL SOUNDTRACK (LP, half-speed master) 12
80s	Mercury HS 9102 504	GREATEST HITS (LP, half-speed master) 12

(see also Godley & Creme, Graham Gouldman, Mindbenders, Mockingbirds, Whirlwinds, Tristar Airbus, Yellow Bellow Room Boom, Peter Cowap, Grumble, Nick Mason & Rick Fenn, Frabjoy & Runcible Spoon, Manchester Mob, Ramases)

TENDER SLIM

60s	XX MIN 702	TENDER SLIM AND COUSIN LEROY (EP). 15

TENDER TONES

69	Crab CRAB 38	Devil Woman/Nobody Cares 7

TEN FEET

66	RCA RCA 1544	Got Everything But Love/Factory Worker 20
67	CBS 3045	Shot On Sight/Losing Game 20

TEN FEET FIVE

65	Fontana TF 578	Baby's Back In Town/Send Me No More Lovin' 30

(see also Troggs)

MINT VALUE £

TEN FOOT BONELESS
88 Fierce FRIGHT 027 Powerslide/Duane Peters Is God (12", yellow or white p/s, with inner) 12
(see also Pooh Sticks)

TENNESSEE JAY BIRDS
51 London L 1007 Sticks And Stones/Trouble Trouble (78) 10

TEN(N)ORS
68 Doctor Bird DB 1152 Massy Massa/CLIVE ALLSTARS: San Sebastian 15
68 Doctor Bird DB 1175 Sufferer (Make It)/Little Things. 15
68 Island WI 3133 Ride Your Donkey/I've Got To Get You Off My Mind 12
68 Island WI 3140 Copy Me Donkey (as Tenors)/The Stage (B-side actually by Ronnie Davis) . . . 15
68 Island WI 3156 Grampa/ROMEO STEWART: While I Was Walking. 18
68 Blue Cat BS 127 Khaki/LEYROY REID: Great Surprise (Pound Get A Blow) 12
68 Big Shot BI 501 Reggae Girl/CLIVE ALLSTARS: Donkey Trot. 12
68 Fab FAB 41 Ride Your Donkey/I've Got To Get You Off My Mind 8
68 Fab FAB 50 Let Go Yah Donkey/ROMEO STEWART: While I Was Walking. 8
69 Big Shot BI 514 You're No Good/Do The Reggae 8
69 Big Shot BI 517 Another Scorcher/My Baby 8
69 Duke Reid DR 2502 Hopeful Village/TOMMY McCOOK: The Village 8
69 Bullet BU 406 Greatest Scorcher/Making Love 6
69 Crab CRAB 26 Baff Boom/Feel Bad. 8
69 Crab CRAB 29 True Brothers/Sign Of The Time. 6
69 Crab CRAB 36 I Want Everything/Cherry. 6
73 Explosion EX 2079 Weather Report/Weather Report — Version 6
73 Pyramid PYR 7000 Money Never Built A Mountain/My World 5
(see also Jennors, Prince Buster, Soul Brothers)

TENPOLE TUDOR
80 Korova KOW 4 Real Fun/What's In A Word (p/s) 4
(see also Sex Pistols)

10,000 MANIACS
84 Reflex RE 1 My Mother The War (Remix)/Planned Obsolescence/
National Education Week (12", p/s) 20
84 Press P 2010 HUMAN CONFLICT #5 (12" EP, gatefold p/s). 30
85 Lyntone LYN 15914 Grey Victory/SIMPLY RED: Something's Burning (33rpm 1-sided
clear flexidisc free with *Jamming!* magazine, issue 29). 12/8
85 Elektra EKR 11 Can't Ignore The Train/Daktari (p/s) 6
85 Elektra EKR 11T Can't Ignore The Train/Daktari/Grey Victory/The Colonial Wing (12", p/s) 12
85 Elektra EKR 19 Just As The Tide Was A-Flowin'/Among The Americans (p/s) 10
86 Elektra EKR 28 Scorpio Rising/Arbor Day (no p/s) 6
87 Elektra EKR 61 Peace Train/The Painted Desert (booklet p/s) 6
87 Elektra EKR 64 Don't Talk/City Of Angels (7" with 12" p/s, with inserts). 6
89 Elektra EKR 93CD Trouble Me (LP Version)/The Lion's Share (LP Version)/Party Of God
(with Billy Bragg) (3" CD, gatefold card sleeve) 8
89 Elektra EKR 93CDX Trouble Me (LP Version)/The Lion's Share (LP Version)/Party Of God
(with Billy Bragg) (3" CD, elephant-shaped card pack). 10
89 Elektra EKR 100TE Eat For Two/What's The Matter Here (Acoustic)/Eat For Two (Acoustic)/
From The Time You Say Goodbye (10", numbered p/s). 7
89 Elektra EKR 100CD Eat For Two/Gun Shy (Acoustic)/Wildheart Flower/
Hello — In There (3" CD, gatefold card sleeve) 8
84 Press P 3001 LP SECRETS OF THE I-CHING (LP, with insert; later re-pressed
in different 'Chinese Chicken' sleeve, some with insert) 40/30
87 Elektra EKT 41 IN MY TRIBE (LP, with free 7" sampler: "What's The Matter Here?"/
X: "See How We Are"/CALL: "In The River" [SAM 390, gatefold p/s]). 12

TEN WHEEL DRIVE (with GENYA RAVAN)
71 Polydor 2066 034 Mornin' Much Better/Stay With Me. 5
69 Polydor 583 577 CONSTRUCTION NO. 1 (LP). 12
70 Polydor 2425 002 BRIEF REPLIES (LP, with Genya Ravan) 12
71 Polydor 2425 065 PECULIAR FRIENDS (LP, with Genya Ravan) 12
(see also Goldie [& Gingerbreads])

TEN YEARS AFTER
68 Deram DM 176 Portable People/The Sounds 7
68 Deram DM 221 Hear Me Calling/I'm Going Home 6
70 Deram DM 299 Love Like A Man (studio)/Love Like A Man (live) (45/33rpm) 7
70 Deram DM 310 Love Like A Man (studio)/Love Like A Man (live) (reissue) 5
71 Deram XDR 48532 She Lies In The Morning/Sweet Little Sixteen (demo only) 12
72 Chrysalis/Philips 6155 006 One Of These Days/Baby Won't You Let Me Rock 'n' Roll You 5
89 Chrysalis CHS 3477 Highway Of Love/Rock 'n' Roll Music To The World (p/s) 5
67 Deram DML/SML 1015 TEN YEARS AFTER (LP, mono/stereo) 35/30
68 Deram DML/SML 1023 UNDEAD (LP, mono/stereo). 30/25
69 Deram DML/SML 1029 STONEDHENGE (LP, gatefold sleeve, mono/stereo) 30/25
69 Deram DML/SML 1052 SSSSH! (LP, gatefold sleeve, mono/stereo) 25
70 Deram DML/SML 1065 CRICKLEWOOD GREEN (LP, gatefold sleeve, initially
with 'Alvin Lee' poster, mono/stereo) 22/18
71 Deram SML 1078 WATT (LP, gatefold sleeve) 20
71 Chrysalis CHR 1001 A SPACE IN TIME (LP) 15
72 Deram SML 1096 ALVIN LEE AND COMPANY (LP) 15
72 Chysalis CHR 1009 ROCK & ROLL MUSIC TO THE WORLD (gatefold sleeve) 12
74 Chrysalis CHR 1060 POSITIVE VIBRATIONS (LP). 12
(see also Alvin Lee, Chick Churchill)

TERMITES (U.K.)
65 Oriole CB 1989 Tell Me/I Found My Place. 20
65 CBS 201761 Every Day Every Day/No-One In The Whole Wide World. 7

TERMITES (Jamaica)

67	Studio One SO 2006	Mercy Mr. Percy/SOUL BROTHERS: Hot And Cold	18
67	Studio One SO 2029	It Takes Two To Make Love/Beach Boy	18
67	Coxsone CS 7008	Sign Up/DELROY WILSON: Troubled Man	15
67	Coxsone CS 7025	Do It Right Now/SUMMERTAIRES: Stay (B-side actually by Gaylads)	15
68	Studio One SO 2040	Mr D.J. (actually by Delroy Wilson)/Tripe Girl (actually by Heptones)	15
68	Coxsone CS 7039	Mama Didn't Know/I Made A Mistake	15
68	Pama PM 729	Push It Up/Two Of A Kind (B-side act. by Clancy Eccles & Cynthia Richards)	8
68	Pama PM 738	Show Me The Way/What Can I Do	8
69	Nu Beat NB 017	Push Push/Girls (actually by Hi Tones)	8
67	Studio One SOL 9003	DO THE ROCK STEADY (LP)	80

(see also L. Sparks, Ken Boothe, Upsetters)

PETE TERRACE

67	Pye International 7N 25427	At The Party/No! No! No!	10
67	Pye International 7N 25440	Shotgun Boo-Ga-Loo/I'm Gonna Make It	12
67	Pye Intl. NPL 28102	BOOGALOO (LP)	20

TERRA COTTA

78	Terra Cotta TC 001	To Be Near You	20

TERRAPLANE

83	City NIK 8	I Survive/Gimme The Money (p/s)	5
84	Epic GA 4936	I Can't Live Without Your Love/Beginning Of The End (gatefold p/s)	6
84	Epic TX 4936	I Can't Live Without Your Love/Beginning Of The End/ Let The Wheels Go Round (12", p/s)	7
85	Epic A 6110	I Survive/All Night And Day (p/s)	5
85	Epic TX 6110	I Survive (You-C Factor Mix)/All Night And Day (12", p/s)	7
85	Epic A 6584	Talking To Myself/Get Your Face Out Of My Dreams (p/s)	4
85	Epic TX 6584	Talking To Myself/Get Your Face Out Of My Dreams (12", p/s)	7
85	Flexi FLX 394/XPS 200	I'm The One (live)/When You're Hot (live) (p/s, flexidisc free with Meat Loaf's 'Bad Attitude' tour programme)	10/5
87	Epic TERRAD 1	If That's What It Takes/Living After Dark (p/s, with free single)	5
87	Epic TERRAP 1	if That's What It Takes/Living After Dark (car-shaped picture disc)	6
87	Epic TERRA 2	Good Thing Going/Night Of Madness (p/s)	6
87	Epic TERRAG 3	Moving Target/When I Sleep Alone/I Survive (live)/ I Can't Live Without Your Love (double pack, gatefold p/s)	6
87	Epic TERRAG 3	Moving Target/When I Sleep Alone/I Survive (live)/ I Can't Live Without Your Love (12", gatefold p/s)	12
86	Epic TERRAQ4	If That's What It Takes (19th Nervous Breakdance Mix) (12", with poster)	12
85	Epic 26439	BLACK AND WHITE (LP)	10
85	Epic 40 26439	BLACK AND WHITE (cassette, with non-LP bonus tracks)	18
87	Epic 460157 1	MOVING TARGET (LP)	10
87	Epic 460157 4	MOVING TARGET (CD)	20

(see also Thunder, Nuthin' Fancy)

LLOYD TERRELL

68	Island WI 3158	My Argument (as Lloyd & Johnny Melody)/JOHNNY MELODY: Foey Man (B-side actually by George Dekker)	40
68	Pama PM 710	Bang Bang Lulu/MRS MILLER: I Never Knew	7
68	Pama PM 740	How Come (actually by Lee Perry)/MRS MILLER: Oh My Lover	8
69	Pama PM 752	Lulu Returns/MRS MILLER: I Feel The Music	8
69	Nu Beat NB 023	Mr Rhya/After Dark	8
70	Pama PM 792	Birth Control/VAL BENNET: Return To Peace	6
70	Bullet BU 434	Exposure/Baby Huey	6
71	Escort ERT 855	One Woman/CHARMERS: What Should I Do (act. by Dave Barker & Charmers)	6
73	Pama PM 863	Big Eight/JUNIOR BYLES: Auntie Lu Lu	6

(see also Charmers, Lloyd Charmers, Lloyd & Johnny, Lloyd & Ken, Lloydie & Lowbites)

TAMMI TERRELL

66	Tamla Motown TMG 561	Come On And See Me/Baby Don'tcha Worry	70
69	T. Motown (S)TML 11103	THE IRRESISTIBLE TAMMI TERRELL (LP)	60

(see also Marvin Gaye & Tammi Terrell)

TAMMI TERRELL/CHUCK JACKSON

69	Marble Arch MAL 1110	THE EARLY SHOW (LP)	15

(see also Chuck Jackson)

TERRI & TERRORS

79	Fresh FRESH 4	Laugh At Me/Laugh At Me (Again) (folded p/s)	5

TERRORVISION

90	(own label)	TERRORVISION: Brand New Toy/Human Error/Pain Reliever/ The Pilgrims Rest (cassette, private issue)	50
91	(own label)	PUMP ACTION SUNSHINE: Urban Space Crime/My House/Jason (cassette, private issue)	50
91	(own label)	TERRORVISION: Blackbird/American TV/Pain Reliever/Human Being (cassette, private issue)	50
92	Total Vegas 12VEGAS 1	THRIVE EP (12" EP)	35
92	Total Vegas CDVEGAS 1	THRIVE EP (CD EP)	40
92	Total Vegas VEGAS 2	My House/Coming Up (p/s)	15
92	Total Vegas 12VEGAS 2	My House/Coming Up/Tea Dance (12", p/s)	20
92	Total Vegas CDVEGAS 2	My House/Coming Up/Tea Dance (CD)	30
93	Total Vegas ATVR 1	Problem Solved/Corpse Fly (p/s)	5
93	Total Vegas 12ATVR 1	Problem Solved/Corpse Fly/We Are The Roadcrew/Sailing Home (12", p/s)	25
93	Total Vegas CDATVR 1	Problem Solved/Corpse Fly/We Are The Roadcrew/Sailing Home (CD)	25
93	Total Vegas VEGAS 3	American TV/Don't Shoot My Dog Again (p/s)	5
93	Total Vegas 12VEGAS 3	American TV/Don't Shoot My Dog Again/Killing Time (12", p/s with poster)	15
93	Total Vegas CDPVEGAS 3	American TV/Psycho Killer/Hole For A Soul (CD)	20
93	Total Vegas VEGAS 4	New Policy One/Pain Reliever (live) (green vinyl, p/s)	6

93	Total Vegas 12VEGASSP 4	New Policy One/Ships That Sink (live)/Problem Solved (live) (12", p/s, with poster)	15
93	Total Vegas CDVEGASSP 4	New Policy One/Ships That Sink (live)/Problem Solved (live) (CD, 1st of 2-CD set)	15
93	Total Vegas CDVEGASSP 4	New Policy One/Psycho Killer/Tea Dance/My House (CD, 2nd of 2-CD set)	15
93	Total Vegas CDVEGASS 6	Oblivion/The Model/Remember Zelda (CD, 1st of 2-CD set)	15
93	Total Vegas CDVEGASS 6	Oblivion/Problem Solved/What D'ya Do That For/Oblivion (CD, 2nd of 2-CD set)	15
94	Total Vegas CDVEGASS 7	Middle Man/I'll Be Your Sister/Wishing Well (CD)	7
92	Total Vegas ATVRLP 1	FORMALDEHYDE (LP, 14 tracks, green vinyl, 500 only)	70
92	Total Vegas ATVRCD 1	FORMALDEHYDE (CD, 14 tracks, 1,000 only)	50
93	Total Vegas VEGASLPS 1	FORMALDEHYDE (reissue LP, 12 tracks, 1,000 copies with 12-page booklet, stickered sleeve & lyric inner)	20
93	Total Vegas BOOT 1	LIVE AT THE DON VALLEY STADIUM (CD, picture disc, 250 promo copies only)	50
94	Total Vegas CDPRIMEDJ 1	PRIME TIME TERRORVISION (CD, picture disc, digipak, promo only)	35

(see also Spoilt Bratz)

TERRY
| 66 | Fontana TF 751 | Spilt Milk/The Way That I Remember Him | 6 |

TERRY, BLAIR & ANOUCHKA
| 89 | Chrysalis CHSCD 3478 | Ultra Modern Nursery Rhyme/Hush Hush Balloo/Love Will Keep Us Together (CD, slimline jewel case) | 10 |
| 89 | Chrysalis CCD 1701 | ULTRA MODERN NUSERY RHYMES (CD) | 18 |

(see also Terry Hall)

CLARK TERRY (& BOB BROOKMEYER)
61	Riverside RLP 12-246	DUKE WITH A DIFFERENCE (LP)	10
65	Fontana TL 5265	TONIGHT (LP, with Bob Brookmeyer)	10
66	Fontana TL 5290	POWER OF POSITIVE SWINGING (LP, with Bob Brookmeyer)	10
66	Fontana TL 5373	MUMBLES (LP)	10
67	Fontana (S)TL 5394	GINGERBREAD MEN (LP, with Bob Brookmeyer)	10
68	Impulse MIPL/SIPL 507	IT'S WHAT'S HAPPENIN' (LP)	10

(see also Coleman Hawkins)

DEWEY TERRY
| 73 | Tumbleweed TW 3502 | CHIEF (LP) | 10 |

(see also Don & Dewey, Don Harris, Harvey Mandel)

GORDON TERRY
| 57 | London REA 1098 | COUNTRY CLAMBAKE (EP) | 35 |

PAT TERRY (GROUP)
| 70s | Myrrh MYR 1031 | PAT TERRY GROUP (LP) | 15 |

SONNY TERRY (TRIO)
53	Parlophone MSP 6017	Hootin' Blues/TOMMY REILLY: Bop! Goes The Weasel	25
53	Parlophone R 3598	Hootin' Blues/TOMMY REILLY: Bop! Goes The Weasel (78)	15
55	Vogue V 2326	Fox Chase/John Henry (78)	10
56	Vogue EPV 1095	SONNY TERRY (EP)	50
55	Vogue LDE 137	FOLK BLUES (10" LP)	25
55	Vogue LDE 165	CITY BLUES (10" LP)	25
58	Melodisc MLP 516	WHOOPIN' THE BLUES (10" LP)	30
58	Topic 10T 30	HARMONICA BLUES (10" LP)	30
65	Topic 12T 30	HARMONICA BLUES (12" LP, reissue)	20
66	Xtra XTRA 5025	SONNY'S STORY (LP)	18
67	Capitol T 20906	WHOOPIN' THE BLUES (LP, reissue)	12
69	Ember CW 136	BLIND SONNY TERRY & WOODY GUTHRIE (LP)	12
69	Xtra XTRA 1064	SONNY TERRY (LP)	15
70	Xtra XTRA 1099	BLUES FROM EVERYWHERE (LP)	15
71	Xtra XTRA 1110	ON THE ROAD (LP, with J.C. Burris)	15

(see also Woody Guthrie)

SONNY TERRY & BROWNIE McGHEE
60	Columbia DB 4433	Talking Harmonica Blues/Rockin' And Whoopin'	20
64	Oriole CB 1946	Dissatisfied Woman/SONNY TERRY: Goin' Down Slow	12
50s	Melodisc EPM7 83	ME AND SONNY (EP)	30
58	Pye Jazz NJE 1060	THE BLUEST (EP)	15
59	Pye Jazz NJE 1073	SONNY TERRY & BROWNIE McGHEE & CHRIS BARBER'S JAZZ BAND (EP)	15
59	Pye Jazz NJE 1074	TERRY and McGHEE IN LONDON PT. 1 (EP)	20
59	Topic TOP 37	HOOTENANNY NEW YORK CITY (EP, with Pete Seeger)	20
61	Top Rank JKP 3007	WORK-PLAY-FAITH-FUN-SONGS (EP)	20
64	Ember EP 4562	SONNY TERRY AND BROWNIE McGHEE (EP)	25
64	Topic TOP 121	R AND B FROM S AND B (EP)	20
64	Realm REP 4002	PAWNSHOP BLUES (EP)	20
64	Vocalion EPV 1274	SONNY TERRY AND BROWNIE McGHEE (EP)	25
65	Vocalion EPV 1279	I SHALL NOT BE MOVED (EP)	25
58	Topic 12T 29	BROWNIE McGHEE AND SONNY TERRY (LP)	22
58	Pye Nixa Jazz NJT 515	SONNY, BROWNIE AND CHRIS (10" LP, with Chris Barber)	25
58	Pye Nixa Jazz NJL 18	SONNY TERRY AND BROWNIE McGHEE IN LONDON (LP)	20
58	London Jazz LTZ-C 15144	BACK COUNTRY BLUES (LP)	35
60	Columbia 33SX 1223	BLUES IS MY COMPANION (LP)	30
61	World Record Club 7379	SONNY TERRY AND BROWNIE McGHEE (LP)	15
61	Vogue LAE 12247	BLUES IS A STORY (LP, also stereo SEA 5014)	25/35
63	Vogue LAE 12266	DOWN SOUTH SUMMIT MEETIN' (LP)	20
63	CBS 52165	BACK COUNTRY BLUES (LP)	20
64	Xtra XTRA 1004	BIG BILL BROONZY/SONNY TERRY/BROWNIE McGHEE (LP)	25
64	Vogue LAE 552	BROWNIE McGHEE AND SONNY TERRY (LP)	25
64	Realm RM 165	BACK COUNTRY BLUES (LP)	15
64	Stateside SL 10076	BLUES HOOT (LP, some tracks by Lightnin' Hopkins)	30

MINT VALUE £

64	Fontana 688 006ZL	LIVIN' WITH THE BLUES (LP)	20
65	Society SOC 1015	BROWNIE & SONNY SING AND PLAY (LP)	12
66	Philips BL 7675	AT THE BUNK HOUSE (LP)	18
66	Verve (S)VLP 5010	GUITAR HIGHWAY (LP, mono/stereo)	18/20
66	Fontana TL 5289	HOMETOWN BLUES (LP)	18
67	Ace Of Hearts (Z)AHT 182	HOMETOWN BLUES (LP, reissue)	12
69	Capitol T 20906	WHOOPIN' THE BLUES (LP)	16
69	Stateside SSL 10291	LONG WAY FROM HOME (LP)	15
69	Marble Arch MAL 843	SONNY TERRY AND BROWNIE McGHEE IN LONDON (LP)	12
70	Fontana SFJL 979	WHERE THE BLUES BEGAN (LP)	15
73	Mainstream MSL 1019	HOMETOWN BLUES (LP, gatefold sleeve)	12

(see also Brownie McGhee, Chris Barber, Pete Seeger, Big Bill Broonzy, Lightnin' Hopkins, Big Joe Turner)

TERRY & JERRY

| 65 | R&B MRB 5009 | People Are Doing It Every Day/Mama Julie | 15 |

TERRY, CARL & DERRICK

| 69 | Grape GR 3012 | True Love/ROY SMITH: Another Saturday Night | 7 |

TERRY SISTERS

57	Parlophone R 4364	It's The Same Old Jazz/Broken Promises	10
57	Parlophone R 4364	It's The Same Old Jazz/Broken Promises (78)	8
58	Parlophone R 4509	Sweet Thing (Tell Me That You Love Me)/You Forgot To Remember	6
58	Parlophone R 4509	Sweet Thing (Tell Me That You Love Me)/You Forgot To Remember (78)	12

TERRY-THOMAS ESQUIRE

56	Decca F 10804	A Sweet Old Fashioned Boy (with Rock 'N' Roll Rotters)/Lay Down Your Arms	15
56	Decca F 10804	A Sweet Old Fashioned Boy/Lay Down Your Arms (78)	10
61	Decca LK 4398	STRICTLY T-T (LP)	20

TESCO BOMBERS

| 82 | Y Y14 | Hernando's Hideaway/Break The Ice At Parties/Girl From Ipanema (p/s) | 5 |

TEST DEPARTMENT

83	Some Bizzare TEST 112	Compulsion/Pulsations (12", p/s)	12
80s	Media City CMC 1	Godaddin (12", p/s, Welsh gig freebie with Brith Gof)	15
91	Catalogue/Jungle CAT 088	Pax Brittanica (Excerpt)/CREAMING JESUS: Charlie Jumps The Bandwagon/MERCURY REV: Dripping/MUTTON GUN: Baby Born With Wooden Arm (flexidisc free with 1/91 issue of *The Catalogue* magazine)	4
82	Test TEST ONE	HISTORY (cassette, with booklet in plastic bag)	25
80s	Pleasantly Surprised PS 5	ECSTASY UNDER DURESS (cassette, in bag with inserts, 2 editions)	20/15
84	Test TEST 33	BEATING THE RETREAT (LP, box set)	15
86	Ministry Of Power MOP 2	THE UNACCEPTABLE FACE OF FREEDOM (LP)	10

JACK TETER TRIO

| 50 | London L 689 | Kansas City Kitty/Just A Little Nightcap (78) | 8 |
| 51 | London L 997 | Here Comes My Ball And Chain/There's A Little White Horse (78) | 10 |

ALAN TEW

| 67 | Decca Phase 4 PFS 4120 | THIS IS MY SCENE (LP) | 15 |

JOE TEX

65	Atlantic AT 4015	Hold What You've Got/Fresh Out Of Tears	10
65	Atlantic AT 4021	You Better Get It/You Got What It Takes	12
65	Sue WI 370	Yum Yum Yum/You Little Baby Face Thing	20
65	Atlantic AT 4027	A Woman Can Change A Man/Don't Let Your Left Hand Know	8
65	Atlantic AT 4045	I Want To (Do Everything For You)/Funny Bone	10
65	Atlantic AT 4058	A Sweet Woman Like You/Close Your Door	10
66	Atlantic AT 4081	The Love You Save/If Sugar Was As Sweet As You	8
66	Atlantic 584 016	S.Y.S.L.J.F.M. (Letter Song)/I'm A Man	6
66	Atlantic 584 035	You Better Believe It/I Believe I'm Gonna Make It	6
67	Atlantic 584 068	Papa Was Too/The Truest Woman In The World	6
67	Atlantic 584 096	Hold What You've Got/A Sweet Woman Like You	6
67	Atlantic 584 102	Show Me/Woman Sees A Hard Time (When Her Man Is Gone)	7
67	Atlantic 584 119	Woman Like That, Yeah/I'm Going And Get It	5
67	Atlantic 584 144	Skinny Legs And All/Watch The One (That Brings The Bad News)	5
68	Atlantic 584 171	Men Are Getting Scarce/You're Gonna Thank Me Woman	5
68	Atlantic 584 212	Go Home And Do It/Keep The One You Got	5
69	Atlantic 584 296	We Can't Sit Down Now/It Ain't Sanitary	5
70	Atlantic 584 318	You're Alright Ray Charles/Everything Happens On Time	5
71	Mercury 6052 067	I Knew Him/Bad Feet	5
72	Mercury 6052 111	Give The Baby Anything/Takin' A Chance	5
72	Mercury 6052 129	I Got 'Cha/Mother Prayer	5
72	Mercury 6052 156	You Said A Bad Word/It Ain't Gonna Work Baby	5
65	Atlantic ATL 5043	THE NEW BOSS (LP)	40
66	Atlantic ATL 587 009	THE LOVE YOU SAVE (LP)	30
67	Atlantic 587 053	I'VE GOT TO DO A LITTLE BETTER (LP)	25
67	Atlantic 587/588 059	THE NEW BOSS (LP, reissue)	18
67	London HA-U 8334	THE BEST OF JOE TEX (LP)	40
67	Atlantic 587/588 079	GREATEST HITS (LP)	15
68	Atlantic 587/588 104	LIVE AND LIVELY (LP)	22
68	Atlantic 587/588 118	SOUL COUNTRY (LP)	20
69	Atlantic 587/588 130	YOU BETTER GET IT (LP)	18
69	Atlantic 588 193	BUYING A BOOK (LP)	15
72	Atlantic K 40239	FROM THE ROOTS CAME THE RAPPER (LP)	12
72	Mercury 6338 093	I GOTCHA (LP)	12

(see also Soul Clan)

TEXAS

| 89 | Mercury TEXCD 1 | I Don't Want A Lover/Believe Me/In Vain (CD, slimline jewel case) | 10 |
| 89 | Mercury TEXCD 2 | The Thrill Has Gone/Nowhere Left To Hide/Dimples (CD, slimline jewel case) | 8 |

MINT VALUE £

89	Mercury TEXCD 3	Everyday Now/Waiting For The Fall/Future Is Promises/Fool For Love (CD, slimline jewel case)	8
89	Mercury TEXCD 4	Prayer For You/I Don't Want A Lover (Live)/Return/ Prayer For You (Acoustic Version) (CD, slimline jewel case)	7
92	Mercury TEXCD 8	Tired Of Being Alone/Thrill Has Gone/In My Heart (12")/ Prayer For You (Remixed by Kenny MacDonald) (CD, digipak)	8
93	Mercury TEXCL10	You Owe It All To Me/I Don't Want A Lover/So Called Friend/Revolution (CD, "Limited edition acoustic CD package", with 3 postcards, card outer pack)	10
99	Mercury NMR 2	THE HUSH (CD, 8" x 8" box with biography and 4 postcards, promo only)	25

TEXANS
| 64 | Columbia DB 7242 | Being With You/Wondrous Look Of Love | 4 |

TEXAS RANGERS
| 57 | HMV 7EG 8387 | WAY OUT WEST (EP) | 10 |

TEXTOR SINGERS
| 54 | Capitol CL 14211 | Sobbin' Women/Remember Me | 10 |

RUDY THACKER & STRINGBEANS
| 62 | Starlite ST45 087 | The Ballad Of Johnny Horton/Tomorrow Is My Last Day | 12 |

JAKE THACKRAY
67	Columbia SCX 6178	LAST WILL AND TESTAMENT (LP)	12
69	Columbia SCX 6345	JAKE'S PROGRESS (LP)	12
71	Note NTS 105	LIVE PERFORMANCE (LP)	12
72	Columbia SCX 6506	BANTUM COCK (LP)	12

THAMESIDERS/DAVY GRAHAM
| 63 | Decca DFE 8538 | FROM A LONDON HOOTENANNY (EP, 2 tracks each) | 30 |
(see also Davy Graham)

THANES
| 87 | D.D.T. DISP 008 | HEY GIRL (EP, p/s) | 4 |
| 87 | D.D.T. DISP 008 | HEY GIRL (12", p/s) | 7 |
(see also Green Telescope)

SISTER ROSETTA THARPE
52	Brunswick 04989	Cain't No Grave Hold My Body Down/Ain't No Room In Church For Liars (78)	15
57	Mercury MT 126	When The Saints Go Marching In/Cain't No Grave Hold My Body Down (78)	10
57	Mercury MT 185	Up Above My Head There's Music In The Air/ Jericho (Joshua Fit The Battle Of Jericho) (78)	15
60	MGM MGM 1072	If I Can Help Somebody/Take My Hand, Precious Lord	6
58	Brunswick OE 9284	GOSPEL SONGS No. 2 (EP)	15
62	Mercury ZEP 10127	GOSPEL SINGER (EP, with Sally Jenkins Singers)	15
64	Mercury 10000MCE	SISTER ROSETTA THARPE (EP)	15
62	MGM MGM-EP 746	SISTER ROSETTA THARPE (EP)	15
57	Mercury MPL 6529	GOSPEL TRAIN (LP)	18
59	Brunswick LAT 8290	GOSPEL TRAIN (LP)	15
61	Mercury MMC 14057	THE GOSPEL TRUTH (LP)	15
(see also Little Richard)

SISTER ROSETTA THARPE & SISTER MARIE KNIGHT
| 51 | Brunswick 04851 | Didn't It Rain/SISTER ROSETTA THARPE: Two Little Fishes And Five Loaves Of Bread (78, with Sam Price Trio) | 12 |
(see also Marie Knight, Rev. Kelsey)

THAT PETROL EMOTION
| 85 | Pink PINKY 4 | Keen/A Great Depression On A Slum Night (p/s) | 4 |
(see also Undertones)

T.H.C. ROLLER
| 94 | Poor Person Prod. PPPR 4 | CHAPTER IN THE LIFE OF T.H.C. ROLLER (LP, handmade sleeve with insert & king-size rolling papers, numbered, 500 only) | 15 |

THEATRE OF HATE
80	S.S. SS 3	Original Sin/Legion (p/s)	5
81	Burning Rome BRR 1	Rebel Without A Brain/My Own Invention (p/s)	4
81	Burning Rome BRR 1	Rebel Without A Brain/My Own Invention (p/s, mispress with 2 B-side labels)	5
85	Bliss TOH 1EP	The Wake/Love Is A Ghost/Poppies/Legion (EP, 33rpm, with T-shirt in stickered pack, some sealed)	10/5
81	S.S. SSSSS 1P	HE WHO DARES WINS — LIVE AT THE WAREHOUSE, LEEDS (LP, white labels, some copies autographed)	12
81	Straight Music TOH 1	LIVE AT THE LYCEUM (cassette)	12
91	Burning Rome BRR 010LP	WESTWORLD (LP, reissue, with 4-track single & letter)	10
(see also Pack, Spear Of Destiny, Senate, Cult, Crisis)

THEE
| 65 | Decca F 12163 | Each And Every Day/There You Go! | 30 |

THEE MIGHTY CAESARS
| 80s | Swag SWG 001 | She's Just Fifteen Years Old/The Swag (1-sided flexidisc) | 6 |
(see also Milkshakes, Prisoners, Billy Childish)

THEM
64	Decca F 11973	Don't Start Crying Now/One Two Brown Eyes	45
64	Decca F 12018	Baby Please Don't Go/Gloria	7
65	Decca F 12094	Here Comes The Night/All For Myself	6
65	Decca F 12175	One More Time/How Long Baby?	10
65	Decca F 12215	(It Won't Hurt) Half As Much/I'm Gonna Dress In Black	10
65	Decca F 12281	Mystic Eyes/If You And I Could Be As Two	10
66	Decca F 12355	Call My Name/Bring 'Em On In	12
66	Decca F 12403	Richard Cory/Don't You Know?	12
67	Major Minor MM 509	Gloria/Friday's Child	12

67	Major Minor MM 513	The Story Of Them (Parts 1 & 2)	15
73	Deram DM 394	Gloria/Baby Please Don't Go (reissue)	5
65	Decca DFE 8612	THEM (EP)	75
65	Decca DFE 8612	THEM (EP, export-only 'band-on-ladder' p/s)	500
65	Decca LK 4700	(THE ANGRY YOUNG) THEM (LP, orig. label, some with flipback sleeve)	80/50
66	Decca LK 4751	THEM AGAIN (LP, original label, some with flipback sleeve)	80/50
70	Decca LK 4700	(THE ANGRY YOUNG) THEM (LP, re-pressing, red label, boxed Decca logo)	18
70	Decca LK 4751	THEM AGAIN (LP, re-pressing, red label, boxed Decca logo)	18
70	Decca (S)PA 86	THE WORLD OF THEM (LP, original issue)	18
78	Sonet SNTF 738	BELFAST GYPSIES (LP, features Them without Van Morrison)	12

(see also Van Morrison, Trader Horne, Taste, Sk'boo, Belfast Gypsies, Moses K. & Prophets, Light, Peter Barden, Jackie McCauley)

THEME MACHINE
81	BBC RESL 104	Themes Ain't What They Used To Be/Lost In A World Of Dreams	4

THEN JERICO
85	Immaculate 12 TJ 1	The Big Sweep/The Big Sweep (Club Mix)/The Rack (12", p/s)	7

THERAPY
72	CBS 69017	ALMANAC (LP)	10
73	Indigo IRS 5124	ONE NIGHT STAND (LP, private pressing)	20

THERAPY?
89	demo cassette	THIRTY SECONDS OF SILENCE (cassette, 100 only)	15
90	demo cassette	MEAT ABSTRACT (cassette sold at gigs, 150 only)	15
90	Multifuckingnational MFN 1	Meat Abstract/Punishment Kisses (p/s, labels on wrong sides, 1,000 only)	15
92	A&M (no cat. no.)	TEETHGRINDER (12", double pack, white labels in presentation pack)	50
92	A&M THX 1	Have A Merry Fucking Christmas: Teenage Kicks/With Or Without You (Xmas gig freebie)	15
92	Wiija WIJ 11	PLEASURE DEATH (mini-LP, 10 white labels)	75+

THERMOMETERS
80	Fokker FEP 100	20th Century Girl/Newtown Refugees/Stole Your Drugs (p/s)	6

THESE ANIMAL MEN
93	Popcor POPCOR 002	WHEELERS DEALERS AND CHRISTINE KEELERS (cassette EP, b/w 5 tracks by S*M*A*S*H, 200 only, photocopied green paper inlay)	5

THE THE
80	4AD AD 10	Controversial Subject/Black And White (p/s)	25
81	Some Bizzare BZS 4	Cold Spell Ahead/Hot Ice (p/s)	25
82	Epic EPC A 2787	Uncertain Smile/Three Orange Kisses From Kazan (p/s, some with insert)	8/7
82	Epic EPC A 13-2787	Uncertain Smile/Three Orange Kisses From Kazan/ Waitin' For The Upturn (12", p/s, some with photo insert)	10/8
82	Epic EPC A 13-2787	Uncertain Smile/Three Orange Kisses From Kazan/ Waitin' For The Upturn (12", yellow vinyl, p/s, some with photo insert)	20/15
83	Epic EPC A 3119	Perfect/The Nature Of Virtue (p/s)	6
83	Epic EPC A 13-3119	Perfect/The Nature Of Virtue (12", p/s)	12
83	Epic A 3710	This Is The Day/Mental Healing Process (p/s)	5
83	Epic A 3710	This Is The Day/Mental Healing Process//Absolute Liberation/ Leap Into The Wind (double pack, gatefold p/s)	10
83	Epic TA 3710	This Is The Day/I've Been Waiting For Tomorrow (All Of My Life) (12", p/s)	5
83	Melody Maker [no cat. no.]	Dumb As Death's Head/SINES: Jonathon (flexidisc with *Melody Maker*)	7/5
83	Epic A 3588	Uncertain Smile/Dumb As Death's Head (p/s)	4
86	Epic PS 215	Sweet Bird Of Truth (Radio Edit) (1-sided, promo only)	7
86	Epic TRUTH D2	Heartland/Born In The New S.A./Flesh And Bones//Perfect/ Fruit Of The Heart (12", p/s, double pack)	8
86	Epic TRUTH Q3	Infected/Infected (Energy Mix)/Disturbed (12", uncensored 'wank' p/s)	12
86	Epic TRUTH T3	Infected/Infected (Energy Mix)/Disturbed//Soul Mining (Remix)/ Sinking Feeling (12", p/s, double pack, with sticker)	10
87	Epic TENSE 1	Slow Train To Dawn/Harbour Lights (p/s, with 2 car stickers)	4
87	Epic CD THE 2	Sweet Bird Of Truth (12" Mix)/Harbour Lights/Sleeping Juice/ Soul Mining (12" Remix) (CD, card sleeve with gauze inner)	7
89	Epic CB EMU 8	The Beat(en) Generation/Angel/Soul Mining (The Previously Un-Released Mix) (3" CD, box set with folded card insert)	7
82	private cassette	PORNOGRAPHY OF DESPAIR (LP, unreleased, cassettes exist)	
83	Epic EPC 25525	SOUL MINING (LP, with inner sleeve, initially with 12" single "Perfect"/"Soup Of Mixed Emotions"/"Fruit Of The Heart")	15
86	Epic EPC 26770	INFECTED (LP, with poster & inner, 1st 25,000 with 'torture' sleeve)	12
94	Epic EPC 478139 0	HANKY PANKY (2 x 10" LP)	15

(see also Matt Johnson, Gadgets)

LLANS THELWELL & HIS CELESTIALS
66	Island WI 262	Choo Choo Ska/Lonely Night (B-side vocal: Busty Brown)	25

THEY MUST BE RUSSIANS
(see under Joe 9T & Thunderbirds)

THEYR (a.k.a. PEYR)
82	Shout XW 1202	THE FOURTH REICH (12" EP)	8

(see also Killing Joke)

THIEVES
79	Arista ARIGV 226	400 Dragons/Headlights (green vinyl)	4

(see also Fairport Convention)

THIEVES LIKE US
80	Earlobe ELS 1	Strike Out/Mind Made (p/s)	4

THIN END OF THE WEDGE
81	Jungle JR 051S	Lights Are On Green (p/s)	30

(see also Damascus)

THINGS
80 Imperial IP 4301   Pieces Of You/Lost Love (p/s) 6
(see also Buzzcocks)

THIN ICE
88 Blag It SJP 858   Freedom Road (p/s) 25

THIN LIZZY
SINGLES
70	Parlophone DIP 513	The Farmer/I Need You (Ireland-only, as Thin Lizzie) 1,000
71	Decca F 13208	NEW DAY (EP, 33rpm, some without p/s) 275/125
72	Decca F 13355	Whiskey In The Jar/Black Boys On The Corner 6
73	Decca F 13402	Randolph's Tango/Broken Dreams (2 versions of A-side:
		matrices ZDR 53384 & ZCPDR 53312) .... each 15
73	Decca F 13467	The Rocker/Here I Go Again 8
74	Decca F 13507	Little Darlin'/Buffalo Gal 8
74	Vertigo 6059 111	Philomena/Sha La La 8
75	Vertigo 6059 124	Rosalie/Half Caste 6
75	Vertigo 6059 129	Wild One/For Those Who Love To Die 8
76	Vertigo 6059 150	Jailbreak/Running Back (p/s) 15
77	Vertigo 6059 177	Dancing In The Moonlight/Bad Reputation (p/s) 10
78	Decca F 13748	Whiskey In The Jar/Vagabond Of The Western World/Sitamoia (p/s) 6
79	Vertigo LIZZY 3	Waiting For An Alibi/With Love (p/s, some with cartoon lyric sheet) 8/5
79	Vertigo LIZZY 4	Do Anything You Want To/Just The Two Of Us (p/s) 5
79	Decca THIN 1	Things Ain't Working Out Down At The Farm/The Rocker (10,000 with p/s) 8
79	Vertigo LIZZY 5	Sarah/Got To Give Up (3 different p/s designs) .... each 7
80	Vertigo LIZZY 6	Chinatown/Sugar Blues (live) (silver lettered p/s) 5
80	Vertigo LIZZY 7	Killer On The Loose/Don't Play Around (p/s) 6
80	Vertigo LIZZY 7 701	Killer On The Loose/Don't Play Around//Got To Give It Up (live)/
		Chinatown (live) (double pack) 6
81	Vertigo LIZZY 8	LIVE KILLERS (EP) 5
81	Vertigo LIZZY 812	LIVE KILLERS (12" EP, with extra track) 8
81	Lyntone LYN 10138/9	Song For Jimmy/GRAHAM BONNET: Night Games/POLECATS: We Say Yeah/
		WAY OF THE WEST: Monkey Love (orange vinyl flexidisc with/without
		Flexipop, issue 10) 12/6
81	Vertigo LIZZY 9	Trouble Boys/Memory Pain (p/s) 5
82	Vertigo LIZZY 10	Hollywood (Down On Your Luck)/Pressure Will Blow (p/s) 5
82	Vertigo LIZZY 10	Hollywood (Down On Your Luck) (10", p/s, 1-sided, existence unconfirmed) ... 10+
82	Vertigo LIZZY PD 10	Hollywood (Down On Your Luck)/Pressure Will Blow (picture disc). 8
83	Vertigo LIZZY 1111/22	Cold Sweat/Bad Habits//Angel Of Death (live)/Don't Believe A Word (live)
		(double pack) 10
83	Vertigo LIZZY 1112	Cold Sweat/Bad Habits/Angel Of Death (live)/Don't Believe A Word (live)
		(12", p/s) 10
83	Vertigo LIZZY 12	Thunder And Lightning/Still In Love With You (live) (p/s). 5
83	Vertigo LIZZY 1212	Thunder And Lightning/Still In Love With You (live) (12", p/s,
		some with poster) 15/8
83	Vertigo LIZZY 13	The Sun Goes Down/Baby Please Don't Go (p/s) 8
83	Vertigo LIZZY 1312	The Sun Goes Down (Remix)/The Sun Goes Down/Baby Please Don't Go
		(12", p/s) 10

LPs
71	Decca SKL 5082	THIN LIZZY (LP, dark blue label, early copies laminated sleeve/later matt) ... 35/25
72	Decca TXS 108	SHADES OF A BLUE ORPHANAGE (LP, gatefold sleeve, dark blue label). 25
73	Decca SKL 5170	VAGABONDS OF THE WESTERN WORLD (LP, dark blue label,
		some with insert). 20/15
76	Decca SKL 5249	REMEMBERING (LP) 12
76	Vertigo 9102 008	JAILBREAK (LP, 'spaceship' label, die-cut gatefold sleeve). 12
83	Vertigo VERL 3	THUNDER AND LIGHTNING (LP, with free 12") 15

(see also Phil Lynott, Wild Horses, Phenomena, Eric Bell Band, Funky Junction, Greedies, John Sykes, Gary Moore)

THIRD & FOURTH GENERATION
72 Punch PH 91   Rudies Medley (actually by Peter Tosh & Soulmates)/Rude Boy — Version 25
(see also Peter Tosh)

THIRD DIMENSION
70 Unity UN 566   Peace And Love/Peace And Love — Version 5

THIRD EAR BAND
69	Harvest SHVL 756	ALCHEMY (LP). 25
70	Harvest SHSP 773	THIRD EAR BAND: ELEMENTS (LP) 22
72	Harvest SHSP 4019	MUSIC FROM MACBETH (LP) 18
76	Harvest SHSM 2007	EXPERIENCES (LP) 10

(see also High Tide, Sounds Nice)

THIRD QUADRANT
82	Rock Cottage (no cat. no.)	SEEING YOURSELF AS YOU REALLY ARE (LP, private pressing,
		wraparound sleeve with handwritten insert, blank white label) 60
88	own label	LAYERED (private cassette, 500 only). 10

THIRD RAIL
67 Columbia DB 8274   Run, Run, Run/No Return 18

THIRD WORLD WAR
71	Fly BUG 7	Ascension Day/Teddy Teeth Goes Sailing (p/s). 6
71	Fly BUG 11	A Little Bit Of Urban Rock/Working Class Man. 4
71	Fly FLY 4	THIRD WORLD WAR (LP) 20
72	Track 2406 108	THIRD WORLD WAR II (LP) 50

(see also Terry Stamp)

13TH CHIME
81	Ellie Jay EJSP 9700	Cuts Of Love/Coffin Maker (poster p/s). 5
81	13th Chime THC 1	Cursed/Dug Up (p/s) 4
82	13th Chime THC 2	Fire/Hide And Seek/Sally Ditch (p/s) 4

13TH FLOOR ELEVATORS

78	Radar/Sound For Industry SFI 347	Reverberation/RED CRAYOLA: Hurricane Fighter Plane (flexidisc free with *Zig Zag* magazine, No. 88) 8/6
78	Radar ADA 13	You're Gonna Miss Me/Tried To Hide (green vinyl) 6
78	Radar RAD 13	THE PSYCHEDELIC SOUNDS OF ... (LP) 15
79	Radar RAD 15	EASTER EVERYWHERE (LP) 15

(see also Roky Erickson, Red Crayola)

31ST OF FEBRUARY

69	Vanguard (S)VRL 19045	THE 31ST OF FEBRUARY (LP) 15

35mm DREAMS

81	More Than This ASA 100	More Than This/The Bearer (foldout p/s) 4
81	More Than This ASA 200	Fasten Your Safety Belts/Corstorphine/Instamatic Dance (p/s) 4

39 LYON ST
(see under Associates)

THIRTY-SECOND TURN-OFF

69	Jay Boy JSL 1	THIRTY-SECOND TURN OFF (LP) 30

(see also Equals)

THIS DRIFTIN'S GOTTA STOP

70s	private pressing	THIS DRIFTIN'S GOTTA STOP (LP) 15

THIS HEAT

80	Piano THIS 1201	Health And Efficiency/Graphic/Varispeed (12", p/s with insert) 8
79	Piano THIS 1	THIS HEAT (LP) 12
81	Rough Trade ROUGH 26	DECEIT (LP, original) 10

THIS MORTAL COIL

83	4AD AD 310	Song To The Siren/16 Days (Reprise) (p/s) 4
83	4AD BAD 310	Song To The Siren/16 Days/Gathering Dust (12", p/s). 7
84	4AD AD 410	Kangaroo/It'll End In Tears (p/s, 2 different designs & label colours, 2,500 of each) .... each 4
86	4AD BAD 608	Come Here My Love/Drugs (10", p/s with inner sleeve) 10
91	4AD TMC 1CD	Extracts From "Blood": Late Night/You And Your Sister/I Come And Stand At Every Door/With Tomorrow (CD, card sleeve, promo only). 25

(see also Cocteau Twins, Modern English, Cindytalk)

THIS 'N' THAT

66	Mercury MF 938	Someday/Loving You 15
67	Strike JH 310	Get Down With It/I Care About You 7

(see also Cleo)

THIS POISON!

87	Reception REC 004	Engine Failure/You;-Think!! (p/s) 5
87	Reception REC 008	Poised Over The Pause Button/I'm Not Asking (p/s) 4
87	Reception REC 008/12	THE FIERCE CRACK EP! (12", p/s) 7

B.J. THOMAS

66	Hickory 45-1395	Never Tell/Billy & Sue. 7
66	Pye International 7N 25374	Mama/Wendy 7
68	Pye International 7N 25467	The Eyes Of A New York Woman/I May Never Get To Heaven. 6
69	Pye International 7N 25487	It's Only Love/You Don't Love Me Anymore (The Train Song) 5
69	Wand WN 1	Raindrops Keep Falling On My Head/Never Had It So Good 5
70	Wand WN 5	I Just Can't Help Believing/Send My Picture To Scranton, PA 5
72	Wand WN 24	Rock And Roll Lullaby/Are We Losing Touch? 5

CARLA THOMAS

61	London HLK 9310	Gee Whiz/For You 18
61	London HLK 9359	A Love Of My Own/Promises. 15
62	London HLK 9618	I'll Bring It On Home To You/I Can't Take It 15
64	Atlantic AT 4005	I've Got No Time To Lose/A Boy Named Tom 10
66	Atlantic AT 4074	Comfort Me/I'm For You 8
66	Atlantic 584 011	Let Me Be Good To You/Another Night Without My Man. 6
66	Atlantic 584 042	B-A-B-Y/What Have You Got To Offer Me. 6
67	Stax 601 002	Something Good (Is Going To Happen To You)/It's Starting To Grow (dark blue label, later light blue). 10/6
67	Stax 601 008	When Tomorrow Comes/Unchanging Love (dark blue label, later light blue) ... 10/6
68	Stax 601 032	Pick Up The Pieces/Separation 5
68	Stax STAX 103	Where Do I Go/I've Fallen In Love 5
69	Stax STAX 112	I Like What You're Doing To Me/Strung Out. 6
69	Stax STAX 131	Unyielding/I've Fallen In Love 5
72	Stax 2025 082	Love Means/You've Got A Cushion To Fall On 5
91	Kent 6T 7	I'll Never Stop Loving/Prophets Band/Peaches Baby 15
67	Stax 589 004	CARLA THOMAS (LP). 25
67	Stax 589 012	THE QUEEN ALONE (LP) 25
69	Stax SXATS 1019	MEMPHIS QUEEN (LP). 22
71	Stax 2363 004	MEMPHIS QUEEN (LP, reissue) 12
72	Stax 2362 023	LOVE MEANS... (LP) 15

(see also Otis Redding & Carla Thomas)

CHARLIE THOMAS (& DRIFTERS)

74	EMI International INT 502	Midsummer Night In Harlem/Lonely Drifter Don't Cry (with Drifters). 5
75	EMI International INT 506	I'm Gonna Take You Home/Run, Run, Roadrunner 10

CLAUDETTE THOMAS

68	Caltone TONE 116	Roses Are Red My Love/YVONNE HARRISON: Near To You. 10

CREEPY JOHN THOMAS

69	RCA RCA 1912	Ride A Rainbow/Moon And Eyes Song. 10
69	RCA SF 8061	CREEPY JOHN THOMAS (LP) 50

(see also Paul Kossoff, Edgar Broughton Band)

DAVID THOMAS & PEDESTRIANS
83	Recommended REDT 7	Didn't Have A (Very) Good Time (1-sided picture disc free with label's quarterly magazine)	6
84	Rough Trade ROUGH 30	THE SOUND OF THE SAND (LP)	10
85	Rough Trade ROUGH 80	MORE PLACES FOREVER (LP)	10

(see also Pere Ubu)

DON THOMAS
76	DJM DJS 10670	Come On Train (Parts 1 & 2)	5

DYLAN THOMAS
50s	Caedmon TCE 151	A WINTER'S TALE (EP)	8

GENE THOMAS
64	United Artists UP 1047	Baby's Gone/Stand By Love	15

HERSAL THOMAS
50	Parlophone R 3261	Suitcase Blues/Hersal Blues (78)	60

IRMA THOMAS
64	Liberty LIB 66013	Breakaway/Wish Someone Would Care	18
64	Liberty LIB 66041	Anyone Who Knows What Love Is (Will Understand)/Time Is On My Side	20
65	Liberty LIB 66080	He's My Guy/True True Love	12
65	Liberty LIB 66095	Some Things You Never Get Used To/You Don't Miss A Good Thing (Until It's Gone)	18
65	Sue WI 372	Don't Mess With My Man/Set Me Free	25
65	Liberty LIB 66106	I'm Gonna Cry Till My Tears Run Dry/Nobody Wants To Hear Nobody's Troubles	20
66	Liberty LIB 66137	Take A Look/What Are You Trying To Do	20
66	Liberty LIB 66178	It's A Man's-Woman's World (Parts 1 & 2)	8
72	Atlantic K 10167	Full Time Woman/She's Taking My Part	5
72	United Artists UP 35402	Time Is On My Side/Anyone Who Knows What Love Is (Will Understand) (reissue)	5
65	Liberty LEP 4035	TIME IS ON MY SIDE (EP)	60
68	Minit MLL/MLS 40004E	TAKE A LOOK (LP)	45
76	Island HELP 29	LIVE (LP)	12

JAMO THOMAS & HIS PARTY BROTHERS ORCHESTRA
66	Polydor BM 56709	I Spy (For The FBI)/Snake Hip Mama	8
69	Polydor 56755	I Spy (For The FBI)/Snake Hip Mama (reissue)	5
69	Chess CRS 8098	I'll Be Your Fool/Jamo Soul	10
71	Mojo 2092 013	I Spy (For The FBI)/Snake Hip Mama (2nd reissue)	4

JIMMY THOMAS
69	Parlophone R 5773	The Beautiful Night/Above A Whisper (withdrawn; demos more common, £75)	125
69	Spark SRL 1035	(We Ain't Looking For) No Trouble/Springtime	5
70	Spark SRL 1040	White Dove/You Don't Have To Say Goodbye	5
72	Jay Boy BOY 67	Where There's A Will/Just Tryin' To Please You	5

(see also Sweet Dreams)

KID THOMAS
70s	JSP 4503	Rockin' This Joint Tonight/Cozy Lounge Blues	6

KID THOMAS/EMANUEL BAND
64	'77' LA 12/26	VICTORY WALK (LP, with Barry Martyn's Band)	30

LEON THOMAS
73	Philips 6369 417	BLUES & SOULFUL TRUTH (LP)	15

NICKY THOMAS
70	Amalgamated AMG 863	Danzella/JOE GIBBS ALLSTARS: Kingstonians Reggae	10
70	Trojan TR 7750	Love Of The Common People/DESTROYERS: Compass	5
70	Trojan TR 7796	God Bless The Children/Red Eye	5
71	Trojan TR 7807	If I Had A Hammer/Lonely Feelin'	6
71	Trojan TR 7830	Tell It Like It Is/B.B.C.	5
70	Trojan TBL 143	LOVE OF THE COMMON PEOPLE (LP)	15

(see also Joe Gibbs)

RAMBLIN' THOMAS
52	Tempo R 51	Jug Head Blues/Hard Dallas Blues (78)	20

(see also Blind Blake)

RAY THOMAS
75	Threshold THS 16	FROM MIGHTY OAKS (LP, with insert)	10
76	Threshold THS 17	HOPES, WISHES & DREAMS (LP)	10

(see also Moody Blues)

RUFUS THOMAS
63	London HLK 9799	Walking The Dog/Fine And Mellow	18
64	London HLK 9850	Can Your Monkey Do The Dog/I Want To Get Married	12
64	London HLK 9884	Somebody Stole My Dog/I Want To Be Loved	12
64	Atlantic AT 4009	Jump Back/All Night Worker	10
66	Atlantic 584 029	Willy Nilly/Sho' Gonna Mess Him Up	7
67	Atlantic 584 089	Jump Back/Walking The Dog	6
67	Stax 601 013	Greasy Spoon/Sophisticated Sissy	7
68	Stax 601 028	Down Ta My House/Steady Holding On	7
68	Stax 601 037	The Memphis Train/I Think I Made A Boo-Boo	7
68	Stax STAX 105	Funky Mississippi/So Hard To Get Along With	5
71	Stax 2025 060	The Breakdown (Parts 1 & 2)	5
71	Stax 2025 080	Do The Funky Penguin (Parts 1 & 2)	5
64	Atlantic AET 6001	DO THE DOG (EP)	30
65	Atlantic AET 6011	JUMP BACK WITH RUFUS (EP)	35
64	London HA-K 8183	WALKING THE DOG (LP)	60
70	Stax SXATS 1033	FUNKY CHICKEN (LP)	22

71	Stax 2363 001	FUNKY CHICKEN (LP, reissue)	12
71	Stax 2362 010	DOING THE PUSH AND PULL LIVE AT P.J.'s (LP)	18
72	Stax 2362 028	DID YOU HEARD ME? (LP)	18
74	Stax STX 1004	CROWN PRINCE OF DANCE (LP)	15

TIMMY THOMAS
73	Mojo 2027 012	Why Can't We Live Together/Funky Me	5
77	T.K. XB 9052	The Magician/Don't Put It Down	5
73	Mojo 2956 002	WHY CAN'T WE LIVE TOGETHER (LP)	15

VAUGHAN THOMAS
70	Page One POF 167	Need You Girl/Come Together	5
70	Page One POF 178	Is This What I Get For Loving You/Since You've Been Mine	5
72	Jam JAL 101	VAUGHAN THOMAS (LP)	20

WAYNE THOMAS
| 67 | Coral Q 72491 | I've Never Known A Lady/My Life's Gonna Change | 6 |

ANDREAS THOMOPOULOS
70	Mushroom 100 MR 1	SONGS OF THE STREET (LP)	40
71	Mushroom 150 MR 4	BORN OUT OF THE TEARS OF THE SUN (LP)	50
	(see also Secondhand)		

BARBARA THOMPSON
| 74 | Explosion EX 2087 | Single Girl/DANDY & COUNT PRINCE MILLER: Version | 6 |

BOBBY THOMPSON
69	Columbia Blue Beat DB 113	That's How Strong My Love Is/Trouble In Town	5
69	Jolly JY 001	That's How Strong My Love Is/Trouble In The Town	6
	(see also Dandy)		

CHERYLE THOMPSON
| 64 | Stateside SS 291 | Teardrops/Black Night | 7 |

CHRIS THOMPSON
| 73 | Village Thing VTS 21 | CHRIS THOMPSON (LP) | 20 |

EDDIE THOMPSON
55	Jazz Today JTE 101	THE FABULOUS EDDIE THOMPSON (EP)	50
57	Nixa NJE 1030	PIANO MOODS VOLUME 6 (EP)	50
60	Ember EMB 3303	PIANO MOODS (LP)	100
60	Tempo TAP 24	HIS MASTER'S JAZZ (LP)	100
60s	77 LEU 12/39	BY MYSELF (LP)	40

ERIC THOMPSON
| 68 | CBS EP 6398 | THE MAGIC ROUNDABOUT NO. 1 (EP) | 8 |
| 68 | CBS EP 6399 | THE MAGIC ROUNDABOUT NO. 2 (EP) | 8 |

HANK THOMPSON (& BRAZOS VALLEY BOYS)
53	Capitol CL 13977	The Wild Side Of Life/Rub-A-Dub-Dub (78)	8
54	Capitol CL 14161	Honky-Tonk Girl/Wake-Up Irene (78)	8
56	Capitol CL 14517	Honey, Honey Bee Ball/Don't Take It Out On Me	12
56	Capitol CL 14517	Honey, Honey Bee Ball/Don't Take It Out On Me (78)	8
56	Capitol CL 14668	I'm Not Mad, Just Hurt/The Blackboard Of My Heart	12
56	Capitol CL 14668	I'm Not Mad, Just Hurt/The Blackboard Of My Heart (78)	10
58	Capitol CL 14869	Li'l Liza Jane/How Do You Hold A Memory	12
58	Capitol CL 14869	Li'l Liza Jane/How Do You Hold A Memory (78)	10
58	Capitol CL 14945	Gathering Flowers/Squaws Along The Yukon	8
58	Capitol CL 14961	I've Run Out Of Tomorrows/You're Going Back To Your Old Ways Again	7
59	Capitol CL 15014	Anybody's Girl/Total Strangers	6
59	Capitol CL 15074	I Guess I'm Getting Over You/I Didn't Mean To Fall In Love	6
60	Capitol CL 15114	A Six Pack To Go/What Made Her Change	15
60	Capitol CL 15156	She's Just A Whole Lot Like You/There My Future Goes (solo)	6
61	Capitol CL 15177	Will We Start It All Over Again/It Got To Be A Habit (solo)	6
62	Capitol CL 15247	The Wild Side Of Life (solo)/Give The World A Smile	6
76	Capitol CL 15877	Rockin' In The Congo/I Was The First One	5
56	Capitol EAP 1028	SONGS OF THE BRAZO VALLEY NO. 1 (EP)	15
57	Capitol EAP1-826	HANK (EP)	15
59	Capitol EAP1-1111	FAVOURITE WALTZES (EP)	12
57	Capitol T 729	HANK THOMPSON'S ALL-TIME HITS (LP)	20
58	Capitol T 975	DANCE RANCH (LP)	20
61	Capitol (S)T 1246	SONGS FOR ROUNDERS (LP)	18
61	Capitol (S)T 1469	THIS BROKEN HEART OF MINE (LP)	18
62	Capitol (S)T 1632	AT THE GOLDEN NUGGET (LP)	15
65	Capitol T 2089	GOLDEN COUNTRY HITS (LP)	15
66	Capitol T 2274	BREAKING IN ANOTHER HEART (LP)	12
68	Capitol T 2826	JUST AN OLD FLAME (LP)	12

JACKIE THOMPSON
| 69 | Direction 58-4521 | Bad Women A Dime A Dozen/Games People Play | 5 |

JOHNNY THOMPSON & ONE-EYED JACKS
| 65 | Ember EMB S 206 | For Us There'll Be No Tomorrow/Soul Chant (some in p/s) | 10/5 |

KAY THOMPSON
| 56 | London HLA 8268 | Eloise/Just One Of Those Things | 25 |
| 56 | London HLA 8268 | Eloise/Just One Of Those Things (78) | 10 |

LINVAL THOMPSON
| 75 | Faith FA 010 | Girl You Got To Run/Run Come Feel | 10 |
| 75 | Faith FA 018 | Jah Redder Than Red/Version | 8 |

LUCKY THOMPSON
| 56 | Vogue V 2388 | But Not For Me/East Of The Sun | 10 |

THOMPSON TWINS

MIKE THOMPSON Jnr.
67   Island WI 3090   Rocksteady Wedding/Flower Pot Bloomers (both with Lyn Taitt & Jets) 20

MOLLIE THOMPSON
66   Asteroid JH 101   SONG NOTES SINGS FROM WORLDS AFAR (LP, private pressing) 40

OWEN THOMPSON
72   Camel CA 103   Must I Be Blue/Version 6

PETER THOMPSON & NTH DEGREE
65   Fontana TF 656   For Me It's All Over/The Way You Used To Do 6

RICHARD THOMPSON
89   Capitol CDCL 550   RECKLESS KIND (CD EP) 7
72   Island ILPS 9197   HENRY THE HUMAN FLY (LP, 'pink rim palm tree' label) 12
81   Elixir LP 1   STRICT TEMPO (LP) 10

RICHARD & LINDA THOMPSON
74   Island WIP 6186   I Want To See The Bright Lights Tonight/When I Get To The Border 5
75   Island WIP 6220   Hokey Pokey/I'll Regret It All In The Morning 5
74   Island ILPS 9305   HOKEY POKEY (LP, 'palm tree' label with lyric insert) 12
75   Island ILPS 9348   POUR DOWN LIKE SILVER (LP, 'palm tree' label with lyrics) 12
75   Island   OFFICIAL LIVE TOUR 1975 (LP, unreleased, test pressings may exist) . . . . 100+
76   Island ICD 8   GUITAR/VOCAL (2-LP, gatefold sleeve) 15
(see also Fairport Convention, Richard Thompson, Sandy Denny, Marc Ellington, Nick Drake, Bunch, Gary Farr, Paul McNeill & Linda Peters)

ROY THOMPSON
67	Columbia DB 8108	Sookie Sookie/Love You Say	8

SIR CHARLES THOMPSON
53	Vogue LDE 032	SIR CHARLES THOMPSON'S ALL STARS WITH CHARLIE PARKER (10" LP)	15
56	Vanguard PPT 12011	AND HIS BAND FEATURING COLEMAN HAWKINS (10" LP)	15

SONNY THOMPSON & HIS RHYTHM & BLUES BAND
52	Vogue V 2143	Real, Real Fine (Parts 1 & 2) (78)	40
53	Esquire 10-320	House Full Of Blues/Creepin' (78)	40
53	Esquire 10-339	Screamin' Boogie/The Fish (78)	40
60	Starlite ST45 008	Screamin' Boogie/The Fish	225

(see also Claude Cloud & Thunderclaps)

SUE THOMPSON
54	Mercury MB 3133	I'm Not That Kind Of Girl/I Long To Tell You (78)	10
61	Polydor NH 66967	Sad Movies/Throwing Kisses	10
62	Polydor NH 66973	Norman/Never Love Again	10
62	Polydor NH 66976	Two Of A Kind/It Has To Be Me	7
62	Polydor NH 66979	Have A Good Time/If The Boy Only Knew	7
63	Polydor NH 66987	What's Wrong Bill/I Need A Harbour	7
62	Fontana 267 244TF	James (Hold The Ladder Steady)/My Hero	10
63	Fontana 267 262TF	Willie Can/Too Much In Love	8
64	Hickory 45-1240	Big Daddy/I'd Like To Know You Better	7
64	Hickory 45-1255	Bad Boy/Toys	10
65	Hickory 45-1284	Paper Tiger/Mama Don't Cry At My Wedding	7
65	Hickory 45-1328	It's Break Up Time/Afraid	10
65	Hickory 45-1340	Just Kiss Me/Sweet Hunk Of Misery	8
65	Hickory 45-1359	I'm Looking For A World/Walkin' My Baby	7
65	Hickory 45-1381	What Should I Do/After The Heartache	6
67	London HLE 10142	Ferris Wheel/Don't Forget To Cry	5
65	Hickory LPE 1507	INTRODUCING KRIS JENSEN AND SUE THOMPSON (EP, 2 tracks each)	20
64	Hickory LPM 102	PAPER TIGER (LP)	30

(see also Kris Jensen)

SUE THOMPSON & BOB LUMAN
63	Polydor NH 66989	I Like Your Kind Of Love/Too Hot To Dance	10
63	Hickory 45-1221	I Like Your Kind Of Love/Too Hot To Dance (reissue)	7

(see also Bob Luman)

THOMPSON TWINS
80	Dirty Discs RANK 1	Squares And Triangles/Could Be He... Could Be You (p/s, different colours)	15
80	Latent LATE 1	She's In Love With Mystery/Fast Food/Food Style (p/s)	15
81	T TEE 1	The Perfect Game/Politics (p/s)	5
82	T TEE 2	Animal Laugh/Anything Is Good Enough/A Dub Product (p/s)	4
82	T TEE 122	Animal Laugh/A Dub Product/Anything Is Good Enough (12", p/s)	8
82	T TEE 5/RANK 3	Runaway/Open Your Eyes (p/s, double pack)	6
83	Arista ARIST 504	Love On Your Side/Love On Your Back//In The Name Of Love/In The Beginning (double pack)	6
83	Arista TWISD 1	Watching/Dangerous (picture disc)	10
83	Arista TWISD 2	Hold Me Now/Let Loving Start (picture disc)	4
84	Arista TWISD 3	Doctor Doctor/Nurse Shark (square-shaped picture disc)	5
84	Arista TWIJP 14/24/34	You Take Me Up/Passion Planet (3 different interlocking shaped pic discs)	each 5
84	Arista TWISD 4	You Take Me Up/Passion Planet (planet-shaped picture disc)	5
84	Arista TWISD 5	Sister Of Mercy/Out Of The Gap (rocket-shaped picture disc)	5
84	Arista TWISD 6	Lay Your Hands On Me/The Lewis Carol (diamond-shaped picture disc)	5
85	Arista TWIN 8	Roll Over/Fools Paradise (p/s, unreleased)	75
85	Arista TWINS 128	Roll Over/Fools Paradise/Roll Over (12", p/s, unreleased)	125
85	Arista TWISD 9	Don't Mess With Doctor Dream/Big Business (baby-shaped picture disc)	5
85	Arista TWIP 7	King For A Day (Extended Mix)/Roll Under (12", picture disc in p/s)	7
87	Arista TWINCD 13	Long Goodbye (Extended)/Dancing In Your Shoes (7" Version)/Hold Me Now (Dance Mix) (CD, gatefold card sleeve with gauze inner)	12
88	Arista 661 808	In The Name Of Love '88 (Single Mix)/(Railroad Mix)/(Railroad Dub)/(Original) (CD)	10
89	Warner Bros W 2819CD	Sugar Daddy/Sugar Daddy (12" Remix)/Sugar Daddy (Sugar House Mix) (3" CD, gatefold card sleeve)	7
82	T TELP 2	SET (LP, with free 7": "Squares And Triangles"/TOM BAILEY: "Weather Station"/BLANKETS: "Modern Plumbing" [T RANK 2])	18
86	fan club	LIVE (LP, signed fan club freebie)	45
84	Arista 610 183	QUICKSTEP AND SIDE KICK (CD)	20
84	Arista 610 106	INTO THE GAP (CD)	20

BILLY THORBURN & HIS STRICT TEMPO MUSIC
56	Parlophone MSP 6227	Jimmy Unknown/Ooh Bang Jiggilly Jang	6
57	Parlophone R 4276	True Love/Singing The Blues	6

GUNILLA THORN
63	HMV POP 1239	Merry-Go-Round/Go On Then	80

TRACEY THORN
82	Cherry Red CHERRY 53	Plain Sailing/Goodbye Joe (p/s)	4

(see also Marine Girls, Everything But The Girl, Grab Grab The Haddock)

DAVID THORNE
62	Stateside SS 141	The Alley Cat Song/The Moon Was Yellow	6
63	Stateside SS 190	One More Fool, One More Broken Heart/Don't Let It Get Away	7
64	Stateside SE 1020	WHAT WILL I TELL MY HEART (EP)	15
63	Stateside SL 10036	THE ALLEY CAT SONGSTER (LP)	30

Ken THORNE Orchestra

KEN THORNE ORCHESTRA
63	HMV POP 1176	"The Legion's Last Patrol" Film Theme/Kisses In The Night	4
68	United Artists ULP 1201	INSPECTOR CLOUSEAU (LP, soundtrack)	25
69	Stateside S(S)L 10271	THE TOUCHABLES (LP, with Nirvana, Wynder K. Frog, et al.)	35

WOODY THORNE
62	Vogue Pop V 9202	Sadie Lou/Teenagers In Love	350

CLAUDE THORNHILL & HIS ORCHESTRA
54	London HL 8042	Pussy-Footin'/Adios	35
54	London HL 8042	Pussy-Footin'/Adios (78)	10
54	London RE-P 1009	CLAUDE THORNHILL GOES MODERN (EP)	18
54	London H-ABP 1019	CLAUDE THORNHILL GOES MODERN (10" LP)	18
54	London H-ABP 1021	DREAM MUSIC (10" LP)	15

EDDIE THORNTON OUTFIT
69	Instant IN 003	Baby Be My Gal/SONNY BURKE OUTFIT: All You	8

WILLIE MAE 'BIG MAMA' THORNTON
54	Vogue V 2284	Hound Dog/Mischievous Boogie (78) (as Willie Mae 'Big Mama' Thornton)	80
65	Sue WI 345	Tom Cat/Monkey In The Barn (as Willie Mae Thornton)	100
69	Mercury SMCL 20176	STRONGER THAN DIRT (LP)	18
78	Vanguard VPC 40001	MAMA'S PRIDE (LP)	15

GEORGE THOROGOOD & DESTROYERS
78	Sonet SON 2148	Can't Stop Lovin'/Homesick Boy	4
78	Sonet SON 2158	Madison Blues/Delaware Slide	4
78	Sonet SON 2169	Cocaine Blues/Move It On Over	4
78	Sonet SON 2171	It Wasn't Me/Who Do You Love	4
79	Sonet SON 2183	SO MUCH TROUBLE (EP)	4
80	Sonet SON 2220	Night Time/The Kids From Philly (title p/s)	4
77	Sonet SNTF 760	GEORGE THOROGOOD AND THE DESTROYERS (LP)	12

BILLY THORPE & AZTECS
65	Parlophone R 5381	Twilight Time/Over The Rainbow	6

THOR'S HAMMER
66	Parlophone DP 565	Once/A Memory (export issue)	150
66	Parlophone DP 567	If You Knew/Love Enough (export issue)	150
66	Parlophone CGEP 62	THOR'S HAMMER (EP, export issue, gatefold p/s, with bonus 45 "If You Knew"/"Love Enough" [CGEP 62])	850

LINDA THORSON
68	Ember EMB S 257	Here I Am/Better Than Losing You (p/s)	40/20

THOSE HELICOPTERS
80	State Of The Art STATE 1	Shark/Eskimo (p/s)	5
81	Lavender LAVENDER 001	Dr. Janov/Technical Smack (p/s)	4

THOSE NAUGHTY LUMPS
79	Zoo CAGE 002	Iggy Pop's Jacket/Pure And Innocent (foldout p/s)	6
80	Open Eye OP-EP 1002	DOWN AT THE ZOO (EP)	6

THOSE OBNOXIOUS TYPES
85	Exoteric EX 2	Love Is Dead/I'm Glad I'm Sick (p/s)	4

THOUGHTS
66	Planet PLF 118	All Night Stand/Memory Of Your Love	65

(see also Tiffany [& Thoughts], Paul Dean & Soul Savages)

THOUGHTS & WORDS
69	Liberty LBF 15187	Morning Sky/Give Me A Reason	4
69	Liberty LBL 83224	THOUGHTS & WORDS (LP)	10

THOUGHTS OF DES COX
69	Morgan MR 4S	Isn't It Nice/It's All Very Strange	4

THRASHER WONDERS
50s	Melodisc MEL 1106	Charity/GOSPEL KEYS: Motherless Child (78)	7
50s	Melodisc MEL 1190	Blind Old Barnabas/Jesus I Love You (78)	7

THREADBARE CONSORT
80s	private pressing	WEARING THIN (LP)	15

THREADS OF LIFE
72	Alco ALC 530	THREADS OF LIFE (LP, actually by Alco)	500

THREATS
82	Rondelet ROUND 22	GO TO HELL (EP)	5
82	Rondelet ROUND 29	Politicians & Ministers/Writing's On The Wall/Deep End Depression (p/s)	5
82	Rondelet ROUND 1229	POLITICIANS & MINISTERS (12" EP)	7

THREE BARRY SISTERS
59	Decca F 11099	Little Boy Blue/My Sweetie's Coming To Call	8
59	Decca F 11099	Little Boy Blue/My Sweetie's Coming To Call (78)	8
59	Decca F 11118	Tall Paul/Till Then	10
59	Decca F 11118	Tall Paul/Till Then (78)	10
59	Decca F 11141	Jo Jo — The Dog Faced Boy/I-Aye Ove-Lay Oo-Yay	8
59	Decca F 11141	Jo Jo — The Dog Faced Boy/I-Aye Ove-Lay Oo-Yay (78)	10
60	Decca F 11201	Spoilsport/Bonnie Prince Charlie	6
60	Decca F 11201	Spoilsport/Bonnie Prince Charlie (78)	15

THREE BELLS
60	Pye 7N 15252	Steady Date/In Between (Wishing I Was Sweet Sixteen)	6
64	Columbia DB 7399	Softly In The Night/He Doesn't Love Me	8

| 65 | Columbia DB 7570 | Someone To Love/Over And Over Again | 6 |
| 66 | Columbia DB 7980 | Cry No More/He Doesn't Want You | 6 |

(see also Satin Bells)

THREE CAPS
66	Atlantic 584 043	I Got To Handle It/Zig-Zagging	7
69	Atlantic 584 251	Cool Jerk/Hello Stranger	7
71	Atlantic 2091 105	Cool Jerk/Hello Stranger (reissue)	5
66	Atlantic 587/588 019	DANCE THE COOL JERK (LP)	25

(see also Capitols)

THREE CHUCKLES
55	HMV 7M 292	Runaround/At Last You Understand	30
55	HMV B 10835	Runaround/At Last You Understand (78)	30
56	HMV 7M 333	Still Thinking Of You/Times Two I Love You	25
56	HMV POP 123	Still Thinking Of You/Times Two I Love You (78)	35
57	HMV POP 292	We're Gonna Rock Tonight/Want You Give Me A Chance	100
57	HMV POP 292	We're Gonna Rock Tonight/Want You Give Me A Chance (78)	50

(see also Teddy Randazzo)

THREE CITY FOUR
| 65 | Decca LK 4705 | THREE CITY FOUR (LP) | 125 |
| 67 | CBS 63039 | SMOKE AND DUST WHERE THE HEART SHOULD HAVE BEEN (LP) | 75 |

(see also Martin Carthy, Leon Rosselson)

THREE COINS
| 70 | Sugar SU 106 | Come And Do The Right Thing/It's So Long | 6 |

3 COLOURS RED
| 97 | Fierce Panda NING 17 | This Is My Hollywood/Hate Slick (p/s) | 5 |

3D
| 84 | Rak RAKH 377 | Never (Revenge Mix) (1-sided, hologram disc, stickered polythene sleeve) | 8 |

THREE DEGREES
65	Stateside SS 413	Gee Baby I'm Sorry/Do What You're Supposed To Do	18
65	Stateside SS 459	Close Your Eyes/Gotta Draw The Line	40
71	Mojo 2092 001	Maybe/There's So Much Love Around Me	5
71	Mojo 2092 002	You're The One/Rose Garden	5
71	Mojo 2092 009	There's So Much Love Around Me/Maybe (reissue)	5
71	Mojo 2092 009	There's So Much Love Around Me/Yours (different B-side)	5
75	Pye International 7N 25671	Sugar On Sunday/Maybe	6
71	Mojo 2916 002	THE THREE DEGREES (LP)	20

THREE DOG NIGHT
69	Stateside-Dunhill SS 8008	Nobody/It's For You	5
70	Stateside-Dunhill SS 8052	Mama Told Me Not To Come/Rock And Roll Widow	6
69	Stateside-Dun. (S)SL 5006	THREE DOG NIGHT (LP)	12
69	Stateside-Dun. (S)SL 5013	SUITABLE FOR FRAMING (LP)	12
70	Stateside-Dunhill SSL 5023	CAPTURED LIVE AT THE FORUM (LP)	12
70	Probe SPBA 6251	IT AIN'T EASY (LP)	12

(see also Danny Hutton)

THREE DOLLS
| 57 | MGM MGM 958 | The Living End/The Octopus Song | 7 |

THREE GOOD REASONS
65	Mercury MF 883	Build Your Love/Don't Leave Me Now	6
65	Mercury MF 899	Nowhere Man/Wire Wheels	7
65	Mercury MF 929	The Moment Of Truth/Funny Kind Of Loving	5

THREE JOHNS
82	CNT CNT 003	English White Boy Engineer/Secret Agent (p/s)	8
83	CNT CNT 011	Pink Headed Bug/Lucy In The Rain (p/s)	7
83	CNT CNT 013	Men Like Monkeys/Two Minute Ape!/Windolene/Marx's Wife/Paris 1941 (12", p/s)	7

THREE KAYES (SISTERS)
| 56 | HMV 7M 401 | Ivory Tower/Mister Cuckoo (Sing Your Song) | 25 |
| 56 | HMV POP 251 | Lay Down Your Arms/First Row Balcony (as Three Kaye Sisters) | 18 |

(see also Kaye Sisters, Frankie Vaughan)

THREE MAN ARMY
72	Pegasus PGS 1	What's Your Name/Travellin'	6
74	Reprise K 14292	Polecat Woman/Take Me Down From The Mountain	5
71	Pegasus PEG 3	A THIRD OF A LIFETIME (LP)	30
73	Reprise K 44254	THREE MAN ARMY (LP)	25
74	Reprise K 54015	THREE MAN ARMY TWO — POLECAT WOMAN (LP)	30

(see also Gun, Baker Gurvitz Army, Adrian Gurvitz, Andy Newman)

THREE PEOPLE
66	Decca F 12473	Have You Ever Been There/Good Times	4
66	Decca F 12514	Suspicions/Easy Man To Find	4
67	Decca F 12581	Got To Find A Reason/Simple Thing Would Be For You To Start Loving Me	4

(see also John Bromley)

THREE PROFESSORS
| 56 | Columbia DB 3845 | Yew Stept Owt Offa Dreme/Vulgar Boatman Rock | 6 |
| 56 | Columbia DB 3845 | Yew Stept Owt Offa Dreme/Vulgar Boatman Rock (78) | 8 |

THREE QUARTERS
| 65 | Columbia DB 7467 | People Will Talk/Love Come A-Tricklin' Down | 5 |
| 65 | Columbia DB 7576 | The Pleasure Girls/Little People | 5 |

THREE'S A CROWD

MINT VALUE £

66	Fontana TF 673	Look Around The Corner/Living In A Dream	10

(see also Embers, Writing On The Wall)

THREE SUNS

55	HMV 7M 297	Perdido/For You	7
55	HMV 7M 346	Cha Cha Joe/Arriverderci Darling (Arriverderci Roma)	7

THREE TOPS

67	Doctor Bird DB 1101	Miserable Friday/This World Has A Feeling	15
67	Studio One SO 2023	Moving To Progress/Love And Inspiration	18
67	Trojan TR 003	It's Raining/Sound Of Music	15
67	Treasure Isle TI 7008	Do It Right/You Should Have Known	15
68	Coxsone CS 7033	A Man Of Chances/HORTENSE ELLIS: A Groovy Kind Of Love	25
68	Coxsone CS 7051	Great Train In '68/You Should Have Known	15
73	Bullet BU 527	Take Time Out/Just Like A Log	8

(see also Dion Cameron & Three Tops, Sir Lord Comic, King Rocky)

THREE WISE MEN

83	Virgin VS 642	Thanks For Christmas/Countdown To Christmas Partytime (p/s)	10

(see also XTC)

THRILLED SKINNY

87	Hunchback HUNCH 001	PIECE OF PLASTIC (12" EP)	7
88	Hunchback HUNCH 002	White Grid/Pinless (flexidisc with stapled b&w p/s & 2nd flexi by Wilderness Children, free with *Sowing Seeds* fanzine, issue 5)	7/5

(see also Wilderness Children)

THRILLERS

68	Blue Cat BS 128	The Last Dance/DELTA CATS: Unworthy Baby	12

(see also Phil Pratt)

THRILLERS

80	Big Bear BB 28	Shooting/To The Top (no p/s)	4

PERCY 'THRILLS' THRILLINGTON

77	Regal Zono. EMI 2594	Uncle Albert — Admiral Halsey/Eat At Home	80
77	Regal Zono. EMC 3175	THRILLINGTON (LP, with inner sleeve)	125
77	Regal Zono. TC-EMC 3175	THRILLINGTON (cassette)	40

(see also Paul McCartney)

THRILLS

66	Capitol CL 15469	No One/What Can Go Wrong	40
79	Grapevine GRP 126	Show The World Where It's At/What Can Go Wrong	6

THROBBING GRISTLE

78	Industrial IR 0003	United/Zyklon B Zombie (p/s)	8
78	Industrial IR 0003/U	United/Zyklon B Zombie (p/s, white or clear vinyl, 1,000 only of each)	15
80	Industrial IR 0003	United/Zyklon B Zombie (longer version) (p/s, reissue, 'Memorial Issue' scratched in matrix)	12
80	Industrial IR 0013	Subhuman/Something Came Over Me (in polythene camouflage bag)	10
80	Industrial IR 0015	Adrenalin/Distant Dreams (Part Two) (in polythene camouflage bag)	10
81	Fetish FET 006	Discipline (live, Berlin)/Discipline (live, Manchester) (12", p/s)	15
76	Industrial IR 0001	BEST OF VOLUME II (private cassette, 50 copies only)	50+
77	Industrial IR 0002	SECOND ANNUAL REPORT (LP, 785 only, white heavy duty sleeve, with questionnaire, xerox strip & 2 stickers)	70
78	Industrial IR 0004	D.O.A. THE THIRD AND FINAL REPORT (LP, 1st 1,000 with calendar & postcard)	20/15
78	Fetish FET 2001	SECOND ANNUAL REPORT (LP, 2,000 only, T.G. 'lightning flash' sleeve, with questionnaire & insert)	18
79	Fetish FET 2001	SECOND ANNUAL REPORT (LP, reissue, glossy sleeve with inserts)	12
79	Industrial IR 0004	D.O.A. THE THIRD AND FINAL REPORT (LP, re-pressing, 1,000 only, banded as 16 equal length tracks)	15
79	Industrial IR 0008	20 JAZZ FUNK GREATS (LP, 5,000 only, 1st 2,000 with b&w poster)	20/12
80	Industrial IR 0009	HEATHEN EARTH (LP, gatefold sleeve, 785 on blue vinyl)	70/12
81	Fetish FET 2001	SECOND ANNUAL REPORT (LP, backwards version, 1st 2,000 in T.G. 'flash' sleeve, later in black & white sleeve)	18/10
81	Fetish FX 1	A BOXED SET (5-LP box set with 28-page booklet & badge, 5,000 only)	80
82	Death 01	MUSIC FROM THE DEATH FACTORY, MAY '79 (LP, 50 only)	100+
82	Power Focus 001	ASSUME POWER FOCUS (LP, 500 only, numbered)	50
82	T.G. 33033	LIVE AT THE DEATH FACTORY, MAY '79 (LP, reissue picture disc, 1,355 only)	20
82	Walter Ulbricht 001	JOURNEY THROUGH THE BODY (LP, 1,000 only)	25
82	Karnage/Illuminated KILL 1	THEE PSYCHICK SACRIFICE (2-LP)	20
84	Illuminated JAMS 35	IN THE SHADOW OF THE SUN (LP, soundtrack)	10
84	Illuminated JAMS 39	THE INDUSTRIAL RECORDS STORY 1976-1981 (LP)	20
84	Casual Abandon CAS 1J	ONCE UPON A TIME (LP)	15
84	Mental Decay 01-1	SPECIAL TREATMENT (LP)	10
80s	Sprut 001	VERY FRIENDLY — THE FIRST ANNUAL REPORT OF T.G. (LP)	15
80s	Industrial IRC 1-IRC 24	24 HOURS (box set of cassettes)	150-200

(see also Psychic TV, Chris Carter, Chris & Cosey, Coil, Sabres Of Paradise)

THROWING MUSES

86	4AD MUSE ONE	Counting Backwards/Say Goodbye/Hook In Her Head (12", no p/s, promo only)	8
87	4AD BAD 701C	Chains Changed/Finished/Reel/Snail Head/Cry Baby Cry (cassette)	6
89	4AD BADD 903	Dizzy/Santa Claus/Mania (live)/Downtown (live) (10", gatefold p/s)	6
92	4AD MUSE TWO	Firepile/Manic Depression/Jak/Rosetta Stone (12", no p/s, promo only)	10
93	4AD CADD 2013	RED HEAVEN (LP, with free live Kristin Hersh LP)	15
93	4AD CADD 2013CD	RED HEAVEN (CD, with free live Kristin Hersh CD)	20
95	4AD CADD 5002CD	UNIVERSITY (CD, in slipcase with postcards)	20

(see also Belly, Tanya Donelly, Kristin Hersh)

HARRY THUMANN
79	Decca FR 13901	Underwater/American Express	4

THUNDER
89	EMI EMS 11	She's So Fine/Girl's Going Out Of Her Head (p/s, some with free patch)	8/5
89	EMI 12EMP 11	She's So Fine/Girl's Going Out Of Her Head/Another Shot Of Love (12", p/s with poster)	10
89	EMI CDEM 1	She's So Fine/Girl's Going Out Of Her Head/Another Shot Of Love (CD)	10
90	EMI EMG 126	Dirty Love/Fired Up (gatefold booklet p/s)	5
90	EMI EMPD 126	Dirty Love/Fired Up (logo-shaped picture disc with insert in PVC sleeve)	8
90	EMI 12EM 126	Dirty Love/Fired Up/She's So Fine (live) (12", p/s with poster)	8
90	EMI CDEM 126	Dirty Love/Fired Up/She's So Fine (live)/Brown Sugar (live) (CD)	8
90	EMI EMS 137	Back Street Symphony/No Way Out Of The Wilderness (box set with badge & postcards)	5
90	EMI 12 EMPD 137	Back Street Symphony/No Way Out Of The Wilderness/An Englishman On Holiday (live) (12", picture disc with insert in PVC sleeve)	8
90	EMI 10EM 148	Gimme Some Lovin'/I Wanna Be Her Slave (10", red vinyl with gatefold booklet)	7
90	EMI 10EM 158	She's So Fine (Full Length Version)/Backstreet Symphony (Live At Donington '90)/I Can Still Hear The Music (10", blue vinyl, gatefold p/s)	7
90	EMI 12EM 158	She's So Fine/Don't Wait For Me (Live At Donington '90)/I Can Still Hear The Music (12", p/s with poster)	7
91	EMI 10EM 175	Love Walked In/Flawed To Perfection (Demo)/World Problems: A Solution (10", p/s, white vinyl)	7
91	EMI 12EMPD 175	Love Walked In (LP Version)/Flawed To Perfection (Demo)/Until My Dying Day (live) (12", picture disc, die-cut p/s)	7
94	EMI EMPD 365	Stand Up/Interview (picture disc, in 12" PVC sleeve with calendar poster)	5
90s	THUNDER 1	She's So Fine/Until My Dying Day/Fired Up (flexidisc with Raw magazine)	5
90s	BENDER 1	Fired Up (live) (flexidisc free with Kerrang! magazine)	5
90	EMI PDEMC 3570	BACK STREET SYMPHONY (LP, picture disc)	12

(see also Terraplane, Nuthin' Fancy)

JOHNNY THUNDER
63	Stateside SS 149	Loop De Loop/Don't Be Ashamed	7
63	Stateside SS 168	Rock-A-Bye My Darling/The Rosy Dance	6
63	Stateside SS 200	Jailer, Bring Me Water/Outlaw	7
63	Stateside SS 229	Hey Child/Everybody Likes To Dance With Johnny	7
64	Stateside SS 337	More, More, More Love, Love, Love/Shout It To The World	7
65	Stateside SS 370	Send Her To Me/Everybody Likes To Dance With Johnny	6
65	Stateside SS 454	Dear John I'm Going To Leave You/Suzie-Q	7
65	Stateside SS 476	Everybody Do The Sloopy/Beautiful	7
66	Stateside SS 499	My Prayer/A Broken Heart	6
63	Stateside SL 10029	LOOP DE LOOP (LP)	40

JOHNNY THUNDER & RUBY WINTERS
67	Stateside SS 2005	Make Love To Me/Teach Me Tonight	7

MARGO THUNDER
75	Capitol CL 15808	Expressway To Your Heart/Hush Up Your Mouth	5

THUNDERBIRDS (U.S.)
55	London HL 8146	Ayuh, Ayuh/Blueberries	75
55	London HL 8146	Ayuh, Ayuh/Blueberries (78)	20

(see also Bert Convy & Thunderbirds, Midnighters)

THUNDERBIRDS (Australia)
61	Oriole CB 1610	Wild Weekend/Rat Race	15
61	Oriole CB 1625	New Orleans Beat/Delilah Jones	15

THUNDERBIRDS (U.K.)
66	Polydor 56710	Your Ma Said You Cried (In Your Sleep Last Night)/Before It's Too Late	40

(see also Chris Farlowe & Thunderbirds)

THUNDERBIRDS (T.V.)
(see under Barry Gray)

THUNDERBOLTS
62	Decca F 11522	Fugitive/Feelin' In A Mood	10

THUNDERBOYS
80	Recent EJSP 9339	Fashion/Someone Like You (p/s)	8

THUNDERCLAP NEWMAN
69	Track 604 031	Something In The Air/Wilhelmina	5
70	Track 2094 001	Accidents/I See It All	5
70	Track 2094 002	Wild Country/Hollywood	5
70	Track 2094 003	The Reason/Stormy Petrel	5
79	Track 2095 002	Wild Country/Hollywood (reissue, p/s)	8
70	Track 2406 003	HOLLYWOOD DREAM (LP)	20

(see also Stone The Crows, One In A Million, Paul McCartney & Wings, Speedy Keen, Andy Newman)

THUNDER COMPANY
70	Columbia DB 8706	Ridin' On The Gravy Train (5.03)/Bubble Drum	35
70	Columbia DB 8706	Ridin' On The Gravy Train (2.35 Edit)/Bubble Drum (demo only)	40

(see also Brian Bennett, Shadows)

THUNDERGROUND
92	Infonet INF 001T	THUNDERGROUND EP (12")	10

THUNDERMUG
73	London HLZ 10411	Africa/Will They Ever	4
72	Axe AXS 502	STRIKES (LP)	10

Johnny THUNDERS

JOHNNY THUNDERS (& HEARTBREAKERS)
78	Real ARE 1	Dead Or Alive/Downtown (p/s)	15
78	Real ARE 3	You Can't Put Your Arms Around A Memory (Edit)/Hurtin' (p/s)	12
78	Real ARE 3T	You Can't Put Your Arms Around A Memory/Hurtin' (12", p/s, blue or pink vinyl, die-cut company sleeve)	10
83	Jungle JUNG 5	VINTAGE '77 (12" EP)	12
84	Jungle JUNG 14P	Get Off The Phone/All By Myself (picture disc)	5
85	Jungle JUNG 23P	Crawfish/Tie Me Up (with Patti Palladin, picture disc)	5
77	Real RAL 1	SO ALONE (LP, with inner sleeve)	12

(see also New York Dolls, Heartbreakers)

THUNDERSTICK
| 83 | Thunderbolt THBE 1002 | FEEL LIKE ROCK'N'ROLL (12" EP, p/s, some with patch) | 10/8 |
| 83 | Thunderbolt THBL 008 | BEAUTY AND THE BEASTS (LP) | 12 |

(see also Samson, Gillan)

THUNDERTHIGHS
| 74 | Philips 6006 386 | Central Park Arrest/Sally Wants A Dress (p/s) | 5 |

THUNDERTHUMBS & TOETSENMAN
| 82 | Polydor POSP 480 | Freedom/Freedom A Gogo (p/s) | 15 |
| 82 | Polydor POSPX 480 | Freedom (Extended Version)/Freedom A Gogo (12", p/s) | 18 |

(see also Level 42, Mark King)

THUNDERTRAIN
| 77 | Jelly JPLP 1 | TEENAGE SUICIDE (LP) | 18 |

THURSDAY'S CHILDREN
| 66 | Piccadilly 7N 35276 | Just You/You Don't Believe Me | 12 |
| 66 | Piccadilly 7N 35306 | Crawfish/Come Softly To Me | 7 |

(see also Phil Cordell)

THYRDS
| 64 | Oak RGJ 133 | Hide 'N' Seek/I've Got My Mojo Working | 200 |
| 64 | Decca F 12010 | Hide 'N' Seek/No Time Like The Present | 40 |

TIARAS
| 63 | Warner Bros WB 92 | You Told Me/I'm Gonna Forget You | 10 |

TICH & QUACKERS
| 65 | Oriole CB 1980 | Santa Bring Me Ringo/Santa's Got Such A Terrible Cold | 8 |

TICKAWINDA
| 75 | Pennine PSS 153 | ROSEMARY LANE (LP) | 300 |

(see also Any Trouble)

TICKETS
| 79 | Bridgehouse BHS 3 | I'll Be Your Pin Up/Guess I Have To Sit Alone (p/s) | 6 |

(see also Wasted Youth)

TICKLE
| 67 | Regal Zonophone RZ 3004 | Subway (Smokey Pokey World)/Good Evening | 175 |

(see also Junior's Eyes, Outsider, Bunch Of Fives)

TICKLERS
| 52 | Melodisc MEL 1214 | Don't Fence Her In/Glamour Gal (78) | 12 |

TIDAL WAVE
| 69 | Decca F 22973 | With Tears In My Eyes/We Wanna Know | 8 |

TIDBITS
| 71 | Fly BUG 12 | Jean Harlow/Vietnam/Six O'Clock Blues | 4 |

PETER TIERNEY & NIGHTHAWKS
| 65 | Fontana TF 547 | Oh How I Need You/That's Too Bad | 6 |

ROY TIERNEY
| 61 | Philips BF 1159 | Cupid/The Lonely One (some in p/s) | 10/6 |
| 61 | Philips BF 1194 | Just Out Of Reach (Of My Two Empty Arms)/Casanova | 6 |

TIERNEY'S FUGITIVES
| 65 | Decca F 12247 | Did You Want To Run Away?/Morning Mist | 12 |

TIFFANIES
| 67 | Chess CRS 8059 | It's Got To Be A Great Song/He's Good For Me | 45 |

TIFFANY (with THOUGHTS)
| 65 | Parlophone R 5311 | I Know/Am I Dreaming | 8 |
| 66 | Parlophone R 5439 | Find Out What's Happening/Baby Don't Look Down (as Tiffany with Thoughts) | 25 |

(see also Thoughts)

TIFFANY SHADE
| 68 | Fontana (S)TL 5469 | TIFFANY SHADE (LP) | 40 |

JIMMY & LOUISE TIG
| 69 | Deep Soul DS 9105 | A Love That Never Grows Cold/Who Can I Turn To | 10 |

TIGER (U.K.)
75	United Artists UP 35848	I Am An Animal/Stop That Machine	5
76	Retreat RTL 6006	TIGER (LP, with inner sleeve)	12
76	EMI EMC 3153	GOIN' DOWN LAUGHING (LP, with inner sleeve)	12

(see also Hackensack, Samson, Brinsley Schwarz, Big Jim Sullivan)

TIGER (Jamaica)
70	New Beat NB 052	Soul Of Africa/Dallas Texas	5
70	New Beat NB 064	Musical Scorcher/Three Dogs Night	5
71	Camel CA 70	Guilty/United We Stand	6

Rare Record Price Guide 2002

71	New Beat NB 075	African Beat/Black Man Land	5
71	New Beat NB 088	Have You Ever Been Hurt/Our Day Will Come	5

(see also Clancy Eccles)

TIGER LILY
75	Gull GULS 12	Monkey Jive/Ain't Misbehavin' (some with p/s)	30/12
77	Gull GULS 54	Monkey Jive/Ain't Misbehavin' (reissue, different p/s)	12/5
80	Dead Good DEAD 11	Monkey Jive/Ain't Misbehavin' (2nd reissue)	6

(see also Ultravox)

TIGERS
69	Polydor 56339	Rain Falls On The Lonely/Smile For Me	4

TIGERS
80	Strike KIK 1	Kidding Stops/Big Expense Small Income (die-cut sleeve)	5
80	Strike KIK 3	Promises Promises/Ska Trekkin' (p/s)	5

TIGERTAILZ
88	M. For Nations MFN 78P	YOUNG AND CRAZY (LP, picture disc)	10
90	M. For Nations MFN 96P	BERSERKER (LP, picture disc)	10

TIGHT LIKE THAT
72	Village Thing VTS 12	HOKUM (LP)	20

TIGHTS
78	Cherry Red CHERRY 1	Bad Hearts/It/Cracked (p/s)	5
78	Cherry Red CHERRY 2	Howard Hughes/China's Eternal (p/s)	4
78	Ch. Red CSP-CHERRY 2	Howard Hughes/China's Eternal (cassette)	10

TIK & TOK
82	Survival SURP 007	Summer In The City/Crisis (picture disc)	5
83	Survival SURP 016	Cool Running/Vile Bodies/Cool Running (TNT mix) (picture disc)	5
83	Survival SURP 020	Screen Me, I'm Yours/Dangerous And Unafraid (picture disc)	5
84	Survival SURP 024	Everything Will Change/Cracking Up (picture disc)	5
84	Survival SURP 027	Higher Ground/Down From The Sky (picture disc)	5
84	Survival SURLP 008	INTOLERANCE (LP, gatefold sleeve)	12
84	Survival SURPP 008	INTOLERANCE (LP, picture disc)	12

TIKKI, TAKI, SUZI, LIES
70	UPC UPC 102	Welcome To My House/I Believe In Love	5
70	UPC UPC 109	Ba-Da-Da-Dum/Dream Stealer	6

TILLER BOYS
79	New Hormones ORG 3	Big Noise From The Jungle/Slaves And Pyramids/What Me Worry? (p/s)	6

(see also Buzzcocks, Pete Shelley, Eric Random)

TILLERMEN
71	Duke DU 109	Be Loving To Me/Judgement Rock	6

(see also Greyhound)

MEL TILLIS
67	London HLR 10141	Life Turned Her That Way/If I Could Only Start Over	6
68	London HA-R 8345	MR. MEL (LP)	20

JOHNNY TILLOTSON
59	London HLA 8930	True True Happiness/Love Is Blind	50
59	London HLA 8930	True True Happiness/Love Is Blind (78)	100
60	London HLA 9048	Why Do I Love You So/Never Let Me Go	30
60	London HLA 9101	Earth Angel/Pledging My Love	30
60	London HLA 9231	Poetry In Motion/Princess, Princess	6
61	London HLA 9275	Jimmy's Girl/His True Love Said Goodbye	6
61	London HLA 9412	Without You/Cutie Pie	8
62	London HLA 9514	Dreamy Eyes/Much Beyond Compare	6
62	London HLA 9550	It Keeps Right On A-Hurtin'/She Gave Sweet Love To Me	8
62	London HLA 9598	Send Me The Pillow You Dream On/What'll I Do	7
62	London HLA 9642	I Can't Help It/I'm So Lonesome I Could Cry	7
63	London HLA 9755	Out Of My Mind/Judy, Judy, Judy	8
63	London HLA 9811	Funny How Time Slips Away/A Very Good Year For Girls	6
63	MGM MGM 1214	Talk Back Trembling Lips/Another You	7
63	MGM MGM 1225	Worried Guy/Please Don't Go Away	6
63	MGM MGM 1235	I'm Watching My Watch/I Rise, I Fall	6
64	MGM MGM 1247	Suffering From A Heartache/Worry	6
64	MGM MGM 1252	She Understands Me/Tomorrow	8
64	MGM MGM 1266	Angel/Little Boy	6
65	MGM MGM 1275	Then I'll Count Again/One's Yours, One's Mine	6
65	MGM MGM 1281	Heartaches By The Number/Your Memory Comes Along	6
65	MGM MGM 1290	Our World/My Gidget	6
66	MGM MGM 1300	Hello Enemy/I Never Loved You Anyway	6
66	MGM MGM 1311	Me Myself And I/Country Boy, Country Boy	6
66	MGM MGM 1319	No Love At All/What Am I Gonna Do	6
68	MGM MGM 1393	Cabaret/If I Were A Rich Man	6
69	London HLU 10281	Tears On My Pillow/Remember When	5
62	London RE-A 1345	JOHNNY TILLOTSON (EP)	30
63	London RE-A 1388	J.T. (EP)	35
63	MGM MGM-EP 788	JOHNNY TILLOTSON (EP)	30
64	MGM MGM-EP 790	JOHNNY TILLOTSON'S HIT PARADE (EP)	30
61	London HA-A 2431	JOHNNY TILLOTSON'S BEST (LP)	60
62	London HA-A 8019	IT KEEPS RIGHT ON A-HURTIN' (LP)	50
65	MGM MGM-C(S) 8005	JOHNNY TILLOTSON SINGS OUR WORLD (LP)	25
66	MGM MGM-C(S) 8025	NO LOVE AT ALL (LP)	25

TILSLEY ORCHESTRA

MINT VALUE £

TILSLEY ORCHESTRA
66	Fontana TF 783	"Thunderbirds" Theme/Theme From "The Power Game"	15
67	Polydor 56150	Mr. Aitch Theme/Cotton Reed	5
67	Fontana (S)TL 5411	TOP T.V. THEMES (LP)	18
69	Fontana SFL 13139	TOP T.V. THEMES (LP, reissue)	12

(see also Electric Banana)

STEVE TILSTON
71	Village Thing VTS 5	AN ACOUSTIC CONFUSION (LP)	20
72	Transatlantic TRA 252	COLLECTION (LP, gatefold sleeve)	12
77	Cornucopia CR 1	SONGS FROM THE DRESS REHEARSAL (LP, with Rupert Hine/John Renbourn)	20
83	TM PROP 4	IN FOR A PENNY IN FOR A POUND (LP, with Peter Bardens)	10

TIMBER
71	Elektra K 12022	Bring America Home/Splinters From Timber	5
72	Elektra K 12042	Outlaw/Song For Two Signs	5
71	Elektra K 42093	BRING AMERICA HOME (LP)	12

TIME
65	Pye 7N 17019	Take A Bit Of Notice/Every Now And Then	40
66	Pye 7N 17146	The First Time I Saw The Sunshine/Annabel	15

TIME
75	B.U.K. BULP 2005	TIME (LP)	45

(see also Spontaneous Combustion)

T.I.M.E. (Trust In Men Everywhere)
69	Liberty LBF 15082	Take Me Along/Make It Alright	4
69	Liberty LBL/LBS 83232	SMOOTH BALL (LP)	35

TIMEBOX
67	Piccadilly 7N 35369	I'll Always Love You/Save Your Love	20
67	Piccadilly 7N 35379	Soul Sauce/I Wish I Could Jerk Like My Uncle Cyril	25
67	Deram DM 153	Walking Through The Streets Of My Mind/Don't Make Promises	12
68	Deram DM 194	Beggin' A Woman That's Waiting	12
68	Deram DM 219	Girl Don't Make Me Wait/Gone Is The Sad Man	12
69	Deram DM 246	Baked Jam Roll In Your Eye/Poor Little Heartbreaker	12
69	Deram DM 271	Yellow Van/You've Got The Chance	12

(see also Bo Street Runners, [Mike] Patto, V.I.Ps)

TIMELORDS
88	KLF 003GG	Gary In The Tardis (Radio)/(Minimal) (white label promo, 500 only)	20
88	KLF 003GG	Gary In The Tardis (Radio)/(Minimal) (12", p/s)	12
88	KLF 003P	Doctorin' The Tardis (Radio)/(Minimal) (car-shaped picture disc)	15
88	KLF 003R	Doctorin' The Tardis (Radio)/Doctorin' The Tardis (Minimal)/Gary Glitter Joins The JAMs (12", 4,000 only, most in stickered black die-cut sleeve, some in full 'Gary Glitter' p/s)	30/8
88	KLF TCD 003	Doctorin' The Tardis (12" mix)/What Time Is Love? (KLF original) (CD)	8
88	KLF CD 003	Doctorin' The Tardis (Radio)/Doctorin' The Tardis (Minimal)/Doctorin' The Tardis (Club Mix)/Doctorin' The Tardis (Video) (CD Video)	30

(see also KLF, Disco 2000, JAMs, Bill Drummond, Orb, Space)

TIME MACHINE
80s	Rip Off RIP 6	Never Met Suzie/Come Dancing/Let Me Tell You	5

TIMES
65	EMI 7ES 24	Ooh Wee/Shepherd Blues/Suzie/Running And Hiding (EP, demo only, no p/s)	60
66	Columbia DB 7804	Think About The Times/Tomorrow Night	20
66	Columbia DB 7904	(She Can't Replace) The Love We Knew/Reconciled	15

TIMES
81	Whaam! WHAAM 2	Red With Purple Flashes/Biff! Bang! Pow! (p/s)	30
82	Art Pop POP 50	Here Come The Holidays (Voici Les Vacances)/Three Cheers For The Sun (A-side as Joni Dee & Times, p/s, some with 'Times' sticker)	15/10
83	Art Pop POP 49	I Helped Patrick McGoohan Escape/The Theme From "Danger Man" (p/s)	12
84	Art Pop POP 46	Boys Brigade/Power Is Forever (p/s)	7
84	Art Pop POP 45	Blue Fire/Where The Blue Begins (p/s)	6
85	Unicorn PHZ 1	London Boys/(Where To Go) When The Sun Goes Down (p/s)	5
90	Caff CAFF 13	Extase/BIFF BANG POW!: Sleep (p/s, with insert)	20
85	Art Pop 43DOZ	BOYS ABOUT TOWN (EP)	10
81	Whaam! BIG 1	POP GOES ART (LP, hand-sprayed sleeve)	35
82	Art Pop ART 20	POP GOES ART! (LP, reissue, hand-sprayed sleeve, some with magazine cuttings taped to plain white cover)	25/20
83	Art Pop ART 19	THIS IS LONDON (LP, white label w/ blue print or black label w/ white print)	18/15
83	Art Pop No. 1	I HELPED PATRICK McGOOHAN ESCAPE (mini-LP)	18
84	Art Pop ART 17	HELLO EUROPE (LP, purple or blue sleeve)	12
85	Art Pop ARTPOP 2	BLUE PERIOD (mini-LP, grey or blue sleeve)	12/10
86	Art Pop ART 16	UP AGAINST IT (LP)	12
86	Art Pop ART 15	ENJOY! (LP, gatefold sleeve)	12
90	Art Pop ART 20	POP GOES ART (LP, 'hand-painted' picture disc reissue, signed)	15

(see also Television Personalities, Teenage Filmstars, O Level, Biff Bang Pow!, L'Orange Mechanik)

TIME ZONE
88	Virgin CDT 29	World Destruction (12" A)/(12" B)/(12" Instrumental Blast) (featuring John Lydon & Afrika Bambaata (3" CD, gatefold card p/s)	7

(see also Public Image Ltd.)

BOBBY TIMMONS
61	Riverside RLP 334	SOUL TIME (LP, with Art Blakey, also stereo [RLP 9334])	15

SALLY TIMMS & DRIFTING COWGIRLS

87	T.I.M. MOT 6	This House Is A House Of Trouble! (w/ Marc Almond)/The Anchor Of Love (p/s) . . 5
87	T.I.M. 12 MOT 6	This House Is A House Of Trouble! (Extended) (with Marc Almond)/
		The Anchor Of Love/Heavenly Gates (12", p/s) 12

(see also Marc Almond, Mekons)

TIMON

| 68 | Pye 7N 17451 | Bitter Thoughts Of Little Jane/Ramblin' Boy . . . . 50 |
| 70 | Threshold TH 3 | And Now She Says She's Young/I'm Just A Travelling Man . . . . 6 |

(see also Tymon Dogg)

TIMONEERS

| 76 | WHM WHM 1919 | ROASTED LIVE (LP) . . . . 20 |

AL TIMOTHY & HIS BAND

| 55 | Decca F 10558 | Gruntin' Blues/You Mad Man! . . . . 7 |

TIM TAM & TURN ONS

| 67 | Island WIP 6007 | Wait A Minute/Ophelia . . . . 15 |

TINA & MEXICANS

| 68 | Pye 7N 17525 | One Love Two/Longing To Hold You . . . . 5 |

TINDERSTICKS

92	Tippy Toe 1	Patchwork/Milky Teeth (p/s, hand-coloured inner sleeve & insert;
		1,000 only, numbered in positive or negative figures [from -500 to 500]) 30
93	Tippy Toe/Ché TIPPY-CHE 2	Marbles/Joe Stumble/For Those.../Benn (10", p/s, stickered PVC sleeve,
		innersleeve & insert, 2,000 only) 15
93	Rough Trade 45rev16	A Marriage Made In Heaven/A Marriage Made In Heaven (Instrumental)
		('singles club' release, p/s, 5,000 only) 20
93	Domino RUG 006	UNWIRED EP: Feeling Relatively Good/Rotweilers And Mace/She/Kooks
		(EP, numbered p/s; 1 copy in 10 with 'Domino' stamp, 1,500 only) 15
93	This Way Up WAY 1811	City Sickness/Untitled/The Bullring (1,500 only) 6
93	This Way Up WAY 1899	City Sickness/Untitled/The Bullring (CD) 12
93	Clawfist XPIG 21	We Have All The Time In The World/GALLON DRUNK: Known Not Wanted
		('singles club' release, p/s, 1,400 only) 25
93	Tippy Toe 003	LIVE IN BERLIN: Raindrops/Tyed (in stamped brown paper bag,
		mail-order/tour release, 1,500 only) 20
94	This Way Up WAY 2811	Kathleen/Summat Moon/Sweet, Sweet Man/E Type Joe (no'd p/s, 5,000 only). . . . 4
94	This Way Up WAY 2888	Kathleen/Summat Moon/Sweet, Sweet Man (10", p/s) 5
94	This Way Up WAY 2899	Kathleen/Summat Moon/Sweet, Sweet Man (CD) 12
94	Kennel Club VTDOG 10	Girl On Death Row/STRANGELOVE: Wolf's Story/GOD MACHINE: The Devil
		Song/BREED: Diamonds Are Forever (10", numbered p/s, free with *Purr*
		magazine, issue 2, 1,500 only) 10/8
95	Sub Pop SP 297	THE SMOOTH SOUND OF TINDERSTICKS: Here/Harry's Dilemma
		(p/s, 3,000 only) 8
95	Sticky STICKY 16	AROUND THE WORLD WITH STICKY RECORDS (picture disc;
		featuring "A Short Time" by Rory Commadore [a.k.a. Tindersticks],
		plus Boy Racer, Heck & Cornershop, 700 only) 12
94	This Way Up WAY 3288	LIVE IN AMSTERDAM (10" LP, brown sleeve) 15
94	This Way Up WAY 3299	LIVE IN AMSTERDAM (CD, numbered brown paper sleeve) 20

PROMOS

93	This Way Up WAY 1755	FIRST ALBUM SAMPLER (CD, card sleeve with 'dancer' postage stamp sticker,
		1000 only) 15
94	This Way Up WAY 3999	TINDERSTICKS (CD, card sleeve, 300 in brown paper envelope hand-sealed
		with red wax) 15
94	This Way Up WAY 4099	SECOND ALBUM SAMPLER (CD, jewel case, 1,500 only) 12
95	This Way Up WAY 4522	Travelling Light/Waiting 'Round You/I've Been Loving You Too Long
		(10", unreleased, 25 white label test pressings only) 30
96	This Way Up WAY 5655	Petites Gouttes D'Eau/Ma Soeur (CD, sampler, 2,000 only) 10
97	This Way Up WAY 6299	CURTAINS (CD, card sleeve in stamped 5" box with booklet, biography,
		1,800 only; 100 copies with 6 black & white photos) 20/18
97	Chop 'Em Out (no cat. no.)	AN INTERVIEW WITH DAVE AND DICKON
		(CD-R, generic inlay, 20 copies only) 30
98	Island CID 8074	TIPPY TOES 1990-1997 (CD, die-cut company card sleeve,
		with incorrect title and corrected sticker "Donkeys 92-97", 150 only) 18
98	Island CID 8074	DONKEYS 92-97 (CD, die-cut company card sleeve, 1,100 only) 15

(see also Asphalt Ribbons)

TINGA (Stewart) & ERNIE (Wilson)

| 69 | Explosion EX 2009 | She's Gone/Old Old Song . . . . 8 |

TINGHA & TUCKER

(see under Century 21)

TINKERBELL'S FAIRYDUST

67	Decca F 12705	Lazy Day/In My Magic Garden 30
68	Decca F 12778	Twenty Ten/Walking My Baby 30
69	Decca F 12865	Sheila's Back In Town/Follow Me Follow 40
69	Decca LK/SKL 5028	TINKERBELL'S FAIRYDUST (LP, unreleased;
		finished copies or test pressings in sleeve) 1,200/700

TINKERS

| 69 | Fontana SFJL 935 | TIL THE WILD BIRDS (LP) . . . . 18 |
| 72 | Argo ZFB 35 | SPRING RAIN (LP) . . . . 20 |

TIN MACHINE

89	EMI USA 10MT 68	Under The God/Sacrifice Yourself/The Interview (10", p/s) 6
89	EMI USA CDMT 68	Under The God/Sacrifice Yourself/The Interview (CD). 8
89	EMI USA MTG 73	Tin Machine/Maggie's Farm (live) (numbered gatefold p/s) 7
89	EMI USA MTPD 73	Tin Machine/Maggie's Farm (live) (shaped picture disc with card insert) 8

TIN MACHINE

89	EMI USA 12MTP 73	Tin Machine/Maggie's Farm (live)/I Can't Read (live)/Bus Stop (live) (12", poster p/s)	8
89	EMI USA CDMT 73	Tin Machine/Maggie's Farm (live)/I Can't Read (live)/Bus Stop (live) (CD)	8
89	EMI USA MTS 76	Prisoner Of Love (Edit)/Baby Can Dance (live) (silver envelope with 4 cards)	7
89	EMI USA MTPD 76	Prisoner Of Love (Edit)/Baby Can Dance (live) (heart-shaped picture disc with printed PVC sleeve & insert)	7
89	EMI USA CDMT 76	Prisoner Of Love (Edit)/Baby Can Dance (live)/Crack City (live)/ Prisoner (LP Version) (CD)	10
91	London LOCDT 305	You Belong In Rock'n'Roll/(Extended Mix)/(Album Version)/Amlapura (Indonesian Version)/Shakin' All Over (live) (CD, round pack with insert)	8
91	London LOCDT 310	Baby Universal/Stateside/If There Is Something/Heaven's In Here (CD, in round tin)	10

(see also David Bowie)

BABS TINO
62	London HLR 9589	Forgive Me/If I Didn't Love You So Much	15
63	London RE-R 1377	FORGIVE ME (EP)	100

MICK TINSLEY
67	Decca F 12544	Let It Be Me/How're You Gonna Tell Me	4

(see also Hedgehoppers Anonymous)

TIN SOLDIERS
93	Detour DR 002	A New Beat/Girlfriend/Get Up And Go (clear vinyl with insert)	6

TINTERN ABBEY
67	Deram DM 164	Beeside/Vacuum Cleaner	120

TIN TIN
69	Polydor 56332	Only Ladies Play Croquet/He Wants To Be A Star	6
70	Polydor 2058 023	Toast And Marmalade For Tea/Manhattan Woman	8
70	Polydor 2058 076	Come On Over Again/Back To Winona	6
71	Polydor 2001 146	Shana/Rocky Mountain	5
71	Polydor 2058 114	Is That The Way/Swans On The Canal	6
72	Polydor 2058 232	Toast And Marmalade For Tea/Cavalry's Coming/Ships On The Starboard	5
72	Polydor 2058 238	Talking Turkey/Cavalry's Coming	5
69	Polydor 2384 011	TIN TIN (LP)	15
72	Polydor 2382 080	ASTRAL TAXI (LP)	15

(see also Steve & Stevie)

TIN TIN
82	WEA TIN 1	Kiss Me/Love's Duet (p/s)	5
82	WEA TIN 1T	Kiss Me (Dub Version)/Love's Duet (Dub) (12", p/s)	10
83	WEA X 9763	Hold It/Blowing Kisses (p/s)	4
83	.WEA X 9763T	Hold It (Extended)/Hold It (Instrumental)/Blowing Kisses//Kiss Me (US Remix)/ Love's Duet/Kiss Me (Instrumental) (12", double pack)	15
84	WEA X 9823T	Kiss Me (U.S. Remix)/Kiss Me (Instrumental)/Love's Duet (12", p/s)	15

(see also Stephen 'Tin Tin' Duffy, Hawks, Lilac Time)

TINY ALICE
72	Kama Sutra 2013 043	Doctor Jazz/The Chocolate Dandies Of 1932/15¢ Hamburger Mama	4
72	Kama Sutra 2319 015	TINY ALICE (LP)	10

TINY TIM
68	Reprise RS 20760	Bring Back Those Rockabye Baby Days	7
68	Reprise RS 23258	Tiptoe Through The Tulips/I Got You Babe	6
68	Reprise RS 20769	Hello Hello/The Other Side	6
69	Reprise RS 20802	Great Balls Of Fire/As Time Goes By	6
69	Reprise RS 20845	Mickey The Monkey/Neighbourhood Children	6
71	Reprise RS 27004	There Will Always Be An England/Bless 'Em All/Long Way To Tipperary/ Have You Seen My Little Sue	5
72	Wand WN 33	Am I Just Another Pretty Face/Movies	5
74	Polydor 2058 485	Happy Wanderer/My Nose Always Gets In The Way	5
68	Reprise RSLP 6292	GOD BLESS TINY TIM (LP)	25
69	Reprise RSLP 6323	TINY TIM'S SECOND ALBUM (LP)	25
69	Reprise RSLP 6351	FOR ALL MY LITTLE FRIENDS (LP)	18

DIMITRI TIOMKIN
54	Vogue Coral Q 2016	The High And The Mighty/Dial M For Murder	15

TINY TOPSY (& CHARMS)
58	Parlophone R 4397	Come On, Come On, Come On/A Ring Around My Finger (with Charms)	50
58	Parlophone R 4397	Come On, Come On, Come On/A Ring Around My Finger (with Charms) (78)	40
58	Parlophone R 4427	You Shocked Me/Waterproof Eyes (solo)	50
58	Parlophone R 4427	You Shocked Me/Waterproof Eyes (solo) (78)	40
61	Pye International 7N 25104	After Marriage Blues/Working On Me Baby (solo)	20

KEITH TIPPETT
69	Polydor 2384 004	YOU ARE HERE, I AM THERE (LP)	60
71	Vertigo 6360 024	DEDICATED TO YOU BUT YOU WEREN'T LISTENING (LP, gatefold sleeve, spiral label)	50
72	RCA SF 8290	BLUEPRINT (LP)	35
76	Steam SJ 104	TNT (LP, with Stan Tracey)	15
77	Vinyl VS 101	WARM SPIRITS, COOL SPIRITS (LP)	12
78	Ogun OGD 003/4	FRAMES (2-LP)	30

(see also Centipede, Ovary Lodge, Nicra)

JULIE TIPPETTS
76	Utopia UTS 601	SUNSET GLOW (LP)	20

(see also Julie Driscoll, Brian Auger, Centipede, Keith Tippett, Elton Dean, Ninesense, Mark Charig)

TIPPIE & CLOVERS
63	Stateside SS 160	My Heart Said/Bossa Nova Baby	15

LESTER TIPTON
80	Grapevine GRP 138	This Won't Change/MASQUERADERS: How	12

TIP TOPS
63	Cameo Parkway P 868	He's Draggin'/Oo-Kook-A-Boo	20

TÍR NA NOG
70	Chrysalis WIP 6090	I'm Happy To Be/Let My Love Grow	5
72	Chrysalis CHS 2001	Lady I Love/Heidi	5
73	Chrysalis CHS 2016	Strong In The Sun/The Mountain & I	5
71	Chrysalis ILPS 9153	TÍR NA NOG (LP)	20
72	Chrysalis CHR 1006	A TEAR AND A SMILE (LP)	20
73	Chrysalis CHR 1047	STRONG IN THE SUN (LP)	15

TITANIC
72	CBS 7278	Sante Fe/Half Breed	5
72	CBS 8185	Rain 2,000/Blond	5
73	CBS 1670	Richmond Express/Heia Valenga	5
71	CBS 64104	TITANIC (LP)	15
72	CBS 64791	SEA WOLF (LP)	12
73	CBS 65661	EAGLE ROCK (LP)	12

TITANS
58	London HLU 8609	Don't You Just Know It/Can It Be	80
58	London HLU 8609	Don't You Just Know It/Can It Be (78)	30

TITUS GROAN
70	Dawn DNX 2503	Open The Door Homer/Woman Of The World/Liverpool (p/s)	15
70	Dawn DNLS 3012	TITUS GROAN (LP, gatefold sleeve)	45

CAL TJADER
65	Verve VS 529	Soul Sauce/Naked City Theme	25
58	Vocalion LAE 556	RITMO CALIENTE (LP, as Cal Tjader Quintet)	12
62	HMV/Verve CLP 1587	IN A LATIN BAG (LP, as Cal Tjader Sextet, also stereo [CSD 1454])	15
65	Vocalion LAE-F 599	GREATEST HITS (LP)	18
65	Verve (S)VLP 9136	SOUL BIRD: WHIFFENPOOF (LP)	15
68	Verve (S)VLP 9192	THE BEST OF CAL TJADER (LP)	15
68	Verve (S)VLP 9215	HIP VIBRATIONS (LP)	15
69	Fontana STL 5527	SOLAR HEAT (LP)	12

TNT
84	Neat NEAT 39	Back On The Road/Rockin' The Night (p/s)	5

TOAD
72	RCA Victor SF 8241	TOAD (LP)	100

TOAD THE WET SPROCKET
79	Sprockets BRS 004	Pete's Punk Song (fold out p/s)	50
80	Sprockets BRS 008	Reaching For The Sky/One Glass Of Whiskey (foldout stapled p/s)	40

RUTH TOBI
69	Concord CON 002	Lazy/That's When I Cry	4

TOBRUK
83	Neat NEAT 32	Wild On The Run/The Show Must Go On (p/s)	7
85	Parlophone R 6093	Falling/Like Lightning (p/s)	4
85	Parlophone 12R 6093	Falling/Like Lightning/Under The Gun (12", p/s)	8
85	Parlophone R 6101	On The Rebound/Poor Girl (p/s)	6
85	Parlophone 12R 6101	On The Rebound/Poor Girl/Falling (Full Length Version) (12", p/s)	7

TOBY JUG
69	private pressing	GREASY QUIFF (LP, with insert)	350

TOBY JUG
71	Decca F 13173	Breakaway Man/Brotherhood	4

TOBY TWIRL
68	Decca F 12728	Harry Faversham/Back In Time	20
68	Decca F 12804	Toffee Apple Sunday/Romeo And Juliet 1968	50
69	Decca F 12867	Movin' In/Utopia Daydream	15

(see also Shades Of Blue)

TODAY'S WITNESS
72	Emblem TDR 345	TODAY'S WITNESS (LP)	40

ART & DOTTY TODD
52	HMV B 10399	Broken Wings/Heavenly — Heavenly (78)	8
58	London HLB 8620	Chanson D'Amour (Song Of Love)/Along The Trail With You	18
58	London HLB 8620	Chanson D'Amour (Song Of Love)/Along The Trail With You (78)	12
59	London HLN 8838	Straight As An Arrow/Stand There, Mountain	18
59	London HLN 8838	Straight As An Arrow/Stand There, Mountain (78)	20

DIANE TODD
58	Decca F 10993	It's A Wonderful Thing To Be Loved/You Are My Favourite Dream	6
58	Decca F 10993	It's A Wonderful Thing To Be Loved/You Are My Favourite Dream (78)	8

EILEEN TODD
54	London HL 8010	Paradise/Ill Wind (78)	10

NICK TODD
57	London HLD 8500	Plaything/The Honey Song	40
57	London HLD 8500	Plaything/The Honey Song (78)	18
58	London HLD 8537	At The Hop/I Do	12
58	London HLD 8537	At The Hop/I Do (78)	10
59	London HLD 8902	Tiger/Twice As Nice	30
59	London HLD 8902	Tiger/Twice As Nice (78)	30

MINT VALUE £

PATSY TODD

68	High Note HS 007	Fire In Your Wire/AL & VIBRATORS: Move Up Calypso	5
69	High Note HS 012	We Were Lovers/Give Me A Chance (B-side with Delano Stewart)	8

(see also Patsy, Stranger & Patsy, Derrick & Patsy)

SHARKEY TODD & MONSTERS

59	Parlophone R 4536	Cool Gool/The Horror Show	18
59	Parlophone R 4536	Cool Gool/The Horror Show (78)	40

(see also Wally Whyton, Vipers [Skiffle Group])

WILF TODD COMBO

64	Blue Beat BB 240	He Took Her Away/Have You Ever Been Lonely	8

WILF TODD & HIS MUSIC

66	Oak WT 101	WILF TODD AND HIS MUSIC (LP)	15

CAMY TODOROW

85	Virgin VS 816	Bursting At The Seams/Don't Stop It, I Like It (with Roger Taylor) (p/s)	18
85	Virgin VS 816-12	Bursting At The Seams (Backroom Version)/Bursting At The Seams (Instrumental)/Don't Stop It, I Like It (12", p/s, with Roger Taylor)	30

(see also Roger Taylor)

TOE-FAT

70	Parlophone R 5829	Working Nights/Bad Side Of The Moon	15
72	Chapter One SCH 175	Brand New Band/Can't Live Without You	10
70	Parlophone PCS 7097	TOE-FAT (LP)	80
70	Regal Zono. SLRZ 1015	TOE-FAT TWO (LP)	75

(see also Cliff Bennett, Uriah Heep, Glass Menagerie)

TOGETHER

68	Columbia DB 8491	Henry's Coming Home/Love Mum And Dad	50

(see also Keith Relf)

TOGETHER

69	Aurora 4278	Memories Of Melinda/Good Morning World	8

TOGGERY FIVE

64	Parlophone R 5175	Bye Bye Bird/I'm Gonna Jump	30
65	Parlophone R 5249	I'd Much Rather Be With The Boys/It's So Easy	30

TOKENS

61	Parlophone R 4790	Tonight I Fell In Love/I Love My Baby	10
61	RCA RCA 1263	The Lion Sleeps Tonight/Tina	5
62	RCA RCA 1279	B'wa Nina (Pretty Girl)/Weeping River	6
62	RCA RCA 1313	I'll Do My Crying Tomorrow/Dream Angel Goodnight	6
62	RCA RCA 1322	Wishing/A Bird Flies Out Of Sight	6
64	Fontana TF 500	He's In Town/Oh Kathy	7
66	Fontana TF 683	I Hear Trumpets Blow/I Could See Me Dancing With You	6
67	Stateside SS 598	Green Plant/Saloogy	6
67	Warner Bros WB 5900	Portrait Of My Love/She Comes And Goes	5
67	Warner Bros WB 7056	It's A Happening World/How Nice?	5
68	Warner Bros WB 7169	Till/Poor Man	5
70	Buddah 2011 011	Don't Worry Baby/Some People Sleep	5
62	RCA RD 27256/SF 5128	THE LION SLEEPS TONIGHT (LP, mono/stereo)	40/60
62	RCA RD 7535	WE THE TOKENS SING FOLK (LP)	20
70	Buddah 2359 007	THE TOKENS (LP)	12

(see also U.S. Double Quartet)

TOKYO BLADE

83	Powerstation OHM 2	Powergame/Death On Main Street (p/s)	8
85	Powerstation LEG 1T	THE CAVE SESSIONS (12" EP)	15

TOKYO ROSE

83	Guardian GRC 270	Dry Your Eyes (p/s)	60

ISRAEL 'POPPER STOPPER' TOLBERT

70	Stax STAX 157	Big Leg Woman/I Got Love	4
71	Stax 2362 020	POPPER STOPPER (LP)	10

HARRY TOLEDO & ROCKETS

77	Spy SPY 001	Busted Chevrolet/Yo Ho/Who Is That Saving Me/John Glenn (33rpm)	4

TOLL

86	Broken Flag BF V7	CHRIST KNOWS (LP, with Tim Gane)	35

(see also Ramleh, McCarthy)

TOM & JERRIO

65	HMV POP 1435	Boo-Ga-Loo/Boomerang	15

TOM & JERRY (cartoon characters)

58	MGM MGM-EP 688	JOHANN MOUSE (EP)	12

TOM & JERRY

59	Gala GSP 806	Baby Talk/PAUL SHELDON: Thank You Pretty Baby (picture labels)	25
63	Pye International 7N 25202	I'm Lonesome/Looking At You	75

(see also Simon & Garfunkel)

TOM & MICK

69	Olga OLE 014	Somebody's Taken Maria Away/Pandemonium	7

TOM CATS

61	Starlite ST45 054	Tom Tom Cat/Big Brother	20

TOMCATS

97	Essex ESSEX 1018LP	THE TOMCATS (LP, with bonus 7": "Seventh Son"/"Walking"/"You Gotta Help"/ "Looking For My Baby" by Second Thoughts [10187])	12

(see also July)

TOMITA
77   RCA Red Seal RL1 1919   THE TOMITA PLANETS SUITE (LP, withdrawn after 1 day)................. 20

LEE TOMLIN
66   CBS 202455   Sweet Sweet Lovin'/Save Me.. 6

ALBERT TOMLINSON
68   Giant GN 28   Don't Wait For Me/LLOYD EVANS: Losing You 60

ROY TOMLINSON
68   Coxsone CS 7056   I Stand For I/MARTIN: I Second That Emotion (actually by Martin Riley)....... 25

TOMMY (Cowan)
72   Dynamic DYN 433   Geraldine/Reverend Leroy.................................. 6
(see also Jamaicans)

TOMMY (McCook) & UPSETTERS
69   Trojan TR 7717   Lock Jaw (actually by Dave Barker)/YARDBROOMS: My Desire 8
(see also Tommy McCook, Upsetters)

TOMORROW
67   Parlophone R 5597   My White Bicycle/Claramont Lake................................. 30
67   Parlophone R 5627   Revolution/Three Jolly Little Dwarfs 30
69   Parlophone R 5813   My White Bicycle/Claramont Lake (reissue) 25
68   Parlophone PMC/PCS 7042   TOMORROW (LP, yellow/black label; mono/stereo) 100/80
76   Harvest SHSP 2010   TOMORROW (LP, reissue)....................................... 15
(see also Keith West, Steve Howe, Twink, Four + One, In Crowd, Syndicats, Aquarian Age, Fairies, Bodast)

TOMORROW COME SOME DAY
69   SNB 97   TOMORROW COME SOME DAY (LP)............................... 450
(see also Ithaca, Friends, Agincourt, Alice Through The Looking Glass, BBC Radiophonic Workshop/Peter Howell)

TOMORROW'S CHILDREN (Jamaica)
67   Island WI 3073   Bang Bang Rock Steady/Rain Rock Steady (some w/same label on both sides) . 12

TOMORROW'S CHILDREN (U.K.)
70   Plexium PXM 17   You're My Baby/Maybe Today 4
71   Plexium PXM 25   Sing A Song/Don't Believe 4
71   Plexium PXM 26   Keep A Little Love In Your Life/My Way Of Living................. 4

TOMPALL & GLASER BROTHERS
68   MGM MGM-C 8082   THROUGH THE EYES OF LOVE (LP)............................. 25

TOMPOT BLENNY
96   Shinkansen SHINKANSEN 2   Thinking Of Ways Of Keeping You Warm/Sleepwaiting For Trains/
Smile Again (p/s, 1,000 only)..................................... 4

TONE DEAF & IDIOTS
80s   Lyntone BLI 1/Angel BL 12   Why Does Politics Turn Men Into Toads/Repatriate The National Front (flexi).... 10
(see also Idiots)

ELEANOR TONER
65   Decca F 12119   All Cried Out/A Hundred Guitars.................................. 7
65   Decca F 12192   Will You Still Love Me Tomorrow/Between The Window And The Phone . 12192 . 7
66   Decca F 12454   Black Rose/Time To Spare Darling 5

TONES ON TAIL
82   4AD BAD 203   A Bigger Splash/Means Of Escape/Copper/Instrumental (12", p/s)........... 8
(see also Bauhaus, Love & Rockets)

TONETTES
62   Island WI 064   Love That Is Real/Pretty Baby 18
(see also Marlene Webber, Lyrics, Don Drummond)

OSCAR TONEY JR.
67   Stateside SS 2033   For Your Precious Love/Ain't That True Love 12
67   Stateside SS 2046   Turn On Your Love Light/Any Day Now 10
67   Stateside SS 2061   You Can Lead Your Woman To The Altar/Unlucky Guy 10
68   Bell BLL 1003   Without Love There Is Nothing/Love That Never Grows Cold 6
68   Bell BLL 1011   No Sad Songs/Never Get Enough Of Your Love 7
69   Bell BLL 1057   Down In Texas/Just For You...................................... 6
72   Capricorn K 17505   Thank You, Honey Chile/I Do What You Wish....................... 6
73   Contempo C 6   Kentucky Bluebird/Everything I Own 5
74   Contempo CS 2002   Is It Because I'm Black/Make It Easy On Yourself................... 5
75   Contempo CS 2043   I've Been Loving You Too Long/For Your Precious Love 5
67   Stateside (S)SL 10211   FOR YOUR PRECIOUS LOVE (LP)................................ 25

TONGUE & GROOVE
69   Fontana STL 5528   TONGUE & GROOVE (LP) 25
(see also Charlatans)

TONIGHT
78   TDS 1   Drummerman/Stroll On By (p/s) 5
78   TDS 2   Money, That's Your Problem/No Sympathy (p/s) 5
78   TDS 4   Wheels/I Can Play Faster Than You Can (p/s) 5
78   TDS 5   Jealousy Kills/Second Hand Man 5
(see also Andy Arthurs, Celia & Mutations)

TERRY TONIK
80   Posh TOFF 1   Just A Little Mod/Smashed And Blocked
(die-cut p/s, some with promo A4 booklet)........................... 100/25

TONTO
74   Polydor 2383 308   IT'S ABOUT TIME (LP) 12
(see also Tonto's Expanding Head Band)

TONTON (MACOUTE)
72	RCA 2190	Summer Of Our Love/Greyhound Lady (as Tonton)	6
71	RCA Neon NE 4	TONTON MACOUTE (LP)	50

TONTO'S EXPANDING HEAD BAND
71	Atlantic 2400 150	ZERO TIME (LP, gatefold sleeve)	25
	(see also Tonto)		

TONY
69	Grape GR 3004	Casa Boo Boo/My Girl	4

TONY & CHAMPIONS
70	Duke DU 90	Eye For An Eye/CHAMPIONS: Broke My Heart — Version	6
	(see also Errol & Champions, Domino Johnson)		

TONY & DENNIS
67	Trojan TR 002	Folk Song/TOMMY McCOOK & SUPERSONICS: Starry Night	30

TONY & GRADUATES
60s	Hit HIT 13	The Statue	50

TONY & HIPPY BOYS
69	Gas GAS 121	Janet/HARMONIANS: Believe Me	6

TONY & HOWARD with DICTATORS
65	Oriole CB 307	Just In Case/Walk Right Out Of The Blues	15

TONY & HOWIE
72	Banana BA 371	Fun It Up/Fun Version	8

TONY & JOE
58	London HLN 8694	The Freeze/Gonna Get A Little Kissin' Tonight	40
58	London HLN 8694	The Freeze/Gonna Get A Little Kissin' Tonight (78)	40

TONY (Tomas) & LOUISE
62	Island WI 059	Ups And Downs/TONY TOMAS: Brixton Lewisham	15
	(see also Tony Washington)		

TONY & TANDY
69	Atlantic 584 262	Two Can Make It Together/The Bitter And The Sweet (with Fleur De Lys)	15
71	Atlantic 2091 075	Two Can Make It Together/Look And Find	6
	(see also Sharon Tandy, Fleur De Lys)		

TONY & TYRONE
70	Ember EMBS 290	Everyday Fun/Whip Your Loving On Me (p/s)	4

TONY & VELVETS
63	Decca F 11637	Sunday/One More Once	6

TONY, CARO & JOHN
72	private pressing	ALL ON THE FIRST DAY (LP, with insert)	350

TONY HENDRIK
69	Pye International 7N 25485	The Grooviest Girl In The World/Majestic World	6

TONY'S ALLSTARS
72	Green Door GD 4041	Rub Up A Daughter/DENNIS ALCAPONE: Daughter Version	5
72	Bullet BU 509	Dub Up A Daughter (as Prince Tony's Allstars)/ DENNIS ALCAPONE: Daughter Version	5
72	Big Shot BI 601	Must Care/L. SPARKS: You Don't Care	6
73	Downtown DT 508	You Don't Say/DENNIS ALCAPONE: Version	8

TONY'S DEFENDERS
66	Columbia DB 7850	Yes I Do/It's Easy To Say Hello	20
66	Columbia DB 7996	Since I Lost You Baby/Waiting For A Call From You	20
	(see also Mike Stuart Span)		

TOOLS
81	Oily SLICK 2	Gotta Make Some Money Somehow/TV Eyes (p/s)	4

TOOLS YOU CAN TRUST
83	Red Energy Dynamo S1.01	Working And Shopping/The Work Ahead Of Us (plain white sleeve with insert)	5
84	Red Energy Dynamo S301	Show Your Teeth/Messy Body Thrust (p/s, with insert)	4
84	Red Energy Dynamo S401	CUT A NEW SEAM (EP)	4
84	Red Energy Dynamo S501	SHARPEN THE TOOLS (12" EP)	7
85	Red Energy Dynamo T7.01	Say It Low/A Blaze Of Shame (12", p/s)	7

STEVE TOOK
(see under Shagrat)

TOOMORROW
70	RCA RCA 1978	You're My Baby Now/Goin' Back (in custom RCA sleeve)	50
70	Decca F 13070	I Could Never Live Without Your Love/Roll Like A River	50
70	RCA LSA 3008	TOOMORROW (LP, soundtrack, with insert)	100
	(see also Olivia Newton-John)		

TOO MUCH
78	Lightning GIL 513	Who You Wanna Be/Another Time Another Place	25
78	Lightning GIL 552	Lick Me One More Time//Be Mine/It's Only For Me (p/s)	25

DAVID TOOP
78	Obscure OBS 48	NEW AND REDISCOVERED MUSICAL INSTRUMENTS (LP, with Max Eastley & Brian Eno)	10
70s	Quartz	WOUNDS (LP, with Paul Burwell)	10
	(see also Brian Eno)		

TOOTS
70	Upsetter US 327	Do You Like It/UPSETTERS: Touch Of Fire	8
	(see also Maytals)		

TOOTS & MAYTALS
(see under Maytals)

TOP NOTES
(see under Nino Tempo & April Stevens)

TOPO D. BILL
70	Charisma CB 116	Witchi Tai To/Jam (some in p/s)	10/7

(see also Bonzo Dog [Doo Dah] Band, Roger Ruskin Spear)

TOPO GIGIO
(see under Century 21)

TOPPERS
57	Brunswick 05678	Stash Pandowski (She's Not Very Much Good For Pretty)/Pots And Pans	4

TINY TOPSY
(see under Tiny)

TOP TOPHAM
69	Blue Horizon 57-3167	Christmas Cracker/Cracking Up Over Christmas	18
70	Blue Horizon 7-63857	ASCENSION HEIGHTS (LP)	100

(see also Fox, Yardbirds)

TORA TORA
80	Mancunian Metal TT 5000	Red Sun Setting/Highway (Shooting Like A Bullet) (p/s)	10
80	Tora TT 5001	Don't Want To Let You Go/Sorry I Broke Your Heart (no p/s)	40

STEVE TORCH
70s	Redball RR 005	Live In Fear/Smoke Your Own (p/s)	5

(BERNIE) TORMÉ (BAND)
78	Jet JET 126	I'm Not Ready/Free (p/s, as Bernie Tormé Band, orange or black vinyl)	8/6
79	Jet JET 137	Weekend/Secret Service/All Night/Instant Impact (as Bernie Tormé Band, p/s) . .	6
80	Island WIP 6586	The Beat/I Want/Bony Maronie (p/s, pink vinyl)	7
81	Fresh FRESH 7	All Day And All Of The Night/What's Next (p/s, also listed as Parole PURL 5) . . .	10
82	Kamaflage KAM 5	America/Chelsea Girls (p/s)	5
82	Kamaflage KAM 8	Shoorah Shoorah/Star//Search And Destroy (live)/Possession (live)	
		(double pack, as Bernie Tormé & The Electric Gypsies)	6
84	Zebra RA 1	I Can't Control Myself/Black Sunday (p/s)	5
84	Zebra RA 2	My Baby Loves A Vampire/Lightning Strikes (p/s)	5
85	Zebra RA 5	All Around The World/Come The Revolution (p/s)	5
82	Kamaflage KAMLP 2	TURN OUT THE LIGHTS (LP, white vinyl)	12
85	Zebra ZEB 6	BACK TO BABYLON (LP, red vinyl, as Tormé)	12
87	Heavy Metal HMRLP 94	DIE PRETTY DIE YOUNG (LP, with bonus 12" [12HM 95], stickered sleeve)	12

(see also Gillan, Split Knee Loons, Girl)

MEL TORME (& MEL-TONES)
SINGLES
56	Vogue Coral Q 72150	Mountain Greenery/Jeepers Creepers	12
56	Vogue Coral Q 72159	Blue Moon/That Old Black Magic	8
56	Vogue Coral Q 72185	Love Is Here To Stay/Goody Goody	7
56	Vogue Coral Q 72185	Love Is Here To Stay/Goody Goody (78)	8
56	London HLN 8305	Lulu's Back In Town/The Lady Is A Tramp	20
56	London HLN 8305	Lulu's Back In Town/The Lady Is A Tramp (78)	8
56	London HLN 8322	Lullaby Of Birdland/I Love To Watch The Moonlight	20
56	London HLN 8322	Lullaby Of Birdland/I Love To Watch The Moonlight (78)	8
56	MGM MGM 922	I Can't Give You Anything But Love/There's No Business Like Show Business . . .	8
56	Vogue Coral Q 72202	All Of You/It Don't Mean A Thing	7
56	Decca F 10800	Walkin' Shoes/The Cuckoo In The Clock (with Ted Heath & His Music)	6
56	Decca F 10809	Waltz For Young Lovers/I Don't Want To Walk Without You	6
57	Vogue Coral Q 72217	My Rosemarie/How (as Mel Torme & Mel-Tones)	7
57	Vogue Coral Q 72217	My Rosemarie/How (as Mel Torme & Mel-Tones) (78)	8
60	Philips PB 1045	The White Cliffs Of Dover/I've Got A Lovely Bunch Of Coconuts	5
61	HMV POP 859	Blue Moon/The Moon Song	5
61	MGM MGM 1144	The Christmas Song/Shine On Your Shoes	6
62	London HLK 9643	Comin' Home Baby/Right Now	12
64	Verve VS 505	Yes Indeed!/Her Face	5

EPs
56	Decca DFE 6384	WALKIN' SHOES (EP)	12
56	MGM MGM-EP 562	VOICE IN VELVET (EP)	12
57	MGM MGM-EP 591	VOICE IN VELVET NO. 2 (EP)	12
58	London Jazz EZ-N 19027	MEL TORME SINGS FRED ASTAIRE PT. 1 (EP)	10
58	London Jazz EZ-N 19028	MEL TORME SINGS FRED ASTAIRE PT. 2 (EP)	10
58	London Jazz EZ-N 19029	MEL TORME SINGS FRED ASTAIRE PT. 3 (EP)	10
58	Philips BBE 12181	TORME MEETS THE BRITISH (EP)	12
59	Coral FEP 2026	MEL TORME SINGS AT THE CRESCENDO PT. 1 (EP)	12
59	Coral FEP 2027	MEL TORME SINGS AT THE CRESCENDO PT. 2 (EP)	12
59	Coral FEP 2028	MEL TORME SINGS AT THE CRESCENDO PT. 3 (EP)	12
63	London REK 1372	MAGIC OF MEL (EP)	15

LPs
55	Vogue Coral LVA 9004	MEL TORME AT THE CRESCENDO (LP)	25
56	Vogue Coral LVA 9032	MUSICAL SOUNDS ARE THE BEST SONGS (LP)	25
56	London Jazz LTZ-N 15009	MEL TORME AND THE MARTY PAICH "DEK-TETTE" (LP)	20
56	London HA-N 2016	IT'S A BLUE WORLD (LP)	20
57	London Jazz LTZ-N 15076	MEL TORME SINGS FRED ASTAIRE (LP)	18
57	Philips BBL 7205	TORME MEETS THE BRITISH (LP)	40
58	HMV CLP 1238	MEL TORME (LP)	15
59	Parlophone PMC 1096	GENE NORMAN PRESENTS MEL TORME AT THE CRESCENDO (LP)	18
60	Parlophone PMC 1114	SONGS FOR ANY TASTE (LP)	20
60	HMV CLP 1315	OLÉ TORMÉ (LP, with Billy May)	15

Mel TORME

60	HMV CLP 1382	BACK IN TOWN (LP, with Mel-Tones) 18
60	HMV CLP 1405/CSD 1330	SWINGS SCHUBERT ALLEY (LP, with Marty Paich Orch., mono/stereo) . . . 18/20
61	HMV CLP 1449/CSD 1349	SWINGIN' ON THE MOON (LP, mono/stereo) 18/20
62	HMV CLP 1584/CSD 1442	MY KIND OF MUSIC (LP, mono/stereo). 18/20
63	London HA-K/SH-K 8021	MEL TORME AT THE RED HILL (LP, with Jimmy Wisner Trio, mono/stereo) . . . 18/20
63	London HA-K 8065	COMIN' HOME BABY (LP) 20
63	Verve (S)VLP 9027	I DIG THE DUKE, I DIG THE COUNT (LP, mono/stereo) 12/15
64	Atlantic ATL/SAL 5005	SUNDAY IN NEW YORK (LP, mono/stereo) 12/15
65	CBS (S) BPG 62250	THAT'S ALL (LP) 12
67	Atlantic Special 590 008	RIGHT NOW! (LP) 12

TORNADOS

62	Decca F 11449	Love And Fury/Popeye Twist 12
62	Decca F 11494	Telstar/Jungle Fever. 5
63	Decca F 11562	Globetrotter/Locomotion With Me (some B-sides credit "Locomotion With You"). . 6
63	Decca F 11606	Robot/Life On Venus 7
63	Decca F 11662	The Ice Cream Man/Theme From "The Scales Of Justice". 8
63	Decca F 11745	Dragonfly/Hymn For Teenagers 8
64	Decca F 11838	Joystick/Hot Pot 8
64	Decca F 11889	Monte Carlo/Blue Blue Beat. 15
64	Decca F 11946	Exodus/Blackpool Rock. 15
65	Columbia DB 7455	Granada/Ragunboneman 20
65	Columbia DB 7589	Early Bird/Stompin' Through The Rye (as Tornados '65) 20
65	Columbia DB 7687	Stingray/Aqua Marina. 40
66	Columbia DB 7856	Pop-Art Goes Mozart/Too Much In Love To Hear 30
66	Columbia DB 7984	Is That A Ship I Hear/Do You Come Here Often 40
62	Decca DFE 8510	THE SOUNDS OF THE TORNADOS (EP) 20
62	Decca DFE 8511	TELSTAR (EP) 20
63	Decca DFE 8521	MORE SOUNDS FROM THE TORNADOS (EP). 25
63	Decca DFE 8533	TORNADO ROCK (EP) 30
63	Decca LK 4552	AWAY FROM IT ALL (LP) 50
72	Decca SPA 253	THE WORLD OF THE TORNADOS (LP) 15
76	Decca REM 4	REMEMBERING…THE TORNADOS (LP) 12

(see also Heinz, Billy Fury, Clem Cattini Ork, Saints, Original Tornados, Roger LaVern & Microns, Saxons, George Bellamy, Gemini, Roger La Vern & Microns)

MITCHELL TOROK

54	London HL 8004	Caribbean/Weep Away (with Louisiana Hayride Band)
		(tri or round centre). 40/30
54	London HL 8048	Hootchy Kootchy Henry (From Hawaii)/Gigolo 50
54	London HL 8048	Hootchy Kootchy Henry (From Hawaii)/Gigolo (78) 10
54	London HL 8083	The Haunting Waterfall/Dancerette (with Louisiana Hayride Band) 50
54	London HL 8083	The Haunting Waterfall/Dancerette (with Louisiana Hayride Band) (78) 10
55	Brunswick 05423	The World Keeps Turning Around/A Peasant's Guitar. 18
55	Brunswick 05423	The World Keeps Turning Around/A Peasant's Guitar (78) 10
56	Brunswick 05586	When Mexico Gave Up The Rhumba/I Wish I Was A Little Bit Younger 20
56	Brunswick 05626	Red Light, Green Light (with Tulane Sisters)/Havana Huddle 20
56	Brunswick 05626	Red Light, Green Light (with Tulane Sisters)/Havana Huddle (78) 10
57	Brunswick 05642	Drink Up And Go Home/Take This Heart 15
57	Brunswick 05642	Drink Up And Go Home/Take This Heart (78) 10
57	Brunswick 05657	Pledge Of Love/What's Behind That Strange Door 15
57	Brunswick 05657	Pledge Of Love/What's Behind That Strange Door (78) 10
57	Brunswick 05718	Two Words (True Love)/You're Tempting Me (with Anita Kerr Quartet) 12
57	Brunswick 05718	Two Words (True Love)/You're Tempting Me (with Anita Kerr Quartet) (78) . . . 10
60	London HLW 9130	Pink Chiffon/What You Don't Know (Won't Hurt You) 12
54	London RE-P 1014	LOUISIANA HAYRIDE (EP, with Louisiana Hayride Band) 50
60	London HA-W 2279	CARIBBEAN (LP) 75

TORPEDO & CARIBBEANS

| 56 | Parlophone MP 143 | Montego Bay/Lazy Jane (78) . . . . 12 |

DONALD TORR

| 69 | CBS 4383 | My Cherie Amour/Never Will I Be . . . . 5 |

MICHELLE TORR

| 66 | Fontana TF 676 | Only Tears Are Left For Me/I Love That Man . . . . 10 |
| 77 | Sonet SON 2104 | I'm Just A Simple Country Girl From France/Une Petite Française (p/s). . . . . . 5 |

GEORGE TORRENCE & NATURALS

| 68 | London HLZ 10181 | Lickin' Stick/So Long Goodbye . . . . 10 |
| 71 | Jay Boy BOY 48 | Lickin' Stick/So Long Goodbye (reissue) . . . . 6 |

CLA(I)RE TORRY

67	Fontana TF 852	The Music Attracts Me/It Takes One To Make The Other Cry (as Claire Terry) 4
67	Fontana TF 878	Unsure Feelings/The End Of A Lifetime (as Claire Terry) 4
69	Decca F 12945	Love For Living/Love Tomorrow, Love Today (as Clare Torry) 4

TORTOISE

| 96 | Duophonic D-UHF-D 12 | Yaus/STEREOLAB: Speedy Car (gig freebie, blue vinyl, p/s, 3,000 only) . . . . 20 |
| 96 | City Slang EFA 04971 | RHYTHMS, RESOLUTIONS & CLUSTERS (LP, clear vinyl) . . . . 30 |

TORTURE

| 81 | Wildebeest WILD 1 | Last Post (no p/s) . . . . 50 |

PETER TOSH

69	Unity UN 525	The Return Of Al Capone/LENNEX BROWN: O Club
		(B-side actually by Lennon Brown) 8
69	Unity UN 529	Sun Valley (as Peter Touch)/HE(A)DLEY BENNETT: Drums Of Fu Manchu 20
71	Bullet BU 486	Maga Dog/THIRD & FOURTH GENERATION: Bull Dog 12

72	Pressure Beat PR 5509	Them A Fe Get A Beatin' (as Peter Touch)/	
		THIRD & FOURTH GENERATION: Version	12
79	Rolling Stones RSR 103	I'm The Toughest/Toughest Version (p/s)	6
79	Rolling Stones RSR 104	Buck In Hamm Palace/The Day The Dollar Die	6
78	Rolling Stones COC 39100	BUSH DOCTOR (LP, with inner sleeve and 'scratch & sniff' sticker)	12

(see also Peter Touch, Bob Marley & Wailers, Cat & Nicky Campbell, Glen Adams)

TOTAL CHAOS

83	Volume VOL 1	There Are No Russians In Afghanistan/Primitive Feeling/	
		Revolution Part 10 (p/s)	5
83	Volume VOL 2	Factory Man/Brixton Prison/She Don't Care/Die (p/s)	5

TOTALLY OUTTA HAND BAND

| 78 | Kilgaron KIL 1 | Teenage Revolution/Too Much Trouble By Far (p/s) | 8 |

TOTNAMITES

| 61 | Oriole CB 1615 | Danny Boy/Spurs Song | 8 |

TOTO

78	CBS S 11-6784	Hold The Line/Takin' It Back (picture disc)	6
82	CBS A 11-2079	Rosanna/It's A Feeling (picture disc)	6
82	CBS A 11-2510	Africa/We Made It (Africa-shaped picture disc)	10
83	CBS A 11-3392	I Won't Hold You Back/Afraid Of Love (picture disc)	6
88	CBS 651 411-2	Stop Loving You/The Seventh One/I'll Be Over You	
		(3" CD & adaptor, 5" case)	8
88	CBS 651 607-2	Pamela/Stay Away/Africa/Rosanna (CD, card sleeve)	8
89	CBS 654 569-3	SOLID GOLD (Pamela/Africa/Hold The Line) (3" CD EP, gatefold card sleeve)	8
84	Polydor 422 8237-7	DUNE (LP, soundtrack, 1 track by Brian Eno)	15

TINA TOTT

| 69 | Pye 7N 17823 | Take Away The Emptiness Too/Burning In The Background Of My Mind | 6 |

DAVE TOTTERDELL

| 77 | Cottage COT 711 | WHITBY BELLS (LP) | 10 |

TOUCH

| 69 | Deram DM 243 | Miss Teach/We Feel Fine | 10 |
| 69 | Deram DML/SML 1033 | THIS IS TOUCH (LP, some with poster) | 80/50 |

TOUCH

80	Ariola ARO 209	When The Spirit Moves You/My Life Depends On You (p/s)	8
80	Ariola ARO 243	Don't You Know What Love Is/My Life Depends On You (p/s)	10
80	Ariola ARO 250	Love Don't Fail Me Now (p/s)	6
80	Ariola ARL 5036	TOUCH (LP)	15

TOUCH

| 88 | Touch T7:45 | Departing Platform 5/Touch Ritual (Radio Cut-Up) (p/s) | 5 |

PETER TOUCH

65	Island WI 211	Hoot Nanny Hoot (actually by Peter Tosh & Wailers)/	
		BOB MARLEY: Do You Remember (actually by Peter Tosh & Wailers)	70
65	Island WI 215	Shame And Scandal (with Wailers)/WAILERS: The Jerk	70
67	Island WI 3042	I Am The Toughest (actually by Peter Tosh & Wailers)/	
		MARCIA GRIFFITHS: No Faith	70
69	Jackpot JP 706	The Crimson Pirate/Moon Duck	8

(see also Peter Tosh, Bop & The Beltone, Glen Adams)

TOUCHED

| 86 | Ebony EBON 27 | Dream Girl (no p/s) | 4 |

TOURISTS

79	Logo GO 350	Blind Among The Flowers/He Who Laughs Last (p/s)	5
79	Logo GO(D) 350	Blind Among The Flowers/He Who Laughs Last//The Golden Lamp/	
		Wrecked (double pack, gatefold p/s)	7
79	Logo GO 360	The Loneliest Man In The World/Don't Get Left Behind (p/s)	5
79	Logo GO(P) 360	The Loneliest Man In The World/Don't Get Left Behind (picture disc)	8
79	Logo GO 370	I Only Want To Be With You/Summer Night (p/s)	4
80	Logo TOUR 1	So Good To Be Back Home/Circular Fever (p/s)	4
80	RCA TOUR 2	Don't Say I Told You So/Strange Sky (p/s)	4
79	Logo LOGO 1018	THE TOURISTS (LP)	10
80	RCA RCALP 5001	LUMINOUS BASEMENT (LP, with yellow vinyl 7":	
		From The Middle Room/Into The Future [FREE 5001, no p/s])	12

(see also Catch, Longdancer, Eurythmics, David A. Stewart, Stewart-Harrison)

TOURS

| 79 | Tours T 1 | Language School/Foreign Girls (printed PVC sleeve) | 5 |
| 79 | Virgin VS 307 | Tourist Information/You Knew (p/s) | 4 |

AL TOUSAN

| 61 | London HLU 9291 | Naomi/Indinna (some copies miscredited to 'Al Pousan') | 10 |

(see also Allen Toussaint)

ALLEN TOUSSAINT

69	Soul City SC 119	We The People/Tequila	10
72	Reprise K 14200	Soul Sister/She Once Belonged To Me	5
72	Reprise K 44202	LIFE, LOVE AND FAITH (LP)	15
75	Reprise K 54021	SOUTHERN NIGHTS (LP)	12

(see also Al Tousan)

CALINE & OLIVER TOUSSAINT

| 78 | Epic S EPC 6334 | The Gardens Of Monaco/Les Jardins De Monaco | 12 |

MINT VALUE £

ROBERTA TOVEY
65	Polydor BM 56021	Who's Who/Not So Old (some in p/s)	40/25

TOWERING INFERNO
95	Island (no cat. no.)	KADDISH (CD in large-format box set with colour booklet & video)	18

TOWER OF POWER
72	Reprise K 16190	Down To The Night Club/You Got To Funkifize	5
73	Reprise K 16278	So Very Hard To Go/Clean Slate	5
73	Reprise K 16211	You're Still A Young Man/Skating On Thin Ice	5
74	Reprise K 16389	Don't Change Horses/Time Will Tell	5
75	Reprise K 16543	It's Not The Crime/Only So Much Time On The Ground	5
73	Reprise K 46223	TOWER OF POWER (LP)	12
74	Reprise K 46282	BACK TO OAKLAND (LP)	12
75	Reprise K 56093	URBAN RENEWAL (LP)	12

JOHNNY TOWERS
62	Philips 326554 BF	The Lonely Man Theme/There's No Place Like Rome	7
63	Philips 326570 BF	This Kind Of Love/My First Romance	6

COLIN TOWN(E)S
78	Virgin VS 204	Full Circle (Main Theme)/Olivia (p/s)	10
80	MCA MCA 643	Breakdown/Working Man (p/s, as Colin Townes)	15
78	Virgin V 2093	FULL CIRCLE (LP, soundtrack, as Colin Towns)	12

(see also Gillan, Samson, Split Knee Loons)

TOWNSEL SISTERS
60	Polydor NH 66954	Will I Ever/I Know	8

ED TOWNSEND
58	Capitol CL 14867	For Your Love/Over And Over Again	6
58	Capitol CL 14927	When I Grow Too Old To Dream/You Are My Everything	6
58	Capitol CL 14927	When I Grow Too Old To Dream/You Are My Everything (78)	8
59	Capitol CL 14976	Richer Than I/Getting By Without You	5
59	Capitol CL 15020	Don't Ever Leave Me/Lover Come Back To Me	5
59	Capitol CL 15072	This Little Love Of Mine/Hold On	5
60	Capitol CL 15141	Don't Get Around Much Anymore/Do Nothin' Till You Hear	5
60	Warner Bros WB 21	Stay With Me (A Little While Longer)/I Love Everything About You	10
59	Capitol EAP1 1091	ED TOWNSEND (EP)	10
59	Capitol T 1140	NEW IN TOWN (LP)	15

ED TOWNSEND
76	Curtom K 56180	NOW (LP)	12

JOHN TOWNSEND
70s	Sweet Folk All SFA 002	NO MUCKING ABOUT (LP)	15

PETE TOWNSHEND
80	Atco K 11486	Let My Love Open The Door/Classified/Greyhound Girl (p/s, with sticker)	5
82	Atco K 11751P	Uniforms/Dance It All Away (picture disc)	6
82	Atco K 11751PT	Uniforms/Dance It All Away (12", picture disc)	7
82	Eva-Tone 623827XS	My Generation/Pinball Wizard (U.S. square flexidisc sewn into U.K. copies of Richard Barnes' *Maximum R&B* book; with/without book)	15/5
89	Virgin VSCD 1198	A Friend is A Friend (3.30)/Man Machines (Extended Mix)/Real World (Can You Really Dance?)/A Friend is A Friend (Album Version 4.45) (3" CD, card p/s)	7
89	Virgin VSCD 1209	I Won't Run Anymore/A Fool Says/Dig (Original Demo Version Recorded November 1987) (3" CD, card sleeve)	7
72	Track 2408 201	WHO CAME FIRST (LP, gatefold sleeve with insert)	15
00	Eel Pie (no cat. no.)	THE LIFEHOUSE CONVERSATIONS (4-CDRs, promo only)	50

(see also Who, Meher Baba, Billy Nicholls, Angie, Elton John)

PETE TOWNSHEND & RONNIE LANE
77	Polydor 2058 944	Street In The City/RONNIE LANE: Annie	5
77	Polydor 2058 944	Street In The City/RONNIE LANE: Annie (12")	12
77	Polydor 2442 147	ROUGH MIX (LP, gatefold sleeve)	15

(see also Who, Ronnie Lane)

TOXIC REASONS
84	Skysaw HANG 1	God Bless America/Destroyer/Can't Get Away (p/s)	7

TOYAH
79	Safari SAFE 15	Victims Of The Riddle/Victims Of The Riddle (Vivisection) (p/s)	4
79	Safari SAP 1	SHEEP FARMING IN BARNET (EP)	5
81	Safari SAFE 28	Ieya/The Helium Song (Spaced Walking) (p/s, white vinyl)	6
81	Safari SAFEP 28	Ieya/The Helium Song (Spaced Walking) (picture disc)	6
81	Lyntone LYN 9899	Sphinx/For You (green vinyl flexidisc with *Flexipop* magazine, issue 8)	8/4
81	Safari SAFEP 38	Thunder In The Mountains/Street Addict (picture disc)	5
81	Safari TOY 2	FOUR MORE FROM TOYAH (EP, with flexidisc "Stand Proud" [FLX 215])	5
81	Safari SAFEX 28	Ieya/The Helium Song (reissue picture disc)	4
82	Safari SAFEX 52	Be Loud Be Proud (Be Heard)/Laughing With The Fools (picture disc)	4
81	Safari VOOR 1	ANTHEM (LP, picture disc)	12

(see also Maneaters)

TOY DOLLS
63	London HLN 9647	Little Tin Soldier/Fly Away	15

TOY DOLLS
81	GBH SSM 005	Tommy Kowey's Car/She Goes To Finos (no p/s, 500 only)	40
81	GRC GRC 104	Tommy Kowey's Car/She's A Working Ticket/Everybody Jitterbug/Teenager In Love/I've Got Asthma (yellow paper p/s, with insert)	30
82	Zonophone Z 31	Everybody Jitterbug/(She's A) Working Ticket (p/s)	15
83	Volume VOL 3	Nellie The Elephant/Dig That Groovy Baby (p/s)	15
83	Volume VOL 5	Cheerio And Toodle Pip/H.O. (p/s)	10

83	Volume VOL 7	Alfie From The Bronx/Hanky Panky (p/s)..................................... 10
84	Volume VOL 10	We're Mad/Deirdre's A Slag (p/s).. 8
84	Volume VOLT 10	We're Mad/Deirdre's A Slag/Rupert The Bear (12", p/s) 12
83	Volume VOL 12	She Goes To Finos/Spiders In The Dressing Room (p/s) 5
83	Volume VOLT 12	She Goes To Finos/Spiders In The Dressing Room/
		Come Back Jackie (12", p/s)... 8
84	Volume VOL 17	James Bond Lives Down Our Street/Olga I Cannot (p/s) 5
86	Volume VOL 21	Geordies Gone To Jail/Idle Gossip (p/s) 4
83	Volume VOLP 1	DIG THAT GROOVE BABY (LP) 10

(see also Showbiz Kids)

TOYS (U.S.)

65	Stateside SS 460	A Lover's Concerto/This Night 6
66	Stateside SS 483	Attack/See How They Run 10
66	Stateside SS 502	May My Heart Be Cast Into Stone/On Backstreet 15
66	Stateside SS 519	Silver Spoon/Can't Get Enough Of You Baby 15
66	Stateside SS 539	Baby Toys/Happy Birthday Broken Heart 12
67	Philips BF 1563	Ciao Baby/I Got Carried Away 6
67	Philips BF 1581	My Love Sonata/I Close My Eyes 8
69	Bell BLL 1053	A Lover's Concerto/Baby Toys 4
66	Stateside (S)SL 10175	THE TOYS SING "A LOVER'S CONCERTO" AND "ATTACK"
		(LP, mono/stereo).. 30/35

TOYS (U.K.)

| 79 | SRT SRTS/79/CUS 345 | My Mind Wanders/The Girl On My Wall/Toytime/I'd Do Anything For You (p/s) .... 5 |
| 79 | Toy TOYS 2 | STILL DANCING (EP, hand-stamped white label, foldaround p/s) .... 5 |

TOYSHOP

| 69 | Polydor 56317 | Say Goodbye To Yesterday/Send My Love To Lucy .... 4 |

TRACE

| 74 | Vertigo 6360 852 | TRACE (LP) .... 10 |
| 75 | Vertigo 6413 080 | BIRDS (LP) .... 10 |

(see also Curved Air)

AL TRACE & HIS LITTLE TRACERS

| 53 | MGM MGM 693 | Mocking Bird Boogie/You're Only A Part-Time Sweetheart (78)............... 6 |

TRACER

| 83 | Mouse Hole TRA 1 | CHANNELLED AGGRESSION EP (p/s) .... 125 |

MARK TRACEY

| 62 | Parlophone R 4944 | Caravan Of Lonely Men/Never Ending (with John Barry & His Orchestra) .... 8 |

STAN TRACEY

58	Vogue LA 160130	STAN TRACEY SHOWCASE (LP).. 80
59	Vogue LA 160155	LITTLE KLUNK (LP, as Stan Tracey Trio) 200
65	Columbia 33SX 1774	JAZZ SUITE (LP, as Stan Tracey Quartet, also stereo SCX 3589) 75
66	Columbia S(C)X 6051	ALICE IN JAZZLAND (LP, as Stan Tracey Big Band)....................... 75
67	Columbia S(C)X 6124	STAN TRACEY... IN PERSON (LP) 50
68	Columbia S(C)X 6205	WITH LOVE FROM JAZZ (LP) 50
69	Ace Of Clubs ACL 1259	LITTLE KLUNK (LP, reissue) 45
69	Columbia S(C)X 6320	WE LOVE YOU MADLY (LP, as Stan Tracey Big Brass) 70
69	Columbia SCX 6358	THE LATIN AMERICAN CAPER (LP, with Big Brass & Woodwind)............. 45
70	Columbia SCX 6385	FREE AN' ONE (LP, as Stan Tracey Quartet) 70
70	Columbia SCX 6413	SEVEN AGES OF MAN (LP, as Stan Tracey Big Band) 45
72	Columbia SCX 6485	PERSPECTIVES (LP as Stan Tracey Trio) 40

(see also New Departures Quartet, Mike Osborne, Neil Ardley, Laurie Johnson)

ZEN TRACEY

| 62 | Decca F 11492 | Shamrocker (Phil The Fluter's Ball)/Two By Two......................... 6 |

TRACK

| 66 | Columbia DB 7987 | Why Do Fools Fall In Love?/Cry To Me .... 12 |

TRACTATUS PHILOSOPHICUS

| 74 | Bent Star √-1 | HUMAN ALGORITHM (LP, some copies with free 3-sided |
| | | flexidisc "I Am Maths"; ½ copy pressed "for external use only") .... 250/150 |

TRACTOR

72	Dandelion 2001 282	Stone Glory/Marie/As You Say....................................... 15
75	UK UK 93	Roll The Dice/Vicious Circle.. 8
81	Cargo CRS 002	No More Rock & Roll/Northern City (p/s, with insert).................... 10
81	Roach RR 2	Average Man's Hero/Big Big Boy (p/s) 5
72	Dandelion 2310 217	TRACTOR (LP) 50

(see also Way We Live)

TRACY

| 66 | Columbia DB 7802 | Don't Hold It Against Me/These Four Walls............................. 8 |

TRACY

69	Columbia DB 8569	Life's Like That/Let Me Love You 5
69	Columbia DB 8637	Follow Me/A City Called Soul 8
71	Columbia DB 8750	Rock Me In The Cradle/Strange Love 6

GRANT TRACY & SUNSETS

61	Ember EMB S 126	Say When/Please Baby Please....................................... 20
61	Ember EMB S 130	Pretend/Love Me 18
62	Ember EMB S 148	The Great Matchmaker/Tears Came Rolling Down 18
62	Ember EMB S 155	Taming Tigers/The Painted Smile 18
63	Decca F 11741	Everybody Shake/Turn The Lights Down, Jenny........................ 15
64	Ember EMB 3352	TEENBEAT (LP) 60

(see also Pete Dello, Honeybus)

MINT VALUE £

TRAFFIC

WENDALL TRACY
58	London HLM 8664	Who's To Know/Corrigidor Rock	30
58	London HLM 8664	Who's To Know/Corrigidor Rock (78)	30

TRADER HORNE
69	Pye 7N 17846	Sheena/Morning Way	10
70	Dawn DNS 1003	Here Comes The Rain/Goodbye Mercy Kelly	7
70	Dawn DNLS 3004	MORNING WAY (LP, with photo & insert)	50

(see also Them, Fairport Convention, Jackie McAuley)

TRADEWINDS
59	RCA RCA 1141	Crossroads/Furry Murray	15
59	RCA RCA 1141	Crossroads/Furry Murray (78)	50

TRADE WINDS
65	Red Bird RB 10020	New York Is A Lonely Town/Club Seventeen	15
66	Kama Sutra KAS 202	Mind Excursion/Little Susan's Dreaming	10

TRAD GRADS
61	Decca F 11403	Runnin' Shoes/Rag-Day Jazz-Band Ball	8

(see also Quarry Men)

TRAFFIC
67	Island WIP 6002	Paper Sun/Giving To You (some in p/s)	15/6
67	Island WIP 6017	Hole In My Shoe/Smiling Phases (some in p/s)	12/6
67	Island WIP 6025	Here We Go Round The Mulberry Bush/Coloured Rain (1st 100,000 in p/s)	12/6
68	Island WIP 6030	No Face, No Name, No Number/Roamin' In The Gloamin' With 40,000 Headmen	7
68	Island WIP 6041	You Can All Join In/Withering Tree (unissued in U.K.)	
68	Island WIP 6041	Feelin' Alright/Withering Tree	8
68	Island WIP 6050	Medicated Goo/Shanghai Noodle Factory	6
74	Island WIP 6207	Walking In The Wind/Walking In The Wind (Instrumental)	6
78	Island IEP 7	HOLE IN MY SHOE (EP, picture disc)	10
67	Island ILP 961/ILPS 9061	MR FANTASY (LP, gatefold sleeve, 1st pressing pink label with black 'circle' logo, mono/stereo)	80/40
68	Island ILPS 9081T	TRAFFIC (LP, gatefold sleeve with stapled-in booklet; pink label with black 'circle' logo, or pink rim label with 'palm tree' logo)	30/15
69	Island ILP(S) 9097	LAST EXIT (LP, pink label with black 'circle' logo, or pink rim label with 'palm tree' logo)	25/15
69	Island ILP(S) 9112	THE BEST OF TRAFFIC (LP, pink rim label with 'palm tree' logo)	15
70	Island ILPS 9081	MR. FANTASY (LP, 2nd pressing, pink rim label with 'palm tree' logo)	15
70	Island ILPS 9116	JOHN BARLEYCORN MUST DIE (LP, gatefold sleeve)	20
71	Island ILPS 9142	LIVE — NOVEMBER '70 (LP, unreleased, may exist as test pressing)	120

(see also Spencer Davis Group, Stevie Winwood, Revolution, Hellions, Dave Mason, Gordon Jackson)

TRAFFIC JAM
67	Piccadilly 7N 35386	Almost But Not Quite There/Wait Just A Minute	225

(see also Status Quo, Spectres)

TRAGICIAN
79	Look LKSP 6411	The Wild The Scared And The Timid (numbered gatefold p/s)	30

PHIL TRAINER
73	BASF 05 19573-5	Beautiful Jim/No No No (p/s)	5
73	BASF BAG 22 29107-3	PHIL TRAINER (LP)	20

(see also Trees)

TRAINSPOTTERS
79	Arista ARIST 290	High Rise/Rock'n'Roll Hall Of Fame (p/s)	5
79	Arista ARIST 320	Unfaithful/Hiring The Hall (no p/s)	4

(see also Mike Read, Just Plain Smith, Just Plain Jones, Micky Manchester, Esprit De Corps)

TRAITS
67	Pye International 7N 25404	Harlem Shuffle/Strange Lips (Start Ole Memories)	12

(see also Roy Head)

ALAN TRAJAN
69	MCA MK 5002	Speak To Me, Clarissa/This Might Be My Last Number	12
69	MCA MKPS 2000	FIRM ROOTS (LP)	80

TRAMLINE
68	Island ILPS 9088	SOMEWHERE DOWN THE LINE (LP, pink label)	45
69	Island ILPS 9095	MOVES OF VEGETABLE CENTURIES (LP, pink label)	50

(see also Whitesnake)

BOBBY LEE TRAMMELL
64	Sue WI 326	New Dance In France/Carolyn	25

TRAMMPS
75	Atlantic K 10664	Hooked For Life/It's Alright	4

TRAMMY (Ron Wilson)
72	Techniques TE 920	Horns Of Paradise/TECHNIQUES ALL STARS: Grass Root	6

TRAMP
69	Young Blood SBY 4	Vietnam Rose/Each Day	10
74	Spark SRL 1107	Put A Record On/You've Gotta Move	7
69	Music Man SMLS 603	TRAMP (LP)	90
73	Spark Replay SRLM 2001	TRAMP (LP, reissue)	40
74	Spark SRLP 112	PUT A RECORD ON (LP)	40

(see also Dave Kelly, Jo-Ann Kelly, Brunning Hall Sunflower Blues Band, Danny Kirwan, Fleetwood Mac)

TRANSATLANTICS
65	Fontana TF 593	Many Things From Your Window/I Tried To Forget	10
65	Fontana TF 638	Stand Up And Fight Like A Man/But I Know	10
65	Mercury MF 948	Don't Fight It/Look Before You Leap	20
65	King KG 1033	Run For Your Life/It's All Over	10
66	King KG 1040	Louie Go Home/Find Yourself Another Guy	10

TRANSMITTERS
78	Ebony EYE 11	Party/0.5 Alive (p/s)	4
78	Ebony EYE 12	Nowhere Train/Uninvited Guest/Persons Unknown (die-cut p/s)	4
79	Step Forward SF 1212	The Ugly Man/The One That Won The War/Free Trade/Curious (12", p/s)	7
70s	Eccentric EX 2 C50	I JAX DUB (cassette)	10
78	Ebony EBY 1002	24 HOURS (LP)	10
81	Heartbeat MB 4	AND WE CALL THIS LEISURE TIME (LP)	10

TRANSPARENT ILLUSION
81	Vortex VEX 001/002	Vortex/Nuclear Release (p/s)	10
82	Vortex VEX 5	Guilty Rich Men (p/s)	10
81	Vortex VEX 3	STILL HUMAN (LP)	20
82	Vortex VEX 4	CHAGRIN RECEIVER (LP)	20

TRANSPARENT THING
97	Wurlitzer Jukebox WJ 25	Quitter/Ada (p/s, 1,000 only)	5

TRAPEZE
69	Threshold TH 2	Send Me No More Letters/Another Day	10
72	Threshold TH 11	Coast To Coast/Your Love Is Alright	10
75	Warner Bros K 16606	Sunny Side Of The Street/Monkey	10
79	Aura AUS 114	Don't Ask Me How I Know/Take Good Care (p/s)	15
80	Aura AUS 116	Running Away/Don't Break My Heart (p/s)	15
69	Threshold THS 2	TRAPEZE (LP)	25
70	Threshold THS 4	MEDUSA (LP)	25
73	Threshold THS 8	YOU ARE THE MUSIC ... WE'RE JUST THE BAND (LP)	18
74	Warner Bros K 56064	HOT WIRE (LP)	15
75	Warner Bros K 56165	TRAPEZE (LP)	15
79	Aura AUL 708	HOLD ON (LP)	15
81	Aura AUL 717	LIVE IN TEXAS ... DEAD ARMADILLOS (LP)	15

(see also Finders Keepers, Montanas, Deep Purple, Glenn Hughes, Judas Priest, Whitesnake)

TRASH
69	Apple APPLE 6	Road To Nowhere/Illusions (initial copies as White Trash, later Trash)	50/20
69	Apple APPLE 17	Golden Slumbers – Carry That Weight/Trash Can	12

(see also Poets, Pathfinders)

TRASHCAN SINATRAS
89	Go! Discs GODX 34	Obscurity Knocks/The Best Man's Fall/Drunken Chours/Who's He? (12", p/s)	12
89	Go! Discs GODCD 34	Obscurity Knocks/The Best Man's Fall/Drunken Chours/Who's He? (CD)	15
90	Go! Discs GODX 41	Only Tongue/Useless Begins With You/Tonight You Belong To Me (12", p/s)	10
90	Go! Discs GODCD 41	Only Tongue/Useless Begins With You/Tonight You Belong To Me (CD)	10
90	Go! Discs GODX 46	Circling The Circumference/My Mistake/White Horses (12", p/s)	12
90	Go! Discs GODCD 46	Circling The Circumference/My Mistake/White Horses (CD)	15
93	Go! Discs GODX 98	Hayfever/Say/Kangaroo Court/Skin Diving (12", p/s)	8
90	Go! Discs 828 2011	CAKE (LP)	20

TRASHMEN
64	Stateside SS 255	Surfin' Bird/King Of The Surf	25
64	Stateside SS 276	Bird Dance Beat/A-Bone	20

MINT VALUE £

TRAVELING WILBURYS

88	Warner Bros W 7732W	Handle With Care/Margarita (gatefold p/s with sticker, some sealed)	10/8
88	Warner Bros W 7732TE	Handle With Care (Extended)/Margarita (10", p/s)	10
88	Warner Bros W 7732T	Handle With Care (Extended)/Margarita (12", p/s)	10
88	Warner Bros W 7732CD	Handle With Care (LP Version)/Margarita/Handle With Care (Extended Version) (3" CD, with adaptor, 5" case)	12
89	Warner Bros W 7637TW	End Of The Line (Extended)/Congratulations (12", p/s, with/without sheet of stickers)	15/10
89	Warner Bros W 7637CD	End Of The Line (Extended Version)/Congratulations (3" CD, gatefold card p/s in PVC sleeve)	15
90	Warner Bros W 9773T	Nobody's Child/DAVE STEWART: Lumière/RINGO STARR: With A Little Help From My Friends (12", p/s)	12
90	Warner Bros W 9773CD	Nobody's Child/DAVE STEWART: Lumière/RINGO STARR: With A Little Help From My Friends (CD)	12
90	Warner Bros W 9523	She's My Baby/New Blue Moon (Instrumental Version) (p/s)	6
90	Warner Bros W 9523T	She's My Baby (LP Version)/New Blue Moon (Instrumental Version)/Runaway (12", p/s)	12
90	Warner Bros W 9523CD	She's My Baby (LP Version)/New Blue Moon (Instrumental Version)/Runaway (CD)	12
91	Warner Bros W 0019	Wilbury Twist/New Blue Moon (Instrumental) (p/s)	7
91	Warner Bros W 0018W	Wilbury Twist/New Blue Moon (Instrumental) (card p/s with 4 postcards)	12
91	Warner Bros W 0019T	Wilbury Twist/New Blue Moon (Instrumental)/Cool Dry Place (12", p/s)	12
91	Warner Bros W 0019CD	Wilbury Twist/New Blue Moon (Instrumental)/Cool Dry Place (CD, silver or black print)	12
88	Warner Bros WX 224W	VOLUME ONE (LP, some with stickered sleeve & sticker inserts)	40/20
88	Warner Bros WX 224CD	VOLUME ONE (CD)	30

(see also George Harrison, Bob Dylan, Roy Orbison, Jeff Lynne, Tom Petty)

TRAVELLING FOLK

70s	Cuchulainn CCHS 1017	TRAVELLING FOLK (LP)	15

PAT TRAVERS

76	Polydor SFI 221/2814 040	Makes No Difference (1-sided flexidisc, promo only, black & white)	15
70s	Polydor	THE PT YOU MISSED (12", LP sampler, promo only, plain red sleeve)	10
77	Polydor Super 2383 436	MAKIN' MAGIC (LP, with inner sleeve)	12
77	Polydor Super 2383 471	PUTTING IT STRAIGHT (LP, with inner sleeve)	12
79	Polydor POLS 1011	GO FOR WHAT YOU KNOW (LP, red vinyl)	12

(see also Nicko McBrain)

TRAVIS

73	A&M AMLS 68120	SHINE ON ME (LP)	35

(see also Paul Travis)

TRAVIS

96	Red Telephone Box PHONE 001	All I Wanna Do Is Rock (10", no'd p/s, 750 only)	30
97	Independiente GOODT 1	The Line Is Fine/All I Want To Do Is Rock/More Than Us/Tied To The 90s (12", promo only)	10
97	Independiente GOOD 1	5 GOOD FEELINGS: The Line Is Fine/All I Want To Do Is Rock/More Than Us/Funny Thing/Tied To The 90s (CD, promo only)	15
97	Ind'nte SAMCD 44992	Good Feeling (1-track CD, promo)	10

MERLE TRAVIS

53	Capitol CL 13985	Gamblers Guitar/Shut Up And Drink Your Beer (78)	8
54	Capitol CL 14051	Green Cheese/Re-Enlistment Blues (78)	10
54	Capitol CL 14110	Jolie Fille (Pretty Girl)/I Can't Afford The Coffee (78)	8
56	Capitol EAP1 032	MERLE TRAVIS GUITAR (EP)	20
57	Capitol EAP2 650	MERLE TRAVIS GUITAR NO. 2 (EP)	15
59	Capitol EAP1 891	BACK HOME (EP)	15
63	Capitol EAP1 1391	WALKIN' THE STRINGS (EP)	15
57	Capitol T 891	BACK HOME (LP)	25
63	Capitol (S)T 1664	TRAVIS! (LP)	18
65	Capitol T 2102	MERLE TRAVIS & JOE MAPHIS (LP)	18

PAUL TRAVIS

75	A&M AMLS 68290	RETURN OF THE NATIVE (LP, with insert)	20

(see also Travis)

TRAVIS & BOB

59	Pye International 7N 25018	Tell Him No/We're Too Young	10
59	Pye International N 25018	Tell Him No/We're Too Young (78)	20
61	Mercury AMT 1142	Baby Stay Close To Me/Give Your Love To Me	6

TRAX FOUR

66	Ace Of Clubs SCL 1216	WINGDING PARTY!!! (LP)	12

JACK TRAYLOR & STEELWIND

73	Grunt FTR 0194	CHILD OF NATURE (LP)	12

TREASURE BOY

67	Trojan TR 010	Love Is A Treasure (actually by Freddie McKay)/TOMMY McCOOK: Zazuka	15

STEVE TREATMENT

78	Rather GEAR 2	5-A-SIDED 45 (EP)	6

(see also Swell Maps)

TREBLETONES

61	Butlin CP 2424	Butlin Holiday/Butlin Holiday	8
63	Oriole CB 1838	In Real Life/Dream Of A Lifetime	10

TREDEGAR

86	Aires CEP 0001	Duma/The Jester (p/s)	25
86	Aires CEP LP 001	TREDEGAR (LP, gatefold sleeve, some embossed)	20/15
91	Sabre Dance SD 001	FIRST DEMOS (cassette, numbered fan club issue)	10

(see also Budgie)

HERBERT BEERBOHM TREE

65	OMY 69	KEEP THOSE DOGS AWAY (EP)	25

TREES

70	CBS 5078	Nothing Special/Epitaph	15
70	CBS 63837	THE GARDEN OF JANE DELAWNEY (LP)	75
71	CBS 64168	ON THE SHORE (LP)	75
87	Decal LIK 12	ON THE SHORE (LP, reissue)	15
87	Decal LIK 15	THE GARDEN OF JANE DELAWNEY (LP, reissue)	15

(see also Casablanca, Juliet Lawson, Trainer)

TREETOPS (U.K.)

67	Parlophone R 5628	Don't Worry Baby/I Remember	7
68	Parlophone R 5669	California My Way/Carry On Living	6
70	Columbia DB 8727	Mississippi Valley/Man Is A Man	5
71	Columbia DB 8799	Without The One You Love/So Here I Go Again	7

TREKKAS

65	Planet PLF 105	Please Go/I Put A Spell On You	45

TREMBLING BLUE STARS

96	Shinkansen SHINKANSEN 1	Abba On The Jukebox/She's Always There (p/s, 1,000 only)	6

TREMELOES

66	Decca F 12423	Blessed/The Right Time	12
66	CBS 202242	Good Day Sunshine/What A State I'm In	7
67	CBS 202519	Here Comes My Baby/Gentlemen Of Pleasure	5
67	CBS 2723	Silence Is Golden/Let Your Hair Hang Down (p/s)	6
67	CBS 2930	Even The Bad Times Are Good/Jenny's Alright (p/s)	6
67	CBS 3043	Be Mine/Suddenly Winter	5
68	CBS Special Products WB 728	Here Comes My Baby/SIMON & GARFUNKEL: The 59th Street Bridge Song (p/s, mail-order only with Pepsi Cola tokens)	6
73	Epic EPC 1399	Ride On/Hands Off	5
73	CBS 1139	Here Comes My Baby/Silence Is Golden (p/s, 'Hall Of Fame Hits' series)	5
68	CBS EP 6402	MY LITTLE LADY (EP)	15
67	CBS (S)BPG 63017	HERE COME THE TREMELOES (LP)	15
68	CBS (S)BPG 63138	THE TREMELOES: CHIP, RICK, ALAN AND DAVE (LP)	15
69	CBS 63547	THE TREMELOES 'LIVE' IN CABARET (LP)	15
70	CBS 64242	MASTER (LP)	15

(see also Brian Poole & Tremeloes, Trems, Chip Hawkes)

TREMORS

80s	Redball RR 0002	Modern World/Smashed Reality (p/s)	4

TREMS

73	Epic EPC 1660	Make It Break It/Movin' On	4

(see also Tremeloes)

TREND

67	Page One POF 004	Boyfriends And Girlfriends/Shoot On Sight	15

TRENDS

63	Piccadilly 7N 35171	All My Loving/Sweet Little Miss Love	10
64	Pye 7N 15644	You're A Wonderful One/The Way You Do The Things You Do	10

(see also Tammy St. John, Freddie Self, Freddie Ryder)

TRENDSETTERS

64	Silver Phoenix 1001	You Don't Care/My Heart Goes	40

TRENDSETTERS

60s	Oak RGJ 999	AT THE HOTEL DE FRANCE (EP)	20

TRENDSETTERS LTD

64	Parlophone R 5118	In A Big Way/Lucky Date	10
64	Parlophone R 5161	Hello Josephine/Move On Over	12
64	Parlophone R 5191	Go Away/Lollipops And Roses	8
65	Parlophone R 5324	You Sure Got A Funny Way Of Showing Your Love/I'm Coming Home	7

(see also King Crimson, Giles Giles & Fripp, Brain)

CHARLES TRENET

58	Columbia SEG 7819	BOUM! (EP)	8

TRENIERS

58	Coral Q 72319	Ooh-La-La/Pennies From Heaven	35
58	Coral Q 72319	Ooh-La-La/Pennies From Heaven (78)	15
58	Fontana H 137	Go! Go! Go!/Get Out Of The Car (featuring Don Hill, Alto Sax)	125
58	Fontana H 137	Go! Go! Go!/Get Out Of The Car (featuring Don Hill, Alto Sax) (78)	50
59	London HLD 8858	When Your Hair Has Turned To Silver/Never, Never	35
59	London HLD 8858	When Your Hair Has Turned To Silver/Never, Never (78)	60

JACKIE TRENT

61	Oriole CB 1711	Pick Up The Pieces/In Your Heart	6
62	Oriole CB 1749	The One Who Really Loves You/Your Conscience Or Your Heart	12
63	Piccadilly 7N 35121	Melancholy Me/So Did I	7
64	Piccadilly 7N 35165	If You Love Me/Only One Such As You	12
64	Pye 7N 15692	Somewhere In The World/I Heard Somebody Say	6
64	Pye 7N 15742	Don't Stand In My Way/How Soon	6

Jackie TRENT

65	Pye 7N 15776	Where Are You Now (My Love)/On The Other Side Of The Tracks	5
65	Pye 7N 15865	When Summertime Is Over/To Show I Love Him	5
65	Pye 7N 15949	It's All In The Way You Look At Life/Time After Time.	6
66	Pye 7N 17047	You Baby/Send Her Away	15
66	Pye 7N 17082	Love Is Me Love Is You/This Time	6
66	Pye 7N 17158	If You Ever Leave Me/There Goes My Love, There Goes My Life	6
67	Pye 7N 17249	Open Your Heart/Love Can Give	6
67	Pye 7N 17323	Your Love Is Everywhere/It's Not Easy Loving You.	6
67	Pye 7N 17415	That's You/Stop Me And Buy One	6
67	Pye 7N 17437	Bye Bye Love (German Version)/Alles Okay (Send Her Away).	6
69	Pye 7N 17693	I'll Be There/Close To You.	5
78	Casino Classics CC 4	You Baby/Send Her Away/FAMILY AFFAIR: Love Hustle	5
65	Pye NEP 4225	WHERE ARE YOU NOW (EP)	15
65	Pye NPL 18125	THE MAGIC OF JACKIE TRENT (LP)	25
67	Pye NPL 18173	ONCE MORE WITH FEELING (LP)	20
67	Pye NPL 18201	STOP ME AND BUY ONE (LP)	22

(see also Family Affair)

TRESPASS
79	Trial CASE 1	One Of These Days/Bloody Moon (p/s)	15
80	Trial CASE 2	Jealousy/Live It Up! (p/s)	15
81	Trial CASE 3	Bright Lights/The Duel/Man And Machine (p/s)	25

TREVOR (Shield)
64	Blue Beat BB 228	Down In Virginia/Hey Little Schoolgirl (with Caribs)	10
68	Blue Cat BS 129	Tender Arms (with Joe White & Glen Brown)/DERMOTT LYNCH: Something Is Worrying Me.	10
68	Blue Cat BS 130	Pretty Girl (with Joe White & Glen Brown)/DERMOTT LYNCH: You Went Away	8
69	Blue Cat BS 153	Everyday Is Like A Holiday/Have You Time (by Trevor & Maytones)	8

TREVOR & KEITH
70	Punch PH 41	The Ark/MINNA BOYS: False Reador (actually titled "Got To Move")	6

(see also Carl Bryan)

T. REX
(see under Marc Bolan /T. Rex; see also Tyrannosaurus Rex)

TRIARCHY
79	SRT/79/CUS 599	Save The Khan/Juliet's Tomb (p/s, 1,000 only)	80
79	Direct NEON 1	Save The Khan/Juliet's Tomb (reissue, p/s)	35
80	Direct NEON 2	Metal Messiah/Sweet Alcohol/Hell Hound On My Trail (p/s)	70

TRIBAN
69	Cambrian CSP 707	Leaving On A Jet Plane/Night In The City	6
71	Decca F 13115	Black Paper Roses/One Way Mirror.	5
69	Cambrian MCT 592	TRIBAN (LP)	25
72	Cambrian	RAINMAKER (LP)	20

TRIBE (U.K.)
66	Planet PLF 108	The Gamma Goochie/I'm Leavin'.	50
67	RCA RCA 1592	Love Is A Beautiful Thing/Steel Guitar	15

TRIBE (U.S.)
66	Polydor 56510	Dancin' To The Beat Of My Heart/Woofin'	12

TRIBE
73	Probe PRO 597	Koke (Parts 1 & 2)	5

TONY TRIBE
69	Downtown DT 419	Red Red Wine/RECO & RUDIES: Blues.	5
69	Downtown DT 439	Gonna Give You All The Love/HERBIE GREY: Why Wait	6

TRICKY DISCO
91	Warp WAP 11	HOUSEFLY EP (12")	8

TRIDENT
84	SRT TRI 1	Destiny (no p/s)	50

(see also Filthy Rich)

TRIFFIDS (U.K.)
65	Fontana TL 5231	THE TRIFFIDS ARE REALLY FOLK (LP)	10

TRIFLE
69	United Artists UP 2270	All Together Now/Got My Thing	6
70	Dawn DNS 1008	Old-Fashioned Prayer Meeting/Dirty Old Town	5
71	Dawn DNLS 3017	FIRST MEETING (LP)	20

(see also George Bean)

PANDIT KANWAR SAIN TRIKHA
71	Mushroom 100 MR 7	THREE SITAR PIECES (LP)	40

TRILOGY
71	Mercury 6338 034	I'M BEGINNING TO FEEL IT (LP)	15

TOMMY TRINDER
59	Fontana H 204	La Plume De Ma Tante/On The Sunny Side Of The Street.	6
59	Fontana H 204	La Plume De Ma Tante/On The Sunny Side Of The Street (78)	15

TRINIDAD ALL STARS
56	Parlophone DP 524	Trouble In Arima/Stone Cold Dead In De Market (78, export issue)	12

TRINIDAD STEEL BAND
51	Melodisc 1185	Caroline/Six String Calypso (78)	8
52	Vogue V 9017	Mango Walk/Take Me (78).	10
52	Vogue V 9018	Ramadin/Johnny (78).	10

TRINITY HOUSE
77   Profile GMOR 146   FLASHBACK THROUGH HISTORY (LP, private pressing, with insert) 50

TRIO
70   Dawn DNLS 3006   TRIO (2-LP, with poster). 35
71   Dawn DNLS 3022   CONFLAGRATION (LP, with poster). 50
76   Dawn DNLS 3072   LIVE AT WOODSTOCK TOWN HALL (LP, with Stu Martin) 15
(see also John Surnam)

TRIPLETS
69   President PT 245   When Lovers Say Goodbye/You Won't See Me Leaving 4

TRIPPERS
66   Pye International 7N 25388   Dance With Me/Keep A-Knockin' 15

TRISHA
65   CBS 201800   The Darkness Of My Night/Confusion. 6

TRISTAR AIRBUS
72   RCA RCA 2170   Travellin' Man/Willie Morgan On The Wing 6
(see also Wimple Winch, 10cc, Hotlegs)

TRIUMVIRAT
74   Harvest SHSP 4030   ILLUSION ON A DOUBLE DIMPLE (LP). 10
75   Harvest SHSP 4048   SPARTACUS (LP) 10

TRIXIE'S BIG RED MOTORBIKE
82   Chew CH 9271   A Splash Of Red/Invisible Boyfriend (white label, stapled foldover p/s) 10
83   Lobby Ludd (no cat. no.)   TRIXIE'S BIG RED MOTORBIKE (EP, plain sleeve with stapled strip) 7
84   Lobby Ludd L 100001   Norman And Narcissus/In Timbuktu (p/s) 8
84   Lobby Ludd L 100002   A Splash Of Red/Invisible Boyfriend (reissue, different p/s) 6
84   Lobby Ludd L 100003   TRIXIE'S BIG RED MOTORBIKE (EP, reissue, stapled p/s) 6
84   Nathan NAT 001   That's The End Of That/CLIVE PIG & LEE VALLEY: As Soon As She's Gone
    (33rpm flexi & sweet with *Wally's Dog* fanzine) 6/4

MARCUS TRO
65   Ember EMB S 203   Tell Me/What's The Matter Little Girl (some in p/s). 10/6
65   Ember EMB 3365   INTRODUCING MARCUS TRO (LP) 30

TROGGS
SINGLES
66   CBS 202038   Lost Girl/The Yella In Me 30
66   Fontana TF 689   Wild Thing/From Home 7
66   Fontana TF 717   With A Girl Like You/I Want You 6
66   Page One POF 001   I Can't Control Myself/Gonna Make You 6
66   Page One POF 010   Any Way That You Want Me/6-5-4-3-2-1 6
67   Page One POF 015   Give It To Me/You're Lyin'. 6
67   Page One POF 022   My Lady/Girl In Black (withdrawn). 35
67   Page One POF 022   Night Of The Long Grass/Girl In Black 6
67   Page One POF 030   Hi Hi Hazel/As I Ride By. 7
67   Page One POF 040   Love Is All Around/When Will The Rain Come 5
68   Page One POF 056   Little Girl/Maybe The Madman? 6
68   Page One POF 064   Surprise Surprise/Marbles And Some Gum? 7
68   Page One POF 082   You Can Cry If You Want To/There's Something About You 7
68   Page One POF 092   Hip Hip Hooray/Say Darlin'! 6
69   Page One POF 114   Evil Woman/Sweet Madeline 6
69   Page One POF 126   Wild Thing/I Can't Control Myself 7
70   Page One POF 164   Easy Lovin'/Give Me Something 7
70   Page One POF 171   Lover/Come Now 7
70   Page One POF 182   The Raver/You 7
71   DJM DJM 248   Lazy Weekend/Let's Pull Together 7
72   Jam JAM 25   Wild Thing/With A Girl Like You/Love Is All Around 5
72   Pye 7N 45147   Everything's Funny/Feels Like A Woman 7
73   Pye 7N 45244   Listen To The Man/Queen Of Sorrow 7
73   Pye 7N 45295   Strange Movies/I'm On Fire 8
75   Penny Farthing PEN 861   Good Vibrations/Push It Up To Me. 6
75   Penny Farthing PEN 884   Wild Thing (Reggae Version)/Jenny Come Down 6
75   Penny Farthing PEN 889   Summertime/Jenny Come Down 6
75   Penny Farthing PEN 901   (I Can't Get No) Satisfaction/Memphis, Tennessee 6
76   Penny Farthing PEN 919   I'll Buy You An Island/Supergirl 5
77   Penny Farthing PEN 929   Feeling For Love/Summertime 5
78   Raw RAW 25   Just A Little Too Much/The True Troggs Tapes (p/s) 6
84   10 TENY 21   Every Little Thing/Blackjack And Poker/With A Girl Like You (picture disc) 5

EPs
67   Page One POE 001   TROGGS TOPS (EP) 20
67   Page One POE 002   TROGGS TOPS VOLUME TWO (EP) 35
67   Page One   TRACK A TROGG (EP, unreleased)
81   DJM DJS 6   TROGGS TAPES (EP, double pack) 10

LPs
66   Fontana (S)TL 5355   FROM NOWHERE — THE TROGGS (LP, mono/stereo). 35/40
66   Page One POL 001   TROGGLODYNAMITE (LP) 45
67   Page One FOR 001   THE BEST OF THE TROGGS (LP) 25
67   Page One POL(S) 003   CELLOPHANE (LP, mono/stereo) 40/50
68   Page One POL 1   THE TROGGS ON TOUR (LP, export issue) . . . . 150+
68   Page One FOR 007   THE BEST OF THE TROGGS VOLUME TWO (LP) 30
68   Page One POL(S) 012   MIXED BAG (LP). 100
69   Page One POS 602   TROGGLOMANIA (LP) 35
70   DJM Silverline DJML 009   CONTRASTS (LP, original issue). 25
(see also Reg Presley, Chris Britton, Ronnie Bond, Ten Feet Five)

MINT VALUE £

CHUCK TROIS & AMAZING MAZE
68 Action ACT 4517 Call On You/Woodsman 10

TROJAN
88 GI GILP 444 MARCH IS ON (LP) 15

TROJANS
58 Decca F 11065 Man I'm Gonna Be/Make It Up 15
58 Decca F 11065 Man I'm Gonna Be/Make It Up (78) 20

TROLL BROTHERS
73 SRT SRT 73316 You Turn Me On/Turn Out The Lights (p/s) 10

TROMBONES UNLIMITED
66 Liberty LIB 55874 Daydream/The Phoenix Love Theme (Senza Fine) 4
66 Liberty LBY 1350 YOU'RE GONNA HEAR FROM ME (LP) 10

TRONICS
61 Fontana H 348 Cantina/Pickin' & Stompin' 12

TRONICS
78 Tronics T 001 Suzie (actually "Suzie's Vibrator")/Favourite Girls (plain sleeve with inserts) 8
79 Tronics T 002 Time Off/Goodbye (p/s) 8
81 Alien ALIEN 18 Shark Fucks/Time Off (p/s, with insert) 5
81 Lyntone Love Backed By Force/(tracks by Dancing Did & Instant Automatons,
flexidisc with *Chainsaw* fanzine, issue 12) 4
83 Red Rhino RED 3 Wild Cat Rock/Tonight (p/s) 4
82 Press PRESS 1 TRANZISTER SISTER (12" EP) 8
80 Tronics T 003 THE TRONICS (cassette) 10
81 Tronics T 004 WHAT'S THE HUBBUB BUBB (cassette) 10
81 Alien BALIEN 3 LOVE BACKED BY FORCE (LP) 10
(see also Les Zarjaz)

TROOPERS
57 Vogue V 9087 Get Out/My Resolution 500
57 Vogue V 9087 Get Out/My Resolution (78) 70

TROOPS OF TOMORROW
82 Troops TROOPS 1 TROOPS OF TOMORROW (12" EP) 7
(see also Vibrators, Fallen Angels)

TROPIC SHADOWS
72 Big Shot BI 603 Our Anniversary/Anniversary (Version) 6

ARCHIBALD TROTT
64 Black Swan WI 407 Get Together/Just Because 12
(see also Baba Brooks)

TROUBADORS/TROUBADOUR SINGERS
57 London HLR 8469 Fascination/Midnight In Athens 15
58 London HLR 8541 The Lights Of Paris/The Flaming Rose 12
58 London RE-R 1135 THE TROUBADORS (EP) 10
58 London HA-R 2095 THE TROUBADORS IN SPAIN (LP) 15
58 London HA-R 2106 THE TROUBADORS IN THE LAND OF THE GIPSIES (LP) 15
58 London HA-R 2114 THE TROUBADORS IN ROME (LP) 15
58 London HA-A 2121 THE TROUBADORS IN HAWAII (LP) 15
60 London HA-R 2249 THE TROUBADORS IN PARIS (LP) 15
66 London SH-F 8275 SING OUT BIG (LP, as Troubadour Singers, stereo) 15
(see also Jane Morgan)

BOBBY TROUP
54 Capitol CL 14219 Julie Is Her Name/Instead Of You 8
54 Capitol LC 6660 BOBBY TROUP (10" LP) 18

BOB TROW QUARTET
54 London HL 8082 Soft Squeeze Baby/I Went Along For The Ride 30
54 London HL 8082 Soft Squeeze Baby/I Went Along For The Ride (78) 10

ROBIN TROWER
78 Chrysalis CHS 2247 It's For You/My Love/In City Dreams (p/s, red vinyl) 5
81 Chrysalis CHS 2497 What It Is/Into Money (p/s, clear vinyl) 5
73 Chrysalis CHR 1039 TWICE REMOVED FROM YESTERDAY (LP) 12
74 Chrysalis CHR 1057 BRIDGE OF SIGHS (LP) 12
75 Chrysalis CHR 1073 FOR EARTH BELOW (LP) 12
(see also Paramounts, Procol Harum, Jack Bruce & Robin Trower)

TROY & T-BIRDS
61 London HL 9476 Twistle/Take Ten 12

DORIS TROY
63 London HLK 9749 Just One Look/Bossa Nova Blues 18
64 Atlantic AT 4011 What'cha Gonna Do About It/Tomorrow Is Another Day 10
65 Atlantic AT 4020 Please Little Angel/One More Chance 10
65 Atlantic AT 4032 Heartaches/You'd Better Stop 10
65 Cameo Parkway C 101 I'll Do Anything (He Wants Me To)/But I Love Him 60
68 Atlantic 584 148 Just One Look/What'cha Gonna Do About It 7
68 Toast TT 507 I'll Do Anything (Anything He Wants Me To)/Heartaches 7
70 Apple APPLE 24 Ain't That Cute/Vaya Con Dios (some with p/s) 15/5
70 Apple APPLE 28 Jacob's Ladder/Get Back 8
71 Mojo 2092 011 I'll Do Anything (He Wants Me To)/But I Love Him (reissue) 6
73 Mojo 2092 062 Baby I Love You/To My Father's House 5
74 People PEO 112 Stretchin' Out/Don't Tell Your Mama 5
65 Atlantic AET 6007 WATCHA GONNA DO ABOUT IT (EP) 55
70 Apple SAPCOR 13 DORIS TROY (LP) 30

MINT VALUE £

73	Mojo 2956 001	THE RAINBOW TESTAMENT (LP, with Gospel Truth)	25
74	Polydor 2464 001	JUST ONE LOOK (LP)	15
74	People PLEO 12	STRETCHING OUT (LP)	15
92	Apple SAPCOR 13	DORIS TROY (LP, reissue, gatefold sleeve with bonus 12" [SAPCOR 132])	12

WILLIAM TRUCKAWAY
69	Reprise RS 20842	Bluegreens On The Wing/Besides Yourself	5

TRUFFLE
81	Chesnut NUT 6	Round Tower (p/s)	150

TRUTH
65	Pye 7N 15923	Baby Don't You Know/Come On Home	12
65	Pye 7N 15998	Who's Wrong/She's A Roller	15
66	Pye 7N 17035	Girl/Jailer Bring Me Water	8
66	Pye 7N 17095	I Go To Sleep/Baby You've Got It	25
66	Deram DM 105	Jingle Jangle/Hey Gyp (Dig The Slowness)	40
67	Decca F 12582	Walk Away Renee/Fly Away Bird	15
68	Decca F 22764	Seuno/Old Ma Brown	18

TRUTH & BEAUTY
74	Rak RAK 181	Tuff Little Surfer Boy/Touch-a Touch-a Touch Me	6

TRUTH CLUB
70s	Le Ray LR 1 EJSP 9597	Sleight/FOTE: Lost Toy (p/s)	4

TRUTH OF TRUTHS
71	Oak OR 1001	TRUTH OF TRUTHS (LP)	22

TRYDAN
80	Sain SAIN 77S	Mods A Rocers/Di-Waith, Di-'Fynedd	4

TANIA TSANAKLIDOU
78	EMI EMI 2797	Charlie Chaplin (English)/Charlie Chaplin (Greek)	12

T.S.O.L.
82	Alt. Tentacles VIRUS 10	WEATHERED STATUES (EP)	6

T2
70	Decca SKL 5050	IT'LL ALL WORK OUT IN BOOMLAND (LP)	50
97	Essex 1019LP	T2 (LP)	10

(see also Flies, Cross & Ross)

ERNEST TUBB (& HIS TEXAS TROUBADORS)
51	Brunswick 04783	Rose Of The Mountains/Kentucky Waltz (78)	8
52	Brunswick 04933	Walking The Floor Over You/Somebody's Stolen My Money (78)	10
56	Brunswick 05527	Thirty Days/Answer The Phone (triangular centre)	35
56	Brunswick 05527	Thirty Days/Answer The Phone (78)	12
56	Brunswick 05587	So Doggone Lonesome/If I Never Have Anything Else	18
56	Brunswick 05587	So Doggone Lonesome/If I Never Have Anything Else (78)	10
50s	Decca BM 31214	What Am I Living For/Goodbye Sunshine, Hello Blues (export issue)	15
55	Brunswick OE 9148	COUNTRY DOUBLE DATE (EP)	20
58	Brunswick OE 9372	THE DADDY OF 'EM ALL PT. 1 (EP)	20
58	Brunswick OE 9373	THE DADDY OF 'EM ALL PT. 2 (EP)	20
58	Brunswick OE 9374	THE DADDY OF 'EM ALL PT. 3 (EP)	20
56	Brunswick LA 8736	JIMMIE RODGERS SONGS (10" LP)	35
57	Brunswick LAT 8161	FAVOURITES (LP)	20
58	Brunswick LAT 8260	THE DADDY OF 'EM ALL (LP)	20
59	Brunswick LAT 8292	THE IMPORTANCE OF BEING ERNEST (LP)	20
60	Brunswick LAT 8313	THE ERNEST TUBB STORY VOLUME ONE (LP)	15
60	Brunswick LAT 8314	THE ERNEST TUBB STORY VOLUME TWO (LP)	15
60	Brunswick LAT 8349	THE ERNEST TUBB RECORD SHOP (LP)	20
66	Brunswick LAT 8627	MY PICK OF THE HITS (LP)	20

(see also Red Foley & Ernest Tubb)

JUSTIN TUBB
54	Brunswick 05302	Somebody Ughed On You/Something Called The Blues (78)	10
67	RCA Victor RCA 1585	But Wait There's More/The Second Thing I'm Gonna Do	6
64	RCA RCX 7133	JUSTIN TUBB (EP)	30
63	Ember CW 100	STAR OF THE GRAND OLE OPRY (LP)	12
64	Ember CW 110	THE MODERN COUNTRY MUSIC SOUND OF JUSTIN TUBB (LP)	12

TUBES
79	A&M AMSP 7423	Prime Time/No Way Out (picture disc)	4
79	A&M AMS 7423	Prime Time/No Way Out (p/s, 7 different coloured vinyl editions)	each 4
79	A&M AMS 7423	Prime Time (promo box of 7 different coloured vinyl editions & picture disc)	30
79	A&M AMS 7462	TV Is King/Telecide (p/s, yellow vinyl)	4

TUBEWAY ARMY
78	Beggars Banquet BEG 5	That's Too Bad/Oh! I Didn't Say (p/s)	10
78	Beggars Banquet BEG 8	Bombers/O.D. Receiver/Blue Eyes (p/s)	10
79	Beggars Banquet BEG 17T	Down In The Park/Do You Need The Service?/ I Nearly Married A Human 2 (12", p/s)	25
79	Beggars Banquet BEG 18	Are "Friends" Electric?/We Are So Fragile (p/s, push out centre)	6
79	Banquet Banquet BEG 18P	Are "Friends" Electric?/We Are So Fragile (picture disc, with insert)	10
79	Banquet Banquet SPC 4	Are "Friends" Electric?/We Are So Fragile (cassette in cigarette-pack style box)	8
79	Beggars Banquet BACK 2	That's Too Bad/Oh! Didn't I Say/Bombers/Blue Eyes/O.D. Receiver (double pack, gatefold p/s)	5
79	Beggars Banquet BACK 2	That's Too Bad/Oh! Didn't I Say/Bombers/Blue Eyes/O.D. Receiver (double pack, gatefold p/s, mispressed 2nd disc omits "O.D. Receiver")	20
85	Beggars Banquet BEG 92E	TUBEWAY ARMY VOL. 1 (12" EP, with "That's Too Bad [Alternate Mix]", yellow vinyl)	10
85	B. Banquet BEG 123E	TUBEWAY ARMY VOL. 2 (12" EP, red or black vinyl)	8/10

TUBEWAY ARMY

85	B. Banquet BEG 124E	TUBEWAY ARMY VOL. 3 (12" EP, blue or black vinyl) 8/10
78	Beggars Banquet BEGA 4	TUBEWAY ARMY (LP, blue vinyl, g/fold stickered sleeve, some w/ badge). . . . 45/40
79	Beggars Banquet BEGA 4	TUBEWAY ARMY (LP, reissue, white stickered sleeve). 12
79	Beggars Banquet BEGA 7	REPLICAS (LP, with large black & white poster). 20
85	B. Banquet BEGC 7879	TUBEWAY ARMY 1978/1979 (cassette only) 12

(see also Gary Numan, Paul Gardiner)

BESSIE TUCKER
55	HMV 7EG 8085	BLUES BY BESSIE (EP). 30

BILLY JOE TUCKER
61	London HLD 9455	Boogie Woogie Bill/Mail Train 60

CY TUCKER
63	Fontana TF 424	My Prayer/High School Dance (with Earl Preston & TTs) 12
64	Fontana TF 470	I Apologise/Let Me Call You Sweetheart 10
65	Fontana TF 534	My Friend/Hurt 10

(see also Earl Preston & TTs)

ORRIN TUCKER
50	London L 556	I Need Lovin'/Everybody Loves My Baby (78). 8

SOPHIE TUCKER
54	Mercury MG 20035	MY DREAM (LP) 18
54	Mercury MG 20046	CABARET DAYS (LP) 18
54	Mercury MPL 6000	LATEST AND GREATEST SPICY SAUCY SONGS (LP) 15
56	Mercury MPL 6503	CABARET DAYS (LP, reissue) 12
57	Brunswick LAT 8144	THE GREAT SOPHIE TUCKER (LP) 18
57	Mercury MPL 6513	BIGGER AND BETTER THAN EVER (LP). 15

TOMMY TUCKER
64	Pye International 7N 25238	Hi-Heel Sneakers/I Don't Want 'Cha. 12
64	Pye International 7N 25246	Long Tall Shorty/Mo' Shorty. 12
64	London HLU 9932	Oh! What A Feeling/Wine Bottles 30
69	Chess CRS 8086	Hi-Heel Sneakers/I Don't Want 'Cha (reissue) 8
64	Pye Intl. NEP 44027	HI HEEL SNEAKERS (EP) 35

WINSTON TUCKER
73	Explosion EX 2083	I'm A Believer/You'll Be Mine. 5

(see also Winston Groovy)

TUCKY BUZZARD
71	Capitol CL 15687	She's A Striker/Heartbreaker 5
73	Purple PUR 113	Gold Medallions/Fast Bluesy Woman 7
77	Purple PUR 134	Gold Medallions/Superboy Rock 'N' Roller '73'. 7
73	Purple TPSA 7510	ALRIGHT ON THE NIGHT (LP) 20
73	Purple TPSA 7512	BUZZARD (LP) 20

(see also End)

TUDOR LODGE
71	Vertigo 6059 044	The Lady's Changing Home/Back To The Good Times We Had 12
71	Vertigo 6360 043	TUDOR LODGE (LP, foldout textured sleeve, spiral label) 125

TUDOR MINSTRELS
66	Decca F 12536	Love In The Open Air/A Theme From "The Family Way". 18

TUESDAY'S CHILDREN
66	Columbia DB 7978	When You Walk In The Sand/High And Drifting 12
66	Columbia DB 8018	High On A Hill/Summer Leaves Me With A Sigh 12
67	King KG 1051	A Strange Light From The East/That'll Be The Day 15
67	Pye 7N 17406	Baby's Gone/Guess I'm Losin' You 10
68	Pye 7N 17474	In The Valley Of The Shadow Of Love/Ain't You Got A Heart 7
68	Mercury MF 1063	She/Bright-Eyed Apples. 5

(see also Warm Sounds)

T.U.F.F.
80s	SONO 001	We've Got A Hot One (Speed Mix) (unreleased, white label promos only) 20

(see also Hard Corps)

TUFF GONG ALLSTARS
72	Punch PH 114	You Should Have Known Better (actually by The Wailing Souls)/Known Better . . 10

(see also Wailing Souls)

TULIPS
74	Explosion EX 2091	Mocking Bird/DES ALL STARS: Version 6

LEE TULLY
57	London HL 8363	Around The World With Elwood Pretzel (Parts 1 & 2) (gold or silver print). . . . 70/40
57	London HL 8363	Around The World With Elwood Pretzel (Parts 1 & 2) (78). 12

TUNDRA
70s	Greenwich Village GVR 208	THE KENTISH SONGSTER (LP). 12
78	Sweet Folk & C. SFA 078	A KENTISH GARLAND (LP, gatefold sleeve). 25

TUNE ROCKERS
58	London HLT 8717	The Green Mosquito/Warm Up. 25
58	London HLT 8717	The Green Mosquito/Warm Up (78) 55

TUNEWEAVERS
57	London HL 8503	Happy Happy Birthday Baby/PAUL GAYTEN: Yo, Yo, Walk 165
57	London HL 8503	Happy Happy Birthday Baby/PAUL GAYTEN: Yo, Yo, Walk (78). 50

(see also Paul Gayten)

TUNIC
96	Love Train PUBE 09	Tick Tock/Malteaser Sunset (p/s, 1,000 only). 4
97	Love Train PUBE 16	Also Ran/There's Too Much Sea On This (Here) Planet (p/s, 1,000 only) 4

Rare Record Price Guide 2002

PADDY TUNNEY

65	Topic 12T 139	A WILD BEES NEST (LP, blue label, later reissued) 15/10
66	Topic 12T 153	IRELAND HER OWN (LP, with Arthur Kearney, Frank Kelly & Joe Tunney, blue label, later reissued) 15/10
66	Topic 12T 165	THE IRISH EDGE (LP, blue label, later reissued) 15/10

TURBO

| 80 | Cargo CRS 004 | STALLION (EP, p/s)................................... 100 |
| 82 | Turbo CUS 1261 | Charged For Glory (no p/s) .... 8 |

BRUCE TURNER

54	Columbia SCMC 9	Falling Leaves/I Wished On The Moon (export issue)............. 6
60	Melodisc MEL 1551	Nuages/My Guy's Come Back 5
60s	Seventy Seven 77EPEU 1	ORIGINAL MUSIC FROM THE FILM LIVING JAZZ (EP) 8
62	Storyville SXP 2025	BRUCE TURNER AND HIS JUMP BAND (EP) 8
63	Philips 433 627 BE	JUMPING FOR JOY NO. 1 (EP) 15
63	Philips 433 627 BE	JUMPING FOR JOY NO. 2 (EP) 15
63	77 EP/EU 1	LIVING JAZZ (EP)............................ 10
55	Jazz Today JTL 2	BRUCE TURNER SHOWCASE (LP) 18
61	77 LEU 12/2	JUMPIN' AT THE N.F.T. (LP) 12
64	Philips BL 7590	GOING PLACES (LP) 20

DENNIS TURNER

| 62 | London HL 9537 | Lover Please/How Many Times .... 12 |

GORDON TURNER

| 70 | Charisma CAS 1009 | MEDITATION (LP)............................... 30 |

IKE TURNER

72	United Artists UP 35411	Lawdy Miss Clawdy/Tacks In My Shoes/ Soppin' Molasses (with Family Vibes)................... 5
84	Fleetville FV 303	New Breed Part 1/New Breed Part 2 5
60s	Ember EMB 3395	IKE TURNER ROCKS THE BLUES (LP) 25
72	United Artists UAG 29362	BLUES ROOTS (LP) 12
75	DJM DJSLM 2010	FUNKY MULE (LP) 12
	(see also Ike & Tina Turner)	

IKE & TINA TURNER

SINGLES

60	London HLU 9226	A Fool In Love/The Way You Love Me 12
61	London HLU 9451	It's Gonna Work Out Fine/Won't You Forgive Me................... 15
64	Sue WI 306	Gonna Work Out Fine/Won't You Forgive Me (reissue)........... 15
64	Sue WI 322	The Argument/Poor Fool 15
64	Sue WI 350	I Can't Believe What You Say/My Baby Now 20
65	Warner Bros WB 153	Finger Poppin'/Ooh Poo Pah Doo 15
65	Sue WI 376	Please, Please, Please/Am I A Fool In Love 18
66	London HLU 10046	River Deep — Mountain High/I'll Keep You Happy 5
66	Warner Bros WB 5753	Tell Her I'm Not Home/Finger Poppin'................ 7
66	HMV POP 1544	Anything You Wasn't Born With/Beauty Is Just Skin Deep 18
66	London HLU 10083	A Love Like Yours (Don't Come Knockin' Every Day)/Hold On Baby 7
66	Stateside SS 551	Goodbye, So Long/Hurt Is All You Gave Me 8
66	Warner Bros WB 5766	Somebody (Somewhere) Needs You/(I'll Do Anything) Just To Be With You 18
67	HMV POP 1583	I'm Hooked/Dust My Broom........................ 30
67	London HLU 10155	I'll Never Need More Than This/Save The Last Dance For Me........ 8
68	London HLU 10189	So Fine/So Blue Over You 7
68	London HLU 10217	We Need An Understanding/It Sho' Ain't Me............. 7
69	London HLU 10242	River Deep — Mountain High/Save The Last Dance For Me.......... 5
69	Minit MLF 11016	I'm Gonna Do All I Can/You've Got Too Many Ties That Bind......... 8
69	London HLU 10267	I'll Never Need More Than This/A Love Like Yours 7
69	Liberty LBF 15223	Crazy 'Bout You Baby/I've Been Lovin' You Too Long 8
70	Liberty LBF 15303	Come Together/Honky Tonky Women 5
70	A&M AMS 783	Make 'Em Wait/Everyday I Have To Cry 10
70	Harvest HAR 5018	The Hunter/Bold Soul Sister 8
70	Liberty LBF 15367	I Want To Take You Higher/Contact High 5
71	Liberty LBF 15432	Proud Mary/Funkier Than A Mosquito's Tweeter............. 5
71	A&M AMS 829	River Deep — Mountain High/Oh Baby 7
71	United Artists UP 35245	Ooh Poo Pah Doo/I Wanna Jump.................. 5
72	United Artists UP 35373	Feel Good/Outrageous................................ 5

EPs

64	Sue IEP 706	THE SOUL OF IKE AND TINA TURNER (EP) 125
65	Warner Bros WEP 619	THE IKE AND TINA TURNER SHOW (EP).................. 40
66	Warner Bros WEP 620	SOMEBODY NEEDS YOU (EP) 40

LPs

65	Warner Bros WM 8170	THE IKE AND TINA TURNER SHOW (LP)................. 30
65	London HA-C 8248	THE GREATEST HITS OF IKE & TINA TURNER (LP) 35
66	Ember EMB 3368	THE IKE AND TINA TURNER REVUE (LP) 22
66	Warner Bros W 1579	THE IKE AND TINA TURNER SHOW (LP)............. 22
66	London HA-U/SH-U 8298	RIVER DEEP MOUNTAIN HIGH (LP) 30
67	Warner Bros WB 5904	THE IKE AND TINA TURNER SHOW VOL. 2 (LP) 22
69	London HA-U/SH-U 8370	SO FINE (LP, with Fontella Bass)................ 20
69	Liberty LBS 83241	OUTTA SEASON (LP) 18
69	Minit MLS 40014	IN PERSON (LP) 18
69	Warner Bros ES 1810	GREATEST HITS (LP) 12
70	Liberty LBS 83350	COME TOGETHER (LP) 15
70	Harvest SHSP 4001	THE HUNTER (LP) 25
71	Liberty LBS 83455	WORKIN' TOGETHER (LP) 12

Ike & Tina TURNER

71	Liberty LBS 83468/9	LIVE IN PARIS (LP).	12
71	Capitol E-ST 571	HER MAN...HIS WOMAN (LP)	12
71	United Artists UAD 60005/6	WHAT YOU HEAR IS WHAT YOU GET (LP).	12
72	United Artists UAG 29256	NUFF SAID (LP)	12
73	Mojo 2916 020	PEACHES (LP, with tracks by Ikettes)	12

(see also Ike Turner, Tina Turner, Ikettes)

JESSE LEE TURNER

59	London HLL 8785	The Little Space Girl/Shake, Baby, Shake	50
59	London HLL 8785	The Little Space Girl/Shake, Baby, Shake (78)	60
60	London HLP 9108	I'm The Little Space Girl's Father/Valley Of Lost Soldiers	30
60	Top Rank JAR 303	That's My Girl/Teenage Misery	15
60	Top Rank JAR 516	Do I Worry (Yes I Do)/All Right, Be That Way	12
62	Vogue V 9201	The Voice Changing Song/All You Gotta Do Is Ask	12

(BIG) JOE TURNER

51	Parlophone DP 265	Roll 'Em Pete/Goin' Away Blues (with Pete Johnson) (78, export only)	50
56	London HLE 8301	Corrine Corrina/Morning, Noon And Night (triangular or round centre)	325/75
56	London HLE 8301	Corrine Corrina/Morning, Noon And Night (78)	45
56	London HLE 8332	Boogie Woogie Country Girl/The Chicken And The Hawk	650
56	London HLE 8332	Boogie Woogie Country Girl/The Chicken And The Hawk (78)	60
57	London HLE 8357	Lipstick, Powder And Paint/Rock A While (gold label print, later silver)	375/250
57	London HLE 8357	Lipstick, Powder And Paint/Rock A While (78)	60
60	London HLE 9055	Honey Hush/Tomorrow Night	45
60	London HLK 9119	My Little Honey Dripper/Chains Of Love	45
65	Atlantic AT 4026	Midnight Cannonball/Baby I Still Want You	15
56	London REE 1047	KING AND QUEEN OF RHYTHM AND BLUES (EP, 2 tracks by Ruth Brown)	150
57	London REE 1111	PRESENTING JOE TURNER (EP, initially tri-centre, later round centre)	175/125
57	London Jazz LTZ-K 15053	BOSS OF THE BLUES (LP, also stereo SAH-K 6019)	75/90
59	London HA-E 2173	ROCKIN' THE BLUES (LP)	100
60	London Jazz LTZ-K 15205	BIG JOE RIDES AGAIN (LP, also stereo SAH-K 6123)	65/75
60	London HA-E 2231	BIG JOE IS HERE (LP)	75
64	Realm RM 207	JOE TURNER SINGS THE BLUES VOL. 1 (LP)	20
64	Realm RM 229	JOE TURNER SINGS THE BLUES VOL. 2 (LP)	20
65	CBS 52229	JOE TURNER SINGS THE BLUES VOL. 2 (LP, reissue)	15
65	Fontana 688 802 ZL	JUMPIN' THE BLUES (LP)	25
67	Atlantic Special 590 006	BOSS OF THE BLUES (LP)	18
68	Stateside (S)SL 10226	SINGING THE BLUES (LP)	22
70	Philips SBL 7911	THE REAL BOSS OF THE BLUES (LP)	15
74	Atlantic K 40525	HIS GREATEST RECORDINGS (LP).	12

(see also Pete Johnson, Meade Lux Lewis, Pete Johnson, Albert Ammons, Sonny Terry & Brownie McGhee)

JOE TURNER/RUTH BROWN

56	London REE 1047	KING AND QUEEN OF R&B (EP, 2 tracks each)	175

(see also Ruth Brown, Big Joe Turner)

JOE TURNER & PETE JOHNSON GROUP

56	Emarcy ERE 1500	JOE TURNER & PETE JOHNSON GROUP (EP)	40

(see also Pete Johnson, Big Joe Turner)

MEL TURNER (& Bandits)

61	Melodisc MEL 1580	Let Me Hold Your Hand/I'll Be With You In Apple Blossom Time (with Bandits)	18
62	Columbia DB 4791	Daddy Cool/Swing Low Sweet Chariot (with Bandits)	12
63	Columbia DB 4963	Don't Cry/I Need	6
63	Columbia DB 7076	I Can't Stand Up Alone/Doing The Ton (with Mohicans)	6
63	Carnival CV 7003	Mohican Crawl/White Christmas	7
66	Island WI 276	Welcome Home Little Darlin'/C'est L'Amour	10
70	United Artists UP 35121	Jungle Harlem/Runaway	5

NIK TURNER

(see under Inner City Unit, Sphynx, Hawkwind)

PRECIOUS CLARENCE TURNER

67	Saga SOC 1041	BOOGIE WOOGIE EXPLOSIONS (LP)	10

SAMMY TURNER

59	London HLX 8918	Lavender Blue (Dilly, Dilly)/Sweet Annie Laurie	15
59	London HLX 8918	Lavender Blue (Dilly, Dilly)/Sweet Annie Laurie (78)	35
59	London HLX 8963	Always/Symphony	10
59	London HLX 8963	Always/Symphony (78)	35
60	London HLX 9062	Paradise/I'd Be A Fool Again	10
62	London HLX 9488	Raincoat In The River/Falling	18
60	London HA-X 2246	LAVENDER BLUE MOODS (LP)	60

SIMON TURNER

73	UK UKAL 1003	SIMON TURNER (LP)	15

SPYDER TURNER

67	MGM MGM 1332	Stand By Me/You're Good Enough For Me	20
74	Kwanza K 19502	Since I Don't Have You/Happy Days	5

TINA TURNER

78	United Artists UP 36513	Sometimes When We Touch/Earthquakes And Hurricanes	5
82	Virgin VS 500	Ball Of Confusion/Ball Of Confusion (Instrumental) (with B.E.F.) (p/s)	8
83	Capitol 12CLP 316	Let's Stay Together/I Wrote A Letter (12", picture disc)	8
84	Capitol CLP 325	Help/Rock'n'Roll Widow (picture disc)	7
84	Capitol CLP 338	Better Be Good To Me/When I Was Young (picture disc)	7
84	Capitol CL 343	Private Dancer/Nutbush City Limits (p/s)	5
85	Capitol CLP 364	We Don't Need Another Hero/(Instrumental) (picture disc)	8
86	Capitol CLP 338	Break Every Rule/Girls (picture disc)	7
86	Capitol CLX 430	Two People/Havin' A Party (p/s, with poster)	6
87	Capitol CLD 439	What You Get Is What You See/Tina Turner Montage (box set)	6

87	Capitol 7CLD 439	What You See Is What You Get/Take Me To The River//	
		Tina Turner Montage Mix (Parts 1 & 2) (double pack)	7
87	Capitol CLP 452	Break Every Rule/Girls (picture disc)	7
87	Capitol CL 459	Paradise Is Here/The Midnight Hour (p/s, with tour poster)	5
87	Capitol CLP 459	Paradise Is Here/The Midnight Hour (picture disc)	7
87	Capitol 12 CLP 459	Paradise Is Here/The Midnight Hour (12", picture disc)	8
88	Capitol CDCL 484	Addicted To Love (live)/Overnight Sensation (live)/Legs (live) (CD)	7
89	Capitol CLS 543	The Best/Undercover Agent For The Blues (p/s, pack with 6 postcards)	5
89	Capitol CDCL 543	The Best/Undercover Agent For The Blues/Bold And Reckless (CD)	7
89	Capitol 12 CLP 553	I Don't Wanna Lose You/Not Enough Romance (12", picture disc)	7
89	Capitol CDCL 553	I Don't Wanna Lose You/Stronger Than The Wind/Not Enough Romance/	
		We Don't Need Another Hero (Thunderdome) (CD)	7
90	Capitol CLPD 593	Be Tender With Me Baby/Be Tender With Me Baby (live) (picture disc)	5
91	10 FLX 2007-1	A Change Is Gonna Come (Excerpt) (with B.E.F.) (flexidisc, p/s, from	
		"Music Of Quality And Distinction Vol 2", promo only)	5
85	Capitol TINAP 1	PRIVATE DANCER (LP, picture disc)	12
89	Capitol CDESTU 2103	FOREIGN AFFAIR (CD, deluxe passport package)	15
99	EMI CDIN 127	INTERVIEW (CD, card sleeve with cues insert, promo only)	25

(see also Ike & Tina Turner, Eric Clapton)

TITUS TURNER

60	London HLU 9024	We Told You Not To Marry/Taking Care Of Business	20
61	Oriole CB 1611	Pony Train/Bla Bla Cha Cha Cha	18
61	Parlophone R 4746	Sound-Off/Me And My Lonely Telephone	20
61	Blue Beat BB 32	Miss Rubberneck Jones/Way Down Yonder	12

ZEB TURNER

51	Vogue V 9002	Chew Tobacco Rag/No More Nothin' (78)	20

TURNING SHRINES

86	Temple TOPY 7	FACE OF ANOTHER (12" EP)	7

TURNSTYLE

68	Pye 7N 17653	Riding A Wave/Trot	125

TURQUOISE

68	Decca F 12756	53 Summer Street/Tales Of Flossie Fillett	30
68	Decca F 12842	Woodstock/Saynia	30

(see also Ewan Stephens)

STANLEY TURRENTINE

76	Fantasy FTC 131	Have You Ever Seen The Rain/Tommy's Tune	5
78	Fantasy FTC 149	Papa'T (Parts 1 & 2)	5
78	Fantasy FTC 162	Disco Dancing/Heritage	5
66	Fontana TL 5300	TIGER TAIL (LP)	15
72	Polydor 2383 111	FLIPPED — FLIPPED OUT (LP)	12
72	CTI CTL 2	SUGAR (LP)	12
73	CTI CTL 8	CHERRY (LP, with Milt Jackson)	12
77	Fantasy FT 535	NIGHTWINGS (LP)	12
78	Fantasy FT 551	WHAT ABOUT YOU (LP)	12

(see also Milt Jackson & Stanley Turrentine, Astrud Gilberto)

TURTLES

65	Pye International 7N 25320	It Ain't Me Babe/Almost There	8
66	Pye International 7N 25341	Let Me Be/Your Ma Said You Cried (In Your Sleep Last Night)	8
66	Immediate IM 031	You Baby/Wanderin' Kind	12
66	London HLU 10095	Can I Get To Know You Better/Like The Seasons	7
67	London HLU 10115	Happy Together/We'll Meet Again	6
67	Pye International 7N 25421	Let Me Be/Almost There	6
67	London HLU 10135	She'd Rather Be With Me/The Walking Song	6
67	London HLU 10153	You Know What I Mean/Rugs Of Woods And Flowers	7
67	London HLU 10168	She's My Girl/Chicken Little Was Right	7
68	London HLU 10184	Sound Asleep/Umbassa The Dragon	8
68	London HLU 10207	The Story Of Rock And Roll/Can't You Hear The Cows	7
68	London HLU 10223	Elenore/Surfer Dan	6
69	London HLU 10251	You Showed Me/Buzz-Saw	7
69	London HLU 10279	You Don't Have To Walk In The Rain/Come Over	6
69	London HLU 10291	Love In The City/Bachelor Mother	6
67	Pye Intl. NEP 44089	IT AIN'T ME BABE (EP)	40
67	London HA-U 8330	HAPPY TOGETHER (LP)	30
68	London HA-U/SH-U 8376	THE TURTLES PRESENT THE BATTLE OF THE BANDS (LP)	30

(see also Flo & Eddie)

RITA TUSHINGHAM & LYNN REDGRAVE

68	Stateside SS 2081	Smashing Time/Waiting For My Friend	7

TUSKAN RAIDERS

95	Clear CLR 410(X)	Bantha Trax (12", p/s, some on clear vinyl)	20/15

(see also Mu-Ziq)

TU-TONES

51	London L 1079	Oh You Million Dollar Doll/Don't Fence Me In (78, as Lee Monti's Tu-Tones)	8
59	London HLW 8904	Still In Love With You/Saccharin Sally	100
59	London HLW 8904	Still In Love With You/Saccharin Sally (78)	50

WESLEY & MARILYN TUTTLE

55	Capitol CL 14291	Jim, Johnny And Jonas/Say You Do	8

T.V. & TRIBESMEN

66	Pye International 7N 25375	Barefootin'/Fat Man	15

T.V. PERSONALITIES

(see under Television Personalities)

T.V. PRODUCT
79	Limited Edition TAKE 3	Nowhere's Safe/Jumping Off Walls/PRAMS: Me/Modern Man (folded p/s)	8

(see also Mission)

TV 21
80	Powbeat AAARGH! 1	Playing With Fire/Shattered By It All (foldout p/s)	12
80	Powbeat AAARGH! 2	Ambition/Ticking Away/This Is Zero (foldout p/s)	15
81	Deram DM 442/DMF 442	Snakes And Ladders/Artistic Licence/Ambition/ Playing With Fire (double pack single, p/s)	5

(see also DNV, Shake)

SHANIA TWAIN
95	Mercury MERCD 433	Any Man Of Mine/Raining On Our Love/God Ain't Gonna Getcha For That/Still Under The Weather (CD)	18
98	Mercury 568 493 2	You're Still The One (Radio Edit)/I'm Outta Here (Mutt Lange Remix)/You Win My Love (Mutt Lange Remix)/You're Still The One (Radio Edit with intro) (CD)	8
98	Mercury 566 119 2	When (Radio Edit)/You're Still The One (Soul Solution Edit)/ (Extended Club Mix)/Don't Be Stupid (You Know I Love You) (CD, some with poster)	10/8
99	Mercury 562 264 2	Man! I Feel Like A Woman (Original Version) (CD, digipak, with lyrics, withdrawn)	15
99	NMC PILOT 54	ON THE WAY (CD, withdrawn)	18

TWELFTH NIGHT
73	Acorn CF 239	TWELFTH NIGHT (EP)	8

TWELFTH NIGHT
80	Twelfth Night TN 001	THE FIRST 7" ALBUM ("The Cunning Man"/"Für Helene") (p/s)	30
80s	Revolution REV 009	Eleanor Rigby/East Of Eden (p/s)	7
86	Virgin/Charisma CB 424	Shame/Blue Powder Monkey (p/s)	5
86	Virgin/Charisma CBY 424	Shame/Blue Powder Monkey (picture disc)	8
86	Virgin/Charisma CB 424-12	Shame (Full Mix)/Shame (7")/Blue Powder Monkey (12", p/s)	8
86	Virgin/Charisma CBY 424-12	Shame (Full Mix)/Shame (7")/Blue Powder Monkey (12", picture disc)	10
86	Virgin/Charisma CB 425	Take A Look/Blondon Fair (p/s)	4
86	Virgin/Charisma CB 425-12	Take A Look (Album Version)/Take A Look (Part 4)/ Blondon Fair (Ext.) (12", p/s)	8
80	Twelfth Night TN 001	TWELFTH NIGHT (cassette)	15
81	Twelfth Night TN 002	LIVE AT THE TARGET (LP)	12
82	Twelfth Night TN 003	SMILING AT GRIEF (cassette)	10
83	Twelfth Night TN 006	FACT AND FICTION (LP)	10
84	Music For Nations MFN 18	LIVE AND LET LIVE (LIVE AT THE MARQUEE) (LP)	10
84	Music For Nations MFN 36	ART & ILLUSION (mini-LP)	10
86	Charisma CASG 1174	X (LP, fold-out cover)	10

20th CENTURY FOX ORCHESTRA
65	Stateside SS422	Those Magnificent Men In Their Flying Machines/Arizona	6

25 RIFLES
79	25 Rifles TFR 1	World War 3/Revolution Blues/Hey Little/Dance 'Bout Now (12", stamped sl.)	12

23 JEWELS
79	Temporary TEMP 1	You Don't Know Me/Playing Bogart (white labels, plain sleeve with photocopied insert)	5
80	Temporary TEMP 2	WELTSCHMERZ A GO-GO! (EP, white label)	4

23RD TURNOFF
67	Deram DM 150	Michael Angelo/Leave Me Here	40

(see also Kirkbys, Jimmy Campbell, Rockin' Horse)

23 SKIDOO
81	Pineapple PULP 23	Ethics/Another Baby's Face (p/s)	8
81	Fetish FE 10	Last Words/Version (promo only, no p/s)	15
81	Fetish FE 11	The Gospel Comes To New Guinea/Last Words (12", p/s)	10
82	Fetish FP 20	Tearing Up The Plans/Just Like Everybody/Gregouka (12", p/s)	8
85	Illuminated ILL 2812	Coup/Version (In The Palace) (12", p/s)	8
82	Fetish FM 2008	SEVEN SONGS (mini-LP)	12

(see also Current 93)

TWICE AS MUCH
66	Immediate IM 033	Sittin' On A Fence/Baby I Want You	7
66	Immediate IM 036	Step Out Of Line/Simplified	7
66	Immediate IM 039	True Story/You're So Good	10
67	Immediate IM 042	Crystal Ball/Why Don't They All Go Away And Leave Me Alone	10
66	Immediate IMLP/IMSP 007	OWN UP (LP)	35
69	Immediate IMCP 013	THAT'S ALL (LP)	35

TWIGGY
67	Ember EMB S 239	Beautiful Dreams/I Need Your Hand In Mine (some in p/s)	15/8
67	Ember EMB S 244	When I Think Of You/Over And Over (some in p/s)	15/8
71	Bell BLL 1158	Zoo Do Zoo Song/Little Pleasure Acre (as Twiggy & Friends)	5
72	Columbia DB 8853	A Room In Bloomsbury (with Chistopher Gable)/You Are My Lucky Star/ All I Do Is Dream	5
76	Mercury 6007 100	Here I Go Again/In Love Together (p/s)	5
78	Mercury 6007 175	Falling Angel/Virginia	5
72	Ember SE 8012	TWIGGY & THE GIRLFRIENDS (LP)	18
72	Columbia SCXA 9251	THE BOYFRIEND (LP, soundtrack, with Christopher Plummer)	12

TWIGGY & ANNIE
66	Columbia DB 7799	Some Do, Some Don't/With Open Arms	7

TWILIGHTS (U.S.)
65	London HLU 9992	Take What I Got/She's There	12

TWILIGHTS (Australia)
66	Columbia DB 8065	Needle In A Haystack/I Don't Know Where The Wind Will Blow Me	12
67	Columbia DB 8125	What's Wrong With The Way I Live/It's Dark	12
68	Columbia DB 8396	Cathy, Come Home/The Way They Play	15

TWILIGHT ZONERZ
79	ZIP/Dining Out ZERO ZERO 1	ZERO ZERO ONE (EP, various silk-screened in red & hand-coloured p/s, signed & numbered)	15
80	ZIP/Dining Out ZIP 002	Brighton Rock/Diversion (p/s)	6

(see also Occult Chemistry)

TWINK (& FAIRIES)
78	Chiswick SWT 26	Do It '77/Psychedelic Punkeroo/Enter The Diamonds (12", p/s, with Fairies)	7
70	Polydor 2343 032	THINK PINK (LP, with some insert)	120/80
70	Polydor 2343 032	THINK PINK (LP, red vinyl with insert)	300
91	Twink LP 2	ODDS & BEGINNINGS (LP, with insert, numbered & signed, some on red vinyl, 1,500 only)	10/15

(see also Pretty Things, Pink Fairies, Fairies, Tomorrow, Aquarian Age, Rings, Mick Farren, Magic Muscle)

TWINKLE (Ripley) (U.K.)
64	Decca F 12013	Terry/The Boy Of My Dreams	6
65	Decca F 12076	Golden Lights/Ain't Nobody Home But Me	6
65	Decca F 12139	Tommy/So Sad	8
65	Decca F 12219	Poor Old Johnny/I Need Your Hand In Mine	10
65	Decca F 12305	The End Of The World/Take Me To The Dance	10
66	Decca F 12464	What Am I Doing Here With You?/Now I Have You	12
69	Instant IN 005	Micky/Darby And Joan	7
74	Bradleys BRAD 7418	Days/Caroline (as Twinkle Ripley)	7
82	EMI 5278	I'm A Believer/For Sale (p/s)	5
65	Decca DFE 8621	TWINKLE — A LONELY SINGING DOLL (EP)	50

(see also Bill & Coo, Silkie Davis)

TWINKLE & HOT ROD ALL STARS (Jamaica)
70	Torpedo TOR 3	Jook Jook/Graduate	6

TWINKLE BROTHERS
70	Jackpot JP 731	Shu Be Du/All My Enemies Beware	8
70	Jackpot JP 740	Miss World/Take What You've Got	8
70	Jackpot JP 741	Sweet Young Thing/Grandma	8
71	Jackpot JP 768	Do Your Own Thing/BOY WONDER: They Talk About Love	18
71	Green Door GD 4007	Miss Labba Labba/The Best Is Yet To Come	7
71	Big Shot BI 593	You Took Me By Suprise/You Took Me By Surprise — Version (both sides actually by Tony Brevitt)	10
71	Big Shot BI 600	It's Not Who You Know/I Need Someone	7
71	Tropical AL 002	Love Sweet Love/HERON ATTAR: Poor Man's Life	7
72	Sioux SI 003	Happy Song/Little Caesar	6
73	Camel CA 106	Room Full All Full/Version	6
73	Magnet MG 033	Mother And Wife/Version	5
73	Pama PM 876	Push It Inna/Village Ram	6
75	Faith FA 007	Friends/No Big Thing	5
75	Faith FA 022	Mother And Wife/GENE RONDO: Impossible Dream	5

(see also Busty Brown, Sammy Jones)

TWINS
73	Downtown DT 511	Rastafari Ruler/TYRONE TAYLOR: Yesterday	5

TWINSET
67	Decca F 12629	Tremblin'/Sneakin' Up On You	8

TWIN-TONES
58	RCA RCA 1040	Jo Ann/Before You Go	45
58	RCA RCA 1040	Jo Ann/Before You Go (78)	25

TWIN TUNES QUINTET
58	RCA RCA 1046	The Love Nest/Baby Lover	12
58	RCA RCA 1046	The Love Nest/Baby Lover (78)	20

TWIST
79	Polydor 2059 156	This Is Your Life/Life's A Commercial Break (p/s)	6
79	Polydor POSP 84	Ads/Rebound (p/s)	6
79	Polydor 2383 552	THIS IS YOUR LIFE (LP)	20

TWISTED ACE
81	Heavy Metal HEAVY 9	Firebird/I Won't Surrender (p/s)	10

TWISTED SISTER
82	Secret SHH 137-12	RUFF CUTS (12" EP, p/s)	10
83	Atlantic A 9827P	The Kids Are Back/Shoot 'Em Down (shaped picture disc)	8
83	Atlantic A 9792	You Can't Stop Rock 'n' Roll/Let The Good Times Roll (live)/I Feel So Fine (poster p/s)	4
84	Atlantic A 9634T	I Wanna Rock/Burn In Hell (live)/SMF (live) (12", poster p/s)	7
86	Atlantic A 9478D	Leader Of The Pack/I Wanna Rock (p/s, with free single)	5
86	Atlantic A 9478I	Leader Of The Pack/I Wanna Rock (gatefold p/s with poster)	4
86	Atlantic A 9478P	Leader Of The Pack/I Wanna Rock (shaped picture disc)	6
85	Atlantic 781 275-1P	COME OUT AND PLAY (LP, picture disc)	12

TWISTERS
60	Capitol CL 15167	Turn The Page/Dancing Little Clown	8
62	Aral/Windsor PSA 106	Peppermint Twist Time/Silly Chilli	12

MINT VALUE £

CONWAY TWITTY

78s

57	Mercury MT 173	Shake It Up/Maybe Baby (78)	60
58	MGM MGM 992	It's Only Make Believe/I'll Try (78)	12
59	MGM MGM 1003	The Story Of My Love/Make Me Know You're Mine (78)	25
59	MGM MGM 1016	Hey Little Lucy! (Don'tcha Put No Lipstick On)/When I'm Not With You (78)	35
59	MGM MGM 1029	Mona Lisa/Heavenly (78)	40
59	MGM MGM 1047	Rosaleena/Halfway To Heaven (78)	60

SINGLES

58	MGM MGM 992	It's Only Make Believe/I'll Try	6
59	MGM MGM 1003	The Story Of My Love/Make Me Know You're Mine	7
59	MGM MGM 1016	Hey Little Lucy! (Don'tcha Put No Lipstick On)/When I'm Not With You	7
59	MGM MGM 1029	Mona Lisa/Heavenly	6
59	MGM MGM 1047	Rosaleena/Halfway To Heaven	7
60	MGM MGM 1056	Lonely Blue Boy/My One And Only You	8
60	MGM MGM 1066	What Am I Living For/The Hurt In My Heart	7
60	MGM MGM 1082	Is A Blue Bird Blue/She's Mine	7
60	MGM MGM 1095	What A Dream/Tell Me One More Time	7
60	MGM MGM 1108	Whole Lotta Shakin' Goin' On/The Flame	10
61	MGM MGM 1118	C'est Si Bon/Don't You Dare Let Me Down	7
61	MGM MGM 1129	The Next Kiss/Man Alone	7
61	MGM MGM 1137	It's Drivin' Me Wild/Sweet Sorry	8
62	MGM MGM 1152	Tower Of Tears/Portrait Of A Fool	10
62	MGM MGM 1170	Comfy An' Cozy/Unchained Melody	8
62	MGM MGM 1187	I Hope I Think I Wish/The Pick Up	10
63	MGM MGM 1201	Handy Man/Little Piece Of My Heart	10
63	MGM MGM 1209	She Ain't No Angel/Got My Mojo Workin'	10
63	HMV POP 1258	Go On And Cry/She Loves Me	7
68	MGM MGM 1404	It's Only Make Believe/Mona Lisa	5
70	MCA MU 1120	That's When She Started To Stop Loving You/I'll Get Over Losing You	5
70	MCA MU 1132	Hello Darlin'/Girl At The Bar	5
72	MCA MMU 1149	Lead Me On/One's On The Way/You're Looking At Country (with Loretta Lynn)	5
72	MCA MMU 1150	I Can't See Me Without You/I Wonder What She'll Think About Me Leaving/After The Fire Is Gone	5
72	MCA MU 1169	I Can't Stop Loving You/Since She's Not With The One She Loves	5
73	MCA MU 1223	You've Never Been This Far Before/You Make It Hard	5
75	MCA MCA 180	As Soon As I Hang Up The Phone/A Lifetime Before (with Loretta Lynn)	5
75	MCA MCA 197	I See The Want-To In Your Eyes/The Girl From Tupelo	5
75	MCA MCA 211	Don't Cry Joni/Touch The Hand	5

EPs

58	MGM MGM-EP 684	IT'S ONLY MAKE BELIEVE (EP)	60
59	MGM MGM-EP 698	HEY LITTLE LUCY (EP)	60
60	MGM MGM-EP 719	SATURDAY NIGHT WITH CONWAY TWITTY (EP)	60
60	Mercury ZEP 10069	I NEED YOUR LOVIN' (EP)	175
60	MGM MGM-EP 738	IS A BLUEBIRD BLUE? (EP)	60
61	MGM MGM-EP 752	THE ROCK 'N' ROLL STORY (EP)	75

LPs

59	MGM MGM-C 781	CONWAY TWITTY SINGS (LP)	75
60	MGM MGM-C 801	SATURDAY NIGHT WITH CONWAY TWITTY (LP)	75
60	MGM MGM-C 829	LONELY BLUE BOY (LP)	75
63	MGM MGM-C 950	R AND B '63 (LP)	50
68	MCA MUP(S) 342	HERE'S CONWAY TWITTY (AND HIS LONELY BLUE BOYS) (LP)	15
68	MGM C/CS 8100	THE ROCK AND ROLL STORY (LP)	40
69	MCA MUPS 363	NEXT IN LINE (LP)	15
69	MCA MUPS 386	DARLING, YOU KNOW I WOULDN'T LIE (LP)	12
70	MCA MUP(S) 404	I LOVE YOU MORE TODAY (LP)	12
70	MCA MUP(S) 412	TO SEE MY ANGEL CRY (LP)	12
71	MCA MUPS 426	FIFTEEN YEARS AGO (LP)	12
71	MCA MUPS 429	WE ONLY MAKE BELIEVE (LP, with Loretta Lynn)	12
72	MCA MUPS 443	I WONDER WHAT SHE'LL THINK ABOUT ME LEAVING (LP)	12
74	MCA MCF 2547	LOUISANA WOMAN/MISSISSIPPI MAN (LP, with Loretta Lynn)	12
74	MCA MCF 2557	YOU'VE NEVER BEEN THIS FAR BEFORE (LP)	12

(see also Loretta Lynn)

TWO & A HALF

66	CBS 202248	Midnight Swim/Faith	7
66	CBS 202404	Questions/In Harmony	6
67	CBS 202526	The Walls Are High/Love You	6
67	Decca F 22672	Suburban Early Morning Station/Just Couldn't Believe My Ears	15
67	Decca F 22715	I Don't Need To Tell You/Christmas Will Be Round Again	12

TWO HELENS

88	Sharko TUFT-57	Silver And Gold/XV Rhythm/Gun (p/s, with sticker insert)	6
86	Sharko SHARKO 2 TUFT-4	REFLECTIONS IN RED (LP)	10

TWO KINGS

65	Island WI 240	Rolling Stone/SUFFERER: Tomorrow Morning (B-side act. by Frank Cosmo)	18
65	Island WI 249	Hit You Let You Feel It/Honey I Love You (both sides actually by Fugitives)	15

TWO MAN SOUND

78	Miracle M12	Que Tal America/Brazil O Brazil (12")	8

TWO MUCH

67	Fontana TF 858	Wonderland Of Love/Mister Money	5
68	Fontana TF 900	It's A Hip Hip Hippy World/Stay In My World	8

TWO-NINETEEN (2.19) SKIFFLE GROUP

57	Esquire 10-497	Freight Train Blues/Railroad Bill (78)	20
57	Esquire 10-502	I'm A-Lookin' For A Home/When The Saints Go Marching In (78)	20
57	Esquire 10-509	In The Valley/Tom Dooley (78)	20
57	Esquire 10-512	Where Can I Go?/Roll The Union On (78)	20
57	Esquire 10-515	This Little Light Of Mine/Union Maid (78)	25
57	Esquire EP 126	TWO-NINETEEN SKIFFLE GROUP (EP)	30
57	Esquire EP 146	TWO-NINETEEN SKIFFLE GROUP (EP)	40
58	Esquire EP 176	TWO-NINETEEN SKIFFLE GROUP (EP)	45
58	Esquire EP 196	TWO-NINETEEN SKIFFLE GROUP (EP)	50

TWO OF CLUBS

| 64 | Columbia DB 7371 | The Angels Must Have Made You/True Love Is Here | 12 |

TWO OF EACH

| 67 | Decca F 12626 | Every Single Day/I'm Glad I Got You | 6 |
| 68 | Pye 7N 17555 | The Summer Of Our Love/Saturday Morning | 5 |

2.3

| 78 | Fast Products FAST 2 | Where To Now?/All Time Low (p/s) | 4 |

TWO SPARKS

| 72 | Moodisc HM 113 | Run Away Girl/When We Were Young | 6 |

(see also Carl Bryan, Winston Wright)

TWO THIEVES & A LIAR

| 87 | Lyntone LYN 18236/DEB 5 | Shackles And Chains/DUB SEX: Tripwire (flexidisc with *Debris* mag, issue 13) | 8/6 |

ARLYNE TYE

| 59 | London HLL 8825 | The Universe/Who Is The One | 18 |
| 59 | London HLL 8825 | The Universe/Who Is The One (78) | 20 |

TYGERS OF PAN TANG

79	Neat NEAT 03	Don't Touch Me There/Burning Up/Bad Times (p/s)	12
80	MCA MCA 582	Don't Touch Me There/Burning Up/Bad Times (p/s, reissue)	8
80	MCA MCA 612	Rock'n'Roll Man/All Right On The Night/Wild Man (p/s)	5
80	MCA MCA 634	Suzie Smiled/Tush (p/s)	5
80	MCA MCA 644	Euthanasia/Straight As A Die (p/s)	5
81	MCA MCA 672	Hellbound/Bad Times//Bad Times/Don't Take Nothin' ('The Audition Tapes' double pack)	6
81	MCA MCA 692	The Story So Far/Silver And Gold/All Or Nothing (p/s)	5
81	MCA MCA 723	Don't Stop By/Slave To Freedom (p/s)	5
81	MCA MCAT 723	Don't Stop By/Slave To Freedom (12", p/s)	8
81	MCA MCA 755	Love Don't Stay/Paradise Drive (p/s)	5
81	MCA MCA 759	Do It Good/Slip Away (no p/s)	25
81	MCA MCA 769	Love Potion No. 9/The Stormlands (p/s)	4
81	MCA MCAP 769	Love Potion No. 9/The Stormlands (picture disc)	6
82	MCA MCA 777	Rendezvous/Life Of Crime (white vinyl, p/s)	6
82	MCA MCA 777	Rendezvous/Life Of Crime (red or blue vinyl, p/s)	5
82	MCA MCA 777	Rendezvous/Life Of Crime (p/s or poster p/s)	4/5
82	MCA MCA 790	Paris By Air/Love's A Lie (poster p/s or standard p/s with earring) each	5
82	MCA MCAP 790	Paris By Air/Love's A Lie (picture disc)	5
82	MCA MCA 798	Making Tracks/What You Saying (p/s)	4
82	MCA MCAT 798	Making Tracks (Extended Remix)/What You Saying (12", p/s)	8
82	MCA MCA 759	Do It Good/Slip Away (p/s)	4
80	MCA MCF 3075	WILD CAT (LP)	10
81	MCA MCF 3104	SPELLBOUND (LP)	10
81	MCA MCF 3123	CRAZY NIGHTS (LP, stickered sleeve, with bonus 12")	15
84	MCA MCLC 1780	CRAZY NIGHTS (cassette, reissue, with 2 bonus tracks: "The Stormlands" & "Slip Away")	12

(see also John Sykes)

TYLA GANG

| 76 | Stiff BUY 4 | Styrofoam/Texas Chainsaw Massacre Boogie (die-cut printed sleeve) | 5 |
| 78 | Beserkley BSERK 16 | MOONPROOF (LP, yellow vinyl, with insert) | 12 |

(see also Ducks Deluxe)

BIG 'T' TYLER

| 57 | Vogue V 9079 | King Kong/Sadie Green | 140 |
| 57 | Vogue V 9079 | King Kong/Sadie Green (78) | 60 |

BONNIE TYLER

83	CBS WA 3338	Gonna Get Better/Faster Than The Speed Of Night (picture disc)	4
83	CBS/Kellogg's KELL 3	Total Eclipse Of The Heart/ADAM ANT: Puss In Boots (promo freebie, no p/s)	6
86	CBS QA 6867	If You Were A Woman/Under Suspicion (poster p/s)	4
88	CBS CD BEST 1	The Best/The Fire Below/Under Suspicion (CD, card sleeve)	7
88	CBS 651 516-8	Hide Your Heart/I'm Not Foolin'/Under Suspicion/Total Eclipse Of The Heart (3" CD, with adaptor, 5" case)	7

(see also Shakin' Stevens & Bonnie Tyler)

JIMMY TYLER & HIS ORCHESTRA

| 56 | Parlophone MSP 6215 | Fool 'Em Devil/Stardust | 15 |

(Alvin) RED TYLER & GYROS

| 60 | Top Rank JAR 306 | Junk Village/Happy Sax | 12 |

TERRY TYLER

| 61 | Pye International 7N 25119 | A Thousand Feet Below/Answer Me | 6 |

TEXAS T. TYLER

| 59 | Parlophone GEP 8788 | COUNTRY ROUND-UP (EP) | 25 |
| 67 | London HA-B 8322 | MAN WITH A MILLION FRIENDS (LP, as T. Texas Tyler) | 25 |

MINT VALUE £

TOBY TYLER
89	Archive Jive TOBY 1	The Road I'm On (Gloria) (mail-order issue, no'd p/s, 1-sided, 1,500 only)	10
93	Zinc Alloy ZAR CD 9006	THE MAXIMUM SOUND SESSION (CD)	20

(see also Marc Bolan)

TYMES
63	Cameo Parkway P 871	So Much In Love/Roscoe James McClain	8
63	Cameo Parkway P 884	Wonderful Wonderful/Come With Me To The Sea (some in p/s)	18/8
64	Cameo Parkway P 891	Somewhere/View From My Window	8
64	Cameo Parkway P 908	To Each His Own/Wonderland Of Love	8
64	Cameo Parkway P 919	The Magic Of Our Summer Love/With All My Heart	7
64	Cameo Parkway P 924	Here She Comes/Malibu	75
64	Cameo Parkway P 933	The Twelfth Of Never/Here She Comes (existence unconfirmed)	75+
69	Direction 58-3903	People/The Love of Ivy	6
69	Direction 58-4450	If You Love Me Baby/Find My Way	6
71	CBS 7250	Someone To Watch Over Me/She's Gone (featuring George Williams)	6
63	Cameo Parkway P 7032	SO MUCH IN LOVE (LP)	45
69	Direction 8-63558	PEOPLE (LP, mono or stereo)	20
78	London HAU 8516	CAMEO PARKWAY SESSIONS (LP)	15

ROB TYNER & HOT RODS
77	Island WIP 6418	'Till The Night Is Gone (Let's Rock)/Flipside Rock (p/s)	4

(see also MC 5, Eddie & Hot Rods)

TYPHOONS
63	Embassy WB 577	Sweets For My Sweet/LES CARLE: You Can Never Stop Me Loving You	5
63	Embassy WB 589	Surf City/I Want To Stay Here	8
63	Embassy WB 607	Glad All Over/Money	5
64	Embassy WB 642	The House Of The Rising Sun/It's All Over Now	5
64	Embassy WB 660	One Way Love/Sha-La-La	5

(see also Bud Ashton, Ray Pilgrim, Mike Redway, Starlings)

TYPHOONS
81	Bohemian BO 1	Telstar/In Fae A Brothin' (p/s)	5

(see also Ruts)

TYRANNOSAURUS REX
68	Regal Zonophone RZ 3008	Debora/Child Star (with promo only p/s, some with insert)	325/300
68	Regal Zonophone RZ 3008	Debora/Child Star	25
68	Regal Zonophone RZ 3011	One Inch Rock/Salamanda Palaganda (with promo only p/s, some with insert)	325/300
68	Regal Zonophone RZ 3011	One Inch Rock/Salamanda Palaganda	40
69	Regal Zonophone RZ 3016	Pewter Suitor/Warlord Of The Royal Crocodiles	40
69	Regal Zonophone RZ 3022	King Of The Rumbling Spires/Do You Remember (with promo only p/s)	375
69	Regal Zonophone RZ 3022	King Of The Rumbling Spires/Do You Remember	40
70	Regal Zonophone RZ 3025	By The Light Of A Magical Moon/Find A Little Wood	40
72	Magni Fly ECHO 102	Debora/One Inch Rock/The Woodland Bop/The Seal Of Seasons (p/s)	8
82	Old Gold OG 9234	Debora/One Inch Rock (1,000 mispressed with "Beltane Walk" on B-side)	5
91	Tyrannosaurus Rex TYR 1	Sleepy Maurice/1968 Radio Promos (Tyrannosaurus Rex Appreciation Society release, 2,000 only, p/s with card insert)	8
68	Regal Zonophone (S)LRZ 1003	MY PEOPLE WERE FAIR AND HAD SKY IN THEIR HAIR BUT NOW THEY'RE CONTENT TO WEAR STARS ON THEIR BROWS (LP, with lyric sheet, m/s)	60/30
68	Regal Zonophone TA-LRZ 1003	MY PEOPLE WERE FAIR AND HAD SKY IN THEIR HAIR BUT NOW THEY'RE CONTENT TO WEAR STARS ON THEIR BROWS (reel-to-reel tape, mono)	30
68	Regal Zonophone (S)LRZ 1005	PROPHETS, SEERS AND SAGES, THE ANGELS OF THE AGES (LP, with lyric sheet, textured sleeve, mono/stereo)	50/30
69	R. Zonophone (S)LRZ 1007	UNICORN (LP, gatefold sleeve, original with blue label; mono/stereo)	50/30
70	R. Zonophone (S)LRZ 1007	UNICORN (LP, gatefold sleeve, later issue with red label; mono/stereo)	40/25
70	R. Zonophone SLRZ 1013	A BEARD OF STARS (LP, some with lyric sheet)	40/25
72	Fly TOOFA 3/4	MY PEOPLE WERE FAIR AND HAD SKY IN THEIR HAIR BUT NOW THEY'RE CONTENT TO WEAR STARS ON THEIR BROWS/PROPHETS, SEERS AND SAGES, THE ANGELS OF THE AGES (2-LP, reissue)	15

(see also Marc Bolan/T. Rex, John's Children, Dib Cochran & Earwigs, Shagrat)

LLOYD TYRELL
(see under Lloyd Terrell)

TYSONDOG
83	Neat NEAT 33	Eat The Rich/Dead Meat (p/s)	7
85	Neat NEAT 46	Shoot To Kill/Hammerhead (p/s)	6
85	Neat NEAT 4612	Shoot To Kill/Hammerhead/Changeling/Back To The Bullet (12", p/s)	10
86	Neat NEAT 56	School's Out (p/s)	7

TYTAN
82	Kamaflage KAM 6	Blind Men And Fools/The Ballad Of Edward Case (p/s)	15
82	Kamaflage KAMA 6	Blind Men And Fools/The Ballad Of Edward Case (12", p/s)	15
85	Metal Masters METALP 105	ROUGH JUSTICE (LP)	18

JUDIE TZUKE
78	Rocket ROKN 541	For You/Sukarita	6
78	Rocket XPRES 2	For You/Sukarita (reissue, p/s)	6
79	Rocket XPRES 17	Stay With Me Till Dawn/New Friends Again (p/s)	10
82	Chrysalis CHS 2617	I'm Not A Loser/Run On Luck (picture disc)	4
85	Legacy LGY 22	I'll Be The One/Falling (p/s, with postcards)	6
85	Legacy LGYT 25	Love Like Fire (Club Mix)/(Backing Track)/Love Like Fire (12")	7
89	Polydor PZCD 31	We'll Go Dreaming (Single Version)/Everything Will Come/Dangerous Toys/We'll Go Dreaming (Remix) (CD, card sleeve)	7
89	Polydor PZ 46	Let Me Be The Pearl/All They Can Do Is Talk/Love Is Not For Sale (12", p/s)	7

(see also Tzuke & Paxo, Zookie)

TZUKE & PAXO
76	Good Earth GD 12	These Are The Laws/It's Only Fantasies	20

UFFINGTON
| 83 | Plant Life | CHRONICLES OF THE WHITE HORSE (LP) | 10 |

U.F.O.
70	Beacon BEA 161	Shake It About/Evil	20
70	Beacon BEA 165	Come Away Melinda/Unidentified Flying Object	18
70	Beacon BEA 172	Boogie For George/Treacle People	15
71	Beacon BEA 181	Prince Kajuku/The Coming Of Prince Kajuku	15
73	Chrysalis CHS 2024	Give Her The Gun/Sweet Little Thing (unreleased in U.K.)	
74	Chrysalis CHS 2040	Doctor Doctor/Lipstick Traces	6
77	Chrysalis CHS 2146	Alone Again Or/Electric Phase	7
78	Chrysalis CHS 2241	Only You Can Rock Me/Cherry/Rock Bottom (p/s, with frisbee offer)	5
78	Chrysalis CHS 2241	Only You Can Rock Me/Cherry/Rock Bottom (p/s, clear/red vinyl)	6
79	Chrysalis CHS 2287	Doctor Doctor (live)/On With The Action (live)/Try Me (p/s, clear vinyl)	6
79	Chrysalis CHS 2318	Shoot Shoot (live)/Only You Can Rock Me (live)/I'm A Loser (live) (p/s, clear vinyl)	5
79	Chrysalis CHS 2399	Young Blood/Lights Out (p/s, red vinyl)	5
80	Chrysalis CHS 2454	Couldn't Get It Right/Hot 'n' Ready (live) (p/s, clear vinyl)	5
81	Chrysalis CHS 2482	Lonely Heart/Long Gone (p/s, clear vinyl with patch)	5
81	Chrysalis CHS 2576	Let It Rain/Heel Of A Stranger/You'll Get Love (p/s, clear vinyl)	5
81	Chrysalis CHS 12 2576	Let It Rain/Heel Of A Stranger/You'll Get Love (12", p/s)	8
82	Chrysalis CHS 2607	Back Into My Life/The Writer (p/s)	4
82	Chrysalis CHSP 2607	Back Into My Life/The Writer (picture disc)	7
83	Lyntone LYN 12821	Blinded By A Lie (edit)/Diesel In The Dust (edit)/When It's Time To Rock (edit) (flexidisc with/without *Metal Fury* magazine, issue 12)	10/7
83	Chrysalis CHS 2672	When It's Time To Rock/Everybody Knows (p/s, with patch)	4
83	Chrysalis CHS 2672	When It's Time To Rock/Everybody Knows (picture disc)	5
83	Chrysalis CHS 12 2672	When It's Time To Rock/Everybody Knows/Push It's Love (12", p/s)	7
85	Chrysalis UFOP 1	This Time/The Chase (shaped picture disc)	7
91	Essential ESS X 2009	One Of Those Nights/She's The One/Long Gone ('91 Version) (CD)	8
70	Beacon BEAS 12	U.F.O. 1 (LP)	30
72	Beacon BEAS 19	FLYING (LP)	30
74	Chrysalis CHS 1059	PHENOMENON (LP, green label, matt sleeve)	12
77	Chrysalis CHR 1127	LIGHTS OUT (LP)	12
78	Chrysalis CDL 1182	OBSESSION (LP, with poster)	12
82	Chrysalis CHR 1360	MECHANIX (LP, with poster)	12
82	AKA AKP 2	LIVE IN JAPAN 1971 (LP, picture disc)	12

(see also Michael Schenker Group)

LESLIE UGGAMS
58	Columbia DB 4160	The Ice Cream Man/I'm Old Enough	7
58	Columbia DB 4160	The Ice Cream Man/I'm Old Enough (78)	10
59	Philips PB 954	One More Sunrise (Morgen)/The Eyes Of God	6
59	Philips PB 954	One More Sunrise (Morgen)/The Eyes Of God (78)	10
59	Philips PB 999	The Carefree Years/Lullaby Of The Leaves	6
60	Philips PB 1063	Inherit The Wind/Love Is Like A Violin	6
61	Philips PB 1124	Sixteen Going On Seventeen/My Favourite Things	5
60	Philips BBL 7370	THE EYES OF GOD (LP)	15

UGLY CUSTARD
| 70 | Kaleidoscope KAL 100 | UGLY CUSTARD (LP) | 50 |

(see also Hungry Wolf, Alan Parker, Rock Machine)

UGLYS
65	Pye 7N 15858	Wake Up My Mind/Ugly Blues	30
65	Pye 7N 15968	It's Alright/A Friend	15
66	Pye 7N 17027	A Good Idea/The Quiet Explosion	25
66	Pye 7N 17178	End Of The Season/Can't Recall Her Name	30
67	CBS 2933	And The Squire Blew His Horn/Real Good Girl	50
69	MGM MGM 1465	I See The Light/Mary Cilento	600

(see also Steve Gibbons, Balls, Lemon Tree, Move, Trevor Burton)

U.K. BONDS
| 65 | Polydor BM 56061 | The World Is Watching Us/I Said Goodbye To The Blues | 6 |
| 66 | Polydor BM 56112 | Anything You Do Is Alright/The Last Thing I Ever Do | 6 |

U.K. DECAY
79	Plastic PLAS 001	U.K. Decay/Car Crash/PNEUMONIA: Exhibition/Coming Attack (folded p/s)	18
81	Plastic PLAS 002	BLACK EP (p/s, reissue has slightly different p/s)	6/5
81	Fresh FRESH 12	For My Country/Unwind Tonight (foldout card p/s)	4
81	Fresh FRESH 26	Unexpected Guest/Dresden (p/s, some with badge)	6/4
81	Fresh FRESH 33	Sexual/Twist In The Tale (poster p/s)	4
82	C. Christi CHRIST ITS 1	Rising From The Dread/Testament/Werewolf/Jerusalem Over (The White Cliffs Of Dover) (12", p/s with insert)	8

(see also Pneumonia)

U.K.s
| 64 | HMV POP 1310 | Ever Faithful, Ever True/Your Love Is All I Want | 12 |
| 64 | HMV POP 1357 | I Will Never Let You Go/I Know | 12 |

ULTRAVOX

U.K. SUBS

78	City NIK 5	C.I.D./Live In A Car/B.I.C. (p/s, clear, red, blue, green or orange vinyl; also black vinyl)	7/5
79	City/Pinnacle NIK 5/PIN 22	C.I.D./Live In A Car/B.I.C. (p/s, reissue, black vinyl)	4
79	Gem GEMS 5	Stranglehold/World War/Rockers (p/s, red vinyl)	5
79	Gem GEMS 10	Tomorrow's Girls/Scum Of The Earth/Telephone Numbers (p/s, blue vinyl)	6
79	Gem GEMS 14	She's Not There/Kicks/Victims/The Same Thing (p/s, green vinyl)	5
80	Gem GEMS 23	Warhead/The Harper/I'm Waiting For The Man (p/s, brown vinyl)	5
80	Gem GEMS 30	Teenage/Left For Dead/New York State Police (p/s, pink or orange vinyl)	4/5
80	Gem GEMS 42	Party In Paris/Fall Of The Empire (p/s, yellow vinyl)	4
81	Gem GEMS 45	Keep Runnin' (Till You Burn)/Perfect Girl (p/s, blue vinyl)	4
82	Ramkup CAC 2	Party In Paris (1-sided fan club single, no p/s, 500 only)	25
81	Gem GEMEP 45	KEEP RUNNIN' EP (Keep Runnin' [Till You Burn]/Ice Age/Perfect Girl/Party In Paris [French Version])	5
82	Abstract ABS 012	SHAKE UP THE CITY (EP, red vinyl)	4
82	Chaos LIVE 009	LIVE AT GOSSIPS (EP, cassette)	6
79	Gem GEMLP 100	ANOTHER KIND OF BLUES (LP, blue vinyl, with innersleeve)	12
80	Gem GEMLP 106	BRAND NEW AGE (LP, clear vinyl)	10
80	Gem GEMLP 111	CRASH COURSE LIVE (LP, purple vinyl, 15,000 w/export 12" [GEMEP 1])	15/10
81	Gem GEMLP 112	DIMINISHED RESPONSIBILITY (LP, red vinyl with inner sleeve)	10
82	Abstract AABT 300	RECORDED '79-'81 (LP, blue vinyl with free stencil)	10
86	RFB RFBLP 2	IN ACTION (LP, green vinyl, 5,000 only)	10
80s	Link Classics CLINK 4	ENDANGERED SPECIES (LP, red vinyl, 1,500 only)	10

(see also Charlie Harper, Urban Dogs)

U.K. TOUPEE

79	Syrup Of Figs WIG 003	You're Not Bald, Just Taller Than Your Hair/Comb On Over ('gingery' p/s)	50

JAMES 'BLOOD' ULMER

81	Rough Trade RT 045	Are You Glad To Be In America?/T.V. Blues (p/s)	4

PETER ULRICH

90	Cornerstone PTD 001	Taqaharu's Leaving/Evocation (12", p/s)	7

ULTIMATE SPINACH
68	MGM MGM-C(S) 8071	ULTIMATE SPINACH (LP)	40
68	MGM MGM-C(S) 8094	BEHOLD AND SEE (LP)	50

ULTRAFUNK
74	Contempo CS 2001	Living In The City/Who Is He And What Is He To You	5
74	Contempo CS 2023	Freddy Mack/Kung Fu Man	5
75	Contempo CS 2020	Sweet F.A./Use Me	6
76	Contempo CX 14	Gotham City Boogie/Sunrise	6
76	Contempo CX 14	Gotham City Boogie/Sunrise (12")	8
77	Contempo CS 2071	Sting Your Jaws (Parts 1 & 2)	5
75	Contempo CLP 509	ULTRAFUNK (LP)	25

ULTRASOUND
98	Nude NUD 33T	Best Wishes/Kurt Russell/Black Hole (10", p/s)	8

ULTRA VIOLENT
83	Riot City RIOT 25	CRIME FOR REVENGE (EP)	5

ULTRA VIVID SCENE
89	4AD BAD 906	Mercy Seat/Codine/H Like In Heaven/Mercy Seat (LP Version) (12", uncut p/s [most copies die-cut])	20
89	4AD AD 908	Something To Eat/H Like In Heaven (no p/s, freebie, 1,000 only)	8
90	4AD AD 0016	Special One/Kind Of Drag (no p/s)	6
90	4AD UVS 1	Staring At The Sun/Three Stars (12", no p/s, promo only)	8
92	4AD UVS 2	Medicating Angels/Mirror To Mirror (12", no p/s, promo only)	8

(see also Crash)

ULTRAVOX
77	Island WIP 6375	Dangerous Rhythm/My Sex (initially no p/s, later with p/s)	4/8
77	Island WIP 6392	Young Savage/Slip Away (p/s)	5
77	Island WIP 6404	Rockwrock/Hiroshima Mon Amour (p/s)	5
77	Island IEP 8	RETRO (EP, 33rpm)	6
78	Island WIP 6454	Slow Motion/Dislocation (p/s)	5
78	Island 12WIP 6454	Slow Motion/Dislocation (12", p/s, translucent vinyl)	10
78	Island WIP 6459	Quiet Men/Cross Fade (p/s)	7
78	Island 12WIP 6459	Quiet Men/Cross Fade (12", p/s, white vinyl)	10
80	Chrysalis CHS 2441	Sleepwalk/Waiting (p/s, clear vinyl)	6
80	Chrysalis CHS 2481	Vienna/Passionate Reply (p/s, clear vinyl)	8
80	Chrysalis CHS 12-2481	Vienna/Passionate Reply/Herr X (12", p/s)	10
80	Chrysalis CHS 2457	Passing Strangers/Face To Face (p/s, clear vinyl)	5
80	Chrysalis CHS 12-2457	Passing Strangers/Face To Face/King's Lead Hat (12", p/s)	7
81	Island WIP 6691	Slow Motion/Quiet Men (p/s)	4
81	Island DWIP 6691	Slow Motion/Dislocation//Quiet Men/Hiroshima Mon Amour (Remix) (double pack)	6
81	Island WIP 6691	Slow Motion/Quiet Men (cassette)	6
81	Chrysalis CHS 2522	All Stood Still/Alles Klar (p/s, clear vinyl)	5
81	Chrysalis CHS 12-2522	All Stood Still/Alles Klar/Keep Talking (12", p/s)	7
81	Chrysalis CHS 2550	The Thin Wall/I Never Wanted To Begin (p/s, clear vinyl)	5
81	Chrysalis CHS 12-2550	The Thin Wall/I Never Wanted To Begin (12", p/s)	7
81	Chrysalis CHS 2559	The Voice/Paths And Angels (p/s, clear vinyl)	5
81	Chrysalis CHS 12-2559	The Voice/All Stood Still/Private Lives/Paths And Angels (12", p/s, clear vinyl)	7
81	Fan Club	The Voice (live)	10
82	Chrysalis CHS 12-2639	Reap The Wild Wind/Hosanna (12", p/s)	7
82	Chrysalis CHS 2557	Hymn/Monument (p/s, clear vinyl)	4
82	Chrysalis CHS 12-2557	Hymn/Monument (12", p/s, clear vinyl)	7
83	Chrysalis VOX 1	We Came To Dance/Overlook (picture disc)	4
84	Chrysalis UVX 1	Dancing With Tears In My Eyes/Building (12", clear vinyl, g/fold p/s & poster)	7
84	Chrysalis UV 3	Love's Great Adventure/White China (p/s, clear vinyl with booklet)	4
84	Chrysalis UV 3	Love's Great Adventure/White China (picture disc)	4
86	Chrysalis UV 4	Same Old Story/3 (picture disc)	4
86	Chrysalis UV 5	All Fall Down/Dreams (p/s, with free single)	5
77	Island ILPS 9449	ULTRAVOX (LP, gatefold sleeve)	10
77	Island ILPS 9505	HA! HA! HA! (LP, with 7" "Quirks"/"Modern Love" [WIP 6417] & inner sleeve)	12
82	Chrysalis PCDL 1394	QUARTET (LP, marbled picture disc)	12
84	Chrysalis CDL 1459	LAMENT (LP, screen-printed sleeve)	10
84	Chrysalis PCDL 1459	LAMENT (LP, picture disc)	12
85	Chrysalis UTV 1	THE COLLECTION (LP, with bonus 12")	10
86	Chrysalis CCD 1545	U-VOX (CD)	25

(see also Tiger Lily, John Foxx, Midge Ure, Helden)

MIYOSHI UMEKI
58	Mercury MT 188	The Mountains Beyond The Moon/Ooh What Good Company We Could Be (78, with Red Buttons)	8
58	Mercury 7MT 203	Sayonara/On And On	5
58	Mercury MT 203	Sayonara/On And On (78)	8

UNBELIEVABLE TRUTH
90s	label	Buildings (CD)	15

UNCLE DOG
72	Signpost SGP 752	River Road/First Night	4
72	Signpost SG 4253	OLD HAT (LP)	15

(see also Carol Grimes)

UNCLE JOHN'S BAND
80	Ellie Jay EJSP 9422	DIFFERENT GAME (LP, private pressing)	18

UNCOMMUNITY
85	Black Dwarf BDBG 1	Brutality Of Fact/Wall Of Sleep (Soundtrack)/The Price Of Your Entry Is Sin (card sleeve, 525 only, numbered, hand-painted labels, with insert)	25

(see also McCarthy)

UNDEAD
82	Riot City RIOT 7	It's Corruption/Undead (p/s)	5
82	Riot City RIOT 15	VIOLENT VISIONS (EP)	5
84	City 006	KILLING OF REALITY (LP, lyric insert)	15

UNDERDOGS
83	Riot City RIOT 26	EAST OF DACHAU (EP)	5

UNDERGRADS
66	Decca F 12492	Looks Like It's Gonna Be My Year/Calling You	6

UNDERGROUND
69	Major Minor SMCP 5014	BEAT PARTY (LP)	15

(see also Madeline Bell)

UNDERGROUNDS
72	High Note HS 061	Skavito/Savito	12

UNDERGROUND SET
70	Pantonic PAN 6302	UNDERGROUND SET (LP)	35

UNDERGROUND SUNSHINE
69	Fontana TF 1049	Birthday/All I Want Is You	7

UNDERNEATH
86	él GPO 17	THE IMP OF THE PERVERSE (EP)	15
86	él GPO 17T	THE IMP OF THE PERVERSE (12" EP)	15
86	él ACME 9	LUNATIC DAWN OF THE DISMANTLER (LP)	15

(see also Karl Blake, Shock Headed Peters, Lemon Kittens)

UNDERTAKERS
63	Pye 7N 15543	Everybody Loves A Lover/Mashed Potatoes	15
63	Pye 7N 15562	What About Us/Money	15
64	Pye 7N 15607	Just A Little Bit/Stupidity	15

(see also 'Takers, Jackie Lomax)

UNDER THE SUN
79	Redball RR 010	UNDER THE SUN (LP)	35

UNDERTONES
78	Good Vibrations GOT 4	TEENAGE KICKS (EP, pink poster p/s; later white)	10/8
78	Sire SIR 4007	TEENAGE KICKS (EP, reissue)	5
79	Sire SIR 4010	Get Over You/Really Really/She Can Only Say No (p/s)	7
79	Sire SIR 4015	Jimmy Jimmy/Mars Bars (green vinyl, printed PVC sleeve & insert; also p/s)	5/4
79	Sire SIR 4022	Here Comes The Summer/One Way Love/Top Twenty (p/s)	4
79	Sire SIR 4024	You've Got My Number (Why Don't You Use It!)/Let's Talk About Girls (p/s)	4
80	Sire SIR 4038	My Perfect Cousin/Hard Luck (Again) (p/s)	4
80	Sire SIR 4042	Wednesday Week/Told You So (p/s)	4
83	Ardeck ARDS 1	Teenage Kicks/Emergency Cases (2-track reissue, p/s)	4
83	Ardeck 12ARDS 1	TEENAGE KICKS (EP, 12", reissue)	7
83	Ardeck 12ARDS 6	My Perfect Cousin/Hard Luck (Again)/I Don't Wanna See You Again (12", p/s)	7
81	Ardeck ARDS 8	It's Going To Happen!/Fairly In The Money Now (p/s)	4
81	Ardeck ARDS 9	Julie Ocean/Kiss In The Dark (p/s)	4
82	Ardeck ARDS 10	Beautiful Friend/Life's Too Easy (p/s)	4
83	Ardeck ARDS 11	The Love Parade/Like That (p/s)	4
83	Ardeck 12 ARDS 11	The Love Parade/You're Welcome/Crises Of Mine/ Family Entertainment (12", p/s)	7
83	Ardeck ARDS 12	Got To Have You Back/Turning Blue (p/s)	4
83	Ardeck 12 ARDS 12	Got To Have You Back/Turning Blue/Bye Bye Baby Blue (12", p/s)	7
83	Ardeck ARDS 13	Chains Of Love/Window Shopping For New Clothes (p/s)	5
94	Dojo TONES 1	TEENAGE KICKS (EP, 2nd reissue, green vinyl, no'd poster p/s, 2,000 only)	4
79	Sire SRK 6071	UNDERTONES (LP, black & white cover, without "Teenage Kicks" & "Get Over You" & different version of "Here Comes The Summer" to reissue)	10
80	Sire SRK 6088	HYPNOTISED (LP, with cardboard mobile)	10
83	Ardeck ARD 104	THE SIN OF PRIDE (LP, mispressing with different tracks: "Bittersweet" & "Stand So Close")	40

(see also Feargal Sharkey, That Petrol Emotion)

UNDERWATER HAIRDRESSERS
79	Sassoon VIDAL 1	Swimmin' With The Wimmin/Underneath The Driers (p/s, with 'Henna' sachet)	475

(see also Dodo Resurrection)

UNDERWORLD
92	Tomato PLUM 2001	Mother Earth/Mother Earth (FM Mix)/The Hump/ The Hump (Groove Without A Doubt Mix) (12", p/s)	70
93	Boys Own BOIX 13	Mmm... Skyscraper I Love You/Mmm... Skyscraper I Love You (Telegraph 6.11.92)/Mmm... Skyscraper I Love You (Jam Scraper) (12", p/s)	30
93	Boys Own BOIXCD 13	Mmm... Skyscraper I Love You/Mmm... Skyscraper I Love You (Telegraph 6.11.92)/Mmm... Skyscraper I Love You (Jam Scraper) (CD)	30
93	Boys Own Collect 002	Rez/Cowgirl (12", company sleeve)	10
93	Boys Own Collect 002P	Rez/Cowgirl (12", glossy pink sleeve, pink vinyl, white label)	60
94	Junior Boys Own JB 017	Spikee/Dogman Go Woof (12", p/s)	10

(see also Lemon Interrupt, Freur)

UNDISPUTED TRUTH
71	Tamla Motown TMG 776	Save My Love For A Rainy Day/Since I Lost You	7
71	Parlophone TMG 776	Save My Love For A Rainy Day/Since I Lost You (mispress on Parlophone)	10
71	Tamla Motown TMG 789	Smiling Faces Sometimes/You Got The Love I Need	7
72	Tamla Motown TMG 818	Superstar/Ain't No Sun Since You've Been Gone	5
74	Tamla Motown TMG 897	Help Yourself/What It Is	5
76	Whitfield K 16804	You + Me = Love (Parts 1 & 2)	5
76	Whitfield K 16804	You + Me = Love (Parts 1 & 2) (12")	7

72	T. Motown STMA 8004	FACE TO FACE WITH THE TRUTH (LP)	12
72	T. Motown STML 11197	THE UNDISPUTED TRUTH (LP)	12
73	T. Motown STML 11240	THE LAW OF THE LAND (LP)	15
75	T. Motown STML 11277	DOWN TO EARTH (LP)	12
75	T. Motown STMA 8023	COSMIC TRUTH (LP)	12
75	T. Motown STML 12009	HIGHER THAN HIGH (LP)	12
77	T. Motown STML 8029	BEST OF THE UNDISPUTED TRUTH (LP)	12

UNDIVIDED
| 74 | Decca F 13522 | Listen To The World/Harder They Come | 4 |
| 74 | Decca SKL 5168 | LISTEN TO THE WORLD (LP) | 10 |

UNEXPLORED BEATS
| 95 | Unexplored Beats UXB 001 | Skool Beats/Inner Life (12") | 15 |

(see also Black Dog)

UNICORN
| 70 | Hollick & Taylor HT 1258 | Going Home/Another World | 30 |

UNICORN
71	Transatlantic BIG 138	P.F. Sloan/Going Back Home	5
72	Transatlantic BIG 509	Cosmic Kid/All We Really Want To Do	5
71	Transatlantic TRA 238	UPHILL ALL THE WAY (LP)	15
74	Charisma CAS 1092	BLUE PINE TREES (LP)	12

UNIFICS
| 68 | London HLR 10231 | Court Of Love/Which One Should I Choose | 8 |

UNION GAP
(see under Gary Puckett & Union Gap)

UNIQUE
| 83 | Prelude TA 3707 | What You Got Is What Is I Need/What You Got Is What Is I Need (Instrumental) (12") | 7 |

UNIQUES (featuring Joe Stampley)
| 65 | Pye International 7N 25303 | Not Too Long Ago/Fast Way Of Living | 50 |
| 66 | Pye Intl. NPL 28094 | UNIQUELY YOURS (LP) | 80 |

UNIQUES
67	Collins Downbeat CR 002	Dry The Water/I'm A Fool For You	30
67	Island WI 3070	People Rock Steady/I'm Trying To Find A Home (credited to Roy Shirley)	22
67	Island WI 3084	Gypsy Woman/KEN ROSS: Wall Flower	18
67	Island WI 3086	Let Me Go Girl/SOULETTES: Dum Dum	18
68	Island WI 3087	Never Let Me Go/HENRY III: Won't Go Away	18
68	Island WI 3106	Speak No Evil/GLAN ADAMS: That New Girl	18
68	Island WI 3107	Lesson Of Love/DELROY WILSON: Til I Die	18
68	Island WI 3114	Build My World Around You/LLOYD CLARKE: I'll Never Change	18
68	Island WI 3117	Give Me Some More Of Your Loving/VAL BENNETT: Lovell's Special	18
68	Island WI 3122	My Conversation/SLIM SMITH: Love One Another	18
68	Island WI 3123	The Beatitude/KEITH BLAKE: Time On The River (actually "Time & The River")	18
68	Island WI 3145	Girl Of My Dreams/LESTER STERLING: Tribute To King Scratch	18
68	Trojan TR 619	Watch This Sound/Out Of Love	10
68	Trojan TR 645	A-Yuh/Just A Mirage	10
68	Blue Cat BS 126	Girls Like Dirt/GLEN ADAMS: She Is Leaving	12
69	Gas GAS 117	Too Proud To Beg/Love And Devotion	8
69	Nu Beat NB 034	Crimson And Clover/What A Situation	8
69	Nu Beat NB 037	I'll Make You Love Me/Lover's Prayer	8
69	Unity UN 527	The Beatitude/My Conversation	8
69	Trojan TRL 15	ABSOLUTELY THE UNIQUES (LP)	50

(see also Slim Smith, Melodians, Lloyd Charmers, Tommy McCook)

UNIQUES
| 72 | Trojan TR 7852 | Mother And Child Reunion/Corner Hop | 4 |
| 72 | Trojan TR 7866 | Lonely For Your Love/LIONS DEN: Chick-A-Bow | 4 |

(see also Pioneers)

UNITED SONS OF AMERICA
| 71 | Mercury 6338 036 | GREETINGS FROM THE U.S. OF A. (LP) | 10 |

UNITED STATES DOUBLE QUARTET
| 67 | Stateside SS 590 | Life Is Groovy/Split | 5 |

UNITED STATES OF AMERICA
| 68 | CBS 3745 | Garden Of Earthly Delights/Love Song For The Dead Che | 15 |
| 68 | CBS (S) 63340 | UNITED STATES OF AMERICA (LP, mono/stereo) | 30 |

UNITED STATES OF EXISTENCE
| 87 | Bam Caruso OPRA 081 | Gone/PAUL ROLAND: Madam Guillotine (jukebox issue, company sleeve) | 5 |

UNIT 4 + 2
64	Decca F 11821	The Green Fields/Swing Down Chariot	15
64	Decca F 11994	Sorrow And Pain/The Lonely Valley	12
65	Decca F 12071	Concrete And Clay/When I Fall In Love	6
65	Decca F 12144	(You've) Never Been In Love Like This Before/Tell Somebody You Know	5
65	Decca F 12211	Hark/Stop Wasting Your Time	7
65	Decca F 12299	You've Got To Be Cruel To Be Kind/I Won't Let You Down	7
66	Decca F 12333	Baby Never Say Goodbye/Rainy Day	8
66	Decca F 12398	For A Moment/Fables	10
66	Decca F 12509	I Was Only Playing Games/I've Seen The Light	10
67	Fontana TF 834	Too Fast, Too Slow/Booby Trap	15
67	Fontana TF 840	Butterfly/A Place To Go	12
67	Fontana TF 891	Loving Takes A Little Understanding/Would You Believe What I Say? (as Unit)	8
68	Fontana TF 931	You Ain't Goin' Nowhere/So You Want To Be A Blues Player	12

MINT VALUE £

69	Fontana TF 990	I Will/3.30	30
65	Decca DFE 8619	UNIT 4 + 2 (EP)	40
65	Decca LK 4697	UNIT 4 + 2 — FIRST ALBUM (LP)	60
69	Fontana SFL 13123	UNIT 4 + 2 (LP)	50

(see also Roulettes, Tom Sawyer, Capability Brown, Argent)

UNIVERSAL INDICATOR
92	Rephlex TB-303	1-BLUE (12")	20
92	Rephlex TR-606	2-RED (12")	20
93	Rephlex MC-202	3-YELLOW (12")	12
95	Rephlex SH-101	4-GREEN (7", 10" + 12" in bag, all green vinyl)	22

(see also Kosmik Kommando)

UNIVERSALS
| 67 | Page One POF 032 | I Can't Find You/Hey You | 30 |
| 67 | Page One POF 049 | Green Veined Orchid/While The Cat's Away | 12 |

(see also Chris Lamb & Universals, Gidian, Lace, Gary Walker & Rain, Plastic Penny)

U.N.K.L.E.
95	Mo' Wax MW 028	THE TIME HAS COME EP (12" EP, picture disc, later black vinyl)	10/12
97	Mo' Wax MW 069L	Berry Meditation (12", clear etched vinyl promo, sealed/unsealed)	20/10
97	Mo' Wax MW 070	Rock On (12")	15
98	Mo' Wax MW 085CDX	Psyence Fiction (CD, gatefold card sleeve)	18

UNKNOWNS
| 66 | London HLU 10082 | Melody For An Unknown Girl/Peith's Song | 6 |

UNLIMITED TOUCH
| 83 | Prelude PRL 25294 | YES, WE'RE READY (LP) | 10 |

UNTAMED
64	Decca F 12045	So Long/Just Wait	40
65	Parlophone R 5258	Once Upon A Time/I'm Asking You	60
65	Stateside SS 431	I'll Go Crazy/My Baby Is Gone	45
66	Planet PLF 103	It's Not True/Gimme Gimme Some Shade	45

(see also Lindsay Muir's Untamed)

UNTAMED YOUTH
| 79 | Hardcore HAR 001 | Untamed Youth/Runnin' Wild (p/s, 1,000 only) | 15 |

UNTOUCHABLES (Jamaica)
68	Blue Cat BS 137	Prisoner In Love/EDWARD RAPHAEL: True Love	12
68	Trojan TR 613	Tighten Up/ROY SHIRLEY: Good Ambition	8
70	Upsetter US 345	Same Thing All Over/UPSETTERS: It's Over	10
70	Upsetter US 350	Knock On Wood/UPSETTERS: Tight Spot	10
71	Bullet BU 460	Can't Reach You/CARL DAWKINS: Natural Woman	7
73	Bread BR 1113	Pay For The Wicked/Pay For The Wicked – Version (actually titled "Pray For The Wicked")	5

(see also Inspirations, Dave Barker, Leroy Reid)

UNTOUCHABLES (U.K.)
| 80 | Fried Egg EGG 2 | Keep On Walking/Keep Your Distance (p/s) | 5 |

UNTOUCHABLES (U.S.)
85	Stiff BUY 221	Free Yourself/Lebanon (shaped picture disc, various designs)	each 6
85	Stiff BUY 227	I Spy For The F.B.I./Whiplash (picture disc)	5
85	Stiff DBUY 240	What's Gone Wrong/The Lonely Bull/The General/Tropical Bird (double pack, p/s, shrinkwrapped with stickered white label 7" [no p/s])	5

UNWANTED
77	Raw RAW 6	Withdrawal/1978/Bleak Outlook (p/s)	20
77	Raw RAWT 6	Withdrawal/1978/Bleak Outlook (12", no p/s, reissue)	12
78	Raw RAW 15	Secret Police/These Boots Are Made For Walking (p/s)	8
78	Raw RAW 30	Memory Man/Guns Of Love (unissued)	

(see also Psychedelic Furs)

STANLEY UNWIN
| 61 | Golden Guinea GGE 0088-4 | FAIRY STORYS (EP) | 10 |
| 61 | Pye NPL 18062 | ROTATEY DISKERS WITH UNWIN (LP) | 15 |

UPBEATS
58	London HLU 8688	Just Like In The Movies/My Foolish Heart	20
58	London HLU 8688	Just Like In The Movies/My Foolish Heart (78)	15
59	Pye International 7N 25016	You're The One I Care For/Keep Cool Crazy Heart	8
59	Pye International 7N 25016	You're The One I Care For/Keep Cool Crazy Heart (78)	8
59	Pye International 7N 25028	Teenie Weenie Bikini/Satin Shoes	8
59	Pye International N 25028	Teenie Weenie Bikini/Satin Shoes (78)	20

PHIL UPCHURCH COMBO
61	HMV POP 899	You Can't Sit Down (Parts 1 & 2)	20
66	Sue WI 4005	You Can't Sit Down (Parts 1 & 2) (reissue)	18
66	Sue WI 4017	Nothing But Soul/Evad	22
72	Blue Thumb ILPS 9219	DARKNESS, DARKNESS (LP)	15

ROBERT UPCHURCH
| 74 | Phil. Intl. PIR 2652 | The Devil Made Me Do It/Glad You're Mine | 6 |

UPCOMING WILLOWS
| 65 | Island WI 182 | Jonestown Special/SHENLEY DUFFAS: La La La | 18 |
| 65 | Island WI 184 | Red China/SHENLEY DUFFAS: You Are Mine | 18 |

(see also Shenley Duffas)

UPP
| 75 | Epic EPC 80625 | UPP (LP) | 10 |
| 76 | Epic EPC 81322 | THIS WAY (LP) | 10 |

(see also Clark-Hutchinson)

UPROAR

82	Beat The System RAW 1	Rebel Youth/No More War/Fallen Angel/Victims (p/s)	5
83	Lightbeat RAW 2	DIE FOR ME (EP)	5
83	Volume VOL 9	NOTHING CAN STOP YOU (EP)	5
80s	Beat The System BTSLP 1	AND THE LORD SAID LET THERE BE UPROAR (LP)	25

UPSETTERS

65	Island WI 223	Country Girl/Strange Country (both sides actually by Ossie & Upsetters)	25
65	Rio R 70	Walk Down The Aisle/So Bad	12
66	Doctor Bird DB 1034	Wildcat/I Love You So	15

(see also Ossie & Upsetters, Dave Barker)

UPSETTERS

69	Duke DU 11	Eight For Eight/Stand By Me (B-side actually by Inspirations)	10
69	Camel CA 13	Taste Of Killing/My Mob	8
69	Punch PH 18	Return Of The Ugly/I've Caught You	8
69	Punch PH 19	Dry Acid/REGGAE BOYS: Selassie	8
69	Punch PH 21	Clint Eastwood/Lennox Mood	6
69	Upsetter US 300	Eight For Eight/You Know What I Mean (B-side actually by Inspirations)	10
69	Upsetter US 301	Return Of Django/Dollar In The Teeth	5
69	Upsetter US 303	Ten To Twelve/LEE PERRY: People Funny Fi True	10
69	Upsetter US 307	Night Doctor/TERMITES: I'll Be Waiting	10
69	Upsetter US 309	Kiddyo/Endlessly (both sides actually by Silvertones)	10
69	Upsetter US 310	A Dangerous Man From MI5/WEST INDIANS: Oh Lord	10
69	Upsetter US 313	Live Injection/BLEECHERS: Everything For Fun	10
69	Upsetter US 315	Cold Sweat/Pound Get A Blow (B-side actually by Bleechers)	8
70	Upsetter US 317	Vampire/BLEECHERS: Check Him Out	8
70	Upsetter US 318	Soulful I/MILTON HENRY: Bread And Butter	8
70	Upsetter US 321	Drugs And Poison/Stranger On The Shore	10
70	Upsetter US 325	Kill Them All/Soul Walk	10
70	Upsetter US 326	Bronco/One More	10
70	Upsetter US 332	Na Na Hey Hey/Pick Folk Kinkyest	10
70	Upsetter US 333	Granny Show/Version	10
70	Upsetter US 334	Fire Fire/Jumper	10
70	Upsetter US 335	The Pillow/Grooving	10
70	Upsetter US 336	Self Control/The Pill	10
70	Upsetter US 338	Fresh Up/Toothaches	10
70	Upsetter US 342	Dreamland/BOB MARLEY: Version Of Cup	30
70	Upsetter US 343	Sipreano/Ferry Boat	10
70	Upsetter US 346	Bigger Joke/Return Of The Vampire	10
70	Upsetter US 349	Upsetting Station (actually plays "Did Your Grave" by Bob Marley & Wailers)/UPSETTERS: Justice (Instrumental)	25
70	Upsetter US 352	Heart And Soul/Zig Zag	10
70	Spinning Wheel SW 100	Haunted House/Double Wheel	12
70	Spinning Wheel SW 101	The Miser/CHUCK JUNIOR: Do It Madly	12
70	Spinning Wheel SW 102	The Chokin' Kind/CHUCK JUNIOR: Penny Wise	10
70	Spinning Wheel SW 103	Land Of Kinks/O'NEIL HALL: This Man	10
70	Trojan TR 7748	Family Man/Mellow Mood	7
70	Trojan TR 7749	Capo/Mama Look	7
70	Punch PH 27	The Result/Feel The Spirit	10
71	Bullet BU 461	All Combine (Parts 1 & 2)	8
71	Bullet BU 499	Beat Down Babylon/JUNIOR BYLES: Version	7
71	Upsetter US 353	Illusion/Big John Wayne (as Upsetters & King Teddy)	12
71	Upsetter US 361	Capasetic (actually "Copasetic" by Lord Comic)/All Africans (actually "Don't Cross The Nation" by Little Roy)	10
71	Upsetter US 365	Earthquake/JUNIOR BYLES: Palace Called Africa	10
71	Upsetter US 370	Dark Moon/DAVID ISAACS: You'll Be Sorry	8
72	Upsetter US 385	French Connection/Version	8
72	Upsetter US 387	Festival Da Da/JUNIOR BYLES: Version	7
72	Upsetter US 393	Crummy People/BIG YOUTH: Moving — Version	8
72	Upsetter US 394	Water Pump (Parts 1 & 2)	8
72	Randy's RAN 523	Nebuchadnezzer/JUNIOR BYLES: King Of Babylon	7
72	Punch PH 109	Hail To Power/JUNIOR BYLES: Pharaoh Hiding	7
73	Upsetter US 396	Puss Sea Hole/WINSTON GROOVY: Want To Be Loved	8
73	Upsetter US 397	Jungle Lion/Freak Out Skank	10
73	Upsetter US 398	Cow Thief Skank (with Charlie Ace)/7 3/4 Skank	12
73	Downtown DT 499	Black Ipa/Ipa Skank	12
73	Downtown DT 506	Sunshine Showdown/Sunshine Version	12
73	Downtown DT 512	Tighten Up Skank/Mid-East Rock	12
73	Downtown DT 513	Sucky Skank/Yucky Skank	15
74	Count Shelly CS 052	San-San/OSBOURNE GRAHAM: Baby Don't Go	7
74	Dip DL 5031	Enter The Dragon/JOY WHITE: Lady Lady	8
74	Dip DL 5032	Rebels Train/Rebels Dub	8
75	Dip DL 5054	Cane River Rock/Riverside Rock	7
75	Dip DL 5056	I Man Free/King Burnett: Version	7
75	Dip DL 5073	Key Card/Domino Game	7
69	Pama Special PSP 1014	CLINT EASTWOOD (LP)	45
69	Trojan TTL 13	THE UPSETTER (LP)	25
69	Trojan TRL 19	THE RETURN OF DJANGO (LP)	25
70	Trojan TTL 28	SCRATCH THE UPSETTER AGAIN (LP)	35
70	Trojan TBL 119	THE GOOD, THE BAD AND THE UPSETTERS (LP)	35
70	Trojan TBL 125	EASTWOOD RIDES AGAIN (LP)	35
70	Pama SECO 24	THE MANY MOODS OF THE UPSETTERS (LP)	35

UPSETTERS

71	Trojan TBL 166	AFRICA'S BLOOD (LP, actually a various artists collection) 25
71	Trojan TBL 167	BATTLE AXE (LP) 25
74	Trojan TRLS 70	DOUBLE SEVEN (LP) 25

(see also Lee Perry, Ossie & Upsetters, Hippy Boys, Bob Marley/Wailers, Family Man, Tommy McCook, Max Romeo, Melodians, Lord Creator, Dennis Alcapone)

UPSETTING BROTHERS
| 71 | Supreme SUP 229 | Not You Baby/DREAD LOCK ALL-STARS: Baby (Version) . . . . 6 |

UPTOWNERS
| 64 | London HLU 9877 | If'n/Search Is Over . . . . 7 |

URBAN CLEARWAY
| 70 | Torpedo TOR 21 | Open Up Wide (Parts 1 & 2) . . . . 4 |

URBAN DISTURBANCE
| 79 | Rok ROK V/VI | Wild Boys In Cortinas/V.I.P.s: Can't Let You Go (no p/s) . . . . 6 |

URBAN DOGS
82	Fallout FALL 008	New Barbarians/Speed Kills/Cocaine (p/s) 5
82	Fallout FALL 011	Limo Life/Warhead (p/s) 5
88	Fallout FALL LP 12	URBAN DOGS (LP) 10
88	Fallout FALL CLP 12	URBAN DOGS (cassette, with 2 extra tracks) 10

(see Hanoi Rocks, U.K. Subs, Charlie Harper, Vibrators)

URCHIN
| 77 | DJM DJS 10776 | Black Leather Fantasy/Rock & Roll Woman (in promo p/s) . . . . 100 |
| 78 | DJM DJS 10850 | She's A Roller/Long Time No Woman (in promo p/s) . . . . 75 |

(see also A.S.A.P., Iron Maiden)

URCHINS
| 66 | Polydor BM 56145 | I Made Her That Way/'Twas On A Night Like This . . . . 4 |

URIAH HEEP
70	Vertigo 6059 037	Lady In Black/Simon The Bullet Freak (unissued in U.K.)
71	Bronze WIP 6111	Look At Yourself/Simon The Bullet Freak 6
72	Bronze WIP 6126	The Wizard/Gypsy 6
72	Bronze WIP 6140	Easy Livin'/Why 6
73	Bronze BRO 7	Stealin'/Sunshine 6
74	Bronze BRO 10	Something Or Nothing/What Can I Do 5
75	Bronze BRO 17	Prima Donna/Shout It Out 5
76	Bronze BRO 27	One Way Or Another/Misty Eyes 5
76	Bronze BRODJ 1	One Way Or Another/Misty Eyes (promo only p/s, 750 copies) 20
77	Bronze BRO 37	Wise Man/Crime Of Passion 5
77	Bronze BRO 47	Free Me/Masquerade (p/s) 6
78	Bronze BRO 62	Come Back To Me/Cheater 5
82	Bronze BRO 143	THE ABOMINOG JUNIOR (EP, p/s) 6
83	Bronze BROP 166	Lonely Nights/Weekend Warriors (picture disc) 8
83	Bronze BROG 168	Stay On Top/Playing For Time//Gypsy/Easy Livin'/Sweet Lorraine/
		Stealin' (double pack, gatefold p/s) 7
85	Portrait WA 6103	Rockerama/Back Stage Girl (shaped picture disc) 10
88	Castle Comms. CD3-16	URIAH HEEP (CD EP, 5,000 only) 10
70	Vertigo 6360 006	VERY 'EAVY... VERY 'UMBLE (LP, gatefold sleeve, spiral label) 30
71	Vertigo 6360 028	SALISBURY (LP, gatefold sleeve, spiral label) 30
71	Bronze ILPS 9142	VERY 'EAVY... VERY 'UMBLE (LP, reissue) 15
71	Bronze ILPS 9152	SALISBURY (LP, reissue) 15
71	Bronze ILPS 9169	LOOK AT YOURSELF (LP, 'mirror' sleeve) 15
89	Legacy LLP 120	RAGING SILENCE (LP, picture disc) 12

(see also Gods, Head Machine, Natural Gas, Spice, King Crimson, John Lawton, Grand Prix)

URUSEI YATSURA
95	Modern Ind. MIR 001	Pampered Adolescent/BLISTERS: A Dull Thought In Itself
		(burgundy vinyl, p/s, 500 only) 25
95	Ché CHÉ 38	Siamese/Lo-Fi (orange & grey vinyl, p/s) 6
95	Love Train PUBE 08	Kernel/Teendream (p/s, 1,000 only) 6

US
| 70s | Jeff Wayne Music SD 015 | You're OK With Us/Tomorrow (p/s, promo for Johnson Wax) . . . . 10 |

(see also David Essex, Randells)

U.S. DOUBLE QUARTET
| 67 | Stateside SS 590 | Life Is Groovy/Split . . . . 7 |
| 67 | BT Puppy BTS 45524 | Life Is Groovy/Split (reissue) . . . . 4 |

(see also Tokens, Kirby Stone 4)

USE
| 90 | Skakin Street HUP 014 | And Then/Typical Values Grover . . . . 5 |

USERS
77	Raw RAW 1	Sick Of You/(I'm) In Love With Today (p/s, some numbered on rear) 15/7
77	Raw RAWT 1	Sick Of You/(I'm) In Love With Today (12", no p/s) 12
78	Warped WARP 1	Warped 45: Kicks In Style/Dead On Arrival (p/s, 5,000 only, numbered) 8

US FOLK
| 65 | Eyemark EMS 1001 | Funny Old World/Dives . . . . 6 |

U.S. SKY
(see under Sky)

U.S. T-BONES
65	Liberty LIB 55836	No Matter What Shape/Feelin' Fine 8
66	Liberty LIB 55867	Sippin'n'Chippin'/Moment Of Softness 10
66	Liberty LIB 55951	The Proper Thing To Do/Tee-Hee-Hee 10

PETER USTINOV

50	Parlophone R 3612	Mock Mozart (with Anthony Hopkins, Harpsichord)/Phoney Folk-Lore (78)	10
53	Parlophone MSP 6012	Mock Mozart (with Anthony Hopkins, Harpsichord)/Phoney Folk-Lore	10

(see also Peter Sellers)

UT

80s	Catalogue CAT 075/3	Griller/MEKONS: Amnesia (square flexidisc with *The Catalogue* magazine)	5

UTOPIA (Germany)

73	United Artists UAG 29438	UTOPIA (LP)	20

(see also Amon Düül II)

UTOPIA (U.S.)

80	Island IEP 12	I JUST WANT TO TOUCH YOU (EP)	4
77	Bearsville K 55514	RA (LP, with lyric inner & pyramid insert)	10
82	Epic EPC 25207	UTOPIA (LP, with free 5-track EP)	10

(see also Todd Rundgren)

U2

IRISH PRESSINGS

79	CBS 7951	U2: THREE (Out Of Control/Stories For The Boys/Boy-Girl) (p/s, black vinyl)	30
80	CBS 7951	U2: THREE (Out Of Control/Stories For The Boys/Boy-Girl) (p/s, white vinyl)	350
80	CBS 7951	U2: THREE (Out Of Control/Stories For The Boys/Boy-Girl) (p/s, orange vinyl)	90
80	CBS 7951	U2: THREE (Out Of Control/Stories For The Boys/Boy-Girl) (p/s, yellow vinyl)	75
80	CBS 7951	U2: THREE (Out Of Control/Stories For The Boys/Boy-Girl) (p/s, brown vinyl mispressing, fewer than 50 copies exist)	900
81	CBS 12-7951	U2: THREE (12" EP, with no'd sticker, orange CBS sleeve, 1,000 only)	350
81	CBS 12-7951	U2: THREE (12" EP, reissue, plain black sleeve, slightly different labels)	35
85	CBS 40-7951	U2: THREE (cassette, reissue)	20
80	CBS 8306	Another Day/Twilight (Demo Version) (p/s, yellow vinyl)	70
80	CBS 8306	Another Day/Twilight (Demo Version) (p/s, orange vinyl)	90
80	CBS 8306	Another Day/Twilight (Demo Version) (p/s, white vinyl)	150
80	CBS 8306	Another Day/Twilight (Demo Version) (p/s, black vinyl, initially with postcard designed by Bono)	300/45
80	CBS 8687	11 O'Clock Tick Tock/Touch (p/s, yellow vinyl)	50
80	CBS 8687	11 O'Clock Tick Tock/Touch (p/s, orange vinyl)	150
80	CBS 9065	I Will Follow/Boy-Girl (live) (p/s, yellow vinyl)	50
80	CBS 9065	I Will Follow/Boy-Girl (live) (p/s, orange vinyl)	80
80	CBS 9065	I Will Follow/Boy-Girl (live) (p/s, white vinyl)	180
80	CBS 9065	I Will Follow/Boy-Girl (live) (p/s, brown vinyl, less than 50 copies)	900
82	CBS PAC 1	4 U2 PLAY (4 x 7", each in p/s, black vinyl)	90
82	CBS PAC 1	4 U2 PLAY (4 x 7", each in p/s, yellow vinyl)	350
80s	CBS PAC 2	PAC 2 (4 x 7" with p/s in plastic wallet)	50
80s	CBS PAC 3	PAC 3 (4 x 7" with p/s in plastic wallet)	50

UK PRESSINGS

80	Island WIP 6601	11 O'Clock Tick Tock/Touch (p/s)	18
80	Island WIP 6630	A Day Without Me/Things To Make And Do (p/s)	18
80	Island WIP 6656	I Will Follow/Boy-Girl (live) (p/s)	15
81	Island WIP 6679	Fire/J. Swallo (p/s)	12
81	Island UWIP 6679	Fire/J. Swallo//11 O'Clock Tick Tock (live)/The Ocean (live)/Cry (live)/ The Electric Co. (live) (double pack, single p/s)	15
81	Island WIP 6733	Gloria/I Will Follow (live) (p/s)	15
82	Island WIP 6770	A Celebration/Trash, Trampoline And The Party Girl (p/s)	25
83	Island WIP 6848	New Year's Day/Treasure (Whatever Happened To Pete The Chop) (p/s)	6
83	Island WIP 6848	New Year's Day/Treasure (Whatever Happened To Pete The Chop) (p/s, mispressing, B-side plays Martha Reeves, Motown label)	50
83	Island UWIP 6848	New Year's Day/Treasure (Whatever Happened To Pete The Chop)// Fire (live)/I Threw A Brick Through A Window (live)/A Day Without Me (live) (double pack, single p/s, black inners)	15
83	Island 12WIP 6848	New Year's Day/Treasure (Whatever Happened To Pete The Chop)/ Fire (live)/I Threw A Brick A Day Without Me (12", p/s)	12
83	Island IS 109	Two Hearts Beat As One/Endless Deep (p/s)	6
83	Island ISD 109	Two Hearts Beat As One/Endless Deep//New Year's Day (U.S.A. Remix)/ Two Hearts Beat As One (U.S.A. Remix) (p/s, double pack)	15
83	Island 12IS 109	Two Hearts Beat As One (Club Mix)/New Year's Day/ Two Hearts Beat As One (U.S Remix) (12", p/s)	12
84	Island IS 202	Pride (In The Name Of Love)/Boomerang 2 (Vocal) (p/s)	5
84	Island ISP 202	Pride (In The Name Of Love)/Boomerang 2 (Vocal) (picture disc)	30
84	Island ISD 202	Pride (In The Name Of Love)/4th Of July//Boomerang I (Instrumental)/ Boomerang 2 (Vocal) (double pack, gatefold p/s)	12
84	Island CIS 202	Pride (In The Name Of Love)/Boomerang I/4th Of July/Boomerang 2/ A Celebration (cassette)	18
84	Island 12IS 202	Pride (In The Name Of Love)/4th Of July/Boomerang 2 (12",white p/s)	8
84	Island 12ISX 202	Pride (In The Name Of Love)/Boomerang I/Boomerang 2/ 11 O'Clock Tick Tock/Touch (Full Length Version) (12", blue p/s)	18
85	Island ISD 220	The Unforgettable Fire/A Sort Of Homecoming (live)/Love Comes Tumbling/ Sixty Seconds In Kingdom Come/The Three Sunrises (double pack, gatefold p/s)	10
85	Island ISP 220	The Unforgettable Fire/A Sort Of Homecoming (live) (logo-shaped pic disc)	40
85	Island 12IS 220	The Three Sunrises/The Unforgettable Fire/A Sort Of Homecoming (live)/ Love Comes Tumbling/Bass Trap (12", p/s)	8
87	Island CIS 319	With Or Without You/Luminous Times (Hold Onto Love)/ Walk To The Water (cassette)	5
87	Island 12IS 319	With Or Without You/Luminous Times (Hold Onto Love)/ Walk To The Water (12", p/s)	8
87	Island CID 319	With Or Without You/Luminous Times (Hold Onto Love)/ Walk To The Water (CD, gatefold card p/s)	18

U2

87	Island CIS 328	I Still Haven't Found What I'm Looking For/Spanish Eyes/ Deep In The Heart (cassette) 5
87	Island 12IS 328	I Still Haven't Found What I'm Looking For/Spanish Eyes/ Deep In The Heart (12", p/s) 8
87	Island IS 340	Where The Streets Have No Name/Silver And Gold/The Sweetest Thing (p/s, paper label) 6
87	Island CIS 340	Where The Streets Have No Name/Race Against Time/Silver And Gold/ The Sweetest Thing (cassette). 5
87	Island 12IS 340	Where The Streets Have No Name/Race Against Time/Silver And Gold/ The Sweetest Thing (12", p/s with "Silver And Gold" lyric insert) 18
87	Island CID 340	Where The Streets Have No Name (edit)/Race Against Time/Silver And Gold/ The Sweetest Thing (CD, gatefold p/s) 18
88	Island IS 400	Desire/Hallelujah Here She Comes (non-gatefold p/s) 5
88	Island CIDP 400	Desire/Hallelujah Here She Comes/Desire (Hollywood Remix) (CD, picture disc) 15
88	Island CIDP 402	Angel Of Harlem (Remix)/A Room At Heartbreak Hotel/Love Rescue Me (Live At Smile Jamaica Concert London Oct '88) (CD, picture disc) 12
88	Island CIDX 402	Angel Of Harlem (Remix)/A Room At Heartbreak Hotel/Love Rescue Me (live) (3" CD, long box, U.S. import with stickered U.K. matrix number) 20
88	Island U2 PK 1	THE JOSHUA TREE SINGLES (4 x 7"s in PVC wallet with 'obi' band) 18
89	Island CIDP 411	When Love Comes To Town/Dancing Barefoot/When Love Comes To Town (Live From The Kingdom Mix) (with BB King)/God Part II (The Hard Metal Dance Mix) (CD, picture disc) 12
89	Island CIDX 411	When Love Comes To Town/Dancing Barefoot/When Love Comes To Town (Live From The Kingdom Mix) (with Little Richard)/God Part II (The Hard Metal Dance Mix) (as U2 with B.B. King) (3" CD, long box, U.S. import with stickered U.K. matrix number) 20
89	Island ISB 422	All I Want Is You (Edit)/Unchained Melody (in numbered tin box) 15
89	Island CIS 422	All I Want Is You (Edit)/Unchained Melody (cassette) 5
89	Island 12IS 422	All I Want Is You (Full Version)/Unchained Melody/Everlasting Love (12", p/s) 8

89	Island 12 ISB 422	All I Want Is You (Full Version)/Unchained Melody/Everlasting Love (12", p/s, box set with 4 prints)	12
89	Island CIDP 422	All I Want Is You (4.14)/Unchained Melody/Everlasting Love/ All I Want Is You (Full Version) (CD, picture disc)	15
91	Island 12IS 509	Mysterious Ways (4.04)/(Solar Plexus Extended Club Mix 7.01)/ (Apollo 440 Magic Hour Remix)/(Tabla Motown Remix)/ (Solar Plexus Club Mix) (12", p/s, withdrawn)	10
92	Island 12IS 525	Even Better Than The Real Thing/Salomé/Where Did It All Go Wrong/ Lady With The Spinning Head (UVI) (Extended Dance Mix) (12", with giant "Zoo TV" poster)	15
92	Island REAL U2	Even Better Than The Real Thing (Perfecto Mix)/(Trance Mix)/ (Sexy Dub Mix) (12", title sleeve)	8
92	Island CREAL 2	Even Better Than The Real Thing (Perfecto Mix)/(Sexy Dub Mix)/ (Apollo 440 Stealth Sonic Remix)/(V16 Exit Wound Remix) (A440 Vs. U2 Instrumental Remix) (CD)	8
92	Island CIDX 550	Who's Gonna Ride Your Wild Horses (Temple Bar Edit)/Paint It Black/Salomé (Zooromancer Remix)/Can't Help Falling In Love (Triple Peaks Remix) (CD, picture disc, tri-fold digipak with 4 prints, some sealed)	25/18
93	Island CIDX 578	Stay (Faraway, So Close!)/Slow Dancing/Bullet The Blue Sky (live)/ Love Is Blindness (live) (CD, 'The Live Format', foldout digipak)	15
93	Island CID 578	Stay (Faraway, So Close!)/I've Got You Under My Skin (as Frank Sinatra & Bono)/Lemon (Bad Yard Club)/Lemon (Perfecto Mix) (CD, 'The Swing Format')	15
96	Island 12IST 649	Discothèque/Holy Joe (Garage Mix) (12", barcoded p/s, poster)	15
96	Island CID 649	Discothèque/Holy Joe (Garage Mix)/Holy Joe (Guilty Mix) (CD, jewel case, withdrawn)	30
97	Island 12IS 684	Mofo (Mother's Mix)/Mofo (House Flavour Mix)/Mofo (Romin Mix)/Mofo (Phunk Force Mix)/Mofo (Black Hole Dub) (12", die-cut p/s, 2,000 only)	15

PROMO-ONLY SINGLES

80	Island WIP 6601	11 O'Clock Tick Tock/Touch (p/s, 'A' label)	35
80	Island WIP 6630	A Day Without Me/Things To Make And Do (p/s, 'A' label)	35
80	Island WIP 6656 DJ	I Will Follow (Special Edited DJ Version) (1-sided, company sleeve)	50
81	WIP 6679	Fire (Radio Edit) (1-sided, p/s)	35
81	WIP 6733	Gloria (Radio Edit) (1-sided, p/s)	35
84	Island U2 2	Wire/Bad/The Unforgettable Fire (12", black die-cut sleeve)	45
88	Island 12ISX 400	Desire (9.23 Hollywood Remix) (12", 1-sided, custom black p/s, 800 only)	30
88	Island U2V 7	EXCERPTS FROM RATTLE AND HUM (In God's Country [live]/Hawkmoon 269/ Bad [live]/God Part II/With Or Without You [live]) (CD, card gatefold sleeve)	50
88	Island IS 319	With Or Without You/Luminous Times (Hold Onto Love)/Walk To The Water/ With Or Without You (Video) (CD Video, withdrawn, less than 100 copies)	400
89	Island 12 ISX 411	U2 3D DANCE MIXES: When Love Comes To Town (Live From The Kingdom Dance Mix)/God Part II (Hard Metal Dance Club Mix)/ Desire (Hollywood Remix 5.23) (12" EP, custom sleeve)	35
90	Island RHB 1	Night And Day (Twilight Remix)/Steel String Mix) (12", p/s, numbered, 4,000 copies only)	60
91	Island U2-3	OCTOBER 1991: I Will Follow/Pride (In The Name Of Love)/God Part II/ Where The Streets Have No Name) (CD EP, 250 only)	300
91	Island IS 500B	Alex Descends Into Hell (unreleased, test pressings only, pink handwritten label, no p/s)	60
92	Island 12 IS 515B	Lady With The Spinning Head (UVI)/Satellite Of Love (12", unreleased, test pressings only, with press release, white label, no p/s)	80
92	Island 12IS 550DJ	Salomé (Zooromancer Remix 8.02)/Can't Help Falling In Love (Mystery Train Dub 8.20) (12", black die-cut sleeve, 1,000 only)	75
92	Island REAL 1	Even Better Than The Real Thing (The Perfecto Mix)/Even Better Than The Real Thing (Trance Mix)/Even Better Than The Real Thing (Sexy Dub Mix) (12", black die-cut sleeve with title sticker)	25
92	Island REAL 2DJ	Even Better Than The Real Thing (The Perfecto Mix-Radio Edit) (2-sided radio promo, some with p/s)	25/15
93	Island NUMJB 1	Numb (2-sided jukebox issue, large centre hole, no p/s)	15
93	Island NUMCD 1	Numb (CD, 1-track with lyric inner, 250 only)	60
93	Island 12LEM DJ 1	Lemon (Bad Yard Club)/(Momo Beats)/(Version Dub)/(Serious Def Dub)// (Perfecto Mix)/(Trance Mix) (12", double pack, p/s, 1,000 only, numbered with press sheets; discs sometimes sold individually - without outer sleeve - @ £25 each)	90
93	Island LEMCD 1	Lemon (Radio Edit) (CD, 1-track, with lyric inner)	30
95	Island 12 MELON 1	MELON (Salomé [Zooromancer Remix]/Lemon [Bad Yard Club Mix]/ Numb [The Soul Assassins Mix]/Numb [Gimme Some More Dignity Mix]) (12" EP, 800 only)	20
95	Atlantic A 7131	Hold Me, Thrill Me, Kiss Me, Kill Me/Themes From Batman Forever (black vinyl, jukebox issue, large centre hole, no p/s)	12
96	Island PRECD 1	U2 PREVIOUSLY: Lemon/Mysterious Ways/One/Desire/I Still Haven't Found What I'm Looking For (CD, card sleeve)	30
97	Island ISJB 649	Discothèque/Holy Joe (Garage Mix) (jukebox issue, large centre hole, no p/s)	10
97	Island ISD(X) 649 D(J)	Discothèque (Howie B Hairy B Mix)/Discothèque (Hexidecimal Mix)// Discothèque (DM Deep Extended Club Mix)/Discothèque (DM Deep Beats Mix)/ Discothèque (DM Tec Radio Mix)/Discothèque (DM Deep Instrumental Mix)// Discothèque (Single Version)/Discothèque (David Holmes Mix) (3 x 12" in silver title sleeve with pink, orange & blue inners; no barcode or front sticker)	35
97	Island DISCO 1	Discothèque (Radio Edit) (CD, 1-track, jewel case)	12
97	Island	Discothèque (Hexidecimal Remix — Radio Edit) (CDR, 1-track, jewel case)	90
97	Island ISJB 658	Staring At The Sun/North And South Of The River (jukebox issue, large centre hole, no p/s)	8
97	Island 12IS 658DJ	Staring At The Sun (Monster Truck Mix)/Staring At The Sun (Lab Rat Mix)/ Staring At The Sun (Sad Bastard's Mix) (12, p/s)	20

U2

MINT VALUE £

97	Island ISJB 664	Last Night On Earth (Single Mix)/Last Night On Earth (First Night In Hell Remix) (jukebox issue, large centre hole, no p/s)	8
97	Island 12IS 664DJ	Last Night On Earth (First Night In Hell Remix)/Happiness Is A Warm Gun (The Gun Mix)/Pop Muzik (Pop Mart Mix)/Happiness Is A Warm Gun (The Danny Sabre Mix) (12", p/s)	25
97	Island MUZIK 1	Pop Muzik (Pop Mart Mix — Radio Edit) (CD, 1-track, picture disc, jewel case, 250 only)	50
97	Island ISJB 673	Please/Where The Streets Have No Name (live) (jukebox issue, large centre hole, no p/s)	8
97	Island PLEASE CD 1	Please (Single Edit)/Please (Single Version) (CD, plain disc with handwritten title, no inlay, less than 200 pressed)	75
97	Island PLEASE CD 1	Please (Single Edit)/Please (Single Version) (CD, 2-track, yellow graphics on disc, jewel case)	20
97	Island ISJB 684	If God Will Send His Angels (Single Vesion)/Sunday Bloody Sunday (live from Sarajevo) (jukebox issue, large centre hole, no p/s)	8
97	Island 12MOFO 1	Mofo (Phunk Force Mix)/Mofo (Black Hole Dub)/Mofo (Romin Remix) (12", orange label, orange & silver die-cut title sleeve)	30
97	Island 12MOFO 2	Mofo (Mother's Mix)/Mofo (House Flavor Mix) (12", pink label, pink & silver die-cut title sleeve, 250 only)	40
97	Island 12MOFO 3	Mofo (Explicit Mix) (12", 1-sided, stamped white label, plain black die-cut sleeve, 200 only)	125
97	Island 12MOFO 3	Mofo (Explicit Mix)/Mofo (Explicit Mix) (12", 2-sided misspressing [same track both sides], stamped white label, plain black die-cut sleeve)	180
97	Island MOFOCD 1	Mofo (Album Version) (CD, 1-track, card sleeve, export issue [to Mexico])	120
97	Island MOFOCD 2	Mofo (Phunk Force Mix) (CD, 1-track, jewel case, export issue [to Mexico])	120
98	Island SWEET CD 1	Sweetest Thing (CD, 1-track)	12
98	Island SWEET CIDDJ 727	Sweetest Thing/Twilight (Live)/An Cat Dubh (Live)/Stories For Boys Out Of Control (Live) (CD, die-cut sleeve)	45
99	Columbia XPCD 1206	BONO & WYCLEF JEAN: New Day (Edit)/New Edit (Version) (CD, card sleeve)	12
00	Island GROUND CD 1	The Ground Beneath Her Feet/The Million Dollar Hotel Movie Trailer (CD-ROM, card sleeve, blue die-cut slipcase)	40

ALBUMS

80	Island ICT 9646	BOY ('1+1' cassette)	25
81	Island ICT 9680	OCTOBER ('1+1' cassette)	25
83	Island PILPS 9733	WAR (LP, picture disc, beware of counterfeits with ILPS cat. no.)	65
83	Island ICT 9733	WAR ('1+1' cassette)	40
85	Island CID 112	WAR (LP, pink cover lettering)	18
91	Island U2-8	ACHTUNG BABY (LP, with 10 art prints)	30
95	Island MELONCD 1	MELON (REMIXES FOR PROPAGANDA) (CD, 9-track compilation, card sleeve, fan club issue, 20,000 only; some sealed with *Propaganda* No. 21)	35/25

PROMO-ONLY ALBUMS

83	Island U2 1	UNDER A BLOOD RED SKY — A DIALOGUE WITH U2 LIVE (LP, custom sleeve, with cue sheet, numbered, 1,000 only)	50
87	Island U2-6	THE JOSHUA TREE (CD, LP & cassette in black/gold 'pizza' box set)	180
87	Island U2 6-1 — U2 6-5	THE JOSHUA TREE COLLECTION Red Hill Mining Town/Where The Streets Have No Name//Trip Through Your Wires/Running To Stand Still/I Still Haven't Found What I'm Looking For/One Tree Hill//Exit/Mothers Of The Disappeared//In God's Country/Bullet The Blue Sky (5 x 7" set, in black box, 250 only)	350

(The above singles sell for around £20-£25 individually, except for U2 6-2, £35)

87	Island U2 6-1 — U2 6-5	THE JOSHUA TREE COLLECTION (5 x 7" black box set, with U2 6-1 mispressed with "Red Hill Mining Town" both sides, less than 50 copies)	900
87	Island U2CLP 1	THE U2 TALKIE: A CONVERSATION WITH LARRY, BONO, ADAM & THE EDGE (LP, music & interview with Dave Fanning for "The Joshua Tree")	45
87	Island U2CC 1	THE U2 TALKIE (cassette)	20
87	Island BOU2 1	CASSETTE SAMPLER (cassette, 17-track instore 'best of' compilation)	30
88	Island U2-7	RATTLE AND HUM (CD, LP & cassette in flight case with leather tag, 250 only)	1000
89	Island U2 2D1	U2 2 DATE (LP, 8-track hits compilation)	25
91	Island U2-8	ACHTUNG BABY (CD, cassette in 'User's Kit', including map/poster, torch, key ring, spanner & screwdriver in printed green nylon kit bag)	500
97	Island CID U2 10	POP (CD, in large cube-shaped picture box set, with prismatic pen & custom notepad)	250
97	Island POP 1	U2 TALK POP (CD, interview with Dave Fanning, card sleeve)	40
97	Island POP 2	U2 TALK POP (CD, interview with Dave Fanning, card sleeve, same tracks as POP 1)	40
97	Island POP 3	U2 TALK POP (CD, interview with Dave Fanning, card sleeve, same track as POP 1)	40
98	Island CIDDU211	THE BEST OF THE 'B' SIDES 1980-1990 (2-CD, discs marked 'A' and 'B', in card sleeves with gold slipcase)	50
98	Island BXU2 11	THE 'BEST OF' COLLECTION 1980-1990 (14 x 7" singles, 2-CDs, 16-page booklet, in gold box, 2,000 copies only)	375
00	Island MDM CD1	THE MILLION DOLLAR HOTEL (CD, card sleeve)	30

(see also Bono & Gavin Friday, Frank Sinatra & Bono, The Edge, Adam Clayton & Larry Mullen, Passengers, Clannad)

UV POP

82	Pax PAX 9	Just A Game/No Song Tomorrow (individually screen-printed p/s, at least 2 different designs/colours)	each 8
85	Flowmotion FM 007	Anyone For Me/Hands To Me (p/s)	5
85	Flowmotion FM 007	Anyone For Me/Hands To Me (12", p/s, with 4 extra tracks)	10

(see also Cabaret Voltaire)

U.V.X.

93	Magic Eye EYET 10	Elevator (12", purple vinyl)	10

UZI

70	Beacon BEA 152	Morning Train/Where Were You Last Night	5

VACELS
65   Pye International 7N 25330   Can You Please Crawl Out Your Window/I'm Just A Poor Boy 12

VAGABONDS
63   Island ILP 916   PRESENTING THE FABULOUS VAGABONDS (LP) 70
(see also Jimmy James & Vagabonds, Jamaica's Own Vagabonds)

VAGINA DENTATA ORGAN
80s WSNS 004   Cold Meat: Sex Star I/II (12", picture disc)............................. 20
87   Temple TOPY 012   MUSIC FOR HASHASINS (LP) 30

VAGRANTS
66   Fontana TF 703   I Can't Make A Friend/Young Blues.................................... 50

VALADIERS
63   Oriole CBA 1809   I Found A Girl/You'll Be Sorry Someday 550

RICKY VALANCE
60   Columbia DB 4493   Tell Laura I Love Her/Once Upon A Time 6
60   Columbia DB 4543   Movin' Away/Lipstick On Your Lips 8
61   Columbia DB 4586   Jimmy's Girl/Only The Young 8
61   Columbia DB 4592   Why Can't We/Fisherboy 7
61   Columbia DB 4680   Bobby/I Want To Fall In Love 10
61   Columbia DB 4725   I Never Had A Chance/It's Not True 8
62   Columbia DB 4787   Try To Forget Her/At Times Like These 8
62   Columbia DB 4864   Don't Play No. 9/Till The Final Curtain Falls 8
65   Decca F 12129   Six Boys/Face The Crowd 10
76   Valley VLY 001   RICKY VALANCE (EP, no p/s)................................... 25
(see also Jason Merryweather)

VAL & V's
67   CBS 2780   Do It Again A Little Bit Slower/For A Rainy Day 7
67   CBS 2956   I Like The Way/With This Theme................................. 7
68   CBS 3316   This Little Girl/Dreamer 6

JERRY VALE
58   Philips PB 826   Goodbye Now/This Is The Place (with Mary Mayo).................. 6
59   Philips PB 963   The Moon Is My Pillow/The Flame.............................. 12
59   Philips PB 963   The Moon Is My Pillow/The Flame (78) 5
65   CBS 201727   Have You Looked Into Your Heart/Andiamo....................... 5
66   CBS 202347   Dommage Dommage/It's Magic................................ 5
67   CBS 202252   I've Lost My Heart Again/Somewhere 5
74   CBS 80420   JERRY VALE SINGS 16 GREATEST HITS OF THE 60s (LP) 12

RITCHIE VALENS
58   Pye International 7N 25000   Come On Let's Go/Dooby Dooby Wah............................ 120
58   Pye International N 25000   Come On Let's Go/Dooby Dooby Wah (78) 160
59   London HL 8803   Donna/La Bamba 20
59   London HL 8803   Donna/La Bamba (78)....................................... 125
59   London HL 7068   Donna/La Bamba (export issue) 25
59   London HL 8886   That's My Little Suzie/Bluebirds Over The Mountains (tri or round centre) ... 30/20
59   London HL 8886   That's My Little Suzie/Bluebirds Over The Mountains (78) 165
62   London HL 9494   La Bamba/Ooh, My Head 20
66   Sue WI 4011   Donna/La Bamba (reissue, unreleased)
67   President PT 126   Donna/La Bamba (reissue) 6
59   London RE 1232   RITCHIE VALENS (EP, initially triangular centre, later round centre)....... 150/100
61   London HA 2390   RITCHIE (LP) 75
64   London HA 8196   HIS GREATEST HITS (LP) 55
67   President PTL 1001   I REMEMBER RITCHIE VALENS (LP)............................ 20
79   London HA-R 8535   RITCHIE VALENS (LP) 12

CATERINA VALENTE
60   Polydor NH 66816   Malaguena/Secret Love 10
60   Polydor NH 66953   The Breeze And I (Andalucia)/Side By Side 8
60   Decca F 11306   Till/Amour... 5
61   Decca F 11321   Canto De Ossanha/The Breeze And I (Andalucia) 5
63   Decca F 11621   La Malaguena/Together 5
69   Decca F 22881   Hare Krishna/Canto De Ossanha................................ 5
62   London Globe GEB 7001   FRENESI (EP).. 10
63   Polydor EPH 20 282   CATERINA VALENTE (EP) 8
63   Decca DFE 8544   MY HAHWAIIAN MELODY (EP)................................ 7
60   Decca LK 4350   RENDEZVOUS WITH CATERINA (LP) 20
60   Polydor LPHM 46.065   COSMOPOLITAN LADY (LP) 20
61   Polydor LPHM 46.310   CATERINA CHERIE (LP)...................................... 20
61   RCA RD 27216/SF 5099   SUPERFONICS (LP) 18
62   Decca LK/SKL 4508   GREAT CONTINENTAL HITS (LP) 15
63   Decca LK/SKL 4537   VALENTE IN SWINGTIME (LP) 15
64   Decca LK 4604   VALENTE ON TV (LP)....................................... 15
64   Decca LK/SKL 4630   I HAPPEN TO LIKE NEW YORK (LP) 20
65   Decca LK/SKL 4646   VALENTE & VIOLINS (LP) 18

DINO VALENTI
68	CBS 65715	DINO (LP)	30

(see also Quicksilver Messenger Service)

BILLY VALENTINE
55	Capitol CL 14320	It's A Sin/Your Love Has Got Me (Reelin' And Rockin')	50
55	Capitol CL 14320	It's A Sin/Your Love Has Got Me (Reelin' And Rockin') (78)	8

DICKIE VALENTINE (& STARGAZERS)
78s
55	Decca F 10628	Christmas Alphabet/Where Are You Tonight? (78)	8
57	Decca F 10906	Puttin' On The Style/Three Sides To Every Story (78)	8
59	Pye Nixa N 15192	Venus/Where? (In The Old Home Town) (78)	10
59	Pye N 15202	A Teenager In Love/My Favourite Song (78)	10
59	Pye N 15221	One More Sunrise (Morgen)/You Touch My Hand (78)	8

SINGLES
54	Decca F 10346	Endless/I Could Have Told You	30
54	Decca F 10394	The Finger Of Suspicion Points At You (with Stargazers)/Who's Afraid (Not I, Not I, Not I)	30
54	Decca F 10394	The Finger Of Suspicion Points At You (with Stargazers)/Who's Afraid (Not I, Not I, Not I) (78)	8
54	Decca F 10415	Mister Sandman/Runaround	35
55	Decca F 10430	A Blossom Fell/I Want You All To Myself (Just You)	18
55	Decca F 10484	Ma Cherie Amie/Lucky Waltz	15
55	Decca F 10493	I Wonder/You Too Can Be A Dreamer	15
55	Decca F 10517	Hello Mrs. Jones (Is Mary There?)/Lazy Gondolier	12
55	Decca F 10549	No Such Luck/The Engagement Waltz	12
55	Decca F 10628	Christmas Alphabet/Where Are You Tonight?	25
55	Decca F 10645	The Old Pi-Anna Rag/First Love	15
55	Decca F 10667	Dreams Can Tell A Lie/Song Of The Trees	10
56	Decca F 10714	The Voice/The Best Way To Hold A Girl	10
56	Decca F 10753	My Impossible Castle/When You Came Along	8
56	Decca F 10766	Day Dreams/Give Me A Carriage With Eight White Horses	8
56	Decca F 10798	Christmas Island/The Hand Of Friendship	12
56	Decca F 10820	Dickie Valentine's Rock 'N' Roll Party Medley (Parts 1 & 2)	10
57	Decca F 10874	Chapel Of The Roses/My Empty Arms	7
57	Decca F 10906	Puttin' On The Style/Three Sides To Every Story	8
57	Decca F 10949	Long Before I Knew You/Just In Time	7
57	Decca F 10950	Snowbound For Christmas/Convicted	8
58	Decca F 11005	Love Me Again/King Of Dixieland	8
58	Decca F 11020	In My Life/Come To My Arms	6
58	Decca F 11066	Take Me In Your Arms/An Old-Fashioned Song	6
59	Pye Nixa 7N 15192	Venus/Where? (In The Old Home Town)	7
59	Pye 7N 15202	A Teenager In Love/My Favourite Song	7
59	Pye 7N 15221	One More Sunrise (Morgen)/You Touch My Hand	6
60	Pye 7N 15255	Standing On The Corner/Roundabout	6
60	Pye 7N 15294	Once, Only Once/A Fool That I Am	6
61	Pye 7N 15336	How Unlucky Can You Be/Hold Me In Your Arms	6
61	Pye 7N 15366	Climb Ev'ry Mountain/Sometimes I'm Happy	5
61	Pye 7N 15381	Shalom/I'll Never Love Again	6
70	Polydor 56372	Fool Of A Man/Primrose Jill	6

EPs
55	Decca DFE 6236	SWING ALONG WITH DICKIE VALENTINE (EP)	12
56	Decca DFE 6279	PRESENTING DICKIE VALENTINE (EP)	15
56	Decca DFE 6363	ONLY FOR YOU (EP)	12
57	Decca DFE 6427	DICKIE GOES DIXIE (EP)	12
57	Decca DFE 6429	STANDARDS (EP)	12
58	Decca DFE 6529	WITH VOCAL REFRAIN BY DICKIE VALENTINE (EP)	15
59	Decca DFE 6549	BELONGING TO SOMEONE (EP)	12
59	Pye NPL 24120	DICKIE VALENTINE HIT PARADE (EP)	12

LPs
54	Decca LF 1163	PRESENTING DICKIE VALENTINE (10" LP)	30
55	Decca LF 1211	HERE IS DICKIE VALENTINE (10" LP)	25
56	Decca LF 1257	OVER MY SHOULDER (10" LP)	25
58	Decca LK 4269	WITH VOCAL REFRAIN BY... (LP)	20
61	Ace Of Clubs ACL 1082	DICKIE (LP)	15
67	Philips BL 7831	AT THE TALK OF THE TOWN (LP)	20

JACK VALENTINE
55	MGM SPC 8	Dressing Up My Heart/Song Of The Bandit (export issue)	12

VALENTINES (U.S.)
60	Ember EMB S 123	Hey Ruby/That's How I Feel	60

VALENTINES (Jamaica)
67	Doctor Bird DB 1065	Blam Blam Fever/BABA BROOKS: The Scratch	12

VALENTINO
75	Gaiee GAE 101	I Was Born This Way/Liberation	5

ANNA VALENTINO
57	London HLD 8421	Calypso Joe/You're Mine	25
57	London HLD 8421	Calypso Joe/You're Mine (78)	20

DANNY VALENTINO
59	MGM MGM 1049	Stampede/(You Gotta Be A) Music Man	25
60	MGM MGM 1067	Biology/A Million Tears	12
60	MGM MGM 1109	Pictures/Till The End Of Forever	10

MARK VALENTINO
63	Stateside SS 148	The Push And Kick/Walking Alone	8
63	Stateside SS 186	Do It/Hey You're Looking Good	8
63	Stateside SS 233	Jivin' At The Drive In/Part Time Job	18

VALENTINOS
68	Soul City SC 106	It's All Over Now/Tired Of Livin' In The Country	12
68	Stateside SS 2137	Tired Of Being Nobody/The Death Of Love	7
71	Polydor 2058 090	Don't Raise Up Your Hands In Anger/Stand Up And Be Counted	5
68	Soul City SCM 001	THE VALENTINOS/THE SIMS TWINS (LP, with Sims Twins)	25

(see also Bobby Womack)

VALERIE (The Rock 'N' Roll Youngster)
56	Columbia DB 3832	Tonight You Belong To Me/The Man Who Owns The Sunshine	12

DANA VALERY
64	Decca F 11881	This Is My Prayer/Would I Love You Again (Tien Va Pas)	6

VALHALLA
84	Neat NEAT 36	Jack/Still In Love With You (p/s)	5

JOE VALINO (& GOSPELAIRES)
57	HMV POP 283	The Garden Of Eden/Caravan	15
58	London HLT 8705	God's Little Acre/I'm Happy With What I've Got (with Gospelaires)	12
58	London HLT 8705	God's Little Acre/I'm Happy With What I've Got (78, with Gospelaires)	15
60	Columbia DB 4406	Hidden Persuasion/Back To Your Eyes	5

VALJEAN (At The Piano)
62	London HLL 9593	Till There Was You/The Eighteenth Variation	6
63	London HLL 9659	Mewsette (From "Gay Purr-Ee")/Mr Mozart's Mash	6
63	London RE-L 1366	MR MOZART'S MASH (EP)	12

VALKYRIES
64	Parlophone R 5123	Rip It Up/What's Your Name?	18

DIORIS VALLADARES ORCHESTRA
64	Island IEP 703	AUTHENTIC MERINGUE (EP)	10
64	Island ILP 910	LET'S GO LATIN (LP, withdrawn)	30

MARCOS VALLE
68	Verve	SAMBA '68 (LP)	18

RUDY VALLEE
54	HMV 7MC 8	The Whiffenpoof Song/Taps (export issue)	8

VALLEY OF ACHOR
75	Dovetail DOVE 18	A DOOR OF HOPE (LP, gatefold sleeve)	25

(see also Achor, Wine Of Lebanon)

VALLEY YOUTH CHORALE
63	London HLU 9818	The Little Bell/Do You Hear What I Hear	6

FRANKIE VALLI
66	Philips BF 1467	(You're Gonna) Hurt Yourself/VALLI BOYS: Night Hawk	7
66	Philips BF 1512	You're Ready Now/Cry For Me	12
66	Philips BF 1529	The Proud One/Ivy	5
67	Philips BF 1556	Beggin'/Dody	5
67	Philips BF 1580	Can't Take My Eyes Off You/The Trouble With Me	5
67	Philips BF 1603	I Make A Fool Of Myself/September Rain	5
68	Philips BF 1634	To Give (The Reason I Live)/Watch Where You Walk	5
69	Philips BF 1795	The Girl I'll Never Know/A Face Without A Name	5
70	Philips 320 226 BF	You're Ready Now/Cry For Me (reissue)	5
74	Private Stock PVT 1	My Eyes Adored You/Watch You Walk	5
67	Philips (S)BL 7814	SOLO (LP)	15
69	Philips SBL 7856	TIMELESS (LP)	15
75	Mowest MWS 7007	INSIDE YOU (LP)	12
77	Private Stock PVLP 1029	LADY PUT THE LIGHT OUT (LP)	12

FRANKIE VALLI & FOUR SEASONS
71	Warner Bros K 16107	Whatever You Say/Sleeping Man	10
72	Tamla Motown TMG 819	You're A Song/Sun Country	5
72	Mowest MW 3002	The Night/When The Morning Comes	7
73	Mowest MW 3003	Walk On, Don't Look Back/Touch The Rainchild	5
75	Mowest MW 3024	The Night/When The Morning Comes (reissue)	5
72	Mowest MWSA 5501	CHAMELEON (LP)	12

(see also Four Seasons, Wonder Who)

JUNE VALLI
53	HMV B 10568	Crying In The Chapel/Love Every Moment You Live (78)	8
53	HMV JO 324	Why Don't You Believe Me/A Shoulder To Weep On (78, export issue)	8
54	HMV 7M 245	I Understand (Just How You Feel)/Old Shoes And A Bag Of Rice	10
54	HMV 7M 259	Tell Me, Tell Me/Boy Wanted	10
55	HMV 7M 284	Wrong, Wrong, Wrong/Ole Pappy Time	8
56	HMV 7M 347	Por Favor (Please)/The Things They Say	8
59	Mercury AMT 1034	The Answer To A Maiden's Prayer/In His Arms	6
59	Mercury AMT 1048	An Anonymous Letter/Bygones	6
60	Mercury AMT 1091	Apple Green/Oh! Why	6
61	Mercury AMT 1130	I Guess Things Happen That Way/Tell Him For Me	6
62	HMV POP 1062	Hush Little Baby/Afraid	4

VALUES
66	Ember EMB S 211	Return To Me/That's The Way	35

MINT VALUE £

VALVES
77	Zoom ZUM 1	Robot Love/For Adolfs Only (p/s)	15
77	Zoom ZUM 3	Tarzan Of The Kings Road/Ain't No Surf In Portobello (p/s)	12
79	Albion DEL 3	I Don't Mean Nothing At All/Linda Vindalco (p/s)	7

VAMP
68	Atlantic 584 213	Floatin'/Thinkin' Too Much	25
69	Atlantic 584 263	Green Pea/Wake Up And Tell Me (withdrawn)	100

(see also Sam Gopal, Viv Prince, Clark-Hutchinson)

VAMPIRES
59	Parlophone R 4599	Swinging Ghosts/Clap Trap	15

VAMPIRES
68	Pye 7N 17553	Do You Wanna Dance/My Girl	8

ILA VAN
71	Patheway PAT 104	No Good Jim/Flying Solo Tomorrow	4
74	Pye Intl. DDS 108	Can't Help Loving Dat Man/I've Got The Feeling	4

PAUL VANCE
66	Pye International 7N 25387	Dommage, Dommage/Sexy	6

TOMMY VANCE
66	Columbia DB 7999	You Must Be The One/Why Treat Me This Way	6
66	Columbia DB 8062	Off The Hook/Summertime	7

HARRY VANDA
69	Polydor 56357	I Love Marie/Gonna Make It	6

(see also Easybeats)

VAN DER GRAAF GENERATOR
69	Polydor 56758	People You Were Going To/Firebrand	200
70	Charisma CB 122	Refugees/The Boat Of Millions Of Years	35
72	Charisma CB 175	Theme One/W (some with p/s)	25/5
76	Charisma CB 297	Wondering/Meurglys III	8
76	Charisma PRO 002	Wondering (Song)/Wondering (Heroics) (promo only)	25
70	Charisma CAS 1007	THE LEAST WE CAN DO IS WAVE TO EACH OTHER (LP, pink label, original mix, matrices read: CAS 1007 A/B, gatefold sleeve, some with poster)	45/25
70	Charisma CAS 1007	THE LEAST WE CAN DO IS WAVE TO EACH OTHER (LP, pink label, remix, matrices read: CAS 1007 A+G/B+G, gatefold sleeve; some with poster)	30/15
70	Charisma CAS 1027	H TO HE, WHO AM THE ONLY ONE (LP, pink label, gatefold sleeve)	15
71	Charisma CAS 1051	PAWN HEARTS (LP, gatefold sleeve, pink label, some with insert)	25/15
72	Charisma CS 2	1968-71 (LP, pink label)	12
75	Charisma CAS 1109	GODBLUFF (LP, with inner sleeve)	12
76	Charisma CAS 1116	STILL LIFE (LP)	12
76	Charisma CAS 1120	WORLD RECORD (LP)	12
80	Charisma BG 3	REPEAT PERFORMANCE (cassette, with extended "The Clot Thickens")	12

(see also Peter Hammill, Long Hello, Juicy Lucy, Misunderstood)

MAMIE VAN DOREN
58	Capitol CL 14850	Something To Dream About/I Fell In Love (promos in p/s)	20/7
58	Capitol CL 14850	Something To Dream About/I Fell In Love (78)	8

EARL VAN DYKE (& SOUL BROTHERS)
64	Stateside SS 357	Soul Stomp/Hot 'N' Tot	75
65	Tamla Motown TMG 506	All For You/Too Many Fish In The Sea (as Earl Van Dyke & Soul Brothers)	60
70	Tamla Motown TMG 759	Six By Six/All For You (matt black label, later shiny)	8/5
72	Tamla Motown TMG 814	I Can't Help Myself/How Sweet It Is (To Be Loved By You) (& Soul Brothers)	5
65	Tamla Motown TML 11014	THAT MOTOWN SOUND (LP)	100

(see also Van Dykes)

GULLIVER VAN DYKE
69	Vogue VRS 7034	Set Me Free/The Day Has Gone	4

LEROY VAN DYKE
61	Mercury AMT 1166	Walk On By/My World Is Caving In	5
62	Mercury AMT 1173	A Big Man In A Big House/Faded Love	6
62	Mercury AMT 1183	I Sat Back And Let It Happen/A Broken Promise	6
65	Warner Bros WB 5650	It's All Over Now Baby Blue/Just A State Of Mind	6
66	Warner Bros WB 5807	You Couldn't Get My Love Back/Fool Such As I	6
67	Warner Bros WB 5777	Almost Persuaded/Less Of Me	6
62	Mercury MMC 14101	WALK ON BY (LP)	40
63	Mercury MMC 14118	MOVIN' VAN DYKE (LP)	40

VANDYKE & BAMBIS
64	Piccadilly 7N 35180	Doin' The Mod/All I Want Is You	10

VAN DYKE PARKS
(see under 'P')

VAN DYKES
66	Stateside SS 504	No Man Is An Island/I Won't Hold It Against You	15
66	Stateside SS 530	I've Gotta Go On Without You/What Will I Do	20

(see also Earl Van Dyke)

LON & DERREK VAN EATON
73	Apple APPLE 46	Warm Woman/More Than Words (some in p/s)	40/15
75	A&M AMS 7157	Wildfire/Music Lover	5
75	A&M AMS 7178	Dancing In The Dark/All You're Hungry For Is Love	5
73	Apple SAPCOR 25	BROTHER (LP, gatefold sleeve, some with insert)	45/35

VAN DER GRAAF GENERATOR

NICK VAN EEDE
78	Barn 201 4128	Rock'n'Roll Fool/Ounce Of Sense	6
79	Barn BARN 003	All Or Nothing/Hold On To Your Heart	7
79	Barn BARN 008	I Only Want/Dicing	7

(see also Drivers)

VANGELIS
75	BBC BBC 1	Heaven And Hell/Alpha (with or without BBC logo on p/s)	5
76	RCA RCA 2762	Pulstar/Alpha	8
78	RCA PB 5064	To The Unknown Man (Part 1)/To The Unknown Man (Part 2) (p/s)	6
79	RCA PC 5208	Pulstar/Dervish D/Spiral/Alpha (12", p/s)	8
79	Polydor POSP 57	The Long March (Part 1)/The Long March (Part 2)	5
80	Polydor 2059 251	Don't Be Foolish/Doesn't Matter (by Peter Marsh & Vangelis, no p/s)	6
81	RCA RCA 71	Heaven And Hell – 3rd Movement/Alpha	5
84	BBC RESL 144	Frame Of The Day: BBC Snooker Themes (To The Unknown Man) (p/s)	5
88	Arista 111 767	Will Of The Wind/Intergalactic Radio Station (p/s)	5
88	Arista 611 767	Will Of The Wind/Metallic Rain/Intergalactic Radio Station (12", p/s)	7
88	Arista 661 767	Will Of The Wind/Metallic Rain/Intergalactic Radio Station (CD)	10
75	RCA RS 1025	HEAVEN AND HELL (gatefold sleeve)	12
76	Polydor 2489 113	L'APOCALYPSE DES ANIMAUX (LP, TV soundtrack)	25
81	Polydor POLS 1026	CHARIOTS OF FIRE (LP, soundtrack, gatefold sleeve)	20
83	Polydor BOX 1	CHARIOTS OF FIRE (LP, soundtrack, box set)	20
89	Polydor VGPK 1	THEMES (LP, 'display pack')	15

(see also Aphrodite's Child, Forminx, Cosmic Baby, Jon & Vangelis)

VAN HALEN
78	Warner Bros K 17107	You Really Got Me/Atomic Punk	5
78	Warner Bros K 17162	Runnin' With The Devil/Eruption	5
79	Warner Bros K 17371	Dance The Night Away/Outta Love Again	7
79	Warner Bros K 17371P	Dance The Night Away/Outta Love Again (picture disc)	10
80	Atlantic HM 10	Runnin' With The Devil/D.O.A. (reissue, p/s)	4
80	Warner Bros K 17645	And The Cradle Will Rock/Everybody Wants Some	4
85	Warner Bros W 9199T	Hot For Teacher/Little Dreamer/Hear About It Later (12", p/s)	8
86	Warner Bros W 8740P	Why Can't This Be Love/Get Up (shaped picture disc with plinth, stickered PVC sleeve)	10
86	Warner Bros W 8642P	Dreams/Inside (car-shaped picture disc with stand, stickered PVC sleeve)	12
88	Warner Bros W 7816TW	When It's Love/Apolitical Blues (12", silver foldout p/s)	8
88	Warner Bros W 7816TP	When It's Love/Apolitical Blues (12", picture disc)	8
88	Warner Bros W 7816CD	When It's Love/Apolitical Blues/When It's Love (Edit)/Why Can't This Be Love (3" CD, with adaptor, 5" case)	8
89	Warner Bros W 7565CD	Feels So Good (Remix/Edit)/Sucker In A 3-Piece/Best Of Both Worlds (live) (3" CD, gatefold card sleeve)	8

(see also David Lee Roth, Sammy Hagar)

CHERRY VANILLA
77	RCA PB 5053	Punk/Foxy Bitch (title sleeve)	10
78	RCA PL 25122	BAD GIRL (LP)	12
79	RCA PL 25217	VENUS DE VINYL (LP)	15

VANILLA FUDGE
67	Atlantic 584 123	You Keep Me Hanging On/Take Me For A Little While	5
67	Atlantic 584 139	(Illusions Of My Childhood) Eleanor Rigby (Parts 1 & 2)	6
68	Atlantic 584 179	Where Is My Mind?/The Look Of Love	7
69	Atlantic 584 257	Shotgun/Good Good Lovin'	6
69	Atlantic 584 276	Some Velvet Morning/Thoughts	5
67	Atlantic 587/588 086	VANILLA FUDGE (LP)	18
68	Atlantic 587/588 100	THE BEAT GOES ON (LP)	18
68	Atlantic 587/588 110	RENAISSANCE (LP)	18
69	Atco 228 020	NEAR THE BEGINNING (LP)	15
70	Atco 228 029	ROCK 'N' ROLL (LP)	15

(see also Beck Bogert & Appice, Cactus)

MINT VALUE £

VANITY FARE
68	Page One POF 075	I Live For The Sun/On The Other Side Of Life	6
68	Page One POF 100	Summer Morning/Betty Carter	5
69	Page One POF 117	Highway Of Dreams/Waiting For The Downfall	6
69	Page One POF 142	Early In The Morning/You Made Me Love You	5
69	Page One POLS 010	THE SUN, THE WIND AND OTHER THINGS (LP)	25

(see also Avengers)

THIJS VAN LEER
73	CBS 65589	INTROSPECTION (LP)	10

(see also Focus)

TEDDY VANN
60	London HLU 9097	Cindy/I'm Waiting	18

ORNELLA VANONI
67	Decca F 22703	Only Two Can Play/Can I?	7

DAVE VAN RONK
65	Stateside SL 10153	INSIDE (LP)	12

ROB VAN SPYK
70s	private pressing	FOLLOW THE SUN (LP)	40

(see also Stonefield Tramp)

TOWNES VAN ZANDT
73	United Artists UAS 29442	THE LATE GREAT TOWNES VAN ZANDT (LP)	15

VAPORS
79	United Artists BP 321	Prisoners/Sunstroke (p/s)	4

PETER VARDAS
59	Top Rank JAR 173	He Threw A Stone/Checkerboard Love	7
59	Top Rank JAR 173	He Threw A Stone/Checkerboard Love (78)	10

VARDI & HIS ORCHESTRA
62	London HLR 9518	Ballad Of A Soldier Theme/Exodus Theme	6

VARDIS
79	Redball RR 017	100 MPH (EP)	100
80	Castle C QUEL 2/100 MPH	Out Of The Way/If I Were King (plain brown sleeve)	8
80	Logo VAR 1/FREE 1	Let's Go/Situation Negative//100 MPH/Out Of The Way (p/s, double pack)	5
80	Logo VAR 2/VARFREE 2	Too Many People/The Lion's Share//Blue Rock (I Miss You)/Dirty Money (p/s, double pack, with insert)	5
81	Logo VAR 3	Silver Machine/Come On (die-cut sleeve)	5
81	Logo VAR 4	All You'll Ever Need/If I Were King/Jumping Jack Flash (p/s)	5
81	Logo GO 408	Gary Glitter pt. 1/To Be With You (p/s)	7
85	Big Beat NS 103	Standing In The Road/Freezing History (p/s)	5
85	Big Beat NST 103	Standing In The Road/Freezing History (12", p/s)	7
80	Logo MOGO 4012	100 MPH (LP, initially with poster)	15/12
81	Logo LOGO 1026	THE WORLD'S INSANE (LP, with insert)	12
82	Logo LOGO 1034	QUO VARDIS (LP, with free 45 "Situation Negative"/"Jeepster"/"Too Many People"/"Steamin' " [VARFREE 1])	15
83	Razor RAZ 3	THE LION'S SHARE (LP)	12

VARIATIONS (U.K.)
65	Immediate IM 019	The Man With All The Toys/She'll Know I'm Sorry	10
69	Major Minor MM 638	Crimson And Clover/She Couldn't Dance	5

VARIATIONS (U.S.)
75	UK USA 10	Sayin' It And Doin' It Pts I & II	4

VARICOSE VEINS
78	Warped WARP 1	INCREDIBLE (EP, mail-order only, no p/s, 200 only)	60

(see also Perfect Disaster, Orange Disaster, Architects Of Disaster)

REG VARNEY
68	CBS 3742	Jingling Rag/Reg's Rag Kitten On The Keys/Russian Rag/12th Street Rag	6
73	Columbia DB 8977	Best Pair Of Legs On The Buses/Come On And Tickle My Fancy	6
73	Columbia SCX 6518	THIS IS REG VARNEY (LP)	18

SYLVIE VARTAN
65	RCA Victor RCA 1490	One More Day/I Made My Choice	10
65	RCA Victor RCA 1495	Another Heart/Think About You	10
79	RCA PB 1578	I Don't Want The Night To End/Distant Shores (p/s, coloured vinyl)	5
65	RCA Victor RCX 7165	SYLVIE VARTAN (EP)	75

VARUKERS
81	Tempest/Inferno HELL 1	Protest And Survive/No Scapegoat (p/s)	6
82	Tempest/Inferno HELL 4	DON'T WANNA BE A VICTIM (EP)	6
83	Riot City RIOT 27	Die For Your Government/All Systems Fail (p/s)	7
83	Riot City RIOT 29	Led To The Slaughter/The End Is Nigh (p/s)	7
83	Riot City RIOT 31	ANOTHER RELIGION ANOTHER WAR (12" EP)	10
84	Rot ASS 16	MASSACRED MILLIONS (12" EP)	12
83	Riot City CITY 005	BLOODSUCKERS (LP)	10
84	Attack ATTACK 001	PREPARE FOR THE ATTACK (LP)	15

VASELINES
87	53rd & 3rd AGARR 10	Son Of A Gun/Rory Rides Away/You Think You're A Man (12", die-cut sleeve)	20
88	53rd & 3rd AGARR 17	Dying For It/Molly's Lips (p/s)	10
88	53rd & 3rd AGARR 17T	Dying For It/Molly's Lips/Teenage Superstars/Jesus Wants Me For A Sunbeam (12", p/s)	15
88	53rd & 3rd AGARR 17CD	Dying For It/Molly's Lips/Teenage Superstars/Jesus Wants Me For A Sunbeam (CD)	15
90	53rd & 3rd AGAS 7	DUM DUM (LP)	15

(see also Pastels, BMX Bandits)

VASHTI

65	Decca F 12157	Some Things Just Stick In Your Mind/I Want To Be Alone.	35
66	Columbia DB 7917	Train Song/Love Song	22

(see also Vashti Bunyan)

RAY VASQUEZ

61	Starlite ST45-055	Nothing Ever Changes My Love For You/Easy To Love	4
61	Starlite STEP 17	IN THE STILL OF THE NIGHT (EP)	8

DENNY VAUGHAN

53	Parlophone R 3657	Forevermore/Take It Off (78)	8

(see also Nancy Reed)

FRANKIE VAUGHAN

78s

53	HMV B 10435	My Sweetie Went Away/Strange (78)	8
53	HMV B 10498	Too Marvellous For Words/No Help Wanted (78)	8
53	HMV B 10529	Look At That Girl/Send My Baby Back To Me (78)	8
53	HMV B 10550	Bye Bye Baby/False-Hearted Lover (78)	8
53	HMV B 10560	Hey Joe/So Nice In Your Arms (78)	8
53	HMV B 10599	Istanbul (Not Constantinople)/Cloud Lucky Seven (78)	8
54	HMV B 10635	The Cuff Of My Shirt/Heartless (78)	8
54	HMV B 10655	She Took/From The Vine Came The Grape (78)	8
54	HMV B 10712	Jilted/Do Do Do Do Do Do Do It Again (78, with Alma Cogan)	8
54	HMV B 10733	Out In The Middle Of The Night/Crazy 'Bout Ya Baby (78)	8
54	HMV B 10766	My Son, My Son/Cinnamon Sinner (Selling Lollipop Lies) (78)	8
54	HMV B 10783	Happy Days And Lonely Nights/Danger Signs (78)	8
55	HMV B 10845	Too Many Heartaches/Unsuspecting Heart (78)	8
55	Philips PB 423	Tweedlee-Dee/Give Me The Moonlight, Give Me The Girl (78).	8
55	Philips PB 438	Wildfire/That's How A Love Song Was Born (78)	8
55	Philips PB 482	Why Did The Chicken Cross The Road/Something's Gotta Give (78).	8
55	Philips PB 511	Seventeen/Meet Me On The Corner (78)	8
56	Philips PB 544	My Boy Flat Top/Stealin' (78)	8
56	Philips PB 559	Rock Candy Baby/This Is The Night (78)	8
57	Philips PB 775	Kisses Sweeter Than Wine/Rock-A-Chicka (78)	8
58	Philips PB 793	We're Not Alone/Can't Get Along Without You (78).	8
58	Philips PB 865	Am I Wasting My Time On You/So Happy In Love (78)	8
59	Philips PB 895	That's My Doll/Love Is The Sweetest Thing (78)	8
59	Philips PB 896	Honey Bunny Baby/The Lady Is A Square (78)	8
59	Philips PB 913	Come Softly To Me/Say Something Sweet To Your Sweetheart (78)	15
59	Philips PB 930	The Heart Of A Man/Sometime Somewhere (78)	12
59	Philips PB 931	Walkin' Tall/I Ain't Gonna Lead This Life (78)	15
57	Rainbow/Weekend	The Truth About Me (5" 78, mail-order only, some with mailer)	20/15

SINGLES

53	HMV 7M 167	Istanbul (Not Constantinople)/Cloud Lucky Seven	30
54	HMV 7M 182	The Cuff Of My Shirt/Heartless	15
54	HMV 7M 252	My Son, My Son/Cinnamon Sinner (Selling Lollipop Lies)	15
54	HMV 7M 270	Happy Days And Lonely Nights/Danger Signs	25
55	HMV 7M 298	Too Many Heartaches/Unsuspecting Heart	15
57	Philips JK 1002	Garden Of Eden/Priscilla (jukebox issue)	30
57	Philips JK 1014	What's Behind That Strange Door/Cold, Cold Shower (jukebox issue)	15
57	Philips JK 1022	These Dangerous Years/Isn't This A Lovely Evening (jukebox issue)	15
57	Philips JK 1030	Gotta Have Something In The Bank, Frank/Single (with Kaye Sisters, jukebox issue)	15
57	Philips JK 1035	Kisses Sweeter Than Wine/Rock-A-Chicka (jukebox issue)	18
57	Philips PB 775	Kisses Sweeter Than Wine/Rock-A-Chicka	15
58	Philips PB 793	We're Not Alone/Can't Get Along Without You	6
58	Philips PB 825	Kewpie Doll/So Many Women	6
58	Philips PB 834	Wonderful Things/Judy	5
58	Philips PB 865	Am I Wasting My Time On You/So Happy In Love	5
59	Philips PB 423	Give Me The Moonlight, Give Me The Girl/Happy Go Lucky	15
59	Philips PB 895	That's My Doll/Love Is The Sweetest Thing	5
59	Philips PB 896	Honey Bunny Baby/The Lady Is A Square	5
59	Philips PB 913	Come Softly To Me/Say Something Sweet To Your Sweetheart (& Kaye Sisters)	6
59	Philips PB 930	The Heart Of A Man/Sometime Somewhere	5
59	Philips PB 931	Walkin' Tall/I Ain't Gonna Lead This Life	5
60	Philips PB 985	What More Do You Want/The Very Very Young.	5
60	Philips PB 1054	Kookie Little Paradise/Mary Lou	6
60	Philips PB 1066	Milord/Do You Still Love Me? (some in p/s)	8/5
61	Philips PB 1195	Tower Of Strength/Rachel	5
61	Philips BF 1215	Don't Stop, Twist!/Red Red Roses	5
62	Philips BF 1233	I'm Gonna Clip Your Wings/Travellin' Man	5
62	Philips 326 542BF	Hercules/Madeleine (Open The Door)	5
63	Philips 326 566BF	Loop De Loop/There'll Be No Teardrops Tonight	5
63	Philips BF 1280	You're The One For Me/I Told You So.	5
64	Philips BF 1310	Alley Alley Oh/Gonna Be A Good Boy Now	5
64	Philips BF 1373	Susie Q/I'll Always Be In Love With You	6
65	Philips BF 1460	Wait/There Goes The Forgotten Man	7

EPs

56	Philips BBE 12022	FRANKIE VAUGHAN (EP)	12
57	HMV 7EG 8245	MISTER ELEGANT (EP)	12
57	Woman's Own P 117 2E	SWINGIN' (EP)	8
57	Philips BBE 12111	FRANKIE VAUGHAN (EP)	10
59	Philips BBE 12299	HEART OF A MAN (EP)	10
61	Philips BBE 12484	LET ME SING AND I'M HAPPY (EP, also in stereo SBBE 9071)	12/15
61	Philips BBE 12485	LET ME SING AND I'M HAPPY NO. 2 (EP, also in stereo SBBE 9072)	12/15
61	Philips BBE 12486	LET ME SING AND I'M HAPPY NO. 3 (EP, also in stereo SBBE 9073)	12/15

Frankie VAUGHAN

LPs

57	Philips BBL 7198	HAPPY GO LUCKY (LP)	20
58	Philips BBL 7233	THE FRANKIE VAUGHAN SHOWCASE (LP)	20
59	Philips BBL 7330	AT THE LONDON PALLADIUM (LP, also on stereo SBBL 511)	15
61	Philips BBL 7482	LET ME SING — AND I'M HAPPY! (LP, also stereo SBL 629)	15/18
61	Philips BBL 7490	WARM FEELING (LP, also stereo SBBL 645)	15/18

(see also Kaye Sisters, Alma Cogan & Frankie Vaughan, Marilyn Monroe)

MALCOLM VAUGHAN

55	HMV 7M 317	More Than A Millionaire/Take Me Back Again	10
55	HMV 7M 338	With Your Love/Small Talk	12
56	HMV 7M 389	Only You (And You Alone)/I'll Be Near You	8
56	HMV POP 250	St. Therese Of The Roses/Love Me As Though There Were Tomorrow	8
57	HMV POP 303	The World Is Mine/Now	8
57	HMV POP 325	Chapel Of The Roses/Guardian Angel	8
57	HMV POP 381	What Is My Destiny/Oh! My Papa	8
58	HMV POP 419	My Special Angel/The Heart Of A Child	7
58	HMV POP 459	To Be Loved/My Loving Arms	6
58	HMV POP 502	Ev'ry Hour, Ev'ry Day Of My Life/Miss You	6
58	HMV POP 538	More Than Ever (Come Prima)/A Night To Remember	6
58	HMV POP 538	More Than Ever (Come Prima)/A Night To Remember (78)	8
59	HMV POP 590	Willingly/Wait For Me	5
59	HMV POP 590	Willingly/Wait For Me (78)	8
59	HMV POP 687	You'll Never Walk Alone/The Holy City	5
59	HMV POP 687	You'll Never Walk Alone/The Holy City (78)	12
60	HMV POP 600	Oh, So Wunderbar/For Everyone In Love	5
60	HMV POP 600	Oh, So Wunderbar/For Everyone In Love (78)	15
57	HMV 7EG 8272	SINCERITY IN SONG (EP)	12
58	HMV 7EG 8377	SINCERITY IN SONG VOL. 2 (EP)	10
59	HMV 7EG 8453	SINCERITY IN SONG VOL. 3 (EP)	10
60	HMV GES 5785	HELLO MALCOLM VAUGHAN NO. 1 (EP, stereo)	10
60	HMV GES 5793	HELLO MALCOLM VAUGHAN NO. 2 (EP, stereo)	10
60	HMV GES 5799	REQUESTS FOR MALCOLM VAUGHAN (EP, stereo)	10
59	HMV CLP 1284	HELLO, MALCOLM VAUGHAN (LP)	18

ROY VAUGHAN BOOGIE TRIO

50	Jazz Parade B 3	Oval Boogie/Rumble Boogie (78)	10

SARAH VAUGHAN

78s

50	MGM MGM 331	Tenderly/I'll Wait And Pray (78)	7
51	MGM MGM 388	I'm Gonna Sit Right Down And Write Myself A Letter/I'm Thru With Love (78)	8
55	Mercury MB 3205	My Funny Valentine/How Important Can It Be (78)	8
55	Philips PB 455	Summertime/I Cried For You (78)	8
57	Mercury MT 151	Poor Butterfly/Whatever Lola Wants (Lola Gets) (78)	8
57	Mercury MT 176	Band Of Angels/Please Mr Brown (78)	8
58	Mercury MT 198	My Darling, My Darling/Bewitched (78)	8
58	Mercury MT 212	Padre/Spin Little Bottle (78)	8
58	Mercury MT 222	Too Much, Too Soon/What's So Bad About It (78)	10
59	Mercury AMT 1010	Everything I Do/I Ain't Hurtin' (78)	12
59	Mercury AMT 1029	Cool Baby/Are You Certain? (78)	20
59	Mercury AMT 1057	Broken-Hearted Melody/Misty (78)	35

SINGLES

58	Mercury 7MT 198	My Darling, My Darling/Bewitched	7
58	Mercury 7MT 212	Padre/Spin Little Bottle	7
58	Mercury 7MT 222	Too Much, Too Soon/What's So Bad About It	7
59	Mercury AMT 1010	Everything I Do/I Ain't Hurtin'	6
59	Mercury AMT 1029	Cool Baby/Are You Certain?	7
59	Mercury AMT 1044	Careless/Separate Ways	6
59	Mercury AMT 1057	Broken-Hearted Melody/Misty	7
59	Mercury AMT 1080	You're My Baby/Eternally	5
59	Mercury AMT 1087	Don't Look At Me That Way/Sweet Affections	5
60	Columbia DB 4491	Ooh! What A Day/My Dear Little Sweetheart	5
60	Columbia DB 4511	If I Were A Bell/Teach Me Tonight (with Count Basie & Joe Williams)	5
60	Columbia DB 4542	Serenata/Let's	5
63	Columbia DB 4990	My Favourite Things/Great Day	5
69	Mercury AMT 1107	The Boy From Ipanema/The Fever (p/s)	5

EPs

56	London RE-U 1065	SARAH VAUGHAN SINGS (EP, with John Kirby's Orchestra)	15
57	Emarcy YEP 9507	SARAH VAUGHAN (EP)	10
57	Mercury MEP 9511	SARAH VAUGHAN HIT PARADE (EP)	10
57	Mercury MEP 9519	SARAH VAUGHAN HIT PARADE NO. 2 (EP)	10
59	Mercury ZEP 10011	SONGS FROM SARAH (EP)	10
59	Mercury ZEP 10030	AFTER HOURS AT THE LONDON HOUSE (EP)	10
59	Mercury ZEP 10041	SARAH WITH FEELING (EP)	10
60	Mercury ZEP 10054	SMOOTH SARAH (EP)	10
60	Mercury ZEP 10087	LIVE FOR LOVE (EP, also stereo SEZ 19006)	10/15
62	Mercury ZEP 10115	NO COUNT BLUES (EP, also stereo SEZ 19023)	10/15

LPs

55	Oriole/Mercury MG 26005	IMAGES (10" LP)	20
56	London HB-U 1049	SARAH VAUGHAN SINGS (10" LP, with John Kirby & His Orchestra)	20
56	Emarcy EJL 100	IN THE LAND OF HI FI (10" LP)	20
56	Philips BBL 7082	SARAH VAUGHAN (LP)	15
56	Mercury MPT 7503	MAKE YOURSELF COMFORTABLE (10" LP)	20
57	Mercury MPT 7518	IMAGES (10" LP, reissue)	15
57	Emarcy EJL 1258	SASSY (LP)	15

MINT VALUE £

57	Mercury MPL 6522	SINGS GREAT SONGS FROM HIT SHOWS PART 1 (LP)	15
57	Philips BBL 7165	LINGER AWHILE (LP)	15
57	Mercury MPL 6523	SINGS GREAT SONGS FROM HIT SHOWS PART 2 (LP)	15
57	Mercury MPL 6525	SINGS GEORGE GERSHWIN VOL. 1 (LP)	12
57	Mercury MPL 6527	SINGS GEORGE GERSHWIN VOL. 2 (LP)	12
58	Mercury MPL 6532	WONDERFUL SARAH (LP)	15
58	Emarcy EJL 1273	SWINGIN' EASY (LP)	12
58	Mercury MPL 6540	IN ROMANTIC MOOD (LP)	15
58	Mercury MPL 6542	AT MISTER KELLY'S (LP)	15
59	Mercury CMS 18011	SINGS GEORGE GERSHWIN VOL. 1 (LP, stereo reissue of MPL 6525)	15
59	Mercury CMS 18012	SINGS GEORGE GERSHWIN VOL. 2 (LP, stereo reissue of MPL 6527)	15
59	Mercury MMC 14001	AFTER HOURS AT THE LONDON HOUSE (LP)	12
59	Mercury MMC 14011	VAUGHAN AND VIOLINS (LP, also stereo CMS 18003)	12/15
60	Mercury MMC 14021	NO COUNT SARAH (LP)	12
60	Mercury MMC 14024	GREAT SONGS FROM HIT SHOWS PART 1 (LP, reissue of MPT 6522)	12
60	Mercury CMS 18019	GREAT SONGS FROM HIT SHOWS PART 1 (LP, stereo reissue of MPT 6522)	12
60	Mercury MMC 14026	GREAT SONGS FROM HIT SHOWS PART 2 (LP, reissue of MPT 6523)	12
60	Mercury CMS 18023	GREAT SONGS FROM HIT SHOWS PART 2 (LP, stereo reissue of MPT 6523)	12
60	Columbia 33SX 1252	DREAMY (LP, also stereo SCX 3324)	12/15
61	Mercury MMC 14059	CLOSE TO YOU (LP, also stereo CMS 18040)	12/15
62	Columbia 33SX 1340	THE DIVINE ONE (LP, also stereo SCX 3390)	12/15
62	Columbia 33SX 1360	COUNT BASIE — SARAH VAUGHAN (LP, also stereo SCX 3403)	12/15
64	Mercury 20011 MCL	SASSY SWINGS THE TIVOLI (LP)	12
65	Mercury 20042 MCL	MY HEART SINGS (LP)	12
60s	Mercury MG 25188	THE DIVINE SARAH (LP)	12

SARAH VAUGHAN & BILLY ECKSTINE

57	Mercury MT 164	Passing Strangers/The Door Is Open (78)	8
59	Mercury AMT 1020	Alexander's Ragtime Band/No Limit	6
59	Mercury AMT 1020	Alexander's Ragtime Band/No Limit (78)	15
59	Mercury AMT 1071	Passing Strangers/SARAH VAUGHAN: Smooth Operator	7
69	Mercury MF 1082	Passing Strangers/Always	4
56	MGM MGM-EP 561	DEDICATED TO YOU (EP)	10
59	MGM MGM-EP 690	BILLY ECKSTINE AND SARAH VAUGHAN (EP)	10
59	Mercury 10025 MCE	PASSING STRANGERS (EP)	10
60	Mercury 10027 MCE	TOGETHER AGAIN (EP)	10
61	Mercury ZEP 10108	BEST OF BERLIN VOL. 1 (EP, also stereo SEZ 19016)	10/15
58	Mercury MPL 6530	THE BEST OF IRVING BERLIN (LP)	18
60	Mercury MMC 14035	THE BEST OF IRVING BERLIN (LP, reissue)	12

(see also Billy Eckstine)

BILLY VAUGHN (& HIS ORCHESTRA)

78s

55	London HL 8112	Melody Of Love/Joy Ride (78)	8
55	London HLD 8205	The Shifting Whispering Sands (Parts 1 & 2) (with Ken Nordine) (78)	7
56	London HLD 8238	Theme From 'The Threepenny Opera'/I'd Give A Million Tomorrows (78)	6
56	London HLD 8319	When The Lilac Blooms Again/Autumn Concerto (78)	6
56	London HLD 8342	Petticoats From Portugal/La La Colette (78)	8
57	London HLD 8417	The Ship That Never Sailed/Little Boy Blue (78)	8
57	London HLD 8511	Johnny Tremain/Naughty Annetta (78)	12
57	London HLD 8522	Raunchy/Sail Along Silvery Moon (78)	10
58	London HLD 8612	Tumbling Tumbleweeds/Trying (78)	12
58	London HLD 8680	Sail Along Silvery Moon/The Singing Hills (78)	10
58	London HLD 8703	La Paloma/Here Is My Love (78)	15
58	London HLD 8772	Cimarron (Roll On)/You're My Baby Doll (78)	20
59	London HLD 8797	Blue Hawaii/Tico Tico (78)	25
59	London HLD 8859	Your Cheatin' Heart/Lights Out (78)	25
59	London HLD 8920	All Nite Long/Blues Stay Away From Me (78)	30
59	London HLD 8952	Morgen (One More Sunrise)/Sweet Leilani (78)	25
59	London HLD 8996	(It's No) Sin/After Hours (78)	25

SINGLES

55	London HL 8112	Melody Of Love/Joy Ride (gold label print)	30
55	London HLD 8205	The Shifting Whispering Sands (Parts 1 & 2) (with Ken Nordine) (gold print)	15
56	London HLD 8238	Theme From 'The Threepenny Opera'/I'd Give A Million Tomorrows (gold label print, later with silver label print)	15/10
56	London HLD 8319	When The Lilac Blooms Again/Autumn Concerto (gold print, later silver)	15/8
56	London HLD 8342	Petticoats From Portugal/La La Colette (gold print, later silver)	15/8
57	London HLD 8417	The Ship That Never Sailed/Little Boy Blue (with Ken Nordine)	12
57	London HLD 8511	Johnny Tremain/Naughty Annetta (as Billy Vaughn's Orchestra & Chorus)	12
57	London HLD 8522	Raunchy/Sail Along Silvery Moon	10
58	London HLD 8612	Tumbling Tumbleweeds/Trying	10
58	London HLD 8680	Sail Along Silvery Moon/The Singing Hills	6
58	London HLD 8703	La Paloma/Here Is My Love	6
58	London HLD 8772	Cimarron (Roll On)/You're My Baby Doll	6
59	London HLD 8797	Blue Hawaii/Tico Tico	6
59	London HLD 8859	Your Cheatin' Heart/Lights Out	6
59	London HLD 8920	All Nite Long/Blues Stay Away From Me	6
59	London HLD 8952	Morgen (One More Sunrise)/Sweet Leilani	6
59	London HLD 8996	(It's No) Sin/After Hours	6
60	London HLD 9152	Look For A Star/He'll Have To Go	6
61	London HLD 9259	Theme From 'The Sundowners'/Old Cape Cod	6
61	London HLD 9279	Wheels/Orange Blossom Special	6
61	London HLD 9380	Blue Tomorrow/Red Wing	6
61	London HLD 9423	Berlin Melody/Theme From 'Come September'	6
62	London HLD 9507	Everybody's Twisting Down In Mexico/Melody In The Night	6
62	London HLD 9541	Chapel By The Sea/A Lover's Guitar	6
62	London HLD 9568	Continental Melody/Born To Be With You	6

Billy VAUGHN

62	London HLD 9578	A Swingin' Safari/Summertime	6
63	London HLD 9675	Meditation/Release Me	6
63	London HLD 9735	Happy Cowboy/Sukiyaki	6
64	London HLD 9865	Blue Tango/Boss	6

EXPORT SINGLES

60	London HL 7093	Red Sails In The Sunset/Harbour Lights	10
60	London HL 7094	Brazil/Perfidia	10
60	London HLD 7107	La Paloma/Green Fields	10

EPs

57	London RE-D 1083	THE GOLDEN INSTRUMENTALS NO. 1 (EP)	10
57	London RE-D 1084	THE GOLDEN INSTRUMENTALS NO. 2 (EP)	10
59	London RE-D 1189	SAIL ALONG SILVERY MOON (EP)	10
60	London RE-D 1248	THEMES FROM BILLY VAUGHN (EP)	8
61	London RE-D 1285	BILLY VAUGHN (EP)	8
62	London RE-D 1329	BILLY VAUGHN PLAYS THE HITS NO. 1 (EP)	8
62	London RE-D 1330	BILLY VAUGHN PLAYS THE HITS NO. 2 (EP)	8
63	London RE-D 1352	SWINGIN' SAFARI (EP)	10
63	London RE-D 1380	HAPPY COWBOY (EP)	8
63	London RE-D 1395	SIXTY-TWO'S GREATEST HITS (EP)	8
65	Dot DEP 20004	THE GREAT BILLY VAUGHN (EP)	8

LPs

56	London HB-D 1048	MELODIES OF LOVE (10" LP)	25
57	London HA-D 2025	THE GOLDEN INSTRUMENTALS (LP, also stereo SAH-D 6018)	15/20
57	London HA-D 2045	SWEET MUSIC AND MEMORIES (LP)	12
57	London HA-D 2072	INSTRUMENTAL SOUVENIRS (LP)	12
58	London HA-D 2090	MELODIES IN GOLD (LP)	12
58	London HA-D 2120	SAIL ALONG SILVERY MOON (LP, also stereo SAH-D 6037)	12/15
58	London HA-D 2129	PLAYS THE MILLION SELLERS (LP, also stereo SAH-D 6003)	12/15
59	London HA-D 2151	LA PALOMA (LP, also stereo SAH-D 6009)	12/15
59	London HA-D 2178	BILLY VAUGHN PLAYS (LP)	12
59	London HA-D 2195	CHRISTMAS CAROLS (LP)	12
59	London HA-D 2201	BLUE HAWAII (LP)	12
60	London HA-D 2209	GOLDEN HITS (LP, also stereo SAH-D 6056)	12/15
60	London HA-D 2241	GOLDEN SAXOPHONES (LP, also stereo SAH-D 6070)	12/15
60	London HA-D 2251	MUSIC FOR THE GOLDEN HOURS (LP, also stereo SAH-D 6075)	12/15
60	London HA-D 2256	A SUMMER PLACE (LP, also stereo SAH-D 6080)	12/15
60	London HA-D 2278	LINGER AWHILE (LP, also stereo SAH-D 6096)	12/15
60	London HA-D 2292	LOOK FOR A STAR (LP, also stereo SAH-D 6104)	12/15
61	London HA-D 2304	GREAT GOLDEN HITS (LP, also stereo SAH-D 6114)	12/15
61	London HA-D 2324	HIT PARADE (LP, also stereo SAH-D 6127)	12/15
62	London SAH-D 6228	GREATEST STRING BAND HITS (LP, stereo)	15

(see also Hilltoppers, Ken Nordine)

MORRIS VAUGHN

69	Fontana TF 1031	My Love Keeps Growing/Make It Look Good	15

VAZZ

85	CRV 5401	Breath/Violent Silence (in folder & bag with postcards & inserts)	5

V.D.U.'s

79	Thin Sliced	Don't Cry For Me/Little White Lie/Holiday Romances (p/s)	6

(see also Boys Wonder)

CHUCK VEDDER

59	London HL 8951	Spanky Boy/Arriba	25
59	London HL 8951	Spanky Boy/Arriba (78)	35

BOBBY VEE

SINGLES

60	London HLG 9179	Devil Or Angel/Since I Met You, Baby	20
61	London HLG 9255	Rubber Ball/Everyday	8
61	London HLG 9316	More Than I Can Say/Stayin' In	6
61	London HLG 9389	How Many Tears/Baby Face	7
61	London HLG 9438	Take Good Care Of My Baby/Bashful Bob	6
61	London HLG 7111	Take Good Care Of My Baby/Bashful Bob (export issue)	25
61	London HLG 9459	Love's Made A Fool Of You/Susie-Q	12
61	London HLG 9470	Run To Him/Walkin' With My Angel	6
62	Liberty LIB 55388	Run To Him/Walkin' With My Angel (reissue)	8
62	Liberty LIB 55419	Please Don't Ask About Barbara/I Can't Say Goodbye	7
62	Liberty LIB 55451	Sharing You/At A Time Like This	6
62	Liberty LIB 10046	A Forever Kind Of Love/Remember Me, Huh?	7
63	Liberty LIB 10069	The Night Has A Thousand Eyes/Tenderly Yours	6
63	Liberty LIB 55530	Bobby Tomorrow/Charms	6
63	Liberty LIB 10124	Stranger In Your Arms/Yesterday And You	6
64	Liberty LIB 10141	She's Sorry/Buddy's Song	10
64	Liberty LIB 55700	Hickory, Dick And Doc/I Wish You Were Mine Again	8
65	Liberty LIB 10197	Keep On Trying/Cross My Heart	8
65	Liberty LIB 10213	True Love Never Runs Smooth/Hey Little Girl	8
65	Liberty LIB 55828	Run Like The Devil/Take A Look Around Me	10
66	Liberty LIB 55877	Look At Me Girl/Save A Love	8
67	Liberty LIB 10272	Like You've Never Known Before/Growing Pains	8
67	Liberty LIB 15016	Come Back When You Grow Up/Let The Four Winds Blow	6
67	Liberty LIB 15042	Beautiful People/I May Be Gone	6
68	Liberty LBF 15058	Maybe Just Today/You're A Big Girl Now	6
68	Liberty LBF 15096	Medley, My Girl - Hey Girl/Take Good Care Of My Baby	6
68	Liberty LBF 15134	Do What You Gotta' Do/Thank You	6
69	Liberty LBF 15178	(I'm Into Looking For) Someone To Love Me/Sunrise Highway	6
69	Liberty LBF 15234	I'm Gonna Make It Up To You/Let's Call It A Day	8

MINT VALUE £

69	Liberty LBF 15305	Electric Trains And You/In And Out Of Love	8
70	Liberty LBF 15370	Woman In My Life/No Obligations	6
70	Liberty LBF 15420	Sweet Sweetheart/Rock'n'Roll Music And You	6
73	United Artists UP 35516	Take Good Care Of My Baby/Every Opportunity (as Robert Thomas Velline)	6
76	Mint CHEW 4	(I'm) Lovin' You/Sayin' Goodbye	5
78	United Artists UP 36370	Well All Right/Something Has Come Between Us	5

EPs

61	London RE-G 1278	BOBBY VEE NO. 1 (EP)	30
61	London RE-G 1299	BOBBY VEE NO. 2 (EP)	30
61	London RE-G 1308	BOBBY VEE NO. 3 (EP)	30
61	London RE-G 1323	BOBBY VEE NO. 4 (EP)	35
61	London RE-G 1324	HITS OF THE ROCKIN' 50's (EP)	35
62	Liberty LEP 2053	SINCERELY (EP)	25
63	Liberty LEP 2084	JUST FOR FUN (EP, 2 tracks by Bobby Vee, 2 by Crickets)	22
63	Liberty LEP 2089	A FOREVER KIND OF LOVE (EP)	25
63	Liberty (S)LEP 2102	BOBBY VEE'S BIGGEST HITS (EP, mono/stereo)	25/30
63	Liberty (S)LEP 2116	BOBBY VEE MEETS THE CRICKETS (EP, mono/stereo)	25/40
64	Liberty LEP 2149	BOBBY VEE MEETS THE CRICKETS VOL. 2 (EP)	25
64	Liberty LEP 2181	NEW SOUNDS (EP)	40
65	Liberty LEP 2212	BOBBY VEE MEETS THE VENTURES (EP, with Ventures)	30

LPs

61	London HA-G 2320	BOBBY VEE SINGS YOUR FAVOURITES (LP)	80
61	London HA-G 2352	BOBBY VEE (LP, also stereo SAH-G 6152)	60/80
61	London HA-G 2374	WITH STRINGS AND THINGS (LP, also stereo SAH-G 6174)	60/75
61	London HA-G 2406	SINGS HITS OF THE ROCKIN' 50s (LP, also stereo, SAH-G 6206)	60/75
61	London HA-G 2428	TAKE GOOD CARE OF MY BABY (LP, also stereo, SAH-G 6224)	50/60
61	Liberty (S)LBY 1004	TAKE GOOD CARE OF MY BABY (LP, reissue)	30/35
62	Liberty (S)LBY 1084	BOBBY VEE RECORDING SESSION (LP, mono/stereo)	35/40
62	Liberty (S)LBY 1086	BOBBY VEE MEETS THE CRICKETS (LP, mono/stereo)	25/35
62	Liberty (S)LBY 1112	BOBBY VEE'S GOLDEN GREATS (LP, mono/stereo)	35/40
63	Liberty (S)LBY 1139	THE NIGHT HAS A THOUSAND EYES (LP, mono/stereo)	35/40
63	Liberty (S)LBY 1147	BOBBY VEE MEETS THE VENTURES (LP, with Ventures)	35/40
63	Liberty (S)LBY 1188	I REMEMBER BUDDY HOLLY (LP, mono/stereo)	35/40
65	Liberty (S)LBY 1263	BOBBY VEE LIVE! ON TOUR (LP, mono/stereo)	30/35
67	Liberty (S)LBY 1341	LOOK AT ME GIRL (LP)	22
68	Liberty LBL/LBS 83112E	JUST TODAY (LP)	20
68	Sunset SLS 50022	BOBBY VEE (LP)	12
69	Liberty LBL/LBS 83130E	DO WHAT YOU GOTTA DO (LP)	20
69	Sunset SLS 50050	A FOREVER KIND OF LOVE (LP)	12
73	United Artists UAS 29457	NOTHIN' LIKE A SUNNY DAY (as Robert Thomas Velline) (LP, with inner lyric sleeve)	12
74	United Artists UAD 60055/6	BOBBY VEE LEGENDARY MASTERS (2-LP, with booklet)	15

(see also Crickets, Ventures)

VEE VV

85	Cathexis CRV 5455	Kindest Cut/Romance Is Over (p/s, with A4 folder in zip-lock bag)	6
87	Debris DEB 4	Romance is Over/THAT TED: Long Expected One And Twenty (flexidisc, with *Debris* magazine)	6/4
80s	Blam	Love Canal (flexidisc, foldout p/s, free with *BLAM* fanzine)	6/4

V8

| 85 | Music Factory MF 104 | Lonely Days | 25 |

ALAN VEGA

81	Celluloid WIP 6744	Jukebox Babe/Lonely (p/s)	8
81	Celluloid 12WIP 6744	Jukebox Babe/Lonely (12", p/s)	15
88	Sniffin' Rock SR 009	WACKO WARRIOR/(track by African Headcharge) (with *Sniffin' Rock* fanzine No. 12)	10
81	Ze/Island ILPS 9692	COLLISION DRIVE (LP)	15

(see also Suicide, Future Pilot AKA Alan Vega, Angel Corpus Christi & Dean Wareham)

SUZANNE VEGA

86	A&M CDQ 320	Left Of Centre/Undertow/Cracking (live) (CD, foldout inlay)	10
87	A&M VEGCD 2	Tom's Diner/Left Of Centre/Tom's Diner (live)/Luka (live) (CD, foldout inlay)	7
87	A&M VEGCD 3	Solitude Standing/Ironbound-Fancy Poultry/Marlene On The Wall (live)/Some Journey (live) (CD, foldout inlay)	7

JAKE VEGAS' NAKED KISS

| 93 | Camden Town GNAR 004 | Jake's Flower Garden/Swamp Child | 5 |

VEHICLE

| 71 | Deram DM 342 | Mr. Organ Grinder/Cloudy Day | 4 |

JORGE VEIGA & MARIO AUGUSTO

| 61 | HMV POP 918 | Brigitte Bardot/Tenha Pena De Min | 5 |

VEIN

(see under Intra Vein)

VEJTABLES

| 65 | Pye International 7N 25339 | I Still Love You/Anything | 20 |

MARTHA VELEZ

69	London HLK 10266	It Takes A Lot To Laugh/Come Here Sweet Man	6
69	London HLK 10280	Tell Mama/Swamp Man	6
72	Blue Horizon 2096 010	Boogie Kitchen/Two Bridges	15
69	London HA-K/SH-K 8395	FIENDS AND ANGELS (LP)	25
70	Blue Horizon 7-63867	FIENDS AND ANGELS AGAIN (LP)	50
76	Sire 9103 252	ESCAPE FROM BABYLON (LP)	12

MINT VALUE £

CAETANO VELOSO
| 71 | Famous SFM 1002 | CAETANO VELOSO (LP) | 12 |

VELOURS
| 77 | MGM 2006 603 | I'm Gonna Change/Don't Pity Me | 5 |

(see also Fantastics)

VELVELETTES
64	Stateside SS 361	Needle In A Haystack/Should I Tell Them?	30
65	Stateside SS 387	He Was Really Sayin' Something/Throw A Farewell Kiss	45
65	Tamla Motown TMG 521	Lonely Lonely Girl Am I/I'm The Exception To The Rule	100
66	Tamla Motown TMG 580	These Things Will Keep Me Loving You/Since You've Been Loving Me	22
65	Tamla Motown TMG 595	He Was Really Sayin' Something/Needle In A Haystack (narrow label print)	15
67	Tamla Motown TMG 595	He Was Really Sayin' Something/Needle In A Haystack (later pressing)	8
71	Tamla Motown TMG 780	These Things Will Keep Me Loving You/Since You've Been Loving Me (reissue)	5
72	Tamla Motown TMG 806	Needle In A Haystack/I'm The Exception To The Rule	5

VELVET HUSH
| 68 | Oak RGJ 648 | Broken Heart/Lover Please | 125 |

(see also Factory [Oak label])

VELVET OPERA
69	CBS 4189	Anna Dance Square/Don't You Realize	7
70	CBS 4802	Black Jack Davy/Statesboro' Blues	7
70	Spark SRL 1045	She Keeps Giving Me These Feelings/There's A Hole In My Pocket	6
69	CBS 63692	RIDE A HUSTLER'S DREAM (LP)	40

(see also Elmer Gantry's Velvet Opera, Stretch, Hudson-Ford, Johnny Joyce)

VELVETS
61	London HLU 9328	That Lucky Old Sun/Time And Time Again	20
61	London HLU 9372	Tonight (Could Be The Night)/Spring Fever	20
61	London HLU 9444	Laugh/Lana	20
61	London RE-U 1297	VELVETS (EP)	125

VEL-VETS
| 74 | Disco Demand DDS 109 | I Got To Find Me Somebody/What Now My Love | 5 |

VELVETTES
| 64 | Mercury MF 802 | He's The One I Want/That Little Boy Of Mine (some in p/s) | 15/8 |

VELVETT FOGG
| 69 | Pye 7N 17673 | Telstar '69/Owed To The Dip | 10 |
| 69 | Pye NSPL 18272 | VELVETT FOGG (LP, laminated sleeve; beware of non-laminated counterfeits) | 50 |

(see also Ghost)

VELVET UNDERGROUND
71	Atlantic 2091 008	Who Loves The Sun?/Sweet Jane	15
73	MGM 2006 283	Candy Says/I'm Waiting For The Man/Run Run Run (as Lou Reed & Velvet Underground)	8
73	Atlantic K 10339	Sweet Jane/Rock And Roll	8
67	Verve (S)VLP 9184	THE VELVET UNDERGROUND AND NICO (LP, single sleeve, mono/stereo)	80/50
68	Verve (S)VLP 9201	WHITE LIGHT WHITE HEAT (LP, 'skull' sleeve, mono/stereo)	80/45
69	MGM MGM-CS 8108	THE VELVET UNDERGROUND (LP)	40
71	Atlantic 2400 111	LOADED (LP)	15
71	MGM 2315 056	THE VELVET UNDERGROUND AND NICO (LP, reissue, gatefold sleeve)	15
71	MGM Select 2353 022	THE VELVET UNDERGROUND (LP, reissue, gatefold sleeve)	12
71	MGM Select 2353 024	WHITE LIGHT WHITE HEAT (LP, reissue)	12
72	MGM Select 2683 006	ANDY WARHOL'S VELVET UNDERGROUND (2-LP)	15
72	Atlantic K 30022	LIVE AT MAX'S KANSAS CITY (LP)	12
73	Polydor 2383 180	SQUEEZE (LP)	12

(see also Lou Reed, Nico, John Cale)

VENDORS
| 64 | Domino Studios (no cat. no.) | Don't Leave Me Now/Twilight Time/Take Your Time/Peace Pipe (acetate, private pressing, 12 copies only) | 500+ |

(see also 'N Betweens, Slade)

VENEICE
| 72 | London HLU 10372 | Stepchild/18 Days | 4 |

VENGERS
| 63 | Oriole CB 1879 | Shake And Clap/Shakedown | 12 |

VENOM
81	Neat NEAT 08	In League With Satan/Live Like An Angel, Die Like An Devil (p/s)	12
82	Neat NEAT 13	Bloodlust/In Nomine Satanas (p/s)	12
82	Neat NEAT 13	Bloodlust/In Nomine Satanas (purple vinyl)	50
83	Neat NEAT 27	Die Hard/Acid Queen (p/s, some with poster)	12/8
83	Megaforce LOM 1/NEAT 27	Die Hard/Acid Queen (picture disc, export issue, 1,000 only)	18
84	Neat NEAT 38	Warhead/Lady Lust (p/s)	5
84	Neat NEATP 38	Warhead/Lady Lust (p/s, mauve vinyl)	15
84	Neat NEAT 3812	Warhead/Lady Lust/Gates Of Hell (12", p/s)	8
85	Neat NEATP 43	Manitou/Woman (picture disc)	10
85	Neat NEATSHAPE 43	Manitou/Woman (shaped picture disc)	12
85	Neat NEATC 43	Manitou/Woman/Dead Of Night/Dutch Radio Interview (cassette)	15
85	Neat NEAT 4312	Manitou/Woman/Dead Of Night (12", p/s)	12
85	Neat NEATS 47	Nightmare/Satanarchist (shaped picture disc)	18
85	Neat NEATSC 47	Nightmare/Satanarchist/F.O.A.D./Radio Intro To Warhead/Warhead (live)/Venoms (cassette)	7
85	Neat NEAT 4712	Nightmare/Satanarchist/F.O.A.D./Warhead (live) (12", 'face' p/s)	12
85	Neat NEAT 4712	Nightmare/Satanarchist/F.O.A.D./Warhead (live) (12", p/s, withdrawn)	18

VENOM

VENTURES

MINT VALUE £

67	Liberty LIB 55967	Strawberry Fields Forever/Endless Dream	7
68	Liberty LBF 15075	Flights Of Fantasy/Pandora's Box	12
70	Liberty LBF 15221	Hawaii Five-O — Theme/Higher Than Thou	10
71	United Artists UP 36316	Theme From 'Shaft'/Tight Fit	6
72	United Artists UP 35326	Joy/Cherries Jubilee	5
73	United Artists UP 35574	Skylab/Little People	7
75	United Artists UP 35951	Hawaii Five-O/Higher Than Thou (reissue)	5
75	United Artists UP 36009	Superstar Revue (Parts 1 & 2)	5
77	United Artists UP 36223	Starsky And Hutch/Charlie's Angels	6

EPs

61	London REG 1279	THE VENTURES (EP)	20
61	London REG 1283	THE VENTURES (EP, export issue)	20
61	London REG 1288	RAM-BUNK-SHUSH! (EP)	22
62	London REG 1326	ANOTHER SMASH (EP)	22
62	London REG 1328	COLOURFUL VENTURES (EP)	20
62	Liberty LEP 2058	TWIST WITH THE VENTURES (EP)	20
62	Liberty LEP 2131	SMASH HITS (EP)	20
63	Liberty LEP 2104	THE VENTURES PLAY TELSTAR AND LONELY BULL (EP)	20
64	Liberty LEP 2174	THE VENTURES PLAY COUNTRY GREATS (EP)	20
65	Liberty LEP 2212	BOBBY VEE MEETS THE VENTURES (EP, with Bobby Vee)	30
66	Liberty LEP 2250	SECRET AGENT MEN (EP)	25

ORIGINAL LPs

61	London HA-G 2340	THE VENTURES (LP, also stereo SAH-G 6143)	35/45
61	London HA-G 2376	ANOTHER SMASH (LP, also stereo SAH-G 6176)	30/40
61	London HA-G 2409	THE COLOURFUL VENTURES (LP, also stereo SAH-G 6209)	30/40
62	Liberty LBY 1002	WALK DON'T RUN (LP)	22
62	London HA-G 2429	TWIST WITH THE VENTURES (LP, also stereo SAH-G 6225)	30/40
62	Liberty LBY 1072	TWIST PARTY (LP)	22
63	Liberty (S)LBY 1110	GOING TO THE VENTURES DANCE PARTY! (LP, mono/stereo)	25/30
63	Liberty (S)LBY 1147	BOBBY VEE MEETS THE VENTURES (LP, with Bobby Vee)	35/40
63	Liberty (S)LBY 1150	SURFING (LP, mono/stereo)	22/25
64	Liberty (S)LBY 1169	LET'S GO! (LP, mono/stereo)	18/22
64	Liberty (S)LBY 1189	THE VENTURES IN SPACE (LP, mono/stereo)	20/25
65	Liberty (S)LBY 1228	WALK DON'T RUN — VOL. 2 (LP, mono/stereo)	20/25
65	Liberty (S)LBY 1252	KNOCK ME OUT (LP, mono/stereo)	18/22
65	Liberty (S)LBY 1270	ON STAGE (LP, mono/stereo)	18/22
66	Liberty (S)LBY 1274	VENTURES A-GO GO (LP, mono/stereo)	15/20
66	Liberty (S)LBY 1285	THE VENTURES' CHRISTMAS ALBUM (LP, mono/stereo)	20/25
66	Liberty (S)LBY 1297	WHERE THE ACTION IS! (LP, mono/stereo)	15/18
66	Liberty (S)LBY 1323	GO WITH THE VENTURES (LP, mono/stereo)	15/18
67	Liberty (S)LBY 1345	GUITAR FREAKOUT (LP, mono/stereo)	15/18
67	Liberty (S)LBY 1372	SUPER PSYCHEDELICS (LP, mono/stereo)	15/18
67	Liberty (S)LBY 1375	THE BEST OF THE VENTURES (LP, mono/stereo)	15/18
68	Liberty LBL/LBS 83046E	GOLDEN GREATS (LP, mono/stereo)	15/18
68	Liberty LBL/LBS 83085E	GREAT PERFORMANCES VOL. 1 (LP)	15
68	Liberty LBL/LBS 83092E	$1,000,000 WEEKEND (LP)	15
68	Liberty LBL/LBS 83124E	LONELY BULL (LP)	15
68	Liberty LBX 2	VENTURES SAMPLER (LP)	15
68	Sunset SLS 50012E	GUITAR GENIUS (LP)	12
68	Sunset SLS 50045E	RUNNIN' STRONG (LP)	12
68	Liberty LBL/LBS 83138E	FLIGHTS OF FANTASY (LP)	15
69	Liberty LBL/LBS 83164E	THE HORSE (LP)	15
69	Liberty LBL/LBS 83193E	UNDERGROUND FIRE (LP)	15
70	Liberty LBL/LBS 83175	MORE GOLDEN GREATS (LP, mono/stereo)	15/12
70	Liberty LBL/LBS 83279	SWAMP ROCK (LP, mono/stereo)	15/12
70	Liberty C 1077	VENTURES 10TH ANNIVERSARY (cassette)	12
71	United Artists UAS 29249	BEST OF POP SOUNDS (LP, export issue)	15
72	United Artists UAS 29280	THEME FROM 'SHAFT' (LP)	12
72	United Artists UAS 29340	THE VENTURES PLAY THE CLASSICS — "JOY" (LP, omits "One Fine Day", stickered sleeve)	12
73	United Artists UAD 6051/2	LEGENDARY MASTERS (2-LP, gatefold sleeve, booklet insert)	15
76	Sunset SLS 50386	THE VERY BEST OF THE VENTURES (LP)	12
83	Valentine VAL 8054	THE VENTURES TODAY (LP)	12
90	See For Miles SEE 292	THE EP COLLECTION (LP)	12

REISSUE LPs

68	Liberty LBL/LBS 83015E	ON STAGE (LP, mono/stereo)	12/15
68	Liberty LBL/LBS 83033E	SUPER PSYCHEDELICS (LP, mono/stereo)	15
68	Liberty LBL/LBS 83089E	GUITAR FREAKOUT (LP, mono/stereo)	12/15
68	Liberty LBL/LBS 83116E	I LIKE IT LIKE THAT (LP, reissue of "A-Go Go", diff. sleeve, mono/stereo)	12/15
68	Liberty LBL/LBS 83123E	WALK DON'T RUN (LP, reissue, different sleeve, mono/stereo)	12/15
68	Liberty LBL/LBS 83125E	LET'S GO! (LP, different sleeve, mono/stereo)	12/15
68	Liberty LBL/LBS 83126E	OUT OF LIMITS (LP, reissue of "In Space", different sleeve, mono/stereo)	12/15
68	Liberty LBL/LBS 83127E	KNOCK ME OUT (LP, different sleeve, mono/stereo)	12/15

CD

86	Castle Comm. CCDCD 156	THE VENTURES COLLECTION (CD)	15

(see also New Ventures, Bobby Vee)

VENUS & RAZORBLADES

77	Spark SRL 1153	I Wanna Be Where Where The Boys Are/Dogfood (numbered p/s)	4
77	Spark SRL 1156	Punk-A-Rama/Alright You Guys	4
78	Spark SRL 1159	Workin' Girl/Midnight	4

JOE VENUTI

50	Parlophone DP 205	Raggin' The Scale/LOUIS ARMSTRONG: I'm In The Market For You (78, export issue)	10

BILLY VERA
68   Atlantic 584 196   With Pen In Hand/Good Morning Blues 4

BILLY VERA & JUDY CLAY
68   Atlantic 584 164   Storybook Children/Really Together 6
69   Atlantic 584 293   Reaching For The Moon/Tell It Like It Is 5
68   Atlantic 588 158   THE STORYBOOK CHILDREN (LP) 15
     (see also Judy Clay)

JOHN VERITY BAND
74   Probe SPB 1087   JOHN VERITY BAND (LP). 12
     (see also Argent)

TIM VERLANDER
72   Midas MR 007   TIM VERLANDER (LP, with booklet). 30

VERMILION
78   Illegal ILM 0010   Angry Young Women/Nymphomania/Wild Boys (p/s) 10
79   Illegal ILS 0015   I Like Motorcycles/The Letter (p/s) 8
     (see also Menace)

VERN & ALVIN
69   Blue Cat BS 167   Everybody Reggae/Another Fool. 10
69   Big Shot BI 525   Old Man Dead/G.G. RHYTHM SECTION: Reggae Me 8
     (see also Maytones)

VERN & SON
71   G.G. GG 4523   Little Boy Blue/TYPHOON ALL STARS: Little Boy Blue — Version 6
     (see also Maytones)

LARRY VERNE
60   London HLN 9194   Mr. Custer/Okeefenokee Two Step. 8
61   London HLN 9263   Mr. Livingstone/Roller Coaster 8

LYN VERNON
60   Top Rank JAR 323   Woodchoppers Ball/Caravan 6

MIKE VERNON
72   Blue Horizon 2096 007   Let's Try It Again/Little Southern Country Girl 20
71   Blue Horizon 2931 003   BRING IT BACK HOME (LP, textured sleeve with insert) 90

VERNON BURCH
75   United Artists UP 35838   Ain't Gonna Tell Nobody/Loving You Gets Better With Time. 4

VERNONS GIRLS
58   Parlophone R 4497   Lost And Found/White Bucks And Saddle Shoes 20
58   Parlophone R 4497   Lost And Found/White Bucks And Saddle Shoes (78) 10
59   Parlophone R 4532   Jealous Heart/Now Is The Month Of Maying 15
59   Parlophone R 4532   Jealous Heart/Now Is The Month Of Maying (78) 15
59   Parlophone R 4596   Don't Look Now But/Who Are They To Say? 15
60   Parlophone R 4624   We Like Boys/Boy Meets Girl 12
60   Parlophone R 4654   Madison Time (with Jimmy Saville)/The Oo-We 10
61   Parlophone R 4734   Ten Little Lonely Boys/Anniversary Song. 8
61   Parlophone R 4832   Let's Get Together/No Message. 8
62   Decca F 11450   Lover Please/You Know What I Mean 6
62   Decca F 11495   The Loco-motion/Don't Wanna Go 6
62   Decca F 11549   Funny All Over/See For Yourself 6
63   Decca F 11629   Do The Bird/I'm Gonna Let My Hair Down. 6
63   Decca F 11685   He'll Never Come Back/Stay-At-Home. 6
63   Decca F 11781   Tomorrow Is Another Day/Why Why Why 8
64   Decca F 11807   We Love The Beatles/Hey Lover Boy. 12
64   Decca F 11887   Only You Can Do It/Stupid Little Girl 8
64   Decca F 12021   It's A Sin To Tell A Lie/Don't Say Goodbye 6
62   Decca DFE 8506   THE VERNONS GIRLS (EP) 30
58   Parlophone PMC 1052   THE VERNONS GIRLS (LP) 60
     (see also Krimson Kake, Wilde Three, Jimmy Saville, Lee Francis, Samantha Jones, Breakaways)

LILI VERONA
54   HMV 7MC 13   Massa Johnny/Hoggin' In The Cocoa (export issue). 12
56   Melodisc MEL 1383   French Lesson/Pica Now (78, with Gulf Stream Calypso Boys). 12

VERSATILE NEWTS
80   Shanghai No. 2   Newtrition/Blimp (p/s, stamped white label) 25
     (see also Felt)

VERSATILES
68   Island WI 3142   Teardrops Falling/Someone To Love 15
68   Amalgamated AMG 802   Just Can't Win/LEADERS: Sometimes I Sit Down Down And Cry 10
68   Crab CRAB 1   Children Get Ready/Someone To Love 8
69   Big Shot BI 520   Worries A Yard/VAL BENNETT: Hound Dog Special 8
69   Crab CRAB 5   Spread Your Bed/Worries A Yard 8
69   Amalgamated AMG 854   Lu Lu Bell/Long Long Time 8
74   Dip DL 5039   Cutting Razor/UPSETTERS: Black Belt Jones 8
     (see also Pioneers, Soul Sisters)

VERSATILES
70   New Beat NB 060   Pick My Pocket/FREEDOM SINGERS: Freedom 7
71   Nu Beat NB 076   Give To Me/TIGER: With Hot 6

VERUKAS
     (see under Varukers)

MINT VALUE £

VERVE

92	Hut HUT 12	All In The Mind/One Way To Go (p/s) 5
92	Hut HUT 16	She's A Superstar (Edit)/Feel (p/s) 7
92	Hut HUTEN 21	GRAVITY GRAVE EP (Gravity Grave [Edit]/Endless Life/ She's A Superstar [Live at Clapham Grand]) (10", p/s)..................... 10
92	Strange Fruit SFPMA 214	HUT — THE PEEL SESSIONS (10", p/s) 7
92	Strange Fruit SFMCD 214	HUT — THE PEEL SESSIONS (CD) 8
93	Hut HUTUS 1/YARDCD 1	THE VERVE EP (Gravity Grave [Edit]/A Man Called Sun/She's A Superstar [Edit]/Endless Life/Feel) (CD, export issue to U.S., 3,000 issued in U.K.) 8
93	Hut HUTEN 29	Blue/Twilight/Where The Geese Go/No Come Down (10", p/s)............... 12
93	Hut HUT 35	Slide Away/Make It 'Til Monday (pink vinyl, p/s)....................... 6
97	Hut HUTTR 82	Bitter Sweet Symphony (James Lavelle Remix)/(James Lavelle Instrumental Remix) (12", stickered plain die-cut sleeve, promo only) 15
97	Hut HUTTP 82	Bitter Sweet Symphony (Extended Version)/(M.S.G. Mix)/(Instrumental) (12", plain die-cut sleeve, promo only) 8
97	Hut HUTLH 92	Lucky Man/Never Wanna See You Cry (jukebox issue, no p/s)................ 7
93	(no label) FLEXI 1	Make It 'Til Monday (Glastonbury '93) (clear vinyl stickered flexi w/ magazine) . 15
95	Hut DGHUT 27	A NORTHERN SOUL (CD, foldout digipak with postcards) 15
97	Hut HUTLPX 45	URBAN HYMNS (2-LP, with inners sleeves, printed outer mailer, 5,000 only) ... 20
97	Hut CDPHUT 45	URBAN HYMNS (CD, ribbon-tied black gatefold sleeve, promo only) 40
93	Jolly Roger JOLLY ROGER 2	VOYAGER 1 (LP, official bootleg, blue vinyl, 1,000 only).................. 70

VERY THINGS

84	Reflex RE 5	The Bushes Scream While My Daddy Prunes/Shearing Machine (p/s) 4
80s	Corp. Christi CHRISTITS 2	The Gong Man/The Colours (Are Speaking To Me) (foldout p/s) 4

(see also Cravats)

V FOR VENDETTA

(see under David J.)

VHF

80	Lion PAW 1	Heart Of Stone (no p/s) 50

VIBES

84	Big Beat SW 99	Can You Feel.../The Underestimated Man/Double Decker Bus/ Mini Skirt Blues/Stranger In The House (p/s) 5

VIBRATIONS

61	Pye International 7N 25107	The Watusi/Wallflower 18
64	London HLK 9875	My Girl Sloopy/Daddy Woo Woo 15
66	Columbia DB 7895	Canadian Sunset/The Story Of A Starry Night 15
67	Columbia DB 8175	Pick Me/You Better Beware 18
67	Columbia DB 8318	Talkin' 'Bout Love/One Mint Julep 12
68	Direction 58-3511	Love In Them There Hills/Remember The Rain 10
67	Columbia SX 6106	NEW VIBRATIONS (LP) 40
69	Direction 8-63644	GREATEST HITS (LP) 25
72	RCA SF 8254	THE VIBRATIONS (LP) 15

(see also Jayhawks)

VIBRATORS (Jamaica)

66	Doctor Bird DB 1036	Sloop John B/Amour 15

(see also Al & Vibrators, Wilbert Francis & Vibrators)

VIBRATORS (U.K.)

76	RAK RAK 245	We Vibrate/Whips And Furs (no p/s) 5
76	RAK RAK 246	Pogo Dancing/The Pose (no p/s, as Vibrators with Chris Spedding)........... 6
77	RAK RAK 253	Bad Times/No Heart (unreleased)
77	Epic EPC 5302	Baby Baby/Into The Future (p/s) 5
77	Epic EPC 5565	London Girls/Stiff Little Fingers (live) (p/s)................................... 7
78	Epic EPC 6137	Automatic Lover/Destroy (p/s)................................... 4
78	Epic EPC 6393	Judy Says (Knock You On The Head)/Pure Mania (p/s)................... 7
80	Rat Race RAT 2	Gimme Some Lovin'/Power Cry (live) (p/s, in slightly different colours) 5
80	Rat Race RAT 4	Disco In Moscow/Take A Chance (p/s, with various coloured writing) 6
77	Epic EPC 82097	PURE MANIA (LP) 12
78	Epic EPC 82495	V2 (LP, with inner lyric sleeve)................................... 15

(see also John Ellis, Chris Spedding, Nazis Against Fascism, Substitute, Troops Of Tomorrow, Urban Dogs)

VICE CREEMS

78	Tiger GRRRR 1	Won't You Be My Girl?/01-01-212 (gatefold p/s) 8
79	Zig Zag ZZ22 001	Danger Love/Like A Tiger (p/s) ; 7

VICEROYS

67	Island WI 3095	Lip And Tongue/DAWN PENN: When Am I Gonna Be Free................... 30
67	Coxsone CS 7031	Magadown/RICHARD ACE: Don't Let The Sun Catch You Crying............ 20
67	Studio One SO 2016	Lose And Gain (as Voiceroys)/SOUL BROTHERS: Honey Pot 18
67	Studio One SO 2025	Shake Up/NORMA FRAZER: Telling Me Lies............................. 18
68	Studio One SO 2064	Last Night/Ya Ho 18
68	Blue Cat BS 121	Fat Fish/OCTAVES: You're Gonna Lose................................ 15
69	Studio One SO 2077	Things A-Come To Bump/LYRICS: Old Man Say 18
69	Punch PH 3	Jump In A Fire/Give To Get (as Voiceroys) 8
69	Crab CRAB 12	Work It/You Mean So Much To Me (B-side actually by Paragons) 8
69	Crab CRAB 27	Death A-Come (actually by Lloyd Robinson)/MATADOR ALLSTARS: The Sword . 6
70	Bullet BU 441	Chariot Coming/SYDNEY ALLSTARS: Stackata 6
70	Bullet BU 444	Power Control/SLICKERS: Dip Dip 6
70	Bullet BU 450	Come On Over/SYDNEY ALLSTARS: Version 6
70	Bullet BU 453	Fancy Clothes/BIGGIE: Jack And Jill 12
71	Bullet BU 470	Rebel Nyah/Feel The Spirit................................... 6
73	Harry J. HJ 6658	Chucky (Parts 1 & 2) 5
74	Harry J. HJ 6669	Wheel & Jig (Parts 1 & 2)................................... 5

(see also Richard Ace, Interns [Jamaica], Derrick Morgan, Vincent Gordon, Hub)

VICE SQUAD

80	Riot City RIOT 1	Last Rockers/Living On Dreams/Latex Love (p/s, with poster)	8
81	Riot City RIOT 2	Resurrection/Young Blood/Hurricane (p/s)	6
82	Riot City RIOT 12 1/2	SINGLES (12" EP)	8
82	Zonophone Z 26	Out Of Reach/Sterile/Out Of Reach (p/s)	5
82	Zonophone Z 30	Rock 'n' Roll Massacre/Stand Strong And Proud/Tomorrow	5
83	Anagram ANA 16	Black Sheep/New Blood (p/s)	4
83	Anagram 12 ANA 16	Black Sheep/New Blood/The Pledge (12", p/s)	7
84	Anagram ANA 22	You'll Never Know/What's Going On (p/s)	4
84	Anagram 12 ANA 22	You'll Never Know/What's Going On/The Times They Are A Changin' (12", p/s)	7
85	Anagram ANA 26	Teenage Rampage/High Spirits (p/s)	4
80s	Vice Squad Fan Club	EVIL (EP, flexidisc)	12
81	Zonophone ZEM 103	NO CAUSE FOR CONCERN (LP)	10
82	Zonophone ZEM 104	STAND STRONG STAND PROUD (LP)	10

(see also Sex Aids)

VICE VERSA

80	Neutron NT 001/PX 1092	MUSIC 4 (EP, poster p/s)	12

(see also ABC, Liza Strike)

VICIOUS PINK (PHENOMENA)

82	Mobile Suit Corp. CORP 1	My Private Tokyo/Promises (p/s)	5
82	Mobile Suit Corp. CORP 12	My Private Tokyo (Long Version)/(Remix)/Promises (12", p/s)	12
83	Warehouse WARE 1	Je T'Aime (Moi Non Plus)/In The Swim (p/s)	5
83	Warehouse WARE 1T	Je T'Aime (Moi Non Plus) (12" Disco Version)/In The Swim (12", p/s)	10
85	EMI PINKP 1	Fetish/Spooky Situation (shaped picture disc, as Vicious Pink)	5

(see also Soft Cell)

MIKE VICKERS (ORCHESTRA)

65	Columbia DB 7657	On The Brink/The Puff Adder (as Mike Vickers & Orchestra)	25
66	Columbia DB 7825	Eleventy One/The Inkling	7
66	Columbia DB 7906	Morgan — A Suitable Case For Treatment/Gorilla Of My Dreams (as Mike Vickers Orchestra)	10
67	Columbia DB 8171	Air On A G-String/Proper Charles (as Mike Vickers Orchestra)	6
67	Columbia DB 8281	Captain Scarlet And The Mysterons/Kettle Of Fish	18
68	Columbia S(C)X 6180	I WISH I WERE A GROUP AGAIN (LP)	25

(see also Manfred Mann, Baker Street Philharmonic)

SUE VICKERS

72	Threshold TH 8	Loving You The Way I Do/Take Me With You	4

MACK VICKERY

60	Top Rank JAR 420	Fantasy/Hawaiian Stroll	8

VICKY

67	Philips BF 1565	Colours Of Love (Love Is Blue)/Who Can Tell	10
67	Philips BF 1599	Sunshine Boy/Tell Me	8
68	Philips BF 1631	Dance With Me Until Tomorrow/Give Me Your Hand	7

(see also Vicky Leandros)

VICKY & JERRY

60	HMV POP 715	Don't Cry/A Year Ago Tonight	12

VICTIM

78	Good Vibrations GOT 2	Strange Things By Night/Mixed Up World (wraparound p/s)	5
79	TJM TJM 13	THE VICTIM (EP, unreleased)	
79	TJM TJM 14	Why Are Fire Engines Red/I Need You (p/s, unissued)	
80	TJM TJM 15	The Teen Age/Junior Criminals/Hung On To Yourself (p/s)	6
80	Illuminated ILL 1	The Teen Age/Junior Criminals/Hung On To Yourself (p/s, reissue)	4

VICTIMIZE

79	I.M.E. IME 1	Baby Buyer/Hi Rising Failure (folded p/s)	20
80	I.M.E. IME 2	Wh?r? Did Th? Mon?y Go (p/s)	20

VICTIMS OF CHANCE

70	Stable SLE 8004	VICTIMS OF CHANCE (LP)	35

VICTIMS OF PLEASURE

80	P.A.M. VOP 1	When You're Young/If I Was/Sporting Pastimes (p/s)	12
81	Rialto RIA 2	Slave To Fashion/On The Game (p/s)	4
82	Rialto RIA 7	Jack And Jill/Red Moon (p/s)	4
82	Rialto RIA 11	When You're Young (p/s)	4

VICTIMS OF VICTIMISATION

87	Death DEAD 2	Kill Or Be Killed/As A Doornail (p/s)	18

TONY VICTOR

62	Decca F 11459	Dear One/There Was A Time	20
63	Decca F 11626	Thinking Of You/Hokey Cokey	8
63	Decca F 11708	In The Still Of The Night/Money	8

VICTORIA

71	Atlantic 2091 084	Tule's Blues/Helplessly Hoping	5
71	Atlantic 2400 176	VICTORIA (LP)	20
71	Mojo 2466 008	SECRET OF THE BLOOM (LP)	35

VICTORIANS

64	Liberty LIB 55693	Oh What A Night For Love/Happy Birthday Blue	10

VICTORS

65	Oriole CB 1984	Take This Old Hammer/Answer's No	7

VICTORS

69	High Note HS 019	Reggae Buddy/Easy Squeeze	8
71	Escort ERT 846	Me A Tell Yuh/LLOYD'S ALL-STARS: More Echo	6

VIDELS
| 60 | London HLI 9153 | Mister Lonely/I'll Forget You | 45 |

VIEWERS
| 80 | Fire Exit LOCK 1 | Accident/Pen Friend (p/s) | 4 |

VIGILANTES
| 61 | Pye International 7N 25082 | Eclipse/Man In Space | 15 |

(PAUL) VIGRASS
68	RCA RCA 1755	New Man/Curly	6
69	RCA RCA 1800	Suzie/Funky Piano Joe (as Vigrass)	5
69	RCA RCA 1857	Free Lorry Ride/Flying	5
70	RCA RCA 1911	Stop/Like It Never Was	5

VIKINGS
63	Island WI 035	Maggie Don't Leave Me/Henchmen (both actually with Victor Wong)	18
63	Island WI 065	Hallelujah/Helpin' Ages (actually by Maytals)	18
63	Island WI 075	Six And Seven Books Of Moses/Zacions (actually by Maytals)	18
63	Island WI 101	Never Grow Old/Irene (actually by Maytals)	18
63	Island WI 107	Just Got To Be/You Make Me Do (actually by Maytals)	18
63	Island WI 117	Fever/Cheer Up (actually by Maytals)	18
64	Island WI 167	Daddy/It's You (actually by Maytals)	30
64	Black Swan WI 423	Down By The Riverside/This Way	18
64	Black Swan WI 428	Treat Me Bad/Sitting On Top	18
64	Black Swan WI 430	Come Into My Parlour/I Am In Love	18

(see also Maytals, Flames [Jamaica], Bonnie & Skitto)

VIKINGS
| 66 | Alp 595 011 | Bad News Feeling/What Can I Do | 18 |

CLAUDIO VILLA
| 60s | Centra SP 4024 | Addio... Addio/Twist A Napoli (p/s) | 5 |

VILLAGE
| 69 | Head HDS 4002 | Man In The Moon/Long Time Coming | 35 |

(see also Peter Bardens, Quiver)

VILLAGE IDIOTS
| 66 | Piccadilly 7N 35282 | Laughing Policeman/I Know An Old Lady | 4 |

VILLAGE PEOPLE
| 77 | DJM DJS 10817 | San Francisco/Fire Island (12") | 7 |

VILLAGERS/PARCEL OF ROGUES
| 73 | Deroy (no cat. no.) | PARCEL OF FOLK (LP, private pressing, with insert, existence unconfirmed) | 70 |

VILLAGE SOUL CHOIR
| 70 | Direction 58-4969 | Catwalk/Country Walk | 4 |

VILLAGE STOMPERS
| 63 | Columbia DB 7123 | Washington Square/Turkish Delight | 6 |

CATERINA VILLALBA
| 60 | Ember EMB S 104 | Quando La Luna/Amore Fantastico (p/s) | 7 |

JOE VINA
| 59 | Top Rank JAR 251 | Marina/That's Alright | 6 |

RAE VINCE & VINCENTS
| 64 | Piccadilly 7N 35211 | One Fine Day/Little Girl, I'm Sad | 4 |

GENE VINCENT (& BLUE CAPS)
78s
56	Capitol CL 14599	Be-Bop-A-Lula/Woman Love (78)	15
56	Capitol CL 14628	Race With The Devil/Gonna Back Up, Baby (78)	25
56	Capitol CL 14637	Bluejean Bop/Who Slapped John? (78)	18
57	Capitol CL 14681	Jumps, Giggles And Shouts/Wedding Bells (Are Breaking Up That Old Gang Of Mine) (78)	30
57	Capitol CL 14693	Crazy Legs/Important Words (78)	30
57	Capitol CL 14722	Bi-I-Bickey-Bi, Bo-Bo-Go/Five Days, Five Days (78)	30
57	Capitol CL 14763	Lotta Lovin'/Wear My Ring (78)	25
57	Capitol CL 14808	Dance To The Bop/I Got It (78)	25
58	Capitol CL 14830	Walkin' Home From School/I Got A Baby (78)	40
59	Capitol CL 15053	Right Now/The Night Is So Lonely (78)	150

(The above 78s are credited to Gene Vincent & Blue Caps)

SINGLES
56	Capitol CL 14599	Be-Bop-A-Lula/Woman Love	30
56	Capitol CL 14628	Race With The Devil/Gonna Back Up, Baby	80
56	Capitol CL 14637	Bluejean Bop/Who Slapped John?	50
57	Capitol CL 14681	Jumps, Giggles And Shouts/Wedding Bells (Are Breaking Up That Old Gang Of Mine) (promo copy in p/s)	100
57	Capitol CL 14681	Jumps, Giggles And Shouts/Wedding Bells (Are Breaking Up That Old Gang Of Mine)	90
57	Capitol CL 14693	Crazy Legs/Important Words (promo copy in p/s)	100
57	Capitol CL 14693	Crazy Legs/Important Words	90
57	Capitol CL 14722	Bi-I-Bickey-Bi, Bo-Bo-Go/Five Days, Five Days (promo copy in p/s)	100
57	Capitol CL 14722	Bi-I-Bickey-Bi, Bo-Bo-Go/Five Days, Five Days	80
57	Capitol CL 14763	Lotta Lovin'/Wear My Ring	35
57	Capitol CL 14808	Dance To The Bop/I Got It	45
58	Capitol CL 14830	Walkin' Home From School/I Got A Baby (promo copy in p/s)	60
58	Capitol CL 14830	Walkin' Home From School/I Got A Baby	25

MINT VALUE £

58	Capitol CL 14868	Baby Blue/True To You 25
58	Capitol CL 14908	Rocky Road Blues/Yes I Love You, Baby 25
58	Capitol CL 14935	Git It/Little Lover 25
59	Capitol CL 14974	Say Mama/Be Bop Boogie Boy 20
59	Capitol CL 15000	Who's Pushin' Your Swing/Over The Rainbow 15
59	Capitol CL 15035	Summertime/Frankie And Johnnie 12
59	Capitol CL 15053	Right Now/The Night Is So Lonely. 12
59	Capitol CL 15099	Wild Cat/Right Here On Earth 10
60	Capitol CL 15115	My Heart/I've Got To Get You Yet 10

(The above singles are credited to Gene Vincent & Blue Caps. Later 45s were solo, unless otherwise stated.)

60	Capitol CL 15136	Pistol Packin' Mama (as Gene Vincent & Beat Boys)/Weeping Willow 10
60	Capitol CL 15169	Anna-Annabelle/Ac-Cent-Tchu-Ate The Positive. 12
61	Capitol CL 15179	Maybe/Jezebel 12
61	Capitol CL 15185	If You Want My Lovin'/Mister Loneliness 12
61	Capitol CL 15202	She She Little Sheila/Hot Dollar 12
61	Capitol CL 15215	I'm Going Home (To See My Baby)/Love Of A Man. 10
61	Capitol CL 15231	Unchained Melody/Brand New Beat (with Blue Caps) 12
62	Capitol CL 15243	Lucky Star/Baby Don't Believe Him (with Dave Burgess Band) 15
62	Capitol CL 15264	Be-Bop-A-Lula/The King Of Fools (with Charles Blackwell Orchestra) 15
63	Capitol CL 15290	Held For Questioning/You're Still In My Heart (with Charles Blackwell Orch.) . . . 15
63	Capitol CL 15307	Rip It Up/High Blood Pressure (unissued, demo copies only) 225
63	Capitol CL 15307	Crazy Beat/High Blood Pressure 30
63	Columbia DB 7174	Temptation Baby/Where Have You Been All My Life. 18
64	Columbia DB 7218	Humpity Dumpity/A Love 'Em And Leave 'Em Kinda Guy 18
64	Columbia DB 7293	La-Den-Da Den-Da-Da/The Beginning Of The End 18
64	Columbia DB 7343	Private Detective/You Are My Sunshine (as Gene Vincent & Shouts) 18
66	London HLH 10079	Bird Doggin'/Ain't That Too Much 30
66	London HLH 10099	Lonely Street/I've Got My Eyes On You 25
68	Capitol CL 15546	Be-Bop-A-Lula/Say Mama 12
69	Dandelion S 4596	Be-Bop-A-Lula '69/Ruby Baby 10
70	Dandelion S 4974	White Lightning/Scarlet Ribbons (For Her Hair) 12
71	Kama Sutra 2013 018	The Day The World Turned Blue/High On Life (some with large centre). 10
73	Spark SRL 1091	Story Of The Rockers/Pickin' Poppies (push-out or solid centre) 8
74	BBC BEEB 001	Roll Over Beethoven/Say Mama/Be-Bop-A-Lula '71 (push-out or solid centre). . . 8
77	Capitol CL 15906	Say Mama/Lotta Lovin'/Race With The Devil 6
81	Capitol CL 203	She She Little Sheila/Say Mama/Dance To The Bop (p/s) 5
87	Nighttracks SFNT 001	Nighttracks (Distant Drums/Be-Bop-A-Lula) (p/s, promo only with insert) 12

EPs

58	Capitol EAP 1-985	HOT ROD GANG (EP). 60
59	Capitol EAP 1-1059	A GENE VINCENT RECORD DATE (EP) 60
60	Capitol EAP 3-1059	A GENE VINCENT RECORD DATE PART 3 (EP) 60
61	Capitol EAP 1-20173	IF YOU WANT MY LOVIN' (EP) 60
62	Capitol EAP 1-20354	RACE WITH THE DEVIL (EP) 60
63	Capitol EAP 1-20461	TRUE TO YOU (EP) 65
64	Capitol EAP 1-20453	THE CRAZY BEAT OF GENE VINCENT NO. 1 (EP) 60
64	Capitol EAP 2-20453	THE CRAZY BEAT OF GENE VINCENT NO. 2 (EP) 60
64	Capitol EAP 3-20453	THE CRAZY BEAT OF GENE VINCENT NO. 3 (EP) 60
69	EMIdisc (no cat. no.)	LIVE & ROCKIN' (EP, fan club issue, mail-order, 99 only) 225
79	Rollin' Danny RD 1	RAINY DAY SUNSHINE (EP, L.A. 1969 demos, 500 only). 15
81	Magnum Force MFEP 003	RAINY DAY SUNSHINE (EP, reissue) 12

ALBUMS

56	Capitol T 764	BLUEJEAN BOP! (LP, originally with turquoise labels; later rainbow) 80/60
57	Capitol T 811	GENE VINCENT AND THE BLUECAPS (LP, turquoise or rainbow labels) 80/60
58	Capitol T 970	GENE VINCENT ROCKS! & THE BLUECAPS ROLL (LP, originally with turquoise labels, later rainbow labels) 80/60
59	Capitol T 1207	SOUNDS LIKE GENE VINCENT (LP) 60
59	Capitol T 1059	A GENE VINCENT RECORD DATE (LP). 60
60	Capitol (S)T 1342	CRAZY TIMES! (LP, mono/stereo) 50/80
63	Capitol T 20453	THE CRAZY BEAT OF GENE VINCENT (LP) 55
64	Columbia 33SX 1646	SHAKIN' UP A STORM (LP, as Gene Vincent & Shouts) 55
65	Music F. Pleasure MFP 1053	CRAZY TIMES (LP, reissue) 12
67	London HA-H 8333	GENE VINCENT (LP) 45
67	Capitol T 20957	THE BEST OF GENE VINCENT (LP, 'rainbow' label) 20
68	Capitol ST 21144	THE BEST OF GENE VINCENT VOLUME 2 (LP 'rainbow' label) 22

(The Capitol compilations listed above may exist with later label designs. These would be worth half the values listed.)

70	Dandelion 63754	I'M BACK AND I'M PROUD (LP, gatefold sleeve) 30
71	Kama Sutra 2316 005	THE DAY THE WORLD TURNED BLUE (LP). 22
71	Kama Sutra 2316 009	IF YOU COULD ONLY SEE ME TODAY (LP) 22
72	Regal Starline SRS 5117	PIONEERS OF ROCK VOLUME 1 (LP) 12
74	Regal Starline SRS 5177	THE KING OF FOOLS: PIONEERS OF ROCK VOLUME 4 (LP) 12
74	Capitol ST 11287	THE BOP THAT JUST WON'T STOP. 12
81	Capitol E-ST 26223	THE SINGLES ALBUM (LP, with bonus "Vintage Vincent" EP [PSR 458]) 12
87	Charly BOX 108	GENE VINCENT: THE CAPITOL YEARS '56-'63 (10-LP box set with 36-page booklet; later remastered and reissued with slimmer box, 1989). 60
90	EMI CDGV 1	THE GENE VINCENT BOX SET (Complete Capitol & Columbia Recordings, 1956-64) (6-CD set). 50

VINCENT UNITS

81	Y Y 8	Carnival Song/Everything Is Going To Be All Wrong (p/s) 4
81	Y Y 8	Carnival Song/Everything Is Going To Be All Wrong (cassette). 8

CAROLE VINCI

78	EMI EMI 2801	Vivre/Souffire Et Sourire 12

JOEY VINE

65	Immediate IM 017	Down And Out/The Out Of Towner 18

MINT VALUE £

VINEGAR JOE

72	Island WIP 6125	Never Met A Dog/Speed Queen Of Ventura	5
72	Island WIP 6148	Rock'n'Roll Gypsies/So Long	5
73	Island WIP 6174	Black Smoke From The Calumet/Long Way Round	5
72	Island ILPS 9183	VINEGAR JOE (LP)	18
72	Island ILPS 9214	ROCK 'N ROLL GYPSIES (LP, gatefold sleeve)	12
73	Island ILPS 9262	SIX STAR GENERAL (LP, gatefold sleeve)	12

(see also Dada, Robert Palmer, Elkie Brooks)

EDDIE 'MR. CLEANHEAD' VINSON

51	Vogue V 2023	Queen Bee Blues/Jump And Grunt (78)	30
64	Riverside RLP 3302	BACK DOOR BLUES (LP)	30
72	Philips 6369 406	THE ORIGINAL CLEANHEAD (LP)	15

(see also Wynonie Harris)

V. VINSTRICK & J.J. ALLSTARS

68	Doctor Bird DB 1167	Love Is Not A Game/CINDERELLA: The Way I See You	15

BOBBY VINTON

61	Fontana H 307	Little Lonely One/Corrine Corrina	12
62	London HLU 9592	I Love You The Way You Are/CHUCK & JOHNNY: You Are My Girl	12
62	Columbia DB 4878	Roses Are Red/You And I	6
62	Columbia DB 4900	Rain Rain Go Away/Over Over	6
63	Columbia DB 4961	Trouble Is My Middle Name/Let's Kiss And Make Up	6
63	Columbia DB 7015	Over The Mountain/Faded Pictures	6
63	Columbia DB 7052	Blue On Blue/Those Little Things	6
63	Columbia DB 7110	Blue Velvet/Is There A Place	12
63	Columbia DB 7179	There! I've Said It Again/The Girl With The Bow In Her Hair	6
64	Columbia DB 7240	My Heart Belongs To Only You/Warm And Tender	6
64	Columbia DB 7303	Tell Me Why/Remembering	6
64	Columbia DB 7348	Clinging Vine/Imagination Is A Magic Dream	6
64	Columbia DB 7422	Mr Lonely/The Bell That Couldn't Jingle	15
65	Columbia DB 7514	Long Lonely Nights/Satin	6
65	Columbia DB 7628	Don't Go Away Mad/Lonely Girl	6
65	Columbia DB 7731	What Colour Is A Man/Love Of Infatuation	6
66	Columbia DB 7808	Satin Pillows/Careless	6
66	Columbia DB 7922	Dum De Da/The Exodus Song	6
67	Columbia DB 8114	Coming Home Soldier/Don't Let My Mary Go Around	6
67	Columbia DB 8319	Please Love Me Forever/Miss America	6
68	Columbia DB 8346	Just As Much As Ever/Another Memory	6
68	CBS 3636	Halfway To Paradise/(My Little) Christie	6
68	CBS 3897	I Love How You Love Me/Little Barefoot Boy	6
69	CBS 4451	Days Of Sand And Shovel/So Many Lonely Girls	6
69	CBS 4910	My Elusive Dreams/Over And Over	6
70	CBS 5106	No Arms Can Ever Hold You/I Love How You Love Me	6
62	Columbia SEG 8212	YOUNG IN HEART (EP)	22
64	Columbia SEG 8363	SONGS OF CHRISTMAS (EP)	25
63	Columbia 33SX 1517	SINGS THE BIG ONES (LP)	25
63	Columbia 33SX 1566	BLUE ON BLUE (LP)	25
63	Columbia 33SX 1611	MY HEART BELONGS TO ONLY YOU (LP)	25
65	Columbia 33SX 1649	TELL ME WHY (LP)	25

MATT VINYL

77	Housewife's Choice	Useless Tasks (p/s)	8

VIOLATORS (U.K.)

82	No Future OI 9	Gangland/Fugitive (p/s, with insert)	10
82	No Future OI 19	Summer Of '81/Live Fast Die Young (p/s)	10
83	Future FS 2	Life On The Red Line/Crossing The Sangsara (p/s)	6

VIOLENT FEMMES

84	Rough Trade RT 147	Ugly/Gimme A Car (p/s)	4
84	Rough Trade RTT 147	Ugly/Gimme A Car/Gone Daddy Gone/Good Feeling (12", p/s)	7
83	Rough Trade ROUGH 55	VIOLENT FEMMES (LP, with inner sleeve)	10

VIOLENTS

63	HMV POP 1130	Alpen Ros/Ghia	12

VIOLENT THIMBLE

67	Polydor 56217	Gentle People (Parts 1 & 2)	6

VIPERS (SKIFFLE GROUP)

56	Parlophone R 4238	Ain't You Glad/Pick A Bale Of Cotton	15
56	Parlophone R 4238	Ain't You Glad/Pick A Bale Of Cotton (78)	8
57	Parlophone R 4261	Don't You Rock Me Daddy-O/10,000 Years Ago	18
57	Parlophone R 4261	Don't You Rock Me Daddy-O/10,000 Years Ago (78)	8
57	Parlophone R 4286	Jim Dandy/Hi Liley, Liley Lo	15
57	Parlophone R 4286	Jim Dandy/Hi Liley, Liley Lo (78)	8
57	Parlophone R 4289	The Cumberland Gap/Maggie May	15
57	Parlophone R 4289	The Cumberland Gap/Maggie May (78)	8
57	Parlophone R 4308	Streamline Train/Railroad Steam Boat	12
57	Parlophone R 4308	Streamline Train/Railroad Steam Boat (78)	8
57	Parlophone R 4351	Homing Bird/Pay Me My Money Down	12
57	Parlophone R 4351	Homing Bird/Pay Me My Money Down (78)	10
57	Parlophone R 4371	Skiffle Party Medley (Parts 1 & 2)	12
57	Parlophone R 4371	Skiffle Party Medley (Parts 1 & 2) (78)	10
58	Parlophone R 4393	Baby Why?/No Other Baby (as Vipers)	20
58	Parlophone R 4393	Baby Why?/No Other Baby (as Vipers) (78)	12
58	Parlophone R 4435	Make Ready For Love/Nothing Will Ever Change (My Love For You) (as Vipers)	12

58	Parlophone R 4435	Make Ready For Love/Nothing Will Ever Change (My Love For You) (78)	15
58	Parlophone R 4484	Summertime Blues/Liverpool Blues (as Vipers)	25
58	Parlophone R 4484	Summertime Blues/Liverpool Blues (as Vipers) (78)	35
57	Parlophone GEP 8615	SKIFFLE MUSIC VOL. 1 (EP)	20
57	Parlophone GEP 8626	SKIFFLE MUSIC VOL. 2 (EP)	20
57	Parlophone GEP 8655	SKIFFLING ALONG WITH THE VIPERS (EP)	25
57	Parlophone PMD 1050	COFFEE BAR SESSION (10" LP)	50
86	Rollercoaster ROLL 2011	COFFEE BAR SESSION (LP)	12

(see also Jet Harris & Tony Meehan, Shadows, Wally Whyton, Sharkey Todd & Monsters)

VIPERS
78	Mulligan LUNS 718	I've Got You/No Such Thing (p/s)	10

VIPPS
66	CBS 202031	Wintertime/Anyone	40

(see also V.I.P.s)

V.I.P.s
64	RCA RCA 1427	Don't Keep Shouting At Me/She's So Good	50
66	Island WI 3003	I Wanna Be Free/Don't Let It Go	30
67	Island WIP 6005	Straight Down To The Bottom/In A Dream	30

(see also Vipps, Art, Spooky Tooth, Felder's Orioles, Timebox, Patto, Baron & His Pounding Piano, Keith Emerson)

V.I.P.s
78	Bust SOL 3	MUSIC FOR FUNSTERS (EP)	15
79	Rok ROK V/VI	Can't Let You Go/URBAN DISTURBANCE: Wild Boys In Cortinas (no p/s)	6
80	Gem GEMS 43	I Need Somebody To Love (Could It Be You?)/One More Chance// Stuttgart Special/Who Knows/Janine (double pack, stickered p/s)	5

(see also Mood Six, Jed Dmochowski)

VIRGIL BROTHERS
69	Parlophone R 5787	Temptation 'Bout To Get Me/Look Away	6
69	Parlophone R 5802	Good Love/When You Walk Away	5

VIRGINIANS
63	Pye International 7N 25175	Limbo Baby/Greenback Dollar	7

VIRGINIA TREE
75	Minstrel 0001	FRESH OUT (LP)	30

(see also Shirley Kent, Ghost)

VIRGINIA WOLF
86	Atlantic A 9459	Waiting For Your Love/Take A Chance (p/s)	10

VIRGINIA WOLVES
66	Stateside SS 563	Stay/B.L.T.	20

VIRGIN PRUNES
81	Baby BABY 001	TWENTY TENS (EP)	8
81	Rough Trade RT 072	In The Greylight/War/Moments Of Mine (Despite Straight Lines) (1st issue in blue p/s with insert, later in black p/s without insert)	6/4
81	Rough Trade RT 090	A New Form Of Beauty Part Two: Come To Daddy/Sweet Home Under White Clouds/Sad World (10", p/s, 33rpm)	7
81	Rough Trade RT 091T	A New Form Of Beauty Part Three: The Beast (Seven Bastard Suck)/ The Slow Children (Abbagal)/Brain Damage/No Birds To Fly (12", p/s)	7
81	Rough Trade RT 089-091	A NEW FORM OF BEAUTY (7"/10"/12" box set)	22
82	Rough Trade RT 106	Pagan Lovesong/Dave-id Is Dead (p/s)	4
82	Rough Trade 12 RT 106	Pagan Lovesong (Vibe Akimbo)/Pagan Lovesong/Dave-id Is Dead (12", p/s)	7
82	Rough Trade RT 119	(What Shall We Do When) Baby Turns Blue/Yeo (p/s)	4
82	Rough Trade RTT 119	(What Shall We Do When) Baby Turns Blue/Yeo/Chance Of A Lifetime (12", p/s)	7
87	Baby BABY 011	HERESIE (10", double pack, gatefold p/s, 1st 1,000 on clear vinyl)	10/7

(see also Gavin Friday, Bono & Gavin Friday)

VIRGIN SLEEP
67	Deram DM 146	Love/Halliford House	30
68	Deram DM 173	Secret/Comes A Time	30

VIRTUE
85	Other OTH 1	We Stand To Fight (p/s)	20

VIRTUES (U.S.)
59	HMV POP 621	Guitar Boogie Shuffle/Guitar In Orbit	15
59	HMV POP 637	Flippin' In/Shufflin' Along	18
59	HMV POP 637	Flippin' In/Shufflin' Along (78)	50

VIRTUES (Jamaica)
65	Island WI 196	Your Wife And Mother/Amen (actually with Ambassadors)	12
68	Doctor Bird DB 1164	High Tide/RUPIE EDWARDS & VIRTUES: Burning Love	10

(see also Lloyd & Devon)

FRANK VIRTUOSO ROCKETS
56	Melodisc MEL 1393	Toodle-Oo Kangaroo/Hop-Skip-Jump Mambo (78)	15
56	Melodisc MEL 1386	Rollin' And A-Rockin'/Rock — Good Bye Mambo (78)	25
58	Melodisc MEL 1386	Rollin' And A-Rockin'/Rock — Good Bye Mambo (red label, tri centre, export issue)	25
58	Melodisc MEL 1386	Rollin' And Rockin'/Toodle-Oo Kangaroo (green label, round centre)	12

VISAGE
79	Radar ADA 48	Tar/Frequency 7 (p/s)	10
81	Polydor POSP 293	Visage (Remix)/Second Steps ('mirror', 'cowboy' or 'melting face' sleeve)	each 5
82	Polydor POSPP 441	Night Train/I'm Still Searching (picture disc)	6
82	Polydor POSPP 523	Pleasure Boys/The Anvil (picture disc)	8
82	Polydor POSPX 523	Pleasure Boys (Dance Mix)/The Anvil (Dance Mix) (12", 800 only)	18

MINT VALUE £

82	Polydor POSPV 523	Der Amboss (12", 1-sided, stickered plain black sleeve & labels, promo only) . . .	15
88	Polydor 080 012-2	Mind Of A Toy/We Move (Dance Mix)/Frequency 7 (Dance Mix)/	
		Mind Of A Toy (Video) (CD Video)	18
83	Polydor VIS 1	FADE TO GREY (DANCE MIX PROMO) (LP, stamped white sleeve, promo only) . .	12

(see also Steve Strange, Midge Ure, Ultravox, Rich Kids)

TONY VISCONTI
79	Regal Zonophone RZ 3089	I Remember Brooklyn/Sitting In A Field Of Heather	5

(see also Dib Cochran & Earwigs)

VISCOUNTS (U.S.)
59	Top Rank JAR 254	Harlem Nocturne/Dig	15
60	Top Rank JAR 388	The Touch (Le Grisbi)/Chug-A-Lug	15
60	Top Rank JAR 502	Night Train/Summertime	12
65	Stateside SS 468	Harlem Nocturne/Dig (reissue)	12
61	Top Rank JKP 3005	VISCOUNTS ROCK (EP)	80

VISCOUNTS (U.K.)
60	Pye 7N 15249	That's All Right/Rocking Little Angel	10
60	Pye 7N 15287	Shortnin' Bread/Fee-Fi-Fo-Fum	7
61	Pye 7N 15323	Money (Is The Root Of All Evil)/One Armed Bandit	7
61	Pye 7N 15344	Banned In Boston/Moonlight Promises	6
61	Pye 7N 15356	Joe Sweeney/Honey Come On And Dance With Me	6
61	Pye 7N 15379	Who Put The Bomp (In The Bomp, Bomp, Bomp)/What Am I Saying.	7
62	Pye 7N 15414	Mama's Doin' The Twist/I'm Going But I'll Be Back	6
62	Pye 7N 15431	One Of The Guys/Dear Mary Brown.	6
62	Pye 7N 15445	Everybody's Got A Ya Ya/Lot Of Livin' To Do.	6
62	Pye 7N 15479	That Stranger Used To Be My Girl/Silent Night	6
63	Pye 7N 15510	Don't Let Me Cross Over/I'm Coming Home	6
63	Pye 7N 15536	It's You/I'll Never Get Over You.	6
63	Columbia DB 7146	I Don't Care What People Say/Roll On Little Darlin'	6
64	Columbia DB 7253	Where Do You Belong/Kiss Me	6
64	Columbia DB 7436	Sally/On Broadway	5
60	Pye NEP 24132	VISCOUNTS' HIT PARADE (EP)	30

(see also Gordon Mills)

VISIONS
69	Grape GR 3009	Captain Hook/The Girl	6

(see also King Horror)

VISITORS
78	NRG SRTS/NRG 002	Take It Or Leave It/No Compromise (no p/s)	20

VISITORS
80	Departure RAPTURE 1	Empty Rooms/Orcadian Visitors (foldover p/s).	7
81	Rational RATE 2	Compatability/Poet's End (foldover p/s)	4

VISITORS
87	Sha La La	Goldmining/MAGIC SHOP: It's True (flexidisc, p/s,	
	BA BA BA BA BA 8	free with *Simply Thrilled* & other fanzines)	7/5

VITAL DISORDERS
85	Lowther International VD 3	Some People/Xmas Island Calypso (hand-screened p/s)	4

MIROSLAV VITOUS
79	Warner Bros K 17448	New York City/Basic Laws (12")	7

AMOR VIVI
70	Big Shot BI 534	Dirty Dog/Round And Round The Moon	7

VIVIENNE
57	HMV 7EG 8290	VIVIENNE (EP)	8

VIXEN
88	EMI MTPD 48	Edge Of A Broken Heart/Charmed Life (shaped picture disc)	7
89	EMI MTS 48	Edge Of A Broken Heart/Charmed Life (p/s, reissue, with backstage pass)	4
89	EMI 12 MTP 48	Edge Of A Broken Heart (Extended Version)/Charmed Life/	
		Edge Of A Broken Heart (12", p/s with poster)	7
89	EMI 12 MTS 48	Edge Of A Broken Heart/Love Made Me (live)/Cryin' (live) (12", p/s)	8
88	EMI MTG 60	Crying/Desperate (gatefold p/s).	4
88	EMI MTPD 60	Crying/Desperate (shaped picture disc)	7
88	EMI MTP 60	Crying/Desperate/Edge Of A Broken Heart (12", poster p/s)	7
91	EMI MTS 66	Love Made Me (Remix)/Give It Away (p/s, with postcards).	4
91	EMI MTPD 66	Love Made Me (Remix)/Give It Away (shaped picture disc with insert)	7
88	EMI MTL 1028	VIXEN (LP, early copies play extra track "Charmed Life", withdrawn)	20

VLADO & ISOLDA
84	Ariola 106 500	Ciao Amore (English)/Ciao Amore (Croatian)	10

VOGUES (U.K.)
66	Columbia DB 7985	Younger Girl/Lies	12

(see also Llan)

VOGUES (U.S.)
65	London HLU 9996	You're The One/Some Words	10
66	London HLU 10014	Five O'Clock World/Nothing To Offer You	10
66	King KG 1035	Magic Town/Humpty Dumpty	8
68	Reprise RS 20766	My Special Angel/I Keep It Hid	6
68	Reprise RS 20686	Turn Around Look At Me/Then	6
69	Reprise RS 20788	Till/I Will	6
69	London HLG 10247	Five O'Clock World/You're The One	7
69	Reprise RS 20820	Earth Angel/P.S. I Love You	6
69	Reprise RS 23366	No, Not Much/You Were Too Good To Me	6
69	Reprise RS 20844	Green Fields/Easy To Say	5

MINT VALUE £

66	King KGL 4003	MEET THE VOGUES (LP)	25
66	King KGL 4006	FIVE O'CLOCK WORLD (LP)	20
69	Reprise RSLP 6314	TURN AROUND, LOOK AT ME (LP)	15
69	Reprise RSLP 6326	TILL (LP)	15

VOICE
| 66 | Mercury MF 905 | Train To Disaster/Truth | 140 |

(see also Karl Stuart & Profile, Profile, Miller Anderson)

VOICEROYS
(see under Viceroys)

VOICES
| 56 | Beltona BL 2667 | Rock And Roll Hit Parade Medley (Parts 1 & 2) | 10 |
| 56 | Beltona BL 2667 | Rock And Roll Hit Parade Medley (Parts 1 & 2) (78) | 20 |

VOICES OF EAST HARLEM
70	Elektra 2101 013	Right On Be Free/Gotta Be A Change — Oh Yeah	6
70	Elektra 2101 018	No No No/Music In The Air	5
70	Elektra 2469 007	RIGHT ON BE FREE (LP)	20

VOICES OF VICTORY
| 54 | Vocalion V 1040 | Trusting In Jesus?/Jesus Lifted Me (78) | 15 |

VOIDS
| 66 | Polydor BM 56073 | Come On Out/I'm In A Fix | 35 |

WES VOIGHT
| 59 | Parlophone R 4586 | I'm Movin' In/I'm Ready To Go Steady | 100 |

VOIZ
| 77 | Pilgrim/Grapevine GRA 110 | BOANERGES (LP, with insert) | 15 |

HOWARD VOKES COUNTRY BOYS
62	Starlite STEP 27	HOWARD VOKES COUNTRY BOYS (EP)	20
63	Starlite STEP 37	MOUNTAIN GUITAR (EP)	20
67	Starlite GRK 508	HOWARD VOKES COUNTRY BOYS (EP; reissue, with sleeve sticker over original catalogue number)	12

VOLCANOES
| 84 | Volcanic VOLC 1 | Strangers In The Night/Murder U.S.A. (p/s) | 4 |

VOLCANOS
61	Philips PB 1098	Ruby Duby Du/Redhead	15
61	Philips PB 1113	Tightrope/Great Imposter	15
62	Philips PB 1246	Polaris/Scotch Mist	12
60	Philips BBE 12432	THE VOLCANOS (EP)	80

VOLUMES
62	Fontana 270 109TF	I Love You/Dreams	60
63	London HL 9733	Teenage Paradise/Sandra	50
68	Pama PM 755	I Just Can't Help Myself/One Way Lover (unreleased, test pressings only)	300

VOLUNTEERS
| 63 | Parlophone R 5088 | Farther Along/Little David | 6 |

(see also Karol Keyes)

VONTASTICS
| 66 | Chess CRS 8043 | Day Tripper/My Baby | 15 |
| 67 | Stateside SS 2002 | Lady Love/When My Baby Comes Back Home | 25 |

VON TRAP FAMILY
| 80 | Woronzow W 001 | Brand New Thrill/Dreaming/No Reflexes (p/s, 500 only) | 35 |

(see also Bevis Frond)

VOOMINS
| 65 | Polydor 56001 | If You Don't Come Back/March Of The Voomins | 12 |

VOX POP
| 93 | Detour DR 007 | Cor Blimey/Pretty Impossible (p/s, some on purple vinyl) | 8/5 |

VOXPOPPERS
58	Mercury 7MT 202	The Last Drag/Wishing For Your Love	40
58	Mercury MT 202	The Last Drag/Wishing For Your Love (78)	30
58	Mercury MEP 9533	VOXPOPPERS (EP)	125

VOYAGER
| 85 | Fighting Cock | Run Away Heart/Don't Hold Back (p/s) | 12 |

V2
78	Bent SMALL BENT 1	Speed Freak/Nothing To Do/That's It (800 only, later reissued on red vinyl)	10
79	TJM TJM 1	Man In The Box/When The World Isn't There (12", p/s)	15
79	TJM TJM 6	Is Anybody Out There? (unissued)	
70s	Groove	Gee Whiz It's You/Face In The Crowd (p/s, stamped white labels)	15

VULCANS
| 73 | Trojan TRLS 53 | STAR TREK (LP) | 18 |

VULCAN'S HAMMER
| 73 | Brown BVH 1 | TRUE HEARTS AND SOUND BOTTOMS (LP, with insert) | 550 |

VULTURES
| 79 | Rubber Connection SP 522 | Time Let's Go/Is This A Man (p/s, with insert & sticker) | 6 |

VULTURES
| 88 | Narodnik NRK 006T | Good Thing/You're Not Scared/What I Say/Jack The Ripper (12", p/s) | 7 |

VYE
| 80 | Dead Good DEAD 8 | Five Hours 'Til Tonight/Right Girl, Wrong Time/Til Dawn (p/s, with insert) | 4 |

WACKERS
63	Oriole CB 1902	I Wonder Why/Why Can't It Happen To Me	12
64	Piccadilly 7N 35195	Love Or Money/Hooka Tooka	8
64	Piccadilly 7N 35210	The Girl Who Wanted Fame/You're Forgetting	8

ADAM WADE
60	Top Rank JAR 296	Tell Her For Me/Don't Cry, My Love	7
60	Top Rank JAR 370	Ruby/Too Far	7
60	HMV POP 764	I Can't Help It/I Had The Craziest Dream	6
60	HMV POP 787	Speaking Of Her/Blackout The Moon	6
60	HMV POP 807	In Pursuit Of Happiness/For The Want Of Your Love	7
61	HMV POP 843	Take Good Care Of Her/Sleepy Time Gal	6
61	HMV POP 896	Point Of No Return/The Writing On The Wall	6
61	HMV POP 913	As If I Didn't Know/Playin' Around	6
61	HMV POP 942	Tonight I Won't Be There/Linda	6
62	HMV POP 966	Cold Cold Winter/Preview Of Paradise	6
62	HMV POP 996	Prisoner's Song/Them There Eyes	6
62	Columbia DB 4891	I'm Climbin'/They Didn't Believe Me	5
63	Columbia DB 4962	There'll Be No Teardrops Tonight/Here Comes The Pain	5
63	Columbia DB 4986	Don't Let Me Cross Over/Rain From The Skies	5
63	Columbia DB 7045	Why Do We Have To Wait So Long/They Say	5
63	Columbia DB 7165	Does Goodnight Mean Goodbye/Julie	5
60	HMV 7EG 8620	AND THEN CAME ADAM (EP)	18
64	Columbia SEG 8316	FOUR FILM SONGS (EP)	18
61	HMV CLP 1451	ADAM AND EVENING (LP)	30

CLIFF WADE
69	Morgan Bluetown BT 1S	You've Never Been To My House/Sister	10

JOHNNY WADE
60	HMV POP 757	Funny Thing/Shadow Love	6

WELLINGTON WADE
63	Oriole CB 1857	Let's Turkey Trot/It Ain't Necessarily So	18

(see also Ian & Zodiacs)

ADRIAN WAGNER
74	Atlantic K 50082	DISTANCES BETWEEN US (LP, with Robert Calvert)	15
78	Charisma CAS 1135	THE LAST INCA (LP, with booklet)	12

(see also Robert Calvert)

ROBERT WAGNER
57	London HLU 8491	Almost Eighteen/So Young	22
57	London HLU 8491	Almost Eighteen/So Young (78)	25

CHUCK WAGON
79	A&M AMS 7450	Rock 'n' Roll Won't Go Away/The Spy In My Face (p/s, black or purple vinyl)	10

(see also Dickies)

PORTER WAGONER
67	RCA Victor RCA 1586	The Cold Hard Facts Of Life/You Can't Make A Heel Toe The Mark	6
64	RCA Victor RCX 7157	A LITTLE SLICE OF LIFE (EP)	15
64	RCA Victor RCX 7158	Y'ALL COME (EP)	15
64	RCA Victor RD 7693	THE BLUE GRASS STORY (LP)	20
65	RCA Camden CDN 5128	AN OLD LOG CABIN FOR SALE (LP)	12

WAH! (HEAT)
81	Inevitable INEV 001	Better Scream/Joe (wraparound p/s in poly bag)	6
81	Inevitable INEV 004	Seven Minutes To Midnight/Don't Step On The Cracks (p/s, different colour sleeves)	4
81	Eternal SLATE 1	Forget The Down!/The Checkmate Syndrome (p/s, as Wah!)	4
80s	WEA	OFFICIAL BOOTLEG (LP)	10

(see also Faction)

WAIKIKIS
61	Palette PG 9025	Hawaii Tattoo/Waikiki Welcome	5
65	Pye Intl. NPL 28060	HAWAII BEACH PARTY (LP)	12
65	Pye Intl. NPL 28063	MERRY CHRISTMAS IN HAWAII (LP)	12
65	Pye Intl. NPL 28072	LOLLIPOPS AND ROSES (LP)	12
66	Pye Intl. NPL 28081	A TASTE OF HAWAII (LP)	12

WAILERS (U.S.)
59	London HL 8958	Tall Cool One/Road-Runner	15
59	London HL 8958	Tall Cool One/Road-Runner (78)	75
59	London HL 8994	Mau-Mau/Dirty Robber (tri centre, later round)	125/75
59	London HL 8994	Mau-Mau/Dirty Robber (78)	120
64	London HL 9892	Tall Cool One/Road-Runner (reissue)	10

WAILERS (Jamaica)
(see under Bob Marley)

WAILING COCKS
78	Bird's Nest BN 116	Rockin' Youth/Stand Up For Peace	5
78	Bird's Nest BN 121	Listen To The Wailing Cocks/Listen To The Wailing Cocks	5

WAILING SOULS

70	Banana BA 305	Row Fisherman Row/Thou Shalt Not Steal	10
70	Banana BA 307	Back Out/Pack Your Things	10
71	Banana BA 335	Walk Walk Walk/KING SPORTY: Love Me — Version (B-side actually by Denis Alcapone)	20
71	Green Door GD 4014	Harbour Shark/Harbour Shark — Version	15
72	Punch PH 106	Dungeon (as Wailing Soul)/NORA DEAN: Kiss Me Honey	35

(see also Denis Alcapone, Tuff Gong All Stars)

WAILING WAILERS

(see under Bob Marley & Wailers)

CHERRY WAINER

58	Pye 7N 15161	Itchy Twitchy Feeling/Cerveza	12
58	Pye N 15161	Itchy Twitchy Feeling/Cerveza (78)	8
58	Pye 7N 15170	Valencia/Blue Cha Cha	10
58	Pye N 15170	Valencia/Blue Cha Cha (78)	8
59	Pye 7N 15197	The Happy Organ/Spanish Marching Song	7
59	Pye N 15197	The Happy Organ/Spanish Marching Song (78)	8
59	Pye 7N 15217	The Song Of Lotus Lee/Iced Coffee	6
59	Pye N 15217	The Song Of Lotus Lee/Iced Coffee (78)	10
59	Top Rank JAR 253	I'll Walk The Line/Saturday Night In Tia Juana	8
60	Columbia DB 4528	Happy Like A Bell (Ding Dong)/Money (That's What I Want)	25
63	Honey Hit TB 128	Sleepwalk/Red River Rock (with Red Price Combo, some with p/s)	10/5
59	Pye NEP 24099	CHERRY WAINER (EP)	25
60	Top Rank BUY 042	WALTZES IN SPRINGTIME (LP)	18

(see also Red Price Combo)

PHIL WAINMAN

65	Columbia DB 7615	Hear Me A Drummer Man/Hear His Drums	10
68	Fontana TF 978	Going Going Gone/Hey Paradiddle	5

LOUDON WAINWRIGHT III

71	Atlantic 2400 103	ALBUM I (LP)	18
72	Atlantic K 40107	ALBUM I (LP, reissue)	12
72	Atlantic K 40272	ALBUM II (LP)	15

WAITING FOR THE SUN

78	Profile GMOR 167	WAITING FOR THE SUN (LP, private pressing)	100

(see also After The Fire)

TOM WAITS

79	Asylum K 12347	Somewhere/Red Shoes By The Drugstore	5
86	Island ISD 260	In The Neighbourhood/Singapore//Tango Till They're Sore/Rain Dogs (double pack, p/s)	5
73	Asylum SYM 9007	CLOSING TIME (LP, with insert)	18
74	Asylum SYM 9012	THE HEART OF SATURDAY NIGHT (LP)	15
75	Asylum SYSP 903	NIGHTHAWKS AT THE DINER (2-LP, gatefold sleeve)	18
76	Asylum K 53030	CLOSING TIME (LP, reissue)	12
76	Asylum K 53035	THE HEART OF SATURDAY NIGHT (LP, 'door' label)	12
77	Asylum K 53050	SMALL CHANGE (LP, 'sky' label)	12
77	Asylum K 53068	FOREIGN AFFAIRS (LP, with inner sleeve)	12
79	Asylum K 53088	BLUE VALENTINE (LP, gatefold sleeve)	12
80	Asylum K 52252	HEARTATTACK AND VINE (LP, with inner sleeve)	12
81	Elektra K 52316	BOUNCED CHEQUES (LP)	12
86	WEA 960 321-1	THE ASYLUM YEARS (2-LP, gatefold sleeve)	15
99	Epitaph 6457 251	MULE CONVERSATIONS (CD, p/s, jewel case, promo only)	20

(see also Roy Orbison)

WAKE

69	Pye 7N 17813	Angelina/So Happy	12
70	Carnaby CNS 4010	Live Today Little Girl/Days Of Emptiness	12
70	Carnaby CNS 4014	Boys In The Band/To Make You Happy	12
70	Carnaby CNS 4016	Noah/To Make You Happy	12
71	Carnaby 6151 001	Linda/Got My Eyes On You	12
70	Carnaby CNLS 6005	23.59 (LP)	75

WAKE

82	Scan SCN 01	On Our Honeymoon/Give Up (p/s in bag)	20
84	Scan 45/Factory FAC 88	Talk About The Past/Everybody Works So Hard (p/s)	5
84	Scan 45/Factory FAC 8812	Talk About The Past/Everybody Works So Hard (12", p/s)	8
89	Sarah SARAH 21	Crush The Flowers/Carbrain (p/s)	7
90s	Sarah SARAH 48	Major John/Lousy Pop Group (p/s)	7
83	Factory FACT 60	HARMONY (LP)	15
91	Factory FACT 130	HERE COMES EVERYBODY (LP)	15
90s	Sarah SARAH 602	MAKE IT LOUD (LP)	15
90s	Sarah SARAH 618	TIDAL WAVE OF HYPE (LP)	15

JIMMY WAKELY

51	Capitol CL 13446	Telling My Troubles To My Old Guitar/My Heart Cries For You (78)	8
51	Capitol CL 13523	When You And I Were Young Maggie Blues/Fool's Paradise (78, with Margaret Whiting)	8
52	Capitol CL 13716	Missing In Action/Star Of Hope (78)	8
52	Capitol CL 13787	A Four-Legged Friend/There's A Cloud In My Valley Of Sunshine (78, with Bob Hope)	8
52	Capitol CL 13812	I Went To Your Wedding/Pale Moon (78)	8
53	Capitol CL 13923	A Bushel And A Peck/Gomen-Nasai (Forgive Me) (78, with Margaret Whiting)	8
53	Capitol CL 14121	My Heart Knows/Tennessee Church Bells (78, with Margaret Whiting)	8
56	Vogue Coral Q 72125	Are You Mine? (with Ruth Ross)/Yellow Roses	12

MINT VALUE £

56	Vogue Coral Q 72125	Are You Mine? (with Ruth Ross)/Yellow Roses (78)	10
56	Brunswick 05542	Are You Satisfied? (with Gloria Wood)/Mississippi Dreamboat	12
56	Brunswick 05542	Are You Satisfied? (with Gloria Wood)/Mississippi Dreamboat (78)	8
56	Brunswick 05563	Folsom Prison Blues/That's What The Lord Can Do	15
56	Brunswick 05563	Folsom Prison Blues/That's What The Lord Can Do (78)	10
57	Brunswick LAT 8179	SANTA FE TRAIL (LP)	20

(see also Karen Chandler, Bob Hope, Margaret Whiting)

RICK WAKEMAN (Band)

73	A&M AMS 7061	Catherine/Anne	5
75	A&M AMS 7206	Love's Dream/Orpheus' Song	6
75	A&M/Lyntone LYN 3176/7	Wagner's Dream/Love's Dream/Count Your Blessings (with 2 tracks by Roger Daltrey, flexidisc free with *19* magazine)	10/5
79	A&M AMS 7435	Birdman Of Alcatraz (Theme From 'My Son My Son')/Falcons De Neige (p/s)	5
79	A&M AMS 7436	Animal Showdown/Sea Horses (p/s)	5
79	A&M AMSP 7436	Animal Showdown/Sea Horses (picture disc, in PVC sleeve)	6
79	A&M AMS 7497	Swan Lager/Woolly Willy Tango	4
80	A&M AMS 7510	I'm So Straight I'm A Weirdo/Do You Believe In Fairies? (p/s)	4
80	WEA K 18354	The Spider/Danielle (some with p/s, 2,000 only)	8/4
71	Polydor 2460 135	PIANO VIBRATIONS (LP, with John Schroeder Orchestra)	18
73	A&M AMLH 64361	THE SIX WIVES OF HENRY VIII (LP, gatefold sleeve, early copies have continuous run-off groove)	10
74	A&M QU-84361	THE SIX WIVES OF HENRY VIII (LP, gatefold sleeve, quadrophonic mix)	20
74	A&M AMLH 63621	JOURNEY TO THE CENTRE OF THE EARTH (LP, gatefold booklet sleeve)	10
75	A&M AMLH 64515	THE MYTHS & LEGENDS OF KING ARTHUR & THE KNIGHTS OF THE ROUND TABLE (LP, gatefold sleeve, 12-page booklet)	10
75	A&M AMLH 64546	LISZTOMANIA (LP, soundtrack)	12
89	A&M RWCD 20	RICK WAKEMAN: 20TH ANNIVERSARY (4-CD box set, 1,000 only)	50

(see also Strawbs, Yes, Dib Cochran & Earwigs, Steve Howe, Jon Anderson)

ANTON WALBROOK

53	Parlophone MSP 6002	La Ronde De L'Amour/BERLIN 'SYMPHONIKER' ORCHESTRA: The Blue Waltz	7
54	Parlophone MSP 6099	Always Young/It Only Took A Minute	7
54	Parlophone MSP 6100	Strike Another Match/Man Is Man	7

JERRY WALD

| 60 | London HLU 8909 | Sheba/Moon Over Miami (unissued) | |

HOWARD WALES

(see under Jerry Garcia)

WALHAM GREEN EAST WAPPING CARPET CLEANING RODENT & BOGGIT EXTERMINATING ASSOCIATION

| 68 | Columbia DB 8426 | Sorry Mr. Green/Death Of A Kind | 50 |

ANNA WALKER & CROWNETTES

| 69 | Pama PM 768 | You Don't Know/Billy Joe | 6 |

BILLY WALKER (U.K.)

60	Philips PB 1001	Forever/Changed My Mind	7
64	Decca F 11917	My Heart Cries For You/Little On The Lonely Side	6
65	Columbia DB 7724	A Certain Girl/I Don't Wanna Fall In Love	7

BILLY WALKER (U.S.)

| 66 | London HLU 10060 | Million And One/Close To Linda | 6 |

BOOTS WALKER

| 69 | London HLP 10265 | No One Knows/Geraldine | 6 |

CLINT WALKER

| 60 | Warner Bros WEP 6006 | INSPIRATION (EP, also stereo WSEP 2006) | 12/18 |

DAVID WALKER

| 68 | RCA RCA 1664 | Ring The Changes/Keep A Little Love | 20 |

(see also Paradox)

GARY WALKER (& RAIN)

66	CBS 202036	You Don't Love Me/Get It Right	10
66	CBS 202081	Twinkie-Lee/She Makes Me Feel Better	6
68	Polydor 56237	Spooky/I Can't Stand To Lose You (as Gary Walker & Rain)	10
69	Philips BF 1740	Come In You'll Get Pneumonia/Francis (as Gary Walker & Rain)	40
74	United Artists UP 35742	Hello How Are You/Fran	5
66	CBS EPS 5742	HERE'S GARY (EP)	35

(see also Walker Brothers, Paul & Ritchie & Cryin' Shames, Badfinger, Universals)

GRAHAM WALKER SOUND

| 69 | Saga EROS 8126 | FAMOUS TV THEMES (LP) | 10 |

JACKIE WALKER

| 58 | London HLP 8588 | Oh Lonesome Me/Only Teenagers Allowed | 225 |
| 58 | London HLP 8588 | Oh Lonesome Me/Only Teenagers Allowed (78) | 50 |

JERRY JEFF WALKER

| 68 | Atlantic 584 200 | Mr Bojangles/Round And Round | 4 |
| 71 | Atlantic 2466 007 | BEIN' FREE (LP) | 10 |

JIMMY WALKER

| 53 | Lyragon J 706 | A Fine Romance/Hallelujah (78) | 8 |

JOHN WALKER

67	Philips BF 1593	Anabella/You Don't Understand Me	8
67	Philips BF 1612	If I Promise/I See Love In You	6
68	Philips BF 1655	I'll Be Your Baby Tonight/Open The Door Homer	6
68	Philips BF 1676	Kentucky Woman/I Cried All The Way Home	6

MINT VALUE £

68	Philips BF 1724	Woman/A Dream	5
69	Philips BF 1758	Yesterday's Sunshine/Little One	5
69	Carnaby CNS 4004	Everywhere Under The Sun/Traces Of Tomorrow	5
70	Carnaby CNS 4009	True Grit/Sun Comes Up	5
70	Carnaby CNS 4012	Cottonfields/Jamie	5
70	Carnaby CNS 4017	Over And Over Again/Sun Comes Up	5
67	Philips (S)BL 7829	IF YOU GO AWAY (LP)	30
69	Carnaby CNLS 6001	THIS IS JOHN WALKER (LP)	25

(see also Walker Brothers, John & Scott Walker, Johnny & Judy)

JOHN & SCOTT WALKER

66	Philips BE 12597	SOLO JOHN — SOLO SCOTT (EP, 2 tracks each)	10

(see also Walker Brothers, Scott Walker, John Walker, Scott Engel)

JUNIOR WALKER & ALL STARS

65	Tamla Motown TMG 509	Shotgun/Hot'Cha	30
65	Tamla Motown TMG 520	Do The Boomerang/Tune Up	45
65	Tamla Motown TMG 529	Shake And Fingerpop/Cleo's Back	22
66	Tamla Motown TMG 550	Cleo's Mood/Baby You Know It Ain't Right	18
66	Tamla Motown TMG 559	Road Runner/Shoot Your Shot (original small label print, later large)	12/6
66	Tamla Motown TMG 571	How Sweet It Is (To Be Loved By You)/Nothing But Soul (small label print)	12
67	Tamla Motown TMG 571	How Sweet It Is (To Be Loved By You)/Nothing But Soul (later pressing)	6
66	Tamla Motown TMG 586	Money (That's What I Want) (Parts 1& 2)	15
67	Tamla Motown TMG 596	Pucker Up Buttercup/Any Way You Wanna	18
68	Tamla Motown TMG 637	Come See About Me/Sweet Soul	8
68	Tamla Motown TMG 667	Hip City (Parts 1 & 2)	12
69	Tamla Motown TMG 682	Home Cookin'/Mutiny	10
69	Tamla Motown TMG 691	Road Runner/Shotgun	5
69	Tamla Motown TMG 712	What Does It Take (To Win Your Love)/Brainwasher	5
70	Tamla Motown TMG 727	These Eyes/I've Got To Find A Way To Win Maria Back	8
70	Tamla Motown TMG 750	Do You See My Love (For You Growing)/Groove And Move	7
72	Tamla Motown TMG 824	Walk In The Night/Right On Brothers And Sisters/ Gotta Hold On To This Feeling (maxi-single)	5
73	Tamla Motown TMG 840	Take Me Girl, I'm Ready/I Don't Want To Do Wrong	5
73	Tamla Motown TMG 857	Way Back Home (Vocal)/Way Back Home (Instrumental)	8
73	Tamla Motown TMG 857	Way Back Home (Vocal)/Way Back Home (Instrumental)/Country Boy (reissue)	5
73	Tamla Motown TMG 872	Wholly Holy/Peace And Understanding Is Hard To Find	5
74	Tamla Motown TMG 889	Don't Blame The Children/Soul Clappin'	5
74	Tamla Motown TMG 894	Gotta Hold On To This Feeling/I Ain't Going Nowhere	5
76	Tamla Motown TMG 1027	I'm So Glad/Dancin' Like They Do On Soul Train (as Jr. Walker)	5
66	Tamla Motown TME 2013	SHAKE AND FINGERPOP (EP)	35
65	Tamla Motown TML 11017	SHOTGUN (LP)	40
66	T. Motown (S)TML 11029	SOUL SESSION (LP, mono/stereo)	35/40
66	T. Motown (S)TML 11038	ROAD RUNNER (LP, mono/stereo)	30/35
69	T. Motown (S)TML 11097	HOME COOKIN' (LP)	25
69	T. Motown (S)TML 11120	JUNIOR WALKER'S GREATEST HITS (LP, original with flipback sleeve)	15
70	T. Motown (S)TML 11140	THESE EYES (LP)	22
70	T. Motown STML 11152	LIVE (LP)	18
70	T. Motown STML 11167	A GASSSSSSSSSSS! (LP)	18
72	T. Motown STML 11198	RAINBOW FUNK (LP)	15
72	T. Motown STML 11211	MOODY JR. (LP)	15
73	T. Motown STML 11234	PEACE AND UNDERSTANDING IS HARD TO FIND (LP)	12
75	T. Motown STML 11274	JR. WALKER AND THE ALL STARS (LP)	12
76	T. Motown STML 12018	HOT SHOT (by Jr. Walker)	15
76	T. Motown STML 12033	SAX APPEAL (by Jr. Walker)	15
76	Motown STML 12048	WHOPPER BOPPER SHOW STOPPER (by Jr. Walker)	12

KARL WALKER & ALLSTARS

66	Rymska RA 103	One Minute To Zero/Don't Come Back (both sides actually featuring Tommy McCook & Supersonics)	35

(see also Kent Walker, Ernel Braham)

KENT WALKER

68	Fab FAB 53	When You Going To Show Me How/Come Yah Come Yah	8

(see also Karl Walker, Ernel Braham)

ROB WALKER

71	Upsetter US 366	Run Up Your Mouth (actually by Stranger Cole)/UPSETTERS: Mouth Version	6
71	Jackpot JP 761	Hear My Heart/Puppet On A String	6

(see also Stranger Cole, Tommy McCook)

RONNIE WALKER

69	Stateside SS 2151	It's A Good Feeling/Precious	15
75	Polydor 2006 578	Magic's In The Air/They Can't Say Hello	5

SCOTT WALKER

67	Philips BF 1628	Jackie/The Plague	8
68	Philips BF 1662	Joanna/Always Coming Back To You	8
69	Philips BF 1793	Lights of Cincinnati/Two Weeks Since You've Gone	7
71	Philips 6006 168	I Still See You/My Way Home	7
73	Philips 6006 311	The Me I Never Knew/This Way Mary	6
73	CBS 1795	A Woman Left Lonely/Where Love Has Died	6
74	CBS 2521	Delta Dawn/We Had It All	6
84	Virgin VS 666	Track 3/Blanket Roll Blues (p/s)	5
67	Philips MCP 1006	GREAT SCOTT (cassette EP)	20
67	Philips (S)BL 7816	SCOTT (LP, mono/stereo)	18/22
68	Philips BL 7840	SCOTT 2 (LP, mono, originally with signed portrait)	25/15
68	Philips SBL 7840	SCOTT 2 (LP, stereo, originally with signed portrait)	35/20
68	Ember EMB LP 3393	LOOKING BACK WITH SCOTT WALKER (LP, mono or stereo)	25
69	Philips SBL 7882	SCOTT 3 (LP, gatefold sleeve)	35

Scott WALKER

69	Philips SBL 7900	SCOTT WALKER SINGS SONGS FROM HIS TV SERIES (LP)	18
69	Philips SBL 7910	THE BEST OF SCOTT WALKER VOL. 1 (LP)	18
69	Philips SBL 7913	SCOTT 4 (LP)	45
70	Philips 6308 035	'TIL THE BAND COMES IN (LP)	50
72	Philips 6308 120	THE MOVIEGOER (LP)	40
73	Philips 6308 148	ANY DAY NOW (LP)	40
73	CBS 65725	STRETCH (LP)	25
74	CBS 80254	WE HAD IT ALL (LP)	20
76	Philips 6625 017	SPOTLIGHT ON SCOTT WALKER (2-LP)	18
73	Philips 6382 052	THIS IS SCOTT WALKER VOL. 2 (LP)	12
73	Philips 6850 013	THE ROMANTIC SCOTT WALKER (LP, Audio Club issue)	35
70s	Philips 6856 022	TERRIFIC (LP, Audio Club issue, reissue of "Scott 2" with different tracks)	40
81	Zoo ZOO 2	FIRE ESCAPE IN THE SKY — THE GODLIKE GENIUS OF SCOTT WALKER (LP)	20
81	Philips 6359 090	SINGS JACQUES BREL (LP)	12
95	Fontana SWINT 1	TILT INTERVIEW CD (CD, promo only)	25

(see also Scott Engel, Scott Engel & John Stewart, John & Scott Walker, Walker Brothers, Routers)

T-BONE WALKER

54	London HL 8087	The Hustle Is On/Baby Broke My Heart (78)	40
65	Liberty LIB 12018	Party Girl/Here In The Dark	15
63	London REP 1404	TRAVELLIN' BLUES (EP)	80
54	Capitol LC 6681	CLASSICS IN JAZZ (10" LP)	50
63	Capitol T 1958	T-BONE WALKER (LP)	40
65	M F P MFP 1043	THE BLUES OF T-BONE WALKER (LP)	30
65	Liberty LBY 4047	SINGS THE BLUES (LP)	45
66	Liberty LBY 3057	SINGING THE BLUES (LP)	45
68	MCA MUPS 331	THE TRUTH (LP)	18
68	Stateside S(S)L 10223	STORMY MONDAY BLUES (LP)	25
69	Stateside S(S)L 10265	FUNKY TOWN (LP)	25
73	Reprise K 94001	VERY RARE (2-LP)	18
74	Atlantic K 40131	T-BONE BLUES (LP)	15

WENDY WALKER

63	Decca F 11573	Window Shopping/Ain't A Boy In The World	6
63	Decca F 11671	Boys Will Be Happy/Casanova	6

WALKER BROTHERS

65	Philips BF 1401	Pretty Girls Everywhere/Doin' The Jerk	12
65	Philips BF 1409	Love Her/The Seventh Dawn	8
65	Philips BF 1428	Make It Easy On Yourself/But I Do	6
65	Philips BF 1454	My Ship Is Coming In/You're All Around Me	6
66	Philips BF 1473	The Sun Ain't Gonna Shine Anymore/After The Lights Go Out	6
66	Philips BF 1497	(Baby) You Don't Have To Tell Me/My Love Is Growing	6
66	Philips BF 1514	Another Tear Falls/The Saddest Night In The World	7
66	Philips BF 1537	Deadlier Than The Male/Archangel	7
67	Philips BF 1548	Stay With Me Baby/Turn Out The Moon	7
67	Philips BF 1576	Walking In The Rain/Baby Make It The Last Time	7
76	GTO GT 42	No Regrets/Remember Me	5
76	GTO GT 67	Lines/First Day	5
77	GTO GT 78	We're All Alone/Have You Seen My Baby	6
78	GTO GT 230	The Electrician/Den Haague (p/s)	6
78	GTO GT 295	Shutout/The Electrician/Nite Flights/Fat Mama Kick	5
66	Philips BE 12596	I NEED YOU (EP)	15
67	Philips BE 12603	THE WALKER BROTHERS (EP, probably unreleased)	
67	Philips MCP 1004	THE HITS OF THE WALKER BROTHERS & DUSTY SPRINGFIELD (cassette EP)	12
65	Philips BL 7691	TAKE IT EASY WITH THE WALKER BROTHERS (LP)	18
66	Philips (S)BL 7732	PORTRAIT (LP, initially with photo insert)	22/15
67	Philips (S)BL 7770	IMAGES (LP)	15
67	Philips DBL 002	THE WALKER BROTHERS STORY (2-LP)	18
68	Wing WL 1188	THE FABULOUS WALKER BROTHERS (LP)	15

(see also Scott Walker, Scott Engel, John Walker, John & Scott Walker, Gary Walker [& Rain], Routers)

WALKIE TALKIES

79	Sire SIR 4023	Rich And Nasty/Summer In Russia (p/s)	6

(see also Pauline Murray & Invisible Girls, Mission)

WALKING FLOORS

80s	My Death Telephone TEL 1	No Next Time/Removal (foldover p/s)	8

FRED WALKING-STICK & ELECTRIC WIRELESS ORCHESTRA

61	Pye 7N 15390	Well I Ask Yew/Ain't She Sweet	4

DENNIS WALKS

68	Amalgamated AMG 816	Having A Party/GROOVERS: Day By Day	10
68	Blue Cat BS 144	Belly Lick/DRUMBAGO & BLENDERS: The Game Song	10
69	Bullet BU 402	Heart Don't Leap/CLARENDONIANS: I Am Sorry	7
69	Bullet BU 408	Love Of My Life/Under The Shady Tree	7
71	Moodisc HM 101	Time Will Tell/Under The Shady Tree	6
74	Magnet MG 062	Don't Play That Song/Version	5

(see also I Roy)

SHELTON WALKS

73	Bullet BU 550	No Money No Friend/BOB MAC ALL STARS: Money Dub	5
74	Dip DL 5026	One Of Us Will Weep/KING EDWARDS ALL STARS: Version	5

WALL

79	Small Wonder SMALL 13	New Way/Suckers/Uniforms (p/s)	5
79	Small Wonder SMALL 21	Exchange/Kiss The Mirror (p/s)	5
80	Fresh FRESH 17	Ghetto/Another New Day (p/s)	4
81	Fresh FRESH 27	Hobby For A Day/Redeemer/8334 (p/s)	4

(see also Ski Patrol)

MAX WALL
51	Polygon P 1028	Take It Easy/Me And My Tune (78)	10
73	York YR 203	The Fiddley Foodle Bird/Story Of The Fiddley Foodle Bird	5
75	DJM DJS 10352	Why Should I Care/Devil Bomb	5
77	Stiff BUY 12	England's Glory/Dream Tobacco (p/s)	5

REM WALL & HIS GREEN VALLEY BOYS
60	Top Rank JAR 324	Heartsick And Blue/One More Time	7

ERROL WALLACE
69	Escort ES 817	Bandit/ASTON BORROT: Family Man Mood (actually by Aston "Family Man" Barrett)	6

GIG WALLACE & HIS ORCHESTRA
60	Philips PB 981	Rockin' On The Railroad/Show Me The Way To Go Home	8
60	Philips PB 981	Rockin' On The Railroad/Show Me The Way To Go Home (78)	25

IAN WALLACE
61	Parlophone R 4726	I Can't Do My Bally Bottom Button Up/In Other Words	6

JERRY WALLACE
54	Polygon P 1133	Dixieanna/Runnin' After Love (78)	15
58	London HL 8719	With This Ring/How The Time Flies	18
58	London HL 8719	With This Ring/How The Time Flies (78)	30
58	London HL 7062	With This Ring/How The Time Flies (export issue)	10
59	London HLH 8943	Primrose Lane/By Your Side	8
59	London HLH 8943	Primrose Lane/By Your Side (78)	35
60	London HLH 9040	Little Coco Palm/Mission Bell Blues	8
60	London HLH 9110	You're Singing Our Love Song To Somebody Else/King Of The Mountain	8
60	London HLH 9177	Swingin' Down The Lane/Teardrop In The Rain	7
61	London HLH 9264	There She Goes/Angel On My Shoulder	7
61	London HLH 9363	Life's A Holiday/I Can See An Angel	7
62	London HLH 9630	Shutters And Boards/Am I That Easy To Forget	7
64	London HLH 9914	Even The Bad Times Are Good/In The Misty Moonlight	7
65	Mercury MF 853	Time/Rainbow	6

SIPPIE WALLACE
67	Storyville 671 198	SIPPIE WALLACE SINGS THE BLUES (LP)	18

WALLACE BROTHERS
64	Sue WI 334	Precious Words/You're Mine	22
65	Sue WI 355	Lover's Prayer/Love Me Like I Love You	25
67	Sue WI 4036	I'll Step Aside/Hold My Heart For A While	25
67	Sue ILP 950	SOUL CONNECTION (LP)	140

WALLACE COLLECTION
69	Parlophone R 5764	Daydream/Baby I Don't Mind	8
69	Parlophone R 5793	Fly Me To The Earth/Love	8
70	Parlophone R 5844	Serenade/Walk On Out	8
69	Parlophone PMC/PCS 7076	LAUGHING CAVALIER (LP)	18
70	Parlophone PCS 7099	WALLACE COLLECTION (LP)	15

'FATS' WALLER (& HIS RHYTHM)
SINGLES
50	London L 808	Laughin' Cryin' Blues/JAMES P. JOHNSON: Roumania (78)	8
51	HMV JO 205	It's A Sin To Tell A Lie/Come Down To Earth My Angel (78, export issue)	7
51	London L 1032	Cow Cow Boogie/TEDDY WEATHERFOOD: Sugar Foot Stomp (78)	7
52	HMV JO 291	I'm On A See-Saw/As Long As The World Goes 'Round (78, export issue)	7
53	HMV 7M 128	My Very Good Friend The Milkman/Shortnin' Bread	10
53	HMV 7M 157	A Good Man Is Hard To Find/The Girl I Left Behind Me	8
53	HMV 7M 142	Honey Hush/You've Been Reading My Mail	10
54	HMV 7M 208	You've Been Taking Lessons In Love/I've Got A New Lease Of Life	8
54	HMV 7M 244	By The Light Of The Silvery Moon/Romance A La Mode (with Deep River Boys)	10
54	HMV 7M 244	By The Light Of The Silvery Moon/Romance A La Mode (78)	8
60	RCA RCA 1189	Dinah/When Somebody Thinks You're Wonderful	5

EPs
54	HMV 7EG 8022	FATS WALLER AND HIS RHYTHM (EP)	8
54	HMV 7EG 8042	FATS WALLER AND HIS RHYTHM (EP)	8
54	HMV 7EG 8054	FATS WALLER AND HIS RHYTHM (EP)	8
55	HMV 7EG 8078	FATS WALLER AND HIS RHYTHM (EP)	8
55	HMV 7EG 8098	FATS WALLER (EP)	8
56	HMV 7EG 8148	FATS WALLER AND HIS RHYTHM (EP)	8
56	HMV 7EG 8191	SWINGING AT THE ORGAN (EP)	8
57	HMV 7EG 8212	FATS WALLER (EP)	8
57	HMV 7EG 8242	FATS WALLER AND HIS RHYTHM (EP)	8
57	HMV 7EG 8255	FATS WALLER AND HIS RHYTHM (EP)	8
58	HMV 7EG 8304	FATS WALLER IN LONDON NO. 1 (EP)	8
58	HMV 7EG 8341	FATS WALLER IN LONDON NO. 2 (EP)	8
59	RCA RCX 1010	FATS WALLER (EP)	8
59	RCA RCX 1053	YOUR FEET'S TOO BIG (EP)	10
60	HMV 7EG 8602	FATS WALLER IN LONDON NO. 3 (EP)	8

LPs
53	London AL 3507	REDISCOVERED FATS WALLER SOLOS (10" LP)	25
53	HMV DLP 1008	FAVOURITES (10" LP)	20
53	HMV DLP 1017	PLAYS AND SINGS (10" LP)	20
54	HMV DLP 1056	RHYTHM AND ROMANCE WITH FATS WALLER (10" LP)	15
54	London AL 3521	FATS AT THE ORGAN (10" LP)	20
54	London AL 3522	JIVIN' WITH FATS (10" LP)	20
55	HMV DLP 1082	FUN WITH FATS (10" LP)	15

MINT VALUE £

55	HMV CLP 1036	THOMAS "FATS" WALLER NO. 1 (LP)	12
55	HMV CLP 1042	THOMAS "FATS" WALLER NO. 2 (LP)	12
56	HMV DLP 1111	YOUNG FATS WALLER (10" LP)	15
56	HMV DLP 1118	FAVOURITES NO. 2 (10" LP)	15
57	HMV DLP 1138	SPREADIN' RHYTHM AROUND (10" LP)	20
57	RCA RD 27047	FATS 1935-1937 (LP)	15
58	RCA RC 24041	FATS 1938-1942 (10" LP)	15
59	RCA Camden CDN 131	THE REAL FATS WALLER (LP)	12
60	RCA RD 27185	HANDFUL OF KEYS (LP)	12

(see also Louisiana Sugar Babies, Deep River Boys, James P. Johnson)

GORDON (WALLER)

68	Columbia DB 8337	Rosecrans Boulevard/Red, Cream And Velvet	8
68	Columbia DB 8440	Every Day/Because Of A Woman	7
68	Columbia DB 8518	Weeping Annaleah/The Seventh Hour	7
69	Bell BLL 1059	I Was A Boy When You Needed A Man/Lady In The Window	5
70	Bell BLL 1106	You're Gonna Hurt Yourself/Sunshine	5
72	Vertigo 6360 069	GORDON (LP, as Gordon, gatefold sleeve, spiral label)	70

(see also Peter & Gordon)

BOB WALLIS & HIS STORYVILLE JAZZMEN

60	Top Rank JAR 331	Bluebird/Captain Morgan	6
60	Top Rank JAR 365	Madison Time/Bonne Nuit, Ma Cherie	6
60	Pye Jazz 7NJ 2039	Jingle Bells/Chinatown, My Chinatown	5
61	Pye Jazz 7NJ 2043	I'm Shy Mary Ellen I'm Shy/Three Live Wires	6
61	Pye Jazz 7NJ 2048	Come Along Please/Bobbin' Along	6
57	77 EP 10	NEW ORLEANS JAM SESSION VOLUME 1 (EP)	25
60	Pye Jazz NJE 1079	BOB WALLIS STORYVILLE JAZZMEN (EP)	10
60	Pye Jazz NJE 1085	BOB WALLIS PLAYS (EP)	12
62	Storyville SEP 368	BOB WALLIS STORYVILLE JAZZMEN (EP)	10
59	77 Records 77LE 12/2	THE RAVING SOUNDS OF BOB WALLIS (LP)	50
60	Top Rank BUY 023	EVERYBODY LOVES SATURDAY NIGHT (LP)	30
61	Pye Jazz NJL 27	OLE MAN RIVER (LP)	40
61	Pye Jazz NJL 30	TRAVELLIN' BLUES (LP)	25
62	Pye Jazz NJL 41	THE WALLIS COLLECTION (LP)	20

BOB WALLIS & SANDY BROWN

| 62 | Pye Jazz 7NJ 2060 | Oh Didn't It Rain/In A Little Spanish Town | 6 |

LARRY WALLIS

| 77 | Stiff BUY 22 | Police Car/On Parole (with p/s or die-cut company sleeve) | 5/4 |

(see also Pink Fairies, Subs, Deviants, Shagrat, Peter Wyngarde)

SHANI WALLIS

60	Philips PB 1019	Sixteen Reasons (Why I Love You)/Forever, Forever	7
60	Philips PB 1076	Where's The Boy/And Now	6
63	Decca F 11632	My Heart Cries For You/All Over Again	6
67	London HLR 10125	Look Of Love/Let Your Love Come Through	6
68	London HLR 10225	As Long As He Needs Me/Where Is Love	6
59	Philips BBE 12337	SHANI WALLIS (EP)	8
61	Vivitone 45EP 3001	CABARET TIME (EP)	10
67	London HA-R 8324	I'M A GIRL (LP)	18
67	London HA-R/SH-R 8338	LOOK TO LOVE (LP)	18

(see also Kirchin Band)

WALL OF SLEEP

| 95 | Woronzow WOO 24 | WALL OF SLEEP (LP, with insert) | 12 |

WALLY BROTHERS

| 74 | Explosion EX 2090 | The Man Who Sold The World/Version | 4 |

WALRUS

70	Deram DM 308	Who Can I Trust?/Tomorrow Never Comes	15
71	Deram DM 323	Never Let My Body Touch Ground/Why?	12
71	Deram SML 1072	WALRUS (LP)	40

JAMES WALSH GYPSY BAND

| 79 | RCA PB 1403 | Cuz It's You Girl/Bring Yourself Together (withdrawn, demo-only) | 20 |

JOE WALSH

| 73 | Probe PRO 600 | Rocky Mountain Way/(Daydream) Prayer | 4 |
| 74 | Probe PRO 611 | Meadows/Book Ends | 4 |

(see also James Gang, Eagles)

SHEILA WALSH & CLIFF RICHARD

83	DJM SHEIL 1	Drifting/It's Lonely When The Lights Go Out (p/s)	5
83	DJM SHEIL 100	Drifting/It's Lonely When The Lights Go Out (picture disc)	10
83	DJM SHEILT 1	Drifting/It's Lonely When The Lights Go Out (12", p/s)	8
83	DJM SHEILT 100	Drifting/It's Lonely When The Lights Go Out (12", picture disc)	12
83	DJM DJF 20581	DRIFTING (LP, with inner sleeve, as Sheila Walsh)	10
84	Sparrow BIRD 152	TRIUMPH IN THE AIR (LP, with lyric sheet, as Sheila Walsh)	10
85	Sparrow BIRD 165	DON'T HIDE YOUR HEART (LP, with lyric sheet, as Sheila Walsh)	10

(see also Cliff Richard)

BURT WALTERS

| 68 | Trojan TR 636 | Honey Love/KING CANNONBALL BRYAN: Thunderstorm | 10 |

(see also Lee 'Scratch' Perry)

DAVE WALTON

66	CBS 202057	Love Ain't What It Used To Be/Tell Me A Lie	7
66	CBS 202098	Every Window In The City/I've Left The Troubled Ground	5
67	CBS 202508	After You There Can Be Nothing/Can I Get It From You	6

WALTONES

87	Medium Cool MC 004	Downhill/Closest To (p/s)	4
88	Medium Cool MC 016	The Deepest/Failing In Love (p/s, with Clint Boon)	4
80s	Zine 10	She Looks Right Through Me (Demo Version)/HEPBURNS: Where You Belong (flexidisc with *Zine* fanzine, issue 10)	6/5

TRAVIS WAMMACK

65	Atlantic AT 4017	Scratchy/Fire Fly	20
72	United Artists UP 35412	Whatever Turns You On/Slip Away	5
73	United Artists UP 35468	So Good/Darling, You're All That I Need	5

WANDERER

59	Top Rank JAR 183	The Happy Hobo/True True Happiness	6
59	Top Rank JAR 183	The Happy Hobo/True True Happiness (78)	30

WANDERERS (U.S.)

60	MGM MGM 1102	I Could Make You Mine/I Need You More	35
61	MGM MGM 1169	As Time Goes By/There Is No Greater Love	18
64	United Artists UP 1020	Run Run Senorita/After He Breaks Your Heart	22
(see also Ray Pollard)			

WANDERERS (Jamaica)

69	Trojan TR 7721	Wiggle Waggle/Jaga Jaga War	6

WANDERERS (U.K.)

81	Polydor POSP 239	Ready To Snap/Beyond The Law (no p/s)	8
81	Polydor POSP 284	The Times They Are A'Changin'/Little Bit Frightening (no p/s)	8
81	Polydor POLS 1028	ONLY LOVERS LEFT (LP)	20
(see also Lords Of The New Church, Stiv Bators, Dead Boys)			

WANGLERS

79	Matchbox Classics MC 5	KICKIN' OUT FOR THE COAST (EP, white label, yellow or red stickered foldover p/s)	10

DEXTER WANSEL

86	Streetwave SWAVE 9	Life On Mars (Parts 1 & 2) (12", p/s)	8
78	Phil. Intl. PIR 82786	VOYAGER (LP)	20

WAR

71	Liberty LBF 15443	Sun Oh Son/Lonely Feelin'	6
71	United Artists UP 35281	All Day Music/Get Down	6
72	United Artists UP 35327	Slippin' Into Darkness/Nappy Head	5
73	United Artists UP 35469	The World Is A Ghetto/Four Cornered Room	5
73	United Artists UP 35521	The Cisco Kid/Beetles In The Bag	5
73	United Artists UP 35576	Gypsy Man/Deliver The Word	5
74	United Artists UP 35623	Me And Baby Brother/In Your Eyes	5
75	United Artists UP 35836	Why Can't We Be Friends/In Mazatlan	5
76	Island WIP 6267	Low Rider/So	5
77	MCA MCA 339	Galaxy/Version (12")	8
71	Liberty LBG 83478	WAR (LP)	15
72	United Artists UAS 29269	ALL DAY MUSIC (LP)	15
73	United Artists UAS 29400	THE WORLD IS A GHETTO (LP)	12
73	United Artists UAG 29521	DELIVER THE WORD (LP)	12
74	United Artists UAD 60067/8	WAR LIVE! (2-LP)	15
75	United Artists UAG 29843	WHY CAN'T WE BE FRIENDS (LP)	12
76	Island ILPS 9413	GREATEST HITS (LP)	12
77	Island ILPS 9507	PLATINUM FUNK (LP)	12
78	MCA MCF 2822	GALAXY (LP)	12
79	MCA MCG 4001	THE MUSIC BAND (LP)	12
79	MCA MCF 2804	YOUNGBLOOD (LP, soundtrack)	12
(see also Eric Burdon & War)			

BILLY WARD & HIS DOMINOES

53	Parlophone R 3789	Don't Thank Me/Rags To Riches (78)	50
54	Parlophone MSP 6112	Three Coins In The Fountain/Lonesome Road	150
54	Parlophone R 3882	Three Coins In The Fountain/Lonesome Road (78)	45
56	Brunswick 05599	St. Therese Of The Roses/Home Is Where You Hang Your Heart	40
56	Brunswick 05599	St. Therese Of The Roses/Home Is Where You Hang Your Heart (78)	10
57	Brunswick 05656	Evermore/Half A Love (Is Better Than None)	20
57	Brunswick 05656	Evermore/Half A Love (Is Better Than None) (78)	12
57	London HLU 8465	Stardust/Lucinda	25
57	London HLU 8465	Stardust/Lucinda (78)	10
57	London HLU 8502	Deep Purple/Do It Again	25
57	London HLU 8502	Deep Purple/Do It Again (78)	10
58	London HLU 8634	Jennie Lee/Music, Maestro, Please	30
58	London HLU 8634	Jennie Lee/Music, Maestro, Please (78)	40
59	London HLU 8883	Please Don't Say 'No'/Behave, Hula Girl	18
59	London HLU 8883	Please Don't Say 'No'/Behave, Hula Girl (78)	45
58	London REU 1114	BILLY WARD & HIS DOMINOES (EP)	175
58	Parlophone PMD 1061	BILLY WARD & HIS DOMINOES FEATURING CLYDE McPHATTER (10" LP)	700
58	London HA-U 2116	YOURS FOREVER (LP)	50
(see also Dominoes, Clyde McPhatter, Jackie Wilson)			

CHRISTINE WARD

66	Decca F 12339	The Face Of Empty Me/Girl I Used To Know	12

CLARA WARD & HER SINGERS

65	Stateside SS 474	Gonna Build A Mountain/God Bless The Child	6

CLIFFORD T. WARD

72	Dandelion 2001 327	Carrie/Sidetrack	10
72	Dandelion 2001 382	Coathanger/Rayne	7
73	Charisma CB 212	Wherewithal/Thinking Of Something To Do	5

Clifford T. WARD

74	Charisma CB 233	Jayne/Maybe I'm Right	6
75	Charisma CB 248	Jigsaw Girl/Cellophane	5
75	Philips 6006 490	No More Rock'n'Roll/Gandalf	5
76	Philips 6006 542	Ocean Of Love/Tomorrow Night	5
77	Mercury 6007 132	Up In The World/Not Waving, Drowning (Revisited)	5
77	Mercury 6007 149	I Got Lost Tonight/Detriment (p/s)	7
77	Mercury LUV 1	Someone I Know/If I Had Known (gatefold p/s)	8
80	WEA K 18294	Convertible/Taking The Long Way Round (no p/s)	7
81	WEA K 18426	The Best Is Yet To Come/Lost Again (no p/s)	7
81	WEA K 18486	Contrary/Climate Of Her Favour (no p/s)	7
84	Philips 880 550 7	Messenger/Where Do Angels Really Come From (p/s)	8
86	Tembo TML 114	Cricket/Computer (no p/s)	10
86	Tembo TML 123	Sometime Next Year/Turbo (p/s)	8
72	Dandelion 2310 216	SINGER SONGWRITER (LP)	15
73	Charisma CAS 1006	HOME THOUGHTS (LP)	15
75	Charisma CAS 1098	ESCALATOR (LP)	12
75	Philips 9109 500	NO MORE ROCK'N'ROLL (LP)	12
75	Philips 9109 216	WAVES (LP)	12
77	Mercury 9109 605	NEW ENGLAND DAYS (LP, with insert)	12
84	Philips 814 777	BOTH OF US (LP, with insert)	15
86	Tembo TMB 111	SOMETIME NEXT YEAR (LP)	15
92	Ameless AME 101	LAUGH IT OFF (LP, first 100 with inserts)	15/12

(see also Secrets, Simon's Secrets, Martin Raynor & Secrets)

DALE WARD
64	London HLD 9835	Oh Julie/Letter From Sherry	12

HEDLEY WARD TRIO
50	HMV B 9911	Enjoy Yourself/Women (78)	8
50	HMV B 9951	Three Wheels On The Wagon/M-I-S-S-I-S-S-I-P-P-I (78)	8
55	Melodisc MEL 1344	Rock Around The Clock/Who Dat Up There (78)	12
56	Melodisc MEL 1352	Who's Sorry Now/Big Ears (78)	10
56	Melodisc MEL 1387	Steamboat Rock/My Baby's Got Such Lovin' Ways (78)	25

ROBIN WARD
63	London HLD 9821	Wonderful Summer/Dream Boy	12

TERRY WARD with BUMBLIES
65	Fontana TF 558	Gotta Tell/When I Come To You	6

SHEELAGH WARDE
59	Top Rank JAR 131	Let Mr. Maguire Sit Down/The Golden Jubilee	6
59	Top Rank JAR 131	Let Mr. Maguire Sit Down/The Golden Jubilee (78)	12

WARDENS
70s	SNO PEAS TIC 001	Lust Like This/Do So Well (with insert, no p/s)	4

WARD SINGERS
56	London Jazz EZ-C 19024	THE FAMOUS WARD SINGERS (EP)	20
56	London Jazz LZ-C 14013	THE FAMOUS WARD SINGERS (10" LP)	18

WARDS OF COURT
67	Deram DM 127	All Night Girl/How Could Say One Thing	15

LEON WARE
77	Motown STML 12050	MUSICAL MASSAGE (LP)	15

WARHORSE
71	Vertigo 6059 027	St. Louis/No Chance	12
70	Vertigo 6360 015	WARHORSE (LP, spiral label, gatefold sleeve)	30
72	Vertigo 6360 066	RED SEA (LP, spiral label, gatefold sleeve)	30

(see also Deep Purple, Nic Simper's Fandango)

FRED WARING & HIS PENNSYLVANIANS
59	Capitol CL 14981	Dry Bones/Way Back Home	5
55	Brunswick OE 9194	THE BALLAD OF DAVY CROCKETT (EP)	12
51	Brunswick LAT 8011	LISTENING TIME (LP)	15
53	Brunswick LA 8625	WALT DISNEY FILM SONGS (10" LP)	18
54	Brunswick LA 8651	A SONG OF EASTER (10" LP)	15
54	Brunswick LA 8678	SONGS OF INSPIRATION (10" LP)	15
54	Brunswick LA 8693	'TWAS THE NIGHT BEFORE CHRISTMAS (10" LP)	15
55	Brunswick LA 8704	HARMONIZIN' THE OLD SONGS (10" LP)	15
55	Brunswick LAT 8068	FOR LISTENING ONLY (LP)	12

RAY WARLEIGH
69	Philips (S)BL 7881	RAY WARLEIGH'S FIRST ALBUM (LP)	22

(see also John Mayall's Blues Breakers, Alexis Korner)

OZZIE WARLOCK & WIZARDS
59	HMV POP 635	Juke Box Fury/Wow!	12

(see also Tony Osbourne)

WARM
78	Warm 2001	It's The Kooler/Teenage Space Queen (p/s)	5
78	Warm SMS 001/2001/S	THE DEMO TAPES (EP, double pack)	10
78	Warm WARM 2003	Floosie/Chewing Gum Sue/Bye Bye It's Blues/Sometimes (p/s)	4

JOHNNY WARMAN
78	Ring O' 2017 112	Head On Collision/London's Burning/Mind Games (some in p/s)	20/10
78	Ring O' 2339 202	HOUR GLASS (LP, Germany only; unreleased in U.K.)	
81	Rocket TRAIN 17	WALKING INTO MIRRORS (LP)	10

WARM DUST
71	Trend 6099 002	It's A Beautiful Day/Worm Dance	10
70	Trend TNLS 700	AND IT CAME TO PASS (2-LP)	40
71	Trend 6480 001	PEACE FOR OUR TIME (LP)	40

WARM EXPRESSION
70	Columbia DB 8672	Let No Man Put Asunder/The Holy City	7

WARM JETS
79	RSO RSO 47	Big City Boys/Mr Natural (p/s)	4
81	Bridgehouse BHS 1	Sticky Jack/Shell Shock (p/s)	5

WARM SENSATION
69	Columbia DB 8568	I'll Be Proud Of You/The Clown	5

(see also Ivy League)

WARM SOUNDS
67	Immediate IM 058	Sticks And Stones/Angeline	12
67	Deram DM 120	The Birds And Bees/Doo-Dah	12
68	Deram DM 174	Nite Is A-Comin'/Smeta Mergaty	25

(see also Denny Gerrard, Tuesday's Children, Open Road)

HERB & BETTY WARNER
59	Felsted AF 114	Slowly/'BUGS' BOWER GROUP: Slowly	6
59	Felsted AF 114	Slowly/'BUGS' BOWER GROUP: Slowly (78)	10

JACK WARNER
68	MFP MFP 1278	YER CAN'T 'ELP LAUGHIN' (LP)	12

JACK WARNER with TOMMY REILLY
58	Oriole CB 1426	An Ordinary Copper/On The Way Up	7
58	Oriole CB 1426	An Ordinary Copper/On The Way Up (78)	10

FLORENCE WARNER
73	Epic EPC 1626	For No Good Reason/Remember	5
75	Epic EPC 3817	Anyway I Love You/Dreamer	5
73	Epic EPC 80077	FLORENCE WARNER (LP)	18

GALE WARNING
56	Pye N 15061	Heartbreak Hotel/Met Rock (78)	18
56	Oriole CB 1349	Rock Those Crazy Skins/I Need Your Love (78)	18

WARP
70s	Warped WPD 001	Do The Warp/(ECT: Here In Britain)/Fable/White (p/s)	5

WARP NINE
75	Stax STXS 2030	Theme From 'Star Trek'/Para Song One	4

ALMA WARREN
56	Parlophone MSP 6200	Stealin'/Now And Forever	7

ELLIE WARREN
83	PRT 7P 263	Shattered Glass/Killer Touch	20

FRAN WARREN
52	MGM MGM 548	What Is This Thing Called Love/One For The Wonder (78)	8
59	MGM MGM 1008	Shame/As Long As You Believe Me	6
59	MGM MGM 1008	Shame/As Long As You Believe Me (78)	15

GUY WARREN OF GHANA
59	Brunswick 05791	Monkies And Butterflies/An African's Prayer (with Rod Saunders)	6
59	Brunswick 05791	Monkies And Butterflies/An African's Prayer (78, with Rod Saunders)	10
69	Columbia SCX 6340	AFRO-JAZZ (LP, as Guy Warren Of Ghana)	25
72	Regal Zono. SLRZ 1031	THE AFRICAN SOUNDS OF GUY WARREN OF GHANA (LP)	25

SHORTY WARRENT & HIS WESTERN RANGE
52	London L 1125	I Thought She Was Local/You're Breaking The Only Heart (That Truly Loves You) (78)	15

WARRIOR
72	Eden LP 27	INVASION! (LP, private pressing, plain white sleeve & label, some handwritten, 100 only)	175

(see also Howard Jones)

WARRIOR
80	Goodwood GM 12326	TROUBLE MAKER (LP)	120

WARRIÖR
80	Rambert RAM ONE	Don't Let It Show/The Lord's Prayer/Silver Lady (10", p/s)	75

WARRIOR
80	Rainbow RSL 132	LET BATTLE COMMENCE (LP, private pressing, 500 only)	50

WARRIOR
84	Warrior WOO 2	Breakout/Dragon Slayer/Take Your Chance (paper sleeve)	30
83	Warrior WOO 1	FOR EUROPE ONLY (mini-LP)	20

WARRIORS
64	Decca F 11926	Don't Make Me Blue/You Came Along	40

(see also Hans Christian, Jon Anderson)

WARRIORS
79	Object OM 07	Martial Time/Martial Law (p/s)	4

WARRIORS
82	Ensign ENVY 6001	BEHIND THE MASK (LP)	10

MINT VALUE £

WARSAW PAKT

78	Island PAKT 1	Safe And Warm/Sick And Tired (a few with p/s)	20/10
77	Island ILPS 9515	NEEDLE TIME (LP, numbered stamped mailer p/s, with insert)	15
79	Stuff Central	SEE YOU IN COURT (cassette only)	20

DEE DEE WARWICK

65	Mercury MF 860	Do It With All Your Heart/Happiness	12
65	Mercury MF 867	We're Doin' Fine/You Don't Know	12
65	Mercury MF 890	Gotta Get Hold Of Myself/Another Lonely Saturday	12
66	Mercury MF 909	A Lover's Chant/Worth Every Tear I Cry	22
65	Mercury MF 937	I Want To Be With You/Alfie	7
65	Mercury MF 953	Yours Till Tomorrow/I'm Gonna Make You Love Me.	7
67	Mercury MF 974	When Love Slips Away/House Of Gold	12
68	Mercury MF 1061	I'll Be Better Off (Without You)/Monday, Monday.	15
69	Mercury MF 1084	Foolish Heart/Thank God.	6
69	Mercury MF 1125	That's Not Love/It's Not Fair	6
70	Atlantic 2091 011	She Didn't Know (She Kept On Talking)/Make Love To Me.	5
70	Atlantic 2091 037	If This Was The Last Song/I'm Only Human	5
71	Atlantic 2091 057	Cold Night In Georgia/Searching.	5
71	Atlantic 2091 092	Suspicious Minds/I'm Glad I'm A Woman	5
75	Private Stock PVT 13	Get Out Of My Life/Funny How Places Change	5
66	Mercury 10036 MCE	WE'RE DOING FINE (EP)	25
71	Atco	TURNIN' AROUND (LP)	20

DIONNE WARWICK

SINGLES

63	Stateside SS 157	Don't Make Me Over/I Smiled Yesterday	12
63	Stateside SS 191	This Empty Place/Wishin' And Hopin'.	12
63	Stateside SS 222	Please Let Him Love Me/Make The Music Play (withdrawn, existence unconfirmed)	12+
63	Pye International 7N 25223	Please Let Him Love Me/Make The Music Play (reissue)	6
64	Pye International 7N 25234	Anyone Who Had A Heart/The Love Of A Boy	5
64	Pye International 7N 25241	Walk On By/Anytime Of Day	5
64	Pye International 7N 25256	You'll Never Get To Heaven/A House Is Not A Home	5
64	Pye International 7N 25265	Reach Out For Me/How Many Days Of Sadness	5
65	Pye International 7N 25290	You Can Have Him/Don't Say I Didn't Tell You.	5
65	Pye International 7N 25302	Who Can I Turn To/That's Not The Answer	5
65	Pye International 7N 25310	(Here I Go Again) Looking With My Eyes/Only The Strong, Only The Brave	5
65	Pye International 7N 25316	Here I Am/They Long To Be Close To You	5
65	Pye International 7N 25338	Are You There (With Another Girl)/If I Ever Make You Cry.	5
66	Pye International 7N 25357	In Between The Heartaches/Long Day, Short Night	5
66	Pye International 7N 25368	A Message To Michael/Here Where There Is Love.	6
66	Pye International 7N 25378	Trains And Boats And Planes/Don't Go Breaking My Heart.	5
66	Pye International 7N 25395	Another Night/Go With Love	5
67	Pye International 7N 25424	Alfie/The Beginning Of Loneliness	5
67	Pye International 7N 25428	The Windows Of The World/Walk Little Dolly	5
67	Pye International 7N 25435	I Say A Little Prayer/Window Wishin'	5
68	Pye International 7N 25445	(Theme From) The Valley Of The Dolls/Zip-A-Dee-Doo-Dah	5
68	Pye International 7N 25457	Do You Know The Way To San Jose?/Let Me Be Lonely	6
68	Pye International 7N 25474	Who Is Gonna Love Me?/(There's) Always Something There To Remind Me	5
75	Warner Bros WB 16530	Take It From Me/Sure Thing	6
75	Warner Bros K 16595	Move Me No Mountain/We'll Burn Our Bridges Behind Us	5
85	Arista ARIST 638	That's What Friends Are For (as Dionne Warwick & Friends [Elton John, Gladys Knight & Stevie Wonder])/Two Ships Passing In The Night (p/s)	5
85	Arista ARIST 12638	That's What Friends Are For/That's What Friends Are For (Instrumental) (as Dionne Warwick & Friends [Elton John, Gladys Knight & Stevie Wonder])/ Two Ships Passing In The Night (12", p/s)	10

EPs

64	Pye Intl. NEP 44024	IT'S LOVE THAT REALLY COUNTS (EP)	10
64	Pye Intl. NEP 44026	DON'T MAKE ME OVER (EP)	10
65	Pye Intl. NEP 44039	WISHIN' AND HOPIN' (EP)	10
65	Pye Intl. NEP 44044	DIONNE (EP).	10
65	Pye Intl. NEP 44046	FOREVER MY LOVE (EP).	10
65	Pye Intl. NEP 44049	WHO CAN I TURN TO? (EP)	10
66	Pye Intl. NEP 44051	HERE I AM (EP)	10
66	Pye Intl. NEP 44067	MESSAGE TO MICHAEL (EP).	10
66	Pye Intl. NEP 44073	WINDOW WISHIN' (EP).	10
66	Pye Intl. NEP 44077	I JUST DON'T KNOW WHAT TO DO WITH MYSELF (EP).	10
67	Pye Intl. NEP 44083	I LOVE PARIS (EP)	10
68	Pye Intl. NEP 44090	DO YOU KNOW THE WAY TO SAN JOSE? (EP)	10

LPs

64	Pye Intl. NPL 28037	PRESENTING DIONNE WARWICK (LP)	15
64	Pye Intl. NPL 28046	MAKE WAY FOR DIONNE WARWICK (LP)	15
65	Pye Intl. NPL 28055	THE SENSITIVE SOUND OF DIONNE WARWICK (LP)	15
66	Pye Intl. NPL 28071	HERE I AM (LP)	15
66	Pye Intl. NPL 28076	DIONNE WARWICK IN PARIS (LP)	15
67	Pye Intl. NPL 28096	HERE WHERE THERE IS LOVE (LP)	15
68	Pye Intl. N(S)PL 28114	VALLEY OF THE DOLLS (LP).	15
75	Warner Bros K 56178	TRACK OF THE CAT (LP)	12

WASHBOARD RHYTHM KINGS

56	HMV 7EG 8101	WASHBOARD RHYTHM KINGS (EP)	20

WASHBOARD SAM

72	RCA RD 8274	FEELING LOWDOWN (LP, with Big Bill Broonzy & Memphis Slim)	12

(see also Big Bill Broonzy, Memphis Slim)

DIONNE WARWICK

DINAH WASHIMGTON

ALBERT WASHINGTON & KINGS
67	President PT 137	Doggin' Me Around/A Woman Is A Funny Thing	6
68	President PT 182	I'm The Man/These Arms Of Mine	6
68	President PT 227	Woman Love/Bring It On Up	7
69	President PT 242	Turn On The Bright Lights/Lonely Mountain	7
73	President PT 391	Rome, GA/Telling All Your Friends	5

BABY WASHINGTON
64	Sue WI 302	That's How Heartaches Are Made/Doodlin'	30
64	Sue WI 321	I Can't Wait Until I See My Baby/Who's Gonna Take Care Of Me	30
65	London HLC 9987	Only Those In Love/Ballad Of Bobby Dawn	18
68	United Artists UP 2247	Get A Hold Of Yourself/Hurt So Bad	18
69	Atlantic 584 299	I Don't Know/I Can't Afford To Lose Him	10
70	Atlantic 584 316	Breakfast In Bed/What Becomes Of A Broken Heart	10
73	People PEO 105	Just Can't Get You Out Of My Mind/You're Just A Dream	5
74	People PEO 107	I've Got To Break Away/Can't Get Over You	5
66	London HA-C 8260	THAT'S HOW HEARTACHES ARE MADE (LP)	45
66	London HA-C 8292	ONLY THOSE IN LOVE (LP)	45
68	United Artists SULP 1217	WITH YOU IN MIND (LP)	40

(see also Baby Washington/Wilbert Harrison)

BABY WASHINGTON & DON GARDNER
73	People PEO 101	Forever/Baby Let Me Get Close To You	5
74	People PLEO 13	LAY A LITTLE LOVIN' ON ME (LP)	12

(see also Don Gardner & Dee Dee Ford)

BABY WASHINGTON/WILBERT HARRISON
71	Joy JOYS 191	BATTLE OF THE GIANTS (LP)	15

DINAH WASHINGTON
52	Oriole CB 1130	Mad About The Boy/I Can't Face The Music (78)	25
54	Oriole CB 1266	My Man's An Undertaker/Since My Man Has Gone And Went (78)	15
54	Oriole CB 1279	Fat Daddy/TV Is The Thing (78)	15
54	Mercury MB 3132	Until Sunrise/Am I Blue (78)	10
54	Mercury MB 3160	Dream/I Don't Hurt Anymore (78)	12
55	Mercury MB 3188	Teach Me Tonight/Wishing Well (78)	8
55	Mercury MB 3207	That's All I Want From You/You Stay On My Mind (78)	8
56	Mercury MT 124	Cat On A Hot Tin Roof/The First Time (78)	20
59	Mercury AMT 1051	What A Diff'rence A Day Made/Come On Home	8
59	Mercury AMT 1069	Unforgettable/Nothing In The World	6
60	Mercury AMT 1105	This Bitter Earth/I Understand	6
60	Mercury AMT 1119	Love Walked In/I'm In Heaven Tonight	6
61	Mercury AMT 1125	We Have Love/Looking Back	6
61	Mercury AMT 1162	September In The Rain/Wake The Town And Tell The People	7
62	Mercury AMT 1170	Tears And Laughter/If I Should Lose You	5
62	Mercury AMT 1176	Such A Night/Dream	5
63	Columbia DB 7049	Soulville/Let Me Be The First To Know	10
56	Emarcy EJT 501	AFTER HOURS WITH MISS D. (10" LP)	30
57	Emarcy EJL 1255	DINAH (LP)	22
57	Mercury MPL 6519	SINGS THE BEST IN BLUES (LP)	18
59	Top Rank RX 3006	THE BLUES (LP, with Betty Roche)	15
60	Mercury MMC 14030	WHAT A DIFF'RENCE A DAY MADE (LP)	18
60	Mercury MMC 14048	THE UNFORGETTABLE DINAH WASHINGTON (LP)	18
61	Mercury MMC 14063	I CONCENTRATE ON YOU (LP, also stereo CMS 18043)	15/18
61	Mercury MMC 14107	SEPTEMBER IN THE RAIN (LP)	15
62	Mercury MMC 14085	FOR LONELY LOVERS (LP)	15
62	Mercury MMC 14099	TEARS AND LAUGHTER (LP)	15
65	Fontana FJL 125	DINAH! (LP)	12

(see also Brook Benton & Dinah Washington)

ELLA WASHINGTON
69   Monument MON 1030   He Called Me Baby/You're Gonna Cry, Cry, Cry 8

GENO WASHINGTON & RAM JAM BAND
66   Piccadilly 7N 35312   Water/Understanding 7
66   Piccadilly 7N 35329   Hi! Hi! Hazel/Beach Bash. 6
66   Piccadilly 7N 35346   Que Sera Sera/All I Need 6
66   Piccadilly 7N 35359   Michael/Hold On To My Love 6
67   Piccadilly 7N 35392   She Shot A Hole In My Soul/I've Been Hurt By Love 8
67   Piccadilly 7N 35403   Tell It Like It Is/Girl I Want To Marry. 7
67   Pye 7N 17425   Different Strokes/You Got Me Hummin'. 6
68   Pye 7N 17570   I Can't Quit Her/Put Out The Fire Baby 6
68   Pye 7N 17649   I Can't Let You Go/Bring It To Me Baby 8
69   Pye 7N 17745   My Little Chickadee/Seven Eleven. 6
71   Pye 7N 45019   Alison Please/Each And Every Part Me. 6
71   Pye 7N 45085   Feeling So Good/Would You Believe My Little Chickadee 5
66   Piccadilly NEP 34054   HI (EP) 20
68   Pye NEP 24293   DIFFERENT STROKES (EP). 20
68   Pye NEP 24302   SMALL PACKAGE OF HIPSTERS (EP). 25
66   Piccadilly NPL 38026   HAND CLAPPIN', FOOT STOMPIN', FUNKY-BUTT . . . LIVE! (LP). 25
67   Piccadilly N(S)PL 38032   HIPSTERS, FLIPSTERS, FINGER-POPPIN' DADDIES! (LP). 25
68   Piccadilly N(S)PL 38029   SHAKE A TAIL FEATHER! (LP) 25
68   Pye N(S)PL 18219   LIVE! — RUNNING WILD (LP) 20
(see also Ram Jam Band, Ram John Holder, Ram Holder Brothers, Dave Greenslade)

GEORGE E. WASHINGTON
64   Fontana TF 510   Spare A Thought For Me/Words Of Love. 4

GROVER WASHINGTON JR.
73   Kudu KUS 4001   Inner City Blues/Ain't No Sunshine. 5
75   Kudu KUDU 924   Mister Magic/Black Frost 5
76   Kudu KUDU 930   Knucklehead (Parts 1 & 2) 5
72   Kudu KUL 1   INNER CITY BLUES (LP) 12
72   Kudu KUL 5   ALL THE KING'S HORSES (LP, original issue) 12
73   Kudu KULD 501   SOUL BOX (LP) 12
75   Kudu KU 20   MISTER MAGIC (LP). 12
75   Kudu KU 24   FEELS SO GOOD (LP) 12
76   Kudu KU 32   A SECRET PLACE (LP) 12

JERRY WASHINGTON
75   Contempo CS 2040   Right Here Is Where You Belong/In My Life I Haved Loved 4
75   Contempo CLP 517   RIGHT HERE IS WHERE YOU BELONG (LP) 10

KENNETH WASHINGTON (& CHRIS BARBER BAND)
67   CBS 202494   If I Had A Ticket/They Kicked Him Out Of Heaven
        (with Chris Barber & T-Bones). 10
67   CBS 202592   Gimme That Old Time Religion (with Chris Barber Band)/
        Just A Closer Walk With Thee 5
(see also Chris Barber)

NORMAN T. WASHINGTON
68   Pama PM 730   Same Thing All Over/You've Been Cheating 5
68   Pama PM 741   Tip Toe/Don't Hang Around 6
69   Punch PH 11   Oh Happy Day/Spinning. 6
70   Gas GAS 159   It's Christmas Time Again/If I Could See You 6
70   Punch PH 26   Sweeter Than Honey/1,000 Pearls 6
70   Punch PH 31   Last Goodbye/Mother's Pride 6

SHERI WASHINGTON & BAND
57   Vogue V 9070   I Got Plenty/Ain't I Talkin' To You Baby 400
57   Vogue V 9070   I Got Plenty/Ain't I Talkin' To You Baby (78) 70

SISTER ERNESTINE B. WASHINGTON
50   Melodisc MEL 1101   God's Amazing Grace/Where Could I Go But To The Lord (78) 15
55   Melodisc EPM 7-52   SISTER ERNESTINE WASHINGTON (EP). 15

TONY WASHINGTON (& HIS D.C.s)
63   React EA 002   Crying Man/Please Mr. DJ 15
63   Island WI 068   Something Gotta Be Done/TONY & LOUISE: I Have Said. 15
64   Sue WI 327   Show Me How (To Milk A Cow)/Boof Ska 20
64   Fontana TF 478   Surely You Love Me/Man To Man 10
65   Black Swan WI 459   But I Do/Night Train (as Tony Washington & His D.C.s) 18
65   Black Swan WI 460   Dilly Dilly/Night Train (as Tony Washington & His D.C.s) 18
(see also Tony & Louise)

WASHINGTON D.C.s
64   Ember EMB S 190   Kisses Sweeter Than Wine/Where Did You Go 12
66   CBS 202226   32nd Floor/Whole Lot More 12
67   CBS 202464   Seek And Find/I Love Gerald Chevin The Great (some in p/s). 60/30
69   Domain D 9   I've Done It All Wrong/Anytime 8
(see also Dave Clark Five, Freedom)

WASP
75   EMI EMI 2253   Melissa/Little Miss Bristol 20
(see also Brian Bennett, Shadows)

W.A.S.P.
84   Music For Nations
       PKUT 109   Animal (Fuck Like A Beast)/Show No Mercy (shaped picture disc,
       pig's head or codpiece designs) 15
84   M. F. Nations 12KUT 109   Animal (Fuck Like A Beast)/Show No Mercy (12", p/s, black vinyl,
       U.K. issue pressed in France) 7

84	M. F. Nations 12KUT 109	Animal (Fuck Like A Beast)/Show No Mercy (12", gold, white, clear or red vinyl, U.K. issue pressed in France)	40/20/25/15
84	Capitol CLP 336	I Wanna Be Somebody/Tormentor (Rageways) (p/s)	6
84	Capitol 12 CLP 336	I Wanna Be Somebody/Tormentor (Rageways) (12", picture disc)	12
84	Capitol CL 344	Schooldaze/Paint It Black (poster p/s)	6
84	Capitol 12 CL 344	Schooldaze/Paint It Black (12", p/s)	10
85	M. For Nations PIG 109	Animal (Fuck Like A Beast)/Show No Mercy (12", reissue, picture disc)	8
85	Capitol CLP 374	Blind In Texas/Savage (shaped picture disc)	10
85	Capitol 12 CL 374	Blind In Texas/Savage/I Wanna Be Somebody (live) (12", p/s)	8
86	Capitol CLD 388	Wild Child/Mississippi Queen//On Your Knees/Hellion (double pack)	7
86	Capitol 12CL 388	Wild Child/Mississippi Queen (12", p/s)	10
86	Capitol CLP 432	9.5 N.A.S.T.Y./Easy Living (shaped picture disc)	8
87	Capitol CL 469	I Don't Need No Doctor/Widowmaker (live) (p/s, blood pack)	6
87	Capitol CLS 469	I Don't Need No Doctor/Widowmaker (live) (p/s, coloured vinyl)	4
87	Capitol CLB 469	I Don't Need No Doctor/Widowmaker (live) (p/s, with backstage pass)	7
87	Capitol 12 CLP 469	I Don't Need No Doctor/Widowmaker (live)/Sex Drive (12", poster p/s)	7
88	Capitol 12 CL 458	Scream Until You Like It (Theme From 'Ghoulies II')/Shoot From The Hip (live)/ Sleeping In The Fire (Acoustic Version) (12", p/s)	8
88	Capitol 12 CLP 458	Scream Until You Like It (Theme From 'Ghoulies II')/Shoot From The Hip (live)/ Sleeping In The Fire (Acoustic Version) (12", picture disc)	7
89	Capitol CLP 521	Mean Man/Locomotive Breath (shaped picture disc)	6
89	Capitol CLM 521	Mean Man/Locomotive Breath (purple vinyl 'Means Test Pack' with badge)	4
89	Capitol CLG 521	Mean Man/Locomotive Breath/For Whom The Bell Tolls (12", gatefold sleeve)	8
89	Capitol CLPD 534	The Real Me/The Lake Of Fools (shaped picture disc)	6
89	Capitol CLPD 546	Forever Free (Eagle Edit)/L.O.V.E. Machine (Live '89) (die-cut pic. disc)	8
89	Capitol 12 CLS 546	Forever Free (Eagle Edit)/L.O.V.E. Machine (Live '89)/ Blind In Texas (Live '89) (12", poster p/s)	8
89	Capitol ESTPD 2087	HEADLESS CHILDREN (LP, picture disc)	12

WASPS
77	4-Play FOUR 001	Teenage Treats/She Made More Magic (p/s)	6
77	NEMS NES 115	Can't Wait 'Til '78/MEAN STREET: Bunch Of Stiffs (p/s)	8
78	RCA PB 5137	Rubber Cars/This Time (p/s)	5

WASTE
86	Morterhate MORT 21	NOT JUST SOMETHING TO BE SUNG (EP, foldout p/s)	5

WASTELAND
79	Ellie Jay/Disaster EJSP 9261	WANT NOT EP (p/s, 2000 only)	25
80	Invicta INV 014	Friends, Romans, Countrymen/Leave Me Alone (p/s, 1,000 only)	25

WATCH COMMITTEE
68	Philips BF 1695	Throw Another Penny In The Well/Now I Think The Other Way	5

WATERBOYS
83	Chicken Jazz CJ 1	A Girl Called Johnny/The Late Train To Heaven (p/s)	4
83	Chicken Jazz CJT 1	A Girl Called Johnny/Ready For The Monkey House/Somebody Might Wave Back/Out Of Control (Another Pretty Face John Peel Session) (12", p/s)	7
85	Ensign 12 ENY 520	The Whole Of The Moon (Extended)/Medicine Jack/Spirit (Extended)/ The Girl In The Swing (live) (12", p/s, later in die-cut sleeve)	8/5

(see also DNV, Another Pretty Face, Funhouse, Last Chant)

WATERFALL
76	Bob FRR 001	FLIGHT OF THE DAY (LP, private pressing)	60
79	Avada AVA 104	THREE BIRDS (LP, with insert)	30
81	Gun Dog GUN 003LP	BENEATH THE STARS (LP, private pressing)	30

WATER FOR A THIRSTY LAND
74	MRA P 100	WATER FOR A THIRSTY LAND (LP, with insert)	20

WATER INTO WINE BAND
73	Myrrh MYR 1004	HILL CLIMBING FOR BEGINNERS (LP, brown or white cover, with insert)	80/60
76	CJT 002	HARVEST TIME (LP, private pressing)	250

WATERLOO & ROBINSON
76	Cube BUG 67	My Little World/Carry On	5

WATER PISTOLS
76	State STATE 38	Gimme That Punk Junk/Soft Punk (p/s, with insert)	10

WATERPROOF CANDLE
68	RCA RCA 1717	Electrically Heated Child/Saturday Morning Repentance	10

ETHEL WATERS
66	World Record Club T 949	ETHEL WATERS (LP)	12

FREDDIE WATERS
71	Buddah 2011 059	Singing A Song/I Love You, I Love You, I Love You	4
75	Mint CHEW 2	Groovin' On My Baby's Love/Kung Fu And You Too	4

MUDDY WATERS
53	Vogue V 2101	Walkin' Blues/Rollin' Stone Blues (78)	60
54	Vogue V 2273	Hello Little Girl/Long Distance Call (78)	60
55	Vogue V 2372	Honey Bee/Too Young To Know (78)	60
65	Chess CRS 8001	My John The Conquer Root/Short Dress Woman	12
65	Chess CRS 8019	I Got A Rich Man's Woman/My Dog Can't Bark	10
69	Chess CRS 8083	Let's Spend The Night Together/I'm A Man	7
69	Python P 04	Country Boy/All Night Long (99 copies only)	35
55	Vogue EPV 1046	MUDDY WATERS WITH LITTLE WALTER (EP)	150
56	London RU-E 1060	MISSISSIPPI BLUES (EP)	150
63	Pye Intl. NEP 44010	MUDDY WATERS (EP)	30
65	Chess CRE 6006	I'M READY (EP)	50
66	Chess CRE 6022	THE REAL FOLK BLUES VOL. 4 (EP)	40

59	London Jazz LJZ-M 15152	THE BEST OF MUDDY WATERS (LP)	60
61	Pye Jazz NJL 34	AT NEWPORT (LP)	30
64	Pye Intl. NPL 28038	MUDDY WATERS — FOLK SINGER (LP)	25
64	Pye Intl. NPL 28040	THE BEST OF MUDDY WATERS (LP)	30
64	Pye Intl. NPL 28048	MUDDY SINGS BIG BILL (LP)	25
65	Chess CRL 4513	AT NEWPORT (LP, reissue)	20
66	Chess CRL 4515	THE REAL FOLK BLUES (LP)	25
67	Chess CRL 4525	MUDDY, BRASS AND THE BLUES (LP)	25
67	Marble Arch MAL 661	AT NEWPORT (LP, 2nd reissue)	12
67	Chess CRL 4529	SUPER BLUES (LP, with Little Walter & Bo Diddley)	25
67	Marble Arch MAL 723	MUDDY SINGS BIG BILL (LP, reissue)	12
68	Chess CRL 4537	THE SUPER SUPER BLUES BAND (LP, with Howlin' Wolf & Bo Diddley)	35
68	Bounty BY 6031	DOWN ON STOVALL'S PLANTATION (LP)	20
69	Chess CRL 4542	ELECTRIC MUD (LP)	20
69	Chess CRL 4553	AFTER THE RAIN (LP)	25
69	Chess CRL 4556	FATHERS AND SONS (LP)	25
69	Polydor 236 574	BLUES MAN (LP)	15
69	Python PLP 12	MUDDY WATERS (LP, 99 copies only)	35
69	Python PLP 18	MUDDY WATERS VOLUME 2 (LP, 99 copies only)	35
69	Python PLP 19	MUDDY WATERS VOLUME 3 (LP, 99 copies only)	35
70	Syndicate Chapter SC 001/2	BACK IN THE EARLY DAYS (2-LP)	30
70	Syndicate Chapter SC 002	GOOD NEWS (LP)	15
70	Sunnyland KS 100	VINTAGE MUDDY WATERS (LP, gatefold sleeve with inserts, 99 copies only)	35
71	Chess 6671 001	McKINLEY MORGANFIELD AKA MUDDY WATERS (LP)	18
72	Black Bear LP 901	RARE LIVE RECORDINGS VOL. 1 (LP)	25
72	Black Bear LP 902	RARE LIVE RECORDINGS VOL. 2 (LP)	25
72	Black Bear LP 903	RARE LIVE RECORDINGS VOL. 3 (LP)	25
72	Chess 6310 121	THE LONDON SESSIONS (LP)	15
74	Chess 6310 129	CAN'T GET NO GRINDIN' (LP)	15
77	Blue Sky SKY 81853	HARD AGAIN (LP)	12

(see also Little Walter, Howlin' Wolf, Bo Diddley, Luther 'Georgia Boy Snake' Johnson)

ROGER WATERS

84	Harvest HAR 5228	5.01 AM (The Pros And Cons Of Hitch-Hiking)/ 4.30 AM (Apparently They Were Travelling Abroad) (p/s)	5
84	Harvest 12HAR 5228	5.01 AM (The Pros And Cons Of Hitch-Hiking)/4.30 AM (Apparently They Were Travelling Abroad)/4.33 AM (Running Shoes) (12", p/s)	8
84	Harvest HAR 5230	5.06 AM (Every Stranger's Eyes)/4.39 AM (For The First Time Today) (p/s)	15
87	EMI EM 6	Radio Waves/Going To Live In L.A. (Demo) (p/s)	6
87	EMI 12EM 6	Radio Waves (Remix)/Going To Live In L.A. (Demo)/ Radio Waves (7" Version) (12", p/s)	7
87	EMI CDEM 6	Radio Waves (Remix)/Going To Live In L.A. (Demo)/ Radio Waves (7" Version) (CD)	10
87	EMI EM 20	Sunset Strip/Money (live) (unissued; Europe-only)	
87	EMI EM 37	The Tide Is Turning (After Live Aid)/Money ('live') (p/s)	6
87	EMI CDEM 37	The Tide Is Turning (After Live Aid)/Money ('live')/Get Back To Radio (Demo Recording) (CD)	10
90	Mercury MER 332	Another Brick In The Wall Part 2/Run Like Hell (p/s)	4
90	Mercury MERCD 332	Another Brick In The Wall Part 2 (Edit)/Run Like Hell (Potsdamer Mix)/ Another Brick In The Wall Part 2 (Full Version) (CD)	7
90	Mercury MER 336	The Tide Is Turning/Nobody Home (p/s)	4
90	Mercury MERCD 336	The Tide Is Turning (Album Version)/Nobody Home/The Tide Is Turning (7" Version) (CD)	7
90	Mercury 878 147-2	PIECES FROM THE WALL: Another Brick In The Wall Part 2 (Edit)/Young Lust (Edit)/Run Like Hell/In The Flesh? (CD, promo only)	20
92	Columbia 658 139 0	What God Wants Part I (Video Edit)/Nobody Home/What God Wants Part I (Album Version) (p/s)	4
92	Columbia 658 139 5	What God Wants Part I (Video Edit)/What God Wants Part I (Album Version)/ What God Wants Part III (CD)	7
92	Columbia 658 139 9	What God Wants Part I (Video Edit)/What God Wants Part I (Album Version)/ What God Wants Part III (CD, box set with prints)	12
92	Columbia 658 819 2	The Bravery Of Being Out Of Range/What God Wants Part I/ Perfect Sense Part I (CD)	8
70	Harvest SHSP 4008	MUSIC FROM THE FILM "THE BODY" (LP, with Ron Geesin, green labels, with Waters/Geesin photos)	18
70	Harvest SHSP 4008	MUSIC FROM THE FILM "THE BODY" (LP, with Ron Geesin, black labels)	12
87	EMI KAOS DJ 1	RADIO KAOS (LP, 'banded' radio promo, custom sleeve)	25
92	Columbia COL 4687610	AMUSED TO DEATH (2-LP, blue vinyl, with booklet)	18

(see also Pink Floyd, Ron Geesin)

LAL & MIKE WATERSON

73	Trailer LER 2076	BRIGHT PHOEBUS (LP)	15

WATERSONS

65	Topic 12T 125	NEW VOICES (LP, blue label, with Harry Boardman & Maureen Craik)	15
65	Topic 12T 136	FROST AND FIRE (LP, blue label)	15
66	Topic 12T 142	WATERSONS (LP, blue label)	15
66	Topic 12T 167	A YORKSHIRE GARLAND (LP, blue label)	15

LOVELACE WATKINS

67	Fontana TF 879	I Apologise Baby/You Can't Stop Love	8
72	Uni UNLS 119	LOVE IS (LP)	15
72	York FYK 404	LOVE MAKES THE WORLD GO ROUND (LP)	15

DILYS WATLING

64	Philips BF 1305	Don't Say You Love Me/Now's The Time	6
65	Philips BF 1393	I'm Over You/Act Like A Lady	5
69	Pye 7N 17791	Have Another Dream On Me/Sweet Darlin'	6

DOC WATSON

64	Fontana TFL 6045	DOC WATSON (LP)	18
65	Fontana TFL 6055	DOC WATSON & SON (LP)	18
72	Vanguard VSD 9/10	ON STAGE (2-LP)	15

EARL WATSON

61	Ember EMB S 129	Nightmare/That Old Black Magic	6

JOHN L. WATSON (& HUMMELFLUGS)

64	Pye 7N 15746	Looking For You/Dance With You	6
65	Piccadilly 7N 35233	Standing By/I'll Make It Worth Your While	6
70	Deram DM-R 285	A Mother's Love/Might As Well Be Gone (solo)	7
70	Deram SML 1061	WHITE HOT BLUE BLACK (LP)	25

(see also Web)

JOHNNY WATSON & KAMPAI KINGS

60	Oriole CB 1532	Moshi, Moshi, Anone!/ABDULLA & HIS LITTLE BAND: Fatima's Theme	5
60	Oriole CB 1532	Moshi, Moshi, Anone!/ABDULLA & HIS LITTLE BAND: Fatima's Theme (78)	30

JOHNNY 'GUITAR' WATSON

76	Fantasy FTC 124	I Don't Need A Lone Ranger/You Can Stay But The Noise Must Go	4

(see also Larry Williams & Johnny 'Guitar' Watson)

NEVILLE WATSON

73	Magnet MG 013	Rasta Army/Version	4

WAH WAH WATSON

76	CBS 4691	Love Ain't Something You Get For Free/Bubbles	4
76	CBS 81582	ELEMENTARY (LP)	10

(see also Larry Williams & Johnny 'Guitar' Watson)

BEN WATT

81	Cherry Red CHERRY 25	Cant/Aubade/Tower Of Silence (p/s)	5
83	Cherry Red CHERRY 55	Some Things Don't Matter/On Box Hill (p/s)	4
82	Cherry Red 12CHERRY 36	SUMMER INTO WINTER (12" EP, with Robert Wyatt, p/s)	7

(see also Everything But The Girl)

LU WATTERS & AND HIS YERBA BUENA JAZZ BAND

56	Vogue V 2125	Muskrat Rumble/Frankie And Johnny	5
56	Vogue V 2315	High Society/Aunt Hagar's Blues	5
50s	Vogue EPV 1053	LU WATTERS (EP)	8
50s	Vogue EPV 1130	LU WATTERS JAZZ BAND (EP)	8
50s	Good Time Jazz EPG 1169	LU WATTERS YERBA BUENA JAZZ BAND (EP)	8
50s	Columbia CLEF SEB 10049	LU WATTERS YERBA BUENA JAZZ BAND (EP)	8
50s	Columbia CLEF SEB 10064	LU WATTERS YERBA BUENA JAZZ BAND (EP)	8
52	Vogue LDE 009	LU WATTERS AND HIS JAZZ BAND (10" LP)	15
53	Good Time Jazz LP 8	LU WATTERS YERBA BUENA BAND VOL. 1 (10" LP)	18
53	Good Time Jazz LAG 12030	LU WATTERS YERBA BUENA BAND VOL. 2 (10" LP)	15
53	Good Time Jazz LAG 12035	LU WATTERS YERBA BUENA BAND VOL. 3 (10" LP)	15
54	Good Time Jazz LDG 038	LU WATTERS JAZZ BAND VOL. 1 (10" LP)	15
55	Columbia Clef 33C 9004	LU WATTERS AND HIS YERBA BUENA JAZZ BAND (10" LP)	15
56	London HB-U 1061	LU WATTERS — 1947 (10" LP)	15
57	Columbia Clef 33C 9036	DIXIELAND JAMBOREE (10" LP)	15

WATTS 103RD STREET RHYTHM BAND

(see under Charles Wright & Watts 103rd Street Rhythm Band)

CHARLIE WATTS

93	Continuum CDCTUM 103	My Ship/You Got To Me Head (CD)	15
86	CBS 450 253-1	LIVE AT FULHAM TOWN HALL (LP, as Charlie Watts & His Orchestra, with insert)	10
91	UFO UFO 2 LP	FROM ONE CHARLIE (10" LP, box set with book & Charlie Parker photo, some signed)	25/20

(see also Rolling Stones, People Band, Rocket 88)

NOBLE 'THIN MAN' WATTS (& HIS BAND)

57	London HLU 8627	Hard Times (The Slop)/Midnight Flight (with His Rhythm Sparks)	50
57	London HLU 8627	Hard Times (The Slop)/Midnight Flight (with His Rhythm Sparks) (78)	40
64	Sue WI 347	Noble's Theme/JUNE BATEMAN: I Don't Wanna	25
60s	XX MIN 717	NOBLE 'THIN MAN' WATTS AND WILD JIMMY SPURRILL (EP)	15

(see also Wild Jimmy Spurrill)

WATUSI WARRIORS

59	London HL 8866	Wa-Chi-Bam-Ba/Kalahari	12
59	London HL 8866	Wa-Chi-Bam-Ba/Kalahari (78)	5

WAVES

82	Armageddon AS 021	Nightmare/Hey War Pig (p/s)	4
82	Albion ION 1037	Brown Eyed Son/She Loves To Groove (p/s)	4

(see also Kimberley Rew)

NANCY WAYBURN

65	Warner Bros WB 5646	The World Goes On Without Me/Listen To My Heart	8

WAYFARERS

61	Decca F 11370	Whistle Down The Wind/Think Of A Stranger	5

WAYGOOD ELLIS

67	Polydor 56729	I Like What I'm Trying To Do/Hey Lover	15

(see also Fleur-De-Lys)

ALVIS WAYNE

63	Starlite ST45 104	Don't Mean Maybe, Baby/I'd Rather Be With You	450

ARTIE WAYNE

52	London L 1164	Rachel/Tonight Or Never (78)	15

BOBBY WAYNE

51	London L 924	When The Wind Was Green/Buffalo Billy (78)	20
51	London L 968	Immaculate Mother/Mother At Your Feet Is Kneeling (78)	12
51	London L 972	Runnin' Around/Always You (78)	15
51	London L 973	Wild Card/Let Me In (78)	15
51	London L 1077	I Am Free/How Long Is Forever (78)	15
51	London L 1078	If You Turn Me Down/Let's Make Up Your Mind (78)	15
55	Mercury MB 3151	They Were Doin' The Mambo/A String Of Broken Hearts (78)	8

(see also Teresa Brewer)

BOBBY WAYNE

| 65 | Pye International 7N 25315 | Ballad Of A Teenage Queen/River Man | 10 |

CARL WAYNE (& VIKINGS)

64	Pye 7N 15702	What's A Matter Baby/Your Loving Ways (as Carl Wayne & Vikings)	40
65	Pye 7N 15824	This Is Love/You Could Be Fun (as Carl Wayne & Vikings)	35
70	RCA RCA 2032	Maybe God's Got Something Up His Sleeve/Rosanna	6
72	RCA RCA 2177	Imagine/Sunday Kind Of Love	5
72	RCA RCA 2257	Take My Hands For A While/Sweet Seasons	5
72	RCA SF 8239	CARL WAYNE (LP)	15

(see also Charlie Wayne, Move, Ace Kefford Stand, Cheetahs, Acid Gallery, Keith Powell [& Valets])

CHARLIE WAYNE

| 82 | Jet JET 7022 | Colourful Lady/MOVE: Aerial Pictures (p/s) | 4 |

(see also Carl Wayne, Move)

CHRIS WAYNE & ECHOES

| 60 | Decca F 11231 | Lonely/Counting Girls | 10 |

JEFF WAYNE

| 69 | Columbia S(C)X 6330 | TWO CITIES (LP, soundtrack) | 30 |

(see also Ran-Dells)

JERRY WAYNE

| 60 | Vogue V 9169 | Half-Hearted Love/Ten Thousand Miles | 20 |

PAT WAYNE (& BEACHCOMBERS)

63	Columbia DB 7121	Go Back To Daddy/Jambalaya	15
63	Columbia DB 7182	Roll Over Beethoven/Is It Love?	15
64	Columbia DB 7262	Bye Bye Johnny/Strictly For The Birds	15
64	Columbia DB 7417	Brand New Man/Nobody's Child	12
65	Columbia DB 7603	Come Dance With Me/I Don't Want To Cry (solo)	7
65	Columbia DB 7739	My Friend/Tomorrow Night (solo)	6
66	Columbia DB 7944	The Night Is Over/Hombre (solo)	7

RICK(Y) WAYNE (& OFF-BEATS)

60	Triumph RGM 1009	Chick A'Roo/Don't Pick On Me (with Fabulous Flee-Rakkers)	40
60	Top Rank JAR 432	Chick A'Roo/Don't Pick On Me (unreleased)	
60	Pye 7N 15289	Make Way Baby/Goodness Knows (as Ricky Wayne & Off-Beats)	30
65	Oriole CB 306	Say You're Gonna Be My Own/It's A Crying Shame (as Rick Wayne)	12
65	CBS 201764	In My Imagination/Don't Ever Share Your Love (as Rick Wayne)	8

(see also [Fabulous] Flee-Rekkers)

TERRY WAYNE

57	Columbia DB 4002	Matchbox/Your True Love	20
57	Columbia DB 4002	Matchbox/Your True Love (78)	12
57	Columbia DB 4035	Plaything/Slim Jim Tie	20
57	Columbia DB 4035	Plaything/Slim Jim Tie (78)	15
58	Columbia DB 4067	All Mama's Children/Forgive Me	20
58	Columbia DB 4067	All Mama's Children/Forgive Me (78)	15
58	Columbia DB 4112	Oh! Lonesome Me/There's Only One You	15
58	Columbia DB 4112	Oh! Lonesome Me/There's Only One You (78)	25
58	Columbia DB 4205	Little Brother/Where My Baby Goes	12
58	Columbia DB 4205	Little Brother/Where My Baby Goes (78)	30
59	Columbia DB 4312	Brooklyn Bridge/She's Mine	20
58	Columbia SEG 7758	TERRIFIC (EP)	100

THOMAS WAYNE

59	London HLU 8846	Tragedy/Saturday Date	30
59	London HLU 8846	Tragedy/Saturday Date (78)	30
59	London HL 7075	Tragedy/Saturday Date (export issue)	18

WAYS & MEANS

66	Columbia DB 7907	Little Deuce Coupe/The Little Old Lady From Pasadena	12
66	Pye 7N 17217	Sea Of Faces/Make The Radio A Little Louder	15
68	Trend TRE 1005	Breaking Up A Dream/She	15

WAY WE LIVE

| 71 | Dandelion DAN 8004 | A CANDLE FOR JUDITH (LP, gatefold sleeve, also listed as K 49004) | 100 |

(see also Tractor, Beau)

WEAPON

| 80 | Weapon WEAP 1 | It's A Mad Mad World/Set The Stage Alight (p/s) | 30 |
| 81 | Virign WEAPONE | It's A Mad Mad World/Set The Stage Alight (12", p/s, reissue) | 25 |

(see also Headbangers, Paddy Goes To Hollyhead, Wildfire)

WEASELSNOUT

| 72 | Weaselsnout WUS 140 | UNSUNG LIES (LP, private pressing) | 150 |

WEATHER

| 69 | Philips BF 1734 | Look In My Eyes/Running Forward | 4 |
| 69 | Philips BF 1819 | Jamboree Special/Two Peculiar People | 4 |

ALFIE WEATHERBY
58 Columbia DC 729   49 Juke Boxes/Why Am I Crying? (78, export issue) 25

WEATHERMEN
71 B&C BC 147   Honey Bee (Keep On Stinging Me)/Anarchy Rock 5
(see also Jonathan King)

WEATHER PROPHETS
86 Creation CRE 029D   Almost Prayed/Your Heartbeat Breathes Life Into Me//Stones In My Passway/
                             Downbound Train (double pack, gatefold p/s) 5
88 Creation CRELP 033   JUDGES, JURIES AND HORSEMEN (LP, with bonus 7": Stepping Lightly
                             On The Ancient Path/Odds And Ends [CREFRE 2, no p/s]) 10
(see also Loft)

WEATHER REPORT
71 CBS 64521   WEATHER REPORT (LP) 12
72 CBS 64943   I SING THE BODY ELECTRIC (LP) 12
73 CBS 65532   SWEETNIGHTER (LP) 12
74 CBS 80027   MYSTERIOUS TRAVELLER (LP) 12
(see also Joe Zawinul)

OSCAR WEATHERS
71 Mojo 2092 006   Spoilers/You Want To Play 4

WEAVERS
59 Top Rank JAR 120   Wild Goose Grasses/Meet The Johnson Boys 6
59 Top Rank JAR 120   Wild Goose Grasses/Meet The Johnson Boys (78) 8
57 Vanguard PPL 11006   AT THE CARNEGIE HALL (LP) 15
57 Vanguard PPL 11011   ON TOUR (LP) 15
59 Top Rank RX 3008   AT HOME (LP) 15
61 Brunswick LAT 8357   BEST OF THE WEAVERS (LP) 12
62 Fontana TFL 6011   WEAVERS' ALMANAC (LP) 12
(see also Pete Seeger)

WEB
68 Deram DM 201   Hatton Mill Morning/Conscience 20
68 Deram DM 217   Baby Won't You Leave Me Alone/McVernon Street 20
69 Deram DM 253   Monday To Friday/Harold Dubbleyew 20
68 Deram SML 1025   FULLY INTERLOCKING (LP) 100
70 Deram SML 1058   THERAPHOSA BLONDI (LP) 90
70 Polydor 2383 024   I SPIDER (LP) 100
(see also John L. Watson [& Hummelflugs], Samurai, Greenslade)

DEAN WEBB
59 Parlophone R 4549   Warm Your Heart/Hey Miss Fannie 25
59 Parlophone R 4587   The Rough And The Smooth/Streamline Baby 25

DON WEBB
60 Coral Q 72385   Little Ditty Baby/I'll Be Back Home 130

GEORGE WEBB DIXIELANDERS
56 Decca DFE 6351   AND HIS DIXIELANDERS (EP) 18
50s Melodisc EPM7 70   THE GEORGE WEBB DIXIELANDERS (EP) 10

JILLA WEBB
56 MGM SP 1180   You Gotta Love Me Now/What Do You Think It Does To Me? 7

JIM(MY) WEBB
68 CBS 3672   I Keep It Hid/I Need You (as Jim Webb) 10
71 Reprise RS 20978   P.F. Sloan/Psalm One-Five-O 5
73 Reprise K 14279   Campo De Encino/Once In The Morning 5
68 CBS (S) 63335   JIM WEBB SINGS JIM WEBB (LP, as Jim Webb) 25
71 Reprise RSLP 6421   WORDS AND MUSIC (LP, with insert) 20
71 Reprise K 44101   WORDS AND MUSIC (LP, reissue) 15
72 Reprise K 44134   AND SO ON (LP) 18
72 Reprise K 44173   LETTERS (LP) 18
74 Asylum SYL 9014   LAND'S END (LP, with inner sleeve) 15
77 Atlantic K 50370   EL MIRAGE (LP, with inner sleeve) 15
(see also Strawberry Children, Glen Campbell)

JOHN WEBB
86 Numa NU 14   The Experiment Of Love/Cry Of The Sea (p/s) 7
86 Numa NUM 14   The Experiment Begins/Cry Of The Sea/The Experiment Of Love (12", p/s) 10

JOHNNY WEBB
56 Columbia DB 3805   Dig/Glendora 8
57 Columbia DB 3904   The Song Of The Moonlight/Give Me More 8
60s Melodisc MEL 1617   Travelin' Man/Hold Back The Town (some with p/s) 12/5

LIZBETH WEBB
53 HMV 7M 140   I've Never Been In Love Before/If I Were A Bell 4

PETA WEBB
73 Topic 12TS 223   I HAVE WANDERED IN EXILE (LP, blue label) 30
(see also Oak)

ROGER WEBB (& HIS TRIO)
64 Parlophone PMC 1233   JOHN, PAUL AND ALL THAT JAZZ (LP) 12
71 Columbia DB 8803   Strange Report/Summer Fancy 12
82 Chandos SBR 102   The Gentle Touch/Arthur's Theme (no p/s) 6
84 Chips CH 1104   Hammer House Of Horror/Cover Up Theme (p/s) 12

SKEETER WEBB
55 Parlophone CMSP 32   Was It A Bad Dream/Your Secret's Not A Secret Anymore (export issue) 15

SONNY WEBB & CASCADES

64	Oriole CB 1873	You've Got Everything/Border Of The Blues	35
64	Polydor NH 52158	You've Got Everything/Border Of The Blues (reissue)	12

MARLENE WEBBER

70	Bamboo BAM 33	My Baby/BRENTFORD ALLSTARS: You Gonna Hold Me (Version)	8
71	Ackee ACK 120	Natengula/Natengula-Kera (as Merlin Webber)	6
71	Ackee ACK 122	Cumbaya/Hail-Hi Freedom (as Merlin Webber)	6
71	Smash SMA 2322	Hard Life/COLLINS ALL STARS: Version Life (as Merlene Webber)	6
71	Trojan TR 7815	Stand By Your Man/CLANCY ECCLES: Credit Squeeze	6

(see also Webber Sisters, Tonettes)

WEBBER SISTERS

67	Island WI 3109	My World/ALVA LEWIS: Lonely Still	60

(see also Delroy Wilson)

WEBS

68	London HLU 10188	This Thing Called Love/Tomorrow	8

WEBSPINNERS

73	Buddah 2011 150	Spider Man — Theme/Goin' 'Cross Town	6

BEN WEBSTER

55	Columbia CLEF 33CX 10014	MUSIC FOR LOVERS (LP)	35
65	Fontana FJL 126	INTIMATE! (LP)	80
66	Verve VLP 9100	BEN WEBSTER'S BIG SOUND (LP)	12
69	Ember CJS 822	BEN WEBSTER AT EASE (LP)	30
70	Fontana FJL 316	BIG BEN TIME (LP)	40
72	Philips 6308 101	WEBSTER'S DICTIONARY (LP)	75

CHASE WEBSTER

64	Hickory 45-1283	Life Can Have Meaning/Where Is Your Heart	5

DEENA WEBSTER

68	Parlophone R 5699	You're Losing/Wish You Were Here	8
68	Parlophone R 5721	Your Heart Is Free Just Like The Wind/Queen Merka And Me	5
68	Parlophone R 5738	Scarborough Fair/The Water Is Wide	5
69	Parlophone R 5798	Joey/It's Alright With Me	5
68	Parlophone PMC/PCS 7052	TUESDAY'S CHILD (LP)	25

WEDDING PRESENT

85	Reception REC 001	Go Out And Get 'Em Boy/(The Moment Before) Everything's Spoiled Again (p/s, 500 only, a few with poster & badge)	30/20
85	City Slang CSL 001	Go Out And Get 'Em Boy/(The Moment Before) Everything's Spoiled Again (reissue, different foldout p/s, 1,000 only)	10
86	Reception REC 002	Once More/At The Edge Of The Sea (p/s, 3,500 only)	8
86	Reception REC 002/12	DON'T TRY AND STOP ME MOTHER (12" EP, combines REC 001 & 002)	8
86	Reception REC 003	This Boy Can Wait/You Should Always Keep In Touch With Your Friends (p/s, matrix numbers: 003 A2 & 003 B1)	6
86	Reception REC 003	This Boy Can Wait/You Should Always Keep In Touch With Your Friends (p/s, mispress both sides play B-side, matrix numbers: 003 A1 & 003 A2)	5
86	Reception REC 003/12	This Boy Can Wait (Extended)/You Should Always Keep In Touch With Your Friends/Living And Learning (12", p/s)	8
87	Reception REC 005	My Favourite Dress/Every Mother's Son/Never Said (p/s, white vinyl, 3,000 only, 2,000 of which free with "George Best" LP)	6
87	Reception	A Million Miles/What Did Your Last Servant Die Of? (DJ promo, 200 only)	8
87	Reception REC 006	Anyone Can Make A Mistake/All About Eve (p/s)	4
87	Reception REC 006/C	Anyone Can Make A Mistake/All About Eve/Getting Nowhere Fast (cassette, shrinkwrapped with badge)	5
88	Reception REC 010X	Davni Chasy/Katrusya (promo only)	6
88	House Of Dolls HOD 004	Unfaithful (Peel Session)/TRUDY: Living On A Moon/HUNTERS CLUB: Little Sister/CLAYTOWN TROUPE: Real Life (no p/s, free with *House Of Dolls* mag)	5
89	M'night Music DONG 39 CD	Pourquoi Es Tu Devenue Si Raisonable? (CD, unreleased)	
89	RCA	Davni Chasy/Katrusya (promo only)	10
90	RCA PB 43403	Brassneck/Don't Talk, Just Kiss (custom hand-painted p/s, 3,000 only)	6
92	RCA PB 45185	Blue Eyes/Cattle And Cane (p/s)	8
92	RCA PB 45183	Go Go Dancer/Don't Cry No Tears (p/s)	5
92	RCA PB 45181	Three/Think That It Might (p/s)	5
92	RCA PB 45311	Silver Shorts/Falling (p/s)	5
92	RCA PB 45313	Come Play With Me/Pleasant Valley Sunday (p/s)	5
92	RCA PB 45315	California/Let's Make Some Plans (p/s)	4
92	RCA PB 10115	Flying Saucer/Rocket (p/s)	4
92	RCA PB 10117	Boing/The Theme From Shaft (p/s)	4
92	RCA PB 10116	Loveslave/Chant Of The Ever-Growing Skeletal Family (p/s)	4
92	RCA PB 11691	Sticky/Go Wild In The Country (p/s)	4
92	RCA PB 11692	The Queen Of Outer Space/UFO (p/s)	4

(A box for the above 11 singles [plus PB 11693] was available separately at gigs.)

87	Reception LEEDS 1	GEORGE BEST (LP, 2,000 only with white vinyl 7": My Favourite Dress/ Every Mother's Son/Never Said [REC 005] & inner sleeve; later with bonus black vinyl 7" or 12" edition)	12/10
88	Reception LEEDS 2	TOMMY (LP, 1,000 signed by band, with poster & inner sleeve)	15
88	Reception REC 010	UKRAINSKI VISTUPI V JOHNA PEELA (10" mini-LP, withdrawn)	10

(see also Pop Guns)

WEDGEWOODS

64	Pye 7N 15642	September In The Rain/Gone Gone Away	6
65	Pye 7N 15846	Peace/Summer Love	6

BUDDY WEED & HIS ORCHESTRA

57	Vogue V 9075	The Kent Song/For Love	20
57	Vogue V 9075	The Kent Song/For Love (78)	12

BERT WEEDON

78s

56	Parlophone R 4178	The Boy With The Magic Guitar/Flannel-Foot (78)	10
57	Parlophone R 4256	Theme From ITV's '$64,000 Question'/Twilight Time (78)	8
57	Parlophone R 4315	The Jolly Gigolo/Soho Fair (78)	8
57	Parlophone R 4381	Play That Big Guitar/Quiet, Quiet, Ssh! (78)	10
58	Parlophone R 4446	Big Note Blues/Rippling Tango (78)	10
59	Top Rank JAR 117	Guitar Boogie Shuffle/Bert's Boogie (78)	12
59	Top Rank JAR 121	Sing Little Birdie/The Lady Is A Tramp (78)	8
59	Top Rank JAR 122	Petite Fleur/My Happiness (78)	8
59	Top Rank JAR 123	Charmaine/It's Time To Say Goodnight (78)	8
59	Top Rank JAR 136	Teenage Guitar/Blue Guitar (78)	15
59	Top Rank JAR 210	Jealousy/Tango, Tango (78)	10
59	Top Rank JAR 211	Stardust/Summertime (78)	10
59	Top Rank JAR 221	Nashville Boogie/King Size Guitar (78)	20

SINGLES

56	Parlophone MSP 6242	The Boy With The Magic Guitar/Flannel-Foot	18
57	Parlophone R 4256	Theme From ITV's '$64,000 Question'/Twilight Time	15
57	Parlophone R 4315	The Jolly Gigolo/Soho Fair	15
57	Parlophone R 4381	Play That Big Guitar/Quiet, Quiet, Ssh!	10
58	Parlophone R 4446	Big Note Blues/Rippling Tango	10
59	Saga SAG 2906	Fifi/Cat On A Hot Tin Roof (as Bert Weedon & Rag Pickers)	15
59	Top Rank JAR 117	Guitar Boogie Shuffle/Bert's Boogie	7
59	Top Rank JAR 121	Sing Little Birdie/The Lady Is A Tramp	5
59	Top Rank JAR 122	Petite Fleur/My Happiness	5
59	Top Rank JAR 123	Charmaine/It's Time To Say Goodnight	5
59	Top Rank JAR 136	Teenage Guitar/Blue Guitar	6
59	Top Rank JAR 210	Jealousy/Tango, Tango	5
59	Top Rank JAR 211	Stardust/Summertime	5
59	Top Rank JAR 221	Nashville Boogie/King Size Guitar	6
60	Top Rank JAR 300	Big Beat Boogie/Theme From 'A Summer Place' (some with p/s)	8/5
60	Top Rank JAR 360	Twelfth Street Rag/Querida	5
60	Top Rank JAR 415	Apache/Lonely Guitar	6
60	Top Rank JAR 517	Sorry Robbie/Easy Beat	6
61	Top Rank JAR 537	Ginchy/Yearning	5
61	Top Rank JAR 559	Mr. Guitar/Eclipse	5
61	Top Rank JAR 582	Ghost Train/Fury	5
61	HMV POP 946	China Doll/Red Guitar	5
62	HMV POP 989	Twist A Napoli/Twist Me Pretty Baby	5
62	HMV POP 1043	Some Other Love/Tune For Two	5
62	HMV POP 1077	South Of The Border/Poinciana	5
63	HMV POP 1141	Night Cry/Charlie Boy	10
63	HMV POP 1216	Dark Eyes/Black Jackets	5
64	HMV POP 1248	It Happened In Monterey/Lonely Night	5
64	HMV POP 1302	Gin Mill Guitar/Can't Help Falling In Love	5
64	HMV POP 1355	Tokyo Melody/Theme From 'Limelight'	5
65	HMV POP 1387	Twelve String Shuffle/Colour Him Folksy	5
65	HMV POP 1485	High Steppin'/East Meets West	5
66	HMV POP 1535	Kick Off/McGregor's Leap	5
67	HMV POP 1592	Stranger Than Fiction/Malaguena	5
60s	Grosvenor GRS 1015	Watch Your Step/Safe And Sound (as Bert Weedon Quartet with Roy Edwards)	5

EPs

56	Esquire EP 56	WAXING THE WINNERS (EP)	25
59	Selmer Amplifiers	DEMONSTRATION RECORD WITH DAVID GELL (EP)	10
61	Top Rank JKP 3008	WEEDON WINNERS (EP)	15
64	HMV 7EG 8856	GUITAR MAN (EP)	15

LPs

60	Top Rank BUY 026	KINGSIZE GUITAR (LP)	35
61	Top Rank 35/101	HONKY TONK GUITAR (LP)	30
70	Fontana 6438 009	THE ROMANTIC GUITAR OF BERT WEEDON (LP)	12
70	Fontana 6438 031	ROCKIN' AT THE ROUNDHOUSE (LP)	12

(see also George Chisholm, Craig Douglas, Ragpickers)

WEE THREE
| 73 | People PEO 104 | Get On Board/Get On Board (Instrumental) | 4 |

WEE WILLIE & WINNERS
| 74 | Action ACT 4624 | Get Some/A Plan For The Man | 12 |
| 74 | People PEO 116 | I Don't Know What You Got But I Know What I Need (Parts 1 & 2) | 5 |

WEEZER
94	Geffen GFS 85	Undone: The Sweater Song/Mykel And Carli/Susanne/Holiday (p/s)	6
94	Geffen GFSCD 85	Undone: The Sweater Song/Mykel And Carli/Susanne/Holiday (CD)	8
95	Geffen GFS 88	Buddy Holly/Jamie (p/s)	6
95	Geffen GFSV 95	Say It Ain't So (Remix)/No One Else (Live & Acoustic)/Jamie (10", p/s)	7
95	Geffen GEF 24629	WEEZER (LP)	15

WE FIVE
65	Pye International 7N 25314	You Were On My Mind/Small World	6
66	Pye International 7N 25346	Let's Get Together/Cast Your Fate To The Wind	7
66	Pye Intl. NEP 44056	LET'S GET TOGETHER (EP)	40
65	Pye Intl. NPL 28067	YOU WERE ON MY MIND (LP)	35

WE 4
| 67 | HMV POP 1603 | Pretty Flowers/I'll Make You A Miracle | 4 |
| 69 | Major Minor MM 593 | Candy Floss Man/Perry Park | 4 |

FRANN WEIGLE
| 50 | London L 551 | Rockin' Chair/My Diary Of Broken Dreams (78) | 12 |

MINT VALUE £

BRUCIE WEIL
53	London L 1203	Little Boy Blues/God Bless Us All (78)	12

BOB WEIR
72	Warner Bros WB 7611	One More Saturday Night/Cassidy	5
72	Warner Bros K 46165	ACE (LP)	15

(see also Grateful Dead, Kingfish, Bobby & Midnites)

FRANK WEIR & HIS ORCHESTRA
54	Decca F 10271	The Happy Wanderer/From Your Lips	8
54	Decca F 10291	The Bandit/By Candlelight	7
55	Decca F 10384	The Cuckoo Cries/Misty Islands Of The Horizons	7
55	Decca F 10435	Theme From 'Journey Into Space'/Serenade To An Empty Room	8
55	Decca F 10646	I'm A Little Echo (with Eula Parker)/Castles In The Air	5
59	Oriole CB 1523	Swinging Ghosts/The Cool Spectre	5
60	Oriole CB 1559	Caribbean Honeymoon/Farewell My Love	7
63	Philips 326 560 BF	Manhunt/Chant Of The Jungle (as Frank Weir & Werewolves)	5
55	Decca LF 1208	PRESENTING FRANK WEIR AND HIS SAXOPHONE (10" LP)	15

(see also Bill Darnell, Vera Lynn, Janie Marden)

NORRIS WEIR (& JAMAICANS)
70	Duke DU 85	Hard On Me (with Jamaicans)/TOMMY COWAN & JAMAICANS: Please Stop The Wedding	6
74	Dragon DRA 1030	Reggay Revolution/Version	5
75	Horse HOSS 81	Dr. Honey/Honey Dub	5

(see also Jamaicans)

WEIRD STRINGS
80	Velvet Moon VM 1	Oscar Mobile/Ancient Square (foldover p/s)	10
80	Ace ACE 009	Criminal Cage/Mi££ionaire (p/s)	8

(see also Paul Roland, Beau Brummel, Midnight Rags)

FRANK WEISS
71	Stax 2362 011	WEISS TO MEMPHIS (LP)	12

WEKNOWWHEREYOULIVE
95	white label	Mental Hygiene/Draped (1-sided gig freebie)	5

(see also Wonder Stuff, Eat)

BRUCE WELCH
74	EMI EMI 2141	Please Mr. Please/Song Of Yesterday	60

(see also Marvin, Welch & Farrar; Shadows, Cliff Richard)

ELIZABETH WELCH
80	Industrial IR 002	Stormy Weather/Ya're Blase (p/s)	10

HONEE WELCH
69	London HLU 10288	I'm Gonna Try/It's My Girl	6

KEN & MITZIE WELCH
62	London RE-R 1275	A PIANO, ICE BOX AND BED (EP)	10

LENNY WELCH
60	London HLA 9094	You Don't Know Me/I Need Someone	6
62	London HLA 9601	Taste Of Honey/Old Cathedral	7
63	London HLA 9810	Since I Fell For You/Are You Sincere	6
64	London HLA 9880	Ebb Tide/Congratulations Baby	6
64	London HLR 9910	If You See My Love/Father Sebastian	6
65	London HLR 9981	Darling Take Me Back/Time After Time	10
65	London HLR 9991	Two Different Worlds/I Was There	6
65	London HLR 10010	Run To My Lovin' Arms/Coronet Blue	10
66	London HLR 10031	Rags To Riches/I Want You To Worry	6
70	Major Minor MM 707	Breaking Up Is Hard To Do/Got To See If I Can Get My Mommy To Come Back Home	5
75	Mainstream MSS 307	When There's No Such Thing As Love/The Minx	5
66	London HA-R/SH-R 8267	TWO DIFFERENT WORLDS (LP)	20
66	London HA-R 8290	RAGS TO RICHES (LP)	20

TIM WELCH
60	Columbia DB 4529	Weak In The Knees/A Boy And A Girl In Love	6

WELFARE STATE
78	Look LKLP 6347	WELFARE STATE SONGS (LP, with insert)	60

LAWRENCE WELK ORCHESTRA
56	Vogue Coral Q 72140	Chain Gang/The Poor People Of Paris	7
56	Vogue Coral Q 72141	The 'Threepenny Opera' Theme/Rock And Roll Waltz	7
57	Vogue Coral Q 72233	Pizzicato Waltz/Whispering Heart	6
57	Vogue Coral Q 72256	Around The World In 80 Days/Ten Little Trees	7
61	London HLD 9261	Calcutta (Nicolette)/Melodie D'Amour	6
64	Dot DS 16697	The 'Addams Family' Theme/Apples And Bananas	20

PAUL WELLER (MOVEMENT)
SINGLES
91	Freedom High FHP 1	Into Tomorrow/Here's A New Thing (p/s, with or without 'Paul Weller Movement' on label)	12
91	Freedom High FHPC 1	Into Tomorrow/Here's A New Thing (cassette)	10
91	Freedom High FHPT 1	Into Tomorrow/Here's A New Thing/That Spiritual Feeling/ Into Tomorrow (8-Track Demo) (12", p/s)	18
91	Freedom High FHPCD 1	Into Tomorrow/Here's A New Thing/That Spiritual Feeling/ Into Tomorrow (8-Track Demo) (CD)	40
92	Go! Discs GOD 86	Uh Huh Oh Yeh/Fly On The Wall (paper or plastic labels, p/s)	7
92	Go! Discs GODX 86	Uh Huh Oh Yeh/Arrival Time/Fly On The Wall/Always There To Fool You (12", p/s)	10

92	Go! Discs GODCD 86	Uh Huh Oh Yeh/Fly On The Wall/Arrival Time/Always There To Fool You (CD, digipak)... 12
92	Go! Discs GOD 91	Above The Clouds/Everything Has A Price To Pay (paper or plastic labels, p/s)... 6
92	Go! Discs GODX 91	Above The Clouds/Everything Has A Price To Pay/All Year Round (live)/Feeling Alright (12", p/s).. 8
92	Go! Discs GODCD 91	Above The Clouds/Everything Has A Price To Pay/All Year Round (live)/Feeling Alright (CD, digipak).. 12
93	Go! Discs GOD 102	Sunflower/Bull-Rush — Magic Bus (p/s)... 6
93	Go! Discs GODX 102	Sunflower/Kosmos SXDub 2,000/Bull-Rush — Magic Bus (live)/That Spiritual Feeling (New Mix) (12", p/s).. 8
93	Go! Discs GODCD 102	Sunflower/Kosmos SXDub 2,000/Bull-Rush — Magic Bus (live)/That Spiritual Feeling (New Mix) (CD, digipak)... 12
93	Go! Discs GOD 104	Wild Wood/Ends Of The Earth (p/s)... 5
93	Go! Discs GODMC 104	Wild Wood/Ends Of The Earth (cassette)... 4
93	Go! Discs GODT 104	Wild Wood/Ends Of The Earth (10", p/s, with poster)..................................... 10
93	Go! Discs GODCD 104	Wild Wood/Ends Of The Earth (CD, sealed with 5 postcards).......................... 15
94	Go! Discs GOD 107	THE WEAVER EP (The Weaver/This Is No Time/Another New Day/Ohio [live]) (p/s)... 5
94	Go! Discs GODMC 107	THE WEAVER EP (cassette)... 4
94	Go! Discs GODT 107	THE WEAVER EP (10", numbered sticker on p/s).. 10
94	Go! Discs GODCD 107	THE WEAVER EP (The Weaver/This Is No Time/Another New Day/Ohio [live]) (CD, digipak)... 12
94	Go! Discs GOD 111	Hung Up/Foot Of The Mountain (live from Royal Albert Hall 23.11.93)/The Loved/Kosmos (Lynch Mob Bonus Beats) (p/s).. 5
94	Go! Discs GODMC 111	Hung Up/Foot Of The Mountain (live from Royal Albert Hall 23.11.93)/The Loved/Kosmos (Lynch Mob Bonus Beats) (cassette)............................... 4
94	Go! Discs GODX 111	Hung Up/Foot Of The Mountain (live from Royal Albert Hall 23.11.93)/The Loved/Kosmos (Lynch Mob Bonus Beats) (12", p/s)................................... 8
94	Go! Discs GODCD 111	Hung Up/Foot Of The Mountain (live from Royal Albert Hall 23.11.93)/The Loved/Kosmos (Lynch Mob Bonus Beats) (CD, digipak).............................. 10
94	Go! Discs GOD 121	Out Of The Sinking/Sunflower (Lynch Mob Dub)/Sexy Sadie (p/s)..................... 5
94	Go! Discs GODMC 121	Out Of The Sinking/Sunflower (Lynch Mob Dub)/Sexy Sadie (cassette)............ 4
94	Go! Discs GODX 121	Out Of The Sinking/Sunflower (Lynch Mob Dub)/Sexy Sadie (12", p/s)............. 7
94	Go! Discs GODCD 121	Out Of The Sinking/Sunflower (Lynch Mob Dub)/Sexy Sadie (CD).................... 8
96	Go! Discs GOD 143	Out Of The Sinking (LP Version)/I Shall Be Released/Broken Stones (live radio)/ Porcelain Gods (live radio) (no'd p/s, with postcard).............................. 4
96	Go! Discs GODCD 143	Out Of The Sinking (LP Version)/I Shall Be Released/Broken Stones (live radio)/Porcelain Gods (live radio) (CD)... 7

ALBUMS

95	Go! Discs 850 070-7	STANLEY ROAD (LP, 6 x 7" in box set with booklet)..................................... 25
95	Go! Discs 828 620-2	STANLEY ROAD (CD, 12" box set with booklet)... 20

PROMOS & FREEBIES

92	Go! Discs	Kosmos (12")... 20
93	no label (WELLER+ F1)	The Loved (blank clear 1-sided flexi free with *The Big Issue* mag)........... 12/5
93	Go! Discs PWBCD 1	Wild Wood (The Sheared Wood Remix) (CD, no inlay)................................... 15
94	Go! Discs PN PCD 2	Sexy Sadie (1-track CD, available via mail order with 1st 500 copies of "Highlights & Hang-Ups" video).. 20
95	Go! Discs PW-G-CD 1	Into Tomorrow/Wild Wood/Out Of The Sinking (CD, free with *The Guardian Guide* magazine)... 5
95	Go Discs SPLINT 1	Walk On Gilded Splinters (12", 1-sided white label)....................................... 60
95	Go Discs LYNCH 1	Whirlpools End (Lynch Mob Mix) (12", 1-sided white label, stamped 1-sided white label, 500 only)... 60
97	Island ISJB 666	Brushed/Shoot The Dove (jukebox issue, no p/s)... 7
97	Island	Heavy Soul (1-sided).. 50
99	Island 12 IS 734DJ	Wild Wood (Sheared Wood Remix) (12", 1 sided white label, promo only)... 15
89	EMI Mus. Pub. CDWELLER 3	THE SONGS OF PAUL WELLER 1982-1988 (CD, 10-track sampler)......... 100
95	Go! Discs (no cat. no.)	CD SAMPLER (CD, given away in queue for 100 Club secret gig, 200 only)..... 40
96	Go! Discs PWRT 1	PEACOCK SUIT (CD, 7-track picture disc, no p/s)... 25
97	Island PAUL-CD 1	WILD WOOD TO HEAVY SOUL (CD, 8-track sampler)................................. 35
97	Southern Songs WELLER 1	PAUL WELLER (LP, white label, live at Hayward Gallery)............................... 60
97	Island PW ICD 1	HEAVY SOUL (box set, including CD "Paul Weller Interview", EPK, 5 cards & insert)... 850
97	Island KINGS 1	KINGS ROAD (CD sampler, 350 only)... 40
98	Island CLASSICD 1	MODERN CLASSICS (CD, 5-track sampler, card sleeve, promo only).......... 25
99	Island INTCD 3	IN CONVERSATION (CD, interview, gatefold card p/s, promo only)............... 30

(see also Jam, Style Council)

ORSON WELLES

59	Top Rank TR 5001	The Courtroom Scene From The Film 'Compulsion' (both sides) (some in p/s)... 10/6

(see also Manowar)

NICK WELLINGS & SECTION

77	The Label TLR 011	You Better Move On/Punk Funk... 6

BOBBY WELLINS

78	Vortex VS1	LIVE JUBILATION (LP).. 40
78	Vortex VS2	DREAMS ARE FREE (LP)... 40

BOBBY WELLS

68	Beacon 3-102	Let's Copp A Groove/Recipe For Love (yellow or green label)................. 7/5
79	Grapevine GRP 124	Be's That Way Sometimes/Recipe For Love.. 5

HOUSTON WELLS (& MARKSMEN)

62	Parlophone R 4955	This Song Is Just For You/Paradise.. 8
62	Parlophone R 4980	Shutters And Boards/North Wind.. 8
63	Parlophone R 5031	Only The Heartaches/Can't Stop Pretending... 8
63	Parlophone R 5069	Blowing Wild (The Ballad Of Black Gold)/Crazy Dreams......................... 8

Houston WELLS

64	Parlophone R 5099	Anna Marie/Moon Watch Over My Baby	8
64	Parlophone R 5141	Galway Bay/Livin' Alone (as Houston Wells & Outlaws)	8
65	Parlophone R 5226	Blue Of The Night/Coming Home (solo)	6
68	CBS 3572	Teach Me Little Children/Does My Ring Hurt Your Finger	5
63	Parlophone GEP 8878	JUST FOR YOU (EP)	75
64	Parlophone GEP 8914	RAMONA (EP)	90
64	Parlophone PMC 1215	WESTERN STYLE (LP)	55

(see also Marksmen, Outlaws)

JEAN WELLS
71	Mojo 2092 023	After Loving You/Puttin' The Best On The Outside	6
70	Sonet SNTF 606	WORLD! HERE COMES JEAN WELLS (LP)	25

JOHNNY WELLS
59	Columbia DB 4377	Lonely Moon/The One And Only One	8
67	Parlophone R 5559	Wondering Why/Guess I'm Dumb	5

JUNIOR WELLS
66	Delmark DS 9612	Hoodoo Man Blues (blue label)	20
66	Delmark DS 628	Southside Blues Jam (blue label)	10
68	Mercury MF 1056	Girl You Lit My Fire/It's A Man Down There	7
66	Delmark DJB 1	BLUES WITH A BEAT (EP)	25
60s	XX MIN 715	JUNIOR WELLS (EP)	15
68	Fontana (S)TFL 6084	IT'S MY LIFE BABY (LP)	30
68	Vanguard SVRL 19011	COMING AT YOU (LP, also stereo, VSD 79262)	25/22
68	Vanguard SVRL 19028	IT'S MY LIFE BABY (LP, reissue)	15
68	Mercury SMCL 20130	YOU'RE TUFF ENOUGH (LP)	15
71	Delmark DS 628	SOUTHSIDE BLUES JAM (LP)	12
75	Delmark DS 635	JUNIOR WELLS ON TAP (LP)	12

(see also Buddy Guy)

KITTY WELLS
64	Brunswick 05920	I Gave My Wedding Dress Away/I've Thought Of Leaving You	6
55	Brunswick OE 9149	KITTY SINGS (EP)	20
61	Brunswick LAT 8361	KITTY'S CHOICE (LP)	18
64	Brunswick LAT 8575	QUEEN OF COUNTRY MUSIC (LP)	15
65	Brunswick LAT 8601	ESPECIALLY FOR YOU (LP)	15
65	Brunswick LAT 8621	LONESOME SAD AND BLUE (LP)	15
66	Brunswick LAT/STA 8646	SINGS SONGS MADE FAMOUS BY JIM REEVES (LP, mono/stereo)	15/18
66	Brunswick LAT 8659	COUNTRY ALL THE WAY (LP, mono/stereo)	15/18
67	Brunswick LAT 8683	LOVE MAKES THE WORLD GO ROUND (LP)	15

MARY WELLS
62	Oriole CBA 1762	You Beat Me To The Punch/Old Love	45
63	Oriole CBA 1796	Two Lovers/Operator	40
63	Oriole CBA 1829	Laughing Boy/Two Wrongs Don't Make A Right	45
63	Oriole CBA 1847	Your Old Standby/What Love Has Joined Together	45
63	Stateside SS 242	You Lost The Sweetest Boy/What's Easy For Two Is So Hard For One	18
64	Stateside SS 288	My Guy/Oh Little Boy	7
64	Stateside SS 316	Once Upon A Time (with Marvin Gaye)/What's The Matter With You, Baby	25
65	Stateside SS 372	Ain't It The Truth/Stop Takin' Me For Granted	12
65	Stateside SS 396	Use Your Head/Everlovin' Boy	10
65	Stateside SS 415	Never Never Leave Me/Why Don't You Let Yourself Go	10
65	Stateside SS 439	He's A Lover/I'm Learnin'	10
65	Stateside SS 463	Me Without You/I'm Sorry	10
68	Stateside SS 2111	The Doctor/Two Lovers' History	7
66	Atlantic AT 4067	Dear Lover/Can't You See (You're Losing Me)	18
66	Atlantic 584 054	Me And My Baby/Such A Sweet Thing	8
67	Atlantic 584 104	Hey You Set My Soul On Fire/Coming Home	6
70	Direction 58-4816	Dig The Way I Feel/Love Shooting Bandit	5
72	Atlantic K 10254	Dear Lover/Can't You See (You're Losing Me) (reissue)	5
65	Tamla Motown TME 2007	MARY WELLS (EP)	60
63	Oriole PS 40045	TWO LOVERS (LP)	65
63	Oriole PS 40051	BYE BYE BABY (LP)	80
64	Stateside SL 10095	SINGS MY GUY (LP)	40
65	Stateside SL 10133	MARY WELLS (LP)	35
65	Tamla Motown TML 11006	MY BABY JUST CARES FOR ME (LP)	45
66	Stateside S(S)L 10171	LOVE SONGS TO THE BEATLES (LP)	30
66	Tamla Motown TML 11032	GREATEST HITS (LP)	25
68	Stateside S(S)L 10266	SERVIN' UP SOME SOUL (LP)	25
68	Atlantic 587 049	THE TWO SIDES OF MARY WELLS (LP)	18
69	T. Motown (S)TML 11102	VINTAGE STOCK (LP, unissued)	
70	Regal Starline SRS 5040	MY GUY (LP)	12

(see also Marvin Gaye)

ALEX WELSH & DIXIELANDERS
55	Decca F 10538	I'll Build A Stairway To Paradise/Eccentric	5
55	Decca F 10557	Blues My Naughtie Sweetie Gives To Me/Shoe Shiner's Blues	5
55	Decca F 10607	As Long As I Live/New Orleans Stomp	10
55	Decca F 10651	Sugar/Smiles	5
55	Decca F 10652	What Can I Say After I Say I'm Sorry/Hard-Hearted Hannah	5
61	Columbia DB 4686	Tansy/Memphis March	6
55	Decca DFE 6254	DIXIELANDERS AT THE RFH (EP)	10
55	Decca DFE 6283	AND HIS DIXIELAND BAND (EP)	18
55	Decca DFE 6315	MUSIC FROM PETE KELLY (EP)	20
62	Columbia SEG 8143	WELSH WAILS (EP)	25
66	Strike JHE 201	ALEX WELSH ENTERTAINS (EP)	35
58	Nixa NJT 516	THE MELROSE FOLIO (LP)	15
59	Columbia 33SX 1219	MUSIC OF THE MAUVE DECADE (LP)	35

MINT VALUE £

61	Columbia 33SX 1322	IT'S RIGHT HERE FOR YOU (LP)	35
62	Columbia 33SX 1429	ECHOES OF CHICAGO (LP)	35
66	Strike JHL 102	STRIKE ONE (LP)	25
68	Columbia SX 6213	AT HOME WITH... (LP)	18
69	Columbia SX 6333	AND HIS BAND '69 (LP)	35
70	Columbia SCX 6376	DIXIELAND PARTY (LP)	30
71	Polydor 2460-123	TRIBUTE TO LOUIS ARMSTRONG VOL. 1 (LP)	35
71	Polydor 2460-124	TRIBUTE TO LOUIS ARMSTRONG VOL. 2 (LP)	35
71	Polydor 2460-125	TRIBUTE TO LOUIS ARMSTRONG VOL. 3 (LP)	35
72	Black Lion BLP 12109	IF I HAD A TALKING PICTURE (LP)	18
72	Black Lion BLP 12112	AN EVENING WITH... VOL. 1 (LP)	35
72	Black Lion BLP 12113	AN EVENING WITH... VOL. 2 (LP)	35
72	Black Lion BLP 12115/6	IN CONCERT (2 LP)	18
75	Black Lion BLP 12120	BAND SHOWCASE VOL. 1 (LP)	25
76	Black Lion BLP 12121	BAND SHOWCASE VOL. 2 (LP)	30
76	Black Lion BLP 12131	DIXIELAND PARTY (LP)	40
76	Black Lion BLP 12161/2	SALUTE TO SATCHMO (2 LP)	45

DANNY WELTON
| 60 | Coral Q 72409 | Boogie Woogie/To Each His Own | 6 |

WENDY & LEMMY
| 82 | Bronze BRO 151 | Stand By Your Man/No Class/Masterplan (p/s) | 7 |

(see also Plasmatics, Motörhead)

WENDY & LISA
87	Virgin VS 999	Waterfall/The Life (p/s)	4
87	Virgin VS 999-12	Waterfall/The Life/To Trip Is To Fall (12", p/s)	8
88	Virgin CDEP 16	Sideshow/Chance To Grow/Waterfall/Sideshow (Extended Version) (CD)	7
89	Virgin VSCD 1156	Are You My Baby/Happy Birthday/Honeymoon Express/ Are You My Baby (12" Mix) (3" CD, card sleeve)	8
89	Virgin VSCD 1175	Lolly Lolly (According To Prince)/Hip Hop Love/Lolly Lolly (Random Dance Mix) (3" CD, card sleeve)	8
89	Virgin VSCD 1194	Satisfaction (Remix)/Stay/Satisfaction (12" Dance Mix)/ Satisfaction (12" Dance Mix) (3" CD, card sleeve)	8
89	Virgin VSCD 1223	Waterfall '89 (Alice & Sundial Seven)/(Psychedelic Teepee Twelve)/ Always In My Dreams/Waterfall (Original Version) (3" CD, card sleeve)	7
90	Virgin VSTY 1272	Strung Out (G-String Mix)/Strung Out/Stones And Birth (12", picture disc in p/s with poster)	7
90	Virgin VST 1280	Rainbow Lake (12" Mix)/Rainbow Lake (No Voices) (12", box set with poster)	7
90	Virgin VSCDX 1337	Don't Try To Tell Me/Are You My Baby (12" Mix)/Lolly Lolly (Dance Mix) (CD, in video-shaped box with 3 prints)	8

(see also Prince)

WE'RE TIRED
77	Deadline DEADS 8	My Life's On The Line/Against All Odds (p/s)	20
77	Deadline DEADS 11	Guide Me Through Hell/Time Is Against Me (p/s)	25
78	Deadline DEADS 15	Over The Edge/Anal Retentive (p/s, as We're Tired & We're Proud)	8
77	Deadline DEADLP 2	FIND THE PRICE IN TIME (LP)	50

WERLWINDS
| 61 | Columbia DB 4650 | Winding It Up/Dig Deep | 15 |

HOWARD WERTH & MOONBEAMS
| 74 | Charisma CB 225 | Lucinda/Johan | 5 |
| 75 | Charisma CAS 11004 | KING BRILLIANT (LP) | 12 |

(see also Audience)

BRIAN WESKE
| 62 | Oriole CB 1723 | In The Midst Of The Crowd/All Mine Alone | 7 |
| 62 | Oriole CB 1776 | 24 Hours In A Day/Where Does The Clown Go | 7 |

FRED WESLEY & J.B.s
73	Polydor 2066 322	Doing It To Death/Everybody Got Soul (with J.B.s)	5
74	Mojo 2093 025	J.B. Shout/Back Stabbers (with J.B.s)	5
80	RSO RSO 67	Houseparty/I Make Music (solo)	6
80	RSO RSO 67	Houseparty/I Make Music (12", solo)	12
74	Polydor 2391 125	DAMN RIGHT, I AM SOMEBODY (LP, with J.B.s)	35
74	Polydor 2391 161	BREAKIN' BREAD (LP, with J.B.s)	25

(see also James Brown, J.B.s)

WES MINSTER FIVE
| 64 | Carnival CV 7017 | Shakin' The Blues/Railroad Blues | 10 |
| 65 | Carnival CV 7019 | Sticks And Stones/Mickey's Monkey | 10 |

(see also Maynell Wilson, Dave Greenslade)

FRANK WESS
| 64 | Fontana TL 5291 | THE AWARD WINNER (LP) | 12 |

ADAM 'BATMAN' WEST
| 76 | Target TGT 111 | Batman And Robin/The Story Of Batman | 7 |

DODIE WEST
64	Decca F 12046	Goin' Out Of My Head/Is He Feeling Blue	8
65	Piccadilly 7N 35239	In The Deep Of The Night/Rovin' Boy (some in p/s)	12/7
65	Piccadilly 7N 35261	Thinking Of You/And Love Will Come	7
66	Piccadilly 7N 35287	Make The World Go Away/Who Does He Think He Is	7
68	Philips BF 1698	Living In Limbo/Birdie Told Me	6

KEITH WEST
| 67 | Parlophone R 5623 | Excerpt From "A Teenage Opera"/MARK WIRTZ ORCHESTRA: Theme From "A Teenage Opera" | 5 |
| 67 | Parlophone R 5651 | Sam (From "A Teenage Opera")/MARK WIRTZ'S MOOD MOSAIC: Thimble Full Of Puzzles (promos in art sleeve) | 15/6 |

Keith WEST

68	Parlophone R 5713	On A Saturday/The Kid Was A Killer	30
72	Parlophone R 5957	Excerpt From "A Teenage Opera"/Sam (From "A Teenage Opera")	5
73	Deram DM 402	Riding For A Fall/Days About To Rain	6
74	Deram DM 410	Havin' Someone/Know There's No Livin' Without You	6
81	Video VID 02	Excerpt From "A Teenage Opera"/Count On Me (p/s)	5

(see also Tomorrow, Four + One, In Crowd, Mark Wirtz)

LESLIE WEST
69	Bell SBLL 126	MOUNTAIN (LP)	20
75	RCA RS 1009	THE GREAT FATSBY (LP)	12
76	Phantom PHS 701	LESLIE WEST BAND (LP)	12

(see also Jolliver Arkansas, Mountain, West Bruce & Laing)

MAE WEST
67	Stateside SS 2021	Twist And Shout/Day Tripper	12
73	MGM 2006 203	Great Balls Of Fire/Men	6
56	Brunswick LAT 8082	THE FABULOUS MAE WEST (LP)	30
67	Stateside (S)SL 10197	WAY OUT WEST (LP)	20
73	Polydor 2315 207	GREAT BALLS OF FIRE (LP)	15

SPEEDY WEST & JIMMY BRYANT
55	Capitol EAP1 520	TWO GUITARS COUNTRY STYLE PT. 1 (EP)	25
55	Capitol EAP2 520	TWO GUITARS COUNTRY STYLE PT. 2 (EP)	25
53	Capitol LC 6619	CAPITOL PRESENTS SPEEDY WEST & JIMMY BRYANT (10" LP)	30
55	Capitol LC 6694	TWO GUITARS COUNTRY STYLE (10" LP)	30

TABBY WEST
58	Capitol CL 14861	All That I Want/If You Promise Not To Tell	5

WEST AFRICAN RHYTHM BOYS
50s	Melodisc HI 1	Calar O/Y B Club	5
50s	Melodisc HI 2	Iwa D'arekere/Ero Ya Kowawo	5
58	Melodisc MEL 1505	Ominira/Gbonimawo	5
59	Melodisc MEL 1513	We Have It In Africa/Aye Wa Adara	5
60	Melodisc MEL 1567	Nigeria Odowoyin/Asikoloto	5
60	Melodisc MEL 1568	Nigeria Koniset/Jekafo Ju Agbawo	5

MIKE WESTBROOK (CONCERT BAND)
69	Deram DM 234	A Life Of Its Own/Can't Get It Out Of My Mind	6
70	Deram DM 286	Requiem/Hooray	6
70	Deram DM 311	Magic Garden/Original Peter (with Norma Winstone)	6
67	Deram DML 1013	CELEBRATION (LP, as Mike Westbrook Concert Band)	100
68	Deram DML/SML 1031	RELEASE (LP)	50
69	Deram SML 1047	MARCHING SONG VOL. 1 (LP)	60
69	Deram SML 1048	MARCHING SONG VOL. 2 (LP)	60
70	Deram SML 1069	LOVE SONGS (LP, as Mike Westbrook Concert Band with Norma Winstone)	60
71	RCA SER 5612	TYGER: A CELEBRATION OF WILLIAM BLAKE (LP, with insert)	120
72	RCA Neon NE 10	MIKE WESTBROOK'S METROPOLIS (LP, gatefold sleeve)	60
72	Cadillac SGC 1001	LIVE (LP, private pressing)	35
75	RCA SF 8433	CITADEL/ROOM 315 (2-LP, with John Surman)	35
75	Transatlantic TRA 323	LOVE/DREAM & VARIATIONS (LP)	25
76	Transatlantic TRA 312	PLAYS FOR THE RECORD (LP)	20
78	Original ORA 001	GOOSE SAUCE (LP)	20
78	Original ORA 002	PIANO (LP)	20
79	RCA PL 25252	MAMA CHICAGO (LP)	20
80	Original ORA 203	WESTBROOK BLAKE (LP)	35
82	Original ORA 309	THE CORTEGE (LP)	35
83	Westbrook LWN 1	A LITTLE WESTBROOK MUSIC (LP)	40
88	Venture VEB 13	LONDON BRIDGE IS BROKEN DOWN (LP)	20

(see also Solid Gold Cadillac, John Surman, Norma Winstone)

WEST, BRUCE & LAING
73	RSO 2090 113	Dirty Shoes/Backfire	5
73	CBS 65314	WHY DONTCHA (LP)	15
73	RSO 2394 107	WHATEVER TURNS YOU ON (LP)	15
74	RSO 2394 128	LIVE 'N' KICKIN' (LP)	18

(see also Jack Bruce, Leslie West, Mountain)

WEST COAST CONSORTIUM
67	Pye 7N 17352	Some Other Someday/Looking Back	6
68	Pye 7N 17482	Colour Sergeant Lillywhite/Lady From Baltimore	15

WEST COAST DELEGATION
67	Deram DM 113	Reach The Top/Mr. Personality Man	8

WEST COAST KNACK
67	Capitol CL 15497	I'm Aware/Time Waits For No One	12

WEST COAST POP ART EXPERIMENTAL BAND
68	Reprise RSLP 6298	A CHILD'S GUIDE TO GOOD AND EVIL (LP)	75

WEST END (Austria)
83	Epic A 3388	Hurricane (English)/Hurricane (German) (unissued, promo only)	4

WEST END (U.K.)
80s	Continental TIN 001	The Servant/Fiction (p/s)	4

JOHNNY WESTERN
60	Philips PB 1030	The Ballad Of Paladin/The Guns Of Rio Muerto (B-side with Richard Boone)	6

WESTERNAIRES ORCHESTRA with CURLY WILLIAMS
57	Brunswick 05692	Walking Alone In A Crowd/Sweet Talk (Won Her Loving Heart)	6

WEST FIVE
65	HMV POP 1396	Congratulations/She Mine	25
65	HMV POP 1428	Someone Ain't Right/Just Like Romeo And Juliet	12
66	HMV POP 1513	If It Don't Work Out/Back To Square One	7

(see also Ferris Wheel)

WEST INDIANS
68	Doctor Bird DB 1121	Right On Time/Hokey Pokey	12
68	Doctor Bird DB 1127	Falling In Love/I Mean It	12
69	Camel CA 16	Strange Whisperings/CARL DAWKINS: Hard To Handle	8
71	Dynamic DYN 413	Never Gonna Give You Up/REBELLIOUS SUBJECTS: Never Give Up	7

(see also Prunes, Kilowatts, Upsetters)

CLIVE WESTLAKE
68	Fontana TF 940	199 Days/From The Beginning To The End	4

JILL WESTLAKE
58	Columbia DB 4132	Sharin'/Over And Over Again	8
58	Columbia DB 4132	Sharin'/Over And Over Again (78)	10

KEVIN WESTLAKE & GARY FARR
68	Marmalade 598 007	Everyday/Green	8

(see also Gary Farr & T-Bones, T-Bones, Blossom Toes, B.B. Blunder)

WESTMORELITES
70	Clandisc CLA 217	Zion/CLANCY ECCLES & DYNAMITES: Revival	6

(see also Minstrels)

GLEN WESTON
68	Columbia DB 8328	With This Ring/Liane	4

KIM WESTON
64	Stateside SS 359	A Little More Love/Go Ahead And Laugh	75
65	Tamla Motown TMG 511	I'm Still Loving You/Just Loving You	80
65	Tamla Motown TMG 538	Take Me In Your Arms (Rock Me A Little While)/Don't Compare Me With Her	50
66	Tamla Motown TMG 554	Helpless/A Love Like Yours	50
67	MGM MGM 1338	I Got What You Need/Someone Like You	12
67	MGM MGM 1357	That's Groovy/Land Of Tomorrow	12
68	MGM MGM 1382	Nobody/You're Just The Kind Of Guy	18
69	Major Minor MM 619	From Both Sides Now/We Try Harder	5
70	Major Minor MM 683	Danger, Heartbreak Dead Ahead/I'll Be Thinking	8
75	Tamla Motown TMG 1000	Do Like I Do/MARVELETTES: Finders Keepers, Losers Weepers	25
65	Tamla Motown TME 2005	KIM WESTON (EP)	85
66	Tamla Motown TME 2015	ROCK ME A LITTLE WHILE (EP)	175
67	MGM MGM-C(S) 8055	FOR THE FIRST TIME (LP)	50
71	Stax 2362 021	KIM KIM KIM (LP)	25

(see also Johnny Nash & Kim Weston, Marvin Gaye & Kim Weston)

PETE WESTON
70	Gas GAS 146	Something Sweet/BIM & BAM: Love Letters	5
70	Punch PH 28	In The Mood (& His Band)/Slide Mongoose (actually "Sly Mongoose")	6

(see also I Roy)

WEST ONE
88	Que Q 9	California '69/Eurotrash (gig freebie, white label)	12
	80s private cassette	WEST ONE (cassette)	10

WEST POINT SUPERNATURAL
67	Reaction 591 013	Time Will Tell/Night Train	12

WESTSIDE
74	People PEO 111	Running In And Out Of My Life/Highway Demon	5

WESTWIND
70	Penny Farthing PEN 737	Love Is A Funny Sort Of Thing/Breakout	7
70	Penny Farthing PELS 505	LOVE IS (LP)	75

WESTWORLD
86	private pressing	Sonic Boom Boy/Sonic Boom Beat/Mix Me Up (12", hand screen-printed sleeve, handwritten label)	10

WE THE PEOPLE
66	London HLH 10089	He Doesn't Go About It Right/You Burn Me Up And Down	80

WE THREE TRIO
65	London HLA 9966	Baby The Rain Must Fall/Shine For Me	6
67	Fontana TL 5308	THE WE THREE TRIO (LP)	15

WET WET WET
86	Lyntone/Jamming!	I Can Give You Everything/FLOOR: Hold On (flexidisc free with *Jamming!* magazine)	15/7
87	Precious JEWEL 312	Wishing I Was Lucky (Metal Remix)/Words Of Wisdom/ Still Can't Remember Your Name (12", p/s)	8
87	Precious JWLD 3	Wishing I Was Lucky (Remix)/Words Of Wisdom/Wishing I Was Lucky (Metal Mix)/I Still Can't Remember Your Name (12", double pack)	15
87	Precious JWLS 4	Sweet Little Mystery/Don't Let Me Be Lonely Tonight (shaped picture disc)	12
87	Precious JEWEL 412	SWEET LITTLE MYSTERY EP (12", PVC 'wet cover')	20
87	Precious JEWEL 5	I Remember/I Don't Believe (unreleased)	
87	Precious JEWEL 512	I Remember/I Don't Believe (12", unreleased)	
87	Precious JEWEL 6	Angel Eyes (Home And Away)/We Can Love (box set with calendar)	12
87	Precious JWLMC 6	Angel Eyes (Home And Away)/We Can Love/Angel Eyes (Extended) (cassette)	4
87	Precious JWLCD 6	Angel Eyes (Home And Away — Full Length Version)/We Can Love/ Home And Away (Original Demo — 7" Version) (CD)	12
88	Precious JEWEL 777	Temptation/Bottled Emotions (Keen For Loving) (gatefold/booklet p/s)	6

88	Precious JWLCD 7	Temptation (Extended)/Bottled Emotions/I Remember (Extended)/ Heaven Helps Us All (CD)	12
88	Precious 080 476-2	Temptation (Extended Version)/I Remember (Extended Version)/Bottled Emotions (Keen For Loving)/Heaven Help Us All (CD Video)	20
88	Lyntone/No. 1	Sweet Little Mystery/Interview With *No. 1* (flexidisc with/without mag)	6/4
89	Precious JWL M/T/G/N 9	Sweet Surrender/This Time (live) (poster pack of each member)	each 4
89	Precious JWLCD 9	Sweet Surrender/This Time (live)/H.T.T.D.T.G.T./ Sweet Surrender (Extended Mix) (CD)	8
89	Precious JWPD 10	Broke Away/You've Had It/And Now For Something Completely Different (picture disc)	5
89	Precious JWCD 10	Broke Away (Original Version)/You've Had It (Club Mix)/ Sweet Surrender (Club Mix) (CD, some as picture disc)	10/8
90	Precious JWLM 11	Hold Back The River/Keys To Your Heart (4 different picture sleeves)	each 4
90	Precious JEWEL 1122	Hold Back The River/Keys To Your Heart/With A Little Help From My Friends (live) (12", gatefold p/s with booklet)	7
90	Precious JWCD 11	Hold Back The River/Keys To Your Heart/With A Little Help From My Friends (live) (CD)	7

WE UGLY DOGS

| 67 | BT Puppy BTS 45537 | First Spring Rain/Poor Man | 4 |

W. GIMMICS

| 65 | Polydor EPH 27 125 | HOT RODS (EP, manufactured in Europe) | 60 |

WHALE FEATHERS

| 71 | Blue Horizon 2431 009 | WHALE FEATHERS (LP) | 50 |

WHALES

| 68 | CBS 3766 | Come Down Little Bird/Beachcomber | 8 |

WHAM!

82	Innervision IVL A 2442	Wham Rap! (Enjoy What You Do) (Special Club Remix)/(Special U.S. Mix) (p/s, 1st pressing, paper label, songwriting credit: "Panos/Ridgeley")	7
82	Innervision IVL A 2442	Wham Rap! (Enjoy What You Do) (Social Mix)/(Unsocial Mix) (p/s, paper label, songwriting credit: "Michael/Ridgeley")	4
83	Innervision IVL A 2442	Wham Rap! (Enjoy What You Do) (Special Club Remix)/(Special U.S. Mix) (reissue, red & blue title p/s)	5
82	Innervision IVL A 13-2442	Wham Rap! (Enjoy What You Do) (Special Club Remix)/(Special U.S. Mix) (12", paper label, p/s, "Panos/Ridgeley" or "Michael/Ridgeley" songwriting credit)	12/7
82	Innervision IVL A 13-2442	Wham Rap! (Enjoy What You Do) (Social Mix)/(Unsocial Mix) (12", initially in p/s, later in plain black die-cut sleeve)	15/7
82	Innervision IVL A 2442	Wham Rap! (Enjoy What You Do) (Special Club Remix)/(Special U.S. Mix) (12", reissue, red & blue title p/s)	12
83	Innervision IVL A 13-2766	Young Guns (Go For It)/Going For It (12", p/s)	10
83	Innervision IVL A 3143	Bad Boys/Bad Boys (Instrumental) (poster p/s)	8
83	Innervision IVL WA 3143	Bad Boys/Bad Boys (Instrumental) (picture disc)	12
83	Innervision IVL WA 3613	Club Tropicana/Blue (Armed With Love) (picture disc)	15
84	Epic TA 4440	Wake Me Up Before You Go-Go/Wake Me Up (Instrumental)/ A Ray Of Sunshine (12", poster p/s)	20
84	Epic QA/WA 4743	Freedom/Freedom (Instrumental) (George Michael- or Andrew Ridgeley-shaped picture disc in wallet, PVC gatefold sleeve; each or as set)	18/30
85	Epic QTA 4949	Everything She Wants (U.S. Remix)/Last Christmas (The Pudding Mix) (12", reissue, A-sides reversed, some w/ stickered p/s & free calendar)	15/7
85	Epic WTA 6716	I'm Your Man (Extended Stimulation)/Do It Right (Instrumental)/ I'm Your Man (A Capella) (12", picture disc)	10
85	Epic WHAMT 1	Last Christmas/Blue (Armed With Love) (live)/Everything She Wants (12", p/s)	7
86	Epic FIN 1	The Edge Of Heaven/Battlestations//Where Did Your Heart Go/ Wham Rap '86 (double pack, gatefold p/s)	4
89	Epic 654 915-3	Wake Me Up Before You Go-Go/Freedom/The Edge Of Heaven (3" CD, 'Solid Gold Classics' series)	15
83	Epic (no cat. no.)	Bad Boys/(track by other artist) (no p/s, free with 'KP Crisps' offer)	7
84	Epic KELL 4	Club Tropicana/HERBIE HANCOCK: Rock It (no p/s, promo only, free with 'Rice Krispies' offer)	7
84	Epic (no cat. no.)	Merry Xmas From Wham (fan club Christmas single, no p/s)	15
86	Epic EPC 450 125-4	THE 12" TAPE (cassette)	10
86	Epic WHAM 2	THE FINAL (2-LP box, gold vinyl picture discs, with sealed T-shirt, calendar, pencil, note-pad and no'd certificate)	75
84	Innervision CDIVL 25328	FANTASTIC (CD)	60
84	Epic CDEPC 86311	MAKE IT BIG (CD)	60

(see also George Michael, Pepsi & Shirley)

PEETIE WHEATSTRAW

| 69 | Matchbox SDR 191 | THE DEVIL'S SON IN LAW (LP) | 20 |
| 69 | Matchbox SDR 192 | THE HIGH SHERIFF FROM HELL (LP) | 20 |

BILLY ED WHEELER

64	London HLR 9920	On The Outside (Lookin' In)/The Right Foot In His World	7
65	London HLR 9950	Ode To The Little Brown Shack Out Back/Sister Sara	7
65	London HAR/SHR 8221	MEMORIES OF AMERICA (LP)	15

KENNY WHEELER & JOHN DANKWORTH ORCHESTRA

| 68 | Fontana STL 5494 | WINDMILL TILTER (LP) | 125 |
| 70s | Incus 10 | SONG FOR SOMEONE (LP) | 125 |

(see also Johnny Dankworth, Elton Dean)

WHEELS

| 65 | Columbia DB 7682 | Gloria/Don't You Know | 100 |
| 66 | Columbia DB 7827 | Bad Little Woman/Road Block (mispressing, demos & a few issues play "Call My Name" on B-side) | 90 |

66	Columbia DB 7827	Bad Little Woman/Road Block	325
66	Columbia DB 7981	Kicks/Call My Name	90

(see also James Brothers, Yellow Dog, Demick & Armstrong)

WHEELS OF TIME
67	Spin SP 62008	1984/So Long	30

WHERE FORTUNE SMILES
(see under John Surman)

WHERE'S LISSE
81	Glass GLASS 008	Talk Takes Too Long/You Stole My Gun (p/s)	5
82	Glass GLASS 014	Tutorial Single (p/s)	4

WHICHWHAT
69	Beacon BEA 127	Gimme Gimme Good Lovin'/Wonderland Of Love	7
69	Beacon BEA 131	Why Do Lovers Break Each Other's Heart/When I See Her Smile	5
69	Beacon BEA 133	In The Year 2525/Parting	5
69	Beacon BEA 144	I Wanna Be Free/It's All Over Again	5
70	Beacon BEA 169	Vietnam Rose/Shame And Solution	5
70	Beacon BEAS 14	WHICHWHAT'S FIRST (LP)	35

WHIPPING BOY
80s	Liquid LQ 4	Favourite Sister/Safari (no p/s)	4

WHIRL
87	Playroom PLAYD 112	Heaven Forbid/Mister Strikes Back/As Soon As/In A Dream (12", p/s)	7
89	The Sound Of Spasm 2	Bizarre Love Triangle/CROCODILE RIDE: Shimmer (33rpm flexi, foldover p/s)	4

WHIRLWIND
78	Chiswick NS 25	Hang Loose/Together Forever (p/s)	6
78	Chiswick NS 42	I Only Wish (That I'd Been Told)/Ducktails (unissued)	
78	Chiswick CHIS 103	I Only Wish (That I'd Been Told)/Ducktails (p/s)	5
79	Chiswick CHIS 117	You Got Class/Losing To You (unissued in U.K.; France-only)	
80	Chiswick CHIS 122	Heaven Knows/Cruisin' Around (p/s)	5
80	Chiswick CHIS 127	Stayin' Out All Night/Running Wild (p/s)	
80	Chiswick PSR 447	Midnight Blue/Honey Hush/Such A Fool/Stayin' Out All Night (promo only)	8
78	Chiswick CH 4	BLOWIN' UP A STORM (10" mini-LP)	12
78	Chiswick WIK 7	BLOWIN' UP A STORM (LP, with 2 extra tracks)	12
80	Chiswick CWK 3012	MIDNIGHT BLUE (LP)	12

WHIRLWINDS
64	HMV POP 1301	Look At Me/Baby Not Like You	50

(see also Mockingbirds, Graham Gouldman, 10cc)

NANCY WHISKEY (& HER SKIFFLERS)
57	Oriole CB 1394	He's Solid Gone/Ella Speed (as Nancy Whiskey & Her Skifflers)	18
57	Oriole CB 1394	He's Solid Gone/Ella Speed (as Nancy Whiskey & Her Skifflers) (78)	20
58	Oriole CB 1452	Hillside In Scotland/I Know Where I'm Goin'.	12
58	Oriole CB 1452	Hillside In Scotland/I Know Where I'm Goin' (78)	15
59	Oriole CB 1485	The Old Grey Goose/Johnny Blue.	10
59	Oriole CB 1485	The Old Grey Goose/Johnny Blue (78)	20
65	Fontana TF 612	Bowling Green/I'm Leaving Today	7
67	CBS 3090	Freight Train/The Game	7
57	Topic 7T 10	NANCY WHISKEY SINGS (7" LP)	30
57	Oriole MG 10018	THE INTOXICATING MISS WHISKEY (10" LP, with Chas McDevitt Skiffle Group)	50

(see also Chas McDevitt Skiffle Group)

WHISPERS
71	Mojo 2916 003	THE WHISPERS (LP)	20
74	Contempo CRM 106	THE WHISPERS (LP)	12
74	Janus 9104 400	WHISPERS GETTIN' LOUDER (LP)	12

WHISTLER
71	Deram SML 1083	HO-HUM (LP)	25

WHISTLING WILLIE
68	Duke DU 8	Penny Reel/Soul Tonic	6

(see also Neville, Neville Willoughby)

SHARON WHITCOMB & FRED
72	RA RALP 6011	SPICE OF LIFE (LP)	20

IAN WHITCOMB
65	Capitol CL 15382	This Sporting Life/Fizz	6
65	Capitol CL 15395	You Turn Me On/Poor But Honest	10
65	Capitol CL 15418	N-N-Nervous!/The End	6
66	Capitol CL 15431	Good Hard Rock/High Blood Pressure	7
66	Stateside SS 573	Where Did Robinson Crusoe Go With Friday/Poor Little Bird)	6
73	Ember NR 5065	YOU TURN ME ON (LP, with Jimmy Page & John Paul Jones)	50

BARRY WHITE
67	President PT 139	All In The Run Of A Day/Don't Take Your Love From Me	8

BRIAN WHITE & MAGNA JAZZ BAND
62	HMV CLP 1534	BRIAN WHITE AND THE MAGNA JAZZ BAND (LP)	150

(see also Magna Jazz Band)

BUKKA WHITE
66	Fontana 688 804 ZL	SKY SONGS (LP, with Big Willie)	25
66	CBS Realm 52629	BUKKA WHITE (LP)	45
69	Blue Horizon 7-63229	MEMPHIS HOT SHOTS (LP)	60
69	Sonet SNTF 609	THE LEGACY OF THE BLUES VOL. 1 (LP, with insert)	12

MINT VALUE £

DANNY WHITE
67	Sue WI 4031	Keep My Woman Home/I'm Dedicating My Life	30
74	MCA MU 155	Cracked Up Over You/Taking Inventory	6

DUKE WHITE
63	Island WI 084	It's Over/Forever	20
64	Black Swan WI 442	Be Wise/BABA BROOKS: Musical Workshop	20
65	Black Swan WI 444	Sow Good Seeds/BABA BROOKS BAND: Bus Strike	20

GEORGIA WHITE
54	Vocalion V 1038	Was I Drunk?/Moonshine Blues (78)	20

IAN WHITE
70	private pressing	IAN WHITE (LP)	25

JAY WHITE
56	London RE-F 1045	FAR-AWAY PLACES VOL. 1 (EP)	10

JEANETTE WHITE
69	A&M AMS 761	Music/No Sunshine	20

JOE WHITE
64	R&B JB 137	Sinners (as Joe White & Maytals)/ROLAND ALPHONSO: King Solomon	15
64	Ska Beat JB 180	Punch You Down (with Chuck)/TOMMY McCOOK: Cotton Tree	25
64	Island WI 145	When Are You Young/Wanna Go Home	18
64	Island WI 159	Hog In A Co Co/SKATALITES: Sandy Gully	18
64	Island WI 166	Downtown Girl/RICHARD BROS.: You Are My Sunshine (B-side is actually "Cool Smoke" by Don Drummond)	18
65	Island WI 201	Low-Minded People (as Chuck & Joe White)/Irene	18
66	Doctor Bird DB 1001	Every Night (with Chuck)/BABA BROOKS & HIS BAND: First Session	15
66	Doctor Bird DB 1024	My Love For You/SAMMY ISMAY & BABA BROOKS BAND: Cocktails For Two	15
66	Doctor Bird DB 1043	So Close (as Joe White & Della)/BABA BROOKS & HIS BAND: Eighth Games	15
67	Doctor Bird DB 1069	Rudies All Around/Bad Man	15
67	Doctor Bird DB 1080	Lonely Nights/I Need You	15
67	Doctor Bird DB 1090	I Need A Woman/Hot Hops	15
68	Blue Cat BS 108	Way Of Life (actually by Lyn Tait & Jets)/I'm So Proud	25
68	Blue Cat BS 119	Try A Little Tenderness/LYN TAITT & CARL BRYAN: Tender Arms	10
68	Blue Cat BS 130	Pretty Girl/DERMOTT LYNCH: You Went Away	10
69	Sugar ESS 102	My Guiding Star/If I Needed Someone	6
70	Sugar SU 103	Yesterday/I Am Free	6
70	Trojan TR 7742	So Much Love/Maybe Now	6
70	Trojan TR 7768	I'm Going To Get There/RUPIE EDWARDS ALLSTARS: Kinky Funky Reggae	6
70	Big BG 301	This Is The Time/The Other Day	6
71	Big BG 309	Baby I Care/Ain't Misbehavin'	6
72	Songbird SB 1072	Trinity/SCOTTY: Monkey Drop	12
72	Dynamic DYN 440	Kenyatta/RECORDING BAND: Version	12
73	Gayfeet GS 202	If It Don't Work Out/BABA BROOKS BAND: Ki Salaboca	8
73	Harry J. HJ 6648	Joe White (Mrs. Jones)/Joe White (Mrs. Jones) – Version (song actually titled "Me And Mrs Jones")	5
77	Ultra PFU 1002	Give And Take (On Both Sides)/Roots Dub	5
70s	Magnet MGT 006	SINCE THE OTHER DAY (LP)	18

(see also Chuck, Rue Lloyd)

JOSH WHITE
50	Jazz Parade B 10	I Want You And I Need You/One Meat Ball (78)	10
50	Jazz Parade B 11	The Blind Man Stood On The Road And Cried/St. James Infirmary (78)	10
50	Jazz Parade B 12	Got A Head Like A Rock/No. 12 Train (78)	15
50	London L 739	Take A Gal Like You/Wanderings (78)	8
50	London L 810	Like A Natural Man/The Foggy, Foggy Dew (78)	8
50	London L 828	I'm Gonna Move To The Outskirts Of Town/Hard Time Blues (78)	8
50	London L 907	T.B. Blues/Molly Malone (78)	10
50	Melodisc MEL 8008	Mean Mistreatin' Woman/Baby Baby (12" 78)	15
51	Melodisc MEL 1145	Fare Thee Well/Outskirts Of Town (78)	10
51	Melodisc MEL 1146	House I Live In/When I Lay Down (78)	8
51	Melodisc MEL 1155	Dupree/Miss Otis Regrets (78)	8
51	Vogue B 10	I Want You And I Need You/One Meat Ball (78)	8
51	London L 1028	On Top Of Old Smoky/Black Girl (with Bill Hill's Orchestra & Stargazers) (78)	8
51	London L 1138	Barbara Allen/The Lass With The Delicate Air (78)	8
52	London L 1142	Lonesome Road/He Never Said A Mumblin' Word (78)	10
52	London L 1143	Call Me Darling/I Want You, I Need You (78)	20
52	London L 1144	Waltzing Landing/Apples, Peaches And Cherries (78)	20
52	London L 1161	Free And Equal Blues (Parts 1 & 2) (78)	12
54	London L 907	T.B. Blues/Molly Malone (78, silver label reissue)	10
57	Pye NJE 1057	BLUES AND... PART 1 (EP)	12
57	Pye NJE 1058	BLUES AND... PART 2 (EP)	12
57	Pye NJE 1059	BLUES AND... PART 3 (EP)	12
57	HMV 7EG 8465	THE JOSH WHITE STORIES (EP)	15
58	Mercury YEP 9504	SOUTHERN BLUES (EP)	15
64	Storyville SEP 388	STORYVILLE BLUES ANTHOLOGY VOL. 8 (EP)	12
64	Mercury 10006 MCE	JOSH WHITE (EP)	15
51	London H-APB 1005	A JOSH WHITE PROGRAM (10" LP)	20
52	Brunswick LA 8562	BALLADS AND BLUES (10" LP)	18
54	Brunswick LA 8653	BALLADS AND BLUES VOL. 2 (10" LP)	18
54	London H-APB 1032	JOSH WHITE SINGS — VOL. 2 (10" LP)	18
54	Mercury MG 25014	SONGS BY JOSH WHITE (10" LP)	18
55	London H-APB 1038	JOSH COMES A-VISITIN' (10" LP)	18
56	Nixa Jazz Today NJL 2	BLUES AND... (LP)	18
58	HMV CLP 1159	JOSH WHITE STORIES VOLUME 1 (LP)	15
58	HMV CLP 1175	JOSH WHITE STORIES VOLUME 2 (LP)	15

MINT VALUE £

62	Storyville SLP 123	JOHN HENRY, BALLADS, BLUES AND OTHER SONGS (LP)	15
60s	Storyville SLP 175	BLUES SINGER AND BALLADEER (LP)	12
62	Mercury MMC 14102	AT THE TOWN HALL (LP)	15
62	HMV CLP 1588	JOSH WHITE LIVE! (LP)	15
62	Golden Guinea GGL 0160	EMPTY BED BLUES (LP)	12
62	Golden Guinea GGL 0205	CHAIN GANG SONGS, SPIRITUALS AND BLUES (LP)	12
64	Mercury 20039 MCL	THE BEGINNING (LP)	18
64	Ace Of Hearts AH 65	JOSH WHITE (LP)	15
65	Mercury 20067 MCL	I'M ON MY OWN WAY (LP)	15
65	Saga SOC 988	JOSH WHITE AND CARL SANDBURG (LP)	12
67	MFP MFP 1139	GOOD MORNING BLUES (LP)	12
69	Decca SPA 44	THE WORLD OF JOSH WHITE (LP)	12
70	Marble Arch MAL 1208	IN MEMORIAM (LP)	12

(see also Teddy Moss/Josh White)

JOSH & BEVERLEY WHITE
| 64 | Realm REP 4003 | BEVERLEY & JOSH WHITE JNR (EP) | 12 |

K.C. WHITE
72	Dynamic DYN 434	Man No Dead/Man No Dead — Version	6
73	Green Door GD 4056	First Cut Is The Deepest/No Good Girl	5
73	Technique TE 929	Anywhere But Nowhere/Bush In Session	6

KITTY WHITE
51	Brunswick 04726	Paradise/You're Tired Of Me (78)	8
51	Capitol CL 13549	I'm Playing With Fire/It Pays To Advertise (78)	8
54	London HL 8102	Jesse James/Scratch My Back (B-side with Dave Howard)	40
54	London HL 8102	Jesse James/Scratch My Back (78, B-side with Dave Howard)	20

LENNY WHITE
| 75 | Atlantic K 50213 | VENUSIAN SUMMER (LP) | 10 |

LOUISA JANE WHITE
| 69 | Philips BF 1810 | When The Battle Is Over/Blue Ribbons | 8 |
| 70 | Philips BF 1834 | How Does It Feel/Truth In My Tears | 5 |

SHEILA WHITE
| 66 | CBS 202465 | Misfit/Switch Off The Night | 6 |

TAM WHITE
67	Decca F 12711	World Without You/Someone You Should Know (unreleased)	
68	Decca F 12849	Waiting Till The Night Comes Around/Girl Watcher	5
69	Deram DM 261	That Old Sweet Roll/Don't Make Promises	6
70	Middle Earth MDS 104	Lewis Carroll/Future Thoughts	8
70	Middle Earth MDLS 304	TAM WHITE (LP)	25

(see also Buzz, Boston Dexters)

TERRY WHITE & TERRIERS
| 59 | Decca F 11133 | Rock Around The Mailbags/Blackout | 45 |
| 59 | Decca F 11133 | Rock Around The Mailbags/Blackout (78) | 45 |

TONY JOE WHITE
68	Monument MON 1024	Soul Francisco/Whompt Out On You	5
69	Monument MON 1031	Polk Salad Annie/Aspen Colorado	6
69	Monument MON 1036	Willie And Laura Mae Jones/Baby Scratch My Back	5
68	Monument LMO/SMO 5027	BLACK AND WHITE (LP)	15
70	Monument LMO/SMO 5035	TONY JOE WHITE CONTINUED (LP)	15
70	Monument SMO 5043	TONY JOE (LP)	15
71	Warner Bros WS 1900	TONY JOE WHITE (LP)	15
71	Warner Bros K 46068	TONY JOE WHITE (LP, reissue)	12
72	Warner Bros K 46147	THE TRAIN I'M ON (LP)	15
73	Warner Bros K 46229	HOME-MADE ICE CREAM (LP)	15
73	Warner Bros K 56149	THE BEST OF TONY JOE WHITE (LP)	15

TREVOR WHITE
| 76 | Island WIP 6291 | Crazy Kids/Movin' In The Right Direction (some with p/s) | 10/5 |

(see also Sparks, Radio Stars)

WHITE DUCK
72	Uni UN 541	Billy Goat/Really	6
73	Uni UN 555	Honey, You'll Be Alright/Carry Love	5
72	Uni UNLS 123	WHITE DUCK (LP)	12
73	Uni UNLS 129	IN SEASON (LP)	12

WHITE ELEPHANT
| 70s | White Elephant RIOCH 1 | CITY WALLS (LP, with other artists) | 10 |

RICK WHITEFIELD
| 71 | Horse HOSS 10 | Hey Mama/Ride Baby Ride | 4 |

WHITEFIRE
| 78 | Whitefire 98DB 001 | SUZANNE (EP) | 50 |

WHITE HEAT
80	Valium VAL 1	Nervous Breakdown/Sammy Sez (p/s)	8
80	Valium VAL 02	Finished With The Fashions/Ordinary Joe (p/s, with insert)	10
81	Valium VAL 03	City Beat/It's No Use (Young Ones) (p/s)	10
82	Valium VALP 101	IN THE ZERO HOUR (LP)	18

WHITEHOUSE
80	Come Org. WDC 881004	BIRTHDEATH EXPERIENCE (LP)	100
80	Come Org. WDC 881005	TOTAL SEX (LP)	100
80	Come Org. WDC 881007	ERECTOR (LP, different coloured vinyls)	80
81	Come Org. WDC 881010	DEDICATED TO PETER KÜRTEN, SADIST AND MASS SLAYER (LP, some on coloured vinyl, some in custom sleeve)	80

WHITEHOUSE

81	Come Org. WDC	GREAT WHITE DEATH (LP)	65
81	Come Org. WDC 881013	BÜCHENWALD (LP)	70
81	Come Org. WDC 881017	NEW BRITAIN (LP)	100
81	Come Org. WDC 881020	LIVE ACTION 1 (cassette)	20
80s	Come Org. WDC 881022	LIVE ACTION 2 (cassette)	20
80s	Come Org. WDC 881027	PSYCHOPATHIA SEXUALIS (LP, clear or black vinyl)	120
80s	Come Org. WDC 883033	RIGHT TO KILL — DEDICATED TO DENNIS ANDREW NEILSEN (LP, & inserts)	70
80s	Come Org. WDC	150 MURDEROUS PASSIONS (LP, with Nurse With Wound)	75

(Many of the above LPs were issued in customised white card sleeves & were later available in a generic 'Peter Kürten' sleeve, originally used for the 2nd pressing of the 'Peter Kürten' LP. This latter design was also used for counterfeits. There may also be various coloured vinyl variations of the above LPs, worth around the same value. Listed below are cassettes, which may sell for more if complete with inserts or magazine. Some of the Live Action releases were videos.)

80s	Come Org. WDC 883044	RADIO INTERVIEWS/LIVE ACTION 9 USA VOL. I	12
80s	Come Org. WDC 883046	LIVE ACTION 13 USA VOL. III.	12
80s	Come Org. WDC 883047	LIVE ACTION 14 USA VOL. IV	12
80s	Come Org. WDC 883048	LIVE ACTION 15/LIVE ACTION 16 USA VOL. V	12
80s	Come Org. WDC 883049	LIVE ACTION 20 USA VOL. VI	12
80s	Come Org. WDC 883050	LIVE ACTION 22/LIVE ACTION 23	12
80s	Come Org. WDC 883052	USA REHEARSAL	12
80s	Come Org. WDC 883053	LIVE ACTION 24/LIVE ACTION 25	12
80s	Come Org. WDC 883055	LIVE ACTION 26	12
80s	Susan Lawley 1	CREAM OF THE SECOND COMING (2-LP)	15

(see also Come, Nurse With Wound, New Order, Skullflower, Konstruktivits)

WHITE LIGHTNING

84	Wild Party PP 1000	This Poison Fountain/Hypocrite (no p/s, 1,000 only)	40
90	Workshop JOB LP 2	MIDNIGHT APPROACHES (LP)	15

(see also Static)

WHITE NOISE

75	Virgin VDJ 2	An Extract From White Noise 2. (promo only)	5
69	Island ILPS 9099	AN ELECTRIC STORM (LP, pink label)	35
75	Virgin V 2032	WHITE NOISE 2 (LP)	20

WHITE ON BLACK

74	Saydisc SDL 251	WHITE ON BLACK (LP)	30

WHITE PLAINS

70	Deram DM 280	My Baby Loves Lovin'/Show Me Your Hand	5
70	Deram DM 291	Today I Killed A Man I Didn't Know/I've Got You On My Mind	5
70	Deram DM 315	Julie Do Ya Love Me/I Need Your Everlasting Love	5
71	Deram DM 325	Every Little Move She Makes/Carolina's Comin' Home	5
71	Deram DM 332	When You Are A King/The World Gets Better With Love	6
71	Deram DM 340	Gonna Miss Her Mississippi/I'll Go Blind	5
72	Deram DM 348	I Can't Stop/Julie Anne	5
72	Deram DM 365	Dad You Saved The World/Beachcomber	5
73	Deram DM 371	Step Into A Dream/Look To See	5
74	Deram DM 415	Ecstasy/A Simple Man	5
76	Bradley BRAD 7609	Summer Nights/Wildest Dreams	5
70	Deram SML 1067	WHITE PLAINS (LP)	25
71	Deram SML 1092	WHEN YOU ARE A KING (LP)	25

(see also Edison Lighthouse, David & Jonathan, Kestrels, Brotherhood Of Man, Peter's Faces, Carter-Lewis & Southerners, First Class, Ivy League)

WHITE RABBIT

69	NEMS 56-4165	Ain't That Something/I'll Do The Rest	4

WHITESNAKE

78	EMI International INEP 751	SNAKEBITE (EP, white vinyl, p/s; later black vinyl with no p/s)	each 10
78	EMI International INT 568	Lie Down/Don't Mess With Me (no p/s)	5
79	EMI International INT 578	The Time Is Right For Love/Come On (live) (no p/s)	5
79	United Artists BP 324	Long Way From Home/Trouble (live)/Ain't No Love In The Heart Of The City (live) (p/s)	4
80	United Artists BP 352	Fool For Your Loving/Mean Business/Don't Mess With Me (some in luminous p/s)	8/5
80	United Artists BP 381	Ain't No Love In The Heart Of The City (live)/Take Me With You (live) (p/s)	4
80	United Artists 12BP 381	Ain't No Love In The Heart Of The City (live)/Take Me With You (live) (12", p/s).	7
82	Liberty BP 416	Here I Go Again/Bloody Luxury (p/s)	4
82	Liberty BPP 416	Here I Go Again/Bloody Luxury (picture disc)	10
82	Liberty BP 12416	Here I Go Again/Bloody Luxury (12", p/s)	7
82	Liberty BP 418	Love An' Affection/Victim Of Love (withdrawn)	30
83	Liberty BP 420	Guilty Of Love/Gambler (p/s)	4
83	Liberty BPP 420	Guilty Of Love/Gambler (shaped picture disc)	10
83	Liberty BP 12420	Guilty Of Love/Gambler (12", p/s)	7
84	Liberty BP 423	Standing In The Shadows/All Or Nothing (US Mix) (p/s, with patch)	4
84	Liberty BPP 423	Standing In The Shadows/All Or Nothing (US Mix) (picture disc)	6
85	Liberty BP 424	Love Ain't No Stranger (US Album Mix)/Slow 'N' Easy (US Album Mix) (p/s)	4
85	Liberty BP 12 424	Love Ain't No Stranger (US Album Mix)/Slow 'N' Easy (US Album Mix) (12", p/s).	7
87	EMI EMIW 5606	Still Of The Night/Here I Go Again (p/s, white vinyl with poster)	8
87	EMI 12 EMIS 5606	Still Of The Night (Extended)/Here I Go Again '87/You're Gonna Break My Heart Again (12", p/s with sticker)	7
87	EMI 12 EMIP 5606	Still Of The Night/Here I Go Again/You're Gonna Break My Heart Again (12", picture disc)	10
87	EMI EMP 3	Is This Love/Standing In The Shadows '87/Need Your Love So Bad '87 (shaped picture disc, all mispressed with 2 tracks, some with 3rd track on bonus white label 7")	10/6
87	EMI EMX 3	Is This Love/Standing In The Shadows '87/Need Your Love So Bad '87 (poster p/s)	4

87	EMI 12EMW 3	Is This Love/Standing In The Shadows '87/Need Your Love So Bad '87/ Still Of The Night (CD, card sleeve)	8
87	EMI CDEM 3	Is This Love/Standing In The Shadows '87/Need Your Love So Bad '87 (12", p/s, white vinyl)	8
87	EMI EMP 35	Here I Go Again '87 (US remix) (poster p/s, 1-sided, B-side etched)	4
87	EMI 10EMI 35	Here I Go Again '87 (US remix)/Guilty Of Love (10", p/s, white vinyl)	8
88	EMI EM 23	Give Me All Your Love/Fool For Your Loving (p/s, white vinyl with insert)	4
88	EMI 12EM 23	Give Me All Your Love/Fool For Your Loving/Don't Break My Heart Again (12", p/s, white vinyl)	7
88	EMI 12EMP 23	Give Me All Your Love/Fool For Your Loving/Don't Break My Heart Again (12", picture disc)	8
88	EMI CDEM 23	Give Me All Your Love/Fool For Your Loving/Here I Go Again (USA Single Remix) (CD)	7
89	EMI EMP 123	Fool For Your Loving (7" Version)/Slow Poke Music (p/s, with poster)	4
89	EMI 12EMS 123	Fool For Your Loving/Slow Poke Music/Walking In The Shadows Of The Blues (live) (12", p/s, white vinyl)	7
90	EMI EMPD 128	The Deeper The Love/Judgement Day (picture disc, with insert)	5
90	EMI 12EMS 128	The Deeper The Love/Judgement Day/Sweet Lady Luck (12", p/s, white vinyl)	7
90	EMI EMPD 150	Now You're Gone (Remix)/Wings Of The Storm (shaped picture disc with plinth)	7
90	EMI 12EMS 150	Now You're Gone (Remix)/Kitten's Got Claws/Cheap And Nasty (12", gatefold p/s with booklet)	7
78	EMI Intl. INS 3022	TROUBLE (LP, grey or pink innersleeve)	each 12
82	Liberty LBGP 30354	SAINTS AN' SINNERS (LP, picture disc)	15
84	Liberty LBGP 240 000 0	SLIDE IT IN (LP, picture disc, U.S. mixes)	18
87	EMI EMC 3528	WHITESNAKE 1987 (LP, embossed sleeve, with innersleeve)	10
87	EMI EMCP 3528	WHITESNAKE 1987 (LP, picture disc)	15
89	EMI EMCDJ 1013	SLIP OF THE TONGUE (LP, with track by track interview, promo only)	20

(see also David Coverdale, Deep Purple, Rainbow, Roger Glover, Bernie Marsden, Jon Lord, Phenomena, Cozy Powell, Young & Moody Band, Company, Snafu, Bogdon, Forcefield, Gogmagog, Tramline, National Health)

WHITE SPIRIT

80	Neat NEAT 05	Back To The Grind/Cheetah (p/s)	7
81	MCA MCA 638	Midnight Chaser/Suffragettes (p/s)	30
81	MCA MCA 652	High Upon High/No Reprieve/Arthur Guitar (no p/s)	15
80	MCA MCF 3079	WHITE SPIRIT (LP, with lyric insert)	20

(see also Gillan, Iron Maiden)

WHITE SS

| 78 | White SS CIA 72 | Mercy Killing/I'm Not One (live) (p/s) | 25 |

WHITE TRASH

| 69 | Apple APPLE 6 | Road To Nowhere/Illusions (early copies as White Trash, later Trash) | 35/18 |

(see also Trash, Poets, Stone The Crows)

WHITE ZOMBIE

| 89 | Caroline CAROL 1457 | God Of Thunder/Love Razor/Disaster Blaster 2 (12", withdrawn) | 35 |

(see also Rob Zombie)

DAVID WHITFIELD

54	Decca F 10242	The Book/Heartless (gold label, triangular centre)	18
54	Decca F 10327	Cara Mia/Love, Tears And Kisses (with Mantovani Orchestra)	18
54	Decca F 10355	Smile/How, When Or Where (B-side with Mantovani Orchestra)	10
54	Decca F 10399	Santo Natale/Adeste Fideles	12
55	Decca F 10458	Beyond The Stars/Open Up Your Heart (with Mantovani Orchestra)	15
55	Decca F 10515	Ev'rywhere/Mama	15
55	Decca F 10562	The Lady/Santa Rose Lea Rose	7
55	Decca F 10596	I'll Never Stop Loving You/Lady Of Madrid	7
55	Decca F 10627	When You Lose The One You Love/Angelus (with Mantovani Orchestra)	8
56	Decca F 10690	My September Love/The Rudder And The Rock	8
56	Decca F 10769	My Son John/My Unfinished Symphony	8
57	Decca F 10833	The Adoration Waltz/If I Lost You	8
57	Decca F 10864	I'll Find You/I'd Give You The World	8
57	Decca F 10890	Without Him/Dream Of Paradise	5
57	Decca F 10931	Ev'rything/Martinella	5
58	Decca F 10978	Cry My Heart/My One True Love (with Mantovani Orchestra)	5
58	Decca F 11018	On The Street Where You Live/Afraid	5
58	Decca F 11039	The Right To Love/That's When Your Heartaches Begin	5
58	Decca F 11079	This Is Lucia/Love Is A Stranger	5
59	Decca F 11101	Willingly/William Tell	5
61	Decca F 11336	Scottish Soldier/Scotland The Brave (withdrawn, export only)	100
62	HMV POP 1015	Impossible/As Long As You Love Me	6
63	HMV POP 1180	You Belong In Someone Else's Arms/This Heart Of Mine	8
77	Denman Discs DD 105	Land Of Hope And Glory/When You Lose The One You Love (p/s, fan club issue, with Carlton & District Male Voice Choir)	20
55	Decca DFE 6225	CARA MIA (EP)	12
56	Decca DFE 6342	DAVID WHITFIELD NO. 1 (EP)	10
57	Decca DFE 6400	DAVID WHITFIELD NO. 2 (EP)	10
58	Decca DFE 6434	DAVID WHITFIELD NO. 3 (EP)	10
62	Decca STO 158	ALONE (EP, stereo)	15
54	Decca LF 1165	YOURS FROM THE HEART (10" LP)	25
58	Decca LK 4242	WHITFIELD FAVOURITES (LP)	18
58	Decca LK 4270	FROM DAVID WITH LOVE (LP)	18
60	Decca LK 4348/SKL 4094	MY HEART AND I (LP, mono/stereo)	15/18
61	Decca LK 4384/SKL 4126	ALONE (LP, mono/stereo)	1518
60s	Philips	HEY THERE (LP)	20

JUNE WHITFIELD

| 53 | Philips PB 137 | Seven Lonely Days/Dancing With Someone (78) | 8 |
| 53 | Philips PB 195 | Diamonds Are A Girl's Best Friend/Bye Bye Baby (78) | 12 |

MINT VALUE £

WILBUR WHITFIELD
57	Vogue V 9078	P.B. Baby/The One I Love.	400
57	Vogue V 9078	P.B. Baby/The One I Love (78)	70

(see also Little Wilbur & Pleasers)

LEONARD WHITING
65	Pye 7N 15943	Piper/That's What Mama Says	20

MARGARET WHITING
50	Capitol CL 13348	Home Cooking/Blind Date (78, with Bob Hope)	8
55	Capitol CL 14213	My Own True Love/Can This Be Love (triangular centre)	15
55	Capitol CL 14242	Heat Wave/Come Rain Or Shine (triangular centre)	15
55	Capitol CL 14307	Stowaway/All I Want Is All There Is And Then Some (triangular centre)	15
55	Capitol CL 14348	A Man/Mama's Pearls (triangular centre)	15
55	Capitol CL 14375	Lover, Lover/I Kiss You A Million Times (triangular centre)	15
56	Capitol CL 14527	I Love A Mystery/Bidin' My Time	8
56	Capitol CL 14591	Old Enough/Day In — Day Out	7
56	Capitol CL 14647	True Love/Haunting Love.	7
57	Capitol CL 14685	The Money Tree/Maybe I Love Him	7
57	London HLD 8451	Kill Me With Kisses/Speak For Yourself, John.	18
57	London HLD 8451	Kill Me With Kisses/Speak For Yourself, John (78)	15
58	London HLD 8562	I Can't Help (If I'm Still In Love With You)/That's Why I Was Born	15
58	London HLD 8562	I Can't Help (If I'm Still In Love With You)/That's Why I Was Born (78)	15
58	London HLD 8662	Hot Spell/I'm So Lonesome I Could Cry	15
58	London HLD 8662	Hot Spell/I'm So Lonesome I Could Cry (78).	20
66	London HLD 10078	Nothing Lasts Forever/The Wheel Of Hurt	7
67	London HLD 10114	Just Like A Man/The World Inside Your Arms	7
68	London HLU 10196	Faithfully/Am I Losing You.	5
68	London HLU 10227	Maybe Just Once More/Can't Get You Out Of My Mind.	5
53	Capitol LC 6585	CAPITOL PRESENTS MARGARET WHITING (10" LP).	25
56	Capitol LC 6811	MARGARET WHITING (10" LP)	25
58	London HA-D 2109	GOIN' PLACES (LP)	30
61	HMV CLP 1418/CSD 1339	SINGS THE JEROME KERN SONGBOOK VOL. ONE (LP, mono/stereo)	15/18
61	HMV CLP 1419/CSD 1340	SINGS THE JEROME KERN SONGBOOK VOL. TWO (LP, mono/stereo)	15/18
61	London HA-D 2321	JUST A DREAM (LP)	25
67	London HA-U/SH-U 8317	THE WHEEL OF HURT (LP)	18
67	London HA-U 8332	MAGGIE ISN'T MARGARET ANYMORE (LP)	18

(see also Jimmy Wakely, Bob Hope, Dean Martin)

RAY WHITLEY
65	HMV POP 1473	I've Been Hurt/There Is One Boy	50

BOBBY WHITLOCK
72	CBS 65109	BOBBY WHITLOCK (LP)	12
73	CBS 65301	RAW VELVET (LP)	15

(see also Derek & Dominoes)

SLIM WHITMAN
78s
53	London L 1186	How Can I Tell/Love Song Of The Waterfall (78, gold label print)	10
53	London L 1191	My Love Is Growing Stale/Bandera Waltz (78, gold label print)	15
53	London HL 1191	My Love Is Growing Stale/Bandera Waltz (78, re-pressing, silver label print)	20
53	London L 1194	Restless Heart/Song Of The Old Water Wheel (78, gold label print).	8
53	London L 1206	My Heart Is Broken In Three/Cold Empty Arms (78, gold label print).	12
54	London HL 1186	How Can I Tell/Love Song Of The Waterfall (78, re-pressing, silver label print)	12
54	London L 1226	North Wind/Darlin' Don't Cry (78, gold label print)	8
54	London HL 1226	North Wind/Darlin' Don't Cry (78, re-pressing, silver label print)	8
54	London HL 8018	Stairway To Heaven/Lord, Help Me To Be As Thou (78).	15
54	London HL 8039	Secret Love/Why (78)	10
54	London HL 8061	Rose Marie/We Stood At The Altar (78, gold label).	7
54	London HL 8080	Beautiful Dreamer/Ride Away (78).	8
57	London HLP 8416	Curtain Of Tears/Smoke Signals (78).	10
58	London HLP 8590	A Very Precious Love/Careless Hands (78).	12
58	London HLP 8642	Candy Kisses/Tormented (78)	10
58	London HLP 8708	Wherever You Are/At The End Of Nowhere (78)	15
59	London HLP 8835	I Never See Maggie Alone/The Letter Edged In Black (78).	25

SINGLES
54	London L 1149	Indian Love Call/China Doll	30
54	London HL 1149	Indian Love Call/China Doll (re-pressing with different prefix)	18
54	London L 1214	There's A Rainbow In Every Teardrop/Danny Boy	35
54	London HL 1214	There's A Rainbow In Every Teardrop/Danny Boy (re-pressing)	20
54	London L 1226	North Wind/Darlin' Don't Cry	40
54	London HL 1226	North Wind/Darlin' Don't Cry (re-pressing with different prefix)	25
54	London HL 8018	Stairway To Heaven/Lord, Help Me To Be As Thou	60
54	London HL 8039	Secret Love/Why	30
54	London HL 8061	Rose Marie/We Stood At The Altar	15
54	London HL 8080	Beautiful Dreamer/Ride Away	25
54	London HL 8091	The Singing Hills/I Hate To See You Cry	25
55	London HL 8125	When I Grow Too Old To Dream/Cattle Call	25
55	London HL 8141	Haunted Hungry Heart/Roll On, Silvery Moon.	25
55	London HLU 8167	I'll Never Stop Loving You/I'll Never Take You Back Again	25
55	London HLU 8196	Song Of The Wild/You Have My Heart	25
56	London HLU 8230	Tumbling Tumbleweeds/Tell Me.	20
56	London HLU 8252	I'm A Fool/My Heart Is Broken In Three.	22
56	London HLU 8287	Serenade/I Talk To The Waves	20
56	London HLU 8327	Dear Mary/Whiffenpoof Song.	25

| 56 | London HLU 8350 | I'm Casting My Lasso Towards The Sky/There's A Love Knot In My Lariat | 30 |
| 57 | London HLP 8403 | I'll Take You Home Again Kathleen/Careless Love | 15 |

(The above singles were originally issued with gold label print & tri-centres; later round-centre and/or silver label print copies are worth half these values.)

57	London HLP 8416	Curtain Of Tears/Smoke Signals (silver label print)	12
57	London HLP 8420	Gone/An Amateur In Love (gold label print)	25
57	London HLP 8434	Many Times/Warm, Warm Lips	12
57	London HLP 8459	Lovesick Blues/Forever	12
57	London HLP 8518	Unchain My Heart/Hush-A-Bye	12
58	London HLP 8590	A Very Precious Love/Careless Hands	12
58	London HLP 8642	Candy Kisses/Tormented	10
58	London HLP 8708	Wherever You Are/At The End Of Nowhere	10
59	London HLP 8835	I Never See Maggie Alone/The Letter Edged In Black	8
59	London HLP 8896	What Kind Of God (Do You Think You Are)/A Tree In The Meadow (unissued)	
60	London HLP 9103	Roll, River, Roll/Twilla Lee	6
61	London HLP 9302	Vaya Con Dios/Ramona	6
64	Liberty LIB 66040	I'll Hold You In My Heart/No Other Arms, No Other Lips	5
65	Liberty LIB 66103	Reminiscing/Mansion On The Hill	5
65	Liberty LIB 12013	Remember Me (I'm The One Who Loves You)/Virginia	5
65	Liberty LIB 12020	More Than Yesterday/Broken Down Merry-Go-Round	5
66	Liberty LIB 66181	A Travelin' Man/I Remember You	5
66	Liberty LIB 66212	One Dream/Jerry	5
67	Liberty LIB 66226	What's The World A-Comin' To/You Bring Out The Best In Me	5
68	Liberty LBF 15066	Cool Water/Down In The Valley	5
69	Liberty LBF 15198	My Happiness/Rose Marie	5
69	Liberty LBF 15220	Stranger On The Shore/Star Of Hope	5
70	Liberty LBF 15394	My Heart Has A Mind Of Its Own/How Could I Not Love You	5
70	Liberty LBF 15430	Snowbird/How Could I Not Love You	5
71	United Artists UP 35277	I Climbed The Mountain/Jerry	5
73	United Artists UP 35493	Got The All Overs For You (All Over Me)/I'll See You When	5
74	United Artists UP 35728	Happy Anniversary/What I Had With You	5
75	United Artists UP 35775	Honeymoon Feeling/Foolish Question	6
75	United Artists UP 36017	When You Were Sweet Sixteen/How Could I Not Love You	5
76	United Artists UP 36072	Everything Leads Back To You/Angel In An Apron	5
76	United Artists UP 36110	Caramia/It's Your Day Today	5
76	United Artists UP 36161	Mr Ting-A-Ling (Steel Guitar Man)/Silver Spurs	6
77	United Artists UP 36220	Una Paloma Blanca/Somewhere My Love	5
77	United Artists UP 36287	Home On The Range/I'm So Lonesome	5
79	United Artists UP 36491	Ghost Riders In The Sky/Carolina Moon	5
80	Liberty BP 377	That Silver Haired Daddy Of Mine/If I Could Dream (p/s)	5
81	Liberty BP 394	When/Till We Meet Again (p/s)	6
82	Liberty BP 408	Can't Help Falling In Love With You/Open Up Your Heart Again, Kathleen (p/s)	6
84	Epic EPC A 4304	Blue Bayou/Blue Memories (p/s)	5
84	Epic EPC A 4695	Four Walls/Trying To Outrun The Wind (p/s)	5

EPs

54	London RE-P 1006	SLIM WHITMAN AND HIS SINGING GUITAR (EP, at least 8 different colour sleeves, with matt or gloss finish & various label designs)	10-15
55	London RE-P 1042	SONG OF THE WILD (EP)	15
56	London RE-P 1064	SLIM WHITMAN VOL. 2 PT. 1 (EP)	15
56	London RE-P 1070	SLIM WHITMAN VOL. 2 PT. 2 (EP)	15
57	London RE-P 1100	SLIM WHITMAN VOL. 2 PT. 3 (EP)	15
59	London RE-P 1199	SLIM WHITMAN SINGS (EP, triangular silver-top centre, later round)	15/12
60	London RE-P 1258	SLIM WHITMAN SINGS No. 2 (EP)	15
63	London RE-P 1360	THE WAYWARD WIND (EP)	15
64	Liberty LEP 4018	IRISH LOVE SONGS THE SLIM WHITMAN WAY (EP)	12
65	Liberty LEP 4027	SLIM WHITMAN SINGS MORE IRISH SONGS (EP)	12
66	Liberty LEP 4046	A SATISFIED MIND (EP)	15

LPs

54	London H-APB 1015	SLIM WHITMAN & HIS SINGING GUITAR (10" LP, gold or silver label print)	50/40
56	London HA-U 2015	SLIM WHITMAN & HIS SINGING GUITAR VOL. 2 (LP)	40
59	London HA-P 2139	SLIM WHITMAN SINGS (LP)	25
59	London HA-P 2199	SLIM WHITMAN SINGS VOL. 2 (LP)	25
60	London HA-P 2343	SLIM WHITMAN (LP)	25
61	London HA-P 2392	JUST CALL ME LONESOME (LP)	25
62	London HA-P 2443	SLIM WHITMAN SINGS VOL. 3 (LP, also stereo SAH-P 6232)	25/30
62	London HA-P 8013	SLIM WHITMAN SINGS VOL. 4 (LP)	22
63	London HA-P 8059	HEART SONGS AND LOVE SONGS (LP)	22
63	London HA-P 8093	I'M A LONELY WANDERER (LP)	22
64	Liberty LBY 3032	YODELING (LP)	15
65	Liberty LBY 3034	COUNTRY SONGS, CITY HITS (LP)	15
65	Liberty LBY 3054	THE BEST OF SLIM WHITMAN VOL. 1 (LP)	12
66	Liberty LBY 3060	THE BEST OF SLIM WHITMAN VOL. 2 (LP)	15
66	Liberty LBY 3067	REMINISCING (LP)	12
66	Liberty LBY 3003	IRISH SONGS (LP)	12
67	Liberty (S)LBY 3079	A TRAVELIN' MAN (LP)	12
67	Liberty (S)LBY 3086	A TIME FOR LOVE (LP)	20
67	Liberty LBY 3092	THE BEST OF SLIM WHITMAN VOL. 3 (LP)	20
67	Liberty LBL/LBS 83039	15TH ANNIVERSARY (LP)	12
68	Liberty LBL/LBS 83064	GREAT PERFORMANCES (LP)	12
68	Liberty LBL/LBS 83093	COUNTRY MEMORIES (LP)	12
68	Liberty LBL/LBS 83109	COOL WATER (LP)	12
68	Sunset SLS 50003	A LONESOME HEART (LP)	12
68	Liberty LBL/LBS 83113	IN LOVE THE WHITMAN WAY (LP)	12
68	Sunset SLS 50044	UNCHAIN YOUR HEART (LP)	12
69	Liberty LBS 83182E	HAPPY STREET (LP)	12
69	Liberty LBS 83244	STRAIGHT FROM YOUR HEART (LP)	12

Slim WHITMAN

70	Liberty LBS 83390	TOMORROW NEVER COMES (LP).	12
70	Sunset SLS 50153	LOVE SONGS OF THE WATERFALL (LP).	12
71	Sunset SLS 50219	GOD'S HAND IN MINE (LP)	12
71	United Artists UAS 29151	SNOWBIRD (LP).	12
71	Sunset SLS 50283	CHRISTMAS ALBUM (LP)	12
72	United Artists UAS 29305	IT'S A SIN TO TELL A LIE (LP).	12
73	United Artists UAS 29433	I'LL SEE YOU WHEN (LP).	12
73	United Artists UAG 29488	25TH ANNIVERSARY CONCERT (LP)	128
76	Sunset SLS 50384	I'LL WALK WITH GOD (LP).	12

MARVA WHITNEY

70	Polydor 2001 036	This Girl's In Love With You/He's The One.	10
72	Mojo 2092 041	Daddy Don't Know About The Sugar Bear/We Need More	6
69	Polydor 583 767	IT'S MY THING (LP)	90

(see also James Brown)

TIM WHITSETT

64	Sue WI 318	Macks By The Tracks/Shine	22

TIM WHITSETT/STICKS HERMAN

60s	Range JRE 7002	RHYTHM & BLUES (EP).	25

PAUL WHITSUN JONES & WALLAS EATON & HOLLAND

65	Oriole CB 1991	Shake It Baby/Instant Marriage	6

WHITSUNTIDE EASTER

77	Pilgrim/Grapevine GRA 109	NEXT TIME YOU PLAY A WRONG NOTE...MAKE IT A SHORT ONE (LP, gatefold sleeve).	150

ROGER WHITTAKER (& COMPANIONS)

62	Fontana H 358	The Charge Of The Light Brigade/Keep It A Secret	7
62	Fontana 267 217TF	Steel Men/After The Laughter	7
63	Fontana 267 258TF	Butterfly/Times Is Tough	7
63	Fontana TF 393	The Sinner/Settle Down (as Rog Whittaker & Companions).	7
64	Fontana TF 437	Mud Puddle/Acre Of Wheat (as Rog Whittaker & His Companions).	7

(see also Hank & Mellowmen)

TOMMY WHITTLE (& HIS QUARTET)

54	Esquire 10-408	Martini/Yesterdays (78)	8
56	Esquire 10-468	How High The Moon/Lester Leaps In (78).	8
57	HMV POP 379	The Finisher/Cabin In The Sky (as Tommy Whittle & His Quartet)	5
55	Esquire EP 37	TOMMY WHITTLE QUINTET (EP).	8
56	Esquire EP 37	TOMMY WHITTLE QUINTET (EP).	10
58	HMV 7EG 8325	TOMMY WHITTLE QUARTET (EP)	40
54	Esquire 20-028	WAXING WITH WHITTLE (LP).	15
55	Esquire 20-048	TOMMY WHITTLE QUINTET (LP).	50
56	Esquire 20-061	SPOTLIGHTING TOMMY WHITTLE (LP).	75
56	Esquire 20-068	LULLABY & RHYTHM (LP).	125
60	Tempo TAP 27	NEW HORIZONS (LP).	12
60s	Ember EMB 3305	EASY LISTENING (LP).	75

WHIZZ KIDS

79	Dead Good DEAD SIX	P.A.Y.E./99% Proof/National Assistance/Cheek To Cheek (p/s, with insert)	10
80	Ovation OVS 1213	Suspect No. 1/Coma Life (ps)	8

WHO

SINGLES

65	Brunswick 05926	I Can't Explain/Bald Headed Woman	15
65	Brunswick 05935	Anyway Anyhow Anywhere/Daddy Rolling Stone.	20
65	Brunswick 05944	My Generation/Shout And Shimmy	10
66	Brunswick 05951	Circles/Instant Party (unreleased)	
66	Reaction 591 001	Substitute/Instant Party (withdrawn).	15
66	Reaction 591 001	Substitute/Circles (withdrawn).	20
66	Reaction 591 001	Substitute/WHO ORCHESTRA: Waltz For A Pig (B-side actually by Graham Bond Organisation).	25
66	Brunswick 05956	A Legal Matter/Instant Party	20
66	Brunswick 05956	The Kids Are Alright/The Ox (mispressing, wrong catalogue number)	25
66	Brunswick 05965	The Kids Are Alright/The Ox	25
66	Reaction 591 004	I'm A Boy/In The City	6
66	Brunswick 05968	La-La-La-Lies/The Good's Gone	30
66	Reaction 591 010	Happy Jack/I've Been Away.	6
67	Track 604 002	Pictures Of Lily/Doctor, Doctor	5
67	Track 604 006	The Last Time/Under My Thumb	35
67	Track 604 011	I Can See For Miles/Someone's Coming	6
68	Track 604 023	Dogs/Call Me Lightning	10
68	Track 604 024	Magic Bus/Dr. Jekyll And Mr Hyde	6
69	Track 604 027	Pinball Wizard/Dogs Part Two	4
70	Track 604 036	The Seeker/Here For More.	5
70	Track 2094 002	Summertime Blues/Heaven And Hell	7
70	Track 2094 004	See Me, Feel Me/Overture From 'Tommy' (withdrawn)	15
71	Track 2094 009	Won't Get Fooled Again/Don't Know Myself (p/s).	15
71	Track 2094 009	Won't Get Fooled Again/Don't Know Myself (white label, different matrix no.).	4
71	Track 2094 012	Let's See Action/When I Was A Boy (black label)	4
72	Track 2094 102	Join Together/Baby Don't You Do It (black label)	4
73	Track 2094 106	The Relay/Waspman	4
73	Track 2094 115	5.15/Water.	4
75	Polydor 2001 561	Overture/See Me Feel Me/Listening To You (from "Tommy" soundtrack, p/s)	4
76	Polydor 2058 803	Substitute/I'm A Boy/Pictures Of Lily (12", company sleeve).	7
78	Polydor WHO 1	Who Are You?/Had Enough (p/s, paper label).	4
79	Polydor WHO 2	Long Live Rock/I'm The Face/My Wife (withdrawn, blank run-off groove)	5

THE WHO

79	Polydor WHO 2	Long Live Rock/I'm The Face/My Wife ('Strawberry' etch on run-off groove) 4
80	Polydor WHO 3	5.15/I'm One (p/s) 4
82	Polydor WHOP 6	Athena/A Man Is A Man (picture disc) 5
82	Polydor WHOPX 6	Athena/A Man Is A Man/Won't Get Fooled Again (12", picture disc) 7
82	Polydor WHOPX 6	Athena/A Man Is A Man/Won't Get Fooled Again (12", picture disc, mispressing, plays "Why Did I Fall For That"). 15
89	Polydor POCD 907	My Generation/Substitute/Baba O'Riley/Behind Blue Eyed (CD, card sleeve). . . . 10
89	Polydor POCD 917	Won't Get Fooled Again (Extended Version)/Bony Maronie/Dancing In The Street/Mary-Anne With The Shaky Hand (CD, card sleeve) 10

EXPORT SINGLES

66	Brunswick 05956	A Legal Matter/Instant Party (with Scandinavian p/s). 80
68	Decca AD 1001	My Generation/Shout And Shimmy (some in p/s) 125/60
68	Decca AD 1002	A Legal Matter/Instant Party 50
72	Track 2094 102	Join Together/Baby Don't You Do It (p/s, for Spain) 15

PROMO SINGLES

69	Track PRO 1	The Acid Queen/We're Not Gonna Take It (existence unconfirmed)
69	Track PRO 2	Go To The Mirror!/Sally Simpson 40
69	Track PRO 3	I'm Free/1921 40
69	Track PRO 4	Christmas/Overture 40

EPs

66	Reaction 592 001	READY STEADY WHO (EP) 40
70	Track 2252 001	EXCERPTS FROM "TOMMY" (EP, 33rpm) 15
83	Reaction WHO 7	READY STEADY WHO (EP, reissue). 10

LPs

65	Brunswick LAT 8616	MY GENERATION 100
66	Reaction 593 002	A QUICK ONE. 50
67	Track 612 002	THE WHO SELL OUT (mono, 500 with stickered sleeve & poster) 200/40
67	Track 613 002	THE WHO SELL OUT (stereo, 500 with stickered sleeve & poster) 250/50
68	Track 612/613 006	DIRECT HITS (mono/stereo) 25/20
69	Track 613 013/014	TOMMY (2-LP, fold-out glossy gatefold sleeve, with no'd 12-page booklet). 20

70	Track 2406 001	LIVE AT LEEDS (foldout sleeve with 12 inserts including poster; blue or red print on sleeve)	15
70	Track 2407 008	BACKTRACK 8: A QUICK ONE (mono budget reissue)	10
70	Track 2407 009	BACKTRACK 9: SELL OUT (stereo budget reissue)	10
70	Track 2407 014	BACKTRACK 14: THE OX	20
70	Track 2856 001	WHO DID IT? (mail-order only, withdrawn)	350
71	Track 2408 102	WHO'S NEXT	10
71	Track 2406 006	MEATY, BEATY, BIG AND BOUNCY (gatefold sleeve)	10
71	Track 2406 006	MEATY, BEATY, BIG AND BOUNCY (gatefold sleeve, mispressed, plays "The Seeker" instead of "Magic Bus")	25
72	Track 2406 007	TOMMY PART ONE	10
72	Track 2406 008	TOMMY PART TWO	10
73	Track 2657 002	TOMMY (2-LP, fold-out matt gatefold sleeve, with 12-page booklet)	15
73	Track 2657 013	QUADROPHENIA (2-LP, original with 22-page photo booklet, matt labels)	15
74	Track 2406 116	ODDS AND SODS (cut-away braille sleeve, with poster & lyric sheet)	12
75	Polydor 2490 129	THE WHO BY NUMBERS (numbered sleeve)	10
81	Polydor 2675 216	PHASES (9-LP box set, stickered cover)	100

(see also High Numbers, Pete Townshend, Roger Daltrey, John Entwistle, Keith Moon, Kenney Jones, Graham Bond Organisation, Rigor Mortis, McEnroe & Cash)

WHO'S GEORGE

80	Impact ACT 1	Didn't Catch Your Name/Stand Up (p/s)	5
85	Impact ACT 2	Shu Shu/I'm Not Leaving (p/s)	4
86	Impact ACT 3	Who's George/Forever (poster p/s)	4

WALLY WHYTON (& VIPERS)

59	Parlophone R 4585	Don't Tell Me Your Troubles/It's All Over You	8
60	Parlophone R 4630	All Over This World/Got Me A Girl	6
60	Pye 7N 15304	It's A Rat Race/Marriage Of Convenience/95% Of Me Loves You (with Sally Miles)/You're Going To Be Caught (as Wally Whyton & Vipers)	6
61	Piccadilly 7N 35089	Little Red Pony/Christmas Land	6
68	Fontana TF 960	Gentle On My Mind/Ballad Of The Bol Weevil	5
69	Fontana TF 994	Wichita Lineman/Leave Them A Flower	5
69	Fontana TF 1030	Jig Alone/Out On The Road	5
68	Fontana STL 5476	IT'S ME, MUM (LP)	12
70	Fontana STL 5535	LEAVE THEM A FLOWER (LP)	12

(see also Vipers, Sharkey Todd & Monsters)

INIA TE WIATA

57	HMV POP 301	Banana Boat Song/Call Of The Sea	5
59	HMV POP 572	The Twelth Of Never/Yellow Bird (78)	10

WICHITA FALL

69	Liberty LBS 83208	LIFE IS BUT A DREAM (LP)	12

WICHITA TRAIN WHISTLE

68	Dot DOT 111	Don't Cry Now/Tapioca Tundra (unissued)	
68	Dot (S)LPD 516	MICHAEL NESMITH PRESENTS THE WICHITA TRAIN WHISTLE SINGS (LP)	25

(see also Michael Nesmith)

WIDOWMAKER

76	Jet JET 766	On The Road/Pin A Rose On Me	5
76	Jet JET 767	When I Met You/Pin A Rose On Me	5
76	Jet JET 782	Pin A Rose On Me/On The Road	5
76	Jet 2310 432	WIDOWMAKER (LP)	12
77	United Artists UAG 30038	TOO LATE TO CRY (LP)	12

(see also Luther Grosvenor, Steve Ellis, Huw Lloyd Langton)

WIGGANS

61	Blue Beat BB 29	Rock Baby/Let's Sing The Blues	12

PERCY WIGGINS

67	Atlantic 584 113	Book Of Memories/Can't Find Nobody	6

SPENCER WIGGINS

67	Stateside SS 2024	Uptight Good Woman/Anything You Do Is Alright	10
70	Pama PM 794	I'm A Poor Man's Son/That's How Much I Love You	12

WILBURN BROTHERS

59	Brunswick 05799	That Silver-Haired Daddy Of Mine/A Boy's Faithful Friend	8
59	Brunswick 05799	That Silver-Haired Daddy Of Mine/A Boy's Faithful Friend (78)	8
59	Brunswick LAT 8291	SIDE BY SIDE (LP)	18
61	Brunswick LAT 8501	CITY LIMITS (LP)	15
62	Brunswick LAT 8507	FOLK SONGS (LP)	15
67	Brunswick LAT 8686	COOL COUNTRY (LP)	14

WILD & WANDERING

86	Iguana VYK 14	2,000 LIGHT ALES FROM HOME (12" EP, with insert)	50

(see also Pop Will Eat Itself)

WILD ANGELS

68	Major Minor MM 569	Nervous Breakdown/Watch The Wheels Go Round	18
69	B&C CB 114	Buzz Buzz/Please Don't Touch	8
70	B&C CB 123	Sally-Ann/Wrong Number, Try Again	8
71	B&C CB 145	Three Nights A Week/Time To Kill	7
72	Decca F 13308	Jo-Jo Ann/My Way	6
72	Decca F 13356	Beauty School Dropout/Midnight Rider	6
73	Decca F 13334	Running Bear/Sussin'	5
73	Decca F 13412	Greased Lightning/Born To Hand-Jive/Beauty School Dropout	5
73	Decca F 13456	Clap Your Hands And Stamp Your Feet/Wild Angels Rock'n'Roll	5
70	B&C BCM 101	LIVE AT THE REVOLUTION (LP)	15
70	B&C BCM 102	RED HOT'N'ROCKIN' (LP)	15
72	Decca SKL 5134	OUT AT LAST (LP)	12

WILD BEASTS
79	Fried Egg EGG 2	Minimum Maximum/Another Noun (p/s)	4
80	Ring Piece CUS 886	Last One Of The Boys/We're Only Monsters (p/s)	5
81	Warped BEND 1	Life Is A Bum/Mary Lou/The Limit (p/s)	5

WILDCATS
59	London HLT 8787	Gazachstahagen/Billy's Cha Cha	15
59	London HLT 8787	Gazachstahagen/Billy's Cha Cha (78)	15
59	London HLT 8907	Dancing Elephants/King Size Guitar (unreleased)	

JACK WILDE
69	Elektra EKSN 45068	Apple Pie Mother And The Flag/Ballad Of Baby Browning	4

KIM WILDE
83	Rak 12 RAK 365	Dancing In The Dark (Extended)/Dancing In The Dark (Instrumental) (12", p/s, with poster)	10
84	MCA KIMP 1	The Second Time/Lovers On A Beach (picture disc)	12
84	MCA KIMP 2	The Touch/Shangri-La (shaped picture disc)	10
85	MCA KIMP 3	Rage To Love/Putty In Your Hands (shaped picture disc)	10
87	MCA KIMX 6	Say You Really Want Me (Video Remix)/Say You Really Want Me (7" Version) Don't Say Nothing's Changed (12", p/s)	7
88	MCA KIM X7	Hey Mister Heartache (Kilowatt Remix)/Hey Mister Heartache/ Tell Me Where You Are (12", p/s)	8
88	MCA DKIM 7	Hey Mister Heartache (Extended)/Tell Me Where You Are/You Keep Me Hangin' On/Another Step (Closer To You) (Extended Version) (CD, 4th track w/Junior)	12
88	MCA KIMB 8	You Came/Stone (box set)	5
88	MCA KIMX 8	You Came (Shep Pettibone Mix)/You Came (Extended) (12", p/s)	7
88	MCA DKIM 8	You Came (Extended)/You Came (7" Version)/Stone (5" CD, unreleased)	
88	MCA DIM 8	You Came (Extended)/You Came (7" Version)/Stone (3" CD)	12
88	MCA KIMX 9	Never Trust A Stranger (Sanjazz Mix)/Wotcha Gonna Do/ Never Trust A Stranger (Extended) (12", p/s)	7
88	MCA DKIM 9	Never Trust A Stranger (Extended Version)/You Came (Pettibone Mix)/ Wotcha Gonna Do? (CD)	12
88	MCA KIMB 10	Four Letter Word/She Hasn't Got Time For You ('88) (numbered box set)	5
88	MCA DKIM 10	Four Letter Word/She Hasn't Got Time For You ('88)/Four Letter Word (Extended Version) (CD)	7
89	MCA KIMR 11	Love In The Natural Way/You'll Be The One Who'll Lose (poster p/s)	4
89	MCA DKIMT 11	Love In The Natural Way (7" Version)/You'll Be The One Who'll Lose/ Love In The Natural Way (Extended Version) (CD, picture disc)	12
90	MCA DKIMT 14	I Can't Say Goodbye (Edit)/Sanjazz Megamix/I Can't Say Goodbye (CD)	7
82	Fame FA 413 130-1	SELECT (LP, withdrawn reissue)	10
86	MCA MCF 3339	ANOTHER STEP (LP, 'map' sleeve, withdrawn)	10
86	MCA DMCF 3339	ANOTHER STEP (CD, 'map' sleeve, withdrawn)	15

MARTY WILDE (& WILDCATS)
78s
57	Philips PB 750	Honeycomb/Wild Cat (as Marty Wilde & Wildcats) (78)	20
58	Philips PB 781	Love Bug Crawl/Afraid Of Love (78)	30
58	Philips PB 804	Sing, Boy, Sing/Oh-Oh, I'm Falling In Love Again (with Wildcats) (78)	25
58	Philips PB 835	Endless Sleep/Her Hair Was Yellow (as Marty Wilde & Wildcats) (78)	10
58	Philips PB 850	My Lucky Love/Misery's Child (as Marty Wilde & Wildcats) (78)	15
58	Philips PB 875	No One Knows/The Fire Of Love (78)	20
59	Philips PB 902	Donna/Love-a, Love-a (78)	30
59	Philips PB 926	A Teenager In Love/Danny (78)	35
59	Philips PB 959	Sea Of Love/Teenage Tears (78)	40
59	Philips PB 972	It's Been Nice/Bad Boy (78)	50
60	Philips PB 1002	Johnny Rocco/My Heart And I (78)	75

SINGLES
57	Philips JK 1028	Honeycomb/Wild Cat (as Marty Wilde & Wildcats) (jukebox issue)	45
58	Philips PB 804	Sing, Boy, Sing/Oh-Oh, I'm Falling In Love Again (with Wildcats)	35
58	Philips PB 835	Endless Sleep/Her Hair Was Yellow (as Marty Wilde & Wildcats)	12
58	Philips PB 850	My Lucky Love/Misery's Child (as Marty Wilde & Wildcats)	8
58	Philips PB 875	No One Knows/The Fire Of Love	10
59	Philips PB 902	Donna/Love-a, Love-a, Love-a	8
59	Philips PB 926	A Teenager In Love/Danny	8
59	Philips PB 959	Sea Of Love/Teenage Tears	6
59	Philips PB 972	It's Been Nice/Bad Boy	6
60	Philips PB 1002	Johnny Rocco/My Heart And I	7
60	Philips PB 1022	The Fight/Johnny At The Crossroads	10
60	Philips PB 1037	I Wanna Be Loved By You/Angry	7
60	Philips PB 1078	Little Girl/Your Seventeenth Spring	6
61	Philips PB 1101	Rubber Ball/Like Makin' Love	6
61	Philips PB 1121	When Does It Get To Be Love/Your Loving Touch	6
61	Philips PB 1161	Hide And Seek/Crazy Dream	6
61	Philips PB 1191	Tomorrow's Clown/The Hellions	6
61	Philips PB 1206	Come Running/Ev'ryone	7
62	Philips PB 1240	Jezebel/Don't Run Away	6
62	Philips 326 546BF	Ever Since You Said Goodbye/Send Me The Pillow You Dream On	6
63	Columbia DB 4980	Lonely Avenue/Brand New Love	6
63	Philips 326 579BF	No! Dance With Me/Little Miss Happiness	6
63	Columbia DB 7145	Save Your Love For Me/Bless My Broken Heart	6
64	Columbia DB 7198	When Day Is Done/I Can't Help The Way I Feel	6
64	Columbia DB 7285	Kiss Me/My, What A Woman	6
64	Decca F 11979	The Mexican Boy/Your Kind Of Love	7
66	Philips PB 1490	I've Got So Used To Loving You/The Beginning Of The End	6
68	Philips BF 1632	By The Time I Get To Phoenix/Shutters And Boards	6
68	Philips BF 1669	Abergavenny/Alice In Blue	5

Marty WILDE

69	Philips BF 1753	All The Love I Have/Any Day	5
69	Philips BF 1783	Endless Sleep/Donna	5
69	Philips BF 1815	Shelley/Jump On The Train (with Deke Leonard)	6
70	Philips BF 1839	No Trams To Lime Street/Prelude To Old Age	5
71	Philips 6006 126	Busker/It's So Real	5
72	Magnet MAG 15	I Love You/She's A Mover	5
82	Kaleidoscope KRLA 2003	In Dreams/Hard To Find, Easy To Love (p/s)	5

EPs
57	Philips BBE 12164	PRESENTING MARTY WILDE (EP)	45
58	Philips BBE 12200	MORE OF MARTY (EP)	40
59	Philips BBE 12327	SEA OF LOVE (EP)	40
60	Philips BBE 12385	VERSATILE MR. WILDE (EP)	45
60	Philips BBE 12422	MARTY WILDE FAVOURITES (EP)	40
62	Philips BBE 12517	COME RUNNING (EP)	40
63	Philips BE 433 638	MARTY (EP)	40

LPs
59	Philips BBL 7342	WILDE ABOUT MARTY (LP)	40
60	Philips BBL 7380	MARTY WILDE SHOWCASE (LP)	35
60	Philips BBL 7385	THE VERSATILE MR. WILDE (LP, also stereo SBBL 570)	35/40
69	Philips SBL 7877	DIVERSIONS (LP)	15
70	Philips 6308 010	ROCK 'N' ROLL (LP)	15
74	Philips 6308 102	GOOD ROCKING — THEN AND NOW (LP)	12

(see also Wilde Three, Brian Bennett, Shadows, Keith Shields, Capricorn, Deke Leonard)

RICH WILDE
79	Dead Good DEAD 5	The Lady Wants To Be Alone/The Lady Wants To Be A Clone (p/s)	4

WILDER BROTHERS
57	HMV POP 365	I Want You/Teenage Angel	200
57	HMV POP 365	I Want You/Teenage Angel (78)	50

WILDERNESS CHILDREN
88	Choabie/Flexi DOSS 1	There's A Good Time A-Comin'/On The West Coast (33rpm flexi, foldover p/s) & Thrilled Skinny flexi, with *Sowing Seeds* fanzine, issue 5, all in PVC bag)	7/5

(see also Thrilled Skinny)

WILDERNESS ROAD
74	Dawn DNLS 3057	WILDERNESS ROAD (LP, unissued)	

WILDE THREE
65	Decca F 12131	Since You've Gone/Just As Long	45
65	Decca F 12232	I Cried/Well Who's That?	55

(see also Marty Wilde, Justin Hayward, Vernons Girls)

WILDFIRE
84	Mausoleum GUTS 8405	Jerusalem/Fight Fire With Fire (p/s)	5
83	Mausoleum SKUL 8307	BRUTE FORCE AND IGNORANCE (LP)	25
83	Mausoleum SKUL 8338	SUMMER LIGHTNING (LP, with insert)	15

(see also Weapon)

WILD FLOWERS
84	No Future FS 11	Melt Like Ice (p/s)	8
84	Reflex RE 2	Things Have Changed (Which Should Have Stayed The Same)/Second Thought (p/s)	7
88	House Of Dolls HOD 003	That Ain't It/MEDICINE FACTORY: Everyman/OUTSIDERS: Satellite Evangelist (Demo)/UNDERNEATH WHAT?: Pointed ID (no p/s, with *House Of Dolls* mag)	6/4

(see also Mighty Lemon Drops)

WILDHEARTS
92	East West YZ 669T	MONDO AKIMBO A-GO-GO (12" EP, with inner sleeve)	35
92	East West YZ 669TX	MONDO AKIMBO A-GO-GO (12" EP, white vinyl, with inner sleeve)	40
92	East West YZ 669CD	MONDO AKIMBO A-GO-GO (CD EP)	35
93	East West YZ 773	Greetings From Shitsville/The Bullshit Goes On (p/s, brown vinyl, with insert)	6
93	East West YZ 784 T	TV Tan/Show A Little Emotion/Dangerlust/Down On London (12", p/s)	8
93	East West YZ 784CD	TV Tan/Show A Little Emotion/Dangerlust/Down On London (CD)	8
94	East West YZ 794	Caffeine Bomb/Girlfriend's Clothes (p/s, green vinyl, with insert)	6
94	East West YZ 794 T	Caffeine Bomb/Girlfriend's Clothes/Shut Your Fucking Mouth And Use Your Fucking Brain/And The Bullshit Goes On (12", p/s)	15
94	East West YZ 794 CD	Caffeine Bomb/Girlfriend's Clothes/Shut Your Fucking Mouth And Use Your Fucking Brain/And The Bullshit Goes On (CD, digipak)	15
93	East West SAM 1262	Suckerpunch/CLAWFINGER: War Fair (Brixton Academy gig freebie)	35
94	East West YZ 828TE	Suckerpunch/Beautiful Thing You/Two-Way Idiot Mirror/29 x The Pain (10", p/s, 1-sided, etched)	8
94	East West YZ 828CD	Suckerpunch/Beautiful Thing You/Two-Way Idiot Mirror/29 x The Pain (CD)	8
95	East West SAM 1555	NAIVETY PLAY (CD, promo only)	18
92	East West 509 91202-1	DON'T BE HAPPY... JUST WORRY (LP, as 2 x 12", with inner sleeves)	18
92	East West 509 91202-2	DON'T BE HAPPY... JUST WORRY (2-CD, with bonus track "Anti-Dance Mixes" of "Mondo Akimbo A-Go Go" tracks)	22
94	East West 509 99039-2	FISHING FOR LUCKIES (CD, 6-track mini-album, fan club/mail-order only)	40
95	East West 0630-12850-1	FISHING FOR MORE LUCKIES (LP, reissue, with 3 extra tracks "Underkill", "Saddened" & "I Wanna Go Where The People Go [Early Version]", unreleased)	60
95	East West 0630-12850-4	FISHING FOR MORE LUCKIES (cassette, reissue, with 3 extra tracks, unreleased)	45
95	East West SAM 1582	LIVING ON A LANDMINE: THE SINGLES 1993-95 (CD, 6-track sampler, promo only, card p/s)	18

(see also Honeycrack)

WILD HONEY
72	Mam MAM 97	He's My Sugar/People Of The Universe	4
72	Mam MAM 154	Baby Don't You Know Anymore/He's My Sugar (featuring Tina Charles)	4

(see also Tina Charles)

WILD HORSES

79	EMI International INTS 599	Criminal Tendencies/The Rapist (p/s)	5
80	EMI EMI 5047	Face Down/Dealer (p/s)	4
80	EMI EMI 5078	Fly Away/Blackmail (p/s, white vinyl)	6
80	EMI 12EMI 5078	Fly Away/Blackmail (12", p/s, white vinyl)	7
81	EMI EMI 5149	I'll Give You Love/Rocky Mountain Way (p/s)	5
81	EMI EMI 5149	I'll Give You Love/Rocky Mountain Way//The Kid/On A Saturday Night (double pack, gatefold p/s)	5
81	EMI EMI 5199	Everlasting Love/The Axe (no p/s)	4
80	EMI EMC 3326	WILD HORSES (LP, with inner sleeve)	12
81	EMI EMC 3368	STAND YOUR GROUND (LP, with inner sleeve)	12

(see also Thin Lizzy, Motörhead, Rainbow, Dio)

WILD INDIANS

84	Hullaballoo! HA! 001	Love Of My Life/The Biggest Man/Maybe (p/s)	5
80s	Having Fun IP 001	Stolen Courage/POP WALLPAPER: The Great Adventure (flexidisc, gatefold p/s)	4

WILD MAGNOLIAS

75	Barclay BAR 30	Smoke My Peace Pipe/Handa Wanda	5
75	Barclay BAR 34	They Call Us Wild/Jumalaka Boom Boom	6
75	Barclay 80 529	THE WILD MAGNOLIAS 1 (LP, gatefold sleeve)	18
75	Barclay 90 033	THEY CALL US WILD (LP, gatefold sleeve)	20

WILD OATS

63	Oak RGJ 117	WILD OATS (EP)	750+

WILD ONES

64	Fontana TF 468	Bowie Man/Purple Pill Eater	40

WILD SILK

68	Polydor 56256	Poor Man/Stop Crying	5
69	Columbia DB 8534	(Vision In A) Plaster Sky/Toymaker	10
69	Columbia DB 8611	Help Me/Crimson And Gold	8

WILD SWANS

82	Zoo CAGE 009	The Revolutionary Spirit/God Forbid (unissued, stamped white label, no p/s)	12
82	Zoo CAGE 009	The Revolutionary Spirit/God Forbid (12", p/s)	8
82	Zoo CAGE 009	The Revolutionary Spirit/God Forbid (12", p/s, with 'The Lament Of Icarus' painting in top right of front sleeve, withdrawn)	15

(see also Lotus Eaters, Care)

WILD THING

69	Elektra EKSN 45076	Old Lady/Next To Me	5
70	Elektra EKS 74059	PARTYIN' (LP)	15
71	Elektra 2410 003	PARTYIN' (LP, reissue)	12

WILD TURKEY

72	Chrysalis CHS 2004	Good Old Days/Life Is A Symphony	5
72	Chrysalis CHR 1002	BATTLE HYMN (LP, gatefold sleeve)	15
73	Chrysalis CHR 1010	TURKEY (LP)	15

(see also Jethro Tull, Babe Ruth, Man, Whitesnake)

WILD UNCERTAINTY

66	Planet PLF 120	Man With Money/Broken Truth	40

WILD WALLY

70	Concord CON 1003	I GO APE (LP)	15

WILDWEEDS

67	Chess CRS 8065	It Was Fun While It Lasted/Sorrow's Anthem	7

WILD WILL'S BLUE WASHBOARD BOYS

71	Flyright LP 4701	BABY YUM YUM (LP)	12

WILFRED & MILLICENT

65	Island WI 190	The Vow/I'll Never Believe In You	12

(see also Jackie [Edwards] & Millie [Small])

MIKE WILHELM

76	Zigzag/United Artists ZZ 1	MIKE WILHELM (LP, sold via Zigzag magazine)	25

(see also Charlatans, Flamin' Groovies)

ROBERT WILKINS

60s	Piedmont PLP 13162	REV ROBERT WILKINS (LP)	25

ROGER WILKINS

70	Spokane SPL 1002	BEFORE THE REVERENCE (LP)	40

ARTHUR WILKINSON ORCHESTRA

65	HMV 7EG 8919	BEATLE CRACKER SUITE (EP)	8

COLM C.T. WILKINSON

78	RSO RSO 009	Born To Sing/The Simple Things In Life	4

JESS WILLARD

51	Capitol CL 13443	If You've Got The Money I've Got The Time/RED MURREL: Ernest Tubb's Talking Blues (78)	10

WILLETT FAMILY

62	Topic 12T 84	THE ROVING JOURNEYMAN (LP, blue label with booklet)	20

AL WILLIAMS

80	Grapevine GRP 136	I Am Nothing/Brand New Love	12

ANDY WILLIAMS

78s

56	London HLA 8284	Walk Hand In Hand/Not Any More (78)	15
56	London HLA 8315	Canadian Sunset/High Upon A Mountain (78)	8
56	London HLA 8360	Baby Doll (From The Film)/Since I've Found My Baby (78).	8
57	London HLA 8487	Lips Of Wine/Straight From My Heart (78).	10
58	London HLA 8587	Are You Sincere/Be Mine Tonight (78)	10
58	London HLA 8710	Promise Me, Love/Your Hand, Your Heart, Your Love (78).	15
59	London HLA 8784	Hawaiian Wedding Song/House Of Bamboo (78)	10
59	London HLA 8957	Lonely Street/Summer Love (78).	15
59	London HLA 9018	The Village Of St. Bernadette/I'm So Lonesome I Could Cry (78).	30

SINGLES

56	London HLA 8284	Walk Hand In Hand/Not Any More	30
56	London HLA 8315	Canadian Sunset/High Upon A Mountain (gold or silver label print)	30/20
56	London HL 7013	Canadian Sunset/High Upon A Mountain (export issue)	10
56	London HLA 8360	Baby Doll (From The Film)/Since I've Found My Baby (gold or silver print)	35/20
57	London HLA 8399	Butterfly/It Doesn't Take Very Long	20
57	London HLA 8437	I Like Your Kind Of Love/Stop Teasin' Me	18
57	London HLA 8487	Lips Of Wine/Straight From My Heart	18
58	London HLA 8587	Are You Sincere/Be Mine Tonight.	15
58	London HL 7034	Are You Sincere/Be Mine Tonight (export issue)	10
58	London HLA 8710	Promise Me, Love/Your Hand, Your Heart, Your Love	12
59	London HLA 8784	Hawaiian Wedding Song/House Of Bamboo	8
59	London HLA 8957	Lonely Street/Summer Love	7
59	London HLA 9018	The Village Of St. Bernadette/I'm So Lonesome I Could Cry	6
60	London HLA 9099	Wake Me When It's Over/We Have A Date	6
60	London HLA 9241	Don't Go To Strangers/You Don't Want My Love.	6
61	London HLA 9348	The Bilbao Song/How Wonderful To Know	6
63	CBS AAG 138	Can't Get Used To Losing You/The Days Of Wine And Roses	5
67	CBS CBS 2675	Music To Watch Girls By/The Face I Love	6
72	CBS 8197	(Love Theme From) The Godfather/In The Summertime (p/s).	5

EPs

57	London RE-A 1088	ANDY WILLIAMS' BIG HITS (EP)	20
57	London RE-A 1102	ANDY WILLIAMS' BIG HITS No. 2 (EP).	25
63	London RE-A 1394	ANDY WILLIAMS' BEST (EP)	15

LPs

57	London HA-A 2054	ANDY WILLIAMS SINGS STEVE ALLEN (LP)	30
58	London HA-A 2113	ANDY WILLIAMS SINGS RODGERS AND HAMMERSTEIN (LP)	30
59	London HA-A 2203	TWO TIME WINNERS (LP)	30
60	London HA-A 2238	LONELY STREET (LP)	18
62	London HA-A 8005	ANDY WILLIAMS' BEST (LP)	15
63	London HA-A 8090	UNDER PARIS SKIES (LP)	18
73	CBS CQ 30797	YOU'VE GOT A FRIEND (LP, quadrophonic)	15
73	CBS CQ 31303/Q 64869	LOVE THEME FROM "THE GODFATHER" (LP, quadrophonic)	15
73	CBS CQ 31625	ALONE AGAIN (NATURALLY) (LP, quadrophonic)	12

AUDREY WILLIAMS

56	MGM SP 1179	Ain't Nothing Gonna Be All Right No How/Livin' It Up And Havin' A Ball	15
56	MGM MGM 911	Ain't Nothing Gonna Be All Right No How/Livin' It Up And Havin' A Ball (78).	10

(see also Hank Williams)

BIG JOE WILLIAMS

57	Jazz Collector JEN 3	A MAN SINGS THE BLUES (EP).	12
57	Jazz Collector JEN 4	A MAN SINGS THE BLUES VOLUME 2 (EP)	12
67	Delmark DJB 4	ON THE HIGHWAY (EP)	12
60s	XX MIN 700	BIG JOE WILLIAMS (EP)	10
63	Esquire 32-191	BLUES ON HIGHWAY 51 (LP)	35
63	'77' LA 12-19	PINEY WOODS BLUES (LP)	25
64	CBS BPG 63813	CLASSIC DELTA BLUES (LP).	15
64	Storyville SLP 158	PORTRAITS IN BLUES VOLUME 4 (LP).	18
64	Storyville SLP 163	PORTRAITS IN BLUES VOLUME 7 (LP).	18
65	Fontana 688 800 ZL	TOUGH TIMES (LP).	18
66	Xtra XTRA 1033	BIG JOE WILLIAMS (LP)	25
66	Bounty BY 6018	BACK TO THE COUNTRY (LP)	25
66	Society SOC 1020	BIG JOE, SONNY, BROWNIE, LIGHTNIN' (LP, with Lightnin' Hopkins, Sonny Terry & Brownie McGhee).	12
69	Storyville 618 011	DON'T YOU LEAVE ME HERE (LP).	18
69	Liberty LBL/LBS 83207	HAND ME DOWN MY OLD WALKING STICK (LP)	20
69	Xtra XTRA 5059	LIVE AT FOLK CITY (LP)	12
70	RCA Intl. INTS 1087	CRAWLIN' KING SNAKE (LP).	18
72	Sonet SNTF 635	THE LEGACY OF THE BLUES VOL. 6 (LP, with insert)	12
72	Delmark DS 627	NINE STRING GUITAR (LP)	12

(see also Poor Joe Williams)

BILLY WILLIAMS (QUARTET)

78s

54	Vogue Coral Q 2012	Sh'Boom/Whenever Wherever (78)	18
54	Vogue Coral Q 2039	The Honeydripper/Love Me (as Billy Williams Quartet) (78)	20
56	Vogue Coral Q 72149	A Crazy Little Palace/Cry Baby (as Billy Williams Quartet) (78)	10
56	Vogue Coral Q 72180	Pray/You'll Reach Your Star (78)	10
57	Vogue Coral Q 72222	Follow Me/Shame, Shame, Shame (as Billy Williams Quartet) (78)	20
58	Coral Q 72303	Don't Let Go/Baby, Baby (as Billy Williams Quartet) (78).	8
58	Coral Q 72316	Steppin' Out Tonight/There I've Said It Again (as Billy Williams Quartet) (78).	10
58	Coral Q 72331	I'll Get By/It's Prayin' Time (78)	10
59	Coral Q 72359	Nola/Tied To The Strings Of Your Heart (78)	15

| 59 | Coral Q 72369 | Goodnight Irene/Red Hot Love (78) | 25 |
| 59 | Coral Q 72377 | Telephone Conversation/Go To Sleep, Go To Sleep, Go To Sleep (78, with Barbara McNair) | 15 |

SINGLES

54	Vogue Coral Q 2039	The Honeydripper/Love Me (as Billy Williams Quartet)	40
56	Vogue Coral Q 72149	A Crazy Little Palace/Cry Baby (as Billy Williams Quartet)	40
56	Vogue Coral Q 72180	Pray/You'll Reach Your Star	18
57	Vogue Coral Q 72222	Follow Me/Shame, Shame, Shame (as Billy Williams Quartet)	25
57	Vogue Coral Q 72241	Butterfly/The Pied Piper	25
57	Vogue Coral Q 72266	I'm Gonna Sit Right Down And Write A Letter/Date With The Blues	15
57	Vogue Coral Q 72295	Got A Date With An Angel/The Lord Will Understand	30
58	Coral Q 72303	Don't Let Go/Baby, Baby (as Billy Williams Quartet)	20
58	Coral Q 72316	Steppin' Out Tonight/There I've Said It Again (as Billy Williams Quartet)	45
58	Coral Q 72331	I'll Get By/It's Prayin' Time	15
59	Coral Q 72359	Nola/Tied To The Strings Of Your Heart	8
59	Coral Q 72369	Goodnight Irene/Red Hot Love	20
59	Coral Q 72377	Telephone Conversation/Go To Sleep, Go To Sleep, Go To Sleep (with Barbara McNair)	18
60	Coral Q 72402	I Cried For You/Lover Of All Lovers	12
60	Coral Q 72414	Begin The Beguine/For You	7

LPs

58	Coral LVA 9092	BILLY WILLIAMS (LP)	35
60	Coral LVA 9120	HALF SWEET HALF BEAT (LP)	25
61	Coral LVA 9139	THE BILLY WILLIAMS REVUE (LP)	25

(seee also Barbara McNair)

BOBBY WILLIAMS

| 68 | Action ACT 4509 | Baby I Need Your Love/Try It Again | 20 |
| 73 | Contempo C 17 | Let's Jam/You're My Baby | 6 |

CHRIS WILLIAMS & HIS MONSTERS

| 59 | Columbia DB 4383 | The Monster/The Eton Boating Song | 25 |
| 60 | Triumph RGM 1003 | Kicking Around/Midnight Rocker (unissued; white label demo copies only) | 250+ |

CINDY WILLIAMS

| 67 | Parlophone R 5648 | They Talk About Us/Did He Call Today Mama | 6 |

CLARENCE WILLIAMS (& HIS WASHBOARD BAND)

50	Jazz Collector L 32	New Down Home Rag/Squeeze Me (78)	8
54	Columbia SCM 5134	High Society/Left All Alone With The Blues	15
54	Columbia DB 3513	High Society/Left All Alone With The Blues (78)	10
58	Fontana TFE 17053	TREASURE OF NORTH AMERICAN MUSIC VOLUME 3 (EP)	15
59	Parlophone GEP 8733	CLARENCE WILLIAMS' WASHBOARD BAND (EP)	15
64	Jazz Collector JEL 18	JAZZ ORIGINATORS (EP)	12
54	London AL 3526	CLARENCE WILLIAMS AND HIS ORCHESTRA (10" LP)	20
55	Columbia 33S 1067	BACK ROOM SPECIAL (10" LP)	20
57	London AL 3561	CLARENCE WILLIAMS AND HIS ORCHESTRA VOL. 2 (10" LP)	20
60	Fontana TFL 5087	SIDNEY BECHET MEMORIAL (LP)	15
62	Philips BBL 7521	CLARENCE WILLIAMS VOL. 1: 1927-1935 (LP)	15

CLIVE WILLIAMS

| 70s | Rock Steady Rev. REVR 6 | Take Good Care Of My Baby/RICO: In Loving Memory Of Don Drummond | 5 |

COOTIE WILLIAMS

| 67 | Transatlantic | SOLID GOLD TRUMPET OF 67 (LP) | 10 |

DAN WILLIAMS & HIS ORCHESTRA

| 55 | London CAY 110 | Donkey City/SHAW PARK CALYPSO BAND: Take Her To Jamaica | 10 |
| 55 | London CAY 110 | Donkey City/SHAW PARK CALYPSO BAND: Take Her To Jamaica (78) | 10 |

DANNY WILLIAMS

59	HMV POP 624	Tall A Tree/I Look At You	8
59	HMV POP 655	So High — So Low/My Own True Love	8
59	HMV POP 703	Youthful Years/It Doesn't Matter	8
60	HMV POP 803	A Million To One/Call Me A Dreamer	7
61	HMV POP 839	We Will Never Be As Young As This Again/Passing Breeze	7
61	HMV POP 885	The Miracle Of You/Lonely	7
61	HMV POP 932	Moon River/A Weaver Of Dreams	5
62	HMV POP 968	Jeannie/It Might As Well Be Spring/Unchain My Heart	5
62	HMV POP 1002	The Wonderful World Of The Young/A Kind Of Loving	5
62	HMV POP 1035	Tears/Tiara Tahiti	5
63	HMV POP 1112	My Own True Love/Who Can Say?	6
63	HMV POP 1150	More/Rhapsody	6
63	HMV POP 1172	The Wild Wind/Once Upon A Time	6
63	HMV POP 1203	A Day Without You/Secret Love	6
63	HMV POP 1236	How Do You Keep From Crying?/Now The Day Is Over	6
63	HMV POP 1263	White On White/After You	7
64	HMV POP 1305	Today/Lonely In A Crowd	6
64	HMV POP 1325	The Seventh Dawn/The World Around Me	6
64	HMV POP 1372	Forget Her, Forget Her/Lollipops And Roses	12
65	HMV POP 1388	The Roundabout Of Love/I Wanna Be Around	6
65	HMV POP 1410	Go Away/Masquerade	7
65	HMV POP 1455	Lovely Is She/Gone And Forgotten	6
65	HMV POP 1487	And So We Meet Again/Violets For Your Furs	6
66	HMV POP 1506	I've Got To Find That Girl Again/Throw A Little Lovin' My Way	10
66	HMV POP 1522	Don't Just Stand There/Now And Then	7
66	HMV POP 1560	Rain (Falling From The Skies)/I'm So Lost	7
67	Deram DM 149	Never My Love/Whose Little Girl Are You (with inverted matrix, later re-pressed with matrix correct way up)	12/6
68	Deram DM 199	Everybody Needs Somebody (I Need You)/They Will Never Understand	6

Danny WILLIAMS

62	HMV 7EG 8748	HITS OF DANNY WILLIAMS (EP)	12
62	HMV 7EG 8763	DANNY WILLIAMS SWINGS WITH TONY OSBORNE (EP)	12
63	HMV 7EG 8800	"THE DAYS OF WINE AND ROSES" AND OTHER FILM FAVOURITES (EP)	12
61	HMV CLP 1458/CSD 1369	DANNY (LP, mono/stereo)	18/22
61	HMV CLP 1521	MOON RIVER AND OTHER TITLES (LP)	20
62	HMV CLP 1605/CSD 1471	SWINGING FOR YOU (LP, mono/stereo)	18/25
66	HMV CLP/CSD 3523	ONLY LOVE (LP)	25
66	Woman's Privilege AZ 3	ROMANCE WITH DANNY WILLIAMS (LP, mail-order via *Woman* magazine)	18
67	Deram DML 1017	DANNY WILLIAMS (LP)	20

DEL WILLIAMS
72	Grape GR 3027	Searching For Your Love/G.G. ALL STARS: Searching (Version)	6

DELROY WILLIAMS
71	Trojan TR 7813	Down In The Boondocks/Baby Make It	6

EDDIE WILLIAMS & LITTLE SONNY WILLIS
60s	XX MIN 707	GOING TO CALIFORNIA (EP)	15

GEORGE WILLIAMS
69	Bullet BU 405	No Business Of Yours/Mast It Up (actually titled "Mash It Up")	7

GEORGE WILLIAMS & HIS ORCHESTRA
55	Vogue Coral Q 72053	The Rompin' Stomper/Knock-Out Choo-Choo	6

GRANVILLE WILLIAMS ORCHESTRA
67	Island WI 3062	Hi-Life/More	10
67	Island ILP 971	HI-LIFE (LP)	55

(see also Silvertones)

HANK WILLIAMS (& HIS DRIFTING COWBOYS)

78s
50	MGM MGM 269	Lovesick Blues/Wedding Bells (78)	10
51	MGM MGM 381	Moanin' The Blues/The Blues Come Around (78)	10
51	MGM MGM 405	Dear John/Fly Trouble (78)	10
51	MGM MGM 454	Hey, Good Lookin'/Howlin' At The Moon (78)	10
51	MGM MGM 459	Cold, Cold Heart/I'm A Long Gone Daddy (78)	10
52	MGM MGM 471	I Can't Help It (If I'm Still In Love With You)/Baby, We're Really In Love (78)	10
52	MGM MGM 483	Why Don't You Love Me/I'd Still Want You (78)	10
52	MGM MGM 505	Honky-Tonk Blues/I'm Sorry For You, My Friend (78)	10
52	MGM MGM 527	Long Gone Lonesome Blues/Half As Much (78)	10
52	MGM MGM 553	Nobody's Lonesome For Me/Mind Your Own Business (78)	10
52	MGM MGM 566	Jambalaya (On The Bayou)/Settin' The Woods On Fire (78)	10
53	MGM MGM 585	I'll Never Get Out Of This World Alive/I Could Never Be Ashamed Of You (as Hank Williams & His Drifting Cowboys) (78)	12
53	MGM MGM 609	Kaw-Liga/Take These Chains From My Heart (& His Drifting Cowboys) (78)	10
53	MGM MGM 630	I Saw The Light/ARTHUR 'GUITAR BOOGIE' SMITH: Recitation Sonny Smith: In Memory Of Hank Williams (78)	12
53	MGM MGM 652	Ramblin' Man/I Won't Be Home No More (78)	10
53	MGM MGM 666	My Bucket's Got A Hole In It/Let's Turn Back The Years (78)	10
53	MGM MGM 678	Window Shopping/You Win Again (78)	12
54	MGM MGM 704	Weary Blues (From Waitin')/I Can't Escape From You (78)	12
54	MGM MGM 733	There'll Be No Teardrops Tonight/Crazy Heart (78)	12
54	MGM MGM 768	I'm Satisfied With You/I Ain't Got Nothin' But Time (78)	12
55	MGM MGM 799	I'm Gonna Sing/California Zephyr (78)	15
56	MGM MGM 889	The First Fall Of Snow/Someday You'll Call My Name (78, withdrawn)	
56	MGM MGM 896	Your Cheatin' Heart/A Teardrop On A Rose (78)	15
56	MGM MGM 921	There's No Room In My Heart (For The Blues)/I Wish I Had A Nickel (78)	15
56	MGM MGM 931	Blue Love (In My Heart)/Singing Waterfall (78)	20
57	MGM MGM 942	Low Down Blues/My Sweet Love Ain't Around (78)	18
57	MGM MGM 957	Rootie Tootie/Lonesome Whistle (78)	18
57	MGM MGM 966	Leave Me Alone With The Blues/With Tears In My Eyes (78)	18

SINGLES
53	MGM SP 1016	I'll Never Get Out Of This World Alive/I Could Never Be Ashamed Of You (as Hank Williams & His Drifting Cowboys)	45
53	MGM SP 1034	Kaw-Liga/Take These Chains From My Heart (& His Drifting Cowboys)	40
53	MGM SP 1049	Ramblin' Man/I Won't Be Home No More	35
53	MGM SP 1048	My Bucket's Got A Hole In It/Let's Turn Back The Years	35
54	MGM SP 1067	Weary Blues (From Waitin')/I Can't Escape From You	35
54	MGM SP 1085	There'll Be No Teardrops Tonight/Crazy Heart	35
54	MGM SP 1102	I'm Satisfied With You/I Ain't Got Nothin' But Time	35
56	MGM SP 1163	The First Fall Of Snow/Someday You'll Call My Name (unreleased)	
56	MGM MGM 921	There's No Room In My Heart (For The Blues)/I Wish I Had A Nickel	25
56	MGM MGM 931	Blue Love (In My Heart)/Singing Waterfall	25
57	MGM MGM 942	Low Down Blues/My Sweet Love Ain't Around	25
57	MGM MGM 957	Rootie Tootie/Lonesome Whistle	22
57	MGM MGM 966	Leave Me Alone With The Blues/With Tears In My Eyes	22
66	MGM MGM 1309	You Win Again/I'm So Lonesome I Could Cry	10
66	MGM MGM 1322	Kaw-Liga/Let's Turn Back The Years	7

EPs
54	MGM MGM-EP 512	HANK WILLIAMS AND HIS DRIFTING COWBOYS (EP, company sleeve)	25
54	MGM EPC 7	HANK WILLIAMS (EP, export issue)	30
55	MGM MGM-EP 551	JUST WAITIN' (EP, as Luke The Drifter, company sleeve, later p/s)	20/30
56	MGM MGM-EP 569	I SAW THE LIGHT (No. 1) (EP, company sleeve, later p/s)	15/20
57	MGM MGM-EP 582	HONKY TONKIN' (EP)	20
57	MGM MGM-EP 608	I SAW THE LIGHT (No. 2) (EP)	20
57	MGM MGM-EP 614	HONKY TONK BLUES (EP)	20
58	MGM MGM-EP 639	SONGS FOR A BROKEN HEART (No. 1) (EP)	20
58	MGM MGM-EP 649	SONGS FOR A BROKEN HEART (No. 2) (EP)	20

Hank WILLIAMS

58	MGM MGM-EP 675	HANK'S LAMENTS (EP)	20
60	MGM MGM-EP 710	THE UNFORGETTABLE HANK WILLIAMS (EP)	20
60	MGM MGM-EP 726	THE UNFORGETTABLE HANK WILLIAMS (No. 2) (EP)	20
60	MGM MGM-EP 732	THE UNFORGETTABLE HANK WILLIAMS (No. 3) (EP)	20
61	MGM MGM-EP 757	HANK WILLIAMS FAVOURITES (EP)	20
63	MGM MGM-EP 770	THE AUTHENTIC SOUND OF THE COUNTRY HITS (EP)	20

LPs

52	MGM MGM-D 105	HANK WILLIAMS SINGS (10" LP, company sleeve, later p/s)	40/55
53	MGM MGM-D 119	HANK WILLIAMS AS LUKE THE DRIFTER (10" LP, company sleeve, later p/s)	35/45
55	MGM MGM-D 137	HANK WILLIAMS MEMORIAL ALBUM (10" LP)	35
56	MGM MGM-D 144	MOANIN' THE BLUES (10" LP)	40
58	MGM MGM-D 150	SING ME A BLUE SONG (10" LP)	40
58	MGM MGM-D 154	THE IMMORTAL HANK WILLIAMS (10" LP)	40
59	MGM MGM-C 784	THE UNFORGETTABLE HANK WILLIAMS (LP)	25
60	MGM MGM-C 811	THE LONESOME SOUND OF HANK WILLIAMS (LP)	25
60	MGM MGM-C 834	WAIT FOR THE LIGHT TO SHINE (LP)	22
62	MGM MGM-C 893	ON STAGE (LP)	18
63	MGM MGM-C 956	THE SPIRIT OF HANK WILLIAMS (LP)	20
66	MGM MGM-C 8019	MAY YOU NEVER BE ALONE (LP)	18
66	MGM MGM-C 8020	IN MEMORY OF HANK WILLIAMS (LP)	16
66	MGM MGM-C 8021	I'M BLUE INSIDE (LP)	18
66	MGM MGM-C 8022	LUKE THE DRIFTER (LP)	15
66	MGM MGM-C 8023	THE MANY MOODS OF HANK WILLIAMS (LP)	16
67	MGM MGM-C(S) 8031	THE LEGEND LIVES ANEW (LP)	12
67	MGM MGM-C(S) 8038	MORE HANK WILLIAMS AND STRINGS (LP)	12
67	MGM MGM-C 8040	LOVE SONGS, COMEDY AND HYMNS (LP)	18
68	MGM MGM-C(S) 8057	I WON'T BE HOME NO MORE (LP)	12
68	MGM MGM-C(S) 8075	HANK WILLIAMS AND STRINGS VOL. 3 (LP)	12
70	MGM MGM-CS 8114	THE ESSENTIAL HANK WILLIAMS (LP)	12
74	MGM 2683 046	ON STAGE VOLUMES 1 & 2 (2-LP)	15
76	MGM 2353 128	LIVE AT THE GRAND OL' OPRY (LP)	12
79	World Records SM 551-556	THE LEGENDARY HANK WILLIAMS (6-LP box set)	25

(see also Audrey Williams)

HANK WILLIAMS & HANK WILLIAMS Jr.

65	MGM MGM-C 1008	SINGING TOGETHER (LP)	15

HANK WILLIAMS Jr.

63	MGM MGM 1223	Long Gone Lonesome Blues/Doesn't Anybody Know My Name	7
63	MGM MGM 1242	Goin' Steady With The Blues/Guess What, That's Right, She's Gone	6
64	MGM MGM 1254	Endless Sleep/My Bucket's Got A Hole In It	6
65	MGM MGM 1276	Mule Skinner Blues/I Went To All That Trouble	6
66	MGM MGM 1294	You're Ruinin' My Life/Pecos Jail	5
66	MGM MGM 1299	Cold Cold Heart/Is It That Fun To Heart Someone	5
66	MGM MGM 1316	Standing In The Shadows/It's Written All Over Your Face	5
64	MGM MGM-C 996	YOUR CHEATIN' HEART (LP)	12
67	MGM MGM-C(S) 8049	MY OWN WAY (LP)	10
70	MGM MGM-CS 8116	LIVE AT COBO HALL, DETROIT (LP)	10

(see also Connie Francis)

JABBO WILLIAMS

50	Jazz Collector L 51	Jab Blues/Pratt City (78)	8

JEANETTE WILLIAMS

69	Action ACT 4534	Stuff/You Gotta Come Through	7
70	Action ACT 4557	Hound Dog/I Can Feel A Heartbreak	7

(LITTLE) JERRY WILLIAMS

65	Cameo Parkway C 100	Baby You're My Everything/Just What Do You Plan To Do About It	25
74	Pye Disco Demand DDS 102	If You Ask Me/Yvonne (as Jerry Williams)	4

(see also Swamp Dogg, Brooks & Jerry)

JIMMY WILLIAMS

65	Atlantic AT 4042	Walking On Air/I'm So Lost	8

JOE WILLIAMS

59	Columbia SCD 2116	Party Blues (Parts 1 & 2)	5
60	Columbia DB 4560	Somebody/One Is A Lonesome Number	5
60	Columbia SEG 8001	EVERYDAY I HAVE THE BLUES (EP)	12
60	Columbia SEG 8016	JOE SINGS THE BLUES (EP)	12
56	London HB-C 1065	JOE WILLIAMS SINGS (10" LP)	25
57	HMV CLP 1109	THE GREATEST (LP)	20
58	Columbia 33SX 1087	A MAN AIN'T SUPPOSED TO CRY (LP)	20
60	Columbia 33SX 1229	JOE WILLIAMS SINGS ABOUT YOU (LP, also stereo SCX 3308)	12/15
60	Columbia 33SX 1253	THAT KIND OF WOMAN (LP, also stereo SCX 3325)	12/15

(see also Count Basie)

JOHN WILLIAMS (U.K.)

67	Columbia DB 8128	She's That Kind Of Woman/My Ways Are Set	10
67	Columbia DB 8251	Flowers In Your Hair/Can't Find Time For Anything Now	10
67	Columbia SX 6169	JOHN WILLIAMS (LP)	100

(see also Maureeny Wishfull)

JOHN WILLIAMS (U.K.)

84	Island IS 155	Paul McCartney's Theme From 'The Honorary Consul'/Clara's Theme (p/s)	12

JOHN WILLIAMS ORCHESTRA (U.S.)

76	MCA MCA 220	'Jaws' Theme (Parts 1 & 2)	5
78	Arista ARIST 177	'Close Encounters Of The Third Kind' (Parts 1 & 2) (p/s)	5
82	MCA MCA 800	Theme From 'E.T.'/Over The Moon (p/s)	5

John WILLIAMS Orchestra

66	Stateside S(S)L 10187	HOW TO STEAL A MILLION (LP)	40
83	MCA MCA 70000	E.T. — THE EXTRA TERRESTRIAL (LP, box set with booklet & poster)	75
83	MCA CAC 70000	E.T. — THE EXTRA TERRESTRIAL (cassette, box set with booklet & poster)	40

JOHNNY WILLIAMS

73	Epic S EPC 1007	Slow Motion/Shall We Gather By The Water	5
73	Epic S EPC 1547	Put It In Motion/It's So Wonderful	5
73	Contempo C 20	Just A Little Misunderstanding/Your Love Controls My Mind	5

KENNETH WILLIAMS

63	Decca DFE 8548	EXTRACTS FROM PIECES OF EIGHT AND ONE OVER THE EIGHT (EP)	10
66	Decca DFE 8671	KENNETH WILLIAMS IN SEASON (EP)	12
67	Decca LK 4856	ON PLEASURE BENT (LP)	20
70	Regal Starline SRS 5034	THE BEST OF RAMBLING SYD RUMPO (LP)	12
70	Decca PA/SPA 64	THE WORLD OF KENNETH WILLIAMS (LP, mono/stereo)	15

(see also Rambling Syd Rumpo, Tony Hancock)

KENNY WILLIAMS

77	Decca FR 13731	You're Fabulous Babe/Give Me My Heart	6

LARRY WILLIAMS

57	London HLN 8472	Short Fat Fannie/High School Dance	30
57	London HLN 8472	Short Fat Fannie/High School Dance (78)	12
58	London HLN 8532	Bony Moronie/You Bug Me Baby	25
58	London HLN 8532	Bony Moronie/You Bug Me Baby (78)	10
58	London HLU 8604	Dizzy Miss Lizzy/Slow Down	35
58	London HLU 8604	Dizzy Miss Lizzy/Slow Down (78)	30
59	London HLU 8844	She Said "Yeah"/Bad Boy	25
59	London HLU 8844	She Said "Yeah"/Bad Boy (78)	40
60	London HLU 8911	I Can't Stop Loving You/Steal A Little Kiss	20
60	London HLU 8911	I Can't Stop Loving You/Steal A Little Kiss (78)	60
60	London HLM 9053	Baby, Baby/Get Ready	20
65	Sue WI 371	Strange/Call On Me	15
65	Sue WI 381	Turn On Your Lovelight/Dizzy Miss Lizzy	15
68	MGM MGM 1447	Shake Your Body Girl/Love, I Can't Seem To Find It	8
59	London RE-U 1213	LARRY WILLIAMS (EP)	100
65	Sue ILP 922	LARRY WILLIAMS ON STAGE (LP)	50
70s	Specialty SNTF 5025	SLOW DOWN (LP)	12

LARRY WILLIAMS & JOHNNY 'GUITAR' WATSON

65	Decca F 12151	Sweet Little Baby/Slow Down	15
67	Columbia DB 8140	Mercy, Mercy, Mercy/A Quitter Never Wins	35
76	Epic EPC 4421	Too Late/Two For The Price Of One	6
65	Decca LK 4691	THE LARRY WILLIAMS SHOW (LP, with Stormsville Shakers)	50

(see also Johnny 'Guitar' Watson, Philip Goodhand-Tait [& Stormville Shakers])

LENNY WILLIAMS

78	ABC 4198	Choosing You/Trust In Me	4

LEONA WILLIAMS

74	Fountain FB 303	LEONA WILLIAMS AND HER DIXIE BAND (LP)	12

LEW WILLIAMS

50s	London (no cat. no.)	Cat Talk (1-sided, orange label demo-only)	40

LLOYD WILLIAMS

66	Doctor Bird DB 1051	Sad World/TOMMY McCOOK'S BAND: A Little Bit Of Heaven	15
68	Treasure Isle TI 7029	Funky Beat/Goodbye Baby	15
68	Doctor Bird DB 1135	Wonderful World (with Tommy McCook)/TOMMY McCOOK & SUPERSONICS: Mad Mad World	15
70	Bamboo BAM 41	I'm In Love With You/Little Girl	10

LORETTA WILLIAMS

66	Atlantic 584 032	Baby Cakes/I'm Missing You	20

LUTHER WILLIAMS ORCHESTRA

61	Limbo XL 101	Early In The Morning/Little Vilma	5
61	Melodisc MLP 12-125	TROPICAL RHYTHMS OF JAMAICA (LP)	15

MARY LOU WILLIAMS

53	London L 1174	Laughing Rag/Rag Of Rags (78)	10
54	Felsted ED 82011	Autumn In New York/En Ce Tempa-La (78)	10
64	Sue WI 311	Chuck-A-Lunk Jug (Parts 1 & 2)	25
55	Vogue EPV 1042	DON CARLOS MEETS MARY LOU WILLIAMS (EP)	10
56	Parlophone GEP 8567	AT THE PIANO (EP)	8
56	Columbia SEG 7608	MARY LOU WILLIAMS (EP)	8
50s	Esquire EP 66	MARY LOU WILLIAMS QUARTET (EP)	12
53	Vogue LDE 022	PLAYS IN LONDON (10" LP)	20
54	Esquire 20-026	PIANO PANORAMA (10" LP)	20
55	Felsted EDL 87012	IN PARIS (10" LP)	18

MAURICE WILLIAMS (& ZODIACS)

60	Top Rank JAR 526	Stay/Do You Believe (as Maurice Williams & Zodiacs)	10
61	Top Rank JAR 550	I Remember/Always	12
61	Top Rank JAR 563	Come Along/Do I	15
61	Top Rank JKP 3006	STAY WITH MAURICE WILLIAMS & THE ZODIACS (EP)	125

(see also Gladiolas)

MIKE WILLIAMS

66	Atlantic 584 027	Lonely Soldier/If This Isn't Love	8

OTIS WILLIAMS & HIS CHARMS

55	Parlophone CMSP 36	Ivory Tower/In Paradise (export issue)	275
56	Parlophone MSP 6239	Ivory Tower/In Paradise	425
56	Parlophone R 4175	Ivory Tower/In Paradise (78)	18

ROBBIE WILLIAMS

56	Parlophone R 4210	One Night Only/It's All Over	325
56	Parlophone R 4210	One Night Only/It's All Over (78)	25
57	Parlophone R 4293	Walkin' After Midnight/I'm Waiting Just For You	400
57	Parlophone R 4293	Walkin' After Midnight/I'm Waiting Just For You (78)	60
58	Parlophone R 4495	The Secret/Don't Wake Up The Kids	60
58	Parlophone R 4495	The Secret/Don't Wake Up The Kids (78)	80
62	Parlophone R 4860	The Secret/Two Hearts	50

(see also Charms)

PAT WILLIAMS ORCHESTRA
74	Capitol CL 15797	Police Story Theme/Magician Theme	5

PAUL WILLIAMS
73	Sonet SNTF 654	DELTA BLUES SINGER (LP)	15

PAUL WILLIAMS
72	A&M AMS 889	Old Fashioned Love Song/Waking Up Alone	5
72	A&M AMS 7006	Simple Man/My Love And I	5
72	A&M AMLH 64327	JUST AN OLD FASHIONED LOVE SONG (LP, with booklet)	12
72	A&M AMLH 64367	LIFE GOES ON (LP)	12

PAUL WILLIAMS BIG ROLL BAND/SET
64	Columbia DB 7421	Gin House/Rockin' Chair (as Paul Williams Big Roll Band)	18
65	Columbia DB 7768	The Many Faces Of Love/Jumpback (as Paul Williams & Zoot Money Band)	20
68	Decca F 12844	My Sly Sadie/Stop The Wedding (as Paul Williams Set)	10

(see also Zoot Money's Big Roll Band, John Mayall's Bluesbreakers, Alan Price [Set], Juicy Lucy)

PAULETTE WILLIAMS
77	Fantasy FTC 140	Dancin'/What's Left To Say	4

PAULINE WILLIAMS
73	Explosion EX 2084	My Island/My Island (Version)	4

POOR JOE WILLIAMS
60	Collector JEN 3	A MAN SINGS THE BLUES (EP)	15
60	Collector JEN 4	A MAN SINGS THE BLUES VOL. 2 (EP)	15

(see also Big Joe Williams)

RANNY/RONNY WILLIAMS
69	Bullet BU 426	Summer Place (with Hippy Boys)/Big Boy	7
69	Gas GAS 120	Throw Me Corn (as Ronny Williams)/HIPPY BOYS: Temptation	7
69	Unity UN 526	Ambitious Beggar/Pepper Seed	7
70	Punch PH 32	Smile/Musical I.D.	7

(see also Winston Reed)

RITA WILLIAMS
58	Oriole CB 1417	Looking For Someone To Love/Love Me Forever	8
58	Oriole CB 1417	Looking For Someone To Love/Love Me Forever (78)	8

ROBBIE WILLIAMS
97	Chrysalis CDCHR 6127	LIFE THRU A LENS (CD with hidden track)	15
98	Chrysalis 4978372	I'VE BEEN EXPECTING (CD with 2 hidden tracks)	15

PROMOS
96	RCA FREELX 1	Freedom '96 (Radio Edit)/Freedom '96 (Full Length Version) (jukebox issue)	8

MINT VALUE £

96	RCA PROPERDJ 1	Freedom '96 (Radio Edit)/Freedom '96 (Full Length Version)	
		(CD, test pressing, no text on disc)	20
97	Chrysalis CHSLH 5055	Old Before I Die/Making Plans For Nigel (jukebox issue)	10
97	Chrysalis CDCHSDJ 5055	Old Before I Die (CD, withdrawn, different sleeve)	12
97	Chrysalis CHSLH 5063	Lazy Days/Teenage Millionaire (jukebox issue)	8
97	Chrysalis CDCHSDJ 5063	Lazy Days (CD)	8
97	Chrysalis CHSLH 5068	South Of The Border/Cheap Love Song (jukebox issue)	8
97	Chrysalis 12CHSDJ 5068	South Of The Border (remixes) (12", stickered black sleeve)	10
97	Chrysalis 12CHSDJS 5068	South Of The Border (remixes) (12", stickered white sleeve)	10
97	Chrysalis CDCHSDJ 5072	Angels (Edit) (CD)	10
97	Chrysalis CDCHSDJS 5072	Angels/Walk This Sleigh (CD)	10
98	Chrysalis 12CHSDJD 5080	Let Me Entertain You (remixes) (12", double-pack)	20
98	Chrysalis CDCHSDJ 5080	Let Me Entertain You (CD)	10
98	Chrysalis CHSCH 5099	Millennium/Angels (jukebox issue)	8
98	Chrysalis CDCHSDJ 5099	Millennium (CD, title sleeve)	10
98	Chrysalis CDCHSDJ 5100	No Regrets (Album version)/No Regrets (edit)	10
99	Chrysalis CHSLH 5107	Strong/Antmusic (jukebox issue)	8
99	Chrysalis CDCHSDJ 5107	Strong (CD, green title sleeve)	10
99	Chrysalis CDCHSDJ 5122	She's The One/It's Only Us (CD, grey title sleeve)	10
99	Chrysalis CDCHSDJX 5122	It's Only Us/She's The One (CD, grey title sleeve)	10
97	Chrysalis RWEPK 01	THE EPK CD (interview and excerpts from "Life Thru A Lens")	30
98	Chrysalis CDPP 080	I'VE BEEN EXPECTING YOU (metal case with album CD, interview disc in	
		digipak, EPK video in p/s, gold press release and photos)	200

(see also Take That)

ROBERT PETE WILLIAMS
63	'77' LA 12-17	THOSE PRISON BLUES (LP)	20
70s	Blues Beacon 1932 101ST	SUGAR FARM (LP)	15
72	Saydisc AMS 2002	ROBERT PETE WILLIAMS (LP)	15
73	Sonet SNTF 649	LEGACY OF THE BLUES (LP)	12

ROBERT PETE WILLIAMS/ROOSEVELT SYKES
67	'77' LEU 12-50	BLUES FROM THE BOTTOM (LP)	15

(see also Roosevelt Sykes)

ROBERT WILLIAMS
90	Blast First FU8	CHROME, FIRE AND SMOKE (2-LP, picture disc, 1000 only)	35

ROGER WILLIAMS
55	London HLU 8214	Autumn Leaves/Take Care	15
56	London HLU 8341	Two Different Worlds (with Jane Morgan)/I'll Always Walk With You	18
56	London HLU 8341	Two Different Worlds (with Jane Morgan)/I'll Always Walk With You (78)	8
57	London HLU 8379	Anastasia/A Serenade For Joy	10
57	London HLR 8422	Almost Paradise/For The First Time I've Fallen In Love	8
57	London HLR 8516	Till/Big Town	7
58	London HLR 8572	Arrivederci Roma/The Sentimental Touch	7
58	London HLR 8643	Indiscreet/Young And Warm And Wonderful	6
58	London HLR 8690	Near You/The Merry Widow Waltz	6
58	London HLR 8758	The World Outside (Warsaw Concerto)/Piano Concerto No. 1 (Tchaikovsky)	5
59	London HLR 8820	The Key To The Kingdom/Dearer Than Dear	5
59	London HLR 8820	The Key To The Kingdom/Dearer Than Dear (78)	8
59	London HLR 8857	Mockin' Bird Hill/Memories Are Made Of This	6
59	London HLR 8857	Mockin' Bird Hill/Memories Are Made Of This (78)	10
59	London HLR 8986	Mary's Boy Child/O Mio Babbino Caro (Oh! My Beloved Father)	5
59	London HLR 8986	Mary's Boy Child/O Mio Babbino Caro (Oh! My Beloved Father) (78)	15
57	London RE-R 1090	AT THE PIANO (EP)	8
57	London RE-R 1107	AT THE PIANO — VOL. 2 (EP)	8
58	London RE-R 1131	MUSIC OF THE MASTERS (EP)	8
57	London HA-R 2057	SONGS OF THE FABULOUS FIFTIES VOL. 1 (LP)	15
57	London HA-R 2058	SONGS OF THE FABULOUS FIFTIES VOL. 2 (LP)	15
58	London HA-R 2089	THE BOY NEXT DOOR (LP)	12
58	London HA-R 2096	SONGS OF THE FABULOUS FORTIES VOL. 1 (LP, stereo SAH-R 6035)	12
58	London HA-R 2097	SONGS OF THE FABULOUS FORTIES VOL. 2 (LP, stereo SAH-R 6036)	12

(see also Jane Morgan)

SAM WILLIAMS
78	Grapevine GRP 116	Love Slipped Thru' My Fingers/TOWANDA BARNES: You Don't Mean It	6

SMITTY WILLIAMS
62	MGM MGM 1167	The Cure/Oh Seymour	8

SONNY WILLIAMS
59	London HLD 8931	Bye Bye Baby Goodbye/Lucky Linda	25
59	London HLD 8931	Bye Bye Baby Goodbye/Lucky Linda (78)	40

SPARKIE WILLIAMS (1958 Champion Talking Budgerigar)
58	Parlophone R 4475	Sparkie Williams — Jailbird/Sparkie The Fiddle	7

SYLVIAN WILLIAMS
69	Big Shot BI 532	Sweeter Than Honey/Son Of Reggae	6
69	Big Shot BI 533	This Old Man/When Morning Comes	6

TEX WILLIAMS
50	Capitol CL 13312	Birmingham Bounce/Artistry In Western Swing (78)	8
50	Capitol CL 13424	Talking Boogie/Tamburitza Boogie (with His Western Caravan) (78)	8
51	Capitol CL 13217	Ham 'N Eggs/Cowpuncher's Waltz (78)	8
54	Brunswick 05327	River No Return/Dawn In The Meadow	15
54	Brunswick 05341	This Ole House (with Rex Allen)/They Were Doin' The Mambo	15
55	Brunswick 05393	Money/If You'd Believe Me	12
56	Brunswick 05516	Be Sure You're Right (And Then Go Ahead)/Old Betsy	7

MINT VALUE £

57	Brunswick 05684	Talkin' To The Blues/Every Night (with Anita Kerr Singers)	12
60	Top Rank JAR 330	The Keeper Of Boothill/Bummin' Around	10
55	Brunswick OE 9147	ALL THE GREATS (EP)	15
61	Capitol (S)T 1463	SMOKE, SMOKE, SMOKE! (LP)	15

(see also Roberta Lee, Rex Allen)

TONY WILLIAMS

61	Reprise RS 20019	Sleepless Nights/Mandolino Mandolino	8
61	Reprise RS 20030	My Prayer/Miracle	8
63	Philips BF 1282	How Come/When I Had You	8
60	Mercury MMC 14027	A GIRL IS A GIRL IS A GIRL (LP)	30
61	Reprise R 6001/	SINGS HIS GREATEST HITS (LP, mono/stereo)	20/18
	ST R9 6006		

(see also Platters, Linda Hayes)

TONY WILLIAMS' LIFETIME

69	Polydor 583 574	EMERGENCY! (2-LP, gatefold sleeve)	40
70	Polydor 2425 019	TURN IT OVER (LP)	20
71	Polydor 2425 065	EGO (LP)	12

(see also Lifetime, John McLaughlin)

TONY WILLIAMS

| 78 | CBS 83338 | JOY OF FLYING (LP) | 10 |

WINSTON WILLIAMS

70	Jackpot JP 733	D.J.'s Choice/SLIM SMITH: Can't Do Without It (B-side actually titled "Lesson/Story Of Love" by Uniques)	8
70	Jackpot JP 743	The People's Choice/BOBBY JAMES: Let Me Go Girl	8
71	Jackpot JP 757	Love Version/SLIM SMITH: Ball Of Confusion	8

BOBBY WILLIAMSON

| 54 | HMV 7MC 26 | Sh-Boom/Love March (export issue) | 12 |

CLAUDE WILLIAMSON

| 54 | Capitol KC 65003 | All God's Chillun Got Rhythm/Woody 'N' You | 6 |

DUDLEY WILLIAMSON

| 67 | Doctor Bird DB 1117 | Coming On The Scene/Anything You Want | 25 |

(see also Dudley & Attractions)

ROBIN WILLIAMSON

| 72 | Island HELP 2 | MYRRH (LP) | 15 |
| 78 | Criminal STEAL 4 | AMERICAN STONEHENGE (LP) | 12 |

(see also Incredible String Band, Vashti Bunyan)

SONNY BOY WILLIAMSON (I)/BIG BILL BROONZY

| 65 | RCA Victor RD 7685 | BIG BILL BROONZY/SONNY BOY WILLIAMSON (LP) | 50 |

SONNY BOY WILLIAMSON (I)

| 69 | Matchbox SDR 169 | SONNY BOY AND HIS PALS (LP) | 25 |
| 70 | RCA Intl. INTS 1088 | BLUEBIRD BLUES (LP) | 15 |

SONNY BOY WILLIAMSON (II)

63	Pye International 7N 25191	Help Me/Bye Bye Bird	12
64	Pye International 7N 25268	Lonesome Cabin/The Goat	12
65	Sue WI 365	No Nights By Myself/Boppin' With Sonny Boy	18
66	Chess CRS 8030	Bring It On Home/Down Child	10
66	Blue Horizon 45-1008	From The Bottom/Empty Bedroom	60
64	Pye Intl. NEP 44037	SONNY BOY WILLIAMSON (EP)	20
65	Chess CRE 6001	HELP ME (EP)	25
66	Chess CRE 6013	IN MEMORIAM (EP)	25
66	Chess CRE 6018	REAL FOLK BLUES VOL. 2 (EP)	22
64	Pye Intl. NPL 28036	DOWN AND OUT BLUES (LP)	30
64	Storyville SLP 158	PORTRAITS IN BLUES, VOL. 4 (LP)	25
65	Chess CRL 4510	IN MEMORIAM (LP)	25
66	Storyville SLP 170	THE BLUES OF SONNY BOY WILLIAMSON (LP)	25
66	Fontana 670 158	PORTRAITS IN BLUES, VOL. 4 (LP, reissue)	18
67	Storyville 671 170	THE BLUES OF SONNY BOY WILLIAMSON (LP, reissue)	18
67	Marble Arch MAL 662	DOWN AND OUT BLUES (LP, reissue)	12
68	Marmalade 607/608 004	DON'T SEND ME NO FLOWERS (LP, with Brian Auger & Jimmy Page)	40
74	Rarity RLP 1	THE LAST SESSIONS — 1963 (LP)	25

(see also Ottilie Patterson)

SONNY BOY WILLIAMSON (II) & YARDBIRDS

65	Fontana TL 5277	SONNY BOY WILLIAMSON & THE YARDBIRDS (LP)	100
68	Fontana SFJL 960	SONNY BOY WILLIAMSON & THE YARDBIRDS (LP, reissue, different sleeve)	30
71	Philips 6435 011	SONNY BOY WILLIAMSON & THE YARDBIRDS (LP, 2nd reissue)	15

(see also Yardbirds, Brian Auger)

STU WILLIAMSON

| 56 | London Jazz LZ-N 14030 | SAPPHIRE (10" LP) | 15 |

WILLIE (Francis) & LLOYD (Lindsay)

| 71 | Camel CA 80 | Marcus Is Alive/GLADIATORS: Freedom Train | 7 |

(see also Willie Francis)

WILLIE & WHEELS

| 77 | ABC ABC 4184 | Skateboard Craze/Do What You Did (p/s) | 7 |

FOY WILLING & THE RIDERS OF THE PURPLE SAGE

| 59 | Columbia SEG 7834 | COWBOY NUMBER 1 (EP) | 8 |
| 59 | Columbia SEG 7855 | COWBOY NUMBER 2 (EP) | 8 |

DORIS WILLINGHAM
69	Jay Boy BOY 1	You Can't Do That/Lost Again	10

CHUCK WILLIS
57	London HLE 8444	C.C. Rider/Ease The Pain	60
57	London HLE 8444	C.C. Rider/Ease The Pain (78)	40
57	London HLE 8489	That Train Has Gone/Love Me Cherry	50
57	London HLE 8489	That Train Has Gone/Love Me Cherry (78)	25
58	London HLE 8595	Betty And Dupree/My Crying Eyes	50
58	London HLE 8595	Betty And Dupree/My Crying Eyes (78)	25
58	London HLE 8635	What Am I Living For/Hang Up My Rock And Roll Shoes	40
58	London HLE 8635	What Am I Living For/Hang Up My Rock And Roll Shoes (78)	30
58	London HL 7039	What Am I Living For/Hang Up My Rock And Roll Shoes (export issue)	20
59	London HLE 8818	My Life/Thunder And Lightning	35
59	London HLE 8818	My Life/Thunder And Lightning (78)	40
59	Fontana TFE 17138	CHUCK WILLIS WAILS (EP)	225
65	Atlantic ATL 5003	I REMEMBER CHUCK WILLIS (LP)	50
69	Atlantic 588 145	I REMEMBER CHUCK WILLIS (LP, reissue)	18

HAL WILLIS
68	President PT 197	The Lumberjack/Klondike Mike	10

LLOYD WILLIS
70	Pressure Beat PR 5502	Mad Rooster (Parts 1 & 2)/As Far As I Can See (actually "The Wicked Must Survive" by Reggae Boys)	8
70	Unity UN 543	Ivan Hitler The Conqueror/The Splice	15

(see also Dynamic Gang, Urie Aldridge)

RALPH WILLIS
54	Esquire 10-370	Lazy Woman Blues/Goodbye Blues (78)	25
54	Esquire 10-380	Old Home Blues/Salty Dog (78)	25
61	Esquire EP 241	RALPH WILLIS (EP)	40
60s	XX MIN 703	RALPH WILLIS (EP)	15
60s	XX MIN 711	RALPH WILLIS (EP)	15

SLIM WILLIS
65	R&B MRB 5004	Running Around/No Feeling For You	18

TIMMY WILLIS
72	United Artists UP 35352	Mr. Soul Satisfaction/I'm Wondering	4
73	Epic EPC 1309	Give Me A Little Sign/Don't Want To Set Me Free	4

WILLIS BROTHERS
67	London HLB 10132	Bob/Show Her Lots Of Gold	6

NEVILLE WILLOUGHBY
72	Duke DU 140	Wheel And Tun Me/Hey Mama	4

(see also Neville, Whistling Willie)

WILLOWS
56	London HLU 8290	Church Bells May Ring/Baby Tell Me	900
56	London HLU 8290	Church Bells May Ring/Baby Tell Me (78)	125

(see also Tony Middleton)

BOB WILLS & HIS TEXAS PLAYBOYS
51	MGM MGM 455	'Tater Pie/Ida Red Likes The Boogie (78)	12
53	MGM MGM 613	Snatchin' And Grabbin'/I Want To Be Wanted (78)	12

BOB WILLS with TOMMY DUNCAN
60	London HL 7102	Heart To Heart Talk/What's The Matter With The Mill (export issue)	12

MICK WILLS
88	Woronzow WOO 9	FERN HILL (LP)	18
97	Acme AC 8013LP	THE MAGIC GARDEN (LP, foldover gatefold sleeve in poly bag)	12

VIOLA WILLS
68	President PT 108	Lost Without The Love Of My Guy/I Got Love	6
68	President PT 150	Together Forever/Don't Kiss Me Hello And Mean Goodbye	6
68	President PT 152	I've Got To Have All Of You/Night Scene	5
68	President PT 154	You're Out Of My Mind/Any Time	5
74	Goodear EAR 103	Run To The Nearest Exit/Day In The Life Of A Woman	5
86	Streetwave MKHAN 66	Dare To Dream/Both Sides Now (12", p/s)	7
74	Goodear EARLH 5002	SOFT CENTRES (LP)	12

WILMER & DUKES
68	Action ACT 4500	Give Me One More Chance/Get It	8

ADA WILSON
79	Ellie Jay EJSP 9288	In The Quiet Of My Room/I'm In Control Here (p/s)	10
80	Barn BARN 012	In The Quiet Of My Room/I'm In Control Here (no p/s, reissue)	5
80	Rockburgh ROCS 224	Head In The Clouds/It Doesn't Have To Be (p/s, with Keeping Dark)	4
85	Thin Sliced TSR 5	In The Quiet Of My Room (New Version)/In The Quiet Of My Room (p/s)	4

(see also Strangeways)

AL WILSON
68	Liberty LBF 15044	Do What You Gotta Do/Now I Know What Love Is	15
68	Liberty LBF 15121	The Snake/Who Could Be Lovin' You	15
69	Liberty LBF 15236	Shake Me Wake Me/I Stand Accused	5
69	Liberty LBF 15257	Lodi/By The Time I Get To Phoenix	5
75	Bell BLL 1436	The Snake/Willoughby Brook	5
69	Liberty LBS 83173	SEARCHING FOR THE DOLPHINS (LP)	18
74	Bell BELLS 247	LA LA PEACE SONG (LP)	12

BRIAN WILSON (& MIKE LOVE)

66	Capitol CL 15438	Caroline, No/Summer Means New Love	15
67	Capitol CL 15513	Gettin' Hungry/Devoted To You (as Brian Wilson & Mike Love)	12
88	Sire W 7814 CD	Love And Mercy (LP Version)/One For The Boys (LP Version)/	
		He Couldn't Get His Poor Old Body To Move (3" CD)	7
88	Sire W 7787 CD	Night Time (LP Version)/One For The Boys/	
		Being With The One You Love (3" CD)	7

(see also Beach Boys, Date With Soul, American Spring)

CLIVE WILSON

| 64 | R&B JB 144 | Mango Tree/Midnight In Chicago | 15 |

DELROY WILSON

63	Island WI 097	Naughty People/I Shall Not Remove	18
63	Island WI 103	One, Two, Three/Back Biter	18
63	Island WI 116	You Bend My Love/Can't You See	18
63	R&B JB 108	Lion Of Judah/Joe Liges	15
63	R&B JB 128	Prince Pharoah/Don't Believe Him	15
63	R&B JB 132	Squeeze Your Toe/Sugar Pie	15
64	Black Swan WI 405	Spit In The Sky/Voodoo Man	18
64	Black Swan WI 420	Goodbye/Treat Me Good	18
64	R&B JB 148	Lover Mouth/Every Mouth Must Be Fed	15
64	R&B JB 168	Sammy Dead/CYNTHIA & ARCHIE: Every Beat	15
65	Island WI 205	Pick Up The Pieces/Oppression	18
66	Doctor Bird DB 1022	Give Me A Chance/(It's) Impossible	15
66	Island WI 3013	Dancing Mood/SOUL BROTHERS: More And More	18
67	Island WI 3033	Riding For A Fall/Got To Change Your Ways	18
67	Island WI 3037	Ungrateful Baby/ROY RICHARDS: Hopeful Village Ska	18
67	Island WI 3039	Close To Me/SOUL BROTHERS: Hi-Life	18
67	Island WI 3050	Get Ready/ROY RICHARDS: Port-O-Jam	18
67	Studio One SO 2009	Won't You Come Home Baby/PETER & HORTENSE: I've Been Lonely	18
67	Studio One SO 2014	Mother Word/HEPTONES: Fat Girl	18
67	Studio One SO 2019	Never Conquer/Run For Your Life	18
67	Studio One SO 2031	I'm Not A King/HEPTONES: Take Me (B-side actually by Soul Vendors)	18
68	Island WI 3099	This Old Heart Of Mine/GLEN ADAMS: Grab A Girl	25
68	Island WI 3127	Once Upon A Time/I Want To Love You (B-side actually with Stranger Cole)	20
68	Coxsone CS 7064	True Believer/MARSHALL WILLIAMS: College Girl	20
68	Studio One SO 2040	Mr. D.J./HEPTONES: Tripe Girl	18
68	Studio One SO 2046	Rain From The Skies/How Can I Love Someone	18
68	Studio One SO 2057	Feel Good all Over/I Like The Way You Walk	18
69	Studio One SO 2074	Easy Snappin'/WEBBER SISTERS: Come On	18
69	High Note HS 011	Put Yourself In My Place/It Hurts	8
69	High Note HS 015	I'm The One Who Loves You/AFROTONES: If I'm In A Corner	8
69	High Note HS 022	Your Number One/I've Tried My Best	8
69	High Note HS 028	Good To Me/What Do You Want Me To Do	8
69	Camel CA 15	Sad Mood (actually by Ken Parker)/STRANGER COLE: Give It To Me	7
70	Trojan TR 7740	Show Me The Way/BEVERLEY'S ALLSTARS: Version	7
70	Trojan TR 7769	Gave You My Love/BEVERLEY'S ALLSTARS: Version	6
70	Summit SUM 8503	Got To Get Away/BEVERLEY'S ALLSTARS: Version	6
70	Joe JRS 11	Don't Play That Song (with Reaction)/BOSS ALL STARS: Just One Look	7
70	Unity UN 559	Drink Wine, Everybody/Someone To Call My Own	6
71	Smash SMA 2317	I Am Trying/COLLINS ALLSTARS: Version	6
71	Smash SMA 2318	Satisfaction/Satisfaction Version (B-side with Alton Ellis)	7
71	Smash SMA 2323	What It Was/LLOYD CLARKE: Chicken Thief	7
71	Jackpot JP 763	Better Must Come/BUNNY LEE'S ALLSTARS: Better Must Come — Version	7
71	Jackpot JP 769	Cool Operator/I'm Yours	6
71	Jackpot JP 770	Try Again/AGGROVATORS: Try Again — Version	6
71	Jackpot JP 780	Keep Your Love Strong/Nice To Be Near	6
71	Jackpot JP 781	Peace And Love/JEFF BARNES: Who's Your Brother	6
71	Banana BA 333	Just Because Of You/I Love You Madly	8
72	Banana BA 367	You Keep On Running (& U Roy)/LARRY'S ALL STARS: Running Version	6
72	Bullet BU 520	Hear Come The Heartaches (actually "Here Come The Heartaches")/	
		You'll Be Sorry	6
72	Jackpot JP 792	Who Cares/HUGH ROY JUNIOR: Who Cares — Version	6
72	Jackpot JP 795	The Same Old Song/Stay By Me	6
72	Jackpot JP 804	Cheer Up/Loving You	5
72	Spur SP 2	Adis Ababa/KEITH HUDSON: Rudie Hot Stuff	25
73	Downtown DT 501	Pretty Girl/JOE GIBBS & PROFESSIONALS: Face Girl	10
73	Grape GR 3038	Can I Change My Mind/Just Because	6
73	Green Door GD 4060	Ain't That Peculiar/What Is Man	8
73	Smash SMA 2336	Trying To Wreck My Life/Live And Learn	15
74	Faith FA 006	Love Got Me Doing Things/PHIL PRATT ALL STARS: Version	4
74	Harry J. HJ 6667	What Will Happen To The Youth Of Today/Baby Don't Do It	5
75	Fab FAB 266	Dancing Mood/Version	8
64	R&B JBL 1112	I SHALL NOT REMOVE (LP)	100
68	Coxsone CSL 8016	GOOD ALL OVER (LP)	90
72	Trojan TRLS 44	BETTER MUST COME (LP)	18
73	Big Shot BILP 102	CAPTIVITY (LP)	18

(see also Hortense & Delroy, Joe Liges, Roy Richards, Soul Brothers, Dennis Alcapone, Stranger Cole, Uniques, Soul Vendors)

DENNIS WILSON (& RUMBO)

70	Stateside SS 2184	Sound Of Free/Lady (as Dennis Wilson & Rumbo)	35
77	Caribou CRB 5663	River Song/Farewell My Friend	5
77	Caribou CRB 81672	PACIFIC OCEAN BLUE (LP, gatefold sleeve, some on blue vinyl)	18/12

(see also Beach Boys)

MINT VALUE £

DOYLE WILSON with JIMMY LACEY & BAND
| 58 | Vogue Pop V 9117 | Hey-Hey/You're The One For Me | 400 |
| 58 | Vogue Pop V 9117 | Hey-Hey/You're The One For Me (78) | 120 |

EDDIE WILSON
| 62 | Oriole CB 1780 | Dankeschoen-Bitteschoen-Wiederschoen/Rheinlaender Waltz | 8 |

EDDIE WILSON
| 69 | Action ACT 4536 | Shing-A-Ling Stroll/Don't Kick The Teenager Around | 8 |
| 70 | Action ACT 4555 | Get Out On The Street/Must Be Love | 6 |

EDITH WILSON
| 60s | Fountain FB 302 | 1921-1922 WITH JOHNNY DUNN'S JAZZHOUNDS (LP) | 15 |

ERNEST ('SOUL') WILSON
67	Studio One SO 2032	Money Worries/SOUL VENDORS: Pe Da Pa	20
68	Studio One SO 2058	If I Were A Carpenter/SOUL VENDORS: Frozen Soul	30
68	Coxsone CS 7044	Storybook Children (as Ernest 'Soul' Wilson)/LITTLE FREDDIE:	
		After Laughter (B-side actually by Freddie McGregor)	25
68	Coxsone CS 7059	Undying Love/SOUL VENDORS: Tropic Isle	20
69	Amalgamated AMG 837	Private Number/GLEN ADAMS: She's So Fine	10
69	Crab CRAB 9	Private Number/Another Chance	6
69	Crab CRAB 17	Freedom Train/STRANGER COLE: You Should Never Have To Come	7
69	Crab CRAB 21	Just Once In My Life (with Freddy)/GLEN ADAMS: Mighty Organ	6
76	Fab FAB 280	Storybook Children/SOUND DIMENSION: Version	8

(see also Tinga & Ernest)

ERNEST WILSON & FREDDY (McGregor)
70	Crab CRAB 45	Sentimental Man/It's A Lie	6
70	Unity UN 564	Love Makes The World Go Round/Love (Version Instrumental)	6
71	Gas GAS 168	What You Gonna Do About It/DOBBY DOBSON: Halfway To Paradise	6
71	Jackpot JP 765	Let Them Talk/The Truth Hurts	6

FRANK WILSON
| 79 | Tamla Motown TMG 1170 | Do I Love You (Indeed I Do)/Sweeter As The Days Go By (promos in p/s) | 20/15 |

FRANK WILSON & CAVALIERS
| 64 | Fontana TF 505 | Last Kiss/That's How Much I Love You | 12 |

GADDY WILSON
| 60 | Philips PB 980 | Nothin' At Night/I'll Never Be Myself Again (78) | 15 |

GARLAND WILSON
| 53 | HMV 7M 122 | Just You, Just Me/Sweet Georgia Brown | 6 |

JACK WILSON QUARTET
| 64 | London HA-K/SH-K 8170 | THE JACK WILSON QUARTET (LP, featuring Roy Ayers) | 25 |
| 66 | Vocalion LAE-L 603 | RAMBLIN' (LP) | 30 |

(see also Roy Ayers)

JACKIE WILSON
78s
57	Vogue Coral Q 72290	Reet Petite/By The Light Of The Silvery Moon (78)	12
57	Coral Q 72290	Reet Petite/By The Light Of The Silvery Moon (78, 2nd pressing)	10
58	Coral Q 72306	To Be Loved/Come Back To Me (78)	12
58	Coral Q 72332	I'm Wanderin'/As Long As I Live (78)	20
58	Coral Q 72338	We Have Love/Singing A Song (78)	20
58	Coral Q 72347	Lonely Teardrops/In The Blue Of The Evening (78)	50
59	Coral Q 72366	That's Why/Love Is All (78)	50
59	Coral Q 72372	I'll Be Satisfied/Ask (78)	60
59	Coral Q 72380	You Better Know It/Never Go Away (78)	75
59	Coral Q 72384	Talk That Talk/Only You, Only Me (78)	80

SINGLES
57	Vogue Coral Q 72290	Reet Petite/By The Light Of The Silvery Moon	20
57	Coral Q 72290	Reet Petite/By The Light Of The Silvery Moon (2nd pressing)	12
58	Coral Q 72306	To Be Loved/Come Back To Me	18
58	Coral Q 72332	I'm Wanderin'/As Long As I Live	18
58	Coral Q 72338	We Have Love/Singing A Song	18
58	Coral Q 72347	Lonely Teardrops/In The Blue Of The Evening	18
59	Coral Q 72366	That's Why/Love Is All	15
59	Coral Q 72366	That's Why/Love Is All (mispressing, B-side plays "You Better Know It")	12
59	Coral Q 72372	I'll Be Satisfied/Ask	12
59	Coral Q 72380	You Better Know It/Never Go Away	12
59	Coral Q 72384	Talk That Talk/Only You, Only Me	12
60	Coral Q 72393	Doggin' Around/The Magic Of Love	12
60	Coral Q 72407	A Woman, A Lover, A Friend/(You Were Made For) All My Love	10
60	Coral Q 72412	Alone At Last/Am I The Man	10
61	Coral Q 72421	The Tear Of The Year/My Empty Arms (withdrawn B-side, demos only)	50
61	Coral Q 72424	The Tear Of The Year/Your One And Only Love	10
61	Coral Q 72430	Please Tell Me Why/(So Many) Cute Little Girls	10
61	Coral Q 72434	I'm Comin' On Back To You/Lonely Life	10
61	Coral Q 72439	You Don't Know What It Means/Years From Now	10
61	Coral Q 72444	The Way I Am/My Heart Belongs To Only You	10
62	Coral Q 72450	The Greatest Hurt/There'll Be No Next Time	10
62	Coral Q 72453	Sing (And Tell The Blues So Long)/I Found Love (B-side with Linda Hopkins)	10
62	Coral Q 72454	I Just Can't Help It/My Tale Of Woe	10
63	Coral Q 72460	Baby Workout/What Good Am I Without You	10
63	Coral Q 72464	Shake A Hand/Say I Do (as Jackie Wilson & Linda Hopkins)	10
63	Coral Q 72465	Shake! Shake! Shake!/He's A Fool	12
63	Coral Q 72467	Baby Get It/The New Breed	10
64	Coral Q 72474	Big Boss Line/Be My Girl	10

MINT VALUE £

64	Coral Q 72476	Squeeze Her — Tease Her (But Love Her)/Give Me Back My Heart	10
65	Coral Q 72480	Yes Indeed!/When The Saints Go Marching In (with Linda Hopkins)	12
65	Coral Q 72481	No Pity (In The Naked City)/I'm So Lonely	12
65	Coral Q 72482	I Believe I'll Love On/Lonely Teardrops	12
66	Coral Q 72484	To Make A Big Man Cry/Be My Love	12
66	Coral Q 72487	Whispers/The Fairest Of Them All	12
67	Coral Q 72493	(Your Love Keeps Lifting Me) Higher And Higher/I'm The One To Do It	12
67	Coral Q 72496	Since You Showed Me How To Be Happy/The Who-Who Song	15
68	MCA MU 1014	For Your Precious Love/Uptight (Everything's Alright) (with Count Basie)	5
68	Decca AD 1008	For Your Precious Love/Uptight (Everything's Alright) (export issue)	20
69	MCA Soul Bag BAG 2	(Your Love Keeps Lifting Me) Higher And Higher/Whispers (Gettin' Louder)	5
69	MCA Soul Bag BAG 7	Since You Showed Me How To Be Happy/Chain Gang	5
69	MCA MU 1104	Since You Showed Me How To Be Happy/The Who-Who Song (reissue)	5
69	MCA MU 1105	Helpless/Do It The Right Way	5
70	MCA MU 1131	(Your Love Keeps Lifting Me) Higher And Higher/Whispers (Gettin' Louder) (reissue)	5
72	MCA MU 1160	I Get The Sweetest Feeling/Soul Galore	6
73	Brunswick BR 3	Beautiful Day/What'cha Gonna Do About Love	6
75	Brunswick BR 18	I Get The Sweetest Feeling/(Your Love Keeps Lifting Me) Higher And Higher	5
75	Brunswick BR 23	Whispers (Gettin' Louder)/Reet Petite	5
75	Brunswick BR 28	Don't Burn No Bridges/Don't Burn No Bridges (Instrumental) (with Chi-Lites)	5

EPs

59	Coral FEP 2016	JACKIE WILSON (EP, triangular or round centre)	75/60
60	Coral FEP 2043	THE DYNAMIC JACKIE WILSON (EP, triangular or round centre)	75/60

LPs

58	Coral LVA 9087	HE'S SO FINE (LP)	100
59	Coral LVA 9108	LONELY TEARDROPS (LP)	100
60	Coral LVA 9121	SO MUCH (LP)	80
60	Coral LVA 9130	JACKIE SINGS THE BLUES (LP)	100
60	Coral LVA 9135	MY GOLDEN FAVOURITES (LP)	60
61	Coral LVA 9144	A WOMAN, A LOVER, A FRIEND (LP)	85
61	Coral LVA 9148	YOU AIN'T HEARD NOTHIN' YET (LP)	60
62	Coral LVA 9151	BY SPECIAL REQUEST (LP, also stereo SVL 3018)	60/70
62	Coral LVA 9202	BODY AND SOUL (LP)	50
63	Coral LVA/SVL 9209	JACKIE (LP, mono/stereo)	50/60
63	Coral LVA/SVL 9214	THE WORLD'S GREATEST MELODIES (LP, mono/stereo)	50/60
66	Coral LVA 9231	SPOTLIGHT ON JACKIE WILSON (LP)	50
66	Coral LVA/SVL 9232	SOUL GALORE (LP, mono/stereo)	50/65
67	Coral LVA 9235	WHISPERS (LP)	40
68	MCA MUP(S) 304	HIGHER AND HIGHER (LP)	15
68	MCA MUP(S) 333	TWO MUCH (LP, with Count Basie & His Orchestra)	12
69	MCA MUPS 361	I GET THE SWEETEST FEELING (LP)	12
70	MCA MUPS 405	DO YOUR THING (LP)	20
73	Brunswick BRLS 3001	YOU GOT ME WALKIN' (LP)	12
73	Brunswick BRLS 3004	GREATEST HITS (LP)	12
75	Brunswick BRLS 3016	THE VERY BEST OF JACKIE WILSON (LP)	12

(see also Billy Ward & Dominoes, Clyde McPhatter, Count Basie, Chi-Lites, Linda Hopkins)

JACKIE WILSON/CLYDE McPHATTER

62	Ember JBS 705	Tenderly/CLYDE McPHATTER: Harbour Lights	225
62	Ember NR 5001	MEET BILLY WARD & THE DOMINOES (LP, 1 side each)	120

(see also Clyde McPhatter)

JOE WILSON

71	Pye International 7N 25550	Sweetness/When A Man Cries	5

LALA WILSON

(see under Alexander Jackson & Turnkeys)

MARI WILSON & IMAGINATIONS

80	GTO GT 274	Love Man/If That's What You Want (p/s)	6
81	Compact Org. PINK 1	Dance Card/She's Had Enough Of You (p/s)	4
82	Compact Org. PINK 2	Beat The Beat/Glamourpuss (p/s)	4

MARTY WILSON & STRAT-O-LITES

58	Brunswick 05750	Hey! Eula/Hedge-Hopper	15
58	Brunswick 05750	Hey! Eula/Hedge-Hopper (78)	6

MAYNELL WILSON & WESTMINSTER FIVE

64	Carnival CV 7014	Hey Hey Johnny/Baby	7
67	CBM CBM 001	Motown Feeling/Mean Ole World	6

(see also Wes[t]minster Five)

MURRY WILSON

67	Capitol CL 15525	Plumber's Tune/Love Won't Wait	6
67	Capitol (S)T 2819	THE MANY MOODS OF MURRY WILSON (LP)	20

(see also Beach Boys)

NANCY WILSON

64	Capitol CL 15343	The Best Is Yet To Come/Never Let Me Go	5
65	Capitol CL 15378	Don't Come Running Back To Me/Love Has Many Faces	5
65	Capitol CL 15412	Where Does That Leave Me/Gentle Is My Love	10
66	Capitol CL 15443	Power Of Love/Rain Sometimes	5
66	Capitol CL 15466	You've Got Your Troubles/Uptight (Everything's Alright)	15
67	Capitol CL 15508	Don't Look Over Your Shoulder/Mercy, Mercy, Mercy	10
68	Capitol CL 15536	You Don't Know Me/Ode To Billie Joe	5
68	Capitol CL 15547	Face It Girl It's Over/The End Of Our Love	25
75	Capitol CL 15810	You're Right As Rain/There'll Always Be Forever	5
62	Capitol EAP1 20604	SECOND TIME AROUND (EP)	10
64	Capitol EAP4 2082	TODAY, TOMORROW, FOREVER (EP)	10

MINT VALUE £

62	Capitol (S)T 1767	HELLO YOUNG LOVERS (LP, mono/stereo)	12/15
63	Capitol (S)T 1828	BROADWAY — MY LOVE (LP, mono/stereo)	12/15
63	Capitol (S)T 1934	HOLLYWOOD — MY WAY (LP, mono/stereo)	12/15
63	Capitol (S)T 2012	YESTERDAY'S LOVE SONGS (LP, mono/stereo)	12/15
64	Capitol (S)T 2082	TODAY, TOMORROW, FOREVER (LP)	15
65	Capitol (S)T 2136	THE NANCY WILSON SHOW (LP)	15
65	Capitol (S)T 2155	HOW GLAD I AM (LP)	15
65	Capitol (S)T 2321	TODAY— MY WAY (LP)	15
65	Capitol (S)T 2351	GENTLE IS MY LOVE (LP)	15
66	Capitol (S)T 2433	FROM BROADWAY WITH LOVE (LP)	15
66	Capitol (S)T 2495	A TOUCH OF TODAY (LP)	15
66	Capitol (S)T 2555	TENDER LOVING CARE (LP)	15
67	Capitol (S)T 2634	NANCY — NATURALLY (LP)	15
67	Capitol (S)T 2757	LUSH LIFE (LP)	12
68	Capitol (S)T 2844	WELCOME TO MY LOVE (LP)	12
69	Capitol (S)T 2909	EASY (LP)	12
69	Capitol (S)T 2970	SOUND OF NANCY WILSON (LP)	12

NANCY WILSON & CANNONBALL ADDERLEY

63	Capitol EAP4 1657	NANCY WILSON & CANNONBALL ADDERLEY (EP)	8
62	Capitol (S)T 1657	NANCY WILSON & CANNONBALL ADDERLEY (LP, mono/stereo)	12/15

(see also Cannonball Adderley)

PEANUTS WILSON

58	Coral Q 72302	Cast Iron Arm/You've Got Love	400
58	Coral Q 72302	Cast Iron Arm/You've Got Love (78)	125
76	MCA MCA 240	Cast Iron Arm/You've Got Love (reissue)	5

PHIL WILSON

87	Creation CRE 036D	Waiting For A Change/Even Now/Down In The Valley/Love In Vain (double pack)	5
89	Caff CAFF 3	Better Days/You Won't Speak (p/s, with insert, handwritten label)	12

(see also June Brides)

REUBEN WILSON

74	People PEO 109	I'll Take You There/Cisco Kid	5
76	Chess 6078 700	Got To Get Your Own (Parts 1 & 2)	12
72	Blue Note BST 84295	ON BROADWAY (LP)	15
72	Blue Note BST 84317	LOVE BUG (LP)	12
72	Blue Note BST 84343	BLUE MODE (LP)	12
73	People PLEO 01	CISCO KID (LP)	12
74	People PLEO 20	THE SWEET LIFE (LP)	12

RON WILSON

68	Island WI 3112	Dread Saras/DAVID BROWN: All My Life	15

(see also Winston Scotland, Douglas Brothers)

SHARK WILSON & BASEMENT HEATERS

71	Ashanti ASH 400	Make It Reggae/Version	6

SMILEY WILSON

60	London HLG 9066	Running Bear/Long As Little Birds Fly	50

TIMOTHY WILSON

73	Decca F 13432	Phoney People/Shine	6

TONY WILSON

69	Bell BLL 1081	Baby, I Love, Love I Love You/Come Back To My Lonely World	5
77	Bearsville K 15530	Anything That Keeps You Satisfied/I Can't Leave It Alone	5
76	Bearsville K 55513	I LIKE YOUR STYLE (LP)	12

(see also Hot Chocolate)

TREVOR WILSON

65	Ska Beat JB 207	You Couldn't Believe/You Told Me You Care	15

WILSON-GALE & CO.

80	Jet JET 156	I Wanna Stay (p/s)	4
80	Jet JET LP 233	GIFT-WRAPPED SET (LP, with insert)	10

(see also E.L.O.)

GABY WILTON & CHARLIE ACE

72	Bullet BU 511	Babylon Falling/CHARLIE ACE: Make It Love	6

JOHNNY WILTSHIRE & HIS TREBLETONES

59	Oriole CB 1494	If The Shoe Fits/Cha Cha Choo Choo	30
59	Oriole CB 1494	If The Shoe Fits/Cha Cha Choo Choo (78)	40

TEACHO WILTSHIRE

57	Oriole CB 1376	Coffee Break/Shut-Eye (78)	12

(see also Annie Ross)

WIMPLE WINCH

66	Fontana TF 686	What's Been Done/I Really Love You	150
66	Fontana TF 718	Save My Soul/Everybody's Worried 'Bout Tomorrow	190
67	Fontana TF 781	Rumble On Mersey Square South/Typical British Workmanship	100
67	Fontana TF 781	Rumble On Mersey Square South/Typical British Workmanship (mispressing, B-side plays "Atmospheres")	325

(see also Just Four Men, Four Just Men, Pacific Drift, Cheeter, Tristar Airbus)

LEM WINCHESTER & BENNY GOLSON

59	Esquire 32-142	WINCHESTER SPECIAL (LP)	25

WIND

85	Proto ENA 126	For Everyone/Für Alle/Fire And Ice (p/s)	4

KAI WINDING
64	Verve VS 501	Baby Elephant Walk/Experiment In Terror	5
65	Verve VS 512	Comin' Home Baby/More	7
55	London LTZ-N 15003	K AND J.J. (LP, with J.J. Johnson Quintet)	15
61	Parlophone PMC 1138	SLIDE RULE (LP, with J.J. Johnson Quintet)	12

(see also Dizzy Gillespie, J.J. Johnson Quintet)

WIND IN THE WILLOWS
68	Capitol CL 15561	Moments Spent/Friendly Lion	15
68	Capitol ST 2956	WIND IN THE WILLOWS (LP)	20

(see also Debbie Harry, Blondie)

WINDMILL
70	MCA MK 5024	Such Sweet Sorrow/I Can Fly	5
70	MCA MK 5045	Wilbur's Things/Two's Company	5

BARRY WINDOW
70	Baf BAF 7	I Thank You/End Of Our Road	5

WINDOWS
78	Skeleton SKL 008	Re-Arrange/Over Dub (p/s)	5
81	Skeleton SKULP 2	UPPERS ON DOWNERS (LP, with inserts)	10

(see also Mutants)

BARBARA WINDSOR
63	HMV POP 1128	Sparrows Can't Sing/On Mother Kelly's Doorstep	8
67	Parlophone R 5629	Don't Dig Twiggy/Swinging London	8
70	UPC UPC 101	When I Was A Child/What A Right Carry On	6
72	Decca F 13323	Grin And Bare It/Cheeky Sorta' Bird	6

WINDY & CARL
95	Enraptured RAPT 4501	Emerald/Fragments Of Time And Space (500 in hand-painted p/s, 300 in tracing paper sleeve)	8/4
96	Enraptured RAPT 4509	Christmas Song/GRIMBLE GRUMBLE: Odyssey And Oracle (no'd p/s, coloured vinyl, 350 only)	7

WINDY CORNER
73	Deroy DER 977	THE HOUSE AT WINDY CORNER (LP, private pressing)	500

WINE OF LEBANON
76	Dovetail DOVE 46	WINE OF LEBANON (LP)	20

(see also Achor)

WINGS
(see under Paul McCartney & Wings)

WINGS OVER JORDAN
51	Vogue V 303	Deep River/Old Ship Of Zion (78)	10

PETE WINSLOW & KING SIZE BRASS
73	BBC 103S	GIRL ON THE TESTCARD (LP)	12

WINSTON
60s	Holyground	WINSTON SINGS (EP)	10

WINSTON (Richards) & BIBBIE (Seaton)
63	R&B JB 115	Lover Man/LESTER STIRLING: Gravy Cool	15

WINSTON (Francis) & CECIL (Locke)
70	Banana BA 306	United We Stand/SOUND DIMENSION: Sweet Message	8

WINSTON & ERROL
71	Punch PH 74	There Is A Land/Goodnight My Love	6

WINSTON & FAY
64	Blue Beat BB 272	Fay Is Gone (actually by Buster & Winston)/MONARCHS: Sauce And Tea (B-side actually by Movers)	12

WINSTON & GEORGE
66	Pyramid PYR 6002	Denham Town/Keep The Pressure On	10

WINSTON (Groovy) & PAT (Rhoden)
68	Trojan TR 605	Pony Ride/Baby You Send Me	8
71	Bullet BU 475	The Same Thing For Breakfast/Sweeter Than Honey	6

(see also Winston Tucker)

WINSTON & ROY
62	Blue Beat BB 80	Babylon Gone/COUNT OSSIE ON AFRICAN DRUMS: First Gone	15

WINSTON & RUPERT
70	Bullet BU 425	Come By Here/Somebody	6
70	Moodisc HM 106	Musically Beat/Let Me Tell You Girl	6

(see also Eternals)

WINSTON (Richards) & TONETTES
65	Ska Beat JB 225	You Make Me Cry/CHECKMATES: Invisible Ska	18

JIMMY WINSTON (& HIS REFLECTIONS)
66	Decca F 12410	Sorry She's Mine/It's Not What You Do (But The Way That You Do It)	150
76	Nems NEMS 12	Sun In The Morning/Just Wanna Smile (solo)	5

(see also Small Faces, Winston's Fumbs, Spheres)

ERIC WINSTONE (& HIS) ORCHESTRA
64	Pye 7N 15603	"Dr. Who" Theme/Pony Express	12
73	Avenue AVINT 1005	PLAYS 007 (LP)	18

NORMA WINSTONE
72	Argo ZDA 148	EDGE OF TIME (LP)	70

(see also Mike Westbrook, Michael Garrick)

MINT VALUE £

WINSTONS
69	Pye International 7N 25493	Colour Him Father/Amen, Brother	10
69	Pye International 7N 25500	Love Of The Common People/Wheel Of Fortune	5

WINSTONS & M-SQUAD
71	Green Door GD 4003	Carroll Street/Carroll Street — Version (B-side act. by Ansel Collins/M-Squad)	5

WINSTON'S FUMBS
67	RCA RCA 1612	Real Crazy Apartment/Snow White	225

(see also Small Faces, Jimmy Winston & His Reflections, Yes, Spheres, Federals)

EDGAR WINTER (GROUP)
71	Epic EPC 7269	Where Would I Be/Good Morning Music (as Edgar Winter's White Trash)	5
72	Epic EPC 7550	Keep On Playin' That Rock'n'Roll/Dying To Live	5
70	CBS 64083	ENTRANCE (LP, as Edgar Winter)	15
71	CBS 64298	EDGAR WINTER'S WHITE TRASH (LP)	15
72	CBS 67244	ROAD WORK (2-LP)	15
73	CBS EQ 31584/Q 65074	THEY ONLY COME OUT AT NIGHT (LP, quadrophonic)	12

JOHNNY WINTER
69	CBS 4386	I'm Yours And I'm Hers/I'll Drown In My Tears	5
69	Liberty LBF 15219	Rollin' And Tumblin'/Bad Luck And Trouble	6
70	CBS 4795	Johnny B. Goode/I'm Not Sure	5
70	CBS 5358	Rock 'N' Roll Hoochie Koo/21st Century Man	5
71	CBS 7227	Jumping Jack Flash/Good Morning Little School Girl	5
69	CBS 63619	JOHNNY WINTER (LP)	30
69	Liberty LBL/LBS 83240E	THE PROGRESSIVE BLUES EXPERIMENT (LP)	18
70	CBS 66231	SECOND WINTER (2-LP, 3-sided)	20
70	Buddah 2359 011	FIRST WINTER (LP)	15
70	CBS 64117	JOHNNY WINTER AND... (LP)	15
71	CBS 64289	JOHNNY WINTER AND... LIVE (LP)	15
73	CBS 65484	STILL ALIVE AND WELL (LP)	12
74	CBS CQ 32188/Q 65484	STILL ALIVE AND WELL (LP, quadrophonic)	15

(see also Johnny & Jammers)

PAUL WINTER
69	A&M AMLS 942	WINTER CONSORT (LP)	12

HUGO WINTERHALTER ORCHESTRA
54	HMV 7M 273	Land Of Dreams/Song Of The Barefoot Contessa	6
56	HMV POP 241	Canadian Sunset/This Is Real (with Eddie Haywood)	7
60	RCA RCA 1164	'Summer Place' Theme/Blue Strings (78)	12

DON WINTERS
60	Brunswick 05827	Someday Baby/That's All I Need	12

LIZ WINTERS & BOB CORT SKIFFLE GROUP
57	Decca F 10878	Freight Train/Love Is Strange	15
57	Decca F 10878	Freight Train/Love Is Strange (78)	12
57	Decca F 10899	Maggie May/Jessamine	12
57	Decca F 10899	Maggie May/Jessamine (78)	12
57	Decca DFE 6409	LIZ WINTERS AND BOB CORT (EP)	20

(see also Bob Cort Skiffle Group)

LOIS WINTERS
56	London HLD 8266	Japanese Farewell Song/JAN GARBER & HIS ORCHESTRA: My Dear	25
56	London HLD 8266	Japanese Farewell Song/JAN GARBER & HIS ORCHESTRA: My Dear (78)	12

MIKE & BERNIE WINTERS
57	Parlophone R 4384	How Do You Do?/Does My Baby?	10
57	Parlophone R 4384	How Do You Do?/Does My Baby? (78)	8
59	Parlophone R 4538	For Me and My Gal/Your Own Home Town	6
59	Parlophone R 4538	For Me and My Gal/Your Own Home Town (78)	12
66	CBS 202458	That Man Batman/Insky Spinsky Spider (some with p/s)	15/8
71	Decca F 13255	You're My Little Boy/How Do You Do	5
72	Philips 6006 254	How I Love Them Old Songs/Everywhere There Is Love	5

RUBY WINTERS
68	Stateside SS 2090	I Want Action/Better	20
79	Creole CR 171	Baby Lay Down/Lovin' Me Is A Full Time Job	8
79	Creole CR 174	Back To Love/I've Been Waiting For You All My Life	8

WYOMA WINTERS
54	HMV 7M 222	Where Can I Go Without You?/Won't You Give A Repeat Performance	6
54	HMV 7M 260	Toy Balloon/Shish Kebab	6

STEVIE WINWOOD
77	Island WIP 6394	Time Is Running Out/Penultimate Zone (12", pre-release sleeve)	10
80	Island IPR 2040	While You See A Chance/Vacant Chair (12", pre-release sleeve)	8
80	Island WIP 6655	While You See A Chance/Vacant Chair (p/s)	5
80	Island CWIP 6655	While You See A Chance/Vacant Chair (cassette, 5,000 only)	8
81	Island WIP 6747	There's A River/Two Way Stretch (p/s)	5
86	Island IS 294	Freedom Overspill/Spanish Dancer (p/s, with bonus cassette of LP highlights & interview [SW 2])	6
86	Island 12 ISD 294	Freedom Overspill (Liberty Mix)/(LP Version)/Spanish Dancer (12", stickered g/fold p/s & t/p 7" "Low Spark Of High-Heeled Boys"/"Gimme Some Lovin'")	10
88	Virgin VST 1085	Roll With It (12" Mix)/The Morning Side/Roll With It (7" Version) (12", g/fold p/s)	8
91	Virgin VSCDX 1317	I Will Be Here/Don't You Know What The Night Can Do (live)/In The Night Of Day (CD, velvet box with family tree and print)	8
86	Island SWCLP 1	A CONVERSATION WITH (LP, promo interview on "Back In The High Life" LP)	12

87	Island SWWLP 1	IN CONVERSATION (LP, promo interview on "Chronicles" LP)	12
87	Island SW 1/2/3	BACK IN THE HIGH LIFE (3 x 7" set, each in p/s, promo only)	20
87	Island	CHRONICLES (5 x 7" box set, promo, 500 only)	30

(see also Winwood Kabaka Amoa, Anglos, Spencer Davis Group, Traffic, Blind Faith, Yamashta Winwood etc.)

WINWOOD/KABAKA/AMAO

| 73 | Island HELP 14 | AIYE-KETA THIRD WORLD (LP) | 15 |

(see also Stevie Winwood)

WIPEOUT

| 82 | M&L MNL 2/ACE 37 | Baby Please Don't Go/Two-O-Five/Crawdaddy/Should A' Known Better (p/s) | 4 |
| 83 | Out OUT 1A/B1 | NO SWEAT (LP) | 15 |

WIPERS

| 84 | Psycho PSYCHO 22 | IS THIS REAL? (LP, with lyric insert) | 10 |
| 84 | Psycho PSYCHO 23 | YOUTH OF AMERICA (LP) | 10 |

WIRE

77	Harvest HAR 5144	Mannequin/Feeling Called Love/12XU (p/s)	12
78	Harvest HAR 5151	I Am The Fly/Ex-Lion Tamer (p/s)	8
78	Harvest HAR 5161	Dot Dash/Options R (p/s)	8
79	Harvest HAR 5172	Outdoor Miner/Practice Makes Perfect (p/s, some on white vinyl)	8/5
79	Harvest HAR 5187	A Question Of Degree/Former Airline (p/s)	7
79	Harvest HAR 5192	Map Ref 41° N 93° W/Go Ahead (p/s)	6
79	Harvest SPSLP 299	154 (12", p/s, white label sampler with insert & press release; beware of counterfeits)	30
81	Rough Trade RT 079	Our Swimmer/Midnight Bahnhof Cafe (p/s)	7
83	Rough Trade RTT 123	Crazy About Love/Second Length (Our Swimmer)/Catapult 30 (12", p/s, 2 different sleeve colours) each	10
89	Mute MUTE 87	Eardrum Buzz/The Offer (p/s, clear vinyl, withdrawn)	12
77	Harvest SHSP 4076	PINK FLAG (LP, with lyric inner)	15
78	Harvest SHSP 4093	CHAIRS MISSING (LP, 1st 10,000 with lilac lyric inner sleeve)	12
79	Harvest SHSP 4105	154 (LP, with inner lyric sleeve & bonus 7" EP: "Song 2"/"Get Down [Parts I & II]"/ "Let's Panic"/"Later"/"Small Electric Piece" [PSR 444, no p/s])	12
84	Rough Trade ROUGH 29	DOCUMENT AND EYEWITNESS (LP, with free 12" EP [ROUGH 2912])	15
84	Rough Trade COPY 004	DOCUMENT AND EYEWITNESS (cassette, in special box)	15
84	Rough Trade COPY 004	DOCUMENT AND EYEWITNESS (cassette with bonus 12" EP tracks)	10
86	Pink PINKY 7	PLAY POP (mini-LP)	8
89	Mute STUMM 66	IBTABA (IT'S BEGINNING TO AND BACK AGAIN) (LP, with 4 postcards & signed print)	18

(see also Colin Newman, Cupol, Gilbert & Lewis, Dome, A.C. Marias [A.C.])

MARK WIRTZ (ORCHESTRA & CHORUS)

68	Parlophone R 5668	(He's Our Dear Old) Weatherman (From "A Teenage Opera")/ Possum's Dance	15
68	Parlophone R 5683	Mrs. Raven/Knickerbocker Glory	7
69	CBS 4306	My Daddie Is A Baddie/I Love You Because	5
69	CBS 4539	Caroline/Goody, Goody, Goody	5
64	World Record Club T 452	TEN AGAIN (LP, by Belle Gonzalez & Russ Loader, Wirtz as producer)	25

(see also Mood Mosaic, Keith West, Sweet Shop, Philwit & Pegasus, Mark Rogers & Marksmen, Belle Gonzalez, Russ Loader, Zion De Gallier, Elmer Hockett's Hurdy Gurdy, Steve Flynn, Fickle Finger, Matchmaker)

WISDOM

| 76 | Crystal CR 026 | Nefertiti/What-Cha-Gonna-Du-About You | 8 |

NORMAN WISDOM

52	Columbia DB 3161	I Don't 'Arf Love You/Narcissus (The Laughing Record) (78, with Joyce Grenfell)	8
54	Philips PB 259	Young At Heart/Just To Be With You (78)	8
54	Philips PB 299	They Didn't Believe Me/So Nice To Dream (78)	8
54	Philips PB 374	Please Opportunity/You Were Meant For Me (78)	8
54	Philips PB 381	Take A Step In The Right Direction/I'll Always Love You (78)	8
56	Columbia SCM 5222	Two Rivers/Boy Meets Girl (with Ruby Murray)	12
57	Columbia DB 3864	Up In The World/Me And My Imagination	8
57	Columbia DB 3903	The Wisdom Of A Fool/Happy Ending	10
59	Top Rank JAR 246	Follow A Star/Give Me A Night In June	8
61	Columbia SCD 2160	Narcissus (The Laughing Record)/I Don't 'Arf Love You (with Joyce Grenfell)	10
69	CBS 4569	Where Do I Go From Here?/Just Like The Day	5
56	Columbia SEG 7612	NORMAN WISDOM (EP)	15
57	Columbia SEG 7687	NORMAN AND RUBY (EP, with Ruby Murray)	12
59	Top Rank JKP 2052	FOLLOW A STAR (EP)	15
58	Columbia 33SX 1085	NORMAN WISDOM IN "WHERE'S CHARLEY?" (LP)	22
60s	Wing WL 1216	I WOULD LIKE TO PUT ON RECORD (LP)	15

(see also Ruby Murray)

WISE BOYS

| 60 | Parlophone R 4693 | Why, Why, Why/My Fortune | 8 |

WISE GUYS

| 60 | Top Rank JAR 271 | (Little Girl) Big Noise/As Long As I Have You | 12 |

MAC WISEMAN

55	London HLD 8174	The Kentuckian Song/Wabash Cannon Ball	50
55	London HLD 8174	The Kentuckian Song/Wabash Cannon Ball (78)	15
56	London HLD 8226	My Little Home In Tennessee/I Haven't Got The Right To Love You	50
56	London HLD 8226	My Little Home In Tennessee/I Haven't Got The Right To Love You (78)	20
56	London HLD 8259	Fireball Mail/When The Roses Bloom Again	50
56	London HLD 8259	Fireball Mail/When The Roses Bloom Again (78)	30
57	London HLD 8412	Step It Up And Go/Sundown	375
57	London HLD 8412	Step It Up And Go/Sundown (78)	50
59	London HL 7084	Jimmy Brown The Newsboy/I've Got No Use For Woman (export issue)	35

			MINT VALUE £
56	London RE-D 1056	SONGS FROM THE HILLS (EP)	35
58	London RE-D 1147	SONGS FROM THE HILLS VOL. 2 (EP)	35
60	London RE-D 1242	SONGS FROM THE HILLS VOL. 3 (EP)	35
56	London HB-D 1052	SONGS FROM THE HILLS (10" LP)	60
60	London HA-D 2217	GREAT FOLK BALLADS (LP)	40

TREVOR WISHART
78	private pressing	RED BIRD: A POLITICAL PRISONER'S DREAM (LP, with insert)	20
79	private pressing	BEACH SINGULARITY AND MENAGERIE (LP, with insert)	20

WISHBONE ASH
70	MCA MK 5061	Blind Eye/Queen Of Torture	6
72	MCA MKS 5097	No Easy Road/Blowin' Free	6
73	MCA MUS 1210	So Many Things To Say/Rock'n'Roll Widow	5
74	MCA MCA 165	Hometown/Persephone	5
75	MCA MCA 176	Silver Shoes/Persephone	6
76	MCA/SFI 263	Outward Bound/Runaway/Mother Of Pearl/You Rescue Me (flexidisc, with/without "New England" tour programme)	12/5
77	MCA MCA 291	Phoenix/Blowin' Free/Jail Bait (p/s)	5
78	MCA MCA 392	You See Red/Bad Weather Blues (live) (p/s)	5
78	MCA 12MCA 392	You See Red/Bad Weather Blues (12", p/s)	7
79	MCA MCA 518	Come On/Fast Johnny (p/s)	5
80	MCA MCA 549	Living Proof/Jail Bait (live) (p/s)	5
80	MCA MCA 577	Helpless (live)/Blowin' Free (live) (p/s)	5
80	MCA MCAT 577	Helpless (live)/Blowin' Free (live) (12", p/s)	7
81	MCA MCA 695	Underground/My Mind Is Made Up (p/s)	5
81	MCA MCA 726	Get Ready/Kicks On The Street (p/s, some with patch)	8/5
81	MCA MCL 14	Get Ready/Kicks On The Street (p/s, alternate issue)	5
82	AVM WISH 1	Engine Overheat/Genevieve (p/s)	5
82	AVM 1002	No More Lonely Nights/Street Of Shame (no p/s)	5
88	I.R.S. IRM 164	In The Skin/Tangible Evidence (p/s)	5
89	I.R.S. EIRS 104	Cosmic Jazz/T-Bone Shuffle (p/s)	5
89	I.R.S. EIRS T104	Cosmic Jazz/T-Bone Shuffle/Bolan's Monument (12", p/s)	10
70	MCA MKPS 2014	WISHBONE ASH (LP, gatefold sleeve, black label)	18
71	MCA MDKS 8004	PILGRIMAGE (LP, gatefold sleeve, black label)	15
72	MCA MDKS 8006	ARGUS (LP, gatefold sleeve, black label)	15
73	MCA MDKS 8011	WISHBONE FOUR (LP, gatefold sleeve, black label, with poster & lyrics)	15

(Red/brown, red/yellow & red/pink label copies of the above LPs may exist, and would be worth the same as these values.)

74	MCA MCSP 254	LIVE DATES (2-LP, gatefold sleeve)	15
74	MCA MCG 2585	THERE'S THE RUB (LP)	12
78	MCA MCG 3528	NO SMOKE WITHOUT FIRE (LP, with stickered sleeve & inner, with single "Come In From The Rain"/"Lorelei" [PSR 431])	12
80	MCA MCG 4012	LIVE DATES II (LP, gatefold sleeve, with live bonus LP)	15
82	AVM ASH 1	TWIN BARRELS BURNING (LP)	12
85	Neat NEAT 1027	RAW TO THE BONE (LP)	20
85	Neat NEATP 1027	RAW TO THE BONE (LP, picture disc, unissued)	

(see also Home)

WISHFUL THINKING
66	Decca F 12438	Turning Round/V.I.P.	7
66	Decca F 12499	Step By Step/Looking Around	5
67	Decca F 12598	Count To Ten/Hang Around Girl	6
67	Decca F 12627	Peanuts/Cherry Cherry	6
67	Decca F 22673	Meet The Sun/Easier Said Than Loving You	7
68	Decca F 22742	Alone/Vegetables (export issue)	7
68	Decca F 12760	It's So Easy/I Want You Girl	5
72	B&C CB 169	Lu La Le Lu/We're Gonna Change All This	5
72	B&C CB 184	Clear White Light/Hiroshima	5
67	Decca SKL 4900	LIVE VOL. 1 (LP)	30
71	Charisma CAS 1038	HIROSHIMA (LP)	20

WISHING STONES
86	Head HEAD 2	Beat Girl/Two Steps Take Me Back (p/s)	6
87	Head HEAD 6	New Ways/House Is Not A Home (p/s)	4
87	Head HEAD 612	New Ways/Wildwood/Hold Up/A House Is Not A Home (12", p/s)	7

(see also Loft)

WITCHES BREW
80s	Pussy PU 016	Angeline (p/s)	20

WITCHFINDER GENERAL
81	Heavy Metal HEAVY 6	Burning A Sinner/Satan's Children (p/s)	30
82	Heavy Metal 12HM 17	Soviet Invasion/Rabies/R.I.P. (live) (12", p/s)	35
83	Heavy Metal HEAVY 21	Music/Last Chance (p/s)	12
83	Heavy Metal HMPD 21	Music/Last Chance (picture disc)	8
82	Heavy Metal HMRLP 8	DEATH PENALTY (LP, red vinyl)	15
82	Heavy Metal HMRPD 8	DEATH PENALTY (LP, picture disc)	15
83	Heavy Metal HMRLP 13	FRIENDS OF HELL (LP, clear vinyl)	12
83	Heavy Metal HMRPD 13	FRIENDS OF HELL (LP, picture disc)	12

WITCHFYNDE
79	Rondelet ROUND 1	Give 'Em Hell/Gettin' Heavy (p/s)	5
80	Rondelet ROUND 4	In The Stars/Wake Up Screaming (p/s)	6
83	Expulsion OUT 3	I'd Rather Go Wild/Cry Wolf (p/s)	18
80	Rondelet ABOUT 1	GIVE 'EM HELL (LP)	12
80	Rondelet ABOUT 2	STAGE FRIGHT (LP)	12
83	Expulsion EXIT 5	CLOAK AND DAGGER (LP)	12
83	Expulsion PEXIT 5	CLOAK AND DAGGER (LP, picture disc)	15
84	Mausoleum SKULL 8352	LORDS OF SIN (LP, gatefold sleeve, with bonus 12" [Cloak & Dagger/I'd Rather Go Wild/Moon Magic/Give 'Em Hell])	12

BILL WITHERS

71	A&M AMS 845	Everybody's Talkin'/Harlem	6
71	A&M AMS 858	Ain't No Sunshine/Harlem	5
72	A&M AMS 7004	Lean On Me/Better Off Dead	5
72	A&M AMS 7038	Use Me/Let Me In Your Life	6
73	A&M AMS 7055	Kissing My Love/I Don't Know	5
73	A&M AMS 7068	Look What I Found/The Lady Is Waiting	6
73	A&M AMS 7080	Ain't No Sunshine/Harlem/Grandma's Hands	6
72	A&M AMLH 68107	STILL BILL (LP)	15
71	A&M AMLS 65002	JUST AS I AM (LP)	12
73	A&M AMLD 3001	LIVE AT CARNEGIE HALL (2-LP)	15
74	A&M AMLH 68230	'JUSTMENTS (LP)	12
75	Sussex LPSX 10	BEST OF BILL WITHERS (LP)	12

JIMMY WITHERSPOON

78s

54	Parlophone R 3914	It/Highway To Happiness (78)	40
54	Parlophone R 3951	Oh Boy/I Done Told You (78)	40
54	Vogue V 2261	Failing By Degrees/New Orleans Woman (78)	40
54	Vogue V 2295	Who's Been Jivin' With You/Rain, Rain, Rain (78)	40
56	Vogue V 2060	Big Fine Girl/No Rollin' Blues (78)	40
56	Vogue V 2356	Jump, Children/Take Me Back Baby (78)	40

SINGLES

54	Parlophone MSP 6125	It/Highway To Happiness	45
54	Parlophone MSP 6142	Oh Boy/I Done Told You	45
56	Vogue V 2060	Big Fine Girl/No Rollin' Blues	40
62	Vogue V 2420	When The Lights Go Out/All That's Good	40
64	Stateside SS 304	Evenin'/Money Is Getting Cheaper	12
64	Stateside SS 325	I Will Never Marry/I'm Coming Down With The Blues	12
64	Stateside SS 362	You're Next/Happy Blues	12
65	Stateside SS 429	Come Walk With Me/Oh How I Love You	12
65	Stateside SS 461	Love Me Right/Make My Heart Smile Again	12
66	Stateside SS 503	If There Wasn't Any You/I Never Thought I'd See The Day	12
66	Verve VS 538	It's All Over But The Crying/If I Could Have You Back Again	7
67	Verve VS 553	Past Forty Blues/My Baby's Quit Me	6
71	Probe PRO 526	Handbags And Gladrags/It's Time To Live	5
75	Capitol CL 15828	Fool's Paradise/Reflections	5

EPs

61	Vogue EPV 1269	JIMMY WITHERSPOON AT MONTEREY (EP)	30
61	Vogue EPV 1270	JIMMY WITHERSPOON AT MONTEREY No. 2 (EP)	30
64	Vocalion EPVH 1278	JIMMY WITHERSPOON (EP)	20
65	Vocalion EPVH 1284	OUTSKIRTS OF TOWN (EP)	20
66	Vocalion VEH 170158	FEELING THE SPIRIT VOL. 1 (EP)	20
66	Vocalion VEH 170159	FEELING THE SPIRIT VOL. 2 (EP)	20

LPs

59	London Jazz LTZ-K 15150	NEW ORLEANS BLUES (LP, with Wilbur de Paris)	25
60	Vogue LAE 12218	SINGIN' THE BLUES (LP)	25
61	Vogue LAE 12253	AT THE RENAISSANCE (LP, with Gerry Mulligan)	20
64	Society SOC 968	SINGS THE BLUES (LP)	12
64	Stateside SL 10088	EVENIN' BLUES (LP)	30
65	Stateside SL 10105	BLUES AROUND THE CLOCK (LP)	35
65	Fontana 688 005 ZL	THERE'S GOOD ROCKIN' TONIGHT (LP)	25
65	Stateside SL 10114	SOME OF MY BEST FRIENDS ARE BLUES (LP)	35
65	Stateside SL 10139	BLUE SPOON (LP)	30
65	Vogue VRL 3005	JIMMY WITHERSPOON IN PERSON (LP)	25
66	Ember EMB 3369	JIMMY WITHERSPOON (LP)	20
67	Fontana (S)TL 5382	'SPOON SINGS AND SWINGS (LP)	30
67	Verve (S)VLP 9156	BLUE POINT OF VIEW (LP)	20
67	Transatlantic PR 7300	EVENIN' BLUES (LP, reissue)	15
68	Transatlantic PR 7356	SOME OF MY BEST FRIENDS ARE THE BLUES (LP, reissue)	15
68	Stateside (S)SL 10232	LIVE (LP)	25
68	Verve (S)VLP 9181	BLUES IS NOW (LP, with Brother Jack McDuff)	18
68	Verve (S)VLP 9216	SPOONFUL OF SOUL (LP)	18
68	Transatlantic PR 7418	SPOON IN LONDON (LP)	18
68	Transatlantic PR 7475	BLUES FOR EASY LIVERS (LP)	15
69	Stateside SSL 10289	THE BLUES SINGER (LP)	20
69	Ember CJS 820	SINGS THE BLUES AT THE RENAISSANCE (LP, reissue, with Gerry Mulligan)	18
69	Polydor Intl. 623 256	BACK DOOR BLUES (LP)	18
71	Probe SPB 1031	HANDBAGS AND GLADRAGS (LP)	12

(see also Eric Burdon & Jimmy Witherspoon, Brother Jack McDuff)

JIMMY WITHERSPOON/HELEN HUMES

60	Vogue EPV 1198	RHYTHM AND BLUES CONCERT (EP, 2 tracks each)	80

(see also Helen Humes)

BITTER WITHY

69	Nevis NEVIS R005	SAMPLER (LP)	20

WITNESSES

60s	Herald ELR 1076	THE WITNESSES (EP)	125

WIZARD'S CONVENTION

76	RCA RS 1085	WIZARD'S CONVENTION (LP, with insert)	15

(see also Deep Purple, Roger Glover, Jon Lord, David Coverdale, Ray Fenwick)

WIZZARD

73	Warner Bros K 16336	I Wish It Could Be Christmas Every Day/Rob Roy's Nightmare (gatefold p/s, withdrawn)	10
73	Harvest HAR 5079	I Wish It Could Be Christmas Every Day/Rob Roy's Nightmare (reissue, gatefold p/s with Harvest sticker over Warner Bros. logo)	10

MINT VALUE £

74	Warner Bros K 16357	Rock'n'Roll Winter/Dream Of Unwin (gatefold p/s)	5
74	Warner Bros K 16434	This Is The Story Of My Love (Baby)/Nixture	5
75	Jet JET 758	Rattlesnake Roll/Can't Help My Feelings	5
76	Jet JET 768	Indiana Rainbow/The Thing Is This (This Is The Thing) (as Roy Wood's Wizzard) (some in p/s)	10/5
76	Harvest HAR 5106	See My Baby Jive/Angel Fingers/Ball Park Incident	6
84	Harvest HAR 5173	I Wish It Could Be Christmas Every Day/See My Baby Jive (reissue, gatefold p/s, record credits Wizzard, sleeve credits Roy Wood)	4
88	Counterpoint CDEP 12	Are You Ready To Rock/Rock'n'Roll Winter/SLADE: How Does It Feel/ Far Far Away (CD)	7
73	Harvest SHSP 4025	WIZZARD BREW (LP, with lyric insert)	15
74	Warner Bros K 56029	INTRODUCING EDDY AND THE FALCONS (LP, gatefold sleeve with poster)	12

(see also Roy Wood, Balls, Idle Race, Grunt Futtock)

WKGB
79	Fetish FET 002	Non-Stop/Ultra Marine (p/s)	6

MAX WOISKI & WEST INDIAN ORCHESTRA
58	Columbia DC 718	Matrugador/ALBERTO GEMERTS: Contestacion A Confession (78, export issue)	10

(DARRYL WAY'S) WOLF
73	Deram DM 378	Wolf/Spring Fever	8
73	Deram DM 395	A Bunch Of Fives/Five In The Morning	8
73	Deram DM 401	Two Sisters/Go Down	8
73	Deram SDL 14	CANIS LUPUS (LP, as Darryl Way's Wolf, gatefold sleeve)	20
73	Deram SML 1104	SATURATION POINT (LP, as Darryl Way's Wolf)	20
74	Deram SML 1116	NIGHT MUSIC (LP)	18
78	Island ILPS 9550	CONCERTO FOR ELECTRIC VIOLIN (LP)	12

(see also Curved Air, King Crimson, Marillion)

WOLF
82	Chrysalis CHS 2592	Head Contact/Rock'n'Roll (p/s, clear vinyl)	10
82	Chrysalis CHS 12 2592	Head Contact/Rock'n'Roll/Soul For The Devil (12", p/s)	15

WOLF
81	Gremlin GREM 73	See Them Running (no p/s)	80

RICHARD WOLFE & HIS ORCHESTRA
60	London HLR 9143	Banjo Boy/Voila	7

WOLFETONES
65	Fontana STL 5244	THE FOGGY DEW (LP)	12

WOLFGANG PRESS
83	4AD (no cat. no.)	Kings Of Soul (Crowned Mix)/(De-Throned Mix)/(7" Mix) (12", same both sides, no p/s, promo only, 50 copies pressed)	15
84	4AD BAD 409	SCARECROW: Desire/Respect/Ecstasy (12" EP)	10
85	4AD BAD 502	WATER: Tremble (My Girl Doesn't)/My Way/The Deep Briny/Fire-Eater (12" EP)	8
87	4AD BAD 702C	Big Sex/The Wedding/The Great Leveller/That Heat/God's Number (cassette)	4
83	4AD CAD 308	BURDEN OF MULES (LP)	10
94	4AD CADD 4016CD	FUNKY LITTLE DEMONS (CD, with free remix CD)	20

(see also Mass, Models)

WOLFHOUNDS
86	Pink PINKY 14	The Anti-Midas Touch/Restless Spell (p/s)	4
86	Legend LEG 100/ LYN 18042	Rats On A Raft/RAZORCUTS: Sad Kaleidoscope (flexidisc, free with *The Legend* & other fanzines, 500 only)	5/4

WOLFRILLA
71	Concord CON 015	Song For Jimi/Come Tomorrow	4

WOOLLY WOLSTENHOLME
80	Polydor 2374 165	MAESTOSO (LP)	12

(see also Barclay James Harvest)

WOLVES
64	Pye 7N 15676	Journey Into Dreams/What Do You Mean	10
64	Pye 7N 15733	Now/This Year Next Year	20
65	Pye 7N 17013	At The Club/Distant Dreams	18
66	Parlophone R 5511	Lust For Life/My Baby Loves Them	50

BOBBY WOMACK
68	Minit MLF 11001	Broadway Walk/Somebody Special	10
68	Minit MLF 11005	What Is This?/What You Gonna Do	7
68	Minit MLF 11010	Fly Me To The Moon/Take Me	5
69	Minit MLF 11012	California Dreamin'/Baby You Oughta Think It Over	5
72	United Artists UP 35339	That's The Way I Feel About 'Cha/Come, L'Amore	5
72	United Artists UP 35375	Woman's Gotta Have It/If You Don't Want My Love	5
73	United Artists UP 35456	Harry Hippie/I Can Understand It (some in p/s)	10/5
73	United Artists UP 35512	Across 110th Street/Hang On In There (as Bobby Womack & Peace)	6
73	United Artists UP 35565	Nobody Wants You When You're Down And Out/ I'm Through Trying To Prove My Love For You	5
74	Jay Boy BOY 75	What Is This?/I Wonder	5
75	United Artists UP 35859	Check It Out/Interlude No. 2	5
76	United Artists UP 36042	Where There's A Will There's A Way/Everything's Gonna Be Alright	5
76	United Artists UP 36098	Daylight/Trust Me	5
79	Arista ARIST 284	How Could You Break My Heart/I Honestly Love You	5
87	Arista RIS 17	How Could You Break My Heart/Give It Up (p/s)	5
87	Arista RIST 17	How Could You Break My Heart/Give It Up/ Mr. D.J. Don't Stop The Music (12", p/s)	12
72	United Artists UAS 29365	UNDERSTANDING (LP)	12
73	United Artists UAS 29451	ACROSS 110TH STREET (LP, soundtrack, with J.J. Johnson)	18

73	United Artists UAS 29306	COMMUNICATION (LP)	12
73	United Artists UAS 29456	FACTS OF LIFE (LP)	12
74	United Artists UAS 29574	LOOKIN' FOR A LOVE AGAIN (LP)	12
75	United Artists UAG 29715	I CAN UNDERSTAND IT (LP)	12
75	United Artists UAG 29762	I DON'T KNOW WHAT THE WORLD IS COMING TO (LP)	12
79	Arista ARTY 165	ROADS OF LIFE (LP)	15

(see also Valentinos, Ted Wood)

WOMB

69	Dot DLP 25933	WOMB (LP)	20
70	Dot DLP 25959	OVERDUB (LP)	25

WOMENFOLK

64	RCA RCA 1439	Turn Around/One Man's Hand	6
65	RCA RCA 1480	My Heart Tells Me To Believe/The Way I Feel	6
65	RCA RD 7704	AT THE HUNGRY I (LP)	15

ALISON WONDER

70	Columbia DB 8667	Once More With Feeling/Black Paper Roses	8

(see also Cheryl St. Clair)

GIRL WONDER

66	Doctor Bird DB 1015	Mommy Out Of The Light/Cutting Wood	15

(LITTLE) STEVIE WONDER

SINGLES

63	Oriole CBA 1853	Fingertips (Parts 1 & 2)	20
63	Stateside SS 238	Workout, Stevie, Workout/Monkey Talk	35
64	Stateside SS 285	Castles In The Sand/Thank You (For Loving Me All The Way)	40
64	Stateside SS 323	Hey, Harmonica Man/This Little Girl	35

(The above singles were credited to Little Stevie Wonder.)

65	Tamla Motown TMG 505	Kiss Me Baby/Tears In Vain	40
65	Tamla Motown TMG 532	High-Heel Sneakers/Music Talk	35
66	Tamla Motown TMG 545	Uptight (Everything's Alright)/Purple Raindrops	10
66	Tamla Motown TMG 558	Nothing's Too Good For My Baby/With A Child's Heart	20
66	Tamla Motown TMG 570	Blowin' In The Wind/Ain't That Asking For Trouble	15
66	Tamla Motown TMG 588	A Place In The Sun/Sylvia	12
67	Tamla Motown TMG 602	Travelin' Man/Hey Love	7
67	Tamla Motown TMG 613	I Was Made To Love Her/Hold Me	6
67	Tamla Motown TMG 626	I'm Wondering/Every Time I See You I Go Wild	6
68	Tamla Motown TMG 653	Shoo-Be-Doo-Be-Doo-Da-Day/Why Don't You Lead Me To Love	5
68	Tamla Motown TMG 666	You Met Your Match/My Girl	7
68	Tamla Motown TMG 679	For Once In My Life/Angie Girl	5
69	Tamla Motown TMG 690	My Cherie Amour/I Don't Know Why I Love You	5
69	Tamla Motown TMG 717	Yester-Me, Yester-You, Yesterday/I'd Be A Fool Right Now	5
70	Tamla Motown TMG 731	Never Had A Dream Come True/Somebody Knows, Somebody Cares	5
70	Tamla Motown TMG 744	Signed, Sealed, Delivered, I'm Yours/I'm More Than Happy (I'm Satisfied)	5
70	Tamla Motown TMG 757	Heaven Help Us All/I Gotta Have A Song	5
71	Tamla Motown TMG 772	We Can Work It Out/Don't Wonder Why (some in p/s)	20/5
71	Tamla Motown TMG 779	Never Dreamed You'd Leave In Summer/If You Really Love Me	5
72	Tamla Motown TMG 798	If You Really Love Me/Think Of Me As Your Soldier	5
84	Tamla Motown TMGT 1368	Do I Do/I Ain't Gonna Stand For It (12", p/s)	8

EPs

64	Stateside SE 1014	I CALL IT PRETTY MUSIC BUT THE OLD PEOPLE CALL IT THE BLUES (EP)	100
65	Tamla Motown TME 2006	LITTLE STEVIE WONDER (EP)	75

LPs

63	Oriole PS 40049	TRIBUTE TO UNCLE RAY (LP)	125
63	Oriole PS 40050	THE TWELVE-YEAR-OLD GENIUS — LIVE (LP)	70
64	Stateside SL 10078	THE JAZZ SOUL OF LITTLE STEVIE WONDER (LP)	80

(The above EPs and LPs were credited to Little Stevie Wonder.)

65	Stateside SL 10108	HEY, HARMONICA MAN (LP)	90
66	T. Motown (S)TML 11036	UPTIGHT (EVERYTHING'S ALRIGHT) (LP, mono/stereo)	25/30
67	T. Motown (S)TML 11045	DOWN TO EARTH (LP, mono/stereo)	30/35
68	T. Motown (S)TML 11059	I WAS MADE TO LOVE HER (LP)	25
68	T. Motown (S)TML 11075	GREATEST HITS (LP)	15
68	T. Motown (S)TML 11085	SOMEDAY AT CHRISTMAS (LP)	30
69	T. Motown (S)TML 11098	FOR ONCE IN MY LIFE (LP)	20
69	T. Motown (S)TML 11128	MY CHERIE AMOUR (LP)	15
70	T. Motown STML 11150	STEVIE WONDER 'LIVE' (LP)	12
70	T. Motown STML 11164	'LIVE' AT THE TALK OF THE TOWN (LP)	12
70	T. Motown STML 11169	SIGNED, SEALED AND DELIVERED (LP)	12
71	T. Motown STML 11183	WHERE I'M COMING FROM (LP)	15

(The above albums originally came with flipback sleeves; see also Diana Ross, Dionne Warwick)

WONDER BOY

69	Jackpot JP 703	Sweeten My Coffee (actually by Slim Smith)/MISTER MILLER: Cherry Pink	7
69	Jackpot JP 705	Love Power (actually by Slim Smith)/PAT KELLY: Since You Are Gone	7
71	Jackpot JP 764	Just For A Day/He Ain't Heavy	6
71	Concord CON 015	Just For A Day/He Ain't Heavy	7

(see also Slim Smith, Pat Kelly)

WONDER BOY

75	Ackee ACK 546	Pressure (Parts 1 & 2)	4

WONDERLAND

68	Polydor 56539	Poochy/Moscow	10

ALICE WONDERLAND

63	London HLU 9783	He's Mine/Cha Linde	8

WONDER STUFF

MINT VALUE £

87	Far Out GONE ONE	It's Not True.../A Wonderful Day/Like A Merry-Go-Round/Down Here (EP, p/s)	45
87	Far Out GONE 002	Unbearable/Ten Trenches Deep (some with p/s)	15/6
87	Far Out GO BIG 002	Unbearable/Ten Trenches Deep/I Am A Monster/Frank (12", p/s)	8
88	Polydor GONE 3	Give Give Give Me More More More/A Song Without An End (p/s)	6
88	Polydor GONEX 3	Give Give Give Me More More More/A Song Without An End/ Meaner Than Mean/Sell The Free World (12", p/s)	8
88	Polydor GONECD 3	Give Give Give Me More More More/A Song Without An End/ Meaner Than Mean/Sell The Free World (CD)	10
88	Polydor 080 582-2	Give Give Give Me More More More (video)/A Song Without An End/ Meaner Than Mean/Sell The Free World (CD Video)	10
88	Polydor GONECD 4	A Wish Away/Jealousy/Happy-Sad/Goodbye Fatman (CD)	10
88	Polydor GONECD 5	It's Yer Money I'm After Baby/Astley In The Noose/Ooh, She Said/ Rave From The Grave (CD)	10
89	Polydor GONE 6	Who Wants To Be The Disco King?/(same) (promo only, with dayglo p/s)	10
89	Polydor GONEX 6	Who Wants To Be The Disco King?/Unbearable (live)/No For The 13th Time (live)/Ten Trenches Deep (live) (12", p/s, with inner p/s)	8
89	Polydor GONECD 6	Who Wants To Be The Disco King? (Remix)/Unbearable (live)/No For The 13th Time (live)/Ten Trenches Deep (live) (CD)	8
89	House Of Dolls HOD 011	Who Wants To Be The Disco King? (King Of Disco Megamix)/PRUDES: Christmas/SANDKINGS: Colourblind/WORLD MUSIC: Stop Playing With My Heart (no p/s, free with *House Of Dolls* magazine)	6/4
89	Polydor GONECD 7	Don't Let Me Down Gently/It Was Me Don't Let Me Down Gently (Extended Version) (CD)	7
89	Polydor GONECD 8	Golden Green/Get Together/Gimme Some Truth (CD)	7
87	Far Out	A HANDFUL OF SONGS (private cassette)	20
87	Polydor	A HANDFUL OF SONGS (cassette, promo only, different to above)	15
88	Polydor GONECD 1	THE EIGHT-LEGGED GROOVE MACHINE (CD, mispressed with "Wish Away" printed on front cover)	30

(see also Weknowwhereyoulive)

WONDERWHEEL
(see under Gary Wright)

WONDER WHO

65	Philips BF 1440	Don't Think Twice, It's Alright/Sassy	7
66	Philips BF 1504	On The Good Ship Lollipop/You're Nobody Till Somebody Loves You.	7
67	Philips BF 1600	Lonesome Road/FOUR SEASONS: Around And Around	7

(see also Four Seasons, Frankie Valli)

ROYCE WONG

65	Blue Beat BB 301	Everything's Gonna Be Alright/Hang Your Head And Cry	12

ANITA WOOD

62	London HLS 9585	I'll Wait Forever/I Can't Show You How I Feel	20
64	Sue WI 328	Dream Baby/This Happened Before	18

BOBBY WOOD

64	Pye International 7N 25264	I'm A Fool For Loving You/My Heart Went Boing! Boing! Boing!	8

BRENTON WOOD

67	Philips BF 1579	Oogum Boogum Song/I Like The Way You Love Me	6
67	Liberty LBF 15021	Gimme Little Sign/I Think You Got Your Fools Mixed Up	6
68	Liberty LBF 15065	Baby You Got It/Catch You On The Rebound	5
68	Liberty LBF 15103	Some Got It, Some Don't/Me And You	5
70	Pye International 7N 25522	Great Big Bundle Of Love/Can You Dig It	10
71	United Artists UP 35266	Gimme Little Sign/I Think You Got Your Fools Mixed Up (reissue)	5
73	Epic EPC 1383	Another Saturday Night/Attempted Love	5
67	Liberty LBL/LBS 83088E	GIMME A LITTLE SIGN (LP)	20

CHUCK WOOD

67	Big T BIG 104	Seven Days Too Long/Soul Shing-A-Ling	10
68	Big T BIG 107	I've Got My Lovelight Shining/Baby You Win	10
71	Mojo 2092 010	Seven Days Too Long/Soul Shing A Ling (reissue)	5

DEL WOOD

52	London L 1141	Ragtime Melody/Rainbow (78)	8
53	London L 1188	Twelfth Street Rag/Pickin' And Grinnin' (78)	8
54	London HL 8036	Ragtime Annie/Backroom Polka	35
54	London HL 8036	Ragtime Annie/Backroom Polka (78)	10
54	London RE-P 1007	RAGTIME PIANO (EP)	15
57	RCA RD 27011	DOWN YONDER (LP)	12

GLORIA WOOD

53	Capitol CL 13947	Hey, Bell Boy/Anybody Hurt? (78)	8

RONNIE WOOD

74	Warner Bros K 16463	I Can Feel The Fire/Breathe On Me	7
75	Warner Bros K 16618	If You Don't Want Me Love/I've Got A Feeling	7
76	Warner Bros K 16679	Big Bayou/Sweet Baby Mine	7
79	CBS 7785	Seven Days/Come To Realise	7
92	Continuum 12210-2	Show Me/Breathe On Me (CD, with Ronnie Wood print, signed & no'd, in black card case tied with ribbon, 600 only)	45
74	Warner Bros K 56065	I'VE GOT MY OWN ALBUM TO DO (LP, with insert)	15
75	Warner Bros K 56145	NOW LOOK (LP)	15
76	Atlantic K 50308	MAHONEY'S LAST STAND (LP, soundtrack, with Ronnie Lane)	15
79	CBS 83337	GIMME SOME NECK (LP, with inner sleeve)	12

(see also Faces, Rolling Stones, Jeff Beck, Ted Wood)

ROY WOOD

72	Harvest HAR 5048	When Gran'ma Plays The Banjo/Wake Up	7
75	Jet JET 754	Oh What A Shame/Bengal Jig (cartoon p/s)	5

75	Jet JET 761	Look Thru' The Eyes Of A Fool/Strider (some copies miscredited as "Looking Thru' The Eyes Of A Fool")	6/5
76	Jet JET 785	Any Old Time Will Do/The Rain Came Down On Everything	5
77	Warner Bros K 16961	The Stroll/Jubilee (p/s, by Wizzo Band)	5
77	Warner Bros K 17028	I Never Believed In Love/Inside My Life (as Roy Wood & Annie Haslam)	7
78	Warner Bros K 17094	Dancin' At The Rainbow's End/Waiting At This Door (p/s, as Wizzo Band)	5
79	Automatic K 17459P	(We're) On The Road Again/Saxmaniacs (picture disc)	5
80	Cheapskate CHEAP 6	Rock City/Givin' Your Heart Away (p/s, as Roy Wood's Helicopters)	5
80	Cheapskate CHEAP 12	Sing Out The Old/Watch This Space	5
81	EMI EMI 5156	Green Glass Windows/The Driving Song (p/s, as Roy Wood's Helicopters)	5
81	EMI EMI 5203	Down To Zero/Olympic Flyer (p/s)	6
82	Speed SPEED 5	O.T.T./Mystery Song (B-side actually "California Man [live]" by Wizzo Band)	5
84	Harvest HAR 5173	I Wish It Could Be Christmas Every Day/WIZZARD: See My Baby Jive (g/f p/s)	5
85	Legacy LEGACY 32	Sing Out The Old... Bring In The New (Vocal)/(Instrumental) (p/s)	5
87	Jet JET 7048	One-Two-Three/Oh What A Shame (gatefold p/s)	5
76	Harvest SHDW 408	THE ROY WOOD STORY (2-LP)	15
82	Speed SPEED 1000	THE SINGLES (LP, initially without "I Wish It Could Be Christmas Everyday")	12

(see also Wizzard, Gerry Levine & Avengers, Mike Sheridan, Danny King['s Mayfair Set], Move, ELO, Renaissance [UK], Rockers, Birds)

TED WOOD

76	Penny Farthing PEN 891	Am I Blue/Shine (B-side features Rod Stewart, Ronnie Wood, Gary Glitter & Bobby Womack)	8

(see also Temperance Seven)

VICTORIA WOOD

70s	EMI SCX 6716	LIVE (LP)	15

WOODEN HORSE

72	York SYK 526	Pick Up The Pieces/Wake Me In The Morning	8
73	York SYK 543	Wooden Horses/Typewriter And Guitar	8
72	York FYK 403	WOODEN HORSE (LP)	125
73	York FYK 413	WOODEN HORSE II (LP, withdrawn, some with sleeve)	175/100

(see also Fox)

WOODEN O & GUESTS

69	Middle Earth MDLS 301	A HANDFUL OF PLEASANT DELITES (LP)	75

WOODENTOPS

84	Food FOOD 002	Plenty/Have You Seen The Lights (p/s)	5
84	Food SNAK 002	Plenty/Have You Seen The Lights/Everybody (12", p/s)	7
86	Rough Trade RT 178D	Love Affair With Everyday Living/Why//Move Me/Well Well Well (double pack, gatefold p/s)	4

(see also Upset, Innocents)

KEN WOODMAN & HIS PICCADILLY BRASS

66	Strike JLH 101	THAT'S NICE (LP)	25

WOODPECKERS

64	Decca F 11835	The Woodpecker/You Can't Sit Down	8
65	Oriole CB 311	Hey Little Girl/What's Your Name	15

CAROL WOODS

72	Ember EMB S 319	We'll Sing The Sunshine/I Wonder What Will Happen	5
72	Ember NR 5059	OUT OF THE WOODS (LP)	15

DANNY WOODS

72	Invictus INV 532	Everybody's Tippin'/Roller Coaster	6

DONALD WOODS & EARL PALMER BAND

58	Vogue V 9107	Memories Of An Angel/That Much Of Your Love	450
58	Vogue V 9107	Memories Of An Angel/That Much Of Your Love (78)	75

GAY WOODS

84	Rewind REW 18	Something's Gotten Hold Of My Heart/Cellophane Rain (p/s)	4

(see also Gay & Terry Woods, Woods Band, Steeleye Span, Sweeney's Men)

GAY & TERRY WOODS

77	Polydor 2058 810	Save The Last Dance For Me/One More Time	6
78	Rockburgh ROCS 202	We Can Work This One Out/Piece Of Summer (p/s)	5
75	Polydor 2383 322	BACKWOODS (LP)	35
76	Polydor 2383 375	THE TIME IS RIGHT (LP, with lyric insert)	35
76	Polydor 2383 406	RENOWNED (LP, with lyric insert)	35
78	Rockburgh ROC 104	TENDER HOOKS (LP, with lyric insert)	18

(see also Woods Band, Gay Woods, Steeleye Span, Sweeney's Men)

NICK WOODS

62	London HLU 9621	Ballad Of Billy Budd/Don't Let Me Down	7

PHIL WOODS

55	Esquire 20-055	NEW JAZZ QUINTET (10" LP)	15

WOODS BAND

71	Greenwich GSLP 1004	THE WOODS BAND (LP, gatefold sleeve)	70
77	Rockburgh CREST 29	THE WOODS BAND (LP, reissue in different sleeve)	15

(see also Gay & Terry Woods)

EDWARD WOODWARD

69	Columbia DB 8547	Only A Fool/Independent Man	6
70	DJM DJS 211	Grains Of Sand/Thing Called Love	5
70	DJM DJS 218	This Man Alone/Today I Killed A Man	5
71	DJM DJS 232	The Way You Look Tonight/The Tide Will Turn For Rebecca	5
71	DJM DJS 249	It Had To Be You/Watch What Happens	5
70	DJM DJLPS 405	THIS MAN ALONE (LP)	12
71	DJM DJLPS 418	IT HAD TO BE YOU (LP)	12

Maggie WOODWARD

MAGGIE WOODWARD
| 59 | Vogue V 9148 | Ali Bama/Zulu Warrior | 12 |
| 59 | Vogue V 9148 | Ali Bama/Zulu Warrior (78) | 25 |

BRIAN WOOLEY
| 58 | Esquire EP 170 | BRIAN WOOLEY'S JAZZMEN (EP) | 10 |
| 58 | Esquire EP 190 | WILD 'N WOOLEY (EP) | 12 |

SHEB WOOLEY
51	MGM MGM 439	Hoot Owl Boogie/Country Kisses (78)	20
54	MGM MGM 757	Panama Pete/Blue Guitar (78)	15
55	MGM SP 1130	38-24-35/I Flipped	18
55	MGM MGM 824	38-24-35/I Flipped (78)	15
55	MGM SPC 5	Hill Billy Mambo/I Go Outa My Mind (export issue)	25
58	MGM MGM 981	The Purple People Eater/I Can't Believe You're Mine	20
58	MGM MGM 981	The Purple People Eater/Recipe For Love (2nd pressing, different B-side)	10
58	MGM MGM 981	The Purple People Eater/I Can't Believe You're Mine (78)	12
58	MGM MGM 997	Santa And The Purple People Eater/Star Of Love	8
58	MGM MGM 997	Santa And The Purple People Eater/Star Of Love (78)	25
59	MGM MGM 1017	Sweet Chile/More	8
60	MGM MGM 1081	Luke The Spook/My Only Treasure	10
61	MGM MGM 1132	The Wayward Wind/Bars Across The Windows	8
61	MGM MGM 1147	That's My Pa/Meet Mr. Lonely	12
62	MGM MGM 1162	Laughing The Blues/Somebody Please	10
65	MGM MGM 1257	Hootenanny Hoot/Old Joe Rag	7
65	MGM MGM 1263	Blue Guitar/Natchez Landing	6
56	MGM MGM-EP 540	JEST PLAIN, WILD AND WOOLEY (EP)	40
61	MGM MGM-C 859	SONGS FROM THE DAY OF RAWHIDE (LP)	18
62	MGM MGM-C 903	THAT'S MY MA AND THAT'S MY PA (LP)	18
63	MGM MGM-C 945	SPOOFING THE BIG ONES! (LP)	18
63	MGM MGM-C 955	TALES OF 'HOW THE WEST WAS WON' (LP)	18

(see also Ben Colder)

CHARLIE WOOLFE
| 68 | NEMS 56-3675 | Dance Dance Dance/Home | 12 |

(see also At Last The 1958 Rock & Roll Show)

WOOLIES
| 67 | RCA RCA 1602 | Who Do You Love?/Hey Girl | 30 |

WOOLLY
| 72 | RCA RCA 2297 | Golden Golden/Sugar Daddy Song | 4 |
| 73 | Mooncrest MOON 10 | Sunshine Souvenirs/Living And Loving You | 4 |

WOOLLY FISH
| 70 | Plexium PXM 16 | Way You Like It/Sound Of Thick | 5 |

BRENDA WOOTTON
71	Sentinel SENS 1006	PASTIES & CREAM (LP, with John The Fish)	25
73	Sentinel SENS 1016	CROWDY CRAWN (LP, with Richard Gendall)	20
74	Sentinel SENS 1021	NO SONG TO SING? (LP, with Robert Bartlett, private pressing with lyric inner sleeve)	18
76	Sentinel SENS 1031	STARRY-GAZEY PIE (LP, with Robert Bartlett)	20

WORD
| 83 | Word WORD 001 | Colour It!/Recurring | 4 |

WORDBUG
| 91 | Boss Tuneage BOSSTAGE6 | LOSING IT ALL (LP, also listed as Home 4, with insert) | 18 |

WORK
| 81 | Woof WOOF 2 | I Hate America/Fingers & Toes/Duty (p/s, clear vinyl) | 5 |
| 82 | Recommended | SLOW CRIMES (LP, with insert) | 12 |

(see also Art Bears)

JIMMY WORK
56	London HLD 8270	When She Said "You All"/There's Only One You	60
56	London HLD 8270	When She Said "You All"/There's Only One You (78)	20
56	London HLD 8308	You've Gotta Heart Like A Merry-Go-Round/Blind Heart	45
56	London HLD 8308	You've Gotta Heart Like A Merry-Go-Round/Blind Heart (78)	20
55	London RE-D 1039	COUNTRY SONGS — WORK STYLE (EP)	50

WORKFORCE
| 80s | WF WF 1 | The Right To Work/Holy Moses (p/s) | 4 |

WORKS
| 72 | London HLU 10360 | Orange Medley (Music Inspired By "A Clockwork Orange")/Sweet Charity | 5 |

WORLD
| 70 | Liberty LBF 15402 | Angelina/Come Out Into The Open | 6 |
| 70 | Liberty LBG 83419 | LUCKY PLANET (LP, gatefold sleeve) | 18 |

(see also Neil Innes, Bonzo Dog [Doo-Dah] Band)

WORLD COLUMN
| 76 | Capitol CL 15852 | So Is The Sun/It's Not Right | 5 |

WORLD DOMINATION ENTERPRISES
| 85 | Karbon KAR 008 | Asbestos Lead Asbestos/Beats Baby Hi (p/s) | 8 |

(see also Danny & Dressmakers)

WORLD OF OZ
68	Deram DM 187	The Muffin Man/Peter's Birthday	12
68	Deram DM 205	King Croesus/Jack	8
69	Deram DM 233	Willow's Harp/Like A Tear	12
69	Deram DML/SML 1034	THE WORLD OF OZ (LP)	40

(see also David Kubinec)

WORLD OF TWIST
92	Caff CAFF 16	The Sausage/Skidding Into Love/Space Rockit (p/s, with insert)	8

WORRYING KYNDE
67	Piccadilly 7N 35370	Call Out The Name/Got The Blame	45

JOHNNY WORTH
57	Columbia DB 3962	Let's Go/Just Because	8
57	Columbia DB 3962	Let's Go/Just Because (78)	8
58	Embassy WB 312	Tom Dooley/GORDON FRANKS: Hoots Mon	5
58	Embassy WB 312	Tom Dooley/GORDON FRANKS: Hoots Mon (78)	8
59	Embassy WB 315	It's Only Make Believe/Chantilly Lace	5
59	Embassy WB 315	It's Only Make Believe/Chantilly Lace (78)	8
59	Embassy WB 317	I Got Stung!/Baby Face	5
59	Embassy WB 317	I Got Stung!/Baby Face (78)	8
59	Embassy WB 325	(All Of A Sudden) My Hearts Sings/High School Confidential	5
59	Embassy WB 325	(All Of A Sudden) My Hearts Sings/High School Confidential	8
59	Embassy WB 329	Donna/A Pub With No Beer	5
59	Embassy WB 329	Donna/A Pub With No Beer (78)	8
59	Embassy WB 335	A Fool Such As I/Idle On Parade	5
59	Embassy WB 335	A Fool Such As I/Idle On Parade (78)	8
59	Embassy WB 338	Mean Streak/Fort Worth Jail	5
59	Embassy WB 338	Mean Streak/Fort Worth Jail (78)	8
59	Embassy WB 347	Living Doll/Lonely Boy	5
59	Embassy WB 347	Living Doll/Lonely Boy (78)	10
59	Embassy WB 354	Sal's Got A Sugar Lip/Just A Little Too Much	5
59	Embassy WB 354	Sal's Got A Sugar Lip/Just A Little Too Much (78)	10
59	Embassy WB 359	Sea Of Love/BUD ASHTON: Sleep Walk	5
59	Embassy WB 359	Sea Of Love/BUD ASHTON: Sleep Walk (78)	10
59	Embassy WB 369	Oh Carol/What Do You Want?	5
59	Embassy WB 369	Oh Carol/What Do You Want? (78)	10
59	Embassy WB 376	Pretty Blue Eyes/Way Down Yonder In New Orleans	5
59	Embassy WB 376	Pretty Blue Eyes/Way Down Yonder In New Orleans (78)	8
59	Embassy WB 379	Poor Me/A Voice In The Wilderness	5
59	Embassy WB 379	Poor Me/A Voice In The Wilderness (78)	10
60	Embassy WB 389	Handy Man/GORDON FRANKS: Beatnik Fly	5
60	Embassy WB 389	Handy Man/GORDON FRANKS: Beatnik Fly (78)	10
60	Embassy WB 393	Someone Else's Baby/Footsteps	5
60	Embassy WB 393	Someone Else's Baby/Footsteps (78)	12
60	Embassy WB 413	How About That/Nine Times Out Of Ten	5
60	Embassy WB 413	How About That/Nine Times Out Of Ten (78)	15
60	Oriole CB 1545	Nightmare/Hold Me, Thrill Me, Kiss Me	7
60	Oriole CB 1545	Nightmare/Hold Me, Thrill Me, Kiss Me (78)	20
62	Columbia DB 4811	You Know What I Mean/All These Things	6
	(see also Barry Kendall)		

MARION WORTH
60	London HL 7089	Are You Willing, Willie/This Heart Of Mine (export issue)	18
60	London HL 7097	That's My Kind Of Love/I Lost Johnny (export issue)	18

STAN WORTH ORCHESTRA
63	London HLU 9703	Roman Holiday/Wiggle Wobble Walkers	7

WRANGLERS
64	Parlophone R 5163	Liza Jane/It Just Won't Work	50
	(see also Kenny Bernard, Kenny & Wranglers)		

LINK WRAY (& HIS RAY MEN)
58	London HLA 8623	Rumble/The Swag (as Link Wray & His Ray Men)	25
58	London HLA 8623	Rumble/The Swag (as Link Wray & His Ray Men) (78)	30
63	Stateside SS 217	Jack The Ripper/The Black Widow	18
64	Stateside SS 256	The Sweeper/Weekend	15
65	Stateside SS 397	Good Rockin' Tonight/I'll Do Anything For You	18
71	Polydor 2066 120	Fire And Brimstone/Jukebox Mama	5
73	Polydor 2066 320	Lawdy Miss Clawdy/Shine The Light	5
73	Virgin VS 103	I'm So Glad, I'm So Proud/Shawnee Tribe	5
76	Virgin VS 142	I Know You're Leaving Me Now/Quicksand	5
78	Chiswick NS 32	Batman Theme/Hidden Charms (unissued, demos probably exist)	15+
64	Stateside SE 1015	MR. GUITAR (EP, sleeve credits Link Ray)	75
71	Polydor 2489 029	LINK WRAY (LP)	18
71	Union Pacific UP 002	THERE'S GOOD ROCKIN' TONIGHT (LP)	20
73	Virgin V 2006	BEANS & FATBACK (LP)	15
73	Polydor 2391 063	BE WHAT YOU WANT TO (LP)	12
74	Polydor 2391 128	THE LINK WRAY RUMBLE (LP)	12

RAY WRAY QUARTET
62	Salvo SLO 1808	When Your Lover Has Gone/A Song Is Born	18

WRECKERS
64	Granta GR 7EP 1010	THE WRECKERS' SOUND (EP)	100

WRECKLESS ERIC
77	Stiff BUY 16	Whole Wide World/Semaphore Signals (p/s)	5
78	Stiff BUY 25	Reconnez Cherie/Rags And Tatters (p/s, yellow vinyl)	5
78	Stiff BUY 34	Take The Cash/Girlfriend (p/s)	5
79	Stiff S12 BUY 49	Hit And Miss Judy/I Need A Situation/Let's Go To The Pictures (12", orange vinyl, die-cut p/s)	10
78	Stiff SEEZ B6	WRECKLESS ERIC (10" LP, brown vinyl)	10
78	Stiff SEEZ 9	THE WONDERFUL WORLD OF WRECKLESS ERIC (LP, black vinyl)	10
78	Stiff SEEZ B9	THE WONDERFUL WORLD OF WRECKLESS ERIC (LP, green vinyl)	10
78	Stiff SEEZ P9	THE WONDERFUL WORLD OF WRECKLESS ERIC (LP, picture disc & insert)	12
	(see also Len Bright Combo)		

MINT VALUE £

JENNY WREN
| 66 | Fontana TF 672 | Chasing My Dreams All Over Town/A Thought Of You | 60 |
| 66 | Fontana TF 772 | The Merry-Go-Round (Is Slowing You Down)/Take A Walk Bobby | 10 |

JENNY WREN
| 79 | RK RK 1017 | I've Danced With A Man/Bring Down The Curtain | 4 |

DAVID WRENCH
| 97 | Ochre OCH-PRO 002 | The Ballad Of The Christmas Tree And Silver Birch (1-sided mailing list freebie, 500 only) | 5 |

BIG JOHN WRENCHER
| 75 | Big Bear BB 4 | BIG JOHN'S BOOGIE (LP) | 12 |

WRIGGLERS
| 68 | Giant GN 26 | The Cooler/You Cannot Know | 12 |
| 68 | Blue Cat BS 106 | Get Right/If I Did Look | 10 |

(see also Wrigglers)

BETTY WRIGHT
68	Atlantic 584 216	Girls Can't Do What The Guys Do/Sweet Lovin' Daddy	6
72	Atlantic K 10143	Clean Up Woman/I'll Love You Forever	5
72	Atlantic K 10190	Is It You Girl/Cryin' In My Sleep	5
72	Atlantic K 40364	I LOVE THE WAY YOU LOVE (LP)	15

CHARLES WRIGHT & WATTS 103rd STREET RHYTHM BAND
69	Warner Bros WB 7250	Do Your Thing/A Dance, A Kiss And A Song	6
69	Warner Bros WB 7298	Till You Get Enough/Light My Fire	5
70	Warner Bros WB 7365	Love Land/Sorry Charlie	5
70	Warner Bros WB 7417	Express Yourself/Living On Borrowed Time	6
72	Jay Boy BOY 71	Spreadin' Honey/Charley (as Watts 103rd Street Rhythm Band)	8
70s	Warner Bros	EXPRESS YOURSELF (LP)	20

DALE WRIGHT
58	London HLD 8573	She's Neat/Say That You Care (as Dale Wright & Rock-Its)	200
58	London HLD 8573	She's Neat/Say That You Care (as Dale Wright & Rock-Its) (78)	60
59	Pye International 7N 25022	That's Show Biz/That's My Gal (as Dale Wright & Wright Guys)	50
59	Pye International N 25022	That's Show Biz/That's My Gal (as Dale Wright & Wright Guys) (78)	75

EARL WRIGHT
| 75 | Capitol CL 15825 | Thumb A Ride/Like A Rolling Stone | 5 |

GARY WRIGHT('S WONDERWHEEL)
71	A&M AMS 812	Get On The Right Road/It Takes A Little Longer	5
71	A&M AMS 826	Get On The Right Road/Over You Now	5
71	A&M AMS 852	Stand For Our Rights/Can't See The Reason	5
72	A&M AMS 888	I Know It's Right	5
72	A&M AMS 7034	Ring Of Changes/Somebody (as Wonderwheel)	5
71	A&M AMLS 2004	EXTRACTIONS (LP)	15
72	A&M AMLS 64296	FOOTPRINT (LP)	15
72	A&M AMLH 64362	RING OF CHANGES (LP, as Wright's Wonderwheel; unissued, test pressings only)	50

(see also Spooky Tooth, Magic Christians, Thomas F. Browne)

GEORGE WRIGHT
| 54 | Parlophone MSP 13 | (The Gang That Sang) Heart Of My Heart/Whistling Blues (export issue) | 15 |

GINNY WRIGHT (& TOM TALL)
55	London HL 8119	Indian Moon/Your Eyes Feasted Upon Her (solo)	40
55	London HL 8119	Indian Moon/Your Eyes Feasted Upon Her (solo) (78)	20
55	London HL 8150	Are You Mine?/Boom Boom Boomerang (with Tom Tall)	30
55	London RE-U 1035	COUNTRY SONGS VOL. 2 (EP, with Tom Tall)	40

(see also T. Tommy Cutrer & Ginny Wright, Tom Tall)

IAN WRIGHT
| 93 | M&G MAGCD 45 | Do The Right Thing (7" Version)/(Rollo — 2-1 Up Mix)/(Second To None Mix)/(Rollo Dub Mix)/(Air Max Mix)/(Rollo 1-0 Down Mix) (CD, slimline jewel case) | 10 |

(see also Pet Shop Boys)

MILTON WRIGHT & TERRA SHIRMA STRINGS
| 77 | Grapevine GRP 103 | I Belong To You/The Gallop | 5 |

NAT WRIGHT
| 59 | HMV POP 629 | Anything/For You My Love | 50 |

OTIS WRIGHT
69	High Note HS 033	Man Of Galilee/Take Up The Cross	6
67	Doctor Bird DLM 5005	PEACE PERFECT PEACE (LP)	50
67	Doctor Bird DLM 5006	IT WILL SOON BE DONE (LP)	50
60s	Coxsone TLP 1001	OVER IN GLORYLAND (LP)	50

O.V. WRIGHT
65	Vocalion VP 9249	You're Gonna Make Me Cry/Monkey Dog	15
66	Vocalion VP 9255	Poor Boy/I'm In Your Corner	12
66	Vocalion VP 9272	Gone For Good/How Long Baby	12
67	London HLZ 10137	8 Men 4 Women/Fed Up With The Blues	8
68	Sue WI 4043	What About You/What Did You Tell This Girl Of Mine	25
68	Action ACT 4505	Oh Baby Mine/Working Your Game	15
69	Action ACT 4527	I Want Everyone To Know/I'm Gonna Forget About You	12
65	Vocalion VEP 170165	CAN'T FIND TRUE LOVE (EP)	60
68	Island ILP 975	8 MEN, 4 WOMEN (LP)	60

OWEN WRIGHT
| 70 | Banana BA 310 | Wala Wala (actually by Burning Spear)/JERRY & FREEDOM SINGERS: Got To Be Sure (B-side actually by Horace Andy) | 12 |

RICK WRIGHT
78	Harvest SHVL 818	WET DREAM (LP, gatefold stickered sleeve)	12

(see also Pink Floyd, Zee)

RITA WRIGHT
68	Tamla Motown TMG 643	I Can't Give Back The Love I Feel For You/Something On My Mind	20
71	Tamla Motown TMG 791	I Can't Give Back The Love I Feel For You/Something On My Mind (reissue)	6

RITA WRIGHT
78	Jet UP 36382	Love Is All You Need/Touch Me, Take Me	12

RUBEN WRIGHT
66	Capitol CL 15460	Hey Girl/I'm Walking Out On You	20

RUBY WRIGHT
53	Parlophone MSP 6025	Till I Waltz Again With You/When I Gave You My Love (with Charlie Gore)	30
54	Parlophone MSP 6073	Bimbo/Boy, You Got Yourself A Gal	30
54	Parlophone MSP 6133	Santa's Little Sleigh Bells/Toodle-oo To You	18
55	Parlophone MSP 6150	What Have They Told You?/I Had The Funniest Feeling	18
56	Parlophone MSP 6209	I Fall In Love With You Ev'ry Day/Do You Believe?	18
59	Parlophone R 4556	Three Stars/I Only Have One Lifetime	10
59	Parlophone R 4556	Three Stars/I Only Have One Lifetime (78)	50
59	Parlophone R 4589	You're Just A Flower From An Old Bouquet/Sweet Night Of Love	8
59	Parlophone GEP 8785	THE THREE STARS GIRL (EP)	45

SAMUEL E. WRIGHT
73	Paramount PARA 3035	There's Something Funny Going On/300 Pounds Of Hunger	4

SANDRA WRIGHT
89	Demon FIEND 198	WOUNDED WOMAN (LP)	10

STEVE WRIGHT
59	London HLW 8991	Wild, Wild, Woman/Love You	200
59	London HLW 8991	Wild, Wild, Woman/Love You (78)	125

SYREETA WRIGHT
72	Mowest MWS 7001	SYREETA (LP)	12

WINSTON WRIGHT
69	Doctor Bird DB 1308	Five Miles High/CARL DAWKINS: Only Girl	12
69	Camel CA 32	Power Pack/TWO SPARKS: Throwing Stones	7
69	Explosion EX 2003	Barefoot Brigade/Slippery	15
69	Trojan TR 7701	Moonlight (Lover) Groover/SENSATIONS: Everyday Is Just A Holiday	7
70	Trojan TR 7715	Moon Invader (with Tommy McCook)/RADCLIFF RUFFIN: You Got To Love Me	7
70	Trojan TR 7775	Meshwire (with Tommy McCook)/BARONS: Darling Please Return	7
70	Explosion EX 2011	Flight 404/LLOYD & ROBIN: Gawling Come Down (B-side actually "Higher Than The Highest Mountain" by Monty Morris)	15
70	Explosion EX 2015	Funny Girl/Funny Girl Version II	6
70	Duke DU 62	Poppy Cock (with J.J. All Stars)/CARL DAWKINS: This World And Me (B-side actually "Satisfaction")	7
70	Bamboo BAM 60	Reggae Feet/DON DRUMMOND: Royal Flush (B-side act. titled "The Rocket")	10
70	High Note HS 040	Soul Pressure/Seed You Sow (with Gaytones)	7
70	Moodisc MU 3501	Musically Red (with Maudie's Allstars; actually also with Count Sticky)/RHYTHM RULERS: Bratah	7
70	G.G. GG 4504	It's Been A Long Time/PAULETTE & GEE: Feel It More And More	6
70	Techniques TE 907	Top Secret/Crazy Rhythm	8
71	Upsetter US 378	Example (with 3rd & 4th Generation)/UPSETTER: Version	6
71	Duke DU 111	Silhouettes/That Did It	6
71	Camel CA 71	Silhouettes/That Did It	6

(see also Ethiopians, John Holt, J.J. Allstars, Slickers)

ZACHARIAH WRIGHT
70s	Bamboo BAM 403	Lumumba Limbo/Green, Red and Gold	8

WRIT
66	Decca F 12385	Did You Ever Have To Make Up Your Mind/Solid Golden Teardrops	6

WRITING ON THE WALL
69	Middle Earth MDS 101	Child On A Crossing/Lucifer Corpus	25
73	Pye 7N 45251	Man Of Renown/Buffalo	15
69	Middle Earth MDLS 303	THE POWER OF THE PICTS (LP)	150
95	Pie & Mash PAM 003	RARITIES FROM THE MIDDLE EARTH (LP, 500 only)	12
95	Tenth Planet TP 017	CRACKS IN THE ILLUSION OF LIFE (LP, gatefold sleeve)	12
96	Tenth Planet TP 018	BURGHLEY ROAD (LP, 1,000 only)	12

(see also Three's A Crowd)

W12 SPOTS
70s	Shepherds Bush SB 1	Sid Never Did/COSMIC PUNKS: 99 Years (no p/s)	12

WURZEL
87	GWR GWR 4	Bess/People Say I'm Crazy (p/s)	7
87	GWR GWT 4	Bess/People Say I'm Crazy/Midnight In London/E.S.P. (12", p/s)	10

(see also Motörhead)

JOHNNY WYATT
68	President PT 109	This Thing Called Love/To Whom It May Concern	5

ROBERT WYATT
74	Virgin VS 114	I'm A Believer/Memories	5
77	Virgin VS 115	Yesterday Man/Sonia	6
82	Rough Trade RT 115	Shipbuilding/Memories Of You (reissue, foldout p/s)	5
70	CBS 64189	THE END OF AN EAR (LP)	18
74	Virgin V 2017	ROCK BOTTOM (LP)	12
75	Virgin V 2034	RUTH IS STRANGER THAN RICHARD (LP)	12
82	Rough Trade ROUGH 35	NOTHING CAN STOP US (LP, early pressing without "Shipbuilding")	12

(see also Soft Machine, Matching Mole, Centipede, Ben Watt)

RICHARD ('POPCORN') WYLIE

| 63 | Columbia DB 7012 | Brand New Man/So Much Love In My Heart (as Richard Wylie) | 20 |
| 77 | Grapevine GRP 100 | Rosemary What Happened (Parts 1 & 2) (as Richard 'Popcorn' Wylie) | 5 |

BILL WYMAN

74	Rolling Stones RS 19112	Monkey Grip Glue/What A Blow	6
74	Rolling Stones RS 19115	White Lightning/Pussy	7
76	Rolling Stones RS 19119	A Quarter To Three/Soul Satisfying	5
76	Rolling Stones RS 19120	Apache Woman/Soul Satisfying	8
81	Polydor POSP 297	Green Ice Theme/Cloudhoppers (p/s)	12
81	Polydor POSP 259	Tenderness (Maria Muldaur)/Noche De Amor	7
74	Rolling Stones COC 59102	MONKEY GRIP (LP)	15
76	Rolling Stones COC 59105	STONE ALONE (LP)	15
81	A&M AMLSP 68540	BILL WYMAN (LP, picture disc)	15
81	Polydor POLS 11031	GREEN ICE (LP, soundtrack)	15
83	Ripple (no cat. no.)	DIGITAL DREAMS (LP, soundtrack, promo only)	100
	(see also Rolling Stones, End)		

WYNDER K. FROG

66	Island WI 280	Turn On Your Lovelight/Zooming	20
66	Island WI 3011	Sunshine Superman/Blues For A Frog	12
67	Island WIP 6006	Green Door/Dancing Frog	12
67	Island WIP 6014	I Am A Man/Shook Shimmy & Shake	15
68	Island WIP 6044	Jumping Jack Flash/Baldy	10
67	Island ILP 944/ILPS 9044	SUNSHINE SUPERFROG (LP, white label)	50
68	Island ILP 982/ILPS 9082	OUT OF THE FRYING PAN (LP, pink label)	30
	(see also Keef Hartley Band, Miller Anderson, Fair Weather, Grease Band)		

MARTYN WYNDHAM-READ

70	Trailer LER 2009	NED KELLY AND THAT GANG (LP, white label, later 'highway' label)	18/12
71	Trailer LER 2028	MARTYN WYNDHAM-READ (LP)	15
73	Argo ZFB 82	HARRY THE HAWKER IS DEAD (LP)	25
75	Trailer LER 2092	MAYPOLES TO MISTLETOE (LP)	12
77	Broadside BRO 128	ENGLISH SPORTING BALLADS (LP, 1 side by High Level Ranters, 2000 only)	20
	(see also A.L. Lloyd)		

TAMMY WYNETTE

68	CBS 3594	D-I-V-O-R-C-E/Don't Make Me Now	4
69	CBS 3961	Stand By Your Man/I Stayed Long Enough	4
73	CBS EQ 30658	WE SURE CAN LOVE EACH OTHER (LP, quadrophonic)	10
	(see also George Jones, David Houston & Tammy Wynette)		

PETER WYNGARDE

70	RCA Victor RCA 1967	La Ronde De L'Amour/The Way I Cry Over You	25
70	RCA Victor PW 1	"Commits" Rape/The Way I Cry Over You (LP sampler, promo only)	40
70	RCA Victor SF 8087	PETER WYNGARDE (LP, gatefold sleeve)	120
	(see also Larry Wallis, Tyrannosaurus Rex)		

ALBERT WYNN CREOLE JAZZ

| 52 | Vocalion V 1018 | Down By The Levee/Parkway Stomp (78) | 8 |

SANDY WYNNS

| 65 | Fontana TF 550 | Touch Of Venus/Lovers' Quarrel | 165 |

MARK WYNTER

60	Decca F 11263	Image Of A Girl/Glory Of Love	7
60	Decca F 11279	Kickin' Up The Leaves/That's What I Thought	7
61	Decca F 11323	Dream Girl/Two Little Girls	7
61	Decca F 11354	Exclusively Yours/Warm And Willing	7
61	Decca F 11380	Girl For Ev'ry Day/The Best Time For Love	8
62	Decca F 11434	Heaven's Plan/In Your Heart	10
62	Decca F 11467	Angel Talk/I Love Her Still	10
62	Pye 7N 15466	Venus In Blue Jeans/Please Come Back To Me	6
62	Pye 7N 15492	Go Away Little Girl/That Kinda Talk	5
63	Pye 7N 15511	Aladdin's Lamp/It Can Happen Any Day	6
63	Pye 7N 15525	Shy Girl/Because Of You	6
63	Pye 7N 15554	Running To You/Don't Cry	8
63	Pye 7N 15577	It's Almost Tomorrow/Music To Midnight	5
64	Pye 7N 15595	The Boy You're Kissin'/I Learned A Lot From You	6
64	Pye 7N 15626	Only You/It's Love You Want	6
64	Pye 7N 15658	Answer Me/I Wish You Everything	6
64	Pye 7N 15686	Love Hurts/Can't Help Forgiving You	6
64	Pye 7N 15716	Forever And A Day/And I Love Her	6
65	Pye 7N 15771	Can I Get To Know You Better/Am I Living A Dream	8
65	Pye 7N 15861	Someday You'll Want Me To Want You/Here Comes Summer	6
65	Pye 7N 15994	Babe I'm Gonna Leave You/The Very Thought Of You	6
66	Pye 7N 17051	Before Your Time/Something About You	6
66	Pye 7N 17122	We'll Sing In The Sunshine/Pencil And Paper	5
66	Pye 7N 17214	You Made Me What I Am/Oh Girl	6
68	Pye 7N 17438	Please Love Me Tender/The Best Thing In My Life	6
68	Pye 7N 17651	She's A Woman/Bless Your Little Heart	6
60	Decca DFE 6674	MARK TIME (EP)	40
63	Pye NEP 24176	IT'S MARK TIME (EP)	30
64	Pye NEP 24185	WYNTER TIME (EP)	30
61	Decca LK 4409	THE WARMTH OF WYNTER (LP)	40
64	Golden Guinea GGL 0250	MARK WYNTER (LP)	15
65	Ace Of Clubs ACL 1141	MARK WYNTER (LP)	30
67	Marble Arch MAL 647	MARK WYNTER (LP)	12
	(see also Joe Brown & Mark Wynter)		

GAIL WYNTERS

| 67 | London HLE 10144 | Snap Your Fingers/Find Myself A New Love | 6 |

JOHNNY X & THE SINGIN' SWINGIN' EIGHT
63   Fontana TF 408 — Lemonade/Come Closer Melinda. 10

STAVROS XARHAKOS
73   Columbia DB 9025 — The Lotus Eaters Theme/Ta Trena Pou Fyghan 5

X-AXIS
93   Detour DR 005 — The Wild Bunch/Deep Dark City 8

X-CALIBURS
65   CBS 201805 — We Will Love/Swing That Chariot. 6
65   Mercury MF 941 — You'll Find Out/That's What Happens (possible as Xcalibres) 6

X-CELLS
81   Snotty Snail NEL COL 4 — Freedom Man/SCHIZOID: Nowhere To Go (p/s) 6
81   Snotty Snail NEL COL 5 — Schizoid (p/s) 5

X-CERTS
78   Zama — Feeling The Groove (p/s) 8
81   Recreational PLAY 1 — Together/Untogether (p/s, with lyric insert). 4

X-DREAMYSTS
78   Good Vibrations GOT 5 — Right Way Home/Dance Away Love (p/s) 5
79   Polydor 2059 129 — Bad News/Money Talks (p/s) 4
80   Polydor 2059 235 — I Don't Wanna Go/Silly Games (p/s). 4
80   Polydor 2059 252 — Stay The Way You Are/Race Against Time (p/s). 4
80   Polydor 2442 181 — X-DREAMYSTS (LP) 10

X-E-CUTORS
80   Rok ROK 13/14 — Too Far To Look Inside My Head/X-FILMS: After My Blood (die-cut co. sleeve) . . . 5

X-EFFECTS
80   Pre-Fab ZO-2 — 19 (French Gymnastics)/Female Pulse (p/s) 4

XERO
83   Brickyard XERO 1 — Oh Baby/Hold On (2-track issue, p/s) 20
83   Brickyard XERO 1 — Oh Baby/Hold On/Lone Wolf (3-track issue, p/s). 10
83   Brickyard XERO 1T — Oh Baby/Hold On/Lone Wolf (12", plain card sleeve with sticker, withdrawn) . . . 15
(see also Bruce Dickinson, Iron Maiden)

XILES
65   Xiles XIL 004 — Our Love Will Never End/The Only People In This World 20

XIT
72   Rare Earth RES 107 — I Was Raised/End 5
73   Rare Earth RES 111 — Reservation Of Education/Young Warrior 5
72   Rare Earth SREA 4002 — PLIGHT OF THE RED MAN (LP) 18

XL5
63   HMV POP 1148 — XL5 (Zero G)/Caviare 15
63   HMV 7EG 8802 — FIREBALL AND OTHER TITLES (EP, 2 tracks by Don Spencer) 40

XL5's
80   Fourplay FOUR 004 — Fireball/Misirlou 8

X-MAL DEUTSCHLAND
83   4AD AD 311 — Incubus Succubus II/Vito (p/s, some with "Vito" listed as A-side) 20/7

X-MEN
84   Creation CRE 006 — Do The Ghost/Talk (foldaround p/s in bag, orange/blue or yellow/green p/s) 5
85   Creation CRE 013 — Spiral Girl/Bad Girl (foldaround p/s in poly bag). 4

X-O-DUS
79   Factory FAC 11 — English Black Boys/See Them A-Come (12", dark grey textured p/s, later light grey p/s). 8

XPOZEZ
80s Fight FIGHT 1 — SYSTEMS KILL (EP). 6
82   Red Rhino RED 15 — 1,000 Marching Feet/Terminal Case (p/s) 5
83   Sexual Phonograph SPH 2 — (Be My) New York Doll/It's All Been Done Before (p/s) 4

X-RAYS
59   London HLR 8805 — Chinchilla/Out Of Control. 30
59   London HLR 8805 — Chinchilla/Out Of Control (78) 60

X-RAY SPEX
77   Virgin VS 189 — Oh Bondage, Up Yours/I Am A Cliche (some in p/s) 15/4
77   Virgin VS 189-12 — Oh Bondage, Up Yours/I Am A Cliche (12", company sleeve). 10
78   EMI International INT 553 — The Day The World Turned Day-Glo/Iama Poseur (p/s, 15,000 orange vinyl) . . . 8/5
78   EMI International INT 563 — Identity/Let's Submerge (p/s, initially on pink vinyl) 6/4
78   EMI International INT 573 — Germ Free Adolescents/Age (p/s). 4
79   EMI International INT 583 — Highly Inflammable/Warrior In Woolworths (p/s, initially on red vinyl) 6/4
78   EMI Intl. INS 3023 — GERM FREE ADOLESCENTS (LP, with lyric inner sleeve) 15
90s EMI Intl. INS 3023 — GERM FREE ADOLESCENTS (LP, orange vinyl reissue) 12
(see also Poly Styrene, Mari Elliott, Essential Logic)

MINT VALUE £

XS DISCHARGE

| 80 | G. Marxist COMMINIQUE 3 | Across The Border/Frustration (p/s) | 8 |
| 80 | Groucho Marxist WH 3 | Life's A Wank (p/s) | 8 |

XS ENERGY

78	World WRECK 1	Eighteen/Jenny's Alright/Horrorscope! (numbered foldover yellow or green p/s, stamped white labels)	15
79	Dead Good DEAD 1	Eighteen/Jenny's Alright/Horrorscope! (reissue, 'National Souvenir Issue', different foldover p/s, stamped white labels)	10
79	Dead Good DEAD 1	Eighteen/Jenny's Alright/Horrorscope! (no p/s, stamped white sleeve & yellow printed labels)	8
79	Dead Good DEAD 3	Use You/Imaginary (p/s)	7

XTC

77	Virgin VS 188	Science Friction/She's So Square (unreleased, in picture sleeve)	1,000
77	Virgin VS 188	Science Friction/She's So Square (unreleased, no picture sleeve)	50
77	Virgin VS 188-12	3D EP (12" version of the above, p/s)	10
78	Virgin VS 201	Statue Of Liberty/Hang On To The Night (p/s)	6
78	Virgin VS 209	This Is Pop?/Heatwave (p/s)	6
78	Virgin VS 231	Are You Receiving Me/Instant Tunes (p/s)	5
79	Virgin VS 259	Life Begins At The Hop/Homo Safari (30,000 clear vinyl, PVC sleeve & insert)	6
79	Virgin VS 259	Life Begins At The Hop/Homo Safari (p/s)	4
79	Virgin VS 282	Making Plans For Nigel/Bushman President (Homo Safari Series No. 2)/Pulsing, Pulsing (initially with game-board p/s with playing pieces)	6/4
79	Smash Hits HIT 002	Ten Feet Tall/SKIDS: The Olympian (33rpm red flexidisc with Smash Hits)	8/5
80	Virgin VS 322	Wait Till Your Boat Goes Down/Ten Feet Tall (U.S. Version) (p/s)	5
80	Virgin VS 365	Generals And Majors/Don't Lose Your Temper (p/s)	4
80	Virgin VS 365	Generals And Majors/Don't Lose Your Temper//Smokeless Zone/The Somnambulist (double pack)	6
81	Virgin VS 372	Towers Of London/Set Myself On Fire (live) (p/s)	4
81	Virgin VS 372	Towers Of London/Set Myself On Fire (live)//Battery Brides (live)/Scissor Man (double pack)	6
81	RSO RSO 71	Take This Town/RUTS: Babylon's Burning (p/s)	6
81	Virgin VS 384	Sgt. Rock (Is Going To Help Me)/Living Through Another Cuba/Generals And Majors (1st 20,000 in poster p/s, with stickered p/s sleeve)	6/4
81	Virgin VS 407	Respectable Street/Strange Tales, Strange Tails/Officer Blue (p/s)	4
82	Virgin VS 462	Senses Working Overtime/Blame The Weather/Tissue Tigers (The Arguers) (initially in foldout poster p/s)	5/4
82	Virgin VS 462-12	Senses Working Overtime/Egyptian Solution (Homo Safari Series No. 3)/Blame The Weather/Tissue Tigers (12", p/s)	7
82	Lyntone LYN 11032	Looking For Footprints (flexidisc free with Flexipop magazine, issue 16; on red, blue, green or yellow vinyl)	8/5
82	Virgin VS 482	Ball And Chain/Punch And Judy/Heaven Is Paved With Broken Glass (p/s)	4
82	Virgin VS 482-12	Ball And Chain/Heaven Is Paved With Broken Glass/Punch And Judy/Cockpit Dance Mixture (12", p/s)	7
82	Virgin VS 490	No Thugs In Our House/Chain Of Command/Limelight/Over Rusty Water (9" die-cut gatefold p/s)	8
83	Virgin VS 553	Great Fire/Gold (p/s, with outer p/s)	6
83	Virgin VSY 606	Wonderland/Jump (picture disc)	6
83	Virgin VS 613	Love On A Farmboy's Wages/In Loving Memory Of A Name/Desert Island/Toys (double pack)	7
84	Virgin VS 709	All You Pretty Girls/Washaway (p/s, with outer die-cut p/s)	5
84	Virgin VS 721	This World Over/Blue Overall (p/s, with postcards)	5
87	Virgin VSY 912	The Meeting Place/The Man Who Sailed Around His Soul (clear vinyl with printed PVC sleeve)	6
87	Virgin CDEP 3	Dear God/Homo Safari/Bushman President/Egyptian Solution/Mantis On Parole/Frost Circus/Procession Toward Learning Land (CD, gatefold card sleeve)	10
88	Virgin CDT 9	Senses Working Overtime/Egyptian Solution (Homo Safari Series No. 3)/Blame The Weather/Tissue Tigers (The Arguers) (3" CD, card sleeve)	7
89	Virgin VSCD 1158	Mayor Of Simpleton/Ella Guru/Living In A Haunted Heart/The Good Things (3" CD, gatefold card sleeve)	12
89	Virgin VSCD 1177	King For A Day (7" Version)/King For A Day (12" Version)/My Paint Heroes (Home Demo)/Skeletons (Home Demo) (3" CD, 'crown' pack)	12
89	Virgin VSCD 1201	The Loving/Cynical Days/The World Is Full Of Angry Young Men (3" CD card sleeve)	7
92	Virgin VSCDG 1415	The Ballad Of Peter Pumpkinhead/Wardance/My Bird Performs (demo)/Always Winter Never Christmas (demo) (CD, digipak)	7
92	Virgin	Wrapped In Grey (p/s, withdrawn, 2,000 only)	100
78	Virgin V 2095	WHITE MUSIC (LP, with black inner sleeve)	10
78	Virgin V 2108	GO 2 (LP, with insert, 1st 15,000 with bonus 12" EP: "Go +")	15
79	Virgin V 2129	DRUMS AND WIRES (LP, with gatefold insert, 1st 15,000 with free 7": "Chain Of Command"/"Limelight" [VDJ 30])	12
80	Virgin V 2173	BLACK SEA (LP, with green paper outer sleeve & lyric insert)	10
84	Virgin V 2251	WAXWORKS (LP, with bonus LP, "Beeswax")	12
84	Virgin V 2325	THE BIG EXPRESS (LP, circular sleeve & lyric inner)	10
88	Virgin CDVT 2581	ORANGES AND LEMONS (LP, as 3-CD single box set)	12

(see also Mr Partridge, Barry Andrews, Three Wise Men, Dukes Of Stratosphere, Johnny Japes & His Jesticles, Colonel, Spys)

XTRAVERTS

78	Spike SRTS SP 001	Blank Generation/A-Lad-In-Sane (no p/s)	70
78	Rising Sun RS 1	Police State/PLASTIC PEOPLE: Demolition (p/s, multi-coloured vinyl)	50
81	Xtraverts XTRA 001	Speed/1984 (white labels, 'photo' or 'no photo' foldout poster p/s)	40
97	Bin Liner RUBBISH LP001	SO MUCH HATE (LP, 1,000 only, 1st 500 in printed carrier bag)	15/12

XYMOX

| 85 | 4AD BAD 504 | A Day/Stranger (12", p/s) | 12 |

YACHTS

77	Stiff BUY 19	Suffice To Say/Freedom Is A Heavy Wine (p/s) 4
78	Radar ADA 23	Look Back In Love (Not In Anger)/I Can't Stay Long (p/s, blue vinyl) 5
78	Radar ADA 25	The Yachting Type/Hypnotising Lies (p/s) 4
79	Radar ADA 36	Love You, Love You/Crazy People (p/s, orange vinyl) 5
79	Radar ADA 42	Box Zoz/Permanent Damage (p/s) 4
79	Radar ADA 49	Now I'm Spoken For/Secret Agent (p/s) 4
77	Radar ADA 52	There's A Ghost In My House/Revelry/The Yachting Type (p/s) 4
80	Radar ADA 57	IOU/24 Hours From Tulsa (p/s) 4
79	Radar RAD 19	THE YACHTS (LP, with live 7" "Suffice To Say"/"On And On" [SAM 98, p/s]) 12

(see also Big In Japan)

YA HO WA 13

83	Psycho PSYCHO 2	GOLDEN SUNRISE (LP, 319 copies only, different coloured vinyls, some on black vinyl without sleeve) 60

(see also Seeds)

YAKS

65	Decca F 12115	Yakety Yak/Back In '57 15

YAMASHTA/WINWOOD/SHRIEVE/SCHULZE/DIMEOLA

78	Island IPR 2014	Crossing The Line (live)/Winnerloser (live) (12", p/s) 7
78	Island ILPS 9387	GO (LP, with 7" booklet) 12

(see also Stevie Winwood, Suntreader)

YAMASUKIS

71	Dandelion DAN 7004	Yamasuki/Aieaoa (p/s, also listed as K 19003) 5

YANA

56	HMV POP 252	Climb Up The Wall/If You Don't Love Me 15
57	HMV POP 340	Mr. Wonderful/Too Close For Comfort 12
58	HMV POP 481	I Need You/I Miss You Mama 10
58	HMV POP 481	I Need You/I Miss You Mama (78) 8
58	HMV POP 546	Papa And Mama/In The Morning 10

JIMMY YANCEY

54	HMV 7EG 8062	JIMMY YANCEY (EP) 20
55	HMV 7EG 8083	JIMMY YANCEY (EP) 20
58	Vogue EPV 1203	YANCEY'S PIANO (EP) 20
54	London AL 3525	JIMMY YANCEY — A LOST RECORDING DATE (10" LP) 25
56	Vogue LDE 166	JAZZ IMMORTALS VOLUME 2 (10" LP) 30
68	Atlantic 590 018	LOWDOWN DIRTY BLUES (LP) 15
72	Gannet 5137	JIMMY AND MAMA YANCEY (LP) 12

MAMA YANCEY/DON EWELL

57	Tempo LAP 7	MAMA YANCEY-DON EWELL (10" LP) 30

(see also Don Ewell)

ZALMAN YANOVSKY

67	Kama Sutra KAS 209	As Long As You're Here/Ereh Er'uoy Sa Gnol Sa (unreleased)
67	Pye International 7N 25438	As Long As You're Here/Ereh Er'uoy Sa Gnol Sa 6
71	Kama Sutra 2316 003	ALIVE AND WELL IN ARGENTINA (LP) 15

(see also Mugwumps, Lovin' Spoonful)

YARDBIRDS

64	Columbia DB 7283	I Wish You Would/A Certain Girl 20
64	Columbia DB 7391	Good Morning Little Schoolgirl/I Ain't Got You 20
65	Columbia DB 7499	For Your Love/Got To Hurry 8
65	Columbia DB 7594	Heart Full Of Soul/Steeled Blues 6
65	Columbia DB 7706	Evil Hearted You/Still I'm Sad (some copies with A-side miscredited to "Samwell-Smith & McCartney") 5
66	Columbia DB 7848	Shapes Of Things/You're A Better Man Than I 6
66	Columbia DB 7848	Shapes Of Things/Still I'm Sad (mispressing) 40
66	Columbia DB 7928	Over, Under, Sideways, Down/Jeff's Boogie 15
66	Columbia DB 8024	Happenings Ten Years Time Ago/Psycho Daisies 30
67	Columbia DB 8165	Little Games/Puzzles 30
68	Columbia DB 8368	Goodnight Sweet Josephine/Think About It (unreleased; acetates only) 225
83	Edsel E 5005	Over, Under, Sideways, Down/Psycho Daisies (p/s) 4
84	Edsel E 5007	Rack My Mind/Jeff's Boogie (p/s) 4
64	Columbia SEG 8421	FIVE YARDBIRDS (EP) 80
67	Columbia SEG 8521	OVER UNDER SIDEWAYS DOWN (EP) 165
64	Columbia 33SX 1677	FIVE LIVE YARDBIRDS (LP, 1st pressing, blue/black label, flipback sleeve) 60
69	Columbia 33SX 1677	FIVE LIVE YARDBIRDS (LP, 2nd pressing, black/silver label, flipback sleeve) ... 18
66	Columbia SCXC 28	HAVING A RAVE UP WITH THE YARDBIRDS (LP, export issue) 80
66	Columbia S(C)X 6063	YARDBIRDS (LP, 1st pressing, blue/black label, flipback sleeve, mono/stereo) 35/40
69	Columbia S(C)X 6063	YARDBIRDS (LP, 2nd pressing, black/silver label, flipback sleeve) 15
70	Columbia S(C)X 6063	YARDBIRDS (LP, 3rd pressing, black/silver label, non-flipback sleeve; some sleeves misprinted without front cover illustration) 15/12

MINT VALUE £

71	Regal Starline SRS 5069	REMEMBER... THE YARDBIRDS (LP)	12
84	Charly BOX 104	SHAPES OF THINGS (LP, box set)	30

(see also Eric Clapton, Jeff Beck, Jimmy Page, Keith Relf, Reign, Stairway, Sonny Boy Williamson & Yardbirds, Shoot)

PER YARROH
88	HMV PY 1	Laughing Inside/Laughing Inside (p/s, promo only; actually by Roy Harper)	7

(see also Roy Harper)

TOM YATES
67	CBS BPG 63094	SECOND CITY SPIRITUAL (LP, as Thomas Yates)	60
72	President PTLS 1053	LOVE COMES WELL ARMED (LP, with booklet)	25
77	Satril SATL 4007	SONG OF THE SHIMMERING WAY (LP, with insert)	25

YAZOO
83	Mute L12 YAZ 003	Nobody's Diary/Situation (12", numbered p/s)	10

(see also Depeche Mode, Alison Moyet, Erasure)

YAZZ
89	Big Life BLBXLP 1	THE WANTED REMIXES (mini-LP, with insert, autographed, 50 only)	15

Y BLEW
67	Qualiton QSP 7001	Maes 'B'/Beth Sy'n Dod Rhyngom Ni (p/s)	10

YEAH YEAH NOH
84	In Tape IT 008	Cottage Industry/Bias Binding/Tommy Opposite (p/s)	5
84	In Tape IT 010	Beware The Weakling Lies/Startling Pillow Case And Why? (p/s)	4
85	In Tape IT 012	Prick Up Your Ears/Brown Shirt/TERRY & GERRY: Bias Binding (p/s)	4

YEAR ONE
69	Major Minor MM 660	Eli's Comin'/Will You Be Staying After Sunday	5

YEH YEH
85	Berlin BRS 001	You Will Pay/7 Bells (1st pressing in grey p/s)	5

YELLO
81	Do It DUN 11	Bimbo/I.T. Splash (p/s)	8
82	Do It DUN 13	Bostich/She's Got A Gun (Instrumental) (p/s)	7
82	Do It DUNIT 13	Bostich/Downtown Samba/She's Got A Gun/Daily Disco (12", p/s)	12
82	Do It DUN 18	She's Got A Gun/Glue Head (p/s)	6
82	Do It DUNIT 18	She's Got A Gun/The Evening's Young/There Is No Reason (12", p/s)	10
82	Do It DUN 23	Pinball Cha Cha/Smile On You (p/s)	6
82	Do It DUNIT 23	Pinball Cha Cha/Smile On You (12", p/s)	15
83	Stiff PBUY 176	I Love You/Rubber West (3-D picture disc, with glasses)	7
83	Stiff BUYIT 176	I Love You (Extended)/Swing/Bostich (12", p/s)	7
83	Stiff BUY 191	Lost Again/Base For Alec (p/s)	8
83	Stiff DBUY 191	Lost Again/Base For Alec//Let Me Cry/She's Got A Gun (double pack)	8
83	Stiff BUYIT 191	Lost Again/Base For Alec/No More Words/Pumping Velvet (12", p/s)	7
85	Elektra EKR 1	Vicious Games/Blue Nabou (p/s)	5
85	Elektra EKR 1T	Vicious Games (Extended)/(Instrumental)/Blue Nabou (12", p/s)	8
85	Elektra EKR 17T	Desire/Oh Yeah (Indian Summer Version) (12", p/s)	7
85	Elektra EKR 17T	Desire/Oh Yeah (Indian Summer "Stella Suite Part 2"/Oh Yeah/ XS (First Ever Version) (12", double pack, some sealed)	20/18
86	Mercury MERDP 218	Goldrush/She's Got A Gun (live at Palladium N.Y.)/I Love You/ Desire (double pack, unreleased)	
86	Mercury MERX 218	Goldrush/Goldrush II/She's Got A Gun (live) (12", p/s)	7
86	Mercury MERXD 218	Goldrush/Goldrush II/She's Got A Gun (live)//Pinball Cha-Cha/ Vicious Games (12", double pack)	10
86	Mercury MERX 235	Vicious Games (Vicious Remix)/Live At The Roxy (Highlights) (12", p/s)	7
87	Mercury MERXR 253	The Rhythm Divine (Version Two)/Dr. Van Steiner (Instrumental)/The Rhythm Divine (Original 7" Version) (12", p/s, as Yello featuring Billy MacKenzie)	40
87	Mercury YELLR 112	The Race (The Pits Mix)/Oh Yeah (Dance Mix) (12", p/s)	7
87	Mercury YELCD 1	The Race (13.22)/La Habanera (CD, black & yellow card sleeve)	7
87	Mercury YELCD 1	The Race (13.22)/La Habanera (CD, individually silk-screened card sleeve, various colours)	10
87	Mercury 080 528-2	The Race (Extended Version)/Another Race (Magician's Version)/ The Race (Video) (CD Video)	12
88	Mercury YELLR 212	Tied Up In Mind/I Love You/Tied Up In Fantasia/Wall Street Bongo (12", individually silk-screen p/s)	7
88	Mercury YELCD 2	Tied Up In Life/Tied Up (7" Version)/Oh Yeah/Wall St. Bongo (CD)	7
88	Mercury 080 644-2	Tied Up In Red (Video)/Wall St. Bongo/Third Of June (CD Video)	12
89	Mercury YELLO 312	Of Course I'm Lying/Oh Yeah (Dance Mix)/The Yello Metropolitan Mixdown 1989 Pt. 1 (12", gatefold p/s)	7
89	Mercury YELLO 322	Of Course I'm Lying/Bostich/The Yello Metropolitan Mixdown 1989 Pt. 2 (12", p/s)	7
89	Mercury YELCD 3	Of Course I'm Lying/Oh Yeah (Dance Mix)/The Yello Metropolitan Mixdown 1989 Pt. I (CD, card p/s in outer box)	8
89	Mercury YELCD 32	Of Course I'm Lying/Bostich/The Yello Metropolitan Mixdown 1989 Pt. II (CD, card p/s in outer box)	8
89	Mercury 080 832-2	Third Of June/Alhambra/Otto Di Cantania/Of Course I'm Lying (Video) (CD Video)	12
89	Mercury YELCD 4	Blazing Saddles (Latinohouse Remix)/I Love You (Emilio Pasquez Rubberband Mix)/The Rhythm Divine/Blue Nabou (CD, card sleeve with heat sensitive sticker)	10
90	Mercury YELCD 5	Rubberbandman (Extended Version)/(Single Version)/Sweet Thunder (CD, with wrap-around yellow rubber face)	8
81	Do It RIDE 8	CLARO QUE SI! (LP, pink sleeve)	12
83	Stiff SEEZ 48	YOU GOTTA SAY YES TO ANOTHER EXCESS (LP, with bonus white label 12": "I Love You"/"Lost Again"/"You Gotta Say To Another Excess [remix]"/"Pumping Velvet")	20

87	Mercury MERH 100	ONE SECOND (LP, with bonus 12" in p/s: "Call It Love (Trego Snare Version) 2"/"Santiago [live at Roxy New York]")	18
88	Mercury 836 778-1	FLAG (LP, HMV competition issue, 100 only)	100
95	Urban 527 728-2	HANDS ON YELLO: THE UPDATES (2-CD, withdrawn)	50

(see also Associates)

YELLOW
70	CBS 4869	Roll It Down The Hill/Living A Lie	15

YELLOW BALLOON
67	Stateside SS 2008	Yellow Balloon/Noollab Wolley	10
68	Stateside SS 2124	Stained Glass Window/Can't Get Enough Of Your Love	6

YELLOW BELLOW ROOM BOOM
68	CBS 3205	Seeing Things Green/Easy Life	15

(see also 10cc, Frabjoy & Runcible Spoon)

YELLOW MAGIC ORCHESTRA
79	Alfa ALF 2145	Rydeen/Absolute Ego Dance (white vinyl, stickered sleeve)	7
79	A&M AMSP 7447	Tong Poo/Cosmic Surfin' (12", p/s, yellow vinyl)	10
80	A&M JAPAN 2	Nice Age/Rydeen (p/s, yellow vinyl)	7
80	A&M AMS 7502	Computer Game/Firecracker/Technopolis (yellow vinyl, PVC sleeve)	7
80	A&M AMS 7559	Behind The Mask/Yellow Magic (p/s, yellow vinyl)	7
80	A&M AMSX 7559	Behind The Mask/Tong Poo/La Femme (12", p/s)	8
81	A&M AMSP 8104	Tighten Up/Rydeen (12", p/s)	8
80	A&M LH 68516	MULTIPLIES (LP, yellow vinyl)	12

(see also Ruichi Sakamoto)

YELLOW PAGES
68	Page One POF 090	Here Comes Jane/Ring-A-Ding	6

(see also Mirage)

YELLOW PAYGES
70	UNI UNS 516	Follow The Bouncing Ball/Little Woman	8
71	UNI UNS 534	Birds Of A Feather/Lady Friend	5

YELLOWSTONE & VOICE
72	Parlophone R 5965	The Flying Dutchman/Philosopher	5
72	Regal Zonophone RZ 3065	Thinking About You And Me/Grandmother Says	5
73	Regal Zonophone RZ 3073	Memories/Well Hello	5
72	Regal Zono. SRZA 8511	YELLOWSTONE & VOICE (LP)	18

YEMM & YEMEN
66	Columbia DB 8022	Black Is The Night/Do Blondes Really Have More Fun	10

YES
69	Atlantic 584 280	Sweetness/Something's Coming	35
69	Atlantic 584 298	Looking Around/Everydays (unreleased; demos may exist)	100+
70	Atlantic 584 323	Time And A Word/The Prophet	50
70	Atlantic 2091 004	Sweet Dreams/Dear Father	30
71	Atlantic 2814 003	I've Seen All Good People (a) Your Move/Starship Trooper (a) Life Seeker (promo only)	75
72	no cat. no.	Siberian Khatru/And You And I (white label promo)	50
74	Atlantic K 10407	Roundabout/And You And I	5
77	Atlantic K 10985	Going For The One/Parallels (unreleased, copies may exist)	40+
77	Atlantic K 10985T	Going For The One (Extended)/Parallels (12", unreleased, copies may exist)	40+
77	Atlantic K 10999	Wondrous Stories/Parallels (12", blue vinyl, p/s)	8
77	Atlantic K 11047	Going For The One/Awaken Part I (12", p/s)	8
78	Atlantic K 11184	Don't Kill The Whale/Abiline (p/s)	5
83	Atco B 9817P	Owner Of A Lonely Heart/Our Song (blue, black or grey shaped picture disc)	8
83	Atco B 9817C	Owner Of A Lonely Heart/Our Song (cassette)	40
70s	Lyntone LYN 2536	Interview/Five Songs (free with 80-page Yes songbook)	40/25
69	Atlantic 588 190	YES (LP, red/plum label with lyric insert)	22
70	Atlantic 2400 006	TIME AND A WORD (LP, red/plum label, with lyric insert)	20
71	Atlantic 2400 101	THE YES ALBUM (LP, red/plum label, gatefold sleeve)	20
71	Atlantic 2401 019	FRAGILE (LP, red/plum label, gatefold sleeve with booklet)	20
77	Atlantic DSK 50379	GOING FOR THE ONE (LP, as 3 x 12" singles, promo only)	75
80	Atlantic K 50842	CLASSIC YES (LP, with bonus 7" "Roundabout"/"Your Move" [SAM 141])	15

(see also Jon Anderson, Hans Christian, Syn, Syndicats, Winston's Fumbs, Warriors, Federals, Peter Banks, Flash, Asia, Rick Wakeman, Steve Howe, Anderson Bruford Wakeman & Howe, Refugee, Chris Squire)

YETTIES
69	Acorn CF 203	FIFTY STONE OF LOVELINESS (LP)	25
70	Argo ZFB 16	KEEP A-RUNNIN' — IT'S THE YETTIES (LP)	12
71	Argo ZFB 32	OUR FRIENDS (LP)	15
72	Argo ZFB 38	DORSET IS BEAUTIFUL (LP)	12
73	Argo ZFB 86	ALL AT SEA (LP)	12

JOHN YLVISAKER
68	Avantgarde AV 107	COOL LIVIN' (LP)	60

YOBS
77	NEMS NES 114	Run Rudolph Run/The Worm Song (p/s)	7
78	Yob YOB 79	Silent Night/Stille Nacht (p/s)	7
81	Safari YULE 1	Rub-A-Dum-Dum/Another Christmas (p/s)	6
82	Fresh FRESH 41	Yobs On 45/The Ballad Of Warrington (p/s)	6
80	Safari RUDE 1	CHRISTMAS ALBUM (LP)	15

(see also Boys)

MAHARISHI MAHESH YOGI
67	Liberty LBS 83075E	MAHARISHI MAHESH YOGI (LP)	20

MINT VALUE £

YOLANDA
60 Triumph RGM 1007 With This Kiss/Don't Tell Me Not To Love You 25
(see also Kenny Graham & His Satellites)

YO LA TENGO
95 Duophonic Super 45s Evanescent Psychic Pez Drop/STEREOLAB: Long Hair Of Death
      DS 45-10 (gig single, fluorescent yellow vinyl,
          plain white stickered card sleeve, 3,000 only). 20
96 Earworm WORM 4 Blue — Green Arrow/Watching The Sun Set On Johnny Carson
          (2,000 only, 100 in handmade p/s) 12/8

NOLA YORK
64 HMV POP 1326 I Don't Understand/Here I Stand 5
66 Philips BF 1527 A Whole Lotta Lovin'/You Just Didn't Wanna Know 6
66 Philips BF 1527 Whole Lotta Lovin'/You Just Didn't Wanna Know 5
67 Philips BF 1582 Photographs/He's Looking At Her 5
67 Philips BF 1606 There's So Much Love All Around Me/Sleeping Boutique 5
68 Philips BF 1714 Ciao Baby/We'll Get To Heaven 7
(see also Bow Bells)

PETE YORK PERCUSSION BAND
73 Decca TXS 109 PERCUSSION BAND (LP, with Ian Paice, gatefold sleeve) 25
(see also Spencer Davis Group, Hardin & York, Deep Purple)

RUSTY YORK
58 Parlophone R 4398 Peggy Sue/Shake 'Em Up Baby (unissued, demos only) 450
(see also Bonnie Lou & Rusty York)

STEVE YORK'S CAMELO PARDALIS
73 Virgin V 2003 MANOR LIVE (LP) 10
(see also Elkie Brooks, Boz Scaggs, Lol Coxhill, Graham Bond, Mike Patto)

YORK BROTHERS
54 Parlophone CMSP 5 Why Don't You Open The Door?/You're My Every Dream Come True
          (export issue) 20
54 Parlophone CMSP 22 Strange Town/Three O'Clock Blues (export issue) 20
55 Parlophone DP 419 Deep Within My Heart/I'll Leave The Door Open (78, export issue) 10
55 Parlophone DP 421 That's All I Want From You/A Chip On Your Shoulder (78, export issue) 10
56 Parlophone DP 515 Don't Leave Me With The Yum Yum Blues/Why Did You Have To Go
          (78, export issue) 10
57 Parlophone DP 527 Lightning Struck My Heart/I'll See It Happen To You (78, export issue) 10
58 Parlophone GEP 8736 COUNTRY AND WESTERN (EP). 40
58 Parlophone GEP 8753 COUNTRY AND WESTERN NO. 2 (EP). 40

DENNIS YOST & CLASSICS IV
70 Liberty LBF 15357 Funniest Thing/Nobody Loves You But Me 4

YOU & I
73 Grape GR 3055 Morning Has Broken/Don't Take Love For A Game 4

YOU KNOW WHO GROUP
65 London HLR 9947 Roses Are Red My Love/Playboy 15

CHRIS YOULDEN
73 Deram DM 377 Nowhere Road/Standing On The Corner 5
73 Deram SML 1099 NOWHERE ROAD (LP) 25
74 Deram SML 1112 CITY CHILD (LP) 25
(see also Savoy Brown)

BARRY YOUNG
65 Dot DS 16756 One Has My Name (The Other Has My Heart)/Show Me The Way. 6

BILLY YOUNG
72 Atlantic K 10277 The Sloopy/Same Old Thing Again 6
72 Jay Boy BOY 55 I'm Available/Sweet Woman 5

BILLY YOUNG/LIZZIE MILES
56 HMV 7EG 8178 THE BLUES THEY SANG (EP, with Jelly Roll Morton) 25

BOB YOUNG
86 Making Waves SURF 115 Mean Girl/Living On An Island (p/s) 5
86 Making Waves SPRAY 104 (TEX AXILE RIDES AGAIN) IN QUO COUNTRY (LP) 12
(see also Status Quo, Young & Moody Band)

BRETT YOUNG (& GHOST SQUAD)
63 Pye 7N 15578 Guess What/It Just Happened 8
64 Pye 7N 15641 Never Again/You Can't Fool Me (as Brett Young & Ghost Squad) 8

DARREN YOUNG
63 Parlophone R 4919 My Tears Will Turn To Laughter/I've Just Fallen For Someone 18
(see also Johnny Gentle)

DESI YOUNG
70 Pressure Beat PB 5504 News Flash/JOE GIBBS & DESTROYERS: News Flash — Version. 12

EVE YOUNG (& SNOOKY LANSON)
50 London L 659 But Me, I Love You/Comanchie Rose (78) 10
50 London L 751 Beloved, Be Faithful (with Snooky Lanson)/I'm In The Middle Of A Riddle
          (with Snooky Lanson) (78) 8
50 London L 774 Squeeze Me/Somewhere, Somehow, Someday (78) 8
50 London L 800 An Ordinary Broom (with Snooky Lanson)/Sometime (with Stuart Foster) (78) . . . 8
51 London L 874 Sentimental Music/I Still Feel The Same About You (78) 10
51 London L 892 Just For Tonight/Would I Love You (78) 10
(see also Snooky Lanson)

FARON YOUNG

78s

55	Capitol CL 14336	Live Fast, Love Hard, Die Young/Forgive Me, Dear (78)	10
56	Capitol CL 14574	If You Ain't Lovin' (You Ain't Livin')/All Right (78)	10
56	Capitol CL 14655	I've Got 5 Dollars And It's Saturday Night/You're Still Mine (78)	10
57	Capitol CL 14735	The Shrine Of St. Cecilia/He Was There (78)	8
57	Capitol CL 14762	Love Has Finally Come My Way/Moonlight Mountain (78)	8
57	Capitol CL 14793	Honey Stop! (And Think Of Me)/Vacation's Over (78)	12
58	Capitol CL 14822	Snowball/The Locket (78)	10

SINGLES

55	Capitol CL 14336	Live Fast, Love Hard, Die Young/Forgive Me, Dear	30
56	Capitol CL 14574	If You Ain't Lovin' (You Ain't Livin')/All Right	25
56	Capitol CL 14655	I've Got 5 Dollars And It's Saturday Night/You're Still Mine	25
57	Capitol CL 14735	The Shrine Of St. Cecilia/He Was There	12
57	Capitol CL 14762	Love Has Finally Come My Way/Moonlight Mountain	10
57	Capitol CL 14793	Honey Stop! (And Think Of Me)/Vacation's Over	15
58	Capitol CL 14822	Snowball/The Locket	10
58	Capitol CL 14860	I Can't Dance/Rosalie (Is Gonna Get Married)	15
58	Capitol CL 14891	Every Time I'm Kissing You/Alone With You	10
58	Capitol CL 14930	I Hate Myself/That's The Way I Feel	7
59	Capitol CL 14975	Last Night At A Party/A Long Time Ago	7
59	Capitol CL 15004	That's The Way It's Gotta Be/We're Talking It Over	7
59	Capitol CL 15050	I Hear You Talkin'/Country Girl	7
59	Capitol CL 15093	Face To The Wall/Riverboat	6
60	Capitol CL 15133	I'll Be Alright (In The Morning)/Your Old Used To Be	6
60	Capitol CL 15151	Is She All You Thought She'd Be/There's Not Any Like You Left	6
60	Capitol CL 15173	Forget The Past/A World So Full Of Love	6
61	Capitol CL 15197	Hello Walls/Congratulations	6
62	Mercury AMT 1198	The Yellow Bandana/How Much I Must Have Loved You	6

EPs

57	Capitol EAP1 778	SWEETHEARTS OR STRANGERS PT. 1 (EP, with Country Deputies)	18
57	Capitol EAP2 778	SWEETHEARTS OR STRANGERS PT. 2 (EP, with Country Deputies)	18
58	Capitol EAP3 778	SWEETHEARTS OR STRANGERS PT. 3 (EP, with Country Deputies)	18
63	Capitol EAP1 1549	HELLO WALLS (EP)	18

LPs

58	Capitol T 1004	OBJECTS OF MY AFFECTION (LP)	22
59	Capitol T 1096	THIS IS FARON YOUNG (LP)	22
64	Mercury 20026MCL	STORY SONGS FOR COUNTRY FOLK (LP)	18
64	Mercury 20025MCL	COUNTRY DANCE FAVOURITES (LP)	18
65	Capitol (S)T 2037	YOUNG'S MEMORY LANE (LP)	15
66	Capitol (S)T 1876	ALL-TIME GREAT HITS OF FARON YOUNG (LP)	12

GEORGIE YOUNG & ROCKIN' BOCS

| 58 | London HLU 8748 | Nine More Miles/The Sneak | 12 |
| 58 | London HLU 8748 | Nine More Miles/The Sneak (78) | 15 |

HARRY YOUNG

| 65 | Dot DS 16756 | Show Me The Way/One Has My Name | 10 |

JESSE COLIN YOUNG

| 79 | Elektra K 12346 | Rave On/Slow And Easy | 4 |

(see also Youngbloods)

JIMMY YOUNG

54	Decca F 10232	A Baby Cried/Remember Me	18
54	Decca F 10406	Give Me Your Word/Lonely Nightingale	15
55	Decca F 10444	These Are The Things We'll Share/Don't Go To Strangers	12
55	Decca F 10483	If Anyone Finds This, I Love You/The Sand And The Sea	12
55	Decca F 10502	Unchained Melody/Help Me Forget	20
55	Decca F 10597	The Man From Laramie/No Arms Can Ever Hold You	20
55	Decca F 10640	Someone On Your Mind/I Look At You	15
56	Decca F 10694	Chain Gang/Capri In May	15
56	Decca F 10736	Rich Man, Poor Man/The Wayward Wind	12
56	Decca F 10774	More/I'm Gonna Steal You Away	12
57	Decca F 10842	Lovin' Baby/My Faith, My Hope, My Love	8
57	Decca F 10875	Round And Round/Walkin' After Midnight	8
57	Decca F 10925	Man On Fire/Love In The Afternoon	7
57	Decca F 10948	Deep Blue Sea/Harbour Of Desire	7
58	Columbia DB 4100	Love Me Again/A Very Precious Love	5
58	Columbia DB 4147	Her Hair Was Yellow/The State Of Happiness	5
58	Columbia DB 4176	Volare (Nel Blu Dipinto Di Blu)/Beats There A Heart So True?	5
58	Columbia DB 4211	There! I've Said It Again/I Could Be A Mountain	5
55	Pye NEP 24004	JIMMY YOUNG SINGS (EP)	15
56	Decca DFE 6277	PRESENTING JIMMY YOUNG (EP)	15
57	Decca DFE 6404	JIMMY YOUNG (EP)	15
55	Decca LF 1200	PRESENTING JIMMY YOUNG (10" LP)	40
57	Decca LK 4219	THE NIGHT IS YOUNG (LP)	25
58	Columbia 33SX 1102	YOU (LP)	15

JOE E. YOUNG & TONIKS

68	Toast TT 502	Life Time Of Lovin'/Flower In My Hand	6
69	Toast TT 514	Good Day Sunshine/Life Time Of Lovin'	5
68	Toast (S)TLP 1	SOUL BUSTER! (LP)	15

JOHNNIE YOUNG

| 67 | Polydor BM 56199 | Every Christian Lion/Epitaph To Mr. Simon Sir | 4 |

JOHNNY YOUNG

67	Decca F 22548	Step Back/Cara Lyn (as Johnny Young & Kompany)	8
67	Decca F 22636	Lady/Good Evening Girl	5
68	RCA RCA 1826	Always Thinking Of You/Dreaming Country (as Johnny Young Four)	5

JOHNNY YOUNG

| 70 | Blue Horizon 7-63852 | FAT MANDOLIN (LP) | 70 |

KAREN YOUNG

65	Mercury MF 943	I'm Yours, You're Mine/Are You Kidding	6
65	Pye 7N 15956	We'll Start The Party Again/Wonderful Summer	6
68	Major Minor MM 584	Too Much Of A Good Thing/You Better Sit Down	8
69	M. Minor MMLP/SMLP 66	SINGS NOBODY'S CHILD AND 13 OTHER GREAT SONGS (LP)	15

KATHY YOUNG & INNOCENTS

61	Top Rank JAR 534	A Thousand Stars/Eddie My Darling	30
61	Top Rank JAR 554	Happy Birthday Blues/Someone To Love	20
	(see also Innocents)		

LEON YOUNG STRINGS

| 64 | Pye 7N 15646 | This Boy/Glad All Over | 15 |

LESTER YOUNG (QUINTET)

56	Vogue V 2362	New Lester Leaps In/She's Funny That Way	6
56	Vogue V 2384	You're Driving Me Crazy/East Of The Sun	6
57	Columbia LB 16654	Encore/Too Marvellous For Words (with Buddy Rich)	5
56	Vogue EPV 1127	LESTER YOUNG (EP)	10
55	Felsted EDL 87014	BATTLE OF THE SAXES (10" LP)	15
55	Columbia Clef 33C 9001	LESTER YOUNG WITH THE OSCAR PETERSON TRIO (10" LP)	15
56	Columbia Clef 33C 9015	LESTER YOUNG (10" LP)	15
56	Columbia Clef 33CX 10031	THE PRESIDENT, LESTER YOUNG (LP)	15
56	Columbia Clef 33CX 10054	THE JAZZ GIANTS '56 (LP)	15
57	Columbia Clef 33CX 10070	PRES (LP)	15
58	London Jazz LTZ-C 15132	BLUE LESTER (LP)	15
59	HMV CLP 1302	PRES AND TEDDY (LP, with Teddy Wilson)	15
59	Fontana TFL 5064	LESTER YOUNG MEMORIAL ALBUM VOL. 1 (LP, with Count Basie)	12
60	Fontana TFL 5065	LESTER YOUNG MEMORIAL ALBUM VOL. 2 (LP, with Count Basie)	15
62	Stateside SL 10002	LESTER YOUNG & KANSAS CITY 5 (LP)	15
65	Fontana TL 5260	PREZ (LP)	12
66	Fontana FJL 128	LESTER YOUNG LEAPS AGAIN (LP)	12
	(see also Count Basie, Coleman Hawkins & Lester Young, Oscar Peterson)		

LLOYD YOUNG

72	Bullet BU 500	Bread And Butter/SHALIMAR ALLSTARS: Version	10
72	Duke DU 135	Soup/J.J. ALLSTARS: Version	20
72	Green Door GD 4037	Shalimar Special/G. MAHTANI ALLSTARS: Version	6
72	Techniques TE 917	High Explosion/ANSELL COLLINS: Version	6
	(see also Carey & Lloyd)		

MIGHTY JOE YOUNG

| 72 | Sonet SNTF 633 | THE LEGACY OF THE BLUES VOL. 4 (LP) | 12 |
| 72 | Delmark DS 629 | BLUES WITH A TOUCH OF SOUL (LP, blue label) | 15 |

NAUGHTILY YOUNG

| 79 | Juve JUVE 002 | No Memory, Just A Forgettory/Not Purple, But Porpil (p/s) | 8 |

NEIL YOUNG

69	Reprise RS 23405	The Loner/Everybody Knows This Is Nowhere	10
70	Reprise RS 20861	Oh Lonesome Me (Long Version)/Sugar Mountain	10
70	Reprise RS 23462	Down By The River (edit)/Cinnamon Girl (alternate mix)	6
70	Reprise RS 20958	Only Love Can Break Your Heart/Birds	5
71	Reprise RS 23488	When You Dance I Can Really Love/After The Goldrush	5
72	Reprise K 14167	Old Man/The Needle And The Damage Done	5
73	Reprise SAM 15	Don't Be Denied/Love In Mind/Last Dance (p/s, 1-sided, promo only sampler for "Time Fades Away" LP)	20
74	Reprise K 14350	Southern Man/Till The Morning Comes/After The Goldrush/Heart Of Gold (special sleeve)	5
74	Reprise K 14360	Walk On/For The Turnstiles	4
76	Reprise K 14416	Looking For A Love/Sugar Mountain	4
76	Reprise K 14431	Don't Cry No Tears/Stupid Girl	6
77	Reprise K 14482	Like A Hurricane (edit)/Hold Back The Tears	4
78	Reprise K 14493	Four Strong Winds/Motorcycle Mama	4
79	Reprise K 14498	Hey Hey, My My (Into The Black)/My My, Hey Hey (Out Of The Blue) (p/s)	4
83	Geffen GEF 2781	Little Thing Called Love/We R In Control (p/s)	4
83	Geffen GEF 3581	Wonderin'/Payola Blues (p/s)	4
86	Geffen GEF 7	Weight Of The World/Pressure (p/s)	4
86	Geffen GEF 7T	Weight Of The World (Extended Remix)/Pressure (12", p/s)	8
90	Reprise W 2776	Rockin' In The Free World (live)/Rockin' In The Free World (p/s)	4
90	Reprise W 2776CD	Rockin' In The Free World (live)/Cocaine Eyes/Rockin' In The Free World (CD)	8
93	Reprise PRO 808	The Needle And The Damage Done (from "Unplugged")/Love Is A Rose (from "Decade") (CD, promo only)	8
93	Columbia XPCD 308	My Back Pages/All Along The Watchtower/Knocking On Heaven's Door (CD, promo only)	8
93	Geffen NYCD 1	LUCKY THIRTEEN ALBUM SAMPLER (Ain't It The Truth/Depression Blues/This Note's For You) (CD, promo only)	15
94	Reprise WO 242CD	Philadelphia/Such A Woman/Stringman (CD)	8
69	Reprise RSLP 6317	NEIL YOUNG (LP, with/without name on front of sleeve)	35/50
69	Reprise RSLP 6349	EVERYBODY KNOWS THIS IS NOWHERE (LP)	20

70	Reprise RSLP 6383	AFTER THE GOLDRUSH (LP, gatefold sleeve with lyric insert) 20
71	Reprise K 44059	NEIL YOUNG (LP, reissue) 12
71	Reprise K 44073	EVERYBODY KNOWS THIS IS NOWHERE (LP, reissue) 12
71	Reprise K 44088	AFTER THE GOLDRUSH (LP, reissue, gatefold sleeve with lyric insert) 12
72	Reprise K 54005	HARVEST (LP, thick cardboard gatefold sleeve with insert) 15
72	Reprise K 64015	JOURNEY THROUGH THE PAST (2-LP, soundtrack, fold-out sleeve & inners) . . 20
73	Reprise K 54010	TIME FADES AWAY (LP, with lyric insert) 15
74	Reprise K 54014	ON THE BEACH (LP, with inner sleeve) 60
75	Reprise K 54040	TONIGHT'S THE NIGHT (LP, gatefold sleeve with inner sleeve & insert) 15
75	Reprise K 54057	ZUMA (LP, with inner sleeve & lyric insert) 15
77	Reprise K 54088	AMERICAN STARS AND BARS (LP, with inner sleeve) 12
79	Reprise K 54105	RUST NEVER SLEEPS (LP, with inner sleeve & lyric insert) 12
79	Reprise K 64041	LIVE RUST (2-LP, with inner sleeves) 20
80	Reprise K 54109	HAWKS & DOVES (LP, with inner sleeve) 15
85	Geffen GEF 26377	OLD WAYS (LP) 15
94	Reprise SAM 1310	FOR THE TURNTABLES (CD, promo only) 18

(see also Buffalo Springfield, Crosby Stills Nash & Young, Stills-Young Band, Crazy Horse)

RALPH YOUNG

55	Brunswick 05466	The Man From Laramie/The Bible Tells Me So 15
55	Brunswick 05500	Bring Me A Bluebird/A Room In Paris 10
56	Brunswick 05605	The Legend Of Wyatt Earp/Do You Know? 10

(see also Jack Pleis)

ROGER YOUNG

66	Columbia DB 7869	Sweet, Sweet Morning/Whatcha Gonna Give Me? 20
66	Columbia DB 8092	No Address/It's Been Nice 60

ROY YOUNG (BAND)

59	Fontana H 200	Just Keep It Up/Big Fat Mama 18
59	Fontana H 200	Just Keep It Up/Big Fat Mama (78) 10
59	Fontana H 215	Hey Little Girl/Just Ask Your Heart 12
59	Fontana H 215	Hey Little Girl/Just Ask Your Heart (78) 15
60	Fontana H 237	I Hardly Know Me/Gilee 15
60	Fontana H 247	Taboo/I'm In Love. 10
61	Fontana H 290	You Were Meant For Me/Plenty Of Love (as Roy Young & Hunters) 12
61	Ember EMB S 128	Four And Twenty Thousand Kisses/Late Last Evening. 10
70	RCA RCA 2031	Granny's Got A Painted Leg/Revolution (as Roy Young Band) 5
72	MCA MKS 5080	Rag Mama Rag/Give It All To You. 5
70	RCA SF 8161	ROY YOUNG BAND (LP). 15

SUSANNAH YOUNG

67	Philips BF 1559	Lazy Afternoon/Here's That Rainy Day 5
67	Philips BL 7728	SWEETEST SOUNDS (LP) 12

TERRY YOUNG

60	Pye 7N 15321	Partners/Maverick 5
61	Pye 7N 15416	Someone New/Now, Forever And A Day 5
62	Pye 7N 15416	They Took John Away/Joe's Been A-Gittin' There 5

TOMMIE YOUNG

73	Contempo C 12	Everybody's Got A Little Devil In Their Soul/Do You Still Feel The Same Way 4
73	Contempo C 23	She Don't Have To See You/That's All Part Of Loving Him 4
74	Contempo CLP 501	DO YOU STILL FEEL THE SAME WAY (LP) 10

VICKI YOUNG

54	Capitol CL 14144	Riot In Cell Block Number Nine/Honey Love (78) 8
55	Capitol CL 14228	Heart Of Stone/Tweedlee Dee (triangular centre) 20
55	Capitol CL 14228	Heart Of Stone/Tweedlee Dee (78) 10
55	Capitol CL 14281	Live Fast, Love Hard, Die Young/Zoom, Zoom, Zoom (triangular centre) 18
55	Capitol CL 14281	Live Fast, Love Hard, Die Young/Zoom, Zoom, Zoom (78) 10
56	Capitol CL 14528	Steel Guitar/Bye Bye For Just A While 10
56	Capitol CL 14528	Steel Guitar/Bye Bye For Just A While (78). 10
56	Capitol CL 14653	Spanish Main/Tell Me In Your Own Sweet Way (with Joe 'Fingers' Carr) 10
56	Capitol CL 14653	Spanish Main/Tell Me In Your Own Sweet Way (with Joe 'Fingers' Carr) (78). 8
56	Capitol EAP1 593	VICKI YOUNG (EP) 35

(see also Joe 'Fingers' Carr)

VICTOR YOUNG & HIS SINGING STRINGS

54	Brunswick 05320	The High And The Mighty/The Song From 'The Caine Mutiny' (I Can't Believe That You're In Love With Me) 6
54	Brunswick 05337	Lisa (The "Rear Window" Theme)/Smile (Theme From 'Modern Times') 6
54	Brunswick 05350	Moonlight And Roses/Magnificent Obsession 6
55	Brunswick 05386	You, My Love (From 'Young At Heart')/Passion Tango (From 'Passion') 6
55	Brunswick 05448	Cherry Pink And Apple Blossom White/The World Is Mine 7
55	Brunswick 05479	The Toy Tiger/Autumn Leaves 6
55	Brunswick 05498	Tall Men (adapted from 'Cindy')/Theme From 'The Left Hand Of God'. 6
56	Brunswick 05579	Love Theme From 'The Proud And Profane' (To Love You)/East Of Eden – Theme . 6
53	Brunswick LAT 8029	CINEMA RHAPSODIES (LP). 15

YOUNG AL CAPONE

71	Green Door GD 4012	Girl Called Clover/Girl Called Clover (Version) 6

YOUNG & MOODY (BAND)

77	Magnet MAG 87	Chicago Blue/Warm Winds 5
79	Fabulous JC 1	The Devil Went Down To Georgia/You Can't Catch Me 5
79	Fabulous JC 3	All The Good Friends/Playing Your Game (p/s) 6
81	Bronze BRO 120	These Eyes/I Won't Let Go (p/s). 6
81	Bronze BRO 130	Don't Do That/How Can I Help You Tonight (p/s, featuring Lemmy and Linda & Coleen Nolan). 6
77	Magnet MAG 5015	YOUNG AND MOODY (LP, with lyric insert, as Young & Moody). 12

(see also Bob Young, Whitesnake, Snafu, Cozy Powell, Motörhead, Nolan Sisters)

YOUNG BLOOD

68	Pye 7N 17495	Green Light/Don't Leave Me In The Dark.	15
68	Pye 7N 17588	Just How Loud/Masquerade	10
68	Pye 7N 17627	Bang-Shang-A-Lang/I Can't Stop	10
69	Pye 7N 17696	The Continuing Story Of Bungalow Bill/I Will	10

(see also Cozy Powell, Ace Kefford Stand, Big Bertha)

YOUNG BLOOD

| 84 | Landslide LAND 1 | FIRST BLOOD (12" EP, p/s) | 7 |

YOUNGBLOODS

69	RCA RCA 1821	Darkness, Darkness/On Sir Francis Drake	6
69	RCA RCA 1877	Get Together/Beautiful	5
70	RCA RCA 1955	Darkness Darkness/On Sir Francis Drake (reissue)	5
71	Warner Bros WB 7445	Hippie From Olena/Misty Roses	5
69	RCA SF 8026	ELEPHANT MOUNTAIN (LP)	18
70	Warner Bros WS 1878	ROCK FESTIVAL (LP)	15
70	RCA LSA 3012	THE BEST OF THE YOUNGBLOODS (LP)	12
71	Warner Bros K 46100	RIDE THE WIND (LP)	15
72	RCA Victor SF 8218	SUNLIGHT (LP)	15

(see also Jesse Colin Young)

YOUNG BUCKS

| 77 | Blueport BLU 1 | Get Your Feet Back On The Ground/Cold, Cold Morning (p/s) | 6 |

YOUNG DISCIPLES

| 90 | Talkin' Loud TLKX 2 | Get Yourself Together/Young Disciples Theme (12", p/s) | 8 |

YOUNGFOLK

| 68 | President PT 136 | Lonely Girl/Joey | 8 |

YOUNG FOLK

| 72 | Midas MR 001 | RIBBLE VALLEY DREAM (LP) | 45 |

YOUNG FREDDIE

| 70 | Camel CA 38 | Drink And Gamble/LENNOX BROWN & HUE ROY: King Of The Road | 6 |

(see also Freddie McGregor)

YOUNG GROWLER & CALYPSO RHYTHM KINGS

| 66 | Columbia DB 7870 | Amy The Sunbather/Sweet Trinidad | 6 |
| 66 | Columbia DB 7958 | "V" For Victory/Be Nice To Women | 6 |

YOUNG-HOLT TRIO

| 67 | Coral Q 72489 | Wack Wack/This Little Light Of Mine | 18 |

YOUNG-HOLT UNLIMITED

69	MCA MU 1053	Soulful Strut/Country Slicker Joe	6
72	MCA MU 1159	Just Ain't No Love/Love Makes A Woman.	5
69	MCA MUP(S) 368	SOULFUL STRUT (LP)	20

(see also Ramsey Lewis Trio)

YOUNG IDEA

66	Columbia DB 7961	The World's Been Good To Me/It Can't Be	7
66	Columbia DB 8067	Gotta Get Out Of The Mess I'm In/Games Men Play	6
67	Columbia DB 8132	Peculiar Situation/Just Look At The Rain	6
67	Columbia DB 8205	With A Little Help From My Friends/Colours Of Darkness	6
67	Columbia DB 8284	Mister Lovin' Luggage Man/Room With A View.	5
68	M. For Pleasure MFP 1225	WITH A LITTLE HELP FROM MY FRIENDS (LP)	12

YOUNG JESSIE

| 58 | London HLE 8544 | Shuffle In The Gravel/Make Believe | 275 |
| 58 | London HLE 8544 | Shuffle In The Gravel/Make Believe (78) | 50 |

YOUNG MARBLE GIANTS

80	Rough Trade RT 043	Final Day/Radio Silents/Cakewalking/(uncredited 4th track) (p/s)	6
81	Rough Trade RT 059	TESTCARD (EP)	6
80	Rough Trade ROUGH 8	COLOSSAL YOUTH (LP, original issue)	10

(see also Jah Scouse)

YOUNG MC

| 88 | Delicious Vinyl BRW 120 | KNOW HOW (12", EP) | 25 |

YOUNG ONES

| 63 | Decca F 11705 | How Do I Tell You/Baby That's It | 8 |

YOUNG RASCALS

65	Atlantic AT 4059	I Ain't Gonna Eat My Heart Out Anymore/Slow Down	8
66	Atlantic AT 4082	Good Lovin'/Mustang Sally	7
66	Atlantic 584 024	You Better Run/Love Is A Beautiful Thing	12
66	Atlantic 584 050	Come On Up/What Is The Reason	12
66	Atlantic 584 067	Too Many Fish In The Sea/No Love To Give	6
67	Atlantic 584 081	I've Been Lonely Too Long/If You Knew.	12
67	Atlantic 584 085	I Ain't Gonna Eat My Heart Out Anymore/Good Lovin'	5
67	Atlantic 584 111	Groovin'/Sueno	5
67	Atlantic 584 128	A Girl Like You/It's Love	5
67	Atlantic 584 138	How Can I Be Sure/I Don't Love You Anymore	5
68	Atlantic 584 161	It's Wonderful/Of Course	8
66	Atlantic 587/588 012	THE YOUNG RASCALS (LP)	20
67	Atlantic 587/588 060	COLLECTIONS (LP)	18
67	Atlantic 587/588 074	GROOVIN' (LP)	22

(see also Rascals, Joey Dee & Starlighters)

YOUNG SATCH
70	Black Swan BW 1401	Bonga Bonga Bonga/HI-TALS: Ram Buck	10

YOUNG SISTERS
62	London HLU 9610	Casanova Brown/My Guy	10

YOUNG SOULS
69	Amalgamated AMG 844	Why Did You Leave/Main A Wail	8

YOUNG TRADITION
74	Argo AFW 115	The Shepherd's Hymn/The Boar's Head Carol	6
68	Transatlantic TRAEP 164	CHICKEN ON A RAFT (EP)	20
66	Transatlantic TRA 142	THE YOUNG TRADITION (LP)	25
67	Transatlantic TRA 155	SO CHEERFULLY ROUND (LP)	25
68	Transatlantic TRA 172	GALLERIES (LP, with Dave Swarbrick)	25
68	Transatlantic TRASAM 13	THE YOUNG TRADITION SAMPLER (LP)	15
73	Transatlantic TRASAM 30	GALLERIES REVISITED (LP, reissue)	12

(see also Dave Swarbrick, Peter Bellamy)

YOUNG TURKS
66	CBS 202353	Duel At Diablo/Our Lady From Maxim's	6

YOUNG WORLD SINGERS
64	Brunswick 05916	Ringo For President/A Boy Like That	6

YOUTH
66	Polydor 56121	As Long As There Is Your Love/Your One And Only Love	10

YOUTH
69	Deram DM 226	Meadow Of My Love/Love Me Or Leave Me	4

YOUTH
84	Illuminated JAMS 36	THE EMPTY QUARTER (LP)	18
85	Illuminated JAMS 41	YOUTH AT THE DIORAMA (LP)	12

(see also Killing Joke, Brilliant, Fireman)

JOHNNY YOUTH
69	Grape GR 3002	Darling It Won't/HIP CITY BOYS: Moon Train	6

YOUTH VALLEY CHORALE
63	London HLU 9818	Do You Hear What I Hear/Little Bell	4

YOU'VE GOT FOETUS ON YOUR BREATH
81	Self Immolation WOMB 07	Wash It All Off/333 (p/s)	20
81	Self Imm. WOMB OYBL-1	DEAF (LP)	50
81	Self Imm. WOMB OYBL-2	ACHE (LP)	50

(see also Foetus, Philip & His Foetus Vibrations, Scraping Foetus Off The Wheel)

LES YPER SOUND
67	Fontana TF 880	Too Fortiche/Psyche Rock	25
69	Philips TFE 8004	MASS FOR THE PRESENT TIME (LP)	85

Y TRWYNAU COCH
70s	Record. Sqwar RSROC 1	WASTOD AR Y TU FAS (BANANAS) (EP)	8
78	Recordian Sqwar RSROC 002	Merched Dan 15 (I Often Think Of Girls Under 15)/Byw Ar Arian Fy Rhieni/Mynd I'r Capel Mewn Levis/Ail Ddechre	20
80s	Record. Coch OCHR 2198	RHEDEG RHAG Y TORPIDOS (LP)	15

JOHNNY YUKON
60	Top Rank JAR 347	Made To Be Loved/Magnolia	6

TIMI YURO
61	London HLG 9403	Hurt/I Apologise	12
62	London HLG 9484	Smile/I Believe (B-side with Johnnie Ray)	12
62	Liberty LIB 55410	Satan Never Sleeps/Let Me Call You Sweetheart	10
62	Liberty LIB 55469	What's A-Matter Baby (Is It Hurting You)/Thirteenth Hour	15
63	Liberty LIB 55519	The Love Of A Boy/I Ain't Gonna Cry No More	18
63	Liberty LIB 55587	Make The World Go Away/Look Down	10
63	Liberty LIB 55634	Gotta Travel On/Down In The Valley	6
64	Liberty LIB 10177	Hurt/Be Anything (But Be Mine)	8
64	Mercury MF 826	If/I'm Afraid The Masquerade Is Over	6
65	Mercury MF 848	You Can Have Him/Could This Be Magic	10
65	Mercury MF 859	Get Out Of My Life/Can't Stop Running Away	30
65	Mercury MF 903	Once A Day/Pretend	6
65	Mercury MF 949	Turn The World Around The Other Way/Just A Ribbon	6
66	Mercury MF 978	Cuttin' In/Why Not Now	6
68	Liberty LBF 15092	Something Bad On My Mind/Wrong	7
68	Liberty LIB 15142	I Must Have Been Out Of My Mind/Interlude	18
68	Liberty LIB 15182	It'll Never Be Over For Me/As Long As There Is You	175
65	Liberty LEP 2214	TIMI YURO: SOUL! (EP)	25
66	Liberty LEP 2253	MAKE THE WORLD GO AWAY (EP)	22
62	London HA-G 2415	TIMI YURO (LP)	60
62	Liberty LBY 1042	SOUL! (LP)	22
63	Liberty (S)LBY 1154	WHAT'S A-MATTER BABY (LP)	20
64	Liberty LBY 1192	MAKE THE WORLD GO AWAY (LP)	20
64	Mercury 20032 MCL	THE AMAZING YURO (LP)	18
65	Liberty LBY 1247	HURT (LP)	25
66	Liberty (S)LBY 1275	LET ME CALL YOU SWEETHEART (LP)	20
66	Liberty (S)LBY 1290	THE BEST OF TIMI YURO (LP)	15
68	Liberty LBL/LBS 83115	GREAT PERFORMANCES (LP)	12
68	Liberty LBL/LBS 83128	TIMI IN THE BEGINNING (LP)	15
69	Liberty LBS 83198E	SOMETHING BAD ON MY MIND (LP)	30
69	Mercury SMWL 21010	TALENTED TIMI (LP)	15

(see also Johnnie Ray)

(HELMUT) ZACHARIAS

57	Polydor BM 6058	Rock 'N' Roll "Roll-Mops" Rock/Barock 'N' Roll Rock (with Hot Club) (78)	8
60	Polydor NH 66635	Never On Sunday (Jamais Le Dimanche)/Theme From 'The Apartment') (as Zacharias).	5
64	Polydor NH 52341	Tokyo Melody/Teatime In Tokyo	5
65	Polydor 236 809	PLAYS THE HITS OF THE BEATLES (LP).	12

JOHN ZACHERLE

58	London HLU 8599	Dinner With Drac Part 1/Dinner With Drac — Conclusion.	35
58	London HLU 8599	Dinner With Drac Part 1/Dinner With Drac — Conclusion (78)	35

(see also Dave Appell & Applejacks)

ZAGER & EVANS

69	RCA 1860	In The Year 2525 (Exordium & Terminus)/Little Kids	5
69	RCA SF 8056	2525 (LP)	15

ZAKARRIAS

71	Deram SML 1091	ZAKARRIAS (LP)	250

ALEX ZANETIS

71	Moodisc HM 102	Guilty/JOLLY BOYS: Do Fe Do.	6

TOMMY ZANG

59	HMV POP 611	Break The Chain/I'll Put A String On Your Finger	10
62	Polydor NH 66955	I'm Gonna Slip You Offa My Mind/Every Hour, Every Day	8
62	Polydor NH 66957	Hey, Good Lookin'/With Love (For You).	12
62	Polydor NH 66960	Take These Chains From My Heart/Truly, Truly	8
62	Polydor NH 66977	I Can't Hold Your Letters (In My Arms)/She's Getting Married	8
62	Polydor NH 66980	Just Call My Name/I Love You Because	10

ZAPP

80	Warner K 17712	More Bounce To The Ounce/Brand New Player.	4
80	Warner K 17712T	More Bounce To The Ounce/Brand New Player (12")	7

FRANK ZAPPA/MOTHERS OF INVENTION

SINGLES

66	Verve VS 545	It Can't Happen Here/How Could I Be Such A Fool (as Mothers Of Invention)	30
67	Verve VS 557	Big Leg Emma/Why Don't You Do Me Right (as Mothers Of Invention)	30
71	Reprise K 14100	Tears Began To Fall/Junier Mintz Boogie (as Mothers Of Invention)	30
71	United Artists UP 35319	What Will This Evening Bring Me This Morning?/Daddy, Daddy, Daddy.	30
74	Discreet K 19201	Cosmic Debris/Uncle Remus.	8
74	Discreet K 19202	Don't Eat The Yellow Snow/Camarillo Brillo	8
79	CBS 7261	Dancin' Fool/Baby Snakes.	8
80	CBS 7950	Joe's Garage/Catholic Girls.	6
80	CBS 7950	Joe's Garage/BOB DYLAN: When You Gonna Wake Up (mispressing).	30
80	CBS 8652	I Don't Wanna Get Drafted/Ancient Armaments (p/s)	6
81	CBS A 1622	You Are What You Is/Harder Than Your Husband (p/s)	6
81	CBS A 12-1622	You Are What You Is/Pink Napkins/Harder Than Your Husband/ Soup 'N Old Clothes (12", picture disc)	15
81	CBS XPS 147	Shut Up 'N' Play Yer Guitar/Variation On The C. Santana Secret (p/s, issued free with "Ship Arriving Too Late To Save A Drowning Witch" LP).	6
82	CBS A 2412	Valley Girl/Teenage Prostitute (p/s)	6
84	EMI EMI 5499	Baby Take Your Teeth Out/Stevie's Spanking (p/s)	8
93	Zappa Records 12 FRANK 102	Valley Girl/You Are What You Is (12", p/s)	8
91	Zappa Records 12 FRANK 101	Stairway To Heaven/Bolero (12", p/s).	8

LPs: VERVE ORIGINALS

66	Verve (S)VLP 9154	FREAK OUT! (as Mothers Of Invention, mono/stereo, single disc)	50/40
67	Verve (S)VLP 9174	ABSOLUTELY FREE (as Mothers Of Invention, mono/stereo)	40/25
68	Verve (S)VLP 9199	WE'RE ONLY IN IT FOR THE MONEY (as Mothers Of Invention, gatefold sleeve, mono/stereo).	40/25
68	Verve (S)VLP 9223	LUMPY GRAVY (gatefold sleeve, mono/stereo)	40/30
69	Verve (S)VLP 9237	CRUISING WITH RUBEN AND THE JETS (as Mothers Of Invention, mono/stereo).	35/25
69	Verve (S)VLP 9239	MOTHERMANIA — THE BEST OF THE MOTHERS (as Mothers Of Invention, mono/stereo)	30/20

LPs: VERVE REISSUES

71	Verve/Polydor 2683 004	FREAK OUT (2-LP)	30
72	Verve/Polydor 2317 034	WE'RE ONLY IN IT FOR THE MONEY (gatefold sleeve)	25
72	Verve/Polydor 2317 035	ABSOLUTELY FREE (gatefold sleeve).	25
72	Verve/Polydor 2317 046	LUMPY GRAVY (gatefold sleeve).	25
72	Verve/Polydor 2317 047	MOTHERMANIA — THE BEST OF THE MOTHERS	30
73	Verve/Polydor 2352 017	MOTHERMANIA — THE BEST OF THE MOTHERS (2nd reissue)	30
73	Verve/Polydor 2317 069	CRUISIN' WITH RUBEN AND THE JETS (gatefold sleeve).	35
75	Verve/Polydor 2352 057	ROCK FLASHBACKS (LP)	15

LPs: ORIGINAL REPRISE/WARNERS/DISCREET ISSUES

70	Reprise RSLP 6356	HOT RATS (1st pressing, pink, gold & green 'riverboat' label, gatefold sl.)	30
70	Reprise RSLP 6356	HOT RATS (2nd pressing, tan 'riverboat' label, gatefold sleeve)	25

70	Reprise RSLP 6370	BURNT WEENY SANDWICH (as Mothers Of Invention,
		1st pressing, pink, gold & green 'riverboat' label, gatefold sleeve) 20
70	Reprise RSLP 2028	WEASELS RIPPED MY FLESH (as Mothers Of Invention, tan 'riverboat' label) ... 20
70	Reprise RSLP 2030	CHUNGA'S REVENGE (tan 'riverboat' label, green or red gatefold sleeve). 25/20
71	Reprise K 44150	FILLMORE EAST, JUNE 1971 (as Mothers Of Invention) 20
72	Reprise K 44179	JUST ANOTHER BAND FROM L.A. (as Mothers Of Invention, g/fold sleeve)..... 20
72	Reprise K 44203	WAKA/JAWAKA (Hot Rats) 15
72	Reprise K 44209	THE GRAND WAZOO (gatefold sleeve) 15
73	DiscReet K 41000	OVER-NITE SENSATION (as Mothers Of Invention, gatefold sleeve) 15
74	DiscReet K 69201	ROXY AND ELSEWHERE (2-LP, as Mothers Of Invention,
		gatefold sleeve) 15
74	DiscReet K 49201	APOSTROPHE (') (no lyric insert) 15
75	DiscReet K 59207	ONE SIZE FITS ALL (as Mothers Of Invention, gatefold sleeve) 15

*(First pressings of the above LPs were issued **without** Warner Bros logo on label or sleeve; copies with Warners logos are post-1975 pressings worth £6-£8 each.)*

76	Warner Bros K 56298	ZOOT ALLURES (LP) 12
77	DiscReet K 69204	ZAPPA IN NEW YORK (LIVE) (2-LP, with & without reference to
		"Punky's Whips") 25
77	DiscReet K 69204	ZAPPA IN NEW YORK (LIVE) (2-LP, "Punky's Whips" listed on
		sleeve but not on label or LP) 25
77	DiscReet K 69204	ZAPPA IN NEW YORK (LIVE) (2-LP, plays "Punky's Whips",
		listed on sleeve but not on label) 50
78	DiscReet K 59210	STUDIO TAN 12
78	DiscReet K 59211	SLEEP DIRT 12
78	DiscReet K 59212	ORCHESTRAL FAVORITES 12

LPs: REPRISE

71	Reprise K 44078	HOT RATS (tan 'riverboat' label, gatefold sleeve) 15
71	Reprise K 44083	BURNT WEENY SANDWICH (tan 'riverboat' label) 15
71	Reprise K 44019	WEASELS RIPPED MY FLESH (tan 'riverboat' label) 20
71	Reprise K 44020	CHUNGA'S REVENGE (tan 'riverboat' label, gatefold sleeve). 20

(The above LPs were issued without Warner Bros logo on label or sleeve; post-1975 pressings with logos are worth £6-£8 each.)

OTHER LPs

69	Transatlantic TRA 197	UNCLE MEAT (2-LP, as Mothers Of Invention) 20
71	United Artists UDF 50003	200 MOTELS (2-LP, with booklet & poster, as Frank Zappa &
		Mothers Of Invention) 40
79	CBS 88339	SHEIK YERBOUTI (2-LP, gatefold sleeve printed with lyrics) 15
79	CBS 86101	JOE'S GARAGE ACT 1 (gatefold sleeve, lyric insert) 12
79	CBS 88475	JOE'S GARAGE ACTS 2 & 3 (2-LP, gatefold sleeve, lyric insert) 15
81	CBS 88560	YOU ARE WHAT YOU IS (2-LP, gatefold sleeve, lyric insert) 15
81	CBS 88516	TINSELTOWN REBELLION (2-LP, gatefold sleeve with lyrics) 15
81	CBS 66368	SHUT UP 'N' PLAY YER GUITAR (3-LP box set, with inner sleeves). 30
82	CBS 85804	SHIP ARRIVING TOO LATE TO SAVE A DROWNING WITCH (with bonus 7"
		"Shut Up 'N' Play Yer Guitar"/"Variation On The C. Santana Secret" [XPS 147]) .. 15
83	CBS 25251	THE MAN FROM UTOPIA 12
84	EMI EL 2701531	BOULEZ CONDUCTS ZAPPA: 'THE PERFECT STRANGER'................ 12
84	EMI	FRANCESCO ZAPPA (with inner sleeve). 15
84	EMI 2402943	THING-FISH (3-LP, box set, with libretto). 35
86	EMI EN 352	JAZZ FROM HELL 15
86	EMI EC 3507	FRANK ZAPPA MEETS THE MOTHERS OF PREVENTION (European version) ... 12
95	Simply Vinyl SLVP 0024	WEASELS RIPPED MY FLESH (180gm vinyl) 12
95	Simply Vinyl SLVP 0025	BURNT WEENY SANDWICH (gatefold sleeve, 180 gm vinyl) 12

LPs: EMI REISSUES

84	EMI EMC 3500	THE MAN FROM UTOPIA 12
84	EMI EMC 3501	SHIP ARRIVING TOO LATE TO SAVE A DROWNING WITCH (with inner sl.). 15
84	EMI FZAP1	JOE'S GARAGE ACTS 1, 2 & 3 (3-LP, box set, inner sleeves only, with libretti) .. 30
84	EMI E5 0021	TINSELTOWN REBELLION (2-LP, gatefold sleeve, printed with lyrics). 15
84	EMI	SHEIK YERBOUTI (2-LP, gatefold sleeve, printed with lyrics). 15
84	EMI	SHUT UP 'N' PLAY YER GUITAR (3-LP box set, with inner sleeves). 30
84	EMI EN 2402343	THEM OR US (2-LP, gatefold sleeve, printed with lyrics) 15

LPs: ZAPPA

84	Zappa Records ZAPPA 1	FREAK OUT (2-LP, gatefold sleeve, some in single sleeve £35). 15
80s	Zappa Records ZAPPA 5	LONDON SYMPHONY ORCHESTRA VOLUME II 15
88	Zappa Records ZAPPA 6	GUITAR (2-LP, gatefold sleeve) 15
88	Zappa Records ZAPPA 7	YOU CAN'T DO THAT ON STAGE ANYMORE SAMPLER (2-LP, gatefold sl.) 15
88	Zappa Records ZAPPA 14	BROADWAY THE HARD WAY (gatefold sleeve with inner sleeve)............ 15
90	Zappa Records ZAPPA 30	THEM OR US (2-LP, gatefold sleeve, printed with lyrics) 15
90	Zappa Records ZAPPA 20	JOE'S GARAGE ACTS 1, 2 & 3 (3-LP , box set, original sleeves, with libretti).... 30
91	Zappa Records ZAPPA 28	SHEIK YERBOUTI (2-LP, gatefold sleeve without lyrics)................. 15
91	Zappa Records ZAPPA 35	BURNT WEENY SANDWICH (gatefold sleeve). 12
91	Zappa Records ZAPPA 37	ZAPPA IN NEW YORK (LIVE) (2-LP, plays "Punky's Whips", listed on label,
		but not on sleeve) 15
91	Zappa Records ZAPPA 42	SHIP ARRIVING TOO LATE TO SAVE A DROWNING WITCH 12
92	Zappa Records ZAPPA 39	ROXY AND ELSEWHERE (2-LP, as Mothers Of Invention, g/fold lyric sleeve).... 15

(see also Flo & Eddie, Jeff Simmons, Wild Man Fischer, Captain Beefheart, John Lennon, Geronimo Black)

ZAP POW

72	Harry J HJ 6650	Lottery Spin/Lottery Spin — Version. 6
73	Trojan TR 7886	Nice Nice Time/Version 6
73	Trojan TR 7741	This Is Reggae Music/Break Down The Barriers. 5
73	Blue Mountain BM 1027	This Is Reggae Music/Break Down The Barriers. 5
74	Island WIP 6181	This Is Reggae Music/Break Down The Barriers. 5

LES ZARJAZ

| 85 | Creation CRE 014 | One Charming Nyte/My Baby Owns A Fallout Zone (foldover p/s, poly bag) ..... 8 |
| 86 | Kaleid. Sound KS 104 | INTER BLOCK ROCK (12" EP). .... 7 |

(see also Tronics)

LENA ZAVARONI
80   Galaxy GY 177   Will He Kiss Me Tonight?/Dream Come True. 8

JOE ZAWINUL
71   Atlantic 2400 151   ZAWINUL (LP) 12
(see also Weather Report)

PETE ZEAR
80   (no label) matrix: 22-1   Tomorrow's World/Fast Food (stamped white label, with insert, numbered) 10
(see also Ruts, Rat Scabies)

ZED
79   Initial IRC 003   VISIONS OF DUNE (LP) 12

ZEE
84   Harvest HAR 5277   Confusion/Eyes Of A Gypsy (p/s) 8
84   Harvest HAR 125277   Confusion (Extended Mix)/Eyes Of A Gypsy (Dub) (12", p/s). 10
84   Harvest SHSP 2401 018 IDENTITY (LP, with inner sleeve) 15
84   Harvest SHSP 2401 018 IDENTITY (cassette, with extra track) 15
(see also Rick Wright)

ZEITGEIST
80   Enchaine ENC 1   Shake-Rake/Sniper (p/s) 4

ZENITH SIX
56   Tempo A 145   Climax Rag/The Chant. 5
57   Tempo A 159   Mahogany Hall Stomp/Cannon Ball Blues 5
56   Decca DFE 6255   THE ZENITH SIX AT THE ROYAL FESTIVAL HALL (EP) 10
56   Tempo EXA 42   THE ZENITH SIX (EP) 10
57   Tempo EXA 58   THE ZENITH SIX (EP) 10

SI ZENTNER ORCHESTRA
62   Liberty LIB 55374   (Up A) Lazy River/Shufflin' Blues 6
64   Liberty LIB 10169   The James Bond Theme/Bond's 007 Theme 7
63   Liberty LBY 1164   RHYTHM PLUS BLUES (LP). 12

ZEPHYR
70   Probe SPB 1006   ZEPHYR (LP) 35
(see also Tommy Bolin)

ZEPHYRS
63   Decca F 11647   What's All That About/Oriental Dream. 30
64   Columbia DB 7199   I Can Tell/Sweet Little Baby 25
64   Columbia DB 7324   A Little Bit Of Soap/No Message 25
64   Columbia DB 7410   Wonder What I'm Gonna Do/Let Me Love You Baby 25
65   Columbia DB 7481   She's Lost You/There's Something About You 25
65   Columbia DB 7571   I Just Can't Take It/She Laughed 25

ZERO
75   BEEB 014   Angels Theme/Truckin'. 5

ZERO FIVE
65   Columbia DB 7751   Dusty/Just Like A Girl 7

ZEROS
77   Small Wonder SMALL 2   Hungry/Radio Fun 5
79   Rok ROK XV/XVI   What's Wrong With A Pop Group/ACTION REPLAY: Decisions
                            (die-cut co. sleeve). 6

ZERO ZERO SEVEN
80s Scanlite BOND 1   Message From Bond/James Bond Theme (p/s) 4

ZERO ZERO SEVEN BAND
65   Marble Arch MAL 590   JAMES BOND THRILLERS (LP). 12

MONICA ZETTERLUND
59   Columbia SEG 8015   SWEDISH SWEET (EP). 20
58   Columbia 33CSX 20   SWEDISH SENSATION (LP, export only) 25

Z'EV
82   Fetish FE 13   Wipeout!/Element L. (p/s). 10

WARREN ZEVON
76   Atlantic K 13060   I'll Sleep When I'm Dead/Mohammed's Radio 5
78   Atlantic K 13111   Werewolves Of London/Tenderness On The Block. 5

ZIMM & DEE DEE
71   Green Door GD 4006   You've Got A Friend (actually by Winston Francis & Donna Hinds)/
                            GROOVERS: Cheep 6
(see also Winston Francis)

TUCKER ZIMMERMAN
69   Regal Zonophone RZ 3020   The Red Wind/Moondog. 5
69   Regal Zono. (S)LRZ 1010   TEN SONGS BY TUCKER ZIMMERMAN (LP). 18
72   Village Thing VTS 13   TUCKER ZIMMERMANN (LP). 20

ZIOR
71   Nepentha 6129 002   Za Za Za Zilda/She's A Bad Bad Woman 15
71   Nepentha 6129 003   Cat's Eyes/I Really Do 15
71   Nepentha 6437 005   ZIOR (LP, gatefold sleeve) 50
(see also Monument, Cardboard Orchestra)

ZIPPERS
64   Hickory 45-1252   My Sailor Boy/Pretend You're Still Mine 7

ZODIAC
68   Elektra EKL 4009   COSMIC SOUNDS (LP, also stereo EKS 74009) 25

ZOMBIES

ZODIAC MOTEL
87	Swordfish SWF 1	The Story Of Roland Flagg (1-sided promo, white label, foldover p/s)	10
87	Swordfish SWF 004	Sunshine Miner/Crescendo (p/s)	8
87	Swordfish ZOMO 1	Sunshine Miner/Crescendo/Inside My Mind/Sugarblood (12", p/s)	7
87	Swordfish ZOMO 2	Crystal Injection/I Can Only Give You Everything/Destiny Ranch/ Stephanie Blue (12", p/s)	7
87	Swordfish SWFLP 001	THE STORY OF ROLAND FLAGG (LP)	10

ZODIACS
57	Oriole CB 1383	Why Don't They Understand/The Game Of Love (78)	20
58	Oriole CB 1432	The Yum-Yum Song/Secrets	5
58	Oriole CB 1432	The Yum-Yum Song/Secrets (78)	20

ZAC ZOLAR & ELECTRIC BANANA
84	Butt FUN 5	Take Me Home/James Marshall	4

(see also Pretty Things, Phil May, Fenmen, Electric Banana)

ROB ZOMBIE
98	Geffen GFS 22367	Dragular/Halloween (picture disc)	5
98	Geffen GFS 22367	Dragular/Dragular (remix) (picture disc)	5

(see also White Zombie)

ZOMBIES
64	Decca F 11940	She's Not There/You Make Me Feel Good	6
64	Decca F 12004	Leave Me Be/Woman	8
65	Decca F 12072	Tell Her No/What More Can I Do	8
65	Decca F 12125	She's Coming Home/I Must Move	10
65	Decca F 12225	Whenever You're Ready/I Love You	10
65	Decca F 12296	Is This The Dream/Don't Go Away	10
66	Decca F 12322	Remember You/Just Out Of Reach	12
66	Decca F 12426	Indication/How We Were Before	12
66	Decca F 12495	Gotta Get A Hold Of Myself/The Way I Feel Inside	12
67	Decca F 12584	Goin' Out Of My Head/She Does Everything For Me	12
68	Decca F 12798	I Love You/The Way I Feel Inside	12
67	CBS 2960	Friends Of Mine/Beechwood Park	25
67	CBS 3087	Care Of Cell 44/Maybe After He's Gone	25
68	CBS 3380	Time Of The Season/I'll Call You Mine	25
65	Decca DFE 8598	THE ZOMBIES (EP)	80
65	Decca LK 4679	BEGIN HERE (LP)	100
68	CBS (S)BPG 63280	ODESSEY AND ORACLE (LP, mono/stereo)	75/40
73	Epic EPC 65728	TIME OF THE ZOMBIES (2-LP)	25
65	RCA RD 7791	BUNNY LAKE IS MISSING (LP, soundtrack)	75

(see also Unit Four Plus Two, Argent, Neil MacArthur, Colin Blunstone)

ZONES
78	Zoom ZUM 4	Stuck With You/No Angels (p/s)	4
78	Arista ARTIST 205	Sign Of The Times/Away From It All	4

(see also Slik, PVC 2)

ZOO
70	Major Minor SMLP 74	ZOO (LP)	12
71	Barclay 521172	ZOO (LP)	15

ZOOKIE
77	DJM DJS 10796	Judie Judie Hold On/I Couldn't Be You	8
78	DJM DJS 10866	Bubbles/Don't Rock Me	8

(see also Judie Tzuke, Tzuke & Paxo)

ZOOT
(see under Zoot Simms)

ZORRO
| 79 | Bridgehouse BHEP 1 | 'Arrods Don't Sell 'Em/Soldier Boy/Starflight (some with p/s) | 25/8 |

ZORRO FIVE
| 70 | Decca F 23042 | Reggae Shhh!/Reggae Meadowlands | 4 |

ZOSKIA
84	All The Madmen MAD 8	Rape/Thank You (p/s)	5
85	Temple TOPY 005	Be Like Me (12", p/s, transparent vinyl)	12
86	All The Madmen MADT 8	Rape/Black Action (12", p/s)	6

ZOSKIA MEETS SUGARDOG
| 84 | Temple TOPYS 021 | J.G. (unissued, white label promos only) | 8 |

ZOUNDS
81	Crass 4219844/3	Can't Cheat Karma/War/Subvert (gatefold p/s, with poster)	8
81	Rough Trade RT 069	Demystification/Great White Hunter (p/s)	6
82	Rough Trade RT 094	Dancing/True Love (p/s)	6
82	Not So Brave NSB 001	LA VACHE QUI RIT (EP, with poster)	8
82	Rough Trade RT 098	More Trouble Coming Every Day/Knife (p/s)	6
80s	Recommended RR 14.15	Ménage (12.59) (1-sided, other side printed, foldout sleeve in PVC sleeve)	8
84	Rough Trade ROUGH 31	THE CURSE OF ZOUNDS (LP)	15

ZUIDERZEE
| 66 | CBS 202062 | (You're My) Soul And Inspiration/Please Don't Call Me | 5 |
| 66 | CBS 202235 | Peace Of Mind/Provocative Child | 7 |

ZYGOAT
| 74 | Polydor 2058 124 | Catching A Thief/Letitia's Song | 4 |
| 74 | Polydor 2383 270 | ELECTROPHON (LP) | 15 |

ZZEBRA
74	Polydor 2058 446	Zardoz/Amusofi	5
75	Polydor 2058 579	Mr. J/Put The Light On Me	5
74	Polydor 2383 296	ZZEBRA (LP)	12
75	Polydor 2383 326	PANIC (LP)	12

(see also John McCoy, Gillan)

ZZ TOP
72	London HLU 10376	Francene/Down Brownie	15
74	London HLU 10458	Beer Drinkers And Hell Raisers/La Grange	10
75	London HLU 10475	La Grange/Just Got Paid	15
75	London HLU 10495	Tush/Blue Jean Blues	10
76	London HLU 10538	It's Only Love/Asleep In The Desert	8
77	London HLU 10547	Arrested For Driving While Blind/Neighbour, Neighbour	12
77	London HLU 10547	Arrested For Driving While Blind/Neighbour, Neighbour (mispressing, B-side plays Ray Charles' "I Can See Clearly Now")	15
79	Warner Bros K 17647	Cheap Sunglasses/Esther Be The One	8
80	Warner Bros K 17576	I Thank You/A Fool For Your Stockings (p/s)	8
83	Warner Bros W 9693	Gimme All Your Lovin'/If I Could Only Flag Her Down (p/s)	4
83	Warner Bros W 9693P	Gimme All Your Lovin'/Jesus Just Left Chicago/Arrested For Driving While Blind/Heard It On The X (12", p/s)	7
83	Warner Bros W 9693T	Gimme All Your Lovin'/If I Could Only Flag Her Down (car-shaped picture disc)	15
84	Warner Bros W 9334	T.V. Dinners/Cheap Sunglasses (p/s)	5
84	Warner Bros W 9334T	T.V. Dinners (Full Length)/Cheap Sunglasses (12", p/s)	8
84	Warner Bros W 9334T	T.V. Dinners (Full Length)/Cheap Sunglasses//Legs (Metal Mix)/A Fool For Your Stockings (12" double pack)	10
84	Warner Bros W 9576	Sharp Dressed Man/I Got The Fix (p/s)	5
84	Warner Bros W 9576T	Sharp Dressed Man/I Got The Fix/La Grange (12", p/s, some shrinkwrapped with sticker)	8
85	Warner Bros W 2001	Sleeping Bag/Party On The Patio (p/s)	5
85	Warner Bros W 2001F	Sleeping Bag/Party On The Patio//Sharp Dressed Man/I Got The Fix (p/s, sealed, stickered double pack)	10
85	Warner Bros W 2001P	Sleeping Bag/Party On The Patio ('sphinx'-shaped picture disc)	10
85	Warner Bros W 2001P	Sleeping Bag/Party On The Patio (shaped pic-disc, part 1 of interlocking set)	25
85	Warner Bros W 2001DP	Sleeping Bag/Party On The Patio ('sleeping bag'-shaped picture disc)	10
85	Warner Bros W 2001T	Sleeping Bag/Party On The Patio/Blue Jean Blues (12", p/s)	10
86	Warner Bros W 2002	Stages/Hi-Fi Mama (p/s)	5
86	Warner Bros W 2002BP	Stages/Hi-Fi Mama (shaped pic-disc, part 2 of interlocking set)	8
86	Warner Bros W 2002T	Stages (Extended Mix)/Stages/Hi-Fi Mama (12", p/s)	8
86	Warner Bros W 2003	Rough Boy/Delirious (p/s)	5
86	Warner Bros W 2003FP	Rough Boy/Delirious (shaped pic-disc, part 3 of interlocking set, some shrinkwrapped with bonus 12")	30/20
86	Warner Bros W 2003T	Rough Boy/Delirious/Legs (12", p/s with poster)	8
86	Warner Bros W 8946	SUMMER HOLIDAY EP: Beer Drinkers And Hell Raisers/I'm Bad, I'm Nationwide/Tush/Got Me Under Pressure (p/s)	5
86	Warner Bros W 8515	Velcro Fly/Can't Stop Rockin' ('86 Remix)/Woke Up With Wood (with velcro zipper)	4
72	London SH-U 8433	RIO GRANDE MUD (LP, original issue)	12
73	London SH-U 8459	TRES HOMBRES (LP, original issue)	12
75	London SH-U 8482	FANDANGO! (LP, original issue)	12
76	London LDU 1	TEJAS (LP, original foldout sleeve)	12
83	Warner Bros W 3774	ELIMINATOR (LP, with bonus stickered p/s 12" "Legs [Metal Mix]")	18
85	Warner Bros W 3774P	ELIMINATOR (LP, picture disc)	12
87	Warner Bros 925 661-2	ZZ TOP'S FIRST ALBUM/RIO GRANDE MUD/TRES HOMBRES/FANDANGO/TEJAS/EL LOCO (3-CD set of 1st 6 LPs, with booklet)	35

ZZY
91	Zebedee MAGICD 06	Is This The Last Time?/Heading For The Light (Of The Soul) (CD)	15
93	Zebedee MAGICD 17	Six Months From Freedom/Six Months From Freedom (You Think)/Six Months From Freedom (Don't Think, Act) (CD)	10
97	Zebedee BONG 002	False Dawn/Deep Despair/Wasted Life (CD, sunken text on black p/s)	7

Various Artists

VARIOUS ARTISTS 50s/60s EPs
(alphabetical by title)

A

56	Decca F 10752	ALL STAR HIT PARADE (Dickie Valentine/Joan Regan/Winifred Atwell/ Dave King/Lita Roza/David Whitfield)	12
57	Decca F 10915	ALL STAR HIT PARADE No. 2 (Johnston Bros/Bill Cotton/Jimmy Young/ Max Bygraves/Beverley Sisters/Tommy Steele)	10
63	Pye NEP 24168	ALL STAR HIT PARADE (Kenny Ball/Chris Barber Jazz Band/Joe Brown/ Lonnie Donegan Skiffle Group/Mary Wynter)	12
64	Pye NEP 24172	ALL STAR HIT PARADE VOL. 2 (Joe Brown/Petula Clark/Julie Grant/ Benny Hill/Mark Wynter)	12
64	Decca DFE 8571	AMERICAN COUNTRY JUBILEE NO. 1 (Ray Phillips/Autrey Inman/ Marvin McCullough/Billy Parker)	12

B

57	Philips BBE 12148	THE BELLS ARE RINGING (Tony Bennett/Vic Damone/De John Sisters/ Jo Stafford)	10
60s	Melodisc EPM7 115	BEST OF BLUEGRASS (COUNTRY STRINGS) (Bill Browning/Buzz Busby/ Country Gentlemen/Williams Brothers)	10
58	Philips BBE 12225	BEST WISHES FOR CHRISTMAS (Beverley Sisters/David Hughes/ Wally Scott Orchestra)	8
59	Mercury ZEP 10024	THE BIG BAND SOUND (Quincy Jones/Ralph Marterie Orchestra)	8
63	Concert Hall BPC 717	THE BIG BEAT (Bob Miller & Millermen/Al Saxon/Roy Young/Duffy Power)	20
65	Embassy WT 2008	THE BIG FOUR (Jaybirds/Redd Wayne/Les Carle/Joan Baxter)	10
65	Embassy WT 2011	THE BIG FOUR (Jaybirds/Terry Brandon/Les Carle/Typhoons)	10
66	Fontana TF 17469	THE BIG FOUR (Dave Dee Dozy Beaky Mick & Tich/Spencer Davis Group/ Mindbenders/Pretty Things)	10
56	Philips BBE 12021	THE BIG FOUR (Roy Hamilton/Frankie Laine/Mitch Miller Orchestra/ Something Smith & Redheads)	12
56	Philips BBE 12040	THE BIG FOUR NO. 2 (Mindy Carson/Don Cherry/Frankie Laine/Jo Stafford)	12
56	Philips BBE 12088	THE BIG FOUR NO. 3 (Shirley Bassey/Ronnie Carroll/David Hughes/ Anne Shelton)	10
56	Philips BBE 12091	THE BIG FOUR NO. 4 (Rosemary Clooney/Doris Day/Four Lads/Frankie Laine)	12
57	Philips BBE 12114	THE BIG FOUR NO. 5 (Shirley Bassey/Ronnie Carroll/Anne Shelton/ Frankie Vaughan)	10
57	Philips BBE 12139	THE BIG FOUR NO. 6 (Shirley Bassey/Ronnie Carroll/Kaye Sisters/ Frankie Vaughan)	10
57	Philips BBE 12145	THE BIG FOUR NO. 7 (Tony Bennett/Doris Day/Guy Mitchell/Johnnie Ray)	12
57	Philips BBE 12158	THE BIG FOUR NO. 8 (Shirley Bassey/Robert Earl/Kaye Sisters/Steve Martin)	10
58	Philips BBE 12165	THE BIG FOUR NO. 9 (Robert Earl/Anne Shelton/Joyce Shock/ Frankie Vaughan & Kaye Sisters)	10
58	Philips BBE 12190	THE BIG FOUR NO. 10 (Jimmy Lloyd/Robert Earl/Kaye Sisters/Anne Shelton)	10
59	Philips BBE 12288	THE BIG FOUR NO. 11 (Shirley Bassey/Kaye Sisters/Frankie Vaughan/ Marty Wilde)	10
59	Philips BBE 12336	THE BIG FOUR NO. 12 (Frankie Laine/G. Mitchell/Johnnie Ray/Leslie Uggams)	12
66	Philips BBE 12593	THE BIG FOUR (Roger Miller/Four Seasons/Dusty Springfield/Walker Bros)	10
64	Fontana TFE 18010	BLOWIN' IN THE WIND (withdrawn; Bob Dylan/Joan Baez/Pete Seeger)	50
60s	Range JRE 7005	BLUEGRASS (Coney Carver/Freeman Ervin)	8
59	Fontana TFE 17081	THE BLUES (Danny Barker/Jimmy Giuffre/Jo Jones/Pee Wee Russell)	8
61	Pieces Of 8 PEP 605	THE BLUES (Big Bill Broonzy/Josh White)	10
64	Pye Intl. NEP 44029	THE BLUES VOL. 1 PT. 1 (John Lee Hooker/Muddy Waters/Sonny Boy Williamson/Jimmy Witherspoon)	20
64	Pye Intl. NEP 44035	THE BLUES VOL. 1 PT. 2 (Howling Wolf/Buddy Guy/Little Walter/ Muddy Waters)	20
66	Chess CRE 6011	THE BLUES VOL. 2 PT. 1 (Otis Rush/Chuck Berry/John Lee Hooker/ Little Walter)	20
64	Pye Intl. NEP 44038	BLUES FESTIVAL (Sugar Pie De Santo/Willie Dixon/Sonny Boy Williamson/ Howlin' Wolf)	25
63	Columbia SEG 8226	BLUES ON PARADE NO. 1 (Jimmy Cotton/Brownie McGhee/ Roosevelt Sykes/Sonny Terry)	15
56	HMV 7EG 8178	THE BLUES THEY SANG (Lizzie Miles/Billy Young & Jelly Roll Morton)	18
61	Pye NEP 24142	BYE BYE BIRDIE (Brook Brothers/Patti Brook/Joe Brown/Jimmy Justice/ Kids/Viscounts)	12
61	RCA RCX 205	BREAKFAST AT TIFFANY'S (Henry Mancini)	20
61	Philips BBE 12472	BYE BYE BIRDIE NO. 1 (original cast; Marty Wilde et al.; stereo SBBE 9064)	10/12
61	Philips BBE 12473	BYE BYE BIRDIE NO. 2 (original cast; Marty Wilde et al.; stereo SBBE 9065)	10/12
61	Philips BBE 12474	BYE BYE BIRDIE NO. 3 (original cast; Marty Wilde et al.; stereo SBBE 9066)	10/12
61	Philips BBE 12475	BYE BYE BIRDIE NO. 4 (original cast; Marty Wilde et al.; stereo SBBE 9067)	10/12

C

63	Cameo Parkway CPE 552	CAMEO BIG FOUR (Bobby Rydell/Chubby Checker/Dovells/Orlons)	15
59	Mercury ZEP 10014	CHA CHA FOR NOW (Jan August/Sil Austin/Jerry Murad's Harmonicats)	8
62	Topic TOP 74	THE COLLIERS' RANT (Louis Killen/Johnny Handle/Colin Ross)	10
53	Columbia SCD 2008	COLUMBIA CAVALCADE (Marie Benson/Steve Conway/Beverley Sisters/ Teddy Johnson/Steve Race/Johnny Brandon/Ronnie Ronalde/Ensemble)	8

MINT VALUE £

JOHNNY CASH

60s	Range JRE 7001	COUNTRY AND WESTERN (Jim Chriss/Bob Strack/Jimmy Strickland)	8
60s	Range JRE 7004	COUNTRY AND WESTERN (Gabe Dean/Jimmy Dry/Rex Dario)	8
60	Top Rank JKP 2055	COUNTRY AND WESTERN EXPRESS VOL. 1 (Bill Alex Dixie Drifters/ Jenny Herrill/Elmer Snodgrass/Musical Pioneers)	8
60	Top Rank JKP 2056	COUNTRY AND WESTERN EXPRESS VOL. 2 (Jack Chambers & Rainbow Boys/Ralph Hodge & Hodges Brothers Band)	8
60	Top Rank JKP 2063	COUNTRY AND WESTERN EXPRESS VOL. 4 (Claude Gray/Eddie Noack)	8
60	Top Rank JKP 2065	COUNTRY AND WESTERN EXPRESS VOL. 6 (Tony Douglas/James O'Gwynn)	15
63	CBS AGG 20033	COUNTRY AND WESTERN HITS VOL. 1 (Carl Butler/Lester Flatt & Earl Scruggs/Lefty Frizzell/Stonewall Jackson/Ray Price)	8
64	CBS AGG 20041	COUNTRY AND WESTERN HITS VOL. 2 (Johnny Cash/Lester Flatt & Earl Scruggs/Lefty Frizzell/Marty Robbins)	10
65	Hickory LPE 1505	COUNTRY AND WESTERN SHOWCASE VOL. 2 (Roy Acuff/Wilma Lee/ Stoney Cooper)	8
57	Philips BBE 12149	COUNTRY AND WESTERN SPECTACULAR (George Morgan/Ray Price/ Mel Tillis/Marty Robbins)	12
59	Mercury ZEP 10038	COUNTRY AND WESTERN TRAIL BLAZERS NO. 1 (Connie Hall/ James O'Gwynn/Jimmy Skinner/Charlie Walker)	12
60	Mercury ZEP 10052	COUNTRY AND WESTERN TRAIL BLAZERS NO. 2 (Bill Clifton & Dixie Mountain Boys/George Jones)	12
60	Mercury ZEP 10080	COUNTRY AND WESTERN TRAIL BLAZERS NO. 3 (James O'Gwynn/ Connie Hall)	10
60s	Heritage 105	THE COUNTRY BLUES	50
58	RCA RCX 107	COUNTRY GUITAR VOL. 1 (Bonnie, Jim Edward & Maxine Brown/ Hank Locklin/Jim Reeves/Hank Snow)	10
58	RCA RCX 110	COUNTRY GUITAR VOL. 2 (Skeeter Davis/Don Gibson/Jim Reeves/Hank Snow)	12
59	RCA RCX 127	COUNTRY GUITAR VOL. 5 (Eddy Arnold/Browns/Skeeter Davis/ Johnny & Jack/Hank Snow/Porter Wagoner)	10
59	RCA RCX 141	COUNTRY GUITAR VOL. 6 (Hank Locklin/Eddy Arnold/Browns/Hank Snow/ Porter Wagoner/Johnny & Jack)	10
59	RCA RCX 147	COUNTRY GUITAR VOL. 8 (Browns/Don Gibson/Hawkshaw Hawkins/ Johnny & Jack/Jim Reeves)	10
59	RCA RCX 159	COUNTRY GUITAR VOL. 9 (Hank Locklin/Gail Davis/Skeeter Davis/Jimmy Driftwood/Jim Reeves)	12
59	RCA RCX 176	COUNTRY GUITAR VOL. 10 (Hank Locklin/Skeeter Davis/Hawkshaw Hawkins/Johnny & Jack/Sons Of The Pioneers/Hank Snow)	12
59	RCA RCX 177	COUNTRY GUITAR VOL. 11 (Browns/Eddy Arnold/Jack Clement/Hank Snow)	10
60	RCA RCX 185	COUNTRY GUITAR VOL. 12 (Eddy Arnold/Hawkshaw Hawkins/Jim Reeves/ Hank Snow/Porter Wagoner)	10
62	RCA RCX 7105	COUNTRY GUITAR VOL. 16 (Bill Monroe & Blue Grass Boys/Monroe Bros)	12
63	Decca DFE 8522	COUNTRY JUBILEE VOL. 1 (Sonny Miller/Ray Phillips/Ott Stephens/ Sonny Williams)	10
63	Decca DFE 8523	COUNTRY JUBILEE VOL. 2 (Kendall Hayes/Margie Laffery/ Lonesome Pine Fiddlers/Marvin McCullough)	10

D

56	Mercury MEP 9509	DAMN YANKEES (Rusty Draper/Vic Damone/Patti Page/Sarah Vaughan) 10
54	Capitol EAP1 518	DANCE CRAZE (Ray Anthony/Pee Wee Hunt/Stan Kenton) 10
60s	XX MIN 706	DARK MUDDY BOTTOM (Jimmy Slim/Good Jelly Bess/Lightning Leon/
		Little Red Walters/Willie B.) 15
58	MGM MGM-EP 652	DEEP IN MY HEART Excerpts (Rosemary Clooney/Vic Damone/Tony Martin/
		Jane Powell/Helen Traubel) 8
50s	Poydras 102	DEPRESSION BLUES. 25
63	Decca DFE 8520	DISCS-A-GO GO (Karl Denver/Billy Fury/Jet Harris/Vernons Girls) 50
60s	Jan & Dil JR 450	DOWN HOME BLUES — SIXTIES STYLE (Lightning Leon/Jerry McCain/
		Little Red Walters) 25
60s	XX MIN 709	DOWNHOME HARP (Kid Thomas/Eddie Hope/Jerry McCain). 15
59	Fontana TFE 17146	DRUMBEAT (Lana Sisters/Adam Faith/Bob Miller & Millermen/
		Sylvia Sands/Roy Young). 35

E

65	Edinburgh S.C. ESC 02	EDINBURGH STUDENTS CHARITIES APPEAL (33rpm, die-cut paper p/s;
		Athenians/Avengers/Ray & Archie Fisher/Lynn & Kathy) 50
66	Edinburgh S.C. ESC 03	EDINBURGH STUDENTS CHARITIES APPEAL (33rpm,
		Athenians/Gear System/Old Bailey's Jazz Advocates) 60
60	Felsted ESD 3083	AN EVENING AT LA POUBELLE (Curly Hamner/Ben Dalida/Wackadous) 8
67	Philips P 160E	EXQUISITE FORM (freebie; Dave Dee, Dozy, Beaky, Mick & Tich/Herd/
		Walker Brothers/Dusty Springfield). 12

F

59	Jazz Collector JEL 12	THE FEMALE BLUES VOL. 1 (Ida Cox/Ma Rainey) 15
60	Jazz Collector JEL 14	THE FEMALE BLUES VOL. 2 (Bertha Henderson/Rosa Henderson) 15
64	Jazz Collector JEL 22	THE FEMALE BLUES VOL. 3 (Ma Rainey/Trixie Smith). 15
64	Pye Intl. NEP 44030	FESTIVAL OF THE BLUES NO. 1 (Willie Dixon/Buddy Guy/Muddy Waters/
		Sonny Boy Williamson) 18
58	Parlophone GEP 8694	FLUTE COCKTAIL (Bill Doggett/Johnny Pate Quartet). 10
66	HMV 7EG 8911	FOLKSOUND OF BRITAIN (Cyril Tawney/Lewis Johns/John Steele) 8
63	Ember EMB EP 4530	FOOL BRITANNIA (Peter Sellers/Dan Massey/Anthony Newley/Joan Collins/
		Maureen Lipton). 10
57	Philips BBE 12140	FOUR GREAT MOVIE THEMES (V. Damone/Hi-Lo's/Frankie Laine/Jerry Vale) 12
68	CBS WEP 1138	FOUR YOU (Gary Puckett, Johnny Mathis, Simon & Garfunkel, Tremeloes) 8
63	Decca DFE 8538	FROM A LONDON HOOTENANNY (Davy Graham/Thamesiders) 15

G

59	MGM MGM-EP 703	GIRLS AND MORE GIRLS (June Allyson/Ava Gardner/Judy Garland/
		Kathryn Grayson). 8
67	Down with the Game 202	GOD DON'T LIKE IT 25
67	Down with the Game 203	GOD DON'T LIKE IT VOLUME 2 25
60s	XX MIN 707	GOING TO CALIFORNIA (Little Sonny Willis/Eddie Williams) 15
59	Philips BBE 12318	GREAT COUNTRY AND WESTERN HITS (Johnny Cash/Johnny Horton/
		Stonewall Jackson/Carl Smith) 15
66	Pye Intl. NEP 45054	THE GREATEST ON STAGE (Maxine Brown/Chuck Jackson/Shirelles/
		Dionne Warwick). 15
67	CBS WEP 1131	GREAT SCREEN THEMES (John Barry/Percy Faith & His Orchestra) 8
63	London RE-U 1393	GROUP OF GOODIES (Marcie Blane/Kokomo/Bill Black's Combo/
		Ernie Maresca) 30
59	Mercury ZEP 10010	GROUPS GALORE (Del Vikings/Mark IV/Diamonds/Hi-Liters) 125
56	Philips BBE 12077	GUYS AND DOLLS (Frankie Laine/Rosemary Clooney/
		Jo Stafford/Jerry Vale) 10

H

64	Hickory LPE 1500	HICKORY SHOWCASE VOL. 1 (Roy Acuff/Wilma Lee/Stoney Cooper). 10
64	Hickory LPE 1501	HICKORY SHOWCASE VOL. 2 (Bobby Lord/Bob Luman) 20
64	Hickory LPE 1504	HICKORY SHOWCASE VOL. 3 (Bobby Lord/Bob Luman) 20
57	Capitol EAP1 852	HIT CALYPSOS (Andrews Sisters/Nat 'King' Cole/Stan Kenton/
		Lord Flea Calypsonians) 10
55	MGM MGM-EP 525	HIT THE DECK — SOUNDTRACK EXCERPTS (Tony Martin/Jane Powell/
		Debbie Reynolds). 8
55	MGM MGM-EP 526	HIT THE DECK — SOUNDTRACK EXCERPTS (Tony Martin/Jane Powell/
		Anne Miller/Vic Damone) 8
65	Pye NEP 24213	THE HITMAKERS NO. 1 (Searchers/Kenny Ball Jazzmen/Dixie Cups/
		Dionne Warwick). 10
65	Pye NEP 24214	THE HITMAKERS NO. 2 (Honeycombs/Tony Jackson/Kinks/Shangri-La's) 22
65	Pye NEP 24215	THE HITMAKERS NO. 3 (Chuck Berry/Julie Grant/Rockin' Berries/
		Sandie Shaw) 12
66	Pye NEP 24241	THE HITMAKERS VOL. 1 (Ivy League/Tommy Quickly/Sandie Shaw/
		Sounds Orchestral) 10
66	Pye NEP 24242	THE HITMAKERS VOL. 2 (Chuck Berry/Kinks/Sue Thompson/Shangri-La's) 12
66	Pye NEP 24243	THE HITMAKERS VOL. 3 (Kinks/Lancastrians/Rockin' Berries/Searchers) 12
66	Piccadilly NEP 34100	THE HITMAKERS (Petula Clark/Kenny Ball/Anita Harris/Honeycombs). 8
66	Pye Intl. NEP 44065	HITMAKERS INTERNATIONAL (Fontella Bass/James Brown/Petula Clark/
		Lovin' Spoonful). 20
56	Mercury MEP 9003	HIT PARADE VOL. 1 (Georgia Gibbs/Platters/Crew Cuts/Patti Page) 18
56	Mercury MEP 9510	HIT PARADE VOL. 2 (Sarah Vaughan/Ralph Marterie/Patti Page/Crew Cuts) 18
57	Brunswick OE 9340	HIT PARADE (Rex Allen/Peggy Lee/Jeri Southern/Victor Young Orchestra) 10
58	Brunswick OE 9450	HIT PARADE NO. 2 (Carmen Cavallaro/Four Aces/Grandpa Jones/
		Jack Pleis & His Orchestra) 12
65	Decca DFE 8648	HITS VOL. 1 (Chris Andrews/Fortunes/Hedgehoppers Anonymous/
		Jonathan King). 8
65	Decca DFE 8649	HITS VOL. 2 (Lulu/Chris Andrews/Marianne Faithull/Fortunes). 15

MINT VALUE £

65	Decca DFE 8653	HITS VOL. 3 (Pinkerton's Assorted Colours/St. Louis Union/Mexicans/ Paul & Barry Ryan)	12
66	Decca DFE 8662	HITS VOL. 4 (Dave Berry/Val Doonican/Joy Marshall/Crispian St. Peters)	10
66	Decca DFE 8663	HITS VOL. 5 (Animals/Los Bravos/Alan Price Set/Small Faces)	12
66	Decca DFE 8667	HITS VOL. 6 (Jonathan King/Lulu/Alan Price Set/Small Faces)	12
67	Decca DFE 8675	HITS VOL. 7 (Ronnie Aldrich/Val Doonican/Bachelors/Small Faces)	12
55	Capitol EAP1 482	HITS FROM CAN CAN (Les Baxter Orchestra/Nat 'King' Cole/Gordon MacRae/ Kay Starr)	8
62	Mercury ZEP 10133	HITSVILLE! (Brook Benton/Crew Cuts/Phil Philips/Diamonds)	25
59	Coral FEP 2034	HITSVILLE VOL. 1 (Buddy Holly/McGuire Sisters/Betty Madigan/Billy Williams)	50
59	Coral FEP 2035	HITSVILLE VOL. 2 (Lennon Sisters/Art Lund/Teresa Brewer/Jackie Wilson)	35
65	Tamla Motown TME 2001	HITSVILLE U.S.A. NO. 1 (Marvin Gaye/Brenda Holloway/Carolyn Crawford/ Eddie Holland)	70
66	Post War Blues 100	HOBOS AND DRIFTERS	40

I

65	Chess CRE 6010	IN CROWD (Radiants/Ramsey Lewis Trio/Little Milton/Billy Stewart)	20
56	Mercury MEP 9503	ITEMS FROM GUYS AND DOLLS (Richard Hayes/Kitty Kallen/Frankie Laine/ David Le Winter)	12
59	Mercury ZEP 10001	IT'S CHA CHA TIME (Jan August & Richard Hayman Orchestra/Jerry Murad's Harmonicats/Hi Liters/Ray Marterie Orchestra)	8
56	Columbia SEG 7639	IT'S GREAT TO BE YOUNG — FILM TUNES (Ruby Murray/Coronets/ Ray Martin Orchestra/Mr Dingle)	8
62	Pye Jazz NJE 1083	IT'S TRAD, DAD — FILM SOUNDTRACK (Bob Wallis/Kenny Ball & His Jazzmen)	10

J

| 67 | Natchez NEP-701 | THE JUG BANDS VOLUME 1 | 15 |
| 64 | Columbia SEG 8337 | JUST FOR YOU (Peter & Gordon/Freddie & Dreamers) | 18 |

K

63	Lyntone LYN 347/348	KEELE RAG RECORD (flexidisc; Rhythm Unlimited & Halettes/Keele Quintet)	15
64	Lyntone LYN 508/509	KEELE RAG RECORD No. 2 (flexidisc; Escorts/Lance Harvey & Kingpins/ Keele Row; some in die-cut sleeve)	30/25
65	Lyntone LYN 765/766	KEELE RAG RECORD (flexidisc; Bob Wilson/Changing Times/ Lance Harvey & Kingpins/Incas)	40
56	London RE-E 1047	THE KING AND QUEEN OF R&B (Ruth Brown/Joe Turner)	175
61	RCA Victor RCX 203	KINGS OF THE BLUES VOL. 2 (Jazz Gillum/Big Maceo/Washboard Sam/ Sonny Boy Williamson)	12
61	RCA Victor RCX 204	KINGS OF THE BLUES VOL. 3 (Arthur Big Boy Crudup/Furry Lewis/ Poor Joe Williams)	15
59	Top Rank 45-TR 5004	KING SIZE (maxi-single; Craig Douglas/Sheila Buxton/Bert Weedon)	10
55	Mercury EP-1 3160	KISMET (Vic Damone/Georgia Gibbs/Ross Bagdasarian)	10
60	Warner Bros WEP 6010	KOOKIE STARS OF SEVENTY SEVEN SUNSET STRIP (Joannie Sommers/Eddie Byrne/Connie Stevens)	15

L

66	Holyground HG 111	THE LAST THING ON MY MIND (EP, 99 copies only)	50
59	Top Rank JKR 8008	LET'S GO NO. 1 (Jimmy Lee/Johnny Hines/Treetoppers)	12
59	Top Rank JKR 8012	LET'S GO NO. 2 (Johnny Hines/Billy Mack/Victors/Ted & Ray)	15
60	Philips BBE 12414/ SBBE 9031	LET'S MAKE LOVE — FILM SOUNDTRACK (Yves Montand/Marilyn Monroe/ Frankie Vaughan; mono/stereo)	25/30
57	London RE-D 1075	LONDON HIT PARADE NO. 1 (Tab Hunter/Hilltoppers/Pat Boone/ Fontane Sisters)	20
57	London RE-P 1096	LONDON HIT PARADE NO. 2 (Fats Domino/Slim Whitman/Ken Copeland/ Roy Brown)	80
58	London RE-D 1097	LONDON HIT PARADE NO. 3 (Pat Boone/Gale Storm/Tab Hunter/Jim Lowe)	20
58	London RE-D 1130	LONDON HIT PARADE NO. 4 (Pat Boone/Nick Todd/ Bonnie Guitar/Hilltoppers)	20
58	London RE-D 1136	LONDON TOPPERS NO. 2 (Pat Boone/Nick Todd/Tab Hunter/Jim Lowe)	20
58	London RE-P 1137	LONDON TOPPERS NO. 2 (Slim Whitman/Fats Domino/Ricky Nelson/ Ernie Freeman)	75
58	London RE-D 1145	LONDON HIT PARADE NO. 5 (Pat Boone/Fontane Sisters/Frank De Rosa)	15

M

59	Jazz Collector JEL 2	THE MALE BLUES VOL. 1 (Georgia Slim/Walter Roland)	15
59	Jazz Collector JEL 4	THE MALE BLUES VOL. 3 (Blind Blake/Ramblin' Thomas)	15
59	Jazz Collector JEL 5	THE MALE BLUES VOL. 4 (Tall Tom/Pinewood Tom)	15
59	Jazz Collector JEL 8	THE MALE BLUES VOL. 5 (Blind Lemon Jefferson/Buddy Boy Hawkins)	15
60	Jazz Collector JEL 10	THE MALE BLUES VOL. 6 (Hound Head Henry/Frankie Jaxon)	15
60	Jazz Collector JEL 13	THE MALE BLUES VOL. 7 (Blind Lemon Jefferson/Ed Bell)	15
61	Jazz Collector JEL 24	THE MALE BLUES VOL. 8 (Blind Lemon Jefferson/Leadbelly)	15
67	Piccadilly NEP 34100	MAXWELL HOUSE PRESENTS HITMAKERS (Kenny Ball/Petula Clark/Honeycombs/Anita Harris)	8
57	Decca DFE 6408	MERRY CHRISTMAS (Dave King/Mantovani Orchestra/Dickie Valentine/ David Whitfield)	12
60	MGM MGM-EP 749	MGM EVERGREENS (Billy Eckstine/Tommy Edwards/Lennie Hayton/ Sam 'The Man' Taylor & Catmen)	12
69	Middle Earth MDE 201	MIDDLE EARTH (Writing On The Wall/Wooden O/Arcadium) (promo only, 33rpm, no p/s)	40
64	RCA RCX 7159	MONTH'S BEST FROM THE COUNTRY AND WEST (Eddy Arnold/Bobby Bare/George Hamilton IV/Connie Smith)	10
64	RCA RCX 7162	MONTH'S BEST FROM THE COUNTRY AND WEST VOL. 2 (Skeeter Davis/Bobby Bare/Don Gibson/Jim Reeves/Hank Snow)	10
64	RCA RCX 7171	MONTH'S BEST FROM THE COUNTRY AND WEST VOL. 3 (Eddy Arnold/Archie Campbell/Porter Wagoner/Dottie West)	10

65	RCA RCX 7172	MONTH'S BEST FROM THE COUNTRY AND WEST VOL. 4 (Bobby Bare/Jim Edward Brown/Willie Nelson/Connie Smith) 10
65	RCA RCX 7178	MONTH'S BEST FROM THE COUNTRY AND WEST VOL. 5 (Bobby Bare/Norma Jean/Porter Wagoner/Connie Smith) 10
65	RCA RCX 7181	MONTH'S BEST FROM THE COUNTRY AND WEST VOL. 6 (Don Gibson/ Bobby Bare/Carl Belew/George Hamilton IV/Hank Locklin/Dottie West) 10
67	RCA RCX 7186	MONTH'S BEST FROM THE COUNTRY AND WEST VOL. 7 (Waylon Jennings/ Stu Phillips/Connie Smith/Dottie West) 10
60s	Jan & Dil TR 451	MORE DOWN HOME BLUES (Good Jelly Boss/Juke Boy Bonner/ Papa Lightfoot/Snooky Prior) 25
60	Philips BBE 12348	MOST HAPPY FELLA HITS (Doris Day/Four Lads/Frankie Laine/Jo Stafford) 10
64	Stateside SE 1021	MOVIE MUSIC (John Barry/Artie Butler/Eddie Heywood/Bill Ramal Combo) 15
60s	Mercury YARD 002	MUSIC FOR 5 AM (promo for Yardley; Hollies & others) 12

N

56	Vogue EPV 1106	NEGRO SPIRITUALS (Original Five Blind Boys/Sensational Nightingales) 15
64	Vocalion EPVP 1271	NEGRO SPIRITUALS (Dixie Hummingbirds/Sensational Nightingales) 15
64	Vocalion EPVP 1276	NEGRO SPIRITUALS (Five Blind Boys/Spirits Of Memphis) 15
66	Tamla Motown TME 2014	NEW FACES FROM HITSVILLE (Jimmy Ruffin/Chris Clark & Lewis Sisters/ Tammi Terrell/Monitors) 175
57	Pye NEP 24052	NIXA HIT PARADE NO. 1 (Gary Miller/Pet Clark/Lonnie Donegan/John Frazer) . . . 12
58	Pye NEP 24064	NIXA HIT PARADE NO. 2 (Pearl Carr & Teddy Johnson/Petula Clark/ Lonnie Donegan Skiffle Group/Colin Hicks & Cabin Boys) 20
58	Pye NEP 24071	NIXA HIT PARADE NO. 3 (Marion Ryan/Gary Miller/Lonnie Donegan/ Edmund Hockridge) 12
58	Pye NEP 24078	NIXA HIT PARADE NO. 4 (Marion Ryan/Pet Clark/Joe Henderson/Gary Miller) . . . 12
58	Pye NEP 24082	NIXA HIT PARADE NO. 5 (Petula Clark/Lonnie Donegan Skiffle Group/ Marion Ryan/Bill Shepherd Orchestra) 12
58	Pye NEP 24090	NIXA HIT PARADE NO. 6 (Lita Roza/Petula Clark/Lonnie Donegan Skiffle Group/Joe Henderson) 12
59	Pye NEP 24100	NIXA HIT PARADE NO. 7 (Lita Roza/Petula Clark/Lonnie Donegan Skiffle Group/Edmund Hockridge) 12

O

65	Columbia SEG 8413	ON THE SCENE (Downliners Sect/Animals/Cherokees/Cheynes/ Georgie Fame/Yardbirds) 60
63	MGM MGM-EP 787	ORIGINAL HITS (Tommy Edwards/Johnny Ferguson/Jimmy Jones/ Conway Twitty) 40
63	London RE-K 1390	THE ORIGINAL HITS (Drifters/Ritchie Barrett/Coasters/Ben E. King) 40
65	Atlantic AET 6006	ORIGINAL HITS VOL. 2 (Barbara Lewis/Coasters/Solomon Burke/Drifters) 30
62	Ember EMB 4522	ORIGINAL RHYTHM AND BLUES HITS (Jesse Belvin/Ray Charles/ Linda Hayes/Jimmy McCracklin/Johnny Moore Blazers) 50
55	Pye Jazz NJE 1043	ORIGINS OF SKIFFLE (Isla Cameron/Guy Carawan/Peggy Seeger) 15
57	Columbia SEG 7669	OUR CHOICE (Eddie Calvert/Michael Holliday/Ruby Murray) 10
68	Apple (no cat. no.)	OUR FIRST FOUR (Beatles/Mary Hopkin/Jackie Lomax/Black Dyke Mills Band; 4 x 7" in presentation pack, including Apple R 5722, APPLE 2, APPLE 3 & APPLE 4]; each mounted in PVC pocket on printed dayglo card insert, in 10" x 12" card or plastic outer box) 1,250

P

55	London RE-A 1036	THE PAJAMA GAME (Archie Bleyer Orchestra/Stephen Douglas/ Douglas & Dorothy Evans/Arthur Malvin) 12
55	Decca DFE 6147	PARADE OF STARS (Joan Regan/Edmundo Ros & Stargazers/ Dickie Valentine/Stargazers) 10
58	Pye NEP 85000	POPS GO STEREO (Marion Ryan/Tony Osborne Orch./Bill Shepherd Orch.) 12
68	CBS Spec. Prod. WEP 1135	POPSTER PACK (Georgie Fame/Anita Harris/Peddlers/Simon & Garfunkel) 7

R

67	Action ACT 002 EP	RAG GOES MAD AT THE MOJO (33rpm; Joe Cocker's Blues Band/ Tangerine Ayr Band/Pitiful Souls/Delroy Good Good Band; in conjunction with Sheffield University rag magazine *Twikker*) 75
56	Vogue EPV 1113	RHYTHM AND BLUES (Dominoes/Swallows) 275
60s	Range JRE 7002	RHYTHM AND BLUES (Sticks Herman/Tim Whitsett) 18
60s	Range JRE 7006	RHYTHM AND BLUES (Harry Lewis/Tommy Wills) 15
63	Stateside SE 1008	RHYTHM AND BLUES (Jimmy Reed/John Lee Hooker) 20
64	Stateside SE 1009	R&B CHARTMAKERS (Martha/Vandellas/Miracles/Marvin Gaye/Marvelettes) . . . 65
64	Stateside SE 1018	R&B CHARTMAKERS NO. 2 (Miracles/Kim Weston/Supremes/Marvelettes) 70
64	Stateside SE 1022	R&B CHARTMAKERS NO. 3 (Marvin Gaye/Darnells/Eddie Holland/ Martha & Vandellas) 70
64	Stateside SE 1025	R&B CHARTMAKERS NO. 4 (Supremes/Eddie Holland/Temptations/ Contours) 65
60	Vogue EPV 1198	RHYTHM AND BLUES CONCERT (Helen Humes/Jimmy Witherspoon) 80
64	Pye Intl. NEP 44021	RHYTHM AND BLUES SHOWCASE VOL. 1 (Don & Bob/Dale Hawkins/ Clarence Henry/Larry Williams) 25
64	Pye Intl. NEP 44022	RHYTHM AND BLUES SHOWCASE VOL. 2 (Jimmy McCracklin/ Muddy Waters/Little Walter/Howlin' Wolf) 25
57	Vogue VE 170111	ROCK AND ROLL (Mister Google Eyes August/Louis Jones Rock & Roll Band/Walter Price Rock & Roll Band/Clarence Gatemouth Brown) 150
62	Capitol EAP1 20197	ROUND-UP (Tommy Collins/Farmer Boys/Ferlin Husky/Texas Bill Strength) 15
60	Top Rank JKP 2060	RUSHING FOR PERCUSSION (Preston Epps/Sandy Nelson) 40

S

| 60s | S.A.U.C.C. PR 5462 | ST. ANDREWS UNIVERSITY CHARITIES CAMPAIGN (20th Century Sounds/ Steve Hall & Roosters/Black Ring; no p/s) . . . . 50 |
| 63 | Decca DFE 8541 | SEA SHANTIES (FROM A LONDON HOOTENANNY) (Redd Sullivan/Lou Killen/Bob Davenport) . . . . 8 |

MINT VALUE £

64	Lyntone LYN 738/739	SHEFFIELD UNIVERSITY RAG RECORD (flexidisc; Vantennas/Dave Allen Band/ Addy Street Five/Los Caribos; die-cut sleeve)	40
55	Columbia SEG 7528	SHOUT FOR JOY (Pete Johnson/Albert Ammons/Meade Lux Lewis)	25
63	London RE-P 1403	SINGING THE BLUES (Ernie K-Doe/Showmen/Jesse Hill/Chris Kenner)	60
58	MGM MGM-EP 671	SINGING IN THE RAIN (Debbie Reynolds/Gene Kelly/Donald O'Connor)	8
58	Decca DFE 6485	SIX FIVE SPECIAL (Jackie Dennis/ Joan Regan/Diane Todd/Dickie Valentine)	25
58	Pye NEP 24076	SIX HIT SONGS FROM MY FAIR LADY (Lita Roza/Petula Clark/Ray Ellington/ Gary Miller/Max Miller/Marion Ryan)	8
62	Pye NEP 24158	SOME PEOPLE (Eagles/Valerie Mountain)	8
66	Lyntone LYN 995	THE SOUND OF THE STARS (flexidisc with Disc And Music Echo; with/without mag & envelope/stamp)	20/10
65	Keele Rag/Lyntone LYN 951/952	SOUNDS OF SAVILE (flexidisc; Hipster Image/London Apprentices/ Tom & Brennie; some in die-cut sleeve)	60/45
55	Decca DFE 6147	STAR PARADE (Stargazers/Edmundo Ros Orchestra/Joan Regan & Squadronaires/Dickie Valentine)	12
60s	208 Radio Luxembourg	STAR SOUVENIR GREETINGS (flexidisc)	15
60	Mercury ZEP 10088	SURPRISE PACKAGE (Ben Hewitt/Diamonds)	100
59	Top Rank JKR 8007	SWEET BEAT (Lee Allen Band/Fred Parris/Cindy Mann/Mellokings)	40
58	Capitol EAP1 1026	SWINGIN' DRUMS (Billy May & His Orchestra/ Earl Palmer & His Orchestra)	10

T

63	Oriole EP 7080	TAKE SIX (Mark Peters' Silhouettes/Ian & Zodiacs/Faron's Flamingos/Earl Preston & T.T.s/Rory Storm & Hurricanes/Sonny Wade & Cascades)	60
59	Mercury ZEP 10015	TEAR IT UP (Boyd Bennett Orchestra/Red Prysock/Hi-Liters)	125
57	Mercury MEP 9522	TEEN-AGE ROCK (Red Prysock/Rusty Draper/Chuck Miller/Crew Cuts)	100
58	RCA RCX 111	TEENAGE TOPS (Ray Peterson/Jimmy Dell/Marlin Greene/Barry De Vorzon)	35
64	Ember EMB 4540	TEEN SCENE '64 (Dave Clark Five/Ray Singer/Washington D.C.s)	45
67	CBS Special Products WEP 1126	THEMES FROM JAMES BOND FILMS (John Barry Orchestra/Mertens Brothers Style/Percy Faith)	10
58	Brunswick OE 9425	THEY SOLD A MILLION NO. 9 (Bobby Helms/Four Aces/Jerry Lewis/ Kitty Kallen)	20
59	Brunswick OE 9426	THEY SOLD A MILLION NO. 10 (Andrews Sisters/Four Aces/Ink Spots/ Mills Brothers)	10
59	Brunswick OE 9427	THEY SOLD A MILLION NO. 11 (Ink Spots/Louis Jordan & His Tympany Five/ Mills Brothers/Weavers)	18
59	Brunswick OE 9431	THEY SOLD A MILLION NO. 15 (Four Aces/Bill Haley & His Comets)	20
60s	Argo EAF 66	THROUGH THE LOOKING GLASS (SCENES FROM) (soundtrack)	10
57	Decca DFE 6411	TOPS IN POPS NO. 1 (Beverley Sisters/Bob Cort Skiffle Group/Terry Dene/ Tommy Steele)	18
58	Decca DFE 6467	TOPS IN POPS NO. 3 (Jackie Dennis/D. King/Southlanders/David Whitfield)	15
59	Decca DFE 6583	TOPS IN POPS NO. 7 (Beverley Sisters/Ted Heath & His Music/ Lord Rockingham's XI/Tommy Steele)	12
63	Stateside SE 1004	TOP TEEN DANCES (Johnnie Morisette/Huey 'Piano' Smith & Clowns/ Al Brown's Tunetoppers/Spartans)	22
57	Parlophone R 4356	TOP TEN SPECIAL (Jim Dale/King Brothers/Vipers Skiffle Group)	12
67	Pye NEP 24276	TOP T.V. THEMES (Cyril Stapleton/Ron Grainer Orchestra/Barry Gray Orchestra/Eliminators/Johnny Keating & Z Men)	15
60	Fontana TFE 17265	TREASURES OF NORTH AMERICAN NEGRO MUSIC VOL. 6 (Reverend J.C. Burnett/Reverend J.M. Gates/Reverend W. Mosley)	12
65	Century 21 MA 105	T.V. CENTURY 21 THEMES (David Graham/Sylvia Anderson/Peter Dyneley/ Barry Gray Orchestra/Gary Miller/Eric Winstone Orchestra)	15
64	Decca DFE 8585	T.V. THEMES (Andrew Oldham Orchestra/Ted Heath Music/ Ron Grainer Music/Cyril Stapleton Orchestra)	40
66	Decca DFE 8661	T.V. THEMES (Magicians/Frank Chacksfield Orchestra/Larry Page Orchestra)	8
69	M.C.P.S. ATV 1	T.V. THEMES: A GIFT FROM PASCALL MURRAY (Laurie Johnson Orch. et al.; Pascal Fruits promo presented by Pete Murray)	10
66	Pye NEP 24244	T.V. THEMES 1966 (Laurie Johnson Orchestra/John Schroeder Orchestra/ Cyril Stapleton Orchestra)	12
62	Starlite STEP 31	TWIST OFF (Wayne Farmer/Medallions/Charles Perrywell/Piano Slim/ Teenbeats/Dellos)	150
62	Starlite STEP 29	TWIST ON (Mighty Trojans/Dee Dee Gaudet/Dixie Lee/ Percy & The Rocking Aces)	150

V

| 65 | Vogue VRE 5002 | VOGUE SURPRISE PARTIE (Petula Clark/Jean Jacques Debout/ Francoise Hardy/Michel Paje) | 12 |

W

59	RCA RCX 128	WAGON TRAIN (Shorty Long/Prairie Chiefs/Sons Of The Pioneers)	8
69	Apple CT 1	WALLS ICE CREAM PRESENTS (Mary Hopkin/Iveys/Jackie Lomax/ James Taylor; with/without p/s)	35/10
65	Liberty LEP 4036	WE SING THE BLUES (Jesse Hill/Ernie K. Doe/Aaron Neville/Benny Spellman)	30
64	Fontana TFE 18009	WITH GOD ON OUR SIDE (withdrawn; Bob Dylan/Joan Baez/Pete Seeger)	50
66	Chess CRE 6009	WITH THE BLUES (Eddie Boyd Blues Combo/Buddy Guy)	30

Y

64	Fontana TFE 18011	YE PLAYBOYS AND PLAYGIRLS (withdrawn; Bob Dylan/Joan Baez/ Pete Seeger)	50
68	Chess CRE 6026	YOUR CHESS REQUESTS (Fontella Bass/Tony Clarke/Mitty Collier/ Billy Stewart)	30
57	Mercury MEP 9525	YOUR CHOICE (Hal Mooney Orchestra/Chuck Miller/Sarah Vaughan/ Florian Zabach)	20
58	Mercury MEP 9532	YOUR CHOICE NO. 2 (Ralph Marterie Orchestra/Patti Page/ Platters/Myoshi Umeki)	12

UNTITLED EP

60s	Coxsone SCE 1	(no p/s, 33rpm; Gaylads/Hugh Godfrey/Glen & Dave/Roy Richards/ Cables/Richard Ace)	50

70s/80s/90s VARIOUS ARTISTS SINGLES & EPs
(alphabetical by title)

A

90	Metro Music DWM-1	ABSLOM DAAK — DALEK KILLER (Mark Ayres/Dominic Glynn/ The Slaves Of Kane) (square flexi, with/without *Doctor Who Magazine*)	8/4
85	Lyntone LYN 16705	ALTERNATIVE TOP OF THE POPS (flexidisc, spoken word)	8
91	Apple APP 1	APPLE EP (Mary Hopkin/Billy Preston/ Jackie Lomax/Badfinger; laminated p/s)	4
91	Apple TC-APP 1	APPLE EP (Mary Hopkin/Billy Preston/Jackie Lomax/Badfinger; cassette)	4
91	Apple CDAPP 1	APPLE EP (Mary Hopkin/Billy Preston/Jackie Lomax/Badfinger; CD, apple-shaped card sleeve or standard jewel case)	each 10
95	Sticky STICKY 16	AROUND THE WORLD WITH STICKY RECORDS (Rory Commadore [a.k.a. Tindersticks]/Boy Racer/Heck/Cornershop, picture disc, 700 only)	12

B

83	Secret SHH 138	BACK ON THE STREET (p/s; Skin Disease/Angela Rippon's Bum/Venom/ Strike/East End Badoes)	5
78	Good Vibrations GOT 7	BATTLE OF THE BANDS (double pack, no'd p/s; Idiots/Rudi/Outcasts/Spider)	5
80	Vinyl Drip DRIP 001	BLACKPOOL ROX (p/s; Membranes/Section 25/Syntax/Kenneth Turner Set)	8
79	Skeleton SKL 002	THE BLANK TAPES VOL. 1 (folded p/s; Attempted Moustache/Junk Act/ Geisha Girls/Zorkie Twins)	8
81	Secret SHH 126	BOLLOCKS TO CHRISTMAS (p/s; Business/4-Skins/Gonads/Max Splodge)	12
80s	Secret	BRITANNIA WAIVES THE RULES (12", p/s; Exploited/Chron Gen/Infa Riot)	8
94	Fierce Panda NING 04	BUILT TO BLAST (double pack, p/s; Green Day/Flying Medallions/Fabric/ Understand/China Drum/Joeyfat)	6
80	Crass 421984/5	BULLSHIT DETECTOR (12", p/s; A.P.F. Brigade/Alternative/Amebix/ Clockwork Criminals/Counter Attack/Crass/Frenzy Battalion/Fuck The CIA/ Icon/Reputations In Jeopardy/Sceptics/Sinyx/Speakers/Andy T.)	8

C

95	Spangle SPANG 001	CLUB SPANGLE EP (p/s; Marion et al.)	10
97	SKAM 0161	COMPILATION (CD, Skam & V/VM artists)	18
80s	No Future	A COUNTRY FIT FOR HEROES (12", p/s)	8
80s	No Future	A COUNTRY FIT FOR HEROES VOL. 2 (12", p/s)	7
94	Fierce Panda NING 02	CRAZED AND CONFUSED (p/s; Supergrass/Ash et al.)	15

D

71	Dandelion DS 7001	DANDELION (die-cut sleeve; Principal Edwards Magic Theatre/Stackwaddy/ Siren/The Way We Live)	10
89	Decoy FART 3	DECOY (gig freebie; Mega City Four/Les Thugs/Hard-Ons/Bomb Disneyland)	7
86	BBC ZRSL 193	DOCTOR WHO (cassette, holographic inlay; Dominic Glynn/Mankind/ BBC Radiophonic Workshop)	8
86	BBC 12RXL 193	DOCTOR WHO (12", holographic p/s; Dominic Glynn/Mankind/ BBC Radiophonic Workshop)	12
87	BBC RESL 193	DOCTOR WHO (p/s, reissue; Dominic Glynn/Mankind)	4

E

79	Fast Products FAST 9B	EARCOM 2 (12", p/s; Joy Division/Thursdays/Basczax)	12
79	Fast Products FAST 9C	EARCOM 3 (double pack, gatefold p/s with colour postcard insert; D.A.F./Middle Class/Noh Mercy/Stupid Babies)	5
78	Stiff FREEBIE 2	EXCERPTS FROM STIFF'S GREATEST HITS (promo only sampler, 33rpm)	10

F

78	Factory FAC 2	A FACTORY SAMPLE (double pack, p/s, in plastic bag, with 5 stickers; Joy Division/Cabaret Voltaire/Durutti Column/John Dowie; beware of counterfeits)	40/30
81	Pax PAX 1	5 MILES TO MIDNIGHT (12", p/s; Brothers/Doormen/I Scream/Mortuary In Wax)	7
91	Fontana FONT 1	THE FONTANA SINGLES BOX SET VOLUME 1 — HITS AND RARITIES (12-single box set, with 12 inserts)	30
91	Fontana FONT 2	THE FONTANA SINGLES BOX SET VOLUME 2 — HITS AND RARITIES (12-single box set, with 12 inserts)	30
79	Heartbeat PULSE 4	4 ALTERNATIVES (p/s; 48 Hours/Joe Public/Numbers/X-Certs)	8
80	Con (no cat. no.)	THE FOUR EPs (cassette; Mark Perry et al.)	15
92	Kerrang! K/EMI 1	4 PLAY (with issue 397 of *Kerrang!*)	5
96	Ché CHE 059	4 TRACK 3 BAND TOUR EP (p/s, Mogwai/Urusei Yatsura/Backwater, 50 only)	25
82	Albion FREEBIE 1	FREEBIE 1 (square flexidisc; Robyn Hitchcock/Cosmopolitans/ Motor Boys Motor/dB's)	6
94	Fierce Panda NING 05	FROM GREER TO ETERNITY (double pack, p/s; Lush/Ivy/Solar Race/ Splendora/Jale/Fuzzy)	8

G

72	Chess 6145 011	GENESIS — THE BEGINNINGS OF ROCK	10
80s	Illuminated 12 PDS 85	GET THAT SNARE! (12", p/s; D.A.F./400 Blows)	7
70	Village Thing VTSX 1000	THE GREAT WHITE DAP (Wizz Jones/Sun Also Rises/Ian A. Anderson/ Pigsty Hill Light Orchestra)	25

H

80	Groucho Marxist COMMUNIQUE 2	HA! HA! FUNNY POLIS (PAISLEY ROCKS AGAINST RACISM) (p/s; Defiant Pose/Fegs/Urban Enemies/XS Discharge)	6

MINT VALUE £

81	Lyntone 12570/1	HAPPY CHRISTMAS FROM THE STARS (flexi free with *Smash Hits*; Abba/Adam Ant/Duran Duran/Jam/Police, et al.)	5
71	Abreaction ABR 001	HART ROCK (Brass Alley/Yellow/Trilogy/Lucas Tyson) (no p/s)	30
85	The Hit HOT 001	THE HIT (p/s; Style Council/Simply Red/Redskins/Jesus & Mary Chain; free with *The Hit* magazine issue 1)	6/4
89	Hometown Atrocities 1	THE HOMETOWN ATROCITIES EP (wraparound p/s, either 'glossy', or 'kylie'; Headless Chickens/Jackson Penis/Beaver Patrol/Mad At The Sun)	150/200
88	House Of Dolls HOD 002	HOUSE OF DOLLS (no p/s; Cardiacs/Orange Cartest/In Two A Circle/ Decadent Few; free with *House Of Dolls* magazine)	6/4
88	House Of Dolls HOD 003	HOUSE OF DOLLS (no p/s; Wild Flowers/Medicine Factory/Outsiders/ Underneath What?; free with *House Of Dolls* magazine)	6/4
88	House Of Dolls HOD 004	HOUSE OF DOLLS (no p/s; Wedding Present/Trudy/Hunters Club/ Claytown Troupe; free with *House Of Dolls* magazine)	6/4
88	House Of Dolls HOD 006	HOUSE OF DOLLS (no p/s; Gaye Bykers On Acid/Creaming Jesus/ Junior Manson Slags/3D Echo; free with *House Of Dolls* magazine)	6/4
89	House Of Dolls HOD 007	HOUSE OF DOLLS (no p/s; New Model Army/Every New Dead Ghost/ Sandmen/Chalk Garden; free with *House Of Dolls* magazine)	6/4
89	House Of Dolls HOD 009	HOUSE OF DOLLS (no p/s; Pop Will Eat Itself/Wild Poppies/Blow Up/ Godspeed; free with *House Of Dolls* magazine)	6/4
89	House Of Dolls HOD 010	HOUSE OF DOLLS (no p/s; Sugarcubes/Host/Murrumbidgee Whalers/ Shark Taboo; free with *House Of Dolls* magazine)	6/4
89	House Of Dolls HOD 011	HOUSE OF DOLLS (no p/s; Wonder Stuff/Prudes/Sandkings/World Of Music; free with *House Of Dolls* magazine)	6/4
75	Solid Sender SEP 100	HOUSTON JUMP (James Widemouth Brown & His Orchestra/Henry Hayes Four Kings & Carl Campbell/Goree Carter & Hepcats)	10

I

97	B. Banquet Random 2.2	I DIE, YOU DIE (12", green vinyl promo, die-cut sleeve, 1200 only; Greenhaus/ Mike Dearborn/Dave Clarke)	10
86	Pink PINKY 11	IF IT SMELLS IT SELLS (12", die-cut sleeve with inner & label insert; Jamie Wednesday/Wolfhounds/McCarthy/Rumblefish)	7
78	Radar SAM 88	INTERNATIONAL ARTISTS (13th Floor Elevators/Red Crayola/ Lost & Found/Golden Dawn; Red Crayola Hope & Anchor gig freebie with *Howdy From Texas The Lone Star State* magazine)	12/8
83	Future FUTURE 1	THE INVISIBLE FRAME (p/s, Blitz/And Also The Trees & others)	7

L

79	Decca FR 13864	THE LONDON BOYS (p/s; David Bowie/Small Faces/Birds/Dobie Gray)	7
73	Ronco MR EP 001	LONG LIVE ROCK (no p/s; Billy Fury/Eugene Wallace/Wishful Thinking)	15
87	Barracuda Blue 12UTA 9	LUNACY IS LEGEND (12", p/s; Times/Necessitarians/Nikki Sudden)	8

M

71	Track 2094 011	MAXI TRACK RECORD (John's Children/Crazy World Of Arthur Brown/ Thunderclap Newman/Jimi Hendrix; withdrawn blue sleeve crediting Pete Townshend as producer)	100
71	Track 2094 011	MAXI TRACK RECORD (John's Children/Crazy World Of Arthur Brown/ Thunderclap Newman/Jimi Hendrix; red & white sleeve with press pack, also maroon & gold sleeve without press pack)	50/7
86	MM Vinyl Conflict 1	MELODY MAKER EP (with magazine)	4
97	Begg. Banquet Random 2.1	METAL (12", red vinyl promo, die-cut sleeve, 1200 only; Robert Armani)	10
85	Davy Lamp DL 1	MINERS BENEFIT (numbered plain white sleeve; Newtown Neurotics/ Respect/Real By Real/Austin's Shirts)	6
97	V/VM VVMT4	MISSINGTOE & WHINE (EP, 500 only)	15
95	Fierce Panda NING 15	MORTAL WOMBAT (double pack, p/s; Super Furry Animals/Baby Bird/ Panda/Mexican Pets/Harvey's Rabbit/Spare Snare)	10
75	Happy Time HT12	MUSIC FROM THUNDERBIRDS AND DOCTOR WHO (p/s)	7
80	EMI 12EMI 5074	MUTHA'S PRIDE (12", p/s; Wildfire/Quartz/White Spirit/Baby Jane)	20

N

| 80 | Neutron NT 003 | 1980! THE FIRST FIFTEEN MINUTES EP (gatefold p/s with inserts; Vice Versa/Clock DVA/I'm So Hollow/Stunt Kites) | 15 |

O

| 82 | Neat NEAT 25 | ONE TAKE NO DUBS (12", p/s; Black Rose/Hellanbach/Alien/Avenger) | 12 |
| 97 | V/VM VVMT4 | PRIVILEGED FRAMES FOR REFERENCE (12" EP, p/s, 450 only) | 20 |

R

93	Raptor RAP 1	RAPTOR PRESENTS ... (12", p/s, 500 only; Ash/Buttlip/Marrow Bone/Fat)	50
82	Recommended RR-8.9	RECOMMENDED RECORDS SAMPLER (Peter Blegvad/Homosexuals/Faust/ R. Stevie Moore; 1-sided, foldout p/s, clear vinyl, silk-screened PVC cover)	10
78	Virgin VR 08 10274/ SHOL 2550	RECORD MIRROR (no p/s; Tangerine Dream/XTC/Motors/U-Roy; with 2nd EP "The State Disco Party" & *Record Mirror* magazine)	7
91	Epic HOT 1	RED HOT & DANCE (4 x 12" promo box set with insert, sticker and condom)	18
94	Fierce Panda NING 03	RETURN TO SPLENDOUR (double pack in foldover p/s with insert in poly bag, 1,000 only; Bluetones et al.)	20
77	Rollercoaster RRCEP 00002	ROCKABILLY HOP (test pressings only)	15
83	Consett Music Project RD 1	ROCK AND DOLE (Obnoxious Tartus/Decade Waltz/Task Force)	25
92	Melody Maker MMI	ROLLERCOASTER EP (CD, Blur/Jesus & Mary Chain/Dinosaur Jr./ My Bloody Valentine; 2,000 only)	10
80	Energy NRG 1	ROOM TO MOVE (p/s; Big Self/Outcasts/Shock Treatment/Vipers)	7

S

| 95 | Atol ATOL 02 | S4C MAKES ME WANT TO SMOKE CRACK VOL. 1 (500 only, Catatonia et al.) | 25 |
| 81 | Springtime RARA 1001 | THE SECRET POLICEMAN'S OTHER BALL (Sting/Phil Collins/Bob Geldof) (10", promo only sampler) | 15 |

MINT VALUE £

94	Fierce Panda/ Damaged Goods NING 01	SHAGGING IN THE STREETS (double pack, wraparound p/s in poly bag, 1,000 only; S*M*A*S*H/Blessed Ethel/Mantaray/Done Lying Down/ These Animal Men/Action Painting!) 12
93	Duophonic DS 45-05/06	SHIMMIES IN SUPER 8 (double pack), 1 disc green vinyl, other white vinyl, numbered in poly bag, 800 with tri-foldout p/s, 400 also with sticker & 2 inserts; Stereolab/Huggy Bear/Darlin'/Colm) .... each 35
80	Sleep 'N' Eat	SLEEP 'N' EAT (includes Originators) 6
80s	Smash Hits	SMASH HITS INTERVIEW PACK (4 flexidiscs in envelope sleeve; Duran Duran/Spandau Ballet/Boy George/Frankie Goes To Hollywood) 10
88	Sniffin' Rock SR 003	SNIFFIN' ROCK PRESENTS (no p/s; Senseless Things/Crazyhead/Birdhouse; free with *Sniffin' Rock*, issue 9) 5/4
86	Broken Flag BF F1	THE SOFT VOLCANO ERUPTS (flexidisc; Controlled Bleeding/Kehamas Curse/ Uncommunity/Nails Of Christ/Cananes/Ramleh) 7
95	Fierce Panda NING 18	SONGS ABOUT PLUCKING (double pack, p/s; Number One Cup/Magoo/ Bennet/American TV Cops/Chopper/Bis) 5
73	Sounds (SH 0999)	SOUNDS PRESENTS FROM POLYDOR'S 'THE GUITAR ALBUM' (flexidisc with *Sounds* magazine; Eric Clapton & others) 8/6
79	Groucho Marxist WH 1	SPECTACULAR COMMODITY (p/s; Mental Errors/Mod Cons/ Poems/Sneex/XS Discharge) 7
70s	Stiff BUY 1-10	STIFF BOX SET NO. 1 (10 x 7" box set) 35
70s	Stiff BUY 11-20	STIFF BOX SET NO. 2 (10 x 7" box set) 35
88	Underground (no cat no)	STRUM + DRUM (Wedding Present & others) (cassette with *Underground* magazine, issue 13) 8/6
95	Fierce Panda NING 10	SUZI QUATRO LIVES IN CHELMSFORD (p/s; Ligament/Scarfo/Joeyfat) 5

T

95	Ankst CD 061	TRISKAIDEKAPHILIA (CD, Super Furry Animals/Catatonia et al.) 15
83	White Noise WN 3	THIS IS WHITE NOISE (p/s; Skrewdriver/Brutal Attack/Die Hards/A.B.H.) 35
82	Total Noise TOT 1	TOTAL NOISE # 1 (Business/Blitz/Dead Generation/Gonads) 10

U

86	Underground 7	UNDERGROUND RHYTHM AND NOISE (cassette with *Underground* issue 7) ... 8/6
80s	Fierce FRIGHT/SFTRI 38	AN UNHOLY MONTAGE (200 only [100 U.K./100 U.S.], coloured vinyl with numbered insert) 25
81	Lyntone LYN 10138/9	UNTITLED EP (orange vinyl flexidisc with/without *Flexipop* No. 10; Way Of The West/Thin Lizzy/Graham Bonnet /Polecats) 12/6
96	SKAM MASK 1	UNTITLED (12", custom sleeve, 100 only; Freeform/Funkstorung/ Boards Of Canada/Jega) .... 100+
97	SKAM MASK 2	UNTITLED (12", custom sleeve, 350 only; Hellinterface/Funkstorung/Bola/ Jega/Intron) 50
96	V/VM VVMT1	UPLINK DATA TRANSMISSIONS (12" EP, with 'data sheets', 250 only) 25

W

98	B.Banquet Random 2.3	WARRIORS (12", blue vinyl promo, die-cut sleeve, 1200 only; Dave Angel/ Liberator DJs/Steve Stoll) 8
98	B.Banquet Random 2.4	WE ARE GLASS (12", clear vinyl promo, die-cut sleeve, 1200 only; Claude Young/ Alex Hazzard/Peter Lazonby) 8
80	Fuck Off FEP 001	WEIRD NOISE (p/s, white labels; Danny & Dressmakers/The Door & The Window/Instant Automatons/012/Sell-Outs) 5
75	Solid Sender SEP 101	WEST SIDE CHICAGO 10
77	MPL MPL 1	WE'VE MOVED! (Wings/Gene Vincent/Frank Sinatra et al., promo only excerpts sampler, some with press pack) 175/125
84	Rather/Seventeen GEAR 17	WHAT A NICE WAY TO TURN SEVENTEEN NO. 2 (p/s; Swell Maps & others; with magazine) 12

U

96	V/VM VVMT 1	UP LINK DATA TRANSMISSIONS (12" EP, with insert) 20

Y

80s	Wonderful World Of	YOU ARE NOT ALONE (p/s; Oi Polloi/Hex/Stalag 17/Symbol Of Freedom) 5

UNTITLED EPs & SINGLES

73	Buddah 2011 164	(Shangri-La's/Tradewinds/Ad Libs) 5
87	Metal Hammer METAL 1	(Paul Samson's Empire/Chariot/Heavy Pettin'/Strangeways; some with *Metal Hammer* magazine) 6/4

VARIOUS ARTISTS LPs & COMPILATIONS
(alphabetical by title)

A

70	ATP 102	THE ABBEY TAVERN 15
88	Woronzow WOO 6	ACID JAM (with insert) 20
69	Action ACLP 6005	ACTION PACKED SOUL 30
85	United Dairies UD 012	AN AFFLICTED MAN'S MUSICA BOX (3 different editions, 1st in gatefold sleeve) 45/20
70	Pama PMP 2004	AFRICAN MELODY 25
70s	Contempo 2870 311	AFRO ROCK FESTIVAL 12
70	Atlantic 2464 013	THE AGE OF ATLANTIC 12
66	Stateside SL 10172	AN ALBUM FULL OF SOUL 30
69	Key KL 002	ALIVE! 20
84	Creation CRELP 001	ALIVE IN THE LIVING ROOM 15
70	Talisman STAL 5013	ALL FOLK TOGETHER 20

VARIOUS ARTISTS LPs & COMPILATIONS

MINT VALUE £

84	Whaam! BIG 8	ALL FOR ART... AND ART FOR ALL	30
71	Utd. Artists UDX 201/202	ALL GOOD CLEAN FUN (2-LP)	20
83	Neat NEAT 102A/B	ALL HELL LET LOOSE	20
61	Blue Beat BBLP 801	ALL STARS — JAMAICAN BLUES	250
70	Speciality SPE 6609	ALL THE BLUES ALL THE TIME	15
62	Golden Guinea GGL 0162	ALL THE HITS BY ALL THE STARS	12
58	Pye Nixa NJT 509	ALL THE WINNERS (10")	12
76	Riva RVLP 2	ALL THIS AND WORLD WAR TWO (2-LP, box set with booklet)	15
58	Parlophone PMD 1064	ALL TIME COUNTRY AND WESTERN HITS (10")	25
68	Topic 12T 189	ALONG THE COALY TYNE (original sleeve)	12
90	Sound Of Spasm CLANG 4	ALVIN LIVES IN LEEDS	10
79	United Artists UAR 101	ALPHA OMEGA (2-LP)	15
73	Polydor 2460 186	AMERICAN BLUES LEGENDS '73	12
74	Big Bear BEAR 1	AMERICAN BLUES LEGENDS 1974	10
75	Big Bear BEAR 8	AMERICAN BLUES LEGENDS 1975	10
63	Polydor LPHM 46 397	AMERICAN FOLK BLUES FESTIVAL (also stereo SLPHM 237 597)	15/18
70s	Rare Records 2	AMERICAN FOLK BLUES FESTIVAL 1962	15
64	Fontana TL 5204	AMERICAN FOLK BLUES FESTIVAL 1963	18
65	Fontana TL 5225	AMERICAN FOLK BLUES FESTIVAL 1964	18
66	Fontana TL 5286	AMERICAN FOLK BLUES FESTIVAL 1965	18
66	Fontana (S)TL 5389	AMERICAN FOLK BLUES FESTIVAL 1966 (mono/stereo)	20/30
70	CBS 63912	AMERICAN FOLK BLUES FESTIVAL 1969	12
70s	Lorimar/CBS 70172	AMERICATHON	12
70s	Skeleton SKLLP 1	AND THE DANCE GOES ON	12
80s	Pleasantly Surprised PS 2	THE ANGELS ARE COMING (2-cassette, with booklet)	25
83	No Future MPUNK 8	ANGELS WITH DIRTY FACES	12
60s	'77' 77LA 12/13	ANGOLA PRISON SPIRITUALS	12
80	Alt. Capitalists ACC 007	ANOTHER CRACK IN THE VOID (C60 cassette)	10
69	Immediate IMAL 03/04	ANTHOLOGY OF BRITISH BLUES VOLUME 1 (2-LP, gatefold sleeve)	25
69	Immediate IMAL 05/06	ANTHOLOGY OF BRITISH BLUES VOLUME 2 (2-LP, gatefold sleeve)	25
64	London HA-K/SH-K 8174	APOLLO SATURDAY NIGHT (mono/stereo)	40/50
93	Art ART 2CD	APPLIED RHYMIC TECHNOLOGY (CD)	30
93	Art ART 4CD	APPLIED RHYMIC TECHNOLOGY (CD)	20
80s	Ram RAMLP 001	THE ART OF SOLVING PROBLEMS (with insert)	10
74	Ashanti SHAN 106	ASHANTI SHOWCASE	12
69	Atco 228 021	ATCO BLOCKBUSTERS	12
69	Atlantic 587/588 180	ATLANTIC BLOCKBUSTERS	12
65	Atlantic ATL 5020	ATLANTIC DISCOTHEQUE	30
60s	Atlantic AP 2	ATLANTIC IS SOUL	15
60s	Atlantic AC 3	ATLANTICLASSICS	25
74	Horse HRLP 705	ATLANTIC ONE	12
67	Pye NPL 18198	AT LAST THE 1948 SHOW	15
64	Decca LK 4597	AT THE CAVERN	60
85	Sweatbox AMO 5	AUDIO VISUAL — ABSTRACT MAGAZINE NO. 5 (printed PVC sleeve)	15
85	Sweatbox SAM 006	AUDIO VISUAL — ABSTRACT MAGAZINE NO. 6 (embossed plastic wallet, with inner & magazine)	15
80	Aura BAUL 601	AURAL WAX	10
70	Beacon SBEAB 9	AUTHENTIC CHICAGO BLUES	18
72	Windmill WMD 124	AUTHENTIC CHICAGO BLUES	18
66	RCA RD 7776	AUTHENTIC COWBOYS & THEIR WESTERN FOLKSONGS	12
64	Stateside SL 10107	AUTHENTIC SKA	45
64	Stateside SL 10068	AUTHENTIC RHYTHM AND BLUES	35
79	Heartbeat HB 1	AVON CALLING — THE BRISTOL COMPILATION (with poster)	12
80	K-Tel NE 1100	AXE ATTACK (early copies with demo of Iron Maiden's "Running Free")	12
80s	Flaccid FLAC 1	AYLESBURY GOES FLACCID	12
74	Deroy DER 1052	AYRSHIRE FOLK (LP, private pressing)	30

B

82	V.U. VU 502	BABY DON'T JUMP	10
79	Fuck Off 1	BACK TO SING FOR FREE AGAIN SOON (C90 cassette)	15
70	Track 2407 001	BACKTRACK ONE	12
70	Track 2407 002	BACKTRACK TWO	12
70	Track 2407 006	BACKTRACK SIX	18
70	Track 2407 007	BACKTRACK SEVEN	12
54	London AL 3535	BACKWOODS BLUES (10")	45
62	Fontana 688 200 ZL	BALLIN'	15
79	JSP 1005	BANDERA ROCKABILLIES	12
68	Pama PMLP 4	BANG BANG LULU	20
60	Melodisc 12-115	BANJO BREAKDOWN	10
63	Realm RM 182	BANJO JAMBOREE SPECTACULAR	12
60s	Envoy VOY 9158	BANJO STORY	10
64	Storyville 670 155	BARRELHOUSE BLUES AND BOOGIE-WOOGIE VOLUME 1	15
65	Storyville 670 183	BARRELHOUSE BLUES AND BOOGIE-WOOGIE VOLUME 2	15
65	Storyville SLP 213	BARRELHOUSE BLUES AND BOOGIE-WOOGIE VOL. 3	15
59	Fontana TFR 6018	BARRELHOUSE, BOOGIE WOOGIE AND BLUES (10")	20
58	Vogue Coral LRA 10022	BARRELHOUSE PIANO (10" LP)	20
59	Vogue Coral LRA 10023	BARRELHOUSE PIANO VOLUME 2 (10" LP)	20
58	Fontana TFL 5001	BASIE, BROWN AND BENNIE	12
83	London CAVE 1	THE BATCAVE — YOUNG LIMBS AND NUMB HYMNS	10
71	Trojan TBL 167	BATTLE AXE	20
71	B&C BCM 103	BATTLE OF THE BANDS VOL. 1	15
64	Melodisc MLP 12-192	BATTLE OF THE GIANTS	15
53	MGM MGM-D 115	A BATTLE OF JAZZ: HOT VERSUS COOL (10")	15
71	BBC REC 118	BBC's FOLK ON TWO PRESENTS NORTHUMBRIAN FOLK	20
69	Beacon BEAB 1	BEACON BRINGS IT TO YOU	12
71	Revival RVS 1004	BEALE STREET MESS AROUND	12

MINT VALUE £

84	Well Suspect SUSS 1	THE BEAT GENERATION AND THE ANGRY YOUNG MEN	12
76	United Artists UDM 101/2	THE BEAT MERCHANTS (2-LP)	15
87	Pink PINKY 15	BEAUTY	10
80s	Porrit's Hill PHEW 2	BECKET HOUSE	12
77	Impulse IS/BED/123	BEDROCK — ALTOGETHER BEDROCK LP (private pressing)	12
68	Elektra EUK 262	BEGIN HERE (also stereo EUKS 7262)	15
78	Rip Off ROLP 1	BELFAST ROCKS	20
71	Delmark DS 622	BELL'S BLUES HARP.	12
68	Bell MBLL 102	BELL'S CELLAR OF SOUL VOLUME 1.	18
69	Bell MBLL 107	BELL'S CELLAR OF SOUL VOLUME 2.	18
69	Bell MBLL 117	BELL'S CELLAR OF SOUL VOLUME 3.	18
69	Bell MBLL/SBLL 111	THE BEST FROM BELL	12
69	Bell MBLL/SBLL 124	THE BEST FROM BELL VOLUME 2	12
78	Stiff ODD 2	BE STIFF (TOUR '78 OFFICIAL RELEASE) (promo only)	12
78	Stiff DEAL 1	BE STIFF ROUTE '78 (with 16-page booklet & biographies, etc.)	12
70s	Storyville 671 188	THE BEST OF THE BLUES.	15
67	United Artists LAS 29021	THE BEST OF BOND (mono)	15
69	United Artists UAS 29021	THE BEST OF BOND (stereo)	15
85	Kamaflage	BEST OF BRITISH	10
65	Xtra XTRA 1031	THE BEST OF BRITISH FOLK	15
69	Pama SECO 18	THE BEST OF CAMEL	25
76	Epic EPC 81224	THE BEST OF OKEH VOL. I	12
76	Epic EPC 81532	THE BEST OF OKEH VOL. II.	12
69	President PTL 1016	THE BEST OF PRESIDENT VOLUME 1	12
69	President PTL 1036	THE BEST OF PRESIDENT VOLUME 2	12
67	Xtra XTRA 1053	BEST OF SCOTTISH FOLK	12
83	Statik STATLP 14	THE BEST OF YOUR SECRET'S SAFE WITH US.	15
86	Pork CUISINE 2	BEWARE THE BACON SLICER (cassette)	10
82	Open Door OD 001	BEYOND THE RIVER	10
87	Imaginary ILLUSION 001	BEYOND THE WILDWOOD — A TRIBUTE TO SYD BARRETT	10
73	Attack ATLP 1011	BIG BAMBOO.	20
60	Fontana TFL 5080	THE BIG BEAT!.	35
64	London HA-B 8199	THE BIG 'D' JAMBOREE	20
78	Giorno GPS	BIG EGO.	20
69	Minit MLL/MLS 40007E	THE BIG ONE.	18
71	Wand WCS 1005	BIG SIXTEEN GOLDEN OLDIES	12
79	London SHY 8527	BIG SOUND FOR A SMALL WORLD	10
72	CBS 64844	THE BIG SUR FESTIVAL	10
78	World Record Club SH 279	BING CROSBY AND FRIENDS	10
70	Pama SECO 32	BIRTH CONTROL	18
70	Matchbox SDX 207/8	BLACK DIAMOND EXPRESS TO HELL (2-LP)	25
60	Columbia 33SX 1244	BLACKPOOL NIGHTS	25
58	HMV CLP 1167	BLACK SLACKS AND BOBBY SOCKS	200
70	Ember SE 8009	BLACK SOUL EXPLOSION	12
70	CBS 52796	BLACK WHITES AND BLUES	18
83	Quiet QLP 3	BLOOD ON THE ROQ (withdrawn).	10
68	Coxsone CSP 1	BLUE BEAT SPECIAL	25
66	RCA Victor RD 7786	BLUEBIRD BLUES	18
63	Stateside SL 10021	THE BLUEGRASS HALL OF FAME	15
65	London HA-B 8227	BLUEGRASS HALL OF FAME VOL. 2	15
64	London HA-B 8118	BLUEGRASS SPECTACULAR	12
62	Columbia 33SX 1417	THE BLUES	40
68	Marble Arch MAL 804	THE BLUES	12
64	Pye Intl. NPL 28030	BLUES VOL. 1.	15
64	Pye Intl. NPL 28035	BLUES VOL. 2.	15
64	Pye Intl. NPL 28045	BLUES VOL. 3.	15
64	Chess CRL 4003	BLUES VOL. 4.	20
65	Chess CRL 4512	BLUES VOL. 5.	20
67	Marble Arch MAL 664	BLUES & SOUL	12
68	Immediate IMLP 014	BLUES ANYTIME VOL. 1	20
68	Immediate IMCP 015	BLUES ANYTIME VOL. 2	20
68	Immediate IMLP 019	BLUES ANYTIME VOL. 3	20
70	Xtra XTRA 1105	THE BLUES ARE ALIVE AND WELL	12
65	Fontana TFL 6048	THE BLUES AT NEWPORT 1964 PART 1.	20
69	Saga FID 2165	BLUES AT SUNRISE.	12
66	London HA-S 8265	THE BLUES CAME DOWN FROM MEMPHIS	50
73	Flyright LP 504	BLUES CAME TO CHAPEL HILL	12
65	Storyville SLP 176	BLUESCENE USA: VOLUME 1 — CHICAGO	18
65	Storyville SLP 177	BLUESCENE USA: VOLUME 2 — LOUISIANA BLUES	18
65	Storyville SLP 181	BLUESCENE USA: VOLUME 3 — BLUES ALL AROUND MY BED	18
67	Storyville SLP 180	BLUESCENE USA: VOLUME 4 — MISSISSIPPI BLUES.	18
71	Python PLP-KM 17	BLUES — CHICAGO STYLE (LP).	25
60	Philips BBL 7369	BLUES FELL THIS MORNING	45
73	Polydor 2383 257	BLUES FOR MR. CRUMP.	25
72	Transatlantic TRASAM 25	BLUES FOR YOUR POCKET	12
69	Chess CRLS 4558	BLUES FROM BIG BILL'S COPACABANA	18
69	Python PLP 6	BLUES FROM CHICAGO (99 copies only).	35
70	Python PLP 9	BLUES FROM CHICAGO VOL. 2 (99 copies only).	35
71	Python PLP 15	BLUES FROM CHICAGO VOL. 3 (99 copies only)	35
60s	Heritage 1004	BLUES FROM MAXWELL STREET (99 copies only)	40
71	Pye Intl. NPL 28142	BLUES FROM THE BAYOU.	18
72	Saydisc SDM 226	BLUES FROM THE DELTA	20
71	Python PLP 21	BLUES FROM THE WINDY CITY (99 copies only)	35
77	Flyright LP 4713	BLUES FROM THE WINDY CITY.	12
63	Stateside SL 10076	BLUES HOOT.	20
57	Pye Nixa NJL 8	(ALAN LOMAX PRESENTS) BLUES IN THE MISSISSIPPI NIGHT	15

MINT VALUE £

60s	Sunflower (no cat. no.)	BLUES IS MY COMPANION (99 copies only)	35
60s	Sunflower (no cat. no.)	BLUES KEEP FALLING (99 copies only)	35
64	Joy JOYS 177	BLUES JAM	12
69	Blue Horizon 7-66227	BLUES JAM AT CHESS (2-LP)	50
69	Immediate IMLP 024	BLUES LEFTOVERS	15
67	Saydisc Match. SDM 142	BLUES LIKE SHOWERS OF RAIN	70
68	Saydisc Match. SDM 167	BLUES LIKE SHOWERS OF RAIN VOLUME 2	70
65	Decca LK 4681	BLUES NOW	40
72	Blues Obscurities BOV 1	BLUES OBSCURITIES VOL. 1: SOUTHERN BLUES/DARK MUDDY BOTTOM (plain cover with photocopied inserts)	30
72	Blues Obscurities BOV 2	BLUES OBSCURITIES VOL. 2: LONESOME HARMONICA	30
72	Blues Obscurities BOV 3	BLUES OBSCURITIES VOL. 3: WEST COAST BLUES	30
72	Blues Obscurities BOV 4	BLUES OBSCURITIES VOL. 4: ONE RAINY MORNING	30
72	Blues Obscurities BOV 5	BLUES OBSCURITIES VOL. 5: SOMETHING'S GONE WRONG	30
72	Blues Obscurities BOV 6	BLUES OBSCURITIES VOL. 6: COMING BACK HOME	30
72	Blues Obscurities BOV 7	BLUES OBSCURITIES VOL. 7	30
72	Blues Obscurities BOV 8	BLUES OBSCURITIES VOL. 8	30
72	Blues Obscurities BOV 9	BLUES OBSCURITIES VOL. 9	30
72	Blues Obscurities BOV 10	BLUES OBSCURITIES VOL. 10	30
74	London HA-U 8454	BLUES OBSCURITIES VOL. 1: DARK MUDDY BOTTOM (reissue)	18
74	London HA-U 8455	BLUES OBSCURITIES VOL. 2: LONESOME HARMONICA (reissue)	18
74	London HA-U 8456	BLUES OBSCURITIES VOL. 3: STRETCHIN' OUT	18
69	Mercury SMXL 77	BLUES PACKAGE '69	10
69	Highway 51 H 102	BLUES PEOPLE	50
68	Matchbox SDR 146	BLUES PIANO	15
72	Atlantic K 40404	BLUES PIANO — CHICAGO PLUS	22
68	Kokomo K 1001	A BLUES POTPOURRI (99 copies only)	50
71	Rarities (Tony's Records)	BLUES RARITIES VOL. 1 (2-LP)	25
69	Atlantic Special 590 019	THE BLUES ROLL ON (reissue of "Southern Folk Heritage: The Blues Roll On")	12
69	Poppy PYM 11001	BLUES ROOTS VOLUME ONE	22
66	Decca LK 4748	BLUES SOUTHSIDE CHICAGO	45
71	Python PLP 16	BLUES TODAY — SOUTHERN STYLE (99 copies only)	35
71	Polydor 2675 007	BOMBERS	15
65	Topic 12T 128	BONNY LASS COME O'ER THE BURN	12
73	Storyville SLP 229	BOOGIE WOOGIE BOYS	12
70s	Milestone MLP 2009	BOOGIE WOOGIE RARITIES	15
60s	Storyville 670184	BOOGIE WOOGIE TRIO	12
55	London AL 3544	BOOGIE WOOGIE WITH THE BLUES (10")	40
69	Pama SECO 17	BOSS REGGAE	60
74	Eron 002	BOTH SIDES OF THE DOWNS (with insert)	25
80	Aardvark STEAL 2	BOUQUET OF STEEL (blue vinyl with 27-page booklet)	15
87	GWR GBS 1	BRISTOL CUSTOM BIKE SHOW 1986 (some with poster)	15/12
81	Bristol Recorder BR 002	THE BRISTOL RECORDER VOL. 2 (with magazine booklet)	20
82	Bristol Recorder BR 003	THE BRISTOL RECORDER VOL. 3 (with magazine booklet)	12
93	EMI CD 502046	BRITISH BEAT BEFORE THE BEATLES 1955/56 (CD)	18
93	EMI CD 502047	BRITISH BEAT BEFORE THE BEATLES 1957 (CD)	18
93	EMI CD 502048	BRITISH BEAT BEFORE THE BEATLES 1958 (CD)	18
93	EMI CD 502049	BRITISH BEAT BEFORE THE BEATLES 1959 (CD)	18
93	EMI CD 502050	BRITISH BEAT BEFORE THE BEATLES 1960 (CD)	18
93	EMI CD 502051	BRITISH BEAT BEFORE THE BEATLES 1961 (CD)	18
93	EMI CD 502052	BRITISH BEAT BEFORE THE BEATLES 1962 (CD)	18
68	Island ILP 966/ILPS 9066	BRITISH BLUE-EYED SOUL	40
67	Tamla Motown TML 11055	BRITISH MOTOWN CHARTBUSTERS (mono, flipback sleeve)	20
69	T. Motown STML 11055	BRITISH MOTOWN CHARTBUSTERS (stereo reissue, flipback sleeve)	15
68	T. Motown (S)TML 11082	BRITISH MOTOWN CHARTBUSTERS VOL. 2 (original, flipback sleeve)	15
93	Hammer (no catalogue no.)	BRITISH OI! — WORKING CLASS ANTHEMS	12
70	Trojan TBL 106	BRIXTON CAT	15
80	CBS 31845	BROADWAY MAGIC VOLUME 2: THE GREAT PERFORMERS	12
64	Decca LK 4598	BRUM BEAT	80
64	Dial DLP 1	BRUM BEAT	70
79	Big Bear BRUM 1	BRUM BEAT — LIVE AT THE BARREL ORGAN (2-LP, with inserts)	20
80	MCA MCF 3074	BRUTE FORCE	20
70	Buddah 2349 008	BUDDAH IN MIND	12
72	Flyright LP 106	BULL CITY BLUES	15
66	Decca LK 4734	BUMPER BUNDLE	22
69	Island IDP 1	BUMPERS (2-LP)	15
77	Stiff SEEZ 2	A BUNCH OF STIFF RECORDS	12
79	Cherry Red ARED 2	BUSINESS UNUSUAL (with *Zig Zag* small labels catalogue)	10
81	Autumn AU 2	BUSTED AT OZ	20
84	Dambusters DAM 003	BUTTONS AND BOWS VOLUME 1 (2-LP)	20
84	Dambusters DAM 006	BUTTONS AND BOWS VOLUME 2 (2-LP)	18

C

56	Columbia 33S 1083	CABARET NIGHT IN PARIS	12
57	Columbia 33S 1099	CABARET NIGHT IN PARIS No. 4	12
57	Columbia 33S 1105	CABARET NIGHT IN PARIS No. 5	12
72	Topic 12TS 219	CANNY NEWCASSEL (with booklet, blue label)	20
67	Bounty BY 6035	CAN'T KEEP FROM CRYING (TOPICAL BLUES ON THE DEATH OF PRESIDENT KENNEDY)	20
78	Capitol CAPS 1025	CAPITOL SOUL CASINO	12
71	Trojan TBL 171	CARIBBEAN DANCE FESTIVAL (wraparound paper sleeve)	12
73	Flyright LP 505	CAROLINA COUNTRY BLUES	15
81	Secret SEC 2	CARRY ON OI!	12
73	Nottingham Festival FEST 2	CASTLE ROCK	125
65	Capitol T2340	CAT BALLOU AND OTHER MOTION PICTURE SONGS (Frankie De Vol/Nat 'King' Cole/Stubby Kaye)	15

MINT VALUE £

77	CBS 82401	CBS ROCKABILLY CLASSICS VOL. 1	12
78	CBS 82993	CBS ROCKABILLY CLASSICS VOL. 2	12
79	CBS 83911	CBS ROCKABILLY CLASSICS VOL. 3	12
81	Rough Trade/NME COPY 1	C-81 (mail-order cassette via *NME*)	10
86	NME 022	C-86 (mail-order cassette via *NME*)	10
86	NME 022	C-86 (LP, promo only for above cassette, 500 pressed)	20
80s	Cerne CERNE 123	THE CERNE BOX SET (3-LP box set; Nurse With Wound/Current 93/ Sol Invictus; with 3 inserts)	40
60	Chappell 672-677	CHAPPELL RECORDED MUSIC (library issue)	20
60	Chappell 678-682	CHAPPELL RECORDED MUSIC (library issue)	20
71	Chess 6671 102	CHARLIE PARKER MEMORIAL CONCERT	12
60s	Columbia	CHARTBUSTERS USA	25
73	Checker 6445 150	CHESS GOLDEN DECADE VOL. 1: THE EARLY 50s	12
73	Checker 6445 151	CHESS GOLDEN DECADE VOL. 2: 1956 TAKE IT EASY GREASY	12
73	Checker 6445 152	CHESS GOLDEN DECADE VOL. 3: 1957 DIMESTORE PONYTAIL	12
74	Chess 6445 153	CHESS GOLDEN DECADE VOL. 4: 1958-1959 BOOK OF LOVE	12
74	Chess 6445 154	CHESS GOLDEN DECADE VOL. 5: 1959-1961 GOOD MORNING LITTLE SCHOOLGIRL	12
74	Chess 6445 202	CHESS GOLDEN DECADE VOL. 6: 1961-1962 TALKIN' TRASH	12
74	Chess 6445 203	CHESS GOLDEN DECADE VOL. 7: 1963-1965 HIGH HEEL SNEAKERS (gatefold sleeve)	15
74	Chess 6445 204	CHESS GOLDEN DECADE VOL. 8: 1965-1966 THE IN CROWD	12
78	Chess 9124 213	CHESS ROCKABILLIES	12
64	Chess CRL 4004	CHESS STORY VOL. 1	30
65	Chess CRL 4516	CHESS STORY VOL. 2	30
72	Delmark DL 624	CHICAGO AIN'T NOTHING BUT A BLUES BAND	12
60s	Vanguard VSD 79217	CHICAGO BLUES VOLUME 2	12
66	Fontana TFL 6068	CHICAGO/THE BLUES/TODAY	20
66	Fontana TFL 6069	CHICAGO/THE BLUES/TODAY VOLUME 2	20
66	Fontana TFL 6070	CHICAGO/THE BLUES/TODAY VOLUME 3	20
69	Vanguard SVRL 19020	CHICAGO/THE BLUES/TODAY VOLUME 1	22
69	Vanguard SVRL 19021	CHICAGO/THE BLUES/TODAY VOLUME 2	22
69	Vanguard SVRL 19022	CHICAGO/THE BLUES/TODAY VOLUME 3	18
68	Sunflower ET 1401	THE CHICAGO HOUSE BANDS (99 copies only)	35
70s	JSP 1004	CHICAGO JUMP	12
69	Kokomo K 1005	CHICAGO SESSIONS VOLUME 1 (99 copies only)	45
70	Flyright LP 4700	CHICKEN STUFF	15
94	Relics CFSD 3	CHOCOLATE SOUP FOR DIABETICS Vol. (CD)	15
58	Philips BBR 8112	CHRISTMAS (10")	15
73	United Artists UDX 205/6	CHRISTMAS AT THE PATTI (2 x 10", gatefold sleeve)	18
68	Chess CRLS 4541	CHRISTMAS DEDICATION	18
81	Ze/Island ILPS 7017	A CHRISTMAS RECORD (LP, initially white vinyl, then black)	each 10
82	Ze/Island ILPS 7022	A CHRISTMAS RECORD (LP, 'improved 1982 edition', blue border on sleeve instead of black)	10
63	London HA-U 8141	A CHRISTMAS GIFT FOR YOU (plum label, later black label)	40/18
72	Speciality SNTF 5015	CITY BLUES	12
80s	White Elephant RIOCH 1	CITY WALLS — A SOUTHAMPTON COMPILATION (with insert)	12
70	Charisma CAS 1008	CLASSICAL HEADS	12
55	London AL 3559	CLASSIC JAZZ PIANO (10")	25
52	Capitol LC 6559	CLASSICS IN JAZZ: PIANO ITEMS (10")	15
52	Capitol LC 6561	CLASSICS IN JAZZ: THE MODERN IDIOM (10")	15
52	Capitol LC 6562	CLASSICS IN JAZZ: DIXIELAND STYLE (10")	15
53	Capitol LC 6579	CLASSICS IN JAZZ: TRUMPET STYLISTS (10")	15
53	Capitol LC 6582	CLASSICS IN JAZZ: SAX STYLISTS (10")	15
53	Capitol LC 6598	CLASSICS IN JAZZ: COOL AND QUIET (10")	15
69	Atlantic 587 167	CLASSIC RHYTHM AND BLUES	12
89	Cavern FAB 1964	CLASS OF '64 (CD)	15
70s	Waldo's DS 005	CLEANING UP THE MUSIC BIZ	12
85	Pusmort 0012-02	CLEANSE THE BACTERIA	20
72	Pegasus PS 1	CLOGS (FOLK SAMPLER) (with insert)	12
90s	Distronics ITCD 3	THE CLOSING PARTY — IN THE CITY LIVE UNSIGNED (CD)	50
72	Pegasus PS 2	CLUB FOLK VOLUME ONE	12
72	Pegasus PS 3	CLUB FOLK VOLUME TWO	12
70	Trojan TBL 159	CLUB REGGAE VOLUME ONE	12
71	Trojan TBL 164	CLUB REGGAE VOLUME TWO	12
71	Trojan TBL 178	CLUB REGGAE VOLUME THREE	12
72	Trojan TBL 188	CLUB REGGAE VOLUME FOUR	12
70	Trojan TTL 54	CLUB ROCK STEADY	25
68	W.I.R.L. ILP 965	CLUB ROCK STEADY '68	50
67	W.I.R.L. ILP 948	CLUB SKA '67	45
67	W.I.R.L. ILP 956	CLUB SKA '67 VOL. 2	45
80	Island IRSP 4	CLUB SKA '67	12
70	Trojan TTL 48	CLUB SKA VOLUME ONE	18
70	Trojan TTL 51	CLUB SKA VOLUME TWO	25
68	Island ILP 964	CLUB SOUL	30
67	Elektra EUK 253	A COLD WIND BLOWS	15
65	Tamla Motown TML 11001	A COLLECTION OF 16 TAMLA MOTOWN HITS	40
67	Tamla Motown TML 11043	A COLLECTION OF 16 ORIGINAL BIG HITS VOL. 4	30
67	Tamla Motown TML 11050	A COLLECTION OF 16 ORIGINAL BIG HITS VOL. 5	25
68	T. Motown (S)TML 11074	A COLLECTION OF 16 ORIGINAL BIG HITS VOL. 6	20
69	T. Motown (S)TML 11092	A COLLECTION OF 16 ORIGINAL BIG HITS VOL. 7 — THE MOTOWN SOUND	20
70	T. Motown (S)TML 11130	A COLLECTION OF 16 ORIGINAL BIG HITS VOL. 8	15
75	Chicago 202	COLLECTORS BLUES SERIES VOL. 1	20
75	Chicago 205	COLLECTORS BLUES SERIES VOL. 2	20
75	Chicago 210	COLLECTORS BLUES SERIES VOL. 3	20
75	Chicago 212	COLLECTORS BLUES SERIES VOL. 4	20

VARIOUS ARTISTS LPs & COMPILATIONS

75	Chicago 213	COLLECTORS BLUES SERIES VOL. 5.	20
54	London AL 3514	COLLECTORS' ITEMS VOLUME ONE (10")	15
54	London AL 3533	COLLECTORS' ITEMS VOLUME TWO (10")	15
56	London AL 3550	COLLECTORS' ITEMS VOLUME THREE (10")	15
86	Color Disc COLORS 4	COLOR SUPPLEMENT (400 only)	15
73	Ronco MSD 2005	COMMAND PERFORMANCE	15
84	T.P.S.U. TPSU 0001	COMMUNICATE!!!! LIVE AT THAMES POLY (2-LP, with booklet)	15
85	Company Classics	COMPANY CLASSICS NO. 3 (cassette, no cat. no.)	10
72	Apple STCX 3385	THE CONCERT FOR BANGLA DESH (3-LP box set, with booklet)	22
70	Transatlantic TRASAM 14	THE CONTEMPORARY GUITAR SAMPLER.	12
70	Transatlantic TRASAM 15	CONTEMPORARY GUITAR SAMPLER VOL. 2	12
64	Decca LK 4664	CONVERSATION WITH THE BLUES.	60
57	Tempo TAP 10	COOL MUSIC FOR A HOT NIGHT – MOOD MUSIC IN THE MODERN MANNER.	25
72	Wicksteed WCKLP 02	CORBY CATCHMENT AREA (private pressing)	500
78	ABC ABCL 5247	COTTON PICKIN' ROCK.	12
80s	Third Mind TMLP 09	COULD YOU WALK ON THE WATER	10
64	London HA-B 8145	COUNTRY & WESTERN GOLDEN HIT PARADE VOL. 1.	15
64	London HA-B 8146	COUNTRY & WESTERN GOLDEN HIT PARADE VOL. 2.	15
60	Philips BBL 7410	COUNTRY AND WESTERN REQUESTS.	12
62	Philips BBL 7552	COUNTRY AND WESTERN REQUESTS VOL. 2	12
63	Mercury 20015 MCL	COUNTRY AND WESTERN ROUND UP	12
60	Storyville SLP 129	THE COUNTRY BLUES	15
73	Speciality SNTF 5014	COUNTRY BLUES	15
60s	Saydisc Roots RL 334	COUNTRY BLUES OBSCURITIES VOLUME 1	15
66	Stateside SL 10170	COUNTRY COUSINS	15
56	Brunswick LA 8729	COUNTRY FAVOURITES VOL. ONE (10")	25
65	London HA-B 8243	COUNTRY GUITAR HALL OF FAME.	15
64	London HA-B 8198	THE COUNTRY MUSIC FESTIVAL	12
66	London HA-B 8263	COUNTRY MUSIC FESTIVAL VOL. 2	12
66	London HA-B 8287	COUNTRY MUSIC FESTIVAL VOL. 3	12
63	Stateside SL 10017	THE COUNTRY MUSIC HALL OF FAME.	15
63	London HA-B 8076	COUNTRY MUSIC HALL OF FAME VOL. 1.	12
63	London HA-B 8077	COUNTRY MUSIC HALL OF FAME VOL. 2.	15
64	London HA-B 8156	COUNTRY MUSIC HALL OF FAME VOL. 3.	12
64	London HA-B 8157	COUNTRY MUSIC HALL OF FAME VOL. 4.	12
65	London HA-B 8216	COUNTRY MUSIC HALL OF FAME VOL. 5.	12
65	London HA-B 8217	COUNTRY MUSIC HALL OF FAME VOL. 6.	12
66	London HA-B 8283	COUNTRY MUSIC HALL OF FAME VOL. 7.	12
66	London HA-B 8284	COUNTRY MUSIC HALL OF FAME VOL. 8.	12
67	London HA-B 8328	COUNTRY MUSIC HALL OF FAME VOL. 9.	12
67	London HA-B 8329	COUNTRY MUSIC HALL OF FAME VOL. 10.	12
68	London HA-B 8354	COUNTRY MUSIC HALL OF FAME VOL. 11.	12
68	London HA-B 8355	COUNTRY MUSIC HALL OF FAME VOL. 12.	12
65	London HA-B 8206	THE COUNTRY MUSIC MEMORIAL ALBUM	12
62	Stateside SL 10003	COUNTRY MUSIC SPECTACULAR	12
63	Starlite STLP 15	COUNTRY MUSIC U.S.A. (reissued as GRK 605)	15/12
64	London HA-B 8185	COUNTRY MUSIC U.S.A.	12
65	London HA-B 8224	COUNTRY MUSIC WHO'S WHO	12
59	Capitol T 1179	THE COUNTRY'S BEST.	12
69	Pama ECO 2	CRAB – GREATEST HITS	25
80	Rabid/Absurd LAST 1	THE CRAP STOPS HERE.	10
60	Fontana TFL 5103	THE CREAM OF 'TAKE IT FROM HERE' (also stereo SFL 534)	12
60s	Saydisc Roots RL 332	CREAM OF THE CROP.	12

D

90	Wau! Mr Modo WAMLP 002	DANCEBUSTERS VOLUME ONE	10
90	Wau! Mr Modo WAMCD 002	DANCEBUSTERS VOLUME ONE (CD)	15
81	2-Tone CHRTT 5004	DANCE CRAZE (with poster)	15
68	H. Note/B. Shot BSLP 5002	DANCING DOWN ORANGE STREET	50
81	NME 001	DANCIN' MASTER (cassette via *NME* magazine, mail-order only)	10
76	Dark Horse DH 1 (DHSAM 1)	DARK HORSE RECORDS '76 (promo only sampler, stickered sleeve & inner)	40
91	Liquid Noise LIQ 1	THE DARK SIDE OF THE POOL	12
71	Dawn DNLB 3024	DAWN TAKEAWAY CONCERT	12
79	Dead Good DEAD 4	DEAD GOOD'S DEAD GOODS.	12
78	Virgin VD 2508	DEAD ON ARRIVAL (glow-in-the-dark vinyl with poster)	10
83	Debut LPMAG 6	DEBUT — ISSUE 6 (gatefold sleeve with magazine).	10
66	Highway 51 H 100	DECADE OF THE BLUES — THE 1950's (99 copies only).	50
66	Highway 51 H 104	DECADE OF THE BLUES — THE 1950's VOLUME 2 (99 copies only).	40
54	Decca LF 1160	DECCA SHOWCASE VOL. 3 (10")	15
55	Decca LF 1265	DECCA SHOWCASE VOL. 5 (10")	18
65	London HA-B 8249	DECK OF CARDS.	12
71	United Artists UAS 29153	DEEPER INTO THE VAULTS	12
69	Topic 12T 188	DEEP LANCASHIRE — SONGS OF BALLADS OF THE INDUSTRIAL NORTH-WEST (blue label)	12
70	Polydor 2673 001	DEEP OVERGROUND POP	15
70	Stax SXATS 1037	THE DEEP SOUL OF STAX	12
71	Flyright LP 102	DEEP SOUTH COUNTRY BLUES.	15
80	Deleted DEC 009	DELETED FUN TIME (cassette)	15
80s	NME	DEPARTMENT OF ENJOYMENT (cassette, mail-order only via *NME*)	10
68	Deram SML 1027	THE DERAM GOLDEN POPS SAMPLER.	100
67	Island ILP 955	DERRICK HARRIOTT'S ROCK (SKA) STEADY PARTY	150
72	Trojan TTL 54	DERRICK HARRIOTT'S ROCKSTEADY PARTY (reissue)	35
80s	Yankhi 01	DEVASTATE TO LIBERATE.	15
75	Echo ECR 008	DICK SAUNDERS' 10TH ANNUAL RALLY	10
70	Mercury 6641 006	DIMENSION OF MIRACLES	15
57	RCA RC 2400	DISCTIONARY OF JAZZ (10")	12

MINT VALUE £

80	DinDisc DONE 1	DINDISC 1980 (with free 20"x 20" game)	10
69	Minit MLL/MLS 40005	DIRT BLUES	25
70	BBC REC 65M	DISC A DAWN	25
67	Island ILP 943	DOCTOR SOUL	45
82	BBC 2-LP-22001	DOCTOR WHO COLLECTOR'S EDITION (2-LP, with poster)	30
80s	Pleasantly Surprised PS 12	DOCUMENT (cassette)	18
89	DELI 03	DONDE ESTA LOS INSECTS? (cassette)	10
79	Object Music OBJ 014	DO THE MARU	10
82	Compact Org. PACT 6	DO THEY MEAN US (2-LP, box set with inserts & poster)	15
89	EMI EE 3530	THE DOTTED LINE (HERE)	10
89	EMI TCEE 3530	THE DOTTED LINE (HERE) (cassette)	10
89	EMI EE 3531	THE DOTTED LINE (THERE)	10
89	EMI TCEE 3531	THE DOTTED LINE (THERE) (cassette)	10
70	Python PLP	DOWNHOME BLUES (99 copies only)	35
70	Python PLP 14	DOWNHOME BLUES VOLUME 2 (99 copies only)	35
71	Python PLP 22	DOWNHOME BLUES VOLUME 3 (99 copies only)	35
73	Speciality SNTF 5024	DOWNHOME BLUES	12
71	Flyright LP 4703	DOWN IN HOGAN'S ALLEY	15
67	Down With The Game 200	DOWN WITH THE GAME VOLUME 1	30
67	Down With The Game 201	DOWN WITH THE GAME VOLUME 2	30
68	Down With The Game 203	DOWN WITH THE GAME VOLUME 3	30
68	Down With The Game 204	DOWN WITH THE GAME VOLUME 4	30
68	Down With The Game 205	DOWN WITH THE GAME VOLUME 5	30
68	Down With The Game 206	DOWN WITH THE GAME VOLUME 6	30
67	Island ILP 954	DR. KITCH	35
82	Beggars Banquet BEGA 35	DR. RHINO AND MR HYDE	12
80s	Pleasantly Surprised PS 6	DREAMS AND DESIRES (cassette, in bag)	15
72	Ember EMB 3413	A DROP OF THE HARD STUFF	12
60	Columbia SCX 3359	DRUM NIGHT AT BIRDLAND	12
68	Island ILP 976	THE DUKE AND THE PEACOCK	45
69	Trojan TTL 8	DUKE REID'S GOLDEN HITS	20
67	Island ILP 958	DUKE REID'S ROCK STEADY	150
70	Trojan TTL 53	DUKE REID'S ROCK STEADY (reissue)	40
69	BBC REC 35S	DUNGEON FOLK	12
73	Dragon HELP 9	DYNAMIC SOUNDS OF JAMAICA VOL. 1	15

E

70	Matchbox SDR 199	EARLY BLUES VOLUME 1: SKOODLE-UM-SKOO	18
70	Matchbox SDR 206	EARLY FOLK BLUES VOLUME 2: HOMETOWN SKIFFLE	18
70	Middle Earth MDLS 20	EARTHED	40
80	Dead Good GOOD 1	EAST (with inner & stickered sleeve)	18
73	Southern Sound SD 200	EAST VERNON BLUES	30
63	Decca LK 4546	EDINBURGH FOLK FESTIVAL VOLUME 1	25
63	Decca LK 4563	EDINBURGH FOLK FESTIVAL VOLUME 2	25
83	Fried Egg FRY 2	E(GG)CLECTIC 1	10
55	Philips BBR 8046	EIGHT EVERGREENS (10")	15
86	Bam Caruso KIRI 044	THE ELECTRIC CRAYON SET	15
75	Island/Transatlantic FOLK 1001	ELECTRIC MUSE — THE STORY OF FOLK INTO ROCK (4-LP box set with booklet)	45
89	A.I.P. AIP 10052	ELECTRIC SUGARCUBE FLASHBACKS Vol. 4	10
85	Push PUSH 001	ELEGANCE, CHARM AND DEADLY DANGER	20
80s	Master BBSLP 007	ELEMENTALS	20
80s	Extract XX 001	ELEPHANT TABLE ALBUM	10
57	Philips BBR 8115	ELLA, LENA, BILLIE AND SARAH (10")	15
71	Island IDLP 1	EL PEA (pink rim label)	15
57	Brunswick LAT 8166	ENCYCLOPAEDIA OF JAZZ ON RECORDS VOL. 1 — JAZZ OF THE TWENTIES	12
57	Brunswick LAT 8167	ENCYCLOPAEDIA OF JAZZ ON RECORDS VOL. 2 — JAZZ OF THE THIRTIES	12
57	Brunswick LAT 8168	ENCYCLOPAEDIA OF JAZZ ON RECORDS VOL. 3 — JAZZ OF THE FORTIES	12
57	Brunswick LAT 8169	ENCYCLOPAEDIA OF JAZZ ON RECORDS VOL. 4 — JAZZ OF THE FIFTIES	12
83	Psycho PSYCHO 1	ENDLESS JOURNEY VOL. 1 (numbered)	22
83	Psycho PSYCHO 3	ENDLESS JOURNEY VOL. 2 (numbered)	18
83	Psycho PSYCHO 19	ENDLESS JOURNEY VOL. 3 (numbered)	18
83	Essence Rare	ESSENCE RARE (C60 cassette)	10
89	Gee Street GEE A 002	ETERNITY PROJECT ONE	20
89	Gee Street GEE ACD 002	ETERNITY PROJECT ONE (CD)	25
67	Speciality SPE 6601	EVERY DAY I HAVE THE BLUES	15
72	Blue Horizon 2683 007	THE EXCELLO STORY (2-LP)	75
68	Amal. AMGLP 2002	EXPLOSIVE ROCKSTEADY	45
66	Xtra XTRA 5004	EZZ-THETIC	12

F

80s	Facet	FACET 1 (C60 cassette with magazine)	10
83	Factory Benelux FBN 27	FACTORY BENELUX GREATEST HITS	10
72	Carnival 2941 201	FADED PICTURE BLUES	12
67	Elektra EUK 259	FANTASTIC FOLK	12
64	Topic 12T 110	FAREWELL NANCY (blue label)	15
78	Lightning LIP 2	FAREWELL TO THE ROXY	10
80s	Come Org. WDC 881021	FASHIONED TO A DEVICE BEHIND A TREE	80
76	Polydor 2475 605	A FEAST OF IRISH FOLK	12
68	Zeus CF 201	FESTIVAL AT TOWERSEY	50
63	Pye Intl. NPL 28033	FESTIVAL OF THE BLUES	22
67	Marble Arch MAL 724	FESTIVAL OF THE BLUES (reissue)	12
61	Melodisc 12-116	FIDDLIN' COUNTRY STYLE	12
89	Fire FIRE CD 19	15 FLAMING GROOVIES (CD, promo only)	15
60s	Melodisc MS 4	15 OLDIES BUT GOODIES	15
65	Sue ILP 920	50 MINUTES & 24 SECONDS OF RECORDED DYNAMITE!	50

MINT VALUE £

72	Warner Bros K 66013	FILLMORE: THE LAST DAYS (3-LP box set with poster & booklet)	30
72	CBS 63816	FILLMORE WEST	12
88	Re-Elect/President NIXON 4	THE FINAL COUNTDOWN	10
65	London HA-B 8205	FINGERS ON FIRE	15
60	HMV CLP 1358/CSD 1298	FINGS AIN'T WOT THEY USED TO BE	25
64	London HA-B 8117	FIRE ON THE STRINGS	12
69	Music Man	FIREPOINT — A COLLECTION OF FOLK BLUES	90
73	Spark SRLM 2003	FIREPOINT — A COLLECTION OF FOLK BLUES (reissue)	30
71	CBS 66311	THE FIRST GREAT ROCK FESTIVALS OF THE 70s: ISLE OF WIGHT AND ATLANTA (3-LP)	30
58	Esquire 20-091	THE FIRST MODERNS (10")	12
57	Esquire 20-089	THE FIRST NATIONAL SKIFFLE CONTEST (10")	50
56	Mercury MPT 7512	FIRST ROCK 'N' ROLL PARTY (10")	100
80s	Alt. Tentacles VIRUS 22	FLEX YOUR HEAD	10
64	Blue Beat BBLP 803	FLY FLYING SKA	300
69	Atlantic 588 184	FLYING HIGH (record club edition)	15
76	Eron ERON 012	FOLK AT THE BLACK HORSE	15
76	Flams/Wounded WR 1068	FOLK AT THE CHEQUERS (private pressing)	15
64	Ember NR 5015	FOLK BLUES SONG FEST	20
66	Elektra EUK 251/2	FOLK BOX (2-LP)	15
66	Waverley ZLP 2067	FOLK FAVOURITES	12
69	World Rec. Club ST 890	FOLK FESTIVAL	20
76	Transatlantic TRA 324	FOLK FESTIVAL (2-LP)	20
60	Top Rank 35/070	FOLK FESTIVAL AT NEWPORT 1959 VOLUME 1	15
60	Top Rank 35/071	FOLK FESTIVAL AT NEWPORT 1959 VOLUME 2	15
60	Top Rank 35/072	FOLK FESTIVAL AT NEWPORT 1959 VOLUME 3	15
62	Fontana TFL 6000	FOLK FESTIVAL AT NEWPORT (VOL. 1)	15
62	Fontana TFL 6004	FOLK FESTIVAL AT NEWPORT (VOL. 2)	15
62	Fontana TFL 6009	FOLK FESTIVAL AT NEWPORT (VOL. 4)	15
63	Pye Intl. NPL 28033	FOLK FESTIVAL OF THE BLUES	18
73	Windmill WMD	FOLK HERITAGE	30
82	Fuck Off (no cat. no.)	FOLK IN HELL (cassette)	15
70s	Nottingham Festival FEST 1	FOLK NOTTINGHAM STYLE	100
65	Decca LK 4783	FOLK NOW	20
70	BBC REC 955	FOLK ON FRIDAY	20
71	Talisman STAL 5019	FOLK PHILOSOPHY	20
63	Golden Guinea GGL 0265	THE FOLK SCENE	12
66	Folkscene SSP 001	FOLK SCENE (LP, private pressing)	150
61	Topic 12T 157	THE FOLK SONGS OF BRITAIN — SONGS OF COURTSHIP	15
61	Topic 12T 158	THE FOLK SONGS OF BRITAIN VOL. 2 — SONGS OF SEDUCTION	15
61	Topic 12T 159	THE FOLK SONGS OF BRITAIN VOL. 3 — JACK OF ALL TRADES	15
61	Topic 12T 160	THE FOLK SONGS OF BRITAIN VOL. 4 — CHILD BALLADS 1	15
61	Topic 12T 161	THE FOLK SONGS OF BRITAIN VOL. 5 — CHILD BALLADS 2	15
61	Topic 12T 194	THE FOLK SONGS OF BRITAIN VOL. 6 — SAILORMEN AND SERVINGMAIDS	15
61	Topic 12T 195	THE FOLK SONGS OF BRITAIN VOL. 7 — FAIR GAME AND FOUL	15
61	Topic 12T 196	THE FOLK SONGS OF BRITAIN VOL. 8 — A SOLDIER'S LIFE FOR ME	15
61	Topic 12T 197	THE FOLK SONGS OF BRITAIN VOL. 9 — SONGS OF CEREMONY	15
61	Topic 12T 198	THE FOLK SONGS OF BRITAIN VOL. 10 — SONGS OF ANIMAL	15
		(Each of the above 10 LPs came with blue labels and a booklet.)	
69	Topic	THE FOLK SONGS OF BRITAIN VOLS. 1-10 (10 x LP box set)	100
61	Topic TPS 201	TOPIC SAMPLER No. 6 — FOLK SONGS	12
57	HMV DLP 1143	FOLK SONG TODAY (SONGS AND BALLADS OF ENGLAND AND SCOTLAND) (10")	25
65	HMV CLP 1910	FOLKSOUND OF BRITAIN	18
71	Nicro K 220971	FOLK UPSTAIRS	80
91	Food TCFOOD 34	FOOD XMAS PARTY 1991 (cassette, 2,000 only)	20
63	Ember CEL 902	FOOL BRITANNIA	15
80s	Martyrwell M. MARY 141	FOOLS RUSH IN WHERE ANGELS DARE TO TREAD	10
82	Kent KENT 001	FOR DANCERS ONLY (LP, coloured vinyl)	10
83	Kent KENT 002	FOR DANCERS ALSO (For Dancers Only Vol. 2) (LP, yellow vinyl)	10
79	Rocket DIAL 1	499 2139 (with inner sleeve)	10
65	Decca LK 4695	FOURTEEN — THE LORD'S TAVERNERS' ALBUM	35
80	Defensive PACT 1	FOUR WAYS OUT	10
70	Bamboo BLP 205	FREEDOM SOUNDS	40
81	Fresh FRESH LP 8	A FRESH SELECTION	10
72	Trojan TRL 51	FROM BAM BAM TO CHERRY OH BABY	15
80	Disques/Crepuscule TWI 007	FROM BRUSSELS WITH LOVE (cassette, in pouch with booklet)	20
86	Disques/Crepuscule TWI 007	FROM BRUSSELS WITH LOVE (2-LP reissue, with inner sleeves)	15
70	Liberty LBS 83321	FROM THE BAYOU	15
70	Liberty LBS 83278	FROM THE VAULTS	15
80s	New European BADVC 666	FROM TORTURE TO CONSCIENCE (with insert)	20
71	Cutty Wren	FROST LANE	50
86	Record Mirror RM 5	FRUITCAKES & FURRY COLLARS	10
70	Trojan TBL 137	FUNKY CHICKEN	15
87	Urban	(JAMES BROWN'S) FUNKY PEOPLE VOL. 1	12
87	Urban URBLP 14	(JAMES BROWN'S) FUNKY PEOPLE VOL. 2	12
70	Bamboo BLP 206	FUNKY REGGAE	50
82	Come Org. WDC 881021	FÜR ILSE KOCH (some on red vinyl)	80/60
70	Ember	FUTURE STAR EXPLOSION	12
80s	Third Mind TMLP 15	FUTURE TENSE VOL. 1	10

G

69	Pama ECO 4	GAS — GREATEST HITS	25
66	Doctor Bird DLM 5001	GAYFEET	80
52	Brunswick LA 8544	GEMS OF JAZZ VOL. 1 (10")	15
52	Brunswick LA 8561	GEMS OF JAZZ VOL. 1 (10")	15

MINT VALUE £

55	HMV DLP 1039	GENE NORMAN PRESENTS JUST JAZZ (10")	20
72	Chess 6641 047	GENESIS — THE BEGINNINGS OF ROCK (4-LP box set with booklet)	50
73	Chess 6641 125	GENESIS — MEMPHIS TO CHICAGO (4-LP box set with booklet)	50
75	Chess 6641 174	GENESIS — SWEET HOME CHICAGO (4-LP box set with booklet)	50
69	Kokomo K 1004	GEORGIA GUITARS 1927-1938 (99 copies only)	45
67	Coxsone CSL 8007	GET READY ROCK STEADY	100
60s	Riverside RLP 12-106	GIANTS OF BOOGIE WOOGIE	15
69	Pama SECO 20	A GIFT FROM PAMA	25
71	Wand WCS 1003	THE GIRLS WITH SOUL	12
72	Revelation REV 1/2/3	GLASTONBURY FAYRE REVELATIONS — A MUSICAL ANTHOLOGY (3-LP, poster sleeve with booklets, pyramid & printed polythene bag)	85
66	Columbia SX 6062	GO!	50
80s	Touch & Go TG 11	GOD'S FAVOURITE DOG	20
72	Flyright LP 103	GOIN' AWAY WALKING	15
70	Python LP 1	GOIN' BACK TO CHICAGO (99 copies only)	35
70	Warner Bros WS 1874	GOING HOME	12
60s	Heritage 1003	GOING TO CALIFORNIA (99 copies only)	35
68	Decca LK 4931	GOIN' UP THE COUNTRY	15
69	Oliver & Boyd SBN 05 002118/9	THE GOLDEN BIRD (2-LP)	30
64	Columbia 33SX 1664	GOLDEN GOODIES VOL. 1.	35
69	Columbia 33SX 1672	GOLDEN GOODIES VOL. 2.	35
69	Roulette RCP 1000	GOLDEN GOODIES VOL. 1.	20
69	Roulette RCP 1001	GOLDEN GOODIES VOL. 2.	20
59	Philips BBL 7331	GOLDEN HITS	18
60	Philips BBL 7422	GOLDEN HITS VOL. 2.	15
61	Philips BBL 7581	GOLDEN HITS VOL. 3.	18
57	Capitol T 830	THE GOLD RECORD (blue label)	12
72	Chess 2CH 50030	THE GOLDEN AGE OF RHYTHM & BLUES (2-LP)	15
88	53rd & 3rd AGAS 3	GOOD FEELINGS	10
75	Eron 004	GOOD FOLK OF KENT (with insert)	40
65	Atlantic ATL 5004	GOOD OLD FIFTIES	35
68	Elek. EUK 260/EUKS 7260	GOOD TIME MUSIC (U.K. version of "What's Shakin' ", gold or red label)	40/30
72	CBS 67234	GOSPEL SOUND (2-LP)	20
59	Brunswick LAT 8290	GOSPEL TRAIN	15
64	London HA-B 8172	GRAND OLE OPRY SPECTACULAR VOL. 1.	15
64	London HA-B 8173	GRAND OLE OPRY SPECTACULAR VOL. 2.	15
73	Greasy Truckers GT 4997	GREASY TRUCKERS — LIVE AT DINGWALLS DANCE HALL (2-LP with insert)	15
73	United Artists UDX 203/4	GREASY TRUCKERS PARTY (2-LP, gatefold sleeve)	25
72	Vanguard VSD 25/26	GREAT BLUESMEN (2-LP)	18
54	London AL 3530	THE GREAT BLUES SINGERS (10")	30
60s	Riverside RLP 12-121	THE GREAT BLUES SINGERS	22
80s	Direct DH 1005	THE GREAT BRITISH BEAT VOL. 2 (cassette via Direct Hits fan club)	10
75	D. Demand DDDDLP 5002	GREAT DISCO DEMANDS	12
55	HMV DLP 1025	GREAT ELLINGTON SOLOISTS (10")	25
70	Trojan TBL 111	GREATER JAMAICA	20
72	Vanguard VSD 17/18	THE GREATEST FOLK SINGERS OF THE SIXTIES (2-LP)	15
75	Brunswick BRLS 3006	GREATEST HITS.	10
81	Street Level/Fuck Off	THE GREATEST HITS (MUSIC 4 PLEASURE) (cassette)	10
64	Stateside SL 10075	THE GREATEST GOSPEL SONGS OF OUR TIME	18
67	Doctor Bird DLM 5009	GREATEST JAMAICAN BEAT	90
66	Pye Intl. NPL 28052	THE GREATEST ON STAGE	12
72	Vanguard VSD 35/36	THE GREATEST SOUNDS OF WOODY GUTHRIE (2-LP)	15
65	RCA RD/SF 7755	GREAT MOMENTS IN JAZZ — NEWPORT JAZZ FESTIVAL 1964	12
54	HMV DLP 1054	GREAT TRUMPET SOLOISTS (10")	25
79	Pilgrim MRT 1001	GREENBELT LIVE	10
85	Crashed METALPS 107	GREEN METAL	30
60	Columbia 33SX 1296	GRETSCH DRUM NIGHT AT BIRDLAND (also stereo SCX 3359)	12
71	Bamboo BDLP 215	GROOVING WITH BAMBOO	40
69	Direction 8-63452	GROOVY BABY	15
63	Realm RM 149	GROUP BEAT '63	35
63	London HA-U 8086	GROUP OF GOODIES	35
64	World Record Club TP 444	GROUP '64	12
78	Virgin VCL 5001	GUILLOTINE (10" mini-LP, with inner sleeve)	10
60s	Storyville SLP 166	GUITAR BLUES	15
73	Transatlantic TRA 271	GUITAR WORKSHOP (2-LP)	20
71	Sunnyland KS 102	GULF COAST BLUES (99 copies only)	35
80s	Situation Two SITU 17	GUNFIRE AND PIANOS (with inner)	12
80s	Situation Two SITC 17	GUNFIRE AND PIANOS (cassette)	10
69	Trojan TTL 16	GUNS OF NAVARONE	18
69	Liberty LBX 3	GUTBUCKET	20
68	Island ILP 977	GUY STEVENS' TESTAMENT OF ROCK AND ROLL	25
71	Wand WCS 1002	THE GUYS WITH SOUL	12

H

58	Oriole MG 20033	HAIL VARIETY!	12
70	Probe PSS 1	HANDLE WITH CARE	12
88	HandMade (no cat. no.)	HANDMADE FILMS MUSIC — THE 10TH ANNIVERSARY (CD, promo only)	100
68	Immediate IMLYIN 2	HAPPY TO BE PART OF THE INDUSTRY OF HUMAN HAPPINESS	15
77	VJM VLP 40	HARD LUCK BLUES	15
77	Revival RVS 1009	HARD TIMES BLUES	12
74	Decca DPA 3009/10	HARD UP HEROES 1963-68 (2-LP, gatefold sleeve)	15
56	London AL 3553	HARLEM PIANO ROLL (10")	20
72	Carnival 2941 001	HARPIN' ON IT	12
71	Harvest SHSS 3	HARVEST BAG	12

MINT VALUE £

TOMMY STEELE

69	Harvest SPSLP 118	HARVEST SAMPLER OF THE INITIAL FOUR JUNE RELEASES (promo only)....	80
63	Reprise R 50001	HAVE YOURSELF A MERRY LITTLE CHRISTMAS.	15
71	Sunnyland KS 101	HAVIN' A GOOD TIME — CHICAGO BLUES ANTHOLOGY (99 copies only).	35
66	Polydor 582 701	HEADLINE NEWS.	15
87	Play Hard	HEAD OVER EARS (with *Debris* fanzine)	12/10
70	Transatlantic TRASAD 18	HEADS AND TALES (2-LP).	15
71	Vertigo 6360 045	HEADS TOGETHER, FIRST ROUND (gatefold sleeve, spiral label).	20
81	Heavy Metal HMR LP 1	HEAVY METAL HEROES	30
82	Heavy Metal HMR LP 7	HEAVY METAL HEROES VOLUME 2	25
81	Epic EPC 88558	HEAVY METAL — MUSIC FROM THE MOTION PICTURE (2-LP, gatefold sleeve with inserts)	15
68	Trojan TRL 6	HERE COMES THE DUKE	35
65	Pye NPL 18121	HERE COME THE GIRLS	15
80s	Temps Modernes LTMV:XI	HEURES SANS SOLEIL.	25
69	Pama PSP 1002	HEY BOY HEY GIRL.	30
80	Rockburgh ROC 111	HICKS FROM THE STICKS.	12
58	Melodisc MLP 518	HIGHLIFE: AUTHENTIC WEST AFRICAN MUSIC VOL. 1 (10").	12
58	Melodisc MLP 519	HIGHLIFE: AUTHENTIC WEST AFRICAN MUSIC VOL. 2 (10").	12
59	Parlophone PMD 1085	HIGHWAY TO HEAVEN (10").	15
57	Capitol T 793	THE HISTORY OF JAZZ VOL. 1 — N'ORLEANS ORIGINS.	12
57	Capitol T 794	THE HISTORY OF JAZZ VOL. 2 — THE TURBULENT TWENTIES	12
57	Capitol T 795	THE HISTORY OF JAZZ VOL. 3 — EVERYBODY SWINGS.	12
57	Capitol T 796	THE HISTORY OF JAZZ VOL. 4 — ENTER THE COOL.	12
68	Atlantic 587 094	HISTORY OF RHYTHM AND BLUES — VOL. 1, THE ROOTS 1947-52	12
68	Atlantic 587 095	HISTORY OF RHYTHM AND BLUES — VOL. 2, THE GOLDEN YEARS 1953-55	12
68	Atlantic 587 096	HISTORY OF RHYTHM AND BLUES — VOL. 3, ROCK 'N' ROLL 1956-57	12
68	Atlantic 587 097	HISTORY OF RHYTHM AND BLUES — VOL. 4, THE BIG BEAT 1958-60	12
68	Atlantic 587 140	HISTORY OF RHYTHM AND BLUES — VOL. 5	12
68	Atlantic 587 141	HISTORY OF RHYTHM AND BLUES — VOL. 6	12
69	Bamboo BDLP 203	HISTORY OF SKA VOLUME ONE.	50
88	PWL HFCD 4	HIT FACTORY — THE BEST OF STOCK, AITKEN & WATERMAN VOL. 2 (CD, with exclusive mix of Kylie Minogue's "I Should Be So Lucky", etc)	20
64	Pye NPL 18108	THE HITMAKERS.	20
65	Pye NPL 18115	THE HITMAKERS VOL. 2.	20
69	Marble Arch MAL 1259	THE HITMAKERS (reissue)	12
57	Pye Nixa NPT 19015	HIT PARADE OF 1956 (10")	22
59	Pye Nixa NPT 19032	HIT PARADE OF 1958.	15
80s	Hits & Corruption HAC 1	HITS AND CORRUPTION (with cassette).	10
66	Marble Arch MAL 650	HITS FROM THE IVY LEAGUE, THE ROCKIN' BERRIES & THE SORROWS	12
77	Stiff FIST 1	HITS — GREATEST STIFFS (with 7", Max Wall's "England's Glory" [BUY 12])	12
65	Tamla Motown TML 11019	HITSVILLE U.S.A.	30
67	Stax 589 005	HIT THE ROAD STAX	15
81	United Dairies UD 05	HOISTING THE BLACK FLAG.	60
64	Ace Of Hearts AH 68	HOLLYWOOD SINGS: THE BOYS.	12
64	Ace Of Hearts AH 69	HOLLYWOOD SINGS: THE BOYS AND THE GIRLS.	12
56	London D 93076	HOMAGE TO DJANGO REINHARDT (10")	12

MINT VALUE £

81	Interior Music IM 011	HOMMAGE A DURAS	10
62	Golden Guinea GGL 0129	HONEY HIT PARADE	12
74	Melodisc 12-216	HONEYS	25
80	Oval OVLM 5003	THE HONKY TONK DEMOS	10
52	Capitol LC 6544	HONKY TONK PIANO (10")	15
60s	Riverside RLP 8806	HONKY TONK TRAIN (with booklet)	22
64	Stateside SL 10079	HOOTENANNY AT THE TROUBADOUR	12
63	Decca LK 4544	HOOTENANNY IN LONDON	20
63	Fontana 688 009ZL	HOOTENANNY SATURDAY NIGHT	20
64	Waverley ZLP 2025	HOOT'NANNY SHOW VOLUME 1	12
64	Waverley ZLP 2032	HOOT'NANNY SHOW VOLUME 2	12
78	Warner Bros K 66077	THE HOPE AND ANCHOR FRONT ROW FESTIVAL (2-LP)	15
71	Pama PMP 2006	HOT NUMBERS	20
71	Pama PMP 2009	HOT NUMBERS VOLUME TWO	20
77	WEA M 100	HOT PLATTER CORDON BLEU (available via *Melody Maker*)	20
70	Trojan TBL 128	HOT SHOTS OF REGGAE	20
72	Hot Wax SHW 5008	HOT WAX GREATEST HITS	12
69	Track 613 016	THE HOUSE THAT TRACK BUILT (gatefold sleeve)	25
69	Blue Horizon PR 45/46	HOW BLUE CAN WE GET (2-LP, gatefold sleeve with insert)	35

I

69	Liberty LBL/LBS 83252	I ASKED FOR WATER ... AND SHE GAVE ME GASOLINE	60
80	TJM TJM 11	IDENTITY PARADE	12
85	EMI TAPE 1/Some Bizzare EJ26 0663 1	IF YOU CAN'T PLEASE YOURSELF, YOU CAN'T PLEASE YOUR SOUL (with inner sleeve, insert & file; cassette)	15/10
69	Immediate IMLYIN 1	IMMEDIATE LETS YOU IN	15
86	Food BITE 4	IMMINENT VOL. 4	12
67	Parlophone PMC 7024	I'M SORRY, I'LL READ THAT AGAIN	18
70	Highway 51 H-104	I'M YOUR COUNTRY MAN (99 copies only)	40
77	United Artists UAS 30101	IMPERIAL ROCKABILLIES	12
79	United Artists UAS 30173	IMPERIAL ROCKABILLIES VOL. 2	12
80	United Artists UAS 30312	IMPERIAL ROCKABILLIES VOL. 3	12
95	Dig The Fuzz DIG LP 1	INCREDIBLE SOUND SHOW STORIES VOL. 1 — TECHNICOLOUR MILKSHAKE	10
96	Dig The Fuzz DIG LP 4	INCREDIBLE SOUND SHOW STORIES VOL. 2 — WHEN THE TANGERINE STRIKES TWELVE (orange vinyl, gatefold sleeve)	10
66	CBS/Denson Shoes	THE IN CROWD (shoe offer compilation)	25
69	Trojan TTL 15	INDEPENDENT JAMAICA	25
67	Fontana TL 5426	INDIAN MUSIC	12
79	Object Music OBJ 002	INDISCRETE MUSIC — DUBIOUS COLLABORATION (500 only)	10
84	Illuminated JAMS 39	THE INDUSTRIAL RECORDS STORY 1976-1981	20
80s	United Dairies UD 015	IN FRACTURED SILENCE	35
95	RCA 74321 315501	IN FROM THE STORM — THE MUSIC OF JIMI HENDRIX (LP, picture disc)	15
63	Colpix PXL 459	IN LONDON (Elizabeth Taylor/John Barry, mono/stereo)	40/50
69	T. Motown (S)TML 11124	IN LOVING MEMORY (TRIBUTE TO MRS LOUCYE G. WAKEFIELD)	50
70	Blue Horizon PR 37	IN OUR OWN WAY (OLDIES BUT GOODIES)	30
70	Ember EMB 34111	IN REGGAE TIME	12
80	Island IRSP 2	INTENSIFIED	10
88	Secret Heart 1008	IN THE BEGINNING — TOMMY STEELE (with insert, 1,000 only)	12
66	Ember FA 2034	IRELAND'S GREATEST SOUNDS: FIVE TOP GROUPS FROM BELFAST'S MARITIME CLUB	50
64	Decca LK 4633	IRISH FOLK NIGHT	15
63	Topic 12T 86	THE IRON MUSE (blue label with lyric insert, later reissued)	15/10
79	Rationale RATE 8	IRRATIONALE (cassette, in bag with booklet)	35
61	Oriole MG 20046	IT'S ALL HAPPENING HERE	12

J

69	Amalgamated CSP 3	JACKPOT OF HITS	25
77	Policy Wheel PW 4593	JACKSON BLUES BOYS	12
68	Blue Cat BCL 1	JAMAICAN MEMORIES	60
64	Atlantic 587 075	JAMAICA SKA (colour 'Dancers' sleeve)	45
67	Atlantic 587 075	JAMAICA SKA (reissue, orange sleeve)	30
68	Flyright LP 3502	JAMBALAYA ON THE BAYOU — VOLUME 1	20
69	Flyright LP 3503	JAMBALAYA ON THE BAYOU — VOLUME 2	20
72	Utd. Artists UAS 60027/8	THE JAMES BOND COLLECTION (2-LP, with booklet)	25
84	Situation 2 SITU 11	JAMMING! A NEW OPTIMISM	10
72	Rolling Stones COC 39100	JAMMING WITH EDWARD	18
55	Columbia Clef 33CX 10008	JAM SESSION	12
61	HMV/Utd Artists CSD 1381	JAZZ ALIVE — A NIGHT AT THE HALF NOTE	12
56	Tempo TAP 5	JAZZ AT THE FLAMINGO	25
55	Columbia 33CX 10078	JAZZ AT THE PHILHARMONIC, 1955 VOL. 1	12
55	Columbia 33CX 10079	JAZZ AT THE PHILHARMONIC, 1955 VOL. 2	12
50s	Columbia SLJS 1	JAZZ EXPLOSION	12
72	Decca ECS 2114	JAZZ IN BRITAIN 1968-1969	25
62	Parlophone PMC 1195	JAZZ IN THE MAKING	12
84	Streetsounds MUSIC 1	JAZZ JUICE	30
85	Streetsounds SOUND 1	JAZZ JUICE (reissue)	25
86	Streetsounds SOUND 4	JAZZ JUICE 2	20
86	Streetsounds SOUND 5	JAZZ JUICE 3	20
86	Streetsounds SOUND 6	JAZZ JUICE 4	20
87	Streetsounds SOUND 8	JAZZ JUICE 5	18
87	Streetsounds SOUND 9	JAZZ JUICE 6	18
87	Streetsounds CDSND 9	JAZZ JUICE 6 (CD)	15
88	Streetsounds SOUND 10	JAZZ JUICE 7	18
88	Streetsounds CDSND 10	JAZZ JUICE 7 (CD)	15
88	Streetsounds SOUND 11	JAZZ JUICE 8	15

88	Streetsounds CDSND 11	JAZZ JUICE 8 (CD)	15
88	Streetsounds SOUND 12	JAZZ JUICE 9	15
88	Streetsounds CDSND 12	JAZZ JUICE 9 (CD)	15
57	London AL 3562	JAZZ OF THE ROARING TWENTIES VOL. 2 (10")	15
58	Philips BBL 7184	JAZZ OMNIBUS	12
63	VJM LC 6	JAZZ PANORAMA OF THE SIXTIES	12
58	Vogue LAE 12097	JAZZ PIANISTS GALORE	12
57	London AL 3565	JAZZ PIANO RARITIES (10")	20
55	Columbia Clef 33C 9007	JAZZ SCENE (10")	15
55	Columbia Clef 33C 9008	JAZZ SCENE VOL. 2 (10")	15
62	Parlophone PMC 1177	JAZZ SOUNDS OF THE 20s VOL. 4: BLUES SINGERS & ACCOMPANISTS	15
56	Vogue LAE 12038	JAZZ WEST COAST	12
57	Vogue LAE 12061	JAZZ WEST COAST VOLUME 2	12
58	Vogue LAE 12115	JAZZ WEST COAST VOLUME 3	12
61	Vogue LAE 12235	JAZZ WEST COAST VOLUME 5	12
77	Decca DPA 3035/3036	THE JOE MEEK STORY (2-LP)	30
60	Top Rank 35/064	JOHN HAMMOND'S SPIRITUALS TO SWING VOLUME 1	12
60	Top Rank 35/065	JOHN HAMMOND'S SPIRITUALS TO SWING VOLUME 2	12
69	BBC REC 52S	JOHN PEEL PRESENTS TOP GEAR	30
70	BBC REC 68M	JOHN PEEL'S ARCHIVE THINGS	20
60	HMV CLP 1327	A JUG OF PUNCH (also issued as XLP 50003)	30
60s	Ace Of Hearts AH 163	JUGS AND WASHBOARDS	15
67	RCA Victor RD 7893	JUGS WASHBOARDS AND KAZOOS	15
70s	Eric's ERICS 008	JUKEBOX AT ERIC'S	10
76	RCA RS 1066	JUMPING AT THE GO GO	18
77	Policy Wheel PW 459-1	JUMPING ON THE HILL	12
64	R&B JBL 1111	JUMP JAMAICA WAY	175
69	RCA Intl. INT 1014	JUST A LITTLE BIT OF SOUL	12
79	Kick KK 1	JUST FOR KICKS	25
80s	Quiet QLP 1	JUST WHEN YOU THOUGHT IT WAS... QUIET!	10

K

59	Capitol T 1057	K.C. IN THE 30's	20
72	Joy JOYS 223	KEEP THE FAITH VOL. 1 (LP)	12
72	Joy JOYS 224	KEEP THE FAITH VOL 2. (LP)	12
72	Joy JOYS 225	KEEP THE FAITH VOL 3. (LP)	12
81	White Witch	KENT ROCKS (200 only)	150
54	HMV DLP 1048	KEYBOARD KINGS OF JAZZ (10")	25
72	Key	KEY COLLECTION (with insert)	15
70	Trojan TBL 140	KING SIZE REGGAE	25
77	Chrysalis CHR 1137	THE KING OF ELFLAND'S DAUGHTER	10
68	Polydor 623 273	KINGS OF RHYTHM AND BLUES	12
60s	Gryphon 13159	KINGS OF THE TWELVE STRING GUITAR	20
71	Flyright LP 101	KINGS OF THE TWELVE STRING GUITAR (reissue)	15
60s	Saydisc Roots RL 333	KINGS OF MEMPHIS TOWN 1927-1930	15
94	Mercury 522 476-1	KISS MY ASS (red, white or blue vinyl)	12

L

79	The Label TRLP 002	THE LABEL SOFA	10
79	The Label TRLP 002S	THE LABEL SOFA ('translumar defractor' 3D picture disc, stickered PVC sleeve)	35
79	Cherry Red ARED 4	LABELS UNLIMITED	10
83	Fetish FR 2011	THE LAST TESTAMENT (with inner, stickered sleeve)	18
87	Other OTH 10	LAST WARRIOR	25
68	Island ILP 986	LEAPING WITH MR LEE (by Bunny Lee All Stars)	150
66	Blue Horizon LP 2	LET ME TELL YOU ABOUT THE BLUES	350
60s	Polydor SLPHM 237 622	LET'S DO THE TWIST, HULLY GULLY, SLOP, SURF, LOCOMOTION, MONKEY	20
66	Neshoba N 11	LET'S GO DOWN SOUTH (99 copies only)	50
58	Brunswick LAT 8271	LET'S HAVE A PARTY	20
81	Alt. Tentacles VIRUS 4	LET THEM EAT JELLYBEANS (with lyric poster)	15
74	Sonet SNTX 1	LEGACY OF THE BLUES SAMPLER	12
80s	Third Mind/Abstract	LIFE AT THE TOP	25
81	WEA K 58412	LIFE IN THE EUROPEAN THEATRE	12
82	Magnum Force MFLP 006	LIGHT UP THE DYNAMITE	10
68	Transatlantic TRASAM 2	LISTEN HERE!	15
83	Polydor ROCK 2	A LITTLE BIT OF LIGHT RELIEF	12
81	NEMS NEL 6020	LIVE AND HEAVY	10
80	BUN 01	LIVE AT BUNJIES (gatefold sleeve with insert)	30
74	Key KL 021	LIVE AT SPREE	20
77	NEMS NEL 6013	LIVE AT THE VORTEX	15
65	Fontana TL 5240	LIVE AT THE WHISKEY A-GO-GO	12
68	Big Shot BBTL 4000	LIVE IT UP	60
64	Embassy WLP 6065	LIVERPOOL BEAT	15
65	Ember NR 5028	LIVERPOOL TODAY — LIVE AT THE CAVERN	30
64	CBS Realm RM 209	LIVIN' WITH THE BLUES	15
70	Trojan TBL 135	LOCH NESS MONSTER	20
68	Pye NSPL 18241	THE LONDON POPS ORCHESTRA	10
87	4AD CAD 703D	LONELY IS AN EYESORE (cardboard pack with book)	30
87	4AD CADX 703	LONELY IS AN EYESORE (CD, LP & cassette, in wooden box with etching, screen print & video, 100 only)	200
78	Chiswick CH 5	LONG SHOTS, DEAD CERTS & ODDS ON FAVORITES — CHISWICK CHARTBUSTERS VOL. 2	10
91	Holyground HG 121	LOOSE ROUTES (2-LP, gatefold foldover sleeve)	30
65	Storyville 616002	LOUISIANA PRISON BLUES	12
69	Pama PSP 1001	A LOVELY DOZEN	25

M

76	Cornish Legend CLM 1	MADE IN CORNWALL (with insert)	25
58	Pye Nixa Jazz NJL 13	(LEONARD FEATHER PRESENTS) MAD THAD	12
70s	Object Music OBJ 003	A MANCHESTER COLLECTION	10
88	Bop BC V001	MANCHESTER, NORTH OF ENGLAND (white labels only)	10
70	Trojan TBL 129	MAN FROM CAROLINA	18
70	CBS 52798	MA RAINEY AND THE CLASSIC BLUES SINGERS	15
69	Marmalade 643 314	MARMALADE — 100% PROOF	15
68	President PTL 1002	MAR-V-LUS SOUND OF R&B AND SOUL MUSIC	15
72	WEA K 60029	MAR-Y-SOL (2-LP)	15
72	Village Thing VTSAM 16	MATCHBOX DAYS	25
78	CBS 82670	MAX'S KANSAS CITY (LP)	12
66	CBS Special Prod. WSR 853	McDONALDS ALL-STAR FAVOURITES	10
69	Liberty LBL/LBS 83190	ME AND THE DEVIL	40
69	Atco 228 023	MEMPHIS GOLD	12
64	London HA 8129	MEMORIES ARE MADE OF HITS VOL. 1	25
64	London HA 8130	MEMORIES ARE MADE OF HITS VOL. 2	25
64	London HA 8131	MEMORIES ARE MADE OF HITS VOL. 3	25
64	London HA 8138	MEMORIES ARE MADE OF HITS VOL. 4	25
64	London HA 8148	MEMORIES ARE MADE OF HITS VOL. 5	25
64	London HA 8171	MEMORIES ARE MADE OF HITS VOL. 6	25
64	London HA 8189	MEMORIES ARE MADE OF HITS VOL. 7	25
65	London HA 8213	MEMORIES ARE MADE OF HITS VOL. 8	25
54	Vogue Coral LVC 10008	MERRY CHRISTMAS (10")	18
69	T. Motown (S)TML 11126	MERRY CHRISTMAS FROM MOTOWN (mono/stere)	20/18
60s	Capitol T 9030	MERRY CHRISTMAS TO YOU	15
75	United Artists USD 305/6	MERSEY BEAT 1962-1964 (2-LP, with newspaper insert & inner sleeves)	15
85	Neat NEAT 1014	METAL BATTLE	10
80	BBC REH 397	METAL EXPLOSION	20
83	Ebony EBON 1	METAL FATIGUE	10
80	EMI EMC 3318	METAL FOR MUTHAS	15
80	EMI EMC 3337	METAL FOR MUTHAS VOL. 2	15
84	Roadrunner RR 9084	METAL MACHINE	10
83	Ebony EBON 8	METAL MANIAXE	10
83	Ebony EBON 14	METAL PLATED	10
83	Ebony EBON 11	METAL WARRIORS	10
81	Virgin OVEDC 5	METHODS OF DANCE (cassette with 5 extra tracks)	10
80	MGM 2315 394	THE MGM ROCKABILLY COLLECTION	12
56	Nixa Jazz Today NJL 3	MIDNIGHT AT NIXA	12
66	Atlantic 587 021	MIDNIGHT SOUL	15
69	Storyville 616 009	MIDNIGHT SPECIAL	12
62	Brunswick LAT 8401	MIDNIGHT JAMBOREE (also stereo STA 3061)	12
56	London AL 3554	MIDWESTERN JAZZ (10")	15
66	Xtra XTRA 1047	THE MIKE RAVEN BLUES SHOW	20
69	Transatlantic TRASAM 5	THE MIKE RAVEN BLUES SAMPLER	20
72	Polydor	MILL VALLEY JAM SESSION	12
60	Coral LVA 9126	MILLION-AIRS	18
80	Pipe PIPE 2	MINIATURES (with poster insert, 500 only)	15
80	Pipe PIPE 2	MINIATURES (cassette with mini-booklet insert, 100 only)	30
86	Word WST R 9661	MISSION ENGLAND VOLUME 2	10
71	Trojan TBL 174	MISS LABBA LABBA REGGAE	20
60	Top Rank BUY 028	MR. BLUE	30
60s	Bounty BY 6025	MODERN CHICAGO BLUES	30
69	London HAB 8380	MODERN COUNTRY HITS OF TODAY VOL. 1	12
69	London HAB 8381	MODERN COUNTRY HITS OF TODAY VOL. 2	12
55	HMV DLP 1022	MODERN JAZZ PIANO (10")	20
56	Tempo TAP 2	MODERN JAZZ SCENE 1956	20
53	Esquire 20-011	MODERN MIXTURE VOLUME ONE (10")	15
79	Bridge House BHLP 003	MODS MAYDAY '79 (original issue)	10
73	Stax STX 1029	MONTREUX FESTIVAL 1973	12
70	Trojan TTL 31	MOONLIGHT GROOVER	20
80	Danceville	THE MOONLIGHT TAPES	12
70	Liberty LBS 83377	MORE FROM THE VAULTS	12
80	Island IRSP 3	MORE INTENSIFIED	10
62	HMV CLP 1583	MORE OF YOUR FAVOURITE TV AND RADIO THEMES	15
68	Marble Arch MAL 813	MORE RHYTHM AND BLUES	12
65	private pressing	MORE SINGING AT THE COUNT HOUSE	30
72	Island HELP 5	MORRIS ON	10
81	cassette	MORROCCI KLUNG! (cassette, some in printed 5" x 9" mailing envelope)	20/12
80	Conventional CON 013	MOTHER OF A PUNK (cassette)	12
86	Iguana VYK LP 11	MOTOR CITY 9 (with booklet)	15
65	Tamla Motown TML 11007	THE MOTORTOWN REVUE LIVE	80
66	Tamla Motown TML 11027	THE MOTORTOWN REVUE IN PARIS	75
70	T. Motown (S)TML 11127	THE MOTORTOWN REVUE LIVE	15
69	T. Motown (S)TML 11121	MOTOWN CHARTBUSTERS VOL. 3 (original with flipback sleeve)	12
70	T. Motown STML 11162	MOTOWN CHARTBUSTERS VOL. 4 (original with flipback sleeve)	12
74	T. Motown STML 11270	MOTOWN CHARTBUSTERS VOL. 9 (green vinyl)	12
72	Tamla Motown STMA 8005	MOTOWN DISCO CLASSICS VOL. 2	12
66	Tamla Motown TML 11030	MOTOWN MAGIC	30
68	Tamla Motown TML 11064	MOTOWN MEMORIES (flipback sleeve)	40
68	Tamla Motown TML 11077	MOTOWN MEMORIES VOL. 2	40
70	T. Motown STML 11143	MOTOWN MEMORIES VOL. 3	40
72	Tamla Motown STML 11200	MOTOWN MEMORIES	15
80	Tamla Motown	MOTOWN MOD CLASSICS VOL. 1	12
80	Tamla Motown	MOTOWN MOD CLASSICS VOL. 2	12

MINT VALUE £

72	Tamla Motown TMSP 1130	THE MOTOWN STORY (5-LP box set)	25
83	Tamla Motown TMSP 6019	THE MOTOWN STORY — THE FIRST 25 YEARS (box set)	20
77	Mountain PSLP 200	MOUNTAIN ROCKS INTO '77 (Mountain label sampler, promo only)	20
75	Tangent TNGM 199D	THE MUCKLE SINGS — CLASSIC SCOTS BALLADS (2-LP with booklet)	15
53	London AL 3503	MUGGY, TESCH AND THE CHICAGOANS (10")	15
57	Pye NJL 11	MURDERER'S HOME	15
71	Mushroom 100 MR 16	THE MUSHROOM FOLK SAMPLER	30
57	Brunswick LAT 8201	MUSIC FOR THE BOYFRIEND — HE REALLY DIGS ROCK'N'ROLL	45
57	Brunswick LAT 8202	MUSIC FOR THE BOYFRIEND — HE REALLY DIGS JAZZ	12
57	Brunswick LAT 8205	MUSIC FOR THE BOYFRIEND — THE FEMININE TOUCH	12
66	Fountain Press KPM/ACW 1	MUSIC FOR YOUR MOVIES	12
73	Charisma CADS 101	MUSIC FROM FREE CREEK (2-LP)	20
71	Trojan TBL 170	MUSIC HOUSE	12
71	Trojan TBL 177	MUSIC HOUSE VOLUME TWO	12
70	Disques Vogue VRLS 3043	LA MUSIQUE PROGRESSIVE	12
81	Ze ISSP 4001	MUTANT DISCO (3 x 12" box set, numbered, 2,000 only)	10
77	EMI NUT 4	MY GENERATION	10

N

73	Enterprise ESAM 100	THE NAME OF THE GAME	10
71	Eden LP 43	NAPTON FOLK CLUB (private pressing, 100 only)	35
62	London HA-B 8003	NASHVILLE SATURDAY NIGHT	12
63	London HA-B 8028	NASHVILLE STEEL GUITAR	12
71	Music F. Pleasure MFP 1432	NAT, DEAN AND FRIENDS	10
69	Bamboo BLP 201	NATURAL REGGAE VOLUME ONE	50
70	Bamboo BLP 204	NATURAL REGGAE VOLUME TWO	50
81	4AD CAD 117	NATURES MORTES — STILL LIVES (export issue)	60
80s	Musique Brut BRV 002	NECROPOLIS, AMPHIBIANS AND REPTILES: THE MUSIC OF ADOLF WOLFLI	20
70s	Bounty BY 6012	NEGRO FOLKLORE FROM TEXAS STATE PRISON	20
57	Vogue LAE 12033	NEGRO SPIRITUALS	20
87	Broken Flag BF V8	NEVER SAY WHEN	40
72	Atlantic K 20024	THE NEW AGE OF ATLANTIC	12
80	Logo MOGO 4011	NEW ELECTRIC WARRIORS	20
53	London AL 3509	NEW ORLEANS HORNS (10")	15
56	London AL 3557	NEW ORLEANS HORNS VOLUME 2 (10")	15
67	Ace Of Hearts AH 140	NEW ORLEANS MEMORIES	12
74	Flyright LP 4708	NEW ORLEANS R&B VOLUME 1	15
74	Flyright LP 4709	NEW ORLEANS R&B VOLUME 2	15
60s	'77' 77LA 12/16	NEW ORLEANS TODAY	12
60s	'77' 77LA 12/29	NEW ORLEANS TODAY VOL. 2	12
65	Fontana TFL 6038	NEWPORT BROADSIDE — TOPICAL SONGS AT THE NEWPORT FOLK FESTIVAL 1963	25
65	Fontana TFL 6041	NEWPORT FOLK FESTIVAL EVENING CONCERT VOL. 1	25
65	Fontana TFL 6050	NEWPORT FOLK FESTIVAL VOL. 1	12
57	Philips BBL 7147	NEWPORT JAZZ FESTIVAL	12
57	Philips BBL 7152	NEWPORT JAZZ FESTIVAL	12
80s	Lakeland	NEW SONGS FOR MUTANTS: A LAKELAND COMPILATION	10
77	Vertigo 6300 902	NEW WAVE	10
72	Flyright LP 4706	NEW YORK CITY BLUES	15
55	London AL 3541	NEW YORK JAZZ OF THE ROARING TWENTIES (10")	15
72	Flyright LP 4707	NEW YORK RHYTHM AND BLUES	15
69	Island IWP(S) 6	NICE ENOUGH TO EAT (pink label)	12
57	Vanguard PPL 11004	A NIGHT AT THE APOLLO	15
88	Bam Caruso KIRI 025	NIGHTMARES IN WONDERLAND (RUBBLE VOL. 3) (LP)	12
88	Bam Caruso RUBBLE CD 2	NIGHTMARES IN WONDERLAND (RUBBLE VOL. 3) (CD)	15
69	Blue Horizon 7-63210	THE 1968 MEMPHIS COUNTRY BLUES FESTIVAL	40
50s	Tempo TAP 11	N.J.F. THIRD BRITISH FESTIVAL OF JAZZ	12
81	NMX	NMX: LIVE AT SHEFFIELD (cassette)	20
68	Spark SRLM 107	NO INTRODUCTION	20
82	ZG Music No. 5	NOISE FEST (cassette)	12
69	Trojan TTL 14	NO MORE HEARTACHES	20
70	Polydor 545 017	NON STOP SOUL	25
69	Regal Starline SRS 5013	NO ONE'S GONNA CHANGE OUR WORLD	18
64	Concert Hall AM 2339	NORTHUMBRIAN MINSTRELS	25
60	Fontana TFL 5123	NOTHIN' BUT THE BLUES (gatefold sleeve)	25
71	CBS 66278	NOTHING BUT THE BLUES (2-LP, Blue Horizon pressings may also exist)	35/50+
79	Giorno GPS	THE NOVA CONVENTION	20
70	Decca Nova SPA 72	NOVA SAMPLER	15
70s	Warm PFLP 201	NOVA-VAGA	15
79	A&M AMLE 68505	NO WAVE ('pizza' picture disc)	12
79	A&M AMLE 68505	NO WAVE (orange, mauve or blue vinyl)	each 10
69	Pama ECO 6	NU BEAT — GREATEST HITS	25
73	Elektra K 62012	NUGGETS (Original Artyfacts From The First Psychedelic Era 1965-1968) (2-LP, gatefold sleeve)	40
80s	Numa NUMA 1004	NUMA RECORDS YEAR 1 (with bonus Italian 12" "My Dying Machine")	15

O

69	Liberty LBS 83234	OAKLAND BLUES	20
80	Object Music OBJ 006	OBJECTIVITY	10
79	Rok ROK LP 001	ODD BODS, MODS AND SODS	30
58	Parlophone PMC 1072	OH BOY!	45
78	Raw RAWLP 2	OH NO IT'S MORE FROM RAW	15
72	Music F. Pleasure MFP 1416	OH! WHAT A CARRY ON	12
80	EMI ZIT 1	OI! — THE ALBUM (initially mail-order only from Sounds magazine)	30
87	Link LP 23	OI! GLORIOUS OI!	12

MINT VALUE £

84	Syndicate SYNLP 4	OI! OF SEX	12
83	Secret SEC 5	OI! OI! THAT'S YER LOT	15
75	Super Beeb BELP 004	OLD GREY WHISTLE TEST	12
64	Stateside SL 10094	OLDIES R & B	35
68	Big Shot BBTL 4001	ONCE MORE	60
69	Marmalade 643 314	100% PROOF	10
73	Charisma CLASS 3	ONE MORE CHANCE	12
63	Columbia 33SX 1536	ONE NIGHT STAND	40
63	Stateside SL 10065	ON STAGE LIVE!	40
69	Atco 228 009/010	ON STAGE — LIVE (2-LP)	18
73	Xtra XTRA 1133	ON THE ROAD AGAIN	30
64	Columbia 33SX 1662	ON THE SCENE	60
84	Sane	ON THE STREETS	12
87	Globe Of Bulbs LSD 5	OOZING THROUGH THE OZONE LAYER (cassette)	10
80s	Interior Music IM 005	OPERATION TWILIGHT	10
63	Stateside SL 10024	OPRY TIME IN TENNESSEE	15
65	Allegro ALL 778	ROY ORBISON SINGS (some tracks by Jerry Lee Lewis, Tommy Roe; black or blue label)	12
65	Ember FA 2005	ROY ORBISON AND OTHERS (with 4 tracks by Orbison)	12
67	Polydor 236 216	ORIGINAL AMERICAN FOLK BLUES FESTIVAL	15
64	Rio RLP 1	THE ORIGINAL COOL JAMAICAN SKA	60
70	Mercury SMCL 20182	ORIGINAL GOLDEN HITS OF THE GREAT BLUES SINGERS	12
73	Prince Buster PB 10	ORIGINAL GOLDEN OLDIES VOLUME 2	18
70	Mercury SMCL 20183	ORIGINAL GOLDEN RHYTHM AND BLUES HITS VOLUME 1	15
60	London HA-G 2308	THE ORIGINAL HITS	35
61	London HA-G 2339	THE ORIGINAL HITS VOL. 2	35
67	Ember SPE 6602	THE ORIGINAL SOUND OF DETROIT	15
68	United Artists ULP 1182	ORIGINAL SOUNDTRACKS OF HITS MUSIC	15
64	Vocalion VA 8017	ORIGINAL SURFIN' HITS	50
52	Vogue LDE 006	ORIGINATORS OF MODERN JAZZ (10")	12
62	London HA-U 2404	OUR SIGNIFICANT HITS	50
65	Ace Of Hearts AH 72	OUT CAME THE BLUES	18
67	Ace Of Hearts AH 158	OUT CAME THE BLUES VOLUME 2	18
71	Coral CP 58	OUT CAME THE BLUES (reissue)	12
80	Inferno INFERNO 001	OUT ON THE FLOOR TONIGHT	10
76	ABC ABCL 5192	OUT ON THE STREETS AGAIN	12

P

64	Golden Guinea GGL 0268	PACKAGE TOUR	20
68	Topic 12T 176	PADDY IN THE SMOKE (original sleeve & blue label)	12
65	Blue Beat BBLP 804	PAIN IN MY BELLY	150
55	London HA-A 2001	THE PAJAMA GAME	15
67	Island ILP 945	PAKISTANI SOUL SESSION	25
61	Parlophone PMC 1134	PARADE OF THE POPS	15
57	HMV DLP 1076	PARIS TU N'A PAS CHANGÉ	12
85	LIL LP2	PARKSIDE STEELWORKS	75
68	Studio One SOL 9009	PARTY TIME IN JAMAICA	80
78	BFD BFD 5019	PEBBLES VOL. 2	10
66	Decca LK 4824	PENTHOUSE MAGAZINE PRESENTS THE BEDSIDE BOND	25
83	Psycho PSYCHO 6	THE PERFUMED GARDEN	15
80s	Psycho PSYCHO	THE PERFUMED GARDEN II	15
81	Cherry Red BRED 15	PERSPECTIVES AND DISTORTION (gatefold sleeve)	15
76	RSO 2479 167	PETER AND THE WOLF	10
73	Phase 4 SPA 213	PHASE 4 WORLD OF SPY THRILLERS	12
86	Streetsounds PHST 1986	THE PHILADELPHIA YEARS (14-LP box set)	80
72	Apple APCOR 24	PHIL SPECTOR'S CHRISTMAS ALBUM (reissue of "A Christmas Gift For You")	25
75	Warner Bros K 59010	PHIL SPECTOR'S CHRISTMAS ALBUM (2nd reissue, some with poster)	18/12
80	Phil Spector Intl. 2307 015	PHIL SPECTOR '74/'79	12
67	Riverside RLP 4501	PIANO BLUES 1927-1933	20
70s	Storyville 671 187	PIANO BLUES	12
77	Magpie PY 4401	PIANO BLUES VOLUME 1: PARAMOUNT 1929-30	12
77	Magpie PY 4402	PIANO BLUES VOLUME 2: BRUNSWICK 1928-30	12
77	Magpie PY 4403	PIANO BLUES VOLUME 3: VOCALION 1928-30	12
77	Magpie PY 4404	PIANO BLUES VOLUME 4: THOMAS FAMILY 1925-1929	12
78	Magpie PY 4405	PIANO BLUES VOLUME 5: POSTSCRIPT 1927-1933	12
78	Magpie PY 4406	PIANO BLUES VOLUME 6: WALTER ROLAND 1933-1935	12
78	Magpie PY 4407	PIANO BLUES VOLUME 7: LEROY CARR 1930-1935	12
78	Magpie PY 4408	PIANO BLUES VOLUME 8: TEXAS SEAPORT 1934-1937	12
79	Magpie PY 4409	PIANO BLUES VOLUME 9: LOFTON/NOBLE 1935-36	12
79	Magpie PY 4410	PIANO BLUES VOLUME 10: TERRITORY BLUES 1934-41	12
80	Magpie PY 4411	PIANO BLUES VOLUME 11: TEXAS SANTA FE 1934-1937	12
80	Magpie PY 4412	PIANO BLUES VOLUME 12: THE BIG FOUR 1933-1941	12
80	Magpie PY 4413	PIANO BLUES VOLUME 13: CENTRAL HIGHWAY 1933-1941	12
80	Magpie PY 4414	PIANO BLUES VOLUME 14: THE ACCOMPANISTS 1933-41	12
81	Magpie PY 4415	PIANO BLUES VOLUME 15: DALLAS 1927-1929	12
81	Magpie PY 4416	PIANO BLUES VOLUME 16: CHARLIE SPAND 1929-1931	12
82	Magpie PY 4417	PIANO BLUES VOLUME 17: PARAMOUNT VOL. 2 1927-32	12
82	Magpie PY 4420	PIANO BLUES VOLUME 20: BARRELHOUSE YEARS 1928-33	12
82	Magpie PY 4421	PIANO BLUES VOLUME 21: UNISSUED BOOGIE 1938-1945	12
72	Delmark DL 626	PIANO BLUES ORGY	12
56	Vogue Coral LVA 9069	PIANO JAZZ — BARRELHOUSE AND BOOGIE WOOGIE	15
70s	Horse HRLP 704	PICK HITS	12
70	Harvest SHSS 1/2	PICNIC — A BREATH OF FRESH AIR (2-LP)	15
60s	Decca SKL 4084	PIECES OF EIGHT	12
72	Flyright LP 104	PIEDMONT BLUES	15
82	Cherry Red PZRED 41	PILLOWS AND PRAYERS (picture disc in printed PVC sleeve)	12

VARIOUS ARTISTS LPs & COMPILATIONS

60	HMV CLP 1362/XLP 50004	A PINCH OF SALT — BRITISH SEA SONGS OLD AND NEW	30
53	London AL 3506	PIONEERS OF BOOGIE WOOGIE (10")	30
54	London AL 3537	PIONEERS OF BOOGIE WOOGIE VOLUME TWO (10")	30
73	Trojan TBL 203	PIPELINE	15
81	K-Tel NE 1134	THE PLATINUM ALBUM	12
70s	Flyright LP 4711	PLAY MY JUKEBOX	12
81	P. Surprised KLARK 002	PLEASANTLY SURPRISED — AN HOUR OF ELOQUENT SOUNDS (cassette)	20
71	Argo ZPR 264/5	POETRY AND JAZZ IN CONCERT 250	15
86	NME 021	POGO A GOGO (cassette, mail-order via 'NME')	10
56	Mercury MPT	POP PARADE VOL. 1 (10")	18
56	Mercury MPT	POP PARADE VOL. 2 (10")	18
57	Mercury MPT 7519	POP PARADE VOL. 3 (10")	18
57	Mercury MPT 7523	POP PARADE VOL. 4 (10")	18
57	Mercury MPT 7525	POP PARADE VOL. 5 (10")	30
70	Polydor 2682 001	POP PARTY	12
68	Polydor 236 517/8/9	POP PARTY! (3-LP in box)	40
83	Fall Out FALL 032	POSH HITS VOL. 1	10
65	Post War Blues PWB 1	POST WAR BLUES: CHICAGO (99 copies only)	35
66	Post War Blues PWB 2	POST WAR BLUES: MEMPHIS ON DOWN (99 copies only)	35
67	Post War Blues PWB 3	POST WAR BLUES: EASTERN AND GULF COAST STATES (99 copies only)	35
68	Post War Blues PWB 4	POST WAR BLUES: TEXAS (99 copies only)	35
68	Post War Blues PWB 5	POST WAR BLUES: DETROIT (99 copies only)	35
60s	Post War Blues PWB 6	POST WAR BLUES: WEST COAST (99 copies only)	35
60s	Post War Blues PWB 7	POST WAR BLUES: THE DEEP SOUTH (99 copies only)	35
69	Python PWBC 1	POST WAR COLLECTOR SERIES VOL. 1 (99 copies only)	35
63	Stateside SL 10046	PREACHIN' THE BLUES	18
86	Premonition PREM 5	PREMONITION ART CONSTRUCT (cassette)	10
86	Premonition	PREMSPEAK (cassette magazine, no cat. no.)	10
80	4AD BAD 11	PRESAGES (mini-LP, green/pink or brown sleeve)	15/20
79	Preseli PRE 001	PRESELI FOLK (private pressing with insert)	30
70	Kokomo K 1006	PRE-WAR TEXAS BLUES (99 copies only)	45
74	RSO SINGL 1	PRIME CUTS (10" mini-LP)	12
83	C.B.C. 2	PRIME CUTS	10
60s	Jazz Collector JGN 1001	PRIMITIVE PIANO	20
87	A&M AMA 3906	PRINCE'S TRUST 10TH ANNIVERSARY BIRTHDAY PARTY (2-LP, with Paul McCartney 7": "Long Tall Sally"/"I Saw Her Standing There" [p/s, FREE 21])	15
63	London HA-B 8062	PRISONERS' SONGS	15
88	Bam Caruso KIRI 098	PROFESSOR JORDAN'S MAGIC SOUND SHOW (RUBBLE 10)	12
79	Blueprint BLUSP 1	PROTOTYPES	10
90	United Dairies UD 134	PSILOTRIPITAKA (3-LP [UD 01, 03 & 04], with bonus LP "Registered Nurse" [UD 00], 1,000 only, 30 in 'leather bondage' bag)	250/60
90	United Dairies UD 134CD	PSILOTRIPITAKA (3-CD [UD 01, 03 & 04], with bonus CD "Registered Nurse" [UD 00CD], 1,000 only, 30 in 'leather bondage' bag)	250/60
91	Delerium DELP 005	PSYCHEDELIC SAUNA (2-LP, 500 numbered on multi-coloured vinyl)	15
65	Sue ILP 919	PURE BLUES VOLUME ONE	40
83	Guardian GRC 2162	PURE OVERKILL	10
73	Purple TPSS 1	PURPLE PEOPLE	10
85	Color Disc COLORS 2	PURPLE TWILIGHT (400 only)	20
94	Blueye Dog PURR 2	PURR 2 (10", with Purr book)	12
68	Island ILP 978	PUT IT ON, IT'S ROCK STEADY	35
71	Pye PSA 6	PYE SALES SAMPLER (sampler for Pye & Dawn releases; 99 copies only, with release sheet)	20

Q

68	Stateside S(S)L 10209	A QUARTET OF SOUL	15
70	Trojan TBL 136	QUEEN OF THE WORLD	20
50s	Vogue LAE 12031	THE QUINTET OF THE YEAR	12

R

85	NME 014	RAGING SPOOL (cassette)	10
85	Rouska RANT 001	RAGING SUN	10
69	Polydor 236 514	RAGS, REELS AND AIRS	12
54	London AL 3515	RAGTIME PIANO ROLL (10")	20
54	London AL 3523	RAGTIME PIANO ROLL VOLUME 2 (10")	20
55	London AL 3542	RAGTIME PIANO ROLL VOLUME 3 (10")	20
57	London AL 3563	RAGTIME PIANO ROLL VOLUME 4 (10")	20
84	Womad WOMAD 001	RAINDROPS PATTERING ON BANANA LEAVES	10
76	Phil Spector Intl. 2307 008	RARE MASTERS VOL. 1	18
76	Phil Spector Intl. 2307 009	RARE MASTERS VOL. 2	12
78	Polydor 2482 274	RARE TRACKS	12
69	United Artists (S)UX 1214	RAVE	15
74	Mooncrest CREST 17	RAVE ON	12
73	Attack ATLP 1012	RAVE ON BROTHER	12
67	Ace Of Clubs ACL 1220	RAW BLUES (also stereo SCL 1220)	18
77	Raw RAWLP 1	RAW DEAL (black & white sleeve & red/blue label)	12
79	Raw RAWLP 1	RAW DEAL (reissue, yellow/black sleeve & green/white label)	10
74	GM GML 1008	READING FESTIVAL '73	12
83	Mean MNLP 82	READING ROCK VOL. 1 (2-LP)	20
64	Decca LK 4577	READY, STEADY, GO!	40
68	Pama PMLP 3	READY STEADY GO ROCKSTEADY	25
64	Decca LK 4634	READY, STEADY, WIN	45
80s	Weird	REALLY WEIRD (C90 cassette)	10
65	Stateside SL 10112	THE REAL R & B	35
80s	Recloose Org. LOOSE 12	R.O. (RECLOOSE ORGANISATION) (picture disc with insert)	20
82	Recommended 104	RECOMMENDED SAMPLER	15

MINT VALUE £

79	Destiny DS 10001	THE RECORD COLLECTOR	20
70	CBS 52797	RECORDING THE BLUES	18
65	Red Bird RB 20-102	RED BIRD GOLDIES	40
81	WEA K 58344	RED HOT ROCKABILLIES (with innersleeve)	12
69	Down Town TTL 11	RED, RED WINE VOL. 1	12
70	Trojan TBL 115	REGGAE FLIGHT 404	15
68	Big Shot BIL 3000	REGGAE GIRL	50
69	Pama ECO 3	REGGAE HITS '69 VOL. 1	20
69	Pama ECO 11	REGGAE HITS VOL. 2	20
69	Pama PTP 1001	REGGAE HIT THE TOWN	30
68	Studio One SOL 9007	REGGAE IN THE GRASS	90
71	Trojan TBL 181	REGGAE JAMAICA	12
71	Bamboo BDLP 208	REGGAEMATIC SOUNDS	50
70	Trojan TBL 144	REGGAE MOVEMENT	20
72	Trojan TBL 189	REGGAE POWER VOLUME TWO	15
70	Trojan TBL 130	REGGAE REGGAE REGGAE	15
71	Trojan TBL 176	REGGAE REGGAE REGGAE VOLUME TWO	15
70	London HA-J 8411	REGGAE REVOLUTION (unissued)	
70	London LGJ/ZGJ 101	REGGAE REVOLUTION	10
69	Coxsone CSP 2	REGGAE SPECIAL	25
70	Trojan TBL 151	REGGAE STEADY GO	15
68	Coxsone CSL 8017	REGGAE TIME	90
72	Ashanti ANB 201	REGGAE TIME	12
71	Pama PMP 2012	REGGAE TO REGGAE	25
69	Pama PSP 1004	REGGAE TO UK WITH LOVE	25
80s	Ré 0101	RE RECORDS QUARTERLY VOL. No. 1 (with book)	15
84	Anagram GRAM 17	REVENGE OF THE KILLER PUSSIES (BLOOD ON THE CATS # 2) (multi-coloured pink vinyl)	10
91	Pop God PGLP 09	REVOLUTION NO. 9	10
91	Pop God PGCD 09	REVOLUTION NO. 9 (CD)	15
64	Decca LK 4616	RHYTHM AND BLUES	60
67	Marble Arch MAL 726	RHYTHM AND BLUES	12
64	Golden Guinea GGL 0280	RHYTHM AND BLUES VOL	20
64	Golden Guinea GGL 0351	RHYTHM AND BLUES VOL. 2	12
69	Liberty LBL 83216	RHYTHM AND BLUES VOLUME 1: END OF AN ERA	20
70	Liberty LBL 83328	RHYTHM AND BLUES VOLUME 2: SWEET 'N' GREASY	20
64	Golden Guinea GGL 0293	RHYTHM AND BLUES ALL STARS	12
69	Minit MLL/MLS 40008E	RHYTHM AND BLUES CLASSICS	20
69	Minit MLL/MLS 40009E	RHYTHM AND BLUES CLASSICS VOL. 2	18
63	CBS Realm RM 101	R&B GREATS VOLUME 1	20
64	CBS Realm RM 175	R&B GREATS VOLUME 2	20
64	Mercury MCL 20019	RHYTHM AND BLUES PARTY	40
76	Philips 6436 028	RHYTHM AND BLUES PARTY (reissue)	15
73	Tamla Motown STML 11232	RIC TIC RELICS	18
68	Coxsone CSL 8015	RIDE ME DONKEY	90
69	Trojan TTL 18	RIDE YOUR DONKEY	20
81	A&M NUKE 1	RIGHT AFTER THIS... ALRIGHT? (promo only)	10
86	SMP/Inferno SINLP 3	THE RIGHT TRACK	12
55	Vogue Coral LRA 10023	RIVERBOAT JAZZ (10" LP)	15
71	London SHU 8245	RIVERTOWN BLUES	20
61	London HA-A 2338	ROCK-A-HITS	75
57	London HB-C 1067	ROCK 'N' ROLL (10")	65
59	London HA-E 2180	ROCK AND ROLL FOREVER	65
60	HMV DLP 1204	ROCKET ALONG — NEW BALLADS ON OLD LINES (10")	15
70s	Flynight FLY 662	ROCKIN' ACCORDION	10
58	Decca LF 1300	ROCKIN' AT THE '2 I'S' (10")	50
59	London HA-E 2167	ROCKIN' TOGETHER	70
77	KPM KPM 1196	ROCK ON (library edition)	60
71	Polydor 2682 002	ROCK PARTY (2-LP)	15
69	Decca LK 5002	ROCK STEADY	15
69	Pama PMLP 7	ROCKSTEADY COOL	30
68	Coxsone CSL 8013	ROCKSTEADY COXSONE STYLE	90
80	Guardian GRC 80	ROKSNAX	50
85	Rollercoaster ROLL 2008	ROLLERCOASTER ROCKERS VOLUME 1	10
80	Rapid Eye Movement	ROOM NOISE (cassette)	15
68	Atlantic Special 590 019	ROOTS OF THE BLUES	12
82	Guardian GRC 130	ROXCALIBUR	40
77	Harvest SHSP 4069	THE ROXY LONDON W.C.2 (JAN - APR 77) (with inner bag)	12
77	Harvest TC-SHSP 4069	THE ROXY LONDON W.C.2 (JAN - APR 77) (cassette)	10
91	Bam Caruso KIRI 084	RUBBLE 15: 5000 SECONDS OVER TOYLAND	15
81	Naive NAIVE 2	RUPERT PREACHING AT A PICNIC (handmade sleeve)	15
69	Xtra XTRA 1035	RURAL BLUES (2-LP)	22
69	Liberty LBL 83213	RURAL BLUES VOLUME 1: GOIN' UP THE COUNTRY	20
69	Liberty LBL 83214	RURAL BLUES VOLUME 2: SATURDAY NIGHT FUNCTION	20
70	Liberty LBL 83329	RURAL BLUES VOLUME 3: DOWN HOME STOMP	20

S

70	Transworld SPLP 101	SAMANTHA PROMOTIONS (orange cover, private pressing, a few with poster)	600
70	Transworld SPLP 102	SAMANTHA PROMOTIONS (purple cover, private pressing, a few with poster)	600
60	Parlophone PMC 1130	SATURDAY CLUB	40
64	Decca LK 4583	SATURDAY CLUB	35
67	Atlantic Special 590 007	SATURDAY NIGHT AT THE APOLLO (reissue of "Apollo Saturday Night")	20
63	Brunswick LAT/STA 8520	SATURDAY NIGHT AT THE GRAND OLE OPRY	15
70	CBS 52799	SAVANNAH SYNCOPATORS	15

MINT VALUE £

81	Suspect SU S3	SCENE OF THE CRIME.	50
65	Columbia 33SX 1730	SCENE '65	70
69	Bamboo BDLP 202	A SCORCHA FROM BAMBOO	50
80s	Barc. Towers SUPLP 2004	SCOTTISH KULTCHUR	12
68	CBS 63288	SCREENING THE BLUES	20
81	Airship AP 342	SEASIDE ROCK (2-LP, with insert)	20
66	Topic TPS 205	TOPIC SAMPLER No. 7 — SEA SONGS & SHANTIES	12
80	Statik 01	SECOND CITY STATIK — A GLASGOW COMPILATION	10
92	Imaginary ILLUSION 34	SECONDS OUT ROUND ONE — LIVE HIT THE NORTH SESSIONS (with bonus promo Boo Radleys/Scorpio Rising 12" [FREE 004]).	12
80s	Come Org. WDC 881008	THE SECOND COMING (various coloured vinyls)	60
84	Davies LP-D2 VOR 8	A SECRET LIVERPOOL (1-sided cardboard sleeve or 2-sided normal sleeve)	25/20
81	Island 12WIP 6598	THE SECRET POLICEMAN'S BALL (THE MUSIC) (mini-LP).	8
86	Dolebusters	SEE YOU LATER AGITATOR (cassette in 7" sleeve, no cat. no.).	10
68	Elektra EUK 261	SELECT ELEKTRA (also stereo EUKS 7261)	30
80s	Uniton UO 28	A SENSE OF BEAUTY	10
80	Kathedral KATH 1	SENT FROM COVENTRY (with booklet)	15
68	Atlantic 587 109	SHAKE, RATTLE AND ROLL	15
81	Albion/Shake SHAKE 1	SHAKE TO DATE.	10
81	In Phaze	SHED SOUNDS SAMPLER (cassette)	15
80s	NME	SHELTER (mail-order via 'NME')	10
74	Eron 003	SHEPWAY FOLK (with insert)	30
78	Virgin VCL 5003	SHORT CIRCUIT — LIVE AT THE ELECTRIC CIRCUS (10"; orange, yellow, blue or black vinyl)	80/50/15/8
78	Virgin VCL 5003	SHORT CIRCUIT — LIVE AT THE ELECTRIC CIRCUS (10"; black vinyl with free John Dowie EP [VED 1004])	12
87	ABC NOSE 15	SICK SICK SICK (Various Artists)	12
60s	Chess CRL 4519	SING A SONG OF SOUL	20
57	RCA Camden CDN 147	SINGIN' THE BLUES.	12
79	Sire SMP 1	THE SIRE MACHINE TURNS YOU UP.	12
57	Parlophone PMC 1047	SIX-FIVE SPECIAL	45
76	BBC REB 252	SIX-FIVE SPECIAL	12
71	Pama PMP 2015	16 DYNAMIC REGGAE HITS	18
72	Trojan TBL 191	16 DYNAMIC REGGAE HITS	18
66	Island ILP 930	SKA AT THE JAMAICA PLAYBOY CLUB (gatefold sleeve)	200
67	Coxsone CSL 8003	SKA-A-GO-GO	90
66	Doctor Bird DLM 5000	SKA-BOO-DA-BA	90
67	Studio One SOL 9000	SKA TO ROCKSTEADY	80
60s	Page One FOR 006	SKA'S THE LIMIT	18
68	Ace Of Clubs ACL 1250	SKIFFLE	30
81	Beggars Banquet BEGA 31	SLIPSTREAM — THE BEST OF BRITISH JAZZ FUNK (2-LP)	15
80s	Inevitable INEVLP 1	SMALL HITS AND NEAR MISSES	10
82	RSB 1	THE SNOOPIES ALBUM (THE LAST REMAINS OF A RICHMOND VENUE) (numbered with inserts, 1,000 only)	15
67	Polydor 583 064	SOCK IT TO 'EM	15
60s	Solar	THE SOLAR BOX SET	40
70s	United Artists LBR 1007	SOLD ON SOUL	15
71	Bamboo BDLP 212	SOLID GOLD	50
66	Atlantic ATL 5048	SOLID GOLD SOUL	18
67	Atlantic 587 058	SOLID GOLD SOUL VOL. 2	18
75	Disco Demand DDLP 5002	SOLID SOUL SENSATIONS	12
81	Some Bizzare BZLP 1	THE SOME BIZZARE ALBUM.	12
72	South. Preservation SPR 1	SOME COLD RAINY DAY	25
75	Flyright LP 114	SOME COLD RAINY DAY (reissue)	15
65	Lestar LLP 101	SOME FOLK IN LEICESTER (private pressing).	30
70	Pama PMP 2003	SOMETHING SWEET FROM THE LADY	30
84	EMI TOPCAT 1	SOMETIMES A GREAT NOTION.	10
72	Argo ZDA 147	SONGS AND MUSIC OF THE REDCOATS	15
60	Topic 12001	SONGS AGAINST THE BOMB	12
77	private pressing	SONGS AT A SUSSEX FEAST	12
79	EMI NUT 18	SONGS LENNON AND McCARTNEY GAVE AWAY	12
67	Fontana STL 5436	SONGS OF GRIEF AND GLORY.	12
69	Liberty LBX 4	SON OF GUTBUCKET	20
76	Harvest SHSM 2012	SON OF MORRIS ON	12
83	Syndicate SYNLP 3	SON OF OI!.	15
85	Natalie LIE 2	SONS FOR JOBS FOR THE BOYS.	10
72	Probe SPB 1061	SOUL BIBLE.	12
69	Direction (S)PR 28	SOUL DIRECTION	15
69	Page One POS 608	SOULED AGAIN	12
69	Polydor 584 163	SOUL FEVER	15
60s	Minit MLL 40011E	SOUL FOOD	20
69	Soul City SCB 1	SOUL FROM THE CITY.	25
70	Specialty SPE 6606	SOUL FROM THE VAULTS	12
74	Trojan TRL 65	SOULFUL REGGAE	15
70	Polydor 583 757	SOUL GOLD.	15
72	Avco 6467 251	SOUL — IN THE BEGINNING	12
68	Trojan TRL 3	SOUL OF JAMAICA	35
68	Polydor Special 236 213	SOUL PARTY	12
69	Pama PMLP 8	SOUL SAUCE FROM PAMA	22
69	Polydor 236 554	SOUL SELLER	15
70s	United Artists UAL 229018	SOUL SENSATION	12
66	Stateside SL 10186	SOUL SIXTEEN.	35
66	Sue ILP 934	SOUL '66	45
67	CBS BPG 62965	SOUL SOUNDS.	15
67	HMV CLP 3617	SOUL SOUNDS OF THE 60s	25
67	Stateside SL 10203	SOUL SUPPLY	35

86	SMP/Inferno SIMLP 4	SOUL TIME	12
65	Pye Intl. NPL 28061	THE SOUND OF BACHARACH	20
68	President PTL 1008	THE SOUND OF SOUL	12
72	United Artists UAS 29215	SOUND OF THE CITY	12
79	Grapevine GRAL 1001	SOUND OF THE GRAPEVINE	20
64	Stateside SL 10077	THE SOUND OF THE R&B HITS	35
69	Joy JOY 125	SOUNDS LIKE SKA	12
78	Sonet SNTF 806	SOUTHEND ROCK	10
69	London HAK 8405	SOUTHERN COMFORT	30
80s	Spectrum ASPEC 001	SOUTHERN COMFORT	50
60s	Saydisc Roots RL 328	SOUTHERN SANCTIFIED SINGERS	15
61	London Jazz LTZ-K 15209	SOUTHERN FOLK HERITAGE VOLUME 1: SOUNDS OF THE SOUTH	18
61	London Jazz LTZ-K 15210	SOUTHERN FOLK HERITAGE VOLUME 2: BLUE RIDGE MOUNTAIN MUSIC	18
61	London Jazz LTZ-K 15211	SOUTHERN FOLK HERITAGE VOLUME 3: ROOTS OF THE BLUES	18
61	London Jazz LTZ-K 15209	SOUTHERN FOLK HERITAGE VOLUME 7: THE BLUES ROLL ON	18
54	London AL 3529	SOUTHSIDE CHICAGO JAZZ (10")	15
71	Python PLP 10	SOUTHSIDE CHICAGO (99 copies only)	35
70	CBS Special Prod. WSR 932	SPARKLING COLOUR (multicoloured vinyl)	12
58	Tempo TAP 17	SPEAK LOW — MORE MUSIC IN THE MODERN MANNER	25
85	Music For Nations MFN 54	SPEED KILLS	10
73	Tempo TMP 9001	SPIN A MAGIC TUNE	15
57	Pye Nixa NPT 19019	SPIN WITH THE STARS — SELECTION NO. 2 (10")	18
57	Pye Nixa NPT 19021	SPIN WITH THE STARS — SELECTION NO. 3 (10")	18
65	Fontana TL 5243	SPIRITUAL AND GOSPEL FESTIVAL	15
59	Top Rank 35/064	SPIRITUALS TO SWING VOLUME 1	20
59	Top Rank 35/065	SPIRITUALS TO SWING VOLUME 2	20
82	WEA K 58415	A SPLASH OF COLOUR	15
72	CBS 67203	STARS OF THE APOLLO THEATRE (2-LP)	15
69	RCA RD 7921/2	THE STARS OF THE GRAND OLE OPRY (2-LP)	15
62	Liberty LBY 1001	THE STARS OF LIBERTY	25
57	Decca LF 1299	STARS OF THE 6.5 SPECIAL (10")	50
66	London HA-B 8269	STARS OF THE STEEL GUITAR	12
71	MFP MFP 5157	STARS SING LENNON AND McCARTNEY	12
84	Broken Flag BF V5	STATEMENT	40
84	Pleasantly Surprised PS 3	STATE OF AFFAIRS (cassette, in poly bag with foldout booklet & insert)	20
85	Statik POL 274	STATIK COMPILATION ONE (2-LP)	20
69	Stax XATS 1007	STAX SOUL EXPLOSION	15
70s	Stax STXH 5004	THE STAX STORY (VOL. 1)	12
70s	Stax STXH 5005	THE STAX STORY (VOL. 1)	12
67	Stax 589 010	THE STAX/VOLT SHOW VOL. 1	15
67	Stax 589 011	THE STAX/VOLT SHOW VOL. 2	15
78	Stiff GET 1	STIFFS LOVE STIFFS	12
60	Topic 10T 59	STILL I LOVE HIM	12
84	ABC ABCLP 3	STOMPING AT THE KLUB FOOT VOL. 1	10
84	ABC ABCLP 4	STOMPING AT THE KLUB FOOT VOL. 2	10
84	ABC ABCLP 8	STOMPING AT THE KLUB FOOT VOL. 3 & 4 (2-LP)	15
69	CBS 66218	THE STORY OF THE BLUES (2-LP)	15
70	CBS 66232	THE STORY OF THE BLUES VOLUME 2 (2-LP)	20
70	Pama PMP 2002	STRAIGHTEN UP	20
71	Pama PMP 2007	STRAIGHTEN UP VOLUME TWO	20
71	Pama PMP 2014	STRAIGHTEN UP VOLUME THREE	20
72	Pama PMP 2017	STRAIGHTEN UP VOLUME FOUR	20
77	Beggars Banquet BEGA 1	STREETS	12
80s	Streetsounds	STREETSOUND ELECTRO (box set)	60
83	Streetsounds ELCST 1	STREETSOUND ELECTRO 1	10
83	Streetsounds ELCST 2	STREETSOUND ELECTRO 2	10
84	Streetsounds ELCST 3	STREETSOUND ELECTRO 3	10
84	Streetsounds ELCST 4	STREETSOUND ELECTRO 4	10
79	Open Eye OE LP 501	STREET TO STREET — A LIVERPOOL ALBUM	20
81	Open Eye OE LP 502	STREET TO STREET — A LIVERPOOL ALBUM VOL. 2	10
81	Decca SKIN 1	STRENGTH THROUGH OI!	50
85	Wonderful World WOWLP 3	STRENGTH THROUGH OI! (reissue)	20
80s	Private Pressing CFCEPI	STUFF THE NEIGHBOURS, PLAY IT LOUD (p/s, in poly bag, with fanzine)	12
81	Chick CHR 001	SUBWAY (clear vinyl)	15
80s	INST-4	SUCK	12
65	Sue ILP 919	SUE SAMPLER RECORD FOR CLUBS (promo, no sleeve, typed labels with detail sheet)	100
65	London HA-C 8239	THE SUE STORY	40
65	Sue ILP 925	THE SUE STORY!	45
69	United Artists UAS 29028	THE SUE STORY (reissue)	15
66	Sue ILP 933	THE SUE STORY VOL. 2	45
66	Sue ILP 938	THE SUE STORY VOL. 3	50
76	Giorno GPS	SUGAR, ALCOHOL & MEAT	20
75	Island ISS 1	SUMMER '75 (promo only sampler)	15
66	Reprise R 5031	THE SUMMIT	50
86	Sun/Charly BOX 105	SUN RECORDS: THE BLUES YEARS (9-LP box with booklet)	60
81	Sunset Gun	SUNSET GUN (cassette with Sunset Gun fanzine)	15
68	Ember NR 5038	SUNSTROKE	20
73	Philips 6369 416	SUPER BLACK BLUES	15
81	Stuff S4	SUPERCOMPILATION (cassette)	10
69	Blue Horizon (S)PR 31	SUPER DUPER BLUES	20
70	Polydor 2485 002	SUPERGROUPS	12
70	Polydor 2485 003	SUPERGROUPS VOL. 2	12
68	Pye Intl. NPL 28107	SUPER SOUL	18
74	People PLEO 24	SUPER SWEET SOUL	12
64	Vocalion VA 8018	SURF BATTLE	40
71	Blue Horizon 7-66263	SWAMP BLUES (2-LP)	50

MINT VALUE £

68	Stateside S(S)L 10243	SWEET SOUL SOUNDS	25
68	Coxsone CSL 8018	SWING EASY	90
68	Saga FID 2136	SWINGING SAGA	15
58	Tempo TAP 21	SWINGIN' THE BLUES	20
93	Tenth Planet TP 002	SYDE TRYPS ONE (numbered, 500 only)	15
93	Tenth Planet TP 004	SYDE TRYPS TWO … FROM THERE TO UNCERTAINTY (numbered, 500 only)	15
93	Tenth Planet TP 006	SYDE TRYPS THREE (numbered, 500 only)	15
94	Tenth Planet TP 008	SYDE TRYPS FOUR (numbered, 500 only)	15
96	Tenth Planet TP 024	SYDE TRYPS SIX (numbered, gatefold sleeve, 1,000 only)	12

T

72	Rubber RUB 001	TAKE OFF YOUR HEAD AND LISTEN	15
71	A&M Mayfair AMLB 51029	TAKE ONE	12
86	Subway Org. SUBORG 001	TAKE THE SUBWAY TO YOUR SUBURB (mini-LP, red or yellow sleeve)	8
85	no label/cat. no.	TAKING THIS PLACE APART (cassette)	10
78	Grapevine GRAL 1000	TALK OF THE GRAPEVINE	20
65	London HA-B 8250	THE TALL 12	12
67	London HA-B 8315	THE TALL 12 VOL. 2	12
80	Fuck Off (no cat. no.)	TAPEZINE 2 (cassette)	15
70s	REL RELP 466	TARTAN ALBUM (tartan picture disc)	12
58	Capitol T 1009	TEENAGE ROCK (turquoise or 'rainbow' label)	45/40
63	Stateside SL 10020	TENNESSEE GUITAR	15
56	Nixa Jazz Today NJL 4	TENORAMA	12
77	Talisman STAL 1051	10 YEARS ON — THE UNIVERSAL FOLK CENTRE (LP)	20
70s	Fountain FV 205	TEXAS BLUES	15
69	Highway 51 H 103	TEXAS-LOUISIANA BLUES (99 copies only)	50
62	Ace Of Clubs ACL 1108	THANK YOUR LUCKY STARS	25
63	Golden Guinea GGL 0190	THANK YOUR LUCKY STARS	15
63	Decca LK 4554	THANK YOUR LUCKY STARS VOLUME 2	35
72	Dandelion 2485 021	THERE IS SOME FUN GOING FORWARD (some with poster)	18/12
69	Action ACLP 6009	THESE KIND OF BLUES VOL. 1	30
81	TTFTC 001	THE THING FROM THE CRYPT (I NEARLY DIED LAUGHING)	10
80	Decca DPA 3087/8	THEY CALLED IT ROCK'N'ROLL (2-LP)	15
57	Tempo TAP 11	THIRD BRITISH FESTIVAL OF JAZZ	12
80s	Come Org. WDC 881021	33 FÜR ILSE KOCH (some on red vinyl)	70
68	Minit MLL/MLS 40002	THIRTY-THREE MINITS OF BLUES AND SOUL	20
83	2-Tone CHR TT 5007	THIS ARE 2-TONE (with free poster, green or pink sleeve)	15
64	Island ILP 910	THIS IS BLUE BEAT (unreleased, white labels may exist)	200+
69	Island IWP 5	THIS IS THE BLUES	25
69	Chess CRL 4540	THIS IS CHESS	15
72	Peg PS 2	THIS IS FOLK VOL. 1	12
72	Peg PS 3	THIS IS FOLK VOL. 2	12
76	Loma/Warners K 56265	THIS IS LOMA VOL. 1	15
76	Loma/Warners K 56266	THIS IS LOMA VOL. 2	12
76	Loma/Warners K 56267	THIS IS LOMA VOL. 3	12
76	Loma/Warners K 56268	THIS IS LOMA VOL. 4	12
76	Loma/Warners K 56269	THIS IS LOMA VOL. 5	12
76	Loma/Warners K 56270	THIS IS LOMA VOL. 6	12
63	Oriole PS 40047	THIS IS MERSEYBEAT VOL. 1	60
63	Oriole PS 40048	THIS IS MERSEYBEAT VOL. 2	60
80	Grapevine GRAL 1002	THIS IS NORTHERN SOUL	20
69	Pama PSP 1003	THIS IS REGGAE	25
73	Island ILPS 9251	THIS IS REGGAE MUSIC	12
71	Pama PMP 2005	THIS IS REGGAE VOLUME TWO	20
71	Pama PMP 2008	THIS IS REGGAE VOLUME THREE	20
72	Pama PMP 2016	THIS IS REGGAE VOLUME FOUR	20
60s	Island IWP 3	THIS IS SUE!	22
60	Philips BBL 7356	THIS WONDERFUL WORLD OF JAZZ	12
63	RCA RD/SF 7608	THE THREE GREAT GUYS (Paul Anka, Sam Cooke & Neil Sedaka)	25
70	Saydisc Matchbox SDR182	THOSE CAKEWALKIN' BABIES FROM HOME	20
80s	Extract XX 002	THREE MINUTE SYMPHONIE	10
66	Allegro ALL 807	THUNDERBALL AND OTHER SECRET AGENT THEMES	15
69	Trojan TTL 1	TIGHTEN UP (orange label)	18
69	Trojan TTL 7	TIGHTEN UP VOLUME TWO	15
69	Trojan TTL 7	TIGHTEN UP VOLUME TWO (pink Island label with different track listing & sleeve)	40+
71	CBS SPR 52	TOGETHER!	12
84	Dog Breath WOOF 12LP	TOO LOUD TO SCREAM	10
64	Ember FA 2018	TOP OF THE POPS	12
64	Golden Guinea GGL 0277	TOP 10 HITS, ORIGINAL ARTISTS	15
63	Golden Guinea GGL 0196	TOP TV THEMES	15
60s	Marble Arch	TOP TV THEMES	12
72	Studio 2 TWO 391	TOP TV THEMES AND COMMERCIALS	15
82	Zoo ZOO 4	TO THE SHORES OF LAKE PLACID (gatefold sleeve with 4-page booklet)	18
64	Topic TPS 114	TOPIC SAMPLER NO. 1 — FOLK SONGS (blue label)	12
66	Topic TPS 145	TOPIC SAMPLER NO. 2 — FOLK SONGS (blue label)	12
66	Topic TPS 166	TOPIC SAMPLER NO. 3 — MEN AT WORK (blue label)	12
66	Topic TPS 168	TOPIC SAMPLER NO. 4 — FROM ERIN'S GREEN SHORE (blue label)	12
72	Topic TPSS 221	TOPIC SAMPLER NO. 8 — ENGLISH GARLAND (blue label)	15
56	Tempo TAP 4	TOP TRUMPETS	12
80s	Beat The System	TOTAL ANARCHY	10
83	Touch M2	TOUCH MERIDIANS 2 (cassette, in pouch with inserts)	10
55	Decca LK 4088	TRADITIONAL JAZZ AT THE ROYAL FESTIVAL HALL	20
55	Decca LK 4100	TRADITIONAL JAZZ AT THE ROYAL FESTIVAL HALL VOL. 2	15
56	Tempo LAP 8	TRADITIONAL JAZZ SCENE (10")	12
56	Tempo TAP 1	TRADITIONAL JAZZ SCENE 1956	12
72	United Artists	THE TRANSPORTS (2-LP, with book)	60

MINT VALUE £

88	Flicknife SHARP 2045	TRAVELLERS AID TRUST (2-LP, with booklet)	15
76	Eron 006	TRAVELLING FOLK (with insert)	25
70	RCA Intl. INTS 1175	TRAVELLING THIS LONESOME ROAD	12
61	'77' LA 12-2	A TREASURY OF FIELD RECORDINGS VOLUME 1	20
61	'77' LA 12-3	A TREASURY OF FIELD RECORDINGS VOLUME 2	20
61	Embassy WLP 6041	TRIBUTE TO CLIFF	15
60s	Embassy WLP 6034	TRIBUTE TO ELVIS	15
64	Columbia 33SX 1635	TRIBUTE TO MICHAEL HOLLIDAY	25
72	CBS 64861	A TRIBUTE TO WOODY GUTHRIE PART 1 (gatefold sleeve)	12
69	Key KL 003	TRIBUTE TO YOUTH PRAISE	40
80	Skeleton SKL LP 1	A TRIP TO THE DENTIST (with insert)	15
61	Parlophone PMC 1139	TRIPLE TREAT	20
71	Trojan TBL 172	TROJAN REGGAE PARTY	15
72	Trojan TALL 1	THE TROJAN STORY (3-LP set)	15
50s	Esquire 32-036	TROMBONE BY THREE	12
71	Revival RVS 1007	TROUBLE IN MIND... (GEORGIA BLUES)	12
67	Riverside RLP 8802	TUB JUG WASHBOARD BANDS	20
74	Melodisc 12-193	12 BIG HITS	20
74	Melodisc 12-217	12 CARAT GOLD	20
60s	Envoy VOY 9159	12 STRING STORY	12
66	London HA-F/SH-F 8285	THE TWELVE-STRING STORY — GUITAR SOLOS	15
83	VCL VCLP 007	21ST ANNIVERSARY INSTRUMENTAL ALBUM	12
95	XL LP 176	25TH CHAPTER	10
65	Ember EMB 3359	25 YEARS OF RHYTHM & BLUES HITS	20
63	Philips BL 7578	TWIST AT THE STAR-CLUB, HAMBURG	50

U-V

68	BBC REC 28M	ULSTER'S FLOWERY VALE	20
88	Link LINKLP 053	UNDERGROUND ROCKERS	10
69	Island ILP 993/ILPS 9093	THE UNFOLDING OF THE BOOK OF LIFE VOL. 1	20
69	Island ILP 994/ILPS 9094	THE UNFOLDING OF THE BOOK OF LIFE VOL. 2 (unissued)	
89	Unicorn PHZA 23	UNICORN 3 — INTO THE LIGHT	10
70s	Flyright FLY 577	UNISSUED CHICAGO BLUES	12
69	Pama ECO 7	UNITY'S GREATEST	25
80	Safari UPP 1	UPPERS ON THE SOUTH DOWNS (original issue without Purple Hearts)	12
68	Atlantic 588 122	UPTOWN SOUL	15
88	Urban URBLP 15	URBAN ACID	15
77	Speciality SNTF 5023	URBAN BLUES	12
69	Liberty LBL 83215	URBAN BLUES VOLUME 1: BLUES UPTOWN	20
70	Liberty LBL 83327	URBAN BLUES VOLUME 2: NEW ORLEANS BOUNCE	20
80	Pungent PUN 1	URBAN DEVELOPMENT (cassette, with/without Fumes fanzine)	20/12
72	Village Thing VTSAM 15	US	12
50s	Audubon AAM	VAUDEVILLE (10")	20
70	VJM VLP 30	VAUDEVILLE BLUES	15
78	Attrix RB 03	VAULTAGE '78 (TWO SIDES OF BRIGHTON) (originally hand-screened sleeve, later with insert)	12/10
71	Trojan TBL 175	VERSION GALORE VERSION TWO	15
73	Trojan TBL 200	VERSION GALORE VERSION THREE	15
72	Trojan TBL 182	VERSION TO VERSION	15
73	Trojan TBL 206	VERSION TO VERSION VOLUME THREE	15
70	Vertigo 6499 407/8	VERTIGO ANNUAL 1970 (2-LP, set no.: 6657 001)	25
55	Philips BBR 8071	VISIT TO JAZZLAND (10")	12
55	Philips	VISIT TO JAZZLAND NO. 2 (10")	12
56	Philips BBR 8098	VISIT TO JAZZLAND NO. 3 (10")	12
80s	Recommended RM 01	VOICES, NOTES AND NOISE	15

W

70s	Object Music OBJ 007	WAITING ROOM	10
62	Columbia 33SX 1385	WAKEY WAKEY	25
85	Psycho PSYCHO 35	THE WAKING DREAM	15
64	Pye Intl. NPL 28041	WALKING BY MYSELF	30
64	Pye Intl. NPL 28044	WALKING THE BLUES	25
73	Flyright LP 503	THE WALKING VICTROLA	12
81	Phil Spector Intl. WOS 001	WALL OF SOUND (9-LP box set)	45
78	CBS WOW 100	THE WAR OF THE WORLDS (boxed 2-LP, book & poster)	15
63	Ace Of Hearts AH 55	WASHBOARD RHYTHM	15
70s	Polydor 218 006	WAY INTO THE 70'S	12
78	Bridgehouse BHLP 001	A WEEKEND AT THE BRIDGEHOUSE E16 (with bonus 12" EP)	30
85	Music For Nations MFN 49	WELCOME TO THE METAL ZONE (2-LP)	18
59	Coral LVA 9096	WE LIKE GIRLS	20
59	Coral LVA 9098	WE LIKE GUYS	20
71	Wand WCS 1004	WE'RE LEAVIN' IT UP TO YOU	12
63	London HA-P 8061	WE SING THE BLUES	60
65	Liberty LBY 3051	WE SING THE BLUES	45
65	Sue ILP 921	WE SING THE BLUES!	45
72	Syndicate Chapter SC 005	WE THREE KINGS	15
70	Trojan TTL 34	WHAT AM I TO DO	20
80s	Rather/17 RATHER 13	WHAT A NICE WAY TO TURN SEVENTEEN NO. 3 (with magazine)	12
80s	Seventeen SEVENTEEN 6	WHAT A NICE WAY TO TURN SEVENTEEN NO. 6 (with magazine)	12
68	Elektra EKS 7304	WHAT'S SHAKIN' (reissue of "Good Time Music")	15
80	S & T	WHERE THE HELL IS LEICESTER? (with bonus single & booklet)	15
87	Sunrise A 40111 M	WHERE WOULD YOU RATHER BE TONIGHT?	10
83	Kamera KAM 14	THE WHIP (with insert)	20
79	London Bomp DHS-Z 3	WHO PUT THE BOMP? (2-LP, gatefold sleeve)	15
70	Trojan TBL 131	WHO YOU GONNA RUN TO	25
72	private pressing	WHOLLY GRAIL	25
61	Philips BBL 7430	WINNERS OF DOWNBEAT'S INTERNATIONAL CRITICS' POLL 1960	12

66	Dot DLP 3535	WIPE OUT	15
76	RCA RS 1085	WIZARD'S CONVENTION (with insert)	12
82	Womad WOMAD 001	WOMAD: RAINDROPS CLATTERING ON BANANA LEAVES	15
67	RCA Victor RD 7840	WOMEN OF THE BLUES	20
81	Stiff FREEB 3	WONDERFUL TIME OUT THERE (Xmas freebie)	12
81	Glass GLASS 010	THE WONDERFUL WORLD OF GLASS	15
70s	Readers Digest RDS 6704	WONDERLAND OF SOUND (10-LP set)	30
70	Atlantic 2663 001	WOODSTOCK (3-LP in foldout sleeve with inners)	20
71	Atlantic 2657 003	WOODSTOCK II (2-LP)	15
96	Magna Carta MA 9010/2	WORKING MAN (LP)	15
63	London HA-P 8099	A WORLD OF BLUES	30
69	Decca (S)PA-R 14	THE WORLD OF BLUES POWER	12
70	Decca (S)PA 63	THE WORLD OF BLUES POWER VOL. 2	12
73	Decca SPA 263	THE WORLD OF BLUES POWER VOL. 3	18
69	Pama SECO 19	A WORLD OF BULLET	25
71	Decca SPA 156	WORLD OF CONTEMPORARY FOLK	12
71	Argo SPA-A 132	THE WORLD OF FOLK	15
71	Decca SPA 124	THE WORLD OF SOUL POWER	12
72	Decca SPA 217	WORLD OF T.V. THEMES	12
70s	United Nations 88 888 DY	WORLD STAR FESTIVAL	12
78	Yuk NE 1023	THE WORLD'S WORST RECORD SHOW (multi-coloured vinyl)	12
89	Woronzow WOO 10	WORONZOID (2-LP, with insert)	15
69	Decca (S)PA 34	WOWIE ZOWIE! — THE WORLD OF PROGRESSIVE MUSIC	15
84	Creation CRELP 002	WOW, WILD SUMMER! (original with £2.99 price & white background)	10

Y-Z

92	Strange Fruit SFPMA	THE YEAR OF THE SPECTACLE: The Hut Recordings Peel Sessions (10" LP)	10
70s	P. Spec. Intl. PSI 2307 007	YESTERDAY'S HITS TODAY	12
69	Island IWPS 2	YOU CAN ALL JOIN IN (pink label)	12
70	Trojan TBL 142	YOU CAN'T WINE	15
69	Trojan TTL 9	YOU LEFT ME STANDING	20
78	Stiff DEAL 1	YOU'RE EITHER ON THE TRAIN OR OFF THE TRAIN (promo only, with booklet)	12
62	HMV CLP 1565	YOUR FAVOURITE TV AND RADIO THEMES	15
63	HMV CLP 1676	YOUR FAVOURITE TV AND RADIO THEMES (VOL. 3)	15
66	HMV CLP 3521	YOUR FAVOURITE TV AND RADIO THEMES (VOL. 5)	15
71	Bamboo BDLP 211	YOUR JAMAICAN GIRL	50
82	Statik STATLP 7	YOUR SECRET'S SAFE WITH US (2-LP)	20
84	Zulu ZULU 6	THE ZULU COMPILATION	20
80s	Relentless R 101	!!?!... A TASTER	12

TV & FILM SOUNDTRACK LPs
(alphabetical by title, composers/artists in brackets)
(N.B. Only the first issues of soundtracks by the Beatles and Elvis Presley are listed below: for later repressings see their individual entries.)

A

73	United Artists UAS 29451	ACROSS 110TH STREET (J.J. Johnson & Bobby Womack)	20
70	Paramount SPFL 260	THE ADVENTURERS (Antonio Carlos Jobim)	15
73	Bell BELLS 228	ADVENTURES OF BARRY MACKENZIE (Peter Best)	12
62	RCA RD 7512	ADVISE AND CONSENT (Jerry Fielding)	15
64	Parlophone PMC 1230	A HARD DAY'S NIGHT (Beatles) (1st pressing, with "The Parlophone Co. Ltd" label rim copy & "Sold In The UK..." text; mono, with mid-sized "mono" lettering on front cover)	35
64	Parlophone PCS 3058	A HARD DAY'S NIGHT (Beatles) (1st pressing, with "The Parlophone Co. Ltd" label rim copy & "Sold In The UK..." text; stereo, with mid-sized "stereo" lettering on front cover)	60
70	MCA MKPS 2010	AIRPORT (Alfred Newman)	12
67	United Artists (S)ULP 1172	AFRICA ADDIO (Riz Ortolani)	20
66	United Artists (S)ULP 1151	AFTER THE FOX (Burt Bacharach/Hollies)	35
60	Philips BBL 7429	THE ALAMO (also stereo SBBL 599) (Dimitri Tiomkin)	12/15
56	Nixa NPT 19010	ALEXANDER THE GREAT (Mario Nascimbene) (10"; beware of counterfeits)	200
72	Impulse IMPL 8050	ALFIE (Sonny Rollins)	35
69	MGM CS 8112	ALFRED THE GREAT (Ray Leppard)	150
72	Warner Bros K 56009	ALICE'S ADVENTURES IN WONDERLAND (John Barry) (gatefold sleeve)	15
79	20th Century/RCA T 593	ALIEN (Jerry Goldsmith)	15
61	Fontana STFL 591	ALL NIGHT LONG (Dave Brubeck/Johnny Dankworth, et al.)	30
71	Buddah 2318 034	ALL THE RIGHT NOISES (Melanie)	15
65	Reprise R 6151	AMERICANIZATION OF EMILY (Johnny Mandel)	20
76	Polydor 2383 405	AMERICANS (John Barry)	20
65	RCA RD 7732	THE AMOROUS ADVENTURES OF MOLL FLANDERS (John Addison)	35
57	Brunswick LAT 8175	ANASTASIA (Alfred Newman)	15
60	Philips SBBL 514	ANATOMY OF A MURDER (Duke Ellington)	15
76	BBC REB 236	ANGELS AND 15 OTHER BBC TV THEMES (Alan Parker, et al.)	15
50s	MGM CD 1	ANNIE GET YOUR GUN (musical) (10") (Betty Hutton, et al.)	12
72	Polydor 2383 109	ANTONY AND CLEOPATRA (John Scott) (foldout sleeve)	35
56	Brunswick LAT 8118	ANYTHING GOES (Bing Crosby, et al.)	12
60	London HA-T 2287	THE APARTMENT (Adolph Deutsch)	15
76	Polydor 2489 113	L'APOCALYPSE DES ANIMAUX (Vangelis)	15
79	Elektra K 62025	APOCALYPSE NOW (2-LP)	15
69	CBS 70054	APRIL FOOLS (Marvin Hamlisch)	15
58	London HA-D 2078	APRIL LOVE (Pat Boone/Shirley Jones/Lionel Newman Orchestra)	15
66	RCA Victor RD 7817	ARABESQUE (Henry Mancini)	18
57	Brunswick STA 3008	AROUND THE WORLD IN EIGHTY DAYS (Victor Young)	12
66	Fontana FJL 135	L'ASCENSEUR POUR L'ECHAFAUD/FEMME DISPARAISSANTE (Miles Davis/Art Blakey [1 side each])	45

MINT VALUE £

54	HMV DLPC 1	AS LONG AS THEY'RE HAPPY (Jack Buchanan) (10")	50
87	Illegal ILP 017	ATHENS, GA. — INSIDE/OUT (R.E.M.)	12
67	Pye NPL 18198	AT LAST THE 1948 SHOW (TV soundtrack)	12
67	Marble Arch MAL 695	THE AVENGERS AND OTHER FAVOURITES (Laurie Johnson)	40

B

66	Fontana TL 5306	BABY, THE RAIN MUST FALL (Elmer Bernstein)	35
62	Pye Intl. NPL 28020	BARABBAS (Mario Nascimbene)	15
68	Stateside (S)SL 10260	BARBARELLA (Bob Crewe/Charles Fox)	75
67	London HA-D 8337	BAREFOOT IN THE PARK (Neal Hefti)	25
75	Warner Bros K 56189	BARRY LYNDON (Leonard Rosenman)	15
66	Stateside S(S)L 10179	BATMAN (Nelson Riddle) (TV show music)	50
89	W.B./Paisley Park WX 281P	BATMAN (Prince) (picture disc, die-cut sleeve)	20
89	W.B./Paisley Park 925 978-2	BATMAN (Prince) (CD, picture disc in 'Bat' tin with booklet)	20
89	W.B./Paisley Park 927 489-2	BATMAN (Prince) (CD, picture disc)	15
69	United Artists UAS 29019	BATTLE OF BRITAIN (Ron Goodwin)	15
66	Warner Bros W 1617	BATTLE OF THE BULGE (Benjamin Frankel)	25
60	Columbia 33SX 1225	BEAT GIRL (John Barry/Adam Faith)	40
57	London HAP 2056	BEAU JAMES (Joseph Lilley)	15
64	RCA Victor RD 7679	BECKET (dialogue only)	15
68	Decca LK/SKL 4923	BEDAZZLED (Peter Cook/Dudley Moore)	100
70	Island ILPS 9140	BE GLAD FOR THE SONG HAS NO ENDING (Incredible String Band)	12
60	Capitol W/SW 1435	BELLS ARE RINGING (André Previn) (mono/stereo)	15/18
73	Ronco RR 2006	THE BELSTONE FOX (Laurie Johnson) (gatefold sleeve)	18
72	Tamla Motown STML 11220	BEN (Michael Jackson)	12
60	MGM MGM-C(S) 802	BEN HUR (Miklos Rozsa) (box set with hardback book; mono/stereo)	15/20
70	Stateside SSL 10311	BEYOND THE VALLEY OF THE DOLLS (Stu Phillips/Strawberry Alarm Clock)	90
66	Stateside S(S)L 10188	THE BIBLE (Toshiro Mayuzumi)	15
75	Music For Pleasure MFP 50227	BIG BOND MOVIE THEMES (Geoff Love) (2 different sleeves; 1st design with front-facing Roger Moore illustration)	each 15
59	London HA-T 2142	THE BIG COUNTRY (Jerome Moross) ('sun' cover)	20
61	HMV CSD 1408	THE BIG COUNTRY (Jerome Moross) ('cast' cover)	12
68	MGM MGM-C(S) 8066	BIGGEST BUNDLE OF THEM ALL (Riz Ortolani/Eric Burdon)	25
86	MCA MCF 3328	BIGGLES (Stanislas/Deep Purple/Motley Crue et al.)	18
69	United Artists (S)ULP 1228	THE BIG GUNDOWN (Ennio Morricone)	15
68	Studio Two TWO 257	THE BIG THEMES (Hugo Winterhalter)	12
77	Warner Bros K 56375	BILITIS (gatefold sleeve) (Francis Lai)	12
67	United Artists (S)ULP 1183	BILLION DOLLAR BRAIN (Richard Rodney Bennett)	25
71	Warner Bros WS 1926	BILLY JACK (Mundell Lowe, et al.)	15
88	CBS 461 002-1	BIRD (Charlie Parker, et al.)	12
73	Polydor 2490 117	BLACK CAESAR (James Brown)	35
62	Stateside SL 10026	BLACK NATIVITY (Alex Bradford)	20
72	Pye NSPL 18376	BLOOMFIELD (Johnny Harris)	12
66	MGM MGM-C(S) 8039	BLOW-UP (Herbie Hancock/Yardbirds)	75
68	Dot (S)LPD 508	BLUE (Manos Hadjidakis)	30
78	MCA MCF 2836	BLUE COLLAR (Jack Nitzsche/Captain Beefheart/Ry Cooder, et al.)	12
61	RCA RD 27238/SF 5115	BLUE HAWAII (Elvis Presley) (black/silver label, mono/stereo)	18/30
60s	RCA Victor RD 27238	BLUE HAWAII (Elvis Presley) (black/silver label, also stereo SF 5115)	15/25
66	RCA RD 7795	BOEING BOEING (Neal Hefti)	25
68	MCA MUPS 360	BOOM! (John Barry/Georgie Fame)	70
68	Warner Bros W 1742	BONNIE AND CLYDE (Charles Strouse)	20
66	MGM MGM-C(S) 8010	BORN FREE (John Barry/Matt Monro)	18
70	Paramount SPFL 263	BORSALINO (Claude Bolling)	15
58	RCA RD 27054	BOTH ENDS OF THE CANDLE (Gogi Grant)	15
71	CBS 70078	THE BOY NAMED CHARLIE BROWN (Rod McKuen)	15
57	Brunswick LAT 8193	BOY ON A DOLPHIN (Hugo Friedhoffer)	40
79	A&M AMLH 64731	THE BOYS FROM BRAZIL (Jerry Goldsmith)	12
77	United Artists UAG 30097	A BRIDGE TOO FAR (John Addison) (gatefold sleeve)	12
80	MCA MCF 2013	BUCK ROGERS IN THE 25th CENTURY (Stu Phillips)	12
72	Bell BELLS 209	THE BURGLARS (Ennio Morricone)	15
66	RCA RD 7791	BUNNY LAKE IS MISSING (Paul Glass/Zombies)	40
65	Liberty LBY 1246	BURKE'S LAW (Herschel/Burke/Gilbert) (TV series music)	15
70	A&M AMLS 963	BUTCH CASSIDY AND THE SUNDANCE KID (Burt Bacharach)	15
63	RCA Victor RD/SF 7580	BYE BYE BIRDIE (musical) (Charles Strouse)	18/22

C

56	Philips BBR 8104	CALAMITY JANE (Doris Day/Howard Keel) (10")	20
66	RCA Victor RD/SF 7820	CALIFORNIA HOLIDAY (Elvis Presley) (black/red dot labels, mono/stereo)	18/22
53	Brunswick LA 8603	CALL ME MADAM (Ethel Merman) (10")	12
69	Stateside (S)SL 10276	CANDY (Dave Grusin/Steppenwolf, et al.)	20
60	Capitol SW 1301	CAN CAN (Nelson Riddle)	12
69	MCA MUPS 380	CAN HIERONYMUS MERKIN EVER FORGET MERCY HUMPPE AND FIND TRUE HAPPINESS? (Anthony Newley)	15
60	Delyse DL 3057/DLS 6057	CAPTAIN HORATIO HORNBLOWER (Robert Farnon) (mono/stereo)	60/75
55	Brunswick LAT 8057	CARMEN JONES (Harry Belafonte, et al.)	20
64	MGM MGM-C 984	THE CARPETBAGGERS (Elmer Bernstein)	15
64	London HA-A/SH-A 8219	THE CARPETBAGGERS (Elmer Bernstein)	15
76	MCA MCSP 278	CAR WASH (2-LP, gatefold sleeve) (Rose Royce/Pointer Sisters)	12
67	RCA Victor RD/SF 7874	CASINO ROYALE (Burt Bacharach/Herb Alpert/Dusty Springfield) (mono/stereo)	50/60
66	United Artists (S)ULP 1140	CAST A GIANT SHADOW (Elmer Bernstein/Vince Hill)	15
71	Polydor 2383 035	CATCH MY SOUL (P.J. Proby/P.P. Arnold, et al.)	15
65	Columbia SX 1756	CATCH US IF YOU CAN (Dave Clark Five)	35
62	F'tana TFL 5170/STFL 585	CHANNEL THRILL: THE T.V. THRILLER THEMES (Johnny Gregory)	12/15
62	Warner Bros WS 8177	THE CHAPMAN REPORT (Leonard Rosenman)	15
63	RCA SF 7620	CHARADE (Henry Mancini)	30
63	MGM MGM-C 969	THE CHARGE IS MURDER (John Green)	20

MINT VALUE £

68	United Artists SULP 1189	THE CHARGE OF THE LIGHT BRIGADE (John Addison/Manfred Mann)	15
81	Polydor POLS 1026	CHARIOTS OF FIRE (Vangelis) (gatefold sleeve)	20
83	Polydor BOX 1	CHARIOTS OF FIRE (Vangelis) (box set)	20
66	CBS (S)BPG 62665	THE CHASE (John Barry) (mono/stereo)	30/40
69	Polydor 583 736	CHE! (Lalo Schifrin)	15
69	United Artists UAS 29049	CHICAGO, CHICAGO (Henry Mancini)	15
67	Fontana TL 5417	CHIMES AT MIDNIGHT (Angelo Lavagnino)	50
74	ABC ABCL 5068	CHINATOWN (Jerry Goldsmith)	20
68	United Artists (S)ULP 1200	CHITTY CHITTY BANG BANG (Sherman Brothers) (gatefold sleeve)	15
50s	Columbia OL 5190	CINDERELLA (Oliver Wallace) (also stereo OS 2005)	12
50s	Columbia OL 6330	CINDERELLA (Oliver Wallace) (remake, also stereo OS 2730)	12
73	Pye Intl. NSPL 28193	CINDERELLA LIBERTY (John Williams)	12
68	RCA Victor RD/SF 7917	CLAMBAKE (Elvis Presley) (black/red dot labels, mono/stereo)	20/25
81	CBS 73588	CLASH OF THE TITANS (Laurence Rosenthal)	12
74	Buddah BDLP 4010	CLAUDINE (Curtis Mayfield/Gladys Knight)	12
63	Stateside S(S)L 10044	CLEOPATRA (Alex North)	15
72	Warner Bros K 46127	A CLOCKWORK ORANGE (Walter Carlos)	12
85	IMS MILCH 014	CODENAME WILDGEESE (Eloy)	12
73	Purple TPSM 2001	COLDITZ BREAKPOINT! (TV soundtrack)	12
65	Fontana (S)TL 5259	THE COLLECTOR (Maurice Jarre)	25
78	MGM 2315 398	COMA (Jerry Goldsmith)	12
67	MGM MGM-C(S) 8058	THE COMEDIANS (Laurence Rosenthal)	15
72	Pye NSPL 18389	CONCERTO FOR HARRY — SOMETHING TO HIDE (Roy Budd)	40
71	Philips 6332 033	CONTINENTAL CIRCUS (Gong)	30
62	Parlophone PMC 1194	THE COOL MIKADO (John Barry Seven/Frankie Howerd, et al.)	80
67	Brunswick AXA 4544	COUNTESS FROM HONG KONG (Charles Chaplin) (with booklet)	15
74	RCA Victor APL 1 0270	COUNTRY GENTLEMEN (Henry Mancini)	15
70	Capitol E-ST 640	CROMWELL (Frank Cordell)	15
70	Word WST 5550	THE CROSS & THE SWITCHBLADE (Ralph Carmichael)	25
77	EMI EMA 782	CROSS OF IRON (Ernest Gold) (gatefold sleeve)	15
80	CBS 70182	CRUISING (various artists)	12
73	Buddah 2318 091	CURTIS IN CHICAGO (Curtis Mayfield/Impressions/Jerry Butler, Gene Chandler, Leroy Hutson) (TV soundtrack, gatefold sleeve)	12
68	Stateside (S)SL 10222	CUSTER OF THE WEST (Bernardo Segall)	40

D

62	Fontana TFL 5184	DANGEROUS FRIENDSHIPS (Art Blakey, et. al.)	18
70	RCA SF 8138	DARLIN' LILI (Henry Mancini) (gatefold sleeve)	15
74	Phase 4 Stereo PFS 4339	THE DAY OF THE LOCUST (John Barry)	18
67	Stateside (S)SL 10217	THE DAY THE FISH CAME OUT (Mikis Theodorakis)	15
68	Stateside (S)SL 10263	DEADFALL (John Barry/Shirley Barry)	40
79	EMI EMC 3256	DEATH ON THE NILE (Nino Rota)	12
74	CBS 80546	DEATH WISH (Herbie Hancock)	25
68	Stateside (S)SL 10259	DECLINE AND FALL... OF A BIRDWATCHER (Ron Goodwin)	100
77	Casablanca CAL 2018	THE DEEP (John Barry/Donna Summer)	15
55	MGM MGM-C 755	DEEP IN MY HEART (Howard Keel/Vic Damone, et al.)	12
73	Warner Bros K 46214	DELIVERANCE (Eric Weissberg)	15
58	London HA-D 2111	DESIRE UNDER THE ELMS (Elmer Bernstein)	18
63	Colpix PXL 440	DIAMOND HEAD (John Williams)	20
76	Bradley BRADS 8002	DIAMONDS (Roy Budd)	60
71	United Artists UAS 29216	DIAMONDS ARE FOREVER (John Barry/Shirley Bassey)	18
59	Top Rank RX 3016	THE DIARY OF ANNE FRANK (Alfred Newman)	60
83	Ripple (no cat. no.)	DIGITAL DREAMS (Bill Wyman) (promo only)	100
68	MGM MGM-C(S) 8048	DIRTY DOZEN (Frank de Vol) (yellow label)	15
67	Stateside S(S)L 10214	DOCTOR DOLITTLE (Lionel Newman) (foldout sleeve)	20
62	Columbia 33SX 1446	DON'T KNOCK THE TWIST (Chubby Checker/Gene Chandler, et al.)	25
67	RCA Victor RD/SF 7892	DOUBLE TROUBLE (Elvis Presley) (black/red dot labels, mono/stereo)	18/22
67	CBS S 63189	DR. FAUSTUS (Mario Nascimbene/Cambridge College Choir) (g/fold sleeve)	75
65	United Artists (S)ULP 1097	DOCTOR NO (Monty Norman) (mono/stereo)	18/20
69	Capitol EST 672	THE DOUBLE DECKERS (TV soundtrack)	25
70s	Music For Pleasure	DOUGAL AND THE BLUE CAT	12
87	Crammed MTM 14	DOWN BY LAW (John Lurie)	15
74	Studio Two TWO 500	DRACULA (HAMMER PRESENTS...) (Christopher Lee) (gatefold sleeve)	15
70	President PTLS 1068	DRAKE'S DREAM (Paul Jones)	12
83	Charisma CAS 1158	THE DRAUGHTSMAN'S CONTRACT (Michael Nyman)	20
74	RCA RD/SF 7846	DROP DEAD... DARLING (Dennis Farnon)	12
59	Parlophone PMCL 1101	DRUMBEAT (Adam Faith/John Barry Seven, et al.)	60
60	HMV CLP 1352/CSD 1296	DRUM CRAZY (THE GENE KRUPA STORY) (Leith Stevens) (mono/stereo)	12/15
66	United Artists (S)ULP 1141	DUEL AT DIABLO (Neal Hefti)	15
58	Decca LF 1308	THE DUKE WORE JEANS (Tommy Steele) (10")	15
84	Polydor 422 8237-7	DUNE (LP, Toto, 1 track by Brian Eno)	15

E

75	MCA MCF 2580	EARTHQUAKE (John Williams)	15
56	MGM D 140	EASTER PARADE/SINGIN' IN THE RAIN (Judy Garland/Gene Kelly) (10")	25
69	Stateside-Dunhill SSL 5018	EASY RIDER (Steppenwolf/Jimi Hendrix/Byrds, et al.)	15
54	Brunswick	THE EGYPTIAN (Alfred Newman)	40
61	MGM MGM-C 876	EL CID (Miklos Rosza) (also stereo [CS 6048])	12/15
67	Columbia S(C)X 6155	EL DORADO (Nelson Riddle)	25
73	United Artists UAS 29486	ELECTRA GLIDE IN BLUE (James William Guercio)	15
69	RCA Victor RD/SF 8011	ELVIS ("TV Special", mono)	12
74	Warner Bros K 56084	EMMANUELLE (Pierre Bachelet)	15
76	Warner Bros K 56231	EMMANUELLE 2 (Francis Lai)	12
57	Vogue Coral LVA 9063	END AS A MAN (Kenyon Hopkins)	30
74	DJM DJLPS 431	ENGLAND MADE ME (John Scott)	12
74	Warner Bros K 46275	ENTER THE DRAGON (Lalo Schifrin)	25
84	Alt. Ten. VIRUS 30	ERASERHEAD (with insert)	20

MINT VALUE £

76	EMI EMC 3148	ESCAPE FROM THE DARK (Ron Goodwin)	25
63	Parlophone PMC 1198	THE ESTABLISHMENT (Peter Cook, et al.)	15
82	MCA MCFP 3160	E.T. (THE EXTRA TERRESTRIAL) (John Williams) (picture disc)	12
83	MCA MCA 70000	E.T. — THE EXTRA TERRESTRIAL (John Williams) (box set, with booklet & poster)	50
83	MCA CAC 70000	E.T. — THE EXTRA TERRESTRIAL (John Williams) (cassette, box set, with booklet & poster)	25
67	Brunswick LAT 8678	AN EVENING WITH BORIS KARLOFF AND FRIENDS	35
61	London HA-T 2362	EXODUS (Ernest Gold)	12
74	Warner Bros K 56071	THE EXORCIST (Jack Nitzsche, et al.)	20
71	Ember NR 5057	EXPERIENCE — THE ORIGINAL SOUNDTRACK (Jimi Hendrix) (g/fold sleeve)	12
72	Deram SML 1095	EXTREEMS (Tony Klinger & Michael Lyons)	25
78	CBS 70163	EYES OF LAURA MARS (Artie Kane/Babs Streisand)	12

F

57	Capitol LCT 6139	A FACE IN THE CROWD (Tom Glazer) (10")	20
64	CBS (S)BPG 62277	FALL OF THE ROMAN EMPIRE (Dimitri Tiomkin)	15
67	Decca LK/SKL 4847	THE FAMILY WAY (Paul McCartney/George Martin) (mono/stereo)	75
60	Top Rank 30/003/4/5	FANTASIA (various classical pieces) (3-LP, with book)	30
58	Capitol LCT 6162	A FAREWELL TO ARMS (Mario Nascimbene)	15
67	MGM MGM-C(S) 8053	FAR FROM THE MADDING CROWD (Richard Rodney Bennett)	25
68	London HA-U/SH-U 8358	THE FASTEST GUITAR ALIVE (Roy Orbison)	35
67	Stateside S(S)L 10213	FATHOM (Johnny Dankworth)	40
73	Pye NSPL 18398	FEAR IS THE KEY (Roy Budd)	60
70	United Artists UAS 29118	FELLINI-SATYRICON (Nino Rota)	12
65	Columbia 33SX 1693	FERRY CROSS THE MERSEY (Gerry & Pacemakers/Cilla Black/Fourmost) (also stereo SCX 3544)	25/35
63	CBS SBPG 62148	55 DAYS AT PEKING (Dimitri Tiomkin/Andy Williams)	18
72	RCA Victor SF 8127	FILM THEMES A-Z (Henry Mancini)	12
66	Columbia S(C)X 6079	FINDERS KEEPERS (Cliff Richard) (with inner sleeve, mono/stereo)	15/20
68	Warner Bros WF(S) 2550	FINIAN'S RAINBOW (Fred Astaire, et al.)	20
57	Brunswick LAT 8194	FIRE DOWN BELOW (Arthur Benjamin)	40
84	MCA MCF 3233	FIRESTARTER (Tangerine Dream)	12
78	United Artists UAS 30181	F-I-S-T (Bill Conti)	12
67	RCA Victor RD/SF 7875	A FISTFUL OF DOLLARS (Ennio Morricone)	20
68	RCA Victor RD 7994	A FISTFUL OF DOLLARS/FOR A FEW DOLLARS MORE/ THE GOOD, THE BAD AND THE UGLY (Hugo Montenegro)	12
70	RCA Camden CDS 1052	A FISTFUL OF DOLLARS/FOR A FEW DOLLARS MORE (Ennio Morricone)	12
72	United Artists UAS 29345	A FISTFUL OF DYNAMITE (Ennio Morricone)	15
71	CBS 70091	FIVE EASY PIECES (Tammy Wynette, et al.)	12
59	London SH-U 6044	THE FIVE PENNIES (Danny Kaye, et al.) (gatefold sleeve)	12
65	RCA Victor RD 7723	FLAMING STAR AND SUMMER KISSES (Elvis Presley) (black labels, later orange)	100/350
75	Chrysalis CHR 1081	FLASH FEARLESS V THE ZORG WOMEN PARTS 5 & 6 (Alice Cooper, Elkie Brooks, et al.)	15
85	Heavy Metal HMI PD 29	FLASHPOINT (Tangerine Dream) (picture disc)	15
85	Heavy Metal HMXD 29	FLASHPOINT (Tangerine Dream) (CD, playable [most copies faulty])	50
61	Golden Guinea GGL 0092	THE FLINTSTONES (TV soundtrack)	15
66	Hanna Barbera HLP 8	THE FLINTSTONES IN S.A.S.F.A.T.P.O.G.O.B.S.Q.A.L.T. (TV soundtrack)	15
62	Brunswick LAT 8392	FLOWER DRUM SONG (Nancy Kwan, et al.) (also stereo STA 3054)	12/18
64	Ace Of Clubs ACL 1166	FLYING CLIPPER (Riz Ortolani)	25
63	MGM MGM-C/CS 6068	FOLLOW THE BOYS (Connie Francis) (mono/stereo)	15/20
62	MGM MGM-C 882	THE 4 HORSEMEN OF THE APOCALYPSE (André Previn)	12
65	Ember NR 5029	FOUR IN THE MORNING (John Barry) (mono/stereo)	40/60
74	T. Motown STML 11269	FOXY BROWN (Willie Hutch)	15
66	RCA Victor RD/SF 7793	FRANKIE AND JOHNNY (Elvis Presley) (black/red dot labels, mono/stereo)	18/22
64	Fontana TL 5208	FREEDOM ROAD (Madeleine Bell, et al.) (TV production)	15
71	Paramount SPFL 269	FRIENDS (Elton John)	12
72	Fantasy FAN 9406	FRITZ THE CAT (Bo Diddley/Billie Holiday, et al.)	35
63	United Artists (S)ULP 1052	FROM RUSSIA WITH LOVE (John Barry/Matt Monroe) (mono/stereo)	22/25
60	London HA-T 2257	THE FUGITIVE KIND (Kenyon Hopkins)	15
66	RCA RD 7860	FUNERAL IN BERLIN (Konrad Elfers)	25
63	RCA Victor RD/SF 7609	FUN IN ACAPULCO (Elvis Presley) (black/silver label, mono/stereo)	18/22
68	CBS 70044	FUNNY GIRL (Barbra Streisand) (gatefold sleeve)	12
73	CBS SQ 30992/Q 70044	FUNNY GIRL (Barbra Streisand) (quadrophonic)	15
75	Arista ARTY 101	FUNNY LADY (Barbra Streisand) (gatefold sleeve)	15

G

65	Liberty (S)LBY 1261	GENGHIS KHAN (Dusan Radic) (mono/stereo)	20
56	Vogue Coral LVA 9003	GENTLEMEN MARRY BRUNETTES (Robert Farnon)	25
53	MGM MGM-D 116	GENTLEMEN PREFER BLONDES (Marilyn Monroe, et al.) (10")	75
65	Mercury 20061 MCL	GENTLE RAIN (Luis Bonfa & Deodato)	15
70	RCA SF 8137	GETTING STRAIGHT (Ronald Stein)	12
57	Capitol LCT 6122	GIANT (Dimitri Tiomkin)	15
60	RCA RD 27192/SF 5078	G.I. BLUES (Elvis Presley) (black/silver label, mono/stereo)	15/30
66	MGM MGM-C(S) 8034	GIRL FROM U.N.C.L.E. (Jerry Goldsmith & Teddy Randazzo)	45
65	RCA Victor RD/SF 7714	GIRL HAPPY (Elvis Presley) (black/red dot labels, mono/stereo)	18/25
68	Polydor 583 714	GIRL ON A MOTORCYCLE (Les Reed)	60
63	RCA Victor RD/SF 7534	GIRLS! GIRLS! GIRLS! (Elvis Presley) (black/silver labels, mono/stereo)	18/22
54	Brunswick LA 8647	THE GLENN MILLER STORY (10")	15
66	United Artists SULP 1120	THE GLORY GUYS (Riz Ortolani)	15
72	Paramount SPFA 7003	THE GODFATHER (Nino Rota) (gatefold sleeve)	12
75	ABC ABCL 5128	THE GODFATHER — PART 2 (Nino Rota) (gatefold sleeve)	12
58	London HA-T 2125	GOD'S LITTLE ACRE (Elmer Bernstein)	30
72	Mother MO 4001	GOLD (MC5/David McWilliams, et al.)	35
74	Philips 9299 225	GOLD (Elmer Bernstein)	15
72	United Artists UAG 29421	GOLDEN AGE OF HOLLYWOOD MUSICALS (various artists) (foldout, pop-up sleeve)	15

MINT VALUE £

73	United Artists UAS 29576	THE GOLDEN VOYAGE OF SINBAD (Miklos Rozsa)	15
64	United Artists (S)ULP 1076	GOLDFINGER (John Barry/Shirley Bassey) (mono/stereo)	22/25
67	MGM MGM-C(S) 8056	GONE WITH THE WIND (Max Steiner)	12
64	Decca LK 4673	GONKS GO BEAT (Lulu/Nashville Teens/Graham Bond, et al.)	100
68	United Artists (S)ULP 1197	THE GOOD, THE BAD AND THE UGLY (Ennio Morricone)	15
61	HMV CSD 1386	GOODBYE AGAIN (Georges Auric)	12
65	Stateside SL 10126	GOODBYE CHARLIE (André Previn)	12
69	Warner Bros W(S) 1786	GOODBYE COLUMBUS (Charles Fox/Association)	18
70	DJM DJLPS 408	GOODBYE GEMINI (Christopher Gunning)	40
69	MGM MGM-CS 8113	GOODBYE MR. CHIPS (Leslie Bricusse) (g/fold sl., initially with book form)	15
68	CBS (S) 70042	THE GRADUATE (Simon & Garfunkel) (original issue, blue label, laminated sleeve, mono/stereo)	18/15
66	MGM MGM-CS 8037	GRAND PRIX (Maurice Jarre)	15
53	HMV ALP 1071	THE GREAT CARUSO (Mario Lanza)	18
63	United Artists (S)ULP 1041	THE GREAT ESCAPE (Elmer Bernstein) (mono/stereo)	18
77	Arista SPARTY 1013	THE GREATEST (Michael Masser/George Benson)	12
65	United Artists SULP 1093	THE GREATEST STORY EVER TOLD (Alfred Newman)	15
65	RCA RD 7759	THE GREAT RACE (Henry Mancini)	40
71	Pye NSPL 18373	GREAT SONGS AND THEMES FROM GREAT FILMS (Roy Budd)	75
75	MCA MCF 2707	THE GREAT WALDO PEPPER (Henry Mancini)	15
68	United Artists SULP 1220	GREAT WESTERN FILM THEMES (Various Artists)	15
81	Polydor POLS 11031	GREEN ICE (Bill Wyman)	15
84	Warner Bros K 925 120-1	GREYSTOKE — THE LEGEND OF TARZAN LORD OF THE APES (John Scott)	12
70	Polydor 2384 021	GROUPIE GIRL (Opal Butterfly/English Rose, et al.)	20
67	RCA RD/SF 7899	GUNN (Henry Mancini)	18
63	Philips BBL 7500	THE GUNS OF NAVARONE (Dimitri Tiomkin) (also stereo SBBL 646)	12/15
69	RCA SF 8025	THE GURU (Ustad Vilayet Khan)	12
73	Ace Of Hearts AH 137	GUYS AND DOLLS	15
62	Warner Bros WM/WS 8120	GYPSY (Rosalind Russel, et al.)	15

H

67	RCA Victor RB/SB 6735	HALF A SIXPENCE (Tommy Steele, et al.) (gatefold sleeve)	15
65	United Artists SULP 1106	THE HALLELUJAH TRAIL (Elmer Bernstein)	15
75	Contour 2870 437	THE HANGED MAN (Bullet) (TV soundtrack)	40
68	United Artists SULP 1204	HANG 'EM HIGH (Dominic Frontiere)	15
70	United Artists UAS 29084	THE HAPPY ENDING (Michel Legrand)	18
56	Philips BBL 7100	HAPPY HOLIDAY (Jo Stafford)	15
65	RCA Victor RD/SF 7767	HAREM HOLIDAY (Elvis Presley) (black/red dot labels, mono/stereo)	15/20
65	Warner Bros W 1599	HARLOW (Neal Hefti)	25
66	United Artists (S)ULP 1154	HAWAII (Elmer Bernstein)	15
80s	PRT/Chips CHILP 1	HAWK THE SLAYER (Harry Robertson) (gatefold sleeve)	15
68	RCA RD/SF 8051	HEAD (Monkees) (mono/stereo)	55/45
93	Lightning LIGCD 5001	HEAD (CD) (Monkees)	15
73	CBS 70125	THE HEARTBREAK KID (Garry Sherman/Arrival)	12
73	Fantasy FT 516	HEAVY TRAFFIC (various artists)	15
72	Reprise K 44168	THE HEIST (Quincy Jones/Little Richard)	15
74	Tamla Motown TML 11260	HELL UP IN HARLEM (Edwin Starr)	20
65	Parlophone PMC 1255	HELP! (Beatles) (1st pressing, with "The Gramophone Co. Ltd" & "Sold In The UK…" label text; mono, with "mono" in outline type on front cover)	40
65	Parlophone PCS 3071	HELP! (Beatles) (1st pressing, with "The Gramophone Co. Ltd" & "Sold In The UK…" label text; stereo, with "stereo" in outline type on front cover)	50
67	United Artists (S)ULP 1186	HERE WE GO ROUND THE MULBERRY BUSH (Spencer Davis/Traffic/Andy Ellison)	25
59	Capitol T 1160	HEY BOY! HEY GIRL! (Louis Prima/Keely Smith, et al.)	20
62	Columbia 33SX 1421	HEY, LET'S TWIST (Joey Dee, et al.)	12
83	A&R FILM 001	HIGH ROAD TO CHINA (John Barry)	20
56	Capitol (S)LCT 6116	HIGH SOCIETY (Frank Sinatra, et al.)	12
70	Columbia SCX 6443	HIS LAND (Cliff Richard/Cliff Barrows)	60
71	Atlantic 2400 137	HOMER (Led Zeppelin/Buffalo Springfield, et al.)	12
67	United Artists ULP 1161	THE HONEY POT (John Addison)	15
59	London HA-T 2197	THE HORSE SOLDIERS (David Buttolph)	30
62	MGM MGM-C 915/CS 6061	HOW THE WEST WAS WON (Alfred Newman)	12
65	United Artists (S)ULP 1098	HOW TO MURDER YOUR WIFE (Neal Hefti)	30
68	CBS (S)BPG 63276	HOW TO SAVE A MARRIAGE AND RUIN YOUR LIFE (Michel Legrand)	18
72	Atlantic K 40371	HOW TO STEAL A DIAMOND IN FOUR UNEASY LESSONS (Quincy Jones)	15
61	Stateside S(S)L 10187	HOW TO STEAL A MILLION (John Williams)	40
61	Golden Guinea GGL 0069	HUCKLEBERRY HOUND (TV soundtrack)	12
67	United Artists SULP 1162	HOW TO SUCCEED IN BUSINESS WITHOUT REALLY TRYING (Frank Loesser)	15
67	RCA Victor RD/SF 7877	HURRY SUNDOWN (Hugo Montenegro)	25

I

69	MGM MGM-C(S) 8101	ICE STATION ZEBRA (Michel Legrand)	20
70	United Artists UAS 29044	IF IT'S TUESDAY THIS MUST BE BELGIUM (Walter Scharf)	15
67	Brunswick LAT/STA 8689	I'LL NEVER FORGET WHAT'S 'ISNAME (Francis Lai)	25
65	United Artists ULP 1105	I'LL TAKE SWEDEN (Bob Hope/Frankie Avalon, et al.)	12
68	RCA Victor RD/SF 7931	IN COLD BLOOD (Quincy Jones)	40
80	Atlantic K 50753	INFERNO (Keith Emerson)	12
65	RCA RD 7707	IN HARM'S WAY (Jerry Goldsmith)	18
67	Stateside S(S)L 10207	IN LIKE FLINT (Jerry Goldsmith)	50
81	Warner Bros K 56901	INSIDE MOVES (John Barry/Eagles et al.)	12
68	United Artists ULP 1201	INSPECTOR CLOUSEAU (Ken Thorne/Liz Taylor)	25
69	RCA Victor RD/SF 7990	INTERLUDE (Georges Delarue/Timi Yuro)	25
62	Colpix PXL 427	THE INTERNS (Leith Stevens)	20
67	United Artists (S)ULP 1181	IN THE HEAT OF THE NIGHT (Quincy Jones/Ray Charles)	50
65	CBS BPG 62530	THE IPCRESS FILE (John Barry) (mono only)	60
84	Illuminated JAMS 35	IN THE SHADOW OF THE SUN (Throbbing Gristle)	12
63	United Artists SULP 1051	IRMA LA DOUCE (Andre Previn)	15

66	CBS (S)BPG 62843	IS PARIS BURNING? (Maurice Jarre)	25
69	Paramount SPFL 256	THE ITALIAN JOB (Quincy Jones/Matt Monroe)	80
63	RCA Victor RD/SF 7565	IT HAPPENED AT THE WORLD'S FAIR (Elvis Presley) (black/silver label, mono/stereo)	18/22
63	Columbia 33SX 1533	IT'S ALL HAPPENING (Tommy Steele/Shane Fenton, et al.) (also stereo SCX 3486)	15/22
63	Philips BL 7609	IT'S ALL OVER TOWN (Frankie Vaughan/Springfields, et al.)	12
63	United Artists (S)ULP 1053	IT'S A MAD MAD MAD MAD WORLD (Ernest Gold)	20
62	Columbia 33SX 1412	IT'S TRAD, DAD! (Helen Shapiro/Gene Vincent, et al.)	25
65	Decca LK 4677	I'VE GOTTA HORSE (Billy Fury/Bachelors, et al.)	40
59	London LTZ-T 15160	I WANT TO LIVE (Johnny Mandel)	30

J

72	United Artists UAD 60027/8	THE JAMES BOND COLLECTION (John Barry) (2-LP, with booklet)	25
57	Capitol LCT 6140	THE JAMES DEAN STORY (Leith Stevens)	25
71	Capitol E-SW 621	JANE EYRE (John Williams)	12
83	MCA MCF 3194	JAWS 3-D (Alan Parker)	12
54	Brunswick LA 8671	JAZZ THEMES FROM "THE WILD ONE" (Leith Stevens) (10")	30
62	HMV CLP 1582	JESSICA (Mario Nascimbene)	15
77	Pye NSPH 28504	JESUS OF NAZARETH (Maurice Jarre) (gatefold sleeve)	15
73	Reprise K 64017	JIMI HENDRIX — SOUNDTRACK RECORDINGS FROM THE FILM (2-LP)	15
68	Stateside (S)SL 10264	JOANNA (Rod McKuen/Mike Sarne)	15
71	Mercury 6338 029	JOE (Bobby Scott/Jenny Butler)	12
73	JSD JSD 100	JOHN SCOTT DEMONSTRATION RECORD	50
72	Reprise K 64015	JOURNEY THROUGH THE PAST (Neil Young) (2-LP, fold-out cover with inner sleeves)	20
77	Polydor/EG 2302 079	JUBILEE (Adam & Ants/Brian Eno, et al.)	12
61	HMV CLP 1545	JUDGMENT AT NUREMBURG (Ernest Gold)	20
66	RCA RD 7788	JUDITH (Sol Kaplan)	12
67	Fontana (S)TL 5317	JULIET OF THE SPIRITS (Nino Rota)	40
69	Buena Vista BVS 4041	JUNGLE BOOK (Sherman Brothers)	12
63	Decca LK 4524	JUST FOR FUN (Tornados/Karl Denver, et al.)	40
64	Decca LK 4620	JUST FOR YOU (Applejacks/Merseybeats, et al.)	40
70	Monument LMO/SMO 5031	JUSTINE (Jerry Goldsmith)	15

K

71	MGM 2315 019	KELLY'S HEROES (Lalo Schifrin/Mike Curb)	12
66	United Artists (S)ULP 1139	KHARTOUM (Frank Cordell)	40
72	Polydor 2383 102	KIDNAPPED (Roy Budd/Mary Hopkin)	35
58	RCA RD 27088	KING CREOLE (Elvis Presley) (black/silver labels)	35
76	Reprise K 54090	KING KONG (John Barry) (with poster)	15
61	MGM MGM-CS 6043	KING OF KINGS (Miklos Rozsa)	20
58	Capitol LCT 6165	KINGS GO FORTH (Elmer Bernstein)	15
66	Fontana (S)TL 5302	KING RAT (John Barry)	40
54	MGM MGM-C 753	KISS ME KATE (Howard Keel, et al.)	20
64	RCA Victor RD/SF 7645	KISSIN' COUSINS (Elvis Presley) (black/red dot labels, mono/stereo)	18/22
65	United Artists ULP 1104	THE KNACK (AND HOW TO GET IT) (John Barry)	50
54	Brunswick LA 8668	KNOCK ON WOOD (Danny Kaye) (10")	15
69	Stateside (S)SL 10277	KRAKATOA: EAST OF JAVA (Frank De Vol)	15
74	Warner Bros K 46271	KUNG FU (TV soundtrack) (with inner sleeve)	12

L

61	RCA RD 27202	LA DOLCE VITA (Nino Rota) (gatefold sleeve)	50
63	Ace Of Hearts AH 70	THE LADY AND THE TRAMP (Peggy Lee)	25
72	HMV CSD 3728	LADY CAROLINE LAMB (Richard Rodney Bennet)	12
69	Stateside S(S)L 10267	LADY IN CEMENT (Hugo Montenegro)	35
73	Tamla Motown TMSP 1131	LADY SINGS THE BLUES (Diana Ross) (2-LP, with brown inner sleeves)	15
71	United Artists UAS 29120	THE LANDLORD (Al Kooper)	15
72	CBS 70115	THE LAST PICTURE SHOW (Jo Stafford/Tony Bennett, et al.)	15
72	MGM 2315 072	THE LAST RUN (Jerry Goldsmith/Steve Lawrence)	15
73	United Artists UAS 29440	LAST TANGO IN PARIS (Gato Barbieri)	20
71	Probe SPB 1027	THE LAST VALLEY (John Barry) (some with insert)	40/35
63	Pye Intl. NPL 28023	LAWRENCE OF ARABIA (Maurice Jarre)	12
85	United Artists 86002	LEGEND (Jerry Goldsmith)	25
71	M. F. Pleasure MFP 50034	THE LEGEND OF FRENCHIE KING (Francis Lai)	35
81	RCA RCALP 5212	THE LEGEND OF THE LONE RANGER (John Barry)	12
74	Warner Bros K 56085	THE LEGEND OF THE 7 GOLDEN VAMPIRES (James Bernard/Peter Cushing)	18
64	Stateside S(S)L 10058	THE LEOPARD (Nino Rota)	30
70	Apple PXS 1	LET IT BE (Beatles) (box set, 1st pressing, dark green label, red Apple logo on LP rear sleeve & white inner, with Get Back book housed in black card tray ['PXS 1' not listed on package])	225
70	Apple PCS 7096	LET IT BE (Beatles) (2nd pressing, green Apple logo on rear sleeve, plain white inner)	15
60	Philips BBL 7414/SBBL 592	LET'S MAKE LOVE (Marilyn Monroe/Yves Montand/Frankie Vaughan)	35/50
79	Warner Bros K 56751	LIFE OF BRIAN (Monty Python) (with inner sleeve)	12
59	Philips SBBL 565	LI'L ABNER (Nelson Riddle)	12
64	Columbia SX 1626	LILIES OF THE FIELD (Jerry Goldsmith)	20
69	CBS 70049	THE LION IN WINTER (John Barry)	30
66	MGM MGM-CS 8029	THE LIQUIDATOR (Lalo Schifrin)	30
75	A&M AMLH 64546	LISZTOMANIA (Rick Wakeman/Roger Daltrey)	12
73	United Artists UAS 29475	LIVE AND LET DIE (George Martin/Wings) (gatefold sleeve)	15
87	Warner Bros 925 616-1	THE LIVING DAYLIGHTS (John Barry)	12
87	Warner Bros 925 616-2	THE LIVING DAYLIGHTS (John Barry) (CD)	60
76	MGM 2315 376	LOGAN'S RUN (Jerry Goldsmith)	15
62	MGM MGM-C 896	LOLITA (Nelson Riddle)	25
67	Polydor 583 014	LONG DUEL (Patrick John Scott)	20
63	Stateside S(S)L 10045	THE LONGEST DAY (dialogue only)	20

MINT VALUE £

83	CES CES 1001	THE LONG GOOD FRIDAY (Francis Monkman) (numbered sleeve with insert, black label print, 2,000 only)	100
83	CES CES 1001	THE LONG GOOD FRIDAY (Francis Monkman) (re-pressing, with insert, blue label print, 500 only)	175
84	CES CES 1001	THE LONG GOOD FRIDAY (Francis Monkman) (3rd pressing, with insert, blue label print, 5,000 only)	50
89	Silva Screen FILM 020	THE LONG GOOD FRIDAY (Francis Monkman) (reissue)	18
89	Silva Screen FILM 020	THE LONG GOOD FRIDAY (Francis Monkman) (CD)	20
65	MGM C/CS 6079	LOOKING FOR LOVE (Connie Francis)	18
70	CBS 70073	LOOT (Keith Mansfield/Steve Ellis)	25
65	Colpix PXL 521	LORD JIM (Bronislau Kaper)	20
69	Uni UNLS 103	LOST MAN (Quincy Jones)	20
70	CBS 70067	LOVE CIRCLE (Ennio Morricone)	40
57	RCA RC 24001	LOVING YOU (Elvis Presley) (10", silver spot label)	100
64	RCA Victor RC 24001	LOVING YOU (Elvis Presley) (10"; black/silver label, mono)	75
57	MGM MGM-D 141	LOVELY TO LOOK AT (Howard Keel, et al.) (10")	12

M

77	MCA MCF 2828	MACARTHUR (Jerry Goldsmith)	15
73	Tamla Motown STMA 8003	THE MACK (Willie Hutch)	15
69	RCA Victor SF 8017	MACKENNA'S GOLD (Quincy Jones/Jose Feliciano)	20
69	Warner Bros WS 1805	THE MADWOMAN OF CHAILLOT (Michael Lewis)	20
70	Pye Intl. NSPL 28133	THE MAGIC CHRISTIAN (Ken Thorne/Badfinger, et al.)	40
71	BBC Roundabout 8	MAGIC ROUNDABOUT (TV soundtrack)	12
54	Brunswick LAT 8045	MAGNIFICENT OBSESSION (Frank Skinner)	12
65	MGM MGM-C 995	THE MAGNIFICENT SHOWMAN (Dimitri Tiomkin)	15
76	Atlantic K 50308	MAHONEY'S LAST STAND (Ronnie Lane & Ron Wood)	15
63	Ace Of Clubs ACL 1135	MAIGRET (Ron Grainer) (TV series music)	15
66	CBS SBPG 62525	MAJOR DUNDEE (Daniele Amfitheatrof)	15
67	United Artists SULP 1155	A MAN AND A WOMAN (Francis Lai)	15
66	Brunswick LAT/STA 8651	A MAN COULD GET KILLED (Bert Kaempfert)	20
67	RCA RB 6712/3	A MAN FOR ALL SEASONS (2-LP, dialogue only)	35
59	Top Rank 35/043	MAN FROM INTERPOL (Tony Crombie) (TV series music)	20
66	RCA Victor RD 7758	THE MAN FROM U.N.C.L.E. (Hugo Montenegro)	40
64	Stateside S(S)L 10087	MAN IN THE MIDDLE (Lionel Bart & John Barry)	50
72	Warner Bros K 46126	MAN IN THE WILDERNESS (Johnny Harris)	12
56	Brunswick LAT 8101	THE MAN WITH THE GOLDEN ARM (Elmer Bernstein)	25
74	United Artists UAS 29671	THE MAN WITH THE GOLDEN GUN (John Barry/Lulu)	12
63	Stateside S(S)L 10048	MARILYN (Marilyn Monroe) (mono/stereo)	25/30
65	HMV CLP 1794/CSD 1564	MARY POPPINS (Sherman Brothers)	12
72	MCA MUPS 441	MARY QUEEN OF SCOTS (John Barry)	30
70	CBS 70072	M*A*S*H (Johny Mandel)	15
70	United Artists UAS 29122	MASTER OF THE ISLANDS (Henry Mancini)	15
69	Philips SBL 7876	MAYERLING (Francis Lai)	60
64	United Artists SULP 1059	McLINTOCK (Frank De Vol)	15
80	Polydor POLD 5034	McVICAR (Roger Daltrey) (clear vinyl)	12
71	Polydor 2383 043	MELODY (Bee Gees, Richard Hewson, et al.)	12
69	CBS 70061	ME, NATALIE (Henry Mancini/Rod McKuen)	15
57	London HA-P 2076	MEN IN WAR (Elmer Bernstein)	35
58	Capitol T 1016	MERRY ANDREW (Danny Kaye)	40
76	EMI SLCW 1033	THE MESSAGE (Maurice Jarre) (gatefold sleeve)	12
65	MGM MGM-C(S) 8001	MICKEY ONE (Stan Getz & Eddie Sauter) (with booklet, mono/stereo)	18/20
69	United Artists UAS 29043	MIDNIGHT COWBOY (John Barry/Nilsson/Elephant's Memory) (orange/pink label)	18
66	Mercury MCL 20072	MIRAGE (Quincy Jones)	25
61	HMV CLP 1481	THE MISFITS (Alex North)	35
68	Dot (S)LPD 503	MISSION: IMPOSSIBLE — MUSIC FROM THE TV SERIES (Lalo Schifrin)	35
54	Oriole MG 25181	MISS SADIE THOMPSON (George Duning) (10")	30
66	Fontana TL 5347	MODESTY BLAISE (Johnny Dankworth)	50
70	Paramount SPFL 259	THE MOLLY MAGUIRES (Henry Mancini)	12
69	Paramount SPFL 255	MONTE CARLO OR BUST! (Ron Goodwin)	40
79	United Artists UAG 30247	MOONRAKER (John Barry/Shirley Bassey)	12
69	Columbia SCX 6346	MORE (Pink Floyd) (laminated flipback sleeve, 'couple facing west' photo on green-tinted rear sleeve)	25
70s	Columbia SCX 6346	MORE (Pink Floyd) (laminated non-flipback sleeve, 'couple facing west' photo on black-tinted rear sleeve)	18
70s	Columbia SCX 6346	MORE (Pink Floyd) (laminated non-flipback sleeve, 'couple facing east' photo on black-tinted rear sleeve)	30
72	Ember NR 5061	MORE EXPERIENCE (Jimi Hendrix)	12
69	Paramount SPFL 252	MORE 'MISSION: IMPOSSIBLE' (Lalo Schifrin)	35
60	MGM MGM-C(S) 857	MORE MUSIC FROM BEN-HUR (Miklos Rozsa)	15/20
66	RCA Victor RD 7832	MORE MUSIC FROM 'THE MAN FROM U.N.C.L.E.' (Hugo Montenegro)	30
62	MGM	MORE MUSIC FROM 'MUTINY ON THE BOUNTY' (Bronislau Kaper)	20
68	MGM MGM-C(S) 8063	MORE THAN A MIRACLE (Piero Piccioni)	15
65	Columbia S(C)X 6303	MRS BROWN YOU'VE GOT A LOVELY DAUGHTER (Herman's Hermits) (mono/stereo)	15/12
77	Pye NSPH 19	MUPPET SHOW VOL. 1 (TV soundtrack) (gatefold sleeve)	12
78	Pye NSPH 21	MUPPET SHOW VOL. 2 (TV soundtrack)	12
62	MGM MGM-CS 6060	MUTINY ON THE BOUNTY (Bronislau Kaper)	20
64	RCA RD 7847	MURDERERS' ROW (Lalo Schifrin)	35
74	EMI EMC 3054	MURDER ON THE ORIENT EXPRESS (Richard Rodney Bennet)	15
72	Harvest SHSP 4019	MUSIC FROM MACBETH (Third Ear Band)	15
70	Harvest SHSP 4008	MUSIC FROM THE BODY (Ron Geesin & Roger Waters) (black labels)	12
70	Harvest SHSP 4008	MUSIC FROM THE BODY (Ron Geesin & Roger Waters) (photos/green labels)	18
62	Warner Bros WS 8066	THE MUSIC MAN (Robert Preston, et al.)	12
85	Cloud Nine CN 4002	MYSTERIOUS ISLAND (Bernard Herrman)	25

N

70	United Artists UAS 29108	NED KELLY (Shel Silverstein/Mick Jagger/Waylon Jennings)	20
61	London HA-T 2309	NEVER ON SUNDAY (Manos Hadjidakis)	12
72	Bell BELLS 202	NICHOLAS AND ALEXANDRA (Richard Rodney Bennet)	15
81	MCA MCF 3107	NIGHTHAWKS (Keith Emerson)	12
67	RCA RD 7848	NIGHT OF THE GENERALS (Maurice Jarre)	20
65	MGM MGM-C 994	NIGHT OF THE IGUANA (Benjamin Frankel)	15
69	United Artists (S)ULP 1235	THE NIGHT THEY RAIDED MINSKY'S (Charles Strouse)	20
62	Decca LK 4527	NINE HOURS TO RAMA (Malcolm Arnold)	100
70	Capitol ESW 475	NORWOOD (Al De Lory/Glen Campbell)	12
68	Dot (S)LPD 507	NO WAY TO TREAT A LADY (American Breed)	20
88	CBS 651379 6	NUTS (Barbra Streisand)	15

O

72	Harvest SHSP 4020	OBSCURED BY CLOUDS (Pink Floyd) (rounded sleeve)	18
76	Phase 4 Stereo PF5 4381	OBSESSION (Bernard Herrman)	15
83	A&M AMLX 64967	OCTOPUSSY (John Barry/Rita Coolidge)	12
83	A&M 394 967-2	OCTOPUSSY (John Barry) (CD)	100
68	Dot (S)LPD 514	THE ODD COUPLE (Neal Hefti)	20
60	London HA-T 2220	ODDS AGAINST TOMORROW (John Lewis)	12
75	MCA MCF 2591	ODESSA FILE (Andrew Lloyd Webber/Perry Como)	12
64	Stateside S(S)L 10056	OF LOVE AND DESIRE (Ronald Stein)	12
95	Rex Mundi REX 230	OH! WHAT A LOVELY SHAG (Jack Kane, Milla Jovovich, et al.)	55
69	Paramount SPFL 251	OH! WHAT A LOVELY WAR (Alfred Ralston, et al.) (gatefold sleeve)	15
73	RCA Victor SF 8366	OKLAHOMA CRUDE (Henry Mancini)	15
70	Starline SRS 5019	OLIVER IN THE OVERWORLD (Freddie Garrity)	15
73	Warner Bros K 46227	O LUCKY MAN! (Alan Price) (gatefold sleeve)	18
70	CBS 70075	ON A CLEAR DAY YOU CAN SEE FOREVER (Barbra Streisand) (gatefold sleeve)	15
75	Fantasy FTA 3004	ONE FLEW OVER THE CUCKOO'S NEST (Jack Nitzsche) (gatefold sleeve)	15
69	United Artists UAS 29020	ON HER MAJESTY'S SECRET SERVICE (John Barry) (foldout sleeve)	30
59	Columbia 33SX 1208	ON THE BEACH (Ernest Gold)	40
60	London HA-T 2222	ON THE BEACH/FILMS THEMES FROM HOLLYWOOD (various artists)	12
54	HMV DLP 1059	ORCHESTRA WIVES (Glenn Miller) (10")	15
70	Fontana SFJL 950	ORFEU NEGRO (BLACK ORPHEUS) (Luis Bonfa/Antonio Carlos Jobim)	15
66	CBS (S)BPG 62684	THE OSCAR (Percy Faith/Tony Bennett)	15
69	RCA SF 8014	OTLEY (Stanley Myers/Don Partridge)	15
66	Stateside S(S)L 10174	OUR MAN FLINT (Jerry Goldsmith)	50
76	Warner Bros K 56286	THE OUTLAW JOSEY WALES (Jerry Fielding)	15
86	MCA MCF 3310	OUT OF AFRICA (John Barry/Al Jarreau)	15
71	CBS 70081	THE OWL AND THE PUSSYCAT (Blood, Sweat & Tears)	15

P

69	Paramount SPFL 257	PAINT YOUR WAGON (Nelson Riddle) (gatefold sleeve)	12
58	Philips BBL 7197	THE PAJAMA GAME (Doris Day, et al.)	12
63	Warner Bros WM 8141	PALM SPRINGS WEEKEND (Frank Perkins)	20
74	EMI EMC 3020	PAPILLON (Jerry Goldsmith)	15
66	RCA Victor RD/SF 7810	PARADISE, HAWAIIAN STYLE (Elvis Presley) (black/red dot labels, mono/stereo)	18/22
61	HMV CLP 1499	PARIS BLUES (Duke Ellington)	15
61	Warner Bros WS 8044	PARRISH (Max Steiner/George Creely)	20
73	CBS S 69042	PAT GARRETT & BILLY THE KID (Bob Dylan)	12
70	Stateside SSL 10302	PATTON (Jerry Goldsmith)	15
65	Mercury 20063 SML	THE PAWNBROKER (Quincy Jones)	25
66	Philips (S)BL 7782	THE PEKING MEDALLION (Georges Garvarentz/Dusty Springfield)	30
67	Ember NR 5040	THE PENTHOUSE (John Hawksworth)	50
60	Pye Intl. NPL 28015	PEPE (Bobby Darin/Judy Garland, et al.)	12
71	Pye NSPL 18365	PERCY (Kinks)	18
70	Warner Bros WS 2554	PERFORMANCE (Mick Jagger/Jack Nitzsche/Randy Newman, et al.)	30
71	CBS 64816	THE PERSUADERS (John Barry)	15
59	RCA RD 27123/SF 5033	PETER GUNN (Henry Mancini)	15
55	Philips BBL 7059	PETE KELLY'S BLUES (Sammy Cahn, Matty Matlock, et al.)	12
55	Ace Of Hearts AH 26	PETE KELLY'S BLUES (Peggy Lee, Ella Fitzgerald)	12
79	Gem GEM 102	PHANTASM (Fred Myrow & Malcolm Seagrave)	12
62	United Artists ULP 1016	PHAEDRA (Mikis Theodorakis)	12
55	Brunswick LAT 8120	PICNIC (George Duning)	25
76	United Artists UAS 30012	THE PINK PANTHER STRIKES AGAIN (Henry Mancini)	15
68	Philips SBL 7858	PLAYTIME/LES VACANCES DE MR. HULOT/JOUR DE FETE/COURS DU SOIR/MON ONCLE (Jaques Tati, et al.)	35
85	CBS 70265	PORKY'S REVENGE (George Harrison/Dave Edmunds et al.)	12
57	Capitol LCT 6141	THE PRIDE AND THE PASSION (Georges Antheil)	15
69	Stateside (S)SL 10278	THE PRIME OF MISS JEAN BRODIE (Rod McKuen/Mike Redway)	15
86	Bam Caruso WEBA 066	THE PRISONER (Ron Grainer, et al.) (fan club issue, gatefold sleeve with inner sleeve, booklet, membership form, map & poster)	35
66	HMV CLP/CSD 3623	PRIVILEGE (Paul Jones & Mike Leander)	15
69	RCA SF 8072	THE PRODUCERS (John Morris)	15
69	United Artists UAS 29005	A PROFESSIONAL GUN (Ennio Morricone)	30
67	RCA Victor RD/SF 7876	THE PROFESSIONALS (Maurice Jarre)	50
60	Contemporary LAC 12293	THE PROPER TIME (Shelly Manne)	15
68	Stateside S(S)L 10248	PRUDENCE AND THE PILL (Bernard Ebbinghouse)	15

Q

71	Sonet SNTF 622	QUIET DAYS IN CLICHY (Country Joe McDonald)	12
66	CBS (S)BPG 62869	THE QUILLER MEMORANDUM (John Barry/Matt Monro) (mono/stereo)	30/4

R

88	Silva Screen FILM 033	RAGGEDY RAWNEY (Michael Kamen)	22
88	Silva Screen FILM 033	RAGGEDY RAWNEY (Michael Kamen) (CD)	20
71	Columbia SCX 6447	THE RAGING MOON (Stanley Myers/Blue Mink)	12
71	Reprise K 44159	RAINBOW BRIDGE (Jimi Hendrix) (matt gatefold sleeve, 'steamboat' label)	12
75	Dart ARTS 65376	RANSOM (Jerry Goldsmith)	50
67	United Artists (S)ULP 1184	RED AND BLUE (Vanessa Redgrave)	40
72	Paramount SPFL 275	THE RED TENT (Ennio Morricone)	12
70	CBS 70068	THE REIVERS (John Williams)	12
76	United Artists UAS 30007	THE RETURN OF A MAN CALLED HORSE (Laurence Rosenthal)	12
75	RCA Red Seal RS 1010	THE RETURN OF THE PINK PANTHER (Henry Mancini)	15
67	United Artists (S)ULP 1156	RETURN OF THE SEVEN (Elmer Bernstein)	15
78	United Artists UAS 30176	THE REVENGE OF THE PINK PANTHER (Henry Mancini)	12
69	United Artists ULP 1226	REVOLUTION (Quicksilver Messenger Service/Steve Miller, et al.)	20
70	United Artists UAS 29137	RIDER IN THE RAIN (Francis Lai)	20
68	MGM MGM-C(S) 8079	THE RISE AND FALL OF THE THIRD REICH (Lalo Schifrin)	20
53	Brunswick LA 8578	ROAD TO BALI (Bob Hope, Bing Crosby) (10")	30
62	Decca LKR 4427	THE ROAD TO HONG KONG (Robert Farnon/Bob Hope & Bing Crosby)	12
67	Decca LK/SKL 4892	ROBBERY (Johnny Keating)	15
54	Brunswick LAT 8031	THE ROBE (Alfred Newman) (gold label)	20
64	Reprise R 2021	ROBIN AND THE SEVEN HOODS (Nelson Riddle)	30
61	RCA RD 27233	ROCCO AND HIS BROTHERS (Nino Rota)	18
57	Mercury MPT 7527	ROCK ALL NIGHT (Platters, Norah Hayes, et al.) (10")	175
67	Polydor 583 013	ROCKET TO THE MOON (John Scott)	80
57	Brunswick LAT 8162	ROCK, PRETTY BABY (Henry Mancini/Rod McKuen)	100
87	Ode RHVX 1	ROCKY HORROR BOX SET (Richard O'Brien) (4-LP box, with inserts, numbered)	30
87	Ode RHBXLP 1	ROCKY HORROR BOX SET (Richard O'Brien) (4-LP box, with different inserts to above)	25
75	Ode ODE 78332	THE ROCKY HORROR PICTURE SHOW (Richard O'Brien) (Original Soundtrack)	12
90	Ode RHBXCD 1	THE ROCKY HORROR PICTURE SHOW — 15TH ANNIVERSARY (Richard O'Brien, et al.) (4-CD box)	45
77	MCA MCF 2813	ROLLERCOASTER (Lalo Schifrin)	12
68	Dot (S)LPD 519	ROSEMARY'S BABY (Kryzstophe Komeda)	35
65	Parlophone PMC 1262	ROTTEN TO THE CORE (New Jazz Voices)	12
64	RCA Victor RD/SF 7678	ROUSTABOUT (Elvis Presley) (black/red dot labels, mono/stereo)	18/22
64	Capitol (S)T 1771	ROUTE 66 (Nelson Riddle) (TV show)	15
66	United Artists ULP 1147	THE RUSSIANS ARE COMING THE RUSSIANS ARE COMING (Johnny Mandel)	15
71	MGM 2315 028	RYAN'S DAUGHTER (Maurice Jarre) (gatefold sleeve)	12

S

72	RCA SF 8211	SACCO AND VANZETTI (Ennio Morricone/Joan Baez)	12
53	Brunswick LA 8604	SALOMÉ (George Duning) (10")	50
68	United Artists SULP 1202	SALT AND PEPPER (Johnny Dankworth/Sammy Davis Jr)	15
67	Stateside S(S)L 10198	THE SAND PEBBLES (Jerry Goldsmith)	15
65	Mercury MCL 20065	THE SANDPIPER (Johnny Mandel)	20
58	Philips BBL 7216	SATCHMO THE GREAT (Louis Armstrong)	12
59	Philips BBL 7335	SAY ONE FOR ME (Bing Crosby)	12
68	United Artists (S)ULP 1190	THE SCALPHUNTERS (Elmer Bernstein)	15
78	Polydor 2480 429	SCOUSE THE MOUSE (Ringo Starr/Adam Faith, et al.) (stickered sleeve with printed competition insert)	80
78	Polydor 3194 429	SCOUSE THE MOUSE (Ringo Starr/Adam Faith, et al.) (cassette)	50
70	CBS 70077	SCROOGE (Leslie Bricusse) (musical, gatefold sleeve)	12
80	EMI EMC 3340	THE SEA WOLVES (Roy Budd/Matt Monroe)	18
56	HMV ALP 1365	SERENADE (Mario Lanza)	12
78	A&M AMLZ 666000	SGT. PEPPER'S LONELY HEARTS CLUB BAND (Bee Gees/Peter Frampton, et al.) (2-LP, pink vinyl, gatefold embossed sleeve with inners & poster)	15
62	Reprise R 2013	SERGEANTS 3 (Billy May)	30
73	Paramount SPFL 296	SERPICO (Mikis Theodorakis)	18
64	United Artists ULP 1072	THE SEVENTH DAWN (Riz Ortolani)	15
74	United Artists UAS 29763	THE SEVENTH VOYAGE OF SINBAD (Bernard Hermann)	25
71	Stax 2659 007	SHAFT — ORIGINAL SOUNDTRACK (Isaac Hayes) (2-LP, gatefold sleeve)	15
73	Probe SPB 1077	SHAFT IN AFRICA (Johnny Pate/Four Tops)	25
74	ABC ABCL 5035	SHAFT IN AFRICA (Johnny Pate/Four Tops) (reissue)	15
72	MGM 2315 115	SHAFT'S BIG SCORE! (Gordon Parks/O.C. Smith/Isaac Hayes)	20
66	CBS BPG 62755	SHAKESPEARE WALLAH (Satyajit Ray)	15
68	Philips SBL 7867	SHALAKO (Robert Farnon)	25
80	Warner Bros K 56827	THE SHINING (Bela Bartok et al.)	12
69	MGM MGM-CS 8103	SHOES OF THE FISHERMAN (Alex North)	12
53	MGM MGM-D 104	SHOWBOAT (Howard Keel, et al.) (10")	12
74	Capitol CAPS 1018	SHUT DOWN (Beach Boys/Surfaris, et al.)	12
70	Stateside SSL 10307	THE SICILIAN CLAN (Ennio Morricone)	20
72	MCA MUPS 458	SILENT RUNNING (Pete Schikele/Joan Baez)	15
66	RCA RD 7792	THE SILENCERS (Elmer Bernstein/Vikki Carr)	30
58	MGM MGM-C 760	SILK STOCKINGS (Fred Astaire)	12
58	Capitol T 929	SING, BOY, SING (Tommy Sands)	45
58	MGM D 140	SINGIN' IN THE RAIN/EASTER PARADE (Gene Kelly/Judy Garland) (10")	25
66	MGM MGM-C(S) 8011	THE SINGING NUN (Debbie Reynolds)	15
78	Charisma CAS 1139	SIR HENRY AT RAWLINSON END (Vivian Stanshall) (with insert)	20
64	United Artists ULP 1071	633 SQUADRON (Ron Goodwin)	15
69	RCA SF 8010	SKIDOO (Nilsson)	18
74	Polydor 2442 126	SLADE IN FLAME (Slade)	12
73	Polydor 2391 084	SLAUGHTER'S BIG RIP-OFF (James Brown)	12
59	Top Rank RX 3022	SLEEPING BEAUTY	12
93	Epic Soundtrax 473594-1	SLEEPLESS IN SEATTLE (Marc Shaiman)	12

73	CBS 70127	SLEUTH (John Addison)	12
69	NEMS 6-70059	THE SMASHING BIRD I USED TO KNOW (Bobby Richards)	20
68	Stateside S(S)L 10224	SMASHING TIME (John Addison)	30
70	Pye NSPL 18348	SOLDIER BLUE AND OTHER THEMES (Roy Budd)	85
60	London HA-T 2221	SOLOMON AND SHEBA (Mario Nascimbene)	15
59	Capitol LCT 6180	SOME CAME RUNNING (Elmer Bernstein)	25
59	London HA-T 2176	SOME LIKE IT HOT (Marilyn Monroe) (also stereo SAH-T 6040)	55/80
67	RCA RD 7845	SONGS FROM THE SWINGER (Marty Paich)	30
74	Rapple APL1 0220	SON OF DRACULA (Nilsson/Ringo Starr) (fold-out sleeve)	15
65	CBS (S)BPG 62558	THE SONS OF KATIE ELDER (Elmer Bernstein/Johnny Cash)	30/40
68	Columbia SAX 9001	SOUNDS AND SONGS OF LONDON (various artists)	
		(gatefold sleeve with booklet)	15
73	CBS 70123	SOUNDER (Taj Mahal)	12
69	RCA Victor SF 8024	THE SOUTHERN STAR (Matt Monro/Georges Garvarentz)	25
58	London HA-D 2079	SPANISH AFFAIR (Daniele Amfitheatrof)	50
76	Atlantic K 56248	SPARKLE (Curtis Mayfield/Aretha Franklin)	12
61	Brunswick LAT 8393	SPARTACUS (Alex North) (gatefold sleeve)	25
68	RCA Victor RD/SF 7957	SPEEDWAY (Elvis Presley) (black/red dot labels, mono/stereo)	20/25
67	RCA RD 7787	THE SPY WHO CAME IN FROM THE COLD (Sol Kaplan)	30
77	United Artists UAG 30098	THE SPY WHO LOVED ME (Marvin Hamlisch) (gatefold sleeve)	12
68	CBS 62919	THE SPY WITH THE COLD NOSE (Riz Ortolani)	35
66	Fontana TL 5354	STAGECOACH (Jerry Goldsmith)	30
68	Stateside S(S)L 10233	STAR! (Julie Andrews, et al.)	12
55	Philips BBL 7007	A STAR IS BORN (Judy Garland)	15
79	CBS 70174	STAR TREK — THE MOTION PICTURE (Jerry Goldsmith)	15
77	20th C. BTD 541	STAR WARS (John Williams) (2-LP, with insert)	15
62	London HA-D 2453	STATE FAIR (Pat Boone/Bobby Darin, et al.)	
		(musical, also stereo SAH-D 6241)	12/15
69	CBS 70062	STILETTO (Sid Ramin)	25
61	MGM MGM-C 864	THE SUBTERRANEANS (André Previn)	15
84	Warner Bros 9239901	SUDDEN IMPACT AND THE BEST OF DIRTY HARRY (Lalo Schifrin et al.)	20
63	Columbia 33SX 1472	SUMMER HOLIDAY (Cliff Richard) (with inner sleeve, mono)	15
63	Columbia SCX 3462	SUMMER HOLIDAY (Cliff Richard) (stereo, with inner sleeve,	
		initially with green labels, later with blue/black labels)	30/20
71	Warner Bros K 46098	SUMMER OF '42 (Michel Legrand)	12
57	London HA-R 2077	THE SUN ALSO RISES (Hugo Friedhofer)	20
70	Avco Embassy 6466 002	SUNFLOWER (Henry Mancini)	15
55	HMV DLP 1104	SUN VALLEY SERENADE (Glenn Miller)	15
62	Golden Guinea GGL 0106	SUPERCAR — FLIGHT OF FANCY (Barry Gray/Edwin Astley)	40
72	Buddah 2318 065	SUPERFLY (Curtis Mayfield)	15
73	Buddah 2318 087	SUPER FLY T.N.T. (Osibisa)	30
64	Stateside SL 10089	SURF PARTY (Astronauts, Routers, et al.)	40
79	EMI EMC 3222	SUSPIRIA (Goblin)	12
78	Warner Bros K 56541	THE SWARM (Jerry Goldsmith)	25
69	MCA MUCS 133	SWEET CHARITY (Shirley MacLaine, et al.)	25
57	Brunswick LAT 8195	SWEET SMELL OF SUCCESS (Elmer Bernstein)	15
68	Stateside S(S)L 10250	THE SWEET RIDE (Pete Rugolo)	15
68	CBS 70043	THE SWIMMER (Marvin Hamlisch)	15
65	MGM MGM-C 8012	THE SWINGIN' SET (Dave Clark Five/Animals, et al.)	30
66	Mercury 20057 SMCL	SYLVIA (David Raksin)	15

T

70	Pye NSPL 18353	TAKE A GIRL LIKE YOU (Stanley Myers/Foundations)	15
73	EMI EMC 3016	TAKE ME HIGH (Cliff Richard) (some with poster)	25/15
67	RCA RB 6711	THE TAMING OF THE SHREW (dialogue only)	15
57	Vogue Coral LVA 9070	TAMMY (Frank Skinner/Debbie Reynolds)	40
63	United Artists ULP 1025	TARAS BULBA (Franz Waxman)	25
76	Arista ARTY 132	TAXI DRIVER (Bernard Herrman)	30
69	T. Motown (S)TML 11110	T.C.B. (Supremes/Temptations, et al.) (laminated gatefold sleeve)	15
58	London HA-D 2074-5	THE TEN COMMANDMENTS (Elmer Bernstein) (2-LP)	40
66	United Artists ULP 1144	THE TEN COMMANDMENTS (Elmer Bernstein) (reissue, single disc)	12
73	Ronco MR 2002/3	THAT'LL BE THE DAY (David Essex/Billy Fury, et al.) (2-LP)	18
71	RCA Victor SF 8162	THAT'S THE WAY IT IS (Elvis Presley)	12
75	CBS 80575	THAT'S THE WAY OF THE WORLD (Earth, Wind & Fire)	12
79	Arista SPART 1088	THAT SUMMER (Boomtown Rats/Elvis Costello et al.) (yellow vinyl, g/fold sl.)	12
63	Parlophone PMC 1197	THAT WAS THE WEEK THAT WAS (Millicent Martin, et al.)	
		(also stereo PCS 3040)	15
59	Coral LVA 9102	THEMES FROM HORROR MOVIES (Dick Jacobs)	25
55	Brunswick LAT 8059	THERE'S NO BUSINESS LIKE SHOW BUSINESS (Marilyn Monroe, et al.)	22
70	United Artists UAS 29128	THEY CALL ME MISTER TIBBS (Quincy Jones)	50
69	Philips SBL 7898	THEY CAME TO ROB LAS VEGAS (Georges Gavarentz)	70
70	Stateside SSL 10305	THEY SHOOT HORSES, DON'T THEY? (John Green)	20
73	Elektra K 46239	THE THIEF WHO CAME TO DINNER (Henry Mancini)	18
78	United Artists UAG 30208	THE THIRTY-NINE STEPS (Ed Welch)	12
58	MGM MGM-C 761	THIS COULD BE THE NIGHT (George Stoll)	12
68	United Artists SULP 1218	THOMAS CROWN AFFAIR (Michel Legrand)	30
65	Stateside SL 10136	THOSE MAGNIFICENT MEN IN THEIR FLYING MACHINES (Ron Goodwin)	30
73	Bell BELLS 235	THE THREE MUSKETEERS (Michel Legrand)	18
54	Capitol LC 6665	THREE SAILORS AND A GIRL (Gordon MacRae, et al.) (10")	30
85	Cloud Nine CN 4003	THREE WORLDS OF GULLIVER (Bernard Herrmann)	25
65	United Artists (S)ULP 1110	THUNDERBALL (John Barry) (mono/stereo)	22/25
67	United Artists (S)ULP 1159	THUNDERBIRDS ARE GO! (Barry Gray/Cliff Richard & Shadows)	
		(mono/stereo)	80/100
67	Pye NPL 18154	TILL DEATH DO US PART (TV soundtrack)	12
69	Polydor 583 717	TILL DEATH DO US PART (Wilfred Burns)	15
72	RCA SF 8253	TIME FOR LOVING (Michel Legrand/Dusty Springfield, et al.)	12

MINT VALUE £

Year	Label & Cat No	Title	Value
80	RSO 2685 145	TIMES SQUARE (2-LP) (Talking Heads/Ramones, et al.)	15
63	MGM MGM-C 934	TO KILL A MOCKINGBIRD (Elmer Bernstein)	15
64	United Artists SULP 1062	TOM JONES (John Addison)	15
59	MGM MGM-C 772	TOM THUMB (Russ Tamblyn)	15
68	Instant INLP 002	TONITE LET'S ALL MAKE LOVE IN LONDON (Pink Floyd/Chris Farlowe, et al.)	100
70	RCA LSA 3008	TOOMORROW (with insert)	100
64	United Artists ULP 1079	TOPKAPI (Manos Hadjidakis)	15
70	Marble Arch MALS 1359	TOP TV SOUNDTRACK THEMES	15
67	Fontana (S)TL 5446	TO SIR, WITH LOVE (Ron Grainer/ Lulu/Mindbenders)	45
69	Stateside S(S)L 10271	THE TOUCHABLES (Ken Thorne/Nirvana/Wynder K. Frog, et al.)	35
74	Philips 6612 040	A TOUCH OF CLASS (John Cameron)	12
74	Stax STXH 5001	TOUGH GUYS (Isaac Hayes)	12
75	Warner Bros K 56102	THE TOWERING INFERNO (John Williams)	12
66	Polydor 582 004	THE TRAP (Ron Goodwin)	35
60	Pye Nonesuch PPLD 206	THE TRIAL OF LADY CHATTERLEY (drama/documentary)	12
67	United Artists ULP 1176	TRIPLE CROSS (Georges Garvarentz)	20
73	T. Motown STML 11225	TROUBLE MAN (Marvin Gaye)	18
74	Stax STXD 4001/2	TRUCK TURNER (Isaac Hayes) (2-LP)	15
70	Capitol E-ST 263	TRUE GRIT (Elmer Bernstein/Glen Campbell)	15
72	Studio Two TWO 392	TAKE A BREAK: THEMES FROM THE TOP TV COMMERCIALS (Robert James)	12
61	Fontana TFL 5110	T.V. WESTERN THEMES (also stereo STFL 538) (Johnny Gregory)	10/12
69	Polydor 583 728	TWISTED NERVE/LES BICYCLETTES DE BELSIZE (Les Reed/Barry Mason, Bernard Herrman)	100
76	Decca SKL 5345	THE TWISTER	20
69	Columbia S(C)X 6330	TWO CITIES (Jeff Wayne)	30
67	RCA RD/SF 7891	TWO FOR THE ROAD (Henry Mancini)	18
63	United Artists ULP 1027	TWO FOR THE SEESAW (André Previn)	15
71	United Artists UDF 50003	200 MOTELS (Frank Zappa) (2-LP, with booklet & poster)	25
70	MCA MKPS 2013	TWO MULES FOR SISTER SARA (Ennio Morricone)	15
69	MGM MGM-C(S) 8078	2001: A SPACE ODYSSEY (Various Classical)	12
85	A&M AMA 5038	2010 (David Shire/Andy Summers)	12
62	Columbia 33SX 1482	TWO TICKETS TO PARIS (Joey Dee)	20

U

Year	Label & Cat No	Title	Value
67	RCA RB 6708	ULYSSES (Stanley Myers) (with insert)	15
60	London HA-T 2258	THE UNFORGIVEN (Dimitri Tiomkin)	18
84	Epic EPC 70251	UP THE CREEK (William Goldstein/Beach Boys)	12
68	Fontana (S)TL 5460	UP THE JUNCTION (Manfred Mann)	30
70	Fontana 6852 005	UP THE JUNCTION (Manfred Mann) (reissue)	15
69	Stax (S)XATS 1005	UPTIGHT (Booker T & MGs)	15

V

Year	Label & Cat No	Title	Value
73	Philips 6303 075	THE VALACHI PAPERS (Riz Ortolani)	15
68	Stateside (S)SL 10228	VALLEY OF THE DOLLS (André Previn/John Williams)	15
71	London SH-U 8420	VANISHING POINT (Delaney & Bonnie/Sam & Dave, et al.)	15
82	MGM 2315 437	VICTOR, VICTORIA (Henry Mancini)	20
63	Colpix PXL 516	THE VICTORS (Sol Kaplan)	20
59	RCA SF 5092	VICTORY AT SEA (Richard Rogers)	12
85	Parlophone BOND 1	A VIEW TO A KILL (John Barry/Duran Duran)	12
58	London HAT 2118	THE VIKINGS (Mario Nascimbene)	50
68	Dot (S)LPD 515	VILLA RIDES (Maurice Jarre)	15
63	MGM MGM-C 951/CS 6074	THE VIPs (Miklos Rozsa)	20
73	RCA Victor SF 8379	VISIONS OF EIGHT (Henry Mancini)	15
66	United Artists (S)ULP 1126	VIVA MARIA! (Georges Delerue) (mono/stereo)	30/40
67	United Artists ULP 1185	VIVRE POUR VIVRE (LIVE FOR LIFE) (Francis Lai)	15

W

Year	Label & Cat No	Title	Value
60	Mercury MMC 14033	WAGON TRAIN (Stanley Wilson, et al.)	25
62	MGM MGM-C 891	WALK ON THE WILD SIDE (Elmer Bernstein)	18
66	Brunswick STA 8636	THE WAR LORD (Jerome Moross)	45
73	Charisma DCS 10	WAR OF THE WORLDS (Orson Welles)	12
85	London YEAR 2	WATER (Mike Moran/George Harrison, et al.)	12
70	Paramount SPFL 266	WATERLOO (Nino Rota)	12
67	United Artists (S)ULP 1173	THE WAY WEST (Bronislau Kaper)	12
75	MCA MCF 2759	W.C. FIELDS AND ME (Henry Mancini)	12
67	Virtuoso TPLS 13010	WELLES RAISES KANE (Bernard Herrman)	30
64	Piccadilly N(S)PL 38011	WHAT A CRAZY WORLD (Joe Brown/Susan Maughan/Marty Wilde)	22
64	Golden Guinea GGL 0272	WHAT A CRAZY WORLD (Joe Brown/Susan Maughan/Marty Wilde) (reissue)	15
64	Stateside SL 10090	WHAT A WAY TO GO! (Nelson Riddle)	12
66	RCA SF 7818	WHAT DID YOU DO IN THE WAR, DADDY? (Henry Mancini)	18
66	RCA RD 27103	WHATEVER LOLA WANTS (Tab Hunter, et al.)	12
65	United Artists ULP 1096	WHAT'S NEW PUSSYCAT? (Burt Bacharach/Tom Jones/Manfred Mann, et al.)	20
66	MGM MGM-C(S) 8006	WHEN THE BOYS MEET THE GIRLS (Connie Francis/Herman's Hermits) (mono/stereo)	15/18
69	MGM MGM-C(S) 8102	WHERE EAGLES DARE (Ron Goodwin)	15
69	Paramount SPFL 254	WHERE'S JACK? (Elmer Bernstein/Mary Hopkin)	15
66	United Artists (S)ULP 1166	WHIPLASH WILLIE (André Previn)	15
67	United Artists (S)ULP 1168	THE WHISPERERS (John Barry)	35
77	A&M AMLH 64614	WHITE ROCK (Rick Wakeman)	12
67	Warner Bros W 1656	WHO'S AFRAID OF VIRGINIA WOOLF? (Alex North)	25
98	Trunk BARKED 4	THE WICKER MAN (Giovanni) (with inserts, some red vinyl)	50/30
57	London HA-N 2023	WILD BILL HICKOCK AND JINGLES ON THE SANTA FE TRAIL (TV s/track)	18
69	Warner Bros WS 1814	WILD BUNCH (Jerry Fielding)	40
71	Warner Bros K 46035	WILD BUNCH (Jerry Fielding) (reissue)	15
78	A&M AMLH 64730	THE WILD GEESE (Roy Budd)	20
68	Capitol (S)T 5099	WILD IN THE STREETS (Les Baxter/Gurus) (original issue, black label, rainbow rim)	18

MINT VALUE £

71	MGM 2315 062	WILD ROVERS (Jerry Goldsmith)	12
83	Chrysalis CHR 1453	WILD STYLE (various artists)	20
71	Paramount SPFL 274	WILLY WONKA AND THE CHOCOLATE FACTORY (Leslie Bricusse)	12
75	Arista ARTY 111	THE WIND AND THE LION (Jerry Goldsmith)	15
75	MCA MCF 2712	WINDOW IN THE SKY (Charles Smith/Olivia Newton John)	12
65	HMV CLP 1930	WINNIE THE POOH (Walt Disney)	12
87	Filmtrax MOMENT 110	WITHNAIL AND I (David Dundas)	35
78	MCA MCSP 287	THE WIZ (Diana Ross/Michael Jackson, et al.) (gatefold sleeve with booklet & poster)	15
57	MGM MGM-C 757	THE WIZARD OF OZ (Judy Garland, et al.)	40
67	Capitol (S)T 2800	WOMAN TIMES SEVEN (Riz Ortolani)	30
64	Columbia SX 1628	WONDERFUL LIFE (Cliff Richard) (gatefold sleeve with inner, also stereo SCX 3515)	15/25
63	MGM MGM-C 944	THE WONDERFUL WORLD OF THE BROTHERS GRIMM (Leigh Harline/David Rose)	12
68	Apple (S)APCOR 1	WONDERWALL MUSIC (George Harrison) (with insert & black inner sleeve, mono/stereo)	60/30
70	Atlantic 2663 001	WOODSTOCK (Jimi Hendrix/Who/Joe Cocker, et al.) (3-LP, fold-out sleeve)	20
60	RCA RD 27198	THE WORLD OF SUZIE WONG (George Duning)	15
57	Brunswick LAT 8174	WRITTEN ON THE WIND/FOUR GIRLS IN TOWN (Frank Skinner)	20

Y

65	MGM MGM-C 997	THE YELLOW ROLLS-ROYCE (Riz Ortolani)	15
69	Apple PMC 7070	YELLOW SUBMARINE (Beatles) (1st pressing, laminated flipback sleeve with red lines above & below rear liner note & black inner; with "Sold In The UK..." label text; mono)	250
69	Apple PCS 7070	YELLOW SUBMARINE (Beatles) (1st pressing, laminated flipback sleeve with red lines above & below rear liner note & black inner; with "Sold In The UK..." label text; stereo)	75
61	Golden Guinea GGL 0081	YOGI BEAR TV SERIES (TV soundtrack)	12
69	CBS (S) 70045	YOU ARE WHAT YOU EAT (Tiny Tim/Electric Flag, et al.)	12
71	Ember NR 5055	YOU CAN'T HAVE EVERYTHING (Joe Parnello/Bobby Scott)	12
57	Brunswick LAT 8170	YOU CAN'T RUN AWAY FROM IT (George Duning)	12
79	MCA MCF 2804	YOUNGBLOOD (War)	15
66	Philips (S)BL 7792	YOUNG GIRLS OF ROCHEFORT (Michel Legrand)	15
57	Brunswick LAT 8252	THE YOUNG LIONS (Hugo Friedhofer)	35
61	Columbia 33SX 1384	THE YOUNG ONES (Cliff Richard) (with inner sleeve, also stereo SCX 3397)	18/35
72	HMV CSDA 9002	YOUNG WINSTON (Alfred Ralston) (gatefold sleeve)	15
67	United Artists (S)ULP 1171	YOU ONLY LIVE TWICE (John Barry)	20
65	MGM MGM-CS 6081	YOUR CHEATIN' HEART (Hank Williams Jr.)	18
67	Kama Sutra KLP 402	YOU'RE A BIG BOY NOW (Lovin' Spoonful)	20

Z

69	CBS 70057	Z (Mikis Theodorakis)	12
70	MGM MGM CS 8120	ZABRISKIE POINT (Pink Floyd/Jerry Garcia/Kaleidoscope, et al.)	18
71	Probe SPB 1026	ZACHARIAH (Country Joe & Fish/James Gang, et al.)	12
64	Ember NR 5012	ZULU (John Barry) (yellow/orange label, flipback sleeve)	30

ORIGINAL STAGE SHOW
& RADIO CAST RECORDING LPs
(alphabetical by title)

A

64	Columbia SX 1676	ALADDIN AND HIS WONDERFUL LAMP (g/fold sleeve, also stereo SCX 3522)	18/22
70	Argo ZTA 501-2	ALICE IN WONDERLAND (2-LP)	20
71	RCA SER 5618	AMBASSADOR	20
82	Key LP 4	ANDY CAPP	15
70	CBS 70053	ANNE OF GREEN GABLES	15
50	Brunswick LAT 8002	ANNIE GET YOUR GUN	15
58	Capitol LCT 6150	ANNIE GET YOUR GUN	12
70	CBS 70052	ANN VERONICA	15
60s	Studio Two TWO 233	ARCADIANS	15

B

66	Columbia S(C)X 6009	BABES IN THE WOOD (mono/stereo)	15/18
60s	RCA Intl. INT 1037	BANDWAGON	12
59	Decca SKL 4136	BELLE — OR THE BALLAD OF DOCTOR CRIPPEN	15
58	Philips BBL 7201	BELLS ARE RINGING	12
64	Capitol (S)W 2191	BEN FRANKLIN IN PARIS	12
65	Parlophone PMC 1238	BEYOND OUR KEN	20
61	Parlophone PMC 1145	BEYOND THE FRINGE	15
74	CBS 70133	BILLY (gatefold sleeve, with lyric sheet)	15
70	Music F. Pleasure MFP 1091	BITTERSWEET	15
60s	M. For Pleasure MFP 1263	BLESS THE BRIDE	12
62	HMV CLP 1569/CSD 1441	BLITZ! (mono/stereo)	18/15
50s	HMV	THE BOYFRIEND (10")	15
63	Decca LK 4564	THE BOYS FROM SYRACUSE	15
63	Parlophone PMC 1190	BRIDGE ON THE RIVER WYE (also stereo PCS 3036)	15/20
61	Philips ABL 3383	BYE BYE BIRDIE — LONDON CAST (g/fold sleeve, also stereo SABL 205)	20/22

C

50s	Columbia KOS 3040	CABARET	15
69	CBS (S)BRG 70039	CABARET	15

MINT VALUE £

64	Melodisc MLP 12-146	CALYPSO CARNIVAL	15
64	HMV CLP 1756/CSD 1559	CAMELOT	12
60s	CBS (S)BRG 70009	CAMELOT	12
60s	Encore	CAN CAN	40
64	Decca LK/SKL 4596	THE CANTERBURY TALES	12
65	Pye N(S)PL 18408	THE CARD	30
50	Brunswick LAT 8006	CAROUSEL	12
71	Polydor 2383 035	CATCH MY SOUL — THE ROCK-OTHELLO	15
66	CBS (S)BPG 62627	CHARLIE GIRL	15
67	Columbia S(C)X 6103	CINDERELLA	20
64	Decca LK 4559	CINDY-ELLA	12
66	Decca LK/SKL 4810	COME SPY WITH ME	15
59	HMV CLP 1298	THE CROOKED MILE	15

D

75	Warner Bros K 56186	DAD'S ARMY	12
70	CBS 70063	DAMES AT SEA	20
57	HMV CLP 1108	DAMN YANKEES	12
60s	RCA Intl. INTS 1049	DANCING YEARS	12
60s	Studio Two TWO 188	DANCING YEARS	12
63	RCA RD/SF 7598	DANCING YEARS	12
65	Decca LK/SKL 4675	DIVORCE ME, DARLING	12
62	Decca LK 4413/SKL 4145	DO RE MI	12
61	RCA RD 27228/SF 5107	DO RE MI	15

E

78	Astoria 1	ELVIS (P.J. Proby) (sold at performances of "Elvis" show)	30
78	MCA MOG 3527	EVITA (silver sleeve)	12
58	Pye NPL 18016	EXPRESSO BONGO	18

F

60	MGM MGM-C 871	THE FANTASTICS	12
60	Decca SKL 4092	FINGS AIN'T WOT THEY USED TO BE	12
64	Reprise F(S) 2015	FINIAN'S RAINBOW — REPRISE REPERTORY THEATRE PRESENTS	15/18
59	Capitol SW 1321	FIORELLO!	12
60	HMV CSD 1305	FLOWER DRUM SONG	15
60	HMV CLP 1366	FOLLOW THAT GIRL	25
63	Ember CEL 902	FOOL BRITANNIA (radio show)	15
66	Parlophone PMC 7014	FOUR DEGREES OVER	12
57	Oriole MG 20016	FREE AS AIR	15
64	Parlophone PCS 3065	FUNNY GAME POLITICS	15
64	Capitol (S)W 2059	FUNNY GIRL (Original Broadway Cast) (mono/stereo)	12
60s	Ember NR 5039	A FUNNY THING HAPPENED ON THE WAY TO THE FORUM	15

G

72	Bell BELLS 203	GODSPELL	15
64	Capitol (S)W 2124	GOLDEN BOY	15
71	Columbia SCXA 9252	GONE WITH THE WIND (gatefold sleeve)	15
57	HMV CLP 1103	GRAB ME A GONDOLA	15
68	Instant INLP 003	GULLIVER'S TRAVELS (withdrawn)	40
53	Brunswick LAT 8022	GUYS AND DOLLS	12
64	Reprise F(S) 2016	GUYS AND DOLLS — REPRISE REPERTORY THEATRE PRESENTS	15/18
70s	RCA Red Seal SER 5686	GYPSY (gatefold sleeve)	15

H

68	RCA RD/SF 7959	HAIR (Broadway)	12
69	Polydor 583 043	HAIR (London)	12
63	Decca LK/SKL 4521	HALF-A-SIXPENCE	12
70s	Groovy STP 3	HANGAHAIR	10
57	Oriole MG 20014	HARMONY CLOSE	15
65	RCA Victor RD/SF 7768	HELLO, DOLLY! (with insert)	20
64	Pye NPL 18100/NSPL 83022	HIGH SPIRITS	30
60	Fontana TFL 5104	HITS FROM THE GANG SHOWS!	12
70	CBS BRG 70027	HOUDINI — MAN OF MAGIC	20
63	RCA RD/SF 7564	HOW TO SUCCEED IN BUSINESS WITHOUT REALLY TRYING	20

I

83	CBS Cameo 32265	I CAN GET IT FOR YOU WHOLESALE	12
68	RCA Victor RD/SF 7938	I DO! I DO!	18
60s	Oriole PS 40062	INSTANT MARRIAGE	30
76	EMI EMC 3139	IRENE	12

J

68	CBS 66207	JACQUES BREL IS ALIVE AND WELL AND LIVING IN PARIS (2-LP)	20
75	MCA MCF 2726	JEEVES	50
74	RSO 2394 141	JOHN, PAUL, GEORGE, RINGO AND BERT	10
66	HMV CLP/CSD 3591	JORROCKS	15
56	Philips	JOYCE GRENFELL REQUESTS THE PLEASURE	12

K

53	Brunswick LAT 8026	THE KING AND I	12
64	Reprise F(S) 2017	KISS ME KATE — REPRISE REPERTORY THEATRE PRESENTS	12/15

L

60	Capitol SW 1240	LITTLE MARY SUNSHINE	12
64	Pye NSPL 83023	LITTLE ME	12
59	Decca LK 4320	LOCK UP YOUR DAUGHTERS	12
73	Reflection RL 306	LONESOME STONE	22

MINT VALUE £

M

64	Decca LK/SKL 4643	MAGGIE MAY (mono/stereo)	15/18
72	Columbia SCX 6504	MAID OF THE MOUNTAINS	12
60s	CBS (S) 70051	MAME	12
68	London HA-R/SH-R 8362	MAN OF LA MANCHA	12
59	HMV CLP 1275	MARIGOLD	12
68	Studio Two TWO 234	THE MERRY WIDOW (radio musical)	15
61	Oriole MG 20054	MINE FAIR SADIE	20
60	HMV CLP 1365	THE MOST HAPPY FELLA!	20
68	CBS 70048	MR. & MRS.	18
57	Brunswick LAT 8184	MR. WONDERFUL	12
50s	Capitol W 990	THE MUSIC MAN	15

N

| 72 | Ace Of Clubs ACL 1238 | A NIGHT OF MUSIC HALL | 25 |
| 63 | Decca LK/SKL 4576 | NO STRINGS | 20 |

O

63	Decca LK/SKL 4542	OH! WHAT A LOVELY WAR	12
50	Brunswick LAT 8001	OKLAHOMA	12
60	Decca LK 4359	OLIVER! (also stereo SKL 4105)	15
60	World Record Club TP 151	OLIVER!	20
61	HMV CLP 1459/CSD 1370	OLIVER! (mono/stereo)	35/50
60	London HA-T 2286	ONCE UPON A MATTRESS	12
80	Warner Bros K 56850	ONE MO' TIME	12
61	Decca LK 4393/SKL 4133	ONE OVER THE EIGHT (mono/stereo)	18/22
61	Decca LK 4395/SKL 4134	ON THE BRIGHTER SIDE	15
67	CBS	ON THE LEVEL	12
63	CBS 60005	ON THE TOWN	45
65	Parlophone PCS 3066	OUR MAN CRICHTON	12

P

65	CBS BPG 62598	PASSION FLOWER HOTEL	35
60s	Ace Of Clubs ACL 1112	PERCHANCE TO DREAM	15
63	Parlophone PMC 1198	PETER COOK PRESENTS THE ESTABLISHMENT	12
65	RCA RD 7722	PETER PAN	12
69	Philips SBL 7916	PHIL THE FLUTER	35
74	Fontana SFL 13190	PHIL THE FLUTER	12
60s	Philips (S)AL 3431	PICKWICK (gatefold sleeve)	18
59	Decca LK 4337	PIECES OF EIGHT	15
77	MCA MCF 2826	THE POINT	15
60	Melodisc MLP 12-117	PREACHIN', PRAYIN', SINGIN' AND SHOUTIN' GOSPEL	15
64	London HA-U/SH-U 8201	THE PRINCE AND THE PAUPER	12
78	EMI EMC 3233	PRIVATES ON PARADE	25
69	United Artists UAS 29075	PROMISES, PROMISES	15

R

65	HMV CLP 1820/CSD 1575	ROBERT AND ELIZABETH	15
75	UK UKAL 1015	THE ROCKY HORROR SHOW (London Cast)	15
75	UK UKMC 1015	THE ROCKY HORROR SHOW (cassette, London Cast)	12
74	Ode ODE 77026	THE ROCKY HORROR SHOW (U.S. Roxy Cast)	15
83	Ode OSVD 77026	THE ROCKY HORROR SHOW (picture disc, reissued in 1987)	15

S

57	Oriole MG 20004	SALAD DAYS	12
70	Capitol E-ST 337	SALVATION	15
58	Pye NPL 18011	SHARE MY LETTUCE	12
59	Philips ABL 3370	THE SOUND OF MUSIC (gatefold sleeve)	12
61	HMV CLP 1453/CSD 1365	THE SOUND OF MUSIC	12
60s	Philips 632 303 BL	SPACE IS SO STARTLING	20
61	Decca LK 4408/SKL 4142	STOP THE WORLD I WANT TO GET OFF	12
67	Wing WL 1172	SUMMER SONG	20
67	CBS (S)BRG 70035	SWEET CHARITY	15

T

60	Fontana TFL 5103	TAKE IT FROM HERE (excerpts from radio show, also stereo STFL 534)	15
60	Capitol SW 1492	TENDERLOIN	12
63	Parlophone PMC 1197	THAT WAS THE WEEK THAT WAS (also stereo PCS 3040)	15
67	World Record Club SH 849	THOROUGHLY MODERN MILLIE	15
72	Decca SKL 5137	TOM BROWNE'S SCHOOLDAYS	15
69	Columbia S(C)X 6330	TWO CITIES (Jeff Wayne)	25
66	United Artists (S)ULP 1116	TWANG (Lionel Bart/James Booth)	12

V

| 63 | Decca LK/SKL 4536 | VIRTUE IN DANGER | 12 |

W

64	Decca LK/SKL 4610	WAIT A MINIM	15
65	HMV CLP 1834/CSD 1587	THE WAYWARD WAY	25
54	Parlophone PMD 1011	WEDDING PARIS (10")	25
61	HMV CLP 1467	WILDEST DREAMS	15
56	HMV DLP 1125	WILD GROWS THE HEATHER (10")	30

Y

| 68 | RCA SB 6792 | THE YOUNG VISITORS | 20 |
| 67 | MGM MGM-C(S) 8045 | YOU'RE A GOOD MAN, CHARLIE BROWN | 12 |

Z

| 69 | Philips 600-287 | ZITA | 50 |

RECORD COLLECTOR'S
BACK ISSUES

A COMPLETE INDEX TO ALL ARTISTS
FEATURED IN PREVIOUS ISSUES

THE ARTISTS, SUBJECTS AND LABELS COVERED IN **RECORD COLLECTOR** ARE LISTED IN ALPHABETICAL ORDER BELOW ON THE FOLLOWING PAGES.

NOTE: ISSUES 1-37, 160 & 184 ARE ALL OUT-OF-PRINT

Indexes to the U.K. SOUL, SPECIAL PRESSINGS and COLLECTABLE INDIE SINGLES series listings are printed at the end of the main listing. The issue in which artists/groups/labels appeared is shown by the number in brackets after each entry. Issues up to and including No. 46 are A5 size, and issues from No. 47 onwards are A4 size.

All the discographies are UK RELEASES ONLY unless stated otherwise. The values were current at the time each issue was published. (*) indicates the discography is unpriced.

For full details of the cost of Back Issues, please see a current issue of RECORD COLLECTOR or write to:

THE MAGAZINE EDITOR, RECORD COLLECTOR,
45 ST. MARY'S ROAD, EALING, LONDON W5 5RQ

RECORD COLLECTOR

June 1984
No.58

For all serious collectors of :-
RARE RECORDS, POP MEMORABILIA, ETC.

95p

SLADE

JOHNNY CASH

ALEXIS KORNER

THOMPSON TWINS

JOHN'S CHILDREN

ETTA JAMES

WITH DISCOGRAPHIES & VALUES

MAY 1986
No. 81

RECORD COLLECTOR

For all serious collectors of :-
**RARE RECORDS, POP
MEMORABILIA, ETC.**

£1.20

TOP
200 MOST
COLLECTABLE
ARTISTS

JOHN
Lennon
RARITIES

SHAKIN'
STEVENS

THE MOODY BLUES'
UK SINGLES

RAINBOW

LONNIE MACK

PHIL OCHS

GLAM ROCK

ALMA COGAN

JOHNNY DUNCAN

THE DAMNED

WITH DISCOGRAPHIES
AND VALUES

RECORD COLLECTOR

Jan. 1987
No. 89

For all serious collectors of :-
RARE RECORDS, POP
MEMORABILIA, ETC.

£1.30

PAUL McCARTNEY TOO MANY VERSIONS?

BRUCE SPRINGSTEEN

RONNIE HAWKINS

BUTTERFIELD BLUES BAND

THEM

THE LEAVES

1960s REVIVAL TOUR

COLLECTABLE CDs

PET SHOP BOYS

STATUS QUO-1962-72

WITH DISCOGRAPHIES AND VALUES

RECORD COLLECTOR

OCTOBER 1991
No.146

For all serious collectors of:
RARE RECORDS, CDs,
POP MEMORABILIA, etc.

£1.95

£2,000 OF ALBUMS TO BE WON

BEATLES U.K. and U.S. SINGLES

KISS

GENESIS
JOHN PEEL INTERVIEW
THE PIXIES
JERRY LEE LEWIS
JOHNNY BURNETTE

MADONNA TOP 200 RARITIES

INTRODUCTION TO RECORD COLLECTING

RECORD COLLECTOR
JANUARY 1994
No. 173

For all serious collectors of:
RARE RECORDS, CDs, VIDEOS,
POP MEMORABILIA, etc.

£2.10
DM 13.80
N FI 10.75

A CONSUMER'S GUIDE TO COLLECTING
PINK FLOYD

70,000
RECORDS
IN NEW
PRICE GUIDE!

ROLLING STONES
BERT JANSCH
FRANKIE LYMON
CAPTAIN SCARLET
TOP OF THE POPS

LEVELLERS

R.E.M.
MARK KNOPFLER
ALBUMS OF THE YEAR

MEAT LOAF

RECORD COLLECTOR

OCT. 1995
No. 194

For all serious collectors of:
RARE RECORDS, CDs, VIDEOS,
POP MEMORABILIA, etc.

£2.40
DM 15.50
H.Fl 11.50

BRITPOP NOW!

COSTELLO ON COSTELLO
THE LAST TEN YEARS
EDWYN COLLINS
VELVET UNDERGROUND
PAUL McCARTNEY

GRATEFUL DEAD

ELVIS IN THE 70s

FLEETWOOD MAC
CHARLIE RICH
THE CLASH
JACKSON 5
ED BALL
TOWERING INFERNO

MUNGO JERRY
RUFUS THOMAS

U2 continued overleaf

BRITISH PSYCHEDELIA GUIDE

This series of collectable British psychedelic records is in alphabetical order:

U.K. SOUL RELEASES

This series of collectable soul singles on U.K. labels is in alphabetical order. Each month, the feature contains a brief guide to the most valuable records on the respective label(s). The issue number is in brackets before the label name.

RECORD COLLECTOR'S GRADING SYSTEM

In order to assist everyone who buys and sells rare discs, Record Collector magazine has originated a set of standards for the condition of second-hand records, cassettes and CDs. Anyone buying or selling records through the magazine must use our conditions to state what amount of wear and tear the disc, its sleeve and/or contents have been subject to. The seven standard condition categories, and a description of what each one means, are listed below:

MINT: The record itself is in brand new condition with no surface marks or deterioration in sound quality. The cover and any extra items such as the lyric sheet, booklet or poster are in perfect condition. Records advertised as Sealed or Unplayed should be Mint.

EXCELLENT: The record shows some signs of having been played, but there is very little lessening in sound quality. The cover and packaging might have slight wear and/or creasing.

VERY GOOD: The record has obviously been played many times, but displays no major deterioration in sound quality, despite noticeable surface marks and the occasional light scratch. Normal wear and tear on the cover or extra items, without any major defects, is acceptable.

GOOD: The record has been played so much that the sound quality has noticeably deteriorated, perhaps with some distortion and mild scratches. The cover and contents suffer from folding, scuffing of edges, spine splits, discoloration, etc.

FAIR: The record is still just playable but has not been cared for properly and displays considerable surface noise; it may even jump. The cover and contents will be torn, stained and/or defaced.

POOR: The record will not play properly due to scratches, bad surface noise, etc. The cover and contents will be badly damaged or partly missing.

BAD: The record is unplayable or might even be broken, and is only of use as a collection-filler.

CDs & CASSETTES: As a general rule, CDs and cassettes either play perfectly — in which case they are in Mint condition — or they don't, in which case their value is minimal. Cassette tape is liable to deteriorate with age, even if it remains unplayed, so care should be taken when buying old tapes. CDs are difficult to grade visually: they can look perfect but actually be faulty, while in other cases they may appear damaged but still play perfectly. Cassette and CD inlays and booklets should be graded in the same way as record covers and sleeves. In general, the plastic containers for cassettes and CDs can easily be replaced if they are broken or scratched, but card covers and digipaks are subject to the same wear as record sleeves.

RECORD COLLECTOR'S GRADING READY RECKONER

This Ready Reckoner will help you work out the value of a record in any condition. For example, if you see a disc which is valued at £10 in Mint condition, but which you consider to be in only Very Good condition, then you can consult the Ready Reckoner and find out the appropriate price for the record — in this case, £5. As very few collectors are interested in records in Poor or Bad condition, we consider that any disc worth less than £10 in Mint condition is effectively worthless in Poor or Bad condition.

Mint	EX	VG	Good	Fair	Poor	Bad
1,000	800	500	300	150	80	25
500	400	250	150	75	40	12
300	240	150	90	45	25	8
250	200	125	75	38	20	6
200	160	100	60	30	15	5
150	120	75	45	22	25	4
125	100	60	38	18	12	3
100	80	50	30	15	8	2.50
75	60	35	22	10	6	2
50	40	25	15	8	4	1.50
40	32	20	12	6	3	1
30	25	15	9	4.50	2.50	—
25	20	12	7.50	3.50	2	—
20	16	10	6	3	1.50	—
15	12	8	4.50	2.25	1.25	—
12	10	6	3.50	1.75	1	—
10	8	5	3	1.50	—	—
8	6	4	2.50	1.25	—	—
7	5	3.50	2	1	—	—
6	4.50	3	1.75	—	—	—
5	4	2.50	1.50	—	—	—
4	3.25	2	1.25	—	—	—
3	2.50	1.50	1	—	—	—
2	1.75	1	—	—	—	—

ABBREVIATIONS
USED IN THIS GUIDE

act . . . . actually	mag. . . . . magazine
alt. . . . . alternative	no. . . . . number
b&w . . . . black and white	no'd . . . . numbered
cass. . . . . cassette	p/s . . . . picture sleeve
cat. no. . . . catalogue number	pic disc. . . . . picture disc
CD. . . . . compact disc	pt(s) . . . . part(s)
co. . . . . company	sl. . . . . sleeve
d/pack . . . . double pack	st. . . . . stereo
dble. . . . . double	stkr . . . . sticker
diff. . . . . different	t/p . . . . test pressing
edn. . . . . edition	vers. . . . . version
EP . . . . extended-play record	vol. . . . . volume
ext. . . . . extended	w/ . . . . with
flexi . . . . flexidisc	w/l . . . . white label
g/f(old) . . . . . . gatefold sleeve	2-CD . . . . double CD
inst . . . . instrumental	2-LP. . . . . double LP
intl. . . . . international	2 x 45 . . . . . two 45rpm singles
LP . . . . . long-playing record	3-LP. . . . . triple LP
m/s . . . . mono/stereo	78 . . . . 78rpm single

IMPORTANT RECORD COMPANY ABBREVIATIONS

Amalgam . . . . Amalgamated
B. Banquet. . . . . Beggars Banquet
B'full/Brains . . . . Bucketfull Of Brains
Col . . . . Columbia
Elek . . . . Elektra
Font . . . . Fontana
L.T.T. Slaughter . . . . Lambs To The Slaughter
M. For Nations . . . . Music For Nations
MFP . . . . Music For Pleasure
M. Minor. . . . . Major Minor
Parl. . . . . Parlophone
PSI . . . . Phil Spector International
Pye Intl . . . . Pye International
R. Digest . . . . Readers Digest
Regal Zono . . . . Regal Zonophone
R. Stones. . . . . Rolling Stones
S'side. . . . . Stateside
St. Tones. . . . . Street Tones
Sweet Folk & C. . . . . Sweet Folk And Country
T. Motown . . . . Tamla Motown
UA. . . . . United Artists
W. Bros . . . . Warner Brothers
WRC. . . . . World Record Club